Who's Who in the West

Biographical Reference Works
Published by Marquis Who's Who

Who's Who in America

- Who's Who in America supplements:
  - Who's Who in America Index by Geographic Location and Professional Area
  - Who's Who in America College Alumni Directory
  - Who's Who in America Birthdate Index

Who's Who in the World

Who Was Who in America

- Historical Volume (1607-1896)
- Volume I (1897-1942)
- Volume II (1943-1950)
- Volume III (1951-1960)
- Volume IV (1961-1968)
- Volume V (1969-1973)
- Volume VI (1974-1976)
- Volume VII (1977-1981)

Who Was Who in American History—Arts and Letters

Who Was Who in American History—The Military

Who Was Who in American History—Science and Technology

Who's Who in the Midwest

Who's Who in the East

Who's Who in the South and Southwest

Who's Who in the West

Who's Who in Frontier Science and Technology

Who's Who of American Women

Who's Who in Finance and Industry

Who's Who in American Law

World Who's Who in Science

Directory of Women in Marquis Who's Who Publications

Marquis Who's Who Publications/Index to All Books 1984

- Volume 1: Alphabetic
- Volume 2: Geographic

Professional Publications
from Marquis Who's Who

Directory of Medical Specialists

Biographical Directory of the Computer Graphics Industry

Biographical Directory of Online Professionals

Who's Who in the West®

Including Alaska, Arizona, California, Colorado, Hawaii, Idaho, Montana, Nevada, New Mexico, Oregon, Utah, Washington, and Wyoming; and in Canada, the provinces of Alberta, British Columbia, and Saskatchewan.

19th edition
1984-1985

MARQUIS
Who'sWho

Marquis Who's Who, Inc.
200 East Ohio Street
Chicago, Illinois 60611 U.S.A.

Library of Congress Catalog Card Number 49-48186
International Standard Book Number 0-8379-0919-8
Product Code Number 030289

Manufactured in the United States of America

Table of Contents

Preface

The nineteenth edition of *Who's Who in the West* is the most recent compilation of biographical information on men and women of distinction whose influence is concentrated in the western sector of North America. Such individuals are of decided reference interest locally and nationally.

The volume contains approximately 19,000 names from the western region of the United States including Alaska, Arizona, California, Colorado, Hawaii, Idaho, Montana, Nevada, New Mexico, Oregon, Utah, Washington, and Wyoming, and from the Canadian provinces of Alberta, British Columbia, and Saskatchewan. Assiduously reviewed, revised, and amended, the nineteenth edition offers up-to-the-minute coverage of a broad range of Westerners based on position or individual achievement.

The persons sketched in this volume represent virtually every important field of endeavor. Included are executives and officials in government, business, education, religion, the press, civic affairs, the arts, cultural affairs, law and other fields. This edition also includes significant contributors in such areas as contemporary art, music, and science.

In the great majority of cases, the biographees have furnished their own data, thus assuring a high degree of accuracy. In some cases, Marquis staff members compile the data through careful and independent research. Sketches prepared in this manner are denoted by an asterisk. As in previous editions, biographees are given the opportunity to review prepublication proofs of their sketches to make sure they are correct.

Marquis Who's Who editors exercise the utmost care in preparing each biographical sketch for publication. Occasionally, however, errors do occur despite all precautions taken to minimize such occurrences. Users of this directory are requested to draw the attention of the publisher to any errors found so that corrections can be made in a later edition.

The question often is asked, "How do people get into a Who's Who volume?" Name selection is based on one fundamental principle: reference value.

Biographees of *Who's Who in the West* can be classified into two basic categories: (1) Persons who are of regional reference importance to colleagues, librarians, researchers, scholars, the press, historians, biographers, participants in business and civic affairs, and others with specific or general inquiry needs; (2) Individuals of national reference interest who are also of such regional or local importance that their inclusion in the book is essential.

There is a minimum of duplication of names between this volume and *Who's Who in America.* In recognition of the complementary relationship between the two Marquis publications, this edition of *Who's Who in the West* contains a listing of all those biographees of the western region whose sketches appear in the forty-second edition of *Who's Who in America.*

In the editorial evaluation that resulted in the ultimate selection of the names in this directory, an individual's desire to be listed was not sufficient reason for inclusion. Only occupational stature or achievement in a field within the western region of North America influenced selection.

The nineteenth edition of *Who's Who in the West* carries on the tradition of excellence established in 1899 with the publication of the first edition of *Who's Who in America.* The essence of that tradition is reflected in the continuing effort at Marquis Who's Who to produce reference works that are responsive to the needs of their users throughout the world.

Standards of Admission

The foremost consideration in selecting biographees for *Who's Who in the West* is the extent of an individual's reference interest. Such reference interest is judged on either of two factors: (1) the position of responsibility held, or (2) the level of significant achievement attained.

Admissions based on the factor of position include:

Members of the U.S. Congress

Federal judges

Governors of states covered by this volume

Premiers of Canadian provinces covered by this volume

State attorneys general

Judges of state and territorial courts of highest appellate jurisdiction.

Mayors of major cities

Heads of major universities and colleges

Heads of leading philanthropic, educational, cultural, and scientific institutions and associations

Chief ecclesiastics of the principal religious denominations

Principal officers of national and international businesses

Others chosen because of incumbency or membership

Admission based on individual achievement is based on objective qualitative criteria. To be selected, a person must have attained conspicuous achievement. The biographee may scarcely be known in the local community but may be recognized in some field of endeavor for noteworthy accomplishment.

Key to Information in this Directory

❶ **ASHTON, HARDY AMES,** ❷ lawyer; ❸ b. Topeka, Aug. 3, 1922; ❹ s. Samuel Taylor and Bertha (Hanson) A.; ❺ m. Nancy Roudebush, June 20, 1943; ❻ children: Marilyn Ashton Heim, Barbara Anne, Eugene Maurice. ❼ B.A., Pa. State U., 1943; J.D., Syracuse U., 1948. ❽ Bar: Calif. 1948, U.S. Supreme Ct. 1956. ❾ Assoc. Prine, Belden and Coates, Sacramento, 1948-55; mem. Johnson, Randolph, Sikes and Bord, 1955—, sr. ptnr., 1957—; legal cons. Sacramento Urban League. ❿ Commr. Sutter County Park Dist., 1967-68; mem. planning com. Arroyo Seco Redevel. Project, Sacramento, 1970—; bd. dirs. Hargrave Inst. ⓫ Served with U.S. Army, 1944-45. ⓬ Named Man of Yr., Sacramento C. of C., 1969. ⓭ Mem. ABA, Calif. Bar Assn., Sacramento Bar Assn., Am. Judicature Soc., Order of Coif. ⓮ Democrat. ⓯ Episcopalian. ⓰ Clubs: Twelve Trees Country, Tuesday Luncheon, Lions (Sacramento). ⓱ Author: Urban Renewal and the Law, 1969. ⓲ Home: 3080 Grant St Sacramento CA 95814 ⓳ Office: 10 Saint Paul St Sacramento CA 95822

Key

❶ Name
❷ Occupation
❸ Vital Statistics
❹ Parents
❺ Marriage
❻ Children
❼ Education
❽ Certifications
❾ Career
❿ Civic and Political Activities
⓫ Military Record
⓬ Awards
⓭ Professional and Association Memberships
⓮ Political Affiliation
⓯ Religion
⓰ Clubs (including lodges)
⓱ Writings and Special Achievements
⓲ Home Address
⓳ Office Address

The biographical listings in *Who's Who in the West* are arranged in alphabetical order according to the first letter of the last name of the biographee. Each sketch is presented in a uniform order as in the sample sketch above. The many abbreviations used in the sketches are explained in the Table of Abbreviations.

Table of Abbreviations

The following abbreviations and symbols are frequently used in this Directory.

*(An asterisk) following a sketch indicates that it was researched by the Marquis Who's Who editorial staff and has not been verified by the biographee.

A.A. Associate in Arts
AAAL American Academy of Arts and Letters
AAAS American Association for the Advancement of Science
AAHPER Alliance for Health, Physical Education and Recreation
AAU Amateur Athletic Union
AAUP American Association of University Professors
AAUW American Association of University Women
A.B. Arts, Bachelor of
AB Alberta
ABA American Bar Association
ABC American Broadcasting Company
AC Air Corps
acad. academy, academic
acct. accountant
acctg. accounting
ACDA Arms Control and Disarmament Agency
ACLU American Civil Liberties Union
ACP American College of Physicians
ACS American College of Surgeons
ADA American Dental Association
a.d.c. aide-de-camp
adj. adjunct, adjutant
adj. gen. adjutant general
adm. admiral
adminstr. administrator
adminstrn. administration
adminstrv. administrative
ADP automatic data processing
adv. advocate, advisory
advt. advertising
A.E. Agricultural Engineer (for degrees only)
A.E. and P. Ambassador Extraordinary and Plenipotentiary
AEC Atomic Energy Commission
aero. aeronautical, aeronautic
aerodyn. aerodynamic
AFB Air Force Base
AFL-CIO American Federation of Labor and Congress of Industrial Organizations
AFTRA American Federation TV and Radio Artists
agr. agriculture
agrl. agricultural
agt. agent
AGVA American Guild of Variety Artists
agy. agency
A&I Agricultural and Industrial
AIA American Institute of Architects
AIAA American Institute of Aeronautics and Astronautics
AID Agency for International Development
AIEE American Institute of Electrical Engineers
AIM American Institute of Management
AIME American Institute of Mining, Metallurgy, and Petroleum Engineers
AK Alaska
AL Alabama
ALA American Library Association
Ala. Alabama
alt. alternate
Alta. Alberta
A&M Agricultural and Mechanical
A.M. Arts, Master of
Am. American, America
AMA American Medical Association
A.M.E. African Methodist Episcopal
Amtrak National Railroad Passenger Corporation
AMVETS American Veterans of World War II, Korea, Vietnam
anat. anatomical
ann. annual
ANTA American National Theatre and Academy
anthrop. anthropological
AP Associated Press
APO Army Post Office
Apr. April
apptd. appointed
apt. apartment
AR Arkansas
ARC American Red Cross
archeol. archeological
archtl. architectural
Ariz. Arizona
Ark. Arkansas
ArtsD. Arts, Doctors of
arty. artillery
ASCAP American Society of Composers, Authors and Publishers
ASCE American Society of Civil Engineers
ASHRAE American Society of Heating, Refrigeration, and Air Conditioning Engineers
ASME American Society of Mechanical Engineers
assn. association
assoc. associate
asst. assistant
ASTM American Society for Testing and Materials
astron. astronomical
astrophys. astrophysical
ATSC Air Technical Service Command
AT&T American Telephone & Telegraph Company
atty. attorney
AUS Army of the United States
Aug. August
aux. auxiliary
Ave. Avenue
AVMA American Veterinary Medical Association
AZ Arizona

B. Bachelor
b. born
B.A. Bachelor of Arts
B.Agr. Bachelor of Agriculture
Balt. Baltimore
Bapt. Baptist
B. Arch. Bachelor of Architecture
B.A.S. Bachelor of Agricultural Science
B.B.A. Bachelor of Business Administration
BBC British Broadcasting Corporation
B.C., BC British Columbia
B.C.E. Bachelor of Civil Engineering
B.Chir. Bachelor of Surgery
B.C.L. Bachelor of Civil Law
B.C.S. Bachelor of Commercial Science
B.D. Bachelor of Divinity
bd. board
B.E. Bachelor of Education
B.E.E. Bachelor of Electrical Engineering
B.F.A. Bachelor of Fine Arts
bibl. biblical
bibliog. bibliographical
biog. biographical
biol. biological
B.J. Bachelor of Journalism
Bklyn. Brooklyn
B.L. Bachelor of Letters
bldg. building
B.L.S. Bachelor of Library Science
Blvd. Boulevard
bn. battalion
B.&O.R.R. Baltimore & Ohio Railroad
bot. botanical
B.P.E. Bachelor of Physical Education
br. branch
B.R.E. Bachelor of Religious Education
brig. gen. brigadier general
Brit. British, Brittanica
Bros. Brothers
B.S. Bachelor of Science
B.S.A. Bachelor of Agricultural Science
B.S.D. Bachelor of Didactic Science
B.S.T. Bachelor of Sacred Theology
B.Th. Bachelor of Theology
bull. bulletin
bur. bureau
bus. business
B.W.I. British West Indies

CA California

CAA Civil Aeronautics Administration
CAB Civil Aeronautics Board
Calif. California
C.Am. Central America
Can. Canada, Canadian
CAP Civil Air Patrol
capt. captain
CARE Cooperative American Relief Everywhere
Cath. Catholic
cav. cavalry
CBC Canadian Broadcasting Company
CBI China, Burma, India Theatre of Operations
CBS Columbia Broadcasting System
CCC Commodity Credit Corporation
CCNY City College of New York
CCU Cardiac Care Unit
CD Civil Defense
C.E. Corps of Engineers, Civil Engineer (in firm's name only or for degree)
cen. central (To be used for court system only)
CENTO Central Treaty Organization
CERN European Organization of Nuclear Research
cert. certificate, certification, certified
CETA Comprehensive Employment Training Act
CFL Canadian Football League
ch. church
Ch.D. Doctor of Chemistry
chem. chemical
Chem.E. Chemical Engineer
Chgo. Chicago
chirurg. chirurgical
chmn. chairman
chpt. chapter
CIA Central Intelligence Agency
CIC Counter Intelligence Corps
Cin. Cincinnati
cir. circuit
Cleve. Cleveland
climatol. climatological
clin. clinical
clk. clerk
C.L.U. Chartered Life Underwriter
C.M. Master in Surgery
C.&N.W.Ry. Chicago & Northwestern Railway
CO Colorado
Co. Company
COF Catholic Order of Foresters
C. of C. Chamber of Commerce
col. colonel.
coll. college
Colo. Colorado
com. committee
comd. commanded
comdg. commanding
comdr. commander
comdt. commandant
commd. commissioned
comml. commercial
commn. commission
commr. commissioner
condr. conductor
Conf. Conference
Congl. Congregational, Congressional
Conglist. Congregationalist
Conn. Connecticut
cons. consultant, consulting
consol. consolidated
constl. constitutional
constn. constitution
constrn. construction
contbd. contributed
contbg. contributing
contbn. contribution
contbr. contributor
Conv. Convention
coop. cooperative
CORDS Civil Operations and Revolutionary Development Support
CORE Congress of Racial Equality
corp. corporation, corporate
corr. correspondent, corresponding, correspondence
C.&O.Ry. Chesapeake & Ohio Railway
C.P.A. Certified Public Accountant
C.P.C.U. Chartered property and casualty underwriter
C.P.H. Certificate of Public Health
cpl. corporal
CPR Cardio-Pulmonary Resuscitation
C.P.Ry. Canadian Pacific Railway
C.S. Christian Science
C.S.B. Bachelor of Christian Science
CSC Civil Service Commission
C.S.D. Doctor of Christian Science
CT Connecticut
ct. court
ctr. center
CWS Chemical Warfare Service
C.Z. Canal Zone

d. daughter
D. Doctor
D.Agr. Doctor of Agriculture
DAR Daughters of the American Revolution
dau. daughter
DAV Disabled American Veterans
D.C., DC District of Columbia
D.C.L. Doctor of Civil Law
D.C.S. Doctor of Commercial Science
D.D. Doctor of Divinity
D.D.S. Doctor of Dental Surgery
DE Delaware
dec. deceased
Dec. December
def. defense
Del. Delaware
del. delegate, delegation
Dem. Democrat, Democratic
D.Eng. Doctor of Engineering
denom. denomination, denominational
dep. deputy
dept. department
dermatol. dermatological
desc. descendant
devel. development, developmental
D.F.A. Doctor of Fine Arts
D.F.C. Distinguished Flying Cross
D.H.L. Doctor of Hebrew Literature
dir. director
dist. district
distbg. distributing
distbn. distribution
distbr. distributor
disting. distinguished
div. division, divinity, divorce
D.Litt. Doctor of Literature
D.M.D. Doctor of Medical Dentistry
D.M.S. Doctor of Medical Science
D.O. Doctor of Osteopathy
D.P.H. Diploma in Public Health
D.R. Daughters of the Revolution
Dr. Drive, Doctor
D.R.E. Doctor of Religious Education
Dr.P.H. Doctor of Public Health, Doctor of Public Hygiene
D.S.C. Distinguished Service Cross
D.Sc. Doctor of Science
D.S.M. Distinguished Service Medal
D.S.T. Doctor of Sacred Theology
D.T.M. Doctor of Tropical Medicine
D.V.M. Doctor of Veterinary Medicine
D.V.S. Doctor of Veterinary Surgery

E. East
ea. eastern (use for court system only)
E. and P. Extraordinary and Plenipotentiary
Eccles. Ecclesiastical
ecol. ecological
econ. economic
ECOSOC Economic and Social Council (of the UN)
E.D. Doctor of Engineering
ed. educated
Ed.B. Bachelor of Education
Ed.D. Doctor of Education
edit. edition
Ed.M. Master of Education
edn. education
ednl. educational
EDP electronic data processing
Ed.S. Specialist in Education
E.E. Electrical Engineer (degree only)
E.E. and M.P. Envoy Extraordinary and Minister Plenipotentiary
EEC European Economic Community
EEG electroencephalogram
EEO Equal Employment Opportunity
EEOC Equal Employment Opportunity Commission

EKG electrocardiogram
E.Ger. German Democratic Republic
elec. electrical
electrochem. electrochemical
electrophys. electrophysical
elem. elementary
E.M. Engineer of Mines
ency. encyclopedia
Eng. England
engr. engineer
engring. engineering
entomol. entomological
environ. environmental
EPA Environmental Protection Agency
epidemiol. epidemiological
Episc. Episcopalian
ERA Equal Rights Amendment
ERDA Energy Research and Development Administration
ESEA Elementary and Secondary Education Act
ESL English as Second Language
ESSA Environmental Science Services Administration
ethnol. ethnological
ETO European Theatre of Operations
Evang. Evangelical
exam. examination, examining
exec. executive
exhbn. exhibition
expdn. expedition
expn. exposition
expt. experiment
exptl. experimental

F.A. Field Artillery
FAA Federal Aviation Administration
FAO Food and Agriculture Organization (of the UN)
FBI Federal Bureau of Investigation
FCA Farm Credit Administration
FCC Federal Communication Commission
FCDA Federal Civil Defense Administration
FDA Food and Drug Administration
FDIA Federal Deposit Insurance Administration
FDIC Federal Deposit Insurance Corporation
F.E. Forest Engineer
FEA Federal Energy Administration
Feb. February
fed. federal
fedn. federation
FERC Federal Energy Regulatory Commission
fgn. foreign
FHA Federal Housing Administration
fin. financial, finance
FL Florida
Fla. Florida
FMC Federal Maritime Commission
FOA Foreign Operations Administration
found. foundation
FPC Federal Power Commission
FPO Fleet Post Office
frat. fraternity
FRS Federal Reserve System
FSA Federal Security Agency
Ft. Fort
FTC Federal Trade Commission

G-1 (or other number) Division of General Staff
Ga., GA Georgia
GAO General Accounting Office
gastroent. gastroenterological
GATT General Agreement of Tariff and Trades
gen. general
geneal. genealogical
geod. geodetic
geog. geographic, geographical
geol. geological
geophys. geophysical
gerontol. gerontological
G.H.Q. General Headquarters
G.N. Ry. Great Northern Railway
gov. governor
govt. government
govtl. governmental
GPO Government Printing Office
grad. graduate, graduated
GSA General Services Administration
Gt. Great
GU Guam
gynecol. gynecological

hdqrs. headquarters
HEW Department of Health, Education and Welfare
H.H.D. Doctor of Humanities
HHFA Housing and Home Finance Agency
HHS Department of Health and Human Services
HI Hawaii
hist. historical, historic
H.M. Master of Humanics
homeo. homeopathic
hon. honorary, honorable
Ho. of Dels. House of Delegates
Ho. of Reps. House of Representatives
hort. horticultural
hosp. hospital
HUD Department of Housing and Urban Development
Hwy. Highway
hydrog. hydrographic

IA Iowa
IAEA International Atomic Energy Agency
IBM International Business Machines Corporation
IBRD International Bank for Reconstruction and Development
ICA International Cooperation Administration
ICC Interstate Commerce Commission
ICU Intensive Care Unit
ID Idaho
IEEE Institute of Electrical and Electronics Engineers
IFC International Finance Corporation
IGY International Geophysical Year
IL Illinois
Ill. Illinois
illus. illustrated
ILO International Labor Organization
IMF International Monetary Fund
IN Indiana
Inc. Incorporated
ind. independent
Ind. Indiana
Indpls. Indianapolis
indsl. industrial
inf. infantry
info. information
ins. insurance
insp. inspector
insp. gen. inspector general
inst. institute
instl. institutional
instn. institution
instr. instructor
instrn. instruction
intern. international
intro. introduction
IRE Institute of Radio Engineers
IRS Internal Revenue Service
ITT International Telephone & Telegraph Corporation

JAG Judge Advocate General
JAGC Judge Advocate General Corps
Jan. January
Jaycees Junior Chamber of Commerce
J.B. Jurum Baccolaureus
J.C.B. Juris Canoni Baccalaureus
J.C.D. Juris Canonici Doctor, Juris Civilis Doctor
J.C.L. Juris Canonici Licentiatus
J.D. Juris Doctor
j.g. junior grade
jour. journal
jr. junior
J.S.D. Juris Scientiae Doctor
J.U.D. Juris Utriusque Doctor
jud. judicial

Kans. Kansas
K.C. Knights of Columbus
K.P. Knights of Pythias
KS Kansas
K.T. Knight Templar
Ky., KY Kentucky

La., LA Louisiana
lab. laboratory
lang. language
laryngol. laryngological
LB Labrador
lectr. lecturer
legis. legislation, legislative
L.H.D. Doctor of Humane Letters
L.I. Long Island
lic. licensed, license
L.I.R.R. Long Island Railroad
lit. literary, literature
Litt.B. Bachelor of Letters
Litt.D. Doctor of Letters
LL.B. Bachelor of Laws
LL.D. Doctor of Laws
LL.M. Master of Laws
Ln. Lane
L.&N.R.R. Louisville & Nashville Railroad
L.S. Library Science (in degree)
lt. lieutenant
Ltd. Limited
Luth. Lutheran
LWV League of Women Voters

m. married
M. Master
M.A. Master of Arts
MA Massachusetts
mag. magazine
M.Agr. Master of Agriculture
maj. major
Man. Manitoba
Mar. March
M.Arch. Master in Architecture
Mass. Massachusetts
math. mathematics, mathematical
MATS Military Air Transport Service
M.B. Bachelor of Medicine
MB Manitoba
M.B.A. Master of Business Administration
MBS Mutual Broadcasting System
M.C. Medical Corps
M.C.E. Master of Civil Engineering
mcht. merchant
mcpl. municipal
M.C.S. Master of Commercial Science
M.D. Doctor of Medicine
Md, MD Maryland
M.Dip. Master in Diplomacy
mdse. merchandise
M.D.V. Doctor of Veterinary Medicine
M.E. Mechanical Engineer (degree only)
ME Maine
M.E.Ch. Methodist Episcopal Church
mech. mechanical
M.Ed. Master of Education
med. medical
M.E.E. Master of Electrical Engineering
mem. member
meml. memorial
merc. mercantile
met. metropolitan
metall. metallurgical
Met.E. Metallurgical Engineer
meteorol. meteorological
Meth. Methodist
Mex. Mexico
M.F. Master of Forestry
M.F.A. Master of Fine Arts
mfg. manufacturing
mfr. manufacturer
mgmt. management
mgr. manager
M.H.A. Master of Hospital Administration
M.I. Military Intelligence
MI Michigan
Mich. Michigan
micros. microscopic, microscopical
mid. middle (use for Court System only)
mil. military
Milw. Milwaukee
mineral. mineralogical
Minn. Minnesota
Miss. Mississippi
MIT Massachusetts Institute of Technology
mktg. marketing
M.L. Master of Laws
MLA Modern Language Association
M.L.D. Magister Legnum Diplomatic
M.Litt. Master of Literature
M.L.S. Master of Library Science
M.M.E. Master of Mechanical Engineering
MN Minnesota
mng. managing
Mo., MO Missouri
moblzn. mobilization
Mont. Montana
M.P. Member of Parliament
M.P.E. Master of Physical Education
M.P.H. Master of Public Health
M.P.L. Master of Patent Law
Mpls. Minneapolis
M.R.E. Master of Religious Education
M.S. Master of Science
MS, Ms. Mississippi
M.Sc. Master of Science
M.S.F. Master of Science of Forestry
M.S.T. Master of Sacred Theology
M.S.W. Master of Social Work
MT Montana
Mt. Mount
MTO Mediterranean Theatre of Operations
mus. museum, musical
Mus.B. Bachelor of Music
Mus.D. Doctor of Music
Mus.M. Master of Music
mut. mutual
mycol. mycological

N. North
NAACP National Association for the Advancement of Colored People
NACA National Advisory Committee for Aeronautics
NAD National Academy of Design
N.Am. North America
NAM National Association of Manufacturers
NAPA National Association of Performing Artists
NAREB National Association of Real Estate Boards
NARS National Archives and Record Service
NASA National Aeronautics and Space Administration
nat. national
NATO North Atlantic Treaty Organization
NATOUSA North African Theatre of Operations
nav. navigation
N.B., NB New Brunswick
NBC National Broadcasting Company
N.C., NC North Carolina
NCCJ National Conference of Christians and Jews
N.D., ND North Dakota
NDEA National Defense Education Act
NE Nebraska
NE Northeast
NEA National Education Association
Nebr. Nebraska
NEH National Endowment for Humanities
neurol. neurological
Nev. Nevada
NF Newfoundland
NFL National Football League
Nfld. Newfoundland
N.G. National Guard
N.H. NH New Hampshire
NHL National Hockey League
NIH National Institutes of Health
NIMH National Institute of Mental Health
N.J., NJ New Jersey
NLRB National Labor Relations Board
NM New Mexico
N.Mex. New Mexico
No. Northern
NOAA National Oceanographic and Atmospheric Administration
NORAD North America Air Defense
NOW National Organization for Women
Nov. November
N.P.Ry. Northern Pacific Railway
nr. near
NRC National Research Council
N.S., NS Nova Scotia
NSC National Security Council
NSF National Science Foundation
N.T. New Testament
NT Northwest Territories
numis. numismatic

NV Nevada
NW Northwest
N.W.T. Northwest Territories
N.Y., NY New York
N.Y.C. New York City
NYU New York University
N.Z. New Zealand

OAS Organization of American States
ob-gyn obstetrics-gynecology
obs. observatory
obstet. obstetrical
O.D. Doctor of Optometry
OECD Organization of European Cooperation and Development
OEEC Organization of European Economic Cooperation
OEO Office of Economic Opportunity
ofcl. official
OH Ohio
OK Oklahoma
Okla. Oklahoma
ON Ontario
Ont. Ontario
ophthal. ophthalmological
ops. operations
OR Oregon
orch. orchestra
Oreg. Oregon
orgn. organization
ornithol. ornithological
OSHA Occupational Safety and Health Administration
OSRD Office of Scientific Research and Development
OSS Office of Strategic Services
osteo. osteopathic
otol. otological
otolaryn. otolaryngological

Pa., PA Pennsylvania
P.A. Professional Association
paleontol. paleontological
path. pathological
P.C. Professional Corporation
PE Prince Edward Island
P.E.I. Prince Edward Island (text only)
PEN Poets, Playwrights, Editors, Essayists and Novelists (international association)
penol. penological
P.E.O. women's organization (full name not disclosed)
pfc. private first class
PHA Public Housing Administration
pharm. pharmaceutical
Pharm.D. Doctor of Pharmacy
Pharm. M. Master of Pharmacy
Ph.B. Bachelor of Philosophy
Ph.D. Doctor of Philosophy
Phila. Philadelphia
philharm. philharmonic
philol. philological
philos. philosophical
photog. photographic
phys. physical
physiol. physiological
Pitts. Pittsburgh
Pkwy. Parkway
Pl. Place
P.&L.E.R.R. Pittsburgh & Lake Erie Railroad
P.O. Post Office
PO Box Post Office Box
polit. political
poly. polytechnic, polytechnical
PQ Province of Quebec
P.R., PR Puerto Rico
prep. preparatory
pres. president
Presbyn. Presbyterian
presdl. presidential
prin. principal
proc. proceedings
prod. produced (play production)
prodn. production
prof. professor
profl. professional
prog. progressive
propr. proprietor
pros. atty. prosecuting attorney
pro tem pro tempore
PSRO Professional Services Review Organization
psychiat. psychiatric
psychol. psychological
PTA Parent-Teachers Association
ptnr. partner
PTO Pacific Theatre of Operations, Parent Teacher Organization
pub. publisher, publishing, published
pub. public
publ. publication
pvt. private

quar. quarterly
q.m. quartermaster
Q.M.C. Quartermaster Corps.
Que. Quebec

radiol. radiological
RAF Royal Air Force
RCA Radio Corporation of America
RCAF Royal Canadian Air Force
RD Rural Delivery
Rd. Road
REA Rural Electrification Administration
rec. recording
ref. reformed
regt. regiment
regtl. regimental
rehab. rehabilitation
rep. representative
Rep. Republican
Res. Reserve
ret. retired
rev. review, revised
RFC Reconstruction Finance Corporation
RFD Rural Free Delivery
rhinol. rhinological
R.I., RI Rhode Island
R.N. Registered Nurse
roentgenol. roentgenological
ROTC Reserve Officers Training Corps
R.R. Railroad
Ry. Railway

s. son
S. South
SAC Strategic Air Command
SALT Strategic Arms Limitation Talks
S.Am. South America
san. sanitary
SAR Sons of the American Revolution
Sask. Saskatchewan
savs. savings
S.B. Bachelor of Science
SBA Small Business Administration
S.C., SC South Carolina
SCAP Supreme Command Allies Pacific
Sc.B. Bachelor of Science
S.C.D. Doctor of Commercial Science
Sc.D. Doctor of Science
sch. school
sci. science, scientific
SCLC Southern Christian Leadership Conference
SCV Sons of Confederate Veterans
S.D., SD South Dakota
SE Southeast
SEATO Southeast Asia Treaty Organization
sec. secretary
SEC Securities and Exchange Commission
sect. section
seismol. seismological
sem. seminary
s.g. senior grade
sgt. sergeant
SHAEF Supreme Headquarters Allied Expeditionary Forces
SHAPE Supreme Headquarters Allied Powers in Europe
S.I. Staten Island
S.J. Society of Jesus (Jesuit)
S.J.D. Scientiae Juridicae Doctor
SK Saskatchewan
S.M. Master of Science
So. Southern
soc. society
sociol. sociological
S.P. Co. Southern Pacific Company
spl. special
splty. specialty
Sq. Square
sr. senior
S.R. Sons of the Revolution

SS Steamship
SSS Selective Service System
St. Saint, Street
sta. station
stats. statistics
statis. statistical
S.T.B. Bachelor of Sacred Theology
stblzn. stabilization
S.T.D. Doctor of Sacred Theology
subs. subsidiary
SUNY State University of New York
supr. supervisor
supt. superintendent
surg. surgical
SW Southwest

TAPPI Technical Association of Pulp and Paper Industry
Tb Tuberculosis
tchr. teacher
tech. technical, technology
technol. technological
Tel.&Tel. Telephone & Telegraph
temp. temporary
Tenn. Tennessee
Ter. Territory
Terr. Terrace
Tex. Texas
Th.D. Doctor of Theology
theol. theological
Th.M. Master of Theology
TN Tennessee
tng. training
topog. topographical
trans. transaction, transferred
transl. translation, translated
transp. transportation
treas. treasurer
TV television
TVA Tennessee Valley Authority
twp. township
TX Texas
typog. typographical

U. University
UAW United Auto Workers
UCLA University of California at Los Angeles
UDC United Daughters of the Confederacy
U.K. United Kingdom
UN United Nations
UNESCO United Nations Educational, Scientific and Cultural Organization
UNICEF United Nations International Children's Emergency Fund
univ. university
UNRRA United Nations Relief and Rehabilitation Administration
UPI United Press International
U.P.R.R. United Pacific Railroad
urol. urological
U.S. United States
U.S.A. United States of America
USAAF United States Army Air Force
USAF United States Air Force
USAFR United States Air Force Reserve
USAR United States Army Reserve
USCG United States Coast Guard
USCGR United States Coast Guard Reserve
USES United States Employment Service
USIA United States Information Agency
USMC United States Marine Corps
USMCR United States Marine Corps Reserve
USN United States Navy
USNG United States National Guard
USNR United States Naval Reserve
USO United Service Organizations
USPHS United States Public Health Service
USS United States Ship
USSR Union of the Soviet Socialist Republics
USV United States Volunteers
UT Utah

VA Veterans' Administration
Va., VA Virginia
vet. veteran, veterinary
VFW Veterans of Foreign Wars
V.I., VI Virgin Islands
vice pres. vice president
vis. visiting
VISTA Volunteers in Service to America
VITA Volunteers in Technical Service
vocat. vocational
vol. volunteer, volume
v.p. vice president
vs. versus
Vt., VT Vermont

W. West
WA Washington (state)
WAC Women's Army Corps
Wash. Washington (state)
WAVES Women's Reserve, U.S. Naval Reserve
WCTU Women's Christian Temperance Union
we. Western (use for court system only)
W. Ger. Germany, Federal Republic of
WHO World Health Organization
WI, Wis. Wisconsin
W.I. West Indies
WSB Wage Stabilization Board
WV West Virginia
W.Va. West Virginia
WY Wyoming
Wyo. Wyoming

YK Yukon Territory (for address)
YMCA Young Men's Christian Association
YMHA Young Men's Hebrew Association
YM & YWHA Young Men's and Young Women's Hebrew Association
Y.T. Yukon Territory
YWCA Young Women's Christian Association
yr. year

zool. zoological

Alphabetical Practices

Names are arranged alphabetically according to the surnames, and under identical surnames according to the first given name. If both surname and first given name are identical, names are arranged alphabetically according to the second given name. Where full names are identical, they are arranged in order of age—with the elder listed first.

Surnames, beginning with De, Des, Du, however capitalized or spaced, are recorded with the prefix preceding the surname and arranged alphabetically, under the letter D.

Surnames beginning with Mac and Mc are arranged alphabetically under M.

Surnames beginning with Saint or St. appear after names that begin Sains, and are arranged according to the second part of the name, e.g. St. Clair before Saint Dennis.

Surnames beginning with Van, Von or von are arranged alphabetically under letter V.

Compound hyphenated surnames are arranged according to the first member of the compound. Compound unhyphenated surnames are treated as hyphenated names.

Parentheses used in connection with a name indicate which part of the full name is usually deleted in common usage. Hence Abbott, W(illiam) Lewis indicates that the usual form of the given name is W. Lewis. In such a case, the parentheses are ignored in alphabetizing. However if the name is recorded Abbott, (William) Lewis, signifying that the entire name William is not commonly used, the alphabetizing would be arranged as though the name were Abbott, Lewis.

Who'sWho in the West

AADAHL, JORG, management consultant; b. Trondheim, Norway, June 16, 1937; came to U.S., 1966; s. Ottar P. and Gurli (Lockra) A.; M.Sc.M.E., Tech. U. Norway, 1961; M.B.A., U. San Francisco, 1973; m. Inger R. Holst, July 13, 1973; children—Erik, Nina. Research fellow Tech. U. Norway, Trondheim, 1961-62; mgr. arc welding devel. NAG, Oslo, 1964-66; mfg. engr. Varian Assos., Palo Alto, Calif., 1966-67; bus. mgr. United Airlines, San Francisco, 1974-75, sr. systems analyst, 1977-81; strategic planning specialist Magnex Corp., San Jose, 1981-82; owner, pres. Internat. Contacts & Cons., San Mateo, Calif., 1976—. Recipient Certificate of Honor, San Francisco Bd. Suprs., 1973. Mem. Am. Inst. Indsl. Engrs. (sr.), Leif Erikson League (pres. 1973), Assn. M.B.A. Execs., Norwegian Soc. Profl. Engrs. Club: Young Scandinavians (v.p. 1971). Author: Strength Analysis, Welded Structures, 1967, 81; contbr. articles in various fields to profl. jours.; editor Nordic Highlights, 1972. Home and Office: 1707 Monticello Rd San Mateo CA 94402

AADLAND, DONALD INGVALD, engr.; b. Britton, S.D., Apr. 20, 1936; s. Ingvald Martin and Mabel Laverne (Hickok) A.; B.S. in Engring. Physics, S.D. State U., 1959; m. Georgia Doris Miller, Jan. 1957; children—Elizabeth, Donald, Kirsten, Danon, Darren. Electronic engr., govt. electronics div. Motorola, Inc., Scottsdale, Ariz., 1962-66, project mgr., 1966-69, sect. mgr. semicondr. div., 1970; prin. Donald I. Aadland Engrs., Scottsdale, 1971—; instr. math. Allen Hancock Jr. Coll., 1960-62. Served as lt. USAF, 1959-62. Mem. Am. Soc. Heating, Refrigerating and Air Conditioning Engrs., ASME, Am. Inst. Aeros. and Astronautics. Designer solar air conditioning systems and equipment, exptl. energy generation devices, ultrasonic systems and transducers, biomass powered elec. generation systems. Home: 8420 E Crestwood Way Scottsdale AZ 85253 Office: PO Box 340 Scottsdale AZ 85252

AADLAND, RICHARD ORVILLE, vocational educator; b. Pierpont, S.D., Jan. 9, 1933; s. Orville and Gertrude W. (Deeks) A.; B.S., No. State Coll., S.D., 1958; M.B.A., U. Hawaii, 1968. Instr., Mount Vernon (S.D.) High Sch., 1958-60, Wayne (Nebr.) city schs., 1960-61, Cannon's Internat. Bus. Coll., Honolulu, 1962-63, St. Louis High Sch., Honolulu, 1963-68, chmn. dept. bus., 1963-68; instr. Leeward Community Coll., Pearl City, Hawaii, 1968—, chmn. bus. edn. div., 1968-70, 80—, acting assoc. dean spl. programs and community services, 1976, program dir. Coll. Theater, 1980—. Mem. Hawaii State Commn. on Manpower and Full Employment, 1977—, chmn., 1983-84; mem. Hawaii State Adv. Com. on Vocat. Edn., 1977—, chmn., 1983-84; patron Hawaii Ballet Theatre for Youth. Served with U.S. Army, 1953-55. Mem. Nat. Bus. Edn. Assn., Western Bus. Edn. Assn., Am. Vocat. Assn. (Hawaii del. 1971), Hawaii Bus. Edn. Assn. (treas. 1979-81, pres. 1983-84), Am. Acctg. Assn., Hawaii Practical Arts and Vocat. Assn. (treas. 1965—), Classroom Educators in Bus. and Office Edn., Hawaii State Theater Council, Beta Gamma Sigma, Alpha Psi Omega, Pi Omega Pi. Home: 1692 Komo Mai Dr Pearl City HI 96782 Office: 96-045 Ala Ike Pearl City HI 96782

AAKER, DAVID A., marketing executive, educator; B.S. in Mgmt., MIT, 1960; M.S. in Ops. Research, Stanford U., 1967, Ph.D. in Bus. Adminstrn., 1969. Cost engr., sales engr., product sales mgr. Tex. Instruments, Inc., Houston, 1960-65; asst. prof. sch. bus. adminstrn. U. Calif.-Berkeley, 1968-72, assoc. prof., 1972-76, prof., 1976-81, J. Gary Shansby prof. mktg. strategy, 1981—; chmn. Mktg. and Internat. Bus. Group, 1982—; vis. speaker, Tokyo and Osaka, 1975, 77, 79, 83, Hakone, Japan, 1979. Mktg. Sci. Inst. grantee, 1980; Ford Found. fellow, 1967-68. Mem. Am. Mktg. Assn., Assn. Consumer Research, Inst. Mgmt. Scis. Author: Developing Business Strategies; editor: (with George S. Day) Consumerism: Search for the Consumer Interest, 4th edit., 1982; (with John G. Myers) Advertising Management: An Analytical Approach, 2d edit., 1982; (with George S. Day) Marketing Research, 2d edit., 1983; editor: Readings in Advertising Management, 1975; Multivariate Analysis in Marketing: Theory and Applications, 1981; co-author: Modern Marketing, 1980; editor Jour. Mktg., 1981—; editorial bd. Current Issues and Research in Advt., 1979—, Pub. Policy Issues in Mktg., 1980—, Mktg. Sci., 1980—, Jour. Advt. Research, 1981—; contbr. articles to profl. jours. Home: 18 Eastwood Dr Orinda CA 94563 Office: Sch Bus Adminstrn U Calif Berkeley CA 94720

AAMOTH, GERALD (JERRY) RODERICK, mech. and design engr.; b. Bismarck, N.D., Nov. 8, 1935; s. Milton R. and Alma B. (Sayler) A.; grad. Stockton Jr. Coll., 1953; student Stockton Coll., 1953-55, DeVry Tech. Inst., 1965; cert. West Valley Jr. Coll., 1964; m. Wanda Jean Chandler, July 10, 1957; children—Gregory Roderick, Norman Tracy, Eric Jeffery, Jason Edward. Engr. drafting specialist Lockheed Missile & Space Co., Sunnyvale, Calif., 1960-63, 65-67; chief draftsman, asso. engr. Electronics Assos., Inc., Palo Alto, Calif., 1967-69; account exec. Mgmt. Recruiters, San Jose, Calif., 1969-70; sr. designer Kaiser Aerospace & Electronics, Palo Alto, 1970-71, Video Logic Corp., Sunnyvale, 1973-74; sr. elec. designer Omron Systems, Sunnyvale, 1971-73; sr. mech. design engr. Novus div. Nat. Semiconductor, Sunnyvale, 1974-76, Atari Inc., Sunnyvale, 1976-79; pres. Outhouse Enterprises, Fremont, Calif., 1970—; dir. mech. design, sr. partner Design Four, Inc., Campbell, Calif., 1980-81; sr. mech. engr. corp. staff USI: Internat., Brisbane, Calif., 1983—. Head coach Fremont Football League, also bd. dirs., div. coordinator, coaches selection com.; trainer Woodbadge and Acorn, Boy Scouts Am., past mem. youth and adult leadership corps; mem. adv. panel Congressman McAlister. Mem. Am. Soc. Metals, Soc. Plastic Engrs., Soc. Mfg. Engrs., Am. Radio Council, Profl. and Tech. Cons. Assn., C. of C. Democrat. Patentee electromech. mechanisms. Home and Office: 47625 Wabana Common Fremont CA 94539

AANDRES, VIOLET SCHROCK, artist; b. Vancouver, Wash., July 14, 1943; d. Liscomb Edward and Helen Arlene (Swanson) Schrock; B.A. in Anthropology, Wash. State U., 1968. Counselor, Napoleon Hill Found., Boulder, Colo.; social worker Del. Home and Hosp., Smyrna, 1968-69; guest artist West Colo. Center for Arts, Grand Junction, 1977; dir. Draw '82, nat. juried show; art workshop coordinator Master Artists in Colo.; exhibited in one-woman shows of watercolors at Boulder Art Center, 1974, Club Santiago, Manzanillo, Mex., 1977, West Colo. Center for Arts, 1977, Tamarron, Durango, Colo., 1977, Blue Door Gallery, Taos (N.Mex.) Inn., 1977, Woman's Bank, Denver, 1981, Denver Nat. Bank, 1982, others; group shows include Boulder Public Library, 1976, U. Okla. Internat. Tng. Center, Colima, Mex., 1974, 75, 76, Albatross Gallery, Boulder, 1975-77, Red Rocks Campus-Community Coll. Denver, 1977, Arvada (Colo.) Center for Arts, 1977, Wonderland Hill Center, 1979, 80, Highland Bldg., Boulder, 1980; represented in permanent collections U. Okla. Internat. Tng. Center, Wonderland Hill, Boulder, State of Colo., Green peace Maui-Labaina, Chautauqua Collection. Bd. dirs. Boulder Art Center. Recipient Gold Seal award Craig Spring Art Gala, 1975, 77, Mem. Am. Watercolor Soc. (asso.), Boulder Art Assn. (pres., Juror's award, ann. show 1980). Address: PO Box 365 Nederland CO 80466

AARON, BURL DAVID, supply officer; b. Temple, Tex., Sept. 14, 1943; s. Urbane and Willie Mae (Linkous) A.; m. Angelina Evelina Silva de Neives, Mar. 14, 1968; m. 2d, Jeri Lynn Honeycutt, Feb. 18, 1971; children—Whitney Paige, Matthew Wheeler. Student Temple Jr. Coll., 1968-69; B.B.A., Campbell Coll., 1973. Bus. analyst Dun & Bradstreet, Inc., Raleigh, N.C., 1969-71, Norwich Mills, Inc., Clayton, N.C., 1974; with VA, Asheville, N.C., 1974-75, Tuskegee, Ala., 1975-77, Marion, Ill., 1977-78, Bedford, Mass., 1978-79, Fort Lyon, Colo., 1979—. Served with USN, 1964-68. Mem. Jaycees. Methodist. Club: Lions. Home: 353 F St PO Box 6 Fort Lyon CO 81038 Office: VA Med Center Fort Lyon CO 81038

AARON, ROY HENRY, lawyer, motion picture theatre company executive; b. Los Angeles, Apr. 8, 1929; s. Samuel Arthur and Natalie (Krakauer) A.; m. Theresa Gesas, Dec. 20, 1953; 1 dau., Jill T. B.A., U. Calif.-Berkeley, 1951; LL.B., U. So. Calif., 1956. Bar: Calif. 1957. Mem. firm Pacht, Ross, Warne, Bernhard & Sears, Inc., Los Angeles, 1957-79, of counsel, 1979—; sr. v.p., gen. counsel Plitt Theatres, Inc. and Plitt Theatre Holdings, Inc., Los Angeles, 1978-80, pres., chief operating officer, 1980—, also dir.; lectr. Calif. Continuing Edn. of Bar; lectr. continuing legal edn. Loyola U. Law Sch., Los Angeles. Trustee, mem. exec. com. Vista Del Mar Child-Care Service, 1968-80, Reiss-Davis Child Study Center, 1977-80; bd. dirs. Jewish Fedn. Council Greater Los Angeles, 1970-75; vice chmn. lawyers div. United Crusade Campaigns, 1971, 72. Served with USAF, 1951-53. Fellow Am. Bar Found.; mem. ABA, State Bar Calif., Los Angeles County Bar Assn. (trustee 1977—, v.p. 1979-80, pres. 1981-82), Beverly Hills Bar Assn., Women Lawyers Los Angeles, U. So. Calif. Law Alumni Assn., Legion Lex, U. Calif. Alumni Assn., Found. Motion Picture Pioneers, Order of Coif. Mem. editorial bd. U. So. Calif. Law Rev., 1954-56. Office: 1925 Century Park E Suite 300 Los Angeles CA 90067

AASHEIM, STEPHEN EDWARD, consulting engineering firm executive; b. Kirkland, Wash., Feb. 21, 1946; s. Helmer T. and Gladys H. (Ona) A.; m. Carol Anne Honenberger, Sept. 5, 1968; children—Bryan L., Kari L. B.S.C.E., Wash. State U.; M.S., Stanford U., 1972. Registered profl. engr., Oreg., Idaho, Colo. Project engr. Enjay Chem. Co., Baytown, Tex., 1968-71; project engr. CH2M Hill, Corvallis, Oreg., 1972-76, div. mgr., Boise, Idaho, 1976-81, water, wastewater div. mgr., Denver, 1981—. Named Young Engr. of Yr., Idaho Soc. Profl. Engrs., 1981. Mem. Am. Water Works Assn., Nat. Soc. Profl. Engrs., Water Pollution Control Fedn. Republican. Lutheran. Club: Metropolitan. Office: CH2M Hill PO Box 22508 Denver CO 80222

ABARBANEL, GAIL, social service administrator, educator; b. Los Angeles, Apr. 17, 1944; d. Sam and Sylvia (Cramer) Pbarbanel; m. Stephen P. Klein, Jan. 31, 1975. B.A. magna cum laude, UCLA, 1966; M.S.W., U. So. Calif., 1968. Lic. clin. social worker. Clin. social worker Mental Health Agy., Los Angeles, 1968-74; founder, dir. Rape Treatment Center and Dept. Social Services Santa Monica (Calif.) Hosp. Med. Center, Los Angeles, 1974—; cons., educator in field. Bd. dirs. Clare Found., 1975-77; active Am. Cancer Soc., 1975-79; Child Trauma Council, 1978-81; Sr. Health Center, 1981-82. Recipient Woman of Year Leadership award YWCA, 1980, 82; Status of Women award AAUW, 1978; Nat. Outstanding Achievement award Am. Cancer Soc., 1977; named Outstanding Alumni U. So. Calif., 1979. Fellow Soc. for Clin. Social Work; mem. Nat. Assn. Social Workers (agy. of year award 1977), Nat. Orgn. for Victim Assistance, Women in Health, Phi Beta Kappa, Pi Gamma Mu. Contbr. articles on rape treatment, crime prevention, edn. of health profls. to profl. jours.; author successful legislation to change rape laws. Office: 1225 15th St Santa Monica CA 90404

ABARBANELL, GAYOLA HAVENS, financial advisor, consultant; b. Chgo., Oct. 21, 1939; d. Leonard M. and Lillian L. (Leviten) Havens; m. Burton Abarbanell, June 1, 1967 (div. 1972); children—Jeffrey and Dena Reddick. Student, UCLA, 1975, San Joaquin Coll. Law, 1976-77. Lic. real estate broker, Calif.; lic. life ins. broker, Calif., Wash., Nev., N.Y., Ill. Postal clk., Van Nuys, Calif., 1966-69; regional mgr. Niagara Cyclo Massage, Fresno, Calif., 1969-72; owner, mgr. AD Enterprises, Fresno, 1972-73; agt., Field supr. Equitable of Iowa, Fresno, 1973-74; rep. Ciba Pharms., Fresno, 1976-76; owner, operator Creativity Unltd., Fresno, 1975-76; fin. Advisor Univ. Securities Corp., Los Angeles, 1976—; lectr. seminars for civic orgns. Past nat. CR coordinator NOW. Recipient award Women in Ins., 1972; Top Producer award Univ. Club-Univ. Securities, 1980, 81, 82, No. 1 Producer, 1982, 83. Mem. Bus. and Profl. Assn. Los Angeles, Central Calif., Bus. and Profl. Assn., ACLU, So. Calif. Women for Understanding, Gay Acad. Union, Nat. Gay Task Force. Democrat. Jewish. Co-author: Guidelines to Feminist Consciousness Raising, 1975. Home and Office: 1181 Hi Point St Los Angeles CA 90035

ABBA, MARTINA, social worker; b. Spokane, July 3, 1943; d. Louis M. and Mary M. (Schumacher) A.; registered technician St. Joseph's Sch. of X-Ray Tech., 1965; B.S. magna cum laude in Social Work, Carroll Coll., Helena, Mont., 1975; M.S. summa cum laude in Social Work, Eastern Wash. U., 1981. Joined Dominican Sisters, Roman Cath. Ch., 1961; x-ray technician Mt. Carmel Hosp., Colville, Wash., 1965-70, head dept., 1965-70; dept. head pastoral care Holy Family Hosp., Spokane, 1975-76; social worker Sts. of Spokane, 1976—; pastoral minister 2 rural chs., Spokane Diocese; cons. and lectr. in field. Bd. dirs. E. Wash. Epilepsy Soc., 1975-80, Child Abuse, Spokane, 1977-79. Recipient Acad. and Community Service award Eastern Wash. U., 1981. Mem. Nat. Assn. Social Workers, Wash. Assn. Social Workers, Nat. Assn. Radiol. Technicians, Wash. Assn. Hosp. Trustees. Democrat. Home: Box 760 Kettle Falls WA 99141

ABBOTT, ELLEN MARGARET, nurse, educator; b. Howard, S.D., Oct. 8, 1920; d. Albert Herman and Stanley Elizabeth (Ziegler) Groth; m. G. Sawyer Abbott, Aug. 13, 1941 (dec.); children—Caroline M., Catherine E. R.N., Bishop Clarkson Hosp. Sch. of Nursing, 1941; B.S.N., U. Nebr., 1947; B.A., San Diego State U., 1957, M.A., 1964. Staff nurse, then head nurse pediatrics Bishop Clarkson Hosp., Omaha, 1943-46; nurse pub. schs., Omaha, 1946-47; office nurse, San Diego, 1947-54; instr. nurse aide edn. program, Grossmont Union High Sch. Dist., La Mesa, Calif., 1955-57, instr. vocat. nursing program, 1957-60, dir. health occupations edn., vocat. nursing edn. program, 1960—. Pres., Lung Assn. of San Diego and Imperial Counties, 1973-74, bd. of dirs. 1969-75, chmn. rev. com., 1973-74; mem. vocat. edn. steering com. Project Focus, Calif. Dept. of Edn., 1975-79; mem. state allied health com. Comprehensive Health Planning, 1973-75, chmn. nursing edn. com., 1975-76, mem. nursing edn. articulation com., 1973-80. Recipient Appreciation award, Calif. Dept. Edn., 1978; Health Service Award, Health Systems Agy. of San Diego and Imperial Counties, 1980; hon. life membership, Northmont Elem. Sch. PTA, 1957; named Vol. of Year, Lung Assn. of San Diego and Imperial Counties, 1975. Mem. Am. Vocat. Assn. (life mem., program chmn. post-secondary edn. dept. 1972-73, chmn. 1973-74; charter mem. policy and planning com. for health occupations div., 1966-74, program co-chmn. nat. conv. 1975-79, outstanding service award 1979), Calif. Dirs. Vocat. Edn. (program co-chmn. conv. 1975), Calif. Vocat. Assn. (woman of yr. 1973), Assn. Calif. Sch. Adminstrs., Heartland Sch. Adminstrs., Grossmont Adminstrs. Assn., Nat. Council of Adminstrv. Women in Edn., San Diego Council of Adminstrv. Women in Edn., Calif. Assn. of Vocat. Edn. (state treas. 1980-83), Calif. Assn. Health Careers Educators (hon. life), Calif. Vocat. Nurse Educators, San Diego County Adult Adminstrs. Assn., Calif. League for Nursing, Soroptimist Internat. (woman of accomplishment 1979). Contbr. numerous articles to profl. jours. Office: Grossmont Health Careers Ctr 5345 Timken St La Mesa CA 92041

ABBOTT, ISABELLA AIONA, biologist; b. Hana, Maui, Hawaii, June 20, 1919; d. Loo Yuen and Annie Patseu (Chung) Aiona; A.B., U. Hawaii, 1941; M.S., U. Mich., 1942; Ph.D., U. Calif., Berkeley, 1950; m. Donald P. Abbott, Mar. 3, 1943; 1 dau., Ann Kaiue Abbott Conner. Prof. biology Stanford U., 1972-82; G.P. Wilder prof. botany U. Hawaii, 1978—; vis. research biologist and tchr., Japan and Chile. Co-recipient N.Y. Bot. Garden award for best book in botany, 1978. Mem. Internat. Phycological Soc. (treas. 1964-68), Western Soc. Naturalists (sec. 1962-64, pres. 1977), Phycological Soc. Am., Brit. Phycological Soc., Hawaiian Bot. Soc. Author: (with G.J. Hollenberg) Marine Algae of California, 1976; contbr. articles to profl. jours. biologist; b. Hana, Maui, Hawaii, June 20, 1919; d. Loo Yuen and Annie Patseu (Chung) Aiona; A.B., U. Hawaii, 1941; M.S., U. Mich., 1942; Ph.D., U. Calif., Berkeley, 1950; m. Donald P. Abbott, Mar. 3, 1943; 1 dau., Ann Kaiue Abbott Conner. Prof. biology Stanford U., 1972-82; G.P. Wilder prof. botany U. Hawaii, 1978—; vis. research biologist and tchr., Japan and Chile. Co-recipient N.Y. Bot. Garden award for best book in botany, 1978. Mem. Internat. Phycological Soc. (treas. 1964-68), Western Soc. Naturalists (sec. 1962-64, pres. 1977), Phycological Soc. Am., Brit. Phycological Soc., Hawaiian Bot. Soc. Author: (with G.J. Hollenberg) Marine Algae of California, 1976; contbr. articles to profl. jours. Office: Dept Botany U Hawaii Honolulu HI 96822

ABBOTT, JOHN PAUL, pvt. investigation and security co. exec.; b. San Diego, June 1, 1952; s. Cecil John and Fonda Catherine A.; A.A., Grossmont Coll., San Diego, 1976; m. Elizabeth Anne Pecsi, Oct. 29, 1979. Asso. Red Carpet Realtors, San Diego, ops. supr. Baker Industries, San Diego, 1974-77; area dir. mgr. Burns Internat. Security, Los Angeles, 1977-79; ops. mgr. Blake, Moffitt Towne, San Diego, 1979-80; corp. dir. mktg. Woodson Enterprise, San Diego, 1980-82; gen. mgr. Pedus Security Services, Inc., San Diego, 1982—; cons. Bd. dirs. First Luth. Ch., El Cajon, Calif., 1974-75. Served with USAF, 1970-71. Mem. Nat. Assn. Credit Mgmt., San Diego Wholesale Credit Assn., No. Calif. Audio Soc., Sherlock Holmes Soc. Club: So. Calif. Chess Players. Home: 6741 Rolando Knolls Dr La Mesa CA 92041 Office: 3443 Caminodel Rio S #319 San Diego CA 92108

ABBOTT, JOHN RODGER, elec. engr.; b. Los Angeles, Aug. 2, 1933; s. Carl Raymond and Helen Catherine (Roche) A.; B.S. with honors, UCLA, 1955; M.S., U. So. Calif., 1957; m. Theresa Andrea McQuaide, Apr. 20, 1968. Advanced study engr. Lockheed Missile Systems, Los Angeles, 1955-56; radar systems engr. Hughes Aircraft Co., Los Angeles, 1956-59; devel. engr. Garrett Airesearch Co., Los Angeles, 1959-63, instr. plant tng. program, 1962-63; asst. project engr. Litton Industries, Los Angeles, 1963; space power systems engr. TRW Systems, Los Angeles, 1963-65; engr. specialist Los Angeles Dept. Water and Power, 1965—; frequency coordination chmn. Region X, Utilities Telecommunications Council, 1977-79, sec.-treas. Utilities Telecommunication Council, 1979-80; instr. electronics course Los Angeles City Schs., 1965-66, Birmingham High Sch., Van Nuys, Calif. Registered profl. engr., Calif. Mem. IEEE, Am. Radio Relay League (Pub. Service award 1971), Tau Beta Pi. Contbr. articles to profl. jours. Office: PO Box 66 Newhall CA 91322

ABBOTT, L. K., broadcasting exec.; b. Mesquite, Nev., Apr. 28, 1920, s. Myron D. and Martha Ann (Burgess) A.; m. Mary M. Cottam, Sept. 25, 1940; children—Kathy Lynn, Gregory L. Student, Dixie Jr. Coll., broadcasting mgmt. Harvard U. Office mgr. Standard Oil Co. Calif., Las Vegas; Salt Lake City; dir. Asian affairs Bonneville Internat. Corp., Salt Lake City. Pres., Utah Spl. Olympics, Salt Lake Sister Cities; v.p. Utah Cerebral Palsy; trustee Internat. Visitors. Name Vol. of Yr.; recipient Spark Plug of Yr. award; recipient 2 Humanitarian awards Readers Digest. Hon. mem. Chukyo TV staff, Nagoya, Japan, Nagano Broadcasting System, Nagano. Republican. Mormon. Various broadcasting positions including film editor, dir.; now v.p. KSL-TV. Home: 1530 Jamestown Dr Salt Lake City UT 84121 Office: Bonneville Internat Corp 130 Social Hall Ave Salt Lake City 84111

ABBOTT, ROBERT DEAN, psychologist, educator; b. Twin Falls, Idaho, Dec. 19, 1946; s. Charles Dean and Billie June (Moore) A.; m. Sylvia Patricia, Dec. 16, 1967; children—Danielle Jennifer, Matthew Jason. B.A. summa cum laude (Calif. State scholar), Calif. Western U., 1967; M.S., U. Wash., 1968, Ph.D., 1970. Asst. prof. Calif. State U., Fullerton, 1970-73, assoc. prof., 1973-75; prof. edn. measurement U. Wash., 1975—; cons. to numerous pub. schs. dists., fed. grant agys. Mem. Am. Psychol. Assn., Psychometric Soc., Am. Statis. Assn. Methodist. Club: Sandpoint Country (Seattle). Author: Elementary Multivariate Analysis: Applications of Basic Structure, 1982; research, numerous publs. in field. Office: Edn DQ-12 U Wash Seattle WA 98195

ABBOTT, RUSSELL JOSEPH, computer scientist; b. Bklyn., Mar. 1, 1942; s. Samuel and Lillian (Ginsberg) A.; B.A., Columbia U., 1962; M.A., Harvard U., 1963; Ph.D., U. So. Calif., 1973. Mem. tech. staff Gen. Electric Center Advanced Studies, Santa Barbara, Calif., 1965-67; mem. tech. staff project MAC, MIT, 1967-68; sr. mem. tech. staff Xerox Data Systems Co., El Segundo, Calif., 1968-70; prof. computer sci. Calif. State U., Northridge, 1973—; vis. prof. Far East div. IBM World Trade Corp., 1978; cons. Info. Sci. Inst., 1973-75, Aerospace Corp., 1978—. NASA summer faculty fellow, 1976, 77. Mem. Assn. Computing Machinery (chpt. chmn. 1977-78, founding chmn. spl. interest group office automation), IEEE (cert. appreciation 1976), Assn. Computational Linguistics, Topanga Center Human Devel. (past sec.-treas., encounter group leader), Los Angeles World Affairs Council, Mensa. Author, editor in field. Home: 19832 Labrador St Chatsworth CA 91311 Office: Dept Computer Sci Calif State Univ Northridge CA 91330

ABBOTT, STANLEY EUGENE, editor, newspaper exec.; b. Hutchinson, Kans., July 22, 1942; s. Harold Seth and Dorothy Elizabeth (Dicus) A.; B.A., Calif. State U., Los Angeles, 1965; m. Trudie Thomas, Apr. 13, 1962 (div. 1972); m. 2d, Jeanne O'dell, Mar. 16, 1975; children—April-Ambre, Robson, Ellen. With Anchorage Daily News, 1965-82, reporter, 1965-66, sports editor, 1966, Sunday editor, 1967, mng. editor, 1968-71, exec. editor, 1971-82; with Columbia Missourian, 1982—; instr., city editor U. Mo. Sch. Journalism. Served with Alaska Air N.G., 1967-72. Club: Alaska Press (pres.). Home: 1417 F St Anchorage AK 99501 Office: Pouch 6616 Anchorage AK 99502

ABBOTT, STEPHEN JEROME, educator; b. Sheridan, Wyo., Feb. 28, 1928; s. Robert Franklin and Lily Margaret (Johnson) Darke; B.A with honors, U. Wyo., 1955; M.A., San Diego State U., 1964; postgrad. (teaching fellow 1969-74), U. Oreg., 1969-78; m. Jo Ann Sprinkle, Sept. 4, 1954; children—Stephen Paul, Jere Ann, Mark Jerome, Jo Alene. Tchr., Laramie (Wyo.) City Schs., 1955-58, Sweetwater Union High Sch. Dist., Chula Vista, Calif., 1959-69; faculty Southwestern Community Coll., Chula Vista, 1968; reading instr., supr. student teaching U. Oreg., Eugene, 1969-74; instr. reading Lane Community Coll., Eugene, 1969-75; elem. reading specialist Eugene (Oreg.) Pub. Schs., Dist. 4J, 1975-81, Edgewood Elem. Sch., 1975-83, Harris Elem. Sch., 1982—; faculty edn./reading and supr. student tchrs. U. Oreg. Coop. Program, 1978—. Precinct worker Democratic Party, 1977-78, 79-80, participant Weaver re-election campaign, 1978, 80. Served with USN, 1945-49, USNR, 1950-52. Mem. NEA, Oreg. Edn. Assn., Eugene Edn. Assn., Internat. Reading Assn., Oreg. Reading Assn., Emerald Empire Council of Internat. Reading Assn. (pres. 1980-81, Ruth Gould award 1982), Assn. Children with Learning Disabilities, Assn. Supervision and Curriculum Devel., Am. Ednl. Research Assn., Phi Delta Kappa, Christian Educators Assn. Am., Navy League. Home: 30701 Koinonia Rd Eugene OR 97405 Office: 1150 E 29th Ave Eugene OR 97405

ABBOTT, WILTON ROBERT, aerospace engr.; b. Campbell, Calif., Jan. 19, 1916; s. Ernest A. and Audrey (Keesling) A.; student San Jose State Coll., 1933-35; B.S., U. Calif., Berkeley, 1937; postgrad. Stanford U., 1937-38; M.S., Iowa State U., 1942, Ph.D., 1945; m. Pearl Honeychurch, Sept. 2, 1938; children—Wilton R., Mary Louise, Mark R. Asst., Stanford U., 1937-38; engr. Remler Co., Ltd., San Francisco, 1938-39, Gen. Elec. Co., 1939-40; asst. prof. to assoc. prof. Iowa State U., Ames, 1940-46; asst. prof. U. Calif., Berkeley, 1946-51; research specialist N. Am. Aviation, Downey, Calif., 1951-57; sr. cons. engr. Lockheed Missiles & Space Co., Sunnyvale, Calif., 1957—, chief devel. engr. Agena spacecraft; program chmn. Reliability and Maintainability Symposium, 1970. Trustee, Linfield Coll., 1977—, chmn. vis. com. natural scis., 1980—. Recipient cert. of excellence Gemini Agena Target Vehicle Program, 1966. Mem. IEEE (life sr.), Reliability Soc., Systems, Man and Cybernetics Soc. (sr.), Sigma Xi, Eta Kappa Nu, Tau Beta Pi. Baptist. Club: Masons. Contbr. articles to profl. jours.; patentee in field. Office: B538 D 6223 PO Box 504 Sunnyvale CA 94086

ABBOUD, A. ROBERT, oil company executive; b. Boston, May 29, 1929; s. Alfred and Victoria (Karam) A.; B.S. cum laude, Harvard U., 1951, LL.B., 1956, M.B.A., 1958; m. Joan Grover, June 11, 1955; children—Robert, Jeanne Frances, Katherine Jane. Asst. cashier First Nat. Bank of Chgo., 1960-62, asst. v.p., 1962-64, v.p., 1964-69, sr. v.p., 1969-72, exec. v.p., 1972-73, vice chmn. bd., 1973-74, dep. chmn. bd., 1974-75, chmn. bd., 1975-80; pres., chief operating officer Occidental Petroleum Corp., Los Angeles, 1980—; dir. Hart Schaffner & Marx, Inland Steel Co. Served with USMCR, 1951-53. Clubs: Econ., Chicago, Comml.; Barrington Hills Country. Office: Occidental Petroleum Corp 10889 Wilshire Blvd Los Angeles CA 90024

ABDELNOUR, CHARLES GABRIEL, city official; b. Calif., Feb. 12, 1938; s. Gabriel George and Mary Nicola (Shalhoob) A.; 1 son, Nicholas. B.A., San Diego State Coll., 1960; postgrad. U. So. Calif., 1960-63, Calif. Western U. Law Sch., 1963-65; J.D., Western State U., 1974. Cert. mcpl. clk. Project control adminstr. Hughes Aircraft Co., 1966-67; law clk., field rep. Legal Aid Soc. San Diego, Inc., 1967-68; account exec. First Calif. Co., 1969-70; adminstr. Catholic Community Services, Diocese of San Diego, 1970-72, dir. Legal Services Program, Padre Hidalgo Center, San Diego, 1972-74; asst. dir. community relations dept. City of San Diego, 1974-76, exec. asst. to city councilman, 1976-77, city clk., 1977—. Mem. Mayor's Election Task Force Com., San Diego County Voting Systems Task Force; exec. chmn. COMBO; bd. govs. United Cerebral Palsy Found. San Diego County; chmn. community relations adv. com. U. San Diego; v.p., bd. dirs. Legal Aid Soc. San Diego, 1972-76; mem. State Atty. Gen.'s Adv. Com.; mem. Cath. Diocese Polit. Awareness Com.; mem. Corps Execs., Sm. Bus. Adminstrn. Bd. dirs. Sr. Citizens Med. Clinic. Mem. Spanish Speaking Polit. Assn., NAACP, San Diego State Coll. Alumni Assn. (dir. 1st v.p.), San Diego Stock and Bond Club. Syrian Orthodox Antiochian. Office: 202 C St 12th Floor San Diego CA 92101

ABDUL-KARIM, KAMAL WADIH, med. instruments co. exec.; b. Aramoun, Lebanon, Mar. 11, 1940; came to U.S., 1973, naturalized, 1980; s. Wadih Yousuf and Alice Nicola (Shehadeh) Abdul-K.; B.A., Am. U. Beirut, 1962, M.A., 1972; A.M., U. Ill., 1976, Ph.D., 1980; m. Leila Amoun, Aug. 8, 1964; children—Imad, Raja. Instr., Beirut Bapt. Sch., 1962-63; instr. Arabian Am. Oil Co., Abqaiq, Saudi Arabia, 1963-69; instr. Nazarene High Sch., Beirut, 1969-71; instr. Haigazian Coll., Beirut, 1971-72; instr. Lebanese U., Beirut, 1972-73; teaching asst. U. Ill., Urbana, 1975-80; adj. faculty Pepperdine U., Malibu, Calif., 1980; mng. dir. Biomed Instruments, Inc., Fullerton, Calif., 1981—; mng. dir. Inst. Public Adminstrn., Riyad, Saudi Arabia, summer 1970; program dir. TESL, German Cultural Mission, Beirut, summer, 1971. Fellow Linguistics Soc. Am.; mem. Phi Kappa Phi. Home: 6435 Bothwell Rd Reseda CA 91335 Office: 1020 S Raymond B Fullerton CA 92631

ABEL, ALLAN BERNARD, mgmt. cons.; b. Williams, Calif., Dec. 22, 1924; s. Allen and Consuelo (Benham) A.; student U. Calif., Berkeley, 1943-50, Golden Gate Coll., 1947, Instituto Cultural Mexicano-Americano, Guadalajara, Mexico, 1961; m. Maria Socorro; children—Allan Bernard, Allen Raymond, Sonya. Practice in Reno, 1954-69, Las Vegas, 1969—; investment adviser, tax cons., rare coinbroker, 1963-67; asso., bus. cons. Bus. Consultants, Inc., bus. and mgmt. cons. in 11 Western states and Mexico, 1967—; pres. SUMCO, Inc.; officer, dir. Centro de Vivienda para Retirados, S.A., Abel de Mexico., S.A.; sec.-treas. Magic Valley Enterprises, Inc.; sec.-treas. Central Devel. Co., Las Vegas, also dir.; sec. Gastrox Constrn. Co., Las Vegas. Agt., Nev. Gaming Control Bd., Nev. Gaming Commn., 1956; dir. So. Nev. conf. Pop Warner Jr. Football, 1st v.p., 1981—; mem. nat. com. Young Democrats Clubs Am., 1955-57, bd. dirs., 1957-59; mem. exec. bd. Clark County Dem. Central Com., 1970—; mem. Nev. State Dem. State Central Com., 1970—, vice chmn., 1957-58; gen. mgr. retirement housing project, Mexico, 1965-67; pres. chpt. 15 Mother Earth News; state chmn. com. select del. Humphrey; chmn. Lucy Branch Kidney Fund; counselor Family Abuse Center; pres. Flame Soccer Club; dir. Las. Las Vegas Under 23 Select Soccer Team; Lic. pub. accountant, Nev. Mem. Nat. Soc. Pub. Accountants, U. Calif. Alumni Assn. (life), Inst. Indsl. Relations Alumni Assn., Internat. Platform Assn., Am. Numis. Assn. Democrat. Spaceite. Clubs: Calif. 23 (Berkeley); Tower and Flame, Daily Californian, Am. Soc. Jalisco. Pub.: Nev. Report. Research on problems of aged living in fgn. country, 1963-64. Home: 712 Ann Dr Las Vegas NV 89107 Office: 953 E Sahara Las Vegas NV 89104

ABEL, RICHARD WAYNE, mktg. communications cons.; b. San Luis Obispo, Calif., July 4, 1941; s. John William and Olive Mae (Bickmore) A.; B.F.A., Cornell U., 1963; M.F.A., U. Hawaii, 1966. Advt. trainee Persons Advt., N.Y.C., 1963-64; campaign dir. Am. Cancer Soc., San Francisco, 1966-67; instr. theatre Occidental Coll., Los Angeles, 1967-69; pres., owner COMM/COORD, Los Angeles, 1969-72; dir. communications TRAN Corp., El Segundo, Calif., 1972-74; communications cons., Laguna Beach, Calif., 1974—. Co-founder, sec. bd. dirs. Nautical Heritage Mus.; founder Heritage Players; capt. California, ofcl. Tallship ambassador State of Calif. Address: 1089 Miramar St Laguna Beach CA 92651

ABEL, TORY ELLEN, advertising sales executive; b. Los Angeles, Mar. 23, 1950; d. Leonard M. and Charlotte R (Helfman) Abel. B.A. in Bus. Adminstrn., Woodbury U., 1973. Sales, then property mgr., Joseph Magnin Co., Los Angeles, 1968-75; account mgr. James K. Levitt and Assocs., Los Angeles, 1975-79; mgr. W.W. Dotts, Inc., Newport Beach, Calif., 1979-82; account mgr. Archtl. Digest mag., Los Angeles, 1982—. Mem. Los Angeles Advt. Club (Toys for Tots Com.), Los Angeles Mag. Reps. (publicity coordinator). Office: Archtl Digest 5455 Wilshire Blvd Los Angeles CA 90036

ABELAR, INA MAE, equipment technician; b. Jay Em, Wyo., July 18, 1926; d. Merritt Lyle and Leeta May (Worthen) Cameron; B.A., Calif. State Poly. U., 1978; m. Michael Sandoval Abelar, Nov. 17, 1951 (div. 1966); children—Debora Jean, Michelle Elaine, Randolph Lee. Lumber estimator Keith Brown Bldg. Supply, Salem, Oreg., 1946-48; with Whiting-Mead Bldg. Supply, Vernon, Calif., 1949-51, Trojan Lumber Co., Burbank, Calif., 1952-55; bookkeeper Jerry Kalior Bookkeeping Systems, North Hollywood, Calif., 1959-66; with Calif. State Poly. U., Pomona, 1967—, supervising equip. technician II dept. physics, 1979—, mem. campus staff council, 1970—, chmn., 1977-78. Deaconess, Upland Christian Ch., 1978—. Mem. Mu Phi Epsilon. Democrat. Office: 3801 W Temple St Rm 8-238 Pomona CA 91768

ABELL, GEORGE OGDEN, astronomer, educator; b. Los Angeles, Mar. 1, 1927; s. Theodore Curtis and Annamarie (Ogden) A.; B.S., Calif. Inst. Tech., 1951, M.S., 1952, Ph.D., 1957; m. Lois Everson, June 16, 1951; children—Anthony Alan, Jonathan Edward; m. 2d, Phyllis Fox, Mar. 10, 1972. Lectr., Griffith Observatory, 1951-60; observer Nat. Geog. Soc.-Palomar Obs. Sky Survey, 1953-56; mem. faculty dept. astronomy UCLA, 1956—, prof., 1967—, chmn. dept., 1968-75; vis. prof. U. Edinburgh, 1976-77; Shapley vis. prof. Am. Astron. Soc.; guest investigator Max-Planck Instutut für Physik und Astrophysik, Munich, 1966-67; cons. in field; mem. faculty Summer Sci. Program, 1960-67, 76—; prin. investigator TV series Understanding Space and Time, 1977-80. Served with AUS, 1945-46. Mem. Internat. Astron. Union (pres. Commn. Cosmology 1979-82), Am. Astron. Soc. (past councilor), Astron. Soc. Pacific (past pres.), AAAS (councilor), Royal Astron. Soc., Com. for Sci. Investigations of Claims of Paranormal. Author: Exploration of the Universe, 4th edit., 1982; Realm of the Universe 1976, 2d edit., 1980; Drama of the Universe, 1978; mem. editorial bd. Skeptical Inquirer, Prometheus Book; contbr. articles to profl. jours. Office: Dept Astronomy UCLA Los Angeles CA 90024

ABELS, RICHARD HUGH, advertising executive; b. Pitts., Apr. 16, 1951; s. Gerald Oscar and Margery (Faigen) A. B.S. in Mktg., Pa. State U., 1973. Market research analyst Nat. Assn. Realtors, Chgo., 1974-75; advt. acct. exec. Albert J. Rosenthal & Co., Chgo., 1975-77, Tathan-Laird & Kudner, Chgo., 1977-79; account supr. Point Communications, Denver, 1979-80; dir. mktg. Telemation Prodns., Denver, 1980-82; account supr. Marsteller Inc., Denver, 1982—; pub. speaker. Mem. health and phys. edn. com., aquatics com. Jewish Community Ctr., Denver. Mem. Denver Ad Fedn., Am. Mktg. Assn. Record reviewer Pickin' mag., 1975-77. Office: 5500 S Syracuse Circle 200 Denver CO 80111

ABELS, ROBERT FREDERICK, educator; b. W. Palm Beach, Fla., Nov. 18, 1926; s. John Frederick and Nelly (Bulfin) A.; B.S., U.S. Naval Postgrad. Sch., 1965; M.B.A. in Fin., U. West Fla., 1971; m. Shirley Mae Larsen, May 31, 1953; children—Robert Frederick, Steven John, Richard Alan. Enlisted in U.S. Navy, 1944, commd. ensign, 1949, advanced through grades to comdr., 1963; aviator in Korea and Vietnam; dir. Naval Officer Candidate Sch., Pensacola, Fla., 1966-68; ret., 1969; sr. math. tchr. Skyline High Sch., Lemon Grove, Calif., 1976—; tax counselor, real estate salesman. Decorated Bronze Star, Air medal, Commendation medal; Vietnamese Cross Gallantry. Mem. Nat. Assn. Tax Consultors. Republican. Lutheran. Address: 10633 Canyon Lake Dr San Diego CA 92131

ABENDROTH, GEORGE HARRY, product safety engineer; b. Phila., Oct. 15, 1954; s. Harry William and Catherine Elizabeth (Snovel) A.; m. Susan Burrough, Sept. 23, 1978; children—Gregory, George. B.M.E., Villanova U., 1976; M.S. in Systems Mgmt., U. So. Calif., 1981; cert. Hazard Control Mgr., 1981, Product Safety Mgr., 1981. Product safety engr. FMC Corp., Colmar, Pa., 1976-79, Santa Clara, Calif., 1979—. Mem. System Safety Soc., Am. Soc. Safety Engrs., Human Factors Soc., ASME, Pi Tau Sigma. Republican. Roman Catholic. Clubs: De Laveaga GC (Santa Cruz, Calif.). Home: 440 N Winchester Blvd Apt 110 Santa Clara CA 95050 Office: FMC Corp CEL Santa Clara CA 95052

ABERCROMBIE, JOHN IVAN, power equipment manufacturing company executive; b. Seattle, Jan. 21, 1926; s. Leslie Luzon and Winnona (Allen) A.; m. Linda Ruth Thiessen, Apr. 6, 1962; 1 son, John Eric. Grad. in bus. adminstrn. Wash. State Coll., 1949. Spl. agt. Kemper Ins. Co., Seattle, 1949-55; salesman Tri-Western, Inc., Portland, Oreg., 1955-65; pres. Timberland Distbrs., Inc., Portland, 1965-76, ABCO Power Equipment Co., Portland, 1976—. Served with USMCR, 1944-46, 50-51. Mem. Power Equipment Dealers Assn. (pres. 1981-83). Republican. Roman Catholic. Home: 19166 S W Olson Ave Lake Oswego OR 97034 Office: ABCO Power Equipment Co 1212 S E Powell Blvd Portland OR 97202

ABERCROMBIE, LEE ROY, JR., financial executive; b. San Francisco, Aug. 26, 1929; s. Lee Roy and Cora May (Maaske) A.; m. Mary Katherine Kinney, Aug. 22, 1980; 1 son, John David. B.A., Stanford U., 1950, M.B.A., 1952. Asst. controller, asst. treas. FMC Corp., San Jose, Calif. and Chgo., 1954-73; treas., v.p. fin. Morrison-Knudsen Co. Inc., Boise, Idaho, 1973—; dir. First Idaho Corp. Dir., chmn. fin. com. Blue Cross Health Services Idaho; dir., pres. Boise Family YMCA; vice chmn. Idaho State Endowment Fund bd.; dir. Boise C. of C., Ada County United Way, Boise chpt. ARC and Regional Blood Ctr.; trustee Coll. Idaho. Served with USN, 1952-54. Mem. Fin. Exec. Inst., Nat. Assn. Accts. Republican. Presbyterian.

ABERCROMBIE, STANLEY ARMSTRONG, safety specialist, consultant, writer/editor; b. Brockton, Mass., Mar. 25, 1911; s. George Albert Jr. and Ethel Evernia (Armstrong) A.; m. Margaret Gardiner Smith, Aug. 24, 1935; children—David Armstrong, Betsey Barker Abercrombie Myrick. B.A., Dartmouth Coll. 1934; postgrad. Pa. State Coll., 1936; M.A., N.Y.U., 1940; postgrad. Am. U., 1946. Research asst. Bur. St. and Hwy. Traffic Research, Harvard U., 1936-37; driver clinic officer Wichita (Kans.) Police Dept., 1937-39; asst. teaching fellow Center Safety Ed., N.Y.U., 1939-40; driver ed. tchr. McKinley High Sch., Wash., 1940-42; bus. analyst automotive supply rationing div. OPA, Washington, 1942-44; with Nat. Commn. Safety Edn., NEA, Wash., 1946—, assoc. exec. sec., 1962-70; area program mgr. Office Alcohol Countermeasures, Nat. Hwy. Traffic Safety Adminstrn., U.S. Dept. Transp., Washington, 1970-72, hwy. safety mgmt. specialist, San Francisco, 1972-78, ret. 1978; sec. Nat. Inst. Traffic Tng.; research subcom. adv. council Pres. Com. Traffic Safety; mem. Accident Prevention Research Study sec. NIH, USPHS, HEW; prin. investigator Pilot Study Sch.-Age Accidents and Ed.; co-prin. Study of Sch. Bus Safety; mem. com. Standard Method Recording and Measuring Work Injury Experience; com. alt. Standard Practice Occupational and Edn. Eye and Face Protection; chmn. Com. Inspection Procedures Sch. Buses; adv. com. Sch. Bus Safety; chmn. Traffic Ed. and tng. com.; mem. Nat. Com. Uniform Traffic Laws and Ordinances; chairperson Ninth Nat. Conf. Sch. Transp. Served as lt., USNR, 1944-46. Recipient U.S. Public Health Service Research Grant, 1961. Mem. NEA, Am. Acad. Safety Ed., Transp. Research Bd., NRC, Nat. Acad. Sci., Veterans Safety, Am. Soc. Safety Engrs. Democrat. Contbr. numerous articles to profl. jours. and confs. in field. Home and Office: 100 Font Blvd 5-C San Francisco CA 94132

ABERG, SIV MARTA, actress, real estate broker, interior designer; b. Gavle, Sweden, Mar. 7, 1942; s. Ragnar Malte and Gertrud Helena (Martinelle) A.; came to U.S., 1964, naturalized, 1964; B.A., Gavle Hogre Allmana Laroverk, 1961; diploma Swedish Spl. Sch. Sci. Cosmetology, 1962. Beauty specialist, cons. Stockholm, 1962-64; Miss Sweden, 1964, runner-up to Miss Europe, 1964, runner-up to Miss Universe, 1964; performer films, TV, TV commls., 1964—; Hollywood Star of Tomorrow, 1967; interior designer Beverly Hills, Calif., 1971—. Mem. Screen Actors Guild, AFTRA, Internat. Platform Assn., Krishnamurti Found. Home: PO Box 1721 Beverly Hills CA 90213

ABERNATHY, SANDRA MARSHALL, microcomputer coordinator, educator; b. North Hollywood, Calif., Dec. 22, 1934; d. Charles Hunt and Ethel Monteith (Low) Marshall; m. George Henry Abernathy, Dec. 28, 1955; children—George Hunt, Katherine Jean, Robert Lloyd, Patricia Ann. B.S. in Biology, U. Calif.-Davis, 1957; M.A., N.Mex. State U., 1968, Ph.D. in Ednl. Adminstrn., 1982. Tchr. pub. schs., Las Cruces, N.Mex., 1967-80; research asst., U. N.Mex., Las Cruces, 1980-82; personnel researcher Forward Area Alerting Radar, Ft. Bliss, Tex., 1981-82; coordinator microcomputer inservice sequence Las Cruces Pub. Schs., 1982; instr. curriculum and instrn. dept. N.Mex. State U., Las Cruces, 1982, instr. ednl. mgmt. and devel. dept., 1983—, program coordinator, Ednl. Mgmt. and Devel. Dept. Inst., 1982—, assoc. project dir. Presch. Handicapped Personnel, Regular Adminstrn. Tng. Project, 1982—, budget Edn. Research Ctr., 1982—; cons. in program evaluation, statis. analysis, software revs. Mem. Assn. for Supervision and Curriculum Devel., Am. Ednl. Research Assn., Council for Exceptional Children, Internat. Reading Assn., Rocky Mountain Ednl. Research Assn., Alpha Delta Kappa, Phi Delta Kappa, Phi Kappa Phi. Republican. Presbyterian. Clubs: N.Mex. Profl. Engrs. Aux., Faculty Wives. Author: (with T. J. Pettibone, D. R. Byrne, D. G. Ferguson) What Selected Groups of New Mexicans Are Saying About Education, 1982; contbr. papers to profl. confs. Home: Star Route Box 30 Mesilla Park NM 88047 Office: EMD Inst Box 3N N Mex State U Las Cruces NM 88003

ABERNETHY, DAVID BEAVEN, political science educator; b. Columbia, Mo., Apr. 23, 1937; s. Bradford Sherman and Mary Jean (Beaven) A; m. Julia Bourne Griffith, June 16, 1962 (dec.); children—Bruce Davenport, Bradford Beaven; m. 2d, Susan Getman, Aug. 23, 1980. B.A. in Govt., Harvard U., 1959, Ph.D. in Govt., 1966; M.A. in Philosophy, Politics, and Econs. (E.J. Noble Leadership award), Oxford U., 1961. Asst. prof. polit. sci. Stanford (Calif.) U., 1965-70, assoc. prof., 1970-80, prof., 1980—; vis. lectr. polit. sci. Univ. Coll., Dar es Salaam, Tanzania, 1968-69; chmn. Stanford Faculty Senate, 1981-82; assoc. dean undergrad. studies, 1976-78. Active First Presbyn. Ch., Palo Alto, Calif. Recipient Chase prize for Ph.D. dissertation, Harvard U., 1965; Dean's award Stanford U., 1976-77; Fgn. Area fellow, 1963-65; Danforth Grad. fellow, 1959; Ford Found. fellow, 1972-73. Mem. African Studies Assn. (editorial bd. African Studies Rev.), Am. Polit. Sci. Assn., Phi Beta Kappa. Democrat. Author: The Political Dilemma of Popular Education: an African Case, 1969. Office: Dept Polit Sci Stanford U Stanford CA 94305

ABERNETHY, JOHN LEO, educator; b. San Jose, Calif., Mar. 6, 1915; s. Elmer Robert and Margaret May (Scott) A.; B.A., U. Calif. at Los Angeles, 1936; M.S., Northwestern U., 1938, Ph.D., 1940. Instr., U. Tex., 1940-42, asst. prof., 1942-44, asso. prof., 1944-45; fellow Northwestern U., 1946; mem. faculty Washington and Lee U., 1948-49; mem. faculty Calif. State U., 1947-59, asso. prof., 1957-59; research asso. U. Calif. at Los Angeles, 1959-69; prof. chemistry Calif. State Poly. U., Pomona, 1969—. Fulbright fellow San Marcos U., Lima, Peru, 1962-63. Adv. Intervarsity Christian Fellowship, 1956-59. Mem. Am. Chem. Soc., Am. Sci. Affiliation, Calif. Assn. Chemistry Tchrs. (editor proc. 1966—), Sigma Xi (club pres.), Alpha Chi Sigma, Phi Lambda Upsilon. Author: Principles of Organic Chemistry, 1949; editorial bd. Jour. Chem. Edn., 1956—; contbr. articles to chem. jours. Research on stereochem. control exerted by enzyme papain. Home: Chandler Terr 2555 6th St LaVerne CA 91750

ABERNETHY, RODNEY ELMER, ophthalmologist; b. Spokane, Wash., Aug. 6, 1921; s. Elmer R. and Margaret (Scott) A.; A.B., U. Calif., 1944, M.D., 1946; postgrad. Harvard U., 1948-49; m. Elizabeth Naftzger, Apr. 21, 1945; children—Robert Norton, David Scott, Pamela, Janet. Intern, Franklin Hosp., San Francisco, 1947-48; resident VA Hosp., San Francisco, 1949-51, U.S. Naval Hosp., Oakland, Calif., 1951; practice medicine specializing in ophthalmology, San Mateo, Calif., 1953—; mem. staff Mills, Peninsula, Chope Gen. hosps.; sec., mem. exec. com. Mills Meml. Hosp., 1963; clin. asst. prof. ophthalmic surgery Stanford U., 1960—. Pres., Community Council San Mateo County, 1961-62, chmn. health sect., 1956-58, v.p., 1959-61, mem. bd., 1963-65; mem. bd. San Mateo County office Bay Area Welfare Planning Assn., 1966-67; nat. trustee Amigos de las Americas, 1969-78, tng. dir. Peninsula chpt., 1969-74, med. dir. Peninsula chpt., 1974—. Served with USNR, 1944-46, lt. (j.g.) M.C., 1951-53. Diplomate Am. Bd. Ophthalomology. Fellow Am. Acad. Ophthalmology, A.C.S.; mem. San Mateo County Med. Soc. (chmn. public health com. 1965-69). Home: 305 Ascot Rd Hillsborough CA 94010 Office: 215 N San Mateo Dr San Mateo CA 94401

ABKEMEIER, MARYANN, accountant; b. St. Louis, Oct. 30, 1932; d. Herman Joseph and Crescentia Marie (Ganss) A. Student St. Louis U., 1959-60, Miss Hickey's Bus. Sch., St. Louis, 1960; cert. data processing principles Ward Sch. IBM, St. Louis, 1962. Office mgr., purchasing agt. Abkemeier Dairy Co., St. Louis, 1950-64; acctg. asst. Mo. Research Labs., St. Louis, 1964-66; purchasing agt. Jill's Bakery, Inc., Albuquerque, 1966-69; corp. sec. Southwestern Skyways, Inc., Albuquerque, 1969-71; adminstrv. asst. to v.p. sales Midland Glass Co., Inc., St. Louis, 1971-72; office mgr., internal acct. Seligman & Thomas, Inc., Albuquerque, 1972-77, PBS, Inc., Albuquerque, 1978-80; internal acct. Downey & Sisneros, P.A., C.P.A.s, Santa Fe, 1980—. Co-founder, treas. LaNueva Federated Republican Women, 1983—; mem. Bernalillo County Rep. Central Com., 1977-81, N.Mex. State Rep. Central Com.,

1979-81; mem. Legis. Study Com. on Criminal Justice, 1977; co-chmn. Santa Fe County reelection campaign U.S. Sen Harrison H. Schmitt, 1982; bd. dirs. Santa Fe Econ. Opportunity Corp., 1982-83. Mem. Santa Fe C. of C., Nat. Assn. Exec. Females (network dir. 1982—), Capital City Bus. and Profl. Women (1st v.p. 1983-84), Am. Bus. Women's Assn., Santa Fe Writers Group, Santa Fe Hist. Soc. Author: (with Laura Robertson) Stand Against the Wind, A Biographical Sketchbook of New Mexico Women, 1977. Office: 350 E Palace Ave Santa Fe NM 87501

ABLES, ERNEST DAVID, wildlife educator, natural resource administrator; b. Hugo, Okla., Jan. 13, 1934; s. Ernest Elmer and Annie May (Cooper) A.; m. Juanita Covington, July 20, 1960; children—Christopher David, Brian Allen. B.S. in Zoology, Okla. State U., 1961; M.S. in Wildlife Mgmt., U. Wis.-Madison, 1964, Ph.D. in Wildlife Ecology, 1968. Cert. wildlife biologist. Asst. prof., assoc. prof. Tex. A&M U., 1968-73; prof. Coll. of Forestry, Wildlife and Range, U. Idaho, Moscow, 1973-74, assoc. dean for academics, 1974-82, head fish and wildlife dept., 1982—; cons. Coll. of Agr., South Korea, 1977; instr. Peoples Republic of China, 1980. Served with U.S. Army, 1954-57. Named outstanding tchr. Coll. Forestry, 1974; recipient Disting. Faculty award Phi Kappa Phi, 1983. Mem. Wildlife Soc. (outstanding publ. award, Tex. chpt. 1977), Am. Soc. Mammalogists, Audubon Soc., Sigma Xi. Democrat. Baptist. Contbr. articles to sci. jours.

ABLES, PAUL, insurance executive; b. San Diego, Dec. 29, 1925; s. Paul and Jane (Reeves) A.; m. Gwendolyn Grace Wade, Nov. 26, 1949; 1 son, Joseph. B.S., Northwestern U., 1946. Asst. treas. Pacific Ins. Co., Ltd., Hawaii, 1966-70, treas. 1970-71, v.p., treas. 1971-81, exec. v.p., 1981, pres. 1981—. Served to lt. j.g. USN, 1943-46. Mem. Fin. Execs. Inst., Hawaii Insurers Council, Hawaii Ins. Rating Bur. Baptist. Clubs: Elks, Navy League, Oahu Country, Mid Pacific Country, Plaza. Office: 841 Bishop St Honolulu HI 96813

ABOUAF, JEFFREY RONALD, lawyer, artist; b. Oakland, Calif., Aug. 9, 1949; s. Morris and Bette Rose (Simon) A.; B.A. with honors, Brandeis U., 1971; J.D., U. Calif., San Francisco, 1974; M.F.A. in Painting, Calif. Coll. Arts and Crafts, 1977. Co-author first course on basic legal techniques for visual artists Bay Area Lawyers for the Arts, San Francisco, 1975; dir. Percy W. Gallery, Oakland, Calif., 1976; lectr. Bay Area Lawyers for the Arts, 1975-80; admitted to Calif. bar, 1974; pvt. practice law, Oakland, 1976—; bus., employee benefit, estate ins. planner Prudential Ins. Co. Am. San Francisco, 1978-82; exhibited in group shows: Calif. State Expn. (3d pl.), Sacramento, 1975, Springville (Utah) Mus. Art, 1976, Nat. Watercolor Soc., Los Angeles, 1976, San Francisco Bar Assn. Ann. Competition (winner), 1979. Bd. dirs. Bay Area Lawyers for the Arts, 1976-78, dir. edn., 1976-79, adv. bd., 1979—. Calif. Coll. Arts and Crafts painting scholar, 1976; named Jr. Assn. of Yr., Prudential Ins. Co. Am., San Francisco, 1979. Mem. Nat. Watercolor Soc., Calif. Bar Assn., Nat. Assn. Life Underwriters, San Francisco Assn. Life Underwriters, Alameda County Bar Assn. Contbr. articles to profl. jours. Office: 436 14th St Suite 1303 Oakland CA 94612

ABOU-SAYED, AHMED SAIED, mechanical engineer; b. Cairo, Dec. 1, 1946; s. Saied Ibrahim and Shams Ali (Hassan) Abou-S.; m. Kadreya Foad El-Hinday, Aug. 19, 1969; children—Hatem, Omar. B.Sc. in Engring. with 1st class honors, Cairo U., 1967; M.Sc. in Applied Mechanics, Brown U., Ph.D. in Engring., 1975. Staff research engr. Terra Tek, Inc., Salt Lake City, 1975-76, head applied mechanics, 1976-77, dir. resource tech., 1977-80, v.p., 1981—; dir., v.p. Pioneer Oil and Gas, Inc., 1980-81; cons. UN, 1978—. Mem. ASME, Soc. Petroleum Engrs., Soc. Engring. Sci., Am. Acad. Mechanics, Internat. Soc. Rock Mechanics, Sigma Xi. Contbr. numerous articles to profl. jours. Office: 400 Wakara Way Salt Lake City UT 84108

ABRAHAM, CAROL JEANNE, ceramicist; b. Phila., 1949. Student Tyler Sch. Art, 1964-67, Boston Mus. Sch. Fine Arts, 1967-71; B.S., Tufts U., 1971; M.F.A., Rochester Inst. Tech., 1973; postgrad. Penland Sch. Crafts, 1975. Works exhibited in permanent collections: Rochester (N.Y.) Inst. Tech., Mus. Ceramics, Bassano del Grappa, Italy, Renwick Gallery, Smithsonian Instn., Washington, Brigham Young U., So. Utah State Coll., Cedar City; exhibits: Renwick Gallery, 1975, Tweed Mus. Art, Duluth, Minn., 1981, Celebration, Spokane, Wash., 1981, Interfaith Forum Religious Art and Architecture, 1981, League N.H. Craftsmen, Manchester, 1981, State U. Mus. Art., University Park, Pa., 1981, Fletcher Brownbuilt Pottery Exhibit, Auckland, N.Z., 1981, many others; one-woman shows: Fine Arts Ctr., Burbank, Calif., 1981, 2d Crossing Gallery, Valley City, N.D., 1981, group exhibits: Ga. State U., Atlanta, 1980-81, Orange County Art Assn., Brea, Calif., 1980, Skidmore Coll. Art Gallery, 1981, Corrier Gallery, Manchester, N.H., 1981, Fletcher Brownbuilt Gallery, N.Z., 1981; instr. Framingham (Mass.) Pub. Schs., 1970, Boston Pub. Schs. System Pilot Sch., 1970, Boston State Coll., 1971, Rochester Inst. Tech., 1972-73; asst. prof. ceramics and sculpture So. Utah State Coll., Cedar City, 1975-77, El Camino Coll., Torrance, Calif., 1980-81. Recipient 3d prize Long Beach Art Assn., 1980; Burbank Fine Arts Fedn. grantee, 1981; Purchase award 2d Crossing Gallery, 1981. *

ABRAHAM, SOL ZALMAN, cons. hosp. adminstrn.; b. Czernowitz, Austria, Nov. 14, 1909; s. Nehemiah and Fannie Leah (Finkelstein) A.; came to U.S., 1921, naturalized, 1940; student Coll. City N.Y., 1927-29; m. Ardis L. Jester, Sept. 15, 1937 (dec. Mar. 1943); m. Daisy B. Jones, June 29, 1946 (dec. Sept. 1959). Asst. bus. mgr. Nat. Jewish Hosp., Denver, 1935-45, asst. adminstr., 1945-72, asso. adminstr., 1972-73, dir. spl. services, 1973-75; Cons. in adminstrv. services, 1975—. Pres., Denver Area Sanatorium Council, 1953; chmn. Emily Griffith Opportunity Sch. for Instl. Housekeeping. N.Y. State Regents scholar, 1927. Fellow Am. Coll. Hosp. Adminstrs. (life), Royal Soc. Health; mem. Am., Colo. pub. health assns., Am., Colo., Midwest hosp. assns., Met. Denver Hosp. Council, Assn. Western Hosps., Am. Lung Assn., Historic Denver, Smithsonian Assos., English Speaking Union. Club: Direct Mail (pres. 1955) (Denver). Contbr. articles to profl. jours. Home: 1020 15th St Denver CO 80202 Office: 3800 E Colfax Ave Denver CO 80206

ABRAHAMSSON, BERNHARD JOSEF, educator; b. Stockholm, Sweden, Mar. 11, 1930; s. Jacob Leopold and Lea Leiserovna (Molvidson) A.; came to U.S., 1959, naturalized, 1976; Master Mariner, Mcht. Marine Acad. Stockholm, 1953; B.B.A., CCNY, 1962; M.Sc., U. Wis., 1964, Ph.D., 1966; m. Varda Katz, Oct. 6, 1958; children—Yael Birgit, Nili Ingrid, Sheila Margit. Staff economist IMF, Washington, 1965-68; asso. prof. econs. U. Alaska, 1968-69; asso. prof. Grad. Sch. Internat. Studies, U. Denver, 1969—; adviser Econ. Research Centre, U. Singapore, 1969; sci. dir. Israel Shipping Research Inst., Haifa, 1971-73; dir. Gas Requirements Agy., Denver Research Inst., U. Denver, 1975-78; vis. prof., research fellow Canadian Marine Transp. Centre, Dalhousie U., Halifax, N.S., 1978-79; cons. on shipping and energy to various orgns., agys. and fgn. govts. Served with Swedish Naval Res., 1953-59. Mem. Am. Econ. Assn., Nat. Assn. Bus. Economists, N.Y. Acad. Scis. Author: Strategic Aspects of Seaborne Oil, 1974; Changing Economics of World Energy, 1976; Energy Conservation and Changing Economic Growth, 1978; International Ocean Shipping: Current Concepts and Principles, 1980; contbr. articles to econs. and shipping publs. Home: 9181 E Berry Ct Englewood CO 80111 Office: Grad Sch Internat Studies U Denver Denver 80210

ABRAMOVICE, BEN, hospital administrator, educator; b. Chgo., Dec. 12, 1932; s. Norman Wolf and Rose (Kushner) A. B.A., U. Calif., 1954; M.B.A., U. Chgo., 1960. Exec. dir. Home for Jewish Parents, Oakland, Calif., 1981; exec. adminstr. Laguna Honda Hosp., San Francisco 1981—; del. White House Conf. on Aging; instr. Golden Gate U. Bd. dirs. Berkeley Law Found. Served with U.S. Army 1958. Mem. Calif. Assn. Homes for Aging Pres. citation 1979, past pres.).

ABRAMS, HOWARD (CHUCK), advertising executive; b. N.Y.C., June 27, 1954; s. Philip and Gloria (Sherr) A. B.A., U. Md., 1976; M.B.A., U. Mich., 1978. Intern, Presdl. Mgmt. Program, Washington, 1978-79; media buyer Leo Burnett Co., Chgo., 1979-80; media planner Schneider, Parker, Jakuc, Boston, 1980-81; media supr. Cunningham & Walsh, San Francisco, 1981-82; media dir. Wilton, Coombs & Colnett, San Francisco, 1982—. Office: Wilton Coombs & Colnett 855 Front St San Francisco CA 94111

ABRAMS, JANE ELDORA, artist, educator; b. Eau Claire, Wis., Jan. 2, 1940; children—John, Joan. B.S., U. Wis.-Stout, Menomonie, 1962, M.S., 1967; M.F.A. with distinction, Ind. U., Bloomington, 1971. One-woman shows: Evansville Mus. Arts and Scis., 1982; group shows: U. Colo. Fine Arts Gallery, 1983, Port of History Mus., Phila., 1983; works represented in permanent collections U.S. Embassy, London, Ind. U. Mus. Fine Arts, U. Ill., Potsdam U., U. Dallas, Tex. Tech U., Minot (N.D.) State U., Mus. N. Mex., Santa Fe, U. N.Mex. Mus. Fine Arts, East Carolina U., Greenville, N.C., La. State U., Baton Rouge, U. Ky., Louisville, Prudential Life Ins. Co., N.J.; instr. art U. Wis.-Stout, 1967-69; guest artist printmaking Ind. U., summer 1976; assoc. prof. printmaking U. N.Mex., Albuquerque, 1971—; guest artist, lectr. La. State U., East Carolina U., U. Colo., U. Ariz., Pima Coll., Tucson. Ford Found grantee, 1979, Tamarind Inst. grantee, 1973. Address: 7811 Guadalupe Trail Albuquerque NM 87107

ABRAMS, JEFFREY KLEIN, architect; b. N.Y.C., Mar. 16, 1943; s. Seymour Henry and Madeline Rose (Klein) A.; B.A. cum laude, Trinity Coll., 1965; M.Arch., Yale, 1969; m. Carol Ann Viens, June 29, 1970; children—Lisa Louise, Noah Seymour. Architect various firms in Denver, 1969-72; campus planner U. Colo., 1972-73; pvt. practice architecture and constrn., Boulder, Colo., 1973—. Recipient award for design Wood, Inc., 1974, 77. Works include Center of Hope, world's first solar heated ch. Office: 2305 Canyon Blvd Boulder CO 80302

ABRAMSON, ARTHUR CHARLES, human relations organization administrator; b. N.Y.C., July 8, 1948; s. Ely and Muriel Hyacinth (Freidus) A.; m. Debbie Kay Gonzales, July 17, 1976. B.A., Queens Coll., 1970; M.A., UCLA, 1971, Ph.D., 1981. Asst. prof. polit. sci. Calif. State U.-Northridge, 1975-78; asst. area dir. Am. Jewish Com., Los Angeles, 1979-80, dir. Wash. State area, Seattle, 1980-83; community relations dir. Jewish Fedn. Greater Houston, 1983—. Mem. World Without War Council, Am. Polit. Sci. Assn., Middle East Inst. Democrat. Home: 6306 Coachwood Houston TX 77035 Office: Jewish Fedn Greater Houston Houston TX 77096

ABRAMSON, EDWARD E., psychologist, educator; b. Bklyn., July 7, 1944; s. Morris B. and Helen (Landau) A.; m. Alina Margarita Rosette, Dec. 21, 1968; children—Anne K. Jeremy D. B.A., SUNY-Stony Brook, 1965; Ph.D., Cath. U. Am., Washington, 1970. Lic. psychologist, Calif. Asst. prof. dept. psychology Calif. State U.-Chico, 1970-75, assoc. prof., 1975-79, prof., 1979—; vis. clin. psychologist Guy's Hospital, London, 1978. Mem. Butte County Mental Health Adv. Bd., 1973-78. Mem. Am. Psychol. Assn., Assn. Advancement Behavior Therapy, Western Psychol. Assn. Author: Behavioral Approaches to Weight Control, 1977; contbr. articles to profl. jours. Office: Dept Psychology Calif State U Chico CA 95929

ABRAMSON, IRWIN, tax consultant, accountant; b. Bklyn., May 27, 1935; s. Sidney Victor and Mae A.; m. Barbara Abramson, Aug. 7, 1960; children—Alisa, Michael. B.B.A., CCNY, 1956; LL.B., Bklyn. Law Sch., 1960; postgrad. NYU Law Sch., 1961-63. Bar: N.Y. 1961, C.P.A., N.Y., N.J., Calif. Acct., tax ptnr. Edward Isaacs & Co., N.Y.C., 1961-81; tax ptnr. Morgen & Co., C.P.A.s, Los Angeles, 1981—; cons. tax and estate planning. Served with M.C., U.S. Army, 1958-64. Mem. ABA, Am. Soc. C.P.A.s, N.Y. State Soc. C.P.A.s, Calif. Soc. C.P.A.s (exec. com.). Democrat. Jewish. Home: 11309 Quail Creek Rd Northridge CA 91326 Office: Morgen & Co 1925 Century Park East Suite 880 Los Angeles CA

ABRAMSON, JOHN DONALD, health care exec.; b. Richmond, Va., Nov. 20, 1939; s. Edward Lincoln and Alice Cecelia (Walls) A.; A.A., Coll. Marin, 1960; B.S., U. Calif. at Berkeley, 1963; M.B.A., Golden Gate U., 1979; m. Yvonne Marsh, May 26, 1968. Staff accountant L. H. Penney & Co., C.P.A.'s, 1963-65; internal auditor, programmer/analyst, project leader Permanente Services, Inc. div. Kaiser-Permanente Med. Care Program, 1965-71; mgr. systems and procedures Kaiser Found. Health Plan, 1971-83, planner, 1983—. C.P.A., Calif. Mem. Assn. Systems Mgmt., Nat. Microfilm Assn., Calif. Soc. C.P.A.'s, Calif. Alumni Assn. Club: Castlewood. Home: 7494 Sedgefield Ave San Ramon CA 94583 Office: 3505 Broadway Oakland CA 94611

ABREU, WANI ELIZABETH WYNNE, optometrist, educator; b. Los Angeles, Apr. 30, 1953; d. Robert Emmitt and Edith Elizabeth (Patterson) Wynne; m. Kenneth Ernest Abreu, Sept. 15, 1979. B.A., Occidental Coll., 1974; O.D., U. Calif.-Berkeley, 1978. Health services instr., credential in optometry, Calif. Assoc. optometrist, Santa Rosa, Calif., 1980-81, San Mateo, Calif., 1981, Marin County, Calif., 1981-82; optometrist Kaiser Permanente Med. Group, 1980-82, optometrist, South San Francisco, Calif., 1982—; mem. faculty paraoptometric tng. program Merritt Coll. Mem. Calif. Optometric Assn., Am. Optometric Assn., Nat. Optometric Assn. Office: 1200 El Camino Real South San Francisco CA 94080

ABRUZZO, BENJAMINE LAWRENCE, real estate developer, balloonist; b. Rockford, Ill., June 9, 1930; s. Louis and Mary (Ginestra) A.; m. Patricia Steer, June 6, 1952; children—Louis, Benny, Mary Pat, Richard. B.S. in Bus. Adminstrn., U. Ill., 1952. With Sandia Corp., Albuquerque, 1956-59; chmn. and pres. Sandia Peak Ski Co., Tram Co., and Utility Co., 1975—; chmn. and pres. Alvarado Realty Co., Albuquerque, 1975—; dir. N.Mex. Fin. Corp., Sandia Fed. Savings and Loan. Served to 1st. lt. USAF, 1952-54 Mem. Albuquerque C. of C. (dir.). Republican. Roman Catholic. Completed first TransAtlantic balloon crossing (with Newman and Maxie Anderson), 1978; first balloon crossing of Pacific Ocean with Larry Newman, Ron Clark and Rocky Aoki, 1981; (world record for time and distance; spl. gold medal from U.S. Congress; FAA award; French Grande medal; Nat. Geographic Soc. gold medal; FAI gold air medal; French sports medal; subject of TV documentaries and book). Home: 9 Sandia Heights Dr NE Albuquerque NM 87122 Office: 10 Tramway Loop NE Albuquerque NM 87122

ABSHER, HENRY JERRELL, educator; b. Comanche, Okla., May 5, 1914; s. Lewis Olvie and Lucindy Elizabeth (Turner) A.; m. Hazel Maurine Proctor; children—Harold, Richard, Phyllis, Terry, Henry Jerrell, David. B.S., Okla. State U., 1957, M.S., 1959; Teaching cert., Okla., Tex., Ariz. Elem. tchr., Okla., 1936-42; tchr. high sch., Clifton, Ariz., 1945-47; instr. engring. drawing, Okla. State U., 1948-49, 56-58; tchr. Shidler (Okla.) High Sch., 1949-50, Miami (Okla.) High Sch., 1958-76; dir. bldg. trades program Labette Community Jr. Coll., Parsons, Kans., 1976-79; instr. drafting Eastern Ariz. Coll., Thatcher, 1980-81; tchr. drafting, organizer computer-aided drafting program Lamson Bus. Coll., Tucson, 1981—. Mem. NEA, Am. Vocat. Assn., Okla. Vocat. Assn., Okla. Edn. Assn., Iota Lambda Sigma (life). Democrat. Baptist. Patentee drafting instrument. Home: 960 N Independence Ave Tucson AZ 85748 Office: 5320 E Pima St Tucson AZ 85712

ABSHIER, DORCEY GWYNNE, nuclear engineer, engineering physicist; b. Wichita, Kans., July 16, 1925; s. Dorcey D. and Leona (Gwynne) A.; B.S., U. Okla., 1948, M.Engring. Physics, 1950; m. Gene Eileen Bond, Jan. 12, 1955 (dec.); children—Stephen (dec.), Holly, Michelle, Dorcey, David. Applications engr. Indsl. Nucleonics Corp., Columbus, 1954; prin. engring. physicist Battelle Meml. Inst., 1954-55; sr. nuclear engr. Gen. Dynamics Corp., Ft. Worth, 1956-58; lead engr. Chance Vought Aircraft, Dallas, 1958-60; staff engr., systems div., Bendix Corp., Ann Arbor, Mich., 1960; design specialist Gen. Dynamics Astronautics, San Diego, 1960-63; specialist Research, Space and Information Systems div. N.Am., Aviation, Downey, Calif., 1963-68; mem. tech. staff Astronautics div. N.Am. Rockwell, Anaheim, Calif., 1968-69; sr. engring. scientist McDonnel Douglas Astronautics Co., Huntington Beach, 1972-73; mem. tech. staff Rockwell Internat., 1974-78, Lockheed Calif. Co., Burbank, 1978-82, Northrop Corp., 1982—. Commr., Buena Park Parks and Recreation Commn.; chmn. Buena Park Beautification Com. Pres. Girls' Club North Orange County. Served with AUS, 1944-46, 51-53. Mem. AIAA, Am. Nuclear Soc., Cryogenics Soc. Am., Bellehurst Community Assn., Am. Phys. Soc., IEEE, Sci. Research Soc. Am. Mason. Club: Los Coyotes Country. Home: 4910 St Andrews Circle Buena Park CA 90621 Office: Northrop Corp Hawthorne CA

ABSHIRE, LYNN THOMAS, computer systems specialist; b. Twin Falls, Idaho, June 10, 1944; s. Joyce and Viola Magdelene (Bitner) Abshire; m. Marcia Louis Jensen, June 18, 1967; children—Mark, Timothy; m. 2d, Barbara Ann McCune, Apr. 23, 1977; 1 son, Matthew. A.Engring., Oreg. Tech. Inst., 1967. Research and devel. technician Conic Corp., San Diego, 1967-69; sr. technician, process control programmer Union Carbide, San Diego, 1969-70; programmer, data processing mgr. Solitron Devices, San Diego, 1970-74; sr. research and devel. systems programmer General Automation, Anaheim, Calif., 1974-75; data processing mgr. VTN Corp., Irvine, Calif., 1975-83; tech. support mgr. DMA Communications, Inc., Anaheim, 1983—. Served with USN, 1961-65. Republican. Home: 27861 Perales St Mission Viejo CA 92692 Office: DMA Communications Inc 3150 E LaPalma Ave Anaheim CA 92806

ABT, BRUCE ALAN, clin. psychologist; b. Buffalo, Aug. 17, 1940; s. Gerald N. and Emma C. (Schaupp) A.; B.A. in History, Hamilton Coll., Clinton, N.Y., 1962; postgrad. U. Madrid (Spain), 1960-61; M.B.A., Columbia U., 1964; Ph.D. in Clin. Psychology, U. Tenn., Knoxville, 1975; m. Evet S. Loewen, June 12, 1973. Asst. account exec. Compton Advt. Agy., N.Y.C., 1965; various assignments to aide of Ambassador William Blair, Manila, 1965-68; staff Model Cities Program, San Francisco, 1968-70; cons. urban community devel. programs, 1970-71; clin. intern Palo Alto (Calif.) VA Hosp., 1975; group therapist San Jose (Calif.) Hosp., 1975-78, TERRAP, 1979-80; therapist supr. Women's Community Clinic, San Jose, 1978-80, employee assistance programs, 1980—; practice clin. psychology, Sunnyvale, Calif., 1977—; mem. faculty West Valley Community Coll., 1976, San Jose State U., 1976, 78, Foothill Community Coll., 1978; lectr. univs. and Am. Inst. Banking; host weekly radio program Sta. KXRX, San Jose, 1980. Served with USAR, 1964. Lic. psychologist, Calif. Mem. Am. Psychol. Assn., Calif. Psychol. Assn. Office: 877 W Fremont Ave Suite K5 Sunnyvale CA 94087

ABUL-HAJ, SULEIMAN KAHIL, pathologist; b. Jordan, Apr. 20, 1925; s. Sheik Khalil and S. Buteina (Oda) Abul-H.; B.S., U. Calif. at Berkeley, 1949; M.S., U. Calif. at San Francisco, 1951, M.D., 1955; m. Elizabeth Abood, Feb. 11, 1948; children—Charles, Alan, Cary; came to U.S., 1946, naturalized, 1955. Intern, Cook County Hosp., Chgo., 1955-56; resident U. Calif. Hosp., San Francisco, 1949, Brooke Gen. Hosp., 1957-59; chief clin. and anatomic pathology Walter Reed Army Hosp., Washington, 1959-62; asso. prof. U. So. Calif. Sch. Medicine, Los Angeles, 1963—; sr. surg. pathologist Los Angeles County Gen. Hosp., 1963; dir. dept. pathology Community Meml. Hosp., Ventura, Calif., 1964-80, Gen. Hosp. Ventura County, 1966-74; dir. Pathology Service Med. Group, 1970—; cons. Calif. Tumor Tissue Registry, 1962—, Camarillo State Hosp., 1964-70, Tripler Gen. Hosp., Hawaii, 1963-67, Armed Forces Inst. Pathology, 1960—. Bd. dirs. Tri-Counties Blood Bank, Am. Cancer Soc. Served to maj., M.C., U.S. Army, 1956-62. Recipient Borden award Calif. Honor Soc., 1949; Achievement cert. Surgeon Gen. Army, 1962. Fellow Am. Soc. Clin. Pathologists, Coll. Am. Pathologists; mem. AMA, N.Y. Acad. Sci., Internat. Coll. Surgeons, AAAS, Calif. Soc. Pathologists, Calif. Med. Assn., Internat. Platform Assn., World Affairs Council. Clubs: Commonwealth of Calif. (San Francisco); Jonathan. Contbr. articles to profl. jours. Research in cardiovascular disease, endocrine, renal, skin diseases, also cancer. Home: 105 Encinal Way Ventura CA 93001 Office: 147 N Brent St Ventura CA 93003

ABUSAIDI, MOHAMMAD SALEH, writer; b. Kerman, Iran, Sept. 21, 1921; came to U.S., 1969; s. Abdullah and Roghieh A.; Licentiate in Law, Tehran U., 1941; M.A. (Fulbright scholar), Columbia U., 1954; Ph.D., U. Oreg., 1972; m. Ezzat Heravi, Mar. 25, 1943; children—Sara, Maryam, Ali. Pres., Abadan (Iran) Inst. Tech., 1960-62; dir. Iranian Petroleum Co., 1965-68; counselor, asso. dir. Parent-Tchr. Community Tng. Center, Eugene, Oreg., 1971-74; faculty U. Oreg., Eugene, Southwestern Oreg. Community Coll., Coos Bay, Oreg., Lane Community Coll., Eugene, 1974-79; counselor, 1972-75. Mem. Am. Psychol. Assn., Oreg. Psychol. Assn., Assn. Humanistic Psychology. Author: Child Guidance, 1955; The De-Formed I and Re-Formed I, 1980; translator: Problem of Lasting Peace (Herbert Hoover and Hugh Gibson), 1949; Reconstruction in Philosophy (John Dewey), 1958; Child Psychology (Arthur T. Jersild), 1968. Address: PO Box 1735 Eugene OR 97440

ACHESON, LOUIS KRUZAN, JR., aerospace engr.; b. Brazil, Ind., Apr. 2, 1926; s. Louis Kruzan and Irene Ruth (Morrison) A.; B.S. in E.E., Case Inst. Tech., 1946; Ph.D. in Theoret. Physics, M.I.T., 1950; m. Hyla Armstrong Cook, July 12, 1958; children—Mary Ruth, William Louis. Mem. tech. staff Hughes Aircraft Co., Los Angeles, 1950—, sr. scientist Systems Labs., Space and Communications Group, 1960—; with Inst. Def. Analyses, Washington, 1958-59. Mem. Am. Phys. Soc., Am. Geophys. Union, AIAA, Brit. Interplanetary Soc., AAAS, Soc. Gen. Systems Research, Mensa, Sigma Xi, Tau Beta Pi, Eta Kappa Nu, Theta Tau, Sigma Chi. Clubs: Worldview Exploration Seminar, Unity-in-Diversity Council, World Federalists, Bertrand Russell Soc. Contbr. to profl. publs. Home: 17721 Marcello Pl Encino CA 91316 Office: Hughes Aircraft Co PO Box 92919 Los Angeles CA 90009

ACHTEL, ROBERT ANDREW, pediatric cardiologist; b. Bklyn., May 5, 1941; s. Murray and Amelia (Ellian) A.; B.A., Adelphi U., 1963; M.D., U. Cin., 1967; m. Erica Noel Woods, Mar. 10, 1963; children—Bergen Alison, Roland Hugh. Intern, Cin. Children's Hosp., 1967-68;

resident in pediatrics Yale U., 1968-69, fellow in pediatric cardiology, 1969-71; clin. instr. pediatrics U. Calif.-Davis, 1972-73, clin. asst. prof., 1977—; asst. prof. pediatrics, U. Ky., 1973-76; dir. pediatric ICU, Sutter Meml. Hosp., Sacramento, 1977—, dir. pediatric Cardiology, 1982—, chmn. instl. rev. com., 1981—; chmn. dept. pediatrics Mercy Hosp., Sacramento, 1981—, dir. pediatric ICU, 1982—. Served as major M.C., USAF, 1971-73. Recipient grants from Heart Assn., U. Ky. Tobacco and Health Research Found. Diplomate Am. Bd. Pediatric Cardiology. Mem. Am. Heart Assn. (dir. Sacramento chpt., mem. councils congenital heart disease and atherosclerosis and cardiovascular surgery), Am. Coll. Chest Physicians, Am. Acad Pediatrics, SW Pediatric Cardiology Soc., So. Soc. Pediatric Research. Contbr. articles in cardiovascular research. Office: 5301 F St Suite 316 Sacramento CA 95819

ACHTERBERG, DEBORAH LAMB, hosp. adminstr.; b. Lindsay, Calif., Sept. 11, 1949; d. John and Margueritte Myrtle (Lamb) Tolan; student Porterville Coll., 1975-77; m. Jerald Albert Achterberg, Dec. 25, 1971; children—Jerald Christopher, Amy Elizabeth. Clk., Lindsay Dist. Hosp., 1969-70, purchasing agt., 1970-75; dir. purchasing Sierra View Dist. Hosp., Porterville, Calif. 1977—. Mem. Calif. Assn. Hosp. Purchasing Agts. (certified; v.p. 1977, pres. 1978). Mem. Assemblies of God. Club: Toastmasters. Home: 875 N Homassel St Lindsay CA 93247 Office: 465 W Putnam St Porterville CA 93257

ACKER, MARTIN HERBERT, educator, psychotherapist; b. N.Y.C., Dec. 15, 1921; s. Irving and Rose Martha (Katz) A.; m. Joan Elise Robinson, Apr. 29, 1948; children—Michael Christopher, David Jonathon, Steven Anthony; m. 2d, Julia Ann Payne, Feb. 14, 1976. Ph.D., NYU, 1963. Lic. psychologist, Oreg. Prof. counseling and psychology U. Oreg., Eugene, 1961—, chmn. counseling, 1963-68; vis. prof. Fed. City Coll., Washington, 1968-69, U. Victoria, B.C., 1974; psychotherapist, Eugene, Oreg., 1974—. Mem. adv. com. Lane County Oreg. Adult Corrections; bd. dirs. Lane Mental Health Ctr., DeBusk Meml. Clinic, 1983. Served to 1st lt. U.S. Army, 1943-46. Recipient NYU Founders Day award, 1963. Mem. Am. Personnel and Guidance Assn. (bd. dirs. 1967-68), Soc. Sci. Study Sex, Oreg. Psychol. Assn., Am. Rehab. Counselors Assn. (pres. 1968-69). Club: Friars. Home: 1310 Barber Dr Eugene OR 97405 Office: 1761 Alder St Eugene OR 97403

ACKERMAN, FRANK EDWARD, artist, museum curator; b. Los Angeles, Jan. 3, 1933. Student Sch. Allied Arts, Glendale Coll., Chouinard Art Inst. Works exhibited in permanent collections: U. Utah, Logan, Hunt Collection Fine Arts, Fullerton, Calif., Vincent Price Collection, Beverly Hills, Calif.; commns.: Antartica Series, USN, Washington, 1967, Alaska, Alaskan C. of C., 1969, Vietnam War Meml., County of Los Angeles Ct. of Flags, 1973, Gen. Omar Bradley, Patriotic Hall, Los Angeles, 1975; group shows: Am. Embassy, Acapulco, Mex., 1960, U.S. Naval World Tour, 1970, NAD, N.Y.C., 1973; one-man shows: Brand Library Fine Arts, Glendale, Calif., 1973, Royal Watercolor Soc., London, 1975; illustrator County of Los Angeles, 1956-63, graphic artist, 1966-68, head graphic artist, 1968-70, art dir., 1970-80; chief exhibitor Mus. Natural History, Los Angeles, 1980—; instr. watercolor Rex Brandt Sch. Painting, Corona del Mar, Calif., 1955-56; pvt. instr., Los Angeles, 1961-65; Recipient Painting of Yr. award Ebell Club, Los Angeles, 1963; award of Merit, Home Savs. and Loan, 1964; Watercolor award Calif. Nat. Watercolor Soc., 1971. Mem. West Coast Watercolor Soc., Nat. Watercolor Soc. (1st v.p., pres. Calif. 1968-70), Soc. South Pole, Internat. Inst. Arts and Letters (Switzerland). Illustrator: Earthquake Report on Los Angeles County, 1973; End of the Era, 1975. Office: Natural History Mus Los Angeles County 900 Exposition Blvd Los Angeles CA 90007*

ACKERMAN, GERALD MARTIN, art educator; b. Alamada, Calif., Aug. 21, 1928; s. Alois Martin and Eva May (Sadler) A. B.A. U. Calif.-Berkeley, 1952; student U. Munich (Ger.), 1956-58; Ph.D., Princeton U., 1964. Instr., Bryn Mawr (Pa.) Coll., 1960-64; asst. prof. Stanford U., 1964-70; prof. art history Pomona Coll., Claremont, 1971—; Fullbright prof. U. Leningrad, 1980. Mem. Société de L'Histoire d'art francais, Deutsche verein fur Kunstwissenschaft, Coll. Art Assn. Author: Thomas Eakins and his Parisian Masters, Gazette des Beaux-Arts, 1969. Home: 360 S Mills Ave Claremont CA 91711 Office: Pomona Coll Art Dept Claremont CA 91711

ACKERMAN, JOHN TRYON, utility co. exec.; b. Cleve., Aug. 12, 1941; s. William Tryon and Lillian Edith (Lancaster) A.; B.S. in Engring. (Harry and Mabel F. Leonard Tuition scholar), U. N.Mex., 1968; M.S. in Utility Mgmt. (Electric Utility Mgmt. Program fellow), N.Mex. State U., 1971; m. Katherine Murphy Pooler, May 1, 1965; children—Joseph Daniel, William Clay, Michael Eric. Design and devel. engr. Gen. Electric Co., Binghamton, N.Y., 1968-71; with Public Service Co. N.Mex., Albuquerque, 1971—, asst. to pres., 1976-78, dist. v.p., 1978-81, v.p. div. ops., 1981—; bd. dirs. Open Pit Mining Assn., 1974-76; mem. N.Mex. Multiple Use Adv. Bd., Bur. Land Mgmt., 1975-77; Vice pres. bd. dirs. Albuquerque Assn. Children with Learning Disabilities, 1976-77, pres. bd., 1978; corp. chmn. United Way of Greater Albuquerque, 1978, bd. dirs. exec. com., 1979, v.p. bd. dirs., 1980, 82 pres., 1981; mem. steering com. Albuquerque Community Leadership Devel., 1980-81; nat. assoc. Boys Clubs Am., 1981—. Served with USN, 1960-64. Registered profl. engr., N.Mex. Mem. Nat. Soc. Profl. Engrs., IEEE, Am. Mgmt. Assn., Albuquerque C. of C. (dir. 1980-81), Eta Kappa Nu (life). Republican. Roman Catholic. Home: 5309 Queens Ct Albuquerque NM 87109 Office: Alvarado Sq Albuquerque NM 87158

ACKLEN, GERALD GILL, journalist; b. Portland, Oreg., Dec. 9, 1907; s. Gerald Jasper and Josephine (Gill) A.; B.S., U. Oreg., 1942; m. Ruth Dinges, Sept. 7, 1940; children—Ruthann Acklen de la Vega, Linda Jo Acklen Chieffo, Gerald Craig, Daniel William. Sch. prin., Grants Pass, Oreg., 1942-45; life ins. underwriter Mut. of N.Y., Grants Pass, 1945-69; wire editor Daily Courier, Grants Pass, 1950-61, sports and city editor, 1961-63, regional editor, sports, 1963-65, sports, 1963-77, hist. editor, 1977—; news corr. for AP, also for UPI, 1950-76, Oreg. Jour., 1942-82, Oreg. Sports, 1950-76; publicity dir. So. Oreg. Horse Racing Assn., 1978-81. Pres., Josephine County Diabetes Assn., 1976-79, program chmn., 1979—; bd. dirs. Oreg. affiliate Am. Diabetes Assn., 1981-1 bd. dirs. Josephine County Community Concert Assn., 1946-68, pres., 1961-64; scoutmaster Boy Scouts Am., Grants Pass, 1942-45, mem. troop com., 1945-48; mem. ofcl. bd. Methodist Ch., 1959-65, 70-82. Home: 1250 Oak View Dr Grants Pass OR 97526 Office: PO Box 1468 Grants Pass OR 97526

ACUFF, GREGORY MITCHELL, management consultant; b. Houton, Aug. 31, 1948; s. Norbert Herschell and Muriel Maxine (Cochran) A.; B.S., USAF Acad., 1971; M.B.A., U. So. Calif., 1978; Systems program mgmt. officer SAMSO, El Segundo, Calif., 1977-78; staff fin. analyst Ford Aerospace and Communications Corp., Palo Alto, Calif., 1978-79; adminstrv. mgr. GTE Sylvania, Mountain View, Calif., 1979-80; mgmt. cons., Gregory M. Acuff & Assos., Sunnyvale, Calif., 1980-82, Humphreys & Assocs., Newport Beach, Calif., 1983—. Served with USAF, 1971-78. Mem. Am. Mgmt. Assn. Presbyterian. Address 1633 Albatross Dr Sunnyvale CA 94087

ACUNA, CELIA PACHECO, educational administrator, educator, consultant; b. Tijuana, Mex., Jan. 10, 1952; d. Francisco G. and Leobarda P. Acuña. B.A. in Spanish with honors, San Diego State U., 1973, M.A., 1977; postgrad. U. San Francisco, 1978—. Tchr. Kimball Sch., National City, Calif., 1974-77; dist. bilingual resource tchr. Nat. Sch. Dist., National City, 1977-79; vice prin. El Toyon Elem. Sch., National City, 1979-80; acting prin. Las Palmas Elem. Sch., National City, 1981; prin. La Mirada Elem. Sch., San Isidro, Calif., 1981—; instr. dept. multicultural edn. San Diego State U.; cons. linguametrics; cons. dept. edn., San Diego, Recipient cert. of achievement San Diego Dept. Edn., 1980; A.M.A.E. recognition award for service to Chicano community; Outstanding Young Educator award Chula Vista C. of C. Jaycees, 1983, Tchr. of Yr. award La Prensa, San Diego, 1983. Mem. Assn. Calif. Sch. Adminstrs., S.W. Adminstrs. (v.p. 1982-83, pres.-elect 1983-84), AAUW, Hispanic Women in Mgmt., Delta Kappa Gamma. Democrat. Roman Catholic. Club: San Ysidro Women's. Co-author: Kimball Reading Management System; Paso por Paso-Bilingual Multicultural Curriculum Handbook. Office: 222 Avenida de la Madrid San Ysidro CA 92073

ADAIR, JAY CARLTON, broadcasting executive; b. Evanston, Ill., Jan. 6, 1946; s. Claude and Ruby (Lemke) A. Student, U. Wis.-Madison, 1964-67; student U. So. Calif., 1970, UCLA, 1974; B.A., Calif. Western U., 1979, M.B.A., 1982. Mgr., Meeker T.V., San Francisco, 1974-78; v.p. sta. relations Meeker T. V., 1978-79, v.p. West Coast ops., Los Angeles, 1979-81; mgr. West Coast Network Sales, CBS Radio Network, Hollywood, Calif., 1981-82; mgr. West Coast sales Broadcast Week, Beverly Hills, Calif., 1982—; co-owner Sta. KLRB-FM, Carmel, Calif., 1977-80; co-chmn. TVB/LA, 1980. lectr. in field. Served with USMCR and USNR, 1967-74. Mem. Hollywood Radio and TV Soc. Republican. Lutheran. Clubs: Olympic, Commonwealth. Office: 101 N Robertson St Suite 206 Beverly Hills CA 90211

ADAM, LAVERN LESTER, magnetic design executive; b. Leola, S.D., July 2, 1943; s. Fred John and Viola (Mehlhaff) A.; m. Barbara Jane Hammrich; children—Jim Dean, Kay Lee. Student in Indsl. Mgmt., North Orange Jr. Coll., 1970-71. Trainee Honeywell-Deburring, Gardena, Calif., 1963-66; prodn. control expeditor Indsl. Tectonics, Compton, Calif., 1966-68; materials mgr. Permag Pacific, Los Angeles, 1968-71; quality control mgr. MPC, Irvine, Calif., 1971-72; pres., chmn. bd. A Z Industries Inc., Temecula, Calif., 1972—; lectr. in field. Mem. career activities bd. Lake Elsinore High Sch. Mem. Temecula C. of C. Republican. Lutheran. Magnetic designer for major corps. throughout U.S. Office: 28065 Diaz Rd Temecula CA 92390

ADAM, RENNIE LAIRD, newspaper publishing company executive; b. Lompoc, Calif.; s. Kenneth Laird and Harriet Hall (McCollum) A.; m. Sara Kay Stratford, Dec. 9, 1947; children—Rennie L., Christopher M.; m. 2d, Karen Lee Stevenson, Feb. 7, 1981. B.A. in Journalism, U. So. Calif., 1970. Advt. salesman, 1970-72; co-pub. Lompoc (Calif.) Record Publs., Inc., 1972-78; co-pub. Adam Bros. Publs., Inc., Breckenridge, Colo., 1978-80, pub., chmn. bd., 1980—; mktg. cons. Breckenridge Music Inst. Served with USNR, 1965-67. Mem. Colo. Newspaper Pubs. Assn. Republican. Episcopalian. Publs. include: summit County Jour., Schuss, Summer Mountain Mag., Good Cents. Home: 200 Primrose-Winterpoint Apt 14 Breckenridge CO 80424 Office: Adam Bros Publs Inc PO Box 98 Breckenridge CO 80424

ADAM, STEPHEN FERENC, electrical engineer; b. Budapest, Hungary, Feb. 28, 1929; s. Stephen and Gizella (Mihaly) A.; came to U.S., 1957, naturalized, 1963; diploma Mech. Engr., Techn. Inst. Budapest, 1951, M.E.E., 1954; Sc.D. in Elec. Engring., 1965; m. Edith E. Tschurtz, Sept. 11, 1965. Research engr. Research Inst. for Telecommunications, Budapest, 1952-56; devel., engr. Hewlett-Packard Co., Palo Alto, Calif., 1957-62, project mgr., 1962-66, engring. sect. mgr. research and devel., 1966-80, research and devel. engr., sect. mgr. microwave semiconductor div., San Jose, 1980-83; instr. elec. engring., Foothill Coll., 1960-69; mem. exec. com. Conf. on Precision Electromagnetic Measurements. Fellow IEEE; mem. Microwave Theory and Techniques Soc. (pres.), Quantumelectronics and Applications Soc., Instrumentation and Measurements Soc., Electron Devices Soc., Internat. Electro Tech. Commn. Roman Catholic. Author: Microwave Theory and Applications, 1969; contbr. articles to profl. jours. Home: 1413 Brookmill Rd Los Altos CA 94022 Office: 3000 Hanover St MS/20BY Palo Alto CA 94303

ADAMCIN, JULIE CAMP, home economist, b. Riverside, Calif., Oct. 3, 1947; d. Donald James and Esther Elizabeth (Ryan) Camp; m. Peter Lawrence Adamcin, 1982. B.S., Okla. Bapt. U., 1969; M.S., U. Ariz., 1978. 4-H extension agt. Pima County Extension Service, Tucson, 1970—. Mem. Am. Home Econs. Assn., Nat. Assn. Extension 4-H Agts., Nat. Assn. Extension Home Economists. Roman Catholic. Office: 131 W Congress Tucson AZ 85701

ADAMS, ARTHUR RAYMOND, manufacturing company executive, marketing consultant; b. Hiawatha, Kans., Apr. 30, 1909; s. George Raymond and Grace Helena (Davis) A.; widowed; children—Ann, Carolyn, Peter, Sharon. B.A., Stanford U., 1931. Ptnr., Rite Hardware Co., Glendale, Calif., 1936-46; pres., chmn. bd. Adams Rite Mfg. Co., City of Industry, Calif., 1946—; pres., chmn. bd. Adams Rite Industries, Inc., Glendale, 1972-81; pres., chmn. bd. Raymond Mgmt. Co., Pasadena, 1981—. Mem. World Affairs Council, Town Hall, Internat. Visitors Council, Cal Tech Assn.; trustee, life mem. bd. Claremont McKenna Coll. Mem. NAM, Assn. Astronautics and Aeros. Republican. Christian Scientist. Clubs: Oakmont Golf, Verdugo (Glendale), Internation (Los Angeles).

ADAMS, CARMEN BOITEL, poetess; b. Bklyn., Apr. 3, 1920; d. Ringgold Raphael and Emma May (Phillips) Boitel; student Katherine Gibbs Secretarial Sch., N.Y.C., 1934; m. Hugh Thomas Adams, Aug. 11, 1950. Pvt. sec. Arnold Serton Export Co., N.Y.C., 1938-46, Anglo-Calif. Nat. Bank, Modesto, 1947-50; worked with Cuban refugee children, Portland, Oreg., 1962; tchr. class in Am. naturalization to Mexicans in Phoenix. Mem. Am. Poetry League, Nat. League Am. Pen Women, Ariz. Poetry Soc., Maj. Poets. Author: Twenty Little Lyrics, 1970; Quite Reflections, 1971, rev. edit., 1974; The Music of Life, 1978; contbr. to Ideals mag., also poetry mags. Home: 345 W Cambridge Ave Phoenix AZ 85003

ADAMS, CHARLES ARTHUR, city ofcl., fin. exec.; b. Caldwell, Idaho, July 25, 1933; s. John Woodrow and Eileen (Vail) A.; B.A., Coll. Idaho, 1962; m. Susan Rae Donovan, Jan. 30, 1960; children—Michael C., Teresa M. Sales mgr. Hoppins Ins. Agy., Nampa, Idaho, 1961-63; auditor Indsl. Indemnity Ins. Co., Boise, Idaho, 1964-65, Argonaut Ins. Co., Portland, 1966-67; br. mgr. Am. Mut. Ins. Co., Portland, 1968-70; underwriting mgr. Alaska Pacific Assurance Co., Juneau, 1970-73; pres. A.I.M. Ins. Inc., Anchorage, 1973-78, sr. v.p. A.I.M. Internat., Tokyo, 1975-78, pres. parent co. A.I.M. Corp., 1977-78; fin. dir. City of Homer (Alaska), 1979-80, Municipality of Anchorage, 1980—. Vol. in corrections State of Alaska, 1981. Served with AUS, 1955-58; ETO. Mem. Am. Legion, Homeowners Warranty Council (v.p. Alaska chpt. 1976-78), Resource Devel. Council Alaska, Porsche Club Am., Alaska Council Sports Car Clubs (dir. 1976-78), Alaska World Affairs Council. Clubs: K.C., Toastmasters (Summit Club Speaker of Year 1969). Designer, adminstr. ins. Wrap Up for Trans-Alaska Pipeline, 1970-73. city ofcl., fin. exec.; b. Caldwell, Idaho, July 25, 1933; s. John Woodrow and Eileen (Vail) A.; B.A., Coll. Idaho, 1962; m. Susan Rae Donovan, Jan. 30, 1960; children—Michael C., Teresa M. Sales mgr. Hoppins Ins. Agy., Nampa, Idaho, 1961-63; auditor Indsl. Indemnity Ins. Co., Boise, Idaho, 1964-65, Argonaut Ins. Co., Portland, 1966-67; br. mgr. Am. Mut. Ins. Co., Portland, 1968-70; underwriting mgr. Alaska Pacific Assurance Co., Juneau, 1970-73; pres. A.I.M. Ins. Inc., Anchorage, 1973-78, sr. v.p. A.I.M. Internat., Tokyo, 1975-78, pres. parent co. A.I.M. Corp., 1977-78; fin. dir. City of Homer (Alaska), 1979-80, Municipality of Anchorage, 1980—. Vol. in corrections State of Alaska, 1981. Served with AUS, 1955-58; ETO. Mem. Am. Legion, Homeowners Warranty Council (v.p. Alaska chpt. 1976-78), Resource Devel. Council Alaska, Porsche Club Am., Alaska Council Sports Car Clubs (dir. 1976-78), Alaska World Affairs Council. Clubs: K.C., Toastmasters (Summit Club Speaker of Year 1969). Designer, adminstr. ins. Wrap Up for Trans-Alaska Pipeline, 1970-73. Home: 2270 Lake George Dr Anchorage AK 99504 Office: Pouch 6-650 Anchorage AK 99502

ADAMS, CLARENCE EDWIN, city ofcl., personnel adminstr.; b. San Diego, Apr. 12, 1941; s. Clarence F. and Daisy M. (Bruno) A.; student City Coll., San Diego, 1959-60, U. Pacific, 1960-61, San Diego City Coll., San Diego State U., 1972; m. Brenda Joyce Jenkins, Nov. 19, 1961; children—Robin Rochelle, Rhonda Terrell. Rehab. aide San Diego Service Center, 1967-68; asst. dir. Mgmt. Council, San Diego, 1968; dir. Stomp Out Stumblers, San Diego, 1970-71; dir. met. dept. San Diego dist. United Methodist Union, 1968-71; personnel analyst City of San Diego, 1972—; mem. Human Relations Commn. San Diego County, chmn. personnel com., 1973; chmn. adv. council Dept. Human Resources Devel., San Diego, 1968-73; coordinator talk show Sta. KSDO-TV, 1972-73. mem. steering com. Mayor's Council on Youth Opportunity, 1968-73, vice chmn., 1969-70; mem. Urban Coalition Law and Justice Task Force, 1967—; adv. bd. San Diego CORE: chmn. adv. bd. Youth Opportunity Center, San Diego, 1968-71; adv. bd. Co-op Area Manpower Planning System, 1969—. Mem. Urban League (community edn. com. 1969—), NAACP (exec. bd. 1970-73, chmn. community coordination com. 1972-74). Club: Men's Social and Charity (v.p. 1973). Home: 2302 Blackton Dr San Diego CA 92105 Office: 202-C St San Diego CA 92101

ADAMS, CLINTON, painter, educator; b. Glendale, Calif., Dec. 11, 1918; s. Merritt Cooley and Effie (Mackenzie) A.; Ed.B., UCLA, 1940, M.A., 1942; m. Mary Elizabeth Atchison, Jan. 9, 1943; 1 son, Michael Gerald. Represented in collections Bklyn. Mus., Art. Inst. Chgo., Pasadena Art. Mus., Grunwald Center Graphic Arts, Mus. Modern Art, Los Angeles County Art Museum, and others; instr. art UCLA, 1946-48, asst. prof., 1948-54; prof. art, head dept. U. Ky., also dir. Art Gallery, 1954-57; prof. art, head dept. U. Fla., 1957-61; dean Coll. Fine Arts, U. N.Mex., Albuquerque, 1961-76, assoc. provost, dean faculties, 1976-77; dir. Tamarind Inst., 1970—; asso. dir. Tamarind Lithography Workshop, Los Angeles, 1960-61, program cons., 1961-70. Mem. Coll. Art Assn. (program chmn. 1963), Nat. Council Fine Arts Deans (chmn. 1956-67), Mid-Am. Coll. Art Assn. (pres. 1973). Author: (with Garo Antreasian) The Tamarind Book of Lithography: Art and Techniques, 1970; Fritz Scholder: Lithographs, 1975; American Lithographers, 1900-1960: The Artists and Their Printers, 1983; editor: The Tamarind Papers, 1974—.

ADAMS, DAVID BENNION, psychologist; b. Salt Lake City, May 21, 1945; s. Ferrell Harrison and Maurine (Bennion) A.; B.A., U. Utah, 1968, M.S. (Kappa Sigma fellow), 1972, Ph.D. in Psychology cum laude, 1976; m. Kathy Jean Hulbert, Aug. 18, 1972. Staff psychologist Granite Mental Health Center, 1972-74; dir. Juvenile Alcohol Program, 1974-75; clin. supr. Adolescent Residential Treatment Center, 1974-79; pvt. practice clin. psychology, Salt Lake City, 1976—, also clin. dir. Am. Community Youth Services, 1979-82, Intermountain Youth Care, 1982—; instr. U. Utah, Brigham Young U. Local dist. del. Democratic Party, 1972. Served with USAR, 1963-71. Lic. and cert. psychologist, Utah; cert. marriage and family counselor, Utah. Mem. Am. Psychol. Assn., Utah Psychol. Assn., Utah Psychologists in Pvt. Practice, Zero Population Growth, Friends of the Earth, Sierra Club, Utah Assn. Juvenile and Adult Corrections, Kappa Sigma. Presbyterian. Contbr. articles to profl. jours. Home: 1371 E 1300 S Salt Lake City UT 84105 Office: 14 E 2700 S Salt Lake City UT 84115

ADAMS, DONALD FREDERICK, mech. engr.; b. Streator, Ill., Sept. 25, 1935; s. Fred Mathew and Margaret Ann (Doerr) A.; B.S. in Mech. Engring., U. Ill., 1957, Ph.D. in Theoretical and Applied Mechanics, 1963; M.S. in Mech. Engring., U. So. Calif., 1960; m. Roberta Ann Rush, June 22, 1957; children—David, Daniel, Douglas, Jayne. Engr. mech. design group Northrop Aircraft, Inc., Hawthorne, Calif., 1957-60; part-time instr. U. Ill., 1960-63; supr. mechanics of materials group Aeronutronic div. Applied Research Labs., Philco-Ford Corp., Newport Beach, Calif., 1963-67; mem. tech. staff RAND Corp., Santa Monica, Calif., 1967-72; prof. mech. engring. U. Wyo., Laramie, 1972—; faculty participant NSF summer program, 1974; cons. to govt. and industry. Recipient Outstanding Faculty Mem. award U. Wyo., 1973; grantee NSF, NASA, U.S. Army, U.S. Navy, also industry; registered profl. engr., Wyo. Mem. Soc. Automotive Engrs. (Teetor award 1978), Soc. Exptl. Stress Analysis, ASME, Am. Acad. Mechanics, AIAA, ASTM, Am. Soc. Engring. Edn., Soc. Advanced Materials and Process Engrs., Nat. Soc. Profl. Engrs., Wyo. Soc. Profl. Engrs., Wyo. Engring. Soc., Sigma Xi, Pi Tau Sigma, Tau Beta Pi, Sigma Tau. Author 100 articles, reports; reviewer various jours. Home: 421 S 19th St Laramie WY 82070 Office: Mech Engring Dept Univ Wyo Laramie WY 82071

ADAMS, DOUGLAS KENT, sales engr.; b. Schenectady, Mar. 26, 1920; s. Lee Francis and Ruth Idel (Mussen) A.; B.S., Pa. State U., 1941; m. Sidney Johnson, July 14, 1968; children—William, Mary, Carolyn, Richard, Claude, James. Application engr., motor dept. Gen. Electric Co., Schenectady, 1945-53, product planner, 1954-56, product specialist, indsl. sales div., Denver, 1956-60, sales engr., 1961—. Fin. sec. Youth Unltd. Christian Club, 1973-76 78, services staff chmn., 1979. Served to maj. USAAF, 1941-45. Registered profl. engr., Colo. Mem. IEEE, Colo. Mining Assn., Coal Mining Inst., Triangle Frat. Republican. Baptist. Home: 2505 Cherry St Denver CO 80207 Office: 201 University Blvd Denver CO 80206

ADAMS, EDWIN CARROLL, electronics engineer; b. Chgo., Aug. 9, 1927; s. Edward and Esther (Mecsery) A.; m. Lillian Uebel, Sept. 4, 1948; children—Donald Edward, Nancy Adams Richards. B.S. in Electrical Engring., Ill. Inst. Tech., 1955. Engring. asst. Ill. Testing Labs., Chgo., 1949-51; devel. engr. Motorola Inc., Chgo., 1951-57; sr. engr. Cook Research Labs., Morton Grove, Ill., 1957-60; project engr. Zenith Radio Corp., Chgo., 1960-65; engr. mgr. Sierra Research Corp., Buffalo, 1965-79; engr. mgr. Thermal Tech. Lab., Buffalo, 1979-80; prin. engr. Sperry Univac, Salt Lake City, 1980—. Served with USN, 1945-46. Mem. IEEE, AIAA, Assn. Unmanned Vehicle Systems, Assn. Old Crows. Presbyterian. Patentee Doppler target simulator, 1967. Home: 8744 Acorn Ln Sandy UT 84092 Office: 322 N 22nd West Salt Lake City UT 84116

ADAMS, ELDON EUGENE, retail/wholesale business executive; b. Brawley, Calif., Sept. 8, 1944; s. Elwood Eugene and Pauline (Striker) A.; m. Bettie Ann Keyfauver, July 16, 1966; children—Michael Trevor, Brad Everett. B.S., Calif. State Poly. U., Pomona, 1968. C.P.A., Calif. Staff acct. Deloitte, Haskins & Sells, C.P.A.s, 1968-71, sr. acct., 1971-74, mgr., 1974-79; pres. W. J. Vogel Co., Inc., Brawley, Calif., 1979—; dir. Imperial County Pvt. Industry Council, Inc. Chmn., Citizens Adv. com. to Brawley Community Redevel. Agy., 1981; trustee Pioneers Meml.

Hosp. Found., 1982—. Mem. Am. Inst. C.P.A.s, Calif. Soc. C.P.A.s, Brawley C. of C. (dir. 1981—). Republican. Club: Lions (v.p.) (Brawley, Calif.). Home: 183 Julia Dr Brawley CA 92227 Office: 860 Main St Brawley CA 92227

ADAMS, GAIL HAYES, interior designer, exec.; b. Bronxville, N.Y., Nov. 18, 1944; d. Samuel Eugene and Kathryn Minnette (Hayes) A.; m. Gilbert Johnson, Oct. 25, 1968; m. 2d, Joy Martin Goodfarb, Nov. 5, 1978. B.S. in Fine Arts, Ariz. State U., 1967. Interior designer Mehagians Furniture Galleries Co., Phoenix, 1967-1979; pres., interior designer Gail Adams Interiors, Ltd., Phoenix, 1979—; v.p. Rocky Mt. region, Am. Soc. Interior Designers, 1981-82. Active Phoenix Art Mus.; mem. steering com. Ariz. Theatre Co. Mem. Am. Soc. Interior Designers (cert., pres. Ariz. N. chpt. 1979-80, v.p. Rocky Mountain region 1981-82). Home and Office: 110 E San Miguel Phoenix AZ 85012

ADAMS, GARY BORAH, criminal justice educator; b. Boise, Idaho, Jan. 25, 1940; s. William and Lois Liberty (McRoberts) A.; m. Joyce Lucile Frost, Aug. 6, 1961; children—Susan, Neal, Gordon. A.B., Coll. Idaho, 1968; M. Pub. Adminstrn., U. So. Calif., 1970, D. Pub. Adminstrn., 1973. Program officer Delinquency Control Inst., U. So. Calif., Los Angeles, 1970-72; mem. faculty Calif. State U., Long Beach, 1972—, now prof. dept. criminal justice, exec. dir. Center for Criminal Justice Research and Tng., 1980—, chmn. bd. dirs. Forty Niner Shops, Inc., 1980—. Mayor City of Sierra Madre, Calif., 1979-80; trustee Pasadena Community Coll., 1979—, pres., 1981—; mem., chmn. Calif. Statewide Curriculum Articulation Com., Criminal Justice, 1978—. Contbr. numerous articles and reviews to profl. publs. Office: California State University Dept Criminal Justice 1250 Bellflower Blvd Long Beach CA 90840

ADAMS, GEORGIA S. WEIN (MRS. JOSEPH JOHN ADAMS), educator, author; b. Ortonville, Minn., May 23, 1913; d. John Frederick and Ella (Merry) Wein; A.B., U. So. Calif., 1933, M.S., 1935, Ph.D., 1941; postgrad. U. Chgo., Claremont Grad. Sch.; m. Joseph John Adams, Sept. 7, 1946;children—Margaret Adams Cross, Jo-Ann, Joseph, Mary. Research asst., research dir. Pasadena City Schs., 1936-51; instr. Muir Coll., 1951-52, 53-54; lectr. Claremont Grad. Sch., 1953—; prof. edn. Calif. State U., Los Angeles, 1954—; assessment coordinator Nat. Dissemination and Assessment Ctr. in Bilingual Edn.; vis. prof. U. Hawaii, summer 1959, 67; dir. Evaluation Teaching Team Project, Ford Found.; coordinator ednl. founds., 1964-67; cons. Project Teach, Office Edn. Project, A Reading Program for Mexican-Am. Children, Orientation and Mobility Skills for The Blind. Recipient of Outstanding Prof. award Calif. State Coll., 1969. Fellow Am. Psychol. Assn.; mem. Internat. Council Psychologists (sec.-gen. 1979-82), Am. Ednl. Research Assn., Phi Beta Kappa, Pi Lambda Theta (nat. v.p. 1963-67, 69-70, nat. pres. 1970-73, Disting. Pi Lambda Thetan award 1980). Author: Exploring the World of Work, 1937; Evaluating Group Guidance Work in Secondary Schools, 1945; California Test in Social and Related Sciences, 1947, 54; Measurement and Evaluation for the Elementary School Teacher, 1954; Measurement and Evaluation for the Secondary School Teacher, 1956; Social Relationships in the Classroom, 1958; California Survey Tests, 1958; Measurement and Evaluation in Education and Psychology, 1964, Spanish edit., 1970; contbg. author Ency. Ednl. Research. Home: 2772 N Lake Ave Altadena CA 91001 Office: 5151 State University Dr Los Angeles CA 90032

ADAMS, HUGH BARNETT, energy company executive; b. Bardwell, Ky., Apr. 20, 1929; s. Jay B. and Willie Alma (Edwards) A.; m. Billie Jean Norris, Jan. 20, 1951; children—Rodney B., Steven W. A.A., Community Coll. Denver, North Denver, 1972; B.S., Met. State Coll., Denver, 1975; M.A., Colo. State U., 1977. Instr. Community Coll. Denver, 1969-79; asst. dir. occupational studies and mining tng. Colo. Mountain Coll., Glenwood Springs, Colo., 1979-80; safety and skills tng. coordinator Rocky Mountain Energy Co., Broomfield, Colo., 1980—. Served with USNR, 1948-54. Mem. Am. Soc Tng. and Devel., Am. Welding Soc., Am. Vocat. Assn., Colo. Vocat. Assn. (Leadership award 1975). Democrat. Baptist. Club: Masons. Office: 10 Longs Peak Dr Broomfield CO 80020

ADAMS, JACK EDWON, interior designer; b. Abiline, Tex., Sept. 21, 1941; s. Robert Edison and Audrea May A.; m. Merrily Ray Pokorny, June 7, 1969; children—Felicity Ann, Andrew Robert. B.S., U.S. Mil. Acad., 1963; student Am. U., 1965; B.S., Art Center, 1971. Designer, Richard Crowell Asso., Honolulu, 1971-74; dir. interior design Media 5 Architects, Honolulu, 1974-76; designer Dale Keller Assocs., Los Angeles, 1976-77; pres., dir. design Adams Design, Inc., Honolulu, 1977—. Active Honolulu Acad. Arts, Honolulu Symphony Soc. Served to capt. U.S. Army, 1959-63. Mem. Am. Soc. Interior Designers (cert., dir. Hawaii chpt. 1979). Clubs: Kailua Racquet, Chaine de Rotisseurs, Masons, Shriners. Contbr. articles to profl. publs. Home: 2710 Puuhonua Honolulu HI 96822 Office: 1415 Kalakaua Ave Suite 204 Honolulu HI 96826

ADAMS, JAMES LOWELL, mech. engr., educator; b. Rialto, Calif., Mar. 6, 1934; s. Frank Lowell and Jean Adele A.; B.S., Calif. Inst. Tech., 1955; M.S., Stanford U., 1959, Ph.D., 1961; m. Marian Player; children—Robert Lowell, Daniel Thomas. Research asso. Stanford U., 1958-61, sr. engr. and engring. group supr. Jet Propulsion Lab., 1961-66, asso. prof. mech. engring., 1966-71, prof., 1971—, dir. design div., 1968-73, chmn. dept. indsl. engring. and engring. mgmt., 1973-76, asso. dean acad. affairs Sch. Engring., 1973—, chmn. program in values, tech., sci. and society, 1982—; cons. to industry, govt. Served with USAF, 1955-57. Registered profl. engr., Calif. Mem. ASME, Am. Soc. Engring. Edn., Sigma Xi, Tau Beta Pi. Author: Conceptual Blockbusting, 2d edit., 1980. Home: 740 Santa Ynez Stanford CA 94305 Office: Stanford U Stanford CA 94305

ADAMS, JAMES PATRICK, health care services administrator; b. Cedar City, Utah, Aug. 6, 1940; s. L. Sturman and Anne (King) A. B.A. in Polit. Sci. and Econs., U. Colo., 1969, Ph.D. in Polit. Sci., 1981. Instr. dept. polit. sci. U. Colo., Boulder, div. social scis., Denver, div. continuing edn., Boulder and Denver, 1971-81; adj. asst. prof. dept. polit. sci. U. Colo., Boulder, 1981-82, instr. div. continuing edn., 1982; instr. Inst. Gerontology and dept. econs., U. Denver, 1982; dir. planning Beth Israel Hosp. and Geriatric Ctr., Denver, 1975—; research assoc. Ctr. Pub. Policy Research dept. polit. sci. U. Colo., Boulder, 1983-84; dir. Denver Mobility; 1982; participant Am. Hosp. Assn. and Can. Hosp. Assn. joint ann. conf., 1980. Mem. Denver Sub-Area Council, Central N.E. Colo. Health Systems Agy., 1978-80, mem. Long-Term Care Adv. Com., 1979-80; participant Nat. Council on Aging ann. confs., 1978, 79; participant N. Am. Conf. Jewish Communal Services and N. Am. Assn. Jewish Homes, Housing for Aging, 1980, 82; mem. site-visit, tng. coms. U. Wash., Seattle, 1979, Abbott-Northwestern Hosp., Mpls. Age and Opportunity Ctr., 1976; cons. Colo. Sr. Lobby, 1982; cons. various partisan and non-partisan election campaigns, 1968-78. Mem. Am. Polit. Sci. Assn., Acad. Polit. Sci., Am. Pub. Health Assn., Soc. Hosp. Planning, Am. Hosp. Assn., Ctr. for Study of Presidency, Greenpeace Found., Audubon Soc. Democrat. Contbr. articles on aging to newspapers, jours.

ADAMS, JESSE LORAINE, sch. adminstr.; b. Santa Maria, Calif., Feb. 22, 1942; s. Ralph Harry and Hilda Cora (Howard) A.; B.S. cum laude, Brigham Young U., 1965, M.S., 1966, Ph.D., 1975. Tchr. English, pub. schs. Santa Maria, Calif., 1965-67, instr. sociology Brigham Young U., Provo. Utah, 1967-72; counslor, elementary schs. Alpine Sch. Dis., Provo, 1972-76, diagnostician, 1976-77, coordinator spl. edn., 1977—. Bd. dirs. Utah Valley Care and Tng. Center; del. Utah County Republican Conv. Mem. Am. Personnel and Guidance Assn., Am. Sch. Counselors Assn. Mem. Ch. Jesus Christ Latter-day Saints. Home: 721 N 1100 E St Provo UT 84601 Office: 50 N Center St American Fork UT 84003

ADAMS, JO-ANN MARIE, computer systems analyst; b. Los Angeles, May 27, 1949; d. Joseph John and Georgia S. (Wein) A.; A.A., Pasadena City Coll., 1968; B.A., Pomona Coll., 1970; M.A., Calif. State U., Los Angeles, 1971. Secondary tchr. South Pasadena (Calif.) Unified Schs., 1970-71; appraiser Riverside County (Calif.) Assessor's Office, 1972-74; systems and procedures analyst Riverside County Data Processing Dept., 1974-76, supervising systems analyst, 1976-79; systems analyst computer Boeing Computer Services Co., Seattle, 1979-81; sr. systems analyst Thurston County Central Services, Olympia, Wash., 1981—; instr. Riverside City Coll., 1977-79. Chairperson legis. task force Riverside/San Bernardino chpt. NOW, 1975-76, chpt. co-chairperson, 1978; mem. ethics com. Calif. NOW Inc., 1978; alt. del. Calif Democratic Caucus, 1978. Mem. NOW, Nat. Abortion Rights Action League, Nat. Assn. Female Execs., Assn. Systems Mgrs., Am. Mgmt. Assn., Nat. Assn. Computing Machinery, Pomona Coll. Alumni Assn., U.S. Olympic Soc. Home: 12313 98th Ave E Puyallup WA 98373 Office: 2000 Lakeridge Dr SW Olympia WA 98502

ADAMS, JOHN WILLIAM, systems research and products co. exec., mgmt. cons.; b. Chgo., Feb. 23, 1923; s. Frank Alexander and Ruth Ella (Haas) A.; B.A., Pomona Coll., 1947; postgrad. Yale U., 1947-48; m. Suzanne Marie Joy, Dec. 27, 1942 (dec.); children—John Shepherd, Bradford Lee; m. 2d, Barbara Lou Hamilton, Sept. 2, 1979. Dir. public relations, producer spl. films 20th Century-Fox Film Corp., Beverly Hills, Calif., 1948-53; mgr. Bur. Occupations, UCLA, 1953-56; asst. to pres., dir. univ. relations Rand Corp., Santa Monica, Calif., 1957-62; dir. adminstrn., engring. div. Aerospace Corp., El Segundo, Calif., 1962-65; with Gen. Research Corp. (now Flow Gen. Inc.), Santa Barbara, Calif., 1965—, asst. to chmn., dir. public and fin. relations and advt., 1975—, semi-ret., 1979—; chmn. bd. Adams Group, Inc., mgmt. cons., 1979—. Served with USAAF, 1942-46. Decorated Air medal. Republican. Episcopalian. Clubs: Santa Barbara, Santa Barbara Polo and Racquet; Coral Casino Beach. Home: 642 Calle de Los Amigos Santa Barbara CA 93105 Office: 5383 Hollister Ave Santa Barbara CA 93111

ADAMS, KATHLEEN, publishing company executive, freelance writer; b. Soap Lake, Wash., May 12, 1951; d. Dale Hartley and Theda June (Edmunds) A. B.A. in Journalism, Colo. State U., Ft. Collins, 1972. Legal asst. H. William Lyle, P.C., Tucson, 1972-78; v.p. editorial div. Continental Communications Group, Inc., Denver, 1978—; mem. faculty Pima Community Coll., Tucson, 1974-75. Campaign worker Ariz. gubernatorial campaign, Tucson, 1974; vol. Ptnrs., Denver, 1978-80; mem. Am. Med. Ctr. for Cancer Research, Denver. Mem. Nat. Assn. Legal Assts. (bd. dirs. 1976-78), Nat. Assn. Female Execs., Am. Assn. Ind. Investors, Rocky Mountain Direct Mail Mktg. Assn., Bank Mktg. Assn. Mem. Ch. of Religious Science. Co-author: Fica-$ave Implementations Manual, 1979. Office: Continental Communications Group Inc 12500 W Cedar Dr Lakewood CO 80228

ADAMS, KENNETH DALE, psychologist, educator; b. Cloud Chief, Okla., Feb. 9, 1929; s. Alvin Rowe and Leona Sarah (Carpenter) A.; m. E. El Wanda Janes; 1 son, K. Dale. B.S. in Math., Southwestern State U., 1950; M.Ed. in Adminstrn and Guidance, U. Okla., 1957, Ph.D. in Counseling Psychology, 1982. Cert. psychologist, counselor, adminstr., tchr. Math tchr., Cowden, Okla., 1948-49, Mountain View, Okla., 1949-57; math tchr., counselor S. Kitsap Schs., Port Orchard, Wash., 1957-64, psychologist, 1965-70, adminstr., 1970-82; profl. counselor and psychologist Sound Counseling Services, Port Orchard, 1980—; adj. prof. counseling Central Wash. State U., Ellenburg, Seattle Pacific U., 1967-82. Active Democratic legis. campaign, 1982. Recipient NDEA Counseling Insts. awards 1961, 62, 63, 64. Mem. Am. Personnel and Guidance Assn., Wash. State Counseling and Guidance Assn., Am. Mental Health Counselors Assn., Wash. Mental Health Counselors Assn., Phi Delta Kappa. Democrat. Methodist. Clubs: Bremerton Yacht, Elks. Home: 2422 Parkwood Dr SE Port Orchard WA 98366 Office: Sound Counseling Services 502 High Ave S-203 Port Orchard WA 98366

ADAMS, MARGARET BERNICE, anthropologist, museologist, historian, art historian; b. Toronto, Ont., Can., Apr. 29, 1936; d. Robert Russell and Kathleen Olive (Buffin) Adams; m. Alberto Enrique Sanches-Quinonez, Nov. 30, 1956 (div.). B.A. in Anthropology and Art History, San Jose State U., 1971; M.A. in Anthropology, U. Utah, 1972; Museology intern Milton H. de Young Mus., San Francisco, 1970-71; staff asst. Civic Art Gallery of San Jose, Calif., 1971, Utah Mus. of Fine Art, Salt Lake City, part-time, 1972; lectr. U. Calif.-Santa Cruz, 1972-74; instr., part-time, Cabrillo Coll., Calif., 1973, Monterey (Calif.) Peninsula Coll., 1973—; mus. chief curator, dir., historian Presidio of Monterey (Army) Mus. and Ft. Ord Mus., 1974—; guest curator Monterey Peninsula Mus. of Art, Monterey, 1974—; cons. in field. Mem. Monterey Peninsula Mus. of Art Assn., Pacific Grove Art Center, Monterey History and Art Assn., Am. Anthrop. Assn., Assn. Applied Anthropology, Am. Assn. Museums, Am. Archeol. Assn. Author catalogues including: Chronology of World Events in Pueblo (Indian) Times, 1974; American Indian Arts, 1975; Skystone and Silver: Southwestern Indian Jewelry, 1982; Spider Woman's Daughters: 20th Century Navajo Weavers, 1982. Home: 363 Hillcrest Ave Pacific Grove CA 93950 Office: Presidio of Monterey Army Mus Presidio of Monterey Monterey CA 93940 also 7th Infantry Div and Ft Ord Mus Ford Ord CA 93941

ADAMS, M. B., govt. ofcl.; b. Weathers, Okla., Feb. 14, 1923; s. William D. and Maude Sarah (Smith) A.; A.A., Diablo Valley Coll., Pleasant Hill, Calif., 1954; diploma Pacific Coast Banking Sch., 1963; m. Martha Dolores Schmidt, Mar. 16, 1952; children—Jennifer Gail, Melissa Louise, Michael Bruce. With Bank Am., N.T.&S.A., Concord, Calif., 1949-51, Pacific Gas & Electric Co., Concord, 1951-55; asst. nat. bank examiner Office of Comptroller of the Currency, Treasury Dept., 1955, dep. regional adminstr. nat. banks, Atlanta, 1967-74, regional adminstr. nat. banks, Portland, Oreg., 1974—. Served with USAAF, 1943-45. Republican.

ADAMS, MARION ROBERT, JR., feed and seed dealer; b. Springfield, Oreg., Oct. 2, 1923; s. Marion Robert and Ida (Carson) A.; student U. Oreg., 1941; m. Bobbie Jean Taylor, Sept. 21, 1947; children—Marion Robert, Amy Carol, Sandra Lynn, Richard Arthur. Owner/mgr., Adams Feed & Seed, Springfield, 1941—, now pres. Councilman, City of Springfield, 1974-80; bd. dirs. Lane Regional Air Pollution Authority, 1974-80, acting dir., 1979; bd. dirs. Met. Wastewater Mgmt. Commn., 1975-80. Served with AUS, 1943-45. Mem. Am. Legion. Republican. Home: 1306 "N" St Springfield OR 97477 Office: 3545 Marcola Rd Springfield OR 97477

ADAMS, NORMAN JOSEPH, economist, corporate mergers broker; b. Los Angeles, Feb. 21, 1930; s. Joseph O'Neil and Florence Mary (Michalek) A.; B.S., U. So. Calif., 1951; diploma Oxford U., 1953; postgrad. Harvard U., 1956; Ph.D., U. Karachi (Pakistan), 1958; m. Julia Jewell, Oct. 16, 1960; children—Darlene, Janet. Pres., Adams & Co., mergers and aquisitions, Los Angeles. Office: Adams & Co 6290 Sunset Blvd Los Angeles CA 90028

ADAMS, PATRICIA ANNE, office automation specialist; b. Boston, Mar. 28, 1947; d. Robert Edward and MaryAnne (Strebe) A. Student Rochester Bus. Inst., 1966-67. With Xerox Corp., Rochester, N.Y., Dallas and St. Louis, 1970-76; nat. mktg. support rep. mgr. Jacquard Systems, Santa Monica, Calif., 1976-78; regional mktg. support rep. mgr., product specialist Basic Four Corp., Tustin, Calif., 1978-80; office automation specialist Prime Computer Inc., Irvine, Calif., 1980—. Home: 3700 Plaza Dr Bldg E Apt PH7 Santa Ana CA 92704 Office: 2102 Business Center Dr Suite 115 Irvine CA 92715

ADAMS, PHILIP, lawyer; b. Los Angeles, July 18, 1905; s. Thaddeus Lafayette and Lena (Kelly) A.; student Pomona Coll., 1924-27; J.D., Hastings Coll. Law, U. Calif., 1938; LL.D. (hon.), Ch. Div. Sch. of Pacific, Berkeley, Calif., 1965; m. Alice Rahman, 1933; children—Stephen, Judith, Deborah, Kate; m. 2d, Elaine Margaret Anderson, 1968. Purser, Panama Mail S.S. Line, 1928-29; profl. investigator, 1930-38; admitted to Calif. bar, 1938; individual practice law, San Francisco, 1938—; atty. U.S. Govt., 1942-46; instr. domestic relations Golden Gate Law Sch., 1971-72. Dir., Children's Protective Soc., 1939-44, United Cerebral Palsy Assn., San Francisco, 1952-72, Assn. for Mental Health, San Francisco, 1952—, United Bay Area Crusade, 1955-61, United Community Fund, San Francisco, 1957-62, San Francisco State Coll., 1964-69, Am. Democratic Action; Resolve of Calif., 1980—; trustee Ch. Div. Sch. of Pacific, 1951-76; nat. v.p. Episcopal Evang. Fellowship, 1952-61; chancellor Episcopal Diocese of Calif., 1960-67; dep. Episcopal Gen. Conv., 1946-70; pres. bd. trustees Grad. Theol. Union, Berkeley, 1963-66. Fellow Am. Acad. Matrimonial Lawyers (dir. No. Calif. chpt. 1968—); mem. Am. (chmn. com. on adoption, family law sect. 1959-60), Calif., San Francisco bar assns., Lawyers Club San Francisco (gov. 1956), Am. Acad. Polit. and Social Sci., San Francisco Symphony Assn., San Francisco Chamber Soloists, Soc. Genealogists (London). Clubs: Villa Taverna, Commonwealth. Author: Adoption Practice in California, 1956. Home: 2170 Jackson St San Francisco CA 94115 Office: Mills Bldg San Francisco CA 94104

ADAMS, ROBERT MORFORD, JR., lawyer; b. Duluth, Minn., Feb. 13, 1916; s. Robert M. and Cherrill (McNeill) A.; m. Elizabeth Sweet, Mar. 23, 1940 (dec. Aug. 1980); children—Robert M., Clifford S., Richard M.; m. 2d, Joyce Halley, June 14, 1981. A.B., Stanford U., 1937, LL.B., 1940. Bar: Calif. 1941, U.S. Supreme Ct. 1958. Practice law, San Francisco, 1941—; assoc. McCutchen, Olney, Mannon & Greene, 1941-47, Athearn, Chandler & Farmer, Hoffman & Angell, 1947-50; ptnr. Angell & Adams, 1950-62, Angell, Adams and Holmes, 1962-70, Busterud, Draper & Adams, 1970-72, Draper, Adams & Huntington P.C., 1973-75, Draper, Adams & Zacher P.C., 1975-76, Cotton, Seligman & Ray, 1976-79; sole practice, 1979—. Chancellor, Protestant Episcopal Diocese Calif., 1973—. Served with USNR, 1942-45. Mem. ABA, Bar Assn. San Francisco, Am. Judicature Soc., AIME (assoc.), Engrs. Club San Francisco, Phi Beta Kappa, Theta Delta Chi, Phi Alpha Delta. Clubs: Bohemian, San Francisco Golf (San Francisco). Home: 529 W Poplar St San Mateo CA 94402 Office: 235 Montgomery St Suite 2500 San Francisco CA 94104

ADAMS, RONALD LYNN, mechanical engineering educator, consultant; b. Hillsboro, Oreg., Apr. 27, 1948; s. Charles Clifford and Nellie Marie (Beckner) A.; B.S. in M.E., Oreg. State U., 1970, Ph.D., 1977; M.S. in Aeros. and Astronautics, M.I.T., 1971; m. Judy Anne Shelton, Aug. 12, 1967; children—Wendi L., Ronald L. Research engr. M.I.T., Aerophysics Lab., Cambridge, 1972, staff mem. M.I.T. Lincoln Labs., 1977-79; asst. prof. mech. engring. Oreg. State U., Corvallis, 1979-83, assoc. prof., 1983—. Served to 1st lt. USAF, 1972-75. Decorated Air Force Commendation medal; registered profl. engr., Oreg. Mem. AIAA, ASME (treas. Willomette Valley sect. 1983-84, reviewer Jour. Heat Transfer 1981—), Air Force Assn., Sigma Xi. Contbr. articles to profl. jours.; reviewer Am. Inst. Chem. Engrs. Jours., 1979-80, NSF Heat Transfer div., 1981—, Internat. Jour. Powder Tech., 1982—, Internat. Jour. Heat and Mass Transfer, 1982—. Office: Dept Mech Engring Oreg State Univ Corvallis OR 97331

ADAMS, SUSAN LORRAINE, interior design and facility planner; b. Glendale, Calif., Feb. 7, 1949; d. Richard and Virginia (Blum) A. A.A., Los Angeles City Coll., 1969; B.A. in Design, Calif. State U., 1972. With Dexion, Inc., 1972-73, Group Attec, 1973-75, Calif. Constrn. Mgmt. Co., 1975-76, DMJM, Los Angeles, 1976-77, Leach, Cleveland, Hayakawa & Barry, Beverly Hills, Calif., 1977-78, Hughes Aircraft, El Segundo, Calif., 1978-79, Fabco, Los Angeles, 1978-79; cons., project designer, 1979-81; cons. sr. interior designer and project coordinator Greenlaw Design Assocs., Glendale, Calif., 1981-82; design cons., Los Angeles, 1982—. Recipient Newman award in journalism, 1966, others. Mem. Calif. Bus. Women's Network, Am. Soc. Engrs. and Architects, Order of Amaranth. Unity Ch. Home: 554 Oleander Dr Los Angeles CA 90042 Office: 3010 Worthen Ave Los Angeles CA 90039

ADAMS, THOMAS COOPER, forest economist; b. San Francisco, Nov. 4, 1918; s. Frank and Amy B. (Hill) A.; B.S., U. Calif. at Berkeley, 1940, A.B., 1941; M.A., U. Mich., 1951, Ph.D., 1952; m. Laura May Kopp, Mar. 17, 1957; children—Anne Adams Abegglen, Sally Adams Kropf. Forest economist Pacific Northwest Forest and Range Expt. Sta., U.S. Forest Service, Portland, Oreg., 1952-54, 57—; asst. prof. Sch. Forestry, Oreg. State U., Corvallis, 1955-57. Vice commodore Portland Sea Scouts, Boy Scouts Am., 1970-73. Served to lt. comdr. USNR, 1941-47. Mem. Soc. Am. Foresters (chpt. chmn. 1962), Am. Econ. Assn., Am. Agrl. Econs. Assn., Regional Sci. Assn., Am. Forestry Assn. Episcopalian (vestryman 1971-73). Home: 7640 SE 28th Ave Portland OR 97202 Office: 809 NE 6th Ave Portland OR 97232

ADAMS, THOMAS FRANCIS, SR., educator; b. Springfield, Mo.; s. Charles Henry and Marguerite Elizabeth (Kibbe) A.; B.S., Calif. State U., Long Beach, 1968, M.S. in Criminology, 1972; postgrad. UCLA, 1968-72; student San Francisco Conservatory of Music, 1948; children—Thomas, Norina, Brian. Profl. entertainer, restaurant mgr., chef, Calif. and U.S., 1946-54; police lt. Santa Ana (Calif.) Police Dept., 1954-68; prof., dept. chmn. criminal justice Santa Ana Coll., 1970—; dir. T.A.D., profl. services, Santa Ana, 1975—; criminal justice cons.; pvt. investigator, polygraph examiner; mgr. amateur community theater and coll. theater prodns. Served with USN, 1944-46. Mem. Calif. Assn. Police Tng. Officers, Calif. Assn. Adminstrs. of Justice Educators, Aircraft Owners and Pilots Assn., Internat. Assn. Polygraph Examiners. Author textbooks: Training Officers Handbook, 1964; Law Enforcement, An Introduction to the Police Role in the Community, 1968; Police Patrol, Tactics and Techniques, 1971; Criminal Justice Readings, 1972; Law Enforcement: An Introduction to Police Role in Criminal Justice System, 1972; Introduction to Administration of Justice, 1975; Criminal Justice Organization and Management, 1974; Introduction to Administration of Justice, 1975, 80; Police Field Operations, 1983; lic. pilot. Home: PO Box 6471 Santa Ana CA 92706 Office: Santa Ana College 17th and Bristol Santa Ana CA 92706

ADAMS, VICKI PORTER, computer publications specialist; b. Wheeling, W. Va., Apr. 10, 1939; d. Clyde Scott and Helen (McClure) Porter; m. Theodore Cecil Adams, Nov. 20, 1971. B.E., Waynesburg Coll., 1961; postgrad. W.Va. U., 1962. Elem. tchr. Los Angeles Bd. Edn., 1961-63; tchr. jr. high sch. Thousand Oaks (Calif.) Unified Sch. Dist., 1963-66; computer programmer System Devel. Corp., Santa Monica, Calif., 1966-70; sr. programmer NCR Corp., San Diego, 1971-75; mem. staff testing Litton Mellonics, San Diego, 1975-76; mgr. tech. publs. TRW Communications, San Diego, 1976-78; sr. cons. publs. specialist NCR

Corp., 1978—; cons., writer, speaker in field. Pub. relations mem. Crime Victims Fund, DAR. Recipient Cert. of Achievement scholarship Nat. U., San Diego, 1982. Mem. Calif. Press Women (v.p., editor, bd. dirs., four writing awards 1980, five awards 1981), Nat. Fedn. Press Women, Nat. Writer's Club, Women in Data Processing, Nat. Assn. Female Execs., San Diego Writers/Editors Guild. Republican. Methodist. Contbr. articles to mags. Home: 4461 Moraga Ave San Diego CA 92117 Office: 11010 Torreyana Rd San Diego CA 92121

ADAMS, WILLIAM, psychologist, publisher; b. Montreal, Que., Can., June 26, 1946; came to U.S. 1955, naturalized, 1965; s. Allen William and Jean Elizabeth (Moore) A.; m. Deborah Ann Wallace, July 25, 1977. B.A., Western Wash. U., 1968, M.S., 1969; Ph.D., U. Wis.-Milw., 1972. Lectr., U. Wis.-Milw., 1972-73; research fellow in psychology Cornell U., 1973-74; asst. prof., chmn. dept. psychology Coll. Idaho, 1974-77; lectr. univ. coll. U. Md., 1977-79; pub. Psycholog. Press, Seattle, 1979—. Mem. Am. Psychol. Assn., Western Psychol. Assn. Author: The Experience of Teaching and Learning: A Phenomenology of Education, 1980. Office: Psychol Press PO Box 5435 Seattle WA 98105

ADAMS, WILLIAM BESLEY, JR., general insurance company executive; b. Portland, Oreg., Feb. 5, 1947; s. William Besley and Ruthe (Rolle) A.; B.S., U. Oreg., 1971; J.D., Lewis and Clark Coll., 1974. Assoc. group legal dept. Standard Ins. Co., Portland, 1975-77; adminstrv. head employment agy. and farm labor div. State of Oreg., Portland, 1977-79; pension cons. Retirement Plans, Inc., Portland, 1979-80; producer, ptnr. W.R. Reed & Co., Portland, 1980-83; assoc. Leonard Adams Co., Beaverton, Oreg., 1983—. Dir. research Multnomah County Republicans. Served with USMC, 1966-68. Mem. Nat. Assn. Pension Cons., Am. Mgmt. Assn. Episcopalian. Clubs: Mazama, Multnomah Athletic, Oreg. Rd. Runners, Ducks Unltd., Trumpeters, Lincoln. Contbr. articles to profl. jours. Home: 4635 SE 44th Ave Portland OR 97206 Office: 11420 SW Canyon Rd Beaverton OR 97005

ADAMS, WILLIAM MANSFIELD, seismologist, educator; b. Kissimmee, Fla., Feb. 19, 1932; s. Shirah Devoy and Olive (Goding) A.; A.B. (Univ. scholar), U. Chgo., 1951; B.A., U. Calif., 1953; M.S. (Gulf scholar), St. Louis U., 1955, Ph.D., 1957; M.B.A., Santa Clara U., 1964; postgrad. Mass. Inst. Tech., 1967-70; m. Roberta Kay Blackwell, July 23, 1955; children—William Mansfield, Jonathan Blackwell, Christopher Daniel; m. Naoko Nakashizuka, 1976; children—Henele Iitaka, Alden Fernald. Instrument man Shell Oil Co., Merced, Calif., 1953; geophys. trainee Stanolind Oil Co., New Orleans, 1953, Western Geophys. Co., Rankin, Tex., 1954; tech. officer Govt. Can., Ottawa, 1956; chief seismologist Geotech. Corp., Laramie, Wyo., 1957-59; program tech. dir. U. Calif., Livermore, 1959-62; pres. Planetary Scis., Inc., Santa Clara, Calif., 1962-64; seismologist U. Hawaii, Honolulu, 1965—, also prof. geophysics; exchange prof. Ind. U., Bloomington, 1975-76; UNESCO expert seismology Internat. Inst. Seismology and Earthquake Engring., Bldg. Research Inst., Tokyo, 1971-72; vis. fellow Co-op. Inst. Research in Environ. Scis., U. Colo., Boulder, 1970-71; mem. vis. faculty Atlantic Marine and Environ. Lab., NOAA, Miami, Fla., 1979-80; cons. Del E. Webb, Kahuku Point, Oahu, Hawaii, 1969, Oceanic Properties, Lanai City, Lanai, Hawaii, 1969, C. Brewer Co., Punaluu, Hawaii, 1970, 74. Fulbright grantee, 1956-57; NATO grantee Internat. Inst. Geothermal Research, Pisa, Italy, 1973. Mem. Am. Geophys. Union, Geol. Soc. Am., Seismol. Soc. Am. (editor Bull. 1962-65), Acoustical Soc. Am., Soc. Exploration Geophysicists, AAUP, European Assn. Exploration Geophysicists, Sigma Xi. Contbr. numerous articles to profl. jours. Patentee in field. Home: 3872 Jewel Ave Las Vegas NV 89121 Office: 2525 Correa Rd Honolulu HI 96822

ADAMSEN, JOHN RUSSELL, training company executive; b. Seattle, June 18, 1939; s. Arthur Harry and Juanita Katheryn (Day) A.; student Everett (Wash.) Jr. Coll., Edmonds (Wash.) Community Coll.; m. Vickey Joy Averitt, Nov. 26, 1977; 1 dau., Teresa Lynette. With John Fluke Mfg. Co., 1962-66, test technician, Mountlake Terrace, Wash., 1968-69, mfg. engr., 1969-74, tng. specialist, sales tng. mgr., from 1974—; founder, pres. tng. co., Bothell, Wash. Served with U.S. Army, 1957-60. Mem. Am. Soc. Tng. Ofcls. (chpt. treas. 1978). Republican. Lutheran. Address: 1118 164th St SE D101 Bothell WA 98012

ADAMS-JOHNSON, PAULA ANTOINETTE, systems specialist; b. Bluefield, W.Va., July 13, 1935; d. John William and Steavie (Mitchell) A.; m. Robert DePriest Johnson, May 1, 1957 (div. Feb. 1962); children—Robert Anthony, Steven Dominic, Stacy Antoinette. B.A., Howard U., 1956. Claims rep. Social Security Adminstrn., 1956-57; computer programmer USAF, systems analyst, then logistics mgmt. specialist, 1978-83, program coordinator systems acquisition, career mgmt. program for civilians Space Div., El Segundo, Calif., 1983—. Mem. Black Employment Program Com. Recipient Outstanding Performance awards USAF, 1976, 81; Sustained Superior award, 1964, 83. Mem. Delta Sigma Theta, Howard U. Alumni Assn. Republican. Roman Catholic. Home: 20530 Anza Ave Apt 215 Torrance CA 90503

ADAMSON, LARRY ROBERTSON, lawyer; b. Tucson, Mar. 17, 1935; s. Harold D. and Manie (Robertson) A.; B.S. in Bus. Adminstrn., U. Ariz., 1957; J.D., U. San Francisco, 1969; LL.M. in Taxation, NYU, U., 1970; m. Florence Obad, May 31, 1969; children—Robby, Michael. Accountant various C.P.A. firms, San Francisco, 1961-69; admitted to Calif. bar, 1970, U.S. Tax Ct. bar, 1970, Ariz. bar, 1971; with firm Fish, Briney, Duffield, Miller, Young & Adamson, P.C. and predecessors, Tucson, 1970—; lectr. community and profl. groups. Mem. Tucson Airport Authority, 1978—; bd. dirs., sec. Santa Cruz Valley Health Found., 1977-81; bd. dirs. Tucson Symphony Soc., 1980—, sec., 1982-84; mem. planned giving com. Up With People, 1981, Ariz. Sonora Desert Mus., 1981—, Tucson Med. Ctr., 1982—. Served to comdr. USNR, 1957-60. Mem. ABA, Ariz. Bar Assn., Pima County Bar Assn., State Bar Calif., Am. Inst. C.P.A.s, Ariz. Soc. C.P.A.s, Calif. Soc. C.P.A.s, Am. Assn. Atty.-C.P.A.s (chpt. pres. 1980—), So. Ariz. Estate Planning Council (dir. 1975-84, pres. 1982-83), Navy League. Clubs: Old Pueblo, Tucson Country, Rotary (dir., 1975-77) (Tucson). Office: Suite 711 Transam Bldg Tucson AZ 85701

ADAN, SUZANNE RAE, artist; b. Woodland, Calif., Feb. 12, 1946; d. Raymond and Myrtle Irene (Cook) Adan; m. Michael Keith Stevens, July 14, 1945. B.A., Calif. State U.-Sacramento, 1969, M.A., 1971. Lic. community coll. tchr., Calif. Instr. art Am. River Coll., Sacramento, 1975, 1976; one woman shows: Sierra Coll., Rocklin, Calif., 1966, WOMANSPACE, Los Angeles, 1974, Candy Store Gallery, Folsom, Calif., 1978, Betsy Rosenfield Gallery, Chgo., 1983; group shows include: Crocker Art Mus., Sacramento, 1968, 72, 73, 75, 80, 81, Candy Store Gallery, Folsom, Calif., 1971, 75, 76, 80, 81, San Francisco Art Inst., 1970, 72, San Francisco Mus. Modern Art, 1971, 78, Whitney Mus. Am. Art, N.Y., 1973, Richmond (Calif.) Art Center, 1980, Hansen Fuller Goldeen Gallery, San Francisco, 1980, Joseph Chowning Gallery San Francisco, 1982, Betsy Rosenfield Gallery, Chgo., 1982. Recipient Crocker Art Mus. Ayling Watercolor award, 1968, Purchase award, 1973, Hardison, Komatsu, Ivelich & Tucker award, 1980. Mem. Calif. Art Assn., Artists Equity Assn. Democrat. Publications: ARTS mag., 1970, Whitney Mus. AM. Art, catalog, 1973, Goodfellow Catalog of Wonderful Things, 1977, 1981, Welcome to the Candy Store catalog, 1981. Home: 3977 Rosemary Circle Sacramento CA 95821

ADDINGTON, HAROLD WALLACE, cons. petroleum engr.; b. Ridgeville, Ind., Sept. 28, 1917; s. Russel Wilson and Nora Viola (Billman) A.; B.A., Internat. Bus. Coll., 1938; diploma in petroleum engring. Colo. Sch. Mines, 1943; m. Carol Jean Hass, Dec. 23, 1967; children—Gary Kent, Pamela Kay. Accountant, Standard Oil Co. Ind., 1938-39; petroleum engr. Calif. Co., Denver and New Orleans, 1946-52; drilling and prodn. supt. Bay Petroleum Corp., Calgary, Alta., Can., 1952-53; sales and service mgr. Mud Control Labs., Denver, 1953-54; v.p., dir. Anschutz Drilling Co., Denver, 1954-58; pres. H.W. Addington & Assos., Inc., Denver, 1958—. Served with C.E., U.S. Army, 1943-46. Mem. Am. Petroleum Inst., Soc. Petroleum Engrs. of AIME, Rocky Mountain Assn. Geologists, Ind. Petroleum Assn. Mountain States, Soc. Ind. Profl. Earth Scientists, Rocky Mountain Oil and Gas Assn., Rocky Mountain Petroleum Pioneers, Denver Petroleum Club. Republican. Methodist. Clubs: Valley Country, Heather Ridge Country. Home: 2783 S Xanadu Way Aurora CO 80014 Office: 620 Petroleum Bldg 110-16th St Denver CO 80202

ADDIS, THOMAS HOMER, III, professional golfer; b. San Diego, Nov. 30, 1945; s. Thomas H. and Martha J. (Edwards) A.; student Foothill Jr. Coll., 1963, Grossmont Jr. Coll., 1965; m. Susan Tera Buckley, June 13, 1966; children—Thomas Homer, IV, Bryan Michael. Head golf profl., mgr. Sun Valley Golf Course, La Mesa, Calif., 1966-67; asst. golf profl. Singing Hills Golf Course, El Cajon, Calif., 1967-69, head golf profl., dir. golf ops., 1969—; area cons. Nat. Golf Found.; gen. chmn. Nat. Jr. Golf championship U.S. Golf Assn., 1973; lectr. Bd. dirs. San Diego County Open, West Coast Golf Conf. and Mdse. Show, El Cajon Pony Baseball, 1981-82; trustee Calif. State Open, pres., 1980-83. Mem. Profl. Golfers Assn. (pres. San Diego chpt. 1978-79, v.p. chpt. 1980-81; sec. So. Calif. sect. 1978-79, pres. sect. 1980-82; speaker, assn. coordinator bus. schs. and seminars; named Profl. of Yr., So. Calif. sect. 1979, Nat. Golf Day Contbrn. Leader, So. Calif. sect. 1973-76, 79; Horton Smith award So. Calif. sect. 1980-81, Nat. Horton Smith award 1981, Resort Merchandiser of Yr., So. Calif. sect. 1978; ofcl. del. nat. meeting 1978, 79, 80-81, 82, mem. nat. bd. control 1978-83, membership com. 1978, 79; nat. edn. com. 1980-83, mem. jr. world championship com.), Nat. Amputee Golf Assn. (hon. mem.), San Diego Jr. Golf Assn. (dir.). Club: Singing Hills Tennis. Author articles. Office: 3007 Dehesa Rd El Cajon CA 92021

ADDISON, ROBERT MARION, pharmacist; b. Big Spring, Tex., Nov. 30, 1950; s. F. M. and Mary Frances (Smith) A.; B.S. in Pharmacy, Southwestern Okla. State Coll., 1973; m. Terry Lynn Bryant, Aug. 20, 1976. Pharmacist, T. Roy Barnes Drugry, Tulsa, 1973, D.M. Cogdell Meml. Hosp., Snyder, Tex., 1973; pharmacist, mgr. Damron Drug Co., Muleshoe, Tex., 1973-74; pharmacist, propr. mgr. Addison Drug, Ft. Sumner, N.Mex., 1975—; v.p. L&A Newspapers, Inc., 1982—; cons. pharmacist to Pecos Valley Nursing Home, Ft. Sumner, 1975-82, Ft. Sumner Med. Office, 1977-82; dir. Drug Abuse Edn., U. N.Mex., 1971-72. Mem. Eastern Plains Comprehensive Health Planning Bd., 1975-76, Airport Zoning Bd., Ft. Sumner, 1977—; mem. Ft. Sumner Bd. Edn., 1980—, sec., 1983—; chmn. DeBaca County March of Dimes; comdg. officer Ft. Sumner squadron CAP, 1982—. Mem. Am. Pharm. Assn., N.Mex. Pharm. Assn. (counselor 1983—), Aircraft Owners and Pilots Assn., Muleshoe Jaycees (Spoke award 1974, dir. 1974-75), Ft. Sumner C. of C. (dir. 1975-79), Ft. Sumner Jaycees (pres. 1977, state dir. 1978), Assn. Retarded Citizens (vice chmn. 1977—), Kappa Kappa Psi. Democrat. Mem. Ch. of Christ. Club: Lions (v.p. 1975-76, pres. 1977-78, 80-81), Masons (32 deg.), Rotary (pres. 1977-78, exchange officer 1978—). Home: PO Drawer 550 Fort Sumner NM 88119 Office: 323 Sumner Ave Fort Sumner NM 88119

ADDOMS, ROBERT BRIAND, development engineer; b. San Diego, July 30, 1931; s. John Fillmore and Josephine (Briand) A.; children—Maricela, Raul, Roberto. B.S., UCLA, 1959, Ph.D., 1971; M.S., San Diego State Coll., 1964. Mech., aeros. and marine engring. positions, 1959-77, devel. engr. Airesearch indsl. div. Garrett Automotive Products Corp., Torrance, Calif., 1977—. Served with U.S. Army, 1951-52. Mem. AIAA. Contbr. articles to profl. jours. Office: 3201 Lomita Blvd Torrance CA 90505

ADELMAN, IRMA GLICMAN, economist, educator; b. Cernowitz, Rumania, Mar. 14, 1930; came to U.S., 1949, naturalized, 1955; d. Jacob Max and Raissa (Ettinger) Glicman; m. Frank L. Adelman, Aug. 16, 1950 (div. 1979); 1 son, Alexander. B.S., U. Calif.-Berkeley, 1950, M.A., 1951, Ph.D., 1955. Teaching assoc. U. Calif.-Berkeley, 1955-56, instr., 1956-57, lectr. and asst. prof., 1957-58, prof. econs. and agrl. econs., 1979—; vis. asst. prof. Mills Coll., Oakland, Calif., 1958-59; acting asst. prof. Stanford U., 1959-61, asst. prof., 1961-62; assoc. prof. Johns Hopkins U., Balt., 1962-65; prof. econs. Northwestern U., Evanston, Ill., 1966-72; prof. econs. U. Md., College Park, 1972-78; cons. UN, 1962-63, AID, 1963—, Internat. Bank, N.Y.C., ILO, Geneva, 1973—. Center for Advanced Study Behavioral Scis. fellow, 1970-71. Fellow Am. Acad. Arts and Scis., Econometric Soc.; mem. Social Sci. Assembley, Nat. Acad. Scis., Am. Econs. Assn. (exec. com., v.p. 1969), Am. Statis. Assn. Author: Theories of Economic Growth and Development, 1961; (with A. Pepelasis and L. Mears) Economic Development: Analysis and Case Studies, 1961; (with Eric Thorbecke) The Theory and Design of Economic Development, 1966; (with C.T. Morris) Society, Politics and Economic Development: A Quantitative Approach, 1967; (with C.T. Morris) Practical Approaches to Development Planning: Korea's Second Five-Year Plan, 1969; (with C.T. Morris) Economic Development and Social Equity in Developing Countries, 1973; (with Sherman Robinson) Planning for Income Distribution, 1977. Home: 10 Rosemont Ave Berkeley CA 94708 Office: Dept Agr and Natural Resources U Calif Berkeley CA 94720

ADELMAN, JONATHAN REUBEN, political science educator, consultant; b. Washington, Oct. 30, 1948; s. Benjamin and Kitty (Sandler) A.; m. Aliza Kolker, June 8, 1969 (div. Aug. 1976); m. 2d, Nancy Sloane, Jan. 9, 1983. B.A., Columbia U., 1969, M.A., 1972, M. Philosophy, 1974, Ph.D., 1976. Vis. asst. prof. Columbia U., N.Y.C., 1977; vis. asst. prof. U. Ala., Tuscaloosa, 1977-78; asst. prof. Grad. Sch. Internat. Studies U. Denver, 1978—; sr. research analyst Sci. Applications, Inc., Denver, 1981—. Mem. Denver Com. Fgn. Relations, 1980—. Charles Phelps Taft fellow U. Cin., 1976-77; Am. Philos. Soc. grantee, 1980. Mem. Am. Polit. Sci. Assn., Am. Assn. Advancement Slavic Studies, Inter-Univ. Sem. Armed Forces and Soc. Democrat. Jewish. Author: The Revolutionary Armies, 1980; editor: Communist Armies in Politics, 1982; contbr. numerous articles in field to profl. jours. Home: 6336 S Florence Way Englewood CO 80111 Office: Grad Sch Internat Studies U Denver Denver CO 80210

ADELMAN, RAYMOND DAVID, pediatric nephrologist; b. Canton, Ohio, Sept. 30, 1941; s. Samuel Seymour and Dora Rebecca (Freed) A.; B.A., Johns Hopkins U., 1962, M.D., 1966; 1 son, Aaron. Intern in pediatrics Albert Einstein Coll. Medicine, Bronx (N.Y.) Mcpl. Hosp. Center, 1966-67, resident, 1967-69; fellow in pediatrics, renal-electrolyte div. U. Calif., San Francisco, 1971-73; asst. prof. pediatrics, also dir. pediatric nephrology U. Calif., Davis, 1974-81, asso. prof. pediatrics, 1979—; cons. in field. Served with M.C., U.S. Army, 1969-71. Diplomate Am. Bd. Pediatrics, Am. Bd. Pediatric Nephrology; lic. physician N.Y. State, Md., Calif. Mem. Internat., Am. socs. nephrology, Internat., Am. socs. pediatric nephrology, Soc. Pediatric Research, Western Soc. Pediatric Research, No. Calif. Acad. Pediatrics, Sacramento Pediatric Soc., Am. Fedn. Clin. Research, Internat. Soc. Clin. Enzymology. Researcher juvenile hypertension, drug toxicity, nutrition. Home: 1545 38th St Sacramento CA 95819 Office: Dept Pediatrics U Calif at Davis Med Center 4301 X St Sacramento CA 95817

ADELSON, MERVYN LEE, film production company executive; b. Los Angeles, Oct. 23, 1929; s. Nathan and Pearl (Schwarzman) A.; ed. Menlo Park Jr. Coll.; m. Gail Kenaston, 1974; children from previous marriage—Ellen, Gary, Andrew. Pres., Market Town Builders, Las Vegas, 1957-63; partner Paradise Builders, Las Vegas, 1958-60; pres. Paradise Devel. Co., Las Vegas, from 1960; v.p. Realty Holdings, Inc., Las Vegas, from 1976; pres. Rancho La Costa, Inc., Carlsbad, from 1963; chmn. bd. Lorimar Prodns., Inc., Culver City, Calif., 1967—. Mem. Am. Film Inst., Acad. Motion Pictures. Clubs: La Costa Country, Las Vegas Country. Office: Lorimar Prodns Inc 3970 Overland Ave Culver City CA 90230*

ADELSTONE, JEFFREY ALA, accountant, tax law specialist, educator; b. Los Angeles, Feb. 15, 1947; s. James and Joyce S. (Waldman) A.; m. E. Ruth Wilcox, Apr. 6, 1968; children—Kimberley, Stacey, Toni. B.S., U. Ariz., 1969; M.Edn., 1971. Cert. Jr. Coll. Instr., Ariz; cert. instr. Ariz. Dept. Real Estate, accredited Accreditation Council for Accountancy, enrolled to practice, IRS. Tchr., Tucson High Sch., 1969-72; instr. Pima Community Coll., Tucson, 1970-78; pres., owner Adelstone Tax & Acctg. Service, Tucson, 1970—. Active Republican Task Force. Mem. Nat. Soc. Pub. Accountant (mem. fed. taxation com.), Nat. Assn. Enrolled Agents (dir.), Ariz. Soc. Practicing Accountants (dir. credit union, pres. Tucson chpt.), Central Ariz. Soc. Enrolled Agents (dir.), U.S. C. of C., Ariz. C. of C., Tucson Better Bus. Bur., Nat. Fedn. Ind. Bus. Contbr. articles to profl. jours. Office: Adelstone Tax Service 165 Sarnoff St Tucson AZ 85710

ADEN, CHARLES LYNN, steel company executive; b. Denver, Oct. 29, 1949; s. Everett Lee and Carrie Louise Aden; student Ottawa U., 1967-68; B.S., U. No. Colo., 1971; m. Kathle Jo Edgar, June 7, 1969; children—Mark Louise, Denise Renee. Vice pres., estimator Lomax Steel Co., Broomfield, Colo., 1973; constrn. cost estimator Marshall Steel Service Co., Arvada, Colo., 1973-76, v.p., gen. mgr., 1976-80; cost estimator Denver Plant Zimmerman Metals, Inc., 1980-81, mktg. mgr., sr. cost estimator Brighton div. (Colo.), 1981-82; owner, pres. CLA & Assocs., 1982—; condr. estimating seminar Denver chpt. Women in Constrn., 1976. Mem. Am. Soc. Profl. Estimators (cert. constrn. cost estimator; chpt. pres. 1977, nat. trustee 1978-79, editor nat. newsletter 1980-82, Chpt. Estimator of Yr. 1979, Nat. Estimator of Yr. 1980), Metal Fabricators Inst., Colo. Subcontractors Assn. (v.p. 1973-74), Aircraft Owners and Pilots Assn., Colo. Pilots Assn. Republican. Baptist. Home: 10760 Brighton Rd Henderson CO 80640

ADERTON, JANE REYNOLDS, lawyer; b. Riverside, Calif., Dec. 22, 1913; d. Charles Low and Verna Mae (Marshall) Reynolds; B.S. in Merchandising, U. So. Calif., 1935; J.D., Southwestern U., 1965; m. Thomas Radcliffe Aderton, Oct. 16, 1964; children (by previous marriage)—Marshall Johnson, Jeannette Johnson Townsend. Jud. sec. to Dist. Ct. Appeal, Los Angeles, 1960-65; admitted to Calif. bar, 1968; practiced in Beverly Hills, 1968-79, Riverside, 1979—; assoc. firm Wyman, Bautzer, Rothman & Kuchel, 1970-79; del. Calif. Bar Conf., 1976, 77, 78. Mem. Founders' Club, Riverside Community Hosp., 1980—; mem. Women's Aux., Salvation Army, 1981—, pres., 1983; bd. govs., 1983—. Mem. Am., Calif., Riverside, Beverly Hills (bd. govs. 1976-79, chmn. del. to Calif. Bar Conf. 1978) bar assns., Riverside Art Alliance, Soroptimist Internat., Phi Alpha Delta, Pi Beta Phi (pres. alumni club Riverside 1981-83). Clubs: Victoria Country (Riverside, Calif.); Newport Harbor Yacht (Newport Beach, Calif.). Home: 5190 Stonewood Dr Riverside CA 92506 Office: Riverside CA

ADKINS, RALPH WELDON, water and land consultant; b. La Junta, Colo., Nov. 11, 1917; s. Clyde and Sallie (Bailey) A.; m. Barbara Belle Brumley, Dec. 7, 1945; children—Ralph Weldon, Anita Gail. B.S. in Civil Engring., Colo. State U., 1943; grad. Alexander Hamilton Inst., 1949. Registered profl. engr., Colo. With U.S. Grazing Service, Grand Junction, Colo., 1939-41; dir. water ops. C F & I Steel Corp., Pueblo, Colo., 1943-83; pres. Ralph Adkins & Assoc. Inc., water and land cons., 1983—; lectr. Pres. Carter's Water Round Table, Denver, 1977. dir., v.p. Union Ditch & Water Co.; dir. Fremont Irrigating Ditch Co. Served to lt. (j.g.), USN, 1944-46. Mem. Colo. Water Congress, Nat. Water Resources Assn., Pueblo C. of C., Colo. State Honor Alumni. Republican. Baptist. Clubs: Rotary (pres. Pueblo chpt. 1977), Kiwanis (pres. Steel City chpt. 1957), Masons. Home: 3210 Quintin St Pueblo CO 81005 Office: C F & I Steel Corp PO Box 316 Pueblo CO 81002

ADKINS, RONALD VERN, educational administrator; b. Huntington, W.Va., Feb. 16, 1939; s. Archie Hobert and Amelia Bay (Eaton) A.; m. Sharon Kaye Estep, Mar. 20, 1965; children—Darrett Bruce, Jason Edwin. B.A., George Washington U., 1963; M.A., Marshall U., 1965; postgrad. U. Denver, 1972-74. Chmn. social studies div. Shenandoah Coll., Winchester, Va., 1965-67; chmn. history dept., honors dir. Huron (S.D.) Coll., 1967-73; Eastern regional dir. admissions U. Denver, 1974-76; dir. admissions U. Puget Sound, Tacoma, 1977-78, dir. acad. advising, 1978—. Vice pres. Univ. Pl. Gifted Child Assn.; mem. Tacoma Youth Symphony. Named Outstanding Young Man in S.D., 1969. Mem. Nat. Acad. Advising Assn. (bd. dirs.), Am. Coll. Personnel Assn., Acad. Affairs Adminstrs. Democrat. Presbyterian. Club: Univ. Pl. Soccer (pres.). Contbg. historian Ideas in Action, 1976; editor Upper Midwest Regional Honors Council newsletter, 1969-71; contbr. articles to profl. jour. Office: 1500 N Warner Tacoma WA 98416

ADLEMAN, WENDY WOODS, television journalist; b. Newark, Nov. 16, 1952; d. Julian Jonathan and Eileen Margaret (Woods) A. Student Wilkes Coll., 1970-72; B.A. in Film, Syracuse U, 1976. Anchor reporter Sta. WIXT, Syracuse, N.Y., 1975-81; corr. Cable News Network, San Francisco, 1981-82; reporter Sta. KGO-TV, San Francisco, 1982, corr. Silicon Valley, 1983—; lectr. in field. Recipient Best Environ. Reporting award Central N.Y. Environment Assn., 1979; Best Reporting under Deadline Pressure award Syracuse Press Club, 1980, Best Investigative Reporting award, 1981. Mem. AFTRA, Nat. Assn. Broadcast Employees and Technicians, Acad. TV Arts and Scis., Nat. Assn. Female Execs. Democrat. Roman Catholic. Clubs: Apple Corp., Sierra (San Francisco). Author screenplays. Home: 538 30th Ave San Francisco CA 94121 Office: Sta KGO-TV 277 Golden Gate Ave San Francisco CA 94102

ADLER, CHARLES SPENCER, psychiatrist; b. N.Y.C., Nov. 27, 1941; s. Benjamin H. and Anne (Greenfield) A.; m. Sheila Noel Morrissey, Oct. 8, 1966. B.A., Cornell U., 1962; M.D., Duke U., 1966. Intern, Tucson Hosps. Med. Edn. Program, 1966-67; psychiat. resident U. Colo. Sch. Medicine, Denver, 1967-70; practice medicine specializing in psychiatry and psychosomatic medicine, Denver, 1970—; chief div. psychiatry Rose Med. Center, 1982—; co-founder Applied Biofeedback Inst., Denver, 1972-75; prof. pro tempore Cleve. Clinic, 1977. Recipient Award of Recognition, Nat. Migraine Found., 1981; N.Y. State regents scholar, 1958-62. Diplomate Nat. Bd. Med. Examiners, Am. Bd. Psychiatry and Neurology. Mem. AMA, Am. Psychiat. Assn., Am. Assn. Study Headache, Am. Acad. Psychoanalysis, Biofeedback Soc. Am., Colo. Psychiatry Soc., Biofeedback Soc. Colo. (pres. 1977-78). Jewish. Author: (with Gene Stanford and Sheila M. Adler) We Are But a Moment's Sunlight, 1976; Psychiatric Aspects of Headache, 1983; contbr. chpts. to books, articles to profl. jours.; mem. adv. bd. Cephalalgia: an Internat. Jour. of Headache. Home: 955 Eudora St Suite 1607 Denver CO 80220 Office: 955 Eudora St Suite 1605 Denver CO 80220

ADLER, ERWIN ELLERY, lawyer; b. Flint, Mich., July 22, 1941; s. Ben E. and Helen M. Adler; B.A. with distinction, U. Mich., 1963, LL.M., 1967; J.D., Harvard Law Sch., 1966; m. Stephanie Ruskin, June 8, 1967; children—Lauren Michelle, Michael Benton, Jonathan Scott. Admitted to Calif. bar, 1967; assoc. Pillsbury, Madison & Sutro, San Francisco, 1967-73; assoc. Lawler, Felix & Hall, Los Angeles, 1973-76, ptnr., 1977-82; ptnr. Rogers & Wells, 1982—. Bd. dirs. Hollywood Civic Opera Assn., 1975-76; gen. counsel Children's Scholarship, Inc., Los Angeles, 1978-80. DeWaters Found. fellow, 1965-67. Mem. ABA (vice chmn. appellate advocacy com. 1982—), Calif. Bar Assn., Phi Beta Kappa, Phi Kappa Phi. Jewish. Club: Los Angeles Athletic. Office: 700 S Flower St Los Angeles CA 90017

ADLER, JOHN STANLEY, lawyer, educator; b. Bronx, N.Y., Apr. 7, 1948; s. Milton Philip and Martha (Weinberg) A.; m. Jacqueline Brenda Brookler, July 8, 1973; children—Allison Jessica, Marc Jordan. A.B. in Polit. Sci., Case Western Res. U., 1968, M.A. in Polit. Sci. (teaching asst.), 1969; M.A. in Edn., NYU, 1971; J.D., U. San Diego, 1974, Lic. tchr., Common Branches, N.Y.C. Bar: Calif. 1974, Research cons., pub. relations Edward Howard & Co., Cleve., 1967-69; teaching asst. dept. polit. sci. Case Western Res. U., Cleve., 1969; tchr. Manpower Devel. Tng. Ctr., Bklyn., 1969-70, Pub. Sch. 173, N.Y.C. Bd. Edn., 1970-71; assoc. Brundage, Williams & Zellmann, San Diego, 1974-76; sole practice, San Diego, 1976-81; ptnr. Adler and Gniatkowski, San Diego, 1981—. Instr. law Western State U., Nat. U. Sch. Law; adv. com. Labor Mgmt. Relations Ctr., U. San Diego Sch. Law. Pres. San Diego Jewish Acad., San Diego and La Jolla; bd. dirs. United Jewish Fedn., San Diego; mem. civil rights panel Anti-Defamation League, San Diego. Served to capt. Army N.G., 1971-80. Recipient award Excellence Labor Law, Brundage, Williams & Zellman, U. San Diego Law Sch., 1973; Am. Jurisprudence Book award U. San Diego, 1973. Mem. ABA, Calif. Bar Assn., San Diego County Bar Assn., N. San Diego County Bar Assn., Indsl. Relations Research Assn. (San Diego chpt.). Democrat. Clubs: San Carlos Swim and Racquet (San Diego). Contbr. articles to legal jours.; mem. U. San Diego Law Rev., 1974. Office: Adler and Gniatkowski 530 B St Suite 2001 San Diego CA 92101

ADLER, LAUREL ANN, educational administrator, consultant; b. Cleve., Sept. 6, 1948; d. Clarence Linsley and Margaret Ann (Roberts) Wheeler; m. Thomas Jay Johnson, June 6, 1981; children—David, Anthony, Jennifer. B.A., U. Calif.-Irvine, 1968; M.A., Calif. State U.-Los Angeles, 1972; Ed.D., U. La Verne, 1980. Audlt Edn. adminstr. Hacienda La Puente Unified Sch. Dist., 1972-79; dir. career and vocat. edn. El Monte Union High Sch. Dist., 1979—; instr. Calif. State U.-Los Angeles, 1979-81; cons. Trust Ty. Pacific Islands, 1979—. Active El Monte Coordinating Council. Recipient Nat. Vol. Action award 1974; Calif. Consortium Ind. Study Recognition award of Outstanding Ednl. Program, 1983, Calif. Sch. Adminstrs. award, 1981; named Citizen of Yr., La Puente C. of C., 1977, Outstanding Vocat. Educator, Hoffman Ednl. Systems, 1983. Mem. Assn. Calif. Sch. Adminstrs., Internat. Reading Assn., Assn. Supervision and Curriculum Devel., Calif. Consortium Ind. Study, Phi Delta Kappa. Club: Soroptomist. Author: A Self Evaluation Model for Micronesian Education Programs, 1980; pub. Essential English for Micronesians, Beginning, 1980; Essential English for Micronesians, 1980; Reading Exercises for Micronesians, 1980; contbr. articles to profl. jours. Home: 2212 Vista Rd La Habra Heights CA 90631 Office: 3537 Johnson Ave El Monte CA 91731

ADLER, NANCY ELINOR, psychologist, educator; b. N.Y.C., July 26, 1975; d. Alan and Pauline (Bloomgarden) Adler; m. Arnold Schiff Milstein, June 29, 1975; 1 dau., Julia Rose. B.A., Wellesley Coll., 1968; M.A., Harvard U., 1971, Ph.D., 1973. Teaching fellow, tutor Harvard U., Cambridge, Mass., 1969-72; asst. prof. U. Calif.-Santa Cruz, 1972-76, assoc. prof., 1976-77, assoc. prof., San Francisco, 1977—, asst. vis. research psychologist Inst. Personality Assessment and Research, Berkeley, 1976; cons. Planned Parenthood Santa Cruz, San Francisco, Almeda; bd. dirs. ETR Assocs., Santa Cruz. Woodrow Wilson fellow, 1968; NSF Found. fellow, 1968-72; U. Calif. Regents' fellow, 1974. Fellow Am. Psychol. Assn. (health psychology and population and environ. psychology divs.); mem. Soc. Exptl. Social Psychology, Internat. Assn. Applied Psychology. Author numerous articles and book chpts. Office: 1350 3d Ave San Francisco CA 94143

ADLER, STUART OWEN, computer systems specialist; b. N.Y.C., Mar. 27, 1935; s. Millard D. and Sydell L. (Levine) A.; B.S., N.Y. U., 1957; m. Marilyn Cynthia Leitner, Oct. 27, 1957; children—Deborah Ann, Michael Evan, Lorraine Carol Systems programmer N.Y. Life Ins. Co., 1957-59; competitive analyst Univac, 1960; systems engr. IBM Corp., 1960-69; prin. mem. tech. staff Xerox Corp., 1969-71; computer systems cons., 1972-75; systems specialist Western Bancorp Data Processing Co., 1976-77; sr. systems analyst Litton Energy Control Systems, 1977-79; systems analyst Worplex Corp., 1979-80; pres. Adler Computer Tech., Woodland Hills, Calif., 1980—; cons. computer systems selection to profls. and small bus. Pres. Temple Solael Mr. and Mrs. Club. Mem. Woodland Hills C. of C. Author programming systems. Home: 23035 Gainford St Woodland Hills CA 91364 Office: 21777 Ventura Blvd Suite 269 Woodland Hills CA 91364

ADRIAN, CHARLES RAYMOND, political science educator, consultant; b. Portland, Oreg., Mar. 12, 1922; s. Harry Raymond and Helen Katherine (Petersen) A.; m. Audrey Jean Nelson, Apr. 2, 1946; children—Kristin, Nelson. B.A., Cornell Coll., 1947, LL.D. (hon.), 1973; M.A., U. Minn., 1948, Ph.D., 1950; postgrad. (Fund for Advancement Edn. fellow) U. Copenhagen, 1954-55. Asst. prof. Wayne U., 1949-55; asst. prof. to prof. Mich. State U., East Lansing, 1955-66, chmn., 1963-66; prof. polit. sci. U. Calif.-Riverside, 1966—, acad. asst. to acad. v.p., 1973-74, chmn., 1966-70; adminstrv. asst. to Gov. of Mich., 1955-56; cons. Mich. Constl. Conv., 1961-62, McGraw-Hill Book Co., 1962-66, ABC, 1966—. Mem. Meridian Twp. (Mich.) Planning Commn., 1959-63, Riverside (Calif.) Environ. Protection Commn., 1977-79. With USAAF, 1943-46. Mem. Am. Polit. Sci. Assn., Western Polit. Sci. Assn., Am. Soc. Pub. Adminstrn., Nat. Mcpl. League. Methodist. Club: Victoria (Riverside). Author: (with O.P. Williams) Four Cities, a Study in Comparative Policy Making, 1963; (with E.S. Griffith) A History of American City Government, the Formation of Traditions, 1976; Governing Urban America, 5th edit., 1977; State and Local Governments, 4th edit., 1978; other books and articles. Home: 6767 Rycroft Dr Riverside CA 92506 Office: Dept Polit Sci U Calif Riverside CA 92521

ADUJA, PETER AQUINO, lawyer, business exec.; b. Vigan, Philippines, Oct. 19, 1920; came to U.S., 1927, naturalized, 1944; s. Dionicio and Francisca (Aquino) A.; B.A., U. Hawaii, 1944; J.D., Boston U., 1951; m. Melodie Cabalona, July 31, 1949; children—Jay, Rebecca. Admitted to Hawaii bar, 1953; individual practice law, Hilo, Hawaii, 1953-60, Honolulu, from 1960; dep. atty. gen. State of Hawaii, 1957-60; judge Hawaii Dist. Ct., 1960-62; prin. broker A.A.P. Realty, Inc., Honolulu, 1970—; pres. Aduja Corp., Las Vegas, Nev., 1972—; pres. Travel-Air Internat., Honolulu, 1975—; mem. Hawaii Ho. of Reps., 1954-56, 67-74; del. Hawaii Constl. Conv., 1968; sec.-treas. Melodie Aduja, Inc., 1979—. Troop #50 committeeman Aloha council Boy Scouts Am., 1959—; active ARC; bd. dirs. Salvation Army Adult Rehab. Center, Honolulu, 1965—, Goodwill Industries, Honolulu, 1972 Advison Corp., Ilocos Surians, 1980—. Served with U.S. Army, 1944-46. Mem. Bar Assn. Hawaii, Hawaii Bd. Realtors. Democrat. Methodist. Home: 49 Niniko Pl Honolulu HI 96817 Office: 2046 N King St Honolulu HI 96819

ADY, LINDA JANE, sales executive; b. Caldwell, Idaho, July 14, 1950; d. Elvin L. and Francis J. (Howell) Ballou; m. Thomas P. Ady, Dec. 27, 1969; 1 son, Thomas E. B.A., Sonoma State U., 1978. Sales rep. Hansel Ford, Santa Rosa, Calif., 1978, gen. sales mgr., 1982—; fin./ins. mgr. Henry Curtis Ford, Petaluma, Calif., 1980, sales mgr., 1980-82. Address: 3075 Corby Ave Santa Rosa CA 95401

AESCHLIMAN, JOHN HAMUEL, public relations agency executive; b. Memphis, Jan. 6, 1932; s. John and Helen Maria (Smith) A.; m. Ava B. Arnold (div.); children—David, Dana, Creed. B.A. in English, Memphis State U., 1951. Editor employee publs. GENESCO, Nashville, 1952-57; copy editor Nashville Banner, 1957-58; bus. editor Press-Scimitas, Memphis, 1958-59; pub. relations mgr. Internat. Harvester Co., Memphis, 1960-64, editor employee publs., Chgo., 1964-69, pub. relations mgr. western region, Oakland, Calif., 1969-74; pres., chief exec. officer PR3, Menlo Park, Calif., 1974-83; ptnr. Aeschliman & Eklund, Los Gatos, Calif., 1983—. Served with USAF, 1951-52. Mem. Pub. Relations Soc. Am. Republican. Club: San Francisco Press. Home: 387 Waverly St Menlo Park CA 94025 Office: Aeschliman & Eklund 179 Belwood Gateway Los Gatos CA 95030

AFFELDT, ARNO MARCUS, JR., steel mill sales executive; b. San Bernardino, Calif., Nov. 16, 1927; s. Arno Marcus and Evelyn Rose (Roberts) A.; m. Cora Nell Watkins, June 25, 1949; children—Arno Marcus, III, Laura Allison, Bruce Lawrence, Sherry Ann. B.A., U. Calif.-Berkeley, 1950; LL.B., LaSalle U., Chgo., 1971. Export trader Otis, McAllister Co., San Francisco, 1951-52; with Kaiser Steel Corp., various locations, 1953-70, Internat. Mill Service, Fontana, Calif., 1971-73; with Marathon Steel Co., Los Angeles, 1974—, mgr. mill sales, Phoenix, 1978—; industry rep. to trade assns.; speaker in field. Served with U.S. Navy, 1946-47. Mem. Concrete Steel Reinforcing Inst., Phoenix C. of C., Pi Kappa Alpha. Republican. Congregationalist. Home: 8576 Via De Dorado E Scottsdale AZ 85258

AFFLECK, JULIE KARLEEN, accountant; b. Upland, Calif., Dec. 23, 1944; d. Karl W. and Juliette O. (Oppegaard) Hall; m. William J. Affleck, Aug. 29, 1964; children—Stephen, Tamara. B.S. in Bus., U. Colo., 1967; M.S.B.A., U. Denver, 1972. C.P.A., Colo. Cost acct. IBM, Boulder, Colo., 1967-71; audit supr. Ernst & Whinney, Denver, 1972-79, Rosemary E. Weiss & Co., Denver, 1979-80; ptnr. Affleck, Businga & Assocs., Denver, 1980—; prin. Julie K. Affleck, C.P.A., Denver, Colo., 1982—; tchr. Colo. Soc. C.P.A.s., U. Denver; dir. Better-Way Electric, Inc. Vice pres., bd. dirs. Bal Swan Children's Ctr. for Handicapped, Broomfield, Colo. Mem. Am. Inst. C.P.A.s., Colo. Soc. C.P.A.s., Am. Soc. Women Accts. (pres. chpt. 1980-81), Women Bus. Owners Assn. (treas., dir.), Colo. Fiscal Mgrs. Assn. Republican. Lutheran. Home: 3913 W 12 Ave Ct Broomfield CO 80020

AGALIDI, SANDA, art critic; b. Bucharest, Romania, Nov. 6, 1939; d. Emil and Sultana A.; M.A. in History of Art, Fine Arts Inst., Bucharest, 1969; M.F.A., U. Calif., San Diego, 1976. Editor, Documentation Center of Romanian Acad. Social Scis., Bucharest, 1969-71; researcher Inst. of Art History of Romanian Acad. Social Scis., 1971-73; free-lance art critic, Los Angeles, 1976—. Home: 936 N Orange Grove Ave Los Angeles CA 90046

AGARDY, FRANKLIN JOSEPH, engineering executive, forensic scientist; b. N.Y.C., Mar. 23, 1933; s. Alexander and Ella A.; m. Grace S. Ferber, Jan. 21, 1955 (div.); children—Jonathan Fredric, Harrison Andrew; m. 2d, Louise F. Ehman, Feb. 17, 1979. B.C.E., CCNY, 1955; M.S. in San. Engring., U. Calif.-Berkeley, 1958, Ph.D. in San. Engring., 1963. Prof. civil engring. San Jose State U., 1962-71; v.p. URS Research Co., San Mateo, Calif., 1971-73, exec. v.p., 1973-74, pres., 1974—; v.p. URS Corp., San Mateo, 1974-79, v.p., group exec., 1980—; pres. URS Engrs.; expert witness forensic sci. and engring.; guest lectr. colls. and univs. Served to capt. USPHS, 1962—. Mem. Am. Water Works Assn. (George A. Elliott Meml. award Calif.-Nev. sect. 1973, Water Utility Edn. award 1974), Water Pollution Control Fedn., Nat. Fire Protection Assn., Am. Mgmt. Assn., Profl. Services Mgmt. Assn. Republican. Lutheran. Home: 610 Edinburgh St San Mateo CA 94402 Office: 155 Bovet Rd San Mateo CA 94402

AGATHANGELIDES, DEMETRIOS, horticulturist, landscape contractor; b. Patris Veria, Greece, Oct. 26, 1937; s. Gregory Theodore and Elpida (Hourouzidou) A.; came to U.S., 1958, naturalized, 1966; grad. Am. Farm Sch., Greece, 1956; student Ricks Coll., 1958-60, Utah State U., 1960-63; m. Diane Moser, Aug. 10, 1963; children—Angela, Athena. Orchard field foreman Ray Dewey Orchards, Emmett, Idaho, 1963-64; asst. to orchard mgr. F.H. Hoque, Emmett, Idaho, 1964-65; research asst. plant sci. dept. Utah State U., Logan, 1965-73; propr., mgr. Greek Gardens, North Logan, Utah, 1974—, pres., 1975—. Scout leader Cache Valley council Boy Scouts Am., 1965-74; pres. Utah State U. Classified Employees, 1974. Named Employee of the Year, Utah State U., 1974. Mem. Am. Assn. of Nurseryman, Utah Assn. of Nurseryman (dir. 1975-78). Mormon. Home: 1798 N 12 E Logan UT 84321 Office: Greek Gardens 2015 N Main North Logan UT 84321

AGERBEK, SVEN, mech. engr.; b. Soerabaya, Dutch Indies, Aug. 2, 1926; s. Niels Magnus and Else Heidam (Nielsen) Agerbek-Poulsen; came to U.S., 1958, naturalized, 1964; M.S.M.E., Tech. U., Denmark, 1952; LL.B., LaSalle Extension U., 1967; postgrad. U. Calif. at Los Angeles, 1969; m. Helen Hadsbjerg Gerup, May 30, 1963; 1 son, Jesper. With Danish Refrigeration Research Inst., Copenhagen, 1952; engr. B.P. Oil Co., Copenhagen, 1952-54; refrigeration insp. J. Lauritzen, Copenhagen, 1954-56; engr. Danish-Am. Gulf Oil Co., Copenhagen, 1956-58; instr. Ohio U., Athens, 1958-60; asst. prof. Calif. State Poly. Coll., San Luis Obispo, 1960-62; prin. engr. environment dept. Ralph M. Parsons Co., Los Angeles, 1962-73; engring. supr. Bechtel Power Co., Norwalk, Calif., 1973—. Served with Danish underground movement, World War II. Registered profl. engr., Calif., Ohio, Fla. Mem. Am. Soc. Heating, Refrigeration and Air Conditioning Engrs., Danish Engring. Soc. Lutheran (past mem. ch. council, pres. sch. bd.). Home: 16428 Santa Bianca Dr Hacienda Heights CA 91745 Office: 12400 E Imperial Hwy Norwalk CA 90650

AGGARWAL, UMA NANDAN, tool company executive; b. Amritsar, India, July 15, 1944; s. Trilok Chand and Raj Rani (Goyaz) A.; m. Pawan Rekha Gupta, Nov. 22, 1971; children—Amit, Anjali. B.Tech., Indian Inst. Tech., Bombay, 1966; M.E., U. Calif.-Berkeley, 1969; M.B.A., U. Chgo., 1976. Ops. research analyst Armour & Co., Chgo., 1969-71; assoc., cons. Theodore Barry & Assocs., Los Angeles, 1971-72; mgr. mgmt. systems Axia Inc., Oakbrook, Ill., 1973-77; v.p., gen. mgr. Jensen Tools Inc. subs. Axia Inc., Phoenix, 1977-83, corp. v.p. Axia Inc., 1983—. Office: 7815 S 46th St Phoenix AZ 85040

AGLER, CHARLES FREDERICK, psychiatrist; b. Denver, Apr. 17, 1932; s. Charles Dee and Edna Marion (Ayres) A.; A.A., U. Calif. at Los Angeles, 1954, B.A., 1954, M.D., 1958. Rotating intern U.S. VA Gen. Med. and Surg. Hosp., West Los Angeles, Calif., 1958; resident psychiatry U.S. VA Neuropsychiat. Hosp., West Los Angeles, 1959-62; asst. surgeon USPHS, St. Elizabeth's Hosp., Washington, 1962-64; staff psychiatrist childrens unit Napa (Calif) State Hosp., 1964-65, 66-67, St. Elizabeth's Hosp., 1965-66; instr. clin. psychiatry George Washington U. Sch. Medicine, 1965-66; chief Mental Retardation Program, Community Mental Health Services, San Francisco, 1967-70, 72-79, dir. Psychiat. Clinic, Youth Guidance Center, 1969-70, dir. Child Psychiat. Clinic, 1970-72; practice medicine specializing in psychiatry, San Francisco, 1967—. Cons., Calif. Dept. Mental Hygiene Conf. Local Mental Health Dirs., 1969-75; therapist San Francisco Parole Outpatient Clinic, 1972—. Bd. dirs. San Francisco Coordinating Council for Mental Retardation, 1967-70. Mem. Am., No. Calif. psychiat. assns. Contbr. articles to profl. jours. Home and office: 2700 15th Ave San Francisco CA 94127

AGNOST, FRANK PETER, publishing executive, editor; b. Chgo., June 14, 1918; s. Peter and Effie (Kellar) A.; m. Mildred Corby, Aug. 31, 1940; children—Frank Peter, Adrienne Pennisi; m. 2d, Melissa Caravellas, Sept. 24, 1970. Student U. Calif.-Berkeley, 1940. Commr. dept. pub. welfare City and County of San Francisco, 1951-58; copy boy, reporter, asst. fgn. editor, then asst. to pub. San Francisco Chronicle, 1940-61; pres. Falcon Assocs. Inc., San Francisco, 1961—; editor, pub. Hellenic Jour., San Francisco, 1975—. Served to capt. USAAF, 1942-46. Decorated Gold Cross, Order of Phoenix (Greece), Meml. Medal 1971, Archon, Order of St. Andrew, Ecumenical Patriarchate (Constantinople), recipient Award of Honor, United Greek Orthodox Charities N.Y., 1971; Disting. Service Award, Greek Orthodox Archdiocese N.Y., 1976; Axion award Hellenic Am. Profl. Soc. of San Francisco, 1978; Extraordinary Community Service award Calif. Assembly, 1982; medal of St. Paul, Greek Orthodox Archdiocese, 1982. Mem. ASCAP, Am. Legion, Clubs: San Francisco Press, Bohemian, Masons, Ahepa. Home: 1170 Sacramento St San Francisco CA 94108 Office: Falcon Assocs 522 Commercial St San Francisco CA 94111

AGOGINO, GEORGE ALLEN, anthropologist; b. West Palm Beach, Fla., Nov. 18, 1920; s. Andrew and Beulah Mae A.; B.A., U. N.Mex., 1948, M.A., 1951; Ph.D., Syracuse U., 1958; postgrad. Harvard U., 1962-63; m. Mercedes Merner, Dec. 1, 1952; children—Alice, Karen. Asst. prof. anthropology Syracuse (N.Y.) U., 1956-58, U. S.D., 1958-59, U. Wyo., 1959-61; Wenner-Gren postdoctoral fellow Harvard U., Cambridge, Mass., 1961-62; asso. prof. Baylor U., Waco, 1962-63; asso. prof. anthropology Eastern N.Mex. U., Portales, 1963—, dir. Indian Inst, 1963—, Anthropology Mus., Blackwater Draw Mus. and Miles Mus., 1967—, chmn. dept. anthropology, 1963-80, dir. spl. programs, 1972-73, dir. humanities div., 1973-74. Served with Signal Corps, U.S. Army, 1942-46. Recipient Pres.'s award Eastern N.Mex. U., 1971; numerous research grants. Fellow Explorers Club, Am. Anthrop. Assn., AAAS, Instituto Interamericana. Republican. Author monographs in field; contbr. numerous articles on anthropology, primitive religion, folklore to profl. jours. Office: Dept Anthropology Eastern N Mex U Portales NM 88130

AGUAS, JAY MICHAEL, labor relations adminstr.; b. Hawthorne, Calif., Mar. 11, 1950; s. Valentino Rea and Mary Louise (Greenwood) A.; B.A. in History, Calif. Poly. U., 1972; m. Linda Anne Lozano, Jan. 22, 1972; children—Aaron Lynne, Lauren Marie. With Calif. State Personnel Bd., Sacramento, 1972-77; coordinator employment practice State and Consumer Services Agy., Sacramento, 1977-78; labor relations adminstr. Gov.'s Office of Employee Relations, Sacramento, 1978—. State treas. Cafe de Calif., Hispanic civil rights orgn. Recipient Spl. awards Cafe de Calif. and Gov.'s Office Minority Relations. Mem. Indsl. Relations Assn. No. Calif., No. Calif. Football Ofcls. Assn. Democrat. Home: 5875 13th St Sacramento CA 95822 Office: 1115 11th St Sacramento CA 95814

AGUIAR, ALBERT VALADO, marketing consultant, educator; b. Chico, Calif., Jan. 1, 1935; s. Manuel Vierra and Mary Alice (Valado) A.; m. Cynthia Keep, Feb. 23, 1963; children—Sharon, Paul, Laura; m. 2d Donna Almquist, April 19, 1980; 1 son, Matthew. B.A., Calif. State U.-Chico, 1956; M.B.A., Golden State U., 1968. With various retailing firms, Stockton, Calif. and Los Angeles, 1956-57; with Macys, 1962-80, sr. v.p., 1972-80; pres. Albert V. Aguiar & Assoc., Lafayette, Calif., 1980—; dir. grad. mktg. program Golden State U., San Francisco, 1980—; lectr. in field. Mem. Calif. Coastal Council, Contra Costa County Taxpayers Assn. Served with U.S. Army, 1957-59. Mem. Acad. Mktg. Sci., Western Mktg. Educator's Assn., Soc. for Office-Based Surgery. Republican. Roman Catholic. Author: How to Market Your Professional Services, 1983. Contbr. articles to profl. jours. Office: 3507 Mt Diablo Blvd Suite B Lafayette CA 94549

AGUILAR, ROBERT, educational administrator, sociology educator; b. El Paso, Tex., June 26, 1936; s. Juan and Margarita (Marquez) A.; m. Gloria Garcia, Dec. 18, 1958; children—Tony, Bobby. A.A. in Social Sci., Porterville Coll., 1958; B.A. in Edn., Calif. State U.-Fresno, 1960; M.A. in Adminstrn. and Instrn., San Jose State U., 1972; Ed.D. in Adminstrn. and Curriculum, U. of Pacific, 1978. Gen. edn. teaching credential elem., secondary, adminstrn., Calif. Rockefeller Found. fellow Ctr. for Edn. Leadership, Los Angeles, 1979; Tchr. elem. and secondary schs., Delano, Calif., 1959-69; dir. ednl. counseling services Wasco (Calif.) City Schs., 1969-70; dir. Region I, Migrant Edn., Supt. Schs., Santa Clara County, San Jose, Calif., 1970-73; asst. prin. instrn. Visalia (Calif.) Unified, Redwood High Sch., 1973-75; dir. spl. programs Stockton (Calif.) Unified, 1975-76; dir. spl. services consortium Supt. Schs. Tulare County, Visalia, 1976-80; supt. Richgrove (Calif.) Sch. Dist., 1980-83, Earlimart Sch. Dist., 1983—; tech. cons. Office Edn., Washington; speaker in field. mem. Visalia Sch. Dist. Bd. Edn.; mem. Gov.'s Commn. Block Grants Pub. Edn.; mem. Commn. Tchr. Preparation and Licensing. Mem. Visalia Human Relations Commn.; bd. dirs. Calif. Easter Seal Soc.; bd. dirs. Kings View Found., vice chmn., 1979-81. Served to sgt. U.S. Army, 1953-56. Recipient Disting. Service award Delano Tchr. Assn., 1962; Service to Youth award Optimist Internat. Visalia, 1966; Meritorious Service award N. Kern/S. Tulare Hosp. Dist., 1972. Mem. Assn. Calif. Sch. Adminstrs. (pres.-elect 1983—), Calif. Sch. Bd. Assn., Nat. Assn. Elem. Sch. Prins., Assn. Mexican Am. Educators (Calif. pres. 1971-72), Assn. Supervision and Curriculum Devel., Phi Delta Kappa (Tulare County dir. 1980-82), Nat. Assn. Bilingual Edn. Roman Catholic. Clubs: Lions, Boys, YMCA Quarterback. Contbr. articles to profl. jours.; spl. cons. Calif. History state textbook, 1983. Home: 3119 W Harvard Dr Visalia CA 93277 Office: Earlimart Sch Dist 785 Center St Earlimart CA 93219

AGUILAR, ROBERT P., U.S. dist. judge; b. Madera, Calif., Apr. 15, 1931; B.A., U. Calif., Berkeley, 1954; J.D., Hastings Coll. Law, San Francisco, 1958; Admitted to Calif. bar, 1960, U.S. Supreme Ct. bar, 1966; partner Aguilar & Edwards, San Jose, Calif., 1960—; judge U.S. Dist. Ct., No. Dist. Calif., San Francisco, 1980—. Mem. Regional Criminal Justice Planning Bd., 1974—; chmn. Santa Clara County (Calif.) Juvenile Justice Commn., 1975; mem. Santa Clara County Drug Abuse Task Force, 1974. Mem. Calif. Trial Lawyers Assn., Santa Clara County Criminal Trial Lawyers Assn., Am. Bar Assn., Calif. Bar Assn., Santa Clara County Bar Assn. (pres. 1972). Office: 450 Golden Gate Ave San Francisco CA 94102*

AGUILERA, DONNA CONANT, research psychologist; 3 Kinmundy, Ill.; d. Charles E. and Daisy L. (Frost) Conant; m. George Limon Aguilera, Feb. 17, 1948; children—Bruce Allen, Craig Steven. R.N., Gordon Keller Sch. Nursing, 1947; B.S., U. Calif. at Los Angeles, 1963, M.S., 1965; Ph.D., U. So. Calif., 1974. Teaching asst. U. Calif. at Los Angeles, 1965, grad. research asst., 1965-66; prof. Calif. State U. at Los Angeles, 1966-81; vis. prof. UCLA, 1982—; mem. Def. Adv. Com. of Women in the Services, 1978-82; cons. crisis intervention Didi Hirsch Community Mental Health Center, Los Angeles, 1967-82; NIH fellow U. So. Calif., 1972-75; originator, project dir. Project Link, Lab. for Ind. Nursing Knowledge, Calif. State U. Recipient award Council Specialists in Psychiat. and Mental Health, 1982. Fellow Am. Acad. Nursing (sec.

1976-77, pres. 1977-78, nat. maternal child health research grants rev. com. 1982—), Acad. Psychiat. Nurse Specialists, Internat. Acad. Electric Psychotherapists (pres. elect 1983); mem. Am. Nurses Assn., Am. Psychol. Assn., Faculty Women's Assn., Am., Calif. psychol. assns., AAUP, Alpha Tau Delta, Sigma Theta Tau. Career tchr. appointee NIMH, 1965-66. Author: Crisis Intervention: Theory and Methodology, 1974, 3d edit., 1978 (pub. in Spanish, French, German, Finnish, Hebrew and Japanese), 4th edit. (book of yr.), 1982; Review of Psychiatric Nursing, 1977, 7th edit., 1978; Crisis Intervention: Therapy for Emotional Crises, 1982; contbr. articles to profl. publs. Home: 3924 Dixie Canyon Ave Sherman Oaks CA 91423 Office: UCLA Ctr Health Scis Los Angeles CA 90024

AGUIRRE, VUKOSLAV ENEAS, engineering executive; b. Santiago, Chile, Nov. 2, 1941; s. Eneas and Tonka Vinca (Domic) A.; m. Emma Jeannette Bendana, Nov. 15, 1970; children—Sergio Eneas, Tonka Lily. B.S., U.S. Mil. Acad., 1964; M.S., U. Ill., 1965, postgrad, 1966-67. Profl. engr. Colo., D.C., Ill., Md., Mich., Pa., Utah, Wyo., Chile. Project engr. Ackenheil Assocs., Pitts., 1965-69; soil specialist Harza Internat. Co., Chgo., 1969-70; project mgr. Law Engrng. Testing Co., Washington, 1971-74; pres., dir. Colo. Testing Labs., Denver, 1974-75; pres. Geotek Inc., Denver, 1975-76; individual cons., 1976-77; pres., owner Aguirre Engrs. Inc., Englewood, Colo., 1977—. Mem. Internat. Soc. Soil Mechanics and Found. Engrng., ASCE, Colo. Cons. Engrs. Council, Internat. Soc. Rock Mechanics. Roman Catholic. Author: (with Earl G. Plenty) A Survey of Personnel Practices of Firms Located in Central Illinois, 1967. Office: 13276 E Fremont Pl Englewood CO 80112

AGUZZI-BARBAGLI, DANILO LORENZO, educator; b. Arezzo, Italy, Aug. 1, 1924; s. Guglielmo and Marianna (Barbagli) A.; came to U.S., 1950; Dottore in Lettere, U. Florence (Italy), 1949; Ph.D., Columbia, 1959. Instr., asst. U. Chgo., 1959-64; asso. prof. Tulane U., New Orleans, 1964-71; prof. U. B.C., Vancouver, 1971—. Mem. Fulbright-Hayes final scholarship com., 1970—; adviser on scholarship application Can. Council, 1972-75. Newberry Library fellow, Chgo., 1974, Folger Shakespeare Library fellow, Washington, 1975. Fellow Am. Philos. Soc.; mem. Newberry Library Assn., Dante Soc. Am., Italian Honor Soc. (regional rep.), Accademia Petrarca, Medieval Soc. Am., Renaissance Soc. Am., Modern Lang. Assn., AAUP, Am. Assn. Tchrs. Italian. Author: Critical Edition of Della Poetica of Francesco Patrizi, 3 vols., 1969, 70, 71, 72; Critical Edition of Francesco Patrizi's Lettere ed opuscoli inediti, 1975; contbr. articles to profl. jours. Home: 485 Walsh Rd Atherton CA 94025 Office: U BC Vancouver BC V6T 1W5 Canada

AHEARN, JOHN JOSEPH, JR., recreation devel. exec.; b. Albany, N.Y., May 11, 1939; s. John Joseph and Elizabeth (Cronin) A.; student Cornell U., 1957-59; B.S., Albany Coll. Pharmacy, 1963; m. Dorothea Katherine Bannigan, Nov. 30, 1963; children—John Joseph III, Christopher B., Michael P., Katherine C. Apprentice pharmacist, store mgr. Ahearn Pharmacies, Johnstown, N.Y., 1963-66, v.p., gen. mgr., 1966-68, pres., 1968-71; regional mgr. Clinton Mdse. Co., Rochester, N.Y., 1971-72; pres., founder Sleeping Giant Enterprises, Steamboat Springs, Colo., 1972-73; with Steamboat Ski Corp., Steamboat Springs, 1973-82, dir. mktg., 1975-77, v.p. mktg., 1977-81, v.p. real estate, 1981-82; pres. Ahearn & Assocs., tourism cons., 1982—; chmn. mktg. com. Colo. Ski Country, U.S.A., 1978. Bd. dirs. Johnstown YMCA, 1968-71; regional chmn. membership drive N.Y. State Conservation Council, 1971. Named Brand Name Retailer of Yr. by Brand Names Found., 1970. Mem. Steamboat Springs Chamber Resort Assn. (pres.), Steamboat Springs Transp. Study (com. chmn. 1977). Republican. Roman Catholic. Club: Steamboat Springs Winter Sports (pres. 1978). Home: PO Box 1604 Steamboat Springs CO 80477 Office: PO Box 1178 Steamboat Springs CO 80477

AHERN, ARLEEN FLEMING (MRS. GEORGE I. AHERN), librarian, educator; b. Mt. Harris, Colo.; B.A. in Sociology, U. Utah, 1943; M.A., U. Denver, 1962; postgrad. U. Colo., 1967; m. George I. Ahern. Library asst. Salt Lake City AFB, 1943; acquisitions librarian Colo. Women's Coll., (name changed to Temple Buell Coll. 1966-73), Denver, 1959-82, also assoc. prof. librarianship; acting dir. library U. Denver, 1982—. Mem. Adult Edn. Council Denver, Mountain Plains Adult Edn. Council. Mem. Am. (com.), Mountain Plains (spl. rev. com. 1973—), Colo. (chmn. scholarship com., sec. coll. and univ. div., v.p. 1969-70, pres. 1971—) library assns., League Women Voters, Soc. Am. Archivists, Colo. Council Library Devel. (adv. com. to revise Colo. library planning), AAUP. Club: Altrusa (v.p. 1969, bd. 1972—, chmn. Expts. in Friendship 1973).

AHERN, THOMAS EDWARD, JR., lawyer; b. Cambridge, Mass., Jan. 11, 1920; s. Thomas Edward and Nora (McLean) A.; A.B. cum laude, Harvard U., 1941, LL.B., 1944; m. Virginia Holmes Hinch, Feb. 2, 1946; children—Sharon Ann, Mary Helen, Joan Nora, Thomas Edward III. Admitted to N.Mex. bar, 1945; since practiced in Albuquerque; mem. firm Wilson & Ahern, 1947-54, Wilson, Ahern & Montgomery, 1954-70, Ahern, Montgomery & Albert, 1970-72, Ahern & Montgomery, 1972—; chmn. Legal Aid to Indigents Com., 1966-67; mem. N.Mex. Bd. Bar Commrs., 1969-76; adj. prof. Law Sch., U. N.Mex., 1973-74, also vis. lectr. Mem. N.Mex. Arts and Crafts Bd., 1966-69; chmn. Fine Arts Adv. Bd., 1974—; div. capt. Community Fund; vice-chmn. Met. Boundaries Commn., 1967-78; chmn. ethics and grievance com. State of N.Mex., 1971-72, chmn. new admissions com., 1974-75, chmn. auditing com., 1974-75, mem. N.Mex. Jud. Council, 1969-73, chmn., 1971-73. Mem. N.Mex. State Bar (pres. 1972-73), Am. (standing com. on profl. discipline 1973-74, com. on membership 1974-76), Albuquerque (pres. 1964-65, dir. 1962-64) bar assns. Clubs: Elks, Country (Albuquerque). Editor Albuquerque Bar Jour., 1960-62. Home: 2437 Pueblo Bonito NW Albuquerque NM 87107 Office: 1401 University Blvd NW Albuquerque NM 87102

AHERN, THOMAS SNOWDEN, computer consulting firm executive; b. Balt., Sept. 18, 1941; s. David Foran and Florence Steele (Hoff) A.; m. Bonnie Anne Dunning, July 6, 1968; 1 dau., Julianne Lee; m. 2d, Euphemia Anna Doodeman; May 7, 1977. B.A., Johns Hopkins U., 1963. Sr. systems analyst Litton Industries, Sunnyvale, Calif., 1967-68; systems cons. Control Data Corp., Honolulu, 1968-69; sr. cons. mgmt. cons. services Ernst & Ernst, San Francisco, 1969-71; cons. Profls. for Computing, San Francisco, 1971-74; dir. Source EDP, McLean, Va., 1974-77; founder, pres. Systems Careers, San Francisco, 1977—; pres., founder Systems Results, San Francisco, 1978—. Pres. 66 Cleary Ct. Condominium Owners Assn., 1979—. Served to lt. (j.g.) USNR, 1963-67. Mem. Assn. Systems Mgmt., Johns Hopkins U. Alumni Assn. (pres. No. Calif. chpt. 1979—). Home: 66 Cleary Ct San Francisco CA 94109 Office: Systems Careers 558 Sacramento St San Francisco CA 94111

AHLGREN, GIBSON-TAYLOR, savings bank executive; b. Memphis, Sept. 7, 1940; s. Frank Richard and Nona Elizabeth (Alley) A. B.S., U. Md., 1967; J.D., Western State U., San Diego, 1978. Legis. clk. U.S. Senate, Washington, 1963-67, spl. asst., 1970-71; legis. rep. Associated Gen. Contractors, Washington, 1971-73, San Diego, 1973-74; campaign dir. Brown for Gov. Calif., 1974; mgmt. cons. Ahlgren, Peters & Assocs., La Jolla, Calif., 1975-77; v.p., dir. pub. affairs Gt. Am. Fed. Savs. Bank, San Diego, 1977—; dir. Calif. Gen. Mortgage Service, Inc. Bd. dirs. San Diego Coalition, Western Water Found.; chmn. Gt. Am. Fed. Savs. Govt. Action Com. Served to lt. USN, 1967-70; Vietnam. Mem. Pub. Relations Soc. Am., Pub. Relations Club San Diego. Clubs: San Diego Press; La Jolla Democratic. Office: 600 B St San Diego CA 92183

AHLUWALIA, HARJIT SINGH, physicist; b. Bombay, India, May 13, 1934; came to U.S., 1968, naturalized, 1975; s. Sewa Singh and Jaswant Kaur A.; B.Sc. with honors, Panjab U., Hoshiarpur, India, 1953, M.Sc., 1954; Ph.D. (Univ. Merit scholar), Gujarat U., Ahmedabad, India, 1960; m. Manjit Kaur Pal, Nov. 29, 1964; children—Suvinder Singh, Davinder Singh. Sr. research fellow Phys. Research Lab., Ahmedabad, India, 1954-62; tech. assistance expert UNESCO, Paris, 1962-63; research asso. S.W. Center Advanced Studies, Dallas, 1963-64; vis. prof. IAEA, Vienna, Austria, 1965-67; sci. dir. Lab de Fisica Cosmica, La Paz, Bolivia, 1965-67; vis. prof. Pan Am. Union, Washington, 1967-68; asso. prof. physics U. N. Mex., 1968-73, prof., 1973—; nat. rep. of Bolivia on profl. groups, 1966-69; rapporteur XIV Internat. Conf. Cosmic Rays, Munich, W. Ger., 1975; gen. sec. High Energy Cosmic Ray Group, Solar Traveling Interplanetary Phenomena subcom. Internat. Council Scientific Unions, 1976—. Panjab U. Merit scholar, 1948-53; NSF grantee, 1963-65, 68—; USAF grantee, 1964-68; Sandia Corp. grantee, 1969-72; NASA grantee, 1972-77. Mem. Am. Astron. Soc., AAAS, AAUP, Am. Geophys. Union, Am. Meteorol. Soc., Am. Phys. Soc., IEEE, Calcutta Math. Soc., Internat. Astronomical Union, Sigma Xi. Democrat. Sikh. Contbr. numerous articles to profl. jours. Home: 13000 Cedar Brook NE Albuquerque NM 87111 Office: Dept Physics and Astronomy U N Mex 800 Yale Blvd NE Albuquerque NM 87131

AHMANSON, WILLIAM HAYDEN, savs. and loan and ins. holding co. exec.; b. Omaha, Oct. 12, 1925; s. Hayden W. and Aimee (Talbod) A.; B.S., UCLA, 1950; LL.D. (hon.), Creighton U., 1972; m. Gloria June Gamble, July 10, 1964; children—Mary Jane, Patricia Ann, Amy Catherine, Dorothy, Joanne, Kimberly. With H. F. Ahmanson & Co., Los Angeles, 1950—, chief exec. officer, 1969—, chmn. bd., 1969—; pres. Nat. Am. Ins. Co., Omaha, 1966-75, chmn., 1975—; chmn. Home Savs. & Loan Assn., 1969—, Stuyvesant Ins. Group, Allentown, Pa., 1974—, Nat. Am. Ins. Co. Calif., Nat. Am. Life Ins. Co. Calif., Nat. Am. Title Ins. Co. Mem. Founders of Music Center, Los Angeles; bd. dirs. Hosp of Good Samaritan; trustee, v.p. Ahmanson Found., Los Angeles, 1952—; trustee Greater Los Angeles Zoo Assn., Los Angeles County Museum Art, Calif. Inst. Arts bd. visitors UCLA. Served with USNR. Clubs: Wilshire Country, Chevalier Du Tastevin, Jonathan. Office: 3731 Wilshire Blvd Los Angeles CA 90010*

AHMED, SALEEM, agronomist; b. Nagpur, India, Dec. 28, 1939; emigrated to Pakistan, 1950; came to U.S., 1973; s. Khan Bahadur Syed Izzuddin and Hamida A.; B.Sc. in Geology and Chemistry with honors, U. Karachi (Pakistan), 1960, M.Sc. in Geology, 1961; Ph.D. in Soil Sci. (East-West Center scholar), U. Hawaii, Honolulu, 1965; m. Carol Yasuko Matsumoto, Aug. 23, 1963; children—Aisha Akiko, Seema Sueko. Lectr. in geology U. Karachi, 1965-66; with Esso Pakistan Fertilizer Co. Ltd., Karachi, 1966-73, regional agronomist, Lahore, 1967-70, tech. services adv., 1970-73; research asso. Resource Systems Inst., East-West Center, Honolulu, 1973—; cons. AAAS, Asian Devel. Bank, govt. of Pakistan, also multinat. agribus. firms. Founder Garden Rd. Community Youth Center, Karachi, 1959-61; gen. sec. Karachi U. Students Assn., 1960-61, East-West Center Students Assn., 1962-63; bd. dirs. Kokohead Community Assn., Honolulu, 1974-75; mem. exec. council Kamiloiki Community Assn., Honolulu, 1979-81; v.p. Honolulu Children Opera Chorus, 1982—; convenor, v.p. U.S. Com. for Justice for Palestinians, 1982—. Recipient Most Outstanding Student of Yr. award Karachi U., 1961, East-West Center, 1963. Mem. AAAS, Am. Soc. Agronomy, Internat. Soil Sci. Soc., Council Agrl. Sci. and Tech. Muslim. Contbr. articles to profl. jours.; edited procs. various confs., symposia; developer statis. procedure for internat. agronomic research. Office: East-West Center 1777 East-West Rd Honolulu HI 96848

AHRENDT, KENNETH MARTIN, educator; b. Chgo., May 25, 1931; s. Martin Lester and Mildred Margaret (Byrnes) A.; m. Jean Highley, Dec. 15, 1962; children—Thomas Kevin, Julie Anne. B.A., Ariz. State U., 1959, M.A., 1962; Ed.D., U. B.C., 1969. Tchr. elem. schs., Wash., 1959-62; tchr. remedial reading Phoenix Union High Sch. Dist., 1962-67; dir. reading Study Skills Ctr., U. B.C., Vancouver, 1969-71; chmn. reading dept. Oreg. State U., Corvallis, 1972-79, assocs. prof., 1971—; asst. prof. U. B.C., 1969-71. Mem. Internat. Reading Assn., Oreg. Reading Assn., Nat. Reading Conf., Kappa Delta Pi, Phi Alpha Theta, Phi Delta Kappa. Republican. Episcopalian. Club: Elks. Contbg. author: Reading Research Revisited, 1983; Community College Reading Programs, 1976; The Content Teacher and Reading Strategies, 1977. Home: 3675 NW Lincoln St Corvallis OR 97330 Office: Sch Edn Oregon State U Corvallis OR 97331

AHRENS, RICHARD WILLIAM, electronic engr.; b. N.Y.C., Apr. 7, 1932; s. Henry Richard and Virginia (Payne) A.; B.A., Bowdoin Coll., 1953; B.S., U. Calif. at Berkeley, 1961; m. Nancy Emery Grove, May 7, 1955 (div. Oct. 1965); children—Richard Bruce, Julie Grove; m. 2d, Joanna Hanson Bassett, Nov. 27, 1976; 1 dau., Elizabeth Anne Bassett. Engr., Alfred Electronics, Palo Alto, Calif., 1961-62; with Singer Bus. Machines, San Leandro, Calif., 1963-73, sr. engr., 1969-73; sr. engr. Diablo Systems, Hayward, Calif., 1973-79, planning mgr., 1979-81; planning mgr. Xerox Corp., Hayward, 1981—; cons. work in elec. safety, 1965-73. Maj., CAP, Oakland, Calif., 1965—, squadron comdr., 1979—. Served to 1st lt. USAF, 1953-57. Mem. Mensa (asst. sec. 1969-71, treas. 1981—), Alpha Tau Omega. Republican. Episcopalian. Clubs: No. Calif. Model T Ford (v.p. 1973-74); No. Calif. Rolls-Royce Owners (sec. 1976-79, chmn. 1980-82); Alameda (Calif.) Flying. Home: 4235 Norton Ave Oakland CA 94602 Office: 26250 Industrial Blvd Hayward CA 94545

AHUJA, JAGDISH CHAND, mathematics educator; b. Rawalpindi, W. Pakistan, Dec. 24, 1927; came to U.S., 1966, naturalized, 1972; s. Nihal Chand and Iashwardai (Chhabra) A.; m. Sudarshan Sachdeva, May 18, 1955; children—Naina, Anita. B.A., Banaras U., 1953, M.A., 1955; Ph.D., U. B.C., 1963. Sr. math. tchr. D.A.V. High Sch., Nairobi, Kenya, 1955-56; tchr. math., Tanzania, 1956-58; teaching asst. U. B.C., 1958-61, teaching fellow, 1961-63, stats. lab. instr., 1959-61, lectr. stats., 1961-63; asst. prof. math. U. Calgary, 1963-66; assoc. prof. math. Portland State U., 1966-69, prof. math., 1969—. Mem. Am. Statis. Assn., Inst. Math. Stats. Contbr. articles to profl. jours.; referee profl. jours., reviewer profl. jours. Home: 9914 SW 30th Ave Portland OR 97219 Office: Dept Math Portland State U PO Box 751 Portland OR 97207

AHVAKANA, ULAAG (LAWRENCE REYNOLD AHVAKANA), sculptor, glassblower; b. Fairbanks, Alaska, July 8, 1946. Student of Allen Houser at Inst. Am. Indian Arts, 1966-69, Cooper Union Sch. Art, 1969-70, R.I. Sch. Design. Works exhibited in permanent collections: Port Authority Bldg., N.Y.C., Visual Arts Ctr. Alaska; commns.: Wolf Dancer (welded steel sculpture), Inst. Am. Indian Arts, 1969; Dancers (welded steel sculpture), Calista Corp., Settlers Bay Lodge, Wassilla, Alaska, 1976; dedication plaque North Slope Borough Barrow, Alaska, 1977, bronze sculpture, 1980; group shows: Bklyn. Mus., 1971, Squash Blossom Gallery, Vail, Colo., 1980, Artique, Anchorage, 1981, Sacred Circle Gallery Am. Indian Arts, 1981, Inst. Am. Indian Arts, N.Mex., 1981, Santa Fe Festival Arts, 1981, many others; represented in permanent collections: Newark Mus., Am. Fedn. Arts, N.Y.C., Bowers Mus., Santa Ana, Calif. Bd. dirs. Visual Art Ctr. Alaska, 1975-77; commd. mem. Anchorage Hist. and Fine Arts, 1976; pres. Raven's Bones Found., 1977—; artist in residence/glass blowing and sculpture Community of Barrow, 1972-74; artist in residence/sculpture Visual Arts Ctr. Alaska, 1975-77; instr. sculpture and glass Inst. Am. Indian Arts, Santa Fe, 1977-78; instr. Pratt Art Ctr., 1980. Recipient award in Glass, Earth, Fire and Fiber Show, Anchorage Hist. and Fine Arts Mus., 1974; 1st in Wood, All-Alaska Juried Art Show, 1976; 1st in Sculpture, Native Arts Invitational, Chevron Corp., 1977; others. Office: Inst Am Indian Arts 1369 Cerrillos Rd Santa Fe NM 87501*

AI, STEVEN C., business executive; b. Honolulu, Dec. 19, 1953; s. David C. and Lani C. A.; m. Nancy Suzanne, Sept. 8, 1979. B.A. in Bus. Adminstrn., Whittier Coll., 1976; M.B.A., U. Denver, 1979. Acct., Mayor's Office, City of Los Angeles, 1976; loan analyst internat. div. Union Bank, Los Angeles, 1977-78; v.p. retail div. City Mill Co. Ltd., Honolulu, 1979—, also sec., dir. Mem. Retail Mchts. Hawaii (dir. 1983). Office: PO Box 1559 Honolulu HI 96806

AIELLO, D. ROBERT, clinical psychologist; b. Los Alamos, Feb. 28, 1952; s. William Peter and Elizabeth Ann (Maroney) A.; m. Deborah Anne Brogden, Mar. 29, 1980. A.B. with honors, Hamilton Coll., 1973; M.A., N.Mex. State U., 1975; Ph.D. (Fellow), Bowling Green State U., 1978. Clin psychologist Los Lunas (N.Mex.) Hosp., 1977-79; psychol. cons. Dist. IV Area Mental Health Bd., Roswell, N.Mex., 1979-81; clin. psychologist Guidance Ctr. Lea County, Hobbs, N.Mex., 1981—, Lea Regional Hosp., Hobbs, 1982—; adj. fac. mem. Coll. of SW and N. Mex. Jr. Coll., Hobbs. Mem. N.Mex. Gov.'s. subcom. aging, long term care, 1981—; bd. dirs. Option, Inc., Hobbs, 1982—. Mem. Am. Psychol. Assn., Am. Personnel and Guidance Assn., Rocky Mountain Psychol. Assn., Psi Chi. Democrat. Baptist. Presenter numerous papers to profl. convs.; contbr. articles to profl. jours. Office: 920 W Broadway St Hobbs NM 88240

AIGNER, DENNIS JOHN, educator; b. Los Angeles, Sept. 27, 1937; s. Herbert Lewis and Della Geraldine (Balasek) A.; children—Mitchell, Annette, Anita, Angela. Student UCLA, 1955-58; B.S., U. Calif.-Berkely, 1959, M.A., 1962, Ph.D., 1963. Math. statistician U.S. Dept. Agr., Forest Service, Berkeley, Calif., 1960-62; asst. prof. econs. U. Ill., 1962-66, dir. Computer Lab., 1964-66, assoc. prof., 1966-67; assoc. prof. econs. U. Wis.-Madison, 1967-70, dir. programming and computation service, 1967-73, prof. econs., 1970-77; summer vis. prof. econs. U. Hawaii, 1970; Fulbright research scholar, vis. prof. Center for Ops. Research & Econometrics, Universite Catholique de Louvain, Belgium, 1970-71; resident cons. Rand Corp., Santa Monica, Calif., spring, 1976; prof. econs. U. So. Calif., Los Angeles, 1976—, chmn. dept. econs., 1979—; cons. in field. H.I. Romnes Faculty fellow, U. Wis., 1976; NSF grantee, 1968, 70, 71, 73, 79; Fulbright scholar, 1970. Fellow Econometric Soc.; mem. Am. Statis. Assn., Am. Econs. Assn. Contbr. articles to profl. jours. Home: 16044 Aiglon St Pacific Palisades CA 90272 Office: Dept Econs Univ So Calif Los Angeles CA 90089

AIKAWA, JERRY KAZUO, physician, educator; b. Stockton, Calif., Aug. 24, 1921; s. Genmatsu and Shizuko (Yamamoto) A.; A.B., U. Calif., 1942; M.D., Wake Forest Coll., 1945; m. Chitose Aihara, Sept. 20, 1944; 1 son, Ronald K. Intern, asst. resident N.C. Baptist Hosp., 1945-47; NRC fellow in med. scis. U. Calif. Med. Sch., 1947-48; NRC, AEC postdoctoral fellow in med. scis. Bowman Gray Sch. Medicine, 1948-50, instr. internal medicine, 1950-53, asst. prof., 1953; established investigator Am. Heart Assn., 1952-58; exec. officer lab. service Univ. Hosps., 1958-61, dir. lab. services, 1961-83, dir. allied health program, 1969—, pres. med. bd., 1980—, asso. dean for clin. affairs, acting head div. lab. medicine and clin. pathology, 1980-83; asst. prof. U. Colo. Sch. Medicine, 1953-60, asso. prof. medicine, 1960-67, prof., 1967—, prof. biometrics, 1974—. Fellow A.C.P.; mem. Western Soc. Clin. Research, So. Soc. Clin. Research, Soc. Exptl. Biology and Medicine, Am. Fedn. Clin. Research, AAAS, Central Soc. Clin. Research, A.M.A., Assn. Am. Med. Colls., Phi Beta Kappa, Sigma Xi, Alpha Omega. Home: 619 S Poplar Way Denver CO 80224 Office: 4200 E 9th Ave Denver CO 80262

AIKEN, LEWIS ROSCOE, JR., psychologist, educator; b. Bradenton, Fla., Apr. 14, 1931; s. Lewis Roscoe and Vera Irene (Hess) A.; m. Dorothy Ree Grady, Dec. 16, 1956; children—Christopher, Timothy. B.S., Fla. State U., Tallahassee, 1955, M.A., 1956; Ph.D., U. N.C., Chapel Hill, 1960. Assoc. prof. psychology U.N.C., Greensboro, 1960-65; prof. Guilford Coll., Greensboro, 1966-74, Sacred Heart Coll., Belmont, N.C., 1974-76, U. Pacific, Stockton, Calif., 1977-79, Pepperdine U., Malibu, Calif., 1979—. Served to sgt. USMC, 1951-54. Fla. Lewis scholar, 1949-51, 54-56; Emory U. fellow, 1957-58; Nat. Acad. Scis.-NRC postdoctoral resident research assocs., 1963-64; U.S. Office Edn. postdoctoral fellow, 1968-69. Fellow Am. Psychol. Assn.; mem. Am. Ednl. Research Assn., Sigma Xi. Author: General Psychology 1969; Psychological and Educational Testing, 1971; Psychological Testing and Assessment, 1976, 3d edit., 1982; Later Life, 1978, 2d edit., 1982; contbr. articles to profl. jours.

AIKEN-KINTZ, SARAH JUDITH, hospital administrator b. Vancouver, Wash., Mar. 23, 1947; d. Lorn Herbert and Janet Bernadine Hutchins (Hingston) Aiken; m. Campbell H.D. Kintz, Oct. 21, 1980. B.A. in Mgmt. Psychology, Marylhurst U., 1980; postgrad. U. Portland, 1981—. With St. Vincent Hosp. and Med. Center, Portland, Oreg., 1981—, dir. mgmt. systems 1983—. Mem. Am. Soc. Tng. and Devel. (pres. Oreg. chpt. 1982), Inst. Managerial and Profl. Women, Am. Mgmt. Assn., Am. Hosp. Systems Soc., Am. Hosp. Assn. Democrat. Jewish. Club: City Portland. Office: 9205 SW Barnes Rd Portland OR 97225

AINBINDER, ARLENE GAIL, fin. adminstr.; b. Detroit, July 6, 1945; d. Hyman and Lillian Ainbinder; B.S. in Mgmt., Pepperdine U., 1981, M.B.A., 1982; 1 son, Todd. Fin. adminstr. So. Calif. Inst. Architecture, Santa Monica, 1977—. Mem. Calif. Assn. Student Fin. Aid Adminstrs., Western Assn. Student Fin. Aid Adminstrs. Office: 1800 Berkeley St Santa Monica CA 90404

AINSLIE, RICHARD GEORGE, life insurance agent; b. Los Angeles, Apr. 4, 1916; s. Edgar and Elizabeth (Chesney) A.; B.S., Purdue U., 1939, M.S., 1940; postgrad. U. So. Calif., 1943-44; children—Paul R., Susan C. Instr., coach Purdue U., W. Lafayette, Ind., 1939-40; instr., head football and basketball coach Whitman Coll., Walla Walla, Wash., 1940-42; safety engr. Consol. Steel., Wilmington, Calif., 1942-44; recreation dir. AirService Command, Fairfield, Ohio, 1944-46; head football coach Wittenberg Coll., Springfield, Ohio, 1946; prof., basketball-baseball coach Creighton U., Omaha, 1947-48; agt. Minn. Mut. Life Ins. Co., Los Angeles, 1948-58, gen. agt., 1958—, field council, 1961, 63, 75, 76. Chmn. war and bond drive Patterson Field, Ohio, 1944-46, Community Chest and Red Cross drive, 1945-46. Named outstanding profl. salesman Am., 1967-68; registered profl. disability and health ins. underwriter. Mem. Million Dollar Round Table (life and qualifying, honor roll, 1952-83), Internat. Assn. Health Underwriters (leading producers Round Table, Health, Life and Qualifying 1969-83, nat. quality award 1955-81), Los Angeles Life Underwriters Assn., Life Ins. and Trust Council Los Angeles, Nat. Football Found. and Hall of Fame, Purdue Alumni Assn. (life), Internat. Srs. Amateur Golf Soc. (N.Y.C. chpt.). Clubs: Los Angeles Athletic, Oakmont Country (Glendale), Elks. Contbr. articles in field to pubs. Home: 3000 Country Club Dr Glendale CA 91208 Office: 3000 Country Club Dr Glendale CA 90039

AINSWORTH, LEONARD DWAIN, city water treatment official, technical writer; b. Taft, Calif., Aug. 26, 1937; s. Glenn Meredith and Ruth Adrienne (Taylor) A.; m. N. Elaine Thompson, July 24, 1965; children—Timothy Scott, Dwain Irwin, Heidi Jean, Michelle Anne. B.S., U. Nev., 1962. Chemist, treatment supt. City of Santa Barbara (Calif.),

1965-71; tng. officer Calif. Dept. Health, Santa Barbara and San Diego, 1971-74; water treatment supr. City of Escondido (Calif.), 1974-78; gen. mgr. Silverlake Water Co., Reno, 1978-79; tech. writer Calif. Sect. Am. Water Works Assn., 1979—; water treatment supt. City of Oceanside (Calif.), 1982—; instr. Calif. community colls., 1965—; contractual tech. writer tng./instructive materials, 1979—. Served with USNR, 1959-61. Mem. Am. Water Works Assn., Exptl. Aircraft Assn. Contbr. articles to profl. jours.

AINSWORTH, RANDALL LEE, portrait photographer; b. Aberdeen, Wash., June 12, 1950; s. Arnold Ned and Carmen Hazel (Simbe) A.; A.A., Grays Harbor Coll., Aberdeen, 1970; student U. Wash., Seattle, 1970-71. Photographer, 1971-78; owner, photographer, Randall Ainsworth Photography; instr. local amateur photographers. Recipient numerous awards in photography. Mem. Profl. Photographers Am., Profl. Photographers Wash., Southwest Profl. Photographers Wash. Baptist. Contrbr. articles to profl. jours. Home and Office: 605 W Wishkah Aberdeen WA 98520

AIRHEART, FRANKLIN BENJAMIN, manufacturing company executive; b. San Francisco, Apr. 12, 1930; s. Ted S. and Dorothy (DeDici) A.; B.S., U. So. Calif., 1956; children—Eric Jeffery, Erin June. Asst. project engr. Lockheed Aircraft, Burbank, Calif., 1956-57; chief engr., v.p. engring. Airheart Products, Inc., Van Nuys, Calif., 1957-67; v.p. engring. Hurst/Airheart, Chatsworth, Calif., 1967-72, exec. v.p., 1972-78; pres. Am. Dibranetics, Inc., Pacoima, Calif., 1978-83; gen. mgr. Brake div. Alston Engring., Sacramento, 1983—. Served to 1st lt. AUS, 1952-54. Recipient Nat. Office Mgmt. award, 1956. Mem. Soc. Automotive Engrs. Republican. Patentee in field. Office: 6291 Warehouse Way Sacramento CA 95826

AITKEN, ROBERT GEORGE, physicist; b. S.I., N.Y., Dec. 27, 1944; s. Robert Peters and Marjorie Dorothea (Jackson) A.; B.S., Fordham U., 1966; M.S., Northwestern U., 1971; Ph.D., U. Ill., 1979. Research asso., then vis. asst. prof. U. Houston, 1978-80; asst. prof. physics U. Colo., Colorado Springs, 1980—. Mem. Am. Phys. Soc., Colo. Assn. Sci. Tchrs. Home: 905 Crosstrail Dr Colorado Springs CO 80906 Office: Physics Dept Univ Colo Colorado Springs CO 80933

AJIFU, RALPH KANICHI, state senator; b. Kaneohe, Hawaii, June 26, 1926; m., 6 children. Agr. loan officer 1st Hawaiian Bank; mem. Hawaii Ho. of Reps., 1967-78; mem. Hawaii State Senate. Chmn., State Land Use Commn.; mem. State Bd. Agr. and Conservation; mem. Hawaii Constl. Conv., 1968; chmn. Windward Oahu Soil and Water Conservation Dist., 1964—; chmn. Windward Fair, 1970; dir., sec. K-Bay Farms, 1974. Chmn. Future Farmers of Am.-Young Farmers Found. Office: PO Box 402 Kaneohe HI 96744*

AKAKA, ABRAHAM KAHIKINA, clergyman; b. Honolulu, Feb. 21, 1917; s. Kahikina and Annie (Kahoa) A.; student U. Hawaii, 1934-37, LL.D. (hon.), 1980; B.A., Ill. Wesleyan U., 1939; B.D., U. Chgo., 1943, D.D., 1958; L.H.D. (hon.), Salem Coll., 1959; LL.D. (hon.), U. Pacific, 1978; m. Mary Louise Jeffrey, July 22, 1944; children—Fenner-Marie Akaka Gilding, Pualani Suzanne Akaka Kallstrom, Sarah Kahikina, Sandra Komokana, Jeffrey Lee. Ordained to ministry United Ch. of Christ, 1944; pastor W. Kauai Larger Parish Council, Hawaii, 1943-45, Central Maui, Hawaii, 1945-54, Haili Ch., Hilo, Hawaii, 1954-57, Kawaiahao Ch., Honolulu, 1957—; chaplain Hawaiian Senate, 1958-60; vesper speaker Oberlin U. series, 1965. Organizer Friends of Kamehameha Schs., 1968; pres. Kahului Town Assn., 1950-54; trustee Mauna Olu Community Coll., Hawaii, 1952-54; regent U. Hawaii, 1961-63. Named Father of Yr. in Religion, Honolulu, 1958; recipient numerous awards including. Citizen of Yr. award Civitan Clubs Hawaii, 1962, Salesman of Yr. award Sales and Market Execs. Hawaii, 1963, Ke Alii Pauahi award Kamehameha Schs., 1963, Nat. Soc. Arts and Letters award, 1965, Community Speaker of Yr. award Pacific Speech Assn., 1966, Good Citizenship medal SAR, 1970. Office: Kawaiahao Church Honolulu HI 96813

AKAKA, DANIEL KAHIKINA, congressman; b. Honolulu, Sept. 11, 1924; m. Mary Mildred Chong; children—Millannie, Daniel Kahikina, Gerard, Alan, Nicholas. B.Ed., profl. cert., M.Ed., U. Hawaii, 1948-66. Tchr., 1953-60; vice prin., 1960; prin., 1963-71; program specialist, 1968-71; dir., 1971-74; dir., spl. asst. in human resources, 1975-76; mem. 95th-98th Congresses from Hawaii. Bd. dirs. Hanahauoli Sch.; mem. Act 4 Ednl. Adv. Commn., Library Adv. Council; scholarship com. Na Hookama O Pauahi, Kamehameha Schs.; mem. Manpower and Full Employment Commn.; minister of music Kawaiahao Ch. Served with U.S. Army, 1945-47. Democrat. Office: 2301 Rayburn House Office Bldg Washington DC 20515*

AKAMATSU, MURIEL, management consultant; b. Norborne, Mo., Aug. 24, 1945; d. Edward M. and Clara A. (Miller) List. A.B. in Art, U. Mo., 1968, A.M. in Journalism, 1972; Ed.D. in Indsl. Edn., W. Va. U., 1979; accredited pub. relations profl. Extension info. specialist Center Extension and Continuing Edn., W. Va. U./U.S. Dept. Agr., Morgantown, 1973-76, extension publs. specialist, 1976-77; coordinator off-the-job safety Gulf Oil Corp., Pitts., 1977-79, sr. health and safety communications analyst, 1979-80; mgr. safety info. services Kaiser Aluminum and Chem. Corp., Oakland, Calif., 1980-82; cons. in mgmt. safety, Oakland, 1982—. Mem. Am. Soc. Profl. Engrs., Am. Soc. Safety Engrs., Am. Soc. Tng. and Devel., Internat. Assn. Bus. Communications (Golden Triangle award, 1978), Ops. Research Soc. Am. Club: Toastmasters. Contbr. numerous articles to mags. and newspapers. Home and office: 6479 Ascot Dr Oakland CA 94611

AKAWIE, THOMAS FRANK, artist, educator; b. N.Y.C., Feb. 22, 1935. Student Los Angeles City Coll., 1953-56; B.A. in Art History, U. Calif.-Berkeley, 1959, M.A. in Painting, 1963. Works exhibited in permanent collections: Milw. Art Ctr., Ithaca (N.Y.) Coll. Art. Mus., Oakland (Calif.) Mus., Williams Coll. Mus., Williamstown, Mass.; group shows: Whitney Mus. Am. Art, N.Y.C., 1969, San Francisco Mus. Modern Art, 1976, Nat. Collection Fine Arts, Smithsonian Instn., Washington, 1977; one-man shows: LaJolla (Calif.) Mus. Art, Calif., 1967, Palace of the Legion of Honor, San Francisco, 1972, San Jose (Calif.) Mus. Art, 1977, 4th Triennial-India 78 Inc., Thailand and Iran, 1978, Calif. Visionary painting, Japan, 1978, Herbert F. Johnson Mus. Art, Cornell U., Ithaca, N.Y., 1980. Asst. prof. painting and drawing UCLA, 1965-66; lectr. painting and drawing U. Calif.-Berkeley, 1972-73; instr. spray-painting and drawing San Francisco Art Inst., 1966—. Recipient Los Angeles All-City Exhibit award, 1965; 1st prize Ana Downey Mus. Invitational, 1966; 1st prize Jack London Art Exhibit, Oakland, 1969. Office: San Francisco Art Inst 800 Chestnut St San Francisco CA 94133*

AKE, MONTIE RALPH, hotel exec.; b. San Angelo, Tex., July 10, 1931; s. William Raleigh and Lorraine (Elliott) A.; B.S., Lamar U., 1949, B.A., 1953. Trainee, front office mgr. Sheraton Corp. Am., St. Louis, 1956-61; sales mgr. Tan-Tar-A Resort, Osage Beach, Mo., 1962-63, gen. mgr., 1963-69, v.p., 1969-78; exec. v.p. Glenwood Manor Motor Hotel, Overland Park, Kans., 1978-80; gen. mgr. Rancho Bernardo Inn, San Diego, 1981—; past sec.-treas., dir., v.p. Dickinson Operating Co., Dickinson, Inc.; sec.-treas. Le Jardin, Inc.; dir. M.D.H. Theatre Corp. Sustaining mem. Gt. Rivers council Boy Scouts Am. Past pres., bd. dirs. Lake Ozarks Assn., 1967-77. Served with U.S. Army, 1953-55. Mem. Am. Hotel-Motel Assn. (past dir.), Greater Kansas City Restaurant Assn. (dir.), Greater Kansas City Hotel Assn. (dir.), Kans. Hotel and Motel Assn. (dir.), San Diego Conv. and Visitors Bur., Kans. Cavalry (col.), AMKO Assn. (dir.), San Diego C. of C. Republican. Presbyterian. Clubs: Variety Internat. (2d asst. barker), Rotary of Rancho Bernardo. Address: 12761-82 Camino de la Broccia San Diego CA 92128

AKERS, DARREL LEE, editorial cartoonist; b. Norman, Okla., Nov. 21, 1944; s. Robert Lee and Rosemary (Brown) A.; A.A., Napa Coll., 1970; postgrad. Solano Coll., 1972-77; m. Jo Ann Jeffrey, Sept. 24, 1965; children—Sandra Elizabeth, Christine Louise. Naval architecture technician Mare Island (Calif.) Naval Shipyard, 1967-75; editorial cartoonist Vacaville (Calif.) Reporter, 1973—, Paradise Post, Calif., 1978-80, Morning Herald, Yuba City, Calif., 1978-79; sr. engring. asso. Sperry Corp., Benicia, Calif., 1978—. Founder, pres. Theatre Machine, Vacaville, 1973—. Served with USAF, 1963-67. Recipient award for editorial cartoon Nat. Newspaper Pubs., 1975; pub. service cert. Lions Club, 1977, Upper Solano Assn. for Retarded Children, 1978; award for cartoons Citizens for Law and Order, 1982, award for cartoons Solano Taxpayers Assn., 1982. Mem. No. Calif. Cartoon and Humor Assn., Am. Film Inst., C. of C., Dramatists Guild/Authors League Am. Lutheran. Club: Elks. Author plays: Night of the Anemic Vampire, 1975; 1776 Plus Tax, 1976; Hanky Panky, 1978; Up in Arms, 1982. Home and Office: 402 Chelan Dr Vacaville CA 95688

AKHAVAN, SIAMAK HOSSEIN, advertising agency executive, international trade specialist; b. Tehran, Iran, Sept. 16, 1953; came to U.S. 1982; s. Khalil and Mahin Bano (Tabrizian) A.; m. Nina Saffari, 1978; children—Ali Reza, Amir Hossein. B.S. in Econs., U. Utah, 1975. Owner, chief exec. officer, Acier, Ltd., Tehran, 1975—; owner, operator Siamk H. Akhavan Trading Co., Tehran, 1976—; owner, chief exec. officer Pertide, Tehran, 1977—; chief exec. officer Tradeworx, Salt Lake City, 1982—; owner, chief exec. officer Adworx, Salt Lake City, 1982—. Office: 450 S 900 E Suite 303 Salt Lake City UT 84102

AKI, JAMES HAJIME, state senator; b. Honolulu, Sept. 10, 1936; s. Walter Dang and Lillian (Ushigusa) A.; m. Faye Reiko Hayashi; children—Michelle, Clayton, Bradley, Collette. B.A., U. Hawaii, 1959. Mem. Hawaii Ho. of Reps., from 1976; now Hawaii state senator; chmn. com. youth and elderly affairs, from 1976. Served to pvt., USAR, 1957-66. Democrat. Office: Hawaii State Senate State Capitol Bldg Room 216 Honolulu HI 96813

AKIMA, HIROSHI, elec. engr.; b. Tokyo, Nov. 20, 1925; s. Yoshio and Chiyo (Sato) A.; B.Eng., Tokyo U., 1947, D.Eng., 1961; came to U.S., 1965, naturalized, 1972; m. Mieko Miyasawa, Dec. 15, 1955; children—Kiyoshi, Hiroko. Research ofcl. Radio Research Labs. Japanese Ministry Posts and Telecommunications, Koganei-shi, Tokyo, 1947-65; elec. engr. Nat. Telecommunications and Info. Adminstrn., Inst. Telecommunication Scis., Dept. Commerce, Boulder, Colo., 1965—. Recipient Outstanding Authorship awards Dept. Commerce, 1977, 81. Mem. IEEE (sr.), Sigma Xi. Contbr. articles to profl. jours. Home: 2880 20th St Boulder CO 80302 Office: 325 Broadway Boulder CO 80303

AKINS, FAREN RAY, psychologist; b. Tulsa, Nov. 30, 1950; s. Lelan Ray and Virginia Belle (Munk) A.; B.A. magna cum laude, U. Tulsa, 1972; M.A., U. Ariz., 1974, Ph.D., 1976; m. Dianna Jane Marie Lyell, Aug. 31, 1976. Research asso. NRC, NASA-Ames Research Center, Moffett Field, Calif., 1976 78; research asso. U. Santa Clara (Calif.), 1978-80; clin. psychologist Mental Health Guidance Clinic Juvenile Hall, Santa Clara County, San Jose, Calif., 1980—; instr. DeAnza Community Coll., Cupertino, Calif., 1976 , U. Santa Clara (Calif.), 1977, Calif. Sch. Profl. Psychology, Berkeley, Calif., 1978. Recipient Research awards U. Tulsa Research Council, 1972, NSF, 1972, Sigma Xi, 1973, NIMH, 1974, 75, 76, NRC, 1976-78, NASA, 1978-81; Omicron Delta Kappa scholar, 1971, Sigma Chi scholar, 1971, John W. Henry Meml. scholar, 1972, Herman E. Demund Found. fellow, 1974-76. Mem. Am. Psychol. Assn., AAAS. Author: Study Guide for Introduction to Psychology: Explorations and Applications, 1977; Study Guide for Essentials of Psychology, 1979; Study Guide for Introduction to Psychology: Explorations and Applications, 1980; Non-Human Primate Behavior Development: An Abstracted Bibliography, 1980; Early Parent-Child Separation: An Abstracted Bibliography, 1981; The Hospitalized Child: An Abstracted Bibliography, 1981; The Bereaved Child: An Abstracted Bibliography, 1981; Human Problems in Extended Spaceflight, 1982. Home: 1342 Glen Dell Dr San Jose CA 95125 Office: 840 Guadelope Pkwy San Jose CA

AKINS, GEORGE CHARLES, jewelry co. exec.; b. Willits, Cal., Feb. 22, 1917; s. Guy Brookins and Eugenie (Swan) A.; A.A., Sacramento City Coll., 1941; m. Jane Babcock, Mar. 27, 1945. Accountant, auditor Calif. Bd. Equalization, Dept. Finance, Sacramento, 1940-44; controller-treas. DeVons Jewelers, Sacramento, 1944-73, v.p., controller, 1973-80, v.p., chief fin. officer, 1980—, also dir.; individual accounting and tax practice, Sacramento, 1944—. Accountant, cons. Mercy Children's Hosp. Guild, Sacramento, 1957-77. Served with USAAF, 1942. Mem. Soc. Calif. Pioneers, Nat. Soc. Pub. Accountants, U.S. Navy League, Calif. Hist. Soc., English Speaking Union, Drake Navigators Guild, Internat. Platform Assn., Mendocino County Hist. Soc. Democrat. Roman Catholic. Clubs: Commonwealth of Calif., Comstock. Contbg. author: Portfolio of Accounting Systems for Small and Medium-Sized Business, 1968, rev., 1977. Home: 4417 Marion Ct Sacramento CA 95822 Office: 1910 29th St Sacramento CA 95816

AKITA, RICHARD MITSUO, electronics engr.; b. Honolulu, Nov. 13, 1939; s. Mitsuyoshi and Tomoyo (Sueoka) A.; B.S. in Math., Oreg. State U., 1961; M.S.E.E., Naval Postgrad. Sch., 1968; m. Gwen Harumi Tateno, June 14, 1964; children—Michael T., Andrea N. Electronics engr. command and control div. Naval Ocean Systems Center, 1970-77, supervisory engr., br. head navigation systems br., 1977—; instr. engring. Calif. Community Colls., 1977—. Mem. sch. site council Wangeheim Jr. High Sch., 1978-80. Served with USN, 1961-70. Mem. IEEE, Sigma Xi. Republican. Club: Lions. Home: 1738 Sorrel Ct Carlsbad CA 92008 Office: Naval Ocean Systems Center Code 8244 San Diego CA 92152

AKIYAMA, KAZUYOSHI, condr.; b. Tokyo, Jan. 2, 1941; student Toho Sch. Music; m. Keiko Akiyama; children—Masayoshi, Tomoyoshi, Makiko. Conducting debut with Tokyo Symphony Orch., 1964, permanent condr., 1964—; prin. condr. Osaka Philharmonic, 1967-78, prin. guest condr., 1979—; asst. condr. Toronto Symphony, 1968-69; music dir. Tokyo Symphony, 1968—; resident condr., music dir. Vancouver (B.C., Can.), 1972—; music dir. Am. Symphony Orch., 1973-78; toured U.S., Japan, Europe with Vancouver Symphony Orch., Toho String Orch., New Japan Philharmonic, Tokyo Symphony Orch.; prin. guest condr. Am. Symphony Orch., 1978—; guest condr. numerous orchs. including Balt. Symphony Orch., Boston Symphony, Cin. Symphony Orch., Cleve. Orch., Detroit Symphony Orch., Los Angeles Philharmonic, Montreal Symphony Orch., San Francisco Symphony Orch., San Diego Symphony Orch., Toronto Symphony Orch., N.Y. Philharmonic. Recipient Torii Music prize for outstanding contbn. to devel. and advancement of classical music in Japan, 1975. Recorded with Vancouver Symphony Orch., Japan Philharmonic Orch., Tokyo Symphony Orch., Osaka Philharmonic Orch., Yomiuri Symphony Orch. Address: Vancouver Symphony Orch 400 E Broadway Vancouver BC V5T 1X2 Canada*

ALAGIA, JAY SHAMJIBHAI, civil, structural engineer, consultant; b. India, Sept. 30, 1933; s. Shamjibhai and Narmada (Patel) A.; m. Jasummati Jayantilal Balubhai Patel, Nov. 30, 1954; children—Parul, Ila, Neal. B.S. in Civil Engring, Bombay State U., 1954; M.S. in Structural Engring, U. Ill., 1956. Cert. structural engr., Ariz. Calif.; cert. civil engr., Calif. Bridge designer Sverdrup & Parcel, Inc., St. Louis, 1956-57, 1958-59; lectr., structural engring, India, 1957-58; structural designer, Fruin-Colnon, St. Louis, 1959-60; structural engr.-in-charge Scholer & Fuller Architects, 1960-62; engr. Magadini-Alagia Assos., Phoenix, 1962-75, prin., exec. v.p., 1975—. Mem. Structural Engrs. Assn. Ariz. (dir.); Natl. Soc. Profl. Engrs; Am. Concrete Inst.; Ariz. Cons. Engrs. Assn. Republican. Club: Kiwanis. Office: 1133 East Missouri Phoenix AZ 85014

ALAMEDA, RUSSELL RAYMOND, JR., radiologic technologist, X-ray service company executive; b. San Jose, Calif., Oct. 13, 1945; s. Russell Raymond and Rose Margaret (Manzone) A.; m. Gayle Evileen Allison, Feb. 16, 1969 (div. 1975); children—Lynda Rae, Anthony David. Student San Jose City Coll., 1963-65. Served with U.S. Navy, 1966-75; x-ray technician VA Hosp., Palo Alto, Calif., 1975-78; office mgr., radiologic tech. orthopedic surgery Mountain View (Calif.) Hosp., 1978—; owner, operator Ren-Tech, San Jose, 1982—. Recipient Mallinckrodt Outstanding Achievement award Mallinckrodt Corp., 1971. Mem. Am. Registry of Radiologic Technologists, Calif. Radiologic Technologists, DAV. Republican. Lutheran. Home: 165 Blossom Hill Rd SP76 San Jose CA 95123 Office: Mountain View Hosp 2500 Hospital Dr Suite 7 Mount View CA 94040

ALAND, KENT MERREL, hosp. adminstr.; b. Pocatello, Idaho, Jan. 2, 1943; s. Montee Levi and Phyllis Helen (Egley) A.; B.S., Brigham Young U., 1968; M.P.H., UCLA, m. Sharon Chadwick, Nov. 18, 1966; children—Terri Lyn, Trevor Montee, Troy Ernest, Timothy Kent. Resident hosp. adminstr. Santa Monica Hosp. Med. Center, 1969-70; adminstr. USPHS Hosp. Philadelphia, Miss., 1970-71, USPHS Hosp., Winslow, Ariz., 1971-73; project dir. Utah cost improvement project Utah State Div. Health, Salt Lake City, 1973-74, dir. div. health Office Program Devel., 1974-78; dir. personnel and purchasing American Fork (Utah) Hosp., 1978-81; adminstr. Kane County Hosp., Kanab, Utah, 1981—; cons. in field. Del. County Conv., 1975-76; chmn. dist. fin. com. Boy Scouts Am., 1976; mem. Granite Community Zoning Com. Recipient award Winslow Hosp., 1973, Master-M-Men Service pin, 1973; Outstanding Performance award for service to youth of Ch. of Jesus Christ of Latter-day Saints, 1973; Superior Work Performance award U.S. Asst. Surg. Gen., 1971. Licensed Salt Lake Bd. Realtors; HEW grantee. Mem. Am., Utah hosp. assns. Republican. Mormon. Club: Kiwanis (sec. 1981, bd. dirs. 1982). Home: PO Box 221 Kanab UT 84741

ALBACH, CARL RUDOLPH, cons. elec. engr.; b. Bayonne, N.J., Feb. 21, 1907; s. George J. and Mary (Bollier) A.; E.E., Rensselaer Poly. Inst., 1928; M.A., U. Buffalo, 1939; m. Anne Avery, Sept. 15, 1934 (dec.), children—Lyndon Carl, Karen Joy Albach Antikajian. Engaged as plant engr. AT&T, Buffalo and N.Y.C., 1928-38; engr. U.S. Engrs. Office, Buffalo, 1942-44; dial office engr. Western Electric Co., Chgo., 1944-47; elec. designer for state capitol and exec. bldgs., Los Alamos Auditorium, pub. schs. and govt. bldgs. W.C. Kruger Co., Santa Fe, 1947-50; cons. elec. engr. labs. and bldgs. at various govt. bases, schs., chs., hosps., U. N.Mex. Women's dormitory, student union, music, drama, concert hall U. N.Mex., Albuquerque Civic Auditorium, Santa Fe, 1950-73; elec. engring. cons. U. N.Mex., 1955-70, lectr. illumination, 1957-64, 72; elec. and lighting cons. sch. plant planning com. N.Mex. Edn. Dept., 1963-70; past vice chmn. N.Mex. Bd. Profl. Engrs.; mem. Sweet's Nat. Adv. Bd., 1965-70, Statutes of Limitations Commn., 1966-67; mem. N.Mex. Elect. Code Com., 1967-76. Mem. devel. council Rensselaer Poly. Inst. Fellow Am. Cons. Engrs. Council (life), Illuminating Engring. Soc. (past chmn. N.Mex. chpt., vice chmn. 4th, 18th intermountain regional conf., nat. dir. 1962-64, mem. nat. allied arts com. 1957-64, Meritorious Service award); mem. IEEE (life), Cons. Engrs. Council N.Mex. (pres. 1956-58, dir. 1958-59, 61-64, 66-67, exec. dir. 1967). Contbr. articles to profl. jours. Address: PO Box 4235 Santa Fe NM 87501

ALBANY, JAMES SMITH, III, financial manager; b. Chester, Pa., Mar. 27, 1952; s. James Smith, Jr., and Mildred (Harrison) A. B.B.A., Roanoke Coll., 1974; M.B.A., Coll. William and Mary, 1976. Accounts receivable mgr. Story's Express, 1976-77; internal auditor Alco Standard Corp., 1978-81; mgr. system devel. and analysis Carpenter/Offutt Paper Co., Inc., Long Beach, Calif., 1981-82, mgr. spl. projects, 1982-83, mgr. corp. acctg., 1983—; operator tax return service; cons. Active Jr. Achievement, 1982. Mem. Inst. Internal Auditors (cert.), Nat. Assn. Accts. Republican. Episcopalian. Office: PO Box 940 Long Beach CA 90801

ALBERS, JAMES ARTHUR, engineering executive; b. Alton, Ill., Oct. 5, 1941; s. Arthur John and Elisabeth Ann (Wickenhauser) A.; m. Theresa Ann Bock, Dec. 26, 1964; children—James, Joseph. B.S. in Aero. Engring., Parks Coll., St. Louis, 1962; M.S. in Engring. Sci., U. Toledo; Ph.D. in Mech. Engring., Mich. State U., East Lansing, 1971; M.B.A. in Mgmt., Golden Gate U., San Francisco, 1979. Chief Propulsion Systems, NASA Dryden, Edwards AFB, Calif., 1977-78; candidate exec. devel. program, NASA Hdqrs., Washington, 1979-80; chief project engring. office NASA Dryden, 1980-81; asst. chief Dryden Aero. Projects, NASA Ames Center, Moffett Field, Calif., 1981—; mem. faculty Calif. State U., 1976-79. Recipient spl. achievement award NASA Lewis, Cleve., 1974; Equal Opportunity award NASA Dryden, 1976; Group Achievement Award, YF-12 symposium team, 1978. Mem. AIAA, Air Force Assn. Roman Catholic. Author reports; contbr. articles to profl. jours. Home: 3555 Sunnyhaven Dr San Jose CA 95117 Office: NASA Ames MS-210-5 Moffett Field CA 94035

ALBERSHEIM, PETER, educator; b. N.Y.C., Mar. 30, 1934; s. Walter Julius and Alberta (Green) A.; B.S., Cornell U., 1956; Ph.D., Calif. Inst. Tech., 1959; m. Joyce Elizabeth Johnson, June 9, 1958; children—Renée, Jim, Stephi. NSF postdoctoral research fellow Swiss Fed. inst. Tech., Zurich, Switzerland, 1959; instr. biology Harvard, Cambridge, Mass., 1960-61, asst. prof., 1961-64; asso. prof. biochemistry, dept. chemistry U. Colo., Boulder, 1964-67, prof., 1967—, also prof. molecular, cellular, developmental biology, 1970—; Dupont lectr. Tex. A&M U., 1978; vis. prof. U. Tex., 1978; vis. disting. prof. U. Hawaii, 1978; cons. Celanese, 1981—, Monsanto, 1976-82, Weyerhaeuser, 1981-82. Recipient Robert L. Stearns award U. Colo., 1979; NIH grantee, 1960-65, NSF grantee, 1966-67, 71-82, Dept. Energy grantee, 1964—, Herman Frasch Found. grantee, 1972-77, Rockefeller Found. grantee, 1975—, USDA grantee, 1975-80; Storer Life Scis. lectr. U. Calif. at Davis, 1977. Fellow AAAS; mem. Am. Chem. Soc., Am. Soc. Biol. Chemists, Am. Soc. Plant Physiology (mem. exec. com. 1978-81; Charles A. Shull award 1973), Biochem. Soc., Am. Phytopathol. Soc., Sigma Xi, others. Author: (with others) Twenty-six Afternoons of Biology - An Introductory Lab Manual, 1966. Contbr. over 145 articles to profl. jours.; mem. editorial bds. Jour. Biol. Chemistry; referee other jours. Home: 1440 Bellevue Dr Boulder CO 80302

ALBERSTONE, DALE STUART, lawyer; b. Los Angeles, Oct. 8, 1951; s. Marvin Howard and Barbara M. (Chudacoff) A.; B.A. cum laude in Psychology, Calif. State U., Northridge, 1973; J.D., Loyola U., 1976; student U. Paris, Sorbonne, 1972, Oxford (Eng.) U., 1974. Admitted to Calif. bar, 1976, U.S. Supreme Ct. bar, 1980, U.S. Dist. Ct. bar, 1983; clk. firm Magana, Cathcart & McCarthy, Los Angeles, 1974-76; asso. firm Caras & Evangelatos, Los Angeles, 1976—; of counsel firm Magana, Cathcart, McCarthy & Pierry, Los Angeles,

1980—; settlement officer Los Angeles Superior Ct., 1977-79; judge pro tem Los Angeles Municipal Ct., 1981—. Notary public, Calif.; lic. pilot, real estate broker. Mem. Am., Los Angeles County, Beverly Hills, Century City bar assns., Los Angeles Trial Lawyers Assn., Assn. Trial Lawyers Am., Psi Chi. Democrat. Jewish. Club: Magic Castle, Hollywood, Calif. Contbr. numerous monthly articles to real estate and landlord/tenant magazines. Office: Caras & Evangelatos 1801 Ave of the Stars Suite 810 Los Angeles CA 90067

ALBERT, EDWARD GEOFFREY, consulting aerospace systems engineer; b. Staten Island, N.Y., Nov. 12, 1931; s. William Henry and Alice Sargent (Merrick) A.; A.B., Wagner Coll., 1953; postgrad. U. N.Mex., 1954; M.S., NYU, 1960; m. Stella L. Girten, Jan. 3, 1977; children by a previous marriage—James E., Bruce H. With, U.S. Weather Bur., Satellite Center, Suitland, Md., 1959-66, OIC, TIROS I, II and III joint data teams, 1960-61, NIMBUS Data Utilization mgr., 1962-65; chief GSFC Project Office ESSA, Rockville, Md., 1966-69; chief spacecraft systems Nat. Oceanic and Atmospheric Adminstrn., Greenbelt, Md., 1969-74; with NASA, 1974-81, SMS/GOES Spacecraft mgr., Palo Alto, Calif., 1974-76, TDRSS systems engr., Redondo Beach, Calif., 1977-80, LANDSAT western region mgr., Santa Barbara, Calif., 1980-81; cons., 1981—. Guest lectr. on meteorol. satellites U. Md., 1965-68. Served with USAF, 1953-57. Mem. AAAS, Am. Meteorol. Soc., Smithsonian Assn., Met. Opera Guild, San Francisco Opera Guild, Friends Am. Ballet. Contbr. articles in field to profl. jours. Home: 714 St Andrews Way Lompoc CA 93436

ALBERT, FRANCOIS LOUIS, interior designer; b. Vitre, Ille et Vilaine, France, Sept. 1, 1924; s. Francis Xavier and Louise (Guibe) A. Student Beaux Arts, Rennes, 1941-44, Ille et Vilaine, 1945-48, Beaux Arts Paris, 1948-52. Ptnr., Maison Gonet, Paris, 1948-52; interior designer Bonyges Lakeshore, Oakland, Calif., 1956-58, Andreasen-Oakland, 1958-61, Carson Furniture Co., Carson City, Nev., 1962-65, M.J. Sloane Co., San Jose, Calif., 1965-66; owner, designer Francois Albert Co., San Francisco, 1966—. Served with French Army, 1944-45. Mem. Am. Soc. Interior Designers. Democrat. Roman Catholic. Office: 407 Jackson St San Francisco CA 94111

ALBERT, MARLENE FRANCES, counselor; b. Vallejo, Calif., May 4, 1935; d. Leo Meyer and Halcyon Edith (Bialkin) Liberman; B.A., U. Calif., Berkeley, 1957; M.A., San Jose State U., 1969; m. Richard Albert, Aug. 18, 1957; children—Sharon, John, Robert. Jr. high sch. tchr. Lafayette (Calif.) Sch. Dist., 1958, Hermosa Beach (Calif.) Sch. Dist., 1958-61; dir. planned parenthood, N. Santa Clara County, Calif., 1970-73; staff counselor, community affairs cons. Wilson Center, Santa Clara, Calif., 1974-75; marriage and family therapist Alameda Counseling and Training Center, San Jose, Calif., 1975—; instr. parenting courses El Camino Hosp.; cons. in stress mgmt. Stay Well Program Control Data Corp., 1980—; acad./vocat. counselor Wilcox High Sch., Santa Clara, 1976-79; counselor/cons. marriage and family course Sch. Age Mothers' Program, Fremont High Sch. Dist., 1975-76. Mem. Santa Clara County Child and Adolescent Adv. Commn., 1976-82; adv. bd. Male's Place, San Jose, 1977-79, Wilson House, Santa Clara, 1977-79; mem. early childhood edn. com. Stocklmeir Sch., Cupertino Sch. Dist., 1973-75, mem. health edn. com., 1972-74; mem. edn. com., cons. staff Resources Center for Women, Palo Alto, Calif., 1973-74; adv. bd., mem. Inst. Human Sexuality, Planned Parenthood, Santa Clara County, 1971-73; bd. dirs. Our Health Clinic, Palo Alto, 1971-73; edn. dir. Santa Clara County unit Am. Cancer Soc., 1979—. Lic. marriage, family and child counselor, Calif. Home: 565 Croyden Ct Sunnyvale CA 94087

ALBERT, ROBERT S., psychologist, educator; b. Dallas, May 23, 1927; s. Sydney and Peggy (Schwartz) A.; m. Julie C. Maehling, Dec. 30, 1961; children—Jess, John. B.A., Vanderbilt U., 1950; M.A., U. Tex.-Austin, 1952; Ph.D., Boston U., 1957. Lic. clin psychologist, Calif., Asst. prof. Boston U., 1955-57, Emory U., Atlanta, 1957-58; asst. prof. to assoc. prof. Skidmore Coll., Saratoga Springs, N.Y., 1961-64; assoc. prof. U. Conn., Storrs, 1964-65; research assoc. Mass. Mental Health Center, 1958-61; assoc. prof. to prof. psychology Pitzer Coll., Clarement Grad. Sch., 1965—, research dir., The Achievement of Eminence, 1977. Served with U.S. Marine Corps., 1945. Grantee Robert Sterling Clark Found., 1977, MacArthur Found., 1981. Mem. Am. Psychol. Assn., AAAS, Nat. Assn. Gifted Children. Author: (with others) The Prevention of Hospitalization; editor: Eminence and Genius; contbr. articles to profl. jours. Office: Pitzer Coll Claremont CA 91711

ALBERT-HOWARD, FIORENZA COSSERIA, utility co. exec.; b. Rome, Oct. 5, 1936; d. Spartaco Claudio and Isolina Ester Alberti; came to U.S., 1971, naturalized, 1979; B.A. in Civil Engring., U. Rome, 1957, M.A. in Statistics, 1959, Ph.D. in Statistics, 1961; m. John Moeur Anderson, Oct. 9, 1976 (dec.); 1 dau. by previous marriage, Paolina Italia Amadio; m. Nicholas Christopher Howard, Apr. 12, 1982. With IMB Italia, Turin, Italy and Boblingen, Germany, 1963-64, Olivetti Inc., Milan, Italy, 1964; software programmer Gen. Electric Co., Milan, 1964, systems analyst, 1964; census expert Inst. Stats. Italy, 1971-72; tech. planner, quality assurance coordinator 1st Nat. Bank Ariz., Phoenix, 1972-73; systems analyst, data processing tng. coordinator So. Calif. Edison, Rosemead, 1973-77, rate structure engr., 1977-79; software and tech. support head Radar Systems Group, Hughes Aircraft Co., El Segundo, Calif., 1979-80; mgr. software operating systems Continental Airlines Co., El Segundo, 1980—; 81; DBA supr. B.C. Telephone Co., Vancouver, B.C., Can., 1981—. Bd. dirs. assurance com. Lowell Elementary Sch., Long Beach, Calif., 1974-80; exec. adviser Jr. Achievement, Long Beach and Lakewood, Calif., 1975-79, recipient citation, 1975-76. Recipient Cert. of Appreciation Regional Occupation Center, Long Beach, 1976; So. Calif. Edison Co., 1976. Mem. IEEE (sr.), Engring. Mgmt. Soc. (officer, adminstrv. com. 1982—), Assn. Computing Machinery, Soc. Women Engrs. (sr.; editor newsletter 1978-79, pres. Los Angeles chpt. 1979-80, chmn. Career Planning Conf. 1979, job opportunity chmn.), Patrons Italian Culture (dir.). Roman Catholic. Club: Pilots Internat. (treas. Long Beach 1979-80, Calif. dist. area leader for internat. relations). Author: The Punched Card System, 1967; The Computer System, 1968; Systems Analysis and Information Systems, 1969. Home: 7027 Fielding Ct Burnaby BC V5A 1Y4 Canada Office: 15-3777 Kingsway Burnaby BC V5H 3Z7 Canada

ALBERTS, CECIL DARWIN, speech pathologist, publisher; b. Winnipeg, Man., Can., Jan. 26, 1916; came to U.S., 1922, naturalized, 1932; s. Sergis and Nina (Balter) A.; B.S., U. Southern Calif., 1950, M.S., 1963; m. Edith Hatfield, 1951; children—Laurence, Jessica. With Torrance (Calif.) Unified Sch. Dist.; speech pathologist Calif. Elks Assn., Auburn, Calif.; speech pathologist Pleasanton (Calif.), Joint Sch. Dist.; mgr. Spin-a-test Publ. Co., Danville, Calif. Served with U.S. Army, 1942-45. Mem. Am. Speech and Hearing Assn., Internat. Reading Assn. Patentee in ednl. games. Address: 3177 Hogarth Dr Sacramento CA 95827

ALBERTS, DAVID SAMUEL, physician; b. Milw., Dec. 30, 1939; s. Benjamin Bernard and Esther (Tonkens) A.; B.S., Trinity Coll., Hartford Conn., 1962; M.D., U. Va., Charlottesville, 1966; m. Heather Axelrod, June 16, 1963; children—Timothy Alexander, Sabrina. Intern, U. Wis. Hosps., Madison, 1966-67; clin. asso. Nat. Cancer Inst., Balt., 1967-69; internal medicine resident U. Minn., Mpls., 1969-71; med. oncology fellow clin. pharmacology U. Calif., San Francisco, 1971-73, asst. prof. medicine, 1974-75; asso. prof. medicine and pharmacology U. Ariz., Tucson, 1975-82, prof., 1982—; dir. fellowship program sect. hematology-oncology U. Ariz. Oncologic Drug Com., FDA, 1980—; chmn. oncologic drug com. FDA, 1981—. Served with USPHS, 1967-69. Recipient faculty tng. award Pharm. Mfg. Assn., 1972. Mem. Am. Assn. Cancer Research, Am. Soc. Clin. Pharmacology and Therapeutics (chmn. hematology and oncology sect. 1981—), Internat. Soc. Preventive Oncology, Am. Soc. Clin. Oncology, Am. Fedn. Clin. Research, Phi Beta Kappa.

ALBERTSON, WILLIAM LEON, broker; b. Wheeling, Mo., Aug. 26, 1906; s. William Robert and Blanche (Gillispie) A.; student University Place, Lincoln, Nebr., 1922; m. Frances A. Lee, Oct. 20, 1966. Real estate broker, San Bernardino, Calif., 1929—. Mem. Calif. Atty. Gen.'s Adv. Council, 1972—. Res. sheriff officer San Bernardino County, Calif. Mem. Calif. Real Estate Assn., San Bernardino Realty Bd. Home: 841 Mountain View Ave San Bernardino CA 92401 Office: 459 4th St San Bernardino CA 92401

ALBI, FRED ANTHONY, lawyer, real estate broker; b. Denver, Sept. 15, 1940; s. Fred Peter and Milly C. (Carbone) A.; B.A., Regis Coll., Denver, 1962; J.D., U. Denver, 1965; m. Mary Carole Dispense, June 23, 1962; children—Christine Marie, Michelle Mary, Cynthia Ann. Admitted to Colo. bar,; inheritance tax analyst inheritance tax div. Colo. Dept. Law, 1965-66; asso firm Hindry & Meyer, P.C., Denver, 1967-70, stockholder, dir., 1971-78, also sec., treas.; sec., shareholder, dir. firm Wegner & Fulton, P.C., 1978-81; owner, broker Albi Properties, 1982—; partner Carbone Investment Co.; dir. A. Carbone & Co., Dealer Hardware Supply, Inc.; lectr. Continuing Legal Edn. in Colo., Inc.; instr. Shwayder Real Estate Acad. Bd. govs., exec. com., planned giving com., Regis Coll., named Man of Yr., 1962; mem. instnl. rev. bd. AMC Cancer Research Ctr. and Hosp. Mem. Am., Colo. (probate trust council 1974-75, chmn. estate and trust adminstrn. com. 1974), Denver bar assns., Rocky Mountain Estate Planning Council (sec.). Republican. Roman Catholic. Clubs: Denver Athletic, Bull Bears (Denver). Dir. CPC Newsletter sect. Colo. Lawyer, 1975-76. Home: 7154 E Jarvis Pl Denver CO 80237 Office: Suite 2300 1st National Bank Bldg Denver CO 80293

ALBRECHT, CAROL LEE, human resources consultant; b. Cleve., June 28, 1947; d. Byron Joseph and Janet Carol (Ramsey) A.; B.A. cum laude, Milton Coll., 1970; M.S.W., U. Wis., 1972. Program dir. Nev. Div. Mental Health, Las Vegas, 1973-74; state planner Gov.'s Council on Devel. Disabilities, Phoenix, 1974-77; specialist for Persons with Handicaps for Gov.'s Office, Phoenix, 1977-79; human resources cons. United Mgmt. Systems, Inc. of Ariz., Phoenix, 1979; exec. dir. Cactus Industries, 1981—; cons. Nat. Gov.'s Assn., 1979—; State of Ariz. rep. at White House Conf. on Handicapped Individuals, 1976, mem. Gov.'s Com. on Employment of Handicapped. HEW fellow, 1970-71; recipient Citation of Merit, Gov. of Ariz., 1977. Mem. Ariz. Affirmative Action Assn., Ariz. Congress for Action, Young Execs. Assn. Contbr. articles to profl. jours. Home: 2934 W Juniper Phoenix AZ 85023 Office: 4120 N 38th Dr Phoenix AZ 85019

ALBRECHT, RICHARD RAYMOND, aircraft manufacturer executive; b. Storm Lake, Iowa, Aug. 29, 1932; s. Arnold L. and Catherine (Boettcher) Al.; m. Constance Marie Berg, June 16, 1957; children—John Justin, Carl Arnold, Richard Louis, Henry Berg. B.A. in Chemistry, U. Iowa, 1958, J.D., 1961. Bar: Wash. 1961. Assoc. Perkins, Coie, Stone, Olsen & Williams, Seattle, 1961-67, ptnr., 1968-74; gen. counsel U.S. Treasury, 1974-76; v.p., gen. counsel, sec. The Boeing Co., Seattle, 1976-81, v.p. fin., contracts and internat. bus., 1981—; dir. Wash. Mut. Savs. Bank. Served with U.S. Army, 1955-58. Recipient Seattle-King County Outstanding Citizen award 1968-69; Alexander Hamilton award U.S. Treasury Dept. 1976. Mem. ABA, Wash. State Bar Assn., Seattle-King County Bar Assn., Am. Judicature Soc., Order of Coif, Delta Kappa. Club: Rainier, Editor: Iowa Law Rev.

ALBRECHT, RUTH, educator; b. Wittenberg, Mo.; d. Frank and Johanna (Bregas) A.; B.S., Washington U., St. Louis, 1934; M.A., U. Chgo., 1946, Ph.D., 1951. Lectr. psychology Ind. U., 1947; lectr. child psychology U. Kans., 1947; research asst. U. Chgo., 1947-48, research assoc., 1948-50; research prof. Auburn Research Found. and Sch. Home Econs., Ala. Poly. Inst. (now Auburn U.), 1951-57; prof., head dept. family life Coll. Arts and Sci., U. Fla., Gainesville, 1957-60, prof. sociology, 1960-75; mem. council on aging U. Calif., San Diego, 1976-79; human devel. cons. Inter-Univ. Sch. Study, 1949. Trustee, Fla. Council Aging, v.p., 1962-64, 74-75; bd. dirs. Nat. Council Family Relations, 1963-66. Fellow Am. Gerontol. Soc. (sec. psychol. and social scis. sect. 1960-63, chmn. 1963-65), AAAS, Am. Sociol. Assn. (sec. family sect. 1967-70); mem. So. Sociol. Soc. (chmn. problems of aging sect. 1965-66, exec. bd. 1969-72, 1st v.p. 1973-74), World Fedn. Mental Health, Southeastern Council Family Relations (editor newsletter 1959-61), Pi Lambda Theta, Alpha Kappa Delta. Author: (with R.J. Havighurst) Older People, 1953; Aging in a Changing Society, 1962; (with E.W. Bock) Encounter: Love, Marriage and Family, 1972, rev. edit., 1975; also articles in sci. jours. Home: 1399 9th Ave San Diego CA 92101

ALBRIGHT, JOANN MARIE, college official; b. Denver, Oct. 23, 1941; d. Nicholas L. and Ruth K. Van Soest; m. Morris G. Albright. B.A., Central Coll., 1963; grad. U. Iowa, 1965; postgrad. U. Iowa, U. Denver. Team leader Oakdale Hosp., 1965-68; placement specialist Ft. Logan (Colo.) Health Ctr., 1968-69; dir. counseling and placement U. Denver, 1970—. Recipient K Book award, U. Denver; named Outstanding Adminstr., U. Denver. Mem. Am. Personnel and Guidance Assn., Am. Coll. Personnel Assn., Nat. Vocat. Guidance Assn., Am. Soc. Tng. and Devel. (chmn positions, bd. assignments com.). Office: Counseling Placement Center U Denver Denver CO 80208

ALBRIGHT, LEWIS E., industrial psychologist, educator, consultant; b. Detroit, Sept. 23, 1931; s. W. Wayne and Ada S. (Snyder) A.; children—Susan, Ann. B.S. in Psychology, Northwestern U., 1953; M.A. in Psychology, U. Mo.-Columbia, 1954; Ph.D., Purdue U., Lafayette, Ind., 1956. Diplomate Am. Bd. Profl. Psychology, Research asst. to dir. employee relations research Standard Oil Co. (Ind.), Chgo., 1956-66; mgr. manpower planning and devel. to corp. dir. tng. and devel. Kaiser Aluminum & Chem. Corp., Oakland, Calif., 1966-82; cons. in pvt. practice; cons. de Recat & Assocs., Inc., San Francisco, 1982—; instr. U. Calif. extension, 1976—; cons. U.S. Dept. Labor, 1968-72. Mem. tng. adv. com. United Way Campaign, San Francisco, 1981. Served with Ill. N.G., 1950-53. Fellow Am. Psychol. Assn. (fellow); mem. Am. Soc. Tng. and Devel., Sigma Xi. Author: The Use of Psychological Tests in Industry, 1963; contbg. author: Handbook of Personnel and Industrial Relations, 1979. Office: 150 Post St 740 San Francisco CA 94108

ALCANTARA, THEO, conductor; b. Cuenca, Castile, Spain, 1941; student Real Conservatorio de Musica, Madrid; grad. Akademie Mozarteum, Salzburg, Austria, 1964; m. Susan Alcantara; children—Rafael, Carlos. Conducting debut with Teatro de la Zarzuela, Madrid; condr. Frankfurt Opera Theatre Orch., 1964-66; dir. orchs. U. Mich., Ann Arbor, 1968-73; music dir., condr. Grand Rapids Symphony, 1973-78; music dir., prin. condr. Phoenix Symphony Orch., 1978—; music dir., condr. Music Acad. of West Summer Festival, Santa Barbara, Calif., 1981—; guest condr. numerous orchs. including: Teatro Colon, Buenos Aires, Met. Opera, Pitts. Opera, Washington Opera, Am. Symphony, orchs. of Paris, Berlin, Madrid, Barcelona, Mexico City, Montevideo, New Orleans, Detroit, Pitts. Recipient Lili Lehman medal; silver medal Dimitri Mitropoulous Internat. Conducting Competition, 1966; Disting. Service award Mich. Found. for the Arts, 1977. Office: Phoenix Symphony Orch 6328 N 7th St Phoenix AZ 85014*

ALCORN, SAMUEL, insurance brokerage executive; b. Phila., May 31, 1927; s. David and Emily Sarah (Stewart) A.; children—Janet Elaine, Shelia Ann. Student Temple U., 1948-52; B.S. in Bus. Adminstrn., Washington U., St. Louis, 1955. Underwriter Wasau Ins. Cos., Phila., 1947-52, br. underwriting mgr., St. Louis, 1952-57, Los Angeles, 1957-59; mktg. mgr. Kuhrts, Cox & Brander, Los Angeles, 1959-63; v.p. mktg. Bayly, Martin & Fay, Los Angeles, 1963-73, v.p. then sr. v.p. Corp. Staff, 1973—, now sr. v.p. ops. and internat. devels.; dir. S & H Ins. Cos., Universal Security Ins. Co. Served to cpl. USAAF, 1945-47. Mem. Soc. Chartered Property & Casualty Underwriters (publs. com., dir. Orange Empire chpt.), Ins. Ednl. Assn (chmn. 1981-82), Am. Inst. for Liability & Property (trustee), Ins. Inst. Am. (trustee). Presbyterian. Clubs: University (Los Angeles), Back Bay (Newport Beach), Masons. Contbr. articles to ins. trade publs. Home: 24662 Linda Flores St Laguna Hills CA 92633 Office: Bayly Martin & Fay Internat Inc 660 Newport Ctr Dr Suite 1000 Newport Beach CA 92660

ALCORN, TROY GENE, clergyman; b. Sulphur Springs, Tex., Aug. 4, 1930; s. Mahlon Winifield and Quincy Blanche (Shrode) A.; m. Bobbie Yvonne McCrady, Sept. 1, 1950; children—Karen L. Havens, Chris Alan Alcorn, Gayle M. Haggard, Cynthia J. Morris. B.A., East Tex. State U., 1952; postgrad. Indsl. Coll. Armed Forces, 1972-73. Commd. U.S. Air Force, 1952, advanced through grades to col., 1971, ret., 1976; ordained to ministry, Christian Assembly, 1974; asst. pastor Christian Assembly, Vienna, Va., 1976-77, pastor, Colorado Springs, Colo., 1977—; mem. adv. bd. Mission to Am., Humble, Tex., Community Care Ctr., Colorado Springs, Christian Homes, El Paso, Tex. Decorated Legion of Merit with oak leaf cluster, Meritorious Service medal, Air Force Commendation medal. Home: 3812 Templeton Gap Rd Colorado Springs CO 80907 Office: 3812 Templeton Gap Rd Colorado Springs CO 80907

ALDEN, GARY WADE, art conservator; b. Somerville, N.J., May 18, 1951. B.A., U. Chgo., 1973; postgrad. Oberlin Coll., 1973-76, Intermus. Conservatory Assn. Tng. Program and study with Richard D. Buck, 1973-76, cert. of conservatory, 1976. Conservator, Intermus. Conservatory Assn. Intermus. Lab., Oberlin, 1976-77; chief conservator Balboa Art Conservatory Ctr., San Diego, 1977-78, dir., 1978—. Mem. Am. Inst. Conservation of History and Artistic Works, Western Assn. Art Conservators (sec./treas.); assoc. Internat. Inst. Conservation. Office: Balboa Art Conservation Ctr PO Box 3755 San Diego CA 92103*

ALDERA, ROBERT LAWRENCE, photographer; b. Los Angeles, Sept. 11, 1943; s. Larry S. and Dorothy (Jenning) A.; A.A., Pasadena City Coll., 1963. Cert. profl. photographer. Photographer, U.S. Navy, 1964-67; worked with master craftsman Phil Chairs, Pasadena, Calif., 1970-75; owner 9 studios, Alfa Color, 1976-81, Aldera Studio, 1981—. Recipient profl. photography awards. Mem. Profl. Photographers West, Profl. Photographers Calif., Profl. Photographers Am., Wedding Photographers Internat. Home: 9036 Arcadia Ave #2 San Gabriel CA 91557

ALDERETE, RAUL, optometrist; b. Chgo., May 21, 1955; s. Eustacio and Valerie (Escobedo) A.; m. Patricia Jean Allen, Sept. 22, 1979. Student in biology, Met. State Coll., 1975; D. Optometry, B.S. in Physiol. Optics, So. Calif. Coll. Optometry, 1979. Cert. optometrist, Colo., Calif. Pvt. practice as assoc. Sam Zebelman, O.D., specializing in visual therapy, pediatric vision, Lakewood, Colo., 1979-80; pvt. practice as assoc. C.E. Johnson, O.D., specializing in contact lenses, Denver, 1980—; mem. external audit team Health Scis. Edn. Jefferson County (Colo.) Pub. Schs., 1983. Active various gubernatorial, congl. and mayoral campaigns. Recipient Collard-Rose Optical Lab. Ophthalmic Dispensing award So. Calif. Coll. Optometry, 1978. Mem. Colo. Optometric Assn. (legis. com.), Am. Optometric Assn. Democrat. Roman Catholic. Home: 8440 Clarabelle Dr Arvada CO 80002 Office: 1555 Welton St Denver CO 80202

ALDERMAN, GRADY, professional football team executive; b. Detroit, Dec. 10, 1938; m. Nancy Alderman; children—Robbie, Christy. Player, Detroit Lions Nat. Football League, 1960, Minn. Vikings, 1961-74; acct. Deloitte, Haskins & Sells, Bloomington, Minn., 1963-79, mgr. office, 1970-79; dir. planning and develop. Minn. Vikings, 1979-81; gen. mgr. Denver Broncos Nat. Football League, 1981—; commentator Minn. Vikings broadcasts, 1976-80; player Super Bowl, 1970, 74, 75. Named Outstanding Lineman Gem City Bowl All-Star Game, 1959, All-Catholic All-Am., 1959. Office: Denver Broncos 5700 Logan St Denver CO 80216

ALDERMAN, MINNIS AMELIA, business executive; b. Douglas, Ga., Oct. 14, 1928; d. Louis Cleveland and Minnis (Wooten) Alderman; A.B., State Coll. for Women Ga., 1949; M.A., Murray State U., 1960; postgrad. (scholar) in clin. psychology U. Utah. Camp counselor, Camp Sloan, Conn., summer 1949; music dir. Umatilla (Fla.) pub. sch., 1949-50, Campbell High Sch., Fairburn, Ga., 1950-54; music and drama dir., tchr. English and speech Wells (Nev.) High Sch., 1954-59; tchr. English and history Sinking Fork Sch., Hopkinsville, Ky., 1960; counselor White Pine High Sch., Ely, Nev., 1960-68; psychologist Nev. Personnel, Ely Mental Health Center, 1969-75, Nev. Job Service, 1975-79; owner Minisizer, exercise salon, 1969-71, Mini-Mimeo, mimeographing service, 1969—, Knit Knook, knitting supplies, 1970—, Gift Gamut, 1977—, Trip and Travel; pvt. instr. piano, violin and voice, 1983—; instr. psychology, guidance and counseling Murray State U., summers 1961, 62; instr. guidance and counseling U. Nev. Extension, 1963-66; sec.-treas. Great Basin Enterprises, 1969-71. Bd. dirs. RSVP, 1973-75; test supr. Coll. Entrance Exam. Bd. and Am. Coll. Testing, 1960-68; dir. Ret. Sr. Citizens Vol. Program, 1973-74; originator White Pine Sr. Citizens Program, White Pine Sr. Citizens Center, White Pine Rehab. Center, Creative Crafts Assos. Pres., 1976—, White Pine County Mental Health Assn., 1960-63, 78—; mem. Mental Health State Com., 1963-66; bd. dirs. White Pine County Fed. Employee's Credit Union, 1961-69, pres., 1963-69; mem. Nev. Gov.'s Commn. Mental Health, 1964-66, Gov.'s Commn. Status of Women, 1968—, Counselors on Alcoholism, Addictions and Related Dependencies, 1974—; sec.-treas. White Pine Rehab. Tng. Center, 1970-75; vice chmn. Gt. Basin Health Council, 1973-76; chmn. White Pine Council Alcoholism and Drug Abuse, 1976-79; bd. dirs. White Pine chpt. ARC, 1978—, Nev. Assn. Hwy. Safety Leaders, 1977—; bd. dirs., band dir. Sacred Heart Sch., 1982—; bd. dirs. White Pine Community Concert Assn., 1965—, pres., 1967-68; dir. Ely Community Choir, 1975—; choir dir. Ely Methodist Ch., 1960—, lay speaker, 1967—, council on ministries, 1970—, lay leader, 1977—; mem. Meth. Conf. Council on Status and Role of Women, 1981—. Mem. NEA (life), Nev. Edn. Assn., AAUW (pres. 1964-65; area rep. edn. 1965-67, state implementation chmn. in edn. 1967-69, state area adviser 1969-73, state handbook pub. 1972-77), Nev. State Employees Assn. (chpt. sec.-treas. 1969-70), Nat. Fedn. Bus. and Profl. Women's Clubs (pres. Nev. 1972-73, parliamentarian Ely 1973-77), UDC, NOW, Common Cause, DAR, Am. Personnel and Guidance Assn. (state membership chmn. 1963-65, 67-68) Nat. Assn. Women Deans and Counselors, Internat. Platform Assn., Nat. Assn. Women Execs., Nat. Fedn. Ind. Bus. Dist. (dist. chmn. 1971—), Am. Fedn. Women's Clubs (dist. pres. 1970-74, state chmn. status of women 1974-76), Mensa (test adminstr. 1965—), Delta Kappa Gamma (state 1st v.p. 1967-68, pres. 1969-71, parliamentarian 1971-73, chpt. pres. 1968-72, parliamentarian 1974-76), Phi Sigma, Beta Sigma Phi (chpt. sponsor 1970-72). Clubs: Knife and Fork (pres. 1970-71), Ely Women's (pres. 1969-70). Author articles and booklets. Home: 945 Ave H East Ely NV 89315 Office: 1280 Ave F East Ely NV 89315

ALDRICH, DANIEL GASKILL, JR., univ. chancellor; b. Northwood, N.H., July 12, 1918; s. Daniel Gaskill and Marian (Farnum) A.; B.S., U. R.I., 1939, D. Sc. (hon.), 1960; M.S., U. Ariz., 1941; Ph.D., U. Wis., 1943; D.H.L., U. Redlands, U. Wis., Chapman Coll., Nat. U.; m. Jean Hamilton, Aug. 23, 1941; children—Daniel Gaskill, Elizabeth, Stuart Hamilton. Research chemist U. Calif. Citrus Expt. Sta., Riverside, 1943-55; chmn. dept. soils and plant nutrition U. Calif.-Davis and Berkeley, 1955-59, univ. dean agr. Berkeley, 1959-62, now chancellor U. Calif.-Irvine; dir. Pacific Mut. Co. Mem. exec. bd. Orange Empire council Boy Scouts Am.; active Girl Scouts U.S.A.; bd. dirs. Big Brothers Orange County, Orange County Philharmonic Soc., Big Bros. Am., Stanford Research Inst., Internat. Vol. Services; trustee Pacific Sch. Religion, Fund for Theol. Edn., Pilgrim Place; hon. sponsor Orange County Soc. Crippled Children. Served as maj., inf. AUS; lt. col. Res. Mem. AAAS (past pres. Pacific div.), Western Soc. Soil Sci. (pres.), Am. Soc. Agronomy (dir.), Nat. Acad. Scis. (agrl. edn. policy com., commn. on edn. in agr. and nat. resources), Nat. Assn. State Univs. and Land-Grant Colls., Soil Conservation Soc., Soil Sci. Soc. Am., Am. Soc. Hort. Sci. Mem. United Ch. of Christ.

ALDRICH, DAVID LAWRENCE, public relations executive; b. Lakehurst Naval Air Sta., N.J., Feb. 21, 1948; s. Clarence Edward and Sarah Stiles (Andrews) A.; m. Benita Susan Massler, Mar. 17, 1974. B.A. in Communications, Calif. State U.-Dominguez Hills, 1976. Pub. info. technician City of Carson (Calif.), 1973-77; pub. relations dir./adminstrv. asst. Calif. Fed. Savs., Los Angeles, 1977-78; v.p., group adv. Hill & Knowlton, Los Angeles, 1978-81; v.p., mgr. Ayer Pub. Relations western div. N.W. Ayer, Los Angeles, 1981—. Served with USAF, 1968-72. Mem. Japan-Am. Soc. Democrat. Club: Los Angeles Athletic. Home: 4751 D La Villa Marina Marina del Rey CA 90291 Office: NW Ayer Inc 707 Wilshire Blvd Los Angeles CA 90017

ALDRICH, ELMER CLARE, ret. environ. cons.; b. Eureka, Calif., June 13, 1914; s. Clarence Ulysses and Lillian Frances (Dickinsen) A.; B.A. in Biol. Scis., U. Calif., Berkeley, 1937, M.A., 1939; m. Jane Nold, July 19, 1941; children—Janet Claire, Marjorie Frances. Wildlife technician, ranger naturalist U.S. Nat. Park Service, summers 1937-39; with State of Calif., 1940-72, supr. conservation Div. Beaches and Parks, 1949-58, exec. officer Calif. Public Outdoor Recreation Plan Com. for Legislature, 1958-60, chief Div. Recreation, 1960-64, mgr. statewide planning br. Calif. Dept. Parks and Recreation, 1968-72; environ. planning cons., Sacramento, 1972-82; chmn. Sacramento region Bikeway Action Com., 1968-75; chmn. Calif. State Adv. Com. Significant Natural Areas, 1980—. Served with USNR, 1942-46. Mem. Am. Inst. Park Execs., Nat. Recreation Assn., Sierra Club (past v.p., dir.), Audubon Soc. (past chpt. pres.), Nature Conservancy, Calif. Park and Recreation Soc., Calif. Conservation Council (Merit award 1954), Calif. Natural Areas Coordinating Council (dir.), League to Save Lake Tahoe, Sigma Xi, Phi Sigma. Author papers in field. Address: 5631 Camellia Ave Sacramento CA 95819

ALDRICH, MICHAEL RAY, orgn. exec.; b. Vermillion, S.D., Feb. 7, 1942; s. Ray J. and Lucile W. (Hamm) A.; A.B., Princeton, 1964; M.A., U. S.D., 1965; Ph.D., SUNY, 1970; m. Michelle Cauble, Dec. 26, 1977. Fulbright tutor Govt. Arts and Commerce Coll., Indore, Madhya Pradesh, India, 1965-66; founder Lemar Internat., 1966-71; mem. faculty Sch. Critical Studies, Calif. Inst. Arts, Valencia, 1970-72; workshop leader Esalen Inst., San Francisco, 1972; co-founder, co-dir. AMORPHIA, Inc., The Cannabis Coop., non-profit nat. marijuana research and reform group, Mill Valley, Calif., 1969-74; exec. curator Fitz Hugh Ludlow Meml. Library, San Francisco, 1974—. Freelance writer, photographer, lectr., cons. on drug research, and sociolegal reform specializing in drug laws and history to various colls., drug confs., publishers, service groups; cons. Commn. of Inquiry into Non-Med. Use of Drugs, Ottawa, Ont., 1973; research aide, select com. on control marijuana Calif. Senate, 1974. Bd. dirs. Ethno-Pharmacology Soc., 1976—. Calif. Marijuana Initiative, 1971-74; mem. nat. adv. bd. Nat. Orgn. for Reform of Marijuana Laws, 1976—. Author: The Dope Chronicles 1850-1950, 1979; co-author: High Times Ency. of Recreational Drugs, 1978; editor: Marijuana Review, 1968-74, Ludlow Library Newsletter, 1974—, contbg. author Cocaine Handbook, 1981, mem. editorial rev. bd. Jour. Psychoactive Drugs, 1981—; contbg. editor High Times, 1979—; contbr. articles to profl. publs. Office: PO Box 99346 San Francisco CA 94109

ALDRICH, ROBERT ANDERSON, physician; b. Evanston, Ill., 1917; M.D., Northwestern U., 1944; m. Marjorie Duttenhofer, 1940; children—Robert Anderson, Stephen M., Frederick G. Intern, Evanson Hosp., 1943-44; resident pediatrics U. Minn. Hosps., 1946-48, sr. fellow pediatrics, 1948-49; instr. pediatrics U. Minn. Grad. Sch., 1951; asso. staff Mayo Clinic, Rochester, Minn., 1949-50, cons. pediatrics, 1950—; asst. prof. pediatrics U. Oreg. Med. Sch., 1951-53, asso. prof., 1953-56; prof. pediatrics U. Wash., Seattle, 1956-63, 64—, chmn. dept., 1956-62, head div. human ecology dept. pediatrics, 1964-70; dir. health resources study center, 1966-70; dir. Nat. Inst. Child Health and Human Devel., NIH, Bethesda, Md., 1963-64; v.p. for health affairs U. Colo., 1970-75, prof. pediatrics and prof. preventive medicine and comprehensive health care Sch. Medicine, 1970-80, emeritus prof. medicine and comprehensive health care, 1980—; clin. prof. pediatrics U. Wash., 1980—. Mem. Pres.'s. Com. on Mental Retardation, 1966-72, vice chmn., 1966-72; chmn. Gov.'s Council on Mental Health and Mental Retardation, 1968-70. Served to lt. (s.g.), M.C., USNR, 1944-46. Diplomate Am. Bd. Pediatrics, 1951. Mem. King County Med. Soc., Soc. Pediatric Research, Am. Acad. Pediatrics, Am. Pediatrics Soc. Home: 5101 NE 41st St Seattle WA 98105

ALDRICH, THOMAS ALBERT, brewing company executive; b. Rosebud, Tex., Nov. 30, 1923; s. John Albert and Georgia Opal (Hilliard) A.; m. Virginia Elaine Peterson, Mar. 1, 1944; children—Sharon Elaine Aldrich Lingis, Pamela Kay Aldrich Williams, Thomas Charles. Student Tex. A&M U., 1942-43, U. Chgo., 1943-44; B.A., George Washington U., 1961, M.S., 1968. Enlisted U.S. Air Force, 1943, commd. 2d lt., 1944, advanced through grades to maj. gen., 1974; dir. war plans Mil. Airlift Command, Scott AFB, Ill., 1968-69, comdr. 9th Weather Reconaissance Wing, 1969-70, vice comdr. USAF Air Weather Service, Scott AFB, 1970-71, comdr., 1973-74, comdr. U.S. Forces Azores, 1971-73, chief of staff plans Mil. Airlift Command, Scott AFB, 1973-75, comdr. 22d Air Force, Travis AFB, Calif., 1975-78, ret., 1978; v.p., corp. rep. Anheuser-Busch Cos., Inc., Sacramento, 1978—; dir. Mktg. Resources Internat. Corp., 1981—. Decorated D.S.M., Legion of Merit with oak leaf cluster. Mem. U.S. Brewers Assn., Calif. Mfrs. Assn. (dir. 1979—). Republican. Presbyterian. Club: North Ridge Country (Sacramento). Home: 1355 Commons Dr Sacramento CA 95825 Office: Anheuser-Busch Cos Inc Suite 126 1451 River Park Dr Sacramento CA 95815

ALDRIDGE, NOEL HENRY, radiologist; b. Durban, S.Africa, Dec. 19, 1924; s. Percy Verey and Isaleine (Wilson) A.; came to U.S., 1955, naturalized, 1967; M.B., Ch.B., U. Cape Town (S.Africa), 1951; D.M.R.D., Roy Coll., London, 1955; L.M.C.C., Royal Coll. Can., 1958, m. 2d, Annette Von Abele, Jan. 20, 1973; children by previous marriage—Anthony Mark, Andrea Marie; m. 3d, Theresa Horton, Dec. 19, 1981. Intern, Groot Schuur Hosp., Cape Town, 1951-52; asst. govt. pathologist, Cape Town, 1952-53; sr. house officer Leeds (Eng.) Gen. Hosp., 1953-55; postgrad. tng. Karolinska Sjukhusset, Stockholm, 1955; fellow Johns Hopkins Hosp., 1955, instr. radiology, 1956; asso. radiologist, instr. Victoria Hosp.-U. Western Ont., 1956-59; clin. fellow in radiology Mass. Gen. Hosp. and Harvard Med. Sch., 1960-61, asso. radiologist, 1961-62; radiologist with pvt. group, Seattle, 1962-63; dir. dept. radiology Stevens Meml. Hosp., Edmonds, Wash., 1963—; pres. Stevens Radiologists, Inc. Diplomate Am. Bd. Radiology. Fellow Royal Coll. Physicians Can.; mem. AMA, Canadian, Brit., Wash. State med. assns., King County Med. Soc., Am. Coll. Radiology, Royal Coll. Radiologists (London), Brit. Inst. Radiology, Canadian Assn. Radiologists, Johns Hopkins Radiologic Alumni Assn., Wash. State Radiologic Assn., Coll. Physicians and Surgeons of B.C., Coll. Physicians and Surgeons of Ont., Aircraft Owners and Pilots Assn., Wash. Pilots Assn., Am. Forestry Assn., Wildlife Fedn., Les Amis du Vin. Episcopalian. Club: Elks. Contbr. articles to profl. jours. Office: Dept Radiology Stevens Meml Hosp Edmonds WA 98020

ALDRIDGE, SUSAN COCKINGS, city official; b. Dodgeville, Wis., Nov. 24, 1951; d. Kenneth Gordon and Mary Patricia (Davis) Cockings; m. M. Gene Aldridge, June 16, 1981. A.A., Madison Area Tech. Coll., 1971; B.A., Colo. Women's Coll., 1977; cert. field adminstrn. U. Denver, 1982. Research assoc. Community Health Problem-Solving Ctr., Swedish Med. Ctr., Englewood, Colo., 1973; v.p. internat. health planning and policy research Aldridge & Assocs., Denver, 1974-78; planner, aging services div. Denver Regional Council Govts., 1978-80, dir. div., 1980—. Mem. policy bd. United Way, 1980-84; bd. dirs. Nat. Assn. Area Agys. on Aging, 1982-84; chmn. fiscal com. Colo. Assn. Area Agys. on Aging, 1981-83. Recipient Recognition award Gov. Lamm, 1981. Office: 2480 W 26th Ave Suite 200 B Denver CO 80211

ALEJANDRE, EDWARD FIDEL, artist; b. Van Nuys, Calif., May 18, 1948; s. Fidel Aldama and Alice (Anthony) A.; B.A. in Spanish, Calif. State U., Northridge, 1971, B.A. in Art, 1973. Tchr., Norwalk LaMirada (Calif.) Unified Schs., 1973-79, Los Angeles Unified Sch. Dist., 1979—; researcher, rendering Victorian and hist. bldgs. Mem. Hist. Soc. So. Calif., Los Angeles Hist. Soc., Los Angeles Conservancy, N. Univ. Park Community Assn., Soc. Archtl. Historians, Glendale Art Soc. Home: 2307 Wayne Ave Los Angeles CA 90027

ALESHIRE, MERLE J., aerospace corp. exec.; b. Carthage, Ill., Dec. 30, 1933; s. Howard and Eula Juanita (Payne) A.; B.S., Fresno State Coll., 1960; M.S., UCLA, 1971; Ph.D., U.S. Internat. U., 1979; m. Dorothy Ann Ikerd, May 2, 1958; children—Benton, Brett, Barron. Chief engr. systems analysis Gen. Dynamics Corp., San Diego, 1974-77, mgr. ops. research, 1977-79, mgr. advanced programs, 1979-80, dir. research, devel., bidding, proposals, 1980-82, dir. program devel., 1982—; cons. Nat. Acad. Sci., 1977-82, Nat. Security Indsl. Assn., 1975-83, Am. Def. Preparedness Assn., 1976-83. Pres., Bd. Edn. Escondido Union Sch. Dist., 1974-75, 78-79; bd. dirs. Boys' and Girls' Club, 1972-79, pres., 1975-76; vice chmn. Palomar council Boy Scouts Am., 1970-71; hon. life mem. PTA. Served with AUS, 1954-56. Recipient David Rist prize Mil. Ops. Research Soc., 1979, Man and Boy award Boys' Club Am., 1975. Mem. Navy League, Air Force Assn., Nat. Security Indsl. Assn., Am. Def. Preparedness Assn., Assn. Old Crows, Ops. Research Soc. Am., Assn. Unmanned Vehicles, Am. Assn. Sch. Adminstrs., Aircraft Owners and Pilots Assn., Nat. Mgmt. Assn., Nat. Sch. Bds. Assn., Am. Legion, SAR, Phi Delta Kappa. Republican. Clubs: Meadow Lake Country, Flyers Inc., Funbirds Flying, Elks. Co-developer Tomahawk cruise missile. Home: 925 Mills St Escondido CA 92027 Office: Gen Dynamics Corp PO Box 85357 San Diego CA 92138

ALEWINE, MARTIN ANSEL, JR., airforce officer; b. Taylors, S.C., Aug. 15, 1932; s. Martin Ansel and Mattie May (Hallum) A.; m. Mary Lou Lewis, June 15, 1957; children—Martin Ansel III, Brian Keith, Pamela. B.Ceramic Engring., Clemson U., 1954; grad. Air Force Squadron Officer Sch., 1958, Air Force Command and Staff Coll., 1970, Indsl. Coll. of Armed Forces, 1976. Commd. 2d lt. U.S. Air Force, 1954, advanced through grades to col., 1978; programs officer Air Force Systems Command, Andrews AFB, Md., 1970-73; dir. indsl. material mgmt. Hdqrs., Air Force Contract Mgmt. Div., Kirtland AFB, N.Mex., 1973-78, chief, systems support div., 1978-80; dir. mgmt. services A.F. Wright Aero. Labs. Wright-Patterson AFB, Ohio, 1980-81; chief program control office, Air Force Weapons Lab. Kirtland AFB, 1981—. Decorated Legion of Merit, Meritorious Service medal, Air Force Commendation medal. Mem. Assn. Old Crows, Air Force Assn., Ret. Officers Assn. Baptist. Home: 3013 Charleston St NE Albuquerque NM 87110

ALEX, ADAM JOSEPH, JR., engineering company executive; b. Los Angeles, Aug. 9, 1928; s. Adam J. and Mable M. (Reynolds) A.; m. Jacquiline Elaine Qualls, July 27, 1968; 1 son, Mark Van; stephchildren—Jeffrey Lloyd Raikes, Carol E. Raikes. A.S. in Design Engring., Pasadena Sch. Design, 1952. Aerospace design cons. Douglas Aircraft Co., Santa Monica, Calif., 1951-58, Boeing Airplane Co., Seattle, 1963-66, Lockheed Aircraft Co., Burbank, Calif., 1967; pres. A.J. Alex Design and Devel. Co., Los Angeles, 1967—; dir. engring Cal-Tool Corp., Inglewood, Calif., 1972—. Served to sgt. U.S. Army, 1947-49. Recipient numerous company excellence awards. Democrat. Club: Men's 2d Ave. (Los Angeles). Home: 4246 9th Ave Los Angeles CA 90008 Office: Cal-Tool Corp 111 S Hindry Ave Inglewood CA 90301

ALEXANDER, ARTHUR JACOB, research economist, consultant; b. Carbondale, Pa., Oct. 6, 1936; s. Howard R. and Sylvia (Eisner) A.; m. Elaine Averich, Aug. 25, 1963; children—Sarah, Jonathan. B.S., MIT, 1958; M.S., London Sch. Econs., 1966; Ph.D. in Econs., Johns Hopkins U., 1969. Systems analyst IBM, Poughkeepsie, N.Y., 1960-63; cons. to industry, Ronald Brech Ltd., London, 1964-65; economist Council of Econ. Advisors, White House, Washington, 1966; research economist Rand Corp., Santa Monica, Calif., 1968—, assoc. head econs. dept., 1977—; research assoc. Internat. Inst. Strategic Studies, London, 1976-77; mem. Army Sci. Bd.; faculty, adv. bd. Rand Grand Inst.; cons. U.S. Govt. Served with U.S. Army, 1959-60. Mem. Am. Econ. Assn., Internat. Inst. for Stretegic Studies, Am. Assn. for Advancement of Slavic Studies. Club: Random Runners. Office: 1700 Main St Santa Monica CA 90406

ALEXANDER, CHARLES JUNIOR, engineering company executive; b. Kirksville, Mo., Jan. 2, 1936; s. Charles Thomas and Arveta Helena (Kapfer) A.; B.S. in Mech. Engring., U. Colo., 1962, postgrad., 1963-64; m. Shirley Maxine James, Sept. 20, 1957; children—Jewell Ann, Charles Len, James Russell, Christine Kay. Draftsman, chief draftsman, mech. engr. Coors Porcelain Co., Golden, Colo., 1956-64, project mgr., engring. supr., 1968-71; sr. market specialist Corning Glass Works (N.Y.), 1964-68; v.p. Blair-Alexander Engring. Co., Inc., Denver, 1971-77, pres., 1978—, also chmn. bd. Class chmn. U. Colo. alumni fund, 1976-77; chmn. fin. com. United Meth. Ch., 1970-78. Recipient outstanding sr. machine design award U. Colo., 1961. Mem. ASME, Am. Foundryman's Soc., Nat. Mgmt. Assn. (leadership award 1975, pres. Rocky Mountain chpt. 1974-75), Rocky Mountain Gas Assn. (pres. 1977-78, chmn. tech. com.), Pi Tau Sigma, Sigma Tau. Republican. Clubs: Kiwanis Internat. (treas. Applewood Club 1977-78, v.p. 1978-79, pres.-elect 1980-81, pres. 1981-82; Mt. Vernon Country. Home: 2200 Willow Ln Lakewood CO 80215 Office: 1109 Harlan St Denver CO 80214

ALEXANDER, EARL BETSON, soil scientist; b. Piqua, Ohio, Apr. 15, 1932; s. Earl Betson and Verda (Youtsey) A.; m. Andrea Lopez, 1964; children—Verda Ann, John Betson, Alexa Kay. B.A., Ohio State U., 1954, M.S., 1955, Ph.D., 1970. With Engring. Sci. Inc., Oakland, Calif., 1962; tech. officer FAO, Nicaragua and Colombia, 1963-67; teaching assoc. Ohio State U., Columbus, 1967-70; assoc. soil sci. U. Nev.-Reno, 1970-72; sr. resource analyst Resource Devel. Assocs., Honduras, 1972-74; soil scientist U.S. Dept. Agr. Forest Service, Redding, Calif., 1958-61, Yreka, Calif., 1975-76, San Francisco, 1976—. Served with USN, 1955-57. Mem. Soil Sci. Soc. Am., Internat. Soc. Soil Sci., Profl. Soil Scientists Assn. Calif., Am. Quaternary Assn., Assn. Am. Geographers, Soil Conservation Soc. Am., Calif. Native Plant Soc., Sigma Xi. Contbr. articles to profle jours. Home: 1714 Kasba St Concord CA 94518 Office: US Dept Agriculture Forest Service 630 Sansome St San Francisco CA 94111

ALEXANDER, EDWARD JAMES, health care adminstr.; b. Denver, Sept. 8, 1938; s. William A. and Flora Margaret (Forsyth) A.; A.B., Yale U., 1960; postgrad. Law Sch., U. Denver, 1960-61; m. Jane Ingeborg Harris, Aug. 20, 1960; children—Edward James, William Harris. Tchr., Graland Country Day Sch., Denver, 1960-64; commd. fgn. service officer State Dept., 1964; polit. officer, Kampala, Uganda and Tunis, Tunisia, 1964-70; asst. adminstr. St. Luke's Hosp., Denver, 1972-79, v.p. Presbyn./St. Luke's Med. Center, Denver, 1979—; cons. Vail Valley Med. Center; dir. Human Services, Inc., 1980-82. Bd. dirs. Am. Coop. Sch. Tunis, 1964-65, Denver Med. Library, 1982—; pres., bd. dirs. St. Luke's Community Found., 1982—; mem. council Mile High chpt. ARC, 1977-82. Mem. Colo. Hosp. Assn., Leadership Denver Assn., Colo. Yale Assn. (dir.). Democrat. Episcopalian. Clubs: Denver Country, Denver Athletic. Office: 1601 E 19th Ave Denver CO 80218

ALEXANDER, FRED SHARPE, III, architect, general contractor; b. Houston, July 21, 1941; s. Fred Sharpe and Bessie Grace (Tauber) A.; m. Carolyn Ann Comptom, Apr. 16, 1966; 1 dau., Katherine Rene; m. 2d, Susan Elinor Hjertman, June 11, 1977; 1 son, Zachary Lee. Student Tex. A&M U., 1960; B.Arch., Tex. Tech. Coll., 1967. Registered architect, Colo., N.Mex., Ariz., Wyo., Kans. Draftsman archtl. firms, Denver, 1967-72; project architect W. C. Muchow Assocs., Denver, 1970-72; prin. Alexander Assocs. Architects, Denver, 1972—; pres. Constrn. 4 Inc., Denver, 1976—; sec-treas. Comml. Design Assocs., Denver, since 1981—; pres. Alexander Industries; instr. U. Colo.-Denver Grad. Sch., 1975-77. Active Boy Scouts Am., 1968-73. Mem. AIA (sec. Denver chpt. 1976), Am. Water Works Assn., Nat. Council Archtl. Registration Bds., Eastern Rockies Rugby Football Union (sec. 1975-77). Republican. Home: 1193 S Biscay St Aurora CO 80017 Office: Constrn 4 Inc 8200 E Pacific Pl Suite 204 Denver CO 80231

ALEXANDER, JOHN DAVID, college administrator; b. Springfield, Tenn., Oct. 18, 1932; m. Catharine Coleman, 1956; children—Kitty, John, Julia. B.S., Southwestern at Memphis, 1953; postgrad. Louisville Presbyterian Theol. Sem., 1953-54; Ph.D., Oxford (Eng.) U., 1957; LL.D. (hon.) U. So. Calif., 1970, Occidental Coll., 1970, Centre Coll. of Ky., 1971. Instr., asst. prof., assoc. prof. Old Testament, San Francisco Theol. Sem., 1957-65; pres. Southwestern at Memphis, 1965-69; pres. Pomona Coll., Claremont, Calif., 1969—; Am. sec. Rhodes Scholarship Trust, 1981—. Bd. dirs. Am. Council on Edn., 1981—; mem. Nat. Commn. on Acad. Tenure, 1971-72, Panel of Gen. Profl. Edn. of the Physician, Assn. Am. Med. Colls., 1982—; trustee Tchrs. Ins. and Annuity Assn., 1970—, Woodrow Wilson Nat. Fellowship Found., 1978—, Webb Sch., Claremont, 1970-72; dir. Gt. Western Fin. Corp., 1973—, Brit. Inst., 1979—, Community Supported TV So. Calif, KCET, Inc., 1979—; bd. dirs. Louisville Presbyn. Theol. Sem., 1966-69. Rhodes Scholar, Christ Ch. Coll., Oxford U., 1954. Mem. Assn. Am. Colls. (commn. on liberal learning 1967-69, chmn. commn. on instl. affairs 1970-73), So. Assn. Colls. and Schs. (exec. council of commn. on colls. 1969), Am. Council on Edn. (dir. 1981—), Am. Oriental Soc., Soc. Bibl. Lit., Soc. for Religion in Higher Edn., Los Angeles Area C. of C. (dir. 1972-73). Phi Beta Kappa, Phi Beta Kappa Alumni So. Calif. (pres. Alpha Assn. 1974-76), Omicron Delta Kappa. Clubs: Bohemian (San Francisco); California, University (Los Angeles); Century Assn. (N.Y.C.); Zamorano. Office: Pomona Coll 333 College Way Claremont CA 91711

ALEXANDER, LOUIS EDGAR, advertising director; b. Batesville, Ind., Dec. 7, 1947; s. John Joseph and Virginia Winifred (Carr) A.; m. Jacqueline Elizabeth Walker, Jan. 1, 1982. B.A., Ind. U., 1971. Reporter-photographer Greensburg (Ind.) Daily News, 1966-70; reporter-photographer Record, Louisville, 1971-74; mng. editor Daily Herald, Monongahelo, Pa., 1974-76; pub. Democrat Messenger, Waynesburg, Pa., 1976-79; advt. dir. The Press, Ypsilanti, Mich., 1979-82; advt. dir. Herald-Republic, Yakima, Wash., 1982—. Home: 206 N 72d St Yakima WA 98908 Office: 114 N 4th St Yakima WA 98909

ALEXANDERSON, GERALD LEE, mathematician; b. Caldwell, Idaho, Nov. 13, 1933; s. Albert William and Alvina (Gertlar) A. B.A., U. Oreg., 1955; M.S., Stanford U., 1958. Instr. math. U. Santa Clara (Calif.), 1958-62, asst. prof., 1962-68, coordinator honors program, 1965-67, asso. prof., 1968-72, prof., 1972—, Michael and Elizabeth Valeriote prof., 1979—, chmn. dept., 1967—, dir. div. math. and natural scis., 1981; lectr. Stanford U., summers 1958, 59, at Geneva, 1964, 65; asso. dir. William Lowell Putnam Math. Competition, 1975—. Trustee U. Santa Clara, 1979—. Recipient U. Santa Clara Spl. Recognition award, 1978. Mem. Am. Math. Soc., Math. Assn. Am. (sec.-treas. No. Calif. sect. 1967-70, chmn. 1971-72, nat. bd. govs. 1975-78; com. on undergrad. program 1977—, com. on Dolciani Math. expn. series 1977-82, mem. Cons. Bur. 1982—), Fibonacci Assn. (pres. 1980—), Phi Beta Kappa, Sigma Xi, Pi Mu Epsilon, Pi Delta Phi, Phi Eta Sigma. Author: Functional Trigonometry, 1961, rev. edit., 1971; (with A.P. Hillman) Algebra and Trigonometry, 1963; Algebra Through Problem Solving, 1966; First Undergraduate Course in Abstract Algebra, 1973, rev. edit., 1983; asso. editor Two-Yr. Coll. Math. Jour., 1979—, Am. Math. Monthly, 1983—; contbr. articles to math. jours. Home: 1133 Highland Ave Santa Clara CA 95050

ALEXIS, JODY RAE, real estate broker, lawyer; b. Langdon, N.D., Mar. 2, 1940; d. Raymond and Ada (Widwick) Armstrong; student Stephens Coll., 1959-61; B.A., U. Nebr., 1963; M.A., U. Colo., 1968; J.D., U. Denver, 1971; div.; 1 son, Clark Kendall. Asst. dir. USO, Colorado Springs, Colo., 1964-65; asst. to dir. adminstrn. Aircraft Mechanics, Inc., Colorado Springs, 1965-67; pub. relations dir. Red Ram of Am. Corp., Colorado Springs, 1967-70, The Woodmar Corp., 1971; admitted to Colo. bar, 1971; exec. dir. Rocky Mountain Land Devel. Assn., Denver, 1970-74; pres. Alexis & Assocs., Denver, 1974—; individual practice law, Denver, 1974—; broker assoc. Premier Assocs. Denver Ltd., 1979—; cons. Indian Mountain Corp., 1977—; br. mgr. Kentwood Co., 1982—; dir. Colo. Mgmt. Rocky Mountain Log Homes Inc., Designs Internationale, Alexis & Foley Assos. Bd. dirs. Colo. Conventions and Reservations, 1974—; chmn. Denver Art Mus. Mem. Denver Center for Performing Arts, Jr. Symphony Guild. Republican. Roman Catholic. Home: 1313 Williams St Denver CO 80218 Office: 2 Steele St Denver CO 80206

ALFARO, FELIX BENJAMIN, physician; b. Managua, Nicaragua, Oct. 22, 1939; came to U.S., 1945, naturalized, 1962; s. Agustin Jose and Amanda Julieta (Barillas) A.; student (State scholar) U. San Francisco, 1958-59, 61-62; M.D., Creighton U., 1967; m. Carmen Heide Meyer, Aug. 14, 1965; children—Felix Benjamin, Mark. Clk., Pacific Gas & Electric Co., San Francisco, 1960-61; intern St. Mary's Hosp., San Francisco, 1967; resident Scenic Gen. Hosp., Modesto, Calif., 1970; practice family medicine, Watsonville, Calif., 1971—; active staff Watsonville Community Hosp., 1971—. Served to capt., M.C., U.S.

Army, 1968-69. Lic. physician, Nebr., La., Calif. Diplomate Am. Bd. Family Practice. Mem. AMA, Calif. Med. Assn., Santa Cruz County Med. Soc., 38th Parrallel Med. Soc. of Korea. Republican. Roman Catholic. Office: 30 Brennan St Watsonville CA 95016

ALI, MIR KURSHEED, mathematician; b. Hyderabad, India, Apr. 16, 1926; s. Mir Warris and Haleema (Begum) A.; came to U.S., 1961, naturalized, 1974; B.Sc., Osmania U., Hyderabad, 1947, M.A., 1949; M.S., Mont. State U., 1964; Ph.D., Wash. State U., 1968; m. Mohammadi Begum, Jan. 13, 1952; 2 children. Lectr. math. City Coll. Hyderabad, 1949-52; lectr. math. Sci. Coll., Saifabad, India, 1952-58, head dept., 1958-61; part-time faculty Mont. State U., 1961-64; instr. Wash. State U., 1964-66, part-time faculty, 1966-68; mem. faculty Calif. State U., Fresno, 1968—, prof. math., 1975—; vis. prof. Abadan (Iran) Inst. Tech., 1976-77. NSF fellow, 1965; Edwin W. Rice fellow, 1966. Mem. Am. Math. Soc., Math. Assn. Am., Soc. Muslim Scientists U.S. and Can., World Affairs Council. Author articles. Office: Dept Math Calif State Univ Fresno CA 93740

ALIBRANDI, JOSEPH FRANCIS, business exec.; b. Boston, Nov. 9, 1928; s. Paul and Anna (Amdndolia) A.; B.S. in Mech. Engring., M.I.T., 1952; m. Lambertha A. Araskiewicz, May 12, 1957; children—Paul, Ann-Marie, Carolyn. With Fairchild Engring. and Airplane Corp., 1951; mgr. indsl. engring. dept. Raytheon Co., 1952-56, asst. mgr., Lowell (Mass.) plant, 1956-58, mgr., 1958-62, ops. mgr., 1962-65, v.p., gen. mgr., 1965-68, sr. v.p., gen. mgr., 1968-70; with Whittaker Corp., Los Angeles, 1970—, exec. v.p., dir., 1970, pres., chief exec. officedr, 1970—; dir. Fed. Res. Bank San Francisco, 1973-76, chmn., 1977-79; dir. Daniel, Mann, Johnson & Mendenhall. Mem. corp. vis. com. Sloan Sch. Mgmt., M.I.T., 1972; chmn. Mass. State Colls. Bldg. Authority, 1968-70; trustee Mass. State Colls., 1967-69; chmn. bus. adv. council UCLA, 1976, dir. internat. student center, 1977—; mem. bd. councilors Sch. Bus. Adminstrn., U. So. Calif., Los Angeles, 1977—. Served with U.S. Army, 1946-48. Mem. C. of C. of U.S. (internat. policy com. 1978—), Calif. C. of C. (dir.), Los Angeles Area C. of C. (dir.), Los Angeles World Affairs Council (dir. 1980—), Navy League (life), Air Force Assn. (life). Office: 10880 Wilshire Blvd Los Angeles CA 90024*

ALIESAN, JODY, poet, researcher, educator; b. Kansas City, Mo., Apr. 22, 1943; d. John David and Minerva Anna (Elliss) Armstrong. B.A., Occidental Coll., 1965; M.A., Brandeis U., 1966, postgrad., 1966-68. Asst. prof. Miles Coll., Birmingham, Ala., 1968-69; N.E. soliciting editor Norvec Pub. Co., Washington, also cons., writer Am. Urban Systems, Washington, and press rep., congl. researcher Nat. Vietnam Moratorium Com., Washington and Chgo., 1969-70; writer; researcher Women's Commn., U. Wash., 1970-71; co-dir. communications U. Wash. YWCA, 1971-72; with Puget Consumers Coop., Seattle, 1973-78; extension lectr. U. Wash. Continuing Edn., 1974-75; grantee, mgr. Urban Homestead Demonstration Project, Dept. of Energy, Seattle, 1971-81; also columnist Seattle Times, 1980-81; asst. to dir. Sch. of Art, U. Wash., 1979-83; poet; books include: as if it will matter, 1978; Soul Claiming, 1975; chapbooks include: To Set Free, 1972; Thunder in the Sun, 1971; recs. include: You'll Be Hearing More from Me, 1971; broadsides include: Empty Bowl Press, The Seal Press, Jawbone Press; poetry represented in periodicals, books and anthologies, Mem. Seattle City Women's Commn., 1971-72; internal coordinator Friends of Discovery Park, 1975; coordinator vols. Citizens for Fair Employment, 1978. Nat. Merit scholar, 1961; Woodrow Wilson fellow, 1965; Woodrow Wilson intern, 1968; performance grantee Seattle Arts Commn., 1973; Nat. Endowment Arts writing fellow, 1978; King County Arts Commn. Work-in-Progress grantee, 1979; Seattle Arts Commn. grantee, 1982, poet-in-residence, 1983. Mem. Phi Beta Kappa.

ALIOTO, ROBERT FRANKLYN, supt. schs.; b. San Francisco, Nov. 22, 1933; s. Michael P. and Evelyn (Blohm) A.; A.A., Hartnell Coll., 1953; B.E., San Jose State Coll., 1958, M.A., 1961; Ed.D., Harvard U., 1968; m. Dominica A. Devuel, June 28, 1980; children—Deborah Ann, Robert Franklyn, David R., Diane A. Tchr. elementary and jr. high schs., Greenfield, Calif., 1956-60; prin. Carneros Elementary Sch., Napa, Calif., 1960-62; supt. Shurtleff Elementary Sch. Dist., Napa, 1962-65; dir. Inst. Tng. Selected Tchrs. Liaison Role, Harvard U., 1966-67; supt. schs. Pearl River (N.Y.) Sch. Dist., 1966-71, Yonkers (N.Y.) City Sch. Dist., 1971-75, San Francisco City and County Sch. Dist., 1975—; adminstrv. asst. Center for Research and Devel. on Ednl. Differences, Harvard U., Cambridge, Mass., 1965-66; Pres., Greenfield Little League, 1956-59; bd. dirs. Napa County Easter Seals, 1961-63. Served with AUS, 1953-55. Mem. Rockland County Pub. Sch. Athletic League (pres. 1969-70), Pearl River Bd. Trade. Club: Rotary. Author: (with J. A. Jungherr) Operational PPBS for Education, 1971. Home: 24 Dellbrook Ave San Francisco CA 94131

ALISKY, MARVIN, political science educator; b. Kansas City, Mo., Mar. 12, 1923; s. Joseph and Bess June (Capp) A.; student St. Mary's U., Tex., 1940-42; B.A., U. Tex., Austin, 1946, M.A., 1947, Ph.D., 1953; cert. Instituto Tecnologico, Monterrey, Mex., 1951; m. Beverly Kay, June 10, 1955; children—Sander Michael, Joseph. News corr. S.W. and Latin Am., NBC, 1947-49, Midwest, 1954-56; news corr. NBC and Christian Sci. Monitor, Latin Am., 1957-72; asst. prof. Ind. U., 1953-57; assoc. prof. journalism and polit. sci. Ariz. State U., Tempe, 1957-60, prof. polit. sci., 1960—, founding chmn. dept. mass communications, 1957-65, founding dir. Ctr. Latin Am. Studies, 1965-72; vis. fellow Princeton U., 1963-64, Hoover Inst., Stanford, 1978; Fulbright prof. Cath. U., Lima, Peru, 1958, U. Nicaragua, 1960; researcher U.S.-Mex. Interparliamentary Conf., Baja, Calif., 1965; cons. U. Rochester, 1981—, Ctr. for Futures Research, U. So. Calif., 1982—. Bd. dirs. Gov.'s Ariz.-Mex. Commn., 1975—, Ariz. Acad. Town Hall, 1981, Tempe Pub. Library, 1974-80; U.S. del. UNESCO Conf., Quito, Ecuador, 1960; U.S. State Dept. lectr., Costa Rica, Peru, Argentina and Chile, 1983. Served as ensign USNR, 1944-45. Fellow Hispanic Soc. Am., 1962; mem. Am. Polit. Sci. Assn., Western Polit. Sci. Assn., Latin Am. Studies Assn., Pacific Coast Council Latin Am. Studies (dir.), Inter-Am. Press Assn., Inter-Am. Broadcasters Assn., Assos. Liga de Municipios de Sonora, Friends of Mex. Art, Sigma Delta Chi. Author: Governors of Mexico, 1965; Uruguay: Contemporary Survey, 1969; The Foreign Press, 1964, 70; Who's Who in Mexican Government, 1969; Political Forces in Latin America, 1970; Government in Nuevo Leon, 1971; Government in Sonora, 1971; Peruvian Political Perspective, 1975; Historical Dictionary of Peru, 1979; Historical Dictionary of Mexico, 1981; Latin America Media: Guidance and Censorship, 1981; Global Journalism, 1983; contbr. numerous articles to profl. jours. and mags. Home: 44 W Palmdale St Tempe AZ 85282 Office: Arizona State University Tempe AZ 85287

ALKANA, RONALD LEE, neuropsychopharmacologist, psychobiologist; b. Los Angeles, Oct. 17, 1945; s. Sam Alkana and Madelyn Jane Davis; student UCLA, 1963-66; Pharm.D., U. So. Calif., 1970; Ph.D., U. Calif., Irvine, 1975; m. Linda Anne Kelly, Sept. 12, 1970; 1 son, Alexander Philippe Kelly. Postdoctoral fellow Nat. Inst. Alcohol Abuse and Alcoholism, U. Calif., Irvine, 1974-76; resident asst. dir. div. neurochemistry, dept. psychiatry and human behavior U. Calif., Irvine, 1976; asst. prof. pharmacy (pharmacology) U. So. Calif., Los Angeles, 1976-82, assoc. prof. pharmacy (pharmacology and toxicology), 1982—. Recipient various scholarships and grants. Mem. Soc. Neurosci., Am. Coll. Clin. Pharmacology, Am. Soc. Pharmacology and Exptl. Therapeutics, Internat. Soc. Biomed. Research on Alcoholism, Research Soc. Alcoholism, AAAS, Sigma Xi, Phi Delta Chi. Contbr. chpts. to books, articles to profl. jours. Office: 1985 Zonal Ave Los Angeles CA 90033

ALKUS, STEPHEN ROBERT, clinical psychologist; b. Los Angeles, Oct. 31, 1943; s. Robert E. and Mary (McKinney) A. B.A. in Psychology, Stanford U., 1965; M.A. in Clin. Psychology, UCLA, 1973, Ph.D., 1977. Lic. clin. psychologist, Calif. Clin. psychology trainee UCLA Psychology Clinic, 1970-71, Sepulveda (Calif.) VA Hosp. Day Treatment Center, 1971-72; intern in clin. psychology Student Mental Health Service, UCLA, 1972-73, fellow in clin. psychology Neuropsychiat. Inst., 1973-75, staff clin. psychologist and coordinator child study program dept. psychology, 1977-80; dir. Y.S.P. Psychol. Services, Costa Mesa, Calif., 1979-81; dir. clin. tng. Y.S.P., Inc., Costa Mesa, 1978—; cons. to schs. and profl. orgns.; pvt. practice clin. psychology, Newport Beach, Calif., 1980—. Recipient Outstanding Teaching award UCLA, 1976. Mem. Am. Psychol. Assn., Nat. Registry Health Service Providers, ACLU. Democrat. Office: 200 Newport Center Dr Suite 204 Newport Beach CA 92660

ALLABASHI, VASIL WILLIAM, sales corporation executive; b. Southbridge, Mass., Feb. 2, 1936; s. Christo and Mary (Pochari) A.; m. Carolyn Marie Gehres; m. 2d, Donna Ruth Margritz, May 14, 1981; stepchildren—Lynn R. Kriegsmann, Kimberly Kay Kriegsmann, Karol Lynn Kriegsmann. B.B.A. Baylor U., 1960. Agt. Prudential Life Ins. Co., 1960-63, div. mgr., 1963-65; gen. agt. Paul Revere Life Ins. Co., Cleve., 1965-69; gen. agt. Lincoln Nat. Life Ins. Co., Denver, 1969-73; pres. Lincoln Nat. Sales Corp. of Colo.-Wyo., Englewood, Colo., 1973—; chmn. agy. head adv. council, 1980—. Served as cpl. USMC, 1954-56. Recipient Presdl. citation Paul Revere Life Ins. Co., 1967; Pres.'s trophy Lincoln Nat. Life, 1975, 78, 80, 81, 82. Mem. Gen. Agents and Mgrs. Assn. (pres. 1976-77), Nat. Assn. Life Underwriters, Denver Assn. Life Underwriters, Million Dollar Roundtable. Club: Masons.

ALLAN, ROBERT MOFFAT, JR., foundation executive; b. Detroit, Dec. 8, 1920; s. Robert M. and Jane (Christman) A.; m. Harriet Spicer, Nov. 28, 1942; children—Robert M. III, Scott, David, Marilee. B.S., Stanford U., 1941; postgrad. Stanford Grad. Sch., 1941-42; M.S., UCLA, 1943; postgrad. Loyola Law Sch., 1947-50. Economist research dept. Security First Nat. Bank, 1942; exec. Marine Ins., 1946-53; asst. to pres., work mgr. Zinsco Elec. Products, 1953-55, v.p., dir., 1956-59; asst. to pres. The Times-Mirror Corp., 1959-60, corp. v.p., 1961-64; pres., dir. Cyprus Mines Corp., 1964-67; pres. Litton Internat., 1967-69; pres. U.S. Naval Postgrad. Sch. Found., Monterey, Calif., 1969—, prof. internat. mgmt., 1969—. Bd. dirs.-trustee U.S. Naval Acad.; trustee Boys Republic, Pomona Grad. Sch., Claremont Grad. Sch., Del Monte Forest Homeowners. Served with USAF, 1942-45. Recipient award Helms Athletic Found., 1947, 49; named Outstanding Businessman of Yr., Los Angeles, Nat. Assn. Accts., 1966; elected to Sailing Hall of Fame, 1969; recipient Meritorious Service award U.S. Navy, 1976; named Monterey Inst. Fgn. Studies trustee and sr. fellow, 1976. Mem. Mchts. and Mfrs. Assn. (dir.), Intercollegiate Yachting Assn. (regional dir. 1940-55), Phi Gamma Delta, Phi Delta Phi. Clubs: Newport Harbor Yacht (commodore 1962), Trans-Pacific Yacht, N.Y. Yacht, Monterey Country. Home: 2980 Cormorant Rd Pebble Beach CA 93953 Office: US Naval Postgrad Sch Monterey CA 93940

ALLARD, DAVID LEE, financial marketing corporation executive; b. Wausau, Wis., Mar. 23, 1936; s. Lee Wilfred and Elvi Marion (Mattila) A.; m. Barbara Ann Bohmer, July 4, 1959; children—Stephen, Elizabeth, Catherine, Michael, Amy. B.S. in Engring., U.S. Naval Acad., 1958. C.L.U.; cert. fin. planner. Personnel rep. Gen. Motors, Milw., 1963-65, salaried personnel supr., Detroit, 1965-68; with Mink-Hanson & Assocs., Monterey, Calif., 1968-69; with Pvt. Planning Corp. (predecessor to Fin. Mktg. Corp.), Carmel, Calif., 1969—, pres., chmn., 1971—; bd. regents Coll. for Fin. Planning, Denver, 1972-75, 78-79, part time acting pres., mem. exec. com. Pres. bd. dirs. Hidden Valley Music Seminars, 1975; treas. All Saints Day Sch., 1977; chmn. Monterey Peninsula United Way Campaign, 1979; chmn. Secretariat of Monterey Diocese Cursillo, 1979; mem. Working Group of Region XI Cursillo, 1983. Served to lt. USN, 1958-63. Mem. Inst. Cert. Fin. Planners (charter), Internat. Assn. Fin. Planners (charter), Soc. C.L.U.s. Republican. Roman Catholic. Office: 100 Clock Tower Pl Suite 220 PO Box 22130 Carmel CA 93922

ALLARD, KERMIT LEE, accountant; b. Ft. Collins, Colo., Sept. 5, 1946; s. Amos Wilson and Sibyl Jean A.; m. Ann Elizabeth Desch, Jan. 16, 1947; children—Karen, Jana. B.S. Colo. State U., 1972. C.P.A., Wyo. Ptnr. McGladrey Henrickson & Co., Cheyenne, Wyo., 1975—; cons. in field. Sec./treas. Symphony and Choral Soc. Cheyenne; mem. Republican Precinct Com., Cheyenne; treas. Rainbow Trail Lutheran Camp, Hillside, Colo. Served with U.S. Army, 1967-70; Vietnam. Mem. Am. Inst. C.P.A.s, Mcpl. Fin. Officers Assn., Wyo. Soc. C.P.A.s (sec./treas., v.p.-elect). Clubs: Dean's U. Wyo, Elks. Home: 915 Ponderosa Rd Cheyenne WY 82009 Office: 1 Rocky Mountain Plaza Cheyenne WY 82001

ALLARD, WAYNE A., state senator, veterinarian; b. Ft. Collins, Colo., Dec. 12, 1943; m. Joan Malcolm, Mar. 23, 1967; children—Cheryl, Christie. D.V.M., Colo. State U., 1968. Veterinarian, Allard Animal Hosp.; mem. Colo. State Senator, 1982—; health officer Loveland (Colo.). Chmn. United Way; active 4-H Found. Mem. Loveland C. of C., AVMA, Colo. Vet. Medicine Assn., Latimer County Vet. Medicine Assn. (past pres.), Bd. Vet. Practitioners (charter mem.), Am. Animal Hosp. Assn. Methodist. Office: State Capitol Denver CO 80203*

ALLDREDGE, ROBERT LOUIS, mfg. co. exec.; b. Johnston City, Ill., Feb. 11, 1922; s. Samuel and Mary Elizabeth (Kreie) A.; B.S. in Chem. Engring., U. Denver, 1942; m. Shirley Alice Harrod, Dec. 15, 1944; children—Alice Louise, Mark Harrod. Research assoc. E.I. DuPont de Nemours & Co., Eastern Lab., Gibbstown, N.J., 1942-44; engring. research assoc. Manhattan Project, Los Alamos (N.Mex.) Sci. Lab., 1944-46; chem. engr. Denver Research Inst., U. Denver, 1946-50; pres. Alldredge & McCabe, Denver, 1950-81; pres. Serpentix Conveyor Corp., Denver, 1969-81; dir. Beryl Ores Co., Broomfield, Colo. Served with C.E., U.S. Army, 1944-46. Mem. Nat. Soc. profl. Engrs. (founding mem. Colo. div.), U. Denver Alumni Assn. (dir. 1965-72), Am. Chem. Soc., Profl. Engrs. Colo., AAAS, Sigma Alpha Epsilon. Methodist. Contbr. articles to profl. jours. Home: 130 Pearl St 1108 Denver CO 80203 Office: 1550 S Pearl St Denver CO 80210

ALLEN, BYRON SEDRIC, JR., physician; b. Center, Tex., Mar. 23, 1923; s. Byron Sedric and Thelma (Daugherty) A.; student S.W. Mo. State Tchrs. Coll., 1942-43, U. Houston, 1944-47; M.D., Tulane U., 1951; m. Alice Harrison, Aug. 21, 1947; children—Kathryn, Byron John, Diane. Intern, Fresno County (Calif.) Gen. Hosp., 1951-52, resident in obstetrics, 1952-53; gen. practice medicine and surgery, Fresno, Calif., 1953-63, Apple Valley Calif., 1963—; pres. med. staff St. Mary Desert Valley Hosp., Apple Valley, 1982-83; med. staff Victor Valley Hosp., Victorville, Calif., 1966—; vis. attending staff dept. family practice San Bernardino (Calif.) County Med. Center, 1973-76; guest lectr. in hypnosis Fresno State Coll., 1960-63; asst. prof. family medicine La. State U., 1976-77, clin. asst. prof., 1978—. Served with USAAF, 1941-43. Named Outstanding Family Physicians in San Bernardino County, 1981-82; recipient Gierman-McKee Meml. award San Bernardino County Med. Ctr., 1982. Diplomate Am. Bd. Family Practice. Fellow Am. Acad. Family Physicians; mem. AMA, Calif. Acad. Family Physicians (chpt. pres. 1961, 80-81, del. Congress of Dels. 1982—), Calif. Med. Assn., San Bernardino County Med. Soc. (sec. 1976—, dir. 1972-83), Calif. Med. Assn. (del. 1974-80). Club: Rotary (pres. 1972—, Man of Year 1973). Home: 19004 Munsee Rd Apple Valley CA 92307 Office: 18327 Hwy 18 Apple Valley CA 92307

ALLEN, CAROL ANNETTE, educator; b. Oshkosh, Nebr., Feb. 9, 1937; d. Frank Ellsworth and Helen Matilda (Curtis) Robinson; A.A., American River Coll., 1969; B.S. in Bus., Calif. State U., Sacramento, 1972, M.A. in Bus. Edn., 1976; m. Norman Eugene Allen, Sept. 2, 1956; children—Susan Michele, Michael Jon, Cheryl Janette, Jeffrey Scott. Sec., First Trust Co., Lincoln, Nebr., 1956-57; tchr., chmn. dept. LaVista High Sch., Orangevale, Calif., 1972-76; cons., presenter Secretarial Seminars, U. Calif., Davis, 1972-76; lectr. on adminstrv. services, and word processing Calif. State U., Sacramento, 1976—; cons. in field. Ruling elder Celtic Cross Presbyn. Ch., Citrus Heights, Calif., 1976-79, chmn. Christian edn. com., 1977-79. Named Outstanding Bus. Edn. Student, Calif. State U., Sacramento, 1972, Nat. Bus. Edn. Assn. Honor Grad., 1972. Mem. Calif. Bus. Edn. Assn. (Commendation 1981), Nat. Bus. Edn. Assn., Am. Bus. Communications Assn., Internat. Word Processing, AAUW, Theta Alpha Delta. Republican. Clubs: Bus. Edn., Job's Daus. Office: 6000 J St Sacramento CA 95819

ALLEN, CEDRIC MERLIN, architect; b. Pullman, Wash., Sept. 18, 1914; s. Karl P. and Frankie (Stevens) A.; B.S. in Archtl. Engring., Wash. State U., 1937; m. Arleen Taylor, June 17, 1937; children—Karl C., Sue Lorraine, Neill J. Draftsman, coll. architect Wash. State U., 1936-37; draftsman archtl. firms, Boise, Idaho, 1937-40; architect Boise-Payette Lumber Co., 1940-48; tchr. Boise High Sch., 1943-44; individual practice architecture, Pocatello, Idaho, 1948—. Mem. Pocatello Planning Zoning Com., 1967-68; bd. dirs. Pocatello Indsl. Lands, Inc., 1975-77, pres., 1978; mem. Bannock County Waterways Bd., 1977-79. Served to lt. (j.g.) USN, 1944-46; CBI, ETO. Mem. AIA, Theta Chi. Clubs: Elks, Pocatello Golf and Country, Idaho State U. Century. Architect: Mini Dome, Idaho State U., also student union bldg., various other halls; bldgs. and residence halls Ricks Coll.; public sch. bldgs., Pocatello; sch., dormitory, chapel and dining hall Idaho Youth Ranch. Home: 160 S 17th St Pocatello ID 83201 Office: 222 E Center St Pocatello ID 83201

ALLEN, CLIFFORD WARREN, JR., elec. engr.; b. Memphis, July 16, 1941; s. Clifford Warren and Geraldine (Crosby) A.; B.S. in Elec. Engring., U. Tenn., 1964; m. Peggy Cox, Oct. 24, 1964; children—Debra Page, Cynthia Michele. Engr., Griffith C. Burr Cons. Engr., Memphis, 1964-65; process engr. Jackson (Miss.) glass plant Gen. Electric Co., 1965-69; chief elec. engr. Baifield Industries, Shreveport, 1969-70; sr. project engr. Masonite Corp., Laurel, Miss., 1970-73; site facilities mgr. Tex. Instruments Inc., Dallas, 1973-78, corp. staff real estate and constrn., Colorado Springs, Colo., 1978-81; site facilities mgr. NCR Corp., Colorado Springs, 1981—; pres. CWAJ & Assocs., freelance photography, 1981—. Chmn. bd. Colorado Springs Texins Assn. Inc., recreation orgn., 1980-81; advanced 1st aid instr. ARC, 1980— CPR instr., 1980—; mem. Nat. Ski Patrol, 1981—. Registered profl. engr., Miss., Tex.; master electrician, Colo. Mem. Colorado Springs Execs. Assn. Republican. Lutheran. Club: Sertoma. Home: 560 Grey Eagle Dr Colorado Springs CO 80919

ALLEN, DAVID, educator; b. Los Angeles, Aug. 10, 1919; B.A., Long Beach State Coll., 1957; M.A., Los Angeles State Coll., 1958; Ed.D., U. Calif. at Los Angeles, 1962; m. Lucille Mary Scott, May 22, 1944; children—Bruce Robert, Bonnie Lynn. Line service mechanic Pan Am. World Airways, 1946-56; instr. Los Angeles Trade-Tech. Coll., 1952-56; spl. supr. Bur. Indsl. Edn., Calif. Dept. Edn., 1956-60; supr. trade-tech. tchr. edn. U. Calif. at Los Angeles, 1960—, lectr. Sch. Edn., 1962—, asso. dir. Div. Vocat. Edn., 1967—; cons. ednl. adv. com. Calif. Instn. for Men, Ventura Sch. for Girls, 1961—, Nat. Council Vocat. Edn., 1967; dir. nat. conf. curriculum devel. in vocat. and tech. edn. U.S. Office Edn., 1969. Served with USNR, 1944-46. Recipient citation of service Dept. Corrections State of Calif., 1966, certificate of award FAA, 1967, Presdl. Distinguished Service and medal award for aviation research FAA-Dept. Transp., 1971; named Man of Year, Aviation Technician Edn. Council, 1969; Calif. Ships award. Fellow Soc. Licensed Aircraft Engrs. and Technologists Gt. Britain; mem. Am. Vocat. Assn., Calif. Indsl. Edn. Assn. (past treas.), Nat. Soc. Study of Edn., Epsilon Pi Tau (Laureate citation 1965), Phi Delta Kappa. Author: Handbook for Beginning Teachers, 1957; A Guide for Developing Electronic Courses, 1958; Simulation and Program Development Strategies, 1967; Automatic Controls, An Instructor's Guide, 1962; Polysensory Learning Through Multi-Media Instruction in Trade and Technical Education, 1968; Air Traffic Control, A Feasibility Study, 1970; Curriculum Development for Inhalation Therapy, 1971; Clean Air Through Automotive Emission Center, 1972; Analysis and Synthesis for a Vocational Student Information System, 1972; Suggested Models for Solutions to Current Vocational Education Problems, 1972; A Survey of Text Materials Used in Aviation Maintenance Schools, 1974; A Survey of the Aviation Mechanics Occupation, 1974; Principles of Adult, Vocational, and Technical Education, 1975; Social and Academic Characteristic Assessments of Black Inner-City High School Students; An Analysis of Alternatives for Payment to States under Public Law 94-482, 1978; Principles and Practices of Vocational Education, 1979; The Instructional Processes in Vocational Education, 1980; A Guide for Professional Development, 1981; contbr. articles to profl. jours., chpt. to yearbook. Home: 8437 Truxton Ave Los Angeles CA 90045

ALLEN, DAVID CHARLES, audiovisual technician; b. Syracuse, N.Y., Jan. 15, 1944; s. Charles Robert and Jane Loretta (Doolittle) A.; m. Mary Ann Stanke, June 15, 1968; children—Meredith Rae, Amelia Kathrine, Carl James. B.Tech. Edn., Nat. U., San Diego, 1983, postgrad., 1983-84. Dir. retail sales Nat. U. Alumni Assn., 1981-83; audiovisual technician Grossmont Union High Sch. Dist., La Mesa, Calif., 1983—. Coordinator mil. outreach Worldwide Marriage Encounter; mem. Presdl. Task Force; mem. Congl. Adv. Com. Vets. Benefits. Served with USN, 1961-81. Mem. Am. Soc. Tng. and Devel., Am. Vocat. Assn., D.A.V., U.S. Navy League, Vietnam Vets. Assn., San Diego Zool. Soc. Republican. Roman Catholic. Club: K.C. Home: 8318 Blossom Hill Dr Lemon Grove CA 92045 Office: 1100 Murray Dr La Mesa CA 92041

ALLEN, DAVID RUSSELL, lawyer; b. Oak Park, Ill., July 30, 1942; s. Paul C. and Lucille (Meyer) A.; m. Penny Grieb, Aug. 27, 1966; children—Todd, Travis. B.A., Stanford U., 1964; J.D., U. So. Calif., 1968. Bar: Calif. 1969. Ptnr. Atherton & Allen, San Diego and Chula Vista, Calif., 1969-81, Atherton, Allen, Mason, Cannon & Geerdes, Chula Vista and San Diego, 1982—. Chmn. bd. trustees community Congl. Ch., Chula Vista, 1981; trustee Chula Vista Community Hosp., 1981—; com. chmn. Cub Scout Pack 885, San Diego County council Boy Scouts Am., 1981, com. chmn. Boy Scout Troop 885, 1983. Served to lt. USNR, 1964-65. Mem. State Bar Calif., San Diego Bar Assn., South Bay Bar Assn. Republican. Congregationalist. Clubs: Rotary (pres. Chula Vista 1976-77), Internat. Wine & Food Soc. (chmn. Chula Vista Br. 1983). Office: 345 F St Suite 200 Chula Vista CA 92010

ALLEN, DENIS MCGEE, educator, poet, engr.; b. Evanston, Ill., June 2, 1944; s. Donald McGee and Joan (Drangas) A. Student U. Minn., 1963, Palomar Coll., 1964, Chapman Coll., 1965, Orange Coast Coll., 1965, Daley Coll., 1978; B.A. in English Lit., U. Ill., 1969; M.S. in Occupational Edn., Chgo. State U., 1978. Tchr., Indsl. Skill Center, Electronic Industries Assn., Chgo., 1969-74, founder, dir. Color TV Service Center, 1974-80; faculty Matanuska-Susitna Community Coll., U. Alaska, 1980, adj. faculty Anchorage Community Coll., 1981; chief engr. Radio KSKA, Anchorage, 1980—; cons. Alaska Skill Center. Vol.

tchr. handicapped swimming Ravenswood YMCA, 1974; vol. tchr. Lawrence Hall Home for Boys, 1977; vol. Am. Cancer Soc. Walk-A-Thon, 1979. Served with USMC, 1962-66. Lic. pvt. pilot; lic. radio operator; teaching cert., Ill., Alaska; cert. broadcast engr. Mem. AAAS, IEEE, Soc. Broadcast Engrs., Am. Radio Relay League (life), Chgo. Tchrs. Union, Am. Fedn. Tchrs., Suburban Amateur Repeater Assn., Aircraft Owners and Pilots Assn., Exptl. Aircraft Assn., Soc. Radio Operators (officer), Amateur Radio Satellite Corp. Club: Midwest Sled Dog; Anchorage Amateur Radio; DX Century (award). Contbr. poetry to mags. Home: Star Route 1762 Eagle River AK 99577 Office: KSKA Public Radio 4101 University Dr Anchorage AK 99508

ALLEN, DOUGLAS ROWAN, real estate mgmt. co. exec.; b. Toledo, Mar. 1, 1941; s. William Trousdale and Virginia (Rowan) A.; B.S., Hampden Sydney Coll., 1963; M.B.A., Rutgers U., 1968; m. Karen Wine, June 20, 1970; children—Douglas Rowan, Kristin Wine. Cons. Peat, Marwick & Mitchell, 1968-71; controller Fred C. Sproul, Inc., Oceanside, Calif., 1971-72; exec. v.p. Andrews & Co., Denver, 1972-75; pres. Allen Assos., Denver, 1975—. Served with USNR, 1963-67. Mem. Colo. Soc. C.P.A.s, Am. Inst. C.P.A.s, Inst. Real Estate Mgmt., Colo. Apt. Assn. (pres.), Denver C. of C. Congregationalist. Clubs: Tennis World, Brown Palace. Office: 5211 S Quebec St Englewood CO 80111

ALLEN, DUANE ARTHUR, accountant; b. Flint, Mich., Feb. 13, 1940; s. Elton J. and Lora (Harris) A.; m. Sally Yvonne George, June 8, 1963; children—Elizabeth, Julie, Gregory. B.A., U. Mich., Ann Arbor, 1966, M.B.A., 1966. C.P.A., Mich., Ariz. Audit supv. Ernst & Whinney, Detroit, 1966-72; ptnr. Walker & Armstrong C.P.A.s, Phoenix, 1972-79; ptnr. Allen & Chew C.P.A.s, Scottsdale, Ariz., 1979—; instr. Ariz. C.P.A. Found. for Edn. and Research; mem. spl. investigating com. Ariz. State Bd. Accountancy. Bd. dirs. Scottsdale Girls Club, 1979-83; pres. 8th Dist. U. Mich. Alumni Clubs, 1983. Recipient Disting. Service award Scottsdale Girls Club, 1983; cert. of Service Ariz. State Bd. Accountancy, 1976, 77, 79. Mem. Am. Inst. C.P.A.s, Mich. Assn. C.P.A.s, Ariz. Soc. C.P.A.s, Retail Fin. Execs., Planning Execs. Inst. Mem. Republican Presdl. Tax Force. Methodist. Club: Sunrise Kiwanis (pres.). Office: Allen & Chew CPAs 7045 3d Ave Scottsdale AZ 85251

ALLEN, EDWARD JOSEPH, exec. photographer; b. San Francisco, Nov. 20, 1934; s. Joseph Peter Alpe and Lena Carolina Agnesa. Cert. Profl. Photographer, 1979. Newspaper photographer, Las Vegas, 1955-60; now pres. Allen Photographers, Inc., Las Vegas, So. Nev. News Bur., Inc., Las Vegas; treas. Nev. Photo Merchandising, Las Vegas, pres. MGM Grand Hotel Photo Studios, Las Vegas and Reno; mng. dir. Internat. Photographics Corp., Las Vegas. Mem. Profl. Photographers Assn. Am., Photo Mktg. Assn., Assn. Profl. Color Labs. Republican. Roman Catholic. Office: 3141 Ind Rd Las Vegas NV 89109

ALLEN, EDWARD RAYMOND, educator, accountant; b. Indpls., Sept. 30, 1913; s. Edward L. and Emmeline (Rice) A.; B.S. in Commerce, Drake U., 1950, M.A. in Accounting, 1951; m. Norma D. M. Brennan, May 10, 1941. Asst. prof. bus. adminstrn. Parsons Coll., Fairfield, Iowa, 1952-56; faculty Coll. of Idaho, Caldwell, 1956—, prof. bus. adminstrn., 1956-73, head dept., 1962-70, chmn. dept., 1970-73, emeritus, 1973—, vis. lectr., 1976—; practicing C.P.A., Caldwell, 1958—. Served to capt. AUS, 1942-46; lt. col. Res. ret. Decorated Bronze Star with 1 palm; C.P.A., Iowa, Idaho. Mem. Am. Inst. C.P.A.s, Idaho Soc. C.P.A.s (dir., regional v.p. 1958-61, mem. standards of practice com. 1974—, chmn. com. 1980—), AAUP (past pres. Coll. of Idaho chpt.), C. of C., Pi Kappa Phi. Clubs: Elks. Contbr. articles to profl. jours. Home: PO Box 336 Caldwell ID 83606

ALLEN, GARY KING, civil engineering consultant; b. Buffalo, June 27, 1944; s. Howard W. and Ethel M. (King) A.; m. Catherine Reardon, July 12, 1969; children—Matthew W., Sarah A. B.S. in Civil Engring., Clarkson Coll. Tech., 1966; M.B.A. with distinction, Nat. U., San Diego, 1977. Sr. engr. Boeing Co., Seattle, 1966-73; lead engr. Rohr Industries, Chula Vista, Calif., 1974-78; specialist engr. RHO Co., Bellevue, Wash., 1978-82; sr. specialist on assignment to Lockheed Corp., Burbank, Calif., 1982—. Mem. nat. adv. bd. Am. Security Council, 1970-76. Recipient Pride in Excellence award Boeing Co., 1980. Mem. AIAA, Lutheran. Home: 27764 Laurel Creek Valencia CA 91355 Office: Lockheed Aircraft Corp PO Box 551 Burbank CA 91520

ALLEN, GARY MICHAEL, investment banking company executive; b. Columbus, Ohio, May 21, 1943; s. Harry Ethan and Mildred Lola (Perfect) A.; m. Gayle Delene Bogovich, Aug. 8, 1981. B.M.E., Ohio State U., 1966, M.B.A., 1969; postgrad. U. Wash., 1969-73. Staff supr. AT&T, Cin., 1960-67; teaching asst. U. Wash., 1969-73; asst. prof. U. Oreg., 1973-74; pres. D. O. Mills Inc., Sacramento, 1974-80, also dir.; pres. G.T.M. Inc., San Diego, 1980—, also dir.; exec. v.p., dir. Lectrocon Inc., San Diego, 1982—; dir., pres. Data Base Concepts, Inc., San Diego, 1983—; dir. Metrum Inc., San Diego; cons. Jeffrey Mfg. Co., 1969. Named Small Businessman of Yr., Calif. SBA, 1978; recipient award Journey for Prospective, 1970. Mem. Sacramento C. of C., Nat. Restaurant Assn., Am. Econ. Soc., ASME, Sigma Pi. Republican. Methodist. Editor: Financial Management (Robert Higgins), 1972.

ALLEN, GREGORY EARL, psychotherapist; b. Tunis, Tunisia, Mar. 2, 1954; came to U.S., naturalized, 1954; s. George Herbert and Etty (Lumbroso) A.; m. Christine Anne Kahawhitta, Mar. 29, 1981; children—Erik, Jason, Trevor. B.A., U. Del., 1977; M.A. summa cum laude, Pepperdine U., 1980; postgrad. Internat. Coll., 1982—. Lic. marriage, family and child therapist, Calif. Counselor Portals House, Los Angeles, 1978; team counselor Life Adjustment Team, Santa Monica, Calif., 1979; assoc. dir. residential services A Touch of Care, Malibu, Calif., 1980; program dir. Huntington Inglewood Manor, Los Angeles, 1981; sr. assoc. McInay & Assocs. Ctr. for Psychotherapy and Counseling, Torrance, Calif., 1981-83; pvt. practice counseling, 1983—; counselor local high schs. and jr. high schs. Recipient award of distinction Portals House. Mem. Assn. Profl. Guidance Activities. Methodist. Research in dreams. Office: 216 Avenida del Norte Redondo Beach CA 90277

ALLEN, HOWARD NORMAN, cardiologist; b. Chgo., Nov. 19, 1936; s. Herman and Ida Gertrude (Weinstein) A.; B.S., U. Ill., 1958, M.D., 1960; m. Lynda Roye Kendrick, Oct. 2, 1967; children—Michael Daniel, Jeffrey Scott. Intern, Los Angeles County Gen. Hosp., 1960-61; resident in internal medicine Wadsworth VA Hosp., Los Angeles, 1961, 64-66, NIH fellow in cardiology Cedars-Sinai Med. Center, Los Angeles, 1966-67; Markus Found. fellow in cardiology St. George's Hosp., London, 1967-68; dir. cardiac care unit Cedars of Lebanon Hosp. div. Cedars-Sinai Med. Center, Los Angeles, 1968-74, dir. Cardiac Noninvasive Lab., 1972—; attending physician cardiology service Sepulveda (Calif.) VA Hosp., 1972—; asst. prof. medicine U. Calif., Los Angeles, 1970-76, asso. prof. medicine, 1976—; cons. Sutherland Learning Assos., Inc., 1970-75. Served to capt. M.C., U.S. Army, 1962-63. NSF fellow, 1958. Diplomate Nat. Bd. Med. Examiners, Am. Bd. Internal Medicine with subsplty. in cardiovascular disease. Fellow A.C.P., Am. Coll. Cardiology, Council Clin. Cardiology of Am. Heart Assn.; mem. Am. Heart Assn.-Greater Los Angeles Affiliate (chmn. fall symposium com. 1978, chmn. emergency cardiac care planning and coordinating com. 1980—, chmn. program com. 1981—, dir. 1979—), Alpha Omega Alpha, Pi Kappa Epsilon, Phi Lambda Kappa. Author chpts. in books and articles on myocardial infarction, echocardiography, mitral valve prolapse syndrome, cardiovascular emergencies. Office: 8700 Beverly Blvd Los Angeles CA 90048

ALLEN, HOWARD PFEIFFER, utility company executive; b. Upland, Calif., Oct. 7, 1925. B.A., Pomona Coll., 1948; J.D., Stanford U. 1951. Bar: Calif. 1952, U.S. Supreme Ct. 1958. Asst. prof., asst. dean dept. law Stanford U. (Calif.), 1951-54; spl. rep. So. Calif. Edison Co., Rosemead, 1954-55, asst. to v.p., 1955-59, spl. counsel, 1959-62, v.p., 1962-71, sr. v.p., 1971-73, exec. v.p., 1973-80, pres., dir., 1980—; dir. Calif. Fed. Savs. and Loan, Republic Corp., ICN Pharms. Inc., PSA Inc., Pacific S.W. Airlines, Computer Scis. Corp., MCA Inc., Assoc. So. Investment Co., Mono Power Co. Bd. dirs. Los Angeles Civic Light Opera, Los Angeles County Mus. Art, Los Angeles County Fair Assn., Calif. Council for Environ. and Econ. Balance, NCCJ; vice chmn. exec. com. Los Angeles Olympic Organizing Com. Mem. Am. Judicature Soc., ABA, Calif. State Bar, Los Angeles County Bar Assn., San Francisco Bar Assn., Pacific Coast Elec. Assn. (dir.), Los Angeles Area C. of C. (dir. 1969-81, pres. 1978, chmn. 1979), Phi Beta Kappa. Address: 2541 Mountain Ave Claremont CA 91711

ALLEN, IRWIN, motion picture writer, producer, dir.; b. N.Y.C.; s. Joseph and Eva (Davis) A.; student CCNY, Columbia U. Radio news commentator KLAC, Hollywood, Calif.; syndicated newspaper columnist, motion picture editor Atlas Features Syndicate, Hollywood; lit. agt. motion picture; TV producer, commentator, Hollywood; prodn. exec. Double Dynamite; asso. producer Where Danger Lives; co-producer A Girl in Every Port; producer, dir., screenplay writer The Sea Around Us; producer Dangerous Mission, When Time Ran Out; writer, producer, dir. Animal World; producer, dir., co-writer screenplay The Story of Mankind; producer, co-writer The Big Circus; producer, dir., co-writer The Lost World, Voyage to the Bottom of the Sea, Five Weeks in a Balloon, City Beneath the Sea; producer, dir. action sequences Poseidon Adventure, The Towering Inferno; producer, dir. The Swarm, 1978, Beyond the Poseidon Adventure; creator, producer TV series Voyage to the Bottom of the Sea, Lost in Space, The Time Tunnel, Land of the Giants, Swiss Family Robinson, Code Red; producer TV movies Adventures of the Queen, The Time Travelers, Flood, Fire, The Return of Captain Nemo, Hanging by a Thread, Cave-In, The Night the Bridge Fell Down, The Memory of Eva Ryker. Recipient Academy award for The Sea Around Us; Internat. Laurel award Motion Picture Exhibitors; Blue Ribbon award for excellent motion picture prodn. Box Office mag. (5 times); Merit award So. Calif. Fedn. Women's Clubs (5 times); U.C. named NATO Producer of Year, Fox Showman of Year. Club: Tamarisk Country (Palm Springs, Calif.). Office: Columbia Pictures Burbank CA 91505

ALLEN, JACQUELYN MAY (HINSON), guidance conselor; b. Los Angeles, Nov. 6, 1943; d. John Richard and Ida May (Townsend) Hinson; B.A., U. Redlands, 1965; M.A., Berkeley Baptist Div. Sch., 1969; M.S., Calif. State U., Hayward, 1972; m. James William Allen, Dec. 19, 1970; children—Julene May, Jason William. Missionary, tchr. English as 2d lang., El Salvador, U. Mexico, 1966-67; dir. Christian edn. youth Valley Bapt. Ch., Walnut Creek, Calif., 1967-68; tchr. Foothill Intermediate Sch., Walnut Creek, 1968-72; counselor, dir. Cross-Age teaching program, summer sch. prin. Thornton Jr. High Sch., Fremont, Calif., 1972-74; career counselor, chmn. dept. Mission San Jose High Sch., Fremont, 1974-79, psychologist, 1980—, mgmt. cons., 1981—; guest instr. Christian edn. Mexican Bapt. Sem., Mexico; therapist Fremont Inst. Transactional Analysis. Vice pres. Parent Tchr. Club, 1974-75. Recipient Outstanding Young Educator award Fremont Jr. C. of C., 1974-75; lic. marriage, family and child counselor. Mem. Am., Calif. assns. personnel and guidance, No. Calif. Fgn. Lang. Assn., Nat. Future Woman's Assn., Am. Personnel and Guidance Assn., Fremont Sch. Adminstrs. Assn. (treas. 1975), Fremont Counseling and Guidance Assn. (pres. 1975-77), Calif. Assn. Marriage and Family Counselors, Am. Sch. Counselor Assn. (local chairperson Nat. Leadership Devel. Conf. 1983), Calif. Sch. Counselors Assn. (area II rep. 1977-79, sec. 1979-81, pres.-elect 1981-82, pres. 1982-83), Delta Kappa Gamma (editor newsletter), Alpha Mu Gamma. Democrat. Presbyterian. Home: 45917 Paseo Padre Pkwy Fremont CA 94538

ALLEN, JAMES, civil engr.; b. Alton, Ill., Apr. 18, 1940; s. Ernest Levi and Ellen Ruth (Reed) A.; B.S. in Civil Engring., U. Ill., 1967; postgrad. U. Alaska, 1970-78. Prin., James Allen, P.E., Anchorage, 1974-80; prin. Franklin & Allen, cons. engrs., Anchorage, 1980—. Registered profl. engr., Alaska, Utah, Wash. Mem. ASCE, Am. Concrete Inst., Alaska Soc. Profl. Engrs., Profl. Engrs. in Pvt. Practice, Constrn. Specifications Inst., Am. Arbitration Assn., Earthquake Engring. Research Inst., Soc. Am. Mil. Engrs. Home: Star Route A Box 1721-B Anchorage AK 99507 Office: 1813 E 1st St Suite 207 Anchorage AK 99501

ALLEN, JAMES A., editor, publisher, rancher; b. Burlington, Kans., Sept. 26, 1932; s. L. H. and Agnes R. (Sylvester) A.; m. Lydia M. Kelly, June 30, 1951; children—Donald R., Cynthia J., Kelly J., Sarah K. B.S. in Bus. Adminstrn., Emporia State U., 1954. Reporter, Burlington (Kans.) Daily Republican, 1950-51; reporter, advt. salesman, Emporia (Kans.) Gazette, 1951-53; mgr. classified Garden City (Kans.) Telegram, 1954-55; account exec. Klamath Falls (Oreg.) Herald and News, 1955-67, advt. dir., 1967-76, editor, pub., 1977—. Campaign chmn. United Way of Klamath Basin, 1978, pres., 1981; bd. dirs. Klamath County Econ. Devel. Corp. Mem. Klamath County C. of C. (bd. dirs.). Republican. Presbyterian. Club: Rotary (pres. 1982-83). Office: Klamath Falls Herald and News Klamath Falls OR 97601

ALLEN, JAMES LOVIC, JR., humanist, educator; b. Atlanta, Jan. 2, 1929; s. James Lovic and Effie Grace (Schell) A.; B.A., Tulane U., 1953, M.A., 1954; Ph.D., U. Fla., 1959; m. Barbara Foster, June 13, 1953 (div.); children—Melinda Sue, Algernon Foster. Instr. English, U. Tenn., 1954-56; asst. prof. English, Stephen F. Austin State U., Nacogdoches, Tex., 1959-60; asso. prof. English, U. So. Miss., Hattiesburg, 1960-63; asso. prof. English, U. Hawaii, Hilo, 1963-69, prof., 1969—; vis. prof. English, Stephen F. Austin State U., 1970-71, U. Tenn., 1976-77. Served with USN, 1946-49. So. Fellowship Fund grantee, 1956-58. Mem. AAUP, MLA, Am. Com. Irish Studies, Can. Assn. Irish Studies, Internat. Assn. Study Anglo-Irish Lit., Phi Beta Kappa. Democrat. Unitarian. Author: Locked In: Surfing for Life, 1970; editor: Yeats Four Decades After: Some Scholarly and Critical Perspectives, 1979; Yeats's Epitaph: A Key to Symbolic Unity in his Life and Work, 1982. editorial bds. 20th Century Lit., Yeat's Eliot Rev.; contbr. articles to profl. publs.; researcher W.B. Yeats. Home: 2405 Kalanianaole Ave Apt 304 Hilo HI 96720 Office: U Hawaii 1400 Kapiolani Ave Hilo HI 96720

ALLEN, JOHN KELSEY, zoologist; b. Sacramento, Dec. 6, 1950; s. Kirke Monroe and Elizabeth (Newman) A.; B.S., U. Calif., Berkeley, 1973, Ph.D. Candidate, 1975. Staff research assoc. U. Calif. Bodega Marine Lab., 1974-77; teaching asso. U. Calif., Berkeley, after 1977; now supr. San Francisco Internat. Airport. U. Calif. Regents fellow, 1973-74, U. Calif. Earle C. Anthony fellow, 1974-75, Edwin Pauley fellow, 1975-76, Henry Luce fellow, 1978-79. Mem. Western Soc. Malacologists, Western Soc. Naturalists, Soc. Systematic Zoology, Sierra Club, Sigma Xi. Contbr. articles to profl. jours. Home: 30 Monte Vista Rd Orinda CA Office: PO Box 8602 San Francisco CA 94128

ALLEN, JOHN MAXWELL, JR., life insurance executive; b. Battle Creek, Mich., June 5, 1947; m. Judith Gayle Jones, Nov. 29, 1980. s. John Maxwell and Beverly (Corlett) A.; B.A., St. Ambrose Coll., Davenport, Iowa, 1970, Am. Coll., Bryn Mawr, Pa. 1978. With N.Y. Life Ins. Co., 1970—, asst. mgr., San Francisco, 1974-80, gen. mgr., Campbell, Calif., 1980—. C.L.U. Mem. Nat. Assn. Life Underwriters, Gen. Agts. and Mgrs., Assn. (dir.), Am. Soc. C.L.U.s, Nat. Assn. Securities Dealers. Republican. Roman Catholic. Club: San Francisco Tennis. Address: 1901 S Bascom Ave Suite 701 Campbell CA 95008

ALLEN, LEXIS MAC FADDEN, curriculum consultant; b. London, Mar. 31, 1937; d. Harry Alexander and Ruth Gloria (Lawlor) Mac Fadden; came to U.S., 1939; m. John Armstrong Hendricks, July 16, 1961; 1 son, Jonathan Armstrong; m. 2d, David Allen, Mar. 31, 1979. B.A. in History, Pomona Coll., 1958; postgrad. U. Calif.-Berkeley, 1958-59; M.A. in Elem. Edn., U. Nev.-Las Vegas, 1970. Cert. tchr., Calif., adminstr., Nev. Tchr., Nev. and Calif., also team leader Tchr. Corps, 1970-72; curriculum writer, cons. Lang. Arts Clark County Sch. Dist., Las Vegas, 1974—; cons. educator Harcourt, Brace, Jovanovich; cons. in field. Active Assistance League Las Vegas. Mem. Assn. Supervision and Curriculum Devel., Nat. Council Tchrs. English, Phi Delta Kappa, Kappa Delta Pi. Republican. Club: Mesquite (past pres. jr. club). Author: (with Frances Van Wert) The Write Way, 1981; Wits, Whys and Wonders, 1983. Home: 4889 W Montara Circle Las Vegas NV 89121 Office: 600 N 9th St Las Vegas NV 89101

ALLEN, LOUIS ALEXANDER, management consultant; b. N.S., Can., Oct. 8, 1917; s. Nathan and Emma (Greenberg) A.; m. Ruth Ellen Graham, Aug. 25, 1946; children—Michael, Ace, Steven, Terry, Deborah. B.S., Wash. State U., 1941. Cert. mgmt. cons., 1974. Mgmt. positions Aluminum Co. Am., 1945-49; tng. dir. Koppers Co., Inc., 1949-53; dir. mgmt. study The Conf. Bd., N.Y.C., 1953-56; dir. orgn. planning Booz-Allen & Hamilton, Chgo., 1956-58; pres., chmn. Louis Allen Assocs., Inc., Palo Alto, Calif., 1958—; vis. lectr. Stanford U., 1961, 64, U. Pitts., 1949-50, NYU, 1953-56, U. Chgo., 1956-58; exec. in residence Wash. State U., 1982. Served to maj. USAF, 1942-45. Decorated Legion of Merit; recipient McKinsey award, 1964. Mem. Inst. Mgmt. Cons., Acad. Mgmt. Author: Improving Staff and Line Relationships, 1955; Management and Organization, 1958; The Professional Manager's Guide, 1961 The Management Profession, 1964; Australian Aboriginal Art, 1972; Professional Management: New Concepts and Proven Practices, 1973; Time before Morning: Art and Myth of the Australian Aborigines, 1975; Making Managerial Planning More Effective, 1982; contbr. numerous articles to profl. jours. Office: 3600 W Bayshore Rd Palo Alto CA 94303

ALLEN, PHILIP SHYRL, govt. systems engr.; b. Paonia, Colo., Feb. 4, 1935; s. F. Ernest and T. Blanche (Knight) A.; B.A. in Physics, Friends U., 1955; B.S. in Elec. Engring., State U. Iowa, 1957; m. R. Cathern Rankin, June 13, 1964; 1 dau., Lorinda. Flight test engr. Pacific Missile Test Center, Point Mugu, Calif., 1958-66, asst. mgmt. info. officer, 1966-72, airborne software systems engr., 1972—. Mem. Aircraft Owners and Pilots Assn., Nat. Hist. Soc., IEEE (sec.-treas. engring mgmt. group 1970-71, vice chmn. 1971-72, chmn. 1972-73), Mensa, Sigma Xi, Tau Beta Pi. Mem. Friends Ch. (treas. 1963-70). Club: Toastmasters (sec. 1964, pres. 1965). Author: Rights, Riots and Responsibility, 1975. Home: 815 Yucca St Port Hueneme CA 93041 Office: Pacific Missile Test Center Code 1223 Point Mugu CA 93042

ALLEN, PHYLLIS ADELLE GRISHAM, public relations and fund raising executive; b. Stockton, Calif., Aug. 11, 1927; d. Clarence William and Norma Grace (Collins) Grisham; children—Carole Hilles, Susan Allen Yonas, Stephen, Thomas, Patrica Allen Ruff. Student Long Beach City Coll., 1945-46, U. Oreg., 1957, Portland State U., 1967. Women's dir., broadcaster KMED Radio and TV, Medford, Oreg., 1957-65; copywriter, account exec. Parma Advt., Portland, Oreg., 1965-66; sec.-treas., account exec. Williams Advt. and Pub. Relations, Portland, 1966-68; pub. relations dir. United Fund, Akron, Ohio, 1969-70; asso. pub. relations dir. Akron Gen. Med. Center, 1972-73; exec. dir. Akron Gen. Devel. Found., 1973-80; dir. community relations and devel. Children's Hosp. of San Francisco, 1980-83; dir. resource devel. Scripps Meml. Hosps., La Jolla, Calif., 1983—. Recipient 1st place Pillsbury invitational recipe contest for food editors, 1964. Fellow Nat. Assn. Hosp. Devel.; mem. Pub. Relations Soc. Am. (accredited). Home: 355 Sea Forest Ct Del Mar CA 92014 Office: Scripps Meml Hosps 9888 Genesee Ave La Jolla CA 92038

ALLEN, R. GARY, architect; b. N.Y.C., Sept. 13, 1928; s. Rembert Gary and Dorothy (Sigman) A.; student George Washington U., 1949; B.Arch., Pratt Inst., 1958; m. Nancy Creighton McAvoy, Aug. 23, 1974. Architect, Philip C. Johnson & Assos., N.Y.C., 1958-62, Carson, Lundin & Shaw, N.Y.C., 1962-63, Tucker, Sadler & Bennett, San Diego, 1963-64; v.p., dir. design Frank L. Hope & Assos., San Diego, 1964-76; prin. Gary Allen, architect, Del Mar, Calif., 1976—. Served with U.S. Army, 1953-55. Mem. AIA. Designer, San Diego Stadium (AIA nat. honor award 1969), Nat. Cash Register Computer Plant, San Diego, Creative Arts Bldgs., San Diego City Coll. (AIA, Am. Assn. Sch. Adminstrs. award 1973), Naval Ocean Systems Center, San Diego (Merit award Naval Facilities Engring. Command 1976), Western Med. Inst. Research, Presidio, Calif., Mesa Coll. Music and Life Scis. Bldg., San Diego, Hemet Valley (Calif.) Hosp. Nursing and Diagnostic Addition, Cuyamaca Community Coll., Linkabit Corp., Torrey Pines Center, La Jolla, Calif., Cashman Sports-Cultural-Conv. Complex, Las Vegas. Home: 750 Hoska Dr Del Mar CA 92014 Office: 1307 Stratford Ct Del Mar CA 92014

ALLEN, REX WHITAKER, architect; b. San Francisco, Dec. 21, 1914; s. Lewis Whitaker and Maude Rex (Allen) A.; A.B., Harvard U., 1936, M.Arch., 1939; m. Bettie June Crossfield, Nov. 6, 1971; children—Alexandra, Frances L., Mark B., Susan M. Asso., Research and Planning Assos., N.Y.C., 1939-42; design engr. Camloc Fastener Corp., N.Y.C., 1942-45; chief design Isadore Rosenfield, Architect, N.Y.C., 1945-48; project architect Blanchard & Maher, Architects, San Francisco. 1949-52; prin. Rex Whitaker Allen, AIA, San Francisco, 1953-60; pres. Rex Allen-Drever-Lechowski Architects, San Francisco, 1961—; prin. works include Dameron Hosp., Stockton, Calif., French Hosp., San Francisco, Roseville (Calif.) Dist. Hosp., Highland Gen. Hosp., Oakland, Calif., Mercy San Juan Hosp., Carmichael, Calif., Meml. Hosp., Modisto, Calif., Woodland (Calif.) Meml. Hosp., St. Francis Hosp., San Francisco, Dominican Santa Cruz (Calif.) Hosp., Alta Bates Hosp., Berkeley, Calif., Sacred Heart Gen. Hosp., Eugene, Oreg., St. Joseph Hosp. West, Mt. Clemens, Mich., outpatient dept. Boston City Hosp., Commonwealth Health Ctr., Saipan. Fellow AIA (pres. 1969-70), fellow Royal Archtl. Inst. Can. (hon.); mem. Am. Assn. Hosp. Planning (pres. 1970-71), Fedn. Pan Am. Archtl. Assns. (v.p. 1980—), Internat. Hosp. Fedn., Assn. Western Hosps., Internat. Union Architects Public Health Work Group, Calif. Hosp. Assn. Clubs: Harvard (N.Y.C. and San Francisco). Author: Hospital Planning Handbook, 1976; also articles. Office: 425 Battery St San Francisco CA 94111

ALLEN, RICHARD HUGH, engineering and construction executive; b. Rochester, N.Y., Jan. 25, 1947; s. Hugh Carlton and Teresa Mary (Herman) A.; B.S. in Civil Engring., U. Detroit, 1969; M.S. in Constrn. Mgmt., U. N.Mex., 1971. Engr. in tng. N.Y. State Dept. Transp., Rochester, 1966, 67, 69; grad. teaching asst. civil engring. dept. U. N.Mex., Albuquerque, 1969-70; structural engr. Cottrell, Vaughan & Assos., Albuquerque, 1971-74, v.p., partner, 1974-78; v.p., partner Design Profls., Inc., Albuquerque, 1978—. Registered profl. engr., N.Mex., Wyo. Mem. Nat. Soc. Profl. Engrs. (chmn. profl. engr. in constrn. 1977-78; Young Engr. of Year 1979), Am. Soc. Valve Engrs.,

ASCE, Soc. Am. Mil. Engrs., N.Mex. Soc. Profl. Engrs. (Young Engr. of Year 1978, Engr. of Yr. award Albuquerque chpt. 1979). Republican. Roman Catholic. Club: Elks. Office: 4301 Carlisle Blvd NE Albuquerque NM 87107

ALLEN, RICHARD LEE, physician; b. Bloomfield, Iowa, Feb. 4, 1927; s. Roy Melvin and Ruth (Hutchings) A.; M.D., B.A., U. Iowa, Iowa City, 1952; m. Ruth Harig Behrman, Feb. 25, 1970; children—Richard L., Steven K., Larry M., Jon P. Intern, City Hosp., St. Louis, 1952-53; practice medicine, Bloomfield, 1958-68, Las Vegas, 1968—; chief of staff Valley Hosp., 1976-79, bd. govs., 1972-77; profl. v.p. So. Nev. Drug Abuse Council, 1972-77; team physician Western High Sch., Las Vegas, 1969—. Served with M.C., USNR, 1953-58. Mem. AMA, Nev. Med. Assn., Clark County Med. Assn. Methodist. Club: Masons. Home: 811 Kenny Way Las Vegas NV 89107 Office: 710 Shadow Ln Las Vegas NV 89106

ALLEN, ROBERT WILLARD, electronics executive, consultant; b. Detroit, Feb. 4, 1931; s. Issac Newton and Effie Marian (Cruikshank) A.; m. Luckie Cherie Allen, Dec. 6, 1952; children—Sheree Lynn, Robert James, Stacey Cherie, Milton George. B.B.A., Wayne State U., 1960, M.B.A., 1964; Ph.D. in Adminstrn., U. Calif.-Irvine, 1978. Mgr. operational analysis office Ford Motor Co., Dearborn, Mich. and Newport Beach, Calif., 1960-73; lectr. Calif. State U.-Fullerton, 1973-77; asst. dean Grad. Sch. Mgmt., U. Calif.-Irvine, 1978-79, now tchr., Seminar leader; v.p. adminstrn. EECO, Inc., Santa Ana, Calif., 1979—. Served to lt., USNR, 1950-54; Korea. Mem. Acad. Mgmt. Republican. Contbr. articles profl. jours., chpt. in book; author: (with L.W. Porter) Organizational Influence Processes, 1982. Office: 1601 Chestnut St Santa Ana CA 92701

ALLEN, ROSS ROUNDY, education educator, researcher; b. Salt Lake City, Jan. 21, 1928; s. William Berry and Rebecca May (Roundy) A.; m. Maunne Neilson; children—Raquel Allen Mittelstadt, Connie Allen Skidmore, Kim Allen Robinson, Ross R., Trent K., Heather Allen Knowles. B.S. in Math. with honors, English, U. Utah, 1952, M.S. in Ednl. Adminstrn., 1955, Ed.D. Supervision with distinction, in Secondary Edn. 1962, Cert. tchr., Colo., Utah. Tchr. pub. schs., Colo., Utah, 1952-57; registrar, dir. admissions Brigham Young U., Hawaii, 1957-63, head dept. secondard edn., 1963-66; head dept. secondary edn. Utah State U., Logan, 1966-68, prof. edn., 1968—; research assoc. Far West Lab. Ednl. Research; David O. McKay lectr. Brigham Young U., 1965; Fulbright lectr., Laos, 1974-75. Mem. Hawaii State Sch. Bd., 1962-66; bishop Ch. of Jesus Christ of Latter Day Saints, 1968-74. Served with USAF, 1946-49. Named Outstanding Prof., Utah State U., 1979, Internat. Prof. of Yr., Internat. Student Assn., 1981; recipient Outstanding Service award United Basin Ctr. Continuing Edn., 1982. Mem. NEA, Assn. Supervision and Curriculum Devel., Utah Council Tchrs. of Math., Nat. Council Tchrs. of Math., Assn. Ednl. Devel. Systems, Nat. Council Tchr. Edn. and Profl. Standards, Phi Kappa Phi, Phi Delta Kappa. Mormon. Clubs: Kiwanis Internat. (pres. 1980-81), Kiwanis (Logan). Author: Metrics for Teachers: Quick and Easy, 1982; (textbook): Know Your Utah, 1960. Editor: Seminar Topics in Secondary Education, 1970; Issues in School Measurement and Evaluation, 1971. Contbr. articles to profl. jours. Home: 1110 N Rose St Logan UT 84321 Office: Utah State U UMC 28 Logan UT 84322

ALLEN, SANDRA ELAINE, insurance agency executive; b. Houston, Feb. 12, 1947; d. Clyde Beecher and Marjorie Lee (Skeen) Skidmore; m. Charles Gilbert Walters, Sept. 10, 1965 (div.); children—Steven, Carren, Christa; m. 2d, Brandon B. Allen, July 9, 1983. Student Orange Coast Coll., Costa Mesa, Calif., 1966-67. Rating technician Providence Washington Ins. Co., Anchorage, 1976-79; exec. dir. Ind. Ins. Agts. & Brokers of Alaska, 1981; Mktg. and casualty supr. Rollins Hurdick Hunter, Anchorage, 1979—. Active Anchorage Civic Opera, 1980—; active Anchorage Area Task Team-Ctrs. Network-EST Tng. Mem. Ins. Women Anchorage (dir.), NOW, Nat. Assn. Female Execs. Editor quar. newsletter Ind. Ins. Agts and Brokers of Alaska, Inc., 1981. Home: 8383 Country Woods Ct Anchorage AK 99502 Office: 840 K St Suite 101 Anchorage AK 99501

ALLEN, STANLEY EDWARD, JR., electrical engineer; b. San Francisco, Dec. 27, 1929; s. Stanley Edward and Honora Anne (Stouky) A.; m. Marilyn Camille Craig, Aug. 29, 1954; children—Michael Robert, Kim Natalie Cifelli. B.S. in Elec. Engring., U. Calif.-Berkeley, 1954. Communications engr. San Francisco shipyard, 1954-56; project engr. Gen. Electric Microwave Lab., Palo Alto, Calif., 1956-57; Lewis & Kaufman, Los Gatos, Calif., 1957-58; engring. mgr., program mgr., project engr. Varian Assocs., Palo Alto, 1958—. Served to sgt. USMC, 1948-52. Sr. mem. IEEE. Clubs: E Clampus Vitus, Elks (Quincy, Calif.). Home: 1783 Kimberly Dr Sunnyvale CA 94087 Office: 611 Hansen Way Palo Alto CA 94303

ALLEN, TERRIL DIENER, author; b. Douglas, Okla., Aug. 13, 1908; d. David M. and Clara (Cline) Diener; A.B., Phillips U., 1929; M.A., B.D. cum laude, Yale U. Div. Sch., 1935; postgrad. U. Okla., 1940, Columbia U., 1941-42, NYU, 1958-59, Stanford U., 1968, U. Calif.-Santa Cruz, 1968; student UCLA, 1965; m. Don Bala Allen, 1941. Student work dir. med. schs., Chgo., 1929-32; editor Young People's Materials, Presbyn. Ch., Phila., 1936-39; established, dir. written arts dept. Inst. Am. Indian Arts, Santa Fe, 1963-68; dir. communications project elem. and secondary schs. Bur. Indian Affairs, 1968—; asso. staff specialist Indian affairs, lectr. Coll. V, U. Calif.-Santa Cruz, 1969-74; prof. Chapman Coll., 1975—; free-lance author, 1940—; contract author motion pictures, filmstrips Family Films, Hollywood, Calif., after 1960; free lance creative writing cons. elem. and secondary schs. Recipient Disting. Alumus award Phillips U., 1970. Mem. Authors League, Contemporary Authors, Western Writers Am. Presbyterian. Author: (with Don Bala Allen) Doctor in Buckskin, 1951; Troubled Border, 1954; Ambush at Buffalo Wallow, 1956; Prisoners of the Polar Ice, 1961; Tall As Great Standing Rock, 1963; Navahos Have Five Fingers; Vol. 68 Civilization of the American Indians Series, 1963, 2d edit., 1981; Doctor, Lawyer, Merchant, Chief, 1965; Miss Alice and the Cunning Comanche, 1959; And Now Tomorrow, 1952; (with Emerson Blackhorse Mitchell) Miracle Hill, 1967; Not Ordered By Man, 1967; Writing to Create Ourselves, 1969; editor: Arrow I, 1969, Arrow II, 1970, Arrow III, 1971, Arrow IV, 1972, Arrow V, 1973; Arrow VI, 1974; The Whispering Wind, Anthology of American Indian Poetry, 1972; Arrows Four, 1974; Writing to Create Ourselves, 1982; (with Gloria Diener Autry) The Color-Coded Allergy Cookbook, 1983. Home: PO Box 2775 Carmel CA 93921

ALLEN, THOMAS GORMAN, radiologist; b. Pasadena, Calif., Aug. 22, 1935; s. Fred Jerome and Helen Marie (Gorman) A.; B.S., Loyola U. of Los Angeles, 1957; M.D., U. So. Calif., 1961; m. Marilyn Consuelo Marcus, July 2, 1960; children—Lisa Marie, Maria Therese, Julie Anne, Jennifer Davila. Intern, Los Angeles County-U. So. Calif. Med. Center, 1961-62, resident in radiology, 1963-65; radiologist, Huntington Meml. Hosp., Pasadena, 1966—, dir. dept. diagnostic ultrasound, 1972—; clin. instr. radiology, U. So. Calif. Mem. Am., Calif., Los Angeles County med. assns., Am. Inst. Ultrasound in Medicine, Am. Coll. Radiology, Los Angeles Radiol. Soc., Radiol. Soc. of So. Calif., Alpha Omega Alpha. Roman Catholic. Home: 1155 Arden Rd Pasadena CA 91106 Office: 100 Congress St Pasadena CA 91105

ALLEN, TRAVIS ARTHUR, lab. adminstr.; b. Fort Smith, Ark., May 29, 1924; s. De Witt and Mary Gladys (McGowan) A.; student Santa Barbara State Coll., 1943, Kans. State Tchrs. Coll., 1944, U. N.Mex., 1954-59; m. Bette Luedtke, 1981; children—David C., Rhonda G., Lisa C., Janene C., Tina C. Supr. modification sect. Sandia Nat. Lab., Albuquerque, 1948-58, supr. secondary standards lab., 1958-62, supr. apprentice tng., 1962-67; v.p., gen. mgr. Product Design, Inc., Albuquerque, 1968-70; supr. photochem. lab. Sandia Nat. Labs., Albuquerque, 1970—; cons., tchr. Albuquerque Tech. Vocat. Inst., 1964-74. N.Mex. insp.-gen., lt. col. CAP, 1955-57. Served with USAAF, 1943-46. Recipient IR-100 award Indsl. Research Panel, 1976. Mem. Soc. Advancement Process Engring., Inst. Printed Circuits, Med. Aids Research Found., Mensa, DAV. Republican. Lutheran. Club: Masons. Patentee in field; inventor hot air solder leveler for printed circuit manufacture. Home: 9422 Cordova St NE Albuquerque NM 87112 Office: Sandia Nat Lab 1473 Box 5800 Albuquerque NM 87185

ALLEN, WAYNE FRANCIS, hospital administrator; b. Manhattan, Kans., Mar. 22, 1933; s. Jesse F. and Ruth D. (Morris) A.; m. Verla M. Allen, Apr. 15, 1955; children—Teri L., Michael D. B.A. in Econs., Washburn Coll., 1959. Dir. data processing County of Santa Barbara, Calif. 1961-62, City of Buena Park, Calif. 1962-67; dir. data processing St. Francis Med. Center, Lynwood, Calif., 1967-71, bus. mgr., 1971-74, sr. v.p., 1974—. Bd. dirs. ARC, Los Angeles. Served with USMC 1951-54. Mem. Hosp. Fin. Mgmt. Assn., Health Care Execs. So. Calif., Lynwood C. of C. (dir. 1982-83). Clubs: Rotary, Elks. Office: 3630 E Imperial Hwy Lynwood CA 90262

ALLEN, WILLIAM EUGENE, lawyer; b. Vincennes, Ind., Feb. 8, 1933; s. Lloyd Laverne and Lillian Elizabeth (Rupe) A.; B.S. in Law, Western State U., 1976, J.D., 1978; m. Carolyn Ann Horner, Nov. 14, 1952; children—Catherine, Cheryl, William Eugene. Design engr. Technomics, Inc., Santa Monica, Calif., 1966-67; project coordinator aerospace div. ITT, San Fernando, Calif., 1967-69; dir. engring. Digital Sci. Corp., San Diego, 1969-74, controller, dir. adminstrn., 1974-79; ops. mgr. COHU, Inc., 1979-82; chief operating officer Helle Engr., Inc., 1982; atty. Hubka & Hubka, 1982—; adj. prof. Western State U. Coll. Law, 1983; admitted to Calif. bar. Served with U.S. Army, 1953-55. Recipient Outstanding Alumnus award Lincoln High Sch., Vincennes, 1973; cert. of appreciation Jet Propulsion Lab., Space Sci. Div., 1965. Mem. Am. Bar Assn., San Diego County Bar Assn., Am. Trial Lawyers Assn., Am. Electronics Assn., Western State U. Alumni Assn. (dir.). Home: Poway CA 92064 Office: 5837 El Cajon Blvd San Diego CA 92115

ALLEN, WILLIAM RICHARD, economist; b. Eldorado, Ill., Apr. 3, 1924; s. Oliver Boyd and Justa Lee (Wingo) A.; A.B., Cornell Coll., Iowa, 1948; Ph.D., Duke U., 1953; m. Frances Lorraine Swoboda, Aug. 15, 1948; children—Janet Elizabeth, Sandra Lee. Faculty, Washington U., St. Louis, 1951-52; faculty UCLA, 1952—, prof., 1963—; vis. prof. Northwestern U., 1952, U. Wis., 1964, U. Mich., 1965, So. Ill. U., 1969, Tex. A. and M. U., 1971-73; cons. Dept. Commerce, 1962; v.p. Found. Research in Econs. and Edn., 1971-73; pres. Internat. Inst. Econ. Research, 1974—; radio and TV commentator. Served with USAAF, 1943-46. Social Sci. Research Council grantee, 1950-51, 62; Ford Found. grantee, 1958-59, 72-74; NSF grantee, 1965-66; Earhart Found. grantee, 1972, 74-75. Mem. Western Econ. Soc. (pres. 1970-71), So. Econ. Soc. (v.p. 1978-79), History of Econs. Soc. (v.p. 1974-75), Phi Beta Kappa. Author: (with others) Foreign Trade and Finance, 1959, Essays in Economic Thought, 1960, University Economics, 3d edit., 1972, Exchange and Production, 3d edit., 1983; International Trade Theory, 1965; Midnight Economist, 1982; mem. adv. bd. History of Polit. Economy, 1969-83, Social Sci. Quar., 1975—; contbr. articles to profl. jours. Home: 11809 Allaseba Dr Los Angeles CA 90066

ALLEN, WILLIAM THOMAS, ins. exec.; b. Kellerton, Iowa, June 4, 1935; s. Albert Johnson and Rohma (Jackson) A.; B.S.C., U. Iowa, 1957; M.S., LaVerne Coll., 1977; grad. Command and Gen. Staff Coll., 1973, Indsl. Coll. Armed Forces, 1975; m. Jan Meisels, Mar. 14, 1980; children—Tami Lynette, William Lawrence. With N.Y. Life Ins. Co., 1957; with Bankers Life Ins. Co., various locations, 1958—, regional claims mgr., 1967-75, regional dir. group claims, Woodland Hills, Calif., 1975—; v.p., dir. HSA Los Angeles County Inc., 1978-81. Served to lt. Inf., U.S. Army, 1957-58. Recipient Civic award City of Redondo Beach, 1978. Mem. Los Angeles Life and Accident Claim Assn. (pres. 1972), Res. Officers Assn. (pres. 1972), 63d Inf. Div. Assn. (pres. 1972), Health Ins. Assn. Am. (state council), Life Mgmt. Inst. Soc. So. Calif. Methodist. Club: Lake Lindero Country. Office: 21031 Ventural Blvd Woodland Hills CA 91364

ALLENBRAND, ROBERT LEROY, ret. pub. edn. ofcl.; b. Wilkie, Sask., Can., May 2, 1917; s. Leroy Elsworth and Amy Catherine (Cline) A.; came to U.S., 1959, naturalized, 1971; certificate in Religious Edn., Alta Bible Inst., 1940; B.A., Warner Pacific Coll., 1961; M.Ed., Oreg. State U., 1963; m. Ida Maier, Nov. 5, 1946; children—James Walter, Robert Wayne, Patricia Dawn, Marvin John. Lay ch. worker Ch. of God, Paradise Valley, Alta., Can., 1946-49, Chilliwack, B.C., Can., 1949-52; salesman Eaton's of Can., Chilliwack, B.C., 1953-59; psychometrist Portland (Oreg.) Pub. Schs., 1965-70; evaluation and research specialist, coordinator edn. goals devel. project Multnomah County (Oreg.) Edn. Service Dist., 1970-80; cons. work release program Chilliwack, 1953-55. Mem. Am. Personnel and Guidance Assn., Am. Edn. Research Assn., NEA. Democrat. Author stories and articles for children's ch. lit. Home: 2605 SE 48th Ave Portland OR 97206

ALLEY, HAROLD PUGMIRE, weed scientist, educator; b. Cokeville, Wyo., Mar. 26, 1924; s. Willis David and Della Young (Pugmire) A.; B.S. in Agronomy, U. Wyo., 1949, M.S., 1955; Ph.D. in Bot. Sci., Colo. State U., 1965; m. Nadra Jeanne Dayton, June 22, 1946; children—Eva Lynette, Willis David. Tchr. vocat. agr. coach La Grange (Wyo.) High Sch., 1949-55; mem. faculty U. Wyo., Laramie, 1955—, prof. weed sci., 1966—, extension weed scientist, 1960—. Served with AUS, 1942-46. Recipient George Humphrey award U. Wyo., 1980. Mem. Weed Sci. Soc. Am. (hon. mem.; Outstanding Extension Worker award 1975), AAAS, Western Soc. Weed Sci. Mormon. Club: Elks. Author research papers in field. Home: 1121 Reynolds St Laramie WY 82070 Office: Plant Sci Div Univ Wyo Laramie WY 82071

ALLIES, VICTORIA ROSSINI, electronics development consultant, chemical engineer; b. Southington, Conn., May 27, 1950; d. Leon and Lillian (Wanagus) Rossini; m. James M. McCarron, June 18, 1980; stepchildren—James Roy, Dolores, Lynn. Student Middlebury Coll., 1968-70; B.A. with honors, U. Conn., 1972, M.S., 1979; M.B.A., U. Phoenix, 1980. Adhesive chemist Loctite Corp., Newington, Conn., 1972-76, adhesives engr., 1976-78; market devel. mgr. laminated materials dept. Gen. Electric, Coshocton, Ohio, 1978-79; chem. process engr. ITT-Courier Terminal Systems, Inc., Tempe, Ariz., 1979-80; sr. chem. process engr., environ. engring. supr. Digital Equipment Corp., Tempe, 1980-82; pres. Tng. 'n' Tech., Inc., Tempe, 1982—; pub., owner TNT Press, 1983—; sec.-treas. MCW Assocs., Inc., 1983—; instr. chemistry Maricopa Community Coll., Phoenix 1981—. Mem. Am. Chem. Soc., Ariz. Printed Circuit Bd. Assn., Soc. Women Engrs. Patentee on temporary bonding adhesives. Home: 11455 S Half Moon Dr Phoenix AZ 85044 Office: 815 S Hohokam Dr Tempe AZ 85281

ALLINA, EDWARD FRANCIS, health care executive; b. St. Louis, June 27, 1952; s. Stanley and Gerry (Francis) A. B.S.E.E., Devry Inst., 1976. With Gen. Electric Med. Systems, San Diego, 1976-80; Western regional mgr. Medtronics Med. Data Div., San Diego, 1980—. Recipient 12 profl. awards Gen. Electric, others. Mem. Field Service Mgrs. Assn., IEEE, Am. Water Ski Assn. Club: San Diego Mission Bay Boat and Ski. Patentee in field. Home: 7110 Barker Way San Diego CA 92119 Office: 2550 N 5th Ave San Diego CA 92109

ALLING, WILLIAM RENNIE, manufacturing company executive; b. Lynbrook, N.Y., Aug. 4, 1940, s. Howard and Hazel Mae (Rennie) A.; m. Kathryn Mary Gordon, Aug. 19, 1957; children—Aaron, Adam, Diane. Nat. mktg. mgr. Singer Co., Sunnyvale, Calif., 1969-72; dir. sales and bus. devel. Lear Cos., Reno, 1973-74; v.p., gen. mgr. Luminoptics div. Universal Mfg. Corp., San Ramon, Calif., 1974—. Deacon, All Saints Lutheran Ch., Danville, Calif. Served with USAF, 1957-61. Mem. Illuminating Engring. Soc. Office: 12903 C Alcosta Blvd San Ramon CA 94526

ALLISON, WILLIAM ANDREW, civil engr.; b. Galesburg, Ill., Feb. 3, 1919; s. Raymond Andrew and Ruth Madora (Dunsworth) A.; B.C.E., Oreg. State U., 1946; m. Clara Loretta Weisgerber, Oct. 7, 1941; children—Donald, Judith, David, Jerry, Richard, Susan, William Andrew. With U.S. Army Corps Engrs., 1941-46, 46-64; commd. 2d lt., 1941, advanced through grades to lt. col., 1952; ret., 1964; constrn. engr. Boyle Engring., Santa Ana, Calif., 1964-71; claims engr., dist. engr. Aviation div. Alaska Dept. Transp., Anchorage, 1971-77, chief constrn. engr., 1977-81, chief design engr., 1981, chief engr., 1981—; dir. Allison Products, Inc., McMinnville, Oreg. Decorated Bronze Star. Registered profl. engr., Alaska, Oreg., Calif. Fellow ASCE (specifications com. constrn. div.); mem. Soc. Am. Mil. Engrs. Roman Catholic (chmn. ch. bldg. com. 1977—). Home: 3131 W 100th Ave Anchorage AK 99502 Office: Pouch 6900 Anchorage AK 99502

ALLISON-HATCH, TIMOTHY WHITING, educator; b. Mpls., July 22, 1948; s. Francis Whiting and Augustine Pardee (Shaw) H.; B.A. in History, Occidental Coll., 1971; postgrad. Brandeis U., 1973; M.A. in Teaching, Northwestern U., 1978; m. Susan Allison. Vol., Peace Corps, 1974-77; tchr. Center for Self-Directed Learning, New Trier High Sch E., Winnetka, Ill., 1977-78; tchr., chmn. social sci. dept. Mayfield Sr. Sch., Pasadena, Calif., 1978—; mem. acad. services com. Calif. Assn. Ind. Schs. Coe fellow, 1980. Mem. Nat. Council Social Studies (religion in schs. adv. com.), Calif. Council Social Studies, Assn. Supervision and Curriculum Devel. Democrat. Mennonite. Club: Foothill Cycle. Home: 231 S Catalina Ave Apt 1 Pasadena CA 91106 Office: 500 Bellefontaine St Pasadena CA 91105

ALLNUTT, FRANKLIN LLOYD, publisher, TV producer, writer; b. Peoria, Ill., Apr. 16, 1940; s. William Lloyd and Gertrude Gwendolyn (Cook) A.; B.A. in Radio, TV and Film, U. Denver, 1965; m. Ruth Ann Cutler, Mar. 30, 1967; children—Garrett Franklin, Theodore William, Lara Ruth. Public relations mgr. WED (Walt Disney) Enterprises, Inc., Burbank, Calif., and Denver, 1962-69; owner, mgr. Allnutt Advt., Newport Beach, Calif., also Denver, 1969—; pres. Christian Resource Communications, Inc., Orange, Calif., 1976-77; gen. mgr. Here's Life Pubs., Inc., San Bernardino, Calif., 1977-79; exec. dir. Charles E. Blair Found., Denver, 1980-81; pres. Frank Allnutt Co., 1983—; writer; books include: Kissinger: Man of Destiny, 1975; After the Omen, 1976; The Force of Star Wars, 1977; (novel) The Peacemaker, 1977; Infinite Encounters, 1978; In Search of a Superman, 1979; (with Josef Korbel) In My Enemy's Camp, 1976; (with Bill Bright) A Movement of Miracles, 1977, The Holy Spirit, 1980; (with John Galvin) Salvation for a Doomed Zoomie, 1983; Unlocking the Mystery of the Force, 1983. Served with USNR, 1958-61. Office: Box 879 Evergreen CO 80439

ALLRED, MYRLE TAYLOR, educational travel executive; b. Salina, Utah, Jan. 26, 1945; d. Vearl D. and Nita (Pierce) Taylor; m. Sherral Jay Allred, Sept. 2, 1967; children—Kelly Jay, Anna Marie, Michael Reed. A.S., So. Utah State Coll., 1965; B.S. in Bus. Edn., U. Utah, 1967. Dir. admissions Fgn. Study League, Salt Lake City, 1967-72; dir., stockholder Internat. Consortium of Edn., Salt Lake City, 1972-80; v.p., corp. sec. Am. Internat. Cultural Heritage, Salt Lake City, 1980—. Pres. Stake Young Women; tchrs. aide West Jordan Elem. Sch.; leader Cub Scouts; mem. West Jordan City Community Devel. Council; former mem. campaign com. West Jordan City Mayor; past mem. adv. council Westvale Elem. Sch. Mormon. Author: American International Cultural Heritage Handbook, 1981. Home: 7480 S 2540 W West Jordan City UT 84084 Office: 302 W 5400 S 108 Salt Lake City UT 84107

ALLRED, SHERMAN B., civil engr.; b. Worland, Wyo., Feb. 7, 1943; s. Howard Zeller and Shirley Mae (Shulze) A.; student Sheridan Coll., 1961, Air Force Acad., 1963, Utah State U., 1964-65; B.S. in Edn., Chadron State Coll., 1970; m. Rebecca Gwendolyn Straight, Mar. 11, 1966; children—Enoch Travis, Eric Troy. Engring. technician III, Wyo. Hwy. Dept., 1963-68; tchr. high sch., Manderson, Wyo., 1970-72, Ten Sleep, Wyo., 1973-76; surveyor, engr. John W. Donnell Assos., Worland, Wyo., 1976—. Mem. Ten Sleep Vol. Fire Dept.; scoutmaster Boy Scouts Am. Served with USAF, 1962-63. Mem. Profl. Land Surveyors Wyo. (charter; dir.), Wyo. Cons. Engrs. and Surveyors, Am. Congress Surveying and Mapping. Republican. Mem. Ch. Jesus Christ of Latter-day Saints. Home: PO Box 201 102S 6th St Basin WY 82410 Office: PO Box 638 1701 Big Horn Ave Worland WY 82401

ALLSHOUSE, ROBERT J., state senator, life ins. underwriter; b. Cambridge, Ohio, Oct. 9, 1918; student Ohio State U., 1939-40; m. Joan Allshouse; children—Dan, Tana. Life ins. underwriter Minn. Mutual Life Ins. Co.; mem. Aurora City (Colo.) Council, 1967-71; mem. Colo. Senate, 1972—, vice chmn. edn. com. 52d Gen. Assembly. pres. Aurora Parks Bd.; mem. Met. Water Study and Annexation Boundary Commn. Served with U.S. Army, 1941-45. Republican. Lutheran. Clubs: Jaycees (past pres.), Optimist, Sertoma. Office: 84 A Nome Way Aurora CO 80012*

ALMARAZ, JAMES WILLIAM, optometrist; b. Chgo., Mar. 24, 1950; s. William Daniel and Shirley Lenore (Johnson) A.; m. Joyce Jean Straatman, Dec., 1971; children—Brian, Amy. A.A. in Aviation Tech., So. Ill. U., 1970, B.S. in Biology, 1974; B.S. in Optometry, So. Calif. Coll. Optometry, 1978, O.D., 1978. Lic. optometrist, Calif. Assoc. Dr. A. I. Stolper O.D., Oxnard, Calif., 1978-79; practice optometry, Big Bear Lake, Calif., 1980—. Pres. bd. dirs. Big Bear Valley Guidance Ctr. Recipient Good Samaritan award Tri-Counties Optometric Soc., 1979. Mem. Am. Optometric Assn., Calif. Optometric Assn., Orange Belt Optometric Soc., Coll. Optometrists in Vision Devel. Club: Lions (hon.) Big Bear Lake. Office: PO Box 2820 Big Bear Lake CA 92315

ALMAZAN, MIRANTE AISON, art director; b. Philippines, Sept. 3, 1951; came to U.S., 1973; s. Pablo S. Almazan and Irene Aison; A.F.A., Feati U., 1973, B.F.A., 1976. Art dir. Entertainment Rev., San Francisco, 1974-76, TL Enterprises, Agoura, Calif., 1976—. Recipient Best in Field award Western Publs. Assn., 1978. Home: 243 E Wilbur Rd 105 Thousand Oaks CA 91360 Office: 29901 Agoura Rd Agoura CA 91301

ALMER, EUGENE RICHARD, psychiatrist; b. Tuttle, N.D., Aug. 28, 1932; s. Daniel and Mary (Maier); M.D., Kans. U., 1958; m. Elizabeth Brandon; children—Shelley, Courtney. Intern, St. Luke's Hosp., Kansas City, Mo., 1958-59; resident Nebr. Psychiat. Inst., Omaha, 1959-61; sr. asst. resident Henry Phipps Clinic, Balt., 1963-64, asst. psychiatrist out patient dept., 1964-65, psychiatrist, 1965-66, supr. Phipps Afternoon Clinic, 1964-66; clin. psychiat. cons. Ostler Med. Clin. Adult Evaluation Clinic, Johns Hopkins Hosp., Balt., 1964-66; cons. forensic psychiatry

Crownsville (Md.) State Hosp., 1964-65; psychiat. cons., supervising psychiatrist Spring Grove State Hosp., Cantonsville, Md., 1965-66; practice medicine specializing in psychiatry, Phoenix, 1966—; med. dir. Narcotics Addiction Rehab. Act, St. Joseph's Hosp., Phoenix, 1969-71; staff Good Samaritan, Camelback hosps., Phoenix, 1966—; instr. psychiatry Johns Hopkins, Balt., 1964-66. Served to capt. M.C., U.S. Army, 1961-63. Office: 7110 E McDonald Dr Suite B-1 Scottsdale AZ 85253

ALMGREN, HOWARD HANS, san. engr.; b. Chgo., May 1, 1938; s. Hans and Edna (Risberg) A.; m. Jeanette Elizabeth Treat, Sept. 30, 1972. B.S. with distinction in Civil Engring., Northwestern U., 1961; M.S. in San. Engring., U. Calif.-Berkeley, 1962, Ph.D. in Engring., 1966. Registered profl. engr., Calif., Ariz., Hawaii; diplomate Am. Acad. Environ. Engrs. Project engr. U. Calif.-Berkeley, 1963-66; postgrad. research fellow Norwegian Govt., project engr. Norwegian Inst. Water Research, Oslo, 1966-69; project engr. Santee County Water Dist., Santee, Calif., 1969-72; cons. Govt. of Singapore, 1972-73; sr. san. engr. Boyle Engring. Corp., Newport Beach, Calif., 1973-74; cons. san. engr. in pvt. practice, La Jolla, Calif., 1974-80; prin. engr. Neste, Brudin & Stone, Inc., San Diego, 1980—; lectr. San Diego State U., 1974-75. Mem. ASCE, Am. Water Works Assn., Water Pollution Control Fedn., Am. Pub. Works Assn., Sigma Xi, Tau Beta Pi, Chi Epsilon. Home: 2075 Caminito Circulo Sur La Jolla CA 92037 Office: 10920 Via Frontera San Diego CA 92128

ALPAUGH, PATRICIA KAY, psychologist, educator; b. Pomona, Calif., May 3, 1947; d. John William and Betty Beatrice (Rothrock) Haines. B.A., Occidental Coll., 1969; M.A., U. So. Calif., 1975, Ph.D., 1977. Probation officer Marion County (Ind.) Juvenile Ct., Indpls., 1970-71; vol. coordinator Hathaway Home for Children, Los Angeles, 1971-73; ednl. therapist, psychol. asst. Learning Center, Arcadia, Calif., 1973; counselor Arcadia Free Clinic, 1973-77; psychology trainee Andrus Gerontology Center Clinic, U. So. Calif., Los Angeles, 1973-76, psychology intern, 1974-78, dir. peer counseling program, adult counseling ctr., 1976-78; psychology intern Ingleside (Calif.) Mental Health Ctr., 1976-77; pvt. practice marriage and family counseling, Pasadena, Calif., 1977—, clin. psychologist, 1979—; asst. prof. Fuller Theol. Sem. Mem. Am. Psychol. Assn., Gerontol. Soc., Calif. State Psychol. Assn., Los Angeles Psychol. Assn. Contbr. articles to profl. jours. Office: 1730 Huntington Dr Suite 202A S Pasadena CA 91030

ALPER, THEODORE JOSEPH, ins. exec.; b. Chgo., July 24, 1945; s. Harold Morris and Clara Bernice (LaPidus) A.; A.A., City Coll. of San Francisco, 1966; m. Laurie Susan Sigrand, Oct. 29, 1967; children—Jennifer Lynn, Jason Daniel. Sales merchandiser Standard Fruit & S.S., Co., San Francisco, 1969-71; dist. sales agent Prudential Ins. Co., San Francisco, 1971-73, mgr., Menlo Park, Calif., 1973-77; pres. Diablo Mortgage Ins. Assos., Danville, Calif., 1977—, Diablo Mortgage Assn. Served with USAF, 1967-68. Elected to Western Leaders Roundtable, Prudential Ins. Co., 1972. Mem. Life Underwriters Assn., Mt. Diablo Assn. Million Dollar Roundtable. Mem. Temple Isaiah, Lafayette, Calif. Home: 4103 Sugar Maple Dr Danville CA 94526 Office: PO Box 575 San Ramon CA 94583

ALPERIN, JEFFREY PETER, advertising executive; b. N.Y.C., Oct. 2, 1953; s. Milton and Phyllis Elaine (Seretean) A.; m. Bernardine Brandis, Mar. 27, 1982. B.A. in Psychology, Syracuse U., 1975; M.B.A., U. So. Calif., 1978. Asst. buyer Abraham and Strauss, Bklyn., 1975-76; account exec. Grey Advt., Inc., Los Angeles, 1979-81, sr. account exec., 1981, account supr., 1981-83, v.p., account supr., 1983—. Mem. Advt. Club Los Angeles, Beta Gamma Sigma; U. So Calif. Alumni Assn., M.B.A. Assn. Office: Grey Advt Inc 3435 Wilshire Blvd Suite 5 Los Angeles CA 90010

ALPERIN, MORTON, aero. research dir.; b. N.Y.C., June 19, 1918; s. Simon and Evelyn (Rose) A.; M.S., Calif. Inst. Tech., 1947, Ph.D., 1950; m. Elayne Patricia Bogen-Fisher, Nov. 2, 1974; children—Terry Michael, James Jeffrey. Mem. sci. advisory bd. U.S. Air Force, Washington, 1944-50, dir. advanced studies Office Sci. Research, Pasadena, Calif., 1950-56; aero. cons., La Canada, Calif., 1956-67; pres., tech. dir. Flight Dynamics Research Corp., Van Nuys, Calif., 1967—. Editor: Vistas in Astronautics, vol. 1, 1958, vol. 2, 1959; contbr. articles to tech. publs.; patentee in field. Home: 6000 Lockhurst Dr Woodland Hills CA 91367

ALPERN, HARVEY L., cardiologist; b. Los Angeles, June 1, 1938; s. Sander and Rose A.; B.A., Pomona Coll., 1960; m. Barbara; 1 son, David. M.D., U. So. Calif., 1964. Diplomate Am. Bd. Internal Medicine, Am. Bd. Cardiovascular Disease. Intern, Cedars of Lebanon Hosp., Los Angeles, 1964-65; resident in internal medicine and cardiology, Cedars-Sinai Hosp., Los Angeles, 1965-68; fellow in cardiology, St. George's Hosp., London, 1968-69; practice medicine specializing in cardiology and internal medicine, Los Angeles, 1969—; asst. clin. prof. medicine UCLA; sec. dept. medicine Cedars-Sinai Med. Center, 1978, now clin. chief Cardiac rehab.; chief of staff Century City Hosp., 1979-81. Bds. dirs. Los Angeles Heart Assn., 1974-76, Profl. Standards Rev. Orgn. Area XXV, 1978-81. Fellow Am. Coll. Cardiology, Am. Heart Assn (council on clin. cardiology); mem. AMA, Calif. Med. Assn., Los Angeles County Med. Assn. (pres. Beverly Hills dist. 1982-83), Los Angeles Soc. Internal Medicine, Los Angeles Cardiac Soc., Los Angeles County Heart Assn. Contbr. articles on cardiology to profl. publs. Office: 2080 Century Park E Los Angeles CA 90067

ALPERS, JOHN HARDESTY, JR., air force officer; b. Richmond, Va., Sept. 7, 1939; s. John Hardesty and Laura Elizabeth (Gaylor) A.; m. Sharon Kay Kurrle, May 1, 1971; 1 son, John Hardesty III. B.S., U. Colo., 1963; M.B.A., InterAm. U., 1969; postgrad. USAF Squadron Officers Sch., 1968-69, USAF Command and Staff Coll., 1976-78, USAF Air War Coll., 1978-79. Commd. 2d lt. U.S. Air Force, 1964, advanced through grades to lt. col., 1979; SAC B-52 navigator, P.R., 1967-70; squadron weapon systems officer Ubon RTAFB, Thailand, 1970-71, radar strike officer Linebacker II strike plans officer, 1972; prisoner of war, Hanoi, 1972-73; asst. wing weapons officer Seymour-Johnson AFB, N.C., 1971-72, wing command post officer, controller, 1973-74; asst. prof. aerospace studies AFROTC, U. Ariz., Tucson, 1974-78; asst. div. chief aviation sci. USAF Acad., Colorado Springs, 1978-79, spl. asst. to commandant, 1979-80, dep. div. chief plans, policy and standardization/evaluation, 1980-83; ret., 1983; lectr. in field. Served with USCG, 1961-63. Decorated D.F.C. (2), Bronze Star, Air Medal, Air Force Commendation medal, Purple Heart (2). Mem. Air Force Assn., U.S. Strategic Inst., Red River Valley Fighter Pilots Assn., Arnold Air Soc., Nam-POWS, Inc., Scabbard and Blade, Pi Kappa Alpha. Republican. Address: Overlook Ln Boulder Heights Boulder CO 80302

ALPERS, W. FRANK, baritone; b. Los Angeles, Apr. 10, 1924; s. Benjamin Francis and Lora Audrey (Cipson) A.; m. Roberta Vern Johns, Dec. 17, 1948; children—Sharon Vern, Debra Lynne. Student Los Angeles City Coll., 1941-42, 46-47, Art Center Sch., 1947-48, Ohio U., 1943, Calif. State U.-Los Angeles, 1950-52, Mt. San Antonio Coll., 1955-56. Soloist, Ralph Carmichael Singers, 1950-60; soloist, Laymen Singers, 1947—, Roger Wagner Chorale, 1955-58, Old Fashioned Revival Hour, 1950-60, Haven of Rest Radio, 1969-76, The King is Coming telecast, What's Your Question telecast, Teaching the Bible radio broadcast World Phophetic Ministry, Colton, Calif., 1976—; choral dir. Baptist chs., Greater Los Angeles area, 1947-77. Served with U.S. Army, 1943-46; ETO. Named Best Male Vocalist, Nat. Evang. Film Found., 1972. Mem. Am. Fedn. TV and Radio Artists, Am. Guild Mus. Artists. Republican. Baptist. Club: Kiwanis. Home: 244 S Wilbur Ave Covina CA 91724 Office: PO Drawer 907 Colton CA 92324

ALPERSTEIN, ARNOLD, lawyer; b. N.Y.C., Sept. 28, 1925; s. Herman and Ray A.; LL.B., U. Mo., 1950; children from previous marriage—Donald Wayne, Ellen Sue. Admitted to Colo. bar, 1951, U.S. Supreme Ct., 1965; atty. Nat. Farmers Union, 1950-52, Anti Defamation League, 1953; mem. firm Alperstein, Alperstein and Forman, P.C. and predecessors, Denver, 1953—; adj. lectr. U. Denver Coll. Law; guest lectr. Colo. Trial Lawyers Assn. Mem. Democratic Nat. Com., 1968-76, exec. com., 1972-76; dep. dist. atty. 1st Judical Dist. Colo., 1956-60. Served with AUS, 1943-46. Decorated Air medal. Fellow Colo. Bar Found.; mem. Am., 1st Jud. Dist. (past pres.), Colo. (gov., exec. com.), Denver bar assns., Colo. State Ofcls. Compensation Commn. (chmn. 1981), Colo. Trial Lawyers Assn., Am. Trial Lawyers' Assn., Internat. Soc. Barristers, Am. Judicature Soc. Jewish. Club: Denver Athletic. Office: 155 S Madison St #330 Denver CO 80209

ALPERT, LINDA M., nurse, administrator; b. Boston, Jan. 25, 1941; d. Sidney M. and Blanche (Kaplan) Omansky.; B.S.N., U. Ariz., 1963; children—Sandra, Jeffrey. Staff nurse Handmaker Nursing Home, 1964; staff relief nurse Tucson Med. Center, 1967-68, nurse recruiter, 1968-70, head nurse cystic fibrosis center, 1970-76, head nurse, dir. chest clinic and allergy clinic, 1976-82; adminstr., dir. Pulmonary Care Center, Good Samaritan Med. Center, Phoenix, 1982—; program coordinator Ariz. Chest Symposium, 1971-82; mem. adv. com. Sch. Respiratory Therapy, Pima Community Coll., 1979—. Bd. dirs. Tucson chpt. Cystic Fibrosis Found., 1971-82, Parents Asthma Network. Mem. Ariz. Nurses in Mgmt., Am. Thoracic Soc., Ariz. Thoracic Soc., Continuity of Care Assn. (bd. dirs.), Jewish Bus. and Profl. Women (bd. dirs.), Sigma Theta Tau. Jewish. Club: Soroptimist. Home: 5900 E Thomas Rd Apt E225 Scottsdale AZ 85251 Office: 1111 E McDowell Rd Phoenix AZ 85006

ALPERT, SUMNER, aerospace company executive; b. Boston, Sept. 24, 1922; s. Max L. and Flora (Effross) A.; m. Esther Kabatznick, June 6, 1944; children—David H., Dan J., Theodore S. B.S., Northeastern U., 1944; M.S., Case Inst. Tech., 1949; M.B.A., San Diego State U., 1968. Registered profl. engr., Calif. Aero. research scientist NASA Lewis Lab., Cleve., 1944-51; mgr. aerospace and indsl. products Solar Turbines, Inc., San Diego, 1951-69; v.p. mktg. and contracts Aeronca, Inc., Middletown, Ohio, 1969-72; pres. Murdock div. CCI Corp., Irving, Tex., 1972-73, v.p. turbo products Marquardt div., Van Nuys, Calif., 1973-75; v.p., gen. mgr. rotary compressor div. Chgo. Pneumatic Tool Co., Franklin, Pa., 1975-80; dir. strategic planning HR Textron Inc., Valencia, Calif., 1980—. Dir., chmn. by-laws com. Calif. Democratic Council, editor bull., 1956-62. Fellow ASME; mem. AIAA, Soc. Automotive Engrs., Planning Execs. Inst., Mensa. Home: 15833 Castlewoods Dr Sherman Oaks CA 91403 Office: HR Textron Inc 25200 W Rye Canyon Rd Valencia CA 91355

ALQUIST, ALFRED E., state senator; b. Memphis; m. Mai Alquist; 1 son, Alan. Educated Southwestern U. Former mem. Calif. State Assembly; mem. Calif. State Senate, 1966—, chmn. fin. com., mem. govt. orgn. and energy and pub. utilities coms. Candidate for lt. gov. State of Calif., 1970; mem. Little Hoover Commn.; mem. Calif. Seismic Safety Commn., Com. Sci. and Tech.; trustee Good Samaritan Hosp. Served with Air-Sea Emergency Rescue Service, USAAF, 1942-44. Mem. Nat. Conf. State Legislators, Am. Legion. Democrat. Clubs: Commonwealth, Elks. Home: 777 N 1st St Apt 245 San Jose CA 95112 Office: California State Senate Sacramento CA 95814*

ALSADI, AKEEL, economist, consultant; b. Baghdad, Iraq, Apr. 23, 1936; came to U.S., 1966; s. Hany Saeed and Nouria Jasim (Altimimi) A.; m. Maria Rosillo Alvarez de Toledo, Feb. 18, 1973. B.A. with honors in Bus. and Econs., U. Baghdad, 1962; M.A. summa cum laude in Econs., U. So. Calif., 1969, Ph.D., 1972. Cert. chief adminstrv. officer, Calif. Asst. adminstr. Civil Service Commn., Baghdad, 1958-62; lectr. Sch. Econ. and Bus., U. Baghdad, 1962-67, also lectr. dept. econs. and stats.; lectr. U. So. Calif., Los Angeles, 1969-71; asst. prof. San Diego State U., 1971; cons. World Bank, Washington, 1972-73, economist, 1973-80; pvt. practice cons. economist, Monterey, Calif., 1980-83; chief tech. adviser on planning and agrl. policy UNDP/FAO, Islamabad, Pakistan, 1983—; lectr. in field Mem. Am. Econ. Assn., Western Econ. Assn., Assn. for Comparative Econ. Studies, U. So. Calif. Nation's Capital Alumni Club, Phi Beta Kappa, Omicron Delta Epsilon. Author: Applications of Statistics, 1965; contbr. articles in field to profl. jours. Home and Office: 984 Portola Dr Monterey CA 93940

ALSTON, LELA RUTH, educator, state senator; b. Phoenix, June 26, 1942; d. Virgil Lee and Frances Mae (Koonse) Mulkey; B.S., U. Ariz., 1967; M.S., Ariz. State U., 1971; children—Brenda, Charles. Tchr., Wakefield Jr. High Sch., 1967-68, West Phoenix High Sch., 1968—; mem. Ariz. Senate, 1977—. Mem. NEA, Am. Home Econs. Assn., Am. Vocat. Assn. Office: Capitol Bldg Senate Wing Phoenix AZ 85007

ALTAMIRANO, BEN D., merchant, ins. agt., state senator; b. Silver City, N.Mex., Oct. 17, 1930; s. Ramon and Eloisa P. (Davila) A.; student Western N.Mex. U.; m. Nina Melendrez, July 24, 1949; children—Yolanda, Benjamin, Paul. Owner, operator Benny's Market Baskets, Silver City, 1949-78, C.H. Pennington Fashions, 1971—; ins. agt. TBA Ins. Co., Dallas, Coastal States Ins. Co., Atlanta; founder, chmn. bd. Silver City Savs. & Loan Assn.; mem. N.Mex. Senate, 1970—. Mem. City Council Silver City; county commr. Served with U.S. Army, 1946-48. Democrat. Roman Catholic. Office: 201 Bullard St Silver City NM 88061*

ALTAMURA, MICHAEL VICTOR, physician; b. Bklyn., Sept. 28, 1923; s. Frank and Theresa (Inganamorte) A.; B.S., L.I. U., 1949; M.A., Columbia U., 1951; D.O., Kirksville Coll., 1961; M.D., Calif. Coll. Medicine, 1962; m. Emily Catherine Wandell, Sept. 21, 1948; children—Michael Victor, Robert Frank. Intern, Los Angeles County Gen. Hosp., 1961-62; practice medicine specializing in family practice, Sunnyvale, Calif., 1962—; staff El Camino Hosp., chief family practice dept., 1972-73; preceptor family practice Stanford Sch. Medicine, 1972-73, clin. asst. prof., 1974-81, clin. assoc. prof., 1982—; preceptor family practice Davis (Calif.) Sch. Medicine, 1974-75. Served to 1st lt. AUS, 1942-45, 51-53; ETO. Recipient Order of Golden Sword, Am. Cancer Soc., 1973. Diplomate Am. Bd. Family Practice. Fellow Am. Acad. Family Physicians (pres. Santa Clara County chpt. 1972-73), Royal Soc. Health, Am. Geriatric Soc.; mem. AMA, Calif., Santa Clara County socs., Internat. Platform Assn. Republican. Lutheran. Author: (with Mary Falconer and Helen Behnke) Aging Patients: A Guide for Their Care. physician; b. Bklyn., Sept. 28, 1923; s. Frank and Theresa (Inganamorte) A.; B.S., L.I. U., 1949; M.A., Columbia U., 1951; D.O., Kirksville Coll., 1961; M.D., Calif. Coll. Medicine, 1962; m. Emily Catherine Wandell, Sept. 21, 1948; children—Michael Victor, Robert Frank. Intern, Los Angeles County Gen. Hosp., 1961-62; practice medicine specializing in family practice, Sunnyvale, Calif., 1962—, staff El Camino Hosp., chief family practice dept., 1972-73; preceptor family practice Stanford Sch. Medicine, 1972-73, clin. asst. prof., 1974-81, clin. assoc. prof., 1982—; preceptor family practice Davis (Calif.) Sch. Medicine, 1974-75. Served to 1st lt. AUS, 1942-45, 51-53; ETO. Recipient Order of Golden Sword, Am. Cancer Soc., 1973. Diplomate Am. Bd. Family Practice. Fellow Am. Acad. Family Physicians (pres. Santa Clara County chpt. 1972-73), Royal Soc. Health, Am. Geriatric Soc.; mem. AMA, Calif., Santa Clara County socs., Internat. Platform Assn. Republican. Lutheran. Author: (with Mary Falconer and Helen Behnke) Aging Patients: A Guide for Their Care. Office: 500 E Remington St Sunnyvale CA 94087

ALTCHULER, DANIEL LEONARD, podiatrist; b. Los Angeles, Sept. 21, 1946; s. Soloman I. and Florence A. Altchuler; A.A., Santa Monica City Coll., 1966; B.S. in Bus. Adminstrn., Calif. State U., Long Beach, 1969; B.S. in Basic Med. Scis., Calif. Coll. Podiatric Medicine, 1973, D.P.M., 1975; m. Eileen Louise Haworth, July 27, 1970. Practice podiatric sports medicine, Santa Monica, Calif., 1978—; clin. instr. podiatric medicine Calif. Coll. Podiatric Medicine, 1978; podiatric cons. Los Angeles Naturite Track Club, 1979, Los Angeles Shaklee Track Club, 1980, Calif. Walkers, 1980, Wilts Athletic Club, 1981, Los Angeles Puma Energizer's Track Club. Fellow Am. Coll. Foot Orthopedists, Am. Acad. Podiatric Sports Medicine; mem. Am. Coll. Sports Medicine, Am. Podiatry Assn., Calif. Podiatry Assn., Los Angeles Podiatry Assn., Am. Med. Joggers Assn., Am. Chiropractic Joggers Assn., Athletics Congress of U.S., Nat. Running and Fitness Assn., U.S. Olympic Soc. Office: 1243 7th St Santa Monica CA 90401

ALTER, EDWARD THOMAS, state ofcl.; b. Glen Ridge, N.J., July 26, 1941; s. E. Irving and Norma (Fisher) A.; B.A. in Banking and Fin., U. Utah, 1966, M.B.A., 1967; m. Patricia Olsen, Mar. 21, 1975; children—Christina Lyn, Ashly Ann, Darli Lee. Sr. acct. Touche Ross & Co., 1968-72; asst. treas. U. Utah, 1972-80; treas. State of Utah, Salt Lake City, 1981—. Mem. Utah Republican Central Com., Rep. Exec. Com., 1981—. Served with U.S. Army, 1959-60. C.P.A., Calif., Utah. Mem. Am. Inst. C.P.A.s, Utah Bond Club (pres.), Utah Money Market Club. Office: 215 State Capitol Salt Lake City UT 84114

ALTER, GERALD L., corp. exec.; b. Rensselaer, Ind., Aug. 24, 1910; s. Leslie and Lettie (Willis) A.; student Bus. Coll., 1927-28; m. Margaret A. Davis, Sept. 15, 1929; children—Judith Ann (dec.), John Edward. Clk. and office mgr., 1929-35; bldg. contractor, 1936-45; real estate broker and ins. agt., 1946—; pres. Alter Realty & Ins., Leads, Inc., investments, Darpco, Inc., investments, Alter Ins. Agy., Inc., REMCO Real Estate Mgmt. Co., Alter Devel. Co.; pres. Developers & Builders. Chmn. Torrance Planning Commn. 1982-83; former bd. dirs. Harbor Area United Way. Mem. Torrance-Lomita-Carson Bd. Realtors (pres. 1978, v.p. 1980, 81), Calif. Assn. Realtors (dir. 1978-81), Nat. Assn. Realtors, Torrance C. of C. (past dir.), Am. Legion. Republican. Clubs: OX-5 (pioneer airman), Rotary. Home: 709 Madrid Ave Torrance CA 90501 Office: 2305 Torrance Blvd Torrance CA 90501

ALTFELD, MERWIN RICHARD, artist, manufacturer's representative; b. Elyria, Ohio, Sept. 19, 1913; s. Otis Charles and Kate Gertrude (Klein) A.; m. Mildred Frances Kirschbaum, June 23, 1936; children—Linda Voorsanger, Pamela Malone. B.A., Case Western Res. U., 1934; postgrad. U. So. Calif., 1966-68. Cert. tchr., Calif. One-man shows: Calif. State U., Sacramento, 1978, SUNY, Alfred, 1979, Nylander Mus., Caribou, Maine, 1979; Loyola U., New Orleans, 1980, Santa Monica Library (Calif.), 1983; group shows include: San Diego Mus., 1963, Swedish Mus., Stockholm, 1972, NAD, N.Y.C., 1972, Watercolor U.S.A., Springfield, Mass., 1973, Palm Desert Mus., Palm Springs, Calif., 1974; represented in permanent collections: Queen Mary ship, Long Beach, Calif., Brugger Collection, Los Angeles; gen. mgr. Ford's Drug Stores, Buffalo, 1940-47; owner Merwin R. Altfeld & Assocs., Los Angeles, 1948—. Big bro. Jewish Big Bros., Los Angeles, 1965-74; bd. dirs. Artists for Ednl. Action, Los Angeles, 1978-82. Recipient Am. Traditional awards, 1955; Santa Monica ann. award, 1964; Delmar ann. graphics award 1964, Westwood ann. award, 1963, Nat. Watercolor Soc. award, 1974. Mem. Los Angeles Contemporary Art Gallery, Westwood Centre of Arts (pres. 1965), Hollywood Press Club, Hollywood Media Assn. Nat. Watercolor Soc. (pres. 1972). Democrat. Jewish. Home: 18426 Wakecrest Dr Malibu CA 90265

ALTHERR, LAWANDA, hospital administrator; b. Ajo, Ariz., Jan. 27, 1926; d. Jesse Hoyt and Mayme Ellen (Amerson) Smith; m. Robert Kenneth Altherr, Aug. 5, 1946 (div.); children—Gary, Larry, Gregory, Brenda, Bryan, Robert. Assoc. in Nursing, Phoenix Coll., 1970; B.S. in Nursing, Ariz. State U., 1975; M.Vocat. Edn., U. No. Ariz., 1978. Staff nurse surg. intensive care unit Maricopa County Gen. Hosp./Maricopa Med. Center 1970-72, inservice instr. 1973-75, dir. tng. and devel. 1975—, dir. bio-medical communication dept. 1980—; mem. nursing adv. com. Ariz. State U. Mem. Nat. League Nursing, Ariz. Vocat. Assn. Home: 1307 W Thomas St Phoenix AZ 85013 Office: 2601 E Roosevelt St Phoenix AZ 85008

ALTIG, DUANE KEITH, educator; b. Mitchell, S.D., Jan. 12, 1934; s. Vern Everett and Dorothy Mae (Nellor) A.; B.S., Portland (Oreg.) State Coll., 1959; M.S. in Geography, Portland State U., 1972; m. Lucia Rodriquez, May 18, 1956; children—Luis, Julian, Juanita, Dean, Duane. Tchr., Prineville (Oreg.) Sch. Dist., 1960-67; tchr., athletic dir., coach Parkrose Sch. Dist. 3, Portland, 1967—; cons. in field. Vice pres. Oreg. Jaycees, 1964. Served with AUS, 1953-56. Mem. NEA, Assn. Supervision and Curriculum Devel., Oreg. Edn. Assn., Oreg. High Sch. Coaches Assn., Parkrose Faculty Assn., Gamma Theta Upsilon. Republican. Roman Catholic. Co-editor: Energy and Man's Environment, 4 vols., 1978; author articles, curriculum simulation games. Home: 310 NE 147th St Portland OR 97230 Office: 11717 NE Shaver St Portland OR 97220

ALTIG, WILLIAM WARD, physician; b. Denver, May 11, 1905; s. Jerome B. and Amy B. (Ward) A.; student Bible Inst. Los Angeles, 1927, U. So. Calif., 1932; M.D., Loma Linda U., 1937; m. Marie Shetler, July 19, 1935; children—Richard W., Donald W., Robert K. Intern Baroness Erlanger Hosp., Chattanooga, 1937; gen. practice medicine, San Gabriel, Calif., 1939-40, Long Beach, Calif., 1940-45, Downey, Calif., 1945-66; dir. emergency dept. Long Beach Community Hosp., 1966-73, Mercy Gen. Hosp., Santa Ana, Calif., 1973-78; clinic physician charge emergency dept. Long Beach Navy Base, 1978—. Tchr. Sch. Missionary Medicine, Los Angeles, 1958-66; organizer Christian Med. Soc., Los Angeles, 1964, Mission Clinic, Union Rescue Mission, Los Angeles, 1964. Mem. Am., Calif., Los Angeles med. assns., Emergency Room Physicians. Mem. Brethren Ch. (pres. sch. bd. Long Beach 1948-52). Home: 16400 Saybrook Ln Huntington Beach CA 92649

ALTMAN, ADELE ROSENHAIN, physician; b. Tel Aviv, Israel, June 4, 1924; came to U.S., 1933, naturalized, 1939; d. Bruno and Salla (Silberzweig) Rosenhain; B.S., U. Mich., 1944; M.D., N.Y. Med. Coll., 1949; m. Emmett Altman, Sept. 3, 1944; children—Brian R., Alan L., Karen D. Intern, Queens Gen. Hosp., N.Y.C., 1949-51; resident Hosp. for Joint Diseases, N.Y.C., 1951-52, Roosevelt Hosp., N.Y.C., 1955-57; clin. instr. radiology Downstate Med. Center, SUNY, Bklyn., 1957-61; asst. prof. radiology N.Y. Med. Coll., N.Y.C., 1961-65, asso. prof., 1965-68; asso. prof. radiology U. Okla. Health Sci. Center, Oklahoma City, 1968-78; asso. prof Dept. Radiology, U. N.Mex. Sch. Medicine, Albuquerque, 1978—. Diplomate Am. Bd. Radiology. Fellow Am. Coll. Angiology, N.Y. Acad. Medicine; mem. Am. Coll. Radiology, Am. Roentgen Ray Soc., Assn. Univ. Radiologists, Radiol. Soc. N. Am. Clubs: Hadassah, B'nai B'rith Women. Author: Radiology of the Respiratory System: A Basic Review, 1978; contbr. articles to profl. jours. Office: Dept Radiology Univ N Mex Sch of Medicine Albuquerque NM 87131

ALTMAN, DAVID, aerospace consultant; b. Paterson, N.J., Feb. 13, 1920; s. Hyman P. and Frieda (Dombroff) A.; m. Beverly Adlis, Nov. 27, 1947; children—Jody, Jan, Rick. A.B., Cornell U., 1940; Ph.D., U.

Calif.-Berkeley, 1943. Assoc. chemist U. Calif. Radiation Lab., 1943-45; chief chemist Jet Propulsion Lab., Calif. Inst. Tech., Pasadena, 1945-56; mgr. vehicle tech. lab. Aeronutronic Systems, Newport Beach, Calif., 1956-59; sr. v.p. chem. systems div., Sunnyvale, Calif., 1959-81, cons., 1981—. Home: 1670 Oak Ave Menlo Park CA 94025

ALTMAN, SHELDON, veterinarian; b. Denver, May 15, 1937; s. Sam Bernard and Bessie (Radetsky) A.; B.S. in Biol. Sci., Colo. State U., 1959, D.V.M., 1961; m. Arlene Barbara Heller, Aug. 23, 1959; children—Susan Wendy, Howard William, Eden Debra. With Newmark Animal Hosp., 1961-62, Lockhart Animal Hosp., 1964; founder, operator Universal City Pet Clinic, North Hollywood, Calif., 1965-70, merged with M.S. Animal Hosps., Inc., Burbank, 1970—, v.p., 1970—; dir. vet. research and cons. acupuncture research project, pain control unit UCLA, 1975-80; prof. Chinese medicine U. Oriental Studies Sch. Chinese Medicine; lectr. vet. acupuncture. Bd. dirs. Emek Hebrew Acad. Served with AUS, 1962-64. Recipient Disting. Service award B'nai B'rith, 1968. Mem. AVMA, So. Calif. Vet. Med. Assn., Calif. Vet. Med. Assn. (chmn. acupuncture-alternative therapies 1977—), Am. Animal Hosp. Assn., Am. Veterinarians for Israel (chpt. pres. 1972-73), Assn. Orthodox Jewish Scientists, Internat. Vet. Acupuncture Soc. (dir.), Center for Chinese Medicine, Acad. Vet. Cardiology, Acupuncture Research Inst., Colo. State U. Alumni Assn., Nat. Assn. Vet. Acupuncture (dir. research), Phi Kappa Phi, Phi Zeta, Beta Beta Beta. Jewish (pres. congregation 70-71, dir. 1964—). Author: Introduction to Acupuncture for Animals; mem. sci. adv. bd. Calif. Veterinarian. veterinarian; b. Denver, May 15, 1937; s. Sam Bernard and Bessie (Radetsky) A.; B.S. in Biol. Sci., Colo. State U., 1959, D.V.M., 1961; m. Arlene Barbara Heller, Aug. 23, 1959; children—Susan Wendy, Howard William, Eden Debra. With Newmark Animal Hosp., 1961-62, Lockhart Animal Hosp., 1964; founder, operator Universal City Pet Clinic, North Hollywood, Calif., 1965-70, merged with M.S. Animal Hosps., Inc., Burbank, 1970—, v.p., 1970—; dir. vet. research and cons. acupuncture research project, pain control unit UCLA, 1975-80; prof. Chinese medicine U. Oriental Studies Sch. Chinese Medicine; lectr. vet. acupuncture. Bd. dirs. Emek Hebrew Acad. Served with AUS, 1962-64. Recipient Disting. Service award B'nai B'rith, 1968. Mem. AVMA, So. Calif. Vet. Med. Assn., Calif. Vet. Med. Assn. (chmn. acupuncture-alternative therapies 1977—), Am. Animal Hosp. Assn., Am. Veterinarians for Israel (chpt. pres. 1972-73), Assn. Orthodox Jewish Scientists, Internat. Vet. Acupuncture Soc. (dir.), Center for Chinese Medicine, Acad. Vet. Cardiology, Acupuncture Research Inst., Colo. State U. Alumni Assn., Nat. Assn. Vet. Acupuncture (dir. research), Phi Kappa Phi, Phi Zeta, Beta Beta Beta. Jewish (pres. congregation 70-71, dir. 1964—). Author: Introduction to Acupuncture for Animals; mem. sci. adv. bd. Calif. Veterinarian. Home: 5647 Wilkinson Ave North Hollywood CA 91607 Office: 2723 W Olive St Burbank CA 91505

ALTRINGER, PAULETTE B., metallurgist; b. Salt Lake City, Jan. 28, 1948; d. Connie Paul and Orva Velda (Schultz) Bogdanow; B.Metall. Engrng. (Jackling scholar, Sterling scholar), U. Utah, 1970, M.Engring. Adminstrn., 1982. Metallurgist, U.S. Bur. Mines, Salt Lake City, 1970-73, group supr.-metallurgist, 1975—; statistician (engring.) EPA, Las Vegas, 1973-75; Congl. fellow for Dept. Interior, Am. Polit. Sci. Assn., 1982-83. Recipient Indsl. Research IR-100 award, 1981. Mem. AIME, AAAS. Contbr. articles to profl. jours. Office: US Bur Mines 729 Arapeen Dr Salt Lake City UT 84108

ALTROCK, RICHARD CHARLES, astrophysicist; b. Omaha, Dec. 20, 1940; s. Raymond John and Ada Ann (Baumann) A.; B.S. in Physics and Math., U. Nebr., 1962; Ph.D. in Astro-Geophysics, U. Colo., 1968; m. Janice Carol Reed, Mar. 23, 1963 (div. 1977); children—Craig Edward and Christopher Raymond (twins); m. 2d, Sally K. Neidig, Mar. 10, 1979; 1 dau., Kristin Ann. Research asst. U. Nebr., Lincoln, 1959-61, teaching asst., 1962; mathematician U.S. Army Engrs., Omaha, 1962; grad. asst. High Altitude Obs., Boulder, Colo., 1963-67; astrophysicist Air Force Geophysics Lab., Sacramento Peak Obs., Sunspot, N.Mex., 1967—, work unit mgr., 1976—, contract mgr., 1976—; co-investigator NASA solar optical telescope, 1981—; vis. research fellow U. Sydney (Australia), 1971-72; proposal reviewer NASA, 1978, NSF, 1980—. Bd. govs. N.Mex. Civil Liberties Union, 1974-76. Woodrow Wilson fellow, 1962-63; High Altitude Obs. fellow, 1962-63; Australian Commonwealth Sci. and Indsl. Research Orgn. travel grantee, 1971-72. Fellow AAAS; mem. Internat. Astron. Union, Am. Astron. Soc., Am. Geophys. Union, Astron. Soc. of Pacific, ACLU, Sigma Xi, Pi Mu Epsilon, Phi Beta Kappa, Delta Phi Alpha, Phi Gamma Delta. Contbr. articles to profl. jours. Home: PO Box 645 Cloudcroft NM 88317 Office: Sacramento Peak Observatory Sunspot NM 88349

ALTUS, GRACE THOMPSON, psychologist, educator; b. Santa Barbara, Calif., Jan. 6, 1924; d. James Roderick and Mary Augusta (Merriman) Thompson; m. William David Altus, Dec. 24, 1951; children—Martha Helen, Elizabeth Diane, Deborah Elaine. B.A., Santa Barbara (Calif.) State Coll., 1944; M.A., U. Calif.-Berkeley, 1947, Ph.D., 1949; postgrad. Tchrs. Coll., Columbia U., 1949. Tchr., Redlands (Calif.) Jr. High, 1944-46; sch. psychologist Santa Barbara County (Calif.) Schs., 1949-53, dir. guidance, 1953-56; sch. psychologist Goleta (Calif.) Union Sch. Dist., 1966—. Recipient Allan D. Wilson Jr. Meml. award, 1947-48. Fellow Am. Psychol. Assn., AAAS; mem. NEA, Calif. Assn. Psychologist and Psychometrists. Clubs: Channel City Women's Forum (charter mem.); Sierra; Faculty Women U. Calif., Santa Barbara (pres. 1957-58). Contbr. articles in field to profl. jours. Home: 767 Las Palmas Dr Santa Barbara CA 93110 Office: 401 N Fairview Ave Goleta CA 93117

ALVAREZ, JANET LANDIS, research co. exec.; b. Bklyn., Nov. 8, 1930; d. James N. and Lucile (Nichols) Landis; A.B., U. Calif., Berkeley, 1952; postgrad. Mass. Inst. Tech., 1953-54; m. Luis W. Alvarez, 1958; children—Donald, Helen. Researcher labs. U. Calif., 1954-65; v.p. Optical Research & Devel. Co., 1966-75, pres., 1976-81; also dir.; pres. Schwem Instruments, 1982—, also dir.; dir. Humphrey Instruments Inc., 1976-80. Bd. dirs. Nueva Day Sch., 1975—. Mem. Phi Beta Kappa, Sigma Xi. Home: 131 Southampton Ave Berkeley CA 94707 Office: 3305 Vincent Rd Pleasant Hill CA 94523

ALVAREZ, JOSEPH IGNATIUS, air force officer; b. Buckholtz, Tex., Feb. 1, 1924; s. Jesse Anton and Martha (Alonzo) A.; m. Ruby M. Welch, June 25, 1949; children—Charles, Raymond, Patrick, Jonathan, Josette. B.S., Baylor U., 1951; postgrad. U. Md., 1961-62, U. S.C., 1973; cert. tchr. Tex., Alaska, Iceland. Commd. officer U.S. Air Force, 1951, advanced through grades to lt. col., 1977; acctg. and fin. officer, Denver, 1951-61; comptroller, San Bernardino, 1962-69; acct., auditor Gen. Acctg. Office, Denver, 1970-78, acct., 1979—. Decorated A.F. Commendation medal, Bronze Star. Mem. Am. Soc. Comptrollers. Democrat. Roman Catholic. Office: 4444 AFAFC/TCRCN Denver CO 80279

ALVAREZ, LUIS W., physicist; b. San Francisco, June 13, 1911; s. Walter C. and Harriet S. (Smyth) A.; B.S., U. Chgo., 1932, M.S., 1934, Ph.D., 1936, Sc.D., 1967; Sc.D., Carnegie-Mellon U., 1968, Kenyon Coll., 1969, Notre Dame U., 1976, Ain Shams U., Cairo, 1979; m. Geraldine Smithwick, 1936; children—Walter, Jean; m. 2d, Janet L. Landis, 1958; children—Donald, Helen. Research asso., instr., asst. prof., asso. prof. U. Calif., 1936-45, prof. physics, 1945-78, prof. emeritus, 1978—, asso. dir. Lawrence Radiation Lab., 1954-59, 75-78; radar research and devel. Mass. Inst. Tech., 1940-43, Los Alamos, 1944-45; dir. Hewlett Packard Co. Recipient Collier Trophy, 1946; Medal for Merit, 1948; John Scott medal, 1953; Einstein medal, 1961; Nat. Medal of Sci., 1964; Michelson award, 1965; Nobel prize in physics, 1968; Wright prize, 1981; named Calif. Scientist of Year, 1960; named to Nat. Inventors Hall of Fame, 1978. Fellow Am. Phys. Soc. (pres. 1969); mem. Nat. Acad. Scis., Nat. Acad. Engring., Am. Philos. Soc., Am. Acad. Arts and Scis., Phi Beta Kappa, Sigma Xi; asso. mem. Institut D'Egypte. Office: Dept Physics U Calif Berkeley CA 94720

ALVAREZ, RODOLFO, sociology educator, consultant; b. San Antonio, Oct. 23, 1936; s. Ramon and Laura (Lobo) A.; m. Edna R. S. Alvarez, June 25, 1960; children—Anica, Amira. B.A., San Francisco State U., 1961; cert. European Studies, Inst. for Am. Univs., Aix-en-Provence, France, 1960; M.A., U. Wash., 1964, Ph.D., 1966. Teaching fellow U. Wash., Seattle, 1963-64; asst. prof. Yale U., New Haven, 1966-72; vis. lectr. Wesleyan U., Middletown, Conn., 1970; assoc. prof. UCLA, 1972-80, prof., 1980—, dir. Chicano Studies Research Ctr., 1972-74, founding dir. Spanish Speaking Mental Health Research Ctr., 1973-75. Pres. ACLU of So. Calif., 1980, 81; bd. dirs. Mexican Am. Legal Def. and Ednl. Fund, 1975-79; mem. adv. commn. on housing 1984 Olympic Organizing Com., 1982—; chmn. bd. dirs. Narcotics Prevention Assn., Los Angeles, 1974-77; mem. bilingual adv. com. Children's TV Workshop, N.Y.C., 1979-82; pres. Westwood (Calif.) Democratic Club, 1977-78; candidate rep. Nat. Dem. Platform Com., Washington, 1976; alt. del. Nat. Dem. Conv., N.Y.C., 1976. Served to sgt. USMC, 1954-57. Recipient citation for meritorious service for devel. of Nat. Fed. Offenders Rehab. and Research Program, State of Wash., 1967. Mem. Internat. Sociol. Honor Soc. (pres. 1976-79), Am. Sociol. Assn. (mem. council 1982—), Soc. Study of Social Problems (bd. dirs. 1982—), Pacific Sociol. Assn. (mem. council 1979-83), Marines Meml. Club. Author: Discrimination in Organizations: Using Social Indicators to Manage Social Change, 1979; Racism, Elitism, Professionalism: Barriers to Community Mental Health, 1976; mem. editorial bd. Social Sci. Quar., 1971—. Office: Dept Sociology UCLA Los Angeles CA 90024

ALVAREZ, WILLIAM ANTONIO, psychiatrist; b. Argentina, Oct. 27, 1931; s. Anastasio and Irene Isabel (Hormig) A.; came to U.S., 1957, naturalized, 1970; M.D. magna cum laude, U. Buenos Aires, 1954, postgrad., 1955. Intern, Bon Secours Hosp., Balt., 1957-58; resident psychiatry R.I. Med. Center, Howard, Spring Grove State Hosp., Catonsville, Md., Child Study Center Md., Balt., 1958-61; mem. staff Broughton Hosp., Morganton, N.C., 1961-62, Sanatorium Bellevue, Kreuzlingen, Switzerland, 1962-63; psychiatrist, researcher Ministry of Labor, Health and Housing, Georgetown, Guyana, 1963; chmn. psychiat. residents Queen's U. dept. psychiatry, Alcoholism Addiction Research Found. of Ont., Kingston, 1964-65; dir. psychiat. services V.I. Dept. Health, 1965-68; chief inpatient psychiatry VA Med. Center, Long Beach, Calif., 1968—; asst. clin prof. dept. psychiatry and human behavior U. Calif. at Irvine, 1968—; vis. prof. Faculty of Medicine, U. Hanoi (Vietnam), 1980—; chmn. V.I. Sanity Bd., 1967; bd. advisers Community Psychology Clinic, Long Beach State U., 1970—, lectr. psychology, 1972. Diplomate Am. Bd. Psychiatry and Neurology. Mem. Am. (pres. Art Assn. 1970-71, 74-75, 79-80), Canadian psychiat. assns., AMA, V.I. Med. Soc., Royal Buddhist Soc. (London), Educators to Africa Assn. (N.Y.C.), Nat. Cat Protection Soc. Mem. Ch. of Universal Brotherhood (minister). Internat. editor Erasmus, Internat. Jour. of Psychiatry and Humanism, 1966; reviewer Jour. Psychiatry in Medicine, 1971; contbr. articles profl. jours. Home: PO Box 14357 Long Beach CA 90803 Office: 5901 E 7th St Long Beach CA 90822

ALVERSON, ROBERT MADISON, computer-communications marketing executive; b. Albertville, Ala., Aug. 4, 1946; s. William Joseph and Mary Helen (Ford) A.; m. Sandra Marie Pazanin, Aug. 25, 1979. B.S. in Agrl. Engring., Purdue U., 1970; postgrad. in environ. engring. Ohio State U., 1971; M.B.A., U. Chgo., 1979. Registered engr.-in-tng., Ala.; lic. pvt. pilot. Engring. research assoc. Sperry Rand Corp., New Holland, Pa., 1970-73; product research mgr. Agrl. Equipment div. Internat. Harvester Co., Chgo., 1973-76, mgr. mktg. program devel., 1976-77, mgr. bus. research and corp. planning, 1977-78, mgr. strategy research and devel. and corp. planning, 1978-79, dir., gen. mgr. corp. advanced harvesting systems, 1979-82; mgr. mktg. installed base accounts Rolm Corp., Santa Clara, Calif., 1982—; engring./research conferee on major agrl. equipment product coms. Mem. Am. Soc. Agrl. Engrs., Am. Mgmt. Assn., Am. M.B.A. Assn., Aircraft Owners and Pilots Assn., Sigma Xi. Clubs: Chgo. Young Execs., U. Chgo. Execs., 401. Author tech. papers; patentee in field. Office: 4900 Old Ironsides Dr Santa Clara CA 95050

ALVERSON, STEVEN ROBERT, aeronautics scientist, airport planner; b. Huntington, N.Y., July 7, 1958; s. Robert W. and Marjory J. (Schweizer) A.; m. Patricia Tayeko, Nov. 14, 1982. B.S. in Aero., Dowling Coll., Oakdale, N.Y., 1981. Coordinator project devel. Aviation Cons., Inc., Manhasset, N.Y., 1980-81; technician PRC Speas, Lake Success, N.Y., 1980-81, sr. technician, 1981-82; planner PRC Engring., Orange, Calif., 1982—. Mem. AIAA, Nat. Aero. Assn., Aero Club of So. Calif. Republican. Lutheran. Office: 972 Town and Country Rd Orange CA 92667

ALVES, HAROLD GEORGE, safety engineer; b. Yonkers, N.Y., Feb. 2, 1946; s. Manuel and Ann (Madry) A.; m. Linda Crosby, Mar. 1, 1965; children—Troy P., Harold R. A.S., No. Westchester Inst. Tech., 1964; A.A., Pima Coll., 1976. Mechanic, Pima Mine, Tucson, 1969-74, mech. supr., 1974-75, asst. safety engr., 1975-78; mgr. tng. Kaiser Steel Corp., Eagles Mountain, Calif., 1978-79; safety engr. Pima Mining Co., Tucson, 1979-80; sr. safety engr. Allen Corp. Am., Orlando, Fla., 1980-81; with Bechtel Civil & Minerals, Inc., San Francisco, 1981—. Pres., Home Owners Assn. of Orlando, 1980-81. Served with USAF, 1965-60. Recipient U.S. Dept. Labor award for improvement safety and health of miners, 1979. Mem. Am. Soc. Safety Engrs., Nat. Safety Council (exec. com. 1977—). Contbr. articles to profl. jours.; patentee in field. Office: Bechtel Civil & Minerals Inc PO Box 3965 San Francisco CA 94119

ALVISO, PATRICIA ANN, market research executive; b. Omaha, July 2, 1935; d. James H. and Kathryn E. (LaForrest) McCrea; divorced; children—Jan A. Ratzlaff, Kimberly Kay Rudolf. B.A. Fresno State U., 1961. Elem. tchr. Fresno Unified Sch. Dist., 1969-71; ptnr. Polimar Research, Fresno, 1959-72; pres. AIS Mkt. Research, 1972—; lectr. various area colls. Chmn. Pvt. Indsl. Council, vice chmn. Multi-Jurisdictional Pvt. Indsl. Council; mem. bus. adv. com. Calif. State U.-Fresno, 1982; bd. dirs. displaced Homemakers. Mem. Market Research Assn.; Am. Market Research Assn., Fresno Advt. Fedn. (dir., v.p.), Fresno City and County C. of C., Fresno Bus. and Profl. Women. Home: 5689 N 5th St Fresno CA 93710 Office: AIS Market Research 6115 N 1st St Suite 102 Fresno CA 93710

ALY, RAZA, microbiologist, educator; b. Quetta, Pakistan, June 3, 1935; s. Farman and Jan (Mohammed) A.; came to U.S., 1960, naturalized, 1977; B.Sc., U. Panjab, Pakistan; M.S., U. Mich, 1962, M.P.H., 1965; Ph.D., U. Okla., 1969; m. Naheed Bashir, Sept. 24, 1958 (div.); children—Hassan, Tanya. Lectr., San Francisco State U., 1970-75; asst. research microbiologist U. Calif., San Francisco, 1969-73, asst. prof., 1973-77, asso. prof. microbiology dermatology, 1977—, also mem. com. fgn. scholars; bd. dirs. Psoriasis Research Assn. Grantee NASA, 1974-77, NIH, 1973—. Mem. Am. Acad. Microbiologists, Soc. Investigative Dermatology, Acad. of Dermatology, Am. Soc. Microbiology (pres. No. Calif.), AAAS, Internat. Soc. Human and Animal Mycology. Author: Clinical Skin Microbiology, 1978; editor: Bacterial Interference, 1982; co-editor: Skin Microbiology: Relevance to Clinical Infection, 1981; also articles. Home: 412 Countyview Dr Mill Valley CA 94941 Office: Univ Calif San Francisco CA 94143

AMADEO, JOSEPH MARTIN, publishing company executive; b. San Jose, Calif., Dec. 2, 1953; s. Samuel Martin and Marth Allice (Holub) A.; m. Deborah Jeanne Dudley, Dec. 26, 1979; children—Tony, Luciana. Student pub. schs., Campbell, Calif. Traffic dir., sales asst., prodn. dir., disc jockey Sta. KOME, San Jose, 1971-74; engrng. technician Litronix, Inc., Cupertino, Calif., 1974-76; advt./mktg./promotion dir. BAM mag., Oakland, Calif., 1976—, v.p. BAM Network, 1981—. Office: BAM Mag 5951 Canning St Oakland CA 94609

AMADOR, RAYMOND ANDREW, aerospace engineer; b. Bogota, Colombia, Aug. 3, 1952; came to U.S., 1955; s. Raymond Howell and Ursula Julie (Wolf) A.; B.S. in Mech. Engring., Tulane U., 1974; M.S. in Aero/Astro (Hughes Aircraft Co. fellow), Stanford U., 1975; m. Margaret Marie Yvonne Ruiterman, June 24, 1978; children—Raymond Michael, Steven Andrew. Mem. tech. staff space and communications group Hughes Aircraft Co., El Segundo, Calif., 1975-76, electro-optical and data systems group, Culver City, Calif., 1976-77; staff engr. Santa Barbara Research Center, Goleta, Calif., 1977-80, sr. staff engr., lectr. advanced tech. edn. program, 1980-82, tech. sect. head, 1983; pres. AMHOF Engring. Assocs., Goleta, 1982—; cons. in field. Mem. AIAA, The Planetary Soc. Republican. Roman Catholic. Club: Cathedral Oaks Tennis. Author papers in field. Office: PO Box 1426 Goleta CA 93016

AMARINO, NEAL THOMAS, pub. relations/advt. exec.; b. New Brunswick, N.J., Mar. 23, 1936; s. John Joseph and Rosina Grace (Tennerali) A.; B.S., Utah State U., 1959; postgrad. NYU Sch. Bus., 1978; m. Martha Ann Peterman, June 13, 1964; children—Neal Thomas, Susan Ruth. Account exec. Laman Advt., Denver, 1960-64; dir. news bur. Frontier Airlines, Denver, 1964-72; mgr. pub. relations Johns-Manville Corp., Denver, 1972-83; v.p. Schenkein Assocs. Pub. Relations/Advt., Englewood, Colo., 1983—; cons. in field. Bd. dirs. Adv. Council for Handicapped, Boulder County, Colo.; active Nat. Alliance Businessmen, Easter Seal Soc., Bal Swan Children's Center, Boys Clubs Am. Served with U.S. Army, 1959-60. Mem. Pub. Relations Soc. Am. (Silver Anvil award 1979, dir. Colo. chpt.), Denver C. of C., Ducks Unltd., Sigma Phi Epsilon. Republican. Roman Catholic. Club: Denver Press. Home: 14704 Fenton St Broomfield CO 80020 Office: 16 Inverness Pl E Englewood CO 80112

AMBERG, HERMAN ROBERT, environmental engineer; b. Frankfurt, Germany, Feb. 10, 1920; s. Joseph Carl and Rosina (Volk) A.; m. Martha Taylor, Aug. 2, 1948; children—Carlton Stark, Karen Louise Pike, David C. B.S. in Chem. Engring., Syracuse U., 1943; M.S., Ph.D., Rutgers U., 1952. Research chem. engr. Johns Manville Research Ctr., Finderne, N.J., 1946-48; West Coast regional engr. Nat. Council Air and Stream Improvement, Oreg. State U., Corvallis, 1951-56; mgr. chem. and biol. research Central Research Div., Crown Zellerbach Corp., Camas, Wash., 1956-71, dir. corp. environ. services, 1971—; mem. Nat. Council Air and Stream Improvement operating and research coms. Contbr. numerous articles to sci. jours. Served with USN, 1944-46. Recipient Pacific Northwest Pollution Control Assn. Achievement award, 1971. Fellow Am. Inst. Chemists; mem. Am. Inst. Chem. Engrs., Am. Chem. Soc., TAPPI (recognition award 1974), Air Pollution Control Assn., N.Y. Acad. Sci., ASCE, Water Pollution Control Fedn., AAAS, Am. Water Works Assn., Sigma Xi.

AMDOR, ROBERT CLINTON, national park manager; b. Miami, Fla., Feb. 20, 1943; s. Burdett Charles and Winifred Offord (Long) A.; m. Judy Maxine Kirby, June 18, 1961; children—S. James Eric, S. Christopher Paul; m. 2d, Kathleen Faye Stubbs, July 13, 1980. Student Ga. Mil. Coll., Dade County Jr. Coll., U. Ky., Wash. U. Pres. Master Coating Corp., 1964-67; park guide Nat. Capital Park, 1967-68; supervisory park technician Jefferson Nat. Expansion Meml., 1968-72; supervisory park ranger Golden Spike Nat. Hist. site, 1972-73; supervisory park ranger Ft. Vancouver Nat. Hist. Site, 1973-76; chief interpretation and resource mgmt Castillo de San Marcos and Fort Matanzas Nat. Monuments, 1976-80; supt. Whitman Mission Nat. Hist. Site, Walla Walla, Wash., 1980—. Recipient Spl. Achievement award Nat. Park Service, 1972. Mem. Assn. Nat. Park Rangers, Heritage Preservation Found., C. of C. Pioneer and Hist. Soc. Republican. Clubs: Rotary, Elks. Home and Office: Rural Route 2 Box 247 Walla Walla WA 99362

AMERONGEN, GERARD JOSEPH, Canadian provincial assembly speaker and member; b. Winnipeg, Man., Can., July 18, 1914; s. Maximilian Ernest and Maria (Waas) Taets von Amerongen; m. Elizabeth Helen Fetherstonhaugh, Dec. 6, 1943; children—Mary, Peter, Margaret, Monica, Helen, Michael, Elizabeth, John. B.A., U. Alta. (Can.), 1943, LL.B., 1944. Bar: Alta. 1946; created queen's counsel, 1966. Mem. Legis. Assembly Alta. for Edmonton-Meadowlark, Edmonton, 1971—, speaker, 1971—, chmn. legis. internship adv. and selection com., chmn. members' services com.; rep. of Can. provinces on exec. com. Commonwealth Parliamentary Assn., 1981—. Pres. Progressive Conservative Assn. Alta; mem. nat. exec. Progressive Conservative Assn. Can.; founding dir. Alta. Can. Native Friendship Centre, personnel dir.; bd. dirs. Edmonton hosps. Mem. Law Soc. Alta. Office: 325 Legis Bldg Edmonton AB T5K 2B6 Canada

AMES, A. E. LYN, nurse; b. Macomb, Ill., Apr. 25, 1949; d. Clark Earl and Betty Amelia (Hegstrom) A.; hon. grad. in biology Santa Fe Community Coll., 1975; hon. grad. cert. operating room technician U. Fla., 1974; grad. in health care adminstrn. UCLA, 1980; B.S./B.A. summa cum laude, U. Redlands, 1982; postgrad. in nursing Pasadena City Coll., 1982. Water safety instr. Bushnell (Ill.) Recreation Assn., 1965-72; operating room technician specialist Shands Teaching Hosp. and Clinics, Gainesville, Fla., 1973-78; asso. dir. logistics and materials mgmt. Cedars-Sinai Med. Center, Los Angeles, 1978-81; operating room nurse St. Luke Hosp., Pasadena, Calif., 1981—. Water safety instr. Internat. Red Cross, Am. Heart Assn., Heart Assn. Greater Los Angeles. Mem. Am. Soc. for Hosp. Purchasing and Materials Mgmt., Am. Soc. for Hosp. Central Service Personnel, Assn. Surg. Technologists. Contbr. articles to profl. jours. Office: St Luke Hospital Washington and Altadena Sts Pasadena CA

AMES, ROBERT KENNETH, chem. engr.; b. Seattle, June 20, 1929; s. Kenneth Ames and Velva Marie (Miller) A.; B.S. in Chem. Engring., U. Wash., 1958; m. Janet Anne Haltom, Aug. 25, 1962; children—Kenneth Carl, Helen Marie, David Haltom. Research engr. Boeing Co., Seattle, 1958-72, mgr., 1972-78; exec. dir. Waste Conversion Co., Seattle, 1978-80; dir. Reflux Ltd., Seattle, 1980—. Served with USN, 1952-54. Mem. ASME (crew systems com.), AIAA (life scis. and systems tech. com.), Soc. Automotive Engrs., Kappa Sigma. Episcopalian. Patentee in field. Office: 3522 W Government Way Seattle WA 98199

AMES, WILLIAM CLARK, ednl. adminstr.; b. Macomb, Ill., July 11, 1950; s. Clark Earl and Betty Amelia (Hegstrom) A.; B.A., Knox Coll., 1972; M.S., Western Ill. U., 1974; Ph.D., Ariz. State U. Asst. to dean students, instr. human interaction Knox Coll., Galesburg, Ill., 1974-75; instr. human interaction, counselor edn. Western Ill. U., Macomb, 1974-75; resident area coordinator Western Carolina U., Cullowhee, N.C., 1975-77; dir. Sahuaro Complex, Ariz. State U., Tempe, 1977-78, dir. housing office vending programs, 1978-79, asst. dir. housing-adminstrn., 1979-80, grad. asso. for student leadership programs, 1980-81, research asso., office of pres., 1981-82; asst. to chancellor Maricopa Community Coll., Phoenix, 1982—. Mem. Western Carolina

Council on Alcohol and Use and Abuse, 1975-77. NSF grantee, 1970-72; recipient Leadership award Elks Ill., 1968; Robert Cunningham Taylor Jr. scholar, 1968-72. Mem. Nat. Assn. student Personnel Adminstrs., Am. Personnel and Guidance Assn., Am. Coll. Personnel Assn., Am. Council Univ. Housing Officers, Southeastern Assn. Housing Officers, Smithsonian Inst. (asso.), Knox Coll., Western Ill. U. alumni assns. Contbr. articles to student personnel jours. Home: 734 W 2d Pl Mesa AZ 85201 Office: 3910 E Washington St Phoenix AZ 85034

AMEZCUA, CHARLIE ANTHONY, counselor, educator; b. Los Angeles, Sept. 1, 1928; s. Carlos and Inez (Nunez) A.; B.A., UCLA, 1958; M.S., Calif. State U., Los Angeles, 1961; m. Kathleen Joyce Greene, Mar. 7, 1964; children—Colleen Alvita, Charles Anthony. Student psychologist Rancho Los Amigos Hosp., Downey, Calif., 1959-60; instr. in psychology East Los Angeles Coll., 1962-72, asst. prof. counseling, 1972-74, assoc. prof. counseling, 1974—, prof. psychology, 1980—, spl. edn. counselor, 1981—, coordinator vet. affairs, 1972—; personnel asst. Los Angeles City Sch. Dist., 1963-64; counselor Youth Tng. and Employment Project, Los Angeles, 1965-66, counseling supr., 1966, project dir., 1966-67; counseling psychologist VA, Los Angeles, 1967-70; dir. Head Start, Los Angeles County Econ. and Youth Opportunities Agy., 1970-71; bd. dirs. Tng. and Research Found., Child and Family Resources Centers; lectr. counselor edn. Calif. State U., Los Angeles. Mem. Calif. Gov.'s Adv. Com. on Children and Youth, 1966-67; judge blue ribbon panel Nat. Acad. TV Arts and Scis., 1966-76. Served with USN, 1948-52; Korea; cert. community coll. counselor, supr.-adminstrn., jr. coll. teaching in psychology. Mem. Am. Psychol. Assn., Calif. State Psychol. Assn., Assn. Chicano Educators, Calif. Assn. Post-Secondary Educators of the Disabled, Nat. Assn. Vets. Program Adminstrs., Western Psychol. Assn. Democrat. Home: 8348 Fable Ave Canoga Park CA 91304 Office: 1301 Brooklyn Ave Monterey Park CA 91754

AMIEL, ELLIOT, security systems co. exec.; b. Alexandria, Egypt, June 18, 1951; came to U.S., 1958, naturalized, 1963; s. Isaac I. and Judith A.; B.S. in Acctg., Bklyn. Coll., 1973; M.B.A. in Fin., St. John's U., 1978; m. Barbara Sue Bloom, May 26, 1975; 1 son, Eric Lee. Staff acct. Meml. Sloan-Kettering Cancer Center, N.Y.C., 1973-75; cost control supr. Prudential Bldg. Maintenance Co., N.Y.C., 1975-77; fin. analyst Am. Dist. Telegraph Co. (ADT Security Systems), N.Y.C., 1977-78, regional controller Los Angeles region, 1978-80, controller Western group, 1981—. Mem. Am. Mgmt. Assn., Omicron Delta Epsilon. Home: 51 Redrock Ln Phillips Ranch CA 91766 Office: 500 S Shatto Pl Los Angeles CA 90020

AMINI, FARIBORZ, med. educator; b. Tehran, Iran, July 23, 1930; s. Mirza and Farkhondeh (Rezai) A.; came to U.S., 1949, naturalized, 1963; B.S. in Math. with highest honors, U. Calif. at Berkeley, 1953; M.D., U. Calif. at San Francisco, 1957; m. Elizabeth Ann Cunningham, Feb. 5, 1972; children—Kim Shareen, Lisa Roshan, Dawn Parvaneh, Ariana Shaheen, Christina Maheen, Elita Farine. Intern, Detroit Receiving Hosp., 1957-58; research fellow Cancer Research Inst., U. Calif. at San Francisco, 1958-59; resident in psychiatry Neuropsychiat. Inst., U. Mich., Children's Psychiat. Hosp., 1959-62; fellow in child psychiatry U. Calif. at Los Angeles Neuropsychiat. Inst., 1962-63; psychoanalytic tng. San Francisco Psychoanalytic Inst., 1964-71, mem. faculty, 1973—; mem. faculty Langley Porter Neuropsychiat. Inst., U. Calif. at San Francisco, 1963—, clin. prof., dir. youth service dept. psychiatry, 1970-77, dir. residency tng. dept. psychiatry, 1976-81, dir. out-patient dept., 1977—, dir. hosp. and clinics, 1981—, pres. exec. med. bd.; vis. lectr. Boalt Hall, U. Calif. at Berkeley, 1965, also Sch. Criminology; cons. Aid to Retarded Children San Francisco, Family Life Edn. and Parent Edn. programs, San Francisco, Foster Parent Program, San Francisco, 1975, others. Diplomate Am. Bd. Psychiatry and Neurology. Fellow Am. Psychiat. Assn.; mem. No. Calif. Psychiat. Soc., San Francisco Psychoanalytic Inst. and Soc. (pres.), Phi Beta Kappa, Sigma Xi, Nu Sigma Nu. Contbr. numerous articles to profl. jours. Home: 202 Lagunitas Rd Ross CA 94957 Office: 401 Parnassus Ave San Francisco CA 94143

AMIOKA, WALLACE SHUZO, ret. petroleum co. exec.; b. Honolulu, June 28, 1914; s. Tsurumatsu and Reye (Yoshimura) A.; B.A., U. Hawaii, 1966, M.B.A., 1968; m. Ellen Misao Honda, Aug. 9, 1942; children—Carol L. Amioka Price, Joanne M. Amioka Chikuma. With Shell Oil Co., 1931—, fin. services mgr., Honolulu, 1973-77; lectr. econs. U. Hawaii, 1969-79. Mem. Honolulu Police Commn., 1965-73, vice chmn., 1966, 68, chmn., 1971; U.S. civil adm. Ryuku Islands, 1950-52. Mem. City and County of Honolulu Charter Commn., 1981-82; bd. dirs. Honolulu Symphony Soc., 1968. Served with M.I., AUS, 1944-48. Mem. M.I. Service Vets. (pres. 1981-82), Hawaii C. of C. (chmn. edn. com. 1963-64, chmn. pub. health com. 1966-67), Phi Beta Kappa, Phi Kappa Phi. Clubs: Hui 31, Hui Aikane, Honolulu Police Old Timers. Home: 4844 Matsonia Dr Honolulu HI 96816 Office: 1451 S King St Honolulu HI 96814

AMIRTHARAJAH, APPIAH, environmental engineer, educator; b. Colombo, Sri Lanka, April 4, 1940, came to U.S. 1976. s. Arumugam and Sinnamma (Sinniah) A; m. Uma Hymavati, July 13, 1968; children—Rajeevan, Mohana. B.S. in Engring., U. Ceylon, 1963; M.S., Iowa State U., 1970, Ph.D., 1971. Registered profl. engr., Mont. Resident, project and designs engr. Dept. Water Supply, Ceylon, 1963-74; chief engr. Nat. Water Supply Bd., Sri Lanka, 1975-76; vis. prof. univs. in Sri Lanka, 1973-76; asst., then assoc. prof. Mont. State U., Bozeman, 1976-79, prof., coordinator environ. engring. programs, 1979—. Fulbright scholar, 1968-69; research fellow Iowa State U., 1969-71; research grantee NSF, 1980-83. Mem. Am. Water Works Assn. (nat. research com. on coagulation), ASCE (acting editor Jour. Environ. Engring.), Water Pollution Control Fedn., Internat. Assn. Water Pollution Research, Pub. Service Engrs. Assn. (v.p. 1974), Phi Kappa Phi, Sigma Xi. Hindu Contbr. papers to profl. jours. Home: 1104 W Koch St Bozeman MT 59715 Office: Dept Civil Engring Mont State U Bozeman MT 59717

AMIS, DOUGLAS KEITH, educator, mgmt. cons., marriage counselor; b. Valparaiso, Fla., Nov. 4, 1948; s. William Frank and Victoria (Bingham) A.; A.B., U. San Francisco, 1971, M.A., 1975, 77, 79, M.M.F.C., 1980, Ed.D., 1982; M.F.A., N.Y. U., 1973; D.B.A., W. Colo. U., 1977; Ph.D., Columbia Pacific U., 1981; Program dir., bd. dirs. Inst. Theatre Studies, City of Pleasanton (Calif.) Dept. Recreation, artistic dir. plays Pleasanton Playhouse, 1971-74; asst. prof. communication arts, program adviser mass media studies program U. San Francisco, 1974-82, dir. spl. events, 1974-75, adminstrv. asst. to dean arts and sci., acting dir. co-op. fine arts program, 1975-76, asst. to dean Coll. Liberal Arts and Scis., edn. adminstr. Fromm Inst. for Lifelong Learning, 1976-77; sr. partner Amis, Amis, Davis & Liebrentz, 1975-82; mgmt. cons. Clayton Williams & Co., San Francisco, 1982—. Trustee, Lincoln U., San Francisco 1979-82. Recipient James J. Gill award U. San Francisco, 1971, Fr. Fred Speiler award, 1982. Mem. Am. Mgmt. Assn., Am. Psychol. Assn. Am. Assn. Higher Edn. Democrat. Presbyterian. Club: New York Univ. Home: Apt 103 629 Arguello Blvd San Francisco CA 94118 Office: 150 Post St Suite 620 San Francisco CA 94108

AMIS, WILLIAM FRANK, food co. exec.; b. Flat Lick, Ky., Jan. 29, 1921; s. Robert Stevens and Clair Stella (Hibbard) A.; A.B., U. San Francisco, 1976, M.A. in Indsl. Labor Relations, 1978; m. Victoria Bingham, Apr. 20, 1942; children—Billie Lynn, Douglas Keith. Enlisted U.S. Army Air Force (now U.S. Air Force), 1940, commd. chief warrant officer, 1950, advanced through grades to sr. chief warrant officer 1965; computer sci. officer Air Force Hdqrs., 1954-58; dir. statis. service, 4th Air Force Hdqrs., 1958-60; ret., 1960; mgr. data processing United Bay Area Crusade, San Francisco, 1960-61; mgr. data processing Mother's Cake Cookie Co., Oakland, Calif., 1961—; sr. partner Amis Amis Davis & Liebrienz, mgmt. cons.'s, Oakland, 1973—; pres., also dir. Pleasanton Gardens, Calif., 1964—, Pleasanton Greens, 1969-73. Chmn. human resources commn. City of Pleasanton, 1965-68, recipient Outstanding award, 1969. Mem. Data Processing Mgrs. Assn. (certified data processing), Am. Inst. Profl. Engrs. Republican. Presbyterian. Home: 4137 Silver St Pleasanton CA 94566 Office: 810 81st Ave Oakland CA 94604

AMMAN, JOHN CHARLES, accountant; b. Colorado Springs, Colo., Mar. 15, 1935; s. George Clarence and Mary Charlotte (Wilson) A.; m. SaraAnn Cameron, Sept. 6, 1958; children—Bradford Kevin, Bruce Cameron, Barry Douglas. B.S. in Acctg., Colo. U., 1957; M.B.A., Denver U., 1962. C.P.A., Colo. With Arthur Andersen & Co., 1961—, audit mgr., Denver, 1966-71, ptnr., 1971—, mng. ptnr., Salt Lake City, 1975-77, mng. ptnr., Denver, 1977—. Past chmn. alumni adv. council U. Colo. Bus. Sch.; mem. adv. council Acctg. Sch., mem. adv. council Bus. Sch., U. Denver; bd. dirs., past pres. Bow-Mar Owners, Inc.; bd. dirs. Denver Partnership; bd. dirs., past treas. Artreach; mem. council Western Regional Council; mem. adv. council Colo. Uplift. Served with Security Agy., U.S. Army, 1957-60. Mem. Am. Inst. C.P.A.s, Colo. Soc. C.P.A.s, Wyo. Soc. C.P.A.s, Utah Assn. C.P.A.s, Denver C. of C. (chmn. retirement plan trustees), Beta Alpha Psi (mem. nat. adv. forum). Republican. Clubs: Univ., Denver, Rotary (Denver); Colo. Elephant; Cherry Hills Country (Englewood, Colo.); Garden of Gods (Colorado Springs, Colo.); Alta (Salt Lake City); Masons. Mem. editorial adv. council Jour. of Accountancy, 1974-77. Office: Arthur Andersen & Co 717 17th St Suite 1900 Denver CO 80202

AMMIRATI, JOSEPH FRANK, JR., botany educator; b. Dunsmuir, Calif., Jan. 10, 1942; s. Joseph Frank and Emma Maria Pasquina (Manfredi) A.; m. Roberta Jean Gleason, Jan. 29, 1966; children—Stephanie May, Joseph Frank III, Anthony James. A.B. in Biology, San Francisco State U., 1965, M.A., 1967; Ph.D. in Botany, (Emma J. Cole fellow), U. Mich., 1972. Research mycologist U.S. Dept. Agr., Beltsville, Md., 1973-74; asst. prof. botany U. Toronto, Mississauga, Ont., 1974-79; asst. prof. U. Wash., Seattle, 1979-81, assoc. prof., 1981—. NSF intern, 1973-74; Nat. Research Council Can. grantee, 1975-80; U. Wash. grantee, 1979-81; U.S. Office Naval Research investigator, 1980-82; NSF grantee, 1981-84. Mem. AAAS, Am. Inst. Biol. Scis., Am. Mus. Natural History, Assn. Systematics Collections, Mycological Soc. Am., Mycological Soc. San Francisco, Mycological Soc. Toronto, N.Am. Mycological Asso., Puget Sound Mycological Soc., Sigma Xi. Author: (with others) The Poisonous Mushrooms of Canada, 1983; contbr. articles to profl. jours.; editor: Mycology Guidebook, 1982, co-editor: Arctic and Alpine Mycology, 1982. Address: Dept Botany U Wash Seattle WA 98195

AMMONS, CAROL HAMRICK, psychologist, editor; b. Tampa, Fla., Feb. 22, 1927; d. Joe Fred and B. Carolyn (Patton) Hamrick; m. R.B. Ammons, August, 1949; children—W. Carl, R. Bruce III, S.M. Douglas, M.M. Elizabeth, Richard L.M., A. Stephanie, A. Gleny. B.A., H.S. Newcomb Coll. Women, Tulane U., 1947; M.A., Tulane U., 1949; Ph.D., U. Ky., 1955. Lic. psychologist, Mont. Research asst. Tulane U., 1949-49; instr. U. Louisville, 1949-55, clin. asst. dir., 1949-55; editor Perceptual and Motor Skills, Missoula, Mont., 1949—, Psychol. Reports, 1955—; cons. in field. U. Ky. fellow, 1951-53. Mem. Am. Psychol. Assn., AAAS, Psychometric Soc., AAUW, LWV. Contbr. articles to profl. jours. Home: 411 Keith Ave Missoula MT 59801 Office: PO Box 9229 Missoula MT 59807

AMMONS, ROBERT BRUCE, psychologist, publisher, educator; b. Denver, Feb. 27, 1920; s. Bruce and Margaret Ann (Gates) A.; m. Carol Hamrick, Aug. 29, 1949; children—Carl, Bruce, Douglas, Elizabeth, Richard, Stephanie, Glenyss. B.A., San Diego State U., 1939; M.A., U. Iowa, 1941, Ph.D., 1946. Lic. psychologist, Mont. Instr. Syracuse U., 1946; asst. prof. U. Denver, 1946-48; asst. prof. Tulane U., 1948-49, U. Louisville, 1949-55; assoc. prof. U. N.D., 1956-57; prof. U. Mont., Missoula, 1957—. Chmn. solar div. Am. Assn. Variable Star Observers, 1980. Fellow Am. Am. Psychol. Assn.; mem. Rocky Mountain, Psychol. Assn., Midwest Psychol. Assn., Mont. Psychol. Assn., Brit. Psychol. Assns., Am. Statis. Assn., Cheiron Soc., Coll. Sports Medicine, Psychonomic Soc., Sigma Xi. Co-editor, pub. Psychol. Reports, 1955—, Perceptual and Motor Skills, 1949—; contbr. articles to profl. jours. Home: 411 Keith Ave Missoula MT 59801 Office: U Mont Missoula MT 59812

AMMONS, RONALD GENE, retail jewelry company executive, energy company executive; b. Knoxville, Tenn., Oct. 5, 1939; s. Harry Eugene and Helen Marie (Jones) A.; m. Sylvia Jane Tipton, Nov. 23, 1962; 1 dau., Kimberly Paige. Student U. Tenn., 1957-60, Ctr. for Exec. Devel., Ariz. State U., 1978. Gen. mgr. Fogarty Jewelers, Knoxville, 1965-68; owner Campus Jewelers, Knoxville, 1968-70; dist. jewelry supr. J.B. Hunter Dept. Stores, Tenn. and Fla., 1970-73; jewelry merchandiser Modern Merchandising Inc., Phoenix, Denver, 1973-81, corp. jewelry dir., Mpls., 1982-83; v.p. M.A.C. Resources Inc., Littleton, Colo., 1981—. Chmn. com. U.S. Senatorial Bus. Adv. Bd.; pres. sch. bd. Silver State Bapt. Sch., Denver, 1981, 82. Republican.

AMODEO, JOHN, marriage, family and child counselor; b. Bklyn., Nov. 17, 1949; s. Ben and Mary (Giammarino) A. M.A. in Clin. Psychology, Lone Mountain Coll., 1979; Ph.D., Calif. Inst. Transpersonal Psychology, Menlo Park, Calif., 1981. Lic. marriage, family and child counselor Calif. Instr. Holistic Life Inst., San Francisco, 1977-81; pvt. practice in psychotherapy, Mill Valley and San Francisco, 1980—; coordinator Focusing, Marin, Sonoma counties; program coordinator U. Without Walls; tutor Internat. Coll. Mem. bd. advs. Inst. Research in Spirituality Mem. Assn. Transpersonal Psychology, Am. Personnel and Guidance Assn. Contbr. editor: Yoga Jour.; contbr. articles to profl. publs. Home and Office: 328 Summit Ave Mill Valley CA 94941

AMODEO, JOHN ANDREW, civil engineer; b. Bklyn., Mar. 10, 1948; s. Andrew and Anna (Bartiromo) A.; m. Judith Frances Smorto, June 1, 1974; m. 2d Julie Anne LaBella, Nov. 10, 1979; 1 son, Michael. B.C.E., CCNY, 1970. Registered profl. engr., N.Y., Calif. Civil engr. City of N.Y., 1970-79; asst. chief engr. Vista (Calif.) Irrigation Dist., 1979—. Mem. Calif. Profl. Engring. Soc., N.Y. State Profl. Engr. Soc., Am. Water Works Assn. Republican. Roman Catholic. Clubs: Toastmasters (Vista), Westwood. Home: 18128 Valladares Dr San Diego CA 92127 Office: 202 W Connecticut Ave Vista CA 92083

AMONIC, ROBERT STEPHAN, plastic and reconstructive surgeon; b. N.Y.C., Sept. 17, 1937; B.A., UCLA, 1960, M.D., 1963. Intern, Yale-New Haven Med. Center, 1963-64, resident in surgery, 1964-65; resident UCLA-Harbor Hosp., 1965-68; resident in plastic surgery UCLA, 1970-73; practice medicine specializing in plastic and reconstructive surgery, Santa Monica, Calif., 1973—; mem. staff St. John's, Santa Monica, UCLA Hosps.; asst. clin. prof. UCLA Med. Sch. Served to maj. M.C., USAF, 1968-70. Diplomate Am. Bd. Plastic Surgery. Mem. ACS, Am. Soc. Plastic and Reconstructive Surgeons, Am. Soc. Aesthetic Plastic Surgery, Calif. Soc. Plastic Surgeons, Bay Surg. Soc., Calif. Med. Assn., Los Angeles County Med. Assn. Contbr. articles med. jours. Office: 2001 Santa Monica Blvd Suite 790W Santa Monica CA 90404

AMOROSO, FRANK, communication systems engr.; b. Providence, July 31, 1935; s. Michele and Angela Maria Barbara (D'Uva) A.; B.S. in Elec. Engring., Mass. Inst. Tech., 1958, M.S., 1958; postgrad. Purdue U., 1958-60; postgrad. math. (fellow) U. Turin (Italy), 1964-65. Sr. engr. Edgerton, Germehausen, and Grier, Inc., Boston and Wake Island, 1958; instr. elec. engring. Purdue U., 1958-59; research engr. Melpar, Inc., Roxbury, Mass., 1959; research engr. Mass. Inst. Tech. Instrumentation Lab., Cambridge, 1960, Litton Systems Advanced Devel. Lab., Waltham, Mass., 1960-61; engr. Melpar Applied Sci. Div., Watertown, Mass., 1961; mem. tech. staff RCA Labs. David Sarnoff Research Center, Princeton, N.J., 1962-64, Mitre Corp., Bedford, Mass., 1966-67; sr. applied mathematician Collins Radio Co., Newport Beach, Calif., 1967-68; communication systems engr. N.Am. Rockwell Corp., El Segundo, Calif., 1968-71, Northrop Electronics div., Palos Verdes Peninsula, Calif., 1971-72, Hughes Aircraft Co., Fullerton, Calif., 1972—. Tchr. Transcendental Meditation program; exec. gov. Age of Enlightenment. Served to 1st lt. AUS, 1961-62. Recipient RCA Labs. award, 1964. Registered profl. engr., Calif. Mem. IEEE (sr.). Contbr. articles to profl. jours. and mags. Advanced open water Scuba diver. Home: 271-D W Alton St Santa Ana CA 92707 Office: Hughes Aircraft Co Fullerton CA 92634

AMOUREUX, MARGARET TINNER, educational administrator, educator; b. Springfield, Ohio, Aug. 26, 1925; d. John Clement and Hilda Susan (Waters) Tinner; m. Alvie Benton, Nov., 1946; m. 2d, Louis P. Amoureux, Apr. 6, 1956; children—Antoinette Sekou, Evelyn Ali, Phillippe. B.S., Langston U., 1944; M.B.A., Ind. U., 1951; postgrad. Washington U., Fla. A&M U., Morgan State Coll., Calif. State U.-Hayward, San Francisco State U., U. Calif.-Berkeley. Tchr., asst. registrar, sec. to dean Bethune-Cookman Coll., Daytona Beach, Fla., 1945-50; tchr. pub. schs., St. Louis, 1951-52; tchr. Castlemont High Sch., Oakland, Calif., 1962-73, N. Peralta Community Coll., Oakland, 1973-75, Merritt Coll., Oakland, 1975-79; dir. govtl. relations and grantsmanship Oakland Unified Sch. Dist., 1979—; cons. Creative Timed Writing, 1975; edn. editor Calif. Voice Newspaper, 1969; corr. Calif. Voice and Sun-Reporter, 1976, 80. Mem. Alameda County Democratic Central Com., 1972-74, alt., 1974-76; mem. Calif. State Dem. Central Com., 1974-76; alt. del. Dem. Nat. Conv., 1972; vice chmn. Black Women Organized for Polit. Action, mem. exec. com., chmn. polit. Action Com.; vice chmn. central com. Calif. Dem. Black Caucas, 1979-81, treas., 1981—; mem. Mayor's Transition Team, 1977-78; chmn., mem. Affirmative Action Com., Oakland Pub. Schs., 1977-79; mem. employment and tng. commn., City of Oakland; mem. 5th Dist. Med. Quality Rev. Bd., State of Calif. Recipient Congressman Ronald V. Dellums award, 1982; Cert. Recognition, City of Berkeley. Mem. Assn. Supervision and Curriculum Devel., Am. Assn. Sch. Adminstrs., United Adminstrs of Oakland, Calif. Student Aid Commn., Bay Area Black Women United, NAACP, Am. Mgmt. Assn., Alpha Kappa Mu, Delta Pi Epsilon.

AMPARAN, MARIA ELENA, personnel exec.; b. Los Angeles, Aug. 19, 1945; d. John S. and Concepcion (Mendez) A.; A.A., East Los Angeles Coll., 1967; B.A. in Journalism, Calif. State U., Los Angeles, 1969. Sec., coordinator press and publicity Sta. KNBC, 1969-70; prin. public relations rep. model cities program East N.E. neighborhood City of Los Angeles, 1970-72; public info. aide Housing Authority, Los Angeles, 1972; editor So. Calif. Rapid Transit Dist., 1972-73; coordinator dept. community services County of Los Angeles, 1973-76; employment specialist Kaiser Permanente Med. Care Program, Los Angeles, 1976-79; personnel supr. McDonald's Corp., San Diego, 1979—. Vol., coordinator Youth Motivation Task Force, 1976-79; mem. employer adv. com. Career Planning Center, Inc., 1978-79. Recipient commendation award Los Angeles County Bd. Supervisors. Mem. Personnel Mgmt. Assn. San Diego, Personnel Mgmt. Assn. of Aztlan (chairperson ad hoc placement com., pres. San Diego chpt. 1982—, nat. publicity chmn. 1982—), Profl. Women's Journalism Soc., Beta Phi Gamma. Democrat. Roman Catholic. Office: 8840 Complex Dr Suite 300 San Diego CA 92123

AMRINE, WILLIAM FREDERICK, accountant, rancher; b. Springfield, Ohio, Sept. 11, 1949; s. Robert Yost and Sally (Harbel) A.; m. Jesse A. Poore, Aug. 15, 1970; children—W. Brett, Sidney C., Robert Y. B.A., U. Mont., 1969; M.S., U. Ark., 1974. C.P.A., Mont. Lectr. acctg. U. Mont., Missoula, 1975; mng. dir. Hoven, Vervick & Amrine P.C., C.P.A.s, Missoula, 1976—. Active Easter Seals, Telethon; mem. Missoula Horse Council. Served with USN, 1969-74. Mem. Am. Inst. C.P.A.s (pres Missoula chpt.), Missoula C. of C., Sigma Chi. Clubs: Back Country Horseman, Exchange, Masons. Home: 301 N Ave E Missoula MT 59801 Office: Hoven Vervick & Amrine PC 111 N Higgins Suite 401 Missoula MT 59802

AMSTER, GLENN JAY, lawyer; b. N.Y.C., Nov. 17, 1949; m. Shelly Cynthia Shapiro, Sept. 17, 1978. B.A., Syracuse U., 1971; J.D., Washington U., St. Louis, 1978. Bar: Wash. 1978, U.S. Dist. Ct. (we. dist.) Wash. 1978. Assoc., Hillis, Phillips, Cairncross, Clark & Martin, P.S., Seattle, 1978—. Mem. ABA, Wash. State Bar Assn., Seattle-King County Bar Assn., Seattle-King County Mcpl. League, Order of Coif. Contbr. articles to legal jours. Office: Hillis Phillips et al 403 Columbia St Seattle WA 98104

AMUNDSON, GARY MARK, physician; b. Sheridan, Wyo., July 4, 1949; s. Henry Mark and Lola Wayve (Brown) A.; B.A., Union Coll., 1971; M.D., Loma Linda U., 1974; m. Connie Lucas, June 24, 1979. Intern straight pediatrics Cedars-Sinai Med Center, Los Angeles, 1974-75, resident in diagnostic radiology, 1975-78; adj. instr. pediatric radiology UCLA, 1978-79, asst. prof. dept. radiology sect. pediatrics, 1980-82; pediatric radiologist, chief div. ultrasonography Alta. Children's Hosp., Calgary, 1982—; fellow pediatric radiology Case Western Res. U., Cleve., 1979-80. Mem. Soc. Pediatric Radiology. Democrat. Seventh-Day Adventist. Home: 4 Strathclair Rise SW Calgary AB T3H 1G4 Canada Office: 1820 Richmond Rd SW Calgary AB T2T 5C7 Canada

ANAND, SURESH CHANDRA, physician; b. Mathura, India, Sept. 13, 1931; s. Satchit and Sumaran (Bai) A.; came to U.S., 1957, naturalized, 1971; M.B., B.S., King George's Coll., U. Lucknow (India), 1954; M.S., U. Colo., 1962; m. Wiltrud, Jan. 29, 1966; children—Miriam, Michael. Fellow pulmonary diseases Nat. Jewish Hosp., Denver, 1957-58, resident in chest medicine, 1958-59, chief resident allergy-asthma, 1962-63; intern Mt. Sinai Hosp., Toronto, Ont., Can., 1962-63, resident in medicine, 1963-64, chief resident, 1964-65, demonstrator clin. technique, 1963-64, U. Toronto fellow in medicine, 1964-65; research asso. asthma-allergy Nat. Jewish Hosp., Denver, 1967-69; clin. instr. medicine U. Colo., 1967-69; pres. Allergy Assos. & Lab., Ltd., Phoenix, 1974—. Mem. Camelback Hosp. Mental Health Center Citizens Adv. Bd., Scottsdale, Ariz.; mem. council Phoenix Symphony; mem. Ariz. Opera Co. Diplomate Am. Bd. Allergy and Immunology. Fellow ACP, Am. Coll. Chest Physicians, Am. Acad. Allergy, Am. Coll. Allergists, Am. Assn. Clin. Immunology and Allergy; mem. AMA, Ariz. Med. Assn., Maricopa County Med. Soc., West Coast Soc. Allergy and Immunology, Ariz. Soc. Allergists, N.Y. Acad. Scis., World Med. Assn., Internat. Assn. Asthmology, Assn. Care of Asthma, Ariz. Thoracic Soc., Nat. Geog. Soc., Smithsonian Instn., Phoenix Art Mus. Clubs: Sertoma Internat., Paradise Valley Tennis. Contbr. articles in field to profl. jours. Office: 2200 W Bethany Home Rd Phoenix AZ 85015 also 1006 E Guadalupe Rd Tempe AZ 85283

ANANE-SEFAH, JOHN CAMARA, physician; b. Bepong, Ghana, June 27, 1941; came to U.S., 1963, naturalized, 1979; s. Sam Kwabena Mireku and Akua (Gyafo) Mawu; B.S., Yale U., 1967; M.D., Harvard U., 1970; m. Patricia Anne Lawrence, June 2, 1973; children—Jason, John. Intern in surgery U. Colo., Denver, 1970-71, resident in surgery, fellow in trauma medicine, 1971-75; practice medicine specializing in gen. and vascular surgery; pres. Mid-County Surg./Med. Group, Inc., 1983—; mem. staffs Dominican Hosp., Community Hosp., Watsonville Hosp. Diplomate Am. Bd. Surgery. Fellow ACS, Royal Soc. Medicine (London), Internat. Coll. Surgeons, Internat. Acad. Proctology; mem. Santa Cruz C. of C. Contbr. articles to profl. jours. Office: 603 Capitola Ave Capitola CA 95010

ANARGYROS, NEDRA FLORENCE HARRISON, cytotechnologist; b. N.Y.C., Dec. 3, 1915; d. Leverette Roland and Florence Martha (Pickard) Harrison; student Emerson Coll., 1936; cert. in cytology U. Calif., San Francisco, 1957; m. Spero Drosos Anargyros, Oct. 21, 1940 (div. 1969). Supr. cytology San Francisco Gen. Hosp., 1957—. Mem. Am. Soc. Clin. Pathologists (affiliate mem.), Am. Soc. for Cytotech. (affiliate mem., cert. cytologist), Women Flyers of Am., DAR (1st regent La Puerta de Oro chpt., San Francisco), Nat. Soc. Colonial Dames of Calif., Huguenot Soc. of Calif. Republican. Christian Scientist. Club: Presidents of Mercer U. (Macon, Ga.). Home: 2503 Clay St San Francisco CA 94115 Office: 22nd and Potrero Sts San Francisco CA 94110

ANARGYROS, SPERO, sculptor; b. N.Y.C., Jan. 23, 1915; s. Drosos Speros and Martha Gustafson (Carlson) A.; m. Maria Ester de Mendez, Feb. 26, 1982. Scholarship student Art Students League, 1934-35, Master Inst. United Arts, 1935-36; travel study, Europe, North Africa, Mexico, C.Am. With Overseas Project 19, N.E. Africa, 1942-44. Exhibited in group shows NAD, 1938-40, 53-56, 59, 77, 78, Archtl. League N.Y., Pa. Acad. Fine Arts, 1940, Calif. State Fair, 1952, 53, DeYoung Mus., San Francisco, 1953-62, Erickson Gallery, Palo Alto, 1972, Rosicrusian Egyptian Mus., San Jose, Calif., 1972, Nat. Sculpture Soc. Ann. (award 1978), 1975, 77, 78; one man shows Houston Gallery, 1968, Corpus Christi Gallery, 1968; exhibited Bronze Greek Fisherman, Nat. Sculpture Soc. 50th Ann., N.Y.C., 1983; works include Redwood bas-relief Pacific Mut. Life Ins. Bldg., San Francisco, 1955, bronze bas-relief Main Office Bldg., First Western Bank, San Francisco, 1957; seal of City and County of San Francisco on Hall of Justice Bldg., 1960; Hawaii Statehood Medallion, Russell Varian Portrait Plaque on Physics Lab., Stamford U., 1962, Lawrence Mario Giannini, Bank of Am. Medallion, Gold Gate Bridge Medallion, 1962; bronze base relief Crocker Citizens Nat. Bank, San Mateo, 1967; Alaska Centennial coin, 1967; San Diego Coronado Bay Bridge Medallion, 1969; marble portrait Benjamin Franklin on facade of Franklin Savs. Bldg., San Francisco, 1964; Am. Negro Commemorative Coin, 1969; restored all sculpture on Palace of Fine Arts, San Francisco, 1965-66; life-size lion sculptures for Chinatown Branch of Honk Kong Bank, San Francisco, 1967; heroic monument Pedro Martinez, K.C.S.S., Guam, 1972; Yellowstone Park Centennial Commemorative Coin, Nat. Commemorative Soc., 1972; portrait bust William Bechtel, San Francisco, 1973, of Clarence Berry U. Alaska, 1973, Risen Christ figure, Guam; medallion for Calif. Hist. Soc., 1974; over life-size bronze of Pedro C. Lujan, Guam, meml. bust of Jack Robinson and Jockey of Year trophy Bay Meadows Race Track, Calif., 1974; 25th anniversary medallion Sta. KGO-TV, Calif., 1974; master model Twin Bicentennial Commemorative Medallion, San Francisco and U.S.A., 1976; bronze bas-relief plaques for the Eagle, Alaska Monument to N.W. passage of 1905, 1976; recreated 4 heroic size groups in cast stone for restoration of State Capitol Bldg., Sacramento, 1981-82; also numerous portrait busts, and heads, medals including Mrs. Edward Goldie, Mrs. William W. Mein, Edwin Herring, Sen. Ernest Gruening of Alaska, Mr. and Mrs. J. Garcia Lourdes. Recipient Best Sculpture award Acad. Artists Assn., 1959, John Spring Founders award Nat. Sculpture Soc., 1975. Fellow Internat. Inst. Arts and Letters, Nat. Sculpture Soc. (Council Am. Artist Socs. prize 1978); life mem. Art Students League N.Y. Club: Bohemian (San Francisco). Address: 541A Tunnel Ave PO Box 522 Brisbane CA 94005

ANASTIO, JOHN JAMES, business executive; b. Danbury, Conn., Mar. 10, 1940; s. James and Sophie (Zangas) A.; m. Harriet D. Efthimiou, Aug. 19, 1967; children—Christa, Elaine. B.S., Bowling Green U., 1961; M.B.A., Suffolk U., 1965. Sales and mktg. rep. Gen. Foods, White Plains, N.Y., 1962-65; nat. sales mgr. Hunt-Wesson Foods, Fullerton, Calif., 1965-76; pres. Old Nev. Enterprises, Las Vegas, 1976-78; exec. v.p. CHB Foods, Terminal Island, Calif., 1978-82; chief exec. officer Sun Harbor Industries, San Diego, 1982—. Served with U.S. Army, 1961. Home: 401 Fiesta Pl Fullerton CA 92635 Office: 2251 San Diego Ave Suite 216 San Diego CA 92110

ANAYAM, TONEY, gov. N. Mex.; b. Moriarty, N. Mex., Apr. 29, 1941; m. Elaine. Student Highlands U.; B.S., Georgetown U., 1963; J.D., Am. U., 1967. Asst. to Senator Dennis Chavez; exec. asst. U.S. Dept. State; legis counsel to Senator Joseph Montaya, 1966-69; adminstrv. asst. to former N.Mex. Gov. Bruce King, 1971; county atty. Santa Fe, asst. dist. atty. 1st Jud. Dist.; atty gen. N.Mex., 1975-78; gov. N.Mex., 1983—; sr. ptnr. Anaya, Strumor, Gonzales & Truman, Santa Fe. Democrat. Roman Catholic. Office: Office of Governor State Capitol Santa Fe NM 87503*

ANCELL, MARY KATHERINE ZIEG, property renovation company executive; b. Lincoln, Nebr., Apr. 10, 1943; d. Henry J. and Lydia B. Zieg; m. Ivan D. Ancell, Oct. 15, 1966. B.A., U. Iowa, 1966; M.A., Stanford U., 1974, Ph.D., 1978. Instr., U. Pa. Sch. Dental Medicine, 1969-70, project dir. NIH, 1970-72; instr. biol. scis. div. Foothill Coll., 1972-73; cons., subject matter expert NIH, San Francisco, 1970-74; research asst. Stanford (Calif.) Ctr. for Research and Devel. in Teaching, 1973-74; prin. operator Ancell Properties, Woodside, Calif., 1973—; owner Paradox Interiors, Woodside, Calif., 1978—; owner Paradox Assocs., div. Paradox Interiors, 1981—. Active, Woodside-Atherton Aux. to Children's Hosp. at Stanford. Recipient Recognition award Alpha Kappa Gamma, 1966; Certificates of Appreciation, Am. Assn. Dental Schs., 1972-76; grantee Div. Health Manpower, NIH, 1970; Recognition award Periodontics Dept. of U. Pa. Sch. Dental Medicine, 1972. Mem. AAUP, Am. Assn. Dental Schs., Am. Thoroughbred Racing Assn., Friends of Filoli, Peninsula Humane Soc. Office: PO Box 0150 Woodside CA 94062

ANCELL, ROBERT MANNING, publishing executive; b. Phoenix, Oct. 16, 1942; s. Robert Manning and Alice (Lovett) A.; B.A., U. N.Mex., 1971; m. Janet Claire Neuber, Dec. 21, 1966; children—Kevin Robert, Kristin Deann. Reporter, photographer, editor and producer KOB-TV, Albuquerque, 1966-72; sales exec., account mgr. Xerox Corp., Albuquerque and Denver, 1972-78; systems cons. Gen. Dynamics Communications Co., Englewood, Colo., 1978; gen. sales mgr. KRDO-TV, Colorado Springs, 1978-79; pub. Colo. Bus. Mag., Denver, 1980-82, Colo. Bus. Weekly, Denver, 1981-82, Colo. Bus. Directory, 1981-82, Denver Bus. Mag., 1983—; dir. advt. and mktg. Gen. Communications, Inc., Denver, 1982-83; cons. in field. Served with U.S. Army, 1962-64; lt. comdr. USNR, 1971—. Recipient 1st place award N.Mex. Broadcasters Assn. and UPI, 1972; Pres.'s Club award Xerox Corp., 1973, 75, 76. Mem. U.S. Naval Inst., Res. Officers Assn., Naval Res. Assn., Air Force Assn., Denver Advt. Fedn. Republican. Presbyterian. Clubs: Nat. Writer's, Optimists, Denver Press. Contbr. articles to profl. jours. Home: PO Box 387 10018 N Regency Pl Parker CO 80134 Office: 899 Logan Suite 307 Denver CO 80203

ANCELL, WILLIAM JOSEPH, city director of public works; b. Chgo., Oct. 17, 1937; s. Marion Sylvester and Linda Elizabeth (Walker) A.; m. Judith Anne Weeks, Oct. 1, 1961; children—William Joseph, Brian Eugene, Mark Edward. B.C.E., Tri-State Coll., 1959; A.S. in Bus., Lansing Community Coll., 1969-72. Registered profl. engr., Mich., Idaho, Fla. Engr., Monroe County (Mich.) Road Commn., 1959-61; county engr. Muskegon (Mich.) County Rd. Commn., 1961-65; asst. dir. pub. service City of Lansing, Mich., 1968-72; dir. pub. works, Boise, Idaho, 1972—. Served with U.S. Army, 1961. Mem. Idaho Soc. Profl. Engrs. (sec.-treas. S.W. Idaho chpt.), Nat. Soc. Profl. Engrs., Am. Pub. Works Assn. (v.p. Inst. Water Resources, dir. Rocky Mountain chpt.), Assn. Met. Sewerage Agys. mem. Boise Valley Christian Communion. Office: City Hall Boise ID 83701

ANCHOR, CLIFFORD JAMES (MICHAEL KARL ERICKSON), radio sta. mgr.; b. Waterloo, Eng., Aug. 20, 1936; s. James J. and Florence G. (Gilroy) A.; came to U.S., 1960, naturalized, 1966; student U. Toronto (External), 1956-57; 1 adopted son, Herbert William Kateley. Tchr., Metro Toronto (Ont., Can.) Sch. for Retarded Children, 1954-60; mgr. Stas. KAFE-FM and KBCO, San Francisco, 1960-67; dir., chmn. N.Am. Broadcasting Corp., San Francisco, 1963-71; adviser Study on Public Broadcasting, Cambridge Study Public Broadcasting Service/Corp. Public Broadcasting, 1966; advt., public relations cons. Booth-Erickson, San Francisco, 1968-78; mgr. Sta. KRJB-FM, Monte Rio, Calif., 1972—; columnist, asso. editor Russian River News, 1974-77; corr. Sebastopol Times, 1976-77. Mem. Monte Rio Bd. Edn., 1972—; mem. public relations adv. bd. Peace Officers Widows and Orphans Fund Sonoma County, 1976—; mem. 1st Senatorial Dist. Club Sacramento, 1971—; commd. maj. Calif. Army N.G., 1980, advanced to lt. col., 1983, spl. asst. to comdg. gen. 1981—; instr. Los Alamitos Res. Center, 1982. Recipient Public Service awards USN, USAF, U.S. Army, 1963-72; named hon. dep. sheriff Sonoma County, 1972, honored guest City of San Francisco at reception HRH Prince Charles of Britain, 1977. Mem. Nat. Assn. Broadcasters, Armed Forces Broadcasters Assn. (charter life), Police Marksman Assn. (charter), Am. Fedn. Police, Sonoma County Dept. Sheriffs Assn. (hon. life), Radio and TV News Dirs. Assn., N.G. Assn., U.S. Naval Inst. (life), USMC Assn. (life), Vietnam Vets. Am. (hon. assoc.), Monte Rio C. of C. (pres. 1977). Republican. Mem. Ch. of Eng. Clubs: Press (San Francisco); Masons. Office: Radio Sta KRJB-FM Box 250 21900 Siri Rd Monte Rio CA 95462

ANDARY, THOMAS JOSEPH, biochemist; b. Sault Sainte Marie, Mich., Oct. 8, 1942; s. Joseph Boula and Marion (Schwifetti) A. B.S., No. Mich. U., 1966, M.A., 1968; Ph.D., Wayne State U., 1974. Instr. biology No. Mich. U., Marquette, 1967-69; research asso. physiology Wayne State U., Detroit, 1973-76; sr. research scientist, mgr. coagulation research Hyland Labs., Costa Mesa, Calif., 1976-83; dir. quality control Hyland Therapeutics, Glendale, Calif., 1983—; lectr. in field. Recipient Research award Sigma Xi, 1973; NDEA fellow, 1969-72. Mem. Am. Chem. Soc., N.Y. Acad. Sci., Sigma Xi. Roman Catholic. Contbr. over 25 articles to profl. publs. Home: 531 N Canyon Monrovia CA 91016 Office: 4501 Colorado Blvd Los Angeles CA 90039

ANDER, HENRY FRED, electric utility executive, educator; b. Taylor, Tex., Sept. 12, 1947; s. Willard Nathaniel and Daisy Ruth (Sebastian) A.; m. Susan Rae Grieb, June 3, 1978; 1 dau., Janet Rae. B.S. in Indsl. Engring., U. Houston, 1970; M.S. in Ops. Research, U. Calif.-Berkeley, 1971; Ph.D. in Stats., Tex. A&M U., 1977. Instr., Inst. Stats., Tex. A&M U., College Station, 1975-77; asst. prof. dept. quantitative systems Ariz. State U., Tempe, 1977-79; supr. ops. analysis Salt River Project, Phoenix, 1979-80, supr. corp. planning, 1981—. Mem. Am. Statis. Assn., Ops. Research Soc. Am., Inst. Mgmt. Sci. Contbr. in field. Office: 1521 N Project Dr Tempe AZ 85281

ANDERBERG, ROY ANTHONY, journalist; b. Camden, N.J., Mar. 30, 1921; s. Arthur R. and Mary V. (McHugh) A.; A.A., Diablo Valley Coll., 1975; m. Louise M. Brooks, Feb. 5, 1953; children—Roy, Mary. Enlisted USN, 1942, commd. officer, 1960, ret., 1970; waterfront columnist Pacific Daily News, Agana, Guam, 1966-67; pub. relations officer Naval Forces, Mariana Islands, 1967; travel editor Contra Costa (Calif.) Times, 1968-69; entertainment and restaurant editor Concord (Calif.) Transcript, 1971-75; entertainment editor Contra Costa Advertiser, 1975-76; free-lance non-fiction journalist, 1976—. Mem. U.S. Power Squadron, DAV, Ret. Officers Assn., Am. Legion, VFW, U.S. Submarine Vets. World War II Assn. Democrat. Clubs: Martinez Yacht; Contra Costa Press; Toastmasters. Home: 2720 Lyon Circle Concord CA 94518 Office: Box 52 Concord CA 94522

ANDERJACK, GEORGE MICHAEL, museum director; b. Perth Amboy, N.J., Mar. 7, 1945; s. George Francis-Xavier and Helen (Yaskowsky) A.; m. Kathleen Leslie McCarthy, Aug. 14, 1980; children—Helana Theresa, Anna Sophia. B.S., Seton Hall U., 1966; postgrad. U. Del., 1973; B.Arch., U. Idaho, 1981. Instr., Perth Amboy (N.J.) High Sch., 1966-72; dir. Sandwich Glass Mus. (Mass.), 1972-73; exec. dir. Nez Perce County Hist. Soc., Lewiston, Idaho, 1976-81, Ventura County Hist. Soc., Ventura, Calif., 1981—. Served to capt. U.S. Army, 1967-80. Decorated Bronze Star medal. Mem. Am. Assn. Museums, Am. Assn. State and Local History, Nat. Trust Hist. Preservation. Clubs: Rotary, Optimists, Exchange (Ventura).

ANDERLE, CARL F., interior designer; b. Portland, Oreg., Aug. 2, 1922; s. Carl and Rose (Bigej) A. B.Interior Architecture, U. Oreg., Eugene, 1952. Interior designer House of Harlow, Portland, 1952-58; Interior designer Jordans Interiors Ltd., Vancouver, B.C., mgr. design services, 1972—. Served with USAF, 1942-46. Mem. Interior Design Inst. B.C., Interior Designers Can., Am. Soc. Interior Designers. Lutheran. Home: 1145 Eyremount Dr W Vancouver BC Canada Office: Jordans Interiors Ltd 1470 W Broadway Vancouver BC V6H 1H4 Canada

ANDERS, CAROL LOUISE, infection control consultant; b. Fresno, Calif., July 22, 1948; d. David and Viola May (Wommack) Carter; m. Bob Anders, Dec. 21, 1968. B.S.N., Fresno State Coll., 1970; M.Nursing Edn. with honors, Calif. State U.-Fresno, 1975; Cert. Hosp. Epidemiology with honors, U. Calif.-San Diego, 1982. Infection control nurse St. Mary's Hosp., San Francisco, 1978-82; instr. nursing Fresno Community Coll., 1976-78; patient educator Fresno Community Hosp., 1975-77; clin. instr., staff nurse Fresno Community Hosp., 1970-75; infection control cons., Waianae, Hawaii, 1982—; condr. workshops in field. Poster Session Travel scholar, 1982. Mem. Assn. for Practitioners of Infection Control. Contbr. articles to profl. jours.

ANDERSEN, BARBARA DORIS, manufacturing company executive; b. Mineola, N.Y., Aug. 25, 1946; d. Frederick W. and Ruth W. (Trebing) A.; m. John Patterson III, Nov. 30, 1968 (div.); 1 son, Andrew Oliver. B.S., U. Vt., 1968. Sales promotion mgr. Advalloy, Inc., Palo Alto, Calif., 1968-70; media dir. Anderson-Madison Advt. Firm, Mnpls., 1970-71; mktg. mgr. Getz Bros., Inc., San Francisco, 1971-76; pub. relations dir. Logical Machine Corp., Sunnyvale, Calif., 1976-77; exhibits mgr. Smith-Kline Instruments Co., Sunnyvale, 1977-78; mktg. communications mgr. Durango Systems, Inc., San Jose, Calif., 1978-80; mktg. services mgr. Tandem Computers Co., Cupertino, Calif., 1980—; cons. Andersen Assocs., Cupertino; guest instr., lectr. local colls. Mem. Bus. and Profl. Advt. Assn., Peninsula Mktg. Assn., Peninsula Women in Advt. (dir.), U. Vt. Alumnae Assn., Delta Delta Delta.

ANDERSEN, BRENDA CATHERINE, real estate broker; b. Red Wing, Minn., Feb. 6, 1942; d. Andreas F. and Loretta (Redding) A.; m. Richard Joseph Gabrych, Apr. 27, 1963; children—Kasha Ann, Richard Andersen; m. Charles Vincent Genthe, Feb. 21, 1981. Tchr., librarian John Marshall High Sch., Rochester, Minn., 1964-66; reference librarian Monterey County Library System, Salinas, Calif., 1966-68; librarian Am. Sch. Japan, Tokyo, 1968-77; dir. community resources data bank project Calif. State U.-Chico/United Way Butte County, 1977-79; agt., broker Century 21 Baker & Assocs., Chico, 1979—. Shasta Elem. Sch. rep. for Adv. Com. for Local Gifted Edn., 1982—; bd. dirs. Human Care Resources for Butte County, 1980—. Named Alpha Die-Hard Salesperson of Yr., Alpha Realty, 1982. Mem. Chico Bd. Realtors, Calif. Assn. for Gifted, Nat. Assn. Realtors, Calif. Assn. Realtors, No. Counties Exchangers. Republican. Home: 407 W Shasta St Route 6 Chico CA 95926 Office: 2260 Esplanade St Chico CA 95926

ANDERSEN, BRENT MERRILL, mech. engr.; b. Bell, Calif., Sept. 18, 1940; s. Kenneth Merrill and Margaret Jeanne (Rowley) A.; B.S. in Mech. Engring., Heald Engring. Coll., 1969; m. Judith DiAnne Meadows, May 30, 1976. Sr. designer Hexcel Corp., Dublin, Calif., 1966-67; project engr. Mother's Cake & Cookie Co., Oakland, Calif., 1969-72; staff engr. Clorox Co., Pleasanton, Calif., 1972-74, plant engr., Tampa, Fla., 1974-75; engring. mgr. Kingsford Co., Louisville, 1975-76, plant engr., Springfield, Ore., 1976-78, region engr., 1978—. Councilor, bd. dirs. Horizons Youth Program, 1974-75. Served with Security Agy., U.S. Army, 1962-65. Mem. Am. Inst. Plant Engrs., Nat. Rifle Assn. Republican, Baptist. Office: Kingsford Co 3315 Marcola Rd Springfield OR 97477

ANDERSEN, ERNEST CHRISTOPHER, lawyer; b. Minden, Nebr., Sept. 10, 1909; s. Dines Peter and Marie (Jensen) A.; m. Audrey Etta Robertson, Sept. 10, 1954; 1 dau., Elaine Carolyn Andersen Smith; 1 stepson, Albert Henry Whitaker. J.D., U. Denver, 1952, B.S. in Bus. Adminstrn., 1956. Bar: Colo. 1954, U.S. Supreme Ct. 1960. With U.S. Treasury Dept., Denver, 1935-39; accountant, Denver, 1939-41; with Civilian Prodn. Adminstrn., Denver, 1946-49; dep. state auditor Colo., 1949-51; with U.S. Commerce Dept., Denver, 1951-52; mgmt. cons., Denver, 1953-54; individual practice law, Denver, 1955-56; asst. dir. GAO, Los Angeles, 1957-58, Denver, 1959, Washington, 1960-69, cons., 1969-75; individual practice law, Denver, 1969-75, Cedaredge, Colo., 1975—; of counsel firm Robert P. Horen, P.C., Denver, 1977—; mem. faculty U. Denver, 1948-56; mcpl. judge Cedaredge, 1977—; exec. in residence Tulane U., spring 1973. Bd. dirs. Delta Montrose Electric Assn., 1976—, Colo.-Ute Electric Assn., 1980—. Served to lt. col. U.S. Army, 1941-46. Recipient Meritorious Service award GAO, 1968. Republican. Presbyterian. Clubs: Masons, Shriners. Home: 1856 Road 2375 Cedaredge CO 81413 Office: PO Box 747 Cedaredge CO 81413-0747

ANDERSEN, IRENE, company executive; b. Nov. 26, 1950; d. John A. and Agnes Purselley; m. Mark N. Andersen, Mar. 23, 1974. B.A. in Communications, Brigham Young U., 1974. With Datagraphix div. Gen. Dynamics Co., San Diego, 1978-80; mktg. communications mgr. Hydro Products div. Honeywell, San Diego, 1980—. Mem. Internat. Assn. Bus. Communicators (News Story Excellence award 1979). Club: Toastmasters. Home: 10684 Esmeraldas Dr San Diego CA 92124 Office: Hydro Products Div Honeywell PO Box 2528 San Diego CA 92112

ANDERSEN, SHIRLEY ANN, educator; b. Centertown, Mo., Nov. 2, 1929; d. Edward Elmer and Olive W. (Wagner) Keso; m. Kenwood Martin Andersen, Oct. 10, 1958; children—Maureen Kaye, Teresa Louise. B.S., Okla. A & M U., 1950, M.S., 1955; postgrad. Colo. State U., U. No. Colo., Adams State U., Cert. vocat. tchr., Okla., Nebr., Colo. Tchr. home econs. Perkins (Okla.) High Sch., 1950-52, Marlow (Okla.) High Sch., 1952-55; instr. food and nutrition U. Nebr., Lincoln, 1955-59, tchr. home econs. Potter (Nebr.) High Sch., 1960-61, Dalton (Nebr.) High Sch., 1962-68, Sterling (Colo.) High Sch., 1968—; judge local, state contests; mem. Extension Service Adv. Bd., North Central Evaluation Teams. Mem. Am. Vocat. Assn., Colo. Vocat. Assn., Colo. Edn. Assn. NEA, South Platte Edn. Assn., Delta Kappa Gamma, Omicron Nu. Republican. Lutheran. Club: Order of Eastern Star (Sterling, Colo.). Office: Sterling High Sch Bengal Blvd Sterling CO 80751

ANDERSON, ALDON J., judge; b. 1917; B.A., U. Utah, 1939, J.D., 1943. Admitted to Utah bar, 1943; chief judge U.S. Dist. Ct. Dist. Utah, Salt Lake City, 1978—. Office: US Dist Ct 251 US Courthouse and Post Office Salt Lake City UT 84101*

ANDERSON, ARMOUR A., paper company executive; b. Twin Falls, Idaho, Aug. 27, 1920; s. Carl Nathaniel and Victoria Sofia (Ragnar) A.; m. Jackie K. Mullinix, June 12, 1971; children—Armour, John Carl, Douglas Ryan. B.S. in Bus., U. Idaho, 1942. Partner Wholesale Paper and Supply Co., Twin Falls, Idaho, 1946, pres., owner, 1967—. Council mem. Coll. So. Idaho Mid Mgmt.; mktg. mgmt. mem. Magic Valley Rehab. Mem. Internat. San. Supply Assn., Idaho Employers Council, Idaho Assn. Commerce and Industry, Twin Falls C. of C., Beta Theta Pi. Clubs: Rotary, Elks.

ANDERSON, ARTHUR ROLAND, civil engr.; b. Tacoma, Wash., Mar. 11, 1910; s. Eivind and Aslaug (Axness) A.; B.S., U. Wash., 1934; M.S., Mass. Inst. Tech., 1935, D.Sc., 1938; J.D. (hon.), Gonzaga U., 1983; m. Barbara Hinman Beck, June 5, 1938; children—Martha Anderson Slocumb, Karl, Richard, Elisabeth Anderson Zerzan, Deborah Anderson Ray. Mem. staff MIT, Cambridge, 1936-38, 39-41, mem. ednl. council, 1954—; design engr. Klonne Steel Co., Dortmund, Germany, 1938-39; head tech. dept. Cramp Shipyard, U.S. Navy Bur. Ships, Phila., 1941-46; cons. civil engr., Stamford, Conn., 1946-51; co-founder Concrete Tech. Corp., Tacoma, 1951, sr. v.p., 1956—; pres. Anderson Enterprises Corp., Tacoma, 1957—; vis. lectr. U. Wash., 1954-55; chmn. bd. Anderson, Birkeland, Anderson & Mast, Engrs., Inc. (now ABAM Engrs. Inc.), Tacoma, 1951-77. Pres. Puget Sound (Wash.) Sci. Fair, 1954-58; mem. Tacoma Public Utility Bd., 1954-69, chmn., 1968-69; mem. Pacific Lutheran U. Collegium, 1976—; mem. vis. com. U. Wash.; mem. Wash. State Council for Post-Secondary Edn., 1977—. Registered profl. engr., Wash., Conn., B.C., Can.; named Alumnus Summa Laude Dignatus, U. Wash., 1980. Mem. Am. Concrete Inst. (hon. mem.; dir. 1962-69, pres. 1966-67, Constrn. Practice award 1962, Alfred E. Lindau medal 1970, Roger Corbetta award 1974, Charles S. Whitney award 1975, Turner medal 1977, Arthur J. Boase award 1979), ASCE (life mem., mem. tech. com. 1963-66, T.Y. Lin award 1971), Soc. Exptl. Stress Analysis (charter), ASTM, Nat. Soc. Profl. Engrs., Soc. Naval Architects and Marine Engrs., Internat. Assn. Bridge and Structural Engrs. (hon.), Prestressed Concrete Inst. (pres. 1970-71), N.E. Coast Shipbuilders and Engrs., Japan Concrete Inst. (hon.), Fedn. Internat. de la Precontrainte (F.I.P. medal 1974), Comité European de Beton, Nat. Acad. Engring., Sigma Xi, Chi Epsilon, Beta Gamma Sigma, Tau Beta Pi. Contbr. numerous articles in tech. of concrete and research on welded steel ships to profl. jours.; patentee in field. Home: 502 Tacoma Ave North Tacoma WA 98403 Office: 1123 Port of Tacoma Rd Tacoma WA 98421

ANDERSON, ARTHUR WESLEY, JR., physician; b. Cumberland, Iowa, June 26, 1924; s. Arthur Wesley and Marguerite Louise (Hanson) A.; B.A., Nebr. Wesleyan U., 1947; M.D., U. Nebr., 1951; m. Hazelmari Clinkerbeard, Dec. 26, 1972; children—Mark, Janis. Intern, Grace Hosp., Detroit, 1951-52; resident Topeka State Hosp., 1955-57, asst. sect. chief, 1957-58; fellow Menninger Sch. Psychiatry, Topeka, 1955-57;

cons. Winfield (Kans.) State Hosp., 1957-58; staff psychiatrist Agnews State Hosp., San Jose, Calif., 1958-60, teaching cons., 1960-66; med. dir. Adult and Child Guidance Clinic Santa Clara County, San Jose, 1960-62; pvt. practice medicine specializing in psychiatry, San Jose, 1962—; psychiat. cons. IBM Corp., San Jose, 1963-73; dir. psychiat. services Good Samaritan Hosp., San Jose, 1972—; lectr. U. Santa Clara Sch. Law, 1977-80. Mem. Santa Clara County exec. com. Nat. Safety Council; bd. dirs. Friends Outside, 1981—, Santa Clara County Profl. Service Rev. Orgn., 1982. Served with USN, 1952-55. Diplomate Am. Bd. Psychiatry and Neurology. Fellow Am. Psychiat. Assn., Royal Soc. Health; mem. AMA, Calif. Med. Soc. (utilization com., com. alcoholism and drug abuse, com. on well-being of physicians), Santa Clara County Med. Assn., No. Calif. (chmn. govt. in psychiatry com.), Santa Clara County psychiat. assns. Democrat. Episcopalian. Club: Commonwealth. Office: Good Samaritan Hosp 2425 Samaritan Dr San Jose CA 95124

ANDERSON, BARBARA ANN, nurse; b. Delphos, Ohio, Mar. 8, 1954; d. William John and Agnes Marie (Wehri) Ulm; m. Alfred Kahalelauniu Anderson, Oct. 22, 1977; 1 dau., Corinne. Diploma in nursing St. Vincent Hosp., 1975; postgrad. St. Joseph's Coll., Windham, Maine, 1982—. Cert. community health nurse Am. Nurses Assn. Staff nurse St. Vincent Hosp., Toledo, 1975-76; community nurse City of Toledo Community Health Services, 1976-77; nurse Upjohn Home Health Agy., Honolulu, 1977—, nursing supr., 1979—. Mem. Nat. Assn. Female Execs., Am. Bus. Women's Assn.

ANDERSON, BARBARA LOUISE, library director; b. San Diego, Jan. 5, 1933; d. Lorenzo and Louise (Morgan) A.; 1 son, Sean Allen. B.S., San Diego State U., 1954; M.L.S., Kans. State Teachers Coll., 1955. Br. librarian Los Angeles Pub. Library, 1956-59; br. librarian, reference, young adult librarian San Diego Pub. Library, 1959-64; librarian U.S. Army, Europe, 1964-69; coordinator Serra Reference Project, Serra Regional Library System, San Diego, 1969-71; head readers services Riverside (Calif.) City and County Pub. Library, 1972-74; county librarian San Bernardino County (Calif.) Library, 1974—. Bds. dirs. Inland Empire Symphony, 1982—, Riverside Mental Health Assn., 1975-79. Mem. ALA, Calif. Library Assn., Black Caucus of Calif. Library Assn., Congress of Pub. Library Systems (pres. elect 1983), Calif. County Librarians Assn., Calif. Soc. Librarians (pres. 1974-75), AAUW (pres. Riverside Br. 1976-77), NAACP, Bus. and Profl. Women San Bernardino. Democrat. Baptist. Contbr. articles to publs. in field. Office: 104 W 4th St San Bernardino CA 92415

ANDERSON, B(ENARD) HAROLD, educator; b. Greeley, Colo., Mar. 21, 1935; s. Benard Joel and Ethel Frances (Robinson) A.; B.S., Colo. State U., 1957, M.Ed., 1963; Ph.D., Ohio State U., 1966; m. Joyce Yvonne Lira, June 10, 1961; children—Tod Allen, Brett Benard. Instr. vocational agr., Cortez, Colo., 1958-63; research asso. Nat. Center Vocat. Edn., Columbus, Ohio, 1964-65; asst. state supr. Colo. State Bd. Vocat. Edn., 1965-66; asso. prof. Colo. State U., Ft. Collins, 1966-73, prof., head dept., 1973—. Cons. Mont. State Dept. Edn., 1970. Utah State Dept. Edn., 1972. Chmn. Pub. Sch. Parents Adv. Com., 1971-73; chmn. legis. com. pub. sch. Parent Tchr. Orgn., 1971-73; chmn. Am. Inst. Coop. Summer Inst. Young Farmers, 1971. Recipient Charles Shepardson award for teaching Colo. State U., 1972. Mem. Am. Assn. Tchr. Educators in Agr. (pres. 1972-73), Nat. Soc. Study Edn., Am., Colo. vocat. assns., Nat., Colo. vocat. agr. tchrs. assns., U. Council Vocat. Edn. (pres. 1978-79), Colo. Assn. Vocat. Adminstrs., Colo. Schoolmasters Club, Alpha Zeta, Alpha Tau Alpha, Phi Kappa Phi, Gamma Sigma Delta, Phi Delta Kappa, Alpha Delta Epsilon, Omicron Tau Theta, Iota Lambda Sigma. Author: Planning and Conducting Cooperative Work Experience Progress, 1965; Learning Through Experience in Agricultural Industry, 1978. Editor Agr. Edn. Round-up, 1963-64, 66-69, Am. Assn. Tchr. Educators in Agr. Newsletter, 1971-72. Home: 3316 Canadian Pkwy Fort Collins CO 80524

ANDERSON, CARL WILLIAM, lawyer; b. Chgo., Mar. 15, 1901; s. Charles Oscar Fredrick and Ada Augusta (Johnson) A.; A.B., Stanford U., 1926, J.D., 1928; m. Audrey Marion Regan, Aug. 15, 1931. Admitted to Calif. bar, 1928; practiced in Burlingame, Calif., 1928—; tchr. comml. law San Mateo Coll., 1929; atty. for San Mateo County Pub. Adminstr., 1935-37; appeals agt. Selective Service, 1938-46; city atty. San Carlos (Calif.), 1942-51; atty. Crippled Children Soc., San Mateo County, 1939, dir., 1940—, pres., 1963-65; dir., chief counsel Hillsborough Estates, Labco, Inc., Landon Pools, Landon Acceptance Corp., San Joaquin Bldg. & Loan Assn., 1929-33. Atty., founder Peninsula Humane Soc., San Mateo County, 1951, dir., 1951-75; pres. Internat. Students Com., 1964-66; campaign mgr. dist. atty. San Mateo County, 1934-35; atty., pub. adminstr., 1933-36; bd. dirs. Hillsborough Homeowners Assn., 1977-81. Recipient Presidential awards SSS, 1939-45; Congressional medal, 1946; plaques Rotary Club, 1972, Humane Soc., 1975; Paul Harris fellow, 1978; Calif. State award for service Easter Seal Soc., 1982. Mem. Internat. Platform Assn., Am., San Mateo bar assns., State Bar Calif. (chmn. disciplinary com. 1932-46), San Mateo County Trial Lawyers Assn., Theta Chi. Republican. Clubs: Bombay Bicycle, Capitol Hill, Masons, Shriners, Jesters, Eagles, Elks. Home: 30 Stonepine Rd Hillsborough CA 94010 Office: 1450 Chapin St Burlingame CA 94010

ANDERSON, CAROLINE ANNE, marketing executive, consultant; b. Belfast, No. Ireland, Jan. 21, 1947; d. James Joseph and Christina Toman; m. James Hugh Anderson, June 17, 1968; children—Keeli, Christina. Student Queens U., Belfast, 1965-67. Dir. mktg. and research Reef Corp., San Francisco, 1973-75; owner, operator Carole Anderson Mktg., Orinda, Calif., 1975—; mktg. cons.; condr. career seminars. Named Salesperson of Yr., Basic Accessories Corp., 1981. Mem. Nat. Assn. Female Execs., Internat. Entrepreneurs Assn. Republican. Roman Catholic. Republican.

ANDERSON, CHARLES EDWARD, lawyer; b. Milw., Aug. 14, 1941; s. Edward Walter and Edna Alice A.; m. Sally J. Moriarity, Aug. 29, 1964; children—Erika, Seth. B.B.A., U. Wis., 1964, J.D., 1966. Bar: Wis. 1966, U.S. Ct. Appeals (10th cir.) 1970, U.S. Ct. Appeals (9th cir.) 1972. N.Mex. 1974, U.S. Dist. Ct. N.Mex. 1974, U.S. Tax Ct. 1974, U.S. Supreme Ct. 1974. Tax atty. Arthur Andersen & Co., Milw., 1967-70; trial atty. appellate sect. tax div. Dept. Justice, Washington, 1970-74; tax atty., ptnr. Schlenker, Parker, Wellborn & Anderson, Albuquerque, 1974-77; sole practice, Albuquerque, 1977—; adj. prof. law U. N.Mex. Served to 1st lt. USAF, 1967-70. Mem. ABA. Republican. Club: Albuquerque Rotary. Home: 7522 Bear Canyon Rd NE Albuquerque NM 87109 Office: 200 Lomas St NW Suite 1210 Albuquerque NM 87103

ANDERSON, CRAIG STEPHEN, engineering firm executive; b. Long Beach, Calif., July 20, 1946; s. Andy Q. and Clara E. (Ross) A.; m. Susan L. Gardner, Aug. 7, 1971; children—Jeffery, April, Kari. Student Long Beach City Coll., 1964-65, 66-67; B.S. in Indsl. Tech., Calif. Poly. State U., San Luis Obispo, 1969; M.S. in Mgmt. Sci., West Coast U., 1976. Mfg. engr. Robertshaw Controls, Anaheim, Calif., 1970-73; indsl. engr. U.S. Divers Co., Santa Ana, Calif., 1973-74; mfg./facilities engring. mgr. Anaconda Co., Anaheim, 1974-78; v.p. Reel Grobman & Assocs., Santa Ana, Calif., 1978—, co. v.p., 1982—. Mem. Soc. Mfg. Engrs., Am. Inst. Indsl. Engrs. Republican. Office: Reel Grobman & Assos 3720 S Susan St Santa Ana CA 92704

ANDERSON, DAN ROGERS, economist; b. Geneva, Ill., Dec. 12, 1951; s. John Rogers and Clara Idele (Brelsford) A.; m. Jane Frances Stricklin, June 15, 1974. B.A. in Math. and Econs., Blackburn U., 1974; M.S. in Econs., Ariz. State U., Tempe, 1976. Economist dept. econ. security, State of Ariz., Phoenix, 1975—, research supr., 1977-80, sr. economist, 1980—; cons. in field. Recipient U.S. Dept. Labor internship award, 1979. Mem. Am. Econ. Assn., Western Regional Sci. Assn., Omicron Delta Epsilon. Contbr. articles to profl. jours. Office: PO Box 6123-733A Phoenix AZ 85005

ANDERSON, DARRELL EDWARD, psychologist, educator; b. Coleridge, Nebr., May 2, 1932; s. Roy Blenton and Ruby Grace (Cisney) A.; m. Violeta Salazar, Sept. 3, 1951; children—Robert, James, Timothy. A.B., York Coll., 1953; Ph.D., U. Nebr., 1958. Cert. psychologist, N.Mex. Counselor, asst. prof. U. Nebr., Lincoln, 1957-59; asst. prof. psychology Wittenberg U., 1959-61; chief psychologist Weld County Mental Health Ctr., Greeley, Colo., 1961-62; asst. prof. U. No. Colo., 1962-66, assoc. prof., 1966-70, prof., 1970-77, chmn. dept. psychology, 1972-77; prof. counselor edn., chmn. dept. counselor edn. U. N.Mex., 1977—. Mem. Am. Psychol. Assn., Am. Personnel and Guidance Assn., Assn. Counselor Edn. and Supervision, Rocky Mountain Psychol. Assn., Rocky Mountain Assn. Counselor Edn. and Supervision, N.Mex. Psychol. Assn., N.Mex. Personnel and Guidance Assn. Home: 9712 Admiral Emerson NE Albuquerque NM 87111 Office: U N Mex Albuquerque NM 87131

ANDERSON, DAVID ARTHUR, public relations executive; b. Kenosha, Wis., Feb. 24, 1955; s. Donald E. and Doris E. (Young) A. Student U. Wis.-Parkside, 1973; B.A., U. Wis.-Madison, 1977. Outdoor recreation instr. YMCA, Denver, 1978; with pub. relations dept. Denver Children's Mus., 1978-79, Rocky Mountain Am. Automobile Assn., Denver, 1979-81; mgr. communications Purgatory Resort, Durango Ski Corp. (Colo.), 1982—; author, freelance writer. Mem. Rocky Mountain Ski Writers Assn., Ski Writers Assn. So. Calif. Author: Colorado Mini Tours and Mystery Tours, 1981; weekly travel columnist Denver Post, Colorado Springs Gazette-Telegraph, 1979-81; contbr. articles to Colo. Visitor Rev., Conventioner Mag., The Traveler Mag., Evergreen Canyon Courier, Rocky Mountain Motorist. Home: 9772 County Rd 250 Durango CO 81301 Office: Purgatory Resort Durango Ski Corp PO Box 666 Durango CO 81301

ANDERSON, DAVID CHARLES, public relations executive, recording official; b. Framingham, Mass., Nov. 8, 1955; s. Richard A. and Betsey A. (Brown) A. B.A in Pub. Relations and Journalism, Utica Coll. of Syracuse U., 1977. With A.J. Lazarus Assocs., N.Y.C., 1977-79, Gilbert, Whitney & Johns, Morristown, N.J., 1979-80, Bozell & Jacobs, Union, N.J., 1980-81; account exec. Regis McKenna, Inc., Phoenix, 1981—. Mem. Pub. Relations Soc. Am. Producer, performer recording group xex. Home: 4341 N 24th St Apt 127 Phoenix AZ 85016 Office: 2747 E Camelback Rd Suite 222 Phoenix AZ 85106

ANDERSON, DONALD MEREDITH, banker; b. Milan, Minn., Feb. 19, 1928; s. Meredith A. and Lydia M. (Helseth) A.; m. Marvel Sundal, March 25, 1961 (dec.); 1 dau., Karen. B.A., U. Minn., 1950; M.B.A., Harvard U., 1952; postgrad. Grad. Banking Sch., Madison, Wis., 1965-67, U. So. Calif. Managerial Policy Inst., 1976. Vice-pres. comml. lending and corr. banking Northwestern Nat. Bank Mpls., 1958-69; v.p. lending Santa Barbara Nat. Bank (Calif.), (named changed to Santa Barbara Bank & Trust Co.), 1969-71, pres., 1971—; dir. Blue Cross So. Calif., Gen. Telephone Calif. Pres., Coleta Valley Hosp., 1979-80; bd. dirs. Pacific Coast Sch. Banking; gen. campaign chmn., pres. United Way, 1980-81; bd. dirs., v.p., Mission Council, Boy Scouts Am., 1977-80; mem. adv. bd. St. Vincent Sch., 1976-80; bd. dirs. Trinity Lutheran Ch., 1970-74, pres., 1973-74; bd. dirs. YMCA, 1971-80, v.p., 1977-80, campaign chmn., 1980. Served to 1st lt. USAF, 1952-53. Mem. Western Ind. Bankers Assn. (bd. dirs.), Am. Bankers Assn., Calif. Bankers Assn., Nat. Alliance Bus. (former bd. dirs., Tri-County Met. chmn.), So. Calif. Ind. Bankers (former bd. dirs.). Clubs: La Cumbre Golf and Country (former bd. dirs., pres.), Rotary. Home: 957 Via Los Padres Santa Barbara CA 93111 Office: 1021 Anacapa St Santa Barbara CA 93101

ANDERSON, DONALD NORTON, JR., elec. engr.; b. Chgo., Aug. 15, 1928; s. Donald Norton and Helen Dorothy (Lehmann) A.; B.S., Purdue U., 1950, M.S., 1952. With Hughes Aircraft Co., Culver City, Calif., 1952—, sect. head, sr. project engr., 1960-65, tech. mgr. Apollo program, 1965-66, mgr. visible systems dept., 1966-69, 70-73, project mgr., 1969-70, mgr. space sensors lab., 1973-79, mgr. space electro-optical systems labs., 1979-80, mgr. space electro-optical systems labs., 1980—. Recipient Apollo Achievement award, 1970; Robert J. Collier Landsat award, 1974. Mem. Research Soc. Am., Nat. Speleological Soc., Am. Theatre Organ Soc., Sigma XI (sec. Hughes Labs. br. 1974-75), Eta Kappa Nu, Sierra Club. Home: 2625 Topanga Skyline Dr Topanga CA 90290 Office: 2000 E El Segundo El Segundo CA 90245

ANDERSON, DONNA LOUISE, association executive; b. Scottsburg, Ind., Mar. 6, 1933; d. Guy Victor and Mable Emaline (Hester) Green; m. Glenn Wallace Green, June 27, 1953; children—Deborah Jo Green Guthrey, Daniel James, Dale Jeffrey; m. 2d, Coulter G. Anderson, Nov. 22, 1967; children—Machiel Lea Anderson Bain, Coulter Lance, Earidith Eugene. Student Ind. U., 1950-52, Gila Pueblo Coll., 1967—; grad. U.S. C. of C. Inst. Orgn. Mgmt., 1979. Asst. pub. Banner Publs., Pekin, Ind., 1947-62; editor Copper Belt Printing and Pub., Globe, Ariz., 1963-69; sec. to city mgr., producer city publs., City of Globe, 1971-72; mgr. Globe C. of C., 1972—; location sec. 20th Century Fox in Globe, 1969. Mem. Ariz. Tourism Adv. Council; bd. dirs. Ariz. Intra-State Tourism com.; sec. Globe-Miami Town Hall; mem. com. Boy Scouts Am.; sec.-treas. Gila County Fair Com., YMCA capital improvement drive; mem. Ariz. Acad.; bd. dirs. Gila County Hist. Soc.; sec.-treas. com. protection multiple use land. Mem. Ariz. C. of C. (dir.), Ariz. Chamber Execs. Assn., U.S. Jr. C. of C. (hon. life). Methodist. Club: Gila County Cowbelles. Author: Honor the Past, Mold the Future, 1976. Home: Russell Rd Globe AZ 85501 Office: 1450 N Broad St Globe AZ 85501

ANDERSON, DORRANCE I., dentist; b. Blue Earth, Minn., Jan. 30, 1917; s. Orville Jay and Clara (Havnen) A.; B.S., Iowa State U., 1941; D.D.S., U. Minn., 1949; m. Katherine Elizabeth Erickson, May 12, 1943; children—Michael Jon, Thomas Jay. Store mgr., plant worker Hap's Ice Cream Co., Phila., 1936-37; jr. marketing specialist U.S. Dept. Agr., Los Angeles, 1941-42; commd. officer USPHS, 1949-53; practice dentistry, Santa Barbara County, Calif. 1953—. First World brother, World Brotherhood Exchange, 1960; founder dental clinics in Madagascar, 1960, Kathmandu, Nepal, 1961; served at Lambarene, Gabon, Africa, 1962, 63, Peru, South Am., 1964, on S.S. Hope, Conakry Guinea, Africa, 1965, New Guinea jungles, 1967, Mellon Hosp., Haiti, 1969, Sierra Leone, 1969, Sarawak, 1970, Korea, 1971; served with Rotary 3-H programs, Bataan, 1981, Mex., 1982, Sumatra, 1983. Mem. Vols. for Internat. Tech. Assistance. Served as aviator USNR, 1942-45. Recipient Alumni Merit award Iowa State U., 1969. Mem. ADA (life), Calif. Dental Assn., Res. Officers Assn., Naval Res. Assn., Ret. Officers Assn., Explorers Club (N.Y.C.). Lutheran. Clubs: Adventurers (Los Angeles); Rotary (pres. club 1969-70; dist. gov. 1972-73), Channel City (Santa Barbara). Pioneer dental missionary to Island of Madagascar, Nepal. Home: 2251 Camino del Rosario Santa Barbara CA 93108 Office: 824 Maple Ave Carpinteria CA 93013

ANDERSON, EDGAR, educator; b. Tukums, Latvia, June 17, 1920; s. Voldemar and Emilija Alma (Kaneps) A.; Historian, U. Riga (Latvia), 1939-44; postgrad. U. Wurzburg (Germany), 1946-49, U. Leiden (Netherlands), 1948; Ph.D. in History, U. Chgo., 1956; m. Ligita Apinis, June 19, 1958; children—Raymond Edgar, Philip Rudolf. Came to U.S., 1949, naturalized, 1956. Lectr. U. Extension Wurzburg, 1945-49; asst. dept. mgr. Sharp & Dohme, 1950-52; instr. Lake Forest (Ill.) Coll., 1953-57; prof. history Calif. State U., San Jose, 1957—; lectr., Europe, 1949, 50, 56, 57, 67, 71, 73, 75, 77, 79, 81, 83, W.I., S.Am., 1957, 59, 60, 74, 76, 78, 80, 82, Australia, N.Z., 1967, Israel, 1983; gen. chmn. 2d Internat. Conf. Baltic Studies; leader hist., archaeol. expdn., Trinidad, Tobago, 1960, co-leader, 1979; disting. prof. Livingston U., 1969. Named Outstanding Educator in Am., 1972, Outstanding Prof., San Jose State U., 1974-75, Pres.' scholar, 1981. Mem. Am. Hist. Assn., AAUP, Am. Assn. Slavic Studies, Soc. Advancement Scandinavian Study, Assn. for Advancement of Baltic Studies (pres. 1972-73), Am. Acad. Polit. Sci., Inst. Caribbean Studies, Baltisches Forschungsinstitut (Germany), Phi Kappa Phi (Disting. Acad. Achievements award 1978), Tau Kappa Epsilon. Author: Western World, Western Horizon, 1949; Cross-Road Country Latvia, 1953; History of Latvia; 1914-20, 1967; Tobago, 1962; Die militarische Situation der Baltischen Staaten, 1969; The Ancient Couronians in Africa, 1970; The Ancient Couronians in America and the Colonization of Tobago, 1971; The United States and the Soviet Union in the 1980s, 1981; History of Latvia, 2 vols., 1982-83; editor-in-chief Latvian Ency., 1979; contbr. numerous articles to profl. jours., chpts. to books, also Ency. Brit., Harvard Ency. Am. Ethnic Groups. Hist. research in U.S., Eng., France, Germany, Holland, W.I., Italy, Spain, Pacific, USSR, Scandinavian and Baltic states. Home: 2571 Booksin Ave San Jose CA 95125

ANDERSON, EDWARD GUSTAV, engring. co. exec.; b. Seattle, Feb. 25, 1920; s. Edward Gustav and Elsie Magdalena (Pust) A.; B.S., U. Wash., 1942; M.E., Tex. A&M Coll., 1950; M.S., Stanford U., 1955; m. Virginia Leona Case, June 13, 1942; children—Edward Gustav Anderson III, Cheryl J. Anderson Ney. Commd. 2d lt. U.S. Army, 1942, advanced through grades to col., 1965; engr. I Corps Group, Korea, 1966-67; dir. U.S. Army Engr. Topographic Labs., Ft. Belvoir, Va., 1967-68; comdr. U.S. Army Topographic Command, Washington, 1970-71; dir. Def. Mapping Def. Topographic Center, Washington, 1971-72; ret., 1972; asso., mgr. aerial mapping div. Bovay Engrs. Inc., Albuquerque, 1973-81. Bd. govs. Goodwill Industries, 1979. Decorated Legion of Merit (4); named Albuquerque Engr. of Yr., 1980. Mem. Nat. Soc. Profl. Engrs., Am. Soc. Photogrammetry, ASCE, Am. Soc. Mil. Engrs., N.Mex. Soc. Profl. Engrs. Republican. Clubs: Masons, Shriners, Kiwanis. Contbr. articles to profl. jours. Home: 7513 Bear Canyon Rd NE Albuquerque NM 87109 Office: 3125 Carlisle Blvd NE Albuquerque NM 87110

ANDERSON, EILEEN R., municipal official; b. Bell, Calif., Oct. 18, 1928; d. Elmer F. and Ellen S. (Martini) Pulling; m. Clifford F. Anderson, Oct. 10, 1950; children—Mark Alexander, Patricia Manulani Anderson Dauterman, Lorita Ellen Anderson Naipo. B.A., U. Hawaii, 1950, postgrad. in bus. adminstrn., 1972-73. Personnel technician Hawaii Dept. Personnel Services, 1956-61; mgmt. analyst Hawaii Dept. Budget and Fin., 1961-64, program evaluation analyst, 1970-72, acting chief program evaluation br., 1972-73, chief of budget, planning and mgmt. div., 1974, dir. fin., 1974-80; tech. cons. Pub. Employees Compensation Appeals Bd., 1964-65; personnel mgmt. services technician City and County of Honolulu Dept. Civil Service, 1965-66; legis. analyst Hawaii Office Legis. Auditor, 1966-70; legis. analyst City and County of Honolulu Office of Council Services, 1973-74, mayor City and County of Honolulu, 1981—; chmn. pension task force Nat. Govs. Assn., 1979-80. Mem. budget and allocations com., bd. dirs. Aloha United Way; mem. adv. council Liliuokalani Trust, 1979-80, bd. dirs. Aloha council Boy Scouts Am., Hawaii Imin Centennial Corp.; mem. Honolulu Symphony, Hawaii Muscular Dystrophy Assn., ARC, Citizens Against Noise, Kaneohe Community Sr. Citizens Council, Grandmothers Club Hawaii, Mental Health Assn. Hawaii; mem. Hawaii vol. com. U.S. Savs. Bond Program. Named Woman of Yr. for 1980, Hawaii Bus. Mag. Mem. Am. Soc. Pub. Adminstrs. (program chmn. Hawaii chpt.), Pub. Personnel Assn. (pres. Hawaii chpt. 1965-66), Bus. and Profl. Women, U.S. Conf. Mayors, Ala Moana Jaycees. Democrat. Episcopalian. Clubs: Oahu Country, Waialae Country; Plaza, Honolulu, Hawaii Yacht, Kaneohe Yacht. Office: 530 S King St Honolulu HI 96813

ANDERSON, EVANS LELAND, educator; b. Upsala, Minn., Sept. 26, 1914; s. Carl Martin and Agda (Otelia) A.; diploma St. Cloud (Minn.) State U., 1934; B.A., Gustavus Adolphus Coll., 1938; M.A., U. Minn., 1939; Ed.D., U. Denver, 1951; m. Virginia Elaine Steinberger, Mar. 7, 1944; 1 dau., Anita Elaine. Tchr., Upsala (Minn.) Consol. Sch., 1935-37; dir. tchr. tng. Waldorf Coll., Forest City, Iowa, 1939-42; asso. prof. gen. and applied psychology St. Cloud State U., 1946-50, 51-54; prof. cdnl. psychology San Diego State U., 1954—; cons. in field. Served with U.S. Army, 1942-46. Mem. Am. Psychol. Assn., Calif. Tchrs. Assn., NEA, Am. Legion, Pi Kappa Delta, Kappa Delta Pi, Phi Delta Kappa, Pi Gamma Mu, Psi Chi. Lutheran. Club: Kiwanis. Author: Successful Teaching, 1972. Home: 4650 60th St San Diego CA 92115 Office: San Diego State Univ Coll Edn San Diego CA 92182

ANDERSON, FLORENCE ROSAMOND, aerospace co. exec.; b. San Francisco, Dec. 31, 1911; d. Gustave Emil and Nellie Elizabeth (Bengtson) Anderson; A.B., U. Calif., Los Angeles, 1933, M.A., 1938; postgrad. U. Calif., 1957-58. Instr. aircraft navigation for USN, Calif. Polytechnic Coll., San Luis Obispo, 1943-46; lectr. mathematics dept. U. So. Calif., Los Angeles, 1946-50; group leader numerical analysis Northrop Aircraft Co., Hawthorne, Calif., 1950-52; instr. math. dept. El Camino Coll., El Camino, Calif., 1952-53; mem. tech. staff Rockwell Internat., Los Angels, 1953-77, ret. Mem. Am. Math. Soc., Math. Assn. of Am., Assn. for Computing Machinery, AAUW, Pi Mu Epsilon. Presbyterian. Home: 5225 Onaknoll Ave Los Angeles CA 90043

ANDERSON, FLOYD M., psychologist, educator; b. Springville, Utah, Apr. 21, 1923; s. Thomas L. and Ellen E. (Whitmore) A.; B.A., Brigham Young U., 1950; Ed.D., Columbia U., 1956; m. Alice Ann Wilkinson Mangum, Mar. 23, 1974; children by previous marriage—Jennifer, Alicia, Devin Lincoln. Marriage counselor Lucas County Domestic Relations Ct., Toledo, 1953-56; lectr. U. Toledo, 1954-56; asso. prof. human devel. and family relationships Brigham Young U., Provo, Utah, 1956-61; exec. dir. Am. Inst. Family Relations, Hollywood, Calif., 1961-63; pres. Calif. Family Guidance Center, Los Angeles, 1963-74; sr. lectr. U. So. Calif., Los Angeles, 1963-68; vis. prof. Calif. State U., Los Angeles, 1967-74; lectr. U. Utah Sch. Medicine, 1974-75; psychologist, marriage counselor, Salt Lake City, 1974—; pres. High Country Sales & Devel. Corp., 1975—; cons. Utah County Juvenile Ct., 1958-61; adminstrv. adviser Utah State Dept. Pub. Welfare, 1957; mem. med. adv. bd. Los Angeles Planned Parenthood Assn., 1969-71. Bd. dirs. Sawyer Bus. Sch., Westwood, Calif., 1967-68; chmn. Friends of Children's Center Bd., 1977-78; mem. Utah Legis. Task Force on Family Ct., 1978—; chmn. com. children and youth Mental Health Assn. Utah. Served with USAAF, 1943-45. Grant Found. fellow, 1953. Fellow Am. Assn. Marriage and Family Counselors (chmn. admissions com. so. Calif. area 1968-70); mem. So. Calif. (v.p. 1964-65), Utah (exec. bd. 1976-78) assns. marriage and family counselors, Am. Psychol. Assn., Calif. Psychol. Assn. (com. family life 1967-70), Utah Psychol. Assn. (legis. chmn. 1976-79), Utah Psychologist in Pvt. Practice (pres. 1982-83), Utah Mental Health Assn. (chmn. com. on children and youth 1982-83), Assn. Humanistic Psychology. Republican. Mem. Ch. of Jesus Christ of Latter-day Saints. Home: 2180 Parleys Terr Salt Lake City UT 84109 Office: 1354 East 33d South Salt Lake City UT 84016

ANDERSON, GEORGE CORLISS, aerospace engring. mgr.; b. Los Angeles, Dec. 3, 1921; s. Gustave Emil and Nellie Elizabeth (Bengtson) A.; B.S. in Applied Physics, U. Calif., Los Angeles, 1949; m. Edna Dorothy Westergard, Aug. 2, 1952; 1 dau., Judith Annette Anderson Hindes. Research engr. sound and acoustics Don Lee Broadcasting System, Hollywood, Calif., 1948-51; engring. mgr. field dir., asst. to exec. v.p. N.Am. Aviation, Inc., Downey, Calif., 1951-64; engring. dir. Saturn II/Apollo program Space div. N.Am. Rockwell, Inc., Downey, 1964-72; engring. mgr. strategic missile systems Autonetics div. Rockwell Internat. Corp., Anaheim, Calif., 1972—; cons. acoustics and electronics; instr. math. and electronics Compton (Calif.) Coll., 1952-55; comml. airplane pilot. Served with USNR, 1944-46. Recipient Apollo program achievement award NASA, 1969. Mem. Am. Inst. Physics, Acoustical Soc. Am., Aircraft Owners and Pilots Assn., Am. Radio Relay League. Republican. Presbyterian. Clubs: East Whittier Radio, Autonetics Radio, Airventurers So. Calif. Patentee precision frequency regulator. Home: 14462 Linda Vista Dr Whittier CA 90602 Office: 3370 Miraloma Ave Anaheim CA 92803

ANDERSON, GEORGE DAVIDSON, accountant; b. Deerlodge, Mont., June 6, 1922; s. William and Florence (Cheeley) A.; m. Norma Gottula, Sept. 1, 1946; children—David L., Debi Farley, Richard G. B.A., Stanford U., 1947. C.P.A., Mont. Ptnr., Med Anderson & Co., Helena, Mont., 1950-57, Anderson & Zur Muehlen, Helena, 1957-79; pres. Anderson Zur Muehlen & Co., Helena, 1979—; dir. Mont. Power Co. Mem. exec. com. Pres.'s Pvt. Sector Survey on Cost Control, 1982-83. Served to capt. USAAF, 1942-45. Decorated D.F.C., Air medal. Mem. Am. Inst. C.P.A.s (chmn. 1981-82, dir.), Mont. Soc. C.P.A.s. Lutheran. Home: 1631 Highland St Helena MT 59601 Office: Box 1147 Helena MT 59624

ANDERSON, GEORGE MARTIN, pharmacist; b. Brule, Nebr., May 28, 1928; s. George Myrl and Delores Marie (Halligan) A.; B.S. in Pharmacy, U. Colo., 1954; m. Annette E. Girmann, June 12, 1949; children—Michael G., Philip C., Martin L. Partner, pharmacist Anderson Drugs Inc. (3 stores), Boulder, Colo., 1955-70; dir. pharmacy Community Hosp., Boulder, 1970—; clin. instr. U. Colo., Boulder, 1976—; mem. Colo. State Bd. Pharmacy, 1974-79, v.p., 1975-77, pres., 1977-79. Bd. dirs. Boulder Pow Wow, 1977-81. Served with USAF, 1948-49. Mem. Colo. Soc. Hosp. Pharmacists (pres.), Tri-County Pharm. Assn. (pres. 1971-72), Boulder County Pharm. Assn. (pres. 1957-58), Colo. Pharm. Assn. (pres.), Nat. Assn. Bds. Pharmacy. Republican. Methodist. Clubs: Elks, Masons. Home: 4750 Ricara Dr Boulder CO 80303 Office: 1100 Balsam St Boulder CO 80302

ANDERSON, GLENN M., Congressman; b. Hawthorne, Calif., Feb. 21, 1913; B.A., U. Calif., Los Angeles; m. Lee Dutton; children—Melinda, Evan, Glenn Michael. Mayor, councilman City of Hawthorne, 1940-43; mem. Calif. State Assembly, 1943-51; lt. gov. Calif., 1959-67; regent U. Calif., 1959-67; mem. 91st-97th Congresses from 32d Calif. Dist., mem. Public Works and Transp. com., chmn. surface transp. subcom., mem. Mcht. Marine and Fisheries com.; mem., chmn. Calif. State Lands Commn., 1959-67; trustee Calif. State Colls., 1961-67; former mem. Commn. of the Califs., Calif. Council on Urban Growth (also first chmn.); past chmn. Calif. Interstate Coop. Commn. Served in U.S. Army, World War II. Mem. Am. Legion, DAV, AMVETS. Clubs: Elks, Kiwanis, Native Sons of the Golden West, Redmen. Address: 2329 Rayburn House Office Bldg Washington DC 20515*

ANDERSON, GORDON M., petroleum company executive; b. 1932. B.S. in Mech. Engring., U. So. Calif., 1954. With Santa Fe Drilling Co. subs., Alhambra, Calif., 1954—, derrickman, 1954, driller, supt., zone mgr., 1958, v.p. 1967-68, exec. v.p., 1968-70, pres., 1970, corp. sr. v.p. and pres. Santa Fe Drilling Co. div. Santa Fe Internat. Corp., 1974, pres. and chief operating officer Santa Fe Internat. Corp., 1980—, also dir. Office: Santa Fe Internat Corp 100 S Fremont Ave Alhambra CA 91802*

ANDERSON, HAROLD PAUL, historian, archivist, bank executive; b. Darby, Pa., Oct. 4, 1946; s. Harold P. and Mary Ann A.; m. Kathleen E. Coyle, Sept. 6, 1969; children—Kathryn Erin, Kelly Rose. B.A., Villanova U., 1968; M.A., Ohio State U., 1969, Ph.D., 1978. Teaching and research fellow Stanford U., 1973-75; archives and library specialist Hoover Instn., Stanford, Calif., 1975-77; asst. archivist dept. history Wells Fargo Bank, N.A., San Francisco, 1977-79, pub. relations officer and corp. archivist dept. history, 1979, asst. v.p. and corp. archivist dept. history, 1979—; lectr. Stanford U., 1981—; bd. dirs. Nat. Council on Pub. History, 1981—. Mem. Am. Hist. Assn., Orgn. Am. Historians, Soc. Am. Archivists. Office: 475 Sansome St San Francisco CA 94111

ANDERSON, HERSCHEL VINCENT, librarian; b. Charlotte, N.C., Mar. 14, 1932; s. Paul Kemper and Lillian (Johnson) A.; B.A., Duke U., 1954; M.S., Columbia U., 1959. Librarian, Bklyn. Public Library, 1954-59; asst. bookmobile librarian King County Public Library, Seattle, 1959-62; asst. librarian Longview (Wash.) Public Library, 1962-63; librarian N.C. Mus. Art, Raleigh, 1963-64; audio-visual cons. N.C. State Library, Raleigh, 1964-68; dir. Sandhill Regional Library, Rockingham, N.C., 1968-70; asso. state librarian Tenn. State Library and Archives, Nashville, 1970-72; unit dir. Colo. State Library, Denver, 1972-73; state librarian S.D. State Library, Pierre, 1973-80; dir. Mesa (Ariz.) Public Library, 1980—; dir. Bibliographical Center for Research, Denver, 1974-80, v.p., 1977; v.p. Western Council State Libraries, 1978, pres., 1979; mem. Ariz. State Library Adv. Council, 1981-84, chmn., 1982-83; mem. Maricopa County Library Council, 1981—, sec., 1981-82, pres., 1983-84. Served with AUS, 1955-57. Mem. ALA, S.D. (Librarian of Yr. 1977, hon. life 1980), Mountain Plains (pres. 1974, dir. 1974-77), Ariz. library assns., Chief Officers of State Library Agys. (dir. 1974-76), Phi Kappa Psi. Episcopalian. Club: Mesa Kiwanis (dir. 1981—). Office: Mesa Public Library Mesa AZ 85201

ANDERSON, HUGH RIDDELL, space physicist, educator; b. Iowa City, June 16, 1932; s. William Arthur and Ann Maria (Riddell) A.; m. Isabel Hamer Smith, Feb. 4, 1955; Wendy Hilland, Apr. 1, 1972; children—Jennifer Ann, Shelby Lorraine, Ian Arthur. B.A., U. Iowa, 1954, M.S., 1958; Ph.D., Calif. Inst. Tech., 1961. Scientist, Jet Propulsion Lab., Pasadena, 1962-65; prof. physics, Rice U., Houston, Tex., 1965-81; sr. research scientist Sci. Applications, Inc., Seattle, 1981—. Served with USAFR, 1960-62. Mem. Am. Geophys. Union, AIAA. Contbr. articles to profl. jours. Office: Sci Applications Inc 13400 B Northrup Way Suite 36 Bellevue WA 98005

ANDERSON, IVAN DELOS, fine arts painter, printmaker; b. Yankton, S.D., Feb. 13, 1915; s. Albert and Elizabeth (Cooper) A.; B.A., Yankton Coll., 1937; cosmetology degree Poly. Coll., Los Angeles, 1939; m. Bette Stanley, Feb. 19, 1944; 1 son, Greg. Designer, Ivan of Hollywood, Beverly Hills, Calif., 1938-40, House of Westmore, Hollywood, Calif., 46-47; v.p. Nutri-Tonic Corp., Hollywood, 1948-59; one man shows: Falco Gallery, Sherman Oaks, Calif., 1967, Haggenmaker Gallery, Los Angeles, 1974, Cagle Galleries, Lubbock, Tex., 1974, Norton Simon's Hunt-Wesson, Fullerton, Calif., 1974, Huney Gallery, San Diego, 1975, The Gallery, Catalina Island, Calif., 1975, Expressions Gallery, Newport Beach, Calif., 1976, Moulton Playhouse, Laguna Beach, Calif., 1977; group shows: Festival of Arts, Laguna Beach, 1973-74, Chaffey Coll., Cucamonga, Calif., 1974, Art-A-Fair Festival, Laguna Beach, 1975, 76, 77, Laguna Beach Mus., 1974, 75, 76, Soc. Am. Impressionists, Scottsdale, Ariz., 1984; represented in permanent collections: Roy Rogers Mus., Victorville, Calif., Library of Congress, Los Angeles Children's Hosp., Los Angeles Mus., Mus. Modern Art, N.Y.C., Kaiser Found., Los Angeles, Hunt Wesson Co., Fullerton, Calif., Buffalo Bill Hist. Center Mus., Cody, Wyo., also represented in numerous pvt. collections including Pres. Ronald Reagan, John Wayne estate, Mary Picford estate; paintings commnd. for posters include: Hopalong Cassidy, 1976, Catalina Island Casino, 1977, Laguna Beach, Calif., 1977; paintings for Anderson's Children of World Serigraph series include Secrets, Mother and Child, Beach Buddies, Boy with Stick, Baby Brown Eyes and Pinkie. Served with AC, U.S. Army, 1941-46. Recipient 43 awards including Gold Trophy Grand Nat., 1940, Best Portrait of Year award Wilshire Ebel Club, 1967, Best of Show, Catalina Festival Arts, 1967, Grand prize Meth. Ch., Los Angeles, 1969, Wrigley award P.K. Wrigley, 1968, 1st prize Catalina Art Festival, 1976. Mem. Soc. Am. Impressionists, Art-a-Fair. Author, illustrator: Creative Hairshaping and Hairstyling (Best Litho Textbook of Year award Am. Lithography Soc.), 1947; Hairstyling, 1948. Home and Studio: 1060 Flamingo Rd Laguna Beach CA 92651

ANDERSON, J. BLAINE, judge; b. Trenton, Utah, Jan. 19, 1922; s. Leslie Howard and Theo Ellen (Stocking) A.; student U. Idaho, 1940-41, U. Wash., 1945-46; LL.B., U. Idaho, 1949; J.D. (hon.), Lewis and Clark Coll., 1978; m. Grace Little, Nov. 14, 1944; children—J. Eric, J. Blaine, Leslie Ann, Dirk Brian. Admitted to Idaho bar, 1949, practiced in Blackfoot, 1949-71; partner firm Furchner and Anderson, and predecessor law firms, 1955-71; U.S. dist. judge Dist. Idaho, Boise, 1971-76; U.S. circuit judge U.S. Ct. Appeals, 9th Circuit, 1976—. Chmn. Idaho Air Pollution Commn., 1959-60. Served with USCG, 1942-45. Fellow Am. Coll. Trial Lawyers; mem. ABA (mem. ho. of dels. 1959-60, 64-71, gov. 1971-74, mem. council gen. practice sect. 1962-66, 70-71, mem. adv. bd. editors Jour. 1969-71), Idaho State Bar (bd. commrs. 1958-61, pres. 1960-61, chmn. unauthorized practice of law com. 1955-58), S.E. Idaho Dist. Bar (pres. 1957-58), Am. Judicature Soc. (dir. 1961-66), Am. Coll. Probate Counsel. Office: US Court Bldg 550 Fort St Boise ID 83724

ANDERSON, JACK BUDD, tax lawyer, accountant, writer, television commentator; b. Omaha, Nebr., Sept. 12, 1946; s. L.M. and V. A. (Carlson) A.; m. Sandra J. Sheffer, Sept. 3, 1972 (div.). J.D., U. Denver, 1972; LL.M. in Taxation, NYU, 1980. Bar: Colo., Calif., Nebr. 1972; C.P.A., Colo., Calif., N.Y. Tax mgr. Peat, Marwick, Mitchell and Co., Denver N.Y.C. and Los Angeles, 1974-82; tax ptnr. Cogswell & Wehrle, Attys. at Law, Denver, 1982—. Office: Cogswell & Wehrle Attys At Law 1660 Lincoln St Suite 1910 Denver CO 80264

ANDERSON, JACK CARTER, psychotherapist, consultant; b. Dallas, Mar. 5, 1936; s. George Lester and Velma Vasser (Dixon) A. B.A., So. Meth. U., 1958; M.A., Pepperdine U., 1963. Registered marriage, family and child counselor, Calif. Music dir. Mark Wilson Enterprises, Hollywood, Calif., 1960-65; clin. psychologist Orange County (Calif.) Probation Dept., Santa Ana, 1963-69; Wash. State dir. Nat. Council on Crime & Delinquency, Seattle, 1969-71; pvt. practice psychotherapy, 1972—; sr. ptnr. Madison Group, Seattle, 1972—; cons. to corps. Mem. Am. Psychol. Assn., Nat. Assn. Marriage and Family Counselors. Democrat. Club: Wash. Athletic (Seattle). Appearances on radio and TV; contbr. articles to jours., mags., newspapers. Office: 2820 E Madison Seattle WA 98112

ANDERSON, JACK JOE, communications executive; b. Lipan, Tex., Oct. 22, 1928; s. William Amon and Tommie Lucille (Roberts) A.; B.A., San Jose State U., 1965, M.A., 1967; postgrad. in bus. adminstrn. Pepperdine U., Los Angeles; m. Maria I. Kamantauskas, Mar. 13, 1976; children—Mark, Douglas, Craig. Asst. mgr. edn. systems Lockheed Missiles & Space Co., Sunnyvale, Calif., 1966-69; v.p. Learning Achievement Corp., San Jose, Calif., 1969-74; mgr. instrnl. systems Ford Aerospace & Communications Corp., Pasadena, Calif., 1974-83; pres. Anderson & Assocs., Alta Loma, Calif., 1983—. Cons. tng. programs and systems, 1969-74. Served with USAF, 1946-66. Decorated 2 Air Force commendation medals; recipient nat. award for tng. program design Indsl. TV Assn., 1974. Mem. Am. Mgmt. Assn., Am. Soc. Tng. and Devel. Contbr. tech. and gen. instrnl. materials in field. Office: 9155 Carriri Ct Alta Loma CA 91701

ANDERSON, JAMES LEROY, insurance company executive; b. Wichita, Kans., Dec. 18, 1943; s. Harold and Freda (Windhorst) A.; m. Carolyn Thompson, Oct. 25, 1980; children—Raif, Ingrid. B.S., Fort Hays Kans. State Coll., 1965. Regional supr. Travelers Ins. Co., 1965-75; pres. Nat. Am. Ins. Co. Calif., Lakewood, 1975-82; exec. v.p., chief operating officer Stuyvesant Life Ins. Co. & Nat. Am. Ins. Co. N.Y., Allentown, Pa., 1980-82; pres., chief exec. officer Hosp. Underwriters Inc. Pasadena, Calif., 1982—; chmn., chief exec. officer Physician and Surgeons Underwriting Corp., Pasadena. Recipient Gen. Ins. cert. Ins. Inst. Am., 1970. Mem. Young Pres.'s Orgn., Alpha Kappa Psi. Republican. Lutheran. Home: 1259 Glenclaire Dr Walnut CA 91789 Office: Hosp Underwriters Inc 301 E Colo Blvd Pasadena CA 91101

ANDERSON, JAMES MARVIN, financial executive; b. Portland, Oreg., Apr. 16, 1942; s. Harvey Howard and Dorothy Hazel (Raymond) A.; B.S.B.A., Portland State U., 1976; postgrad. U. Idaho, 1977; m. Marsha Kay Mills, July 6, 1963; children—Deborah Jill, James Neal. Jr. acct. Portland Gen. Electric Co., 1963-66, acct., 1967-71, internal audit mgr., 1972-74, asst. controller, 1975-80; treas./controller Beartooth Coal Co., Portland, 1978-80; v.p. adminstrv. services N.W. Energy Services Co., Bellevue, Wash., 1980-81, v.p. fin. and adminstrn., 1982—. Served with Oreg. N.G., 1963-68. Cert. mgmt. acct., 1977. Mem. Nat. Assn. Accts. (chpt. pres. 1977-78), Inst. Mgmt. Accts. N.W. Electric Light and Power Assn. Republican. Lutheran. Home: 14845 SW Beard Rd Beaverton OR 97007 Office: PO Box 1090 Kirkland WA 98033

ANDERSON, JANIS CLARE, marketing official; b. Salem, Oreg., Dec. 9, 1946; d. Gerald D. and Margaret R. (Driscoll) Kendall; m. Donald A. Anderson, Sept. 17, 1966 (div.); children—Stephen Kendall, Scott Christopher. A. Mgmt. and Supervision, Portland Community Coll., 1979; B.S. in Mgmt., Marylhurst Coll., 1981. Sec. to comptroller Highline Sch. Dist., Seattle, 1966-68; with Mktg. Support div. Westinghouse Electric Corp., Portland, Oreg., 1972—. Mem. Meeting Planners Internat. (past v.p. Oreg. chpt., past dir.), Parents Without Ptnrs. (dir.), Network (past v.p. programs, now mem. at large, dir.). Office: 5901 SW Macadam Ave Portland OR 97201

ANDERSON, JAY ENNIS, biologist, educator; b. Logan, Utah, Oct. 18, 1937; s. Fred and Viola May (Lovell) A.; m. Phyllis Ann Noel, June 13, 1959; 1 son, Jay Daniel. B.S., Mont. State U., 1959; M.S., Syracuse U., 1967, Ph.D. in Botany, 1971. High sch. biology tchr. Deer Lodge, Mont., 1964-68; staff cons. biol. scis. curriculum study Boulder, Colo., 1971-74; research assoc. dept. chem. engring. U. Colo., Boulder, 1974-75; asst. prof. dept. biology Idaho State U., Pocatello, 1975-81, assoc. prof., 1982—; cons. Unified Sci. and Math. for Elem. Schs. project Edn. Devel. Ctr., Newton, Mass., 1974-77. Served with U.S. Army, 1959-62. Mem. AAAS, Ecol. Soc. Am., Am. Inst. Biol. Scis., Soc. Range Mgmt. Contbr. numerous articles to profl. jours. Office: Box 8007 Idaho State U Pocatello ID 83209

ANDERSON, JENNIFER, food and nutrition extension specialist, educator; b. Ripon, Yorkshire, Eng., Nov. 29, 1943; d. Ralph Mehew and Annie Kathleen Bates; m. Oren Paul Anderson, Mar. 20, 1967; children—Craig Rolf, Neil Owen. Student Leicester Coll. Domestic Sci., Eng., 1961; M.S. in Human Nutrition, Colo. State U., 1977. Registered Dietitian. Dietitian, head supr. Northwestern U. Food Service, Evanston, Ill., 1965-68; clin. dietician Univ. Hosp., Bergen, Norway, 1969-70; extension specialist EFNEP, Colo. State U., Ft. Collins., 1977-81, food and nutrition specialist, instr. dept. food sci. and nutrition, Colo. State U., 1982—; cons., lectr. Bd. dirs. Colo. Heart Assn., dir., co-author Healthy Heart Program. Recipient Colo. Dairy Council Nutrition Edn. award, 1982-83. Mem. Am. Dietetic Assn., Soc. Nutrition Edn., Am. Home Econs. Assn. News columnist Denver Post; contbr. numerous articles to profl. jours.

ANDERSON, JEROME TAYLOR, biomedical engineer; b. Arcata, Calif., July 20, 1942; s. Donald Chester and Hazel Marie (Taylor) A. A.B., Humboldt State U., 1965, postgrad. Calif. State U., 1965-67, U. Calif.-San Francisco Med. Ctr., 1973. Cert. clin. engr., biomed. equipment technician. Bioengr. Automated Health Systems, Burlingame, Calif., 1970-71; biomed. engr. Apollo 14 Recovery Team, 1971; med. service mgr. SIMCO Electronics, Santa Clara, Calif., 1971-73; biomed. engr. Marin Gen. Hosp., Greenbrae, Calif., 1973-75; regional mgr. Shared Biomed. Engring. Services, Tustin, Calif., 1975-77; dir. biomed. engring. St. Joseph Hosp., Orange, Calif., 1977—; cons. in field. Served with USPHS, 1965-70. Calif. Heart Assn. fellow, 1963; San Mateo County Heart Assn. grantee, 1959. Mem. Assn. Advancement Med. Instrumentation, Am. Soc. Hosp. Engring., Nat. Fire Protection Assn. Republican. Presbyterian. Club: Bahia Corinthian Yacht (Newport Beach, Calif.). Contbr. articles to profl. jours. Home: 613 1/2 Narcissus Ave Corona Del Mar CA 92625 Office: 1100 W Stewart Dr Orange CA 92667

ANDERSON, JILL MARIE, data processing supervisor; b. Albuquerque, Oct. 16, 1956; d. Robert L. and Eileen M. (Brunner) Anderson. B.S. cum laude in Mgmt. Sci., Kean (N.J.) Coll., 1976; postgrad. U. Tex. 1982—. Mem. acctg. dept. Prudential Life Ins. Co., Newark, 1976-80; programmer/analyst Phillips Uranium Co., Albuquerque, 1980-82; data processing ops. supervisor Phillips Petroleum Co., Odessa, Tex., 1982—; tchr. ballooning Freedom U., Albuquerque. Mem. Albuquerque Aerostat Ascension Assn., Balloon Fedn. Am. Republican. Roman Catholic. Home: 5050 Tanglewood #2308 Odessa TX 79762 Office: 4001 Penbrook Odessa TX 79762

ANDERSON, JOAN BROWNELL, economics educator; b. Colorado Springs, Colo., Oct. 15, 1938; d. John Wesley and Emily Margarite (Baer) Brownell; m. Fredric Clifford Anderson, July 1, 1961; children—Carolyn Anne, Fredric Brownell, Jo Ellen. B.A. in Econs., San Diego State U., 1960; M.A., Stanford U., 1961; Ph.D. in Econs., U. Calif.-San Diego, 1971. Lectr., San Diego State U., 1961-64, 71-81; teaching asst. U. Calif.-San Diego, 1965-68; sr. economist Calif. Border Area Resource Ctr., 1979-81; asst. prof. econs. U. San Diego, 1981-83, assoc. prof., 1983—; pub. speaker. Fellow Stanford U., 1960; recipient award for outstanding student Wall Street Jour., 1960; Regional Employment Tng. Consortium grantee, 1979. Mem. Am. Econs. Assn., Western Econs. Assn., Assn. Borderland Scholars. Democrat. Presbyterian. Club: Altrusa. Author: Directory of U.S. Border Data and Information, 1980; contbr. articles to profl. jours., chpts. in books. Office: Sch Bus U San Diego Alcala Park San Diego CA 92110

ANDERSON, JOAN MAE, aerospace engineering manager; b. Seattle, May 10, 1934; d. Grant Merrifield and Lottie Adele (Deck) Merrifield; married. B.S. in Physics, U. Wash., 1957; M. Ed. in Sci. Edn., U. Utah, 1962; M.S. in Physics, Purdue U., 1966. Tchr. Seattle Sch. Dist. 1, 1957-67; systems analyst Fed. Electric Corp., ITT, Vandenberg AFB, Calif., 1967-72, sr. engr., 1972-75, supr., 1975-80, mgr. dept. program support, 1980—. NSF scholar, grantee. Mem. Nat. Mgmt. Assn., AIAA (chmn. Vandenberg sect.), Soc. Photo-Optical Instrumentation Engrs. Office: PO Box 5728 RO400 Vandenberg AFB CA 93437

ANDERSON, JOHN RANDOLPH, counseling psychologist; b. Bluefield, Va., Nov. 27, 1916; s. Reece Campbell and Flora (Bowling) A.; B.S., Roanoke Coll., 1938; M.S., Va. Poly. Inst., 1950; m. Margaret Ruth Dennis, Mar. 9, 1941; children—Linda Gail Anderson Couchman, Randolph Campbell. Tchr., asst. prin. Va. Public Schs., 1939-42; assoc. dir. counseling and placement Va. Poly. Inst., Blacksburg, 1947-64; counseling psychologist Clemson (S.C.) U., 1964—; dir. Va. State Mental Health Center. Mem. Blacksburg City Council, 1961-62, vice mayor, 1962-64. Served to lt. (j.g.), USNR, 1942-45. Recipient Meritorious Achievement award Directory of Ednl. Specialists, 1970. Mem. New River Valley (Va.) Mental Health Assn. (pres.), Am. Acad. Polit. and Social Sci., Am. Personnel and Guidance Assn., Nat. Vocat. Guidance Assn. Lutheran. Club: Lions. Contbg. author: The Clearing House, 1959; contbr. articles to profl. jours. Home: 1038 Via Terrado Tucson AZ 85710

ANDERSON, JOSEPH JAMES, librarian; b. Dubuque, Iowa, June 28, 1932; s. George James and Agnes Irene (Melroy) A. B.A., St. Mary's U., 1953; M.L.S., U. Calif.-Berkeley, 1961. Library asst. Bolt Hall Sch. Law Library, U. Calif.-Berkeley, 1960-61; sr. tech. librarian Lockheed Missiles & Space Co., Van Nuys, Calif., 1961-64; mgr. tech. processing sect. tech. library Ampex Corp., Redwood City, Calif., 1964-67; dir. ref. services div. Nev. State Library, Carson City, 1967-70, Nev. state librarian, Carson City, 1970—, state hist. records coordinator, 1979—. Chmn. Western States Adv. Council Continuing Edn., 1974-76; mem. Western States Commn. on Higher Edn., 1970-77; sec.-treas. Western Council State Libraries, 1977—; chmn. Nev. Elementary and Secondary Edn. Act Title II Council, 1971-76. Served to lt. comdr., USNR, 1954-66. Mem. ALA, Nev., Calif., Mountain Plains (v.p., pres.-elect 1979-81), Spl. library assns., Nev. Environ. Edn. Council. Republican. Roman Catholic. Home: PO Box 1693 Carson City NV 89701 Office: Nevada State Library Capitol Complex Carson City NV 89710

ANDERSON, JUDITH JAN, home economics educator, receptionist; b. Cascade, Idaho, June 15, 1955; d. Dale Vernon and Audrey Isabella (Harvey) A. A.A. in Gen. Sci., Cottey Coll.; B.S. (Mary Hall Niccolls scholar, PEO scholar) in Home Econs., U. Idaho, 1977. Cert. secondary edn., vocat. home econs. tchr., Idaho. Substitute tchr. pub. schs., Boise and Meridian, Idaho, 1978—; co-mgr. Vans Catering Co., Boise, 1978—; tchr. home econs. Meridian Jr. High Sch., 1977—; receptionist week-end Sta. KTVB-TV; mem. adv. com. spl. edn. curriculum, Meridian. Mem. PEO, Phi Beta Kappa, Phi Upsilon Omicron, Kappa Alpha Theta (alumni chpt. officer). Republican. Methodist. Club: Jobs Daughters. Home: 5271 Sorrento Dr Boise ID 83704 Office: Meridian Jr High Sch 1507 W 8th St Meridian ID 83642

ANDERSON, JULIA ESTHER, nursing adminstrator, cons.; b. Butte, Mont., Oct. 20, 1929; d. John K. and Julia (Peterson) Visnes; m. Dennett Asa Anderson, Apr. 16, 1952; children—D. John, Leslie Jo Burr. B.S. with Honors, U. Utah, 1966, M.S., 1968; cert. R.N. St. Lukes Hosp., and Nursing Sch., Boise, Idaho, 1950; cert. nurse midwife. Staff nurse hospitals in Idaho and Utah, 1950-65; clin. specialist LDS Hosp., Salt Lake City, 1969-75; asst. dir. nursing 1975—; mem. clin. faculty U. Utah Coll. Nursing; cons. Ob-Gyn. to corporate hospitals. Mem. Am. Coll. Nurse Midwifery, Nursing Assn. Am. Coll. Ob-Gyn, Internat. Childbirth Edn. Assn., Nat. Perinatal Assn. Contbr. articles to profl. jours. Home: 4821 Oak Terr Salt Lake City UT 84117 Office: LDS Hosp 325 8th Ave Salt Lake City UT 84113

ANDERSON, KAREN EMILY, educator; b. The Calles, Oreg., Apr. 21, 1945; d. Joseph Jacob and Grace Emily (Day) Meistrell; m. Joseph Russell Anderson, June 12, 1965; children—Joseph Lloyd, Timothy David. Student Wright State U., 1969; B.S. in Home Econs., Oreg. State U., 1970; postgrad. U. N.Mex., 1979, 82—. Cert. tchr., N.Mex. Nursery sch. tchr. Lollipop House Day Care Ctr., Dayton, Ohio, 1966-67; sci. tchr. Mad River Township Schs., Dayton, 1967-69; kindergarten tchr. Mary Moppetts Day Care Ctr., Albuquerque, 1977; substitute tchr. Albuquerque Pub. Schs., 1978-79; home econs. tchr. McKinley Middle Sch., Albuquerque, 1980—; sponsor Future Homemakers Am., 1981-82. Program v.p. Protestant Women of the Chapel, Kirtland AFB, 1975-76; Sunday Sch. tchr. Sombra del Monte Christian Ch., 1977-80; Evening Circle chmn. Christian Women's Fellowship, 1979-80, youth group sponsor, 1982—. Mem. Am. Home Econs. Assn., N. Mex. Vocat. Tchrs. Assn., Am. Fedn. Tchrs. Republican. Club: Officer's Wives (Kirtland AFB; contbr. articles to newspaper). Home: 8304 Yeager Dr NE Albuquerque NM 87109 Office: McKinley Middle Sch 4500 Comanche Rd NE Albuquerque NM 87110

ANDERSON, KARL RICHARD, human factors engr.; b. Vinita, Okla., Sept. 27, 1917; s. Axel Richard and Hildred Audrey (Marshall) A.; B.S., Calif. Western U., 1964, M.A., 1966; Ph.D., U.S. Internat. U., 1970; m. Jane Shigeko Hiratsuka, June 20, 1953; 1 son, Karl Richard. Engr. personnel subsystems Atlas Missile Program, Gen. Dynamics, San Diego, 1960-63; design engr. Solar div. Internat. Harvester, San Diego, 1964-66, sr. design engr., 1967-69, project engr., 1970-74, product safety specialist, 1975-78; engring. cons., lectr. Am. Indian Sci. and Engring. Soc. Served to maj. USAF, 1936-60. Registered profl. engr., Calif. Republican. Episcopalian. Home: 5886 Scripps St San Diego CA 92122

ANDERSON, KATHLEEN EASON, counselor, educator; b. Kellogg, Idaho, Feb. 11, 1947; d. Lloyd James and Eula Lorraine (Anderson) Eason; m. James Anton Anderson, Dec. 25, 1968; 1 son, Matthew James. B.A., Boise State U., 1969; M.A., San Jose State U., 1975; postgrad. Coll. Idaho, 1979-80, U. Idaho, 1980-83. Cert. secondary tchr., secondary prin., cert. in pupil personnel, Idaho. Tchr. math. Escambia High Sch., Pensacola, Fla., 1969-70; tchr. math., sci. L.L. Shannon Jr. High Sch., Corpus Christi, Tex., 1970-71; counselor Lowell Scott Jr. High Sch., Meridian, Idaho, 1975-79, Lake Hazel Jr. High Sch., Meridian, 1979-80; counselor Borah High Sch., Boise, Idaho, 1980—, tchr. math., 1983—; mem. Citizens Task Force for Solutions to Overcrowding at Meridian High Sch. Mem. Idaho Edn. Assn., Boise Edn. Assn., NEA, Idaho Sch. counselors Assn. (pres. 1982-83), Am. Sch. Counselor Assn., Idaho Personnel and Guidance Assn., Am. Personnel and Guidance Assn., N.W. Women in Ednl. Adminstrn., Boise State U. Alumni Assn., P.E.O., Phi Delta Kappa. Republican. Methodist. Home: 9573 Telfair Dr Boise ID 83704 Office: 6001 Cassia St Boise ID 83709

ANDERSON, KEITH DOUGLAS, mech. engr.; b. Story City, Iowa, July 24, 1936; s. Everett Vernon and Garnette Esther (Mohler) A.; B.S., Iowa State U., 1958; M.S., U. So. Calif., 1963; postgrad. U. Calif. at Los Angeles, 1959-65; M.S. in Mgmt., LaVerne U., 1978; m. Catherine Prud'homme, Nov. 23, 1973; 1 dau., Karina; stepchildren—Joe, Bob, John. With Caterpillar Tractor Co., Peoria, Ill., 1956-58; thermodynamics engr. Pomona (Calif.) div. Gen. Dynamics, 1959-61, sr. preliminary design engr., 1961-64, design specialist, 1965-72, engring. specialist/project engr., 1972-80, mgr. systems engring. TAMS div. Aerojet Electro Systems, 1980—. Advisor, Order of Arrow, Boy Scouts Am., Pomona, 1971-73, asst. scoutmaster, 1973—, scoutmaster for disadvantaged troop, 1968-72; chmn. So. Calif. Tri-Counties council Boys' Clubs Am., 1975, bd. dirs. West End Boys' Clubs, 1968—, pres., 1972-74, v.p., 1980—; v.p. caretakers First Presbyn. Ch., Upland, Calif., 1976. Recipient Scoutmasters key Boy Scouts Am., 1972; medallion Boys' Clubs Am., 1976. Mem. Am. Def. Preparedness Assn., AIAA, Nat. Mgmt. Assn., ASME. Club: Rotary. Contbr. articles to profl. jours. Home: 2478 Mountain Ave Upland CA 91786

ANDERSON, LEE ROGER, solar, environmental, recreation and site planner; b. Boone, Iowa, July 24, 1945; s. Carl Donald and Hazel Irene (Erickson) A.; m. Linda Jean Parker, May 28, 1966; children—Eric Lee, Tai Denise. B.S. in Landscape Architecture, Iowa State U., 1967, M. Landscape Architecture, 1968. Registered landscape architect Calif. Dept. Consumer Affairs. Designer, draftsman H&F Builders, Ames, Iowa, 1966-68; landscape architect Simonds & Simonds, Pitts., 1968-70, Shasta-Trinity Nat. Forest, Redding, Calif., 1970-73, Klamath Nat. Forest, Yreka, Calif., 1973-81; prin. Designs for Living, Yreka, 1981—; planner nat. recreation area resorts; designer solar houses. Mem. Yreka City Planning Commn., 1976-80. Recipient award for design of children's playground Yreka Lions Club, 1976. Mem. Am. Soc. Landscape Architects, Tau Sigma Delta. Democrat. Club: Rotary. Author: (with others) Visual Absorption Capability, 1979, Visual Management Support Systems, 1979. Office: 2270 Belle Ave Yreka CA 96097

ANDERSON, LEO JOSEPH, internat. mechanization planner; b. Kanwaka, Kans., Aug. 15, 1921; s. Michael Alexander and Helen Marie (O'Brien) A.; student engring. U. Kans., 1939-41, Wichita State U., 1958-59, m. Henrietta Slavens, Oct. 20, 1943; children—Leo Joseph, II, Kathleen Lynn. Planning engr. Kans. Hwy. Commn., 1946-49; elec. supervisory engr. U.S. Army C.E., 1950-52; chief engr. constrn. Hdqrs. SAC, USAF, Omaha, 1952-59; dir. engring. and facilities U.S. Dept. Post Office, 1959-67; dir. process engring. Hdqrs. U.S. Postal Service, 1967-71; pres., chmn. bd. Mechanized Systems Designs Inc., San Diego and Washington, 1971—; chmn. Engrs. in Govt., Kans., 1965-67. Served to capt. AUS, 1942-46. Registered profl. engr., Kans., Calif. Mem. Nat. Soc. Profl. Engrs., Calif. Soc. Profl. Engrs. Democrat. Roman Catholic. Home: 17021 Palacio Pl San Diego CA 92127 Office: 8361 Vickers St Suite 208 San Diego CA 92111

ANDERSON, LLOYD HAROLD, architect; b. Wichita, Kans., Aug. 21, 1945; s. Willard Harold and Ruby Treva Edith (Rymph) A.; B.Arch., U. Colo., 1970; m. Linda Jane Proctor, Dec. 27, 1965; children—Scott Dirk, Tadari Ciel. Designer, Charles Deaton Assos., Denver, 1967-71; chief design architect Bur. Reclamation, Denver, 1971-76; partner Deaton-Anderson Design, furniture and product design Denver, 1975—; dir. design Zuhair Fayez & Assos., Jeddah, Saudi Arabia, 1976-78; pvt. practice overseas design and cons., Lakewood, Colo., 1978—; prin. works in Saudi Arabia and Jordan include Dallah Group Office Bldg., 1977-79, six archaeol. museums, 1977-80, Dur Mosque, 1979, Royal Mountain Retreat, 1979, Air Def. Command Officers Club, 1982, transp. terminals and Comml. devels. for Mecca and Medina, 1981-82. Recipient Emerson Meml. prize Nat. Inst. Archtl. Edn., 1965. Patentee furniture design. Address: 12791 W Jewell Circle Lakewood CO 80228

ANDERSON, LOUISE STOUT, crime analyst; b. Wellsville, N.Y., Aug. 11, 1952; d. Carlton C. and Mary (Gasdik) Stout; m. Leonard M. Anderson, June 2, 1973. B.A. in German Lit., Polit. Sci., Mt. Holyoke Coll., 1974; M.A. in Polit. Sci., San Diego State U., 1977. Cert. community coll. tchr., Calif. Statistician Grossmont Coll., El Cajon, Calif., 1976-78; crime analyst San Diego Police Dept., 1978-80; crime analyst Career Criminal Apprehension Program, Marin County Sheriff's Office, San Rafael, Calif., 1980-83; crime analyst CCAP Unit, Sonoma County Sheriff's Office, Santa Rosa, Calif., 1983—; cons. Search Group Inc. for Automated Crime Analysis. Alumna recruiter Mt. Holyoke Club No. Calif., 1981—. Mem. Am. Polit. Sci. Assn., Assn. Police Planners Research Officers, Calif. Women in Govt. Contbr. articles in field. Office: Sonoma County Sheriff's Office Santa Rosa CA 95604

ANDERSON, LYNDA JULENE, video specialist; b. San Diego, Aug. 8, 1950; d. Sophie Moen. B.A. in Art, U. Calif.-Berkeley, 1974; postgrad. San Francisco State U. Bookkeeper, account adjuster Sears Roebuck & Co., San Diego, Larry Blake's Restaurant, Berkeley; personnel asst. Dept. Pub. Health City of Berkeley, Calif., 1970-73; video asst./clk. typist Calif. Sch. for the Deaf, Berkeley, 1973-75; video specialist, cons. State Compensation Ins. Fund, San Francisco, 1975—; owner, mgr. Moving Moments, Lafayette, Calif., 1982—. Mem. Internat. Indsl. TV Assn., Nat. Assn. Female Execs. Office: 1275 Market St Suite 343 San Francisco CA 94103

ANDERSON, MARGARET LOUISE, lawyer; b. Lincoln, Nebr., Jan. 31, 1948; d. Lew R. and Jean A. J.D., U. San Francisco, 1976; postgrad. Golden Gate U., 1982—. Bar: Calif. 1977. Assoc., Behrens, Nelson & Mackey, Petaluma, 1977-79; ptnr. Anderson & Piotrkowski, Petaluma, 1979-80, Anderson, Piotrkowski & Rosenfield, Petaluma, 1980-82, Anderson & Piotrkowski, Petaluma, 1983—; tchr. family law, paralegal cert. program Sonoma State U., Cotati, Calif., 1980-81. Bd. dirs. Petaluma Symphony and Chorus Assn., 1980-81; mem. Sonoma County Alcoholism Adv. Bd., 1981-82. Mem. ABA, State Bar Calif. (cert. family law specialist), Sonoma County Bar Assn., Calif. Women Lawyers, Inns. of Ct. Soc. Calif., Family Mediation Assn., Assn. Family and Concilation Cts., Am. Orthopsychiat. Assn., NOW. Office: PO Box 2624 Petaluma CA 94953

ANDERSON, MARK RICHARD, sales and marketing executive; b. Springfield, Mass., Apr. 29, 1949; s. Richard F. and Yvette R. (Fisher) A. Student, U. Oreg., 1976-78. Prodn. mgr. Major Mfg. Inc., San Francisco, 1974-76; mgr. Beef & Brew, Beaverton, Oreg., 1977-79; dir. mktg. and sales Group W Cable TV, Lewiston, Idaho, 1981—. Served with USN, 1968-70. Democrat. Lodges: Elks, K.C. Home: PO Box 1382 Lewiston ID 83501 Office: PO Box 876 Lewiston ID 83501

ANDERSON, MARTIN RAY, trust company executive; b. Vicksburg, Mich., Nov. 8, 1946; s. Ray E. and Ruby F. (Draime) Anderson; m. Susan A. Ransom, May 29, 1974; children—Justin R., Aaron R., Ethan S. B.A., Western Mich. U., 1972; J.D., Drake U., 1975. Bar: Iowa 1976, Alaska 1983. Estate analyst Bankers Life Ins. Co., Des Moines, 1976-77; trust officer Am. Trust & Savs. Bank, Dubuque, Iowa, 1977-79, Bankers Trust Co., Des Moines, 1979-80, Valley Nat. Bank of Des Moines, 1980-81; v.p., div. mgr. trust div. First Nat. Bank of Fairbanks (name changed to Alaska Pacific Trust Co. 1983), 1981-83; exec. v.p., gen. mgr. Alaska Pacific Trust Co., Anchorage, 1983—. Served with USAF, 1967-71. Mem. ABA. Office: 101 W Benson Blvd PO Box 900 Anchorage AK 99510

ANDERSON, MARY ANN, educational administrator; b. Burley, Idaho, Nov. 1, 1941; d. Melnot LaVaughn and Afton (Neeley) McBride; m. Larry Gordon Anderson, Nov. 23, 1962. B.S., Utah State U., Logan, 1963; M.A., Calif. State U.-Sacramento, 1979. Tchr., Ctr. Unified Sch. Dist., North Highlands, Calif., 1963-65, 66-69, 73-76, resource specialist, 1976-78, head tchr., 1978-81, vice prin. Arthur S. Dudley Elem. Sch., 1981—; tchr. County Borough of Smethwick (Eng.), 1965-66; Pres., Democratic Women's Club of Sacramento, 1974-75. Mem. Assn. Calif. Sch. Adminstrs., Women in Ednl. Leadership, Nat. Assn. Female Execs., AAUW. Democrat. Contbr. articles to profl. jours. Office: 8000 Aztec Way North Highlands CA 95660

ANDERSON, MAXIE LEROY, mining and exploration company executive; b. Sayre, Okla., Sept. 10, 1934; s. Carl C. and Louise A. (Loughridge) A.; m. Patty L. Nassett, Apr. 21, 1952; children—Michael, Stephanie, Kristian, Timothy. B.S., U. N.D., 1956. Mgr., Ranchers Exploration and Devel. Corp., Albuquerque, 1962—, chief exec. officer, 1963—, dir., 1957—, chmn. bd., 1981—; dir. Bank Securities, Inc., Steam Corp. Am. Trustee St. Joseph Hosp. First gas balloonist to cross the Atlantic Ocean, first to cross the N.Am. continent, first to begin around-the-world flight. Office: Ranchers Exploration Devel Co Box 6217 Albuquerque NM 87107

ANDERSON, MILES HARRISON, ednl. adminstr.; b. Lees Summit, Mo., July 4, 1910; s. Clyde Lycurgus and Zulah (Walker) A.; B.S., U. Calif., Berkeley, 1931, M.A., 1947, Ed.D., 1950; m. Marie Evelyn Harmon, Jan. 9, 1935; children—Miles, Clyde, Penelope. Instr., Napa Jr. Coll., 1941-43; dir. apprenticeship program Calif. State Dept., 1943-52; dir. prosthetic edn. program UCLA Med. Sch., 1952-68, dir. allied health professions curriculum research and devel. program Div. Vocat. Edn., UCLA, 1968-75, clin. instr., 1968-75, dir. emeritus Allied Health Professions Publs., 1975—. Mem. Nat. Rehab. Assn., Am. Vocat. Assn., Congress of Phys. Medicine and Rehab., Calif. Ind. Edn. Assn., U. Calif. Alumni Assn., Phi Delta Kappa. Democrat. Presbyterian. Clubs: Masons, Scottish Rite. Home: 1363 Avenida de Cortez Pacific Palisades CA 90272 Office: UCLA Unex Bldg 10995 Le Conte Ave Los Angeles CA 90024

ANDERSON, MYLES NORMAN, mining and refining metals company executive; b. Flin Flon, Man., Can., Jan. 22, 1931; B.Sc., U. Man.; m. Tania Lorette Babienko; children—Kristopher, Paul, Kathryn. Chmn., chief exec. officer Cominco Ltd., Vancouver, B.C., Can.; v.p., dir. West Kootenay Power & Light Co. Ltd.; dir. Toronto-Dominion Bank, Fording Coal Ltd., Aberfoyle Ltd., Cominco Australian Pty. Ltd., Cominco Binani Zinc Ltd., Cominco Am., Inc., Vestgron Mines Ltd. Mem. Mining Assn. Can. (dir.), Can. Inst. Mining and Metallurgy, Am. Inst. Metall. Engrs., B.C. Profl. Engrs., Mo. Profl. Engrs., Alta. Profl. Engrs., Coal Assn. Can. Clubs: Vancouver, Shaughnessy Golf and Country. Office: Cominco Ltd 200 Granville Sq Vancouver BC V6C 2R2 Canada

ANDERSON, PAUL MAURICE, elec. engr.; b. Des Moines, Jan. 22, 1926; s. Neil W. and Buena Vista (Thompson) A.; B.S. in Elec. Engring., Iowa State U., 1949, M.S., 1958, Ph.D., 1961; m. Virginia Ann Worswick, July 8, 1950; children—William, Mark, James, Thomas. Transmission and distbn. engr. Iowa Public Service Co., Sioux City, 1949-55; mem. faculty Iowa State U., 1955-75; program mgr. Electric Power Research Inst., Palo Alto, Calif., 1975-78; pres. Power Math Assos., Palo Alto, 1978—; faculty chair Ariz. State U., Tempe, 1980—; cons. in field. Served with USAAF, 1944-45. NSF faculty fellow, 1960-61; recipient Faculty citation Iowa State U. Alumni Assn., 1973; Profl. Achievement citation Iowa State U., 1981; registered profl. engr., Iowa, Calif., Ariz. Fellow IEEE; mem. ASME, Conf. Internat. des Grands Reseaux Electriques, Sigma Xi, Phi Kappa Phi, Eta Kappa Nu, Pi Mu Epsilon. Republican. Author: Analysis of Faulted Power Systems, 1973; co-author: Power System Control and Stability, 1977; cons. editor Elec. Power Engring., McGraw-Hill Ency. Sci. and Tech., 1979—. Home: 1236 E Malibu Dr Tempe AZ 85282 Office: PO Box 27535 Tempe AZ 85282

ANDERSON, PAUL NATHANIEL, physician; b. Omaha, May 30, 1937; s. Nels Paul E. and Doris C. (Chesnut) A.; B.A., U. Colo., 1959, M.D., 1963; m. Dee Ann Hipps, June 27, 1965; children—Mary Kathleen, Anne Christen. Intern Johns Hopkins Hosp., 1963-64, resident in internal medicine, 1964-65; research asso., staff asso. NIH, Bethesda, Md., 1965-70; fellow in oncology Johns Hopkins Hosp., 1970-72, asst. prof. medicine, oncology Johns Hopkins U. Sch. Medicine, 1972-76; attending physician Balt. City Hosps., Johns Hopkins Hosp., 1972-76; dir. dept. med. oncology Penrose Cancer Hosp., Colorado Springs, Colo., 1976—; clin. asst. prof. dept. medicine U. Colo. Sch. Medicine, 1976—; dir. Penrose Cancer Hosp., 1979—; med. dir. So. Colo. Cancer Program, 1979—; mem., chmn. treatment com. Colo. Cancer Control and Research Panel, 1980—; prin. investigator Cancer Info. Service of Colo., 1981—; med. dir. Colo. Community Clin. Oncology Program, 1982—. Served with USPHS, 1965-70. Diplomate Am. Bd. Internal Medicine. Mem. Am. Soc. Clin. Oncology, Am. Assn. Cancer Research, Am. Assn. Cancer Insts. (liaison mem. bd. trustees 1982—), Am. Acad. Med. Dirs., Nat. Cancer Inst. (com. for community hosp. oncology program evaluation 1982—), Assn. Community Cancer Centers (chmn. membership com. 1980—, trustee 1981—), AAAS, N.Y. Acad. Scis., Johns Hopkins Med. Soc., AMA, Colo. Med. Soc., El Paso County Med. Soc., Alpha Omega Alpha. Contbr. articles to med. jours. Office: 2215 N Cascade Ave Colorado Springs CO 80907

ANDERSON, PAULINE RACHEL, vocational educator/administrator, curriculum consultant; b. Ephrata, Wash., Feb. 28, 1934; d. John Paul and Marie Margaret (Weber) Simpson; m. James Lind Anderson, Apr. 8, 1956; children—Paul, Eric, Kristin Anderson Pearson, Alisa Anderson Demmert. Student U. Wash., 1952-55; B.A. in Edn., Western Wash. State Coll., 1968. Cert. R.N., Wash., 1956; cert. standard teaching, Wash., 1970, vocat. instr./supr./dir., Wash. 1970. Staff nurse, 1956-64; elem. sch. tchr., 1968-70; instr. practical nursing program Bellingham Vo-Tech Inst., 1970-75, vocat. program. supr., 1975-82, asst. vocat. dir., 1982—. Mem. Wash. State Bd. Practical Nurse Examiners, 1982-87. Mem. Am. Vocat. Assn., Wash. Vocat. Assn., Wash. State Nurses Assn., Am. Nurses Assn., Nat. Council Local Vocat. Adminstrs., Wash. Assn. Vocat. Adminstrs. Club: Soroptimists. Home: 3115 Eldridge Ave Bellingham WA 98225 Office: Bellingham Vocat Tech Inst 3028 Lindbergh Ave Bellingham WA 98225

ANDERSON, RANDAL LEE, agronomist; b. Fargo, N.D., Dec. 11, 1952; s. Lloyd Stanley and Myrtle Evelyn (Tveito) A. B.S., S.D. State U., 1974, M.S., 1976; Ph.D., Wyo. U., 1980. Lic. pesticide applicator. Research asst. U. Wyo., Laramie, 1978-81; agronomist Mont. State U., Sidney, 1981-82, U.S. Dept. Agr., Agr. Research Service, Akron, Colo., 1982—. Mem. Weed Sci. Soc. Am., Am. Soc. Agronomy. Club: Quadrangle Sq. Dancing (Laramie). Contbr. articles to sci. jours.

ANDERSON, RICHARD, business consultant; b. Phila., Aug. 24, 1937; s. James Earl and Ellen (Lawson) A.; student Lincoln Law Sch., Sacramento, 1976; A.A., Sacramento City Coll., 1977; B.A., Calif. State U., Hayward, 1978, postgrad. in pub. adminstrn., 1979; postgrad. New Coll. Calif. Sch. Law, 1978-81; M.P.A., Golden Gate U., 1981; cert. in jr. coll. teaching, Calif.; children by previous marriage—Ashley Benton, Fawhn Lynette. Partner, v.p. Baco Industries, Los Angeles, 1967-70; v.p. Arleo Mfg., Inc., Los Angeles, 1972-73; asst. dir. Los Angeles New Careers Orgn., 1972; pres. Amal. Enterprises, Inc., Beverly Hills, Calif., 1972-76, Anderson Devel. Assn., Sacramento, 1970—; dir. Internat. Minority Bus. Seminar, Sacramento, 1972—; employment agt. Gen. Electric Co., Rockville, Md., 1973—; owner Profit Concepts & Systems Design Co., Sacramento, 1974—; exec. v.p. Fawhn Wholesale Distbg. Co., Sacramento, 1974—. Past chmn. exec. bd. small bus. adv. bd. Calif. Senate Select Com. on Small Bus. Enterprises. Served with USN, 1955-56. Democrat. Baptist. Author: (plays) Twenty Fourth Day, 1966; A Thought of My People, 1977; The Strange Land, 1977; Nostalgia, 1977; Sight and Fancy, 1977; Confluence, 1977; Colloquilism, 1977; Mind Poet, 1977; Themes, 1977. Office: PO Box 160213 Sacramento CA 95816

ANDERSON, RICHARD BRADFORD, economist; b. Mpls., July 31, 1931; s. Francis Xavier and Evelyn (Hanson) A.; B.B.A. magna cum laude, Nat. U., 1977, M.B.A., 1978; D.B.A., U.S. Internat. U., 1981; m. Mary Kathryn Schwenn, Oct. 8, 1971; children—Jacquelyn Sue, Marta Jean, Richard Bradford, Ariana M. Asst. cashier First Nat. Bank San Diego, 1949-62; v.p., cashier Bank La Jolla (Calif.), 1962-64; broker Hayden-Stone & Co., Inc., San Diego, 1965-71; v.p., partner Roberts-Scott & Co., Inc., San Diego, 1971-73; asst. to pres., sec.-treas. Commodore Resources, Inc., San Diego, 1974-75; sr. partner Bradford Anderson Assos., San Diego, 1976-77; partner Schwenn Anderson, Inc., Salt Lake City, 1978—; mem. faculty U.S. Internat. U., San Diego, 1980-81; domestic and internat. cons., 1976—; pres. SLC Energy Resources, 1983—. Pres., San Diego County Young Republicans, 1958; bd. dirs. Mother Goose Parade Assn., 1955-62; chmn. Republicans of La Jolla, 1973-74; maj. U.S. Mormon Bn., 1978-81, nat. donations officer, nat. liaison officer, gen. staff, 1981—; mem. nat. adv. bd. Am. Security Council, 1979-83. Mem. Am. Enterprise Inst. (asso.), Nat. Geog. Soc., Smithsonian Instn. Mormon. Office: 1604 Federal Heights Dr Salt Lake City UT 84103

ANDERSON, RICHARD ERNEST, rancher, ret. engring. co. exec.; b. North Little Rock, Ark., Mar. 8, 1926; s. Victor Ernest and Lillian Josephine (Griffin) A.; m. Mary Ann Fitch, July 18, 1953; children—Vicki Lynn Anderson Shampeny, Lucia Anita. B.S.C.E., U. Ark., 1949; M.S.E., U. Mich., 1959; Registered profl. engr., Mich., Va., Tex., Mont. Commd. ensign U.S. Navy, 1952, advanced through grades to capt., 1968; ret., 1974; v.p. Ocean Resources, Inc., Houston, 1974-77; mgr. maintenance and ops. Holmes & Narver, Inc., Orange, Calif., 1977-78; pres. No. Resources, Inc., Billings, Mont., 1978-81; v.p. Holmes & Narver, Inc., Orange, Calif., 1981-82; owner, operator Anderson Ranches, registered Arabian horses and comml. Angus cows, Bozeman, Mont., 1982—. Bd. trustees Lake Barcroft-Virginia Watershed Improvement Dist., 1973-74; pres. Lake Barcroft-Virginia Recreation Center, Inc., 1972-73. Served with USAAF, 1944-45. Decorated Silver Star, Legion of Merit with Combat V (2), Navy Marine Corps medal, Bronze Star with Combat V, Meritorious Service medal, Purple Heart; Anderson Peninsula in Antarctica named in his honor. Mem. ASCE, Soc. Am. Mil. Engrs. (Morrell medal 1965). Republican. Methodist. Clubs: Billings Petroleum, Elks. Home and Office: 14 Hodgman Canyon Bozeman MT 59715

ANDERSON, ROBERT E., toy manufacturing company executive; b. N.Y.C., 1929; B.A., Brown U., 1959; married. With N.Y. Telephone Co., 1954-56; asso. brand promotion mgr. Procter & Gamble Co., 1956-62; v.p., mgmt. supr. William Esty Co., 1962-63; exec. v.p., dir. Lever Bros. Co., 1963-78; exec. v.p., dir. R.J. Reynolds Tobacco Co., 1976-79; pres., chief operating officer Mattel Inc., 1979—, also dir. Office: Mattel Inc 5150 Rosecrans Ave Hawthorne CA 90250*

ANDERSON, ROBERT JAMES, pharmacist; b. Sacramento, Nov. 15, 1948; s. James William and Ruth Elizabeth (Sterk) A.; m. Jeanne Gail Berry, Sept. 13, 1969; children—James, Kristin. Pharm. D., U. Calif.-San Francisco, 1972. Commd. officer USPHS, 1972, advanced through grades to lt. comdr.; pharmacist NIH, Bethesda, Md., Ft. Yates (N.D.) Indian Hosp., Gallup (N.Mex.) Indian Med. Ctr., 1972-78; dir. pharmacy St. Mary's Hosp., Reno, 1978—. Mem. Am. Soc. Hosp. Personnel, Nev. Pharm. Assn., Nev. Soc. Hosp. Pharmacists. Democrat. Office: 235 W 6th St Reno NV 89520

ANDERSON, ROBERT ORVILLE, industrialist; b. Chgo., Apr. 13, 1917; s. Hugo A. and Hilda (Nelson) A.; B.A., U. Chgo., 1939; m. Barbara Phelps, Aug. 25, 1939; children—Katherine, Julia, Maria, Robert Bruce, Barbara Burton, William Phelps, Beverley. With Am. Mineral Spirits Co., Chgo., 1939-41; pres. Malco Refineries, Inc. (now Hondo Oil and Gas Co.), Roswell, N.Mex., 1941-63; chmn. bd., chief exec. officer Atlantic Richfield Co., Los Angeles; owner Diamond A Cattle Co., Roswell. Mem. Com. Econ. Devel., Nat. Petroleum Council, Washington. Chmn., Aspen Inst. for Humanistic Studies; chmn. Lovelace Found.; trustee Calif. Inst. Tech., U. Chgo., U. Denver. Mem. Am. Petroleum Inst. (dir.). Clubs: Century (N.Y.C.); California (Los Angeles); Metropolitan (Washington); Chicago; Pacific-Union (San Francisco). Home: PO Box 1000 Roswell NM 88201 Office: 515 S Flower St Los Angeles CA 90071*

ANDERSON, ROBERT WILLIAM, architect, engr.; b. Chgo., Sept. 19, 1940; s. Arthur William and Emmy Elizabeth (Larson) A.; B.Arch., U. Ill., 1965, M.S. in Archtl. Engring. (grad. research asst.), 1966; m. Linda Kazman, Aug. 28, 1965; 1 son, Thomas William. Draftsman, Harry I. Larson, Architect, Chgo., 1959-63; project architect Jack Blackman, AIA, Architect, Danville, Ill., 1963; engr. T.Y. Lin & Assos., Chgo., 1964-69; architect Jack D. Pickett, Hinsdale, Ill., 1969-71; architect, engr. Bourn & Dulaney, AIA, Greenwood Village, Colo., 1971-76; asso. architect and engr. Warren A. Flickinger & Assos., Denver, 1976-77; partner Anderson/Klipp, AIA, Denver, 1977-78; pres. Anderson Assos., AIA, Architects-Engrs.-Planners, Denver, 1979—. Lic. architect, Colo., Ill., Mont., Nebr., N.Mex., S.D., Wyo.; lic. structural engr., Colo., Ill. Mem. AIA (corporate), Structural Engrs. Assn. Ill., Am. Concrete Inst., U. Ill. Alumni Assn. (life), Gargoyle Soc. Lutheran. Clubs: Masons, Shriners. Home: 2594 S Nome St Aurora CO 80014 Office: 1582 S Parker Rd Denver CO 80231

ANDERSON, RONALD TRUMAN, writer, consultant; b. Utica, N.Y., Mar. 20, 1933; s. Stanley Truman and Corabelle (Livingston) A.; B.S.B.A., U. Fla., 1955, J.D., 1959; M.S., Fla. State U., 1961, Ph.D., 1966; 1 son, Charles Theodore. Admitted to Fla. bar, 1960; claims rep. State Farm Ins., Tallahassee, 1959-60; asst. dean Law Sch., Fla. State U., 1960-70; exec. v.p. Soc. C.P.C.U.s, Malvern, Pa., 1970-75; owner Mountain Ins., Steamboat Springs, Colo., 1975-83; cons., writer; books include: Insurance Agency Computer Power, 1978; Agent's Legal Responsibility, 1980; Automating Your Agency, 1982; mem. Colo. Ins. Bd., 1977—. C.P.C.U.; C.L.U. Mem. Fla. Bar Assn., Am. Risk and Ins. Assn., Soc. C.P.C.U.s. Democrat. Home and Office: PO Box 77 2114 3005 Trails Edge Rd Steamboat Springs CO 80477

ANDERSON, ROSANNE CARTER, interior designer; b. Salt Lake City, June 17, 1943; d. Wallace E. and Verda L. (Nelsen) Carter; m. Ronald Lee Anderson, June 17, 1960; children—Brian, Steven, Sherrie; A.S. in Interior Design, LaSalle U., 1968. Owner, operator Am. Home Furnishings, Salt Lake City, 1968-71; interior designer J.C. Penney Co., West Valley City, Utah, 1971-73, Shag-Rug-La, West Valley City, 1973-78; owner, operator Rosanne Interiors, Murray, Utah, 1979—. Pres. Welcome Wagon Club, West Valley City. Mem. Women's Info. Network, Meadowbrook Bowling League (pres. 1979-81). Democrat. Baptist. Office: 148 E 5065 Suite 5 Murray UT 84107

ANDERSON, ROY ARNOLD, aerospace co. exec.; b. Ripon, Calif., Dec. 15, 1920; s. Carl Gustav and Esther (Johnson) A.; A.B., Stanford U., 1947, M.B.A., 1949; m. Betty Leona Boehme, June 10, 1948; children—Ross David, Karyn Dale, Debra Elayne, James Patrick. With Westinghouse Electric Corp., 1952-56; mgr. acctg. and fin., then dir. mgmt. controls Lockheed Missiles & Space Co., 1956-65; dir. fin. Lockheed-Ga. Co., 1965-68; asst. treas. Lockheed Aircraft Corp., 1968-69, v.p., controller, 1969-71, sr. v.p. fin., 1971-75, vice chmn. bd., chief fin. and adminstrv. officer, 1975-77, chmn. bd., chief exec. officer, 1977—; dir. Avantek, Santa Clara, Calif., So. Calif. Edison Co., Rosemead, First Interstate Bancorp, Los Angeles, First Interstate Bank Calif., Los Angeles. Served with USNR, 1942-46, 50-52, C.P.A., Calif. Mem. Phi Beta Kappa. Office: 2555 N Hollywood Way Burbank CA 91503

ANDERSON, ROYAL J., advertising agency executive; b. Portland, Oreg., Sept. 12, 1914; s. John Alfred and Martha Marie (Jacobsen) A.; B.A., Albany Coll., 1939; postgrad. U. Oreg., summers 1939-41, Oreg. Inst. Tech., 1940-41; children—Michael, Johnny, Dora Kay, Mark Roy, Stan Ray, Ruth Gay, Janelle A., Jennifer T.; 1 adopted dau., Muoi-Muoi. Corp. cons. Dupont Corp., Beverly Hills, Calif., 1967-68; editor-pub. Nev. State Democrat, Carson City, Nev. State Pub. Observer, Nev. State Congl. Assn., Carson City, 1962-78; pres. Allied-Western Produce Co., Yuma, Ariz., Nev. Dem. Corp., 1966-78; pres. Western Restaurant Corp., 1978-81, Nev. State Sage Co., 1979—, Midway Advt. Co., Environ. Research Corp., 1983—, Mid-City Advt. Agy., 1983—, Nat. Newspaper Found., 1969, 71-76; chmn. bd. Press/Register Daily Newspapers, Foster Mortgage Co., 1983—. Bishop, Ch. of Palms, Mexico. Dep. registrar voters, Washoe County, Nev., 1966. Recipient Heroism award for rescue, 1933. Research fellow, Alaska, 1936. Mem. Am. Hort. Soc., Sparks (pres. 1970-81), Nev. chambers commerce, C. of C. of U.S., Chatso Farm Assn. (pres. 1962-81), Smithsonian Assos., N.Am. C. of C. Execs., Nat. Geog. Soc., Am. Newspaper Alliance (v.p. 1976), Clubs: Kiwanis, Elks, Lions. Designer prefabricated milk carton container, 1933, well water locating under-stream device, 1938. Home: PO Box 4349 North Las Vegas NV 89030 also 5600 E Sundance Ave Las Vegas NV 89116

ANDERSON, SHARON LOUISE TUCCI, corporate human resources official; b. Cleve., Apr. 14, 1945; d. Angelo A. and Evelyn Rose (Delsanter) Tucci; A.B. in Secretarial Sci., U. Dayton, 1966; B.S. in Personnel Mgmt., U. Colo., 1978; m. Andrew G. Anderson, Nov. 27, 1971; children— Nicholas A., Lauren M., Lindsay A. Sec. personnel, Glidden-Durkee, div. SCM, Cleve., 1966-68; statis. analyst personnel, Honeywell, Inc., Denver, 1969-70; personnel asst. Cartridge TV, San Jose, Calif., 1970-71; personnel mgmt. specialist dept. personnel State of Colo., Denver, 1972-77; mgr. employment and placement human resources dept. Samsonite Corp., Denver, 1977—; speaker in field. Active homeowners' assn., publicity chmn., 1974-76; bd. dirs. Passages. Mem. Am. Soc. Personnel Adminstrs., Am. Compensation Assn., Coll. Placement Council. Roman Catholic. Condr. workshops in field. Office: 11200 E 45th Ave Denver CO 80239

ANDERSON, STANLEY HELMER, scientist, educator; b. San Francisco, Aug. 6, 1939; s. Helmer and Tyra (Sahlin) A.; m. Donna A. Lawrence, Feb. 27, 1965; children—Rebecca Gregory. B.S. in Biology, U. Redlands, 1961; Ph.D. in Ecology, Oreg. State U., 1970. Asst. prof. Kenyon (Ohio) Coll., 1970-75; scientist Oak Ridge Assoc. U., 1975-76; chief Sect. Migratory Nongame Birds, Patuxent Research Ctr., (Md.), 1976-80; leader Wyo. Coop. Research Unit, U. Wyo., Laramie, 1980—. Served to lt. USN, 1963-66. Mem. Am. Ornithologist's Union, Ecology Soc. Am., Cooper Ornithol. Soc., Wilson Ornithol. Soc. Author: Environmental Sciences, 1983; contbr. articles to profl. jours. Home: 1062 Arapaho Dr Laramie WY 82070 Office: Room 426 Biol Sci Bldg U Wyo Laramie WY 82071

ANDERSON, STEPHEN HUME, building materials executive; b. Los Angeles, Aug. 28, 1932; s. Carl H. and Edith H. Anderson; m. Jane Louise Cochrane, Feb. 19, 1955; children—Kimberly Ann, Stephen H. Jr., Carl H. II, Lynn Paisley. B.S., U. So. Calif., 1955. Chief exec. officer Modern Materials, Inc. Buena Park, Calif., 1965—. Served to capt. USAAF, 1956-57. Clubs: Los Angeles Country, Jonathon, Big Canyon (Los Angeles); Newport Beach Lodges. Office: 6280 Artesia Blvd Buena Park CA 90620

ANDERSON, STEPHEN JORDAN, optometrist; b. Bend, Oreg., Mar. 8, 1941; s. Roland Norman and Frances Virginia (Jordan) A.; B.S., Pacific U., 1963, D. Optometry, 1964; m. Marianne McKenzie, Oct. 14, 1967. Practice optometry, Hayward, Calif., 1966-68, Castro Valley, 1968-69, Los Altos, 1969—. Chief visual cons. Creative Acad. Remedial Edn. project Cambrian Sch. Dist., San Jose, Calif., 1969-72, also visual cons. Project Spark, Cambrian and Union sch. dists. Served to 1st. lt. AUS, 1964-66. Named Young Optometrist of Year, Calif. Optometric Assn., 1971; recipient award of merit Cal. Assn. Neurologically Handicapped Children, 1972. Fellow Coll. Optometric Vision Devel.; mem. Santa Clara County Optometric Soc. (pres. 1972-74, named Optometrist of Year 1973), Calif. Optometric Assn., Am. Optometric Assn. Presbyterian. Club: Los Altos Rotary (dir. 1972-74, 77—, v.p. 1978-79, pres. 1979-80). Home: 1072 Dartmouth Ln Los Altos CA 94022 Office: 133 2d St Los Altos CA 94022

ANDERSON, STEVEN ALLAN, museum curator; b. Vancouver, Wash., Apr. 15, 1955; s. Edward Allan and Loraine Alma A. B.A., Colo. State U., 1978; postgrad. U. Idaho, 1979. Guide, Pioneer Farm Mus., 1979-80; curator Fort Nisqually Mus., Tacoma, Wash., 1980—. Mem. Am. Assn. State and Local History, Western Interpreter's Assn., Wash. State Hist. Soc. Lutheran. Home and Office: Fort Nisqually Point Defiance Park Tacoma WA 98407

ANDERSON, SUSAN HOLLIDAY, coastal planner, consultant; b. Laconia, N.H., Aug. 23, 1944; d. Edmund Gilmore and Marguerite (Pardee) A. B.A. (scholar), Mt. Holyoke Coll., 1966; M.S. in Marine Affairs (Noyes fellow), U. R.I., 1973. Regional rep. Expt. Internat. Living, Washington, 1968-70; adminstrv. asst. Ocean Affairs Bd., Nat. Acad. Scis., Washington, 1971-72; project coordinator French-Am. Mid-Ocean Study, Woods Hole (Mass.) Oceanographic Inst., 1973-74; marine recreation specialist Marine Adv. Program, U. So. Calif. Sea Grant Program, 1974-78; planner, legal asst. Nossaman, Krueger and Marsh, Los Angeles, 1978-80; coastal planner, project mgr. Moffatt & Nichol, Engrs., Long Beach, Calif., 1980—; cons. spl. projects Can., U.S. Mem. County Los Angeles Beach Adv. Com., 1975-82. Mem. Marine Tech. Soc., Am. Shore and Beach Preservation Assn., Orange County Coast Assn., Calif. Marine Parks and Harbors Assn. (pres. 1980-81). Republican. Episcopalian. Club: Mt. Holyoke So. Calif. Contbr. articles to profl. jours. Office: 250 W Wardlow Rd Long Beach CA 90807

ANDERSON, THEODORE WILBUR, statistician, econometrician; b. Mpls., June 5, 1918; s. Theodore Wilbur and Evelynn (Johnson) A.; Dorothy Fisher, July 8, 1950; children—Robert Lewis, Janet Lynn, Jeanne Elizabeth. Asst. in math. Northwestern U., Evanston, Ill., 1939-40; instr. math. Princeton (N.J.) U., 1941-43, research assoc., 1943-45; research assoc. U. Chgo., 1945-46; instr. math. stats. Columbia U., N.Y.C., 1946-47, asst. prof., 1947-50, assoc. prof., 1950-56, prof., 1956-67, acting chmn. dept. math. stats., 1950-51, 63, chmn., 1956-60, 64-65; prof. stats. and econs. Stanford (Calif.) U., 1967—; Guggenheim fellow U. Stockholm and U. Cambridge, 1947-48; fellow Ctr. for Advanced Study in Behavioral Scis., 1957-58, vis. scholar, 1972-73, 80; Sherman Fairchild Disting. scholar Calif. Inst. Tech., 1980; Columbia U., 1983-84; vis. research prof. econs. NYU, 1983-84. Fellow Am. Acad. Arts and Scis., AAAS, Am. Statis. Assn. (v.p. 1971-73), Econometric Soc., Inst. Math. Stats. (pres. 1963, mem. council), Royal Statis. Soc.; acad. visitor U. London, 1967-68; vis. prof. math U. Moscow, 1968; vis. prof. stats. U. Paris, 1968; acad. visitor London Sch. Econs., 1974-75; Wesley C. Mitchell prof. econs. mem. AAUP, Am. Math. Soc., Indian Statis. Inst., Nat. Acad. Scis., Internat. Statis. Inst., Psychometric Soc. (council of dir.), Bernoulli Soc. for Math. Stats. and Probability, Phi Beta Kappa. Author: An Introduction to Multivariate Statistical Analysis, 1958; The Statistical Analysis of Time Series, 1971; (with Somesh Das Gupta and George P.H. Styan) A. Bibliography of Multivariate Statistical Analysis, 1972; (with Stanley L. Sclove) Introductory Statistical Antalysis, 1974; (with Stanley L. Sclove) An Introduction to the Statistical Analysis of Data, 1978; editor Annals of Math. Stats., 1950-52; mem. editorial bd. Psychometrika, 1954-72; assoc. editor Jour. of Time Series Analysis, 1980—; contbr. articles to statis. jours. Home: 746 Santa Ynez St Stanford CA 94305 Office: Dept Stats Sequoia Hall Stanford U Stanford CA 94305

ANDERSON, TIMOTHY LEE, advertising executive; b. Evanston, Ill., Nov. 17, 1944; s. Ernst Harold and Jane Elnore A.; m. Glenda Veronne, July 15, 1971; 1 son, Luke Hazen. Student Taylor U., 1962-65, Ind. U., 1965-66, Lake Forest Coll., 1971-72, Def. Lang. Inst., 1977. Copy supr. Leo Burnett Advt., Chgo., 1972-75; v.p. client services Buti-Roberts Advt., Chgo., 1975-77; creative supr. Tracy-Locke/BBDO, Dallas, 1977-79, assoc. creative dir., Denver, 1979-81, v.p., dir. direct mktg., 1981—. Served to sgt. USAF, 1967-71. Decorated Air Medal. Mem. Rocky Mountain Direct Mktg. Club (dir.), Direct Mktg. Assn. Contbr. article to profl. jour. Home: 7875 Swaps Trail Evergreen CO 80439 Office: 7503 Marin Dr Englewood CO 80111

ANDERSON, VERNON LEROY, consulting engineer; b. Sunnyside, Wash., Feb. 15, 1934; s. Frederick John and Frances Minerva (Bishop) A.; m. Janet Marie Hanson, June 21, 1958; children—Karol Marie, Jill Teresa, Steven Leroy. B.S. in Agrl. Engring. with honors, Wash. State U., 1957. Registered profl. engr., Idaho, Wash., Oreg. Civil engr. trainee Columbia Basin project Bur. Reclamation, Dept. Interior, 1957-58, hydraulic engr., drainage div. Columbia Basin project, 1958-60, br. engr., asst. irrigation mgr. Franklin field br., Columbia Basin project, 1960-62, asst. regional agrl. engr. N.W. region Bur. Reclamation, 1962-67; agrl. engr. N.W. dist. chem. sales services Collier Carbon and Chem. Corp. div. Union Oil Co. of Calif., Los Angeles, 1967-70; owner, operator Anderson Engring., cons. engr., Sunnyside, Wash., 1971—. Served to capt. U.S. Army Res., 1957-66. Mem. Nat. Soc. Profl. Engrs., Wash. Soc. Profl. Engrs., Am. Soc. Agrl. Engrs., Internat. Conf. Bldg. Ofcls., Am. Concrete Inst., Prestressed Concreta Inst., Post-Tensioning Inst., ASTM, U.S. C. of C., Sunnyside C. of C. Republican. Methodist. Clubs: Lower Valley Golf, Elks (exalted ruler 1976-77, state trustee 1978-82, dist. dep. grand exalted ruler 1982-83), Masons (Sunnyside). Home and Office: 607 Lookout Dr Sunnyside WA 98944

ANDERSON, WESTON ARTHUR, research lab. adminstr.; b. Kingsburg, Calif., Mar. 28, 1928; s. Arthur Edward and Hilma Katherine (Brandvig) A.; B.S., Stanford U., 1950, Ph.D., 1955; m. Jeannette Kirkham Arndt, June 14, 1952; children—Joel Weston, Lucille Hilma. Spl. asst. to dir. CERN, Geneva, Switzerland, 1954-55; research scientist Instrument div. Varian Assos., Palo Alto, Calif., 1955-63, dir. instrument research, 1963-72, dir. Systems and Techniques Lab., 1972—; pres. Royer-Anderson, Palo Alto, 1972—. Mem. Am. Phys. Soc., Am. Assn. Physics Tchrs., IEEE, Optical Soc. No. Calif., Assn. Advancement Med. Instrumentation. Patentee in field. Contbr. articles to profl. jours. Home: 763 LaPara St Palo Alto CA 94306 Office: 611 Hansen Way Palo Alto CA 94303

ANDERSON, WILLIAM DONALD, aerospace engineer and consultant; b. Marysville, Calif., Apr. 22, 1937; s. Donald Ray and Beatrice (Horton) A.; m. Barbara Ann Limbach, Aug., 10, 1959; children—William Scott, Jeffrey Todd, Douglas Craig. B.S., U. Calif.-Berkeley, 1959; M.S., UCLA, 1966; registered profl. engr. Calif. Assoc. engr. Lockheed Calif. Co., Burbank, Calif., 1959-62, design engr., 1962-63, dynamics engr., 1963-66, sr. dynamics engr., 1966-68, research specialist, 1968-69, group engr. dynamics. 1969-72, research and devel. engr., 1972-77, sr. engr. dynamics and aerolastic stability of advanced aerospace vehicles, 1979—; cons. in field Mem. AIAA, Am. Helicopter Soc. Republican. Contbr. articles to profl. jours. Office: 2555 N Hollywood Way PO Box 551 Burbank CA 91520

ANDON, JERAR, cons. engr.; b. Milford, Mass., Feb. 8, 1921; s. Karnig and Zumrout (Khacharian) Andonian; B.M.E., Gen. Motors Inst., 1951; M.S.M.E., Stanford U., 1968; m. Nancy Jane Simons, Aug. 29, 1953. Sr. research engr. Gen. Motors Corp., Warren, Mich. and Santa Barbara, Calif., 1951-63, 65-69; mech. engr. U.S. Naval Civil Engring. Lab, Port Hueneme, Calif., 1964-65; cons. engr. to mfg. and legal firms in Los Angeles, Washington and Santa Barbara, 1969—; vis. lectr. mech. engring. U. Calif., Santa Barbara, 1981—. Served with U.S. Army, 1942-45. Decorated Bronze Star; registered profl. engr., Calif., Mich. Mem. Soc. Automotive Engrs. (Horning Meml. award 1963), ASME, Instn. Mech. Engrs. (Gt. Britain), Tau Beta Pi. Patentee in field. Home and Office: 98 Loma Media Rd Santa Barbara CA 93103

ANDRE, CURT ANTHONY, optometrist; b. Turlock, Calif., Nov. 5, 1953; s. Clarence Anthony and Marvelina Claire (Almeida) A. B.S., U. Calif.-Davis; M.P.H., O.D., U. Calif.-Berkeley, 1977. Practice optometry specializing in pediatric vision and contact lenses, Turlock, Calif., 1977—. Pres. Stanislaus Statesmen; chmn. Turlock City Planning Commn. Mem. Am. Optometric Assn., Calif. Optometric Assn., San Joaquin Optometric Soc., Turlock C. of C. (v.p.). Republican. Roman Catholic. Club: 20/30 (pres. elect). Office: 607 E Olive St Turlock CA 95380

ANDREADIS, NICHOLAS ANDREW, cardiologist; b. Canton, Ohio, Sept. 27, 1948; s. Nicholas Harry and Nina (Rossetti) A.; B.A., Kent State U., 1969; M.D., Creighton U., 1974; m. Barbara Ann Kirkwood, July 4, 1970; children—Tiffany, Peter, Phillip. Intern, Creighton U. and Affiliated Hosps., Omaha, 1974-75, resident and cardiology fellow, 1975-78; practice medicine specializing in cardiovascular diseases, Federal Way and Auburn, Wash., 1978—; mem. staff, dir. non-invasive cardiac lab. Auburn Gen. Hosp., also mem. exec. com., sec.-treas.; staff Tacoma Gen. Hosp. Fellow Am. Coll. Cardiology; Mem. Wash. Med. Assn. (del.), AMA (physicians recognition award 1978-81), Wash. Heart Assn., Am. Soc. Echocardiography, Am. Heart Assn., ACP. Home: 31843 25th Ave SW Federal Way WA 98003 Office: 1715 S 324th Pl #300 Federal Way WA 98003

ANDREOPOULOS, SPYROS GEORGE, writer; b. Athens, Greece, Feb. 12, 1929; s. George S. and Anne Levas) A.; came to U.S., 1953, naturalized, 1962; A.B., Wichita State U., 1957; m. Christiane Loesch Loriaux, June 6, 1958; 1 dau., Sophie. Pub. info. specialist USIA, Salonica, Greece, 1951-53; asst. editorial page editor Wichita (Kans.) Beacon, 1955-59; asst. dir. info. services, editor The Menninger Quar., The Menninger Found., Topeka, 1959-63; dir. communications Stanford U. Med. Ctr. and editor Stanford Medicine, 1983—; editor Sun Valley Forum on Nat. Health, Inc. (Idaho), 1972-83. Served with Royal Hellenic Air Force, 1949-50. Mem. AAAS, Assn. Am. Med. Colls., Nat. Assn. Sci. Writers, Am. Med. Writers Assn., Am. Hosp. Assn., Am. Soc. Hosp. Pub. Relations, Council for Advancement Edn. Co-author, editor: Medical Cure and Medical Care, 1972; Primary Care: Where Medicine Fails, 1974; National Health Insurance: Can We Learn from Canada? 1975; Heart Beat, 1978. Contbr. articles to profl. jours. writer; b. Athens, Greece, Feb. 12, 1929; s. George S. and Anne Levas) A.; came to U.S., 1953, naturalized, 1962; A.B., Wichita State U., 1957; m. Christiane Loesch Loriaux, June 6, 1958; 1 dau., Sophie. Pub. info. specialist USIA, Salonica, Greece, 1951-53; asst. editorial page editor Wichita (Kans.) Beacon, 1955-59; asst. dir. info. services, editor The Menninger Quar., The Menninger Found., Topeka, 1959-63; dir. communications Stanford U. Med. Ctr. and editor Stanford Medicine, 1983—; editor Sun Valley Forum on Nat. Health, Inc. (Idaho), 1972-83. Served with Royal Hellenic Air Force, 1949-50. Mem. AAAS, Assn. Am. Med. Colls., Nat. Assn. Sci. Writers, Am. Med. Writers Assn., Am. Hosp. Assn., Am. Soc. Hosp. Pub. Relations, Council for Advancement Edn. Co-author, editor: Medical Cure and Medical Care, 1972; Primary Care: Where Medicine Fails, 1974; National Health Insurance: Can We Learn from Canada? 1975; Heart Beat, 1978. Contbr. articles to profl. jours. Home: 1012 Vernier Pl Stanford CA 94305

ANDRES, ALLAN ARTHUR, telephone co. exec.; b. San Francisco, Dec. 30, 1943; s. Alvin Adolph and Helen Virginia Andres; B.A., Point Loma Coll., 1970; M.A. in Psychology, Iowa State U., 1977; m. Margaret Elizabeth Johnson, Feb. 1, 1964; children—Dori Lynne, Christopher Allan. Electronic technician Space Gen. Corp., El Monte, Calif., 1964; communications technician Pacific Telephone, Los Angeles, 1964-70, communications mgr., 1970-74, corp. planning mgr., 1977-78; engring. tng. mgr. Am. Tel. & Tel. Co., Lisle, Ill., 1974-76; mktg./sales mgr. Western Electric Co., San Francisco, 1979-82; staff mgr. Pacific Telephone, San Francisco, 1982—. Bd. dirs. Petaluma Elem. and High Sch. Dists., 1980—, pres., 1982-83; bd. dirs. Petaluma Ednl. Found; mem. Selective Service Bd #11, 1982—; chmn. sch. site council McDowell Elem. Sch., 1978-80; res. police officer Petaluma Police Dept., 1977—. Served with USN, 1960-64. Home: 2208 Mari Lane Petaluma CA 94952 Office: Pacific Telephone Co 666 Folsom St Room 980 San Francisco CA 94107

ANDRESON, EVERETT HARLAN, food mktg. cons.; b. Abilene, Kans., Jan. 23, 1907; s. Henry August and Ada Amanda (Goodnow) A.; student Kans. State U., 1923-25, U. Calif. at Los Angeles, 1927, U. Wash., 1927, Stanford U., 1928-29, Advanced Mgmt. Program, Harvard U., 1958; m. Jeanette Rickey, July 30, 1932; children—Francis E., Clara Jean Andreson Kurgan, Arlene Andreson DesJardins. With Gen. Mills, Mpls., 1929-69, sales supr., 1932-33, sales mgr., 1934-36, new products mgr., 1937-48, merchandising mgr., 1948-53, dir. sales, 1953-57, v.p., 1955-69, dir. mktg., 1957-60, dir. trade and customer relations, 1960-69; food mktg. cons., San Diego, 1969—; cons. U.S. Dept. Agr., 1965—; trustee Food Industries Ednl. Council, 1963-69. Mem. adv. council Harvard Bus. Sch., 1958-60; bd. dirs. Shamrock Found., 1950-69; patron Mpls. Soc. Fine Arts. Mem. San Diego Zool. Soc., Kappa Sigma, Kappa Kappa Psi. Republican. Episcopalian. Clubs: R.B. Swim and Tennis, Oaks North. Home: Rancho Bernardo 17046 Tesoro Dr San Diego CA 92128

ANDRESS, VERN RANDOLPH, psychologist, marriage counselor; b. Boulder, Colo., Mar. 29, 1935; s. Victor William and Frances Willette (Boyer) A.; B.A. in Psychology, San Diego State Coll., 1969; M.S. in Clin. Psychology, San Diego State U., 1971; Ph.D. in Psychology, U.S. Internat. U., 1976; m. Monica Pia Heep, Oct. 22, 1960; children—Vivian Monica, Kimberley Dawn. Pres., Beauty Boutique, Inc., 1960-67; counselor San Diego Acad., 1969-70; instr. psychology Loma Linda U., 1970-72, asst. prof., 1972-76, asso. prof., 1976-78, prof., 1979—, chmn. dept., 1977-80, dir. adminstrn. of justice program, 1970—, dean Coll. Arts and Scis., 1980—; cons. Calif. Instn. for Women, Riverside Police Dept., Corona Police Dept., Riverside County Coroner's Office. Mem. Mayor's Com. on Chicano-Police Relations, Riverside, Calif., 1975-76; mem. Grand Terrace (Calif.) Planning Commn., 1978—. Served with AUS, 1954-56. Lic. marriage and family counselor, Calif. Mem. Am. Assn. Suicidology, Internat. Assn. Suicide Prevention, Am. Psychol. Assn., Western Psychol. Assn., Calif. Psychol. Assn., Am. Assn. Marriage and Family Counselors, Calif. Assn. Marriage and Family Counselors, Inland Counties Psychol. Assn., Assn. Adventist Behavioral Scientists, Am. Orchid Soc., Am. African Violet Soc., Gesnariad Soc. Internat., Riverside Geneal. Soc., Grand Terrace C. of C., Sigma Xi. Seventh-day Adventist. Author: The Demographic Distribution of Suicide in Riverside County Between 1965 and 1969, 1976; editor Jour. Assn. Adventist Behavioral Scientists, 1976-80; contbr. numerous articles on suicide to profl. jours. Office: Coll Arts and Scis Loma Linda U Riverside CA 92515

ANDREW, EUGENE JOSEPH, interior designer, consultant; b. Dearborn, Mich., Mar. 4, 1928; s. John and Helen (Bartick) A.; m. Gloria La Mond, June 2, 1929; children—Michele Bonwell, Karen Guiney, Susan Perkins, Nancy Wise. B.A., Wayne State U., 1951. Mgr., designer Crossroad Furniture, Whittier and Newport Beach, Calif., 1960-65; designer Carroll Sagar Co., Newport Beach, 1965-70; owner, design cons. Design Forum Co., Orange, Calif., 1970—. Served with U.S.

Army, 1946-47. Recipient Am. Inst. Designers award, 1973; Alden Carpet Mills Nat. award, 1958, City of Huntington Beach (Calif.) Parade Theme award, 1979. Mem. Am. Soc. Interior Designers. Democrat. Roman Catholic. Office: 290 S Tustin Ave Orange CA 92666

ANDREW, FRED WILLIAM, agribusiness executive; b. Great Neck, N.Y., Jan. 26, 1927; s. Flynn L. and Marian (Herbert) A.; m. Virginia Sherry, June 24, 1950; children—Flynn L., Christine Bond, Kevin S., Keith R., Mark J., Joan T., Jeff T., Tracy M. B.S. magna cum laude in Agronomy, U. Ariz., 1952. Worker to foreman Winmesa Farms, Inc, 1952-57; mgmt. trainee Farmers Investment Co., Appleton Ranch, 1958, mgr. Continental Ranch, 1958-59, mgr., 1959-64; mgr. Bruce Church, Inc., Parker Ranch, 1965-68, gen. mgr. Calif. ops., 1958-70; v.p. prodn. Superior Farming Co., Bakersfield, Calif., 1970, pres., chief exec. officer, 1970—, chmn. bd., 1982—; dir. Fed. Res. Bank of San Francisco; chmn. bd. T.M. Duche Nut Co., Inc. Adv. bd. Calif. State Coll., Bakersfield. Served to 1st lt., AUS, 1944-49. Mem. Calif. Assn. Winegrape Growers (exec. com.). Calif. C. of C., Greater Bakersfield C. of C., (v.p., dir.), C. of C. U.S. Republican. Roman Catholic. Office: PO Box 9999 Bakersfield CA 93389

ANDREW, ROBERT LYNAL, Canadian provincial official; b. Eston, Sask., Can., Apr. 13, 1944; s. Robert Elvin and Elizabeth Ann (Ellis) A.; m. N. Lynne Tunall, Dec. 22, 1964; children—Quinn, Kalen, Sharmen, Dreeson. B.A., U. Sask., 1966, LL.B., 1970. Bar: Sask. With supply and transp. dept. Pacific Petroleums, Calgary, Alta., Can., 1967-68; programmer IBM, Saskatoon, 1968; with personnel dept. Allan Potash Mine, 1969-70; mem. Andrew, Ritter, Chinn, Kindersley, Sask., 1970-80, sr. ptnr., 1973-80; minister of fin. Govt. of Sask., Regina, 1982—. Mem. Eston Town Council, 1972-74. Progressive Conservative. Contbr. articles to parliamentary jours. Office: Govt Sask 312 Legislative Bldg Regina SK S4S 0B3 Canada

ANDREWS, DANA GENE, research engineer, youth advisor; b. Los Angeles, May 26, 1944; s. Elden L. and Marcella I. (Raitt) A.; m. J. Anne Dyar, June 24, 1967; children—Jason E., Christopher C.D., Sarah E. B.S., U. Wash., 1966; M.S., Calif. Inst. Tech., 1967; Ph.D. in Aeros. and Astronautics, Stanford U., 1973. With Boeing Aerospace Co., Seattle, 1967-68, 79—, prin. engr., 1979—; with Boeing Comml. Airplane Co., 1973-79; designer air transp. exhibit Nat. Air and Space Mus., Smithsonian Instn., Washington, 1976. Republican precinct committeeman. Mem. AIAA. Patentee in field. Office: 4826 NE 41st St Seattle WA 98105

ANDREWS, JAMES WARREN, mining engr., land surveyor; b. Fort Collins, Colo., Aug. 26, 1929; s. James Henderson and Lydia Anne (Warren) A.; student Colo. A&M Coll., 1947-48; diploma as engr. of mines Colo. Sch. Mines, 1963; m. Nancy Jean Bailey, Aug. 30, 1959; children—Bradford Warren, Karen Ann. Land surveyor Betchart Engring. Co., Evergreen, Colo., 1963-66; jr. engr. O.W. Walvoord, Inc., Denver, 1966; mining engr. U.S. Bur. Mines, Denver, 1966-73; mine ventilation engr. Mining Enforcement and Safety Adminstrn., Denver, 1973-78, Mine Safety and Health Adminstrn., 1978—; tchr. mine safety Community Coll. Denver, 1974, Nat. Mine Health and Safety Acad., 1977; land surveyor cons.; incorporator, sec. Colo. Central Narrow Gauge Ry. Co., Central City, 1968. Served with USN, 1948-50. Recipient award U.S. Bur. Mines, 1967, Mining Enforcement and Safety Adminstrn., 1975, Mining Safety and Health Adminstrn., 1980; registered profl. land surveyor, Colo., Wyo., profl. safety engr., Calif. Mem. Soc. Mining Engrs. of AIME, Mine Ventilation Soc. S. Africa, Profl. Land Surveyors Colo. (past pres.), Colo. Engring. Council, St. Andrew Soc. Colo., Alpha Tau Omega. Republican. Unitarian. Club: Toastmasters (charter). Home: 1942 Mount Zion Dr Golden CO 80401 Office: PO Box 25367 Denver Federal Center Denver CO 80225

ANDREWS, JESSIE MAE, ret. realtor; b. Richfield, Idaho, Jan. 18, 1918; d. Clyde Osborn and Golda Pearl (Meyer) Ewing; student Santa Maria Jr. Coll., 1936-37; m. Forest Merl Andrews, Apr. 20, 1946. Sec., Kraft Foods, Aberdeen, Idaho, 1963-64; ins. sec., real estate salesman H.T. Breazeal Agy., Rupert, Idaho, 1964-69, real estate broker, 1969-73; asso. broker Bailey-Roberts Realty, Rupert, 1973-74; asso. broker, sec.-treas., co-owner, mgr. Rupert office Big Wood Realty, Inc., 1974-75; broker-owner Trend Realty, Rupert, 1975-80, ret., 1980. Mem. Rupert Uniform Bldg. Codes Appeals Bd., 1974—. Named Woman of Progress, Rupert Bus. and Profl. Women, 1978-79. Mem. Burley-Rupert Bd. Realtors (sec.-treas. 1969-70, dir.), Nat. Inst. Farm and Land Brokers. Methodist (asst. treas. woman's soc. Christian service 1967-68). Home: 817 15th Dr Rupert ID 83350 Office: 638 Fremont St Rupert ID 83350

ANDREWS, L. LEE, public relations manager, consultant, lecturer; b. Wichita, Kans., July 17, 1951; d. Harry Morton and Phyllis Lee (Stephenson) Crandell. B.S. in Journalism, U. Kans., 1973. Accredited bus. communicator. Media specialist Epilepsy Found. Am., Los Angeles, 1977-79; asst. mgr. pub. affairs div. Sunkist Growers, Los Angeles, 1979-82; pub. relations mgr. Allstate Savs., Glendale, Calif., 1982—; guest lectr. UCLA, U. So. Calif. Recipient award of excellence Nat. Council Farmer Coops., 1982; photography award Coop. Editors Assn., 1982. Mem. Internat. Assn. Bus. Communicators (v.p. mem. services Los Angeles chpt.), Pub. Relations Soc. Am. Club: Lemon Men's. Author Sunkist Growers ann. report, 1981, 82. Office: 701 N Brand Blvd Glendale CA 91203

ANDREWS, M(ARVIN) RICHARD, stock broker; b. Santa Maria, Calif., Sept. 11, 1930; s. Marvin and Mildred (Redwine) A.; B.S., Calif. Poly. State U., 1956; m. Joyce Jean Garrity, Aug. 22, 1953; children—Jon Robert, Richard Jerome, Elizabeth Colleen. With Paine, Webber, Jackson & Curtis, Inc., Santa Barbara, Calif., 1956—, v.p., 1970—; pres. Masonic Properties of Santa Barbara, Inc. Div. chmn. United Way; chmn. Calif. Masonic Investment Com.; trustee 1st Presbyterian Ch., gen. treas., 1980. Served with AUS, 1951-52. Honored alumnus Calif. Poly. State U. Sch. Bus., 1980. Mem. Town Hall, Calif. Poly. State U. Alumni Assn. (pres.). Clubs: Commonwealth of Calif., Channel City, Santa Barbara, Masons. Home: 1000 Via Tranquila Santa Barbara CA 93110 Office: 1100 State St Santa Barbara CA 93101

ANDREWS, THOMAS EARL, accountant; b. Payson, Utah, Oct. 19, 1944; s. James Erva and Rita (Schofield) A.; B.S., U. Utah, 1968; M.Acctg., Utah State U., 1975; m. Barbara J. Dover, May 24, 1968; children—Rita Carolin, Thomas E. Mgr. acctg. and systems design Orscheln Farm and Home Supply, Moberly, Mo., 1971-74; instr. Humphrey's Coll., Stockton, Calif., 1975-77, U. Pacific, Stockton, 1977; supervising sr. audit staff Fox & Co., Stockton, 1975-77; mng. partner Roberts, Parker & Andrews, C.P.A.s, Salt Lake City, 1977-81; partner Andrews, Hymas & Co., C.P.A.s, Salt Lake City, 1981—; pres. SRI Co., Salt Lake City, 1980—; v.p. Style Realty, 1978—, Techna Industries, 1977—. Br. pres. Ch. Jesus Christ Latter-day Saints, Key West, Fla., 1969-70. Served with USN, 1968-71, to comdr. USNR, 1971—. C.P.A., Utah. Mem. Res. Officers Assn. (Navy v.p. Utah 1980-81), Utah Assn. Public Accts. (state and local govt. audio com.), Am. Inst. C.P.A.s, Navy Res. Assn. Republican. Home: 7128 Pine Cone St Salt Lake City UT 84121 Office: 875 Beneficial Life Tower 36 S State St Salt Lake City UT 84111

ANDREWS, THOMAS FRANKLIN, historian, educator, univ. ofcl. and dean; b. Lindsay, Calif., Mar. 11, 1937; s. James R. and Mabel (Carmody) A.; A.B., Pasadena Coll., 1962; M.A., U. So. Calif., 1970, Ph.D., 1970; m. Evelyn Mosley, Aug. 22, 1958; children—Karen, Lori, Thomas. Teaching asst. U. So. Calif., Los Angeles, 1963-66, Calif. State Coll., Long Beach, summer, 1964; instr. history Pasadena Coll., 1964-66; Azusa Pacific Coll., summer, 1965; asst. prof. Pasadena Coll., 1967-72, asso. prof., 1972-73; vis. instr. Eastern Nazarene Coll., summer 1970, Calif. State Poly. Coll., Pomona, summer, 1971; asso. prof. Am. history Azusa (Calif.) Pacific Coll., 1973-76, prof., 1976-78, dir. local history-oral history program, 1973-78, dir. of spl. collections, 1975-78, faculty moderator, 1977-78; v.p., acad. dean Westmont Coll., 1979—. Recipient teaching excellence cert. Azusa Pacific Coll., 1978; Am. Philos. Soc. grantee, 1970, Haynes Found. grantee, 1966; recipient Distinguished Service award Atladena Jr. C. of C., 1970; named Most Inspirational Prof., Pasadena Coll., 1971. Mem. Orgn. of Am. Historians, Calif., Utah, So. Calif. hist. socs., Am., Western hist. assns. Editor: English Privateers at Cabo San Lucas: The Descriptive Accounts of Puerto Seguro by Edward Cooke (1712), and Woodes Rogers (1712), with added comments by George Shelvocke (1726) and William Betach (1728), 1979; contbr. articles and reviews on Am. history to scholarly jours.; editorial bd. So. Calif. Quar. Home: 1456 Las Positas Pl Santa Barbara CA 93105

ANDRUS, MELINDA GAYLE, home economics educator; b. Springfield, Mo., Sept. 2, 1955; d. William Lonzo and Hazyl Wynoma (Carter) Andrus. B.S., Brigham Young U., 1978. Microwave cooking demonstrator Huco, Inc., Salt Lake City, 1977-79; tchr. home econs. Beaver (Utah) High Sch., 1978-79, Weber High Sch., Ogden, Utah, 1981-82, Hillcrest High Sch., Midvale, Utah, 1982—; tchr. summer sch. Ogden pub. schs., 1978—; tchr. missionary, Bolivia, 1979-81; staff food coordinator Camp Loll, Boy Scouts Am., 1983. Recipient Profl. Performance and Interpersonal Relationships award Brigham Young U., 1978. Mem. Am. Home Econs. Assn., Utah Assn. Vocat. Home Econs. Tchrs., Am. Vocat. Assn., Utah Home Econs. Assn. Mormon. Office: 7305 S 900 East St Midvale UT 84047

ANEMA, DURLYNN CAROL, university administrator, author; b. San Diego, Dec. 23, 1935; d. Durlin L. and Carolyn L. Flagg; m. Charles J. Anema, Jan. 18, 1955; children—Charlynn Ann, Jay, Richard F. Student Stanford U., 1953-55, U. Calif.-Berkeley, 1955; B.A., Calif. State U.-Hayward, 1968, M.S., 1977; Ed.D., U. Pacific, 1983. Cert. adminstr., supv., Calif. Tchr. journalism, history San Leandro Sch. Dist., 1970-72; tchr. journalism Hayward (Calif.) Unified Sch. Dist., 1972-75, adminstr., 1975-77; adminstr. Lodi Unified Sch. Dist., 1977-80; research asst. U. Pacific, Stockton, Calif., 1980-81, dir. Lifelong Learning, 1981—; cons. social studies, adult learning, 1982—. Pres., PTA, San Leandro, 1961, 63, hon. life mem., 1966; pres. San Leandro Library Bd., 1974, commendation, 1974; bd. dirs. Valley Community Counseling Ctr., 1981—; youth leader Grace Presbyterian Ch., Lodi, 1982—; bd. dirs. econ. edn. com. San Joaquin County, 1982—; mem. exec. com. San Joaquin County Hosp. 125th Anniversary; bd. dirs. San Joaquin County Authors Sumposium. Recipient commendations San Leandro City Council, 1974, 77. Mem. Nat. Council Social Studies, Calif. Council Social Studies, Assn. Calif. Sch. Adminstrs., Am. Assn. Adult and Continuing Edn., Calif. Assn. Re-entry. Author: Don't Get Fired, 1977; Get Hired, 1979; Sharing an Apartment, 1982; California Yesterday and Today, 1983. Home: 1782 W Vine St Lodi CA 95240 Office: Office of Lifelong Learning U Pacific Stockton CA 95211

ANEWALT, ANTHONY, real estate and insurance company executive; b. San Diego, Feb. 4, 1930; s. Henry Philip and Ellen (Cooper) A.; B.A., Stanford, 1951; children—John A., Mary E. Real estate, ins. salesman Hotchkiss & Anewalt, Inc., San Diego, 1952-60, sec.-treas., 1961-69, pres., 1970—. Vice-pres. San Diego County council Boy Scouts Am., 1973-77; v.p. San Diego Taxpayers Assn., 1975-77; pres. Central City Assn., 1977-80, San Diego Bd. Realtors, 1974, chmn. San Diego/Imperial Counties ARC, 1983—; mem. hosp. com. Mesa Vista Psychiat. Found., 1971-76. Served with AUS; PTO. Mem. Apt. and Rental Owners Assn. (pres. 1973), San Diego Bd. Realtors (pres. 1974), Calif. Assn. Realtors (hon. life dir., v.p. 1975), Ind. Ins. Agts. Assn. Clubs: Rotary, University, La Jolla Beach and Tennis. Office: 770 B St Suite 202 San Diego CA 92101

ANGELLO, NANCY BRYAN, ednl. cons.; b. Washington, July 17, 1945; d. Harry C. and Pat Bryan; B.A., Antioch Coll., 1967, M.Ed., U. Wash., 1970; Ph.D. (univ. scholar), Wash. State U., 1980; m. John C. Angello, June 23, 1967; 1 dau., Janine. Tchr., Whitman Jr. High Sch., Seattle, 1967-71; reading coordinator Seattle Public Schs., 1971-75; ednl. cons., Seattle, 1980—; secondary curriculum coordinator Kent (Wash.) Sch. Dist. Mem. Wash. State Tech. Assistance Adv. Bd., 1973-75; bd. dirs. N.W. Regional Ednl. Lab., 1978-81. Mem. Internat. Reading Assn., Wash. Orgn. Reading Devel. (pres. elect 1981-82). Am. Assn. Sch. Adminstrs., Assn. Supervision and Curriculum Devel., Phi Delta Kappa, Delta Kappa Gamma, Phi Lambda Theta. Home: 1724 NW 96th St Seattle WA 9117 Office: 12033 SE 256th St Kent WA 98031

ANGELO, ALBERT CARL, JR., building contractor; b. Vancouver, Wash., Feb. 19, 1949; s. Albert Carl and Katheryn Mae (Beatty) A.; A.A., Clark Coll., Vancouver, 1971; B.S., Wash. State U., 1973. Bldg. contractor, land developer, 1973—; pres., owner A-A Constrn. Co., Vancouver, 1973—; pres. Angelo-Moody Co., 1978—; partner Angelo Investment Co., 1973—, Al, Jr. and Craig Angelo Co., 1973—; past chmn. bd. Wash. State Bank, Vancouver, 1981—; chmn. Vancouver Bldg. Codes Commn., 1976—; vice chmn. Vancouver Planning Commn., 1979—; bd. dirs. Goodwill Industries. Served with USMCR, 1968-70. Mem. Nat. Home Builders Assn., Vancouver Contractors Assn., Vancouver C. of C., Wash. State U. Alumni Assn., Ducks Unlimited. Roman Catholic. Clubs: Multnomah Athletic (Portland, Oreg.); Oxford, Elks (Vancouver); Wash. Racquetball Assn. Office: 1815 D St Vancouver WA 98663

ANGELOFF, DANN V., investment banker; b. Hollywood, Calif., Nov. 15, 1935; B.S. in Fin., U. So. Calif., 1958, M.B.A., 1963; married; 2 daus., 1 son. Trainee, Dean Witter & Co., Inc., Los Angeles, 1957-60; v.p. Dempsey-Tegeler & Co., Inc., Los Angeles, 1960-70; v.p., dir. West Coast corp. fin. dept. Reynolds Securities, Inc., 1970-76; pres., dir. The Angeloff Co., Los Angeles, 1976—; dir., corp. fin. adv. Bobby McGee's U.S.A., Inc., Phoenix, Cathedralite, Capitola, Calif.; dir., chmn. audit com., corp. fin. adv. Golden West Homes, Santa Ana, Calif.; dir. Margaret Hills, Inc., Newport Beach, Calif., Storage Equities, Pasadena, Calif., Marine Nat. Bank, Irvine, Calif., Decade Corp., Los Angeles, Watt Comml. Properties, Inc., Los Angeles, Erisco, Inc., Los Angeles, Bd. dirs. Trojan Club, 1969-73, pres. Trojan Jr. Bd.; membership chmn. U. So. Calif. Assos., 1973—; bd. govs., trustee U. So. Calif., 1979—. Mem. Bond Club Los Angeles, Gen. Alumni Assn. U. So. Calif. (pres.), Commerce Assos. U. So. Calif., Skull and Dagger, Cardinal and Gold, Kappa Beta Phi. Clubs: California, Jonathan, Pacific. Office: 727 W 7th St Los Angeles CA 90017

ANGLEA, RALPH MAYHEW, savings and loan exec.; b. Pueblo, Colo., May 14, 1921; s. William P. and Ethel S. (Mayhew) A.; student So. Colo. State U., 1938-40, Denver U., 1940; Asso. Engring., U. Calif., Berkeley, 1950; postgrad. UCLA, 1970-71; m. Harriette Hopkins, June 30, 1943; children—Robert R., Carolyn Anglea Henderson. Air traffic controller FAA, 1941-55, supr., chief controller, 1956-58, staff air traffic control procedures, ops. and evaluation Los Angeles, 1959-61, spl. projects coordinator nat. and western region, 1962-77; v.p., mng. assoc. State Savs. & Loan, Encino, Calif., 1978—. Mem. Los Angeles World Affairs Council, 1979-82. Recipient Superior and Outstanding awards FAA, 1958-76; named Most Outstanding Account Exec., State Savs. & Loan, 1979. Mem. AIAA, Air Traffic Control Assn., Am. Ordinance Assn. Methodist. Clubs: Lions, Nat. Rocket, Cal Tech Assocs. Office: 15910 Ventura Blvd Suite 710 Encino CA 91436

ANGLIN, RICHARD LEE, JR., legal, engring., econ. energy researcher, cons.; b. Herrin, Ill., July 31, 1945; s. Richard Lee and Helen Yanulavich, A.; B.S. with honors, Case Inst. Tech., 1967; M. Regional Planning, Cornell U., 1969; postgrad. Claremont Grad. Sch., 1974-77; J.D., Loyola Law Sch., Los Angeles, 1981. Bar: Calif., D.C. Systems programming cons., Bluffton, Ohio, 1969-70; project dir. York Planning Corp., N.Y.C., 1970-71; dir. environ. planning J.F. Davidson Assos., Riverside, Calif., 1972-74; pres. AMECUS, Pasadena, Calif., 1974—; mem. tech. staff Jet Propulsion Lab. Calif. Inst. Tech., 1976—; ptnr. Lybrand and Anglin, Los Angeles, 1982—; asso. urban studies U. Calif., Riverside, 1973-76. Martin Co. scholar, 1963-67; recipient Neff prize, 1966; USPHS Environ. Health fellow, 1967-69; John C. Lincoln Inst. fellow, 1974-76; registered profl. engr., Calif., Colo., W.Va. Mem. Am. Bar Assn., ASCE (conf. chmn. 1981), Sigma Xi, Tau Beta Pi, Phi Kappa Phi, Theta Tau, Omicron Delta Epsilon, Phi Alpha Delta. Address: PO Box 5966 Pasadena CA 91107

ANGLIN, ROBERT BRUCE, real estate broker; b. Seattle, Feb. 20, 1925; s. Edward A. and Olga Ann (Zellmer) A.; B.S., U. Wash., 1948; m. Mary Margaret McGullough, July 19, 1948 (dec.); children—Robert Bryce, Bruce Timothy, Julie Ann, David Lloyd. Service rep. U.S. Plywood Corp., Seattle, 1948-58; dist. sales rep. Curtiss-Wright Corp., Seattle, 1958-60; dist. mgr. St. Regis Paper-Panelyte Co., San Francisco, 1960-68; v.p., sales mgr. Continental Pools, Livermore, Calif., 1968-80; Realtor assoc. Real Estate West, Pleasanton, Calif., 1980—. Sustaining mem. Republican Party, 1980—; v.p. Tri Valley Republican Caucus, 1981-82; pres. Pleasanton Community Band, 1976-77; pres. Pleasanton Cultural Arts Council. Served to comdr. USNR, 1944-72, ret. Mem. Calif. Swimming Pool Industry Energy Codes and Legis. Council, Wash. State Producers Council (past pres.), Asso. Gen. Contractors (dir. 1955-58); asso. mem. S. Alameda Bd. Realtors. Republican. Presbyterian. Club: Elks. Contbr. editorial articles on swimming pools to local newspaper. Office: Real Estate West 915C Main St Pleasanton CA 94566

ANKLAM, JAMES RICHARD, pipe manufacturing and sales company sales executive, geophysical engineer, mining engineer, exploitation engineer; b. Tucson, July 26, 1933; s. Joseph Ralph and Jessie (Paddock) A.; m. Markie Katrine Barker, June 18, 1933; children—Deborah Anklam Benedict, James Lawrence, Mark Richard. B.S. in Mining Engring. and Geology with high distinction, U. Ariz., 1955. Explotation engr. Shell Oil Co., Calif., Tex., Utah, N.Mex. and Wyo., 1955-58; sales rep. Johns-Manville, Scottsdale, Ariz., 1958-65, area mgr., western states, San Francisco, 1965-68, dist. mgr., western U.S., San Mateo, Calif., 1969—; mem. statewide water resources com. and legis. subcom. Calif. C. of C. Deacon, Community Presbyn. Ch., Danville, Calif., 1970-73, bd. moderator, 1973, elder, 1981—; co-founder troop Mt. Diablo council Boy Scouts Am., 1971, active council, 1971-83; coach Little League, Danville, Catholic Youth Basketball, Danville; invitational cross country and track ofcl., 50 schs., 1972-83. Named Outstanding Young Men Am., U.S. Jr. C. of C., 1965; recipient Dir.'s award U. Ariz., 1970, Service award Boy Scouts Am., 1980; Baird scholar, 1951-55. Mem. Am. Waterworks Assn., Nat. Assn. Corrosion Engrs., Ariz. Alumni Assn. (dir.), Tau Beta Pi, Theta Tau, Phi Kappa Phi, Phi Gamma Delta. Republican. Clubs: Toastmasters (pres. club 1963-64, area gov. 1965); Elks (Phoenix). Home: 325 Del Amigo Rd Danville CA 94526

ANKRUM, WARD ELWOOD, educator emeritus; b. Danville, Ill., Mar. 2, 1910; s. Wesley Jay and Margaret Elizabeth (Ward) A.; student Wabash Coll., 1929-32; B.S. in Edn., U. Ill., 1934, M.S. in Edn., 1941; student U. Denver, 1942-43; Ed.D., U. Mo., 1951; m. Wilma Mooney Walloch, May 30, 1965. Instr. speech and English, Danville High Sch., 1938-42; ednl. specialist, div. instr. tng. USAAF, 1942-44; instr. speech and English, U. Denver, 1943-44; chmn. English dept. Coronado (Calif.) High Sch., 1944-45; instr. div. communications Stephens Coll., Columbia, Mo., 1945-52, dir. audio-visual library, 1952-57; asso. prof., dir. audio-visual edn. Henderson State U., Arkadelphia, Ark., 1957-63, prof., dir. audio visual edn., 1963-75, prof. emeritus, 1975—; Ford Found. lectr. Ark. A. and M. Coll., 1953; co-dir. Grad. and Undergrad. Credit Workshop, Northeast Mo. State Tchrs. Coll., Kirksville, 1954-58, 62, 64, 66; asst. dir. Ednl. Media Inst. Ark. State Coll., summer 1967; spl. research influence selected TV programs on preservice tchrs. fundamental factors in reading rate acceleration. Charter pres. Columbia (Mo.) Art Theatre Adv. Council, 1955-58; chmn. audiovisual services Mo. P.T.A., 1955-58; del. from Mo. nat. conv. P.T.A., 1957; chmn. audio-visual services Ark. P.T.A., 1958-61; pres. dept. audio visual services Mo. Tchrs. Assn., 1955-56; juror Golden Reel Film Festival, N.Y.C., 1955, juror, chmn. motion pictures in edn., 1956. Mem. Clark County Health Adv. Bd., 1972—. Mem. adv. bd. Wonderland Sch., Arkadelphia, 1970—, pres., 1975—. Mem. Nat. (parliamentarian dept. audio visual instrn. 1960-75), Ark. (pres. Ark. audio visual assn. 1959-61, treas. 1971-75, pres. unit 1973-74, bd. dirs. emeritus 1975—) edn. assns., Ark. Ednl. TV Assn. (v.p. 1961—), Phi Delta Kappa, Tau Kappa Epsilon. Republican. Presbyn. Mason. Co-author: Utilization of Audio-Materials in Missouri, 1955. Contbr. articles to profl. jours. Home: 3920 S Galapago St Englewood CO 80110

ANNERUD, CAROLYN RIEDERER, emergency physician; b. San Antonio, Nov. 17, 1953; d. Joseph Dwight and Paula Jean (Wickward) Riederer; m. Nils Arne Annerud, Aug. 24, 1973 (div.); 1 dau., Kerstin Erika. B.S. in Biology, Walla Walla Coll., 1973; M.D., Loma Linda U., 1977. Intern, White Meml. Med. Ctr., Los Angeles, 1978-79; emergency physician Pacific Physician Services, Loma Linda, Calif., 1979, Barlett Meml. Hosp., Juneau, Alaska, 1980-81, Spectrum Emergency Care, Lake Havasu, Ariz., 1981; med. dir. Critical Air Medicine Air Ambulance Service, San Diego and emergency physician Associated Emergency Physicians Med. Group, 1981—; expdn. physician. Mem. San Diego Zool. Soc., La Jolla Mus. Contemporary Art. Mem. Am. Coll. Emergency Physicians, Alaska Med. Assn., Calif. Med. Assn., Nat. Assn. Female Execs. Home: 3246 I Ashford St San Diego CA 92111 Office: 8665 Gibbs Dr Suite 202 San Diego CA 92123

ANNESTRAND, STIG ALVAR, elec. engr.; b. Husby, Sweden, Sept. 18, 1933; s. August Erik and Frida Linnea (Carlsson) Johansson; M.S., Royal Inst. Tech., Stockholm, 1958; m. Britta Viviann Olsson, June 28, 1958; children—Peter N., Thomas A. Came to U.S., 1967, naturalized, 1972. Lab. engr. Almanna Svenska Elektriska Aktiebolaget, elec. equipment mfg., Ludvika, Sweden, 1958-61, mgr. research, 1962-67; tchr. Tech. High Sch., Borlange, Sweden, 1961-62; elec. engr. Bonneville Power Adminstrn., Dept. Interior, Portland, Oreg., 1967, head high voltage unit, 1967-74, head elec. investigations sect., Vancouver, Wash., 1974-77, chief br. labs., 1977-81, mgr. research and devel., Portland, 1981—. Served with Swedish Army, 1953-54. Recipient 1st prize Portland section IEEE, 1970. Registered profl. engr., Oreg. Fellow IEEE (sr.; active various coms.); mem. Am. Nat. Standards Inst. (chmn. subcom. contamination 1969-75), Internat. Conf. Large High Tension Electric Systems. Club: Toastmasters (pres. 1973). Author: Standard Handbook for Electrical Engineers, 10th edit., 1968. Contbr. articles to profl. publs. Home: 5392 SW Tree St Lake Oswego OR 97034 Office: PO Box 3621 Portland OR 97208

ANNON, JACK STAFFORD, psychologist; b. Chgo., Nov. 26, 1929; s. Dorcey and Marjorie Louise (Sites) A.; B.A. summa cum laude, U. Hawaii, 1966, M.A., 1968, Ph.D., 1971; m. Arvillie Ann Reed, Sept. 16,

1962; children—Jeffrey, Jason, Tyron, Marselene. TV ops. mgr. KGMB-TV, Honolulu, 1952-61; TV prodn. mgr. KHVH-TV, Honolulu, 1961-63; research asst. dept. psychology U. Hawaii, Honolulu, 1967, lectr. edn., 1968, clin. psychologist Counseling and Testing Center, 1968-71, mem. affiliate grad. faculty dept. psychology, 1974—, sr. cons. Sexual Counseling Service, Dept. Obstetrics and Gynecology, 1973—; pvt. practice clin. and forensic psychology, Honolulu, 1971—; cons. Child and Family Services, 1974—; cons. staff dept. psychiatry Queens Med. Center, Honolulu, 1971—; chmn. Bd. Certification Practicing Psychologists State of Hawaii, 1975—; clin. assoc. prof. dept. psychiatry Sch. Medicine, U. Hawaii; dir. Enabling Systems, Inc. Corp. dir. Merry-go-Round Child Care Center, Inc., 1963—. Served with USMC, 1944-48. Diplomate Am. Bd. Forensic Psychology. Clin. mem. Am. Assn. Sex Educators, Therapists and Counselors, Nat. Alliance for Family Life; mem. Am. Psychol. Assn., Hawaii Psychol. Assn. (pres. 1973-75, Disting. Service award), AAAS, Hawaii Assn. Humanistic Psychology, Hawaii Personnel and Guidance Assn., Acad. Psychologists in Marital and Family Therapy, Am. Assn. Marriage and Family Counselors, Behavior Therapy and Research Soc., Soc. Sci. Study of Sex, Soc. Clin. and Exptl. Hypnosis, Assn. Advancement of Behavior Therapy, Phi Beta Kappa, Sigma Xi, Omicron Delta Kappa, Phi Eta Sigma, Phi Kappa Phi, Psi Chi. Author: The Behavioral Treatment of Sexual Problems, 2 vols.; also chpts., articles. Home: 680 Ainapo St Honolulu HI 96825 Office: Suite 909 Queen's Physicians' Office Bldg 1380 Lusitana St Honolulu HI 96813

ANSALDO, OSCAR PICAR, physician; b. Davao City, Philippines, Jan. 15, 1937; came to U.S., 1964, naturalized, 1979; s. Genaro Salamat and Benigna Picar A.; m. Lilia de la Paz, Jan. 29, 1966; children—Maria Vera, Jean Marie, Lisa Mae. Student (Entrance scholar) U. Philippines, 1954-57; M.D., Far Eastern U., 1963. Diplomate Am. Bd. Family Practice. Intern, Mercy Hosp., Hamilton, Ohio, 1964; resident in pathology Swedish Covenant Hosp. and Cook County Hosp., Chgo., 1965-69; fellow in pathology Luth. Gen. Hosp., Park Ridge, Ill., 1970-71; staff physician Wis. VA Hosp., King, 1972-79, acting med. dir., after 1979; ind. med. reviewer nursing homes, Wis., 1976-80; med. dir. Wis. Vets. Home, after 1980; now practicing in Calif. Fellow am. Acad. Family Practice; mem. AMA (Physicians recognition award 1985), Calif. Acad. Family Phyicians, Merced-Maricopa County Med. Soc. Home: 1540 Racquet Club Dr Los Banos CA 93635

ANSBACHER, CHARLES ALEXANDER, condr., musician; b. Providence, Oct. 5, 1942; s. Heinz L. and Rowena Ripin A.; B.A., Brown U., 1965; M. Music, U. Cin., 1968, D.M.A., 1979; 1 son, Henry Lloyd. Asst. condr. Kingsport (Tenn.) Symphony Orch., 1965-66; condr., mus. dir. Middletown (Ohio) Symphony Orch., 1967-70, Colorado Springs Symphony Orch., 1970—; condr. Young Artists Orch. Denver, 1980—; music dir. Rockefeller Found. Apprentice Musicians Program, Cin. Playhouse in Park, 1967; guest condr. Cin. Symphony Orch., Denver Symphony Orch., Frysk Orkest in Leeuwarden, Holland; nat. adv. bd. Avery Fisher awards music, 1974—; Colo. State Festival Council for Centennial-Bicentennial Commn., 1974-76. White House fellow, 1976-77. Mem. Urban League Pike's Peak Region (bd. dirs.), Pike's Peak Musicians Assn. (v.p. 1974—), Condrs. Guild of Am. Symphony Orch. League (chmn. 1979-81), Colo. Council Arts and Humanities, Colorado Springs World Affairs Council (pres. 1981—), Music Educators Nat. Conf. Rotarian. Home: 1431 N Tejon St Colorado Springs CO 80907 Office: Box 1692 Colorado Springs CO 80901

ANSEL, ALAN LEE, surgeon; b. Chgo., Jan. 9, 1947; s. Harvey H. and Dorothy (Russ) A.; B.S. with honors, No. Ill. U., 1968; M.D., Loyola U., Chgo., 1972. Intern, St. Joseph's Hosp. and Med. Center, Phoenix, 1973; resident in surgery Michael Reese Hosp. and Med. Center, Chgo., 1974, Maricopa County Gen. Hosp., Phoenix, 1974-77; fellow in vascular surgery Maricopa County and area hosps., Phoenix, 1978; practice surgery, specializing in peripheral vascular surgery, Phoenix, 1979—; staff Mercy Hosp., Chgo., 1978, Good Samaritan Hosp. and Trauma Center, Phoenix, 1979-80, St. Joseph's Hosp., Phoenix, 1979—, St. Luke's Hosp., Phoenix, 1979—, Doctor's Hosp., 1979—, Maricopa County Gen. Hosp., 1979—, teaching staff, 1979—; teaching staff Phoenix VA Hosp., 1979—. Diplomate Am. Bd. Surgery. Fellow A.C.S.; mem. AMA, Maricopa County Med. Soc., Southwestern Surg. Congress. Club: Peripheral Vascular Surgery. Office: 1010 E McDowell Rd Phoenix AZ 85006

ANSELL, EDWARD ORIN, lawyer, university official; b. Superior, Wis., Mar. 29, 1926; s. H. S. and Mollie (Rudnitzky) A.; m. Hanne B. Baer, Dec. 23, 1956; children—Deborah, William. B.S.E.E., U. Wis., 1948; J.D., George Washington U., 1955. Bar: D.C. 1955, Calif. 1960. Electronic engr. FCC, Buffalo, 1948-51, Washington, 1951-55; patent atty. RCA, Princeton, N.J., 1955-57; gen. mgr. AeroChem Research Labs., Inc., Princeton, 1957-58; patent atty. Aerojet-Gen. Corp., La Jolla, Calif., 1958-63, corp. patent counsel 1963-82, asst. sec., 1970-79, corp. sec. 1979-82, assoc. gen. counsel, 1981-82; dir. patents and licensing Calif. Inst. Tech., Pasadena, 1982—; adj. prof. U. LaVerne Coll. Law, 1972-78; adv. bd. BNA Patent, Trademark and Copyright Jour., 1971-76; spl. advisor U.S. Commn. on Govt. Procurement, task force chmn., 1971. Recipient Alumni Service award George Washington U., 1979. Mem. ABA, Fed. Bar Assn., Am. Patent Law Assn., Los Angeles Patent Law Assn., Soc. Univ. Patent Adminstrs., Licensing Execs. Soc., Assn. Corp. Patent Counsel, AIAA. Contbr. articles to profl. jours. Office: 1201 E California Blvd Pasadena CA 91125

ANSELMI, RUDOLPH THEODORE, construction company executive; b. Rock Springs, Wyo., May 1, 1904; s. Joseph A. and Mary (Menghini) A.; B.S., U. Wyo., 1925, LL.D. (hon.), 1977; m. Shuster, July 10, 1929; children—Mary Lou Anselmi Unguren, Lynn Anselmi Lockhart, Jerl Anselmi Kirk. Pres., mgr. Miners Merc. Co., Rock Springs, 1931-65; exec. v.p. Cheyenne Service Corp., 1973-75; sec.-treas. HMA Realty, KOA Kampgrounds, Rock Springs; dir. North Side State Bank, Wyo., Cheyenne Fed. Savs. & Loan Assn.; sec. Huntley Constrn. Co., Rock Springs. Chmn. exec. com. Wyo. Cancer Soc., 1970-72. Mem. Sch. Bd., Rock Springs, 1936-65, pres., 1942-65; mem. Wyo. Senate, 1937-65; mem. Gov.'s Com. on Edn., 1963-64, Gov.'s Re-orgn. Com., 1967-68, 69-71; state committeeman Democratic party, 1944-66; mem. Legislative Interim Com., 1945-65; chmn. Bd. Equalization Wyo. Tax Commn., 1975—; mem. Wyo. state treas. investment adv. com., 1973-75. Named Distinguished Alumnus, U. Wyo. Coll. Commerce and Industry, 1961-62, Disting. Alumnus, U. Wyo., 1984; recipient Disting. Service award Nat. Govs. Assn., 1980. Mem. Sigma Chi, Phi Kappa Phi. Roman Catholic. Clubs: Elks, Eagles; K.C. (past grand knight); Vocations (pres.), Lions (past pres.) (Rock Springs). Home: 2608 House Cheyenne WY 82001 Office: 2200 Carey St Cheyenne WY 82001

ANSON, MICHAEL A., publisher; b. San Diego, Dec. 11, 1946; s. C. A. and E. R. Anson; B.A. in Journalism, Calif. State U.-Long Beach, 1969; m. Viki Nolan; 1 son, Rory Michael. Rd. test editor Rd. & Track mag., Newport Beach, Calif., 1970-72; asso. editor Car Life mag., Newport Beach, 1969-70; dir. advt. Interpart Corp., El Segundo, Calif., 1972-73; editor Petersen's 4 Wheel & Off-Rd. mag., Los Angeles, 1978-79, pub., 1979—, pub. Pickup, Van & 4 Wheel Drive Mag., 1982—. Mem. Splty. Equipment Marketers Assn., Alfa Romeo Owners Club, SCORE Internat., Sports Car Club Am., Sigma Delta Chi. Author: How to Customize Your Pickup Truck, 1977; contbr. articles to mags.; author TV comedy scripts, 1976-77. Office: 8490 Sunset Blvd Los Angeles CA 90069

ANTHONY, JAMES STEPHEN, psychologist; b. Rochester, Pa., June 3, 1951; s. Stephen James and Helen (Athas) A.; B.A., U. Calif., Berkeley, 1973; M.A., Pepperdine U., 1974; Ph.D., U.S. Internat. U., 1982. Psychologist child psychiatry div. Clinton Valley Center, Pontiac, Mich., 1974-76, Plymouth Center for Human Devel., Northville, Mich., 1976, Lakewood Clinic, Birmingham, Mich., 1974-76; alcoholism counselor East County Accord, El Cajon, Calif., 1980—; psychol. intern, drug edn. coordinator Navy Alcohol Rehab. Center, San Diego, 1979-81; instr. U.S. Internat. U., San Diego, 1977-78. Mem. Am. Psychol. Assn., Calif. State Psychol. Assn., Acad. San Diego Psychologists, San Diego Psychology-Law Soc., Hellenic Profl. Assn. Am. Greek Orthodox. Home: 2447 San Elijo Ave Cardiff by the Sea CA 92007 Office: 130 S Magnolia El Cajon CA 92020

ANTHONY, MARY CARMEL, county law librarian; b. Visalia, Calif., June 3, 1925; d. Francisco Cardoso and Virginia (Cotta) Jacques; student Coll. of Sequoias, 1944-46; cert. 4C's Coll., Fresno, Calif., 1967; m. Jack Gerard Anthony, Nov. 27, 1976. Operator, Pacific Telephone Co., Visalia, 1944-46; sec. State Bd. Equalization, Visalia, 1946-47; clk. typist County Farm Advisors, Visalia, 1947-49, Dept. Motor Vehicles, Visalia, 1968-69; clk. typist II, Juvenile Probation Dept., Visalia, 1969-70; dep. clk. Jury Commrs. Office, Visalia, 1971-73; county law librarian Tulare County, Visalia, 1973—. Active various fund drives. Mem. Public Employees Assn. Tulare County, Am. Assn. Law Libraries, San Joaquin Valley Library System, Asso. Bus. Girls Calif., Kaweah Delta Dist. Hosp. Guild, V.F.W. Roman Catholic. Home: Visalia CA 93291 Office: County Civic Center Room 1 Visalia CA 93291

ANTION, DAVID LEE, marriage counselor, educator; b. Cannonsburg, Pa., May 6, 1937; s. Leo and Freda Marie (David) A.; m. Molly Cope Hammer, Aug. 16, 1959; 1 son, David Stephen. B.A., Ambassador Coll., Pasadena, Calif., 1959; M.S., Calif. State U.-Fullerton, 1977; Ph.D., U. So. Calif., 1983. Ordained to ministry, 1960. Pastor, 1960-65, dist. supt., Akron, Ohio, 1965-69; ch. adminstrn., 1969-72; assoc. prof. sociology and religion Ambassador Coll., 1974-75, dir. coll. relations, 1975-78; v.p. ch. adminstrn., 1972-74; marriage, family and child counselor, Pasadena, 1978—; lectr. marriage communication, 1974-78; dir. fund devel. Kennedy Child Study Center, 1979-80; pres. Antion Enterprises, mktg., fin. planning and human devel., 1980—. Mem. Pasadena C. of C., Calif. Assn. Marriage and Family Counselors. Democrat. Club: Rotary. Author workbooks and cassette programs; contbr. articles to profl. jours. Home: 311 Waverly Dr Pasadena CA 91105

ANTIPORDA, HIPOLITO, surgeon; b. Vigan, Ilocos Sur, Philippines, Jan. 30, 1937; came to U.S., 1962; s. Proceso P. and Felicidad B. A.; M.D., U. Santo Tomas, Manila, 1961; m. Teresa McInerney, May 9, 1964; children—Maria, Catherine, Michael. Intern, Mary Immaculate Hosp., Jamaica, N.Y., 1962-63; resident in surgery Mary Immaculate Hosp., also Bridgeport (Conn.) Hosp., 1963-67; practice medicine specializing in surgery, N.Y.C., 1969-78, Carlsbad, N.Mex., 1979—; mem. staff Guadalupe Med. Center, Carlsbad. Diplomate Am. Bd. Surgery. Fellow ACS, Southwestern Surg. Congress, Am. Soc. Abdominal Surgeons, Soc. Philippine Surgeons in Am.; mem. AMA, N.Mex. Med. Soc., Eddy County Med. Soc. Clubs: Riverside Country, Elks. Office: 2402 W Pierce Suite 3A Carlsbad NM 88220

ANTONELLI, ARTHUR LOUIS, entomologist; b. Vancouver, B.C., Can., Feb. 4, 1944; came to U.S., 1972; s. Ottorino and Audrey (Odlum) A.; B.S. in Biology, Seattle U., 1967; M.S. in Zoology, Central Wash. State Coll., 1969; Ph.D. in Entomology, U. Idaho, 1974; m. Lois Marie Kounkel, Jan. 4, 1980; children—David, Antony, Vincent. Research asst., bio-illustrator dept. biology Seattle U., 1967; teaching asst. Central Wash. State Coll., Ellensburg, 1968-69; instructional asst. entomology U. Idaho, Moscow, 1969-70, grad. asst., 1971-73, research asso., 1973-74; research technologist Wash. State U., Pullman, 1974-76; extension entomologist Wash. State U. Research and Extension Center, Puyallup, 1976—; mem. tech. adv. com. Wash. State Poison Prevention, 1976—; mem. Wash. State Agrl. Pesticide Adv. Bd., 1983—; guest lectr. pest control and entomology to various profl. confs. and workshops, 1976—. Mem. Entomol. Soc. Am., Wash. State Entomol. Soc., Sigma Xi. Roman Catholic. Contbr. articles on insect control to profl. publs. Home: 18008 79th Ave E Puyallup WA 98373 Office: Western Wash Research and Extension Center Puyallup WA 98371

ANTONELLI, SHARON GROMER, home economist, educator; b. Healdsburg, Calif., Jan. 27, 1942; d. Lloyd Marvin and Dorothy Elenore (Davis) Gromer; m. Michael Edward Antonelli, July 3, 1964 (div.); children—Kelly, Michael. M.A. in Home Econs., San Jose State U., 1970. Cert. community coll. tchr. Calif. Instr. consumer edn. Can. Coll., Redwood City, Calif., 1970-72; instr. food and nutrition West Valley Coll., Saratoga, Calif., 1971-74; instr. nutrition San Jose State U., 1974-75; instr. nutrition, child devel., parent-child relationships San Jose City Coll., 1974—; tchr. adult edn. classes in consumer edn. and parent-child relationships. Mem. Calif. Tchr. Assn., Interagy. Nutrition Council Santa Clara County. Democrat. Roman Catholic. Club: Apres Ski (Mountain View), Peninsula Little (Los Altos). Author consumer student workbook, 1975 Home: 2818 Steinhart Ct Santa Clara CA 95051 Office: 2100 Moorpark Ave San Jose CA 95128

ANTONOFF, STEVEN ROSS, educator, university dean, consultant, civic leader; b. Waukon, Iowa, Dec. 14, 1948; s. Ben H. and Florence (Rosenberg) A.; B.S., Colo. State U., 1967; M.A., U. Denver, 1970, Ph.D., 1979. Spl. asst. to dean U. Denver, 1970-71, dean student life, 1971-74, dean Center for Prospective Students, 1974-75, exec. dir. admissions and student affairs, 1975-78, dean admissions and fin. aid, 1978-81, adj. prof. speech communication, 1979—; dir., owner Denver Nuggets Basketball, Inc., 1970-82. Chmn., Mayor's Commn. on Arts, Denver, 1979-81; trustee Congregation Emanuel; chmn. bd. dirs. Hospice of Metro Denver; mem. scholarship com. Mile High Cablevision. Mem. Am. Mgmt. Assn., Internat. Communication Assn., Speech Communication Assn., Am. Assn. Higher Edn., Nat. Assn. Student Personnel Adminstrs., Soc. Profl. Mgmt. Consultants, Nat. Assn. Coll. Admissions Counselors. Office: 425 S Cherry St Suite 710 Denver CO 80222

ANTONOVICH, MICHAEL DENNIS, county official; b. Los Angeles, Aug. 12, 1939; s. Mike and Frances (McColm) A.; student Los Angeles City Coll., Rio Hondo Res. Officer Advanced Tng. Sch., 1978; grad. Pasadena Police Acad., Res. Officer Sch., 1967; B.A., Calif. State U., 1963, M.A., 1967; Instr. govt., history Los Angeles Unified Sch. Dist., 1966-72; dir. George Miller Constrn. Co., Vernon, Calif., 1975—; instr. Calif. State U.-Los Angeles, 1979, Pepperdine U., 1979-80; v.p. Gregg-Gangi Devel., Glendale, Calif., 1979—; mem. Los Angeles Community Coll. Dist. Bd. Trustees, 1969-73; mem. Calif. State Assembly, 1972-78; supr. 5th Dist. Los Angeles County, Los Angeles, 1980—. Mem. Youth for Goldwater State Steering Com., 1964; regional chmn. Reelection Gov. Reagan, 1970; pres. 43rd Assembly Dist. Republican Central Com., 1965-80; mem. Los Angeles County Rep. Central Com., 1966—, youth chmn., 1971-72; mem. Rep. State Central Com. Calif., 1965-80; Los Angeles county co-chmn. Pres. Ford Com., 1976, Reagan for Pres. Com., 1976, 80; alt. del. Rep. Nat. Conv., 1972; mem. Rep. Platform Com., 1976, co-chmn. subcom. human resources, 1979; del. Rep. Nat. Conv., 1976; chmn. Los Angeles County George Deukmejian Gov.'s Campaign, 1982; alumni assn. bd. dirs. Calif. State U.-Los Angeles, 1970-74; bd. govs. Glendale Symphony Orch. Assn., 1973—. Recipient awards including Outstanding Legislator of Yr., Calif. Rep. Assembly, 1973-74, 74-75, 76-77; Statesman of Yr. award Calif. Pro-Life Council, 1976. Mem. Glendale C. of C., Profl. Educators Los Angeles, Secondary Tchrs. Los Angeles, Phila. Soc., Intercollegiate Studies Inst., Blue Key, Sigma Nu (pres.). Lutheran. Clubs: Kiwanis, Elks. Home: 3023 San Gabriel Ave Glendale CA 91208 Office: 500 W Temple St Los Angeles CA 90012

ANTONUCCIO, DAVID OLIVER, psychologist; b. Palo Alto, Calif., July 3, 1953; s. Oliver John and Sally (Calvo) A. B.A. in Psychology and Econs., Stanford U., 1975; M.A. in Clin. Psychology, U. Oreg., 1979, Ph.D., 1980. Cert. psychologist, Nev. Intern in clin. psychology VA Med. Ctr., Lyons, N.J., 1977-78; clinic coordinator dept. psychology U. Oreg., 1978-80; crisis team coordinator VA Med. Ctr., Reno, 1981-82, asst. coordinator Mental Hygiene Clinic, 1981—; asst. prof. dept. psychiatry U. Nev. Med. Sch., Reno, 1981—; mem. U. Nev. Speakers Bur., 1981—. U. Oreg. fellow, 1976-77, 78-80; USPHS trainee, 1975-76. Mem. Am. Psychol. Assn., Assn. Advancement Behavior Therapy, Western Psychol. Assn. Democrat. Roman Catholic. Contbr. articles to profl. jours. Office: Mental Hygiene Clinic VA Med Ctr Reno NV 89520

ANZ, REG DEAN, architect; b. Clifton, Tex., Jan. 21, 1942; s. Edward Walter and Elizabeth Helen (Holman) A.; student U. Tex., Arlington, 1960-62, B.S. in Archtl. Studies, Austin, 1965; m. Patrice Ann Niehaus, Jan. 9, 1977; children—Adrian Van, Marisa Santana. Project architect Envirodynamics Inc., Dallas, 1971-72, Dahl/Braden/Jones/Chapman, Dallas, 1973-74, Dan Dworsky, Beverly Hills, Calif., 1974; asso. Martin Stern, Jr., Beverly Hills, 1975-79, Maxwell Starkman, Beverly Hills, 1979-83. Lic. architect, Tex., Calif. Mem. AIA (corp.), Constrn. Specifications Inst., Am. Arbitration Assn., Nat. Council Archtl. Registration Bds. (cert.). Supervising architect M.G.M. Grand Hotel, Reno, 1977-78; project architect Sahara Hotel & Casino, Las Vegas and Atlantic City, 1978-79; project dir. Sheraton Grande Hotel, Los Angeles, 1979-83. Office: 1008 5th St Santa Monica CA 90403

ANZALONE, BARBARA JEAN, computer manufacturing company official; b. Huntington, W.Va., Dec. 10, 1950; d. Bill E. and Mary C. Stewart; accounting diploma Heald Bus. Coll., 1969; B.S.B.A. candidate U. Phoenix; m. John Anzalone, June 17, 1972. Accounts receivable adminstr., mgr. Manpower, Inc., Monterey, Calif., 1969-74; supr. word processing CTB/McGraw-Hill, Monterey, 1975-76; mgr. word processing Sambo's Restaurants, Santa Barbara, Calif., 1976-77, dir. adminstrn., 1977-79; head adminstrn. GTE, Los Gatos, Calif., 1980-81; mgr. adminstrn. Triad Systems Corp., Sunnyvale, 1981—. Recipient Regional Occupational Program. Outstanding Service award, 1976. Mem. Am. So. Calif. Micrographics Assn., Office Automation Exchange (dir.). Office: 1252 Orleans Dr Sunnyvale CA 94086

ANZURES, RICHARD EDWARD, steel co. ofcl.; b. Silver City, N.Mex., Aug. 5, 1949; s. Ernest Baca and Minnie (Diaz) A.; B.A. in Math. and Acctg. (Univ. scholar), Western N.Mex. U., 1970. With C F & I Steel Corp., Pueblo, Colo., 1972—, sales tax acct., 1972-78, asst. cashier, 1978-81, cashier, 1981—. Served with Army N.G., 1970-78. Mem. Nat. Assn. Accts. (bd. dirs. Pueblo-Colorado Springs chpt. 1973-74, sec. 1974-75). Roman Catholic. Club: Jaycees (bd. dirs. Pueblo chpt. 1976-77, Dir. of Yr. 1977). Home: 418 Colorado Ave Pueblo CO 81004

APARTON, JEROME, insurance agency executive; b. San Francisco, Apr. 28, 1927; s. Lawrence Harold and Sally A.; m. Nancy Joan Low, Dec. 19, 1970; children—Craig Arthur, Bruce Jerome, Victoria Nancy. B.A., U. Calif.-Berkeley, 1950; postgrad. Stanford U. Bus. Sch., 1969, Columbia U. Bus. Sch., 1966. With Chubb & Son, 1952-70, regional v.p., 1966-69, nat. sales dir., 1969-70; with Johnson & Higgins, San Francisco, 1970-78; v.p. Clifton & Co., San Francisco, 1978—, sr. v.p., dir. risk mgmt., co. dir., 1978—. Served with USNR, 1944-46. Decorated Purple Heart, Air medal. Mem. Am. Inst. for Property and Liability Underwriters, Soc. Ins. Brokers, Nat. Assn. Ins. Brokers, Ins. Agts. and Brokers Calif. (chmn. legis. com. 1976-82), San Francisco C. of C. (new bus. com. 1970-75). Recipient Legis. award Soc. Ins. Brokers, 1978. Clubs: University, Tiburon Peninsula. Contbr. articles to profl. jours. Office: Clifton & Co Suite 1700 3 Embarcadero Center San Francisco CA 94111

APILADO, MYRON, university administrator; b. Chgo., May 18, 1933; s. Inosencio Tadina and wuth Moselle (Mays) M.; m. Sherri Ann Mitchell, Oct. 21, 1972; children—Mariano, Kea, Kelli, Mnthony, Adam. B.A., U. Md., 1971; M.A. Ball Snate U., 1973: Ed.D., U. S.D., 1976. Cert. sch. psychologist, Iowa. Mem. exec. com. Community Counseling Program, Torrejon, Spain, 1972; chmn. Ednl. Grad. Orgn. U. S.D., 1974, instr., 1975, asst. prof., 1976; dean student devel. Peru ZNebr. State Coll., after 1976; now v.p. student affairs, Olympia, Wash. Pres., Nemaha County Mental Health Assn., after 1980; mem. adv. com. Region V Mental Health, Alcoholism and Drug obuse Program, 1981-82. Served with USAF, 1953-73. Decorated Bronze Star. Mem. Am. Psychol. Assn., Am. Personnel and Guidance Assn., Phi Delta Kappa. Address: 3205 Wilderness Dr Olympia WA 98501

APONTE, GLORIA JEAN, human services executive, consultant; b. Tempe, Ariz., Mar. 13, 1951; d. George Richard and Petra (Equrrola) A.; m. Anthony R. Garcia, July 1, 1967 (div. 1973); children—Paul, Ramona R. Student U. Calif.-Riverside, 1973-74, Calif. State U.-San Bernardino, 1980; A.A., San Bernardino Valley Coll., 1975. Cert. mental health worker. Retail clk. May Co., 1969-70; program coordinator, counselor aide Mental Health Assn., 1970-73; probation aide Riverside (Calif.) Dept. Probation, 1973-74; sr. counselor Colton (Calif.) Drug Abuse Program, 1975-77; project dir. Los Padrinos of So. Calif., Inc., 1977-82, mem., 1983—; program mgr., field specialist Women in Community Services/Job Corps, San Bernardino, Calif., 1982—; cons. program mgmt., referrals, recruitment. Com. rep. Assembly Dist. 66, 1981—; past 4-H adviser, leader Boy Scouts Am.; San Bernardino County commr. for Status of Women. Mem. Affirmative Action of San Bernardino Unified Dist. Democrat. Roman Catholic.

APP, JOHN O'NEAL, pension funding consultant; b. Hammond, Ind., Nov. 24, 1938; s. John Maximilian and Lurline Elizabeth (Burch) A.; B.A., Brown U., 1961; m. Janet Manderson, June 22, 1979; children—John Maximilian III, Konrad Alexandre, Friedrich Wilhelm. Agt., Underwriters Nat. Assurance Co., Orange, Calif., 1969-74; owner, operator John O. App and Assos., pension cons., Newport Beach, Calif., 1974-78; pres., chief exec. officer Corp. Pension Funding, Inc., Laguna Hills, Calif., 1978—. Mem. Orange County (Calif.) Bd. Edn., 1974-78, v.p., 1978; pres. Dana Point (Calif.) Pacific Ocean Found., 1978-83. Served to maj. USMC, 1962-67. Named Outstanding Area Gov., Toastmasters Internat. Founders Dist., 1974. Mem. Internat. Assn. Fin. Planners, Orange County Marine Inst. Office: 25200 E La Paz Rd Suite 217 Laguna Hills CA 92653

APPEL, KAREN WAGGONER, vocational educator, consultant; b. Natchez, Miss., Dec. 9, 1940; d. William Comer and Nadine Lucille (Milligan) Waggoner; m. Robert Reid Prentice, Sept. 19, 1963; children—Katrina W. Prentice Parker, Robert Reid, Ricarda N.; m. 2d, Richard Ralph Appel, July 31, 1978. B.S. in Textiles and Clothing, Iowa State U., 1963; postgrad. No. Ill. U., 1963-64, U. Minn., 1965, Colo. State U., 1975, U. Mex., 1960; M.S. in Home Econs. Edn., U. Wyo., 1978, Ed.D. in Vocat. Edn., 1982. Tchr. pub. schs., Mpls., 1964-67, Denver, 1967-70; tchr. adult edn. Kadena Air Base, Okinawa, Japan, 1970-73; tchr. Kelly Walsh High Sch., Natrona County Sch. Dist. #1, Casper, Wyo., 1979—; mem. dist. curriculum adv. council; cons. changing families; lectr. in field. Leader Girl Scouts U.S.A. 1965-67, 80—; leader Boy Scouts Am., 1979; layreader St. Stephens Episcopal Ch., 1979—. Mem. NEA, Natrona County Classroom Tchrs. Assn., Wyo. Edn. Assn., Wyo. Vocat. Assn., Am. Home Econs. Assn., Phi Kappa Phi, Phi Delta Kappa (newsletter editor). Republican. Contbr. articles to profl. jours. Home: 3301 Arroyo Dr Casper WY 82604 Office: Kelly Walsh High Sch 12th and Nottingham Sts Casper WY 82601

APPEL, KEITH KENNETH, painter, printmaker, sculptor; b. Bricely, Minn.; s. Leon Valarius and Leona (Salley) A.; m. Darlene Marie (Appel,) Aug. 6, 1960; children—Beth Marie, Mary Patronella. B.A., B.S., M.S., Mankato State Coll.; postgrad. Ohio State U., 1967-68. Tchr. art Anchorage Sch. Dist., 1960-67, art dir., 1968-70; assoc. prof. art U. Alaska-Anchorage, 1970-81, chmn. dept. art, 1978-80; exhibited in one-man shows, including: Alaska State Museum, Juneau, 1970, traveling exhibit to 12 galleries outside of Alaska, 1974-75, Anchorage Hist. and Fine Arts Mus., 1970, 75, Artique Gallery, Anchorage, 1974, 75, Artworks Gallery, Fairbanks, Alaska, 1976, Art Inc. Gallery, Anchorage, 1977-80, The Gathering, Ketchikan, Alaska, 1980, 82, The Artique, Anchorage, 1982; numerous group exhbns., including: All Alaska Juried Exhibit, 1960-83, represented in permanent collection: All Alaska Juried Exhibit; various sculpture commns.; juror for numerous local, state exhbns.; bd. dirs. Alaska Council on Arts, 1976-80. Bd. dirs. Anchorage Hist. and Fine Arts Mus., 1969-70, Visual Arts Ctr. Alaska, 1974-77. Served with U.S. Army, 1957-58. Recipient Print award All Alaska Juried Exhibit, 1966, 67, 71, 73, Mel Kohler award for painting, 1966, 71, 73, Juror's Choice award, 1967, 70, 71, 75, Gov.'s award, 1971, Ceramics award, 1971, Mixed Media award, 1983, First Place award Exxon Juried Exhibit, 1973, Sculpture award Alaska State Arts Council, 1977; Alaska State Council on Arts grantee, 1969, 71; U. Alaska-Anchorage research grantee, summer 1980. Mem. Alaska Artists Guild (pres. 1965-66).

APPEL, MARTIN SHERMAN, lawyer; b. Chgo., Mar. 15, 1933; s. Philip T. and Pearl (Goldman) A.; m. Audrey Blumenthal, Aug. 29, 1954; children—Lynne, Leslie, Leanne, Richard. B.S., Northwestern U., 1953, J.D., 1956. Bar: Ill. 1956, Calif. 1958; C.P.A., Ill., Calif. C.P.A. Godow & Lawrence, Chgo., 1953-56; assoc. Law Offices of Max Swerin, Chgo., 1956-58; tax mgr. Arthur Andersen & Co., Los Angeles, 1958-62; v.p. Ring Bros., Los Angeles, 1962; mem. Pacht, Ross, Warne, Bernhard & Sears, Inc., Los Angeles, 1962-82; prin. Rudin, Richman & Appel, Beverly Hills, Calif., 1982—; dir. Independence Bank, Los Angeles; lectr. in field. Mem. Vikings, 1977—, Jewish Fedn. Council Greater Los Angeles Branch, U.S. Olympic Com.; chmn. Bur. Synagogue Affairs; bd. dirs. Jewish Community Found. Recipient Outstanding Service award Los Angeles Jr. C. of C., 1965. Mem. ABA, Los Angeles Bar Assn., Beverly Hills Bar Assn., Calif. Bar Assn. (chmn. personal income tax com.). Republican. Club: Hillcrest Country. Author publs. in field. Home: 607 N Elm Dr Beverly Hills CA 90210 Office: Rudin Richman & Appel Penthouse 9601 Wilshire Blvd Beverly Hills CA 90210

APPELT, GLENN DAVID, pharmacologist, educator; b. Yoakum, Tex., Aug. 24, 1935; s. Leonard William and Josephine Mildred (Ohnhauser) A.; m. Jennifer S. McNew, Feb. 2, 1983. B.S. in Pharmacy, U. Tex., Austin, 1957, M.S. in Pharmacy (Armour fellow), 1959; Ph.D., U. Colo., 1963. Teaching asst. Sch. Pharmacy U. Tex., Austin, 1957-60, asst. prof. pharmacology, 1963-67; research asso., lectr., instr. Sch. Pharmacy, U. Colo., Boulder, 1960-63, assoc. prof., 1967-78, prof., 1978—, asst. dean student affairs, 1977-82; registered pharmacist, retail and hosp. pharmacies, Austin, 1957-60; cons. pharmacology O'Connor Products Co., Redford, Mich., Menley James Labs., Phila.; mem. profl. adv. bd. Herb Research Found., 1983—. Recipient Outstanding Prof. award U. Colo. Sch. Pharmacy, 1977. Mem. Am. Pharm. Assn., Acad. Pharm. Scis., Am. Assn. Colls. Pharmacy, Sigma Xi, Rho Chi, Kappa Psi. Democrat. Contbr. book chpt., articles in biochem. pharmacology to profl. and pharm. edn. publs. Home: 2990 Regis Dr Boulder CO 80303 Office: Ekeley W181 Univ Colorado Boulder CO 80309

APPERSON, MARJORIE MAY, newspaper exec.; b. San Francisco, Apr. 22, 1929; d. John Philip and Jessie Lucille (Earl) Sampson, B.A., Stanford, 1950; div.; children—Virginia, April, John. Co-pub., editor So. Siskiyou Newspapers, 1950—; panelist Western Newspaper Found. Seminar, 1975. Mem. Mt. Shasta Planning Commn., 1966-70, chmn., 1969; mem. Overall Econ. Devel. Planning Com. Siskiyou County (Calif.), 1970; mem. archtl. adv. com. Siskiyou County Planning Commn., 1974—. Mem. AAUW, Calif. Newspaper Pubs. Assn. (dir. 1977-79, 80—, govt. affairs com. 1977—, exec. com. 1983—, pres. Mid-Valley unit 1976), Calif. Press Assn. Home: PO Box 394 Mount Shasta CA 96067 Office: PO Box 127 Mount Shasta CA 96067

APPLBAUM, RONALD LEE, university administrator; b. Charleroi, Pa., Dec. 14, 1943; s. Irwin and Marion (Caplan) A.; m. Susan Joy, July 4, 1968; 1 son, Lee David. B.A., Calif. State U.-Long Beach, 1965, M.A., 1966. Asst. prof. Calif. State U.-Long Beach, 1969-73, assoc. prof., 1973-78, prof., 1978-82, assoc. dean, 1976-77, dean humanities, 1977-82; v.p. acad. affairs Pan Am. U., Edinburg, Tex., 1982—. Contbr. articles to profl. publs. Mem. AAUP, Phi Kappa Phi. Office: Pan Am U Edinburg TX 78539

APPLEBEE, WILLIAM ROBERT, newspaper publisher; b. Iowa City, Iowa, Aug. 22, 1936; s. Kenneth O. and Sadie E. Applebee; grad. Iowa Wesleyan Coll., 1959; m. Katherine R. Payne, Sept. 9, 1956; children—William K., Julie A., Jennifer L., Jessica E. Gen. mgr. Grand Forks (N.D.) Herald Daily Newspaper, 1966-73; pres., pub. Niles (Mich.) Daily Star, 1973-77; gen. mgr. Bradenton (Fla.) Herald, 1977-79; gen. mgr. Pasadena (Calif.) Star-News, 1979-81, pub., 1981—. Mem. Inland Daily Press Assn., Am. Newspaper Pubs., Assn., Calif. Press Assn., C. of C. Republican. Club: Athletic (Pasadena). Office: Twin Coast Newspapers 525 E Colorado St Pasadena CA 91109*

APPLEGATE, RICHARD DUANE, newspaper advt. mgr.; b. Pontiac, Ill., July 30, 1932; s. Clyde Eugene and Gladys Irene (Evans) A.; B.S., U. Ill., 1957; postgrad. (Am. Legion scholar), Nat. U. Mexico, 1955; m. Martha Gerda Doden, Sept. 13, 1953; children—Janet, David, Kathryn. Retail advt. rep. Fullerton (Calif.) Daily News-Tribune, 1957-61; with San Diego Union & Evening Tribune, 1961—, automotive editor and mgr., 1968-80. Copley News Service contbr. Mem. media panel Motor Trend's Golden Wheels Awards, San Diego, 1974-75. Served with USNR, 1951-52. Mem. San Diego C. of C. Exec. Club, Alpha Delta Sigma. Home: 6712 Carthage San Diego CA 92120 Office: PO Box 191 350 Camino de la Reina San Diego CA 92112

APPLEMAN, WAYNE DOUGLAS, state official; b. Wausau, Wis., July 8, 1937; s. Wilbur Ross and Alberta Marie (Kohlenbach) A.; B.A., Ohio Wesleyan U., 1959; postgrad. Ohio State U., 1960-61; m. Penelope Ann Sears, Dec. 21, 1959; children—Todd Douglas, Scott Douglas. Mem. personnel staff Nationwide Ins. Co., Columbus, Ohio, 1961-66; corp. tng. dir. Am. Investment Co., St. Louis, 1966-68; mgr. manpower devel. The Vendo Co., Kansas City, Mo., 1969-70; with Calif. Personnel Bd., Sacramento, 1971-81, mgr. mgmt. devel. mgr. instrl. design, coordinator regional tng. ctrs., 1976-81; mgr. quality of worklife Calif. Dept. Personnel Adminstrn., 1981-82, chief mgmt. and staff devel., 1983; chmn. adv. group, dept. mgmt. and supervision Sierra Coll., 1977-80. Campaign mgr. Sacramento State Employees United Way, 1975; elder Presbyterian Ch., 1979-81; bd. dirs. Center for Mgmt. Devel., Fairfield, Calif., Intergovtl. Tng. and Devel. Center, San Diego, Mgmt. Devel. Inst., Oakland, Calif., Valley Regional Tng. Center, Fresno, Calif., Channel Coast Tng. Center, Santa Barbara, Calif., S.W. Regional Tng. Center, Carson, Calif. Mem. Am. Soc. Tng. and Devel. (local chpt. co-founder 1971, chpt. pres. 1975, asst. regional v.p. 1977-78, mem. nat. task force on communication 1978, chmn. regional selection and devel. com. 1979, nat. com. on ethics 1979, asst. regional v.p. adminstrn. 1981-82, Torch award for disting. contbn. to profession 1979), Sacramento Quality Circle Facilitator Network (founder, chief facilitator). Republican. Office: 1116 9th St Lower Level Sacramento CA 95814

APPLETON, DAVID TENEYCK, strategic planner; b. Santa Fe, Oct. 27, 1929; s. Norman Roy and Mary Carolyn (TenEyck) A.; B.S. in Elec. Engring., U. Colo., 1951; postgrad. UCLA, 1957-67; m. Geraldine Mae Booker, Feb. 10, 1952; children—Carolyn Mae, Katharine Ann. With Westinghouse Electric Corp., Balt., 1952-62; with Def. & Space Systems group TRW, Redondo Beach, Calif., 1962—, mgr. Bus. Plans and Programs group, 1974—. Registered profl. engr., Tex. Mem. IEEE. Republican. Lutheran. Home: 1246 W 18th St San Pedro CA 90731 Office: TRW One Space Park Redondo Beach CA 90278

APPLETON, JAMES ROBERT, university administrator; b. North Tonawanda, N.Y., Jan. 20, 1937; s. Robert Martin and Emma (Mollnow) A.; A.B., Wheaton Coll., 1958; M.A., Mich. State U., 1962, Ph.D., 1965; m. Carol Koelsch, Aug. 8, 1959; children—Steven, Jon, Jennifer. Grad. asst. Mich. State U., East Lansing, 1960-63, asso. dir. residence hall programs, 1963-65, vis. lectr. Coll. Edn., 1969, 72; asso. dean students Oakland U., Rochester, Mich., 1965-68, dean for student life, 1968-69, asso. prof. behavioral scis., 1969-72, v.p. student affairs, 1969-72; asso. prof. dept. higher and post secondary edn. Sch. Edn., U. So. Calif., Los Angeles, 1972—, v.p. student affairs, 1972-82, v.p. devel., 1982—; accreditation cons. U. Calif., Boston U., Denver U., Fuller Sem. Elder, St. Peters By The Sea Presbyn. Ch., Rancho Palos Verdes, Calif., 1973—. Served to lt. U.S. Army, 1958-60. Selected by Change and Am. Council on Edn. as 1 of 100 Young Leaders of Am., 1978. Mem. Nat. Assn. Student Personnel Adminstrs. (nat. pres. 1974-75, nat. exec. com. 1969-76), Council for Advancement Small Colls., AAUP, Phi Kappa Phi. Author: (with Channing M. Briggs and James J. Rhatigan) Pieces of Eight: The Rites, Roles, and Styles of the Dean, 1978; contbr. articles on higher edn. to profl. publs. Home: 29370 Quailwood Dr Rancho Palos Verdes CA 90274 Office: 201 Student Union U So Calif Los Angeles CA 90007

ARAKAKI, WAYNE SHINEI, insurance underwriter; b. Honolulu, July 3, 1932; s. Kama and Unto A.; B.B.A., U. Hawaii, 1954; m. Muriel S. Teruya, Mar. 30, 1963; children—Scott, Dwight. Vice-pres. United Ind. Ins. Agys., Inc., Honolulu, 1955-74; v.p. Nat. Mortgage & Finance Co., Ltd., Honolulu, 1974—; v.p. Island Ins. Co., Ltd., Honolulu, 1974—; vice-pres. Tradewind Ins. Co. Ltd., Honolulu, 1974—; assoc. in risk mgmt. Chartered Property and Casualty Underwriter. Mem. Soc. Chartered Property and Casualty Underwriters. Club: Mariners Cove Bay. Office: 1022 Bethel St Honolulu HI 96813

ARANT, DAVID EUGENE, real estate broker, educator; b. Southgate, Calif., Apr. 17, 1935; s. Francis Marian and May Laveigh (Morris) A.; B.S., Pepperdine U., 1957; M.S., U. So. Calif., 1960; children—Brenda, Bradford. Treas., Vet. Escrow Co., Inc., Los Angeles, 1958-61; prof. accounting Los Angeles Met. Coll. of Bus., 1961-66; prof. mgmt. Los Angeles Harbor Coll., 1966—; founder Synthicomp, Acctg. Service, Lomita, Calif., 1978—; owner, Realtor, operator Dave Arant Realty, Lomita, 1979—. VA grantee, 1972, 74. Mem. Calif. Real Estate Assn., Am. Mgmt. Assn., Delta Pi Epsilon, Pi Gamma Mu, Alpha Gamma Sigma. Republican. Home: 1890 Peninsula Verde Dr Lomita CA 90717

ARBELBIDE, SYLVIA JEAN, geologist; b. Weiser, Idaho, June 7, 1951; d. Ollie Marion and Betty Lou (Kilpatrick) A. Student Boise State Coll., 1969-71; B.S. in Geol. Sci., U. Wash., 1973. Underground geologist Magma Copper Co., Superior, Ariz., 1973-75; area geologist Bur. Land Mgmt., Golden, Colo., 1975-77, dist. geologist, Canon City, Colo., 1977-78, state office geologist, Denver, 1978-80; phys. scientist Bur. Mines, Denver, 1980—. Mem. Jefferson Symphony Guild, 1977—, NOW, 1981—, LWV, 1983—, Nat. Abortion Rights Action League, 1981—. Mem. AIME, Colo. Sci. Soc., Assn. Women Geoscientists, Women in Mining, Internat. Class Laser Assn. (Quebec), Rocky Mountain Laser Assn. (Denver). Author: (with Robert B. O'Sullivan, Frances Wahl-Pierce) Preliminary Geologic Map of the McCarthy Gulch Quadrangle, Rio Blanco and Garfield Counties, Colorado, 1981; (with Gary R. Peterson) Availability of Alumnium in Market-Economy Countries, 1983. Home: 364 Goldco Circle Golden CO 80403 Office: 20 Denver Federal Ctr Denver CO 80225

ARBOLEDA-FLOREZ, JULIO ERNESTO, psychiatrist; b. Pto Wilches, Colombia, Feb. 7, 1939; s. Julio and Carmen (Arboleda) Duque; M.D., U. Nacional, Bogota, 1964; D.Psychiatry, U. Ottawa (Can.), 1970; fellow in forensic psychiatry U. Toronto, 1970-71; m. Nelly Ramirez, Jan. 6, 1964; children—Julio, Mimi. Intern in Cali, Colombia, 1963; resident in psychiatry Royal Ottawa Hosp., Ottawa Civic Hosp., Nat. Def. Med. Center, 1967-70; chief forensic unit Royal Ottawa Hosp., 1971-75; clin. dir. Regional Psychiat. Centre, Abbottsford, B.C., 1975-77; dir. forensic services Calgary (Alta.) Gen. Hosp., 1977—; dir. forensic psychiatry So. Alta. Regional Services, 1980—; asso. prof. psychiatry U. Calgary, 1977-81, prof., 1981—; cons. law firms, courts, fed. govt., Ont. and Alta. govts. Chmn. Riverside group Boy Scouts, Ottawa, 1974; mem. Calgary Sch. Council, 1980; mem. Law Reform Commn. Can., 1976; Latin Am. rep. Internat. Council Prison Medicine, 1979—. Recipient grants Ministry Justice Can., 1979-80, 80-81. Fellow Royal Coll. Physicians and Surgeons Can., Am. Psychiat. Assn.; mem. Can. Med. Assn., Can. Psychiat. Assn., Can. Criminology Assn., Am. Acad. Psychiatry and Law, Internat. Platform Assn., Can. Civil Liberties Assn., Amnesty Internat. Mem. editorial bd. Internat. Jour. Offender Therapy, 1978, Internat. Jour. Law and Psychiatry, 1981; cons. Jour. Criminology, 1980—; contbr. articles to profl. jours. Roman Catholic. Office: Psychiatry Dept Calgary Gen Hosp 841 Centre Ave E Calgary AB Canada

ARBUCKLE, ERNEST COMINGS, bus. exec.; b. Lee, N.H., Sept. 5, 1912; s. Frank Albert and Ernestine C. (Weeden) A.; A.B., Stanford U., 1933, M.B.A., 1936; Dr. honoris causa U. Centroamericana, 1970; LL.D., Golden Gate U., 1973; m. Katherine Norris Hall, Dec. 10, 1942; children—Ernest C., Joan, Katherine, Susan. Personnel specialist Standard Oil of Calif., 1937-41, orgn. analyst, 1945-46; dir. procurement, asst. to pres. Golden State Co., Ltd., 1946-50; exec. v.p. Pacific Coast div. W.R. Grace & Co., 1950-58; dean Grad. Sch. Bus., Stanford U., 1958-68, now dean emeritus; chmn. bd. Stanford Research Inst., 1966-70, dir.; chmn. Wells Fargo Bank, San Francisco, 1968-77, now dir.; chmn. Saga Corp., Menlo Park, Calif., 1978-81, chmn. exec. com., 1982; dir. Owens-Ill., Inc., Hewlett-Packard Co., Utah Internat. Inc., A. Johnson & Co., Inc.; mem. adv. com. Export-Import Bank U.S., 1972-75. Mem. Commn. on White House Fellows, 1964-68; mem. Adv. Com. on Pvt. Enterprise in Fgn. Aid, 1964-65; mem. Pres.'s Commn. on Internat. Trade and Investment Policy, 1970-71; mem. industry adv. council Dept. Def., 1969-72; mem. Trilateral Commn., 1973-77; bd. dirs. Bay Area Council, Inc., chmn., 1976-77; trustee Stanford U., 1954-58, 68-76, Packard Found., 1970—, Calif. Acad. Scis., 1979—. Served as lt. comdr. USNR, 1941-45. Decorated Silver Star; recipient Freedoms Found. award, 1950; Adminstrv. Excellence award Stanford Bus. Sch. Assn., 1968; Bus. Leadership award U. Mich. Grad. Sch. Bus. Adminstrn., 1969; Disting. Achievement medal Stanford Athletic Bd., 1971; Bus. Statesman award Harvard Bus. Sch. Alumni Assn., 1975. Republican. Clubs: Pacific Union, Bohemian. Home: 12 Arastradero Rd Menlo Park CA 94025 Office: One Saga Ln Menlo Park CA 94025

ARBUTHNOT, GUY LANE, III, engineering laboratory administrator; b. Anniston, Ala., Oct. 6, 1936; s. Guy Lane a and Eileen Marie (Packard) A.; B.S. in Physics, U. Miss., 1959; m. JoAnn Johnston, July 18, 1958; children—Becky Ann Arbuthnot Korgenski, Debbie Ann, Guy Lane. Physicist U.S. Navy Mine Def. Lab., Panama City, Fla., 1961-62; mem. tech. staff TRW, Cape Canaveral, Fla., 1962-69, mgr. TRW, Houston, 1969-74, staff engr. TRW Space Park, Redondo Beach, Calif., 1974-81, lab. mgr. TRW, Ogden, Utah, 1975-81, program mgr. TRW Space Park, 1981—; faculty Fla. Inst. Tech. and U. Miss. Exec. advisor Jr. Achievement; coach Little League baseball; coach NASA area football. Recipient Apollo achievement award, Skylab award; registered profl. engr. Mem. Am. Def. Preparedness Assn., Air Force Assn., Soc. Logistical Engrs., Ogden Logistics Assn. Republican. Presbyterian. Club: Alpha Tau Omega. Electromechanical patentee; developer lunar descent mission techniques. Home: 4680 W 141st St Hawthorne CA 90250

ARCE, RAUL ALBERT, management engineer, consultant; b. San Jose, Costa Rica, Oct. 14, 1957; s. Raul and Marie Eugenia (Valverde) A. B.B.A., U. N.Mex., 1983. Inventory control Meth. Hosp., Bklyn., 1976-77; med. records technician Presbyn. Hosp., Albuquerque, 1977-79, statis. technician, 1979-80; mgmt. engr. SW Community Health Services, Albuquerque, 1980—; cons. systems analysis, standards setting, computerization. Mem. Am. Inst. Indsl. Engrs., Hosp. Mgmt. Systems Soc., N.Mex. Hosp. Assn. Club: Am. Youth Soccer Orgn. (coach). Contbr. article to profl. jour. Home: 601 Academy NE Albuquerque NM 87109 Office: 1100 Central SE Albuquerque NM 87106

ARCHDEACON, JOHN ROBERT, orthopedic surgeon; b. N.Y.C., Aug. 1, 1919; s. Thomas Francis and Mary (O'Connor) A.; m. Molly Taylor Sinclair, Sept. 18, 1948; children—Patricia Archdeacon Holland, Douglas, John, Richard, Moira, Kenneth. student Fordham U., 1939-41; M.D., N.Y.U., 1950. Diplomate Am. Bd. Orthopedic Surgeons, Am. Bd. Preventive Medicine. Served with USAAF, 1942-45; commd. 1st lt. USAF, 1952, advanced through grades to col., 1965; intern St. Lukes Hosp., N.Y.C., 1950-51; resident orthopedic surgery N.Y. U.-Bellevue Med. Center, 1955-59; chief orthopedic surgery Carswell AFB Hosp., Ft. Worth, 1959-61; dir. orthopedic pathology course Armed Forces Inst. Pathology, 1963-64; chief of surgery, cons. to surgeon gen. Maxwell Air Force Hosp., Ala., 1964-66; chief profl. services, sr. med. adviser Air Evacuation Squadron, USAF Hosp., Clark Hosp., Philippines, 1966-68, hosp. comdr., 1967-68; hosp. comdr. 78th USAF Hosp., Hamilton AFB, Calif., 1968-69; ret., 1969; practice medicine, specializing in orthopedic surgery, Los Gatos-Saratoga, Calif., 1969—. Decorated D.F.C., Air medal with 3 oak leaf clusters, Air Force Commendation medal, Legion of Merit. Fellow ACS, Am. Acad. Orthopedic Surgeons, Am. Coll. Preventive Medicine; mem. Am., Calif. med. assns., Santa Clara County Med. Soc., Brit. Assn. Aviation Med. Examiners. Office: 800 Pollard Rd Los Gatos CA 95030

ARCHER, CARROLL LAVERNE, optometrist; b. Vandalia, Mich., Jan. 27, 1908; s. Elmer Joseph and Edith Bess (Brown) A.; O.D., Monroe Coll., 1948; m. Harriett Evelyn Wiley, Oct. 15, 1974. Clk., U.S. Post Office, Chgo., 1928-63; optometrist, Maywood, Ill., 1948-73. Served with USAAF, 1943-45. Mem. West Suburban Optometric Soc. (sec.-treas. 1952-53, treas. 1954-65, v.p. 1966), Sch. Dist. 89 Bowling League (sec.-treas. 1970-71, sec. 1971-73), Kappa Phi Delta. Address: 841 W Acadia Dr Tucson AZ 85706

ARCHER, GUY PHILIP DODSON, lawyer; b. N.Y.C., Jan. 18, 1943; s. Robert Palin and Dorothy Louise (Dodson) A.; B.A. with honors, Wesleyan U., 1965; J.D., Columbia U., 1968; m. Jeanne B. Graham; children—Kristen, Gina, Richard, Brandon. Bar: N.Y. 1968, Hawaii 1974. Asso. firm Marshall, Bratter, Greene, Allison & Tucker, N.Y.C., 1969-72; ptnr. firm Langa & Archer, Wailuku, Maui, Hawaii, 1975-76; pvt. practice law, Kula, Hawaii, 1977-80, Wailuku, Maui, 1981; dep. corp. counsel County of Maui, 1981—; br. mgr. Hawaii Escrow & Title Inc., Maui, 1974; legis. counsel NORML, N.Y.C., 1972-73. George F. Baker scholar, 1961-65; Davenport fellow, 1964. Mem. Am. Bar Assn. Hawaii Bar Assn., Maui County Bar Assn. Democrat Conglist. Home: 2761 Keikilani St Pukalani Maui HI 96788 Office: 200 S High St County Bldg Wailuku Maui HI 96793

ARCHER, JOHN SKIDMORE, civil engr.; b. Phila., Nov. 10, 1923; s. John Blazer and Hattie Leo (Skidmore) A.; B.S. in Civil Engring., W.Va. U., 1944; M.S. in Civil Engring., M.I.T., 1948, Sc.D., 1950; m. Evelyn Eleanor Beatty, Dec. 23, 1944; children—John Beatty, Evelyn Eleanor, Nathan Charles, Philip James, Rosemary Rene. Bridge draftsman B.& O. R.R., 1944-46; bridge designer State Road Commn. W.Va., 1946-47; research asso. M.I.T., Cambridge, 1950-51, asst. prof. civil engring. dept., 1951-55; project structures engr. Gen. Dynamics Corp., Ft. Worth, 1955-60; lectr. dept. civil engring. So. Meth. U., Dallas, 1955-60; mgr. dynamics dept. engring. mech. lab. TRW/S&TG, Redondo Beach, Calif., 1960-65, asst. mgr. spacecraft engring. div. mech. engring. lab., 1966—; lectr. dept. civil engring. U. So. Calif., Los Angeles, 1960-63; lectr. structural dynamics and analysis UCLA, 1961-63, 65, 66; guest lectr. U. Wis., 1968, Cornell U., 1968; guest participant Joint U.S.-Japanese Symposium on Matrix Structural Analysis, Tokyo, 1969; speaker. Registered profl. engr., Tex., Calif. Mem. ASCE (com. exptl. analysis 1956-59, chmn. com. electronic computation 1961-64), AIAA, Sigma Xi, Tau Beta Pi, Phi Kappa Alpha. Mormon. Club: King Harbor Yacht. Contbr. articles on structural analysis, advanced composite materials and precision spacecraft antenna reflectors to engring. jours.; patentee in field. Home: 30827 Rue Valois Rancho Palos Verdes CA 90274 Office: TRW/DSSG R5/2231 One Space Park Redondo Beach CA 90278

ARCHER, RICHARD JOSEPH, lawyer; b. Virginia, Minn., Mar. 24, 1922; s. William John and Margaret Leanore (Duff) A.; A.B., U. Mich., 1947, J.D., 1948; m. Kristina M. Hanson, Jan. 29, 1977; children—Alison P., Cynthia J. Admitted to Calif. bar, 1949, U.S. Supreme Ct. bar, 1962, Hawaii bar, 1982; ptnr. Morrison and Foerster, San Francisco, 1954-71, Sullivan, Jones and Archer, San Francisco, 1971-81, Archer Rosenak & Hanson, San Francisco, 1981—. Served with USN, 1942-45. Decorated Bronze Star. Mem. Am. Law Inst., Am. Coll. Trial Lawyers, Am. Bar Assn., ACLU, Am. Soc. Internat. Law. Republican. Clubs: Stock Exchange, Bankers (San Francisco). Home: 3110 Bohemian Hwy Occidental CA 95465 Office: 130 Sutter St San Francisco CA 94104

ARCHIBALD, JAMES KELLY, JR., mining engineer; b. Butte, Mont., Apr. 8, 1949; s. James Kelly and Cynthia Louise (Hester) A.; m. Lynn Marie Markovich, Sept. 12, 1970; children—James Kelly III, Ryan Edward. B.S., Mont. Coll. Mineral Sci. and Tech., 1971. Registered profl. engr., Idaho. U.S. mineral examiner U.S. Forest Service, N.W. region, 1978-80; sr. mining engr. Anaconda Minerals Co., Yerington, Nev., 1980-81; adminstr. bus. devel. Occidental Oil Shale, Inc., Grand Junction, Colo., 1981-82; corp. adminstr. U.S. Synthetic Fuels Corp. Proposal, Cathedral Bluffs Shale Oil Co., Grand Junction, 1982—; chmn. ad hoc com. on oil shale leasing Am. Mining Congress, 1981-82. Mem. allocations com. United Way, 1982—. Mem. AIME, N.W. Mining Assn. Republican. Club: Elks. Home: 2311 Apricot Ct Grand Junction CO 81501 Office: 751 Horizon Ct PO Box 2687 Grand Junction CO 81502

ARCHIBALD, KENT M., optometrist; b. Rexburg, Idaho, July 25, 1947; s. Don Carlos and Vera (Manwaring) A.; A.S., Ricks Coll., 1969; student Brigham Young U., 1966, 69; B.S., Pacific U., 1972, O.D., 1974; m. Elaine Ball, June 21, 1969; children—Gregory, Jeffrey, Samuel, Wendy, Tyler, Michael. Optometrist, Optometry Clinic Rexburg, 1976—; pres. Superior Optical, Inc., Vision Center, P.A. Served with U.S. Army, 1974-76. Fellow Am. Acad. Optometry. Mormon. Club: Kiwanis (dir. 1978-81, pres. 1980-81). Contbr. articles to profl. jours. Home: 245 Apache Ave Rexburg ID 83440 Office: 76 Professional Plaza Rexburg ID 83440

ARCHIBALD, WILLIAM EDDIE, mfg. co. exec.; b. Gillette, Wyo., Apr. 6, 1940; s. U. Staley and Pearl Marguerite Archibald; student Tulane U., 1958-60; B.S. in Elec. Engring., U. Wyo., 1963, M.S., 1967; postgrad. U.S. Internat. U., 1968-70, U. Ariz., 1971-73; m. Carolyn Antoinette Brown, June 24, 1963; children—Patrick William, Cynthia Lee. Test equipment engr. Convair div. Gen. Dynamics, San Diego, 1967-70; test equipment engr., product engr., product design engr., pilot prodn. mgr., mfg. engring. mgr., systems mfg. mgr. Burr-Brown Research Corp., Tucson, 1971-79; ops. mgr. Granville-Phillips Co., Boulder, Colo., 1979-82; product assurance mgr. Data Products div. Burr-Brown Corp., Tucson, 1982—. Served to 1st lt. U.S. Army, 1963-65. Mem. Am. Soc. Quality Control. Republican. Office: PO Box 11400 Tucson AZ 85734

ARCINIEGA, REBECA ESTRADA, word processing adminstr., cons.; b. Mexico City, Mex., May 8, 1953; came to U.S., 1972; d. Marino Estrada and Dolores Rodriguez Estrada; A.S., Brigham Young U., 1978, B.S., 1980; m. Julio Arciniega, July 28, 1972; children—Brenda, Israel, David, Benjamin. Exec. sec. Colegio Vista Hermosa, Mexico City, 1969-71; bilingual sec. dept. instructional research and evaluation Brigham Young U., Provo, Utah, 1973-74; word processing operator McKay Inst. Research and Evaluation, Provo, 1975-78; word processing dir., 1979—. Mem. Internat. Word Processing Assn., Am. Mgmt. Assn. Mormon. Home: 444 N 100 W Provo UT 84601 Office: Box 7238 Brigham Young Univ Provo UT 84602

ARD, BEN NEAL, JR., psychologist, educator; b. Dallas, Dec. 6, 1922; s. Ben Neal and Maudie Lou (Yeatts) N.; 1 dau., Beth Levin. B.A., UCLA, 1947; M.S., Oreg. State U., 1954; Ph.D., U. Mich., 1962. Lic. psychologist, Calif., marriage family and child counselor, Calif. Asst. prof. Mich. State U., 1956-59; teaching fellow U. Mich., 1960-62; prof. psychology Central Mich. U., 1960-63; prof. counseling San Francisco State U., 1963—. Mem. Calif. Assn. Marriage and Family Therapy (past pres.), Am. Assn. Marriage and Family Therapy (dir.), Am. Psychol. Assn., Soc. Sci. Study of Sex, Am. Assn. Sex Educators, Counselors and Therapists. Author: Treating Psychosexual Dysfunction, 1974; Rational Sex Ethics, 1978; editor: Counseling and Psychotherapy, 1975; co-editor: Handbook of Marriage Counseling, 1976. Home: 125 Cambon Dr #M-B San Francisco CA 94132 Office: 595 Buckingham Way Suite 454 San Francisco CA 94132

ARDLEY, HARRY MOUNTCASTLE, mathematical statistician, operations research consultant; b. Oakland, Calif., Jan. 22, 1926; s. Harry Mountcastle and Anne Alvina (Meyer) A.; m. Jane Partridge, June 24, 1948; children—David Michael, Douglas Mountcastle, Mary Elizabeth. A.B., U. Calif.-Berkeley, 1950, postgrad., 1950-51, 58-59, 62-63. Econ. statistician U.S. Dept. Commerce, Washington, 1951-53; math. statistician Pacific Telephone, San Francisco, 1953-59, gen. statistician, San Diego, 1959-63, supr. math. and statis. research, San Francisco, 1963—. Active citizens com. to establish Foothill Coll., 1957-58, San Francisco Symphony Assn.; exec. com. Santa Clara County Democratic Council, 1957-59; pres. Palo Alto-Stanford Dem. Club., 1965; Greenmeadow Community Assn., 1969. Served with USAAF, 1943-46. Mem. Am. Statis. Assn. (pres. San Francisco Bay Area chpt. 1981-82), Ops. Research Soc. Am., Inst. Mgmt. Sci. Club: Sierra (San Francisco). Home: 352 Parkside Dr Palo Alto CA 94306 Office: 85 2d St Room 816 San Francisco CA 94105

ARENBERG, IRVING KAUFMAN, otologist; b. E. Chicago, Ind., Jan. 10, 1941; s. George Isadore and Ada Yetta (Field) A.; B.A. in Zoology, U. Mich., 1963, M.D., 1967; m. Carol Ann Rakita, May 31, 1964; children—Daniel Kaufman, Michael Harrison, Julie Gayle. Intern in surgery Wesley Meml. Hosp., Chgo., 1967-68; asst. resident in surgery St. Luke's Hosp., St. Louis, 1968-69; NIH fellow Washington U. Sch. Medicine, St. Louis, 1969-70; resident in otolaryngology Barnes Hosp., St. Louis, 1970-74, NIH clin. fellow neuro-otology, 1974-75; vis. scientist Swedish Med. Research Council, U. Uppsala, 1975-76; asst. prof. U. Wis. Med. Sch. and Hosps., 1976-80; clin. asso. prof. U. Colo. Med. Sch., Denver, 1980—; chief otolaryngology service VA Hosp., Madison, 1976-80; dir. Internat. Meniere's Disease Research Inst., U. Wis. Hosps., 1976-80; with Colo. Otologic Research Center, Porter Meml. Hosp.-Swedish Med. Center, Denver, 1980—; cons. Denver Surg. Developments, Inc., Storz Instrument Co., Ergo Instrument Co., Denver Biomaterials Inc. Served to lt. comdr. M.C., USNR, 1963-74. NINDS spl. tchr. investigator awardee, 1971-76. Diplomate Am. Bd. Otolaryngology. Fellow ACS, Am. Acad. Ophthalmology and Otolaryngology (research award 1969-70, 72, 74, 75), Internat. Coll. Surgeons; mem. AMA (Physician's Recognition award 1971, 74, 77, 82), Triologic Soc., Barany Soc., Politzer Soc., Prosper Meniere Soc. (founder, exec. dir.), Assn. Research Otolaryngology. Jewish. Asso. editor AMA Archives Otolaryngology, 1968-81; mem. editorial bd. Am. Jour. Otology, 1978—; contbr. over 200 articles to med. jours. Office: Colo Ear Clinic 950 E Harvard Ave Suite 200 Denver CO 80210

ARENDT, HAROLD JOSEPH, JR., educator; b. St. Paul, Minn., Nov. 23, 1923; s. Harold Joseph and Alfretta (Philpott) A.; B.S., U. Oreg., 1955, M.S., 1959; student Oreg. State U., 1942-46, U. Minn., 1968, U. Denver, 1969; m. Karen Adele Lee, June 25, 1955; children—Martin Lee, Terrence Royal, Brian Karl. Logging operator, Sweet Home, Oreg., 1942-50; topog. surveyor U.S. Forest and Range Expt. Sta. div., Oreg., 1950-51; head chmn. Oreg. State Hwy. Dept., Gold Beach, 1952-53; supr. farm ops. H.J. Arendt Sons, Aurora, Oreg., 1950-70; chmn. dept. English, history Benson Poly. Sch., Portland, Oreg., 1958-67, dir. ednl. media, 1967—; cons. ednl. innovation; specialist dissemination vocat. info., ednl. micrographics. Active Boy Scouts Am. Area capt. Republican party, 1964-68, precinct chmn., 1963-65. Served with AUS, 1948-49, 51-52. Decorated Purple Heart medal. Mem. ALA, Assn. Ednl. Communications and Tech., Oreg. Assn. Sch. Librarians, Oreg., Nat. edn. assns., Oreg. Instructional Media Assn., Bible Study Fellowship (sec.). Lutheran (deacon 1963-66, dir. edn. 1969—). Home: 1140 SE 141st Ave Portland OR 97233 Office: 546 NE 12th Ave Portland OR 97232

ARENSMAN, ELTON EUGENE, civil engr.; b. Kinsley, Kans., Mar. 15, 1932; s. Henry William and Elsie Lydia (Lippoldt) A.; B.S. in Civil Engring., Kans. State U., 1954; m. Marilynn June Russell, Aug. 28, 1953; children—Michael Gene, Russell Kim, Kevin Keith, Diana Marie. Engr., Stearns-Roger Corp., Denver, 1954-61; chief structural engr. Ken White Co., Denver, 1962-65; asst. chief structural engr. Smith, Hinchman & Grylls, Detroit, 1966-72; pres. Architect Assos., Inc., Southfield, Mich., 1973-77; dept. chief engr. Morison-Knudsen Co., Inc., Boise, Idaho, 1978—; dir. Ridge View Farms, Inc.; dir. Disciples of Christ Non-Profit Housing Inc. Registered profl. engr., Idaho, Colo., Mich., Wyo., N.Mex.; cert. Nat. Council Engring. Examiners. Mem. Structural Engrs. Assn. Idaho, Nat. Soc. Profl. Engrs., Kansas State U. Alumni Assn. Republican. Club: Theta Xi. Home: 5044 Mountain View Dr Boise ID 83704 Office: PO Box 7808 Boise ID 83729

ARENTZ, SAMUEL SHAW, consulting mining and metallurgical engineer, mine operator; b. Los Angeles, Mar. 9, 1913; s. Samuel Shaw and Harriet Johnson (Keep) A.; m. Mary Alice Meagher, Feb. 5, 1940; children—Mary Catherine, Susan, Samuel, Nicholas, Margaret. B.S. in Mining Engring., U. Nev., 1934. Registered profl. engr., Nev., Utah. Assayer-engr., foreman-supt. Snyder Mines, Mercur, Utah, 1934-38; supervising engr. Rico Argentine Co. (Colo.), 1938; mill supt., Ima Mines Co., May, Idaho, 1939, resident mgr., 1939-41; engr.-supt., mgr. Combined Metals Reduction Co., Pioche, Nev. and Salt Lake City, 1941-54; cons. engr., mine operator, Salt Lake City, 1954—; owner Samuel S. Arentz, Mining Engrs., Salt Lake City, 1955-83; pres. Armet Co., Salt Lake City, 1955—, Escalante Silver Mines Co., Salt Lake City, 1972—; dir. Ranchers Exploration, Salt Lake City. Bd. regents U. Nev., 1948-52; trustee Holy Cross Hosp., Salt Lake City, 1976-83. Mem. AIME, (past chmn. Nev. and Utah sects.), Mining and Metallurgy Soc. Am. Republican. Presbyterian. Clubs: Alta, Salt Lake Country, Mount Moriah 2 (Salt Lake City). Contbr. articles to mining jours.

ARGENZIO, SALVATORE VICTOR, jeweler; b. N.Y.C., July 8, 1902; s. Andrew and Nancy (Giliberti) A.; Ph.D. (hon.), Calif. Western U., 1975; student pub. schs. N.Y.C.; m. Margaret Anne Henderson, Jan. 7, 1947 (dec. 1981); children—Robert Alan, Judith Anne, Victor James. Clk. jewelry Wathen & Co., Denver, 1918-25; co-owner, Argenzio Brothers Jewelers, Denver, 1925-66, chmn. bd., 1966—; diamond cons.; diamond historian Zale Corp., Dallas. Cellist, Denver Symphony, 1924-44. Recipient Non-Fiction book award Colo. Authors League, 1975, Lead Mag. Article award Nat. Writers Club, 1958. Mem. Retail Jewelers Assn., Nat. Writers Club, Colo. Authors League (Juvenile Book award 1978), Authors Guild Inc., Authors League Am., Nat. Writers Club. Clubs: Denver Athletic, Masons, Shriners. Author: Fascination of Diamonds, 1967; Diamonds Eternal, 1975; Crystal Clear, 1977; Gems and Gyps, 1983. Home and Office: 520 Clermont St Denver CO 80220 Died Aug. 1983.

ARGUE, JOHN CLIFFORD, lawyer; b. Glendale, Calif., Jan. 25, 1932; s. John Clifford and Catherine Emily (Clements) A.; m. Leah Elizabeth Moore, June 29, 1963; children—Elizabeth Anne, John Michael. A.B., Occidental Coll., 1953; LL.B., U. So. Calif., 1956. Bar: Calif. 1957. Ptnr. Argue & Argue, Los Angeles, 1958-59; ptnr. Flint & MacKay, Los Angeles, 1960-72; sr. ptnr. Argue, Freston, Pearson, Harbison & Myers, Los Angeles, 1972—; dir. First Bus. Bank, LAACO, Inc., Trust Services Am. Chmn. Verdugo Hills Hosp., 1979; chmn. Am. Heart Assn., 1981; pres. So. Calif. Com. for Olympic Games, 1972—, founding chmn. Los Angeles Olympic Organizing Com., 1978-79, now vice chmn.; trustee, mem. investment com. Pomona Coll. Served with AUS, 1957-58. Mem. Town Hall (dir., v.p.), World Affairs Council, Central City Assn. (dir.), Los Angeles Hdqrs. City Assn., Newcomen Soc. N.Am., So. Calif. Golf Assn. (pres. 1980), Los Angeles Area C. of C. (chmn. Olympic com.), Phi Delta Phi, Alpha Tau Omega. Clubs: Chancery (sec.), Rotary of Los Angeles, 100 Club, Lincoln, Twilight, California (pres.), Oakmont Country (pres. 1971), Flint Canyon Tennis, Riviera Country (gen. chmn. PGA Championship 1983), Los Angeles Athletic. Office: 626 Wilshire Blvd Suite 1000 Los Angeles CA 90017

ARGYROS, GEORGE L., professional baseball team owner, business executive; b. Detroit; m. Judie. Student Mich. State U.; B.A., Chapman Coll., 1959. Pres. Arnel Devel. Co., Santa Ana, Calif.; chmn. Arnel Mgmt. Co., Santa Ana; owner Seattle Mariners, 1981—. Commr. selection com. Baseball's Revenue Sharing Com.; bd. dirs. Am. League; dir. Comml. Financing Services, Newport Bancorp, Coast Thrift and Loan. Trustee, Chapman Coll. Office: Arnel Devel Co 505 N Tustin Ave Santa Ana CA 92705*

ARIAS, ALFONSO VINCENT, JR., accountant; b. Los Angeles, Oct. 9, 1940; s. Alfonso V. and Molly R. (Hernandez) A.; m. Joan Elizabeth Hazuka, Apr. 10, 1941; children—Kimberly Arias Pebbles, Jill Ann. B.S., Calif. State U.-Northridge, 1968; student U. So. Calif., 1961-63. C.P.A., Calif., 1968. Assoc., Peat, Marwick, Mitchell & Co., Los Angeles, 1965-78, ptnr., 1978-80; ptnr. Hurley, Silberman & Zimmerman, San Diego, 1980-81; mng. ptnr. Arias & Fitzgerald, San Diego, 1981—. Active Nat. Football Found. and Hall of Fame, LaJolla Mus. Contemporary Art, Juvenile Diabetes Found., Ducks, Unltd. Mem. Am. Inst. C.P.A.s, Calif. Soc. C.P.A.s (dir. San Diego chpt.), Nat. Assn. Accts., Estate Planning Council San Diego. Democrat. Roman Catholic. Clubs: LaJolla Beach and Tennis, LaJolla Tennis, Torrey Pines Kiwanis, San Diego City. Office: 5030 Camino de la Siesta Suite 401 San Diego CA 92108

ARIAS, LUIE GUILLERMO, architect; b. San Jose, Costa Rica, May 23, 1950; came to U.S., 1965, naturalized, 1971; s. Louis G. and Emilia B. de A.; student UCLA extension, summer 1969, Coll. Data Processing, 1968-69; B.Arch. and Environ. Design, Calif. Poly. U., San Luis Obispo, 1975; m. Maureen Arias; 1 son, Louie Eduardo. Archtl. draftsman Maxwell Starkman, Assos., Beverly Hills, Calif., 1972; engr. Rockwell Internat., Calif., 1975-77; job capt. Richard Huston, Architect, Anaheim, Calif., 1977-78; design mgr. Associated Archtl. Design Group, San Gabriel, Calif., 1978-82; adminstrv. coordinator Krieger Co., Pico Rivera, Calif., 1982—; cons. land planner, comml., indsl. and residential architecture and constrn.; rep. at public hearings. Recipient awards Rotary, 1968, City of Monterey, 1974; fed. grantee, 1970; Italian archtl. program grantee, 1974. Mem. Nat. Engrs. and Profls. Assn., Orgn. Latin Am. Architects, Nat. Assn. Latino Elected and Apptd. Ofcls. (founding), Constrn. Specifications Inst. Home: 584 Vista Rambla Walnut CA 91789

ARIMA, SUMIYASU, engineering manager; b. Seattle, July 14, 1934; s. Sumio and Fujio (Nishinaka) A.; m. Colleen L. McGuire, Oct. 28, 1967; 1 dau. Lynn. Student Olympic Coll., Bremerton, Wash., 1952-54; B.S.E.E., Seattle U., 1959. Elec. engr. Puget Sound Naval Shipyard, 1952-59; gen. engr., supr. shipbldg. U.S. Navy, Seattle, 1959-67; sr. civilian engr. David Taylor Naval Ship Research and Devel. Ctr., Bremerton, Wash., 1967—. Mem. Internat. Hydrofoil Soc., AIAA, Japanese Am. Citizens League. Roman Catholic. Home: 15005 NE 65th St Redmond WA 98052 Office: care Puget Sound Naval Shipyard Bremerton WA 98314

ARISTOV, OLEG, chief respiratory therapist; b. Kiev, Russia, Mar. 14, 1929; s. Andrey and Maria (de Nolcken) A.; m. Asta Tersky, Sept. 15, 1956; children—Natalia, Andrey. Student U. Buffalo, 1962-63. Chief respiratory therapist Buffalo (N.Y.) Gen. Hosp. (Greene and Kallogg Inc.), Buffalo, 1958-63; respiratory therapist UCLA Hosp., 1963-65; day shift and tech. supr., 1965-69, chief respiratory therapist, 1969—. Active Russian Am. Cultural Soc., Congress Russian Ams., St. John of Kronstad Found., v.p. Council Holy Virgin Mary Russian Orthodox Cathedral. Mem. Am. Assn. Respiratory Therapy, Calif. Assn. Respiratory Therapy, UCLA Adminstrs. and Suprs. Assn. Republican. Club: Movie Travel, Los Angeles. Contbr. paper to profl. jour.

ARIYOSHI, GEORGE RYOICHI, state ofcl.; b. Honolulu, Mar. 12, 1926; s. Ryozo and Mitsue (Yoshikawa); A.; student U. Hawaii, 1944-45, 47; B.A., Mich. State U., 1949; J.D., U. Mich., 1952; LL.D. (hon.), U. Philippines, 1975, U. Guam, 1975, Mich. State U., 1979; D.Hum. (hon.), U. Visayas (Philippines), 1977; m. Jean Miya Hayashi, Feb. 5, 1955; children—Lynn Miye, Todd Ryozo, Donn Ryoji. Admitted to Hawaii bar, 1953; practiced in Honolulu, 1953-70; lt. gov. Hawaii, 1970-73, acting gov., 1973-74, gov., 1974—. Mem. Ter. Hawaii Ho. of Reps., 1954-58, Ter. Hawaii Senate, 1958, Hawaii State Senate, 1959-70; chmn. Senate Ways and Means Com., 1963-64, Senate majority leader, 1965-66, majority floor leader of State Senate, 1969-70; chmn. Western Govs.' Conf., 1977-78. Chmn. small bus. div. Community Chest, 1963; mem. bd. mgrs. YMCA, 1955-57; pres. Pacific Basin Devel. Council, 1980-81. Served with M.I. Service, AUS, 1945-46. Recipient Disting. Alumni award Mich. State U., 1975, U. Hawaii, 1975. Mem. Am. (ho. of dels. 1969), Hawaii (pres. 1969) bar assns., Hawaii Bar Found. (charter mem., pres. 1969). Democrat. Club: Military Intelligence Service Vets (pres. 1968-69). Home: Washington Pl Honolulu HI 96813 Office: State Capitol Honolulu HI 96813

ARKIN, MICHAEL BARRY, lawyer, rancher; b. Washington, Jan. 11, 1941; s. William Howard and Zenda Lillian (Liebermann) A.; m. Carol Lee Altman, Aug. 26, 1962 (div.); children—Tracy Renee, Jeffrey Harris, Marcy Susan; m. 2d, Gay Callan, July 3, 1982; 1 child, Chatom Callan. A.A. George Washington U., 1961; B.A. in Psychology, U. Okla., 1962, J.D., 1965. Bar: Okla. 1965, Calif. 1970, U.S. Supreme Ct. 1968, U.S. Ct. Claims 1968, U.S. Tax Ct. 1970, U.S. Ct. Appeals (3d, 5th, 6th, 9th and 10th cirs.). Trial atty. Tax Div., U.S. Dept. Justice, Washington, 1965-68, appellate atty., 1968-69; ptnr. Surr & Hellyer, San Bernardino, Calif., 1970-79; mng. ptnr. Wied, Granby, Alford & Arkin, San Diego, 1979-82, Lorenz, Alhadeff, Fellmeth & Arkin, San Diego, 1982; resident mng. ptnr., chmn. bus. and tax depts. Finley, Kumble, Wagner, Heine, Underberg, Manley & Casey, San Diego, 1983—. Bd. dirs. Legal Aid Soc. San Bernardino, 1970-73, pres. 1974-75; bd. dirs. Am. Cancer Soc., San Bernardino Area Mental Health Assn., 1972-75. Recipient Meritorious Service to Community award San Bernardino County Bd. Suprs., 1973. Mem. Calif. Bar Assn., Okla. Bar Assn. San Diego County Bar Assn. (past dir., sec., treas.), ABA. Democrat. Jewish. Contbg. poetry to anthology. Home: Chatom Ranch San Andreas CA 95249 Office: Finley Kumble et al 1010 Second Ave 9th Floor San Diego CA 92101

ARMACOST, GEORGE HENRY, educator; b. Upperco, Md., May 6, 1905; s. Joshua Franklin and Matilda Frances (Nolte) A.; A.B., Dickinson Coll., 1926, LL.D., 1947; student Johns Hopkins, summers 1926, 27, 30; A.M., Columbia U., 1930, Ph.D., 1940; L.H.D., Coll. of Osteo. Phys. and Surgery (Los Angeles), Denison U., 1957, U. Redlands, 1970; m. Verda Gay Hayden, June 14, 1933; children—Peter Hayden, Michael Hayden, Samuel Henry, Mary Cole. Tchr. sci. Kane (Pa.) High Sch., 1926-29; asso. in secondary edn. Tchrs. Coll., Columbia U., 1930-32, mem. staff summer sessions, 1931-37; prin. Kane High Sch. 1932-36, Shore Sch. Euclid, Ohio, 1936-37; asso. prof. edn. Coll. of William and Mary, 1937-42, prof., 1942-45, acting dean of men, 1943-45, dir. summer sch. and chmn. dept. of edn., 1944-45; pres. U. Redlands (Calif.), 1945-70, pres. emeritus, 1970—, chmn. profl. studies div. Alderson-Broaddus Coll., 1971-73. Adv. bd. Bank Am. in Redlands; mem. San Bernardino County Grand Jury, 1976-77. Mem. accreditation com. Calif. State Bd. Edn.; mem. W.Va. Adviser's Council Tchr. Edn., 1972-73. Mem. bd. So. Calif. Bapt. Conv., pres., 1960-61; trustee Berkeley Bapt. Div. Sch.; bd. dirs. A.K. Smiley Pub. Library, Plymouth Village Redlands. Mem. Lincoln Shrine Assn. (pres.), Ind. Colls. So. Calif. (pres. 1953-55), Western Colls. Assn. (pres. 1954-55), Council Protestant Colls. and Univs. (pres. 1963), Assn. Ind. Calif. Colls. and Univs. (pres. 1966-68), NEA, Nat. Assn. Deans and Advisors of Men, Nat. Council for Social Studies, Phi Beta Kappa (pres. So. Calif. alumni 1960-62), Kappa Delta Pi, Phi Delta Kappa, Omicron Delta Kappa. Clubs: Rotary, Redlands Country. Author: High School Reports, 1940; (with others) Whose Emblem Shines Afar, 1983. Home: 650 Palo Alto Dr Redlands CA 92373

ARMACOST, SAMUEL HENRY, bank executive; b. Newport News, Va., 1939. Ed. Denison U., Stanford U. Pres., chief exec. officer Bank Am. N.T. & S.A., San Francisco, Bank Am. Corp.; dir. Standard Oil Calif. Office: Bank Am Ctr 555 California St San Francisco CA 94104*

ARMENTROUT, STEVEN ALEXANDER, physician; b. Morgantown, W.Va., Aug. 22, 1933; s. Walter W. and Dorothy (Gasch) A.; A.B., U. Chgo., 1953, M.D., 1959; m. Barbara Jean Lamson, July 18, 1977; children—Marc, Susan, Sandra, Nancy, Julie, Chris, Victor. Intern, U. Hosp., Cleve., 1959-60; resident in medicine, fellow Am. Cancer Soc., Western Res. U. Hosp., 1960-63; project dir. USPHS, 1963-65; asst. prof. Case Western Res. U. Med. Sch., 1965-71; mem. faculty U. Calif. Med. Sch., Irvine, 1971—, prof. medicine, chief div. hematology/oncology, 1978—, also dir. program in oncology. Mem. Am. Assn. Cancer Research, AAUP, A.C.P., Am. Cancer Soc. (chmn. bd. dirs. 1973), AMA, Am. Soc. Clin. Oncology, Am. Soc. Hematology, Orange County Med. Assn., Am. Soc. Internal Medicine, Calif. Med. Assn. Researcher in multiple sclerosis. Office: 101 City Dr S Orange CA 92668

ARMIJO, JACQULYN DORIS, interior designer; b. Gilmer, Tex., July 2, 1938; d. Jack King and Iris Adele (Cook) Smith; children—John, Christy, Mike. Student North Tex. State Coll., U. N.Mex. Profl. model, 1961-75; sec. State Farm Ins., Albuquerque, 1965-71; life ins. agt. Mountain States, Albuquerque, 1980; owner Interiors by Jacqulyn, Albuquerque, 1961—; cons., lectr. in field. Mem. Alby Little Theatre, fund raiser for Old Town Hist. Com., Arthritis Fund. Mem. Am. Soc. Interior Design. Republican. Roman Catholic. Club: Albuquerque Jr. Women's. Home: 509 Chamiso Ln NW Albuquerque NM 87107 Office: Interiors by Jacqulyn 509 Chamiso NW Albuquerque NM 87107

ARMISTEAD, JAY DAVID, communications and mgmt. cons.; b. Littlefield, Tex., July 1, 1951; s. J. Davis and Cora Francis (Bell) A.; B.A. in Zoology, Tex. Tech U., 1973; postgrad. U. Tex. Med. Br., Galveston, 1973-74; m. Suzanne Priscilla Weiner, Aug. 15, 1977. mental tng. coach Ariz. State U., 1980-81; pres. Nova Communication, Inc., Austin, Tex., 1979—, Advance Mgmt. Assocs., Inc., Austin, 1978—, Futuretrends Found., Inc., 1982—; adj. faculty Antioch Coll. West, San Francisco, 1976-77; mem. faculty Burklyn (Vt.) Bus. Sch., 1979; cons. on mgmt. and communications U Calif.-Berkeley Men's Swimming Team, 1978-80. Author: The Nova Communication Personal Organizer, 1979; The Wholesport Whitepaper, 1980. Address: 8200 Mopac Expressway Suite 295 Austin TX 78759

ARMISTEAD, ROBERT ASHBY, JR., research and development company executive; b. Roanoke, Va., Feb. 7, 1940; s. Robert A. and Lucille Denis (Owen) A.; B.S. in Physics (Disting. Grad.; Jackson-Hope medal award), Va. Mil. Inst., 1962; M.S. in Physics (AEC spl. fellow), 1963, Ph.D. in Nuclear Sci. (Oak Ridge Grad. fellow), 1966; M.B.A., U. Santa Clara (Calif.), 1973; m. Mona Carole Thornhill, Dec. 28, 1965; children—Robert Ashby, Wade Owen, Clay Thornhill. Mem. research staff Oak Ridge Nat. Lab., 1964-66; project officer Def. Nuclear Agy., Washington, 1966-68; mgr. radiation and solid state physics dept. Stanford Research Inst., Menlo Park, Calif., 1968-76; founder, pres., chief exec. officer, chmn. bd. Advanced Research & Applications Corp. (ARACOR), Sunnyvale, Calif., 1976—; dir. Sierra Nuclear Corp., N.Mex. Capital Corp.; cons. in field. Served to capt. USAR, 1966-68. Mem. Am. Phys. Soc., IEEE, Am. Assn. Physicists in Medicine, Am. Electronics Assn. Author papers in field, chpts. in books. Office: 1223 E Arques Ave Sunnyvale CA 94086

ARMON, NORMA, educational company producer, writer, editor; b. Mexico, July 22, 1937; came to U.S. 1977; d. Abraham and Gertrude (Cohen) Kreimerman; m. Moises Itzkowich, Dec. 17, 1955 (div. 1971); children—Ricardo, Rebeca, Carla. B.A. in English, U. of Americas,

1955; B.A. in Spanish Lit., Nat. U. Mex., 1968, M.A., 1970, Ph.D. in Linguistics, 1976; student London (Eng.) U., 1974, Cambridge (Eng.) U., 1980. Prof. linguistics and lit. Nat. U. Mex., 1968-76; writer, producer Mundo Latino, Spanish Internat. Network, Los Angeles, 1977-79; pres., Sispi Prodns., Inc., Los Angeles, 1979—; dir. curriculum devel. Summit, Inc., Los Angeles, 1980-82; creative dir. Eye Contact; editor-in-chief, Metamorphoses quar.; books include: Charles Dickens, 1970, Computers For Those Over Forty, 1983. Office: 1755 Seaview Trail Los Angeles CA 90046

ARMSTEAD, ROBERT LOUIS, physicist; b. Blair, Nebr., Nov. 5, 1936; s. Louis Clifford and Florence Sutherland (Curtis) A.; B.S., U. Rochester, 1958; Ph.D., U. Calif., Berkeley, 1965; m. Mary R. Armstead, Aug. 12, 1961; children—Karen, Janet. Mem. faculty dept. physics Naval Postgrad. Sch., Monterey, Calif., 1964—, asso. prof., 1971—. Mem. Am. Phys. Soc. Home: PO Box 6491 Carmel CA 93921 Office: Dept Physics Naval Postgrad Sch Monterey CA 93940

ARMSTRONG, C(AROL) JOYCE, secretarial service company executive, civic worker; b. Cortez, Colo., Dec. 17, 1948; d. Gaylord Norris and Evelyn Marguerite (Gilman) Gardner; m. Richard William Armstrong, Dec. 28, 1968; children—Robin Allegra, Jeremy Israel. Student Grace Bible Inst., Omaha, 1966-67, Ariz. Bible Coll., Phoenix, 1967-68. Unit clk. Good Samaritan Hosp., Phoenix, 1969-70, John C. Lincoln Hosp., Phoenix, 1970-71; ward clk. Southwest Meml. Hosp., Cortez, Colo., 1977-78, nursing adminstrn. sec., 1978-81; owner, operator Et Cetera Secretarial Services, Cortez, Colo., 1981—; also profl. pianist, vocalist. Coordinator spl. folks Assn. Retarded Citizens of Colo., Durango, 1981—, chmn. spl. edn. adv. com. Cortez Dist., Colo. Mem. Profl. Secretaries Internat. Assn. Club: Civitan (bull. editor 1982-83). Contbr. articles to newspapers.

ARMSTRONG, CHRISTINE, consultant; b. Los Angeles, June 23, 1952; d. Robert P. and Helen C. (Brooks) A. B.S., U. Ariz., 1974; M.A., Ohio State U., 1976; J.D., U. Puget Sound, 1982. Bar: Wash. 1983. Labor relations rep. Ford Motor Co., Lima, Ohio, 1976-78; profl. relations adminstr. Rockwell Internat. Corp., Los Angeles, 1978-79; employee service adminstr. Energy Services Co., Seattle, 1980-82; cons. human relations, systems devel., Seattle, 1982—. Active NOW, Wash. Women United. Home: 17249 NE 15th Pl Bellevue WA 98008 Office: PO Box 901 Bellevue WA 98004

ARMSTRONG, CLARA JULIA EVERSHED (MRS. ROLLIN S. ARMSTRONG), ret. coll. adminstr.; b. Murray, Utah, Aug. 25, 1911; d. Elmer B. and Lenora K. (Tripp) Evershed; student Henager Bus. Coll., 1936-37; m. Rollin S. Armstrong, Sept. 29, 1956; foster children—Maxwell Rollin, Ruth Elizabeth, Robert Neil, Philip Samuel. Office mgr., credit mgr. D.N. & E. Walter & Co., Salt Lake City, 1937-48; with Latter Day Saints Bus. Coll., Salt Lake City, 1948-77, sec., 1948-52, fgn. student adviser, 1952-55, vet. coordinator, 1952-55, rehab. counselor, 1952-55, registar, 1955-62, sec.-treas., 1962-76; vol. worker, 1976—. Mem. Ch. of Jesus Christ of Latter-day Saints (pres. Ward Mut. Improvement Assn. 1941-45). Home: 35 F St Salt Lake City UT 84103 Office: 411 E South Temple Salt Lake City UT 84111

ARMSTRONG, CLEVE ERLING, optometrist; b. Spoken, Wash., June 30, 1942; s. John Erling and Anna Loise (Funk) A.; m. Sharon K. Herb, June 5, 1966 (div.); 1 dau., Bethany Ann. B.S. in Natural Sci., Pacific U., 1964, O.D., 1965, M.S. in Physiol. Optics and Exptl. Psychology, 1969; M.P.H. in Environ. Health and Community Health Adminstrn., U. Tex.-Houston, 1971. Lic. optometrist, Colo. Asst. prof. U. Houston, 1968-72; sr. research scientist Tech. Inc., Manned Spacecraft Ctr., Houston, 1969; exec. dir. Colo. Optometric Ctr., Denver, 1972-74; pvt. practice optometry specializing in spl. problems, Lafayette, Colo., 1974—; cons. Am. Optometric Assn. Served to capt. U.S. Army, 1966-68; Vietnam. Mem. Am. Optometric Assn., Colo. Optometric Assn. Club: Colo. Mountain. Author NASA and mil. publs. on radiation injuries, vision in space, 1967-69; author continuing edn. publs. Office: 801 S Public Rd Lafayette CO 80026

ARMSTRONG, DEBORAH ANNE, personnel representative; b. Detroit, Sept. 23, 1954; d. Walter Alex and Dolores (Alder) Wosik. B.S. with honors, Mich. State U., 1977, M.A. with high honors, 1981. Phys. edn. instr. St. Roberts, Detroit, 1978-79; instr. Glen Riley Sch. Gymnastics, Pontiac, Mich., 1978-79; resident advisor Mich. State U., East Lansing, 1979-80, asst. hall dir., 1980-81, hall dir., 1981-82; personnel rep. Gen. Mills Inc., Lodi, Calif., 1982—. Sponsored exec. United Way of San Joaquin County, 1982. Mem. Am. Soc. Tng. and Devel., Am. Soc. Personnel Adminstrn. Office: PO Box 230 Lodi CA 95240

ARMSTRONG, DICKWIN DILL, assn. exec.; b. Muncie, Ind., Aug. 18, 1934; s. Colby C. and Elizabeth A. (Houck) A.; m. Janice A. Flora, June 2, 1957; children—Brent D., Stacey J. B.S., Ind. U., 1956. Chief exec. officer Madison (Ind.) C. of C., 1959-61, Frankfort, Ind., 1961-63, Marion, Ind., 1963-66, Lakeland, Fla., 1966-80, Portland, Oreg., 1980—; mem. faculty Ctr. for Continuing Edn., U.S. C. of C., 1975—. Bd. dirs. Nat. Alliance Bus., Oreg. Joint Council for Econ. Edn., Found. for Oreg. Research and Edn. Served to capt. U.S. Army, 1957-59. Mem. Am. C. of C. Execs. (dir.), Oreg. Chamber Execs. (dir.), Sigma Alpha Epsilon. Republican. Methodist. Clubs: Masons, Shriners, Rotary. Home: 5722 SW Windson Ct Portland OR 97221 Office: 824 SW 5th Ave Portland OR 97204

ARMSTRONG, GENE LEE, aerospace co. exec.; b. Clinton, Ill., Mar. 9, 1922; s. George Dewey and Ruby Imald (Dickerson) A.; B.S. with high honors, U. Ill., Urbana, 1948, M.S., 1951; m. Lael Jeanne Baker, Apr. 3, 1946; children—Susan Lael, Roberta Lynn, Gene Lee. With Boeing Aircraft, 1948-50, 51-52; chief engr. astronautics div., corp. dir. Gen. Dynamics, 1954-65; chief engr. systems integration and engring. div. TRW/DSSG, Redondo Beach, Calif., 1956—. Served to 1st lt. USAAF, 1942-45. Decorated Air medal; recipient alumni awards U. Ill., 1965, 77; registered profl. engr., Calif. Mem. Am. Math. Soc., AIAA, Nat. Mgmt. Assn., Am. Def. Preparedness Assn., Am. Legion, VFW. Club: Masons. Contbr. chpts. to books, articles to profl. publs. Home: 5242 Bryant Circle Westminster CA 92683 Office: One Space Park Bldg E1 Room 5029 Redondo Beach CA 90278

ARMSTRONG, JAMES EDWARD, accountant; b. Boonville, N.C., May 17, 1940; s. Carl E. and Lucy C. (Ceaser) A.; m. Stacia Moore, June 7, 1968; children—Danielle, Michael. B.B.A. in Acctg., U. Denver, 1971. C.P.A., Colo., Mo. Staff acct. Arthur Andersen & Co., Denver, 1970-72; ptnr.-in-charge audit dept. Ashby, Armstrong, Johnson & Co., 1973-80, adminstrv. and audit ptnr., 1980—. Bd. dirs. 9 Who Care; treas. Mile High council Girls Scouts USA, Urban League Met. Denver. Served with USAF, 1959-62. Mem. Colo. State Bd. Accountancy, Am. Inst. C.P.A.s, Colo. Soc. C.P.A.s, Nat. Assn. Black Accts. Democrat. Baptist.

ARMSTRONG, JAMES THOMAS, building systems company executive; b. Los Angeles, Dec. 13, 1938; s. James Floyd and Mary Louise (Harris) A.; student Santa Rosa Jr. Coll., 1956-57, San Francisco City Coll., 1958-59, U. Calif., 1964-65; m. Virginia Carol Williams, Nov. 4, 1972; children—Alyson Louise, James Floyd, Dawn Lynn, Victoria Ruth. Research, devel. Speedspace Corp., Santa Rosa, Calif., 1966-68; engring. mgr. Trus-Joist Calif. Corp., Santa Rosa, 1968-69; owner, cons. Armstrong & Assos., Santa Rosa, 1969-71; ops. mgr. Pacific State Components, Sonoma, Calif., 1971-72; pres. Creative Bldg. Systems, Santa Rosa, Calif., 1972—. Active YMCA, 1969—, asst. chief Indian Guides, 1969-70. Served with C.E., AUS, 1957. Mem. Forest Products Research Soc., Am. Inst. Bldg. Design, North Coast Builders Exchange, Beta Phi Beta. Developer FHA-approved criteria for manufactured wood building system. Office: 714 Mendocino Ave 2d Floor Santa Rosa CA 95401 also PO Box 3432 Santa Rosa CA 45402

ARMSTRONG, JAN ROBERT, lawyer; b. Harrington, Wash., Mar. 10, 1953; s. Dean H. and Margery L. (Knapp) A.; m. Gail L. Gravbrot, Mar. 20, 1955. B.B.A. cum laude, Wash. State U., 1975; J.D., U. Wash., 1978. Bar: Wash. 1978, U.S. Dist. Ct. (ea. dist.) Wash. 1980. Ptnr., Lawless & Armstrong, Attys. at Law, Richland, Wash., 1978-82, Armstrong & Klym, Richland, 1982-83, Armstrong, Klym & Waite, Attys. at Law, Richland, 1983—. Mem. Wash. State Bar Assn., ABA, Benton-Franklin County Bar Assn. Home: 1905 W 37th St Kennewick WA 99336 Office: Armstrong Klym & Waite 1200 Jadwin Ave Suite 502 Richland WA 99352

ARMSTRONG, JOHN DAVID, II, physician; b. Topeka, Aug. 6, 1938; s. John David and Mary LaMerle (Sayler) A.; B.A., U. Kans., 1962, M.D., 1966; m. Margaret Lois French, Sept. 4, 1960; children—John David, Jason Allen, Judson Sayler. Intern, St. Luke's Hosp., Kansas City, Mo., 1967; resident Edward Mallinckrodt Inst., Washington U. Sch. Medicine, Barnes Hosp., St. Louis, 1967-69, Edward Mallinckrodt radiology fellow, 1969-70; asst. prof. Washington U. Sch. Medicine, 1970-71; asst. prof. diagnostic radiology U. Utah, Salt Lake City, 1973-77, assoc. prof., 1977-83, prof., 1983—; head chest sect., chief radiology VA Hosp., Salt Lake City, 1973-78; research fellow U. London Hammersmith Hosp., 1978-79. Surgeon, vol. fireman Rockville (Md.) Vol. Fire Dept., 1971-73; mem. exec. com. Greater Salt Lake council Boy Scouts Am., Salt Lake City, 1975-77; coach, referee Am. Youth Soccer Assn., Salt Lake City, 1977—; vol. Hospice of Salt Lake. Served to lt. comdr. U.S. Navy, 1971-73. Named Outstanding Prof. for excellence and dedication in teaching U. Utah, 1977. Diplomate Am. Bd. Radiology. Fellow Am. Thoracic Soc.; mem. Am. Coll. Radiology, Am. Coll. Chest Physicians, Assn. Univ. Radiologists, Royal Coll. Radiology (London), Phi Delta Theta. Presbyterian (elder). Contbr. articles to profl. jours. Home: 3346 Enchanted Hills Dr Salt Lake City UT 84121 Office: U Utah Medical Center Salt Lake City UT 84132

ARMSTRONG, RAMSEY CLARK, aircraft and automobile component mfg. co. exec.; b. Muskogee, Okla., Nov. 29, 1915; s. Ramsey Clark and Frances (Whaley) A.; m. Frances Jean Hoskins, Feb. 4, 1938; children—Ramsey Clark IV, Sally Bess (Mrs. Roger Miller). Vice-pres. Texasteel Mfg. Co., Ft. Worth, 1937-44; prodn. mgr. Rheem Mfg. Co., Houston, 1944-45; pres. Welex, Inc., Ft. Worth, 1945-50; chmn. bd. dirs. Sierracin Corp., Sylmar, Calif., 1952-76; ret., 1976. Clubs: Balboa Yacht, Irvine Coast Country. Patentee electrically heated automobile windshields, heat reflecting archtl. glazing. Home: 4601 Surrey Dr Corona del Mar CA 92625

ARMSTRONG, ROBERT WEAVER, lawyer; b. Burbank, Calif., Oct. 6, 1923; s. Merritt Harold and Leila May (Smith) A.; B.A., Pepperdine Coll., 1947; J.D., U. So. Calif., 1950; m. Maybelle Stewart, June 1, 1944 (div. Feb. 1955); children—Sandra Armstrong Brush, Patricia Armstrong Smoot, John, Robert; m. 2d, Eleanor Bolton, Apr. 15, 1960; 1 son, Raymond. Admitted to Calif. bar, 1951, U.S. Supreme Ct. bar, 1958; practiced in Huntington Park, Calif., 1951-70; partner firm Armstrong & Wilbur, 1951-70, Armstrong, Veron & Wilbur, Downey, Calif., 1970-77, Armstrong Wilbur Knoll, Ratcliffe & Perkins, 1977—; tchr. English, Atlantic City High Sch., 1945-46; lectr. law extension sch. Los Angeles City Schs., 1960-61; lectr. seminars and symposia, N.Y.C., 1976—. Mem. Republican Central Com., Los Angeles County, Calif., 60; nat. dir. Jaycees, 1957-58. Served to capt. USMCR, 1943-45, 50-51. Certified criminal law specialist, Calif. Mem. Am., Los Angeles County bar assns., Criminal Cts. Bar, Nat. Assn. Criminal Trial Lawyers, Am. Judicature Soc., Calif. Attys. for Criminal Justice, Legion Lex, Los Angeles Trial Lawyers. Episcopalian. Clubs: Calif. Yacht, 4th of July Yacht, Catalina Island (commodore 1975). Home: 5226 Marina Pacifica Dr S Long Beach CA 90803 Office: 9701 S Lakewood Blvd Downey CA 90240

ARMSTRONG, ROGER JOSEPH, cartoonist, educator; b. Los Angeles, Oct. 12, 1917; s. Roger Dale and Elizabeth Theresa (Eliason) A.; m. Jacquelyn Joy West, 1970 (div.); 1 dau., Julie Ann Vance. Student Pasadena City Coll., 1932-38, Chouinard Art Inst., 1938-40, 48-50. Illustrator, writer children's books and comic books Western Pub. Co., 1940-49; cartoonist Ella Cinders comic strip United Feature Syndicate, 1950-60; cartoonist, writer Napoleon and Uncle Elby comic strip Times Mirror Syndicate, 1950-61; cartoonist Little Lulu comic strip Western Pub. Co., 1964-66; dir. Laguna Beach (Calif.) Mus. Art, 1963-66; instr. Laguna Beach Sch. of Art, 1967—; cartoonist Scamp comic strip Walt Disney Prodns., 1978—; mem. faculty Orange Coast Coll., Costa Mesa, Calif., 1980—; one-man shows include: Ettinger Gallery, Laguna Beach, 1980-82, Challis Galleries, Laguna Beach, 1982, Anaheim (Calif.) Cultural Ctr., 1983; group shows include: Dalzen Hatfield Galleries, Los Angeles, 1975, Desert Mus., Palm Springs, Calif., 1981; represented in permanent collections including: Laguna Beach Art Mus. Served with U.S. Army, 1944. Recipient 1st prize for oil painting Pico Rivera Festival of Arts, 1967; 1st Bicentennial award for meritorious achievement Cypress (Calif.) Coll., 1976. Mem. Nat. Watercolor Soc., Artists Equity, Nat. Cartoonists Soc., Comic Artists Profl. Soc. Home: 34202 Del Obispo Apt 24 Dana Point CA 92629 Office: Laguna Beach Art School 2222 Laguna Canyon Rd Laguna Beach CA 92651

ARMSTRONG, WALLACE DOWAN, JR., data processor; b. Los Angeles, Feb. 9, 1926; s. Wallace Dowan and Vina Edith (Kreinbring) A.; B.S. cum laude, U. So. Calif., 1951; postgrad. U. Oslo (Norway), 1955; 1 son, Erik Bentung. Supr. accounting Ramo Wooldridge Corp., 1955-60; mgr. programmers, systems analyst Aerospace Corp., El Segundo, Calif., 1960-80, mgr. bus. systems, 1980—. Served with USMCR, 1944-46, 51. Mem. Data Processing Mgmt. Assn. Home: 25713 Crest Rd Torrance CA 90505 Office: 2350 E El Segundo Blvd El Segundo CA

ARMSTRONG, WILLIAM L., senator; b. Fremont, Nebr., 1937; s. William L. and Dorothy (Steen) A.; m. Ellen M. Eaton, July 15, 1962; children—Anne Elizabeth, William. Pres., Radio Sta. KOSI AM-FM, Aurora, Colo., 1959—; mem. 93d-95th Congresses, 5th Dist. Colo.; mem. U.S. Senate from Colo., 1979—; mem. Colo. Senate, 1965-72, majority leader, 1969-72; mem. Colo. Ho. of Reps., 1963-64, mem. com. on appropriations, 1963-64, mem. com. state affairs, 1963-64; mem. Arapahoe County Central Com., Colo. Republic Central Com., 1962-72; mem. Colo. Rep. Platform and Resolutions Com., 1966; chmn. Colo. Rep. Platform Drafting Com., 1968; chmn. Colo. Nixon for Pres. Com., 1968. Bd. govs., exec. com. Metro Denver Urban Coalition, 1969-72; bd. dirs. Denver Organizing Com. for the XII Winter Olympic Games, 1971-72, Adams County-Aurora unit Am. Cancer Soc., 1972. Recipient Distinguished Service award Aurora Jr. C. of C., 1970; named one of three Outstanding Young Men in Colo., State Jaycees, 1970. Mem. A.P. Broadcasters Assn. (dir. 1971-72, v.p. 1972). Office: 311 Steele St Suite 103 Denver CO 80206 also 528 Hart Senate Office Bldg Washington DC 20510

ARNDT, ROLF-DIETER, radiologist, educator, author; b. Bremerhaven, Germany, Dec. 14, 1941; s. Ernst and Lieselotte (Falk) A.; came to U.S., 1952, naturalized, 1957; B.A., Occidental Coll., 1964; M.D., U. Calif., Los Angeles, 1968; m. Peggy Sue Sander, June 24, 1966; children—Ava Lee, Lisa Ann. Intern, Wadsworth VA Hosp., Los Angeles, 1968-69; resident U. Calif. Center Health Scis., Los Angeles, 1972-74, asst. prof. radiology, 1974-75, asst. clin. prof. radiology, 1975—; staff radiologist St. John's Hosp. and Health Center, Santa Monica, Calif., 1975—, mem. cleft palate team. Served with USN, 1970-72. Diplomate Am. Bd. Radiology. Mem. Am., Calif., Los Angeles County med. assns., Am. Coll. Radiology, Calif., Los Angeles County radiol. socs., Phi Beta Kappa. Contbr. articles to profl. jours.; author books. Office: 1328 22d St Santa Monica CA 90404

ARNELL, WALTER JAMES WILLIAM, engineering educator, consultant; b. Farnborough, Eng., Jan. 9, 1924; s. James Albert and Daisy (Payne) A.; came to U.S., 1953, naturalized, 1960; Aero. Engr., Royal Aircraft Establishment, 1946; B.Sc., U. London, 1953, Ph.D., 1967; M.A., Occidental Coll., Los Angeles, 1956; M.S., U. So. Calif., 1958; m. Patricia Catherine Cannon, Nov. 12, 1955; children—Sean Paul, Victoria Clare, Sarah Michele Arnell. Lectr., Poly. and Northampton Coll. Advance Tech., London, 1948-53; instr. U. So. Calif., Los Angeles, 1954-59; asst. prof. mech. engring. Calif. State U., Long Beach, 1959-62, assoc. prof., 1962-66, prof., 1966-71, chmn. dept. mech. engring., 1964-65, acting chmn. div. engring., 1964-66, dean engring., 1967-69; researcher Ctr. for Engring. Research, affiliate faculty dept. ocean engring. U. Hawaii, 1970-74; vis. prof. systems and indsl. engring. U. Ariz., 1981—; pres. Lenra Assocs. Ltd., 1973—. Chmn., project mgr. Hawaii Environ. Simulation Lab., 1971-72. Trustee Rehab. Hosp. of the Pacific, 1975-79. Asso. fellow Royal Aero. Soc.; mem. AIAA, Am. Soc. Exptl. Stess Analysis, Am. Soc. Metals, AAUP, Am. Psychol. Assn., Soc. Engring., Psychology, Human Factors Soc., Psi Chi, Alpha Pi Mu, Tau Beta Pi, Phi Kappa Phi, Pi Tau Sigma. Contbr. articles to profl. jours. Home: 4491 E Ft Lowell Tucson AZ 85712

ARNESEN, ARNE URBANE, educator; b. Springfield, Vt., Oct. 24, 1921; s. Otto Harold and Ida May (Richardson) A.; B.S. in Phys. Edn., U. Wis., 1947; M.Ed., Springfield (Mass.) Coll., 1954; m. Marguerite Leonora Manley, July 24, 1943; children—Kay E., Arne E., Gene S., Guy S., Ann L. Grad. asst. track and field coaching Springfield Coll., 1947-48; instr. phys. edn. M.I.T., 1948-57, head field event coach, 1948-57, head freshman and varsity soccer coach, 1953-57; asso. prof. phys. edn. U.S. Air Force Acad., 1978—, head soccer coach, 1957-62, head track and field coach, 1957-75, head cross country coach, 1962-77, asst. chief instrn. for phys. edn., 1980—. Served with USAAF, 1942-46. Decorated 6 Air medals, D.F.C. Mem. Internat. Track and Field Coaches Congress, U.S. Soccer Coaches Assn., U.S. Track and Field Coaches Assn., U.S. Cross Country Coaches Assn. Club: 325th Checkertail Clan (chmn. ann. reunion 1977). Contbr. articles to profl. jours. Home: 4130 Old Ranch Rd Colorado Springs CO 80908 Office: AHPI US Air Force Acad USAF Academy CO 80840

ARNETT, MAHLON EDWARD, II, management consultant; b. Pasadena, Calif., Apr. 15, 1942; s. Mahlon Edward and Martha (Rhijnsberger) A.; m. Roberta R. Hunt, Oct. 31, 1970; children—Hubert Dale, Megan Elisa Nichelle, Mahlon Edward. B.A., Occidental Coll., 1964. Cert. shopping ctr. mgr.; cert. mktg. dir.; lic. realtor, Calif. With Bullocks Dept. Stores, Calif., 1965-69; property mgr. Coldwell Banker, Los Angeles, 1969-72; v.p. First Nat. Bank Albuquerque, 1974-76; gen. mgr. Aetna Life & Casualty, Hartford, Conn., 1977-78, Halcyon Ltd., Hartford, 1979-81; v.p. Halcyon Leasing & Mgmt. Inc., Mountain View, Calif., 1981—. Author: Christmas Village, 1978; Harrison A. Hare Esquire, 1979. Exec. dir. Conn. 4-H Found., 1981; dir. Lace Mus., Mountain View. Mem. Internat. Council Shopping Ctrs. (state dir. 1975-76; Maxi award 1977). Club: Lions. Office: 2540 California St Mountain View CA 94040

ARNETT, RUSSELL EUGENE, lawyer; b. Oak Park, Ill., July 28, 1927; s. Roy E. and Evelyn (Hall) A.; student Central Coll., 1946-48; LL.B., Northwestern U., 1951; m. Betty J. Epps, Aug. 7, 1954; children—April, Heather, Hans. Admitted to Alaska bar, 1955, since practiced in Anchorage; U.S. commr., Nome, Alaska, 1952. Pres. Anchorage Republican Club, 1957. Served with USNR, 1945-46. Mem. Alaska (bd. govs.), Anchorage (past pres.) bar assns. Home: Star Route Box 2043 Anchorage AK 99507 Office: 1016 W 6th Ave Suite 300 Anchorage AK 99501

ARNETT, THOMAS ROY, real estate exec.; b. Virden, N.Mex., July 14, 1941; s. Thomas Marvin and June (Patten) A.; A.A., Mesa Community Coll., 1963; student Eastern Ariz. Coll., 1959, Brigham Young U., 1963-64, No. Ariz. U., 1965-66; grad. Realtors Inst., 1973; m. Sheryl Sampson, June 24, 1966; children—Melanie, Anjanette, Greg, Amy, Scott. Owner, mgr. Payson (Ariz.) Roundup Newspapers, 1969-70; escrow officer Transamerica Title Co., Scottsdale, Ariz., 1968; mgr. Farnsworth Realty Brokerage Co., Mesa, Ariz., 1969-78, v.p., 1978—. Mem. planning coms. City Mesa; bishop Ch. Jesus Christ Latter-day Saints, 1977—, counselor to bishop, 1974-77. Mem. Ariz. Interscholastic Assn., Nat. Bd. Realtors, Ariz. Assn. Realtors, Mesa Chandler Tempe Bd. Realtors. Republican. Club: Sertoma. Office: 6053 E University St Mesa AZ 85205

ARNEY, REX ODELL, lawyer, state senator; b. Ashland, Ky., Jan. 11, 1940; s. Harold Leat and Frances (Odell) A.; student U. Mich., 1958-59; B.A., U. Wyo., 1962, M.A., 1963; J.D., U. Ill., 1968; m. Marion Carroll Roberts, July 23, 1979; children—Dana, Jill, Michele, Ryan. Instr., Black Hawk Coll., Moline, Ill., 1963-65; admitted to Wyo. bar, 1968; partner firm Redle, Yonkee & Arney, Sheridan, Wyo., 1968—; mem. Wyo. Ho. of Reps., 1973-77, senator Wyo. Senate, 1977—. Mem. Am. Bar Assn., Am. Judicature Soc., Am. Trial Lawyers Assn. Republican. Episcopalian. Clubs: Elks, Lions. Office: 319 W Dow St Sheridan WY 82801

ARNEY, WILLIAM RAY, sociology educator, researcher; b. Charlotte, N.C., Sept. 18, 1950; s. John Wilson and Grace (Kuhn) A.; m. Deborah Henderson Jan. 2, 1972; 1 son, John Arthur. B.A., U. Colo., 1971, M.A., 1972, Ph.D., 1974. Asst prof. sociology Dartmouth Coll., Hanover, N.H., 1974-80, assoc. prof., 1980-81; adj. asst. prof. community and family medicine Dartmouth Med. Sch., 1979-82; mem. sociology Faculty Evergreen State Coll., Olympia, Wash., 1981—. Univ. fellow U. Colo., 1972; NEH fellow, 1977; Whiting Found. fellow, 1979; Nat. Insts. Health grantee, 1975. Mem. Am. Sociol. Assn., Am. Statis. Assn., Phi Beta Kappa. Mem. Christian Ch. (Disciples of Christ). Author: Power and the Profession of Obstetrics, 1982; (with Bernard J. Bergen) The New Medical Revolution: Taming the Last Great Beast, 1984; contbr. articles to profl. jours. Home: 526 N Rogers St Olympia WA 98502 Office: L 2102 Evergreen State Coll Olympia WA 98505

ARNHYM, ROLFE GUNTHER, chamber of commerce executive; b. Berlin, Germany, June 17, 1930; came to U.S., 1936, naturalized, 1939; s. Albert A. and Leni H. (Mottek) A.; m. June K. Darley, Oct. 24, 1954; children—Kathryn, Carolyn. B.S., U.S. Mil. Acad., 1953; M.B.A., Fla. Tech. U., 1975; postgrad. George Washington U., 1971-72. Commd. 2d lt., U.S. Army, 1953, advanced through grades to lt. col., 1974, ret., 1974; pres. Mid. Fla. Cons., Orlando, 1974-75; program mgr. Xerox/Electro-Optical Systems, Pasadena, 1975-78; exec. v.p. Pasadena C. of C., 1978—. Adv. bd. Am. Cancer Soc., Salvation Army. Decorated Legion of Merit, Air medal, Army Commencation medal. Mem. Am. C. of C. Execs., Calif. C. of C. Execs. (dir.), M.B.A. Assn. Republican. Club: Rotary. Home: 2743 San Angelo Dr Claremont CA 91711 Office: 11 W Del Mar St Suite 201 Pasadena CA 91105

ARNO, CARMEN JOSEPH, JR., employee leasing co. exec.; b. Syracuse, May 16, 1944; s. Carmen J. and Rose (Corso) A.; A.A.A., Auburn Coll., 1970; student Syracuse U., UCLA Extension, LaSalle U.; 1 son, Michael Dean. Acct., Green & Green Public Accts., Syracuse, 1967; controller P.E.A.C.E., Inc., Syracuse, 1968-71; v.p. fin. AMPCO Auto Parks, Inc., Los Angeles, 1971-74; pres. Paystaff Inc., Long Beach, Calif., 1980—, Calif. Bus. Devel. Corp., Long Beach, 1974—, Am. Bus. Developers, Inc., Long Beach, 1981—. Served with USN, 1963-67. Mem. Nat. Assn. Tax Consultants, Am. Extrepreneurs Assn., Am. Mgmt. Assn., Nat. Assn. Accts. Roman Catholic. Home: 17372 Drey Ln Huntington Beach CA 92647 Office: 4201 Long Beach Blvd Bldg 403 Long Beach CA 90807

ARNOLD, CARRIE KAREN, artist, art dir.; b. Greeley, Colo., May 25, 1944; d. James P. and Dorothy Adeline (Sweet) Forman; student Colo. State Coll. at Greeley, 1961-62; m. Samuel P. Arnold, 1971. Mgr. ABC Copy Service, Denver, 1962-65; draftswoman Iraola Drafting Service, Denver, 1965-67; owner Carrie's Copy & Color Service, Denver, 1967-71; owner The Fort Restaurant, Morrison, Colo., 1971-76, Arnold & Co., Denver, 1971-82, computer systems mgr., dir., 1982—; commd. New Year's card Sri Lanka, 1974; pub. relations cons. Colo. Open Space Council, 1973; preliminary exhibits design Ash Hollow (Nebr.) State Park. Program chmn. Opera on Tuesday, Denver Lyric Opera Guild, Jr. Symphony Guild, Soc. Scribes N.Y., Western History Assn., Colo. Calligraphers Guild. Republican. Congregationalist. Address: 2221 S Fillmore St Denver CO 80210

ARNOLD, EVERETT WILFORD, education and business consultant, foremer community college administrator; b. White Salmon, Wash., July 8, 1921; s. Wilford Merriet and Grace May (Nickols) A.; B.B.A. in Personnel Mgmt., U. Wash., 1949; Ed.M. in Bus. Edn., Oreg. State U., 1962, postgrad., 1968-70; m. Jane Elizabeth Myers, June 12, 1948; children—David Everett, Dean Robert. With First Nat. Bank Oreg., Portland, 1950-52, McKales Corp., Portland, 1952-58; tchr. Beaverton (Oreg.) Sch. Dist. 48, 1958-64, Portland Sch. Dist. 1, 1964-68; dir. Maywood campus Mt. Hood Community Coll., Gresham, Oreg., 1970-82; cons. in field. Trustee Woodland Park Hosp., 1981—. Served with USAAF, 1942-46. Vocat. Leadership Devel. fellow, 1968-69; named Oreg. Bus. Edn. Tchr. of Year, 1968. Mem. Nat. Bus. Edn. Assn., Am. Vocat. Assn., Oreg. Bus. Edn. Council (a founder), Oreg. Bus. Edn. Assn. (pres. 1968-69), Phi Delta Kappa (pres. 1983-84). Republican. Methodist. Home and office: 2673 SW Orchard Ct Gresham OR 97030

ARNOLD, JOHN MILLER, biomedicine researcher, educator; b. St. Paul, Oct. 6, 1936; s. Arthur Henry and Lucile (Miller) A.; divorced; 1 dau., Kathrine Elizabeth. B.A., U. Minn., 1958, Ph.D., 1963. Mem. staff Am. Mus. Natural History, 1963-64; asst. prof. Iowa State U., 1965-67; instr., trustee, chmn. Marine Biol. Lab., U. Hawaii, 1967—, now prof. biomed. research, acting dir. Kewalo Marine Lab., 1973 vis. prof. Silliman U., Philippines, 1982. NSF fellow, 1962; Am. Mus. Natural History fellow, 1963-64; Sigerfoos fellow, 1961; recipient E.G. Conklin award, 1960; Nautilus research corp. grantee. Mem. Marine Biol. Lab., AAAS, Am. Inst. Biol. Scis., Am. Soc. Devel. Biologists, Am. Soc. Cell Biology, Western Soc. Naturalists. Contbr. numerous articles to profl. jours. Office: Kewalo Marine Lab 41 Ahui St Honolulu HI also Marine Biol Lab Woods Hole MA

ARNOLD, JONATHAN HARTLEY, clinical psychologist, educator; b. San Francisco, June 21, 1949; s. Hartley and Adele (Burton) A.; m. Glory Kash, Dec. 16, 1973; 1 son, Stephen Kash. B.A. in Religious Studies, U. Calif.-Santa Barbara, 1972, M.Ed. in Counseling Psychology, 1974; M.A. in Theology, Fuller Theol. Sem., 1977; Ph.D. in Clin. Psychology, 1978. Lic. clin. psychologist, Calif. Counselor, Santa Barbara (Calif.) Schs., 1973-74; research asst. Child Devel. Clinic, Pasadena, Calif., 1974-77; mgmt. cons. Assocs. for Behavior Change, San Francisco, 1979-80; pvt. practice clin. psychology, San Mateo, Calif., 1980—; asst. prof. Simpson Coll., San Francisco, 1979—; adj. prof. Azusa Pacific U., San Jose, Calif., 1980—. Mem. profl. adv. bd. San Mateo County Suicide Prevention Clinic. Served alt. mil. duty Calif. State Dept. Corrections, 1970-72. Mem. Am. Psychol. Assn. Contbr. chpt. to book and articles to profl. jours. Office: 334 N San Mateo Dr San Mateo CA 94401

ARNOLD, KENNETH JAMES, lawyer, pub. co. exec., author; b. Brighton, Colo., Sept. 10, 1927; s. Kenneth Wilburt and Frances Irene (Lloyd) A.; student U. Paris, 1950-51, U. Rabat (Morocco), 1951-52; A.B., U. Calif., Berkeley, 1949, M.A., 1950, J.D., San Francisco, 1958. Admitted to Calif. bar, 1959; pvt. practice law, San Francisco, 1959-60, 63—, Sacramento, 1960-62; research atty. Calif. Supreme Ct., Sacramento, 1960-62, Calif. Ct. Appeals 1st Appellate Dist., San Francisco, 1958-60; owner Law Book Service Co., San Francisco, 1969—; asst. sr. editor-in-chief Matthew Bender & Co., San Francisco, 1963-81, staff author, 1981—; lectr. in field, 1972-81; cons. to Calif. State Jud. Council, 1970—, Calif. Center Jud. Edn. and Research, 1974—, Calif. Coll. Trial Judges, 1975, McGeorge Coll. Law, U. Pacific, 1975-80; mem. Calif. Legal Forms Com., 1971-73. Bd. dirs. PRIDE Found., San Francisco, 1974-77. Served with AUS, 1952-55. Mem. State Bar Calif., Criminal Cts. Bar Assn. No. Calif., Hastings Alumni Assn., San Francisco Gem and Mineral Soc., Friends of Animals Inc., Soc. Individual Rights, 1964-77. Author: California Courts and Judges Handbook, 1968, 73, 75, 76, 77, 79, 81, 82; California Justice Court Manual, 1971 supplement; (with others) California Points and Authorities I-XII, 1964-66; (with others) California Forms of Pleadings and Practice, 48 vols., 1966—; (with others) California Legal Forms, 25 vols., 1967-69; Commencing Civil Action in California, 1975, and supplements; (with others) California Family Law Practice, 6 vols., 1977-78, Civil Actions in California, 5 vols., 1982—; other manuals and handbooks; feature writer Barclays Law Monthly, 1979-82; editor Vector Mag., 1965-67. Home: 369 Harvard St San Francisco CA 94134 Office: 450 Sansome St San Francisco CA 94111

ARNOLD, LINDA JOAN, mgmt. and communication cons.; b. N.Y.C., Jan. 26, 1943; d. Samuel and Dorothy (Jacobson) Moss; R.N., Lenox Hill Hosp. Sch. Nursing, 1964; B.S., Columbia U., 1968; M.S., U. Calif., San Francisco, 1975; m. Michael Arnold, Nov. 15, 1969. Staff, Lenox Hill Hosp., N.Y.C., 1964-68, head nurse, 1968-71; dir. nursing Cathedral Hill Med. Center, San Francisco, 1971-73; asst. dir. nursing Samuel Merritt Hosp., Oakland, Calif., 1975-78, dir. nursing service, 1978-81; mgmt. and communication cons., 1981—; asst. clin. prof. U. Calif., San Francisco, 1976—. Mem. adv. com. health services mgmt. program Golden Gate U., 1977-79; mem. adv. com. health services adminstrn. program St. Mary's Coll., Moraga, Calif., 1977-79. Mem. Nat. League for Nursing, Am. Soc. Nursing Service Adminstrs., Calif. League Nursing, Calif. Soc. Nursing Service Adminstrs. (dir. 1980—, sec. 1980-82), Sigma Theta Tau. Home: 21 Worth St San Francisco CA 94114

ARNOLD, MAXWELL, advertising agency executive, writer; b. San Francisco, Feb. 18, 1919; s. Max and Lela (Klein) A.; m. Patricia Schulman, Oct. 6, 1950; children—Jane Sarah, Caroline Lela, Oliver Maxwell. A.B. magna cum laude in English, Stanford U., 1948. Mem. staff Guild, Bascom and Bonfigli, San Francisco, 1953-65, Dancer Fitzgerald Sample, San Francisco, 1965-69, Maxwell Arnold Agy., San Francisco, 1970-81; pres., chmn. Maxwell Arnold, Jackson and Smyth, 1981—; lectr. Stanford U., U. Calif.-Berkeley; cons. Stanford Ann. Fund, Nat. Acad. Arts and Scis. Bd. dirs. No. Calif. Service League, Pub. Media Ctr., San Francisco. Served with USNR, 1942-46. Recipient Humanities Prize Stanford U., 1946. Mem. Am. Assn. Advt. Agys., San Francisco C. of C., French Am. C. of C., San Francisco Advt. Club. Democrat. Jewish. Clubs: Cercle d l'Union, Alliance Francaise. Author: numerous short stories to mags; contbr. articles to advt. jours.

ARNOLD, RUTH CAROLYN, psychiatric rehabilitation administrator; b. Boston, Aug. 12, 1949; d. Louis Anthony and Marguerite Rose (O'Connor) A.; m. Louis Terry Sicotte, Sept. 25, 1948. Student Bryn Mawr Coll., 1967-68; B.A., Bennington Coll., 1971. Teaching asst. Spl. Edn. Dist. Lake County (Ill.), Gurnee, 1972-74; with Mental Health Center Boulder County, Inc., Boulder, Colo., 1974—, psychiat. rehab. counselor/asst. workshop coordinator, 1974-76, team leader vocat. rehab. services, 1976—; cons. devel. vocat. services, Colo., Mont., Idaho. Bd. dirs. Ctr. for People with Disabilities, Boulder, 1975—. Mem. NOW, Nat. Assn. Female Execs. Office: WATshop 5741 Arapahoe St Boulder CO 80403

ARNOLD, SHEILA, state legislator; b. N.Y.C., Jan. 15, 1929; d. Michael and Eileen (Lynch) Keddy; coll. courses; m. George Longan Arnold, Nov. 12, 1960; 1 son, Peter; 1 son by previous marriage, Michael C. Young; stepchildren—Drew, George Longan, Joe. Mem. Wyo. Ho. of Reps., 1978—, mem. com. mines, minerals and indsl. devel., hwys. and transp. Former mem., sec. Wyo. Land Use Adv. Coms.; past pres. Democratic Women's Club, Laramie; past vice-chmn. Albany County Dem. Central Com.; past mem. Dem. State Com. Mem. Laramie Area C. of C. (pres. 1982; Top Hand award 1977), LWV. Episcopalian. Clubs: Faculty Women's (past pres.), Zonta, Laramie Women's, Cowboy Joe. Office: Capitol Bldg Cheyenne WY 82002

ARNOLD, STEVEN LELAND, physician/actor; b. Bronx, Apr. 7, 1950; s. Herbert Joseph and Jeanette (Wetter) A. A.B., SUNY, 1971; M.D., U. Miami, 1976, M.S., 1978. Intern Cedars-Sinai Med. Center, Los Angeles, 1976-77; resident in family practice Northridge (Calif.) Hosp. Found., 1977-79; practice medicine, specializing in family practice and emergency medicine, Century City, Calif., 1979—; emergency rm. physician Granda Hills Hosp., 1977; football team physician Cleve. High Sch., 1977, Hollywood High Sch., 1983—; emergency room physician Westpark Hosp., 1978, Rio Hondo Hosp., 1979, Los Angeles New Hosp., 1979, Pacioma Luth. Hosp., 1979, Riverside Hosp., 1979; tech. advisor MGM Studios, Chips, 1981; cons. physician ABC, Inc.; med. dir. Med. Hypnosis Center, Los Angeles, 1977-79; lectr. in field. Bd. dirs. Heart Care Inst. Beverly Hills, 1979—, Acute Care Med. Group, Inc., 1979—; mem. med. adv. bd. Medic Alert Found. Internat., 1980—; spokesman Los Angeles Medic Alert, 1980-82; mem. nat. adv. council Press Edn.-Govt. Found., 1980—; founder, chmn. Nat. Emergency Care Mo., and Nat. Emergency Care Week., 1980—, preceptor dept. family medicine UCLA, 1980-82. Mem. Los Angeles Olympic Med. Adv. Commn.; med. dir 10K Run for Soviet Jewry, 1980—. Recipient Letter of Recognition, Blood Pressure Alert, 1975; U. Miami Family Practice award, 1976; diplomate Am. Bd. Family Practice. Fellow Am. Acad. Family Physicians, Am. Med. Student Assn., Calif. Acad. Family Physicians, So. Med. Assn., Family Practice Soc. U. Miami Sch. Medicine, Los Angeles County Med. Assn., AMA (adv. bd. motion pictures, TV and radio), Calif. Med. Assn., Am. Heart Assn., Am. Coll. Sports Medicine, Calif. Council Against Health Fraud, Century City C. of C., Beverly Hills C. of C., Psi Chi, Phi Delta Epsilon. Contbr. articles to profl. jours. Office: 2080 Century Park E Suite 1206 Los Angeles CA 90067

ARNOLD, TERRY SUTTON, systems engring. co. exec.; b. Colorado Springs, Colo., Jan. 13, 1945; s. Robert Elwyn and Frances Langley (Sutton) A.; student Harvey Mudd Coll., 1962-65; M.S.C.S., West Coast U., 1978; m. Martha Goddard Welch, Oct. 9, 1976. Mem. tech. staff TRW Systems Group, 1966-72; cons. computer architectures, Los Angeles, 1969-72; co-founder, v.p. engring. Merdan Group, San Diego, 1971—, dir., 1972—, sec., 1972-76; instr. computer sci. West Coast U., 1979—. Mem. IEEE Computer Soc., Assn. Computing Machinery, Mensa, Sports Car Club Am. (named Rookie of Yr., 1971, co-driver Mexican nat. rally champion 1971, So. Pacific div. rally champion 1971). Patentee in chem. engring. Home: 2640 B St San Diego CA 92102 Office: PO Box 20217 San Diego CA 92120

ARNOLD, WALTER FRANK, adminstrv. mech. engr.; b. Rochester, N.Y., Nov. 2, 1920; s. Ernst and Margaret (Charcholla) A.; B.S. in Metall. Engring., U. Ill., 1942; m. Ione Stroud, Dec. 28, 1953; 1 dau., Jan. Asst. metallurgist Syming Gould Corp., Rochester, N.Y., 1942-43; sect. leader, metallurgy, Los Alamos (N.Mex.) Sci. Lab., 1943-53; asst. assoc. dir. engring., Lawrence Livermore Lab., Livermore Calif., 1953—. Mem. civil def. advisory com. City of Pleasanton (Calif.), 1961, Mem. master plan com., 1962, mem. appeal bd., 1964-66, mem. planning commn., 1966-69, mem. zoning ordnance com., 1967; bd. govs. County of Alameda (Calif.), 1962-64. Recipient commendation City of Pleasanton, 1969; registered profl. engr., Calif. Mem. ASME, Soc. Mfg. Engrs. Democrat. Lutheran. Home: 841 Abbie St Pleasanton CA 94566

ARNOLD, WILLIAM WRIGHT, III, hospital administrator; b. Long Beach, Calif., Dec. 10, 1948; s. William Busey and Virginia Eloise (Moore) A.; m. Joan Doell, Dec. 18, 1971; children—Brandon Wright, Justin Menefee. B.A. in English and Bus., U. Wash., 1972; M.H.A., UCLA, 1974. Asst. adminstr. Santa Barbara (Calif.) Cottage Hosp., 1975-79; asst. dir. Stanford U. Hosp., Palo Alto, Calif., 1979-82, assoc. dir., 1982—. Bd. dirs. St. Joseph's Hosp., San Francisco. Mem. Am. Coll. Hosp. Adminstrs. Office: 300 Pasteur Dr C-204 Palo Alto CA 94305

ARNOLD, WILMA JEAN, aerospace corporation manager; b. Detroit, July 11, 1952; d. William Henry and Geneva Vivian (Shaw) A.; 1 dau., Donna Louise Bellamy. B.S., U. Akron, 1974; M.A., U. No. Colo., 1977. Tchr., Wooster (Ohio) City Schs., 1974-75, Sheridan Sch. Dist., Englewood, Colo., 1975-76, Cherry Creek Sch. Dist., Englewood, 1975-76, coordinator, 1977-79; job devel. specialist Rehab. Specialists, Inc., Denver, 1979; mgr. employment practices and coll. relations Ball Aerospace Systems Div., Boulder, 1979—. Mem. adv. council U. Colo., Boulder, 1980—; adv. mem. Urban League Met. Denver, 1982—; bd. dirs. N.E. Denver Women's Resource Ctr.; Goodwill Industries, 1971—. Recipient Rocky Mountain Women at Work award, 1983; U. Colo. Disting. Service award, 1983. Mem. Am. Assn. Affirmative Action (dir. Region VIII), Am. Assn. Female Execs., Bus. adv. Council Jefferson County, Boulder County Pvt. Industry Council, Colo. Black Women for Polit. Action, Zeta Phi Beta. Democrat. Home: 2984 S Argonne St Aurora CO 80013 Office: PO Box 1062 Boulder CO 80306

ARNST, ALBERT, editor, forester; b. Portland, Oreg., July 9, 1909; s. David and Alwina (Lorenz) A.; B.S. in Forestry, Oreg. State U., 1931; m. Della Coleen Irwin, May 1, 1939; children—Audrey Karen, Robert Craig, Rosemary. Forester, Forest Service, U.S. Dept. Agr., Portland, Oreg., 1931-35, Medford, Oreg., 1935-36, Lakeview, Oreg., 1937, public info. officer, Washington, 1962-75, with Soil Conservation Service, Dayton, Spokane and Sedro-Woolley, (all in Wash.), 1937-45, Corvallis and Portland, Oreg., 1941-43; sales rep Skagit Steel & Iron Works, Sedro-Woolley, 1945-46; public info. rep. Weyerhaeuser Co., Tacoma, 1946-52; editor Timberman mag., Portland, 1952-53; editor Miller Freeman Publs., Portland, 1954-62; mng. editor Western Conservation Jour., Portland, 1975-82. Fellow Soc. Am. Foresters (50-yr. mem.); mem. Soil Conservation Soc. Am., Internat. Assn. Bus. Communicators (Rodney Adair Meml. award 1978, pres. 1962, 71, 79, named Communicator of Yr. 1966 nat. Pres.'s award 1983), Nat. Press Club, Nat. Assn. Govt. Communicators, Willamette Writers. Democrat. Clubs: Lions, Foggy Bottom (pres. 1971) (Washington). Contbr. articles on forestry to profl. jours. Address: 2430 NE Stanton Portland OR 97212

ARONOFF, CAROL ARMSTRONG, city librarian; b. Denver, Dec. 3, 1945; d. William F. and Barbara J. (Strong) Armstrong; m. Richard N. Aronoff, Apr. 29, 1978. B.A., UCLA, 1967, M.L.S., 1968. Reference librarian Santa Monica (Calif.) Pub. Library, 1968-72, head borrowers' services, 1972-74, city librarian, 1974—. Mem. gen. adv. bd. Santa Monica Coll., 1975—; elder Bel Air Presbyn. Ch., 1979-81, deacon, 1983-84; mem. adv. council UCLA Library Sch., 1981—; chmn. Met. Co-op. Library System, 1979. Mem. ALA, Calif. Library Assn. (pres. 1982, chmn. forum coordinating com. 1976-77), Congress Calif. Pub. Library Systems (chmn. 1980), League Calif. Cities (revenue and taxation policy com. 1983—), Freedom to Read Found. Republican. Office: Santa Monica Pub Library 1343 6th St Santa Monica CA 90401

ARONOFSKY, ALLAN MARVIN, water treatment professional; b. San Francisco, July 15, 1949; s. Norman and Ann Sylvia (Levitsky) A.; m. Suzanne Joan Collins, May 6, 1972; children—Gina, Deborah. Student City Coll. San Francisco, 1967-68, Ohlone Coll., 1974, 75. Lic. water treatment plant operator, Calif. Jr. stationary engr. San Francisco Water Dept., 1974-75; plant operator Alameda County (Calif.) Flood Control Dist., 1975-76; water treatment plant operator Alameda County Water Dist., 1976—; pres. bd. Lake Vera Mut. Water Co. Trustee, United Way of Bay Area; chmn. property mgmt. com. Alameda-Contra Costa council Camp Fire, Inc., Nevada City, Calif. Recipient cert. of appreciation Alameda-Contra Costa council Camp Fire, Inc., 1982. Mem. Am. Waterworks Assn., Bay Area Waterworks Assn. Office: 38050 Fremont Blvd Fremont CA 94536

ARONSON, HILLEL SAMUEL, accountant; b. Mpls., Apr. 12, 1931; s. David and Bertha (Friedman) A.; m. Diane Fern Weinberg, Apr. 6, 1952 (div.); children—Naomi Palmor, Debra Isaac, Esther, Judith, Jacqueline. B.B.A., U. Minn., 1951; M.Hebrew Lit., Jewish Theol. Sem., 1957. C.P.A., Calif. Contract termination officer Aeroquip Corp., Los Angeles, 1957-59; staff acct. Gold, Mason & Wilder, Beverly Hills, Calif., 1959-61, Orrin Kabaker & Co., Los Angeles, 1961-62; ptnr. Elmer Fox, Westheimer & Co. and predecessor cos. Orrin Kabaker & Co., Kabaker, Aronson & Leve, Westheimer, Fine, Berger & Co., Los Angeles, 1963-77; tax ptnr. Touche, Ross & Co., Los Angeles, 1977—. Bd. dirs. United Synagogue Am., v.p. Pacific S.W. region, 1968-76; bd. dirs. Temple Beth Am, v.p., 1977-79; bd. dirs. Akiba Acad., 1968—, pres. 1971-74; bd. dirs. U. Judaism, 1971—, chmn. audit and budget com.; bd. dirs. Jewish Fedn. Council Greater Los Angeles, 1980—, treas. 1981—, chmn. audit and fiscal mgmt. com. 1981—, vice chmn. bur. Jewish edn., mem. budget and planning com. Mem. Am. Inst. C.P.A.s, Calif. Soc. C.P.A.s, Beverly Hills Estate Planning Council (pres. 1977-78). Democrat. Jewish. Office: Touche Ross & Co 3700 Wilshire Blvd Los Angeles CA 90010

ARONSON, WILLIAM JORDAN, obstetrician, gynecologist; b. Boston, Apr. 30, 1930; s. Hyman Arnold and Esther Rhoda (Davidson) A.; A.B., Harvard, 1951; M.S., Mass. Inst. Tech., 1953; M.D., Columbia, 1963; m. Gisele Ellen Leiser, May 30, 1962; children—Peter Anthony, Neal Gregory. Intern, Harbor Gen. Hosp., Torrance, Calif., 1963-64; resident Stanford (Calif.) U. Hosp., 1964-67, mem. staff, 1967—; practice medicine, specializing in obstetrics and gynecology, Palo Alto, Calif., 1967—; clin. asso. prof. Stanford U. Sch. Medicine, 1975—. Served with USNR, 1953-57. Diplomate Am. Bd. Obstetrics and Gynecology. Fellow Am. Coll. Obstetricians and Gynecologists; mem. Am. Fertility Soc., Pacific Coast Fertility Soc., Peninsula Gynecologic Soc., San Francisco Gynecologic Soc., Santa Clara County Med. Soc. Home: 570 Coleridge Ave Palo Alto CA 94301 Office: 900 Welch Rd Palo Alto CA 94304

ARRIGA, DALE JOSEPHINE, optician; b. Binghamton, N.Y., Nov. 6, 1954; d. Parker B. and Verna J. (Roscoe) Raphael; m. Rudy Arriga, Apr. 26, 1976; 1 dau., Carolyn Alicia. Student So. Calif. Coll. Optometry, Cerritos Coll., 1981—. Lic. optician, Calif. Lab. asst. Vista Labs Phoenix, 1976; optometrist asst. Dr. Rogoway, Stonewood, Downey, Calif., 1977-80; optician, mgr. Drs. Fishberg & Golstone, Norwalk, Calif., 1980-82; optician, mgr. Frame & Lens, Long Beach, Calif., 1982—; vision screener community schs. Mem. Am. Optometric Assn. (paraoptometric sect.). Roman Catholic. Home: 13329 Bixler St Downey CA 90240 Office: Frame & Lens 5305 E 2d St Suite 103 Long Beach CA 90803

ARRIOLA, DAVID BRUCE, hotel marketing executive; b. Winnemucca, Nev., June 18, 1950; s. Mario M. and Barbara M. (Metcalf) A.; m. Elizabeth S. Peterson, Apr. 28, 1979. B.A. U. Nev., Reno, 1973; postgrad., Ariz. State U., 1979. Dir. pub. relations Mt. Rose Resort, Reno, Nev., 1971-73; dir. mktg. Heavenly Valley Ski Resort, Lake Tahoe, Calif., 1973-75; dir. mktg. Crested Butte (Colo.) Devel. Corp., 1975-77; gen. sales mgr. Best Western Internat., Inc., Phoenix, Ariz., 1977—. Mem. Fiesta Bowl Com., 1983-84. Mem. Phoenix Valley of the Sun Visitors and Conv. Bur. (mktg. com. 1981-83), Am. Bus. Assn. (travel adv. com. 1982—). Republican. Office: Best Western Internat 6201 N 24th Pkwy Phoenix AZ 85064

ARRIS, DAN M., educator, school counselor; b. Nigeria, July 28, 1937; s. Dogo M. and Ugoro A. (Tamida) A.; married; 1 dau., Melissa. B.S., Bethany Bible Coll., Santa Cruz, Calif., 1970; M.A., San Francisco State U., 1976; Ph.D. in Ednl. Psychology, U. San Francisco, 1983. Cert. tchr., counselor Calif. Documentation clk. States Steamship Co., San Francisco, 1970-74; dir. metro-services Golden Gate council Camp Fire Girls Inc., San Francisco, 1974-77; tchr. San Francisco Unified Sch. Dist., 1977-79; counselor Challenge to Learning, San Francisco, 1979-81; asst. dir. Rainbow Sch., Daly City, Calif., 1981—. Mem. Am. Personnel and Guidance Assn., Calif. Personnel and Guidance Assn. Democrat. Author: (autobiography) A Dauntless Journey.

ARROW, KENNETH JOSEPH, economist; b. N.Y.C., Aug. 23, 1921; s. Harry I. and Lillian (Greenberg) A.; B.S. in Social Sci., CCNY, 1940; M.A., Columbia U., 1941, Ph.D., 1951, D.Sc., D.Sc. (hon.), M.A. (hon.), Harvard U., 1968; LL.D. (hon.), U. Chgo., 1967, CUNY, 1972, Hebrew U. Jerusalem, 1975, U. Pa., 1976; D.Social and Econ. Scis. (hon.), U. Vienna (Austria), 1971; D.Social Scis. (hon.), Yale U., 1974; Doctor (hon.), Université René Descartes, Paris, 1974; Dr.Pol. (hon.), U. Helsinki, 1976; m. Selma Schweitzer, Aug. 31, 1947; children—David Michael, Andrew. Research asso. Cowles Commn. for Research in Econs., 1947-49; asst. prof. econs. U. Chgo., 1948-49; acting asst. prof. econs. and statistics Stanford U., 1949-50, asso. prof., 1950-53, prof. econs. and statistics, ops. research, 1953-68; prof. econs. Harvard U., 1968-74, James Bryant Conant univ. prof., 1974-79; exec. head dept. econs. Stanford U., 1954-56, acting exec. head dept., 1962-63, Joan Kenney prof. econs. and prof. ops. research, 1979—; economist Council Econ. Advisers, U.S. Govt., 1962; cons. RAND Corp. Served as capt. AUS, 1942-46. Social Sci. Research fellow, 1952; fellow Center for Advanced Study in the Behavioral Scis., 1956-57; fellow Churchill Coll., Cambridge, Eng., 1963-64, 70, 73; Guggenheim fellow, 1972-73. Recipient John Bates Clark medal Am. Econ. Assn., 1957; Alfred Nobel Meml. prize in econ. scis., 1972. Fellow Am. Acad. Arts and Scis. (v.p. 1979-81), Econometric Soc. (v.p. 1955, pres. 1956), Am. Statis. Assn., Inst. Math. Stats., Am. Econ. Assn. (exec. com. 1967-69, pres. 1973); mem. Nat. Acad. Scis., Internat. Soc. Inventory Research (pres.), Am. Philos. Soc., Inst. Mgmt. Scis. (pres. 1963, chmn. council 1964), Finnish Acad. Scis.

(fgn. hon.), Brit. Acad. (corr.), Western Econ. Assn. (pres. 1980-81), AAAS (chmn. sect. K, 1982—). Author: Social Choice and Individual Values, 1951; Essays in the Theory of Risk Bearing, 1971; The Limits of Organization, 1974; co-author: Mathematical Studies in Inventory and Production, 1958; Studies in Linear and Nonlinear Programming, 1958; Time Series Analysis of Inter-industry Demands, 1959; Public Investment, The Rate of Return and Optimal Fiscal Policy, 1971; General Competitive Analysis, 1971; Studies in Resource Allocation Processes, 1977. Office: Dept Econs Stanford U Stanford CA 94305

ARTERBURN, JAMES DAVID, hosp. adminstr.; b. Sandwich, Ill., Aug. 18, 1942; s. James Brown and Norma Lee (Nelson) A.; B.S., U. Nebr., 1964; M.P.A., San Diego State U., 1972; M.P.H., UCLA, 1975; m. Doris Yvonne Klein, July 13, 1968; children—James Eric, Mathew Christopher. Budget analyst Chief Adminstrv. Office County of Los Angeles, 1970-71; asst. adminstr. Rancho Los Amigos Hosp., Downey, Calif., 1971-74; asst. adminstr. Orthopaedic Hosp., Los Angeles, 1974-80, v.p. adminstrv. affairs, 1980-82, exec. v.p., 1982—. Bd. dirs. United Way Credit Union, 1975-81; fund raiser Torrance-S. Bay YMCA, 1978-79. Served with USN, 1964-69. Mem. Assn. Western Hosps., Health Care Execs. So. Calif., Am. Coll. Hosp. Adminstrs. Lutheran. Office: 2400 S Flower St Los Angeles CA 90007

ARTHUR, GREER MARTIN, JR., maritime container leasing firm executive; b. Champaign, Ill., Feb. 15, 1935; s. Greer Martin and Olive Loretta (Simard) A.; m. Veronica Lattman, Nov. 30, 1968; children—Alexandra, Vincent, Tanya, Greer III. B.A., Lafayette Coll., 1956; LL.B., Columbia U., 1960. Account exec. tng. program Young & Rubicam, 1957-58; assoc. Havens, Wandless, Stitt & Tighe, N.Y.C., 1961-62; mgmt. cons. McKinsey & Co., 1962-66; asst. to v.p. internat. Scovil Mfg. Co., Waterbury, Conn.; internat. market mgr. Scovil France, Paris, market mgr. Hamilton Beach div. Scovil, Waterbury, 1967-69; pres., chief exec. officer SSI Container Corp., subs. Itel Corp., San Francisco, 1969-73; pres., chief exec. officer, dir. Trans Ocean Leasing Corp., San Bruno, Calif., 1973—. Treas., trustee Phillips Brooks Sch., Menlo Park, Calif., 1980—; mem. Lafayette Coll. Nat. Council, 1980—. Mem. Assn. Corp. Growth, Bus. Edn. Council, Inst. Internat. Container Lessors, N.Y. State Bar (pres. 1982-84), Young Pres. Orgn. Clubs: Bankers, World Trade (San Francisco); Club at World Trade Center (N.Y.C.). Office: 851 Traeger Ave San Bruno CA 94066

ARTHUR, JEANNE LENORE, lawyer; b. Los Angeles, Apr. 21, 1939; d. James Leland and LeNora (Barba) A.; B.A., Stanford U., 1964; J.D., U. Santa Clara, 1967. Admitted to Calif. bar, 1967; assoc. Morton P. MacLeod, Los Altos, Calif., 1968-70, Skornia, Rosenblum & Gyemant, Palo Alto, Calif., 1970-72; pvt. practice law, Palo Alto, 1972-82; ptnr. Arthur, Pennix & Thompson, Palo Alto, 1983—. Mem. adv. com. Community Found. Santa Clara County, 1975—. Mem. State Bar Calif. (com. public affairs 1979—, chmn. 1982-83), Am., Santa Clara County (trustee 1974-75, 77-78, treas. 1981), Palo Alto Area (pres. 1977-78) bar assns., Peninsula Estate Planning Council (dir. 1973-76), Palo Alto Fin. Planning Forum (pres. 1975-76). Assoc. editor: U. Santa Clara Law Rev., 1966-67. Office: 385 Sherman Ave Palo Alto CA 94306

ARTHUR, JOHN SCRIPTURE, thoracic and vascular surgeon; b. Rome, N.Y., Nov. 30, 1942; s. William Maurice and Ruth Priscilla (Scripture) A.; A.B., Dartmouth Coll., 1964; M.D., Albany Med. Coll., 1968; m. Ellen Doris Creeley, Apr. 29, 1967; children—Kelly Allison, Rachael Kimberly, Jason Andrew, Rebecca Susan, Benjamin Douglas, Sara Gamble, Luke William. Intern in surgery U. Wash. Affiliated Hosps., 1968-69, resident in gen., thoracic and cardiovascular surgery, 1969-75; practice medicine specializing in thoracic and vascular surgery, Bremerton, Wash., 1977—; mem. staff Harrison Meml. Hosp., Bremerton. Served with M.C., USN, 1975-77. Diplomate Am. Bd. Surgery. Mem. U. Wash. Surg. Soc., Kitsap County Med. Soc. Club: Bremerton Tennis and Swim. Office: 1225 Campbell Way Suite 101 Bremerton WA 98310

ARTHUR, PAUL KEITH, electronic engr.; b. Kansas City, Mo., Jan. 14, 1931; s. Walter B. and Frieda J. (Burckhardt) A.; m. Joy N. Lim, Apr. 26, 1958; children—Gregory V., Lia F. Student Ohio No. U., 1947, Taylor U., Upland, Ind., 1948-49; B.S.E.E., Purdue U., 1956; postgrad. N.Mex. State U., 1957-78; Registered profl. engr., N.Mex. With White Sands Missile Range, N.Mex., 1956—, electronic engr. field engring. group missile flight surveillance office, 1956-60, chief field engring. group, 1960-62, project engr. Pershing weapon system Army Missile Test and Evaluation Directorate, 1962-74, chief high altitude air def. projects br., 1974-82, chief air def. materiel test div., 1982—, mem. exec. devel. group. Active Mil Gracias Soc. Served with USN, 1949-53; served to capt. USNR, 1954—. Decorated Meritorious Service medal U.S. Navy; Navy Achievement medal. Mem. Am. Def. Preparedness Assn. (past pres.), AIAA (past vice chmn.), Assn. Old Crows (dir.), Naval Res. Assn., Res. Officers Assn. (pres. 1983-84), Am. Soc. Naval Engrs., Naval Inst., Purdue Alumni Assn. (past pres.), N.Mex. State U. Alumni Assn., Sierra Club, Bujutsukan Acad. Martial Arts. Author numerous plans and reports on weapon system tests and evaluation. Home: 2050 San Acacio Las Cruces NM 88001

ARTHUR, RICHARD JOSEPH, financial executive; b. Logansport, Ind., Dec. 19, 1924; s. Robert Jamieson and Mary (Grady) A.; m. Marilyn Anita Horn, 1956; m. 2d, Donna Elizabeth Braunecker, Oct. 4, 1967; children—Susan, Terry, Mala, Kevin, Mary. Mgmt. trainee Coast Fed. Savs. and Loan Assn., 1953-57; v.p., dir. chief fin. officer World Savs. and Loan Assn., Lynwood, Calif. and TransWorld Fin. Co., Los Angeles, 1957-75; pres., asst. mgr. Mercury Savs. and Loan Assn., Huntington Beach, Calif., 1975-80; pres., mng. officer, dir. Palm Springs Savs. and Loan Assn. (Calif.), 1980—. Mem. Calif. Savs. and Loan League (dir.), Fin. Mgrs. Soc. Savs. Insts. (past nat. pres.). Office: 103 N Palm Canyon Dr Palm Springs CA 92262

ARTIS, EDWARD ALLEN, mortgage and financing consultant, educator; b. Highland Park, Ill., July 9, 1945; s. Edgar and Lenore (Healy) A.; student U. Calif., Berkeley, 1966-68, Glendale Community Coll., 1974; LL.D. (hon.), U. Saigon, 1972. Dist. mgr. Jr. Achievement So. Calif., N. Hollywood, 1973-75; realtor asso. Stevenson, Dilbeck Inc. Realtors, Glendale, Calif., 1975-78; asst. treas. Advance Mortgage Corp., Van Nuys, Calif., 1976-78; exec. v.p., prin. Classic Fin. Corp., Panorama City, Calif., 1978-79; prin., chief exec. officer Ed Artis & Assos., mortgage brokerage, real estate devel., syndications, Glendale, 1979—; fin. cons. Western Fin. Diversified Ltd., Encino, Calif., 1981—; prof. real estate fin. Los Angeles City Coll., 1980—. Bd. dirs. Nat. Research Found. on Aging, 1975-80; lifetime benefactor John F. Kennedy Spt. Warfare Mus., Ft. Bragg, N.C. Served as Spl. Forces Green Beret, U.S. Army, 1963-73. Decorated Silver Star (3), D.F.C., Bronze Star (3), Purple Heart (3); recipient Distinguished Service award City of Concord, Calif., 1972; named an Outstanding Young Man, Calif. Jaycees, 1971, Calif. Humanitarian of Yr., 1973. Mem. Calif. Jaycees (spl. presdl. asst. on child abuse 1974-76, pres. internat. USA Mexico Border Fedn. 1974), Glendale C. of C., Calif. Assn. Realtors, Nat. Assn. Realtors, Calif. Mortgage Bankers Assn., Assn. Profl. Mortgage Women, Glendale Bd. Realtors, Glendale Days of Verdugos Assn., Am. Fedn. Tchrs. Republican. Address: 24343 Vanowen St Canoga Park CA 91307

ARTUSY, RAYMOND LONGINO, consulting geologist, consulting economist; b. Galveston, Tex., July 25, 1916; s. Max and Lena (Magee) A.; A.B., U. So. Calif., 1937, M.S., 1939; A.B., St. Mary's U., San Antonio, 1952; postgrad. (Stanolind fellow 1952-54) La. State U., 1952-55, Ph.D., 1960; post doctoral studies in Econs., U. Colo., 1964-68; m. Jane Burks Cox, Oct. 7, 1937; 1 son, Max. Research geologist Tidewater Assn. Oil Co., 1937-38; sr. research geologist Union Producing Co., 1939-41; pilot Pan Am. World Airways, 1945-47; capt. AVIANCA, 1946-47; regional geologist Ryan, Hays & Burke, 1949-50; asst. prof. geology St. Mary's U., San Antonio, 1950-52; asst. prof. Tex. Christian U., Ft. Worth, 1955-56; v.p. Univ. Oil & Gas Corp., Houston, 1956-57; asst. prof. geology N.Y. U., N.Y.C., 1957-59; chief geologist Dorfman Prodn. Co., Dallas, 1959-61; pvt. cons. geologist, Boulder, Colo., and Galveston, Tex., VAM Co., from 1950; prof. econs. Black Hills State Coll., Spearfish, S.D., from 1970; asso. prof. econs. No. State Coll., Aberdeen, S.D., 1968-70; research asso. geology Pa. State U., 1961-62; fellow geography U. Calif., Berkeley, 1962-63; lectr. U. Oreg., Eugene, 1963-64. Bd. govs. St. Mary's U., San Antonio, 1953-62. Served to maj. with USAF, 1941-45, 47-49. Decorated D.F.C. Mem. Am. Assn. Petroleum Geologists, Soc. Econ. Paleontologists and Mineralogists, Paleontol. Soc., Geol. Soc. Am., Am. Assn. U. Profs., Assn. Am. Geographers, Air Force Assn., Am. Geog. Soc., Nat. Rifle Assn., N.Y. Acad. Scis., Am. Econs. Assn., Va. Mil. Inst. Alumni Assn. No. Calif. (v.p. 1979—), Sigma Xi, Alpha Tau Omega, Phi Delta Kappa, Phalanx Frat. Republican. Baptist. Mason, Eagle. Home: 1920 Latham St Mountain View CA 94040 Deceased July 26, 1982.

ARUNDEL, IAN BRESSON, art dealer; b. Mitchell, S.D., Feb. 22, 1914; s. Charles Henry and Mary Porter (Bresson) A.; student U. Mich., 1934-37; m. Millie Lewis Waugh, Nov. 8, 1952; children—Ann Waugh, Colin Waugh. Restorer paintings and art objects, Detroit, 1937-43; dealer antique art, conservator, Los Angeles, 1945-52; art dealer, appraiser, Los Angeles, 1952—; expert primitive tribal art, appraiser U.S. govt.; exhibited tribal art in group shows at Santa Barbara (Calif.) Mus. Art, Los Angeles County Mus. Art, Miami U., Pomona Coll., U. Calif. at Fullerton, Otis Art Inst. Served with AUS, 1943-45. Fellow Am. Inst. for Conservation Historic and Artistic Works; mem. Smithsonian Instn., Brit. Mus. Soc., Archives Am. Art, Mus. Alliance Los Angeles County Mus., Victorian Soc. Office: 3921 SW Dakota St Portland OR 97221

ARY, BONNITA ELLEN, bookkeeper, govt. ofcl.; b. Walden, Colo., July 26, 1932; d. Burney Grover and Maude Velisa (Bulis) Dowdell; m. Leo D. Ary, Aug. 16, 1950 (div.); children—Kristy L. Ary Ackerson, R. Craig. Student pub. schs., Jackson County, Colo.; cert. med. asst. Am. Assn. Med. Assts. Sec., Mountain Park REA, Walden, 1950-51; dep. treas. Jackson County, Walden, 1955-61, registrar of vital stats., 1965—; med. asst., Walden, 1961-66; bus. mgmt. assn. U.S. Forest Service, Walden, 1966—; bookkeeper for small businesses, 1950—. Mem. Walden Sch. Bd., 1971-79; chmn. fin. bd. North Park Community United Meth. Ch., 1980—. Recipient cert. of merit U.S. Forest Service, 1978, 81. Home: 496 McKinley St Walden CO 80480 Office: 612 5th St Walden CO 80480

ARZONETTI, WILLIAM JOHN, advertising company executive; b. Mt. Vernon, N.Y., Aug. 3, 1931; s. Nicholas Joseph and Rose Pauline (Graziano) A.; m. Marie Milani, June 28, 1954; m. 2d, Lois Ann Caldwell, Apr. 29, 1978; children—Rosemarie, Nicholas, Lee. B.A. in Fine Arts, Pratt Inst., 1956. Art dir. Daniel & Charles, N.Y.C., 1960-63; art dir. McCann-Erickson, N.Y.C., 1963-64; v.p., art dir. Doyle, Dane Bernbach, N.Y.C., 1964-77; v.p., art dir. McDonald & Little, Atlanta, 1977-78; sr. v.p., creative dir. Doyle, Dane Bernbach (Milici-Valenti Advt.), Honolulu, 1979—. With U.S. Army, 1951-54. Recipient Gold Medal, N.Y. Art Dirs. Club, 1965, Atlanta Art Dirs. Club, 1978, Honolulu Advt. Fedn. show, 1981; Advt. Age's 100 Best TV Commercials, 1965. Mem. Honolulu Advt. Fedn. (chmn. awards com. 1981), Am. Advt. Fedn. (judge students advt. competition).

ARZOUMANIAN, ARAM S., electromech. engr.; b. Cairo, Mar. 16, 1917; came to U.S., 1966, naturalized, 1974; s. Sarkis and Makrouhi (Melkonian) A.; French baccalaureat in Math., Coll. St. Joseph, Cairo, 1936; Electromech. Engr. (Master's degree) with mention excellent, Poly. Inst., Yerevan, Armenia, 1952; m. Daraklian Rosa, Oct. 1, 1950; children—Sarkis, Margaret. Sr. engr. designer Electrotech. Plant, Yerevan, 1952-57; chief engr. Research and Devel. Inst. of Computers, Yerevan, 1957-66; sr. project engr. Bryant Computer Products, Walled Lake, Mich., 1966-67; mem. tech. staff Dataproduct Corp., Woodland Hills, Calif., 1968—, now advance developer spl. projects. Mem. Evereg Fenesse Ednl. Soc. (pres. central com.). Developer disc printer for banking ops.; developed 1st memory magnetic drum with flying heads, USSR, 1962; contbr. tech. papers to profl. publs.; patentee in field. Home: 24326 Caris St Woodland Hills CA 91367 Office: Dataproducts Corp 6250 Canoga Ave Woodland Hills CA 91365

ASANO, FAYE HIROMI, foodservice specialist; b. Sacramento, Sept. 26, 1955; d. Hiroko Asano. B.S. in Food Sci. and Nutrition, Colo. State U., 1977. Summer cons. child nutrition Colo. Dept. Edn., 1976; foodservice cons. E. Central Bd. Coop. Ednl. Services, Limon, Colo., 1977-79; No. Colo. nutrition educator Dairy Council Inc., Thornton, Colo., 1979-81; Colo.-Wyo. foodservice specialist Western Dairyfarmers' Promotion Assn., Thornton, 1981—. Mem. Colo.-Wyo. Restaurant Assn., Home Economists in Bus., Am. Home Econ. Assn., Am. Dietetic Assn., Colo. Sch. Food Service Assn., Am. Sch. Food Service Assn. Democrat. Buddhist. Office: 12450 N Washington Thornton CO 80241

ASANO, TAKASHI, environ. engr.; b. Sapporo, Japan, Feb. 7, 1937; s. Hiroshi and Hideko (Yanagida) A.; came to U.S., 1963, naturalized, 1969; B.S., Hokkaido U., 1959; M.S. in Engring., U. Calif. at Berkeley, 1965; Ph.D., U. Mich., 1970; m. Holly Asano. Engr., Maruzen Engring., Inc., Japan, 1959-63; engr. State of Calif. Dept. Water Resources, 1965-67; asst. prof. dept. civil engring. Mont. State U., Bozeman, 1972-75; asso. prof. dept. civil engring. Wash. State U., Pullman, 1975-78; with Office Water Recycling, Calif. Water Resources Control Bd., Sacramento, 1978—; research in unit processes of environ. engring. NATO fellow Cambridge (Eng.) U., 1977; registered profl. engr., Calif., Mich., Wash. Mem. Am. Assn. Environ. Engring. Profs., ASCE, Water Pollution Control Fedn. Club: Backyard Wilderness Program. Author: (with R.L. Sanks) Land Treatment and Disposal of Municipal and Industrial Wastewater, 1976. Home: 1125 Dartmouth Pl Davis CA 95616 Office: Office Water Recycling Calif Water Resources Bd PO Box 100 Sacramento CA 95801

ASAY, E. VERL, state senator; b. Castle Dale, Utah, Apr. 21, 1922; s. Joseph Edward and Susan Sariah (Johnson) A.; ed. public schs.; m. La Vaun Heaton, Sept. 7, 1942; children—Verla, Kaye, Sharon, Joseph. With Verl Asay Industries, Salt Lake City; mem. Utah Senate, 1979—. Served with U.S. Army, 1942. Mormon. Home: 4857 S 1950 W Salt Lake City UT 84118 Office: 3480 S 500 W Salt Lake City UT 84115

ASBAHR, ROGER LEE, counselor, therapist; b. Corvallis, Oreg., June 21, 1950; s. Lynn E. and Vera F. (Reger) A.; m. Molly O'Hearn, Dec. 25, 1982. B.A. in Social Scis., Marylhurst Coll., 1981; M.S. in Counseling, Western Oreg. State Coll., 1982. Cert. Nat. Bd. Cert. Counselors. Part-time instr. Linn Benton Community Coll., Corvallis, 1978—; pvt. practice counseling Asbahr & Assoc., Corvallis, 1979—; dir. Cascade Hypnosis and Counseling Ctr. Vol. Community Outreach, Corvallis, 1981—, Oreg. State U. Exptl. Coll. Mem. Am. Personnel and Guidance Assn., Oreg. Personnel and Guidance Assn., Assn. Humanistic Edn. and Devel., Am. Mental Health Counselors Assn. Office: 1873 NW King Blvd Corvallis OR 97330

ASBELL, CHARLES WARREN, agronomy educator, university administrator; b. Corona, Calif., Nov. 1, 1934; s. Ferriss Edward and Clara Ellen (Hughes) A.; m. Marilyn Ann Ewers, Aug. 19, 1955; children—Caryn E., Tracie L., Kimberly A. B.S., Oreg. State U., 1957; M.S., U. Calif.-Riverside, 1966, Ph.D., 1976. Staff research assoc. U. Calif.-Riverside, 1957-78; assoc. prof. agronomy plant and soil sci. dept. Calif. State Poly. U.-Pomona, 1978-81, assoc. dean Sch. Agr., 1981—. Vice pres. bd. dirs. Riverside Christian Day Sch., Woodcrest Christian High Sch. Mem. Am. Phytopathol. Soc., Am. Soc. Agronomy. Republican. Contbr. articles to profl. jours. Home: 16207 Olive Ave Riverside CA 92504 Office: Sch Agr Calif State Poly U 3801 W Temple Blvd Pomona CA 91768

ASCHER, ANN FINE, interior design firm executive; b. Stamford, Conn., June 2, 1939; d. Joseph and Adele (Abzug) Fine; student Barnard Coll., 1957-58, Coll. William and Mary, 1958-59; A.B., UCLA, 1962; postgrad. Chouinard Art Inst., 1965-66; m. Everett Ascher, June 25, 1958; 1 dau., Allison. Founder, pres. Ann Ascher Interiors, Los Angeles, 1965—; sec. Sonatina Music, Inc.; mem. adv. bd. Am. Internat. Bank, Los Angeles; dir. Ruthanne Music Co., Inc. Bd. govs. Coro Assos., 1977—; sec., bd. dirs. So. Calif. Center for Non Profit Mgmt., 1978—; founder, mem. Blue Ribbon 400 of Los Angeles Music Center; mem. adv bd. undergrad. and grad. interior design dept. Woodbury U., Los Angeles; sec. Founders Club of City of Hope, 1976-77; chmn. bd. dirs. So. Calif. Center Non-Profit Mgmt. 1982-83, active polit. fund raising; mem. President's Adv. Council on Pvt. Sector Initiatives, 1983—. Mem. World Affairs Council, Town Hall. Republican. Contbr. articles to profl. jours. Office: Ann Ascher Interiors 201 S Beverly Glen Blvd Los Angeles CA 90024

ASCHER, EVERETT S., music company executive; b. N.Y.C., Apr. 3, 1936; s. Morton and Ruth (Klein) A.; m. Ann Fine, June 25, 1958; 1 dau., Allison. B.A., U. Rochester, 1957. Pres., Regent Recorded Music, Emil Ascher, Inc., Los Angeles, 1959—; vice-chmn. Westwood Bancorp., Los Angeles, 1982-84. Trustee U. Rochester; v.p., bd. dirs. Los Angeles Chamber Orch.; founder Los Angeles Music Ctr.; mem. Citizens Adv. Commn. for 1984 Olympics; bd. dirs. Homby-Westwood Property Owners Assn. Served to lt. (j.g.) USN, 1957-59. Mem. ASCAP, Western Los Angeles Regional C. of C. (v.p.), Music Ctr. Frat. of Friends (charter). Republican. Club: Regency (Los Angeles). Office: 6255 Sunset Blvd Suite 911 Los Angeles CA 90028

ASEBEDO, MERRI LOUISE, educator; b. Amherst, Tex., Oct. 5, 1953; d. Lazaro and Guadalupe (Martinez) Asebedo; m. Stephen R. Griego, June 24, 1977; 1 son, Scot Jeremy; m. 2d, Edward William Piorkowski, Mar. 26, 1983. B.S., U. N.Mex., 1976; postgrad. No. Ariz. U. Tchr. bus. edn. Albuquerque Job Corps, 1976-78; tchr. home econs. Socorro (N.Mex.) High Sch., 1978—. Mem. N.Mex. Home Econs. Assn., N.Mex. Vocat. Assn., Socorro Classroom Tchrs. Assn. Republican. Baptist. Office: Socorro High Sch Socorro NM 87801

ASH, EDWARD BRADLEY, marketing analyst; b. Pasadena, Calif., Nov. 17, 1930; s. Edward F. and Dorothy N. (Nash) A.; A.A. in Engring., Pasadena City Coll., 1946-51; B.S., UCLA, 1953; advanced nuclear engring. degree (AEC scholar) Oak Ridge Sch. Reactor Tech., 1954; m. Barbara Ann Knowles, Aug. 28, 1954; children—Gary, Carol. Research engr. Electric Boat Corp., Groton, Conn., 1954-55; with Atomic Internat. div. N.Am. Rockwell Corp., Canoga Park, Calif., 1955-73, mgr. fast breeder reactor engring., 1965-73, sr. engring. exec., corp. staff Rockwell Internat., 1973-78, dir. advanced programs Rockwell Energy Systems Group, Canoga Park, 1978-82, dir. market analysis Rockwell Space Ops., 1982—; adj. prof. dept. engring. UCLA, 1972-74; instr. nuclear course M.I.T., Cambridge, 1970. Com. chmn. Boy Scouts Am., Canoga Park, 1966-68. Registered profl. engr. Mem. Am. Nuclear Soc. Tech. Mktg. Soc. Am. Contbr. articles to profl. jours. Patentee in field. Office: 2230 E Imperial Hwy El Segundo CA 90245

ASH, JAMES WILLIAM, educator; b. Lebanon, Tenn., Dec. 6, 1935; s. James Oliver and Marjorie Valentine (McLaughlin) A.; A.A., Cumberland U., 1962; B.S., Middle Tenn. State U., 1964; M.A., San Jose State U., 1969; m. Jacklyn Rene Stratton, June 17, 1958; children—Dana Lynn, Lisa Ann, James Travis. Tchr. Santa Clara (Calif.) Unified Schs., 1964—, teaching v.p., 1971-73; pub. Santa Clara Am. newspaper, 1980-82. Active Mission City Democrats, 1968—, pres., 1968-70; asso. mem. Santa Clara County Dem. Central Com., 1969; chmn. Santa Clara Civil Service Commn., 1977-78; mem. Santa Clara Planning Commn., 1980-81, Santa Clara City Council, 1981—; pres. Tri-Cities Little League, 1975-76. Served with USN, 1954-58. Mem. United Tchrs. of Santa Clara (bd. dirs., 1971-72, Unified Schs. Needs Assessment Com., 1970-73, Edn. Policies and Planning Com., 1977—), Am. Legion (comdr. Post 419 1979-80). Baptist. Home: 3746 Hillsdale Ct Santa Clara CA 95051 Office: 1250 Pomeroy Ave Santa Clara CA 95051

ASHBAUGH, BARBARA ELAINE, insurance company advertising executive; b. Zanesville, Ohio, Oct. 4, 1950; d. Wayne and Helen (Rohrer) A.; m. Richard Carl Bossert, Dec. 12, 1971 (div.). B.A., Wittenberg U., 1972; postgrad. Foothill Coll., 1975, Skyline Coll., 1977, Mt. Union Coll., 1968. Supr. licensing Alliance AAA Club (Ohio), 1972-73; mgr. catering dept. Can. Tavern Corp., Sunnyvale, Calif., 1973-74; supr. mktg. and adminstrv. services Houghton Mifflin Co., Palo Alto, Calif., 1974-81; mgr. graphic communications Calif. Casualty Co., San Mateo, Calif., 1981—. Active Russian Hill Forum. Mem. San Francisco Advt. Club., Kappa Delta. Office: Calif Casualty Co 1900 Alameda de las Pulgas San Mateo CA 94403

ASHBY, HAL, film dir.; b. 1936. Film editor with Norman Jewison on films The Cincinnati Kid, The Russians Are Coming, The Russians Are Coming, In the Heat of the Night; asso. producer The Thomas Crown Affair, Gaily, Gaily; film dir. The Landlord, Harold and Maude, The Last Detail, Shampoo, Bound for Glory, Coming Home, Being There, Second Hand Hearts, Lookin' To Get Out. Recipient Acad. Award nominations for The Russians Are Coming (editor), Coming Home (dir.), In the Heat of the Night (editor), Bound for Glory (best picture), Coming Home (best picture). Office: care Green & Reynolds 1900 Ave of Stars Los Angeles CA 90067*

ASHBY, LUCIUS ANTONE, JR., accountant; b. Des Moines, Feb. 1, 1944; s. Lucius Antone Sr. and Ruth Mildred (Moore) A.; 1 dau., Felicia. B.S. in Bus., U. Colo., 1969; postgrad. Harvard U., 1982. C.P.A., Colo., Wash., Minn. Mgmt. trainee Grant Western Sugar, 1968-69; sr. acct. Arthur Anderson & Co., Denver, 1969-72; mng. ptnr. Ashby, Armstrong, Johnson & Co., Denver, 1973—; past pres. State of Bd. of Accountancy; chmn., past dir. Nat. Assn. Minority C.P.A. firms. Former treas. Colo. State Democratic Party; bd. dirs. Salvation Army. Served with U.S. Army, 1961-64. Recipient Nat. Assn. Black Accts. Achievement award, Barney Ford award for bus. achievement, entrepreneur award. Mem. Leadership Denver Assn., Colo. Soc. C.P.A.s (bd. dirs.), Partnership Inc. (dir.), Am. Inst. C.P.A.s, Denver C. of C. (past dir.). Home: 3861 Rosemary Way Denver CO 80237 Office: Ashby Armstrong Johnson & Co 655 Broadway Suite 800 Denver CO 80203

ASHE, C. CLYDE, data processing company executive; b. Harlem, Mont., May 1, 1934; s. Edward C. and Sarah B. (Taylor) A.; m. Armeda A. Brim, Nov. 24, 1952; children—Michael C., Linda L. Atwood. Grad. cert., Am. Inst. Banking. Commd. Joined U.S. Navy, 1952; served in Middle East, 1954; served on patrol and tng. mission, Vietnam, 1961-62; duty in Japan, 1962, resigned, 1966; v.p. First Nat. Bank of Oreg.,

Portland, Western Bancorp Data Processing Co., El Segundo, Calif., 1974-78; dir. customer support Am. Data, Portland, 1978—. Mem. Assn. Systems Mgmt (sec., treas. conf. com. 1983), Data Processing Mgmt. Assn. (past pres.). Club: Toastmasters (past pres. Datamasters). Home: 1721 SE Jacquelin Dr Hillsboro OR 97123 Office: 4550 SW Macadam Ave Portland OR 97201

ASHER, EUGENE LEON, historian, educator; b. Cleve., Nov. 23, 1929; s. Samuel H. and Dorothy Denise (LePon) A.; A.B., UCLA, 1952, M.A., 1955, Ph.D., 1958; postgrad. (Fulbright fellow) U. Paris, 1956-57, U. Toulouse, 1957; m. Bonnie Jane Anderson, June 9, 1956; children—Allyson Elizabeth, Christine Marie. Asst. prof. history U. Wichita (Kans.), 1957-59; mem. faculty history Calif. State U.-Long Beach, 1959-67, 71—, prof., chmn. dept. history, 1971-76, exec. asst. to pres., 1976-80, exec. officer, 1980—; exec. dir. KLON-FM public radio, 1981—; dir. Am. Hist. Assn. History Edn. Project, 1968-75; prof. history Ind. U., Bloomington, 1969-71. Pres., Casa Dorado Mng. Agt. Inc., Palm Springs, Calif., 1975. Vice chmn. Long Beach Am. Revolution Bicentennial Commn., 1973-76; co-chmn. history adv. panel, mem. Calif. State Social Scis. Commn., 1965-68; chmn. Joint Anglo-U.S. Commn. Confs. History, Dept. State, 1972-75. Trustee Sloan Found. Notre Dame U. Program. Am. Council Learned Socs. fellow, 1962-63, 66-67; Social Sci. Research Council grantee, 1962, 66-67; HEW grantee, 1969-75. Mem. Soc. History Edn. (chmn bd. 1972-78), Am. Hist. Assn., Nat. Council Social Studies, Orgn. Am. Historians, Societe d'Histoire Moderne et Contemporaine, Phi Beta Kappa Alumni Assn. (council Calif. 1979—, v.p. 1982—). Author: The Resistance to the Maritime Classes: the Survival of Feudalism in the France of Colbert, 1960: (with others) A Framework for the Social Sciences: Report of the Statewide Social Science Study Commission, 1968. Contbr. articles to profl. publs.; producer film: Oil: The Pioneering Years, 1978. Home: 38 58th Pl Long Beach CA 90803 Office: Office of Pres Calif State U Long Beach CA 90840

ASHER, JAMES EDWARD, cons. forester, engr.; b. Los Angeles, July 22, 1931; s. John Edward and Dorothy (Ingraham) A.; student Pasadena City Coll., 1949-50; B.S., Oreg. State U., 1954; m. Marilyn Lee Struebing, Dec. 28, 1953; children—Lynne Marie, Laure Ann. With U.S. Forest Service, San Bernardino (Calif.) Nat. Forest, summers 1950-53, forester, 1956-57; prin. James E. Asher, ACF, Cons. Forester, 1957—; capt., bn. chief, asst. chief, fire prevention officer Crest Forest Fire Protection Dist., Crestline, Calif., 1960-69, chief, 1969-71; forester Big Bear div. Golden State Bldg. Products, Redlands, 1972, timber mgr., 1972-74; mem. profl. foresters exam. com. Calif. Bd. Forestry, 1978—, vice chmn., 1982—; mem. Calif. Forest Pest Control Action Council. Vol. firewarden State of Calif., 1967—. Served with AUS, 1954-56. Recipient certificate of merit Nat. Fire Protection Assn., San Bernardino Mountains Assn.; Resolution of Commendation, County Bd. Suprs.; Forester of Year award So. Calif. sect. Soc. Am. Foresters, 1977; others. Registered profl. forester, registered profl. engr., Calif.; lic. pest control advisor, pest control operator, Calif. Mem. So. Calif. Assn. Foresters and Fire Wardens, Soc. Am. Foresters (chmn. licensing and ethics com. So. Calif. sect., chmn. elect So. Calif. 1983), Assn. Cons. Foresters, Internat. Soc. Arboriculture, Sierra-Cascade Logging Conf., Am. Forestry Assn., Tau Kappa Epsilon. Presbyterian. Club: Masons. Contbr. articles to profl. Office: PO Drawer N Lake Arrowhead CA 92352

ASHER, LAWRENCE JOSEPH, advertising executive; b. Seattle, Oct. 30, 1951; s. Lester Joseph and Sally (Lewis) A. B.A. in Sociology and Communications summa cum laude, U. Wash., 1973. Creative dir. Solkover Davidge & Jenkins, Seattle, 1974-77; sr. copywriter Ehrig & Assocs., Seattle, 1977; v.p., creative supr. John Brown & Ptnrs., Seattle, 1977-81; pres., co-creative dir. Asher Camuso & Gibbs, Seattle, 1981—. Trustee Seattle Ctr. Found., 1982—. Recipient Best in the West Competition Sweepstakes for best newspaper ad, 1980; Advt. Club of N.Y. Andy award 1980, 81; Western Art Dirs. Club West Coast Show 77 gold award for radio. Mem. Am. Advt. Fedn. (Addy awards 1977, 81). Creative work featured in Communications Arts Mag., 1981, ann. exhbn. catalogs. Home: 2146 N 38th St Seattle WA 98103 Office: Asher Camuso & Gibbs 633 Yesler Way Seattle WA 98104

ASHER, ROBERT JOSEPH, mfg. co. exec.; b. New Orleans, Aug. 6, 1944; s. Luther Leon and Shirley Mae (Covington) A.; B.S., Calif. State U., Long Beach, 1967; postgrad. U. So. Calif., 1967-68; m. Patricia Arlene Hernandez, July 1, 1972. Ops. analyst G.L. Collins Corp., Long Beach, 1967-69, applications engr., 1970-72, mktg. and sales mgr., 1972-77; gen. mgr. Pacific Air Industries, Santa Monica, Calif., 1978—; v.p., gen. mgr. AirCert Inc., Santa Monica, 1979-80; materials control mgr. Hartwell Corp., Placentia, Calif., 1980—. Mem. Am. Prodn. and Inventory Control Soc. Home: 1878 Molino Ave Signal Hill CA 90804 Office: 900 S Richfield Rd Placentia CA 92670

ASHFORD, ROBERT LOREN, data processor; b. Salina, Kans., Aug. 3, 1936; s. Robert Andrew and Mildred Nerissa (Hallam) A.; B.S., U. Md., 1960; m. Donna Jean Fox, Mar. 30, 1973; children—Kelly Jean, Jennifer Anne. Systems engr. IBM Corp., 1960-67; dir. data processing Gibbons & Reed Co., 1967-71; regional systems mgr. Basic Four Corp., 1971-74; dir. mfg. systems Gen. Automation Co., 1974-76; pres. Mfg. Mgmt. Systems, Huntington Beach, Calif., 1976-78; mgr. bus. systems div. EG&G, Inc., Idaho Falls, Idaho, 1978-80; pres. Bus. Automation, Inc., Idaho Falls, 1980-82; exec. v.p. Internat. Electronic Machinery Inc., Ft. Collins, Colo., 1982—. Served with USAF, 1956-60. Mem. Data Processing Mgmt. Assn., Assn. Computing Machinery. Republican. Presbyterian. Club: Elks. Home: PO Box 7050 Fort Collins CO 80525 Office: PO Box 1818 Fort Collins CO 80522

ASHFORTH, ALDEN, musician, educator; b. N.Y.C., May 13, 1933; m. Nancy Ann Regnier, June 12, 1956 (div. 1980); children—Robyn Richardson, Melissa Adams, Lauren Elizabeth. A.B., Oberlin Coll., 1958; Mus.B., Oberlin Conservatory, 1958; M.F.A., Princeton U., 1960, Ph.D., 1971. Instr., Princeton (N.J.) U., 1961, Oberlin (Ohio) Coll., 1961-65, NYU, 1965-66, Manhattan (N.Y.) Sch. Music, 1965; lectr. CUNY, 1966-67; asst. prof. music UCLA, 1967-72, assoc. prof., 1972-80, prof., 1980—, coordinator electronic music studio, 1969—; composer numerous works including: (piano solo) Piano Sonata, 1955, (violin and piano) Fantasy-Variations, 1959, (flute solo) Pas Seul, 1974, (harpsichord solo) St. Bride's Suite, 1983; producer, recorder New Orleans Jazz including, New Orleans Parade: The Eureka Brass Band Plays Dirges and Stomps, 1952, Doc Paulin's Marching Band, 1962, Last of the Line: The Eagle Brass Band, 1982. Contbr. articles to profl. jours. Office: Music Dept UCLA Los Angeles CA 90024

ASHLEY, ANNE, data processing official, consultant; b. Glen Ridge, N.Y., May 5, 1942; d. Walter Quay and Virginia Anne Ashley; m. James Lee Hieronymus, May 30, 1964 (div.). B.S. in English, U. Mich., 1964. Research engr. Gen. Dynamics, San Diego, 1964-66; systems engr. Control Data, 1966-67; sr. systems programmer Cornell U., 1968-71; mgr. operating systems Stanford (Calif.) Linear Accelerator Ctr., 1971-75; systems programming mgr. Western States Bank, San Francisco, 1975-77; mgr. systems devel. and support Boole & Babbage, Sunnyvale, Calif., 1977-79, 79-80; pvt. cons., San Mateo, Calif., 1979-81; systems cons. mgr., mgr. benchmark and performance analysis Amdahl Corp., Sunnyvale, Calif., 1980—, also mgr. Performance Evaluation Ctr., dir. user group mgmt. liaison. Active San Francisco Sex Info. Mem. Am. Mgmt. Assn., Assn. Systems Mgrs., IBM User Groups. Democrat. Club: Decathelon. Composer and lyricist MVS Is Breaking My Heart (song), 1975. Home: 20 Medway Rd Woodside CA 94062 Office: Amdahl Corp MS116 PO Box 470 Sunnyvale CA 94086

ASHLEY, IRVIN ESTER, JR., rehab. center exec.; b. Osceola, Ark., Jan. 18, 1939; s. Irvin Ester and Mary Helen (Woodard) A.; B.S., U. Ark., Fayetteville, 1960, M.Ed., 1966; certificate in phys. therapy Sch. Phys. Therapy, Baylor U., 1964; Ed.D., U. Ill., Urbana, 1969; m. Sylvia Anne Morris, Aug. 19, 1966; children—Mark Edward, James Tod. Phys. therapist Baylor U. Med. Center, Dallas, 1963-65; research asst. vocat. edn. U. Ark., Fayetteville, 1965-66; instr., research asso. vocat. edn. U. Ill., Champaign, 1966-69; dir. vocat. edn. Eastern N.Mex. U., Roswell, 1969-70; rehab. specialist N.Mex. Rehab. Center, Roswell, 1970-72, exec. dir., 1972—. Mem. N.Mex. Steering Com. for Rehab. Coordination; bd. dirs. Chaves County Mental Health Center; co-chmn. Integrated Health Services Com. for S.E. N.Mex.; chmn. N.Mex. adv. bd. health occupational edn. N.Mex. Dept. Edn., 1970-72; N.Mex. rep. regional adv. bd. Tex. Inst. Research and Rehab., Houston; regional field rep., survey cons. Commn. on Accreditation of Rehab. Facilities, Chgo. Served with adminstrn.-aviation supply, USMC, 1960-63. Named Adminstr. of Yr., Nat. Student Nurse Assn., Eastern N.Mex. U., 1971. Mem. Nat. Rehab. Assn. (v.p. N.Mex. chpt. 1973), Internat. Assn. Rehab. Facilities, Phi Delta Kappa. Office: D St at E Eyman St RIAC Roswell NM 88201

ASHMEAD, HARVE DEWAYNE, nutritionist, executive consultant; b. Brigham City, Utah, June 6, 1944; s. Harvey Harold and Allez (Morrill) A.; m. Eugele Baird, June 24, 1966; children—Stephen, Jilane, Brett, Angelique, Heidi. B.S., Weber State Coll., 1969; Ph.D., Pacific Inst., 1970; Ph.D. magna cum laude (scholar), Donsbach U., 1981. Cert. nutritional, dietary cons. With Ch. Jesus Christ of Latter Day Saints, Paris, 1963-66; v.p. Albion Labs., Odgen, Utah, 1966-71, exec. v.p., Clearfield, Utah, 1971-82, pres., 1982—. Dir. several corps.; guest lectr. Adv. Fruit Heights City (Utah); pres. PTA; adv. bd. Donsbach U. Mem. Am. Soc. Animal Sci., Am. Coll. Nutrition, Am. Acad. Applied Health Scis., AAAS, Clearfield C. of C. (dir.), Delta Sigma Pi. Mormon. Author: Chelated Mineral Nutrition, 1981; Mineral Absorption Mechanisms, 1981; Chelated Mineral Nutrition in Plants, Animal and Man, 1982; A New Era in Plant Nutrition, 1982; contbr. numerous articles to profl. jours. Office: 101 N Main St Clearfield UT 84015

ASHTON, WENDELL JEREMY, publisher; b. Salt Lake City, Oct. 31, 1912; s. Marvin Owen and Rae (Jeremy) A.; B.S. magna cum laude, U. Utah, 1933; LL.D., Westminster Coll., 1980; m. Marian Reynolds, Apr. 24, 1940 (dec. Mar. 1963); children—Wendy Jane (Mrs. Neil Christiansen), Susan, Ellen (Mrs. J. Robert Van Orman), Marged, Owen, Kay; m. 2d, Belva Barlow, June 26, 1964; 1 dau., Allyson Louise. Reporter, Salt Lake City Telegram, 1931-34; asso. editor Millennial Star, London, Eng., 1935-36; salesman for bldg. materials co., 1936-42; gen. sec. Sunday Schs., Ch. of Jesus Christ of Latter Day Saints, 1942-46; mng. editor Deseret News, Salt Lake City, 1947-48; v.p. Gillham Advt., Inc., Salt Lake City, 1951-72; mng. dir. pub. communications Ch. of Jesus Christ of Latter Day Saints, 1972-77; pub. Deseret News Pub. Co., Salt Lake City, 1978—; partner Oneida Investment Co., 1952—; chmn. bd. Salt Lake br. Fed. Res. Bank San Francisco, 1979—. Pres., chief exec. officer Utah Symphony, 1966—; pres. Sons Utah Pioneers, 1946-47; chmn. Utah Cancer Crusade, 1964; v.p. Great Salt Lake council Boy Scouts Am., 1957-60; vice chmn. Utah Bicentennial Commn. for Am.'s Ind., 1972—; state adv. com. Citizens for Better Utah, 1968—; mem. Utah Travel Commn., 1975—; bd. govs. LDS Hosp., 1975—, Stevens Henager Coll., 1957-72, Deseret Utah Art Found., 1974—; adv. bd. dept. journalism U. Utah, 1967—; mem. nat. adv. bd. Brigham Young U. Coll. Bus., 1972—; exec. com. Utahns Against Pornography, 1976—; bd. dirs. Newspaper Agy. Corp. Recipient Distinguished Alumni award U. Utah, 1968, Service to Journalism award, 1967; Silver medal Am. Advt. Fedn., 1967; Silver Beaver award Boy Scouts Am., 1957; Meritorious Service award Dept. Communications, Brigham Young U., 1975; Disting. Service award U. Utah Coll. Bus., 1979. Mem. Salt Lake Area C. of C. (bd. govs. 1976-79, 1st v.p., pres. 1978-79), Sigma Nu (Utah Hall of Fame 1976), Republican. Mem. Ch. of Jesus Christ of Latter Day Saints (stake pres. 1960-62; regional rep. of 12, 1967-73). Author: (with Ab Jenkins) Salt of the Earth, 1939; Theirs is the Kingdom, 1945; Voice in the West, 1950; It's Your Life to Enjoy, 1955; In Your Own Image, 1959; Bigger Than Yourself, 1965; To Thine Own Self, 1972. Office: 30 E 1st S Salt Lake City UT 84110

ASHUCKIAN, EDWARD S., dentist; b. Fresno, Calif., July 7, 1912; s. Sahag and Yeran (Barberian) A.; student Fresno State Coll., 1930-32; D.D.S., U. Calif.-San Francisco, 1936;; m. Venus Shahbazian, Jan. 1, 1939; 1 dau., Susan Lee (Mrs. Arthur Van Diggelen). Pvt. practice gen. dentistry, Alameda, Calif., 1937-82. Mem. adv. health bd., Alameda, 1954-58, adv. bd. Alameda Boys Club, 1960-72; pres. Mr. and Mrs. Soc., St. Vartan Armenian Ch., 1980. Served to maj. Dental Corps, AUS, 1943-46. Mem. Am. Dental Assn., Am. Legion. Mem. Armenian Ch. Clubs: Elks (exalted ruler 1960-61), Rotary (pres. Alameda 1975-76). Patentee artificial tooth. Office: 600 Fortress Isle Alameda CA 94501

ASHWORTH, BRENT FERRIN, lawyer, corporation executive; b. Albany, Calif., Jan. 8, 1949; s. Dell Sheperd and Bette Jean (Brailsford) A.; B.A., Brigham Young U., 1972; J.D., U. Utah, 1975; m. Charlene Mills, Dec. 16, 1970; children—Amy Josephine, John Dell, Matthew Ferrin, Samuel Mills, Adam Parrish, David Alden, Emily Bette. Admitted to Utah bar, 1977; asst. county atty. Carbon County (Utah), 1975-76; asso. firm Frandsen & Keller, Price, Utah, 1976-77; v.p., sec., gen. counsel Nature's Sunshine Products, Inc. (formerly Amtec Industries, Inc.), Spanish Fork, Utah, 1977—. City councilman, Payson, Utah, 1980-82, acting mayor, 1982; mem. Payson Planning Commn., 1980-81; dir., counsel Carbon County Nursing Home, 1975-76; bishop Ch. Jesus Christ of Latter-day Saints, 1980-82, high councilman, Stake mission pres., 1983—; chmn. Utah County crusade com. Am. Cancer Soc., 1981—. Named One of Outstanding Young Men of Am., Jaycees, 1982. Mem. Southeastern Utah Bar Assn. (past sec.), Assn. Trial Lawyers Am., Utah State Bar Assn., Am. Bar Assn., U. Utah Alumni Assn., SAR, Phi Kappa Phi, Phi Eta Sigma. Republican. Home: 1965 N 1400 East Provo UT 84604 Office: 1655 N Main St Spanish Fork UT 84660

ASHWORTH, DELL SHEPHERD, architect; b. Salt Lake City, July 20, 1923; s. Paul P. and Jane (Ferrin) A.; student Brigham Young U., 1940-42, 47; B.A., U. Calif.-Berkeley, 1949; m. Bette Brailsford, Dec. 21, 1946 (dec. Mar. 1977); children—Brent, Mark, Anne, Christopher; m. 2d, Faughn Montague, Dec. 10, 1977. Pres., TAG - the Ashworth Group, Inc., TAG Devel. Co.; propr. Dell S. Ashworth & Assocs., architect, 1977—, Intermountain Panel Brick Co., B. Ashworth Shop, Costa Mesa, Calif.; dir. Provo Internat. Corp., Educare Corp. Active Provo Dist. com. Boy Scouts Am., 1956-60; chmn. City Planning Commn., Provo, 1961-66; mem. Utah County Planning Adv. Com.; dir. Provo Indsl. Devel. Corp. Served with USNR, 1942-46. Mem. Provo C. of C. (pres. 1969), SAR (chaplain Utah Valley chpt., pres. 1978-79, Utah pres. 1981). Mem. Ch. of Jesus Christ of Latter-day Saints (bishop). Club: Kiwanis (past pres.). Archtl. works include Payson City Center, Nephi City Center, Juab County Center, Nephi, Utah, Springville Art Gallery Addition, Payson High Sch., Millard High Sch., Springville High Sch., City Center, Provo, City Center and Library, Orem, Utah, Jefferson Center, Springville, Utah, Edgemont Plaza, Provo, Utah. Home: 1211 E 2080 N PO Box 479 Provo UT 84601 Office: 36 E 400 North PO Box 479 Provo UT 84603

ASHWORTH, KEITH, state senator; b. Kimberly, Nev., Sept. 4, 1924; student Butler U., U. Utah; m. Colleen Christensen; children—Glen, Kenneth, Brian. Public adminstr. for Clark County, 1950-54; public acct., corp. v.p. govt.-community relations Del Webb Hotels, Sahara-Nev. Corp.; mem. Nev. Assembly, 1967-76, speaker, 1973-75, chmn. Clark County del., 1977; mem. Nev. Senate, 1977—, chmn. legis. commn., 1969-70. Mem. Nev. Adv. Council for Manpower Tng. and Career Edn.; mem. Multistate Tax Compact Commn. for State of Nev.; bd. dirs. Boys' Club of Clark County; mem. Las Vegas Youth Adv. Council, 1955-60. Served with USAF, World War II. Mem. Nat. Conf. State Legislatures (chmn. transp. com. 1976-77), Western Conf. Council of State Govts. (chmn.-elect 1978-79, chmn. 1980-81), Nat. Soc. Public Accts., Nev. Soc. Public Accts. (pres. 1957-59), Greater Las Vegas C. of C. (past dir.), Las Vegas Jaycees (pres. 1957). Democrat. Clubs: Rotary (pres. 1973), Masons, Shriners. Office: PO Box 7548 Las Vegas NV 89101*

ASIANO, BETTY TIMBLIN, pharmacist; b. Port Clinton, Ohio, Jan. 29, 1927; d. William Clyde and Nena Elmay (Bower) Timblin; B.S. in Pharmacy, Ohio State U., 1948; m. William Edward Asiano, Sept. 13, 1948; children—Mark William, Jane Ellen, William Timblin. Pharmacist, Wendt Bristol Co., Columbus, Ohio, 1948-50, Webb & Rogers Pharmacy, San Rafael, Calif., 1951-53; relief pharmacist Central Pharmacy, Sausalito, Calif., also Marin City (Calif.) Pharmacy, 1953-65, Village Pharmacy, Mill Valley, Calif., 1965-68, Rutherfords Pharmacy, Mill Valley, 1975-78; pharmacist Strawberry Pharmacy, Mill Valley, 1975—. Pres. Peter Pan chpt. Children's Home Soc., 1958-60; treas. Reed Dist. PTA Club, 1964, Redwood High Sch. PTA, 1970-72, Northgate Group, Marin Art and Garden Center, 1976-79. Mem. Am., Calif., Marin County pharm. assns., Chi Omega (pres. 1970-72). Club: Tiburon Peninsula. Address: 222 Martinique Ave Tiburon CA 94920

ASKEVOLD, DAVID MARIUS, artist, educator; b. Conrad, Mont., Mar. 30, 1940; s. Severra Marius and Katherine Irene (Hartin) A.; student U. Mont., 1958-63; cert. Bklyn. Mus. Sch. Art, 1964; B.F.A., Kansas City Art Inst., 1968; m. Christina Dawn Ritchie, Dec. 7, 1974; 1 son, Jesse Ben. Exhibited in one-man shows including: Art & Project Gallery, Amsterdam, Holland, 1972, Paul Maenz Gallery, Cologne, West Germany, 1972, Jack Wendler Gallery, London, 1972, Yvon Lambert Gallery, Paris, 1972, John Gibson Gallery, N.Y.C., 1977; exhibited in group shows including: Mus. Modern Art, N.Y.C., 1970, Wallraf-Richarz Mus., Cologne, 1974, Autumn Festival, Paris, 1973, Israel Mus., Jerusalem, 1977, Los Angeles Inst. Contemporary Art, 1977; represented in permanent collection: Van Abbe Mus., Eindhoven, Holland; mem. faculty N.S. Coll. Art and Design, 1968-75, U. Calif., Irvine, 1976-77, Calif. Inst. Arts, 1977-78. Can. Council Artists grantee, 1973, 75. Home: 709 Millwood Ave Venice CA 90291

ASKEW, STEPHEN EDWARD, refrigeration and air conditioning company executive; b. Los Angeles, Jan. 24, 1937; s. Peter and Mary Clare (Morgan) A.; student Calif. State Poly. Coll., 1956; m. Diane Beverly Firlotte, Jan. 26, 1957; children—Mark Kevin, Stephanie Lyn, Kristen Edward. Mech. engr. Lockheed Aircraft Co., Burbank, Calif., 1956; dir. tech. sales Missimers, Inc., Los Angeles, 1956-60; pres. Thermal Products, Inc., Los Angeles, 1960—, also Askew Mgmt., Inc.; partner Askew Investment Partnership, Los Angeles; dir. Thermal Products, Inc., Los Angeles. Pres. Glendale Crescent Campfire Girls, 1969; mgr. Little League Baseball, 1958-70; chmn. area United Way, Glendale, Calif., 1967-68; chmn. fund drive YMCA, Glendale, 1968-70; pack chmn. Verdugo Hills council Boy Scouts Am., 1965-66. Recipient Presdl. Recognition award Campfire Girls, 1969, Community Leadership award City of Glendale, 1967, Gov's. award Calif. Jr. C. of C., 1967. Mem. Air Conditioning and Refrigeration Wholesalers (dir. 1970, pres. 1975), Refrigeration Service Engrs. Soc. (ednl. chmn. 1965-66), ASHRAE, Refrigeration Engrs. and Technicians Assn., Balboa Power Squadron, Glendale Jr. C. of C. (pres. 1966). Republican. Clubs: Verdugo (Glendale); Bahia Corinthian Yacht (fleet capt. 1982-83) (Newport Beach, Calif.). Lahaina Yacht (Hawaii). Home: 1891 Derby Dr Santa Ana CA 92705 Office: 16924 Marquardt Ave Cerritos CA 90701

ASKEY, ROBERT JAMES, mayor; b. Lincoln, Nebr., Dec. 26, 1929; s. Hollis Ash and Mabel Louise (Fuesler) A.; m. Jacqueline Ruth McClure, May 27, 1967; children—David Richard, Steven James. B.A., U. Nebr., Lincoln, 1951. With Stas. KOLN, KFOR, KFOR-TV, Lincoln, 1949-65; with Sta. WNAX, Yankton, S.D., 1966; with Sta. KLMO-AM-FM, Longmont, Colo., 1967-70; with Stas. KHOW, KBTR, KAAT, KDEN, KOA-AM-FM-TV, Denver, 1970-75; mem. Longmont City Council, 1975-79, mayor City Longmont, 1979-81; narrator numerous – talking books – for Library of Congress, Washington, 1975—; free-lance narrator audio visual prodns. Bd. dirs. Platte River Power Authority, 1979-81; mem. Longmont Pub. Library Bd., 1970-75; mem. adv. bd. Longmont Career Devel. Ctr., 1977—. Mem. AFTRA, Screen Actors Guild, Actors Working for an Actors' Guild, Alpha Epsilon Rho. Republican. Methodist. Clubs: Masons, Shriners. Home: 2025 Longs Peak Ave Longmont CO 80501

ASKIN, LEON, director, actor, producer, writer; b. Vienna, Austria, Sept. 18, 1907; s. Samuel and Malvine (Susman) Aschkenasy; came to U.S., 1940, naturalized, 1943; grad. New Sch. for Dramatic Arts (later called Reinhardt-Seminar), Vienna, 1927; postgrad. Columbia U., summer 1951; m. Annelies Ehrlich, Apr. 12, 1955; 1 stepdau., Irene Hartzell. Actor, Dumont Playhouse, Dusseldorf, Germany, 1927; cabaret dir., writer, actor, Paris, 1933-35, Vienna, 1935-38; author motion pictures including Rappel Immediat, Paris, 1938-40; artistic dir. Washington Civic Theater, 1940-42, including Troilus and Cressida (Shakespeare) (Most Outstanding Prodn. 1941); Broadway actor and dir., 1946-52, staged Faust for Goethe Festival, 1948-49, played Shylock in Merchant of Venice, 1952; appeared in over 55 motion pictures including: The Robe, 1953, One, Two, Three, 1962, Guns for San Sebastian, 1967, Do Not Disturb, 1966, Going Ape, 1980, The Horror Star, 1981, Airplane II; starred as Gen. Burkhalter in Hogans Heroes, TV series, 1966-71; star TV series Kotan, Vienna, 1982; dir. West Coast plays: St. Joan (Bernard Shaw), 1954, Julius Caesar (Shakespeare), 1960, The Egg (Felicien Marceau), 1975, Fever in the Brain (Marvin Aron), 1980; played Othello (in German), Hamburg and Berlin (award Die Welt), 1957; tchr. modern play analysis Am. Theater Wing, 1946-47, directing Dramatic Workshop, N.Y.C., 1947-48; founder Actors Equity Community Theater, 1948; chmn. various coms. Actors Equity Library Theatre, 1947-52; hon. life dir. Equity Library Theatre. Organized Nat. Artist award to Fred Astaire, 1978, Henry Fonda, 1979, Bob Hope, 1980, Jimmy Stewart, 1981, Roger L. Stevens, 1983. Served to sgt. USAAC, 1942-45. Recipient cert. of spl. commendation Bd. Trustees Calif. Mus. Sci. and Industry, 1980; Ehren Medaille der Stadt (Vienna), 1983. Mem. Actors Equity (dir. West Coast advisory com. 1952-55), Screen Actors Guild (dir. 1973), AFTRA, Acad. Motion Picture Arts and Scis. (select com. fgn. films), Acad. TV Arts and Scis., Am. Nat. Theatre and Acad. West (nat. bd. dirs. 1978—, chmn. bd. 1976-78, pres. 1979-81, chmn. bd. 1981—, pres. emeritus 1983—). Contbr. articles to ANTA West News Letter, Los Angeles Times, essays to U. Hamburg Arbeitastelle fur Exilliteratur; editor in chief Army Orientation Digest, 1944-45 (15 citations for outstanding work). Home: 625 N Rexford Dr Beverly Hills CA 90210 Office: 9777 Wilshire Blvd Suite 900 Beverly Hills CA 90212

ASKIN, RICHARD HENRY, JR., broadcasting co. exec.; b. Flushing, N.Y., Feb. 11, 1947; s. Richard H. and Anne Margaret A.; B.A. in

Econs., Rutgers U., 1969; M.A. in Communications, U. Tex., 1971; M.B.A. in Fin., Fordham U., 1976; m. Carol Ann Reilly, Aug. 16, 1969; children—Jennifer Leigh, Michael Richard. Sales rep. Proctor & Gamble Distbg. Co., Jericho, N.Y., 1969; account exec. CableRep, Inc., N.Y.C., 1973-74, WNBC-TV Nat. Broadcasting Co., N.Y.C., 1974-75, NBC-TV, NBC, N.Y.C., 1975-76, sales mgr. KNBC-TV, Los Angeles, 1976-79, dir. sales, 1979—; partner Breckford Group. Served to 1st lt. Adj. Gen. Corps, U.S. Army, 1971-73. Decorated Army Commendation medal; Alcoa fellow, 1969-70. Mem. Hollywood Radio and TV Soc., Advt. Industry Emergency Fund (pres., bd. dirs.), Alpha Rho Alumni Assn., Chi Psi. Republican. Roman Catholic. Home: 1288 Westwind Circle Westlake Village CA 91361 Office: 3000 W Alameda Ave Burbank CA 91523

ASKIN, WALTER MILLER, artist, educator; b. Pasadena, Calif., Sept. 12, 1929; s. Paul Henry and Dorothy Margaret (Miller) A.; B.A., U. Calif.-Berkeley, 1951, M.A., 1952; postgrad. Ruskin Sch. Drawing and Fine Art, Oxford; m. Doris Mae Anderson, Sept. 16, 1950; 1 dau., Nancy Carol Oudegeest. Asst. curator edn. Legion of Honor Mus., San Francisco, 1953-54; prof. art Calif. State U., Los Angeles, 1956—; vis. artist Pasadena Art Mus., 1962-63, U. N.M., 1972, Calif. State U., Long Beach, 1974-75, Cranbrook Acad. Art, Michigan, 1978, Ariz. State U., Tempe, 1979, Art Center Athens Sch. Fine Arts, Mykonos, Greece, 1973, Kelpra Studio, London, 1969, 73; numerous exhbns. including one-man shows Kunstlerhaus, Vienna, Austria, 1981, Santa Barbara Mus. Art, 1966, Hellenic-Am. Union, Athens, Greece, 1973, Hank Baum Gallery, San Francisco, 1970, 74, 76, Ericson Gallery, N.Y.C., 1978, Abraxas Gallery, Calif., 1979, 80, 81; chmn. visual arts panel Commn. on Presdl. Scholars. Trustee Baxter Art Gallery, Calif. Inst. Tech., 1980—, Graphic Arts Council, Los Angeles County Mus. Art, 1980—. Recipient Outstanding Prof. award Calif. State U., 1973, Artists award Pasadena Arts Council, 1970, also over 50 awards in competitive exhns. art. Mem. Coll. Art Assn. Am. Home: 846 Bank St South Pasadena CA 91030 Office: 26 W Dayton St Pasadena CA 91105

ASLAM, MUHAMMAD, plant physiology researcher; b. Pakistan, Apr. 4, 1943; came to U.S., 1966; s. Barkat and Sardaran (BiBi) Ali; m. Riffat Yasmin, Oct. 3, 1971; children—Affifa, Aniqa, Adeel. B.S., West Pakistan Agrl. U., 1959, M.S., 1965; Ph.D., U. Calif.-Davis, 1970. Lectr. in agronomy U. Agr., Faisalabad, Pakistan, 1971-73, postdoctoral fellow biology dept. McMaster U., Hamilton, Ont., Can., 1974-75; research assoc. crop sci. dept., U. of Guelph (Ont.), 1975-77; postgrad. plant physiologist Plant Growth Lab., U. Calif.-Davis, 1977-79, staff research assoc., 1980—; vis. fellow Agr. Can. Research Sta., Harrow, Ont., Can., 1979-80. Mem. Am. Soc. Agronomy, Am. Soc. Crop Sci., Am. Soc. Plant Physiologists. Contbr. articles to profl. jours. Home: 933 Bienville St Davis CA 95616 Office: Plant Growth Lab U Calif Davis CA 95616

ASMUNDSON, VIGFUS ANTHONY, lawyer, investor; b. Sacramento, Aug. 28, 1936; s. Vigfus Samundur and Aline Mary (McGrath) A.; m. Ruth Lane Uy, Oct. 6, 1973; children—Alinia, Irena, Vigdis, Sigrid. Student U. Calif.-Davis, 1954-56; B.A. in Polit. Sci., U. Calif.-Berkeley, 1958; LL.B., Harvard U., 1961. Bar: Calif. 1962. Assoc. Diepenbrock, Plant & Hannegan, Sacramento, 1963-69, ptnr., 1970-71; sole practice, Sacramento, 1971-82; assoc. Lawyer, Downey, Brand, Seymour & Rohwer, Sacramento, 1983—; prof. corps. law U. Pacific, Sacramento, 1963-67. Mayor, City of Davis, 1970-72. Served with USAR, 1961-67. Named Young Man of Yr. Jaycees, 1972. Mem. Sacramento County Bar Assn., Yolo County Bar Assn., Calif. Bar Assn., Calif. Trial Lawyers Assn., Harvard Law Sch. Assn., Library Assocs. U. Calif.-Davis, Phi Beta Kappa. Republican. Roman Catholic. Home: 545 Miller Dr Davis CA 95616 Office: Downey Brand et al 555 Capitol Mall Suite 1050 Sacramento CA 95814

ASTARABADI, ZAID A., real estate broker; b. Baghdad, Iraq, Sept. 20, 1942; came to U.S., 1960, naturalized, 1973; s. Assad Allah and Shamsa A.; m. Janice Susan Jackson, Dec. 21, 1968; 1 son, Jeffery J. B.S., U. Calif.-Berkeley, 1966; M.B.A., Calif. State U., Fresno, 1970; B.A., Am. Grad. Sch. Internat. Mgmt., Phoenix, 1971; Middle East mgr. Borg-Warner Internat. Corp., various locations, 1972-76; mgmt. trainee Honeywell Inc., Ft. Washington, Pa., 1976-77; v.p. fin. 41 Corp., Alpaugh, Calif., 1977-79; pres. Z. Astarabadi Assos., Newport Beach, Calif., 1979—; investment cons. Mem. Alpha Kappa Psi, Sigma Pi. Republican. Office: 3 Corporate Plaza Newport Beach CA 92660

ASTRACHAN, MAX, emeritus educator; b. Rochester, N.Y., Mar. 30, 1909; s. Israel and Lottie (Goldman) A.; A.B., U. Rochester, 1929; A.M., Brown U., 1930, Ph.D., 1935; m. Regina Hyman; children—Gerald, David, Judith. Dept. chmn. Antioch Coll., Yellow Springs, Ohio, 1935-49; prof. stats., chmn. dept. U.S. Air Force Inst. Tech., 1949-60; mathematician Rand Corp., Santa Monica, Calif., 1960-65; dir. edn. and tng. inst. Am. Soc. Quality Control, Milw., 1965-67; emeritus prof. mgmt. sci. Sch. Bus. Calif. State U., Northridge, 1967-81. Mem. Am. Soc. Quality Control (Eugene L. Grant award, 1979), Am. Statis. Assn., Phi Beta Kappa, Sigma Xi. Office: 18111 Nordhoff St Northridge CA 91330

ASWANI, PRAKASH, engineering executive; b. Nawabshah, Pakistan, Mar. 5, 1943; s. Gangaram N. and Kalawanti G. (Raichandani) A.; m. Shakuntala P. Jethmalani, July 30, 1971; children—Prashant, Aparna. B.S. with honors in Physics, U. Delhi, 1963; B.S. in Elect. Engring., Madras Inst. Tech., 1966; M.B.A., Ind. No. Grad. Sch., 1980. Test engr. Meril Ltd., Bombay, India, 1966-71; sr. product engr. Adcor Electronics Inc., Atlanta, 1972-78; mgr. Test Ctr., Burroughs Corp., Plymouth, Mich., 1978-80; pres., chief exec. officer Microtest Systems Inc., Sunnyvale, Calif., 1981—; mgmt. cons. Mem. Am. Mgmt. Assn. (exec. con.). Home: 1596 Lewiston Dr Sunnyvale CA 94087 Office: 1188 Bordeaux Dr Sunnyvale CA 94086

ATAIE, ATA JENNATI, oil products mktg. exec.; b. Mashad, Iran, Mar. 15, 1934; s. Hamid Jennati and Mohtaram (Momeni) A.; came to U.S., 1957, naturalized, 1969; B.S. in Agr., Fresno (Calif.) State U., 1964; B.A. in Econs., San Francisco State U., 1966; m. Judith Garrett Bush, Oct. 7, 1961; children—Ata Jennati, Andrew J. Mktg. exec. Shell Oil Co., Oakland, Calif., 1966-75; pres. A.J. Ataie & Cos., Concord, Calif., 1975—; chmn. bd. Am. Heritage Oil Co., Moraga, Calif., 1976—, Am. Value Inc., 1976—. Served as 2d lt. Iranian Army, 1953. Mem. Nat. Petroleum Retailers Assn. Democrat.

ATCHISON, CARLA JOAN, political scientist; b. Denver, May 24, 1948; d. Lowell Chrysler and Jerry Louise (Stephens) A. B.A., Willamette U., 1970; M.A., U. Colo., 1972. Teaching asst. U. Colo., Boulder, 1971-72, lectr., 1976—; vis. instr. U. Denver, 1980. Recipient George M. Putnam award in Journalism, 1969; NSF predoctoral trainee, 1970-71; U. Colo. doctoral fellow 1980-81. Mem. Am. Polit. Sci. Assn., Acad. Polit. Sci., Phi Beta Kappa, Alpha Lambda Delta, Pi Gamma Mu, Alpha Kappa Nu, Dobro Slovo. Presbyterian. Club: Order Eastern Star. Home: 527 S York St Denver CO 80209

ATEN, NANCY K(AY), educator; b. Mpls., Apr. 24, 1947; s. Ralph Wallace and Jeanette Florence (Anderson) Kopacek; m. Vern Eugene Lund, Dec. 15, 1968; m. William Andrew Aten, May 10, 1975. Student Calif. State Poly. U., 1965-69; B.A. in Biol. Sci., Calif. State U.-Fresno, 1971. Standard secondary teaching credential, Calif. Lab. asst. Calif. State Poly. U., 1967-69; jr. high sch. tchr. Kit Carson Elem. Sch. O, Hanford, Calif., 1972-76; tchr. English, West Hills Community Coll., Coalinga, Calif., 1976-77; tchr. math. 8th grade Thomas Jefferson Jr. High Sch., Madera, Calif., 1977—; instr. sci. U. Calif.-Santa Cruz, summer 1979; travel cons. Gateway Travel, Madera, 1977—; leader workshops in activating integration of math. and sci. Bd. dirs. Pismo Coast Village, Inc. (Calif.), 1977-81, PTA, Madera, 1977—; mem. edn. com. Madera C. of C., 1981—; mem. Madera County (Calif.) Affirmative Action Com., 1981—; chmn. planning com., bd. dirs. United Way Madera, 1982—; precinct capt. various local campaigns. Recipient Service award Pismo Coast Villge Bd. Dirs., 1982; NSF grantee, 1981. Mem. NEA, Calif. Tchrs. Assn. (treas. Fresno-Madera County Service Ctr. council), Madera Unified Tchrs. Assn. (pres. 1981-83), Assn. Supervision and Curriculum Devel., Nat. Council Tchrs. Math., Calif. Math. Council, Math-Sci. Network Earthwatch, AAUW, Madera Republican Women. Lutheran. Club: Panoche Guild of Valley Children's Hosp. (pres. 1980) (Kerman, Calif.). Author: Patterns and Symmetry Around Us, 1983. Grade 8 Math Enrichment Activites, 1983; co-producer film: Madera County: Land of Varied Resources, 1983. Home: 522 Willis Ave Madera CA 93637 Office: 1407 Sunset Ave Madera CA 93637

ATENCIO, EDDIE, educational administrator; b. Fairview, N.Mex., Aug. 8, 1947; s. Jose Elifar and Gregorita Linda A.; m. Helen Amada Herrera, June 6, 1970; children—Linda Marie, Eddie Joe. B.A., N.Mex. Highlands U., 1974, M.B.A., 1975. Security guard N.Mex. State Hosp., Las Vegas, 1971-77; tchr. bus. edn., high sch., Mosquero, N.Mex., 1977-79; tchr. vocat. edn. Vocat. Tech. Inst., Springer (N.Mex.) Satellite Night Sch., 1979; tchr., prin. Roy (N.Mex.) High Sch., 1979—. Served with USMC, 1965-69; Vietnam. Mem. N.Mex. Assn. Secondary Sch. Prins., Am. Vocat. Assn., N.Mex. Middle Sch. Assn. Sch. Prins., Nat. Bus. Tchr. Edn. Soc., VFW, NEA (local pres.). Democrat. Roman Catholic. Club: Eagles.

ATHA, GEORGE CRAWFORD, petroleum geologist; b. Fairmont, W.Va., Nov. 25, 1902; s. William Hunter and Jessie Julia (Dougan) A.; student in geology Ohio State U., 1922, Muskingum Coll., 1927; m. Gladys R. Wray, Apr. 7, 1948. Civil engr., Sebring, Fla., 1927; salesman, mgr. real estate, Lorain, Ohio, 1927-28; staff Midwest Rc '28 Co., Roswell, N.Mex., 1928-29; staff City of Palo Verde Estates (Calif.), 1929-30; pres. Hiawatha Exploration Co., San Marino, Calif., 1947—; pvt. practice petroleum geologist San Marino, 1947—. Mem. Internat. Oil Scouts. Club: Long Beach Petroleum, Elks (life), Los Angeles Athletic. Inventor geophys. equipment. Address: 2221 California Blvd San Marino CA 91108

ATHERLEY, WILLIAM JOHN, accountant; b. San Francisco, Dec. 16, 1942; s. Henry John and Eleanor McKenzie (Aitken) A.; B.A., Stanford U., 1964; postgrad. U. Oreg., 1968-70, U. Calif. at Berkeley, 1976. Auditor, Peat, Marwick Mitchell & Co., San Francisco, 1970-71, Foremost-McKesson Inc., San Francisco, 1971-73, Coopers & Lybrand, San Francisco, 1973-75, Kaiser Aluminum & Chem. Corp., Oakland, Calif., 1975-76; controller Chinese Hosp., San Francisco, 1976—. Served with Army Nat. Guard, 1964. C.P.A., Calif. Mem. Hosp. Financial Mgmt. Assn., Stanford Alumni Assn. Republican. Home: 2450 Octavia St Apt 2C San Francisco CA 94109 Office: 845 Jackson St San Francisco CA 94133

ATHERTON, ALEXANDER SIMPSON, newspaper executive; b. Honolulu, Mar. 29, 1913; s. Frank Cooke and Eleanore Alice (Simpson) A.; B.A., Dartmouth, 1936; m. LeBurta Marie Gates, Oct. 8, 1941; children—Burta Lee, Frank Cooke II, Marjory Gates. With Hawaiian Trust Co., Honolulu, 1954-66, asst. v.p., 1958-66; pres. Honolulu Star-Bull., 1963—; pres. Guam Publs.; dir. Hawaiian Trust Co., Castle & Cooke, Inc. Pres. Mid-Pacific Inst., 1955—; past campaign chmn. Honolulu Community Chest. Trustee Hawaii Loa Coll., Atherton Family Found.; bd. dirs. Africare, Inc., Honolulu Zoo, Bishop Mus. Mem. Navy League U.S., Royal Philatelic Soc. London, Theta Delta Chi. Republican. Mem. United Ch. Christ. Clubs: Pacific, Adventurers, Waialae Country, (Honolulu); Collectors (N.Y.C.). Office: Gannett Pacific Corp PO Box 3080 Honolulu HI 96802*

ATHERTON, ARLENE RUTH, financial planner; b. Redlands, Calif., May 3, 1956; d. Jaheel Arlie and Donna Ruth Gillmore. Cert. fin. planner Coll. Fin. Planning; registered investment advisor. Registered rep. Waddell & Reed, Inc., 1975-80, dist. mgr., 1980-81; registered rep. FSC Securities Corp., Santa Clara, Calif., 1982—; pres. Atherton Advisers, Inc., Santa Clara, 1982—. Mem. Internat. Assn. Fin. Planning, Inst. Cert. Fin. Planners, Women's Entrepenuers. Republican. Contbg. fin. editor: Santa Clara Mag., 1982. Office: 1333 Lawrence Expressway Suite 253 Santa Clara CA 95051

ATIYEH, VICTOR, gov. Oreg.; b. Portland, Oreg., Feb. 20, 1923; student U. Oreg., 1941-43; m. Dolores Hewitt. Pres. Atiyeh Bros., Inc., Portland, to 1979, dir., 1979—; mem. Oreg. Ho. of Reps. and Oreg. Senate, 1959-78, senate Republican leader, 1971-78; gov. state of Oreg., Salem, 1979—. Chmn. nat. task force on Indian edn. Edn. Commn. of States; higher edn. liaison Western Govs.' Conf. and Western Interstate Commn. Higher Edn.; del. Republican Nat. Conv., 1968, 72, 76, mem. platform com., 1968, 72; pres. Columbia-Pacific council Boy Scouts Am., pres. Western Region Area I, 1978, mem. nat. bd. exploring. Mem. Nat. Govs. Assn. (vice-chmn. natural resources and environ. mgmt. com., mem. internat. trade and fgn. relations com.). Episcopalian. Home: 796 Winter St Salem OR 97301 Office: Office of Gov State Capitol Salem OR 97310

ATKIN, SPENCER WYATT, state senator, businessman; b. Arcadia, La., Aug. 16, 1923; s. Spencer Wyatt and Daisy (Marshall) A.; m. Donetta Jo Reeves, 1931; 1 son, Spencer Bert. Student Northwestern La. Coll., 1941-42. Owner ins. and fin. bus., Alamogordo, N.Mex., 1950; automobile dealer Studebaker, Edsel and Dodge, 1959-74; investor, Alamogordo, 1952; dir. 1st Nat. Bank of Alamogordo, 1962; mem. N.Mex. State Senate from Otero County, 1980—. Chmn. Otero County Democratic Party, 1952-72, 74-78; city police judge Alamogordo, 1954-68; mem. Regional Housing Authority, adv. com. Interstate 70. Dir. Sch. for Retarded Children, Alamogordo, 1976-79. Lodges: Elks, Masons, Moose. Home: Box 228 Alamogordo NM 88310 Office: New Mexico State Senate Santa Fe NM 87503*

ATKINS, GORDON LEE, architect; b. Calgary, Alta., Can., Mar. 5, 1937; s. Grant Lee and Dorothy (Atkins) Kearl; B.Arch., U. Wash., Seattle, 1960; m. Constance Joan Lecoq, Mar. 21, 1956; children—Lisa Dawn, Laura Celine, Drew Gordon, Ryan Blake, Murray Kyle, Seth Myer. Design architect R.R. Campbell & Assos., Seattle, 1958-60, Green, Blankenstein, Russell & Assos., Winnipeg, 1960-61; free lance designer, 1961; partner Alton McCaul Bowers, 1961-62; pvt. practice architecture, Calgary, 1962—; pres., prin. Gordon Atkins & Assos., Architects, Ltd., 1977—; works include Calgary Centennial Planetarium (2d place design award 1964), Indian Friendship Center Calgary (Urban Design award), 1980, residences, schs.; works displayed Nat. Gallery, 1967, 69; sessional instr. Mt. Royal Coll., So. Alta. Inst. Tech.; lectr. U. Calgary; academician Royal Canadian Acad. Art. Mem. Mid-Can. Devel. Corridor Conf. Recipient faculty medal for excellence in design U. Wash., 1960, Massey medal, 1967, award of excellence Canadian Architects Yearbook, 1968, 80, Gov. Gen.'s medal for Stoney Adminstrn. Bldg., 1982, numerous other archtl. awards. Mem. Royal Archtl. Inst. Can., Alta. Assn. Architects (pres. Calgary chpt. 1964; Practice Profile award 1981). Mormon. Author: Plywood World, 1970. Contbr. articles to profl. jours. Office: 1909 17th Ave SW Calgary AB T2T OE9 Canada

ATKINS, WILLIAM RONALD, hotel exec.; b. Mound City, Mo., May 14, 1933; s. William Stanley and Alta May (Hagloch) A.; m. Beverly Joan Lynn, Aug. 6, 1950 (div.); children—Jacqua Lyn, Brian Allan, Koby Vaughn, Dawn Michelle. Cert. in bus. adminstrn. La Salle Extension U., Chgo., 1968. Asst. mgr. hardware dept. Sears Roebuck & Co., Battle Creek, Mich., 1954-57; sr. illustrator art dept., manuals and statistics div. Clark Equipment Co., Battle Creek, 1957-62; ptnr., mgr. Duncan's Oak Hills restaurant and motel, Mayer, Ariz., 1962-80; pres. D&A Enterprises Inc., Mayer, 1980—. Mem. Mayer Unified sch. dist. bd., 1968-78, pres., 1972-74, bd. dirs. Yavapai County (Ariz.) br. Ariz. Sch. Bds. Assn., 1974-78; fire chief Mayer vol. fire dist. Served with Mich. N.G., 1951-55. Recipient VFW Aux. Commendable Service award, 1974-79. Mem. Nat. Restaurant Assn., Ariz. Fire Fighters Assn., Ariz. Fire Chiefs, Nat. Fire Chiefs Assn. Democrat. Baptist. Clubs: Mayer Centennial Lions (Charter), Soc. Preservation and Encouragement Barber Shop Quartette Singing in Am. (past pres. Prescott chpt.). Office: PO Box 97 Mayer AZ 86333

ATKINS, WILLIAM THEODORE, retired insurance executive; b. Lebanon, Pa., May 14, 1918; s. William Theodore and Edna Marie (Phillips) A.; B.S., Central YMCA Coll., 1945; J.D., DePaul U., 1949; m. Katherine Malinda Shank, Apr. 25, 1942 (dec. June 1973); children—Karen Jean, Judith Ann, William Theodore III; m. 2d, Elena Garcia Ramsey, Sept. 29, 1974; 1 step-dau., Sarah Ramsey Kerns. Admitted to Ill. bar, 1950, Calif. bar, 1960; surety claim adjuster Continental Casualty Co., Chgo., 1940-52; regional surety claim mgr. Mfrs. Casualty Pacific Nat. Fire Ins. Co., Chgo., 1952-56, nationwide surety claim mgr., Phila., 1956-57, San Francisco, 1957-59; bond claim supr. United Pacific Ins. Group (now United Pacific-Reliance Ins. Cos.), Tacoma Wash., 1960-63, v.p. claims, 1963-75, v.p., legal counsel, 1975-80, v.p., assoc. counsel, 1980-81; v.p. United Pacific Life Ins. Co., 1963-78, v.p., sec., 1978-80, v.p., sec., assoc. counsel, 1980-81; v.p. Reliance Ins. Co., 1971-81. Trustee, 1st pres. bd. Meth. Found. N.W., 1966-69; pres. Kauai Concert Assn., 1982—. Mem. ABA (vice chmn. fidelity and surety com.), Pacific Claim Execs. Assn. (pres. 1966-67), Scribes, Nat. Assn. Ind. Ins. Adjusters (chmn. N.W., nat. adv. councils 1965-67). Presbyterian. Club: Tacoma. Home: 5867 Haaheo Pl Kapaa HI 96746

ATKINSON, SALLY ANN, graphologist; b. Lafayette, Ind., June 19, 1932; d. Myrl Herbert and Merta Marie (Lawler) Bolds; student Purdue U., 1949-52, Rutgers U., 1963; diploma Internat. Graphoanalysis Soc., 1973, Master in Graphoanalysis, 1974; proficiency degree World Assn. Document Examiners, 1974; 1 son, William Gregory Wnuck. Engring. aide Boeing Airplane Co., Seattle, 1954-56; engring. graphanalyst Allison div. Gen. Motors Corp., Indpls., 1956-57; freelance artist, N.J., 1958-64, jr. microbiologist Johnson & Johnson Research Corp., Brunswick, N.J., 1960-62; tchr. art Jamesburg (N.J.) Pub. Schs., 1962-64, Wallenpaupack (Pa.) Pub. Schs., 1964-65; freelance artist, tchr., Seattle, Whidbey Island, Wash., 1965-72; pres. Handwriting, Inc., Seattle, 1975-80; asst. to dir. U. Puget Sound, Seattle, 1978-79; profl. handwriting analyst, 1979—; instr. Seattle Central Community Coll., S. Seattle Community Coll., Bellevue (Wash.) Community Coll., 1980—; exec. sec., dir. product devel. Computerized Handwriting Analysis Services, Inc., Seattle, 1981—; expert Wash. State Trial Lawyers Assn., 1981—. Area rep. Wash. Arts Commn., 1969. Wash. State Arts Commn. grantee, 1968. Mem. South Whidbey Arts Assn. (pres., founder 1966-69), Am. Mgmt. Assn., World Assn. Document Examiners, Internat. Graphoanalysis Soc. Seminar jury selection by handwriting analysis approved by Wash. Bar Assn., 1981. Address: 10523 24th Ave NE Seattle WA 98125

ATKINSON, WILLIAM WILDER, lawyer; b. Little Rock, May 18, 1910; s. William Wilder and Mary Byrne (Parrish) A.; B.A., U. N.Mex., 1936; J.D., U. Colo., 1948; m. Josephine Foster, Oct. 20, 1934; children—William Wilder, Richard Foster. Asst. office mgr. Charles Ilfeld Co., 1923-44; admitted to N.Mex. bar, 1948, U.S. Supreme Ct. bar, 1975; practiced in Albuquerque, 1948—, assoc. firm M. Ralph Brown, 1948-51; sole practice, 1951-62; ptnr. firm Hernandez & Atkinson, 1962-70, Hernandez, Atkinson, Kitts, Kelsey & Hanna, 1970-71, Cotter, Hernandez, Atkinson, Campbell, Kelsey & Hanna, 1972-73, Atkinson & Kelsey, 1973—. Mem. Albuquerque City Commn., 1955-63, vice chmn., 1962-63; pres. N.Mex. Mcpl. League, 1962-63; pres. Albuquerque Community Council, 1964-65, mem., 1963-78; chmn. personnel bd. City of Albuquerque, 1964-65; pres. Albuquerque-Bernalillo County Econ. Opportunity Bd. 1967-68; trustee Bernalillo County Mental Health/Mental Retardation Center, 1968-73; del. N.Mex. Constl. Conv., 1969; mem. U. N.Mex. Governance Adv. Com., 1970; bd. dirs. Goodwill Industries N.Mex., 1968—, pres., 1973-76; mem. Human Rights Commn., City of Albuquerque, 1974-82; bd. mem. N.Mex. chpt. NCCJ., 1974-79; mem. exec. com. Presbyn. Hosp. Ctr. Found., 1977-80, mem. Albuquerque Adv. Com. on Transp. for Elderly and Handicapped, 1983—; mem. Gov.'s Task Force on Municipal Finances, 1976. Recipient Distinguished Citizenship award, Albuquerque Jr. C. of C., 1958; Brotherhood award NCCJ, 1972. Mem. ABA, N.Mex., Albuquerque (pres. 1972-73) bar assns., Albuquerque Lawyers Club (pres. 1954); Am. Arbitration Assn., Estate Planning Council Albuquerque, U. N.Mex. Alumni Assn. (dir. 1960-66), Order of Coif, Phi Kappa Phi, Phi Delta Phi. Democrat. Congregationalist. Clubs: Optimist of Albuquerque (pres. 1952-53), Knife and Fork. Home: 1637 Kit Carson Ave SW Albuquerque NM 87104 Office: PO Box 1126 1300 Bank of New Mexico Bldg Albuquerque NM 87103

ATTEBERRY, EDWIN EVERETTE, JR., pipeline co. ofcl.; b. El Paso, Tex., Sept. 21, 1929; s. Edwin Everette and Celesta Pearl (Ridley) A.; A.A., Lee Coll., 1964; m. Virginia Breed, Nov. 6, 1954; children—Gregory Donald, Sherrill Jean, Malcolm Everette. Process operator Baytown refinery Exxon Co., Baytown, Tex., 1951-56; fire and safety supr. Sinclair Petrochems., Channelview, Tex., 1957-69; fire, safety and security supt. Arco Chem. Co., Channelview, 1969-76; fire and safety contingency coordinator Alyeska Pipeline Service Co., Valdez, Alaska, 1976-82, pipeline safety and fire coordinator, 1982—. Chmn., Lake Shadows Civic Club, Crosby, Tex., 1973-74; capt. Vol. Fire Dept., Valdez, 1978-80; reporter Crosby High Sch. Cougars, 1970-76. Served with U.S. Army, 1947-50. Mem. Am. Soc. Safety Engrs., Internat. Synthetic Rubber Safety Assn. (chmn. 1967, 73), Alaska State Firefighters Assn., Tex. Chem. Council (chmn. safety com. 1976), Houston Ship Channel Mut. Aid Firefighting Group (chmn. 1974-76). Democrat. Lutheran. Home: SRA 1002 610 Light House St Anchorage AK 99502 Office: 1835 S Bracaw St Anchorage AK 99502

ATTEBERRY, MARIE GETTY, ednl. adminstr.; b. Phoenix; d. Charles Francis and Goldie Belle (Simmons) Getty; B.A. in Edn., Ariz. State U., Tempe, 1950, M.A. in Edn., 1962, Ed.D. in Ednl. Adminstrn., 1976; div.; children—Katherine Townsend, Joellen Brenton, Richard Brenton. Tchr. Three Ariz. Sch. Dist., Globe and Phoenix, 1950-60, curriculum supr. Roosevelt Sch. Dist. #66, Phoenix, 1960-70, curriculum coordinator Phoenix Elem. Dist. No. 1, 1970-78, facilitator, cons. Phoenix Research Inst. Mgmt. Edn., 1975—; asst. supt. Kingman (Ariz.) Dist. 4, 1978-80; supt. Sacaton (Ariz.) Sch. Dist. No. 18, 1980-81; prin. Casa Grande Elem. Dist., 1981-82; ret., 1982; adj. prof. No. Ariz. U., 1978—. Pres. Wm. C. Jack PTA, 1958-59. Certified in teaching, supervision, adminstrn. and as reading specialist, Ariz. Mem. Am. Assn. Sch. Adminstrs., Ariz. Sch. Adminstrs. Inc. (past pres.), Internat. Reading Assn., Delta Kappa Gamma, Phi Delta Kappa. Home: 1994 E Orion St Tempe AZ 85283

ATTRI, NARINDER SINGH, aircraft mfg. co. exec., mech. engr.; b. Barnala, India, Feb. 9, 1933; came to U.S., 1954, naturalized, 1972; s.

Shamsher S. and Kartar (Kaur) A.; B.A. in Math. and Physics, Panjab U., India, 1953; B.S. in Mech. Engring., Calif. State U., Fresno, 1956; M.S., Kans. State U., 1958; m. Indra Rikhi, May 7, 1960; children—Bindu, Satinder S. Research instr. Kans. State U., 1958; asst. prof. dept. mech. engring. Panjab Engring. Coll., Chandigarh, India, 1958-61; research engr. Hydroelectric Power Commn., Toronto, Ont., Can., 1961-66; research engr. Boeing Comml. Co., Renton, Wash., 1966-70, sr. specialist, 1970-74, sr. group engr. mech. systems, 1974-75; chief engr. Boeing Mil. Airplane Co., Seattle, 1975-79, dep. chief dir. tech., 1979—; spl. adv. to aero. systems div. Air Force Systems Command 1972—. Founding mem. Friends of India, Seattle, 1966-72. Mem. ASME (program chmn. Ont. sect. 1964-66), AIAA (Testing award 1977), Canadian Space Inst., Sigma Xi, Phi Sigma Tau. Contbr. articles on mech. systems and aircraft tech. to profl. jours.; patentee in field. Home: 17106 151 Ave SE Renton WA 98055 Office: PO Box 3999 Seattle WA 98124

ATWELL, LAWRENCE THOMAS, construction equipment company executive; b. Oakland, Calif., June 25, 1938; s. Kenneth Tilden and Maureen (Mullin) A.; m. Constance Marie Evans, Nov. 30, 1941; children—Susan, Michael, Timothy. B.S. in Civil Engring., Gonzaga U., 1961; Assoc. Degree in Transp., U. Mo.-Kansas City, 1966; M.B.A., Xavier U., 1973. Profl. engr., Wyo. Tech. writer Boeing Airplane Co., Renton, Wash., 1961-64; distbn. mgr. Symons Mfg. Co., Des Plaines, Ill., 1964-70, br. mgr., Cin., 1970-73; v.p. Wilson Equipment & Supply Co., Cheyenne, Wyo., 1973-76, pres., 1976—. Active Laramie County Republican Com. Named Wyo. Bus. Person of Year, Future Bus. Leaders Am., 1979. Mem. Associated Equipment Distbrs. (regional dir. 1979-82), Cheyenne C. of C. (dir., pres. 1984). Club: Cheyenne Rotary. Roman Catholic.

ATWOOD, AILEEN HANSEN, nurse, educator; b. Logan, Utah, Feb. 19, 1922; d. Joseph Heber and Eliza Ann (Godfrey) Hansen; B.S.N., U. Utah, 1958; M.S.N., U. Calif., San Francisco, 1966, postgrad., 1977-78; Ed.D., U. San Francisco, 1981; m. William L. Knecht, Oct. 25, 1969; children—Robert Dixon, Charles Thomas. Asst. dir. nursing service Salt Lake City Gen. Hosp., 1958-59; dir. nursing, vocat. edn. Magic Valley Meml. Hosp., Twin Falls, Idaho, 1959-65; asst. adminstr. nursing service and edn. Samuel Merritt Hosp and Sch. Nursing, Oakland, Calif., 1966-78; asst. adminstr. nursing service Children's Hosp., San Francisco, 1978-82; mgmt. cons. Atwood Mgmt. Inc., 1982—; v.p. Peninsula Hosp., Burlingame, Calif.; asst. clin. prof. U. Calif., San Francisco, 1978—. Bd. dirs. San Francisco Health Consortium; mem. Idaho Commn. on Status of Women, 1965; bd. dirs. Far West Sch., 1972-76. Mem. Assn. Western Hosps., East Bay Dirs. Nursing (chmn. 1967-68), Idaho Nurses Assn. (pres. 1964-65), Calif. Soc. Nursing Service Adminstrs., Assn. Holistic Health, Calif. Hosp. Assn., Nat. League Nursing, Calif. League Nursing. Republican. Mormon. Home: 303 Deerfield Dr Moraga CA 94556

ATWOOD, JERRY LEE, architect; b. San Diego, Sept. 30, 1943; s. George H. and Evelyn E. (Trunkenbolz) A.; B.Arch., Ariz. State U., 1967; m. Laura Rebecca Bengtson, June 30, 1980; 1 son, Theodore Owen. Mut. fund security dealer Waddell & Reed, Inc., 1965-71; v.p. Flatow, Moore, Bryan & Fairburn, Architects-Planners, Phoenix, 1968-74; real estate salesman, Ariz., 1976—; pres. Atwood Assos. Architects, Inc., Scottsdale, Ariz., 1974—; pres. Atwood Assos. Contractors, Inc.; vis. lectr. arch. Ariz. State U.; works include Scottsdale Hilton Hotel Additions, Hilton Villas, branches United Bank of Ariz., Gold Dust Village Shopping Center, Grove Office Plaza, Queen Creek Elem. Sch., Starmark Pl. Condominiums, Gilbert Engring. Mfg. Facility, Park Mitchell Office Bldg., Newport Beach. also residences. Served with USNG, 1967-73. Cert. Nat. Council Archtl. Registration Bds.; lic. architect, Ariz., Calif. Mem. AIA (Outstanding Service award, Ariz. Soc. Citation award 1981; nat. urban planning and design com.), Scottsdale Bd. Realtors. Episcopalian. Clubs: La Camarillo Racquet; Rotary (treas.) (Phoenix-Camelback). Office: PO Box 2118 Scottsdale AZ 85251

ATWOOD, MARIE LOUISE, guidance coordinator, educator; b. Los Angeles, Sept. 20, 1938; d. Howard Catlin and Edith Elberta (Tuggy) Atwood. B.A., Westmont Coll., 1960; M.S., Calif. State U.-Los Angeles, 1976. Tchr. social sci. Rosemead (Calif.) High Sch., 1961-76, career guidance coordinator, 1976—. Recipient Outstanding Educator award Santa Anita Industry-Edn. Council, 1980. Mem. Calif. Tchrs. Assn. (WHO award 1978), NEA, Calif. Assn. Work Experience Educators, Calif. Assn. Vocat. Edn., Am. Vocat. Assn., Delta Kappa Gamma Soc. Internat. (chpt. pres.). Presbyterian. Designed model for career edn. in sch. dist.; coordinator dist.-wide curriculum study, proposal and mgmt. plan. Office: Rosemead High Sch 9063 E Mission Dr Rosemead CA 91107

ATWOOD, MARY SANFORD, author; b. Mt. Pleasant, Mich., Jan. 27, 1935; d. Burton Jay and Lillian Belle (Sampson) Sanford; B.S., U. Miami, 1957; m. John C. Atwood, III, Mar. 23, 1957. Author: A Taste of India, 1969. Mem. San Francisco/N. Peninsula Opera Action, Hillsborough-Burlingame Newcomers, Suicide Prevention and Crisis Center, DeYoung Art Mus., Internat. Hospitality Center, Peninsula Symphony, San Francisco Art Mus., Mills Hosp. Assos. Mem. AAUW, Suicide Prevention Aux. Republican. Clubs: Commonwealth of Calif.; St. Francis Yacht. Address: 40 Knightwood Ln Hillsborough CA 94010

ATWOOD, ROBERT BRUCE, editor, publisher; b. Chgo., Mar. 31, 1907; s. Burton H. and Mary Beach (Stevenson) A.; A.B., Clark U., 1929; Litt.D. (hon.), Alaska Methodist U., 1967; D.Journalism (hon.), U. Alaska, Anchorage, 1979; m. Evangeline Rasmuson, Apr. 2, 1932; children—Marilyn Sara Elaine. Reporter Worcester (Mass.) Telegram, 1926-29 and 1934-35, Ill. State Jour., Springfield, 1929-34; editor and pub. Anchorage Times, 1935—. Chmn. Alaska Statehood Com., 1949-59. Hon. Norwegian consul at Anchorage; bd. govs. Am. Polar Soc. Mem. Asso. Press. Am. Newspapers Pubs. Assn., Am. Soc. Newspaper Editors, Allied Daily Newspapers, Anchorage C. of C. (pres. 1944, 48), Nat. Mcpl. League (council), Internat. Press Inst., Pacific N.W. Newspaper Assn., Explorers Club, Nat. Press Club. Sigma Delta Chi. Republican. Presbyterian. Clubs: Masons, Rotary. Home: 2000 Atwood Dr Anchorage AK 99503 Office: 820 4th Ave Anchorage AK 99510 also Box 40 Anchorage AK 99510

ATWOOD, ROSLYN IRENE, insurance underwriter; b. Buffalo, Apr. 22, 1945; d. Edward George Atwood and Lorraine Charlotte Gibson (Winkleman) Atwood. B.A., Chapman Coll., 1971, M.A., 1976; M.A., Pacific Lutheran U., 1974; With MDB Systems, Inc., Orange, Calif., 1972; community counsel Orange Probation Dept., 1970-75; tchr. human relations and psychology Columbia (Mo.) Coll., 1976-77; enlisted as pvt. U.S. Army, 1973, advanced to capt., 1977; with Army Community Services, Ft. Lewis, Wash., 1973-75; recruiting officer WAC, 1976-77; adj. Kaiserlautern Army Depot, W.Ger., 1978, emergency relief officer, 1979-81; field underwriter Mut. of New York Life Ins. Co., Vista, Calif., 1981—. Served with USAR, 1981—. Decorated Army Accommodation medal, Humanitarian Service medal. Mem. Am. Personnel and Guidance Assn., Nat. Assn. Life Underwriter, Nat. Assn. Female Execs., Assn. U.S. Army. Republican. Participant Greek Marathon, Athens, 1980, 21st Support Command Marathon, 1980. Home: 123 Mayfair Oceanside CA 92054 Office: 956 Vale Terr Suite 130 Vista CA 92083

ATWOOD, SETH LANG, venture capital investor, resort developer; b. Rockford, Ill., Feb. 19, 1950; s. Seth Glanville and Patricia Jane (Lang) A.; m. Connie Lynn Kuehl, Mar. 25, 1978; children—Philip Michael, Jordan Seth. Student Stanford U., 1968-72, San Jose City Coll., 1973-74, De Anza Coll., 1975-76. Census supr. U.S. Dept. Commerce, Washington, 1970-72; dep. sheriff, Santa Clara County, San Jose Calif., 1972-78; exec. v.p. Creative Car Corp., Rockford, Ill., 1981—; pres. Clock Tower Inn, Rockford, 1981—; pres. Walley's Hot Springs Resort, Genoa, Nev., 1982—, United Venture Capital, Inc., Incline Village, Nev., 1981—; dir. True Data Corp, Irvine, Calif., Cash Flow Mgmt., Inc. Belmont, Calif., North Lake Tahoe Broadcasting Co., Incline Village. Trustee Orme Sch. Bd. Mem. Nat. Venture Capital Assn., Western Assn. Venture Capitalists, Nat. Assn. Small Bus. Investment Cos. Mgmt. Inst. Republican. Mem. United Ch. Club: Incline Village Rotary (sec. 1981-83). Office: United Venture Capital Inc 923 Incline Way Suite 3 PO Box 5998 Incline Village NV 89450

AUBRY, WILLIAM EDWARD, psychologist, consultant, educator; b. Woodland, Calif., July 1, 1939; s. Bert B. and Dorothy Louise (Boudinot) A.; m. Jeri Anita Aubry; children—Allison, Dawn, Kristie, Michael. B.S., Oreg. State U., 1961, Ed.M., 1963; Ed.D., U. Ariz., 1970. Lic. psychologist, lic. marriage, family and child counselor, Calif.; diplomate Am. Bd. Family Psychology. Counselor, VA, Tucson, 1963-65, Ariz. Div. Vocat. Rehab., 1965-66; counseling psychologist, Humboldt State U., 1966-76, lectr. dept. sociology, anthropology, and social welfare, 1972-76, lectr. dept. psychology, 1976; field supr. and prof. M.A. programs in marriage, family and child counseling U. San Francisco, in Eureka, Crescent City, Redding and Lake Tahoe, Calif., 1974-79, assoc. prof. counselor edn. U. San Francisco, 1977-79; pvt. practice marriage, family and child counseling, 1969—; pvt. practice psychology, 1972—; exec. dir. Profl. Psychology Services, San Diego, 1981; mem. faculty Profl. Sch. Humanistic Studies, 1981; cons. psychologist Personal Profile Cons., Del Mar, Calif., 1982; columnist. Mem. Am. Psychol. Assn., Am. Assn. Marriage and Family Therapists, Am. Soc. Clin. Hypnosis. Author profl. papers; mem. editorial adv. bd. Marriage and Family Counselors Quar., 1975-76. Home: 1050 N Horne Apt 35 Mesa AZ 85203 Office: 500 W 10th Pl Mesa AZ 85201

AUCHINCLOSS, EVA SEED, foundation executive; b. N.Y.C., July 21, 1933; d. Allen Hartley and Eva Standish (Matthews) Seed; widow; children—Eva S. William S., Elizabeth B. B.A., Vassar Coll., 1955. Pres., pub. Schnell Pub. Co., N.Y.C., 1971-72; assoc. pub. Women's Sports Pub. Co., San Francisco, 1974-76; exec. dir. Women's Sports Found., San Francisco, 1976—; cons. Nat. YWCA, Nat Girl Scouts U.S.A., Nat. Explorer Scouts; dir. Nat. Wood Products, Schnell Pub. Co. Recipient Service award Nat. Assn. Girls and Women in Sports. Mem. Women's Forum West. Office: Women's Sports Found 195 Moulton St San Francisco CA 94123

AU COIN, LES, congressman; b. Portland, Oreg., Oct. 21, 1942; s. Francis Edgar and Alice (Atkinson) Au C.; B.A., Pacific U., 1969; m. Susan Swearingen, June 11, 1963; children—Stacy, Kelly. Reporter, editor Redmond (Oreg.) Spokeman, 1964, Portland Oregonian, 1965-66; dir. pub. info. and publs. Pacific U., 1966-73; adminstr. Skidmore, Owings & Merrill, Portland, Oreg., 1973-74; mem. 94th-98th Congresses from 1st Oreg. Dist., mem. Com. on Appropriations. Mem. Oreg. Ho. of Reps., 1971-74, majority leader, 1973-74, chmn. Com. on State and Fed. Affairs, 1973, Com. on Rules, 1974; mem. Govt. Ops. Task Force, Intergovtl. Relations Com., Nat. Legis. Conf., 1973-74, State Emergency Bd., 1973-74. Served with inf., U.S. Army, 1961-64. Named Outstanding Democratic Freshman Legislator, Oreg. Legis. Session, 1971; named 1 of 10 Outstanding Young Men of Am., U.S. Jaycees, 1977. Office: 2159 Rayburn House Office Bldg Washington DC 20515 also 1716 Fed Bldg 1220 SW 3d Ave Portland OR 97204*

AUCUTT, CHARLES HENRY, real estate exec.; b. Mo., July 23, 1934; s. Thomas Mictehll and Blanche Jane (Henry) A.; B.S., U. San Francisco, 1966; diploma Am. Inst. Banking, 1964, Grad. Realtors Inst., 1978; m. Susan Kay Nelson, Sept. 9, 1961; children—Winston Henry, Amy Elizabeth. Trainee, Bank of Am., Stockton, Calif., 1952, 57-58; savs. supr. Wells Fargo Bank, San Francisco, 1958-61; nat. bank examiner Comptroller of Currency, San Francisco, 1961-65; self-employed in investments, 1964-69; asst. v.p., mgr. Valley Nat. Bank, Pacific Grove, Calif., 1969-72; propr. CHA, Inc., Monterey, Calif., 1972—; pres. Monterey County Exchange Counselors. Hon. bd. dirs. Planned Parenthood Monterey County. Served with USAF, 1953-56. Mem. Internat. Real Estate Fedn., Realtors Nat. Mktg. Inst., Farm and Land Inst., Real Estate Syndication and Securities Inst., Nat. Assn. Realtors, Monterey Peninsula Bd. Realtors, Calif. Assn. Realtors, Multiple Listing Service, History and Art Assn. Monterey. Republican. Clubs: Commonwealth (San Francisco); Beach and Tennis (Pebble Beach); Rotary Pacific Grove (past pres.; Rotarian of Year 1973). Home: PO Box 532 Pebble Beach CA 93953 Office: 1011 Cass St Monterey CA 93940

AUDRETSCH, ROBERT WILLIAM, librarian; b. Detroit, Nov. 9, 1941; s. William Sylvester and Catherine Frances (Pultorak) A.; children—William Patrick, Robert William. B.A., Wayne State U., 1969, M.S. in Library Sci., 1970. Reference librarian Southfield (Mich.) Pub. Library, 1970-72; head cataloging dept. Wayne-Oakland Library Fedn., Wayne, Mich., 1972; asst. dir. Warren (Ohio) Pub. Library, 1972-73; dir. Salem (Ohio) Pub. Library, 1973-77, Three Rivers Regional Library Service System, New Castle, Colo., 1978—; mem. faculty Sch. Library Sci., Kent (Ohio) State U., part-time, 1977. Served with U.S. Army, 1964-66. U.S. Office Edn. fellow, 1969-70. Mem. ALA, Mountain-Plains Library Assn., Colo. Library Assn., Colo. Ednl. Media Assn., Nat. Audubon Soc. (v.p. Roaring Fork chpt. 1980-82). Democrat. Clubs: Sierra, Colo. Mountain, Rocky Mountain Road Runners. Editor, compiler: The Salem, Ohio Women's Rights Convention Proceedings, 1976; mem. editorial bd. Rural Libraries, 1981-82; contbr. articles to newspaper and profl. jours. Home: 1308 129 Rd Apt 2A Glenwood Springs CO 81601 Office: PO Box 97 New Castle CO 81647

AUERBACH, EUGENE CHARLES, education company executive; b. Escanaba, Mich., Sept. 4, 1917; s. William and Bessie (Oshinsky) A.; m. Barbara Ann Aiken, Mar. 15, 1941. B.A., UCLA, 1940; M.S., U. So. Calif., 1949, Ph.D., 1957. Gen. secondary credential life diploma, Calif. Tchr.-coordinator Los Angeles High Sch. Dist., 1947-63; syndicated newspaper columnist, 1959-62; v.p., dir. edn. Nat. Systems Corp., 1963-78; sr. v.p., dir. Nat. Edn. Corp., Newport Beach, Calif., 1978—; mng. ptnr. Rolling Mulligan Farms, 1980—, South Coast Oil and Gas, Ltd., 1982—; lectr., vis. prof. U. So. Calif., 1959-64; cons. Calif. Bd. Edn., Calif. Community Coll. advisor Calif. Postsecondary Edn. Commn., 1976-77; mem. Calif. Commn., on Vocat. Edn., 1978-79. Served to 1st lt. USAAF, 1942-45. Decorated DFC Air medal with oak leaf cluster. Mem. Outdoor Writer's Assn. Am., Am. Soc. for Tng. and Devel., Nat. Soc. for Performance and Instrn. Club: Irvine Coast Country (Newport Beach). Author 5 textbooks for N.Am. Corr. Schs., Inc. Home: 272 High Dr Laguna Beach CA 92651 Office: 4361 Birch St Newport Beach CA 92660

AUERBACH, ROGER MICHAEL, labor union executive; b. Bklyn., March 21, 1946; s. George and Helene Janice (Siegel) Auerbach Sparber. B.A., Alfred U., 1968; J.D., Boston U. Law Sch., 1971. Bar: Mass. 1971. Atty., HUD, Boston, 1971-72; buyer, organizer, New Eng. Food Co-op Orgn., Boston, 1973-74; researcher, Oreg. Student Public Interest Research Group, Portland, 1975-76; pres. Oreg. Fedn. Tchrs. AFL-CIO, Portland, 1977—; pres. Oreg. Fedn. Public Employees, AFl-CIO, 1980—; v.p. Oreg. State Indsl. Union Council, AFL-CIO, 1979—; v.p. Pacific NW Labor Coll. Assn., 1977—. Precinct committeeperson Democratic party; mem. community relations com. Jewish Fedn. of Portland; treas. NW Oreg. Health Systems. PO Box 10351 Portland OR 97210

AUERBACH, STEVANNE STOCKHELM, educational administrator, consultant; b. N.Y.C., Sept. 22, 1938; d. Nathan and Jeane Sydney (Rosen) Stockhelm; m. Arthur Auerbach, Nov. 24, 1961 (div. Dec. 1968); 1 dau., Amy Beth.; m. 2d, Don Fink, Feb. 4, 1972 (div. 1980). B.A., Queens Coll., 1960; postgrad. U. Md., 1961-65; M.S., George Washington U., 1965; Ph.D. in Child Devel., Union Grad. Sch., 1973. Tchr. recreation and swimming N.Y. Bd. Edn., 1958-60; tchr. 6th grades, N.Y.C., 1959-60; tchr. 4th grade Haven Elem. Sch., Silver Spring, Md., 1960-61; profl. asst. Am. Personnel and Guidance Assn., Washington, 1961-63; editorial and profl. asst. B'nai B'rith Vocat. Service, Washington, 1963-64; tchr., coordinator mentally retarded children St. John's Devel. Service for Children, Washington, 1965-66; research assoc. analytic study of state legis. for handicapped children Council for Exceptional Children, Washington, 1966-67; ops. coordinator Mid-Atlantic Region Spl. Edn. Instructional Materials Ctr., George Washington U., 1967; tchr. Anthony Bowen Elem. Sch., Washington, 1968; cons. Theatre in Edn. Program, Central Atlantic Regional Ednl. Lab. and Arena Stage, Washington, 1968-69; edn. program specialist evaluation sect., div. compensatory edn., asst. in office of commr. U.S. Office Edn., Washington, 1968-69, child care research and program devel. br. OEO, 1970-71; intern in child devel. Far West Lab., Berkeley, Calif., 1971. Mem. U.S. Nat. Com. Early Childhood Edn. Mem. Council for Exceptional Children (pres. student chpt. Nat. Capital area 1965-66), Am. Personnel and Guidance Assn. (life), Nat. Vocat. Guidance Assn., NEA (pres. student chpt. Queens Coll. 1958-59), Nat. Assn. for Edn. Young Children, Assn. Childhood Edn. Internat., AAUW. Editor: Child Care: A Comprehensive Guide, 4 vols., 1976-79; co-author: Choosing Child Care: A Guide for Parents, 1976, rev., 1980; Confronting the Child Care Crisis, 1979; Whole Child: A SourceBook for Parents, 1980; World of Work and the Family, 1978: The Toy Chest, 1983; contbr. articles to profl. jours., chpts. in books. Office: Inst Childhood Resources 1169 Howard St San Francisco CA 94103

AUGENBLICK, JOHN GILBERT, financial education administrator, consultant; b. Jersey City, May 5, 1947; s. Gilbert Lewis and Maxine (Hillman) A.; m. Frances Nord Green, July 16, 1969; children—John, Edward. B.S. in Humanities and Scis., MIT, 1969; M.A. in Edn. Adminstrn., Columbia U., 1974; Ed.D. in Edn. Adminstrn., U. Rochester, 1981. Tchr., Wilton (Conn.) Pub. Schs., 1969-72; asst. to indsl. engr. Ethan Allen Corp., 1972-73; sr. research assoc. N.J. Commn. Financing Postsecondary Edn., Princeton, N.J., 1975-76; with Edn. Fin. Ctr., Edn. Commn. of States, Denver, 1977—, asst. dir., 1979, dep. dir., 1980, dir., 1981—; pres. Augenblick, Van de Water & Assocs., 1983—; cons. Nat. Inst. Edn., 1978, 79, 81; dir. Port Newark Refrigerated Warehouse, Inc., 1981—. Author edn. reports, papers; contbr. to profl. jours. Home: 2099 Ivy St Denver CO 80207 Office: Box 20276 Denver CO 80220

AUGUST, RICHARD BRUCE, elec. engr., cons.; b. Miami, Fla., June 19, 1952; s. John Joseph and Patricia Adele (Beaton) A.; B.S.E.E., U. So. Calif. 1973; M.S.E.E., M.I.T., 1974; m. Kathleen Leslie Perez, May 15, 1977; 1 son, Richard Bruce II. Pres. SOMED, mfr. med. electronics, 1978—, chmn. bd. SOMED S.A., Mex., 1978—; treas. AAR-O, Inc., 1980—; developer imaging systems for Viking and Voyager Space probes; mem. Viking and Voyager imaging team NASA Jet Propulsion Lab.; developer instrumentation telemetry system USAF Global Positioning System; developer TACFIRE/CCS arty. fire direction system for U.S. Army. Mem. exec. com. Internat. Boxing Hall of Fame, Las Vegas. Served with USNR. Mem. Am. Soc. Engrs. and Architects (former pres.). Contbr. papers to profl. insts. Home: 2680 Monterey Rd San Marino CA 91108

AUGUSTINE, DENNIS F(RANCIS), podiatrist; b. Jersey City, Aug. 26, 1950; s. Frank and Maria (Micalizzi) A.; m. Cecile Weiner, Mar. 25, 1977; 1 son, Jason. Student Northwestern State Coll., Alva, Okla., 1967-69, Wagnar Coll., 1969-70; D.P.M., Ill. Coll. Podiatric Medicine, 1975. Founder, dir., podiatrist Park Ave. Foot Clinic, San Jose, Calif., 1975—; lectr. on ambulatory foot surgery for continuing edn. seminars; lectr. on foot care to numerous sr. citizen ctrs., 1976-82; program coordinator for free sr. citizen foot health screening. Active Council on Aging, San Jose. Recipient Marjorie-Rush Falknor award Ill. Coll. Podiatric Medicine, 1975, award for outstanding service to profession, 1978; commendation San Jose Mayor, 1982. Mem. Acad. Ambulatory Foot Surgery (dir.; Region 8 award for outstanding lectures 1980, Region 4 award for outstanding contbns. to acad. 1981, award for disting. service and dedication to profession 1981, award for excellent sci. representation 1982, award for disting. service and dedication 1982), Am. Acad. Podiatric Sports Medicine, Am. Podiatry Assn., Calif. Podiatry Assn., Central Coast Podiatry Assn., Am. Pub. Health Assn., Am. Soc. Podiatric Angiology, Am. Running and Fitness Assn. Author: How To Market Your Professional Services, 1979; The Foot Care Revolution, How to Walk Away From a Foot Operation On Your Own Two Feet, 1980; med. editor Santa Clara Orgn. Older People Newsletter, Council on Aging.

AULGUR, ROBERT KIRBY, real estate executive; b. Farmington, Mich., July 22, 1929; s. George L. and Clarice M. (Taylor) A.; m. Teri Thompson (div.), Oct. 26, 1977; 1 dau., Christiane. B.A., Mich. State U., 1955; M.B.A., Santa Clara U., 1965. With Edsel div. Ford Motor Co., 1956-58; adminstr. indsl. relations dept. Lockheed Missiles & Space Co., Sunnyvale, Calif., 1958-70; real estate broker, salesman, officer mgr. Dalton Realty, Palo Alto, Calif., 1970-77; owner, mgr. Bob Aulgur Realtors, Palo Alto, 1977—; cons., lectr.; dir. Palo Alto Housing Corp.; mem. Palo Alto Rental Mediation Com. Served to maj USAFR. Mem. Nat. Mgmt. Assn., Palo Alto Real Estate Bd. (dir., Realtor of Yr. 1977). Clubs: Kiwanis, Elks (Palo Alto). Home: 648 Maybell Ave Palo Alto CA 94306 Office: 261 Hamilton Ave Suite 309 Palo Alto CA 94301

AUS, ALFRED BURTON, business executive; b. Portland, Oreg., June 6, 1936; s. Alfred E. and Esther (Westby) A.; divorced: children—A. Michael, Katherine, Kristen, Julie, Elizabeth. Student Lewis and Clark Coll., 1955-56; grad. U.S. Army Command and Gen. Staff Coll., 1974. With Oreg. Typewriter and Recorder, Portland, 1952—, pres., 1966—; pres. Mgrs.' Leasing Co.; expert witness office equipment industry; cons. computer software. Served to col. USAR. Mem. Nat. Office Machine Dealers Assn. (bd. dirs., past pres.). Republican. Lutheran. Club: Rotary (Portland). Office: PO Box 19119 Portland OR 97219

AUSTAD, LORRAINE BLANCHE, interior designer, consultant; b. Las Vegas, Nev., June 21, 1947; d. Willard E. and Phyllis L. (Scott) Baldwin; 1 son, Paul K. B.A. in Design, U. Calif.-Irvine, 1970. Chief designer Dunes Hotel, Las Vegas, 1980-81; project designer Sheraton Hotel, Industry Hills, Calif., 1981; designer Golden Nugget Hotel, Las Vegas and Atlantic City, N.J., 1981-82; cons., South Laguna, Calif., 1968—; cons./designer Le Clarion Hotel, Los Angeles, 1983—. Mem. Am. Soc. Interior Designers, Color Mktg. Group (host regional meeting 1981), chmn. Address: Interiors by Lorraine Austad 31755 S Coast Hwy Suite 306 South Laguna CA 92677

AUSTIN, DONALD STAFFORD, engring. and surveying co. exec.; b. Honolulu, Dec. 2, 1922; s. Herbert Ashford Robertson and Beatrice Margaret (Hancock) A.; student Stanford U., 1941-43; B.S.C.E., U. Hawaii, 1951; m. Ruth Woolley, Aug. 20, 1947; children—Donald Stafford, Margaret, Herbert, Allan. Jr. engr. Hawaiian Airlines, Ltd.,

Honolulu, 1944-47; asst. civil engr. H.A.R. Austin & Assos., Ltd., Honolulu, 1951-57, v.p., treas., 1957-59; pres. Austin, Smith & Assos., Inc., Honolulu, 1959-75; chmn. bd., pres. Austin, Tsutsumi & Assos., Inc., Honolulu, 1975—; instr. dept. engring. U. Hawaii, 1952. Fellow ASCE (recipient Commendation award 1962-66, nat. dir. 1976-79, nat. v.p. 1979-80), Am. Cons. Engrs. Council; mem. Am. Water Resources Assn., Am. Concrete Inst., Am. Water Works Assn., Cons. Engrs. Council Hawaii, Engring. Assn. Hawaii (dir.), Hawaii Water Pollution Control Fedn., Nat. Soc. Profl. Engrs., Soc. Am. Mil. Engrs. (past pres. Honolulu), Water Pollution Control Fedn. Mormon. Club: The Pacific. (Honolulu). Home: 1353 Kainui Dr Kailua HI 96734 Office: 745 Fort St Mall Suite 900 Honolulu HI 96813

AUSTIN, EUGENE HOWARD, writer; b. Poughkeepsie, N.Y., Sept. 1, 1926; s. Eugene Hiram and Florence A.; student Coll. of Sequoias, 1968-72; m. Lucy Mary Ruggiero, Nov. 18, 1950; children—Lucyanne, Eugene John. Free lance writer, poet, 1972—. Mem. Kings County Grand Jury, 1979-80, Kings County Parole Commn., 1980-83. Served with USN, 1943-46, U.S. Army, 1951-57. Mem. Am. Security Council (nat. adv. bd.), Am. Def. Preparedness Assn., U.S. Naval Inst., DAV (life), VFW. Club: K.C. (4th deg.). Home: 8606 La Vaca Way Hanford CA 93230

AUSTIN, JAMES ALBERT, obstetrician and gynecologist, reserve naval officer; b. Phoenix, Sept. 23, 1931; s. Albert Morris and Martha Lumpkin (Mercer) A.; B.A., U. So. Calif., 1952; M.D., George Washington U., 1956; m. Sandra Lee Marsh, Jan. 3, 1979; children—Cynthia Milee, Lauri Jeanne, Wendy Patrice; stepchildren—Kathleen E. Bush, Daniel P. Bush, Jeffery Bush. Intern, resident in obstetrics and gynecology Bethesda (Md.) Naval Hosp., 1956-61; commd. lt. j.g. M.C., U.S. Navy, 1956, advanced through grades to comdr. 1966; service in U.S. and Spain; resigned, 1966, now commodore Res. clin. instr. George Washington U. Sch. Medicine, also Georgetown U. Sch. Medicine, 1966-69; practice medicine specializing in Ob-Gyn, Washington, 1966-69, Phoenix, 1969-78; chief surgery St. Luke's Med. Center, 1971-73, vice chief staff, 1974-75; recalled to active duty as capt., 1978; chief dept. Ob-Gyn, Naval Regional Med. Center, Guam, 1979-81, dir. clin. services, 1979-81; practice medicine, specializing in Ob-Gyn, Coronado, Calif., 1981-83; dir. Ob-Gyn Family Health Program, Salt Lake City; assoc. staff Holy Cross Hosp.; attending staff Salt Lake Surg. Ctr.; past active active staff Coronado Hosp.; cons. Naval Hosp., San Diego; asso. clin. prof. U. Calif., San Diego; cons. surgeon gen. U.S. Navy, 1974—. Bd. dirs. Luke's Men, 1973-74; chmn. Ariz. Med. Polit. Action Com. Served to capt. USNR. Recipient George Washington Honor medal Freedom Found., 1963, 70. Mem. AMA, Ariz. Med. Assn. (dir. 1978—), Am. Coll. Obstetricians and Gynecologists, (triservice rep. to armed forces dist. adv. council 1977-79), Naval Res. Assn. (past nat. surgeon), Assn. Mil. Surgeons U.S., Soc. Med. Cons. to Armed Forces, San Diego Ob-Gyn Soc., Intermountain Microsurg. Soc. Club: Coronado Kiwanis. Address: 791 E Shady Lake Dr Salt Lake City UT 84186

AUSTIN, JAMES ELVYN, mfrs. rep.; b. Modesto, Calif., Dec. 3, 1931; s. James Curry and Mabel (Hansen) A.; B.B.A. in Mktg., San Jose (Calif.) State U., 1953; M.B.A. in Mktg., Pepperdine U., Los Angeles, 1976; m. Jeane Bullok, Sept. 25, 1954; children—James Edward, John Patrick. Dist. mgr. So. Calif., Anderson Electric Co., 1962-65; mktg. and prodn. mgr. Consol. Products Corp., Gardena, Calif., 1965-67; sales and mktg. mgr. Western region Alpha Metals Co., 1967-76; sales mgr. chain div. Western region ACCO (Am. Chain and Cable Co.), Los Angeles, 1976-79; dir. sales and mktg. John Treiber Co., Fountain Valley, Calif., 1979-81; partner Automation Technology, San Jose, Calif., 1981—. Served with U.S. Army, 1954-56. Mem. Sigma Alpha Epsilon (life). Home: 433 Rider Ridge Rd Santa Cruz CA 95065 Office: 1440 Koll Circle Suite 111 San Jose CA 95112

AUSTIN, JO-ANNE JORDAN, artist; b. Springfield, Ohio, Nov. 15, 1925; d. William Conrad and Pauline Nell (McAdams) Jordan; B.A. cum laude, Western Reserve U., 1947; postgrad. Chgo. Acad. Fine Arts, 1947-48; M.F.A., San Diego State Coll., 1956; children—William, Robert, Kathleen, Jill, Audrey. Pub. info. officer San Diego Fine Arts Gallery, 1956-57, tchr., 1954-57; tchr. Santa Barbara (Calif.) schs., 1957-60, owner, dir. Austin Gallery, Santa Barbara, 1966-74, Scottsdale, Ariz., 1975—; one-woman shows Park's Art Gallery, San Jose, Calif., Lucile Fickett Gallery, Los Angeles; exhibited in group shows at Santa Clara U., San Diego State Coll., Fine Arts Gallery San Diego; represented in pub. and pvt. galleries. Tchr. San Diego Art Inst., Fine Arts Gallery San Diego, Santa Barbara schs.; producer film Reflections on Oil (Bronze award N.Y. Internat. Film and TV Festival also Chris award Columbus Film Festival), 1969. Recipient various art awards, San Diego, 1952-56. Mem. Santa Barbara Mus. Art, Art Assn. San Diego, Phoenix Art Mus., Scottsdale Center for Arts, Phi Beta Kappa. Republican. Presbyn. Home: 5117 N 68 Pl Scottsdale AZ 85253 Office: 7103 Main St Scottsdale AZ 85251

AUSTIN, KENNETH MELVIN, psychologist; b. Loma Linda, Calif., Oct. 25, 1931; s. Fred Kenneth and Vada Margaret (VanFleet) A.; m. Joan Lee Faltesek, Sept. 27, 1952 (div.); m. 2d, Cynthia Lorraine Holding, Oct. 24, 1970; 1 dau., Elaine Louise. Ph.D., Calif. Western U., 1975. Lic. psychologist, Calif. Psychologist, County of San Bernardino (Calif.), 1959-65, sr. psychologist, 1966-69, dir. psychol. services, 1970-73, dir. clin. services, 1974-76; pvt. practice, San Bernardino, 1976—. Served to sgt. U.S. Army, 1953-55. Recipient San Bernardino County Bd. Supvs. resolution for 23 yrs. exemplary service, 1976. Mem. Calif. State Psychol. Assn. (ethics com.), Am. Psychol. Assn., Indland So. Calif. Psychol. Assn. (disting. service award 1979). Contbr. articles to profl. jours. Office: 2340 Sierra Way Suite 3 San Bernardino CA 92405

AUSTIN, LORA EVELYN, med. technologist; b. Grand Rapids, Mich., Sept. 6, 1926; d. Carlton and Florence Evelyn (Tyson) Austin; B.A., Olivet Coll., 1948; M.S., Calif. State U., Dominguez Hills, 1981. Intern in med. tech. Butterworth Hosp., Grand Rapids, Mich., 1948-49, staff med. technologist, 1949-52; staff So. Calif. Permanente Med. Group Lab., Los Angeles, 1952—, regional chief immuno-serologist, 1970—; mem. adj. faculty Calif. State U., Dominquez Hills, 1974—. Leader, Campfire Girls, Grand Rapids, Mich., 1949-52; asst. leader Girl Scouts U.S.A., Los Angeles, 1970-81. Recipient Disting. Alumni award Olivet Coll., 1978; lic. med. technologist, Calif., Nat. Cert. Agy. Mem. Am. Soc. Clin. Pathologists (assoc.), Calif. Assn. Med. Lab. Technologists, Am. Soc. Med. Technologists, Olivet Coll. Alumni Assn., Smithsonian Assos., Nat. Wildlife Fedn., Nat. Audubon Soc., Nat. Rifle Assn. Republican. Presbyterian. Home: 10707 Moorpark St Toluca Lake CA 91602

AUSTIN, PATRICIA (PAT) ANN, artist, poet, educator; b. Detroit, Mar. 17, 1937; d. Walter Joseph and Helen (Guzik) Musial; m. Alan Bruce Austin, June 4, 1958. A.B. in English, U. Mich., 1958; B.F.A. in Printmaking, U. Wash., 1970; M.F.A. in Creative Writing, U. Alaska-Anchorage, 1975. Tchr. English, Shelby (Mich.) Pub. Schs., 1959-63; library asst. U. Mich., Ann Arbor, 1964; tchr. English, art Anchorage Sch. Dist., 1965-68; mem. art faculty Anchorage Community Coll., 1972—; pub. Knights Move Publs.-Studio, 1975—; represented in permanent collections: Alaska State Museum and Art Bank (Purchase awards), Anchorage Hist. and Fine Arts Mus. (Purchase awards); works include Governor's Award Presentation Print (commn. 1981); mem. art adv. bd. Anchorage Civic Opera, 1982; panelist selection of pub. art com. Alaska Council on Arts, 1982. Mem. N.W. Print Council (bd.), Alaska Artists Guild. Author catalogue for Contemporary Art from Alaska at Nat. Collection Fine Arts, Smithsonian Instn.: Observations from Inside, 1978; contbr. articles, poems to jours., including Alaska Jour.; subject of biographical article Alaska Jour., 1982; designer logo for Alaska Repertory Theatre, 1976. Home: 7030 Apollo Dr Anchorage AK 99504 Office: Anchorage Community Coll C205B McDonald 2533 Providence Dr Anchorage AK 99504

AUSTIN, SONIA MAXWELL, social worker, cons.; b. Kokomo, Ind., Dec. 15, 1947; d. Charles Clayton and Bernice Louise (Tyrrel) Maxwell. B.Social Work, Washburn U., 1970; M.S.W., U. Kans., 1974. Social work assoc. VA Hosp. Topeka, 1971-72; clin. social worker St. Mary's Hosp., Tucson, 1975-79, dir. social work, 1979—; cons. Can Surmount Program, Cancer Cope; chmn. local service and rehab. com., Am. Cancer Soc., 1982-83. Mem. Nat. Assn. Social Workers (state bd. 1979-81, 82-84), Am. Hosp. Assn., Soc. for Hosp. Social Work Dirs.

AUSTIN, WAYNE GARY, aerospace company executive; b. Mpls., Dec. 21, 1936; s. Theodore Morris and Eloise Ida (Morgan) A.; m. Michiko Hashimoto, May 10, 1965; children—Cassie, Brett. B.A. in Social Sci., Park Coll., 1974; M.A. in Mgmt./Human Relations, Webster Coll., 1975; M.A. in Multicultural Edn., Pepperdine U., 1978. Route salesman Davies Linen Co., San Diego, 1958-60; enlisted U.S. Air Force, 1961, advanced through grades to sr. master sgt., 1980; air traffic controller, 1969-80, ret., 1980; human resources adminstr. TRW, Redondo Beach, Calif., 1980-81, dir. tng. and devel., space and tech. group, 1982—; cons. organizational devel.; tchr. mgmt. courses. Served with USMC, 1954-58. Decorated Meritorious Service medal with 2 oak leaf clusters; Air Force Commendation medal with 3 oak leaf clusters. Mem. Am. Soc. Tng. and Devel., Air Force Sgts. Assn., Pepperdine U. Alumni Assn. Republican. Home: 6541 Klondike Ave Westminster CA 92683 Office: TRW E1/4006 Redondo Beach CA 92078

AUTH, ROBERT R., artist, art educator; b. Bloomington, Ill., Oct. 27, 1926; s. Philip Conrad and Frances Elizabeth (Holtz) A.; m. Alice Faye Auth, June 15, 1979 (div.); children—Christine, Constance, Cindy. B.F.A. in Painting, Ill. Wesleyan U., 1952; M.F.A. in Painting, Wash. State U., 1963. Instr. Burley High Sch., 1960-61, East Jr. High Sch., 1961-67, evening program Boise (Idaho) Jr. Coll., 1967-69, Boise High Sch., 1967—, evening program Coll. Idaho, Caldwell, 1974-75; art supr. Boise Sch. District, Boise, 1981—; one man show: Boise Gallery of Art, 1980; group shows include: U.S. Artrain tour, 1973, Missoula (Mont.) Mus. of Arts, 1975, Boise Gallery of Art, 1976, 54th Ann. Springfield (Utah) Nat. Art Exhbn., 1978; work represented in numerous pub. and corp. collections. Served with USN, 1944-46. Recipient numerous art awards. Mem. Allied Arts Council, Co. Mil. Historians, Idaho Art Assn. (v.p.), Boise Edn. Assn. (bd. dirs.), Boise Gallery of Art Assn. (trustee), Idaho Art Assn. (conf. chmn.). Home: 530 Hillview Dr Boise ID 83702

AUTIO, ARNE RUDY, ceramic artist, art educator; b. Butte, Mont., Oct. 8, 1926; s. Arne Eero and Aiti Autio; m. Lela Ruth Autio, Mar. 17, 1948; children—Arne, Lisa, Lar, Cristofer. B.A. in Art, Mont. State U., 1960; M.F.A. in Sculpture, Wash. State U., Resident artist Archie Bray Found., Helena, Mont., 1952-57, trustee, 1973—; asst. curator Mont. Mus., Helena, 1957; prof. ceramics and sculpture U. Mont., Missoula, 1957—, acting chmn. dept. art, 1968-69, 78-79; artist-in-residence, Arabia, Helsinki, 1981; vis. lectr. U. Helsinki Ateneum, 1982; guest lectr.; condr. workshops; juror various shows; represented in permanent collections Am. Craft Mus., N.Y.C., Archie Bray Found., Arabia Ceramic Co., Helsinki, Contemporary Crafts Assn., Portland, Oreg., Henry Gallery, U. Wash., Seattle, Lannan Found., Palm Beach, Fla., Mont. Mus., Portland Art Mus., San Francisco Mus. Modern Art, Seattle Art Mus., Smithsonian Mus., Toledo Art Mus., Univs. Ariz., Mich., Oreg., Utah, Wichita Art Assn. (Kans.). Bd. dirs. No. Mus. Ariz., Flagstaff, 1976. Served with USN, 1944-46. Recipient Tiffany Found. award, 1963, Am. Ceramic Soc. award, 1978, Mont. Gov.'s 1st ann. arts award, 1980; U. Mont. ceramics research grantee, 1972; Nat. Endowment for Arts craftsman's fellow, 1980. Fellow Am. Crafts Council; mem. Nat. Council on Edn. Ceramic Arts (hon.), Yellowstone Art Ctr. Office: Dept Art U Mont Missoula Mt 59812

AUTRY, ORVON GENE, singer, actor, radio entertainer, broadcasting exec.; b. Tioga, Tex., Sept. 29, 1907; s. Delbert and Elnora (Ozment) A.; grad. Tioga High Sch., 1925; m. Ina Mae Spivey, Apr. 1, 1932 (dec. 1980); m. 2d, Jacqueline Ellam, July 1981. Began as railroad telegraph operator, Sapulpa, Okla., 1925; made first phonograph record of cowboy songs, 1929; radio artist Sta. WLS, Chgo., 1930-34; motion picture actor, 1934—, including film In Old Santa Fe; starred in 88 musical Western feature pictures, 95 half-hour TV pictures; pres., chmn. bd. Calif. Angels; owner TV sta. KAUT-TV, Oklahoma City, radio stas. KMPC, Hollywood, KSFO, San Francisco, KVI-AM and KPLZ-FM, Seattle, KEX and KRRZ, Portland, Oreg., WCXI and WCXI-FM, Detroit. Served with USAAF, 1942-45. Mem. Internat. Footprinters. Clubs: Masons (32 deg.); Shriners; Elks. Has written over 250 songs including That Silver-Haired Daddy of Mine, 1931; You're the Only Star in My Blue Heaven, 1938; Dust, 1938; Tears On My Pillow, 1941; Be Honest With Me, 1941; Tweedle O'Twill, 1942; Here Comes Santa Claus, 1948. Address: care Golden West Broadcasters 5858 W Sunset Blvd PO Box 710 Hollywood CA 90078

AVERILL, DONALD FREDERICK, educator, consultant; b. Los Angeles, Jan. 9, 1938; s. Anthony Michael and Anita Marie (Moser) A.; m. Carol Jean Hules, Aug. 19, 1939; children—Margaret, Kathleen, Donald James. B.A., Calif. State U.-Los Angeles, 1960, M.A., 1965; Ed.D., U. La Verne (Calif.), 1982. Tchr. core math. Norwalk La Mirada pub. schs., 1961-63; tchr., coordinator work experience edn. Whittier (Calif.) Union High Sch. Dist., 1963-72; dir. career edn. Huntington Beach (Calif.) Union High Sch. Dist., 1972-77; vice chancellor ednl. planning and vocat. edn. Coast Community Colls., Costa Mesa, Calif., 1977—; cons., v.p., Alternatives Assocs. Chmn. La Habra (Calif.) Planning Commn., 1982. Served with Air N.G., 1956-62. Named Vocat. Educator of Yr., Calif. Adv. Council Vocat. Edn., 1979. Mem. Assn. Calif. Community Coll. Adminstrs., Calif. Community Coll. Adminstrs. Occupational Edn., Calif. Work Experience Educators. Republican. Roman Catholic. Clubs: Kiwanis (Fountain Valley, Calif.), K.C.; Sertoma (past pres., Seratoman Yr. 1977). Editor Am. Vocat. Assn. Yearbook, 1982; contbr. articles to profl. jours. Office: 1370 Adams Ave Costa Mesa CA 92626

AVERY, ARTHUR WILLIAM, psychologist; b. Wilmington, Del., June 11, 1949; s. Arthur Wolcott and Merylyn Meeks A.; B.A., Pa. State U., 1971, M.S., 1973, Ph.D., 1975. Doctoral fellow Coll. Human Devel., Pa. State U., 1974-75; dir. grad. program human devel. and family studies Tex. Tech. U., Lubbock, 1975-79; prof., dir. Human Devel. Lab., U. Ariz., 1979—. Groves fellow, 1975; NIH grantee, 1980—. Mem. Am. Psychol. Assn., Am. Assn. Marriage and Family Therapy, Nat. Council Family Relations, Groves Conf. Marriage and Family, Phi Beta Kappa, Psi Chi, Alpha Kappa Delta. Contbr. articles to profl. jours. Home: 444 W Orange Grove Rd 915 Tucson AZ 85704 Office: Human Devel Lab U Ariz Tucson AZ 85721

AVERY, CHARLES CARRINGTON, forester, educator; b. Syracuse, N.Y., July 22, 1933; s. Edward Carrington and Elizabeth Amelia (Boorum) A.; B.S., Utah State U., 1961; cert. French, Nat. Sch. Forests and Waters, 1962; M.F., Duke U., 1963; Ph.D., U. Wash., 1972; m. Valeen Tippetts, Sept. 13, 1961; children—Christopher E., Maureen E., Nathan C., Theodore C. Forester, U.S. Forest Service, Wenatchee, Wash., 1961-64; hydrologist U.S. Forest Service, Laramie, Wyo., 1964-66, research hydrologist, Flagstaff, Ariz., 1967-74; asso. prof. forestry No. Ariz. U. Sch. Forestry, 1974-80, prof., 1980—; chmn. No. Ariz. Regional Water Quality Mgmt. Program, 1976-78. Served with U.S. Army, 1953-55. Fulbright fellow, 1961-62. Mem. Ariz.-Nev. Acad. Sci. (pres. 1978-79), Soc. Am. Foresters, Am. Geophys. Union, Ecol. Soc. Am., Sigma Xi, Phi Kappa Phi. Democrat. Mormon. Club: Rotary. Office: Sch Forestry No Ariz U Flagstaff AZ 86011

AVERY, PATRICK LUCAS, chemist; b. Arkansas City, Kans., Oct. 31, 1952; s. John J. and Shirlee (Baier) A.; B.A. in Biology, U. Colo., 1975, B.A. in Chemistry, 1977, M.S. in Environ. Engring., 1983. Hydrologist Water Resources div. U.S. Geol. Survey, Denver, 1977-79; sr. environmentalist Douglas (Conoco) Oil Co., Paramount, Calif., 1980-81; environ. engr. Atlantic Richfield Co.-Watson Refinery, Carson, Calif., 1981—. Mem. Research Soc. N.Am., Am. Chem. Soc., Am. Petroleum Inst., Sigma Xi. Home: 1141 E Carson Long Beach CA 90807 Office: 1801 E Sepulveda Carson CA 90749

AVEY, GARY MICHAEL, publisher; b. Phoenix, June 5, 1940; s. George Mourice and Edith (Barbara Eaton) A.; B.S., Ariz. State U., 1965, postgrad., 1975—; m. Norma F. Barrow, Dec. 8, 1961; children—Marci Lynn, Mark Bradford. Editor, adv. yearbooks Ariz. State U., 1962-64; asst. to pres. Tyler Printing Co., Phoenix, 1963-65; commd. 2d lt. U.S. Army, 1965, advanced through grades to capt., 1968; assigned Cav. Sch., Ft. Knox, Ky.; reconnaissance platoon leader 2d Cav., Bamberg, Ger.; squadron border intelligence officer, Ft. Lewis, Wash.; ret., 1980; asst. Western regional mgr. W.A. Krueger Co., Phoenix, 1969-79; editor Ariz. Hwys. Mag., Phoenix, 1979-83; assoc. pub., exec. v.p. KC Publs., 1983—. Mem. Ariz. Acad. (gov.'s commn. on environ.), Ariz. Hist. Soc., Colo. Antique Gun Collectors Assn., Phoenix Advt. Club, Phoenix Art Dirs. Club, N.Am. Mktg. Com., Office Tourism, Theta Delta Chi. Episcopalian. Club: Rotary Internat. Office: 2039 W Lewis St Phoenix AZ 85009

AVILA, EDWARD EMANUEL, social worker, counselor; b. Vallejo, Calif., Sept. 1, 1937; s. Edward Earnest Avila and Eleanor Theresa (Day) Jenkins; m. Diane Edith Curtis, Jan. 2, 1965; children—Daniel Wayne, Scott Andrew. A.A., Napa Coll., 1957; B.A. in Sociology, Calif. State U.-San Jose, 1959; M.Div., Am. Bapt. Sem. of the West, 1962; M.S. in Counseling Psychology, U. Oreg., 1977. Asst. youth dir. Berkeley (Calif.) YMCA, 1963-64; social worker, caseworker Alameda County Welfare Dept., Oakland, Calif., 1964-71; caseworker, Children's Services Div., Eugene, Oreg., 1971—, child protective services intake screener, 1982—; counselor Eugene Friends Counseling Service, 1973-75, 78-79, Christian Family Service, Eugene, 1980—; pvt. practice counseling, 1980—; facilitator support group for parents. Elder, Lowell (Oreg.) Christian Ch., past chmn. bd., facilitator Sunday Sch. Class; active Sunday Sch. and youth work various chs. Served with USAFR, 1954-60. Mem. Am. Personnel and Guidance Assn. Home: 91972 Lost Valley Ln Dexter OR 97431

AVILA, LIDIA D., school administrator; b. Phoenix; d. Pete A. and Elvira (Duarte) A. M.A. in Edn., NDEA Inst., UCLA-Phillipines, 1964; Ed.D., Ariz. State U., 1980. Cert. elem. tchr., counselor, adminstr. Successively tchr., counselor, coordinator Wilson Sch. Dist., Phoenix, 1958-73, prin., 1973-75; adult edn. tchr., Tempe, Ariz., 1966-68; fed. project reader cons., Phoenix, 1968-72; prin. Glendale Elem. Sch. Dist. (Ariz.), 1976—; textbook cons. Active Robert A Taft Inst. Govt., 1981; del. Inter-Club Council Women's Orgn. Greater Phoenix area; bd. dirs. YWCA, 1968-70. Baylor U. Leadership/Mgmt. Inst. grantee 1980; NDEA grantee, 1968. Mem. Am. Bus. Women's Assn. (Woman of Yr. 1982), Assn. Supervision and Curriculum Devel., Nat. Assn. Elem. Sch. Prins. (participant nat. fellows program), Delta Kappa Gamma, Phi Delta Kappa. Democrat. Roman Catholic. Home: Phoenix AZ Office: 5734 W Glendale Ave Glendale AZ 85301

AWADA, MICHAEL JAMIL, banker; b. Beirut, Lebanon, Jan. 5, 1940; s. Jamil Awada and Fatima Hussein (Nassar) A.; B.A., Patriarchal Coll., Beirut, 1958; M.B.A., Pepperdine U., 1978; m. Jo Ann Reinmiller, Mar. 18, 1972; children—Tarek, Iehad. Mgr. Credit Lyonnais, Beirut, 1960-66; supt. Polietileno, Monterrey, Mexico, 1967-69; with Credit Lyonnais, Beirut, 1970-72; gen. mgr. internat. dept. Security Nat. Bank, Oakland, Calif., 1973-75; v.p. internat. dept. Bank of Boston, Los Angeles, 1975-79; v.p., agt. Multibanco Comermex, S.N.C., Los Angeles, 1979—. Mem. Pacific Rim Bankers Assn., Brazil-Calif. Trade Assn., U.S.-Mexico C. of C., Nat. Assn. Arab-Ams., Arab-Am. Anti-Discrimination Com. Clubs: Toastmasters, Jonathan, Rotary. Contbr. articles to profl. jours. Home: 4785 Galendo St Woodland Hills CA 91364 Office: 515 S Figueroa St 10th Floor Los Angeles CA 90071

AWANI, ALFRED OWUMI, aerospace engineer; b. Warri, Nigeria, Jan. 14, 1952; s. Owumi Gray and Celia Nonekuone (Ebietomere) A.; m. Denise Iola DeVoe, June 21, 1975. B.S. in Aero. Engring., Aerospace Inst., Chgo., 1975; M.S. in Mgmt., Northrop U., Inglewood, Calif., 1978, M.S. in Aerospace Engring., 1977; D.E. in Aerospace Engring., U. Kans., Lawrence, 1981. Asst. prof. Aero-Space Inst., 1978-79; asst. instr. engring. project mgmt. U. Kans., 1980, teaching asst. aircraft flight dynamics, 1979-80; research assoc. NASA Ames Research Ctr., Moffett AFB, Calif., 1980-83; project engr. Hughes Helicopters, Inc., 1983—. Mem. AIAA, Soc. Logistics Engrs., Am. Soc. Aerospace Edn., Assn. M.B.A. Execs., Am. Helicopter Soc., Helicopter Club Am., Sigma Gamma Tau. Anglican. Author textbook on project mgmt., numerous tech. papers; contbr. articles to profl. jours. Home: 4822 Hollow Corner Rd Apt 275 Culver City CA 90230 Office: Hughes Helicopters Inc Bldg 6 M/S C490 Culver City CA 90230

AWEIDA, NAIM SALEH, computer company executive; b. Nablus, Palestine, Dec. 9, 1928; s. Saleh J. and Jameeleh A. (Abbed) A.; came to U.S., 1969, naturalized, 1974; student schs., Haifa, Palestine; m. Aida N. Salfiti, Dec. 17, 1955; children—Rema, Lena, Ramzi, Andy. Auditor, Saba & Co., Haifa, 1946-48; mgr. field ops. Internat. Red Cross Soc., Jordan, 1948-50; project mgr. UN Relief and Works Agy., Jordan, 1950-51; auditor, acct. Arabian Am. Oil Co., Dhahran, Saudi Arabia, 1951-55; with Am. embassy, Amman, Jordan, 1955-67; coordinator Middle East activities Luth. World Relief, Amman, 1967-69; exec. v.p. field ops. div. Storage Tech. Corp., Louisville, Colo., 1969-82, pres., 1982—. Decorated Annahdha medal (Jordan). Home: 7474 Spring Dr Boulder CO 80303 Office: Storage Tech Corp 2270 S 88th St Louisville CO 80028

AWTRY, JOHN H., lawyer, ret. army officer, ins. exec.; b. Quitman, Tex., July 29, 1897; s. Emmett and Elizabeth (Williams) A.; J.D., U. Tex., 1921; m. Nell Catherine Jacoby; 1 dau., Nell Catherine Awtry Gilchrist (dec.). With Fed. Res. Bank of Dallas, 1917-19; with Govt. Savs. Div., Dept. Treasury, 1919-20; admitted to Tex. bar, 1920, U.S. Supreme Ct., Ct. Mil. Appeals bars; partner firm Taylor & Awtry, 1921-23; handled ins. on intra and interstate motor buses and trucks 17 years; pres. First Reins. Co. of Hartford (Conn.), 1936-41, John H. Awtry & Co., Inc., N.Y.C.; owner John H. Awtry & Co., Dallas; commd. officer AUS, 1942; active mil. service, 1942-53; assisted planning, participated in invasion of Europe 1944; on War Dept. Gen. Staff, 1946; chief fraud unit War Dept., Dept. Army, 1946-49; chief (lt. col.) contract and procurement br. Judge Adv. Div., European Command, 1949-50; mem. Army panel Armed Services Bd. Contract Appeals, Office Asst. Sec. Army, Washington; col. (promoted by direct order Pres. U.S.), U.S. Army and U.S. Army Res., ret. 1953; lectr. Leisure World, Laguna Hills, Calif. Decorated Bronze Star medal,

Legion of Merit. Mem. N.Y. So. Soc., 12th Army Group Assn. (life), Judge Advs. Assn., N.Y. State C. of C., Fed., Am., N.Y., Tex. (life), Dallas bar assns., Mil. Order World Wars, Am. Legion (life), Washington Tex. Soc., Fed. Grand Jury Assn., U. Tex. Ex Assn. (life), DAV, Ret. Officers Assn. (life), Lambda Chi Alpha. Baptist. Clubs: Masons (32 deg.), Shriners, High Twelve, Nat. Sojourners, Nat. Exchange (ct. of honor; nat. pres.), Drug and Chem., Downtown Athletic, Bankers of Am. (N.Y.C.); Town (life) (Scarsdale, N.Y.); Scarsdale Golf (Hartsdale, N.Y.); Hartford Comm. Dallas Athletic, Dallas Exchange (life, 1st pres.); Nat. Exchange (ex-pres.); Army and Navy (Washington). Opinions as mem. Armed Services Bd. Contract Appeals in Commerce Clearing House legal publs. Home: 3337-2A Punta Alta Rossmoor Leisure World PO Box 2833 Laguna Hills CA 92653

AWTRY, JOHN HIX, lawyer, ret. army officer, former ins. exec.; b. Quitman, Tex., July 29, 1897; s. Emmett and Elizabeth (Williams) A.; LL.B., U. Tex., 1921, J.D., 1969; m. Nell Catherine Jacoby; 1 dau., Nell Catherine (Mrs. William W. Gilchrist) (dec.). With Fed. Bank of Dallas, 1917-19, Govt. Savs. Div. Treasury Dept., 1919-20; admitted to U.S. Supreme Ct. bar, Tex. bar, also U.S. Ct. Mil. Appeals, U.S. Ct. Claims; with Taylor & Awtry, attys., 1921-23; handled ins. on intra and interstate motor buses and trucks 17 years; pres. First Reins. Co. of Hartford (Conn.), 1936-41; pres. John H. Awtry & Co., Inc., N.Y.C.; owner John H. Awtry & Co., Dallas; commd. officer U.S. Army, 1942-53, advanced through grades to col. by order of Pres.; assisted planning, participated in invasion of Europe as staff mem. 12th and 1st U.S. Army Groups, 1943, 44; mem. Gen. Staff War Dept., 1946; chief fraud unit War Dept., Dept. Army, 1946-49; chief (lt. col.) contract and procurement br. Judge Adv. Div., European Command, 1949-50; mem. Army panel Armed Services Bd. Contract Appeals, Office Asst. Sec. Army, Washington; ret., 1953. Decorated Bronze Star, Legion of Merit; recipient commendation U.S. atty. gen. Mem. N.Y. So. Soc., 12th Army Group Assn. (life), Judge Advs. Assn. (life), N.Y. State C. of C., Fed. (life), Am. (life), Tex. (life), Dallas (life) bar assns., State Bar Tex., Fed. Grand Jury Assn. N.Y., Mil. Order World Wars, Am. Legion, Washington Tex. Soc., U. Tex. Ex-Students Assn. (life), Officers Assn. (life), Am. Assn. Ret. Persons (past pres. Leisure World chpt.), Patriotic Letterwriters Club, Orange County Ret. Officers Club, El Toro-Santa Ana Marine Corps Air Sta. Officers Club, Disabled Officers Assn., Assn. U.S. Army, Nat. Sojourners (life), Lambda Chi Alpha. Republican. Baptist. Mason (32 deg. Shriner). Clubs: High Twelve, Drug and Chemical, Downtown Athletic, Bankers of Am. (N.Y.C.); Town (life) (Scarsdale, N.Y.); Scarsdale Golf (Hartsdale, N.Y.); Hartford; Dallas Athletic (life), Dallas Exchange (1st pres.; life), Nat. Exchange (twice nat. pres.; ct. honor); Army and Navy (Washington); Leisure World Masons, Exchange of Leisure World; Saddleback Valley Masons. Opinions as mem. Armed Services Bd. Contract Appeals pub. in Commerce Clearing House legal Publs. Home: PO Box 2833 3337-2A Punta Alta Rossmoor Leisure World Laguna Hills CA 92653

AWTRY, NELL CATHERINE, real estate executive; b. Dallas, Sept. 29, 1900; d. Henry Hibbler and Laura Jane (Harris) Jacoby; B.A., So. Meth U., 1935; postgrad. Columbia, 1941-42; m. John Hix Awtry, Apr. 24, 1922; 1 dau., Nell C. (Mrs. William W. Gilchrist) (dec.). Real estate saleswoman Prince & Ripley, Scarsdale, N.Y., 1948, Midgeley Parks, Scarsdale, 1949, Cleveland E. Van Wert, Inc., Scarsdale, 1954-60, Julia B. Fee, Inc., Scarsdale, 1960-73. Former mem. Scarsdale Realty Bd., Westchester Realty Bd. Mem. Am. Legion Aux. (vice comdr.), Leisure World Am. Aux., Zeta Tau Alpha. Republican. Baptist. Mem. Order Eastern Star (worthy matron 1961, 67). Clubs: Scarsdale Golf, Dallas Athletic, Leisure World Republican. Author poems and lyrics. Home: 3337-2A Punta Alta Rossmoor Leisure World PO Box 2833 Laguna Hills CA 92653

AXELROD, TODD MICHAEL, investment banker; b. Bklyn., Oct. 25, 1949; s. Herbert Richard and Ruth (Levy) Canvasser; m. Nancy Elizabeth Haag (div. Dec. 8, 1982). B.S., NYU, 1973. Lic. gen. securities prin. Sr. v.p. Bache Halsey Stuart Shields, La Jolla, Calif., 1980-81; pres. Am. Mus. Hist. Documents, Las Vegas, 1981—, exec. dir., 1981—; pres. Western Diversified Equities Corp., Las Vegas, 1982—; pres. TMA Industries Inc., Las Vegas, 1980—, permaTek Inc., Las Vegas, 1980—; adj. prof. fin. U. Nev.-Las Vegas. Mem. Manuscript Soc., Nat. Assn. Securities Dealers. Office: Western Diversified Equities Corp 520 S 4th St Suite 340 Las Vegas NV 89101

AXELSON, JOHN ALLAN, aeronautical engineer; b. San Diego, Sept. 22, 1920; s. Carl Ivan and Ida Christina (Johnson) A.; m. Edna Louise Bellah, June 12, 1945; m. 2d, Shirley Rose Friedrichs, June 5, 1970; children—Christine Adele, Terrence Allan. B.S., U. Calif.-Berkeley, 1942; M.S., Stanford U., 1949. Mech. engr. Ames Aero. Lab., NACA, 1942-59; aero. research engr. NASA, Ames Research Ctr., Moffett Field, Calif., 1960-76, ret., 1976; pvt. contractor, cons., Walnut Creek, Calif. Served to lt. comdr. USNR, 1944-67. Mem. Stanford Alumni Assn. (life), U. Calif. Alumni Assn. (life), AIAA. Democrat. Lutheran. Club: Sons in Retirement, Walnut Creek. Contbr. papers to tech. publs.; patentee in field. Home: 3054 Ebano Dr Walnut Creek CA 94598

AXLINE, STANTON GERALD, physician, medical educator; b. Columbus, Ohio, July 11, 1935; s. Raymond Floyd and Merle Patria (Rader) A.; divorced; children—Thomas Allen, Sheryl Lynne. B.A., Ohio State U., 1956, M.D., 1960. Intern, U. Colo., Denver, 1960-61; resident in internal medicine Stanford U. Med. Ctr., 1961-63, fellow in infectious disease, 1963-65; guest investigator Rockefeller U., N.Y.C., 1967-69; asst. prof. internal medicine Stanford U., 1969-76; assoc. prof. internal medicine U. Ariz., Tucson, 1976-82, chief infectious disease sect, 1977-82; assoc. chief research and devel. VA Med. Ctr., Tucson, 1976-82; med. dir. Virology Research Corp., Beverly Hills, Calif., 1983—. Served as capt. with USAF, 1965-67. Mem. Infectious Disease Soc. Am., Am. Soc. Cell Biology, Am. Assn. Immunologists, Am. Fedn. Clin. Research. Contbr. articles to profl. jours. Home: 845 20th St Apt 201 Santa Monica CA 90403 Office: 8911 Wilshire Blvd Beverly Hills CA 90211

AXTELL, RONALD JAY, police chief; b. San Angelo, Tex., Jan. 6, 1944; s. Jay Milton and Barbara Louise (Bowman) A.; m. Diane Templeton Lundie, Mar. 20, 1965; children—Hallie Diane, Camille Renee Lemons, Jason Lee, Jacqueline Carol Lemons, Joshua Jay; m. 2d Anita Renee Ultch, Aug. 29, 1980. A.S., N.Mex. State U., 1982. With Las Cruces (N.Mex.) Police Dept., 1967—, asst. adminstr., 1973-78, chief of police, 1978—. Bd. dirs. Las Cruces Boys Club, 1974; La Casa Inc., 1982. Served with USNR, 1963-67. Mem. Internat. Assn. Chiefs of Police. Democrat. Methodist.

AYAD, BOULOS AYAD, archaeology educator; b. Egypt, May 3, 1928; came to U.S., 1967, naturalized, 1973; s. Ayad Ayad; B.A., U. Cairo, 1952, M.A., 1957, Ph.D. with honors, 1963; M.A., U. Ain Shams, 1953; M.A., Higher Inst. Coptic Studies, 1960; m. Suzanne E., Feb. 14, 1970; children—Mary, Thereza, Boulos. Asst. prof. U. Utah, 1967-68; asst. prof. U. Colo., Boulder, 1968-72, assoc. prof., 1972-77, prof. archaeology and ancient langs. of Middle East, 1977—, univ. fellow, 1974-75. Mem. African Studies Assn., Sociète d'Archeologie Copte, AAUP, Am. Assn. Tchrs. Arabic, Smithsonian Instn., Soc. Bible Friends. Coptic Orthodox. Author: Coptic Grammar and Texts, 1971; The Jewish-Aramaean Communities in Ancient Egypt, 1975; The Aramaeans in Egypt, 1975; Aramaeans in the Ancient Middle East, 1982; The Four Gospels: Manuscripts from the 13th Century A.D., 1982; The Jewish-Aramaean Civilization and its Relationship to the Ancient Egyptian Civilization, 1982; The Aramaens in the Ancient Middle East 1982; The Four Gospels: Manuscripts Written from the 13th Century A.D., 1982; translator: Book of Job (from Syriac into Arabic), 1975; others; contbr. articles in field to profl. jours. Home: 1332 Scrub Oak Circle Boulder CO 80303 Office: Dept Anthropology Colo Boulder CO 80309

AYALA, RUBEN SAMUEL, state senator; b. Chino, Calif., Mar. 6, 1922; s. Mauricio R. and Erminia (Martínez) A.; student Pomona Jr. Coll., 1941-42; grad. Nat. Electronic Sch., Los Angeles, 1948; m. Irene Morales, July 22, 1945; children—Buddy, Maurice Edward, Gary. City councilman City of Chino, 1962-64, mayor, 1964-66; bd. suprs., 1966-73; chmn. San Bernardino County Bd. Suprs., 1968-72; mem. Calif. Senate, 1974—, chmn. agrl. and water resources com., 1976—, mem. revenue and taxation com., 1973—, mem. transp. com., 1981. Mem. Chino Sch. Bd., 1955-62; chmn. San Bernardino County Health Com., 1968-72, Chino Police Commn., 1964-66, Chino Parks and Recreation Commn., 1962-64; mem. Nat. Alliance of Businessmen Com., Washington, 1970; chmn. W. Valley Planning Agy., 1968-72; mem. steering com. County Hwy. Safety Orgn., 1968-72; bd. dirs. Pomona Freeway Assn., 1968. Served with USMC, World War II; PTO. Recipient Citizen of Year award Chino Valley C. of C., 1970; named Calif. Legislator of Yr., 1980. Mem. Assn. Calif. Water Agys., Assn. Calif. Engrs., Am. Legion, Native Sons of Golden West. Club: Kiwanis. Office: 353 W 6th St Suite 103 San Bernardino CA 92401*

AYER, HARRY WRIGHT, agricultural economist, educator, researcher, consultant; b. Deadwood, S.D., Dec. 5, 1942; s. Darrell Pike and Arthula (Wright) A.; m. Barbara Miller Aug. 15, 1964; children—Jeffrey, Brian, Thomas. B.S., Iowa State U., 1964; M.S., Purdue U., 1967, Ph.D. 1970. Asst. prof. agrl econs. U. Ariz., Tucson, 1970-75, assoc. prof. 75, prof., 1975-76; agrl. economist. Econ. Research Service, U.S. Dept of Agr., 1976-82. Recipient cert. of merit U.S. Dept. Agr., 1981; Rice Estate fellow, 1964; NDEA fellow, 1965-68; Ford Found fellow, 1968-70; Am. Assn Agrl. Economists and Internat. Assn. Agrl Economists fellow, 1973. Mem. Am. Econ. Assn., Am. Agrl. Econ. Assn., Western Agrl. Econ. Assn., Internat. Assn. Agrl. Economists, Western Regional Sci. Assn. Presbyterian. Contbr. articles to profl. jours. Office: Dept of Agrl Econs U Ariz Tucson AZ 85721

AYERS, KEN C., city official; b. Redondo Beach, Calif., Jan. 20, 1939; s. Clark H. and Dorothy (Sneary) A.; m. Dawn Ellen Wilson, Sept. 6, 1957; children—Debra, Kenneth, Denise. Asst. dir. gen. services City of Redondo Beach (Calif.), 1957-70; maintenance supt. City of Palos Verdes Estates (Calif.), 1971-74; dir. pub. services City of Gardena (Calif.), 1974—. Mem. Am. Pub. Works Assn., St. Supts. and Maintenance Assn.

AYERS, RENDALL PAUL, public relations consultant; b. Wichita Falls, Tex., Aug. 25, 1937; s. Richard Kelly and Gertrude Christine (Paul) A.; m. Sara Lee Hoffman, Aug. 27, 1960; children—Sydney Lynn, Reed A. B.A. in Journalism, U. Colo., 1961. Asst. bur. chief AP, Helena, Mont., 1960-61; asst. city editor Denver Post, 1962-67; dist. mgr. Ins. Info. Inst., Denver, 1968-69; pub. relations mgr. Denver div. Safeway Stores, Inc., 1970-74; pres. William Kostka & Assocs., Denver, 1975-80; prin. Rendall Ayers Pub. Relations, Denver, 1980—; lectr. in field. Bd. dirs. Men's Assistance Ctr., 1970-82, pres., 1974-76; bd. dirs. Colo. Heart Assn., 1970—, pres., 1977-78, chmn. Colo. Heart Fund campaign, 1971-73; bd. dirs. Goodwill Industries Denver, 1970—, v.p. 1981—; bd. dirs. Colo. Retail Council; active Mile High United Way. Recipient award Outstanding Reporting, Denver Newspaper Guild, 1966; Outstanding Vol. award Colo. Heart Assn., 1973. Mem. Pub. Relations Soc. Am. (accredited, pres. Colo. chpt. 1978), Pub. Relations Soc. Am. Counselors Acad., Sigma Delta Chi, Denver C. of C., Alpha Delta Sigma. Republican. Unitarian. Clubs: Press, Lakewood Country, Meadow Creek Racquet (Denver). Office: 2480 W 26th Ave Suite 100B Denver CO 80211

AYERS, THEODORE G., aeronautical engineer; b. Valentine, Nebr., Oct. 30, 1935; s. Ted J. and Doris M. (Harms) A.; m. Kathryn Hefina, July 24, 1957; children—David, Kathy Andrew. B. S. in Aero. Engring., Northrop Inst. Tech., 1961. Aerospace engr. NASA Langley Research Ctr., 1961-70, mgr. aerodynamics Advanced Transport Tech. Office, 1970-72, sr. aerospace engr., 1972-76; exchange engr. to NASA Dryden Flight Research Facility, 1974-75, dir. aerodynamics div. 1976-79, chief aero. engring. div., 1979-82, dep. dir. flight ops. Ames Research ctr., 1982—. Trustee Tehachapi Sch. Dist. Served with U.S. Army, 1954-57. Mem. AIAA (charter, tech. com. on aerodynamics). Presbyterian. Contbr. articles to NASA, other profl. publs. Home: 1223 Start Route 2 Tehachapi CA 93561 Office: Code O NASA Edwards CA 93523

AYLER, MAYNARD FRANKLIN, geologist; b. Tacoma, Wash., Oct. 15, 1922; s. Thomas Franklin and Edith (Sivear) A.; student Wash. State U., 1940-43; E.M., Colo. Sch. Mines, 1945, M.S., 1963; m. Marjory Annabelle Loyd, Aug. 25, 1945; children—Corliss Ann, David Franklin. Geologist U.S. Bur. of Reclamation, Denver, 1945-46; geologist The California Co., Lexington, Ky., Denver and New Orleans, 1947-52; mem. faculty Colo. Sch. of Mines, Golden, 1958-63, project mgr. Colo. Sch. Mines Research Inst., Golden, 1968-73; mining engr. U.S. Bur. Mines, Denver, 1961-64, 66—; mining engr. Ill. Inst. Tech. Research Inst., 1964-66; chief geol. sect. Ministry of Industry Govt. of Libya, Tripoli, 1964-66; v.p., treas., dir. Mineral Industries Engrs., Inc., Golden, Colo., 1967-68; minerals cons. Golden, 1952—; v.p. Energy Devel. Cons., 1977; lectr. U. Md., Wheelus AFB, Tripoli, 1965-66. Playing mem., pres. Brico Symphony, Golden Symphony Orch.; playing mem., bd. dirs. Mostly Strauss Orch. Served with AUS, 1946-47. Registered profl. engr., Colo. Mem. Am. Inst. Mining, Metall. and Petroleum Engrs., Am. Assn. Petroleum Geologists, Am. Inst. Profl. Geologists, Am. Def. Preparedness Assn. (dir. Colo.-Wyo. chpt. 1982—), Rocky Mountain Assn. Geology, Am. Geol. Inst., Assn. Profl. Geol. Scientists, Colo. Sch. Mines Alumni Assn. Address: 1315 Normandy Golden CO 80401

AYLWARD, JOHN DAVID, lawyer; b. Chgo., Oct. 11, 1950; s. John Joseph and Josephine Marie (Terrell) Aylward; m. Nancy Ann Radawski, May 19, 1972. B.A., U. Notre Dame, 1972; J.D., Washington U., St. Louis, 1976. Bar: Colo. 1976. Sole practice Ft. Collins, Colo., 1976-78; ptnr. Bye, Gascoyne, & Aylward, Ft. Collins, 1978—. Bd. dirs. Ft. Collins Community Crisis Ctr., 1977-80, Elizabeth Stone Resources Ctr., 1978-81. Mem. ABA, Colo. Bar Assn., Larimer County Bar Assn. Democrat. Roman Catholic. Lodge: Elks. Home: 1020 W Oak St Fort Collins CO 80521 Office: Bye Gascoyne & Aylward PO Box 1905 Fort Collins CO 80522

AYMERICH, MIGUEL, architect, engr.; b. Terrassa, Spain, Apr. 15, 1947; came to U.S., 1970; s. Manuel and Maria Rosa A.; Indsl.-Textile Engr., U. Barcelona, 1968; B.Univ. Studies in Environ. Engring. cum laude, U. Utah, 1974; B.Arch., M.Arch., U. Ariz., 1977; m. Cheryl L. Hogan, Sept. 19, 1970; children—Marc, David E. Project architect Ruth & Going, Inc., San Jose, 1979-81; mgr. design, chief architect Amdahl Corp., Sunnyvale, Calif., 1981—; cons. energy auditor. Recipient award in archtl. design 1st Nat. Bank of Ariz., 1976. Mem. AIA, No. Calif. Solar Energy Assn. Author tech. works in field. Office: 1250 E Arques Ave Sunnyvale CA

AYRAULT, MARGARET WEBSTER, emeritus educator; b. Tonawanda, N.Y., Sept. 8, 1911; d. Miles and (Maud) Eleanor (Webster) A.; A.B., Oberlin Coll., 1933; B.S. in L.S., Drexel Inst. Tech., 1934; M.S. in L.S., Columbia U., 1940. Gen. asst. Drexel Inst. Tech. Library, Phila., 1934; cataloger Pratt Free Library, Balt., 1934-38; asst. reference dept. library Columbia U., 1939-40; head cataloger Carnegie Endowment for Internat. Peace Library, Washington, 1941-43; chief processing sect. library U.S. Dept. Agr., Washington, 1943-50; chief bibliog. control sec. Tech. Library, Naval Ordnance Test Sta., Inyokern, Calif., 1950-51; asst. librarian Bur. Budget, Washington, 1952-54; head cataloging dept. library U. Mich., Ann Arbor, 1954-65; prof. Grad. Sch. Library Studies, U. Hawaii, Honolulu, 1965-75, prof. emeritus, 1976—. Mem. Friends of Library of Hawaii, bd. dirs., 1979—. Mem. ALA (past counselor, exec. bd. resources and tech. services div. 1958-62, orgn. com. 1968-70, Margaret Mann citation 1975), Hawaii Library Assn. (hon.; pres. 1974-75), U. Hawaii Library Assn., AAUP, Phi Beta Kappa, Beta Phi Mu. Contbr. articles to profl. jours. Home: 1434 Punahou St Apt 729 Honolulu HI 96822 Office: Grad Sch Library Studies U Hawaii Honolulu HI 96822

AYRE, JACK KISER, electronic directory publisher; b. Pitts., July 9, 1921; s. Albert J. and Agnes (Kiser) A. Student Drew U., 1939-41; B.A., U. Mich., 1948. Newspaper reporter, Port Chester, N.Y., 1948-50; publicist United Air Lines, Panagra, also several advt. agys., N.Y.C., 1950-60; ins. publ. editor, state colls. publs. mgr., Fairchild Semicondr. publicist in No. Calif., 1960-70; founder Electro Buyers Guide, Sunnyvale, Calif., 1971—. Served with USCGR, 1942-45. Address: 21801 Wright Terr Sunnyvale CA 94087

AYRES, JAMES DALY, advertising executive, consultant; b. Lincoln, Nebr., Sept. 25, 1946; s. Warren Joyce and Harried (Daly) A.; divorced; children—Cortney, Lindsey. Grad., U. Nebr., 1975. Prin. Ayres/Koenig Advt., Inc., Omaha, 1976-81; creative dir. Ayres & Assocs., Omaha, 1981-82; account exec., creative dir. Morin Advt. Co., Omaha, 1982—; cons. in field. Sec. Consumer Credit Counseling Service of Nebr. Served with USMC, 1967-70. Decorated Purple Heart (2). Mem. Omaha Fedn. Advt. (numerous awards), Graphic Artist Guild (bd. dirs.) Republican. Methodist. Club: Rotary Internat. Office: Suite 100 11704 W Center Rd Omaha NE 68144

AZAR, DOUGLAS ALAN, accountant; b. Raton, N.Mex., Oct. 19, 1955; s. Richare S. and Patricia Ann (Hoag) A. B.B.S., U. N.Mex., 1977. C.P.A., N.Mex. Sr. acct. Ernst & Whinney, Albuquerque, 1978-79, ptnr. Azar, Murrielta Co., Albuquerque, 1979-81; ptnr.-in-charge Azar & Assocs., Albuquerque, 1981—; lectr. in field. Mem. Am. Inst. C.P.A.s, N.Mex. Soc. C.P.A.s. Democrat. Roman Catholic. Office: Azar & Assocs 2130 San Mateo St NE Suite F Albuquerque NM 87110

AZAR, SHAKER WILLIAM, mfrs. rep.; b. Trinidad, Colo., Mar., 10, 1911; s. William Habib and Sophia Maggie (Barrack) A.; student U. Colo. at Boulder, 1930-31; m. Laurice Marie Azar, Aug. 10, 1931; 1 dau., Lorraine Joan. Owner, mgr. Azar Grain & Produce Co., Trinidad, 1931-35, Azar Ranches So. Colo. and No. N.Mex., 1931-49, Azar Wholesale Grocery Co., Trinidad and Alamosa, Colo., 1935-55, Blue Ribbon Distbg. Co., Trinidad and Pueblo, Colo., 1935-55; part owner, bd. mem. Trinidad Nat. Bank, 1945-55; owner, mgr. Mode O Day Dress Shops, Trinidad, Walsenburg, Colo., Raton, N.Mex., 1945-49, Easy Washateria & Econo Wash Laundries, Trinidad, 1956-61; part owner Ben Franklin Variety Stores, Hereford, Lubbock, Tex., 1960-63; owner Jefferson Hills Apts., Lakewood, Colo., 1961—, Azar Motor Hotel, Inc., Trinidad, 1976—; owner, mgr. Azar Distbg. Co., Trinidad, 1955—, Ramada Inn, Trinidad, 1965-73. Active various community drives. Mem. city council, Trinidad, 1956-57, mayor, 1958-59. Trustee, pres. Mt. San Rafael Hosp., Trinidad; bd. dirs. City of Trinidad Urban Renewal. Mem. Colo. State (dir. 1956-59), Trinidad, Las Animas County (pres. 1955-56) chambers commerce. Eagle, Elk, Rotarian (pres. 1957-58), K.C. Home: 817 Colorado Ave Trinidad CO 81082 Office: 418 E Main St Trinidad CO 81082

AZIM, DIANE SUSAN, educator; b. Charleston, S.C., Aug. 29, 1955; s. Kaleem and Bonnie (Kooken) A. B.A., Asbury Coll., 1977; M.A., Calif. State U.-Sacramento, 1982, postgrad., 1982—. Tchr., Heritage Sch., Chico, Calif., 1977-78, Tierra Buena Sch., Yuba City (Calif.) Unified Sch. Dist., 1978-79, 79-82; math. tchr., program coordinator, social studies and reading tchr. Barry Sch., 1982—, adv. Calif. Jr. Scholarship Fedn., 1982—. Mem. Assn. Supervision and Curriculum Devel., NEA, Calif. State Edn. Assn., Yuba City Unified Edn. Assn. Home: 1561 Valley View Dr Yuba City CA 95991 Office: 1255 Barry Rd Yuba City CA 95991

BAAB, KENNETH DONALD, marketing executive; b. Greeley, Colo., Mar. 22, 1946; s. Donald S. and Clara I. (Nix) B. B.S. in Bus. Adminstrn., Colo. State U., 1969; grad. U.S. C. of C. Insts. for Orgnl. Mgmt., Republican. Campaign Mgmt. Coll. Asst. exec. dir. Alpha Kappa Lambda, Ft. Collins, Colo., 1969-72; mgr. Campbell County C. of C., Gillette, Wyo., 1972-75; exec. dir. Cheyenne (Wyo.) C. of C., 1975-78; campaign mgr. Ostlund for Gov., Casper, Wyo., 1978; mktg. dir. Taco John's, Cheyenne, 1979-82; pres. Ken Baab Mktg., Ft. Collins, 1983—. Bd. dirs. Cheyenne YMCA; mem. Cheyenne Mayor's Adv. Com. Recipient Pacemaker award Colo. State U. Mem. Wyo. C. of C. Execs. Assn. (pres.), Cheyenne Jogging Club (pres.). Republican. Baptist. Office: Ken Baab Mktg PO Box 1449 Fort Collins CO 80525

BABAYANS, EMIL, internat. trade co. exec.; b. Tehran, Iran, Nov. 9, 1951; s. Hacob and Jenik (Khatchatourian) B.; came to U.S., 1969; B.S., U. So. Calif., 1974, M.S.E.E., 1976; m. Annie Ashjian, June 1977. Pres., Babtech Internat. Inc., Encino, Calif., 1975—. Mem. IEEE, Nat., Calif. socs. profl. engrs., Nat. Pilots Assn., Los Angeles Area C. of C., U. So. Calif. Alumni Assn. Armenian Orthodox. Office: 15910 Ventura Blvd Suite 633 Encino CA 91436

BABBEL, DAVID FREDERICK, economist, educator; b. Salt Lake City, Apr. 12, 1949; s. Frederick William and June (Andrew) B.; m. Mary Jane Babbel, Aug. 27, 1975; children—Tara Nicole, Elise Kiera, Karisa Rose. B.A., Brigham Young U., 1973; M.B.A., U. Fla., 1975, Ph.D., 1978. Economist Econ. Research Service, U.S. Dept. Agr., Washington, 1973-74, Instituto Brasileiro de Mercado de Capitais, Rio de Janeiro, Brazil, 1976-77; prof. fin., ins. and internat. bus. U. Calif.-Berkeley, 1978—; internat. bus. and fin. cons. Fulbright-Hays fellow, 1976-77; Internat. Monetary and Fin. Inst. fellow, 1980-82. Mem. Am. Econ. Assn., Western Econ. Assn., Am. Fin. Assn., Western Fin. Assn. Republican. Mormon. Contbr. articles to profl. jours.

BABBIE, EARL ROBERT, sociologist, educator; b. Detroit, Jan. 8, 1938; s. Herman Octave and Marion Evelyn (Towle) B.; A.B., Harvard U., 1960; M.A., U. Calif.-Berkeley, 1966, Ph.D., 1969; m. Sheila Trimble, May 17, 1965; 1 son, Aaron Robert. Asst. dir. Survey Research Center, U. Calif.-Berkeley, 1967-68; dir. Survey Research Office, U. Hawaii, Honolulu, 1970-73, prof., chmn. dept. sociology, 1973, 77-79, affiliate prof., 1980—; pres., dir. Babbie Enterprises, Inc., Honolulu, 1976—; mem. adv. bd. est, San Francisco, 1976-80, chmn. adv. council Hunger Project, 1978—; bd. dirs. Zero Population Growth, Inc., 1981-82, Holiday Project, 1981—; faculty adv. Breakthrough Found., 1981—. Served to lt. USMC, 1960-63. William Penn Found. grantee, 1973-74; est Found. grantee, 1974-75. Mem. Am. Sociol. Assn., Am. Assn. Pub. Opinion Research. Democrat. Author: To Comfort and to Challenge, 1967; Science and Morality in Medicine, 1970; The Practice of Social Research, 1975, 2d 1979, 3d edit., 1983; Survey Research Methods, 1973; Society by Agreement, 1977, 2d edit., 1980, 3d edit., 1983; Understanding Sociology: A Context for Action, 1981; Social Research for

Consumers, 1982. Home and Office: 91 LaVerne Ave Mill Valley CA 94941

BABBITT, BRUCE E., gov. Ariz.; b. June 27, 1938; B.A. magna cum laude, U. Notre Dame; M.A., U. Newcastle (Eng.), 1963; LL.B., Harvard U., 1965; married. Admitted to Ariz. bar, 1965; individual practice law, Phoenix; atty. gen. Ariz., 1975-78, gov., 1978—; spl. asst. to dir. VISTA, Washington; mem. NAAG com. on antitrust and com. consumer protection. Mem. Phoenix LEAP Commn., chmn. manpower tng. com.; trustee Dougherty Found. Democrat. Office: Gov's Office State Capitol 1800 W Washington St Phoenix AZ 85007*

BABBUSH, HARVEY EDWARD, univ. ofcl.; b. Detroit, Dec. 4, 1928; s. David Charles and Edith Judith B.; B.S., Mich. State U., 1952; M.A., Calif. State U., Long Beach, 1957; m. Elaine Joyce Karasick, Sept. 17, 1950; children—Randall Mark, Wendy Jo, Robert Alan. Tchr., Long Beach Unified Sch. Dist., 1953-56; procedures writer, orgn. planner, tng. supr. N.Am. Aviation, Downey, Calif., 1956-57; employment supr. Ryan Aero., Torrance, Calif., 1957-58; personnel supr., budget dir., asso. dean, dir. Career Planning and Placement Center, Calif. State U., Long Beach, 1958—. Chmn., Long Beach Commn. Econ. Opportunities and Community Relations. Served with U.S. Army, 1946-48. Recipient Calif. Personnel Guidance Assn. Outstanding Service award, 1976; Western Assn. Coll. and Univ. Bus. Officers fellow, 1960-61. Mem. Am. Soc. Tng. and Devel., Western Coll. Placement Assn., Calif. Ednl. Placement Assn., Student Personnel Assn. Calif., Calif. State Coll. Alumni Assn. Author: College Relations and Recruiting, 1982; Finders-Seekers—A Guide To Obtaining a New Job, 1982. Contbr. articles to profl. jours. Office: 1250 Bellflower Blvd Long Beach CA 90840

BABCOCK, DAVID JOHN, software company executive; b. Washington, Feb. 4, 1952; s. Robert Lloyd and Esther Catherine (Ball) B.; B.S. in Computer Scis., Calif. State U., Northridge, 1979; m. Madalyn Alice Martino, June 3, 1976; children—Ann Marie, Thomas Michael, Clare Elizabeth, Theresa Gayle. Computer cons. Calif. State U., Northridge, 1972-74, systems analyst for statewide timesharing system, Computer Center, 1974-77, supr. acad. applications Computer Center, 1977-78; sr. mem. tech. staff MSC engring. dept. ROLM Corp., Santa Clara, Calif., 1979-81, mgr. compiler devel. MSC engring. dept., 1981-82, mgr software devel., 1982—; cons. in field; tchr. high sch. and univ. computer courses, 1972—. Recipient Rensselaer Poly. Inst. award for math. and sci., 1970. Mem. Assn. Computing Machinery. Author: (with Fred Gruenberger) Computing With Mini Computers, 1972; asso. editor Popular Computing, 1972-81. Home: 2151 Port Way San Jose CA 95133 Office: 1 River Oaks Pl San Jose CA 95134

BABCOCK, GARY DANA, state ofcl.; b. Sisseton, S.D., Apr. 8, 1932; s. Dana Bernard and Fern Eve (Jackson) B.; B.A. in Acctg., U. Oreg., 1957; LL.B., Williamette U., 1961; m. Lisa Beatrice Heller, June 3, 1978. Admitted to Oreg. bar, 1961; claims adjuster State Farm Ins., 1961-62; asst. atty. gen. State of Oreg., Salem, 1962-63, asst. public defender, Salem, 1964-67, public defender, 1967—; asst. dist. atty. Marion County (Oreg.), 1963-64. Served with USN, 1950-52. Mem. Nat. Legal Aid and Defenders Assn., Oreg. Bar Assn., Oreg. Public Defenders Assn., U.S. Bar Assn. Office: 1655 State St Salem OR 97310

BABCOCK, MICHAEL JANE ALLEN (MRS. JAMES D. BABCOCK), computer co. exec.; b. Wichita, Kans., Sept. 17, 1926; d. Harry R. and Alma (Garrison) Allen; B.A., Roosevelt U., 1948; postgrad. U. Tex., 1948-49, U. Calif. at Los Angeles, 1960-62; m. James D. Babcock, Aug. 27, 1949 (div. Apr. 1969); 1 dau. Carla Anne. Sec.-treas. Allen-Babcock Computing, Inc., Los Angeles, 1965-67, exec. v.p., 1967-69, pres., 1969-73, also dir.; pres. Mitro Computer Corp., Los Angeles, 1973—. Bd. dirs. Century City Civic Council. Bd. dirs., exec. v.p. Know Found. Mem. Delta Phi Upsilon. Home: 805 San Vicente St Santa Monica CA 90402 Office: Suite 1204 1888 Century Park East Los Angeles CA 90067

BABCOCK, RAYMOND ALBERT, newspaper editor; b. Hawthorne, Calif., Dec. 13, 1930; s. Harry Hudson and Hilda Katherine (Correa) B.; m. Fuchle Yusa, July 6, 1952; 1 child, Tamuko Daeko. Student East Los Angeles Coll., 1960-62. Reporter, East Whittier (Calif.) Rev., 1968-72; city editor Dean Newspapers, Culver City, Calif., 1972-74; with So. Calif. Pub. Co., 1975—, news editor Montebello (Calif.) News, 1978—. Served with U.S. Army, 1950-52. Mem. Southland Art Assn. (best of show, 1st, 2d awards 1982 photography contest). Democrat. Home: 1015 W Cleveland Ave Montebello CA 90640 Office: 2108 W Beverly Blvd Montebello CA 90640

BABCOCK, WILLIS, engr.; b. Waukesha, Wis., May 31, 1922; s. Barney and Helen (Reuter) B.; student Northland Coll., 1941-42, M.I.T., 1945-48, Cornell U., 1948; M.S.M.E., Century U., 1982; m. Elizabeth Anne Zimmerman, Sept. 26, 1947; children—Rudolph, Kathryn, Willis W., Gregory, Janet, Deborah. Chief engr. Domestic Engine and Pump Co., Shippensburg, Pa., 1948-53; chief engr. research and devel. Aurora Pump Co. (Ill.), 1953-59; v.p. engring., exec. v.p., gen. mgr. Carver Pump Co., Muscatine, Iowa, 1959-63, cons., 1963-64; chief engr. Mission Valve & Pump Co., Houston, 1964-66; dir. research and devel. Mech. Equipment Co., New Orleans, 1966-68; program mgr. Battelle N.W. Labs., Richland, Wash., 1968-71; sr. project engr. Emco Wheaton Inc., Conneant, Ohio, 1971-72; chief engr. Sta-Rite Industries, Inc., Delavan, Wis., 1972-77; mgr. engring. Wayne Home Equipment Co., Ft. Wayne, Ind., 1977-80; with Rockwell Internat., Richland, Wash., 1980—. Served with AUS, 1942-45. Mem. ASME, Nat. Soc. Profl. Engrs. Baptist. Home: 3937 Austin St West Richland WA 99352 Office: Rockwell Hanford Ops Richland WA 99352

BABEL, RONALD FREDERICK, city official; b. Lynwood, Calif., Mar. 28, 1946; s. Frederick George and Constance Caroline (DiMaggio) B.; m. Bonita Eva Lafayette, Sept. 8, 1973; 1 dau., Tiffany Constance; A.A., Compton Jr. Coll., 1967. Water maintenance man City of South Gate (Calif.), 1973-76, water foreman, 1976-79; water supt. City of Cerritos (Calif.), 1979—. Mem. Am. Water Works Assn. Office: Civic Center Bloomfield Ave and 183d St Cerritos CA 90701

BABICH, ALAN FRANCIS, computer scientist; b. Sewickley, Pa., Nov. 21, 1943; s. John and Hedwig Joanna (Bitautos) B.; B.S. in Physics, Carnegie Inst. Tech., 1965, M.S. in Elec. Engring., 1966; Ph.D. in Elec. Engring., Carnegie-Mellon U., 1972. With Burroughs Corp., 1971-79, mgmt. systems analyst, Mission Viejo, Calif., 1975, project leader, 1975-79; architect, large systems Basic Four Corp., Tustin, Calif., 1979-83; architect File Net Corp., Costa Mesa, Calif., Mem. Capt. Hook and the Sky Pirates sport parachuting team, Elsinore, Calif., 1974-76. Recipient awards in parachuting accuracy competitions, 1967-72, including 1st place, Tecumseh, Mich., 1970. Mem. IEEE, Assn. Computing Machinery, Mensa, Sigma Xi. Democrat. Office: FileNet Corp 1575 Corporate Dr Costa Mesa CA 92626

BABICH, BETSY MELL MIDDLETON, home economics educator; b. Yuma, Ariz., May 25, 1946; d. Harry Eugene and Marjorie Moore (Platt) Middleton; m. George Babich, Aug. 14, 1971. B.S. in Home Econs., U. Ariz., 1968, M.S. in Secondary Edn., 1972; Ph.D. in Vocat. Edn., Pa. State U., 1982. Cert. tchr., sch. administr., Ariz. Jr. high sch. home econs. tchr. Tucson Unified Sch. Dist., 1968-71, high sch. home econs. tchr., 1971-79, coop. edn. coordinator, 1979-81, occupational edn. resource person, 1981—; cons. State College (Pa.) Area Sch. Dist., Dept. Edn. Home Econs., Harrisburg, Pa., Ariz. Dept. Edn. Home Econs., Phoenix; mem. Ariz. State Adv. Council Bus. Edn., Ariz. State Adv. Council Home Econs. Named Ariz. Home Econs. Tchr. of Year, 1979. Mem. Am. Home Econs. Assn., Ariz. Home Econs. Assn. (pres.-elect), Am. Vocat. Assn., Ariz. Vocat. Assn. (sec.), Tchr. Edn. Council, Nat. Council Adminstrv. Women in Edn. (program chmn., v.p.), Alpha Delta Kappa (treas., pres.), Omicron Nu, Ariz. Agr. and Home Econs. Alumni Councils. Republican. Home: 4058 E Hawthorne Tucson AZ 85711 Office: PO Box 40400 Tucson AZ 85717

BABICH, GEORGE, educator; b. Chgo., Aug. 7, 1945; s. Peter and Jewel B.; A.A., Thornton Jr. Coll., 1965; B.A., U. Ariz., 1969, M.Ed., 1971, Ed.D., 1977; m. Betsy Middleton, Aug. 14, 1971. Tchr., adminstr. schs. in Tucson, 1968-75; teaching asso. U. Ariz., Tucson, 1977; community edn. coordinator, adminstr. Tucson Unified Sch. Dist. Elem. Schs., 1978-80; asst. prof. secondary edn. U. Ariz., Tucson, 1980—; asso. state dir. office of sch. accreditation Ariz. N. Central Assn., 1980—. Mem. Nat. Community Edn. Assn., NEA, Nat. Assn. Advancement Sci., Tucson Edn. Assn., Ariz. Community Edn. Assn., Ariz. Edn. Assn., Ariz. Jr. High/Middle Schs. Assn., So. Ariz. Jr. High/Middle Schs. Assn. (exec. dir. 1980—), Ariz. Sch. Adminstrs. Assn., Ariz. Sci. Tchrs. Assn., Assn. Supervision and Curriculum Devel., Phi Delta Kappa. Club: Pima Education Golf (pres. 1979, 81). Home: 4058 E Hawthorne St Tucson AZ 85711 Office: U Ariz Coll Edn #327 Tucson AZ 85721

BABINGTON, S(TANLEY) DAVID, optometrist; b. Champaign, Ill., Mar. 2, 1944; s. Stanley and Margaret (Hill) B.; m. Linda McDonnell, Feb. 25, 1964; 1 son, David. Student U. Idaho, 1964; B.S., U. Houston, 1970, O.D., 1972. On staff Lovelace Clinic, Albuquerque, 1972-77; practice optometry, Albuquerque, 1977—. Served with USAF, 1962-67. Recipient Boss of Yr. award Am. Bus. Women's Assn., 1983. Mem. Bernalillo County Optometric Assn. (past pres.), Am. Optometric Assn., N.Mex. Optometric Assn. (past sec.). Club: Los Altos Civitan (past pres.). Office: Apple Tree Optical 7520-E Montgomery St NE Suite 6B Albuquerque NM 87109

BABYLON, JOHN RAKESTRAW, economist; b. Sharon, Pa., June 26, 1942; s. Elvan and Eugenia (Ralston) B.; student U. N.C., 1959-60; B.A., Central Mo. State U., 1963; M.A., U. Md., 1965; postgrad. George Washington U., 1964; m. Catherine Nahid, Nov. 20, 1972; children—Jon R., Sahreah C. With Treasury Dept., Washington, 1963, U.S. Tariff Commn., 1963-64, U.S. Bur. Budget, 1965-67; with AID, 1967—, sr. economist AID Mission to Zaire, 1981—; acting alt. dir. Asian Devel. Bank, Manila, 1980-81. Mem. Am. Econ. Assn., AAAS. Contbr. articles to profl. jours. Office: Am Embassy (ID) APO New York NY 09662

BACA, GAIL A. HERSHBERGER, purchasing administrator; b. Pasadena, Calif., Aug. 1, 1948; d. William Patton and Beth Mae Hershberger Student San Francisco State U., 1971. Counselor community services, City of Gardena (Calif.), 1973-79, sr. adminstrv. asst., 1979— Mem. steering com. Gardena Women's Day, 1978-82. Mem. NOW, Internat. City Mgmt. Assn., Am. Soc. Pub. Adminstrs., Pub. Risk Ins. Mgrs. Assn., Calif. Assn. Pub. Purchasing Officers. Democrat. Office: 1700 W 162d St Gardena CA 90247

BACA, SAMUEL LEONARD, accountant; b. Los Angeles, Sept. 19, 1946; s. L.J. and Carmen B.; m. Sharon Dunnagan, Nov. 27, 1974; children—Jennifer, Adam. B.B.A., U. N.Mex., 1972. C.P.A., N.Mex. Ptnr., Baca & Rasmussen, P.C., C.P.A.s, Albuquerque, 1982—. Served with U.S. Army, 1967-69. Decorated Bronze Star. Mem. N.Mex. Estate Planning Council, N.Mex. Soc. C.P.A.s, Am. Inst. C.P.A.s. Republican.

BACA-BARRAGAN, POLLY, state senator, Democratic nat. committeewoman from Colo.; b. La Salle, Colo., Feb. 13, 1941; B.A. in Polit. Sci., Colo. State U., 1962; postgrad. Am. U., 1966-67; children—Monica, Mike. Editorial asst. dept. research and edn. Internat. Brotherhood Pulp, Sulphite and Paper Mill Workers, AFL-CIO, Washington, 1962-65; editor Airline News mag., legis. aide Brotherhood Ry. and Airline Clks., AFL-CIO, Washington, 1966-67; public info. officer Interagy. Com. on Mexican-Ams., The White House, Washington, 1967-68; nat. dep. dir. Viva Kennedy div. Nat. Robert F. Kennedy for Pres. Campaign, Washington, 1968; dir. research services and info. Nat. Council of La Raza, Phoenix, 1968-70; dir. div. Spanish-speaking affairs, spl. asst. to chmn. Dem. Nat. Com., Washington, 1971-72; dir., pres. Bronze Publs., Inc., Denver, 1972-74; mem. Colo. Ho. of Reps., 1975-78, chmn. Dem. caucus, 1977-78, vice chmn. house rules com., 1975-76; mem. Colo. Senate, 1979—; dir. Fed. Home Loan Bank, Topeka, 1979—; mem. nat. adv. council Fed. Savs. and Loan Assns., 1980-81. Mem. exec. com., state sec. Colo. Young Dems., 1960-62; del. or alt. Nat. Dem. Conv., 1974, 76, 78, 80, co-chmn., 1980; Dem. nat. committeewoman from Colo., 1973—; vice chmn. procedures and rules com. Dem. Nat. Com., 1978, mem. compliance rev. com., 1979-80, mem. exec. com., 1977—, vice chmn., 1981—; chmn. Colo. del. to Nat. Dem. Mid-Term Conf., 1978; Rocky Mountain states coordinator Carter/Mondale Presdl. Campaign, 1979; Dem. candidate for U.S. Congress from 4th Dist. of Colo., 1980; mem. Adams County Dem. Central Com., 1973—, Colo. Dem. Exec. Com., 1973—; participant Camp David Domestic Summit, 1979; participant Am. Council Young Polit. Leaders legis. del. to USSR, 1978; mem. policyholders' adv. council Div. State Compensation Ins. Fund, 1975—; trustee St. Mary's Acad., Labor's Community Agy., 1973—; bd. dirs. La Unidad Broadcasting Corp., 1980—, Nat. Inst. for Socio-Econ. Research, 1979—; mem. nat. steering com. Hispanic/Black Dem. Coalition, 1978—, Hispanic Am. Dems., 1978—; mem. nat. adv. bd. Nat. Women's Polit. Caucus, 1978—; mem. Nat. Overseas Edn. Fund of LWV, 1980—; mem. sec.'s adv. com. on rights and responsibilities of women HEW, 1979-81; mem. Colo. Gov.'s Commn. on Public Telecommunications, 1980—, Nat. Women's Employment and Edn., Inc.; mem. adv. bd. Nat. Inst. for Women of Color; participant German Marshall Fund and European Coop. Fund. fgn. policy seminar, Brussels, 1981. Recipient Outstanding Service in State Govt. award Adams County Fiesta Day Com., 1979; cert. of appreciation Colo. Migrant Council, 1979; Salute to Women award Big Sisters of Colo., Inc., 1979; named One of 10 Women of Future, Ladies Home Jour., 1979, One of 80 Women To Watch in '80s, MS mag., 1980, One of 20 New Dem. Faces for '80s, Newsweek mag., 1980. Office: Colo State Capitol Bldg Denver CO 80203*

BACASTOW, JACK LEROY, safety engr.; b. Arkansas City, Kan., Aug. 25, 1925; s. Alvin Hemperly and Mary Esther (Gribble) B.; m. Diane Edith Janicek, Sept. 22, 1951; children—Laurie Jean, Daniel Jack. Student U. Ill., 1946-47, Spartan Sch. Aeros., Tulsa, 1947-48; Los Alamos Grad. Ctr., U. N.Mex., 1960-70; B.S. in Indsl. Engring., N.Mex. State U., 1973. Research technician, pilot plant operator Universal Oil Products, McCook, Ill., 1949-50; research/instrument technician Argonne (Ill.) Nat. Lab., 1950-59; electronics/instrument technician Los Alamos Nat. Lab., 1959-70, staff mem., 1972-79, dep. safety group leader, 1979—. Served with USN, 1943-46; PTO. Registered profl. engr., Calif. Mem. Am. Soc. Safety Engrs. (cert. safety profl.), Am. Ins. Insl. Engrs., IEEE, System Safety Soc., Laser Inst. Am. Democrat. Contbr. articles to profl. jours. Office: Los Alamos Nat Lab Safety Group H-3 Mail Stop P-230 Los Alamos NM 87545

BACCHUS, HABEEB, physician; b. Brit. Guiana, Oct. 15, 1928; came to U.S., 1945, naturalized, 1956; s. Noor and Jumratan (Khan) B.; B.S., Howard U., 1947; M.S., George Washington U., 1948, Ph.D., 1950, M.D., 1954; m. Frances Solarczyk, June 26, 1965; children—Paula Bacchus Robey, Andree Jean Bacchus Scalissi, Jeanne Carol, David Michael, Michael Francis, Julie Shireen. Research analyst NRC, Washington, 1949-51; research asso. dept. physiology George Washington U., Washington, 1950-54, asst. research prof. physiology, 1954-59; intern Sibley Meml. Hosp., Washington, 1954-55; resident in medicine Providence Hosp., Washington, 1955-57, tng. officer in medicine, 1957-69; practice medicine specializing in internal medicine, endocrinology and metabolism, Riverside, Calif., 1969—; asso. chief of medicine Riverside Gen. Hosp., 1969—, asso. clin. pathologist, 1970-75; prof. medicine Loma Linda (Calif.) Sch. Medicine, 1979—. Served with USPHS, 1957-59. Named Tchr. of Year in Medicine, Loma Linda U., 1978; diplomate Am. Bd. Internal Medicine, subbd. endocrinology and metabolism. Fellow A.C.P.; mem. Am. Physiol. Soc., Endocrine Soc., Am. Fedn. Clin. Research, Calif. Med. Assn., Author: Essentials of Gynecologic and Obstetric Endocrinology, 1975; Essentials of Metabolic Diseases and Endocrinology, 1976; Rational Management of Diabetes, 1977; Endocrine and Metabolic Emergencies, 1977; contbr. numerous articles in field to med. jours. Home: 1444 Ransom Rd Riverside CA 92506 Office: 9851 Magnolia Ave Riverside CA 92503

BACCIGALUPPI, ROGER JOHN, agricultural association executive; b. N.Y.C., Mar. 17, 1934; s. Harry and Ethel (Hutcheon) G.; m. Patricia Marie Wier, Feb. 6, 1960; m. 2d, Iris Christine Walfridson, Feb. 3, 1979; children—John, Elisabeth, Andrea and Jason. Student, Coll. of San Mateo, 1953; B.S., U. Calif.-Berkeley, 1956; M.S., Columbia U. Grad. Sch. Bus., 1957. Sales promotion mgr. Maco Mag. Corp., N.Y.C., 1956-57; merchandising mgr. Honig, Cooper & Harrington, San Francisco and Los Angeles, 1957-58, merchandising mgr., account exec., 1958-60, asst. dir. merchandising, 1960-61; sales rep. Calif. Almond Growers Exchange, Sacramento, 1961-64, mgr. advt., sales promotion, 1964-70, v.p. mktg., 1970-73, sr. v.p., 1973-74, exec. v.p., 1974-75, pres., chief exec. officer, 1975—; chmn., dir. Nat. Council Farmer Coops.; bd. dirs. Almond Bd. Calif., Agrl. Council Calif.; Calif. mem. Agrl. Adv. Council Internat. Trade; past mem. Adv. Council Econ. Devel. Bd. dirs. Nat. Alliance Businessmen, Sacramento, 1974-77, Mercy Hosps. Found., 1974-79, Sacramento area chpt. Friends Calif. State R.R. Mus., R.R. Mus.; bd. dirs., exec. com. United Way Sacramento; adv. bd. Berkeley Bus. Sch.; agrl. adv. bd. U. Calif.; mem. mktg. and internat. trade conf. group Nat. Council Farmer Coops. Mem. Calif. C. of C. (internat. trade task force). Office: 1802 C St Sacramento CA 95814

BACH, MARTIN WAYNE, stockbroker, owner antique clock stores; b. Milw., Mar. 30, 1940; s. Jack Baer and Rose (Weiss) B.; B.A., U. Wis., 1963; m. Roberta Sklar, Aug. 19, 1962; children—David Louis, Emily Elizabeth. Stockbroker, J. Barth & Co., Oakland, Calif., 1966-72, v.p., 1970-72; sr. v.p., stockbroker Dean Witter & Co., Oakland, 1972—; founder The TimePeace, Carmel, Calif., 1972-83, San Francisco, 1975—, La Jolla, 1977—; instr. fin. San Leandro (Calif.) Adult Sch., 1970—; breeder, owner thoroughbred race horses. Served to 1st lt., US. Army, 1963-65. Mem. Calif. Thoroughbred Breeders Assn. Jewish. Clubs: East Bay Brokers, B'nai B'rith. Home: 180 Sandringham S Moraga CA 94556 Office: 2150 Valdez St Suite 350 Oakland CA 94556

BACHER, ROSALIE WRIDE, sch. adminstr.; b. Los Angeles, May 25, 1925; d. Homer M. and Reine (Rogers) Wride; A.B., Occidental Coll., 1947, M.A., 1949; m. Archie O. Bacher, Jr., Mar. 30, 1963. Tchr., English, Latin, history David Starr Jordan High Sch., Long Beach, Calif., 1949-55, counselor, 1955-65, Lakewood (Calif.) Sr. High Sch., 1965-66; research asst., counselor Poly. High Sch., Long Beach, 1966-67; counselor, office occupational preparation, vocational guidance sect. Long Beach Unified School Dist., Long Beach, 1967-68; vice prin. Washington Jr. High Sch., Long Beach, 1968-70; asst. prin. Lakewood Sr. High Sch., Long Beach, spring 1970; vice prin. Jefferson Jr. High Sch., Long Beach, 1970—; chmn. vocat. guidance steering com. Long Beach Unified Sch. Dist., 1963—. Mem. Internat. Platform Assn., AAUW, Long Beach Personnel and Guidance Assn. (dir. 1958-60), Long Beach Sch. Counselors Assn. (sec. high sch. segment 1963-64), Phi Beta Kappa, Delta Kappa Gamma (pres. Delta Psi chpt., area dir.; Calif. profl. affairs com. chmn. 1972-74), Phi Delta Gamma (pres. chpt. 1977-78, nat. chmn. bylaws com. 1980-81), Pi Lambda Theta (pres. chpt. 1974-76, v.p. So. Calif. council 1974-76), Phi Delta Kappa (sec. Long Beach chpt. 1977-80). Home: 265 Rocky Point Rd Palos Verdes Estates CA 90274 also 17721 Misty Ln Huntington Beach CA 92649 Office: John Marshall Jr High Sch 5870 E Wardlow Rd Long Beach CA 90808

BACHERT, ROBERT EDWARD, advertising exec.; b. Bellingham, Wash., May 30, 1935; s. Ralph Andy and Rueberta (Whitely) b.; m. Maryanne Brosovich, May 7, 1957; children—Kimberly anne, Kari ann, Jeffery allen. B.A., Western Wash. U., 1959; postgrad. indsl. design, Burnly Sch. Profl. Design, 1960-61; postgrad. in Econ., Corp. Mgmt., U. Wash., 1976. Art dir., designer Univ. Printing, Seattle, 1960-70; pres., creative dir. Gail, Bachert, Leach, Inc., Seattle, 1970—; pres., chmn. bd. Cycle Seafoods, Inc., Seattle; chmn. Cycle World Resources Inc.; pres. R.E. Bachert & Assocs. Chief Seattle Hist. Trust Fund. Served to capt. USMC, 1953-56. Recipient numerous design awards from advt. assns. and graphic publns. Mem. Seattle C. of C., Am. Assn. Advt. Agys., Bus./Profl. Advt. Assn., USMC Support Group, Assn. Wash. Gens., Mag. Pubs. Assn. Republican. Roman Catholic. Home: 18324 84th Pl W Edmonds WA 98020 Office: 3231 Eastlake Ave E Seattle WA 98102

BACHMAN, RICHARD THOMAS, oceanographer; b. Los Angeles, May 10, 1943; s. John Randolph and Elizabeth (Lapsley) B.; B.A., San Diego State U., 1966, postgrad., 1966-68; m. Nancy Merideth Hines, July 8, 1967; children—Richard Randolph, Sarah Catherine. Instr., San Diego State U., 1966-67; oceanographer Naval Ocean Systems Center, San Diego, 1967—. Fellow Geol. Soc. Am. Home: 9162 Brier Rd La Mesa CA 92041 Office: Naval Ocean Systems Center Code 5322 San Diego CA 92152

BACHMANN, JEFFREY CHRISTOPHER, executive; b. Portland, Oreg., Aug. 17, 1946; s. Roland Henry and Blanche Elaine (Fearon) B.; m. Helene G. Gripon, Oct. 19, 1974. B.B.A., Loyola U., Los Angeles, 1968. C.P.A., Calif. Sr. auditor Arthur Andersen & Co., Los Angeles, 1968-72; sr. v.p. fin. Mattel Toys, Hawthorne, Calif., 1972-81; pres. Ixo, Inc., Culver City, Calif., 1981—, also chief exec. officer. Home: 2037 W 35th St San Pedro CA 90732 Office: Ixo Inc 6041 Bristol Pkwy Culver City CA 90230

BACHTOLD, HAROLD ERNEST, investment co. exec.; b. Walla Walla, Wash., July 28, 1912; s. Ernest Frederick and Christine (Retzer) B.; A.A., Sacramento Jr. Coll., 1933; student San Francisco Law Sch., 1935-36; m. Louise Marie Hollingsworth, May 16, 1939; children—Barbara, Patricia, Christine. With So. Pacific Co., San Francisco, 1935-43; public relations Whitaker & Baxter, San Francisco, 1944-45; pres. H.E. Bachtold Co., Inc. subs. Am. Internat. Comml. Corp., N.Y.C. and Calif., 1946-50; exec. sec. Calif. State Assembly Com. on Govt. Reorgn., 1950-53; asst. to speaker Calif. State Legislature, 1953-57; sr. asso. v.p. Dean Witter Reynolds, Inc., Sacramento, 1958—. Bd. regents Calif. Luth. Coll., 1965-68. Mem. San Francisco Press Club. Republican. Lutheran. Club: El Macero Country. Home: 2941 Garden Ct El Macero CA 95618 Office: 455 Capitol Mall Sacramento CA 95814

BACIGALUPA, ANDREA, liturgical artist; b. Balt., May 26, 1923; s. Andrew Louis and Maria Laura (Merolla) B.; m. Ellen Williams, Oct. 9, 1952; children—Gian Andrea, Pier Francesca, Ruan Saire, Chiara Domenica, Daria Concessa. B.F.A., Md. Inst. Fine Arts, Balt., 1950; postgrad. Art Students League, Woodstock, N.Y., Accademia di Belli Arti, Florence, Italy. Owner, Studio of Gian Andrea, Santa Fe, 1954—; designer interior sacred environment for chs. throughout U.S., including

St. Laurence Catherdral, Amarillo, Tex.; works represented in pvt. collections through U.S. and Europe; murals, statues, paintings in pub. bldgs. U.S. and Eng.; cons., lectr liturgical arts. Chmn. arts com. Liturgical Commn. Archdiocese of Santa Fe; mem. bldg. comm. Diocese of Amarillo. Served with AUS, 1943-46; ETO. Recipient Bronze medallion Md. Inst. Fine Arts, 1950; Top award for design of St. Laurence Cathedral, Fort Worth chpt. AIA, 1975; 1st prize Santa Fe Competition for Art in Pub. Places, 1980. Mem. Artists Equity (past pres. Santa Fe chpt.). Author: Santo and Saints' Days, 1972; Journal of An Itinerant Artist, 1977; A Good and Perfect Gift, 1978; The Song of Guadalupana, 1979. Weekly columnist Santa Fe New Mexican; contbr. articles and features to Santa Fe Opera Program, Met. Opera News, Nat. Catholic Reporter, Liturgical Arts Quar., others. Home: 626 Canyon Rd Santa Fe NM 87501

BACKHAUS, RALPH ANDREW, horticulturist, educator, researcher; b. Elizabeth, N.J., Jan. 12, 1951; s. Rolf Richard and Suzanne (Sladek) B. B.S. in Environ. Sci., Rutgers U., 1973; M.S. in Horticulture U. Calif.-Davis, 1975, Ph.D. in Plant Physiology, 1977. Asst. prof. agr. Ariz. State U., 1977-81, assoc. prof., 1981—; research in field physiology of desert plants. NSF grantee, 1982—. Mem. Am. Soc. Hort. Sci., Am. Soc. Plant Physiology. Office: Div of Agr Ariz State U Tempe AZ 85281

BACKLUND, ELIZABETH MAU, psychologist; b. Redding, Calif., Feb. 26, 1921; d. Carl Frederick and Bess (Miles) Mau; 1 son, Carl S. A.B., U. Calif.-Berkeley, 1942, M.A., 1949, postgrad., 1959-61; postgrad. Stanford U., 1954-56, San Jose State U., 1955-58, Western Inst. Group and Family Therapy, 1971. Lic. psychologist, Calif. Cons., Emery Unified Sch. Dist., 1949-50; supervising psychologist, dir. spl. edn. Ceres Elem. Sch. Dist., 1950-53; psychol. cons., supervising psychologist, dir. spl. services Alum Rock Elem. Sch. Dist., San Jose, Calif., 1954-60; staff demonstration program for severely disturbed children and adolescents Contra Costa Mental Health Assn., 1963-68; pvt. practice psychology, Santa Clara County, 1957-63, Walnut Creek, Calif., 1962—; assoc. staff Walnut Creek Hosp., 1972—, supr. psychology interns, 1977—. Mem. Contra Costa County Mental Health Assn., 1961—; condr. workshops Assistance League of Diablo Valley, 1977—. PTA grantee, 1954. Mem. Am. Psychol. Assn., Calif. Psychol. Assn., Nat. Register of Health Service Providers, Internat. Transactional Analysis Assn. Author: (with others) Education of Gifted Children, 1957. Office: 177 La Casa Via Suite 2 Walnut Creek CA 94598

BACKMAN, CARL WARD, sociologist, educator; b. Canandiagua, N.Y., July 1, 1923; s. Carl F. and Edna B. (Ward) B.; m. Shirley L. Bennet, June 25, 1947. B.A., Oberlin Coll., 1948; M.A., Ind. U., 1950, Ph.D., 1954. Mem. faculty U. Nev., Reno, 1951—, prof. sociology, 1967—, chmn. dept. sociology, 1962—; vis. prof. Oxford U. (Eng.), 1974, Cath. U., Netherlands, 1981. Served with AUS, 1943-46. Mem. Am. Sociol. Assn., Am. Psychol. Assn., Pacific Sociol. Assn., West Coast Conf. Small Groups Research, Soc. Exptl. Social Psychology. Author: (with P.F. Secord) Problems in Social Psychology, 1966; (with P.F. Secord) Social Psychology, 2d edit., 1974; contbr. articles to profl. jours. Home: 1335 Hoge Rd Reno NV 89503 Office: U Nev Dept Sociology Reno NV 89557

BACKSTROM, JOHN MARVIN, advertising company executive; b. Biwabik, Minn., Jan. 21, 1940; s. Ralph V. and Marge L. (Gillespie) B.; children—John M., Jeffery R., Jennifer L. Grad., Sales Tng., Inc., 1963. Formerly constrn. worker; with sales dept. Mut. Benefit Life Ins. Co. of Newark, Seattle, 1964-69; with sales dept. Wash. Transit Advt. Sales Co., Seattle, 1969—, pres., ptnr., 1975—; part-owner, operator screen printing co.; guest lectr. advt.-mrkt. sequence at numerous univs. Life mem. Republican Nat. Com. Served with USN, 1958-63. Mem. Seattle Advt. Fedn., Transit Advt. Assn., Seattle-King County Conv. and Visitors Bur., Seattle C. of C. Clubs: Seattle Skeet and Trap, Porsche Club of Am. Office: Washington Transit Advt Co 2600 Western Ave Seattle WA 98121

BACKUS, WALTER JAY, chemical engineer; b. Spokane, Wash., Mar. 13, 1954; s. Walter Elliott and Effie Adeline B.; m. Theresa Griep, Oct. 5, 1955. B.S. in Chem. Engring., Wash. State U., 1977, M.S., 1979. Engr.-in-tng., water treatment plant operator II, Wash. With Boise Cascade, Walla Walla, Wash., 1979—, process engr., 1981-82, prodn. engr., 1982—. Chevron 4-H Achievement scholar, 1972; Inst. Paper Chemistry fellow, 1977. Mem. Am. Inst. Chem. Engrs., TAPPI, Am. Water Works Assn. Clubs: Internat. Soccer (Walla Walla), Appleton Rugby (Wis.). Home: 124 Elliott Pl Walla Walla WA 99362 Office: PO Box 500 Walla Walla WA 99363

BACON, J. RAYMOND, business exec.; b. Chgo., Aug. 11, 1906; s. Elmer Winfield and Alma C. (Romburg) B.; diploma in commerce Northwestern U., 1943; M.A., Western U., 1950; Ph.D. in Bus. Adminstrn. (hon.), Colo. State Christian Coll., 1972; m. Florence I. Burdine, Nov. 5, 1927 (dec. Nov. 1960); 1 dau., Grace Florence (Mrs. John W. Bacher); m. 2d, Margaret Austin, Nov. 30, 1963. Asst. mgr. King Woodworking Co., Chgo., 1926-34; dept. head Montgomery Ward & Co., Chgo. and Albany, N.Y., 1935-40; v.p., gen. mgr. O. D. Jennings & Co., Chgo., 1940-48; exec. v.p. Rockola Mfg. Co., Chgo., 1948-54; pres., treas., dir. F. H. Noble & Co., Chgo., 1954-67; pres., dir. F. H. Noble & Co. (Can.) Ltd., 1956-67; mng. dir. F. H. Noble & Co. (Ireland), Belfast, No. Ireland, 1963-67; pres., dir. Draftette Co., Hemet, Calif., 1967—. Mem. Am. Mgmt. Assn., Soc. for Advancement Mgmt., A.I.M. (asso.), YMCA, Art Inst. Chgo. (life), Hemet C. of C., Calif. Mfrs. Assn. Presbyn. Kiwanian (past pres.). Home: PO Box 895 Hemet CA 92343 Office: 26951 Cawston Ave PO Box 895 Hemet CA 92343

BACON, ROGER LEE, educator; b. Boise, Idaho, Oct. 23, 1939; s. Russell C. and Uvonna (Royle) B.; B.A., U. Oreg., 1964, M.A., 1965; Ph.D., U. Utah, 1972, 76; m. Christine Lee Wright, Dec. 18, 1965; children—Kimberlee, Bryan, Eric, Melissa, Jill. Asst. prof. English, So. Oreg. State Coll., Ashland, 1965-69; teaching fellow U. Utah, Salt Lake City, 1969-72; assoc. prof. English, No. Ariz. U., Flagstaff, 1972—, dir. tech. writing, 1972—; cons. Shipley Assos., 1980—. Served as chaplain, USAFR, 1974—. Mem. Nat. Council Tchrs. English, AAUP, Tech. Writing Tchrs. Assn., Soc. Tech. Communication (sr.), Phi Kappa Phi, Phi Kappa Delta. Mormon. Home: 754 Hilltop Ave Flagstaff AZ 86001 Office: No Ariz Univ PO Box 6032 Flagstaff AZ 86011

BACON, VICKY LEE, lighting services exec.; b. Oregon City, Oreg., Mar. 25, 1950; d. Herbert Kenneth and Lorean Betty (Boltz) Rushford; student Portland Community Coll., 1974-75, Mt. Hood Community Coll., 1976, Portland State Coll., 1979; m. Dennis M. Bacon, Aug. 7, 1971; 1 dau., Randene Tess. With All Electric Constrn., Milwaukie, Oreg., 1968-70; with Lighting Maintenance Co., Portland, Oreg., 1970-78; service mgr. GTE Sylvania Lighting Services, Portland, 1978-80, br. mgr., 1980—. Mem. Nat. Secs. Assn., Illuminating Engring. Soc., Nat. Assn. Lighting Maintenance Contractors. Office: 10775 SW Cascade Blvd Portland OR 97223

BACON, WALTER LAURENCE, III, elec. engr.; b. Phila., Nov. 2, 1912; s. Walter Laurence and Elisabeth V. (Ford) B.; M.S., Calif. Inst. Tech., 1936; m. Ada Gwendolyn Perkin, Aug. 31, 1944; children—Cheryl Elizabeth, Walter Laurence IV. With Tex. Co., 1936-41; sr. staff engr. Gen. Telephone & Electronics Corp. Calif., Pomona, 1947-77; owner Ocean Electronics Research Studies, cons. firm, 1968—. Supr. edn., tng. Retarded Children's Assn. San Gabriel Valley, 1959-65, pres., 1957-58. Served as comdr. USNR, 1942—. Recipient Dr. Elenora Preston award for research, devel. methods in teaching retarded children, 1964. Mem. Am. Inst. E.E. (chmn. communications Los Angeles chpt.), IEEE (chmn. communications soc. profl. group Los Angeles Council, vice chmn. oceanic engring. council 1979—). Contbr. articles to profl. jours. Home: 323 N Elizabeth Ave Monterey Park CA 91754

BADDLEY, BRENT DEGREY, social worker; b. Summit, N.J., Apr. 30, 1930; s. Wallace DeGrey and Melba Grace (Parry) B.; A.S., Weber Coll., 1950; B.S., U. Utah, 1954; M.S.W., 1956; m. Jacqueline M. Morris, Aug. 20, 1954; children—Judy Ann, Douglas, James, Becky. Dist. supr. No. Utah Office Vocat. Rehab., Ogden, 1956-64; asso. prof. sociology and social work Weber State Coll., Ogden, 1965; exec. dir. family counseling service United Way, Ogden, 1966—. Pres., Family Financial Counseling Center, 1974-75; pres. Social Services Coordinating Council Weber County, 1968-69, exec. bd., 1966—; chmn. Weber County Heart Fund Drive, 1961; div. chmn. United Way No. Utah, 1970-75. Bd. dirs. Weber County Tng. Center for Mentally Retarded Children, 1965-73, A.R.C., 1963-66, Multiple Sclerosis Soc., 1960-63. Mem. Am. Assn. Marriage and Family Counselors, Phi Beta Kappa, Phi Kappa Phi. Mem. Ch. Jesus Christ Latter-day Saints. Home: 635 43d St Ogden UT 84403 Office: 2503 Adams Ave Ogden UT 84401

BADER, GERALD LOUIS, JR., lawyer; b. St. Louis, Mar. 15, 1934; s. Gerald Louis and Mabel Adeline (Stephens) B.; A.B., Washington U., 1956; LL.B., U. Mich., 1959; m. Catherine Louise Ince, Aug. 26, 1961 (div. Jan. 1977); children—Gerald Louis III, Stephanie, Cynthia, Carlie, Deborah; m. 2d, Barbara Anne Lien, June 2, 1979. Admitted to Colo. bar, 1960, Mo. bar, 1960, N.Y. bar, 1961; asso. firm White & Case, N.Y.C., 1960-62, 64-65, firm Hodges, Silverstein & Harrington, Denver, 1965-68; partner firm Bader & Cox, and predecessors, Denver, 1969—; asst. sec., dir. Altex Oil Corp., 1971—; dir., v.p., sec. Royal Resources Corp., 1980—; sec., dir. First Charter Bank, 1982—; sec., treas., dir. Rocky Mountain Fuel Co., 1973-77; hearing examiner Colo. Real Estate Commn., 1970-78. Sec., v.p. Consumer Credit Counselling Service, 1966-73, bd. dirs., 1966—; mem. Coop. Endeavor Com., 1968-72, 73-74; sec. Denver County Republican Central Com., 1969-73. Served as 1st lt. Intelligence Service, U.S. Army, 1962-64. Mem. Phi Beta Kappa, Delta Theta Phi, Omicron Delta Gamma, Phi Delta Theta. Roman Catholic. Club: Univ. Office: 1660 17 St Denver CO 80202

BADER, MICHAEL BRUCE, controller; b. Los Angeles, Oct. 7, 1957; s. Martin and Norma Sally (Heimbach) B. B.B.A., Calif. State U.-Fullerton, 1979. C.P.A., Calif. Acct., Broussard Accountancy Corp., Orange, Calif., 1978-80; tax specialist Thomas, Fees & Assocs., C.P.A.s, Tustin, Calif., 1981; controller James R. Glidewell Dental Ceramics Inc., Orange, 1981—; cons. computers for dental labs. Mem. Am. Inst. C.P.A.s, Nat. Acctg. Soc. Republican. Club: Duck. Home: 2501-F7 W Sunflower Ave Santa Ana CA 92704 Office: Glidewell Dental Ceramics Inc 1722 E Rose Ave Orange CA 92704

BADGER, LAURENE LAURITZEN, nurse; b. Salt Lake City, Jan. 24, 1955; d. Vaughn Kent and Lona Mae Stratford (Hyde) Lauritzen; m. Karl Franklin Badger, Dec. 14, 1978 (div.). A.D. in Med. Scis., Brigham Young U., 1975; A.D. in Nursing, Weber State Coll., 1978. Registered nurse, Utah. Registered nurse cons. Procter & Gamble, Salt Lake City, 1980-82, Knoll Pharmaceutical, Salt Lake City, 1983—; nurse St. Mark's Hosp., Salt Lake City, 1976—; Mem. Utah Soc. for Post Anesthesia Nurses. Republican. Mormon. Office: 616 E Cobblestone Ln Midvale UT 84047

BADGLEY, JOHN ROY, architect; b. Huntington, W. Va., July 10, 1922; s. Roy Joseph and Fannie Myrtle (Limbaugh) B.; A.B., Occidental Coll., 1943; M. Arch., Harvard, 1949; postgrad., Centro Internazionale, Vincenza, Italy, 1959; m. Janice Atwell, July 10, 1975; 1 son, Adam; children by previous marriage—Michael, Dan, Lisa, Holly, Marcus. Prin. architect own firm, San Luis Obispo, Calif., 1952-65; chief architect, also planner Crocker Land Co., San Francisco, 1965-80; v.p. Cushman & Wakefield Inc., San Francisco, 1980—; tchr. Calif. State U. at San Luis Obispo, 1952-65. Bd. dirs. Ft. Mason Found. Served with USCGR, 1942-46. Mem. AIA, Am. Arbitration Assn. Oceanic Soc. (trustee). Clubs: St. Francis Yacht, Golden Gate Wine Soc. Home: 1356 Idylberry Rd San Rafael CA 94903 Office: 555 California St San Francisco CA 94104

BADGLEY, THEODORE MCBRIDE, psychiatrist, neurologist; b. Salem, Ala., June 27, 1925; s. Roy J. and Fannie M. (Limbaugh) B.; student Occidental Coll., 1942-44; M.D., U. So. Calif., 1949; m. Mary Bennett Wells, Dec. 30, 1945; children—Justice Badgley O'Neil, Jan Badgley Wolkov, Mona Badgley Covey, Jason Wells, James John, Mary Rose. Intern, Letterman Gen. Hosp., San Francisco, 1949-50, resident psychiatry, 1950-53; resident neurology Walter Reed Gen. Hosp., Washington, 1955-57; practice medicine specializing in psychiatry and neurology, 1957—; commd. lt., M.C., U.S. Army, 1949, advanced through grades to lt. col., 1967; chief mental hygiene consultation service, Fort Gordon, Ga., 1954-55; asst. chief psychiatry service Walter Reed Gen. Hosp., Washington, 1957-59, dir. psychiat. tng., 1957-63, chief psychiatry service, 1959-62, asst. chief dept. psychiatry and neurology, 1962-63; asst. clin. prof. psychiatry Med. Coll. Ga., 1954-55; asso. clin. prof. psychiatry Georgetown U. Sch. Nursing, Washington, 1962-63; chief dept. psychiatry and neurology U.S. Army Gen. Hosp., Landstuhl, Germany, 1963-66; cons. psychiatry Canadian Air Force, Europe, 1964-66; chief psychiatry outpatient service Letterman Gen. Hosp., San Francisco, 1966-67; ret., 1967; practice medicine specializing in med. and forensic neuropsychiatry, Bakersfield, Calif., 1967—; dir. Kern View Community Mental Health Center and Hosp., Bakersfield, 1967-69; pres. Sans Doloroso Inst. Med. Group, Inc., Bakersfield, 1969—. Served with USN, 1943-45. Diplomate Am. Bd. Psychiatry and Neurology. Fellow Am. Psychiat. Assn.; mem. Am. Acad. Clin. Psychiatrists, Kern County Med. Soc. (pres. 1981), Am. Coll. Forensic Psychiatry, Central Calif. Psychiatry Soc. (pres. Kern chpt. 1976—). Office: 1901 Truxtun Ave Bakersfield CA 93301

BADHAM, JOHN MACDONALD, motion picture dir.; b. Luton, Eng., Aug. 25, 1943; s. Henry Lee and Mary Iola (Hewitt) B.; came to U.S., 1945, naturalized, 1950; B.A., Yale U., 1963, M.F.A., 1965; m. Bonnie Sue Hughes, Dec. 28, 1967 (div. 1979); 1 dau., Kelly MacDonald. Asso. producer Universal Studios, 1969-70; asso. producer TV movies Night Gallery, 1969, Neon Ceiling, 1970; asso. producer, dir. The Senator (Emmy award nomination 1971), 1970; dir. numerous episodes of Night Gallery, Police Story, Streets of San Francisco, The Bold Ones, others; motion pictures for TV include: The Law (Emmy nomination 1974, ARD reihe 'das film festival award 1975), 1974, Isn't It Shocking, 1973, Reflections of Murder, 1973, The Impatient Heart (Christopher award), 1971, The Gun (So. Calif. Motion Picture Council award), 1974, The Godchild, 1974; theatrical motion pictures include: The Bingo Long Travelling All Stars and Motor Kings (NAACP image award nomination), 1976, Saturday Night Fever, 1977, Dracula (Grand prize Paris Internat. Sci. Fiction and Fantasy Festival, Best Horror Film award Acad. Sci. Fiction and Fantasy), 1979, Whose Life Is It Anyway?, 1981, Blue Thunder, 1982; War Games, 1982; pres. John Badham Films, Inc.; chmn. bd. JMB Films, Inc.; guest lectr. U. Calif., Loyola Marymount Coll., U. Ala., Amherst Coll., U. So. Calif. Served with U.S. Army, 1963-64. Mem. Dirs. Guild Am., Filmex Soc., Acad. Motion Picture Arts and Scis.

BADHAM, ROBERT EDWARD, Congressman; b. Los Angeles, June 9, 1929; s. Byron Jack and Bess (Kissinger) B.; A.B. in Architecture, Stanford U., 1951; m. Anne Carroll; children—Sharon, Robert, William, Phyllis, Jennifer. Mem. Calif. Assembly, 1962-76; mem. 95th-98th Congresses from 40th Calif. Dist., chmn. Republican study com., Rep. research task force nat. def.; mem. Rep. policy com., armed services com., house adminstrn. com., vice-chmn. congressional travel and tourism caucus; mem. exec. com. Nat. Rep. Congressional Com. Active Boy Scouts. Served to lt. (j.g.) USNR, 1951-54. Mem. Am. Legion, Phi Gamma Delta. Republican. Lutheran. Office: 180 Newport Center Dr Suite 240 Newport Beach CA 92660 also 2438 Rayburn House Office Bldg Washington DC 20515

BADIYI, REZA SAYED, film and television dir.; b. Arak, Iran, Apr. 17, 1930; s. Mehdi Sayed and Nazeneen Bagom (Messy) B.; B.A., Drama Sch. Iran, 1950; Masters in Lit., U. Tehran, 1953; M.A., Syracuse U., 1955; m. Barbara Turner, Apr. 5, 1968; 1 dau., Mina Alexis. Cameraman, Ministry of Culture and Art, Iran, 1953-54, Horizon Prodns., Kansas City, Mo., 1956-60, Robert Altman Co., 1960-64; asso. producer Talent Prodn., N.Y.C., Los Angeles, 1965-67; dir. TV shows including: Mission Impossible, 1969-75, Hawaii Five O, 1968-79, Baretta, 1977-78, Incredible Hulk, 1978-79, Rockford Files, 1977-78, White Water, 1982, Cagney & Lacey, 1982; films include: Carnival of Souls, 1958, Death of a Strangler, Eyes of Charles, 1973, Of Mice and Men, 1981. Recipient gold medal of art, Govt. Iran, 1953. Mem. Dirs. Guild Am., Acad. TV Arts and Scis. Home: 1850 Outpost Dr Los Angeles CA 90068 Office: 9903 Kip Dr Beverly Hills CA 90210

BADSTUEBNER, HANS ALEXANDER, elec. co. exec.; b. Berlin, Germany, Feb. 26, 1916; s. Alexander and Emilie (Luechters) B.; grad. elec. engring., Berlin, Germany, 1938; Ph.D., 1972; m. Vera Ott, Jan. 9, 1939; 1 son, Stefan. Came to U.S., 1960. Asst. to gen. mgr. research and devel. depts. Telefunken GmbH., Leubus and Berlin, Germany, 1942-45; cons. efficiency engring., Berlin, 1945-52; owner Elba Electric Co., Burnaby, B.C., Canada, 1952-60; v.p. prodn. engring. R.M. Hadley Co., Inc., Los Angeles, 1960-64, v.p. charge engring. Baum Electric Co., Inc., Garden Grove, Calif., 1964—; partner Hansera Co., Fullerton, 1969—; cons. Foster-Mathews Electric Co., Fullerton, 1981—. Mem. Am. Mensa Selection Agy. Mem. Soc. Plastic Engrs., Internat. Platform Assn. Mason (Shriner). Inventor in various fields. Home: 1312 Norman Pl Fullerton CA 92631 Office: 114 S Lemon Ave Fullerton CA 92632

BAENDER, MARGARET WOODRUFF, free lance writer; b. Salt Lake City, Apr. 1, 1921; d. Russell Kimball and Margaret Angline (McIntyre) Woodruff; m. Phillip Albers Baender, Aug. 17, 1946 (dec.); children—Kristine Lynn, Charlene Anne, Michael Phillip, Russell Richard. B.A., U. Utah, 1944. In clerical, personnel work various firms, San Francisco, 1970-75; reporter, columnist Valley Pioneer, Danville, Calif., 1975-77; editor Diablo (Calif.) Inferno, 1971-76; author Shifting Sands, 1981, Tail Waggings of Maggie, 1982. Mem. Nat. Writers Club, AAUW, Alpha Delta Pi. Republican. Episcopalian.

BAER, CHAROLD LEE, nursing educator; b. Dover, Ohio, July 15, 1946; d. Harold and Zelda Mae (Frantz) Morris; m. Richard Carl Baer, Sept. 7, 1968. B.S.N., Ohio State U.-Columbus, 1968, M.S.N., 1970, Ph.D., 1977. Staff nurse Ohio State U. Hosps., 1968-69, 70-77; instr. Ohio State U. Sch. Nursing, 1970-74, grad. research assoc., 1974-77; project dir. Ohio Nurses Assn., 1977-78; adj. prof. edn. Portland (Oreg.) State U., 1979—; prof., chmn. dept. adult health and illness Sch. Nursing, Oreg. Health Scis. U., Portland, 1978—. Coordinator lector programs St. Elizabeth Cath. Ch., 1978—. Recipient Research Cash award Ohio State U. Sch. Nursing, 1977; named Outstanding Faculty Mem., Oreg. Health Scis. U. Sch. Nursing, 1981. Mem. Am. Nurses Assn., Am. Assn. Critical Care Nurses, Am. Assn. Nephrology Nurses and Technicians, Nurses Political Action Com. (dir.), Western Soc. Research in Nursing, Oreg. Nurses Assn. (treas.), Sigma Theta Tau, Pi Lambda Theta, Phi Delta Kappa. Democrat. Roman Catholic. Editorial bd. Topics in Clin. Nursing, 1979—, Heart and Lung, 1980—, Nursing Life, 1981—, Critical Care Nurse, 1983. Home: 8039 SW 62d Pl Portland OR 97219 Office: 3181 SW Sam Jackson Park Rd Portland OR 97201

BAER, DANIEL HESS, public relations consultant; b. Chgo., Aug. 2, 1929; s. Stanley F. and Betsy (Hess) B.; m. Shirley Kaufmann, June 16, 1956; children—James, John; m. 2d, Barbara Blumenthal, June 14, 1970. B.S. in Journalism, U. Ill., 1951. Police reporter City News Bur., Chgo., 1947-48; writer News-Gazette, Champaign, Ill., 1949-50; combat corr. 2d Infantry Div., Korea, 1951-52; account exec. Harshe-Rotman, Inc., Chgo., 1953-54; sr. v.p. Western ops. Harshe-Rotman & Druck, Inc., Los Angeles, 1955-71; pres. Daniel H. Baer, Inc., Sherman Oaks, Calif., 1971—; instr. U. So. Calif. Served in U.S. Army, 1951-52. Mem. Pub. Relations Soc. Am. (1st v.p. Los Angeles chpt.), Sigma Delta Chi. Contbr. articles to profl. jours. Home: 3738 Glenridge Dr Sherman Oaks CA 91423

BAER, D(AVID) RICHARD, film archive adminstr.; b. Oakland, Calif., Jan. 18, 1946; s. Oliver Albrecht and Beatrice Faye (Shrager) B.; B.S. in Bus. Adminstrn., UCLA, 1967. Founder, pres. Hollywood Film Archive, 1972—, also dir. Author: The Film Buff's Bible of Motion Pictures, 1915-1972, 1972; The Film Buff's Checklist of Motion Pictures, 1912-1979, 1979. Home: PO Box 48174 Los Angeles CA 90048 Office: 8344 Melrose Ave Hollywood CA 90069

BAER, DORICE BENTLEY, former mus. curator; b. Huntington, Oreg., Sept. 20, 1892; d. John Edward and Mary Elizabeth (Bentley) Kurtz; student Walla Walla Coll., Wash., 1907-08; m. Charles Andrew Baer, May 13, 1912; children—Samuel Edward, Charles William, Patricia Wylie, Mary E. Bookkeeper, Dalles Box & Lumber Co., The Dalles, Oreg., 1909-11; curator Coos-Curry Mus., Simpson Park, North Bend, Oreg., 1964-78. Clk., Election Bd., Coos Bay, Oreg., 1940-64. Mem. D.A.R. (chpt. regent 1946-48), Coos-Curry Pioneer and Hist. Assn. Address: 595 S 12th St Coos Bay OR 97420

BAER, ROBERT JULIUS, check and credit card verification co. exec.; b. Pitts., Oct. 27, 1912; s. Julius and Blanche (Sidenberg) B.; m. Elice Weber, Nov. 25, 1937; children—Theodora Baer Bailey, Ronald W., Jeffrey. Student U. Pitts. Pres. Alemite Co. of Wis., 1952-66; chmn. bd., chief exec. officer TeleCheck Services, Inc., Honolulu, 1966—; speaker on mktg. and motivation, 1945—. Chmn. adv. bd. Salvation Army, Hawaii, 1966; mem. exec. com. Honolulu Retail Bd.; del White House Conf. on Small Bus., 1980. Mem. Internat. Franchise Assn. (pub. relations and trade com.), Honolulu C. of C., Honolulu Sales and Mktg. Execs. Club (life), Internat. Platform Assn. Republican. Christian Scientist. Clubs: Oahu Country, Plaza, Masons, Kiwanis. Home: 64 Niuiki Circle Honolulu HI 96821 Office: 190 S King St Suite 1610 Honolulu HI 96813

BAETZNER, KARL EDWARD, cons. engr.; b. Rochester, N.Y., July 24, 1909; s. Karl Christian and Emma (Wirth) B.; grad. high sch.; m. Frances Hitt, Sept. 3, 1973. With Washington Gas Light Co., Springfield, Va., 1927-74, supt. mains planning, to 1974; mgr. bus. devel. Univ. Sci. Center, Pitts., Falls Church, Va. and Phoenix, 1974-75. Mem. Am. Right of Way Assn. (nat. pres. 1970-71), Am. Gas Assn., Am. Pub. Works Assn., D.C. Road Builders Assn. Club: Manor Country (Rockville, Md.). Contbr. articles to profl. jours. Address: 2502 W Roveen Ave Phoenix AZ 85029

BAGGERLY, EVERETT ELZY, finance company executive; s. Newton and Sarah Elizabeth (Ferguson) B.; B.A., Goddard Coll.; M.Ed., Wayne State U., also Edn. Specialist; m. Bonnie M. Barnette, Mar. 1, 1969;

children by previous marriage—Edward E., Timothy M. Salesman, sales mgr., collector, collection mgr. P.F. Collier & Son, Inc., N.Y.C., 1933-38; collector, collection mgr., credit mgr., operations mgr., dist. mgr. CIT Corp., N.Y.C., 1939-53, gen. mgr., pres. Island Interprises, Inc., Okinawa, 1949-51; mng. dir. Micronesia Nav. Co., Micronesia Metal & Equipment Co., Inc., Trust Ty. of Pacific Islands, 1953-56; owner, pres. Micronesia Investment Co., Guam, Marianas Islands, 1956-59; gen. operations mgr., v.p., cons. urban problems Ford Motor Credit Co., Dearborn, Mich., 1959-71; owner Eastern Calif. Investment Co., pres. Micronesia Investment Co., Inc., owner Everett E. Baggerly Ins. Agy., Victorville, Calif., 1973-74; v.p. adminstrn. Freightliner Credit Corp., Portland, Oreg., 1974-78; gen. mgr. Stewart & Tunno Inc., Portland, 1978—. Chmn. Tax Appeal Bd., Guam, Bd. Equalization, 1957-59; adv. council SAC, 1950-59; mem. Oreg. Wages and Hours Commn., 1975—; treas. Dem. Party of Oreg., 1977—. Mem. bd. advisors City and Country Sch., Bloomfield Hills, Mich., 1961-69. Trustee, v.p. Childrens Internat. Summer Village, 1964-70. Served to capt. USAAF, 1943-45. Mem. Am. Mgmt. Assn., Soc. for Advancement Mgmt., Internat. Soc. Gen. Semantics (v.p., dir.). Am. Legion, People to People, C. of C. (dir.), Am. Humanistic Psychol. Assn., Am. Indsl. Bankers Assn. (dir.), Ops. Research Soc. Am. Clubs: Elks, Kiwanis (pres. 1979—), City, Internat., Royal Rosarian (Knight). Home: 41 da Vinci St Lake Oswego OR 97034

BAGGETT, DEWEY LLOYD, hospital association executive; b. Corpus Christi, Tex., July 25, 1931; s. Dewey and Sophia (Munson) B.; m. Roycelene Matson, Sept. 14, 1957; 1 son, Steven Gregory. B.A. in Econs., U. Tex., 1957; M.B.A., George Washington U., 1967. Cert. assn. exec., 1978. Asst. adminstr. N.W. Tex. Hosp., Amarillo, 1967-68, Bapt. Hosp., Phoenix, 1968-69; dir. registration Am. Hosp. Assn., Chgo., 1970-71, dir. mgmt. services, 1972-73; dir. mgmt. effectiveness program Calif. Hosp. Assn., Sacramento, 1971-72; exec. v.p. Hosp. Council Coordinated Programs, Hosp. Council San Diego and Imperial Counties, 1973—; faculty Nat. U. Grad. Sch., Webster U. Grad. Sch. Served with USN, 1950-54. Fellow Am. Coll. Hosp. Adminstrs.; mem. Am. Soc. Assn. Execs., Am. Mgmt. Assn., Hosp. Fin. Mgmt. Assn., Am. Health Planning Assn. Republican. Baptist. Home: 1749 Tamarack Ave Carlsbad CA 92008 Office: 8305 Vickers St Suite T San Diego CA 92111

BAGGETT, KELSEA KINDRICK, nursing adminstr.; b. Pine Bluff, Ark., Nov. 19, 1937; s. Joe L. and Mildred (Franks) B.; grad. Los Angeles County Gen. Hosp., 1964; A.S., Cypress Coll., 1975; B.S.N., Calif. State U., Fullerton, 1980; m. Roxanna V. Dixon, Jan. 5, 1963; children—Daniel, Sheryl, Noel, Douglas. With Los Angeles County Sheriff's Med. Services, 1964—, dir. nursing, 1976—. Served with USAF, 1956-60. Mem. Nat. League Nursing, Am. Health Care Correctional Assn. Republican. Baptist. Office: 441 Bauchet St Los Angeles CA 90012

BAGLEY, DIANA WOLCOTT, public relations representative, consultant, writer; b. Long Beach, Calif., Nov. 12, 1953; d. Alfred Warren and Helen Emma (Wolcott) B. B.A. in Journalism, Calif. State U.-Long Beach, 1975. Freelance writer, Long Beach, Calif., 1975-77; pub. relations coordinator Pub. Corp. for the Arts, City of Long Beach, 1978-80; mng. editor Performance mag., Long Beach, 1978-80; staff writer Galaxy mag., Long Beach, 1979-83; sr. copywriter Direct Mktg. Corp. Am., Los Angeles, 1980-81; pub. relations rep. Transam. Occidental Life Ins. Co., Los Angeles, 1981—; founder Pub. Relations Network of Long Beach. Recipient Clarion award Women in Communications, 1982. Mem. Pub. Relations Soc. Am., Pacific Coast Press Club (service award 1982, dir., 1st v.p.), Sigma Delta Chi, Zeta Tau Alpha (pres. Long Beach Alumnae chpt. 1977-78, 79-80). Office: 1150 S Olive Suite T-1300 Los Angeles CA 90015

BAGLEY, RONALD LAIRD, air force officer, engineering educator; b. Indiana, Pa., May 31, 1947; s. Ronald Dale and Sarah (MacPherson) B., m. Ellen Louise Isaksen, June 26, 1971; children—Ross Andrew, Melissa Anne. B.S., M.I.T., 1969, M.S., 1971 Ph.D., Air Force Inst. Tech., 1979; postgrad. Air Command and Staff Coll., Maxwell AFB, Ala., 1983—. Commd. U.S. Air Force, 1971, advanced through grades to maj., 1982; instr. U.S. Air Force Acad., 1979-80, asst. prof., 1980-82, assoc. prof., 1982-83, lab. dir. civil engring. and engring. mechanics lab., 1981-83; cons. in field. Decorated Air Force Commendation medal with oak leaf cluster. Mem. ASME. Presbyterian. Contbr. articles to profl. jours.

BAHME, RICHARD BEALE, agronomist, plant ecologist; b. Los Angeles, Dec. 23, 1918; s. John William and Jessie Irene (Beale) B.; m. Anna Hanlin, Aug. 31, 1946; children—Robert Hanlin, John Beale. B.S. in Forest and Range Mgmt., U. Calif.-Berkeley, 1940, M.S. in Plant Physiology and Ecology, 1947, Ph.D. in Soils and Plant Nutrition, 1949. Registered profl. forester, Calif.; lic. nurseryman, Calif., pest control adviser, Calif.; cert. profl. agronomist, soil scientist, crop scientist. Research agronomist E.I. du Pont Co., Sacramento, Calif., 1949-54; chief agronomist Pacific Guano Co., Berkeley, Calif., 1954-58; western regional agronomist Nat. Plant Food Inst., San Francisco, 1958-64; v.p., cons. Uniconsult, Inc., Lafayette, Calif., 1964-67; pres. AgriDevel. Co., Orinda, Calif., 1967—, AgBio Chem, Inc., Orinda, 1967—; owner, mgr. Agridevel. Orchard, Red Bluff, Calif., 1951—; project mgr. Tambo Valley Land Reclamation, Lima, Peru, 1967-71; agrl. cons. Pacific Gas and Electric Co., San Francisco, 1965—. Served to capt. U.S. Army, 1941-46. Mem. Soc. Am. Foresters, Am. Soc. Farm Mgrs. and Rural Appraisers, Am. Soc. Agronomy, Crop Sci. Soc. Am., Calif. Fertilizer Assn. (soil improvement com. 1954—), Am. Soc. Range Mgmt., Am. Chem. Soc., Sigma Xi. Republican. Episcopalian. Clubs: Orinda Country, Lake Almanor Country, San Francisco Press, Lions. Patentee in field; contbr. numerous sci. articles to profl. publs. Home and Office: 3 Fleetwood Ct Orinda CA 94563

BAHN, IRENE ELIZA SCHUYLER, author; b. Borodino, N.Y., June 19, 1895; d. William Scott and Carrie Eugene (Kennedy) Schuyler; A.B., Syracuse U., 1918; m. Chester Bert Bahn, June 25, 1921 (dec. 1962); children—Gilbert Schuyler, Chester Bert, Jerrold Philip. News reporter Syracuse (N.Y.) Jour., 1918-21; free lance poet and news corr. various newspapers, N.Y., Pa., 1921-32; publicity agt. Loew's Theatre, Syracuse, 1932-34, RKO Theatres, Syracuse, 1934-36; vol. publicity agt. various charitable orgns., Malverne, N.Y., 1936-60, Thousand Oaks, Calif., 1960—. Vol., S. Nassau Communities Hosp. Malverne Aux., 1944-62, pres., 1956-57; organizer Save the Name referendum upon incorporation Thousand Oaks, 1964; founding pres. Conejo Valley Hosp. Aux., 1963-68; vol. Los Robles Hosp. Aux., 1968—; founding mem. Conejo Valley Debutantes Ball Com., 1968—; bd. dirs. Conejo Valley Hist. Soc., 1968—, named Dona Conejo, 1970. Recipient Community Service medal Thousand Oaks C. of C., 1963; life mem. Conejo Players, 1976. Mem. AAUW, Alpha Chi Omega. Republican. Presbyterian. Clubs: Conejo Valley Garden (hon. mem. 1975); Las Patronas. Home: 238 Encino Vista Dr Thousand Oaks CA 91362 Mailing Address: 615 Brandywine Dr Newport News VA 23602

BAHR, HOWARD MINER, sociologist, educator; b. Provo, Utah, Feb. 21, 1938; s. A. Francis and Louie Jean (Miner) B.; B.A. with honors, Brigham Young U., 1962; M.A. in Sociology, U. Tex., 1964, Ph.D., 1965; m. Rosemary Frances Smith, Aug. 28, 1961; children—Bonnie Louise, Howard McKay, Rowena Ruth, Tanya Lavonne, Christopher J., Laura L., Stephen S., Rachel M. Research asso. Columbia U., N.Y.C., 1965-68, vis. lectr., summer, 1968; lectr. in sociology N.Y. U., 1967-68, Bklyn. Coll., City U. N.Y., 1967; asso. prof. sociology Washington State U., Pullman, 1968-72, prof., 1972-73, chmn. dept. rural sociology, 1971-73; prof. sociology Brigham Young U., Provo, Utah, 1973—, dir. Family Research Inst., 1977—; vis. prof. sociology U. Va., 1976-77. NIMH grantee, 1968-70, 71-73; NSF grantee, 1971-72, 76-80. Mem. Am. Sociol. Assn., Rural Sociol. Assn., Nat. Council on Family Relations, Southwestern Social Sci. Assn. Mormon. Author: An Introduction to Disaffiliation, 1973; Old Men Drunk and Sober, 1974; Women Alone: The Disaffiliation of Urban Females, 1976; Ethnic Americans, 1979; The Sunshine Widows, 1980; Middletown Families, 1982; Life in Large Families, 1982; All Faithful People, 1983; Divorce and Remarriage, 1983; contbr. articles to profl. jours.; asso. editor Rural Sociology, 1978—, Jour. Marriage and the Family, 1978—. Office: Dept Sociology Brigham Young U Provo UT 84602

BAHR, JEROME FELSHEIM, writer; b. Arcadia, Wis., Oct. 26, 1909; student U. Minn., 1928-29, 31-33; m. Jean Blaney, Feb. 11, 1955; children—Nicholas, Antony; 1 dau. by previous marriage, Tonia Bahr O'Shea. Civilian speech writer U.S. Dept. Def., 1951-58; civilian press officer U.S. Army, Berlin, 1958-64; writer U.S. Office Edn., Washington, 1968-71; free-lance writer, 1971—; books include: All Good Americans, 1937, The Linen Suit and Other Stories, 1957, Wisconsin Tales, 1964, Holes in the Wall, 1970, The Perishing Republic, 1971, The Lonely Scoundrel, 1974, Five Novellas, 1977. Served to maj. USAAF and USAF, 1942-50; CBI. Home: 800 Hillcrest Dr Santa Fe NM 87501

BAHRAMIAN, HAMLET, architect; b. Erevan, Armenia, Aug. 26, 1922; s. Zora and Aroussiak (Mirakian) B.; Engr.-Architect, U. Tehran, 1949. Came to U.S., 1960, naturalized, 1967. Individual practice architecture, Tehran, Iran, 1949-60, Los Angeles, 1968—; with Richard J. Neutra, Los Angeles, 1960-62, Termohlen Empire Corp., Long Beach, Calif., 1964, Robert E. Alexander, Los Angeles, 1965-66. Works include Tehran Hosp., Maragheh (Iran) R.R. Sta., Cinema Flora of Tehran, Shluker residence (Los Angeles). Mem. AIA, Soc. Am. Registered Architects. Home and office: 1014 Meadowbrook Ave Los Angeles CA 90019

BAIL, GRACE SHATTUCK, composer-poet, author, music tchr.; b. Cherry Creek, N.Y., Jan. 17, 1898; d. Frederick John and Clarissa (Richmond) Shattuck; spl. student Meadville Coll. Music, 1911-12; grad. Dana Music Sch. of Youngstown U., 1919; children—Richard, Roland Hornby. Tchr. piano, organ, violin, theory, Beaumont, Calif.; tchr. violin United Brethren Pvt. sch., Cherry Valley. Composer numerous selections including Sleepy Song, Autumn Love, Dreams, Minuet for Two Violins, 23d and 24th Psalms of David, Evening Reverie, A Bird Sings, 465 bible songs, numerous others; songs recorded: Autumn Love, Hushabye. Recipient Poem of Month award, Desert mag., 1961, 62; Edwin Markham Silver Medal, 1961; couplet award, sonnet award Am. Bard, 1967; bronze medal Centro E Scambi; also Internat. Poetry's Shrine Gold medal 1969; 1st prize Calif. Fedn. Chaparral Poets, 1972; award Friendly Way mag., 1972; Sweepstakes prize poems Mich. Poetry Soc., 1972, also certs. of merit. Mem. Nat. League Am. Penwomen (Biennial awards, Nat. Biennial award 1970). Composers, Authors, Artists Am. (nat. dir., award violin solo 1965, 68), Am. Poetry League, Internat., Fla. poetry socs., Poetry Soc. Mich., Mary Carr Moore Manuscript Club (prize winners chpt. Calif. Chaparral Poets). Republican. Methodist. Author books including: Arethusa, 1945; Singing Heart, 1948; Daily Bread, 1952; Phantasy, 1954; Whispering Leaves, 1957; For the Dreamer, 1965; Heartstrings, 1968; Golden Days, 1970; Cantabile, 1975; Shadow Fingers, 1976; Echoes, Sonnets, Little Songs, 1981; poems pub. Orbis, Poet, Christian Writers Soc. Mag.; editor weekly poetry column Daily Record-Gazette, Banning-Beaumont, Calif. Home: 451 E 8th St Beaumont CA 92223

BAILEY, ALTON L., agricultural services educator, farmer; b. Blossom, Tex., Aug. 17, 1928; s. Luke M. and Nora B. (Stevens) B.; m. Madine A. Bailey, Dec. 22, 1951; children—Gary, Steven, Kenneth, Janet. B.S. in Hort., Tex. A&M U.; M.S. in Agrl. Econs., N.Mex. State U. With U.S. Soil Conservation Service, 1951; br. mgr. Southwest Fertilizer & Chem. Co., Pecos, Tex., Anthony, N.Mex. and El Centro, Calif., 1951-58; head agrl. services dept. N.Mex. State U., Las Cruces, 1958-80, coordinator demonstration plot program, coop. extension service, 1980—; farmer. Chmn. Property Rights Com. Dona Ana County, N.Mex.; deacon First Baptist Ch., Anthony. Served to 2d lt. U.S. Army, 1949-50; served to capt. USNG, 1951-57. Mem. Dona Ana County Farm Bur. (v.p.). Republican. Office: Box 3ES Las Cruces NM 88003

BAILEY, BRIAN DENNIS, accountant, author, publisher; b. Tacoma, June 10, 1952; s. Hugh Charles and Elsie Denise (Hinds) B.; B.B.A., Pacific Luth. U., Tacoma, 1975; M.B.A., City U. Seattle, 1982. Owner B.D. Bailey Enterprises, Brian D. Bailey & Assos., Inc., Tacoma, 1975—. Mem. corp. bd., pres. Shekinah Ministries (formerly Christian Helps Inst.), Tacoma; pres. Young Democrats South. Pierce County, 1975-76. Served with USAF, 1971-73. Mem. Full Gospel Businessmen's Fellowship Internat., Christian writers Guild, Grange of Washington State. Home: 10912 S K St PO Box 44757 Tacoma WA 98444 Office: PO Box 44757 Tacoma WA 98444

BAILEY, CHARLES CHRISTOPHER, educator; b. Houston, Feb. 24, 1934; s. Cozbi and Julia Lurline (Edwards) B.; B.A., Golden Gate U., 1969; M.A., U. Calif., Berkeley, 1970; D.H.L., Lincoln U., San Francisco, 1968; 1 dau., Jennifer Loraine. Asso. exec. YMCA sect., Berkeley, 1957-58; ordained to ministry Am. Baptist Chs. of U.S.A., 1957; pastor Allen Temple Bapt. Ch., Oakland, Calif., 1958-69; faculty San Jose City Coll., 1969-70, Coll. of Alameda, 1970-71, Cabrillo Coll., Aptos, Calif., 1971—. Vice pres. Lustre Corp., Redwood City, Calif., 1969. Mem. Am. Polit. and Hist. Socs. Author: The Black Community: A New Strategy, 1975. Home: PO Box 606 Santa Cruz CA 95060 Office: 6500 Soquel Dr Aptos CA 95003

BAILEY, CHARLES HOWARD, optometrist, consultant, educator; b. Logan, W.Va., Jan. 3, 1943; s. Dane Barb and Ruth Hazel (Walker) B.; m. Frangee Marie Vierhelter, Feb. 24, 1968; children—Kevin Charles, Dane Brian. B.S. in Applied Math. magna cum laude, LaSalle Coll., 1974; B.S. in Optometry, O.D., U. Calif.-Berkeley, 1982. Cert. data processor. Asst. dir. Corp. Info. Ctr., Auerbach Corp., Phila., 1968-70; program mgr. First Pa. Bank, Phila., 1970-74; mgr. data processing, Fund/Plan Services, Inc., Phila., 1974-78; supr. mgmt. cons. services Ernst & Whinney, Providence, 1977-78; pvt. practice optometry, St. Helena, Calif., 1982—; assoc. instr. contact lenses U. Calif.-Berkeley. Served with USAF, 1965-68. Recipient Outstanding Achievement award Bausch & Lomb, 1982, J. Harold Bailey award in Adminstrv. Sci., 1982., Contact Lens award Optometry Alumni Assn., 1982. Mem. Am. Optometric Assn., Calif. Optometric Assn., North Bay Optometric Assn. Club: Rotary. Office: 1310 Railroad Ave Saint Helena CA 94574

BAILEY, CLAYTON GEORGE, artist; b. Antigo, Wis., Mar. 9, 1939; s. Clayton Pence and Mary (Pence) B.; m. Betty Graveen, Oct. 11, 1958; children—Kurt Douglas, Robin Lynn, George Gladstone. B.S., U. Wis., 1961, M.S., 1962. Asst. prof. Wis. State U., 1963-67; head ceramic dept. U. S.D., 1967-68; prof. Calif. State U.-Hayward, 1968—, chmn. dept. arts, 1980—; exhibited in shows Mus. Contemporary Crafts, N.Y.C., Everson Mus. Art, Syracuse, Addison Gallery Am. Art, Andover, Mass., Milw. Art Ctr., Walker Art Ctr., Mpls., Art Inst. Chgo., San Francisco Art Inst., Richmond Art Mus., Renwick Gallery, Wash., others; represented in permanent collections U. Wis., Addison Gallery Am. Art, Brooks Meml. Gallery U. Okla., State U. Iowa, Milw. Art Ctr., Hokkoku Shinbun, Korinbo, Japan, Sacramento State Coll., Johnson Found., Racine, Wis., Metromedia Collection, USIA, San Francisco Mus. Art., Mus. Contemporary Crafts, N.Y.C., Mills Coll., Oakland, Calif., USIA, Crocker Gallery, Sacramento, others. Founder, curator Kaolithic curiosities Wonders of the World Mus., Port Costa, Calif. Louis Comfort Tiffany Found. grantee, 1963; Am. Craftsmen's Council grantee, 1963; George Gladstone award, 1970; Piltdown Found. grantee, 1972; Nobel Prize nominee in physics, 1976; NEA grantee, 1979; Nat. Council for Edn. in Ceramic Arts fellow, 1982. Home: PO Box 69 Port Costa CA 94569

BAILEY, CLENTIS WILLIAM, air force officer; b. Kosciusko, Miss., Aug. 7, 1931; s. William Jennings and Addie Bea (Royals) B.; children—Bill, John. B.S. in C.E., Miss. State U., 1953; M.S., George Washington U., 1964; postgrad. Air Command & Staff Coll., 1964, Air War Coll., 1971. Civil engr. Boeing Co., Seattle, 1952; commd. officer USAF, 1953, advanced through grades to col.; chief Space & Reconnaissance Systems div. Air Force Test & Eval. Center, Albuquerque, 1977-83. Decorated Bronze Star medal, Legion of Merit. Mem. Phi Kappa Phi, Tau Beta Pi. Republican. Baptist. Clubs: Masons (Shriner), K.T. Home: 4712 Glenwood Hills Dr NE Albuquerque NM 87111 Office: AFTEC/TES Kirtland AFB NM 87117

BAILEY, DANA KAVANAGH, radiophysicist, research botanist; b. Clarendon Hills, Ill., Nov. 22, 1916; s. Dana Clark and Dorothy (Kavanagh) B.; B.S., U. Ariz., 1937; student Harvard, 1940; B.A. (Rhodes scholar), Queen's Coll., Oxford U., 1940, M.A., 1943, D.Sc., 1967. Astronomer expdn. to Peru for Hayden Planetarium, N.Y.C., 1937; physicist Antarctic expdn. U.S. Antarctic Service, Washington, 1940-41; project engr. Project RAND, Douglas Aircraft Co., Santa Monica, Calif., 1946-48; physicist Nat. Bur. Standards, Washington, 1948-55, physicist, cons., Boulder, Colo., 1959-66; radiophysicist, research botanist Space Environment Lab., Environmental Research Labs., NOAA, Boulder, 1966-76; sci. dir. Page Communications Engrs., Washington, 1955-59. Exchange rep. Brit. Antarctic Survey, 1967-68; research asso. physics Rhodes U., Grahamstown, South Africa, 1970-71; assoc. Gymnosperms U. Colo. Mus., 1972—; internat. chmn. study group internat. radio consultative com. Internat. Telecommunication Union, Geneva, 1956-78. Served from 2d lt. to maj. Signal Corps, AUS, 1941-46. Recipient Arthur S. Flemming govt. award, 1951, Silver medal U.S. Dept. Commerce, 1952, Gold medal, 1956; decorated Legion of Merit. Fellow AAAS, Am. Phys. Soc., Am. Geog. Soc., Royal Astron. Soc., Royal Geog. Soc.; mem. Sci. Research Soc. Am. (past pres. Boulder br.), Am. Geophys. Union, Am. Astron. Soc., Geog. Soc. Lima (hon.), Phi Beta Kappa, Sigma Xi. Clubs: Cosmos (Washington); Explorers (N.Y.C.). Contbr. articles to profl. jours. Home: 1441 Bluebell Ave Boulder CO 80302 Office: U Colo Museum Boulder CO 80309

BAILEY, ELAINE KVES, personnel administrator; b. Sacramento, July 21, 1943; d. George James and Gladys Goldie (Wood) Kves; m. Willard Eugene Bailey, Aug. 12, 1968; children—Stacy, Erik. B.A., in Speech and Communications, Calif. State U.-Sacramento, 1966; M.A. in Mgmt. and Personnel Adminstrn., Central Mich. U., 1978. Trainer, recruiter ARC, Washington, 1966-68; edn. counselor, ctr. dir. U.S. Army, W. Germany, 1969-71; program dir., instr. Hawaii Pacific Coll., Honolulu, 1977-79, mgmt. trainer, cons. Hawaii State Personnel Dept., Honolulu, 1979—; lectr. U. Hawaii—Manoa Coll. Bus. Adminstrn.; Mgmt., Personnel and Indsl. Relations Dept.; pres. Pacific-Rim Mgmt. Assocs. Inc. Mem. local bd. SSS; mem. Neighborhood Bd. 25 Edn., Planning and Zoning com. Mem. Bus. Women's Assn., Women Pacific Assn., AAUW, Honolulu Bd. Realtors, Am. Soc. Tng. and Devel., Nat. Assn. Female Execs., SBA Hawaii, Sigma Iota Epsilon. Clubs: Central Mich. U. Alumni Assn., Mililani Tennis, Am. Overseas Assn. Author numerous tng. and personnel manuals. Home: 94-035 Kuahelani Ave Apt 125 Mililani Town HI 96789 Office: 2404 Maile Way Mail Box C Honolulu HI 96822

BAILEY, HENRY JOHN, III, lawyer, educator; b. Pitts., Apr. 4, 1916; s. Henry J. Bailey II and Lenore Powell Bailey Cahoon; student U.S. Naval Acad., 1934-36; B.A., Pa. State U., 1939; J.D., Yale U., 1947; m. Marjorie Jane Ebner, May 30, 1949; children—George W., Christopher G., Barbara W., Timothy P. Bar: N.Y. 1948, Mass. 1963, Oreg. 1974. Ins. investigator Liberty Mut. Ins. Co., N.Y.C., 1941-42; atty. Fed. Res. Bank of N.Y., N.Y.C., 1947-55; asst. v.p. Empire Trust Co., N.Y.C., 1955-56; atty. legal dept. Am. Bankers Assn., N.Y.C., 1956-62; editor Banking Law Jour., Boston, 1962-65; assoc. prof. law Willamette U., Salem, Oreg., 1965-69, prof., 1969-81, prof. emeritus, adj. prof., 1981—; mem. firm Churchill, Leonard, Brown & Donalson, Salem, 1981-83, of counsel, 1983—; vis. prof. law U. Akron (Ohio) Sch. Law, 1983; cons. and lectr. to bar and banking groups; lectr. Banking Sch. of South, Baton Rouge, 1972, 73, 75. Served to 1st. lt. USAAF, 1942-45; lt. col. Res. ret. Mem. ABA (chmn. subcom. comml. paper 1965-66, 79—), Am. Law Inst., Oreg. State Bar, Lambda Chi Alpha. Author: The Law of Bank Checks, 1960, 4th edit., 1969, 5th edit. and supplements, 1979; Modern Uniform Commercial Code Forms, 1963; (with Clarke and Young) Bank Deposits and Collections, 1972; (with Robert D. Hursh) The American Law of Products Liability, 2d edit., 1974; (with William D. Hawkland) The Sum and Substance of Commercial Paper, 1976; Secured Transactions in a Nutshell, 1976, 2d edit., 1981; Oregon Uniform Commercial Code, 1982; contbr. articles on sales, products liability, comml. paper and secured transactions to legal jours. Home: 4156 Riverdale Rd S Salem OR 97302 Office: 530 Center St NE PO Box 804 Salem OR 97308

BAILEY, JASON SAMUEL, lawyer; b. Portland, Oreg., Jan. 3, 1915; s. John Ora and Verna Alice (Chase) B.; B.S., U. Oreg., 1937, J.D., 1940; m. Vivienne Delta Deane, Aug. 28, 1943; 1 dau., Jayne Deane. Admitted to Oreg. bar, 1940, Calif. bar, 1946; asso. Platt, Henderson, Warner & Cram, Portland, 1940; spl. agt. FBI, U.S. Dept. Justice, Washington, also Juneau, Alaska, 1940-43, San Francisco, 1946-47, Seattle, 1947-48; dep. dist. atty. Multnomah County, Portland, 1948-50; various positions CIA, Washington, 1950-70; judge pro tem Dist. Ct., Portland, 1970; pvt. practice law, Portland, 1971—. Pub. mem. Columbia-Willamette Air Pollution Authority, 1971-72. Served to lt. col. U.S. Army. Decorated Bronze Star. Mem. Oreg. Bar Assn., Calif. Bar Assn., Phi Alpha Delta. Republican. Conglist. Home and Office: 9520 SE 14th St Vancouver WA 98664

BAILEY, JESSE EDWARD, Realtor; b. San Diego, Mar. 26, 1917; s. Jesse Wray and Huldah (Salquist) B.; B.A., San Diego State Coll., 1939; m. Marian Elizabeth Johnson, Jan. 20, 1945; children—Alan Edward, Karen E. Bailey Farley. With San Diego Ind. Newspaper Group, 1940-70, prodn. mgr., 1963-66, gen. mgr., publisher, 1966-70; sales exec. Land Cons. Am., San Diego, 1970-73; realtor Bailey & Assos., La Mesa, Calif., 1973—; pres. Coop. Traders, real estate, San Diego, 1980—. Past bd. dirs. Samarkand, Santa Barbara, Calif., Hearthstone Manor, Folsom, Calif., Homemakers for Children, San Diego; chmn. Mt. Miguel Covenant Ch., 1980; mem. Calif. Covenant Retirement Communities Bd., 1978—; dir. nat. bd. benevolence Evang. Covenant Ch. Am., 1971-75, chmn. nat. social service commn., 1974-75. Served as lt. USNR, World War II. Recipient newspaper circulation mgmt. service awards. Chmn. exec. bd. Mt. Miguel Covenant Village, Spring Valley, Calif., 1964—. Pub. books on history of San Diego. Home: 8645 Butte St La Mesa CA 92041 Office: 8080 La Mesa Blvd Suite 106 La Mesa CA 92041

BAILEY, JIMMY MACK, indsl. engring. exec.; b. DeFuniack Springs, Fla., Nov. 14, 1947; s. Orval Reece and Laura Alma (Oehler) B.; B.S. in Indsl. Engring., Auburn U., 1970; m. Linda Ann Martin, July 31, 1971. Indsl. engr. Tom's Foods Ltd., Corsicana, Tex., 1970-72, systems analyst, Columbus, Ga., 1972-73; mgmt. engr. Lee Meml. Hosp., Ft. Myers, Fla., 1973-75, dir. personnel relations, 1974-75; mgmt. systems engr. Phoenix (Ariz.) Baptist Hosp. and Med. Center, 1975-77, asst. to pres. mgmt. services, 1977-79; v.p. Bapt. Hosps. and Health Systems, Phoenix, 1979—; mem. Central Ariz. Health Systems Agy. Mem. Am. Inst. Indsl. Engrs., Am. Acad. Med. Adminstrs., Am. Coll. Hosp. Adminstrs., Hosp. Mgmt. Systems Soc., Am. Hosp. Assn., Phoenix Jaycees. Democrat. Mem. Ch. of Christ. Home: 3439 E Hatcher Rd Phoenix AZ 85028 Office: 2224 W Northern St Suite 300-D N 20th Ave Phoenix AZ 85021

BAILEY, JOSEPH JOHN, psychiatrist; b. Meridian, Miss., Mar. 13, 1930; s. Joe and Evelyn (Erben) B.; B.S., Miss. State U., 1951, M.S., 1952; M.D., U. Geneva (Switzerland), 1959; m. Barbara Ann Lindenthal, June 10, 1967; children—Mark Thomas, Geoffrey John, Stephen Joseph. Teaching fellow Miss. State U., 1951-52; intern St. Joseph's Hosp., San Francisco, 1960-61; resident psychiatry St. Elizabeth's Hosp., Washington, 1961-63, Neuropsychiat. Inst., UCLA, 1963-64; acting med. dir. Douglas Young Clinic, San Diego, 1964-65; practice medicine specializing in psychiatry, San Diego, 1964—; cons., Superior Ct. County of San Diego, 1973—, Calif. Tchrs. Retirement System, 1974; psychiat. cons. Fed. Met. Correction Ctr., 1974-80. Served with AUS, 1950-52. NIMH grantee, 1965, research grantee Licensed Beverage Industries on Treatment Alcoholism with LSD, 1967. USPHS fellow UCLA, 1963-64. Mem. N.Y. Acad. Scis. Author: The Use of LSD-25 in Psychotherapy and Alcoholism, 1965. Home: 2427 Romney Rd San Diego CA 92109 Office: 4655 Cass St San Diego CA 92109

BAILEY, JOSEPH VERNON, rancher, former community center ofcl.; b. Salt Lake City, June 14, 1923; s. Joseph and Annie (Walker) B.; student U. Utah, 1946-50; B.A., Eastern Wash. State Coll., 1960; m. Juanita Rose Palin, Mar. 19, 1970. Joined U.S. Army, 1943, advanced through grades to lt. col., 1966; chief plans 7th Aradcom, 1965; dir. plans and ops., CamRahn Bay, South Viet Nam, 1967; ret., 1967; sr. adviser Army Res., Washington, 1968; exec. dir. devel. project Flathead Indian Reservation, Dixon, Mont., 1968-70; dir. Am. Indian Community Center, Spokane, from 1970; rancher, owner, operator sheep and livestock bus., Dixon, 1975—. Decorated Silver Star, Purple Heart. Mem. Western Mont. Livestock Assn., Internat. Arabian Horse Assn., Arabian Horse Registry, Pyramid Soc., Arabian Horse Club of Western Mont., Am. Quarter Horse Assn., Mont., Western Mont. Nat. sheep producers assns. Home: Box 12 Dixon MT 59831

BAILEY, KAREN ANN, marketing executive; b. Hobart, Ind.; d. Cecil Alonzo and Florence Elizabeth (Cihonski) Bailey; student Purdue U., 1975-78, Met. State Coll., Denver, 1979-80; B.S. in Bus. Adminstrn., Econs., Regis Coll., 1982. Various clerical positions, Chgo. and Denver, 1975-78; gen. acctg. clk. Adolph Coors Co., Golden, Colo., 1979, property acctg. clk., fin. coordinator, 1979, fin. analyst II, 1979-82, distbr. econs./expansion analyst, 1982-83, Supr. young adult mktg., 1983—. Office: Mktg Dept 331 Adolph Coors Co Golden CO 80401

BAILEY, LEONARD LEE, surgeon; b. Takoma Park, Md., Aug. 28, 1942; s. Nelson Hulburt and Catherine Effie (Long) B.; B.S., Columbia Union Coll., 1960-64; postgrad NIH, 1965; M.D., Loma Linda U., 1969; m. Nancy Ann Schroeder, Aug. 21, 1966; children—Jonathan Brooks, Charles Connor. Intern, Loma Linda U. Med. Center, 1969-70, resident in surgery, 1970-73, resident in thoracic and cardiovascular surgery, 1973-74; resident in pediatric cardiovascular surgery Hosp. for Sick Children, Toronto, Ont., Can., 1974-75; resident in thoracic and cardiovascular surgery Loma Linda U. Med. Sch., 1975-76, asst. prof. surgery, 1976—, asst. prof. pediatrics, 1978—, dir. pediatric cardiac surgery, 1976—. Diplomate Am. Bd. Surgery, Am. Bd. Thoracic Surgery. Mem. Am. Coll. Cardiology, Soc. Thoracic Surgery, Am. Assn. Thoracic Surgery, Western Thoracic Surg. Assn., Western Soc. Pediatric Research, Walter E. McPherson Soc. (clin. investigator of year 1976). Democrat. Seventh-day Adventist. Office: Loma Linda U Med Center Loma Linda CA 92350

BAILEY, PATRICIA SUSAN, physician; b. N.Y.C., Dec. 18, 1943; d. Joel and Ethel (Miller) Salzburg; B.S. magna cum laude, Central Mich. U., 1970, M.A., 1972; M.D., Mich. State U., 1977; m. Del Whan, Mar. 27, 1981. Clin. instr. Mich. State U. Coll. Human Medicine, 1976-77; resident Los Angeles County-Harbor Gen. Hosp., UCLA Med. Center, Torrance, 1977-78; partner, physician in emergency medicine Kaiser-Permanente Hosp., Harbor City, Calif., 1978—; instr. Am. Heart Assn.; clin. instr. U. So. Calif. Coll. Medicine. Trustee, Delta Coll., 1972-74. Mem. Am. Coll. Emergency Medicine, Am. Physicians for Human Rights, Am. Physicians for Social Responsibility, Gay Acad. Union, So. Calif. Women for Understanding, NOW. Jewish. Author: (novel) The Summer of the Flea, 1980; contbr. to Echoes from the Heart (poetry anthology), 1982; contbr. articles to various publs. Office: 1050 W Pacific Coast Hwy Harbor City CA 90710

BAILEY, PEGGY LUCILLE, speech pathologist; b. Spokane, July 1, 1950; d. Lloyd Clift and Betty Jo (Hoppe) B. B.A., Calif. State U.-Long Beach, 1972; M.A., Whittier (Calif.) Coll., 1975. Speech pathologist Baldwin Park (Calif.) Unified Sch. Dist., 1975-77, Irwin Lehrhoff, Ph.D., Assocs., Beverly Hills, Calif., 1975-78, Bernard Landes, Ph.D., Speech Pathology Assocs., Long Beach, Calif., 1977-78; pres. La Habra Rehab. Assocs., Inc., 1977—; dir. speech pathology Whittier Hosp., La Mirada Community Hosp., Sierra Vista Med. Ctr. clin. supr. Biola Coll., La Mirada, Calif. Mem. Am., Calif. speech and hearing assns., Calif. Speech Pathologists and Audiologists in Pvt. Practice, Council Exceptional Children, Exceptional Children's Found. Republican. Office: 2249 W Whittier La Habra CA 90631

BAILEY, RAY THEODORE, mktg. cons.; b. Clifton, N.J., Aug. 26, 1913; s. James Garfield and Anna (Pedersen) B.; grad. high sch.; m. Laura Jean Schanze, Dec. 1, 1948; children—Cynthia, Raymond, James, Gretchen, Guy, Laurie. Editor, pub. 3 Weekly Newspapers, Flemington, N.J., 1943-46; publs. and sales promotion dir. Thermoid Co., Trenton, N.J., 1946; advt. mgr. Borden Foods Co., N.Y.C., 1947-54; mktg. dir. This Week mag., N.Y.C., 1954-60; group mktg. dir. J. Walter Thompson, N.Y.C., 1960-65; v.p. Gift Stars, Inc., Mpls., 1965-77; pres. Luncheon Is Served, Inc., Tucson, 1967-77, chmn. bd., dir., 1967—; chmn. bd. Party Line, Inc., 1968-77; chmn. bd. Internat. Mktg. Assos., Ariz.; chmn. Ariz. Territory Land Investment Co., Good Life Inc.; dir. in charge U.S. and Can., United Survival Products Internat. (U.K.) Ltd.; lectr. univs. including Mich. State U., So. Calif., Cornell U.; del. White House Conf. on Small Bus., 1979; U.S. del., speaker Internat Small Bus. Symposium, Berlin, 1979, 1st World Assembly on Small Bus., New Delhi, 1980; trustee, Nat. Citizens Com. Working with Congress on Paperwork Reduction, 1977-78. Recipient top award for weekly, 1943; gen. excellence award NEA. Mem. Nat. Small Bus. Assn. (trustee, v.p., exec. com.). Home: 7022 Blue Lake Dr Tucson AZ 85715 Office: PO Box 13449 Tucson AZ 85732

BAILEY, RICHARD CLAYTON, historian, author, ret. mus. adminstr.; b. Muskegon, Mich., Apr. 20, 1911; s. Irving Jacob and Blanche Arvilla (Hosler) B.; A.A., Bakersfield Jr. Coll., 1932; student Fresno State U., 1945; m. Dorothy Jean Searles, June 17, 1971; children—Richard Hugh, Joyce Carol. Tchr. pub. schs., Mountain View Dist., Lamont, Calif., 1946-48; asst. dir., edn. dir. Kern County Mus., Bakersfield, Calif., 1948-55, dir. Kern County Mus. and Pioneer Village, 1955-81; instr. local history Bakersfield Community Coll., 1970-80. Chmn. Fort Tejon Restoration Com., 1949-73; mem. Calif. Bicentennial Commn.; mem. Red Rock Canyon Adv. Com., 1969-73; advisor Kern County Heritage Commn., 1976—; treas. Kern County Centennial Com., 1966-68; mem. Kern County Hist. Records Commn. Mem. Am. Assn. Mus. (past pres. Western regional conf.), Calif. Conf. Hist. Socs. (past pres.), Kern County Hist. Soc. Republican. Presbyterian. Clubs: Petroleum Prodn. Pioneers, Death Valley 49ers, Masons. Author: Collector's Choice, 1951; A Heritage of Kern, 1957; Explorations in Kern, 1959; Historic Chronology of Kern County, 1972-79; Heart of the Golden Empire, 1983. Home: 1101 Lomita Bakersfield CA 93307

BAILEY, ROBERT TERRY, landscape contracting company executive; b. Detroit, Oct. 9, 1938; s. Winfield Walter and Florance Marie (Griffen) B.; m. Marilyn Marie Evans, Nov. 8, 1958; children—Deborah Marie, Terry Robert. Student Pierce Coll., Los Angeles. Gen. supt. Valley Crest Landscape-Environ. Industries, Van Nuys, Calif., 1958-68; co-owner Bailey-Sperber, Inc. (doing bus. as Century Landscape Contractors, Hydro West Environ. Seeding, Pacific-Western Irrigation Co.), Agoura, Calif., 1968—. Recipient state landscape awards Calif. Landscape Contractors Assn., 1970, 71, Los Angeles bus. and industry award, 1973-74; Nat. Instl. Landscaping award Mrs. Patricia Nixon, 1973. Mem. Am. Landscape Contractors Assn. (nat. environ. grand award 1976, 80, 82), Am. Assn. Nurserymen. Major projects include UCLA, U. Calif-Irvine, Los Angeles Internat. Airport, freeway systems State of Calif., others.

BAILEY, WALTER ALEXANDER, artist, writer; b. Wayandotte County, Kans.; Oct. 17; s. Richard Alfred and Pauline (Doughty) B.; m. Millicent Garrison, June 15, 1926. Student Leavenworth Bus. Coll., Kans. City Art Inst. Artist, art editor Kansas City Star, 1910-28; artist, art instr., Taos, N. Mex., 1928-32; artist Douglas Aircraft, 1940-41; artist, writer Los Angeles Examiner, 1944-62; art editor Los Angeles Herald Examiner, 1962-67; freelance painter, writer, 1968—; columnist So. Pasadena (Calif.) Rev., 1972-78; one man shows in various cities; numerous commns. Louis Comfort Tiffany Found. fellow, 1924; traveling fellow Jose Drudis Found., 1966; recipient Johann Berthold Jongkind award Frye Mus., 1967, also numerous other awards. Fellow Am. Inst. Fine Arts; mem. Valley Artists' Guild, Scandinavian Am. Art Soc., Calif. Art Club (dir. 1963, 66-67). Clubs: Greater Los Angeles Press, Ensenada, Masons, Shriners. Home: 1417 12th Ave Los Angeles CA 90019

BAILEY, WILLIAM, manufacturing company executive; b. Danville, Va., Mar. 12, 1939; s. William and Mary (Meade) B.; m. Susan Cragg, Jan. 20, 1973; 1 son, Matthew Cragg. B.S., N.C. State U., 1961; M.A., UCLA, 1965; M.B.A., U. Nev., 1981. Research engr. Rocketdyne div. Rockwell Internat., Canoga Park, Calif., 1961-66; mem. tech. staff TRW Systems, Redondo Beach, Calif., 1966-68; mem. tech. staff, staff engr., sect. head, project engr. TRW Systems & Energy, Washington, 1968-78, mgr. field office TRW Energy Engring. div., Las Vegas, Nev., 1978—. Mem. Soc. Petroleum Engrs., Tau Beta Pi, Sigma Pi Sigma, Pi Mu Epsilon. Club: So. Nev. Econ. (dir. 1981—). Contbr. articles to profl. jours. Home: 3040 Robar St Las Vegas NV 89121 Office: 2225 E Flamingo Rd Suite 301 Las Vegas NV 89109

BAIN, CONRAD STAFFORD, actor; b. Lethbridge, Alta., Can., Feb. 4, 1923; s. Stafford Harrison and Jean Agnes (Young) B.; grad. Am. Acad. Dramatic Art, 1948; came to U.S., 1946, naturalized, 1946; m. Monica Marjorie Sloan, Sept. 4, 1945; children—Kent Stafford, Mark Alexander, Jennifer Jean. Broadway appearances include Candide, 1957, Lost in The Stars, 1958, Hot Spot, 1963, Advise and Consent, 1961; Uncle Vanya, 1971; off-Broadway appearances include Iceman Cometh, 1957, Hogan's Goat, 1966, Scuba Duba, 1967, The Kitchen, 1968, Steambath, 1969; film appearances include A Lovely Way to Die, 1967, Who Killed Mary Whats er Name, 1968, Up The Sand Box, 1970, C.H.O.M.P.S., 1979; star TV prodn. Maude, 1971-78, Diff'rent Strokes, 1978—; star TV movie Child Bride of Short Creek, NBC; founder Actors Fed. Credit Union, 1962. Served with Canadian Army, World War II. Mem. Actors Equity Assn. (councilor 1962-76), ANTA West (dir. since 1977). Club: Players (N.Y.C.). Office: 1901 Ave of Stars Los Angelos CA 90067

BAIN, WILLIAN JAMES, JR., architect; b. Seattle, June 26, 1930; s. Willian James and Mildred Worline (Park) B.; m. Nancy Sanford Hill, Sept. 21, 1957; children—David Hunter, Stephen Frazer (dec.), Mark Sanford, John Worthington. B. Arch., Cornell U., 1953. Ptnr. Naramore, Bain, Brady & Johanson (now NBBJ Group), Seattle, 1961—; juror, lectr., U. Wash. and Wash. State U., Bd. dirs. Seattle Symphony Orch., 1974-83. Served to 1st lt. C.E., U.S. Army, 1953-55. Recipient Cert. of Achievement, Port of Whittier (Alaska), 1955, 1st York prize Cornell U., 1949, Charles Goodwin Sands Meml. medal Cornell U., 1953. Fellow AIA; mem. Seattle C. of C. (bd. dirs. 1980-83), Downtown Seattle Assn. (bd. dirs. 1980-83), Urban Land Inst., Nat. Assn. Corp. Real Estate Execs., Nat. Assn. Indsl. and Office Parks, Am. Arbitration Assn. (comml. panel 1975—), Lambda Alpha. Episcopalian. Clubs: Rainier, Wash. Athletic, Rotary, Seattle Tennis. Prin. works include: U.S. Pavilion at Expo '74, Ohio Conv. Ctr., Battelle Meml. Inst. Northwest Research Ctr., Seattle Research Ctr., Honolulu Mcpl. Office Bldg., Bagley Wright Theatre, Four Seasons Olympic Hotel Restoration, AEC Biology and Life Scis. Lab., High Temperature Sodium Facility, Unigard Park Office Complex, Whitman College-Cordiner Hall, Wash. State U. Design Disciplines Bldg., Phys. Scis. Bldg., Port Ludlow Community Plan. Home: 1631 Rambling Ln Bellevue WA 98004 Office: 111 S Jackson St Seattle WA 98104

BAINUM, BRUCE DAVID, psychologist, educator; B. Takoma Park, Md., May 25, 1953; s. Stewart William and Jane Loretta (Goyne) B.; m. Charlene Ann Kubo, Nov. 25, 1979. Diploma Alliance Française, Paris, 1973; Ph.D. in Exptl. Psychology, U. Tenn. Asst. prof. psychology, behavioral sci. dept. Pacific Union Coll., Angwin, Calif., 1979—; research cons. in alcoholism, brain damage, methodology. Mem. Am. Psychol. Assn., Calif. State Psychol. Assn., Psi Chi. Democrat. Adventist. Office: Behavioral Sci Dept Pacific Union Coll Angwin CA 94508

BAIR, THOMAS DEPINNA, educator; b. N.Y.C., Mar. 19, 1922; s. Royden S. and Ruth I. (Farmer) B.; children—Hudson Thomas, John Hamilton. A.B., DePauw U., 1946; M.A., Ind. U., 1947; Ph.D., U. Ill., 1950. Instr., Utica Coll., Syracuse U., 1950-53, Albany Med. Coll., Union U., 1953-56; from asst. prof. to prof. Calif. State U.-Los Angeles, 1956—; sr. lectr. parasitology U. So. Calif., 1964-68; vis. asst. prof. physiology Calif. Coll. Medicine, 1959-64; med. entomologist USPHS, 1951-52; Fulbright vis. prof. in India, 1977-78. Dist. tng. officer, dist. commr., council commr. Upper Mohawk, Ft. Orange and San Gabriel Valley councils Boy Scouts Am., 1950-56, 72—. Served with AUS, World War II; to lt. comdr. Med. Service Corps, USNR, 1958—. Research fellow in physiology Am. Physiol. Soc., 1958, Inter-Am. fellow tropical medicine and parasitology, 1960, Fulbright prof. Nangrahar Med. Faculty, Afghanistan, 1970-71. Mem. Am. Soc. Parasitologists, Helminthological Soc. of Wash., Am. Inst. Biol. Sci., Indian Soc. Parasitologists, Assn. Advancement Bio-Med. Edn., U.S. Power Squadron, Res. Officers Assn. U.S., Sigma Xi, Phi Delta Theta, Alpha Phi Omega. Contbr. articles to profl. jours. Home: 1240 Journey's End Dr La Canada CA 91011 Office: Dept Biology Calif State U Los Angeles CA 90032

BAIRD, BILLIE RUTH, temporary employment services executive; b. Tex., Apr. 4, 1930; d. William Perry and Ruth Lee (Meriwether) Gullett; student Fresno (Calif.) City Coll., San Francisco State U., Calif. State U.; m. William T. Baird, Apr. 11, 1951; children—Deborah R., Lynne A., William T., Kristi A. Jr. acct. Alexander & Alexander, C.P.A.s, Fresno, 1950-60; auditor acctg. Frank Chessman, C.P.A., Fresno, 1962-63; controller San Francisco Floral Co., Fresno, 1963-74; sales rep. Kelly Temporary Service, Fresno, 1975-77; mgr. Am. Temporary Services, Fresno, 1978—; cons. in field. Mem. Nat. Bus. and Profl. Women's Assn., Nat. Assn. Profl. Saleswomen, Am. Soc. Personnel Adminstrn., Women's Network, Women's Trade Club of Fresno County (charter), Fresno C. of C., Beta Sigma Phi. Office: 745 E Locust St Suite 105 Fresno CA 93710

BAIRD, CHARLES FRANCIS, systems engineer; b. Santa Monica, Calif., June 2, 1943; s. Francis Charles and Helene Elizabeth (Ball) B.; B.S. in Engring., San Jose (Calif.) State U., 1974; postgrad. U. Santa Clara (Calif.), 1976; M.B.A., Pepperdine U., 1983; m. Carolyn Frances Benedict, Aug. 18, 1979. Head attitude determination and mission planning sect. System Devel. Corp., Tokyo, 1976-77, mgr. def. meteorol. satellite program support project, Santa Monica, 1977-78; chief architect AFSCF data systems modernization program Hughes Aircraft Co., El Segundo, Calif., 1978-79, mgr., 1979-80; co-mgr. classic wizard support project Ultra Systems Inc., Los Angeles, 1980-83; pres. Lutzky Baird Assocs., 1983—. Served with USAF, 1965-68; Vietnam. Home: 36 Ave 25 Venice CA 90291 Office: 2400 Michelson Dr Irvine CA 92715

BAIRD, HUGH ADAMSON, engring. co. exec.; b. Renfrew, Scotland; s. Andrew and Betty B.; came to U.S., 1923, naturalized, 1942; B.S., Calif. Inst. Tech., 1942, M.S., 1946; m., June 12, 1943; children—Suzanne, Mark. Mem. staff Office Sci. Research and Devel., Calif. Inst. Tech., 1942-45; with C.F. Braun & Co., Alhambra, Calif., 1946—, v.p., 1971-74, exec. v.p., 1974-79, pres., 1979—. Fellow Am. Inst. Chem. Engrs., IAE. Club: Calif. Office: CF Braun & Co 1000 S Fremont Ave Alhambra CA 91802

BAIRD, JOHN NORTHCOTE, legal executive; b. Montreal, Que., Can., Mar. 13, 1940; s. Jack N. and Claire T. (Fortier) B.; m. Christine Hoffman, Aug. 23, 1975; children—Emily-Claire, Christopher John. B.A. in Econs., Concordia U., 1961; B.C.L., McGill U., 1965; postgrad. U. Grenoble (France), 1967. Legal exec. with Liquid Air Corp., San Francisco, 1968—, sec., 1976—. Home: 33 Pacific Ave Piedmont CA 96411 Office: Liquid Air Corp One Embarcadero Center San Francisco CA 94111

BAIRD, JOSEPH ARMSTRONG, JR., architectural historian, educator; b. Pitts., Nov. 22, 1922; s. Joseph Armstrong and Lulu Charlotte (Fuller) B.; B.A., Oberlin Coll., 1944; M.A., Harvard, 1947, Ph.D., 1951. Lectr., instr. U. Toronto (Ont., Can.), 1949-53; faculty U. Calif., Davis, 1953—, prof. dept. art, 1968—; curator, art cons. Calif. Hist. Soc., San Francisco, 1962-63, 68-71; cataloguer Honeyman Collection, Bancroft Library, U. Calif., Berkeley, 1964-65; art cons., owner North Point Gallery, San Francisco, 1972—; vis. prof. U. So. Calif., Los Angeles, 1952, 70, U. Mexico, Mexico City, 1957, U. Oreg., Eugene, 1963; pvt. art cons. mus., civic and hist. orgns.; active lectr. cultural instns. including Toronto Art Gallery, Royal Ont. Mus. Art, numerous mus., univs. U.S.; compiler exhbn. catalogues. Recipient award of Merit, Calif. Hist. Soc., 1961. Mem. Soc. Archtl. Historians, Nat. Trust for Hist. Preservation, Am. Fedn. Arts, Phi Beta Kappa. Author: Time's Wondrous Changes: San Francisco Architecture, 1776-1915, 1962; The Churches of Mexico, 1962; California's Pictoral Lettersheets, 1849-1869, 1967; Historic Lithographs of San Francisco, 1972; The West Remembered, 1973; Wine and the Artist, 1979; (catalogues) Samuel Marsden Brookes: 1816-1892, 1962; Catalogue of Original Paintings, Drawings and Watercolors in the Robert B. Honeyman, Jr. Collection, 1968; Pre-Impressionism: 1860-1869: A Formative Decade in French Art and Culture, 1969; (with Ellen Schwartz) Northern California Art: An Interpretive Bibliography, 1977; editor monographs, exhbn. catalogues including From Frontier to Fire, 1964; Fifteen and Fifty, 1965; China and California, 1966; France and California, 1967; Images of Eldorado (history of Calif. photography), 1975; Theodore Wores: The Japanese Years, 1976; Theodore Wores and the Beginnings of Internationalism in Northern California Art, 1978; From Exposition to Exposition, 1981, others; contbr. articles to profl. jours. Home: 1830 Mountain View Dr Tiburon CA 94920 Office: Art Dept U Cal Davis CA 95616 also 872 N Point St San Francisco CA 94109

BAIRD, MARGARET LUCILLE, school administrator; b. Cox City, Oklahoma, May 5, 1930; d. Albert Frederick and Ethel (Seay) Elliott; m. Lyle Boyd Baird, June 30, 1950; 1 son, Richard Lyle. B.A., Okla. Coll. for Women, 1952, B.S., 1953; M.L.S., U. Okla., 1968; Ph.D., Iowa State U., 1976. Cert. elem. tchr., library media specialist, sch. administr. Tchr., Duncan (Okla.) Pub. Schs., 1954-55; English tchr., librarian Alex (Okla.) Pub. Schs., 1964-69; librarian Southwestern Okla. State U., Weatherford, 1969-71, Southwestern Iowa Community Coll., 1971-73; asst. prof. edn. Eastern N.Mex. U., 1976-82; coordinator elem. edn. Hobbs (N.Mex.) Mcpl. Schs., 1982—. HEW grantee, 1978. Mem. Internat. Reading Assn. (N.Mex. council), Lea County Reading Council, Assn. Supervision and Curriculum Devel., N.Mex. Sch. Adminstrs., Phi Delta Kappa. Baptist. Editor Teaching Learning Rev., 1980-82; contbr. articles to profl. jours. Office: Hobbs Municipal Schs Box 1040 Hobbs NM 88240

BAIRD, ROBERT ROY, real estate exec.; b. Colorado Springs, Colo., Sept. 3, 1937; s. Eldred D. and Alice Eudora (Havens) B.; B.S. magna cum laude, Woodbury U., 1969; postgrad. Calif. State U., Northridge, 1970-71; m. Sally Ann Baird, Oct. 3, 1959; children—J. Brian, Sean Christopher, Robert Roy. Life agt. Manhattan Life Ins. Co., Encino, Calif., 1961-62; v.p. Red Top div. Am. Hosp. Supply Co., Los Angeles, 1962-73; pres. Baird Industries, Inc., Montrose, Calif., 1973-79; pres. Central Security Trust, Glendale, Calif., 1981—; pres. Pension Vest Inc., 1982—; dir. Baird Industries, Inc.; TV talk show host Channel 22, Los Angeles, 1981-83. Lector, St. Bede's Catholic Ch., LaCanada, Calif., 1977-81; mem. Long Beach Redevel. Agy., 1976; chmn. bd. Local 117 Selective Service; dist. chmn. Am. Cancer Soc., 1962; v.p. Lakeview Terrace (Calif.) Little League, 1974. Served with U.S. Army, 1955-57; ETO. Decorated Letter of Commendation; recipient Outstanding State Vice Pres. award Jr. C. of C., 1962, Phi Gamma Kappa award Woodbury U., 1969, Dora E. Kirby award Woodbury Coll., 1969; named Outstanding Mktg. Dir., Red Top, Inc., 1971-73. Mem. Assn. Interior Environmentalists (charter), Calif. Assn. Realtors, U.S. Olympic Volleyball Assn. (charter). Club: Crown City Kiwanis (dir.) (Pasadena, Calif.). Contbg. author: Young Men Can Change the World, 1966. Pioneer Tele Tissue, roller ski poles. Home: 1801 Devon Rd Pasadena CA 91103 Office: 2335 Honolulu Ave Montrose CA 91020

BAISHIKI, SADAO, quality engr.; b. Stockton, Calif., Apr. 26, 1922; s. Toichi and Tsune (Wada) B.; A.A., Coll. of Pacific, 1942; grad. Am. Radio Inst., 1947; student U. Buffalo, 1957, Capitol Radio Engr. Inst., 1963, San Jose State Coll., 1970; m. Midori Barbara Yokoi, Sept. 30, 1944; children—Rodney Sadao, Yukiye. TV trouble shooter Colonial Radio, Buffalo, 1948-49; lab. technician Sylvania Electric Products, Inc., Buffalo, 1950-53, supr. quality control lab., Batavia, N.Y., 1954-57, component engr., 1958-59, mgr. quality control, Santa Cruz, Calif., 1959-61, prodn. mgr., 1962, mgr. vendor quality control, 1963-66, quick reaction prodn. quality control mgr., 1967-69, quality engr., Mountain View, Calif., 1970-78; quality engr. in charge hybrid microcircuit prodn. inspection Aertech subs. TRW, Sunnyvale, Calif., 1978; product engr. Varian Assocs., Santa Clara, Calif., 1979—; instr. Cabrillo Jr. Coll., Santa Cruz, 1959-60, evening sch. Santa Cruz High Sch., 1960-61, San Jose City Coll. (Calif.), 1966-68, mem. adv. bd. for quality control, 1965-66. Pres. PTA Bklyn. Sch., Batavia, N.Y., 1957-58; active Japanese Am. Citizens League, Adult Buddhist Assn. Served with U.S. Army, 1945-46. Registered profl. engr., Calif. Mem. IEEE, IRE, Am. Soc. Quality Control (Sr., cert. quality engr., organizer, chmn. Monterey Bay Area chpt. 1968-72, 82). Republican. Club: Sylvania/GTE Employees Quarter Century. Home: 2-3003 East Cliff Dr Santa Cruz CA 95062 Office: Santa Clara CA

BAIZER, GAYLE SUSAN, merchandiser, designer, illustrator; b. Los Angeles, Nov. 22, 1945; d. Benjamin Nathan and Fania (Gay) B.; B.F.A. with honors, Calif. Inst. Arts, 1968. Freelance illustrator, costume designer, 1968—; tchr. design and illustration UCLA, also Fashion Inst., 1973-77; designer jr. swimwear Catalina, Inc., 1968-69; designer jr. sportswear and swimwear Miss Pat, 1969-72; designer contemporary dresses and sportswear Jantzen, Inc., Los Angeles, 1973-79, merchandizer jrs. sportswear and swimwear, 1979-83; creative mdsg. mgr. Jantzen Tokyo. Recipient Monsanto Co. Student Design award, 1967, Metsovara Internat. Design award, Finland, 1971; Mademoiselle mag. guest exec. editor, 1968; Tommy award for swimwear, 1982; named to Motion Picture Costume Designes guild. Mem. Fashion Group.

BAJAJ, KAMLESH VIJ, real estate investment executive; b. Punjab, India, Feb. 26, 1944; came to U.S., naturalized, 1968; d. Madan Lal and Raj Rani (Sodhi) Vij; m. Ishwar Dutt Bajaj, May 26, 1967; children—Jason, Ashima, Amolika. M.Econs., Punjab U., 1967. Real estate investor, Los Angeles, 1974—; now mng. dir. RKB Investments Co., Downey, Calif. Recipient numerous awards for pub. speaking; named Punjab's number 1 speaker, 1960. Home and Office: 8126 Dinsdale St Downey CA 90201

BAJWA, SAJJAN SINGH, biochemist; b. Village Wirring, Dist. Amritsar City, India, Oct. 14, 1943; s. Harnam Singh and Harnam Kaur B.; Ph.D., Indian Inst. Sci., Bangalore, 1974; m. Raghbir Kaur Hayre, Dec., 1976; 3 sons, Sukhjeet, Ranjeet, Prubhjeet. Postdoctoral fellow Ariz. Med. Center, Tucson, 1974-76; research assoc. Health Sci. Center, San Antonio, 1976-77; sr. research assoc. Sch. Medicine, U. So. Calif., Los Angeles, 1977-79, asst. prof. pathology, 1979-83; health program dir. Tule River Indian Health Center, Inc., Porterville. Mem. AAAS, Am. Heart Assn., Sigma Xi. Contbr. articles to profl. jours. Home: 1121 Birch Dr Porterville CA 93257 Office: Tule River Indian Health Center Inc PO Box 768 Porterville CA 93257

BAKEMAN, CAROL ANN, information services manager, singer; b. San Francisco, Oct. 27, 1934; d. Lars Hartvig and Gwendolyne Beatrice (Zimmer) Bergh; student UCLA, 1954-62; m. Delbert Clifton Bakeman, May 16, 1959; children—Laurie Ann, Deborah Ann. Singer, Roger Wagner Chorale, 1954—, Los Angeles Master Chorale, 1964—; librarian Hughes Aircraft Co., Culver City, Calif., 1954-61; head econs. library Planning Research Corp., Los Angeles, 1961-63; corporate librarian Econ. Cons., Inc., Los Angeles, 1963-68; head econs. library Daniel, Mann, Johnson & Mendenhall, architects and engrs., Los Angeles, 1969-71, corporate librarian, 1971-77, mgr. info. services, 1978—, mgr. services, 1981—. Pres., Creative Library Systems, Los Angeles, 1974—; library cons. ArchiSystems, div. SUMMA Corp., Los Angeles, 1972—, Property Rehab. Corp., Bell Gardens, Calif., 1974-75, VTN Corp., Irvine, Calif., 1974, William Pereira & Assos., 1975. Mem. Assistance League, So. Calif., 1956—, mem. nat. auxilaries com. 1968-72, 75—, mem. nat. by laws com. 1970-75, mem. asso. bd. dirs., 1966-76. Mem. Am. Guild Musical Artists, AFTRA, Screen Actors Guild, Spl. Libraries Assn. (mem. So. Calif. adv. council 1960-73), Assn. Archtl. Librarians, Assn. Info. and Image Mgmt., Adminstrv. Mgmt. Soc., Assn. Records Mgmt. Adminstrs., Los Angeles Master Chorale Assn. (bd. dirs. 1978—). Office: DMJM 3250 Wilshire Blvd Los Angeles CA 90010

BAKER, ALTON FLETCHER, JR., editor, publisher; b. Cleve., Nov. 15, 1919; s. Alton Fletcher and Mildred (Moody) B.; A.B., Pomona Coll., 1942; m. Genevieve Mertzke, 1947 (div. 1975); m. 2d, Jeannette Workman Vollstedt, Feb. 14, 1976; children—Sue Baker Diamond, Alton Fletcher, III, Sarah Moody, Robin Louise. Reporter, Eugene (Oreg.) Register-Guard, 1946-50, mng. editor, 1950-54, editor, 1954—, pub. from 1961, now chmn. bd.; chmn. Oreg. Press Conf., 1973. Chmn. fund drive United Way, Eugene, 1965, pres., 1966-67; bd. dirs., pres. YMCA, Eugene. Served to capt. USAAF, World War II. Mem. Oreg. Newspaper Pubs. Assn. (dir. 1965-70), Am. Soc. Newspaper Editors, Am. Newspaper Pubs. Assn. Republican. Clubs: Eugene Country, De Anza Country. Office: Guard Pub Co 975 High St PO Box 10188 Eugene OR 97440*

BAKER, BERNARD ROBERT, judge; b. Chgo., Apr. 5, 1937; s. Bernard F. and Pearl L. Baker; B.S. in Bus. Adminstrn. (scholar), Northwestern U., Evanston, Ill., 1958; J.D., Ind. U., Bloomington, 1964; m. Caroline Roberta Spanier, Mar. 22, 1958; children—Susan Caroline, Deborah Ann, Pamela Ruth. Admitted to Ind. bar, 1964, Colo. bar, 1968, U.S. Supreme Ct. bar, U.S. Ct. Mil. Appeals bar, U.S. Dist. Ct. bars in Colo. and Ind.; ins. counselor Equitable Life Assurance Co., N.Y.C., 1958-60; claims investigator, supr. AllState Ins. Co., Indpls., 1961-64; assoc. firm Agee & Fann, Colorado Springs, Colo., 1968; chief dep. dist. atty. Office of Dist. Atty., 4th Jud. Dist., Colo., 1969-75; dist. ct. judge Colo. 4th Jud. Dist., Colorado Springs, 1976—. Pres., Citizens Lobby for Sensible Growth; bd. dirs. Salvation Army; bd. dirs. Mental Retardation Found. Served as capt. Judge Adv. Gen.'s Corps, U.S. Army, 1965-67. Decorated Army Commendation medal. Mem. Am. Bar Assn., Colo. Bar Assn., El Paso County Bar Assn., Am. Judicature Soc. Democrat. Methodist. Clubs: Civitan, Sierra (chmn. Pikes Peak chpt.), Moose. Bd. editors Colo. Environ. Law Handbook, 1972—. Office: El Paso County Courthouse Suite 323 20 E Vermijo St Colorado Springs CO 80903

BAKER, CAROL ANN, city ofcl.; b. Charleston, S.C., May 13, 1952; d. Charles Lee and Mamie-Clara (Taylor) B.; B.A., Wake Forest U., 1973. Producer, announcer Sta. WFDD-FM, Winston-Salem, N.C., 1971-73; info. asst. City of Winston-Salem, 1973; info. coordinator Eugene (Oreg.) Parks and Recreation Dept., 1974-78; community relations dir. City of Eugene, 1978-82; Coll./community relations coordinator Linn-Benton Community Coll., Albany, Oreg., 1982—. Bd. dirs. Sponsors, Inc. Mem. Women in Communication, League Oreg. Cities. Democrat. Presbyterian. Office: 6500 SW Pacific Blvd Albany OR 97321

BAKER, CAROL MAUVENE, government official; b. Stillwater, Okla., Dec. 19, 1947; d. James Austin and Almeta M. (Marshall) Baker; student Okla. Christian Coll., 1965-67; B.S., U. Tex.-El Paso, 1969; postgrad. U. N.Mex., 1971, No. Ariz. U., 1976. Dir., El Paso (Tex.) Presch. for Crippled Children, Inc., 1967-69; with Bur. Indian Affairs, 1969—, edn. program adminstr., 1975-79, edn. specialist, Washington, 1980-82, asst. supt. for edn., Crownpoint, N.Mex., 1982—. Bd. dirs. Ford Canyon Youth Ctr., 1977-79. Mem. AM. Mgmt. Assn., Profl. Mgrs. Assn. Primary author of regulations/manuals establishing new fin. acctg. system and personnel system for Bur. Indian Affairs schs. Office: PO Box 328 Crownpoint NM 87313

BAKER, CLIFTON BAKER, engineering and construction executive; b. Harrietsville, Ohio, May 11, 1923; s. Lewis Raymond and Freda Edith (Parks) B.; m. Louise Hodgson, Aug. 20, 1947; children—Peggy Lee, Terrie Sue. B.S., Ohio U., 1943; M.S., Ohio State U., 1947. Registered profl. engr. in 44 states. Jr. structural designer Goodyear Aircraft Co., Akron, Ohio, 1943-44; Austin Co., Cleve., 1945-46; structural designer Design Service Co., Cleve., 1947; sr. structural designer, H.K. Ferguson Co., Cleve., 1947-51, structural group leader, Ft. Detrick, Md., 1951, structural div. chief, project engr., Frederick, Md., 1951-53, staff engr., Cleve., 1953-54, asst. dist. chief engr., Los Angeles, 1954-55, San Francisco, 1955-57, dist. chief engr., Cleve., 1957-59, dir. indsl. bldgs. div., 1959-61, dir. missile div., Los Angeles, 1961-63, v.p., dir., Cleve., 1963-73, pres., 1974-79, chmn. bd., 1979—; group v.p. indsl. ops. Morrison-Knudsen Co., Boise, Idaho; dir. Morrison-Knudsen Internat. Co. Inc., 1979—, Bendy Engrng. Co., 1981—; pres. H.K. Ferguson Engrng. Co., 1961-79; chmn. bd. Hale & Kullgren, 1974-79. Served with U.S. Army, 1944-45. Decorated Bronze Stare (2). Mem. Am. Ordnance Assn., ASTM, ASCE, Nat. Soc. Profl. Engrs., Idaho Soc. Profl. Engrs., Boise Soc. Profl. Engrs. Clubs: Union (Cleve.); Hillcrest Country (Boise); Beavers, Moles, Masons. Home: 4020 Hillcrest Dr Boise ID 83705 Office: One Morrison-Knudsen Plaza PO Box 7808 Boise ID 83729

BAKER, DALE EDWIN, accountant; b. Moline, Ill., Nov. 13, 1946; s. Harold W. and Dorthy B. B.; m. Linda R. Ihrke, July 20, 1968; 1 son, Brian. Founding ptnr. Baker, Kimmeling & Myers, Indpls., 1974-80; ptnr. Ernst & Whinney, Indpls., 1980-81, ptnr. in charge of mgmt. cons. services, Denver, 1982—; founder Medicare Group Appeals by hosps. in 46 states; speaker local, regional, nat. health care meetings. Mem. Am. Inst. C.P.A.s (nat. com.), Healthcare Fin. Mgmt. Assn., Am. Hosp. Assn. Club: Denver Athletic. Home: 2354 Foothills Dr Golden CO 80401 Office: Ernst & Whinney 2400 IntraWest Tower Denver CO 80202

BAKER, DAVID GENE, accountant; b. Oskaloosa, Iowa; s. Marvin Eugene and Florence Marian Baker. B.A. in Econs., Carleton Coll., 1968; M.B.A. in Mgmt., Wharton Sch., U. Pa., 1973. C.P.A., Calif. Auditor Touche Ross & Co., San Francisco, 1973-76; internal audit supr. AMFAC, Inc., San Francisco, 1976-77; controller Golden Gate Equipment Corp., San Francisco, 1977-80; pvt. practice acctg., San Francisco, 1980—. Served to lt. USNR, 1969-73. Mem. Am. Inst. C.P.A.s, Calif. Soc. C.P.A.s. Address: 429 Arkansas St San Francisco CA 94107

BAKER, DAVID KENNETH, coll. pres.; b. Glasgow, Scotland, Oct. 2, 1923; s. David Thomas and Edith (Horner) B.; came to U.S., 1946, naturalized, 1956; B.Sc., McMaster U., 1946; Ph.D., U. Pa., 1953; m. Vivian Christian Perry, Sept. 13, 1947; children—Paul D., Richard R. Prof. physics Union Coll., Schenectady, 1953-65; mgr. profl. personnel, research and devel. lab. Gen. Electric Co., 1965-67; v.p., dean St. Lawrence U., Canton, N.Y., 1967-76; pres. Harvey Mudd Coll., Claremont, Calif., 1976—; cons. NSF. Mem. Am. Inst. Physics, AAUP. Clubs: Rotary; Calif. (Los Angeles); Univ. (Claremont). Author: (with A.T. Goble) Elements of Modern Physics. Office: Pres's Office Harvey Mudd Coll Claremont CA 91711*

BAKER, EDWIN MOODY, newspaper publisher; b. Cleve., Dec. 20, 1923; s. Alton Fletcher and Mildred Elizabeth (Moody) B.; children—Bridget, Amanda Baker Barber, Jonathan. B.S. in Bus. Adminstrn., U. Oreg., 1948. With Eugene (Oreg.) Register-Guard, 1948—, successively advt. mgr., bus. mgr., gen. mgr., pub., pres. Guard Pub. Co.; pres. Times Newspapers, Inc., Beaverton, Oreg., Willamette Newspapers, Inc., Portland, Oreg. Mem. exec. bd. Oregon Trail Council, Boy Scouts Am., 1953—, pres. Region XI Council, 1960-61, chmn. Area I (Northwest) 1971, pres., 1972, mem. nat. exec. bd., 1971-72, nat. adv. council, 1972—; trustee U. Oreg. Found., 1975—; chmn., trustee Eugene Arts Found., 1980—. Served with AUS, World War II. Decorated Bronze Star, Purple Heart, recipient Silver Beaver award, Boy Scouts Am., 1962, Silver Antelope, 1965, Disting. Eagle Scout award, 1982; Pioneer award U. Oreg., named Eugene First Citizen, 1983. Mem. Am. Newspaper Pubs. Assn. (research inst. lab. com. 1978-79), Oreg. Newspaper Pubs. Assn. (dir. 1982-83), U. Oreg. Pres. Assocs. Clubs: Rotary, Country (Eugene); Willow Creek Racquet. Home: 85144 Appletree Dr Eugene OR 97405 Office: Guard Pub Co 975 High St PO Box 10188 Eugene OR 97440

BAKER, ELBERT HALL, II, newspaper publisher; b. Quincy, Mass., July 18, 1910; s. Frank Smith and Gertrude Elizabeth (Vilas) B.; m. Betye Martin, June 27, 1936; children—Suzanne Baker Bethke, Martine Baker Huesman. Student Culver Mil. Acad., 1930, Rensselear Poly. Inst., 1932. With Tribune Pub. Co., Tacoma, 1932—, mgr. classified advt., 1938-40, advt. salesman, 1940-42, 46-50, mgr. circulation, 1950-60, pub., 1960—, pres., 1968-73, chmn., 1973—. Served to capt. inf. U.S. Army, 1942-44. Mem. Am. Newspaper Pub. Assn., Am. Soc. Newspaper Editors, Tacoma C. of C., Sigma Delta Chi, Delta Kappa Epsilon. Episcopalian. Clubs: Tacoma, Tacoma Country and Golf, Rotary (Tacoma); Bohemian (San Franisco). Office: 1950 S State St Tacoma WA 98405

BAKER, FLOYD WAYNE, highway engineer; b. Beaver, Okla., June 4, 1934; s. Clarence Hubert and Myra Amy (Bayliff) B.; m. Myrtle Lou Aldridge, Mar. 27, 1955; children—Lori Ann, Lisa Gaye. Student Yuba (Calif.) Jr. Coll., 1951-53; Chico State Coll., 1953. Lic. real estate agt., Calif. Asst. hwy. engr. Calif. Dept. Transp., Marysville, 1953-63; mgr. hwy. div. Baldwin Contracting Co., Inc., Marysville, 1962—. Served in U.S. Army, 1957-59. Mem. Associated Gen. Contractors of Calif., Marysville C. of C., Real Estate Assn. Democrat. Club: Rotary. Clubs: Peach Tree Country (bd. dirs.), Elks (Marysville). Office: 8th and Yuba Sts Marysville CA 95901

BAKER, FRED GREENTREE, engineering geologist, hydrologist; b. Chgo., July 26, 1950; s. Con J. and Ethel M. (Skowbo) B.; m. Hannah F. Pavlik, Apr. 26, 1976. B.S. in Geology, U. Wis., 1972, M.S. in Soil Sci., 1975; M.S. in Civil Engrng., U. Colo., 1981. Specialist, U. Wis.-Madison, 1975-76; research assoc. Colo. State U., Fort Collins, 1977-78; hydrologist EPA, Denver, 1979-81; hydrogeologist Appropriate Tech. Corp., Boulder, Colo., 1981—. Mem. Am. Geophys. Union, Am. Assn. Petroleum Geologists, Soil Sci. Soc. Am., Colo. Ground Water Assn. Contbr. articles to profl. jours.

BAKER, GEORGE, educator, sculptor; b. Corsicana, Tex., Jan. 23, 1931. Student Coll. of Wooster; B.A., Occidental Coll.; M.F.A., U. Calif. Group shows include Occidental Coll., Los Angeles, Mus. Modern Art, N.Y.C., 1968, Whitney Mus. Am. Art, 1968, 70, Studio Marconi, Milan, Italy, 1970, Springer Gallery, Berlin, 1975; commns. include Internat. Sculptors Symposium Osaka World's Fair, 1970, San Diego State Coll., 1972; represented in permanent collections at Mus. Modern Art, N.Y.C., Mus. Am. Art, N.Y.C., Mus. 20th Century Art, Vienna, Austria, Forest of Sculpture, Hakone, Japan; instr. sculpture U. So. Calif., 1960-64; assoc. prof. sculpture Occidental Coll., 1964—; artist-in-residence West Tex. State U., 1978. Participant Internat. Sculptors Symposium, Osaka, Japan, 1969, Berlin Artist in Residence Program, 1971-72, 75. Office: Occidental College Dept Art 1600 Campus Rd Los Angeles CA 90041

BAKER, GERALD LEWIS (JERRY), advertising executive; b. Evansville, Ind., Mar. 6, 1943; s. Lewis Allen and Dorothy Elloise (Woolsey) B.; m. Sharon Kay Terrill, July 26, 1969; children—Katherine, Matthew. B.S., U. So. Calif., 1966; M.B.A., Long Beach State U., 1968. Dep. dir. Calif. Dept. Commerce, 1972-75; dir. mktg. San Diego Conv. and Visitors Bur., 1975-77; pres. Kaufman, Lansky and Baker Advt., San Diego, 1977—. Bd. dirs. San Diego Civic Light Opera, Lead San Diego, USO. Mem. Pub. Relations Soc. Am. Republican. Methodist. Clubs: City of San Diego, Masons, Scottish Rite, Shriners. Office: 565 Fifth Ave San Diego CA 92101

BAKER, JACK WARREN, physician; b. Westminster, Calif., Nov. 29, 1919; s. Elmer Phillip and Charlotte Louise (Creeper) B.; B.S., La Sierra Coll., 1940; M.D., Loma Linda U., 1944; m. Patricia Gray Scheidell, May 19, 1950 (dec. May 11, 1976); children—Wendy Gray Baker Van Bushkirk, Gayle Lynn Baker Cinnamon, Bambi Dawn Baker Dinsmore; m. 2d, Lavaunge Brazel Oedekerk, Apr. 1, 1978. Intern and resident San Joaquin Gen Hosp., Stockton, Calif., 1943-45; resident Lahey Clinic, Boston, 1945-46; practice gen. medicine, Temple City, Calif., 1947—; founder Temple City Med. Group, 1947-76; mem. staff Community Hosp., San Gabriel, Meth. Hosp., Arcadia, Calif. Served to comdr. USNR, 1954-56. Diplomate Am. Bd. Family Practice. Mem. Am. Acad. Family Practice, Toastmasters (pres. chpt. 1953), Doctors, Dentists, Druggists Assn. Greater San Gabriel Valley (founder, pres. 1962-63), Am., Calif., Los Angeles County (pres. San Gabriel Valley dist. 1962) med. assns. Author: (with Page, Starr and Sprague) A Struggle For Excellence, 1971. Editor: Los Angeles County Med. Assn. Bull., 1968-75. Office: 9822 Las Tunas Temple City CA 91780

BAKER, JOAN MARIAN, city official; b. Balt., Mar. 23, 1936; d. Charles Rowland and Iola (Sellers) Mitchell; m. James H. Baker, June 2, 1956; children—James Charles, Jay Herbert, Jack Marion, Jon William. Student Butler U., Indpls., 1954-55, Macalester Coll., 1955-56, Colo. U., 1980. Cert. mcpl. clk. With Sunlife Assurance Co. of Can., Indpls., 1954-55; with Conrad Sheveland, atty., St. Paul, 1955-56; tax cons. Lawrence Bookkeeping, Indpls., 1966-70; legal sec. City of Northglenn (Colo.), 1975-80, city clk., 1980—. Mem. Colo. Clks. Assn., Internat. Inst. Mcpl. Clks., Women in Mcpl. Govt., Colo. Mcpl. League. Meth. Office: 11701 Community Ctr Dr #204 Northglenn CO 80233

BAKER, JOHN ALBERT, JR., accountant; b. Port Angeles, Wash., July 2, 1919; s. John Albert and Rose (Anderson) B.; B.A., Wash. State U., 1943; m. P. Pasha Prossen, Nov. 25, 1978; children—Raymon Edward, Carlton Crawford, Cameron John, Peggy Melinda, Fred Albert. Sr. acct., audit supr., sr. tax cons. Cameron & Johnstone, Honolulu, 1946-50; partner Cameron, Tennent & Greaney, Honolulu, 1950-51, Baker & Gillette, Honolulu, 1951-65, Coopers & Lybrand, 1965-81; chmn. Pasha Pacific Properties, Inc., 1981—. Served with USMCR, 1943-46. Mem. Nat. Assn. Accountants, Hawaii Soc. C.P.A.s, Hawaii Estate Planning Council, Nat. Tax Assn., Hawaii Bd. of Accountancy (pres.), Am. Inst. C.P.A.s (bd. examiners 1964-68), Nat. Assn. State Bds. Accountancy, Am. Acctg. Assn. Home: PO Box 3919 Honolulu HI 96812

BAKER, KATHLEEN MARY, state govt. ofcl.; b. Butte, Mont., Mar. 25, 1933; d. Hugh I. and Kathleen Mary (Harris) O'Keefe; B.A. in Communications, St. Mary Coll., Xavier, Kans., 1954; m. Nick B. Baker, Sept. 18, 1954 (div. 1970); children—Patrick, Susan, Michael, Cynthia, Hugh, Mardeen. Profl. singer, mem. Kathle Baker Quartet, 1962-72; research cons. Wash. Ho. of Reps., Olympia, 1972-73; info. officer Wash. Employment Security Commn., Seattle, 1973—; freelance writer, composer, producer, 1973—. Founder, pres. bd. Eden, Inc., visual and performing arts, 1975—; public relations chmn. Nat. Women's Democratic Conv., Seattle, 1979, Wash. Dem. Women, 1976—; bd. dirs., public relations chmn. Eastside Mental Health Center, Bellevue, Wash., 1979—. Recipient Black Community award for composition The Beaufort County Jail, Seattle, 1975, Silver medal Seattle Creative Awards Show for composing, directing and producing Rent A Kid, TV public service spot, 1979. Mem. Wash. Press Women. Democrat. Roman Catholic. Author handbook on TV prodn.; composer numerous songs, also producer Job Service spots. Home: 1485 168th Pl NE Bellevue WA 98008 Office: 1601 2d Ave 9th Floor Seattle WA 98101

BAKER, LAURENCE HOLLAND, systems mgmt. cons.; b. Des Moines, Jan. 23, 1933; s. Raymond Francis and Fannie Mildred (Holland) B.; B.S., Iowa State U., 1954; Ph.D., U. Minn., 1961; m. Norma Wray Walters, Aug. 8, 1953; children—Marcia Helen, Brian Joseph. Mgr. computing services Pioneer Hi-Bred, Internat., 1960-69; pres. Pioneer Data Systems, 1969-71; v.p. Cost, Planning & Mgmt., 1971; pres. Evaluation, Systems & Planning, 1972; dir. info. systems Calif. State Univs. and Colls., 1973-80, mgmt. cons., 1980—. Served as 1st lt. arty. AUS, 1955-56. Mem. Assn. Systems Mgmt., Data Processing Mgmt. Assn. (pres. Des Moines 1970-71), COMMON (pres. 1971-72), Assn. Computing Machinery, EDP Auditors Assn., Sigma Xi, Gamma Sigma Delta, Beta Alpha Psi. Club: Los Angeles Athletic. Contbr. articles to data mgmt., computer decisions, systems mgmt., apt. constrn. news, and sci. jours. Address: PO Box 490 Templeton CA 93465

BAKER, MARY, mechanical engineer; b. Madison, Wis., July 30, 1944; d. John Gordon Baker and Elizabeth Theadora (Nelson) B.; m. Wayne Wallace Pfeiffer, July 4, 1974. B.S., U. Wis., 1966; M.S. in Applied Mechanics, Calif. Inst. Tech., Pasadena, 1967, Ph.D. 1972. Registered profl. mech. engr., Calif., 1977. Mem. tech. staff IBM Research Ctr., Yorktown Heights, N.Y., 1972; sr. engr. Rohr Industries, Chula Vista, Calif., 1973-75; mem. sci. staff Systems Science and Software, 1975-77; project mgr., mgr. analytical services, tech. dir. western ops., Structural Dynamics Research Corp., San Diego, 1977—. Mem. ASME, AIAA, Sigma Xi, Phi Kappa Phi, Tau Beta Pi. Contbr. articles to profl. jours. Home: 13864 Boquita Dr Del Mar CA 92014 Office: 11055 Roselle Street San Diego CA 92121

BAKER, RICHARD LEIGH, screening systems company executive; b. Seattle, Jan. 6, 1927; s. Peter Estol and Eleanor Kathleen (Nelson) B.; B.S.E.E., Mont. State U., 1950, B.S.I.E., 1950; M.B.A., U. So. Calif., 1962; m. Betty Ann Payne, Oct. 9, 1954; children—Peter, Lucy, Susan. Field engr. Eastman Oil Well Survey Co., Houston, 1950-51; mgr. design effectiveness ops. Hughes Aircraft Co., Culver City, Calif., 1955-79, mgr. corp. reliability engring., 1978-79; co-founder, pres. Screening Systems, Inc., Rolling Hills Estates, Calif., 1979—; gen. chmn. 1977 ann. meeting Inst. Environ. Scis.; co-chmn. Nat. Conf. and Workshop Environ. Stress Screening of Electronic Hardware, 1979. Served with U.S. Army, 1951-55. Recipient I.R. 100 award, 1980. Fellow Inst. Environ. Sci., Sigma Alpha Epsilon. Republican. Patentee in field. Home: 236 Calle Campesino San Clemente CA 92672 Office: 22642 Lambert St Suite 408 El Toro CA 92630

BAKER, ROBERT ERWIN, accountant; b. Salmon, Idaho, Aug. 26, 1956; s. William Norris and Olena (McDonald) B.; m. Melba June Howell, Aug. 19, 1978; 1 son, William Robert. B.S. in Bus., U. Idaho, 1979. C.P.A., Idaho. Staff acct. Presnell Gage & Co., C.P.A.s, Lewiston, Idaho, 1980-81; treas. City of Salmon, 1982; ptnr. Baker & Baker, C.P.A.s, Salmon and Challis, Idaho, 1981—. Sec.-treas. Lemhi Devel. Com. Mem. Am. Inst. C.P.A.s, Idaho Soc. C.P.A.s. Democrat. Clubs: Rotary, Elks. Home and Office: PO Box 2055 Salmon ID 83467

BAKER, ROBERT M. L., JR., university president; b. Los Angeles, Sept. 1, 1930; s. Robert M.L. and Martha (Harlan) B.; m. Bonnie Sue

Vold, Nov. 14, 1964; children—Robert Randall, Robert M.L., Robin Michele Leslie. B.A., UCLA, 1954, M.A., 1956, Ph.D., 1958. Cons., Douglas Aircraft Co., Santa Monica, Calif., 1954-57; sr. scientist Aeronutronic, Newport Beach, Calif., 1957-60; head Lockheed Aircraft Research Center, West Los Angeles, 1961-64; assoc. mgr. Math. analysis Computer Scis. Corp., El Segundo, Calif., 1964-80; pres. West Coast U., Los Angeles, 1980—; faculty UCLA, 1958-72; dir. Internat. Info. Systems Corp., Pasadena, Calif., Transp. Scis. Corp. Served to maj. USAF, 1960-61. Named Outstanding Young Man of Year, 1965; recipient Dirk Browwer award, 1976. Fellow Am. Astro. Soc., Meteoritical Soc., Brit. Astro. Soc., AIAA; mem. Am. Phys. Soc., Phi Beta Kappa, Sigma Xi, Sigma Pi Sigma. Author: An Introduction to Astrodynamics, 1960; 2d edit., 1967; Astrodynamics-Advanced and Applied Topics, 1967; editor: Jour. Astron. Scis., 1961-76. Home: 8123 Tuscany Ave Playa del Rey CA 90291 Office: 440 Shatto Pl Los Angeles CA 90020

BAKER, STEVEN WILLIAM, entertainment executive; b. Moline, Ill., May 18, 1950; s. Woodrow L. and Ruth V. Baker; B.A. in Am. Civilization, U. Iowa, 1972. Reporter, Quad City Times, Davenport, Iowa, 1973-75; dir. pub. affairs Sta. KRNA, Iowa City, Iowa, 1975-76; owner, gen. mgr. Duck's Breath Mystery Theatre Comedy Troupe, San Francisco, 1976—; regular appearances All Things Considered, Nat. Pub. Radio. Mem. U. Iowa Pres.'s Club Assocs. Recipient Gold award for outstanding comedy group San Francisco Cabaret, 1979. Mem. San Francisco Council Entertainment, Theater Communications Ctr. Democrat. Home and Office: PO Box 22513 San Francisco CA 94122

BAKER, SUZANNE BERKELEY, interior designer; b. Oak Park, Ill., June 12, 1918; d. Lee Charlton and Irma Mathile (Brewer) Budge; A.A., Pine Manor Coll., Chestnut Hill, Mass., 1937; student Chgo. Acad. Fine Arts, 1938; student art appreciation, Paris, 1938-39; m. Frederick Lloyd Baker, Jr., June 1, 1940; children—Frederick Lloyd III, John Bartlett. Apprentice designer Grace Hume Interiors, Janesville, Wis., 1958-64; prin. Suzanne Baker Interiors, Hinsdale, Ill., 1964-76, Solana Beach, Calif., 1976—. Mem. Am. Soc. Interior Designers. Club: Lomas Santa Fe Country (Solana Beach). Address: 712 Solana Circle East Solana Beach CA 92075

BAKER, VICTOR RICHARD, geology educator; b. Waterbury, Conn., Feb. 19, 1945; s. Victor Andrew and Doris Elizabeth (Day) B.; B.S., Rensselaer Poly. Inst., 1967; Ph.D., U. Colo., 1971; m. Pauline Marie Heaton, June 10, 1967; children—Trent Heaton, Theodore William. Hydrologist, geophysicist U.S. Geol. Survey, Albany, N.Y., 1966-67, Denver, 1967-69; city geologist, City of Boulder (Colo.), 1969-71; asst. prof. U. Tex., Austin, 1971-76, assoc. prof., 1976-81; vis. Fulbright sr. research fellow Australian Nat. U., 1979-80; prof. geoscis. U. Ariz., Tucson, 1981—, prof. planetary scis., 1982—. Served to 1st lt. U.S. Army, 1972. Fellow Geol. Soc. Am.; mem. Am. Geophys. Union, Internat. Assn. Sedimentologists, Am. Quaternary Assn., Soc. Econ. Paleontologists and Mineralogists, Nat. Assn. Geology Tchrs., AAAS, Sigma Xi. Author: The Channeled Scabland, 1978; (with John Costa) Surficial Geology, 1981; The Channels of Mars, 1982; editor: Catastrophic Flooding, 1981. Office: Dept Geoscis U Ariz Tucson AZ 85721

BAKER, WILLIAM CHARLES, corporate executive; b. Port Arthur, Tex., May 14, 1933; s. Harry Winters and Martha Emily (Newby) B.; B.B.A., U. Tex., 1955, LL.B., 1957; m. Janice Yeteva Haskin, Jan. 14, 1965; children—William C., Cynthia Carol, Lisa Lanette, Stacy Allison, Catherine Suzanne. Admitted to N.Y. bar, 1960, Tex. bar, 1957, U.S. Supreme Ct. bar, 1962; trial atty. U.S. Dept. Justice, Washington, 1957-59; mem. firm Zock, Petrie, Sheneman & Reid, N.Y.C., 1959-62, Wynne, Jaffe & Tinsley, Dallas, 1962-64; gen. counsel Great S.W. Corp., Arlington, Tex., 1964-67, chmn., pres., 1967-70; pres., dir. Macco Corp., Newport Beach, Calif., 1967-70; partner firm Baker & Caldwell, Newport Beach, 1970-71; prin. B.H. Miller Devel. Co.; partner Baker-Miller & Assocs., Santa Ana, Calif., 1973-76; pres., dir. Del Taco, Inc., Costa Mesa, Calif., 1976-77, chmn. bd., dir., 1977—; Served to capt. USAR. Licensed real estate broker, Calif. Mem. Urban Land Inst., Am. Mgmt. Assn. Clubs: Balboa Bay, Big Canyon Country, Pacific (Newport Beach); Coto de Caza (Trabuco Canyon, Calif.); La Quinta Country (Calif.); Dallas. Home: 1 Oakmont Ln Newport Beach CA 92660 Office: 345 Baker St Costa Mesa CA 92626

BAKER, WILLIAM EARL, JR., lawyer; b. Long Beach, Calif., Aug. 19, 1949; s. William Earl and Muriel Jena (Torfin) B.; AA., Long Beach City Coll., 1969; B.A. in Polit. Sci., U. So. Calif., 1971; J.D., U. Pacific, 1974; m. Paige Merrill, Mar. 11, 1972; children—Merrill Elizabeth, William Earl III. Admitted to Calif. bar, 1974; asso. mem. firm Virtue & Scheck, Newport Beach, Calif., 1974-76; owner Wm. Baker & Assos., Anaheim, Calif., 1976—; owner, broker Trust Deed Center, Inc., Santa Ana, 1979—, Loan Arranger, Inc., Santa Ana, 1975—. Dist. chmn. Orange County council Boy Scouts Am., 1981; trustee Chapman Coll. Athletic Found., 1980—. Landreth Leadership scholar, 1968-69; recipient Lions Club Recognition award, 1977. Mem. Am. Bar Assn., Calif. Bar Assn., Orange County Bar Assn., Kappa Sigma. Democrat. Roman Catholic. Club: Rotary. Office: 3921 E La Palma Suite 100 Anaheim CA 92807

BAKER, WILLIAM SYLVESTER, JR., physician; b. Detroit, June 27, 1914; s. William Sylvester and Laura Mary (Cunningham) B.; B.Sc., U. Detroit, 1935; M.D., Wayne State U., 1940; m. Geraldine Mary Franklin, 1936; children—James Patrick, Diana Louise, Dennis William (twins), Terrence John. Commd. lt. j.g. U.S.Navy, 1941, advanced through grades to capt., 1955; chief obstetrics and gynecol. service Naval Hosp., Camp LeJeune, N.C., 1949-54, San Diego, Calif., 1954-60, Oakland, Calif., 1960-62; exec. officer Naval Hosp., Oakland, Calif., 1962-64; comdg. officer, Jacksonville, Fla., 1964-68; chief outpatient service Naval Hosp., San Diego, 1968-73; ret., 1973; asso. dir. San Diego State U. Health Service, 1973—. Decorated Legion of Merit. Diplomate Am. Bd. Obstetrics and Gynecology. Fellow Am. Coll. Obstetricians Gynecologists; mem. AMA, Obstet. and Gynecol. Assembly So. Calif., Pan Am. Cancer Cytology Soc., San Diego Gynecol. Soc. Contbr. articles profl. jours. Home: 5817 Arboles St San Diego CA 92120 Office: San Diego State University Health Services San Diego CA 92115

BAKES, ROBERT ELDON, state justice; b. Boise, Idaho, Jan. 11, 1932; s. Warren H. and Oral R. (Rich) B.; B.A., U. Idaho, 1954, J.D., 1956; m. Lurlene M. Fisher, Jan. 16, 1959; children—Juliann, Janette (dec.), Colleen, Diane, Rachel. Admitted to Idaho bar, 1956; practiced in Twin Falls, 1959-60, Boise, 1960-71; mem. firm Kiser & Bakes, 1966-69, Bakes, Ward & Bates, 1969-71; instr. law U. Ill. Law Sch., 1956-57; legal counsel State Tax Collector, 1959-61; asst. U.S. atty., 1961-66; justice Idaho Supreme Ct., Boise, 1971—. Mem. Am. Bar Assn. (mem. exec. com. appellate judges conf.), Idaho State Bar Assn. (dir. continuing legal edn. div. 1963-68). Office: 451 W State St Boise ID 83720*

BAKEY, THOMAS, computer graphics consultant. B.S. in Elec. Engring., Northeastern U., 1958, postgrad. in elec. engring., 1960-62. Dir. graphics mktg. Varian Assocs., Palo Alto, Calif., 1971-76; dir. market research and devel. Calma, Sunnyvale, Calif., 1976-81; founder, v.p. Tricad, Campbell, Calif., 1981-83; pres. Tom Bakey and Assocs., CAD Cons., 1983—; lectr. in field. Author several books, numerous articles on computer graphics systems and their application. Home: 1142 Quince Sunnyvale CA 94087

BAKKER, ATY, educator; b. Den Haag, Netherlands, Jan. 4, 1932; came to U.S., 1953, naturalized, 1956; d. Albert and Frederika (Haalboom) Bakker; B.S., Brigham Young U., 1966; M.S., Utah State U., 1970, Ed.S., 1971; Ph.D. in Ednl. Adminstrn., U. Utah, 1973; children—Cindy Rae Bitton Pratt, Joyce Ellen Bitton Close, Michael Edward Bitton. Tchr. home econs., 1966-71; vocat. dir. Intermountain Inter-Tribal Sch., Brigham City, Utah, 1971-80, tchr. supr., 1980—, fed. women's program mgr., tchr. workshops and extension classes Utah State U., Weber State Coll.; 1983-84; mem. Utah Adv. Council Vocat. Edn.; exec. sec. Utah Home Econs. Assn., 1976-83; adv. council Hill AFB EEO, fed. women's programs, extension services, women's work project, vocat. edn. Named Outstanding Field Mgmt. Trainee, Bur. Indian Affairs, 1976; cert. sch. adminstr., Utah, Colo., Ariz., N.Mex., Alaska; recipient Spl. Service award, Outstanding Performance Ratings, Sustained Superior Performance award Bur. Indian Affairs, 1977. Mem. Utah Home Econs. Assn. (Disting. Service award 1980), Am. Home Econs. Assn., Utah Vocat. Assn., Am. Vocat. Assn., AAUW, LWV, YWCA, Federally Employed Women (past chpt. pres.), Utah Assn. Vocat. Home Econs. Tchrs., Equal Rights Coalition of Utah, NOW, League Utah Consumers, Vocat. Indsl. Clubs Am. (adv.). Clubs: Brigham City Golf and Country, Ski, Toastmistress Internat. Home: 408 W 2d South Brigham City UT 84302 Office: PO Box 345 Intermountain Inter-Tribal School Bur Indian Affairs Brigham City UT 84302

BALBACK, GEORGE L., banker; b. Glendive, Mont., July 13, 1946; s. Marvin J. and E. Grace (Kegley) B.; m. Lynn Ann Jones Aug. 20, 1967; 1 dau., Shauna Dalyn. B.S. in Agrl. Bus., Mont. State U., 1968; student Mont. State Real Estate Inst., 1976; student Nat. Comml. Lending Sch., 1979; student Oil, Gas Lending Sch., 1982. Trainee 1st Bank System 1st Nat. Bank, Bozeman, Mont., 1969-70, installment loan officer, 1970-72; real estate loan officer, 1972-74; v.p. First Citizens Bank, Miles City, Mont., 1974-77; asst. v.p. Security Bank, Billings, Mont., 1977-80; pres. Western Bank, Billings, 1980—, also dir. Served with N.G., 1968-74. Mem. Mont. Bankers Assn. (sec.-treas. group 7B), Ind. Bankers Assn., Am. Bankers Assn. Club: Elks. Home: 5541 Gene Sarazen Billings MT 59106 Office: PO Box 20719 Billings MT 59104

BALCH, GLENN MCCLAIN, JR., univ. pres.; b. Shattuck, Okla., Nov. 1, 1937; s. Glenn McClain and Marjorie (Daily) B.; student Panhandle State U., 1958-60, So. Meth. U., summers 1962-64; B.A., S.W. State U. Okla., 1962; B.D., Phillips U., 1965; M.A., Chapman Coll., 1973, M.A. in Edn., 1975, M.A. in Psychology, 1975; Ph.D., U.S. Internat. U., 1978; postgrad. Claremont Grad. Sch., 1968-70, U. Okla., 1965-66; m. Diana Gale Seeley, Oct. 15, 1970; children—Bryan, Gayle, Wesley, Johnny. Ordained to ministry Methodist Ch., 1962; sr. minister First Meth. Ch., Eakly, Okla., 1960-63, First Meth. Ch., Calumet, Okla., 1963-65, Goodrich Meml. Ch., Norman, Okla., 1965-66, First Meth. Ch., Barstow, Calif., 1966-70; asst. dean Chapman Coll., Orange, Calif., 1970-76; v.p. Pacific Christian Coll., Fullerton, Calif., 1976-79; pres. Newport U., Newport Beach, Calif., 1979—; sr. pastor Brea United Meth. Ch., 1978—; edn. cons. USAF, 1974-75; mental health cons. U.S. Army, 1969. Mem. Community Adv. Bd. Minority Problems, 1975; Mayor's rep. to County Dependency Prevention Commn., 1968-69; bd. dirs. For Kid's Sake. Served with USMC, 1956-57. Recipient Eastern Star Religious Tng. award, 1963, 64; named Man of Year, Jr. C. of C., Barstow, 1969; Broadhurst fellow, 1963-65. Mem. Calif. Marriage Therapists Assn., Doctoral Soc. U.S. Internat. U. Lodges: Rotary, Masons, Shriners, Elks. Home 1016 Steele Dr Brea CA 92621 Office: 480 N State College Brea CA 92621

BALCIAR, GERALD GEORGE, sculptor; b. Medford, Wis., Aug. 28, 1942; s. George Paul and Bernice Gertrude (Schmidt) B.; m. Bonnie Kathryn Balciar, Aug. 30, 1963; children—Gerald George, John, Jackie. Taxidermist, 1960-72; wildlife sculptor in bronze and marble, 1973—; group shows include: Anchorage Audubon Soc. Wildlife Art Exhbn. (award), 1983; represented in permanent collections including Wildlife World Mus., Monument, Colo.; works include: 17-foot bronze elk sculpture, 1982. Mem. Nat. Sculpture Soc. (Dr. Hexter prize 1978, Bronze medal 1979, Commendation youth awards 1979, Chilmark award 1983), Soc. Animal Artists (award of merit 1982).

BALCOM, GLORIA DARLEEN, computer adminstrv. and mktg. cons.; b. Porterville, Calif., July 23, 1939; d. Orel A. and Eunice E. Stadtmiller; A.A., El Camino Coll., 1959; student computer sci. Harbor Coll., 1976-77; m. Orville R. Balcom, July 23, 1971; stepchildren—Cynthia Lou, Steven Raymond. Personnel trainee AiResearch div. Garrett Corp., Los Angeles, 1959-60, sales promotion adminstr., 1960-64; sales rep. Volt Temporary Services, El Segundo, Calif., 1965-69, mgr., Tarzana, Calif., 1969-71; co-owner, co-operator Brown Dog Engring., Lomita, Calif., 1972-77; pres., owner, cons. MicroSly Mktg., Lomita, 1977—. Mem. Ind. Computer Cons. Assn. (nat. pub. relations com.), Am. Soc. Profl. and Exec. Women, Nat. Assn. Female Execs., NOW, Common Cause. Club: Torrance Athletic. Home and office: 24521 Walnut St Lomita CA 90717

BALCOM, ORVILLE, engr.; b. Inglewood, Calif., Apr. 20, 1937; s. Orville R. and Rose Mae (Argo) B.; B.S. in Math., Calif. State U., Long Beach, 1958, postgrad., 1958-59; postgrad. UCLA, 1959-62; m. Gloria Stadtmiller, July 23, 1971; children—Cynthia, Steven. Engr., AiResearch Mfg. Co., 1959-62, 64-65; chief engr. Meditron, El Monte, Calif., 1962-64; chief engr. Astro Metrics, Burbank, Calif., 1965-67; chief engr., gen. mgr. Varadyne Power Systems, Van Nuys, Calif., 1968-71; owner, chief engr. Brown Dog Engring., Lomita, Calif., 1971—. Mem. IEEE Computer Group, Independent Computer Cons. Assn. (bd. dirs. Los Angeles chpt. 1981—). Patentee in field. Club: Torrance Athletic. Home: 24521 Walnut St Lomita CA 90717 Office: PO Box 427 Lomita CA 90717

BALCOMB, M. MICHELLE, biology educator; b. Colorado Springs, Colo., July 25, 1927; d. Paul and Gladys Mae (Petit) Michel; m. Kenneth C. Balcomb Jr., Mar. 20, 1976; children—Laura Baker Strong, Scott Petit Baker. B.A., U. Colo., 1959; M.A., 1961, Ph.D., 1964. Grad. asst. U. Colo., 1959-64; asst. prof. Adams State College, Alamosa, Colo., 1964-67; assoc. prof. U. Colo., 1968-70; assoc. prof. biology Colo. Mountain College, Glenwood Springs, 1970-76, prof., 1976—; cons. Aspen Inst. Humanistic Studies, 1972, Colo. State Forest Service, 1972-78; mem. Govs. Sci. Adv. Com., 1975-78; leader ecology study tours. NIH fellow, 1959-61, 61-64; NSF fellow, 1966, 71. Mem. AAAS (exec. officer Southwestern and Rocky Mountain div. 1979—), Am. Inst. Biol. Scis., Nat. Assn. Biology Tchrs., Colo. Biology Tchrs. Assn., Colo.-Wyo. Acad. of Sci., Phi Beta Kappa, Sigma Xi, Phi Sigma. Republican. Episcopalian. Co-author: (with Carol A. Paul) Study Guide and Instructor's Manual for Understanding Biology, 1978; mem. editorial bd. Biology Tchr., 1975-77. Home: 4829 154 Rd Glenwood Springs CO 81601 Office: Colorado Mountain College Spring Valley Campus 3000 County Rd 114 Glenwood Springs CO 81601

BALD, JUNE, accountant; b. Jackson Hole, Wyo., June 3, 1917; d. Clay and Ireta (Winegar) Seaton; m. Ralph Taylor, May 7, 1934 (dec.); children—Donald, Clay O.; m. 2d, Arno A. Bald, Sept. 6, 1972. Treas., dep. Teton County, Wyo., 1936-47; acct. Livingston Motor Co., Jackson, Wyo., 1948-69; owner, mgr. June Bald Acctg., Jackson, 1969—; exec. mgr. Hoback Motel. Mem. Jackson Hole C. of C. Republican. Episcopalian. Clubs: Order Eastern Star, B.P.O. Does. Address: Star Route 23 Jackson WY 83001

BALDERMAN, MORRIS AARON, geologist; b. Chgo., Apr. 3, 1942; s. Arthur James and Iris B.; B.S., UCLA, 1969, M.S. (NSF trainee 1970-71, NDEA Title IV fellow 1971-72), 1972; m. Barbara Louise Renkow, Mar. 29, 1969; children—Mark Daniel, Amy Michelle. Engring. geologist Moore & Taber, Anaheim, Calif., 1969-70, 73, Woodward-McNeill & Assocs., Orange, Calif., 1972; research asst. UCLA, 1970-71; project geologist Fugro Inc., Long Beach, Calif., 1973-77, D'Appolonia Cons. Engrs., Laguna Niguel, Calif., 1978-79; sr. engring. geologist Leighton & Assos., Irvine, Calif., 1979; cons. geologist, Dana Point, Calif., 1979—. Served with U.S. Army, 1963-66. Registered geologist, cert. engring. geologist, Calif. Mem. Geol. Soc. Am., Assn. Engring. Geologists, South Coast Geol. Soc., Sigma Xi. Contbr. articles to profl. jours. Home: 32802 Mermaid Circle Dana Point CA 92629

BALDERSTONE, IRL LA FAYETTE, clergyman, counselor; b. Sturgis, S.D., Dec. 10, 1912; s. Cloy Lurant and Mattie Louise (La Fayette) B.; B.A., Roosevelt U., Chgo., 1957, M.A., 1970; postgrad. Idaho State U., 1960; B.D., Oxford (U.K.) U., 1968, D.D., 1972. Reporter, freelance writer, Calif., Nev., 1932-42; staff expedition Mex. Mayan and Toltec religions, 1942-44; clin. trainee pastoral counseling Elgin (Ill.), St. Charles (Ill.) state hosps., 1945-46; mem. com. ministry and counseling Chgo. Ch. Fedn., 1947-49; chaplain East Moline (Ill.) and Elgin state hosps., also supr. employment counselors Youth Opportunity Centers, Chgo., 1965-68; ordained minister Spiritualist Ch., Albuquerque, 1976, pastor, counselor, 1974—. Active Democratic party. Fellow Internat. Biog. Assn. (Cambridge, Eng.); mem. Internat. Gen. Assembly Spiritualists, Brit. Psychic Soc., Nat. Chaplains Assn., Nat. Rehab. Assn., Am. Personnel and Guidance Assn., Profl. Counseling Assn., Alpha Psi Omega. Author: Recycling Life (poetry). Home: 1310 Mobile Ln Alamogordo NM 88130

BALDESSARI, JOHN ANTHONY, artist; b. National City, Calif., June 17, 1931; s. Anton and Hedvig B.; B.A., San Diego State U., 1953, M.A., 1957; m. Carol Ann Wixom, June 23, 1962; children—Annamarie, Antonio. Asst. prof. U. Calif.-San Diego, 1968-70; faculty Calif. Inst. Arts, Santa Monica, 1970—, prof., 1970—; one-man shows include: Sonnabend Gallery, N.Y.C., Van Abbemuseum, Eindhoven, Holland, Mus. Folkwang, Essen W. Ger., Rudiger Schöttle Gallery, Munich, Sumangallery, Genoa, Italy, 1981—; group shows include: Paula Cooper Gallery, N.Y.C., Los Angeles County Mus. Art, Westkunst, Cologne, W. Ger., 5th Internat. Biennale, Vienna, Austria; represented in permanent collections Mus. Modern Art, N.Y.C., Stedelijk Mus., Amsterdam, Holland, Kunstmuseum, Basel Switzerland, Australian Nat. Gallery. Nat. Endowment for Arts grantee, 1973, 74. Home: 3552 Beethoven St Los Angeles CA 90066 Office: 2001 1/2 Main St Santa Monica CA 90405

BALDIGO, MICHAEL EDWARD, business educator, accountant; b. Milw., Dec. 23, 1944; s. Edward Michael and Marcia (Draves) B.; m. Jean Ruth McGee, June 15, 1966; m. Sandra Anne De Bella, June 7, 1976; 1 son, Matthew Anthony; children by previous marriage—Victoria, Steven, David. Student Santa Rosa Jr. Coll., 1962, U. Calif.-Santa Barbara, U. Calif.-Berkeley, 1962-64, U. Madrid (Spain), 1964; M.B.A., U. Chgo., 1966; postgrad. NYU, 1967-68; M.B.A., Ind. U., 1971; B.A., Edison Coll., 1976, B.S. in Bus. Adminstrn., 1978; Ph.D., Calif. Western U., 1977. C.P.A., Calif.; cert. in mgmt. acctg. Systems analyst Shell Oil Co., N.Y.C., 1966-68; sr. assoc. programmer IBM Corp., N.Y.C., Franklin Lakes, N.J., 1968-73; assoc. prof. mgmt. Sonoma State U., Rohnert Park, Calif., 1975—; instr. data processing Medocino Lake Community Coll., Ukiah, Calif., 1981-82; cons. Named life mem. Calif. Scholarship Fedn. and Nat. Hon. Soc., 1963. Mem. Am. Inst. C.P.A.s, Nat. Assn. Accts. (cert.), Inst. Internal Auditors (cert.), Am. Prodn. and Inventory Control Soc., Assn. Systems Mgmt., Soc. Data Educators (cert.), Western Econs. Assn., Calif. Soc. C.P.A.s, Acad. Internat. Bus., EDP Auditors Assn., Data Processing Mgmt. Assn. (cert.), Beta Gamma Sigma (Alpha chpt.). Democrat. Quaker. Contbr. articles to bus. and profl. jours. Office: Sonoma State U 1801 E Cotati Ave Rohnert Park CA 94928

BALDWIN, ANN, nurse; b. Chattanooga, Dec. 16, 1946; d. Robert Edwin and Emily Ann (Hudson) B. B.S. in Nursing, Vanderbilt U., 1968; M.S., U. Calif.-San Francisco, 1971; Ph.D., U. Mich., 1979. R.N., Mich., Calif. Staff nurse U. Mich., Ann Arbor, 1968-70, asst. prof., 1973-76; asst. prof. U. Calif.-San Francisco, 1979—; nursing cons. Stanford (Calif.) U. Hosp., 1980—; cons. work stress and conflict resolution. Recipient Vanderbilt U. Founder's medal, 1968. Mem. Am. Nurses Assn., Western Soc. Research in Nursing, Am. Soc. Tng. and Devel. Presbyterian. Contbr. articles to profl. jours. Office: Stanford U Hospital Room C 020 Stanford CA 94304

BALDWIN, ELLEN JANE (MRS. HAL WEST), real estate co. exec.; b. N.Y.C.; d. Whitney and Edna Estelle (Bolles) Eckert; student N.Y. Sch. Design, 1956-58, New Sch., CCNY, 1958-60; m. Hal West, Oct. 18, 1968; children (by previous marriage)—Richard A., Suzanne E. Real estate sales agt., 1963-71; owner Baldwin West and Assos., San Rafael, Calif., 1971—. Sec., Marin County (Calif.) Cerebral Palsy, 1962-64; bd. dirs. Margarita Valley Homeowners Assn., 1972—, v.p., 1972-76, pres., 1976—. Cert. residential specialist; grad. Realtors Inst. Mem. Nat. Assn. Realtors, Calif. Assn. Realtors, Realtors Nat. Mktg. Inst., Marin County Bd. Realtors (dir. 1979—), Million Dollar Club (life), Nat. Million Dollar Real Estate Club. Home: 16 Galleon Way San Rafael CA 94903 Office: 200 Northgate One San Rafael CA 94903

BALDWIN, JANICE ELAINE, real estate agent; b. Omaha, Oct. 11, 1934; d. James H. and Frances Cecelia (Hon) Wagner; m. Valder Dee Baldwin, Oct. 9, 1954 (div.). B.A. in Mktg., Western Wash. U.-Bellingham, 1978. Lic. real estate, Wash. Export mgr. Wham-O Mfg., San Gabriel, Calif., 1964-65; sales rep. HPH, Inc., Rosemead, Calif., 1968-74; dir. Personal Advocacy Services, Seattle, 1975-78; buyer The Boeing Comml. Airplane Co., Renton, Wash., 1977-82, real estate agt. Harbin Properties, Seattle, 1983—. Precinct committeeman Democratic Party, Seattle. Mem. Nat. Assn. Female Execs. Office: 105 14th Ave Suite B Seattle WA 98122

BALDWIN, JOHN DAVID, sociology educator; b. Cin., June 24, 1941; s. Herman J. and Helen T. (Scrivner) B.; m. Janice Irene Whiteside, Aug. 26, 1967. B.A., Johns Hopkins U., 1963, Ph.D., 1967. Asst. prof. sociology U. Calif.-Santa Barbara, 1967-72, assoc. prof., 1972-78, prof., 1978—. Dankstipendium fellow, 1963-64, NSF fellow, 1966-67, NIMH grantee, 1969-71, Max-Planck Gesellschaft fellow, 1973; named Prof. of Yr., Univ. Affiliates, 1981-82; recipient disting. scholarship award Pacific Sociology Assn., 1983. Mem. Am. Sociol. Assn., AAAS. Author: Beyond Sociology, 1981; Behavior Principles in Everyday Life, 1981. Home: 1159 Palomino Rd Santa Barbara CA 93105 Office: Dept Sociology U Calif-Santa Barbara Santa Barbara CA 93106

BALDWIN, JOHN EDWIN, chemistry educator; b. Berwyn, Ill., Sept. 10, 1937; s. Francis Miller and Irville (Miller) B.; A.B. summa cum laude, Dartmouth Coll., 1959; Ph.D., Calif. Inst. Tech., 1963; m. Anne Kruesi Nordlander, Sept. 23, 1961; children—Claire Miller, John Nordlander, Wesley Hale. Mem. chemistry faculty U. Ill., 1962-68; prof. chemistry U. Oreg., Eugene, 1968—, dean Coll. Arts and Scis., 1975-80; cons.

Stauffer Chem. Co., Office Sci. and Tech., NIH. Guggenheim fellow, 1967; Sloan fellow, 1966-68; sr. U.S. scientist award Alexander von Humboldt Found., 1974-75. Author: Experimental Organic Chemistry, 1965; also articles. Adv. bd. Organic Reactions.

BALDWIN, JOHN FRANK, civil engr.; b. Winslow, Ariz., July 15, 1941; s. Joy Jesse and Crystal Christina (Danielson) B.; B.S.C.E., Colo. State U., 1962; M.A., U. Phoenix, 1982; m. Fleeta Joyce Rowland, Aug. 5, 1962; 1 son, John Frank. Civil engr. Calif. Dept. Water Resources, 1962-63; flight engr. Pan Am. Airlines, 1968-70; engring. supr. airports City of Phoenix, 1973—; pilot Ariz. ANG, 1970—; pres. Bravo-Alpha, Inc., Phoenix, 1975—; partner Aranda-Baldwin, 1975-80, Aero-Aviation, 1980—, Almaraz-Baldwin, 1980—. Bd. dirs. N.W. YMCA, Phoenix. Served with USAF, 1963-68. Decorated Air medal with 9 oak leaf clusters. Mem. ASCE, Nat. Soc. Profl. Engrs., Structural Engrs. of Ariz., N.G. Assn. U.S., Air Line Pilots Assn. Republican. Club: Ariz. Office: 125 E Washington St Phoenix AZ 85003

BALDWIN, LARELL HARDISON, ins. co. exec.; b. Hanford, Calif., May 12, 1940; s. Leo H. and Bernice (Gash) B.; student Pasadena Coll., 1958-61; grad. Alexander Hamilton Inst. Bus., 1967; m. Kathleen L. Hardison, June 23, 1979; children—Jennifer Lin, Leslie Kari, Richard Allen, Michael Maxwell. Vice-pres. mortgage lending div. Standard Life & Accident Ins. Co. of Okla., Phoenix, 1961-64; sales mgr. Peterson Baby Products Inc., Burbank, Calif., 1964-67; v.p. sales Rotorway Aircraft Corp., Tempe, Ariz., 1967-69; pres. Trans World Arts Inc., San Jose, Calif., 1969-75, Baldwin Assocs. Devel. Corp., Santa Cruz, Calif., 1975-80; ptnr., v.p. Assurance Distbg. Co. Ltd., Santa Ana, Calif., 1979-82; pres. Transassurance Mktg. Co., 1982—; nat. cons. ins. cos.; dir. Am. Acrylic Industries. Home: 8 Deer Trail Way Scotts Valley CA 95066 Office: PO Box 92649 Scotts Valley CA 95066

BALDWIN, LAWRENCE WILLIAM, elec. engr.; b. Kansas City, Mo., Aug. 31, 1914; s. Edgar Derbyshire and Emma Belle (Haberlein) B.; B.S. with honors, Calif. Inst. Tech., 1935, M.S., 1937; m. Carolyn Hollingshead, June 2, 1943 (div. June 1957); children—Lawrence William, Lee Franklin, Carl Smiley, Holly Adair; m. 2d, Verna Spence, Oct. 26, 1957. Range instrumentation coordinator U.S. Naval Air Missile Test Center, Point Mugu, Calif., 1946-51; project engr. Engring. Research Assos., St. Paul, 1951-52, staff engr. Internat. Telemeter Corp., Los Angeles, 1952-54; supr., mem. tech. staff Hughes Aircraft Co., Culver City, Calif., 1954-79, cons., 1979-80; partner C. S. Baldwin Engring., Ltd., 1979—; mem. faculty U. Calif., Berkeley, 1942-45, UCLA, 1953-54; cons. Radiation Lab., 1950. Trustee family trusts. Mem. IEEE (sr.; life), Am. Contract Bridge League (life master, tournament dir.), Maccabees (great comdr. Calif. 1966-82, supreme trustee 1978—). Patentee in field. Home and Office: 7137-38 Shoup Ave Canoga Park CA 91307

BALDWIN, PAMELA BELKNAP, design co. exec.; b. Washington, Mar. 20, 1944; d. Ralph Belknap and Lois Virginia (Johnston) B.; m. David Paul Castellino, Sept. 12, 1981. A.A., Briarcliff Coll., 1964; B.S., Sch. Architecture and Design, U. Mich., 1967; M.B.A., Golden Gate U., 1983. Designer, Scope Corp., Saga Foods, Menlo Park, Calif., 1967-70, Howard Johnson Assocs., AIA, San Francisco, 1970; sr. designer CPC, Chgo., 1970-71; sr. design and assoc. JSA Assocs., Chgo., 1971; sr. designer, project mgr. M. Arthur Gensler & Assocs., San Francisco, 1971-74, Environ. Planning and Research, San Francisco, 1974-75; co-founder, pres., treas. Baldwin/Clarke Assocs., Inc., San Francisco, 1976—; guest lectr. schs. and univs.; competition jurist. Mem. adv. bd. Salvation Army, San Francisco, 1983-86; mem. policy panel Nat. Endowment for Arts/Design Arts Program, 1983—, mem. fellowship panel, 1983— Named one of top 25 female execs. in San Francisco, 1979. Fellow Inst. Bus. Designers (profl., co-chmn. organizing com. No. Calif. chpt. 1974, chpt. pres. 1974-75, nat. trustee 1974, 75, nat. treas. 1975-77, nat. chmn. and pres. 1977-79, pres. nat. jud. council 1981—); mem. Am. Soc. Interior Designers, Jr. League San Francisco. Republican. Congregationalist. Contbr. to publs. including Contract mag., Interior Design mag., Interiors, Designers West, Modern Office Procedures, San Francisco Examiner, San Francisco mag. Office: 700 Sansome St San Francisco CA 94111

BALDWIN, RUSSELL WARNE, artist, educator, gallery administrator; b. San Diego, May 26, 1933; s. Victor Lewis and Carolyn (Odell) B.; children—Sarah, Marc. B.A., M.A., Calif. State U.-San Diego. Exhibited works in one-man shows, the most recent being: Jewish Community Ctr., San Diego, 1975, Casat Gallery, La Jolla, Calif., 1978, La Jolla Museum Contemporary Art, 1981, San Francisco Mus. Modern Art, 1981, Claremont (Calif.) Coll., 1982, Space Gallery, Los Angeles, 1982; group shows include: La Jolla Mus. Contemporary Art (Painting award, Purchase award), Long Beach (Calif.) Mus. Modern Art (Sculpture award), Southwestern Coll., (Purchase award), First Ann. Art Exhbn., San Diego (First Sculpture award), Fine Arts Mus., San Diego (award), Laguna Beach (Calif.) Mus. Modern Art (award), represented in permanent collections: Kelly Found., Los Angeles, San Francisco Mus. Modern Art, Newport Harbor Art Mus., Newport Beach, Calif., Internat. Paper Co. Corp. Collection, N.Y.C., Joseph Hirschorn Collection, Washington, La Jolla Mus. Contemporary Art, San Diego, Santa Barbara Mus. Modern Art, Southwestern Coll., Calif. State U-San Diego, Ahmanson Found., Los Angeles, also numerous pvt. collections; instr. in art, dir. Boehm Gallery, Palomar Coll., San Marcos, Calif., 1965—. Served with USNR. Recipient First Painting award San Diego Art Guild. Mem. La Jolla Mus. Contemporary Art. Subject of articles on art, various publs. Office: 1140 W Mission San Marcos CA 92069

BALK, DAVID EDWARD, educator; b. Monroe, Mich., Oct. 24, 1943; s. Arnold Cornelius and Mildred Violet (Martell) B.; m. Mary Ann Brown, Nov. 5, 1975; 1 dau., Janet Renee. B.A., Immaculate Conception Sem., 1965; M.A., Marquette U., 1970; M.C., Ariz. State U., 1975; Ph.D. (Grad. Coll. fellow, Coll. Edn. grantee, William T. Grant grantee) U. Ill.-Urbana, 1981. Theology instr. Rockhurst Coll., 1967-69; social ethics instr. Riordan High Sch., 1971-72; research specialist Phoenix S. Community Mental Health Ctr., 1975-77, research dir., 1977-78; grad. research asst. U. Ill., 1978-81, vis. asst. prof., 1981, vis. research assoc., 1981-82; dir. program evaluation La Frontera Ctr., Tucson, 1982—. Mem. Am. Psychol. Assn. Contbr. articles to profl. jours. Home: 4244 E 25th St Tucson AZ 85711

BALKANY, THOMAS JAY, physician; b. Miami, Fla., May 1, 1948; M.D., U. Miami, 1972; m. Diane Judith Pielage, 1970; 1 son, Jordan Thomas. Diplomate Am. Bd. Otolaryngology. Intern U. N.Mex. Hosps., Albuquerque, 1972-73; resident in surgery St. Joseph's Hosp., Denver, 1973-74; resident in otolaryngology U. Colo. Med. Ctr., Denver, 1974-77, asst. prof. dept. otolaryngology, 1977-80, clin. asst. prof., 1980; dir. pediatric otolaryngology Denver Children's Hosp., 1978—; head sect. otology and neurotology dept. otolaryngology U. Colo. Health Scis. Ctr., 1978-80; asst. chief otolaryngology sect. Porter Meml. Hosp.-Swedish Med. Ctr., Denver, 1980-81, chief, 1981-82; med. advisor Inter Canyon Rescue Squad, 1977—, Colo. Wilderness Trails, Inc., 1978—; cons. Denver Biomaterials, Inc., 1976—, Indian Health Service, USPHS, 1978-80, Storz Instrument Co., St. Louis, 1980—, Ergo Instrument Co., Granger, Ind., 1980—, 3M Corp., St. Paul, 1981—; mem. task force on new materials Am. Bd. Otolaryngology, 1979—. Fellow Am. Acad. Otolaryngology (self improvement program 1981—), ACS, Internat. Coll. Surgeons; mem. Soc. Univ. Otolaryngologists, Am. Auditory Soc., Barany Soc., Internat. Soc. History of Otolaryngology, Assn. Research in Otolaryngology, Soc. Ear, Nose and Throat Advances in Children, Southwestern Surg. Congress, Colo. Med. Assn., Colo. Found. Med. Care, Denver Med. Soc., Arapahoe Med. Soc. Mem. editorial bd. Am. Jour. Otolaryngology, 1979—; contbr. articles to med. jours. Office: Cole Ear Clinic 950 E Harvard Ave Suite 200 Denver CO 80210

BALKUS, THELMA LOUISE (MRS. JOSEPH F. BALKUS), ret. city ofcl.; b. Denver, Jan. 26, 1915; d. Guy and Mary (Ganschow) Boatwright; student extension courses U. Calif. at Los Angeles, 1938-39; m. Joseph F. Balkus, Feb. 17, 1941; children—Jo Ann Balkus Tanner, Joseph C. With travel bur. Continental Oil Co., Denver, 1936-37; secretarial position, artist Burroughs, Inc., dir. mail advt., Los Angeles, 1937-42; secretarial position Wianko Engring., Pasadena and Davidson Optronics, West Covina, Calif., intermittently 1957-58; city clk. City of Baldwin Park (Calif.), 1958-80, acting chief adminstr., 1962-63, 71; adminstrv. aide Baldwin Park City Council, 1959-76. Sec. Edgewood Family Counseling Agy., Covina, 1963-64; sec. Baldwin Park Personnel Bd., 1964-80; sec. Baldwin Park Charter Study Commn., 1970-71, Baldwin Park Redevel. Agy., 1975-76. Mem. Calif. Democratic State Central Com., 1969-70. Recipient 1st Lady citations Calif. Fedn. Women's Clubs, 1974, Bus. and Profl. Women's Clubs, 1974; named Baldwin Park Citizen of Year, 1979. Mem. Baldwin Park C. of C., Baldwin Park Hist. Soc. (pres. 1970-74), Internat. Inst. Municipal Clks. (certified). Roman Catholic. Club: Women's. Home: 4625 N Harlan Ave Baldwin Park CA 91706

BALL, DOUGLAS SCHELLING, oil, gas and mineral cons.; b. Cheyenne, Wyo., Mar. 5, 1920; s. Max Waite and Amalia (Maeder) B.; P.E., Colo. Sch. Mines, 1943; m. Caroline Marguerite Schmidt, Mar. 12, 1943; children—Richard Neal, Max Waite (dec.), Michael Douglas, Anna Gail. Various positions in refinery constrn. and oil field work, Can. and U.S., 1937-39; geophysics work, Gulf Coast and N. Tex., 1940-42; gas reservoir engr. Phillips Petroleum Co., Panhandle area, 1946-49; mem. firm Max. W. Ball & Douglas Ball, Washington, 1949-55; pres. Ball Assos., Ltd., Washington and Colo., 1955—; co-chmn. tar sands subcom., enhanced recovery com. Interstate Oil Compact Commn., 1969—; dir. Oceanic Exploration Co. Mem. Gilpin County (Colo.) Sch. Bd., 1969-73, pres., 1971-73. Served to 1st lt. U.S. Army, 1942-46. Fellow Geol. Soc. Am.; mem. AAAS, Am. Assn. Petroleum Geologists, Soc. Petroleum Engrs. of Am. Inst. Mining and Metall. Engrs. (chmn. petroleum br. econs. com. 1953), Rocky Mountain Assn. Geologists, Israel Inst. Petroleum and Geophysics (hon.). Republican. Episcopalian. Author: (with Daniel S. Turner) This Fascinating Oil Business, 1966; sr. author: U.S. Bur. Mines Monograph 12, Surface and Shallow Oil-Impregnated Rocks and Shallow Oil Fields in the U.S., 1965; contbr. articles to profl. jours. Home and office: 105 Main St PO Box 8 Black Hawk CO 80422

BALL, FRED DOUGLAS, actor, entertainer; b. Davenport, Iowa; s. Elbert Alvaro and Velma Jean (Beresford) B. B.S. in Edn., Western Ill. U., 1960; M.A., U. Hawaii, 1967; postgrad. U. Seven Seas, 1964. Appeared with KGMB-TV, 1967-73, 12 segments Hawaii 5-0, CBS-TV, 1970-78, C'est Si Bon, Polynesian Palace nightclubs, 1972, 74, Queen Kapiolani Hotel, Honolulu, 1972-79, Sta. KIKV-TV, Honolulu, 1981—; tchr. pub. schs., Ill., 1960-63, Hawaii, 1965-70. Mem. Hawaii Magicians' Soc. (sgt. at arms 1964-65, pres. 1965-66, 68-69), Variety Club (dir. Honolulu chpt. 1971, named Press Guy 1972, 81), Screen Actor's Guild (steering com. Hawaii chpt. 1974, chmn. 1974), Hawaii Council Am. Indian Nations, Am. Humanists Assn., AFTRA (v.p. Hawaii chpt. 1971-74), Am. Guild Variety Artists (del. from Hawaii 1965), Clowns Am., Honolulu Press Club, Internat. Brotherhood Magicians, Internat. Ventriloquists Assn. Home: 4460 Wahinekoa Place Honolulu HI 96821 Office: PO Box 10121 Honolulu HI 96816

BALL, JEAN GAIL LYONS (MRS. EDWIN LEE BALL), Realtor; b. Elizabeth City, N.C., Jan. 17, 1927; d. George Cluster and Dorothy Louise (Tillett) Lyons; student Temple U., 1945; diploma Moore Inst. Design, 1945, Kesley Jenney Coll., 1959, Anthony Schs. Real Estate, 1970; m. Edwin Lee Ball, June 28, 1946; 1 dau., Dianna Lee. Profl. fashion model, singer with various agys. including Neufelt, Phila., Walters, Balt., Powers, San Diego, N.Y.C., Fashionality, San Diego, intermittently, 1942-58; owner, broker Gail Ball & Assos. (formerly Ball Realty), El Cajon, Calif., 1970—, now pres.; pres. Ball/McKinnon, Inc.; owner Dyana's Beauty Salons, El Cajon, 1973—; pres., gen. mgr. Gail Ball & Asociados S.A. de C.V., internat. real estate investment corp., Baja California, Mex., 1980—; broker, gen. partner Internat. Fin. Co., 1980—. Exhibited art in shows at Tivoli Hotel Little Gallery, C.Z. various commns. Mem. Nat. League Am. Pen Women, Inc., El Cajon Valley Bd. Realtors, Cal. Real Estate Assn., Nat. Assn. Real Estate Bds. Realtor; b. Elizabeth City, N.C., Jan. 17, 1927; d. George Cluster and Dorothy Louise (Tillett) Lyons; student Temple U., 1945; diploma Moore Inst. Design, 1945, Kesley Jenney Coll., 1959, Anthony Schs. Real Estate, 1970; m. Edwin Lee Ball, June 28, 1946; 1 dau., Dianna Lee. Profl. fashion model, singer with various agys. including Neufelt, Phila., Walters, Balt., Powers, San Diego, N.Y.C., Fashionality, San Diego, intermittently, 1942-58; owner, broker Gail Ball & Assos. (formerly Ball Realty), El Cajon, Calif., 1970—, now pres.; pres. Ball/McKinnon, Inc.; owner Dyana's Beauty Salons, El Cajon, 1973—; pres., gen. mgr. Gail Ball & Asociados S.A. de C.V., internat. real estate investment corp., Baja California, Mex., 1980—; broker, gen. partner Internat. Fin. Co., 1980—. Exhibited art in shows at Tivoli Hotel Little Gallery, C.Z. various commns. Mem. Nat. League Am. Pen Women, Inc., El Cajon Valley Bd. Realtors, Cal. Real Estate Assn., Nat. Assn. Real Estate Bds. Home: 1787 Hillsdale Rd El Cajon CA 92020 Office: 772 E Washington Ave El Cajon CA 92020

BALL, LINDA JEAN, personnel exec.; b. Rochester, N.Y., Nov. 7, 1948; d. Henry A. and Geraldine I. T. (Cole) Davis; m. Joseph H. Ball, Aug. 13, 1972. B.S. in Bus. Adminstrn., Calif. State U., Northridge, 1970; M.B.A., National U., 1982. Personnel adminstr. ARA Transp., Encino, Calif., 1970-78; benefits/compensation adminstr. Everest & Jennings, Los Angeles, 1978; sr. wage and salary analyst Cubic Corp., San Diego, 1978-82, mgr. wage and salary adminstrn., 1982-83, dir. compensation and benefits, 1983—. Mem. Compensation Practices Assn., Internat. Assn. Personnel Women (founder, past pres. San Diego), Personnel Mgmt. Assn., Career Women's Assn., AAUW. Democrat. Office: 9333 Balboa Ave San Diego CA 92123

BALL, LYLE V., painter; b. Reno, Dec. 24, 1909; s. William and Pearl Ann (Wood) B.; m. Esther M. Flanary, Aug. 9, 1931; children—Phyllis Diane, Larry L. Owner, mgr. The Ball Sign Co., Reno, 1929-69; one man shows: Northeastern Nev. Mus., 1971, 77, Burk Gal'ry, Boulder City, Nev., 1975, Art Mcht., Sisters, Oreg., 1977-80; group shows include: Soc. Western Artists, 1967-70, Death Valley 49ers, 1968-82, Artists Profl. League, N.Y.C., 1971—, Am. Indian and Cowboy Artists, 1976-83, Silver Medallion award Water Colors, 1977; represented in permanent collections: Senate Office Bldg., Washington, Nev. Legislature Bldg., Carson City, Reno City Hall, Las Vegas Art League. Recipient Edgar Surdez award Lodi Art Center, 1968. Mem. Soc. Western Artists (Walter Keane award 1968), Artists Profl. League, Am. Indian and Cowboy Artists (Gold medal nominee 1981, 82). Republican. Presbyterian. Clubs: Odd Fellows, Lions. Home: 181 Bret Harte Ave Reno NV 89509

BALL, WILLIAM, producer, director; b. 1931; A.B., Fordham U.; M.A. (NBC/RCA fellow), Carnegie Inst. Tech.; Ph.D. (hon), Carnegie-Mellon U., 1979. Appearances with Oreg. Shakespeare Festival, 1950-53, Antioch Shakespeare Festival, 1954, Group 20 Players, 1956, San Diego Shakespeare Festival, 1955, Arena Stage, Washington, 1957-58; in Back to Methuselah, Broadway and on tour, 1958; Six Characters in Search of An Author, 1959; Cosi Fan Tutte, 1959; The Inspector General, 1960; Porgy and Bess, 1961; Midsummer Night's Dream, 1963; with off-Broadway N.Y.C. Center Opera Co. in The Misanthrope, The Lady's Not for Burning. The Country Wife, Ivanov, A Month in the Country, 1956-58, Under Milkwood, 1956-61, Six Characters in Search of An Author, 1963; in The Tempest, Stratford (Conn.) Festival, 1964; in Yeoman of the Guard, Stratford, Can., 1964; liberttist, dir. Natalia Petrovna, N.Y.C. Center Opera Co., 1964, Tartuffe for Lincoln Center Repertory Co., 1965. Founder, gen. dir. Am. Conservatory Theatre, 1965—. Recipient Tony award, 1979. Fulbright scholar to Eng., 1953-54; Ford Found. Director's grantee, 1959, commn. for Natalia Petrovna, 1964. Address: 450 Geary St San Francisco CA 94102

BALL, WILLIAM PAUL, physicist, engineer; b. San Diego, Nov. 16, 1913; s. John and Mary (Kajla) B.; A.B., UCLA, 1940; Ph.D., U. Calif., Berkeley, 1952; m. Edith Lucile March, June 28, 1941 (dec. 1976); children—Lura Irene Ball Raplee, Roy Ernest. Projectionist, sound technician studios and theatres in Los Angeles, 1932-41; high sch. tchr., Montebello, Calif., 1941-42; instr. math. and physics Santa Ana (Calif.) Army Air Base, 1942-43; physicist U. Calif. Radiation Lab., Berkeley and Livermore, 1943-58; mem. tech. staff Ramo-Wooldridge Corp., Los Angeles, 1958-59; sr. scientist Hughes Aircraft Co., Culver City, Calif., 1959-64; sr. staff engr. TRW-Def. Systems Group, Redondo Beach, Calif., 1964—. Bd. dirs. So. Dist. Los Angeles chpt. ARC, 1979—. Recipient Manhattan Project award for contbn. to 1st atomic bomb, 1945; registered profl. engr., Calif. Mem. Am. Phys. Soc., Am. Nuclear Soc., AAAS, AIAA, N.Y. Acad. Scis., Torrance (Calif.) Area C. of C. (dir. 1978—), Sigma Xi. Contbr. articles profl. jours. Patentee electron-multiplier vacuum and temperature gauge. Home: 209 Via El Toro Redondo Beach CA 90277 Office: TRW-DSG 1 Space Park Redondo Beach CA 90278

BALLANCE, CHARLEEN ANN, trainer/educator, consultant; b. Marysville, Kans., May 24, 1947; d. Charles Andrew and Dorothy Catherine (Cleavenger) Saylors; m. William Roscoe Ballance, Jan. 18, 1969; children—Charles Ransom, Nicole Lynn. B.S., U. Nebr., 1969; M.A., U. No. Colo., 1979. Audio-visual specialist, Goose Bay, Labrador, Can.; program supr. Pikes Peak Community Coll., Colorado Springs, Colo., 1972-75, coordinator basic skills edn. program, 1978-79; bus. instr., Taipei, Taiwan, 1975-77; dir.-mgr. Colorado Springs Coll. Bus., 1979-80; dir. Career Devel. Ctr., Mgmt. Tng. Inst., Blair Jr. Coll., Colorado Springs, 1980-83; asst. dir. tng. and edn. Penrose Hosp., Colorado Springs, 1983—; tchr. Am. Mgmt. Assn. Mem. Am. Soc. Tng. and Devel. (chpt. pres.), Am. Bus. Women's Assn. Democrat. Roman Catholic. Home: 6945 Defoe Ave Colorado Springs CO 80911 Office: 2215 N Cascade Ave Colorado Springs CO 80907

BALLANTINE, MORLEY COWLES (MRS. ARTHUR BALLANTINE), newspaper publisher; b. Des Moines, May 21, 1925; d. John and Elizabeth (Bates) Cowles; A.B., Ft. Lewis Coll., Durango, Colo., 1975; L.H.D. (hon.), Simpson Coll., Indianola, Iowa, 1980; m. Arthur Ballantine, Jr., July 26, 1947 (dec. Nov. 1975); children—Richard, Elizabeth, William, Helen Ballantine Healy. Pub. (with husband) Durango (Colo.) Herald, 1952—; dir. Cowles Media Co., First Nat. Bank Durango, Des Moines Register & Tribune. Mem. Colo. Anti-Discrimination Commn., 1959-61, Colo. Com. on Ednl. Endeavor, 1959-63, Colo. Commn. on Status of Women, 1973-75; mem. Colo. bd. LWV, 1954-57, Durango bd., 1953-59; pres. S.W. Colo. Mental Health Center, 1964, 65; mem. Colo. Population Adv. Council, 1972-75, Colo. Nat. Hist. Preservation Act, 1968-75, Colo. Land Use Commn., 1975-80; trustee Choate-Rosemary Hall, 1973-81, Fountain Valley Sch., Colorado Springs, 1976—, Simpson Coll., 1981—; pres. Four Corners Opera Assn., 1983—. Recipient 1st pl. award for editorial writing Nat. Fedn. Press Women, 1955; Outstanding Alumna award Rosemary Hall, Greenwich, Conn., 1969, (with husband) Outstanding Journalism award U. Colo. Sch. Journalism, 1967, Disting. Service award Ft. Lewis Coll., Durango, 1970. Mem. Nat. Soc. Colonial Dames, Colo. Press Club. Clubs: Federated Women's (Durango); Mill Reef (Antigua, W.I.). Episcopalian. Home: 175 W Park Ave Durango CO 81301 Office: care Herald Drawer A Durango CO 81301

BALLANTYNE, REGINALD MALCOLM, III, hospital administrator; b. Columbus, Ga., Oct. 2, 1943; s. Reginald M. and Constance Aimee (Martin) B.; B.S., Coll. of Holy Cross, 1965; M.B.A. (Sloan scholar), Cornell U., 1967. Adminstrv. resident Glen Cove (N.Y.) Community Hosp., 1966; coordinator community health tng. programs Office Surgeon Gen. USPHS, New Eng. Region, 1967-70; asst. adminstr. St. Luke's Hosp. Med. Center, Phoenix, 1970-73; adminstr. Meml. Hosp., Phoenix, 1973-74, exec. v.p., 1974-76, pres., trustee, 1976—; mem. steering com. Comprehensive Health Planning Council of Maricopa County (Ariz.), 1970-71; vis. lectr. Yale U., 1968-70, U. Conn., 1968-70, Phoenix Coll., 1971-73; pres. Phoenix Regional Hosp. Council, 1978-79; chmn. bd. Valley Emergency Med. Services, Inc., 1974-77. Mem. adv. bd. Jr. League Phoenix, 1975-77; bd. dirs. Citizens Com. for Better Health, Estate Los Arboles Home Owners Assn.; pres. Florence Crittenton Services of Ariz., 1980-81. Recipient Cert. of Merit award USPHS, 1970. Mem. Am., Ariz. (chmn. bd. 1981-82) hosp. assns., Ariz. Assn. Health and Welfare, Am., Ariz. public health assns., Assn. Western Hosps., Soc. Public Health Edn., Am. Coll. Hosp. Adminstrs., Am. Acad. Med. Adminstrs. (state chmn. 1975-79), Phoenix C. of C. (bus. and govt. div. council 1974—), Commd. Officers Assn. of USPHS, Maricopa County Assn. Med. Edn. (dir. 1975—), Ariz. Coop. Purchasing Assn. (pres. 1975-78), Phoenix Execs. Club. Roman Catholic. Clubs: Rotary (pres. 1979-80), Ariz. Contbr. articles on hosp. adminstrn. to profl. publs. Home: 1252 E Gardenia Dr Phoenix AZ 85020 Office: PO Box 21207 Phoenix AZ 85036

BALLARD, EATON WALLING, dept. store exec.; b. Seattle, June 27, 1911; s. Roy Page and Olive (Murphy) B.; A.B., Stanford U., 1932; M.B.A., Havard U., 1937; m. Beverly Holtenhouse, Dec. 28, 1933; children—Sarah Eaton Ballard Pileggi, Gretchen Ballard Guard, Jonathan Roy. With Marshall Field & Co., Chgo., 1937-38, May Co., Los Angeles, 1939-46; with Carter Hawley Hale Stores, Inc., Los Angeles, 1947—, treas., 1956-63, v.p., 1959-67, exec. v.p., 1967-77, dir., 1956-77, cons., 1977—; dir. Airborne Freight Corp., Am. Mut. Fund, Inc., Christiana Cos., Inc., Fundamental Investors, Inc., Pacific Am. Income Shares; pres. Music Center Operating Co. Chmn. bd. trustees Pacific Oaks Coll.; bd. dirs. Children's Hosp. Los Angeles; trustee Calif. Inst. Arts. Served as lt. USNR, 1943-45. Clubs: Calif., Stock Exchange (Los Angeles). Home: 635 Rockwood Rd Pasadena CA 91105 Office: 550 S Flower St Los Angeles CA 90071

BALLARD, LOCKETT FORD, JR., museum director; b. Cold Springs, N.Y., Aug. 1, 1946; s. Lockett Ford and Charlotte Carr (Morrison) B. B.A., Hamilton Coll., 1968; M.A., Cooperstown U., 1973. Asst. curator Old State Capitol Restoration, Frankfort, Ky., 1973; dir. Litchfield (Conn.) Hist. Soc., 1974-81; exec. dir. Rosemount Victorian House Mus., Pueblo, Colo., 1981—. Mem. Preservation Adv. Bd., Pueblo, 1982—. Served with USN, 1968-72. Mem. Am. Assn. Museums, Am. Assn. for State and Local History, Mountain Plains Mus. Assn., Colo.-Wyo. Assn. Museums. Episcopalian. Office: Rosemount Victorian House Museum PO Box 5259 Pueblo CO 81002

BALLARD, MELVIN RUSSELL, JR., church ofcl.; b. Salt Lake City, Oct. 8, 1928; s. Melvin Russell and Geraldine (Smith) B.; student U. Utah, 1946, 1950-52; m. Barbara Bowen, Aug. 28, 1951; children—Clark, Holly, Meleea, Tamara, Stacey, Brynn, Craig. Sales mgr. Ballard

Motor Co., Salt Lake City, 1950-54; investment counselor, Salt Lake City, 1954-56; founder, owner, mgr. Russ Ballard Auto, Inc., Salt Lake City, 1956-58, Ballar-Wade Co., 1958-67; owner, mgr. Ballard & Co., Salt Lake City, 1962-72; gen. authority Ch. of Jesus Christ of Latter-day Saints, Salt Lake City, 1976—; dir. Foothill Thrift & Loan, Nate-Wade, Inc., Silver King Mines, Inc. (all Salt Lake City); gen. partner N & R Investment, Salt Lake City, 1958—, Ballard Investment Co., Salt Lake City, 1955—. Mem. bd. Salt Lake Jr. Achievement, 1978-80; bd. dirs. Freedoms Found., 1978—, David O. McKay Inst. Edn., 1979—; Served to 1st lt. USAR, 1950-57. Mem. Salt Lake Area C. of C. (gov. 1979—). Republican. Office: 50 E North Temple St Salt Lake City UT 84150*

BALLEN, SAMUEL BERNARD, utility co. exec.; b. N.Y.C., Mar. 3, 1922; s. Max and Monya (Friedman) Biegelaisen; B.B.A., City U. N.Y., 1942; postgrad. Columbia, 1946, U. Okla., 1950, Tex. A. and M. U.; m. Ethel Levine, July 29, 1945; children—Nina, Lois, Joanne, Paula, Lenore, Marta. Oil analyst Lehman Bros. & Wertheim Co., N.Y.C., Dallas, 1945-56; chief officer Elec. Log Services, Inc., Dallas, 1956-69; chmn. bd., chief exec. officer High Plains Natural Gas Co., Santa Fe, 1963—; pres. La Fonda Hotel, Santa Fe, 1969—. Trustee J. Robert Oppenheimer Meml. Com.; bd. dirs. Old Santa Fe Assn. Served with C.E. AUS, 1942-45. Mem. AIME, Dallas Assn. Investment Analysts, SW Assn. Indian Affairs (treas.). Club: Explorers of N.Y. Author: Computer Analysis of Well Logs; Oil Reserves and the Security Analyst. Home: 1020 Old Santa Fe Trail Santa Fe NM 87501 Office: Box 2263 Santa Fe NM 87501

BALLESTEROS, THOMAS RODRIGUEZ, podiatrist; b. Riverside, Calif., June 27, 1951; s. Manuel and Cruz (Rodriguez) B.; B.S., Loyola U., Los Angeles, 1973; B.S. in Medicine, Calif. Coll. Podiatric Medicine, 1975, D.Podiatric Medicine, 1977; m. Patricia La Tendresse, Aug. 26, 1972; children—Doug, Manuel. Pvt. practice podiatry, Riverside, 1977—; mem. med. staff Circle City Hosp. Del., Calif. Conf. Small Bus., 1980; mem. Riverside City Charter Rev. Com. Mem. Am. Podiatry Assn., Calif. Podiatry Assn., Riverside Jaycees (dir.; disting. service award 1982), Riverside C. of C., Hispanic Chamber. Democrat. Roman Catholic. Office: 4009 Brockton St Riverside CA 92501

BALLIET, ALBERT, investment co. exec.; b. Lansford, Pa., Nov. 27, 1927; s. Albert L. and Arlene (Kipp) B.; B.S. in Chemistry, Muhlenberg Coll., 1951; m. Barbara Ann Henritzy, Jan. 28, 1950; children—Linda Louise, Alicia Ann. Chemist, supr. powder line Atlas Powder Co., Richmond, Calif., 1951-60, powder line supr., Joplin, Mo., 1960-62; shift supr., sr. engr., nitroplasticizer plant Aerojet Gen. Corp., Sacramento, 1962-70; pres., dir. Pacific Securities Investment Co., Sacramento, 1974—; sec., dir. Pacific Securities Assocs., 1972-76; dir. Foothill Securities Inc. Served with USAAF, 1946-47. Recipient Pub. Service awards Cordova Park and Recreation Dept. Mem. Internat. Assn. Fin. Planners (pres. Sacramento chpt. 1976-77), Inst. Cert. Fin. Planners, Gideons Internat. Republican. Lutheran. Clubs: Toastmasters, Square Dance. Home: 2521 Zinfandel Dr Rancho Cordova CA 95670 Office: 8915 Folsom Blvd Suite C Sacramento CA 95826

BALLINGER, CHARLES EDWIN, ednl. adminstr.; b. West Mansfield, Ohio, June 3, 1935; s. William E. and Mildred A. (Jester) B.; B.A., DePauw U., 1957; M.A., Ohio State U., 1958, Ph.D., 1971. Asst. supt. curriculum North Canton (Ohio) City Schs., 1964-67; curriculum cons. Franklin County Office of Edn., Columbus, Ohio, 1967-70; ednl. cons. Ohio Dept. Edn., Columbus, 1970-71; curriculum coordinator San Diego County Dept. Edn., San Diego, 1971—; exec. sec. Nat. Council Year-Round Edn. Bd. dirs. San Diego County Adv. Com. Drug Abuse, San Diego County Ecumenical Conf., Citizens Coordinate for Century 3; pres. San Diego chpt. Ams. United Separation of Ch. and State. Mem. Am. Ednl. Research Assn., Assn. Supervision and Curriculum Devel., Phi Delta Kappa. Republican. Methodist. Author: A Drug Education Curriculum: K-12, 1971; Year-Round Education and the High School, 1973. Home: 6312 Caminito Luisito San Diego CA 92111 Office: 6401 Linda Vista Rd San Diego CA 92111

BALLOU, LINDA CAROL, sales manager; b. Enid, Okla., Sept. 15, 1942; d. Charles and Ludie Kirkpatrick; m. James Craig, Aug. 15, 1966; m. 2d, Richard Ballou, May 19, 1979; children—Debra, Kathy, Jack, James, Troy. Student St. Catherine Sch. Nursing, U. Omaha, 1960-63. Cert. profl. med. assn. With Atlantic Richfield, Los Angeles, 1972-74, STP Corp., Ft. Lauderdale, Fla., 1974-75; owner Merle Norman Cosmatics Studio, Thousand Oaks, Calif., 1974-76; sales mgr. Cert. Labs., Beverly Hills, Calif., 1978—; condr. sales seminars. Active Republican Congl. Com., 1981-83. Mem. Peterson C. of C. Office: 8383 Wilshire Blvd Beverly Hills CA 91362

BALOG, JOHN FRANCIS, psychiatrist; b. Detroit, June 23, 1934; s. Paul and Marie (Spicka) B.; student Wayne State U., 1952-54; B.A., U. Mich., 1958, M.D., 1962; m. Lois Dawn Gilpin, June 22, 1963; children—Monica Marie, Teresa Alice. Intern, Sparrow Hosp., Lansing, Mich., 1962-63; resident psychiatry U. Calif. at Los Angeles, 1963-66; practice psychiatry, Pasadena, 1966—; med. dir. psychiat. unit Glendale (Calif.) Adventist Med. Center, 1970-71, mem. exec. com., chief psychiatry, 1975-80, sec.-treas., 1980-81; asst. clin. prof. U. So. Calif., Los Angeles, 1971—; asso. clin. prof. psychiatry Loma Linda (Calif.) U., 1974—; founder Creative Psychiat. Inst., Pasadena, Profl. Diversified Resources, Balog Med. Group; med. dir. Lifestyle Dynamics, Behavioral Medicine Ctr. at Pasadena Community Hosp. Served with AUS, 1954-56. Mem. Am., Los Angeles (pres.) group psychotherapy socs., AMA, Am. Psychiat. Assn., Internat. Transactional Analysis Assn., Biofeedback Soc. Calif. (a founder), Am. Soc. Clin. Hypnosis, Internat. Soc. Clin. and Exptl. Hypnosis. Asso. editor Jour. Med. Hypnoanalysis. Office: 837 S Fair Oaks Ave Pasadena CA 91105

BALOG, KEESY, writer; b. Lorain, Ohio, Aug. 9, 1949; d. George S. and Katherine (Nagy) B.; student Kent (Ohio) State U., 1967-68, 69-71. Reporter, The Lorain Jour., 1970-71; freelance writer, Los Angeles, 1977—; owner Writing a La Carte, Los Angeles, 1980—; v.p. SRW Industries, Los Angeles. Mem. Women in Communications, Author's Guild, Nat. Writers Club.

BALOG (GILLETTE), DAWN LOIS, motivational therapist, nutritionist; b. Lansing, Mich., May 5, 1940; d. Harold James and Edna Alice (Richmond) Gilpin; m. John Francis Balog, June 22, 1963; children—Monica Marie, Teresa Alice. B.A., Immaculate Heart Coll., 1974; M.S., Donsbach U., 1981, Ph.D., 1983. Cert. biofeedback therapist. Program dir. Life Fitness Center, Pasadena, Calif., 1980-83; program dir., co-founder Lifestyle Dynamics, Pasadena, 1983—. Bd. dirs. Immaculate Heart Coll., Los Angeles. Mem. Religious Science Ch. Club: Calif. Inst. Tech. Assocs. (Pasadena). Office: Lifestyle Dynamics 837 S Fair Oaks Suite 200 Pasadena CA 91105

BALOK, ELAINE MARIE, city ofcl.; b. South Bend, Ind., Jan. 10, 1948; d. Lawrence Stephen and Betty Mae (Daugherty) B.; student Mich. State U., 1965-67; B.S., Ind. U., 1969; M.S., Columbia U., 1971; J.D., Western State Law Sch., 1979. Program design specialist Mich. Dept. Mental Health, Traverse City, 1971-73; dir., owner Activity Therapy Cons. Service, N.Y.C. and Traverse City, 1972-78; asst. supt. special transp. City of San Diego, 1978-79, supt. paratransit div., 1979-80, asst. to city mgr., 1980—; admitted to Calif. bar, 1981; cons. U. Calif., Berkeley, also fed., state agencies; guest lectr. N.W. Mich. Coll., San Diego State U. Vice pres. N.W. Mich. Coll. Community Assn., 1973; bd. dirs. Asgard Sheltered Workshop, 1971-73, San Diego County Assn. for Retarded, 1976—, Foster Grandparent Program, San Diego County, 1976-79, Advocates Associated, 1979—. Mem. Nat. Park and Recreation Assn., Internat. Assn. Fin. Planners, Bus. and Profl. Women's Club (v.p. 1973, Young Career Woman of Year 1973), Women's Legal Soc., San Diego Bar Assn. Methodist. Author: Volunteers and the Aged, 1972. Office: 121 Broadway 658 San Diego CA 92101

BALSIGER, DAVID WAYNE, author, lit. agt., advt. agy. exec., educator; b. Monroe, Wis., Dec. 14, 1945; s. Leon C. and Dorothy May (Meythaler) B.; student Pepperdine Coll., Los Angeles, 1964-66. Cypress Jr. Coll., 1966, Chapman Coll. World Campus Afloat, Orange, Calif., 1967-68, Internat. Coll., Copenhagen, Denmark, 1968; B.B.A., Nat. U., San Diego, 1977; L.H.D., Lincoln Meml. U., Harrogate, Tenn., 1977; m. Robyne Lynn Betzsold, July 10, 1982; children by previous marriage—Lisa Atalie, Lori Faith. Teller, trainee Bank Am., Los Angeles, Santa Ana and El Toro, Calif., 1964-66; chief photographer, feature writer Anaheim (Calif.) Bull., 1968-69; publisher, editor Money Doctor, consumer mag., Anaheim 1969-70; media dir. World Evangelism, San Diego, 1970-72; dir. mktg. Logos Internat. Christian, book publishers, Plainfield, N.J., 1972-73; news editor Logos Jour., nat. religious mag., 1972-73; owner Balsiger Lit. Service, Costa Mesa, 1972-77; pres., dir. Master Media, mktg. agy., Costa Mesa, Calif., 1973-75; v.p. communications Donald S. Smith Assocs., advt. agy., Anaheim, Calif., 1975-77, v.p., 1982—; asso. producer, dir. research devel. Sunn Classic Pictures, Inc., Los Angeles and Salt Lake City, 1976-78; owner Writeway Profl. Lit. Assocs., Santa Ana, 1978—; owner Balsiger Enterprises, investments, Costa Mesa, 1978—; pub. Mini Guide Books, Santa Ana, 1979-80; vis. prof. Nat. U., San Diego, 1977-79. Republican candidate for Congress from 38th Calif. dist., 1978, for Costa Mesa City Council, 1980; campaign mgr. James E. Johnson U.S. Senate campaign, 1974; press agt. John G. Schmitz congl. campaign, 1972, Gordon Bishop supr. campaign, Orange County, 1970; press agt. asst. Ronald Reagan for Gov., Calif. statewide, 1966. Mem. World Affairs Council Orange County and San Diego, 1969-70. Assoc. Mem. Calif. Republican Central Com., 1969-70; mem. Calif. Rep. Assembly, 1976-77, Rep. Assocs. Orange County, 1977, 82—; sustaining mem. Rep. Nat Com. Bd. dirs. Chapman Coll. World Campus Afloat, 1967; bd. dirs. Chrisma Ministries. Orange, Calif., 1969-73. Recipient Leadership citation Pepperdine Coll. Alumni Bd., 1965; Vietnam appreciation citation Am. Soldiers in Vietnam, 1966; Key of City of Costa Mesa (Calif.), 1977; George Washington Honor medal Freedom's Found. for film Lincoln Conspiracy, 1978; named writer of month Calif. Writer, 1967; elected to Lit. Hall of Fame, 1977; lic. talent agt., Calif.; lic. real estate agt., Calif.; cert. diamond counselor, Calif. Mem. Nat. Writers Club (profl.), Internat. Assn. Fin. Planners, Religion in Media Assn., Am. Entrepeneurs Assn. Author: The Satan Seller, 1972 (Nat. Religious Best Sellers List 1973); The Back Side of Satan, 1973; Noah's Ark; I Touched It, 1974 (Word and Chrisma Book Club selections 1974-75); One More Time, 1974; It's Good to Know, 1975; In Search of Noah's Ark, 1976 (Nat. Best Sellers List); The Lincoln Conspiracy, 1977 (Nat. Best Sellers List); Beyond Defeat (George Washington honor medal 1979), 1978; On the Other Side, 1978; Mini Guide Books, 1979; Presidential Biblical Scoreboard, 1980; Mistah Abe, 1983. Historian, tech. cons. In Search of Noah's Ark, 1976; dir., co-star Operation Thanks, 1965; hist. research dir., tech. adviser The Lincoln Conspiracy, 1977; researcher The Bermuda Triangle, 1977; adminstrv. researcher NBC-TV series The Life and Times of Grizzly Adams, 1977. Clubs: 552 Hoag Hosp., U.S. Senatorial. Address: PO Box 10428 Costa Mesa CA 92627

BALSTER, CLIFFORD ARTHUR, geologist; b. Monmouth, Iowa, Feb. 27, 1922; s. Delbert Clarence and Tessie (Wilcox) B.; B.S., Iowa State U., 1948, M.S., 1950; postgrad. U. Mo., Oreg. State U.; m. Norma Anne Petersen, June 19, 1943; children—Steven W., Linda J., Gwen K., Kenneth L. Instr. U. Mo., Columbia, 1950-51; stratigrapher Pure Oil Co., Billings, Mont., 1951-54; div. mgr. Am. Stratigraphic Co., Billings, 1954-60; carbonate research group leader Continental Oil Co., Ponca City, Okla., 1960-61; research geologist U.S. Dept. Agr., Corvallis, Oreg., 1961-67; research petroleum geologist Mont. Bur. Mines, Billings, 1967-74; cons. geologist, Billings, 1974-77; exploration mgr. Burlington-No., Billings, 1977-79; cons. geologist, Billings, 1979—; pres. Cana Corp., 1982—. Served with U.S. Army Air Corps, 1942-45. Fellow Geol. Soc. Am.; mem. Am. Assn. Petroleum Geologists, Mont. Geol. Soc. (dir. 1976—), Am. Inst. Profl. Geologists (past pres. Mont. sect.). Club: Masons. Contbr. articles in field to profl. jours. Home: Route 1 Fishtail MT 59028

BALTHASER, JAMES LEE, gas utility ofcl.; b. Fremont, Ohio, Aug. 5, 1948; s. Robert G. and Gwendolyn H. Balthaser; B.Indsl. Engring., Ohio State U., 1971, M.S., 1971; m. Anita Ruth Young, July 14, 1979. Gas supply engr. Consumers Power Co., Jackson, Mich., 1971-72, methods engr. gas distbn. dept., 1972-73; chief of natural gas Public Utilities Commn. Ohio, Columbus, 1975-77, chief of rates, tariffs, 1977-79; dir. state regulation Mountain Fuel Supply Co., Salt Lake City, 1979-82, mgr. regulatory affairs, 1982—. Recipient commendation for service during energy crisis Ohio Gov., 1976-77. Mem. Am. Gas Assn. (rate reform task force 1979-81), Pacific Coast Gas Assn., Tau Beta Pi, Phi Eta Sigma, Alpha Pi Mu. Methodist. Club: Salt Lake Athletic. Home: 7990 S Oak Creek Dr Sandy UT 84092 Office: Mountain Fuel Supply Co 180 E First S Salt Lake City UT 84139

BALTHAZOR, ALBERT, JR., optometrist; b. Fond du Lac, Wis., Jan. 11, 1925; s. Albert Francis and Ernestina Alvina (Smith) B.; m. LaVerne R. Nelson, Aug. 30, 1952; children—Loren, Dean, Michael, Timothy. Student U. Wis., 1942-43, 46-47; O.D., Ill. Coll. Optometry, 1949. Gen. practice optometry, Fond du Lac, 1949-78, Apache Junction, Ariz., 1978-82, Mesa, Ariz., 1982—; cons. Fond du Lac County Mental Health Ctr., 1973-78; vision screening on Seattle Mariners basketball team, U.S. Olympic archery team. Bd. dirs. Fond du Lac County Republican party, 1965-67; county chmn. Wis. Congress Conservatives; mem. sch. bd. Christ the King Sch., Mesa, 1982—. Served with USAF, 1943-46; to capt. USAFR, 1950-58. Fellow Coll. Optometrists in Vision Devel. (state dir.); mem. Am. Optometric Assn., Central Area Optometric Soc. (pres. 1981-82), Optometric Extension Program, Jaycees (Outstanding Mem. Fond du Lac 1961), VFW, Am. Legion. Roman Catholic. Clubs: Lions; KC (Mesa). Home: 1013 N Barkley St Mesa AZ 85203 Office: 8001 E Apache Trail Mesa AZ 85207

BAMFORD, DOUGLAS CHARLES, restaurant chain executive; b. Salem, Oreg., June 5, 1944; s. Edwin Albert and Francis Alice (Douglas) B.; m. Kathryn Williams, June 10, 1967; chidren—Amy Elizabeth, Gregory Douglas. B.A. in History, Willamette U., 1967; M.B.A., Portland State U., 1971. Product promotion mgr. Omark Industries, Portland, Oreg., 1971-72; account exec. David Evans Advt., Portland, 1972-73; dir. mktg. Farrell's Ice Cream div. Marriott Corp., Portland, 1973-76; dir. mktg. Skipper's Seafood Restaurants, Bellevue, Wash., 1976-79, v.p. mktg., 1979—; lectr. Wash. State U. Hotel Restaurant Sch. Mem. March of Dimes Walkathon Com., 1979-83. Served to 2d lt. USAR, 1967-73. Named Nat. Exec. of Yr., 1980, Skipper's, Inc. Mem. Am. Mktg. Assn. (dir. 1975, Seattle chpt. Mktg. Firm of Yr. 1980, Portland chpt. Mktg. Firm of Yr. 1975), Beta Theta Pi. Clubs: Bellevue Athletic, Bellevue Racquet. Office: 14450 NE 29th Place Suite 200 Bellevue WA 98007

BANCROFT, PETER, author, photographer; b. Tucson, May 5, 1916; s. Roy Francis and Lillian (Walker) B.; A.B., U. Calif. at Santa Barbara, 1941; M.S., U. So. Calif., 1947; Ed.D., No. Colo. U., 1957; m. Virginia Pomeroy, Aug. 21, 1940; children—Martha Bancroft Melino, Edward, Robert, Barbara Bancroft Barnard. Tchr., Costa Mesa, Calif., 1941-42; vice prin. pub. schs., Mojave, Calif., 1942-43; supt. schs., Vineland, Calif., 1943-55; dir. student employment No. Colo. State U., Greeley, 1955-56; dir. edn. U.S. Dept. State, Bolivia, 1956-58; prin., Beverly Hills, Calif., 1958-59; supt. schs., Lincoln, Calif., 1959-61, Cajon Valley dist., El Cajon, Calif., 1961-66, Livermore, Calif., 1966-69; prin. Intermediate Sch., Ramona, Calif., 1969-73; field rep. Pala Properties, Inc., Fallbrook, Calif., 1973-75; photographer Hanna Barbera Studios, Hollywood, Calif., 1966. Pres., El Cajon Girl's Club, 1964-65. Bd. dirs. Stockton (Calif.) Symphony Assn., 1960-61. Served with USMCR, 1935-39. Named Prof. of Year, Ministry of People, Bolivia, 1961; personal gem collection winner Am. Fedn. Mineral Socs., 1968, 73. Mem. Calif., Am. adminstrs. assns., Alumni Assn. U. Calif. (pres. 1954). Clubs: Elks, Rotary (pres. local club 1972-73), Grange. Author: World Finest Minerals and Crystals, 1973; also articles. Home: 3538 Oak Cliff Dr Fallbrook CA 92028

BANDER, RICKI SUE, psychologist; b. N.Y.C., May 26, 1953; s. Leslie C. and Leona B. B.A., CCNY, 1975; M.A., Ohio State U., 1977, Ph.D., 1979. Lic. psychologist, Wis., Calif. Staff psychologist U. Wis.-La Crosse, 1979-81; dir. human behavior U. So. Calif.-Calif. Presbyn. Intercommunity Hosp. Family Practice Residency Program, Los Angeles, 1981—; pvt. practice psychology. Mem. Am. Psychol. Assn., Soc. Tchrs. Family Medicine, Western Psychol. Assn. Office: 12401 E Washington Blvd Family Practice Ctr Whittier CA 90602

BANDROWSKI, JAMES FRANCIS, strategic planning executive; b. Providence, Feb. 23, 1948; s. Stanley and Stella B.; B.E., Villanova U., 1969; M.S., N.J. Inst. Tech., 1973; M.B.A., NYU, 1976. Engr., new products coordinator Becton Dickinson & Co., Rutherford, N.J., 1969-73; mgmt. cons. Stone & Webster, N.Y.C., 1973-75; sr. planner Kaiser Industries, Oakland, Calif., 1975-77; pres. Med-A-Tape Co., producer and pub. cassette tapes on sports, 1977—; dir. strategic planning Systron Donner Corp., Concord, Calif., 1978-79; dir. planning Di Giorgio Corp., San Francisco 1979—. Mem. Assn. Corp. Growth, Corp. Planners Assn., Planning Execs. Inst. Republican. Club: Orinda, Epicureans. Home: 260 Summit Rd Walnut Creek CA 94598 Office: 1 Maritime Plaza Suite 2300 San Francisco CA 94111

BANDSMA, JOHN JAMES, purchasing agt.; b. Courtland, Wis., Nov. 6, 1920; s. Paul and Anna B.; B.S., U. Denver, 1945; m. Katherine Tena Tolsma, June 26, 1946; children—Beverly Jean, Nancy Anne, Peggy Joanne. Tax accountant Internat. Trust Co., Denver, 1944-47; partner Bandsma & Son, Denver, 1947-56; purchasing agt., office mgr. O. W. Walvoord Inc., Denver, 1956-60; purchasing agt. Stearns Roger Corp., Denver, 1961-66, St. Luke's Hosp., Denver, 1966-79; sr. purchasing agt., contract adminstr. Morrison-Knudsen Co., Inc., Boise, Idaho, now Burlingame, Calif., 1979—. Treas., bd. dirs. Univ. Hills Christian Nursing Home, 1974-76, pres., 1977-78; bd. dirs. Bethesda Community Mental Health Center, 1979—. Mem. Am. Purchasing Soc. (cert. purchasing profl. exec.), Internat. Materials Mgmt. Soc. (cert. materials mgr.). Home: 631 Comet Dr Foster City CA 94404 Office: 1350 Old Bayshore Hwy Burlingame CA 94010

BANDT, PAUL DOUGLAS, radiologist, educator; b. Milbank, S.D., June 22, 1938; s. Lester H. and Edna L. (Sogn) B.; B.S. in Edn., U. Minn., 1960, B.S. in Medicine, 1966, M.D., 1966; m. Inara von Rostas; children—Douglas, Peggy, Jennifer. Intern, USPHS Hosp., San Francisco, 1966-68, nuclear medicine fellow, 1967-68; resident in radiology Stanford Med. Center, 1969-72; practice medicine, specializing in radiology, Las Vegas, 1972—; mem. staff Desert Springs, So. Nev. Meml. hosps., Las Vegas; adj. prof. radiobiology U. Nev., Las Vegas, 1968-69, adj. prof. radiologic tech., 1973—. Diplomate Am. Bd. Radiology, Am. Bd. Nuclear Medicine. Mem. Am. Coll. Nuclear Medicine, Am. Coll. Radiology, A.M.A., Clark County Med. Soc. (dir. 1974—), Phi Chi, Alpha Omega Alpha. Contbr. articles on radiology to profl. jours. Home: 3812 Topaz St Las Vegas NV 89121 Office: 901 Rancho Ln Las Vegas NV 89106

BANDY, ALICE MARIE, publishing company executive; b. Dayton, Ohio, Aug. 14, 1947; d. Philip C. and Phyllis B. (Walker) Dow; m. G. Thomas Bandy, Feb. 19, 1972. B.A., U. Colo., 1969; M.B.A., Pepperdine U., 1980. Sales asst. Cahners Pub., Los Angeles, 1973-75, office mgr., 1975-76; prodn. asst. Archtl. Digest Mag., Los Angeles, 1976-77; adminstrv. asst. Knapp Press, Los Angeles, 1977-79, adminstrv. mgr., 1979-81, v.p., gen. mgr., 1981-82, pres., 1982—; v.p. Knapp Communications Corp., 1982—. Mem. Direct Mail Mktg. Assn., Assn. Am. Pubs., So. Calif. Book Builders. Office: Knapp Press 5900 Wilshire Blvd Los Angeles CA 90036

BANDY, FREDERICK EARL, lawyer; b. Merced, Calif., May 20, 1949; s. Frederick G. and Kelly Alyne (Daves) B.; m. Rosalie Joan Smith, Feb. 19, 1983. Student Mich. State U., 1967-68; A.B. in Econs., UCLA, 1972; J.D., U. Pacific, 1976. Bar: Calif. 1976. Staff atty. Pub. Defender's Office, Madera, Calif., 1977-81; sole practice, Madera, 1981-82; ptnr. Musso, Cooke, Peterson & Bandy, Madera, 1982—. Mem. Madera County Hist. Soc.; chmn. fin. com. Madera United Methodist Ch., 1980-82, lay leader, 1983. Mem. ABA, Madera County Bar Assn. (pres. 1982, sec. 1978-79), Phi Eta Sigma. Republican. Clubs: Sunrise Rotary, Madera Camera. Office: Musso Cooke Peterson & Bandy 900 E Almond Ave Suite 3B Madera CA 93637

BANGART, GARY LEE, aerospace company executive; b. Billings, Mont., Oct. 1, 1934; s. David Robert and Etta Mae (Straight) B.; B.S.E.E., San Jose State U., 1973; m. Shirley Anne Young, June 8, 1957; children—Kurt Vaughn, Glenn Eric. With RCA Service Co., 1959-61; with Lockeed Missiles and Space Co., Sunnyvale, Calif., 1961—, reliability engr., sr. research engr., group engr. 1964-74, program engring. mgr., 1974-75, 77-78, chief systems engr. advanced devel. programs, 1975-77, 78-80, asst. program mgr., 1980—. Served with USAF, 1953-57. Mem. IEEE, Nat. Mgmt. Assn. Democrat. Baptist. Office: PO Box 504 Sunnyvale CA 94086

BANGERT, HAROLD WALLACE, investment banker; b. Sheldon, N.D., Oct. 12, 1905; s. Charles George and Sarah Elizabeth (Wallace) B.; student, U.N.D., 1923-28; J.D., George Washington U., 1931; m. Mary K. Jeffries, Sept. 5, 1931; 1 son, Charles Jeffries. Admitted to N.D. bar, 1934, D.C. bar, 1931; atty. FTC, Chgo., 1931-33; mem. firm Bangert & Bangert, Fargo, N.D., 1937-76; atty., dist. dir., nat. dir. Price Control Bds. Office Price Adminstrn., Fargo, Chgo., also Washington, 1942-46; organizer, chmn. Statesman Group Inc., Des Moines, 1959-72; organizer, chmn. Bangert & Co. Investment Bankers, San Francisco, 1971-75; dir., chmn. emeritus Bangert, Dawes, Reade, Davis & Thom, San Francisco, 1975—; organizer, dir., chmn. emeritus Am. Life & Casualty Ins. Co., Fargo, N.D., 1949—. Mem. Am., N.D. bar assns., Phi Delta Phi, Delta Tau Delta. Republican. Club: Chicago. Home: 839 Terra California Dr Walnut Creek CA 94595 Office: 1138 Taylor St San Francisco CA 94108

BANGERTER, NORMAN H., building contractor; b. Granger, Utah, Jan. 4, 1933; s. Isabelle (Bawden) B.; m. Colleen Monson; children—Garrett, Ann, Jordan, Blair, Alayne, Adam. Student, U. Utah, Brigham Young U., Pres., Bangerter and Hendrickson Enterprises, Inc., Utah, v.p. B. and H. Real Estate; sec. Dixie-Six Land Devel. Co.; pres. N.H.B. Constrn. Co., West Valley City, Utah; mem. Utah Ho. of Reps., speaker, 1981-84. Served with Armed Forces; Korea. Recipient Outstanding Legislator award V.F.W., 1981; Disting. Service to Home Bldg. Industry award, 1979; Outstanding Businessman award West Valley C. of C. Republican. Mormon. Home: 4059 S Montaia Dr West Valley City UT 84119 Office: 3251 W 4100 South West Valley City UT 84119

BANICK, THEODORE JOHN, aviation safety educator, consultant; b. Chgo., Dec. 11, 1932. M.S. in Safety, U. So. Calif., 1982. Lic. airline transport pilot FAA; cert. safety profl. Commd. 2d lt. U.S. Air Force, 1954, advanced through grades to col., 1980, chief Flight Safety div. Air Force Insp. and Safety Ctr., 1977-80, ret., 1980; teaching assoc. U. So. Calif., Los Angeles, 1980—. Decorated Legion of Merit, D.F.C. with one oak leaf cluster, Air medal with two oak leaf clusters, Meritorious Service medal, Air Force Commendation medal. Mem. Am. Soc. Safety Engrs. (chpt. pres.), Air Safety Investigators. Office: USC Safety Center 63 ABG/DPE Norton AFB CA 90409

BANISTER, JAMES HENRY, JR., aerospace company executive; b. Springfield, Mo., June 18, 1930; s. James Henry and Frances Boyden (Williams) B.; m. Sara Lee Cinegran, Jan. 26, 1956; children—Jeffrey, James, Mark, Robert, Douglas. B.S., MIT, 1951; postgrad. Golden Gate Coll. Sch. Law, 1957-58. Mgr. contract adminstrn. SRI, Inc., Menlo Park, Calif., 1953-54; contracts mgr. Physics Internat., San Leandro, Calif., 1964-68, v.p. adminstrn., 1968-70, sr. v.p. fin. and adminstrn., 1972—; pres. Cintra Inc., Sunnyvale, Calif., 1968-70; dir. Spectromagnetics, Inc., PZ Technology Inc., Cintra Corp.; sec.-treas. Pulsar Products Inc. Served to 1st lt. USAF, 1951-53. Republican. Episcopalian.

BANK, MILTON HAROLD, II, aviation safety and aeronautical engineering educator; b. Brockton, Mass., Aug. 11, 1935; s. Milton Harold and Fern Elaine (Richey) B.; m. Linda Hollis, Apr. 12, 1958; children—Baynes W., Milton H. B.S., U.S. Naval Acad., 1957; B.S. in Aero. Engring., Naval Postgrad. Sch., 1964; Aero. Engr., Stanford U., 1967; M.S., Ga. Tech., 1970, Ph.D., 1971. Registered profl. engr., Calif. Commd. ensign U.S. Navy, 1957, advanced through grades to lt. comdr., 1965; ret. 1968; assoc. prof. aviation safety and aero. engring. Naval Postgrad. Sch., Monterey, Calif., 1971—. Decorated Air Medal with gold stars (2). Mem. AIAA, Systems Safety Soc., Nat. Fencing Coaches Assn. Am., Soc. Exptl. Stress Analysis. Presbyterian. Office: Code 034 BT Naval Postgrad Sch Monterey CA 93940

BANKS, GEORGE WAYNE, JR., holding co. exec.; b. Dallas, Feb. 13, 1951; s. George Wayne and Beverly Dolores (Sikking) B.; student Valley Coll., 1969-71; Pierce Coll., 1971-73; Calif. State Coll., Northridge, 1973-76. With G. W. B. Cos., Los Angeles, 1971—; owner, mgr. Pacific State Plumbing, Los Angeles, 1971—, Food Service, Inc., Carmel, Calif., 1975—; chmn. Internat. Bankshares, Woodland Hills, Calif., 1979—, also dir.; dir. Western Mechanical, Pacific State Plumbing, Food Service Inc., D.B.A. Tech. Cons. Mem. So. Calif. Restaurant Assn., Calif. Contractors Assn., Calif. Young Republicans, Beverly Hills Republican Club. Club: Lincoln. Home: 190 Saddlebow Rd Bell Canyon CA 91307 Office: 6355 Topanga Blvd Woodland Hills CA 91364

BANKS, HAMPDEN OSBORNE, JR., physical chemist; b. N.Y.C., Nov. 12, 1922; s. Hampden Osborne and Muriel Irving (Sage) B.; student Hofstra Coll., 1940-41, Mich. State Coll., 1943-44; B.S. in Inorganic Chemistry, Mo. Sch. Mines and Metallurgy, 1949, M.S. in Phys. Chemistry, 1950; postgrad. Oak Ridge Inst. Nuclear Study, 1957; m. Jean Marie Binks, Oct. 21, 1960. Asso. research chemist Brookhaven Nat. Lab., 1950-56; asst. project mgr. Nuclear div. Martin Co., Balt., 1956-59, asst. mgr. Corporate div., Los Angeles, 1959-60; projects dir. Royal Research Corp., Dublin, Calif., 1960-63; mem. tech. staff F.M.P. Integration Lab., SEID div. TRW Def. and Space Systems Group, Redondo Beach, 1963—. Mem. staff Med. Nuclear Consultants, 1957; advisor Minuteman ICBM, MX and ASMS Missile on-board and ground power systems. Served with USAAF, 1941-43; with AUS, 1943-45; ETO. Mem. Electrochem. Soc., Air Force Assn., Alpha Chi Sigma. Contbr. articles to profl. publs. Patentee chemistry, physics, metallurgy and engring. design fields. Research on missile and oceanographic electric power; developer separation techniques for radioiodine, radiofluorine and radiomagnesium for use in med. and dental nuclear research, prototype cesium generator for deep-ocean power, prototype strontium generator for Arctic weather sta.; discovered cesium borosilicate (safe RTG nuclear fuel). Home: 5102 Cornell Ave Westminster CA 92683 Office: TRW Systems 1 Space Park Redondo Beach CA 90278

BANKS, HARVEY OREN, cons. civil engr.; b. Chaumont, N.Y., Mar. 29, 1910; s. Harry Roseboom and Carrie Ethel (Halliday) B.; B.S.C.E. magna cum laude, Syracuse (N.Y.) U., 1930; M.S., Stanford U., 1955; m. Mary Ida Morgan, Dec. 14, 1934; children—Robert Stephen, Philip Oren, Kimball Morgan. Asst. state engr., then state engr. State of Calif., 1953-56; dir. water resources State of Calif., 1956-60; v.p., then chmn. Leeds, Hill & Jewett, Inc., cons. engrs., San Francisco, 1961-69; pres., owner Harvey O. Banks, Cons. Engr., Inc., Belmont, Calif., 1970-76; pres. water resources div. Camp Dresser & McKee Inc., environ. engrs., Walnut Creek, Calif., 1977-82; pres. Harvey O. Banks, Cons. Engr., Inc., Belmont, Calif., 1983—; chmn. bd. dirs. Systems Assos., Inc., 1970-76; bd. dirs. Belmont County Water Dist., 1972-80; cons., lectr. in field. Served with U.S. Army, 1942-45. Recipient George Arents Pioneer medal Syracuse U., 1961. Diplomate Am. Acad. Environ. Engrs. Fellow Am. Cons. Engrs. Council, ASCE (hon. mem., Royce J. Tipton award 1973, Julian Hinds award 1976); mem. Nat. Acad. Engring., Am. Water Works Assn. (hon.), Water Pollution Control Fedn. Methodist. Home and Office: 3 Kittie Ln Belmont CA 94002

BANKS, HOBART MELVIN, JR., psychologist; b. Muskogee, Okla., Nov. 13, 1925; s. Hobart Melvin and Jamie Ann (Wiley) B.; B.A., U. Minn., 1952, Ph.D., 1959; M.A., U. Calif. at Davis, 1973, Ph.D., 1982; m. Dorothy Elvira Wells, Mar. 26, 1966; 1 dau., Anna Elvira. Clin. psychologist Willmar (Minn.) State Hosp., 1959-61, Sonoma (Calif.) State Hosp., 1961-63, Deuel Vocat. Instn., Tracy, Calif., 1963-67; supr. clin. psychology Calif. Dept. Corrections, Sacramento, 1967-74, asst. dir. psychiat. outpatient clinic dept. corrections, parole and community services div., San Francisco, 1975—; assoc. Children's Hosp., San Francisco, 1980—; cons. Kaiser Found. Research Inst., 1978—. Mem. edn. com. San Francisco Assn. Mental Health, 1968-70. Bd. dirs. St. Lukes Parish Sch., 1973-79; trustee Cathedral Sch. Boys, 1974-80. Served with USAF, 1944-46, 50-51. King Gustav scholar, 1949-50. Mem. Am. Psychol. Assn. (com. on speciality practice and vis. psychologist 1972), Am. Assn. Correctional Psychologists, Psi Chi. Episcopalian. Editorial bd. Criminal Justice and Behavior, 1974—. Home: 2 Amber Dr San Francisco CA 94131 Office: 1050 Ferry Bldg San Francisco CA 94111

BANKS, JAMES ALBERT, educator; b. Marianna, Ark., Sept. 24, 1941; s. Matthew and Lula (Holt) B.; A.A., Chgo. City Coll., 1963; B.E., Chgo. State U., 1964; M.A., Mich. State U., 1967, Ph.D., 1969; m. Cherry Ann McGee, Feb. 15, 1969; children—Angela Marie, Patricia Ann. Elementary tchr. Francis W. Parker Sch., Chgo., 1965-66; asst. prof. edn. U. Wash., Seattle, 1969-71, asso. prof., 1971-73, prof., 1973—, chmn. curriculum and instrn., 1982—; Disting. Scholar lectr. Kent State U., spring 1978, Ariz. State U., summer 1979; mem. com. examiners social studies Ednl. Testing Service, 1974-76; mem. Nat. Adv. Council Ethnic Heritage Studies, U.S. Office Edn., 1975-78; keynote speaker U.S.-Dutch Bicentennial Conf. on Multicultural Edn. and Tchr. Tng., Amersfoort, Netherlands, 1982; lectr. Brit. Acad., 1983. NDEA fellow, 1966-69; Spencer fellow Nat. Acad. Edn., 1973; Kellogg fellow, 1980-83; Rockefeller Found. research fellow, 1980. Mem. Nat. Council Social Studies (dir. 1973-74, v.p. 1980, pres.-elect 1981, pres. 1982, dir. 1983—), Council on Anthropology and Edn., Assn. Supervision and Curriculum Devel. (dir. 1976-80), Social Sci. Edn. Consortium (dir. 1976-79), Am. Ednl. Research Assn. Author: Teaching Strategies for the Social Studies, 2d edit., 1977; Teaching Strategies for Ethnic Studies, 1975, 2d edit., 1979, 3d edit., 1983; Black Self-Concept, 1972; Teaching the Black Experience, 1970; March Toward Freedom: A History of Black Americans, rev. edit., 1978; Teaching Ethnic Studies: Concepts and Strategies, 1973; Multiethnic Education: Practices and Promises, 1977; We Americans: Our History and People, 2 vols., 1982; (with others) Curriculum Guidelines for Multiethnic Education, 1976; Multiethnic Education: Theory and Practice, 1981; also chpts., articles, book revs.; editor: Education in the 80's: Multiethnic Education, 1980; co-editor: Teaching Social Studies to Culturally Different Children, 1971; Teaching the Language Arts to Culturally Different Children, 1971; guest editor Social Edn., 1982, Phi Delta Kappan, 1983; editorial bd. Rev. of Edn., Interracial Books for Children Bull. Home: 1333 NW 200th St Seattle WA 98177

BANKS, JOYCE PERRY (MRS. THURML L. BANKS), research asso.; b. Stillwater, Okla., July 17, 1930; d. Louis William and Lucille (Freeman) Perry; B.A., Fisk U., 1953; m. Thurml L. Banks, June 30, 1955; children—Joyce Lynn, Toni Aileen. Lab. technician Carver Inst., Tuskegee, Ala., 1953-55; research asso. U. Calif. Med. Center, San Francisco, 1955—. Chmn. evening vols. Mt. Zion Hosp., 1970-71; pres. Woman's Aux. to John Hale Med. Soc., 1970-72; chmn. personnel appeals com. U. Calif. Med. Center; bd. dirs. Hamlin Sch., 1973—; pres. bd. dirs. St. Luke's Parish Sch., 1973-79; mem. San Francisco Regional Tumor Found. Research grantee academic research com. U. Calif. Med. Center, 1971. Mem. Nat. Tissue Culture Assn. Democrat. Congregationalist. Clubs: Links (San Francisco); Jack and Jill Am. Contbr. articles to profl. jours. Home: 65 Corte Dorado Kentfield CA 94904

BANKS, RICHARD ALLEN, apparel co. exec.; b. Circleville, Ohio, Apr. 10, 1939; s. Carl E. and Nana L. (Watson) B.; student Ohio Wesleyan U., 1957-59; B.A., Ind. U., 1962; m. Rebecca Ann Robles, Sept. 4, 1971; children—Terri M., Scott H., Matthew R., Benjamin T., Channing R. Ohio, F & R Lazarus, Columbus, Ohio, 1964-66; v.p. mktg. Bobbie Brooks, Cleve., 1969-73; pres. S.F. Gold Co., San Francisco, 1973-75, Harris & Stroh, Hayward, Calif., 1975-77, women's wear div. Levi Strauss, San Francisco, 1980—. Mem. Republican Senatorial Adv. Com.; bd. dirs. Big Bros. of Peninsula. Recipient Outstanding Bus. Achievement award B.R.A.G., N.Y.C., 1980. Republican. Roman Catholic. Club: Bankers (San Francisco). Office: Lewis Plaza 1155 Battery St PO Box 7215 San Francisco CA 94120

BANKS, SHARON ELIZABETH, nurse, educator; b. Pitts., Apr. 5, 1950; d. John C. and Myrtle (Banks) Laughton. B.S. in Nursing, U. Pitts., 1974, M. Nursing, 1980. Critical care nurse Presbyn.-Univ. Hosp., Pitts., 1974-79, relief supr. critical care div., critical care instr., 1979-80; critical care educator Doctors Med. Ctr., Modesto, Calif., 1980-82; critical care nurse Lavina Hosp., Altadena, Calif., 1982—; cons. Doctors Med. Ctr., tchr. CPR, Am. Heart Assn. bd. dirs. Am. Lung Assn. of Valley Lode, 1981-82. Served to lt. (j.g.) USNR, 1983—. Mem. Am. Assn. Critical Care Nurses, Four County Council Educators, Female Execs., Am. Nurses Assn. (dir.). Democrat. Roman Catholic. Address: 280 E Del Mar Blvd Pasadena CA 91101

BANNING, JAMES HOWARD, university administrator, clinical psychologist; b. Horton, Kans., Jan. 24, 1938; s. Howard Thomas and Minnie Mae (Carter) B.; m. Carolyn Sue, Oct. 9, 1959; children—Sherri Sue, Michael James. A.B., William Jewell Coll., 1960; M.A., U. Colo., 1965, Ph.D., 1965. Dir., Univ. Counseling Center, U. Colo., 1968-70; project dir. Western Interstate Commn. for Higher Edn., Boulder, Colo., 1970-73; vice chancellor for student affairs U. Mo., Columbia, 1973-78; v.p. student affairs Colo. State U.-Ft. Collins, 1978—, assoc. prof. psychology, 1978—, assoc. prof. edn., 1979—. Bd. dirs. Ft. Collins (Colo.) Area C. of C. Mem. Am. Psychol. Assn., Nat. Assn. Student Personnel Adminstrn., Environ. Design Research Assn. Co-author monographs; contbr. chpts., numerous articles to profl. publs.; editor Campus Ecology, 1978—. Home: 1901 Bear Ct Fort Collins CO 80525 Office: 108 Adminstrn Colo State U Fort Collins CO 80523

BANTUVERIS, MIKE, consulting company executive; b. Racine, Wis., Dec. 25, 1935; s. Nickolas and Evangeline (Kallis) B.; m. R. Lois Enos, Dec. 30, 1959; children—Susan, Karen. B.B.A., U. Wis., 1963, M.B.A., 1964; postgrad. UCLA, 1978—. Dir. market devel. E&J Gallo Wine Co., Modesto, Calif, 1964-67; dir. long range planning, new enterprise mgr. Gen. Mills Co., Mpls., 1967-70; dir. acquisitions and new bus. devel. Internat. Multifoods, Mpls., 1970-73; v.p., dir. west coast ops. North Star Industries, Los Angeles, 1973-75; pres. founder InterQuest Inc., Woodland Hills, Calif., 1975—; instr. in field; dir. Hogan Holding Co. Served with U.S. Army, 1954-59. Vilas fellow, 1964. Sr. mem. Am. Soc. Appraisers; mem. Planning Execs. Inst., Am. Mgmt. Assn., Phi Beta Kappa, Beta Gamma Sigma, Phi Kappa Phi. Republican. Episcopalian. Office: 5955 DeSoto Ave Suite 256 Woodland Hills CA 91367

BAPTIST, OREN CECIL, energy cons.; b. Uniontown, Kans., Oct. 17, 1912; s. John Oliver and Iva Marie (Jones) B.; grad. Ft. Scott Jr. Coll., 1937; B.S., U. Kans., 1940, postgrad., 1940-41; m. Ellen Marie Bandy, Mar. 1, 1947; 1 dau., Linda Marie (Mrs. William J. Stockton). Asst. engr. U.S. C.E., Albuquerque, 1942-43; geologist-engr. Socony Mobil Oil Co., Bogota, Colombia, 1943-45; petroleum engr. Mobil Oil Co., Casper, Wyo., 1945-47; research engr., supr. U.S. Bur. Mines, Dept. Interior, Laramie, Wyo., 1947-67, research dir., San Francisco, 1967-75; dir. U.S. ERDA, San Francisco, 1975-76; fossil energy cons., 1976—; mem. joint U.S.-Soviet Union team for environ. protection in permafrost, Alaska Pipeline, 1976. Registered profl. engr., Wyo., Calif. Mem. Soc. Petroleum Engrs. (chmn. monograph com. 1969-71, mem. Anthony F. Lucas gold medal award com. 1980-84), Nat. Soc. Profl. Engrs., Am. Assn. Petroleum Geologists, Am. Petroleum Inst., Marin Geneal. Soc., Sigma Xi, Tau Beta Pi. Republican. Methodist. Elk. Club: Commonwealth (San Francisco). Author: The Baptist and Harden Families; co-author: Enhanced Oil Recovery; contbr. articles to profl. jours. Home and office: 396 Montecillo Rd San Rafael CA 94903

BAR, MEYER, elec. engr.; b. Java, Soerabaya, Dutch East Indies, Feb. 22, 1930; s. Moses Meyer and Rachel (Dwek) B.; B.A., U. Calif., Berkeley, 1954; M.S.E.E., U. So. Calif., 1961, Ed.D., 1979; m. Zita Fleur Levine, Sept. 12, 1954; children—Debra Jean, Michael Lawrence. Research engr. Northrop Corp., 1958-60; group leader Ryan Electronics, 1960-61; tech. specialist Autonetics, 1961-68; project mgr. Guidance Tech., Santa Monica, Calif., 1968-69; sr. scientist Signal Galaxies, Northridge, Calif., 1969-70; engring. and fin. cons., Los Angeles, 1971-80; project engr. TRW Systems, Redondo Beach, Calif., 1980—. Mem. Phi Delta Kappa, Delta Epsilon. Jewish. Patentee in field. Office: 1 Space Park Redondo Beach CA 90278

BARANEK, PAUL PETER, agriculturist; b. Wynn, Pa., Feb. 18, 1914; s. Joseph and Sophia (Koltas) B.; B.S., U. Calif. at Davis, 1936, teaching certificate, 1937, M.Edn., 1946; m. Marie Agatha Herzog, Aug. 18, 1937 (dec. 1974); children—Jeanne Marie Baranek Olmstead, Robert Paul, Barbara May Baranek Plaskett, John Peter. Dir. inst. vocat. agr. Escalon (Calif.) High Sch., 1937-42; mgr., operator Delta Dairy, Courtland, Calif., 1942-45; land use specialist Delta dist., Bur. Reclamation, Sacramento, Stockton, Calif., 1946-50; regional weed specialist Bur. Reclamation, Sacramento 1950-53; farm adviser Agrl. Extension Service U. Calif., Madera, 1953-74, agriculturist emeritus, 1974—; cons. research com. Calif. Raisin Adv. Bd., 1958—, grading com. Fed. Raisin Adv. Bd., 1965—; ofcl. judge vine judging contest Future Farmers of Am., (Fresno Calif.) State, 1955-83. Advancement chmn. Sequoia council Boy Scouts Am., 1953-62, counselor, 1953-62. Mem. Am. Soc. Enologists, Young Men's Inst., Alpha Gamma Rho, Alpha Zeta. Democrat. Roman Catholic. Club: Commonwealth California (San Francisco). Contbr. articles to profl. jours. Address: 511 Barsotti Ave Madera CA 93637

BARASCH, STEPHEN BENNETT, architect, interior designer; b. Los Angeles, May 9, 1949; s. Buddy R. and Shirley Lee (Stock) B.; B.Arch. with honors, U. Ariz., 1971; M.Arch., Rice U., 1972; m. Janine Nina Nussbaum, May 7, 1972; children—Shauna, Ross. Archtl. designer William L. Pereira & Assos., Los Angeles, 1969-70; sr. archtl. designer The Oglesby Group, Inc., Dallas, 1972-73; project mgr., sr. architect Flower Mound New Town Ltd., Dallas, 1973-74; postgrad. research Archtl. Assn. London, 1975-76; dir. design Robert L. Carli & Assos., Los Angeles, 1976-77; pres. Barasch Architects and Assos., Inc., Pasadena, Calif., 1977—; vis. lectr. U. Tex., Dallas, 1973-74; mem. design rev. com. Parkside Indsl. Center and City of Pasadena. Mem. AIA, Calif. Council Architects, Tex. Soc. Architects, Tavistock Inst. Human Relations, Environ. Design Research Assn., Nat. Council Archtl. Registration Bds., Pasadena C. of C. (dir.), San Marino Tennis Found. Democrat. Jewish. Author: The Learning Environments Resource Book, 1970; The Social and Behavioral Characteristics of Recreational Facilities Planning, 1972; Recreational Planning for New Communities. Address: 25 N Mentor Ave Pasadena CA 91106

BARASH, ANTHONY HARLAN, lawyer; b. Galesburg, Ill., Mar. 18, 1943; s. Burrel B. and Rosalyne J. (Silver) B.; m. Jean E. Anderson, May 17, 1965; children—Elizabeth, Christopher, Katherine, Andrew. A.B. cum laude, Harvard Coll., 1965; J.D., U. Chgo., 1968. Bar: Calif. 1969. Assoc., Irell & Manella, Los Angeles, 1968-71; assoc. Cox, Castle & Nicholson, Los Angeles, 1971-74, ptnr., 1975-80; ptnr. Barash & Hill, Los Angeles, 1980—; dir. Bank of Beverly Hills, Deauville Restaurants, Inc. Mem. vis. com. U. Chgo. Law Sch., 1982—; trustee Pitzer Coll., 1981—; nat. adv. bd. Ctr. Nat. Policy, 1981—; bd. dirs. Shelter Media, Inc., 1982—. Mem. State Bar Calif., ABA, Los Angeles County Bar Assn., Beverly Hills Bar Assn. (bd. dirs. found. 1979—, bd. govs. 1979-81), Pub. Counsel (dir. 1980—). Clubs: Regency (Los Angeles); Rotary (Century City, Calif.); Harvard of So. Calif. Home: 825 Amalfi Dr Pacific Palisades CA 90272 Office: 2029 Century Park E Suite 2050 Los Angeles CA 90067

BARAT, GEORGE, physician, med. researcher; b. Budapest, Hungary, Apr. 14, 1921; s. Emanuel and Maria I. (von Hauke) B.; came to U.S., 1956, naturalized, 1962; B.A., State Coll. Kolcsey, 1939; Ph.D., Pazmany U., Budapest, 1942, M.D., 1950; m. Susanna Donnenberg, Aug. 5, 1954; children—Adrienne Linda, Lynn Jennifer. Assoc. prof. pathophysiology Pazmany U., Budapest, 1947-50; practice medicine specializing in neuroendocrinology, Budapest, 1951-56, Beverly Hills, Calif., 1960—; ind. research scholar in endocrinology Hungarian Acad. Scis., Budapest, 1951-56; research fellow Thyroid Clinic, U. So. Calif., Los Angeles, 1957, Diabetes Tng. Center, Coll. Med. Evangelists, Los Angeles, 1959-60; cons. psychoneuroendocrinology, Beverly Hills, 1960—; dir. Hufeland Medicobiol. Inst., Los Angeles, 1962-66, Neuroendocrine Research Center, Stress Inst. of Beverly Hills, 1966—; co-chmn. research com. Santa Monica (Calif.) Hosp. Med. Center, 1973-74. Recipient Acad. Scholar award, 1953, 55; Endocrine and metabolism fellow, 1957, NIH research grantee, 1953, 55, 59-60. Fellow Am. Coll. Angiology, Am. Geriatrics Soc., Am. Acad. Psychosomatic Medicine; mem. Internat. Soc. Psychoneuroendocrinology, N.Y. Acad. Scis., Gerontol. Soc. Author: numerous books; contbr. numerous articles on research in neuroendocrinology to profl. jours. Home: PO Box 335 Beverly Hills CA 90210 Office: 435 N Bedford Dr Beverly Hills CA 90210

BARATTA-LORTON, ROBERT, educator; b. Fresno, Calif., June 19, 1939; s. Paul Vernon and Jean (Steinbeck) Lorton; B.A. in Econs. with honors, Stanford U., 1961; M.A. in Edn., U. Calif., Berkeley, 1968; widower. Classroom tchr., tchr. educationally handicapped, Calif., 1966-73; instr. Miller Math. State Specialized Tchr. Improvement Program, also Center Improvement Math. Edn., San Diego, 1971-74; co-founder, 1975, since chmn. bd. dirs., dir. Center Innovation in Edn., Saratoga, Calif.; pres., bd. govs. Center Grad. Coll., Saratoga, 1980—. Served to lt. USNR, 1963-66; Vietnam. Mem. Internat. Reading Assn., Nat. Council Tchrs. Math., Assn. Supervision and Curriculum Devel., Nat. Assn. Edn. Young Children, Council Exceptional Children, Calif. Math. Council. Author: Mathematics. . .A Way of Thinking, 1977. Office: 19225 Vineyard Ln Saratoga CA 95070

BARATTI, JOHN, JR., grocery store owner; b. Marion, Ark., Sept. 13, 1931; s. John and Novelle B. Baratti; B.B.A., Memphis State U., 1953; m. Bettye Sue Wright, Sept. 13, 1955; children—Jon Mark, Susan. Sales rep. E.L. Bruce Co., Memphis, 1953-55; owner Barattis Supermarket, Marion, Ark., 1955—. Alderman, Marion City Council, 1959—; deacon First Assembly of God Ch., West Memphis, 1967—. Served with USNR, 1952-59. Office: Barattis Supermarket 25 Military Rd Marion AR 72364

BARB, JENNIFER JACKSON, family therapist, nurse; b. Tampa, Fla., Aug. 30, 1942; d. Ellis and Clara (Yeomans) Jackson; B.S. in Nursing, Fla. A&M U., 1965; M.A., Chapman Coll., Orange, Calif., 1976; m. Arthur Lee Barb, June 18, 1966; 1 son, Christopher Arthur. Staff and charge nurse Flint-Goodridge Hosp., New Orleans, 1966-68; counselor Chapman Coll. Community Clinic, 1976-77; family counselor A.&R. Assos., Inc., Orange and Los Angeles counties, 1977-80; tchr., counselor regional occupation program nursing asst./med. occupations Santa Ana (Calif. Unified Sch. Dist., 1979-81. Chmn. social services com. Orange County Grand Jury, 1976-77; active local Cub Scouts, 1977-79; treas. Cambridge Elem. Sch. PTA, 1978-79; adv. council Central Orange County YWCA, 1969-80; mem. Inland Urban League. Mem. Am. Assn. Family Therapists, Am. Vocat. Assn., Calif. Assn. Health Career Educators, Delta Sigma Theta. Office: Counseling Center San Bernardino Valley Coll 701 S Mt Vernon Ave San Bernardino CA 92410

BARBADIAN, JOHN CHARLES, hospital personnel administrator; b. Lowell, Mass., July 12, 1947; s. Garabed and Mary (Shakarian) B.; m. Terrie Patricia Goetz, June 30, 1973; children—Matthew, Traci. B.S. in Polit. Sci., Calif. State U.-Los Angeles, 1971, M.S. in Pub. Adminstrn., 1974. Cert. tchr., Calif. Prin. program analyst Los Angeles County Dept. Personnel, 1974-75, lead analyst task force for consolidation of Dept. of Community Devel., 1976-77; asst. dir. personnel Los Angeles County Dept. Health Services, 1977-78; dir. human resources Hollywood Presbyn. Med. Ctr., 1978-81; dir. personnel Hoag Meml. Presbyn. Hosp., Newport Beach, Calif., 1981—. Mem. Hosp. Personnel Mgmt. Assn., Am. Mgmt. Assn., So. Calif. Personnel Mgmt. Assn., Am. Soc. Hosp. Personnel Adminstrs., San Marino C. of C., Calif. State U. Alumni, Sigma Nu. Republican. Presbyterian. Club: Lions (San Marino). Home: 2464 Sherwood Rd San Marino CA 91108 Office: 301 Newport Blvd Newport Beach CA 92663

BARBARA, MAURICE EDWARD, finance company executive; b. N.Y.C., July 25, 1933; s. Salvatore Bruno and Carrie B.; m. Joanna, Oct. 7, 1957; 5 children. B.A. in Banking, NYU, 1950. C.P.A., 1962. Pres., Barlat Loan & Fin. Corp., United Fin. Corp., Santa Clara, Calif., Multi remote Mfg. Inc., Santa Clara, also chief exec. officer; lectr. Served to cpl., U.S.Army, 1953. Mem. Nat. Pub. Accts. Assn., Democrat. Roman

Catholic. Clubs: KC (treas.), Optimists (treas). Patentee wireless remote control. Home: 1180 Flying Fish Foster City CA 94404 Office: 2045 Martin Ave Suite 203 Santa Clara CA 95050

BARBEE, MARY K., educational administrator; b. North Kansas City, Mo., June 15; d. John C. and Virginia E. (Garton) Keenum; children—Mark, Mike, Mary Elizabeth, John Eric. B.A. in Secondary Edn., U. No. Colo.; M.A. in Counseling Edn., U. N.Mex. Tchr. Aspen (Colo.) Sch. Dist.; owner Peppermint Tree Confectionery, Aspen; asst. dean of students U. N.Mex., Albuquerque, 1977—. Pres. Aspen Hist. Soc., 1976-78; mem. exec. com. Nat. Panhellenic Conf., 1977-83, chmn., 1981-83. Mem. Nat. Assn. Women Deans and Counselors, Nat. Assn. Student Personnel Adminstrs., Sigma Sigma Sigma (exec. com.).

BARBER, BERNARD, psychologist; b. Bayonne, N.J., Oct. 7, 1929; s. Morris D. and Rose (Facter) B.; m. Shirley Gottlieb, Jan. 20, 1959; m. 2d Donna J. McGee, Apr. 14, 1979. A.A., Los Angeles City Coll., 1952; B.A., Calif. State U., 1954; Fil. kand, U. Stockholm, 1955; Ph.D., U. So. Calif., 1962. Cert. marriage, family and child counselor; cert. coll. tchr.; cert. psychologist; approved panel provider in psychology for crippled children's services, Calif.; cert. psychologist, Ariz. Rehab. officer in counseling and research Los Angeles County Sheriff's Dept., 1954-55; probation and parole officer U.S. Dist. Cts., 1955-56; social psychologist in labor relations and research Dan Johnston and Assocs., 1956-58; instr. in social psychology, social dynamics of abnormal behavior, Calif. State U., Los Angeles, 1958-59; psychologist in research and devel., psychotherapy, dept. alcoholic rehab. Los Angeles City Pub. Health Dept., 1959-60; pvt. practice clin. and social psychology, Los Angeles and Phoenix, 1959—; dept. psychologist Ariz. Dept. Pub. Safety, Phoenix, 1978-80; cons. psychologist Dept. Justice Bur. Prisons, 1965-67; instr., cons., Santa Monica Coll., 1967-70, Los Angeles County Sheriff's Dept., 1974-78, Simi Valley Police Dept., 1975-78; group instr. in marriage and alternative life styles UCLA, 1975-76; contract psychologist Maricopa County (Ariz.) Sheriff's Office, 1980-81; mem. expert panel U.S. Dist. Ct., 1977. Mem. Am. Psychol. Assn., Calif. State Psychol. Assn., Los Angeles County Psychol. Assn., Ariz. State Psychol. Assn., Maricopa Psychol. Assn., Am. Soc. Clin. Hypnosis. Office: 4614 E Shea Blvd Phoenix AZ 85028

BARBER, CYRIL JOHN, educator; b. Pretoria, South Africa, May 18, 1934; came to U.S., 1962, naturalized, 1976; s. Charles Stanley and Muriel (Radford) B.; B.R.E., Winnipeg (Man., Can.) Bible Coll., 1968, M.Th., Dallas Theol. Sem., 1967; M.A. in L.S., Rosary Coll., 1971; D.Min., Talbot Theol. Sem., 1979; came to U.S., 1962, naturalized, 1976; m. Aldyth Ayleen Aereboe, Apr. 13, 1957; children—Allan Martin, Stephen Marlin. Librarian, chmn. dept. Bible exposition Winnipeg Bible Coll., 1967-69; dir. library Trinity Evang. Div. Sch., Bannockburn, Ill., 1969-72; mem. faculty Rosemead Grad. Sch. Profl. Psychology, La Mirada, Calif., 1972—, dir. library, 1972-77, asst. prof., 1972-75, asso. prof., 1975-80; dir. libraries, prof. Internat. Christian Grad. U., Arrowhead Springs, Calif., 1980—; cons. in field; ordained to ministry Ind. Fundamental Chs. Am., 1963. Mem. ALA, Am. Theol. Library Assn., Royal Soc. Lit., Philos. Soc. Gt. Britain, Calif. Writers Guild, PEN, Beta Phi Mu. Republican. Author numerous books including: The Minister's Library, 1974; Searching for Identity, 1975; Nehemiah and the Dynamics of Effective Leadership, 1976; Vital Encounter, 1979; The Effective Parent, 1979; also articles. Office: PO Box 5181 Hacienda Heights CA 91745

BARBER, DANIEL MAXFIELD, educator; b. Chgo., Aug. 3, 1944; s. Timothy Lawrence and Katharine Jean (McEvoy) B.; B.Ed., U. Miami, 1968, M.A., 1970; Ed.S., Fla. Atlantic U., 1973, Ed.D., 1974. Adminstrv. asst. Center for Urban Studies, U. Miami, Coral Gables, Fla., 1969; exec. dir. S. Fla. Regional Planning Council, Miami, 1970-72; instr. Marymount Coll., Boca Raton, Fla., 1973; asst. dir. Gov.'s Office Manpower and Human Devel., Springfield, Ill., 1974-75; asso. prof. Center for Pub. Policy, Calif. State U., Long Beach, 1975—; Ednl. Policy fellow, 1974-75; research asso. Nat. Acad. Scis.-NRC. Bd. dirs., chmn. mgmt. com. Community Rehab. Industries. Served with U.S. Army Res., 1969-75. Canaveral Press Club scholar, 1966-67. Mem. Am. Inst. Planners, Am. Soc. Public Adminstrn., Calif. Assn. Public Adminstrn. Edn., Western Govtl. Research Assn. Democrat. Presbyterian. Author: Citizen Participation in American Communities, 1981. Home: 306 Coral Reef Dr Apt 53 Huntington Beach CA 92648 Office: Center for Pub Policy Calif State U Long Beach CA 90840

BARBER, JEAN ELAINE, advertising executive; b. Hackensack, N.J., Sept. 16, 1936; d. George Edward and Edna Adelaide (Ahrendt) B. Student, Knox Coll., 1957-58. Asst. editor Locksmith Ledger, Inc., Little Falls, N.J., 1960-68, editor, 1968-70; asst. exec. dir. Assoc. Locksmiths of Am., Kingston, N.Y., 1970, editor, 1971; asst. gen. mgr., dir. advt. Baxter Systems, Inc., El Cajon, Calif., 1972-77, treas., dir. advt., 1977—. Mem. Phi Mu. Home: 9158 Les Rd Santee CA 92071 Office: 1934 John Towers Ave Suite C&D El Cajon CA 92020

BARBER, JOHN RICHARDSON, mechanical engineer; b. Pasadena, Calif., Dec. 21, 1923; s. Daniel Francis and Norma Elizabeth (Richardson) B.; B.Mech.Engring., U. Santa Clara, 1949; m. Sally Buckman, Feb. 20, 1951; children—Kendall, Ann. Project engr. Specialized Instrument Co., Belmont, Calif., 1952-53; projects mgr. Wetmore Hodges & Assos., Redwood City, Calif., 1953-56; cons. engr. Hundley Engring., Cupertino, Calif., 1957; mgr. mech. structural sect. antenna systems lab., Philco-Ford Western Devel. Labs., Palo Alto, Calif., 1958-63; mgr. engring. Dalmo Victor Co., Belmont, Calif., 1964-67; mem. tech. staff Aerospace Corp., El Segundo, Calif, 1967-79; founder JR Barber & Assos., Inc., cons. engrs., Manhattan Beach, Calif., 1979—. Founding pres. Fiesta Gardens Homeowners Assn., San Mateo, Calif., 1954-56. Served with USAAF, 1942-45, USAF, 1951-53. Registered profl. engr. Mem. Soc. Automotive Engrs., Exptl. Aircraft Assn. Republican. Roman Catholic. Patentee antenna aerodynamic spoilers. Club: Nat. Rifle Assn. Home: 405 5th St Manhattan Beach CA 90266 Office: PO Box 3057 Manhattan Beach CA 90266

BARBER, MARIE L., educator; b. Price, Utah, Apr. 3, 1952; d. Ralph A. and Arlene C. Lemon; b. Mark R. Barber, Jan. 17, 1975; children—Flint, Chet, Luke. B.S., Utah State U., 1974. Cert. vocat. home econs. tchr. Home econs. tchr. Davis High Sch., Kaysville, Utah, 1974—; adviser Coll. Family Life, Utah State U., 1979—; mem. textbook adoption com. Utah State Bd. Edn., 1979—. Office: Davis High Sch 325 S Main Kaysville UT 89037

BARBER, MICHAEL ALLEN, air force officer; b. Sedalia, Mo., May 28, 1945; s. Norval Allen and Juanita Kay (Cochran) B.; m. Nancy Joyce Newnum, June 3, 1967; children—Carolyn, Michael, Roy. A.A., Phoenix Coll., 1966; B.S., Ariz. State U., 1968; M.A., Ball State U., 1975. Commd. lt. U.S. Air Force, 1968, advanced through grades to maj., 1980, F-4 weapon system officer, MacDill AFB, Fla., Ubon RTAFB, Thailand, Torrejon Air Base, Spain, 1971-76, C-5A navigator Travis AFB, Calif., 1976-82, 22d Air Force strategic airlift dir., 1982—. Decorated D.F.C. with oak leaf cluster, Air medal with 15 oak leaf clusters, Air Force Commendation medal. Mem. Air Force Assn. Republican. Baptist. Home: 543 Corte Gonzales Vacaville CA 95688

BARBER, ROBERT EDWIN, turbomachinery cons.; b. Long Beach, Calif., July 8, 1932; s. Edwin G. and Doris Rose (Prested) B.; B.S., Oreg. State U., 1957; M.S. in Mech. Engring., Rensselaer Poly. Inst., 1961; m. Margaret Jane Fasnacht, Dec. 16, 1956; children—Catherine Marie, ChrisAnn Robin, Hilary Rose, Kevin Robert. Research engr. United Aircraft Corp., East Hartford, Conn., 1957-62, Sundstrand Aviation, Denver, 1962-66; v.p., engring. cons. Barber-Nichols Engring. Co., Arvada, Colo., 1966—. Mem. Nat. Ski Patrol System, 1962-77. Mem. Gov.'s Air Pollution Variance Bd., 1968-77; mem. Colo. State Engring. Ethical Practices Com., 1967-72, chmn., 1972. Served with USN, 1961-63. Registered profl. engr., Colo., Calif. Mem. Nat. Soc. Profl. Enrs., Soc. Automotive Engrs., ASHRAE. Contbr. articles to profl. jours. Patentee in field. Home: 10795 W 81st St Arvada CO 80005 Office: 6325 W 55th St Arvada CO 80002

BARBER, THOMAS KING, dentist; b. Highland Park, Mich., Sept. 26, 1923; s. Thomas Cassius and Allie Estella (King) B.; B.S., Mich. State Coll., 1945; B.S.D., U. Ill., 1947, D.D.S., 1949, M.S., 1949; m. Margot Jaques, July 12, 1947; children—Margaret, Thomas, Robert. Research asst. U. Ill., 1945-49; instr. pedodontics Marquette U., Milw., 1950-51; instr. pedodontics U. Ill. Coll. Dentistry, 1951-53, asst. prof., 1953-58, assoc. prof., 1958-62, lectr. postgrad. studies, 1958, clin. prof. surgery Coll. Medicine, 1958, assoc. head dept. pedodontics, 1961-65, prof., 1962-69, head dept. pedodontics, 1965-69; prof., chmn. div. pediatric dentistry, prof. pediatrics Sch. Dentistry, UCLA, 1969—, chmn. div. preventive dental scis., chmn. sec. pediatric dentistry, 1971-78, assoc. dean, 1978-80, 81—, acting dean Sch. Dentistry, Ctr. Health Scis., 1980-81; cons. USPHS, ADA, R.W. Johnson Found., Am. Fund Dental Health; cons. VA Hosp., Brentwood, Los Angeles, Vets. Hosp., Wadsworth, Los Angeles, 1972—; examiner Nat. Prevention Demonstration Program, 1977-81; spl. cons. Ednl. Testing Service, Princeton, N.J., 1973-81; cons. AVLINE, Nat. Library Medicine, 1976—; editorial cons. Jour. Dental Edn., 1978—. Mem. bd. edn., Bensenville, Ill., 1964-69; pres. Bensenville Recreation Assn., 1968; sec.-treas. White Pines Civic Assn. Served with U.S. Army, 1941-43, USN, 1943-44. Recipient Disting. Alumnus award U. Ill. Coll. Dentistry, 1977; Named Dentist of Year, Am. Soc. Dentistry for Children, 1980. Fellow Am. Coll. Dentists; mem. Am. Acad. Pedodontics (mem. editorial bd. 1974—, chmn. 1977—, assoc. editor 1978-81), Am. Assn. Dental Editors, Am. Soc. Dentistry for Children (mem. research and review bd. 1974—), ADA (chmn. pedodontics council on sci. session 1973-74), Internat. Assn. Dental Research, Am. Assn. Dental Schs. (mem. curricular guidelines dental care of handicapped com. 1978-79), Calif. Soc. Pediatric Dentists (mem. exec. bd. 1974-80, pres. 1979-80), Ill. Soc. Dentistry for Children (pres. 1950-51), So. Calif. Soc. Dentistry for Children, Calif. Dental Assn. (council dental edn. 1979-82), Associacion Odontiologica Del Peru, Sociedad Peruana Odontopediatria, Societe Francaise de Pedodontie, Beverly Hills Acad. Dentistry, Sigma Xi, Omicron Kappa Upsilon. Mem. editorial bd. Jour. Dentistry for Children, 1968—; contbr. articles to profl. jours.; author: (with L. Luke) Pedodontics, 1982; (with Stewart, Troutman and Wei) Pediatric Dentistry, 1982. Home: 27406 Rainbow Ridge Palos Verdes CA 90274 Office: UCLA Sch Dentistry Los Angeles CA 90024

BARBERA, HENRY RAYMOND, political sociologist, researcher; b. N.Y.C., Dec. 21, 1929; s. John Salvatore and Rosalia Carini (Conigliaro) B.; m. Gabrielle Dorothee Gilbert, Jan. 4, 1953 (div.); children—Scott, Clement; m. 2d, Judith Anne Hartshorne, June 10, 1970; 1 son, Geoffrey. B.A., Hofstra U., 1953; M.A., Columbia U., 1954, Ph.D., 1971. Lectr., Hunter Coll., N.Y.C., 1956-60, instr., 1964-66; research analyst Nat. Opinion Research Ctr., U. Chgo., 1962-64; project dir. Bur. Applied Social Research, Columbia U., N.Y.C., 1966-71; assoc. prof. sociology CCNY, 1971-77; adj. prof. SUNY-Purchase, 1979-82; vis. prof. U. Calif.-Irvine, 1983—; cons. internat. change. Served in U.S. Army, 1946-49. Mem. Am. Sociol. Soc., Am. Polit. Sci. Assn. Author: Rich Nations and Poor in Peace and War, 1973; The Rise of Hope, the Rise of Discontent, 1983. Home: 345 Oak St San Marino CA 91108

BARBOUR, MICHAEL GEORGE, botany educator; b. Jackson, Mich., Feb. 24, 1942; s. George Jerome and Mae (Dater) B.; children—Julie Ann, Alan Benjamin. B.S. in Botany, Mich. State U., 1963; Ph.D. in Botany, Duke U., 1967. Asst. prof. dept. botany U. Calif.-Davis, 1967-71, assoc. prof., 1971-76, prof., 1976—, chmn. botany dept., 1982—; dir. U. Calif. Study Ctr., Jerusalem; vis. prof. botany The Hebrew U., 1979-80. Fulbright fellow, 1964; Guggenheim fellow, 1978. Mem. Brit. Ecol. Soc., Ecol. Soc. Am., Am. Inst. Biol. Scis., Sigma Xi. Democrat. Jewish. Co-author: Coastal Ecology, 1973; Terrestrial Plant Ecology, 1980; Botany, 6th edit., 1982; co-editor; Terrestrial Vegetation of California, 1977; contbr. numerous articles to tech. jours. Home: 2453 Creekhollow Davis CA 95616 Office: Dept Botany U Calif Davis CA 95616

BARCA, GEORGE GINO, winery business executive; b. Sacramento, Jan. 28, 1937; s. Joseph and Annie (Muschetto) B.; m. Maria Sclafani, Nov. 19, 1960; children—Anna, Joseph, Gina and Nina (twins). A.A., Grant Jr. Coll., Lasalle U., 1963. With AeroJet Gen. Corp., Sacramento, 1958-65, United Vintness, Inc., San Francisco, 1960-73; pres., gen. mgr. Barcamerica Corp., Sacramento, 1963—; cons. in field. Named Best Producer of Sales, United Vintness, Inc. Mem. Calif. Farm Bur., Met. C. of C., Better Bus. Bur., Roman Catholic. Club: KC. Developer wine trademarks.

BARCELOUX, PETER MELVIN, fruit grower, credit assn. ofcl.; b. Sacramento, Feb. 4, 1954; s. Reeve Henry and Edith Marie (Allen) B.; B.S., U. Calif.-Davis, 1976; m. Carole Diane Cunha, May 7, 1977; 1 son, Reeve Scott. Environ. storage controller Bell-Carter Foods, Orland, Calif., 1976-77; field rep. Calif. Farm Bur. Fedn., San Jose, 1977-81; mgr. Santa Clara County Farm Bur., San Jose, 1977-81; owner, operator R.B. Orchards, Orland, 1973—; loan officer San Jose Prodn. Credit Assn., 1981—; cons. John Muir Hist. Site, 1975-76; info. officer for Mediterranean Fruit Fly, 1980-81; dir. Food Bank, Inc., 1980—. Mem. spl. task force to study pesticide use Santa Clara County Bd. Suprs., 1981; mem. agrl. water adv. bd., water reuse adv. com. Santa Clara Valley Water Dist.; chmn. Coop. Exentension Adv. Com. Santa Clara County; mem. Santa Clara County Fair Assn., chmn. feature booth com. Recipient Outstanding Achievement award Santa Clara County Farm Bur., 1981. Mem. Glenn County Farm Bur., Santa Clara County Agrl. Round Table, Council Calif. Growers, Internat. Plant Propagators Soc., Calif. Farm Bur. Fedn., Kappa Sigma. Clubs: Commonwealth, Orland Flying (v.p. 1971-81), Achievers, Rotary (pres. 1981-82). Home: 654 Abrigo Ct San Ramon CA 94583 Office: 2025 Gateway Pl San Jose CA 95109

BARCHAS, PATRICIA RUTH, sociologist; b. Chickasha, Okla., July 26, 1934; d. Bill Doherty and Jimmie Ione (Hendricks) Corbitt; B.A., Pomona Coll., 1956; postgrad. U. Chgo., 1961-62; Ph.D., Stanford U., 1971; m. Jack David Barchas, Feb. 9, 1957; 1 son, Isaac Doherty. Faculty, Stanford (Calif.) U., 1971—, dir. program in sociophysiology Lab. of Social Research, asst. prof. sociology and (courtesy) psychiatry and behavioral scis., 1975—; mem. Dept. Mental Health and Developmental Disabilities Research Panel, State of Ill., 1976-81; cons., co-author Nat. Inst. Neurol. Diseases report to Congress on biol. aspects of aggression, 1976; panel mem., co-author Inst. Medicine of Nat. Acad. Scis. report on psychobiol. research and mental health, 1978, biol. aspects of stress, 1980. Grantee, Harry Frank Guggenheim, 1972-73, Nat. Inst. Alcohol Research, 1972-73, Spencer Found., 1977-78; recipient Stanford U. research devel. award, 1971; spl. contract Office Naval Research, 1974, 79-82. Mem. Am. Sociol. Assn., AAAS, N.Y. Acad. Scis., Acad. Behavioral Medicine Research, Soc. Psychophysiol. Research, Soc. Neurosci., Brain Research Assn., European Brain and Behavior Soc., Soc. Personality and Social Psychology. Contbr. articles to profl. publs. Home: 669 Mirada Ave Stanford CA 94305 Office: Dept Sociology Stanford U Stanford CA 94305

BARCHEK, JAMES ROBERT, educational administrator; b. Norwalk, Conn., May 24, 1935; s. John D. and Helen I. (Pesti) B.; m. Ardyce Jean Patchin, Sept. 5, 1956; children—Douglas Alan, Julie Marie. B.A., Portland State U., 1959; M.Ed., Reed Coll., 1962; D.F.A., U. Oreg., 1969. Tchr., Marshall Sr. High Sch., Portland, Oreg., 1958-65; research assoc. Oreg. Curriculum Study Ctr., U. Oreg., 1965-68; lectr., asst. prof. Western Wash. State U., Bellingham, 1968-72; coordinator English, dir. instrn., asst. supt. curriculum and instrn. Kent (Wash.) Sch. Dist., 1972—; cons., author, lectr. Served with U.S. Army, 1953-55. Mem. Nat. Council Tchrs. English (dir.), Wash. State Council Tchrs. English (pres. 1974-76), Assn. Supervision and Curriculum Devel., Internat. Reading Assn., Wash. Assn. Supervision and Curriculum Devel., Wash. Assn. Sch. Adminstrs., Internat. Arthurian Soc. Author: (with others) Language/Rhetoric I, II, 1968, Invention and System, Purpose and Change, The Private I, 1978; (with Lee Odell) Fantasy, 1978; (with G. Petrequin) Individualizing Instruction through Scheduling, 1968; contbr. articles to profl. jours. Home: 28206 112th Ave SE Kent WA 98031 Office: 12033 SE 256th St Kent WA 98031

BARCZAK, EDWARD, indsl. designer; b. Buffalo, Dec. 12, 1922; s. Stanley Martin and Helen (Holtyn) B.; student Buffalo public schs.; m. Phyllis Lowren, June 14, 1947; 1 son, Christopher. With Hoffman Electronics, Los Angeles, 1946-61, Hughes Aircraft, 1951-52, Packard Bell Electronics, 1965-69, Mattel Toys, 1970-72, Pathcom, Inc., Los Angeles, 1973-77; mgr. indsl. design Cetec Vega, El Monte, Calif., 1979-81; cons. corps.; continuing design cons. E & P Assos. Mem. Los Feliz Improvement Assn. Served with USMC, 1942-46. Recipient Leadership award Nat. Mgmt. Assn., 1969. Republican. Office: 2449 N Vermont St Los Angeles CA 90027

BARD, JOHN DELBERT, mortgage banker; b. Kimball, Nebr., May 6, 1944; s. Arthur Elroy and Irene Ruby (Watts) B.; B.S., U. Wyo., 1967, M.Ed., 1975; m. Janet Karen Joslyn, Nov. 22, 1966; children—Brooke Lea, John Linton. Tchr., St. Mary High Sch., Cheyenne, Wyo., 1970-73; tchr., coach Worland (Wyo.) High Sch., 1973-76; spl. rep. Franklin Life Ins. Co., Laramie, Wyo., 1976-78; loan officer Transamerica Mortgage Co., Laramie, 1978-79; br. mgr., v.p. ICM Mortgage Corp., Laramie, 1979—. Served with USNR, 1968-70. Mem. Mortgage Bankers Assn., Nat. High Sch. Athletic Ofcls. Assn., Nat. High Sch. Athletic Coaches Assn., Albany County Ofcls. Assn. (sec.-treas. 1980-81), Wyo. Farm-House Assn. (pres. 1980-84, internat. bd. dirs. 1978-86). Republican. Methodist. Clubs: Internat. Turtles, Elks. Office: PO Box 1585 Laramie WY 82070

BARD, STEVEN, mech. engr.; b. Budapest, Hungary, Mar. 28, 1954; s. Alex and Magda (Steiner) B.; B.S. in M.E., CCNY, 1975; M.S., U. Calif., Berkeley, 1976, Ph.D., 1980; m. Sherry Silberstein, Sept. 19, 1976. Research asst. Lawrence Berkeley (Calif.) Lab. and U. Calif., 1975-80, teaching asst., 1979; sr. engr. Jet Propulsion Lab., Pasadena, Calif., 1980—. Earl C. Anthony Grad. fellow, 1975-76. Mem. AIAA, ASME, Soc. Automotive Engrs., No. Calif. Solar Energy Assn., Sigma Xi, Pi Tau Sigma, Tau Beta Pi. Jewish. Clubs: CCNY Photography (pres. 1974-75), Tennis. Contbr. articles to profl. jours. Home: 320 E Stocker St Glendale CA 91207 Office: Mail Stop 157 102 Jet Propulsion Lab 4800 Oak Grove Dr Pasadena CA 91103

BARDACH, SHELDON GILBERT, lawyer; b. Holyoke, Mass., Sept. 4, 1937; s. Arthur Everett and Ruth (Goodstein) B.; A.B., Bklyn. Coll., 1958; J.D., U. Calif. at Los Angeles, 1961; m. Martha Robson, June 7, 1970; 1 son, Noah Arthur. Admitted to Calif. bar, 1962; practiced in Beverly Hills, Calif., 1962-67, Century City, Calif., 1967—; prin. law offices Sheldon G. Bardach; dir. Century Artists Talent Agy., Beverly Hills, 1981—; spl. counsel to Dade County (Fla.) Grand Jury, 1963; mem. nat. panel arbitrators Am. Arbitration Assn.; arbitrator Los Angeles Superior Ct. Mem. dean's counsel Sch. Law, U. Calif. at Los Angeles, 1968—; bd. govs. Studio Watts Workshop, 1963-71; bd. dirs. Beverly Hills Theatre Guild, 1977—. Recipient Lubin award U. Calif. Sch. Law, 1961; Bancroft-Whitney award, 1961. Mem. State Bar Calif., Am., Beverly Hills (bd. govs. barristers 1964-69), Century City, Los Angeles County bar assns., Am. Trial Lawyers Assn., Comml. Law League Am., Vikings of Scandia, Zeta Beta Tau, Phi Alpha Delta. Democrat. Jewish. Club: Wilt's Athletic (bd. dirs. 1981—) (Los Angeles. Mem. bd. editors Law in Transition Quar., 1967; contbr. articles to profl. jours. Office: 1888 Century Park East Century City CA 90067

BARDACKE, PAUL GREGORY, lawyer, state government official; b. Oakland, Calif., Dec. 16, 1944; s. Theodore Joseph and Frances (Woodward) B.; m. Lauren Elaine Marble, June 21, 1980; children—Julie, Brynn, Francheska. B.A. cum laude, U. Calif.-Santa Barbara, 1966; J.D., U. Calif.-Berkeley, 1969. Bar: Calif. 1969, N.Mex. 1970. Atty., Legal Aid Soc., Albuquerque, 1969-70; assoc. Sutin, Thayer & Browne, Albuquerque, 1970—, ptnr., 1972-82; atty. gen. State of N.Mex., Santa Fe, 1983—; adj. prof. U. N.Mex. Sch. Law; mem. faculty Nat. Inst. Trial Advocacy. Bd. dirs. All Faiths Receiving Home: past bd. dirs. Friends of Art, Legal Aid Soc. Mem. ABA, N.Mex. Bar Assn., Albuquerque Bar Assn., Calif. Bar Assn. Democrat. Office: PO Drawer 1508 Santa Fe NM 87504

BARDIN, JAMES NELSON, civil engr.; b. Charlottesville, Va., Apr. 14, 1926; s. James Cook and Sally Norvell (Nelson) B.; student U. N.Mex., 1948-51, Calif. State U., Long Beach, 1964-65; B.S. in Civil Engring., Tenn. Christian U., 1976; m. Patricia Ann Kascht, Mar. 5, 1956; 1 dau., April Kascht. Served as enlisted man U.S. Marine Corps, 1943-46; commd. 2d lt. U.S. Marine Corps, 1950, advanced through grades to capt., 1953; resigned, 1962; plant engr. Meml. Hosp., Long Beach, Calif., 1962-77, South Bay Hosp., Redondo Beach, Calif., 1977—; sec. AUDEX Corp., 1971. Mem. Am. Inst. Plant Engrs. (cert. plant engr.), Nat. Fire Protection Ass., Soc. Am. Mil. Engrs., Am. Soc. Hosp. Engrs., So. Calif. Hosp. Engrs. Assn., Internat. Assn. Hosp. Security, DAV, Mensa, Intertel. Republican. Episcopalian. Office: South Bay Hosp 514 N Prospect St Redondo Beach CA 90277

BARDIN, MICHAEL D(AVID), public relations executive; b. Berkeley, Calif.; s. David Bardin and Marion Wilma (McConnell) Roller; m. Arlene Carole Greene, Oct. 22, 1966; children—Stephanie Lynn, Laurie Anne. B.A. in Communications and Journalism, Stanford U., 1964; postgrad. in Radio-TV-Film, San Francisco State U., 1964-65. News prodn. asst. sta. KPIX-TV, San Francisco, 1965-66; pub. relations account exec. Phillips-Ramsey, Inc., San Diego, 1969-75, dir. client pub. relations services, 1975—, v.p. pub. relations, 1977—; guest lectr. San Diego State U., Nat. U. Pres. Calif. Ballet Co., 1982, trustee, 1979—; adv. com. San Diego Community Found., 1979—; trustee Mexican-Am. Found., 1971-79; bd. dirs. Travelers Aid Soc., 1979—. Served to lt. USN, 1966-69. Named Man of Distinction, Mexican-Am. Found., 1977, Mem. Pub. Relations San Diego Pub. Relations Profl. of Yr., 1980. Soc. Am. (accredited, pres. San Diego County chpt.), Pub. Relations Club of San Diego (pres. 1978, four awards 1974-78), Pub. Utilities Communicators Assn. Republican. Episcopalian. Club: San Diego Press. Office: 6863 Friars Rd San Diego CA 92108

BARDING, LEWIS DANIEL, stockbroker; b. East Moline, Ill., Mar. 28, 1928; s. Lewis Daniel and Lillian Alice (Braastad) B.; m. Marilyn Marlene Huyett, Mar. 17, 1957; children—Lewis Daniel III, Bradford Huyett. B.A., Tulane U., 1950. Stockbroker Dain, Kalman & Quail,

Davenport, Iowa, 1958-73; 1st v.p., resident mgr. Wagenseller & Durst, San Diego, 1973-82; stockbroker, sr. v.p. J. David Securities, La Jolla, Calif., 1982—; cons. corp. fin. for mergers and acquisitions. Served with CIC, U.S. Army, 1951-53; Korea. Mem. San Diego Corp. Fin. Council, San Diego Stock and Bond Club (pres. 1977), Stockbroker Soc. (chmn. 1976-82), Coronado Navy League, Assn. Former Intelligence Officers. Republican. Home: 5 The Inlet Coronado CA 92118 Office: 1205 Prospect St Suite 550 La Jolla CA 92037

BAREISS, LYLE EUGENE, aerospace engineer; b. Rawlins, Wyo., Nov. 4, 1945; s. Godfrey Matthew and Vera Edith Bareiss; m. Chris Elizabeth Bartlett, Aug. 23, 1969. B.S.M.E., Wyo. U., 1969; postgrad. in indsl. mgmt. Colo. State U., 1970. Assoc. engr. then sr. engr. Martin Marietta Aerospace Co., Denver, 1969-79, sr. group engr. group mgmt., 1980—. Recipient NASA Skylab Achievement award, 1974; NASA New Tech. awards, 1977, 82; Martin Marietta author, performance awardee, 1974, 75, 79, 82. Mem. AIAA (Nat. Thermophysics Com.), Soc. Photo Optical Instrumentation Engrs., Sigma Tau, Omicron Delta Kappa, Sigma Alpha Epsilon. Presbyterian. Lodge: Odd Fellows (Rawlins, Wyo.). Contbr. articles to profl. jours.; architect computer model simulating spacecraft contamination to evaluate US satellite systems. Home: 8031 E Phillips Circle Englewood CO Office: PO Box 179 Denver CO 80201

BARELA, ROBERT, asst. supt. schs.; b. Los Angeles, Oct. 21, 1934; s. Gilbert and Guadalupe B.; B.A. in Edn., Calif. State Coll., Los Angeles, 1960; M.A. in Public Adminstrn., San Jose State Coll., 1966; m. Kathleen Patricia Higgins, Sept. 18, 1954; children—Anne, Michael, Mary Therese, Peter Anthony, Maureen, Thomas Gilbert, Christina. Tchr., coach, vice prin. Encinal-organ Hill Sch. Dist., 1960-65; high sch. prin., coll. instr. George Pepperdine Coll., 1957-69, dir. pupil personnel, 1964; dir. program devel. Santa Clara Office of Edn., 1966-67; dir. civil rights HUD, Dept. Commerce, 1976-78, Dept. Interior Water and Power Resource Office, Denver, 1979-80; pub. Colo. Cornerstone; editor La Luz Publs., Denver, 1973-76, chmn. bd., 1980-83; asst. supt. schs. North Conejo Schs, La Jara Colo., 1983—. condr. ednl. workshop Dominican Republic, 1966. Pres. P.T.A., 1963-64; mem. Morgan Hill County Bd., 1960-63, Lakewood Bd. Edn., 1973-76; del. Colo. Republican Conv., 1974, 76, 78; dist. capt. Jefferson County Rep. party, 1981; mem. Colo. Edn. and Manpower Devel. Com., 1972-74, del. White House Conf. on Youth, 1972. Served with AUS, 1953-55. Decorated U.S. Peace medal; Named Outstanding Prin. of Year, El Rancho Unified Sch. Dist., 1968, Coach of Year, 1976; recipient award Fellowship of Christian Athletes, 1979, Outstanding Achievement award HUD, 1972; award Valley Forge Freedoms Found., 1983. Mem. NEA, NAACP, Am. Legion, Am. GI Forum, Image, Journalists of Am., Internat. Youth Leaders Am. Roman Catholic. Clubs: Rotary (past pres.), Lions, Kiwanis. Author: Though Many We Are One, 1968; The American Creed, 1971; The Civil Rights Creed, 1977; Mornin', 1980. Home: 2064 S Moore Ct Lakewood CO 80227 Office: North Conejos Schools PO Box 72 La Jara CO 81140

BARER, BURL ROGER, creative cons.; b. Walla Walla, Wash., Aug. 8, 1947; s. David and Dorothy (Copeland) B.; student U. Wash., 1969; m. Britt Elin Johnsen, Mar. 2, 1974; 1 dau., Anea Bergen. On-air personality Sta. KJR, Seattle, 1967-68, Sta. KOL, Seattle, 1968-73, Sta. KJR, 1974-76; tchr., cons. Mind Devel., Inc., Seattle, 1973-74, v.p., 1978—; on-air personality creative dir. Barer/McManus, Bellevue, Wash., 1975-77; pres. Barer/Goldblatt & Assos., Bellevue, 1978—; regional v.p. Merklingar Labs., Denver, 1977—; guest lectr.; on-air personality Sta. KYYX, Seattle, 1978-80, Sta. KXA, Seattle, 1981—; dir. B. Barer & Sons, Inc., 1980—; asst. to aux. bd. Continental Bd. Counsellors for Americas, 1980—; pres. Barer Cable Advt., Inc., 1982—. Active Variety Club. Recipient Bob Wiley Creative award, 1977. Mem. AFTRA, Am. Film Inst. Mem. Baha'i faith. Office: 1839 Crestline Dr Walla Walla WA 99362

BARGER, JAMES DANIEL, physician; b. Bismarck, N.D., May 17, 1917; s. Michael Thomas and Mayte (Donohue) B.; m. Susie Belle Helm, 1945 (dec. 1951); m. 2d, Josephine Steiner, May 31, 1952 (dec. 1971); m. 3d, Jane Ray Regan, Apr. 21, 1980; children—James Daniel, Mary Susan, Michael Thomas II, Mary Elizabeth. Student St. Mary's Coll., 1934-35; A.B., U. N.D., 1939, B.S., 1939; M.D., U. Pa., 1941; M.S. in Pathology, U. Minn., 1949. Intern, Milwaukee County Hosp., Wauwatosa, Wis., 1941-42; fellow in pathology Mayo Found., Rochester, Minn., 1941-49; pathologist Pima County Hosp., Tucson, 1949-50, Maricopa County Hosp., Phoenix, 1950-51; chmn. dept. pathology Good Samaritan Hosp., 1951-63; former med. dir. S.W. Blood Bank, Ariz.; asso. pathologist Sunrise Hosp., Las Vegas, Nev., 1964-69, chief pathology dept., 1969—. Served from 1st lt. to maj., AUS, 1942-46. Recipient Sioux award U. N.D. Alumni Assn., 1975, Disting. Physician award Nev. State Med. Assn., 1983. Diplomate Am. Bd. Pathology; registered profl. engr., Calif. Mem. AMA (alt. del.), Nev. Med. Assn. (alt. del.), AAAS, Am. Assn. Pathologists, Soc. Advancement Mgmt., Am. Assn. Clin. Chemists, Am. Assn. for History Medicine, Coll. Am. Pathologists (gov. 1966-72, sec.-treas. 1971-79, v.p. 1979-81, pres.-elect 1980, pres. 1981-83, Pathologist of Yr. 1977), Am. Soc. Quality Control, Am. Mgmt. Assn., Am. Soc. Clinical Pathologists, Am. Cancer Soc. (nat. dir. 1974-80), Nev. Soc. Pathologists, Am. Assn. Blood Banks, Am. Pub. Health Assn., Order of St. Lazarus (comdr.), Sigma Xi. Research in field. Home: 1307 Canosa Ave Las Vegas NV 89105 Office: Sunrise Hosp PO Box 14157 Las Vegas NV 89114

BARGER, WILLIAM JAMES, financial executive, economist; b. Los Angeles, Nov. 1, 1944; s. James Ray and Aylene M. (Skinner) B. A.B., U. So. Calif., 1966; A.M., Harvard U., 1969, Ph.D., 1972. Asst. prof. in econs. U. So. Calif., Los Angeles, 1971-76; economist Bank of Am., Los Angeles, 1976-79, sr. economist, v.p., 1979-81; exec. v.p., dir. corp. devel. Gibraltar Savs. and Loan Assn., Beverly Hills, Calif., 1981—. Assoc., St. John's Hosp. Child Study Ctr., Santa Monica, Calif. Mem. Am. Econ. Assn., Nat. Assn. Bus. Economists. Club: Los Angeles Athletic.

BARGER, WILLIAM PAUL, newspaper publisher; b. Chickasha, Okla., June 21, 1929; s. William Hampton and Eilleene Hadetta (Thomas) B.; m. June Hamm, Jan. 11, 1952; children—Matthew Paul, Lorna Barger Frost. B.S., U. Calif.-Berkeley, 1951, B.A., 1954. News editor San Juan Record, Fair Oaks, Calif., 1954-57; editor, co-pub. Carpinteria (Calif.) Herald, 1957-68; salesman Bill Dawson Realty, Carpinteria, 1968-69; editor, pub. Holbrook (Ariz.) Tribune-News, The Winslow (Ariz.) Mail, 1969—; pres. Navajo County Pub., Inc. Mem. Holbrook City Planning Com. Served to lt. Q.M.C., U.S. Army, 1951-53. Named Man Yr. Holbrook C. of C., 1982. Mem. Sigma Delta Chi. Republican. Baptist. Club: Holbrook Lions (sec.) Home: 791 9th Ave Holbrook AZ 86025 Office: 200 E Hopi Dr Holbrook AZ 86025

BARHAM, DORIS ANN, banker; b. Washington, Jan. 4, 1933; d. Vern Clinton and Thelma Louise (Snelling) Brannock; m. Richard Carroll Barham, Nov. 18, 1950; 1 dau., Carolyn Sue Emshwiller. Cert. legal sec. tng., Ventura Coll., 1966; student LaSalle Extension U., 1970-72; certs. banking courses Am. Inst. Banking, 1963-70. Sec. Govt. Mortgage Ctr., San Diego, 1950-60; escrow officer 1st Nat. Bank of Vista (Calif.), 1961-63; trust officer Bank of Am., Ventura, Calif., 1964-74; trust officer, sr. trust officer Security Pacific Nat. Bank, Ventura, 1974-80, v.p., mgr., Hollywood, Calif., 1981-82, v.p., mgr. Head Office Trust & Agy. Ctr., Pasadena, 1982—; estate planning seminar leader. Mem. Nat. Assn. Bank Women. Republican. Lutheran. Club: Gopher Flats Sportsmen's (Panorama City). Office: Suite 14-46 234 E Colorado Blvd Pasadena CA 91101

BARHAM, JESSE WALTER, city official; b. Salem, Oreg., Feb. 22, 1924; s. Jesse Alba and Esther L. (Dewey) B.; m. Marie Frakes, Dec. 27, 1944; children—Terry A., Bruce L. B.S. in C.E., Oreg. State Coll., 1950. Registered profl. engr., Oreg., Calif. Engring. asst. City of Salem, 1951; city engr. City of Coos Bay (Oreg.), 1952-54, dir. pub. works, 1954-58; city mgr., city engr. City of Coalinga (Calif.), 1959-61; city mgr. Coos Bay, 1961-68; city mgr., Longview, Wash., 1968—. Oreg. chmn. Nat. Library Week, 1967; mem. State Adv. Com. on Library Cooperation; mem. tech. com. Wash. Traffic Safety Commn., 1970-75; chmn. Coalinga Boosters for San Luis Fed. Water Project; mem. Wash. State Solid Waste Com.; pres. Cowlitz-Waukiakum Govt. Conf., 1973, 82. Trustee Seattle Pacific U., 1963—. Served with USMC, 1942-46. Mem. Profl. Engrs. S.W. Oreg. (pres. 1958), Internat. City Mgmt. Assn. (pres. Oreg. 1968, pres. Wash. 1974). Free Meth. (chmn. bd. adminstrn. Oreg. conf. 1963-75), Rotarian. Home: 2938 Madrona Dr Longview WA 98632 Office: City Hall 1575 Broadway Ave Longview WA 98632

BARKAN, PHILIP, educator; b. Boston, Mar. 29, 1925; s. Philip and Blanche (Seifert) B.; B.S., Tufts U., 1946; M.S., U. Mich., 1948; Ph.D., Pa. State U., 1953; m. Hinda Brody, Sept. 5, 1948 (dec. Aug. 1979); children—Ruth, David. Asst. prof. engring. research Pa. State U., 1948-53; mgr. applied physics and mech. engring. Gen. Electric Co., Phila., 1953-77; prof. mech. engring. and design Stanford (Calif.) U., 1977—; cons. to electric power industry. Pres. Middletown (Pa.) Free Library, 1959-61; chmn. bd. Sch. in Rose Valley (Pa.), 1967-68. Served to lt. USNR, 1943-46. Recipient Steinmetz medal Gen. Electric Co., 1973. Registered profl. engr., Pa. Fellow IEEE; mem. Nat. Acad. Engring., Am. Soc. Elec. Engring., ASME, Sigma Xi. Patentee in field. Home: 42 Pearce Mitchell Pl Stanford CA 94305 Office: Mech Engring Dept Design div Stanford U Stanford CA 94305

BARKER, BARRIE WORDEN, avionics operations specialist; b. Quogue, N.Y., Feb. 26, 1945; s. Jay Redfield and Florence (Nesbitt) B.; A.S., Mitchell Jr. Coll., 1964; m. Dianna, Apr. 22, 1978; children—Suzanne, Janet, DeWayne, Holly. Mil. flying ops. Lockheed Calif. Co., Burbank, Calif., 1972—, instr. airborne antisubmarine warfare. Served to lt. USNR, 1964-71. Decorated Air medal. Mem. Engrs. and Scientists Guild. Republican. Innovator use of color in mil. computerized display systems. Home: PO Box 3055 Burbank CA 91504 Office: Lockheed California Co Mil Flying Ops Div PO Box 551 Burbank CA 91520

BARKER, CHERIE ROBERTA, educational administrator, consultant; b. Los Angeles, Apr. 17, 1944; d. Robert Arthur and Beverly Maxine (Edwards) Jahraus; m. Larry J. Barker, Mar. 21, 1964 (div.); children—Danielle Beverly, Jennifer Anne. B.A. in Liberal Studies, San Diego State U., 1978, M.A. in Edn., 1981. Cert. tchr., Calif. Spl. edn. asst. Fallbrook (Calif.) Unified Sch. Dist., 1974-75; counselor asst. Allied Health, Palomar Community Coll., San Marcos, Calif., 1977-80, asst. dir. Gateways Disadvantaged Student Program, 1978-80, dir. Women: New Perspectives, 1980-81, dir. Gender Equity, Women's Ctr. and Student Accountability Model, Vocat. Edn., 1980—; guest lectr., workshop leader Women & Careers Conf.; cons. as devel. officer to small bus. Bd. dirs. Female Opportunities in Constrn., 1981-82; mem. sch. improvement com. San Marcos High Sch. Dist., 1981—; bd. dirs. San Marcos Girls Softball, 1982-83; mem. adv. com. Republican State Central Com. Recipient Women: New Perspectives Exemplary Program award Calif. Community Colls., 1980-81; Calif. Community Colls. grantee, 1980-81, 82-83. Mem. Am. Vocat. Assn., Am. Assn. Women in Community and Jr. Colls., Calif. Assn. Vocat. Educators, Calif. Advocates for Reentry Edn., Nat. Assn. Women in Constrn. Republican. Lutheran. Office: Palomar Comm Coll 1140 W Mission Rd San Marcos CA 92069

BARKER, JOHN MATTHEW, state senator; b. Twin Falls, Idaho, Nov. 29, 1916; s. John H. and Alice (Scully) B.; B.S. in Bus., U. Idaho, 1938; m. Rose Smith, Jan. 3, 1941; children—John (dec.), Rosemary, James, Marianne. Co-owner John M. Barker Realty, Buhl, Idaho, 1938—; pres. Am. Falls Reservoir Dist., Jerome, Idaho, 1957-83; mem. Idaho Senate, 1967—; commr. Edn. Commn. States, Denver, 1970-83. Various mil. decorations, WWII; recipient Silver Beaver award, Boy Scouts Am., 1959; named Legislator of Yr., Cable TV, 1981; named to Idaho Water Users Assn. Hall of Fame, 1979. C.P.C.U., Idaho. Mem. Buhl C. of C. (pres.), Jr. C. of C. (pres.), Nat. Soc. Pub. Accts., Farm and Land Inst. Republican. Presbyterian. Clubs: Rotary (past pres., dist. gov.); Masons, Shriners. Office: Box 549 Buhl ID 83316

BARKER, LEROY N., agronomy educator, plant breeder; b. Brigham City, Utah, Oct. 18, 1928; s. Claude Rufus and Iva (Nelson) B.; m. Sara Ann Workman, Aug. 31, 1956; children—Michael, Dennis, LeAnn, Nanette, Amy. B.S., Utah State U., 1953, M.S., 1956; Ph.D., U. Wis., 1960. Plant breeder Asgrow Seed Co., Sun Prairie, Wis., 1960-65; instr. agronomy Calif. State U.-Chico, 1965-68, asst. prof., 1968-70, prof., 1970—; sr. lectr., plant breeder U. Ife, Ile-Ife, Nigeria, 1968-70; plant breeder U. Wis.-Madison, Rice Researchers, Inc., summers. Active Boy Scouts Am., 1966-68, 70-76; dist. leader, com. chmn. PTO, U. Ife. Served to 1st lt. U.S. Army, 1953-55. Cliff Poole fellow, 1956; U. Wis. research asst., 1956-60. Mem. Am. Soc. Agronomy, Crop Sci. Soc., Calif. Fertilizer Assn., Sigma Xi. Republican. Morman. Assisted in devel. of two new rice varieties. Home: 2964 Alamo Ave Chico CA 95926 Office: Plant & Soil Scis Calif State U Chico CA 95929

BARKER, LINDA RICHTER, public relations counselor; b. St. Louis, Apr. 14, 1947; d. Thomas Eugene and Rachel (Palmer) Richter; m. Paul William Barker, Mar. 30, 1968; 1 son, Philip Webster. B.Journalism, U. Mo., 1969; M.B.A. in Fin., U. Denver, 1983. Staff reporter St. Louis Globe-Democrat, 1970-71; editor MarketPlace mag., Dallas, 1973-74; v.p. corp. communication United Bank Denver, 1974-81; v.p. Hill and Knowlton, Inc., Denver, 1981—; guest lectr. colls. and univs. Active Leadership Denver Assn., 1979—, Downtown Denver, Inc., 1975-81. Recipient Young Woman of Yr. award Denver Bus. and Profl. Women, 1975. Mem. Pub. Relations Soc. Am., Internat. Assn. Bus. Communicators (accredited), Women in Communications, Inc. (headliner of year award Colo. chpt. 1976), Denver C. of C. Home: 2775 S Lansing Way Aurora CO 80014 Office: 909 17th St Suite 505 Denver CO 80202

BARKER, MITCHELL FREDERICK, government public relations official; b. Tulsa, June 29, 1948; s. Albert B. and Dorothy L. (Bashe) B. B. Univ. Studies, U. N.Mex., 1976. News dir. Sta. KBRR-AM, Leadville, Colo., 1976-77, Sta. KAFE-AM-FM, Santa Fe, 1977; pub. affairs asst. U.S. Army Engr. Dist., Albuquerque, 1978-79; seminar asst. VA InterWest Regional Med. Edn. Ctr., Salt Lake City, 1979-80; tech. writer Robins AFB, Ga., 1980-81; pub. affairs specialist U.S. Army Engr. Dist., Walla Walla, Wash., 1981-82; pub. affairs officer Fitzsimons Army Med. Ctr., Aurora, Colo., 1982—. Served with U.S. Army, 1969-73. Recipient Keith L. Ware award for radio prodn. Dept. of Army, 1972. Mem. Pub. Relations Soc. Am., Colo. Soc. Hosp. Pub. Relations, Aurora C. of C. (mil. affairs com.). Unitarian. Home: PO Box 6059 Aurora CO 80045 Office: Pub Affairs Officer Fitzsimons Army Med Ctr Aurora CO 80045

BARKER, PATRICIA LEE, extension home economist; b. Tacoma, Dec. 8, 1933; d. Ernest Lewis and Evalyn (Willard) Miller; m. Richard Charles Barker, June 11, 1956; children—Mark Richard, Bruce Patrick, Karen Elizabeth, Michelle Marie. B.S., Wash. State U., 1956; M.Ed., U. Alaska, 1978. Tchr. adult edn. night classes, Colville, Wash., 1963-66; half-time tchr. Klickitat (Wash.) High Sch., 1966-68; tchr. Bethel (Alaska) High Sch., 1968-70; substitute tchr., sec. Boarding Home Program, Tok, Alaska, 1970-72; extension home economist, dist. coordinator, Coop. Extension Services, Bethel, 1972—. Pres. Council on the Arts, 1974-80; mem. Bethel State Fair Bd., 1971-82; bd. dirs. Receiving Home, 1979-82; bd. dirs., sec. Lower Kuskokwim Sch., 1980-82. Mem. Am. Home Econs. Assn., Nat. Assn. Extension Home Economists, Alaska Extension Assn., N.W. Adult Educators Assn., Epsilon Sigma Phi, Beta Sigma Phi.

BARKER, RICHARD ALEXANDER, indsl. psychologist; b. San Diego, Aug. 11, 1947; s. Alexander Markewich and Donna Lee Barker; B.A. in Psychology, San Diego State U., 1974, M.S. in Indsl. and Organizational Psychology, 1976; m. Julie Ann Akers, Apr. 3, 1971; children—Jaime Lynn, Cory Richard. Statis. analyst U.S. Navy Personnel Research and Devel. Center, San Diego, 1974-75; personnel and testing analyst City of San Diego, 1976; cons. various orgns., 1976-78; employment mgr. Computer Scis. Corp., San Diego, 1978; indsl. psychologist Gen. Dynamics Corp., San Diego, 1978—; instr. music, San Diego City Coll., 1976—; lectr. psychology, mgmt. sci., stats., orgnl. behavior U. Redlands, 1978—; lectr. mfg. engring. San Diego State U., 1983—. Bd. dirs. San Diego Youth Services, Inc., chmn. personnel com., 1978-81. Served with USNR, 1968-69. Mem. Am. Psychol. Assn. (asso.), Computer Automated Systems Assn./Soc. Mfg. Engrs., Nat. Mgmt. Assn., Internat. Assn. Applied Psychology (asso.), Am. Fedn. Musicians, Psi Chi. Home: 7495 Rondel Ct San Diego CA 92119 Office: General Dynamics Electronics Div 5011 Kearny Villa Rd San Diego CA 92123

BARKER, RICHARD CANFIELD, trust company executive; b. N.Y.C., Sept. 22, 1935; s. W. Delmar and Anne (Baker) B.; m. Abbie D. Mustermann, June 29, 1957; children—Anne, Derek; m. 2d, Jennifer E. Peak, Apr. 30, 1977; 1 dau. Jessica. A.B., Brown U., 1957; postgrad. Sch. Bus. Adminstrn., U. Conn., 1964-65. Staff several investment orgns., 1961-65; portfolio mgr., research dir. Conn. Gen. Life Ins. Co., 1965-69; v.p., investment mgr. S.&P. Intercapital, N.Y.C., 1970; portfolio mgr. Capital Guardian Trust Co. div. Capital Group Inc., 1971-72, dir., chmn. investment com., 1981, sr. v.p. 1972—, dir. parent co. Served to lt. USN, 1957-61, USNR, 1962-68. Mem. Security Analysts San Francisco (dir.), Fin. Analysts Fedn. Republican. Episcopalian. Clubs: University, Tiburon Peninsula, Golden Gateway Tennis, Brown U. of No. Calif.; Naval (London).

BARKER, RONALD CLAUDE, lawyer; b. Newton, Utah, Sept. 28, 1927; s. S. W. and Hazel (Larsen) B.; B.S., Utah State U., 1949; LL.B., U. Utah, 1955, J.D., 1967; m. Geraldine C. Phillips, Apr. 15, 1952; children—Stephen, Bart, Luann, Mitchell, Beth, Sterling, Heather, Dawn, Marshall. Admitted to Utah bar, 1956; accountant Jones & Atwood, C.P.A.'s, Ogden, Utah, 1949-50, Burnett & Humphries, C.P.A.'s, Idaho Falls, Idaho, 1950-52; pvt. practice accounting, Salt Lake City, 1952-56, law, 1956—; pres. Salt Lake-Kanab Freight Lines, Salt Lake City, 1956-59; sec. Domestic Credit Corp., 1961-62; dir. University Heights Inc., Harold K. Beecher & Assos. Served with AUS, 1956-57. C.P.A., Utah, Idaho. Mem. Utah Soc. C.P.A.'s, Utah State, Salt Lake County bar assns., Alpha Kappa Psi, Phi Kappa Phi. Mem. Ch. Jesus Christ of Latter-day Saints (stake pres. 1972—). Home: 5655 W 3500 S Salt Lake City UT 84120 Office: 2870 S State St Salt Lake City UT 84115

BARKSDALE, ALMINA ANDERSON, home economics educator; b. Raymond, Alta., Can., May 15, 1922; d. John Forbes and Sarah Elizabeth (Tracy) Anderson; m. Bruce Warren Barksdale, Sept. 10, 1948 (div.); children—Karl, Sydnie Harman. B.S. in Home Econs. Edn., Brigham Young U., 1967; M.S. in Home Econs. Edn., Utah State U., 1980. Tchr. home econs. Granite Sch. Dist., Salt Lake City, 1967-81, supr. home econs., 1981—. Mem. Am. Home Econs. Assn., Utah Home Econs. Assn. (Tchr. of Yr. 1978), Am. Vocat. Assn., Utah Vocat. Assn., NEA, Utah Edn. Assn., Home Econs. Edn. Assn., Salt Lake Council of Women, Women's Legis. Council, Freedoms Found. at Valley Forge, Alpha Delta Kappa, Omicron Nu. Republican. Mormon. Home: 6093 Don Juan Dr Salt Lake City UT 84118 Office: Granite Sch Dist 340 East 3545 South Salt Lake City UT 84115

BARKSDALE, DIXIE LEE BARKER, state and county govt. ofcl.; b. Elsinore, Utah, May 25, 1930; d. Aaron Glen and Fawn Lenore (Braithwaite) Whitney; student Brigham Young U., Provo, Utah, 1956, Utah State U., 1957; m. Bruce W. Barksdale; children—Viviann, Vicki Joan, Whitney Dwain. Pres., gen. mgr. Moab Broadcasting and TV Corp., 1969-77; dir. community devel. Grand County (Utah), Moab, 1976-81; exec. dir. Canyonlands Travel Region, 1976-81; econ. devel. specialist Mountainland Assn. Govts., 1981—; exec. dir. Provo City Planning Commn., 1982—. Bd. dirs. Utah Econ. and Indsl. Devel., Utah Assn. Travel Regions; mem. Moab City Council, 1976-80; chmn. Grand County Democratic Com., 1968-69, Moab Drug and Alcohol Adv. Bd., 1973; mem. multiple-use adv. bd. Bur. Land Mgmt., 1980—. Named Woman of Yr., Epsilon Sigma Alpha, 1960, Friend of Utah, State of Utah, 1978. Mem. Provo C. of C. (indsl. devel. bd. 1981—), Moab C. of C. (pres. 1974-75), Canyonlands Natural History Assn. (chmn. 1979—), Utah Assn. Broadcasters, Utah Indsl. Devel. Execs. Assn. Democrat. Mormon. Club: Moab Women's Lit. (pres. 1959-60). Address: 110 West Pkwy Provo UT 84601

BARLIN, CAROLE ARLENE, ednl. adminstr.; b. Oakland, Calif., Nov. 7, 1935; d. Carl Christian and Leona Lillian (Vielhauer) Barlin; B.A., U. Calif., Berkeley, 1958; M.S., U. Redlands, 1971; 1 dau., Lizette Leona Swanson. Tchr., San Francisco Unified Sch. Dist., 1966-69, Los Angeles County Supt. Schs., 1971-74, asst. prin., 1974-76, prin., 1976, personnel coordinator, 1976—; lectr. —The Profl. Woman—. Mem. Assn. of Calif. Sch. Adminstrs. (officer 1976-82), Assn. of Los Angeles County Sch. Adminstrs. (pres. 1981-82), Women in Ednl. Leadership, Am. Speech and Hearing Assn. Office: 9300 E Imperial Hwy Downey CA 90242

BARLOW, WILLIAM PUSEY, JR., accountant; b. Oakland, Calif., Feb. 11, 1934; s. William P. and Muriel (Block) B.; student Calif. Inst. Tech., 1952-54; A.B. in Econs., U. Calif.-Berkeley, 1956. Acct. Barlow, Davis & Wood, San Francisco, 1960-72, ptnr., 1964-72; ptnr., J.K. Lasser & Co., 1972-77, Touche Ross & Co., San Francisco, 1977-78; self employed acct., 1978—. Fellow Gleeson Library Assos., 1969, pres., 1971-74; mem. Council Friends Bancroft Library, 1971—, chmn., 1974-79; bd. dirs. Oakland Ballet, 1982—. C.P.A., Calif. Mem. Am. Water Ski Assn. (dir., regional chmn. 1959-63, pres. 1963-66, chmn. bd. 1966-69, 77-79, hon. v.p. 1969—), World Water Ski Union (exec. bd. 1961-71, 75-78). Clubs: Grolier (N.Y.C.); Roxburghe (San Francisco); Book of Calif. (dir. 1963-76, pres. 1968-69, treas. 1971-83). Co-author: Collectible Books: Some New Paths, 1979; contbr. articles to profl. jours. Home: 1474 Hampel St Oakland CA 94602 Office: 1330 Broadway Suite 1600 Oakland CA 94612

BARMAN, DOUGLAS DALE, geophysicist; b. Tampa, Fla., Apr. 13, 1926; s. Howard Henry and Evelyn Marie (Schaefer) B.; B.S., St. Louis U. Inst. Tech., 1950; m. Elizabeth Woods, Mar. 31, 1951; children—Mary, Anne, William, Barbara, Robert, Thomas, Douglas M. With Texaco, Inc., Los Angeles, 1950—, dist. geophysicist, 1966-68, sr. geophysicist, 1968-69, asst. div. geophysicist, 1969-79, staff geophysicist, 1979, cons. exploration geophysicist, 1980—; guest lect. geophysics U. So. Calif. and Stanford U., 1975; Dana-Decker lectr. in geophysics U. Redlands, 1980, 81; adv. com. M.S. program in geophysics Calif. State U., Fullerton, 1980, 81. Served with U.S. Army, 1944-46. Registered geophysicst, geologist, Calif. Mem. Soc. Exploration Geophysicists (v.p. 1974, pres. 1981—, gen. chmn. internat. meeting 1972, steering com. internat. meeting 1981 v.p. Pacific sect. 1965-66, pres. Pacific sect. 1966-67, mem. nat. coms.; chmn. nominating com. 1982-83), Am. Petroleum Inst. Republican. Roman Catholic. Office: 3350 Wilshire Blvd Los Angeles CA 90010

BARMANN, BARRY CARROL, psychologist; b. Lakewood, Ohio, Feb. 1, 1955; s. George J. and Marguerite B.; B.A. with honors and distinction in Psychology, Ohio State U., 1976; M.A. in Psychology, U. of Pacific, 1979; postgrad. in psychology U. Calif., Santa Barbara, 1979—. Psychol. asst. Western Res. Psychiat. Habilitation Center, Cleve., 1976-77; inservice tng. instr. Mable Barron Elem. Sch., Stockton, Calif., 1977-78; behavior analyst Tri-Counties Regional Center, Santa Barbara, Calif., 1979—; counselor Counseling Psychology Clinic, U. Calif., Santa Barbara, 1979-80, adminstrv. coordinator, asst. dir., 1980-81, research asst. dept. speech and hearing and dept. edn., 1980-81; behavior analyst Behavior Intervention Service, Stockton, 1977-79; behavior analyst, tng. specialist Cath. Charities Disability Service, Stockton, 1977-79; behavior analyst, cons. Cath. Social Services, Stockton, 1978-79; instr. psychology Santa Barbara City Coll., 1980—, div. continuing edn. extension program, U. Calif., Santa Barbara, 1980-81; research asst. U. of Pacific, Stockton, 1978-79, Stockton State Hosp., 1978-79, Stanford U., 1977-78; cons. Valley Community Mental Health Service, Stockton, 1978-79, Wagner Group Home for Delinquent Teenage Boys, Carpinteria, Calif., 1979-80, spl. edn. units various schs. Santa Barbara, 1979-81. Acad. state travel scholar, U. Calif., Santa Barbara, 1980; Eagle Scout. Mem. Am. Psychol. Assn. and Student Affiliate Group of Div. 17, Assn. for Advancement of Behavior Therapy, Western Psychol. Assn. (travel scholar 1979, 81), Psi Chi (cert. of recognition 1981). Contbr. papers to profl. publs. and confs. Home: 2924 Hermosa Rd Santa Barbara CA 93105 Office: Tri Counties Regional Center 222 E Canon Perdido St Santa Barbara CA

BARNA, LILLIAN CARATTINI, supt. schs.; b. N.Y.C., Jan. 18, 1929; d. Juan and Dolores Elsie Nieves (Alicea) Carattini; A.B. Hunter Coll. 1950; M.A. San Jose State U. 1970; m. Eugene Andrew Barna, July 1, 1951; children—Craig Andrew, Keith Andrew. Tchr., N.Y.C. Sch. Dist. 1950-52; tchr. Whittier (Calif.) Sch. Dist. 1952-54, tchr. high sch. 1954-56; tchr. presch. Long Beach and Los Gatos, Calif., 1958-67; supr. early childhood edn. San Jose (Calif.) Unified Sch. Dist. 1967-72, sch. adminstr., 1972-80, supt. schs., 1980—; cons. in field. Recipient Soroptimist Internat. Woman of Yr. award 1980, Western Region Puertorican Council Achievement award 1980, Assn. Puertorican Profls. Achievement award 1981, Calif. State U. Outstanding Achievement in Edn. award 1982, Woman of Achievement award Santa Clara County Commn. on Status of Women/San Jose Mercury News, Disting. Alumni award San Jose State U. Mem. Nat. Assn. Edn. Young Children, Tchrs. English to Speakers of Other Langs., Women Leaders in Edn., Calif. Reading Assn., Calif. Assn. Women Adminstrs., Assn. Calif. Sch. Adminstrs., Phi Kappa Phi, Delta Zeta. Office: 1605 Park Ave San Jose CA 95126

BARNARD, GEORGE AUGUSTUS, III, electronics engr., engring. co. exec.; b. Worcester, Mass., Jan. 15, 1921; s. George A. and Grace (Roberts) B.; B.S., Harvard U., 1943, postgrad., 1950-51; M.S., Stanford U., 1957; postgrad. U. Hawaii, 1944-45, U. Calif., Berkeley, 1958-59; m. Annette Mildred Bilodeau, June 17, 1949. Electronics engr., Venezuela, Colombia, Fairchild Aerial Surveys, Los Angeles, 1947-48, India, 1951-52, Peru, 1952; electronics engr. Hawaiian Signal Ops. Group, Honolulu, 1948-50; research engr. Stanford Research Inst., Menlo Park, Calif., 1952-58; mgr. advanced product planning Ampex Corp., Redwood City, Calif., 1958-61; instr. in electonics Palo Alto, Menlo Park Pub. Schs., 1954-55; sr. engring. specialist Western Devel. Labs. of Philco Corp., Palo Alto, Calif., 1961-65; mgr. computer advanced planning Comml. Airplane Group, Boeing Co., Seattle, 1965-71; tech. cons. Weyerhaeuser Co., Tacoma, Wash., 1971—; mem. No. Calif. Electronics Apprenticeship Advisory Com., 1954-55. Served to capt., Signal Corps, U.S. Army, 1943-46; PTO. Registered profl. engr., Wash.; lic. amateur radio operator. Mem. IEEE (sr.), Am. Radio Relay League, Sci. Research Soc., Am. Fedn. Info. Processing Socs. (chmn. computer conf. 1962), Le Progres de l'Oceanie. Mgr. circulation San Francisco Engr., 1959-60; contbr. articles to profl. jours.; patentee in field.

BARNARD, LLOYD WAYNE, computer systems executive; b. Moline, Ill., July 13, 1940; s. Lee and Helen Mary (Lockwood) B.; A.A., Blackhawk Coll., 1965; postgrad. U. So. Calif., 1978; m. Roberta Lee Fulton, June 1, 1963; children—Todd Lee, Melissa Mary. Engring. aid Bendix, Davenport, Iowa, 1961-66; engr. Univac div. Sperry Rand, Dayton, Ohio, 1966-68; software specialist Emerson Electric, St. Louis, 1968-71; mgr. systems engring. Northrop Data Systems, Carson, Calif., 1971-78; v.p. Mfrs. Resources and Planning, Inc., 1978-80; pres. Technology Support, Inc., Tustin, Calif., 1980—; mgr. devel. Calcomp, Anaheim, Calif., 1980-82; exec. dir. mgmt. info. systems U. So. Calif., Los Angeles, 1982—. Served with U.S. Army, 1958-61. Office: PO Box 675 Tustin CA 92680

BARNARD, ROBERT LEE, electrical engineer; b. Indpls., May 16, 1945; s. Alva LaRoy and Gladys Mary (Kennedy) B.; B.S. in Elec. Engring., N.Mex. State U., 1969, M.S., 1972; m. Jane Alexandra Armell, Dec. 16, 1966; children—Kathryn Genevieve, Anne Bodwin, Robert Charles. Computer control clk. First Nat. Bank, Las Cruces, N.Mex., 1966-68; programmer N.Mex. State U., 1968-69, mgr. users services, 1969-72; systems analyst cons. Handy & Assos., Las Cruces, 1969-72; dir. data processing Region XIX, Edn. Service Center, El Paso, Tex., 1973-74; chief biometry Cancer Research and Treatment Center, U. N.Mex., Albuquerque, 1974-76; mgr. electronic data processing Colo.-Ute Electric Assn., Montrose, Colo., 1976-81, mgr. fuels and waste products, 1981—. Chmn. bd. Mesilla Valley Christian Ch., Las Cruces, 1971; treas. 1st United Meth. Ch., Montrose, 1977-80; mem. exec. com. Montrose Child Care Center; bd. dirs., sec. Montrose Recreation Dist.; bd. dirs. Spl. Dist. Assn. Mem. Am. Mgmt. Assn., Assn. Computing Machinery, Sigma Tau. Democrat. Methodist. Home: 740 S 2d St Montrose CO 81401 Office: PO Box 1149 Montrose CO 81401

BARNARD, ROLLIN DWIGHT, savs. and loan exec.; b. Denver, Apr. 14, 1922; s. George Cooper and Emma (Riggs) B.; B.A., Pomona Coll., 1943; m. Patricia Reynolds Bierkamp, Sept. 15, 1943; children—Michael Dana, Rebecca Susan Barnard Wulfestieg, Laurie Beth Barnard Kostelecky. Clk., Morey Merc. Co., Denver, 1937-40; partner George C. Barnard & Co., gen. real estate and ins., Denver, 1946-47; v.p. Foster & Barnard, Inc., 1947-53; instr. U. Denver, 1949-53; dir. real estate U.S. Post Office Dept., Washington, 1953-55, dep. asst. postmaster gen., bur. facilities, 1955-59, asst. postmaster gen., 1959-61; pres., dir. Midland Fed. Savs. and Loan Assn., Denver, 1962—; mem. adv. council Fed. Home Loan Bank Bd., 1982; dir. Fed. Home Loan Bank of Topeka, 1965-66, Verex Assurance Inc., 1983—. Mem. nat. council Pomona (Calif.) Coll., 1963—; mem. exec. bd. Denver Area council Boy Scouts Am., 1962-73, adv. bd., 1973—, pres., 1970-71; bd. dirs. Bethesda Found., 1973-82; bd. dirs. Children's Hosp., 1979— treas., 1983—; bd. dirs. Rocky Mountain Child Health Services, Inc., 1982—; trustee Mile High United Fund, 1969-72, Denver Symphony Assn., 1973-74; trustee Morris Animal Found., pres., chmn., 1974-78, trustee emeritus, 1981—; bd. dirs. Pitts. Theol. Sem., 1968-73, YMCA, 1969-71; mem. Greenwood Village (Colo.) Planning and Zoning Commn., 1967-73, chmn., 1969-73; mem. Greenwood Village City Council, 1975-77. Served to capt. AUS, World War II. Nominated one of ten outstanding young men in Am., U.S. Jr. C of C., 1955, 57; recipient Disting. Service award Postmaster Gen. U.S., 1960; Silver Beaver award Boy Scouts Am., 1969; Outstanding Citizen of Yr., Mile Hi chpt. Sertoma Internat., 1982; Colo. Citizen of Yr., Colo. Assn. Realtors, 1982. Mem. Denver Bd. Realtors (v.p., dir. 1949-53), Denver C. of C. (dir. 1964-67, pres. 1966-67), Savs. League Colo. (pres. 1971-72), Fed. Nat. Mortgage Assn. (adv. council 1982-83), Fellowship Christian Athletes (Denver area dir. 1963-76), U.S. League Savs. Instns. (nat. legis. com., dir. 1972-77, exec. com. 1974-77, 79-82, vice-chmn. 1979-80, chmn. 1980-81, SAPEC fin. com. 1983—), Western Stock Show Assn. (dir. 1971—), Colo. Council Econ. Edn. (dir., chmn. bd. 1971-76), Colo. Assn. Commerce and Industry (dir. 1971-76), Downtown Denver Improvement Assn. (pres. 1965), Nu Alpha Phi. Republican. Presbyterian. Clubs: 26 (pres. 1970), Mountain and Plains Appaloosa Horse (pres. 1970-71), Rotary (dir. 1979-81, 2d v.p. 1980), Roundup Riders of the Rockies (dir. 1980, treas. 1982—) (Denver). Home: 3151 E Long Rd Littleton CO 80121 Office: 444 17th St Denver CO 80202

BARNES, BARRY RONALD, educator; b. Berkeley, Calif., Dec. 9, 1939; s. Ronald E. and Kathleen D. (McGagin) B.; A.A., Diablo Valley Coll., 1961; B.A., Calif. State U. at Chico, 1965; M.A., Calif. State U. at Sacramento, 1967; m. Mary Ann Bequette, Aug. 7, 1966; children—Barry Ronald, Jonathan Patrick. Instr. art Coll. of the Siskiyous, Weed Calif., 1967—; asst. prof. extension art Calif. State U. at Chico, 1968—. Participant Nat. Found. for the Humanities seminar, 1971. Mem. Siskiyou County Democratic Central Com., 1972; bd. dirs. Mt. Shasta Union Sch. Dist., 1974 basketball coach Mt. Shasta High Sch., 1982—; bd. dirs. Mt. Shasta Recreation Dist. cubmaster Mt. Shasta council Boy Scouts Am., 1976—. Mem. Soc. for Gen. and Liberal Studies, Coll. Art Assn., Calif. Assn. Community Colls. (bd. dirs. 1981—), Calif. Community and Jr. Coll. Assn. (dir.). Author: How to Build a Kick Wheel. Home: 3525 N Old Stage Rd Mount Shasta CA 96067 Office: College of the Siskiyous 800 College Ave Weed CA 96094

BARNES, BERNICE, sales trainer; b. Ogden, Utah, Dec. 12, 1942; d. Rulon Jay and Claribel (Richardson) Harper; A.S., Weber Coll., 1963; 1 dau., Wendy. Dental adminstr. David O. Hendrickson, Inc., Utah, 1965-76; nat sales rep., sales trainer Patterson Dental Co., 1976-78; cons., sales trainer Am. Optical Co., Southbridge, Mass., 1978—; public speaker ch. orgns. Vol. rest homes and hosps. Recipient Golden Gleaner award Ch. of Jesus Christ of Latter-Day Saints, 1965; recipient certs. of achievement Patterson Dental Co., Am. Optical Co. Mem. Am. Soc. Profl. and Exec. Women, Am. Soc. Tng. and Devel. Home: 11859 Turquoise Fountain Valley CA 92708 Office: 14 Mechanic St Southbridge MA 01550

BARNES, B.J. (BETTY JEAN), educator; b. San Dimas, Calif., Mar. 6, 1921; d. Harold Tinsley and Daisy Linden Caldwell; m. George William Barnes, Jan. 22, 1947; children—Lauren Louise, Jeffrey William, Betsy Jane. B.A., Pomona Coll., 1945; M.A., Claremont Grad. Sch., 1966, Ph.D., 1973. Cert. tchr., Calif., 1963. Tchr., Upland (Calif.) Elem. Sch. Dist., 1962-64, Ontario-Montclair (Calif.) Sch. Dist., 1966-67; staff assoc. Claremont (Calif.) Grad. Sch., 1967-70, program coordinator, 1970-71; mem. faculty Calif. State U.-Fullerton, 1972—, prof. edn., 1982—. Mem. Calif. Assn. Edn. Young Children, Calif. Profs. Early Childhood Edn., Calif. Curriculum Forum, Phi Delta Kappa, Pi Lambda Theta, others. Democrat. Editor: (with Shirley Hill) Young Children and Their Families: Needs of the Nineties, 1982; (with Carolyn Ellner) Schoolmaking: An Alternative in Teacher Education, 1977; contbr. articles, monograph, videotapes. Office: Div Tchr Edn Calif St U Fullerton CA 92634

BARNES, CAROL P., educator, consultant; b. Ann Arbor, Mich., Jan. 21, 1941; d. Reinhold Walter and Ruth Ardillis (McKillen) Pardon; m. Gary Lee Barnes, June 17, 1959; children—Katherine L., Erik Howard. A.B. in Edn., U. Mich., 1962; M.Ed., Wright State U., 1970; Ph.D., Claremont Grad. Sch., 1975. Cert. tchr., Mich., Ohio. Tchr. pub. schs. Mich. and Ohio, 1962-70; lectr. Wright State U., Dayton, Ohio, 1970-72, Claremont Grad. Sch., Calif., 1973-74; asst. then assoc. prof. tchr. edn. and child devel. Calif. State U.-Fullerton, 1975—, coordinator elem. edn., 1978-81, chmn. child devel. program, 1982—; cons. Calif. Dept. Edn. Commn. Tchr. Preparation and Licensing; dir. Calif. Council Edn. Tchrs. Mem. Assn. Supervision and Curriculum Devel. (Calif. exec. council), Calif. Reading Assn., Oreg. Reading Assn., Colo. Reading Assn., AAUP, AAUW, Am. Ednl. Research Assn., Congress Faculty Assns., NEA, Phi Delta Kappa, Kappa Delta Pi, Phi Kappa Phi. Presbyterian. Author: (with others) Studies in College Teaching, 1983; contbr. articles to profl. jours., chpt. in reading text. Office: Tchr Edn Calif State U Fullerton 800 N State College Blvd Fullerton CA 92634

BARNES, DEBRA ANN, public relations executive; b. Chgo., Mar. 25, 1955; d. Roy Dillon and Amelia Frances (Carlomango) B.; B.S. in Journalism with honors, No. Ill. U., 1977. Dir. pub. relations Doctors' Hosp., Modesto, Calif., 1977-79, Mary's Help Hosp., Daly City, Calif., 1979-82; dir. pub. relations/mktg. communications Children's Hosp. Med. Ctr. No. Calif., Oakland, 1982—. Publicity chmn. Oakland City councilwoman re-election campaign, 1983. Recipient Print Festival Publs. award Health Scis. Communication Assn., 1982. Mem. Acad. Hosp. Pub. Relations, Am. Soc. Hosp. Pub. Relations (Nat. MacEchern award 1983), Hosp. Pub. Relations Assn. No. Calif. (sec./officer), Soroptimist Internat. Democrat. Roman Catholic. Author various hosp. publs., designs and coordinates health-related events/displays. Home: 1445 Greenwich #208 San Francisco CA 94109 Office: Children's Hospital Medical Center 51st and Grove Sts Oakland CA 94609

BARNES, GARY LEE, aeronautical engineer; b. Ann Arbor, Mich., Mar. 19, 1940; s. Howard Earle and Alice May (Gary) B.; m. Carol Ann Pardon, June 17, 1959; children—Katherine Lynn, Erik Howard. B.S.E. in Aero. Engring., U. Mich., 1963; M.S.E., Air Force Inst. Tech., 1964. Group leader Fgn. Tech. div. USAF, Dayton, Ohio, 1967-72; sect. head Hughes Aircraft Co., Fullerton, Calif., 1972-75, dept. mgr., 1975-78, mgr. advanced communication systems, 1978-80, mgr. advanced systems lab., 1980-82, assoc. mgr. C3I program mgmt. office, 1982—. Served to capt. USAF, 1963-67. Decorated Legion of Merit. Mem. AIAA, Am. Def. Preparedness Assn. Contbr. articles to profl. jours. Home: 2061 Skyline Dr Fullerton CA 92634 Office: Hughes Aircraft Co 1901 Malvern St Fullerton CA 92634

BARNES, JIMMY DOYLE, oil company executive, educator; b. Bakersfield, Calif., May 20, 1943; s. Doyle B. and Pearlie E. (Davidson) B.; A.A. in Bus. Adminstrn., Bakersfield Jr. Coll., 1964; B.S. in Mktg., Calif. State U.-Fresno, 1966, M.B.A., 1968; Ph.D. in Mktg., U. Oreg., 1972; m. Gaye Madchen Mullhofer, Jan. 6, 1966. Grad. asst. Calif. State U.-Fresno, 1967-68, asst. prof. fin. and industry (part-time), 1968-69; instr. U. Oreg., Eugene, also lectr. prins. of mktg., 1969-71; lectr. Sch. Bus. and Fin., Calif. State U.-Fullerton, 1971-72; v.p. Barnes Core Drilling Co., Bakersfield, 1971—; gen. ptnr., mgr. B & S Oil Co., Bakersfield, 1981—; pres. Tri-Valley Oil & Gas Co., Inc., Bakersfield, 1980-81; prof., chmn. dept. mktg. Calif. State Coll., Bakersfield, 1972—; vis. prof. U. Hawaii, summers 1973-81; cons. mktg. to bus. orgns. Mem. Am. Mktg. Assn., Am. Inst. Decision Scis. (pres. Western region 1978-79), Acad. Mgmt. Author: (with Michael Geurts) Conducting Business in the Pacific Basin, 1976; contbr. over 50 articles on mktg. and bus. adminstrn. to profl. jours. Home: 4300 Woodlake Dr Bakersfield CA 93309 Office: 1350 Roberts Ln Bakersfield CA 93308

BARNES, JOHN BERREL, dentist; b. New Iberia, La., Jan. 15, 1922; s. Paul and Virginia B.; student Morehouse Coll., 1947; D.D.S., Meharry Med. Coll., 1952; LL.B., LaSalle Ext. U., 1965; m. Audra Mae Guyton; children—Audra Yvonne, John Berrel. Practice dentistry, Los Angeles, 1958—. Served with AUS, World War II; served to capt. USAF, 1951-55. Mem. ADA, So. Calif. Soc. Dentistry for Children. Methodist. Office: 12060 S Central Ave Los Angeles CA 90059

BARNES, JOHN FAYETTE, scientist; b. Santa Cruz, Calif., Jan, 28, 1930; s. John Fayette and Bertha Henrietta (Youngman) B.; B.A., U. Calif.-Berkeley, 1951; M.S., U. Denver, 1952; Ph.D., U. N.Mex., 1963, M.Mgmt., 1981; m. Joanne Cecily Lyle, Aug. 28, 1955; children—John Fayette, David Lyle. Staff mem. Los Alamos Sci. Lab., 1953—, asst. group leader, 1968-71, alternate group leader, 1971, group leader, 1971-76, asst. theoretical div. leader, 1976-77, assoc. div. leader, 1977-80, dep. div. leader, 1980-81, dep. assoc. dir. for energy, 1981-82, dep. assoc. dir. physics and math., 1982—; mathematician Research Directorate Air Force Spl. Weapons Center, Albuquerque, 1956-57; mem. research adv. bd. Lab. for Laser Energetics, U. Rochester, chmn., 1981. Active Boy Scouts Am. Mem. Am. Phys. Soc. Republican. Contbr. articles to profl. jours. Home: 13 Village Pl White Rock Los Alamos NM 87544 Office: Physics and Math Directorate Office Los Alamos Nat Lab PO Box 1663 Los Alamos NM 87545

BARNES, MARTIN HILBERT, ins. co. exec.; b. Chgo., Mar. 9, 1922; s. Martin James and Helen Louise (Hilbert) B.; B.S., U. Oreg., 1949; m. Gloria Joan Walsh, Dec. 28, 1946; children—Lynda Marie, Martin Edward, James Austin, Deborah Ann, William Earl. Casualty underwriting supr., mgr. methods and planning, Indsl. Indemnity Co., San Francisco, 1952-70; dir. office services, Gt. Am. Ins. Co., Los Angeles, 1970-73; v.p. adminstrn., Highlands Ins. Co., Houston, 1973-75; adminstrv. mgr., Employee Benefits Ins. Co., Portland, Oreg., 1976-82; sr. v.p. L.M. Radke Assos., Portland, 1982—. Pres. bd. library trustees, Santa Clara, Calif., 1967-70; exec. bd. Mayor's Adv. Com., Los Angeles, 1970-73; dist. chmn. Santa Clara County council Boy Scouts Am., 1968-70, mem. exec. bd. Columbia Pacific council, 1976—, commr., 1978-82. Served with USCG, 1941-46, to comdr. USCGR, 1951-52. Recipient Silver Beaver award Boy Scouts Am., 1978. Mem. Res. Officers Assn., Adminstrv. Mgmt. Soc. Republican. Presbyterian. Club: Elks (charter Lodge 2347). Home: 4123 SW Jerald Way Portland OR 97221 Office: 749 SE Lexington Portland OR 97202

BARNES, MOLLY, art dealer, art critic; b. London, Eng., May 18, 1936; d. John Edmonds and Jane (Moore) Mock; m. Howard G. Barnes, Dec. 7, 1959 (div.); children—Christie Ann, Paul Louis Lloyd. B.A. in Art History, U. Calif.-Berkeley, 1957. With Calif. Arts Commn., 1965; dir. Matisse Gallery, Frank Perls Gallery, Rolf Nelson Gallery, 1965-67; owner, dir. Molly Barnes Gallery, Los Angeles, 1967—; art critic Radio Sta. KFWB, Los Angeles, 1965-70; art critic Hollywood Reporter Mag., 1970—. Founding mem. Mus. Contemporary Art, Los Angeles. Home: 474 S Rodeo Dr Beverly Hills CA 90212 Office: 750 N La Cienega Blvd Los Angeles CA 90069

BARNES, ROBERT PAUL, coll. ofcl.; b. Minot, N.D., Jan. 16, 1934; s. Richard Neil and Erna Margaret (Broeckel) B.; m. Pamela Kay Frantz, Mar. 13, 1976; 1 dau., Claire Margaret. B.A., U. Wash., 1956; M.A., U. Colo., 1963; Ph.D. (Univ. scholar), U. So. Calif., 1967. Tchr. pub. schs., Calif., Ill., 1960-62; lectr. U. of Pacific, 1966; asst. prof. history Western State Coll., Gunnison, Colo., 1966-67, Purdue U., 1967-68; assoc. prof. Central Wash. U., 1968-72; acad. dean N.W. Mo. State U., 1972-75, ednl. cons. and devel. officer, 1975-80; v.p. Rockmont Coll., Denver, 1980-82; v.p. Westmar Coll., 1982—; speaker for civic, profl. groups; mem. Fulbright Selection Com., 1977—. Served with U.S. Army, 1957-58. Central Wash. U. faculty research grantee, 1970-71. Mem. Am. Hist. Assn., Am. Assn. Higher Edn., Conf. Brit. Studies, Faith and History, Christian Stewardship Council, Assn. Instnl. Devel. Officers, Western Social Sci. Assn., Phi Alpha Theta. Republican. Mem. Christian Ch. (Disciples of Christ). Contbr. articles, revs. to profl. jours.

BARNET, ROBERT JOSEPH, cardiologist; b. Port Huron, Mich., Apr. 27, 1929; s. John A. and Ruth Elizabeth (Wittliff) B.; student Port Huron Jr. Coll., summers 1947, 49; B.S. magna cum laude, Notre Dame U., 1954; M.D., Loyola U., Chgo., 1954; m. Helen Kresoja Dec. 8, 1969; children—Benedict, Maria, Antonia, Peter, Elizabeth, Rebecca, Christina, Jacqueline, Ann. Med. intern Boston City Hosp., 1954-55; rotating intern Mercy Hosp., Chgo., 1955; asst. resident in medicine Boston City Hosp., 1958-59; clin. and research fellow in cardiology Children's Med. Center and House of the Good Samaritan, Boston, 1959-60; cons. fellow in rheumatic fever Pediatric Service, Boston City Hosp., 1959-60; cons. fellow in rheumatic fever Mass. State Rheumatic Fever Clinic, 1959-60; research fellow in pediatrics Harvard U., Boston, 1959-60; clin. fellow in cardiology Mass. Meml. Hosps., Boston, 1960-61; physician-in-charge St. Francis Mission Hosp., Solwezi, No. Rhodesia, 1961-62; vis. physician Solwezi Boma Rural Hosp., No. Rhodesia, 1961-62; dir. clinics, asso. in medicine Stritch Sch. Medicine, Loyola U., Chgo., 1962-65; asso. attending physician dept. medicine Cook County Hosp., Chgo., 1962-63, attending physician, 1963-65; practice medicine, specializing in cardiology, Reno, 1965—; mem. med. staff Washoe Med. Center, Reno, 1965—, St. Mary's Hosp., Reno, 1965—; asso. clin. prof. cardiology U. Nev. and asso. dir. Lab. Environ. Patho-Physiology, Desert Research Inst., U. Nev., Reno, 1965-68; dir. CCU, Washoe Med. Center, Reno, 1965-83, chmn. emergency room com., 1967-71, mem. exec. com., 1967-71, 73-78, vice chief dept. medicine, 1969, chief, 1970-71, 78, chief dept. emergency services, 1973-77; cons. cardiologist Disability Determination Unit, State of Nev., 1966—, Crippled Children's Service, 1966-77; cons. in cardiology Reno VA Hosp., 1967—; asst. clin. prof. med. edn. U. Utah, 1968-71; cons. in cardiology Churchill Pub. Hosp., Fallon, Nev., 1969—, Pershing Gen. Hosp., Lovelock, Nev., 1969—; clin. asso. U. Nev., Reno, 1971-72, asso. clin. prof. medicine, 1973-77, prof., 1978—. Served with U.S. Army, 1955-58. Recipient Clin. Faculty Honor award for Outstanding Tchr., Loyola U., 1963-64; licensed physician, Mass., Ill., Calif., Wash., Nev. Diplomate Nat. Bd. Med. Examiners, Am. Bd. Internal Medicine. Fellow ACP (gov. 1980-81), Am. Coll. Cardiology (gov. 1974-77), Am. Coll. Chest Physicians; mem. Am. Soc. Internal Medicine, AMA, Nev., Washoe County med. socs., Am. Fedn. Clin. Research, Nev. Heart Assn. (dir. 1968-81, exec. com. 1968-75, v.p. 1971-73, pres. 1974-75, Common Cause (coordinator No. Nev. 1975-76). Contbr. articles to med. jours. Home: 166 Greenridge Dr Reno NV 89509 Office: 850 Mill St Suite 101 Reno NV 89502

BARNETT, BLAIR MERCER, physician; b. Mpls., Apr. 18, 1938; s. Blair Mercer and Bernardine (Lilyquist) B.; B.A., Washington and Jefferson Coll., 1960; M.D., UCLA, 1964; m. Leanne Carol Sandland, Oct. 7, 1972; children—Karen, Stephanie, Lindsay. Intern, Naval Hosp., Pensacola, Fla., 1964-65; resident Nat. Naval Med. Center, Bethesda, Md., 1965-67; practice medicine, specializing in anesthesiology, Arroyo Grande, Calif., 1975—; chief anesthesia service Paradise Valley Hosp., National City, Calif., 1970-75; chief anesthesia service Arroyo Grande Community Hosp., 1975—, dir., 1978-80. Bd. dirs. Ventura-Santa-Barbara-San Luis Obispo Counties Profl. Standards Rev. Orgn., 1980. Served to lt. comdr. USN, 1964-70. Fellow Am. Coll. Anesthesiologists;

mem. AMA, Calif. Med. Assn., Internat. Anesthesia Research Soc. Inventor cardiac resuscitation mattress, 1978, variable transparency window, 1979, variable pressure endotracheal tube cuff, 1980. Office: 345 S Halcyon Rd Arroyo Grande CA 93420

BARNETT, GEORGE HERSCHEL, ret. judge; b. Detroit, Oct. 6, 1914; s. Bernard and Jeannette (Sindell) B.; A.B., Case Western Res. U., 1937, J.D., 1939; m. Suzanne Price, July 13, 1980; children—Helen Barbara Gold, Jeffrey Alan, Susan Kay Nissenbaum. Bar: Ohio 1939. Practiced law, Paulding, Ohio, 1939-41; atty. War Dept., Cleve. Ordnance Dist., 1941-42; admitted to Calif. bar, 1947; practiced law, San Jose, Calif., 1947-60; judge Municipal Ct. San Jose, 1960-63, Superior Ct., 1963-81; presiding judge Santa Clara County, 1966-67, Juvenile Ct., Santa Clara County, 1975-77; instr. law U. Santa Clara Sch. Law, 1969-71; arbitrator, mediator. Pres. Community Welfare Council Santa Clara County, 1956, Family Service Assn. Santa Clara County, 1957, Goodwill Industries of Santa Clara and San Benito Counties, 1958; v.p., dir. Family Service Assn. Am., 1956-65; former treas., dir. Calif. Assn. Health and Welfare; co-chmn. Santa Clara County chpt. NCCJ, 1964-70; chmn. Israel Bond dr. Santa Clara County, 1962, 75, chmn. profl. div., 1961-68; mem. housing code com. City San Jose, 1957; bd. dirs. San Jose Symphony Assn. (emeritus), Police Activities League; bd. govs. Goodwill Industries Santa Clara County; mem. bd. fellows emeritus U. Santa Clara. Served with AUS, 1942-46. Decorated Bronze Star; named Disting. Citizen City of San Jose, Trial Judge of Year, 1977. Mem. Santa Clara County Bar Assn. (pres. 1958), Calif. Judges Assn., Conf. Conciliation Cts. Jewish (pres. temple 1963-64). Author: West's California Code of Civil Procedure Forms; also articles in field. Home: 12215 Edgecliff Pl Los Altos Hills CA 94022

BARNETT, JAMES KEITH, III, state official, lawyer; b. Burbank, Calif., Nov. 14, 1947; s. James K. and Barbara L. (Keep) B.; m. Marilyn Shuman, Aug. 14, 1971. A.A., Glendale Coll., 1967; B.S., U. Calif.-Berkeley, 1968, M.B.A., 1969; J.D., Cornell U., 1971. Bar: Alaska 1974. Assoc., Ely, Guess, & Rudd, Anchorage, 1974-76; atty. BP Alaska & Sohio Alaska Petroleum Co., Anchorage, 1976-83; dep. commr. Dept. Natural Resources State of Alaska, Anchorage, 1983—; chmn. North-Slope Borough Service Area 10 Utility Bd., Prudhoe Bay, Alaska, 1980-83. Mem. Upper O'Malley Limited Road Service Area, 1978-81; mem. Anchorage Reapportionment Com., 1980; chmn. Anchorage Platting Bd., 1981—; bd. dirs. Anchorage United Way, 1981—. Mem. ABA, Alaska Bar Assn., Anchorage Bar Assn. Contbg. editor Cornell Internat. Law Jour., 1974; contbr. articles to Alaska Mag., 1981. Home: SRA Box 2040 J Anchorage AK 99507 Office: Pouch 7 005 Anchorage AK 99502

BARNETT, MARK ANDREW, rec. studio exec.; b. Jersey City, 1950; s. Lawrence and Shirley (Joseph) B.; student Drew U., Bard Coll., U. Colo. Pvt. music tchr., San Francisco and Boulder, 1967-80; guitarist Black Rose The Carnes-Barnett Band; free-lance producer/arranger; founder The Last Rec. Studio, Ltd., Boulder, 1978—; dean dept. aesthetics and engring. Rocky Mountain Sch. Rec. Music, Boulder, 1980—. First pres., planner Goss Grove Neighborhood Assn., 1973-76; classroom advisor Boulder Public Schs. Mem. ASCAP, Audio Engring. Soc., Rocky Mountain Studio Owners Assn. Contbr. articles to profl. jours. Office: 2539 Pearl St Boulder CO 80302

BARNETT, MICKEY DEE, lawyer; b. Clovis, N.Mex., Mar. 5, 1951; s. Frank H. and Chris K. (Laughlin) B.; B.B.A., Eastern N.Mex. U., 1973; J.D., George Washington U., 1977; m. Jacqueline Elaine Farmer, May 26, 1973; children—Frank Charles, Jennifer Michelle. Legislative aide to Senator Pete V. Domenici, U.S. Senate, 1973-76; admitted to N.Mex. bar, 1977; practiced in Portales, N.Mex., 1977—; mem. N.Mex. Senate, 1981—. Republican. Home: 416 E 18th St Portales NM 88130 Office: PO Drawer 659 Portales NM 88130

BARNETT, RAY HOSMER, elec. engr.; b. Jacksonville, Fla., Oct. 9, 1927; s. Marvin Robert and Grace Amelia (Allen) B.; student U. Miami (Fla.), 1947-48; B.S. in E.E., Colo. U., 1958; m. Sonia Leatrice Shaw, June 30, 1978; children—Thomas, Michael. Electronics engr. U.S. Geol. Survey, Denver, Flagstaff, Ariz., 1954-66, Navy Dept., Washington, 1966-70, U.S. Bur. Mines, Denver, 1970-76; program analyst Nure project office U.S. Dept. Energy, Grand Junction, Colo., 1976—. Served with USN, 1945-46, 48-52; Korea. Democrat. Home: 225 Walnut Ave Grand Junction CO 81501 Office: PO Box 2567 Grand Junction CO 81502

BARNETTE, MACK JAMES THOMAS, accountant; b. Everett, Wash., Dec. 5, 1931; s. Mack Fisher and Janice (Wilmot) B.; m. Marjorie Helen McNeely, May 10, 1958; children Beverly Marjorie, Kevin Mack George, Colleen Heather. B.A., U. Wash., 1954, postgrad., 1961-63. C.P.A., Wash. Acct., Seattle First Nat. Bank, 1949-60; asst. treas. Grange Ins. Assn., Seattle, 1960-65; sec., treas. West Coast Credit Corp., Seattle, 1965-76, also dir.; pvt. practice acctg., Arlington, Wash., 1976—. Del., Republican State Conv., 1960, 78; King County chmn. Conservative Party, 1966. Served with AUS, 1956-57. Mem. Nat. Soc. Public Accts., Arlington C. of C. (treas. 1978-82), Scabbard and Blade. Libertarian. Mem. Unity Ch. of Truth (pres. 1981-83). Contbr. articles to profl. jours. Home: 8234 Interlake Ave N Seattle WA 98103 Office: 518 N Olympic Ave Arlington WA 98223

BARNEY, DOYLE DUANE, constrn. co. exec.; b. Provo, Utah, Mar. 23, 1929; s. Edith Deborah Barney; student public schs.; m. Wanda Robertson, June 21, 1950; children—Carolyn, Patricia, Diana Dee, Duane R., Sandra Joy. Operator heavy cranes for constrn. cos., Utah and Wyo., 1969-80; supt. equipment Jelco Inc. and MK Power Assos., Huntington and Castle Dale, Utah, 1980—. Mayor of Castle Dale, 1974-79; dist. chmn. Boy Scouts Am., 1980-81. Democrat. Mormon. Home: 240 East 1st South Castle Dale UT 84513 Office: Hunter Power Plant Castle Dale UT 84513

BARNEY, KLINE PORTER, JR., environ. cons.; b. Salt Lake City, Dec. 16, 1934; s. Kline Porter and Doris Lyle (Nielsen) B.; B.C.E., U. Utah, 1957; M. Pub. Adminstrn., San Diego State U., 1971; m. Cheryl Kathleen Taylor, June 14, 1957; children—Peter, Suzanne, Cathleen, Patrick, Andrew. Engring. asst. Chgo. Bridge and Iron Co., Salt Lake City, 1955-56; asst. engr. Fallbrook Pub. Utility Dist., San Diego County, Calif., 1960-63; exec. v.p. Engring.-Sci., Inc., Arcadia, Calif., 1963-81, pres., 1981—, also dir. Served to capt. USMC, 1957-60. Registered profl. engr., Calif., 33 other states. Mem. Am. Acad. Environ. Engrs., ASCE, Am. Water Works Assn., Calif. Water Pollution Control Assn., Am. Water Resources Assn., Tau Beta Pi, Chi Epsilon, Phi Eta Sigma. Mormon. Contbr. articles in field to profl. jours. Home: 1235 Oakwood Dr Arcadia CA 91006 Office: Engring-Sci Inc 125 W Huntington Dr Arcadia CA 91006

BARNGROVER, MARY ELIZABETH, sociologist; b. Indpls., Oct. 18, 1953; d. David William Barngrover and Doris Jean Barngrover Small. B.A. in Sociology, Ind. U., 1976; M.S. in Sociology, Utah State U., 1980. Research, adminstrv. asst. dept. sociology, Utah State U., Logan, 1977-79, program adminstr. Affirmative Action/Equal Opportunity Office, 1979-80, acting dir., 1980-81, dir., 1981—; research asst. Women's Ednl. Equity Act Study, 1979-80. Vol. Hospice Cache Valley Program. Mem. Bus. and Profl. Women, Sociologists Women Soc., Am. Assn. Affirmative Action, Am. Soc. Personnel Adminstrn., Nat. Assn. Female Execs., Alpha Kappa Delta. Club: Elks. Office: Utah State U Affirmative Action/Equal Opportunity UMC 14 Logan UT 84322

BARNWELL, DAVID RAY, aerospace financial analyst; b. Amarillo, Tex., Sept. 9, 1953; s. Jasper Clarence and Mary Evelyn (King) B.; m. Maria Milagrosa Bellido, July 7, 1975; 1 dau., Miriam Louise. Student Army and Navy Acad., Carlsbad, Calif., 1971; A.A. in Bus. Adminstrn., Cerritos Coll., Norwalk, Calif., 1979; B.Sc. in Bus. Adminstrn., U. Redlands, 1981. Instr., Cerritos Coll., 1977-79; adjuster Western Thrift and Loan Assn., Long Beach, Calif., 1978-80; prodn. cost analyst, space shuttle orbiter div. Rockwell Internat., Downey, Calif., 1980—, mem. space shuttle speaker's bur., 1981—; chaplain Am. Legion Hollydale Post 723 dept. Calif. Served with USMC, 1970-76. Recipient NASA first shuttle flight achievement award, 1981. Mem. Pub. Policy Com. (Los Angeles sect.), AIAA. Club: Am. Philatelic Soc. Home: 10453 Greenhurst St Bellflower CA 90706 Office: 12214 Lakewood Blvd Downey CA 90241

BARON, JUDITH KAPLAN, career consultant; b. Chgo., Dec. 5, 1952; d. Herman and Mignon (Damond) Kaplan; m. Fred Michael Baron, Mar. 22, 1981. B.S. (with honors), U. Tex.-Austin, 1974; M.S. in Counseling, Tex. A&I U., 1976. Admissions counselor Texas A&I U., Corpus Christi, 1975-76; vocat. counselor, program dir. Occupational Tng. Services, San Diego, 1977—; pres. Judy Kaplan Baron Assocs., La Jolla, Calif., 1978—; cons. Am. Inst. Banking, City of San Diego, Orange County Probation Dept., Gen. Dynamics, County of San Diego; mem. faculty San Diego State U. Extension, San Diego Community Coll. Dist., Nat. U. Mem. Nat. Assn. of Female Execs., San Diego Career Guidance Assn., Am. Personnel and Guidance Assn., Am. Soc. Tng. and Devel. Jewish. Club: Breakfast of Champions. Author: Personnel Selection Interviewing, 1983. Office: 7730 Herschel Ave Suite B La Jolla CA 92037

BARON, JUDITH ROSALYND, interior designer, educator, antique dealer; born Sioux City, Iowa, Nov. 30, 1941; d. Lawrence A. Baron and Adelaide J. (Goldman) B.; m. Jean-Pierre Chaillou, Jan. 1, 1981. B.A., U. Tex., 1963; M.A., So. Meth. U., 1965. Owner, operator Judith Baron Interiors, Larkspur, Calif., 1967—; owner, mgr. Baron-Chaillou Antiques, 1980—; mgr. Antiquarian Traders, San Francisco, 1981, Store of Memories, Tiburon, 1982—; mem. archtl. rev. bd. City of Larkspur; bd. dirs. Marin Heritage; instr. interior Design, San Francisco. Named Best in Show Designers Showhouse, Design Colleagues Group, 1978, Tchr. of Yr., Design Inst., 1972. Mem. Am. Soc. Interior Designers (cert.), Internat. Soc. Interior Designers (cert.), Internat. Fedn. Interior Designers, Network Women of Marin County. Clubs: University Women, Packard Internat. Author: A Designer Travels to Paris, 1980; contbr. articles to publs. Office: 101 Magnolia Ave Larkspur CA 94939

BARON, MELVIN FARRELL, pharmacist, educator; b. Los Angeles, July 29, 1932; s. Leo Ben and Sadie (Bauchman) B.; Pharm.D., U. So. Calif., 1957, M.P.A., 1973; m. Lorraine Ross, Dec. 20, 1953; children—Lynn, Ross. Pharmacist, Shield Pharmacy, Van Nuys, Calif., 1957-73; project dir. Haynes Found. Drug Research Ctr., Los Angeles, 1973-74; assoc. dir. Calif. Alcoholism Found., Los Angeles, 1974-76; pres. Shield Health Care Ctr., Van Nuys, 1977—; cons. Calif. labor mgmt. plan, 1975-76; guest lectr. U. So. Calif. Sch. Pharmacy, 1975-76, asst. prof. clin. pharmacy, 1980—. Pres., Friends of Operation Bootstrap, Los Angeles, 1965-75; service chmn. Am. Cancer Soc., 1978. Named Preceptor of Yr., U. So. Calif. Sch. Pharmacy, 1979, Disting. Alumnus of Yr., 1983. Mem. Pharm. Inst., Am. Soc. Pub. Adminstrn., Am. Pharm. Assn., Calif. Pharm. Assn., So. Calif. Pharm. Assn. Democrat. Jewish. Club: Srs. Track. Home: 16927 Sunset Blvd Pacific Palisades CA 90272 Office: 6705 Valjean Ave Van Nuys CA 91406

BARON, MICHAEL PHILIP, psychologist; b. Bklyn., Oct. 5, 1949; s. Gabriel George and Edith B.; B.A., Syracuse U., 1972; M.A., U. N.Mex., 1974, Ph.D., 1978. Staff devel. specialist N.Y. State Dept. Mental Hygiene, Regional Edn. Center, Syracuse, N.Y., 1972; psychometrist, 2d Jud. Dist. Ct. Clinic, Albuquerque, 1974-75; instr. dept. guidance and counseling U. N.Mex., 1975, psychologist Student Health Center, 1977-82; pvt. practice psychology, 1980—; cons. Bernalillo Pub. Schs., 1981—. Founder, Mid Long Island chpt. Zero Population Growth, 1971. U. N.Mex. fellow, 1975-77. Mem. Am. Psychol. Assn., N.Mex. Psychol. Assn., s.w. Psychol. Assn., Assn. Poetry Therapy (hon.). Club: Scrabble Players (co-dir.). Office: 2109 Altez St NE Albuquerque NM 87112

BARON, SAMUEL JOSEPH, optometrist; b. Butler, Pa., Feb. 18, 1947; s. Alfred Leon and Mary Francis (Marx) B.; m. Ann Elizabeth Gill, Dec. 11, 1971; children—Matthew, Emily, Amanda. B.S., Mass. Coll. Optometry, 1969, O.D., 1971. Diplomate Nat. Bd. Optometry. Clin. instr. Mass. Coll. Optometry, Boston, 1971; asst. chief contact lens clinic Optometric Ctr. N.Y., N.Y.C., 1971-73; dir. vision therapy clinic Colo. Optometric Ctr., Denver, 1973-74; practice optometry, Golden, Colo., 1973—. Mem. Golden C. of C. Club: Golden Lions. Contbr. articles to profl. jours. Home: 13176 W Montana Ave Lakewood CO 80228 Office: 1218 Arapahoe St Golden CO 80401

BARON, SUSAN FRANCES, media exec.; b. London; d. Maurice Bernhard and Linda Lucy (Loftus-Tottenham) B.; came to U.S., 1940, naturalized, 1957; B.A., St. Martin's, London, 1945-48. Research analyst A.C. Nielsen Co., N.Y.C., 1954-59; media buyer/talent supr. Maxon Inc., N.Y.C., 1959-62; mgr. advt. Litchfield (Conn.) Enquirer, 1962-66; sr. buyer Batten, Barton, Durstine and Osborn, N.Y.C., 1966-67, supr. media buying, 1968-69; asst. asso. media dir. Sullivan, Stauffer, Colwell and Bayles/Lintas, N.Y.C., 1967-68; asso. media dir. Norman, Craig and Kummel, N.Y.C., 1970-74; media dir. Grey Advt. Co., San Francisco, 1975-76; media mgr. Olympia Brewing Co. (Wash.), 1977-80; pres. Barons Media Mktg. Co., Seattle, 1980—; lectr. in field. Mem. Mktg. Communications Execs. Internat., Puget Sound Advt. Assn. Address: PO Box 19262 Seattle WA 98109

BAROODY, ROGER ASA, research lab. exec.; b. Utica, N.Y., Nov. 11, 1924; s. Asa Abraham and Ziqua (Albert) B.; B.S. in Mech. Engring., U. Wyo., 1950; m. Mary Waitt Jackson, Sept. 11, 1951; children—Martha Jackson, Elizabeth Anne, Sarah Marie. Mem. tech. staff Sandia Nat. Labs., Albuquerque, 1951-56, sect. supr. project engring., Livermore, Calif., 1956-59, div. supr., 1959-66, dept. mgr. research and devel. testing, 1966—. Mem. machine tool and tech. adv. com. Chabot Coll., Hayward, Calif., 1965—. Served with USNR, 1943-46. Mem. ASME (chmn. Mount Diablo sect. 1969-70). Democrat. Episcopalian. Club: Mason. Home: 607 Bentley Pl Livermore CA 94550 Office: Sandia Nat Labs PO Box 969 East Ave Livermore CA 94550

BAROV, ZDRAVKO, antiquities conservator; b. Sofia, Bulgaria, Mar. 25, 1938; s. Iordan Christov and Tzvetana Popivanova (Tzviatkova) B.; m. Maya Petkova, Feb. 13, 1965; 1 son, Nikolai. M.F.A., Acad. Fine Arts, Sofia, 1957-63; grad. Istituto Centrale del Restauro, Rome, Italy, 1963. Head conservator, research fellow, chief conservator Nat. Inst. for Preservation of the Monuments of Culture, Solfia, 1964-75; head antiquities conservation J. Paul Getty Mus., Malibu, Calif., 1976—; lectr. U. London, Inst. Archaeology; instr. Art Center Coll. Design, Pasadena, Calif.; cons. for conservation of Watts Towers, State of Calif. UNESCO scholar, 1963. Mem. Internat. Inst. for Conservation, Western Assn. Art Conservators. Author: Iordan Barov. Bulgarski Hudojnik, Sofia, 1967; contbr. articles to profl. jours. Office: PO Box 2112 Santa Monica CA 90406

BARR, DONALD ROY, statistician, educator; b. Durango, Colo., Dec. 10, 1938; s. Russell Wesely and Elizabeth Joanette (Grommett) B.; B.A., Whittier Coll., 1960; B.A., Colo. State U., 1962, Ph.D., 1965; m. Loudean Suttle, June 14, 1958; children—Mark Edward, Bryan Michael. Instr., Colo. State U., 1964-65; asst. prof. math. U. Wis., Oshkosh, 1965-66; prof. stats. and ops. research Naval Postgrad. Sch., Monterey, Calif., 1966—; statistician Office of Naval Research, London, 1982-83. Mem. Am. Statis. Assn., Math. Assn. Am., Ops. Research Soc. Am., Royal Statis. Soc., Sigma Xi. Author: College and University Mathematics, 1968; Finite Statistics, 1968, Probability, 1971; Analytic Geometry: A Vector Approach, 1971; Probability: Modeling Uncertainty, 1981; Calculator Statistics, 1983; contbr. articles to profl. jours. Home: 422 Pine Ave Pacific Grove CA 93950 Office: Naval Postgrad Sch Monterey CA 93940

BARR, GEORGE RICHARD, physician; b. Berwick, Pa., Aug. 12, 1942; s. George and Helen Rita (Larko) B.; B.S., Le Moyne Coll., 1964; M.D., State U. N.Y. Upstate Med. Center, 1968; m. Linda Claire Krenzer, Nov. 25, 1965; children—Richard, Kristen. Intern, USPHS Hosp., Balt., 1968-69; resident in ophthalmology Wills Eye Hosp. and Research Inst., Phila., 1971-74, asst. surgeon, 1974-77; clin. asst. U. Conn. Health Sci. Center, 1978-79; practice medicine specializing in ophthalmology, Manteca and Stockton, Calif., 1979—; mem. staff Manteca Hosp., St. Joseph's and Dameron hosps., Stockton. Served with USPHS, 1969-71. Diplomate Am. Bd. Ophthalmology. Fellow A.C.S.; mem. Am. Intraocula-Implant Soc., Wills Eye Ex-Resident Soc., AMA, San Joaquin County Med. Soc., Calif. Opthal. Soc., Am. Acad. Ophthalmology and Otolaryngology.

BARR, JOHN THOMAS, photojournalist; b. Pitts., May 10, 1950; s. Joseph Charles and Sarah Ellen (McIntyre) B.; B.S., Rochester Inst. Tech., 1972; m. Linda Marcelle Dion, Oct. 8, 1977; 1 dau., Elizabeth Sarah. Mng. editor, The Spectator, Hornell, N.Y., 1972-73; staff photographer UPI, Los Angeles, 1973-77, Los Angeles Times, 1977-78; contbg. photographer Washington Post, 1977-79; staff photographer Gamma/Liaison, N.Y.C., 1977-83; photo editor/photographer USA TODAY, Los Angeles, 1983—. Mem. Press Photographers Assn. Greater Los Angeles (1st place award 1979, 80, dir.), Am. Soc. Mag. Photographers, Nat. Press Photographers Assn. Club: Overseas Press of Am. Home: Box 45909 Los Angeles CA 90045 Office: 924 Westwood Blvd Suite 735 Los Angeles CA 90026

BARR, ROBERT DALE, university dean, educator; b. Ft. Worth, Nov. 24, 1939; s. Robert Edward and Leota Oleta (Sanders) B.; m. Beryl Lucas, Aug. 26, 1956; children—Bonny, Brady. B.A., Tex. Christian U., 1961; M.S., North Tex. State U., 1965; Ph.D., Purdue U., 1969. Lifetime profl. certs. secondary social studies and sch. administrn. Social studies tchr., dept. chmn. R.L. Paschal High Sch., Ft. Worth, 1961-65; grad. instr. Purdue U., 1965-67; asst. prof. edn. U. Tex.-Arlington, 1967-69; staff assoc. Nat. Council for Social Studies, Washington, 1969-70; asst. prof., assoc. prof. social studies edn. and secondary edn., dir. alternative schs. grad. program, 1970-77, prof. edn., dir. tchr. edn. and extended services, 1978; vis. prof. Am. Summer Sch. sponsored by U. Fla. and U. New Orleans, U. Innsbruck, Austria, summer 1979; interim dir. Center for Urban and Multicultural Edn., dir. Office Tchr. Edn. and Extended Services, Ind. U., Bloomington, 1980-81; dean Sch. Edn., Oreg. State U., Corvallis, 1982—; co-dir. Nat. Consortium for Options in Pub. Edn., 1971-77; bd. advisors Fielding Inst., Santa Barbara, Calif., 1974—; chmn., mem. publ. bds. Nat. Council for Social Studies, 1970-74; mem. Phi Delta Kappa Task Force on Compulsory Edn. and Transitions for Youth, 1976-77, mem. research team Project Alternative Edn., 1981; dir. project for programmatic evaluation Nat. Inst. Profl. Devel., Santiago, Chile, 1980-81; co-dir. basic edn. project, Lilly Endowment and Indpls. Pub. Schs., 1977-78; developer Ind. U. Weekender Inservice Program for Tchrs., 1978; asst. developer tchr. ctr. proposals Indpls. Pub. Schs., Bartholomew Pub. Schs., Columbus, Ind., 1977, mem. policy bds. for ctrs.; co-planner, participant confs. Nat. Inst. Edn., 1976; cons. in field pub. sch. dists. Ind., Mich., Calif., Can., various cities and states; co-dir. various sch. confs. univs., internat. confs., regional confs.; participant, dir. summer workshops and confs.; speaker in field. Ford Found. Washington fellow, 1969-70; recipient Disting. Achievement award Am. Assn. Colls. for Tchr. Edn., 1975; named to Internat. Invitational Colloquium on Adult Edn., U. Nottingham, 1981. Author: (with James L. Barth and S. Samuel Shermis) Defining the Social Studies, 1977, The Nature of the S Social Studies, 1978; (with Vernon H. Smith and Daniel J. Burke) Alternatives in Education: Freedom to Choose, 1976 (also Japanese transl.), Optional Alternative Public Schools, 1971 (reprinted as School Violence and Vandalism: Model and Strategies for Change, 1975); Values and Youth, 1971; co-editor Changing Schools newsletter, Nat. Consortium for Options in Pub. Edn., 1971-77; producer, editor filmstrip: To Lead a Profession, 1970; contbr. chpts. to books, reports, monographs, articles, revs., editorials to profl. publs. Office: Room 215 Edn Hall Oreg State Univ Corvallis OR 97331

BARR, WARREN PAUL, optometrist; b. Hawthorne, Calif., Dec. 9, 1955; s. Paul Cornelius and Betty Patricia (Warnack) B. A.A., El Camino Coll., 1976; B.S., So. Calif. Coll. Optometry, 1978, O.D., 1980. Optometrist visual electrophysiology clinic Children's Hosp., San Diego, 1979-80, outpatient clinic Los Angeles VA Hosp., 1979-80, Brentwood Neuropsychiat. Hosp., 1980, Low Vision Clinic, 1980; pvt. practice gen. optometry, Hermosa Beach, Calif., 1980—; cons. South Bay Children's Health Ctr. Recipient Gordon Optics award for lens design, 1980. Mem. Am. Optometric Assn., Calif. Optometric Assn., So. Bay Optometric Soc. (dir.), Coll. Optometrists in Vision Devel., Am. Pub. Health Assn., Optometric Extension Program, Hermosa Beach C. of C. (dir.). Contbr. articles to profl. jours. Home: 640 The Village #308 Redondo Beach CA 90277 Office: 1500 Pacific Coast Hwy PO Box 515 Hermosa Beach CA 90254

BARRAD, CATHERINE MARIE, lawyer; b. Moscow, Idaho, Dec. 12, 1953; d. Richard Gary and Hazel Mae (Hollon) Morrison; m. Mark William Barrad, Dec. 29, 1974; 1 son, Joshua Avarm. B.S. in Laws, Western State U., 1979, J.D., 1980. Bar: Calif. 1980, U.S. Dist. Ct. (cen. dist.) Calif. 1982. Customer service rep. Forman-Forman & Assocs., Inc., Lynwood, Calif., 1975-76; office mgr. Apollo Mgmt. Corp., Long Beach, Calif., 1976-78; law clk. Gottlieb, Gottlieb & Stein, Inc., Long Beach, 1978-80; sole practice, Long Beach, 1980—; jud. intern Long Beach Mcpl. Ct., 1979-80, judge pro-tem, 1980—. Mem. ABA, Los Angeles County Bar Assn., Long Beach Bar Assn., Women Lawyers Long Beach (sec. 1981-82, pres. 1983-84), Orange County Women Lawyers, Calif. Trial Lawyers Assn., Greater Long Beach and West Orange County Jewish Fedn. (community relations com. 1982—, chair domestic affairs subcom. 1983—, leadership devel. group 1982—). Democrat. Office: 5212 Katella Ave Suite 103B Los Alamitos CA 90720

BARRAN, NICHOLAS DUDLEY EDWARD, insurance company executive; b. Northampton, Eng., Jan. 17, 1942; came to U.S., 1963, naturalized, 1977; s. Edward Nicholson and Daphne Margaret (Bird) B.; student Sorbonne U., Paris, 1961-62; B.S., UCLA, 1966; m. Feliksa

Pabilionis, Apr. 11, 1964; children—Antony Nicholas, Daniel Nicholas. Divisional fin. dir., dep. mng. dir. Courtaulds Ltd., Eng., 1967-73; asst. treas., dir. mktg. Vaportech Corp., Los Angeles, 1974-79; controller Allied Energy Internat., Beverly Hills, Calif., 1980-81; asst. dir., acctg. services ABC, Inc., Century City, Calif., 1981-83; controller Graham Miller, Inc., 1983—. Councillor London Borough of Islington, 1968-71; gov. St. Aloysius Coll., 1968-69; del. Democratic Nat. Conv., 1978; mem. Los Angeles County Dem. Central Com., 1979—; chmn. 43d Assembly Dist. Council, 1981—; chmn. 22d Senatorial Dist. Council, 1981—. Mem. Inst. Dir. (Eng.), Beta Gamma Sigma. Clubs: Brooks's (London); Windjammers Yacht (treas. 1978-80, fleet capt. 1981). Home: 8740 Willis Ave Panorama City CA 91402 Office: 3435 Wilshire Blvd Suite 2210 Los Angeles CA 90010

BARRERAS, CAROL DIANNE, accountant; b. Atlanta, Aug. 13, 1948; d. Ashley C. and Anne E. Carter; m. Allen J. Barreras, June 30, 1980. B.S. in Acctg., Cameron U., 1979; postgrad. Golden Gate U., 1983. C.P.A., Calif. Staff acct. Woodrow F. Morgan, Pub. Acctg., Vacaville, Calif., 1979-80; tax mgr. Christensen Boler & Co., C.P.A.s, Vacaville, 1980—; acctg. and tax cons. community bus. Mem. Am. Inst. C.P.A.s, Calif. Soc. C.P.A.s, Am. Women's Soc. C.P.A.s. Republican. Seventh-day Adventist. Home: 149 Fairoaks Dr Vacaville CA 95688 Office: 540 W Monte Vista Ave Vacaville CA 95688

BARRETT, ELAINE SWANSON, science educator, textbook consultant; b. Springfield, Mo., Mar. 7, 1953; d. Thomas Florian and Laura Grace (Gross) Swanson; m. W. Louis Barrett, Dec. 22, 1976. B.A. in Biology, Western Wash. U., 1975, B.Ed., 1977, M.Ed., 1982. Sci. tchr. Hyak Jr. High Sch., Bellevue (Wash.) pub. schs., 1977-78, math and sci. dist. project leader, 1978-80, chmn. dept. sci. Highland Jr. High Sch., 1980—; project coordinator Computer 'n' Kids, cons. Addison-Wesley Pubs. Mem. Nat. Sci. Tchrs. Assn., Assn. Supervision and Curriculum Devel., Nat. Council Tchrs. Math. Democrat. Roman Catholic. Developed Addison-Wesley Sci. Tests for 3d-8th grades. Home: 9923 NE 144 Ln 706 Bothell WA 98011 Office: Highland Jr High School 310-102 Ave NE Bellevue WA 98002

BARRETT, EMMETT E(DWARD), college administrator; b. Sioux City, Iowa, Nov. 7, 1916; s. Patrick Daniel and Maria (Mullally) B.; B.A. in Bus. Adminstrn., U. Portland, 1941; m. Viola Bornhorst, Apr. 17, 1944; children—Patricia Barrett Lorenz, Kathleen Barrett Swanberg, Thomas, Elizabeth Reinhardt, Robert, Maureen. Mem. N.Y. Giants profl. football team, 1941-44; contact rep. VA, 1945-47; agt. Nat. Life of Vt., Portland, Oreg., 1948-54; mgr. Mut. Trust Life, Portland, 1955-60; regional mgr. United Founders Life, Portland, 1960-70; exec. v.p. Oreg. Poly. Inst., 1974, pres., exec. officer, 1975—; v.p. U. Portland Columbia Found., 1953-60. Served with AUS, 1943. Mem. All Ireland Cultural Soc. (Portland). Democrat. Roman Catholic. Clubs: Pilot Wheels (pres. 1953, 54, 59), Met. (pres. 1950); Kiwanis (dir. club) (Portland). Home: 2441 N E 61st Ave Portland OR 97213 Office: 812 SW 10th Ave Portland OR 97205

BARRETT, JAMES E., judge; b. Lusk, Wyo., Apr. 8, 1922; s. Frank A. and Alice C. (Donoghue) B.; student St. Catherine's Coll., Oxford, Eng., 1945, Cath. U. Am., 1946; LL.B., U. Wyo., 1949; m. Carmel Ann Martinez, Oct. 8, 1949; children—Ann Catherine Barrett Sandahl, Richard James, John Donoghue. Admitted to Wyo. bar, 1949; mem. firm Barrett and Barrett, Lusk, 1949-67; atty. gen. State of Wyo., 1967-71; judge U.S. Circuit Ct. Appeals, 10th Circuit, 1971—; county and pros. atty. Niobrar County, Wyo., 1951-62; atty. Town of Lusk, 1952-64, Niobrara Sch. Dist., 1950-64. Active Boy Scouts Am.; sec.-treas. Niobrara County Republican Central Com.; bd. dirs. St. Joseph's Children's Hosp., Torrington, Wyo.; trustee ch. Served as cpl. AUS, 1942-45; ETO. Recipient Distinguished Alumni award U. Wyo., 1973. Mem. Cheyenne C. of C., VFW, Am. Legion. Club: Lions. Office: US Ct of Appeals PO Box 1288 Cheyenne WY 82001*

BARRETT, JAMES LEE, screenwriter; b. Charlotte, N.C., Nov. 19, 1929; s. James Hamlin and Anne (Blake) B.; ed. Furman U., Pa. State U., Columbia U., Art Students League; m. Merete Engelstoft, June, 1960; children—Jessica, Penelope, Birgitte, Christian, David. Screenwriter, 1955—; motion pictures include: The D.I. (Marine Corps Combat Corrs. Assn. award), The Greatest Story Ever Told, Bandolero, The Undefeated, Shenandoah, tick...tick...tick, The Cheyenne Social Club (nominee Writer's Guild award), The Green Berets, Something Big, Fools' Parade, Hank, Smokey and the Bandit; TV films include: The Awakening Land (Am. Women in Radio and TV cert. of commendation) Belle Starr, Stubby Pringle's Christmas (nominee Humanities award), The Day Christ Died, Angel City, Mayflower: The Pilgrim Experience; playwright: Shenandoah (Tony award for Best Musical Book). Served with USMC, 1950-52. Mem. Writers Guild Am., Dramatists Guild, Acad. Motion Picture Arts and Scis. Address: PO Box 66 Paso Robles CA 93446

BARRETT, LAWRENCE EARL, corporate executive, engineer; b. Rifle, Colo., Nov. 20, 1928; s. Miles William and Juno Eva (Goldman) B.; m. Charlotte Rice, Mar. 21, 1953; children—Martin, Miles, Nancy, Alice. Petroleum Engr., Colo. School Mines, 1950. Registered profl. engr., Colo. Various field, dist. and div. petroleum engring. assignments Texaco Inc., 1952-68; mgr. Ladd Petroleum Corp., 1968-69, v.p., 1969-78, sr. v.p. ops., 1978-81, sr. v.p. internat. exploration and ops., 1981—. Served to 1st lt. U.S. Army, 1950-52. Mem. Soc. Petroleum Engrs., Rocky Mountain Natural Gas Assn. Home: 6935 Garfield Way Littleton CO 80122 Office: 830 Denver Club Bldg Denver CO 80122

BARRETT, LEWIS RICHARD, JR., personnel official, retired air force officer; b. Des Moines, Iowa, Sept. 8, 1921; s. Lewis R. and Nellie (Keister) B.; m. Betty Jo Weseman, Jan. 11, 1943; children—Emma Jo, Hiordis, Heidi, Sue. Student Grinnell Coll., 1941-43. Commd. lt. U.S. Air Force, 1942, advanced through grades to col., 1969, service in Korea, Vietnam; ret., 1977; dir. personnel procurement, 1974-77; dir. personnel Air Force civilian employees, Weld County, Colo., 1977—. Mem. budget and allocation com. United Way, 1979-81. Decorated Air Medal with 4 oak leaf clusters, Legion of Merit, DFC. Mem. Am. Mgmt. Assn., County Personnel Dirs. Assn., Colo. Pub. Personnel Dirs. Assn. Republican. Congregationalist. Clubs: Rotary, Blue and Gold (co-chmn.). Office: Centennial Center PO Box 758 Greeley CO 80632

BARRETT, MICHAEL GARY, retail food company executive; b. Pasadena, Calif., Jan. 4, 1954; s. Jack Donald and Joyce (Scott) B.; m. Janice Lee Driscoll, Oct. 30, 1982. B.S. in Fin., Brigham Young U., Provo, Utah, 1979; M.B.A., Boise State U., Idaho, 1981. Missionary to Guatemala and El Salvador, Ch. of Jesus Christ of Latter-day Saints, 1973-75; loss control cons. Diversified Risk Mgmt. Services, Boise, 1977-79; program coordinator Boise City Recreation Dept., 1976-77; asst. dir., risk mgmt. Albertson's Inc., Boise, 1980—; exec. adv. to Idaho Bus. Week, 1981. Active, United Way campaign com., Ore-Ida council Boy Scouts Am. Awarded Eagle Scout rank Boy Scouts Am.; recipient Calif. Interscholastic Fedn. Scholar-Athlete award. Mem. Risk and Ins. Mgmt. Soc. (dir. Idaho chpt.), Brigham Young U. Mgmt. Soc., Am. Soc. Safety Engrs. Republican. Mormon. Clubs: Cougar (Brigham Young U.), Bronco (Boise State U.). Home: 7383 Snohomish St Boise ID 83709 Office: PO Box 20 Boise ID 83726

BARRETT, RONALD KEITH, psychologist, educator; b. Bklyn., Aug. 17, 1948; s. Cyril and Dorothy (Addison) B.; B.S., Morgan State U., 1970; M.A., U. Pitts., 1974, Ph.D., 1977. Cert. clin. hypnotist. Program evaluator Right Start, U. Pitts., 1976-77; asst. prof. psychology Calif. State U.-Dominguez Hills, 1977-78; cons. psychologist Inglewood (Calif.) Child Devel. Ctr., 1977-78; cons. Social Service Bur., City of Richmond (Va.) Dept. Public Welfare, 1978; asst. prof. psychology Loyola Marymount U. Los Angeles, 1978—; lectr., cons. in field. Mem. adv. bd. Nat. Council Culture and Art, Inc., N.Y.C., 1980—, Catholic Big Bros., Los Angeles, 1978—. Mem. Assn. Black Psychologists, Am. Psychol. Assn., Black Analysis, Inc., Psi Chi, Alpha Phi Omega. Democrat. Contbr. numerous sci. articles to profl. publs. Home: 200 W Queen St Apt 120 Inglewood CA 90301 Office: Loyola Marymount U Psychology Dept Los Angeles CA 90045

BARRETT, WILLIAM THOMAS, engineering executive; b. Bluefield, Va., Sept. 2, 1931; s. Francis Kyle and Margaret Grace (Jones) B.; student Va. Poly. Inst., 1953, Bluefield Coll., 1953; m. Mary Boyce Edwards, Oct. 2, 1955; children—Julia Lynn, Charles Andrew. Telemetry specialist RCA Services, Inc., Cape Canaveral, Fla., 1953-62; with EG & G, Inc., Las Vegas, 1962—, beginning as engr., reactor engine instrumentation, successively mgr. spl. projects ops., program mgr. spl. projects ops., div. mgr. nuclear rocket devel. sta., 1962-71, gen. mgr. spl. projects div., 1971—; pres., gen. mgr. Spl. Projects Inc., 1983—. Served with USAF, 1949-52. Mem. Assn. Old Crows. Presbyterian. Club: Kiwanis. Home: 1716 Rambla Ct Las Vegas NV 89102 Office: 2755 E Desert Inn Rd Las Vegas NV 89121

BARRICK, LOWELL SUNDE, fisheries engr.; b. Libby, Mont., Mar. 3, 1936; s. Lowell Roscoe and Stella Amanda (Sunde) B.; student Ricks Coll., 1954-55, U. Hawaii, 1955-56, U. Idaho, 1956-59; B.S. in Civil Engring., Utah State U., 1962; M.S. in Engring. Mgmt., U. Alaska, 1977; m. Kay Parkinson, June 23, 1962; children—Burke, Kevin, Kathryn. Hwy. engr. Idaho Dept. Hwys., 1962-64; airport engr. Alaska Div. Aviation, 1964-74; fisheries engr., chief engr. Alaska Dept. Fish and Game, Juneau, 1974—. Pres., Gastineau Channel Little League, 1976-78; search and rescue pilot CAP. Served with USNG, 1952-73. Mem. Assn. Conservation Engrs. (pres. 1980-81), Am. Soc. Engring. Mgmt. (charter), Am. Fisheries Soc., Anglo-Am. Acad. Home: 9505 Mendenhall Loop Rd Juneau AK 99801 Office: Alaska Dept Fish and Game Box 3-2000 Juneau AK 99801

BARRIE, DONALD SHAW, constrn. exec.; b. St. Louis, Oct. 16, 1924; s. Donald Alexander and Ruth (Shaw) B.; student Calif. Inst. Tech., 1946-50, B.S. in Civil Engring., 1950; m. Audrey G. Joly, Nov. 16, 1957; children—Donald Shaw, Bruce Robert, Scott William. With Kaiser Engrs. and Affiliates, 1950—, jr. engr., Wash., 1950-52, resident engr., Calif., 1952-54, constrn. engr., Ohio, 1954-55, gen. supt., New Orleans, 1955-57, asst. constrn. mgr., Calif., 1957-59, gen. constrn. mgr., Can., 1959-63, project mgr., Calif., 1963-69, project mgr., Mo., 1969-70, dept. mgr., Calif., 1971-78, v.p. gen. constrn., Oakland, Calif., 1978—; v.p., gen. mgr. Foothill Electric Corp.; adv. bd. constrn. program San Francisco State U.; invited speaker U. Calif., Berkeley, Stanford U., U. Wis. Served with U.S. Army, 1943-46. Registered profl. engr., Wash.; lic. gen. engring., bldg. and elec. contractor, Calif. Mem. ASCE (chmn. constrn. mgmt. com. 1977-80; com. constrn. productivity), Project Mgmt. Inst. (pres. No. Calif. chpt. 1979-80, chmn. adv. bd. 1981-82), Nat. Acad. Scis. (transp. research bd.). Author: Professional Construction Management, 1978; Directions in Managing Construction, 1981; Planning and Estimating Heavy Construction, 1983; contbr. articles to profl. jours. Home: PO Box 586 Diablo CA 94528 Office: 300 Lakeside Dr Oakland CA 94623

BARRINS, PHYLLIS CAROLINE, hypnotherapist, writer; b. Dyer, Ind., Apr. 9, 1921; d. Frank A. and Catherine M. (Alber) Willy; diploma St. Mary Mercy Hosp. Sch. Nursing, 1942; B.A. in Sociology, Eastern Nebr. Christian Coll., 1971, M.A. in Sociology, 1972, B.A. in Parapsychology, Ph.D. in Psychology, 1973; B.A. in Social Scis., Thomas Edison Coll., 1981; m. Edward Francis Barrins, Sept. 19, 1942; children—Edward, Mary Barrins Roberts, Barbara Barrins O'Shea, Patricia Barrins Schipper, James, Gerard, Janine Barrins Perry. Pvt. duty nurse, Gary, Ind., 1942-45; nursery sch. nurse, Tucson, 1948-50; police officer Pinal County Sheriff's Office, Ariz., 1955-59; staff nurse Tucson Med. Center, 1961-62; supt. nurses El Gran Sanitorium, Tucson, 1962-63; supr. Handmaker Jewish Nursing Home for the Aged, 1963-64; adminstr. Hillcrest Med. Center, Tucson, 1964-65; nurse cons. Blaze Lodge, Tucson, 1965-67; dir. Community Blood and Plasma Service, Tucson, 1967-68; free lance writer, 1968-72; instr. sociology Pima Community Coll., Tucson, 1975; instr. U. Phoenix, 1979-80; pvt. practice family counseling and hypnotherapy, Tucson, 1972—. Mem. Mensa Edn. and Research Found., 1973—. Mem. Am. Sociol. Assn., Assn. Women in Psychology, Hypnotists Examining Council, Hypnotists Union Local 472, Assn. Christian Marriage Counselors, Assn. Advancement of Psychology, Am. Assn. Suicidology, Soc. Advancement of Social Psychology, Fedn. Am. Scientists, Mensa (proctor for testing 1975-82), Soc. Psychol. Study of Social Issues, Internat. Assn. Applied Psychology, AAUP. Roman Catholic. Author: Manual for Hypnotherapy, 1981; co-author, editor: Hypnosis, Its Use in Nursing, A Symposium, 1981; Hypnosis—New Tool in Nursing Care, 1982; contbr. numerous articles on health, nursing and counseling to mags., newspapers and profl. publs.; writer children's stories; asso. editor Geriatric Institutions, 1964-65; editor: Hypnosis in Counseling (E. Arthur Winkler), 1975; book rev. editor Tucson Nite Times, 1978-79. Research on reincarnation. Home: 2023 E Adams St Tucson AZ 85719 Office: 2023 E Adams St Tucson AZ 85719

BARRIOS, MARC, brewing co. mgr.; b. Havana, Cuba, Oct. 1, 1944; came to U.S., 1961; s. Marcos A. and Raquel M. (Rodriguez) B.; student Colo. Inst. Art, 1967; B.A., Loretto Heights Coll., 1973; m. Maria Fuentes, July 12, 1980; children—Kenneth, Alexander. Art dir. Dacey Wolff & Weir Adv. Agy., Colo., 1967-68; pres., creative dir. Barrios & Assocs., Colo., 1968-69; art dir. Hoflund Graphics, Colo., 1969; group mgr. creative services Adolph Coors Co., Golden, Colo., 1969—; graphic cons. Ken Monfort senatorial campaign, 1968. Adv. bd. Community Coll. Denver, 1977—; dir. Real Estate Brokers and Assos., Chgo. Recipient awards Art Dirs. Club N.Y., 1980, Advt. Fedn. of West, 1973, 75 Alfie award, 1973, Nikki award, 1976, 78, Ceba award, 1980, 81. Mem. Denver Advt. Fedn., Art Dirs. Club Denver (award 1973, 74, 80), Point of Purchase Inst. Am. (award 1971, 72, 75, 76, 78, 79, 80, 81). Republican. Methodist. Club: Optimist (dir. Golden and Arvada, Colo. 1971-73). Office: Adolph Coors Co Golden CO 80401

BARROLL, KENNETH COCKE, airline pilot; b. Stockholm, Sweden, Mar. 7, 1939; s. Lawrence Sprague and Clare (Cocke) B. (parents Am. citizens); student Stockholm Tech. Inst., 1960-62; student U. of Air, Santa Barbara, Calif., 1966; m. Ann Sevier Clark, June 12, 1971 (div. 1982). Automotive apprentice engr. Gen. Motors, Rüsselsheim, Germany, 1959, Luton, Eng., 1960-61, Lausanne, Switzerland, 1962; electronic engr. Forslid & Co., Stockholm, 1963-65; cons. Heathkit div. Schlumberger & Co., Stockholm, 1966; flight officer N.W. Orient Airlines, St. Paul, 1967—; freelance comml. and portrait photographer. Mem. Am. Radio Relay League (life), Soaring Soc. Am. (life). Home: Box 228 Seahurst WA 98062 Office: NW Orient Airlines St Paul MN 55111

BARROS, ANNAMARIE VIERRA, health mgmt. cons.; b. San Jose, Calif., Mar. 14, 1932; d. Anthony Clarence and Clara Magdalene (Pacheco) Vierra; B.A., Coll. Holy Names, Oakland, Calif., 1953; M.A., Central Mich. U., 1978; m. Richard Laurence Barros, June 11, 1960. Adminstrv. technologist, Children's Hosp., San Francisco, 1958-65, Good Samaritan Hosp., San Jose, Calif., 1965-74; mgmt. devel. dir. O'Connor Hosp., San Jose, 1974-76; adj. prof. mgmt., grad. program in clin. scis. San Francisco State U., 1975—; owner Health Mgmt. Analysts, Los Gatos, Calif., 1976—; adminstrv. asst. public relations and mktg. Lab. Services, San Jose, 1974-76; adj. prof. Southeastern Mass. U., Central Mich. U.; mem. panel Health Professions Edn. Adv. Council, HEW, 1975-77. Bd. dirs., mem. blood services adv. com. San Jose chpt. ARC, 1980—; pres. bd. Rinconada Hills Homeowners Assn., 1976-79; exec. com. Quota Internat., 1973. Cert. clin. lab. scientist; sec.-treas. Nat. Certification Agy. for Med. Lab. Personnel, 1977-83, v.p., 1983-84. Mem. Am. Soc. Med. Tech. (pres. 1973-74, dir. 1969-75, adminstrv. technologist of year 1973, mem. of year 1978, past pres.'s achievement award 1979), Calif. Soc. Med. Tech. (mem. of year 1969, 78), Am. Mgmt. Assn., Calif. Clin. Lab. Assn., Allied Clin. Lab. Mgmt. Assn., Nat. Assn. Female Execs., AAUW. Roman Catholic. Contbr. articles to profl. and trade jours. Home and Office: 129 Callecita Los Gatos CA 95030

BARROW, NANCY KAY, management consultant, research analyst; b. Chgo., Nov. 30, 1930; d. Norman Eastman and Alelle Maud (Sinclair) Holmes; B.A. magna cum laude, U. Colo., 1970, M.A., 1974, Ph.D., 1976; m. James Harrington Barrow, Oct. 1, 1949; children—Laura Kay, Guy James. Library aide City of Milw., 1948-51; service rep., bus. office supr. Mountain Bell Telephone Co., Denver, 1952-59; cons. Behavorial Scis. Inst., Inc., Golden, Colo., 1976-77; now exec. v.p. Prime Devel. Co., Inc.; research analyst Edn. Commn. of States. Regional co-ordinator Republican Congl. Candidates Orgn. Mem. Am. Psychol. Assn., Colo. Alumni Found., Phi Beta Kappa, Sigma Xi, Am. Contract Bridge League. Home: 11725 W 22d Pl Lakewood CO 80215

BARRUS, WALTER RODGER, safety engineer; b. San Francisco, Mar. 26, 1937; s. Walter Elvin and Gerda Irmgard (Reimer) B.; B.S. in Sociology and Law Enforcement, Brigham Young U., 1974, M.A. in Organizational Behavior, 1975; m. Ellen June Johnson, Dec. 20, 1958; children—Rhonda, Pamela, John Warren, Brenda, Cynthia, Robert Andrew. Final test technician IBM, San Jose, Calif., 1961-63; patrolman Calif. Hwy. Patrol, San Jose and Truckee, 1963-72; dir. coop. edn. Brigham Young U., Provo, 1973-78; dir. indsl. safety and health Utah Tech. Coll., Provo, 1978-81, part-time 1982—; v.p. Corporate Health Systems, Inc., 1982—; cons. Food Processors Inst., Washington, 1981—; cons. Dir. Bail Reform program, Provo, 1973-81, Community Youth Council, Springville, Utah, 1978—; pres. Springville High Sch. PTA, 1978-79. Served with U.S. Navy, 1956-60. Mem. Calif. Assn. Hwy. Patrolman, Am. Soc. Safety Engrs. Republican. Mem. Ch. Jesus Christ of Latter-day Saints. Author: Law Enforcement and Justice Administration: Field Experience Handbook, 1975. Home: 33 N 700 E Springville UT 84663 Office: 36 S State St Suite 1030 Salt Lake City UT 84111

BARRY, JOHN WILLARD, biologist; b. Columbus, Ohio, July 18, 1934; s. George Willard and Sylvia Evelyn (Ward) B.; B.S. in Botany, U. Cin., 1956; postgrad. U. Utah and Brigham Young U., 1961-70; m. Patricia Anne Arends, Dec. 29, 1956; children—Cynthia Shawn, Sandra Sue. Test officer Dugway (Utah) Proving Ground, 1961-65; test dir. Deseret Test Center, Ft. Douglas, Utah, 1965-75; nat. pesticide application specialist U.S. Dept. Agr., Forest Service, Davis, Calif., 1975—. Active in sponsoring and encouraging native Am. artists. Served as officer U.S. Army, 1956-61. Recipient Spl. Act award Dept. Army, 1967; cert. merit Dept. Agr., 1979. Mem. Entomol. Soc. Am., Am. Soc. Agrl. Engrs., Am. Meteorol. Soc., Southwestern Assn. Indian Affairs, U. Calif. Library Assocs. (pres.), Western History Assn. Republican. Lutheran. Author: American Indian Pottery, 1981; also agrl. bulls. and reports; contbr. articles to profl. jours. Co-developer canopy penetration model for planning and evaluating forest spraying. Home: 3123 Beacon Bay Pl Davis CA 95616 Office: 2810 Chiles Rd Davis CA 95616

BARRY, PATRICK JAMES, optometrist; b. Syracuse, N.Y., Aug. 28, 1951; s. James Earl and Helen Elizabeth (Bushey) B.; m. Kathy Ann Krupanski, July 6, 1974; children—Justin Reid, Amanda Nicole. B.S. in Biology, Siena Coll., 1973; B.S. in Optometry, Pa. Coll. Optometry, 1975, O.D., 1977. Lic. optometrist, N.J., Ariz. Sr. optometrist Group Health Med. Assocs., P.C., 1977—. Bd. dirs. Capilla Del Sol Christian Ch., 1982-84; dir., chmn. So. Ariz. Health Fair, Pima County, 1983. Mem. Am. Optometric Assn., Ariz. Optometric Assn., So. Ariz. Optometric Assn. (pres.), Optometric Extension Program. Democrat. Office: 1231 D W Saint Mary's Rd Tucson AZ 85745

BARRY, WILLIAM PARKE, company executive; b. Los Angeles, May 11, 1940; s. Robert J. and La Priel (Parke) B.; student St. Mary's Coll., 1958-60, U. So. Calif., 1962-63; m. Sue Greenleaf, Dec. 2, 1967; children—Steven, Jill. Sales rep. Diamond Nat., Los Angeles, 1963-65, Task Force, Los Angeles, 1965-68; v.p. Barry and Co., Los Angeles, 1970-74, sr. v.p., 1974-83, pres., 1983—; researcher, speaker on Year 2000. Deacon United Presbyn. Ch., 1978—. Served with USNG, 1961-66. Mem. Twentieth Century Round Table, Jonathan Club Los Angeles. Republican. Clubs: San Marino City, Rotary (chmn. Los Angeles 1977-78). Contbr. research paper on plant layout, 1976. Home: 2820 Lorain Rd San Marino CA 91108 Office: 900 Wilshire Suite 900 Los Angeles CA 90017

BARSCH, (GARY) GERHARD RUSSELL, advertising agency executive; b. Compton, Calif., Sept. 21, 1932; s. Gerhard Victor and Alice Mildred (Herndon) B.; m. Nancy Wolcott, Nov. 10, 1956; children—Ruth Anne Barsch Wilson, David Russell. B.S., Los Angeles State Coll., 1964. With Long Beach Ind.-Press Telegram, 1951-52, 56-66; owner/mgr. Ad-Grafic Typographers, Orange County, Calif., 1966—. Served with USNR, 1952-56. Mem. Nat. Composition Assn. Republican. Presbyterian. Club: Masons. Office: Ad-Grafic Typographers Suite H 1228 Village Way Santa Ana CA 92705

BARSH, MAX KING, materials scientist; b. Los Angeles, Feb. 13, 1921; s. Samuel and Ella Rose (Garshfield) B.; A.A., Pasadena City Coll., 1941; B.S., UCLA, 1943, M.S., 1949; Ph.D., U. So. Calif., 1955; predoctoral fellow U. Zurich, Switzerland, 1953-54; m. Carol Lee Segall, Dec. 19, 1948; children—Gregory Stefan, Andrea Lynn, Dayna Ellen. With Aerojet Gen. Corp., 1954—, sr. specialist tech. staff mech. engring. dept. Aerojet Electro Systems Co., Azusa, Calif., 1972—. Former pres. Symphony League Los Angeles County, Claremont Symphony Orch. Assn. Served with USAAF, 1945-47. Mem. AAAS, AIAA, Soc. Mfg. Engrs., Inst. Environ. Scis., Sigma Xi, Phi Lambda Upsilon. Democrat. Contbr. space sci. articles to internat. symposia and tech. jours. Home: 4205 Oak Hollow St Claremont CA 91711 Office: PO Box 296 Azusa CA 91702

BARSHOP, NATHAN, surgeon; b. N.Y.C., Jan. 22, 1913; s. Samuel and Esther (Shiffris) B.; B.A., Baylor U., 1930, M.D., 1934; m. Coe Thelma Fisher, Apr. 27, 1949; children—Deborah, Melanie Coe, Mark Nathan. Intern Baylor U. Hosp., Dallas, 1934-36; resident Los Angeles County Hosp, 1936-40; practice medicine, specializing in surgery, Beverly Hills and Los Angeles, 1940—; chief surgery Mt. Sinai Hosp., Los Angeles, 1948—, chief of staff, 1957-59, 65—, dir., chmn. tumor bd., 1953—; attending surgeon Cedars of Lebanon Hosp., 1947—, Los Angeles County Gen. Hosp., 1947—; asst. prof. surgery U. So. Calif. Coll. Medicine, 1948—. Bd. govs. Cedars of Lebanon Hosp.-Mt. Sinai Hosp. Med. Center, 1961—. Served to maj. M.C., AUS, World War II. Decorated Presdl. Citation with 2 oak leaf clusters. Diplomate Am. Bd. Surgery. Fellow A.C.S.; mem. Beverly Hills Acad. Medicine, Soc. Grad. Surgeons, Pan Am. Med. Assn., Los Angeles Surg. Soc., Phi Delta Epsilon (dist. dep. grand council 1957). surgeon; b. N.Y.C., Jan. 22, 1913; s. Samuel and Esther (Shiffris) B.; B.A., Baylor U., 1930, M.D.,

1934; m. Coe Thelma Fisher, Apr. 27, 1949; children—Deborah, Melanie Coe, Mark Nathan. Intern Baylor U. Hosp., Dallas, 1934-36; resident Los Angeles County Hosp, 1936-40; practice medicine, specializing in surgery, Beverly Hills and Los Angeles, 1940—; chief surgery Mt. Sinai Hosp., Los Angeles, 1948—, chief of staff, 1957-59, 65—, dir., chmn. tumor bd., 1953—; attending surgeon Cedars of Lebanon Hosp., 1947—, Los Angeles County Gen. Hosp., 1947—; asst. prof. surgery U. So. Calif. Coll. Medicine, 1948—. Bd. govs. Cedars of Lebanon Hosp.-Mt. Sinai Hosp. Med. Center, 1961—. Served to maj. M.C., AUS, World War II. Decorated Presdl. Citation with 2 oak leaf clusters. Diplomate Am. Bd. Surgery. Fellow A.C.S.; mem. Beverly Hills Acad. Medicine, Soc. Grad. Surgeons, Pan Am. Med. Assn., Los Angeles Surg. Soc., Phi Delta Epsilon (dist. dep. grand council 1957). Home: 11300 Sunset Blvd Los Angeles CA 90049 Office: 405 N Bedford Dr Beverly Hills CA 94210

BARSHTER, NANCY ELLEN, special education consultant; b. Buffalo, Dec. 30, 1953; d. Sidney and Evelyn Ruth (Greenfield) B. B.A. magna cum laude, Ithaca Coll., 1975; M.Ed., U. Ariz., 1976, Ed.S., 1979. Supr. tchr. credential, Oreg. Resource tchr. Tucson Pub. Schs., 1976-78; supr. M.Ed. field work, dept. spl. edn. U. Ariz., 1978-79; dir. spl. edn. Indian Oasis Sch. Dist., Papago Indian Reservation, Sells, Ariz., 1979-81; evaluation specialist Clackmas County Edn. Service Dist., Marylhurst, Oreg., 1981-82; edn. cons., learning specialist Clatsop County Edn. Service Dist., Astoria, Oreg., 1982—. U. Ariz. scholar, 1975-76; U. Ariz. fellow, 1978-79. Mem. Council Exceptional Children, Council Adminstrs. in Spl. Edn., Council Oreg. Sch. Adminstrs. and Suprs. Home: PO Box 758 Cannon Beach OR 97110 Office: Clatsop County Education Service District 3194 Marine Dr Astoria OR 97103

BARTA, VIRGIL P., research scientist; b. Hudson, Iowa, Feb. 8, 1920; s. James C. and Alice (Pierce) B.; student Reed Coll., 1937-40; B.S., Oreg. State Coll., 1942, D.Sc., 1978; m. Helen May Jones, Sept. 10, 1942; children—Kathleen D., James J., Elisabeth S. Instr., Oreg. State Coll., 1946-47; head photog. dept. Wash. State Coll., 1947-50; dir. graphic arts research dept. Rochester Inst. Tech., N.Y., 1950-55; tech. dir. graphic arts div. Technicolor Corp., Los Angeles, 1955-58; dir graphic scis. research Stanford Research Inst., Menlo Park, Calif., 1958-66, sci. cons., 1966—; pres. Counselors To Tech. Mgmt., Palo Alto, Calif., 1966—, Barta and Assos., Portland, Oreg., 1977—; U.S. rep. 2d Internat. Conf. Printing Research Insts., Stockholm, 1953; speaker 1st Internat. Congress Reprography, Cologne, Germany, 1963, U.S. rep. 2d Congress, Cologne, 1967, London, 1971; U.S. rep. 5th Internat. Interpol Congress, Mexico City, 1969; U.S. rep High Security Conf. of Internat. Security Printers, Montreux, Switzerland, 1982; mem. Research and Engring. Council Graphic Arts Industry, Inc., Washington, 1961-65; mem. research com. Lithographic Tech. Found., Chgo., 1951-65; mem. exec. research com. Graphic Arts Tech. Found., 1966—. Served as maj. Signal Corps., AUS, 1942-45. Decorated Bronze Star with oak leaf cluster, Purple Heart; Croix de Guerre (Belgium); Croix de Guerre (France); recipient Sci. Bronze Plaque award Grafisk Teknik, Svenska Teknologforeningen, 1963. Mem. Tech. Assn. Graphic Arts (pres. 1957-58), Internat. Soc. Sci. Cons., Forensic Sci. Soc., Soc. Info. Display (v.p. 1964-65). Am. Acad. Forensic Scis., Sci. Research Soc. Am., Soc. Photog. Scientists and Engrs., Soc. Am. Mil. Engrs., Am. Soc. Quality Control (sr.), Calif. Check Investigators Assn. (sr.), N.Y., Calif., Oreg. acads. sci., Sigma Xi, Sigma Pi Sigma, Chi Beta Phi. Congregationalist. Home: PO Box 509 Lake Oswego OR 97034

BARTCHY, S(TUART) SCOTT, history educator; b. Canton, Ohio, Nov. 9, 1936; s. Jacques Robert and Dorothy Elizabeth Bartchy; B.A. cum laude, Milligan Coll., 1958; S.T.B., Harvard U., 1963, Ph.D., 1971; postgrad. Christian Theol. Sem., 1959-60, U. Tuebingen (W. Ger.), 1968-69; m. Diane Walker, June 13, 1956; children—Beth, Christopher Walker. Dir., Institut zur Erforschung des Urchristentumns, Tuebingen, 1971-74, 77-79, acting dir., 1969-71; prof. Bibl. hermeneutics Emmanuel Sch. Religion, Johnson City, Tenn., 1976-77; assoc. prof. N.T. and Christian origins, 1974-76; lectr. N.T. studies Protestant Theol. faculty Eberhard Karls Universitaet, Tuebingen, 1971—, vis. assoc. prof. early Christian history UCLA, 1980-82, adj. assoc. prof. history, 1982—; resident N.T. scholar Westwood Christian Found.; Los Angeles, 1979—; disting. lectr. Staley Found., 1974, 76. Recipient award Indpls. Hebrew Congregation, 1960. Mem. Studiorum Novi Testamenti Societas, Soc. Bibl. Lit., Am. Acad. Religion, Cath. Bibl. Assn., Inst. Bibl. Research. Author: Mallon Chresai: First Century Slavery and the Interpretation of I Corinthians 7:21, 1973; mem. editorial com. Gospel in Context: A Dialogue on Contextualization, 1977-79. Office: 10808 Le Conte St Los Angeles CA 90024

BARTELL, JOHN FRANK, ednl. adminstr.; b. Harrisburg, Pa., Aug. 6, 1941; s. Frank John and Dorothy Jane (Mumma) B.; B.S., Grand Canyon Coll., 1963; M.A. in Guidance and Counseling, Ariz. State U., 1967, Ednl. Specialist in Adminstrn. and Supervision, 1973, Ed.D., 1976; children—Jill Ree, Timmy John. Tchr., Cartwright Sch. Dist., Phoenix, 1963-66; tchr., coach Pendergast Sch. Dist., Tolleson, Ariz., 1966-68, prin., 1970-74, supt., 1975; prin. Litchfield Sch. Dist., Litchfield Park, Ariz., 1968-70; coordinator, observation/participation program Ariz. State U., Tempe, 1974-75; prin. Aquilar Sch., Tempe, 1976—; founder, dir., human relations cons. People in Everything Program, 1970—. Mem. Glendale Council for Arts, Glendale Bicentennial Commn., Glendale Parks and Recreation Commn. mem. tchr. edn. adv. com., adminstrv. cons. Cadre, Ariz. State Dept. Edn.; active Boy Scouts Am., Boys' Club, YMCA, teen activities. Recipient Service award Boy Scouts Am., 1974, YMCA, 1974; Disting. Alumnus Service award Grand Canyon Coll., 1974; Early Childhood Edn. award, 1974; S.W. Community Edn. award Ariz. U., 1974; Youth Vol. award Glendale Youth Services Bd., 1973; Ariz. State Fair Hobby award, 1974; Service to Sch. award PTA, 1974; Outstanding Coach award, 1965, 66, 68, 70, Outstanding Tchr. awards, 1966, 68, Outstanding Prin. award, 1973, 74, 80; Am. Educators medal Freedoms Found, 1976; John Hancock award for patriotism Ariz. Congress God and Country, 1975; ABI Bicentennial award, 1976; Community Service award City of Glendale, 1981, 82, 83; Tempe United Way award. Mem. NEA, Ariz. Edn. Assn., Am. Assn. Sch. Adminstrs., Nat. Elementary Sch. Prins., Am. Personnel and Guidance Assn., Assn. Tchr. Educators, Phoenix West Art League, Ariz. State Poetry Soc., Ariz. Sch. Adminstrs., Tempe C. of C., Phi Delta Kappa, Kappa Delta Pi. Club: Optimists. Author: Poems of Life and Nature, 1978; the People in Everything Program-A Positive Approach to Education, 1977. Contbr. articles to profl. jours. Home: 6617 W Georgia Ave Glendale AZ 85301 Office: Aguilar Sch 5800 S Forest Ave Tempe AZ 85283

BARTELL, SELMA DOROTHY CLASSEN, auto distbg. co. exec.; b. Fairview, Okla., Apr. 19, 1906; d. Dietrich John and Helena (Duerksen) Classen; grad. Kern County Jr. Coll., 1924; m. Henry Jacob Bartell, Mar. 1, 1925; children—Lula May, Ruben C., Florence Lucille, Clarence Henry, Lawson Wayne, Henry Lee. Owner, mgr. H.J. Bartell Bardahl Distbrs., Bakersfield, Calif., 1972—. Pres., PTA, 1932, 33, pres. Kern County Home Dept.; v.p. Calif. Farm Bur. Women; Calif. del. Asso. Country Women of the World, 1953; leader 4-H, 1936; pres. Symphony Assos., 1967-68; pianist, Sunday sch. tchr. Mennonite Brethren Ch., 1920-60. Named Woman of Yr., Valley Plaza Mchts. Assn., 1970. Mem. Rosedale Hwy. Bus. Assn. (pres. 1978, treas. 1983), Desk and Derrick Bakersfield (pres. 1966-67). Republican. Home and office: 2001 Calloway Dr Bakersfield CA 93308

BARTELS, JUERGEN E., hotel company executive; b. Swinemuende, Ger., Sept. 14, 1940; s. Herbert and Lilli E. (Wendland) B.; m. Rachel M.P. Villemaire, Mar. 14, 1951. Final, Werner V. Siemens Sch., Hanover, W. Germany, 1956. Vice pres. Commonwealth Holiday Inns Can. Ltd., Can., 1971-76; exec. v.p. Ramada Internat., Brussels, Belgium, 1976-77; pres. Ramada Hotel Group, Phoenix, 1978-83; pres., chief exec. officer Carlson Hospitality Group, Carlson Cos., Inc., Mpls., 1983—; exec. v.p. Ramada Inns, Inc.; mem. Ramada Mgmt. Com. Office: Carlson Cos Inc World Hdqrs Suite 12755 State Hwy 55 Minneapolis MN 55441

BARTH, BERLE IRA, physician; b. Paterson, N.J., Apr. 11, 1929; s. J.H. and Fay (Miller) B.; B.A., Montclair State Tchrs. Coll., 1951; postgrad. U. Denver, 1952-53, U. Colo., 1954-55; M.D., U. Chgo., 1959; m. O. Stephanie Ritz, Aug. 24, 1952; children—David, Geoffrey. Intern, Letterman Hosp., San Francisco, 1959-60; resident Letterman, also Walter Reed hosps., 1960-63; chief of neurology Orange County Med. Center and U. Calif. at Irvine, 1967-70; pvt. practice med. neurology, Orange, Calif., 1967-78; asst. clin. prof. neurology U. Calif. at Irvine, 1969-78, U. Calif.-San Francisco, 1978-81; assoc. prof. medicine Oreg. State U., 1981—, also team physician, dir. sports medicine; instr. neurology U. Colo., 1962-63; chief of neurology, chief dept. internal medicine, chief med. staff Santa Ana Hosp.; cons. to Easter Seal Rehab. Center, Orange, Calif. and Orange County Epilepsy Soc.; mem. guest faculty Calif. State Coll. at Fullerton and Fullerton Jr. Coll.; med. edn. advisor Orange Coast Coll.; pres. Berle I. Barth, M.D., Inc.; cons. U.S. Army; mem. exec. com. Santa Ana Community Hosp. Served to maj. M.C., AUS, 1959-67. Diplomate Nat. Bd. Med. Examiners. Mem. Los Angeles Neurol. Soc., Western Electroencephalography Soc. (trustee), Orange County Neurosurg. Soc. (asso.), Am. EEG Soc., Am. Assn. Electrodiagnosis and EMG, Calif., Orange County med. socs., Calif. Med. Assn., AMA, Western Fedn. Neurol. Sci., Am. Soc. Study of Headache, Orange County Neurol. Soc. Clubs: Toastmasters (pres.). Contbr. articles to profl. jours. Office: PO Box 329 Monroe OR 97456

BARTHELL, JOLENE HUNTEMAN, business educator; b. Dallas, Oct. 25, 1936; d. Paul Albert and Prunella Aldena (Flowers) Hunteman; m. James G. Jordan, Aug. 31, 1957; 1 dau., Paula; m. 2d, Barry L. Barthell, Aug. 11, 1972; children—Robin, Ben, Gregory. B.S., Oklahoma City U., 1958; postgrad. U. Okla., 1962, Eastern N.Mex. U., 1973-74, Adams State Coll., Alamosa, Colo., 1978-79. Cert. profl. educator, N.Mex. Tchr. bus. edn. Blanchard (Okla.) High Sch., 1960-63; instr. Hill's Bus. U., Oklahoma City, 1963-64; tchr. Los Alamos High Sch., 1964—; coordinator coop. vocat. office edn., 1979—; region II advisor Office Edn. Assn., dir., 1981—. Mem. LWV, Valle Escondido (N.Mex.) Home Owners Assn., Los Alamos Edn. Assn., N.Mex. Edn. Assn., NEA, N.Mex. Bus. and Office Edn. Assn. (pres.), Am. Vocat. Assn., AAUW. Democrat.

BARTKUS, RICHARD ANTHONY, mag. pub.; b. Chgo., Mar. 14, 1931; s. Anthony J. and Mary (Petraitis) B.; student U. Ill., 1949-55; m. Betty Ann Luetke, Jan. 2, 1954; children—Susan Kimberly, David Richard. Circulation trainee Chgo. Tribune, 1955-58; asst. advt. mgr. Kilner Pub. Co., Chgo., 1958-59; advt. mgr. Cox Publs., Arcadia, Calif., 1959-60, Bond Pub. Co., 1960, Western advt. mgr., advt. dir., 1969-75, pub. Road and Track, Newport Beach, Calif., 1975—; v.p. CBS Consumer Publs., 1977—. Served with USMC, 1951-53. Club: Univ. Athletic. Home: 18681 Via Torino Irvine CA 92715 Office: 1499 Monrovia St Newport Beach CA 92663

DARTLEBAUGH, CLYDE ALLAN, III, computer services co. exec.; b. Detroit, Feb. 11, 1943; s. Clyde Allan and Eloise V. Bartlebaugh; B.A., Mich. State U., 1968; m. Marsha C. Strom, June 30, 1979. Mem. mgmt. tng. program Gen. Motors Corp., Pontiac, Mich., 1967-69; with Brit. Am. Yacht Corp., 1969-70; cons. Star Internat., Chgo., 1970-72; cons. Kearney Clark & Assos., Chgo., 1972-77; pres. Western Programmers, Inc., Albuquerque, 1978—. Served with USCG, 1966-67. Mem. Digital Equipment Computer Users Soc., Albuquerque C. of C., N.Mex. Assn. Commerce and Industry, Data Processing Mgmt. Assn. Home: 7708 Callow NE Albuquerque NM 87109 Office: 3620 Wyoming NE Albuquerque NM 87111

BARTLETT, BRUCE L., mfg. co. exec.; b. Denver, July 14, 1944; s. Edgar E. and Genevieve J. Bartlett; B.A., Adams State Coll., 1967; M.A., U. Colo., 1971; m. Joyce L. Klein, Mar. 13, 1976; children—Erin A., Christine M., Jason E. Founder, exec. dir. Community Group Homes, Denver, 1971-75; grant adminstr. Com. for Econ. Devel., City of Tucson, 1975-76; city mgr. City of Bethel (Alaska), 1976-77; dir. NW Econ. Devel. Center, Seattle, 1977-78; v.p. Roberge Sheet Metal Inc., Seattle, 1978-79, owner, pres., 1979—; mem. adj. faculty U. Puget Sound. Bd. dirs. King County (Wash.) Assn. for Retarded Citizens, Children's Home Soc. Wash. Mem. Soc. Mfg. Engrs., Internat. City Mgmt. Assn., Wash. Council Crime and Delinquency. Republican. Roman Catholic. Home: 16424 164th Ave NE Woodinville WA 98072 Office: 2922 Western Ave Seattle WA 98121

BARTLETT, HALL, motion picture producer; b. Kansas City, Mo., Nov. 27, 1925; s. Paul Dana and Alice (Hiestand) B.; grad. Yale U., 1942; children—Cathy, Laurie. Propr., Hall Bartlett Prodn., Inc., Los Angeles, 1952—; now pres. Hall Bartlett Films, Johathan Livingston Seagull Mcht. Co., producer, dir. films Navajo, 1952, Crazylegs, Unchained, All the Young Men, Dorango, Zero Hour, The Caretakers, Changes, 1969, Sandpit Generals, Jonathan Livingston Seagull, 1973; producer-dir. Cleo Laine-John Dankworth TV Spl., Zubin Mehta Spl., Children of Sanchez; co-producer, dir. Comeback, 1982. Bd. dirs. Hollywood Greek Theatre; patron Music Center. Served with USNR, 1942-46. Recipient 11 Acad. award nominations, Film Festival awards from Cannes, 1961, 63, Venice, 1959, 65, Edinburgh, 1952, San Sebastian, 1969, Moscow, 1971, NCCJ, 1955, Fgn. Press awards. Mem. Motion Picture Acad. Arts and Scis., Acad. TV Arts and Scis., Friends of Library, Cinema Circulus, Phi Beta Kappa. Presbyterian. Club: Bel-Air Country (Los Angeles). Home: 861 Stone Canyon Rd Los Angeles CA 90024 Office: 9200 Sunset Blvd Suite 908 Los Angeles CA 90069

BARTLETT, J(AMES) KENNETH, chemist; b. Lynden, Wash., Feb. 2, 1925; s. James Pierce and Hazel Gertrude (Harmelink) B.; B.S. in Chemistry, Willamette U., 1949; Ph.D., Stanford U., 1954; m. Patricia Evelyn Curtis, Aug. 21, 1948; 1 dau., Nancy Evelyn. Instr., U. Santa Clara (Calif.), 1953-54; asst. prof. Long Beach (Calif.) State Coll., 1954-56; mem. faculty So. Oreg. State Coll., Ashland, 1956—, prof. chemistry, 1963—, chmn. dept., 1976—; cons. in field. Served with U.S. Army, 1943-46. duPont fellow, 1952-53. Mem. Am. Chem. Soc. Republican. Presbyterian. Author: General Chemistry Experiments, 1976; Identification of Chemical Substances, 1978. Home: 1313 Woodland Dr Ashland OR 97520 Office: Chemistry Dept So Oreg State Coll Ashland OR 97520

BARTLETT, JOHN DONNINGTON, surgeon; b. Bozeman, Mont., Jan. 24, 1932; s. John Donnington and Rae (Anceny) B.; B.S., U. Mich., 1959; M.D., 1963; m. Joanne Beverly Button, Feb. 1, 1958; children—Deborah, Jennifer, Wendy, John. Intern, U. Mich. Med. Sch., Ann Arbor, 1963-64, resident surgery, 1964-68; instr. gen. surgery, 1968-69, asst. prof., 1969-70; vice-chmn. surgery Lovelace Bataan Med. Center, Albuquerque, 1970-74, chmn. med. staff, 1972-74; asso. prof. surgery U. N.Mex., Albuquerque, 1970-77; practice medicine specializing in gen. vascular surgery, Butte, Mont., 1977—. Bd. dirs. Am. Cancer Soc. Served with USN, 1951-55; comdr. USNR, 1982. Fellow A.C.S.; mem. Western, Frederic A. Coller surg. socs., Soc. Academic Surgeons, Endocrine Soc., Assn. Mil. Surgeons U.S., Naval Res. Assn. Club: Rotary. Pharm. research autonomic nervous system. Home: Route 1 Butte MT 59701 Office: 401 S Alabama Butte MT 59701

BARTLETT, LEONARD LEE, advertising executive; b. Mountain Home, Idaho, Jan. 31, 1930; s. Harold Roberts and Alma Martina (Nixon) B.; m. Helen Eugenia Dennison, Oct. 20, 1950; m. 2d, Sue Ann Kipfer, Nov. 5, 1966; children—Linda, Cynthia, Nancy, Pamela, William Charles, Jennifer, Deborah. B.A. in Art, Brigham Young U., 1957. Advt. mgr. Steiner Co., Chgo., 1951-59; acct. mgr., creative dir. Marsteller Inc., Chgo., 1959-67; vice chmn., chmn. exec. com. Cole & Weber, Inc., Seattle, 1967—. Vice pres., bd. dirs. Friends Phila. String Quartet. Served with USAF, 1951-56. Mem. Am. Assn. Advt. Agys. (past chmn. Western region). Republican. Mormon. Clubs: Rainier, Sand Point Golf and Country (Seattle).

BARTLETT, PAUL ALEXANDER, artist, author; b. Moberly, Mo.; s. Robert Alexander and Minnie Lou (Dobson) B.; B.A., Oberlin Coll., 1929; student San Carlos Acad. and Bellas Artes, Mexico, 1942-43; m. Elizabeth Winters, Apr. 19, 1943; 1 son, Steven. One—man shows: N.Y.C. Pub. Library, 1950, U. Calif., 1969, U. Tex., 1972, Ga. Tech. U., 1955, Los Angeles County Mus., 1968, Inst. Mexicano Americano, Mexico City, 1956, Neiman Marcus, Dallas, 1951, Telenews Gallery, Dallas, 1952, San Diego Pub. Library, 1982; exhibitor group shows; pen and ink drawings represented in permanent collection Latin Am. Library, U. Tex., Austin; author: (novel) When the Owl Cries, 1960; (poems) Wherehill, 1976, Spokes for Memory, 1979; (novelette) Adios Mi Mexico, 1979; also short stories in Crosscurrents, Antigonish Rev., Wind, N.Mex. Humanities, Southwest Rev., Dalhousie Rev., Nuestro Mag., Prism Internat., Stories Mag., others. Fellowships from New Sch. Social Research, Huntington Hartford Found., Montalvo Assn., Yaddo, MacDowell Colony, Dorland Mountain Colony; grantee Carnegie Found., Latin Am. Research Found. Paul Alexander Bartlett Archive at Western History Research Center, U. Wyo., Laramie, Bartlett Archive at UCLA Spl. Collections. Editor publs. U. Calif., Santa Barbara, 1965-70, fiction editor U. Calif., Los Angeles, 1968-69; instr. creative writing Ga. State U., 1958-59. Home: 2875 Cowley Way Apt 1302 San Diego CA 92110

BARTLETT, RICHARD JAMES, physician; b. Muskegon, Mich., Apr. 25, 1930; s. Frank Herbert and Lucy Althea (Weeks) B. Student Harvard U., 1948-50; student U. Mich., 1950-51, M.D., 1955. Intern, Chgo. Wesley Meml. Hosp., 1955-56; resident U. Mich. Med. Center, 1958-61, U. Calif., 1961-62; practice medicine specializing in internal medicine and gastroenterology, San Francisco, 1961—; mem. active staff St. Francis Meml. Hosp., San Francisco, chmn. med. dept., 1969-72, chief staff, 1975-77; mem. courtesy staff U. Calif. Med. Center at San Francisco Gen. Hosp.; asso. clin. prof. dept. medicine U. Calif., San Francisco, 1975—; mem. team responsible med. care Sequoias Retirement Community; mem. adminstrv. body Calif. Blue Shield, 1979—; med. adv. Bur. Hearings and Appeals, Social Security Adminstrn., HEW, 1975—; mem. San Francisco Health Found. and Individual Practice Assn.; trustee St. Francis Hosp., 1977—, v.p., 1978—. Mem. nat. council Met. Opera; bd. dirs. Merola Opera Program. Served with USNR, 1971; now capt. Res. (ret.). Diplomate Am. Bd. Internal Medicine. Fellow A.C.P.; mem. AMA, Calif., San Francisco med. socs., Am. (coms.), Calif., San Francisco socs. internal medicine, Calif. Acad. Medicine, Am. Lung Assn. (dir. Calif. chpt. 1980—, treas. 1983—), San Francisco Lung Assn., No. Calif. Soc. Clin. Gastroenterology, Am. Med. Soc. of Vienna, Soc. Med. Friends of Wine, Calif. Thoracic Soc., San Francisco Individual Practice Assn. (dir., sec. 1979—), San Francisco Mus. Art, DeYoung Mus. Soc. and Patrons of Art and Music, Assn. Clin. Faculty U. Calif. Med. Center (council), Calif. Hist. Soc., Marines Meml. Assn., Naval Res. Assn., Res. Officers Assn., Naval Order (council), San Francisco Symphony Assn., Clin. Faculty Assn. U. Calif.-San Francisco Med. Ctr. (treas. 1983—), Nu Sigma Nu. Clubs: Pacific Union, Commonwealth, Olympic, Faculty U. Calif. (San Francisco). Home: 1845 Laguna St San Francisco CA 94115 Office: 909 Hyde St San Francisco CA 94109

BARTLETT, THOMAS EDWARD, research exec.; b. Tulsa, Sept. 3, 1920; s. Michael Leo and Elizabeth (Stadden) B.; B.A., U. Okla., 1942; M.S., Columbia U., 1947; postgrad. Purdue U., 1957-59, U. Fla., 1965, Ariz. State U., 1966. Engr., Montgomery Ward & Co., 1947-48; chief indsl. engr. Bank of Am., 1948-50; mem. tech. staff Hughes Research and Devel., 1950-54, Ramo-Wooldridge, 1954; prof. Purdue U., 1955-63; mem. teaching staff Calif. State Poly. Coll., 1964-65; ops. research cons., 1965-67; dir. ops. research Lester Gorstine Assocs., 1967-68; pres., chmn. bd. dirs. Wyvern Research Assos., Inc., Mill Valley, Calif., 1968—; dir. Jebor, Inc. Served with CIC, U.S. Army, 1942-46. Registered profl. engr., Calif. Mem. Am. Inst. Indsl. Engrs., Inst. Mgmt. Scis., Ops. Research Soc. Am., Fedn. Am. Scientists, Soc. Indsl. and Applied Math., Scis., AAAS, Am. Soc. Personnel Adminstrn., Sigma Xi, Phi Kappa Phi, Phi Kappa Psi. Club: San Francisco Press. Home: 1 Lincoln Dr Sausalito CA 94965 Office: 456-458 Coloma St Sausalito CA 94965

BARTLING, JUDD QUENTON, research corp. exec.; b. Muncie, Ind., July 24, 1936; s. Hubert George and Hildagarde (Good) B.; B.A., U. Calif., 1960, Ph.D., 1969; M.S., Purdue U., 1964; m. Madeline Levesque, June 9, 1973; stepchildren—Mary Johnson, Michael Johnson. Research asst. U. Calif., Riverside, 1965-69; cons. Azak Corp., Chatsworth, Calif., 1969-71, pres., 1971—. Served with U.S. Army, 1960-62. NSF grantee U. Fla., 1969. Research in bus., solid state physics, quantum electronics, electromagnetics and radar. Office: 9738 Nevada St Chatsworth CA 91311

BARTLIT, JOHN RAHN, cryogenic engr.; b. Chgo., June 1, 1934; s. Fred Holcomb and Agnes Marie (Rahn) B.; B.S., Purdue U., 1956; M.S., Princeton, 1957; D.Engring., Yale, 1963; m. Nancy Edith Reynolds, July 2, 1961; children—Jennifer, John. Engr., Calif. Research Corp., Emeryville, 1956, Esso Engring., Linden, N.J., 1957, Am. Cyanamid, Stamford, Conn., 1958, Los Alamos (N.Mex.) Sci. Lab., 1962—; instr. Yale, 1960. State chmn. N.M. Citizens for Clean Air and Water, 1970—; mem. tech. adv. com. for air pollution N.Mex. Environ. Improvement Agy., 1969—; mem. N.Mex. Environ. Inst., 1972—; mem. environ. adv. com. Fed. Energy Adminstrn.; mem. adv. panel on tech. innovation and health, safety and environ. regulation U.S. Congress Office Tech. Assessment, 1979. Recipient Inventions and Contbns. Bd. award NASA, 1971; Citizen Achievement award Rocky Mountain Center on Environment, 1973. Mem. Sigma Xi, Tau Beta Pi. Republican. Home: 113 Monte Rey N Los Alamos NM 87544 Office: Box 1663 Los Alamos NM 87545

BARTO, MILAN ANDREW (DOC), hosp. mgmt. cons.; b. Youngstown, Ohio, Jan. 25, 1928; s. George and Susanna Barto; ed. Youngstown Coll., LaSalle Extension U.; m. June Delores Zetts, June 20, 1953; children—Rick, Joni, Terri, Tim, Jeff. Mgmt. trainee Sears, Roebuck & Co., Youngstown, 1958-60; credit mgr. St. Elizabeth Hosp., Youngstown, 1962-64; bus. mgr. Riverside Hosp., Kankakee, Ill., 1964-66; patient accounts mgr. Stanford (Calif.) U. Med. Center, 1966-68; propr., hosp. accounts systems cons. Barto Associates, Inc., San Jose, Calif., 1969—. Pres., mgr., coach Little League baseball teams, Ohio, Ill. and Calif.; active various youth orgns., 1948-80; chmn. congregation St. John's Ch., Youngstown, 1968; now mem. U.S. Senatorial Bus. Adv. Bd.

Served with Signal Corps, U.S. Army, 1950-52; ETO. Mem. Am. Hosp. Assn., Cath. Hosp. Assn., Am. Assn. Profl. Consultants, United Hosp. Assn., Am. Mgmt. Assn., Hosp. Fin. Mgmt. Assn. (pres. No. Calif. chpt. 1975-76, ann. bd. dirs. award, no. Calif. charter presdl. award, mem. nat. Matrix 1983-84), Follmer award 1977, Reeves award 1980, Muncie award 1980), Assn. Western Hosps., Internat. Consumer Credit Assn., Businessmen's Christian Assn. Clubs: Kiwanis, Optimists. Home: 6351 Wisteria Way San Jose CA 95129 Office: 1135 Saratoga Sunnyvale Rd San Jose CA 95129

BARTOLME, GODFREY RALPH, metal products company executive; b. Chgo., Feb. 2, 1918; s. Max and Tina (Trivisono) B.; B.S., Roosevelt U., 1939; J.D., Marquette U., 1952; m. Barbara Ganser, Aug. 8, 1943; children—Wayne John, Donna Kay, Barbara Ann, Mary Margaret. Unemployment compensation tax auditor U.S. Dept. Labor, Chgo., 1939-41; internal revenue service agt. U.S. Treas. Dept., Chgo., 1946-47; admitted to Wis. bar, 1952, practiced in Milw., 1952-56; with Gen. Electric Co., Milw., 1948-56; with VSI Corp., Pasadena, Calif., 1956—, sr. v.p., 1970—, also dir.; dir. Boulonnerie et Matricage de Precision Blanc, S.A., France, D-M-E Can. Ltd., D-M-E Italiana, S.A., Italy, Société Generade de Capsules S.A., France, Japan D-M-E Co., D-M-E-Comat Ibérica, Partes Para Moldes D-M-E, S.A., Mexico, Talleres de Escoriaza, S.A., Spain, VSI Internat., N.V., Belgium. Served with USAAF, 1942-45. C.P.A., Ill., Wis. Mem. Am., Wis. bar assns., Am. Soc. Corp. Secs., Am. Inst. C.P.A.s, Fin. Execs. Inst. (former dir. Western region). Clubs: Jonathan (Los Angeles); El Niguel Country (Laguna Niguel, Calif.); Springs Country (Rancho Mirage, Calif.). Office: 600 N Rosemead Blvd Pasadena CA 91107

BARTON, ANN ELIZABETH, fin. exec.; b. Long Lake, Mich., Sept. 8, 1923; d. John and Inez Mabel (Morse) Seaton; student Mt. San Antonio Coll., 1969-71, Adrian Coll., 1943, Citrus Coll., 1967, Golden Gate U., 1976, Coll. Fin. Planning, 1980-82; m. H. Kenneth Barton, Apr. 3, 1948; children—Michael, John, Nancy. Tax cons., real estate broker, Claremont, Calif., 1967-72, Newport Beach, Calif., 1972-74; v.p., officer Putney, Barton, Assos., Inc., Walnut Creek, Calif., 1975—; dir., officer Century Fin. Enterprises, Inc., F.F.A. Inc.; registered rep. WZW Fin. Services, Inc. Cert. fin. planner. Mem. Internat. Assn. Fin. Planners, Calif. Soc. Enrolled Agts., Nat. Assn. Enrolled Agts., Nat. Soc. Public Accts., Inst. Cert. Fin. Planners. Office: 1705 N California Blvd Walnut Creek CA 94596

BARTON, GERALD LEE, farming company executive; b. Modesto, Calif., Feb. 24, 1934; s. Robert Paul and Alice Lee (Hall) B.; A.B. with distinction, Stanford U., 1955; m. M. Janet Murray, June 24, 1955; children—Donald Lee, Gary Michael, Brent Richard. Owner, mgr. R.P. Barton Ranch, Escalon, Calif., 1961—; v.p. R.P. Barton Mfg. Co., Escalon, 1963—; chmn. bd. Diamond Walnut Growers Inc., 1976-81, chmn. emeritus, 1981—; chmn. Diamond-Sunsweet Co., Stockton, Calif., 1978-80, Sun Diamond Growers, Inc., 1980-81; vice chmn. Fed. Land Bank, Modesto, Calif., 1976-81; chmn. Growers Harvesting Com., Modesto, 1976-77; mem. pomology research adv. bd. U. Calif.-Davis, 1968—, Walnut Mktg. Bd., San Francisco, 1971-73, 77—. Chmn. bd. edn. Escalon Unified Sch. Dist., 1963-75; vice chmn. San Joaquin County Sch. Bds. Assn., 1965; mem. adv. com. U. Santa Clara Agribus. Inst., 1981—; bd. dirs. Norman Ross Hort. Found., 1981—. Served with AUS, 1956-58. Named Outstanding Young Farmer in San Joaquin County, C. of C., 1965, Farmer of Yr., Escalon C. of C. Mem. Stanford U. Alumni Assn., Delta Chi. Republican. Presbyterian. Home: 31110 E Lee St Escalon CA 95320 Office: 22398 S McBride St Escalon CA 95320

BARTON, PHILLIP, pub. relations exec., journalist; b. New Brighton, Pa., June 18, 1928; s. Arthur Abraham and Veda Naomi (Zeligsohn) Segall; A.A., Los Angeles City Coll., 1964; grad. Rio Hondo Police Acad., 1973; vocat. teaching cert. UCLA, 1975; m. Katherine Ramirez, Mar. 29, 1952; children—Dirck, Jeffery, Katherine, Dane, Dolores. Freelance press and pub. relations cons., actor, announcer, dialectician, Los Angeles, 1954—; former news dir. Sta. KBLA, Sta. KGFJ, PM Newspaper, news anchor-mobile reporter Sta. KHJ; pub. affairs dir. Los Angeles Community Devel. Dept., 1972-81; tchr. broadcasting Columbia Coll., Pasadena City Coll.; past mem. Adv. Com. to Calif. Joint Legis. Com. on Telecommunications; press adviser Senate Subcom. on Med. Edn. and Health Needs; press cons. Los Angeles City/County-Hiroshima Joint Clinic on Atomic Bomb Survivors; specialist res. officer Los Angeles Police Dept. Bd. dirs. Los Angeles area USO. Served with U.S. Maritime Service, 1944, AUS, 1946-47; lt. col. Calif. Mil. Res. Recipient awards Los Angeles County Chief Med. Examiner-Coroner, Los Angeles Bd. Edn., Calif. Senate, Calif. Assembly, Los Angeles City Council, Human Relations Commn., Mayor's Office, Police Dept., Nisei Week Japanese Festival, Comite Mexicano Civico-Patriotico, Calif. Army N.G., USO, others. Mem. AFTRA, Screen Actors Guild. Radio-TV News Assn. So. Calif., Pub. Interest Radio and TV Ednl. Soc. (bd. dirs.), Nat. Geog. Soc. Clubs: Shomrim Soc. So. Calif., Binnacle, Los Angeles Harbor. Office: Los Angeles Police Dept Pub Affairs Sect Parker Center Los Angeles CA 90012

BARTON, PHYLLIS SETTECASE, fine arts appraiser, art writer; b. Dubuque, Iowa, Nov. 5, 1934; d. Joseph T. and Elizabeth Catherine (Gaidzik) Settecase. B.A. in Art History, Calif. State U.-Long Beach, 1978, M.A. in Art History, 1982. Adminstrv. asst. Norton Simon Inc., 1958-65; art cons., Bangkok, Thailand, 1965-67; art editor Santa Ana Register, 1967-68; art agent, publicist, antiques dealer, 1968-76; arts cons., art writer, Rancho Dominguez, Calif., 1976—. Recipient excellence of book design award Printing Industries Am., 1976, 79. Mem. Am. Soc. Appraisers, Nat. League Am. Pen Women (treas.), Illustrators Research Group. Author: Sassone-California, 1973, Cecil C. Bell, 1906-1970, 1976; The Art of Alexander Dzigurski, 1979; contbr. articles to profl. jours.

BARTON, WILLIAM THOMAS, bldg. supplies retail exec.; b. Granger, Utah, Feb. 18, 1933; s. Doran Warr and Beatrice (Orullian) B.; student U. Utah, Utah Tech. U.; m. Laren Sue Larson, May 28, 1958; children—Thomas Kim, Allison, Doran Lynn. Mgr., owner Bartons Builders Mart and treas. Oaken Bucket Enterprises, Granger, Utah, 1956—. Sec., Salt Lake County Republican Party, 1971-75. Mem. Intermountain Hardware and Implement Dealers Assn., Intermountain Ace Dealers Assn., West Valley Area C. of C. (pres. 1977). Mormon. Clubs: Jaycees (pres. Granger 1965, state v.p. 1966, nat. dir. 1967), Lions (past pres.). Office: 3940 W 4100 S Granger UT 84120

BARTON, WILSON RICHARD, chiropractor; b. Salt Lake City, Nov. 2, 1946; s. Wilson Gardner Barton and June Hollist; B.S., Los Angeles Coll. Chiropractic, D. Chiropractic, 1978; m. Eileen K. McPhie, Dec. 30, 1979 (div. July 1980); children—Daniel Elliott, Deborah June, Kristopher Clarence, Melissa Kay. Mem. Am. Chiropractic Assn., Sigma Chi Psi. Libertarian. Club: Rotary. Home: 1845 W 4500 S #132 Roy UT 84067 Office: Suite 23A Harrisville Rd Family Bank Bldg Ogden UT 84404

BARTOO, ALICE JEAN, computer consultant; b. Wichita, Kans., Sept. 4, 1949; d. Glenn Walter and Letha Lee (Long) Ryder; m. Robert Kittleson Reid, Sept. 13, 1968; m. Russell Roger Bartoo, July 4, 1976. Student Portland Community Coll., 1970-71, U. Alaska-Juneau, 1977—. Keypuncher to computer operator Redken Labs., Los Angeles, 1971-75; computer operator U.S. Forest Service, Juneau, 1977; programmer State Alaska, 1977; computer cons., Juneau, 1980—. Republican. club: Big Dipper Square Dance. Home and Office: PO Box 847 Juneau AK 99802

BARTZ, BETTY JEAN, tool manufacturing executive; b. Hobbs, N.Mex.; d. J.E. and Juanita (Shaffer) Bowden; student public schs.; m. Elton M. Kesner, Mar. 6, 1960 (div. Jan. 1977); children—Eva Camille Kesner Wheeler, Guy Gregory; m. 2d, Don Lee Bartz, Feb. 12, 1981. Part-owner H & K Tax Service, Hobbs, 1960-78; tax cons., Hobbs, 1977—; bookkeeper Hobbs Automatic Tool Co. Inc., 1977-80, pres., mgr., 1980—; constrn. foreman Roosevelt Apts. Inc., 1977; cons. Hatco Inc., Roosevelt J.E. Bowden, 1975—. Republican. Methodist. Home: 720 E Green Acres Hobbs NM 88240 Office: Hobbs Automatic Tool Co Inc 3403 Industrial Blvd Hobbs NM 88240

BARUH, MORTON GOLDMAN, liquor co. exec.; b. San Francisco, Mar. 15, 1923; s. Harold F. and Doris (Goldman) B.; student Marin Jr. Coll., 1940-41; San Francisco Inst. Accountancy, 1941-42; m. Marilyn Felix, Aug. 10, 1944; children—Barry F., Terye Baruh Levy, Randie (dec.). Treas., merchandising mgr. Goldman's Store, Oakland, Calif., 1946-53; treas. Goldman's Hayward Inc. (Calif.), 1952-53; v.p. Baruh Liquors, Inc., San Jose, Calif., 1953-60, exec. v.p., 1960-69, pres., 1969-70; v.p. E. Martinoni Co., San Francisco, 1954-69, pres., 1969—, chmn. bd., 1979—; v.p. Goldman's Walnut Creek Inc., Goldman's Alameda Inc., 1958—; pres. James A. Robertson of Wash., Seattle, 1969—; chmn. bd. Am. Constrn. Assos., Menlo Park, Calif., 1962-64. Bd. dirs. Randie Lynn Baruh Research Found. for Leukemia; trustee Leukemia Soc. Am., 1980—. Served with USAAF, 1943-45. Decorated Air medal. Mem. Calif. Wholesale Liquor Distbrs. Assn. (pres. 1969), Calif. Distilled Spirits Rectifiers Assn. (pres. 1973—). Club: Mason. Office: care E. Martinoni Co 543 Forbes Blvd San Francisco CA 94080

BARWICK, WILLIAM ADEN, radio announcer; b. Raleigh, N.C., Mar. 12, 1946; s. George Ira and Mary Bertha (Barber) B.; student Plymouth (N.H.) State Tchrs. Coll., 1964-65, U.S. Army Marine Engring. Sch., Ft. Eustis, Va., 1966-67, N.E. Broadcasting Sch., Boston, 1968-69, Elkins Inst., Denver, 1974-75. Solo performer, vocalist Dunfey Hotels & Motor Inns, Hampton, N.H., 1969-71; research and info. analysis cons. Westfall Assos., Franconia, N.H., 1971-72; newsman, music dir. announcer Sta. WPOR, Portland, Maine, 1974-75; announcer, music dir. Sta. KERE, Denver, 1974-75; announcer, music dir. Sta. WWVA, Wheeling, W.Va., 1975-76; tchr. Ron Bailie Sch. Broadcasting, Denver, 1976-78; prodn. dir., radio announcer Sta. KHOW, Denver, 1977-80, Sta. KYGO, Denver, 1980—. Water safety instr. ARC, 1967-70; scout leader Boy Scouts Am., 1958-60. Served with AUS, 1965-68. Named Country Disc Jockey of Year, Billboard Mag., 1976; Colo. Country Disc Jockey of Yr., Colo. Country Music Found., 1981. Office: 5350 W 20 Ave Denver CO 80214

BARZAGA, GRACIELA ABERION, physician; b. Cavite, Philippines, Oct. 29, 1943; came to U.S., 1969, naturalized, 1976; d. Raul B. and Julita Aberion; M.D., U. Philippines, 1967; m. Ildefonso Barzaga, July 20, 1970; children—Pearl, David, Albert. Intern, Philippine Gen. Hosp., Manila, 1966-67; resident N.Y. U. Inst. Rehab. Medicine, N.Y.C., 1969-72; practice medicine, Stockton, Calif.; med. dir. Phys. Medicine-Rehab. Dept., San Joaquin Gen. Hosp., Stockton, Calif., 1976—. Mem. San Joaquin Med. Soc., Am. Congress of Phys. Medicine and Rehab. Home: 8464 Mason Dr Stockton CA 95209 Office: 2420 N California St Stockton CA 95204

BASHAM, WILLIAM HARRISON, civil engr.; b. Daylight, Tenn., May 25, 1941; s. Flavil L. and Ella Florene (Mitchell) B.; student Calif. State Poly. Coll., 1963; m. Marifrances Renfro, Aug. 4, 1973; children—Barbara Lynn, Gregory William, Marty Eileen. Project job leader Calif. Dept. Transp., San Bernardino, 1963-72; project planner CM Engring. Assos., San Bernardino, 1972-77; v.p., office mgr. W.R. Showalter & Assos., San Bernardino, 1977-78; v.p., office mgr. land devel. CM Engring. Assos., San Bernardino and Vista, Calif., 1978—. Active Boy Scouts Am.; trustee Judson Bapt. Ch., San Bernardino, 1974-75; mem. Vista Land Use Circulation Com., 1981-82. Registered profl. engr., Calif., Ariz., Colo., Nev. Mem. Nat. Soc. Profl. Engrs. Calif. Soc. Profl. Engrs. (1st v.p. San Bernardino-Riverside chpt.), ASCE, Am. Public Works Assn., San Bernardino Hist. Soc., Vista C. of C. (econ. devel. com. 1982—), Nat. Platform Assn. Republican. Home: 1268 Eucalyptus Ave Vista CA 92083

BASIL, DOUGLAS CONSTANTINE, educator; b. Vancouver, B.C., Can., May 30, 1923; s. William and Christina (Findlay) B.; B.Commerce, U. B.C., 1949, B.A., 1949; Ph.D., Northwestern U., 1954; postgrad. London Sch. Econs., 1950; m. Evelyn Margaret Pitcairn, 1950; 1 dau., Wendy Patricia. Instr., Marquette U., 1951-54; asst. prof. Northwestern U., 1954-57; asso. prof. U. Minn., 1957-61; prof. mgmt. U. So. Calif., 1961—; cons. mgmt. devel. Remington Rand Univac, Pepsi-Cola, Mpls. Honeywell, Union Carbide, Am. Can Co., others; cons. long range planning numerous cos.; lectr., Brussels, Caracas, Bogota, Paris, London, others. Served to capt. Canadian Army, 1943-46. Author: Executive Development, 1964; (Paul Cone, John Fleming) Effective Decision Making Through Simulation, 1972; Organacao E Controls Da Pequena Empresa, 1968; La Direccion de la Pequeña Empresa, 1969; Managerial Skills for Executive Action, 1970; Leadership Skills for Executive Action, 1971; Women in Management: Performance, Prejudice, Promotion, 1972; Autorité Personnelle et Efficacité des Cadres, 1972; Conduccion y Liderazgo, 1973; Developing Tomorrow's Managers, 1973, Management of Change, 1974, others. Contbr. articles in field to profl. jours. Home: 2201 Warmouth St San Pedro CA 90732 Office: Grad Sch Bus Adminstrn Los Angeles CA 90007

BASILE, PAUL LOUIS, JR., lawyer; b. Oakland, Calif., Dec. 27, 1945; s. Paul Louis and Roma Florence (Paris) B.; A.B., Occidental Coll., 1968; postgrad. U. Wash., 1968-69; J.D., U. Calif. at Los Angeles, 1971; m. Diane Chierichetti, Sept. 2, 1977. Admitted to Calif. bar, 1972, U.S. Supreme Ct., 1978, U.S. Tax Ct., 1977; assoc. firm Parker, Milliken, Kohlmeier, Clark & O'Hara, Los Angeles, 1971-72; corp. counsel TFI Cos. Inc., Irvine, Calif., 1972-73; individual practice law, Los Angeles, 1973-80; ptnr. firm Basile & Siener, Santa Monica, Calif., 1980—; sec., treas. Roughwater Boats, Inc., Marina del Rey, Calif., 1977—; sec. Souriau, Inc., Valencia, Calif., 1981—, Pernovo, Inc., Sherman Oaks, Calif., 1980—, J.W. Brown, Inc., Santa Monica, Calif., 1983—; v.p., sec. Pvt. Fin. Assocs., Los Angeles, 1983—. Sec., trustee Nat. Repertory Theatre Found., Los Angeles, 1975—, Hippovideo, Los Angeles, 1975-76, Bilingual Found. of Arts, 1978-79; trustee Free Pub. Theatre Found., Los Angeles, 1974-75; bd. dirs. Episcopal City Mission Soc., 1977-79, March of Dimes Birth Defects Found., 1982—, Los Angeles Vol. Action Center, 1978. Mem. Los Angeles Jr. C. of C. (dir. 1975-82, treas. 1978-79, v.p. 1977-79, pres. 1980-81, chmn. 1981-82), Am., Los Angeles County, bar assns., State Bar Calif., English-Speaking Union (dir. Los Angeles br. 1977-80), Occidental Coll. Alumni Assn. (v.p. 1978-79, pres. 1979-80, gov. 1977-81), French-Am. C. of C. (councillor 1979—, v.p. 1980, 82—), Los Angeles C. of C. (dir. 1980-81), English-Speaking Union (dir. 1977-80), Can. Soc. Los Angeles (bd. dirs. 1980-83, sec. 1982-83), Canada Calif. C. of C. (dir. 1983—, 2d v.p. 1983—), Phi Alpha Delta. Democrat. Baptist. Club: University of Los Angeles. Contbr. articles to profl. jours. Home: 5845 Doverwood Dr #204 Culver City CA 90230 Office: 1460 4th St Suite 300 Santa Monica CA 90401

BASILIO, L(EONA) PATRICIA, nuclear medicine technologist; b. San Jose, Calif., Sept. 24, 1949; d. Toribio Tercila and Florence Tillie Ruth (Holman) B.; children—Kristie, Heather, Eric. A.A., Foothill Jr. Coll., 1970; B.A., St. Mary's Coll., Moraga, Calif., 1981. Cert. Am. Registry Radiologic Technologists; cert. nuclear medicine technologist. Staff technologist nuclear medicine El Camino Hosp., Mountain View, Calif., 1970-71; asst. chief technologist nuclear medicine Gould Med. Group, Medesto, Calif., 1971-78; chief technologist nuclear medicine Dominican Hosp., Santa Cruz, Calif., 1979—. Active Monterey Bay council Girl Scouts U.S.A., Brook Knoll PTA. Mem. Soc. Nuclear Medicine, Am. Soc. Radiol. Technologist, NOW. Office: Dominican Hosp 1555 Soquel Dr Santa Cruz CA 95065

BASKER, SETH HENRY, computer co. exec.; b. N.Y.C., Nov. 22, 1946; s. Irving Rubin and Evelyn (Foxman) B.; B.A. in Geology, Hunter Coll., 1969; postgrad. CCNY, 1970, U. Idaho, 1972; m. Sandra J. Basker, Sept. 24, 1978; children—Jacob Dov, Jonathan David. Shipboard geologist Lamont-Dougherty Geol. Obs., Palisades, N.Y., 1968-70; pres. Wildflower, Inc., Pullman, Wash., 1970-76; central regional mgr. N.Y. Times Info. Services, Chgo., 1976-79; v.p. Nordata, Ltd., Seattle, 1979—; v.p. Brookvale Computer Assocs., 1981—. Mem. Am. Mgmt. Assn., Sales Execs. Club, Sierra Club, Three Village Hist. Soc. Clubs: Seattle Mountaineers, Appalachian Mountain, Sidha. Office: 4433 27th Ave W Seattle WA 98199

BASKETT, KIRTLEY MORRISON, mag. writer; b. Mexico, Mo., Oct. 27, 1905; s. Cecil Morrison and Martha Elila (Kirtley) B.; B.J., U. Mo., 1927; m. Clara Hood Newman, June 19, 1946; children—Martha (Mrs. Richard Stuart Scully), Laura (Mrs. Gary Walter Anderegg). Editorial, advt. positions St. Louis Post-Dispatch, Miami (Fla.) Daily News, Pasadena (Calif.) Star News, 1927-30; publicity writer Universal Studios, Universal City, Calif., 1930-32; staff writer Photoplay Mag., Hollywood, Calif., 1932-35; freelance mag. writer contbg. articles to mags. including Liberty, Sat. Eve. Post, Am. Mag., Woman's Home Companion, Redbook, Good Housekeeping, Reader's Digest, Am. Weekly, most mags. in entertainment field, 1935—. Mem. Sigma Nu. Home: 700 Bradford St Pasadena CA 91105

BASKIN, HERBERT BERNARD, computer co. exec., educator; b. N.Y.C., Nov. 24, 1933; s. Jackob and Anna B.; M.E.E., Syracuse U., 1959; one dau., Debby Lynne. Elec. engr. IBM Devel. Lab., 1956-59, mgr. systems research Research Center, 1960-69; prof. elec. engring. and computer scis. U. Calif., Berkeley, 1969-80; pres., founder Computer-Lock Systems Corp., Berkeley, 1972-76; v.p. Western Devel. Center, Datapoint Corp., Berkeley, 1976-81; founder, pres. Gen. Parametrics Corp., Berkeley, 1981—; cons. in field. Served with USCGR, 1957-58. Mem. IEEE. Assn. Computing Machinery, Soc. Info. Display, Sierra Club, Eta Kappa Nu, Sigma Xi. Asso. editor, contbr. articles to profl. publs. Patentee in field. Home: Berkeley CA 94708 Office: 1505 Solano Ave Berkeley CA 94707

BASKURT, F. YUCE, civil engr.; b. Ankara, Turkey, June 30, 1944; s. Esat Arif and Haver Nabi (Ozerdim) B.; came to U.S., 1965; B.S. in Civil Engring., Tex. A & M U., 1969, M.S. in Civil Engring., 1970; m. Ylva Aino Garpne, Nov. 4, 1964; 1 child, Deren Arif. Structural engr. Fluor Corp., Houston, 1970-72; sr. hydraulics engr. Alyeska Pipeline Co., Anchorage, 1972-78; sr. engr. Atlantic Richfield Co., Los Angeles, 1978-80; mgr. engring. System Devel. Corp., Irvine, Calif., 1980-81; mgr. engring. Atlantic Richfield Co., Los Angeles, 1981—. Registered profl. engr., Tex. Mem. ASCE, Chi Epsilon, Tau Beta Phi. Home: 229 W Yale Loop Irvine CA 92714 Office: 515 S Flower St Los Angeles CA 90071

BASS, JOEL LEONARD, artist; b. Los Angeles, Dec. 23, 1942; s. Herbert and Ethyl (Kaye) B.; B.A., Art Center Coll. of Design, Los Angeles, 1967; m. Sydney Joan Littenberg, Jan. 28, 1979. Exhibited in one man shows at Michael Walls Gallery, San Francisco, 1970, 71, 72, Reed Coll., Portland, Oreg., 1971, Cusack Gallery, Houston, 1974, John Berggruen Gallery, San Francisco, 1974, John Doyle Gallery, Chgo., 1974, John Doyle Gallery, Paris, 1975. Galerie Marguerite Lamy, Paris, 1976, Kathryn Markel Fine Arts, N.Y.C., 1977, 78, Janus Gallery, Venice, Calif., 1978-80, Roy Boyd Gallery, Chgo., 1978; exhibited in group shows at Michael Walls Gallery, 1970, Joslyn Art Center, Omaha, 1970, Whitney Mus. Am. Art, N.Y.C., 1971, 73, Oakland (Calif.) Mus., 1971, Govett-Brewster Art Gallery, New Plymouth, N.Z., 1972-73, Pasadena (Calif.) Art Mus., 1972-73, Mus. Modern Art, N.Y.C., 1975, Davison Art Center, Wesleyan Coll., 1975, Mendel Art Gallery, Saskatoon, Sask., Can., 1978; represented in permanent collections at Des Moines Art Center, Ft. Worth Art Center, Greenville (S.C.) County Mus. Art, Whitney Mus. Am. Art, Albright Knox Mus. Art Buffalo, Mus. Modern Art, San Francisco Mus. Art, Oakland Mus., La Jolla Mus. Contemporary Art; instr. Art Center Coll. Design, Los Angeles, 1976—. Nat. Endowment for Arts fellow, 1978—. Jewish. Studio: 239 S Los Angeles St Los Angeles CA 90012

BASS, JOSEPH FRANK, traffic engineer; b. Phenix City, Ala., Jan. 10, 1938; s. Frank and Mary Lou (Sanks) B.; m. Jenean Brantley, Jan. 31, 1959; children—Terence, Steven, Sandra. A.A., Hartnell Coll., 1958; student U. Calif.-Berkeley, 1964-76, Carnegie-Mellon U., 1972, U. Santa Clara, 1978, Harvard U., 1981. Registered profl. engr., Calif.; registered traffic engr., Calif. Draftsman, City of Salinas (Calif.), 1958-61, draftsman City of San Jose (Calif.), 1961-62, civil engr., 1962-67, sr. civil engr., 1967-75, prin. civil engr., 1975-80, dir. dept. traffic ops., city traffic engr., 1980—; mem. Calif. Traffic Control Device Com., 1981—, vice-chmn., 1982—; mem. Afro-Am. Community Services Agy. Fed. grantee, 1972. Mem. Inst. Traffic Engrs. (mem. nat. com. on access control for maj. routes), Santa Clara County Black Concerns Assn., NAACP, Am. Pub. Works Assn., ASCE, No. Calif. Council Black Profl. Engrs., South Bay Traffic Ofcls. Assn., Inst. Traffic Engrs. Democrat. Home: 6025 Susan Ct San Jose CA 95123 Office: 801 N 1st St Room 460 San Jose CA 95110

BASS, LAWRENCE JAMES, dermatologist; b. Detroit, May 31, 1941; s. Clifford Joseph and Mary Johanna (Harty) B.; A.B., U. Ky., 1963; M.D., U. Mich., 1967; m. Carolyn Ann Woodward, Aug. 8, 1964; children—Todd Matthew, Laura Catherine, Gregory Lawrence. Intern, Sacramento County Hosp., 1967-68; resident in dermatology U. Mich. Med. Center, 1970-73, chief resident in dermatology, 1972-73; practice medicine specializing in dermatology, Sacramento 1973—; cons. dermatologist Mercy Hosps., Sutter Community Hosps., U. Calif. at Davis Med. Center, Sacramento; lectr., assoc. clin. prof. dept. dermatology, U. Calif., Davis, 1973, adj. lectr., 1981—, acting chmn., 1975-80. Bd. dirs. Sacramento Ballet Assn., 1974-75, Sutter Research Found., 1978—; Sacramento unit Am. Cancer Soc., 1981—. Served with U.S. Army, 1968-69; Viet Nam. Decorated Bronze Star. Diplomate Am. Bd. Dermatology with spl. competence in dermatopathology Am. Bd. Pathology and Am. Bd. Dermatology; lic. to practice medicine, Calif., Mich., Ind. Mem. AMA, Calif. Med. Assn. (mem. com. on dermatology, com. on med. edn.), Assn. Profs. Dermatology, Am. Acad. Dermatology, Pacific Dermatol. Assn., San Francisco, Sacramento Valley dermatol. socs. Republican. Roman Catholic. Contbr. articles in field. Home: 1622 McClaren Dr Carmichael CA 95608 Office: 5340 Elvas Ave Suite 600 Sacramento CA 95819

BASS, LOUIS NELSON, agronomist, plant physiologist, government official; b. Iola, Kans., Mar. 7, 1919; s. Herbert and Olive (Felker) B.; m. Helen Jane Collins, Nov. 7, 1943; children—Colin David, Nelsa Louise Bass Mullen. B.S., Upper Iowa U., 1940; M.S., U. Iowa, 1943; Ph.D., Iowa State U., 1949; Asst. prof. botany and plant pathology Iowa State U., Ames, 1949-58; plant physiologist Nat. Seed Storage Lab., U.S. Dept. Agr., Ft. Collins, Colo., 1960—. Recipient Alumni Achievement award Upper Iowa U., 1972. Fellow Am. Soc. Agronomy (assoc. editor Jour. 1971-74); mem. Soc. Comml. Seed Technologists, Assn. Ofcl. Seed Analysts (merit award 1975, sci. edn. editor 1962—, pres. 1971-72, mem.

pub. service com. 1962—), Crop Sci. Soc. Am. (ex-officio mem. com. for preservation of genetic stocks 1971—), Am. Soc. Hort. Sci., Internat. Seed Testing Assn. (vice-chmn. seed moisture and storage com. 1974-80, chmn. 1980—), Am. Type Culture Collection, Sigma Xi, Phi Kappa Phi, Gamma Sigma Delta, Epsilon Sigma Phi. Author: (with O.L. Justice) Principles and Practices of Seed Storage, 1978; research on factors affecting seed viability during storage. Home: 1117 Fairview Fort Collins CO 80521 Office: Nat Seed Storage Lab Agr Research Service US Dept Agr Colo State Fort Collins CO 80523

BASSETT, JOHN WALDEN, JR., lawyer; b. Roswell, N.Mex., Mar. 21, 1938; s. John Walden and Evelyn (Thompson) B.; m. Patricia Ann Lubben, May 22, 1965; children—John Walden III, Loren Patricia. A.B., Stanford U., 1960; J.D. with honors, U. Tex., 1964. Bar: N.Mex. 1964, Tex. 1964. Mem. Atwood & Malone, 1964; White House fellow, Washington, 1966-67; mem. Atwood, Malone, Mann & Cooter, P.A., Roswell, 1967—; dir. A. H. Belo Corp., Dallas; dir., vice-chmn. Security Nat. Bank, Roswell. Pres., campaign chmn. United Way of Chaves County, 1973-75; bd. dirs. St. Marys Hosp., Roswell, 1976—, chmn., 1980. Served to 1st lt. U.S. Army, 1961. Mem. ABA, N.Mex. Bar Assn., Tex. Bar Assn. Republican. Episcopalian. Club: Rotary (pres. Roswell 1975). Home: 602 Rosemary Ln Roswell NM 88201 Office: PO Drawer 700 Roswell NM 88201

BASSETT, KIMBROUGH STONE, bus. services co. exec.; b. Evanston, Ill., Jan. 19, 1931; s. Albert Edward and Elizabeth Louise (Stone) B.; B.S., U.S. Naval Acad., 1953; M.B.A., Pepperdine U., 1976; m. Carole Jean Gilchrist, May 21, 1956; children—Leslie Ann, Diane Moran, Kimbrough Stone. With Procter and Gamble Co., Inc., 1958-65, mgr. regional data center, 1958-65; sr. cons. Peat, Marwick, Mitchell & Co., 1966; pres. PC Service Corp., San Francisco and exec. v.p. Pacific Stock Exchange, 1967-73; v.p. Mitchum, Jones & Templeton, Inc., Los Angeles, 1974; v.p. fin. and adminstrn. Monex Internat. Ltd., Newport Beach, Calif., 1975—, pres. Monex Fin. Corp., 1975—; dir. Marlboro Co. Served with USAF, 1953-58. Clubs: Balboa Bay, Palos Verdes Tennis. Home: 1541 Addison Rd Palos Verdes Estates CA 90274 Office: 4910 Birch St Newport Beach CA 92660

BASSFORD, FORREST, livestock publications council director; b. Canton, Okla., Feb. 2, 1906; s. Horace Albert and Vilura (McGinnis) B.; m. Marian Louise Horton, Oct. 12, 1929; children—Marilyn Ann, Karen Lee Bassford Kaytes, Dale Horton. B.S. in Animal Husbandry, Colo. State U., 1929. Field rep. Denver Daily Record Stockman, 1930-34; field rep. Am. Hereford Jour., Kansas City, Mo., 1934-40; v.p. Nelson R. Crow Publs., Los Angeles, Anaheim, Calif. and Denver, 1948-77, gen. mgr., 1956-57; editor, exec. editor, pub., Western Livestock Jour., 1948-77; founding pub. Charolais Jours., Houston, 1977-78; exec. dir. Livestock Publs. Council, Encinitas, Calif. 1974—. Served to Wyo. N.G., 1920-25. Recipient Father of Yr. award Mile Hi CowBelles, Denver, 1973; Spl. Recognition award Am. Polled Hereford Assn., 1974; Honor Alumnus award Colo. State U., Ft. Collins, 1977; Meritorious Service in Communication award Am. Soc. Farm Mgrs. and Rural Appraisers, 1977; Headliner award Livestock Publs. Council, 1981; Alpha Gamma Rho Jerry Litton Meml. award, 1983. Mem. Colo. Cattlemen's Assn. (life), Nat. Cattlemen's Assn., Calif. Cattlemen's Assn., San Diego Cattlemen's Assn., Livestock Merchandising Inst., Western Stock Show Assn. (dir.), Colo. State U. Alumni Assn., Alpha Tau Omega, Alpha Zeta, Pi Delta Epsilon, Scabbard & Blade. Republican. Episcopalian. Home: 927 Elmview Dr Encinitas CA 92024

BASSING, JENNIFER, public relations specialist, writer; b. N.Y.C., July 26, 1944; d. Gregory C. and Violet T. (Fischer) Drobinko; m. Peter J. Bassing, Sept. 14, 1979. B.A., SUNY, 1973; A.A., Foothill Coll., 1968. Dir. pub. relations San Francisco Conservatory Mus., 1975-78; pub. info. officer Peninsula Humane Soc., San Mateo, Calif., 1978-81; animal columnist and feature writer San Mateo Times, 1981-82; dir. pub. relations Guide Dogs for the Blind, Inc., San Rafael, Calif., 1983—; bi-monthly columnist Calif. Veterinarian jour.; writer Internat. Eco Features Syndicate, West Hollywood, Calif., 1983—; corr. Israel Today, Los Angeles, 1983—; cons. pub. relations. Mem. Pub. Relations Soc. Am., Am. Jewish Press Assn., Peninsula Press Club (1st place award best new feature release 1979), Calif. Press Women, Dog Writers' Assn. Am. (1st place award 1982, 83). Contbr. articles to periodicals. Office: Guide Dogs for the Blind Inc PO Box 1200 San Rafael CA 94915

BASSO, JOSEPH, advertising agency executive, computer software developer; b. Chgo., Oct. 21, 1938; s. Sylvan T. and Agnes M. (MacMahon) B.; m. Jeannette L., Jan. 4, 1949; children—Cory, Randall, Ashley. Student Northwestern U., Evanston, 1961. Salesman Admiral Corp., mktg. dept., Chgo., 1961, Babcock Corp., Costa Mesa, Calif., 1963-69; account supr. Durel Advt., Newport Beach, Calif., 1969-72; pres., chief exec. officer Basso & Assocs., Newport Beach, 1972—; advisor Golden West Coll. Bd. dirs. Christian Outreach Mission. Served with USAF, 1956-59. Mem. Affiliated Advt. Agys. Internat. (mktg. adv. bd.). Republican. Clubs: Balboa Bay (Newport Beach), John Wayne Tennis. Office: Basso & Assocs PO Box 8030 3198B Airport Loop Dr Newport Beach CA 92660

BASU, BANAJ KAMAL, engineer; b. Calcutta, India, Aug. 4, 1942; s. Balai Lal and Reba (Paul) B.; came to U.S., 1971; B.S. in Physics with honors, Calcutta U., 1961, B.S.E.E., 1963, M.S.E.E. in Applied Physics, 1964; m. Anjana Roy, Nov. 20, 1969; children—Banajyotsna, Bananjana. Sr. systems engr. Mahindra & Mahindra Ltd., Calcutta, 1964-71; instrumentation and control engr. Heyward Robinson Co., Inc., N.Y.C., 1971-72, Commonwealth Assos., Inc., Jackson, Mich., 1972-74; sr. instrumentation and control engr., project mgr. C.F. Braun & Co., Alhambra, Calif., 1974—. Registered profl. engr., Calif. Mem. IEEE, Instrument Soc. Am. Contbr. articles to profl. jours. Home: 1611 Avenida Entrada San Dimas CA 91773 Office: 1000 S Freemont Ave Alhambra CA 91802

BATASTINI, RALPH CHARLES, diversified company executive; b. Chgo., Aug. 30, 1929; s. Charles and Catherine (Tognotti) B.; B.S. in Bus. Edn., Ill. State U., 1951; M.B.A., U. Chgo., 1957; m. Catherine V. Belt, Sept. 3, 1960; children—Brian J., Lynn Ann. Associated with Joseph T. Ryerson & Son, Inc., Chgo., 1956-57; with Greyhound Corp., 1957—, treas., 1961-66, v.p. fin., 1966-71, dir., 1971—, exec. v.p. fin., 1971-77, vice chmn., 1977-80, mem. exec. office, 1975—, pres., 1980-82, vice chmn., chief fin. officer, 1982—; treas. Greyhound Lines Can. Ltd., 1961-66, now dir.; chmn. bd., dir. Greyhound Leasing & Fin. Corp., 1975—, Greyhound Computer Corp., 1976—, Pine Top Ins. Co., 1977—; dir. Greyhound Lines, Inc., Greyhound Computer Can. Ltd., Greyhound Fin. & Leasing Corp. A.G., Greyhound Leasing & Fin. Can. Ltd., Travelers Express Co., Inc., Armour & Co., Verex Corp., Pansophic Systems Inc. Served to 1st lt. USAF, 1951-55. Decorated D.F.C., Air medal with oak leaf cluster; recipient Alumni Achievement award Ill. State U., 1980. Office: Greyhound Corp Greyhound Tower Phoenix AZ 85077

BATCHELDER, AUGUSTUS HUGH, chemist; b. San Francisco, Dec. 7, 1903; s. John Hugh and Mary (Leech) B.; B.S., U. Calif., 1927; children—George, Paul, James, Ann, John. With research dept. Calif. Ink Co., 1927-30; with petroleum prods. research and devel. Standard Oil of Calif. and Calif. Research Corp., also Chevron Research Co., 1930—, v.p., gen. mgr. labs., 1953-63, pres., 1963-67; v.p. research Standard Oil of Calif., 1968-70. Tech. advisor Calif. Air Resources Bd.; mem. Calif. Air Resources Bd., 1972—. Fellow AAAS; mem. Atomic Indsl. Forum, Coordinating Research Council (bd.), Am. Chem. Soc. (chmn. petroleum div. 1963-64), Am. Ordnance Soc., Faraday Soc., Gordon Research Conf., Soc. Automotive Engrs., Am. Petroleum Inst., Soc. Naval Engrs., Sigma Xi, Phi Lambda Upsilon, Alpha Chi Sigma, Tau Beta Pi. Clubs: Commonwealth, Stock Exchange, Engineers. Home: 5557 Yerba Buena Rd Santa Rosa CA 95405

BATCHELDER, WILLIAM HERBERT, actuary, ins. co. exec.; b. Elkhart, Ind., Sept. 4, 1940; s. William Glenn and Minna Belle B.; student Wabash Coll., 1958-60, Ind. U., 1960-61; B.S. in Bus. Adminstrn., Drake U., 1963; m. Kathryn Eloise Smith, June 24, 1967; children—Karen Louise, William Michael, Karla Jean, Mark Andrew, John Robert, David James. Actuarial trainee Country Life Ins. Co., Bloomington, Ill., 1963-65, asst. actuary, 1965-67, asso. actuary, 1967-74; v.p., actuary Western Farm Bur. Life Ins. Co., Denver, 1974—. Adviser, Jr. Achievement, Bloomington, 1967-72, bd. dirs. Bloomington Area, 1972-74. Fellow Soc. Actuaries; mem. Am. Acad. Actuaries. Republican. Presbyterian. Home: 5546 W Hinsdale Pl Littleton CO 80123 Office: 1200 Lincoln St Denver CO 80203

BATDORF, SAMUEL B(URBRIDGE), physicist; b. Jung Hsien, China, Mar. 31, 1914; s. Charles William and Nellie (Burbridge) B.; A.B., U. Calif.-Berkeley, 1934, A.M., 1936, Ph.D., 1938; m. Carol Catherine Schweiss, July 19, 1940; children—Samuel Charles, Laura Ann. Asso. prof. physics U. Nev., 1938-43; aero. research scientist Langley Lab., NACA, 1943-51; dir. devel. Westinghouse Electric Corp., Pitts., 1951-56; tech. dir. weapons systems Lockheed Missile and Space Co., Palo Alto, Calif., 1956-58; mgr. communication satellites Inst. Def. Analysis, Washington, 1958-59; dir. research in physics and electronics Aeronutronic, Newport Beach, Calif., 1959-62; prin. scientist Aerospace Corp., El Segundo, Calif., 1962-77; adj. prof. engring. and applied sci. UCLA, 1973—. Fellow Am. Phys. Soc., Am. Acad. Mechanics (pres. 1982-83), AIAA; mem. ASME (hon.). Republican. Presbyterian. Contbr. articles to profl. jours. Home: 5536 B Via La Mesa Laguna Hills CA 92653 Office: 6531 Boelter Hall UCLA Los Angeles CA 90024

BATEMAN, MERRY A., public relations coordinator; b. Pensacola, Fla., Dec. 6, 1953; d. Harold B. and Verna P. (Vaughan) Bateman. B. Gen. Studies, U. S.C., 1976; M.A., Goddard Coll., 1979; cert. Radcliffe Pub. Procedures Course, Harvard U., 1982. Exec. editor, pub. Auntie Bellum: A So. Jour. for Women, Columbia, S.C., 1976-79; researcher, editor Am. Friends Service Com., Columbia, 1977-78; sr. copywriter Abbey Press, St. Meinrad, Ind., 1978-79; publs. dir., promotional copywriter Unicover Corp., Cheyenne, Wyo., 1980-81; pvt. practice pub. relations, advt., publs. cons., Denver, 1981—; book packager for 9-Lives Pet Food. Vol. Girl Scouts U.S.A., Office of Youth Alternatives, Cheyenne, Wyo.; chmn. info. com. Civic Ctr. Dedication Week, Cheyenne. Named Dist. Young Career Women of Yr., S.C. Bus. Profl. Women's Clubs, 1978; recipient Spl. Merit Sch. Bell award, S.C. Edn. Assn., 1978; first place employee publs. Carolinas Hosp. Pub. Relations Soc., 1979. Mem. Internat. Assn. Bus. communicators, Soc. Profl. Journalists, Friends of Earth, NOW, Sierra Club. Home and Office: PO Box 4420 Denver CO 80204

BATES, HARLEY RONALD, savings and loan exec., appraiser; b. Portland, Oreg., Aug. 23, 1934; s. Harley Alexis and Hazel Esther (Lucas) B.; m. Margaret Ann Buyalos, Apr. 24, 1959; children—Harley Matthew, Kevin Michael, Jason Andrew. B.A., Lewis and Clark Coll., Portland, Oreg., 1956; grad. diploma Am. Savs. and Loan Inst., 1963. Cert. real estate appraiser Soc. Real Estate Appraisers. Sr. appraiser Benjamin Franklin Savs. & Loan, Portland, Oreg., 1958-63; northwest regional appraisal mgr. Western Savs. & Loan, 1963-67; exec. v.p., dir. Oreg. Trail Savs. & Loan Assn., 1967-82, v.p. First Fed. Savs. of Vancouver, 1982; exec. v.p. Vancouver Fed. Savs. and Loan Assn., 1983—; cons., instr. chmn. bd., elder Christian Ch. of Corbett (Oreg.). Served with U. S. Army, 1956-58. Home: 33730 NE Mershon Rd Corbett OR 97019 Office: 13th St and Broadway Vancouver WA 98666

BATES, JIM, congressman; b. Denver, July 21, 1941; m. Marilyn Brewer, 1971; 1 dau., Jennifer. B.A., San Diego State U., 1975; A.A. (hon.), San Diego City Coll., 1977; D.H.L., (hon.), U. Humanistic Studies, San Diego, 1982. Businessman and banker; mem. 98th Congress from Calif. Mem. San Diego City Council, 1971-74; chmn. San Diego Bd. Suprs., 1975-82; mem. San Diego Met. Transit Devel. Bd., Mental Health Adv. Bd.; bd. commrs. Housing Authority of San Diego, NAACP, Ducks Unltd., Inc., San Diego County Intercultural Council of Arts, San Diego Jaycees, San Diego Mus. Art, Citizens Adv. Com. to Calif. Sch. Nurse Orgn., Hillcrest-Mission Hills Improvement Assn., San Diego Adult Edn.; mem. adv. planning bd. Oak Park Community Council; mem. East San Diego C. of C., Com. of 100; mem. adv. bd. Girls Club; mem. Congress of San Diego Srs., Mid-City Council, Assn. Retarded Persons, Mid-City C. of C. Served with USMC, 1959-63. Democrat. Congregationalist. Office: 1632 Longworth House Office Bldg Washington DC 20515*

BATES, MARY LEE, librarian; b. Ordway, Colo., Aug. 28, 1926; d. James Milton and Grace Bernice Bennett; B.A., Linfield Coll., McMinnville, Oreg., 1948; M. in Librarianship, U. Wash., Seattle, 1968; m. Melvin Lane Bates, Aug. 23, 1947; children—Richard Lane, Katherine Lee, Ronald Martin, Marjorie Ellen. Tchr. schs. in Oreg., 1948-53; librarian Arlington (Oreg.) High Sch., 1962-64, Blue Mountain Community Coll., Pendleton, Oreg., 1963—; vis. prof. U. Oreg. Sch. Librarianship, summers 1971-73; cons. in field. Mem. Task Force for Battered Women, Rootseller Food Coop.; mem. Community Devel. Council; project dir. Oreg. Com. for Humanities; mem. Oreg. Gov.'s Commn. for Women, 1975-78; mem. adv. com. Housing and Neighborhood Improvement; mem. Blue Mountain Community Coordinated Child Care Council, Pendleton Arts Council. Named Pendleton's First Woman Citizen, 1971; recipient Women Helping Women award. Mem. ALA, Pacific N.W. Library Assn. (pres. 1977-78), Oreg. Library Assn. (pres. 1974-75), AAUW (pres. Pendleton br. 1971-72), Common Cause, Oreg. Consumer League, Oreg. Women's Polit. Caucus, Oreg. Fedn. Democratic Women, Umatilla County Hist. Soc., Pendleton C. of C. (chmn. govtl. relations council), LWV. Democrat. Clubs: Pendleton Women's (pres. 1971-72), Altrusa, Soroptimist. Home: PO Box 1091 Pendleton OR 97801 Office: PO Box 100 Pendleton OR 97801

BATES, PHILIP KNIGHT, research adminstrn. cons.; b. Cohasset, Mass., July 2, 1902; s. Edgar Wallace and Minnie Frances (Knight) B.; B.S., MIT, 1924, Ph.D. 1929; m. Eleanor Johnson, July 9, 1929; children—Charles J., Philip K., Bradford. Bacteriologist, Frigidaire Corp., Dayton, Ohio, 1928-32; mgr. research devel. Rexall Co., Boston, Los Angeles, 1936-49; pres. Riker Labs., Los Angeles, 1949-52; gen. mgr. research Carnation Co., Los Angeles, 1952-66; ret., 1966; cons., research adminstrn., Santa Monica, Calif., 1967—; instr. Tufts Med. Dental Sch., Boston U. Med. Sch. Fellow Inst. Food Technologists (pres. 1955-56), Am. Chem. Soc., MIT Club So. Calif. (gov.). Republican. Unitarian. Clubs: Chemists (N.Y.C.); Beach (Santa Monica). Editor, Jour. Agrl. Food Chemistry, 1965-82. Home and office: 363 17th St Santa Monica CA 90402

BATES, ROBERT HINRICHS, political scientist, educator; b. Bklyn., Dec. 5, 1942; s. David Hinrichs and Lucy Lilian (Thomas) B.; m. Margaret Rouse, June 6, 1963; 1 dau., Elizabeth Rouse. B.A. summa cum laude, Haverford Coll., 1964; Ph.D., MIT, 1969. Asst. prof., Calif. Inst. Tech., Pasadena, 1969-75, assoc. prof., 1975-79, prof. polit. sci., 1979—; cons. U.S. AID, World Bank. Recipient Haverford Coll. Kurzman prize, 1964; Social Sci. Research Council grantee, 1970-71, 76-77, 82-83; NSF grantee, 1978-80, 83-85. Mem. Am. Polit. Sci. Assn., African Studies Assn., Phi Beta Kappa. Democrat. Congregationalist. Author: Unions, Parties and Political Development: A Study of Mineworkers in Zambia, 1971; Rural Responses to Industrialization: A Study of Village Zambia, 1976; Agricultural Development in Africa: Issues of Public Policy, 1980; States and Markets in Tropical Africa: The Political Basis of Agricultural Policy, 1981; Essays on the Political Economy of Rural Africa, 1983; contbr. numerous articles to profl. jours. Home: 526 W 12th St Claremont CA 91171 Office: Caltech Dept Humanities and Social Scis Pasadena CA 91125

BATHEN, KARL HANS, oceanographer; b. New Haven, Nov. 28, 1934; s. John H. and Jane H. (Koscinski) B. B.S. in Mech. Engring. cum laude, U. Conn., 1956; postgrad. Orange Coast Coll., 1964, U. Calif.-Davis, 1964-65; M.S., U. Hawaii, 1968, Ph.D., 1970. Research asst. in oceanography U. Hawaii, Oahu, 1966-70, assoc. prof., assoc. researcher, Honolulu, 1971-76, prof., researcher, 1976—; mgr. Dillingham Environ. Co., Honolulu, 1970-71. Served with USAF, 1956-59. Mem. Internat. Assn. Water Pollution Research, Am. Geophys. Union, Am. Water Resources Assn., Marine Tech. Soc., Conservation Council for Hawaii, Underwater Photog. Soc. Am., Sigma Xi. Contbr. articles to profl. jours.

BATISTE, PEARL THERESA, educator; b. Jeanerette, La., Dec. 9, 1930; d. Erris and Pearl (Armelin) Edgerly; B.A., Calif. State U., San Francisco, 1975; M.A. in Edn., U. San Francisco, 1978; M.S. in Pepperdine U., 1979; m. Berwick Batiste, Sept. 12, 1950; children—Michael, Keith, Ronald, Elissa, Ingrid, Patrick. Dir. counseling tng. dept. Amrick Advt., Oakland, Calif., 1976-77; public relations dir. San Francisco Ednl. Found., Oakland, 1977-78; fashion model, instr., substitute tchr. Barbizon Modeling Sch., 1975-76; program and project coordinator Oakland Pub. Schs., 1976—. Mem. Amway Exec. Women Assts., Profl. Woman Exec. Corp. Am., Black Profl. Bus. Women Assts., Nat. Alliance Black Edn. Democrat. Roman Catholic. Club: Fashionnete Social. Author: The Influence of African on American Fashion, 1980. Home: 2509 Tulare Ave El Cerrito CA 94530

BATRA, MOE RADHAKISHEN, civil engineer; b. Karachi, Pakistan, Dec. 4, 1936; s. Radhkakishen N. and Laxmibai R. (Sitlani) B.; m. Brigitte Ruth Montigel, Aug. 18, 1962; children—Rita, Sanjay. Sci. degree U. Bombay, 1959; B.S.C.E., Utah State U., 1962; postgrad. U. Wash., 1962-79. Registered profl. engr., Wash. Design traffic and hydraulic engr. Wash. State Dept. Transp., 1962-74; regional engr. Wash. State Dept. Health, Seattle, 1974—. Mem. Sultan River Basin Com. Recipient Service award Wash. State Dept. Health, 1982. Mem. Am. Water Works Assn. (dir. sub-sect.), ASCE. Club: Nat. Sport (Bombay). Hindu. Home: 9204 40th Ave NE Seattle WA 98115 Office: Dept Health 1312 Smith Tower Bldg Seattle WA 98104

BATT, GEORGE KENNETH, ret. industrialist; b. New Albany, Ind., Oct. 18, 1894; s. George McClelland and Hettie (Markland) B.; student Purdue U., 1913-15; LL.D., Bloomfield Coll. and Sem.; m. Margaret Robinson Dugan, Oct. 11, 1921; children—Peggy Batt Palmer, Mary Batt Taylor. Mem. exec. staff R.H. Macy Co., N.Y.C., 1919-25, becoming 1st asst. controller; v.p., treas., mem. firm Dugan Bros., 1925-62, now ret. dir.; ret. dir. N.J. Bell Telephone Co., Montclair Nat. Bank & Trust Co. (N.J); industry mem. Nat. War Labor Bd., 1943-44, Pres.'s Cost of Living Com., 1943-44; vice chmn. Gov. N.J. War Transp. Commn., Gov. N.J.'s Human Resources Commn. Chmn., Ann Rutgers Bus. Forum, 1950; chmn. citizens council N.J. Jet Port Assn., 1960-61; mayor Montclair, 1944-48; chmn. N.J. Republican Fin. Com., 1945-48; ret. dir. Morristown (N.J.) Meml. Hosp., Bloomfield Coll.; ret. trustee Vineland (N.J.) Tng. Sch. Served to 1st lt., F.A., U.S. Army, 1917-19; AEF. Recipient Man of Year award Notre Dame Alumni Assn., N.J., 1946; named Man of Year in N.J. Agr. and Industry, 1962. Mem. N.J. C. of C. (pres. 1941-43, dir. emeritus), Beta Gamma, Sigma Theta Xi. Presbyterian. Home: 7711 Hillside Dr PO Box 1623 La Jolla CA 92037

BATTAGLIA, RICHARD JOSEPH, designer, development executive; b. Chgo., Nov. 5, 1943; s. Thomas G. and Faythe E. (Schmidt) B. Student Calif. State U.-Long Beach. Pres. Battaglia Assos., Inc., Huntington Beach, Calif.; chmn. bd. Am. West Telephone Co.; pres. Frontier Investment Corp. Served to lt. USN, 1967-70. Designer Entertainment City, theme park, Kuwait, Kuwait, Parques Interama theme park, Buenos Aires, Argentina. Office: 21062 Brookhurst St Suite 208 Huntington Beach CA 92646

BATTIN, JAMES FRANKLIN, U.S. district judge; b. Wichita, Kan., Feb. 13, 1925; s. William Russell and Hannah (McBroom) B.; m. Barbara F. Choate, Aug. 9, 1947; children—Loyce Barbara, Patricia Jean, James Franklin. J.D., George Washington U., 1951. D.C. 1951, Mont. 1953. Practiced in Washington, 1951-52, Billings, Mont., 1952-60; dep. atty. Yellowstone County (Mont.), 1953-55; asst. city atty., Billings, 1955-57, city atty., 1957-59; mem. Mont. Ho. of Reps. 1958-59; mem. 87th-91st congresses 2d Mont. Dist.; U.S. dist judge, 1969-78; chief judge Dist. Ct. Mont., 1978—. Past sec., counsel Billings-Yellowstone County Planning Bd. Served with USNR, 1943-46. Mem. Am. Legion, DeMolay Legion Honor. Republican. Presbyterian. Clubs: Masons, Shriners. Office: 5428 US Courthouse Billings MT 59101

BATTISTICH, VICTOR ANTHONY, psychologist, researcher, consultant; b. Sacramento, Sept. 9, 1952; s. Carl Anthony and Marian Rita (Hansen) B.; m. Martha Susan Montgomery, Jan. 6, 1978; 1 dau., Sarah. B.A. in Psychology with highest honors, Calif. State U.-Sacramento, 1974; M.A. in Personality-Social Psychology, Mich. State U., 1976, Ph.D. in Personality-Social Psychology, 1979. Sr. research assoc. Ctr. for Evaluation and Assessment dept. psychology Mich. State U., 1978-79; vis. asst. prof. dept. psychology and First Coll., Cleve. State U., 1979-80, participant in planning, devel. and implementation of Extended Campus Coll., 1979-80; sr. research assoc. Child Devel. Project, Devel. Studies Ctr., San Ramon, Calif., 1981—; cons. to numerous state, local agys.; lectr. in field. Mem. AAAS, Am. Psychol. Assn., Internat. Assn. for Study Cooperation in Edn., Midwestern Psychol. Assn., Soc. Personality Assessment, Soc. Personality and Social Psychology, Soc. for Psychol. Study Social Issues, Phi Kappa Phi. Contbr. articles to profl. jours.; author profl. papers; occasional reviewer profl. jours. Office: 130 Ryan Ct Suite 210 San Ramon CA 94583

BATTISTONE, SAM D., professional basketball team executive; m. Nan Battistone; 6 children. Owner, pres. Utah Jazz (formerly New Orleans Jazz), NBA, 1973—. Past bd. dirs. Nat. Restaurant Assn., Calif. C. of C., Mission council Boy Scouts Am.; past chmn. Santa Barbara March of Dimes; past nat. chmn. Victor Awards. Recipient Golden Plate award Am. Acad. Achievement, Spirit of Life award as man of yr. City of Hope. Office: Utah Jazz Salt Palace 100 SW Temple Suite 206 Salt Lake City UT 84101*

BATTLE, ROBERT CALVIN, ins. analyst; b. San Francisco, Mar. 27, 1918; s. Calvin Woodward and Anna (Booth) B.; A.B., U. Calif.-Berkeley, 1940; m. Ruth Lennea Olson, June 30, 1944; children—Robert Calvin, William A., Laurie Ann. Ins. broker, San Francisco: Cosgrove and Co., 1943-45, C. W. Battle Co., 1946-51, Emett and Chandler, 1951-58, Alexander and Alexander, 1958-81. Mem. Soc. Ins. Brokers (pres. 1971-72), Nat. Assn. Ins. Brokers (dir. 1972-75). Republican. Contbr. articles in field to publs. Home and Office: 611 Tahos Rd Orinda CA 94563

BATZEL, ROGER ELWOOD, chemist; b. Weiser, Idaho, Dec. 1, 1921; s. Walter George and Inez Ruth (Klinefelter) B.; m. Edwina Lorraine Grindstaff, Aug. 18, 1946; children—Stella Lynne, Roger Edward, Stacy Lorraine. B.S., U. Idaho, 1947; Ph.D., U. Calif.-Berkeley, 1951. Asst. chem. div. leader Lawrence Livermore Lab. (Calif.), 1953-59, head chemistry dept., 1959-67, assoc. dir. for chemistry, 1961-71, assoc. dir. for testing, 1961-64, assoc. dir. for space reactors, 1966-68, assoc. dir. for chemistry and biomed. research, 1969-71, dir. lab., 1971—. Served with USAF, 1943-45. Named to Alumni Hall of Fame, U. Idaho, 1972. Mem. Am. Phys. Soc., Sigma Xi. Club: Commonwealth of Calif. Office: Lawrence Livermore Lab PO Box 808 Livermore CA 94550*

BAUCH, THOMAS JAY, lawyer; b. Indpls., May 24, 1943; s. Thomas and Violet (Smith) B.; m. Ellen L. Burstein. B.S., U. Wis., 1964, J.D., 1966. Admitted to Ill. bar, 1966, Calif. bar, 1979; assoc. firm Lord Bissell & Brook, Chgo., 1966-72; gen. atty., asst. sec. Marcor Inc., Chgo., 1973-75; spl. asst. to Solicitor of Labor, Washington, 1975-77; v.p., gen. counsel Levi Strauss & Co., San Francisco, 1977—; dir. Med. Research Inst.; lectr. Practising Law Inst. Mem. ABA, Chgo. Bar Assn., Am. Assn. Corp. Counsel (bd. dirs.). Clubs: University (San Francisco); Saddle and Cycle, Racquet (Chgo.). Contbr. articles to profl. jours. Home: 54 Alcatraz Belvedere CA 94920 Office: Levi's Plaza San Francisco CA 94106

BAUCUS, MAX, senator; b. Helena, Mont., Dec. 11, 1941; s. John and Jean (Sheriff) B.; B.A., Stanford, 1964, LL.B., 1967. Admitted to D.C. bar, 1969, Mont. bar, 1972; staff atty. Civil Aeronautics Bd., Washington, 1967-69; lawyer SEC, Washington, 1969-71, legal asst. to chmn., 1970-71; practiced in Missoula, Mont., 1971-; mem. 94th and 95th congresses from 1st Dist. Mont., mem. Com. on Appropriations; U.S. senator from Mont., 1978—. Mem. Mont. Ho. of Reps., 1972-74. Acting exec. dir., com. coordinator Mont. Constl. Conv., 1972—. Home: Missoula MT Office: 706 Hart Senate Bldg Washington DC 20510

BAUER, ALBERT N., JR., state senator; b. Lewistown, Mont., June 6, 1928; s. Albert and Florence C. (Hooper) B.; m. Patricia Ellen McQueen, 1953; children—Jerry Sue, James Allyn, Nancy Ellyn. Student Clark Coll., 1948, 54-55; B.S., Portland State Coll., 1957; M.Ed., Oreg. State Coll., 1959. Former mem. Wash. Ho. of Reps from 17th Legis. Dist., now mem. Wash. State Senate. Democratic precinct committeeman Clark County, 1968-70. Served with U.S. Navy, 1948-54; Korea. Mem. Wash. Edn. Assn., Vancouver Edn. Assn., Am. Legion, Wash.-Oreg. Farmers Union. Methodist. Club: Salmon Creek Community. Home: 13611 NE 20th Ave Vancouver WA 98665 Office: Washington State Senate Olympia WA 98504

BAUER, A(UGUST) ROBERT, JR., surgeon; b. Phila., Dec. 23, 1928; s. A(ugust) Robert and Jessie Martha-Maynard (Monie) B.; B.S., U. Mich., 1949, M.S., 1950, M.D., 1954; M. Med. Sci.-Surgery, Ohio State U., 1960; m. Charmaine Louise Studer, June 28, 1957; children—Robert, John, William, Anne, Charles, James. Intern Walter Reed Army Med. Center, 1954-55; resident in surgery Univ. Hosp., Ohio State U., Columbus, also instr., 1957-61; individual practice medicine, specializing in surgery, Mt. Pleasant, Mich., 1962-74; chief surgery Central Mich. Community Hosp., Mt. Pleasant, 1964-65, vice chief of staff, 1967, chief of staff, 1968; clin. faculty Mich. State Med. Sch., East Lansing, 1974; mem. staff St. Mark's Hosp., Salt Lake City, 1974—; individual practice surgery, Salt Lake City, 1974—; clin. instr. surgery U. Utah, 1975—. Trustee, Rowland Hall, St. Mark's Sch., Salt Lake City; mem. Utah Health Planning Council, 1979-81. Served with M.C., U.S. Army, 1954-57. Diplomate Am. Bd. Surgery. Fellow ACS, Southwestern Surg. Congress; mem. AMA, Salt Lake County Med. Soc., Utah med. assns., Utah Soc. Certified Surgeons, Salt Lake Surg. Soc., Royal Soc. Medicine (affiliate), Pan Am. Med. Assn. (affiliate), AAAS (affiliate), Sigma Phi Epsilon, Phi Rho Sigma. Episcopalian. Clubs: University, Zollinger. Contbr. articles to profl. publs., researcher surg. immunology. Office: PO Box 17533 Salt Lake City UT 84117

BAUER, CAROLINE FELLER, educational consultant; b. Washington, May 12, 1935; d. Abraham H. and Alice (Klein) F.; m. Peter A. Bauer, Dec. 21, 1968; 1 dau., Hilary A. B.A., Sarah Lawrence U., 1957; M.L.S., Columbia U., 1958; Ph.D., U. Oreg., 1971. Producer, Caroline's Corner, Oreg. Pub. Broadcasting System, 1973-79; assoc. prof. U. Oreg., Eugene, 1966-79; cons. Ednl. Cons. Assocs., Denver, 1979-81; ednl. cons. Conf. Contractors, Portland, Oreg., 1982—. Recipient Ersted award U. Oreg., 1968; Christopher award The Christophers, 1982. Mem. ALA, Internat. Reading Assn., Nat. Council Tchrs. English, Soc. Am. Magicians, Internat. Brotherhood Magicians. Author: Handbook for Storytellers, 1977: Creative Storytelling Techniques, 1979; My Mom Travels A Lot, 1981; Take a Poetry Break, 1981; This Way to Books, 1983.

BAUER, DANIEL, banker; b. Cleve.; s. Ben J. and Rose (Rocklin) B.; m. Debra L. Rosenthal, Dec. 17, 1972. B.S. summa cum laude, Ohio U., 1971. Account exec. Ketchum Advt., Pitts., 1971-74; v.p., account supr. Milici/Valenti Advt., Honolulu, 1975-80; v.p., dir. corp. communications Bank of Hawaii, Honolulu, 1981-83, dir. mktg. services, 1983—. Bd. dirs. Hawaii Opera Theatre, 1981—, Symphony Guild of Honolulu, 1980—. Mem. Am. Mktg. Assn. (pres. Honolulu 1980-81), Sales and Mktg. Execs. Honolulu (pres. 1983-84).

BAUER, DENNIS KEITH, health care adminstr.; b. Inglewood, Calif., July 8, 1947; s. William Melvin and Emma Ruth (Fernsler) B.; B.S., U. Calif. Sch. Public Health, Los Angeles, 1971, M.P.H., 1972; children—Eric Keith, Wendy Lynn. With Los Angeles County Dept. Health Services, 1972—, adminstrv. asst., 1974-77, dir. ambulatory care Coastal Region, Long Beach, Calif., 1977-80, asst. dir., inspection and audit div., 1980—; cons. Calif. Dept. Health, 1975-78. Served with U.S. Army, 1968-69. Mem. Am. Public Health Assn., Nat. Mgmt. Assn. Republican. Office: Room 805 313 N Figueroa St Los Angeles CA 90012

BAUER, DONALD DEFOREST, radiologist; b. Bklyn., Dec. 31, 1914; s. John Leopold and Marie Rebecca (Jurgens) B.; A.B. (Cramer fellow), Dartmouth, 1937; M.D., McGill U., 1942, M.S., 1943; m. Phyllis E. Witzel, July 23, 1943; children—Phyllis, John, Rebecca, Ann, Donald. Intern, N.C. Bapt. Hosp., Winston-Salem, 1942-43; resident Duke U. Hosp., Durham, N.C., 1943-44, Charles Miller Hosp., St. Paul, 1950-52; practice medicine specializing in radiology, Coos Bay, Oreg., 1952-59, Klamath Falls, Oreg., 1960-69; asso. prof. radiology Oreg. Tech. Inst., Klamath Falls, 1960-69; radiologist (asso.) Queen of Angels Hosp., Los Angeles, 1970-72, Sepulveda VA Hosp., Sepulveda, Calif., 1972-78; asso. clin. prof. radiology U. Calif., Los Angeles, 1972-78; radiologist Hawthorne (Calif.) Community Med. Group, 1973-83, Northridge (Calif.) Community Med. Group, 1978-83, Lomita-Torrance Med. Group (Calif.), 1979-83, Warner-Bristol Med. Group, Anaheim, Calif., 1979-82, Mid-Wilshire Med. Group, Los Angeles; charter bd. dirs. Presbyterian Community Hosp., Klamath Falls. Served with AUS, 1944-47. Fellow Am. Coll. Radiology; mem. Am. Roentgen Ray Soc., Radiol. Soc. N.Am., So. Calif., Calif., Los Angeles County radiol. socs. Clubs: Kiwanis (past pres. Klamath Falls). Author: The Practice of Country Radiology, 1963; Textbook of Radiology for Students and Technicians, 1965; Lumbar Discography and Low Back Pain, 1960. Address: 3531 Valley Meadows Rd Sherman Oaks CA 91403

BAUER, JUDITH ANN, family and marriage counselor, clinical social worker; b. Mpls., May 28, 1947; d. Francis C. and Marion G. Bauer; B.S., U. Minn., 1973; M.S.W., U. Denver, 1975; M.S. in Ednl. Psychology, U. Utah, 1979. Child Psychiat. technician Glenwood Hills Hosp., Golden Valley, Minn., 1970-73; program coordinator Alcohol-driving countermeasures program, Denver, 1975-77; job coach Salt Lake County Employment and Tng. Adminstrn., 1978; psychology intern U. Utah Med. Center, 1977-79; clin. dir. chem. dependency center West Park Hosp., Cody, Wyo., 1979-80; pvt. practice clin. social work, Cody, 1980-82; therapist Aurora Community Mental Health Ctr., 1982—. Mem. AAUW, Nat. Assn. Social Workers, Acad. Cert. Social Workers, Phi Kappa Phi. Home: 1700 Xenia St Denver CO 80220 Office: 1020 S Uvalda St Aurora CO 80010

BAUER, RANDY MARK, mgmt. tng. firm exec.; b. Cleve., Sept. 2, 1946; s. Ralph I. and Gloria P. Bauer; B.S. summa cum laude, Ohio State U., 1968; M.B.A., Kent State U., 1971; m. Sue Dellva, July 4, 1975; children—Sherri, Kevin. Mgmt. auditor Peat Marwick Mitchell & Co., Cleve., 1971-72; mgmt. devel. specialist GAO, Denver, 1972-80; adj. prof. mgmt. Columbia Coll., Denver, 1979—; pres. Leadership Tng. Assos., Denver, 1979—; condr. exec. devel. workshops U. Colo., Denver, 1979—. Recipient Best in 1976 award GAO. Mem. Am. Soc. for Tng. and Devel., Beta Gamma Sigma. Address: 17651 E Crestridge Ave Aurora CO 80015

BAUER, THOMAS PATRICK, aerospace engineer; b. Detroit, July 5, 1954; s. Bruce David and Amelia Marion (Manis) B.; m. Dona Fay, Dec. 28, 1981; 1 son, Scott Patrick. B.S., U. Mich., 1976, M.S., 1977; Ph.D., Calif. Inst. Tech., 1982. Aerospace technician NASA-Johnson Space Ctr., Houston, 1977-78; research asst. Jet Propulsion Lab., Pasadena, 1979-81; mem. tech. staff Aerospace Corp., El Segundo, Calif., 1982—. Mem. AIAA.

BAUGH, L. DARRELL, fin. exec.; b. Prairie Grove, Ark., Oct. 7, 1930; s. Lacey D. and Mary Grace (Brown) B.; B.S. in B.A., U. Ark., 1954; M.S. in B.A., U. Colo., 1960; C.L.U., Am. Coll., 1967, chartered fin. cons., 1983; m. Wileeta Claire Gray, June 15, 1958; children—Adrienne Leigh, John Grayson. With Penn Mut. Life Ins. Co., 1961-71, gen. agt., Sacramento, 1968-71; pres. Nat. Estate Planning Inst., Boulder, Colo., 1974—; lectr. estate planning seminars Colo. State U.; cons. U. Colo. Center for Confs. Mgmt./Tech. Programs, 1975-80; sponsor ednl. programs for profl. estate planners and estate owners. Bd. dirs. Stronghold Youth Found. Served with U.S. Army, 1954-56. Mem. Boulder C. of C., Am. Soc. C.L.U.s, Rocky Mountain C.L.U.s (chmn. grad. studies programs), Boulder County Estate Planning Council (pres. 1972-73), Sacramento Estate Planning Council, Nat. Registry Fin. Planners (interview com.). Contbr. articles to profl. jours. Home: 92 Caballo Ct Boulder CO 80303 Office: 75 Manhattan Dr Boulder CO 80303

BAUGHMAN, GERLAD V(AN), tax consultant; b. Jesup, Iowa, Apr. 25, 1931; s. Edward Glen and Florence Pauline (Parker) B.; m. Virginia Ruth Barnes, Apr. 16, 1965. Student San Diego City Coll., 1954-56, San Diego State Coll., 1957-60. Enrolled agt. IRS. With acctg. dept. Gen. Dynamics, Convair, 1952-63; pvt. tax cons., La Mesa, Calif., 1963—. Served with U.S. Army, 1951-52. Mem. Nat. Assn. Enrolled Agts., Nat. Assn. Pub. Accts., Nat. Notary Assn. Republican. Lutheran. Clubs: Masons, Shriners. Home: 164 Southern Rd El Cajon CA 92020 Office: 9019 Park Plaza Dr Suite K La Mesa CA 92041

BAUGHMAN, RICHARD JOSEPH, scientist; b. Lisbon, Ohio, Sept. 9, 1927; s. James Russell and Mary (Chillik) B.; B.S., Mt. Union Coll., 1950; postgrad. Western Res. U., 1954-56, U. N.Mex., 1962-64; m. Eve Krizay, Sept. 12, 1948; children—Sandra Louise (Mrs. Michael Ian Spitz), Karol Ann. Analytical chemist Harshaw Chem. Co., Cleve., 1950-52, prodn. supr., 1952-54, Crystal growth and shift plant supt., 1954-61; mem. tech. staff Sandia Labs., Albuquerque, 1961—. Counselor Greater Cleve. Council Boy Scouts Am., 1958-61; nat. aquatic examiner YMCA, 1956-61. Bd. dirs. ARC, 1968-70, instr., trainer, 1956—; instr. Nat. Aquatic Sch., 1970-71; pres., chmn. bd. dirs. Albuquerque Softball/ Baseball Hall of Fame, 1983—. Served with USNR, 1945-47. Recipient Hon. Sci. award Bausch & Lomb, 1945. Mem. Am. Ceramic Soc. (life, chmn. N.Mex. sect. 1968), Am. Assn. Crystal Growth, Phi Sigma. Democrat. Methodist. Contbr. articles to profl. jours. Patentee in field. Home: 7309 Dellwood Rd NE Albuquerque NM 87110 Office: Orgn 5154 Albuquerque NM 87185

BAUKNIGHT, GERALD CONRAD, aerospace engr.; b. Columbia, S.C., April 4, 1935; s. Ralph Madison and Anne Marie (Hook) Bauknight; m. Catherine McClain, June 11, 1957; children—Gerald Conrad, Mark McClain, Cecilia Marie. B.S. in Mech. Engring., U. S.C. 1958; M.S. in Aeros. and Astronautics, Purdue U., 1969; grad. Air Command, Staff Coll. U.S. Air Force, 1973; M.S. in Counseling, Guidance, Troy State U., 1973. commd. 2d lt. U.S. Air Force, 1958, advanced through grade to lt. col., 1980; engr. Washington, Sacramento, Cape Canaveral, Fla., and West Lafayette, Ind., 1959-70; planner, researcher Saigon, Viet Nam, Honolulu and Sunnyvale, Calif., 1971-80; ret. 1980; staff engr. Martin Marietta Corp., Sunnyvale, 1980—; mem. faculty dept. aeros. U.S. Air Force Acad.; assoc. Aeros. Adv. Com.; dir. Electex Assocs., Santa Clara, Calif. Pres. Family Edn. Ctrs., Hawaii, 1971-77. Decorated Bronze Star, Meritorious Service Medal, Joint Services Commendation Medal. Mem. AIAA, AAAS, Armed Forces Communications Electronics Assn. (bd. dirs. Santa Clara), Sigma Chi. Republican. Roman Catholic. Clubs: Los Altos Aquatic (bd. dirs. 1978-80), Life Loyal Sig. Home: 654 Cuesta Dr Los Altos CA 94022 Office: 1183 Bordeaux Dr Suite 10 Sunnyvale CA 94086

BAUM, CARL EDWARD, electromagnetic theorist; b. Binghampton, N.Y., Feb. 6, 1940; s. George Theodore and Evelyn Monica (Bliven) B.; B.S. with honors, Calif. Inst. Tech., 1962, M.S., 1963, Ph.D., 1969. Commd. 2d lt. USAF, 1962, advanced through grades to capt., 1967, resigned, 1971, project officer Air Force Weapons Lab., Kirtland AFB, N.Mex., 1963-71, sr. scientist for electromagnetics, 1971—; U.S. del. to gen. assembly Internat. Union Radio Sci., Lima, Peru, 1975, Helsinki, Finland, 1978, Washington, 1981; mem. Commn. B U.S. Nat. Com., 1976—, Commn. E, 1982. Decorated Air Force Commendation medal; recipient research and devel. award USAF, 1970, award Honeywell Corp., 1962. Mem. IEEE (sr.), Electromagnetics Soc. (v.p.), Sigma Xi, Tau Beta Pi. Roman Catholic. Author: (with others) Transient Electromagnetic Fields, 1976; Electromagnetic Scattering, 1978; Acoustic, Electromagnetic and Elastic Wave Scattering, 1980; contbr. articles to profl. publs. Home: 5116 Eastern SE Unit D Albuquerque NM 87108 Office: Air Force Weapons Lab Kirtland AFB NM 87117

BAUM, DWIGHT CROUSE, investment banking executive; b. Syracuse, N.Y., Nov. 21, 1912; s. Dwight James and Katharine Lucia (Crouse) B.; E.E., Cornell U., 1936; M.B.A., Harvard U., 1938; m. Hildagarde Engelhardt, Jan. 17, 1942; children—Dwight J., John E. Asst. to v.p. Mine Safety Appliance Co., Pitts., 1938-40; armament supply officer British Air Commn., Washington, 1940-46; asst. to partner Eastman Dillon & Co., Los Angeles, 1946-47; v.p. First Calif. Co., Los Angeles, 1947-56; gen. partner Eastman Dillon Union Securities & Co., Los Angeles, 1956-71, sr. v.p., 1971-72, also dir.; sr. v.p. Blyth Eastman Dillon & Co., Inc., Los Angeles, 1972-79, adv. dir., 1980—, also dir.; sr. v.p. Paine Webber Jackson & Curtiss, Inc., 1980—; chmn. bd. United Cities Gas Co.; dir. Dominguez Water Corp., Far W. Fin. Corp., Measurex Corp., Far West Savs. & Loan Assn., Vista Capital Corp. Trustee Alice Lloyd Coll. Decorated Order Brit. Empire. Mem. Nat. Assn. Securities Dealers (bd. govs. 1976-79), Los Angeles Soc. Fin. Analysts, IEEE, Pacific Coast Stock Exchange (vice-chmn. 1980-81), N.Y. Stock Exchange (allied mem.), Phi Delta Theta. Clubs: Calif., Bond (Los Angeles). Home: 1011 Oak Grove Ave San Marino CA 91108 Office: 700 S Flower St Los Angeles CA 90017

BAUM, MARJORIE LOUISE, personnel development educator, consultant; b. Seattle, June 10, 1927; d. Bert and Mabelle M. (Sasse) Lundahl; m. Milton R. Baum, June 10, 1951; children—Mary Baum Love, Rebecca L., John C. B.A., Willamette U. 1951; M.S. in Counseling, Oreg. Coll. Edn., 1974; postgrad. Oreg. State U., 1981-83. Cert. counselor, Oreg., 1975. Instr., assertiveness trainer, Chemeketa Community Coll., Salem, Oreg., 1974—; personal growth cons. Active YWCA; chmn. Women's Resource Ctr.; pres. Silverton (Oreg.) Hosp. Aux., 1962-63. Mem. Inst. Mng. and Profl. Women Oreg., Oreg. Ednl. Adminstrs Assn., AAUW (chmn. women's issues, 1982—), Oreg. Council Women's Equity, Oreg. Profl. Guidance Assn., Am. Profl. Guidance Assn. Democrat. Methodist. Contbr. articles to profl. jours. Home: 1795 Summer St SE Salem OR 97302 Office: Chemeketa Community College Salem OR 97302

BAUM, NEAL PATRICK, research scientist; b. Ridley Park, Pa., Aug. 21, 1942; s. George Theodore and Evelyn Monica (Bliven) B.; student Antioch Coll., 1959-60; B.S. in Physics, Lemoyne Coll., 1965; M.S., Syracuse U., 1967, Ph.D., 1970; m. Martha Helen Coleman, June 12, 1971; children—George Patrick, Spencer Earl. Research asso. Syracuse U., 1965-70; postdoctoral research asso. AF Weapons Lab., Nat. Research Council, Kirtland AFB, N.Mex., 1970-71; mgr. instrumentation div. U. N.Mex. Engring. Research Inst., Albuquerque, 1971—; adv. bd. AF, Def. Nuclear Agy. Served with AUS, 1960-62. NSF Research Participation grantee, 1964; recipient invention awards, USAF, 1971. Mem. Laser Inst. Am., Sigma Xi. Republican. Roman Catholic. Research and publs. on solid state theory of metals, optics, instrumentation. Inventor in field. Home: 628 Amherst St SE Albuquerque NM 87106 Office: U NMex Campus PO Box 25 Albuquerque NM 87131

BAUMAN, CHARLES JOSEPH, agribus, and food mfg. co. exec.; b. Altoona, Pa., Nov. 5, 1924; s. Charles Raymond and Anna Margaret (Mullen) B.; B.S. in Civil Engring., U. Notre Dame, 1949; m. Gwendolyn W. Beard, June 9, 1951; children—David, Cheryl, Eric, Mark. Project engr. Walsh Contrn. Co., N.Y.C., 1949-52, Internat. Mineral & Chem. Co., Skokie, Ill., 1953-58; chief engr. Cerro Corp., Santiago, Chile, 1959-62; constrn. mgr. Mobil Chem. Co., Taipei, Taiwan, 1962-63; with Castle & Cooke, Inc., 1964—, mgr. engring. Honduras div., 1964-68, exec. v.p., gen. mgr. Philippines div., 1968-72, Dole Co., Honolulu, 1972-73, v.p. prodn. foods div., San Francisco, 1974-81, corp. v.p., sr. v.p. foods div., Honolulu and San Francisco, 1981—, pres., dir. Dole Philippines, Inc., 1972—; pres., dir. Standard Fruit Corp., Philippines, 1967—. Served with USNR, 1942-46. Registered profl. engr., Ind., Fla. Mem. Pineapple Growers Assn. Hawaii (pres. 1973-74, dir.). Clubs: Manila Polo; San Francisco Tennis. Home: 611 Fairway Circle Hillsborough CA 94010 Office: Castle & Cooke Foods 50 California St San Francisco CA 94111

BAUMAN, EARL WILLIAM, accountant, government official; b. Arcadia, Nebr., Jan. 30, 1916; s. William A. and Gracia M. (Jones) B.; B.S. with honors, U. Wyo., 1938; postgrad. Northwestern U., 1938-39; m. Margaret E. Blackman, Oct. 21, 1940; children—Carol Ann Bauman Ammerman. Earl William. Acct., Haselmire, Cordle & Co., Casper, Wyo., 1939-42; asst. dir. finance VA, Chgo., 1946-49, chief acctg. group, Washington, 1949-52, supr. systems acctg., 1952-55; supervising auditor GAO, Washington, 1955-58; dir. finance, asst. dir. Directorate Acctg. and Financial Policy, Office Asst. Sec. Def., Washington, 1958-63; tech. asst. to comdr. AF Acctg. and Finance Ctr., Denver, 1963-73; mem. investigations staff Ho. of Reps. Appropriations Com., 1953-54; prof. acctg. Benjamin Franklin U., 1960-63; mem. exec. council Army Finance, 1963-64; dir. Real Estate Investment Corp., 1962-64; ptnr. EMB Enterprises, 1973—; chmn. Acctg. Careers Council Colo., 1969-71. Chmn. Aurora Citizens Adv. Budget Com., 1975-76; chmn. fin. and taxation com. Denver Met. Study, 1976-78. Served with AUS, 1942-46; col. Res., now ret. C.P.A. Mem. Am. Inst. C.P.A.s, Wyo. Assn. C.P.A.s, Fed. Govt. Accts. Assn. (nat. v.p. 1972-73, pres. Denver 1973-74), Army Finance Assn., Am. Soc. Mil. Comptrollers, Denver Am. Soc. Mil. Comptrollers (pres. 1968-69), Citizens Band Radio Assn. (pres. 1963), Alpha Kappa Psi, Beta Alpha Psi, Phi Kappa Phi. Club: Columbine Sertoma (pres. 1975-76). Home: 536 Newark Ct Aurora CO 80010

BAUMBACH, HENRY DALE, psychologist, educator, consultant; b. Lodi, Calif., Sept. 13, 1944; s. Henry C. and Loma D. (Schrenk) B.; children—Catherine, Pamela, Christopher, Carrie. B.A., U. Calif.-Riverside, 1969, M.A., 1973, Ph.D., 1975; M.A. in Sociology, Loma Linda U., 1970; postgrad. in psychology, U. Mo., 1970-71. Lic. psychologist, Calif., Idaho. From instr. to asst. prof. psychology Loma Linda U., 1971-75; postdoctoral fellow Stanford U. Sch. Medicine, 1975-78, research assoc., 1978-79; clin. neuropsychologist Idaho Dept. Health and Welfare Adult/Child Devel. Ctr., Lewiston, 1979-81; staff psychologist Napa (Calif.) State Hosp. 1981-83; instr. psychology Ohlone Coll., Fremont, Calif., part-time 1978; spl. cons. clin. neuropsychology San Joaquin Gen. Hosp., Stockton, Calif., 1982—; adj. asst. prof. Chapman Coll., 1982—; clin. neuropsychology cons. Los Medanos Community Hosp., Pittsburg, Calif., 1982—; pvt. practice psychology, Stockton, 1982—; clin. coordinator Pain Mgmt. and Neuropsychology Ctr., Mt. Diablo Hosp. Med. Ctr., Concord, Calif., 1983—. Recipient Chancellor's Patent Fund award U. Calif.-Riverside, 1974; NSF fellow, 1968. Mem. Am. Psychol. Assn., AAAS. Democrat. Contbr. sci. articles to profl. jours. Home: 8132 Camelback Pl Pleasant Hill CA 94523 Office: 2087 Grand Canal Blvd Suite 12 Stockton CA 95207

BAUMER, DAVID AARON, commodities consultant; b. Casablanca, Morocco, Feb. 2, 1953; s. Samuel L. and Rosa (Gibermann) B.; student Wayne State U., 1972-76. Lic. commodities futures trader. Sr. acct. exec. Premex Inc., San Diego, 1977—. Republican. Jewish. Home: 4004 Crystal Dawn Ln Apt 19 San Diego CA 92122 Office: 7670 Opportunity Rd San Diego CA 92111

BAUMGARTEN, RONALD NEAL, lawyer, real estate syndicator and developer; b. Chgo., May 13, 1942; s. Albert and Beatrice (Loseff) B.; m. Aloha Herman, Aug. 27, 1966; children—Brett, Reed, Jaclyn, Blake. B.A. (Edmund James Scholar), U. Ill., 1964, J.D., 1966. Bar: Calif. 1970, U.S. Dist. Ct. for Calif. 1970, U.S. Ct. Appeals 1973, U.S. Supreme Ct. 1975. Clk. firm Low & Stone, Beverly Hills, Calif., 1966-67; gen. counsel, chief ops. officer, dir. Elgin Jewelry Distbrs., Inc., Los Angeles, 1967-72; mem. firm Grobe, Rinestein, Freid & Katz, P.L.C., Beverly Hills, 1972-75; sr. ptnr. Jacobs & Baumgarten, P.L.C., Beverly Hills, 1975-80, Baumgarten & Greene, P.L.C., Santa Monica, Calif., 1980—; chief fin. officer, chmn. bd. J.D. Alexander & Assocs., Inc., Santa Monica, 1980—; asst. prof. law U. San Fernando Valley Coll. Law, 1974; v.p., dir., gen. counsel Variety Club So. Calif., Tent 25, 1974—; founder 1st Bus. Bank, Los Angeles, 1981. Mem. Los Angeles World Affairs Council, 1974—; mem. Los Angeles Olympic Citizens Adv. Com., 1982-84. Mem. ABA, State Bar. Calif., Los Angeles County Bar Assn., Beverly Hills Bar Assn., Santa Monica Bar Assn., Phi Delta Phi.

BAUMGARTNER, ALLAN RODNEY, computer company executive; b. N.Y.C., May 27, 1938; s. John Herbert and Claire Regina (Strobele) B.; B.S., Carnegie Inst. Tech., 1960; m. Dolores Zalewski, Dec. 4, 1975; children—Yvette Selena, Brendon Allan Hans. Product mgr. Westinghouse Electric Corp., Sunnyvale, Calif., 1966-67, data processing devel. mgr., 1967-71; data communications designer Pacific Telephone Co., San

Francisco, 1971-74, internal cons., 1974-78; cons. to advanced communications system AT&T, Morristown, N.J., 1976-77; dir. tech. strategy Nat. Semicondr. Corp., San Diego, 1979-80, dir. software mktg. subs. Nat. Advanced Systems, Inc., Mountain View, Calif., 1980-83, pres. Gyros Systems Corp., San Diego, 1983—; cons. mgmt. and data processing. Served to capt. C.E., U.S. Army, 1960-65. Mem. Data Processing Mgmt. Assn., IEEE, Assn. Data Processing Service Orgns. Republican. Home: 14820 Satanas St San Diego CA 92129 Office: 800 E Middlefield Rd Mountain View CA 94043

BAXTER, CECIL WILLIAM, JR., coll. pres.; b. Stockton, Kans., Aug. 11, 1923; s. Cecil William and Marjorie LaVerne (Fitzpatrick) B.; B.A., Kans. Wesleyan U., 1950; M.B.A., U. Denver, 1954; Ph.D. (Ford Found. fellow, Kellogg Found. fellow), U. Tex., 1967; m. Pat Ann Layman, June 6, 1951; children—Cecil William, Michael Kent, Patrick Alan. Secondary sch. tchr., then secondary sch. prin., 1951-60; bus. mgr. Cottey Coll., Nevada, Mo., 1960-65; dean instrn. Kansas City (Kans.) Community Jr. Coll., 1967-68, Forest Park Community Coll., St. Louis, 1968-70; pres. North Seattle Community Coll., 1970—; mem. faculty U. Wash., Seattle, 1971. Bd. dirs. Sr. Citizens Orgn., Seattle, 1972, Commn. on Colls., Northwest Assn. Schs. And Colls., 1982—. Served with AUS, 1944-46. Mem. Wash. Assn. Marriage and Family Therapy (state bd. dirs.), Phi Delta Kappa. Club: Rotary. Office: 9600 College Way N Seattle WA 98103

BAXTER, JAMES ALBERT, hospital administrator, psychiatrist; b. Fairfield, Mich., Sept. 24, 1926; s. Emmet Glenwood and Ina Lucille (Myers) B.; m. Yvonne Hedwigia Capone, July 1, 1950; children—John, Karen, Lisa, Trisha; m. 2d, Lorraine Ruth Sullivan, Dec. 30, 1978. A.B., Oberlin Coll., 1949; M.Sc., Ohio State U., 1951; M.D., Case-Western Res. U., 1955. Gen. practice medicine, Salem, Oreg., 1959-67; staff psychiatrist Lane County Mental Health Program, Eugene, Oreg., 1969-70; dir. Marion County Mental Health, Salem, Oreg., 1970-75; clin. dir. Eastern Oreg. Co. Mental Health Ctr., Pendleton, Oreg., 1975-78; supr. Eastern Oreg. Hosp. and Tng. Ctr., Pendleton, 1978—. Served to col. Oreg. N.G., 1982—. Mem. Oreg. Med. Assn., Am. Psychiat. Assn., Am. Assn. Mental Deficiency, Nat. Assn. Suprs. State Mental Health Facilities. Republican. Methodist. Club: Rotary. Home: 109 Hospital Dr Pendleton OR 97801 Office: Box A Pendleton OR 97801

BAXTER, RALPH FELIX, b. Hamburg, Germany, Aug. 31, 1925; s. Felix F. and Irmy A. (Muenden) B.; m. Janice Phillips, Aug. 14, 1960; children—David, Eric, Robert. Student Rensselaer Poly. Inst., 1942-43; B.S. in Mech. Engring., U. Calif.-Berkeley, 1949. Staff Gen. Air Conditioning Corp., Los Angeles; 1949-50; group project engr. Rheem Mfg. Co., Los Angeles, 1950-56; asst. to pres., dir. mfg., Revell, Inc., Venice, Calif., 1956-58; v.p. ops. Hunt Food and Industries, Fullerton, Calif., 1959-64; v.p. long range planning, 1964-67; sr. v.p. Avery Internat., Pasadena, Calif., 1967—; dir. Knox Glass. Bd. dirs. Industry Edn. Council Calif., 1974; v.p. Industry Edn. Alliance of Los Angeles, 1974-78; mem. White House fellowship selection com. Western Region, 1978, 79. Mem. Am. Arbitration Assn. (panel arbitrators), Calif. Mfrs. Assn. (dir. 1981—). Home: 1263 N Citrus Dr La Habra CA 90631 Office: 150 N Orange Grove Blvd Pasadena CA 91103

BAYAN, MILAN MARTIN, interior designer; b. N.Y.C., Jan. 21, 1926; s. Martin Stefen and Anna (Baumgartner) B. B.F.A., U. So. Calif., 1951. Designer, Cannell & Chaffin Corp., Los Angeles, 1954-62; owner, Bayan-Allan Interiors, Los Angeles, 1972-76, exec. design dir. Vagabond Hotels, Inc., San Diego, 1977-82; owner Milan M. Bayan Interiors, 1982; exec. v.p. design Vibrant Design, Inc., 1983—. Served with USAF, 1944-46. Mem. Am. Soc. Interior Designers. Democrat. Roman Catholic. Contbr. articles to publs. Home: 3221 Vista Cielo Ln Spring Valley CA 92077

BAYDA, EDWARD DMYTRO, judge; b. Alvena, Sask., Can., Sept. 9, 1931; s. Dymtro Andrew and Mary (Bilinski) B.; m. Marie-Therese Yvonne Gagne, May 28, 1953; children—Paula, Christopher, Margot, Marie-Therese, Sheila, Kathryn. B.A., U. Sask.-Saskatoon, 1951, LL.B. cum laude, 1953. Called to Sask. bar, 1954. Barrister, solicitor, Regina, Sask., Can., 1953-72; justice of Ct. of Queen's Bench for Sask., Regina, 1972-74, justice of the Ct. of Appeal for Sask., Regina, 1974-81; chief justice of Sask., Regina, 1981—. Office: Court House 2425 Victoria Ave Regina SK S4P 3V7 Canada

BAYLE, DEBORAH SPARROW, association executive; b. Ogden, Utah, Aug. 29, 1951; d. Herschel Duell and Carlene Alice (Critchlow) Sparrow; m. Raymond John Etcheverry, July 31, 1974 (div. Sept. 1977); m. F. Robert Bayle, Jr., May 18, 1979; 1 dau., Megan Quinn. Student Weber State Coll., 1969-73. Sec., United Fund of No. Utah, Ogden, 1968-69; office mgr. M & D Sales Inc., Salt Lake City, 1971-74; sec., employee relations rep. Duke U., 1974-76; sec. Salt Lake Area C. of C. 1976-78, dir. spl. projects/community devel., 1978-80, adminstrv. mgr., 1980—. Mem. exec. com. Postal Customer Council Salt Lake Area, 1981-83; vice-chmn. adminstrv. services Utah Bus. Week, 1981—; mem. Salt Lake City Cultural Arts Com., 1978—, Tourism and Convs. Com., 1980—. Mem. Nat. Assn. Female Execs. Club: Oakridge Country. Office: 19 East 200 South Salt Lake City UT 84111

BAYLES, ROBERT SCOTT, advertising executive; b. Los Angeles, July 7, 1953; s. Herbert William and Mona Lee (Roberts) B.; m. Deborah Leigh Berry, July 10, 1976. B.A. in English, Calif. State U.-Chico, 1976; M.A. in English, Calif. State U.-Fullerton, 1979. Mktg. librarian Computer Automation, Irvine, Calif., 1976-77, mktg. communications adminstr. Naked Mini div., 1977-78; tech. writer Aeronutronic div. Ford Aerospace and Communications Corp., Newport Beach, Calif., 1978-79; sales promotion specialist Lexitron div. Raytheon Data Systems, Thousand Oaks, Calif., 1979-81; mgr. cooperative advt. Vector Graphic Inc., Thousand Oaks, 1981—. Mem. Bus. Profl. Advt. Assn. Evangelical. Office: 500 N Ventu Park Rd Thousand Oaks CA 91320

BAYLOR, ROBERT GENE, legal office adminstr.; b. Portland, Oreg., Feb. 7, 1932; s. Jack Preston and Eva Inez (Miralda) B.; B.S., U. Calif.-Berkeley, 1956; M.B.A., Portland State U., 1970; m. Mary Lavonne Grabow, May 21, 1977; children by previous marriage—Barbara, Jeanne, Suzanne. Asst. mdse. mgr. J.C. Penney Co., San Francisco, 1956-60; v.p. fin. Halo Sales Corp., San Francisco and Portland, 1960-64; adminstr. law firm Davies, Biggs, Strayer, Stoel & Boley, Portland, 1964-77; dir. adminstrn. law firm Manatt, Phelps, Rothenberg & Tunney, Los Angeles, 1977—; founder, chmn. Mgmt. and Supervisory Devel. Inst. and M & B Enterprises; pres. Robert G. Baylor & Assocs., law mgmt. firm; mem. vis. faculty Portland Community Coll., San Diego U., univs. Oreg., Minn. and Mich., UCLA, U. So. Calif. Mem. Clackamas County (Oreg.) Land Use Planning Commn., 1962-64. Served with USMCR, 1950-52; Korea. Decorated Bronze Star, Purple Heart. Mem. Assn. Legal Adminstrs., Nat. Assn. Legal Assts. (dir.), Oreg. Legal Secs. (hon.), Internat. Word Processing Assn. Democrat. Clubs: Multnomah Athletic (Portland); Calif. Yacht (Los Angeles). Author papers in field. Home: 4863 Matilija Ave Sherman Oaks CA 91423 Office: 1888 Century Park E Los Angeles CA 90067

BAYNE, MICHAEL ANTHONY, mfg. and devel. engr.; b. Spokane, Feb. 29, 1948; s. William Maitlen and Saralee (Cole) B.; B.S. in Physics, Wash. State U., 1971, M.S. in Surface Physics, 1972; m. Nancy Ann Earley, July 11, 1969; children—Matthew Anthony, Jill Kathleen. Lab. and research asst. dept. physics Wash. State U., Pullman, 1969-72; devel. engr. Battelle Pacific Northwest Labs., Richland, Wash., 1974-79; sr. scientist Exxon Nuclear Co., Inc., Richland, 1979-81; devel. engr. Hewlett-Packard, Vancouver, Wash., 1981—. Mem. West Richland Planning Commn., 1978. Served with U.S. Army, 1972-74. Mem. Am. Vacuum Soc. (chpt. vice-chmn.). Contbr. articles to profl. jours. Home: 12917 NE 20th St Vancouver WA 98664 Office: PO Box C-006 Vancouver WA 98668

BAZANT, STANLEY KENT, utility executive; b. Chgo., Nov. 16, 1936; s. Stanley and Sally (Dennis) B.; m. Marilyn Kay Hackney, Dec. 27, 1958; 1 dau., Pamela Lynn. B.S.E.E., U. N.Mex., 1958. Registered profl. engr., N.Mex. With Plains Electric Generation and Transmission Coop., Albuquerque, 1955—, asst. utility man, 1955,58, relay and electronics engr., 1961-62, adminstrv. asst., 1962-69, ops. and constrn. engr., 1969-72, asst. mgr., 1973-74, gen. mgr., 1975-77, exec. v.p., 1977—; pres. Western Fuels. Vice chmn. N.Mex. Job Tng. and Safety Com.; sec. engring. com., mem. exec. com. 39th Power Pool; former mem. N.Mex. Gov.'s Energy Task Force. Served to 1st lt. USMC, 1959-60; to maj. Res., 1961—. Mem. Rocky Mountain Utility Radio Assn. (past pres.), N.Mex. Rural Electric Assn. (sec.-treas.), Nat. Soc. Profl. Engrs., N.Mex. Soc. Profl. Engrs., U. N.Mex. Letterman's Assn. (former dir.), Nat. Rural Electric Coop. Assn. (power and generation com.), Albuquerque C. of C., Colo. River Energy Distbrs. Assn. (pres.). Democrat. Roman Catholic.

BAZELA, STANLEY ANTHONY, paper company executive; b. Wilmington, Del., Mar. 3, 1929; s. William Adam and Frances (Warych) B.; B.M.E., U. Del., 1950; m. Janet Ann Damai, Mar. 31, 1951; children—Stephen M., Christine M., Kathleen J., Sandra J. Paper mill engr. Scott Paper Co., Mobile, Ala., 1958-62; chief engr. paper machines Rice Barton Corp., Worcester, Mass., 1962-66; mfg. mgr. Garden State Paper Co., Pomona, Calif., 1966-78, mill mgr., 1978—. Served to 1st lt. U.S. Army, 1951-53. Named Outstanding Young Man, Worcester Jr. C. of C., 1964. Mem. ASME, Paper Industry Mgmt. Assn., Internat. Assn. Sci. Paper Makers, TAPPI. Republican. Roman Catholic. Clubs: K.C., Kiwanis. Office: Garden State Paper Co 2205 W Mount Vernon Ave Pomona CA 91766

BAZOVSKY, IGOR, sci. cons.; b. Lucenec, Slovakia, Apr. 13, 1914; s. Louis and Bozena (Fajnor) B.; student Tech. U., Berlin, Germany, 1932-35; Dipl. Ing. in Elec. Engring., German Tech. U., Prague, Czechoslovakia, 1939; m. Drahomira Machacek, Oct. 17, 1939; children—Igor, Eva (Mrs. Donald Booth), John-Louis. Came to U.S., 1957, naturalized, 1962. Engaged in elec. power engring., Europe, 1939-57; research engr. Boeing, Seattle, 1957-59; mgr. reliability engring. United Control Corp., Seattle, 1959-62; chief reliability analyst Raytheon Missile Div., Bedford, Mass., 1962-63; systems reliability mgr. Litton Industries, Woodland Hills, Calif., 1963-66; dir. sci. and cons. div. Genge Industries, Inc., Sherman Oaks, Calif., 1966-69; pres., chief scientist Igor Bazovsky & Assos., Inc., 1969—. Recipient Reliability award IEEE. Am. Soc. for Quality Control, 1963. Registered profl. engr., Wash., Calif. Mem. IEEE Navy League U.S., Am. Nuclear Soc., Am. Def. Preparedness Assn., fellow Inst. Advancement of Engring. Nat. Nat. Soc. Profl. Engrs.; Republican. Lutheran. Author: Reliability Theory and Practice, 1961; co-author, editor: Maintainability Engineering Theory and Practice, 1976. Home: 20305 Oxnard St Woodland Hills CA 91367 Office: 7255 Owensmouth Ave Canoga Park CA 91303

BEACH, ARTHUR O'NEAL, lawyer; b. Albuquerque, Feb. 8, 1945; s. William Pearce and Vivian Lucille (Kronig) B.; B.B.A., U. N.Mex., 1967, J.D., 1970; m. Alex Clark Doyle, Sept. 12, 1970; 1 son, Eric Kronig. Admitted to N.Mex. bar, 1970; asso. firm Smith & Ransom, Albuquerque, 1970-74; asso. firm Keleher & McLeod, Albuquerque, 1974-75, partner, 1976-78, shareholder firm Keleher & McLeod, P.A., Albuquerque, 1978—; teaching asst. U. N. Mex., 1970. Mem. State Bar N.Mex. (unauthorized practice of law com.), Am., Albuquerque (dir. 1978-82) bar assns., State Bar Specialization Bd. Democrat. Mem. Christian Sci. Ch. Home: 2015 Dietz Pl NW Albuquerque NM 87107 Office: PO Drawer AA Albuquerque NM 87103

BEACH, CHARLES KENNETH, mfg. co. exec.; b. Corvallis, Oreg., Dec. 4, 1905; s. Charles Leslie and Ellen (Wallace) B.; B.S., Oreg. State U., 1929, M.S., 1934; Ph.D., Cornell U., 1941; m. Mildred Marley, June 10, 1930; 1 dau., Sallie Lou. Asso. prof., head dept. indsl. edn. La. State U., Baton Rouge, 1935-40; state supr., indsl. tchr. trainer SUNY, Albany, 1941-46; prof. indsl. and labor relations Cornell U., Ithaca, N.Y., 1946-52; dir. mgmt. devel., dir. tng. Arabian Am. Oil Co., Dhahran, Saudi Arabia, 1952-61; exec. devel. advisor Exxon Corp., N.Y.C., 1961-64, dir. exec. devel. and compensation Exxon Chem. Corp., 1964-69; dir. mgmt. devel. and compensation Norris Industries, Long Beach, Calif., 1969—; mgmt. devel. specialist Flying Tigers, Los Angeles, 1981—. Mem. Am. Soc. Tng. and Devel. Republican. Episcopalian. Home: 944 6th St Santa Monica CA 90403 Office: Norris Industries One Golden Shore Long Beach CA 90802

BEACH, JACK GORDON, brewery executive; b. Craik, Sask., Can., May 14, 1941; s. John Lee and Lillian (Spencer) B.; m. Marlene Douglas, June 30, 1961; children—Spencer Lee, Alex Andrea. B.A., U. Calgary, 1963; M.A., U. Edmonton, 1965. Econ. cons. Underwood, McLellan & Assocs., Calgary, Alta., Can., 1966-68; mktg. exec. Booker Bros., McConnel Ltd., London, Eng. and Edmonton, Alta., 1964-66; with Molson Breweries, Vancouver, B.C., 1968—, mktg. mgr., 1972-74, exec. asst. to pres., Montreal, Que., 1974-75, spl. projects mgr., Toronto, Ont., 1975-77, dir. distbn., 1977-81, v.p. mktg., Calgary, 1981-83, pres. Molson Brewery B.C. Ltd., Vancouver, 1983—. Mem. Can. Mfrs. Assn. (dir. B.C.). Clubs: North Shore Winter, Terminal City, Hollyburn Country (Vancouver). Home: 5631 Sumac Pl North Vancouver BC V7R 4T6 Canada Office: 1550 Burrard St Vancouver BC V6J 3G5 Canada*

BEADLE, CLIFFORD R., accountant; b. East St. Louis, Ill., June 11, 1950; s. Clinton M. and Anna A. (Jackson) B.; m. Claudia A. Zlomke, Dec. 29, 1970; 1 dau., Courtney. B.B.A., Wichita State U., 1972. C.P.A., Idaho, Nev. Staff acct. Fox & Co., Wichita, Kans., 1972-73, Boise, Idaho, 1973-78, Las Vegas, Nev., 1978-80, ptnr., audit coordinator, Las Vegas, 1980—. Mem. Am. Inst. C.P.A.s, Nev. Soc. C.P.A.s, Idaho Soc. C.P.A.s, Nat. Assn. Accts. (pres. Las Vegas chpt. 1982-83), Am. Accts. Assn. Office: Fox & Co 300 S 4th St Suite 905 Las Vegas NV 89101

BEAIRD, BYRON BRYANT GRADY, railroad food service adminstr.; b. Apr. 28, 1919; s. Grady Milford and Nancy Isabelle (Bryant) B.; m. Evelyn Ruth Frost, Oct. 18, 1941; children—Richard Charles, John Michael. Student Northwestern U., 1956. Owner Beaird's Cafe, 1936-38; mgr. Rex Cafe, 1939-41; accounting dept. E.I. Du Pont de Nemours & Co. Inc., Wilmington, Del., 1942-43; cost accountant Douglas Aircraft Co., Santa Monica, Calif., 1944-45; maitre d'hotel Ladd's Supper Club, Santa Monica, 1946-49; dining car steward A.C.L. N.Y., N.Y. and Union Pacific R.R., Denver, 1950; supr. dining car and hotel dept., 1964-71, supr. commissary. 1971—; pres., founder Ice Creations Unlimited, Denver, 1970-75; now pres. M-M Investment Co., Los Angeles; mem. A.B.C. Corp.; specialist in buffet and gourmet food display projection, mass feeding systems; holds copyrights on ice sculpture molds, Beaird method coffeemaking. Mem. Griffith Park Hills Republican Assembly, Los Angeles County Rep. Assembly, Calif. Rep. Assembly. Mem. Soc. Geneva, Am. Assn. Individual Investors, Rocky Mountain Restaurant Assn., Rosicrucian Order, Patriots of Am. Bicentennial, Navy League. Methodist. Clubs: Portland Press, Ranch Country, Internat. House, Optimists (pres. Beverly Hills). Home: 10330 Ashton Ave Los Angeles CA 90024 Office: Wilshire Tower Bldg Suite 406 5514 Wilshire Blvd Los Angeles CA 90036

BEAL, BRENDA ULRICH, educator; b. Lockport, N.Y., Nov. 9, 1938; d. Howard Louis and Mary Ruth (Whalen) Ulrich; m. David Russell Beal, Aug. 20, 1960 (div.). Tchr. Newark (N.Y.) Central Sch. Dist., 1960-61, Phelps (N.Y.) Central Sch. Dist., 1961-67; tchr. Union Springs (N.Y.) Central Sch. Dist., 1967-68, coordinator title I, 1968-71; grad. asst. reading ctr. Ariz. State U., Tempe, 1971-73; prof. dept. edn. Humboldt State U., Arcata, Calif., 1973—; prof. No. Ariz. U., Flagstaff, summers 1980, 81, 83; cons. in field. Mem. Citizens Adv. Bd. for Site Decisions, 1981, 82. Mem. AAUW, Internat. Reading Assn., Humboldt Reading Council, Assn. for Supervision and Curriculum Devel., Phi Delta Kappa. Office: HGH Humboldt State U 202C Arcata CA 95521

BEALS, HERBERT KYLE, community planner, historian; b. Portland, Oreg., July 26, 1934; s. James Herbert and Mae Adelia (Thompson) B.; student Reed Coll., 1951-53; B.A., Portland State U., 1958, M.A. in History, 1983; m. Barbara Carol Brown, Mar. 22, 1957; children—Patricia L., Cheryl A., Steven K. Planner, asst. dir. Clackamas County (Oreg.) Planning Dept., Oregon City, 1957-65; community planning cons. Bur. Govt. Research, U. Oreg., Eugene, 1965-70; sr. and prin. planner Columbia Region Assn. Govts., Portland, Oreg., 1970-78; prin. housing planner Met. Service Dist., Portland, 1979-80. Mem. Gladstone City Planning Commn., 1964-67, 72-76; moderator Pacific N.W. Assn. Congl. Christian Chs., 1981-83. Served with AUS, 1953-56. Recipient award for excellence Portland State U., 1983. Mem. Am. Inst. Cert. Planners (dir. 1962-64), Am. Planning Assn., Soc. Hist. Archaeology, Soc. Am. Archaeology, Oreg. Hist. Soc., Oreg. Archeol. Soc. (pres. 1972, 77), Oreg. Numismatic Soc., Phi Alpha Theta. Author: For Honor and Country: The Diary of Bruno Hezeta and the Voyage of the Santiago, 1775, 1984. Illustrator: Wappato Indians (R.F. Jones), 1971; contbr. articles to archeol. jours., numismatic publs. Home: 7005 Valley View Dr Gladstone OR 97027 Office: 527 Hall St SW Portland OR 97201

BEALS, MARK G., educator; b. Irvona, Pa., Aug. 11, 1936; s. George Bylle and Leila Elzeda (Eidell) B.; B.A., Lycoming Coll., 1956; M.A., U. Hawaii, 1958; Ph.D., U. Ariz., 1968. Psychologist, Yakima, Wash., 1961-64; instr. psychology Yakima Valley Coll., 1961-64; asst. prof., coordinator program in spl. edn. No. Ariz. U., Flagstaff, 1966-69; prof., dir. undergrad. curricula, coordinator student teaching and programs for gifted, U. Nev., Las Vegas, 1969—; cons. State of Ariz. Dists. 15, 16, 22, 1970-79; founder, cons. New Horizons Center for Learning, Las Vegas, Nev., 1971—; cons. and lectr. in field. Pres., So. Nev. Epilepsy Assn., Nev. Epilepsy Assn., 1972-75; mem. Com. on Rehab., 1969, Gov.'s Com. on Gifted, 1975, Com. on Accreditation, 1981—, others. Served with U.S. Army, 1944-47. Recipient Gov.'s award, State of Nev., 1968; Epilepsy Found. leadership award, 1975; Award for Leadership to Children, Ariz. Assn. Chronic Lung Disease, 1977. Fellow Menninger Found.; mem. Am. Psychol. Assn., Western Psychol. Assn., Council for Exceptional Children, AAAS, Ednl. Research Assn., Assn. for Retarded Citizens, Orton Soc., Humanistic Psychology Assn., Mensa. Republican. Author: Handbook for Teachers of the Culturally Deprived, 1966; Laughter of Children, 1968 (film); contbr. articles to profl. jours. Office: Dept Spl Edn Univ Nev Las Vegas NV 89154

BEAMER, JO ANN JEAN, forging company executive; b. Dedham, Iowa, June 15, 1939; d. William Columbus and Neva Belle (Randolph) Dennis; m. Michael R. Beamer, July 10, 1973; children—Steven Dean, Donald Lee, Karey Lee Beamer Davidofsky. Student Chaffey Jr. College, U. Nev. Exec. sec. Aerojet Gen. Corp., Azusa, Calif., Nuclear Rocket Devel. Sta., Jackass Flats, Nev., 1959-62, 64-68; exec. sec. safety and test ops. Pan Am. World Airways, Nuclear Rocket Devel. Stat., 1962-64; personnel and safety asst. safety and personnel Survival Systems Co., Ontario, Calif., 1968-71; personnel mgr. Hooker Industries, Ontario, 1971-74; asst. terminal mgr. CMD Transp. Co., Vernon, Calif., 1977-80; personnel mgr. Schlosser Forge Co., Cucamonga, Calif., 1980—; guest speaker Ontario Community Hosp. Active Chino (Calif.) High Sch. Band Boosters. Mem. Nat. Assn. Female Execs., Mchts. and Mfrs. Assn., Personnel Indsl. Relations Assn. Home: 5729 Portsmouth St Chino CA 91710 Office: Schlosser Forge Co 11711 Arrow Route St Cucamonga CA 91730

BEAMER, SCOTT, cons. elec. engr., lectr.; b. Berkeley, Calif., Apr. 2, 1914; s. Joseph H. and Louise (Scott) B.; B.S. in Elec. Engring., U. Calif., 1936; m. Alpha Mae Rogers, Oct. 21, 1939; children—Joan Louise, Scott, Ronald Laurence, Alexander Rogers, Deborah. Jr. elec. engr. Pacific Electric Motor Co., 1938-40; asso. elec. engr. Farm Sect. Adminstrn., U.S. Dept. Agr., 1940-42; cons. engr. with Clyde E. Bentley, 1946-47, Beamer & Tilson, 1949-51; with Beamer/Wilkinson & Assos., 1966-76, Scott Beamer & Assos., 1977—; mem. faculty U. Calif., 1948-63, teaching regular classes architecture and engring. and extension classes at Oakland and San Francisco, 1948-59, also univ. research projects; lighting cons. Bay Area Rapid Transit Dist. Joint Ventures. Former chmn. adv. council Salvation Army Hosp.; former chmn. troop com., mem. exec. council Boy Scouts Am.; former trustee Children's Hosp. Med. Center Found.; bd. dirs. Oakland Mus. Assn.; mem. adv. bd. Ladies Home Soc., Oakland. Served as maj. AUS, Office Chief of Ordnance, 1942-46, in Washington, France and Germany on Proximity Fuse project; mem. O.R.C., 1937-63. Decorated Bronze Star medal, Distinguished Service Wreath, Army Commendation medal. Registered profl. engr., Calif., Nev., Oreg. Fellow Illuminating Engring. Soc.; mem. IEEE (life). Clubs: Rotary (past pres.), Claremont Country, 100 (past dir.). Contbr. articles to profl. jours. Patentee neon dimming transformer; co-author of patent luminous bodies. Home: 36 King Ave Piedmont CA 94611 Office: Scott Beamer & Assos 618 Grand Ave Oakland CA 94610

BEAMER, WILLIAM FRED, research expedition organizer; b. Mt. Airy, N.C., Apr. 2, 1938; B.S. in Engring., N.C. State U., 1960; M.B.A., U. N.C., 1962; m. Sharon Kaye Ehrig, Nov. 2, 1968. Engr., Atomics Internat., Canoga Park, Calif., 1962-68; pres. Beamer Expdns., Canoga Park, Calif., 1968—. Mem. Am. Soc. Primatologists, Internat. Primatological Soc. Organizer, dir. research expdns. in search of Bigfoot, an unidentified primate. Office: PO Box 285 Canoga Park CA 91305

BEAN, LARRY GEORGE, accountant, financial and tax consultant; b. Marengo, Iowa, Feb. 16, 1946; s. George J. and Eunice L. (Haas) B.; m. Margaret Linda Cronbaugh, Dec. 17, 1966; children—Joshua Benjamin, Amber Alissa, Nathan Samuel. B.A. with high honors, U. No. Iowa, 1968. C.P.A., Wyo., Iowa. Staff acct. Haskins & Sells, Colorado Springs, Colo., 1968-69; tax specialist McGladrey, Henrickson & Co., C.P.A.s, Davenport, Iowa, 1969-74, tax ptnr. Casper, Wyo., 1974-80; pvt. practice fin. and tax cons., Casper, 1980—; dir. Converse County Bank, Converse County Capital Corp., Bailey School Supply, Inc., Dale Weaver, Inc., Natural Gas Processors Inc., Thatcher & Sons, Inc., others. Bd. dirs. Big Bros. Am., 1968-69, Babe Ruth League, 1975-78, Nicolaysen Art Mus. Found., Casper YMCA, YMCA Found., Am. Bapt. Chs. of Rocky Mountain Region, Casper Symphony, Wyo. Fed. Tax Com.; mem. U.S. Congl. Award Council, Wyo.; active nat., state Republican Party. Named Outstanding Young Man, U.S. Small Bus. Assn., 1974. Mem. Wyo. Soc. C.P.A.s, Am. Soc. C.P.A.s, Wyo. Estate Planning Council, Casper C. of C. Republican. Baptist. Clubs: Casper Country, Nat. Wildlife, T-Bird Booster, Cowboy Joe. Home: 3115 Bella Vista St Casper WY 82601 Office: PO Box 3732 Casper WY 82602

BEAR, HENRY LOUIS, lawyer; b. Kansas City, Kans., Jan. 8, 1917; s. Max and Mary (Kagon) B.; J.D., U. Mo., 1939; m. Betty J. Isenhart, Jan. 4, 1951; 1 dau., Dinah Lou. Admitted to Mo. bar, 1939, Calif. bar, 1949; law asso. M.W. O'Hern, Kansas City, Mo., 1939-42; partner firm Bear, Kotob, Ruby & Gross, and predecessor, Downey, Calif., 1949—, sr. partner, 1955—; dir. Bank of Irvine; sec., dir. Pyrotronics Corp. Active local Boy Scouts Am., ARC, Community Chest. Served as officer USAAF, 1943-46. Named Man of Year, Lynwood, Calif., 1952. Fellow Am. Coll. Probate Counsel; mem. Am., Mo., Calif., Los Angeles bar assns., Am., Calif. trial lawyers assns. Clubs: Rotary (past pres.), Exec. Dinner (past pres., dir.), Elks (Downey). Author: California Law of Corporations, Partnerships and Associations. Home: 9205 Gainford St Downey CA 90240 Office: 10841 Paramount Blvd Downey CA 90241

BEAR, MORAYE BETTINA, biostatistician; b. Los Angeles, Dec. 13, 1951; d. Albert and Mina (Rosen) B. M.A., Calif. State U.-Northridge, 1975. Cert. jr. coll. tchr., Calif. Statis. analyst Los Angeles County (Calif.), 1975-76, U. So. Calif., Los Angeles, 1976-77, System Devel. Corp., Santa Monica, Calif., 1977-80; sr. biostatistician Cedars-Sinai Med. Ctr., Los Angeles, 1980—; research mgr. Calif. Prevention of Prematurity Project, 1983—. Mem. Am. Statis. Assn.

BEAR, NAOMI REBECCA DUMES, accountant, leadership consultant; b. Clinton, Ind., July 28, 1926; d. Arthur and Jennie Rachael (Rosenberg) Dumes; m. Leon Bear, July 10, 1949; children—David G, Alice S., Marian J. B.A., U. Ariz., 1949, M.Ed., 1955. Dir. student activities Hillel Found., U. Ariz., Tucson, 1958-63, 65-68, program advt. student activities student union activities bd., 1968-72; acct., office mgr. Leon Bear, P.A., P.C., Tucson, 1972—; cons., coordinator leadership workshops, 1980—. Bd. dirs. YWCA, Tucson; program v.p. Hadassah; coordinator Temple Eamanual Chavurah. Mem. AAUW (v.p. state div. membership, branch program, assn. task force, recipient individual mems' grant), Pi Lambda Theta. Democrat. Jewish. Home: 2850 E 3rd St Tucson AZ 85716 Office: Leon Bear Firm 3740 E Speedway St Tucson AZ 85716

BEARD, VICTORIA NANCY, title insurance company executive; b. Seattle, Mar. 19, 1945; d. Walter A. and Nancy (Paksis) Vane; A.A., Coll. San Mateo, 1965; B.A. in Sociology and Psychology, Chico (Calif.) State Coll., 1969. Sales mgr. The Emporium, Palo Alto, Calif., 1963-66; mgr., bus. rep. rehab., Chico, 1969-73; dir. Janet Rea Modeling Sch., Fresno, Calif., 1973-77; Realtor, 1976-77; account mgr., sr. sales exec. specializing in comml. and indsl. sales Ticor Title Ins., 1977-83, v.p., sales mgr., comml. and indsl. div., 1983—; designer women's sportswear. Policewoman, Chico Police Dept., 1969-71. Lic. Realtor, Calif. Mem. Fresno C. of C., Homebuilders Assn. Fresno, Fresno Bd. Realtors (affiliate), Assn. Women in Mgmt. Republican. Office: 320 Lennon Ln Walnut Creek CA 94598

BEARDMORE, GLENN EVERETT, univ. ofcl.; b. Elmdale, Kans., Apr. 22, 1930; s. Everett L. and Eulah L. (Merritt) B.; A.A., Mesa Coll., 1967; B. in Tech., Tex. State Tech. Inst., 1971; B. in Tech. Edn., Nat. U., 1972; M.A., U.S. Internat. U., 1974; Ed.D., Nova U., 1979; m. Gwendolyn Loree Whitfield, Nov. 12, 1950; children—David Eugene, Stephen Leroy. Propr., Mount Hope Produce Co., Mount Hope, Kans., 1948-50; enlisted U.S. Navy, 1950, advanced through grades to master chief petty officer; ret., 1973; v.p. adminstrn. Nat. U., San Diego, 1972—; mem. chancellor Nat. U., Vista, Calif., Evaluation Team for Approval of Schs. to Offer Degrees, State of Calif., 1975—. Bd. dirs. Lifeline Corp., Vista. hon. dep. sheriff San Diego County. Life fellow Am. Biog. Inst.; mem. Am. Soc. Personnel Adminstrn., Western Assn. Coll. and U. Bus. Officers (exec. com.), Personnel Mgmt. Assn. (pres. 1978), Calif. Assn. Fin. Aid Adminstrs., Nat. Mgmt. Assn. (chpt. pres. 1980-81, nat. dir. 1982-83, Silver Knight of Mgmt. award 1981, Gold Knight of Mgmt. award 1983), Vista Am. Soc. Trainers and Developers, El Cajon Blvd. Bus. Assn. (pres. 1978-79), Navy League U.S. (life, pres. North San Diego County council), C. of C. (treas.), Nat. Assn. Student Personnel Adminstrs., Fleet Res. Assn., Nat. U. Alumni Assn. (life mem., asso. dir. 1974—). Club: Rotary. Home: 5556 Nokomis St La Mesa CA 92041 Office: 4141 Camino del Rio South San Diego CA 92108

BEARDSLEY, STEPHANIE ANN, educational administrator; b. Whittier, Calif., June 28, 1948; d. Stephen Timothy and Maxine Cora (Billington) Shanahan; m. Dennis Martin Beardsley, June 6, 1970; 1 dau., Alyce Christine. A.B. in Spanish, U. Calif.-Davis, 1970; M.Ed., Wichita State U., 1972; C.Phil., in Higher Edn. Adminstrn., U. Calif.-Berkeley, 1982. Spanish tchr. Presentation High Sch., San Francisco, 1970-71; resident dir. Regan Hall, U. Calif.-Davis, 1973-75, asst. community housing coordinator, 1975-78, asst. dir. housing-residence life, 1978-81; asst. dean of students Mills Coll., Oakland, Calif., 1981—, also dir. residential and commuting student life.; cons. mgmt. and staff devel. U. Calif. Regents' scholar, 1966-70. Mem. Nat. Assn. Student Personnel Adminstrn., Am. Personnel and Guidance Assn., Am. Coll. Personnel Assn. (directorate body Commn. III). Democrat.

BEARLEY, WILLIAM LEON, computer co. exec.; b. Hays, Kans., June 6, 1938; s. William L. and Wilma M. (Sechrist) B.; B.S., U. Wyo., 1969, M.Ed., 1964; Ed.D., U. La Verne, 1983; M.H.R.D., Univ. Assos. Grad. Sch. Human Resource Devel., 1980; also grad. Lab. Edn. Intern Program; m. Diane Lee Kiser, Dec. 15, 1967. Tchr. math. Baldwin Park Unified Sch. Dist., Baldwin Park, Calif., 1961-64, chmn. dept. math, 1962-64; chmn. math. dept. Citrus Coll., Azusa, Calif., 1965-69, chmn. data processing dept., 1969-80, dir. computing and info. systems, 1972-80; pres. Computer Info. Assocs., Inc., Pasadena, Calif., 1980-82; assoc. prof. Sch. Mgmt., U. LaVerne, 1982—; cons., trainer info. resource mgmt., 1981—. Cert. in data processing Data Processing Mgmt. Assn. Mem. Assn. Systems Mgmt., Am. Soc. Tng. and Devel., Acad. Mgmt., Am. Mgmt. Assn., Am. Guild Organists, Phi Delta Kappa. Author/co-author books and articles in field. Home: 339 N Westridge Ave Glendora CA 91740 Office: U La Verne 1950 3d St La Verne CA 91750

BEARSON, ROBERT, mgmt. cons.; b. Peoria, Ill., June 13, 1923; s. Samuel and Sophia (Katz) B.; student UCLA, 1941-42; B.S., Calif. Inst. Tech., 1947; M.B.A., Harvard U., 1949; m. Marilyn Waldman, Mar. 22, 1956 (div.); children—Lee Waldman, Matt Edward, Dann Alan. Trainee, May Co., Los Angeles, 1949-56, buyer, 1951-54, gen. mgr., Crenshaw, 1954-56, gen. mgr., Lakewood, Calif., 1956-61; v.p., dir. ops., merchandising Unimart, San Diego, 1961-64; div. merchandising adminstr. Bullocks Dept. Store, Los Angeles, 1964-67; exec. v.p. Shelly's Tall Girl Shops, Los Angeles, 1967; mng. dir. ABM Advisors, Long Beach, Calif., 1970—; dir. Golden State Fabrics, San Diego, Mayco Pump Co., Albar Imports, Power Climber (all Los Angeles); sr. instr. UCLA Extension; instr. U. Calif., Irvine. Dist. chmn. Long Beach Area-Los Angeles Area council Boy Scouts Am.; active Long Beach Community Chest, Am. Cancer Soc.; mem. Planning Commn., City of Lakewood; bd. dirs. Lakewood Community Hemodialysis Center, Doctor's Hosp., Lakewood, Jewish Family Service; pres. Temple Israel, Long Beach. Served in USAF, 1943-45. Mem. Greater Lakewood C. of C. (v.p.), Lakewood Center Bus. Men's Assn. (pres.). Democrat. Jewish. Home: 5400 The Toledo #311 Long Beach CA 90803

BEASLEY, BRUCE MILLER, sculptor; b. Los Angeles, May 20, 1939; s. Robert Seth and Bernice (Palmer) B.; student Dartmouth, 1957-59; B.A., U. Calif-Berkeley, 1962; m. Laurence Léaute, May 21, 1973. Sculptor in metal and plastic; one-man shows at Everett Ellin Gallery, Los Angeles, Kornblee Gallery, N.Y.C., Hansen-Fuller Gallery, San Francisco, David Stuart Gallery, Los Angeles, Andre Emmerich Gallery, N.Y.C., De Young Mus., San Francisco, Santa Barbara Mus. Art, Fine Arts Gallery, San Diego; exhibited in group shows at Mus. Modern Art, N.Y.C., Guggenheim Mus., N.Y.C., Albright Knox Gallery, Buffalo, La Jolla (Calif.) Art Mus., Musée d'Art Modern, Paris, San Francisco Mus. Art, Krannert Art Mus. at U. Ill., Jewish Mus., N.Y.C., Luxembourg Gardens, Paris, Calif. Palace of Legion of Honor, De Young Mus., Santa Barbara Art Mus., others; represented in permanent collections Mus. Modern Art, Guggenheim Mus., Musée d'Art Modern, Los Angeles County Art Mus., Univ. Art Mus., Berkeley, Calif., Oakland (Calif.) Mus., Wichita (Kans.) Art Mus., San Francisco Art Commn., Santa Barbara Art Mus., others; major sculpture commns. include State of Calif., 1967, Oakland Mus., 1972, City of San Francisco, 1974, U.S. govt., 1975, City of Eugene (Oreg.), 1974, Sterling Heights, Mich., 1975, Miami Internat. Airport, 1978, State Office Bldg., San Bernardino, 1979, San Francisco Internat. Airport, 1981, Stanford U., 1982, Los Angeles Olympics, 1983. Recipient Andre Malraux purchase award Biennale de Paris, 1961, purchase prize San Francisco Arts Festival, 1967. Home: 322 Lewis St Oakland CA 94607

BEASLEY, IDA LUE, government official; b. Franklin, Heard County, Ga., Dec. 12 1936; d. Solomon and Sarah Ophelia (Daniel) Stricklin; m. Robert Erskine Beasley, Sept. 14, 1957; children—Michelle Yvette, Stephen Erskine, Chayra A. A.A. with honors, Compton Community Coll., 1974; B.A. with distinction, Calif. State U.-Dominguez Hills, 1978. Flex-writer operator VA, 1956-61; clk.-stenographer U.S. Air Force, Los Angeles, 1962, stenographer-sec., Los Angeles, 1968-70; legal stenographer U.S. Atty.'s Office, Los Angeles, 1962-67; stenographer U.S. Customs, Los Angeles, 1970-72, import specialist, 1972-82; spl. agt. Dept. Def. Investigative Services, Gardena, Calif., 1982—; past co-mgr. U.S. Customs Black Emphasis Program, 1980-82; participant Def. Dept. Quality Circle Program. Recipient scholarship Blayton Sch. Acctg., 1954; Disting. Mother Yr. award Brethren Elem. Sch., 1979-80; Black Emphasis Program award U.S. Custom Service, 1982; numerous letters commendation. Mem. Calif. State U. Alumni Assn., Los Angeles Urban League, Am. Legion Women's Aux., Am. Bus. Women's Assn. (pres. Los Angeles chpt. 1983), AAUW, NAACP, Black Womens Corp. (2d v.p.). Democrat. Mem. Christian Ch. Home: 2216 W 156th St Compton CA 90220 Office: 15110 Atkinson Ave Gardena CA 90249

BEASLEY, LEROY B., mathematician, educator; b. Shelley, Idaho, July 31, 1942; s. Lawrence Byington and Grace Vivian (Davis) B.; B.S., Idaho State U., 1964, M.S., 1966; Ph.D. in Math., U. B.C., 1969; m. Debra Anne Schaefer, July 18, 1975; children—Mia Louise, Lisa Nichelle. Instr., Treasure Valley Community Coll., Ontario, Oreg., 1966; spl. instr. math. Boise State U., 1972-75; research assoc. U. Waterloo (Ont., Can.), 1973-83; tchr. Middleton (Idaho) High Sch., 1972-81; asst. prof. math. Utah State U., Logan, 1981—; postdoctoral research fellow U. B.C., 1969; research assoc. Wilfrid Laurier U., 1978-79. NSF research grantee, 1979-80. Served with AUS, 1970-71; Vietnam. Mem. Math. Assn. Am., Am. Math. Soc., Soc. Indsl. and Applied Math., Nat., Idaho, Middleton edn. assns. Club: Masons. Contbr. articles to math. jours. Home: 125 E 700 N Logan UT 84321 Office: Dept Math Utah State U Logan UT

BEATTIE, ROBERT PRIME, ski coach, TV commentator; b. Manchester, N.H., Jan. 24, 1933; s. Robert D. and Katherine P. (Prime) B.; m. Ann Dwinell, Aug. 1956; children—Susan, Robert; m. 2d, Kiki Cutter, 1970; m. 3d, Cheryl Britton, Dec. 8, 1981. B.A., Middlebury Coll., 1955. Head ski coach U. Colo., Denver, 1956-65, asst. football coach, 1956-61; head ski Alpine coach U.S. Ski Team, Aspen, 1961-69; Olympic ski coach, 1964, 68; pres. World Wide Ski Corp., 1969—; sports commentator ABC-TV. Recipient Am. Bell award, 1983. Democrat. Unitarian. Office: PO Box 4580 Aspen CO 81612

BEATTY, BEVERLY WALKER, financial management consultant; b. Ford City, Pa., July 1, 1934; d. Henry S. and Blanche E. (Klingman) Walker; B.S., Indiana U. of Pa., 1956; children—Amy Lynn, Gregory Leigh. With payroll and personnel depts. Green-Gifford Motor Corp., Norfolk, Va., 1956-58; tchr. bookkeeping and bus. English Sharon Hill (Pa.) High Sch., 1958-62; co-owner Sunnyvale (Calif.) Vet. Clinic, 1966-79, bus. mgr., 1966—; accountant Santa Clara Valley Vet. Med. Assn., San Jose, Calif., 1969-74; accountant Santa Clara Valley Vet. Emergency Clinic, San Jose, 1973-74; staff Rosenthal & Weintraub, C.P.A.s, San Jose, Calif., 1976-78; fin. mgmt. cons., Sunnyvale, Calif., 1969—; owner Moonbeam Enterprises, Sunnyvale, 1978—; pres. A/gee Informational Services, Inc., Sunnyvale, 1979—; mng. editor Newsletter of Cares, 1983—; chief fin. officer U.S. Bear Force. Mem. Nat. Assn. Accountants, Nat. Assn. Female Execs., Sunnyvale C. of C., Better Bus. Bur., AAUW. Office: PO Box 2248 Sunnyvale CA 94087

BEATTY, GEORGE LEWIS, surgeon, ret. mil. officer; b. Kiel, Okla., May 20, 1904; s. Robert S. and Rose B. (Lewis) B.; B.S., U. Okla., 1927, M.D., 1929; m. Mary Catherine Cass, June 18, 1948; children—Rosemary (dec.), Robert A., Kathryn Beatty Anderson. Intern Fresno County (Calif.) Hosp., 1929-31; resident in surgery Letterman Gen. Hosp., San Francisco, 1939-41; practice medicine specializing in surgery; instr. S.W. PTO, 1942-44; commd. 1st lt. M.C., U.S. Army, 1932, advanced through grades to col., 1945; comdg. officer 27th Army Gen. Hosp., Philippines, 1945, New Ginea, 1944-45; chief depts. surgery U.S. Army Hosp., Ft. Ord, Calif., 1949-52, Percy Jones Gen. Hosp., Battle Creek, Mich., 1952-53, Tripler Gen. Hosp., Honolulu, 1953-56, Valley Forge Gen. Hosp., Phoenixville, Pa., 1956-57, ret., 1958; mem. surg. staff Holderman Hosp., Vets. Home, Yountville, Calif., 1958-68; chief med. officer Holderman Hosp., 1969-71; ret., 1971; surg. tng. program for interns and residents various hosp., 1939-57. Decorated Bronze Star, Legion of Merit; recipient Distinguished Service citation Calif. State Seante, 1971; diplomate Am. Bd. Surgery. Fellow A.C.S.; mem. AMA, Napa County Med. Soc., Ret. Officers Assn. Club: Marine Meml. Address: 2509 Rollingwood St Napa CA 94558

BEATTY, JAMES D., lawyer, state senator; b. La Junta, Colo., Sept. 3, 1929; B.A., Adams State U., 1951; LL.B., U. Colo., 1956; m. Mary Beatty; children—Bruce, Lila, Bob, Mike. Mem. Colo. Senate. Past pres., charter dir. United Fund; pres. disaster Com., ARC; pres. Ft. Collins (Colo.) Heart unit, Am. Heart Assn.; dir. Colo. Heart Assn.; pres. Larimer County Am. Cancer Soc.; chmn. Larimer County Mental Health Bd.; mem. White House Conf. on Youth, White Conf. on Aging, Ft. Collins Zoning Bd. Appeals, Larimer County Republican Exec. Com. Served to 1st lt. USAF, 1951-53. Mem. Jaycees (past v.p., state gen. legal counsel and parliamentarian). Clubs: Elks, Rotary (past pres., dir. Ft. Collins). Office: PO Box 1336 Fort Collins CO 80522*

BEATTY, JAMES RUSSELL, psychologist, statistician, educator; b. Huntsville, Ala., Nov. 8, 1943; s. Russell and Thelma (Wells) B.; B.A., Franklin Coll. of Ind., 1965; M.S., Ind. State U., 1968; Ph.D. (doctoral fellow), U. No. Colo., 1973; postgrad. Calif. Sch. Profl. Psychology, 1975; m. Ann Lynn Childs, Aug. 31, 1963; children—Kimberly Ann, Lynn Michelle, Susannah Elizabeth. Counselor, Ind. Dept. Corrections, 1965-67; exec. dir. Community Action Program, 1968; asst. prof. psychology Mt. Union Coll., 1968-70; clin. psychologist dir. Union Hosp. Mental Health Clinic, 1969-70; asst. prof., head psychology dept. St. Meinrad Coll., 1970-71; from asst. prof. to prof. mgmt. San Diego State U., 1973—, chmn. dept., 1980—; vis. prof. Econs. Inst., U. Colo., summers 1978-82; internat. speaker, workshop coordinator. Mem. citizens adv. com. Hardy Sch. Dist.; mgr. Little League, v.p., 1981, pres., 1983; mgr. Sr. League; soccer coach and mgr., 1981, 82, 83. Accredited personnel diplomate Am. Soc. Personnel Adminstrs.; cert. Am. Compensation Assn. Mem. Am. Psychol. Assn., Am. Inst. Decision Scis. (program co-chmn. western div. 1980), Acad. Mgmt., Am. Soc. Clin. Hypnosis, Western Acad. Mgmt., Western Psychol. Assn. Presbyterian (elder). Contbr. articles to profl. jours., chpts. to books. Home: 5144 Manhasset Dr San Diego CA 92115 Office: Dept Management San Diego State San Diego CA 92182

BEATTY, PAUL VINCENT, educational administrator; b. Anaconda, Mont., July 19, 1952; s. Matt Patrick and Davida Laura (Coughlin) B.; m. Loralee Marie Lemelin, July 27, 1975; children—Ryan, Dan. B.S. in Edn., Eastern Mont. Coll., 1974; M.A., U. Nev.-Reno, 1976. Dir. Petro Hall, residence halls Eastern Mont. Coll., Billings, 1974, Manzanita, Juniper Halls U. Nev.-Reno, 1974-77; counselor North Toole County High Sch., Sunburst, Mont., 1977-82, Mont. Coll. Mineral Sci. and Tech., 1983—, also fgn. student adviser, dir. orientation. Mem. Am. Personnel and Guidance Assn., Mont. Personnel and Guidance Assn., Nat. Assn. Fgn. Student Affairs, North Toole County Jaycees (McAlpine award 1980-81). Roman Catholic. Lodge: Rotary. Home: 110 Milky Way Butte MT 59701

BEATY, DAVID WILEY, electronics and wildlife telemetry equipment mfg. co. exec.; b. Williams, Ariz., June 27, 1942; s. Clyde W. and Maybell L. (Neer) B.; student elec. engring., Mesa (Ariz.) Community Coll., 1966-68, Ariz. State U., Tempe, 1964-69; m. Betty Roselle Cooley, Aug. 14, 1960; children—David, Robert, Aaron, Amber, Stacy, William, Sophie. Photographer and technician Kolb Bros. Studios, Grand Canyon, Ariz., 1959-60; optical technician Apache Optical Labs., Inc., Mesa, 1960-61; service technician and salesman O.S. Stapley Co., Mesa, 1961-63; elec. engring. technician Govt. Electronics div. Motorola, Inc., Scottsdale, Ariz., 1963-65, reliability engr., 1965-68, quality assurance project mgr., 1968-71, group leader spl. projects sect., 1971-73, sr. engr. surface communications sect., 1973-76; mng. dir. Telonics Inc., Mesa, 1974—, sec., treas., 1978—; guest lectr. wildlife telemetry/instrumentation for continuing edn. seminars, various univs., 1976—. Mem. The Wildlife Soc. (award 1970), Amateur Radio Relay League. Mormon. Patentee inductive bone conduction audio relay system. Office: 932 E Impala Ave Mesa AZ 85204

BEAUMONT, MONA M., artist; b. Paris, Jan. 1, 1927; came to U.S., 1942, naturalized, 1945; d. Jacques Hippolyte and Elsie M. (Didisheim) Marx; B.A., U. Calif.-Berkeley, 1945, M.A., 1946; postgrad. Harvard U., 1945-46, Fogg Mus., Cambridge, 1945-46, Hans Hoffman Studios, N.Y.C., 1946; m. William G. Beaumont, Dec. 20, 1946; children—Garrett, Kevin. One-woman shows at Galeria Proteo, Mexico City, 1960, Gumps Gallery, San Francisco, 1962, 64, 65, Palace of Legion of Honor, San Francisco, 1964, L'Armitiere Gallery, Rouen, France, 1966, Hoover Gallery, San Francisco, 1967, San Francisco Mus. Modern Art, 1968, Galeria Van der Voort, San Francisco, 1969, William Sawyer Gallery, San Francisco, 1972, Palo Alto (Calif.) Cultural Center, 1975, Galerie Alexandre Monnet, Brussels, 1974, Honolulu Acad. Arts, 1980; exhibited in group shows at San Francisco Mus. Modern Art, 1954, 57, 68, San Francisco Art Inst., 1958-74, DeYoung Meml. Mus., San Francisco, 1960-62, Grey Found. Tour of Asia, 1963, Bell Telephone Invitational, Chgo., 1968, Richmond Art Center, 1968, Los A,,geles County Mus. Art, 1973, Galerie Zodiaque, Geneva, 1974, others; represented in permanent collections: Oakland (Calif.) Mus. Art, City and County of San Francisco, Hoover Found., San Francisco, Grey Found., Washington, Bulart Found., San Francisco; also numerous pvt. collections. Recipient Jack London Sq. Ann. Painting award, 1965; Purchase award Grey Found., 1963; Ann. award San Francisco Women Artists, 1966, 68; Purchase award San Francisco Art Festival, 1966; One-Man Show award San Francisco Art Festival, 1975; included in 1982-83, 83-84 Printworld International. Mem. Soc. for Encouragement of Contemporary Art, Bay Area Graphic Arts Council, San Francisco Art Inst., Archives of Am. Art, San Francisco Mus. Modern Art, Delta Epsilon, Delta Chi Alpha. Address: 1087 Upper Happy Valley Rd Lafayette CA 94549

BEAVERS, MARY EISELE, clinical psychologist; b. Chgo., Oct. 3, 1939; d. Charles Wesley and Blanche Mae (Kennell) Eisele; m. David Peter Adam, 1961 (div.); m. 2d, Ronald Beavers, 1969 (div.); 1 son, John Miller Adam. B.A. in History cum laude, Radcliffe Coll., 1962; M.A., U. Ariz., 1970, Ph.D. in Psychology, 1973. Cert. psychologist, Ariz. Clin. psychologist Student Counseling Service, U. Ariz., Tucson, 1972-76, asst. dir., 1976—, acting dir., 1980, dir. univ.-wide honors program, 1980—, lectr. dept. psychology, 1973-75; Ariz. coordinator Catalyst Network for Nat. Women's Info. Co-founder Tucson Gilbert & Sullivan Theatre, 1966, bd. dirs., 1966-71; mem. Ariz. Opera Co. Chorus, 1975—; mem. adminstrv. bd. St. Francis in the Foothills Meth. Ch., 1978-81. Recipient faculty achievement award U. Ariz. Alumni Assn., 1983; NIMH fellow, 1968-69. Mem. Am. Psychol. Assn., Ariz. Psychol. Assn., So. Ariz. Psychol. Assn., Ariz. Group Psychotherapy Soc., Internat. Transactional Analysis Assn., Nat. Collegiate Honors Council. Democrat. Contbr. articles to profl. jours. Office: Honors Program Math Bldg 507 U Ariz Tucson AZ 85721

BEAZLIE, HORACE VAN HOUTEN, mktg. and public relations cons.; b. Newport News, Va., Aug. 26, 1916; s. John Washington and Ethel May (Van Houten) B.; student Union Coll., Cranford, N.J., 1934-37, U. Hawaii, 1973-78; B.B.A., Hawaii Pacific Coll., 1983; m. Natsuko Nakasone, Oct. 2, 1947; children—Mark, David, Karla, Nadine. Purchasing agt. Davis Engring. Corp., 1935-39; expeditor Air Assos., Inc., 1939-40; XP47B project buyer Republic Aviation Corp., 1940-41; dir. procurement Simmonds Aerocessories, Ltd., 1941-44; asst. mgr. machinery sales The Hawaii Corp., 1948-50; v.p., gen. mgr. W.H. Male, Inc. (became McCann-Erickson, Hawaii), 1950-61; mgr. mktg. communications Lewers & Cooke subs., Champion Internat., 1961-67; mgr. community relations Dillingham Corp., Honolulu, 1967-71; adminstr. public info. Hawaiian Electric Co., Inc., Honolulu, 1971-73, dir. public info., 1973-82; mktg. and public relations cons., 1982— cons., lectr. SBA. Chmn. Hawaii Joint Council on Econ. Edn., 1969-70. Served as officer with USNR, 1944-48. Named Hawaii Adman of Year, Am. Advt. Fedn., 1965-66. Mem. Public Relations Soc. Am. (accredited, pres. Hawaii chpt., 1968-69, del. nat. assembly, 1969-71), Internat. Public Relations Assn., Honolulu Press Club. mktg. and public relations cons.; b. Newport News, Va., Aug. 26, 1916; s. John Washington and Ethel May (Van Houten) B.; student Union Coll., Cranford, N.J., 1934-37, U. Hawaii, 1973-78; B.B.A., Hawaii Pacific Coll., 1983; m. Natsuko Nakasone, Oct. 2, 1947; children—Mark, David, Karla, Nadine. Purchasing agt. Davis Engring. Corp., 1935-39; expeditor Air Assos., Inc., 1939-40; XP47B project buyer Republic Aviation Corp., 1940-41; dir. procurement Simmonds Aerocessories, Ltd., 1941-44; asst. mgr. machinery sales The Hawaii Corp., 1948-50; v.p., gen. mgr. W.H. Male, Inc. (became McCann-Erickson, Hawaii), 1950-61; mgr. mktg. communications Lewers & Cooke subs., Champion Internat., 1961-67; mgr. community relations Dillingham Corp., Honolulu, 1967-71; adminstr. public info. Hawaiian Electric Co., Inc., Honolulu, 1971-73, dir. public info., 1973-82; mktg. and public relations cons., 1982— cons., lectr. SBA. Chmn. Hawaii Joint Council on Econ. Edn., 1969-70. Served as officer with USNR, 1944-48. Named Hawaii Adman of Year, Am. Advt. Fedn., 1965-66. Mem. Public Relations Soc. Am. (accredited, pres. Hawaii chpt., 1968-69, del. nat. assembly, 1969-71), Internat. Public Relations Assn., Honolulu Press Club. Office: 337-D Kihapai St Kailua HI 96734

BEBER-VANZO, ALBERT JOHN, architect; b. San Francisco, Apr. 13, 1928; s. Antonio and Angelina (Damele) B.-V.; m. Josephine F.

Stadler, Mar. 12, 1956; children—Paul Martin, David John, Bryan Anthony, Francesca Lyn. Archtl. apprentice Falk & Booth, 1954-58, John Carl Warneke, architect, 1959; with Simpson, Stratta & Assos., architects and engrs., 1959-67; architect Kaiser Found. hosps., research and planning med. centers, 1967-76; hosp. architect N.T. Enloe Meml. Hosp., 1976-79; univ. architect U. Calif., San Francisco, 1979—. Served with AUS, 1950-52. Address: 607 Main St Sausalito CA 94965

BECCUE-BROWN, DIANA LYNN, public relations executive, consultant; b. Denver, Sept. 1, 1955; d. Charles Henry and Helen Eileen (Warner) Beccue; m. Robert Edward Brown, Sept. 26, 1981. B.S. in Home Econs., Colo. State U., 1977. Food technologist Keebler Corp. Mfg. Tech. Center, Denver, 1977-78; consumer cons. Colo. Beef Promotion Bd., Denver, 1979-82; mgr. membership promotion Am. Waterworks Assn., Denver, 1982; acct. supr. pub. relations Sam Lusky Assocs. Inc., Denver, 1982—; specialist food and beverage promotion. Bd. dirs. unit Am. Cancer Soc. Home: 5412 Newton St Denver CO 80221 Office: Sam Lusky Assocs Inc 633 17th St Suite 1616 Denver CO 80202

BECHT, ADELINE CHARLOTTE, counselor, rehabilitation therapist, researcher, consultant; b. Muskegan, Mich., Mar. 11, 1937. B.A. in Psychology, Cascade Coll., 1964; M.Ed. in Counseling and Guidance, Lewis and Clark Coll., 1976; M.A. in Clin. Psychology, U. Oreg., 1982, Ph.D. in Counseling Psychology, 1982, Ph.D. in Clin. Psychology, 1982. Library asst., researcher Tektronix, Inc., Beaverton, Oreg., 1965-72; vis. lectr. deaf specialist tng. program Oreg. Coll. Edn., Monmouth, 1974-80; cons. on deafness, blindness, deaf-blindness, mental health care to the handicapped Riverside Psychiat. Hosp., Portland, 1974—; vis. lectr. Lewis and Clark Coll., Portland, 1971—; founder, exec. dir., dir. programs and program devel. Living Rehab. Ctr. Inc., Portland, 1971-81; practice psychology Portland, 1981—; practicum counselor Wash. State Sch. For Blind, Vancouver, 1976; sponsor, counselor Alcoholics Anonymous, Portland, 1962-70; counselor Hillcrest State Sch. Girls, 1962-65; asst. to social worker White Shield Home for Unwed Mothers, Portland, 1959-64; entertainer instns. for socially and physically handicapped, 1959-64. Recipient Spl. citation Oreg. Gov.'s Com. on Employment of Handicapped 1970, award NCCJ, 1976; Service to Mankind award Sertoma Internat., 1977. Mem. Am. Personnel and Guidance Assn., Am. Psychol. Assn., Internat. Platform Assn. Lodge: Masons. Developed effective methods for communicating with deaf-blind persons. Home and Office: 6108 SE Milwaukee Ave Portland OR 97202

BECHT, PAUL FREDERICK, lawyer, state senator; b. Marshfield, Wis., Sept. 14, 1937; s. Frederick Andrew and Beatrice Isabelle (Murphy) B.; student Marquette U., 1955-56, U. Wis., 1957-58; B.S., Wis. State U., 1961; M.A., U. Ill., 1963; J.D., U. N.Mex., 1977; children—William Andrew, Stephen Irving, Lucinda. Mgmt. systems analyst Sandia Labs., 1962-74; purchasing agt. State of N.Mex., 1968-70; admitted to N.Mex. bar, 1977; gen. counsel Western Holding Co., 1978-79; individual practice law, Albuquerque, 1979—; mem. N.Mex. State Senate, 1973—. Bd. dirs. Drug Addicts Recovery Enterprises, Fellowship Christian Athletes. Mem. Am. Bar Assn., N.Mex. Bar Assn., Assn. Trial Lawyers Am., Am. Legis. Exchange Council, Christian Legal Soc. Republican. Roman Catholic. Club: Elks. Office: 110 Quincy St NE Albuquerque NM 87108*

BECHTEL, STEPHEN DAVISON, JR., engineering executive; b. Oakland, Calif., May 10, 1925; s. Stephen Davison and Laura (Peart) B.; B.S., Purdue U., 1946, Dr. Engring. (hon.), 1972; M.B.A., Stanford, 1948; D.Sc. (hon.), U. Colo., 1981; m. Elizabeth Mead Hogan, June 5, 1948; 5 children. Engring. and mgmt. positions Bechtel Corp., San Francisco, 1941-60, pres., 1960-73, chmn. of cos. in Bechtel group, 1973-80, chmn. Bechtel Group, Inc., 1980—; dir. Hanna Mining Co., IBM Co., So. Pacific Co. Mem. Bus. Council; life councillor, past chmn. Conf. Bd.; mem. Presdl. Com. on Urban Housing, 1967-69; mem. Nat. Indsl. Pollution Control Council, 1970-73, Nat. Productivity Commn., 1971-74; mem. Cost of Living Council, 1973-74; mem. Nat. Commn. Indsl. Peace, 1973-74, Labor-Mgmt. Group, 1974—, Nat. Action Council on Minorities in Engring., 1974—. Trustee, Calif. Inst. Tech. Served with USMC, 1943-46. Decorated officer French Legion of Honor; recipient Disting. Alumnus award Purdue U., 1964; Ernest C. Arbuckle Disting. Alumnus award Stanford U., 1974; Man of Yr., Engring. News-Record, 1974; Outstanding Achievement in Constrn. award Moles, 1977; Disting. Engring. Alumnus award U. Colo., 1979; Herbert Hoover medal, 1981; Chmn.'s award AAES, 1982. Registered profl. engr., N.Y., Mich., Alaska, Calif., Md., Hawaii, Ohio, D.C., Va. Fellow ASCE, Inst. Chem. Engrs. (U.K.) (hon.); mem. Nat. Acad. Engring. (chmn.; fin. com. 1975-77); AIME, Calif. Acad. Scis. (hon. trustee), Chi Epsilon, Tau Beta Pi. Clubs: Pacific Union (San Francisco); Claremont Country (Oakland, Calif.); Cypress Point (Monterey Peninsula, Calif.); Thunderbird Country (Palm Springs, Calif.); Vancouver (B.C.); Ramada (Houston); Bohemian, San Francisco Golf (San Francisco); Links, Blind Brook (N.Y.C.); Augusta (Ga.) National Golf; York (Toronto); Mount Royal (Montreal). Office: 50 Beale St San Francisco CA 94105

BECHTOL, ROBERT CARROLL, surgeon; b. Binghamton, N.Y., May 31, 1917; s. Clarence Miles and Hazel I. (Forse) B.; B.S., U. Ill., 1940, M.D., 1942; m. Sarah Margaret Graham, June 14, 1942; children—Margaret (Mrs. S. J. Tillinghast), Robert Miles, John Frederick. Intern, Los Angeles County Gen. Hosp., 1943; resident in surgery U. Ill. Research Hosp., 1947-50; practice medicine specializing in orthopaedic surgery, Stockton, Calif., 1950-52, Santa Rosa, Calif., 1952—; instr. U. Ill., Chgo., 1947-50; mem. staffs Santa Rosa Meml. Hosp., chmn. dept., 1956; mem. staff Warrack Med. Hosp., Santa Rosa Gen. Hosp., Community Hosp. Sonoma County; clin. asst. Dept. Orthopaedic Surgery Queen's Coll., Dundee, Scotland. Served to capt., AUS, 1943-46. Diplomate Am. Bd. Orthopaedic Surgery. Fellow A.C.S., Internat. Coll. Surgeons; mem. Assn. Am. Physicians and Surgeons, Internat. Arthroscopy Assn., Am. Acad. Orthopaedic Surgeons, Western Orthopaedic Assn., Royal Soc. of Medicine, John Birch Soc., S.A.R., Astron. Soc. Pacific, Am. Defense Preparedness Assn., Alpha Kappa Kappa. Contbr. articles on orthopaedic radiology to med. jours., also chpts. in books. Office: 1154 Montgomery Dr Santa Rosa CA 95405

BECK, CYNTHIA MARIE, food service company executive, personnel trainer; b. Lynwood, Calif., Oct. 30, 1956; d. Herbert Paul and Phyllis Jean (West) Beck. B.A. in Communications, U. Colo., 1978. Sales rep. E & J Gallo Co., Denver, 1978-79; account service rep. Weyerhaeuser Co., San Francisco, 1980-81; mktg. dir. Michel & Pelton Chems. Co., 1981-83; trainer tng. and devel. Saga Corp. Menlo Park, Calif., 1983—; sales trainer careers for women; cons. in field. Exec. advisor Bay Area Jr. Achievement. Mem. Am. Soc. Tng. and Devel. Republican. Mem. Unity Ch. Club: Toastmasters Internat.

BECK, EARL WILBUR, silicone tech. specialist; b. Toledo, Oct. 27, 1925; s. Jacob Wilbur and Linda Elizabeth (Weichel) B.; student Bowling Green State U., 1943-44, U. Notre Dame, 1944-45; B.Ch.E., U. Toledo, 1948; postgrad. San Francisco State Coll., 1960-61; m. Ruth Miller, Sept. 3, 1949; children—Cynthia, Lorraine. Chemist, Dow Chem. Co., 1948-50; lab. supr. Dow Corning Corp., Midland, Mich., 1950-60, applications engr., Elizabethtown, Ky., 1965-68, sr. tech. service and devel. specialist, Costa Mesa, Calif., 1968—; materials engr. Sandia Corp., Livermore, Calif., 1960-65; lectr. on silicone. Served to lt. (j.g.) USNR, 1943-46. Recipient Chem. Engring. Achievement award McGraw-Hill Pub. Co., 1955. Mem. Los Angeles Rubber Group, No. Calif. Rubber Group, Soc. Advancement Materials and Process Engring. Republican. Clubs: Masons, Shriners. Home: 209 Springfield #3 Huntington Beach CA 92648 Office: 18008 Skypark Blvd Irvine CA 92714

BECK, GEORGE RICHARD, real estate investment exec.; b. Hanford, Calif., Jan. 18, 1917; s. George Anthony and Mabel (Strunk) B.; B.S., U. Calif. at Berkeley, 1938; postgrad. Harvard, Mass. Inst. Tech.; m. Mary Elizabeth Russell, Aug. 17, 1940; children—Elizabeth Rae, Richard Russell. Surveyor Kings County, Calif., 1938-40; mineral rights appraiser Kings County, 1940-42; radio engr. Fed. Telephone and Radio Corp., Newark, 1946-50; product devel. engr. Hughes Aircraft Co., Culver City, Calif., 1950-53; program mgr. Bendix Pacific, North Hollywood, Calif., 1954-57; sr. staff radioplane div. Northrop Corp., Van Nuys, Calif., 1958; product engring. mgr. TRW Systems, Redondo Beach, Calif., 1959-70; v.p. administrn. Altrad Corp., Tarzana, Calif., 1970-71; investment mktg. Burreson Investment Co., Inc., North Hollywood, 1971-73; v.p. mktg. Mariel Realty, Inc., Canoga Park, Calif., 1973-76; pres. George Beck & Assocs., Inc., real estate investments, Woodland Hills, Calif., 1976—. Scoutmaster, Boy Scouts Am.; bd. dirs. Valley Youth Cathedral, Inc., Northridge, Calif. Served to lt. comdr. USNR, 1942-46. Mem. IEEE (sr.), Nat. Assn. Realtors, Los Angeles Bd. Realtors, San Fernando Valley Bd. Realtors, Inst. Cert. Bus. Counselors, Calif. Assn. Realtors, Internat. Exchangers Assn., Gideons Internat., Naval Res. Assn., Internat. Platform Assn. Baptist. Contbr. articles to sci. mags. Home: 24153 Gilmore St Canoga Park CA 91307 Office: 6355 Topanga Canyon Blvd Woodland Hills CA 91367

BECK, JOHN ROLAND, biological and business consultant; b. Las Vegas, N.Mex., Feb. 26, 1929; s. Roland Lycurgus and Betty Lind (Shrock) B.; B.S., Okla. A&M Coll., 1950; postgrad. U. Tex., 1954; M.S., Okla. State U., 1957; postgrad. George Washington U., 1965; m. Doris Aliene Olson, Feb. 9, 1951; children—Elizabeth Joan, Thomas Roland, Patricia Lind, John William. Biologist, King Ranch, Tex., 1950-51; wildlife mgmt. fellow Okla. A&M Coll., 1951, asst. instr., 1952-53; instr. physiology U. Tenn., 1954-55; control agt. U.S. Fish and Wildlife Service, N.D., 1953-54, research biologist, Idaho, 1955-57, control biologist, Ohio, 1957-65, Va., 1967-69; dir. Job Corps Center, U.S. Dept. Interior, Okla., 1965-67; v.p. Bio-Serv Corp., Troy, Mich., 1969-78; prin. Biol. Environ. Cons. Services, Phoenix 1978—; pres., lic. operator Ariz. Pest Control, Prescott; partner B & H Devel. Co.; lectr. preventive medicine Ohio Coll. Vet. Medicine, 1957-65; lectr. econ. biology Bowling Green State U., 1958-76; faculty asso. Ariz. State U., 1980—; grain sanitation cons. Ohio Grain and Feed Dealers Assn., 1958-65; mem. Interag. Bd.-U.S. Civil Service Examiners, Dallas, 1965-67; mem. Ohio Gov.'s Com. on Pesticides, 1961-63; chmn. adv. bd. pesticide tech. Ferris State Coll., 1972-76, mem. adv. bd. Sch. Allied Health, 1977-79, mem. pesticide adv. com. Mich. Dept. Agr., 1977-79. Bd. dirs. Braes of Bloomfield, 1970-72, pres., 1971; bd. dirs. Birmingham YMCA, Detroit YMCA. Registered sanitarian, Ariz., Ohio; cert. wildlife biologist. Fellow Explorers Club, Royal Soc. Health (London); mem. Mich. Pest Control Operators Assn. (pres. 1970-72, dir. 1973-76), Nat. Pest Control Assn. (dir. 1972-75, award 1970, chmn. reorgn. com. 1976-78), ASTM (chmn. com. on vertebrate pesticides 1973-78, chmn. Symposium on vertebrate control test methods 1978, chmn. com. pesticides 1980-82), Nat. Environ. Health Assn., Wildlife Soc., Entomol. Soc. Am., Pi Chi Omega (dir. 1972-78, pres. 1977). Republican. Baptist (deacon 1957-75). Clubs: Masons, Rotary (chmn. youth support com. Detroit 1972-73). Contbr. articles to profl. publs.; bus. editor Pest Control mag., 1982—. Home: 3631 W Pasadena Phoenix AZ 85019

BECK, LINDA L., management consultant, realtor; b. Roundup, Mont., Sept. 25, 1940; d. Don E. and Clare Elizabeth (Alexander) Belcher; m. Rick B. Beck, Apr. 8, 1967 (div.). B.S. in Secondary Edn., Eastern Mont. Coll., 1967. Tchr., Omaha Women's Job Corps Ctr., 1967-69; caseworker Cunningham Children's Home, Urbana, Ill., 1969-71; staff cons. Ralston Purina Co., St. Louis, 1971-79; mgr. tng. and devel. div. Van Camp Sea Food Co., San Diego, 1979-81, ptnr. L & L Assocs., Billings, Mont., 1981—; cons., trainer. Mem. Am. Soc. Tng. and Devel. (pres. chpt. 1982-83), Nat. Assn. Profl. Cons. Republican. Roman Catholic. Office: PO Box 2415 Billings MT 59103

BECK, NICHOLS COLER, elementary school principal; b. Koloa Kauai, Hawaii, Dec. 8, 1939; s. Luther Clagett and Virginia (Coler) B.; m. Pam Wilcox, Dec. 29, 1962; children: David, Hobey. B.A., U. So. Calif., 1962; M.Ed., U. Hawaii, 1967. Tchr., Kapaa High and Internat. Sch., 1964-66; instr. Iona Coll., N.Z., 1967-68, Kauai Community Coll., 1970; vice prin. Kapaa High and Internat. Sch., 1970-73; vice prin. Kilauea and Hanalei (Hawaii) Elem. Schs., 1973-77, prin., 1977—. Pres., Hanalei Community Assn., 1970-73; chmn. Northshore Adv. Com., 1981-83; bd. dirs. Hanalei Mus., 1964-83, East Kauai Soil and Water Conservation Dist., 1970-79, Hawaii Mus. Assn., 1976. Recipient Goodyear Environ. Edn. award, 1978. Mem. Assn. Supervision and Curriculum Devel., Nat. Assn. Elem. Sch. Prins., Am. Assn. State and Local History. Club: Hanalei Hawn Civic Canoe.

BECK, RICHARD PAUL, computer co. exec.; b. St. Johnsbury, Vt., May 12, 1933; s. Harold Conrad and Ruth (Taylor) B.; B.S., Babson Coll., 1957, M.B.A., 1960; m. Judith A. McCarthy. Asst. controller Cool-Ray, Inc., Boston, 1960-63; v.p., treas. Controlled Environment, Inc., Whitman, Mass., 1963-68; pres., dir. Particle Tech., Inc., Sunnyvale, Calif., 1968-70; exec. v.p., dir. Apogee Chem. Co., Inc., Richmond, Calif., 1970-71; v.p., treas. MB Assos., San Ramon, Calif., 1971-72; partner San Francisco Cons., 1972-75; prin. Beck & Assos., 1975-76; sr. v.p., treas., dir. HealthGarde Corp., Salt Lake City, 1976-77; exec. v.p., treas. Beehive Internat., Salt Lake City, 1978—. Served with USAF, 1950-54. Home: 1 Payday Dr Box 1256 Park City UT 84060

BECK, ROGER D., public relations counselor, educator; b. Pitts., Oct. 20, 1921; s. Jules D. and Flora M. (Malloy) B.; children—Mark, Andee. Student Law Sch., Southwestern U., 1954-55; H.H.D. (hon.), Los Angeles Coll. Chiropractic, 1979. With various Los Angeles wire services and newspapers, 1945-62; account supr. Harshe-Rotman & Druck, pub. relations, Los Angeles, 1962-67; pres. Roger Beck Pub. Relations, Sherman Oaks, Calif., 1967—; instr. in pub. relations Calif. State U.-Northridge. Mem. citizens adv. council to city councilman, Los Angeles. Served with U.S. N.G., 1940-41, USAAF, 1941-45. Mem. Pub. Relations Soc. Am. (accredited), Greater Los Angeles Press Club, Mensa. Contbr. numerous articles to mags. Home: 17139 Nanette St Granada Hills CA 91344 Office: 4348 Van Nuys Blvd Suite 208 Sherman Oaks CA 91403

BECK, THEODORE RICHARD, chem. engr.; b. Seattle, Apr. 11, 1926; s. Theodore and Gudmunda Elin (Thorarinsdottir) B.; B.S., U. Wash., 1949, M.S., 1950, Ph.D., 1952; m. Ruth Elizabeth Schaumberger, Dec. 1, 1951; children—Randi Marie, Maren Louisa. Research engr. duPont Corp., Deepwater, N.J., 1952-54; group leader Kaiser Aluminum & Chem. Corp., Permanente, Calif., 1954-59; sect. head Am. Potash & Chem. Corp., Henderson, Nev., 1959-61; tech. staff Boeing Co., Seattle, 1961-65; sr. basic research scientist, 1965-72; div. mgr. Flow Research, Inc., Kent, Wash., 1972-75; pres. Electrochem. Tech. Corp., Seattle, 1975—. Guest lectr. U. Wash., 1963-64, research prof., 1972—; cons. Argonne Nat. Labs., 1973—. Bd. dirs. North Cascades Conservation Council, Seattle, 1973—, Seattle Youth Symphony Orch., 1975-79. Mem. AAAS, Am. Chem. Soc. (chmn. Puget Sound sect. 1971), Electrochem. Soc. (div. chmn. 1968-70, dir. 1968-78, pres. 1975-76), Am. Inst. Chem. Engrs. (chmn. South Nev. sect. 1961), Internat. Soc. Electrochemistry (chmn. electrochem. engring. div. 1978—), Nat. Assn. Corrosion Engrs., Sigma Xi, Tau Beta Pi, Phi Lambda Upsilon. Editor corrosion div. Jour. Electrochem. Soc., 1971-75. Contbr. to profl. jours. Patentee in field. Home: 10035 31st Ave NE Seattle WA 98125 Office: 3935 Leary Way NW Seattle WA 98107

BECKER, ARLIE BEACH, assn. exec.; b. Culbertson, Mont., Dec. 15, 1918; s. John Thomas and Ada (Livesay) B.; student Golden Gate Coll., 1948-49, San Francisco State Coll., 1957-58; m. Frances Adelaide Landess, Apr. 18, 1943; children—Lawrence Beach, Bruce Alan. Served as chief storekeeper USN, 1937-56, ret., 1956, instr. Naval ROTC, U. Calif.-Berkeley, 1946-48; real estate broker, 1948—; housing mgr. San Francisco State Coll., 1956-64; staff officer U. Calif.-Berkeley, 1964-75; sec. Calif. Bodies, Ancient and Accepted Scottish Rite, San Francisco, 1977—, sec. Calif. Scottish Rite Found., 1981—. Cubmaster, Boy Scouts Am., 1954. Mem. Calif. Assn. Coll. and Univ. Housing Officers (pres. 1962-63), Am. Legion. Clubs: Masons, Shriners, Commonwealth of Calif., Presidio Army Golf, Nat. Sojourners, Royal Order Jesters, Royal Order Scotland, San Francisco Bible Breakfast. Home: 240 5th Ave San Francisco CA 94118 Office: 2850 19th Ave San Francisco CA 94132

BECKER, CAROL SUE, psychologist, educator; b. Sault Ste. Marie, Mich., July 14, 1942; d. Bernard P. and Violet (Plankey) B. B.A., Mercy Coll. of Detroit, 1964; M.A., Duquesne U., 1968, Ph.D., 1973. Lic. psychologist, Calif. Lectr. psychology Duquesne U., Pitts., 1972-73; asst. prof. clin. psychology Calif. Sch. Profl. Psychology, Berkeley, 1978—; pvt. practice clin. psychology, Berkeley, 1980—; assoc. prof. human devel. Calif. State U.-Hayward, 1973—. Mem. Am. Psychol. Assn., Calif. State Psychol. Assn., Assn. Lesbian and Gay Psychologists, Western Psychol. Assn., Calif. Council on Gerontology and Geriatrics. Home: 6471 Heather Ridge Way Oakland CA 94611 Office: Dept Human Devel Calif State Univ Hayward CA 94542

BECKER, DONALD LEO, pathologist; b. Boulder, Colo., Apr. 12, 1923; s. Frederick E. and Frances E. (Donaldson) B.; B.S., U. Denver, 1943; M.D., U. Colo., 1946; M.S. in Pathology, U. Minn., 1952; m. Katheryn Jenkins, Mar. 18, 1947; children—Alan D., Ann M., Janet M. Intern, Montreal (Que., Can.) Gen. Hosp., 1947-48; chief pathologist Meml. Hosp. Natrona County, Casper, Wyo., 1952—; cons. Carbon County, Campbell County, Converse County meml. hosps.; vis. lectr. U. Wyo. Served with M.C., AUS, 1947-49. Fellow Am. Soc. Clin. Pathologists, Coll. Am. Pathologists; mem. Wyo., Natrona County med. socs., others. Contbr. articles to med. jours. Home: 2915 Nob Hill Dr Casper WY 82601 Office: 1233 E 2d St Casper WY 82601

BECKER, ELEANOR FRIEDMAN, psychologist; b. Bishop, Calif., July 16, 1952; d. Norman H. and Marie (McCain) Friedman. B.A., New Coll. Calif., 1979; M.A., Lewis and Clark Coll., 1982; cert. sexuality and disability ednl. counselor U. Calif.-San Francisco, 1979. Social services counselor Kaiser Hosp., Vallejo, Calif., 1978-79; program mgr. Sho-Craft Sheltered Workshop, Vancouver, Wash., 1980; mental health specialist St. Vincent's Hosp., Portland, Oreg., 1981-82, Cedar Hills Psychiat. Hosp., Portland, 1980-82; mental health specialist for families Tualatin Valley Mental Health Ctr., Cedar Mill, Oreg., 1983—; vocat. rehab. counselor Oreg. State, 1983—; govt. liaison worker Oreg. Mental Health Counselors Assn., Portland. U. Calif.-San Francisco Med. Sch. tuition scholar, 1978. Mem. Oreg. Psychol. Assn., Oreg. Personnel and Guidance Assn., Oreg. Mental Health Counselors Assn. Jewish. Author: Female Sexuality Following Spinal Cord Injury, 1978. Office: 13200 SW Glenn Ct Beaverton OR 97005

BECKER, FREDERICK PAUL, real estate co. exec.; b. Logan, Kans., Sept. 2, 1926; s. Fred and Emma (States) B.; certificate in real estate, U. Calif. at Los Angeles, 1960; m. Neta F. Simpson, Mar. 25, 1954; children—Cynthia Diane, Jerry Lee, Patricia Ann, Frederick Paul. Mgr., Branham Realty Co., Burbank, Calif., 1947-60, mgr. P.W.C. Realtors, Burbank, 1961-68, v.p., 1968-81; v.p. Merrill Lynch Realty, 1981—; lectr. U. Calif. at Los Angeles, 1959-61; instr. Calif. Assn. Realtors, 1960—, Realtors Nat. Mktg. Inst., 1967—. Served with USAAF, World War II. Mem. Calif. Assn. Realtors (v.p. 1971), Burbank Bd. Realtors (pres. 1965). Rotarian. Contbr. articles to profl. jours. Home: 912 Scenic Way Ventura CA 93003 Office: 1501 W Magnolia Blvd Burbank CA 91506

BECKER, GEORGE, JR., educator; b. Stevens Point, Wis., July 21, 1935; s. George Charles and Irene Alvina (Klein) B.; student Wis. State Coll., 1953-56; B.S., U. Minn., 1960; M.S., U. Wis., 1962, Ph.D., 1965; m. Irene Blanche Colvin, Aug. 29, 1964; children—Lisa Anne, Julie Renee, Grant Charles. Asst. prof. biology U. Wis.-Whitewater, 1964-66; asst. prof. biology Met. State Coll., Denver, 1966-69, asso. prof., 1969-72, prof., 1972—, chmn. dept., 1971—. Served with USMCR, 1956-58. Recipient Disting. Service award Met. State Coll., 1978-79. Mem. Am. Inst. Biol. Scis., AAUP, Entomol. Soc. Am., Sigma Xi, Gamma Sigma Delta, Xi Sigma Pi. Author: Introductory Concepts of Biology, 1972; also tech. papers. Home: 2903 S Otis St Denver CO 80227 Office: 1006 11th St Denver CO 80204

BECKER, LARRY EUGENE, dermatologist; b. Sioux City, Iowa, Nov. 8, 1943; s. Lawrence and JoAn Denice (Rembe) B.; B.S. in Zoology, Iowa State U., 1966; M.D., U. Iowa, 1969; m. Dorothy Jean Smith, Aug. 13, 1966; children—Douglas Paul, Bradley David. Commd. 2d lt. M.C., U.S. Army, 1968, advanced through grades to maj., 1972; intern Tripler Gen. Hosp., Honolulu, 1969-70; flight surgeon Ft. Campbell (Ky.) Army Hosp., 1970-71; resident in dermatology Walter Reed Army Med. Center, 1971-74; staff dermatologist William Beaumont Army Med. Center, 1974-76; resigned, 1976; clin. asso. prof. Tex. Tech. U. Med. Sch., 1975-76; asst. prof. medicine U. N.Mex. Med. Sch., 1976-79, asso. prof., 1979—, dir. div. dermatology, 1979—; com. mem. N.Mex. Skin Cancer project, 1978—. Decorated Army Commendation medal. Diplomate Am. Bd. Dermatology (dermatopathology). Fellow Am. Acad. Dermatology, Royal Soc. Tropical Medicine and Hygiene, A.C.P.; mem. Soc. Investigative Dermatology, AMA, Pacific Dermatol. Assn. Republican. Mem. Community Ch. of Sandias. Author or co-author papers in field. Home: PO Box 68 Sandia Park NM 87047 Office: 2701 Frontier St NE Room 268 Surge Bldg Albuquerque NM 87131

BECKER, MADGE JOSEPHINE MOORE, librarian; b. Portland, Oreg., Sept. 1, 1928; d. Jesse William and Madge Johnson (Guthrie) M.; m. Henry C. Becker, Jr., Jan. 30, 1970. B.A., Western Coll. for Women, Oxford, Ohio, 1949; M.S., U. Ill., 1952. Gen. asst. New Castle-Henry County (Ind.) Library, 1949-51; br. librarian Library Assn., Portland, Oreg., 1951-54; br. supr./adminstrv. asst. Yakima Valley Regional Library, Yakima, Wash., 1954-59; field librarian U.S. Army Spl. Services, Germany, 1959-61; county librarian Plumas County, Quincy, Calif., 1961-64; city librarian City of Longview (Wash.), 1964-71, City of Vallejo (Calif.), 1971-74; acting county librarian Solano County, Fairfield, Calif., 1973-74, county librarian, 1974—. Sec., Calif. Inst. Libraries, 1978-79; sec. Solano Library Authority, 1975—; mem. adv. bd. Lower Columbia Community Coll., 1969-70; bd. dirs., pres. bd. Lower Columbia Community Action Council, OEO, 1965-66, 67-69; chmn. North Bay Coop. Library System, Santa Rosa, Calif., 1973-74; active Projects to Advance Creativity in Edn., Cowlitz County, Wash., 1966-70. Recipient Bess Sawhill Robertson award, Western Coll., 1949. Mem. ALA, Calif. Library Assn., Library Adminstrs. No. Calif., Calif. County Librarians Assn., Beta Phi Mu. Club: Soroptimist (pres. 1965-67, 77-78). Office: 1150 Kentucky St Fairfield CA 94533

BECKER, PATRICIA ANN, sales executive; b. Long Beach, Calif., Apr. 26, 1939; d. Ralph W. and Helen K. (Kleffman) Rampton; children—Sean Philip Holland, Scot Farrell Holland, Karen Annette Holland. Student UCLA, 1957-60; B.A. in English, Calif. State Coll., Bakersfield, 1976, M.B.A., 1979. Mktg. asst. Tenneco West, Bakersfield, Calif., 1976-79; regional sales mgr. West Woodfield Farms, Natick, Mass., 1980, Pez Haas, Inc., Orange, Conn., 1980; account exec. Southland Mktg. Co., Los Angeles, 1980; regional sales dir. West Tobler Suchard U.S.A., Ltd., Los Angeles, 1980—. Mem. Swiss Bus. Assn. Club: Toastmasters (past pres.). Office: Tobler Suchard USA Ltd 12021 Wilshire Blvd Suite 223 Los Angeles CA 90025

BECKER, ROBERT ADOLPH, physicist; b. Tacoma, Feb. 10, 1913; s. Adolph Adam and Anna (Hurtienne) B.; m. Dorothy May Wilkins, Sept. 10, 1944; children—Regina Ann, Doreen Maybell, Barbara Jean, Thomas Alan, Jennifer Kathleen. B.S., Coll. Puget Sound, 1935; M.S., Calif. Inst. Tech., 1937, Ph.D., 1941. Asst. physicist, dept. terrestrial magnetism Carnegie Instn., 1941; physicist, head electronics group Nat. Bur. Standards, 1941-43; physicist Manhattan project, U. Calif.-Berkeley, 1943; group leader applied physics lab. U. Wash., 1943-46; asst. prof., assoc. prof., prof. physics U. Ill., Urbana, 1946-60; vis. prof. Calif. Inst. Tech., 1960; dir. space physics lab. Aerospace Corp., El Segundo, Calif., 1960-68, assoc. gen. mgr. lab. ops., 1968-73; cons. physicist, Carmel, Calif. 1973—. Guggenheim fellow, 1958, 59. Fellow Am. Phys. Soc., AAAS, Explorers Club; mem. Am. Astronom. Soc., N.Y. Acad. Scis., Am. Geophys. Union, Planetary Soc. (founding), AIAA, Sigma Xi. Author: Introduction to Theoretical Mechanics, 1954; Space Physics at the Aerospace Corporation, 1968; patentee in weapon devel.; contbr. articles to profl. jours. Address: PO Box 4609 Carmel CA 93921

BECKERMAN, JOSEPH HARRY, pharmaceutical consultant; b. Bklyn., May 31, 1915; s. Solomon and Clara (Lober) B.; Ph.G. in Pharmacy cum laude, Long Island U., 1936; certificate in clin. microscopy and parisitology, Fordham U., 1937; Ph.C., St. John's U., 1937, B.S. cum Laude, 1939; M.Sc., U. So. Calif., 1961, Pharm. D., 1971; m. Gertrude Bender, Feb. 10, 1940; children—Barry, Steve, Carol Ann. Community pharmacy practice, N.Y.C., 1933-44; spl. hosp. rep. Winthrop Labs., Los Angeles, 1946-55; with U. Calif. at Los Angeles Hosp., 1955-77, dir. pharmacy services, 1960-77; exec. v.p. Calif. Soc. Hosp. Pharm., 1977-82; cons. several pharm. firms; lectr. dept. pharmacology U. Calif. at Los Angeles Sch. of Medicine; lectr. pharmacology to dental hygiene students Cerritos Coll. Served with U.S. Army, 1944-46. Recipient William C. Anderson medal, 1936; Lederle Research award, 1958; Giegy Leadership award, 1958; Service awards, Myasthenia Gravis Found., 1964, 72; certificate of merit, U. Calif. at Los Angeles Allied Health Professions project, 1972; Jane Dewey Ellsworth Humanitarian award, Myasthenia Gravis Found., 1975; letter of appreciation, Calif. Army Nat. Guard, 1975; named Calif. Hosp. Pharmacist of Yr., 1974. Mem. Am., Calif. pharm. assns., Am. (pres. 1968-69), So. Calif. (past pres.), Calif. soc. of hosp. pharmacists, Western Pharmacology Soc., Am. Arbitration Assn., Rho Chi, Delta Sigma Theta, Rho Pi Phi. Democrat. Jewish. Contbr. articles to profl. jours. Home: 23137 Village 23 Camarillo CA 93010

BECKET, MARTA, dance mime, painter; b. N.Y.C.; d. Henry and Helen (Neidig) Beckett; studied painting with Antonio Cortizes, dancing with Madame Toscaninni, Caird Leslie, Gluck Sandor, Am. Ballet Sch., Madame DuVal; m. Tom Williams, June 30, 1962. Cartoonist drama page N.Y. Herald-Tribune 1948-49; exhibited paintings Park South Gallery, N.Y.C.; 3 one-man shows; dance mime, appearing in solo concerts for concert assns., colls., univs. throughout nation, 1955—; appeared Town Hall, Carnegie Hall, Radio City Music Hall (N.Y.C.); Broadway appearances in Show Boat, A Tree Grows in Brooklyn, Wonderful Town; founder, dir. Amargosa Opera House, Inc., Death Valley Junction, Calif. Illustrator: glossary for Complete Book of Ballets (Balanchine); Star Performance (Walter Terry). Address: PO Box 602 Death Valley Junction CA 92328

BECKETT, ADELE CECILIA MAAS STEVENS (MRS. GARNER A. BECKETT), civic worker; b. Chgo., May 8, 1900; d. Louis Herman and Mamie (Mayrhofer) Maas; student U. Wash., 1917-18, Washington U., St. Louis, 1922-23; m. Dillon Stevens, Apr. 11, 1918 (dec. Dec. 1953); 1 dau., Barbara (Mrs. John Albert Arnett); m. 2d, Garner A. Beckett, Oct. 28, 1967 (dec. Apr. 1974). Former partner Dillon Stevens & Co. Publicity chmn. John Burroughs Jr. High Sch. P.T.A., 1934, Los Angeles High Sch. P.T.A., 1936-37, Euterpe Opera Reading Club, 1937-38; pres. Glaides, 1946, v.p., 1963; finance chmn. Ebell of Los Angeles, 1955-57, sec. creative writing dept., 1962-63, asst. curator dept., 1971-72, chmn. Writer's Workshop, 1973-81; mem. Friends of Claremont Colls., Calif. Inst. Tech. Assos., Postscripts, Friends of Huntington Library, Around the World Club (rec. sec.). Recipient award for blood bank work A.R.C., 1943, various awards for fiction. Author: Relatively Speaking. Home: 621 San Vicente Blvd Apt 209 Santa Monica CA 90402

BECKETT, JOHN R., business executive; b. San Francisco, Feb. 26, 1918; s. Ernest J. and Hilda (Hansen) B.; A.B., Stanford U., 1939, M.A., 1940; m. Dian Calkin, Nov. 27, 1947 (dec. June 1968); children—Brenda Jean, Belinda Dian; m. 2d, Marjorie Davis Abenheim, July 1969. Valuator, Pacific Gas & Electric Co., 1941-42; utility fin. analyst Duff & Phelps, 1942-43; utility fin. expert SEC, 1943-44; asst. to pres. Seattle Gas Co., 1944-45; investment banker Blyth & Co., 1945-60, v.p., 1955-60; pres. Transam. Corp., 1960-68, chmn. bd., chief exec. officer, 1968-70, chmn. bd., pres., chief exec. officer, 1970-79, chmn. bd., chief exec. officer, 1980-82, chmn. bd., 1982, chmn. exec. com., 1982—, dir., 1960—; dir. Am. Pres. Cos. Inc., Tex. Eastern Corp., Houston, Kaiser Aluminum & Chem. Co., The Clorox Co., Bank Am., NA and SA, BankAm. Corp. Clubs: San Francisco Golf, Pacific Union, Bohemian (San Francisco); Cypress Point (Pebble Beach, Calif.). Home: PO Box 7928 San Francisco CA 94120 Office: 600 Montgomery St San Francisco CA 94111

BECKETT, RALPH LAWRENCE, educator, consultant; b. Salt Lake City, June 6, 1923; s. Louis Stanford and Grace Emily (Feveryear) B.; m. Barbara Miner, June 8, 1946; children—Larry, Carolyn, Stephen. A.B., U. So. Calif., 1950, M.A., 1952, Ph.D., 1968. Cert. Am. Speech and Lang. Assn. Tchr., South Gate High Sch., Los Angeles, 1951-57; asst. prof. Los Angeles Harbor Coll., 1957-68, U. Mo., Columbia, 1968-70; from. assoc. prof. to prof. communicative disorders Calif. State U., Fullerton, 1970—; cons. voice disorders Riley's Speech and Lang. Inst. Office: 800 N State College Blvd Fullerton CA 92634

BECKINGHAM, RAYMOND JOHN HENRY, helicopter co. official; b. Alfold, Sussex, Eng., Aug. 4, 1931; came to U.S., 1967, naturalized, 1977; s. Donald John and Elizabeth Mona (Spooner) B.; A.A. in Mech. Engring., Salisbury Coll. Tech., 1961, A.A. in Prodn. Engring., 1961; B.S. in Mech. Engring., Luton Coll. Tech., 1965; m. Pamela J. Wyatt, Feb. 27, 1954; children—Timothy, Amanda. Airframe designer Brit. Aircraft Corp., 1960-63; sr. designer research and devel. Ripper Robots Ltd., 1963-65; project engr. 3d stage European launcher ognp. Hawker Siddley Dynamics, 1965-66; engr. supr. Rohr Industries Inc., Chula Vista, Calif., 1967-77; mgr. engring. services, program mgmt., fin. mgmt. Hughes Helicopters Inc., Culver City, Calif., 1977—; design cons. light aircraft modification, 1965-66. Served with RAF, 1948-60. Chartered engr., London. Mem. Royal Aero. Soc., Instn. Engring. Designers. Republican. Baptist. Author: Theory of Struts, 1967. Patentee rail car steel sidewall assembly. Home: 15771 Las Lunas Westminster CA 92683 Office: Hughes Helicopters Inc Bldg 6/C68 Centinela and Teale Sts Culver City CA 90230

BECKLEY, ALAN PAUL, graphic arts cons.; b. Spencer, Nebr., Nov. 27, 1937; s. Keith Franklin and Aura (Braithwait) B.; student public schs., also various specialized schs.; m. Virginia Evelyn Rowe, Dec. 26, 1974; 1 dau., Valerie Lynn. Mgr. mktg. tech. support Autologic, Inc., 1976; mgr. mktg. tech. support Atex, Inc., Western region, 1977; dir. mktg. for N.Am., Xenotron, Ltd., 1978; sr. cons. Matrix Assos., Portland, Oreg., 1974—, v.p., gen. mgr., 1974—. Served with USAF, 1955-59. Asso. mem. Oreg. Newspaper Publishers Assn. Republican. Devel. hardware tech. to allow no space band composition on Linotype machines, 1st pre-installation survey process for newspaper computer systems. Address: 4140 NE 137th Ave Portland OR 97230

BECKMAN, ARNOLD ORVILLE, chemist, scientific instrument manufacturing company executive; b. Cullom, Ill., Apr. 10, 1900; s. George W. and Elizabeth E. (Jewkes) B.; B.S., U. Ill., 1922, M.S., 1923; Ph.D., Calif. Inst. Tech., 1928; D.Sci. (hon.), Chapman Coll., 1965; LL.D. (hon.), U. Calif., Riverside, 1969, Loyola U., Los Angeles, 1969; D.Sci. (hon.), Whittier Coll., 1977; LL.D. (hon.), Pepperdine U., 1977; m. Mabel S. Meinzer, June 10, 1925; children—Gloria Patricia, Arnold Stone. Research asso. Bell Telephone Labs., N.Y.C., 1924-26; chem. staff Calif. Inst. Tech., 1926-39; v.p. Nat. Tech. Lab., Pasadena, Calif., 1935-39, pres., 1939-40; pres. Helipot Corp., 1944-58, Arnold O. Beckman, Inc., South Pasadena, Calif., 1946-58; pres. Beckman Instruments, Inc., Fullerton, Calif., 1940-65, chmn. bd., 1965—; dir. Security Pacific Nat. Bank, 1956-72, adv. dir., 1972-75; dir. Continental Airlines, 1956-71, adv. dir., 1971-73. Mem. Pres.'s Air Quality Bd., 1970-74. Chmn. bd. trustees System Devel. Found.; chmn. bd. trustees emeritus Calif. Inst. Tech.; hon. trustee Calif. Museum Found.; trustee Calif. Inst. Research Found., Ear Research Inst., Scripps Clinic and Research Found.; bd. dirs. Hoag Meml. Hosp. Served as pvt. USMC, 1918-19. Benjamin Franklin fellow Royal Soc. Arts. Fellow Assn. Clin. Scientists; mem. Am. Acad. Arts and Scis., Los Angeles C. of C. (dir. 1954-58, pres. 1956), Calif. C. of C. (dir., pres. 1967-68), Nat. Acad. Engring., N.A.M., Am. Inst. Chemists, Instrument Soc. Am. (pres. 1952), Am. Chem. Soc., AAAS, Social Sci. Research Council, Am. Assn. Clin. Chemistry (hon.), Newcomen Soc., Sigma Xi, Delta Upsilon, Alpha Chi Sigma, Phi Lambda Upsilon. Clubs: Jonathan, California, Newport Harbor Yacht. Author articles in field. Patentee in field. Office: Beckman Instruments Inc 2500 Harbor Blvd Fullerton CA 92634

BECKMAN, GLEN LEONARD, consumer and trade show exec.; b. Los Angeles, July 22, 1930; s. Glenn Leonard and Lillian Nell (Etie) B.; m. Karen Marie Nielsen, Aug. 18, 1956 (dec.); 1 dau., Tracy Lynn. Sales and adminstrn. Archtl. Arts, 1955-60; ptnr. Continental Exchange Corp., Los Angeles, 1960-63; v.p. Fortune of Calif., apparel mfg., Los Angeles, 1963-65; exec. dir. Los Angeles chpt. Bldg. Contractors Assn. Calif., 1965-67; pres. Industry Prodns. Am., Los Angeles, 1967-70, Industry Prodns. Am., Los Angeles, 1976—. Served with USN, 1951-54. Recipient commendations mayor Los Angeles, bd. suprs. Los Angeles County, Los Angeles City Council. Mem. Advt. Club Los Angeles, Nat. Assn. Exposition Mgrs., Fgn. Trade Assn. So. Calif. Major shows produced include: Bldg. Products Show So. Calif., Western Invitational Advt. and Sales Promotion Show, Mobile Merchandising Tour of Am., Pool, Garden and Patio Living Show, Profl. Arts, Crafts and Indoor Plants Show, Beckman's Gift Shows of Los Angeles, Houston and Washington. Address: 10992 Ashton Ave Los Angeles CA 90024

BECKMAN, JAMES WALLACE BIM, mktg. exec.; b. Mpls., May 2, 1936; s. Wallace Gerald and Mary Louise (Frissell) B. B.A., Princeton U., 1958; Ph.D., U. Calif., 1973. Pvt. practice econ. cons., Berkeley, Calif. 1962-67; cons. Calif. State Assembly, Sacramento, 1967-68; pvt. practice market research and econs. consulting, Laguna Beach, Calif., 1969-77; cons. Calif. State Gov.'s Office, Sacramento 1977-80; pvt. practice real estate cons., Los Angeles 1980-82; v.p. mktg. Gold-Well Investments, Inc., Los Angeles 1982—. Served to maj. USMC 1958-67. NIMH fellow 1971-72. Mem. Am. Econs. Assn., Am. Statis. Assn., Am. Anthrop. Assn., Am. Mktg. Assn., Nat. Assn. Bus. Economists. Democrat. Presbyterian. Contbr. articles to profl. jours. Home: 1046 N Spaulding Ave Los Angeles CA 90046

BECKMAN, JESSE KARL, educator; b. Sweet, Idaho, June 9, 1931; s. Albert Clarence and Lillian Inez (Hilbert) B.; children—Janet, Sandra, James. B.S., U. Idaho, 1954. Cert. tchr. Tchr. vocat. agr. high schs. in Otis Orchards, Wash., Emmett, Idaho, Forsyth, Mont., Ethete, Wyo. and Lodge Grass, Mt.; tchr. indsl. arts high sch., Emmett, Idaho; tchr. vocat. agr., Colstrip, Mont. Mem. Mont. Vocat. Assn., Am. Vocat. Assn., Mont. Vocat. Agr. Tchrs. Assn., Nat. Vocat. Agr. Tchrs. Assn., Colstrip Faculty Assn. Republican. Clubs: Elks (Caldwell, Idaho); Moose (Colstrip). Home: 116 Olive St Colstrip MT 59323 Office: High Sch Colstrip MT 59323

BECKMAN, LINDA JOYCE, psychologist, educator; b. Detroit, Oct. 6, 1941; d. Max and Bettie Linden; m. Stan Beckman, Jan. 15, 1967. A.B., U. Mich., 1963; M.A., UCLA, 1966, Ph.D. in Psychology, 1969. Research asst. UCLA, 1963-64, 64-68; research psychologist Kirschner Assocs., Los Angeles, 1968-69; lectr. Pierce Coll., Woodland Hills, Calif., 1968-70; staff psychologist Camarillo (Calif.) State Hosp., 1968-72; research psychologist Reiss Davis Child Study Ctr., 1969-71; profl. assoc. East-West Ctr., Honolulu, summer 1979; research affiliate Wadsworth VA Hosp., Los Angeles, 1979—; adj. asst. prof. dept. psychiatry and biobehavioral scis. UCLA Sch. Medicine, 1971-78, adj. assoc. prof., 1978-81, adj. assoc. prof. dept. psychiatry and biobehavioral scis. and div. of behavioral sci. and health edn. UCLA Sch. Pub. Health, 1981—. Nat. Inst. Alcohol Abuse and Alcoholism grantee, 1975—. Fellow Am. Psychol. Assn. (sec.-treas. div. population and environ. psychology 1978-81); mem. AAAS, Am. Pub. Health Assn., Population Assn. Am., Research Soc. Alcoholism, Western Psychol. Assn., Soc. Psychol. Study Social Issues, Gerontol. Soc. Am., Phi Beta Kappa, Phi Kappa Phi. Editor 2 books in field; cons. editor Population and Environment; Behavioral and Social Issues; contbr. articles to profl. jours. Office: Dept Psychiatry UCLA 760 Westwood Plaza Los Angeles CA 90024

BECKMANN, PETR, elec. engr., author, educator; b. Prague, Czechoslovakia, 1924; came to U.S., 1963, naturalized, 1974; B.S. in Elec. Engring., Prague Tech. U., 1949, Ph.D., 1955; Sc.D., Czechoslovak Acad. Scis., 1962. Head of wave propagation dept. Inst. Radio Engring. and Electronics, Czechoslovak Acad. Scis., Prague, 1955-63; prof. elec. engring. U. Colo., 1963-81, prof. emeritus, 1981—; founder Golem Press, 1967. Presdl. appointee Energy Task Force, 1980. Served with RAF, 1942-45. Registered profl. engr., Colo. Fellow IEEE; mem. Am. Nuclear Soc., Health Physics Soc., Sigma Xi. Author 8 books in engring., latest being The Depolarization of Electromagnetic Waves, 1968, Orthogonal Polynomials for Engineers and Physicists, 1973; (non-tech. books) Whispered Anecdotes-Humor from Behind the Iron Curtain, 1969; The Structure of Language, 1972; A History of Pi, 1970; Eco-Hysterics and the Technophobes, 1973; The Health Hazards of Not Going Nuclear, 1976; translator tech. books in Russian, French, German and Czech langs.; pub., editor Access to Energy, monthly newsletter; contbr. articles in field to profl. jours. Address: Access to Energy Box 2298 Boulder CO 80306

BECKMEYER, HAROLD EDWARD, purchasing executive, retired naval officer; b. Yorktown, Tex., Oct. 6, 1920; s. Edward Louis and Ella Isabel (Schneider) B.; m. Honora Horstmann, Oct. 22, 1948; 1 son, James Edward. B.A., Tex. Tech U., 1941; M.B.A., Stanford U., 1953. Cert. purchasing mgr. Acct., Continental Oil Co., Ft. Worth, 1941-42; commd. officer U.S. Navy, 1942, advanced through grades to capt., ret., 1965; mgr. purchasing Watkins Johnson Co., 1965-75, treas., adminstrv. dir., 1976—, also corp. div. Bd. dirs. Palo Alto chpt. ARC, United Way of Santa Clara (Calif.). Mem. Nat. Assn. Purchasing Mgmt., Palo Alto C. of C. (chmn. bd. polit. action com.). Republican. Club: Rotary Internat. (Palo Alto). Home: 490 Pine Ln Los Altos CA 94022 Office: 3333 Hillview Ave Palo Alto CA 94304

BECKSTEAD, RICHARD LEROY, business executive; b. Salt Lake City, Oct. 25, 1929; s. Richard LeRoy and Ada May (White) B.; m. Gay Martinson, Mar. 1, 1958 (div.); children—Richard, Riley, Bruce, Wendy, Trace. B.S. in Acctg., U. Utah, 1954. Security clk., spl. agt. FBI, 1951-54; jr. acct. Wells, Baxter & Miller, Ogden, Utah, 1954-55; asst. sec., asst. treas. Browning Arms & Browning, Morgan, Utah, 1959-69, sec., treas., 1969-75, treas., 1975—. Bd. dirs. Jr. Achievement of Ogden. Mem. Nat. Assn. Credit Mgmt., Nat. Corp. Cash Mgmt. Assn. Presbyterian. Club: Elks. Home: 638 N 1050 West Clearfield UT 84015 Office: Browning Arms & Browning Rt 1 Morgan UT 84050

BECKSTOFFER, WILLIAM ANDREW, agrl. co. exec.; b. Richmond, Va., Nov. 28, 1939; s. Herman Joseph and Rose Marie (Simonpetri) B.; B.S., Va. Tech. Inst., 1961; M.B.A., Dartmouth, 1966; m. Elizabeth Kusterer, June 11, 1960; children—David Michael, Dana Marie, Andrew Tuck, Kristin Anne, Stephen John. Field engr. C & P Bell Telephone Co., Washington, 1961-64; dir. long range planning/acquisition analysis Heublein Inc., Hartford, Conn., 1966-69; v.p. planning United Vintners Co., San Francisco, 1969-70; pres. Vinifera Devel. Corp., subs. Heublein Inc., San Francisco, 1970-73; pres. Vinifera Vineyards, Napa Valley Vineyard Co., Mendocino Vineyard Co., San Francisco, 1973-77, Beckstoffer Vineyards, 1977—. Mem. Napa County Planning, Conservation and Devel. Commn., 1977-81; dirs. N. Bay Prodn. Credit Assn., 1978—; trustee Justin Sienna High Sch., 1980—. Lic. real estate broker, San Francisco, 1976—. Served to 1st lt. U.S. Army, 1961-63. Gulf Oil fellow, 1965-66. Mem. Napa Valley Grape Growers Assn. (pres. 1977-79), Young Presidents Orgn., Confrerie de la Chaine des Rotisseurs. Roman Catholic. Clubs: World Trade, Racquet, Dartmouth. Home: 525 Zinfandel Ln Saint Helena CA 94574 Office: 1127 Pope St Saint Helena CA 94574

BECKWITH, BURNHAM PUTNAM, economist, author; b. Carthage, Miss., Sept. 2, 1904; s. Herbert Henry and Louise Rice (Taylor) B.; widower. B.A., Stanford U., 1926; postgrad., Harvard U. Bus. Sch., 1926-28; Ph.D. in Econs., U. So. Calif., 1932. Instr. Kans. U., 1934-35; prof. econs. U. Ga., 1937-40; economist War Prodn. Bd., 1941-45; economist, statistician, Office Mil. Govt., Berlin, 1946-49. Author: Socialist Economy, 1949; Marginal Cost Price-Output Control, 1955; Religion, Philosophy and Science, 1957; The Next 500 Years, 1967; Government by Experts, 1972; Liberal Socialism, 1974; Radical Essays, 1981; others. Home: 656 Lytton Ave C 430 Palo Alto CA 94301

BECKWITH, DAN REXFORD, loss control representative; b. Battle Creek, Mich., July 17, 1942; s. Carroll John and Alpha Ardele (Pilgrim) B.; children—Anita Lynn, Diane Marie. B.S. in Occupational Safety and Health, Ferris State Coll., 1976. Assoc. safety profl. Am. Bd. Cert. Safety Profls. Loss control rep. Liberty Mut. Ins., Indpls., 1976-77; loss control rep. Gen. Accident Ins. Co., Indpls., 1977-78, Portland, Oreg., 1978-81; special loss control rep. Aetna Ins. Co., Portland, 1981—. Served with U.S. Army, 1959-65. Mem. Am. Soc. Safety Engrs. Adventist. Home: 3975 SW 198th Ave Aloha OR 97007 Office: 6420 SW Macadam Ave Suite 300 Portland OR 97207

BECKWITH, SUSAN, educator, adminstr.; b. Missoula, Mont., Aug. 28, 1936; d. John Keith and Marion Paula (Gunning) B.; m. Donald Wayne Mielke, June 12, 1958 (dec.); children—David Keith, Dorothy Anna. B.A. in Sociology, U. Mont., 1958; M.Ed. in Vocat. Edn., Colo. State U., 1978; postgrad. U. Colo., 1968, Idaho State U., 1969, SUNY, 1970, Montana State U., 1971-81. Tchr., Pub. Schs. Missoula, 1958-65; ednl. cons., asst. dir. Neighborhood Youth Corps, Missoula, 1965-67; chmn. Adult Learning Ctr., Missoula, 1968—; cons. Mont. Jobs Corps; cons. external diploma programs Mont. and Calif. Bd. dirs. Network for Adolescent Pregnancies, 1979—. Recipient Ednl. and Profl. Devel. award Mont. Office Pub. Instrn., 1977-78; named Outstanding Adult Educator of Yr., Mont. Adult Edn. Assn., 1980. Mem. Mont. Adult Edn. Assn. (pres. 1973, 81), Mont. Community Edn. Assn., N.W. Adult Edn. Assn. (dir. 1979-81), Mont. Edn. Assn., NEA, Adult and Continuing Edn. Assn., Delta Kappa Gamma (pres. 1980-82). Democrat. Episcopalian. Home: 1101 W Greenough Dr F-10 Missoula MT 59802 Office: 909 S Ave W Missoula MT 59801

BECRAFT, JERRY RANDALL, training manager; b. Florence, Ariz., Feb. 26, 1952; s. Irvin W. and Katherine (Rankin) B.; m. Gayle Pratt, Jan. 28, 1972; children—Lynnette, Emily, Pamela, Marilyn. B.S. in Indsl. Edn., Brigham Young U., 1974, M.S. in Instructional Sci., 1982. Safety clk., safety engr. Magma Copper Co., San Manuel, Ariz., 1975-79; tng. designer Signetics Corp., Orem, Utah, 1980-82, mgr. tng. resources and documentation, 1982—. Mem. Am. Soc. Tng. and Devel. Mormon. Office: 1275 S 800 E Orem UT 84058

BECZE, THOMAS DAVID, federal regulations compliance specialist, consultant; b. Pitts., June 10, 1948; s. William John and Ethel Ester (Nemeth) B.; m. Carol Lynn Kent, Jan. 30, 1971; children—Christopher Robertson, Bryan Williams. Grad. Bethany Coll., 1970; student Wroxton Coll., Oxford, Eng., 1969; postgrad. Rutgers U., 1970-72, Va. Commonwealth U., 1980-82. Math. tchr., chmn. art dept. St. Peter's High Sch., New Brunswick, N.J., 1970-72; bus. sales rep. Liberty Mut. Ins. Co., East Orange, N.J., 1972-73; prodn. supr., tng. supr. E.R. Squibb & Sons, New Brunswick, 1973-77; sr. fed. regulatory compliance analyst A.H. Robins Co., Richmond, Va., 1977-82; dir. regulatory compliance and tng. Pharm. Tech., Inc., Springfield, Oreg., 1982—; cons. health-care industry; past mem. lecture faculty U. Wis. Extension Services in Pharmacy. Coach Am. Youth Soccer League, 1983. Tokan scholar, Bethany Coll., 1966-70; Pa. Higher Edn. Assistance Agy. scholar for study in Eng., 1969. Mem. Am. Soc. Quality Control, Am. Soc. Tng. and Devel. Republican. Club: Phulgutz Assn. of Eugene. Contbr. articles to pharm. publs. Office: 320 North A St Springfield OR 97477

BEDDOME, CLARENCE JORDAN, bus. and telecommunications cons.; b. Tucson, June 23, 1928; s. Clarence Crawford and Ola (Jordan) B.; diploma in traffic police adminstrn., Northwestern U., 1962; m. Elsie Lucille Salter, June 28, 1950; children—Lawrence Conard, Michael Allen. Mem. Ariz. Hwy. Patrol, 1954-74, maj., asst. chief of adminstrn., 1968-74; ret., 1974; exec. dir. Nat. Law Enforcement Telecommunications Systems, Inc., Phoenix, 1974-78; v.p., gen. mgr., dir. Nat. Safety Products Corp., Phoenix, 1979—; past chmn. Ariz. Privacy and Security Council; former bd. dirs. SEARCH Group, Inc., Sacramento. Served with USN, 1945-53. Mem. Internat. Assn. Chiefs of Police, Am. Fedn. Police Officers. Democrat. Mem. Christian Ch. Clubs: Masons, Shriners, Fraternal Order Police. Home: 4402 W El Camino Dr Glendale AZ 85302 Office: 5340 N 7th St Phoenix AZ 85014

BEDELL, CLYDE, ret. advt. cons.; b. Des Moines, Apr. 25, 1898; s. John Delbert and Mabel Eleanor (Young) B.; student Coe Coll.; m. Florence Evans, June 19, 1926; children—C. Barrie, Jeffrey. Traveling bus. editor for trade mags. and advt. agy. account exec., 1919-24; successively advt. mgr., dir. sales and advt., dir. corp. Butler Bros., 1924-32; account exec. N. W. Ayer, 1933-35; advt. mgr. and author Caleb column Marshall Field & Co., 1936-39; ind. advt. counsel, 1940-41, from 1944; now ret.; now activist Urantia Movement; lectr. Northwestern U. Sch. Commerce, 1938-42; sales promotion mgr. The Fair Store, Chgo., 1942-43; advt. counselor, v.p., dir. Bride-to-Be mag. 1954; pres. Clyde Bedell, Inc., Basic, Inc., Santa Barbara, Calif. Pres. Park Ridge (Ill.) Parent Teachers Assn., 1945-46, Northwestern U. Settlement, 1944-47, Friends of Pub. Library, 1949-50. Recipient Nichols Cup Alpha Delta Sigma, 1954; named to Retail Hall of Fame Nat. Retail Advt. Conf., 1955; named to Advt.'s 50 All Time Greats Alpha Delta Sigma; named All Time Great Nat. Retail Mchts. Assn., 1968. Mem. Newspaper Advt. Execs. Assn. Conglist. Clubs: Commonwealth, Press, Union League (San Francisco); University (Chgo.). Author: Seven Keys to Retail Profits, 1930; How to Write Advertising that Sells, 1940; Shopper's Special, 1941; Let's Talk Retailing, 1946; Precepts and Principles of Advertising that Sells, 1947; Your Advertising —Force or Farce, 1954; Total Selling Service-Furniture, 1963; How to Convert White Space into Advertising that Sells, 1964; Total Selling Service-Music, 1966; Concordex of Urantia Book, 2d edit., 1980. Columnist Nat. Home Furnishings Assn. Reports, 1969-75. Author weekly feature in Advertising Age, 9 yrs. Home: 1850 Folsom St Apt 310 Boulder CO 80302

BEDELL, THOMAS ERWIN, range management educator; b. Santa Cruz, Calif., Dec. 21, 1931; s. Harold Erwin and Muriel Lucille (Copsey) B.; children—Shelley, Kristin, Robin. B.S., Calif. State Poly. Coll., 1953; M.S., U. Calif.-Berkeley, 1957; Ph.D., Oreg. State U., 1966. Extension adviser U. Calif., 1957-63; asst. prof. range mgmt. Oreg. State U., Corvallis, 1966-70, county extension agt., 1973-76, extension rangeland resources specialist, 1976—; assoc. prof. range mgmt. U. Wyo., Laramie, 1970-73. Range mgmt. cons. Served with U.S. Army, 1953-55. Fellow Soc. Range Mgmt. (bd. dirs.); mem. Am. Soc. Animal Sci., Am. Soc. Agronomy, Phi Kappa Phi. Contbr. numerous papers to profl. jours. Home: 120 Wonderly Ln Philomath OR 97370 Office: Oreg State U Corvallis OR 97331

BEDNAR, CHARLES THOMAS, chemist; b. Czechoslovakia, Oct. 20, 1912; s. Karel and Anna (Mrkva) B.; came to U.S., 1956, naturalized, 1961; Ph.M., Charles U., Prague, Czechoslovakia, 1934, Ph.D., 1938; m. Hana V. Susicky, Oct. 29, 1956. Asst. lectr. Charles U., 1938-41; owner Pharm. Mfg., Czechoslovakia, 1936-48; chem. plant mgr. Corona Chems., Sydney, Australia, 1951-56; chief chemist Montrose-Stauffer Chem. Co., Henderson, Nev., 1956-78; lab. mgr. Clark County Community Coll., North Las Vegas, Nev., from 1978. Mem. Am. Chem. Soc. Home: 4204 El Parque Las Vegas NV 89102

BEDNAR, JAMES EDMUND, lawyer; b. Omaha, Oct. 13, 1911; s. James Edmund and Britannia (Daughters) B.; m. Rachel Audrey Hancock, Oct. 15, 1940 (dec.); 1 dau., Lisa; m. 2d, Irene Ann Thomassen, July 31, 1976. A.B., Stanford U., 1932; LL.B., Harvard U., 1935. Bar: Calif. 1936, U.S. Dist. Ct. (so. dist.) Calif. 1937, U.S. Supreme Ct. 1945. Assoc., then ptnr. Musick and Burrell, Los Angeles, 1937-53; ptnr. Jones and Bednar, Los Angeles, 1953-78, Bednar and Russell Inc., Los Angeles, 1978—; dir. Lyon Moving & Storage Co., Preferred Theatres Corp., Hamilton Supply Co.; faculty Southwestern U., 1949-65; mem. panel on constrn. problems Am. Arbitration Assn. Served to capt. AUS, 1943-46. Mem. Los Angeles Bar Assn., ABA. Republican. Methodist. Club: Jonathan (Los Angeles). Home: 4200 Via Dolce Apt 230 Marina del Rey CA 90291 Office: Bednar and Russell Inc 5901 W 3d St Los Angeles CA 90036

BEE, HELEN L(UCILLE), psychologist, author; b. Tacoma, Apr. 27, 1939; d. Austin Edward and Susan Lee (Emmons) B.; m. Geroge Chase Douglas, Mar. 19, 1972 (div.); children—Rex, Arwen. B.A., Radcliffe Coll., 1960; Ph.D. in Psychology, Stanford U., 1964. Asst. prof. psychology Clark U., 1964-65; asst. prof. U. Wash., 1965-70, assoc. prof., 1970-72, sr. research assoc., dept. psychology and Sch. of Nursing, 1979—; cons. in child psychology, Seattle, 1972-79. Trustee Happy Valley Found., Ojai, Calif., 1978—; chmn. bd. trustees Happy Valley Sch., Ojai, 1980—. Mem. Am. Psychol. Assn., Soc. for Research in Child Devel., Nat. Council Family Relations. Author: The Developing Child, 1965, 3d edit., 1981; (with S.K. Mitchell) The Developing Person, 1980; (with others) Invitation to Psychology, 1979, 2d edit., 1983. Contbr. numerous articles to profl. publs. Home: 4535 NE 94th St Seattle WA 98115 Office: CDMRC Residence WJ-10 U Wash Seattle WA 98195

BEEBE, MARJORIE HARTH, museum administrator, educator; b. Cin., Sept. 3, 1943; d. John Edward and Marjorie Catherine (Udry) Harth; m. Richard Olds Swain, Aug. 10, 1968; 1 son, Jason Alexander; m. 2d, William Gerald Beebe, Aug. 20, 1980. B.A. in Art History, Smith Coll., 1965; M. Mus. Practice, U. Mich., 1968, postgrad. (Nat. Mus. Act fellow), 1977—. Curatorial intern Toledo Mus. Art, 1967-68; asst. curator Flint (Mich.) Inst. Arts, 1968-69; asst. drawings collection Royal Inst. Brit. Architects, London, 1969-70; asst. to dir., coordinator mus. practice program U. Mich. Mus. Art, Ann Arbor, 1973-78, assoc. chmn., 1978-80, acting chmn., 1980-81; dir. Galleries of Claremont (Calif.) Colls., 1981—; instr. Mich. State U., East Lansing, 1969, Kenyon Coll., Gambier, Ohio, 1973, U. Mich., Ann Arbor and Flint. Extension, 1968-69, 1973-75, 1975-81, Pomona Coll., Claremont, 1981—. Recipient Rackham award, 1974-75. Mem. Am. Assn. Mus., Coll. Art Assn., Nat. Trust for Hist. Preservation. Author: Galli Bibicna and Juvarra entries, Catalogue of the Drawings Collection Royal Inst. Brit. Architects, Volume 5, 1973; author exhibition catalogues; editor: The Univ. of Mich. Mus. Practice Program: The First Twenty Years. Office: Montgomery Art Gallery Pomona Coll Claremont CA 91711

BEEBE, MARY LIVINGSTONE, curator; b. Portland, Oreg., Nov. 5, 1940; d. Robert and Alice Livingstone. B.A., Bryn Mawr Coll., 1962; postgrad. Sorbonne, U. Paris, 1962-63. Curatorial asst. Fogg Art Mus., Harvard U., Cambridge, Mass., 1966-67; producer Am. Theater Co., Portland State U., 1969-71; dir. pub. relations Sally Judd Gallery, Catlin Gable Sch., Portland, 1971; exec. dir. Portland Ctr. for Visual Arts, 1973-81; dir. Stuart collection U. Calif.-San Diego, La Jolla, 1981—; cons. in field. Mem. art steering com. Portland Devel. Commn., 1977-80; bd. dirs. Henry Gallery, U. Wash., Seattle, 1977-80; project cons. Nat. Research Ctr. for Arts, N.Y.C., 1978-79; bd. dirs. Art Mus. Assn. San Francisco, 1978—; mem. arts adv. bd. Centre City Devel. Corp., San Diego, 1982; arts adv. bd. Port of San Diego; panel mem., cons. Nat. Endowment Arts; juror numerous art shows and exhbns. Nat. Endowment Arts fellow, 1979. Contbr. articles to profl. jours. Office: Stuart Collection U Calif San Diego B-027 La Jolla CA 92093

BEEKMAN, KEITH LORENZ, management consultant; b. Mpls., Sept. 27, 1930; s. Paul Lorenz and Frances Lillian (Hebner) B.; m. Mary Lou Seage, Apr. 1, 1961. B.A. in Econs., Stanford U., 1952, M.B.A., 1954. Asst. to pres. Kern County Land Co., San Francisco, 1956-60; prin. McKinsey & Co., Inc., San Francisco, 1960-71; v.p. Towers, Perrin, Forster & Crosby, Inc., San Francisco, 1971—. Served to 1st lt. USAF, 1954-56. Mem. Hillsborough Homeowners Assn. Republican. Methodist. Clubs: Stanford Golf, San Francisco Comml.

BEEKS, WILLIAM TRULOCK, judge; b. El Reno, Okla., May 5, 1906; s. William Tecumseh and Elsie Jane (Rawles) B.; m. Florence Carlson, Jan. 4, 1929; 1 son, William Trulock, J.D., U. Wash., 1932. Practice, Seattle, 1932-41, 47-61; judge U.S. Dist. Ct. (we. dist.) Wash., Seattle, 1961-73, sr. judge, 1973—; instr. in admiralty law U. Wash., 1954-55. Served to col. U.S. Army, 1942-46. Mem. Maritime Law Assn. U.S., Seattle-King County Bar Assn., Wash. State Bar Assn., ABA, Order of Coif. Clubs: Rainier, Harbor, Wash. Athletic. Lodges: Masons (32 deg.), Shriners. Office: 407 US Courthouse Seattle WA 98104*

BEELER, JOHN GORDON (JAY), public relations and advertising executive, educator; b. Takoma Park, Md., Sept. 30, 1943; s. Samuel Edward and Rieman Louise (Stouffer) B.; m. Anita Rush, Dec. 28, 1968, children—Jeffrey Evan, Janet Lynne, Melinda Jill. B.A. in Radio/TV and Journalism, Calif. State U.-Long Beach, 1970; Asst. pub. relations mgr. Transam. Fin. Corp., Los Angeles, 1970-71; v.p. Bishop & Assocs., Marina del Rey, Calif., 1971-73; dir. pub. relations Hyatt Med. Enterprises, Encino, Calif., 1973-78; pres. Beeler & Assocs., Long Beach, Calif., 1978—; lectr. in field. Chmn. pub. relations Am. Heart Assn., Long Beach. Served with USAF 1962-65. So. Calif. Soc. Hosp. Pub. Relations (past pres.). Club: Pacific Coast Press (1st v.p. 1980—). Home and Office: 1110 Ramillo Ave Long Beach CA 90815

BEEMER, MARLAYNE, petroleum service co. exec.; b. Sedalia, Mo.; d. Fordyce Carlton and Fannie Ethel (Williams) Close; student Central Mo. State U., 1951-52; A.A., Orange Coast Coll., 1973; m. Richard L. Beemer, Feb. 2, 1962; children—Carla, Marla, Lauren, Richard A. With The Real Estaters, Costa Mesa, Calif., 1965-67; artist, 1968-69; acct. Royal Electric Co., Long Beach, Calif., 1970-71; with Santa Fe Engring. & Constrn. Co. div. Santa Fe Internat. Corp., Orange, Calif., 1971—, adminstrv. asst. to pres., 1974—; instr. real estate. Cert. real estate, Calif. Club: Desk and Derrick. Home: 12 Elfin Irvine CA 92714 Office: PO Box 1401 505 S Main St Orange CA 92668

BEFAME, JEANNETTE, reporter, writer; b. Wahpeton, N.D., July 15, 1919; d. Frederick and Sykea (Ashton) Befame; A.B., Stanford, 1941; m. John Allen Sontheimer, Aug. 10, 1968 (dec.); m. 2d, W. Gordon Eustice, May 7, 1976. Reporter, San Francisco News, 1941, Sacramento Union, 1942; now newspaper feature writer-reporter San Jose (Calif.) Mercury-News; radio work, news reporter, interviews, San Francisco, 1947; TV guest appearances, 1956; during World War II wrote newscasts for overseas. One of 10 U.S. dels. Asian-Am. Women Journalist Conf., East-West Center, Hawaii, 1965. First woman to win Edward McQuade Meml. award for outstanding pub. service in journalism, 1955; recipient top reporting award Calif. Fair Competition, 1956; Matrix award Theta Sigma Phi, 1964; Award for Excellence, Calif. Press Women, 1975; award Stanford, 1976. Mem. AAUW, Women in Communications (pres. Palo Alto-San Jose chpt. 1975-76), Stanford Alumni Assn., Nat. Fedn. Press Women, Inc. (chpt. pres.), Theta Sigma Phi (alumni adviser Stanford U. chpt.), Sigma Delta Chi. Club: San Francisco Press. Home: 1560 Plateau Ave Los Altos CA 94022 Office: San Jose Mercury-News San Jose CA 91513

BEGLARIAN, GRANT, composer, found, adminstr.; b. Tiflis, Georgia, USSR, Dec. 1, 1927; came to U.S., 1947, naturalized, 1954; s. Boghos and Arax (Boghosian) B.; Mus.B., U. Mich., 1950, Mus.M., 1952; D. Mus. Arts (Creative Arts fellow 1955-57), 1958; m. Joyce Heeney, Sept. 2, 1950; children—Eve, Spencer. Composer in residence, Cleveland Heights, 1959-60; editor Prentice Hall, Inc., 1960-61; pres. Music Book Assn., 1961-68; field rep., project dir. Ford Found., 1961-68; dean, prof. music Sch. Performing Arts, U. So. Calif., Los Angeles, 1969-81; pres. Nat. Found. for Advancement Arts, Miami, Fla., 1982—; compositions include: String Quartet, Violin Sonata, Cello Sonata, Divertimento for Orch., Sinfonia for Orch., A Hymn for our Times, Diversions, Sinfonia for Strings, To Manitou, Elegy for Cellist; mem. music adv. council Princeton U., music council Yale U., 1974-76, music tng. panel Nat. Endowment Arts. Served with AUS, 1952-54. Recipient Gershwin Composition award, 1959; ASCAP awards, 1965—; grantee Ford Found., 1959, 62, 68. Mem. ASCAP, Internat. Council Fine Arts Deans (pres. 1980-82), Am. Music Center, Coll. Music Soc. Armenian Apostolic. Home: 333 S Windsor Blvd Los Angeles CA 90020

BEHLING, RALPH TITUS, retired dermatologist; b. Buffalo, June 19, 1918; s. Howard G. and Grace Mary (Black) B.; B.S., U. Buffalo, 1940, M.D., 1943; m. Rita Mary Clancy, Nov. 19, 1943; children—James, David, Linda, Marshall, Jenifer. Intern, Buffalo Gen. Hosp., 1943-44, E.J. Meyer Meml. Hosp., 1944-46; practice medicine specializing in dermatology, San Mateo, Calif., 1950—; asst. prof. dermatology U. Calif.-San Francisco, 1955—; dir. Glendale Fed. Savs. & Loan. Served to lt. col., USPHS, 1947-50. Mem. San Mateo C. of C. (dir. 1958—), Calif., Am. med. assns., Pacific Dermatol. Assn., Am. Acad. Dermatology, San Mateo County Med. Soc., San Francisco Dermatology Assn., Dermatology Therapy Assn., Burlington Jr. Cotillion. Republican. Methodist. Clubs: Kiwanis, Elks, Masons (Shriner). Contbr. articles in field to profl. jours. Home: 650 Parrott Dr San Mateo CA 94402

BEHLKE, JANE H., educator; b. Seward, Alaska, Nov. 29, 1925; d. Paul C. and Luella E. (Kelsey) McMullen; m. Charles E. Behlke, Nov. 26, 1953; children—Susan, Carol, James. B.A., Whitman Coll., 1947, M.S., U. Mich., 1949; postgrad. U. Alaska. Cert. tchr., adminstr. Tchr. elem. sch., Seward, Alaska, 1947-52; registrar, dir. admissions U. Alaska, 1952-54; tchr. Univ. Park Elem. Sch., Fairbanks, Alaska, 1967—; elem. sci. resource tchr., 1970-75; condr. worshops. Mem. Fairbanks Pollution Control Commn., 1974-82. Recipient Fairbanks Tchr. of Yr. award, 1977. Mem. NEA-Alaska, Nat. Sci. Tchrs. Assn., Internat. Reading Assn., Delta Kappa Gamma (state pres. 1979-81, internat. profl. affairs com. 1982—). Roman Catholic.

BEHLMER, RUDY H., JR., TV comml. producer-dir.; b. San Francisco, Oct. 13, 1926; s. Rudy H. and Helen Mae (McDonough) B.; student Pasadena Playhouse Coll., 1946-49; student Los Angeles City Coll., 1949-50; 1 son, Curt. TV dir. KLAC-TV, Hollywood, Calif., 1952-56; network TV dir. ABC-TV, Hollywood, 1956-57; TV comml. producer-dir., exec. Grant Advt., Hollywood, 1957-60; exec. producer-dir. KCOP TV, Hollywood, 1960-63; v.p., TV comml. producer-dir. Hollywood office Leo Burnett USA, 1963—. Lectr. on film Art Center Coll. of Design, Pasadena, Calif., 1967-81. Served with AC, USNR, 1944-46. Mem. Dirs. Guild Am. Author: Memo From David O. Selznick, 1972; (with Tony Thomas) Hollywood's Hollywood, 1975; America's Favorite Movies—Behind the Scenes, 1982; co-author The Films of Errol Flynn, 1969; text on Warner Bros. Fifty Years of Film Music, 1973; editor: The Adventures of Robin Hood, 1979, The Sea Hawk, 1982 (Wis./Warner Bros. screenplay series); various articles on aspects of film history. Office: Leo Burnett USA 6255 Sunset Blvd Hollywood CA 90028

BEHM, EDWARD WILLIAM, engineer, retired naval officer; b. Los Angeles, Nov. 23, 1922; s. William Carl and Sarah Elizabeth (George) B.; m. Elizabeth Ann Muir, Jan. 5, 1945; children—Joanne Muir, Cynthia Behm Broadhead. B.S., U.S. Naval Acad., 1944; postgrad. U.S. Naval Postgrad. Sch., 1950. Commd. ensign U.S. Navy, 1944, advanced through grades to capt., 1965—, ret., 1974; sr. project engr. VSE Corp., Alexandria, Va., 1977—. Decorated Navy Meritorious Service medal with star, Commendation medal with star. Mem. Navy League, U.S. Yacht Racing Union, Mil. Order World Wars, U.S. Naval Acad. Alumni Assn., Armed Forces Communication and Electronics Assn. Republican. Clubs: Optimists, Masons, San Diego Naval Sailing.

BEHM, JOANN RUPERT, health executive, nurse, consultant, author; b. Charleston, W.Va., July 29, 1948; d. Rodney Clifton Rupert and Helen Virginia (Price) Goff; m. Jerry William Behm, Apr. 5, 1980; 1 dau., Sarah Elizabeth. B.S., Fla. State U., 1970, M.S. U. Ariz., 1972. Adminstr., Project Clinic, Vacaville, Calif., 1973-74; dir. edn. Pima County Hosp., Tucson, 1974-75; free lance critical care/emergency cons./educator, Palo Alto, Calif., 1975-77; pres. Applied Med. Tng., Inc., Novato, Calif., 1977—; lectr., editor, author, cons. Charter mem., bd. dirs. Bay Area Flying Drs., 1975-80, v.p. U.S. Flying Drs., 1979-80. Served to 1st lt. USAF, 1973-74. HEW trainee, 1971-72. Mem. Am. Assn. Critical Care Nurses (founder, charter mem. San Diego chpt.), Am. Heart Assn. Author: Basic Cardiopulmonary Life Support: Theory and Technique, 1978, 81; Introduction to Basic EKG Interpretation, 1979, 82; Management of Office and Clinic Emergencies, 1977, 83, Serious and Life-Threatening Arrhythmias, 1979, Practical Emergency Pharmacology, 1982. Office: Applied Med Tng Inc PO Box 1547 Novato CA 94948

BEHN, PETER WOLFGANG, architect; b. Munich, Germany, Dec. 12, 1936; s. Fritz and Gerda (Schuster) B.; came to U.S., 1951, naturalized, 1956; m. Kathie Carriegan, June 1974; children—Daniel, Kevin. B.Arch., U. Calif.-Berkeley, 1965; With Whiting Assocs., Rome, 1966-67, Ludovico Quaroni, Rome, 1968; project architect Fisher Friedman, San Francisco, 1970; pvt. practice, Berkeley, Calif., 1971—. Served with USN, 1958-60. Recipient 4 AIA-Sunset Western Home awards; Archtl. Record awards, 1973, 79. Mem. AIA. Designs include residences of Lozano, Schiro, Kay, Baumrind, Behn. Office: 38460 Hwy 1 S PO Box 721 Gualala CA 95445

BEHN, ROGER FREDERICK, educator, librarian; b. Liverpool, Eng., May 15, 1930; s. Frederick Joseph and Constance (Pratt) B.; B.Ed., U. B.C., 1967; diploma in agr. MacDonald Coll. of McGill U., 1954; m. Marion Edith Rose, July 9, 1955; children—Karen, Jeremy. Tchr., librarian, Sch. Dist. 36, Surrey, B.C., Can., 1962-63, Sch. Dist. 24, Chase, B.C., 1963—. Chmn. Cariboo-Thompson Nicola Library System Soc., 1972-73, Thompson Nicola Library System, 1974-75, Cariboo-Thompson Nicola Library System, 1976-81. Alderman, Village of Chase, 1981-82. Served with Royal Corps of Signals, 1949-51. Mem. Canadian, B.C. (pres. 1970-71) sch. librarians assns., Sch. Library Assn. (Eng.), Canadian Power Squadrons, Nat. Model Railroaders Assn., Royal Canadian Legion. Address: Box 353 Chase BC Canada

BEHNEY, CHARLES AUGUSTUS, JR., veterinarian; b. Bryn Mawr, Pa., Nov. 30, 1929; s. Charles Augustus and Victoria Parks (Wythe) B.; B.S., U. Wyo., D.V.M., Colo. State U., 1961; m. Judith Ann Boggs, May 26, 1979; children—Charles Augustus III, Keenan F. Owner, Cochise Animal Hosp., Bisbee, Ariz., 1961—; veterinarian, dir. S.W. Traildust Zoo, Bisbee, 1966—; owner Banning Creek Ranch, Bisbee, 1969—; asso. prof. Cochise Coll. Chmn., Comprehensive Health Planning, Cochise County, Ariz., 1968. Mem. Am. Vet. Med. Assn., Soc. for Breeding Soundness. Democrat. Episcopalian. Rotarian, Elk. Patentee ultrasound device and eye cover for treating infections, apparatus to alter equine leg conformation, external vein clamp, equine sanitation instrument; developer ear implant instrumentation system. Home and office: PO Box 4337 Bisbee AZ 85603

BEHNKE, BRUCE STEPHEN, hospital administrator; b. Detroit, Feb. 10, 1949; s. E. Thomas and Marie (Malje) B.; B.B.A., Wayne State U., 1970; M.H.A., U. Minn., 1972. Asst. hosp. adminstr. Rochester Meth. Hosp. (Minn.), 1972-74, Kaiser Found. Hosp., Los Angeles, 1974-77; asso. hosp. adminstr. Kaiser Found. Hosp., Fontana, Calif., 1978-79; hosp. adminstr. Kaiser Found. Hosp., Bellflower, Calif., 1979—; clin. preceptor various univs. Mem. Am. Coll. Hosp. Adminstrs., Health Care Execs. of So. Calif. Republican. Episcopalian. Office: 9400 E Rosecrans Ave Bellflower CA 90706

BEHNKE, SHARI (DUNKELMAN), research child psychologist, psychometrist; b. Oceanside, N.Y., Oct. 17, 1951; d. Sidney and Shirley Ethel (Elson) Dunkelman; m. John Skinner Behnke, Nov. 1, 1980; 1 son, Zane Howard Dunkelman. B.A., Case Western Res. U., Cleve., 1973; M.Sc., U. Leicester (Eng.), 1975; Ed.M., Harvard Grad. Sch. Edn., 1978. Sch. psychologist Fircrest Sch., Seattle, 1975-77; research asst. Harvard U., 1977-78; instr. Green River Community Coll., Auburn, Wash., 1978-79; child psychology specialist, pregnancy and health program, U. Wash., Seattle, 1979-81; asst. researcher Kamehameha Ednl. Research Inst., Honolulu, 1982—; cons. Maxin Sch., Seattle, 1978. Recipient award U. Wash. Alcoholism and Drug Abuse Inst., 1981-82. Mem. AAUW, Am. Psychol. Assn. Clubs: Harvard (Honolulu); Wash. Athletic (Seattle). Author: Sex Differences in Moral Behavior: A Study of Stereotypes in Children, 1973; contbg. author: Professional Manual: The Pregnancy and Health Program, 1981; co-author Preliminary Clinical Observations of Alcohol-Affected Children, 1980. Home: 177 Ohana St Kailua HI 96734 Office: Kamehameha Ednl Research Inst 1850 Makuakani Honolulu HI 96817

BEHR, FRITZ O., law enforcement exec., administrator; b. Cologne, Germany, Feb. 5, 1933; came to U.S., 1941, naturalized, 1946; s. Fritz and Rose (Wittemann) B.; m. Angela Ann Borace, Sept. 21, 1958; children—Lorraine, Frank, Fred. B.S., CUNY, 1966; J.D. cum laude, St. John's U., 1971; grad. Nat. Acad., FBI, 1972. Bar: N.Y., 1972. Mem. N.Y.C. Police Dept., 1956-77, maj., 1973-77; adminstr. law enforcement services div. Mont. Dept. Justice, Helena, 1977—. Bd. dirs. Grand Street Theatre, Helena, 1982—; mem. commn. on ministry Episcopal Diocese of Mont., 1980—. Served with Army N.G., 1957-63. Recipient Medal of Honor, N.Y.C. Police Dept., 1977. Mem. Rocky Mountain Info. Network (mem. exec. bd. 1981—), Am. Acad. Profl. Law Enforcement, Assn. State Criminal Investigation Adminstrs. Office: Montana Dept Justice 303 Roberts St Helena MT 59620

BEHRENS, BERNICE, city official; b. Portland, Oreg., July 5, 1910; d. Frank Kelly and Anita (Smith) Woodard; B.A. magna cum laude, Stanford U., 1932; m. Jess A. Digman, May 9, 1935 (div. 1939); 1 dau., Diane (Mrs. James F. Dalton); m. 2d, Earl C. Behrens, July 11, 1963. Vice pres. d'Armigene Inc., N.Y.C., 1961-63; merchandising and fashion asst. to pres. Harry Camp Millinery Co., San Francisco, 1943-60; lectr., 1963-69; dir. U.S. Dept. State Reception Center, San Francisco, 1969-77; dep chief protocol City of San Francisco. Mem. Pres. Nixon's Commn. Observance 25th Anniversary UN, 1970. Decorated officer's cross Order Merit (West Germany); comdr. Order Star Italian Solidarity; insignia comdr. Order No. Star (Sweden); officer Order Leopold II (Belgium); officer Order of Isabel la Catholic (Spain); officer Order of Crown (Belgium); Order of Precious Crown (Japan); recipient resolutions San Francisco Consular Corps, 1975, Calif. Senate, 1975, certificate San Francisco Bd. Suprs. Mem. Internat. Visitors Center, People-to-People, Nat. Council Women U.S., Internat. Council Women, UN Assn., World Affairs Council No. Calif., Am. Women for Internat. Understanding (founder, dir.), AAUW, Japan Soc. (dir.), Phi Beta Kappa. Club: Commonwealth of Calif. (bd. govs.). Home: 1201 California St #502 San Francisco CA 94109

BEHRENS, RAYMOND WALTER, ins. co. exec.; b. N.J., July 19, 1933; s. Max Gustau and Jean B.; B.A., Rutgers U., 1955; m. Judith A. Harvey, Nov. 14, 1970 (div.); children—Elizabeth, John. Command officer USAF, 1956, resigned, 1963; brokerage cons. Conn. Gen. Life Ins. Co., Los Angeles, 1964-69, account mgr., 1970—; seminar speaker. Active in charitable fund raising, local community and polit. fund raising. Served with USAF, 1956-63. Recipient awards for profl. achievements Conn. Gen. Life Ins. Co. Republican. Originator design techniques. Home: 27925 Ridgebrook Ct Rancho Palos Verdes CA 90274

BEICKEL, SHARON LYNNE, psychologist, educator, researcher; b. Hanford, Calif., Mar. 1, 1943; d. William Wayne and Kathleen (Haun) B. B.S., Eastern Oreg. State Coll., 1965; M.S. in Human Devel., U. Oreg., 1970, Ph.D. in Counseling Psychology, 1977. Cert. psychologist, Ariz. Tchr. English, Hermiston (Oreg.) High Sch., 1965-66; instr. psychology U. Oreg., Eugene, 1966-69, grad. teaching fellow, 1968-69, research assoc. dept. human devel., 1971-75, clin. supr. DeBusk Counseling Service, 1975-76, intern counseling ctr., 1976-77; psychologist Ariz. State U., Tempe, 1978—, supr. doctoral interns, 1978—; pvt. practice psychology, Tempe, 1978—. Mem. Am. Psychol. Assn., Ariz. Psychol. Assn., Western Psychol. Assn., Ariz. State U. Faculty Women's Assn. Democrat. Home: 1978 E Don Carlos St Tempe AZ 85281 Office: Counseling and Consultation Center Ariz State U Tempe AZ 85281

BEIER, ERNST GUNTER, psychologist, educator; b. Germany, June 26, 1916; s. Paul and Hanna M. (Moses) B.; m. Frances R. Redlich, Sept. 6, 1949; children—Paul, Lisa. B.A. Amherst Coll., 1940; Ph.D. in Psychology, Columbia U., 1949. Lic. psychologist, Utah. Asst. prof. psychology Syracuse U., 1948-53; prof. U. Utah, Salt Lake City, 1953—; researcher in non verbal behavior and stress. Served with U.S. Army, 1943-45. Decorated Silver Battle Star. Fellow Am. Psychol. Assn.; mem. Utah Psychol. Assn. (past pres.), Rocky Mountain Assn. (past pres., pres. elect psychotherapy div.). Club: Petrol. Author: The Silent Language of Psychotherapy, 1966; People Reading, 1976. Contbr. articles to profl. jours. Home: 44 W 3d South Apt 607 Salt Lake City UT 84101 Office: Behavioral Sci Bldg U Utah Salt Lake City UT 84112

BEIGEL, JOAN KAYE, marriage and family counsellor; b. Bronx, N.Y., Dec. 1, 1942; d. Walter and Selma (Berger) Kaye; m. Allan Beigel, Dec. 24, 1962; children—Jennifer, Jill. B.A. in Edn., NYU, 1964, M.A. in Edn., 1968; M.Ed. in Counseling and Guidance, U. Ariz., 1975. Lic. marriage, family and child counselor, Calif. Founder, dir. Ctr. for Family and Individual Counseling, Tucson, 1975—; founder, ptnr. Tucson Transitions, 1981—, Ariz. Employee Assistance Program, Inc., 1982—; instr. U. Ariz., 1978—. Active Exec. Women's Council, Interface, St. Joseph's Hosp.; adv. bd. Com. for Lang. Arts Adoption, Ariz. Bd. Edn. Mem. Am. Personnel and Guidance Assn., Am. Assn. Marriage and Family Therapists, Am. Soc. for Tng. and Devel., Internat. Transactional Assn.

BEIGHLE, DOUGLAS PAUL, lawyer; b. Deer Lodge, Mont., June 18, 1932; s. Douglas Paul and Clarice Janice (Driver) B.; m. Gwendolen Anne Dickson, Oct. 30, 1954; children—Cheryl L., Randall P., Katherine A., Douglas J. B.S. in Bus. Adminstrn., U. Mont., 1954, J.D. with honors, 1958; LL.M. (fellow 1959-60), Harvard U., 1960. Bar: Mont. 1958, Wash. 1959. Law clk. to U.S. dist. judge, 1958-59; practice in Seattle, 1960-80; partner firm Perkins, Coie, Stone, Olsen & Williams, 1967-80; chief legal counsel Puget Sound Power & Light Co., 1970-80; v.p. contracts The Boeing Co., Seattle, 1980-81, v.p. contracts, gen. counsel, sec., 1981—; dir. Puget Sound Power & Light Co. Mem. Hale Adv. Council, 1974-76; trustee Wedgwood Presbyn. Ch., Seattle, 1968-70, Wash. State Research Council, 1981—; bd. dirs. Mental Health/North, 1979—, Jr. Achievement, Inc., 1981—; mem. adv. council Sch. Bus. Adminstrn., U. Mont., 1981—. Served as officer USAF, 1954-56. Mem. ABA, Fed. Energy Bar Assn., Am. Judicature Soc., Mont. Bar Assn., Wash. Bar Assn. (chmn. adminstrv. law sect. 1979), Seattle-King County Bar Assn. Republican. Clubs: Rainier, Seattle Yacht. Contbr. articles to legal jours. Home: 2621 2d Ave Seattle WA 98121 Office: PO Box 3707 Seattle WA 98124

BEIL, DRAKE, management and educational consultant; b. Miami Beach, Fla., Dec. 2, 1949; s. Theodore and Muriel (Feller) B.; m. Judi Iselin, July 2, 1972; children—Joshua Hayden, Dana Malia. B.A. in English, CCNY, 1971; M.Ed., U. Hawaii, 1975, Ed.D. in Curriculm and Instrn., 1981. Coordinator academically talented program Hawaii Dept. Edn., 1978; dir. tng. Survey & Mktg. Services, Inc., Hawaii, 1979-80; assoc. prof., lectr. U. Hawaii, dir. Ednl. Enterprises, 1979—; pres. Trans-Pacific Mgmt. Assocs., Inc., 1980—. Recipient Presdl. Achievement award, 1982. Mem. Am. Soc. Tng. and Devel. (pres. Hawaii chpt.), Internat. Reading Assn., Am. Chess Fedn. Club: Honolulu. Contbr. articles profl. jours. Office: PO Box 27731 Honolulu HI 96827

BEIL, KENNETH EMMON, consulting forester; b. San Diego, Calif., Mar. 20, 1920; s. Emmon Harrison and Nellie Mae (Berg) B.; m. Mary Louise Gordon, Oct. 5, 1946; children—Gordon Kenneth, Judy Ann Beil Eib. B.S. in Forestry, U. Wash., 1942. Registered land surveyor, Wash.; registered forester, Calif. Logging engr. Rayonier, Inc., Forks and Hoquiam, Wash., 1946-48; forester Army-Navy Lumber Agy., Portland (Oreg.) Dist. C.E., 1948-53; forester, logging engr. Nettleton Timber Co., Seattle, 1953-59; v.p., mgr. cons. div. Greenacres, Inc., Seattle, 1959-66; pres. Internat. Forestry Cons., Inc., Seattle, 1966—. Mem. Bellevue Streams Com., 1975-77. Served with USNR, 1944-46. Mem. Assn. Cons. Foresters (1st v.p.), Soc. Am. Foresters, Internat. Soc. Tropical Foresters. Republican. Presbyterian. Office: 220 Hoge Bldg Seattle WA 98104

BEIRIGER, KENNETH NORMAN, investment co. exec.; b. Bedford, Ind., Apr. 30, 1911; s. Edward George and Grace Marble (Van Benthuysen) B.; student Colo. Sch. Mines, 1929; B.A., Woodbury Coll., 1931; m. Mary Louise Sig, Aug. 12, 1937 (dec. 1963); children—Deanna (Mrs. John Simons), Martha (Mrs. Gordon Nedom), Kevin Edward; m. 2d, Marion Rosella Koester Sprague, Apr. 30, 1965. Supr. factory accounting So. Calif. div. Gen. Motors Corp., South Gate, 1936-41; controller Daggett div. Douglas Aircraft Co., Santa Monica, Calif., 1941-45; pub. accountant Hawkins, Warne, Beiriger & Co., Los Angeles, 1946-51; controller Pacific Airmotive Corp., Burbank, Calif., 1951-54, Am. Electronics, Inc., Los Angeles, 1957-61; group controller Gen. Precision, Inc., Glendale, Calif., 1961-64; asst. dir. fin. mgmt. Douglas Aircraft, 1965-69; v.p. San Diego Marine Constrn. Co., 1969-72; v.p., treas. Star & Crescent Investment Co., San Diego, 1972—, also dir.; sec., treas. Star & Crescent Boat Co., 1976—, also dir.; v.p. Star & Crescent Investment Co. of Nev., Las Vegas, 1976—, also dir.; treas., dir. Monticello Nurseries (Fla.), 1980—; sec.-treas. Boulder Beach Co., Las Vegas, 1982—. Mem. Nat. Assn. Accountants, Financial Execs. Inst., Gamma Sigma Pi. Elk. Home: 4324 Mt Helix Highlands Dr La Mesa CA 92041 Office: PO Box 751 570 No Harbor Dr San Diego CA 92112

BEIRNE, HELEN D., former state ofcl.; b. Idaho; postgrad. Stanford U., Syracuse U., Northwestern U.; Ph.D., U. Denver. Adminstr. and clin. dir. Alaska Crippled Children's Assn., 1956-59; mem. Alaska Ho. of Reps., 1969-70, 73-77; commr. Alaska Dept. Health and Social Services, 1978-82. Served as women's med. specialist U.S. Army, Japan. Office: Dept Health and Social Services Alaska Office Bldg Pouch H-01 Juneau AK 99811

BEITELSHEES, CLELAND DALE, phys. scientist; b. Huntington, Ind., Aug. 21, 1919; s. Oscar William and Velma Peace (Mason) B.; B.S., Huntington Coll., 1941; postgrad. Colo. U., 1946-49; m. Frieda Henrieta Sager, Mar. 26, 1943; 1 son, Carl Philip. Asst. chief chemist Rocky Mountain Arsenal, Denver, 1949-52; group leader Dow Chem. Co., Denver, 1952-61; chief chemist Bruesselbach Chem. Co., Denver, 1961-64; phys. scientist Dept. Interior, U.S. Bur. Reclamation, Denver, 1964-74. Pres., B, S & B, Inc., Boulder, Colo., 1963—; in charge of desalting test stas. Office of Saline Water, Dept. Interior, in Colo., N.M., Utah, Nev. and Wyo., 1968-74. Served with AUS, 1941-45. Registered profl. engr., Colo. Mem. Am. Chem. Soc., Boulder Aero. Soc. (pres. 1959-60), Aircraft Owners and Pilots Assn., Alpha Chi Sigma. Home: 3395 N 95th St Boulder CO 80301

BEITELSPACHER, RONALD JAMES, state senator; b. Hoven, S.D., Jan. 24, 1945; s. Albert and Marcelline (Illies) B.; student Santa Ana Coll., 1964-65; children—Diane, Janet. Lineman, Washington Water Power Co., Grangeville, Idaho, 1970—; mem. Idaho Senate, 1980—, Idaho Ho. of Reps., 1979-80; mem. com. human resources Nat. Conf. State Legislatures. Mem. Nat. Rifle Assn. Democrat. Roman Catholic. Club: Lions. Office: Box 405 Grangeville ID 83530*

BEITSCHER, STANLEY, metall. engr.; b. Bklyn., Nov. 19, 1935; s. Jack and Anna (Wieser) B.; Metall. Engr., Colo. Sch. Mines, 1957, Ph.D., 1970; M.S., Rensselaer Poly. Inst., 1961; m. Claudia Beard Smith, Apr. 5, 1981; children by previous marriage—Warren Steven, Deborah Lynn; stepchildren—Christine, Debra, Troy. Mech. metallurgist Gen. Electric Co., Schenectady, 1957-63; asso. scientist Rockwell Internat., Golden, Colo., 1963—; honorarium prof. mech. engring. U. Colo. Named Engr. of Yr., Rocky Flats Plant, Rockwell Internat., 1978. Mem. Am. Soc. Metals (sec. Rocky Mountain chpt. 1978-79, vice chmn. chpt. 1979-80, chmn. chpt. 1980-81, nat. MEI com. 1977-83), Israeli Metall Soc., Colo. Sch. Mines Alumni Assn., Step Family Assn. Colo., Rensselaer Poly. Inst. Alumni Assn. Democrat. Jewish. Club: Rocky Mountain Saab (co-dir.). Contbr. numerous articles on metall. engring. to profl. jours. Home: 8261 Upham Ct Arvada CO 80003 Office: Rockwell Rocky Flats Golden CO 80401

BEKEY, GEORGE ALBERT, electrical engineer, educator; b. Bratislava, Czechoslovakia, June 19, 1928; came to U.S., 1945, naturalized, 1956; s. Andrew and Elizabeth (Magyar) B.; B.S., U. Calif.-Berkeley, 1950; student UCLA, 1946-49, Ph.D., 1962, M.S., 1952; m. Shirley White, June 10, 1951; children—Ronald, Michelle. Research engr. UCLA, 1950-54; dir. computer ctr. Beckman Instruments, Los Angeles, 1955-58; mem. sr. tech. staff TRW Systems, Inc., Los Angeles, 1958-62; faculty U. So. Calif., Los Angeles, 1962—, prof., chmn. dept. elec. engring., 1978—; cons. in field. Served with Signal Corps, U.S. Army, 1954-56. Recipient Disting. Faculty award U. So. Calif., 1979; numerous grants. Fellow IEEE; mem. Soc. Computing Simulation (editor trans.), Biomed. Engring. Soc., AAAS, World Affairs Council. Patentee in field; author: (with W. Karplus) Hybrid Computation, 1968; contbr. articles to profl. jours.; editorial bd. Math. Bioscis., Math. and Computers in Simulation. Office: Dept Elec Engring Univ So Calif Los Angeles CA 90089

BEKOOY, RODGER GEORGE, cons. engring. co. exec.; b. Portland, Oreg., Jan. 10, 1942; s. George and Irene Gwendolyn (Robertson) B.; student Portland State U., 1960-61; B.S. in M.E., Oreg. State U., 1965; m. Susan Alice Bekooy, June 8, 1965; children—Elizabeth, Catherine, Stephanie. Staff engr. Morrison, Funatake & Assos., Inc., Portland, 1970-77; prin. Carson, Bekooy, Gulick & Assos., Inc., Portland, 1977—. Served with U.S. Navy, 1965-70. Registered profl. engr. Oreg. Mem. ASHRAE, Cons. Engrs. Council Am., Nat. Soc. Profl. Engrs., Am. Soc. Plumbing Engrs. Office: 3220 SW 1st Ave Portland OR 97201

BEL, ERNEST FRED, clergyman, psychoanalyst; b. New Orleans, Oct. 23, 1936; s. John Albert and Daisy Miller (Boyd) B.; m. Carolyn Cavitt Pilchard, June 16, 1956; m. 2d, Mary Elizabeth Barnes, Nov. 29, 1980; children—John Boyd, Jeanne Elizabeth. B.A., La. State U., 1958; M. Div., Gen. Theol. Sem., N.Y.C., 1961; postgrad. in humanistic psychology Baden, Switzerland, 1974; grad. C.G. Jung Inst., Zurich, Switzerland, 1975. Ordained priest Episcopal church, 1961; asst. priest Christ Ch. Cathedral, New Orleans, 1961-63; chaplain, asst. headmaster St. Martin's Sch., Metairie, La., 1963-69; pvt. practice in Jungian psychoanalysis, Tiburon, Calif., 1975—; mem. faculty C.G. Jung Inst. San Francisco, 1977—; staff mem. St. Stephen's Episc. ch., Belvedere; mem. clinic staff Sunset Day Treatment Ctr., San Francisco, 1976. Mem. Am. Personnel and Guidance Assn., Internat. Assn. Analytical Psychology. Democrat. Office: 1640 Tiburon Blvd PO Box 718 Tiburon CA 94920

BELAMIDE, ERNEST KIAMZON, mgmt. devel. cons.; b. Philippines, Dec. 11, 1942; came to U.S., 1971; s. Jose J. and Elisea M. (Kiamzon) B.; B.S. in Econs., Ateneo de Manila (Philippines) U., 1964; M.A. in Edn., Loyola-Marymount U., 1972. Instr., Ateneo de Manila High Sch., 1964-68; supr. Blue Cross So. Calif., Los Angeles, 1972-74, personnel devel. specialist, 1974-79; mgr. mgmt. devel. Alpha Therapeutic Corp., Los Angeles, 1980—; pres. UNI, Inc.; facilitator personal growth workshops; tchr. profl. growth. Mem. Am. Soc. Tng. and Devel., Orgn. Devel. Network, Alpha Sigma Nu. Author co. handbooks. Home: Alpha Therapeutic Corp 5555 Valley Blvd Los Angeles CA 90032 Office: 5555 Valley Blvd Los Angeles CA 90032

BELDEN, LOUIS DE KEYSER, investment counsel; b. Indpls., July 11, 1926; s. Louis de Keyser and Frances (Pardue) B.; B.A., Harvard U., 1949; M.B.A., Stanford U., 1951. Security analyst Bank of New York, 1951-52; ptnr. Brundage, Story & Rose, N.Y.C., 1961-66; pres. Wentworth, Belden & Dahl, San Francisco, 1966-75, Belden and Assocs. Investment Counsel, San Francisco, 1975—; regent Fin. Analysts Seminar, 1976-80. Community adviser San Francisco Jr. League, 1977—; pres. Internat. Inst. San Francisco, 1970. Served with AUS, 1944-46. Mem. Investment Counsel Assn. Am. (gov. 1976—). Republican. Episcopalian. Clubs: University, Harvard (N.Y.C.); Stock Exchange, St. Francis Yacht (San Francisco). Home: 1100 Union St San Francisco CA 94109 Office: 2 Embarcadero Center Suite 2910 San Francisco CA 94111

BELDING, HIRAM HURLBURT, III, physician; b. Riverside, Ill., Aug. 15, 1918; s. Hiram Hurlburt and Rose Wright (Merritt) B.; A.B., Dartmouth Coll., 1941; M.D., Northwestern U., 1943; M.S., U. Minn., 1953; m. Nancee Rogers Rielheimer, Dec. 27, 1941; children—Hiram Hurlburt, Lindsay B. (Mrs. T.J. Heaslet), David S., Mark R.; m. 2d, Barbara Carroll Littlefield, Feb. 14, 1973; 1 son, Joel L. Intern, Henry Ford Hosp., Detroit, 1943, resident in surgery, Detroit, 1943-45, Mayo Clinic, Rochester, Minn., 1947-50, asst. to staff in surgery, 1950-51; practice medicine, specializing in surgery, Riverside, Calif., 1951—; asso. prof. surgery Loma Linda U., 1971—; mem. staff Riverside Community Hosp., Riverside Gen. Hosp., Parkview Community Hosp. Pres., Univ. Religious Center, U. Calif., Riverside, 1962-64; mem. Bd. Zoning Adjustment, City of Riverside, 1963; mem. Riverside Planning Commn., 1964-67; mem. Riverside City Council, 1967-71. Served to capt. M.C., AUS, 1945-47. Mem. Riverside County, Calif., Am. med. assns., Tri-County Surg. Assn. So. Calif., Am. Geriatrics Soc., So. Calif. Gastroenterologic Soc., Los Angeles Acad. Medicine, Los Angeles Surg. Soc., Western Surg. Assn., Pacific Coast Surg. Assn., A.C.S., Sigma Xi. Republican. Episcopalian (sr. warden 1960-61). Club: Victoria Club (Riverside). Contbr. articles to profl. jours. Office: 6860 Brochton Ave Riverside CA 92506

BELDING, HIRAM HURLBURT, IV, psychologist; b. Chgo., Nov. 26, 1942; s. Hiram Hurlburt and Nancee Rogers (Rietheimer) B.; m. Margaret Irving, June 25, 1966; children—Wendy Kathleen, Lindsay Cameron. A.A., Riverside City Coll., 1964; B.A. in Psychology, San Jose State U., 1968; M.A. in Human Behavior, U.S. Internat. U., 1971, Ph.D. in Human Behavior, 1975. Lic. clin. psychologist S.C., Calif. Agt. Conn. Mut. Life Ins., Santa Clara, Calif., 1968-68; dep. probation officer aftercare and placement Calif. Probation Dept. Twin Pines Ranch for Boys, Banning, 1968-70; counselor Manaolu campus U.S. Internat. U., Makawao, Maui, Hawaii, 1971-72; instr. psychology Dominican Coll., Racine, Wis., 1972-73; clin. psychologist, owner Psychol. Services San Diego, 1979—; cons. in field. Bd. dirs. Riverside County Employees Assn., 1969. Served to lt. USN, 1974-79. Mem. Am. Psychol. Assn., Clin. Psychology Assn., Clin. Hypnosis Assn., Assn. Advancement Psychology, Am. Group Psychotherapy Assn. Office: 3560 4th Ave San Diego CA 92103

BELIAJUS, VYTAUTAS FINADAR, publisher; b. Lithuania, Feb. 26, 1908; came to U.S., 1923, naturalized, 1940; s. Joseph and Sofia Beliajus. Instr. dance Chgo. Park Dist.-WPA, 1934-39, Sch. Organic Edn., Fairhope, Ala., 1942-44; guest tchr. throughout U.S., Can. and Mex., 1936—, Israel, 1973—; pub. Viltis, A Mag. of Folklore and Folk Dance, Denver, 1942—, Lore mag., 1936-39, Dance and Be Merry, Vol. 1, 1940, Vol. 2, 1941, Lithuanian Folk Dances, 1950, Evening Song: Lithuanian Legends, 1954, Hanukkah Book, 1974, ONA (short stories), 1977; also numerous pamphlets; organizer 1st Lithuanian folk dance club in world, 1933; dir. Atetis Lithuanian Folk Dancers, 1945-50; organized 1st Kolo club in U.S., 1937. Recipient cert. recognition 20th Kolo Festival, San Francisco, 1971, Honor Man of Year award AAHPER, 1972, numerous others. Mem. Colo. Folk Arts Council, Friends Martha Faure Dance Library. Office: PO Box 1226 Denver CO 80201

BELK, JOHN BLANTON, educational organization executive; b. Orlando, Fla., Feb. 4, 1925; s. John Blanton and Jennie (Wannamaker) B.; m. Elizabeth Jane Wilkes, Dec. 11, 1954; children—Virginia Elizabeth, Katherine Wilkes. Student, Davidson (N.C.) Coll., 1943, U. N.C., 1943-45. Aide to congressman U.S. Ho. of Reps., Washington, 1949-50; vol. Moral Re-Armament, exec. dir., to 1968; founder, chmn. bd., pres. Up With People, 1968—. Active Tucson Mus. Art, Tucson Symphony. Served to lt. (j.g.) USN, 1943-45; PTO. Decorated Order of Vasco Nunez de Balboa (Panama), Mem. Zeta Psi. Clubs: Mountain Oyster, Old Pueblo (Tucson); Guaymas (Mexico) Yacht. Home: 2920 Cerrado los Palitos Tucson AZ 85718 Office: 3103 N Campsbell Ave Tucson AZ 85719

BELL, A(LEXANDER) ROBERT LUNDRIGAN, educator; b. Rock Island, Ill., Aug. 9, 1936; s. William and Rosaleigh (Coombs-Lundrigan) B.; student U. Chgo., 1959; B.A., U. Miami, 1960, M.A., 1962; D.D., Brotherhood Ch., Spokane, 1970; Ph.D., U. Md., 1971. Jr. acct. H.L. Davis & Assos., Miami, Fla., 1954-57; research asst. CBS-TV Network, N.Y.C., 1957; asst. to pres. Research Des-Tex, Inc., Miami, 1958-59; publications asst. Domestic Engring. Publs., Chgo, 1959; bibliographic researcher U. Miami, 1960-62; instr. U. Md., 1963, 67-69, also asst. to head dept. English; instr. English, Calif. State U., Long Beach, 1964-67, asst. prof., 1969-73, asso. prof., 1973-78, prof., 1979—, producer ednl. video series, 1972—; v.p. Archive Corp., San Francisco, 1963—; co-founder, dir. Center for Mediaeval & Renaissance Studies. Served with ROTC, U.S. Army, 1951-54. Center for Mediaeval and Renaissance Studies fellow, 1973—; Knights Templar scholar, Vitale scholar. Fellow Anglo Am. Acad.; mem. Mediaeval Acad. Am., Medieval Assn. Pacific Coast, Early English Text Soc., France-Am. Soc., Am. Film Inst. Episcopalian. Club: Order DeMolay. Author: Changes, 1975, Cute Ben, 1976; editor: Comparative Literature Newsletter, 1967—, Studies in Bibliography, 1968—; contbr. articles in field to profl. jours. Office: Calif State U 1250 Bellflower Blvd Long Beach CA 90840

BELL, ARTHUR THOEN, printing co. exec.; b. Santa Monica, Calif., Oct. 28, 1942; s. Arthur Anthony and Audrey Gwendolyn (Larson) B.; B.A. in Social Sci., San Jose State U., 1964; m. Linda Ann Lawson, Aug. 11, 1967; children—Brendy Lynn, Jason Wesley. Salesman, Graphic Press, Los Angeles, 1967-72; gen. mgr. Continwntal Graphics, Los Angeles, 1972-78; v.p., co-owner Colographics, Los Angeles, 1978—; adv. bd. Los Angeles Advt. Ctr.; speaker in field. Mem. Printing Industries Am. (excellence in printing and packaging award 1977). Republican. Clubs: Los Angeles Racquet, Calabasas Golf. Office: 150 N Meyers St Los Angeles CA 90033

BELL, DAVID BISHOP, pediatrician, educator; b. Boise, Idaho, Apr. 11, 1939; s. Walter Godfrey and Georgia Edith (Patterson) B.; m. Lorna Dee MacKinnon, Dec. 27, 1961; children—David Ainslie, Diana Lökke, Malcolm Bishop. B.S., Oreg. State U., 1962; Ph.D. in Pharmacology, U. Colo., 1967, M.D., 1969. Diplomate Am. Bd. Pediatrics. Intern, Children's Orthopedic Hosp., Seattle, 1969-70; resident in pediatrics U. Wash., Seattle, 1969-72; practice medicine specializing in pediatrics, Portland, Oreg., 1974—; mem. staff Emanuel Hosp., 1974—, chmn. dept. pediatrics, 1976—; asst. clin. prof. pediatrics U. Oreg. Health Scis. Ctr., Portland, 1977—. Served to maj. M.C., U.S. Army, 1972-74. Mem. Am. Acad. Pediatrics, Oreg. Med. Assn., Multnomah County Med. Assn., Portland Acad. Pediatrics, North Pacific Pediatric Soc., Oreg. Pediatric Soc. Home: 13747 NE Klickitat Ct Portland OR 97230 Office: 265 N Broadway Portland OR 97227

BELL, EARLIE BOBBIE DELLEY, educator; b. James, Tex., Mar. 24, 1934; d. Earl and Ethel Lee (Crowe) Delley; B.S., Tex. Coll., 1953; M.A., U. Denver, 1968; 1 dau., Marguerite Lynne. Tchr.-counselor, Denver Public Schs., 1960-71, summer sch. coordinator, asst. to prin., 1971-75, diagnostic tchr., 1975—; coordinator Community Study Hall. Team mem. Edn. Participation in Communities, 1969; candidate Colo. Ho. of Reps., 1970; Dem. committeewoman, 1968; active adult edn. tutorial program, 1975. Colo. State Centennial-Bicentennial Commemoration grantee, 1976. Mem. NEA, Colo. Edn. Assn., Denver Classroom Tchrs. Assn., Assn. Supervision and Curriculum Devel., AAUW, Delta Kappa Gamma, Zeta Phi Beta, Nat. Assn. Fashion and Accessory Designers, Nat. Council Negro Women. Baptist.

BELL, FRANKLIN DANIEL, educator; b. Fresno, Calif., Feb. 2, 1928; s. Frank Mayhill and Eva Pearl (Wood) B.; B.A., U. Calif., Santa Barbara, 1953; A.A., Monterey Peninsula Coll., 1951; M.Ed., Oreg. State U., 1957, postgrad., 1974, 75; m. Carol Jean Bedau, June 25, 1950; children—David F., Kenneth D. Tchr. indsl. arts, adult edn. Rosemead (Calif.) High Sch., 1953—, chmn. indsl. arts dept., 1970—; master tchr. trainer in career edn. Rio Hondo Coll., Whittier, Calif., 1971—, mem. indsl. edn. advisory com., 1968—. Merit badge counselor Boy Scouts Am., 1958-75, adviser explorers post, 1960-65; coach Little League, 1958-60; counselor Indian Guides Hi Y, 1959-61. Served with USAAF, 1946-49. Mem. El Monte Union High Sch. Dist. Edn. Assn. (pres. 1972-73), Calif. Indsl. Edn. Assn. (So. sect. indsl. arts tchr. of yr. 1978), Calif. Indsl. Arts Assn. (dir., high sch. rep.), Am. Vocat. Assn., NEA, Nat. Woodcarving Assn., Nat. Rifle Assn., Calif. Fish and Game Hunter Safety Assn. (instr.), Amateur Trap Assn., Calif. Carvers Guild, Calif. Rifle and Pistol Assn. Republican. Presbyterian. Office: 9063 Mission St Rosemead CA 91770

BELL, GEORGE ALFRED, marketing professional; b. Plattsburgh, N.Y., Mar. 14, 1948; s. George Alfred and Marian (Yersley) B.; B.A. in Pub. Relations, San Jose State U., 1978; A.A., Antelope Valley Coll., 1976. Automobile racing driver, 1964-67, 70-72; liaison engr., mem. flight test crew Lockheed-Calif. Co., Palmdale, 1972-75; v.p. Bluemenshein & Bell, Leona Valley, Calif., 1975-77; cons. pub. relations, writer, San Jose, Calif., 1977-81; mgr. mktg. communications Dynatel/3M, Sunnyvale, Calif., 1981-83; account exec. Simon Pub. Relations, Sunnyvale, Calif., 1983—; cons. mktg. communications and research; condr. seminars in high performance driving for law enforcement agys.; designer racing cars and lightweight aircraft, 1964-80. Served with AUS, 1967-70; Vietnam. Decorated Air medal, Army Commendation medal, Purple Heart. Mem. Pub. Relations Soc. Am., Internat. Assn. Bus. Communicators, Bus./Profl. Advt. Assn. (bd. dirs. 1982—, v.p. fin. 1983—),

Soaring Soc. Am., Exptl. Aircraft Assn. Author: Motor Racing' Management, 1975; contbr. numerous articles to mags. Home: 3830 Underwood Dr Apt 4 San Jose CA 95117

BELL, GEORGE LEE, merchant; b. Ogden, Utah, May 2, 1927; s. George and Beatrice (Lee) B.; m. June Brewer, Aug. 4, 1947; children—Gregory S., Christopher J., Dexter L., Corey G., Justin D., Nathan W., Daren R., Allyson. B.S., U. Utah, 1949. Owner, mgr., Bell Co. Janitorial Supply, Ogden, 1963—. Mem. Ogden City Sch. Bd., 1970—, pres., 1974, 77, 81. Served with USN, 1945-46. Mormon. Club: Lions (past pres.). Home: 2557 Jackson Ave Ogden UT 84401 Office: 1776 Wall Ave Ogden UT 84404

BELL, GEORGE LEE, industrial engineer; b. Sacramento, Oct. 17, 1952; s. Harold Lee and Joanna Sue (West) B.; student El Camino Jr. Coll., 1971-72; m. Gail Andrea McCarthy, Dec. 2, 1972; children—Steven, Sean. With Liberty Appliance Co., Torrance, Calif., 1972-73, Honeywell, Inc., Commerce, Calif., 1973-79; indsl. design engr. Litton Energy Control Systems, Chatsworth, Calif., 1979-82; project mgr. Margaux Controls, Inc., San Jose, Calif., 1982—. Mem. ASHRAE. Republican. Baptist. Office: 2302A Lake Forest Dr Suite K Laguna Hills CA 92653

BELL, GORDON WOLF, executive trainer; b. Montreal, Que., Can., Dec. 2, 1938; came to U.S., 1959; s. Leslie and Nettie (Goldman) B. Founder Speak Easy Internat. div. Wolf Gordon Bell & Assocs., Carmel, Calif. Served with U.S. Army, 1962-64. Mem. Nat. Speakers Assn. Office: PO Box 4261 Carmel CA 93921

BELL, JAMES KENTON, educator, author; b. Borger, Tex., Sept. 30, 1937; s. Walter Kenton and Martha Ruth (Blankenship) B.; B.A., U. Calif. at Santa Barbara, 1959; M.A., U. Calif. at Berkeley, 1961; m. Joan Penelope Dunn, Oct. 5, 1957 (div. Aug. 1983); children—Elizabeth Anne, Jonathan Edward-Kenton. Prof. English, Grossmont (Calif.) Coll., 1961-62, Coll. San Mateo (Calif.), 1963—. Author: (with Adrian A. Cohn) Rhetoric in a Modern Mode, 1968; Toward the New America, 1970; Rhetoric 2, 1972; Bell and Cohn's Handbook of Grammar, Style and Usage, 1972; Rhetoric 3, 1976. Home: 2044 Touraine Lane Half Moon Bay CA 94019 Office: 1700 W Hillsdale Blvd San Mateo CA 94402

BELL, JAYNELLE KHAMILLAH, pharmaceutical company official; b. Oakland, Calif., Feb. 26, 1953; d. William Hayes and Genieve Cartwright (Hilton) Jenkins; B.A., U. Calif., Berkeley, 1976; M.B.A. (Basic Edn. Opportunity grantee, Consortium fellow), U. So. Calif., 1979; m. James M. Bell, June 28, 1980; children—Robert, Semaj. Bus. mgr. U. Calif.-Berkeley publ. Blue and Gold, 1975-76; mktg. analyst Oakland Tribune/Gannett Publs., 1976-77; sales rep. Procter & Gamble Co., San Francisco dist., 1979-81; dist. mgr. Drackett Products div. Bristol Myers Corp., Dublin, Calif., 1981—. Participant Big Sister Program, San Francisco, 1974—; voter registrar for Congressional campaign, 1971—. Mem. Nat. Assn. Female Execs., Women in Advt., Nat. Council Negro Women (publicity dir. asst. 1979), LWV. Republican. Methodist. Club: Profl. and Bus. Women's. Editor United Meth. Women newsletter, 1982. Home: 345 Goheen Circle Vallejo CA 94590 Office: Drackett Products div Bristol Myers Corp 11875 Dublin Blvd Suite A 160 Dublin CA 94566

BELL, JOHN FREDERICK, forestry educator; b. Ashland, Oreg., Jan. 7, 1924; s. James Roderick and Lilly (Duvy) B.; m. Myrna Perry, Aug. 2, 1928; children—Cheri, Marilyn, James, Marla. B.S., Oreg. State U., 1949; M.F., Duke U., 1951; Ph.D., U. Mich., 1970. With Oreg. Dept. Forestry, 1949-59; mem. faculty Oreg. State U., Corvallis, 1959—, now prof. forestry. Served with inf. U.S. Army, 1943-46. Mem. Soc. Am. Foresters. Republican. Mormon. Contbr. numerous articles to profl. jours. Office: Dept Forestry Oreg State U Corvallis OR 97331

BELL, LARRY STUART, artist; b. Chgo., Dec. 6, 1939, s. Hyman David and Rebecca Ann (Kriegmont) B.; student Chouinard Art Inst., Los Angeles, 1957-59; married; 2 daus., 1 son. One man exhbns. include: Stedelijk Mus., Amsterdam, 1967, Pasadena Art Mus., 1972, Oakland Mus., 1973, Ft. Worth Art Mus., 1975, Santa Barbara Mus. Art, 1976, Hudson River Mus., 1981, Newport Harbor Art Mus., Newport Beach, Calif., 1982, Milw. Art Mus., 1982, Mus. Fine Arts, Santa Fe, 1982, Detroit Inst. Arts, 1982; group exhbns. include: Los Angeles 6, Vancouver Art Gallery, 1968, Walker Art Center, Mpls., 1968, Mus. Modern Art, N.Y.C., 1965, Jewish Mus., N.Y.C., 1966, Whitney Mus. Am. Art, 1966, Guggenheim Mus., 1967, Tate Gallery, London, 1970, Hayward Gallery, London, 1971, Detroit Inst. Arts, 1973, Nat. Collections Fine Arts, 1975, San Francisco Mus. Modern Art, 1976, Los Angeles County Mus. Art, 1981; represented in permanent collections. Nat. Mus. Am. Art, Washington, Mus. Modern Art, N.Y.C., Whitney Mus. Am. Art, Guggenheim Mus., Los Angeles County Mus. Art, Tate Gallery, Gallery New South Wales (Australia), Centre Georges Pompidou, Paris, City of Denver; instr. sculpture U. South Fla., Tampa, U. Calif. at Berkeley, Calif. State Coll. at Hayward, U. Calif. at Irvine, 1969-73. Copley Found. grantee, 1962; Guggenheim Found. fellow, 1970; Nat. Endowment Arts grantee, 1975. Home: Box 495 Ranchos de Taos NM 87557 Office: Box 4101 Taos NM 87571

BELL, LEO S., physician; b. Newark, Nov. 7, 1913; s. Alexander M. and Marie (Saxon) B.; A.B., Syracuse U., 1934; M.D., 1938; m. Edith Lewis, July 3, 1938; children—Jewyl Linn, David Alden. Intern, N.Y.C. Hosp., 1938, Bklyn. Hosp., 1939-40; resident in pediatrics Sea View Hosp., N.Y.C., 1940-41, N.Y.C. Hosp., 1941-42; practice medicine specializing in pediatrics, San Mateo, Calif., 1946—; mem. staff Mills Meml. Hosp., San Mateo, Peninsula Hosp. & Med. Center, Burlingame, Children's Hosp., San Francisco; asst. clin. prof. pediatrics U. Calif. Med Sch., San Francisco, Stanford Med. Sch. Palo Alto. Bd. dirs. Mills Hosp. Found., San Mateo, San Mateo County Heart Assn. Served to capt. as flight surgeon USAAF, 1942-46. Recipient bronze and silver medals Am. Heart Assn.; diplomate Am. Bd. Pediatrics. Fellow Am. Acad. Pediatrics, Am. Pub. Health Assn.; mem. Calif. Fedn. Pediatric Socs. (pres.), Am. Fedn. Pediatric Socs. (pres.), Calif. Med. Assn., Am. Pub. Health Assn., Air Force Assn., AMA (alt. del. to ho. of dels.), Calif. (ho. of dels.), San Mateo County (sec.-treas.) med. assns., Internat., Hong Kong snuff bottle socs., World Affairs Council San Francisco. Clubs: Peninsula Golf and Country (San Mateo); Commonwealth (San Francisco). Contrb. articles to profl. jours. Home: 220 Roblar Ave Hillsborough CA 94010 Office: 36 San Mateo Dr San Mateo CA 94401

BELL, LLOYD FRANKLIN, computer co. exec.; b. Polk County, Ark., Apr. 9, 1922; s. Benjamin Franklin and Anna Caroline (Woods) B.; B.S., U.S. Naval Acad., 1944; M.S., Stanford, 1952, Ph.D., 1961; m. Rita Lilian Winkler, Nov. 7, 1968; children—John Franklin, Mary Anne Bell Taylor, Celia Frances. Commd. ensign U.S. Navy, 1944, advanced through grades to capt.; ret., 1969; various duties including dir. Naval ASW Data Center, 1965-68, staff Chief of Naval Ops., 1968-69; sr. scientist, dir. Tetra Tech, Inc., San Diego, 1969-76; pres. Tetra Tech Services, Inc., San Diego, 1976—; lectr. math. U. Hawaii, 1961-64. Mem. Ops. Research Soc. Am., Sigma Xi. Home: 2288 Soledad Rancho Rd San Diego CA 92109 Office: 3559 Kenyon St San Diego CA 92110

BELL, MARION WETHERBEE JACK, aerospace co. exec.; b. Wichita Falls, Tex., Aug. 17, 1927; s. Marion Wetherbee and Mamie Louise Verdie (Carpenter) B.; B.S., U.S. Mcht. Marine Acad., 1949; student Ohio State U., 1954-56, Calif. State U., Long Beach, 1977-79; m. Janell Wright MacDonald, Nov. 4, 1950; children—Jan Ellen, Marion Wetherbee Jack, David MacDonald, Heather Anne Louise, Rebecca Lynn, Diana Laurel. Deck officer Alcoa Steamship Co., Mobile, Ala., 1949-54; propulsion system design devel. and test engr. N. Am. Aviation, Inc., Columbus, Ohio, 1954-57, advanced systems project engr., 1957-61; with Rockwell Internat., Downey, Calif., 1962—, asst. chief engr. preliminary design and mission analysis, 1981—. Fellow AIAA (assoc.). Brit. Interplanetary Soc. Mem. Christian Ch. Club: Mason. Home: 3332 Corinna Dr Rancho Palos Verdes CA 90274 Office: Rockwell International 12214 Lakewood Blvd Downey CA 90241

BELL, MICHAEL GEOFFREY, chemist; b. Ashland, Ohio, Aug. 12, 1947; s. Wakeman R. and Frances B. (Bell) B.; B.Chemistry, Western N.Mex. U., 1972. Chemist, U.S. Natural Resources, Mining and Minerals, Silver City, N.Mex., 1970-72; forensic drug chemist N.Mex. State Police Crime Lab., Santa Fe, 1972—. Mem. Midwest Assn. Forensic Sci., Southwestern Assn. Forensic Scientists, Am. Chem. Soc., Nat. Rifle Assn. (life), N.Mex. Rifle and Pistol Assn. Democrat. Methodist. Home: 2922 Camino del Gusto Santa Fe NM 87501 Office: PO Box 1628 Santa Fe NM 87501

BELL, MICHAEL STEVEN, art curator; b. Joplin, Mo., July 4, 1946; s. Vernon L. and Alpha Marie (Russell) B.; m. Michele Ellis, Oct. 29, 1978; children—Shannon, Ororah, Justin, Mercury. B.F.A. (scholar), Calif. Inst. Arts, 1970; M.F.A., U. Ky., 1972. Teaching asst. Calif. Inst. Art, 1970-71, U. Ky., 1971-72; designer Amorphia, Inc., Mill Valley, Calif., 1972; asst. dir. reprodns. dept. Vorpal Gallery, San Francisco, 1973-74; curatorial asst. Oakland (Calif.) Mus., 1975-76, registrar, 1976-80; dir. Midland (Mich.) Art Council, 1980-81; art curator San Francisco Mus. Modern Art, 1981—; exhibited in group shows including: Evansville (Ind.) Mus. Art and Sci., 1971, San Francisco Mus. Modern Art, 1978. Served with USAF, 1963-67. Mem. Art Mus. Assn., Am. Assn. Mus., Internat. Council Museums. Episcopalian. Contbr. poems to various publs. Home: 763 45th Ave San Francisco CA 94121 Office: San Francisco Museum of Modern Art Van Ness and McAllister St San Francisco CA 94102

BELL, PAULA OBRAY, assn. exec.; b. Paradise, Utah, Aug. 18, 1933; d. Ernest S. and Kate (Hawkes) Obray; m. Charles Connell Bell, June 27, 1952; children—Charles Michael, David Paul, Rodney O., Allison. Student Utah State U., 1952, 80—. Legal aid, Logan, Utah, 1951, 55-65; adminstrv. asst. continuing edn. ctr. Utah State U., 1967-70; exec. v.p. Roosevelt (Utah) C. of C., 1973—; real estate salesperson Roosevelt area, 1972—. Chmn. Roosevelt City Econ. Devel. Com.; chmn. Roosevelt Mcpl. Airport Bd.; bd. dirs. Utah Heart Assn., chmn., 1981-82, regional rep.; mem. bd. commrs. Utah Travel Council; mem. adv. bd. Utah State U. Coll. Bus. Utah Festival Arts, Utah Children's Mus.; mem. Utah State Agenda for 80's sterring com.; trustee Utah Council Vols.; past sec.-treas. Republican party, Duchesne County. Named Outstanding Young Woman of Utah, 1976. Mem. Utah State C. of C. (dir., pres. 1977), Utah Airport Owners and Operators Assn. (sec.-treas.). Mormon. Clubs: Bus. and Profl. Women (Woman of Yr. award 1982), Pilot, Socialette, Fedn. Women's. Home: 11 E Lagoon Roosevelt UT 84066 Office: 332 S Second St Roosevelt UT 84066

BELL, ROBERT B., travel agency executive; b. Boston, December 22, 1923; s. Abraham and Sarah (Lewis) B.; divorced; children—Amy Bell Wilder, Susan, Randall, Benjamin. Student Boston U., 1941-43. Pres. Tenneco Advanced Materials, Inc., Boston, 1946-65; pres. Gilford Inc., N.Y.C., 1965-68, chmn. 1968-82; chmn. Wings Travel, Inc., Los Angeles, 1982—; chmn., pres. Relief Printing Corp., Los Angeles and Boston, 1975—; also tchr., cons. Served to 2d lt. U.S. Army, 1943-46. Mem. Am. Mgmt. Assn., Tau Epsilon Phi. Republican. Clubs: Masons, Friars. Inventor 6 roll vinyl calender. Office: 1737 Cordova St Los Angeles CA 90007

BELL, ROSALIND MILLS, insurance company executive; b. Phoenix, Nov. 18, 1945; d. John Clay and Velma (May) Mills; m. Joseph Lawrence Bell, Apr. 26, 1943 (div.); children—Andrew, Michele. B.A. in Math, U. N.Mex., 1967. Statistician to programmer-analyst Amerco U-Haul, Phoenix, 1967-71; programmer-analyst to analyst-programmer Motorola, Phoenix, 1973-76; systems analyst, sr. systems analyst, mgr. ops. Blue Shield, Portland, Oreg., 1976—; systems and programming mgr. Blue Cross-Blue Shield of Oreg., Portland. Mem. Assn. Systems Mgmt. Office: Blue Cross-Blue Shield of Oreg 100 SW Market St Portland OR 97204

BELLAMY, GIL WORTHINGTON, state ofcl.; b. Oregon City, Oreg., July 14, 1943; s. G. Worth and Elsa (Zacker) B.; B.S. (scholar), U. So. Calif., 1965; J.D., Willamette U., 1969; m. Glenice Joy Cook, Aug. 29, 1964; children—Mark, Dirk. Law clk. Oreg. Legis. Counsel Com., 1967-69; admitted to Oreg. bar, 1970; adminstr. Oreg. Traffic Safety Commn., 1969—; adj. prof. Oreg. State U., 1974—; lectr. Coll. Law, Willamette U., 1975—; judge McMinnville Mcpl. Ct., 1976; mem. Group Study Exchange Team to India, 1980. Mem. Salem (Oreg.) Planning Commn., 1978-82; youth legislature cons. YMCA, 1970—; chmn. Oreg. Employees Cancer Crusade, 1980, 82; bd. dirs. Salem Boys' Club, 1979-82; master of ceremonies Salem Jr. Miss Contest, 1979; mem. Presdl. Commn. on Drunk Driving, 1982; exec. dir. Gov.'s Task Force on Driving While Intoxicated, 1982—. Recipient Jr. First Citizen of Salem award, 1976. Mem. Oreg. Bar Assn., Nat. Conf. Gov.'s Hwy. Safety Reps. (dir.), Transp. Research Bd. of Nat. Acad. Scis. Home: 2945 Island View Dr N Salem OR 97303 Office: 400 State Library Bldg Salem OR 97303

BELLAMY, JOHN CARY, engineer; b. Cheyenne, Wyo., Apr. 18, 1915; s. Benjamin Charles and Beth (Cary) B.; B.S. in Civil Engring., U. Wyo., 1936; Ph.M. in Physics, U. Wis., 1938; Ph.D. in Meteorology, U. Chgo., 1947; m. Josephine Johnston, Sept. 21, 1940; children—John Cary, Agnes Louise, Charles Fulton, William Delaney, Mary Elizabeth. With Bellamy & Sons, Engrs., Lamont, Wyo., 1938-41; asst. prof. U. Chgo., 1941-47, dir. Inst. Tropical Meteorology, San Juan, P.R., 1944; asst. dir. Cook Research Labs., Cook Electric Co., Chgo., 1947-59; pvt. practice cons., Barrington, Ill., 1959-60; dir. Natural Resources Research Inst., U. Wyo., Laramie, 1960-70, prof. dept. civil and archtl. engring., 1970-81; Wyo. mem. Western Interstate Nuclear Bd., 1967-77. Served as spl. cons. USAAF, 1943-45. Decorated Medal of Freedom; recipient Losey award, Inst. Aero. Scis., 1944; Disting. Alumni award U. Wyo., 1968; lic. surveyor, profl. engr., Wyo.; lic pvt. pilot. Fellow Am. Meteol. Soc. (dir., cert. cons. meteorologist); mem. Inst. Nav. (pres. Thurlow award, 1946), Am. Geophys. Union, Nat. Soc. Profl. Engrs. (pres. Bellamy chpt.), Am. Inst. Engring. Edn., Wyo. Engring. Soc., Sigma Xi, Phi Kappa Phi, Sigma Tau. Clubs: Laramie Lions (pres., 1980), Sigma Alpha Epsilon (pres. Wyo., 1935). Patentee electromech. devices; contbg. author to books and manuals in field; originator of Bellamy Drift method of navigation; contbr. tech. papers to publs. Home and Office: 2308 Holliday Dr Laramie WY 82070

BELLAN, JOSETTE ROSENTWEIG (MRS. PAUL MURRAY BELLAN), combustion scientist; b. Bucharest, Romania, May 9, 1946; d. Naftali Leizer Rosentweig and Sara (Scvartz) R.; m. Paul Murray Bellan, June 25, 1972; children—Norbert Henry, Leon Marcel. A.E.A., M.S. in Applied Math., U. Scis. of Paris, 1969; M.A., M.S. in Aerospace and Mech. Engring., Princeton U., 1972, Ph.D. (Amelia Earhart fellow), 1974. Mem. research staff Princeton U., 1974-77; scientist Sci. Applications Inc., Los Angeles, 1977-78; engr. specialist Boeing Co., Pasadena, Calif., 1978-80; mem. tech. staff. Jet Propulsion Lab., Pasadena, Calif., 1980—; Recipient Bourse du Troisieme Cycle award U. Scis. of Paris, 1969. Mem. AIAA, ASME (tech. com. on combustion and heat transfer in fires), Combustion Inst. Contbr. articles to profl. jours. Office: 4800 Oak Grove Dr MS 125-159 Pasadena CA 91109

BELLER, GERALD STEPHEN, former ins. co. exec.; b. Phila., Aug. 6, 1935; s. Nathan and Adelaide B. (Goldfarb) B.; C.L.U., Am. Coll., Bryn Mawr, Pa., 1972; m. Nancy R. Nelson, June 8, 1968; children—Fay A., Mark S., Royce W., Merrilee A. Spl. agt. Prudential Ins. Co., San Bernardino, Calif., 1959-62, div. mgr., 1962-66; agy. supr. Aetna Life & Casualty Co., Los Angeles, 1966-69, gen. agt., 1969-77. Active fund-raising drives City of Hope. Served with USAF, 1953-57. Recipient Man of Year award, 1961; Manpower Builders award, 1966-69; Agy. Builders award, 1970-72; Pres.'s Trophy award, 1973-74; Nat. Mgmt. award, 1973-76. Mem. Los Angeles Life Underwriters Assn., Am. Soc. C.L.U.'s. Home: 7025 N Rosemead Blvd San Gabriel CA 91775

BELLER, OSMAN B., physician; b. Istanbul, Turkey, Mar. 5, 1926; s. Bedri and Rabia; B.; came to U.S., 1949, naturalized, 1955; M.D., U. Istanbul, 1974; m. Naomi Burlingame, Feb. 22, 1950; children—Kaplan, Suzan, Sami. Intern, E. Tenn. Bapt. Hosp., Knoxville, 1950-51; resident in surgery Cleve. (Ohio) Clinic, 1951-55; practice medicine specializing in surgery, Pomona, Calif.; pres. Osman B. Beller, M.D., Pomona, Calif., 1956—; mem. staff Pomona Community Hosp., Montclair Doctors Hosp., Park Ave State Hosp. Served to capt. AUS, 1955-57. Diplomate Am. Bd. Surgery. Fellow A.C.S.; mem. Los Angeles Med. Assn., AMA, Tri County Surg. Assn., Republican. Muslim. Home: 3251 Moritz Dr Huntington Beach CA 92649 Office: 1770 N Orange Grove St Pomona CA 91767

BELL-IRVING, HENRY P., lt. gov. British Columbia, Canada. Decorated D.S.O., Order Brit. Empire (OBE), Efficiency Decoration (ED), CD Office: Govt House 1401 Rockland Ave Victoria BC V8S 1V9 Canada

BELLIS, CARROLL JOSEPH, surgeon; b. Shreveport, La.; s. Joseph and Rose (Bloome) B.; B.S., U. Minn., 1930, M.S. in Physiology, 1932, Ph.D. in Physiology, 1934, M.D., 1936, Ph.D. in Surgery, 1941; m. Mildred Darmody, Dec. 26, 1939; children—Joseph, David. Resident in surgery U. Minn. Hosps., 1937-41; mem. staff St. Mary's Hosp., Community Hosp., Long Beach, Calif.; cons. in surgery Long Beach Gen. Hosp.; pvt. practice surgery, Long Beach, 1945—; prof., chmn. dept. surgery Calif. Coll. Medicine. Served to col. M.C., U.S. Army, 1941-46. Recipient Charles Lyman Green prize in physiology, 1934, gold medal Mpls. Surg. Soc. Diplomate Am. Bd. Surgery. Fellow Am. Cancer Inst., A.C.S., Internat. Coll. Surgeons, Am. Coll. Gastroenterology, Am. Med. Writers Assn., Internat. Coll. Angiology (sci. council); mem. Am. Assn. Study of Neoplastic Diseases, Mississippi Valley Med. Soc., N.Y. Acad. Scis., Hollywood Acad. Medicine, Irish Med. Soc., AAAS, Am. Assn. History of Medicine, Alpha Omega Alpha, Sigma Xi, Phi Beta Kappa. Author: Fundamentals of Human Physiology, 1935; A Critique of Reason, 1938; Lectures in Human Physiology, 1960. Contbr. numerous articles in field of surgery, physiology to profl. jours. Home: S Quail Ridge Rd Rolling Hills CA 90274 Office: 1045 Atlantic Ave Suite 1011 Long Beach CA 90813

BELLIS, DAVID JAMES, educator, social agency consultant; b. Nashville, May 1, 1944; s. Carroll Joseph and Helen Louise (Jett) B.; B.A., U. Calif. at Los Angeles, 1966; M.A. (Haynes Found. fellow), U. So. Calif., 1969, Ph.D., 1977; m. Ann Seagreaves, Dec. 23, 1972. Chief research and statis. div. Narcotics Prevention Project, Los Angeles, 1971-73; dir. ops. West End Drug Abuse Control Coordinating Council, Inc., Ontario, Calif., 1973-75; cons. project HEAVY, City of Los Angeles, 1975—; instr. polit. sci. Long Beach (Calif.) City Coll., 1970-79; lectr. in pub. adminstrn. U. So. Calif., 1978-79; lectr. criminal justice Calif. State U., Long Beach, 1978-79; cons. drug abuse Santa Monica Bay Area Drug Abuse Council, 1974—, Calif. Dept. Health, 1975-78, Center for Criminal Justice Calif. State U., Long Beach, 1975—. Dir. econ. planning East Los Angeles Community Union, 1979-80; asst. dir. Youth Gang Services Project, 1980-81, mem. Signal Hill (Calif.) City Council, 1980—, mayor pro tem, 1982, mayor, 1983—. NIMH grantee, 1973. Mem. Am. Acad. Polit. and Social Sci., Am., Western polit. sci. assns., Am. Acad. Arts and Scis. Jewish. Author: (with Kenneth F. Johnson) Mexican Democracy: A Critical View, 1970; (with F. Tennont, P. O'Rourke and W. Wilson) A Study of Third Party Payments, 1975; Heroin and Politicians: The Failure of Public Policy to Control Addiction in America. Home: 2058 Terrace Dr Signal Hill CA 90806

BELL-KING, BARBARA ANNE, management consultant; b. Montgomery, Ala., Apr. 18, 1924; d. Robert M. and Lilli B. (Howard) Mosley; m. William Y. Bell, Feb. 9, 1963; m. 2d, Michael Sebastian King, Jan. 22, 1976; children—Bunny, Sandra, Andra (twins), Richard. B.A., Spelman Coll., 1944; M.S., Pepperdine U., 1973, M.P.A., 1974, M.B.A., 1980; Ph.D., U.S. Internat. U., 1978. Housing adv. City of Berkeley (Calif.), 1960-68; relocation dir. HUD Region IX, San Francisco, 1968-70, dep. dir. HUD, Los Angeles, 1970-72; asst. dir. Mayor's Office Community Devel., Los Angeles, 1973-75; assoc. prof. pub. adminstrn. Pepperdine U., Los Angeles, 1975-80; vis. assoc. prof. U. So. Calif., 1980-82; owner Bell-King Assocs.; mgmt. cons.; bd. dirs. Am. Soc. Tng. and Devel. Bd. dirs. United Way Region IV, Los Angeles. Recipient Achievement and Community Service award Mayor Los Angeles; Meritorious Service to City of Los Angeles award; Acad. Profl. Achievement award Spelman Coll. Nat. Alumnae Assn.; Outstanding Leadership award Am. Soc. Tng. and Devel. (Los Angeles chpt.), 1982. Home: 4631 S Mullen Ave Los Angeles CA 90043

BELLMAN, SAMUEL IRVING, educator; b. El Paso, Tex., Sept. 28, 1926; s. Max and Bessie Pauline (Levenson) B.; m. Jeanne Lisker, Mar. 16, 1952; children—Joel Ethan, Jonathan David. B.A., U. Tex., 1947; M.A., Wayne U., 1951; Ph.D., Ohio State U., 1955. Instr., Fresno (Calif.) State Coll., 1955-57; asst. prof. English, Calif. State Poly. Coll., San Luis Obispo, 1957-59; asst. prof. Calif. State Poly U, Pomona, 1959-62, assoc. prof., 1962-66, prof., 1966—. Mem. Internat. Conf. on Humor, Am. Studies Assn. Democrat. Jewish. Author: Marjorie Kinnan Rawlings, 1974; Constance Mayfield Rourke, 1981; editor: The College Experience, 1962; Survey and Forecast, 1966; contbr. chpts. to books; contbr. poems and articles in field to profl. jours. Office: English Dept Calif State Poly 3801 W Temple Ave Pomona CA 91768

BELLONI, ROBERT CLINTON, judge; b. Riverton, Oreg., Apr. 4, 1919; s. John Edward and Della (Clinton) B.; B.A., U. Oreg., 1941, LL.B. 1951; m. Doris A. Adams, Jan 27, 1946; children—James L., Susan K. Admitted to Oreg. bar, 1951; practiced in Coquille, Oreg., 1951-52. Myrtle Point. Ore., 1952-57; judge Oreg. Circuit Ct., Coos and Curry Counties, Coquille, 1957-67; U.S. dist. judge Dist. Oreg., 1967—, chief judge, 1971-76. Councilman, Myrtle Point, Oreg., 1953-57. Mayor, 1957; chmn. Coos County Democratic Central Com., 1957. Robert C. Belloni Boys Forest Ranch dedicated in his honor by Coos County Bd. Commrs., 1969. Served as 1st lt. AUS, 1942-46. Mem. Am., Oreg. State bar assns., Am. Judicature Soc., Oreg. Juvenile Ct. Judges Assn. (pres. 1963), Circuit Ct. Judges Assn. Oreg. (pres. 1966), 9th Circuit Dist. Judges Assn. (pres. 1980, 81), Sigma Alpha Epsilon, Delta Theta Phi. Episcopalian. Office: 612 US Courthouse Portland OR 97205

BELLPORT, BERNARD PHILIP, cons. engr.; b. LaCrosse, Kans., May 25, 1907; s. Bernard P. and Louise H. (Groves) B.; B.S. in Mining

Engring., Poly. Coll. Engring., Oakland, Calif., 1927; m. Elsy V. Johnson, June 11, 1931 (dec. Mar. 1954); children—Louise Bellport Garcia, Bernard Philip; m. 2d, Mabelle W. Kandolin, Sept. 26, 1955. Mining engr., Western U.S., 1927-28; engr.-geologist St. Joseph Lead Co., 1928-31; with Phoenix Utility Co., 1931-32, Mont. Hwy. Commn., 1932-35; with Bur. Reclamation, 1936-72, regional dir. region 2, Calif., 1957-59, asso. chief engr., Denver, 1959-63, chief engr., 1963-70, dir. design and constrn., 1970-72; practice as engring. cons., 1972—; arbitrator Constrn. Arbitration Panel, State of Calif. Recipient Disting. Service award Dept. Interior; Golden Beaver for engring.; named Man of Year, Am. Pub. Works Assn., 1970; registered profl. engr., Colo. Mem. Nat. Acad. Engring., U.S. Commn. Large Dams (chmn. 1971-72), Internat. Commn. Irrigation, Drainage and Flood Control, ASCE (pres. Colo. 1966), Am. Arbitration Assn., Rossmoor Engrs. Club, Internat. Water Resources Assn., Hon. Order Ky. Cols., Chi Epsilon (hon.). Episcopalian. Clubs: Masons (32 deg.), Shriners, Round Hill Country. Address: 855 Terra California Dr Apt 4 Walnut Creek CA 94595

BELLUCCI, NANCY ROSINE, psychologist; b. Boston, July 12, 1941; d. Antone Adolph and Dorina Florence (Sartorelli) Bellucci. B.A., U. N.H., 1962; M.S., Calif. State U., 1970; Ph.D., Calif. Sch. Profl. Psychology, 1979. Lic. psychologist, Calif. Tchr., Concord (N.H.) High Sch., 1962-65, Meml. High Sch., Manchester, N.H., 1966-67, Colton (Calif.) Unified Sch. Dist., 1967-69; intern, U. Hosp., San Diego, 1978, Southwood Mental Health Center, Chula Vista, Calif., 1978-79; cons. Applied Personal Dynamics, San Diego, 1979-81; sch. psychologist Chula Vista City Sch. Dist., 1971—; pvt. practice psychology, San Diego, 1979—; affiliate staff mem. Southwood Meml. Mental Health Ctr., 1981—, Vista Hill Hosp., 1983—; field placement supr. Calif. Sch. Prof. Psychology, San Diego, San Diego State U., U.S. Internat. U. Named Outstanding Sch. Psychologist, Calif. Assn. Sch. Psychologists and Psychometrists, 1976. Mem. Am. Psychol. Assn., Nat. Assn. Sch. Psychologists, Calif. Psychol. Assn., Western Psychol. Assn., San Diego Acad. Psychologists, San Diego Assn. Sch. Psychologists and Psychometrists (treas. 1976-77), S.W. Personnel and Guidance Assn. (pres. 1974-75). Office: 2615 Camino Del Rio S Suite 300 San Diego CA 92108

BELLUOMINI, FRANK STEPHEN, accountant; b. Healdsburg, Calif., May 19, 1934; s. Francesco and Rose (Giorgi) B.; m. Alta Anita Gifford, June 16, 1967; 1 dau., Wendy Ann. A.A., Santa Rosa Jr. Coll., 1954; B.A. with honors, San Jose State U., 1956. C.P.A., Calif. Staff acct. Hood, Gire & Co., C.P.A.s, San Jose, Calif., 1956-69, ptnr., 1960-66; ptnr. Touche Ross & Co., C.P.A.s, San Jose, 1967—, ptnr.-in-charge San Jose office, 1971—. Mem. adv. bd. Salvation Army, San Jose, 1979-84, San Jose Children's Council, 1982—; trustee Santa Clara County (Calif.) United Way, 1979-83, v.p. planning and allocations, 1981-83. Named Disting. Alumnus, San Jose State U. Sch. Bus., 1978. Mem. Santa Clara County Estate Planning Council (pres. 1979-80), Calif. Soc. C.P.A.s (pres. chpt. 1968-69, state v.p. 1976-77), Am. Inst. C.P.A.s (chmn. state and local govt. com. 1976-79), San Jose State Alumni Assn. (treas. 1960-61, dir. 1961-62, exec. com. 1961-62). Roman Catholic. Club: San Jose Rotary (dir. 1979-81, trustee and treas. San Jose Rotary Endowment 1976-83).

BELMONT, LARRY MILLER, health executive, tree farmer; b. Reno, Nev., Apr. 13, 1936; s. Miller Lawrence and Madeline (Echante) B.; m. Laureen Metzger, Aug. 14, 1966; children—Miller Lawrence, Rebecca Madeline, Amie Echante, Bradley August. B.A. in Psychology, U. Nev., 1962; M.P.H. in Med. Care Orgn. and Areawide Planning, U. Mich., 1968; cert. environ. mgmt. U. So. Calif., 1978; M.P.A., U. Idaho, 1979. Venereal disease program rep. USPHS, Los Angeles and Long Beach, Calif., 1962-63, pub. health advisor Anchorage, Alaska, 1963-64, with health moblzn., Juneau and Anchorage, 1964-67; dep. dir. Wash./Alaska Regional Med. Program, Spokane, 1968-71; dir. Panhandle Health Dist. Coeur d'Alene, Idaho, 1971—; mem. water quality statewide adv. com., Idaho, 1976-77; legis. com. Wash. Pub. Health Service, 1970-71. Bd. dirs., chmn. nominating com. Kootenai Econ. Devel. Council, 1981—; regional coordinator Govs. Com. Vol. Services, 1979-80; chmn. Montessori Adv. Bd., 1975-79; adv. com. Kootenai Council Alcoholism, 1979-80; bd. dirs. North Idaho Spl. Services Agy., 1972-76; chmn. Idaho Conf. Dist. Health Dirs., 1976-79; mem. Water Power Citizens Adv. Com., 1981—; mem. health sci. adv. com. Whitworth Coll., 1983—. Served with U.S. Army, 1956-58. Mem. Idaho Pub. Health Assn. (bd. dirs. 1973-75, treas. 1975-76), Idaho Forest Owners Assn., Idaho Assn. Home Agys. (interim bd. dirs. 1980-81, chmn. legis. com. 1973-76), Nat. Assn. Home Health Agys. (legis. com. 1975-81, chmn. legis. com. 1979-81, bd. dirs. 1978-81), Nat. Assn. Home Care (nominating com. 1982-84, Am. Pub. Health Assn., Wash. Pub. Health Assn. (legis. com. 1970-71), Kootenai County Environ. Alliance, Idaho Conservation League, Ducks Unltd. Democrat. Roman Catholic. Presented papers to confs.; contbr. articles to profl. jours.

BELOK, MICHAEL VICTOR, educator; b. Whiting, Ind., June 22, 1923; s. Michael and Helen (Dobos) B.; B.S., Ind. U., 1948; M.A., Ariz. State U., 1953; Ph.D., U. So. Calif., 1958; m. Georgina Pilkington, July 31, 1965. Lectr. edn. U. So. Calif., 1958; mem. faculty Ariz. State U., Tempe, 1959—, prof. edn., 1968—. Editorial cons. Served with AUS, 1943-46. Fellow Nat. Philosophy Edn. Soc.; mem. History Edn. Soc., Delta Tau Kappa (region chancellor 1968—), Phi Delta Kappa, Kappa Delta Pi. Author: Psychological Foundations of Education, 1964; Approaches to Values in Education, 1967; Forming the American Minds: Early Schoolbooks and Their Compilers 1783-1837, 1973; Explorations in the History and Sociology of Indian Education, 1973; Noah Webster Revisited, 1973; Conflict, Permanency, Change and Education, 1976. Contbg. editor Internat. Rev. History and Polit. Sci., 1968-73; editor Rev. Jour. of Philosophy and Social Scis., 1976; guest editor Parsons and Sociology, 1975; adv. editor Indian Jour. Social Research, 1965-71, others. Home: 1015 W Fairway Dr Mesa AZ 85201

BELT, SARAH JANE, librarian; b. Cumberland, Md., Aug. 5, 1928; d. Francis A. and Anna E. (Barnett) Worth; B.S. in Edn., Millersville State Tchrs. Coll., 1950; M.S. in L.S., Syracuse U., 1956; postgrad. Wenatchee Valley Community Coll., 1972, Central Wash. U., 1975-77; m. Paul Franklin Belt, Feb. 20, 1959; children—Anna Paula, Victor James. Bookmobile librarian Dayton and Montgomery Library, Dayton, Ohio, 1950-53, children's br. librarian, 1953-54; asst. architecture librarian Syracuse (N.Y.) U., 1954-55, edn. librarian, 1955-56; children's librarian Wenatchee and Chelan County Library, Wenatchee, Wash., 1956-58; bookmobile librarian N. Central Wash. Library, 1958-59; substitute tchr. Wenatchee Sch. Dist., 1965-69; nursing sch. librarian Deaconess Hosp., Wenatchee, 1967-71; med. librarian Central Wash. Hosp., Wenatchee, 1972—, coordinator hosp. continuing edn., 1977—; mem. regional adv. council Pacific N.W. Regional Library, 1980-82, chmn., 1981; mem. Wash. Adv. Council on Libraries, 1979-81; sec. treas. N. Central Wash. Pastoral Counseling Center, 1978-80; chmn. Central Wash. Library Service Area, 1981-82. Mem. choir Meth. Ch., 1958—; mem. Wash. Health Info. Planning Group, 1980-82. Assn. Western Hosps. Ednl. and Trust Found. grantee, 1978-79, 80-81. Mem. Wash. State Library Assn. (assembly mem. Wash. library network 1977-79), Med. Library Assn. (chmn. elect Pacific N.W. regional sect. 1983), Wash. Med. Librarians Assn. (award 1980; rec. sec. 1979-80, pres. 1982), Am. Soc. Health, Edn. and Tng., Health Edn. Media Assn., Wash. Assn. for Ednl. Communications Tech., Assn. Western Hosps. (state area rep. hosp. library sect. 1976—), Beta Phi Mu. Club: Soroptimist. Home: 3661 NW Cascade Ave East Wenatchee WA 98801 Office: Central Wash Hosp Ross A Heminger Health Scis Library 1211 Rosewood St PO Box 1887 Wenatchee WA 98801

BELTON, ELEANOR IRMA, manufacturing company executive; b. St. Helena, Calif., Mar. 16, 1926; d. Augustine and Lena (Craviotto) Cravea; b. George G. Belton, June 21, 1948 (div.); children—Linda Marie Valerga, Jeffrey George. B.A. in Bus. Adminstrn., Coll. San Mateo, 1971. With Mfg. and Transmission Corp., San Carlos, Calif., 1957—, now supr. document services, document control. Mem. Lenkurt Recreation Assn., Nat. Micrographics Assn. Democrat. Roman Catholic. Club: Singles Orgn. (San Mateo) Home: Apt 1 2995 Melendy Dr San Carlos CA 94070 Office: 1105 County Rd San Carlos CA 94070

BELTRAMI, ALBERT PETER, county official; b. Sacramento, Feb. 26, 1934; s. Battista and Anastasia B.; A.A., Modesto Jr. Coll., 1953; A.B. in Polit. Sci., U. Calif., Berkeley, 1955, M.A. in Public Adminstrn., 1957; m. Patricia Jean Kearns, July 27, 1957; children—Katharine Clare, Robert Richard. Dep. marshal Modesto (Calif.) Mcpl. Ct., 1955-57; asst. county adminstrv. officer San Luis Obispo County (Calif.), 1960-65; county adminstr. officer Mendocino County (Calif.), 1965—; adv. com. Golden Gate U. Grad. Sch. Public Adminstrn., San Francisco, 1975-80; mem. Calif. N. Coast Regional Water Quality Control Bd., 1972—, vice-chmn., 1982-83, chmn., 1984; adv. com. Calif. Law Enforcement Telecommunications System, 1977—, adv. com. Sonoma State U. Grad. Sch. Public Adminstrn., 1980-84. Chmn. bd. dirs. United Way North Bay, 1984. Served to lt. USNR, 1957-60, comdr. Res., 1981. Mem. Internat. City Mgmt. Assn., Am. Soc. Public Adminstrn., Nat. Assn. County Adminstrs., County Adminstrv. Officers Assn. Calif. (sec.-treas. 1979-80, pres. 1982). Republican. Roman Catholic. Clubs: Commonwealth of Calif.; San Luis Obispo Elks; Ukiah Lions. Home: 145 Mendocino Pl Ukiah CA 95482 Office: Rm 110 Courthouse Ukiah CA 95482

BELTRAMINI, RICHARD F., marketing educator; b. Peoria Ill., Aug. 25, 1949; s. Ambrose J. and Irene A. (Bozza) B.; m. Robin E. Lee, Sept. 2, 1972; 1 dau., Elizabeth L. B.S. cum laude in Communication, U. Ill., 1972, M.S. in Advt., 1973; Ph.D. in Communications, U. Tex., 1980. Product mgr. The Drawing Board, Inc., Dallas, 1975-77; program mgr. Tex. Instruments, Inc. Dallas, 1973-75; copywriter Penta Advt., Inc., Champaign, Ill., 1972-73; asst. prof. mktg. advt. Ariz. State U., Tempe, 1977—; cons. schs., advt. agys. Bd. dirs. Cactus-Pine council Girl Scouts U.S.A.; bd. dirs. Jr. Achievement, United Way. Recipient numerous acad. fellowships and grants. Mem. Am. Mktg. Assn., Am. Acad. Advt., others. Roman Catholic. Contbr. articles to profl. jours. Home: 5924 So Stanley Pl Tempe AZ 85283 Office: Dept Mktg Ariz State U Tempe AZ 85281

BEMIS, KENNETH EATON, real estate investment exec.; b. Stillwater, Minn., June 7, 1918; s. Kenneth Eaton and Ruth (Lovell) B.; student Lawlors Profl. Sch., 1935; m. Martha Grimes, Oct. 20, 1946; children—Dorothy Bemis Marrelli, Kenneth Eaton III. Mem. brother-sister dance team, U.S. and Europe, 1934-40; v.p. Nat. Corp. Am., 1940-58; pres. Bemis Enterprises, Inc., 1958-69; gen. partner, chief exec. Bemis Enterprises, Ltd. and Bemis Mgmt. Co., Denver, 1969—. Republican committeeman, 1980; regional adv. com. Small Bus. Adminstrn., 1971; gen. ball site coordinator Richard Nixon Inaugural Ball, Washington, 1969; disaster coordinator Fed. Disaster Mgmt. Adminstrn., 1980. Served with USAAF, 1944-46. Lic. realtor, Colo.; lic. comml. multi-engine instrumentrated pilot, flight instr. Mem. Colo. Bd. Realtors, Denver Bd. Realtors. Christian Scientist (1st reader 1972-74). Clubs: Capitol Hill (Washington); Garden of the Gods (Colorado Springs); Masons, Shriners (Denver); Optimists (v.p. 1980-81). Holder registered trademarks and patents in field. Home: 2552 E Alameda Ave 122 Denver CO 80209

BENALLY, HERBERT, grantwriter, educator; b. Sweetwater, Ariz., Mar. 16, 1944; s. Hasteen and Ason Bigadii; m. Helen Isabel Begay, Nov. 23, 1965; children—Bert, Valerie, Joseph, Helena, Lehi, Naomi, Moroni. B.A., Ariz. State U., 1969, M.Ed., 1978. Adult edn. instr., Blanding, Utah, 1969-70; adult educator, curriculum writer Navajo Community Coll., Tsalle, Ariz., 1970-73, adult edn. dir., 1973-78, adj. prof., 1979-80; grantswriter Chinle (Ariz.) Sch. Dist., 1979-82; cons. Br. pres. Church of Jesus Christ of Latter Day Saints, Many Farms, Ariz., 1977-78, Chinle, Ariz., 1979-81; adviser Boy Scouts Am., 1977-78; mem. sch. bd., Chinle, 1977-78. Recipient appreciation service award Navajo Community Coll., 1978; Indian Edn. fellow, 1978-80. Mem. Nat. Indian Edn. Assn., Dine Edn. Assn., Nat. Indian Adult Educations Assn., No. Ariz. Bilingual Consortium. Democrat. Home: Star Route 1 Box 41 Teec Nos Pos AZ 86514

BEN-ASHER, M. DAVID, physician; b. Newark, June 18, 1931; s. Samuel I. and Dora Ruth (Kagan) Ben-A.; A.B., Syracuse U., 1952; M.D. (Walter Goodale scholar), U. Buffalo, 1956; m. Bryna Shirley Zeller, Nov. 22, 1956; children—Nancy Beth, Susan Rachel, Jonathan Roy, Judith Ann. Intern, E. J. Meyer Meml. Hosp., Buffalo, 1956-57; resident in internal medicine Jersey City Med. Center, 1957-58; resident in internal medicine Madigan Gen. Hosp., Tacoma, 1960-61, chief resident, 1961-62; practice medicine specializing in internal medicine and nephrology, Tucson, 1964—; attending staff St. Mary's Hosp., Tucson, 1964—, chief staff, 1971-73, trustee, 1978—; cons. staff Tucson Med. Center, 1964—, St. Joseph's Hosp., Tucson, 1964-80, Pima County Hosp., 1964—, Univ. Hosp., 1972—; clin. asso. in medicine U. Ariz., Tucson, 1969—; mem. Ariz. State Bd. Med. Examiners, 1978—. Bd. dirs. Tucson Symphony, 1971-73; bd. dirs. Pima chpt. Ariz. Kidney Found., 1969—, v.p., 1975-78; trustee Congregation Anshei Israel, Tucson, 1967—, v.p., 1977-79, pres., 1979-81. Served to maj. M.C., U.S. Army, 1958-64. Named Physician of Yr., City of Tucson, 1973; A.C.P. traveling scholar, 1969. Fellow A.C.P.; mem. Am., Internat. socs. nephrology, AMA, Ariz. Med. Assn., Pima County Med. Soc. (pres. 1976). Democrat. Jewish. Club: B'nai B'rith. Contbr. articles to profl. jours. Home: 5635 E 7th St Tucson AZ 85711 Office: 4711 N 1st Ave Tucson AZ 85718

BENBASSAT, WILLIAM ALLAN, hosp. adminstr.; b. Los Angeles, Sept. 3, 1950; s. Leon Albert and Violet Lucky (Schenasi) B.; B.A., U. Calif., Irvine, 1972; M.S., UCLA, 1974, D.P.H., 1976. Lectr., U. Calif., Irvine, 1976, lectr. program social ecology, 1976; exec. dir. health edn. and research Los Angeles New Hosp., 1976, exec. dir. med. edn., 1977; exec. dir. Los Angeles Health Edn. and Research Found., 1977; cons. in-service edn. series on sch. health, in-service edn. series on proposal devel. Calif. State Dept. Edn., 1975—; health edn. cons. on curriculum and evaluation sch. dists. So. Calif., 1974—; cons. nutrition edn. project, joint project Calif. State Dept. Edn./U.S. Dept. Agr., 1975—, Newport-Mesa Schs., 1976—, genetics project Calif. State Dept. Edn., 1976—; mem. affiliate faculty Am. Health Assn., Greater Los Angeles, 1978—. Bd. dirs. Los Angeles coastal cities unit Am. Cancer Soc., 1977—. mem. public health edn. com., 1976—. USPHS tng. grantee, 1972-76. Mem. AAHPER, Am. Psychol. Assn., Am. Public Health Assn., Am. Sch. Health Assn., Assn. Advancement Health Edn., Assn. Supervision and Curriculum Devel., Nat. Assn. Edn. Young Children, Soc. Public Health Edn., Calif. Assn. Health, Phys. Edn. and Recreation, Calif. Assn. Edn. Young Children, Calif. Sch. Health Assn., Phi Delta Kappa, Phi Delta Upsilon. Jewish. Author: Health Practice Inventory, 1976. Office: 9701 Wilshire Blvd Suite 700 Beverly Hills CA 90212

BENBOW, RICHARD ADDISON, psychological counselor; b. Las Vegas, Dec. 27, 1949; s. Jules Coleman and Bonnie Ray Benbow; B.S. in Bus. Adminstrn., U. Nev. 1972, M.S. in Counseling, 1974; A.A.S. in Bus. Mgmt. and Real Estate, Clark County Community Coll., 1980; Ph.D. in Clin. Psychology, U. Humanistic Studies, 1983. Cert. tchr., Nev.; lic. real estate broker, Nev. Broker, salesman Bates & Bertges Real Estate, Inc., Las Vegas, 1979-81; owner, mgr. Dick's Hardware, Las Vegas, 1981-82; jud. services officer Mcpl. Ct., City of Las Vegas, 1982, inmate classification technician Detention and Correctional Services, 1982—; stress mgmt. cons. Mem. Biofeedback Soc. Am., Assn. Humanistic Psychology, Nat. Assn. Psychotherapists, Am. Personnel and Guidance Assn., Am. Mental Health Counselors Assn., Am. Acad. Crisis Interveners, Am. Correctional Assn., U.S. Tai Kung Fu Assn. (black belt), Nat. Assn. Underwater Instrs., So. Nev. Bluegrass Soc., Jr. C. of C., U.S. Jaycees (presdl. award of honor 1978-79), Delta Sigma Phi. Democrat. Christian Scientist. Home: 1020 Desert Ln Las Vegas NV 89106 Office: Detention and Correctional Services City of Las Vegas 3100 E Stewart St Las Vegas NV 89101

BENCH, ARNOLD EUGENE, former marine officer, ins. co. exec.; b. Fordland, Mo., Apr. 13, 1925; s. James C. and Zula (Page) B.; B.S., U. Mo., 1949, Ed.M., 1950; M.A., George Washington U., 1970; student Nat. War Coll., 1969-70; m. Ila May Kelley, Aug. 1, 1948; children—Rebecca Anne, David Eugene. Enlisted U.S. Marine Corps, 1943, advanced through grades to 1st sgt., 1950; commd. 2d lt. 1950, advanced through grades to col., 1970; tchr. amphibious warfare, Quantio, Va., 1951-52; chief ops. briefing br., CinC Pac, Hawaii, 1968-69; asst. prof. mil. history and naval sci. Oreg. State U., 1963-66; comdr. inf. bn. 4th Mar Regt., S. Vietnam, 1966-67; planning staff, Pentagon, 1970; amphibious adviser, European theater, 1971; insp. gen., 1972; ret. 73; spl. ins. agt. NW Farm Bur. Ins. Co., Salem, Oreg. and Western Farm Bur. Ins. Co., Denver, 1974—; instr. ins. Oreg. State U., Corvallis, 1975—; guest tchr. high schs. Ruling elder Calvin Presbyn. Ch., Corvallis, 1977—, chmn. worship com., 1977-80, chmn. personnel com., 1978-81. Decorated Silver Star, Legion of Merit, Bronze Star (2), Purple Heart; Cross of Gallantry with palm (2) (South Vietnam); named Rookie of the Year NW Farm Bur. Ins. Co., 1975. Mem. Ret. Officers Assn., DAV, Nat. Wild Life Assn., Small Woodlands Assn., Smithsonian Instn., Nat. Farm Bur. Fedn., Izaac Walton League (pres. Marys Peak chpt. 1976-77), Phi Delta Kappa. Republican. Clubs: Masons, Shriners, Vesuvious Square and Compass (pres. 1956-57). Home: 910 NW Overlook Dr Corvallis OR 97330 Office: 33254 Hwy 99E Tangent OR 97389

BENCHIMOL, ALBERTO, cardiologist, author; b. Belem, Para, Brazil, Apr. 26, 1932; s. Isaac I. and Nina (Siqueira) B.; came to U.S., 1957, naturalized, 1964; B.S., State Coll., Rio de Janeiro, Brazil, 1950; M.D., U. Brazil, 1956; m. Helena Lourdes Levy, Apr. 14, 1962; children—Nelson, Alex. Intern, U. Brazil Med. Center, Rio de Janeiro, 1956-57, resident in medicine, 1957; fellow in medicine U. Kans. Med. Center, Kansas City, 1958-60, Scripps Clinic, La Jolla, Calif., 1960-61; practice medicine specializing in cardiology, La Jolla, now Phoenix; research assoc. Inst. Cardiopulmonary Diseases, Scripps Clinic and Research Found., La Jolla, 1961-63, assoc., 1963-66; dir. Inst. Cardiovascular Diseases, Good Samaritan Med. Center, Phoenix, 1966—; vis. prof. U. Brazil, 1966, Desert Hosp., Palm Springs, Calif., 1971; tutor U. Mo. Sch. Medicine, Kansas City, 1974-77, lectr., 1978-81; prof. in residence U. Oreg., Portland, 1975; vis. prof. Nagasaki U., Japan, 1970, Letterman Gen. Hosp., San Francisco, 1972. Haskell fellow in cardiology, 1957-59. Fellow ACP, Am. Coll. Cardiology, Am. Coll. Chest Physicians, Am. Coll. Angiology; mem. Am., Ariz. heart assns., Am. Physiol. Soc., Western Soc. Clin. Research, AMA, Biol. and Med. Scis. Research Club San Diego, Am. Fedn. Clin. Research. Author: Atlas of Vectorcardiography, 1971; Atlas of Phonocardiography, 1971; Vectorcardiography, 1973; Non-Invasive Diagnostic Techniques in Cardiology, 1977, 2d edit., 1981; Noninvasive Techniques in Cardiology for the Nurse and Technician, 1978; contbr. articles on cardiology and cardiography to profl. jours., chpts. to med. books; editorial bd. Am. Heart Jour., 1968-76, Am. Jour. Cardiology, 1969-76, Catheterization and Cardiovascular Diagnosis, 1974—, Chest, 1974; producer films on cardiography, 1962, 66. Home: 195 E Desert Park Ln Phoenix AZ 85020 Office: 926 E McDowell Rd Phoenix AZ 85006

BENDAT, JULIUS SAMUEL, cons., author; b. Chgo., Oct. 26, 1923; s. Benjamin M. and Frieda (Korn) B.; B.A. cum laude, U. Calif. at Berkeley, 1944; M.S., Calif. Inst. Tech., 1948; Ph.D. in Math., U. So. Calif., 1953; m. Mildred Rosen, July 27, 1947; children—James Russell, Lucinda Ann. Asst. prof. aero. engring. U. So. Calif., Santa Maria, 1948-49; research engr. Northrop Aircraft, Inc., Hawthorne, Calif., 1953-55; sr. staff mem. Thompson Ramo Wooldridge, Inc., Canoga Park, Calif., 1955-62; pres. Measurement Analysis Corp., Los Angeles, 1962-68; v.p. Digitek Corp., Los Angeles, 1968-70; owner J.S. Bendat Co., Los Angeles, 1970—. Served as ensign USNR, 1945-46. Mem. Am. Math. Soc., Math. Assn. Am., Soc. Indsl. and Applied Math., Phi Beta Kappa, Sigma Xi, Pi Mu Epsilon. Author: Principles and Applications of Random Noise Theory, 1958; Measurement and Analysis of Random Data, 1966; Random Data: Analysis and Measurement Procedures, 1971; Engineering Applications of Correlation and Spectral Analysis, 1980. Home: 1231 Casiano Rd Los Angeles CA 90049 Office: 833 Moraga Dr Los Angeles CA 90049

BENDER, BETTY WION, library exec.; b. Mt. Ayr, Iowa, Feb. 26, 1925; d. John F. and Sadie A. (Guess) Wion; student Drake U., Des Moines, 1942-44; B.S., N. Tex. State U., Denton, 1946; M.A., U. Denver, 1957; m. Robert F. Bender, Aug. 24, 1946. Asst. cataloger N. Tex. State U., Denton, 1946-49; cataloger So. Meth. U., Dallas, 1949-51, periodicals librarian, 1952-53, head of acquisitions, 1953-56; reference asst. Ind. State Library, Indpls., 1951-52; librarian Ark. State Coll., State College, 1958-59, Eastern Wash. Hist. Soc., Spokane, 1960-67; reference librarian Spokane Pub. Library, 1968, head circulation dept., 1968-73, library dir., 1973—; vis. instr. U. Denver, summers 1957-60, 63, fall 1959; instr. Whitworth Coll., Spokane, 1962-64; mem. Gov.'s Regional Conf. on Libraries, 1968, Wash. Statewide Library Devel. Council, 1970-71, White House Conf. on Library and Info. Services, 1979, Gov.'s Conf. on Libraries and Info. Services, 1979. Bd. dirs. N.W. Regional Found., 1974-75, Inland Empire Goodwill Industries, 1975-77. AAUW Fellowship named in her honor, 1972. Mem. ALA (chmn. circulation services sect. 1975-76), Pacific N.W. Library Assn. (chmn. circulation div. 1972-75, conv. chmn. 1977), Wash. Library Assn. (dir. 1971-73, treas. 1973-75, 1st v.p., pres. elect 1975-77, pres. 1977-79, chmn. finance com. 1975-77), Wash. Library Network (exec. council 1977-79), Library Adminstrn. and Mgmt. Assn. (chmn. nominating com. 1980-81, mem. com. on orgn. 1980-83), AAUW (pres. Spokane br. 1969-71, Wash. Conv. chmn., mem. state bd. 1964-65, rec. sec. Wash. 1965-67), Spokane and Inland Empire Librarians (dir. 1967-68). Republican. Lutheran. Club: Zonta Internat. (dir. Spokane 1972-73, pres. 1976-77, treas. Dist. VIII Ann. Conf. 1972). Home: 119 N 6th St Cheney WA 99004 Office: W 906 Main Ave Spokane WA 99201

BENDER, BOB GEORGE, materials technologist; b. Watertown, S.D., June 10, 1925; s. George Almon and Ruby Belle (Duryee) B.; B.S. in Ceramic Engring., U. Ill., 1949; completed Modern Bus., Alexander Hamilton Inst., 1964; m. Grace Jadwiga Kowalski, Nov. 29, 1947; children—Bruce G., Carol S., Barbara G., Paul F., Holly M., Dean F. Chief ceramic engr. Rauland Corp., Chgo., 1949-54; sr. glass technologist CBS-Hytron, Newburyport, Mass., 1954-56; mng. head microelectronics dept. Hughes Aircraft Co., Newport Beach, Calif., 1956-67; mgr. packaging engring. Rockwell Internat., Anaheim, Calif., 1967-77; mem. tech. staff Silicon Systems, Tustin, Calif., 1977-79; cons. mem. of engring. staff Xerox Corp., El Segundo, Calif., 1979—; cons. engr. glass to metal sealing. Served with USAF, 1943-45. Mem. Internat. Soc. Hybrid Microelectronics. Republican. Mormon. Contbr. articles to tech. publs.;

patentee bonding procedures in assembly of silicon microcircuits. Home: 11371 Homeway Dr Garden Grove CA 92641 Office: 701 S Aviation Blvd El Segundo CA 90245

BENDER, DOUGLAS FRED, mfg. co. mgr.; b. Wa Keeney, Kans., Sept. 4, 1954; s. George Fredrick and Helena Geraldine (Burch) B.; B.B.A. magna cum laude, Boise State U., 1976; postgrad. J.L. Kellogg Grad. Sch. Mgmt., Northwestern U.; m. Christine Ann Echeverria, June 4, 1977. With Chandler Corp., Boise, Idaho, 1975—, door products mgr., 1978-79, mktg. mgr., 1979—. Direct Mail Mktg. Assn.-Inst. scholar, 1976. Mem. Phi Kappa Phi. Lutheran. Pub. Lumberbuyer, 1979-80. Home: 5701 Millrun Boise ID 83704 Office: 1301 N Orchard Boise ID 83705

BENDER, GARY LEE, accountant; b. Aberdeen, S.D., Oct. 9, 1948; s. Gideon and Dorothy (Malsom) B.; m. Daena Sue Poynor, Dec. 20, 1971; 1 son, Garrett. B.B.A. magna cum laude, Eastern N.Mex. U., 1974. C.P.A., N.Mex. Acct., Elmer Fox & Co., Colorado Springs, Colo., 1975-76, Williams, Faver, Sudduth & Co., Muleshoe, Tex., 1976-77; bus. mgr. Bender Oldsmobile-Cadillac-Datsun, Inc., Clovis, N.Mex., 1977; ptnr. Hager, McKay, Bender & Co., Portales, N.Mex., 1978; owner Gary L. Bender, C.P.A., Portales, 1978—. Pres., Roosevelt County Crimes-toppers, 1979-81; bd. dirs. N.Mex. Christian Children's Home, 1980—, sec.-treas., 1983—; mem. Portales Bd. Econ. Devel., 1982—, vice chmn., 1982. Served with USN, 1967-70. Mem. Am. Inst. C.P.A.s, N.Mex. Soc. C.P.A.s, N.Mex. State Bd. Pub. Accts. (dir.), Nat. Assn. State Bds. Accountancy (surveillance and enforcement com.), Roosevelt County C. of C. (dir., v.p. 1982), Sigma Nu (assoc. treas. alumni 1978-80). Republican. Clubs: Rotary (dir., pres. 1982-83). Home: Route 1 Box 41 B2 Portales NM 88130 Office: PO Box 570 Portales NM 88130

BENDER, HAROLD JAMES, accountant; b. Ellsworth, Kans, July 9, 1921; s. Adolph and Emma (Shanalec) B.; B.S. in Bus. Adminstrn., U. Denver, 1950; m. Margaret June Priebe, May 31, 1952; children—Susan Kay, Joyce Ann, Harold James, Jennifer L. Mem. accounting staff Ralph B. Mayo & Co., Denver, 1950-55, Arthur Young & Co., Denver, 1955-62; pvt. practice accounting, Longmont, Colo., 1962-65, Denver, 1965—; city auditor Castle Rock, Colo., 1964—; county auditor Douglas County, Colo., 1964-69. Pres. Kansas Dist. Walther League, 1948-49. Served to col. U.S. Army, 1942-46; ETO. Recipient Presdl. citation, 1977. Mem. Am. Inst. C.P.A.'s, Colo. Soc. C.P.A.'s, Littleton Hist. Soc., Internat. Platform Assn., Littleton Library Assn., Air Force Acad. Officers Club. Republican. Lutheran. Home: 6289 S Marion Way Littleton CO 80121 Office: 1279 W Littleton Blvd Littleton CO 80120

BENDTZEN, RICHARD HENRY, ins. co. exec.; b. Norwalk, Conn., Aug. 6, 1935; s. Robert A. and Margaret A. (Shepherd) B.; student NYU, 1967, Coll. of Ins., 1969; Assoc. in Mgmt., Ins. Inst. Am., 1976; m. Gail G. Nodine, July 2, 1964, children—Fred, Scott. Claim supr. Hartford Accident & Indemnity, Bridgeport, Conn., 1960-63; loss control mgr. Great Am. Ins. Co., Western Div., Los Angeles, 1963-77, v.p. loss control and premium audit Calif. Casualty Mgmt. Co., San Mateo, Calif., 1977—. Pres., San Mateo Safety Council, 1980-81, chmn. safety and health com. Calif. Workers Compensation Inst., 1976; coach Calif. Youth Soccer Assn.; mgr. S. San Ramon (Calif.) Little League, 1977-80. Served with USAF, 1953-57. Registered profl. engr., Calif.; cert. safety profl. Mem. Am. Soc. Safety Engrs., Casualty Engrs. Assn. Los Angeles (pres. 1976). Home: San Ramon CA 94583 Office: 1900 de las Pulgas St San Mateo CA 94402

BENEDETTO, ROBERT DONALD, health adminstr.; b. N.Y.C., Dec. 23, 1935; s. John B. and Jean (Gallagher) B.; B.A., St. Paul's Coll., Washington, 1958, M.A., 1962; M.S.W. (Dept. Labor grantee 1971), Columbia U., 1972; m. Maryellen Connors, Dec. 16, 1972; children—Michele, James. Dir. outpatient clinic Lawrence (Mass.) Gen. Hosp., 1973-74; clin. coordinator crisis evaluation unit Ventura County (Calif.) Mental Health, 1974-76, adminstrv. dir. hosp. based services, 1976—; instr. Calif. Community colls. Bd. dirs. Cooper Sq. Community Devel. Assn., N.Y.C., 1972-73. Lic. clin. social worker, Calif. Mem. Acad. Cert. Social Workers, Ventura County Council Clin. Social Workers (charter). Democrat. Roman Catholic. Author articles in field. Home: 705 Mercer Ave Ventura CA 93004 Office: 300 Hillmont Ave Ventura CA 93003

BENEDICT, DAVID ROBERT, instructional designer, technical trainer; b. Syracuse, N.Y., July 17, 1952; s. Harrison Berdette and Dorothy May (Riley) B.; m. Esther Lee O'Brien, June 7, 1975 (div.). A.A.S., SUNY-Morrisville, 1972; B.S., SUNY-Buffalo, 1975; postgrad. Calif. State U., 1981-83. Teaching cert., N.Y. Technician, Fred's Sport Motors, Syracuse, 1974-77; instr. Nat. Schs., Syracuse, 1976-77; dist. service mgr., instr. Yamaha Motor Corp., Cudahy, Wis., 1977-79; coordinator edn. programs, Cypress, Calif., 1979-81; sr. tech. tng. analyst Toyota Motor Corp. Torrance, Calif., 1981—. Active Big Brothers/Big Sisters of Orange County, 1982—. Morgan Badgely scholar, 1970. Mem. Am. Soc. Tng. and Devel., Am. Vocat. Assn., Phi Theta Kappa. Club: Outdoor Singles (Orange County). Office: Toyota Motor Corp 19001 S Western Ave Torrance CA 90509

BENEDICT, HARRIS MILLER, plant physiologist; b. Cin., Aug. 13, 1907; s. Harris M. and Florence Stevens (McCrea) B.; m. Helen McLaughlin, Sept. 16, 1948. A.B., U. Cin., 1929, M.A., 1930; Ph.D., U. Chgo., 1932. Assoc. plant physiologist U.S. Dept. Agr., Cheyenne, Wyo. 1934-42, plant physiologist, Salinas, Calif., 1942-49; sr. ecologist AEC Oak Ridge, 1949-50; sr. plant physiologist, then mgr. plant sci. sect., staff scientist, SRI Internat., Menlo Park, Calif., 1950-72, cons. 1972—. Fellow AAAS; mem. Am. Soc. Plant Physiologists, Am. Soc. Agronomy, N.Y. Acad. Scis., Air Pollution Control Assn. (chmn. agrl. tech. com. 1973-74). Republican. Contbr. numerous articles to profl. journals. Home: 408 S Orange Grove Blvd Pasadena CA 91105 Office: PO Box 50046 Pasadena CA 91105

BENEDICT, KAY LOUISE, history museum curator; b. Globe, Ariz., Jan. 21, 1928; d. Eugene Cosby and Zoma (Cooper) Hill; m. Samuel John Benedict, June 12, 1948; children—Bruce John, Jeril Samuel, David Brett. Student Ariz. State U., 1945-48. Sec., San Diego Vocational High Sch., 1944-45, English dept. Ariz. State U., 1945-48, Arlington Cattle Co., Ariz., 1957-58, Benedict Feeding Co., Stanfield, Ariz., 1958—; museum volunteer exhibits Casa Grande Valley Hist. Soc., 1967-77, museum curator 1977—. Treas., exec. com. Ariz. Humanities Council, 1979—; vice chmn. Casa Grande Community Hosp. bd. trustees, 1982—; mem. Casa Grande Silent Witness Com.; sec. Casa Grande Library Bd., 1970-74; sec. Casa Grande Bicentennial Centennial Com., 1974-79; bd. govs. Casa Grande Town Hall, 1972-79; bd. dirs. Am. Cancer Soc., 1963-73, chmn. Am. Field Service, others. Mem. Casa Grande Valley Hist. Soc., Ariz. Hist. Soc., Heritage Found. Ariz., Ariz. Paper and Photograph Conservation Assn., Western History Assn. Presbyterian. Club: Zonta. Home: 912 N Picacho Dr Casa Grande AZ 85222 Office: 110 W Florence Blvd Casa Grande AZ 85222

BENEDIKTER, HELEN CLAIRE, nursing service adminstr.; b. Syracuse, N.Y., May 21, 1939; d. Hans and Marie Antoinette (Doublehöfer) B.; R.N., St. Joseph's Hosp. Nursing, 1960; B.S., Boston Coll., 1962; postgrad. in bus. adminstrn. Calif. State U. at Long Beach. Nurse, Boston, 1960-61; staff nurse Children's Hosp. Med. Center, Boston, 1961-62; asst. dir. nursing evenings St. Joseph's Hosp., Syracuse, N.Y., 1962-66; field rep., research asso., asst. dir., research and edn. Joint Commn. Accreditation Hosps., Chgo., 1966-70; dir. nursing, asso. exec. dir. Long Beach Community Hosp., Long Beach, Calif., 1970—; pres. dirs. of nursing council Hosp. Council So. Calif., 1980; cons. hosps.; leader workshops, seminars in nursing; mem. council on nursing Am. Hosp. Assn., 1979—. Mem. Nat. League for Nursing, Am., Calif. nurses assns. (mem. by-laws com. Calif.), Am. Soc. for Nursing Service Adminstrs. (pres., past bd.). Republican. Episcopalian. Club: Internat. City (1st woman mem.). Contbr. articles in nursing to profl. jours.; mem. editorial bd. Jour. Nursing Adminstrn. Quar., 1977. Home: 5311 Tattershall Ave Westminster CA 92683 Office: 1720 Termino Ave Long Beach CA 90801

BENEFIELD, JAMES ROSS, advt. exec.; b. Ross, Calif., July 14, 1929; s. Glidden and Erma (Moore) B.; m. Judith Anne Lamoure, Nov. 27, 1965; children—Brian, Kerry. B.A. in Journalism, U. Calif.-Berkeley, 1951. Reporter San Francisco Examiner, 1954-56; pub. relations rep. United Airlines, San Francisco, 1956-58; publicity dir. Pacific Area Travel Assn., San Francisco, 1958-60; account exec. Campbell-Ewald Co., San Francisco, 1960-64; v.p. Botsford Ketchum Advt., San Francisco and Tokyo, 1964-69; account supr. Dancer Fitzgerald Sample Advt., San Francisco, 1969-72; pres. Benefield, Levinger & Assocs., Santa Rosa, Calif., 1972—. Pres. Santa Rosa Symphony Assn., 1979-81. Served to lt. USN, 1952-54. Democrat. Roman Catholic. Club: Sonoma County Press (co-founder, pres. 1978-80). Home: 2110 Parrish Dr Santa Rosa CA 95404 Office: 51 E St PO Box 669 Santa Rosa CA 95402

BENELBAS, LEON AMRAM, economist, educator; b. Larache, Morroco, Jan. 29, 1952; s. Samuel and Leah (Tapiero) B.; m. Clara Adrados, Apr. 15, 1981; 1 dau., Helena. Lic. in Econs., U. Barcelona (Spain), 1974, D. Econs., 1979. Asst. prof. econs. U. Barcelona, 1979-82, assoc. prof., 1982; research fellow dept. agrl. and resource econs. U. Calif.-Berkeley, 1980—; advisor in agrl. economy Govt. Catalonia, 1978-80. Fulbright postdoctoral fellow, 1980. Mem. Am. Econ. Assn., Am. Agrl. Econs. Assn. Author: Economia Agraria de Cataluna, 1981; Notas de Politica Agraria, 1982. Home: 1918 Channing Way Apt E Berkeley CA 94704 Office: 207 Giannini Hall Univ Calif Berkeley CA 94720

BENESTAD, AADNE, safety, construction engineer; b. Oslo, Nov. 20, 1943; s. Tor and Solveig Margrete Vefring (Nielsen) B.; m. Ellen D. Boin, Sept. 10, 1968; children—Birgitte Solveig, Tor Frederick. B.S. in Constrn. Engring., Oslo Tech. Coll., 1965. Carpenter Benestad Constrn. Co., Yelm, Wash., 1966; salesman Cee Bee Realty, Olympia, Wash., 1966-67; carpenter Tacoma Carpenters Union Local, 1967-68; ptnr. foreman Benestad, Peden and Strand, Olympia, 1968-69; attendant driver A.A. Ambulance Co., Portland, Oreg., 1969-70; supt. Benestad Constrn. Co., Olympia, 1970; mgr. Thurston Ambulance Co., 1971; first aid instr. Centralia (Wash.) Community Coll., 1970-73; sales service rep. Fire and Safety Equipment Co., Olympia, 1971-73; safety ednl. rep. I Wash. Dept. Labor and Industries, 1973-78; indsl. safety health instr. Grays Harbor Community Coll., Aberdeen, Wash., 1974-78; ptnr., constrn. supr. Benhuff Constrn. Co., Inc., Aberdeen, 1978; first aid. instr. Everett (Wash.) Community Coll., 1978—; safety engr. Austin Co., Everett, 1978-80; constrn. engr. Boeing Comml. Airplane Co., Seattle, 1980-81; loss control mgr. James L. Groves & Co., Everett, 1982—. Med. Mukilteo Sch. Bd.; mem. Aberdeen Police Res.; youth pastor and dir., Sunday sch. tchr., mem. bd., conf. bd. Evang. Covenant Ch., Everett and Aberdeen. Mem. Am. Soc. Safety Engrs. Home: 1016 93d St SW Everett WA 98204 Office: PO Box 5651 Everett WA 98206

BENFIELD, JOHN RICHARD, surgeon; b. Vienna, Austria, June 24, 1931; came to U.S. 1938, naturalized, 1945; s. Richard and Charlotte Lola (Glatter) B.; A.B., Columbia U., 1952; M.D., U. Chgo., 1955; m. Joyce A. Cohler, Dec. 22, 1963; children—Richard L., Robert E., Nancy J. Intern, Columbia-Presbyn. Hosp., N.Y.C., 1955-56; E.H. Andrews fellow in thoracic surgery U. Chgo., 1956-57; chief resident and instr. in surgery U. Chgo. Clinics, 1963-64, resident in surgery, 1956-57, 59-63; asst. prof. surgery U. Wis., 1964-67; asst. prof. UCLA, 1967-69, asso. prof., 1969-72, prof., 1972-76, clin. prof., 1978—; James Utley prof. surgery, chmn. dept. surgery Boston U., 1977; chmn. surgery City of Hope Nat. Med. Center, Duarte, Calif., 1978—; cons. U.S. Naval Med. Center, San Diego, 1968—; mem. sr. staff VA Wadsworth Med. Center, Los Angeles, 1978—. Sec., trustee Univ. Synagogue, Los Angeles, Served as capt., M.C., U.S. Army, 1957-59; Korea. Recipient Christopher award Chgo. Surg. Soc., 1958; Life Ins. Med. Research grantee, 1962-66; Am. Heart Assn. grantee, 1968-71; USPHS grantee, 1971—. Diplomate Am. Bd. Thoracic Surgery (bd. dirs. 1982—). Mem. Am. Surg. Assn., Am. Assn. Thoracic Surgery, Soc. Thoracic Surgeons, Soc. Univ. Surgeons, Pacific Coast Surg. Assn., Soc. Surg. Oncology, Am. Coll. Chest Physicians, A.C.S. (gov. 1982—), Internat. Surg. Soc. Club: Pasadena Athletic. Contbr. numerous articles, chpts. to profl. publs.; editor Current Problems in Cancer, 1975—; editorial bd. Annals of Thoracic Surgery, 1979—. Office: City of Hope Nat Med Center Duarte CA 91010

BENFIELD, WILLIAM RICHARD, pharmacy exec.; b. San Francisco, May 20, 1946; s. Harold R. and Jean A. (Hurlbert) B.; B.S. in Pharmacy, U. Wash., Seattle, 1969; M.S. in Pharmacy Adminstrn., U. Miss., 1974, Ph.D. in Health Care Adminstrn., 1975; m. Ruth Margaret Fletcher, Aug. 26, 1967; children—Ashley Dawn, Morgan Fletcher. Practicing pharmacist, Seattle, 1969-70, San Francisco, 1970-71; teaching asst. U. Miss. Sch. Pharmacy, 1971-74; guest lectr. U. Tenn. Coll. Nursing, 1972-75; mem. faculty U. Tenn. Center for Health Scis., Memphis, 1974-75; sales mgr. drug distbrs. div. Malone and Hyde of Memphis, 1975-77; pres. Diversified Pharm. Interests, Inc., Seattle, 1977—, Downtown Pharmacies, Inc., 1978—, Downtown Delivery, Inc., 1978—. Fellow Royal Philatelic Soc.; mem. Am. Pharm. Assn., Am. Mgmt. Assn., Master Resource Council Internat., Postal History Soc., Essay-Proof Soc., Kappa Psi, Rho Chi. Contbr. articles on pharmacy adminstrn. to profl. jours. Office: 714 Cherry St Seattle WA 98104

BENFORD, GEORGE STUART, JR., mech. engr.; b. Flint, Mich., Nov. 29, 1925; s. George Stuart and Florence Manila (Racette) B.; B.S. in Mech. Engring., Calif. State Poly. U., 1953; m. Dorothy Ellen Wood, Sept. 27, 1947; children—Marsha, Julie, George Stuart III, Theresa, Paula, Kathy Lynn. Engr., Union Sugar Co., Betteravia, Calif., 1953-57; mech. engr. Amalgamated Sugar Co., Ogden, Utah, 1957-71, asst. chief engr., 1971-73, plant engr., Nampa, Idaho, 1973—. Bd. dirs., v.p. Amalgamated Sugar Co. Credit Union, 1974-78. Served with U.S. Army, 1944-46. Mem. ASME, Am. Inst. Plant Engrs., Am. Soc. Sugar Beet Technologists. Republican. Roman Catholic. Home: 427 W Colorado Ave Nampa ID 83651 Office: PO Box 250 Nampa ID 83651

BENGTSON, VERN LEROY, sociologist, gerontologist, educator; b. Lindsborg, Kans., May 2, 1941; A.B., North Park Coll., 1963; M.A., U. Chgo., 1965, Ph.D., 1967. Asst. prof. sociology U. So. Calif., Los Angeles, 1967-70, assoc. prof., 1970-77, chief lab. social orgn. and behavior, 1971-77, prof. sociology, 1977—, dir. gerontology research inst., 1982—; vis. assoc. in sociology Calif. Inst. Tech., 1975-76; vis. prof. sociology U. Stockholm (Sweden), 1979. Fellow Am. Psychol. Assn. (mem. council div. 20 adult devel. and aging, 1975-78), Gerontol. Soc. Am. (pres. behavior and social scis. sect. 1983—); mem. Nat. Council Family Relations, Soc. Study Social Problems, Internat. Assn. Gerontology (9th internat. congress Kiev, Russia 1972, 12th internat. congress Hamburg, Germany 1981). Assoc. editor Sociology of Education; series editor Brooks-Cole Series in Social Gerontology; mem. exec. bd. Sociology and Social Research; mem. editorial bd. Journal of Marriage and the Family, Journal of Gerontology, Sage Family Studies Abstracts, Research of Aging, NCFR Monographs; contbr. numerous articles to profl. jours. and books. Office: Andrus Gerontology Ctr U Southern Calif Los Angeles CA 90089

BENIN, MARY HOLLAND BAKER, sociology educator, consultant; b. Madisonville, Ky., July 15, 1951; d. James G. and Anne (Priest) Baker; m. J. Miller McPherson, May 19, 1973; m. 2d David Budd Benin, Jan. 1, 1983. B.A. in Sociology cum laude, Vanderbilt U., 1972; M.A. U. Nebr., 1974, Ph.D., 1977. Teaching asst. U. Nebr., Lincoln, 1973-75, vis. asst. prof. sociology, 1978-79; instr. Doane Coll., Crete, Nebr., 1977-78; asst. prof. Ariz. State U., Tempe, 1979—; cons. in field; speaker profl. meetings. NSF Undergrad. Research participant, summer 1971; NIMH research trainee, 1975-77; Ariz. State U. faculty grantee, 1980, 81. Mem. Am. Sociol. Assn., Pacific Sociol. Assn. Contbr. articles to profl. jours. Office: Dept Sociology Ariz State U Tempe AZ 85282

BENIOH, TRAVIS NEIL, tribal administrator; b. Cedar City, Utah, Oct. 10, 1953; s. Billy and Mae Judy (Parashonts) B.; m. Lillian L., June 2, 1978; 1 son, Travis Shane. B.A. in Sociology, So. Utah State Coll., Cedar City, 1979. Job developer, counselor Utah Native Am. Consortium, Salt Lake City, 1975; ranger aid Utah State Dept. Forestry, Ogden, 1975; tchr.'s aide Iron County Sch. Dist., Cedar City, 1977-78, night watchman, 1978; ethnic gerontology recruiter Rocky Mountain Gerontology Center, Salt Lake City, 1979; Paiute research asst. So. Utah State Coll., 1979-80; laborer Ron Lewis Constrn. Co., Moapa, Nev., 1980; social services rep. Paiute Indian Tribe of Utah, Cedar City, 1981-82, tribal adminstr., 1982—; chmn. Cedar City Band of Paiutes, 1975-79; vice chmn. Utah Paiute Tribal Corp., 1977-79; mem. Interim Tribal Council, 1980—; vice chmn., dir. Utah Div. Indian Affairs, 1981—. Mem. adv. com. Salt Lake City Bd. Edn.; mem. Am. Indian Services bd. Brigham Young U.; mem. Bd. Indian Affiliates, Orem, Utah. Mormon. Club: Rotary. Author: The Paiute Language for Beginners. Home: 369 W Sunbow Cedar City UT 84720 Office: 600 N 100 E Cedar City UT 84720

BENISON, FRANK J., clin. psychologist; b. Detroit, Mar. 9, 1947; s. Irving G. and Mildred M. (Schwartz) B.; B.S., (NSF scholar), Mich. State U., 1970; Ph.D. in Clin. Psychology, Union Grad. Sch., 1975; m. Pamela Jane Follen, Nov. 28, 1971; 2 sons, Adam Peter, Alexander Martin. Dir. therapy The Rap House, Fenton, Mich., 1970-73; cons. affiliate New Statements Communication and Devel. Cons. Ltd., Que., 1973-76; psychologist Airline Pilots Assn. Internat., Denver, 1975; dir. Personal Growth Labs. West, Littleton, Colo., 1977—, also pvt. practice clin. psychology, Littleton, 1975—. Bd. dirs. Arapaho County div. Am. Cancer Soc., 1975-77. Mem. Am. Psychol. Assn., Colo. Psychol. Assn., Colo. Soc. Profl. Psychologists. Home and Office: 19 Lindenwood Dr Littleton CO 80120

BENITZ, PAUL ANTHONY, investment adviser; b. South Bend, Ind., Jan. 21, 1906; s. William Logan and Eleanor (Howard) B.; B.S., U. Notre Dame, 1927; M.A., Stanford, 1931; postgrad. Columbia, 1932; m. Alberta Sherman, Sept. 28, 1935. Cons. Axe-Houghton Mut. Fund, N.Y.C., 1948-52, Knickerbocker Mut. Fund, N.Y.C., 1948-50; pres. Calif. Mut. Fund, 1966-70, portfolio mgr., 1966-70; pres. Benitz-Lannan Mgmt. Co., 1966-70; self-employed as profl. investment mgr., La Jolla, Calif., 1961—. Granville Garth fellow in polit. economy Columbia, 1931-32. Mem. Financial Analysts Fedn. Contbr. weekly column La Jolla Light and Jour., 1967—. Address: 6515 Muirlands Dr La Jolla CA 92037

BENJAMIN, ANDREA KOPLIN, marketing executive; b. Chgo., Feb. 18, 1955; d. Allen Atlas and Martha Francis (Culbert) Koplin; m. Scott Douglas Benjamin, June 12, 1977. B.A. in Lit., U. Va., 1977; M.B.A., Golden Gate U., 1982. Mgr. pub. relations Budget Rent a Car Corp., Chgo., 1978-80; dir. communications Transam. Corp., San Francisco, 1980-82; dir. mktg. communications Activision, Inc., Mountain View, Calif., 1982—.

BENJAMIN, ARLIN JAMES, physicist; b. Guthrie, Okla., Oct. 9, 1933; s. Harold Dinsmore and Lula Martha (Black) B.; m. Patricia Ann Crabb, Oct. 10, 1964; children—Arlin James, Cynthia Denise, Deborah Dawn. B.S., Sam Houston State Coll, 1955; M.S., Okla. State U., 1957; postgrad. MIT, 1959, Wichita U., 1959-60. Engr. Boeing Co., Wichita (Kans.), 1956-63; lead nuclear engr. LTV Corp., Dallas, 1963-64; ops. research analyst Research Triangle Inst., Research Triangle Park, N.C., 1964-66; sr. ops. research analyst Gen. Dynamics Corp., Ft. Worth, 1966-68; mgr. Control Data Corp., Honolulu, 1968-70; sr. scientist Southwest Research Inst., San Antonio, 1970-78; mgr., prin. scientist Hittman Assocs. Inc., Sacramento, 1978-81; mgr., sr. ops. research analyst The BDM Corp., Ft. Lewis, Wash., 1981—. Mem. Am. Geophys. Union, Am. Nuclear Soc., Am. Phys. Soc., Inst. Physics (London), Phys. Soc. (London), European Phys. Soc., Inst. Mgmt. Sci., Alpha Chi, Pi Gamma Mu. Author articles and sci. papers for profl. jours. Office: PO Box 33284 Fort Lewis WA 98433

BENJAMIN, HERBERT STANLEY, psychiatrist, surgeon, educator; b. Washington, June 7, 1922; s. Joseph and Katie (Lewin) B.; Ph.B., U. Wis., 1943; postgrad. Columbia U., 1948-49, (Fulbright scholar) Sorbonne, U. Paris, 1949-50; M.D., U. Vienna, Austria, 1957, postgrad. Postgrad. Acad. Medicine, 1957-64, certificate in psychosomatic medicine and surgery, 1975; m. Edith Steiner, July 20, 1966; children—Oliver, Alice. Resident guest physician in surgery and urology U. Vienna, 1957-60; intern Cedars of Lebanon Hosp., Los Angeles, 1964-65; resident in psychiatry Cedars-Sinai Med. Center, Los Angeles, 1965-68, chief resident in psychiatry, 1967-68; practice medicine specializing in psychiatry and psychosomatic medicine, Beverly Hills, Calif., 1968—; mem. staffs Cedars-Sinai Med. Center, Westwood Hosp., Beverly Glen Hosp., Encino Hosp. (all Los Angeles); cons. in psychiatry So. Calif. Permanente Med. Group, 1969-70; sr. faculty Cedars-Sinai Med. Center, Los Angeles, 1968—; chmn. internat. seminar in psychosomatic medicine U. Vienna, 1975; asst. prof. psychiatry and behavioral scis. Faculty of Medicine, UCLA, 1982—. Served to lt. (j.g.), USNR, 1943-48. Mem. Am., Calif. psychiat. assns., So. Calif. Psychiat. Soc., Am., So. Calif. socs. adolescent psychiatry, Soc. for History of Medicine, So. Calif. Soc. for Child Psychiatry, Los Angeles Psychoanalytic Study Group, N.Y. Acad. Medicine, Am. Med. Soc. Vienna, AAAS, Pi Gamma Mu. Contbr. numerous articles to encys. Office: 436 N Roxbury Dr Suite 220 Beverly Hills CA 90210

BENJAMIN, LAWRENCE WILLIAM, sales exec.; b. N.Y.C., July 12, 1941; s. Lawrence Christopher and Louise Irene (Gressler) B.; B.Mech. Engring., Pratt Inst., 1965, M.Mech. Engring., 1969; postgrad. Calif. State U.-Northridge, 1972-75; m. Aleta Shari Fierman, June 18, 1966. Mech. engr. U.S. Navy Applied Material Lab., Bklyn., 1965-67; instr. Pratt Inst. Sch. Engring., 1967-68; acoustical cons. Cerami & Assocs., Queens, N.Y., 1968-69; Product mgr. Indsl. Acoustics Co., Bronx, N.Y., 1969-72; product mgr. Am. Air Filter Co., Santa Paula, Calif., 1972-77; gen. sales mgr. Ransco Industries, Oxnard, Calif., 1977—. Pres. Shadow Mountain Tennis Club Home Owners Assn. Recipient Silent Chain Hoist Design award, 1965. Mem. ASME, Inst. Environ. Scis., Am. Mgmt. Assn. Office: 2221 Statham Blvd Oxnard CA 93033

BENJAMIN, WILLIAM EARL, lawyer; b. Kansas City, Mo., Oct. 5, 1942; s. Roger Olney and Mary Elizabeth (Jones) B.; B.A., Johns Hopkins, 1964; LL.B., Yale, 1968; m. Ruth Lee Coombs, Aug. 19, 1967; children—Sharla Ann, Brien Randall. Instr., U. N.C. Inst. of Govt., Chapel Hill, 1968-69; admitted to Colo. bar, 1970; law clk. Colo. Ct. Appeals, Denver, 1970; staff atty. Colo. Rural Legal Services, Greeley and Alamosa, 1971-74; sr. staff atty. Nat. Center for State Cts., Denver, 1974-75; supervising atty. Legal Aid Soc. Met. Denver, 1975-81; sole practice, Boulder, Colo., 1982—. Mem. Colo. State Bar Com. on Availability of Legal Services to Poor and Moderate Incomed, 1971—. Bd. dirs. Weld County Mental Health Assn., 1971-72, Boulder chpt. ACLU, 1981—. Reginald Heber Smith Community Lawyer fellow, 1970-72. Mem. ABA, Colo. Bar Assn. (chmn. com. on availability legal services to poor and moderate incomed 1977-78) bar assns. Home: 3570 Catalpa Way Boulder CO 80302

BENKELMAN, CLAY EDWARD, optometrist; b. Honolulu, Oct. 28, 1950; s. Ward E. and Mary Helen (Lewis) B.; m. Debra Lynn Smith, Aug. 29, 1981; children—Merisa Rae, Brandon Eugene. Student U. Mont., 1971-72; B.S., Mont. State U., 1973; O.D., Pacific U., 1976. Optometrist, U.S. Navy Support Base, Barstow, Calif., 1976-78; ptnr. Bigfork Optometric Group (Mont.), 1978—. Served with USN, 1974-78. Mem. Am. Optometric Assn., Mont. Optometric Assn., C. of C. Republican. Lutheran. Club: Lions. Home: Box 487 Bigfork MT 59911 Office: 120 Village Ln Bigfork MT 59911

BENNACK, FRANK ANTHONY, JR., media company executive; b. San Antonio, Feb. 12, 1933; s. Frank Anthony and Lulu Wardell (Connally) B.; student St. Mary's U., 1956-58, U. Md., 1954-56; m. Luella Smith, Sept. 1, 1951; children—Shelley, Laura, Diane, Cynthia, Julie. Vice pres., pub., editor San Antonio Light, 1967-74; gen. mgr. newspapers Hearst Corp., N.Y.C., 1974-75, exec. v.p., 1975-77, chief operating officer, 1977-79, pres., chief exec. officer, 1979—, also dir.; chmn. bd. Nat. Mag. Co. (U.K.); dir. Allied Stores, Mfrs. Hanover Trust Co., Southwest Forest Industries. Bd. dirs. Newspaper Advt. Bur., 1975-83, William Randolph Hearst Found., The Hearst Found.; life mem. bd. govs. N.Y. Hosp., 1980—; mem. corp. fund com. Lincoln Center for Performing Arts, 1979—; chmn. San Antonio Symphony Soc., 1973-74. Served with U.S. Army, 1954-56. Recipient Brotherhood award NCCJ, 1974; named San Antonio's Outstanding Man of Year, 1973. Mem. Am. Newspaper Pubs. Assn. (dir. 1982—), Tex. Daily Newspaper Assn. (pres. 1973). Roman Catholic.

BENNER, DAVID STEPHEN, civil engr.; b. Grant, Nebr., Aug. 20, 1952; s. Robert Edwin and Evelynne Sandy B.; student Hastings (Nebr.) Coll., 1970-72; B.S. in Civil Engring., U. Wyo., 1975. Engring. aide Forest Service, Sheridan, Wyo., summer 1972, VA, Sheridan, summer 1973, 74; hydraulic engr. Wyo. Hwy. Dept., Cheyenne, 1975—. Lic. profl. engr., Wyo. Mem. ASCE (asso.), U. Wyo. Alumni Assn. (life), Omicron Delta Kappa, Sigma Tau, Tau Beta Pi. Republican. Presbyterian. Home: 7013 Evers Blvd Cheyenne WY 82009 Office: PO Box 1708 Room 231 Cheyenne WY 82001

BENNETT, BRIAN JOSEPH, parochial sch. prin.; b. Rochester, N.Y., Apr. 24, 1949; s. Joseph Eustace and Genevieve (Conlin) B.; B.A. in English, Loyola U., Los Angeles, 1971, J.D., 1975; m. Jeanine Longeway, Aug. 21, 1971; children—Monica Anne, Anne Elizabeth. Tchr., Nativity Sch., Torrace, Calif., 1971-73, St. Jerome Sch., Los Angeles, 1973-75; prin. St. Madeleine Sch., Pomona, Calif., 1975-79, Blessed Sacrament Sch., San Diego, 1979—; leader work shops on sch. law for tchrs. and prins. non-public schs.; policy cons. sch. law Catholic Diocese of Orange (Calif.). Mem. Greater San Diego Traffic Safety Adv. Com., I Love a Clean San Diego Com. Named Outstanding Faculty Mem., Loyola Debate Inst., 1975; recipient awards of merit Cath. Assn. Student Councils, Nat. Multiple Sclerosis Found. Mem. Nat. Cath. Edn. Assn., Assn. Supervision and Curriculum Devel., Calif. Assn. Pvt. Sch. Orgns., San Diego Coll. Area Community Council. Democrat. Roman Catholic. Office: 4551 56th St San Diego CA 92115

BENNETT, CARL ALLEN, research statistician; b. Winfield, Pa., Nov. 22, 1921; s. Charles Noah and Florence Edna (Crabb) B.; m. Myra Elizabeth Schwan, June 17, 1944; children—Carla M., Tamara L. A.B., Bucknell U., 1940, A.M., 1941, Sc.D. (hon.), 1972; M.A., U. Mich., 1942, Ph.D. in Math., 1952. Chemist, supr. quality control Manhattan Project, Tenn. Eastman Corp., Oak Ridge, 1944-46; statistician Hanford Atomic Products Ops., Gen. Electric Co., Richland, Wash., 1947-50, chief statistician, mgr. math. dept., 1961-65; research assoc. stats. Princeton (N.J.) U., 1950-51; vis. prof. stats. Stanford (Calif.) U., 1964; div. mgr. Battelle N.W., Richland, 1965-70 staff scientist Battelle-Human Affairs Research Ctrs., Seattle, 1971—; cons. adv. com. reactor safeguards AEC, 1970—; mem. Nat. Acad. Scis. INRC Adv. Bd. Applied Math., Nat. Bur. Standards, 1969-75, evaluation panel Ctr. Applied Math., 1980—; mem. standing adv. group on safeguards implementation IAEA, 1975-79. Bd. regents Pacific Lutheran U., Tacoma, 1963-72, Collegium, 1976—. Rackham predoctoral fellow, 1946-47. Fellow Am. Statis. Assn. (dir. 1969-71, com. fellows 1974-78, chmn. technometrics mgmt. com. 1967-72, ad hoc com. nuclear regulatory research 1980—), Am. Soc. Quality Control, AAAS; mem. Inst. Nuclear Materials Mgmt., Soc. Risk Analysis, Biometrics Soc. (pres. region 1962-63). Democrat. Lutheran. Author: (with N.L. Franklin) Statistical Analysis in Chemistry and the Chemical Industry, 1954; (with A.A. Lumsdaine) Evaluation and Experiment, 1975; contbr. articles to profl. jours. Home: 11121 SE 59th St Bellevue WA 98006 Office: 4000 NE 41st St Seattle WA 98105

BENNETT, CHARLES LEON, vocational educator, graphic arts consultant; b. Salem, Oreg., Feb. 5, 1951; s. Theodore John and Cora Larena-May (Rowland) B.; m. Cynthia Alice Hostman, June 12, 1976 (div.); m. 2d., Lynn Marie Toland, Aug. 12, 1977; children—Mizzy Marie, Charles David. A.S. in Vocat. Tchr. Edn., Clackamas Community Coll., 1977; A.S. in Gen. Studies, Linn Benton Community Coll., 1979; postgrad. SUNY, 1983—. Tchr. printing Tongue Point Job Corps, Astoria, Oreg., 1979-80, Portland (Oreg.) pub. schs., 1980—; owner, mgr. printing and pub. co., Portland, 1981—. Served with AUS, 1970-72. Mem. Oreg. Vocat. Trade-Tech. Assn. (dept. chmn., pres. graphic arts div., Indsl. Educator of Year 1981-82), Oreg. Vacat. Assn. (Vocat. Tchr. of Year 1982-83), Graphic Arts Tech. Found., In-Plant Printing Mgmt. Assn., Internat. Graphic Arts Edn. Assn., Nat. Assn. Quick Printers, Am. Vacat. Assn., Portland Club Lithographers and Printing House Craftsmen. Democrat. Clubs: Oreg. Athletic (Portland); Elks (Milw.). Home: 6602 SE 97th Ave Portland OR 97266 Office: SE Milwaukie Ave Portland OR 97202

BENNETT, DOLORES B., organization administrator; b. Clarkston, Utah, Oct. 26, 1920; d. Golden L. and Sarah P. Buttars; student Utah State U., 1938-40; m. James Austin Bennett, Sept. 18, 1940; children—James R., Carl R., Calleen, Marilyn, Marvin C. Vice chmn. Republican Party, Cache County, Utah, 1962-68, 1st congressional dist. vice chmn., 1963-66, 69-72; bd. dirs. Utah State Fair, 1964-69, vice chmn., 1967-69; v.p. Utah Fedn. Republican Women, 1971-73, pres., 1973-77, bd. dirs. nat. fedn. 1973-80, co-chmn. fund raising com., 1978-80; v.p. Utah Womens Legislative Council, 1976-77; del. Internat. Women's Year Conf., 1977; mem. City of Logan Zoning and Planning Commn., 1974—, chmn. 1976-78; mem. City of Logan Bd. Adjustments, 1978—; founder, exec. v.p., chmn. awards Utah chpt. Freedom Found. at Valley Forge, pres., 1983. Mormon. Office: 714 N 150th St W Logan UT 84321

BENNETT, DON, state senator, consultant; b. Fresno, Calif., May 6, 1931; m. Beverly Ann Bennett; 3 children. Student San Jose State Coll., U. Md. Indsl. medicine cons.; mem. Alaska Ho. of Reps., 1976-78, Alaska State Senate, 1978—. Served to lt. col., U.S. Army. Home: Box 2801 Fairbanks AK 99707 Office: Alaska State Senate Juneau AK 99811*

BENNETT, GAYMON LAMONT, English educator; b. Portland, Oreg., Mar. 2, 1942; s. Allen Andrew and Adeline Deloris (Gudmundsen) B.; A.B. in English, N.W. Nazarene Coll., 1964; M.A. in Am. Studies, Calif. State U., Los Angeles, 1969; Ph.D. in Am. Studies, Wash. State U., 1982; m. Evelyn Louise Sanner, July 3, 1964; children—Cristina Suzanne, Gaymon Lamont, Maria Akiko. Tchr. English, Homedale (Idaho) High Sch., 1964-66; tchr. English, drama, journalism, social studies Rowland High Sch., Rowland Heights, Calif., 1966-68, 69-71; prof. English and English edn. N.W. Nazarene Coll., 1971—, head dept. English, 1976—; humanist cons. Assn. for Humanities in Idaho. Mem. Nat. Council Tchrs. English, Western Lit. Assn., Am. Studies Assn., Assn. Depts. English. Mem. Ch. of the Nazarene. Office: NW Nazarene Coll Nampa ID 83651

BENNETT, GROVER BRYCE, consulting civil engineer; b. Shelley, Idaho, Apr. 9, 1921; s. Grover T. and Guila (Young) B.; B.S., U. Idaho, 1943; M.S., U. Wash., 1949; m. Barbara A. Beedle, July 30, 1944; children—William G., Rebecca I., Alan B. Jr. constrn. engr. Pan Am Airways, 1943-44; instr. civil engring. Seattle U., 1946-48; asst. prof. civil engring. U. Idaho, 1949-51; materials engr. Idaho Dept. Hwys., 1951-53; asphalt mgr. Shell Oil Co., Sacramento, 1953-54; asst. state hwy. engr. Idaho Dept. Hwys., Boise, 1955-56, state hwy. engr., 1956-64; project mgr. Internat. Engring. Co., Chile, 1964-66, chief hwy. engr., San Francisco, 1966-67, v.p. adminstrn., 1967-68, v.p., gen. mgr., dir., 1968-71, exec. v.p., dir., 1971-83; dep. project dir. Morrison-Knudsen Co., Inc., 1981-83; cons. engr., 1983—. Served with USNR, 1944-46. Registered profl. engr., Idaho, Wash., Calif., Ariz., Hawaii, Alaska. Fellow ASCE; mem. Am. Road Builders Assn. (cert. of recognition 1964), Western (past pres.), Am. (past regional v.p.) assns. state hwy. ofcls., Cons. Engrs. Assn. Calif. (dir.), Nat. Soc. Profl. Engrs. Club: World Trade. Home and Office: 2680 Skyfarm Dr Hillsborough CA 94010

BENNETT, HYRAM, manufacturer's agent; b. Roxbury, Mass., June 28, 1916; s. Harry and Anne (Bennett) Glick; m. Nellie Nelson, Jan. 15, 1943. Student pub. schs., Roxbury. Nat. sales mgr. Varco Products Co., Los Angeles, 1959-63, Omega Power Steering Co., Los Angeles, 1963-64, Alco U-Joints Co., Chgo., 1964-67; mfrs. agt. TR-3 Chem. Corp., Granada Hills, Calif., 1974-82; owner, pres. Hy Bennett & Assocs., Granada Hills, Calif., 1974—. Served to capt. U.S. Army, 1943-53. Republican. Mem. Church of Religious Science. Club: Masons. Home and Office: 13347 Mission Tierra Way Granada Hills CA 91344

BENNETT, JAMES AUSTIN, animal scientist, educator; b. Taber, Alta., Can., Jan. 29, 1915; s. William Alvin and Mary (Walker) B.; came to U.S., 1945, naturalized, 1949; B.S., Utah State U., 1940, M.S., 1941; Ph.D., U. Minn., 1957; m. Dolores Buttars, Sept. 18, 1940; children—James Ralph, Carl Robert and Calleen (twins), Marvin Charles and Marilyn (twins). Livestock asst. Dominion Dept. Agr., Swift Current, Sask., Can., 1941-45; asst. prof. Utah State U., 1945-50, prof. animal sci., 1950-73, 74—, head dept., 1950-73, 74-76, coordinator sheep research Utah State U.-Ministry Agr. Iran, 1973-74. Mem. AAAS, Am. Soc. Animal Sci. Am. Genetic Assn., Sigma Xi. Contbr. numerous articles on animal breeding and genetics to profl. jours. Home: 714 N 150th W Logan UT 84321

BENNETT, JAMES GORDON, pathologist; b. Lee's Summit, Mo., Dec. 14, 1915; s. Ernest Sheridan and Georgia Martha (Shawhan) B.; A.B., Central Meth. Coll., Fayette, Mo., 1935; M.D., Harvard U., 1939; m. Beatrice Elizabeth Babcock, Feb. 17, 1940; children—Nancy Lee von Gnechten, John Edward, Carolyn Babcock, Jean Elizabeth Bishop. Intern, Mary Hitchcock Meml. Hosp., Hanover, N.H., 1940-41, resident in pathology, 1942; fellow in pathology Mayo Found., Rochester, Minn., 1943-44; dir. labs. Firland Sanatorium, Seattle, 1949-56; dir. labs. Kaiser Med. Center, Honolulu, 1959-72, now pathologist; clin. asso. prof. pathology John A. Burns Sch. Medicine, Honolulu. Served to maj. M.C., U.S. Army, 1944-47. Mem. AMA, Hawaii Med. Assn., Am. Soc. Clin. Pathologists, Coll. Am. Pathologists, Internat. Acad. Pathology, Hawaii Soc. Pathologists, Am. Thoracic Soc., Am. Assn. Blood Banks. Unitarian. Clubs: Mid-Pacific Road Runners, Amateur Fencers League Am., Nat. Tennis Assn. Home: 4760 Farmers Rd Honolulu HI 96816 Office: 1697 Ala Moana Honolulu HI 96815

BENNETT, JEAN LOUISE, performing artists' manager; b. Barnsdall, Okla., Apr. 25, 1923; d. John L. and Lillian E. (Turner) Million; children—Johnny Lee Arrowood, Alicia Bennett. Student Colo. State Tchrs. Coll., 1945. Mgr., The Platters singing group, Las Vegas, Nev., 1953—; pres. Five Platters Inc., Las Vegas, 1975—; owner Personality Prodns. Inc., Las Vegas; assoc. of composer-producer Buck Ram, 952—; represented Five Platters Inc. in fed. ct. cases for trade name infringement. Office: Personality Prodns PO Box 39 Las Vegas NV 89125

BENNETT, JOAN ELEANOR, business executive; b. N.Y.C., Mar. 14, 1934; d. Samuel Arthur and Mildred Ethel (Mueller) Gee; children—Barbara Susan. Student Monmouth Coll., N.J., 1962-64, Southwestern Coll., Calif., 1975-77; B.S. in Bus. Edn. and Mgmt. magna cum laude, Brigham Young U.-Hawaii, 1982, postgrad., 1981-82; postgrad. U. Hawaii, 1983. Controller, Young Properties, Inc., 1969-72; acct. Cal-Am. Communities, Inc., 1974-75; office mgr. Florentine Co., 1975-78; personnel dir. Polynesian Cultural Ctr., Laie, Hawaii, 1978-80; spl. instr., advisor student sec. Brigham Young U.-Hawaii, 1980-82; sec.-treas. Golden Trends Enterprises, Inc., Honolulu, 1980—; tchr. spl. edn. Castle High Sch., Kaneohe, Hawaii, 1982—; cons. Mem. Nat. Bus. Educators Assn., Am. Bus. Women's Assn. (nat. v.p. 1976, founder, pres. Koolauloa charter chpt. 1980), Western Bus. Educators Assn., Hawaii Bus. Educators Assn., Nat. Council Tchrs. English, Assn. Supervision and Curriculum Devel. Republican. Mormon. Author: Employment for Youth: Where to Begin?, 1983. Home: 54-179 Kawaeku St Hauula HI 96717

BENNETT, LEWIS TILTON, JR., actor, advertising and communications company executive; b. Manchester, N.H., Jan. 14, 1940; s. Lewis Tilton and Elizabeth (Goodwin) B. B.S. in Bus., Babston Inst., 1961; B.A. in Film, San Francisco State U., 1965. Pres., Bennett, Inc., San Francisco, 1967—, Luxembourg, 1967—; actor in films: Petulia, Guess Who's Coming to Dinner, Bullitt, Zabriski Point, Strawberry Statement, Harold and Maude, Magnum Force, Towering Inferno, Time After Time, also TV commls.; tchr. San Francisco Film Clinic, 1968-71, 74—; also stand-in for film actor Steve Mc Queen; also photographer. Mem. San Francisco Symphony Found., 1967—; del. sponsor San Francisco Internat. Film Festival, 1967, 68, 69. Mem. SAR. Clubs: Olympic, Lakeside Country, Carmel Beach, Commonwealth, West Coast Yacht, Racket, Europe United. Office: 1348 Sacramento St San Francisco CA 94109 also 1647 Hyde Park St Sarasota FL also 20 rue des Roses Luxembourg Luxembourg

BENNETT, LOIS ELAINE, interior designer; b. Los Angeles, Feb. 25, 1953; d. Robert Milton and Barbara Reid (Hinton) Bennett; B.A., Iowa State U., 1974. Interior designer Sharon Brady Interiors, Ames, Iowa, 1974-75, Haber's Furniture, Santa Cruz, Calif., 1976-79; space planner real estate div. GSA, San Francisco, 1980—. Mem. Nat. Trust for Historic Preservation, Smithsonian Instn., Am. Soc. Interior Designers. Office: 525 Market St San Francisco CA 94105

BENNETT, MAX DIAL, medical educator, medical center administrator; b. Clovis, N.Mex., June 30, 1944; s. Reece L. and Lila M. (Boss) B.; m. Pamela Ann Montgomery, Aug. 4, 1965; children—Nolan, Meredith. B.A. in Chemistry, Eastern N.Mex. U., 1966; M.Hosp. Adminstrn., U. Mich., 1968; Ph.D. in Econs., Johns Hopkins U., 1973. Mgr., Portales (N.Mex.) Mcpl. Swimming Pool, 1963-65; asst. prof. econs. Purdue U. 1973-74; v.p. Interstudy, Mpls. 1974; asst. to v.p. health scis. U. N.Mex. 1974-77, assoc. prof. 1977—, planning officer med. ctr., 1977—; mem. Gov.'s Task Force on Rural Med. Practice 1979-81, Gov.'s Task Force on Driving While Intoxicated and Alcohol Abuse 1982—. Mem. Am. Econ. Assn., Am. Pub. Health Assn., Assn. Am. Med. Colls. Democrat. Methodist. Contbr. articles to profl. jours. Home: 7000 Shoshone St NE Albuquerque NM 87110 Office: School of Medicine U New Mexico Albuquerque NM 87131

BENNETT, MICHAEL, distribution exec.; b. Los Angeles, May 12, 1948; s. William Franklin and Elizabeth Louisa (Dilday) B.; m. Lucinda Ball, June 24, 1969; children—Mollie Louisa, Joshua Lincoln. Student U. Calif.-San Diego, 1966-67; B.A. in Econ., UCLA, 1970, postgrad. in Bus., 1970-71. Vice pres. ops. L.B. Ball & Co., Long Beach, Calif., 1970-77, exec. v.p., gen. mgr., 1977—; v.p., owner In-Store Services, Inc. Chmn. bd. Goodwill Industries So. Los Angeles County. Served with USAR, 1969-75. Mem. Am. Mktg. Assn., Am. Mgmt. Assn., Nat. Council Phys. Distbn. Mgmt., Ctr. Futures Research, Nat. Assn. Tobacco Distbrs. (dir., v.p. Young Execs. div.). Club: Kiwanis (v.p. Long Beach). Office: 3100 E 29th St PO Box 989 Long Beach CA 90801

BENNETT, REED W., ret. computer services adminstr.; b. Ogden, Utah, Sept. 1, 1929; s. Phillip John and Maude Miller (Walker) B.; B.A., U. Utah, 1958, M.B.A., 1959; postgrad. U. Chgo., 1964-65; m. Dolores Steiner, May 23, 1981; children—Kelly, Laurie, Tamara, Fredric, Perry, Paula. Prodn. controller Collins Radio Co., 1959; computer systems programmer U.S. Air Force, 1960; systems analyst Hercules, Inc., Baachus, Utah, 1961-62; br. mgr. IRS, Ogden, Utah, 1963-70, mgr. computer services and acctg. div., Fresno, Calif., 1970-82; dir. U.S. Employees Credit Union. Mem. Davis County Recreational Adv. Bd., 1966-70; mem. Fresno Service Center Careers Adv. Bd., 1972—. Served with USAF, 1953-57. Nat. Inst. Public Affairs fellow, 1964. Mem. Data Processing Mgrs. Assn., Fresno Realtors. Republican. Mormon. Club: Elks. Home: 230 S Clovis Ave Fresno CA 93727

BENNETT, ROBERT LOUIS, college administrator; b. Winnett, Mont., July 17, 1925; s. William and Florence B.; m. Jean Kathryn Pierson, Oct. 20, 1971; children—Mary, Jean, James, William, Stephen. B.A., Mont. State Coll., 1950; M.S., Eastern Mont. Coll., 1959; Ed.D., U. Calif.-Berkeley, 1967. Tchr., counselor, Billings, Mont., 1951-60; researcher in ednl. devel. San Mateo (Calif.) High Sch. Dist., 1961-67; coll. adminstr. in resource devel. San Mateo Community Coll. Dist.; project dir. Ford Found. Cooperative Edn. Program, Kellogg Found. Community Coll. Mgmt. by Objectives, U.S. Office Edn. Career Edn. Nat. Demonstration. Served with USN, 1945-46. Mem. Am. Soc. Tng. and Devel., Assn. Calif. Community Coll. Adminstrs. (charter). Author: Identification of Curriculum Strengths and Weaknesses, 1967; An Improved Urban-Suburban Management Model for Community Colleges, 1977; Careers Through Cooperative Work Experience, 1978; Earning and Learning, 1980. Address: 53 Condon Ct San Mateo CA 94403

BENNETT, THOMAS LEROY, JR., psychology educator; b. Norwalk, Conn., Sept. 25, 1942; s. Thomas LeRoy and Gertrude Upson (Richardson) B.; B.A., U. N.Mex., 1964, M.S., 1966, Ph.D., 1968; m. Jacqueline Beekman, Sept. 5, 1972; children—Dean, Shannon, Brian, Laurie. Asst. prof. Calif. State U., Sacramento, 1968-70; assoc. prof., then prof. psychology, physiology and biophysics, Colo. State U., Ft. Collins, 1970—; pvt. practice Ctr. for Stress Mgmt. and Personal Growth, Ft. Collins. Elder, Timnath Presbyn. Ch. Mem. Psychonomic Soc., Sigma Xi. Author: Brain and Behavior, 1977; The Sensory World, 1978; The Psychology of Learning and Memory, 1979; Exploring the Sensory World, 1979; Introduction to Physiological Psychology, 1982; contbr. articles to profl. jours. Home: 213 Camino Real Fort Collins CO 80524 Office: Psychology Dept Colorado State U Fort Collins CO 80523

BENNETT, WILLIAM CHARLES, accountant, educator; b. East Chicago, Ind., June 24, 1952; s. Jerry and Elizabeth B. B.A. in Econs. and Bus., DePauw U., 1974; M.B.A., Washington U., St. Louis, 1976. Acctg. intern IBM Corp., Greencastle, Ind., 1974; adminstrv. asst. Ball Corp., Muncie, Ind., 1973-74; internal auditor Monsanto Corp., Creve Corue, Mo., summer 1975; grad. teaching asst. computer lab. Sch. Bus. Washington U., St. Louis, 1975-76, acctg. tutor, 1975-79; acctg. cons. Inst. of Black Studies, St. Louis, 1978-79; acctg. instr. Mo. Baptist Coll., St. Louis, 1978-79; sr. acct. Ernst & Ernst, C.P.A.s, St. Louis, 1976-79; spl. agt. acctg. FBI, 1979-82; ptnr. Bennett, Hutt & Co., C.P.A.s, Albuquerque, 1982—; adj. asst. prof. acctg., U. N.Mex., 1982—. Bd. dirs. Albuquerque Crime Stoppers Assn.; chmn. supervisory com. Albuquerque U.S. Employees Fed. Credit Union. Recipient Mary McCleod Bethune Community Service award, St. Louis, 1976, East Chicago Recreation Dept. Community Service award, 1976; Consortium for Grad. Studies in Mgmt. fellow, 1974. Mem. Am. Inst. C.P.A.s, N.Mex. Soc. C.P.A.s, Mo. Soc. C.P.A.s, Nat. Assn. Black Accts. (past nat. bd. dirs., achievement award St. Louis 1977, Disting. Achievement award St. Louis 1979), Assn. Govt. Accts. St. Louis (past bd dirs.), Soc. of Former Spl. Agts. FBI, Washington U. Alumni Club, Kappa Alpha Psi (Middle Western Province achievement award 1976, Darryl D. Sharp Achievement award St. Louis 1978). Home: 9301 Shoshone NE Albuquerque NM 87111 Office: 720 Grand NE Albuquerque NM 87102

BENNETT, WILLIAM RICHARDS, premier British Columbia, Canada; b. Kelowna, B.C., Can., Apr. 14, 1932; s. William Andrew Cecil and Annie Elizabeth May (Richards) B.; grad. Kelowna high sch.; m. Audrey Lyne James, Apr. 16, 1955; children—Brad, Kevin, Stephen, Gregory. Operator, owner furniture and appliance store, Kelowna, B.C., Can.; elected Legis. Assembly B.C. from S. Okanagan dist., 1973, premier B.C., 1975—. Mem. Social Credit Party, Kelowna C. of C. (past pres.). Mem. United Ch. Club: Kelowna Toastmasters. Home: Rural Route 1 Pritchard Dr Westbank BC V1Y 7P9 Canada Office: Premiers Office Parliament Bldgs Victoria BC V8V 1X4 Canada

BENNING, ARTHUR E., former sugar company executive; b. Sterling, Colo., 1912; student Yale U. Former chmn. bd., chief exec. officer Amalgamated Sugar Co., Ogden, Utah; past dir. First Security Corp., Utah Power and Light Co. Mem. US Beet Sugar Assn. (former trustee).

BENNINGER, FRED, hotel and casino executive; b. Germany, 1917. Ed. NYU, 1937, U. So. Calif., 1941. Former chmn., chief exec. officer MGM Grand Hotels Inc., Las Vegas, Nev., now chmn. exec. com., 1982—; dir. MGM Film Co. (Calif.), Western Air Lines Inc. Office: MGM Grand Hotels Inc 3645 Las Vegas Blvd S Las Vegas NV 89109*

BENNINGTON, ANNA LAURA, educational administrator; b. Hot Springs, S.D., July 13, 1932; d. Thomas Henry and Myrtle Christine (Christianson) Callan; m. J.T. Bennington, Dec. 19, 1954; 1 son, J.T. B.S.B.A. in Acctg. and Edn., U. Denver, 1954; M.Ed. in Bus. Edn., U. Ariz., 1978. Acct., N.Y. and Denver, 1953-54; tchr., head bus. edn. dept. Tuolumne (Calif.) High Sch., 1954-55; bus. coll. instr., 1958-62; pvt. sec. to dir. purchasing State of Kans., 1963-65; tchr., adminstr. U.S. mil. base high sch. Dept. Def., Eng., 1965-68, tchr. bus. edn., head dept. W.Ger., 1973-76; tchr. bus. edn., coordinator personnel dept., asst. to dir. personnel/supt. Tucson Unified Sch. Dist., 1970-73, inservice trainer, 1976-80, coordinator Experience Based Career Edn. Project, 1976-77; profl. inservice bus. edn. coordinator U. Ariz., Tucson, 1978-82; dir.

competency based vocat. edn., 1982—; instr. Pima Community Coll., Tucson, 1976-82; pres. Bus. Extraordinaire, Inc.; speaker profl. meetings. Project dir. fund raising com. City Panhellenic, Topeka and Tucson; mem. English-Speaking Union Bd., Oxford, Eng.; mem. welfare com., fin. com., membership com., state senate liaison LWV; tchr. Sunday sch., vol. office worker chs. in Kans., Eng., Tucson. Recipient award Anglo-Am. Council, Eng., 1968; Sustained Superior Teaching award Dept. Def., 1975. Mem. Assn. Tchr. Educators, Internat. Word Processing Assn. (treas. chpt. 1981-82), Am. Vocat. Assn., Ariz. Vocat. Assn. (treas. 1981, v.p. 1982), Nat. Bus. Edn. Assn., Nat. Assn. Tchr. Educators for Bus. Edn. (membership com. 1979-80, editorial and publs. com. 1980-81, pres.-elect 1981-82, pres. 1982-83), Western Bus. Edn. Assn., Ariz. Tchrs. Educators Assn. (dir.), Ariz. Bus. Edn. Assn. (Pres.'s award 1982, editor jour. 1982, dir. 1982-83), Internat. Assn. Bus. Edn., Tucson Bus. Educators (pres. 1980-81), Nat. Assn. Vocat. Educators for Spl. Needs Personnel, Mortar Board, Phi Beta Lambda (adv. U. Ariz. chpt. 1980-81), Beta Alpha Psi, Pi Omega Pi, Phi Delta Kappa (treas. U. Ariz. chpt. 1982—), Kappa Delta (past nat. press dir.). Democrat. Episcopalian. Club: Officers' Wives (past pres.; Outstanding Mil. Wife 1967-70). Contbr. articles to profl. jours., newspapers, other publs. Home: 4121 Larrea Ln Tucson AZ 85715 Office: Coll Edn PO Box 308 U Ariz Tucson AZ 85721

BENNINGTON, JAMES LYNNE, physician; b. Evanston, Ill., Apr. 29, 1935; s. Neville L. and Virginia R. (Tudor) B.; student Wooster Coll., 1952-53, Beloit Coll., 1953-55; M.D., U. Chgo., 1959, M.S., 1962; m. Josephine Marie Krussell, June 14, 1959; children—Jeffrey George, William James. Intern, Presbyn.-St. Luke's Hosp., Chgo., 1959-60; resident U. Chgo., 1960-62, Kaiser Hosp., Oakland, 1962-64; practice medicine specializing in pathology, Seattle, 1964-69, Oakland, Calif., 1969-70, San Francisco, 1970—; asso. prof. pathology U. Wash. Med. Sch., Seattle, 1966-69; chmn. dept. pathology King County (Wash.) Hosp., 1966-69, Kaiser Hosp., Oakland, 1969-70, Children's Hosp., San Francisco, 1970—; cons. DuPont Corp.; mem. adv. panel on cost-effectiveness analysis of med. tech. Office of Tech. Assessment, U.S. Congress, 1979-80. Trustee, Cathedral Sch., San Francisco, chmn., 1980—. Served with USPHS, 1964-66. Diplomate Am. Bd. Pathology. Mem. Coll. Am. Pathologists, Am. Assn. Pathologists and Bacteriologists, Am. Soc. Clin. Pathologists, Internat. Acad. Pathology, Royal Soc. of Medicine. Clubs: Univ., Bohemian (San Francisco). Author: Renal Carcinoma, 1977; contbr. articles on pathology to med. jours.; editor Major Problems in Pathology Series, 1970—. Home: 3536 Jackson St San Francisco CA 94118 Office: 3700 California St San Francisco CA 94118

BENNION, DAVID K., structural engr.; b. Vernal, Utah, Jan. 2, 1941; s. Enos L. and Beatrice (Murray) B.; B.S. in Civil Engring., Utah State U., 1968, M.S. in Structural Engring., 1969; m. Susan Blair Daines, July 3, 1968; children—Natalie, Leland. Mgr. Bennion Land Enterprises, Vernal, 1962-68; asst. dept. mgr. CH2M-Hill, cons. engrs., Boise, 1969—, maj. project mgr., 1971—, dept. mgr., 1976-80, v.p. and Boise regional mgr., 1980—. Chmn. subcom. Boise City United Fund, 1974; mem. March of Dimes Walk-A-Thon Com., 1970-74. Registered profl. engr., Idaho Recipient Portland Cement Assn. award, 1974. Mem. ASCE, Nat., Idaho (chmn. state conv. 1973, Outstanding Young Engr., 1976, treas. S.W. chpt. 1978-79, pres.-elect 1979-80, pres. 1980-81) socs. profl. engrs., Structural Engrs. Assn. Idaho (pres. 1978-79), Capitol (dir. 1970-71, v.p. 1972-73, pres. 1973-74, outstanding local pres. award 1974), Idaho (adminstrv. v.p. 1974-75, nat. dir. 1975-76, pres. 1976-77, chmn. bd. 1977-78) jaycees, Leadership Boise, Boise C. of C. (chmn. task force on car pooling), Sigma Chi. Mem. Ch. of Jesus Christ of Latter-day Saints. Author: A Computer Based Algorithm for the Analysis of Continuous Three Dimensional Structural Frames, 1969. Home: 2212 Ridge Point Way Boise ID 83702 Office: 700 Clearwater Ln Boise ID 83702

BENNION, MARILYN ROBINS, educator; b. Vernal, Utah, June, 1934; d. Stan L. and Lila Lois (Chivers) Robins; m. Enos L. Bennion, Oct. 18, 1956; children—Susan Bennion Johnsen, Annette. B.S., Utah State U., 1972. Cert. tchr. Utah. Sec. Civil Service, White Sands (Utah) Missile Range, 1956-58; sec. Thiokol Corp., Brigham City, Utah, 1958-61; bus. edn. tchr. Box Elder High Sch., Brigham City, Utah, 1972—; student tchr. trainer Utah State U. Organizer, advisor sch. chpt. Future Bus. Leaders Am., Utah No. Valley region advisor; mem. Utah Textbook Com., 1981-83, mem. high sch. accreditation team, Northwest region, 1977-78; bd. dirs. Box Elder Office Occupation Ctr., Brigham City. Recipient Sustained Superior Performance award Civil Service, 1958; Outstanding Bus. Student Tchr. award Utah State U., 1972. Mem. NEA, Am. Vocat. Assn., Utah Vocat. Assn., Nat. Bus. Edn. Assn., Utah Bus. Edn. Assn., Box Elder Edn. Assn. (faculty rep.), Future Bus. Leaders Am. (profl., hon.). Republican. Mormon. Club: Civic Improvement. Office: 380 S 600 W Brigham City UT 84302

BENO, JOHN RICHARDSON, clergyman, state senator; b. Council Bluffs, Iowa, Nov. 13, 1931. Student State U. Iowa, Loras Coll., Creighton U., Loyola U., Chgo., Iliff Sch. Theology, U. Denver, St. Thomas Sem.; B.A., M.R.E. Ordained priest Roman Catholic Ch. Mem. Colo. Senate, 1978—, mem. joint budget com., 1983—. Pres. S.W. Liturgical Conf.; sec.-treas. Nat. Fedn. Diocesan Liturgical Commns.; bd. dirs. Colo. Migrant Council; pres. Tri-County War on Poverty; dir. Women's Career Devel. Center; mem. Chicano Democratic Caucus. Mem. ACLU, LWV, Pueblo C. of C., Common Cause. Democrat. Office: 214 State Capitol Bldg Denver CO 80203 also PO Box 11447 Pueblo CO 81001

BENSELL, ARTHUR SUTHERLAND, Indian tribal executive; b. Siletz, Oreg.; s. Arthur and Stella Rose (Sutherland) B.; m. Margaret Louise Egebert; m. 2d, Ruth Montandon; 1 dau., Joan F. Bensell Fisher. A.B., Heidelburg Coll. Tchr., prin., supt. Bur. Indian Affairs, 1934-53; owner, mgr. grocery store, Siletz, Oreg., 1953-74; dir. Siletz Indian alcohol program Lincoln County Mental Health Dept., 1974-81; tribal chmn. Conf. Tribes of Siletz Indians of Oreg., 1975-83, vice chmn., 1983—. Mayor, City of Siletz, 1960-74; bd. dirs. Commn. on Indian Services, New Lincoln Hosp. Mem. Nat. Congress Am. Indians, Oreg. Edn. Assn. Presbyterian. Lodges: Masons, Shriners.

BENSON, DAVID BERNARD, educator; b. Seattle, Nov. 18, 1940; s. Allan I. and Martha (White) B.; B.S. in Engring., Calif. Inst. Tech., 1962, M.S. in E.E., 1963, Ph.D. (NASA fellow), 1967; m. Nancy Elaine Dollahite, Sept. 17, 1962; children—Megan, Bjorn, Nils, Amy, Kjell, Ingri. Research engr. N. Am. Rockwell, Downey, Calif., 1963-64; asst. prof. U. N.C., Chapel Hill, 1967-70; vis. assoc. prof. U. Colo., Boulder, 1976-77; asst. prof. Wash. State U., Pullman, 1970-72, assoc. prof., 1972-79, prof. computer sci., 1979—; vis. computer scientist U. Edinburgh (Scotland), 1983. Precinct chmn. 72nd Precinct, Whitman County, Wash., 1978-82; Whitman County Dem. Conv. del., 1972, 76. NSF grantee, 1969—. Mem. Assn. Computing Machinery, Am. Math. Soc., Am. Assn. Computational Linguistics, IEEE Computer Soc., AAAS, AAUP. Democrat. Mem. Soc. of Friends. Contbr. articles to profl. jours. Home: NE 615 Campus St Pullman WA 99163 Office: Computer Sci Dept Wash State Univ Pullman WA 99164

BENSON, GERALD EDWIN, air force officer; b. River Falls, Wis., May 26, 1945; s. Edwin Carl and Helen Elizabeth (Hawkins) B.; m. Ana Marie Spencer, Aug. 30, 1969; children—Adrian Spencer, Crista Nicole. B.A. in Bus. Adminstrn., Wis. State U.-Superior, 1967; M.S. in Systems Mgmt., U. So. Calif., 1978. Commd. 2d lt. U.S. Air Force, 1969, advanced through grades to maj., 1980; intercept dir., Duluth, Minn., 1969-71; ops. officer, Kuma Jima, Okinawa, 1971-72; chief positional tng., Luke AFB, Ariz., 1972-75; chief acad. tng. USAF Interceptor Weapons Sch., Tyndall AFB, Fla., 1975-78; NORAD insp. gen. team, Colorado Springs, Colo., 1978-80; chief tng. devel. br., air def. Tactical Air Command, Colorado Springs, 1980-81; tng. dir. USAF Acad., Colorado Springs, 1981-82, chief plans and spl. programs div., dep. commandant mil. instrn., since 1982—; Mem. Am. Soc. Tng. and Devel. (bd. dirs. Pikes Peak chpt.). Office: USAF Acad CWIX Colorado Springs CO 80840

BENSON, JACK ALBERT, mech. engr.; b. London, Feb. 8, 1919; s. John and Esther (Fortman) Kolbensen; came to U.S., 1953; Mech.Engring. certificate Wandsworth Tech. Coll. (Eng.), 1935; m. Ivy Lillian Boulden, Aug. 18, 1945. Toolmaker, Ascot Gas Water Heaters Co., London, 1935-38; tool designer Houghton Butcher Co., London, 1938-39, Philips Radio Co., Mitcham, Eng., 1939-42, London Aircraft Prodn., 1942-43, Briggs Motor Bodies Co., Dagenham, Eng., 1943-46; chief tool designer Cossor Radio Co., London, 1946-47; asst. chief draftsman The Design Group, London, 1947-48; chief designer MSE Ltd.-Westminster, London, 1948-51, Cochrane Machine Tool Co., Toronto, Ont., Can., 1951-53; process engr. Ford Aircraft Engine Div., Chgo., 1953-58; materials analyst Hewlett Packard Co., Palo Alto, Calif., 1958—. Certified mfg. engr. Mem. Soc. Plastics Engrs. (dir. color and appearance div. 1977—), Am. Soc. Tool and Mfg. Engrs. (chpt. chmn. 1963), ASME, ASTM, Standards Engrs. Soc. (chpt. sec. 1977), Inst. Gen. Tech. Engrs. (Eng.), U.S. Metric Assn., Am. Inst. Design and Drafting. Mem. Ch. of Eng. Club: Brit. Am. of No. Calif. Contbr. articles to profl. jours.; author: Visual Texture Standard for Plastic Molded Products, 1975. Home: 3670 Pruneridge Ave Santa Clara CA 95051 Office: 1501 Page Mill Rd Palo Alto CA 94304

BENSON, JAMES CARL, accountant; b. Mpls., Aug. 24, 1935; s. Fritz L. and Annie C. (Nordstrom) B.; B.B.S. with distinction, U. Minn., 1960; m. Ruth Ann Backlin, Sept. 10, 1960; 1 dau., Emily Ruthann. Intern, Greyhound Co., 1959, Haskins & Sells, 1960; with Arthur Andersen & Co., San Jose, Calif., 1960—, partner, 1970—. Pres., Trinity Luth. Ch., Oakland; Calif., 1966; pres. W. Valley Aquatic Team, 1980; bd. dirs. Family Services Assn., Alexian Bros. Hosp. Found.; trustee Alexian Bros. Hosp., 1982; mem. planning and allocations com. United Way of Santa Clara County, 1981-82; mem. council Prince of Peace Luth. Ch., 1977-79. C.P.A., Calif., La. Mem. Am. Inst. C.P.A.s, Nat. Assn. Accts., Calif. C.P.A. Soc., Alliance Francaise of Saratoga (treas.), Beta Alpha Psi, Beta Gamma Sigma. Clubs: Kiwanis (dir.), Am. Men's (Brussels); Country (San Jose, Calif.); Country (Saratoga, Calif.). Office: 99 Almaden Blvd San Jose CA 95113

BENSON, JERI, psychologist, educator; evaluation consultant; b. Charleston, S.C., Jan. 19, 1946; d. W.E. and Iris Bethea (Mitchell) Cotton; B.A., M.A.E., U. Fla., Ph.D., 1977. Asst. prof. U. So. Calif., Los Angeles, 1977—; evaluation cons. to sch. dists. and bus. Mem. Am. Ednl. Research Assn. (prize for exemplary evaluation report 1977), Am. Psychol. Assn., Nat. Council Measurement in Edn. Contbr. articles to profl. jours. Office: Dept Ednl Psychology 404 Phillips Hall U So Calif Los Angeles CA 90089

BENSON, KENNETH PETER, forest products company executive; b. Vancouver, B.C., Can., Mar. 1, 1927; s. Lawrence and Clara (Peel) B.; m. Joyce Alice Heino, Nov. 4, 1949; children—David, Sally. C.A., U. B.C., 1953. With Powell River Co., 1955-62, asst. comptroller, 1958-62; comptroller B.C. Forest Products, Ltd., 1962-67, v.p. fin., 1967-72, exec. v.p. ops., 1972-74, sr. exec. v.p., 1974-76, pres., 1976—, chief operating officer, 1976-79, chief exec. officer, 1979—, also dir.; dir. Blandin Paper Co., Donohue St.-Felicien Inc., Finlay Forest Industries Ltd., Western Forest Products Ltd., Pinette & Therrien Mills Ltd.; alt. dir. Council Forest Industries; bd. dirs., mem. exec. com. Forest Indsl. Relations, Pulp and Paper Indsl. Relations Bur.; bd. dirs., chmn. fin. com. Forest Engring. Research Inst. Can. Mem. Can. Forestry Assn. B.C. (dir.), Can. Pulp and Paper Assn. (dir., mem. exec. com.). Club: Vancouver. Home: 6329 Angus Dr Vancouver BC V6M 3P4 Canada Office: Suite 2200 1050 W Pender St Vancouver BC V6E 2X3 Canada

BENSON, RANDY J., religious orgn. adminstr.; b. Pocatello, Idaho, Aug. 4, 1944; s. June Leland and Virginia (Green) B.; B.S., Brigham Young U., 1967; m. Elaine Bitton, Apr. 26, 1963; children—Todd, Brett, Paul, Brandon, Ryan, Saralyn, Rebecca. Mgr., Thom McAn, Provo, Utah, 1964-67; personnel dir. Am. Potato Co., Blackfoot, Idaho, 1967-72; mgr. adminstrn. Am. Micro Systems, Pocatello, 1972-75; dir. tng. and devel. Ch. Jesus Christ of Latter-day Saints, Salt Lake City, 1975—, stake pres., 1982—; sr. partner Results Mgmt., Inc., Salt Lake City, 1980—. Dir., Idaho Employers Council, 1973-75; mem. Idaho State U. Trade and Tech. Sch. Adv. Council, 1970-75; chmn. County Young Republicans, 1969-70, state treas., 1970-71; bd. dirs. Salvation Army, 1974, YMCA, 1974; active Boy Scouts Am. Mem. Am. Soc. Personnel Adminstrn. (past chpt. pres., dist. dir.), Am. Soc. Tng. and Devel. (past dir., exec. v.p. Utah chpt., pres. 1983—), Utah Personnel Assn. (dir.). Home: 3652 Carriage Ln Bountiful UT 84010 Office: 50 E N Temple Salt Lake City UT 84150

BENSON, ROBERT SLATER, child care executive; b. South Bend, June 6, 1942; s. Ernest Birger and Ruth (Kenney) B.; m. Cynthia C. Kappus, June 15, 1974; 1 son, Erik. A.B. magna cum laude, Harvard U., 1964, M.B.A. with high distinction, 1966. Asst. to comptroller Office of Sec. of Def., Washington, 1966-68; Western regional dir. nat. priorities project Nat. Urban Coalition, Washington, 1968-71; pres., chief exec. officer Children's World, Inc., Evergreen, Colo., 1971—; dir. Vicorp, Inc., Snugli, Inc. Pres. Colo. Philharm. Orch., 1982—; mem. Pres.' Commn. for a Nat. Agenda for the 80's, 1980-81. Mem. Nat. Assn. Child Care Mgmt. (treas.), Nat. Assn. Edn. Young Children. Democrat. Club: Rocky Mountain Harvard U. (dir.). Author: (with others) Counterbudget: A Blueprint for Changing National Priorities, 1971; contbr. articles to profl. jours. Office: Box 2290 Evergreen CO 80439

BENSON, THOMAS QUENTIN, lawyer; b. Grand Forks, N.D., Jan. 9, 1943; s. Theodore Quentin and Helen Marie (Winzenberg) B.; m. Mary Mangelsdorf, Aug. 3, 1968; children—Annemarie C., Thomas Quentin II, Mark W. B.A., U. Notre Dame, 1964; J.D., U. Denver, 1967. Bar: Colo. 1967, N.D. 1967, U.S. Dist. Ct. Colo. 1968, U.S. Ct. Appeals (10th cir.) 1974, U.S. Ct. Mil. Appeals 1981. legal counsel Denver Regional Council Govts., 1968-70; assoc. firm Schneider, Shoemaker, Wham & Cooke, Denver, 1970-72; prin. firm Thomas Quentin Benson, Denver, 1972-74, 76—; ptnr. firm Benson & Vernon, Denver, 1974-76. Mem. bd. Am. Health Planning, 1973-77, Mayors Adv. Com. Community Devel., Denver, 1975-78; Republican precinct committeeman, 1972-78; mem. White House Advance for U.S. Pres., 1975; pres. Park Vista-Pine Ridge Homeowners Assn., 1971-73, Ridge Homeowners Assn., 1971-73; mem. parish council Ch. of Risen Christ, 1978-80; pres. M.P.B. Home and Sch. Assn. Serves as comdr. Judge Adv. Gen. Corps. USNR Res. Cited for Leadership, Denver C. of C., 1975-76. Mem. ABA, Colo. (sect. chmn. 1975-78), Denver bar assns., Cath. Lawyers Guild Denver (pres. 1979-80). Roman Catholic. Clubs: U. Notre Dame (pres. 1979-80), Univ. Hills Rotary (program chmn. 1973-76, 78-81 dir. 1976-78), Eastmoor Swim and Tennis (dir. 1973-74, 78-80) (Denver). Office: 1660 S Albion St Suite 400 Denver CO 80222

BENSON, WILLIAM THOMAS, contracting/development company executive; b. Topeka, Oct. 19, 1940; s. George William and Emeline Erwin (Phillips) B.; B.S., U.S. Naval Acad., 1964; M.B.A., Columbia U., 1971; m. V. Mary Kr. Mortgage analyst Conn. Gen. Life Ins. Co., Hartford, 1971-73; investment specialist Coldwell Banker Co., San Jose, Calif., 1974-75; v.p., gen. partner The Koll Co., San Jose, 1976—; instr. U. Calif., Santa Cruz, 1979-80. Bd. mgrs. S.W. YMCA, Los Gatos, Calif., also mem. exec. com.; mem. real estate adv. bd. U. Calif., Santa Cruz; bd. dirs. NCCJ. Served with U.S. Navy, 1964-69. Decorated Air medal. Mem. Assn. South Bay Brokers, Bay Area Exec. Club: Rotary. Home: 13044 Cumberland Dr Saratoga CA 95070 Office: 1651 N First St San Jose CA 95112

BENSUASKI, FERNANDO, financial consultant; b. Sao Paulo, Brazil, Oct. 13, 1949; s. Fernando and Luzia Cruz (Oliveira) B.; m. Margaret E. Smith, Nov. 15, 1972; children—Max, Andrea K. B.A. in Physics, Northwest Nazarene Coll., 1972. Asst. v.p. comml. loans Idaho First Nat. Bank, Boise, 1973-80; pres. Bensuaski & Co., Boise, 1980—. Mem. Am. Bankers Assn., Am. Inst. Banking. Mem. Ch. of Nazarene. Home: 2220 Serene Dr Boise ID 83706 Office: Idaho First Plaza Suite 1103 Boise ID 83702

BENSUSSEN, JANE ODELL, speech pathologist; b. Columbia, Mo., May 15, 1945; d. Joe Sanford and Leeta Dell (Lane) Cunningham; A.A., Stephens Coll., 1965; B.A. with honors, U. Mo., 1967; M.A., U. So. Calif., 1969; m. Gale Kearney Bensussen, Aug. 10, 1968; children—Adrienne Odell, Lane Kearney. Speech pathologist Los Angeles VA Hosp., 1968-70, Los Angeles County Crippled Children's Soc., 1971-74; dir. communication disorders White Meml. Med. Center, Los Angeles, 1974-76; dir. communication disorders Daniel Freeman Hosp. Med. Center, Inglewood, Calif., 1976—. Treas., Nat. Charity League of San Fernando Valley, Calif., 1978-79; mem. adv. bd. Am. Cancer Soc., 1979—. Mem. Calif. Speech Pathologists and Audiologists in Pvt. Practice, Calif. Speech and Hearing Assn., Am. Speech, Lang. and Hearing Assn. Democrat. Methodist. Club: Jr. Auxillary to Lawyers Wives of Los Angeles. Home: 1264 Casiano Rd Bel Air CA 90049 Office: 333 N Prairie Ave Inglewood CA 90301

BENT, MICHAEL WILLIAM, realty company executive, consultant; b. Oakland, Calif., Mar. 7, 1951; s. William Camp and Lorene (Howson) B.; m. Mary Agnes Ruhl, Aug. 30, 1974 (div.); 1 son, J. Donovan. Student Rutgers U., 1969-72. Lic. real estate broker, Colo. Vice-pres. Century 21 Kato & Co., Denver, 1979-80; broker, mgr. Century 21 Hasz & Assocs., Denver, 1980-81; sec. Metro Brokers, Inc., Denver, 1982-83, v.p., 1983—; broker, owner Metro Broker M. Bent Realty & Mgmt. Co., Aurora, Colo., 1981—; dir. Metro Brokers, Inc., Builder-Realtor Council; past pres. Country Club Real Estate, Inc. Mem. Denver Bd. Realtors, Aurora Bd. Realtors, Realtors Nat. Mktg. Inst., Internat. Assn. Fin. Planners. Republican. Roman Catholic. Club: Optimist of Heather Ridge, (pres. 1982—). Home: 6409 S Magnolia Ct Englewood CO 80111 Office: Metro Brokers/M Bent Realty & Mgmt Co 2260 S Xanadu Way Suite 390 Aurora CO 80014

BENTEL, ROBERT BRIGGS, banker; b. San Diego, Sept. 20, 1938; s. Carr Eugene and Gladys (Briggs) B.; B.A., Dartmouth Coll., 1960; M.B.A., Stanford U., 1964; m. Alma Baltodano, Apr. 16, 1966; children—John Carr, Elizabeth Anne. With The Bank of Calif., 1964-81, br. mgr., San Francisco, 1968-69, asst. v.p., mgr. central credit dept., 1969-70, v.p. met. div., 1970-72, v.p., dir. tng., 1972-73, v.p., London, 1973-75, v.p. comml. loan supervision, 1975-76, sr. v.p., div. head loan rev. div., 1976 81; v.p. loan supervision Wells Fargo Bank, N.A., 1981—. Bd. dirs. Vis. Nurse Assn. San Francisco, 1981—. Served with USNR, 1960-62. Mem. Robert Morris Assos. Clubs: Commonwealth of Calif.; Guardsmen. Home: 2900 Ocean Ave San Francisco CA 94132 Office: 394 Pacific St San Francisco CA 94111

BENTIVOGLIO, PAOLA, linguistics educator; b. Genoa, Italy, Aug. 6, 1932; d. Remo and Olga (Pasetto) Adriani, came to U.S., 1978; B.A., U. Central Venezuela, Caracas, 1967; M.A., UCLA, 1980, postgrad., 1980—; children by previous marriage—Luca, Cristiana; m. 2d, Allen I. Neiman, July 21, 1979. Faculty, Inst. Filologia A. Bello, U. Central Venezuela, 1970—, assoc. prof. linguistics, 1980—. Consejo de Desarrollo Cientifico y Humanistico, scholar, 1978-81. Mem. Programa Interam. de Linguistica y Ensenanza de Idioma, Linguistic Soc. Am., Latin Am. Assn. Linguistics and Philology. Contbr. articles to profl. jours.

BENTLEY, EVELYN MARY, tour operator; b. Webster, Pa., May 13, 1930; d. Ernest Leroy and Mary Alice (Patterson) B.; student Pricedale (Pa.) public schs. Gen. acct. U.S. Steel Corp., Pitts., 1949-60; with Braniff Internat. Airways, Kansas City, Mo., and Los Angeles, 1960-73; sales and promotions mgr. Wright Way Tours, Glendale, Calif., 1973-78; dir. outbound tour dept. Bramer Tours, Los Angeles, 1978—. Recipient commendation Peruvian Govt., 1968. Mem. Am. Soc. Travel Agts. Democrat. Presbyterian. Contbr. articles to travel trade publs. Office: 1619 N Cherokee Ave Los Angeles CA 90028

BENTON, DEBRA ANN, management consultant; b. Grinnell, Kans., Dec. 16, 1953; d. Fred H. and Teressa C. (Feldt) B.; m. Alan K. Lovejoy, May 10, 1981. B.S. in Fin. and Econs., Colo. State U., 1974. Account rep. Scott-Fetzer Corp., Ft. Collins, Colo., 1971-74, Control Data Corp., Denver, 1974-76; v.p. Exec. Mktg. Cons., Denver, 1976-78; mng. ptnr. Benton Mgmt. Resources, Denver, 1978—, outplacement cons., 1978—; founder, dir. Teenage Personel Improvement Programs: Model Am. Girl and All Around Girls. Active Hugh O'Brien Youth Found. Mem. Nat. Assn. Bus. and Indsl. Sales Women (exec. dir., founder), Cons. Speakers Bur. (founder), Profl. Sales Persons Am., Colo. Women in Bus. Enterprises, Spl. Opportunities for Women. Republican. Roman Catholic. Author: How to Avoid the Frustration and Anxiety of Trial and Error Job Hunting, 1981; contbr. articles to publs. including Bus. Week, Working Woman, Savvy, Success Unlimited, Personnel Jour., Chem. Bus.

BENTON, DOUGLAS GEORGE, government official; b. Denver, Feb. 4, 1946; s. Nicholas and Dorothy Revilla (Sloan) B. B.A. in Journalism, Colo. State U., 1971; M.P.A., U. Colo., 1981. Electronics technician Colo. Engring. Expt. Sta., Nunn, Stanley Aviation, Denver, 1970-72; bldg. mgmt. asst. Gen. Services Adminstrn., Denver, 1973-74, bldgs. mgr., Casper, Wyo., 1974-78, Colorado Springs, Colo., 1978-79, chief maintenance and utilities sect., Denver, 1979-80, dist. mgr., 1980—. Chmn., Casper Combined Fed. Campaign, 1976-78; bd. dirs. Natrona County United Way. Served in USN, 1965-69. Decorated Navy Commendation medal with Combat V. Mem. Casper Fed. Execs, Council (v.p. 1975-76, pres. 1977). Methodist. Home: 3005 S Xeric Ct Denver CO 80231 Office: GSA Bldg 41 Denver CO 80225

BENTON, KATHRYN M. BRADLEY (MRS. ROBERT E. BENTON), escrow co. exec.; b. Carnegie, Pa.; d. Charles A. and Mary (Halpin) Bradley; student U. Calif. at Los Angeles, 1929-35; m. Robert E. Benton, Sept. 14, 1935 (dec. Sept. 1965); 1 dau., Barbara A. (Mrs. Bernard P. Drachlis). Co-founder, pres. Eagle Rock Escrow Co., Los Angeles, 1962—. Charter exec. sec. United Orgns., 1966-68, N.E. Taxpayers Assn., 1966—. Bd. dirs., sec., founder Robert E. Benton Meml. Found. Mem. Eagle Rock Bus. and Profl. Womens Club, Eagle Rock C. of C., Women's 20th Century Club Eagle Rock. Office: 5012 Eagle Rock Blvd Los Angeles CA 90041

BENTON, PATRICIA, author, musician; b. Westchester County, N.Y., Mar. 20, 1907; d. Louis and Pearl (Asher) Rosenstein; B.A. in Fine Arts, Castle Sch., Tarrytown, N.Y., 1925; diploma in music Westchester

Conservatory Music, 1935; postgrad. Columbia U., 1938-40; m. Arthur Benton, May 17, 1928; 1 dau., Barbara Benton Webster; m. 2d, Nicolai Mednikoff, 1936. Piano soloist; poet, lectr. own poetry, 1952-66; lectr. interrelations of arts; poetry cons. to Ariz. Dept. Pub. Instruction, 1953-60; dir. Ariz. Poetry Day, 1954-64; dir. 1st. Poetry Workshop, Phoenix Pub. Library, 1954-57; narrator weekly poetry program Sta. KDOT, Scottsdale, Ariz., 1956-58; chmn. Ariz. Festival Arts, 1969—; author: Signature in Sand, 1953; Young Corn Rises, 1954; Miracle of Roses, 1953; Medallion Southwest, 1956; Arizona: The Turquoise Land (nominated for Pulitzer prize 1960), 1960; Of the Heart's Own Telling, 1978; author of plays including: Miracle of Roses, 1962; Highlights of Arizona, 1976; contbr. poetry to Ariz. Hwys. and other lit. publs.; producer slide film: Indians of the Turquoise Land, 1958; editor poetry column in The Arizonian, Voices of Sun and Sand, 1955-58. Chmn., Ariz. Festival of Arts, 1979. Elected to Songwriters Hall of Fame. Fellow Royal Soc. Arts, Eng.; mem. Nat. League Am. Pen Women (pres. N.Y. and Ariz. brs.), ASCAP, Am. Guild Composers Authors, Poetry Soc. Am., Nat. Assn. Composers and Conductors, Dramatists Guild, Authors Guild, Nat. Arts Council, Nat. Soc. Arts and Letters (founder, pres. N.Y. and Ariz. chpts.), Composers, Authors and Artists Am. (Ariz. pres. 1975—), Cath. Poetry Soc., Internat. Poetry Archives, Centro Studio Scambi International (hon. v.p. 1955-58), Internat. Platform Assn., Beta Sigma Phi (hon. pres.). Permanent collection of all work at Boston U. Home: 7849 E Glen Rosa Scottsdale AZ 85251 Office: care Frederick Fell Publisher 386 Park Ave New York NY 10016

BENTZ, CLAUDE MARVIN, clin. psychologist, adminstr.; b. Long Beach, Calif., Feb. 21, 1929; s. Claude M. and Vilate (LeCheminant) B.; A.A., Compton City Coll., 1948; B.A., Brigham Young U., 1950; M.A., U. Utah, 1957; Ph.D., U.S. Internat. U., 1974; m. Arvilla Simpson, June 19, 1970; children—Dean, Vilate, Shelby. Psychologist, counselor Lancaster Sch. Dist., 1957-60; clin. psychologist Pasadena (Calif.) Child Guidance Clinic, 1960-61; psychologist Kern County Sch., Bakersfield, Calif., 1961-64; coordinator guidance Supt. Schs. Office, Bakersfield, 1964-67 dir. guidance, 1967-79; staff psychologist Kern View Mental Health Center and Hosp., 1979, chief psychologist, 1979-80; psychol. cons. San Felipe Boys Home, 1969-78; pvt. practice as psychologist and marriage counselor, Bakersfield, 1961—. Tchr. Antelope Valley Coll., 1958-61, Fresno State Coll., Santa Barbara Extension, 1962-74, U. Calif. at Bakersfield, 1971—, Calif. Lutheran Coll., 1975. Vice-chmn. Kern County Human Resources Coordinating Council, 1969-80; pres. Kern County Mental Health Assn., 1971-72, chmn. mental health research com., 1965-71, 72-74; exec. council Bakersfield chpt. Big Bros. Am., 1968—; bd. dirs. Crises Center Hotline, 1970-80, Citizens Orgn. Against Drug Abuse, 1971-74; pres. Kern Child Abuse Prevention Counsel Inc., 1979-80; budget com. United Way, 1971—. Served to lt. U.S. Army, 1950-54. Mem. Am., Western, Calif., Kern County (past pres.) psychol. assns., Assn. Calif. Sch. Adminstrs. (adminstr. region II pupil personnel services 1971-73). Club: Elks. Home: 5207 Kent Dr Bakersfield CA 93306 Office: 3535 San Dimas Sq Suite 24 Bakersfield CA 93301

BENYAS, PAMELA FRAN, clinical researcher; b. Detroit, Sept. 14, 1953; d. Donald Alden and Maxine Miriam (Cohen) B., B.A. magna cum laude, U. So. Calif., 1978; M.A., Calif. Sch. Profl. Psychology, 1980, Ph.D., 1982. Dir. psychol. services Los Feliz Med. Center, Glendale, Calif.; ednl. therapy asst. Cedars Sinai Med. Ctr., Los Angeles, 1978-79; therapist Verdugo Mental Health Clinic, Glendale, Calif., 1979-80; psychology intern Los Angeles Police Dept., 1980-81, Pasadena Guidance Clinics, Inc., 1981-82; psychol. asst. to Nancy Tither, Ph.D., North Hollywood, Calif., 1982—. Mem. Am. Psychol. Assn., Calif. State Psychol. Assn., Assn. Humanistic Psychology, Assn. Women in Psychology, Phi Beta Kappa, Phi Kappa Phi. Democrat. Jewish. Contbr. articles to profl. jours. Office: 4741 Laurel Canyon Blvd Suite 207 North Hollywood CA 91607

BENYO, RICHARD STEPHEN, magazine editor, author, race driver; b. Palmerton, Pa., Apr. 20, 1946; s. Andrew Joseph and Dorothy Rita (Herman) B.; B.A. in English Lit., Bloomsburg (Pa.) State Coll., 1968; m. Jill Wapensky, Apr. 29, 1972 (div. 1979). Mng. editor Times-News, Lehighton, Pa., 1968-72; program dir. Sta. PTVC-TV, Palmerton, 1969-72; editor Stock Car Racing mag., Alexandria, Va., 1972-77; exec. editor Runner's World mag., Mountain View, Calif., 1977—; editorial dir. Skier's World mag., 1980—, Anderson World Books, 1980—, Fit mag., 1981—; v.p. Runner's World Mag. Co., 1982—; editor Corp. Fitness Report, 1982—, Runner's World Quan., 1982—. Mem. racing panel of experts Union 76. Recipient 1st pl. award local column Pa. Newspaper Pubs. Assn., 1972. Mem. Track and Field Writers Am., Assn. Internationale de la Presse Sportive Am. Auto Racing Writers and Broadcasters Assn. (1st place award for tech. writing), U.S. Ski Writers Assn., No. Calif./Nev. Ski Writers Assn., Internat. Motor Press Assn. Democrat. Roman Catholic. Author: The Grand National Stars, 1975; The Book of Richard Petty, 1976; Superspeedway, 1977; Return to Running, 1978; Indoor Exercise Book, 1980; Advanced Indoor Exercise Book, 1981; Sexercise, 1982; editor The Complete Woman Runner, 1978. Home: PO Box 4432 Mountain View CA 94040 Office: 1400 Stierlin Rd Mountain View CA 94042

BENZ, DAVID ABRAHAM, printing company executive; b. Shanghai, China, June 12, 1920; s. Oscar A. and Aida (Mrantz) B.; student pub. schs.; m. Inez Marie Kozuki, Nov. 14, 1953; children—Donna Estelle Benz Goodley, Philip, Gregory, Jeffrey. Reporter Shanghai Evening Post and Mercury, 1937-40; sales mgr. Tongg Pub. Co., Honolulu, 1946-50; exec. v.p. Aloha Airlines, Honolulu, 1949-59, now dir.; pres. Tongg Pub. Co. and subsidiary, Mercantile Printing Co., Honolulu, 1959—; dir. Advertiser Pub. Co. Pres. Hawaii Visitors Bur., 1962-63, Friends of East-West Center, 1965. Served to lt., AUS, 1942-46. Decorated Legion of Merit, Bronze Star. Mem. Nat. Assn. Printers and Lithographers (dir.), Printing Industry of Hawaii (dir., past pres.), Hawaii C. of C. (dir. 1967). Democrat. Mason (Shriner). Clubs: Pacific, Waialae (Honolulu). Home: 3826 Poka St Honolulu HI 96816 Office: 1320 Rycroft St Honolulu HI 96814

BENZING, WALTER CHARLES, electrical company executive; b. N.Y.C., Aug. 28, 1924; s. Frederick Ludwig and Grace Augusta (Engelhart) B.; m. Ruth Elinor McBride, Sept. 11, 1948; children—Steven M., David W., Jeffrey C. B.S., U. Rochester, 1945; M.S., MIT, 1948; Ph.D., Princeton U., 1964. Sr. engr., mgr. chem. engring. research and devel. Merck & Co., Inc., Rahway, N.J., 1952-64; dir. tech. Electronics div. Union Carbide Corp., Mountain View, Calif., 1964-68; v.p., dir. tech. Applied Materials, Inc., Santa Clara, Calif., 1968—; mem. adv. bd. chem. engring. dept. U. Calif.-Berkeley, 1977-82. Served to lt. (j.g.) USNR, 1942-46. Recipient SEMI award Semicondr. Equipment and Materials Inst., 1979. Mem. Am. Chem. Soc., Electrochem. Soc., Am. Assn. Crystal Growth, Am. Inst. Chem. Engrs., Phi Beta Kappa. Club: Decathlon (Santa Clara). Contbr. articles to profl. jours.; patentee in field.

BERAN, WALTER FRANK, accountant; b. The Grove, Tex., Apr. 20, 1926; s. Frank and Selma (Nowotnik) B.; B.B.A. cum laude, Baylor U., 1948; LL.D. (hon.), Calif. Luth. Coll.; m. Annette Lott, May 28, 1948; children—John, James. Acct. Ernst & Whinney, San Antonio, 1948—, ptnr. in charge San Antonio, Austin, Corpus Christi, Laredo, Tex. offices, 1960-65, ptnr. in charge nat. client relations, Cleve., 1965-71, vice-chmn. and regional mng. ptnr. in charge Western regional offices, 1971, mem. mgmt. com., 1971—. Chmn. bd. councilors Sch. Bus. U. So. Calif., 1977—; commr. Calif. World Trade Commn.; sect. chmn. major gifts com. Los Angeles Music Ctr. Unified Fund, chmn. cabinet, 1983-84; trustee Calif. Calif. Mus. Found., Criminal Justice Legal Found.; vice chmn. bd. govs. Performing Arts Council; mem. Music Ctr. Operating Co., Los Angeles; active United Way. Served with U.S. Army, 1944-46. Decorated Purple Heart, Bronze Star; recipient awards City and County of Los Angeles, 1979, Freedoms Found. at Valley Forge, 1979, 82, NCCJ, 1982; C.P.A., Calif. Mem. Los Angeles Area C. of C. (past chmn.), Calif. C. of C. (dir., chmn. state tax com.) Calif. Soc. C.P.A.s., Mchts. and Mfrs. Assn. (bd. dirs.), U. So. Calif. Assocs. (bd. dirs.). Clubs: Los Angeles Country, Calif., Regency. Home: 600 Clinton Pl Beverly Hills CA 90210 Office: 515 S Flower St Los Angeles CA 90071

BERCOVITZ, Z(ACHARIAS) TAYLOR, physician; b. Albuquerque, Apr. 9, 1895; s. Moses and Mary (Bernstein) B.; B.S., U. Chgo., 1920, M.S., 1920, M.D., 1924, Ph.D., 1924; m. Nina Lillian Bierman, Mar. 25, 1923 (dec. Nov. 1974); children—Mary Caroline (Mrs. Harold B. Fohlin, Jr.), Timothy Taylor. Intern Los Angeles Gen. Hosp., 1923-24; practice medicine, specializing in tropical medicine and gastroenterology, N.Y.C., 1934-60, La Jolla, Calif., 1960—; med. missionary U.P. Ch., U.S.A., 1924-34; research fellow N.Y. Postgrad. Med. Sch., 1929-30; physician in charge Parasitology Service Bur. Labs. Dept. Health, N.Y.C., 1934-43; asst. prof. clin. medicine, asso. attending physician U. Hosp., N.Y. U. Med. Center, 1938-60; asso. vis. physician Bellevue Hosp., N.Y.C., 1938-60; mem. med., courtesy staff Doctors Hosp., 1938-60; assoc. vis. physician Welfare Island Hosp., 1938-49; cons. tropical medicine USPHS, Ellis Island, 1938-60; cons. gastroenterology Horton Meml. Hosp., Middletown, N.Y., 1941-60; sr. courtesy staff Roosevelt Hosp., N.Y.C., 1952-60; attending physician VA Hosp., N.Y.C., 1956-60; mem. sr. staff Scripps Meml. Hosp., La Jolla, 1961-75, courtesy cons., 1975—; cons. Palomar Meml. Hosp., Escondido, Cal., Grossmont Hosp.; mem. courtesy staff Sharp Meml. Hosp., Mercy Hosp., San Diego. Served from maj. to lt. col. M.C., AUS, 1943-46. Diplomate Am. Bd. Internal Medicine, also sub-bd. Gastroenterology. Fellow ACP, Am. Therapeutic Soc., Royal Soc. Tropical Medicine and Hygiene (London), Am. Acad. Compensation Medicine (dir.), N.Y. Acad. Medicine, Am. Geriatric Soc., AAAS; mem. Am. Gastroent. Assn., AMA, Am. Soc. Tropical Medicine, Mason (32 deg., K.T., Shriner), Rotarian. Editor: Clinical Tropical Medicine, 1944; Ulcerative and granulomatous colitis, 1973. Contbr. articles to profl. jours. Home and office: 7450 Olivetas Ave La Jolla CA 92037

BERDROW, STANTON K., power company executive; b. Long Beach, Calif., Oct. 4, 1928; s. Earl Lester and Martha Ann B.; m. Rosa R. Rottger, Feb. 22, 1951; children—Nancy, John, Matthew. B.S., Armstrong Coll., Berkeley, Calif., 1950; postgrad. Sch. Bus. Syracuse U., 1951-52. Dist. advt. and sales promotion mgr. The Pennzoil Co., Los Angeles, 1953-59; v.p., mgmt. supr. Batten, Barton, Durstine & Osborn, Inc., San Francisco, 1960-77; v.p., dir. acctg. services Commart Communications, Santa Clara, Calif., 1978-80; mgr. corporate communications Sierra Pacific Power Co., Reno, 1980—. Bd. dirs. No. Nev. unit, Am. Cancer Soc., 1982-83. Served with U.S. Army, 1946-48. Recipient 1st award complete campaign N.Y. Ad Club Nat. Competition, 1976. Mem. Am. Advt. Fedn. (1st award TV nat. competition 1978), Pub. Utility Communicators Assn. (1st award complete campaign 1981), Pacific Coast Electric Assn., Pacific Coast Gas Assn., Assn. Indsl. Advertisers, Reno Advt. Club. Republican. Clubs: Innisfree Beach (Lake Tahoe, Calif.); Rotary. Contbr. articles to profl. jours. Home: 3925 Skyline Blvd Reno NV 89509 Office: PO Box 10100 Reno NV 89520

BERDUX, WILLIAM JAMES, JR., optical instruments manufacturing company executive; b. San Diego, Mar. 13, 1947; s. William James and Beatrice Naomi (Martin) B.; m. Barbara Love, Feb. 14, 1976; children—Sabrina M., Chelsie L. B.S. in Bus. Mgmt., San Diego State U., 1973. Mgmt. trainee Union Bank, San Diego, 1973-73, Los Angeles, 1973, comml. loan officer, San Francisco, 1974-76; pres. B.H.R. Fin. Services, Inc., Los Angeles, 1976-78; div. mgr. Iwasaki Images of Am., Inc., Torrance, Calif., 1978-79; v.p., mng. dir. Argo Industries, Inc., Laguna Hills, Calif., 1979-81; internat. sales and mktg. mgr. Busnell div. Bausch & Lomb, Inc., Pasadena, Calif., 1981—. Served with USAF, 1965-69. Home: 26652 Estanciero Dr Mission Viejo CA 92691

BERESTYNSKI, ADAM STAN, architect; b. Krakow, Poland, May 5, 1927; s. Adam and Kazimiera B.; came to U.S., 1966, naturalized, 1972; M.Sc. in Architecture and City Planning, Polytech. U., Krakow, Poland, 1951; postgrad. U. Katowice (Poland), 1962; m. Magdalena Steinhagen, Oct. 4, 1957; 1 son, Peter. Head dept. architecture and city planning City of Krakow, 1956-64; tchr. architecture and urban design, Kabul, Afghanistan, 1964-66, also cons. urban planning to Royal Afghan Ministry of Pub. Works, 1964-66; sr. planner City of Oklahoma City, 1967-68; regional planner Leslie Properties, Inc., Redwood City, Calif., 1968-69; asso. planner Fremont (Calif.) Dept. of Community Devel., 1969-70; urban designer VTN, Consol., Inc., Irvine, Calif., 1970-76; planning dir. RBF & Assos., Newport Beach, Calif., 1976-81; planner for master plan of Yanbu, Saudi Arabian Parsons Ltd., Yanbu, 1982—. Mem. Tech. Council, Municipality of Krakow, 1960-64. Served with Polish Underground Resistance Army (A.K.), 1944-45. Mem. Soc. Polish Architects, Am. Inst. Planners (asso.), Am. Soc. of Planning Ofcls., AIA (asso.), Assn. Environ. Profls. Prin. works include residential projects, Krakow, 1950-64; master plan for new towns, Kabul, 1964-66, also high rise apt. bldgs., 1965-66; urban studies, Oklahoma City, 1967-68; gen. plans residential and recreational devel., Calif., 1970—. Contbr. numerous articles on art and architecture to profl. jours. Home: 2845 Chillon Way Laguna Beach CA 92651 Office: 1401 Quail St Newport Beach CA 92663

BERG, A(NDREW) SCOTT, writer; b. Norwalk, Conn., Dec. 4, 1949; s. Richard J. and Barbara (Freedman) B.; B.A., Princeton U., 1971. Author: Max Perkins-Editor of Genius (Am. Book award), 1978. Guggenheim fellow, 1982-83. Mem. Authors Guild, Writers Guild, PEN. Club: Century Assn.

BERG, LARRY LEE, political science educator, consultant; b. Ft. Dodge, Iowa, July 30, 1939; s. Carl and Zene M. (Anderson) B.; m. Mary Ellen Randall, June 12, 1960; children—Andrea, Michelle. Student Iowa State U., 1957-59; B.A. in Polit. Sci. and History, U. Iowa, 1962, M.A., 1963; Ph.D., U. Calif.-Santa Barbara, 1972. Lectr. Am. politics U. Calif.-Santa Barbara, 1967-69; instr. U. So. Calif., Los Angeles, 1969-72, asst. prof., 1972-74, assoc. prof., 1975—, dir. Inst. Politics and Govt., Washington Politics Program; cons. bd. govs. Town Hall; cons. Haynes Found. Mem. S. Coast Air Quality Mgmt. Bd., 1983—; mem. Calif. State Adv. Com., U.S. Commn. Civil Rights, 1981—; bd. dirs. Nat. Indian Inst. NDEA fellow, U. Calif.-Santa Barbara, 1963-65; Calif. Energy Resources and Conservation Commn. grantee, 1982; Haynes Found. grantee, 1983; Ahmanson Found. grantee, 1982; grantee Calif. Air Resource Bd., Edison Electric Inst., Bus. Roundtable. Mem. Am. Assn. Polit. Cons. (nat. exec. bd.), Am. Polit. Sci. Assn., AAUP, Internat. Polit. Sci. Assn., So. Calif. Ctr. Edn. in Pub. Affairs, So. Calif. Polit. Sci. Assn., Western Polit. Sci. Assn. Democrat. Co-author: The Supreme Court and Congress: Conflict and Interaction, 1945-68, 1972; Corruption in the American Political System, 1976. Co-editor: The United States and World Energy Sources, 1982. Office: Inst Politics and Govt U So Calif JEF 111 University Park Los Angeles CA 90089

BERG, LAWRENCE WILLIAM, pattern maker, union business official; b. Falconer, N.Y., Dec. 15, 1933; s. Ralph Magnus and Eva (Pearson) B.; m. Shirley Mae Erickson, May 28, 1954; children—Karen Dianne, Kristin Marie. Student pub. schs., Denver, 1951-53. Apprentice Silver Engring. Works, 1953-57; pattern maker Gen. Iron Works, Denver, 1960—; bus. mgr., fin. sec., Denver Assn. of Pattern Makers League N. Am., 1974—. Served with U.S. Army, 1954-56. Mem. Colo. Right to Life, NRA, Am. Foundry Men's Soc. Club: Swedish (Denver).

BERG, PAUL, biochemist, educator; b. N.Y.C., June 30, 1926; s. Harry and Sarah (Brodsky) B.; B.S., Pa. State U., 1948; Ph.D. (NIH fellow 1950-52), Western Res. U., 1952; D.Sc. (hon.), U. Rochester, 1978, Yale U., 1978; m. Mildred Levy, Sept. 13, 1947; 1 son, John. Postdoctoral fellow Copenhagen U., 1952-53; postdoctoral fellow Sch. Medicine, Washington U., St. Louis, 1953-54, Am. Cancer Soc. scholar cancer research dept. microbiology, 1954-57, from asst. to asso. prof. microbiology, 1955-59; prof. biochemistry Stanford U. Sch. Medicine, 1959—, Sam, Lula and Jack Willson prof. biochemistry, 1970, chmn. dept., 1969-74; non-resident fellow Salk Inst., 1973; lectr. Weizmann Inst., 1977; disting. lectr. U. Pitts., 1978; Priestly lectr. Pa. State U., 1978; Shell lectr. U. Calif., Davis, 1978; adv. bd. NIH, NSF, M.I.T.; vis. com. dept. biochemistry and molecular biology Harvard U. Served to lt. (j.g.) USNR, 1943-46. Recipient Eli Lilly prize biochemistry, 1959; V.D. Mattia award Roche Inst. Molecular Biology, 1972; Henry J. Kaiser award for excellence in teaching, 1972; Disting. Alumnus award Pa. State U., 1972; Sarasota Med. awards for achievement and excellence, 1979; Gairdner Found. award; Albert Lasker Basic Med. Scis. award; N.Y. Acad. Scis. award; Nobel prize in chemistry, 1980; named Calif. Scientist of Yr., Calif. Mus. Sci. and Industry, 1963; Harvey lectr., 1972, Lynen lectr., 1977. Mem. Inst. Medicine, Nat. Acad. Scis. (council 1979), Am. Acad. Arts and Scis., Am. Soc. Biol. Chemists (pres. 1974-75), Am. Soc. Microbiology. Editor: Biochem. and Biophys. Research Communications, 1959-68; editorial bd. Molecular Biology, 1966-69; contbr. articles to profl. jours. Office: Stanford Sch Medicine Stanford CA 94305*

BERG, THOMAS ELLIOTT, lawyer; b. Chgo., Nov. 2, 1942; s. Sidney Howard and Layle Rebecca (Weinberg) B.; B.A. cum laude in History, U. Colo., 1964; J.D., Harvard, 1967; m. Mary Elizabeth Berg, Nov. 21, 1979; children—Matthew Alan, Emily Sydney, Eve Christine. Admitted to Colo. bar, 1968; asso. firm Cole, Herbert, Hecox, Tolley & Edwards, and predecessor, Colorado Springs, 1967-70, partner, 1971-72; v.p., gen. counsel. dir. Schuck Corp., Colorado Springs, 1972-77; dir. Schuck Securities Corp., 1972-77, Berniger, Berg & Sterling, 1977—; chmn. Human Relations Commn. Colorado Springs, 1975-77; mem. legal assts. advisory com. El Paso Community Coll., 1973-77; lectr. real estate and real estate securities laws. Bd. dirs. U. Colo. Alumni, Colorado Springs, Ruth Washburn Coop. Nursery Sch., 1973-74, Children Sch., 1972-75; chmn. U.S. Olympics Nat. Sports Festival Torch Lighting Ceremony Com., 1978, 79, 81, 83. Mem. Am., Colo., El Paso County bar assns., Colo. Assn. Homebuilders (legis. com.), Pikes Peak Apt. Assn. (dir.). Home: 2118 Wood Ave Colorado Springs CO 80907 Office: 511 N Tejon Colorado Springs CO 80903

BERGAU, ARTHUR JOHN, ins. agt.; b. Wilbur, Wash., Sept. 13, 1925; s. Otto Max and Marie Margaret Dorothy (Menke) B.; student pub. schs.; m. Beverly Jean Gibbons, July 2, 1949; children—Don Arthur, Kathleen Calfern Marie, Laura Louise, Daniel Glenn. Dist. rep. Lutheran Brotherhood Ins. Co., Missoula, Mont., 1962-68, gen. agent, Grand Blanc, Mich., 1968-71, Billings, Mont., 1971-79, Portland, Oreg., 1979—. Mem. gen. agt.'s advisory com., 1976-79. Served with AUS, 1944-46. Recipient numerous salesmanship awards. C.L.U.; registered rep. Mem. Nat., Mich., Mont., Billings (past pres.), Portland life underwriters assns., Gen. Agents and Mgrs. Assn. (past pres. Billings and Portland), Am. Soc. C.L.U., Portland Estate Planning Council. Democrat. Lutheran. Club: Portland Elks. Office: 6330 SW Beaverton-Hillsdale Hwy Portland OR 97221

BERGE, DALE LEROY, archaeologist; b. Coalinga, Calif., Sept. 5, 1934; s. William H. and Lucille M. (Provost) B.; B.A., Brigham Young U., Provo, Utah, 1961, M.A., 1964; Ph.D., U. Ariz., 1968; m. Geraldine Mitton, June 30, 1961; children—Kurt W., Tara M., Matt J. Mem. staff Ariz. State Museum, Tucson, 1966-68; mem. faculty Brigham Young U., 1968—, prof. anthropology, 1981—, dir. Mus. Peoples and Cultures, 1968—. Served with AUS, 1957-59. Charles Redd fellow, 1979. Mem. Soc. Hist. Archaeology, Soc. Am. Archaeology, Am. Anthrop. Assn., Sigma Xi. Republican. Mormon. Author articles, monograph in field. Office: Allen Hall Anthropology Dept Brigham Young U Provo UT 84602

BERGENDORFF, FRED LAVOY, radio sta. exec.; b. Bremerton, Wash., Feb. 7, 1944; s. Fred R. and Lola M. (Young) B.; B.A., San Diego State U., 1965, postgrad., 1966; postgrad. U. So. Calif., 1973; M.A., Ph.D., Columbia Pacific U., 1982; m. Sharyn Yettra, Sept. 23, 1972. Asst. news dir. San Diego State U., 1965; publicity mgr. Sta. KOGO, San Diego, 1966-68; promotion and advt. dir. Sta. KABC, Los Angeles, 1968-69; dir. advt. and promotion Sta. KNX, Los Angeles, 1969—. Mem. Westminster (Calif.) Environ. and Beautification Com., 1977; bd. dirs. Westminster Pub. Cable TV Authority. Served with USAF, 1968. Recipient over 60 major advt. awards, including Clio award, 11 gold medallions Broadcasters Promo Assn., 11 awards Am. Advt. Fedn., 1st pl. graphics Time Inc. Art Show, Best of Show, Broadcast Designers Assn., Creativity 80 award Art Direction mag. Mem. Broadcasters Promotion Assn. (chmn. 1977, pres.), San Diego State Athletic Found. (dir.), San Diego State Alumni Assn. (life), Advt. Club Los Angeles, Am. Advt. Fedn., ASCAP, Hollywood Radio and TV Soc., Los Angeles, Orange County advt. clubs, So. Calif. Broadcasters Assn. Author: Broadcast Advertising and Promotion, 1983. Home: PO Box 1036 Westminster CA 92683 Office: Sta KNX 6121 Sunset Blvd Los Angeles CA 90028

BERGER, AUGUST WALTER, data processing/manufacturing/material systems consultant, educator; b. Los Angeles, June 23, 1937; s. Alfred and Josephine Marie (Obadahl) B.; B.A., Calif. State U., 1971, M.B.A., 1973; m. Camilla Anne Orndorff, Oct. 5, 1957; children—Lisa Ann, Larry Mark, David Andrew, Karen Marie. Dir. purchasing Exec. Industries, Inc., Anaheim, Calif., 1972-73; dir. material Calif. Computer Products, Inc., Anaheim, 1974-76; ind. mgmt., data processing system cons., Yorba Linda, Calif., 1976—; v.p. Mfrs. Resources and Planning, Inc., Santa Ana, Calif., 1977-79; pres. The Gus Berger Group, Inc., educators and cons. mfg./data processing, Anaheim, 1979—; asst. prof. evenings Calif. State U., Fullerton, 1970-78; lectr. in field. Served with USAF, 1955-59. Mem. Am. Prodn. and Inventory Control Soc. (dir., past pres. Orange County chpt.; participant Internat. Tech. Confs., 1975, 76, 77, 78, 79, 81, 82, chmn. 1980; cert.), Internat. Material Mgmt. Soc. (cert.), Am. Soc. Tng. and Devel. Republican. Contbg. editor: Production and Inventory Handbook; contbr. articles to profl. jours. and nat. trade mags. Developer material mgmt. concepts time bucket w.i.p., rotational inventories, flip-flop bills of material, product profile. Office: 5544 E La Palma Ave Suite 2B Anaheim CA 92807

BERGER, BENNETT MAURICE, sociologist; b. N.Y.C., May 1, 1926; s. Julius and Ethel (King) B.; B.A., Hunter Coll., N.Y.C., 1950; Ph.D., U. Calif., Berkeley, 1958; m. Jean Kirkham Righter, Dec. 9, 1956 (div. 1970); children—Jane, Nora; m. 2d, Chandra Mukerji, 1981; 1 son, Kenneth. Mem. faculty U. Ill.-Urbana, 1959-63, U. Calif.-Davis, 1963-73; prof. sociology U. Calif.-San Diego, 1973—, chmn. dept., 1979—; vis. prof. Harvard U., 1968; cons. in field, 1957—. Served with USMCR, 1944-46. Grantee NIMH, 1970-73, Nat. Endowment Humanities, 1979, 81. Mem. Am. Sociol. Assn., Soc. Study Social Problems, Pacific Sociol. Assn. Author: Working-Class Suburb, 2d edit., 1968,

Looking for America, 1971, The Survival of a Counterculture, 1981. Address: 1376 Summit Ave Cardiff CA 92007

BERGER, JAMES HANK, entertainment mgmt. co. exec.; b. Cleve., July 27, 1951; s. James Henry and Joan Marie (Wertz) Kunberger; student Cooper Sch. Arts, 1971-72; m. Rochelle Kiehl, Apr. 29, 1977. Pres., Berger Enterprises, Inc., Sun Valley, Calif., 1979—; pres. Berger/Manning, Inc., 1980—; pres. Hashell, Inc., 1979—. Served with U.S. Navy, 1968-71. Republican. Address: 7928 Sangamon Sun Valley CA 91352

BERGER, JAMES KENT, cons. engr.; b. Chgo., Apr. 22, 1931; s. Harold Elmer and Ethel Margaret (Doolan) B.; B.S., with honors, U. Calif., Los Angeles, 1958, M.S., 1961; m. Patricia Rae Prom, Mar. 27, 1954 (div. Jan. 1970); 1 dau., Karen Valerie; m. 2d, Iris Jeanette Mixer, Oct. 24, 1975 (div. July 1979); m. 3d, Linda Lee Klotz, Feb. 27, 1982. Mem. tech. staff Hughes Aircraft Co., Culver City, Calif., 1958-61; mgr. advanced projects Librascope Group, Gen. Precision, Inc., Glendale, Calif., 1961-64; sr. staff engr. Ampex Corp., Culver City, Calif., 1964-66; ind. cons. engr., 1966—. Served to 1st lt., USAF, 1950-56. Registered profl. engr., Calif., Mem. IEEE, Aerospace Elec. Soc., Tau Beta Pi. Patentee in field of electronics. Home: 29979 Harvester Rd Malibu CA 90265

BERGER, MARTIN, oil company executive; b. N.Y.C., May 23, 1926; s. Harry and Elizabeth (Gotthelf) B.; m. Helen Cherin, Aug. 3, 1947; children—Henry, Susan, Laura Intfen. B.S. in Physics, Columbia U., 1949. Research physicist Uniroyal, Detroit, 1950-54, Chrysler Corp., Detroit, 1954-56; dir. govt. research labs. Exxon Corp., Linden, N.J., 1956-76; v.p. R&D, Occidental Petroleum Corp., Los Angeles, 1977-81, sr. v.p., 1981-82, exec. v.p. ops. 1982—; pres. Occidental Research Corp., Irvine, Calif., 1976—. Served with USCG, 1943-46. Mem. Indsl. Research Inst., Nat. Conf. Advancement of Research. Jewish. Club: Balboa Bay. Contbr. articles to profl. jours.; patentee in field. Home: 2210 Canyonback Rd Los Angeles CA 90049 Office: 10889 Wilshire Blvd Los Angeles CA 90024

BERGER, MICHAEL EINAR, mechanical engineer; b. Springer, N.Mex., Nov. 26, 1945; s. Fredrick Godfrey and Ila Corean (Woodward) B.; B.S.M.E., U. N.Mex., 1967, M.S.M.E., 1969, Ph.D., 1973; m. Gretchen B. Jordan, Mar. 26, 1983; 1 son, James Michael. Program mgr. Fairchild Space and Electronics Co., Germantown, Md., 1971-74; staff mem. weapons design div. Los Alamos Nat. Lab., 1974-79; program mgr. weapons programs, 1979-80, program mgr. energy security, 1980-82, dep. assoc. dir. alternative energy sources, 1982—; adj. prof. mech. engring. U. N.Mex., 1976-82. Mem. Los Alamos County Planning and Zoning Commn., 1978-79; chmn. Los Alamos County Right to Work Com., 1975-78. NSF fellow, 1969-71; Beck scholar, 1966-67; Mason scholar, 1964-66. Mem. Internat. Solar Energy Soc., ASME, N.Mex. Solar Energy Assn., Pi Tau Sigma, Sigma Tau, Phi Kappa Phi. Republican. Methodist. Home: 825 Calle Majia Santa Fe NM 87501 Office: PO Box 1663 Los Alamos NM 87545

BERGER, OTTO, engr.; b. Vienna, Austria, Feb. 16, 1927; s. Max and Sophie (Lichtman) B.; B.E.E., CCNY, 1950; M.S.E.E., Johns Hopkins U., 1956; Engr., Stanford U., 1969; m. Joyce Brouillette, Sept. 8, 1951. Electro-mech. engr. Martin Co., Balt., 1950-56; electro-mech. group head Vanguard, Cape Canaveral, Fla., 1956-58; guidance and control supr.-Agena, Lockheed Missiles and Space Co., Vandenberg Air Force Base, Calif., 1958-60, engring. mgr. Ranger and Mariner launch vehicles, Cape Canaveral, Fla., 1960-64, sr. staff engr., Sunnyvale, Calif., 1964-82, cons., 1982—. Served with USN, 1945-46. Registered profl. engr., Calif. Asso. fellow AIAA; mem. IEEE, Sigma Xi, Tau Beta Pi, Eta Kappa Nu. Holder patent automatic autopilot analyzer. Home and Office: 216 Creekside Dr Palo Alto CA 94306

BERGERUD, MARLY KAY, educator; b. Minot, N.D., July 27, 1942; d. Winton Ernest and Florence Martha-Carrie (Hall) Balsukot; student U. N.D., 1960-63; B.A., Calif. State U., Fresno, 1965; M.S., U. So. Calif., 1968; 1 son, Christen Erik. Tchr., Brea-Olinda High Sch., Brea, Calif., 1966-70; prof. bus. div., dir. info. systems center Cypress (Calif.) Coll., 1970—; owner Infopro, Los Alamitos, Calif. cons. in field. Mem. Assn. Info. Systems, Internat. Info. Word Processing Assn. (pres. Orange County chpt. 1979-81), AAUP, Calif. Bus. Edn. Assn., NEA, Calif. Tchrs. Assn., Faculty Assn. Calif. Community Colls., Am. Vocat. Assn. Co-author: Word/Information Processing Concepts, 2d edit., 1984; Word Processing: Concepts and Careers, 3d edit., 1984. Home: 5792 Carbeck Dr Huntington Beach CA 92648 Office: 9200 Valley View Cypress CA 90630 also 10641 Los Alamitos Blvd Los Alamitos CA 90720

BERGGREN, MARTHA CHRISTINE, petroleum company executive; b. Manhattan, Kans., Oct. 10, 1952; d. Robert Alan and Fern Florence (Hagenmaier) B. B.S., Kans. State U., 1973; M.B.A., Creighton U., 1977. Systems analyst, assoc. systems analyst InterNorth, Inc., Omaha, 1974-78, sr. systems analyst, Houston, 1978-79; mgr. Denver Data Ctr., 1979-82; sr. systems analyst Milestone Petroleum Inc., Denver, 1982—. Mem. Assn. Systems Mgmt., Mortar Bd. Lutheran. Office: Milestone Petroleum Inc 5613 DTC Parkway Englewood CO 80111

BERGGRUEN, JOHN, art gallery owner; b. San Francisco, June 18, 1943; s. Heinz and Lillian (Zellerbach) B. B.A. in Political Sci., San Francisco State U., 1966. Pres., owner John Berggruen Gallery, San Francisco, 1970—. Mem. Soc. for Encouragement Contemporary Art, San Francisco Mus. Modern Art, Am. Assn. Art Dealers. Club: Calif. Tennis (San Francisco). Office: 228 Grant Ave San Francisco CA 94108

BERGMAN, ARLIE W., lawyer; b. Escondido, Calif., Mar. 20, 1937; s. Orlando Arlie and Annie Esther (Mendenhall) B.; m. Coral E. Rhodes, Jan. 2, 1959; children—Coral Anne, Abigail Esther, Mary Rachel. B.S. in Acctg., San Diego State Coll., 1959; J.D., Calif. Western Sch. Law, 1964. Admitted to Calif. bar, 1965. Atty. Cox, Pendleton & Swan, Hemet, Calif., 1965-66; ptnr. Bergman and Roick, Escondido, Calif., 1966-76, Bergman and Lisi, Escondido, 1976—; lectr. in field; cattle rancher. Served with USMC. Mem. Calif. State Bar, ABA, Calif. Farm Bur., Calif. Cattlemen's Assn. (pres. San Diego County chpt.). Republican. Club: Masons (Consuelo, Escondido). Office: 309 South Maple St Escondido CA 92025

BERGMAN, DANIEL CHARLES, county official, lawyer, educator; b. Corpus Christi, Tex., Aug. 18, 1943; s. Benjamin and Pearl H. B.; m. Susan Lee Axall, Aug. 15, 1965; children—Erica Catherine, Kelli Lorraine. B.S. in Biology, San Diego State U., 1965, M.S., 1971; J.D., U. San Diego, 1975. Bar: Calif. 1976, U.S. Dist. Ct. (so. dist.) Calif. 1976, U.S. Ct. Appeals (9th cir.) 1977; registered sanitarian, Calif., Ill.; cert. community coll. tchr., Calif. Asst. sanitarian, sanitarian San Diego County (Calif.) Dept. Pub. Health, 1968-71, vector ecologist, 1971-72, supervising sanitarian Dept. Health Services, 1972-79, chief div. sanitation/environ. health protection program mgr., 1979-81; environ. health cons. Contra Costa (Calif.) Dept. Health Services, 1981, asst. health services dir. Div. Environ. Health, 1981—; sole practice law, San Diego and Danville, Calif., 1976—; lectr. in field. Recipient Am. Jurisprudence awards. Mem. Am. Pub. Health Assn., Nat. Environ. Health Assn. (Presdl. citation 1977), Calif. Environ. Health Assn. (Presdl. citation 1977, 78), ABA, Calif. State Bar Assn. Office: 2500 Alhambra Ave Martinez CA 94553

BERGMAN, GERALD K., entertainment company executive; b. St. Paul, July 2, 1934; s. E.A. and Kathryn A. (Vien) B.; m. Joan Potter, Sept. 11, 1976, children—Kurt, Virginia. Kenneth, Stephen Cummings, Gretchen Cummings, Carolyn Cummings. B.A.A., U. Minn., 1957. With Continental Ill. Nat. Bank and Trust Co., 1957-82, 2d v.p. nat. div., 1966-68, v.p., 1968, group head met. div., 1969, pres. Continental Ill. Leasing Corp., 1972, sr. v.p., div. head spl. industries divs., 1974, sr. v.p. CICorp., 1980, exec. v.p. CICorp. and parent co., 1981-82; exec. v.p., dir. Twentieth Century-Fox Film Corp.; pres. Twentieth Century-Fox Enterprises; dir. Northwestern Engring. Co., John B. Coleman and Bd. dirs. Lincoln Park Zool. Soc., 1972—; treas. Citizens for Jim Thompson, 1975-82; sec.-treas. bd. dirs. Max McGraw Wildlife Found., 1977-82. Mem. Robert Morris Assos., Sigma Alpha Epsilon. Club: Bankers. Address: PO Box 900 Beverly Hills CA 90213

BERGMAN, JOHN STONEMAN, oil co. exec., petroleum landman; b. Donora, Pa., June 26, 1928; s. John Frederick and Dorcas (Stoneman) B.; B.A., Okla. State U., 1952; postgrad. Oklahoma City U. Law Sch., 1954-56; m. Karen Campbell, Dec. 11, 1959; children—Heidi Karen, John Stoneman. Petroleum Landman Sohio Petroleum Co., La., Okla., Colo., Alta., Can. and Tex., 1954-60; dist. landman Union Tex. Petroleum Co., Denver, 1960-68; div. landman McKnight Petroleum Trust Co., Denver, 1968-72; v.p. land Resources Investment Corp., Denver, 1972—, sr. v.p., 1978—. Served with USAAF, 1943-47, USAF, 1947-48, U.S. Army, 1952-54, col. Res. Decorated Air medal with 5 oak leaf clusters, D.F.C. with oak leaf cluster, Purple Heart with oak leaf cluster, Silver Star, Bronze Star, D.S.C., Meritorious Service medal with oak leaf cluster; recipient Betty McWhorter commendation Desk and Derrick Club of Denver, 1977. Mem. Am. (dir.; Disting. Landman 1975), Denver (Landman of Yr. 1976) assns. petroleum landmen, Rocky Mountain Petroleum Pioneers, Natural Gas Men of Okla., Natural Gas Men of Permian Basin, Res. Officers Assn. Republican. Lutheran. Clubs: Denver Petroleum (dir.), Masons, Shriners. Research on def. and vulnerability of Alaskan Pipeline, 1974. Home: 2370 S Lima St Aurora CO 80014 Office: 1225 17th St 32d Floor Denver CO 80202

BERGMANN, DUANE ALBERT, mech. engr.; b. Los Angeles, Oct. 6, 1938; s. Clarence Audley and Leona Louise B.; B.S. with honors in Mech. Engring., Calif. Poly. U., 1962; M.S. in Mech. Engring., U. So. Calif., 1964; m. Sarah Karen Andersen, Dec. 19, 1959; children—Darren Lee, Lars Erik. Turbomachinery product mgr. Airco Cryogenics Co., Irvine, Calif., 1964-77; v.p. Prestec, Inc., Orange, Calif., 1978; pres. Bergmann Engring., Inc., Glendora, Calif., 1979—. Registered profl. engr., Calif., Okla., Iowa. Mem. ASME, Western Gas Processors Assn. Republican. Episcopalian. Office: Bergmann Engring Inc 220 S Glendora Ave Glendora CA 91740

BERGMANN, JEANNINE ANNE PERSSON, trucking co. mgr.; b. Alameda, Calif., Nov. 11, 1950; d. Ralph Rockwell and Jeannette Jane (Zisa) P.; m. William C. Bergmann. B.A., Calif. State U., Hayward, 1972; postgrad. San Jose State U., 1972-73; cert. occupational safety and health Merritt Jr. Coll., 1973; cert. photography Chabot Jr. Coll., 1976. Clk., Kaiser Sand & Gravel, Pleasanton, Calif., 1971-74, clk. dispatcher, 1974-76, dispatcher, 1976-79, coordinator transport ops., 1979-80, mgr. transport ops., 1980; mgr. aggregate transport ops. Mile & Sons Trucking Service, Inc., Pleasanton, Calif., 1980—. Mem. Women in Constrn. Clubs: Oakland Ski, Powder Hound Ski. Home: 543 Ruby Rd Livermore CA 94550 Office: PO Box 40 Pleasanton CA 94566

BERGRUN, NORMAN RILEY, research and devel. co. exec.; b. Green Camp, Ohio, Aug. 4, 1921; s. Theodore and Naomi Ruth (Stemm) B.; B.S. in M.E., Cornell U., 1943; LL.B., LaSalle Extension U., Chgo., 1955; postgrad Stanford U., 1947, Foothill Coll., 1970-79; m. Claire Michaelson, May 23, 1943; children—Clark, Jay, Joan. Thermodynamicist Douglas Aircraft Co., El Segundo, Calif., 1943-44; research scientist NASA, 1944-56; Polaris project mgmt. team Lockheed Missile and Space Co., Sunnyvale, Calif., 1956-69; dir. mgmt. systems Nielsen Engring. and Research, Mountain View, Calif., 1969-72; chmn. Bergrun Cos., Los Altos Hills, Calif., 1972—; guest lectr. Am. River Coll., Sacramento; cons. in field. served with U.S. Navy, 1944-46. Fellow AIAA (Appreciation for sustained contbns. advancement arts, sci. and tech. of aeronautics and astronautics 1972); mem. Aviation Hall of Fame, Nat. Socs. Profl. Engrs., Calif. Soc. Profl. Engrs., AAAS, Internat. Platform Assn., Am. Film Inst., Tau Kappa Epsilon. Republican. Clubs: Stanford U. Alumni, Cornell U. Alumni. Author: Tomorrow's Technology Today. Contbr. articles in field to profl. jours. Home: 26865 Saint Francis Rd Los Altos Hills CA 94022

BERG-SLOAN, CAROL ANN, dietitian; b. Pasadena, Calif., Apr. 14, 1957; d. Robert Ellsworth and June Katherine B. Student U. Minn., 1975-76, Pasadena City Coll., 1978-79; B.S., Calif. State U.-Los Angeles, 1980. Registered dietitian, Calif. Food service nutrition specialist Calif. Egg Adv. Bd., Upland, 1980-81; corp. dietitian health care div. S.E. Rykoff & Co., Los Angeles, 1981—. Mem. Los Angeles Dietitians in Bus. and Industry (pres. 1982-83), Am. Dietetics Assn., Calif. Dietetics Assn., Greater Los Angeles Nutrition Council. Office: SE Rykoff & Co 761 Terminal St Los Angeles CA 90021

BERGSMAN, BARRY ROEMER, television production and distribution company executive; b. Chgo., Dec. 6, 1936; s. Leon Ashser and Helen Natalie (Roemer) B.; m. Bette Linda Berman, Dec. 19, 1976; 1 son, Jason Ashley. B.S. in Bus., Ind. U.-Bloomington, 1958. Account exec. Sta.-KTTV, Los Angeles, 1961, CBS TV, Los Angeles, 1962-64; pres. Bergsman Co., Beverly Hills, Calif., 1964-68; pres. Baron Enterprises, Inc., Los Angeles, 1968—. Served to lt. U.S. Army, 1958-59. Recipient Internat. Film and TV Festival award, 1982. Mem. Nat. Assn. TV Program Execs. Club: Sand & Sea. Office: 522 S Sepulveda Blvd Los Angeles CA 90049

BERGSTROM, EDITH H., artist; b. Denver; d. William E. and Annabelle (Harrod) Youtsler; m. Erik E. Bergstrom, Mar. 22, 1974. B.A., Pomona Coll., 1963; M.A., Stanford U., 1964. Group shows include: San Diego Watercolor Soc. Internat. 1983 Exhbn. (award), Nat. Watercolor Soc. 1983 Exhbn. (award), Rocky Mountain Nat. Watermedia Exhbn. (Century award of Merit), 1982; pvt. tchr. art; tchr. Palo Alto adult edn. programs; juror watercolor competitions. Mem. Am. Watercolor Soc. (Carl Folke Sahlin award 1983), Nat. Watercolor Soc., Rocky Mountain Nat. Watermedia Soc., West Coast Watercolor Soc., Watercolor West, Santa Clara Valley Watercolor Soc., The Museum Soc., San Jose Mus. Art, Palo Alto Cultural Ctr., Filoli Ctr. Republican. Christian Scientist. Club: Palm Soc.

BERGSUND, RICHARD THEODORE, executive search consultant; b. Elgin, Ill., Nov. 27, 1927; s. Leif H. and Myrtle (Rovelstad) B.; m. Joan Reid, June 28, 1952; children—Sara Leslie, Richard. B.A. in Sociology, Carleton Coll., 1950. Trainee Providence Wash. Ins. Co., 1950, method anal., 1951, office service mgr., 1952-53; pacific region personnel dir. Glens Falls Ins. Group, N.Y., 1954-61, sec. adminstrv. official, 1962-63, corp. personnel and orgn. ofcl., 1964-66; v.p., asst. to pres., 1967-68, v.p. field ops., 1968; pacific regional mgr. INSCO Systems Corp., San Francisco, 1969-73; div. mgr. Inds. Indemnity Co., San Francisco, 1973-77; sr. v.p., sr. ptnr. Leon A. Farley Assocs., San Francisco, 1977—; Served with U.S. Army, 1946-47. Mem. Ins. Forum. Clubs: San Francisco Yacht, San Francisco Comml., Tiburon Peninsula. Home: 55 Seafirth Rd Tiburon CA 94920 Office: Steuart Tower One Market Plaza Suite 1001 San Francisco CA 94105

BERGT, NEIL GRADON, diversified corporation executive; b. Tacoma, Wash., Mar. 22, 1936; s. Percy Leo and Florence Louise (Hall) B.; m. Judith Jo, Dec. 29, 1977; children—Debra, Michael, Karen, Bryan, Kevin, Patrick. Grad. high sch. Bush pilot, Alaska, 1956-70; chmn. bd., chief exec. officer Alaska Internat. Industries, Anchorage, 1971—; chmn. bd., chief exec. officer Western Airlines, 1981-83; dir. Northwest Energy Co., Salt Lake City. Office: 3201 C St Anchorage AK 99503

BERGUM, CHRISTIAN OLSON, constrn. co. exec., architect; b. Los Angeles, Nov. 3, 1953; s. Jarle Albert and Elna Lucille (Hansen) B. Student U. Geneva, 1972; cert. U. Poitiers, 1972-73; student Calif. State U.-Fullerton, 1973; B.A., U. Oreg., 1976, B.Arch., 1976; M.Arch., U. Wash., 1978; Ph.D., U. Pa., 1981. Research asst. architecture dept. U. Wash., Seattle, 1977-78; intern architect McClarty & Johnson, Inc., Architects, Planners, Bellevue, Wash., 1978-79; architect Danielian Assos., Architecture, Planning, Newport Beach, Calif., 1980; v.p. Bergum Constrn. Co., Fullerton, 1976—; pres. Christian Olson Bergum AIA Architecture/Planning, Fullerton, 1980—. Bd. dirs. Bergum Family Found., 1976—. Recipient Energy Research grant U. Wash., 1977; Fulbright Hays professorship U. Jordan, 1981-82. Mem. AIA, Assn. Collegiate Schs. Architecture, Soc. Archtl. Historians, Environ. Research Design Assn., Nat. Assn. Home Builders, Gerontol. Soc. Am. Lutheran. Home: 1330 Dana Pl Fullerton CA 92631 Office: 1023 E Chapman Ave Fullerton CA 92634

BERHALTER, WALTER ANTHONY, lawyer; b. Chgo., July 20, 1946; s. Howard Robert and Marilee A. (Miles) B.; B.A. in Communications, B.A. in Edn., Eastern Wash. State U., 1971, M.B.A., 1977; J.D. (scholar), Gonzaga U., 1978. Bar: Wash. 1980, U.S. Dist. Ct. (ea. dist.) Wash. 1980, U.S. Ct. Appeals (9th cir.) 1982. Tchr., Wash., 1971-75; bus. mgr. M & M Corp., 1978; pres. Brown & Capeloto Tax and Bus. Services, Inc., Moses Lake and Grand Coulee, Wash., 1979—; chmn. bd. Acorn Services Inc., 1980—; gen. partner Acorn 1, 1980—; enrolled agt. IRS, 1979-80; individual practice law, 1980. Bd. regents Gonzaga U., 1976-78; Mem. ABA, Assn. Trial Lawyers Am., Wash. Bar Assn., Nat. Soc. Pub. Accts., Phi Alpha Delta, Phi Theta Kappa, Kappa Delta Pi, Pi Kappa Delta. Clubs: Elks, Eagles, Wash. Athletic, Kiwanis. Author: The Effects of Government Agency Regulation and Procedures on Business, 1977; The Three Little Flashlights, 1977, The Law of Oil and Gas Leasing and Drilling in Wildcat Washington, 1982. Home: 8941 Westover Moses Lake WA 98837 Office: 524 W Broadway Moses Lake WA 98837

BERK, KAREN MAE, state official; b. Bklyn., Mar. 29, 1943; d. Harry and Minerva G. (Liptzen) Sternberg. B.A., UCLA, 1964. Adminstr., Calif. Employment Devel. Dept., Sacramento, 1964—, employment and Tng. programs, 1970-73, mgr., adminstr. program and systems analysis div., 1980—. Mem. Encore of Sacramento, Nat. Council Jewish Women. Recipient Sustained Superior Accomplishment award Employment Devel. Dept. Calif. Mem. Internat. Assn. Personnel in Employment, Sacramento Jewish Bus. and Profl. Women's Assn. Democratic. Home: 1521 University Ave Sacramento CA 95825 Office: 800 Capitol Hall Sacramento CA 95814

BERKE, JUDIE, publisher, editor; b. Mpls., Apr. 15, 1938; d. Maurice M. and Sue (Supak) Kleyman; student U. Minn., 1956-60, Mpls. Sch. Art, 1945-59. Free lance illustrator and designer, 1959—; pres. Berke-Wood, Inc., N.Y.C., 1971-80, Manhattan Rainbow & Lollipop Co. subs. Berke-Wood, Inc., 1971-80; pres. Get Your Act Together, club act staging, N.Y.C., 1971-80; pub., editor The Coordinator, 1982—; head prodn. Advanced Audio Visual Systems; cons. to film and ednl. cos.; guest lectr. various colls. and univs. in Calif. and N.Y., 1973—; writer, illustrator, dir. numerous ednl. filmstrips, 1972—, latest being Focus on Professions, 1974, Focus on the Performing Arts, 1974, Focus on the Creative Arts, 1974, Workstyles, 1976, Wonderworm, 1976, Supernut, 1977; author, illustrator film Fat Black Mack (San Francisco Ednl. Film Festival award), 1970; designer posters and brochures for various entertainment groups, 1963—; composer numerous songs, latest being Time is Relative, 1976, Love Will Live On in My Mind, 1976, My Blue Walk, 1976, You Make Me a Baby, 1982, Let's Go Around Once More, 1983; composer/author off-Broadway musical Street Corner Time, 1978; contbr. children's short stories to various publs., also articles. Trustee The Happy Spot Sch., N.Y.C., 1972—. Mem. Am. Acad. Polit. and Social Sci. Home: 11417 Vanowen St North Hollywood CA 91605

BERKEY, DANIEL STEWART, small business consultant; b. New Brunswick, N.J., June 25, 1941; s. Richard Scott and Dorothy (Hayden) B.; B.A., Lehigh U., 1963; M.B.A., U. Pa., 1970; m. Ann Cabot Richardson, Feb. 22, 1975; 1 dau., Elizabeth Wellington. Systems analyst Thomas J. Lipton, Inc., Englewood Cliffs, N.J., 1970-72; mgmt. cons. Dept. Interior, Washington, 1972-73; spl. asst. to asst. sec. Interior for energy and minerals, 1973-74; exec. asst. rates and regulatory affairs United Gas Pipe Line Co., Houston, 1975-76, mgr. research and devel., 1976-77; cons./owner Gen. Bus. Services, Oakland, Calif., 1977-80; pres. Berkey & Assocs., 1980—. Bd. dirs., treas. Goodwill Industries of Greater East Bay. Served to capt. U.S. Army, 1963-68; Vietnam. Decorated Bronze Star, Army Commendation medal. Mem. SBA (Calif. legis. coordinator 1978—). Republican. Episcopalian. Clubs: Kiwanis (chmn. scholarship found., dir. Oakland chpt.); Wharton (San Francisco). Home: 5100 Proctor Ave Oakland CA 94618 Office: 1845A Berkeley Way Berkeley CA 94703

BERKLAND, JAMES OMER, geologist; b. Glendale, Calif., July 31, 1930; s. Joseph Omer and Gertrude Madelyn (Thompson) B.; A.A., Santa Rosa Jr. Coll., 1951; A.B., U. Calif., Berkeley, 1958; M.S., San Jose State U., 1964; postgrad., U. Calif., Davis, 1969-72; m. Janice Lark Keirstead, Dec. 19, 1966; children—Krista Lynn, Jay Olin. With U.S. Geol. Survey, 1958-64; engring. geologist U.S. Bur. Reclamation, 1964-69; cons. geologist, 1969-72; asst. prof. Appalachian State U., Boone, N.C., 1972-73; county geologist Santa Clara County, San Jose, Calif., 1973—; adj. prof. San Jose State U., 1975-76; mem. evening faculty San Jose City Coll. Treas. Creekside/Park Place Homeowners Group; v.p. West Coast Aquatics, Creekside/Park Place Swim Team; mem. various city and county adv. bds. Registered geologist, Calif.; cert. engring. geologist, Calif. Fellow Geol. Soc. Am.; mem. Assn. Engring. Geologists (past vice chmn. San Francisco sect.), Santa Clara County Engrs. and Architects Assn. (v.p.), San Jose Hist. Mus. Assn., Western Council Engrs., Internat. Platform Assn., Nat. Jogging Assn., Nat. Geog. Soc., Calif. State Employees Assn., Calif. State Firemen's Assn., Youth Sci. Inst. Peninsula Geol. Soc. (past treas.), Earthquake Engring. Research Inst., AAAS, Saber Soc. (co-founder, past pres.), Sigma Xi. Independent Democrat. Contbr. numerous articles to profl. jours.; originator seismic window theory for earthquake prediction. Home: 14927 East Hills Dr San Jose CA 95127 Office: Santa Clara County 70 W Hedding St San Jose CA 95110

BERKLEY, GAIL WINNICK, psychotherapist; b. Detroit, Feb. 21, 1947; d. Lawrence C. and Helen M. (Caner) Winnick. B.A., San Francisco State U., 1970, M.S., 1979, now postgrad. Staff, Work Furlough Program, San Mateo County Jail, Redwood City, Calif., 1978-80; tchr. San Francisco Unified Sch. Dist., 1971-80; couple counselor Mental Health Seminar Tour, No. Council Health Facilities, 1976-79; pvt. practice psychotherapy, San Mateo, Calif., 1982—; self-employed interior designer, 1980—; cons. in field. Active San Mateo Family Services Aux., Mills Meml. Hosp. Aux.; founding sponsor San Francisco Performing Arts Ctr., 1976—; sponsor San Francisco Opera, San Francisco Ballet. Mem. Calif. Assn. Mental Health Counselors, Am.

Counselors Mental Health Assn., Am. Personnel and Guidance Assn., Internat. Reading Assn., Am. Soc. Interior Designers, Am. Assn. Marriage, Family and Child Therapists, Am. Arbitration Assn. (panel arbitrators), Internat. Council Sex Edn. and Parenthood. Club: Commonwealth. Soft sculpture—Bible Walk—wall hangings in Congregation Temple Emanu-El, San Francisco, 1978. Home: 817 Wilmington Rd San Mateo CA 94402 Office: 36 S El Camino Real Suite 304 San Mateo CA 94401

BERKMAN, JACK MARTIN, public relations executive; s. San Francisco, Oct. 13, 1946; s. Sidney Allen and Bella (Dworkin) B. B.A., Calif. State U.-Northridge, 1969. Pub. relations staff Gen. Motors, Detroit, 1969-71; acctg. supr. Herbert H. Rozoff Pub. Relations Counsel, Chgo., 1971-73; nat. dir. pub. relations/dir. sales and mktg. Am. Housing Guild, San Diego, 1973-75; v.p., dir. mktg. Rancho La Costa Properties, San Diego, 1975-76; pres. Berkman & Daniels, San Diego, 1976—; pub. relations lectr. univs., seminar leader. Bd. dirs. San Diego Repertory Theatre; trustee Combined Arts and Edn. Council of San Diego County; active San Diegans, Inc. Named Most Outstanding Citizen, San Diego Jaycees, 1980; recipient cert. of merit Sr. Citizens Community Med. Clinic, Leukemia Soc. Am., Inc. Mem. Pub. Relations Soc. Am., San Diego Bldg. Contractors Assn., Nat. Assn. Real Estate Editors (v.p.), Sigma Delta Chi. Jewish. Club: San Diego Press (exec. bd.). Home: 2842 Dove St San Diego CA 92103 Office: 1717 Kettner Blvd Suite 100 San Diego CA 92101

BERKMAN, JEROME, food service executive, consultant; b. Bronx, N.Y., June 5, 1931; s. Charles and Fanny (Schor) B.; m. Cynthia Gail Lutsky; children—Mark B., David A. B.S. in Bus. Adminstrn., U. Denver, 1953; M.B.A., Pepperdine U., 1973. Registered dietician. Food prodn. mgr. Mountainside Hosp., Montclair, N.J., 1956-59; propr. Beefburger Express Restaurant, Denver, 1959-61; dietary dir. Meml. Hosp., Glendale, Calif., 1961-68; dir. food service Cedars-Sinai Med. Ctr., Los Angeles, 1968—; pres. J. Berkman and Assoc. Food Service Cons. Served with U.S. Army, 1953-56. Recipient Award for Excellence in Food Service, Modern Hosp. Mag., 1963, Ivy award Instns. Mag., 1975, Internat. Silver Plate award Food Mfrs. Assn., 1971, Gold Seal award Nat. Restaurant Assn., 1971. Mem. Am. Dietetic Assn., Silver and Gold Plate Soc, Am. Soc. Food Service Adminstrs., Hosp. Council Dietary Program, Ivy Soc. Contbr. articles to numerous profl. jours. Home: 2003 Manistee Dr La Canada CA 91011

BERKMAN, JOHN WORRALL, mechanical engineer; b. Rochester, Minn., Jan. 29, 1924; s. David Mayo and Frances Kieffer (Scott) B.; m. Jan Westcott Maytum, Feb. 20, 1943; children—Dulcie, Nancy, Joseph; m. 2d, Caroline Julia Teig, Mar. 29, 1959; children—Amelia, John. B.S., U. Minn., 1949; M.S. in Mech. Engring., 1950; registered mech. engr., Minn. Engr., Mayo Clinic, Rochester, Minn., 1950-57; adv. engr. IBM, Rochester, 1957-73; engr. Burroughs Corp., Westlake Village, Calif., 1973-76; sr. staff engr. Applied Magnetics Corp., Goleta, Calif., 1976-78; sr. engr. Cooper-Vision Systems (Cooper Labs.), Irvine, Calif., 1978—. Served with USNR, 1943-45; PTO. Mem. Pi Tau Sigma. Patentee in electromech. field.

BERKOWITZ, NATHANIEL CHARLES, financial consultant; b. Mattoon, Ill., Feb. 12, 1933; s. Abraham I. and Anita (Brady) B.; m. Myra de Hes, Feb. 26, 1961; children—Ethan, Zachary, Ruth. A.B., Harvard Coll., 1953; postgrad. London Sch. Econs., 1954. Mng. dir. N.C. Berkowitz & Co., fin. and mgmt. services and investments, 1958—; dir. Cyclotomics, Inc., Berkeley, Calif. Served to capt. USAF, 1954-57. Mem. AAAS, Navy League (San Francisco council). Club: Harvard (N.Y.). Author: How to Protect Your Small Business Investment, 1960. Home: 78 22d Ave San Francisco CA 94121 Office: 1 Sutter St Suite 800 San Francisco CA 94104

BERLIN, BEATRICE WINN, visual artist, printmaker; b. Phila., May 27, 1922; d. Benjamin and Pauline (Neubauer) Winn; m. Herbert Edward Berlin, Oct. 21, 1945; m. 2d., Warren Joseph Sturmer, Aug. 21, 1971; children—Arlene (dec.), Janice. Student Moore Coll. Art, Phila., Phila. Coll. Art; student Samuel Maitin, Hitoshi Nakazato, Kenjilo Nanao. Lectr. Phila. Print Club, Phila., 1964-68; instr. Intaglio techniques Long Beach Island Ctr. Arts and Sci., N.J., 1970; freelance artist, Pa., 1963-76, Calif., 1976—; represented in pub. collections including Phila. Mus. Art., Bklyn. Art. Mus., N.Y. Public Library, Phila. Main Library, De Cordova Mus., Mass., U. So. Calif., N.J. State Mus., Temple U., Phila., U. Pa., Phila., Lebanon Valley Coll., Pa., Ocean City Cultural Ctr., N.J. Recipient Phila. Water Color Club drawing prize, 1976, 82, Ocean City (N.J.) Boardwalk best in show prize, 1973. Lebanon Valley (Pa.) Coll. purchase prize, 1973, Hazelton (Pa.) Art League purchase prize, 1972, Cheltenham (Pa.) Art Ctr. Nat. Print Exhbn. first prize, 1970. Mem. Am. Color Print Soc., Phila. Watercolor Club, Phila. Print Club, Calif. Soc. Printmakers, Artists Equity Assn. Home and Office: 927 Taylor Ave Alameda CA 94501

BERLINER, ROBERT, lawyer; b. N.Y.C., Aug. 16, 1935; s. Harry and Anna (Sussman) B.; B.S., CUNY, 1956; student DePaul U., 1957-60; J.D., Detroit Coll. Law, 1961; m. Barbara Gail Karch, June 30, 1962; children—Steven Aaron, Julie Ann. Chemist, Sinclair Oil Co. Research Labs., 1956-60; admitted to Mich. bar, 1962, Calif. bar, 1967; patent atty. Ethyl Corp., 1960-65, Bell & Howell Co., 1965-68; mem. firm Nilsson, Robbins, Dalgarn & Berliner, Los Angeles, 1968—. Lectr. patent law UCLA, 1968—; adj. prof. law Southwestern U. Pres. Los Angeles Lung Assn., 1982. Fellow Inst. Advancement Engring.; mem. Am., Los Angeles patent law assns., Am., Los Angeles, San Fernando Valley bar assns., State Bar Calif., State Bar Mich., Los Angeles Council Engrs. and Scientists (legal counsel 1968—), Los Angeles Area C. of C. (legis. chmn. clean air com. 1970—), Los Angeles Central City Assn. (legal com.), Mensa. Home: 3843 Dixie Canyon Ave Sherman Oaks CA 91403 Office: 707 Wilshire Blvd Los Angeles CA 90017

BERLINGERI, RUTH ANN, pharmacist; b. Pasadena, Calif., Nov. 1, 1953; d. Dale Brooks and Elizabeth Mae (Kissack) Eckrote; B.S. in Pharmacy, U. Pacific, 1975; m. Charles P. Berlingeri, June 2, 1979; 1 dau., Rebecca Ann. Intern pharmacist Huntington Pharmacy, Ontario, Calif., 1973-75; 2d pharmacist Clark Drugs, LaVerne, Calif., 1975-77; chief pharmacist Calif. State Poly. U., Pomona, 1977-78; pharmacist N. Rialto Drug, Rialto, Calif., 1979-80; pharmacist Gemmel Pharmacies, Chino and Fullerton, Calif., 1979, asst. mgr., Norco, Calif., 1979—; relief pharmacist Redlands (Calif.) Community Hosp., 1981—. Mem. Am., Calif. (del. 1978-79), Ontario Area (sec. 1978-79) pharm. assns., Lambda Kappa Sigma. Republican. Congregationalist. Club: Jobs Daus. Home: 615 Nottingham Dr Redlands CA 92373

BERMAN, ALAN PHILLIP, business and financial consulting company executive; b. Johannesburg, South Africa, Jan. 28, 1948; came to U.S., 1979; s. Charles and Fay Berman; m. Dianne Kusner, Apr. 2, 1967; children—Craig, Lauren, Stacey, Terri. Law degree U. South Africa, 1966. Law clk. Van Jarsveld & Vickers, attys., Roodepoort, South Africa, 1962-66; sales mgr. Roodepoort Motors, 1967-71; pres., gen. mgr. Roodepoort Motors Datsun, 1971-79, Kyalami Internat. Inc., Los Angeles, 1979—; pres., chief exec. officer Multinat. Cons. Inc., Los Angeles, 1981—, Premier Foods Inc., Los Angeles, 1979—. Mem. Inst. Motor Industry, Nat. Automobile Dealers Assn. (chmn. Johannesburg), Motor Industry Fedn. Jewish. Clubs: Rotary (Roodeport); Killarney Country (South Africa). Contbr. numerous articles on motor trade and fin. to South African periodicals. Home: 1820 Idaho Ave Santa Monica CA 90403 Office: 1666 Corinth St Suite 200 Los Angeles CA 90025

BERMAN, BARUCH, elec. engr.; b. Tel-Aviv, Israel, Nov. 10, 1925; s. Joseph and Sonia (Leoff) B.; B.S. in Elec. Engring., Israel Inst. Tech., 1947, diploma in Engring., 1948; M.S., Columbia, 1957; m. Rose S. Goodman, Sept. 22, 1952; children—Sharon Joy, Orrie Anne. Chief engr. Regulators, Inc., Wyckoff, N.J., 1953-58, Am. Car and Foundry, Paramus, N.J., 1958-62; mgr. indsl. control Elec. Regulator Corp., Norwalk, Conn., 1962-66; project mgr. TRW Systems, Redondo Beach, Calif., 1966-74; asst. gen. mgr., v.p. engring., engineered magnetics div. Gulton Industries, Hawthorne, Calif., 1974-77; mgr. power systems TRW, Redondo Beach, 1977-81; sr. scientist space div. Rockwell Internat., 1981—; pres., Berman Engring., cons., 1966—. Served with Israel Army Def., 1948-53, Brit. Coast Guard, 1944-45. Fellow Inst. Advancement of Engring., IEEE (past chmn. South Bay Harbor sect., awards com. chmn. 1981-83); mem. Nat. Soc. Profl. Engrs., Calif. Soc. Profl. Engrs. (dir.). Patents, publs. in field. Home: 28739 Trailriders Dr Palos Verdes Peninsula CA 90274

BERMAN, GERSHON, clin. psychologist; b. St. Paul, Nov. 3, 1933; s. Lawrence and Frances (Goldberg) B.; A.B., U. Mich., 1954; M.A., Stanford U., 1957, Ph.D., 1963; children—Jenny Leah, Edith Minna, Elizabeth Fernanda. Clin. psychology trainee VA Hosps., Palo Alto, Calif., San Francisco, 1954-57, 58, 59; psychology intern Stanford Hosp., San Francisco, 1957-58; teaching asst. clin. psychology Stanford, 1958-59; clin. psychologist Agnews State Hosp., San Jose, Calif., 1959-65, sr. psychologist, 1965-67; clin. psychologist Kaiser-Permanente Med. Center, Santa Clara, Calif., 1967-75, chief psychologist, 1975—; pvt. practice clin. psychology, San Mateo, Calif., 1964-66, Santa Clara, 1966-78, Palo Alto, 1964—. Mem. Santa Clara County Mental Health Adv. Bd., 1968-79, chmn., 1969-75. Bd. dirs. Calif. Sch. Profl. Psychology, 1974-80, treas., 1976-77, sec., 1977-80. Mem. Am., Calif. Psychol. Assn. (editor newsletter 1968-69, dir. 1973-75), Santa Clara County Psychol. Assn. (sec. 1967-68, pres. 1969-70, treas. 1972-74, chpt. rep. 1973-75), Santa Clara County (dir. 1967-75, pub. affairs chmn. 1967-70, mem. exec. com. 1968-74), Calif. (mem. pub. affairs com. 1967-70) assns. for mental health, Am. Psychology-Law Soc. (bd. dirs. Santa Clara County chpt. 1983—), ACLU No. Calif. (dir. Mid-Peninsula chpt. 1965-69, past vice chmn.), Phi Beta Kappa, Sigma Xi. Phi Eta Sigma, Phi Kappa Phi. Home: 938-57 Clark Ave Mountain View CA 94040 Office: Kaiser-Permanente Med Center 900 Kiely Blvd Santa Clara CA 95051 also 599 College Ave Suite 5 Palo Alto CA 94306

BERMAN, HOWARD L., congressman; b. Los Angeles, Apr. 15, 1941; s. Joseph and Eleanor (Schapiro) B.; B.A. in Internat. Relations, UCLA, 1962, J.D., 1965; m. Axelrod, June 24, 1978; children—Brinley, Lindsey Rose. Mem. Calif. Assembly from West Los Angeles Dist., 1973-82, majority leader, 1973-80, chmn. policy research mgmt. com., 1981; mem. 98th Congress from 26th Dist. Calif. Pres., Calif. Fedn. Young Democrats, 1967-69; mem. regional bd. Anti-Defamation League, Am. Jewish Congress, League of Conservation Voters of Calif., Calif. Fair Housing Council; nat. bd. dirs. Americans for Dem. Action. Named Number 1 Consumer Legislator, Calif. Fedn. Consumers, 1975. Democrat. Jewish. Home: 520 S Sepulveda Blvd Apt 406 Los Angeles CA 90049

BERMAN, LAWRENCE RICHARD, psychologist, educator; b. N.Y.C., Dec. 3, 1946; s. Louis and Lillian (Greenberg) B.; B.A., U. Calif. at Berkeley, 1968; M.S., U. Mass., 1971; Ph.D. in Counseling Studies Profl. Sch. Humanist Studies. Spl. profl. asst. in psychology Agnews State Hosp., San Jose, Calif., 1969; advanced psychology intern Northampton (Mass.) VA Hosp., 1969-70; asst. dir. Bay Area Diagnosis and Treatment Center, San Francisco, 1971-73; exec. dir. Alysan Center, San Jose, 1973-79; dir. youth services Jewish Community Center, Palo Alto, Calif., 1973; instr. psychology Ohlone Coll., Fremont, Calif., 1972—; psychol. cons. Potrero Hill Social Devel. and Edn. Program, San Francisco, 1973-75, Westwood, Fremont, 1974—, Serra Residential Center, Fremont, 1976—, San Andreas Regional Center for Developmentally Disabled, San Jose, 1975—, Santa Clara Pub. Guardian's Office, 1975-79; mem. gender identity adv. com. U. Calif. Med. Center, San Francisco, 1973-76. NSF grantee, 1963; Calif. State scholar, 1964-68, fellow, 1968; NIMH fellow, 1968-69; lic. marriage, family and child counselor; cert. rehab. counselor. Mem. Calif. Scholarship Fedn., Calif. Assn. Marriage and Family Counselors, Am. Psychol. Assn., AAAS. Author: Children's Coloring Projective, 1979. Contbr. articles to profl. jours. Office: 1405 Civic Center Dr Santa Clara CA 95050

BERMAN, MARSHALL, scientist; b. Detroit, June 16, 1939; s. Martin and Esther (Roth) B.; B.S., U. Mich., 1961; Ph.D., Wayne State U., 1968; m. Nancy Elizabeth Thomadsen, Aug. 14, 1966; children—Brandon Michael, Brian Daniel, Brenna Jeanne. Physicist, Chrysler Missile Div., Detroit, 1961-64, Ling-Temco-Vought, Detroit, 1964-65; staff mem. Sandia Corp., Albuquerque, 1969-78, supr. reactor safety studies div., 1978—. Mem. Criminal Justice Com., Albuquerque, 1972-73. Mem. Am. Phys. Soc., Am. Nuclear Soc., Sigma Xi. Home: 4706 Hilltop Pl NE Albuquerque NM 87111 Office: Sandia Nat Labs Kirtland AFB E Albuquerque NM 87185

BERMAN, MELVIN, marketing executive; b. N.Y.C., Apr. 23, 1942; s. Morris and Sophie (Adelman) B.; divorced; children—Martin L., Lisa D. A.A. in Electronics, Los Angeles Valley Coll., 1966; B.S. in Bus., U. Redlands, 1980. Project engr. Commatic Systems, Inc., Chatsworth, Calif., 1969-70; sr. assoc. engr. Litton Data Systems, Van Nuys, Calif., 1970-75; mgr. programs Waugh Controls Corp., Chatsworth, 1975-80, mktg. mgr., 1980—; tchr. tech. sems. Served with AC, USN 1961-65. Sr. mem. Instrument Soc. Am.; mem. So. Calif. Meter Assn. Home: 10954 Marklein Ave Mission Hills CA 91345 Office: 9001 Fullbright Ave Chatsworth CA 91311

BERMAN, NANCY MALLIN, museum administrator; b. Phila., Oct. 20, 1945; d. Philip Isaac and Muriel (Mallin) B.; m. Alan Jonas Bloch, Feb. 3, 1979; 1 dau., Rebecca Berman Bloch. B.A. in Art History, Wellesley, Coll., 1967; M.A. in Jewish Edn., Hebrew Union Coll., 1977. Asst. curator Judaica, Jewish Mus., N.Y.C., 1968-72; curator Lester Aunet Collection, N.Y.C., 1968; prodn. asst. WGBH-TV, Boston, 1967; dir. Skirball Mus., Hebrew Union Coll., Los Angeles, 1972—. Office: 3077 University Ave Los Angeles CA 90007

BERMAN, STANLEY ZISSMAN, physician, educator; b. New Orleans, June 17, 1941; s. Herman and Golda (Kleinfeldt) Zissman; adopted son Leo Berman; student Tulane U., 1959-62; B.S. in Medicine, Northwestern U., 1963, M.D., 1966; m. Leslie Dale Miller, July 7, 1968; children—Jason Lee, Laura Elizabeth. Med. intern Chgo. Wesley Meml. Hosp., 1966-67; resident in internal medicine Mayo Grad. Sch. Medicine, Rochester, Minn., 1969-71; clin. fellow in allergy and immunology Scripps Clinic and Research Found., San Diego, 1971-73; practice medicine specializing in allergy and immunology, Albuquerque, 1973—; mem. asso. staff Lovelace Med. Center, Albuquerque; clin. asso. in medicine dept. of medicine U. N.Mex., Albuquerque, 1973-76, clin. asst. prof. medicine, 1976—; attending physician in internal medicine VA Hosp., Albuquerque, 1974—; courtesy staff Presbyn. Hosp. Center. Served to lt. comdr. USNR, 1967-69. Am. Acad. Allergy grantee, 1973. Diplomate Am. Bd. Internal Medicine, Am. Bd. Allergy and Immunology, Nat. Bd. Med. Examiners. Fellow A.C.P. (sec. N.Mex. chpt. 1979, pres. 1981), Am. Acad. Allergy, Am. Coll. Chest Physicians; mem. Am., Albuquerque and Bernalillo County med. assns., Am. Thoracic Soc. (pres. N.Mex. chpt. 1982), N.Mex. Med. Soc., N.Mex. Allergy Soc. (sec. 1977-78, v.p. 1981-82, pres. 1983—), N.Mex. Lung Assn. (bd. dirs., exec. com. 1977-78), Alpha Epsilon Delta. Contbr. articles on immunology and allergy to profl. jours. and books. Office: Lovelace Med Center 5200 Gibson Blvd SE Albuquerque NM 87108

BERMINGHAM, PETER, mus. dir., curator; b. Buffalo, Nov. 6, 1937; s. Donald Michael and Margaret Anne (Murphy) B.; B.A., U. Md., 1964, M.A., 1968; Ph.D., U. Mich., 1971; m. Eleanor Joan Sigborn, Sept. 5, 1964; children—Christopher, Jason, Alexander, Noelle, Nicholas. Teaching asst. U. Md., College Park, 1965-68, U. Mich., Ann Arbor, 1968-71; asst. prof. art history U. Cin., 1971-72; curator edn. Nat. Collection Fine Arts, Smithsonian Instn., Washington, 1972-78; dir., chief curator U. Ariz. Mus. Art, Tucson, 1978—, adj. prof. art history U. Ariz., 1981-82; mem. mus. policy com. Nat. Endowment Arts, Washington, 1979-81. Served with USAF, 1956-60. Nat. Endowment Humanities tng. fellow, 1968; doctoral fellow, Smithsonian Instn., Washington, 1971-72. Mem. Coll. Art Assn., Am. Assn. Museums, Western Art Mus. Assn. Roman Catholic. Author: Jasper Cropsey: A Retrospective View of America's Painter of Autumn, 1968; The Art of Poetry, 1976; American Art in the Barbizon Mood, 1976; New Deal in the Southwest: Arizona and New Mexico, 1980; Jacques Lipchitz: Sketches and Models, 1982. Home: 3585 E Thimble Peak Tucson AZ 85718 Office: U Ariz Mus Art Tucson AZ 85721

BERNABIE, CARMEN RALPH, personnel and training official; b. Midland, Pa., Nov. 3, 1942; s. Ralph Joseph and Jean Louise (Mosticone) B.; m. Linda Kay Smith, June 4, 1966; 1 dau., Gina Marie. B.S. in Bus. Adminstrn., Butler U., 1974. Mgr. Firestone Tire and Rubber Co., Wichita, Kans., 1966; data processor Crucible Steel Co., Midland, Pa., 1966-68; regional tng. mgr. Burger Chef Systems, Indpls., 1968-78; dir. tng. and personnel Clancy's Inc., Noblesville, Ind., 1978-81; mgr. field tng. Taco Bell div. Pepsico Inc., Irvine, Calif., 1981—. Served with USAF, 1962-66. Mem. Am. Soc. Tng. and Devel., Am. Soc. Personnel Adminstrn., Soc. Performance Instn. Republican. Episcopalian. Home: 12548 Russell Ave Chino CA 91710 Office: 16808 Armstrong Ave Irvine CA 92714

BERNACCHI, RICHARD LLOYD, lawyer; b. Los Angeles, Dec. 15, 1938; s. Bernard and Anne (Belluomini) B. B.S. in Commerce (Nat. Merit Found. scholar) with honors, U. Santa Clara, 1961; LL.B. (Legion Lex scholar, Jerry Geisler Meml. scholar) with highest honors, U. So. Calif., 1964. Bar: Calif. 1964. Ptnr. Irell and Manella, Los Angeles, 1964—. Co-chmn. Regional Transp. Com., 1970-72; lectr. Am. Law Inst., 1972-73; lectr. data processing contracts and law U. So. Calif., Los Angeles, 1972, 78, 81. Served to capt. AUS, 1964-66; PTO. Mem. ABA (mem. adv. com. on edn. 1973-74, chmn. subcom. taxation computer systems of sect. sci. and tech. 1976-78), Los Angeles Bar Assn., Computer Law Assn. (dir. 1973—, chmn. preconf. symposium on law and computers 1974-75, West Coast v.p. 1976-79, sr. v.p. 1979-81, pres. 1981-83), Order of Coif, Scabbard and Blade, Beta Gamma Sigma, Alpha Sigma Nu. Author: (with Gerald H. Larsen) Data Processing Contracts and the Law, 1974. Editor-in-chief U. So. Calif. Law Rev., 1962-64. Office: 1800 Ave of Stars Los Angeles CA 90067

BERNANKE, BEN SHALOM, economist, educator; b. Augusta, Ga., Dec. 13, 1953; s. Philip Richard and Edna Rivy (Friedman) B.; m. Anna Friedmann, May 29, 1978. B.A. summa cum laude, Harvard U., 1975; Ph.D., MIT, 1979. Asst. prof. Stanford U. Sch. Bus., 1979-83, assoc. prof., 1983—; research assoc. Nat. Bur. Econ. Research, Recipient John H. Williams prize, also Allyn Young prize Harvard U., 1975; NSF grad. fellow, 1975-78; Hoover Instn. nat. fellow, 1982-83; Alfred P. Sloan research fellow, 1983-84. Mem. Am. Econ. Assn., Phi Beta Kappa. Contbr. articles to profl. jours. Home: 2850 Devonshire Ave Redwood City CA 94063 Office: Grad School of Bus 273 Stanford U Stanford CA 94305

BERNARD, CHARLES KEITH, urban transportation executive; b. Montreal, Que., Can., Nov. 4, 1938; s. George Farquer and Barbara Dunsmuir (Mac Dougal) B.; m. Sandra Elaine Boyd, Nov. 30, 1968; children—Kevin, Brendan. B.S. in Engring., McGill U., 1961; M.B.A. in Transp., U. Calif.-Berkeley, 1970; postgrad. profl. program urban transp. Carnegie-Mellon U., 1973. Engr. research and devel. Can. Nat. Rys., Montreal, 1961-63; sales and application engr. Ingersoll Rand (Australia) Pty., Ltd., Sydney, 1963-65; project engr. secondary transp. systems for world exhbn. Can. Corp., Montreal, 1965-68; planning engr. Bay Area Rapid Transit Dist., San Francisco, 1970-74, dir. mktg. and research, 1974-75, dir. planning, budgeting and research, 1975-78, staff office gen. mgr., 1978-79, gen. mgr., 1979—. Office: Bay Area Rapid Transit Dist 800 Madison St Oakland CA 94607

BERNARD, J. THOMAS, real estate developer; b. Denver, June 26, 1943; s. C.A. and G.I. Bernard; Engr. Mines, Colo. Sch. Mines, 1966; M.B.A., Boston U., 1970; m. Jacqueline J. Ranthum, Feb. 1, 1969; 1 son, James Abbot. With Bechtel Corp., 1966-67; with Cabot, Cabot & Forbes Co., 1970—, v.p., N.W. gen. mgr., Seattle, 1974—. Mem. Republican Exec. Forum, 1978—; bd. dirs. Bellevue Community Coll. Found., 1981—. Served as officer U.S. Army, 1967-69. Mem. Nat. Assn. Office and Indsl. Parks (pres. Seattle chpt. 1980, bd. dirs. 1982—, chmn. 1983), Bellevue Downtown Assn. (v.p. 1980-81, bd. dirs. 1980—), Bellevue C. of C. (bd. dirs. 1980—), Seattle C. of C. (com. chmn. 1979-80), Soc. Indsl. Realtors (assoc.), Tukwila C. of C., South Snohomish C. of C., Seattle Mcpl. League, Lambda Alpha. Clubs: Bellevue Rotary; Seattle Tennis; Bellevue Athletic. Home: 1421 Shenandoah Dr E Seattle WA 98112 Office: 3350 161st Ave SE Suite 200 Bellevue WA 98008

BERNARD, JEANNE MARIE, thermodynamics engineer; b. Los Angeles, Mar. 10, 1927; d. John Henry and Freida Marie (Engler) Frye; B.S., Calif. State U., Hayward, 1964; M.B.A., Pepperdine U., 1983; children—Anne Hazleton, Patricia George, Mary Bernard, Michael Bernard. Sr. engr. Philco-Ford Corp., Palo Alto, Calif., 1965-67; staff engr. Aerotherm Corp., Mountain View, Calif., 1967-70; research specialist systems engring./launch vehicle systems/spacecraft thermodynamics Lockheed Missile and Space Co., Inc., Sunnyvale, Calif., 1970-77, group engr. advanced vehicle systems thermodynamics, 1977-81, space tech. project engr., 1981-83, mgr. advanced programs info ctr., 1983—. Mem. AIAA, Inst. Environ. Scis., Nat. Mgmt. Assn. Club: Toastmasters (Sunnyvale, Calif.). Office: PO Box 504 Sunnyvale CA 94088

BERNARD, LARRY CRAIG, psychologist; b. Los Angeles, June 10, 1948; s. Jack and Gloria Shirley (Newman) B.; B.A., U. So. Calif., 1970, Ph.D., 1980; M.A., Calif. State U., 1975. Psychology intern Childrens Hosp., Los Angeles, 1979-80, VA Wadsworth Hosp. Med. Center, 1978-79; v.p. Pacific Garment, Inc. (now Nancy Craig Inc.), Los Angeles, 1971-79; psychologist, adolescent med. div. Children's Hosp. of Los Angeles, 1980-81; pvt. practice psychology, Los Angeles, 1981—; vis. asst. prof. psychology U. So. Calif., 1981-82; clin. neuropsychologist Daniel Freeman Meml. Hosp., Inglewood, Calif., 1982—. Mem. Am. Psychol. Assn., Calif. Psychol. Assn., Am. Assn. Sex Educators, Counselors and Therapists, Nat. Acad. neuropsychologists, Internat. Neuropsychol. Soc., Am. Acad. Behavioral Medicine, Soc. Personality Assessment, Blue Key, Alpha Phi Omega. Contbr. articles to profl. jours. Office: 566 S Vicente Blvd Los Angeles CA 90048

BERNARD, THELMA RENE, constrn. co. adminstr.; b. Phila.; d. Michael John and Louise Thelma (Hoffman) Campione; grad. high sch.; m. Gene Bernard, Feb. 17, 1962. Sec., Penn Mut. Life Ins. Co., Phila., 1958-64, Suffolk Franklin Savs. Bank, Boston, 1964-66, Holmes & Narver, Inc., Las Vegas, Nev., 1968-71; constrn. site office mgr. Miles R. Nay, Inc., Las Vegas, 1972-74; adminstrv. asst. to pres. N.W.S.

Constrn. Corp., Inc., Las Vegas, 1974-82, corporate sec., 1982—; gen. mgr., corporate sec. D.A.P., Inc., 1982—. Mem. Nat. League Am. Pen Women (pres. Red Rock Canyon br. 1976-78), Internat. Platform Assn., Nat. Assn. Women in Constrn. (corr. sec. Las Vegas chpt. 1975-77, rec. sec. 1977-78), Humanitarian Soc. Quakertown (Pa.), Antique Valentine Assn. Author: Blue Marsh, 1972; Winds of Wakefield, 1972; Moonshadow Mansion, 1973, 2d edit., 1976, Spanish transl., 1974, German transl., 1977; also song lyrics. Past editor: Cactus Courier; editor/pub. Hoyer Enthusiastic Ladies Mail Assn. Office: 305 W Saint Louis Ave Las Vegas NV 89102

BERNDLMAIER, KARL C. (BRO), counselor; b. N.Y.C., Mar. 23, 1940; s. Karl and Bertha (Kaiser) B. B.A., Iona Coll., 1961; M.S., Chgo. State U., 1970; postgrad. U. San Francisco, 1973-80. Lic. marriage and family counselor, Calif. Professed mem. Congregation Christian Bros., 1957—; cons. to marriage tribunal Diocese of Monterey (Calif.), 1977-80; guidance dir. Palma High Sch., Salinas, Calif., 1970-80, Brother Rice High Sch., Birmingham, Mich., 1980-82; counselor Butte (Mont.) Central High Sch. Diocese of Helena, 1982—. Mem. Am. Assn. Marriage and Family Therapists (clin. mem.), Am. Sch. Counselor Assn., Nat. Vocat. Guidance Assn., Nat. Council Family Relations. Roman Catholic. Club: KC. Home: 17 S Washington St Butte MT 59701 Office: 9 S Idaho St Butte MT 59701

BERNDT, JOYCE NADINE TARLEN, health care executive; b. Wichita, Kans., Feb. 23, 1937; d. Clevelon Jacob and Edna Lucile Dempsey; children—Jame Lynne Tarlen, Daren Jane Tarlen. B.A., U. Calif.-San Jose, 1969. Front office mgr. Pennsula Mortgage Co., San Jose, 1962-64; tchr. vocat. edn. to mentally retarded Joseph McKinnon Sch., San Jose, 1967-78; owner, adminstr. Victoria House and Victoria House Ranch, facility for developmentally disabled adults, Forestville, Calif., 1978—, Victoria House Transp., Forestville, 1979—; pres. bd. dirs. Sonoma County Orgn. Retarded, 1979-81, Becoming Independent, Santa Rosa, Calif., 1979-82; mem. Santa Clara County Com. Sexuality and Devel. Disabilities, 1976-79; mem. exec. com., area coordinator Santa Clara County Spl. Olympics, 1969-81. Mem. Nat. Assn. Women Execs., Calif. Tchrs. Assn., Calif. Assn. Retarded. Democrat. Roman Catholic. Address: 6871 Covey Rd Forestville CA 95436

BERNE, KATRINA H., psychotherapist, educator; b. N.Y.C., Mar. 14, 1947; d. Arthur A. and Claire M. (Beck) B.; children—Karen, Jeffrey. A.B., Douglass Coll., 1968; M.A., Montclair State Coll., 1972; M. Counseling, Ariz. State U., 1979. Art tchr. N.J. pub. schs., 1968-72; free-lance artist, Scottsdale, Ariz., 1972-75; pvt. practice psychotherapy, Mesa, Ariz., 1979—; instr. assertiveness tng., marriage enrichment Mesa Community Coll., 1979—; condr. psychotherapy workshops. Mem. Am. Personnel and Guidance Assn., Ariz. Personnel and Guidance Assn. Office: 123 N Sirrine St Suite 210 Mesa AZ 85201

BERNER, ANDREW JOSEPH, JR., psychologist, psychotherapist, researcher; b. Los Angeles, June 20, 1945; s. Andrew Joseph and Grace Elizabeth (Christy) B. B.A., U. San Francisco, 1967; M.A. (Coll. Student Personnel Inst. fellow 1967-68, Calif. State fellow 1967-68, Western Interstate Commn. on Higher Edn. fellow 1968), 1968, Ph.D., 1981. Cert. marriage, family and child counselor, Calif. Counselor, Antioch Coll., 1972-73, Dominican Coll., 1973-75; asst. to dean Calif. State U.-Long Beach, 1975-76, Harvey Mudd Coll., 1976-78; counselor Chaffey Coll., 1976-80; counseling psychologist Fullerton Coll., 1980—; pvt. practice psychotherapy, Laguna Beach, Calif., 1981—; research assoc. Claremont Ctr. for Devel. Studies; co-founder Laguna Outreach. Mem. Am. Psychol. Assn., Western Psychol. Assn. Democrat. Author: Career Direction and Redirection for Adults, 1979; Providing Student Services for the Adult Learner, 1980. Office: Fullerton Coll 321 E Chapman Fullerton CA 92632

BERNEY, ROBERT E., economist, educator, consultant; b. Walla Walla, Wash., Sept. 13, 1932; s. William Edward and Dorothy Adeline (Smith) B.; m. Marilyn Faye Trimble, Apr. 2, 1955; children—Michael Edward, Peter William, Marybeth Ann, Timothy Grant; B.A. in Bus. Adminstrn., Wash. State U., 1960, M.A. in Econs.; M.S., Ph.D. in Econs. U. Wis., Madison. Asst. prof. econs. Ariz. State U., Tempe, 1964-66; asst. prof. econs. Wash. State U., assoc. prof. econs., 1968-72, prof. econs., 1972—, dir. grad. programs in econs., 1970-78; sr. acad. resident in pub. fin. Adv. Com. on Intergovt. Relations, Washington, 1973-74; chief economist, U.S. SBA, Washington; cons. in field; research officer, Royal Commn. on Taxation, Ottawa, Can., 1963-64. Regional coordinator Ecuminical Inst., Seattle, 1970-73; social concerns chmn. Simpson United Methodist Ch., 1972-73. Served to 1st lt. U.S. Army, 1954-58. Mem. Am. Econ. Assn., Nat. Tax. Assn. Democrat. Author: Tax Structure Variations in the State of Washington, 1970; Review of Public Data Use, 1982. Office: Dept Econs 4860 Wash State U Pullman WA 99164

BERNFIELD, AUDREY ANNE, career counselor; b. Chgo., Nov. 3, 1937; d. Samuel W. and Bernice A. (Oster) Rivkin; m. Merton Bernfield, Sept. 30, 1959; children—Susan, James, Mark. B.A. in Polit. Sci., U. Ill., 1958; M.A. in Counseling, U. Santa Clara, 1976. Cert. counselor K-12. Adminstrv. asst. Booz, Allen and Hamilton, 1958-62; career counselor, 1976-82; dir. advising and career planning, program in human biology Stanford (Calif.) U., 1976—, cons. dept. English, history and econs., 1980-82, coordinator dept. student services Sch. Humanties and Scis., 1982—; profl. in residence St. Lawrence U., 1980. Active NOW, Common Cause, Palo Alto Democratic Club, Planned Parenthood, Citizens Caucus, Stanford Med. Faculty Wives. Mem. Am. Soc. Tng. and Devel., Am. Personnel and Guidance Assn., Am. Coll. Personnel Assn., Am. Vocat. Guidance Assn., Calif. Personnel and Guidance Assn., Calif. Coll. Personnel Assn., Calif. Career Guidance Assn., Counseling and Edn. Alumni Steering Com. (Santa Clara). Club: Stanford Bay Area Profl. Women's. Home: 1661 Hamilton Ave Palo Alto CA 94303 Office: Stanford U Sch Humanities and Scis Bldg 1 Stanford CA 94305

BERNHEIMER, MARTIN, music critic; b. Munich, Germany, Sept. 28, 1936; s. Paul Ernst and Louise (Nassauer) B.; came to U.S., 1940, naturalized, 1946; Mus.B. with honors, Brown U., 1958; student Munich Conservatory, 1958-59; M.A. in Musicology, N.Y.U., 1962; m. Lucinda Pearson, Sept. 30, 1961; children—Mark Richard, Nora Nicoll, Marina and Erika (twins). Free-lance music critic, 1958—; mem. music faculty N.Y.U., 1960-62; N.Y. corr. for Brit. publ. Opera, 1962-65, Los Angeles corr., 1965—; contbg. critic N.Y. Herald-Tribune, 1959-62; asst. music editor Saturday Rev., 1962-65; mng. editor Philharmonic Hall Program, N.Y.C., 1962-65; music editor, chief critic Los Angeles Times, 1965—; faculty Rockefeller program for tng. music critics at U. So. Calif., 1966-71; mem. music faculty UCLA, 1969-75, Calif. Inst. for the Arts, 1975-83, Calif. State U., Northridge, 1978-82. Recipient Deems Taylor award ASCAP, 1974, 78; Pulitzer prize for disting. criticism, 1982. Contbr. articles newspapers, mags. in field, also liner notes for recordings; radio and TV appearances. Office: Los Angeles Times Times-Mirror Square Los Angeles CA 90053

BERNHOFT, THOMAS EDWARD, investment advisor; b. Cavalier, N.D., Dec. 13, 1942; s. Johann Edward and Anna (Haldora) B.; m. Deanna Jane Graybeal, Nov. 9, 1979; children—Thomas Edward, Brian J., Kirstine A., Jennifer M., Jeremy M., Kimberly A. B.A., U. Puget Sound, 1969, M.B.A., 1979; C.P.A., Wash. Stockbroker Dean Witter & Co., Tacoma, 1970-72; auditor Def. Contract Audit Agy., Kent, Wash., 1975-78; instr. acctg. St. Martin's Coll., Lacey, Wash., 1978-80; chmn. Forbes Group, Inc., Tacoma, 1979—; contract mgr. Tacoma Boatbuilding Co., 1980-82; instr. acctg. and fin. U. Puget Sound, Tacoma, 1980-82; v.p., dir. Stephan Johannson & Assocs., Inc., Tacoma, 1982—; investment advisor, prin. Forbes Portfolio Mgmt., Tacoma, 1982—. Mem. Am. Inst. C.P.A.s, Wash. Soc. C.P.A.s, Nat. Acctg. Assn. Republican. Lutheran. Club: Oakbrook Tennis. Office: 1501 Pacific Ave Tacoma WA 98402

BERNICK, JOHN FREDERICK, ins. co. exec.; b. Oskaloosa, Iowa, Sept. 13, 1917; s. Frederick F. and Jennie Emaline (Williams) B.; B.S. in Indsl. Econs., State U. Iowa, 1940; m. June E. Blake, Nov. 30, 1940; children—Patricia Anne, John Williams. In sales Goodyear Tire & Rubber Co., 1940; with Wausau Ins. Co., 1946-82, v.p. mktg., sales and advt., Wausau, Wis., 1966-70, v.p. Pacific Southwest, Los Angeles, 1970-82; founder J.F. Bernick Cons., Inc., ins. and fin. corp. mgmt. services, 1982—; lectr. in field. Chmn. U.S. Census Tract, Marathon County, Wis., 1966-68; bd. dirs., v.p. Greater Los Angeles Safety Council; 1st v.p. Greater Los Angeles Council on Alcoholism. Served with U.S. Army, 1940-45; PTO. Paul Harris fellow, 1980. Mem. Calif. Workers Compensation Inst. (v.p. 1977-80, dir. 1972-80), Am. Mgmt. Assn. (planning council), Ins. Ednl. Assn. (dir. 1978, v.p., treas. 1980), Western Ins. Info. Service (pres. 1979), Calif. Ins. Guarantee Assn. (gov. 1979—), Delta Upsilon, Alpha Phi Omega. Methodist. Clubs: Los Angeles (v.p.), Shriners, Rotary. Contbr. articles to profl. jours.

BERNIE, MARSHALL, warehouse co. exec.; b. Chgo., June 30, 1922; s. David and Esther (Bolton) B.; grad. Wright City Coll., Chgo., 1940; student Lawrence U., Appleton, Wis., 1942; widower; children—Linda, Patricia, Allison. Pres., chief exec. officer M.L. Bernie Co. Inc., Los Angeles, 1946—; dir. Image Interprises; adv. Superior Savs. & Loan Assn., First State Bank (both Los Angeles); mem. adv. com. bus. affairs U.S. Congress. Mem. President's Task Force. Served with USNR, 1942-45. Mem. Nat. Tire Dealers Assn., U.S. Small Bus. Assn. Address: 5012-5016 W Venice Blvd Los Angeles CA 90019

BERNOLFO, JOSEPH EDWARD, JR., investor; b. N.Y.C., Sept. 3, 1911; s. Joseph Edward and Lydia (Wickson) B.; m. Marie Odell, June 20, 1940; children—Joseph Edward III, David W., Gloria Bernolfo Rothwell. B.S., Northwe. U., 1932; LL.D. (hon.), Westminster Coll., 1976. Master, Millbrook Acad., 1935-36, engr. Pantapec Oil, S.Am., 1937-39; engr. Associated Oil & Gas Co., 1939-42; chmn. Bamberger Investment & Exploration Co., 1945-81; pvt. investor, Salt Lake City, 1981—; dir., mem. audit com. Zions Utah Bancorp.; dir. Zions 1st Nat. Bank. Bd. regents U. Utah, 1967-79; chmn. bd. trustees Westminster Coll., 1970-74; bd. dirs. John Ernest and Ruth Eleanor Bamberger Meml. Found., 1961—; Utah state chmn. March of Dimes-Nat. Found., 1968-74. Served to maj. C.E., AUS, 1942-45. Decorated Bronze Star. Republican. Roman Catholic. Clubs: Alta, Salt Lake Country, New State Gun (Salt Lake City). Office: 163 S Main St Salt Lake City UT 84111

BERNSTEIN, AMY J., bank executive, lawyer; b. Worcester, Mass., Feb. 4, 1953; d. Max L. and Dorothy T. (Goodstein) Bernstein; m. Robert F. Goldstein, Dec. 28, 1974. B.A. cum laude, U. Pa., 1974; J.D. cum laude, U. San Francisco, 1977. Bar: Calif. 1974. Research atty. Superior Ct., San Mateo County, Calif., 1974-78; assoc. Levy & Levit, San Francisco, 1979; atty. trust and investment legal dept. Wells Fargo Bank, San Francisco, 1979-80, asst. v.p., counsel, 1980—. Mem. Calif. Bankers Assn. (govtl. affairs com.), Calif. Bar Assn. (trust adminstrn. job com.). Home: 86 San Gabriel Ave San Francisco CA 94112 Office: Wells Fargo Bank 475 Sansome St 10th Floor San Francisco CA 94163

BERNSTEIN, ANNE CAROLYN, psychotherapist, psychology educator; b. N.Y.C., Apr. 8, 1944; d. Alfred J. and Clara (Handelman) B.; m. Conn M. Hallinan, Jan. 16, 1982; 1 son, David Alexander; 3 stepsons, Sean, Antonio, Brian. B.A. magna cum laude, Brandeis U., 1965; Ph.D. (USPHS grantee), U. Calif.-Berkeley, 1973. Psychologist, Family Therapy Inst. of Marin, San Rafael, Calif., 1972-73; psychologist, lectr. Cowell Coll., U. Calif.-Santa Cruz, 1973-75; clin. lectr. family practice residency program, U. Calif.-San Francisco, 1974-76; contract instr. John F. Kennedy U., Orinda, Calif., 1975, Calif. Sch. Profl. Psychology, San Francisco, 1975-77, Calif. State U.-Hayward, 1977; program dir. M.A. in Psychology and Family Reunification, San Francisco Dept. Social Services, Lone Mountain Coll., and U. San Francisco, 1977-81; prof. Wright Inst., Berkeley, Calif., 1981—; psychologist Rockridge Health Plan, Oakland, Calif., 1979—; pvt. practice clin. psychology and psychotherapy, Berkeley, 1974—. Treas., bd. dirs. Children's Rights Group, San Francisco, 1976-83. Mem. Psychotherapy Inst. (mem. coordinating council 1981-82), Am. Family Therapy Assn., Am. Psychol. Assn., No. Calif. Family Therapy Assn., Sex Info. and Edn. Council of U.S., Am. Assn. Sex Educators, Counselors and Therapists, Am. Orthopsychiat. Assn., Soc. for Psychol. Study of Social Issues, Phi Beta Kappa. Author: The Flight of the Stork, 1978, 2d. edit., 1980; contbr. articles to profl. jours., including Parents Mag. Office: 2728 Durant St Berkeley CA 94704

BERNSTEIN, ELMER, composer, conductor; b. N.Y.C., Apr. 4, 1922; s. Edward and Selma (Feinstein) B.; student N.Y. U.; m. Pearl Glusman, Dec. 21, 1946; children—Peter Matthew, Gregory Eames; m. 2d, Eve Adamson, Oct. 25, 1965; children—Emily Adamson, Elizabeth Campbell. Concert pianist, N.Y.C., Phila., Chgo., 1946-50; composer music for UN radio shows, 1949; composer mus. film scores 1950—, including Man with the Golden Arm, The Ten Commandments, The Magnificent Seven, Summer and Smoke, Walk on the Wild Side, To Kill a Mockingbird (Golden Globe award Hollywood Fgn. Press 1962), The Great Escape, The Birdman of Alcatraz, Hud, Sudden Fear, God's Little Acre, Sweet Smell of Success, Desire Under the Elm, Some Came Running, From the Terrace, Love With the Proper Stranger, Baby the Rain Must Fall, The Caretakers, The Sons of Katie Elder, Cast a Giant Shadow, Hawaii, Seven Women, True Grit, The Shootist, National Lampoon's Animal House, Bloodbrothers, Meatballs, Airplane!, Stripes, Going Ape, The Chosen; scores for TV series include Julia, Owen Marshall, Ellery Queen, Serpico. Pres., Young Musicians Found., 1961—. Recipient Motion Picture Exhibitor Laurel awards 1956, 57, 62, Emmy award for best music written for TV, Making of a President, 1964, Acad. award for best original music score for Thoroughly Modern Millie, 1968. Mem. Acad. Motion Picture Arts and Scis. (1st v.p. 1963—), The Thalians (v.p. 1959-62), Screen Composers Assn. (dir.), Composers and Lyricists Guild Am. (pres. 1970—), Nat. Acad. Rec. Arts and Scis. (dir.). Office: care Acad Motion Picture Arts and Scis 8949 Wilshire Blvd Beverly Hills CA 90211*

BERNSTEIN, LEWIS, psychologist; b. Stanhope, N.J., Jan. 28, 1915; s. Philip and Dora (Kaplan) B.; m. Rosalyn Samuel, June 18, 1940; children—Paul Alam, Ellen. B.S., Wayne State U., 1939, M.A., 1941; Ph. D., U. Colo., Boulder, 1951. Diplomate Am. Bd. Profl. Psychology, examiner, 1964-72. Chief clin. psychology sect. VA Med. Ctr., Denver, 1951-59, research cons., 1959-62; dir. psychol. services and research Children's Asthma Research Inst. and Hosp., Denver, 1959-62; chief psychology service VA Med. Ctr., Milw., 1962-77; head psychology sect. dept. psychiatry Med. Coll. of Wis., Milw., 1962-77; clin. prof. dept. psychiatry U. Calif., San Diego, 1978—, vis. prof. dept. psychology, 1978—; vis. prof. Middlesex Hosp. and Med. Sch., London (Eng.), 1972; chmn. Colo. State Bd. Psychologist Examiners, 1961-62; vis. scientist Jackson Meml. Labs., Bar Harbor, Maine, 1958. Served to 1st lt. U.S. Army, 1942-46. Recipient VA commendation, 1975; USPHS grantee, 1957-59, 1959-62, 1961-66. Fellow Am. Psychol. Assn., AAAS; mem. Interam. Soc. Psychology, Psi Chi, Sigma Xi. Author: (with R.S. Bernstein) Interviewing: A Guide for Health Professionals, 3d edit., 1980; (with B.C. Burris) The Contribution of the Social Sciences to Psychotheraphy, 1967; contbr. chpts. to books, articles to profl. jours. Home: 3355 Caminito Gandara La Jolla CA 92037 Office: Dept Psychology U Calif San Diego La Jolla CA 92037

BERNSTEIN, MOREY, manufacturing corporation executive; b. Pueblo, Colo, June 21, 1919; s. Samuel and Celia (Wagner) B.; m. Hazel Doris Higgins, Aug. 1, 1948. B.S. in Econs. with distinction, U. Pa., 1941; postgrad. Columbia U., 1953. Ptnr., Bernstein Bros. Equipment Co., Pueblo, 1941—, Bernstein Bros. Investment Co., Pueblo, 1941—; pres. Bernstein Bros. Machinery Corp., 1946-62; dir. Minnequa Bank, Pueblo, 1951-55; chmn. bd. Double-B, Inc., 1970—, Wholesalers, Inc., 1970—. Chmn., Bernstein Bros. Parapsychology Found., 1969—. Mem. Am. Soc. Psychical Research, Pueblo C. of C. Jewish. Author: The Search for Bridey Murphy, 1956. Patentee instant fence, pronto panels, kwik-lok portable corrals. Home: 1819 Elizabeth St Pueblo CO 81003 Office: Bernstein Bros Equipment Co 134 N Mechanic St Pueblo CO 81003

BERNSTEIN, NORRIS STANLEY, management consultant; b. Los Angeles, Nov. 14, 1929; s. Maurice Edward and Sophie Lillian (Borson) B.; B.A., U. Calif.-Berkeley, 1951; m. Irvene Alva Clayton, Sept. 15, 1951; children—Perri Lynn, Robert Clayton. Ptnr., Bernstein Foods Corp., Seal Beach, Calif., 1951-62, pres., 1962-74, head subs. Nalley Foods div. Curtice-Burns Inc., 1974-76, also head product mktg.; exec. v.p. Funky Foods Inc., Buena Park, Calif., 1976-77; pres. NSB Corp. mgmt. cons., Norris Bernstein, Creative Mktg., 1978—; ptnr. Mrs. Baker's Calif. Cookies, Munich, Ger. Mem. adv. bd. Nat. Bank So. Calif. Bd. dirs. Long Beach Community Hospital, Ennoble Group Ctrs., Harbor Area unit Am. Cancer Soc. Mem. Assn. Dressings and Sauces (chmn. bd. 1973-75), Pres.'s Roundtable, Internat. Mgmt. Cons. (chpt. dir.), U. Puget Sound (chmn., 1978-80. SAG, AFTRA, Long Beach C. of C. Clubs: Rotary, Masons; Internat. City (Long Beach). Home and Office: 9309 Marina Pacific Dr N Long Beach CA 90803

BERNSTEIN, SOL, physician, med. service adminstr.; b. West New York, N.J., Feb. 3, 1927; s. Morris Irving and Rose (Leibowitz) B.; A.B. in Bacteriology, U. So. Calif., 1952, M.D., 1956; m. Suzi Maris Sommer, Sept. 15, 1963; 1 son, Paul. Intern Los Angeles County Hosp., 1956-57, resident, 1957-60; practice medicine specializing in cardiology, Los Angeles, 1960—; staff physician dept. of medicine Los Angeles County Hosp.-U. So. Calif. Med. Center, Los Angeles, 1960—, chief cardiology clinics, 1964, asst. dir. dept. medicine, 1965-72, chief profl. services, Gen. Hosp., 1972-74; med. dir. Los Angeles County-U. So. Calif. Med. Center, 1974; med. dir. of central region Los Angeles County, 1974-78; asso. prof. medicine U. So. Calif. Sch. of Medicine, Los Angeles, 1968—; cons. Crippled Childrens Service, Calif., 1965—. Served with AUS, 1946-47, 52-53. Diplomate Am. Bd. Internal Medicine. Fellow A.C.P., Am. Coll. Cardiology; mem. Am. Fedn. Clin. Research, N.Y. Acad. Sci., Los Angeles, Am. heart assns., Los Angeles Soc. Internal Medicine, Los Angeles Acad. Medicine, Sigma Xi, Phi Beta Phi, Phi Eta Sigma, Alpha Omega Alpha. Contbr. articles on cardiac surgery, cardiology and diabetes to med. jours. Home: 4966 Ambrose Ave Los Angeles CA 90027 Office: 1200 N State St Los Angeles CA 90033

BERNTSON, ERIC, Canadian provincial government executive; b. Oxbow, Sask., Can., May 16, 1941; s. Arthur and Johanna B.; m. Jean Howell; children—Kira, Lee Anne, Roland, Ben. Student U. Calgary. Mem. Sask. Legis. Assembly, Regina, 1975—, minister of agr., dep. premier and govt. house leader. Served with Royal Can. Air Force, Royal Can. Navy. Conservative. Club: Royal Can. Legion. Office: Saskatchewan Legis Assembly Legislative Bldg Room 340 Regina SK S4S 5Z5 Canada

BERO, ANDY ERNEST, fire chief; b. Gary, W.Va., Aug. 26, 1925; s. Florian and Anna (Forgo) Biro; m. Loretta Victoria Seidel, Dec. 8, 1926; children—Mark A., Andrea Giudice; student Flint (Mich.) Jr. Coll., 1946-48. Mem. Gardena (Calif.) Fire Dept., 1956—, fire capt., 1968-73, battalion chief, 1973-75, fire chief, 1975—. Mem. Outstanding Citizen Com., Gardena Friends of Library, 1962-83; pres. Gardena Valley Art Assn., 1963-66. Served with AC, USN, 1943-46. Mem. Calif. Fire Chiefs Assn., Western Fire Chiefs Assn., Internat. Fire Chiefs Assn. Democrat. Roman Catholic.

BEROZ, NEAL STUART, psychotherapist; b. Boston, Feb. 22, 1951; s. Arthur Bernard and Elaine (Goodman) B.; B.S. with honors, Northeastern U., Boston, 1973; M.S., SUNY-Albany, 1978, Ed.S., 1979. Social worker Parsons Child and Family Ctr., Albany, 1973-76; coordinator counseling/tng. Drug Edn. and Counseling Program, SUNY-Albany, 1976-78; outpatient therapist Panhandle Mental Health Ctr., Scottsbluff, Nebr., 1979-81; cons. Area I Office Mental Retardation, Hay Springs, Nebr., 1980-81; cons. Pine Ridge Job Corps, Chadron, Nebr., 1980-81; clin. supr. Alpha House Resdl. Drug Treatment, Portland, Oreg., 1981—; cons. in field. Mem. Am. Psychol. Assn., Am. Personnel and Guidance Assn., Am. Mental Health Counselors Assn. Office: 1325 SW Gibbs Portland OR 97201

BERQUAM, EUGENE MAURICE, educational administrator; b. Moorhead, Minn., Mar. 29, 1946; s. Eugene Douglas and Frances Anabelle (Carney) B.; m. Holly Anne Aldridge, July 3, 1982. B.S., Moorhead State U., 1969; M.S., Western Ill. U., 1974; Ph.D., U. Fla., 1981. Elem. tchr., Jamestown, N.D., 1970-73; grad. asst. Western Ill. U., Macomb, 1973-74; elem. prin., Hardin, Mont., 1974-78; grad. trainee U. Fla., Gainesville, 1978-80; spl. project adminstr. Orange County Schs., Orlando, Fla., 1980-81; elem. prin., Port Angeles, Wash., 1981—. Mem. Developmental Disabilities Adv. Bd., Clallam County, Wash., 1982—. Served with U.S. Army N.G., 1966-72. Mem. Assn. Supervision and Curriculum Devel., Wash. Assn. Sch. Adminstrs., Phi Delta Kappa. Home: 1525 W 7th St Port Angeles WA 98362 Office: Jefferson Sch 218 E 12th St Port Angeles WA 98362

BERRES, FRANCES BRANDES, clinical psychologist; b. Chgo., d. Max and Anna (Gould) Brandes; m. George Berres, July 6, 1941 (dec.); 1 dau., Barbara Lo Monaco. B.A., UCLA, 1937, M.A., 1940, Ph.D., 1967. Head remedial instrn., tchr. English, Huntington Beach (Calif.) High Sch., 1940-44; psychologist, tchr. Fernald Sch., psychology dept. UCLA, 1950-52, assoc. dir., acad. adminstr., lectr. learning disabilities, dept. psychology, 1952-71; coordinator child-related programs info. project Neuropsychiat. Inst., 1971-73; pvt. practice clin. psychology, Santa Monica, Calif., 1976—. Past bd. dirs. Los Angeles Philharm. Soc. Women's Com.; past pres., bd. dirs. Marina del Rey Symphony Soc.; sec. bd. dirs. Internat. Children's Sch. Grantee, State of Calif., Dept. Edn., Div. Compensatory Edn., 1966-69, Office Edn., HEW, 1966-70, NIMH, 1970-75, Office Vice Chancellor, UCLA, 1972. Mem. Am. Psychol. Assn. Author: Deep Sea Adventure Series, 1959, 62, 67, 71, 79; A Survey of Child Related Programs, 1975. Office: 2122 Wilshire Blvd Santa Monica CA 90403

BERRIER, DAVID JEWELL, electrical engineer, aerospace executive; b. Murphysboro, Ill., Mar. 20, 1934; s. Jewell Hilbourne and Thelma Irene (Walker) B.; m. Mary Rose Butcher, Dec. 26, 1954. B.S. in Elec. Engring. (scholar.), U. Ill., 1957. Project engr. Gen. Elec. Corp., Ontario, Calif., 1960-65; engr./scientist/specialist McDonnell Douglas, Long Beach, Calif., 1965-67; staff engr. TRW Systems, Redondo Beach, Calif., 1967-70; program mgr. Hughes Aircraft, Fullerton, Calif., 1970-79; space test program mgr. Aerospace Corp., Los Angeles, 1979—; cons.

aerospace equipment. Active in YMCA, 1964-73, Jr. C. of C., 1964-65, Ontario-Upland, Philharmonic Assn., Los Angeles, 1965-78, Long Beach, 1979—. Served to lt. U.S. Navy, 1957-67. Mem. AIAA, Soc. Flight Test Engrs., Nat. Security Indsl. Assn., Program Mgmt. Inst., Tech. Mktg. Soc. Am., Mensa. Republican. Clubs: Toastmasters (Los Angeles), Aerospace Employees Assn. Travel. Contbr. articles to profl. jours.

BERRISFORD, CHRISTOPHER, headmaster; b. Liphook, Eng., Jan. 27, 1930; s. Edwin Aris and Susan Helena (Claughton) B.; B.A., Oxford U., 1954, M.A., 1957; Ed.M., Harvard, 1962; m. Brenda Margaret Houfton, Mar. 23, 1963 (div.); children—Nicholas, Sara. Came to U.S., 1957, naturalized, 1967. Chmn. history dept. Univ. Sch., Victoria, B.C., Can., 1954-57; asst. headmaster St. Mark's Sch., Dallas, 1957-63, headmaster, 1963-69; headmaster Harvard Sch., North Hollywood, Calif., 1969—. Mem. vis. com. Harvard Sch. Edn., 1964-70; mem. com. on entrance procedures Coll. Entrance Exam. Bd., 1965-66; mem. ind. schs. adv. com. Ednl. Records Bur., 1966-69. Mem. Citizens Com. on Goals for Dallas, 1965-69; vice-chmn. City of Dallas Task Force on Health, 1967-69; trustee Ind. Schs. Overseas, Crossroads Sch., 1971-76, S.W. Outward Bound, 1977-80, Windward Sch.; mem. UCLA Arts Council, 1977-81; dir. Inst. Adminstrv. Leadership, 1980—. Served to 2d lt. Royal Arty., 1948-50. Mem. Nat. Inst. Public Affairs, Headmasters Assn. (sec. 1979-82, pres. 1982-83), Country Day Sch. Headmasters Assn. (pres. 1983-84), Calif. Assn. Ind. Schs. (trustee 1974-77), English Speaking Union (chmn. student exchange 1982-83). Co-author: The Expanding School Environment. Address: 3700 Coldwater Canyon Rd North Hollywood CA 91604

BERRY, ANDREA JILL, food company official; b. Long Beach, Calif., Nov. 21, 1955; d. Herbert Alexander and Dorothy Mildred (Lazenby) B.; 1 dau., Brieanne Lee Berry. A.A., Calif. State U.-Fullerton, 1975; B.A. in History with honors, Calif. State U.-Irvine, 1977. Investigator, interviewer criminal div. Orange County Pub. Defender's Office, Orange, Calif., 1977-78; personnel supr. R.L. Kautz Ins. Mgmt., Irvine, Calif., 1978-79; equal opportunity coordinator Disneyland, Anaheim, Calif., 1980-82; corp. exec. recruiter Hunt-Wesson Foods Inc., Fullerton, Calif., 1982—. Bd. dirs. Orange County Urban League, Dayle McIntosh Ctr. for Disabled; mem. Youth Motivational Task Force Orange County. Mem. AAUW, Nat. Assn. Exec. Females, Inst. Food Technologists, Am. Soc. Personnel Adminstrs., Orange County Equal Opportunity Employers Assn. (dir. 1980—). Democrat. Presbyterian. Office: Hunt-Wesson Foods 1645 W Valencia Ave Fullerton CA 92625

BERRY, BETTY MARIE NEFF, nurse, educator; b. Durkee, Oreg., Oct. 9, 1925; d. Charles Frederick and Blanche Olive (Hickerson) Schuck; R.N., St. Elizabeth Hosp. Sch. Nursing, 1946; postgrad. St. Joseph's Coll., 1978-82, No. Mont. Coll., 1982—; m. John Wesley Berry, June 12, 1981; children by previous marriage—Charles, Susan, Doris, Bill. Obstetrical nurse various hosps., various locations worldwide, 1957-76; instr. Gt. Falls (Mont.) Vo-tech. Center, 1976—. Pres. bd. dirs. Unity Ch., Great Falls, 1976-80; pres. Health Occupations Div., Vocat./Tech. Edn., State of Mont., 1980-82, sec.-treas., 1982—. Mem. Beta Sigma Phi. Democrat. Mem. Unity Ch. of Truth. Club: Soroptomist. Home: 1001 11th St NW Great Falls MT 59404 Office: 2100 16 Ave S Great Falls MT 59405

BERRY, CAROLYN, artist; b. Sweet Springs, Mo., June 27, 1930; d. Charles Thomas and Florence Valora (Harrison) B.; m. Robert E. Becker, Oct. 13, 1974; m. Benjamin Bishop, Oct. 12, 1952; children—Deborah Rachael, Rebecca. Student Columbia (Mo.) Coll., 1948-49; B.A., U. Mo., 1953; postgrad. in spl. edn. Humboldt U., 1969-71. One person shows include: Monterey Peninsula Mus. Art, 1966, 75, Marist Coll., Poughkeepsie, N.Y., 1969, Everywoman, Menlo Park, Calif., 1976, Studio Performance, Palo Alto, Calif., 1980; group exhbns. include: Franklin Furnance, 1980, Sao Paulo Biennale, Brazil, 1981, Women's Caucus For Art, N.Y.C., 1982; represented in permanent collection: Monterey Peninsula Mus. Art, Brandeis U., Waltham, Mass., Marist Coll., Poughkeepsie, Tweed Mus., Duluth, Minn., Ind. Press Archive, Rochester, N.Y., Albrecht Mus., St. Joseph, Mo., Portland (Maine) Sch. Art, Art Inst. Chgo.; dir. Handicapped Activities Unltd., Pacific Grove, Calif., 1971—. Calif. Arts Council grantee, 1980; recipient Best Small Painting award Pacific Grove Mus. Natural History, 1981. Mem. Womens Caucus for the Arts, Internat. Soc. Copier Arts, Women in Arts Found., Nat. Womens Polit. Caucus, NOW. Home: 78 Cuesta Vista Dr Monterey CA 93950 Office: 511 Grand Ave Pacific Grove CA 93950

BERRY, GLENN, educator, artist; b. Glendale, Calif., Feb. 27, 1929; s. B. Franklin and Heloise (Sloan) B.; B.A. magna cum laude, Pomona Coll., 1951; B.F.A. (Honnold fellow), M.F.A., Sch. Art Inst. Chgo., 1956. Faculty, Humboldt State U., Arcata, Calif., 1956-81, prof. art, 1969-81, emeritus, 1981—. Exhibited one-man shows Ingomar Gallery, Eureka, Calif., 1968, Ankrum Gallery, Los Angeles, 1970, Esther Bear Gallery, Santa Barbara, Calif., 1971; exhibited in group shows Palace of Legion of Honor, San Francisco, Pasadena (Calif.) Art Mus., Rockford (Ill.) Coll., Richmond (Calif.) Art Mus., Henry Gallery U. Wash., Seattle; represented in permanent collections at Storm King Art Center, Mountainville, N.Y., Kaiser Aluminum & Chem. Corp., Oakland, Calif., Palm Springs (Calif.) Desert Mus., Hirshhorn Mus., Washington, others; mural Griffith Hall, Humboldt State U., 1978. Mem. Phi Beta Kappa. Home: PO Box 2241 McKinleyville CA 95521

BERRY, GORDON LAVERN, educator; b. Dayton, Ohio, Oct. 7, 1932; s. Marcus and Gertrude Mary (Hughes) B.; B.S., Central State U., 1955; M.S., U. Wis., 1961; Ed.D., Marquette U., 1969; m. G. Juanita Jackson, Mar. 31, 1956; children—Gordon L., Steven Wayne, Cheryl Denise. Counseling psychologist Milw. Tech. Coll., 1965-68; asst. to v.p. acad, affairs Marquette U., 1968-70; asst. dean Grad. Sch. Edn., UCLA, 1970-75; asso. prof. Grad. Sch. Edn., 1975-80, prof., 1980—; Marquette U. Ralph Metcalfe Chair Disting. Lectr.; sr. cons. children's programs CBS TV, N.Y., 1972—; bd. dirs. S.W. Regional Lab., 1976-77. Fanon Research and Devel. Center fellow, Inst. for Social Sci. Research fellow. Mem. Nat. Assn. Sch. Psychologists, Am. Personnel and Guidance Assn., Assn. Supervision and Curriculum Devel., Am. Orthopsychiat. Assn., Phi Delta Kappa, Alpha Phi Alpha. Contbr. articles on counseling psychology, edn., TV, social behavior. Office: U Calif at Los Angeles 405 Hilgard Ave Los Angeles CA 90024

BERRY, JOHN CHARLES, clinical psychologist, educational administrator; b. Modesto, Calif., Nov. 29, 1938; s. John Wesley and Dorothy Evelyn (Harris) B.; A.B., Stanford, 1960; postgrad. Trinity Coll., Dublin, Ireland, 1960-61; Ph.D., Columbia, 1967; m. Arlene Ellen Sossin, Oct. 7, 1978; children—Elise, John Jordan, Kaitlyn. Research assoc. Judge Baker Guidance Center, Boston, 1965-66; psychology asso. Napa State Hosp., Imola, Calif., 1966-67, staff psychologist, 1967-75, program asst., 1975-76; program dir. Met. State Hosp., Norwalk, Calif., 1976-77; asst. supt. Empire (Calif.) Union Sch. Dist., 1977—. Mem. Am. Psychol. Assn., Assn. Calif. Sch. Adminstrs., Sigma Xi. Contbg. author: Life History Research in Psychopathology, 1970. Home: 1308 Lorry Ave Modesto CA 95355 Office: Empire Union Sch Dist 200 G St Empire CA 95319

BERRY, MARCY MAY, dental health service organization executive; b. Wellsville, N.Y., June 18, 1950; d. Marshall Newton and Miriam May (Lingle) Jones; m. Ronald Glenn Berry, Aug. 7, 1967 (div.) 1 dau., Angelia Lynn. Student Chaffey Jr. Coll., Alta Loma, Calif. Jr. clk. N.Y. Life Ins., Los Angeles, 1970-73; jr. acct. FMC Corp., Pomona, Calif., 1973-78; sec. Gen. Med. Ctrs., Anaheim, Calif., 1978-79, service rep., 1979-80; dir. mktg. services Protective Health Providers, San Diego, 1980-81, Dental Health Services, Long Beach, Calif., 1981—. Mem. Nat. Assn. Female Execs. Democrat. Home: 11186 Greenwood Way Ontario CA 91761 Office: 146 E 3d St Long Beach CA 90802

BERRY, MICHAEL B., accountant; b. Buckhannon, W.Va., July 30, 1936; s. Gillette P. and Lucille L. (Taylor) B.; m. Janette Dooley, Aug. 5, 1957; children—Michael, Gillette, Jeffrey. Degree in Acctg., Ariz. State U., 1954-58. C.P.A., Ariz. Ptnr., G.P. Berry & Co., Phoenix, 1958-67; pvt. practice acctg., Phoenix, 1967-74; ptnr. Main Hurdman, C.P.A.s (formerly Main Lafrentz & Co.), Phoenix, 1974—, ptnr., 1983—, ptnr. in charge audit dept., 1983—. Pres. bd. dirs. Boys' Clubs Phoenix, 1976; trustee Doctors Hosp., Phoenix. Recipient Golden Man and Boy award Boys' Clubs Am., 1976. Mem. Am. Inst. C.P.A.s, Ariz. Soc. C.P.A.s. Clubs: Phoenix Country, Ariz. Biltmore Country, Masons, Shriners. Office: 20000 Valley Bank Center Phoenix AZ 85073

BERRY, RICHARD DOUGLAS, architect, educator, urban designer; b. Denver, Oct. 28, 1926; s. Howard Thomas and Susie Ann (Ross) B.; B.A. in Humanities, U. Denver, 1951; B. Architecture, U. Calif.-Berkeley, 1957. Scenic artist, lighting designer Univ. Civic Theatre and Central City Opera Festival, Denver, 1948-49; asso., project dir. Victor Gruen Assos., Architects and Planners, Los Angeles, and New York, 1957-63; mem. faculty U. So. Calif., Los Angeles, 1963—, prof. architecture, 1976—; planning, programming cons. on new community devel., Gen. Electric, 1967-68, U.S. Dept. Housing and Urban Devel., 1973-74; cons. Gen. Electric Found., 1967-68, U. N.C., 1971-73; vis. prof. urban design U. Wash., Seattle, 1969. Served with U.S. Army, 1951-53; Korea. Recipient Research and ednl. grants from several pub. and pvt. orgns.; Urban Design award for downtown Cin. Renewal Plan, editors of Progressive Architecture Mag., 1963. Mem. Am. Inst. Cert. Planners, Am. Planning Assn., AIA (asso. mem.), AAUP, Urban Land Inst. Office: Sch of Architecture Univ of So Calif Los Angeles CA 90089

BERRY, ROBERT ALLEN, health care corp. exec.; b. Nampa, Idaho, Jan. 5, 1932; s. Marion Allen and Clara Carolyn (Schleuter) B.; B.S., U. Oreg., 1954; m. Barbara Beverly Inman, May 17, 1958; children—Steve, Mike. Mgr. profl. relations Blue Cross of Oreg., Portland, 1966-74, exec. dir. Oreg. Found. for Med. Care, 1974—. Loaned exec. United Way, 1965. Served to lt. col. AUS, 1956-57. Mem. Hosp. Fin. Mgmt. Assn. (William G. Follmer award 1972), Am. Med. Peer Rev. Assn., Conf. Oreg. County/State Med. Execs. Democrat. Lutheran. Office: Oreg Found for Med Care 5210 S W Corbett Ave Portland OR 97201

BERRY, WILLIAM BENJAMIN NEWELL, paleontologist; b. Boston, Sept. 1, 1931; s. John King and Margaret Elizabeth (Newell) B.; A.B., Harvard U., 1953, A.M., 1955; Ph.D., Yale U., 1957; m. Suzanne Foster Spaulding, June 10, 1961; 1 son, Bradford Brown. Asst. prof. geology U. Houston, 1957-58; vis. asst. prof. paleontology U. Calif., Berkeley, 1958-60, mem. faculty, 1960—, prof. paleontology, 1968—, dir. mus. paleontology, 1975—. Guggenheim fellow, 1966-67. Fellow Explorers Club; mem. Palentol. Soc., Geol. Soc. Norway. Author: Growth of a Prehistoric Time Scale, 1968; editor U. Calif. Geol. Sci. Series, 1973—; contbr. numerous articles profl. jours. Office: Dept/Museum Paleontology Univ Calif Berkeley CA 94720

BERSELL, ROBERT TOHMS, association executive; b. Chgo., Mar. 22, 1927; s. E. Leonard and Maurine Helen (Tohms) B.; m. Dolores LaCalle, Dec. 1, 1956; children—Michael, Kevin, Sean, Colin, Bridget. B.S.B.A., Northwestern U., 1951; M.Ed., Antioch U., 1979. Membership services dir. Ind. Ins. Agts. N.H., 1978-79; dir. edn. Ind. Ins. Agts. Ill., 1979; exec. v.p. Ind. Ins. Agts. N.Mex., Albuquerque 1979—, also dir. Task Force on Continuing Edn. Ind. Ins. Agts. Am. and mem. Task Force Subcom. on Delivery of Edn. Services; mem. adv. bd. N.H. Ins. Adv. Com. Sigmund Livingston Interfaith fellow, Northwestern U., 1951, numerous awards Jaycees, 1957-64. Mem. Am. Soc. Assn. Execs., Ind. Ins. Agts. Am., N.Mex. Soc. Assn. Execs., Assn. Ind. Ins. Agts. Execs., Northwestern U. Alumni Assn. Roman Catholic. Office: 8015 Mountain Rd Pl NE Albuquerque NM 87110

BERSHON, LAWRENCE CHOLLETT, advertising manager; b. Toledo, July, 21, 1933; s. Albert Lois and Miriam Alice (Chollett) B.; m. Dorrine Bloom, June 3, 1965; children—Eric, Nicole. A.B., Princeton U., 1955. Trainee Benton & Bowles, N.Y.C., 1955, media buyer, 1956-57; media supv. McCann Erickson, N.Y.C., 1958-62; account exec. Ted Bates, N.Y.C., 1963-65; account supr. Grey Advt., N.Y.C., 1965-67; advt. mgr. Atlantic Richfield Co., N.Y.C., 1968-70, media mgr., 1970-76, mgr. advt. services, Los Angeles, 1977—; tchr. Advt. Ctr. Los Angeles; lectr. U. So. Calif., UCLA. Bd. dirs. Advt. Industry Emergency Fund; sec., bd. dirs. Leukemia Soc. Am.; mem. capital fund raising com. Princeton U. Served in U.S. Army, 1956-58. Recipient cert. of merit Leukemia Soc., 1982. Mem. Advt. Club Los Angeles (dir., pres.), Hollywood Radio-TV Soc., Assn. Nat. Advertisers, Am. Advt. Fedn. Republican. Jewish. Office: 515 S Flower St Los Angeles CA 90071

BERSI, ROBERT MARION, university executive; b. Ark., June 4, 1932; s. Mack M. and Angelina (Perona) B.; m. Ann Brakebill, Nov. 17, 1975; 1 dau., Margaret Ann. N.S., U. Pacific, 1958; M.A., Stanford U., 1962, Ph.D., 1965. Research assoc. Stanford (Calif.) U., 1964-66; exec. asst. to pres. Calif. State U.-Dominguez Hills, 1966-70, prof. edn., 1970-75, dean innovative programs, 1971-73, v.p. instl. devel., 1973-75; pres. Western Conn. State Coll., Danbury, 1975-81; chancellor U. Nev. System, Reno, 1980—; mem. exec. com. Conn. Council on Higher Edn. Served with USN, 1952-54. Recipient Carson Black Heritage Assn. award of merit, 1973. Mem. Am. Assn. Sch. Adminstrs., Western Assn. Schs. and Colls., Greater Danbury C. of C. (dir.). Author: Restructuring the Baccalaureate, 1973; mem. editorial adv. bd. Coll. Mgmt. mag. 1973-75; contbr. articles to profl. publs. Office: U Nevada Systems Central Office Office of the Chancellor 405 Marsh Ave Reno NV 89509

BERTAIN, G. JOSEPH, JR., lawyer; b. Scotia, Calif., Mar. 9, 1929; s. George J. and Ellen Veronica (Canty) B.; A.B., St. Mary's Coll. of Calif., 1951; J.D., Cath. U. Am., 1955; m. Bernardine Joy Galli, May 11, 1957; 1 son, Joseph F. Admitted to Calif. bar, 1957, U.S. Supreme Ct. bar, 1969; assoc. firm Joseph L. Alioto, Esquire, San Francisco, 1955-57, 59-65; asst. U.S. atty., No. Dist. Calif., 1957-59; pvt. practice law, San Francisco, 1966—; spl. confidential advisor on jud. selection to Calif. Gov. Reagan, San Francisco, 1967-74. Panel mem. Am. Forum of Air, Washington, 1954-55; chmn. San Francisco Lawyers Com. for Election of Ronald Reagan, 1966, 70, 80; chmn. San Francisco Lawyers Com. for Better Govt., 1980-83; confidential advisor on fed. judiciary to Senator HayaKawa, 1981-82; bd. regents St. Mary's Coll., 1980—. Recipient Signum Fidei award St. Mary's Coll., 1976. Mem. Am., Fed. (del. to 9th circuit jud. conf. 1967-76), Calif. bar assns., Am. Judicature Soc., St. Thomas More Soc. San Francisco, Calif. Acad. of Scis., Mus. Soc., Assn. Former U.S. Attys. and Asst. U.S. Attys. of No. Calif. (past pres.). Roman Catholic. Clubs: Commonwealth, Commercial, Olympic, KC. Editor-in-chief Cath. U. Am. Law Rev., 1954-55, Supreme Ct. Hist. Soc. Office: Union Bank Bldg Suite 955 50 California St San Francisco CA 94111

BERTELSEN, KARYN PICCIONI, educator; b. Standardville, Utah, Nov. 20, 1944; d. John and Edith (Toson) Piccioni; m. Bruce Bertelsen, July 15, 1967; children—Kristy Lee, Kelly Ann. A.S., Coll. Eastern Utah, 1963; B.S., Utah State U., 1967; M.S., Brigham Young U., 1983. Tchr. home econs. Pub. Schs. Sunnymead (Calif.), 1967-68; receptionist, sec., Pitts., 1968-69; tchr. home econs. Helper (Utah) Jr. High Sch., 1969—, tchr. phys. edn., 1971-74; real estate agt. ERA, Price, Utah, 1979-83. Mem. Carbon County Edn. Assn., Utah Edn. Assn., NEA, Utah Vocat. Home Econs. Assn., Delta Delta Delta, Delta Kappa Gamma, LWV. Clubs: Elks, Bus. and Profl. Women. Home: 322 N 5th E Price UT 84501 Office: 130 Uintah St Helper UT 84526

BERTHOLD, EARL FREDERICK, project engr.; b. Canby, Oreg., July 28, 1926; s. Otto Frederick and Eleonora Mathilda (Weleber) B.; B.S. in Bus. Adminstrn., U. Oreg., 1952; m. Joan Claire Pearson, Dec. 28, 1949; children—Pamela Joanne, Martin Otto., Jr. progress engr. Kaiser Engrs., Oakland, Calif., 1952-55, asst. project engr., 1955-61; sr. field engr. Kaiser Engrs., Richland Wash., 1961-63, project engr., Oakland, 1963-83. Served with USAF, 1944-45. Republican. Lutheran. Home: 737 Laurel Dr Walnut Creek CA 94596

BERTHOLD, JANICE ANNETTE, life insurance company executive; b. Boulder, Colo., May 10, 1947; d. Maurice A. and Alice O. Notch; m. Thomas R. Berthold, July 21, 1973; children—Timothy Eugene, Alison Marie. B.A. in English, U. San Francisco, 1969. C.L.U. Life specialist Safeco Life, Burlingame, Calif., 1974-77; brokerage supr. Aetna Life, San Jose, Calif., 1977-80, gen. agt., 1980-83, mktg. mgr., 1983—. Mem. Calif. Senate Adv. Com. on Ins. Recipient Pres.'s Trophy, Aetna Life, 1983; Nat. Mgmt. award Gen. Agts. and Mgrs. Conf., 1983. Mem. San Jose Chartered Life Underwriters Assn., Santa Clara County Estate Planning Council, San Jose Life Underwriters Assn., San Jose Ind. Agts. Assn., Nat. Assn. Life Underwriters. Republican. Roman Catholic. Office: 1150 N 1st St San Jose CA 95112

BERTHOLD, JEANNE SAYLOR, psychologist, nurse, educator; b. Kansas City, Mo., June 4, 1924; d. Carl Richard and Ann Elizabeth (Wolfe) Saylor; divorced. B.S., U. Calif., Berkeley, 1953, M.S. in Psychiat. Nursing, 1955, Ph.D. in Counseling Psychology, 1961. Staff nurse Vis. Nurse Assn., Los Angeles, 1945-46; sch. nurse Los Angeles Bd. Edn., 1946-47; staff asst. Sonoma County Hosp., Santa Rosa, Calif., 1947-51; psychiat. nurse Langley Porter Neuropsychiat. Inst., San Francisco, 1955-61; instr., lectr. Sch. Nursing U. Calif. Med. Center, San Francisco, 1955-61; asst. prof. Francis Payne Bolton Sch. Nursing Case Western Res. U., Cleve., 1961-63, asso. prof., 1963-64, prof., 1964-71, chairperson research group, 1964-67; adj. prof. U. Colo. Sch. Nursing, Denver, 1971-73; prin. investigator, program dir. Western Interstate Commn. for Higher Edn., Regional Program for Nursing, Research and Devel., Boulder, Colo., 1971-73; prof. dept. community and family medicine U. So. Calif. Sch. Medicine, 1973—; dir. nursing research Rancho Los Amigos Hosp., Downey, Calif., 1973-75, dir. nursing research and edn., 1975—; adj. prof. Calif. State U., Long Beach, 1977—. Pres., bd. trustees Am. Nurses Found., 1969-71. Mem. Nat. League Nursing, Am. Psychol. Assn., AAAS, Center Study of Democratic Instns., Inst. Soc., Ethics and the Life Scis., Am. Congress Rehab. Medicine, Assn. Rehab. Nurses, Highland Alumnae Assn., Calif. Alumni Assn., Pi Lambda Theta, Sigma Theta Tau. Mem. editorial bd. nursing research Am. Jour. Nursing, 1969-72, chairperson, 1972-73; contbr. chpts. to books, articles to profl. jours. Office: Rancho Los Amigos Hosp 7601 E Imperial Hwy Rancho Learning Center Downey CA 90242

BERTOZZI, JOANNE MARIE, accountant; b. Pawtucket, R.I., Oct. 22, 1957; d. Peter Anthony and Audrey Jean (Bennett) B.; m. Verle L. Bartels, June 28, 1980 (div.). B.A., Calif. State U.-Stanislaus-Turlock, 1979; postgrad. Golden Gate U., San Francisco. C.P.A., Calif. Staff acct. Bertozzi & Co., C.P.A.s, Modesto, Calif., 1975-81, ptnr. (name changed to Bertozzi, Johnston & Co. C.P.A.s), 1981—. Pres., Modesto Venture Club; mem. Modesto Civic Theatre, Stanislaus county Comm. for Women, Women's Resource Center, Modesto. Mem. Calif. Soc. C.P.A.s, Am. Inst. C.P.A.s. Home: 1820 Scenic Apt 147 Modesto CA 95355 Office: 621 14th St Modesto CA 95353

BERTRAM, PHYLLIS ANN, educator, lawyer; b. Long Beach, Calif., July 30, 1954; d. William Joseph and Ruth Ann (Hoge) B.; B.S., U. So. Calif., 1977; M.B.A., Calif. State U., Long Beach, 1978; J.D., Western State U. Coll. Law, 1982. Bar: Calif. 1982. Instr., lifeguard City of Long Beach, 1972-78; ind. sports ofcl. for high schs. and colls. internat. contests, 1972—; instr. fire sci., seamanship and nav. Long Beach City Coll., 1977—; asst. commr. Met. Conf. Bus. Cons. Bus. Adminstrn., 1978—; asst. commr. So. Calif. Conf. Vol. ARC; cardio-pulmonary resuscitation instr.; mem. Republican Nat. Com. Mem. So. Calif. Basketball Ofcls. Assn., So. Calif. Volley Ball Ofcls. Assn., Swim Ofcls. Assn. (pres. 1978-79), Softball Ofcls. Assn., Assn. M.B.A. Execs., U. So. Calif., Calif. State U. Long Beach alumni assns., Commerce Assos., Delta Theta Phi (treas.). Club: Seal Beach Yacht. Home: 2237 Albury Ave Long Beach CA 90815 Office: 4901 E Carson St Long Beach CA 90808

BERTRAND, WATSON CLARK, mfg. co. exec.; b. Kansas City, Mo., Dec. 7, 1931; s. Lawrence Walter and Frances Evelyn (Smith) B.; student Kalamazoo Coll.; B.A. with honors, Mich. State U., 1957; m. Sarah Louise Beals, June 23, 1956; children—Sandra Kay, Mark Steven, Paul Steven. Sr. accountant Price Waterhouse & Co., Detroit, Los Angeles, 1957-62; asst. div. controller Garrett Corp., Los Angeles, 1962-66; sec.-treas., dir. Info. Devel. Co., Santa Ana, Calif., 1966-69; treas., dir. TRE Corp., Beverly Hills, 1969—. Served with USAF, 1951-55. C.P.A., Calif., Mich. Mem. Delta Sigma Pi. Episcopalian. Home: 2405 N Hathaway St Santa Ana CA 92701 Office: 9460 Wilshire Blvd Beverly Hills CA 90212

BERTSCH, NED ANTHONY, clergyman; b. Portland, Oreg., Sept. 20, 1933; s. LaVerne A. and Velma (Root) B.; B.A., Calif. Bapt. Coll., 1967; M.Div., Golden Gate Bapt. Theol. Sem., 1971; D.Min., Maranatha Bible Sem., 1978; m. Virginia McKoon, Sept. 3, 1966; children—Bryan Anthony, Paul LaVerne. Ordained to ministry So. Baptist Conv., 1966; asst. pastor, Ontario, Calif., 1963-64, Banning, Calif., 1964-66; interim pastor 1st So. Bapt. Ch., Banning, 1966; pastor 1st Bapt. Ch., Hesperia, Calif., 1966-68, Rodeo, Calif., 1968-71, West Santa Rosa (Calif.) Bapt. Ch., 1971-72; mem. staff Campus Crusade for Christ Internat., San Bernardino, Calif., 1972-78, nat. coordinator host family devel., 1973-78; pastor 1st Bapt. Ch., Searless Valley, Trona, Calif., 1978-80; nat. coordinator Am. for Jesus, Campus Crusade for Christ Internat., San Bernardino, 1980—, nat. ch. relations coordinator AGAPE Movement, 1980—; mem. Greg Smith Singers, 1962-63. Served with USAF, 1952-61. Club: Rotary. Office: Campus Crusade for Christ Internat Arrowhead Springs Rd San Bernardino CA 92414

BESSE, RALPH STEPHEN, JR., university agricultural administrator; b. Cheyenne, Wyo., Dec. 26, 1919; s. Ralph Stephen and Helen Margaret (Haines) B.; B.S. in Agronomy, Oreg. State U., 1943, M.Agr., 1971; m. Virginia Monhinweg, June 24, 1945; children—Marilyn, Susan, Joyce. Ofcl. milk tester U. Calif.-Davis, 1939-40; internat. sales mgr. Ferry-Morse Seed Co., Mountain View, Calif., 1946-63; county extension agt. Oreg. State U., Corvallis, 1963-78, extension area supr., 1978-81, assoc. dir. internat. agr., 1981—. Served with USN, 1943-45. Mem. Am. Soc. Agronomy, Council Agrl. Sci. and Tech., Corvallis C. of C. Republican. Methodist. Club: Rotary. Home: 1516 NW 12th St Corvallis OR 97330 Office: Office Internat Agr Oreg State U Corvallis OR 97331

BESSE, ROBERT GALE, food technologist; b. Calgary, Alta., Can., Feb. 11, 1923 (parents Am. citizens); s. Rene A. and Doria (Bray) B.;

student N.Mex. State Tchrs. Coll., 1941-42; B.S., Oreg. State Coll., 1948; m. Mary A. McKay, Sept. 11, 1948; children—Rene A., Madeliene E., Leon J., Alan G., Michele M., Marc, Angelique. Supt., also in quality control Alderman Farms Frozen Foods, Dayton, Oreg., 1948-50, plant supt., 1950-54; chief food technologist Kuner Empson Co., Brighton, Colo., 1954-60; food technologist Northwest Packing Co., Portland, Oreg., 1960-62; food technologist research and devel. Nat. Can Corp., San Francisco, 1962-67, mgr. Pacific Area tech. research service, 1967-70; mgr. tech. services Western Can Co., 1970—; dir. Material Metrics. Pres. St. Gregory's Theatre Guild; vol. hunting safety instr. Calif. Fish and Game Dept., 1972—. Served with Signal Corps, AUS, 1942-45. Mem. Inst. Food Technologists (sec.-treas. Rocky Mountain sect.; exec. com. Oreg. sect.), Confraternity of Christian Doctrine Cath. (pres.), Northwest Canners and Packers, Packaging Inst. (profl. mem.), Nat. Canners Assn. (mem. western lab. adv. com.), No. Calif. Metal Decorating Assn. (pres.), Western Packaging Assn.; Soc. Mfg. Engrs. Club: Elks. Home: 264 Portola Dr San Mateo CA 94403 Office: 1849 17th St San Francisco CA 94103

BESSER, LES, cons. engr.; b. Budapest, Hungary, Aug. 27, 1936; s. L. and A. (Valkar) B.; came to U.S., 1963; B.S. in E.E. and B.A., U. Colo., 1966; M.S. in E.E., U. Santa Clara, 1973; m. Joyce Ann Bogart, Feb. 22, 1969; children—George Scott, Nancy Ann. Project supr. Hewlett Packard Co., Palo Alto, Calif., 1966-69; engring. mgr. Fairchild Semiconductors, Palo Alto, 1970-72, Farinon Elec. Co., San Carlos, Calif., 1974-75; pres. Compact div. Comsat Gen. Integrated Systems, Palo Alto, Calif., 1976—; leader tech. seminars for engrs. and scientists; lectr. UCLA, U. Md.; cons. Recipient IEEE-MIT Application award, 1983. Mem. IEEE (sr.), Eta Kappa Nu, Sigma Tau, Tau Beta Pi. Club: AYSO. Contbr. articles to profl. jours. Contbg. author: Electronic Measurements and Instrumentation, 1971; Computer Aided Design of Microwave Circuits, 1982. Patentee in field; author two interactive circuit optimization computer programs. Home: 1109 Russell Ave Los Altos CA 94022 Office: 1070 E Meadow Circle Palo Alto CA 94303

BESSLER, URSULA MARTA, management service manager; b. Eberswalde, Germany, Nov. 30, 1938; d. Georg Wilhelm and Maria Anna (Lamparter) Bromann; came to U.S., 1957, naturalized, 1962; m. Thomas Ray Bessler, Apr. 24, 1957; children—Joann Ursula, Jacqueline Sue, Michelle Gai. Grad. Hiese Sch. Bus., Frankfurt, Germany, 1956; student Am. Inst. Banking, 1965-70, Am. Mgmt. Assn. Extension Inst., Portland State U., 1980-82. With U.S. Nat. Bank, Portland, Oreg., 1964-72; mktg. analyst, acct. BFG Bank, Frankfurt, Germany, 1972-77; mgr., EEO officer Multnomah-Washington Employment and Tng. Agy., Portland, 1978—. Mem. Internat. Personnel Mgrs. Assn., Nat. Assn. Female Execs. Republican.

BEST, GARY ALLEN, special education educator, consultant; b. Occanside, Calif., July 27, 1939; s. Charles Richard and Vivian Elaine (Misner) B.; m. Shirley J. Seelhammer, Dec. 18; 1 dau., Joanna Elaine. B.A., Calif. State U.-Los Angeles, 1961, M.A., 1965; Ph.D., U. Minn., 1968. Cert. for life in elem. edn., teaching of orthopedically handicapped including cerebral palsy. Classroom tchr. physically handicapped, Los Angeles, 1961-65; instr. spl. edn. U. Minn., 1966-68; prof. spl. edn. Calif. State U.-Los Angeles, 1968—; cons. spl. edn., physically handicapped and sex edn., 1968—; vis. prof. Wis. State U., 1966, Western Mich. U., 1972, U. Victoria, 1970, 74; community adv. com. dept. spl. edn. Calif. State U.-Los Angeles. Bd. dirs. East San Gabriel Valley Hospice, Inc. Recipient Outstanding Prof. award Calif. State U., Los Angeles, 1982 83. Mem. Council Exceptional Children (pres. div. physically handicapped), Am. Assn. Sex Educators, Counselors and Therapists (cert.), Calif. Assn. Profs. Spl. Edn., Calif. Educators of Physically Handicapped. Author: Individuals with Physical Disabilities, an Introduction to Educators, 1978; editor: Selected Readings in Special Education, 1970; contbr. articles to profl. jours., chpts. to books.

BEST, GARY DEAN, historian; b. Estherville, Iowa, Sept. 18, 1936; s. Frederick William and Maxine Avis (Bassett) B.; B.A., U. Hawaii, Manoa, 1968, M.A., 1969, Ph.D., 1973; m. Matsue Ichino, May 2, 1958. Asst. prof. history Sophia U., Japan, 1973-74; Fulbright research prof. Tokyo U., 1974-75; asst. prof. history U. Hawaii, Hilo, 1975-78, assoc. prof., chmn. dept. history, 1978-82, prof., 1982—. Served with USN, 1954-59. Am.-East Asian Relations fellow Am. Hist. Assn., 1973-74; Fulbright scholar, Japan, 1974-75; Nat. Endowment for Humanities grantee, 1976, Nat. Endowment Humanities fellow, 1982-83; vis. scholar Hoover Instn. on War, Revolution and Peace, 1983. Mem. Orgn. Am. Historians, AAUP. Republican. Author: The Politics of American Individualism, 1975; To Free A People, 1982; Herbert Hoover: The Post-Presidential Years, 1983. Office: 1400 Kapiolani St Hilo HI 96720

BEST, JOY MORGAN, home economist; b. Partales, N.Mex., Oct. 21, 1934; d. R.C. Ike and Nell Bruton Morgan; m. Wendell Best, Dec. 29, 1952; children—Barbara Rogers, Monte, Kent, Kyle. B.S., Eastern N.Mex. U., 1970, M.E., 1971. Instr. home econs. Eastern N.Mex. U., 1970-74; home economist Coop. Extension Service, 1977—. Mem. Nat. Assn. Extension Home Economists, Nat. Home Econs. Assn., N.Mex. Assn. Extension Home Economists (pres. 1980-81), PEO, Federated Women's Club. Democrat. Baptist. Office: Coop Extension Service Courthouse B-6 Portales NM 88130

BEST, LOIS VIOLA, retired educator; b. Okla., Sept. 11, 1918; B.E. in Fine Arts, Music Edn., Seattle Pacific U., 1956; m. Harold G. Best; children—Jerry, Judi. Dir. vocal music South Bend (Wash.) Sch. Dist., 1955-57; dir. vocal music Raymond (Wash.) Sch. Dist., 1957-59; asst. dir. music Tacoma (Wash.) Sch. Dist. 10, 1959-78, coordinator fine arts, 1978-82. Bd. dirs. Tacoma Philharm., 1979—. Mem. Wash. Music Educators Assn., Music Educators Nat. Conf., Puget Sound Music Suprs. and Coordinators (pres. 1981-82), Adminstrv. Women in Edn. (treas. 1983—), Sigma Alpha Iota (pres. 1983-84), Delta Kappa Gamma (pres. 1976-78). Home: 2021 Narrows View Circle NW C-124 Gig Harbor WA 98335

BESTWICK, WARREN WILLIAM, constrn. co. exec.; b. Missoula, Mont., June 27, 1922; s. William Andrews and Beatrice Anna (Eddy) B.; student Glendale Coll., 1941, U. Mont., 1942; B.A., U. Wash., 1949; m. Glenette Haas, Sept. 11, 1949; children—Sharon Kaye, Carol Eddy, Jan Marie. Sr. acct. Frederick & Nelson, Seattle, 1950; controller, bus. mgr. Virginia Mason Hosp., Seattle, 1958-64; controller Bumstead Woolford Co., Seattle, 1964-68; controller, treas. Wash. Asphalt Co., Seattle, 1968-72; exec. v.p., sec. treas. Wilder Constrn. Co., Inc., Bellingham, Wash., 1972-77, pres., 1977—, also dir.; dir., pres. Wilder Group, Wilder Constrn. Co., Inc., Thermal Radiation Co., Inc., TRC Thermal Reduction, Ltd.; treas., dir. Vincent Contracting, Inc., May Contracting, Vincent Corp.; trustee Mt. Baker Mut. Savs. Bank, Bellingham; chmn. Area IV advisory bd. Wash. Dept. Commerce and Econ. Devel. Pres. Shuckson Found. Whatcom County. Served to col., pilot USMCR, 1942-74. Decorated D.F.C. (3), Air medal (7). Mem. Assn. Wash. Bus. (dir.), Whatcom County Devel. Council (past dir. and pres.), Bellingham C. of C. (past dir.), Marine Res. Officers Assn. (past dir. Seattle), Res. Officers Assn., Marine Corps League, Associated Gen. Contractors Am., United For Wash., U. Wash. Alumni Assn., Bus. Industry Polit. Action Com. Lutheran. Clubs: Wash. Athletic (Seattle); Bellingham Golf and Country, Bellingham Yacht; Rotary (pres.). Home: 1000 E Toledo St Bellingham WA 98226 Office: 2006 State St N Bellingham WA 98225

BETTENCOURT, EDWARD MANUEL, ednl. adminstr.; b. San Jose, Calif., Dec. 26, 1941; s. Manuel Anthony and Mary Isabel (Azavedo) B.; B.A., San Jose State U., 1963, M.A., 1969; Ed.D., U. Oreg., 1979; m. Connie J. McClure, Aug. 13, 1967; children—Derek McClure, Ryan Edward. Tchr. schs., Calif., 1963-69, W. Ger., 1969-71, Eng., 1971-73; asst. prin. Lakenheath (Eng.) Am. Sch., 1973-75; prin. Copenhagen Am. Sch., 1975-77; prin. elem. sch. W. Verne McKinney Sch., Hillsboro, Oreg., 1980—; asst. prof. U. Oreg., 1977-80. Mem. Nat. Assn. Elem. Sch. Prins., Confedn. Oreg. Sch. Adminstrn., Assn. Supervision and Curriculum Devel., Kappa Delta Pi. Home: 2405 SE Meadow Lark Dr Hillsboro OR 97123 Office: 535 NW Darnielle St Hillsboro OR 97123

BETTES, WILLIAM HENRY, JR., aeronautical engineer; b. Hollywood, Calif., June 2, 1928; s. William H. and Rosella J. B.; B.S., Northrop Inst. Tech., 1961; M.S., Calif. Inst. Tech., 1963; m. Peggy A. O'Neal, 1950; children—Belinda, David; m. 2d, Valeria A. Hamilton, May 24, 1958; children—Kimberly, Brian, Keith. Test project engr. So. Calif. Wind Tunnel, Pasadena, 1956-59; supr. Galcit 10 foot wind tunnel Calif. Inst. Tech., Pasadena, 1960-63, asst. dir., 1964-65, dir., 1966-69, dir. exptl. facilities, 1970—, mgr. grad. aero. labs., 1976—. Served with U.S. Army, 1950-52. Decorated Bronze Star medal. Mem. AIAA, Soc. Automotive Engrs. (chmn. aero. subcom.), Subsonic Aerodynamic Testing Assn. Republican. Office: 205-45 Calif Inst Tech Pasadena CA 91125

BETTS, BARBARA LANG (MRS. BERT A. BETTS), lawyer, rancher; b. Anaheim, Calif., Apr. 28, 1926; d. W. Harold and Helen (Thompson) Lang; B.A., Stanford, 1948; LL.B., Balboa U., 1951; m. Roby F. Hayes, July 22, 1948 (dec.); children—John Chauncey IV, Frederick Prescott, Roby Francis II; m. 2d, Bert A. Betts, July 11, 1962; 1 son, Bruce Harold. Admitted to Calif. bar, 1952, U.S. Supreme Ct. bar, 1978; pvt. practice law, Oceanside, Calif., 1952-68, San Diego, 1960—, Sacramento, 1962—; partner firm Roby F. Hayes & Barbara Lang Hayes, 1952-60; city atty., Carlsbad, Calif., 1959-63; v.p. Isle & Oceans Marinas, Inc., 1970-80, W. H. Lang Corp., 1964-69; sec. Internat. Prodn. Assos., 1968—, Margaret M. McCabe, M.D., Inc., 1977—. Chmn., Traveler's Aid, 1952-53; pres. Oceanside-Carlsbad Jr. Chambrettes, 1955-56; vice chmn. Carlsbad Planning Commn., 1959; mem. San Diego Planning Congress, 1959; v.p. Oceanside Diamond Jubilee Com., 1958; dir. No. San Diego County Chpt. for Retarded Children, 1957-58. Candidate Calif. State Legislature, 77th Dist., 1954; mem. Calif. Dem. State Central Com., 1960-66; co-chmn. 28th Congl. Dist., Dem. State Central Com., 1960-62; alt. del. Dem. Nat. Conv., 1960. Mem. Am. Judicature Soc., Nat. Inst. Mcpl. Officers, Am., Calif., San Diego County bar assns., Oceanside C. of C. (sec. 1957, v.p. 1958, dir. 1953-54, 57-59), AAUW (legislative com. 1958-59; local pres. 1959-60; asst. state legislative chmn. 1958-59), No. San Diego County Assn. Chambers of Commerce (sec.-treas.), Bus. and Profl. Women's Club (So. dist. legislation chmn. 1958-59), D.A.R. (regent Oceanside chpt. 1960-61), San Diego C. of C., San Diego Hist. Soc., Fullerton Jr. Assistance League, U.S. Supreme Ct. Hist. Soc., Calif. Scholarship Fedn., Loyola Guild of Jesuit High Sch., Phi Beta Kappa. Clubs: Soroptimist Internat. (pres. Oceanside-Carlsbad 1958-59, sec. pub. affairs San Diego, Imperial Counties 1954; pres. of pres.'s council San Diego and Imperial counties and Mexico 1958-59), Barristers. Author: (with Bert A. Betts) A Citizen Answers. Office: Betts Ranch PO Box 306 Elverta CA 95626 also 3119-A Howard Ave San Diego CA 92104

BETTS, BERT A., ret. accountant; b. San Diego, Aug. 16, 1923; s. Bert A. and Alma (Jorgenson) B.; B.B.A., Calif. Western U., 1950; m. Barbara Lang; children—Terry Lou, Linda Sue, Sara Ellen, Bert Alan, Randy Wayne, LeAnn, Bruce Harold, Chauncey, Fred, Roby. Accountant John R. Gillette, 1946-48; partner Gillette & Betts, 1949-50; pvt. accounting practice, 1951-54; partner Betts & Munden, Lemon Grove, Calif., 1954-57; sr. partner Bert A. Betts & Co., 1958-59; treas. State of Calif., 1959-67; founder Bert A. Betts & Assos., 1967-77; treas., chief exec. officer Internat. Prodn. Assos., 1968-72; gen. partner Sacramento Mct. Airport Properties No. 4, Ltd., 1970—. Mem. Lemon Grove Sch. Bd., 1954-57. State chmn. Max Baer Heart Fund; state employees chmn. Heart Fund; state employees chmn. Am. Cancer Soc., 1962-64, bd. dirs. County unit, 1963-69, pres., 1967-68, campaign chmn., mem. exec. com., 1965; bd. dirs. Lifetime Communities, Inc. Served as 1st lt., pilot, USAAF, 1942-45. Decorated D.F.C., Air Medal with 4 oak leaf clusters; Louisville award Municipal Finance Officers U.S. and Can., 1963; award Calif. Municipal Treasurers Assn., 1964. C.P.A., Calif. Mem. San Diego Squadron Air Force Assn. (past vice comdr.), Am. Legion, VFW, Native Sons Golden West, N.Y. Municipal Forum, Nat. Assn. State Auditors, Comptrollers and Treasurers, Municipal Finance Officers Assn. of U.S. and Can., Beta Alpha Psi (hon.), Alpha Kappa Psi (hon.). Presbyn. Mason, Eagle. Clubs: Men's (pres.), Lions (treas.) (Lemon Grove); Commonwealth (San Francisco). Home: 441 Sandburg Dr Sacramento CA 95819 also Betts Ranch E Levee Rd Elverta CA 95626

BETTS, JAMES WILLIAM, JR., financial analyst, consultant; b. Montclair, N.J., Oct. 11, 1923; s. James William and Cora Anna (Banta) B.; m. Barbara Stoke, July 28, 1951; 1 dau., Barbara Susan (dec.). B.A., Rutgers U., 1946; M.A., U. Hawaii, 1957. With Dun & Bradstreet, Inc., 1946—, service cons., 1963-64, reporting and service mgr., 1964-65, sr. fin. analyst, Honolulu, 1965—; owner, operator Portfolio Cons. of Hawaii, 1979—. Served with AUS, 1942-43. Mem. Am. Econ. Assn., Western Econ. Assn., Atlantic Econ. Soc. Republican. Episcopalian.

BETTS, WILBUR WARD, engineer, author, historian; b. Rockford, Ill., Aug. 28, 1904; s. Fred Grant and Edith Belle (Beach) B.; B.S. with honors in Mech. Engring., U. Ill., 1935; m. Sarah Elizabeth Farrey, June 2, 1928; children—Mary Edith, Sharon Ann; m. 2nd., Mary Roberta Van DeWalker, Oct. 19, 1970. Design engr. Ingersoll Milling Machine Co., Rockford, 1922-32; asst. sales mgr. Barnes Drill Co., Rockford, 1935-37; sales engr. English & Miller Machinery Co., Detroit, 1937-38; design engr. Farrel Birmingham Gear Corp., Buffalo, 1938-40; group leader Bell Aircraft Corp., Buffalo, 1940-42, W. Coast Engring. rep. B-29 Com., 1942-44; product analyst Webster-Brinkley Co., Seattle, 1944-46; chief engr. Kirsten Pipe Co., Seattle, 1946-48; adminstrn. engr. B47 and Bomarc Functional tests Boeing Co., Seattle, 1948-61; test devel. engr. DynaSoar Gliders, Seattle, 1962, charge test verification saturn booster, New Orleans, 1963-65, adminstrn. engr. 747 airplane, 1965-69; test procedures cons., Seattle, 1969—. Chmn. adv. com. Office of Price Adminstrn., State of Wash., 1944-46. Recipient Bronze Tablet award U. Ill., 1935. Mem. Soc. Automotive Engrs. (25-Yr. Membership award 1969), Am. Indian Profl. Assos., Mayflower Soc., Sons of Union Vets. of Civil War, SAR, Gen. James A. Longstreet Meml. Assn., James Willard Schultz Soc., Jet Pioneers Assn. U.S.A., Phi Eta Sigma, Pi Tau Sigma, Theta Tau, Tau Beta Pi. Methodist. Clubs: Horseless Carriage (pres. 1958), N.W. Intertribal. Contbr. articles to profl. jours. Home: 1317 44th Ave SW Seattle WA 98116 Office: PO Box 3707 13 59 Seattle WA 98124

BEURET, JULES WILLIAM, real estate exec.; b. Jersey City, May 25, 1914; s. Jules and Johanna (Luhrs) B.; B.S., Columbia U., 1935; m. Martha Elizabeth Bucher, Aug. 6, 1937; children—Peter B., Martha Lynn, Christopher W., Stephen G. Sales and marketing exec. Vick Chem. Co., N.Y.C., 1935-40; account exec., v.p. Fuller & Smith & Ross, Inc., Cleve. and Pitts., 1940-59; dir. advt. Magnavox Co., Ft. Wayne, Ind., 1961-62; dir. marketing Pfizer Labs., 1962-65; v.p., dir. marketing services ARA Services, Inc., Phila., 1966-73; corporate v.p., Cummings Realty & Trust Co., Tucson, 1974—, also dir.; cons. marketing. Pres., Tucson Gen. Hosp. Found. Served with USAAF, 1944-45. Mem. Health Industries Assn. (officer, dir. 1971-73), Realtors Mktg. Inst. Home: 111 E Florence Rd Tucson AZ 85704 Office: 1725 N Swan Rd Tucson AZ 85712

BEUTLER, H. LEROY, ins. exec.; b. Emmett, Idaho, May 23, 1927; s. Heber Frederick and Beulah Ann (Aston) B.; student Boise Jr. Coll., 1946; m. Rubye Jeanette Livingston, Mar. 1, 1974; children—Janet, Kathleen, Ann Marie, Karen; stepchildren—Patrick, Dawn, Kathleen, Colleen, Lawson. Asst. chief examiner Idaho Surveying and Rating Bur., Boise, 1947-51; adminstrv. mgr. Gen. Ins. Co., Albuquerque, 1951-56; exec. v.p. Clinton P. Anderson Agy. (merged with Alexander and Alexander, Inc. 1980), Albuquerque, 1956-80, gen. mgr., 1963-80, mng. v.p., 1980-82; v.p. Alexander and Alexander, Inc., 1982—; mem. N.Mex. Ins. Adv. Bd. Mem. Gov.'s Com. Employment of Handicapped. Served with U.S. Navy, 1944-46. Mem. Greater Albuquerque C. of C. (com. chmn.), Newcomen Soc., Albuquerque Ins. Agts. Assn. (past pres.), Ind. Ins. Agts. N.Mex. (past pres.), Nat. Assn. Ind. Ins. Agts. (state nat. dir. 1967-72), N.Mex. Surplus Lines Brokers Assn., Rocky Mountain Territorial Conf. Agts. Adv. Com. Clubs: Albuquerque Petroleum, Knife and Fork, U. N.Mex. Boosters, Rotary, Elks, Masons, Shriners. Democrat. Home: 7500 Tamarron Pl NE Albuquerque NM 87109 Office: PO Box A Albuquerque NM 87103

BEUTLER, LARRY EDWARD, clinical psychologist, psychology educator; b. Logan, Utah, Feb. 14, 1941; s. Edward and Violet Stella (Rasmussen) B.; m. Maria Elena Oro'-Beutler, Feb. 25, 1977; children—Jana Lynne, Kelly Jo, Ian David, Gail Lei. B.S., Utah State U., 1965, M.S., 1966; Ph.D., U. Nebr.-Lincoln, 1970; cert. psychologist Am. Bd. Profl. Psychology. Asst. prof. med. psychology Duke U., Asheville, N.C., 1970-71; asst. prof. Stephen F. Austin State U., 1971-73; assoc. prof. Baylor Coll. Medicine, Houston, 1973-79; prof., chief psychologist U. Ariz. Coll. Medicine, Tucson, 1979—; cons. VA Hosp. Mem. Am. Psychol. Assn., Soc. Psychotherapy Research, Ariz. State Psychol. Assn. Contbr. articles to profl. jours. Home: 2249 E Edison Tucson AZ 85719 Office: U Ariz Coll Medicine Tucson AZ 85724

BEUZEKOM, RICHARD ALLEN, franchise cons. and mktg. co. exec.; b. Balt., June 9, 1940; s. Richard and Jeanne (Monsma) B.; student Calvin Coll., 1958-61; m. Joanne A. Sikkema, July 7, 1961; children—Tamara Jo, Michael Scott. With Olivetti Corp. Am., 1961-73, agy. regional mgr., Indpls., 1964-67, ednl. sales coordinator, N.Y.C., 1967-68, mktg. mgr. of edn., 1968-70, southwestern area mgr., Dallas, 1970-73; gen. mgr. Redman Mobile Homes, Inc., Chandler, Ariz., 1973; western regional mgr. SCM Corp., Phoenix, 1974; pres. Bus. Opportunities of Am., Inc., Mesa, Ariz., 1974—; dir. Grand Canyon State Bank. Chmn. community devel. com. Mesa Community Council, 1978; div. chmn. United Way; mem. Mesa Bd. Zoning and Adjustment, 1979; bd. dirs. Sister City Corp. of Mesa. Mem. Internat. Franchise Opportunities, Nat. Speakers Assn., Mesa C. of C. (pres.). Methodist. Club: Rotary (Mesa). Home: 2115 E Hale St Mesa AZ 85203 Office: 637 E Main St Mesa AZ 85203

BEVAN, DONALD EDWARD, university dean; b. Seattle, Feb. 23, 1921; s. Arthur and Violette B.; B.S., U. Wash., 1948, Ph.D., 1959; postgrad. Moscow U., 1959-60; m. Tanya L. Potapova, Sept. 8, 1971. Sr. fisheries biologist U. Wash., 1955-59, lectr., 1956-61, research asst. prof., 1959-61, research assoc. prof., 1961-64, assoc. prof., 1964-66; assoc. dean Coll. Fisheries, 1965-69, prof., 1966—, dir. Computer Center, 1968-69, asst. v.p. research, 1969-77, adj. prof. Inst. Marine Studies, 1973—, acting dean, 1976-77, assoc. dean, 1977-80, dean, 1980—; pres., dir. Univ. Book Store, Seattle, 1977—; dir. Assoc. Vintners Inc. Served to capt. U.S. Army, 1942-46. Decorated Bronze Star, Purple Heart. Mem. Pacific Region Fisheries Council (sci. and statis. commn.), N. Pacific Fisheries Council, Marine Tech. Soc., U.S.-USSR Pacific Fisheries Negotiations, Am. Inst. Fishery Research Biologists. Contbr. numerous articles to profl. jours. Home: 29801 NE Cherry Valley Rd Duvall WA 98019 Office: A-204 Fisheries Center WH-10 U Wash Seattle WA 98195

BEVERETT, ANDREW JACKSON, merchandising exec.; b. Midland City, Ala., Feb. 21, 1917; s. Andrew J. and Ella Levonic (Adams) B.; B.S., Samford U., 1940; M.B.A., Harvard U., 1942; m. Martha Sophia Landgrabe, May 26, 1951; children—Andrew Jackson III, James Edmund, Faye A. Various exec. positions in corporate planning and mgmt. United Air Lines, Chgo., 1946-66; dir. aviation econs., sr. mktg. and econ. cons. Mgmt. and Econs. Research, Inc., Palo Alto, Calif., 1966-71; sr. economist Stanford Research Inst., Menlo Park, 1971-72; pres. Edy's on the Peninsula stores, 1973-78; real estate broker, cons., Saratoga, Calif., 1979—. Served from ensign to lt. USNR, 1942-46. Mem. Am. Mktg. Assn., Nat. Assn. Realtors, Pi Gamma Mu, Phi Kappa Phi. Club: Toastmasters. Home: 19597 Via Monte Dr Saratoga CA 95070 Office: 12195 Saratoga-Sunnyvale Rd Suite A Saratoga CA 95070

BEVERLY, ROBERT G., state senator, lawyer; b. Belmont, Mass., July 1, 1925; s. William James and Helen (Graham) B.; m. Elizabeth Louise Weisel, 1946; children—William J., Barbara L., Robert Graham, Brian C. Student U. Pitts., 1943, UCLA, 1946-48; LL.B., Loyola U., Los Angeles, 1951. Bar: Calif. Practicing atty., 1952—; mem. Calif. State Assembly from 46th Dist., 1967-76, minority floor leader, 1973-76; mem. Calif. State Senate, 1979—. Mayor, city councilman, Manhattan Beach, Calif., 1958-67; mem. Republican State Central Com.; del. Rep. Nat. Conv., 1972, 80, alt. del., 1976; mem. YMCA. Served to cpl., USMC, 1943-46. Mem. Am. Legion. Home: 1611 S Pacific Coast Hwy Suite 102 Redondo Beach CA 90277 Office: California State Senate Sacramento CA 95814*

BEYERS, ROBERT WEST, news service exec.; b. N.Y.C., Oct. 10, 1931; s. Charles M. and Bernice (West) Gratz; B.A. in Sociology, Cornell U., 1953; m. Alice Mencher, Feb. 5, 1955 (div.); children—William West, Robert Bruce, Amy Jane; m. 2d, Charlotte Kempner Davis, June 20, 1971. Brand asst., advt. dept. Procter & Gamble, Cin., 1954; pub. relations dir. U.S. Nat. Student Assn., Phila., 1954-55; editor Saline (Mich.) Reporter, 1955-56; asst. mng. editor U. Mich. News Service, Ann Arbor, 1956-61; dir. Stanford U. News and Publs. Service, Stanford, Calif., 1961—; trustee Editorial Projects for Edn., 1975—, vice-chmn., 1980—; cons. U.S. Office Edn., HEW, Robert Wood Johnson Found., various univs., others; staff White House Conf. on Higher Edn., 1965; vol. dir. communication and police relations Miss. Summer Project, 1964. Mem. Sigma Delta Chi. Unitarian. Home: 330 Santa Rita Palo Alto CA 94301 Office: Press Courtyard Santa Teresa St Stanford CA 94305

BEYERS, WILLIAM BJORN, educator; b. Seattle, Mar. 24, 1940; s. William and Esther (Svendsen) B.; m. Margaret L. Rice, July 28, 1968. B.A., U. Wash., 1962, Ph.D., 1967. Asst. prof. geography, U. Wash., Seattle, 1967-74, assoc. prof., 1974-81, prof., 1981—; vis. asst. prof. Harvard U., Cambridge, Mass., 1971, Cornell U., Ithaca, N.Y., 1971; cons. in field. NSF grantee, 1978—. Mem. Assn. Am. Geographers, Peace Sci. Soc., Regional Sci. Assn., Am. Econ. Assn. Contbr. articles to profl. jours. Office: Dept Geography DP 10 Univ Wash Seattle WA 98195

BEZAR, GILBERT EDWARD, aerospace and materials manufacturing company executive; b. Phila., May 24, 1930; s. Abraham Bernard and Leah (Hymowitz) B.; m. Norma Jean Davis, Sept. 4, 1964 (dec.); children—Eric David, Robyn Lisa. B.S. in Acctg., Temple U., 1951; M.B.A., UCLA, 1957. With TRW, 1956-62, controller U.S. Polymeric Western div., Santa Ana, Calif., 1962-63, corp. controller, 1963-67, v.p., controller, 1967-72; v.p. fin. Armco-Hitco, Irvine, Calif., 1972-77; v.p. fin. Armco-Nat. Supply Co., Houston, 1977-81; v.p. adminstrn. Armco-Aerospace & Strategiv Materials Group, Irvine, 1981—; teaching fellow UCLA, 1955-57, instr. extension, 1957-62; instr. extension U. Calif.-Irvine, 1963-72. Served to lt. USNR, 1952-55. Mem. Fin. Execs. Inst. Beta Gamma Sigma. Club: Houstonian. Home: 965 Del Mar Ave Laguna Beach CA 92651 Office: PO Box C-19514 Irvine CA 92713

BHAKTA, CHHAGANBHAI BHULABHAI, microbiologist; b. Sarai, India, Oct. 27, 1930; came to U.S., 1954, naturalized, 1972; s. Bhulabhai H. and Dhaniben B.; m. Sarojben Bhakta, June 7, 1954; 1 son, Sanjay. Diploma U. Baroda (India), 1952; grad. O.H. Nazar Ayurvedic Coll., Bombay, India, 1954; A.B., U. Pa., 1956; B.S., Sch. Pub. Health, U. Calif.-Berkeley, 1958; postgrad. Calif. State Coll., San Diego, 1965. Cert. Am. Coll. Pathology. Research fellow Mt. Zion Hosp., San Francisco, 1958-59; pub. health insp. San Francisco Health Dept., 1959; sci. officer Ministry of Health's Leeds Hosp. Bd. (Eng.), 1959-60; bacteriologist in charge Marsh & Baxter, Ltd., Birmingham, Eng., 1961-64; pub. health microbiologist Los Angeles County Health Dept., 1965—. Fellow Royal Soc. Health (Eng.), Am. Pub. Health Assn.; mem. Am. Soc. Microbiologists, Bhakta Soc. U.S. (founder, pres. 1980), So. Calif. Pub. Health Assn., U. Calif., U. Pa. alumni clubs, Shree Ramkabir Bhakta Samja (founder; pres. 1980—). Democrat. Contbr. articles to profl. publs. Home: 1816 W Main St Alhambra CA 91801 Office: 313 N Figueroa St Los Angeles County Health Los Angeles CA 90012

BHANGOO, MAHENDRA SINGH, soil science educator; b. Ayali Kalan, Ludhiana, India, Apr. 15, 1931; came to U.S., 1951; s. Naranjan Singh and Ind Kaur (Mand) B.; m. Surjit Kaur; children—Gurdip, Guri. B.S. in Agr., Agra (India) U., 1950; M.S. in Subtropical Horticulture, UCLA, 1954; Ph.D., Kans. State U., 1957. Cert. profl. soil scientist. Instr. soils Kans. State U.-Manhattan, 1955-57; agronomist Standard Fruit Co., La Ceiba, Honduras, 1958-60, asst. to dir. research, New Orleans, 1960-63; chemist cane sugar refining research U.S. Dept. Agr., New Orleans, 1963-66; prof. soils U. Ark.-Pine Bluff, 1966-76; prof. soil sci. plant sci., mechanized agr. dept., Calif. State U.-Fresno, 1976—; cons. soil fertility, soil relamation, plant nutrition, water quality to farmers. Mem. Am. Soc. Agronomy, Soil Sci. Soc. Am., Soil Conservation Soc. Am., Gamma Sigma Delta, Sigma Xi. Democrat. Sikh. Contbr. articles to profl. jours. Home: 3412 W Palo Alto St Fresno CA 93711 Office: Calif State U Fresno CA 93740

BHATIA, KUMAR GOBINDRAM, mechanical engineer; b. Karachi, India, Apr. 15, 1941; s. Gobindram Ramchand and Rukmani (Gobindram) B.; m. Sunita Kumar, Jan. 18, 1963; children—Prashant, Sumeer. B.S.M.E., Ranchi U., India, 1962; M.S.M.E., U. Va., 1965; Ph.D., Clemson U., 1971. Project engr. W. Va. Pulp and Paper, Covington, Va., 1965-66; mech. engr., Tata-Ebasco cons. engr., Bombay, India, 1966-68; NRC postdoctoral fellow NASA Langley Research Ctr., Hampton, Va., 1971-73; with Boeing Comml. Airplane Co., Seattle, 1973—, now sr. specialist engr. Home: 8241 S E 67th St Mercer Island WA 98040

BHAUMIK, MANI LAL, physicist; b. Calcutta, India, Jan. 5, 1932; s. Gunadhar and Lolita (Pramanik) B.; B.S., U. Calcutta, 1951, M.S., 1953; Ph.D., Indian Inst. Tech., 1958. Came to U.S., 1959, naturalized, 1968. Fellow, UCLA, 1959-63; with Xerox Electro-Optical Systems, Pasadena, 1961-67; with Northrop Research and Tech. Center, Palos Verdes, Calif., 1968—, research dir., 1971—. Lectr. physics Calif. State U.-Long Beach, 1967-69. Fellow Am. Phys. Soc., IEEE. Contbr. articles to profl. jours. Patentee in field. Home: 820 Seco St Pasadena CA 91103 Office: 1 Research Park Palos Verdes Peninsula CA

BHUSHAN, BHARAT, mechanical engineer, research scientist; b. Jhinjhana, India, Sept. 30, 1949; m. Sudha Bhushan June 14, 1975; children—Ankur, Noopur. B.E. with honors in Mech. Engring., Birla Inst. Tech. and Sci. (India); 1970; M.S. in Mech. Engring., MIT, 1971; M.S. in Mechanics, U. Colo., 1973, Ph.D. in Mech. Engring., 1976; M.B.A. in Mgmt., Rensselaer Poly. Inst., 1980. Registered profl. engr., Pa. Program mgr. research and devel. div. Mech. Tech. Inc., Lathom, N.Y., 1976-80; research scientist tech services div. SKF Indusries Inc., King of Prussia, Pa., 1980-81; adv. engr. gen. products div. lab. IBM Corp., Tucson, 1981—. Ford Found. Research fellow, 1970-71; U. Colo. Grad. fellow, 1973-74; Recipient Alfred Noble prize, 1981, George Norlin award U. Colo., 1983. Mem. ASME (Henry Hess award 1980, Burt L. Newkirk award 1983), Nat. Soc. Profl. Engrs., N.Y. Acad. Scis., Sigma Xi, Tau Beta Pi. Contbr. articles to profl. jours. Patentee in field.

BIAETT, HEWITT, lawyer, former railroad exec.; b. Cotton Plant, Ark., Nov. 25, 1914; s. Doddridge Hewitt and Myrtle Louise (Woodruff) B.; student Phoenix Coll., 1934; LL.B., Coll. Law, U. Ariz., 1938; m. Ruthanne Migely, Feb. 8, 1941; children—Doddridge Hewitt III, Julie Jane, Walter M. Admitted to Ariz. bar, 1938, Ill. bar, 1939, Va. bar, 1947; atty. C., B. & Q. R.R., Chgo., 1938-42, commerce atty., 1942-46; gen. atty. C. & O. Ry. Co., 1946-53, gen. solicitor, 1953-58, gen. counsel, 1958-64; gen. atty. P.M. R.R., 1946-47, N.Y.C., & St. L. R.R., 1946-47; v.p. coal traffic and devel. B. & O. R.R., Balt., 1964-70; v.p. Lakefront Dock & R.R. Terminal Co.,1964-70, B. & O. R.R. Co. Chgo. Terminal, 1964-70, S.I. Rapid Transit Ry. Co., 1964-70, Monongahela Ry. Co., 1965-70, Western Pocahontas, Chesapeake Mineral Co., Chesapeake Toledo Corp., Cin. Inter-Terminal R.R. Co., Covington-Cin. Elevated R.R. Transfer & Bridge Co., all 1966-70; pres. Mid-Allegheny Corp., 1965-70, New Gauley Coal Corp., W. Va. & Pitts. Co., Littleton Fuel Co., 1966-70; v.p. Chesapeake and Ohio Railway Co., 1966-69; asso. Biaett & Bahde, Phoenix, 1970—; sec., dir. Gemini Pub. Co., 1978—. Served with USNR, 1944-46. Recipient Phi Delta Phi award, 1938. Mem. U. Ariz. Coll. Law Alumni Assn., Order of Coif. Clubs: Rons, Confederate Air Force. Home: 1301 W Townley Phoenix AZ 85021 Office: 5822 W Glenn Glendale AZ 85301

BIAGGINI, BENJAMIN FRANKLIN, railroad exec.; b. New Orleans, Apr. 15, 1916; s. B.F. and Maggie (Switzer) B.; B.S., St. Mary's of Tex., 1936; grad. Advanced Mgmt. Program, Harvard, 1955; m. Anne Payton, Sept. 9, 1937; children—Connie Sue Biaggini Guittard, Anne Biaggini Krattebol. Chmn., chief exec. officer, dir. So. Pacific Co., also So. Pacific Transp. Co.; chmn. St. Louis Southwestern Ry. Co.; dir. Ticor, Tenneco, Inc. Mem. Nat. Transp. Policy Study Commn., 1976—. Bd. dirs. SRI Internat.; trustee Calif. Inst. Tech., Nat. Safety Council. Mem. Bay Area Council (chmn.), Bus. Council, Calif. C. of C. (pres. 1973), Calif. Roundtable (founder, vice-chmn.), Conf. Bd., Bus. Roundtable. Office: So Pacific Bldg 1 Market Plaza San Francisco CA 94105*

BIAGGIO, MARY KAY, educator, psychologist; b. Chgo., Nov. 4, 1950; d. William Charles and Phyllis Theresa (Weber) B.; Ph.D., Utah State U., Logan, 1977. Counselor, Hillside Sch., Logan, Utah, 1974-76; psychology intern Austin (Tex.) State Hosp., 1976-77; assoc. prof. U. Idaho, Moscow, 1977—, dir. clin. psychology grad. program, 1980—. Mem. Am. Psychol. Assn., Soc. Personality Assessment, Western Psychol. Assn. Contbr. articles in field to profl. jours. Office: Psychology Dept U Idaho Moscow ID 83843

BIANCHI, DONALD ERNEST, college dean; b. Santa Cruz, Calif., Nov. 22, 1933; s. Ernest A. and Florence A. (Foerster) B.; m. Georgia Louise McCush, Sept. 8, 1956; children—Diana, David, William. A.B., Stanford U., 1955, A.M., 1956; Ph.D., U. Mich., 1959. Asst. prof. biology San Fernando Valley State Coll., Northridge, Calif., 1959-63, assoc. prof., 1963-66; prof. Calif. State U., Northridge, 1966—, dean Sch. Sci. and Math., 1973—. Mem. AAAS, Am. Arachnological Soc., Mycological Soc. Am. Author: Cell Biology, 1980, 83. Office: California State University School of Science and Mathematics 18111 Nordhoff St Northridge CA 91330

BIBERMAN, EDWARD, artist; b. Phila., Oct. 23, 1904; s. Joseph and Eva (Goldich) B.; m. Sonja Teresa Dahl, Dec. 5, 1938; 1 dau., Sonya. B.S. in Econs., U. Pa., 1924; postgrad. Pa. Acad. Fine Arts, 1924-26. Numerous one-man shows including Heritage Gallery, Los Angeles, 1955-65, Palm Springs Mus. (Calif.), 1971, Los Angeles Mcpl. Art Gallery, 1971; exhibited in group shows including Mus. Modern Art, N.Y.C., 1930, 32, Corcoran Gallery Art, Washington, 1931, Whitney Mus. Am. Art, N.Y.C., 1936; represented in permanent collections Los Angeles County Mus., Brandeis U., Waltham, Mass., Denn Acad. Fine Arts, Phila., Butler Inst. Am. Art, Youngstown, Ohio, Palm Springs Desert Mus.; lectr. U. Calif., Loyola-Marymount U.; host TV series Sta. KNBC, 1967-68. Recipient award Los Angeles County Mus., 1955; Tupperware fellow, 1957. Mem. Nat. Soc. Mural Painters, Artists for Econ. Action. Democrat. Jewish. Author: The Best Untold, 1954; Time and Circumstance, 1968. Home and office: 3332 Deronda Dr Los Angeles CA 90028

BICK, MICHAEL DAVID, medical manufacturing executive, molecular biologist; b. Stockton, Calif., Jan. 6, 1945; s. Jack Arthur and Pauline Ethel (Jensen) B.; B.A., U. Puget Sound, 1967; Ph.D., U. So. Calif., 1971; m. Sharon Jo Poderis, Feb. 8, 1964; children—Geri Michelle, Michael David. Postdoctoral fellow div. clin. genetics Children's Hosp. Med. Center and dept. biol. chemistry Harvard U. Med. Sch., 1971-74; asst. mem. Roche Inst. Molecular Biology, Nutley, N.J., 1974-78; pres., sci. dir. Pacific Hemostasis Lab., Inc., Bakersfield, Calif., 1978—; dir. Bay Area Hematology Oncology Clin. and Research Lab., Inc. Damon Runyon Cancer Fund fellow, 1971-73; Nat. Inst. Child and Human Devel. fellow, 1969-71; Med. Found. fellow, 1973-74. Mem. Am. Soc. Biol. Chemists, Am. Assn. Blood Banks, N.Y. Acad. Sci., Am. Assn. Clin. Chemists, World Fedn. Hemophilia. Contbr. numerous articles to profl. jours. Home: 3512 Christmas Tree Ln Bakersfield CA 93306 Office: 4100 Easton Dr #8 Bakersfield CA 93309

BICK, RODGER LEE, physician, medical researcher, author; b. San Francisco, May 21, 1942; s. Jack A. and Pauline E. Bick; student U. Calif.-Berkeley; M.D., U. Calif.-Irvine, 1970; m. Marcella, Oct., 1979; 1 dau., Shauna Nicole. children by previous marriage—Michelle, Le Anne Bick. Intern in straight medicine Kern County Gen. Hosp., Bakersfield, Calif., 1970-71, resident in internal medicine, 1971-72; fellow in hematology and med. oncology dept. of medicine U. Calif. Los Angeles Center for the Health Scis., 1972-73; hematology fellow Hyland Labs., Costa Mesa, Calif., 1966-67; practice medicine specializing in hematology/oncology and thrombosis, Santa Monica, Calif., 1974-77; dir. hemostasis and thrombosis research lab. Kern County Gen. Hosp., 1973-74, dir. med. edn., 1973-74, chief med. oncology, 1973-74; attending physician Wadsworth VA Hosp., Los Angeles, 1974—; mem. med. staff St. John's Hosp. and Health Center, Santa Monica, 1974-78, Santa Monica Hosp. and Med. Center, 1974-78, mem. research com., 1975-77; asst. prof. medicine UCLA Center for the Health Scis., 1974—, mem. med. staff, 1974—; asso. prof. Calif. State U.-Bakersfield, 1977—; asso. prof. physiology Wayne State U. Sch. Medicine, Detroit; cons. to Nigeria Hematology Center, Lagos, Nigeria, 1973-75; med. dir. San Joaquin Hematology and Oncology Med. Group, Bakersfield, 1977—; dir. hematology/oncology San Joaquin Community Hosp., Bakersfield. Fellow Am. Coll. Angiology, Internat. Coll. Angiology; mem. Am. Soc. of Clin. Pathologists (dir. coagulation workshop 1974—), A.C.P., Am. Soc. Hematology, Internat. Soc. Hematology, Am. Assn. for Clin. Research, AAAS, Am. Soc. of Mammalolgists, Fedn. of Am. Scientists, Internat. Assn. for Study of Lung Cancer (founding mem. 1974), Am. Geriatrics Soc., N.Y. Acad. Scis., Am. Heart Assn., Nigerian Hematology Soc., Internat. Soc. on Thrombosis and Haemostasis, Am. Cancer Soc., Calif. Coll. Honor Soc. Author: (with others) Modern Concepts and Evaluations of Hemostasis and Thrombosis, 1975, Difficult Diagnosis Problems in Hemostasis and Thrombosis, 1976; Recent Concepts and Developments in Evaluating Disorders of Hemostasis and Thrombosis, 1976; Current Concepts of Hemostasis and Thrombosis, 1976; Basic Concepts of Hemostasis and Thrombosis, 1980; contbr. chpts. in field to books in medicine; contbr. numerous articles on hematology and angiology to med. jours. Home and Office: 2727 Eye Ct Bakersfield CA 93301

BICKAR, BETTY ARLENE, business systems executive; b. Plattville, Colo., Nov. 14, 1931; d. Leslie William and Kathryn Mabel (Rutherford) Clawson; children—Patricia J., Andrew L. Bookkeeper, office mgr. Manes Logging Co., Clallam Bay, Wash., 1958-70; stenographer, prodn. acct. Crown Zellerbach Corp., Sekiu, Wash., 1970-73; bookkeeper, acct., office mgr., A. W. Logging Inc., Corner Bay, Alaska, 1973-79; owner, operator Spectra Northwest, Bellevue, Wash., 1979—. Mem. C. of C. (Seattle, Bellevue), Nat. Assn. Female Execs., Nat. Fedn. Ind. Bus. Home: 12612 S E 30th St Bellevue WA 98005 Office: Spectra Northwest 827 Bellevue Way NE Suite 203 Bellevue WA 98004

BICKEL, DWIGHT FRANKLIN, lawyer, insurance company executive; b. Trilla, Ill., Feb. 1, 1931; s. Melvin and Ethel M. (Hackley) B.; m. Cynthia A. Gross, Aug. 2, 1969; children—Dwight A., Deborah A., Justin D. B.S., U. Ill., 1955, J.D., 1957. Bar: Ill. 1957, Idaho 1958, Hawaii 1981. Asst. atty. gen., Boise, Idaho, 1958-61; exec. v.p. Idaho Investment Corp., Twin Falls, 1963-64; v.p. and sec. Mich. Chem. Corp., Chgo., 1964-67; pres. IUC, Inc., Santa Ana, Calif. and Seattle, 1969-71; sole practice law, Boise, 1971—; dir. Employers Adminstrv. Services, Inc.; lectr. Boise Community Schs. Served with USAF, 1950-54. Mem. Ill. Bar Assn., Hawaii Bar Assn. Club: Masons. Editor: Idaho Real Estate Practice, 1977, 80. Office: 5440 Franklin Rd Suite 101 Boise ID 83705

BICKEL, GEORGE PHILIP, manufacturing executive; b. Phila., Apr. 10, 1926; s. Mahlon Levis and Mary Belle (Evenden) B.; A.B., Harvard Coll., 1947; m. Patricia Louise Warren, Oct. 30, 1948; children—Linda, Scott, Cinthia. With Minn. Mining & Mfg. Co., 1950-83, mgr., Honolulu, 1965-83; dist. mgr. Am. Internat. Co., Honolulu, 1983—. Pres., Portlock Community Assn., Honolulu, 1970. Served to lt. (j.g.) USNR, 1943-47, lt. 1951-53. Mem. Am. C of C. in Japan (dir. 1962-63), Navy League U.S. (pres. Honolulu council 1980-81), Pacific Fleet Submarine Meml. Assn. (chmn. bd. 1980-83). Club: Rotary. (pres. Honolulu 1975-76). Home: 1434 Laamia St Honolulu HI 96821 Office: 1311 Kalani St Honolulu HI 96817

BICKETT, JAMES ALAN, loss control administrator, safety consultant; b. Los Angeles, Apr. 30, 1945; s. James Albert and Lorraine Vivian (Muller) B.; m. Nancy Elaine Basil, Feb. 5, 1965; children—Darcel Nanette, Derek Douglas, Nicole Charmaine. A.A., Los Angeles Pierce Coll., 1971; B.A., Calif. State U.-Northridge, 1974. Assoc. safety profl. sr. prodn. planner Whittaker Corp., Northridge, 1968-73; mfg. mgr. Innovative Security Corp., Northridge, 1973-74; safety cons. State Compensation Ins. Fund, Ventura, Calif., 1974-80; loss control mgr. Safeco Ins. Co., Fountain Valley, Calif., 1980-82; safety cons. Unicare Ins. Co., Irvine, Calif., 1982—. Mem. Nat. Safety Council, Am. Soc. Safety Engrs., Bd. Cert. Safety Profls. Democrat. Office: 2361 Campus Dr Irvine CA 92715

BICKNELL, BYRNA DEE, political scientist, educator; b. Norton, Kans., Sept. 12, 1938; d. Lawrence Roth and Thora Helen (Edson) B.; m. Vitas A. Cataldo, Mar. 7, 1955 (div.); children—Larry C., Paul A., Anthony C., Darci M. A.A., Grossmont Coll., 1975; B.A., San Diego State U., 1979. tchr. and vocat. counselor Calif. Adult guidance specialist Grossmont Coll., El Cajon, Calif., 1972-79; research and organizing coordinator San Diego/Imperial Counties Labor Council, San Diego, 1980-83; instr. San Diego Community Coll., 1981—; cons. in fin. planning and tax preparation. Mem. YWCA program devel. com.; edn. chmn., treas. Coalition Labor Union Women; charter mem., organizing steering com. CONCORD; founding mem. Networking; mem. coordinating counsel Regional Occupational Program; mem. accreditation com. student personnel services Grossmont Coll., mem. Title IX evaluation, grievance coms.; mem. Calif. Assemblyman Chacon's Com. on Minority and Women Entrepreneurs; mem. adv. com. Womens Ctr. and Studies. Mem. Am. Assn. Women in Community Colls., Indsl. Relations Research Assn. (exec. bd.), San Diego Soc. Sex Therapists and Edn. (hon.), Am. Fedn. Tchrs., San Diego Vocat. Guidance Assn., Nat. Ctr. Pub. Service Internship Programs, NOW, Nat. Women's Polit. Caucus. Office: 2496 E St San Diego CA 92102

BIDDLE, DONALD RAY, aerospace co. exec.; b. Alton, Mo., June 30, 1936; s. Ernest Everet and Dortha Marie (McGuire) B.; student El Dorado (Kans.) Jr. Coll., 1953-55, Pratt (Kans.) Jr. Coll., 1955-56; B.S. in Mech. Engring., Washington U., St. Louis, 1961; postgrad. computer sci. Pa. State U. Extension, 1963; certificate bus. mgmt. Alexander Hamilton Inst., 1958; m. Nancy Ann Dunham, Mar. 13, 1955; children—Jeanne Kay Biddle Dionne, Mitchell Lee, Charles Alan. Design group engr. Emerson Elec. Mfg., St. Louis, 1957-61; design specialist Boeing Vertol, Springfield, Pa., 1962; cons. engr. Ewing Tech. Design, Phila., 1962-66; chief engr. rotary wing Gates Learjet, Wichita, Kans., 1967-70; dir. engring. Parsons of Calif. div. HITCO, Stockton, Calif., 1971—. Cons. engr. Scoutmaster, counselor, instl. rep. Boy Scouts Am., St. Ann, Mo., 1958-61; mem. Springfield Sch. Bd., 1964. Mem. Am. Helicopter Soc. (sec.-treas. Wichita chpt. 1969), ASME, Am. Mgmt. Assn., ASTM, Am. Inst. Aeros. and Astronautics, Exptl. Pilots Assn. Republican. Methodist (trustee, chmn. 1974-76). Patentee landing gear designs, inflatable rescue system, glass retention systems, adjustable jack system, cold weather start fluorescent lamp, paper honeycomb core post-process systems. Home: 1140 Stanton Way Stockton CA 95207 Office: 3437 S Airport Way Stockton CA 95206

BIDDLE, WAYNE THOMAS, drilling company executive; b. Miller, S.D., May 13, 1924; s. Clifford Henry and Neva Berniece (Rhodes) B.; m. LaFawn H. Hall, Mar. 20, 1952; children—Belinda G., Barbara G. B.S. in Petroleum Engring., U. Okla., 1948. Engr., Stanolind Oil & Gas Co., Ardmore, Okla., 1948-50; sales engr. Dunigan Tool & Supply Co., Abilene, Tex., 1950-53; dir. mgr. Am. Iron & Machine Works, Denver, 1953-56; vice chmn. Exeter Drilling Co., Denver, 1956—; also dir. Named Man of Month, Western Oil Reporter, 1971. Mem. Internat. Assn. Drilling Contractors (dir.), Ind. Petroleum Assn. Am., Am. Petroleum Inst. Republican. Congregationalist. Clubs: Denver Petroleum (Man of Year 1978), Cherry Hills Country (Englewood); Castle Pine (Castle Rock); Old Baldy (Saratoga, Wyo.). Home: 4001 Nassau Circle Englewood CO 80110 Office: 17th and Broadway Suite 3400 Denver CO 80217

BIDLEMAN, MARY JOSEPHINE, home economist; b. Cin., Nov. 5, 1935; d. August Louis and Wilma Gertrude (Mette) Juniet; B.S., Ariz. State U., 1976; m. William Ellsworth Bidleman, May 30, 1956; children—Marie Angela, Francis Leo, Mary Colette, Donald Valery. Decorator cons. Creative World, Scottsdale, Ariz., 1977; sales coordinator Gen. Semicondr. Industries, Tempe, Ariz., 1978; substitute tchr., Phoenix, 1979; freelance cons., counselor, Tempe, 1979—. Cert. hosp. chaplain aide. Mem. Phoenix Com. against Pornography, 1969; del. White House Conf. Handicapped, 1976; sec. Ariz. Congress for Action, 1977-78; adv. Governor's Conf. Energy, 1979. Recipient nat. award for women returning to edn. PEO, 1975. Mem. Am. Home Econs. Assn., Ariz. Home Econs. Assn., Ariz. Solar Energy Assn., N.Mex. Solar Energy Assn., Nat. Assn. Cath. Chaplains. Republican. Address: 1737 E Manhattan Dr Tempe AZ 85282

BIDWELL, DOROTHY KAY, business executive; b. San Francisco, July 10, 1947; d. Gerald R. and Viola E. (Herker) Danks; m. Dennis A. Riggs, Feb. 10, 1968; 1 dau., Tina L.; m. 2d, John R. Bidwell, Aug. 31, 1973. A.A. in Mgmt., San Diego Evening Coll., 1978. Lic. notary pub., Calif.; lic. pvt. pilot, FAA. Adminstrv. asst. to v.p. theoretical physics SAI, La Jolla, Calif., 1972-75; co-founder, corp. sec. JAYCOR, San Diego, 1975—, also dir. Mem. San Diego Master Chorale and Symphony, 1970—. Mem. Nat. Notary Assn., Nat. Assn. Female Execs., Am. Mgmt. Assns. Republican. Presbyterian. Office: PO Box 85154 11011 Torreyana Rd San Diego CA 92138

BIDWELL, JAMES KERRY, mechanical engineer; b. Akron, Ohio, Apr. 25, 1947; s. James Kenneth and Donna Jean (Hufford) B.; student U. Akron, 1965-66; B.S., U.S. Mcht. Marine Acad., 1970; postgrad. Kent State U., 1971; M.B.A., U. Hawaii, 1975; m. Barbara Anne Beck, June 6, 1970. With U.S. Mcht. Marines, N.Y.C., 1968-70, Babcock & Wilcox Co., Barberton, Ohio, 1971-72, Dillingham Shipyard, Honolulu, 1972-73, Arinc Research Corp., Honolulu, 1974-75, Seaco Inc., Honolulu, 1976, Am. Piping & Boiler Co., Honolulu, 1976, Rigging Internat., Honolulu, 1977; owner James K. Bidwell & Assocs., Honolulu, 1974—, Kailua Kanchoe Comml. Properties, Honolulu, 1979—; gen. mgr. Central Pacific Boiler & Piping Ltd., 1982—; cons. mech. engr. Am. Piping & Boiler Co., 1979-82, others. Pres., Kalama Valley Maintenance Assn., 1976-78. Served to lt., USNR, 1966-82. Lic. gen. contractor, Hawaii; registered profl. engr., Hawaii, Ohio; lic. 3rd asst. engr., U.S. Coast Guard. Mem. Am. Soc. Profl. Engrs., ASME. Republican. Home: 7514 Nakalele St Honolulu HI 96825 Office: 106 Puuhale Rd Honolulu HI 96819

BIEBER, JEANETTE JEAN, business educator, consultant; b. Aberdeen, S.D., July 15, 1937; d. John and Lenora Jean B.; m. Norton Holmes Moses, Aug. 8, 1982. B.S. in Bus. Edn., No. State Coll., Aberdeen, 1960, M.S., 1961; Ed.D. in Adult and Higher Edn., Mont. State U., 1978. Grad. teaching asst. Mont. State U., 1973-75; coordinator Affirmative Action Program, Eastern Mont. Coll., 1973-74, acting dir., 1975, chairperson, prof. bus. edn. and office adminstrn., 1979—. Mem. Mont. Bus. Edn. Assn. (pres. 1975-77), Office Systems Research Assn. (charter), Assn. Info. Systems Profls., Nat. Bus. Edn. Assn., Am. Vocat. Assn., Nat. Soc. Profs. (pres. 1973-74), Alpha Delta Kappa. Editor Western News Exchange, 1978-79; editor: New Directions for Business Education, 1980. Home: 843 Parkhill Dr Billings MT 59102 Office: 1500 N 30th St Eastern Mont Coll Billings MT 59101

BIEGEN, DAVID ALLAN, clin. psychologist; b. Bklyn., July 30, 1940; s. Joseph Henry and Pauline Pearl Biegen; B.S., SUNY, Cortland, 1962; M.S., CCNY, 1964; Ed.D., U. Cin., 1971; children—Michael Allan, Scott Eric. Asso. psychologist Dannemora (N.Y.) State Hosp., 1969-72; prin. psychologist Adirondack Correctional Treatment and Evaluation Center, Dannemora, 1972-75; chief psychologist Ariz. State Prison, Florence, 1974-77; psychologist Maricopa County Juvenile Ct. Center Phoenix, 1977-80; pvt. practice clin. psychology, Phoenix, 1980—. Mem. Am. Psychol. Assn., Ariz. State Psychol. Assn., Maricopa County Soc. Clin. Psychologists, Phoenix Psychoanalytic Soc. Home: 2956 W Sandra Terr Phoenix AZ 85023 Office: 515 W Buckeye Rd Suite 205 Phoenix AZ 85003

BIENEK, GERHARD KLAUS, ecologist, parasitologist; b. Germany, Oct. 20, 1943; came to U.S., 1960, naturalized, 1966; s. Fritz Max and

Hildegard Anna (Werner) B.; B.A. magna cum laude, U. Utah, 1971, Ph.D., 1974; m. Rosemarie Edeltraud Beier, Apr. 29, 1963; children—Klaus, Peter, Diane. Research biologist Govt. of Alta. (Can.), 1974; dir. environ. scis. Surveyer, Nenninger, Chenevert, Alta., 1975-76; dist. environ. coordinator Bur. Land Mgmt., U.S. Dept. Interior, Salt Lake City, 1976-77, Alaska Outer Continental Shelf wildlife biologist, endangered species coordinator, Anchorage and 1977-79, sci. advisor endangered species research, 1977-79; affiliate assoc. prof. ecology U. Alaska, Fairbanks, 1979-80; dir. environ. scis. Northwestern Biol. Cons.'s, Salt Lake City, 1980-81; adj. prof. dir. Alaska/Can. Arctic Expdn., Utah State U. Extension Div., 1981—; expert witness N. Slope Borough, Barrow, Alaska, 1979, endangered species cons. Delta residents, 1980-81. Cub scout master Great Salt Lake council Boy Scouts Am., Salt Lake City, 1976-77, mem. Boy Scout Com., Eagle River, Alaska, 1977-79. Mem. AAAS, Am. Soc. Parasitology, Rocky Mountain Soc. Parasitology, Ecol. Soc. Am., N.Y. Acad. Sci., Sigma Xi, Delta Phi Alpha. Mormon. Author high sch. manuals: Elementary Approach for Resource and Ecology, 1974; Introduction to Ecology, 1975; contbr. writings to sci. publs., govt. reports. Home: 485 K St Salt Lake City UT 84103

BIENIASZ, ROBERT BURBANK, safety engineer; b. Chgo., May 26, 1946; s. Nicholas F. and Helen J. (Zajdel) B.; A.A. Lyons Twp. Jr. Coll., 1966; B.S. in Ceramic Engring., U. Ill., 1969; M.B.A., U. Hawaii, 1975. Lab. technician Lutheran Deaconess Hosp., Chgo., 1966; student engr. Continental Can Co., Chgo., 1967-68; ceramic devel. engr. CHI-VIT div. Eagle Picher Industries, Cicero, Ill., 1969-74; safety engr. U.S. Navy Pub. Works Center, Pearl Harbor, Hawaii, 1977-80, safety mgr. Naval Supply Center, 1980, safety engr. Pacific div. Naval Facilities Engring. Command, 1981—. Recipient Spl. Achievement award, Naval Supply Center, 1980. Mem. Am. Soc. Safety Engrs., Am. Welding Soc., Keramos. Roman Catholic. Address: PO Box 6294 Honolulu HI 96818 Office: Navy Public Works Center Safety Office-Code 20A Pearl Harbor HI 96860

BIENKIEWICZ, BOGUSZ, civil engr.; b. Koszalin, Poland, May 14, 1948; came to U.S., 1976; s. Kazimierz and Jozefa (Baczek) B.; M.S. in Civil Engring., Tech. U. Gdansk (Poland), 1971; Ph.D. in Civil Engring., Colo. State U., 1981. Asst. prof. Tech. U. Gdansk, 1971-76; grad. research asst. civil engring. Colo. State U., Ft. Collins, 1976-79, research assoc., 1980-82, asst. prof., 1982—. Mem. Sigma Xi. Home: 905 W Laurel St Apt 303 Fort Collins CO 80521 Office: Colo State U ERC Foothills Campus Fort Collins CO 80523

BIENVENU, ROBERT CHARLES, lawyer; b. Milw., Dec. 3, 1922; s. Harold John and Nellie (Davidson) B.; A.B., U. Calif., Berkeley, 1947; J.D., McGeorge Coll. Law, U. Pacific, 1953; m. Martha Beard, Mar. 28, 1945 (dec. 1969); children—Susan (Mrs. James Tuttle), Nancy (Mrs. Gary Simas), John; m. 2d, Joyce Marlene Holley, Aug. 13, 1971. State parole officer Dept. Corrections, Sacramento, 1947-54; admitted to Calif. bar, 1954; since practiced in Modesto; mem. firm Hoover, Lacy & Bienvenu, 1954-66; individual practice, 1966—. Pres., Stanislaus County Sch. Bds. Assn., 1968-69; mem. Modesto City Schs. Bd. Edn., 1961-81; mem. Calif. Republican Central Com. 1960-70; bd. dirs. Modesto Symphony Orch., 1966-72, Retarded Children's Soc. Stanislaus County, 1965-70, Am. Cancer Soc., 1955-60. Served with AUS, 1942-45. Mem. State Bar Calif., Am., Stanislaus County bar assns., Am. Trial Lawyers Assn. Clubs: Modesto Racquet. Home: 218 Brook Way Modesto CA 95354 Office: 726 10th St Modesto CA 95354

BIENZ, DARREL RUDOLPH, horticulturist, author, educator; b. Bern, Idaho, Apr. 1, 1926; s. Rudolph Benjamin and Marintha (Derricott) B.; m. Betty Jean Hirschi, June 15, 1950; children—Stephen, Robert, Marianne, Karl, Bart. Student U. Utah, 1946-47; B.S., U. Idaho, Moscow, 1947-50; Ph.D., Cornell U. 1950-54. Research asst. Cornell U., 1950-54; acting asst. prof. U. Idaho, 1954-57; geneticist U.S. Dept. Agr., 1957-59; asst. prof., to prof. Wash. State U., Pullman, 1959—; Fullbright exchange prof. Ege U., Izmir, Turkey, 1967-68; vis. prof. U. Hawaii, 1975; sr. adviser Eastern Islands, Indonesia Edn. project, 1981. Scoutmaster, dist. tng. chmn., dist. chmn. Boy Scouts of Am., 1961-75; bishop Pullman U. ward Ch. of Jesus Christ of Latter-day Saints, 1974-81. Served with AUS, 1945-46. Mem. Am. Soc. Horticultural Sci., Am. Genetic Assn., Am. Horticultural Soc., Internat. Horticultural Soc., Am. Inst. Biological Sci., Sigma Xi, Alpha Zeta. Author: The Why and How of Home Horticulture, 1980; Horticulture for the Homeowner, 1975; Horticulture 101 x Study Guide, 1981; contbr. articles to profl. jours. Home: Rt 2 Box 842 Pullman WA 99163 Office: Horticulture Dept Wash State U Pullman WA 99164

BIERI, CHRISTEL DORIS HESSELSCHWERDT, mfg. co. exec.; b. Karlsruhe, W. Ger., Apr. 29, 1938; came to U.S., 1962; d. Emil and Karolina Hesselschwerdt; m. Jurg H. Bieri, Apr. 21, 1962. B.S. in Langs., U. Geneva (Switzerland); M.A., U. Calif., Berkeley, 1966. Teaching asst. U. Calif., Berkeley, 1964-66, property mgr., 1966-73; bus. co-owner, gen. mgr. Vouvry, Switzerland, 1974-76; co-founder Heliodyne Inc., Richmond, Calif., 1976—, v.p. mktg., 1978—. Mem. No. Calif. Solar Energy Assn. (dir. 1978-80), Internat. Solar Energy Soc. (Am. chpt.), Calif. Solar Energy Industries Assn. Home: 2350 Alva Ave El Cerrito CA 94530 Office: 700 S 4th St Richmond CA 94804

BIERMAN, EDWARD OTTO, physician, ophthalmologist; b. St. Louis, May 26, 1923; s. Max John and Ida (Smolensky) B.; M.Ophthalmology, St. Louis U., 1940, M.D., 1952; m. Shirley Mae Fox, Nov. 27, 1947; children—Ellen Jean, Steven Fox, Rhonda Beth, Susan Jill, James Fox. Intern, St. Louis U., 1947-48, resident, 1948-52; ophthalmologist Ross-Loos Clinic, Los Angeles, 1953-58; practice medicine specializing in ophthalmology, Santa Monica, Calif., 1954—; sr. mem. staff Santa Monica Hosp., 1954—, dir. ophthalmology residency tng. program, 1973-75, sec. joint staff, 1970-73; mem. staff St. John's Hosp., Santa Monica, 1955—; lectr. exhibitor 23d Congress Ophthalmology, Japan; Pan Pacific Ophthalmology Soc. goodwill tour to People's Republic of China, 1978. Chmn. dist. Fund dr. Boy Scouts Am., 1975—. Served with USN, 1942-45, USMC, 1944-52. Fellow Am. Acad. Ophthalmology, Internat. Coll. Surgeons; mem. AMA, Calif., Los Angeles County med. assns., Los Angeles County Ophthal. Soc., Zionist Orgn. Am., Alpha Omega Alpha, Phi Delta Epsilon. Jewish. Club. Rotary. Author religious pamphlets; contbr. articles med. jours. Home: 17179 Avenida De Santa Ynez St Pacific Palisades CA 90272 Office: 1304 15th St Santa Monica CA 90404

BIERSCHBACH, RAYMOND ANTON, insurance company executive; b. Lemmon, S.D., Feb. 15, 1933; s. Nicholas Bernard and Thelma Ursula (Lewis) B.; B.A., State U. Iowa, 1955, M.S., 1957; m. Margaret Jean Benson, Feb. 22, 1963; children—Daniel M., Kimberly M., Catherine J., Kristin R. With Occidental Life Ins. Co. of Calif., Los Angeles, 1960-83, v.p., actuary, 1968-71, exec. v.p., actuary, 1971-73, gen. mgr. European ops., 1973-76, exec. v.p., dir., 1976-83, now dir.; pres. Transam. Internat. Ins. Services, 1983—. Bd. dirs. Catholic Big Brothers of Los Angeles, 1969-70. Served to 1st lt. USAF, 1957-60. Fellow Soc. Actuaries; mem. Los Angeles Actuarial Club, Am. Acad. Actuaries, Actuarial Club of Pacific States. Home: 2111 El Monte Ave Arcadia CA 91006

BIERYLO, JOHN I., builder, developer; b. Cranbury, N.J., July 6, 1941; s. Ignatz and Mary Bierylo; A.B., Rutgers U., 1963. Audit mgr. Coopers and Lybrand, San Francisco, 1967-71; chief fin. officer DiGiorgio Devel. Corp., San Francisco, 1971-77; sr. v.p. Doric Devel., Inc., Alameda, Calif., 1977—, dir., 1977—; dir. Doric Constrn. Co., Inc., Alameda, Doric Realty, Alameda, Harbor Bay Isle Assos., Alameda, Harbor Bay Isle Realty, Alameda. Served to capt. USAF, 1963-67. Mem. Urban Land Inst., Soc. Indsl. Realtors, Real Estate Research Council No. Calif., Am. Inst. C.P.A.'s, Calif. Soc. C.P.A.'s. Clubs: Harbor Bay Isle (dir. 1979—); San Francisco Tennis. Home: 373 Lombard St San Francisco CA 94133 Office: 936 Shorepoint Ct Alameda CA 94501

BIETZ, DUANE STANLEY, surgeon, emergency services dir.; b. Denver, July 1, 1938; s. Reinhold Reinhart and Martha Pearl (Reiswig) B.; M.D., Loma Linda U., 1965; m. Eunice Faith Pietz, June 10, 1965; children—Michal Christina, Matthew Christian. Resident in gen. and thoracic surgery U. Wash., Seattle, 1965-72, HEW grantee, project investigator, trauma tng. materials, 1975-77, mem. faculty med. sch., 1974-75; mem. clin. faculty U. Oreg., Portland, 1976—; practice medicine specializing in thoracic cardiac and vascular surgery, Portland, 1975—; chief trauma service Portland Adventist Hosp., 1980—; postdoctoral fellow in trauma U. Tex. Southwestern Med. Sch., Dallas, 1973-74; cardiac surgery fellow Loma Linda U., 1980; mem. Oreg. Emergency Med. Technician Adv. Bd., 1977-81; pres. Emergency Services Supply NW Inc.; instr. trauma nurse Oreg. Emergency Dept. Nurses Assn.; mem. emergency med. treatment adv. bd. Oreg. Bd. Med. Examiners; mem. com. on categorization N.W. Oreg. Council Hosps.; chmn. civilian com. mil. assistance for safety and traffic 304th Air Force. Served to lt. col. USAFR. Diplomate Nat. Bd. Med. Examiners, Am. Bd. Surgery, Am. Bd. Thoracic Surgery. Fellow ACS, Am. Coll. Cardiology; mem. Portland Surg. Soc., Portland Vascular Soc. (founding), Oreg. Thoracic Soc., Univ. Assn. Emergency Med. Services, Henry N. Harkins Surg. Soc., Multnomah Med. Soc. (chmn. emergency med. services com. 1982—), Am. Trauma Soc. (founding mem.). Office: 10000 SE Main St Suite 408 Portland OR 97216

BIGELOW, DONALD ELLSWORTH, optometrist, public health service officer; b. Holden, Mass., Sept. 19, 1942; d. Chester Ellsworth and Ellen (Sorblom) B.; m. Janice Cole, Jan. 21, 1966; m. 2d, Lois Marie Baldwin, Nov. 15, 1981; children—Andrew E., Christopher N.; stepchildren—Kevin B. Kenan, Kelly M. Kenan. B.S. in Biology, Norwich U., 1964; O.D., Pacific U., 1967. Diplomate Nat. Bd. Examiners in Optometry. Commd. 2d lt. U.S. Army, 1967, advanced through grades to capt., 1967, clin. optometrist Walter Reed Army Med. Ctr., Washington, 1967-68; clin. optometrist, Ft. Richardson, Alaska, 1969-71; chief optical div. U.S. Army Med. Equipment and Optical Sch., Denver, 1972-74, resigned, 1974; commd. officer USPHS, 1974, sr. health services officer, 1979; sr. optometrist Alaska Native Med. Ctr., Anchorage, 1974—; optometric cons. Alaska Area Native Health Service. Mem. Am. Optometric Assn., Alaska Optometric Assn. Office: Alaska Native Med Ctr Box 7-741 Anchorage AK 99510

BIGELOW, JOHN BALDWIN, lawyer, state official; b. N.Y.C., Jan. 31, 1943; s. John Albert and Virginia Ann (Hegarty) B.; A.B. in Econs., U. Calif., Berkeley, 1964; J.D., U. Calif., Hastings Coll. Law, 1967. Admitted to Calif. bar, 1968, Alaska bar, 1969, U.S. Dist. Ct. bar, 1969-75, U.S. Circuit Ct. Appeals bar, 1973, 75, N.Mex. bar, 1975, U.S. Supreme Ct. bar, 1979; Staff atty. Alaska Legal Services Corp., Anchorage and Fairbanks, 1968-69, Contra Costa Legal Services Found., Richmond and Martinez, Calif., 1969-72; asso. firm. Pettit, Evers and Martin, San Francisco, 1973-74, Kegel and McCulloh, P.A., Santa Fe, 1974-77; chief public defender State of N.Mex., Santa Fe, 1978-83, dep. atty. gen., 1983—. Mem. State Bar of N.Mex., Alaska Bar Assn., State Bar of Calif. Office: PO Box 2492 Santa Fe NM 87501

BIGGERS, GLEN EDWIN, plumbing contractor; b. Strawberry Glen, Idaho, Sept. 19, 1924; s. Alvin Claude and Bessie Iola (Greene) B.; student pub. schs., Sacramento; m. Susan Maddrill, June 29, 1980; children—LeRoy Glen, Charlotte Louise Johnson, Cynthia June Hoffman. Pres., owner, operator Biggers Plumbing & Heating, Chico, Calif., 1949-80; pres., owner Gridley Plumbing, Chico, 1958—; owner Biggers Leasing, Chico, 1968—; pres., owner Biggers-Do-It-Yourself Centers, Chico, 1969-79, owner B & P Constrn., Chico, 1978—, Cee-Bee Builders, Chico, 1974—; dir. Joint Apprentice Com., 1976-82, dir. Industry Fund, Area 3, 1974—. Youth dir., Sunday Sch. supt., ch. bd. dir., ch. bldg. fund chmn. First Ch. of the Nazarene; bd. dirs. Salvation Army Adv. Bd., 1969—; investment counselor Anderson Oaks. Recipient Award of Appreciation, Biggers Plumbing Employees, 1980. Mem. Apprenticeship Tng. and Funds (dir.), Calif. Mech. Contractors Assn. (dir. 1979—), Mech. Contractors Central Calif. (pres. 1980—). Republican. Ch. of the Nazarene. Club: Mountain Valley Hunting (pres. 1965—). Home: 975 Naomi Ave Chico CA 95926 Office: 551 Country Dr Chico CA 95926

BIGGERS, ROBERT WHITSON, architect, company executive; b. San Angelo, Tex., Sept. 5, 1951; s. Edgar Whitson and Erma Mardie (Garris) B.; 1 dau., Ashley McCausland. B.F.A., U. N.Mex., 1973, M.Arch. with honors, 1978. Project architect Robbins and Assocs. Architects, Tampa, Fla., 1974-75; grad. asst. U. N.Mex., 1967-77; office mgr. H. William Fanning, Albuquerque, 1977-80; dir. archtl. programming The Burns/Peters Group P.A., Albuquerque, 1981—; interim instr. U. N.Mex., 1980; speaker in field. Patron Albuquerque Little Theater, 1982. Mem. AIA (assoc.), U. N.Mex. Alumni Assn., English Setter Assn. Am., Albuquerque Amateur Softball League, Phi Kappa Phi. Designer logo for Ronald McDonald House, Albuquerque, 1982. Home: 2828 Palo Verde Apt C Albuquerque NM 87112 Office: 8000 Pennsylvania Circle Albuquerque NM 87116

BIGGS, BARBARA ELLEN, clin. psychologist; b. Bayonne, N.J., Aug. 30, 1931; d. Joseph Michael and Sylvia (Rosenthal) Silverman; B.A., Adelphi U., 1953; M.A., NYU, 1954; Ph.D., UCLA, 1971; m. Sidney Sonenblum, Nov. 22, 1973; children—Michael Patrick, Jonathan David. Speech pathologist Upper Darby (Pa.) Sch. Dist., 1954-55; asst. prof. communicative disorders U. Calif., Northridge, 1968-69; dir. acad. studies Student Devel. Ctr., Mt. St. Mary's Coll., 1969-71; vis. prof. psychobiology U. So. Calif., 1971-73; clin. psychologist, marriage, family and child counselor, divorce mediator; co-dir. Center for Interpersonal Studies, Los Angeles, 1971—; supr. UCLA Psychology Clinic, 1981—; cons. Profl. Tng. Workshops for Tchrs., Claremont Colls., Immaculate Heart Coll., Rio Hondo Coll., Center in Amsterdam, Quaesitor in London, 1969-75; cons. St. John's Hosp., VA Outpatient Clinic, Assn. Social Workers, Japanese Counseling Assn., Tokyo, Ctr., Amsterdam, Quaesitor, London, Cold Mountain Inst., Vancouver, B.C., 1969-71; dir. hearing officers tng. program Los Angeles City Atty.'s Office, 1975-76; cons. Clackamas County (Oreg.) Dist. Atty.'s Office, 1976, State Calif. Office Adminstrv. Hearings, 1976; cons. Southwestern U. Law Sch., 1976, Humanistic Law Inst., 1976-78; condr. tng. workshops Beverly Hills Barristers, Calif. Bar Assn.; condr. mediation tng. programs Venice Mar Vista Neighborhood Justice Ctr., City of Los Angeles Landlord-Tenant Mediation Bd., 1978, Wright Inst. Mediation Service, 1983; exhibited in photography shows Gallery La Porte, Los Angeles, 1979-82, Garendo Gallery, 1979-80; Women in Design, 1982, 83. Recipient Public Service award VA, 1966. Mem. state central com. Democratic party, 1964. Mem. Women in Design, Am., Calif., Los Angeles County psychol. assns., Group Psychotherapy Assn. So. Calif. (mem. bd. 1970-74, membership sec. 1972-73), Los Angeles Soc. Clin. Psychologist (pres. 1976). Author: (with Gary Felton) Up From Under-Achievement, 1977; contbr. articles to profl. jours. Home: 1340 Linda Flora Dr Los Angeles CA 90049 Office: 11941 Wilshire Blvd Los Angeles CA 90025

BIGGS, JEANNE MARIE, executive secretary; b. Norristown, Pa., Jan. 26, 1947; d. Raymond J. and Marie Gertrude (Coovert) Macolly; m. Darryl E. Mueller, Aug. 26, 1968; m. 2d Edwin Alan Biggs, Apr. 6, 1979; 1 dau., Gretchen Elizabeth. Student, Mundelein Coll., 1979-80. Sec. to pres. Product Research and Development Corp., Tylersport, Pa., 1964-65; sec. to mgr. tng. and devel. Univac div. Sperry Rand Corp., Blue Bell, Pa., 1965-69, adminstrv. asst., 1967-69; exec. sec. to dir. pub. relations KDI Sylvan Pools, Inc., Doylestown, Pa., 1970-71, sec. to sales mgr., 1971-76; adminstrv. asst. to exec. dir. Probational Vol. Services, Inc., Doylestown, 1977-78; dist. exec. sec. to supt. of Clear Creek County Schs., Idaho Spring, Colo., 1980—, also asst. sec. to Bd. of Edn., Clear Creek County, Idaho Springs. Sec. Georgetown (Colo.) Fasching Ltd.; chmn. Georgetown Soc.'s Silent Auction; Georgetown rep. to St. Paul Winter Carnival. Roman Catholic. Home: 2030 Blue Bird Dr PO Box 744 Georgetown CO 80444 Office: PO Box 370 Idaho Springs CO 80452

BIGLIARDI, MATTHEW PAUL, bishop; b. Charleroi, Pa., Sept. 14, 1920; s. Achille and Regina (Bonaccinni) B.; B.S., U. Calif.-Berkeley, 1950; M.Div., Ch. Div. Sch. of the Pacific, 1953, D.D., 1974; m. Jeanne C. Gross, Feb. 19, 1949; 1 child, Aidan. Ordained priest Protestant Episcopal Ch., 1954; curate Trinity Ch., Seattle, 1953-55; vicar Emmanuel Ch., Mercer Island, Wash., 1955-60; rector, 1960-74; bishop Diocese of Oreg. Lake Oswego, 1974—. Trustee Good Samaritan Hosp., Portland and Corvallis, Oreg., chmn., 1974—; trustee Oreg. Episcopal Schs., chmn. 1974—; trustee Oreg. Heart Assn., 1978-81, Boy Scouts Am., 1978-81, Pres. Bishop's Fund for World Relief, 1979—; trustee Ch. Divinity Sch. of the Pacific, Berkeley, 1983—. Mem. Sigma Xi, Phi Beta Kappa. Address: 11800 SW Military Ln Portland OR 97219

BIGLIERI, EDWARD GEORGE, physician; b. San Francisco, Jan. 17, 1925; s. Ned and (Mignacco) B.; student U. San Francisco, 1942-43, Gonzaga U., 1943-44; B.S. in Chemistry summa cum laude, U. San Francisco, 1948; M.D., U. Calif., 1952; m. Beverly A. Bergesen, May 16, 1953; children—Mark, Michael, Gregg. Intern, U. Calif. at San Francisco Med. Center, also VA Hosp., San Francisco, 1952-54, resident, 1954-56; research physician NIH, 1956-58, also metabolic unit U. Calif., 1958-61, asst. prof. medicine, 1962-65, assoc. prof., 1965-71, prof., 1971—; program dir. gen. clin. research, also chief endocrinology service San Francisco Gen. Hosp., 1962—; NATO vis. scientist, 1983; vis. prof. Monash U., Melbourne, Australia, 1967. Cons. Oak Knoll Naval Hosp., Travis AFB; mem. NIH study sect., 1971-74. Served to lt. (jg) USNR, 1944-46. NIH grantee, 1972-73. Diplomate Am. Bd. Internal Medicine, mem. endocrine test com. 1971-77. Mem. Endocrine Soc., A.C.P., Am. Soc. Clin. Investigation, Am. Heart Assn. (council for high blood pressure research), Assn. Am. Physicians, Western Assn. Physicians, Am. Fedn. Clin. Research. Contbr. articles to profl. jours. Home: 129 Convent Ct San Rafael CA 94901 Office: San Francisco General Hospital San Francisco CA 94110

BIGLIONE, NORMAND JOSEPH, agriculture fertilizer co. exec.; b. Clovis, Calif., Aug. 12, 1925; s. Fred Julius and Kathryne Margaret (Andreis) B.; m. Shirley Jean Goodwin, Aug. 2, 1952; children—Lisa Normande, Normand Joseph. A.B., Calif. State U., 1949, M.A., 1951; postgrad. U. Okla., 1964. Commd. officer U.S. Army, 1951, advanced through grades to col., 1968, ret., 1970; assigned U.S. Army Command and Gen. Staff Coll., 1960-63, prin. staff asst., to U.S. comdr., West Berlin, W.Ger., 1965-67; chief tng. orgn. and readiness br. Policy and Programs Div., Directorate for Civil Disturbance, Washington, 1967-71; v.p., controller Nat. Bank of Agr., Fresno, Calif., 1970-75; exec. Western Farm Services, Shell Oil Co., Fresno, 1975-81; exec. Agr.-Fertilizer Co., Dos Palos, Calif., 1981—, controller, 1983—. Pres., Clovis Ctr.; pres. Fresno County Farm Bur., 1979-80, bd. dirs., 1981—. Decorated Legion of Merit, Bronze Star medal, Army Commendation medal with oak leaf cluster. Mem. Pacific Coast Quarter Horse Racing Assn., Am. Quarter Horse Assn., Sigma Alpha Epsilon. Democrat. Methodist. Clubs: Fresno Appaloosa (pres. 1974-75), Masons. Home: 12895 Auberry Rd Clovis CA 93612 Office: PO Box 1145 Dos Palos CA 93620

BILBRAY, JAMES HUBERT, state senator, lawyer; b. Las Vegas, May 19, 1938; s. James A. and Ann E. (Miller) B.; student Brigham Young U., 1957-58, U. Nev., 1958-60; B.A., Am. U., 1962; J.D., Wash. U., 1964; m. Michaelene Mercer, Jan. 1960; children—Bridget, Kevin, Erin, Shannon. Admitted to Nev. bar, 1965, staff mem. Senator Howard Cannon, U.S. Senate, 1960-64; dep. dist. atty., Clark County, Nev., 1965-68; mem. firm Bilbray, Carelli & Miller, Las Vegas, 1969—; mem. Nev. Senate, 1980—, chmn. taxation com., 1983-84, chmn. interim com. on pub. broadcasting, 1983; dir. Lenoy Corp., Las Vegas, 1968—, pres., 1979-80; alt. mcpl. judge City of Las Vegas, 1978-80. Bd. regents U. Nev. System, 1968-72; mem. nat. council State Govts. Commn. on Arts and Historic Preservation. Named Outstanding Alumni, U. Nev., Las Vegas, 1979. Mem. Nev. State Bar Assn., Clark County Bar Assn., Phi Alpha Delta, Sigma Chi. Democrat. Roman Catholic. Club: Elks. Office: 428 S 4th St Las Vegas NV 89101

BILBY, RICHARD MANSFIELD, fed. judge; b. Tucson, May 29, 1931; s. Ralph Willard and Marguerite (Mansfield) B.; B.S., U. Ariz., 1955; J.D., U. Mich., 1958; m. Ann Louise Borchert, July 6, 1957; children—Claire Louise, Ellen Markley. Admitted to Ariz. bar, 1959, since practiced in Tucson; law clk. to Chief Judge Chambers, 9th Circuit Ct. Appeals, San Francisco, 1958-59; mem. firm Bilby, Thompson, Shoenhair & Warnock, 1959-79, partner, 1967-79; judge U.S. Dist. Ct., Dist. Ariz., Tucson, 1979—; conscientious objector hearing officer Dept. Justice, 1959-62; chmn. Pima County Med.-Legal panel, 1968-70. Mem. Tucson Charter Revision Com., 1965-70; chmn. United Fund Profl. Div., 1968, Spl. Gift Div., 1970; chmn. St. Joseph Hosp. Devel. Fund Drive, 1970. Republican state chmn. Vols. for Eisenhower, 1956; Rep. county chmn. Pima County, Ariz., 1972-74. Past pres. Tucson Conquistadores; bd. dirs. St. Josephs Hosp., 1969-77, chmn., 1972-75. Served with AUS, 1952-54. Fellow Am. Coll. Trial Lawyers; mem. Ariz. Acad., Town Hall (dir. 1976-79). Home: 4717 Brisa Del Sur Tucson AZ 85718 Office: 55 E Broadway Tucson AZ 85701

BILIK, SARA FAYTHE, mental health center executive, consultant; b. N.Y.C., Apr. 15, 1955; d. William and Evelyn B. Student Sorbonne, Paris, 1973-74, Chinese U. Hong Kong, 1979, Les Hautes Etudes Commerciales, Paris, 1978-79; B.A. in French and Philosophy, NYU, 1975, M.B.A., 1980; postgrad. cert. U. Utah, 1981. Adminstrv. asst. Bankers Trust Internat., N.Y.C., 1976-67; mktg. research asst. Corning Glass Ware Internat., Paris, 1978; intern, mktg. asst. ITT World Communications, N.Y.C., 1980-81; dir. mktg. and employee assistance programs Colo. West Regional Mental Health Ctr., Glenwood Springs, 1981—; cons. mktg. and strategic planning non-profit orgns.; speaker nat. assn. meetings. Mem. Garfield County Human Services Council. United Airlines fellow, 1978-79; NYU grad. fellow, 1978-79; recipient Internat. Mgmt. Program award, 1978-79, Lever Bros. Mktg. Excellence award, 1978, N.Y. State Regents award, 1972-75. Mem. Am. Mktg. Assn. Acad. Health Services Mktg., Nat. Council Community Mental Health Ctrs., Assn. Labor-Mgmt. Adminstrs. and Cons. on Alcholism, Inc., Am. Soc. Tng. and Devel. Democrat. Jewish. Author: What an Executive Should Know About Employee Assistance Programs, 1983. Office: PO Box 1580 Glenwood Springs CO 81602

BILLER, ANGIE MARIE, telephone company manager; b. Denver, Mar. 18, 1947; d. Anthony A. and Clara (Mertens) McNulty; m. John J. Lay, Nov. 28, 1981; children—Steve, Stacey. B.A., U. No. Colo., 1969. Customer service rep. Mountain Bell, Denver, 1969-71, bus. office supr., 1971-77, staff mgr. fin. dept., 1977-78, product mgr., 1978—. Founder, pres. Women in Mgmt. Mountain Bell, Denver, 1978-83; bd. dirs. Colo. Women Forward, 1979-80, Denver Women's Career Ctr., 1979-83. Mem. Nat. Assn. Female Execs., AAUW. Democrat. Home: 3835 S

Kalispell St Aurora CO 80013 Office: Mountain Bell 1125 17th St Room 920 Denver CO 80202

BILLET, ARTHUR B., aerospace, marine engineer, consultant; b. Indpls., May 20, 1920; s. Arthur J. and Inza A (Brazington) B.; m. E. Christine Carter, Sept. 19, 1942; children—Thomas A., Carol C. B.S. in Aerospace Engrng., U. Mich., Ann Arbor, 1942. Design engr. Sperry Vickers, Troy, Mich., after 1944, group supr., to 1956, lab. mgr. hydraulic equipment, 1956-63, exec. engr. hydraulic equipment and systems, 1963-67; research specialist 747 hydraulic/mech. systems Boeing Co., 1967-73; systems engr. Teledyne Ryan, San Diego, 1970-73; supr., fluid engr., Rohr Industries/Rohr Marine, Inc., 1973-81; prin. engr. Hydro Products/Honeywell, San Diego, 1981—; led expedition to African desert, Greenland ice cap, Panama jungle to study aircraft environ. for Soc. Automotive Engrs. and USAF, 1962-66; cons. U.S. Dept. of Commerce, 1965-73, USAF, Soc. Automotive Engrs., 1965-70. Served to 1st lt. (pilot) USAF, 1942-44. Decorated Air Medal. Recipient certs. of merit Soc. Automotive Engrs., 1965, 67, 82. Mem. Soc. of Automotive Engrs. (nat. dir. 1976-79, past pres. San Diego sect.), AIAA, Am. Def. Preparedness Assn., Inst. of Environ. Sci. (pres. 1961-62). Contbr. articles to profl. jours. Home: 2322 Via Siena La Jolla CA 92037 Office: 11777 Sorrento Valley Blvd San Diego CA 92121

BILLIGMEIER, ROBERT HENRY, sociologist, educator; b. McClusky, N.D., Jan. 16, 1917; s. Henry and Meta Berta (Masueger) B.; m. Hanny Marie Salirsberg, Jan. 20, 1940; children—Jon Christian, Robin Hanny, Carina. A.B., U. Calif.-Berkeley, 1939, M.A., 1941; Ph.D., Stanford U., 1951. Population analyst U.S. Dept. State, Washington, 1943-45; instr. Stanford U., 1946-50; instr. to prof. sociology U. Calif.-Santa Barbara, 1952—; assoc. dir. U. Calif. Edn. Aboard program, 1964-75. Mem. Am. Hist. Soc., Population Soc. Am., Am. Sociol. Assn. Democrat. Author: Americans from Germany: A Study of Cultural Diversity, 1974; A Crisis in Swiss Pluralism, 1979. Home: 398 Stevens Rd Santa Barbara CA 93105 Office: U Calif Dept Sociology Santa Barbara CA 93106

BILLINGS, ANDREW GLOVER, psychologist; b. New London, Conn., Apr. 8, 1952; s. Charles Ledin and Mary Rabin (Glover) B.; m. Barbara Ann Miller, Mar. 5, 1979. B.A. summa cum laude, U. Conn., Storrs, 1974; Ph.D. in Psychology, U. Vt., Burlington, 1979. Lic. clin. psychologist, Calif. Research psychologist U. Vt. Sch. Medicine, 1978-79; research psychologist dept. psychiatry, Social Ecology Lab., Stanford U. Sch. Medicine, 1979—; psychologist Palo Alto VA Med. Center, 1979—; fellow med. psychology service Med. Center Hosp. Vt., 1977-78. Mem. Am. Psychol. Assn., Soc. Behavioral Medicine, Phi Beta Kappa, Phi Beta Phi. Democrat. Club: West Bay Express. Co-author: The Conceptualization and Measurement of Coping, 1982; contbr. articles to profl. jours. Home: 828 Roosevelt Ave Redwood City CA 94061 Office: Psychiatry TD-114 Stanford U Sch Med Stanford CA 94305

BILLINGS, CHARLES REEMS, psychologist, educator; b. Chgo., Apr. 5, 1943; s. Von D. and Nina Eloise (Sanders) B.; m. Naomi Singer, Feb. 14, 1982; children by previous marriage—Paul Reems, David Aaron. A.A., Coll. Marin, 1963; B.A. in Psychology, San Francisco State U., 1965, M.A. in Psychology, 1967, M.A. in Ednl. Adminstrn., 1971; Ph.D., Calif. Sch. Profl. Psychology, 1974. Lic. psychologist and marriage, family and child counselor, Calif.; diplomate Am. Bd. Profl. Psychology and Am. Bd. Family Psychology. Psychology trainee San Mateo County (Calif.) Community Mental Health, 1967-68; psychologist various schs., Calif. and instr., lectr. Sonoma State Coll. and San Francisco State U., 1969-70; dist. psychologist Shoreline Unified Sch. Dist., Tomales, Calif., 1970-75; pvt. practice marriage, family and child counseling, Larkspur, Calif., 1968—, ednl. psychology, 1971—, psychology, 1976—; mem. faculty Dominican Coll., 1978—, assoc. prof., 1981—, dir. student counseling services, 1982—; psychol. cons. Family Service Agy. Marin, San Rafael, Calif., 1982. Recipient Most Outstanding Research award and Merit cert. Calif. Assn. Sch. Psychologists and Psychometrists, 1976, Appreciation cert. Marin County Supt. Schs. Mem. Acad. Psychologists in Marital, Sex and Family Therapy, Am. Psychol. Assn., Calif. Psychol. Assn., Am. Art Therapy Assn., Marin County Psychol. Assn., Calif. Assn. Marriage and Family Therapists, Marin County Assn. Marriage and Family Therapists, Psi Chi. Contbr. psychol. articles to profl. jours. Address: 60 E Sir Francis Drake Blvd Suite 309 Larkspur CA 94939

BILLINGS, HOLLY LYNN, public relations executive; b. Montebello, Calif., Dec. 17, 1956; d. Edward Everett III and Elizabeth (Weldon) Billings; m. Robert Barton Rasband, July 21, 1978 (div.). B.A. in Communications/Pub. Relations, Calif. State U.-Fullerton, 1979. Pub. relations asst. Presbyn. Hosp./Health Ctr., Whittier, Calif., 1978-79; pub. relations coordinator Aerojet Ordnance Co., Downey, Calif., 1979-80; mktg. communications mgr. Century Data/Xerox Co., Anaheim, Calif., 1980-82; pub. relations account exec. Jansen Assocs., Inc., Irvine, Calif., 1982—. Named Outstanding Editor, Calif. State U., 1979; recipient cert. of excellence Calif. State U., 1979. Mem. Pub. Relations Soc. Am., Los Angeles Press Club. Republican. Contbr. articles to computer related publs. Office: Jansen Assocs 2960 Daimler Irvine CA 92705

BILLINGS, RICHARD BRUCE, economist, educator; b. Waukesha, Wis., Dec. 5, 1938; s. Floyd Henry and Edessa Mary (Burmeister) B.; m. Patricia Christy Barnum, Mar. 31, 1961; children—Stephen, David. B.A. in Econs., U. Ariz., Tucson, 1962, M.A., 1963; Ph.D. in Econs., Claremont Grad. Sch., 1969. Lectr. econs. U. Ariz., 1965—; research economist Ariz. State Legislature, 1969. Mem. Western Tax Assn. (past pres.), Western Regional Sci. Assn., Am. Econs. Assn., Nat. Tax Assn. Democrat. Methodist. Contbr. several articles to profl. jours. Home: 2439 E 7th St Tucson AZ 85719 Office: Dept Econs U Ariz Tucson AZ 85721

BILS, ROBERT FREDERICK, scientist, educator; b. Harvey, Ill., Jan. 10, 1931; s. Frederick Stephen and Grace Esther (Pohlman) B.; student Oberlin Coll., 1949-51; B.S., U. Ill., 1954, M.S., 1958, Ph.D. in Plant Biochemistry, 1960; m. Afrodite Konstans, Aug. 8, 1954; children—Lynne, Julie, Lisa. Teaching asst. botany U. Ill., Urbana, 1956-57, research asst. Electron Microscope Labs., 1957-60; cons. Delco Battery Co., Muncie, Ind., 1957-59; NIH fellow Mass Inst. Tech., Cambridge, 1960-61; asst. prof. biology U. So. Calif., Los Angeles, 1961-66, dir. Electron Microscope Lab., 1961—, asso. prof. 1966-70, prof. biol. sci., cellular and molecular biology, 1970—; asso. dir. Specialized Center of Research Environmental Lung Disease, U. So. Calif.-Rancho Los Amigos Hosp., Downey, 1972-77; cons. Los Angeles Air Pollution Control Dist., 1969-74; cons. to spl. studies sect. Nat. Adv. Environmental Health Sci. Council, 1971-72; vis. prof. Pathologisches Institut, research scientist Lufthygiene Silikose Inst. U. Dusseldorf, 1968-69; vis. prof. research unit for comparative animal respiration U. Bristol, 1976-77. Mem. planning bd. Montebello (Calif.) Unified Sch. Dist., 1966-68. Served with AUS, 1954-56; PTO. Fellow Royal Microscopical Soc.; mem. AAAS, Am. Soc. for Cell Biology, N.Y. Acad. Scis., Electron Microscopy Soc. Am. (chmn. 30th meeting 1972, exec. council 1973-76, dir. technician certification program 1978—), So. Calif. Soc. for Electron Microscopy (pres. 1965), Sigma Xi, Phi Sigma, Pi Alpha Xi. Author: Electron Microscopy, 1974. Contbr. articles to profl. jours. Home: 816 Westmoreland Dr Montebello CA 90640 Office: Dept Biological Sciences University Southern California Los Angeles CA 90007

BILYEU, CHARLES E., educator, state senator; grad. U. Idaho, Redlands U.; m. Diane Bilyeu; children—Brigette, Clark, Valencia. Prof. speech and drama Idaho State U., Pocatello; mem. Idaho Senate from 35th dist., mem. fin. com., transp. com. Democrat. Office: Dept Speech and Drama Idaho State U Pocatello ID 83209*

BINDER, DEBORAH JIL, securities and commodities broker, educator; b. Durango, Colo., Nov. 30, 1949; d. Forest Vernon and Charlene Jacqueline (Woods) Binder. B.A., U. Colo., 1971, M.A., 1977, postgrad. 1980—. Asst. to purchasing agt. U. Colo., Boulder, 1971-72; tchr. English, West End Pub. Schs., Naturita, Colo., 1972-76; tchr., reading specialist, asst. dept. chmn. Jefferson County Pub. Schs., Arvada, Colo., 1976-81; tchr. speed reading U. Colo., Boulder, 1980—; broker Internat. Securities, Denver, 1981-82; v.p., securities broker Mills Fin. Services, Inc., Denver, 1982—; commodities broker Major Trend Futures, Ltd., Denver, 1982—. Regents Honors scholar, U. Colo., 1967. Mem. Nat. Assn. Securities Dealers. Democrat. Episcopalian. Office: Suite B 160 1050 17th St Denver CO 80265

BINDER, JAMES KAUFFMAN, nuclear energy co. exec.; b. Reading, Pa., Nov. 20, 1920; s. Paul Burdette and Edna (Kauffman) B.; B.A., Lehigh U., 1941; M.A., Johns Hopkins U., 1952; profl. cert. in systems mgmt. U. Calif.-San Diego, 1976; A.S. in Data Processing, San Diego Evening Coll., 1979, A.A. in Fgn. Lang., 1979; A.A. in Spanish, Mira Costa Coll., Oceanside, Calif., 1981. Instr. English, Notre Dame U., South Bend, Ind., 1948-49; prof. English, Athens (Greece) Coll., 1950-51; CARE rep., Greece, 1951-52; reporter, staff writer Athens News, 1952-53; dir. lang. tng. World Council Chs. Refugee Service, Athens, 1953-54; co-editor Am. Overseas Guide, N.Y., West Berlin, 1957-58; lectr. English, U. Md. Overseas Program, European and Far East divs., 1958-66; successively supr. Central Info. Center, supt. documents, systems analyst GA Techs., Inc., La Jolla, Calif., 1968—. Recipient Williams Prize, Lehigh U., 1939, 41; Johns Hopkins U. Grad. Sch. Pres. scholar, 1945-48. Roman Catholic. Clubs: Tudor and Stuart, Automobile of So. Calif. Author: The Correct Comedy, 1951; contbg. translator Modern Scandinavian Poetry, 1948; editor: (with Erwin H. Tiebe) American Overseas Guide, 1958.

BINDI, ROBERT VICTOR, podiatrist; b. San Francisco, July 5, 1940; s. Albert and Rose Marie (Miraglia) B.; B.S., St. Mary's Coll., Calif., 1962; B.S., Calif. Coll. Podiatric Medicine, 1966, D.Podiatric Medicine, 1966; m. Maureen McCline; children—Scott, Craig. Practice podiatric medicine, San Jose, Calif., 1967—; mem. Samaritan Podiatry Group, Inc., 1974—; mem. staff Good Samaritan Hosp., San Jose, 1978—, chmn. podiatry div., 1979-81; mem. staff Valley West Gen. Hosp., Los Gatos, Calif., Hazel Hawkins Meml. Hosp., Hollister, Calif., Calif. Podiatry Hosp., San Francisco; instr. Calif. Coll. Podiatric Medicine. Named Podiatrist of Year, Central Coast Podiatric Assts. Assn., 1976; diplomate Nat. Bd. Podiatric Examiners, Am. Bd. Podiatric Surgery. Fellow Am. Coll. Foot Surgeons; mem. Am. Podiatry Assn. (del. 1974-81), Calif. Podiatry Assn. (pres. 1978-79, dir. 1973-80; Podiatrist of Yr. 1982), Calif. Coll. Podiatric Medicine Alumni Assn. (pres. 1981), Central Coast Podiatry Soc. (pres. 1970-72), Sigma Pi Epsilon. Democrat. Club: Civic. Home: 6740 Lookout Bend San Jose CA 95120 Office: 2577 Samaritan Dr Suite 705 San Jose CA 95124

BINDMAN, STEPHEN S., clin. psychologist; b. N.Y.C., Dec. 3, 1932; s. Abraham I. and Cecilia B.; B.A., UCLA, 1957, Ph.D. (USPHS fellow), 1966; m. Terry Holdiman, July 4, 1963; children—Rachel, Daniel. Asst. prof. dept. psychology U. Tex., Austin, 1966-72; partner Psychol. Service Assn. of Westwood, Los Angeles, 1972-78; pvt. practice clin. psychology, Los Angeles, 1978—; asst. clin. prof. psychology UCLA. Mem. Am. Psychol. Assn., Calif. Psychol. Assn., Tex. Psychol. Assn., Soc. Clin. Psychologists Los Angeles, AAAS, Am. Acad. Psychotherapists. Office: 1100 Glendon Ave Suite 2014 Los Angeles CA 90024 also 801 N Tustin Ave Suite 307 Santa Ana CA 92705

BINDRIM, PAUL, psychologist; b. N.Y.C., Aug. 14, 1920; s. Paul Arthur and Caroline B.; B.A., Columbia U., 1941; postgrad. N.Y. Med. Coll., 1941-43; M.A. (scholar), Duke U., 1947; Ph.D., Internat. Coll., 1976. Instr., Finch Coll., 1944-46; research asso. parapsychology lab. Duke U., 1946-47; instr. El Camino Coll., 1948-52, Calif. Inst. Transpersonal Psychology, 1975; pvt. practice psychology, Los Angeles, 1948—; mem. staff Edgemont Hosp., 1975; pres. Group Psychotherapy Assn., 1979—. Duke U. research grantee, 1946-47; lic. psychologist, Calif. Mem. Am. Psychol. Assn., Humanistic Psychology Assn. Republican. Author: Out of Touch (film), 1970; The Use of Nudity as a Psychotherapeutic Procedure, 1968; Outcome Research and Analysis of the Nude Marathon, 1976; Group Therapy: Protecting Privacy, 1980. Office: 2000 Cantata Dr Los Angeles CA 90068

BINEGAR, GWENDOLYN ANN, social worker; b. Phoenix, Sept. 23, 1924; d. Glenn Marvin and Mary Lenore (Cartwright) Redington; B.S. in Sociology, Iowa State U., 1948; M.Social Service, Bryn Mawr Coll., 1967; m. Lewis Albert Binegar, Nov. 2, 1951; children—Glen Albert, Birne Thomas, William Lewis, Alan Martin. Coordinator vols. Santa Barbara Mental Health Service, Lompoc, Calif., 1964; psychiat. social worker Child Study Inst., Bryn Mawr (Pa.) Coll., 1967-71; sr. social worker Ruth Sch. for Girls, Seattle, 1972; staff worker Nat. Assn. Social Workers, Los Angeles, 1973; med. social worker Casa Colina Hosp., Pomona, Calif., 1974; supervising counselor San Gabriel Valley Regional Center, Pomona, 1975-78, program mgr. six Los Angeles County Regional Centers' High Risk Infant Projects, 1978-79; chief case mgmt. services San Diego Regional Center, 1981—. Lic. clin. social worker. Mem. Am. Acad. Certified Social Workers, Am. Assn. on Mental Deficiency, Devel. Disabilities Council San Gabriel Valley (sec. 1976-77), Nat. Assn. Social Workers. Republican. Presbyterian. Co-researcher Roots of Learning Disabilities, 1967-69. Home: 28809 Lilac Rd Valley Center CA 92082 Office: 4355 Ruffin Rd San Diego CA 92123

BINGAMAN, JEFF, atty. gen. N.Mex.; b. El Paso, Tex., Oct. 3, 1943; s. Jess and Beth B.; B.A., Harvard U., 1965; LL.B., Stanford U., 1968. Admitted to N.Mex. bar, 1968; mem. firm Campbell, Bingaman & Black, Santa Fe, 1970-78; asst. atty. gen. N.Mex., 1970-78, atty. gen., 1979—. Mem. legal staff Constl. Conv., 1969. Served with U.S. Army Res., 1968-74. Mem. Am. Bar Assn., N.Mex. Bar Assn., Santa Fe County Bar Assn. Democrat. Office: Office of Atty Gen 237 Don Gaspar Ave PO Drawer 1508 Santa Fe NM 87501

BINGHAM, CHARLES WAYNE, wood products company executive; b. Myrtle Point, Oreg., May 13, 1933; s. Irwin G. and Edna Mae (Sippy) B.; m. Barbara Pahl, June 20, 1959; children—Charles Wayne, Helen Sippy, Deborah Winn, Donald Pahl. A.B., magna cum laude, Harvard U., 1955, LL.B., 1960. Bar: Wash. 1960. Lawyers, Weyerhaeuser Co., Tacoma, Wash., from 1960, chip supply mgr., 1964-65, raw material supply mgr., 1965-67, acting area mgr., Longview, Wash., 1967, mgr. of areas, 1967-68, v.p. wood products and timberlands, 1968-72, sr. v.p. timerlands, wood products and internat., 1972-81, exec. v.p., 1981—; dir. Puget Sound Power & Light Co. Bd. overseers Harvard Coll. Mem. Wash. Export Council, Associated Harvard Alumni (dir.). Office: Weyerhaeuser Co Tacoma WA 98477

BINGHAM, ROBERT, orthopedic surgeon; b. Lafayette, Colo., July 21, 1910; s. William John and Francis (Rice) B.; B.A., U. Redlands, 1932; M.D., U. Colo., 1938; m. Charlotte Martin, Aug. 20, 1936; children—William Charles, Katherine Ruth, Ann Louise. Intern, Hosp. U. Pa., Phila., 1938-40; resident in orthopedic surgery N.Y. Orthopedic Hosp., N.Y.C., 1940-42; practice medicine specializing in orthopedic surgery, Riverside, Calif., 1946-73, Yorba Linda, Calif., 1973-81, Anaheim, Calif., 1982—; med. dir. Nat. Arthritis Med. Clinic, Desert Hot Springs, Calif. Served to maj. M.C., AUS, 1942-46. Fellow AMA. ACS, Am. Coll. Orthopedic Surgeons. Democrat. Presbyterian. Contbr. articles on arthritis, orthopedics, nutrition and clin. research to med. jours. 1000 S Anaheim Blvd Suite 301 Anaheim CA 92805 also 13-630 Mountain View Rd Desert Hot Springs CA 92240

BINGHAM, VERNON LESLIE, agrl. coop. adminstr.; b. Ogden, Utah, Mar. 19, 1919; s. Eugene and Esther (Erickson) B.; student U. Utah, 1938-41; m. Mildred Fern Garn, Dec. 1, 1947; children—Vernon E., Leslie G., Brent G., David E. Membership rep. Federated Milk Producers, Salt Lake City, 1946-49, gen. mgr., 1949-64; dir. mktg. Mich. Milk Producers, Detroit, 1965-70; mktg. and transp. mgr. Mountain Empire Dairymen's Assn., Denver, 1970-74, gen. mgr., 1974—; dir. Western Dairymen's Coop., Inc., Nat. Milk Mktg. Bd., Dairy Research Inc.; bd. dirs., nat. adv. bd. United Dairy Industry Assn. Chmn., Emigration Canyon Zoning and Planning Dist. Salt Lake County, Utah, 1948-50; del. Utah Republican party convs., 1948, 52, 56; trustee Humana Inc., Thornton, Colo., 1981-82, chmn. bd. trustees, 1982—. Served with USAAF, 1942-45. Decorated D.F.C., Air medal with 8 clusters. Mem. Nat. Milk Producers Fedn., Internat. Assn. Agrl. Economists, Nat. Agrl. Mktg. Assn., Hyland Hills Amateur Hockey Assn. (pres. 1975-78). Mem. Ch. Jesus Christ of Latter-Day Saints. Office: 12450 N Washington St Denver CO 80241

BINGHAM-NEWMAN, ANN MARIE, child development educator, family therapist; b. Coronado, Calif., Feb. 14, 1943; d. C. R. and Jane Bell (Bingham) Newman; m. Arthur J. Gonchar, July 11, 1976; children—Rebecca, Andrew, Jonathan. B.S., U. Wis., 1966, M.S., 1971, Ph.D., 1974; M.A., Calif. Family Study Ctr., 1980. Coordinator Early Childhood Study Ctr., U. Wis., Madison, 1971-74; coordinator interdisciplinary child devel. degree program. Calif. State U.-Los Angeles, 1974-82, prof. child devel., home econs, 1974—; cons. Family Therapy Services, Inc., Rancho Cucamonga, Calif., House of Ruth, Claremont, Calif. Mem. Nat. Assn. Edn. Young Children, Soc. Research in Child Devel., Am. Assn. Marriage and Family Therapists, Calif. Assn. Marriage and Family Therapists, Nat. Council Family Relations, Resources for Infant Educators. Author: (with Arthur J. Gonchar) Observational Methods for Psychology Curricula, 1983; contbr. numerous articles to profl jours. Office: 5151 State University Dr Los Angeles CA 90032

BINGLE, EDMUND JOSEPH, SR., electronics engr., educator; b. St. Louis, May 15, 1916; s. Jules Francis and Edith Octavia (White) B.; student Coll. San Mateo, evenings 1950-56; grad. Capitol Radio Engrng. Inst., 1959; m. Jeanette Lucille Schaffhauser, May 24, 1936; children—Edmund Joseph, Richard Charles. Powder mixer-foreman Pacific Ry. Signal Co., Los Gatos, Calif., 1936-42; tchr. piano, Los Gatos, 1940-42; radio electric mechanic United Airlines, San Francisco, 1946-57, instr. electronics, 1943-78; instr. Avionics Coll. San Mateo (Calif.), 1968-70, mem. electronics adv. bd., 1971-78. Chmn. community relations com. United Air Lines Employees Community Fund, 1963-68. Served with USAAF, 1942-45. Mem. Calif. Council Electronics Instr. (pres. 1973), Nat. Avionics Soc. Democrat. Roman Catholic. Club: Skywest Golf (Hayward, Calif.). Home: 750 Glenview Dr Apt 309 San Bruno CA 94066

BINGMAN, STEVEN ANTHONY, construction company executive; b. Union City, Ind., Apr. 16, 1941; s. Ralph Glenn and Hazel Virginia (Rice) B.; B.S. in Constrn., Ariz. State U., 1965; m. Della Ione Hodges, Aug. 4, 1961; children—Delane, Brian. Seaman, Scripps Inst. Oceanography, La Jolla, Calif., 1959-61; estimator Morrison-Knudson Constrn. Co., South Gate, Calif., 1965, Ameron Pipe Products Co., Phoenix, 1965-66; dir. estimating Kitchell Contractors, Inc., Newport Beach, Calif., 1966—; instr. Calif. State U.-Long Beach; condr. seminars. Active local YMCA, Little League Baseball, Big Bros.; bd. dirs. Irvine Youth Basketball League. Named Ariz. Estimator of Year, Ariz. chpt. Am. Soc. Profl. Estimators, 1975; named to Walker's Estimators' Hall of Fame, 1983. Cert. constrn. estimator. Mem. Am. Soc. Profl. Estimators (chpt. pres. 1973; nat. award of merit 1975, 79, nat. pres. 1977, Nat. Estimator of Yr. award 1977), Orange County Builders Assn., Ariz. Sun Ray Divers (past pres.; Diver of Year 1972). Republican. Club: Toastmasters. Home: 5082 Yearling Ave Irvine CA 92714 Office: 5010 Campus Dr Suite 101 Newport Beach CA 92660

BINKERD, EVAN FRANCIS, research executive; b. Lynch, Nebr., Mar. 30, 1919; s. A. A. and Verna (Jones) B.; B.S., Iowa State U., 1942; m. Jerene M. Hallen, Oct. 10, 1942. Research chemist Armour and Co., Chgo., 1942-43, various research positions, 1946-67, dir. research Armour Foods, 1967-71, v.p. research and devel., 1971-78, v.p. Armour & Co., 1978-80; v.p. Picowave Processors, Inc., 1980-83; cons. to pres. Emergent Techs., Inc., 1983—; participant White House Conf. Food, Nutrition and Health; adviser U.S. Codex Alimentarius (FAO-WHO) Commn., advisor foot and mouth disease, Argentina; cons. Found. Chile. Mem. citizenship task force Ariz. Dept. Edn.; pres. Ariz. Found. for Citizenship Edn.; research adv. bd. Calif. Beef Council, 1982—. Served from ensign to lt. USNR, 1943-46. Recipient Distinguished Achievement award Iowa State U., 1974; Alumni Merit award Iowa State U. Club, Chgo., 1975; Indsl. Achievement award Inst. Food Tech., 1979. Fellow Inst. Food Technologists (Hall of Fame 1978, Nicholas Appert medal 1980); mem. Am. Chem. Soc., AAAS, Am. Oil Chemists Soc., N.Y. Acad. Scis., Soc. Chem. Industry, The Westerners (sheriff Scottsdale Corral 1978), Am. Meat Inst. (chmn. sci. com. 1965-73, 77-78), Am. Meat Sci. Assn., Indsl. Research Inst., Calabash Soc., AMA (chmn. food industry adv. com. 1976-77), Agrl. Research Inst., Inst. Food Technologists (exec. com. 1973-76, treas. 1981—), Phoenix Pvt. Industry Council, Research and Devel. Assocs. (chmn. com. on food irradiation 1982—), Western History Assn., Sigma Alpha Epsilon, Phi Tau Sigma. Republican. Methodist. Clubs: Arizona; Chicago Chemists. Patentee in field. Home: 3153 N 48th St Phoenix AZ 85018 Office: PO Box 15209 Phoenix AZ 85060

BINKLEY, CHRISTOPHER HAMILTON, food marketing executive; b. El Paso, Tex., Mar. 18, 1946; s. Hamilton Brown and Merrie Lillian (Parks) B.; m. Lynn Anne McGuigan, Aug. 10, 1968; 1 dau., Lisa Anne. B.A., Northwestern U., 1968; M.S., Sloan Sch. Mgmt., 1971. Marketing research analyst Pillsbury Co., Mpls., 1971-74, marketing asst., 1974-75, mktg. mgr., 1976-78; mktg. mgr. Van de Kamp's Frozen Foods, Long Beach, Calif., 1978-79, group mktg. mgr., 1979-82, dir. mktg., 1982—. Recipient Gen. Host Corp. Chmn's. award, 1982. Republican. Roman Catholic. Home: 1813 Avenida Feliciano San Pedro CA 90732 Office: Van de Kamp's PO Box 1451 Long Beach CA 90801

BINNS, JAMES HAZLETT, JR., entrepreneur; b. Lancaster, Pa., June 5, 1945; s. James Hazlett and Ruamie (Hill) B.; m. Connie Hoffman, Nov. 26, 1971. B.A. magna cum laude, Stanford U., 1967; J.D. magna cum laude, Harvard U., 1973. Bar: Ariz. 1974. Atty. Martori, Meyer, Hendricks & Victor, Phoenix, 1973-74; v.p. Advanced Diagnostic Research Corp., Tempe, Ariz., 1974-76, pres., 1976-82. Adv. council Ariz. State U. Coll. Bus. Adminstrn., 1982—; bd. dirs. Phoenix Meml. Hosp. Found., 1982—; class agt. Stanford U., 1967—. Served to 1st lt., AUS, 1967-69. Mem. ABA, Phi Beta Kappa.

BIONDI, DANIEL DAVID, optical mfg. co. exec.; b. Alton, Ill., Aug. 30, 1951; s. John B. and Martha Theresa (Durham) B.; m. Claudia Clare

Hartman, May 30, 1975; children—Jason Daniel, Jean Paul. Student U. Mo., 1969-72; B.A., Calif. State U., 1978. Optical engr. Space Optics Gen., Inc., Torrance, Calif., 1976-78; pres. Pro-Spec, Inc., Torrance, 1978—. Bd. dirs. Los Angeles City Coll., 1979. Mem. Optical Lab. Assn. Club: Internat. Y's Mens. Home: 3104 Calle Grande Vista San Clemente CA 92672 Office: 1815 205th St Torrance CA 90501

BIRCH, ANTHONY DURNFORD DE GRAY, university controller; b. Ashland, Oreg., Oct. 13, 1939; s. Donald Courtnay and Ruth Dorothy (Ammerman) B.; B.S., Oreg. State U., 1962, M.S., 1969; M.B.A., U. Wash., 1964; m. Janette Mae Heltsley, Dec. 14, 1963; children—Grant Walter de Gray, Cynthia Ann. Engr. trainee Oreg. Hwy. Dept., summers 1959, 60, 61; design progress estimator aero-space div. Boeing Co., Seattle, 1962-63, engring. new bus. estimator, 1963-64; Ford Found. fellow, research asst. U. Wash., Seattle, 1964-65; budget officer Oreg. State U. at Corvallis, 1965-72, asst. dir. instl. research, 1968-72, acting dir. affirmative action, 1971-72, dir. budgets and personnel services, 1972-73; asst. budget dir. Oreg. Dept. Higher Edn., 1973-74; instr. bus. div. Linn-Benton Community Coll., Albany, Oreg., 1970-74; dean adminstrv. services Lane Community Coll., 1974-79; controller Whitman Coll., Walla Walla, 1979—; mem. data elements task force Nat. Center Higher Edn. Mgmt. Systems, Western Interstate Commn. for Higher Edn., 1971-72. Adult leader Boy Scouts Am., 1974-78; bd. dirs. Lane County unit ARC. Served with USCGR, 1957-59. Mem. Nat. (subcom. fed. reporting requirements 1968-71), Western (membership chmn. 1977-79, mem. exec. com. 1978-79, chmn. profl. devel. 1979-81) assns. coll. and univ. bus. ofcls., Beta Gamma Sigma, Kappa Delta Pi, Alpha Kappa Psi, Alpha Delta Sigma, Sigma Phi Epsilon. Clubs: Corvallis Civitan (dir. 1966, pres. 1968, lt. gov. No. Oreg. 1969; bd. dirs. Camp Found. 1967); Eugene Rotary (dir. 1975-79). Contbr. articles to profl. jours. Home: 424 Catherine Walla Walla WA 99362

BIRD, ADREN J., educator; b. Ririe, Idaho, Nov. 17, 1926; s. Thorn O and Grace Aonona (Birch) B.; m. Josephine Puninani Kanekoa, Nov. 27, 1948; children—Kuuipo Bird Grover, Russell, Anela Bird Smith, Kealii, Mahina. Student Ricks Coll., 1952-54; B.S., Brigham Young U., 1955, M.Ed., 1969, Ed.D., 1971. Pub. sch. tchr., 1955, 65-68; chemist FDA, 1955-64; grad. asst. Brigham Young U., 1968-71; headmaster Palm Beach Prep. Schs., Inc., Palm Beach Gardens, Fla., 1971-73; assoc. prof. edn., coordinator secondary edn. Brigham Young U.-Hawaii, Laie, 1973—. Mem. Young Republicans; candidate Hawaii Constnl. Conv.; counselor, mem. rev. bd. Boy Scouts Am. Served with USNR, 1944-46, 50-52. NASA scholar, 1970-71. Mem. Am. Assn. Colls. of Tchr. Edn. (state rep. 1982—), Hawaii Assn. Supervision and Curriculum Devel., DAV, Phi Delta Kappa. Clubs: Lions, Rotary. Author: The Craft of Hawaiian Lauhala Weaving, 1982. Home and Office: PO Box 96 Brigham Young U-Hawaii Laie HI 96762

BIRD, CHARLOTTE SOETERS, public administration analyst; b. Burley, Idaho, July 15, 1947; d. Harold J. and Dorothy L. (Breakey) Soeters; m. Charles A. Bird, June 28, 1969. B.A. in Anthropology, U. Calif.-Davis; M.A. in Pub. Adminstrn., U. Alaska, 1975. Adminstrv. asst. U. Calif.-Davis, 1970-73; analyst State of Alaska Dept. Labor, Juneau, Alaska, 1973-74, adminstrv. asst. tng. specialist Dept. Human Services, 1975-79, budget analyst Office Mgmt. Budget, 1979-82, mgmt. analyst exec. asst. Office Chief Adminstrn., County of San Diego, 1982-83, mgmt. analyst EDP services dept., 1983—. Mem. San Diego Zool. Soc., San Diego Mus. of Man, Nat. Women's Edn. Fund, West Coast Task Force, 1980 Gourmet du Theatre, Old Globe Theater, 1981-83, Spl. Fund Devel. Task Force; mem. fund devel. com. San Diego, Imperial Counties Girl Scouts Am. Mem. Calif. Women in Govt. (program chmn. 1980-81, dir. 1979-83), Am. Soc. Pub. Adminstrn. (chpt. v.p. 1981-83), Women in Mgmt. Democrat. Author job opportunity information booklets Alaska depts. labor and edn., 1974. Office: County of San Diego Dept EDP Services 1600 Pacific Hwy San Diego CA 09101

BIRD, DIANE C., ednl. adminstr.; b. Santo Domingo Pueblo, N.Mex., Dec. 8, 1948; d. Ray and Reycita M. (Quintana) B.; B.A., U. Albuquerque, 1970. Counselor, N.Mex. Ednl. Talent Search, various pueblos, 1970-72; caseworker social services Sandoval County Health and Social Services, Bernalillo, N.Mex., 1972; asst. dir. ednl. opportunity program Calif. State U. at Long Beach, 1972-73; dir. Indian edn. Bernalillo Pub. Schs., 1973-75; counselor N.Mex. Ednl. Opportunity Center, Bernalillo, 1975-77; dir. Ednl. Opportunity Center, No. N.Mex. Community Coll., Espanola, 1977-80; counselor, cons. Indian edn. programs. Pres. N.Mex.-W. Tex. Assn. Student Assistance Programs, 1977-78; bd. dirs. SW Assn. Student Assistance Programs, 1977-78; bd. dirs., vice chairperson Am. Indian Higher Edn. Council, 1977-80. Mem. Am. Personnel and Guidance Assn., Nat. Indian Edn. Assn., Ednl. Opportunities Centers Assn., N.Mex.-Nat. Lawyers Guild, Am. Indian Law Students Assn. Democrat. Home: PO Box 8 Santo Domingo Pueblo NM 87052

BIRD, JANICE MARIE, educational counselor; b. Pampa, Tex., Mar. 31, 1953; d. Albert and Harriet Frances (Cosgrove) B. B.A. in Edn., Northeastern Okla. State U., 1976, M.Ed., 1979. Tchr., Rattan (Oklan.) Pub. Schs., 1976-78; residence counselor Northeastern Okla. State U., Tahlequah, 1978-79; ednl. counselor Coampbell County Sch. Dist., Gillette Wyo., 1979—. Active community choir, 1982-83. Mem. Am. Personnel Guidance Assn., AAUW. Home: 706 S Gillette Ave Gillette WY 82716 Office: Campbell County School District 7th and Gillette Ave Gillette WY 82716

BIRD, ROSE ELIZABETH, chief justice Calif. Supreme Ct.; b. Tucson, Nov. 2, 1936; B.A. magna cum laude, L.I. U., 1958; J.D., U. Calif.., Berkeley, 1965. Admitted to Calif. bar, 1966; clk. to chief justice Nev. Supreme Ct., 1965-66; successively dep. public defender, sr. trial dep., chief appellate div. Santa Clara (Calif.) County Pub. Defender's Office, 1966-74; mem. faculty Stanford U. Law Sch., 1972-74; sec. Calif. Agr. and Services Agy., also mem. gov.'s cabinet, 1975-77; chief justice Calif. Supreme Ct., 1977—; chmn. Calif. Jud. Council, Commn. Jud. Appointments; pres. bd. dirs. Hastings Coll. Law, U. Calif.; bd. councilors U. So. Calif. Law Center. Past mem. Western regional selection panel Pres.'s Commn. White House Fellowships; bd. assos. San Fernando Valley Youth Found. Named Most Outstanding Sr. L.I. U., 1958; Ford Found. fellow, 1960. Democrat. Address: Supreme Ct Calif State Bldg 350 McAllister St San Francisco CA 94102*

BIRD, WILLIAM FREDERICK, dentist; b. Ft. Wayne, Ind., Feb. 20, 1934; B.A., Wabash Coll., 1957; D.D.S., Loyola U., Chgo., 1961; postgrad. U. Kans., 1966-67; M.P.H., Harvard U., 1974, Dr.P.H., 1976; m. Doni Lynn Wingate. Commd. officer USPHS, 1961; dental officer Indian Hosp., Eagle Butte, S.D., 1961-63; gen. practice resident USPHS Hosp., S.I., N.Y., 1967-68; dep. chief dental intern tng. and service unit dental program USPHS Indian Med. Center, Gallup, N.Mex., 1968-69, chief dental services and gen. practice residency tng., 1969-71; chief area dental services br. Aberdeen Indian Health Service Area Office, 1971-73; clin. fellow dept. dental ecology Harvard Sch. Dental Medicine, 1973-74, fellow tchr. preparation program Sch. Public Health, 1973-74; dir. staff devel. dental br. Indian Health Hdqrs. Staff, Albuquerque, 1976-78, dir. dental spl. services sect. and staff devel., dir. dental public health residency program, 1978—; pres. Bird Enterprises Inc., 1981—; edn. cons. Am. Dental Assts. Assn. Recipient USPHS medal, 1968, 81. Diplomate Am. Bd. Dental Public Health. Mem. ADA (nat. continuing dental edn. adv. com.), Commd. Officers Assn. (pres. Aberdeen-Bemidji br. 1971-72), Am. Assn. Public Health Dentists (exec. com. 1979—), Am. Assn. Dental Schs., Los Medicos Volodores, Aircraft Owners and Pilots Assn., Balloon Fedn. Am. Office: Hwy 49 Route 6 Box 9 Los Lumas NM 87031

BIRDLEBOUGH, HAROLD, dentist; b. Yakima, Wash., May 4, 1928; s. Otis Theodore and Elizabeth (Brown) B.; D.D.S., U. Wash., 1959; m. Donna Mae Vensel, June 18, 1977; children—John Michael, Ann Michele, Elizabeth, William Powers, Marcia; stepchildren—Steve Hassenfratz, Nancy Hassenfratz, Keith Fontel. Practice dentistry, Seattle, 1959-61, King County, Wash., 1961—; mem. dental adv. com. Blue Cross Ins. Co. Served with USNR, 1948-52. Mem. Am., Wash. dental assns., Snohomish County Dental Soc., Gen. Acad. Dentistry, U. Wash. Dental Alumni, Soc. Preservation and Encouragement Barbershop Quartet Singing in Am., Delta Sigma Delta, Alpha Delta Phi (1st v.p. local alumni assn., del. nat. constl. conv. 1968). Republican. Episcopalian (sr. warden). Clubs: Kiwanis (v.p. Shoreline chpt.), Elks. Home: 16929 Inglewood Rd NE C-105 Bothell WA 98011 Office: 332 NW Richmond Beach Rd Seattle WA 98177

BIRDSALL, JOHN EDWIN, electronic engring. cons.; b. Los Angeles, June 1, 1937; s. Jack Edwin and Eda Marie (Entner) B.; B.S. in Elec. Engring., Calif. Christian U., 1970, M.S. in Elec. Engring., 1974, Ph.D., 1976; m. Constance Kelly, Feb. 10, 1961; children—Dean Edwin, John Phillip, Yvette Cheyree. Dir. engring. Spectra-Strip Corp., Garden Grove, Calif., 1964-66; div. mgr. Giannini Corp., Whittier, Calif., 1966-68; pres. Reo Data Products, Inc., Westminster, Calif., 1968-75; pres. Zermatt Corp., Crestline, Calif., 1975-80, also chmn. bd.; dir. mktg. Holt Integrated Circuits, Costa Mesa, Calif., 1980—; electronic engring. cons.; dir. Reo Data Products, Inc.; tchr. Calif. Christian U., 1977—; cons. monolithic circuit design, product devel., microprocessor and minicomputer systems; v.p. community news and weather TV channel 3. Served with USN, 1955-58. Mem. Weststate Cons. Assn., AAAS, IEEE, Smithsonian Instn. Clubs: Rotary, Show Valley Ski. Publs. include counting systems for industry, 1975, printing technique, 1969, data printer in naval systems, 1974; inventor spl. printing devices and digital torque instrument. Home: PO Box LB Crestline CA 92325

BIRGE, ROBERT RICHARDS, chemist; b. Washington, Aug. 10, 1946; s. Robert Bowen and Dorothy (Richards) B.; B.S. in Chemistry, Yale U., 1968; Ph.D. in Chemistry, Wesleyan U., Middletown, Conn., 1972; m. Joanne Schwiebert, June 15, 1968; children—Jonathan Richards, David Porter. Postdoctoral research fellow Harvard U., 1972-74, NIH postdoctoral fellow, 1973-75; asst. prof. chemistry U. Calif., Riverside, 1975-81, asso. prof., 1981—; Peter A. Leermakers Meml. lectr. Wesleyan U., 1972; mem. Bice Commn., advisory panel to U.S. Senate on environ. pollution, 1972-73. Served as officer USAF, 1970-72. Recipient Nat. Sci. award Am. Cyanamid Co., 1964; U. Calif. Regents Faculty fellow, 1976; Weingart fellow Calif. Inst. Tech., 1982-83. Mem. Am. Chem. Soc., Am. Phys. Soc., Sigma Xi. Contbr. over 50 articles to profl. jours. Home: 30165 Via de la Mesa Temecula CA 92390 Office: Dept Chemistry U Calif Riverside CA 92521

BIRK, JOHN RICHARD, soft drink co. exec.; b. Boston, Aug. 11, 1951; s. Harold Frank and Jane Tipton B.; student U. Wyo., 1970-71; B.A. in Econs., Colgate U., 1974; m. Susan Arnold, Feb. 9, 1980; 1 son, John Richard. Sales rep. Procter and Gamble, 1975-76, dist. field mgr., 1976, unit mgr., Dallas, 1976-78; mgr. sales devel. mgr. Pepsi-Cola Co., White Plains, N.Y., 1978-80, regional mgr., San Francisco, 1980—. Vice-pres., bd. dirs. Alpha Tau Omega Alumni Corp. Republican. Roman Catholic. Clubs: San Francisco Tennis, Scottsdale Swim and Tennis, Olympic Racquetball, Roton Point Sailing and Tennis. Home: 730 Spring Dr Walnut Creek CA 94598 Office: 1900 Powell St Emeryville CA 94608

BIRK, THOMAS ALLEN, radio station executive; b. Burtonwood RAF Sta., Eng., Aug. 27, 1953; came to U.S., 1954, naturalized, 1971; s. Allen S.T. and Helen Kathleen (Dempsey) B.; m. Constance Sorensen, Aug. 23, 1981. B.A., U. Nebr., 1976; postgrad. Webster Coll., 1982—. Announcer, account exec. KOTD-AM, Plattsmouth, Nebr., 1974; account exec. KFMQ FM, Lincoln, Nebr., 1974-79; gen. sales mgr. KFMG/KAMX, Albuquerque, 1979-82, pres., gen. mgr. KFMG, Inc., 1982—; real estate advt. cons., Lincoln, 1978-79; guest lectr. U. Nebr., Lincoln, Lincoln Sch. of Commerce, 1977-79. Active Big Bros./Big Sisters of Albuquerque. Mem. Alpha Epsilon Rho. Republican. Episcopalian. Office: KFMG Inc 5601 Domingo Rd NE Albuquerque NM 87108

BIRKELAND, PETER WESSEL, geological science educator; b. Seattle, Sept. 19, 1934; s. Ivar Wessel and Marguerite (O'Connor) B.; m. Suzanne J. Franzke, Aug. 28, 1959; children—Karl, Robin. B.S., U. Wash., 1958; Ph.D., Stanford U., 1962. Acting instr., asst. prof. U. Calif.-Berkeley, 1962-67; assoc. prof. to prof. geol. sci. U. Colo., Boulder, 1967—. Served with U.S. Army, 1953-55. Mem. Geol. Soc. Am., Soil Sci. Soc. Am., Am. Quaternary Assn., Internat. Assn. Quaternary Research. Author: (with Larson) Putnam's Geology, 1978; Pedology, Weathering and Geomorphological Research, 1974. Home: 3075 5th St Boulder CO 80302 Office: Dept Geol Sci U Colo Boulder CO 80309

BIRKENSTEIN, LILLIAN RAY, ornithologist; b. Phila., Oct. 9, 1900; d. Morris and Stella (Schloss) Rosenzweig; B.A. (coll. scholar), Wellesley Coll., 1922; student U. Pa., 1920-21, Northwestern U., 1936-37, Instituto Allende (Mexico), 1951-55, Academia Hispana-Americana (Mexico), 1960-68; m. George Ulman Birkenstein, Sept. 2, 1922; children—Dorothy (Mrs. Jose Vidargas), Jean (Mrs. Atlee Washington). Pres., Anker-Holth Mfg. Co., Port Huron, Mich., 1944-51; researcher local Spanish and tribal Indian names of Mexican birds, 1952—; vol. librarian, San Miguel Allende, 1954-64, tchr. ornithology Institute Allende, San Miguel Allende, 1973. Bd. dirs. Public Library San Miguel Allende, 1954-67, Hot Breakfasts for Sch. Children, San Miguel, 1957-61. Mem. San Miguel Allende Audubon Soc. (founder 1967, pres. 1967-71, dir. 1971—), Am. Soc. Mfg. Engrs. (hon. life), Am. Ornithologists Union, Cooper Ornithol. Soc., Linnaean Soc., Wilson Ornithol. Soc., Cornell Lab. Ornithology, Mexican Natural History Soc. (dir. 1972—), Mexican Ornitholog. Soc. (dir.), Internat. Com. for Bird Preservation (treas. Mexican sect. 1968—), Women's Aux. AIME (hon.). Clubs: San Miguel Allende Garden (1st v.p. 1971—); Golf Malanquin. Author: Native Names of Mexican Birds, 1981. Contbr. articles to various publs. Home: Tenerias 45 San Miguel Allende Guanajuato Mexico

BIRKHOFF, WILLIAM NICHOLAS, bus. cons., educator; b. Buffalo, N.Y., Feb. 2, 1945; s. Pierce and Ruth C. (Blass) B.; B.S. in Engring., Clarkson Coll., Potsdam, N.Y., 1968; M.B.A., U. Colo., 1973; m. Anne Lee Trevethan, July 4, 1974. With IBM, Denver, 1970-72; data processing cons. Martin Marietta Co., Denver, 1972-74; instr. El Camino Coll., Los Angeles, 1973-78; mem. faculty Nat. U., San Diego, 1978—; sr. analyst TRW Systems, Los Angeles, 1975-77; project mgr. Gen. Dynamics Western Data Services Center, San Diego, 1977-79, mgr. systems software, 1979—; pres. Colonial Heritage Cons., San Diego, 1977—. Certified data processor (CDP); lic. bus. broker, Calif. Mem. Assn. Computing Machinery, Data Processing Mgmt. Assn., EDP Auditors Assn., Space Park Employees Assn. (treas. 1977), Triangle (advisor 1970). Club: Investment (pres. 1970). Contbr. articles to profl. jours. Home: 16111 Big Springs Way Rancho Bernardo CA 92127 Office: Box 28744 Rancho Bernardo CA 92128

BIRKHOLZ, HAROLD ALVIN, radio engr.; b. Freeport, Ill., Nov. 11, 1923; s. Albert and Grace (Viel) B.; B.S. in Applied Radio Engring., John Brown U., Ark., 1950; m. Betty Belle Brown, Apr. 20, 1951; children—David Mark, Deborah Faith. Missionary, Far Eastern Gospel Crusade, Japan, 1951-53; instr. electronics DeVry Tech. Inst., Chgo., 1953-61; field engr. Kay & Assos., San Diego, 1961-67; project engr. Naval Air Systems Command, Washington, 1967-73; supr. naval air rework facility Naval Air Sta., San Diego, 1973-80, dir. materials engring. lab., 1980-81, logistics mgr., 1981—; pastor Maranatha Baptist Ch., Annandale, Va., 1970; ordained to ministry N.Am. Baptist Conf., 1950. Bd. elders Christian and Missionary Alliance Ch., 1977—; comdr. Awana Youth Assn., 1963—. Served with USNR, 1945-46. Home: 1130 Blackbird St El Cajon CA 92020 Office: Naval Air Rework Facility Naval Air Sta North Island San Diego CA 92135

BIRKITT, JOHN CLAIR, engineer; b. Inglewood, Calif., Aug. 20, 1941; s. Clair Willis and Helene Blanche (Gille) B.; m. Constance Ellen May, June 4, 1966; m. 2d, Linda Ann Aylmer, Sept. 13, 1980; children—Andra, Robert, Danielle. B.S. in Aerospace Engring., Calif. Poly. State U., 1969. Engr., Aerojet Mfg. Co., Fullerton, Calif., 1969-74; with TRW, 1974-83, engr. def. and space systems group, Redondo Beach, Calif., 1974-79, plant mgr. advanced ground systems engring., Long Beach, Calif., 1979-83, test condr. Capistrano test site, San Clemente, Calif., 1975-83; tech. mgr. Ford Aerospace and Communications Corp., Newport Beach, Calif., 1983—. Vice pres., treas., tng. officer El Cariso Vol. Fire Dept., 1978—. Served with USMC, 1959-65. Mem. AIAA, Nat. Assn. Watch and Clock Collectors, Musical Box Soc. Internat. Home: 32536 Ortega Hwy El Cariso Village Lake Elsinore CA 92330 Office: Ford Rd 6/137 Newport Beach CA 92660

BIRKITT, LINDA ANN AYLMER, phys. therapist; b. Oakland, Calif., Feb. 8, 1946; d. William Stanley and Phyllis Jane (King) Aylmer; student U. Md. at Munich, W.Ger., 1967-68; B.S., Calif. State Poly. U., 1963-69; M.A. (HEW scholar), U. So. Calif., 1973; m. John C. Birkitt, Sept. 13, 1980; children—Andra, Robert, Lowell, Daniélle. Staff phys. therapist Valley Presbyn. Hosp., Van Nuys, Calif., 1973-75; chief therapist Ingleside Mental Health Center, Rosemead, Calif., 1975-79; mem. Speakers Bur., 1976-79; lectr. Santa Monica City Coll., 1976-79; asst. chief phys. therapist Alhambra (Calif.) Community Hosp., 1979-81; pvt. practice phys. therapy, San Juan Capistrano, Calif., 1981—. Vol. fire fighter, El Cariso Village, Calif., 1979—; organizer village home owners El Cariso Village, Lake Elsinore, Calif., 1981. Mem. AAUW, Nat. Assn. Female Execs., St. Margaret's PTA. Episcopalian. Research in motivation as a factor in performance of phys. skill, verticality perception distortion in hemiplegic patients. Home: 32536 Ortega Hwy El Cariso Village Lake Elsinore CA 92330 Office: PO Box 1593 San Juan Capistrano CA 92693

BIRKLE, LYDIA SCHRACK BLOEDORN (MRS. DAVID L. BIRKLE), audiologist; b. Orleans, Nebr.; d. Charles F. and Zoe (Schrack) Bloedorn; B.A., U. Denver, 1927, M.A., 1959; m. David L. Birkle, July 2, 1932 (dec. 1957). Tchr. high sch., Platteville, Colo., 1927-31; mgr. clin. audiology Colo. Hearing and Speech Center, Denver, 1959—. Mem. Centurion Club of Deafness Research Found. Mem. Acad. Rehabilitative Audiology, Am. Speech and Hearing Assn., Colo. Speech and Hearing Assn., Am. Auditory Soc., Am. Tinnitus Assn., Pi Beta Phi. Congregationalist. Home: 1901 Leyden St Denver CO 80220 Office: 4280 Hale Pkwy Denver CO 80220

BIRKLER, JOHN LOUIS, physicist; b. Dover, Del., Oct. 28, 1944; s. John Louis and Margaret M. (McGeehan) B.; m. Joan Moore, June 1, 1968; children—John, Megan. B.S. in Physics, Roanoke Coll., Salem, Va., 1967; M.S. in Physics, U.S.C., Columbia, 1969. Sect. head propulsion br. aeronautics design and propulsion div. aviation vehicle tech. dept. Naval Air Devel. Center, 1972-77; sr. tech. staff mem. systems scis. dept. The Rand Corp., Santa Monica, Calif., 1977—. Bd. dirs., chmn. investment com. Rand Employees Fed. Credit Union. Served to comdr. USNR. Mem. AIAA, U.S. Naval Inst. Contbr. articles to profl. jours.

BIRMINGHAM, JOSEPH E., public health administrator; b. Pitts., May 23, 1923; s. Joseph Eugene and Rose Marie (Barzanty) B.; m. Anita L. Loomis, Oct. 25, 1947; children—James P., Thomas E., Richard J., Mary E.; m. 2d, Margaret L. Schell, Oct. 12, 1963. B.S. in Pharmacy, U. Pitts., 1944, M.S. in Hygiene, 1968; M.S., U. Wash., 1960. Chief pharmacy service VA Hosp., Roanoke, Va., 1954-51, Pitts., 1960-66, chief pharmacy service, Seattle, 1951-60, asst. dir., 1970-72, asst. dir., Amarillo, Tex., 1968-70, Los Angeles, 1972-75; dir. VA Med. Center Albuquerque, 1975—; mem. governing body N.Mex. Health Systems Agy.; mem. N.Mex. State Health Coordinating Council; chmn. Albuquerque-Santa Fe Fed. Exec. Bd., 1983—. Bd. dirs. Albuquerque Vis. Nursing Assn. Served with AUS, 1944-46; lt. comdr. USNR, 1953-74 (ret.). Recipient Mgr. of Year award Fed. Exec. Bd., 1982; Outstanding Leadership award Am. Pharm. Assn., 1955; Superior Performance award Fed. Exec. Bd. Los Angeles, 1975. Mem. Am. Coll. Hosp. Adminstrn., Am. Pub. Health Assn., N.Mex. Pub. Health Assn., Am. Pharm. Assn. (pres. Puget Sound chpt.), Fed. Hosp. Execs. Alumni Assn., Fed. Exec. Inst. Alumni Assn., AMA, Albuquerque Area Hosp. Council. Roman Catholic. Clubs: K.C., Elks. Home: 4706 Glenwood Hills Dr NE Albuquerque NM 87111 Office: 2100 Ridgecrest Dr SE Albuquerque NM 87108

BIRN, RAYMOND FRANCIS, historian, educator; b. N.Y.C., May 10, 1935; s. Saul Albert and Celia (Markman) B.; B.A., N.Y. U., 1956; M.A., U. Ill., 1957, Ph.D., 1961; m. Randi Ingebrigtsen, July 18, 1960; children—Eric Stephen, Laila Marie. Faculty, U. Oreg., Eugene, 1961—, asso. prof., 1966-72, prof. history, 1972—, head dept., 1971-78. Mem. adv. screening com. Council for Internat. Exchange of Persons (Fulbright program), 1974-76; mem. fellowship rev. com. Nat. Endowment for Humanities, 1980. Served with AUS, 1959-60. Fulbright research fellow to France, 1968-69; Nat. Endowment for Humanities sr. fellow, 1976-77. Mem. Am. Hist. Assn., Soc. French Hist. Studies, Am. Soc. 18th Century Studies. Author: Pierre Rousseau and the Philosophes of Bouillon, 1964; Crisis, Absolutism, Revolution: Europe, 1648-1789/91, 1977. Adv. editor Eighteenth-Century Studies, 1974—; French Hist. Studies, 1977-80. Contbr. articles to profl. publs. Home: 2140 Elk Ave Eugene OR 97403

BIRNBAUM, LUCIA CHIAVOLA, historian, educator; b. Kansas City, Mo., Jan. 3, 1924; d. Salvatore and Kate (Cipolla) Chiavola; m. Wallace Birnbaum, Feb. 3, 1946; children—Naury, Marc, Stefan. Ph.D., U. Calif.-Berkeley, 1964. Lectr., U. Calif.-Berkeley, 1963-64, research assoc., 1982-83. Asst. prof. history San Francisco State U., 1964-69; adj. prof. U. San Francisco, 1976-78; mem. faculty Feminist Inst., Berkeley, 1981—. Soroptimist fellow, 1955. Mem. Orgn. Am. Historians, Am. Italian Hist. Assn. (pres. Western Regional Chpt. 1978-82), Nat. Women's Studies Assn., Center for Women and Religion of Grad. Theol. Union, Women's Party for Survival. Author: La Religione e le Donne Siculo Americane, 1981; Italian Feminists: A Study of a Socialist Feminism, 1984. Home: 349 Gravatt Dr Berkeley CA 94705

BIRNEY, WILLIAM JOSEPH, lawyer, corporate executive; b. Torrington, Conn., Mar. 29, 1931; s. William Joseph and Lina (Valli) B.; m. Barbara Allen, Aug. 12, 1967; children—William Joseph, Mark Allen. B.A., St. Bonaventure U., 1952; LL.B., Southwestern U., 1960. Dep. city atty. Los Angeles, 1961-62; dep. county counsel Los Angeles County, 1962-68; counsel Vons Grocery Co., 1968—, sec., 1969, gen. counsel,

1973, v.p., 1975—. Mem. ABA, Calif. Bar Assn. Office: 10150 Lower Azusa Rd El Monte CA 91731

BIRON, ANNETTE MAUREEN, youth counselor; b. Hilo, Hawaii, Dec. 6, 1953; d. Maurice Eugene and Rose (Chow) B. B.A., U. Hawaii, 1976; M.S., Eastern Wash. U., 1978. Tutor/counselor Eastern Wash. U., Cheney, 1976-77, teaching asst., 1977-78; social worker Awareness House, Spokane, Wash., 1978-79; child welfare worker Cath. Family Services, Spokane, 1979-83, adolescent pregnancy counselor, 1983—. Youth minister St. Rose of Lima Ch., Cheney, 1978, 79, 82—, parish council mem., 1982—; bd. dirs. Big Bros./Big Sisters, 1978-82. Mem. Am. Personnel and Guidance Assn. Home: 25 N Washington Ct Cheney WA 99004 Office: PO Box 1453 Spokane WA 99210

BISCHOFF, ELMER N., educator, artist; b. Berkeley, Calif., July 9, 1916. B.A., U. Calif.-Berkeley, 1938, M.A., 1939. One-man shows: Arts Club, Chgo., 1980, Contemporary Arts Mus., Houston, 1980; group shows include: Whitney Mus. Am. Art, N.Y., 1959, Mus. Modern Art, N.Y.C., 1962, Tate Gallery, London, 1964, Pitts. Internat. Exhbn., 1967, Osaka World's Fair, 1970, Albright-Knox Art Gallery, Buffalo, 1978; represented in permanent collections: Mus. Modern Art, Whitney Mus. Am. Art, Art Inst. Chgo., New Sch. Art Ctr., N.Y.C., San Francisco Mus. Art. Instr. painting and drawing San Francisco Art Inst., Calif., 1946-52, 56-63; prof. painting and drawing U. Calif., Berkeley, 1963—. Grantee Ford Found., 1959, Nat. Inst. Arts & Letters, 1963. Office: University of California Dept of Art Berkeley CA 94720

BISCHOFF, MARTIN EARL, JR., radiologist; b. Denver, July 6, 1920; s. Martin Earl and Lydia Rebecca (Henshaw) B.; student U. Colo., 1938-39, 40-41, M.D., 1950; B.A., Denver U., 1947; m. Dorothy Ann Skogerson, July 12, 1953 (dec.); children—Martin Earl, Kimberly Joan, Stephanie Ann; m. 2d, Rosemary Russell Look, Nov. 17, 1979. Intern, St. Luke's Hosp., Denver, 1950-51, resident, 1952-54; gen. practice medicine, Denver, 1951-52; resident Swedish Hosp. Tumor Inst., Seattle, 1954-55; asso. radiologist St. Luke's Hosp., Denver, 1955-66; pvt. practice medicine specializing in radiology, Lakewood, Colo., 1966-74; partner, chief dept. radiology, Colo. Permanente Med. Group, Denver, 1974—, mem. exec. com., 1978-81, clin. prof. radiology U. Colo., 1957—; roentgenologist Denver med. dept. United Air Lines, 1966-72. Active age-group swimming and diving AAU, 1965-74; pres. Denver U. Hilltoppers, swimming and diving team, 1967-69. Served to capt. AC, U.S. Army, 1941-45. Decorated D.F.C., Purple Heart, Air medal with 11 oak leaf clusters; recipient Med. Alumni award U. Colo. Sch. Medicine, also Centennial recognition award for meritorious service in radiology. Diplomate Am. Bd. Radiology. Mem. Am. Coll. Radiology, Colo., Rocky Mountain radiol. socs., Colo., Denver med. socs. Home: 4505 S Yosemite #360 Denver CO 80237 Office: 10400 E Alameda Ave Denver CO 80231

BISCHOFF, ROBERT WILLIAM, educational administrator; b. Tacoma, Wash., Jan. 5, 1925; s. Harry Peter and Hazel Isabel (Brasslin) B.; B.A., Pacific Lutheran U., 1950, B.Ed., 1951, M.A., 1958; Ed.D., U. Oreg., 1967; m. Violet D. Schadler, Aug. 16, 1947; children—Bruce R., Joan I., Donald A. Tchr., Tacoma Public Schs., 1950-58, asst. elem. prin., 1958-62, assoc. dir. visually handicapped dept., 1962-64, 66-68; assoc. prof. spl. edn. No. Ill. U., DeKalb, 1968-72; coordinator preschool and vision services Ednl. Service Dist. 189, Mt. Vernon, Wash., 1983—; prin. Utah Sch. for the Blind, Ogden, 1972-83; Utah trustee Am. Printing House for the Blind, 1972-83, mem. ednl. research com., 1978-83; adj. prof. spl. edn. Utah State U., U. Utah, Weber State Coll., Brigham Young U., 1972-83; co-dir. INSITE, 1981-84; cons. Utah State Bd. Edn. Chmn. council of ministries First United Methodist Ch., Ogden, 1975-79, vice chmn. council of adminstrn., 1979-83. Served with U.S. Army, 1943-46. U.S. Office Edn. fellow, 1964-66. Mem. Utah Schs. for Deaf and Blind Edn. Assn., Utah Edn. Assn., NEA, Council for Exceptional Children, Assn. Educators for Visually Handicapped, Am. Assn. Spl. Educators, Phi Delta Kappa. Club: Lions Internat. (Ogden mem. exec. bd. 1975-77). Contbr. articles to profl. jours. Home: 8020 220th St SW Edmonds WA 98020 Office: 330 Pacific Pl Mount Vernon WA 98273

BISH, DANIEL WILLIAM, hosp. adminstr.; b. Oakland, Calif., Aug. 22, 1927; s. Charles Meryl and Margaret Elizabeth (Bush) B.; B.B.A. cum laude, St. Mary's U., San Antonio, 1969; M.S. in Hosp. Adminstrn., Trinity U., San Antonio, 1972; m. Jeannette Louise (Larson), Sept. 1, 1954; children—Elizabeth Jaye, Katherine Kaye. Enlisted in U.S. Army, 1948, advanced through ranks to 1st sgt.; served with med. units in Korea, W. Ger., Vietnam; ret., 1968; health facilities rep. Calif. Dept. Health, San Jose, 1972-73; asst. adminstr. Lanterman State Hosp., Pomona, Calif., 1973—. Decorated Combat Inf. badge, Combat Med. badge, Army Commendation medal with oak leaf cluster. Mem. Assn. Mental Health Adminstrs. Presbyterian. Clubs: St. Mary's U. Century, Masons. Address: 3530 W Pomona Blvd Pomona CA 91766

BISHOP, ANTHONY CLARENCE LEONARD, communication cons.; b. Harrow, Eng., Oct. 5, 1925; came to U.S., 1958, naturalized, 1969; s. Leonard and Lucy (Martin) B.; m. Patricia Kirby, Oct. 24, 1959; 1 son: David Neville Anthony. Personnel mgr. KLM Airlines, Eng., 1956-58; personnel mgr. Capitol Records, Hollywood, Calif., 1960-62; presentations mgr. Douglas Aircraft Co., Santa Monica, Calif., 1962-67; exec. dir. Soc. Logistics Engrs., Manhattan Beach, Calif., 1968-70; adminstr. profl. devel. and edn. McDonnell Douglas Corp., Long Beach, Calif., also St. Louis, 1971-78; edn. and tng. mgr. TRW Info. Services, Orange, Calif., 1978-80; v.p. personal devel. programs T.K. Mira & Assocs., Irvine, Calif., 1980-82; prin. Communications Unltd., Palos Verdes, Calif., 1982—; project mgr. exec. presentations Rocketdyne div. Rockwell Internat., Canoga Park, Calif. Borough councilman, Harrow, 1950-58, sec., conservative majority whip, 1955-58; mem. Orange County United Way Edn. Adv. Com., 1979—. Served with Royal Navy, 1943-46. Fellow Am. Bus. Communication Assn. Episcopal (lay reader). Author: Effective Technical Presentations, 1969. Columnist, On The Right, Palos Verdes Peninsula News, 1980—. Home: 32614 Coastsite Dr D Rancho Palos Verdes CA 90274 Office: Rocketdyne Div Rockwell Internat 6633 Canoga Ave Canoga Park CA 91304

BISHOP, ARLENE JOYCE, corporate foundation executive; b. Oakland, Calif., May 28, 1942; d. Arnold Nicolas and Mildred Carolina (Kwartz) Hamstad; m. Dale Judson Edward Bishop, Sept. 3, 1965 (div.); 1 son, Scott. B.A., U. Calif.-Berkeley, 1963; teaching credential Calif. State U.-Hayward, 1964; postgrad. North Park Theol. Sem., Chgo., 1965-66, Spanish Lang. Inst., San Jose, Costa Rica, 1968-69. Mem. staff Evangl. Covenant Ch., Medellin, Colombia, 1969-75; adminstrv. asst. Crown Life Ins. Co., San Francisco, 1976-77; data processing project coordinator Crown Zellerbach Corp., San Francisco, 1977-79; analyst Indsl. Indemnity Ins. Co., San Francisco, 1979-80; adminstr. The Lowell Berry Found., Oakland, 1980-82; dir. The Consol. Capital Found., Emeryville, Calif., 1982—. Mem. Coro Found. Womens Adv. Bd., Oakland, 1982—. Republican. Clubs: U. Calif. Alumni, Commonwealth (San Francisco). Home: 6076 Thornhill Ct Oakland CA 94611 Office: 1900 Powell St Suite 1000 Emeryville CA 94608

BISHOP, BARRY RHETT, newspaper pub., rancher; b. Stevens Point, Wis., Aug. 7, 1940; s. Rexford Ernest and Bernice Marie (Whiting) B.; student UCLA, 1960-61; B.S., U. Wis., Madison, 1962; postgrad. U Puget Sound, Tacoma, 1963-64, U. Calif., San Jose, 1973-74; m. Gael Lucette Briggs, Oct. 28, 1966; children—Terri, Steve, Heidi, Barbra, Robert. With Stars and Stripes, 1964; editor Wis. State Farmer, 1965; editor, advt. dir. Manawa (Wis.) Adv., 1965-66, editor, pub., owner, 1966-69; editor The Ariz. Currents, writer/reporter Milw. Jour., also editor, pub. Sierra Vista (Ariz.) Herald-Dispatch, 1969-74; editor, pub., owner The Paper, Sierra Vista, 1974—; v.p. Sulphur Springs Valley Elec. Coop.; tchr. journalism Cochise Coll. Bd. dirs. Sierra Vista Bd. Edn.; sec.-treas. Sierra Vista Indsl. Devel. Authority. Chmn. Border Relations Commn., Utilities Commn., City of Sierra Vista; fin. chmn. Catalina council Boy Scouts Am.; cubmaster Pack 464, Sierra Vista, also troop chmn. mem. Gov.'s Commn. Ariz.-Mex.; del. Gov.'s Commn. Small Bus. Served to capt. U.S. Army, 1962-64. Recipient Spoke award Wis. Jaycees; winner numerous nat., state awards including editorial award Wis. br. Am. Automobile Assn., Ariz. Dept. Edn.; named Small Businessman of Year, also Citizen of Yr., City of Sierra Vista, 1979. Mem. Nat. Assn. Advt. Publs., Western Pubs. Assn., Western Newspaper Found., Nat. Newspaper Assn., Wis. Newspaper Assn., Ariz. Newspaper Assn., Wis. Press Photographers Assn., Ariz. Interscholastic Assn., Nat. Sch. Bd. Assn., Sierra Vista C. of C. (pres.), Assn. U.S. Army (corp. mem.), Kappa Sigma. Republican. Mormon. Clubs: Sierra Vista Rotary (pres., gov.'s rep. dist. 550), Lions (past mem. Wis. dist. cabinet), U. Wis. Lettermen's, U. Ariz. Wildcat, Masons. Home: 2500 Quail Run Sierra Vista AZ 85635 Office: 202 E Wilcox Dr Sierra Vista AZ 85635

BISHOP, CAMILLA LINDA, university housing administrator; b. Spokane, Wash., Sept. 4, 1949; d. Roy Harlan and Bess Blanche (Haskin) B. B.A. in Fgn. Langs. and Edn., Wash. State U., 1971, M.A. in Counseling, 1973, doctoral candidate. Tchr., research asst. Wash. State U., Pullman, 1972-73; counselor Lewis-Clark State Coll., Lewiston, Idaho, 1973-76; hall dir. Wash. State U., 1978-79; asst. dir. housing N. Tex. State U., Denton, 1979-81; dir. housing Linfield Coll., McMinnville, Oreg., 1981—; cons. housing systems. Sec. Community Action Com., Lewiston, 1976. Mem. Am. Coll. Personnel Assn. (nat. directorate commn. III, 1982—), Ass. Coll. and Univ. Housing Officers-Internat. (membership com. 1981-82), Am. Personnel and Guidance Assn., N.W. Coll. Personnel Assn., N.W. Assn. Coll. and Univ. Housing Officers-Internat. (program com. 1981-82). Home: 208 W 16th McMinnville OR 97128 Office: Linfield Coll McMinnville OR 97128

BISHOP, CAROL WARD, home economist, educator; b. Sewickley, Pa., July 10, 1936; d. Earl D. and Wilma H. (Obenour) Ward; m. Jack Lynn Bishop, Mar. 29, 1958; children—Lori, Jeffrey. B.S. in Home Econs. and Journalism, Kans. State U., 1958; M.S. in Nutrition, Va. Poly. Inst., 1961. Asst. editor Household Mag., Topeka, Kans., 1958-59; research instr. Va. Poly. Inst., Blacksburg, 1965-67; instr. Modesto (Calif.) Jr. Coll., 1967-70; instr. Solano Community Coll., Suisun City, Calif., 1970-75, head dept. home econs., 1975-78; chmn. div. fine and applied arts, 1978—; cons. Prentice-Hall, McGraw-Hill; mem. Calif. State Nutrition Adv. Com. Found. for Improvement Postsecondary Edn. grantee, 1981-82. Mem. Am. Dietetic Assn., Assn. Calif. Community Coll. Adminstrs. Republican. Office: PO Box 246 Suisun City CA 94585

BISHOP, DORIS JACKSON, govt. ofcl.; b. Rahway, N.J., June 26, 1927; d. Alfred Charles and Ella Mae (Snyder) Jackson; student Parsons Sch. Design, 1945, U. Nev., 1949, Coll. Charleston, 1971-72; m. Frank Davis Bishop (dec.). Statis. officer, mgmt. analyst Naval Supply Center, Charleston, S.C., 1958-73; dep. command EEO officer, Fed. Women's Program coordinator Naval Supply Systems Command, Washington, 1973-75; coordinator, dep. dir. EEO/Fed. Women's Program, Mil. Dist. Washington, U.S. Army, 1975-79; internal EEO program mgr. FHWA, Denver, 1979-80; regional EEO officer Nat. Park Service, Denver, 1980—. Bd. dirs. Amberwick Homeowners Assn., 1980-82, Greenhouse Condominium, Alexandria, Va., 1977-79. Served with USAF, 1951-53. Named Career Woman of Yr., Bus. and Profl. Women, Charleston, 1967; recipient Outstanding Performance awards, U.S. Navy, U.S. Army. Mem. Federally Employed Women, Am. Bus. Women's Assn., Women's Equity Action League, Am. Soc. Public Adminstrn., Navy League U.S. Clubs: Ports of Call Travel, Order Eastern Star. Columnist, Alex Port Packet, weekly, 1977-79. Home: 128 S Holman Way Golden CO 80401 Office: 655 Parfet St Denver CO 80225

BISHOP, JAY LYMAN, organic, indsl. and metall. chemist, chemical engineer, paleographer, translator; b. Salt Lake City, July 7, 1932; s. Marvin James and Klar (Lyman) B.: B.S. with honors, U. Utah, 1953, Ph.D., 1962; m. Geneil True Walton, June 9, 1958; children—Peggy Joy (dec.), Lynn Walton, Janet Gay, Nancy, Deanna True, Linda Elaine, Lyman Michael, Jay Stanley, Michelle. Mechanic, Colonial Sheet Metal Works, 10 years; analytical chemist, 1951-52; lectr. U. Utah, 1960-62; research assoc., then instr. Ariz. State U., 1962-67; vis. lectr. Traveling Sci. Inst., Ariz. Acad. Sci., 1962-66; sr. chemist Ciba-Geigy Corp., Summit, N.J., 1967-71; cons. chemist Bishop Mfg. Co., Bountiful, Utah, 1971—; chief chemist, metallurgist Asso. Smelters Internat., 1973, United Refinery, Inc., 1973-75, U.S. Nat. Metals, Inc., 1975-76; chemist Kennecott Copper Corp., 1972; pres. Western Consultants, 1976—; v.p. Renewed Energy Corp., 1979-81; chem. engr. Tooele Army Depot, 1982—; genealogist, historian, pilot. Active local Boy Scouts Am.; missionary Ch. of Jesus Christ of Latter-day Saints, E. Ger., 1953-56, welfare worker, elder, tchr., 1944—, mem. priesthood exec., 1959—, mem. seventy, 1966-78, high priest, 1978—, ch. organist, 1946—; mem. Salt Lake Mormon Tabernacle Choir, 1976-78. Served with AUS, 1956-57. Mem. AAAS, Sci. Research Soc. N.Am., Assn. Profl. Genealogists, Utah Geneal. Assn. Author, patentee in field. Address: 11 West 900 North Bountiful UT 84010

BISHOP, JEANETTE EILEEN, publisher's representative; b. Boulder, Colo., July 4, 1943; d. Alvin L. and Elberta J. (Quail) B. Student Long Beach City Coll., 1965-69, UCLA, 1975-76, San Francisco State Coll., 1977-79. Adminstrv. asst. TRW Inc., Redondo Beach, Calif., 1963-72; program coordinator in devel./personnel Continental Airlines, Los Angeles, 1972, advt. asst., to 1974; traffic asst. Needham, Harper & Steers/Wet, Los Angeles, 1974-76, talent payment coordinator, 1976; account mgr. Arlt/Stierle Design, San Mateo, Calif., 1976-77; mgr. sales promotion/advt. Hughes Airwest, San Mateo, 1977-79; sr. account exec. Dailey & Assocs., Advt./San Francisco, 1979-80; account mgr. W. W. Dotts, Inc., Newport Beach, Calif., 1980-82; prin. Bishop Co., Marina del Rey, Calif., 1983—. Mem. Calif. Mag. Reps., Los Angeles Advt. Club.

BISHOP, JEFFREY BRITTON, artist, educator; b. Berkeley, Calif., Feb. 18, 1949; s. Amasa Stone and Barbara (Merill) B. B.F.A., Boston U., 1973; diploma Boston Mus. Sch., 1973; M.F.A., U. Wash., 1977. Mem. faculty Cornish Inst. Arts, Seattle; one man shows: Linda Farris Gallery, Seattle, 1980-83, Karl Bornstein Gallery, Santa Monica, Calif., 1981, Seattle Art Mus., 1983, Recipient Betty Bowen Meml. award Seattle Art Mus.; James William Paige travelling fellow, Boston Mus. Sch. Home: 6032 31st NE Seattle WA 98115

BISHOP, JULIA KAY, marketing director; b. Topeka, Sept. 9, 1946; d. Raymond A. and Anna Clara (Freiberger) B. M.B.A., Pepperdine U., 1983. Communications cons. Pacific Telephone, Riverside, Calif., 1966-72; asst. sales promotion mgr. Clark Equipment Co., Benton Harbor, Mich., 1972-75; area sales mgr. ARA Transp. Group, Encino, Calif., 1976-79; account supr. Bozell & Jacobs Advt., Los Angeles, 1979-82; mktg. dir. Sims Roberts Assocs., Hermosa Beach, Calif., 1982—; cons. Advt. chmn. Tour Mgrs. Assn., 1978; mem. Minn. Gov.'s Council on Tourism, 1978. Mem. Sales and Mktg. Execs. Los Angeles, Los Angeles Advt. Women, Women in Communications.

BISHOP, MARY CUNNINGHAM, educator; b. Yuma, Ariz., May 17, 1930; d. Walter and Esther (French) Cunningham; B.A. in Edn., Ariz. State U., 1953; m. Arblee Bishop, Jan. 24, 1959. Tchr. Dunbar Sch., Phoenix Elem. Sch. Dist. No. 1, 1953-70, 71-73, Mary Bethune Sch., 1977-78, Heard Sch., 1978—, mem. Title 1 adv. com., 1972, installer individualized learning program 1973-77, mem. com. to develop dist. tchr. assessment and evaluation instrument, 1976-77; mem. social studies textbook selection com. Ariz. Dept. Edn., 1971-72, mem. Am.-Ariz. History Commn., 1972-73; cons. in devel. dental health ednl. units Ariz. Dept. Health, 1972-73; mem. statewide adv. com. to develop state long-range ednl. goals Ariz. Supt. Public Instrn., 1975-76; vis. prof. dept. edn. Ariz. State U., 1970-71; ednl. cons. to Headstart Program, Sacaton Indian Reservation, 1970-71; cons. participant with Utha System Approach to Individualized Learning, Nat. Assn. Supervision and Curriculum Devel. Active Phoenix Urban League, NAACP, Ariz. Coalition for Change; mem. nat. organizing team sponsored by Martin Luther King, Jr. Center for Social Change, 1978; mem. exec. com. Heard Sch. PTA, 1978—, 1st v.p., 1980—; Mem. NEA (life mem.; mem. Ariz. del. 1970-80, numerous coms., participant Nat. Policy Conf. on Edn. for Blacks 1972), Ariz. Edn. Assn. (chmn. Black Caucus, chmn. minority affairs com., mem. del. assemblies, numerous coms.), Assn. for Supervision and Curriculum Devel., NEA/Black Caucus. Democrat. Baptist. Home: 3303 S Newberry Rd Tempe AZ 85282 Office: 2301 W Thomas Rd Phoenix AZ 85009

BISHOP, MILO ELLIS, financial company executive; b. Buhl, Idaho, Oct. 2, 1939; s. Henry Milo and Gertha Irene B.; m. Marcia A. Morgan, Nov. 25, 1961; children—Bradley James, Laura Ann, Lynnette Carol, Paul Steven. B.S., U. Utah, 1966; M.A., U. N.Mex., 1969; Ph.D., Purdue U., 1972. Trainee, Utah Sch. for the Deaf, Ogden, 1965-66, instr., researcher, 1966-68; asst. prof./research assoc. Nat. Tech. Inst. for the Deaf, Rochester, N.Y., 1972-74, asst. dean, 1974-77, assoc. prof., 1976, assoc. dean, 1977-79, dean, 1979-81; pres. Equi-Fin. Co., Salt Lake City, 1981—; tchr. communications Rochester Inst. Tech., 1973-78; cons. in field. Active Boy Scouts Am.; mem. Greece Central Bd. Edn., 1977-81. Served with U.S. Army, 1958-61. Office of Edn. fellow, 1967; USPHS fellow, 1968-69; Nat. Inst. Neurol. Diseases and Stroke fellow, 1969-71; PTA spl. edn. scholar, 1964-65. Mem. Acoustical Soc. Am., Alexander Graham Bell Assn., Am. Ednl. Research Assn., Am. Instrs. of the Deaf, Conf. Execs. Am. Schs. ceaf, Am. Mgmt. Assn., Am. Speech and Hearing Assn., Acad. Rehabilitative Audiologists, Nat. Sch. Bds. Assn., Soc. Research Adminstrs. Co-author: Mainstreaming Bibliography, 2 Vols.; assoc. editor Hour. Speech and Hearing Research, 1973-75; author: Mainstreaming, Practical Ideas for Education Hearing Impaired Students; contbr. articles to profl. jours. Home: 11466 S High Mesa Dr Sandy UT 84092

BISHOP, TILMAN M., state senator, coll. adminstr.; b. Colorado Springs, Jan. 1, 1933; B.A., M.A., U. No. Colo.; m. Pat Bishop, 1951; 1 son, Barry Alan. Adminstr., dir. student services Mesa Coll., Grand Junction, Colo.; mem. Colo. Senate. Bd. dirs. Boys Club of Grand Junction. Served with U.S. Army. Mem. Am. Sch. Counselors Assn., Am. Personnel and Guidance Assn., Colo. Personnel and Guidance Assn. Clubs: Elks, Lions. Office: Passport II 1433 Williams St Suite 602 Denver CO 80218*

BISKEY, JOHN WESLEY, consulting metallurgical engineer, educator; b. Thief River Falls, Minn., Nov. 6, 1951; s. John Wesley and Alice Mildred (Lindquist) B. B.S. in Metall. Engring., Oreg. State U., 1973, M.S. in Mech. Engring., 1975. Registered profl. engr., Oreg., Wash., Calif. Research assoc. Oreg. Grad. Ctr. Teaching and Research, Beaverton, 1973-77; corrosion engr. N.W. Natural Gas Co., Portland, Oreg., 1977-78; assoc. Talbott, Wong & Assocs., Inc., Portland, 1978-81; v.p. Wong's Forensic & Metall. Engrs., Inc., Portland, 1981—; asst. grad. tchr. Oreg. State U., 1974-75; adj. prof. U. Portland, 1978-79. Mem. Nat. Soc. Profl. Engrs., Profl. Engrs. Oreg., Am. Soc. Metals, Am. Soc. Safety Engrs. Republican. Lutheran. Clubs: Elks, Portland. Home: 4067 Jefferson Pkwy Lake Oswego OR 97034 Office: 321 NW Couch St Portland OR 97209

BISSETT, LESLEY DRUCILLA, financial services company executive; b. Winnipeg, Man., Can., May 26, 1935; d. Richard Rodney and Maybelle Goodwin; m. Frank Weston Bissett, Sept. 30, 1961 (div.) children—John W., Richard L., Thomas. Student pub. schs., Winnipeg. Cert. fin. planner. Featured skater Shipstads & Johnson's Ice Follies, 1957-61; mktg. mgr. University Group, Inc., Long Beach, Calif., 1974-79; regional v.p. Keystone Mass., Inc., Los Angeles, 1979-81; sr. v.p. Integrated Resources Equity Corp., Englewood, Colo., 1981—; dir. Resources Planning, Inc. Mem. Internat. Assn. for Fin. Planning (dir.), Bus. and Profl. Womens Club. Presbyterian. Author: Client Finder, 1982; contbr. articles to fin. jours. Office: 5347 S Valentia Way Englewood CO 80111

BISTLINE, STEPHEN, justice; b. Pocatello, Idaho, Mar. 12, 1921; s. Ray D. and Martha (Faber) B.; LL.B., U. Idaho, 1949; m. Sharon Mooney; children—Patrick, Paul, Arthur, Claire, Susan, Shelley, Diana, Leslie. Admitted to Idaho bar, 1949; individual practice law, Sandpoint, Idaho, 1950-76; justice Idaho Supreme Ct., Boise, 1976—. Served with USN, 1941-45. Office: Supreme Ct Bldg State Capitol Boise ID 83720*

BISWAS, BASUDEB, economics educator; b. Jhowbona, Murshidabad, India, Jan. 1, 1935; came to U.S., 1971; s. Haridayal and Asitbarani Biswas; m. Renuke Biswas, Feb. 21, 1962; children—Mausumi, Sugata. B.A. in Econs. with honors, Presidency Coll., 1954; M.A. in Econs., Calcutta U., 1956; M.A. in Econs., U. Chgo., 1975, Ph.D., 1976. Exec. officer West Bengal Civil Service (India), 1958-59; lectr. econs. Berhampore K.N. Coll., West Bengal, 1960, R.K. Mission Vidyamandira and Asutosh Coll., India, 1960-71; assoc. prof. econs. Utah State U., Logan, 1976—. Ford Found. fellow, 1973-75. Mem. Am. Econ. Assn., Western Econ. Assn., Econometric Soc. Hinduism. Contbr. articles to profl. jours. Home: 380 South West Apt B4 Logan UT 84321 Office: Dept Econs UMC35 Utah State U Logan UT 84322

BITTERMAN, MARY GAYLE FOLEY, state official; b. San Jose, Calif., May 29, 1944; d. John Dennis and Zoe Joyce (Hames) Foley; student Dominican Coll., San Rafael, Calif., 1962-64, Georgetown U., 1964-65; A.B., U. Santa Clara, 1966; M.A., Bryn Mawr Coll., 1968, Ph.D., 1971; m. M.E. Bitterman, June 26, 1967; 1 dau., Sarah Fleming. Lectr. in history U. So. Fla., Tampa, 1969-71; research assoc. in Hawaiian history Hawaii Environ. Simulation Lab., U. Hawaii, Honolulu, 1971-72, project mgr., 1972-74; exec. dir., gen. mgr. Hawaii Public TV, Honolulu, 1974-80; dir. Voice of Am., Washington, 1980-81; dir. Dept. Commerce and Consumer Affairs, State of Hawaii, 1981—; dir. Dillingham Corp. Chmn. bd. govs. East-West Center; mem. adv. council Sea Grant, U. Hawaii; bd. Hawaii Council for Culture and Arts, Honolulu Community Media Council; active U.S.-Japan TV Subcom.; historian Democratic Party of Hawaii, 1973-74, vice chmn., 1973-74, del. nat. Dem. midterm conv., 1974. Recipient Outstanding Young Women of Am. award, 1976, 78; One of 3 Outstanding Young People of Hawaii award, 1977. Mem. Nat. Assn. Ednl. Broadcasters (dir.), Hawaiian, Friends hist. socs., Hawaii Film Bd., Japan Soc., Japan-Am. Soc. Honolulu. Contbr. articles to publs. on ch. history and environ. mgmt. Home: 229 Kaalawai Pl Honolulu HI 96816 Office: PO Box 541 Honolulu HI 96809

BITTERS, ROBERT GEORGE NELSON, electronics co. exec.; b. Cin., Feb. 22, 1932; s. Arthur John and Dorothy May (Manning) B.;

student Los Angeles Pierce Coll., 1962-64, U. Cinn. Coll. Bus. Adminstrn., 1950-53; m. Mary Louise Beckham, July 18, 1953; children—Paula Kay, Bruce Gordon. Material control mgr. Ramo-Wooldridge Corp., Canoga Park, Calif., 1957-61; material mgr. Advanced Communications Inc., Chatsworth, Calif., 1961-64; quality assurance dir. Advanced Communications Inc., 1965-71; quality assurance dir., then v.p., ordnance div. mgr. Networks Electronics Corp., Chatsworth, 1972-78, exec. v.p., gen. plant mgr., 1979—, corp. sec., 1974-76, dir., 1975—. Served with AUS, 1953-55. Mem. Am. Mgmt. Assn., Am. Def. Preparedness Assn., Internat. Platform Assn., Soc. Mfg. Engrs. Baptist. Home: 5440 Quakertown Ave Woodland Hills CA 91364

BIVINS, SUSAN STEINBACH, systems engr.; b. Chgo., June 5, 1941; d. Joseph Bernard and Eleanor Celeste (Mathes) S.; B.S., Northwestern U., 1963; postgrad. U. Colo., 1964, U. Ill., 1965, UCLA, 1971; m. James Herbert Bivins, June 7, 1980. With IBM, 1967—, support mgr. East, White Plains, N.Y., 1977-78, systems support mgr., western region, Los Angeles, 1978-81, br. market support mgr., 1981—. Vol. tchr. computer sci. Calif. Mentally Gifted Minor Programs; vol. Los Angeles Youth Motivation Task Force. Recipient Kranz award Northwestern U., 1963; various engring. and mgmt. awards IBM, 1969—. Mem. Systems Engring. Symposium, Pi Lambda Theta. Developed program to retrieve data via terminal and direct it to any appropriate hardcopy device, 1973. Office: 3424 Wilshire Blvd Los Angeles CA 90010

BIXBY, KATHERINE COSTLOW, orgn. exec.; b. Lusk, Wyo., Feb. 8, 1920; d. Jesse Patrick and Anna (Thompson) Costlow; B.A., Doane Coll., Nebr., 1941; m. E. Rew Bixby, May 30, 1942; children—Patrick, Jean. Pres., Camp Fire Girls, Los Angeles, 1957-58, Vol. Bur. Los Angeles, 1966, Calif. Assn. Health and Welfare, 1969; v.p. USO, Los Angeles, 1962-70, Calif. Mental Health Commn., 1966-69; bd. dirs. United Way, Los Angeles, 1962-70, United Way Calif., 1970-72; exec. dir. Vol. Ctr. of Los Angeles, 1971—. Recipient United Way Gold Key award, 1965, Armed Services Vol. award, 1967, Gold Medallion award, 1968, Koshland award, 1976, Vol. Leadership award, 1963. Mem. Dirs. Volunteers in Agencies, Assn. Vol. Adminstrs. Home: 920 Crestview Ave Glendale CA 92102 Office: 621 S Virgil St Los Angeles CA 90005

BIZE-BOUTTE, SHERYL JUNE, federal government management executive; b. Berkeley, Calif., June 1, 1951; d. Norick Joseph and Emma Lee (Andrews) Bize; m. Anthony Michael Boutte, Apr. 3, 1971; 1 dau., Angela Monique. B.A., Mills Coll., 1973. Asst. to dir. West Oakland (Calif.) Health Ctr., 1971-73; with U.S. Dept. Energy, Oakland, 1973—, program coordinator Office Spl. Asst. for Affirmative Action, 1976-78, program mgr. solar in fed. bldgs. program, 1978-83, chief orgn. and mgmt., 1983—; tchr. Oakland Pub. Schs. Scholars and Achievers Program, 1981-82, Practical Econs. Seminars, 1973-74. Bd. dirs. Vol. Bur. Alameda County, 1973-74, Vols. for Oakland Program, 1975; participant U. Calif. Med. Ctr. Parent Calling Program, 1977, Oakland Concerned Citizens for Urban Renewal, 1980-82. Scholar, Mills Coll., 1969; recipient Spl. Achievement award U.S. Dept. Energy, 1974, 78, 79, Spl. award for superior act, 1981, Spl. citation, 1983. Mem. Mills Coll. Alumnae Orgn., Mills Alumnae Black Caucus, Zeta Phi Beta. Democrat. Office: US Dept Energy Suite 600 1333 Broadway Oakland CA 94612

BJORK, ROBERT ALLEN, psychologist, educator, researcher; b. Hector, Minn., Jan. 30, 1939; s. Oscar and Margaret Josephine (Bjornstad) B.; m. Tele Boveng Triggs, June 10, 1964; m. 2d, Elizabeth Ligon, Sept. 13, 1969; children—Olin, Eric. Student St. Olaf Coll., 1957-58; B.A. in Math. (Evans scholar), U. Minn., 1962; Ph.D. in Psychology (NDEA fellow 1962-65, NSF fellow 1965-66), Stanford U., 1966. Predoctoral instr. Stanford U., 1965-66; asst. prof. psychology U. Mich., 1966-70, assoc. prof., 1970-74, prof., 1974, prof. UCLA, 1974—, vis. asst. prof. Rockefeller U., 1969-70; vis. cons. Bell Labs., 1977-78; lectr. Inst. Mgmt. Studies; cons./lectr. in field. Basketball coach Los Angeles Jr. Basketball Program. Fellow Am. Psychol. Assn.; mem. Psychonomic Soc., Cognitive Sci. Soc., Phi Beta Kappa. Presbyterian. Author. (with William Batchelder and John I. Yellott) Problems in Mathematical Learning Theory, 1966; editor Memory and Cognition, 1981—; contbr. numerous articles to profl. jours.; research in human memory. Office: Dept Psychology UCLA Los Angeles CA 90024

BJURMAN, GEORGE DAVID, investment counselor; b. Pa., Mar. 11, 1906; s. Andrew and Augusta (Bert) B.; B.S., U. Calif., Berkeley, 1930; m. Dorothy Kuhlmeyer, Oct. 10, 1936; children—Susan A., George A. With Wells Fargo Bank, 1930-36; sr. trust investment officer Bank of America, Los Angeles, 1936-46; dir., exec. v.p. fin. Occidental Life Calif., Los Angeles, 1946-70; chmn. bd., chief investment officer George D. Bjurman & Assos., Los Angeles, 1970—. Fellow Fin. Analyst Fedn.; mem. Los Angeles Soc. Fin. Analysts, N.Y. Soc. Fin. Analysts. Republican. Clubs: Los Angeles Country, El Dorado Country, Calif., Mens Garden of Los Angeles, Chevaliers du Tastevin. Office: 10100 Santa Monica Blvd Suite 2300 Los Angeles CA 90067

BLACHER, NORMAN, association executive; b. Denver, Sept. 4, 1925; s. Sidney and Mary (Kaminsky) B.; m. Joan Helen Oak Holt, July 27, 1973; children—Eric, Steven, Mark. B.A. in Econ. and Polit. Sci., Colo. U., 1948; M.A. in Polit. Sci., Stanford U., 1949; postgrad. Columbia U., 1955-61, U. So. Calif., 1961-67. Successively personnel officer, reading asst., field worker U.S. Bur. Budget, 1946-49; tng. program coordinator Bur. Govt. Research, U. Kans., Lawrence, 1949-51; sr. adminstrv. analyst Research and Budget Dept. Kansas City (Mo.), 1951-54; community mgr., Sea Gate (N.Y.), 1954-61; exec. sec. Ventura (Calif.) County Taxpayers Assn., 1961-70; dep. dir. job tng. devel., placement div. Calif. Dept. Human Resources Devel. Sacramento, 1970-72; cons. regional manpower adminstrn. U.S. Dept. Labor, San Francisco, 1972; exec. dir. Ventura County Assn. Govts., 1973—. Mem. adv. com. Ventura County Water Works; commr. Juvenile Justice and Delinquency Prevention Commn., Ventura and Santa Barbara Health Systems Agy.; bd. dirs. Ventura County Symphony. Served in USN, 1944-46; PTO, CBI, Korea. Mem. Am. Acad. Polit. and Social Sci., Am. Pub. Works Assn., Am. Soc. Pub. Adminstrn. (sec. chpt. 1953-54, chmn. mem. com. chpt. 1956-57, council chpt. 1957-58, 68-69), Internat. City Mgrs. Assn., Mcpl. Fin. Officers Assn., Nat. Mcpl. League, Nat. Safety Council. Home: 6170 Balcom Canyon Rd Moorpark CA 93021 Office: Ventura County Assn Govts 800 S Victoria Ave Ventura CA 93009

BLACK, ASHLEY VIRGINIA, distribution company manager; b. Chgo., Mar. 4, 1947; d. Raymond August and Virginia Josephine (Rogers) Isotta. B.A., DePaul U., 1969, M.A., 1970; postgrad. Georgetown U., 1977. Prin. systems engr. City of Chgo., 1971-74; cons. AEC, Germantown, Md., 1974-76; project mgr. Four Phase Systems Co., Cupertino, Calif., 1977-79; mgr. systems planning VWR, Inc., Brisbane, Calif., 1979—; cons. long-range planning computer depts. Mem. San Francisco Zool. Soc., Smithsonian Inst. Mem. Nat. Assn. Female Execs., Bay Area Career Women, NOW, Broadcast Industry Conf. Lodges: Rosicrucian, AMORC. Author screenplays. Office: VWR Inc PO Box 7900 San Francisco CA 94119

BLACK, BAXTER FRANKLIN, III, hosp. adminstr.; b. Washington, Oct. 28, 1935; s. Baxter Franklin and Elia (Wilson) B.; A.B., U. N.C., 1958; M.H.A., Baylor U., 1969; m. Bonnie Lois Black, June 13, 1959; children—Baxter Franklin IV, Frances Elizabeth. Joined U.S. Army, 1958, advanced through grades to lt. col., 1975; asst. adminstr. Silas B. Hays Hosp., Fort Ord, Calif., 1976-78; ret., 1978; assoc. dir. San Joaquin Gen. Hosp., Stockton, Calif., 1978-81; v.p. St. John's Regional Med. Ctr., Oxnard, Calif., 1981—; assoc. prof. hosp. adminstrn. Baylor U., 1976-78. Deacon, First Bapt. Ch. of Ojai. Decorated Legion of Merit, Bronze Star. Mem. Health Care Execs. So. Calif. Healthcare Mgmt. Assn. Club: Masons. Home: 1116 Golden W Ojai CA 93023 Office: St John's Hosp Oxnard CA 93030

BLACK, BRADY BRENT, copywriter; b. Columbus Ohio, Dec. 29, 1948; s. Brady Forest and Edra (Daily) B.; m. Janet Elaine Kruse, Dec. 31, 1982. B.A., Johns Hopkins U., 1970. Jr. copywriter J.M. Korn & Son, Phila., 1972; creative dir. Black, Black and Seitz Agy., Cin., 1975-78; copywriter Botsford Ketchum, San Francisco, 1978-79; sr. copywriter Dancer, Fitzgerald, Sample, San Francisco, 1979-81, Allen and Dorward, 1981-82; creative supr. Visa USA, 1982—. Clio award finalist, 1975, 79, 80, 82; Andy award finalist, 1979, 80, 81, 82. Mem. Am. Film Inst. Office: VISA USA PO Box 8999 San Francisco CA 94128

BLACK, BRIAN WESTON, executive recruiter; b. Newport, R.I., May 18, 1951; s. John W. and Star R. B.; 1 son, Jonathan Weston. B.A. in Geography, Colgate U., 1973; M.B.A., St. Mary's Coll., Moraga, Calif., 1979. Systems engr. Electronic Data Systems, San Francisco, 1976-77; project mgr., systems mgr. Decimus Corp., San Francisco; with Source Edp, San Francisco, 1978—, assoc. dir. Mountain View office, 1979—; owner, operator MTB Video, Inc., Oakland, Calif., 1979—. Libertarian. Presbyterian. Club: Bay. Office: 2063 Landings Dr Mountain View CA 94043

BLACK, CHARLES HENRY, steel company executive; b. Atlanta, Sept. 12, 1926; s. Charles Henry and Elfrida (Peterson) B.; m. Bonnie Nicksic, Feb. 14, 1982; children by previous marriage—Charles Henry, Richard Swanton; stepchildren—Peter Branch, Laura Branch. B.S., U. So. Calif., 1950. Mgr. fin. planning missles and space div. Lockheed Aircraft Corp., Van Nuys, Calif., 1953-57; v.p. fin. profl. group Litton Industries, Inc., Beverly Hills, Calif., 1957-70, treas., 1970—, corp. v.p. and treas., 1976-80; exec. v.p. Gt. Western Fin. Corp., Beverly Hills, 1980-82; sr. v.p. and chief fin. officer Kaiser Steel Corp., Fontana, Calif., 1982—; dir. Investment Co. Am., Fundamental Investors Inc., Interdyne Co.; bd. govs. Pacific Coast Stock Exchange. Trustee, Brentwood Sch. Served with AC, USN, World War II. Mem. Phi Kappa Psi. Clubs: Los Angeles Country, California. Home: 351 Alma Real Pacific Palisades CA 90272

BLACK, COBEY, journalist; b. Washington, June 15; d. Elwood Alexander and Margaret (Beall) Cobey; B.A., Wellesley Coll., 1944; postgrad. U. Hawaii. Exec. sec. to Irene, designer, Metro-Goldwin-Mayer, 1944; actress in W. Ger., 1945-46; women's editor Washington Daily News, 1947-50; columnist Honolulu Star Bull., 1954-65; cons. HEW, Peace Corps, 1960-61; travel editor Bangkok (Thailand) World, 1968-69; columnist Honolulu Advertiser, 1972—; publicist CBS-TV show Hawaii Five-O, 1978; pres. Mandalay Imports Corp. Mem. Hawaii State Commn. on Status of Women, 1978—. Democrat. Episcopalian. Clubs: Nat. Press, Honolulu Press, Royal Bangkok Sports, Outrigger Canoe. Home: 4910 Kahala Ave Honolulu HI 96816 Office: Honolulu Advertiser Honolulu HI 96802

BLACK, CRAIG CALL, museum administrator; b. Peking, China, May 28, 1932 (parents Am. citizens); s. Arthur Proctor and Mary (Nichols) B.; A.B. cum laude (Kellogg fellow), Amherst Coll., 1954, M.A. (Simpson fellow), Johns Hopkins U., 1957; Ph.D. (NIH fellow), Harvard U., 1962; m. Sabra Bowman, Aug. 1954; 1 dau., Lorna Vorn; m. 2d, Constance E. Hockenberry, May 23, 1967; 1 son, Christopher Arthur. Geologist, Okla. Geol. Survey, summer 1956; asst. curator vertebrate fossils Carnegie Mus. Natural History, Carnegie Inst., Pitts., 1960-62, curator vertebrate fossils, 1962-70, dir. mus., 1975-82; dir. Los Angeles Mus. Natural History, 1982—; mem. Nat. Mus. Services Bd., 1982—; assoc. prof. systematics and ecology U. Kans. 1970-72; dir. mus., prof. geoscis. Tex. Tech. U., 1972-75; adj. prof. U. Colo. Mus.; adj. prof. mem. grad. faculty in anthropology and earth scis. U. Pitts.; co-dir. Mus. Mgmt. Inst., U. Calif., Berkeley; trustee Ft. Ligonier Meml. Found., 1979—. Mem. Lubbock Lake site com. Lubbock (Tex.) C. of C., 1973-75. Fellow Linnean Soc., mem. Am. Soc. Mammalogists, Soc. Study Evolution, Geol. Soc. Am., Paleontol. Assn., Paleontol. Soc., Soc. Vertebrate Paleontology (pres. 1970-71), Soc. Systematic Zoologists, Am. Assn. Museums (pres. 1980-82), Assn. Sci. Mus. Dirs., Pitts. Geol. Soc., AAAS, Pa. Humanities Com., Pa. Mus.'s Coalition (mus. data bank com.), Assn. Systematic Collections, Sigma Xi. Club: Cosmos (Washington). Contbr. numerous articles to profl. publs. Home: 777 S Windsor Blvd Los Angeles CA 90007 Office: 900 Exposition Blvd Los Angeles CA 90007

BLACK, DEBORAH ANN, nurse; b. Columbus, Ohio, July 18, 1949; d. Bruce Mohler and Doris Ann (Kempf) Karr; m. George Pierre Black, July 22, 1973. Nurse diploma St. Vincent's Coll. Nursing, Los Angeles, 1971; B.S.N., Oreg. Health Scis. U., 1979; M.S. in Counseling and Edn., Portland State U., 1981. R.N., Calif. Staff nurse, cardiology St. Vincent's Med. Ctr., Los Angeles, 1971-72, charge nurse, 1972; charge nurse Gerald Champion Meml. Hosp., Alamogordo, N.Mex., 1974; charge nurse VA Med. Ctr., Portland, Oreg., 1975-76, staff nurse, 1975—. Served to 1st lt. Nurse Corps, USAF, 1972-74. Mem. Am. Assn. Sex Educators, Counselors and Therapists, Am. Personnel and Guidance Assn. Republican. Methodist. Club: Elks (Beaverton, Oreg.).

BLACK, DONALD BRUCE, lawyer, arbitrator; b. Los Angeles, June 25, 1932; s. Freeman Carleton and Elizabeth (Bergstrom) B.; children—Jeanine Debra, Lawrence Bently. A.B., UCLA, 1954; J.D., U. So. Calif., 1960. Bar: Calif. 1960. Mem. firm Shield and Smith, 1960-72, Williams & Black, Los Angeles, 1972-75; individual practice law as Donald B. Black, Inc., Los Angeles and Laguna Beach, Calif., 1976—; panel judge pro tem Los Angeles Mcpl. Ct. Pres., Parent Tchrs. Council, 1968-70; sec. Betts Found., 1970—, Elliott Found., 1969—. Served with USAF, 1955-56. Mem. Am. Bd. Trial Advocates (nat. pres. 1975-76), Assn. So. Calif. Def. Counsel (pres. 1972-73, joint legislative commns. structure of the judiciary 1974-77, tort reform 1977-79, jud. council adv. com. 1978-81), ABA (chmn. elect com. on econs. of practice), Phi Delta Phi, Delta Tau Delta. Republican. Presbyn. Clubs: Jonathan, Balboa Bay, Calcutta Saddle and Cycle (founding gov. 1971—) (Los Angeles). Office: 615 S Flower St Suite 1900 Los Angeles CA 90017 also 301 Forest Ave Laguna Beach CA 92651

BLACK, GENEVA LEE STANLEY, educator; b. Greentop, Mo., Aug. 31, 1929; d. Harry Cecil and Virginia Mae (Netterfield) Stanley; student N.E. Mo. State U., 1947-49; B.A. with high distinction, Ariz. State U., 1954, M.A., 1960; m. Raymond A. Black, May 28, 1950; children—Joyce Ann Black Wood, Paul James. Tchr., Mendon, Mo., 1949-50, Vandalia, Mo., 1950-52; tchr. Mesa (Ariz.) Public Schs., 1954-55, 57—, now asst. prin.; tchr., primary chmn. Longfellow Sch., Mesa, also sr. faculty rep., cooperating tchr. for student teachers; tchr. Wallace Sch., Des Moines, 1955-56, Porter Sch., Kirksville, Mo., 1956-57; del. Internat. Congress on Comparative Edn., Tokyo, 1980; del. to Mesa Speaks, 1978; student in China, 1980, 82. Mem. Assn. Supervision and Curriculum Devel., NEA, Ariz. Edn. Assn., Mesa Edn. Assn., Assn. Tchr. Edn., Phi Delta Kappa. Republican. Lutheran. Clubs: Am. Bus. Womens Assn. (rec. sec. 1975-77, v.p. 1979-80, membership com. 1980—), Sigma Phi Gamma (pres. Iota Psi chpt.). Author curriculum study guides. Home: 1942 E Fountain St Mesa AZ 85203 Office: 345 S Hall St Mesa AZ 85204

BLACK, HUGH LAWRANCE, lawyer, banker; b. Cleve., Mar. 8, 1942; s. Marion Eckert and Margaret Esther (Blaser) B.; B.A., Coll. of Wooster, 1964; J.D., Case-Western Res. U., 1967. Trust officer Cleve. Trust Co., 1968-70; admitted to Ohio bar, 1968, Fla. bar, 1968, D.C. bar, 1979; staff Coconut Grove Bank, Miami, Fla., 1970-72; asso. firm Kahn & Clein, P.A., North Miami, Fla., 1972-73; asst. city atty. City of North Miami, also city prosecutor, 1972-73; individual practice law, Miami and Palm Beach, Fla., 1973-76; mktg. specialist Wells Fargo Bank, Beverly Hills, Calif., 1976-80; v.p., trust officer Lloyds Bank Calif., 1980—; adj. prof. law Pepperdine U.; lectr. Orange Coast Coll.; cons. in field. Bd. dirs. Coconut Grove Cares Inc., 1972-76; pres. Coconut Grove Assn., 1973-76, also bd. dirs.; trustee Orange (Calif.) YMCA; bd. dirs. Rehab. Inst. Orange County. Mem. Coconut Grove C. of C. (sec. 1972-76, disting. service award 1973), Beverly Hills Estate Planning Council, Newport Harbor C. of C., Am. Bar Assn., Ohio Bar Assn., Fla. Bar Assn., D.C. Bar Assn., Palm Beach County Bar Assn., Newport/Irvine Estate Planning Council. Presbyterian. Author: Florida's Intangible Tax, 1972. Home: 900 Sea Ln Corona del Mar CA 92625

BLACK, JAN KNIPPERS, polit. scientist; b. Lawrenceburg, Tenn., Mar. 10, 1940; d. Ottis J. and Opal (Moody) Knippers; B.A. in Art and Spanish, U. Tenn., 1962; M.A. in Latin Am. Studies, Am. U., 1967, Ph.D. in Internat. Relations, 1975; m. John D. Black, 1967 (dec. 1974); m. 2d, Martin C. Needler, 1976; stepchildren—John D., II, Marc Black, Steve Needler, Dan Needler; 1 foster dau., Mary Marfise. Singer, pianist, 1954-58; comml. artist Sta. WSM-TV, Nashville, 1960; vol. Peace Corps, Chile, 1962-64, mem. staff, 1965; research polit. scientist div. fgn. area studies Am. U., 1968-75, chmn. Latin Am. research team, editor area handbooks for Latin Am., 1975-76; program coordinator State Dept. funded study Latin Am. petroleum policies U. N.Mex., 1976-77, sr. research asso. div. inter-Am. affairs, 1976—, coordinator interdisciplinary courses Latin Am. Inst., research asso. prof. Div. Public Adminstrn., 1979—; mem. faculty World Campus Afloat, 1966, Dag Hammarskjold Coll., 1974, George Mason U., 1975-76; cons. in field; TV appearances include MacNeil-Lehrer Report, 1976. Del., Nat. Young Democrats Conv., 1965, N.Mex. Dem. Conv., 1978; mem. fgn. policy adv. team Dem. Presdl. Campaign., 1972; mem. Mayoral Transition Team, City of Albuquerque, 1977; mgr. various polit. campaigns. Recipient Outstanding Dissertation award Am. U., 1967. Mem. Latin Am. Studies Assn. (chmn. subcom. ethical guidelines 1976-78), Inter-Am. Council Washington (v.p. 1975-76), Am. Polit. Sci. Assn., Internat. Studies Assn., Assn. Borderland Scholars, Phi Kappa Phi. Contbg. author books on Latin Am. and Caribbean, including: The Restless Caribbean, 1979; co-author 17 books in Area Handbook series, 1969-75; author: United States Penetration of Brazil, 1977; editor books on Latin Am. and Caribbean, including: Area Handbook for Cuba, 1976; Area Handbook for Trinidad and Tubago, 1976; contbr. numerous articles to profl. jours., popular publs. Home: 421 Solano Dr SE Albuquerque NM 87108 Office: Latin Am Inst U NMex Albuquerque NM 87131

BLACK, LARRY KIETH, sch. adminstr.; b. Page County Clarinda, Iowa, Sept. 4, 1923; s. James Glenn and Ina Agnus B.; B.A., Ariz. State U., 1961, M.A., 1967; Ph.D., Hamilton Coll., 1974; m. Edith I. Black, Dec. 25, 1948. Auditor tax commn. State of Iowa, 1950-58; field auditor Govway Mens Clothing, Phoenix, 1958-67; tchr. Cartwright Sch., Phoenix, 1961-67, cons., 1967-74, adminstr., 1974—; asst. mgr. Malcolm's Men's Clothing, Phoenix, 1967-71, Boston Men's Clothing, Phoenix, 1971-78; prof. Glendale Community Coll., 1971—; cons. PBSW Edn. Devel. Labs. Served with USAF, 1941-48, USAFR, 1948-61. Decorated Air medal, D.F.C. Mem. Hump Pilots Assn., Am. Fedn. Police, NEA, Ariz. Edn. Assn., Ariz. Adminstrs. Assn., Internat. Reading Assn., Am. Legion, Phi Delta Kappa. Republican. Clubs: Rotary, Shriners, Masons, Oddfellows. Home: 4513 W Hayward Ave Glendale AZ 85031

BLACK, MARJORIE WATKINS, business educator; b. Atlanta, Aug. 30, 1938; d. Thomas Harlan and Helen Coachman (Lockhart) Watkins; m. Bruce Allan Black, July 30, 1959; children—Bruce Harmon, Leigh Helen. B.A., U. Tex.-El Paso, 1959; M.A., N.Mex. State U., 1979, Vocat. cert., N.Mex. Asst. prof. bus. div. San Juan Coll., Farmington, N.Mex., 1969—; corp. sec., dir. Colo. Plateau Geol. Services, Farmington, 1975-80; exec. v.p. Black Oil Inc., Farmington, 1979—. Sec. bd. dirs. San Juan Community Concert Assn.; sec. adminstrv. bd., mem. choir First United Meth. Ch., Farmington. Mem. Am. Vocat. Assn., N.Mex. Vocat. Assn., N.Mex. Bus. Edn. Assn., San Juan Coll. Assn. (pres. 1983-84), Pan Hellenic Assn. (past pres.), Delta Kappa Gamma, Phi Kappa Phi, P.E.O., Delta Delta Delta. Republican. Home: 206 W 38th St Farmington NM 87401 Office: 4601 College Blvd Farmington NM 87401

BLACK, ROBERT CLIFFORD, III, history educator; b. N.Y.C., Feb. 11, 1914; s. Robert Clifford and Beatrice (Cluett) B.; B.A., Williams Coll., 1937; M.A., U. Denver, 1947; Ph.D., Columbia U., 1951; m. Regina Ann Maleham, Sept. 5, 1939; children—Maleham C., R. Clifford, Beatrice (Mrs. Rolland W. Hoverstock), John N., Peter N., James A. Instr. history Rensselear Poly. Inst., Troy, N.Y., 1945-48; instr. history Trinity Coll., Hartford, Conn., 1950-52, assoc. prof., 1952-66; prof. history Colo. Women's Coll., Denver, 1965-79, emeritus, 1979—; lectr. in field. Dist. committeeman West Hartford Republican Com., 1954-66; bd. dirs. Hist. Denver Inc., 1974-76. Served to capt. AUS, 1942-45. Recipient Merit award Am. Assn. State and Local History, 1970. Mem. Am., Can., Conn., Colo. hist. assns., Assn. Am. Historians, Colo. Hist. Soc. (dir. 1969—), Friends of Denver Pub. Library, Alpha Delta Phi., Pi Gamma Mu. Episcopalian. Clubs: Denver Country, Denver, Williams. Author: The Railroads of The Confederacy, 1952; The Younger John Winthrop, 1966; Island in the Rockies, 1969. Home: Sky Valley Ranch Box 488 Tabernash CO 80478

BLACK, ROBERT OWEN, banking administrator; b. Rugby, N.D., Mar. 6, 1949; s. Fabian A. and Elizabeth (Gumeringer) B.; m. Linda Mae Streifel, June 8, 1970; children—Justin Robert, Angela Lynn, Robert Fabian. B.S., U. N.D., 1971; M.P.A., U. Okla., 1976. Adminstrv. asst. to dir. radiology St. Mary's Hosp., Grand Rapid, Mich., 1975-77; dir. adminstrv. services Heartview Found., Mandan, N.D., 1977-81; personnel mgr. Roughrider Drilling Fluids, Inc., Williston, N.D., 1981-82; human resources officer Northwestern Bank, Great Falls, Mont., 1983—; human resources cons., 1982—. Served with U.S. Army, 1971-75. Mem. Am. Soc. Personnel Adminstrn., Am. Soc. Tng. and Devel., Orgn. Devel. Inst. Democrat. Roman Catholic. Home: 3304 Antelope Ln Great Falls MT 59404 Office: 21 3d St N Great Falls MT 59401

BLACK, ROY LEO, optometrist, educator; b. Detroit, Oct. 27, 1927; s. Russell Laroy and Atala Marie (Pruneau) B.; m. Lillian Adeline Salamon, Dec. 26, 1959; children—Aimee, Anne Elizabeth, Jennifer. B.S. in Optometry, U. Calif., 1951, M.S. in Optometry, 1952. Practice optometry, Hayward, Calif., 1953—; mem. faculty U. Calif. Sch. Optometry. Chmn. br. ARC, Hayward. Mem. Am. Optometric Assn., Calif. Optometric Assn. (trustee 1976-78), Alameda Contra-Costa Optometric Soc. (pres. 1974-75, Optometrist of Yr. 1975), Hayward C. of C. (dir. 1978-82). Democrat. Roman Catholic. Club: Lions (pres. 1969-70) (Hayward). Office: 22268 Foothill Blvd Hayward CA 94541

BLACK, WILFORD REX, JR., state senator; b. Salt Lake City, Jan. 31, 1920; s. Wilford Rex and Elsie Isabell (King) B.; m. Helen Shirley; children—Susan, Janet, Cindy, Joy, Peggy, Vanna, Gayle, Rex. Student schools in Utah. Locomotive engr. Rio Grande R.R., 1941-81; mem.

Utah Senate, 1972—, speaker Third House, 1975-76, majority whip, 1977-78, minority leader, 1981—; chmn., vice chmn. United Transp. Union, 1972-78; sec. Utah State Legis. Bd., United Transp. Chmn. bd. Rail Operators Credit Union, 1958—; mission pres. Rose Park Stake Mormon Ch., high priest group leader Rose Park 9th Ward, 1980-83, mem. Rose Park Stake High Council, 1957-63. Served with U.S. Army, 1942-45. Recipient various awards r.r and legis. activities. Democrat. Office: Utah State Senate State Capitol Salt Lake City UT 84114

BLACK, WILLIAM FAULKNER, investment exec.; b. Oklahoma City, Nov. 19, 1933; s. William Harmon and Ruth (Faulkner) B.; B.A., Stanford, 1955; m. Kathleen McCormick, 1956 (div. 1962); 1 dau., Kathleen Serena; m. 2d, Electa Sevier, 1964 (div. 1979); children—Charles Randolph, Alexandra Sevier. Pres., La Jolla Properties (Calif.), 1958-61, 72—, also dir.; pres. First Borrego Finance Co., Borrego Springs, Calif., 1958-61; asst. cashier, asst. v.p., v.p., asst. to pres. Guaranty Bank, Phoenix, 1961-63; pres., dir. Bank of La Jolla, 1963-68; sr. v.p., mem. mgmt. com. So. Calif. 1st Nat. Bank, San Diego, 1968-70; dir. Landowners Oil Assos., Island Farms, Inc., Exec. Express Co. Trustee, former chmn. Scripps Clinic and Research Found.; trustee Menlo Sch. and Coll., Ducks Unltd., San Diego Aerospace Mus., San Diego Mus. Art; mem. adv. bd. Mex. and Am. Found., Inc., San Diego; Commn. of the Californias. Served to 1st lt. USAF, 1956-58. Named one of five Outstanding Young Men, San Diego Jr. C. of C., 1964. Mem. Alpha Tau Omega. Episcopalian. Clubs: La Jolla Beach and Tennis, Cuyamaca, University (San Diego); La Jolla Country; California (Los Angeles); Venice Island (Stockton). Office: 7855 Ivanhoe Ave La Jolla CA 92037

BLACKBURN, WALTER MERLE, librarian; b. Cove, Ark., Sept. 28, 1929; B.S.Ed. Language Arts/Social Science, Oreg. Coll. Edn., Monmouth, 1970, M.S.Edn. Ednl. Media Specialist, 1972; married. Sr. chief yeoman U.S. Navy, 1947-67; librarian Dallas (Oreg.) High Sch., 1971-72; dir. Instructional Materials Center, Redmond High Sch., Redmond, Oreg., 1972. Recipient Freedoms Found. Award, 1961. Mem. Oreg. Ednl. Media Assn., Am. Legion, Nat. Ret. Tchrs. Assn., Fleet Res. Assn. Clubs: Masons, Elks, Good Sam Recreational Vehicle, Red Rock Squares. Home: 715 NW 67th St Redmond OR 97756 Office: 675 SW Rimrock Dr Redmond OR 97756

BLACKHAM, (BILLIE) JEAN TOPOLOVEC, elementary educator, child development adviser; b. Price, Utah, Mar. 27, 1942; d. Henry John and Ruth Esther (Temple) Topolovec; m. Frank Blackham, June 12, 1964; children—Calvin Frank, John Ryan. A.A., Carbon Jr. Coll., 1962; B.A. in Elem. Edn., Utah State U., 1964, M.Ed., 1977. Cert. elem. tchr., Utah. Tchr., project developer, then dir. Toy Lending Library, Murray (Utah) Sch. Dist., 1964-72; parent resource person, then program adviser, Follow Through Responsive Edn. Program, Salt Lake City Sch. Dist., 1971-77; dir. Parent Coop. Pre-sch., West Jordan, Utah, 1974-80; Child Devel. Assoc. adviser to tchrs. Granite Head Start Program, Salt Lake City, 1978-79; Child Devel. Assoc. adviser Ute Headstart, Ft. Duchesne, Utah, 1978—; instr. U. Utah Extension, 1980—. Recipient Service award Ute Tribe, 1981; named Murray (Utah) Bus. and Profl. Woman of Yr., 1968. Mem. NEA, Nat. Assn. Edn. Youth Child.

BLACKHURST, JAMES HERBERT, philosopher, educator; b. Midland, Mich., Mar. 11, 1890; s. William and Mary (Dwyer) B.; student Ferris Inst., 1906-08, Mich. Central Normal Coll., 1910-11, Mich. State Normal Coll., 1912-13; Ph.B., U. Chgo., 1916, M.A. in Edn., 1917; Ph.D. in Edn., Northwestern U., 1923; m. Edna Dee Young, Dec. 23, 1923; children—Bonnie Ellen (Mrs. Francis F. Wilcox), Beverly Elaine (Mrs. Robert E. Scott), Marilynn Lee (Mrs. Ronald L. Hughes), Donna Lenore (Mrs. Daniel T. Winger), James Herbert, William W., Thomas E. Prof. edn. and philosophy Huntington Coll., 1921-23; asst. prof. edn. Purdue U., 1923-25; prof. edn. and philosophy Drake U., 1926-60; editor Univ. Press, Blackhurst Book Co. Inc., Des Moines, 1936-60; freelance teaching, research philosophy, 1960—. Served with U.S. Army, 1917-19; AEF in France. Mem. Iowa Philos. Assn. (pres. 1957), Am. Humanist Assn., Metaphys. Soc. Am., Pi Delta Kappa, Kappa Delta Pi. Author: Directed Observation and Supervised Teaching, 1925; Introducing Education, 1930; Principles of Method, 1936; Euclidean Geometry, Its Nature and Use, 1937; Body-mind and Creativity, 1957; The Philosophical Ground of Democracy and Education, 1975, others; also articles in profl. jours. Home: 3575 Owens St Wheatridge CO 80033 Office: 1901 E 13th Ave Apt 6D Denver CO 80206

BLACKORBY MUELLER, CAROL HILDA, life insurance company executive, educator; b. Helena, Mont., June 23, 1924; d. Stanley Prentice Freeman and Hilda Sophia (Matson) F.; m. Lyle Lee Blackorby, Feb. 18, 1944; children—Richard L., Lynne S., Brian R., Jeffry D. m. 2d, Floyd Kenneth Mueller, Oct. 23, 1982. Student Seattle Pacific Coll., 1942-43 U. Wash., Seattle, 1943-44, Am. Coll. 1976. C.L.U. Brokerage mgr. Mfrs. Life Ins. Co., Spokane, Wash., 1976-83; brokerage mgr Gt. West Life Assurance, 1983—; instr. Spokane Falls Community Coll. Mem. Spokane C.L.U.s (pres. 1979-80), Spokane Assn. Life Underwriters, Spokane Estate Planning Council. Republican. Presbyterian. Club: Am. Contract Bridge League. Office: 202 Columbia Bldg Spokane WA 99201

BLACKSTOCK, DOROTHY LYONS, artist; b. Tacoma, Aug. 4, 1914; d. Frank and Mildred (Potts) Lyons; student Whitman Coll., 1931, Coll. of Puget Sound, 1932, U. Wash., 1933; m. Carl M. Blackstock, July 12, 1942; children—Carl Lyons, Gregory Lee. One man shows State Hist. Mus., Olympia, Wash., Handforth Gallery, Tacoma; exhibited in group shows Seattle Art Mus., Woessner Gallery, Seattle, Frye Art Mus. U. Puget Sound, Frederick and Nelson Little Gallery, Northwest Watercolor Show, traveling exhibit Nat. League Am. Pen Women, 1972; cover artist Seattle Times, Tacoma News Tribune. Art chmn. bd. trustees Music and Art Found., 1961-63. Named Woman of Year in Art, Past Pres.'s Assembly, 1959. Mem. Nat. League Am. Pen Women (br. pres. 1966-68, 1st v.p. 1979-80), Seattle Co-Arts and Quad A Art Club, Fedn. Womens Clubs, Women Painters of Wash. (pres. 1972-74), Seattle Opera Guild, Assistance League Seattle, Windermere Orthopedic Guild. Clubs: Sand Point Country, Womens Educational (pres. 1960-61); Seattle Golf, Inglewood Country, Wash. Athletic. Home: 5520 Coniston Rd NE Seattle WA 98105

BLACKWELDER, RON F., engineering educator, consultant, researcher; b. Pratt, Kans., July 16, 1942; s. Forest A. and Evelyn (Meyer) B.; m. Judy P. Tiefel, Sept. 12, 1965; children—Laura, Sherri. B.S., U. Colo.-Boulder, 1964; postgrad., Technische Hochschule, Munich, W.Ger., 1964-65; Ph.D., Johns Hopkins U., Nsly 1970. Teaching and research asst. Johns Hopkins U., 1967-70; asst. prof. U. So. Calif., Los Angeles, 1970-75, assoc. prof., 1975-79, prof., 1979—; cons. in fluid mechanics, instrumentation and data processing. Guggenhiem fellow, 1976-77; vis. scientist Max Planck Inst., Göttingen, W.Ger., 1976-77; recipient outstanding Faculty Service award U. So. Calif., 1975. Mem. AIAA, Am. Phys. Soc., AAAS, Sigma Xi, Tau Beta Pi. Lutheran. Contbr. articles to profl. jours.; patentee vorticity probe utilizing strain measurements. Office: Dept Aerospace Engring U So Calif Los Angeles CA 90007

BLACKWELL, JERRY EUGENE, business exec.; b. Walnut Springs, Tex., Apr. 17, 1937; s. Paul Willis and Ruth (Hill) B.; B.A., N.Y. U., 1954; postgrad. Pepperdine U.; 1 son, Forest. Editorial researcher Time mag., 1952-54; purchasing clk. Orientalia Inc., N.Y.C., 1954-55; exec. theater mgr. Loews Theatres, N.Y.C., 1956-60; theatre supr. M-G-M, 1960-64; chief exec. Pubs. Group, San Juan, P.R., 1964-67; exec. v.p., dir. Old Tucson Corp., 1973-79; officer, dir. Old West Corp., 1974-79, Fiesta Cabelvision Inc.; partner RFC Partners, Old Pueblo Cablevision; pres., dir. Sepia Pub. Corp. Bd. dirs. Community Orgn. for Drug Abuse, Awareness House; mem. Gov.'s Com. for Mex. Trade Relations, past pres.; mem. Ariz. Civic Theatre; past pres. Palo Verde Found.; mem. Planned Parenthood Assn., Cosanti Found. Arcosanti Festival, Nat. Assn. Pvt. Psychiat. Hosps., Hosp. Fin. Mgmt. Assn. Democrat. Clubs: Old Pueblo, Skyline Country. Home: 5800 W Gates Pass Rd Tucson AZ 85205

BLACKWELL, JOHN ROY, medical center human resources director; management consultant; b. Meyersdale, Penn., Sept. 4, 1920; s. Couryell and Flora Matilda (MacElfish) B.; m. Doris Jeanne Sherwood, Nov. 3, 1943; children—Bonnie J. Blackwell Bermeo, John R., Jr. Student Md. State Tchrs. Coll., 1939; B.S.B.A., Babson Coll., 1956; postgrad. Command and Gen. Staff Coll., Ft. Leavenworth, 1960. Dir. indsl. relations Marquardt Corp., Van Nuys, Calif., 1963-73; partner, mgmt. cons. Global Research Co., Century City, Calif., 1973-74; dir. indsl. relations NMB Corp., Chatsworth, Calif., 1974-75; mgr. labor relations UCLA, 1975-77, dir. human resources UCLA Med. Center, 1977—. Active Republican party. served to col., U.S. Army, 1940-63. Decorated Bronze Star. Mem. Ret. Officers' Assn., Personal Indsl. Relations Assn., Hosp. Personnel Mgrs. Assn., Am. Soc. Personnel Adminstrs. Republican. Clubs: Pearl Harbor Survivors Assn., Inc., Family Motor Coach Assn., Inc. Club: Masons. Contbr. articles to jours. in field. Home: 11471 Tampa Ave #150 Northridge CA 91326 Office: UCLA Med Center 10911 Weyburn St Los Angeles CA 90024

BLACKWELL, LEE ROY, psychologist; b. Piedmont, Mo., Dec. 23, 1945; s. William Toney and Verlie Fay (Allen) B.; B.A., UCLA, 1967; M.A., Ball State U., 1972; Ph.D. (Ednl. Personnel Devel. Act fellow), Fla. State U., 1974; 1 son, Bryan. Grad. teaching fellow Fla. State U., 1972-73; counselor, mem. adj. faculty Wright State U., Dayton, Ohio, 1974-75; clinic coordinator Rutherford-Polk Mental Health Services, Tryon, N.C., 1975-77, Gallia-Jackson-Meigs Community Mental Health Center, Ohio, 1977-78; pvt. practice psychology, Huntington Beach, Calif., 1978—; mem. adj. faculty Pepperdine U., 1979—; asst. clin. prof. dept. psychiatry Neuropsychiat. Inst., UCLA, 1981—. Served to capt. USAF, 1968-72. Mem. Am. Psychol. Assn., Am. Personnel and Guidance Assn., Am. Soc. Clin. Hypnosis. Office: 16052 Beach Blvd Suite 214 Huntington Beach CA 92647

BLACKWELL, VERLIE ALLEN, ins. agt., acct.; b. Piedmont, Mo., Sept. 10, 1921; d. Luther M. and Annie B. (Faulkner) Allen; grad. Nat. Accountants Soc., 1960; m. William Toney Blackwell, Apr. 30, 1940; children—Reginald T., Lee R. Bus. mgr. Plymouth auto dealer, San Gabriel, Calif., 1949-63; co-owner ins. agency, Garden Grove, Calif., 1964—; ops. mgr. So. Bapt. Credit Union, Garden Grove, 1960-81; pres. Blackwell Fin. Mgmt., Inc. Mem. Profl. Ins. Agts. Assn., Inland Soc. Tax Cons., Orange County Credit Union Mgrs. Assn. Republican. Baptist. Club: Toastmasters (area gov.).

BLAHA, JACK WARREN, city ofcl.; b. Cleve., May 12, 1924; s. Roland Fredrick and Otillie Celia (Kliment) B.; B.A., Baldwin-Wallace Coll., 1948; postgrad. Ariz. State U., 1966-67, 64-65; m. Ann Katherine Kovacs, June 21, 1952; 1 dau., Beth Ann. Asst. to customers accounting mgr. Cleve. Electric Illuminating Co., 1948-56; sales rep. large computer systems Univac div. Remington Rand, Inc., Cleve., 1956-58; regional mgr. Alwac Computer Systems, Cleve., 1958-59; systems analyst Basic, Inc., Cleve., 1959-63; br. mgr. Univac Data Processing Center, Phoenix, 1964-66; customer services adminstr., Phoenix 1966—. Adviser, Jr. Achievement, 1953-55; chmn. Community Fund Campaign City of Phoenix Employees Drive, 1972; pres. Central Park W. Assn., Inc., 1971-72; pres. United Meth. Men's Assn.; vice-chmn. adminstrn. bd. Meth. Ch. Served with A.C., USNR, 1943-45. Mem. Data Processing Mgmt. Assn. (dir. Phoenix chpt. 1968-71), Ariz. Water and Pollution Control Assn. (dir. 1971-73, v.p. 1975, pres. 1976-77), Am. Water Works Assn. (dir. 1980—), Water Pollution Control Fedn., City of Phoenix Mcpl. Employees Assn. (dir. 1976-79), Alpha Sigma Phi. Mason. Club: Valley Country (Scottsdale, Ariz.). Home: 113 E El Caminito Rd Phoenix AZ 85020 Office: 125 E Washington St Phoenix AZ 85004

BLAIN, JOHN (JEFF) S., cons. speech, investments; b. Great Falls, Mont., A.B., U. No. Colo., 1967, M.A. in Speech Communication, 1975; m. Paulette A. Mullins, Nov. 26, 1970; children—Jennifer M., Lindsay E., Sarah K. Public relations rep. Chapman Coll., Orange, Calif., 1968; stockbroker Blayson Davis, Denver, 1969; tchr. Boulder (Colo.) Valley Schs., 1970-77; pvt. practice cons. communications and investments, Longmont, Colo., 1977—; speaker in field. Mem. Am. Speech Assn., Denver-Boulder Speakers Bur., Speech Assn. Am., Gallery of Homes Speakers Bur., Alpha Phi Gamma, Pi Kappa Delta (Gold medal for oratory). Lutheran. Clubs: Boulder Jaycees (dir. 1970—), Toastmasters (pres. 1976-77, Eastern Div. lt. gov. 1975), John T. Nothnagle Knights of Round Table. Home: 5657 Gunbarrel Rd Longmont CO 80501 Office: 6700 Lookout Rd Boulder CO 80301

BLAINE, DEVON, public relations exec.; b. Lynwood, Calif., Sept. 16, 1947; d. Harold W. and Ruth Mae (Decho) Schulz; m. Robert Beau Baur, Feb. 1970 (div.). Student UCLA, 1965-66. Owner, founder Blaine Group, Los Angeles, 1975—. Mem. exec. com. White Conf. 1980, 82, Small Bus., Calif. State Conf. Small Bus.; mem. blue ribbon planning com. Calif. State Conf. Small Bus., 1984; mem. Gov. Brown's Small Bus. Adv. Council. Mem. Nat. Small Bus. Assn., Women in Bus., Nat. Assn. Women Bus. Owners (past chpt. pres.), Pub. Relations Soc. Am., Book Publicists So. Calif., Women in Show Bus., Women's Nat. Book Assn., Variety Club, Publicity Club N.Y. Democrat. Lutheran. Office: 7465 Beverly Blvd Los Angeles CA 90036

BLAINE, DOROTHEA CONSTANCE RAGETTÉ, lawyer, b. N.Y.C., Sept. 23, 1930; d. Robert Raymond and Dorothea Ottilie Ragetté; B.A., Barnard Coll., 1952; M.A., Calif. State U., 1968; Ed.D., UCLA, 1978; J.D., Western State U., 1981; postgrad. in taxation Golden Gate U. Mem. tech. staff Planning Research Corp., Los Angeles, 1964-67; asso. scientist Holy Cross Hosp., Mission Hills, Calif., 1967-70; career devel. officer and affirmative action officer County of Orange, Santa Ana, Calif., 1970-74, sr. adminstrv. analyst, budget and program coordination, 1974-78; spl. projects asst. CAO/Spl. Programs Office, 1978-80, sr. adminstrv. analyst, 1980-83; admitted to Calif. bar, 1982; sole practice, 1983—. Bd. dirs. Deerfield Community Assn., 1975—, Orange YMCA, 1975-77. Mem. Orange County Trial Lawyers Assn., Calif. Women Lawyers, Nat. Women's Polit. Caucus, ABA, Calif. Bar Assn., Orange County Bar Assn., Orange County Women Lawyers Assn. ACLU, Delta Theta Phi, Phi Delta Kappa. Office: 270 Newport Center Dr Newport Beach CA 92660

BLAIR, B. WAYNE, accountant; b. Whiteburg, Ky., Nov. 20, 1941; s. Bill K. and Lettie Blair; m. Janice, July 11, 1970; 1 son, Philip. B.C.S. in Acctg., Seattle U., 1968. C.P.A., Wash., 1971. Sr. auditor Coopers & Lybrand, Seattle, 1968-72; controller, sec.-treas. Ruth Ashbrook Bakery Corp., Seattle, 1973-78; regional mgr. Robert Half of Seattle, 1979—. Bd. Govs. Seattle U. Alumni Assn., 1982-84. Served with USN, 1959-69. Mem. Am. Inst. C.P.A.s, Wash. Soc. C.P.A.s, Nat. Assn. Accts. Clubs: Wash. Athletic (Seattle); Alderbrook Golf and Yacht (Union, Wash.); Elks; Rotary.

BLAIR, DAVID WILSON, psychologist; b. Murray, Utah, Oct. 4, 1945; s. Harold William and Shirley Ruth (Wilson) B.; m. Cynthia Brewster, May 14, 1976. B.A., U. Utah, 1964, M.A., 1973, Ph.D., 1980. Lic. psychologist; cert. sch. psychologist, Utah. Guidance counselor, Granite Sch. Dist., Salt Lake City, 1976-77, sch. psychologist 1977-81; supr. psychol. services dept. mental health services, Utah Valley Hosp., Provo, 1981—. Served with USAR, 1963-71. Mem. Am. Psychol. Assn., Utah Psychol. Assn., Utah Assn. Sch. Psychologists. Mormon. Home: 7183 MacIntosh Ln Salt Lake City UT 84121 Office: 388 W 1150 N Provo UT 84601

BLAIR, EDWARD HUMPHREY, historian; b. Leadville, Colo., Dec. 17, 1938; s. Darrell Wayne and Alberta Marie (Burchardt) B.; m. Kay Kimery, Feb. 24, 1966; children—Darrell, Kimery. B.A., U. No. Colo., 1962; M.A., Western State Coll., 1969; postgrad. Union Coll., 1968, Utah State U., 1972. Tchr., chmn. dept. history Lake County Jr. High Sch., 1965-70; curator Healy House State Mus., Leadville, 1970-81; prof. history Colo. Mountain Coll., Leadville, 1972-80; adminstrv. asst. Blair Sales, Montrose, Colo., 1981-82; cons. Nat. Park Service, Colo. Mountain Coll., Colo. Hist. Soc., Saratoga Hist. Soc., Hot Sulphur Springs Hist. Soc., Colo.-Wyo. Assn. Museums. Chmn. Leadville Improvement Assn.; treas., pres. Lake County Pub. Schs. Named to Honor Roll, Colo. Assn. Sch. Bds., 1978. Mem. Am. Assn. State and Local History, Western Writers Am., Colo. Hist. Soc., Colo.-Wyo. Assn. Museums (pres. 1979-80), Lake County Civic Center Assn. (pres. 1970-72). Democrat. Author: (with E. Richard and Linda R. Churchill) Fun with American History, 1966, Fun with American Literature, 1968; Everybody Came to Leadville, 1970; Tubor Family Album, 1974; author: Palace of Ice, 1971; Leadville, Colorado's Magic City, 1980. Dec. Sept. 19, 1982.

BLAIR, JOHN RAY, management consultant; b. Seattle, Jan. 26, 1942; s. Robert M. and Yvonne P. (Schumacher) B.; student U.S. Mil. Acad., 1960-62, Oreg. State U., 1962; B.A., U. Oreg., 1964, postgrad., 1966; postgrad. Stevens Tech. Inst., 1964-65; m. Frances J. Pedersen, Dec. 22, 1962; children—Tod Michael, Teri Michelle. Programmer trainee Bell Telephone Labs., Whippany, N.J., 1964-65; lead programmer Boeing Co., Seattle, 1965-66; mgr., systems analyst, programming supr., tech. writer Oreg. Total Info. System, Eugene, 1966-70; computer ops. mgr., sr. systems analyst Systems Analysis, Inc., Bellevue, Wash., 1970-73; ptnr. in charge mgmt. adv. services Deloitte Haskins & Sells, Honolulu, 1973—. Served with U.S. Army, 1960-62. Mem. Soc. Info. Mgmt., Assn. Ednl. Data Systems, EDP Auditors Assn., Pi Mu Epsilon. Home: 1225 Kahili St Kailua HI 96734 Office: Deloitte Haskins & Sells 745 Fort St Suite 1000 Honolulu HI 96813

BLAKE, BILL CAREY, newspaper company executive; b. Great Falls, Mont., June 30, 1950; s. William H. and Louise D. (Halliett) B.; m. Nancy E. Green, Mar. 21, 1970; children—Brian K., Wendy A. B.A., U. Mont., 1972. Sales mgr. Missoulian, Missoula, Mont., 1975-81; advt., mktg. dir. Times News, Twin Falls, Idaho, 1981—. Mem. Pacific N.W. Newspaper Advt. Execs. Assn. (bd. govs. 1982—), Internat. Newspaper Advt. and Mktg. Execs., Idaho Advt. Fedn. Club: Kiwanis. Office: Times News PO Box 548 Twin Falls ID 83301

BLAKE, DUANE LEROY, educator; b. Gregory, S.D., Aug. 27, 1922; s. Roscoe M. and Gladys V. (Jernberg) B.; B.S., Iowa State U., 1949, M.S., 1956, Ph.D., 1963; m. Marilyn S. Fyffe, Nov. 30, 1974; children—Richard, Barbara, Debra; stepchildren—Jeff, Juli. Tchr. high sch., Iowa Falls, Iowa, 1949-51, Spencer, Iowa, 1951-55; asst. to asso. dean Iowa State U., 1955-57, instr. agrl. edn., 1957-63, asst. prof., 1963-66, asso. prof. Colo. State U., Fort Collins, 1966-72, prof., 1972—, head dept. vocat. edn., 1966-72, head related programs, 1972—; square dance caller and rec. artist, 1955—; cons. edn. and human relations. Served with USN, 1942-46. Mem. Am. Personnel and Guidance Assn., NAACP, Am. Vocat. Research Assn., Am. Research Assn., Am., Colo. vocat. assns., Danforth Found. Assn., Phi Delta Kappa. Democrat. Methodist. Club: Kiwanis (past officer). Author: Golden Nuggets for Career Counseling, 1976; Dynamics of Human Relations in Vocational Education, 1978; contbr. articles to profl. jours. Home: 1300 Parkwood Fort Collins CO 80525 Office: Dept Vocat Edn Colorado State U Fort Collins CO 80523

BLAKE, LARRY JAY, educational administrator; b. Kalispell, Mont., Apr. 25, 1930; s. Morris E. and Leah V. (Kemmis) B.; m. H. Jeane Trippet, July 9, 1953; children—Howard, Kathleen, Richard, Larry, Jay. B.S., U. Wash., 1957, M.S., 1960; Ph.D., U. Ariz., 1967. Registered profl. engr., Wash. Pres., Flathead Valley Community Coll., Kalispell, Mont., 1967-74, Fraser Valley Coll., Chilliwark, B.C., Can., 1974-79, N.C. Community Coll. System, Raleigh, 1979-83, Oreg. Inst. Tech., Klamath Falls, 1983—; cons. Arab Republic of Egypt, 1976—, Alaska Dept. Health, 1963-64; chmn. Pres.'s Nat. Council for Edn. Professions Devel., 1970-73. Mem. Am. Assn. Community and Jr. Colls. (dir. 1972-75), Assn. Can. Community Coll. Adminstrs. (pres. 1972-73). Author: The Character and Significance of Irrigation Return Flows, 1960; Sanitary Waste Disposal for Navy Camps in Polar Regions, 1962; Elements of Engineering for Non-Majors, 1967; State Master Plan for Montana Community Colleges, 1970; contbr. articles to profl. jours. Office: Oreg Inst Tech Klamath Falls OR 97601

BLAKE, RICHARD LEE, physicist/astrophysicist; b. Berkeley Springs, W.Va., Mar. 8, 1937; s. Robert A. and Ica Virginia (Yost) B.; B.S. in Physics, Rensselaer Poly. Inst., 1959; Ph.D., U. Colo., 1968. Astronomer, Naval Research Lab., Washington, 1959-63; asst. prof. astrophysics U. Chgo., 1968-74; astrophysicist Los Alamos (N.Mex.) Sci. Lab., 1974—. Served with USN, 1959-62. Mem. Am. Phys. Soc., Am. Astron. Soc. Contbr. articles to profl. jours. Home: 448 Paige Loop Los Alamos NM 87544 Office: MS 436 Los Alamos Scientific Lab Los Alamos NM 87545

BLAKE, ROBERT WALLACE, aeronautical engineer, consultant; b. Quantico, Va., May 24, 1921; s. Robert and Rosselet Alice (Wallace) B.; m. Ruth Gafney, May 25, 1951. B.S. in Aero. Engring., MIT, 1941; Naval Aviator, U.S. Navy Flight Sch., Pensacola, Fla., 1947; postgrad. Columbia U. Sch. Bus., 1951-52. With Pan Am. World Airways, 1941-82, exec. v.p., gen. mgr. Ariana Afghan Airlines, Kabul, Afghanistan, 1962-65, resident rep. Falcon/Concorde programs, Bordeaux, France, 1965-67, 707/737/747/SST programs, Seattle, 1967-70, staff v.p., N.Y.C., 1970-77, mgr. Westchester County Airport, White Plains, N.Y., 1977-78, resident rep. 727/747 programs, Seattle, 1978-82; internat. cons. aviation, Seattle, 1982—; vis. lectr. N.Y. U., 1942, Princeton U., 1957, MIT, 1974, U. Wash., 1981, Embry-Riddle Aviation U., 1981; dir. AID Staff Houses, Afghanistan, 1963-65. Served with USN, 1944-47. Fellow AIAA (assoc.); mem. Soc. Automotive Engrs., Am. Nuclear Soc., Am. Assn. Airport Execs., Phi Kappa Sigma. Club: Army and Navy (Washington). Home and Office: 900 Warren Ave N Seattle WA 98109

BLAKELEY, ELAINE WEBER, security consultant; b. Freedom, Wyo., May 26, 1929; d. Charles Samuel and Johanna (Bollig) Weber; m. William Blakeley, May 7, 1947 (dec.). Student Henager Bus. Coll., 1947-48, U. Utah, 1948-50. With State of Utah, 1947-82, employer relations cons., 1961-82; security cons. World Security, Salt Lake City, 1981-83. Mem. adv. council Utah Bd. Edn., Salt Lake Bd. Edn., Utah Trade Tech Coll. Mem. Am. Soc. for Tng. and Devel. (life, pres.), Utah Needlecraft Industries Assn. (pres. 1962-72). Home: 794 Monte Del Oro Dr Salt Lake City UT 84107

BLAKELEY, JAMES EDWARD, III, interior designer, mfg. co. exec.; b. Los Angeles, June 15, 1944; s. James Edward and Mary Anna (Carlisle) B.; B.S., Woodbury U., 1968; m. Sharon Heinz, Dec. 31, 1967. Interior designer Elsters & Co., Los Angeles, 1968-69, Bustamante Interiors, Los Angeles, 1968-71; owner, operator James Blakeley Interiors, Los Angeles, 1971—, James Blakeley Design Co., Los Angeles, 1976—; lectr. in field. Mem. Internat. Soc. Interior Designers, Am. Soc. Interior Designers (dir. Los Angeles chpt. 1976-78), Nat. Council Interior Design Qualifications, Illuminating Engring. Soc. Am., Interior Designer Ednl. Soc., Designer Lighting Forum, Internat. Platform Assn. Designer interiors St. Germain Restaurant, Los Angeles, 1972, Elizabeth Arden Salon, Los Angeles, 1971. Contbr. article to profl. jour. Office: James Blakeley Interiors 620 N Sweetzer St Suite 4 Los Angeles CA 90048

BLAKELY, EDWARD JAMES, educational administrator; b. San Bernardino, Calif., Apr. 21, 1938; s. Edward and Josephine (Carter) B.; m. Maaike C. Van Der Sleesen, July 7, 1970; 1 child, Pieta. B.A. with honors, U. Calif.-Riverside, 1960; M.A., U. Calif.-Berkeley, 1964; Ed.D., UCLA, 1971. Mgmt. trainee PT & T, Pasadena, Calif., 1960-61; community devel. worker Internat. Civil Service, Villamozo, Italy, 1965; tng. dir. UCLA, 1966-68; exec. dir. Western Community Action Tng., Inc., San Francisco, 1968-70; spl. asst. to asst. sec. for pub. affairs U.S. Fgn. Service Office, Washington, 1970-71; asst. to chancellor, dir. personnel U. Pitts., 1971-74; assoc. dean applied behavioral scis. U. Calif., Davis, 1974-77, asst. v.p. systemwide adminstrn., 1977—, prof. applied behavioral scis., prof. city and regional planning. Mem. Oakland Employment and Tng. Advisory Commn., 1977-82, Oakland Pvt. Industry Council, 1977-82; participant Calif. Policy Seminar. Served to 1st lt. USAF, 1961-65. Recipient NAACP award outstanding community service, 1970; Civic Service award San Francisco, 1969, City and County San Bernardino, 1980; Rural Service award, 1968. Fellow Internat. Soc. Social Economists; mem. Community Devel. Soc., Social Econs. Soc., Internat. Platform Assn., Alpha Gamma Sigma (life), Phi Delta Kappa. Contbr. articles in field to profl. jours. Office: 750 Univ Hall U Calif Berkeley CA 94720

BLAKEMORE, RICHARD EUGENE, state senator; b. Parsons, Kans., Sept. 21, 1922; s. Jack and Carolyn (Fox) B.; student Pasadena Jr. Coll.; m. Angela Catherine Majerus, Nov. 6, 1958; children—Richard Ralph, Brian Fox, John Russell. Profl. pilot and airport mgr.; mem. Nev. Senate, 1972—, chmn. Select Com. on Public Lands. Mem. Nev. CD Adv. Bd., Nev. Execs. for Econ. Devel. Chmn. Nye County Democratic Central Com., 1962-64, mem., 1968—; mem. Nev. Dem. Central Com., 1962-64; del. Dem. Nat. Conv., 1968. Bd. dirs. Nye County Hosp., 1970. Served with USNR, 1940-46. Mem. Nev. Aviation Trades Assn. (pres. 1968-69), Tonopah C. of C. (pres. 1962-63), V.F.W. (life). Mason (Shriner), Elk, Lion (pres. Tonopah 1964-65). Address: Box 672 Tonopah NV 89049

BLAKEMORE, SUSAN, speech pathologist; b. Manitowoc, Wis., Mar. 5, 1939; d. Erwin Isadore and Francis (Risdon) Kletzien; B.S. in Elementary Edn., U. Wis., Madison, 1961; M.A. in Communicative Disorders, Calif. State U., San Francisco, 1973; m. Joe Clark Blakemore, Oct. 25, 1969. Tchr. kindergarten, pub. schs., Waunakee, Wis., 1961-62; speech pathologist Enterprise Sch. Dist., Redding, Calif., 1973—; pvt. practice speech pathology. Lic. speech pathologist, Calif. Mem. Am. Speech and Hearing Assn. (cert. clin. competence in speech pathology), Calif. Speech and Hearing Assn., Calif. Tchrs. Assn., Little People Am., Fund for Animals, Environ. Action. Home: 945 Deschutes Rd Palo Cedro CA 96073 Office: 1073 Hartnell Ave Redding CA 96001

BLAKESLEE, DIANE PUSEY, financial planning company executive; b. West Chester, Pa., Apr. 12, 1933; d. Norman Solomon and Leona (Ruth) Pusey; m. Earle Bevington Blakeslee, June 11, 1954; children—Samuel, Barbara, David Ruth. Student Hood Coll., 1951-54, Calif. Poly State U., 1966. Cert fin. planner. With Nat. Bank of Avondale (Pa.), 1952, Bank of Am., Chino, Calif., 1954; registered rep. TMI Equities, Newport Beach, Calif., 1971-73, registered prin., br. mgr., 1973-78; registered prin., br. mgr. Walt Becker & Assos., Fresno, Calif., 1978-80; registered prin., owner Blakeslee & Blakeslee, San Luis Obispo, Calif., 1980—; faculty Calif. Poly. State U. Extension, 1979-82, Cuesta Jr. Coll., 1979-80. Bd. dirs. Pvt. Industry Council, 1980—, San Luis Obispo Child Devel. Center, 1978-82; counselor Family Services Orgn., 1978—; mem. choir Arroyo Grande Meth. Ch., 1976-82, fund raiser, 1966-76; active Symphony Guild, 1974-82; sponsor Pony Club, 1978-79; active PTA, 1961-77; bd. regents Coll. Fin. Planners, Denver, 1980—. Mem. Internat. Assn. Fin. Planners, Inst. Cert. Fin. Planners (dir. 19—), Nat. Assn. Life Underwriters, San Luis Obispo Life Underwriters. Republican. Quaker. Clubs: Symphony Guild, Women's Network, Quota Internat. Office: Blakeslee & Blakeslee 1110 California Blvd San Luis Obispo CA 93401

BLAMA, ROBERT JAMES, communications equipment mfg. co. ofcl.; b. Youngstown, Ohio, Oct. 28, 1937; s. Andrew and Ann (Yavorsky) B.; B.S., Youngstown, U., 1961; postgrad. Case Western Res. U. Statistician, U.S. Navy Fin. Ctr., 1962-63; sales rep. IBM, 1963-65; systems analyst/sales rep. Gen. Electric Co., 1965-69; account mgr. Honeywell, Inc., 1969-77; sr. sales rep. Data Gen. Co., 1977-80; dir. Western region Halcyon Communications, Inc., San Jose, Calif., 1980—. Office: 2001 Gateway Pl San Jose CA 95110

BLAMEY, PHILIP, oil co. exec.; b. Calgary, Alta., Can., Dec. 27, 1922; s. Thomas Philip and Ethel (Davies) B.; m. Lois Jean Williams, Dec. 15, 1945; children—Curtis, Richard, Robert. B.A., UCLA, 1947. Staff Union Oil Co., Los Angeles, 1941-68, asst. comptroller, 1968-74, comptroller, 1974-78, v.p. finance, chief fin. officer, 1978—. Served to 1st lt. USAAC, USA 1943-45; ETO; to 1st lt. USAF, 1951-52. Decorated D.F.C., Air medal with two oak leaf clusters. Episcopalian. Clubs: Jonathan (Los Angeles); Hacienda Golf (LaHabra, Calif.). Office: 461 Boyleston St Los Angeles CA 90017

BLANC, FRANCIS LOUIS, ret. govt. ofcl.; b. Knoxville, Tenn., Aug. 22, 1916; s. Olan Randolf and Katherine M. (Underwood) B.; B.S., U. Calif. at Berkeley, 1938, postgrad., 1939-40; m. Fern Adell Gambrell, Jan. 9, 1938; children—Yvonne Marie (Mrs. Thomas K. Burgess), Donna Jean (Mrs. Chris A. Frey). With Calif. Dept. Agr., 1940-75, supr. insect detection survey, Sacramento, 1957-71, supr. pest detection, Sacramento, 1971-75. Served to 1st lt. AUS, 1943-45. Mem. Entomol. Soc. Am., Pacific Coast Entomol. Soc. (pres. 1971), Calif. State Employees Assn., Alpha Zeta, Phi Sigma. Clubs: Northern Calif. Entomology, So. Calif. Entomology. Author: (with Richard H. Foote) The Fruit Flies or Tephritidae of California, 1963. Home: 5309 Spilman Ave Sacramento CA 95819

BLANCHARD, DONALD EMERSON, health ins. co. exec.; b. Denver, July 21, 1924; s. Clyde William and Agnes Pauline (Wolnick) B.; A.B., Yale U., 1948; J.D., U. Denver, 1962; m. Cynthia May Anderson, Dec. 25, 1946; children—James Douglas, Robert William. Sec., gen. mgr. Hurd's Bakeries, Denver, 1948-62; admitted to Colo. bar, 1963; v.p. bus. affairs Colo. Woman's Coll., Denver, 1962-67; v.p., treas. Knox Coll., Galesburg, Ill., 1967-71; chmn. chief exec. officer East West Enterprises (Aurora Downs Race Track), Aurora, Ill., 1969-71; v.p. Sunbeam Corp., Chgo., 1971-75; partner firm Almon, Barsotti & Blanchard, 1975-77; sr. v.p. adminstrn. Blue Cross and Blue Shield Colo., Denver, 1977-82, pres., 1983—; vice chmn. bd. Rocky Mountain Life Ins. Co.; dir. HMO Colo., Inc. Bd. dirs. Denver chpt. ARC, 1958-67. Served with AUS, 1943-45. Mem. Am. Bar Assn., Colo. Bar Assn., Denver Bar Assn., Phi Beta Kappa, Phi Delta Phi. Republican. Lutheran. Club: Denver Kiwanis (past pres.). Author articles in field. Office: 700 Broadway Denver CO 80273

BLANCHARD, NINA, talent agent; b. Greenwich, Conn., July 21; d. John Dean and Mildred Eleanor (Weakley) Blanchard; m. Benjamin James Tomkins, May 28, 1950 (div.). Student El Camino Coll., 1948, Columbia U., 1950. Actress, Los Angeles and N.Y.C., 1948-51; make-up artist NBC-TV, N.Y.C., 1951-58; casting dir., N.Y.C., 1954-55; talent agent, prin. Nina Blanchard Enterprises, Inc. & Nina Blanchard Agency, Los Angeles, 1961—; TV and film UCLA Extension; lectr. in field. Mem. adv. bd Free Arts Clinic Abused Children, Hathaway Home for Children. Mem. Assn. Talent Agents, Acad. TV Arts and Scis., Women in Film, Com. 200. Author: How to Break Into Motion Pictures, Television, Commercials and Modeling, 1978.

BLANCHE, JOHN GORDON, psychologist; b. Vancouver, B.C., Can., Aug. 12, 1947; s. Kenneth P. and Beverly C. (Bronger) B.; m. Patricia L. Gunckel, Aug. 16, 1969; children—Heather, Kevan. A.B., U. So. Calif., 1969, Ph.D., 1976; M.A., Calif. State U.-Los Angeles, 1971. Lic. psychologist, Calif. Sr. cons. psychologist and mgr. test publ. div. Psychol. Services, Inc., Los Angeles, 1975-78; cons. psychologist, sr. cons. psychologist, mgr. Rohrer, Hibler and Replogle, Los Angeles, 1978—. Mem. U. So. Calif. Nat. Championship Football Team, 1968; Rose Bowl Team, 1967, 68, 69. Mem. Am. Psychol. Assn., U. So. Calif. Alumni Assn. Republican. Club: Los Angeles Athletic. Home: 490 Starlight Crest La Canada Flintridge CA 91011 Office: 626 Wilshire Blvd Suite 800 Los Angeles CA 90017

BLANCHET-MACIEL, BARBARA, interior designer; b. Chgo., June 15, 1933; d. Benjamin Klaus and Eleanor Irene (Jarmen) Blanchet; m. David Arnold Maciel, 1980; children—Tara Lyn Way, Machelle Dawn. Student Laguna Beach Sch. Environ. Design, 1970. Owner, mgr. Blanchet Advt. Agy., Newport Beach, Calif., 1964-73; designer Cannel & Chaffin Co., Newport Beach, 1973-74, Arthur Valdes & Co., Newport Beach, 1975; dir. design Splty. Restaurants Inc., Long Beach, Calif., 1976; dir. design W.R. Grace Inc. (El Torito Restaurants), Los Angeles, 1976-78; designer Robert Altevers & Co., Newport Beach, 1978-80; owner-designer Barbara Blanchet Interior Design Co., Pebble Beach, Calif., 1980-82, Ruby Begonia's Interior Design & Antiques, Carmel-by-the-sea, Calif., 1982—. Mem. Am. Horse Show Assn., Nat. Trust Hist. Preservation, Monterey County Hist. Soc., N.Am. Soc. Interior Design, Inst. Bus. Designers. Republican. Home: 14194 Reservation Rd Salinas CA 93908 Office: PO Box 6238 Carmel-by-the-Sea CA 93953

BLANCHETTE, JAMES EDWARD, psychiatrist; b. Syracuse, N.Y., Aug. 28, 1924; s. Joseph M. and Margaret (Vincent) B.; B.A., Syracuse U., 1950, M.D., SUNY-Syracuse Sch. Med., 1953; m. Shirley Ruth Brisco, Sept. 1, 1948 (dec. May 1981). Intern, St. Vincent's Hosp., N.Y.C., 1953-54; resident Patton (Calif.) State Hosp., 1954-55, Met. State Hosp., Norwalk, Calif., 1957-59; pvt. practice psychiatry, Redlands, Calif., 1959—; chief profl. edn. Patton State Hosp., 1960-64, tchg. cons., 1964-69; asst. clin. prof. psychiatry Loma Linda Med. Sch.; mem. staffs San Bernardino Community Hosp., St. Bernadine Hosp. (both San Bernardino); cons. psychiatry Redlands Community Hosp. Served with USAAF, 1945-47. Diplomate Am. Bd. Med. Examiners, Am. Bd. Psychiatry and Neurology. Fellow Am. Psychiat. Assn., AAAS, Pan-Am. Med. Assn.; mem. AMA, Calif. Med. Assn., San Bernardino Med. Soc., Internat. Platform Assn., So. Calif. Psychiat. Soc. (pres. Inland chpt. 1963-64, pres. elect 1982-83), Royal Soc. Health, Am. Med. Soc. Vienna, Phi Mu Alpha Symphonia, Nu Sigma Nu. Home: 972 W Marshall Blvd San Bernardino CA 92405 Office: 236 Cajon St Redlands CA 92373

BLANCHFIELD, KATHLEEN SHARON, rehabilitation counselor, consultant; b. Chgo., Mar. 24, 1944; d. Walter Benjamin and Olive Bernice (Gray) B. B.A., Mundelein Coll., 1971; M.S., Ill. Inst. Tech., 1978. Cert. rehab. counselor. Rehab. coordinator med. dept. Ill. Central Gulf R.R., Chgo., 1978-81; rehab. counselor coordinator Pain Center, Swedish Hosp. Med. Center, Seattle, 1981—; cons. in field. Active NOW. Recipient Pres.'s award Mundelein Coll., 1968. Mem. Nat. Rehab. Assn., Nat. Rehab. Counselors Assn., Am. Personnel and Guidance Assn., Am. Rehab. Counselors Assn., Nat. Assn. Rehab. Profls. in Pvt. Sector. Contbr. article to profl. jour. Office: 702 Summit Ave Seattle WA 98104

BLANCK, WALTER ROBERT, II, univ. adminstr.; b. Greenwood, S.C., Mar. 15, 1945; s. Walter Robert and Corrie Victoria (Morgan) B.; B.A., U. Redlands (Calif.), 1972, M.A. in Human Resources Mgmt., 1980; M.S. in Urban Planning, Calif. Poly. U., 1974; m. Margaret Estelle Toepfer, Aug. 23, 1969; children—Robert Michael, Ryan Matthew, Rebekah Maeve. Asst. dept. sociology U. Redlands, 1971, lectr., 1979—; asst. prof. Sch. Environ. Design, Calif. Poly. U., 1973; city planner City of Ontario (Calif.), 1973-74; urban planner County of San Bernardino (Calif.), 1974-77; adminstr. Calvary Chapel Conf. Center, Twin Peaks, Calif., 1977-79; with Aaron K. Anderson Constrn. Co., Lake Arrowhead, Calif., 1979-80; program dir. M.A. in Mgmt. degree program U. Redlands (Calif.), 1980—; cons. in urban planning and human resources mgmt., 1977—. Served with USN, 1964-68; Vietnam. Recipient Cross Mil. Service, UDC, 1976. Mem. Pi Gamma Mu. Republican. Home: 939 Aaron Redlands CA 92373

BLAND, LAUREL LEMIEUX, cons. firm exec., educator, author; b. Spokane, Wash., Feb. 23, 1926; d. Alfred T. and Bernice K. (Lawrence) LeMieux; A.A., Anchorage Community Coll., 1966; Ed.B. cum laude, U. Alaska, 1968, M.A., 1969; Ph.D., U. N.Mex., 1974; m. Frank H. Schricker, Mar. 30, 1976; children—Daniel Matthew Bland, Laurel Kathleen Bland Eisinger. Tech. asst. Alaska Human Rights Commn., Anchorage, 1967; liaison 2d Jud. Dist., Alaska Legal Services, Nome, 1968; instr. Alaska Meth. U., Anchorage, 1969-73; project dir. spl. hist. and cultural inventory of Imuruk Basin, Alaska, 1969-73; asst. prof. edn. U. Alaska, Fairbanks, 1974; prof. cross-cultural edn. Sheldon Jackson Coll., Sitka, Alaska, 1974-79, now life appointment; exec. dir. Human Environ. Resources Services, Inc., Anchorage and Kennewick, Wash., 1970—; cons. to state and fed. govt. agys., Indian communities and orgns., 1964—. Mem. TriCities Minority Purchasing Council. Mem. Alaska Hist. Soc. Club: Altrusa. Author: (with William Oquilluk) People of Kauwerak, 1973; Northern Eskimos of Alaska, 1972; Alaska Legal Services Field Operation Manual, 1968; Manpower Needs to Construct the Trans-Alaska Pipeline, 1970; Alaska Native Population and Manpower Vol. 1, 1975, Vols. 2, 3, 1978; contbr. numerous articles on social anthropology to profl. publs. and U.S. Office Edn. inter-library system; specialist in EEO research. Home: 1921 W 17th St Kennewick WA 99336 Office: 1921 W 17th St Kennewick WA

BLAND, THOMAS RAYMOND, ins. co. exec.; b. Aleppo Twp., Pa., June 13, 1937; s. Herbert Wesley and Margaret Ann (Wood) B.; B.S., Miami U., Oxford, Ohio, 1959; postgrad. Golden Gate Law Sch., 1977; m. Joan Clair Coffman, Feb. 20, 1960; children—Julie Rae, Douglas Lynn, Laura Joan, Michael Christopher, Heather Robin. With Universal C.I.T. Co., Sandusky, Ohio, 1959-60; mgr. Coll. Life Ins. Co., Bowling Green, Athens, Columbus, and Oxford, Ohio, 1960-69; dir. mktg. Cal-Farm Ins. Co., Berkeley, 1969-79; v.p. mktg. Phila. Life Ins. Co., San Francisco, 1980-81; sr. v.p. mktg. West Coast Life, San Francisco, 1981—; dir. Wesco Securities Inc.; lectr. estate planning U. Calif. C.L.U.; cert. advanced estate planning. Mem. Nat. Assn. Life Underwriters, Oakland-East Bay Chartered Life Underwriters, Phi Kappa Tau. Republican. Episcopalian. Home: 2079 Banbury Rd Walnut Creek CA 94598 Office: 1275 Market St San Francisco CA

BLANK, SHELDON ELMER, chemical researcher; b. Spokane, Wash., Nov. 14, 1949; s. Elmer Jacob and Nina Faye (Kjack) B.; m. Janyce Lee Galbreath, Aug. 8, 1970; children—Ryan, Jeffrey, Michelle. B.S. in Agronomy, Wash. State U.-Pullman, 1972; M.S. in Agronomy, U. Minn.-St. Paul, 1974, Ph.D. in Agronomy, 1976. Field researcher, developer agrl. chems. Monsanto Co., Twin Falls, Idaho, 1976-79, Kennewick, Wash., 1981—, tech. supr., St. Louis, 1979-81. Recipient H. K. Hayes Outstanding Grad. Student award Dept. Agronomy and Plant Genetics, U. Minn., 1974. Mem. Weed Sci. Soc. Am., Western Soc. Weed Sci., Am. Soc. Agronomy (Outstanding sr. grad. 1971), Council Agrl. Sci. Tech. Methodist. Club: Odd Fellows (Kennewick). Speaker profl. meetings. Office: Monsanto Co 3805 S Dennis St Kennewick WA 99336

BLANKENSHIP, DOUGLAS PAUL, devel. co. exec.; b. Ky., Nov. 13, 1944; s. Herbert and Bertie Lee (Smith) B. B.A. in History and Geography, Eastern Ky. U., 1964; M.A. in Adminstrn., U. Ky., 1966, M.A. in Transp., 1967; postgrad. UCLA, 1967-68; Ph.D., Ohio State U., 1969. Instr. high sch., dept. chmn. Pike County Sch. System, Pikeville, Ky., 1964-67; research asso. U. Ky., 1966; sr. transp. systems planner Gen. Motors Corp., Los Angeles, 1967-72; project mgr. market research, asso. transp. planner Orange County Transit Dist., Santa Ana, Calif., 1972—; exec. v.p. transp. systems and mktg. Nat. Transp. Research Corp., Los Angeles, 1976—; owner, pres. Pacific Coast Devel. Co.; guest lectr. U. So. Calif. Active System Task Force for Transit, Citizens Adv. Council, Modeling Task Force. Recipient Enoch Grehan Journalism award, 1964, Outstanding recognition in strategic and Guerrilla warfare gaming, 1968, Electronic Mus. award Los Angeles Mus. chpt., 1969, Creativity Recognition award Internat. Personnel Research, 1972. Mem. Am., So. Calif. mktg. assns., Am. Inst. Planners (asso.), Am. Soc. Planning Ofcls., Assn. Am. Geographers, Los Angeles Geog. Soc., Urban and Regional Info. Systems Assn., Transp. Research Bd. of Nat. Acad. Scis., U. Ky. Alumni Assn. (pres. So. Calif.), Mensa, Kappa Iota Epsilon, Omicron Alpha Kappa. Democrat. Author: The Soviet Union-Expansion at Any Cost, 1969; Theories of World Power and Control, 1969; Multivariate Analysis of Power-A Ten Nation Study, 1969; A Tentative Theory of International Relations, 1969; A Model of International Message Flow, 1970; Cognition Related to Ten Branches of Philosophy, 1966; Human Freedom and Existentialism, 1966; Application of Raul Prebisch's ECLA Rationale to West Indies, 1968; The Nature of Some Geographical Theories, 1967; A Model of Guerrilla Engagements and Its Application, 1966; A Study of Directional Bias in International Lifelines, 1969; A Geographical Analysis of Entropy-Long Range Changes in Settlement Patterns Over Time, 1969. Contbr. articles on transp. system, modeling and quantitative market research to profl. jours. Home: 448 S Alexandria Ave Los Angeles CA 90020

BLANKFELD, HOWARD MARTIN, psychiatrist, educator; b. Bklyn., Sept. 29, 1941; s. Nathan and Stella (Cohen) B.; B.A., Columbia U., 1962; M.D., N.Y.U., 1966; m. Tecca Kaye, June 7, 1964; children—Deborah, David. Intern, Bronx Mcpl. Hosp. Center, 1966-67; resident in psychiatry NYU-Bellevue Med. Ctr., 1967-68, Herrick Meml. Hosp., Berkeley, Calif., 1970-71; fellow in child psychiatry City of Berkeley Mental Health Services, 1971-72, L.I. Jewish-Hillside Med. Ctr., 1972-73; practice medicine specializing in psychiatry, Walnut Creek, Calif., 1974—; staff psychiatrist Alameda County (Calif.) Mental Health Services, 1974-78; med. dir. Fred Finch Youth Center, Oakland, Calif., 1978; mem. staff Walnut Creek Hosp., Gladman Meml. Hosp., Oakland, Calif., 1982—; asst. clin. prof. Langley Porter Psychiat. Inst., U. Calif., San Francisco, 1982—; cons. child psychiatry Contra Costa County Mental Health Services, 1982—. Bd. dirs. We Care Soc., 1982—. Served to lt. comdr. M.C., USNR, 1968-70. Diplomate Am. Bd. Psychiatry and Neurology. Mem. Am. Psychiat. Assn. Office: 177 La Casa Via Walnut Creek CA 94598

BLANKFORT, LOWELL ARNOLD, newspaper publisher; b. N.Y.C., Apr. 29, 1926; s. Herbert and Gertrude (Butler) B.; B.A. in History, Polit. Sci., Rutgers U., 1946; m. April Pemberton; 1 son, Jonathan. Reporter, copy editor L.I. (N.Y.) Star-Jour., 1947-49; columnist London Daily Mail, Paris, 1949-50; copy editor The Stars & Stripes, Darmstadt, Germany, 1950-51, Wall St. Jour., N.Y.C., 1951; bus., labor editor Cowles Mags., N.Y.C., 1951-53; pub. Pacifica (Calif.) Tribune, 1954-59; free-lance writer, Europe, Asia, 1959-61; co-pub., editor Chula Vista (Calif.) Star-News, 1961-78; co-owner Paradise (Calif.) Post, 1977—, Monte Vista (Colo.) Jour., Center (Colo.) Post-Dispatch, Del Norte (Colo.) Prospector, 1978—, Plainview (Minn.) News, St. Charles (Minn.) Press, Lewiston (Minn.) Jour., 1980—, Summit (Colo.) Sentinel, New Richmond (Wis.) News, 1981—. Mem. Calif. Democratic Central Com., 1963. Named Outstanding Layman of Year, Sweetwater Edn. Assn., 1966, Citizen of Year, City of Chula Vista, 1976; Headliner of Yr., San Diego Press Club, 1980. Mem. ACLU (pres. San Diego chpt. 1970-71), Calif. Newspaper Pubs. Assn., Sigma Delta Chi. Contbr. articles on fgn. affairs to newspapers. Home: Old Orchard Ln Bonita CA 92002 Office: 835 3d Ave Chula Vista CA 92010

BLANKS, HERBERT BEVERLY, pest control co. exec.; b. Cleve., Oct. 27, 1915; s. Anthony Faulkner and Dorothy McGee (Welch) B.; B.S. in Forestry, U. Calif.-Berkeley, 1937; postgrad. Civil Affairs Tng. Sch., U. Chgo., 1944; m. Roxana Caroline Holmes, May 26, 1937; children—George Anthony, Herbert Elliot, Donald Allen. With U.S. Forest Service, Tahoe Nat. Forest, 1936-38; park ranger Sequoia Nat. Park, Calif., 1938-42; co-partner Ailing House Pest Control, Carmel, Calif., 1946-73, pres., 1974-80, chmn. bd., 1980—. Scoutmaster Boy Scouts Am., Carmel, 1949-55. Charter mem. City of Carmel Forestry Commn., 1955; planning commr., Carmel, 1955-62, chmn., 1960-61; councilman, Carmel, 1962-70, mayor, 1964-66; mem. Monterey County (Calif.) Local Agy. Formation Commn., 1967-70, chmn., 1967-68. Bd. dirs. Assn. Monterey Bay Area Govts., 1966-70; trustee Harrison Meml. Library, 1971-77. Served with AUS, 1942-46; lt. col. Res. ret. Decorated Bronze Star, Army Commendation medal. Mem. PTA (hon., life), Pest Control Operators Calif. (dir. 1963-64, sec.-treas. Monterey Bay Area dist. 1974-80), Nat. Pest Control Assn. (committeeman 1962-64), Res. Officers Assn. (life), Ret. Officers Assn. (life). Mem. Community Ch. (pres. bd. govs. 1972, 76). Clubs: Commonwealth, Masons (past master Carmel; knight comdr. Ct. of Honor 1975; 33 deg.; treas. Monterey County Scottish Rite club 1972—); Hi-12. Home: PO Box 241 Carmel CA 93921 Office: PO Box 2066 Carmel CA 93921

BLANTON, ANITA LOUISE, home economist; b. Cheyenne, Okla., Nov. 3, 1936; d. John Morris and Dorothy Turbyfill; m. Edward E. Blanton, May 18, 1955; children—Bruce, David. B.S. in Home Econs. Edn., Tex. Tech. U., 1972; M.A. in Pub. Adminstrn., U. N.Mex., 1980. Extension home economist Zuni Indian Reservation, N.Mex., 1973-76; county extension agt. Collingsworth County, Tex., 1976; 4-H home economist Bernalillo County, N.Mex., 1977—. Recipient Disting. Service award N.Mex. Assn. Extension 4-H Agts., 1982; named Outstanding Jaycee-Ette, 1969. Mem. Am. Home Econs. Assn., Nat. Assn. Extension 4-H Agts., Nat. Assn. Extension Home Economists, Albuquerque Home Economists, Epsilon Sigma Alpha, Phi Upsilon Omicron. Republican. Methodist. Home: 2513 Landman NE Albuquerque NM 87112 Office: Extension Office 105 5th NW Albuquerque NM 87102

BLANTON, JOHN ARTHUR, architect; b. Houston, Jan. 1, 1928; s. Arthur Alva and Caroline (Jeter) B.; B.A., Rice U., 1948, B.S. in Architecture, 1949; m. Marietta Louise Newton, Apr. 10, 1953 (dec. 1976); children—Jill Annette Blanton Lewis, Lynette Louise, Elena Diane. With Richard J. Neutra, Los Angeles, 1950-64; pvt. practice architecture, Manhattan Beach, Calif., 1964—; lectr. UCLA Extension, 1967-76, Harbor Coll., Los Angeles, part time, 1970-72. Mem. Capital Improvements Com., Manhattan Beach, 1966, city commr. Bd. of Bldg. Code Appeals. Served with Signal Corps, U.S. Army, 1951-53. Recipient Best House of Year award C. of C., 1969, 70, 71, 83, Preservation of Natural Site award, 1974, design award, 1975. Mem. AIA (contbr. book revs. to jour. 1972—, recipient Red Cedar Shingle/nat. merit award 1979), Soc. Archtl. Historians. Club: Rotary. Six bldgs. included in A Guide to the Architecture of Los Angeles and Southern California. Office: 2100 Sepulveda Blvd Suite 14 Manhattan Beach CA 90266

BLANTON, ROY EDGAR, water treatment operator; b. El Centro, Calif., Apr. 30, 1933; s. William Moses and Annie Estle (Smith) B. B.A. in Bus. Adminstrn. and Econs., La Verne U., 1975. Cert. wastewater treatment plant operator V, Calif. Constrn. insp., operator Conejo Valley San. Co., Thousand Oaks, Calif., 1964-66; water and wastewater treatment supr. Thousand Oaks Utilities Dept., 1966-72; gen. mgr. Goleta (Calif.) San. Dist., 1972-80, Selma-Kingsburg-Fowler County San. Dist., Kingsburg, Calif., 1980—; mem. operator adv. com. Calif. State Water Resources Control Bd., 1979-81. Served with U.S. Army Security Agy., 1952-55, USAF Security Service, 1957-63. Mem. Water Pollution Control Fedn., Calif. Water Pollution Control Assn., Am. Water Works Assn., NRA, Calif. Rifle And Pistol Assn. Club: Rotary (Kingsburg); Elks, Eagles, KC. Office: PO Box 95 Kingsburg CA 93631

BLASCHKE, L. LINDEN, music and advertising consultant; b. Orange, Tex., July 15, 1943; s. Lester Emil and Margaret Anne (Reeves) B. B.A., U. N.Mex., 1965. Music pub. Motown Records, Los Angeles, 1970-73; mng. dir. artists and repertoire ABC Records, Los Angeles, 1973-79; advt. sales mgr. Albuquerque Cable TV, 1981-82; pvt. cons. to music industry and cable TV, Albuquerque, 1983—. Mem. Nat. Assn. Rec. Arts and Scis., ASCAP, Sigma Alpha Epsilon. Democrat. Methodist. Clubs: Westerners Corral (Los Angeles and Albuquerque). Office: 7400 Osuna Rd NE Albuquerque NM 87109

BLASCO-IBANEZ, ALEC MONTGOMERY, photo-journalist; b. Chgo., Mar. 7, 1929; s. Alejandro Serrat and Dalmyra Burnett (Montgomery) Blasco-Ibanez; student U. Notre Dame, 1948-49; Ph.B., U. So. Calif., 1957. Sports editor Maywood-Bell Indsl. Post, editor Bell Gardens Rev. and Post Star, McGiffin Pub. Co., Calif., 1959; asst. dir. U. So. Calif. News Bur., 1960-61; spl. sci. corr. Los Angeles Examiner and Pictorial Living mag., 1961-62; combat corr. and photographer covering NATO, SEATO and U.S. Armed Forces in Europe, Africa, Middle East, S.E. Asia and Far East including graduating from mil. paratrooper schs., U.S. Army 8th Inf. Div. (W. Ger.), West German Republic Army, Fernspaeh 200 Co., and French Fgn. Legion 2d Regt. Etranger Parachutistes (Algeria), S. African Republic 1st Parachute Bn., Bloemfontein, Los Angeles Herald-Examiner and Hearst Headline Service, 1962-66; adminstrv. asst. to Rep. John G. Dow of N.Y. and dir. Dow Peace Mission, South Vietnam, 1967; travel and mil. affairs editor Los Angeles Herald-Examiner and Calif. Living mag., 1968-80; travel editor daily radio program Ports of Call/Word on Travel, Sta. KFAC, classical music sta., 1975-81; covered Am. Floating Arctic ice stas., Arctic Ocean, 1960-62. No. Alaskan Eskimo whaling hunts U. So. Calif. and Arctic Research Lab., 1961; deepest Arctic Ocean ice-pack penetration U.S.S. Burton Island, 1961; deepest Antarctic Ocean ice-pack penetration Marie Byrd Land, U.S.S. Glacier, Antarctica, 1961; 2d expdn. to relocate South Magnetic Pole, Commonwealth Bay, Adelie Land, U.S.S. Burton Island 1962. Chile-Peru trench expdn., U.S.S. Anton Brun, NSF, 1965, 1st to photograph living-fossil Neopolina and possible lost undersea Inca City, 1965; Sargasso Sea expdn., pioneer in deep-sea photography photographing abyssal sea creature Holothurian, Duke U.'s Eastward, 1965; Mayan Sacred Wells (cenotes) expdn., Isla Cozumel and Yucatan Peninsula, 1965; Inter-Am. Geodetic Survey expdn., Peruvian Andes, 1965; 1st corr. to search for Che Guevara, Bolivia, 1965-66; native African music expdn. Dundo Anthrop. Mus., Angola, 1966; lion-human fear response expdn. Gorangoza Nat. Game Preserve, Mozambique, 1966; Mt. Kilimanjaro ski expdn., 1st Westener to ski 19,340-foot peak without oxygen, 1971; helicopter ski expdns. Andes, Colombia and Columbia Mountains, B.C., Can., 1969-76; pres. Silver Spur Enterprises, originator and editor 1 pub. Horses of Kings, Andalusian World, Cowboy mags., also trainer, exhibitor Andalusian stallion Paladin, 1976—. Served with USNR, 1948-53; lt. col. USMCR; officer-in-charge or liaison various assignments in U.S. and with NATO in Greece, Turkey and Italy, 1970-81. Recipient Gold Medal of Merit (Austria), 1972; Gold medal Literary Excellence, Internat. Poets' Shrine and Congress of Am. Poets, 1972; Japanese Govt. travel writing award, 1972; 2d ann. Best Writers award N.Am. and Can., Japanese Nat. Tourist Orgn., 1973; Gen. D. MacArthur Gold medal, 1974. Mem. USMCR Combat Corrs. Assn. (Outstanding Citizen award 1976), USMCR Officers Assn., Appaloosa Horse Club, Am. Andalusian Horse Assn., Internat. Andalusian Horse Assn., Chief Joseph Trail Ride Soc., Explorers Club, Japan Ukiyo-e Soc. (Tokyo). Club: Safari Internat. (Los Angeles). Office: Silver Spur Enterprises 3963 Wilshire Blvd Suite 357 Los Angeles CA 90010

BLATT, MORTON BERNARD, medical illustrator; b. Chgo., Jan. 9, 1923; d. Arthur E. and Hazel B. Student Central YMCA Coll., 1940-42, U. Ill., 1943-46. Tchr., Ray-Vogue Art Schs., Chgo., 1946-51; med. illustrator VA Center, Wood, Wis., 1951-57, Swedish Covenant Hosp., Chgo., 1957-76; med. illustrator Laidlaw Bros., River Forest, Ill., 1956-59; cons., artist health textbooks, 1956-59; illustrator Standard Edn. Soc., Chgo., 1960; art editor Covenant Home Altar, 1972-83, Covenant Companion, 1958-82. Served with USAAF, 1943-44. Mem. Art Inst. Chgo., Assoc. Ch. Press, Evangel. Press Assn. Club: Chicago Press. Illustrator: Atlas and Demonstration Technique of the Central Nervous System, 1961, also numerous med. jours.; illustrator, designer Covenant Hymnal, books, record jackets. Address: PO Box 489 Mill Valley CA 94942

BLATTER, FRANK EDWARD, banker; b. Denver, Jan. 9, 1939; s. Anthony John and Irene Marie (Tobin) B.; B.S., Regis Coll., Denver, 1961; grad. Colo. Sch. Banking, 1966, Sch. Bank Adminstrn., 1973; m. Barbara E. Drieth, Sept. 6, 1959; children—Dean Robert, Lisa Kay, Paul Kelly. Accountant, McMahon, Maddox & Rodriguez, C.P.A.'s, Denver, 1960-63, United Bank Denver, 1963-65; with United Banks Colo., Inc., Denver, 1965—, comptroller, then treas., comptroller, 1969-74, v.p., fin., treas., 1974-79, sr. v.p., treas., 1979-81, exec. v.p., 1981—; chmn. bd., dir., United Bank Arvada, United Mortgage Co., United Bank of Longmont, United Bank of Arapahoe, United Banks Service Co., United Bank Brighton, United Bank Cherry Creek; pres. United Fin. Ctrs., Inc. C.P.A., Colo. Bd. dirs., treas. Denver Catholic Community Services; nat. adv. council Regis. Coll. Mem. Tax Execs. Inst. (chpt. pres. 1972, nat. v.p. 1974), Bank Adminstrn. Inst., Fin. Execs. Inst., Am. Inst. C.P.A.s, Colo. Soc. C.P.A.s. Roman Catholic. Club: Rolling Hills Country. Office: 1700 Lincoln St Denver CO 80217

BLATTNER, ERNEST WILLI, engring. co. exec.; b. Aarau, Switzerland, Apr. 14, 1929; came to U.S., 1957, naturalized, 1970; s. Ludwig and Martha B.; m. Anneke Geurds, May 24, 1958; children—Mark Hermann, Flora Grazia, Elisabeth Rose, Paul Johann. M.S. in Mech. Engring., Swiss Fed. Inst., Zurich, 1953; postgrad. Drexel Inst., 1959-60. Design engr. Brown Boveri Ltd., Baden, Switzerland, 1954-57; engr.-in-charge De Laval Turbine Inc., Trenton, 1957-65; chief engr. Chicago Pneumatic Tool Co., Franklin, Pa., 1965-73; mgr. advanced design EIMCO div. Envirotech Corp., Salt Lake City, 1973-79; mgr. ops. Biphase Energy Systems joint venture Research Cottrell and Transam.-Delaval, Santa Monica, Calif., 1979-81; dir. engring. Mafi-Trench Corp., Santa Maria, Calif., 1981—. Mem. Franklin Water and Waste Authority, 1963-65. Fellow ASME (chmn. Utah sect. 1976-77, mem. regional policy bd. 1977-79). Inventor turbines, compressors. Home: 490 Miles Ave Santa Maria CA 93455 Office: Mafi-Trench Corp 3037 Industrial Pkwy Santa Maria CA 93455

BLATTNER, MEERA MCCUAIG, educator; b. Chgo., Aug. 14, 1930; d. William D. McCuaig and Nina (Spertus) Klevs; B.A., U. Chgo., 1952; M.S., U. So. Calif., 1966; Ph.D., UCLA, 1973; children—Douglas, Robert, William. Research fellow in computer sci. Harvard U., 1973-74; asst. prof. Rice U., 1974-80; asso. prof. applied sci. U. Calif. at Davis, Livermore, 1980—; adj. prof. U. Tex., Houston, 1977—; vis. prof. U. Paris, 1980; program dir. theoretical computer sci. NSF, Washington, 1979-80. NSF grantee, 1977-81. Mem. Soc. Women Engrs., Assn. Computing Machinery (editor SIGACT News), IEEE Computer Soc. Contbr. articles to profl. jours. Office: Dept Applied Sci U Calif Davis/Livermore Livermore CA 94550

BLAUER, AARON CLYDE, biologist, educator; b. Burley, Idaho, Apr. 26, 1939; s. Henry William and Lucile (Woodbury) B.; m. Geaneen Whittle, Sept. 14, 1962; children—Alan, Robert, Lucile, Anthony, Elizabeth, Amy. B.S., Brigham Young U., 1964, M.S. 1965; postgrad. Cornell U., 1965-66, U. Ala., 1973. Lab instr. botany, Brigham Young U., 1962-64; range technician U.S. Forest Service, Uintah Nat. Forest, Utah, summers 1963-64; instr. biology Snow College, Ephraim, Utah, 1966-71, asst. prof. 1971-78, assoc. prof. 1978—; range research technician Intermountain Forest and Range Experiment Sta., Ogden, Utah, summers 1967-73, botanist, summers 1974—. Dist. chmn. Republican party, del. state conv. 1970; mem. Ephraim City Beautification Com., 1977-78, merit badge councilor Boy Scouts Am., 1966—, scoutmaster, 1978, com. mem. 1978-83, unit commr., 1981—; emergency med. technician. NDEA fellow, 1964-65; NSF fellow, 1965; Shell Found. fellow 1965-66; recipient Tchr. of Year award Snow Coll., 1967, 72, 77. Mem. Snow Coll. Teaching Profls., Utah Assn. Acad. Profls., Utah Pub. Employees Assn., Utah Acad. Arts, Sci. and Letters, Am. Hort. and Bot. Soc., Sigma Xi, Phi Eta Sigma, Phi Kappa Phi, Beta Beta Beta. Mormon (high priest, bishop, high councilor). Contbr. numerous articles to profl. journals. Home: 295 North 300 East Box 16-5 Ephraim UT 84627 Office: Biology Dept Snow Coll Ephraim UT 84627

BLAUSTEIN, ARTHUR I., legal center director, writer; b. N.Y.C., Sept. 1, 1933; s. Morris and Esther (Schneider) B. Program exec. Fgn. Policy Assn., 1963-64; dir. legis. and pub. affairs OEO, Northeast, 1965-66, dir. inter-agy. coordination and intergovtl. affairs, 1967-68; dir. Nat. Econ. Devel. and Law Ctr., Berkeley, Calif., 1969—; chmn. Nat. Adv. Council for Econ. Opportunity, 1977-83; chmn. bd. dirs. Ctr. for Rural Studies, 1977-80; council of advisors World Hunger Edn. Service; bd. sponsors Task Force for Democracy, 1981—; chmn. legis. oversight com. Nat. Congress for Community Econ. Devel.; chmn. nat. joint legis. task force Nat. Congress for Community Econ. Devel. Bd. dirs. nat. commn. on law, social action and urban affairs Am. Jewish Congress, 1972—. Served with U.S. Army, 1953-54. Democrat. Author: World War III, Man Against Poverty, 1968; The Star Spangled Hustle, 1972; The American Promise: Equal Justice and Economic Opportunity, 1982; contbr. articles to pubs. Office: 1950 Addison St Berkeley CA 94707

BLAZEK, MARY LOUISE, health physicist; b. Boise, Idaho, Mar. 12, 1944. D. Robert Rudolph and Karen Elizabeth (Wennstrom) Bolliger; m. William James Blazek, Oct. 18, 1969; children—Teresa Marie, Jason Patrick. Student, Bannock Meml. Hosp. Sch. Radiol. Tech., Pocatello, Idaho, 1967-69, Walla Walla Clinic (Wash.), 1969-71, Evergreen State Coll., Olympia, Wash., 1980-81. Cert. nuclear medicine technologist. Tech. services supr., chief nuclear medicine technologist Walla Walla Clinic, 1969-77; nuclear medicine technologist Auburn (Wash.) Gen. Hosp., 1978-79; health physicist State of Wash. Dept. Health Services, Olympia, 1980-81; radiation specialist State of Oreg. Health Div., Portland, 1981—; mem. NRC task force on human use byproduct material. Mem. Am. Registry Radiol. Technologists, Nuclear, Medicine Technology Cert. Bd., Health Physics Soc., Nat. Honor Soc., Conf. Radiation Control Program Dirs. (assoc., chmn. ad hoc com.). Democrat. Episcopalian. Office: Oreg Health Div 1400 SW 5th Ave Room 1012 PO Box 231 Portland OR 97207

BLEDSOE, CARL BEVERLY, state legislator, rancher; b. Aroya, Colo., Oct. 6, 1923; m. Alice Elizabeth Cotellessa, Sept. 14, 1946; children—Robert Carl, Thomas Beverley, Christopher Joel. B.S., Colo. State U., 1949. Rancher, nr. Hugo, Colo., 1949—; mem. Colo. Ho. of Reps., 1972—, speaker, 1981—. Sec., Kit Carson (Colo.) Sch. Bd., 1964-70, pres., 1970-72; sec. Cheyenne County Republican Central Com.; bd. dirs. Colo. Housing, Inc., 1976-77. Mem. Nat. Western Stockshow Assn., Colo. Cattlemen's Assn., Lincoln County Stockmen's Assn., Cheyenne County Cattlemen's Assn., Colo. Farm Bur., Cheyenne County Farm Bur., VFW, Alpha Zeta. Office: Colorado House of Representatives Office of the Speaker State Capitol Denver CO 80203

BLEDSOE, (ELLEN) ALENE, physician; b. Linden, Tex., May 5, 1914; d. Joseph Sidney and Clyde (Harkey) Bledsoe; B.A., Columbia Union Coll., 1941, postgrad; M.D., Loma Linda U., 1950. Intern, Bridgeport (Conn.) Hosp., 1949-50; resident home obstetrics Chgo. Maternity Center, 1950, Jacksonville (Ill.) State Psychiatry Hosp., 1951-52; resident in pathology St. Joseph's Hosp., Marshfield, Wis., 1952-53, Ill. Masonic Hosp., Chgo., 1954, Jewish Hosp., Cin., 1955, Kern County Hosp., Bakersfield, Calif., 1956, Gorgas Hosp., C.Z., 1957, Sacramento Hosp., 1960; gen. practice medicine Skagway, Alaska, 1951; pathologist Mendicino, Calif., 1961-69; regional Cumberland, N.S., Can., 1970-72; quality control physician Cutter's Intake Labs., Stockton and Oakland, Calif., 1974-75; med. dir. Clinica de Salud para Familias, Hollister, Calif., 1975-76; practice medicine specializing in family medicine, Ft. Bragg, Calif., 1978—. Diplomate Am. Bd. Anat. and Clin. Pathology. Fellow Coll. Am. Pathologists, Am. Soc. Clin. Pathologists (emeritus fellow); mem. N.Y. Acad. Scis. (life mem.), Pan-Am. Med. Assn. (diplomate), World Med. Assn. (asso. mem.), Am. Cancer Soc., Am. Heart Assn., Am. Lung Assn., Calif. Acad. Scis. (sr. mem.). Republican. Adventist. Author: Resident's Manual of Clinical Pathology, 1955; contbr. articles on pathology to profl. jours. Home: 33201 Jefferson Way PO Box 729 Fort Bragg CA 95437 Office: 684 S Main Fort Bragg CA 95437

BLEICH, PAMELA ANN, educator, librarian; b. Glendale, Calif., Oct. 3, 1928; d. Gustav Edward and Mildred Charlotte (Wolford) B.; student Compton Coll., 1947-48, U. Redlands, 1948-50; B.A., UCLA, 1951, postgrad., 1951-53; postgrad. U. Md., 1963-64; M.S. in L.S., U. So. Calif., 1955, M.A. in History, 1961, postgrad., 1967-77. Tchr., Long Beach (Calif.) Unified Sch. Dist., 1953, Paramount Jr. High Sch., 1953-55; library coordinator library sect. Instructional Materials Center, Los Angeles Unified Sch. Dist., 1955-61; prof. history and library sci., coordinator Instructional Media Center, Los Angeles Harbor Coll., 1961—; librarian Mannheim Am. High Sch., 1963-65. Pres. San Pedro Bay Hist. Soc., 1975-76; advisor Los Angeles Maritime Mus. Assn., 1976-79; v.p. Friends of Wilmington Public Library, 1980-81; Mem. Los Angeles Mayor's Bicentennial History Team, 1979-81; mem. univ. archives com. Calif. State U., Dominguez Hills, 1982—. Mem. ALA, Calif. Library Assn., Calif. Assn. Sch. Librarians, Calif. Assn. Ednl. Materials and Tech., Assn. Ednl. Communications Tech., NEA (life), AFT, Calif. Hist. Soc., So. Calif. Hist. Soc., Community Coll. Media Assn., U. Calif. Los Angeles, U. So. Calif. alumni assns., English Speaking Union, Beta Phi Mu, Phi Beta Gamma. Democrat. Editor Shoreline, 1974-76; mem. editorial bd. Calif. Librarian, 1958-61; asst. editor, bus. mgr. Calif. Sch. Libraries Quar., 1956-60; contbr. articles to Calif. Hist. Soc. Quar., 1964-66. Student Library Assts. Assn. of Calif. Assn. Sch. Librarians ann. perpetual trophy for exemplary library service named in her honor.

BLESENER, MARY MARGARET, school counselor; b. Northfield, Minn., Mar. 26, 1943; d. Felix Simon and Genevieve Adeline (Petersen) B. B.S., Mankato State Coll., 1965, M.S., 1972. Cert. sch. counselor, Ariz. Tchr. Pub. Schs. Gackel (N.D.), 1965-66, Kenyon (Minn.), 1966-68, Eureka (Nev.), 1969-71; high sch. counselor Pub. Schs. Tuba City (Ariz.), 1972—; tchr. extension classes Yavapai Coll., Tuba City. Mem. Am. Personnel and Guidance Assn., Ariz. Counselors Assn., NEA, Delta Kappa Gamma. Democrat. Roman Catholic. Home: Box 642 Tuba City AZ 86045 Office: Tuba City High Sch Box 67 Tuba City AZ 86045

BLETHEN, JOHN A., publisher; b. Seattle, July 12, 1918; s. Clarance Brettun and Rae (Kingsley) B.; attended Dartmouth; m. Barbara Prentice, Nov. 27, 1948; children—John Prentice, Alden Joseph. Pub., Seattle Times; chmn. bd. Walla Walla (Wash.) Union-Bulletin. Office: Seattle Times Fairview Ave N and John St PO Box 70 Seattle WA 98111*

BLEWETT, ROBERT NOALL, lawyer; b. Stockton, Calif., July 12, 1915; s. Stephen Noall and Bess Errol (Simard) B.; LL.B., J.D., Stanford U., 1936; m. Virginia Weston, Mar. 30, 1940; children—Richard Weston, Carolyn Blewett Lawrence. Admitted to Calif. bar, 1939; dep. dist. atty., San Joaquin County, 1942-46; individual practice law, Stockton, 1946—; pres. firm Blewett, Garretson & Hachman, Stockton, 1971—; dir. various corps. Bd dirs. Family Service Agy., 1960-62, Am. Cancer Soc., 1956-58; v.p. Goodwill Industries, 1965-68; vice chmn. Stockton Sister City Commn., 1969-71; trustee San Joaquin Pioneer Mus., 1974—. Mem. Am. Bar Assn., State Bar Calif., Am. Coll. Probate Counsel, Am. Bar Found., Am. Law Inst. (life), Am. Judicature Soc., Stockton C. of C., Navy League (v.p. 1977—), Delta Theta Phi, Theta Xi. Republican. Clubs: Rotary, Yosemite (Stockton); San Francisco Comml.; Masons, Shriners. Home: 3016 Dwight Way Stockton CA 95204 Office: 141 E Acacia St Stockton CA 95202

BLIDY, CAROL JEAN, ops. analyst; b. Peoria, Ill., May 31, 1944; d. Howard E. and Edna Marjory (Herrmann) Rittenhouse; B.S., Ohio State U., 1967; M.B.A., Pepperdine U., 1979; postgrad. John Marshall Law Sch., 1970-71; m. Peter Stephen Blidy III, July 18, 1971 (div. Sept. 1975). Food technologist Durkee's Famous Foods, Chgo., 1967; sect. head spl. products applications, corp. research and devel. Beatrice Foods, Chgo., 1967-72; research chemist Carageenan application Eastern divisional labs. Stauffer Chem., Dobbs Ferry, N.Y., 1972-73; quality assurance and research and devel. mgr. Western div. Derby House Products, Pfeiffer Foods, Paramount, Calif., 1974-75; corp. quality control staff engr., prodn. supr., asst. packaging supt. oil refinery Hunt-Wesson Foods, Inc., Fullerton, Calif., 1975-79, ops. analyst refinery ops. adminstrn. and planning, 1980—; staff auditor Western div., insp. quality assurance and mfg. Pepsi-Cola Bottling Group, Fountain Valley, Calif., 1979-80. Vol., Ray of Hope; mem. alumni adv. bd. Pepperdine U., 1981—. Ohio State U. scholar, 1972; recipient Outstanding Women in Bus. and Industry award Orange County YWCA, 1980. Mem. Inst. Food Technologists, Cereal Chemists Soc., Dairy Chemists, Am. Oil Chemists Soc., Nat. Assn. Female Execs., Am. Soc. Profl. and Exec. Women. Office: 1645 W Valencia Dr Fullerton CA 92634

BLINDER, MARTIN S., publishing company executive; b. Bklyn., Nov. 18, 1946; s. Meyer and Lillian (Stein) B.; B.B.A., Adelphi U., 1968. Account exec. Bruns, Nordeman & Co., N.Y.C., 1968-69; v.p. Blinder, Robinson & Co., Westbury, N.Y., 1969-73; treas. BHB Prodns., Los Angeles, 1973-76; pub. Martin Lawrence Ltd. Edits., Van Nuys, Calif., 1976—, also dir.; dir. Corp. Art Inc., Visual Artists Mgmt. Corp., Art Consultants Inc.; lectr. bus. symposia; TV and radio appearances. Mem. Democratic Nat. Com.; patron Guggenheim Mus., N.Y.C., Mus. Modern Art, N.Y.C., Los Angeles County Mus. Art, Hirschhorn Mus., Washington, Skirball Mus., Los Angeles, Diabetes Found. of City of Hope, B'nai B'rith Anti-Defamation League; bd. dirs., pres. Research Found. for Crohns Disease. Read into Congl. Record, 1981; recipient resolution of commendation Los Angeles City Council, 1983; State of Calif. resolution for contbn. to arts in Calif., 1983; County of Los Angeles Bd. Suprs. resolution for Contbn. to arts in So. Calif., 1983. Mem. Citizens for Common Sense. Contbr. articles to mags. and newspapers. Office: 7011 Hayvenhurst Ave Van Nuys CA 91406

BLINOFF, MARK, radio broadcaster, educator, writer; b. Concord, Calif., Mar. 29, 1939; s. Gennady Nicholas and Olga (Ladd) B.; m. Sherri Gaye Mudd, June 16, 1973; children—Darrick Sean, Kimberly Kay, Nicholas Mark. B.A., U. Pacific, 1957. Program dir. Sta. KTRE-TV, Lufkin, Tex., 1957-59; mgr. KAYS-TV, Hays, Kans., 1959-61; acct. supr. Sta. KWUN, Concord, Calif., 1961-63; asst. program dir. Sta. KSFO, San Francisco, 1963-65; program dir. Sta. KEX, Portland, 1965-68; program dir. Sta. KMPC, Los Angeles, 1968-79; v.p., gen. mgr. Merv Griffin Radio, Hollywood, Calif., 1979-81; pres. Firebird Communications, Salem, Oreg., 1981—; instr. Grad. Sch. Mgmt. UCLA. Respite care parent Los Angeles Children's Home Soc.; child sponsor Los Angeles Maryvale Orphange; deacon Meth. Ch., Glendale, Calif. Recipient Best Radio Promotion award N.Y. Ad. Club, 1964; Best Radio Comml. award Hollywood Ad Club, 1973; Program Dir. of the Yr. award Billboard Mag., 1978. Author: (with Eric Norberg) Who Put What on the Radio and Why, 1979; Owning and Operating your Own Radio Station, 1982. Office: 1405 E Ellendale St Dallas OR 97338

BLISCHKE, WALLACE ROBERT, statistical educator, consultant; b. Oak Park, Ill., Apr. 20, 1934; s. Walter Henry and Mabel Edna (Schulz) B.; m. Rosemary Case, Sept. 3, 1960; children—Elizabeth Ann, Scott Douglas, m. 2d, Beverly Jean Williams, Dec. 9, 1972; 1 son, Michael Walter; stepchildren—Douglas Paul Satterblom, Carol Jean Williams Satterblom. B.S., Elmhurst Coll., 1956; M.S., Cornell U., 1958, Ph.D., 1961. Post-doctoral fellow N.C. State U., Raleigh, 1961-62; mem. tech. staff Space Tech. Labs., Redondo Beach, Calif., 1962-64; prin. statistician C-E-I-R Inc./Control Data Corp., Beverly Hills, Calif., 1964-71; assoc. prof. stats. dept. decision systems U. So. Calif., Los Angeles, 1972—; cons. statis. analysis Wallace R. Blischke Ph.D., Inc. U.S. Navy Research grantee, 1973—. Mem. Am. Statis. Assn., Inst. Math. Statis., Inst. Mgmt. Scis., Biometric Soc., Internat. Acad. Bus., Indian Inst. Mgmt. Sci. Lutheran. Contbr. articles to profl., tech. jours. Home: 5401 Katherine Ave Van Nuys CA 91401 Office: Sch Bus Adminstrn Univ So Calif Los Angeles CA 90007

BLISH, EUGENE SYLVESTER, trade association administrator; b. Denver, Oct. 9, 1912; s. George Joseph and Lillian Lenox (O'Neill) B.; m. Susan M. Monti, Feb. 21, 1950; children—Eugene A., Mary, Susan Blish McCoy, Julia. B.S.C., U. Notre Dame, 1934. Advt. dir. Colo. Milling and Elevator Co., Denver, 1934-45; advt. and mktg. cons., Denver, 1945-57; asst. exec. dir. Am. Sheep Producers Council, Denver, 1957-74; merchandising rep. Nat. Potato Bd., Denver, 1974—. Mem.

alumni bd. dirs. U. Notre Dame, 1947-49. Clubs: Denver Athletic, Mt. Vernon Country, Denver Notre Dame. Home and Office: 1370 Madison St Denver CO 80206

BLISS, ARTHUR EDMOND, engineer; b. Klamath Falls, Oreg., Sept. 21, 1931; s. Peter Edmond and Lucy Edith (Johns) B.; m. Virginia Rose Garner, June 20, 1953; children—Judith Lynn Bliss Healy, Lori Diane. B.S.E.E., Oreg. State U., 1958. Mgr. test instruments Nat. Semicondr., Santa Clara, Calif., 1965-68; mgr. engring. Varian, Palo Alto, 1968-79; v.p. Benson, Inc., Mountain View, Calif., 1979—. Served with USAF, 1950-54; Korea. Mem. Assn. Computing Machinery, IEEE Computer Soc. Republican. Contbr. papers to profl. jours.; patentee in field. Home: 803 Kilbirnie Ct Sunnyvale CA 94087 Office: 385 Ravendale Dr Mountain View CA 94043

BLISS, AUDREY PRATT (MRS. WALTER ERNEST BLISS), real estate agt.; b. Phila., June 20, 1919; d. Joshua Dickson and Marion Claudine (Grignard) Pratt; student Mills Coll., 1936-37; B.A., U. Colo., 1940; m. Walter Ernest Bliss, Nov. 10, 1945; children—Walter Ernest, Wendy Marie Bliss Martin. Tchr., Schofield Barracks, Hawaii, 1940-41; teller Bank Hawaii, Honolulu, 1942-45; salesman real estate Fearon-Cross, Inc., Honolulu, 1959-60; salesman real estate A.D. Castro & Co., Honolulu, 1960-62, broker, 1962; ind. real estate broker, Honolulu, 1963—; mem. State Ethics Commn., Honolulu, 1971-79, chmn., 1976; active Girl Scouts Am., 1957; div. chmn. Punahou P.T.A., 1957. Bd. dirs. Jr. League Honolulu, 1947, Children's Aid Assn., 1954. Mem. Daus. Hawaii, Hawaiian Mission Children's Soc., Lawyers Wives Hawaii (past dir.), Outdoor Circle, Delta Gamma (del. Panhellenic Council 1967). Club: Garden of Honolulu (dir. 1973-75, 81-82). Home: 44-221A Mikiola Dr Kaneohe HI 96744

BLISS, PATRICIA LOUISE, property manager, owner realty company; b. Atlantic City, Apr. 10, 1947; d. John Patrick and Alice Paula (Vincent) Meyer; m. Jack Leslie Bliss, Dec. 5, 1969. B.S., Calif. State U.-Long Beach, 1972. Recreation dir. City of Torrance, Calif., 1965-80; property and office mgr., owner J & P Realty, Torrance, 1980—. Active in teen run-away program 1776 House, Hermosa, 1975-80. Recipient John Anson Ford award County of Los Angeles, 1970; citation Torrance Unified Sch. Dist., 1975. Democrat. Roman Catholic. Club: South Bay Bird (Torrance). Office: J & P Realty 1024 Crenshaw Torrance CA 90501

BLIWISE, NANCY GOURASH, psychologist, statistical consultant; b. Wilkinsburg, Pa., Apr. 16, 1953; d. Francis and Dorothy Carolyn (Yenick) Gourash; m. Donald Linn Bliwise, Oct. 12, 1980. B.A. summa cum laude, Cleveland State U., 1975; M.A., U. Chgo., 1979, Ph.D., 1982. U. Chgo. fellow, research asst. Sr. Actualization and Growth Encounter Project, Berkeley, Calif., 1978-79; Nat. Inst. Aging trainee, research asst. ethnicity and adaptation in middle and later yrs. Com. on Human Devel., U. Chgo., 1978-79, project dir., 1980-81; program evaluator The Thresholds, Chgo., 1980-81; Nat. Inst. Aging fellow U. Calif.-San Francisco, 1982—; statis. cons. psychiatry dept. Stanford U. Mem. Gerontol. Soc. Am., Am. Sociol. Assn., Assn. Women in Sci. Office: Human Devel and Aging U Calif 745 Parnassus Ave San Francisco CA 94143

BLOCH, E. MAURICE, art historian, curator; b. N.Y.C.; s. Leonard and Rose (Von Auspitz) B.; B.F.A., NYU, 1939, M.A., Inst. Fine Arts, 1942, Ph.D., 1957. Asst. curator Met. Mus. Art, N.Y.C., 1943; instr. U. Mo., Columbia, 1943-44; lectr. NYU, 1945-46, U. Minn., Mpls., 1946-47; prof., curator drawings and prints Cooper Union, N.Y.C., 1949-55; prof. art history UCLA, 1956-81, dir.-curator Grunwald Ctr. for Graphic Arts, 1957-83. Vice pres., dir. Va. Steele Scott Found., Pasadena, Calif., 1977. Recipient Founders Day Award of Achievement, NYU, 1956; Western Heritage award Western Heritage Center and Nat. Cowboy Hall of Fame, 1968, CRB fellow, Brussels, 1951; Am. Council Learned Socs. grantee. Mem. Coll. Art Assn., Assn. Art Hist. So. Calif. Home: 2253 Veteran Ave Los Angeles CA 90064

BLOCH, FELIX, physicist, educator; b. Zurich, Switzerland, Oct. 23, 1905; s. Gustav and Agnes (Mayer) B.; came to U.S., 1934, naturalized, 1939; E.T.H., U. Zurich, 1924-27; Ph.D., U. Leipzig, 1928; D.Sc. (hon.), U. Grenoble, 1959, Oxford U., 1960, U. Jerusalem, 1962, U. Zurich, 1966, Brandeis U., 1976, U. Pavia, 1977; m. Lore C. Misch, Mar. 14, 1940; children—George, Daniel, Frank, Ruth. Docent in physics U. Leipzig, 1932-33; prof. physics Stanford U., 1934-71, prof. emeritus, 1971—; dir. gen. CERN, Geneva, 1954-55. Recipient Nobel prize in physics, 1952. Mem. Am. Phys. Soc. (past pres.), Nat. Acad. Scis., Am. Philos. Soc., Am. Acad. Arts and Scis. Contbr. articles on atomic and nuclear physics to profl. jours. Home: 1551 Emerson Palo Alto CA 94301 Office: Dept Physics Stanford U Stanford CA 94305

BLOCH, FRED EDGAR, architect; b. Cologne, Germany, Apr. 10, 1935; s. Iwan I. and Friederike Else (Meyer) B.; came to U.S., 1945, naturalized, 1950; cert. in architecture with honors Cooper Union, 1957; m. Bridget M. Sullivan; children—Rachell, Yvonne, Steve, Bert. Successively asso., designer, project architect, officer mgr. archtl. firms, N.Y.C., 1953-70; propr. Fred Edgar Bloch & Assos., Architects, Inc., Phoenix, 1970—; pres. Interiors III Inc., Phoenix, 1971—, Bloch Devel. & Constrn. Co. div. Bloch Cos., 1980—. Mem. Phoenix Bonds Com., 1979. Served with USAFR, 1958. Mem. AIA (past chmn. ethics com. Phoenix), Am. Arbitration Assn., Am. Soc. Ch. Architecture, Solar Energy Soc. Am. Club: Kiwanis. Prin. works include The Lakes Apts., Tempe, Ariz., 1972, 7 br. banks 1st Interstate Bank Ariz., 1973-80, Fire Sta. #3, Glendale, Ariz., 1974, computer offices and assembly plant Wordstream, Houston, 1979, S.W. regional offices Century 21 Co., 1981, Ariz. Rehab. Complex, 1981, The Villas on Country Club, Mesa, Ariz., 1982. Office: 5201 N 7th St Phoenix AZ 85014

BLOCH, PAUL DAVID, advt. co. exec.; b. N.Y.C.; s. Max and Albena (Simmons) B.; B.S. in Journalism, Ohio State U.; m. Mary Rose Speziale, Dec. 4, 1965; children—Michael Max, Donna Rose. Vice pres., dir. E.T. Legg & Co., Glendale, Calif., 1967—, Spectacular Sign Corp., Glendale, 1967—; pres. Western Advt., Inc., Paul Bloch. Advt. dir. Freeway Properties, Inc. Pres., Strathmore Village Civic Assn., 1962-64; bd. mem. Greater Manhasset Pres.'s Civic Assn.; mem. bd., col. United Fund Nassau County, N.Y., 1963. Mem. Nat. Acad. Rec. Arts and Scis., Milline Club of So. Calif., Variety Clubs So. Calif., Nat. Football Found. and Hall of Fame (dir. San Fernando Valley chpt. 1978—). Clubs: Big Ten of So. Calif., Ohio State Alumni of So. Calif. (sec.). Contbr. articles in field to mags. Home: 19620 Los Alimos St Chatsworth CA 91311

BLOCK, GENE RAYMOND, engineer, mining company executive; b. St. Louis, Mar. 10, 1937; s. Raymond W. and Janice M. (Stanze) B.; m. Sandra Jeanne Thoms, Dec. 30, 1961; children—Cheryl Ann, Cynthia Ann, David Alan. B.S. in Geol. Engring., St. Louis U., 1960; M.S. in Bus. Adminstrn., Calif. State U.-Los Angeles, 1968. Registered geologists, Calif. Engr., U.S. Forest Service, Yreka, Calif., 1961-62, Los Angeles County Flood Control Dist., 1962-64; property mgr. Livingston-Graham Sand & Gravel Co., El Monte, Calif., 1964-75; mgr. real estate and property devel. Ottawa Silica Co. (Ill.), 1975-78; v.p., property mgr. Conrock Co., Los Angeles, 1978—. Mem. Gov.'s Earthquake Council, 1972, Calif. Seismic Safety Commn., 1975; councilman City of Claremont (Calif.), 1970-75, vice-mayor, 1974-75. Named Vol. of Year, Claremont chpt. ARC, 1969, Ottawa YMCA, 1977. Republican. Roman Catholic. Home: 2788 Westfield Pl Claremont CA 91711 Office: Conrock Co 3700 San Fernando Rd Los Angeles CA 90065

BLOCK, L. CANDACE, sports and fitness promotor, publicist; b. Kansas City, Mo., Feb. 15, 1949; d. James H. and Rae Alene (Vile) B. Student Birkbeck Coll., London, 1970, U. Lausanne (Switzerland), 1970, Sorbonne, Paris, 1969; B.A. in Mass Communications and French, U. Miami, Fla., 1971. Ski instr. Aspen Ski Corps. (Colo.), 1973-76; tennis coordinator Aspen Racquet Club, 1974-76; sports writer, photographer Racquetball Illustrated, 1978; publicist sports Rogers & Cowan, Beverly Hills, Calif., 1979-80; producer George Burns 85th Birthday for Rogers & Cowan, 1980-81; dir. pub. relations Bob Lorsch Group, Hollywood, Calif., 1982; owner, operator Aerobics on Wheels and Time Out/Work Out, 1982—; cons., free lance publicist, writer; v.p. Michelob Light Tennis Tournament, Industry Hills, Calif., 1982. Sport fitness columnist Faces Internat., 1983—.

BLOCK, MICHAEL JOSEPH, research chemist; b. Chgo., June 29, 1942; s. Samuel Albert and Frieda (Kligman) B.; B.S. in Chemistry, U. Mich., 1964; M.A., Harvard U., 1965, Ph.D., 1969; m. Karen Ruth Plotkin, Sept. 19, 1970; children—Laura Miriam, Jeremy Daniel. Research chemist Union Research Center, Union Oil Co. of Calif., Brea, 1968-76, sr. research chemist, 1976-80, supr. carbon and nitrogen chems. research, 1981—. NSF research fellow, 1964-66, NIH fellow, 1966-68. Mem. Am. Chem. Soc., AAAS. Patentee in sulfur and cyanogen chemistry. Office: Union Oil of Calif 376 S Valencia Ave Brea CA 92621

BLOCK, MICHAEL KENT, economics educator; b. N.Y.C., Apr. 2, 1942; s. Philip and Roslyn (Klein) B.; A.B., Stanford U., 1964, A.M. (Univ. fellow), 1969, Ph.D., 1972; m. Carole Arline Polansky, Aug. 30, 1964; children—Robert Justin, Tamara Nicole. Research analyst Bank of Am., San Francisco, 1965-66; research assoc. Planning Assos., San Francisco, 1966-67; asst. prof. econs. U. Santa Clara (Calif.), 1969-72; asst. prof. econs. dept. ops. research and adminstrv. sci. Naval Postgrad. Sch., Monterey, Calif., 1972-74, assoc. prof., 1974-76; research fellow Hoover Instn., Stanford U., 1975-76, sr. research fellow, 1976-81; dir. Ctr. for Econometric Studies of the Justice System, 1977-81; ptnr. Block & Nold, Palo Alto, Calif., 1980-81, Block & Block, Tucson, 1981—; assoc. prof. mgmt. and econs. U. Ariz., Tucson; cons. in field. NSF fellow, 1965. Mem. Am. Econ. Assn., Phi Beta Kappa. Author: (with H.G. Demmert) Workbook and Programmed Guide to Economics, 1974, 77, 80; (with James M. Clabault) Sherman Act Indictments: 1955-80. Contbr. articles to profl. publs. Home: 3452 Camino Esplanade Tucson AZ 85715 Office: Coll Bus and Pub Adminstrn U Ariz Tucson AZ 85721

BLOCK, MITCHELL WILLIAM, filmmaker, educator; b. Columbus, Ohio, June 5, 1950; s. Albert William and Janet B.; B.F.A., N.Y. U., 1972, M.F.A., 1973; M.B.A., Columbia, 1974; Ph.D., U. Calif., Los Angeles, 1978. Owner, operator Mitchell Block Prodns., Los Angeles, 1968—; pres. Direct Cinema Ltd.; filmmaker; documentaries include: That's My Advice to You, 1978, Portrait of Jane, 1979; Speeding?; Greetings from California, 1977; producer over 60 short subjects and commls. including No Lies, 1973; adj. prof. film U. So. Calif., 1979-81, Art Center Coll. Design, Pasadena; cons. ind. filmmakers; lectr. Columbia U., others; panelist Nat. Endowment/Ednl. Film Library Conf., N.Y.C., 1976; mem. short subject br. scholarships and grants com., documentary com. Acad. Motion Picture Arts and Scis. Recipient Emmy award for best community service show, 1976; Nat. Endowment for the Arts grantee, 1976, 77, Bicentennial Filmmaking grantee USIA, 1976; fellow Center for Advanced Studies, Am. Film Inst., 1975-76. Mem. Assn. Ind. Video and Filmmakers (bus. editor The Independent 1979-82, dir. 1978—, treas. 1984), Soc. Cinema Studies, Univ. Film Assn. (editorial bd. Jour., dir. 1978—), Am. Film Inst. Alumni Assn. (v.p., treas. 1982—). Club: Palm Springs Racquet. Contbr. articles to Filmmakers Newsletter, Jour. UFVA, Am. Film, Ednl. Film Library Assn. Home: Box 69589 Los Angeles CA 90069

BLOCK, ROBERT JACKSON, investment banker; b. Seattle, Oct. 20, 1922; s. Max Harry and Esther Ida (Parker) B.; m. Dorothy Wolens, Aug. 11, 1946 (dec.); children—Jonathan, Adam, Daniel, Kenan, Susanna, Mary Judith; m. 2d, Mary Lou Moats, Dec. 26, 1972; children—Melinda Mulvaney, Ned Moats, Christina Moats, Tamara Ingle. Student Stanford U., 1940-43, U. Wash., 1943-44. Asst. to pres. Block Shoe Stores, Inc., Seattle, 1946-56, pres., 1956-58; pres. Columbia-Cascade Securities Corp., Seattle, 1958-77; pres. Nat. Securities Corp., Seattle, 1977-80, chmn., chief exec. officer, 1980—; pres. Block Found., Inc., Century Savs. & Loan Assn.; founding dir. North West Bank (merged with Old Nat. Bank); pres. Area Redevel. Adminstrn., 1961-62; exec. reservist policy secretariat Nat. Def. Exec. Res.; GSA, 1968—. Trustee, former chmn. Puget Sound chpt. Nat. Found. March of Dimes; mem. nat. exec. council Am. Jewish Com.; former mem. Seattle Bd. Park Commrs.; dir. Cornish Inst.; trustee, treas. Pilchuck Sch., Stanwood, Wash.; bd. dirs., treas. Seattle Pub. Library Found., Seattle Psychoanalytic Inst., Travelers Aid Soc.; trustee Puget Sound chpt. Nat. Multiple Sclerosis Soc.; chmn. King County (Wash.) USO Com., 1950-52; chmn. Civic Ctr. Com., Seattle, 1954; co-chmn. Metro Campaign Com., Seattle, 1958; alt. del. Democratic Nat. Conv., 1956; King County co-chmn. Vols. for Stevenson, 1956; elected King County Freeholder, 1967. Mem. Wash. Bar Assn. (fee arbitration panel). Clubs: Wash. Athletic; College (Seattle); Rainier. Home: 1617 E Boston Terr Seattle WA 98112 Office: 500 Union St Seattle WA 98101

BLOCK, ROBERT SHELDON, communications exec.; b. Chgo., Nov. 26, 1927; s. Samuel and Revelle (Rose) B.; m. Carol Schlesinger, Dec. 25, 1950; children—Debra Slotnick, David Lee. B.S., U. Wis., 1975; postgrad. U. Ill., 1948-49, Latin Am. Inst., 1949-50, B.A., 1950. Chief exec. officer Robert Block Advt., Milw., 1955-75, InHouse Systems, Inc., Milw., 1955-75; pres. B & F Broadcasting, Inc., Milw., 1973—; chief exec. officer Telease, Inc., Los Angeles, 1971—; lectr. in field. Served with M.C., U.S. Army, 1945-46. Mem. Western Regional Los Angeles C. of C., Hollywood Radio and TV Soc., World Future Soc., Am. Film Inst., Acad. TV Arts and Scis., Nat. Assn. Broadcasters, U.S. Sports Acad. (past pres., dir. 1973—), Subscription TV Assn., Aircraft Owners and Pilots Assn., Nat. Cable TV Assn., Greater Los Angeles C. of C. Jewish. Clubs: Magic Castle, Masons, Shriners. Patentee in field; author: No Togethers, 1973; 14 Days to Better Faster Reading, 1974; Step-by-Step Cookbook, 1975.

BLOCK, STEPHAN M., bank education specialist, human resource development consultants; b. Chgo., Sept. 10, 1951; s. Arthur Harry and Beatrice Minerva (Friman) B.; B.A. in Psychology, Sociology, UCLA, 1974; M.A. in Communications, San Diego State U., 1977. Counselor, PACE Orgn., Los Angeles, 1973-76; news dir. Sta. KBSQ, Espanola, N.Mex., 1976-78; dir. tng. and interpretation U.S. Nat. Park Service, Grand Canyon, 1978-82; edn. specialist Am. Inst. Banking, Phoenix, 1982—; human resource devel. cons. Mem., coach athletic teams Espanola Valley Community Assn., 1979-80; pres. N. Rim Recreation Assn., 1982. Mem. Am. Soc. Tng. and Devel., Soc. Internat. Edn., Tng. and Research. Contbr. feature articles to mags.

BLOCK, THELMA VERNON, principal; b. San Diego, June 30, 1942; d. Robert and L. Catherine (Crow) Vernon; m. Gary John Block, May 6, 1967 (dec.). B.A., U. Calif.-Riverside, 1964; M.A., San Diego State U., 1981. Tchr., Aloord Unified Schs., Arlington, Calif., 1964-65, LeMesa Spring Valley (Calif.) Sch. Dist., 1965-66; revenue officer IRS, San Diego, 1966-67; tchr. Santee (Calif.) Sch. Dist., 1967-72; columnist Pacific Skipper Mag., Baja, Calif., 1978; substitute tchr. Mountain Empire Unified Sch. Dist., Boulevard, Calif., 1978-79, lead tchr., 1979-82; prin. Biggs Elem. Sch. and Richvale Elem. Sch., Biggs, Calif., 1982—. Mem. exec. bd. Boulevard Fire and Rescue Dist., sec., 1981-82. Mem. Nat. Assn. Female Execs., Assn. Calif. Sch. Adminstrs., Butte County Adminstrs. Assn. Republican. Lutheran. Office: PO Box 397 Biggs CA 95913

BLOCKEY, JOHN EDWARD DE BURGH, property development corporation executive; b. Melbourne, Australia, Oct. 6, 1943; s. Anthony de Burgh and Julia (Casanovas) B.; came to U.S., 1977; m. Sanda Alcorso, June 10, 1971; 1 dau., Clea Suzannah. Asso. Acct., Com.B., U. Queensland, 1967. Audit mgr. Arthur Young & Co., Brisbane and Sydney, Australia, and London, 1962-68; corp. fin. adv. N.M. Rothchild & Sons Ltd., London, 1969-70; fin. controller Security Projects Ltd., Sydney, 1971-76; v.p. Project Devels. Inc., Honolulu, 1977-79; pres. Joanda, Inc., Honolulu, 1980—; dir., part-owner Colour Copy Centres Pty. Ltd., Sydney, 1978—. Mem. Australian Inst. Dirs., Australian Soc. Accts., Real Estate Securities and Syndication Inst. Clubs: Pacific, Honolulu; Royal Sydney Golf, Australian Golf. Home: 22/1487 Hiikala Pl Honolulu HI 96816 Office: Suite 2700 Grosvenor Center 733 Bishop St Honolulu HI 95813

BLODGETT, ELSIE GRACE, association executive; b. Eldorado Springs, Mo., Aug. 2, 1921; d. Charles Ishmal and Naoma Florence (Worthington) Robison; m. Charles Davis Blodgett, Nov. 8, 1940; children—Carolyn Doyel, Charleen Bier, Lyndon Blodgett. Student Warrensburg (Mo.) State Tchrs. Coll., 1939-40; B.A., Fresno (Calif.) State Coll., 1953. Tchr. schs. in Mo. and Calif., 1940-42, 47-72; owner, mgr. rental units, 1965-79; exec. dir. San Joaquin County (Calif.) Rental Property Assn., Stockton, 1970-81; prin. Delta Rental Property Owners and Assocs., 1981—; propr. Crystal Springs Health World, Inc., Stockton, 1980—; bd. dirs. Stockton Better Bus. Bur. Active local PTA, Girl Scouts, Boy Scouts Am.; bd. dirs. Stockton Goodwill Industries. Named (with husband) Mr. and Mrs. Apt. Owner of San Joaquin County, 1977. Mem. Nat. Apt. Assn. (state treas. women's div. 1977-79), Calif. Ret. Tchrs. Assn. Republican. Methodist. Club: Stockton Zonta. Home: 2285 W Mendocino St Stockton CA 95204 Office: 2303 W Alpine Ave Stockton CA 95204

BLODGETT, FORREST CLINTON, educator; b. Oregon City, Oreg., Oct. 6, 1927; s. Clinton Alexander and Mabel (Wells) B.; B.S., U. Omaha, 1961; M.A., U. Mo., 1969; Ph.D., Portland State U., 1979; m. Beverley Janice Buchholz, Dec. 21, 1946; children—Cherine (Mrs. Jon R. Klein), Candis Melis (Mrs. Mark A. Schaeffer), Clinton George. Joined C.E., U.S. Army, 1946, commd. 2d lt., 1946, advanced through grades to lt. col., 1965; ret. 1968; engring. assignments Japan, 1947-49, U.K., 1950-53, Korea, 1955-56, Alaska, 1958-60, Vietnam, 1963; staff engr. 2d Army Air Def. Region, Richards-Gebaur AFB, Mo., 1964-66; base engr. Def. Atomic Support Agy., Sandia Base, N.Mex., 1966-68; bus. mgr., asst. prof. econs. Linfield Coll., McMinnville, Oreg., 1968-73, assoc. prof., 1973—, also trustee; pres. Blodgett Enterprises, Inc.; dir. Valley Community Bank, 1980—. Commr., Housing Authority of Yamhill County (Oreg.), chmn., 1980-83; mem. Yamhill County Econ. Devel. Commn.; bd. dirs. Yamhill County Found., 1983—. Decorated Army Commendation medal with oak leaf cluster; recipient Joint Services Commendation medal Dept. of Def. Mem. Soc. Am. Mil. Engrs. (pres. Albuquerque post 1968), Am. Econ. Assn., Western Econ. Assn., Nat. Retired Officers Assn., Res. Officers Assn. (pres. Marion chpt. 1976), SAR, Pi Sigma Epsilon, Pi Gamma Mu, Omicron Delta Epsilon (Pacific NW regional dir. 1978—). Republican. Episcopalian. Club: Rotary. Office: Linfield Coll McMinnville OR 97128

BLOEDE, VICTOR CARL, lawyer, univ. exec.; b. Woodwardville, Md., July 17, 1917; s. Carl Schon and Eleanor (Eck) B.; A.B., Dartmouth Coll., 1940; J.D. cum laude, U. Balt., 1950; LL.M. in Pub. Law, Georgetown U., 1967; m. Ellen Louise Miller, May 9, 1947; children—Karl Abbott, Pamela Elena. Admitted to Md. bar, 1950, Fed. bar Hawaii, 1958, U.S. Supreme Ct. bar, 1971; practiced in Balt., 1950-64; mem. firm Goldman & Bloede, 1959-64; Md. counsel Seven-Up Bottling Co., Balt., 1958-64; dep. atty. gen. Pacific Trust Ter., Honolulu, 1952-53; asst. solicitor for ters. Office of Solicitor, U.S. Dept. Interior, Washington, 1953-54; atty. U.S. Dept. Justice, Honolulu, 1955-58, asst. gen. counsel Dept. Navy, Washington, 1960-61, 63; asso. prof. U. Hawaii, 1961-63; legal cons. Md. Legis. Council, also Md. Legislature, 1963-64, 66-67; dir. property mgmt. U. Hawaii, 1964-67, house counsel, dir. contracts and grants U. Hawaii System, 1967-82; house counsel U. Hawaii Research Corp., 1970-82; legal counsel Law of Sea Inst., 1978-82; legal cons. Research Corp., U. Hawaii, 1982—. Spl. counsel to Holifield Commn. on Govt. Procurement, 1970-73. Mem. Gov.'s Task Force Hawaii and The Sea, 1969—, Citizens Housing Com., Balt., 1952-64, Bd. govs. Balt. Community YMCA, 1954-64; bd. dirs. U. Hawaii Press, 1964-66, Coll. Housing Found., 1968—; internat. rev. commn. Canada-France-Hawaii Telescope Corp., 1973-82, chmn., 1973, 82. Served with USNR, 1942-45; PTO. Recipient Sea grant for ocean law study, 1970-80. Mem. Am., Balt., Fed., bar assns., Am. Soc. Internat. Law, Nat. Assn. Univ. Attys. Unitarian. Author: Hawaii Legislative Manual, 1962; Maori Affairs, New Zealand, 1964; Oceanographic Research Vessel Operations, Liabilities and Remedies, 1972; Hawaiian Archipelago, Legal Effects of a 200 Mile Territorial Sea, 1973; Copyright—Guidelines to the 1976 Act, 1977; Forms Manual; Inventions: Policy, Law and Procedure, 1982. Writer publs. on legislation and pub. law. Home: 635 Onaha St Honolulu HI 96816

BLOLAND, PAUL ANSON, educator; b. Primrose, Wis., Nov 15, 1923; s. Arthur George and Sarah (Hustad) B.; B.S., U. Wis., 1949, M.S., 1950; Ph.D., U. Minn., 1959; m. Ruth Marion Nolte, Apr. 7, 1951; children—Eric Craig, Peter Brian. Student activities adviser U. Minn., 1950-51, asso. dir. student activities bur., 1953-55, dir., 1955-60, asst. prof. ednl. psychology, 1959-60; dean of students Drake U., Des Moines, 1960-64; dean of students, asso. prof. edn. U. So. Calif., Los Angeles, 1964-69, v.p. student and alumni affairs, 1969-72, prof. edn., 1970—, chmn. dept. counseling. Served with AUS, 1943-46, 1951-52. Mem. Am. Personnel and Guidance Assn. (senate del. 1962-63, mem. com. br. coordination 1963-64, nat. membership com. 1963-65), Am. Coll. Personnel Assn. (program com. 1960-61, commn. advising fgn. students 1963-64, chmn. nat. membership com. 1964-65, mem.-at-large nat. exec. council 1965-66, 67-70, pres.-elect 1969-70, pres. 1970-71), Nat. Assn. Student Personnel Adminstrs. (mem.-at-large and sec. nat. exec. com.), Am. Assn. Higher Edn., Am. Psychol. Assn., Coll. Student Personnel Inst. (exec. com. 1965-66, dir. 1965-69, chmn. acad. council 1967-69), Calif. Coll. Personnel Assn. (v.p. 1976-78, pres.-elect 1980-81, pres. 1981-82), Nat. Vocat. Guidance Assn., Educare, Sierra Club, Iron Cross Skull and Dagger, Blue Key, Alpha Phi Omega, Phi Delta Kappa, Delta Epsilon, Psi Chi, Omicron Delta Kappa. Author: Student Group Advising in Higher Education. Contbr. articles to profl. and mountaineering jours. Home: 27128 Fond du Lac Rd Rancho Palos Verdes CA 90274 Office: U So Calif Los Angeles CA 90007

BLOM, NICOLE JAN, public relations official; b. Seattle, Oct. 3, 1958; d. Daniel Charles and Ellen Lavon (Stewart) Blom. Student Am. Conservatory Theatre, 1978; B.A. in Theatre, U. Wash., 1981. Profl. dancer, actress, Seattle, 1976-80; devel. assoc., pub. relations officer The Bush Sch., Seattle, 1981—. Fund raising co-chmn. Bob Ellis for Wash. State Legislature, 1982. Mem. Pub. Relations Soc. Am., Council for Advancement and Support of Edn. (Case Scholarship for Newcomers in Devel. 1982), Northwest Devel. Officers Assn., Seattle World Affairs Council, U. Wash. Alumni Assn. Gamma Phi Beta Alumni Assn. Clubs: Women's Univ., Junior of Seattle (pres.), Jr. League (Seattle). Home:

2424 Magnolia Blvd W Seattle WA 98199 Office: 405 36th Ave E Seattle WA 98112

BLOMQUIST, CARL ARTHUR, health care association executive; b. Los Angeles, Feb. 2, 1947; s. Carl A. and Delphine M. (Forcier) B.; m. Diane Nunez, May 5, 1973; 1 dau., Kirsten. B.S., U. San Diego, 1969; M.P.H., UCLA, 1973. Asst. v.p. United Calif. Mortgage, 1977-79; asst. adminstr. St. Vincent Med. Ctr., Los Angeles, 1976-77, Northridge Hosp., 1973-76; chief exec. officer Mut. Protection Trust, Los Angeles, 1979—, Coop. Am. Physicians, Inc., Los Angeles, 1979—. Treas., Calif. Health Facilities Authority, 1981—; mem. Calif. Senate Adv. Commn. on Malpractice Ins., 1981—. Mem. Pres.'s Assn., Am. Mgmt. Assn., Am. Soc. Assn. Execs., Hosp. Fin. Mgmt. Assn., Am. Coll. Hosp. Adminstrs. Republican. Roman Catholic. Club: Calif. Yacht.

BLOOM, JOHN PORTER, historian, archivist, editor, educator; b. Albuquerque, Dec. 30, 1924; s. Lansing Bartlett and Maude (McFie) B.; m. Louise Platt, Mar., 1954 (div.); m. 2d, Jo Tice, July 30, 1968; children—Katherine Jassen, John Lansing, Susan Marie. A.B., U. N.Mex., 1947; A.M., George Washington U., 1949; Ph.D., Emory U., 1956. Faculty mem. history Emory U., N. Ga. Coll., Brenau Coll., U. Tex.-El Paso, 1952-60; historian, mus. planner, editor Nat. Park Service, U.S. Dept. Interior, St. Louis and Washington, 1960-64; sr. specialist, editor Nat. Archives, Washington, 1964-80; univ. archivist, editor, dir. Holt-Atherton Pacific Ctr. Western Studies, U. of Pacific, Stockton, Calif., 1981—; cons. Div. Pub. Programs NEH, Nat. Hist. Publs. Records Commn., Va. Hist. Mus. Fedn.; hist. adviser, dir. Joseph Priestley Chapel Assocs., Inc., Sunbury, Pa., 1978-81; dir. Gateway, Inc., Alexandria, Va., 1971-75; chmn. Fairfax County (Va.) History Commn., 1972-73. Served to cpl. USAAF, 1943-45. Recipient Golden Spike award, Westerner's Soc. Mem. Western Hist. Assn. (council 1962-67, 73-77, sec.-treas. 1962-67, v.p. 1973, pres. 1974), Nat. Council Pub. Hist. (steering com. 1980, bd. dirs. 1980-83, co-chmn. program com. 1983—), Westerners Internat., Inc., (pres. 1981-83, pres. Potomac Corral 1974), Council Am.'s Mil. Past (bd. dirs. 1982—), Am. Assn. State and Local Hist., Soc. Am. Archivists, Am. Hist. Assn., Orgn. Am. Historians, Nat. Trust Hist. Preservation, Eastern Nat. Parks Monuments Assn., Soc. Hist. Archaeology, So. Hist. Assn., State Hist. Soc. Colo., Mont. State Hist. Soc., Pioneer Am. Soc., Albuquerque Hist. Soc., Phi Alpha Theta, Pi Gamma Mu. Unitarian-Universalist. Editor: The American Territorial System, 1973; The Territorial Papers of the United States, Wisconsin Territory, 1969, 71; Soldier and Brave, 1973; contbr. articles and book reviews to profl. jours. Home: 1629 Academy Ct Stockton CA 95207

BLOOM, JOHN WARREN, psychologist, educator; b. Cleve., Mar. 15, 1945; s. W. Warren and Audrey R. B.; m. Susan Beth Staley, Apr. 6, 1968; children—Kristi Ann, Lori Beth. B.A., Miami U., Oxford, Ohio, 1967, M.Ed., 1969; Ph.D., Purdue U., 1973. Cert. psychologist, mental health counselor Ariz. Tchr., counselor Mad River Twp. Schs., Dayton, 1967-71; counselor Lindbergh High Sch., St. Louis, 1973-75; asst. prof. Central Mich. U., Mt. Pleasant, 1976, Iowa State U., Ames, 1976-77; assoc. prof. psychology No. Ariz. U., Flagstaff, 1978—. Mem. adminstrv. bd. Trinity Heights United Methodist Ch. Mem. Am. Personnel and Guidance Assn. (chmn. Western region), Am. Mental Health Counselors Assn., Ariz. Counselors Assn. (past pres., Outstanding Mem. award 1982), Lambda Chi Alpha (Disting. Alumni award 1972), Phi Delta Kappa. Author: (with R. Nelson) Choice Awareness: An Innovative Guidance Process, 1975. Home: 3464 NW Ranier Loop Flagstaff AZ 86001 Office: No Ariz U Dept Educational Psychology Box 6002 Flagstaff AZ 86011

BLOOM, MICHAEL EUGENE, communications executive; b. Pittsburg, Calif., Jan. 16, 1947; s. Benjamin Bernard and Mildred (Haims) B.; m. Deborah Ann Bresler, Aug. 6, 1977; children—Benjamin Solomon Bresler, Miriam Hannah Bresler. B.A. in Sociology, U. Calif.-Santa Barbara, 1969, postgrad. elec. engring., 1969-71; M.B.A., Stanford U., 1979. Broadcaster, Sta. KCSB-FM, Santa Barbara, 1964-68, gen. mgr., 1968-69; broadcaster KKIS-AM, Pittsburg, Calif., 1965, KMUZ-FM, Santa Barbara, 1965-67, KTMS-AM-FM, Santa Barbara, 1967-69; mem. tech. staff Gen. Research Corp., Santa Barbara, 1970-72; mgmt. scientist, cons. Sci. Applications, Inc., LaJolla, Calif., 1973-74, Planning and Mgmt. Cons. Corp., Cleve., 1974, Bloom Enterprises, Santa Monica, Calif., 1975-77; retail product planner Crocker Nat. Bank, San Francisco, 1978; dir. corp. devel. Am. TV & Communications Corp., Englewood, Colo., 1979-82, dir. new bus. devel., 1983—; chmn. communications bd. U. Calif.-Santa Barbara; v.p., dir. Intercollegiate Broadcasting System, Inc., 1967-70; founder, dir. U. Calif. Radio Network, 1967-69; chmn. systems standards task force on teletext Nat. Cable TV Assn., 1980-81. Adv. council Coll. Info. Studies, U. Denver, 1982—. Recipient Pres.'s merit award U. Calif., 1965. Mem. IEEE, Assn. MBA Execs., Soc. Cable TV Engrs., Soc. Broadcast Engrs., Nat. Cable TV Assn., U. Calif.-Santa Barbara Alumni Assn. (life), Stanford U. Bus. Sch. Alumni Assn. (program dir. Rocky Mountain chpt. 1982). Author: (with L.A. Sibley) Carrier Current System Design, 1967. Home: 7397 S Hudson Way Littleton CO 80122 Office: 160 Inverness Dr W Englewood CO 80112

BLOOM, MIRIAM KRASNICK, psychoanalyst; b. Chgo., Dec. 22, 1920; d. Sol H. and Anna (Glick) Krasnick; m. Louis R. Bloom, Aug. 22, 1942; children—Robert, Fredi, Steven, Debra. B.S., U. Ill.-Urbana, 1941, M.A., 1955; postgrad. Center for Modern Psychoanalytic Studies, N.Y.C., 1981, Calif. Grad. Inst. Cert. sch. psychologist, tchr. N.Y., Colo.; lic. marriage and family therapist, Calif. Speech pathologist Chgo. Pub. Schs., 1941; tchr., Champaign, Ill., 1942, Hicksville, N.Y., 1955-58; sch. psychologist various N.Y. schs., 1958-75, St. Vrain Schs., Longmont, Colo., 1975-81, coordinator program for emotionally disturbed children, 1978-81; pvt. practice psychoanalysis, Boulder, Colo., 1975—; founder, dir. Colo. Center Modern Psychoanalytic Studies. Mem. Nat. Assn. Accreditation of Psychoanalysis, Am. Psychol. Assn., Colo. Psychol. Assn., Colo. Soc. Sch. Psychologists, Colo. Women in Psychology. Democrat. Jewish. Contbr. articles to profl. jours. Home and Office: 2240 Linden Ave Boulder CO 80302

BLOOM, WILBUR (WIL) WAYNE, JR., real estate development company executive; b. Mpls., July 7, 1932; s. Wilbur Wilford and Hildegarde Amanda (Loman) B.; B.A., Ottawa (Kans.) U., 1954; postgrad. Eastern Baptist Theol. Sem., Phila., 1954-56; m. Dorothy Ann Burns, June 1, 1954; children—Carey Lynn, Jay Kristian, Jon Kirtley. Asst. minister Bala Cynwyd (Pa.) Methodist Ch., 1954-56; sales agt. Nat. Life Ins. Co. of Vt., Phila., 1956; br. mgr. Transam. Title Ins. Co., Phoenix, 1958-64, 67-69; v.p. Mfrs. Tire, Phoenix, 1964-65; account mgr. Allied Brands div. Uniroyal, Inc., 1965-67; dir. ann. fund Ottawa U., 1969-72; v.p. Cannon Devel. Corp., Scottsdale, Ariz., 1972-81; v.p. A.G. Muir Investments, 1981-83; real estate broker Prudential Realty Services, Phoenix, 1983—; mem. adv. bd. Ottawa U. Coll. Without Campus, Phoenix, 1977—; career edn. adv. council Tempe (Ariz.) Area Schs., 1977-79. Served with U.S. Army, 1956-58. Cert. football ofcl., Ariz. Interscholastic Assn. Mem. Public Relations Assn. (v.p. 1971-72), Am. Bapt. Chs./Pacific SW (bd. mgrs. 1974—), Am. Bapt. Chs., U.S.A. (gen. bd. 1978—). Republican. Clubs: Tempe Racquet and Swim, Rotary, Tempe Diablos (exec. v.p. 1969, dir. 1973-78). Home: 3821 S Kenwood Ln Tempe AZ 85282 Office: 4531 N 16th St Phoenix AZ 85016

BLOOMER, LINDA STONE, sales executive, TV broadcaster, writer; b. Atlanta, Nov. 11; student Ferrell Sch. Entertainment Arts, 1960-61, Phoenix Coll., 1960-61, Ga. State U., 1962-63; m. Howard Corbett Bloomer, July 1, 1978. Owner, Acad. Playhouse of Entertainment Arts, Charleston, S.C., 1969-70; promotion mgr. WUSN-TV, Charleston, 1967-69; promotion mgr., broadcaster KPHO-TV, Phoenix, 1970-78; creative dir. KJJJ and KXTC Radio Stas., 1978-79; promotion dir., pub. service dir. Sta. KTAR-KBBC-FM, Phoenix, 1980-81; v.p. sales and promotion Aerolight Flight Devel., Inc., Mesa, Ariz., 1982—; pilot, dir. Services Superstition Mountain Airpark, 1982—; program and advt. dir. Short Excursions in Ariz.; author children's books; contbr. articles to various jours. and publs. including: Phoenix mag., Ariz. Sports News Weekly, Ariz. Host; instr. communication Ariz. State U., 1977. Mem. Broadcast Promotion Assn., Acad. TV Arts and Scis., Am. Women in Radio and TV (past dir.), Phoenix Press Club, LWV, Mu Rho Sigma (life). Editor: Ad-Libber, Phoenix Ad Club, 1975-76. Address: PO Box 2313 Phoenix AZ 85002

BLORE, CHUCK, production company executive, writer; b. Los Angeles, Apr. 10, 1929; s. Charles and Justia V. (Haggin) Blower; m. Patricia Gittings, Oct. 30, 1949; 1 dau., Catherine Ann; m. 2d, Judith Lynn Feldman, Apr. 16, 1978. Deejay, Sta. KGAN, Kingman, Ariz., Sta. KTKT, Tucson, 1949-55; program dir. Sta. KELP, El Paso, 1955-57; program dir. Sta. KFWB (Crowell-Collier Pub. Co.), Los Angeles, 1957-1963; owner, operator Chuck Blore Creative Services, Hollywood, Calif., 1963-1976; ptnr., chmn. bd. Chuck Blore & Don Richman, Inc., Hollywood, 1976—; guest lectr. UCLA, Calif. State U., U. So. Calif.; frequent speaker. Mem. Common Cause, ACLU; founder, patron Los Angeles theater groups. Served with USN, 1946-48. Recipient over 400 major awards in broadcast advt., including Clio, Internat. Broadcast Awards, U.S. Film Festival, Chgo. Film Festival, Anny, Big Apple. Mem. AFTRA, Am. Film Inst., Acad. TV Arts and Scis., Writers Guild, Screen Actors Guild, FILMEX. Democrat. Office: Chuck Blore & Don Richman Inc 1606 N Argyle Ave Hollywood CA 90028

BLOSS, FRED JOHN, mfg. co. exec.; b. Toronto, Ont., Can., Nov. 2, 1920; s. Thomas and Mary A. (Lloyd) B.; student Calif. Inst. Tech., 1941-43; m. Elouise Pyle, Feb. 14, 1942; 1 dau., Cheryl Ann. Exptl. engr. N.Am. Aviation, Inglewood, Calif., 1940-44; pres. Bloss Inc., Bloss Plastics & Engraving (both Pasadena, Calif.), 1946—; plastics cons. Served with inf. AUS, 1944-46; ETO. Decorated Purple Heart. Mem. Pasadena C. of C., Pasadena Sports Ambassadors. Mason (32 deg., Shriner). Home: 1140 Pine Bluff Dr Pasadena CA 91107 Office: Bloss Inc 2785 E Foothill Blvd Pasadena CA 91107

BLOSSER, JOHN HENRY, JR., retail food store exec.; b. Hubbard, Oreg., May 18, 1917; s. John Henry and Elva (Mills) B.; B.S., Oreg. State U., 1941; m. Doris Pratt Gribble, Sept. 28, 1945. Research asst. agrl. econs. Oreg. State Coll., 1942-44; apprentice buyer Safeway Stores, Inc., Portland, Oreg., 1944-45, jr. buyer, Yakima, Wash., 1946-49, sr. buyer, Phoenix, 1950-51, Bakersfield, Calif., 1952-55, Visalia, Calif., 1956-58, mgr., Wapato, Wash., 1959-60, Wenatchee, Wash., 1960—. Chmn. Pub. Phase $350,000 Capital Funds Campaign, 1964-65; chmn. advanced gifts phase United Good Neighbors Fund Drive, 1969. Bd. dirs., pres. Wenatchee Valley YMCA, Wenatchee United Good Neighbors; bd. dirs. Wenatchee Valley Humane Soc., 1977; mem. adv. panel YWCA, Wenatchee, 1976-77; trustee Wenatchee Valley Coll.; sec.-treas. Chelan County Citizens for Sensible Land Use; fin. chmn. for Eastern Wash., Gov.'s Campaign, 1980; chmn. Citizens Com. for Regional Planning, Chelan County, Wash., 1974-75. Mem. Wenatchee Sportsman Assn. (dir. 1962-65), Alpha Zeta, Alpha Gamma Rho. Republican. Conglist. Elk. Club: German Shorthaired Pointer (Seattle). Home: PO Box 62 Wenatchee WA 98801 Office: PO Box 622 Wenatchee WA 98801

BLUBAUGH, DONALD ALAN, city mgr.; b. Waynesboro, Pa., Mar. 8, 1942; s. Max and Alma Florence (White) B.; m. Janet Ann Ergen, May 30, 1964; children—Tracey Lynn, Christopher Alan, Allison Paige. B.A., Shippensburg State Coll., 1964; M. Govt. Adminstrn., U. Pa., 1966. Asst. to city mgr., Riverside, Calif., 1965-69; asst. city mgr., Palm Springs, Calif., 1969-73, city mgr., 1973-79; city mgr., Hayward, Calif., 1979—; instr. govt. Chapman Coll., 1967-69, Coll. of Desert, 1969-73. Fels scholar, 1964, Fels fellow., 1965. Mem. League Calif. Cities (exec. com.), City Mgrs. Assn., Internat. City Mgmt. Assn., Am. Soc. Pub. Adminstrn. Democrat. Roman Catholic. Club: Rotary. Office: 22300 Foothill Blvd Suite 1126 Hayward CA 94541

BLUECHEL, ALAN, state senator, wood structural components manufacturing company executive; b. Edmonton, Alta., Can., Aug. 28, 1924; s. Joseph Harold and Edith (Daly) B.; m. Aylene Louchnan, Nov. 2, 1958; children—Gordon, Turner; m. Jeanne Ehrlichman, Aug. 8, 1981. B.A.Sc. in Elec. Engring., B.A., U. B.C.; postgrad. U. Wash. Vice pres. Loctwall Corp., Kirkland, Wash., 1948-64, pres., 1964—; pres. Crystal Mountain Inn Co., developer condominiums, restaurants, hotels, swimming pools, 1968—; mem. Wash. State Ho. of Reps., 1966-74; mem. Wash. Senate, 1974—, Republican whip, 1979-81, 83, majority whip, 1981-83, mem. rules, ways and means, parks and ecology coms.; speaker various confs., convs., orgns. Mem. Wash. State Land Planning Commn., 1969-73, Wash. State Women's Council, 1976, Spl. Com. on Office State Actuary, 1983; chmn. Wash. State Winter Recreation Commn., 1983, Wash. State Commn. on Environ. Policy, 1983; mem. Juanita Citizens Devel. Council, 1975-79, King County Conservation Com., 1967-69, King County Flood Control Adv. Bd., 1968-70, Com. To Save Sch. Trust Lands, 1975—, St. Edwards Park Adv. Bd., 1977-79, Seattle Symphony Phonathon Fundraisers, 1980, 81, Gov.'s Council on Child Abuse and Neglect, 1983; mem. conservation com. King County Environ. Devel. Commn., 1969-74, numerous other civic orgns. Recipient Outstanding Service award Lake Washington PTSA Council, 1982. Clubs: Mountaineers, Sun Valley Ski, Forelaufer Ski.

BLUEITT, NAOMI RUTH, state agy. adminstr.; b. Weir, Miss., Nov. 2, 1936; d. James A. and Lubertha M. (Eiland) Miller; B.S., Jackson State U., 1959; postgrad. U. Calif.-Riverside, 1971-72, cert. in community coll. teaching, Davis, 1975; cert. of mgmt., Calif. State U.-Long Beach, 1970; m. Essie L. Blueitt, Apr., 1958; children—Dimitri L., Phyllis R., Ray K., Roderick M. With Calif. Dept. Corrections, Sacramento, 1974—, chief departmental safety coordinator, 1975-77, state women's program mgr., 1977—, asst. chief instn. services, 1977-80, assoc. supt., 1980—. Vice pres. Mental Health Assn., San Bernardino, Calif., 1972-74. Mem. Black Advocates in State Service, United Black Correctional Workers Assn., Black Am. Polit. Assn. of Calif., Black Women for Polit. Action, Sacramento Black Women's Network. Office: PO Box 2000 Calif Med Facility Reception Center Vacaville CA 95696

BLUEMLE, ROBERT LOUIS, lawyer; b. Anderson, Ind., Nov. 6, 1933; s. Orville Wesley and Marguerite (Fadely) B.; B.S. with distinction, Ind. U., 1955, M.B.A., 1956; J.D., U. Mich., 1959; children—Tiffany Windsor, Elizabeth Hayden; m. 2d, Carol Gillard Bidstrup, Aug. 6, 1979. Admitted to Ariz. bar, 1959, U.S. Supreme Ct., 1964; practiced in Phoenix, 1961—; partner in charge Phoenix office Furth Fahrner Bluemle & Mason, San Francisco, Washington and Phoenix; atty., fin. analyst SEC, Washington, 1959-61. Bd. dirs. Western Opera Theater, San Francisco, 1975-78, Scottsdale Arts Center Assn., 1974-80; bd. dirs. Valley Shakespeare Theatre, 1979—, pres., 1982; past bd. dirs., pres. Greater Phoenix Summer Festival-Images: USA; bd. dirs. Am. Light Opera Co., Washington, 1960, Friends of Mexican Art, Phoenix, 1973, Jr. Achievement, Phoenix, 1970-73, Southwest Ensemble Theater, 1975, Valley Forward Assn., Phoenix, 1972-75; chmn. Scottsdale Citizens Com. on Cable TV, 1979-82; pres. Shakespeare on the Desert, Phoenix, 1968. Served with USAF, 1959. Mem. Phoenix Soc. Fin. Analysts, Fed., Am. bar assns., State Bar Ariz. (chmn., sec. law com. 1969—), Bar Assn. San Francisco. Clubs: Ariz., Univ. (co-founder, pres. 1967-68), Plaza (Phoenix). Film critic Phoenix Mag., 1977-80. Office: 3443 N Central Ave Phoenix AZ 85012

BLUESTEIN, MARTIN ALLEN, computer scientist; b. Boston, Mar. 27, 1938; s. Arthur Clarence and Evelyn (Goller) B.; B.S.E.E., Northeastern U., 1965; M.S.E.E., UCLA, 1967; postgrad. Calif. Inst. Tech., 1970; m. Barbara Bloom, Dec. 2, 1962 (div. 1974); 1 son, Scott. Jr. exec. tng. program Owens-Ill., 1965-67; tech. liaison mgr. Hughes Aircraft, Calif., 1968-70; mgr. plant diagnostics Burroughs Corp., Calif., 1970-71; mem. advanced research and devel. staff Data Products Co., Calif., 1971-72; sr. mem. tech. staff Xerox Corp., El Segundo, Calif., 1972-73; mgr. microprocessor activities Citicorp, Los Angeles, 1974-75; tech. staff to v.p. Systems Engring. Labs., Ft. Lauderdale, Fla., 1976, Nat. Semicondr., San Diego, 1977-78; founder, pres. The Analytical Group, Inc., San Diego, 1979—; chmn. bd., pres. Real Time Info., Inc., San Diego, 1981—; cons. Jet Propulsion Labs., Pasadena, Calif.; dir. Tag, Inc.; lectr. Control Data Corp., Inst. Advanced Tng. of Data-Pro Corp. Active U. Calif. at Irvine Friends of Univ. Served with USAF, 1956-60. Mem. Assn. Computing Machinery, IEEE (chmn., pres. student br. Northeastern U.). Home: 932 Miramar St Laguna Beach CA 92651

BLUETT, JEAN ESTELLA, home economics educator; b. Dillon, Mont., Mar. 25, 1949; d. John Hansen Anderson and Estella Margurite (Hansen) A.; m. Marc Joseph Bluett, Sept. 5, 1972; 1 son, Jaques Beaufort. B.A. in Home Econs., U. Mont., 1971. Cert. tchr., N.Mex. With GTE Lenkurt, N.Mex., 1972, sales order processing dept. head, 1976-76; tchr. home econs. Belen (N.Mex.) High Sch., 1976—. Mem. Am. Home Econs. Assn., Kappa Omicron Phi. Republican. Lutheran. Office: West Delgado Belen NM 87002

BLUM, CARL WILLIAM, administrator, safety consultant; b. Camden, N.J., May 1, 1940; s. Mattias A. and Helen M. (DuBrink) B.; m. Joan A. DiNicola, Nov. 11, 1962; children—Carl Jr., Alisa, Lynne. Student Wake Forest Coll., Rutgers U.-Camden Extension. Registered profl. engr. Calif. Loss control trainee Camden Fire Ins. (N.J.), 1960-64; loss prevention rep. Crum and Forrester Ins. Co., Phila., 1964-69; supr. St. Paul Fire and Marine Ins. Co., Van Nuys, Calif., 1969-73, mgr., 1973-82, Western regional account mgr. risk mgmt., 1982—; cons. city safety rev. Past pres. Wildwood Homeowners Assn.; past chmn. and planning commr. City of Thousand Oaks, 1977—. Mem. Am. Soc. Safety Engrs., Bd. Registered Profl. Engrs. Calif. Democrat. Roman Catholic. Club: Sunset Hills Men's (exec. bd.). Office: PO Box 9243 Van Nuys CA 91409

BLUM, CHARLES EDWARD, accountant; b. Oceanside, N.Y., Aug. 1, 1949; s. Leo and Adele H. (Herrmann) B.; m. Janet Amy Rosner, Mar. 18, 1973; children—Seth Herrmann, Aaron Charles. A.B., Muhlenberg Coll., 1971; B.S. in Pub. Accounting, Hofstra U., 1973. C.P.A., Ariz. Pvt. practice pub. acctg., Scottsdale, Ariz., 1978—. Mem. Ariz. Soc. C.P.A.s, Tau Kappa Epsilon. Address: 8055 E Indianola Scottsdale AZ 85251

BLUM, JOAN KURLEY, fund raising executive; b. Palm Beach, Fla., July 27, 1926; d. Nenad Daniel and Eva (Milos) Kurley; grad. U. Wash., 1948; m. Robert Cecil Blum, Apr. 15, 1967; children—Christopher Alexander, Martha Jane, Louisa Joan, Paul Helmuth, Danna Carolyn. U.S. dir. Inst. Mediterranean Studies, Berkeley, Calif., 1962-65; asst. dir. U. Calif. Alumni Found., Berkeley, 1965-67; pres. Blum Assocs., San Anselmo, Calif., 1967—; chmn. Internat. Fund Raisers Cert. Examination Com.; mem. faculty U. Calif. Extension (Berkeley, Irvine, Los Angeles, Santa Cruz), Inst. Fund Raising (N.Y.C., Washington, Chgo.), S.W. Inst. Fund Raising of U. Tex., Fund Raising Sch. of U. San Francisco, U.K. Voluntary Movement Group (London). Recipient Golden Addy award Am. Advt. Fedn., 1972; Silver Mailbox award Direct Mail Mktg. Assn., 1973; best ann. giving program Nat. Assn. Hosp. Devel., 1974; Time-Life award Council Advancement Scholarship in Edn., 1975; Si Seymour award Nat. Assn. Hosp. Devel., 1976. Mem. Direct Mktg. Writers Guild, Direct Mail Fund Raisers Assn., Nat. Soc. Fund Raising Execs. (cert., dir.), Nat. Assn. Hosp. Devel., Women Emerging, San Francisco Advt. Club. Contbr. articles profl. jours. Home: Kentfield CA Office: 292 Red Hill San Anselmo CA 94960

BLUM, JOHN ALAN, urologist, educator; b. Bklyn., Feb. 2, 1933; s. Louis J. and Pauline (Kushner) B.; A.B., Dartmouth, 1954; M.D., N.Y. U., 1958; M.S., U. Minn., 1965; m. Debra Merlin Ackerman, June 30, 1957; children—Louis Jeffrey, Alfred Merlin, Jacqueline. Intern, U. Minn. Hosp., Mpls., 1958-59, resident, 1959-64; practice medicine, specializing in urology, Chgo., 1964-66, Mpls., 1966-67, San Diego, 1969—; chmn. dept. urology Mt. Sinai Hosp., Chgo., 1965-66; asst. prof. urology U. Minn., Mpls., 1967; assoc. clin. prof. urology U. Calif., San Diego, 1969—; mem. staff Mercy, Donald Sharp, Children's hosps., San Diego, 1969—, Scripps Hosp., La Jolla, Calif., 1969—. Bd. dirs. Vietnam Vet. Leadership Program. Served to capt. USNR, 1967—; Vietnam. Diplomate Am. Bd. Urology. Fellow A.C.S.; mem. Am., Calif. med. assns., Am. Urol. Assn., San Diego Urol. Soc., San Diego Surg. Soc. (pres. 1977—), Phi Beta Kappa, Sigma Xi, Alpha Omega Alpha. Club: San Diego Yacht. Research in devel. of silicone rubber for urinary tract. Home: 890 Cornish Dr San Diego CA 92107 Office: 3415 6th Ave San Diego CA 92103

BLUM, JOHN PHILLIP, law librarian, state official; b. Warren, Ohio, Apr. 2, 1930; s. Leonard Anthony and M. Dorsey (Gegan) B.; m. Judith K. Arnold, Aug. 24, 1957 (div.); children—John Phillip, Adam Arnold, Jason Peter. B.A., U. N.Mex., 1957; M.A., U. Calif.-Berkeley, 1961, postgrad. Sch. Law, 1967. Curator, Mus. N.Mex., Santa Fe, 1962-65; dir.-curator Ernest Thompson-Seton Meml. Mus. and Library, Cimarron, N.Mex., 1967; dir. N.Mex. Supreme Ct. Law Library, Santa Fe, 1967—, state law librarian, 1967—; sec. N.Mex. Pub. Records Commn., 1967—; mem. N.Mex. Supreme Ct. Com. on N.Mex. Statues, 1975—. Served with USAF, 1948-52. Mem. Am. Assn. Law Libraries (cert. 1971). Home: Rt 1 Box 174 Santa Fe NM 87501 Office: 237 Don Gaspar Supreme Ct Bldg Santa Fe NM 87501

BLUMENTHAL, SUSAN GAIL, soil scientist; b. Marlow, Okla., Oct. 19, 1948; d. Lynn Delbert and Eunice Ervin; B.S. in Agronomy, Tex. A&M U., 1976; 1 dau., Eve Ayala. Soil scientist Soil Conservation Service, Dept. Agr., San Marcos, Tex., 1976-77; soil scientist U.S. Forest Service, Nezperce Nat. Forest, Grangeville, Idaho, 1977-78, Rogue River Nat. Forest, Medford, Oreg., 1978-79, Ashland and Butte Falls Ranger Dists. of Rogue River Nat. Forest, Ashland, Oreg., 1979—. Chairperson membership Siskiyou chpt. Native Plant Soc. Oreg., 1980-81; treas. bd. dirs. So. Oreg. Land Conservancy, 1981; pres. bd. dirs. SUNERGI, non-profit orgn. to promote awareness solar energy tech., Ashland, 1981. Named to Outstanding Young Women Am., U.S. Jaycees, 1980. Mem. Am. Soc. Agronomy, Oreg. State Soc. Soil Scientists, Calif. Forest Soils Council, AAAS, Nat. Assn. Women in Sci., Nature Conservancy Cousteau Soc., Phi Kappa Phi. Author: (with Don Boyer) Organic Amendments in Forest Nursery Management, 1981. Home: Ashland OR 97520 Office: US Forest Service Ashland Ranger Dist 2200 Hwy 66 Ashland OR 97520

BLUMER, JACQUES JAN STEPHEN, medical center administrator; b. Wilmington, Del., Oct. 20, 1943; s. Jacques Arthur Karl and Ruth Edith (Livinghouse) B.; m. Mary Lou Schreck, June 27, 1971; 1 son, Jacques A. B.S., Marshall U.; M.B.A., George Washington U. Health services officer USPHS, Rockville, Md., 1968-70; exec. dir. Health Alliance No. Calif., San Jose, 1971-73; sr. cons. Medicus Systems Corp., Sausalito, Calif., 1974-75; asst. adminstr. Kaiser/Permanente Med. Center, Sacramento, 1975-77, adminstr., 1977—. Mem. Am. Coll. Hosp. Adminstrs., Calif. Hosp. Assn. (trustee 1983—), Golden Empire Health Systems Agy., Sacramento Healthcare Consortium, Sacramento Healthcare Execs. Office: 2025 Morse Ave Sacramento CA 95825

BLUMRICH, JOSEF FRANZ, aerospace engineer; b. Steyr, Austria, Mar. 17, 1913; s. Franz and Maria Theresia (Mayr) B.; m. Hildegard Anna Schmidt-Elgers, Nov. 7, 1935; children—Michael Sebastian, Christoph, Stefan. B.S. in Aero. and Mech. Engring., Ingenieurschule Weimar (Germany), 1934. Engr., Gother Waggonfabrik A.G., Gotha, Germany, 1934-44; ct. interpreter U.S. Mil. Ct., Linz, Austria, 1946-51; dep. chief hydraulics dept. United Austrian Iron and Steel Works, Linz, 1951-59; structural design engr. Army Ballistic Missile Agy., Huntsville, Ala., 1959-61; chief structural engring. br. G.C. Marshall Space Flight Ctr., NASA, Huntsville, 1961-69, chief systems layout br., 1969-74; cons. in field, 1974—. Served with German Army, 1944-45. Recipient Apollo Achievement award NASA, 1969, Exceptional Service medal, 1972. Mem. AIAA, AAAS. Author: The Spaceships of Ezekiel, 1974; Kasskara, 1979; editorial cons. on space sci. and rocketry Scribner-Bantan English Dictionary, 1977; contbr. articles to profl. jours. Patentee in field. Home: 1139 Noria St Laguna Beach CA 92651

BLUNDELL, HARRY, elec. utility exec.; b. Salt Lake City, May 1, 1925; s. Henry James and Eliza Ellen (Terry) B.; B.S. in Philosophy and Math., U. Utah, 1949; postgrad. U. Mich.; m. Beverly Mae Martin, Aug. 26, 1944; children—Martin, James, John, Peter, Amy, Ann, Todd. With Utah Power & Light Co., Salt Lake City, 1949—, successively asst. treas., treas., v.p., sr. v.p., 1949-76, exec. v.p., 1976-79, pres., chief exec. officer, 1979—, dir., 1965—; dir. First Interstate Bank Utah (formerly Walker Bank & Trust Co.), Rio Grande Industries, Inc., D&RGW R.R., Ideal Basic Industries, Inc. Mem. nat. adv. council Utah State U.; mem. adv. council and institutional council Utah Tech. Coll. Served with USNR, 1943-46. Mem. Salt Lake C. of C. (past v.p.), Phi Beta Kappa, Phi Kappa Phi. Clubs: Rotary, Alta. Mormon. Office: 1407 W N Temple St PO Box 899 Salt Lake City UT 84110

BLUNK, JOHN WILLIAM, piano technician, organist; b. Terre Haute, Ind., Mar. 27, 1924; s. John William and Ethel Elizabeth (Jenkins) B.; student Ind. State U., 1942-45; B.S., Chgo. Mus. Coll., 1948. Piano technician Depauw U., Greencastle, Ind., 1948-51, Indpls. Symphony Orch., 1948-51; pvt. practice as piano technician, 1952-62; concert tuner Steinway Co., Indpls., also Portland, Oreg., 1952-74; organist Nat. Basketball League, Western Hockey League, 1970—, Portland Maverick Baseball Team, 1973-77, Western Canadian Hockey League, 1976—, Portland Beaver Baseball Team, Pacific Coast League, Pitts. Pirates Farm Club, 1978—; organist, music dir. Sherwood Oriental Silent Movie Theatre, 1978—; composer, arranger silent movie scores, 1976—; tchr. piano and organ, 1965-72; builder pipe organs for chs. Mem. Am. Theatre Organ Soc. (charter, chmn. Puget Sound chpt. 1964-65), Am. Fedn. Musicians, Internat. Soc. Organ-Builders (asso.). Address: 29765 SW Montebello Dr Wilsonville OR 97070

BLUNT, ROBERT WILLMARTH, mfg. co. exec.; b. Youngstown, Ohio, Oct. 23, 1911; s. George W. and Ruby (Zimmerman) B.; A.B., B.S., Wittenberg U., 1934; m. Dorothy Marie Leubin, Sept. 21, 1935; children—William George, David Willmarth, Robert Lee. Sec. in vocational guidance Wittenberg U., 1934-39; dist. mgr. Mass. Mut. Life Co., Youngstown, 1939-41; bus. mgr. Booz, Allen, Hamilton, N.Y.C., 1941-42; personnel mgr. Ohio Boxboard Co., 1942-45; asst. nat. sales mgr., market analyst Great Lakes Carbon Corp., Los Angeles, 1945-51; chmn. bd. Harborlite Corp., Escondido, Calif., 1951—. Mem. Escondido C. of C. (dir. 1962-63), Blue Key, Beta Theta Pi. Republican. Lutheran. Home: 2686 Canyon Crest Dr Escondido CA 92027 Office: 1450 Simpson Way Escondido CA 92025

BLUTH, ELIZABETH JEAN (BJ), sociology educator, consultant; b. Phila., Dec. 5, 1934; d. Robert Thomas and Catherine Cecelia (Boxman) Gowland; m. Thomas Bluth, Aug. 20, 1960; children—Robert, Richard. B.A. cum laude, Bucknell U., 1957; M.A., Fordham U., 1960; Ph.D., UCLA, 1970. Teaching fellow in research methods Fordham U., N.Y.C., 1957-58; instr. Reading Lab., Phila., 1958-59; instr. history, civics and English, Rosary High Sch., San Diego, 1959-60; instr. sociology Immaculate Heart Coll., Hollywood, Calif., 1960-63, asst. prof., 1963-65; asst. prof. sociology Calif. State U., Northridge, 1965-75, assoc. prof., 1975-79, prof., 1979—; cons. in field. Bd. dirs. L-5 Soc.; adviser United Space Alliance; mem. Citizens Adv. Council on Nat. Space Policy. Recipient Teaching award Alpha Omega, 1974, 66; Disting. Teaching award Calif. State U.-Northridge, 1968; grantee Rockwell Internat., TRW, Lockheed, 1978-80; Cert. appreciation Soc. Am. Mil. Engrs., 1980; fellow Inst. Advancement Teaching and Learning, Calif. State U.-Northridge, 1974. Fellow Inst. Advancement Engring.; mem. Internat. Acad. Astronautics (mem. com. on space econs. and benefits), AIAA (spl. program award Los Angeles sect. 1980), Am. Astron. Soc. (cert. appreciation 1978), Brit. Interplanetary Soc., Am. Soc. Aerospace Edn., Inst. Social Sci. Study Space (acad. adv. bd.), Space Studies Inst., Am. Sociol. Assn., Air Force Assn. Author: Update on Space, 1981; Parsons' General Theory of Action: A Summary of the Basic Theory, 1982; 1982; Space Station Habitability Report, 1983; contbr. articles in field to profl. jours. Office: Dept Sociology Calif State U Northridge CA 91330

BOARD, ROBERT ROY, univ. adminstr.; b. Lewistown, Mont., Sept. 30, 1922; s. William Charles and Irene Anna (Conners) B.; B.S., U. Santa Clara (Calif.), 1947; m. Mary Lu Bush, Feb. 15, 1948; children—Gregory Charles, Bradley Robert. Systems salesman Nat. Cash Register Co., San Francisco, 1947-51; factory rep. Ames Harris Meville Co., San Francisco and Fresno, Calif., 1951-56; systems and interior office salesman Healey & Popovich Co., Fresno, 1956-64; registrar Calif. State U., Fresno, 1964—; systems cons. Mem. Sierra natural resources com. Three Forests Assn.; research asst. Nat. Park Service, Nat. Forest Service. Served with AUS, 1943-46; PTO. Decorated Purple Heart. Mem. Am. Assn. Coll. Registrars, Student Personnel Assn. Calif. Colls., Pacific Assn. Collegiate Registars (program dir. 1975, v.p. 1977—, pres. elect 1978, pres. 1979-80), Sierra Club (chpt. founder). Republican. Presbyn. Clubs: Masons, Kiwanis. Home: 5494 N Roosevelt St Fresno CA 93704 Office: Calif State Univ Fresno CA 93740

BOARMAN, PATRICK MADIGAN, economist, author, research instn. adminstr.; b. Buffalo, Apr. 23, 1922; s. Marcus D. and Virginia (Madigan) B.; A.B., Fordham U., 1943; M.S., Columbia U., 1946; postgrad. (Fulbright fellow) U. Amsterdam, 1949-50, (Ford Found. fellow) U. Mich., 1958, (Gen. Electric Found. fellow) U. Va., 1965; Ph.D. (Earhart fellow) in Econs., U. Geneva, 1965; children—Thomas, Christopher, Jesse, Barbara. Asst. prof. econs. U. Wis., Milw., 1956-62; asso. prof. econs. Bucknell U., Lewisburg, Pa., 1962-67; vis. prof. econs. U. Geneva, 1965-66; prof. econs. L.I. U., N.Y., 1967-72; dir. research Center for Internat. Bus., Pepperdine U., Los Angeles, 1972-75; pres. Patrick M. Boarman Assos., internat. bus. cons., San Diego, 1975—; fgn. corr. CBS in Geneva, 1946-48; dir. Office Cultural Affairs, U.S. Cath. Conf., Bonn, Germany, 1951-55; dir. research U.S. Ho. of Reps. Republican Conf., 1967-68; mgr. econ. research Gen. Electric Co., N.Y.C., 1964-65; mgr. econ. reports, div. econ. analysis, AT&T, N.Y.C., 1969; sr. economist World Trade Inst., N.Y.C., 1971; cons. to sec. U.S. Treasury, 1970; supr. 3d Dist. San Diego County, 1983—. Served with AUS, 1943. Decorated D.S.C. of Order of Merit (Fed. Republic of Germany), 1956. Danforth Tchr. Study grantee, 1959; Relm Found. grantee, 1966. Fellow Royal Econ. Soc. London; mem. Am., Western econ. assns., Nat. Assn. Bus. Economists. Author: Der Christ und die soziale Marktwirtschaft, 1955; Union Monopolies and Antitrust Restraints, 1963; Germany's Economic Dilemma, 1964; The World's Money: Gold and the Problem of International Liquidity, 1965; Trade with China, 1974; (with Hans Schöllhammer) Multi-National Corporations and Governments, 1975; (with David G. Tuerck) World Monetary Disorder, 1976. Translator: Economics of the Free Society (Wilhelm Roepke), 1963. Contbr. numerous articles on pub. finance, internat. and labor econs. to profl. jours. Home and office: 6421 Caminito Estrellado San Diego CA 92120

BOAS, ROGER, city and county ofcl.; b. San Francisco, Aug. 21, 1921; s. Benjamin and Larie (Klien) B.; m. Nancy Lee Magid, July 6, 1958; children—John Roger, Christopher, Anthony, Lucy Anne. A.B., Stanford U., 1942; vis. fellow Nuffield Coll., Oxford (Eng.) U., spring 1982. Pres., Boas Internat. Motors, San Francisco, 1946-76; chief adminstrv. officer City and County of San Francisco, 1977—. Chmn., Calif. Democratic Central Com., 1968-71; mem. Bd. Suprs. City and County of San Francisco, 1962-73. Served to 1st lt. AUS, 1942-45; ETO. Decorated Silver Star, Bronze Star. Producer, moderator weekly ednl. TV program World Press, 1960-76. Office: Room 289 City Hall San Francisco CA 94102

BOBECK, CHARLES JOSEPH, surgeon; b. Cleve., Oct. 7, 1910; s. Frank L. and Anna R. (Hajny) B.; m. Jane Russell Bush, Nov. 22, 1975. B.A., Ohio Wesleyan U., 1932; M.D., U. Rochester (N.Y.), 1936. Diplomate Am. Bd. Surgery. Intern, then asst. resident surgeon Genesee Hosp., Rochester, 1936-38; intern in obstetrics and gynecology Strong Meml. Hosp., Rochester, 1938; practice medicine specializing in surgery, Canandaigua, N.Y., 1938-42, 46-60; resident surgeon Clifton Springs (N.Y.) Sanitarium and Clinic, 1952-55; coroner Ontario County, N.Y., 1946-55; clin. instr. surgery U. Rochester Med. Sch., 1959-60; surgeon Williams Surg. Clinic, Rapid City, S.D., 1960-65; practice gen. surgery, Long Beach, Calif., 1965—; mem. staff Meml., St. Mary's, Long Beach Community hosps., Los Alamitos (Calif.) Gen. Hosp. Served to capt. M.C., AUS, 1942-46; MTO. Decorated Bronze Star, Meritorious Service medal. Fellow ACS, Am. Soc. Abdominal Surgeons, Internat. Coll. Surgeons; mem. Am., Calif., Los Angeles County med. assns., Pan-Pacific Surg. Assn., Long Beach Surg. Soc., Kappa Sigma. Republican. Roman Cath. Club: KC (4 deg.). Contbr. to Jour. Urology. Home: 851 Hillside Dr Long Beach CA 90815 Office: 1703 Termino Ave Long Beach CA 90804

BOBERG, ANNA MARIA, home economics educator; b. Cieszyn, Poland, Feb. 19, 1940; d. William and Emilia J. (Zywczok) Zweck; came to U.S., 1955, naturalized, 1958; m. Walter W. Boberg, June 16, 1962; children—Richard Zweck, Tracy Ann. B.S., Mont. State U., 1963. GED tchr. Army Edn. Ctr., Wildflecken, Germany, 1964-66; tchr. earth sci., home econs. East Jr. High Sch., Casper, Wyo., 1971—; mem. Natrona County Sch. Dist. Sci. Curriculum Com., Home Econs. Curriculum Com. Mem. Grads. Home Econs. (sec. 1972), Natrona County Classroom Tchrs. Assn., Wyo. Edn. Assn., NEA, Wyo. Sci. Tchrs. Assn. LWV, Our Lady of Fatima Council Catholic Women (St. Joseph's Circle), Pi Beta Phi Alumni (pres. 1972). Republican. Roman Catholic. Office: 900 S Beverly St Casper WY 82601

BOBERG, WALTER WILLIAM, geologist; b. Kalispell, Mont., Jan. 8, 1940; s. Walter Harold and Meva Julia (Lapsley) B.; B.S. in Geology, Mont. State U., 1963; M.S., U. Colo., 1970; m. Anna Maria Zweck, June 16, 1962; children—Richard Zweck, Tracy Ann. Exploration geologist Hecla Mining Co., Wallace, Idaho, 1968; teaching asst. U. Colo., Boulder, 1968-70; exploration geologist Gulf Mineral Resources Co., Denver, 1969-70; geologist Anaconda Co., Salt Lake City, 1970; exploration geologist minerals dept. Continental Oil Co., Casper, Wyo., 1970-76, dist. geologist, 1976-77; chief geologist Wold Nuclear Co., Casper, 1977-79; exploration program mgr. Kennecott Exploration, Inc., Casper, 1979-81; ind. geologist, Casper, 1981—. Chmn. sub-com. on water Paradise Valley Civic Com., Casper, 1974-76. Served to capt. AUS, 1963-68. Decorated Army Commendation medal. Mem. Soc. Economic Geologists, AIME, Am. Assn. Petroleum Geologists, Northwest Mining Assn., Wyo. Geol. Assn. (mineral editor field conf. 1978, 2d v.p. 1978-79, pres. 1979-80, Frank A. Morgan Jr. award 1981, editor field conf. 1983), Rocky Mountain Assn. Geologists, Con. Geologists Soc. Petroleum Geology, Wyo. Mining Assn. (chmn. exploration com. 1978, 80-81, dir. 1981—), Soc. Geol. Applied to Mineral Deposits, Minerals Exploration Coalition, Casper C. of C. (chmn. subcom. on legis. affairs mineral industry com. 1977-78, chmn. mineral industry com. 1979-81), Sigma Xi. Contbr. articles to profl. publs. Home: 3810 Plateau Pl Casper WY 82604 Office: 254 N Center St 107 Casper WY 82601

BOBET, BONNIE MAE, marketing communications consultant; b. New Orleans, June 19, 1948; d. Bertram and Hazel Niona (Owen) B.; B.A., Brigham Young U., 1971; M.A., U. Utah, 1974; postgrad. (Union grantee-in-aid 1978-81, Union Guild scholar 1979) Grad. Theol. Union, 1977—. Editor, Center for Studies of Am. West, U. Utah, 1975, asst. thesis editor, 1975; pub. relations coordinator, mgr. editorial services, publs. mgr. Fidelity Savs. and Loan Assn., Oakland, Calif., 1975-82; communications dir. Citicorp Savs., 1982; mktg. communications cons., 1982—; instr. Grad. Theol. Union, 1980-81; cons. editor. Mem. Am. Studies Assn., Am. Acad. Religion, Mormon History Assn., Assn. Mormon Letters, Berkeley Archtl. Heritage Assn., San Francisco Women in Advt., Utah Heritage Found., Utah State Hist. Soc. Office: Grad Theol Union 2465 Le Conte Ave Berkeley CA 94709

BOBROW, DANIEL GUREASKO, computer scientist, researcher; b. N.Y.C., Nov. 29, 1935; s. Jacob J. Bobrow and Ruth (Gureasko) B.; m. Eileen Harriet Melamed, Sept. 21, 1963; children—Kim, Deborah, Jordan; m. 2d, Toni Helene Wagner, Jan. 1, 1982. B.S., Renasalear Poly. Inst.; 1957; S.M., Harvard U., 1958; Ph.D., MIT, 1964. Asst. prof. MIT, 1964-65; v.p. Bolt Beranek & Newman Co., Cambridge, Mass., 1965-72; research fellow Xerox Corp., Palo Alto, Calif., 1972—. Recipient Best Paper award Assn. Computing Machinery, 1974. Mem. Am. Assn. Artificial Intelligence (exec. council), Cognitive Sci. Soc. (governing bd.). Author: Calculus, 1961; Basic Mathematics, 1962; Calculus of Chemistry, 1965; editor: Programming Language LISP, 1968, Representation and Understanding, 1975; editor-in-chief Internat. Jour. Artificial Intelligence, 1979—. Office: 3333 Coyote Hill Rd Palo Alto CA 94304

BOCK, TIMOTHY LOUIS, programmer, analyst; b. Corvallis, Oreg., Mar. 23, 1953; s. Paul John and Eve (Chybova) B.; B.A., Oberlin (Ohio) Coll., 1974; Ph.D., Princeton U., 1980. Engring. analyst, The Aerospace Corp., El Segundo, Calif., 1980-82; sr. analyst Pacific Sierra Research Corp., Los Angeles, 1982—. Fulbright scholar Munich, W. Ger., 1974-75. Office: 12340 Santa Monica Blvd Los Angeles CA 90025

BOCKIUS, RUTH BEAR, nurse, educator; b. Pa., Dec. 19, 1925; d. Weidler R. and Ruth Mary (Jacoby) Bear; A.A. (1st Nat. Bank scholarship award, AMA scholarship award), Phoenix Coll., 1970; B.S.N. (Fed. Nursing grant), Ariz. State U., 1973, M.Ed., 1978; m. Thomas B. Bockius, Jr., Dec. 15, 1946; children—Donna Ruth, Dawn Eileen. Dental asst. to Dr. L. Bairo, Phoenix, 1963-64; licensed practical nurse, dental asst. to Dr. C.W. Sandahl, Phoenix, 1964-68; R.N., staff nurse then asst. charge nurse Phoenix Gen. Hosp., 1970-72, coordinator nursing edn., 1973-77, asst. dir. nurses, 1977-79; instr. Mesa (Ariz.) Community Coll., 1973-80, Glendale Community Coll., 1979-80; health edn. coordinator Samaritan Health Service, Phoenix, 1980-81; dir. patient and community edn. Maryvale Samaritan Hosp., Phoenix, 1981-83, dir. edn., 1983—. Mem. Ariz. Nurses in Mgmt., Ariz. Public Health Assn., Am. Public Health Assn., Am. Assn. Adult and Continuing Edn., Ariz. Assn. Adult and Continuing Edn., Phi Theta Kappa, Phi Kappa Phi. Republican. Lutheran. Home: 2337 W Diana Ave Phoenix AZ 85021 Office: 5102 W Campbell Ave Phoenix AZ 85031

BODDEN, THOMAS ANDREW, lawyer, realtor, educator; b. Lafayette, Ind., Dec. 18, 1945; s. William A. and Dorothy C. (Schlacks) B.; m. Irene S. Hiye, Aug. 9, 1980; children—Wendee, Todd, Christopher. A.B. with honors, Cornell U., 1968; J.D., U. Miami, 1974. Bar: Hawaii 1975, U.S. Dist. Ct. Hawaii 1975. Ptnr. Torkildson, Katz, Jossem & Loden, Honolulu, 1975-81; pres. Thomas A. Bodden Law Corp., Kihei, Hawaii, 1981—; lectr. Nat. Assn. Realtors, Real Estate Securities and Syndication Inst., Hawaii Bar Assn., Hawaii Soc. C.P.A.s, U. Hawaii. Vice-pres. Kihei Community Assn., 1983. Served to lt. USN, 1969-72. Mem. ABA, Nat. Assn. Realtors, Real Estate Securities and Syndication Inst., Navy League U.S. (pres. Maui Council 1983). Club: Rotary. Author real estate and taxation ednl. materials; contbr. articles to profl. jours. PO Box 719 Kihei HI 96753

BODE, FRANCES LOUISE MAINO (MRS. WILLIAM THEODORE BODE), author, lectr.; b. San Luis Obispo, Calif., Mar. 1, 1920; d. Theodore Michael and Eleanor Elizabeth (Hazard) Maino; B.A., Mills Coll., 1940; postgrad. U. Calif. at Berkeley, 1941; M.A., Sacramento State U., 1958; m. William Theodore Bode, Dec. 25, 1942; children—Eleanor Bode Cauldwell, Catherine Bode Appel, William T. II. Tchr., Ceres Union High Sch., 1941-43, Sacramento State Coll., 1957; free-lance tchr. flower arrangement, 1946—; lectr. on flower arrangements to various orgns. throughout U.S. Teaching specialist Ala. Judges Council, 1971, Ohio Judges Council, 1971, Ga. Judges Council, 1978, Judges Council So. Calif., 1978; dir. Sacramento Garden and Art Center, 1958-68, v.p., 1977-79; floriculture coordinator Calif. State Fair, 1981-83. Recipient Exec. Com. award Calif. Expn., 1969, 82; Community Service award Sacramento Soc. for the Blind, 1976; Design award Calif. State Fair, 1978. Mem. Profl. Arrangers No. Calif. (pres. 1968-69), Am. Horticultural Soc., Calif. Writers Club, Garden Writers Assn. Am., Carmichael, Sacramento arrangers guilds, Kingsley Art Club, Nat. Council State Garden Clubs, Am. Guild Flower Arrangers, Calif. State Garden Clubs, Inc., Mignonette Garden Club. Author: Creativity in Flower Arrangement, 1967; New Structures in Flower Arrangement, 1968; Dried Flower Designs, 1975; Designing with Flowers, 1976; contbr. author: Brooklyn Botanic Gardens Handbooks. Contbr. pictures of arrangements to various mags. Home: 2800 Huntington Rd Sacramento CA 95825

BODENHEIMER, EDGAR, lawyer, educator; b. Berlin, Germany, Mar. 14, 1908; came to U.S., 1933, naturalized, 1940; s. Siegmund and Rosi (Maass) B.; J.D., U. Heidelberg, 1933; LL.B., U. Wash., 1937; m. Brigitte M., June 6, 1935; children—Peter H., Thomas S., R. Rosemarie, Brigitte H. Admitted to Wash. bar, 1940; atty. U.S. Dept. Labor, 1940-42; prin. atty. Office Alien Property Custodian, 1942-46; asso. prof. Coll. Law, U. Utah, 1946-51, prof., 1951-66; prof. Sch. Law, U. Calif., Davis, 1966-75, prof. emeritus, 1975—. Fulbright travel grantee, 1953, 59, 73; research grantee Rockefeller Found., 1955-56; Nat. Endowment for Humanities fellow, 1971-72. Mem. Wash. State Bar Assn., Am. Soc. Polit. and Legal Philosophy (v.p., 1970-71), Internat. Assn. Philosophy of Law and Social Philosophy, Fgn. Law Assn., Am. Assn. Comparative Study of Law. Editorial bd. Am. Jour. Comparative Law, 1967-75; author: Treatise on Justice, 1967; Power, Law and Society, 1973; Jurisprudence: The Philosophy and Method of the Law, rev. edit., 1974; Philosophy of Responsibility, 1980; co-author: Introduction to the Anglo-American Legal System, 1980. Home: 542 Miller Dr Davis CA 95616 Office: Sch Law Univ Calif Davis CA 95616

BODENSIECK, ERNEST JUSTUS, mech. engr.; b. Dubuque, Iowa, June 1, 1923; s. Julius Henry and Alma Freida (Sommer) B.; B.Sc. in M.E., Iowa State U., 1943; m. Margery Elenore Sande, Sept. 9, 1943; children—Elizabeth Bodensieck Meyer, Stephen. Project engr. TRW Inc., Cleve., 1943-57; supr. rocket turbomachinery Rocketydyne div. Rockwell Internat., Canoga Park, Calif., 1957-60, supr. nuclear turbomachinery Rocketydyne div., 1964-70; advance gear engr. Gen. Electric Co., Lynn, 1960-64; asst. mgr. engine components Aerojet Nuclear Systems Co., Sacramento, 1970-71; gear and bearing cons. AiResearch div. Garrett Corp., Phoenix, 1971-81; transmission cons. Bodensieck Engring. Co., Scottsdale, Ariz., 1981—. Registered profl. engr., Ariz. Mem. Soc. Automotive Engrs. (various coms.), Aircraft Industries Assn. (various coms.), Am. Gear Mfrs. Assn. (vice chmn. aerospace gear com.), ASME, AIAA, Nat. Soc. Profl. Engrs., Pi Tau Sigma. Lutheran. Patentee in field. Home: 7133 N Via De Alegria Scottsdale AZ 85258

BODENSTEINER, ROBERT VICTOR, alloys manufacturing corporation executive; b. Earlville, Iowa, Sept. 10, 1941; s. Hugo Henry and Ruth Elizabeth (Sherwood) B. B.S. in Mech. Engring., U. Wash., 1970. Registered profl. engr., Wash. Owner, mgr. R. Bodensteiner & Assos., Cons. Engrs., Seattle, 1975-78; sales rep. Dieterich-Post Co. of Wash., Seattle, 1978-81; tech. area mgr. Eutectic Corp., Seattle, 1981—. Chmn., 32d Dist. Republicans, 1978, pres. King County Young Reps., 1979. Served with USNR, 1960-64. Named King County Young Republican of Year, 1977; recipient Spl. Appreciation award Wash. Spl. Olympics, 1981. Mem. Wash. Soc. Profl. Engrs. (chmn. architects and engrs. legis. council 1980-81, legis. chmn. 1981-82). Presbyterian. Club: Engineers (Seattle, pres. 1977-78). Home: 6427 Woodland Pl N Seattle WA 98103 Office: Eutectic Corp 7731 Oakport St Oakland CA 94621

BODILY, DAVID MARTIN, educator; b. Logan, Utah, Dec. 16, 1933; s. Levi Delbert and Norma (Christensen) B.; student Utah State U., 1952-54; B.A., Brigham Young U., 1959, M.A., 1960; Ph.D., Cornell U., 1964; m. Beth Alene Judy, Aug. 28, 1958; children—Robert David, Rebecca Marie, Timothy Andrew, Christopher Mark. Postdoctoral fellow Northwestern U., Evanston, Ill., 1964-65; asst. prof. chemistry U. Ariz., Tucson, 1965-67; asst. prof. fuels engring. U. Utah, Salt Lake City, 1967-70, asso. prof., 1970-77, prof., 1977—, chmn. dept. mining and fuels engring., 1976-82, chmn. dept. fuel engring., 1982—. Mem. Am. Chem. Soc. (chmn. Salt Lake sect. 1975), Catalysis Soc. N.Am., Am. Inst. Mining and Metall. Engrs., Sigma Xi. Mormon. Contbr. articles to profl. jours. Home: 2651 Cecil St Salt Lake City UT 84117 Office: 320 WBB U Utah Salt Lake City UT 84112

BODILY, KEVIN RAY, architect; b. Pocatello, Idaho, Apr. 28, 1950; s. Gaylen Leon and Marie Louise (Davis) B.; m. Carol Sue Jorgensen, Mar. 21, 1981; 1 dau., Erin Marie. B.Arch. with honors, Idaho State U., 1973. Design architect Alpha Engrs., Inc., Pocatello, 1973-76; architect Max L. Call & Assos., Idaho Falls, Idaho, 1976-80, v.p., 1980—, also dir.; works of firm include Ricks Coll. Fine Arts Center, Star Valley Jr. High Sch., Idaho Falls Westside Elem. Sch., Malad City High Sch., Sugar City Thomas D. Kershaw Intermediate Sch. Lic. architect, Idaho, Wyo.; cert. Nat. Council Archtl. Registration Bds. Mem. AIA (Henry Adams Fund cert. of merit 1973; pres. Eastern sect. Idaho chpt. 1981). Mormon. Home: 1439 Fairmont Dr Idaho Falls ID 83401 Office: 990 John Adams Pkwy Idaho Falls ID 83401

BODIN, ARTHUR MICHAEL, psychologist, psychotherapist; b. N.Y.C., July 11, 1932; s. Harry Sabbath and Rose (Kurz) B.; m. Miriam

Irene, June 25, 1961; children—Douglas Adam, Laura June. B.A., Swarthmore Coll., 1954; M.A., N.Y. U., 1957; Ph.D., SUNY-Buffalo, 1965. Lic. psychologist, Calif. Research assoc. Mental Research Inst., Palo Alto, Calif., 1965—, dir. tng. and edn., 1967-69, co-dir. communications and human systems program, 1969-70; pvt. practice psychotherapy, Palo Alto, 1967—; co-founder, sr. clin. psychologist Emergency Treatment Center, Palo Alto, 1975—; assoc., clin. prof. med. psychology, dept. psychiatry U. Calif.-San Francisco; chmn. Calif. Council on Psychiatry, Psychology, Social Work and Nursing, 1980-81; dir. Am. Bd. Forensic Psychology. Recipient Outstanding Contbn. to Psychology award Santa Clara County Psychol. Assn., 1977, Disting. Achievement in New Direction in Family Therapy award Am. Family Therapy Assn., 1981. Mem. Am. Psychol. Assn. (council of reps. 1978-81, 83—), Western Psychol. Assn., Calif. State Psychol. Assn. (pres. 1976-77, Disting. Service award 1978), Assn. Family Therapists No. Calif. (pres. 1970-72), Assn. Advancement Psychology, Nat. Council Family Relations, Am. Psychology-Law Soc. (pres. Santa Clara County chpt. 1982-83). Contbr. numerous chpts., articles to profl. publs.; bd. adv. editors Family Process, 1968—; editorial adv. bd. Jour. Marital and Family Therapy, 1979-82, Psychotherapy in Pvt. Practice, 1982—; editorial bd. Am. Jour. Forensic Psychology, 1982—. Office: Mental Research Inst 555 Middlefield Rd Palo Alto CA 94301

BODINSON, HOLT, conservationist; b. East Orange, N.J., Nov. 14, 1941; s. Earl Herdien and Hermoine (Holt) B.; B.A., Harvard, 1963; m. Ilse Marie Maier, Feb. 29, 1970. Sr. asso. Am. Conservation Assn., Inc., N.Y.C., 1966-70; dir. Office of Policy Analysis, N.Y. State Dept. Environ. Conservation, Albany, 1970-71, dir. div. ednl. services, 1971-77; dir. Ariz.-Sonora Desert Mus., 1977-78; adminstrv. dir. Safari Club Internat./Safari Club Internat. Conservation Fund, Tucson, 1980—. Committeeman, Montgomery Twp. Conservation Commn., 1967-70. Served with arty. AUS, 1964-66. Mem. Stony Brook-Millstone Watershed Assn. (dir.), N.Y. Outdoor Edn. Assn. (dir.), N.Y. State Rifle and Pistol Assn. (dir.). Episcopalian. Club: Harvard of So. Ariz. (dir.). Author: (with Clepper and others) Leaders in American Conservation, 1971. Contbg. editor Jour. Environmental Edn., 1968—; dir. Conservationist mag. 1971-77, N.Y. State Environment newspaper, 1971-74. Home: 4525 Hacienda del Sol Rd Tucson AZ 85718 Office: Suite 1680 5151 E Broadway Tucson AZ 85711

BOECKEL, GENE THOMAS, utility safety supr.; b. Zap, N.D., June 30, 1939; s. Thomas P.F. and Viola (Isaak) B.; student Capitol Comml. Coll., 1958-59, Internat. Corr. Schs., 1978-80, spl. courses; m. Diane Marie Mickelson, Mar. 10, 1963; children—Jeffrey, Jamie, Jodie. Operator trainee Basin Elec. Power Coop., Stanton, N.D., 1965-66, asst. control room operator, 1966, control room operator, 1966-75, shift supr., 1975-78; safety supr., Wheatland, Wyo., 1978—; panelist N.D. Safety Congress, 1975. Pres., Lutheran Ch. Council, 1977; sec. Civic Club, 1975; bd. dirs. Jaycees, 1972, v.p., 1973, Disting. Service award, 1974; v.p. P.T.O., 1970; pres. Park Bd., 1973. Cert. hearing conservationist. Mem. Nat. Safety Council, Am. Soc. Safety Engrs., Nat. Fire Protection Assn. Home: 1456 Mitchell St Wheatland WY 82201 Office: PO Box 1346 Wheatland WY 82201

BOEDING, MARVIN ALEX, clinical psychologist; b. New Hampton, Iowa, Mar. 3, 1948; s. Arnold Aloyius and Hermina Barbara (Rausch) B.; m. Kathleen Elizabeth Keefe, July 21, 1979; children—Scott Alexander, Kristin Elizabeth. B.S. magna cum laude, Loras Coll., 1970; M.S., Colo. State U., 1972, Ph.D., 1975; lic. psychologist, Colo. Staff psychologist Univ. Counseling Ctr., Colo. State U., Fort Collins, 1972-74, instr. dept. psychology, 1974-75; staff psychologist Thompson Sch. Dist. R2-J, Loveland, Colo., 1975-80; clinical psychologist Psychol. Assocs., Loveland, 1980—. Bd. dirs. So. Larimen County Crisis Intervention Service Inc. Mem. Coll. Natural Scis. Alumni Adv. Bd. Colo. State U. Mem. Am. Psychol. Assn., Colo. Psychol. Assn., Colo. Soc. Sch. Psychologists, Phi Beta Kappa. Contbr. articles to profl. jours. Home: 1453 Glenda Ct Loveland CO 80537 Office: 1530 Boise Ave Suite 205 Loveland CO 80537

BOEHM, BARRY WILLIAM, computer scientist, researcher, author; b. Santa Monica, Calif., May 16, 1935; s. Edward George and Katherine Genevieve (Kane) B.; m. Sharla Rita Perrine, July 1, 1961; children—Romney Ann and Tenley Lynn. B.A. in Math., Harvard U., 1957; M.A. in Math, UCLA, 1961, Ph.D. in Math, 1964. Head info. sci. dept., The Rand Corp., Santa Monica, 1959-73; dir. software research, tech. TRW, Redondo Beach, Calif., 1973-82, chief engr. Software Info. Systems div., 1982—; vis. prof. computer sci., UCLA. Mem. NASA Research Adv. Council, 1968-76, 1982—, Def. Sci. Bd. Task Force, 1981-82, Wang Grad. Inst. Nat. Acad. Adv. Com., 1982—. Recipient AIAA Info. Systems award, 1979; U.S. Air Force cert. merit, 1972. Mem. IEEE Computer Soc. (governing bd.), AIAA, (Assn. Computing Machinery. Author: (with Brown, Lipow, et all) Characteristics of Software Quality, 1978; Software Engineering Economics, 1981; (with H. Sackman) Planning Community Information Utilities, 1972; Rocket: Rand's Omnibus Calculator of the Kinematics of Earth Trajectories, 1964. Home: 518 Adelaide Dr Santa Monica CA 90402 Office: TRW DSG One Space Park Dr R-2 1076 Redonda Beach CA 90278

BOEHM, JOSEF FRANZ, wholesale and retail hardware executive; b. Wullenstetten, Ger., Jan. 29, 1944; came to U.S., 1956, naturalized, 1963; s. Franz and Cacilia (Boehm) B.; m. Linda Jean Fults, Aug. 3, 1968; 1 dau., Brigitte. Student pub. schs., Anchorage. With Anchorage Times, 1957-60, Sears, Roebuck & Co., Anchorage, 1960-63; prin. owner, pres. Alaska Indsl. Hardware, Inc., Anchorage, 1963—. Served with Alaska N.G., 1960-63. Office: 2192 Viking Dr Anchorage AK 99501

BOEHMER, CLIFFORD BERNARD, nuclear engr., lawyer; b. St. Louis, Aug. 25, 1927; s. Arthur Herman and Pearl (Schmering) B.; B.S. in Elec. Engring., Washington U., St. Louis, 1952; M.S. in Physics, Drexel U., 1960; LL.B., LaSalle Extension U., 1974; m. Mary Frances Wilson, Aug. 19, 1950 (dec.); children—Richard, Robert, Terry, Sally; m. 2d, Joan Schweitzer Ashbrook, Sept. 5, 1981. Sr. engr. White Rodger Electric Co., St. Louis, 1953-56, Martin Co., Balt., 1956-61; supr. Westinghouse Electric Co., Pitts., 1961-64, 65-67; staff mem. Los Alamos Sci. Lab., Jackass Flats, Nev., 1964-65; mgr. McDonnell Douglas Co., Huntington Beach, Calif., 1967—; mgr. safety Solar One, 10 megawatt solar electric power plant, Barstow, Calif., 1979—; admitted to Calif. bar, 1974, Fed. bar, 1974, Patent and Trademark bar, 1978; individual practice law, El Toro, Calif., 1978—. Pres. Mission Viejo (Calif.) High Sch. Council, 1970-71, Tustin (Calif.) Sch. Dist. Council, 1971-72. Served to 1st lt. U.S. Army, 1946-47, 52-53. Registered profl. engr., Calif. Mem. Orange County Bar Assn. Republican. Roman Catholic. Home: 22945 Leo Ln El Toro CA 92630 Office: 5301 Bolsa Ave Huntington Beach CA 92647

BOEHNKE, HENRY L., pediatrician; b. Eugene, Oreg., July 21, 1928; s. Edwin G. and Florence V. (Thorpe) B.; B.S., U. Oreg., 1953, M.D., 1955; m. Dorothy C. Thomason, July 1, 1951; children—Joan, John, William. Intern Multnomah County, Oreg., 1955-56; resident in pediatrics Doernbecher Children's Hosp., Portland, Oreg., 1955-58; pvt. practice medicine, specializing in pediatrics, Medford, Oreg., 1958—; asso. prof. pediatrics U. Oreg. Med. Sch., 1965—. Served with U.S. Army, 1946-49. Mem. AMA, Oreg. Med. Soc., Am. Acad. Pediatrics. Diplomate Am. Bd. Pediatrics. Republican. Home: 242 Valley View Medford OR 97501 Office: 1025 E Main St Medford OR 97501

BOENISCH, EDMOND WILLIAM, JR., educator, counselor; b. San Antonio, Dec. 17, 1947; s. Edmond William and Mary Margaret (Branecky) B.; m. Linda Gail Powell, Dec. 23, 1969; children—Laura Michelle, Lisa Nicole. B.A. in Sociology, St. Mary's U., 1969; M.S. in Student Personnel and Guidance, E. Tex. State U., 1974; postgrad. U. No. Colo., 1979—. Counselor, instr. and vets. affairs coordinator Laramie County Community Coll., Cheyenne, Wyo., 1974—; stress mgmt. and human devel. cons. Served to capt. USAF, 1969-73; to maj. Air N.G., 1975—. Decorated Bronze Star. Mem. Am. Personnel and Guidance Assn., Am. Coll. Personnel Assn., Wyo. Personnel and Guidance Assn., Colo.-Wyo. Assn. Women Adminstrs. and Counselors. Democrat. Roman Catholic. Author: (with Michele Haney) Stressmap: Finding Your Pressure Points, 1982. Home: 1124 King Ct Cheyenne WY 82007 Office: 1400 E College Dr Cheyenne WY 82007

BOEPPLE, ROLLAND EMERSON, coll. librarian; b. Balt., Dec. 25, 1927; s. John Theuer and Matie Viola (Flessner) B.; A.B., Elizabethtown Coll., 1949; M.L.S., U. So. Calif., 1962; m. Saeko Nakano, Nov. 9, 1958; children—Kathy Elaine, Leslie Ruth. Librarian trainee, then librarian Los Angeles Pub. Library, 1959-62; librarian Douglas Aircraft Co. Engring. Library, Long Beach, Calif., 1962-64, Anaheim (Calif.) Pub. Library, 1964. Philco-Ford Aeronutronic Div. library, 1965-67; dir. library services Santa Ana (Calif.) Coll. Library, 1967—; coordinator library tech. curriculum Santa Ana Coll., 1967—. Mem. Faculty Assn. Calif. Community Colls., Calif. Library Assn., Assn. Calif. Community Coll. Adminstrs., Council on Library Tech. Home: 17972 Larcrest Circle Huntington Beach CA 92647 Office: 17th St at Bristol St Santa Ana CA 92706

BOESEL, RICHARD ERNEST, JR., fin. exec.; b. Port Chester, N.Y., Dec. 15, 1928; s. Richard Ernest and Alice S. (Scatterday) B.; B.A., Brown U., 1952; m. Virginia Nelson, Mar. 28, 1953; children—Douglas, David, John, Elizabeth. Asso., Kuhn, Loeb & Co., N.Y.C., 1952-60; v.p., dir. Hayden, Stone & Co., N.Y.C., 1960-67, v.p., San Francisco, 1971-73; pres., chief exec. officer Am. DualVest Fund, N.Y.C., 1967-68; chmn., pres. Competitive Capital Corp., N.Y.C. and San Francisco, 1968-71; fin. cons., San Francisco, 1973-75; partner Hanson, Boesel & Co., San Francisco, 1975-79; regional v.p. Fidelity Group of Funds, San Francisco, 1980—. Pres., bd. dirs. Center for Attitudinal Healing, Tiburon, Calif., 1979—; bd. dirs. Golden Gate Bridge Hwy. and Transp. Dist., San Francisco, 1981—. Served with U.S. Army, 1946-47. Republican. Clubs: San Francisco Yacht, Belvedere Tennis, Rotary (charter; pres. Tiburon-Belvedere 1978-79). Home: 67 West Shore Rd Belvedere CA 94920 Office: 433 California St San Francisco CA 94104

BOESEN, VICTOR, journalist, author; b. Plainfield, Ind., Sept. 7, 1908; s. Jens Eugene and Helene (Petersen) B.; student U. Mo., 1928-30; m. Nancy Hagedorn, Oct. 2, 1940. Reporter, Wichita (Kans.) Beacon, 1930-31; reporter Chgo. City News Bur., 1931-35; news and commentary writer radio station WBBM, Chgo., 1935-38; reporter Hawthorne (Calif.) Advertiser, 1939-40; news writer KNX radio, Los Angeles, 1941-42; publicist, Beverly Hills, Calif., 1942; roving reporter Skyways Mag., N.Y.C., 1943-45; war corr. Liberty Mag., 1945-46; free-lance writer, 1946—. Mem. Authors Guild, Am. Soc. Journalists and Authors, Overseas Press Club of Am. Author: (with Joseph Karneke) Navy Diver, 1962; They Said It Couldn't Be Done, 1971; From High School Dropout to Space Age Inventor, 1974; Doing Something About the Weather, 1975; (with Florence Curtis Graybill) Edward Sheriff Curtis: Visions of a Vanishing Race, 1976, Edward Sheriff Curtis, Photographer of the North American Indian, 1977, Storm—Irving Krick vs. The U.S. Weather Bureaucracy, 1978; (with Wendy Grad) The Mercedes-Benz Book, 1981. Contbr. articles to numerous publs. Home: 971 Chattanooga Ave Box 244 Pacific Palisades CA 90272

BOGAD, CAROLYN MCWILLIAMS, educational administrator; b. Montebello, Calif., June 22, 1947; d. Carroll W. and O. Fayetta (Jacobs) McWilliams; m. Steven Richard Bogad, Aug. 25, 1968; children—Lesley Meredith, Molly Elizabeth, Neely Kathleen. B.A., U. Calif.-Santa Barbara, 1969, M.A., 1980, postgrad., 1980—. Cert. tchr., adminstr., Calif. Tchr. elem. schs., Calif., 1970-75; supr. tchr. edn., instr. ednl. adminstrn. U. Calif.-Santa Barbara, 1976-82; dir. gen. studies Akiba Acad., Westwood, Calif., 1982-83; prin. Adat Ariel Day Sch., North Hollywood, Calif., 1983—; cons. in ednl. adminstrn. Mem. Am. Ednl. Research Assn., Assn. Supervision and Curriculum Devel., Assn. Calif. Sch. Adminstrs., Calif. Assn. for the Gifted, Internat. Reading Assn., Nat. Assn. Female Execs., Phi Delta Kappa. Home: 11950 Susan Dr Granada Hills CA 91344 Office: 5540 Laurel Canyon Blvd North Hollywood CA 91607

BOGARDUS, WILLIAM BROWER, former government communications executive; b. Torrington, Conn., Apr. 7, 1929; s. De Witt Brower and Henrietta Elizabeth (Burn) B.; student pub. schs., Torrington and El Monte, Calif.; m. Iva Irene Sims, Dec. 16, 1951; children—Karen L. Bogardus Thill, Linda L. Bogardus Waltz, Tracy Allyn, Mark W., Dorene E. Bogardus Dunbar, Lynette A. Chief leased facilities Airways and Air Communications Service, Dept. Air Force, Andrews AFB, Md., Scott AFB, Ill., 1956-61; specialist comml. policy div. Def. Communications Agency, Dept. Def., Washington, 1961-66; dir. U.S. Army Comml. Communications Office, Ft. Huachuca, Ariz., 1967-83; Air Force contracting officer, 1957-61. Served with USAF, 1948-56. Decorated Meritorious Civilian Service medal Dept. Army, 1971, 82. Mem. Armed Forces Communications and Electronics Assn. (1st v.p. Ariz. chpt. 1977-78), N.Y. Geneal. and Biog. Soc., Anneke Jans and Everardus Bogardus Descs. Assn. (pres.). Mormon. Home: 1313 Granada Way Modesto CA 95355

BOGDAN, FABIAN, mech. and elec. engr.; b. Wilkes-Barre, Pa., May 9, 1918; s. Peter Paul and Catherine (Starr) B.; grad. courses Internat. Corr. Schs., 1938-44; m. Edna Alveretta Spray, Jan. 29, 1937; children—James Thomas, Lois Ellen Bogdan Leach. Sheet metal foreman Leo Steadle Co., Kingston, Pa., 1936-40; supt. mfg. Stedco Products, Kingston, 1940-51; chief engr. Diamond Mfg. Co., Wyoming, Pa., 1951-63; chief engr. Diamond Perforated Metals Co., Gardena, Calif., 1963—, also mem. fin. bd., supervisory bd. Mem. Soc. Mfg. Engrs., Am. Soc. Metals. Club: Masons. Contbr. articles to profl. jours. Home: 5438 Lakewood Blvd Lakewood CA 90712 Office: 17915 S Figueroa St Gardena CA 90248

BOGDANOW, NORMAN COLMAN, mktg. exec.; b. Chgo., Nov. 18, 1942; s. Morris D. and Dorothy (Neiderman) B.; student Claremont Men's Coll., 1961-62; B.S., UCLA, 1965; m. Susan Elaine Liebman. Sales mgr. Maddux of Calif., Los Angeles, 1968-69, v.p. mktg., 1969-76; pres. Rinor Mktg. Corp., 1976-77; v.p. ops. Servette Inc., 1977-79, v.p., 1979—; dir. Bel Air Industries, Los Angeles, Norman Farms, Inc., Ind., Parts & Polish, Los Angeles. Vol. counselor probationers Mcpl. Ct. Los Angeles, 1970-73. Served to lt. USNR, 1965-68. Mem. Sales and Mktg. Execs. Los Angeles, Alpha Kappa Psi. Club: Marina City. Home: 349 15th St Santa Monica CA 90402 Office: 5844 E Slauson City of Commerce CA 90040

BOGDON, ROBERT RUSSELL, automobile salesman; b. Tonopah, Nev., Dec. 8, 1943; s. Anthony Charles and Grace Johanna (Elliott) B.; student U. Nev., Reno, 1960-61; m. Phyllis Ruth Taylor, July 13, 1968. With First Nat. Bank Nev., Tonopah, 1961, Nev. Dept. Hwys., Tonopah, 1961; counterman, Bellingers, Elko, Nev., 1966-68; parts mgr. Warren Motor Co., Elko, 1968—, salesman, 1978—; advisor No. Nev. Community Coll., 1967. Served with U.S. Army, 1962-65. Named Medallion mgr. Ford Motor Co., 1970, 71, 77, 80, 81. Mem. Jaycees (numerous offices, pres. 1976-77, dist. dir. Nev. State Jaycees 1977-78, dir. Silver Baron Jaycees 1977—; JCI senator 1980; local, state, nat. awards), Elko C. of C. (dir. 1975-76). Democrat. Roman Catholic. Home: 838 Wilson St Elko NV 89801 Office: 618 Idaho St Elko NV 89801

BOGERT, HOWARD ZABRISKIE, JR., market research executive; investor; b. Dayton, Ohio, May 5, 1935; s. Howard Zabriskie and Ethel Jane (Hitchings) B.; m. Carol Marston, June 18, 1957; children—Jennifer Allice, Becky Angel, Howard Daniel. B.S., Stanford U., 1957; M.S., U. Md., 1960; M.B.A., Santa Clara U., 1978. Research and devel. engr. Fairchild Semicondr., 1960-63; engring. dir. Gen. Micro-Electronics, 1963-67, Am. Micro Systems, 1967-69; pres., founder Internat. Computer Modules, 1969-70; mgr. Siliconix, 1971-72; v.p. engring. Unicom, 1972-75; cons., 1975-78; v.p. Dataquest, Cupertino, Calif., 1978—; dir. Cognos-A. Served to lt. (j.g.), USNR, 1957-60. Mem. IEEE. Republican. Author: Vertical Disintegration, 1978; contbr. articles to profl. jours. Designer first linear integrated circuit; patentee circuit designs. Home: 11247 Terra Bella Dr Cupertino CA 95014 Office: 1290 Ridder Park Dr San Jose CA 95131

BOGGAN, DANIEL, JR., city administrator; b. Albion, Mich., Dec. 9, 1945; s. Daniel and Ruthie Jean (Crum) B.; m. Jacqueline (Boggan,) Oct. 4, 1977 (div.); children—DeVone, Daniel, Dhanthan, Alike. B.A., Albion Coll., 1967; M.S.W., U. Mich., 1968. Clin. supr. West Campus, Starr Commonwealth for Boys, 1968-70; asst. city mgr., Jackson, Mich., 1970-72; dep. city mgr., then city mgr., Flint, Mich.; dir. mgmt. services City of Portland, Oreg., 1976-78; asst. chief adminstrv. officer San Diego County, Calif., 1978-79; adminstr. Essex County, N.J., 1979-81; city mgr., Berkeley, Calif., 1982—; former mem. faculty Jackson Community Coll., Portland State U., Upsala Coll. Bd. dirs. local United Way 1971-72. Recipient Soc. Afro Am. Police award, 1974; named to Outstanding Young Men Am., U.S. Jaycees, 1974. Mem. Internat. City Mgrs. Assn., Am. Mgmt. Assn., NAACP (Outstanding Youth Services award 1965). Democrat. Baptist. Office: 2180 Milvia Berkeley CA 94708

BOGGS, ORVALLE, JR., telecommunications company executive; b. Logan, W. Va., June 9, 1935; s. Orvalle and Lila V.B.; m. Ruth Needle, Feb. 18, 1957; children—Cathy E., Joanne L. B.S. in Vocat. Edn., Calif. State U., 1981; M.B.A. in Telecommunications Mgmt., Nat. U., 1983. Served as enlisted man U.S. Navy, 1952-72; ret., 1972; with Sears Service Ctr., Buena Park, Calif., 1972-75, J.C. Penney Co., Buena Park, 1975-79; tech. tng. instr. and mgr., design and utilization engr. Anderson Jacobson Inc., Anaheim, Calif., 1980—; instr. electronics Long Beach (Calif.) City Coll., 1977—. Mem. Am. Vocat. Edn. Assn. Home: 5734 Apia Dr Cypress CA 90630 Office: Anderson Jacobson Inc 125 W Cerritos Ave Anaheim CA 92805

BOGNAR, CHARLES RALPH, marketing manager; b. Phila., Feb. 2, 1926; s. Charles S. and Anna Bognar. Student Pa. State U., 1957-67; m. Bernadine L. Schantz, Oct. 2, 1948. Tool and model maker in machine shop Franklin Inst. Research Labs., Phila., 1949-55, sr. tech. assoc. friction lubrication div., 1955-70, sr. test engr. utilities services group, 1970-73; mgr. test ops. and co-founder turbo exptl. div. Turbo Research, West Chester, Pa., 1973-75; co-founder Energy Tech., Inc., West Chester, 1975, v.p., dir. mktg., 1975-79; new bus. devel. mktg. spl. services div. Ebasco Services, Inc., N.Y.C., 1979-80, mgr. project devel./mktg. for process indsl. div., Los Angeles, 1980-83, mgr. project devel./mktg. for process indsl. bus. devel. for Pacific S.W. and Hawaii, 1983—. Mem. ASME, Research Engrs. Soc. Am., Sigma Xi. Mem. Christian Ch. Home: 17892 Mann St Irvine CA 92715 Office: 3000 W MacArthur Blvd Santa Ana CA 92704 also World Trade Center New York NY

BOGUE, BRUCE, ins. agt.; b. Los Angeles, Sept. 24, 1924; s. Charles Luther and Viola (Adam) B.; B.A., U. Calif. at Los Angeles, 1947; grad. Inf. Staff and Command Sch. U.S. Army, 1948; m. Tays Myrl Tarvin, Dec. 18, 1945; children—Tays Elizabeth, Charles Luther II. Agt., Mut. Benefit Life Ins. Co., Los Angeles, 1948-55, prodn. mgr., 1955-62; gen. agt. Guardian Life Ins. Co., Los Angeles, 1962—; tchr. ins. UCLA. Precinct capt., poll watcher, hdqrs. chmn., fund raising chmn., campaign chmn. for Rep. party. Served to capt., inf. AUS, 1942-46; ETO. Recipient Man of Affairs award Los Angeles Wilshire Press, Los Angeles Mirror News, 1958. Mem. Million Dollar Round Table (life), Am. Soc. C.L.U.s, Assn. Advanced Life Underwriters, Nat. Assn. Life Underwriters, Gen. Agts. and Mgrs. Assn., Los Angeles Life and Trust Council, U. Calif. at Los Angeles Alumni Assn. (life). Congregationalist. Clubs: Annandale Golf (Pasadena, Calif.); California (Los Angeles). Contbr. articles to profl. jours. Home: 2200 Homet Rd San Marino CA 91108 Office: 3440 Wilshire Blvd Los Angeles CA 90010

BOGUE, DONALD JOSEPH, vocational college president, clergyman; b. Raymond, Wash., Sept. 11, 1930; s. Joseph Alfred and Esther Mable (Peterson) B.; m. Marian Ann Balderston, Aug. 29, 1952; children—Stephen Paul, Debra Renee. Student N.W. Coll., 1948-50, U. Wash., 1947-50; Th.B., Central Bible Coll., 1951; M.A., Pacific Western U., 1977, Ed.D., 1978; Ph.D., Union U., 1978. Ordained to ministry Assembly of God, 1953. Pres. Andon Corp., 1970—, Andon Coll. Vocat. Allied Health, 1970—, B&B Advt. and Mktg., 1974—; owner, Bogue Investment Fund, 1966—; vice chmn. Accrediting Bur. Allied Health Schs., 1979—; cons. to colls. and univs. on allied health and accreditation, San Jose, Calif., 1968—; mem. No. Calif.-Nev. Dist. council Assembly of God; mem. Calif. Postsecondary Edn. Commn., Calif. Dept. Employment Devel. Mgmt. Info. Systems. Mem. Nat. Assn. Allied Health Schs. (exec. bd.), Calif. Assn. Paramed. Schs., Am. Mgmt. Assn., ADA, Health Services Commn. Club: Yosemite. Author: College Cost Survey, 1980, 81-83; How to Teach Teachers to Teach Allied Health, 1982. Office: 1118 N El Dorado St Stockton CA 95202 also 1414 N Winchester Blvd San Jose CA 95128

BOHACHEVSKY, IHOR OREST, mathematician; b. Sokal, Ukraine, Sept. 7, 1928; s. Daniel and Rostyslava Stephania (Nychay) B.; m. Ulana Mary Kebalo, Jan. 28, 1939. B.Aero. Engring. magna cum laude, NYU, 1956, Ph.D. in Applied Math., 1961. Research scientist, adj. assoc. prof. NYU, 1961-63; research engr. Cornell Aero. Lab., Buffalo, 1963-66; prin. research scientist, sr. staff Avco-Everett Research Lab. (Mass.), 1966-68; tech. staff Bellcomm Inc., Washington, 1968-72, Bell Lab. Inc., Murray Hill, N.J., 1972-75; staff Los Alamos Nat. Lab., 1975—. Served with U.S. Army, 1951-53. Recipient W. Bryans medal in engring. mechanics NYU, 1956, NASA Apollo Achievement award, 1969, AT&T cert. of Recognition, 1969; NSF fellow, 1956, 57, 58, 59. Mem. Am. Nuclear Soc., N.Y. Acad. Scis., AIAA, Soc. Indsl. and Applied Math., Signa Xi, Tau Beta Pi. Eastern Rite Catholic. Patentee beam heated linear thera-pinch device for producing hot plasma; contbr. articles to sci. and tech. jours. Home: 829 Pine St Los Alamos NM 87544 Office: Los Alamos Nat Lab Los Alamos NM 87545

BOHAN, JANIS SUE, psychology educator; b. Denver, Mar. 5, 1945; d. Marion Kieth and Fern Mae (Warren) Beebe. B.A. cum laude (NSF undergrad. fellow), U. Denver, 1967; Ph.D. (NDEA fellow), U. Rochester, 1970. Instr. nursing U. Rochester (N.Y.), Med. Center 1969-70; prof. psychology Metropolitan State Coll., Denver, 1970—, dir. Parent Edn. Resource Center, 1978—; cons. in field. Vol. probation counselor Denver County Court, 1971—; mem. Met. State Coll. speakers bur., 1972—; cons. to Rocky Mountain Planned Parenthood, 1973—. Mem. Am. Psychol. Assn., Soc. for Research in Child Devel., NEA, Met.

Child Protection Council, Colo. Advocacy for Children Today (Denver coalition), ACLU, NOW. Home: 28254 Tresine Dr Evergreen CO 80439 Office: Psychology Dept Metropolitan State Coll 1006 11th St Box 54 Denver CO 80204

BOHAN, JOHN FRANCIS, graphic arts educator, administrator; b. Mitchell, S.D., June 26, 1932; s. John Francis and Olga Cornelia (Shields) B.; m. Marilyn Lauris Jacobs, June 30, 1960. Grad. S.D. State U., 1975; M.Ed., Oreg. State U., 1976; Ed.D., Portland State U., 1983. Tchr., Shelton (Wash.), Pub. Schs., 1976-77; owner, Model Printery, Willmar, Minn., 1961-72; instr. graphic arts Clackamas Community Coll., Oregon City, Oreg., 1977—, chmn. dept. pub. service and graphic arts, 1979-81. Pres. Willmar C. of C., 1967, bd. dirs., 1964-67. Mem. Am. Vocat. Assn., Oreg. Vocat. Assn., Internat. Graphic Arts Educators Assn., Portland Club of Printing House Craftsmen. Republican. Roman Catholic. Home: 18701 Madrona Dr Oregon City OR 97045 Office: Clackamas Community Coll 19600 S Molalla Ave Oregon City OR 97045

BOHAN, MARILYN LAURIS (JACOBS), stress counselor, nurse, educator; b. Bowdle, S.D., Feb. 28, 1935; d. Carl Thomas and Rose Mary (Savelsberg) Jacobs; m. John Francis Bohan, July 30, 1961. B.S., Presentation Sch. Nursing, S.D. Northern State Coll., 1961; M.S. in Counseling, Portland State U., 1981. R.N. in S.D., Minn., Wash., Oreg. Program nurse Little Crow Community Council, Willmar, Minn., 1963-72; dir. family planning Interlakes Community Action, Madison, S.D., 1973-74; instr., nurse Shelton (Wash.) Sch. Dist., 1975-76; nurse counselor Community Health, Oregon City, Oreg., 1976-80; dir. Healthwise Stress Counseling Consulting Center, Portland, Oreg., 1981—; cons. Women's Center, 1981—; instr. Clackamas Community Coll., 1981—; tchr. art, choral reading St. Mary's Sch., Willmar, Minn., 1968-70. Chmn., camp nurse Minn. Soc. for Crippled Children & Adults; dir., camp nurse Kandiahi County (Minn.) Assn. for Retarded Children, Willmar, 1965-72; dir. West Central Industries, Willmar, 1968-72; leader Girl Scouts USA, 1967-78; program chmn. Willmar Roundtable Study Club, 1968-72; active Friends of Library, Oregon City, 1982—. Mem. Am. Personnel Guidance Assn., AAUW, Phi Kappa Phi. Author: Psychodrama and the Terminal Patient, 1981.

BOHL, MICHAEL CLIFFORD, newspaper executive; b. Madera, Calif., Aug. 17, 1950; s. Russell Carl and Erma May Bohl; m. Pamela Bennetts, Aug. 28, 1971; children—Amanda, Matthew, Emily. A.A. in Journalism, Bakersfield Coll., 1970; B.S. in Journalism, Calif. Poly. U., 1972. Tech. writer, adminstr. Bechtel Corp., Norwalk, Calif., 1971-73; advt. salesman Oakdale (Calif.) Leader, 1973-75; pub., owner Bohl Newspapers Inc. (Amador Progress-News, Ione and Amador Ledger, Jackson, Calif.), 1975—; part owner Colfax (Calif.) Record, Mother Lode Weekly, Sonora, Calif.; part-time prison guard Calif. Dept. Correction, Sierra Conservation Ctr., Jamestown, Calif., 1974. Mem. Ione Planning Commn., 1980-81; pres. Ione Bus. Assn. Recipient Elk Leadership award, 1968; Calif. Newspaper Pubs. Assn. awards, 1976, 78, 80; Nat. Newspaper Assn. awards 1976, 78-82. Mem. Calif. Newspaper Pubs. Assn. (past pres., dir.), Amador County C. of C. Democrat. Methodist. Clubs: Ione Parlor Native Sons Golden West, Jackson Lions (v.p.). Office: PO Box 606 22 E Main St Ione CA 95640

BOHLMEYER, DELMAR EUGENE, educator; b. Jefferson County, Nebr., Jan. 28, 1937; s. Herman Fred and Malinda Doretta (Hothan) B.; Mus.B. (Anna L. Werner Meml. scholar), U. Nebr., 1958; M.A. in Edn., Ariz. State U., 1966; Edn. specialist, 1970; m. Elaine Lois Morton, Sept. 27, 1958; children—Teresa, Lisa. Music tchr. pub. schs., Exeter, Nebr., 1958-62; music tchr. Duckeye (Ariz.) Union High Sch., 1962-64; music tchr. Phoenix Elementary Sch. Dist. 1, 1964-72, chmn. dept., 1972-79, chmn. dept. fine arts, 1979—. Mem. Ariz. Dept. Edn. Music Adv. Com., 1971-73; choir dir. Encanto Community Ch., Phoenix, 1964-82, deacon, 1978-80; bd. dirs. Ariz. Young Audiences, 1975-79, v.p., 1978—. Mem. Music Educators Nat. Conf., Ariz. Music Educators Assn. (pres. gen. music sect. 1981-83), Am. Orff Schulwerk Assn. (charter mem., pres. Ariz. chpt. 1978-80, nat. exec. bd. 1982—), Sinfonia Profl., Phi Mu Alpha, Phi Delta Kappa. Home: 413 E Fremont Dr Tempe AZ 85282 Office: 125 E Lincoln St Phoenix AZ 85004

BOHMAN, FRANK WILLIAM, rancher; b. Peterson, Utah, Apr. 27, 1918; s. Alfred Fingal and Agda Selina (Fornelious) B.; ed. pub. schs. Rancher, Morgan County, Utah, 1932—; pres. Utah Assn. Soil Conservation Dists., Salt Lake City, 1969—; v.p. Fed. Land Bank Assn., Salt Lake City, 1970-72, pres., 1973—, also dir. Chmn. Morgan County planning and zoning com. Farm Bur., 1940—, pres., 1944-49, bd. dirs., 1949—; county commr. Morgan County, 1975-78, 81-82; bd. dirs. Weber Basin Water Conservancy Dist.; mem. natural resources com. Utah State Farm Bur. Fedn., 1977—. Mem. Soil Conservation Soc. Am. (pres. Utah chpt. 1978—), Am. Soc. Range Mgmt. Democrat. Mem. Ch. of Jesus Christ of Latter-Day Saints (stake mission pres.). Address: RFD 1 Morgan UT 84050

BOHN, DENNIS ALLEN, electronic engineer, consultant, writer; b. San Fernando, Calif., Oct. 5, 1942; s. Raymond Virgil and Iris Elouise (Johnson) B.; m. Christa Adelle Porche', Apr. 6, 1963; (div.); 1 dau., Kira Michelle. B.S.E.E. with honors, U. Calif.-Berkeley, 1972, M.S.E.E. with honors, 1974. Engring. technician Gen. Electric Co., San Leandro, Calif., 1964-72; research and devel. engr. Hewlett-Pakard Co., Santa Clara, Calif., 1973; application engr. Nat. Semicondr. Corp., Santa Clara, 1974-76; engring. mgr. Phase Linear Corp., Lynnwood, Wash., 1976-82; v.p. engring. RANE Corp., Mountlake Terrace, Wash., 1982—; founder TOLECO Systems, Kingston, Wash., 1980. Suicide and crisis ctr. vol., Berkeley, 1972-74, Santa Clara, 1974-76. Served with USAF, 1960-64. Recipient Am. Spirit Honor medal U.S. Air Force, 1961; Math. Achievement award Chem. Rubber Co., 1962-63. Mem. Audio Engring. Soc., Tau Beta Pi. Libertarian. Editor: We Are Not Just Daffodils, 1975; contbr. poetry to Reason mag.; tech. editor Audio Handbook, 1976; contbr. articles to tech. jours.; columnist Polyphony mag., 1981—. Patentee in field. Home: PO Box 401 Kingston WA 98346 Office: 6510 216th St SW Mountlake Terrace WA 98043

BOHN, FRED O., JR., construction co. exec.; b. Chgo., Jan. 22, 1945; s. Fred O. and Marjorie L. (Simpson) B.; B.S. in Fin., Calif. State Poly. U., Pomona, 1971; M.B.A., U. So. Calif., 1976; m. Marsha T. Kipley, Feb. 7, 1970; children—Jeffrey, Marcus, Rochelle. Research assoc. Native Am. Legal Def., Washington, 1971-72; asst. prof. Calif. Poly. U., Pomona, 1972-74; dir., chief exec. officer Execujet Fin. Ltd., London, 1980—; v.p. adminstrn. Comprenetics, Beverly Hills, Calif., 1977-79; pres., chief exec. officer ExecuJet Ltd., Chino, Calif., 1979—, also chmn.; dir. Mountain Pacific Corp. Served with U.S. Army, 1969-70. Mem. Aircraft Owners and Pilots Assn. Republican. Lutheran. Club: South Hills Country (West Covina, Calif.). Office: 7600 Kimball Chino CA 91710

BOHN, RALPH CARL, university dean; b. Detroit, Feb. 19, 1930; s. Carl and Bertha (Abrams) B.; m. Adelle Stanul, Sept. 2, 1951; children—Cheryl, Jeffrey; m. JoAnn Olvera, Feb. 19, 1977; stepchildren—Kathryn McCawn, Kimberly Butler, Gregory Butler. B.S., Wayne State U., 1951, M.Ed., 1954, Ed.D., 1957. Tchr. indsl. edn. Detroit Pub. Schs., 1947-51, 54-55; instr. indsl. edn. Wayne State U., Detroit, 1954-55; prof. indsl. studies San Jose (Calif.) State U., 1956—, chmn. dept. indsl. studies, 1961-69, assoc. dean ednl. services, 1968-70, dean continuing edn., prof. indsl. tech., 1970—; mem. accreditation teams Western Assn. Schs. and Colls. Served to capt. USCGR. Recipient Ship's Citation, Am. Indsl. Arts Assn., 1971, Calif. Indsl. Edn. Assn., 1971; Service awards Am. Vocat. Assn., 1966, 67; Man of Yr. award Am. Council Indsl. Arts Tchr. Edn., 1967. Mem. AIAA, Am. Vocat. Assn., Consortium Profl. Assns., NEA, Nat. Fluid Power Soc., Am. Indsl. Arts Assn. (pres. 1963-64), Am. Council Indsl. Arts Tchr. Edn. (pres. 1964-66), Western Assn. Summer Session Adminstrs. (pres. 1974-75), Nat. Assn. Summer Session Adminstrs., Associated Orgns. Tchr. Edn., Nat. Assn. Indsl./Tech. Tchr. Edn., Calif. Indsl. Edn. Assn., Indsl./Edn. Council Calif., Epsilon Pi Tau, Phi Delta Kappa. Lutheran. Author: (with MacDonald and Miller) Power Mechanics, 1978; (with Silvius) Planning and Organization Instruction, 1976; (with Strasser, Aaron and Eales) Fundamentals of Safety Education, 1967, 2d edit., 1973, 3d edit., 1981; (with MacDonald) Power: Mechanics of Energy Control, 1973, 2d edit., 1983; (with Silvius) Organizing Course Materials for Industrial Education, 1961; indsl. arts editor Am. Vocat. Jour., 1963-66. Office: Office Continuing Edn San Jose State U San Jose CA 95192

BOHNSACK, KURT KARL, zoologist, educator; b. Stuttgart, Germany, Mar. 23, 1920; came to U.S., 1923, naturalized, 1941; s. Rudolf Otto and Johanna Marie (Mauser) B.; B.S., Ohio U., 1946; M.S., U. Mich., 1947, Ph.D., 1954; m. Julie Mary Low, June 15, 1946; children—Linda Mae, Richard Carl, Mary Ellen. Instr. zoology, U. Mich., 1950-51; instr., asst. prof. Swarthmore Coll., 1951-56; from asst. prof. to prof. zoology San Diego State U., 1956—; summer faculties Pa. State U., 1954, 55, Ariz. State U., 1971-73, John Carroll U., 1970, Mich. State U., 1978; researcher Arctic Research Lab., Barrow, Alaska, summers 1961-64. Trustee San Diego Natural History Soc., 1966-79. Served with U.S. Army, 1942-45. Research grantee Arctic Inst., 1962, 63, Oak Ridge Nat. Lab., summers 1956, 57. Fellow AAAS; mem. AAUP, Acarol. Soc. Am., Entomol. Soc. Wash., Western Soc. Naturalists, Audubon Soc., Arctic Inst. N. Am., Sigma Xi. Democrat. Unitarian. Editorial bd. Pedobiologia, 1964—; contbr. articles to profl. publs. Home: 5130 Mesa Terrace La Mesa CA 92041 Office: Zoology Dept San Diego State Univ San Diego CA 92182

BOILY, DAVID LAURENT, sales executive; b. Central Falls, R.I., Sept. 12, 1943; s. Norman Eugene and Eleanor Margaret B.; student Boston Coll., 1967-68, Morris County (N.J.) Community Coll., 1973-74, U. Calif., Santa Barbara, 1976; m. Marie Celeste Maccini, Nov. 28, 1964; children—Matthew David, Christopher Marc, Michael Stephen. Asst. mgr. Ara's Inc., Wellesley, Mass., 1966-68; retail rep. Personal Products div. Warner Lambert, Boston, 1968-69, sales rep., Hartford, Conn., 1969-72, nat. sales trainer, Morris Plains, N.J., 1972-73, nat. asst. sales tng. mgr., 1973-76, retail dist. mgr., Los Angeles, 1976-77, dist. mgr., 1977-82; dist. sales mgr. Personal Products div. Lever Bros. Co., Pleasanton, Calif., 1982—. Gen. mgr. Ventura County Youth Football Conf., 1981, commr., 1982. Served with U.S. Navy, 1962-66. Mem. Am. Soc. Tng. and Devel., Non-Food Merchandisers Assn. of the West, Nat. Rifle Assn., Conejo Cowboy Athletic Assn. (sec. 1978, pres. 1979). Home: 1049 Harvest Circle Pleasanton CA 94566 Office: 5776 Stoneridge Mall Rd Suite 160 Pleasanton CA 94566

BOITANO, JAMES DAVID, lawyer; b. Napa, Calif., May 21, 1927; s. David A. and Teresa (Trabucchi) B.; ed. U. Santa Clara, 1944-45, 47-49; J.D., U. San Francisco, 1951; m. Margaret P. Mahoney, Aug. 27, 1955; children—Sarah M., Mary T. Admitted to Calif. bar, 1952; pvt. practice law, 1952-54; ptnr. Dickenson & Boitano, Napa, 1954-62; dist. atty. Napa County, Calif., 1963-83; pub. adminstr., pub. guardian Napa County, 1969-83; ptnr. Dickenson, Peatman & Fogarty, Napa, 1983—; dir. Imperial Savs. & Loan Assn., 1967-74, mem. North Bay adv. bd., 1974-76. Mem. Calif. State Adv. Bd. for Mentally Disturbed, Napa State Hosp., 1971-77, chmn., 1973-77; bd. dirs. Napa County Legal Assistance Agy., 1967-76, Napa Boys Club, Hanna Boys Center, 1966-69, Napa County A.R.C., 1953-56; bd. dirs. Queen of Valley Hosp. Found., 1974-80, pres., 1976-78; mem. Napa County Republican Central Com., 1954-59, chmn., 1958-59; county chmn. Young Reps., 1953-54, Calif. Young Rep. regional v.p., 1954-55; mem. Calif. Rep. Conv. and Central Com., 1956-58. Served with U.S. Mcht. Marine, World War II. Mem. ABA, Calif. State, Napa County (pres. 1966-67) bar assns., Napa County Mental Health Assn. (pres. 1969-70), Big Bros. of Napa County (dir. 1968-71), Native Sons Golden West (pres. Napa Parlor 1957, grand officer 1958-66, grand pres. 1964-65), Sons of Italy. Clubs: Toastmasters (pres. 1959-60), Elks, KC. Home: 2876 Pinewood Dr Napa CA 94558 Office: 809 Coombs St Napa CA 94559

BOIVIN, SHERMAN BURNS, city ofcl.; b. Petaluma, Calif., Mar. 2, 1916; s. Emile Peter and Elsie Viola (Burns) B.; student Santa Rosa (Calif.) Jr. Coll., 1934-37; A.B. with distinction, Stanford U., 1939, M.A., 1940; postgrad. Am. U., 1940-41, Adj. Gen. Sch. U.S. Army, 1942; m. Phoebe Louise Barnes, Jan. 6, 1951; children—Sharon Boivin Roripaugh, Nancy Boivin Vala, Alan. Mem. staff Bur. Budget, Washington, 1941; planning and evaluation officer CAA, Los Angeles, 1946-52; mgmt. engr. U.S. Navy, Pt. Mugu, Calif., 1952-56; with AEC, 1956-71, asst. mgr. Nat. Reactor Testing Sta., Idaho, 1962-67, dept. asst. mgr. econ. and community affairs, Washington, 1967-71; mem. Joint Coll.-Fed. Service Council So. Calif., 1952-56. Mem. exec. bd. Teton Peaks council Boy Scouts Am., Idaho Falls, Idaho, 1965-67; mem. grand jury County of Sonoma, Calif., 1975-76; chmn. Luther Burbank Property adv. com. City of Santa Rosa (Calif.), 1977—. Served to capt. U.S. Army, 1941-46, to lt. col. USAFR. Nat. Inst. Public Affairs intern, 1940-41. Mem. Nat. Assn. Ret. Fed. Employees (past chpt. pres.), Sonoma County Hist. Soc. (dir. 1979—, pres. 1982—), Sonoma County Geneal. Soc. (past pres.), Calif. Hist. Soc., SAR (past chpt. pres.), Hammer and Coffin Soc., Alpha Gamma Sigma, Pi Sigma Alpha. Republican. Home: 2200 Grace Dr Santa Rosa CA 95404

BOL, DOUGLAS JOHN, psychologist; b. Grandville, Mich., July 31, 1935; s. J. Edward and Jean B. (Putnam) B.; m. Marylin J. Seman, July 31, 1954; children—Gary Douglas, Julie Ann. B.B.A., Western Mich. U., 1963; LL.B., LaSalle U., 1960; M.Div., Grand Rapids Bapt. Sem., 1971; M.Ed., U. Ariz., 1972, Ed.D., 1973; Hon. Sc.D., Hanyang U., Seoul, Korea, 1979. Clin. psychologist in pvt. practice, Tucson, 1970—; pres. Inst. Family Living, 1970—; dir., editor Psychology in the Bible, Radio Broadcast, 1973—; adj. prof. Calif.-Grad. Sch. Theology, 1974—; dir. Ministry program Drew U.; pastoral counselor, 1970—; state chaplain Ariz. Army N.G., 1970—; dir. Computer Data Tronics; adj. prof. San Francisco Theol. Sem.; cons. in field. Active Family Life Council of Pima County. Served with U.S. Army, 1966-70. Decorated D.F.C., Bronze Star (5), numerous others. Mem. Pima County Psychol. Assn., Nat. Alliance for Family Life, Am. Personnel and Guidance Assn., Western Assn. Christians for Psychol. Studies, Am. Psychol. Assn., Assn. for Advancement Psychology, Assn. Clin. Pastoral Edn. Author: Principles and Techniques for Family Harmony, 1976; On Target Living, the Key to Self-Fulfillment, 1977; contbr. Tyndale Family Bible Ency., 1978; contbr. articles to profl. jours. Home: 9249 E 39th St Tucson AZ 85710 Office: 8230 E Broadway Suite W5 Tucson AZ 85710

BOLAK, WILLIAM MICHAEL, dentist; b. Nyack, N.Y., Mar. 29, 1951; s. William J. and Dorothy M. (Rose) B.; m. Diane Robinson, Aug. 14, 1971; children—Kimberly Ann, Lauren Marie. B.A. in Chemistry, Cornell U., 1972; D.M.D., Fairleigh Dickinson U., 1976. Pvt. practice dentistry, Alamogordo, N.Mex. Served to capt. USAF, 1976-79. Mem. ADA, Acad. Gen. Dentistry. Office: 901 Delaware Ave Alamogordo NM 88310

BOLAND, JOHN FRANCIS, JR., lawyer; b. Yonkers, N.Y., July 23, 1915; s. John Francis and Celeste (Kinalley) B.; B.A., Fordham U., 1935, J.D., 1946; m. Jean Clayton Smith, Sept. 15, 1942; children—John Francis III, Richard P., Christopher J., Katherine B., Patricia, Anne, Pegeen. Admitted to N.Y. bar, 1946, Ariz. bar, 1949, also U.S. Supreme Ct.; asso. firm McCarthy & Gaynor, White Plains, N.Y., 1946-48, Boland & D'Antonio, Tucson, 1949-50; partner Evans, Kitchel & Jenckes, Phoenix, 1951—; dir. Apache Powder Co., Tucson, Cornelia & Gila Bend R.R. Served to capt. Signal Corps, AUS, 1941-46. Mem. ABA, Ariz., Maricopa County bar assns., AIME (dir. Ariz. conf.), Am. Mining Congress (cons. labor-mgmt. subcoms.). Clubs: Southwestern Yacht; Ariz. Yacht; Univ. (Phoenix). Home: 1102 E Tapatio Dr Phoenix AZ 85020 Office: 2600 N Central Ave 20th Floor Phoenix AZ 85004

BOLDT, GEORGE HUGO, U.S. dist. judge; b. Chgo., Dec. 28, 1903; s. George F. and Christine (Carstensen) B.; A.B., U. Mont., 1925, LL.B., 1926, LL.D., 1961; grad. Command and Gen. Staff Sch., Ft. Leavenworth, 1943; LL.D., Coll. Puget Sound, 1954; m. Eloise Baird, Nov. 17, 1928; children—Joan (Mrs. Hugh Sobottka), Virginia (Mrs. Thomas Riedinger), George B. Admitted to Mont. bar, 1926, Wash. bar, 1928; asso. W. D. Rankin, Helena, Mont., 1926-27; partner Ballinger, Hutson & Boldt, Seattle, 1928-45, Metzger, Blair, Gardner & Boldt, Tacoma, 1945-53; spl. asst. atty. gen. Wash., 1940, 50. U.S. dist. judge, Western dist. Wash., 1953-71, chief judge, 1971, sr. judge, 1971—; chmn. Pay Bd., Nat. Econ. Stablzn. Program, Washington, 1971-73. Ofcl. U.S. rep. 1st UN Congress on prevention of crime and treatment of offenders, Geneva, Switzerland, 1955; mem. U.S. Jud. Conf. Com. on Adminstrn. of Criminal Law and Standing Com. on Rules of Practice and Procedure for Fed. Cts., mem. adv. com. on appellate rules; Jud. Conf. rep. on sec. state's adv. com. on pvt. internat. law; mem. adv. com. on ops. and appraisal Fed. Jud. Center; trustee U. Mont. Found., 1975-76; trustee U. Puget Sound; chmn. bd. visitors Law Sch., U. Puget Sound, 1972-76. Served as lt. col. AUS, World War II. Mem. Inst. Jud. Adminstrn., Internat. Inst. Juridical Studies (mem. gen. scientific com.), Am. Judicature Soc., Am., Wash. State, Pierce County bar assns., Am. Legion, Am. Law Inst., Sigma Chi. Republican. Presbyterian. Mason (32deg., Shriner). Mem. editorial bd. Manual for Complex and Multidistrict Litigation. US Courthouse Seattle WA 98104*

BOLDUAN, NILS WILLIAM, physician; b. N.Y.C., July 21, 1907; s. Charles Frederick and Adele (Jonssen) B.; A.B., Columbia, 1929; M.D., Cornell, 1933; m. Marie Louise Wagner, Sept. 15, 1937; children—Michael, Jonathan, David; m. 2d, Margaret Bailey, June 24, 1969. Intern, Bellevue Hosp., N.Y.C., 1934-35, resident pediatrics, 1935-37; instr. pediatrics N.Y. U. Med. Sch., N.Y.C., 1935-42; jr. attending physician Lenox Hill Hosp., N.Y.C., 1937-42; med. dir. Scarsdale (N.Y.) Sch. System, 1939-42; practice medicine, specializing in pediatrics, Forest Hills, N.Y., 1939-42, Santa Barbara, Calif., 1946-67; staff Regional Med. Program, Santa Barbara, 1967-72; research physiologist U. Calif. at Santa Barbara, 1969—. Mem. Santa Barbara Health Bd., 1948-55; active Children's Home Soc., 1973-74; chmn. Republican Central com., Santa Barbara, 1954. Served to maj. AUS, 1942-46. Diplomate Am. Bd. Pediatrics. Mem. Santa Barbara County Med. Soc., AMA, Calif. Med. Assn., Los Angeles, SW pediatric socs., Am. Acad. Pediatrics, Mental Health Assn. Santa Barbara (pres. 1975), Santa Barbara Mus. Natural History. Republican. Episcopalian. Contbr. articles in field to med. jours. Home: 2130 Emerson Ave Santa Barbara CA 93103 Office: Univ of Calif at Santa Barbara Goleta CA 93017

BOLEN, JOHN E., art dealer; b. Ft. Gordon, Ga., Aug. 27, 1953; s. James Leon and Peggy Jean (Sandstrom) B.; m. Lynne N. Uyeda, July 25, 1976; children—James L., Katherine L. B.A., UCLA, 1975. Dir., Bolen Gallery Inc., Santa Monica, Calif., 1978—, Los Angeles, 1981—, Bolen Publ., Playa del Rey, Calif., 1979—; cons., tchr., art appraiser. Mem. Art Dealers Assn. Calif. (v.p., dir.), Am. Contract Bridge League. Pub. original graphics, art catalogs, monographs. Office: Bolen Art Gallery 2904 Main St Santa Monica CA 90405

BOLEN, LYNNE N., art dealer; b. San Diego, Feb. 19, 1954; d. Leon R. and Maria N. (Ishida) Uyeda; m. John E. Bolen, July 25, 1976; children—James L. III, Katherine L. B.S., UCLA, 1976, postgrad., 1976-79. Dir., Bolen Gallery Inc., Santa Monica, Calif., 1978—, Los Angeles, 1981—, Bolen Pub., Playa Del Rey, Calif., 1979—. Mem. Art Dealers Assn. Calif. (sec., dir.), Am. Contract Bridge League, Pub. original graphics, art catalogs, monographs. Office: Bolen Gallery Inc 2904 Main St Santa Monica CA 90405

BOLES, JOHN JOSEPH, economist; b. Waterville, Maine, June 3, 1924; s. Thomas and Mary (Saad) B.; B.S., U. Va., 1947, M.A., 1949; Ph.D. (Fulbright prof.), U. Cairo (Egypt), 1952; m. Diane Lindsay Durand, Aug. 27, 1955; children—Thomas, Hilary, Maria, Patricia, Christa. Govt. liaison rep. Arabian Am. Oil Co., Saudi Arabia, 1951-52; instr. econs. Loyola U., 1953-56, asst. prof., 1956-57; asst. prof. econs. Marquette U., Milw., dir. Middle East Inst., 1957-60; economist, Los Angeles, 1961—; Middle East oil economist, govt. affairs dir. Occidental Petroleum Corp., Los Angeles, 1965-75; pres. ISACO, Inc., Ojai, Calif., 1975—. Bd. dirs. St. Jude Hosp. Found., Memphis, Am. Arab Assn. Commerce and Industry Inc. Mem. Am. Econ. Assn., Am. Polit. Sci. Assn. Author: Monetary System of Saudi Arabia; Foreign Trade System of USSR. Contbr. articles to profl. jours. Home: 804 Country Club Rd Ojai CA 93023

BOLES, ROBERT DOWN, realtor; b. Bakersfield, Calif., Dec. 31, 1929; s. Ralph D. and Delia (DeRoos) B.; certificate in Real Estate, U. Calif. Extension at Berkeley, 1962; m. Mary Ellen Chaffin, Mar. 5, 1954; children—Ronald D., Lori D. Gen. sales A.J. Puglizivich Real Estate Co., 1955-57; partner, officer Dome Realty, Inc., 1957-59; partner Boles Branco Realtors, 1959-62; owner Boles Realty, 1962—, South Lake Tahoe, Calif., 1962—; partner BFC Developers, 1963—, Boles & Farr Constrn. & Real Estate Investment Co., 1964— (all Merced, Calif.); pres. Merced Trust Deed & Mfg. Co., 1962—, Tahoe Constrn., Inc., 1972-79, Cargo Properties Inc. Tchr. real estate Adult Edn., Merced, 1960, Merced Jr. Coll., 1962. Chmn., adv. bd. Salvation Army, Merced, 1960-65. Served with USAAF, 1948-52. Mem. Lake Tahoe C. of C. (dir.), Merced County (past pres.), South Lake Tahoe (pres. 1968) bd. realtors, Calif. Real Estate Assn. (state dir.), Nat. Assn. Real Estate Brokers, Real Estate Certificate Inst., Am. Real Estate Assn., Am. Legion. Elk, Mason. Club: Heavenly Valley Ski. Home: PO Box 10780 Zephyr Cove NV 89448 Office: PO Box 10990 Zephyr Cove NV 89448

BOLET, ALBERTO, condr.; b. Havana, Cuba, Sept. 10, 1905; s. Antonio and Adelina (Tremoleda) B.; came to U.S., 1968, naturalized, 1974; studied at Inst. 2d Ensenanza, Havana, 1918-21, Real Conservatorie de Musica, Madrid, 1922-24, Conservatoir de Paris, 1924-26. m. Rosa Suavez, Mar. 3, 1950; children—Alberto, Armando, Adela Maria. Violinist ch. music, various cities; dir. music various theatres Paris, Madrid, Havana; music dir., condr. Philharmonic, Havana, 1952-59, Bilbao (Spain) Symphony, 1963-68; music dir. Long Beach (Calif.) Symphony, 1968-79, Bakersfield, Calif., 1972-75, Rio Hondo Symphony, 1972-76, San Bernardino (Calif.) Symphony, 1976-81, Downey (Calif.) Symphonic Orch., 1980; prof. music Fullerton U., 1971-72. Recipient Caflos M. de Cespedes S.Am. award. Rotarian. Club: Long Beach Torch. Home: 6328 E 5th Long Beach CA 90803

BOLEY, HAL DAVID, naturalist, educator; b. Los Angeles, Mar. 8, 1947; s. Clarence W. and Dorothy L. (Alles) B.; m. Jennifer L., Nov. 23, 1971; children—Lindsay J., Tanner D. B.A. in Biology, Calif. State U., 1970, M.A. in Biology, 1974. Park naturalist, mgr. El Dorado East Regional Park, City of Long Beach, 1969—, outdoor recreation supr.

1979—; instr. Calif. Community Coll., cons. in open space planning. Recipient Biol. Research award So. Calif. Acad. Sci., 1972, Environ. Planning award Calif. Parks and Recreation Soc., 1971. Mem. Alliance Wildlife Rehab. and Edn., Calif. Park and Recreation Soc. Republican. Office: 7550 E Spring St Long Beach CA 90815

BOLGER, BRENNA MERCIER, public relations executive; b. Toledo, Dec. 26, 1942; d. Ray E. and Madalyn (Mercier) B. B.A. magna cum laude, Santa Clara U., 1964. Exec. v.p. Coakley-Heagerty Advt., Santa Clara, Calif., 1962-74; pres., owner PRX, Cupertino, Calif., 1975—; cons. Peninsula Vols., Adult & Child Guidance Clinic, Ctr. for Living with Dying, Am. Lung Assn., Peninsula Oral Sch. for Deaf, Inst. Med. Research, Ind. Aging, Mitty High Sch. Named Women of Achievement, San Jose Mercury News, 1972. Mem. San Jose Mus. Art, San Jose Symphony. Mem. Pub. Relations Soc. Am. (assoc.), Peninsula Press Club, Hosp. Pub. Relations Assn. Roman Catholic. Address: 10350 S DeAnza Blvd Suite 2-H Cupertino CA 95014

BOLIN, RICHARD LUDDINGTON, industrial development consultant; b. Burlington, Vt., May 13, 1923; s. Axel Birger and Eva Madora (Luddington) B.; m. Jeanne Marie Brown, Dec. 18, 1948; children—Richard Luddington, Jr., Douglas, Judith, Barbara, Elizabeth. B.S. in Chem. Engring., Tex. A&M U., 1947; M.S. in Chem.Engring., MIT, 1950. Jr. research engr. Humble Oil & Refining Co., Baytown, Tex., 1947-49; staff mem. Arthur D. Little, Inc., Cambridge, Mass., 1950-56, Carribean office mgr. San Juan, 1957-61, gen. mgr., Mex., 1961-72; pres. Internat. Parks, Inc., Flagstaff, Ariz., 1973—; dir. The Flagstaff Inst., 1976—; dir. Parque Indsl. de Nogales, Nogales, Sonora, Mex. Served with U.S. Army, 1942-46. Club: University (Mex.). Office: PO Box 986 Flagstaff AZ 86002

BOLIN, WILLIAM HARVEY, banker; b. Dallas, Dec. 8, 1922; s. William Harvey and Bertha Adelia (Dickey) B.; m. Emma Jane Davis, July 9, 1949; children—Teresa Bolin Gonzalez, Patricia Bolin Wade. B.A. in Internat. Relations, U. Calif.-Berkeley, 1947; postgrad. Nat. U. Mex., 1948. Trainee, Bank of Am., San Francisco, 1947-56, asst. v.p., 1956-57, br. mgr., Guatemala, 1957-60, asst. v.p. Middle East and Africa div., San Francisco, 1960, v.p. div., 1961, v.p., head Latin Am. div., 1965-68, sr. v.p., 1968-75, exec. v.p. Latin Am. Caribbean div., 1975-81, exec. v.p., head world banking div., San Francisco, 1981, vice chmn., head world banking div., San Francisco, 1982—. Dir. Banca d'America d'Italia. Trustee, Overseas Devel. Council, World Affairs Council; active San Francisco Com. Foreign Relations. Served as capt. U.S. Army, 1942-45; to maj. USAR, 1946-59. Decorated Order Francisco de Miranda (Venezuela). Mem. San Francisco World Trade Assn., Am. Bankers Assn. (chmn. internat. banking div.), Council of Americas and Americas Soc. (dir.), Pan Am. Soc. (dir.), Bankers Assn. Fgn. Trade, Inst. Internat. Fin. (founding mem.). Mem. Ch. of Christ. Clubs: Bankers, Villa, Taverna, World Trade, Commonwealth (San Francisco). Office: Bank Am 555 California St San Francisco CA 94137

BOLINDER, ROBERT DONALD, supermarket exec.; b. Sacramento, Sacramento, Apr. 25, 1931; s. Eldon L. and Rose (Zitting) B.; B.S., Brigham Young U., 1956; M.B.A., U. Calif. at Berkeley, 1958; grad. advanced mgmt. program, Harvard, 1968; m. Trudi S. Beer, June 16, 1954; children—Kurt E., Sonia L., Heidi M., Kari Ann, Tina D., Erik J., Remi S., Clint R. Journalist, typographer No. Sacramento Jour., 1947-50; mgr., accountant Touche, Ross, Bailey & Smart, San Francisco, 1956-65; exec. v.p. adminstrn. and fin., treas. Albertson's Inc., Bosie, Idaho, 1965-72, pres., 1972-80, vice chmn., chief exec. officer, from 1974, now chief fin. and adminstrv. officer; dir. Idaho Power Co.; instr. U. Calif. Extension Sch., Berkeley, 1959-65. Pres. Idaho Taxpayers Assn., Boise, 1974; mem. advisory council Coll. Bus. Brigham Young U., bd. dirs. Bogus Basin Ski Assn., chmn. Boise United Way of Ada County, 1965-67. Served with USAF, 1950-54. C.P.A. Calif., Idaho. Mem. Nat. Assn. Accountants (pres.), Am. Inst. C.P.A.'s, Fin. Execs. Inst., Western Assn. Food Chains (dir.), Greater Boise C. of C. (pres. 1972), Idaho Assn. Commerce and Industry (dir.), Phi Kappa Phi, Beta Alpha Psi, Beta Gamma Sigma. Republican. Mormon. Office: Albertson's Inc 250 Parkcenter Blvd Boise ID 83726*

BOLINGBROKE, ROBERT A., grocery product exec.; b. Rexburg, Idaho, May 2, 1938; s. Delbert Thomas and Ina Leota (Andersen) B.; m. Marilyn Joan Wolfe, Sept. 16, 1961; children—Debbie, Cindy, Tami. Student Dartmouth Coll., 1956-57; B.A., Wash. State U., 1960; M.B.A., Stanford U., 1962. With Clorox Co., Oakland, Calif., 1962—, successively advt. dept. trainee, br. mgr., advt. mgr., gen. mgr. grocery store products Grocery Products Div., Household Products Div., v.p. Kingsland div., v.p. bus. devel., 1983—. Pres. Mt. Diablo council Boy Scouts Am. Mormon. Office: 1221 Broadway Oakland CA 94612

BOLINGER, BRUCE CLYDE, county ofcl.; b. Madison, Wis., Nov. 13, 1936; s. Dwight LeMerton and Louise Ida (Schrynemakers) B.; B.A. (Falk Found. grantee), Pomona Coll., 1958; M.A., UCLA, 1960; postgrad. U. So. Calif., 1967-70. Instr. dept. social sci. Santa Monica (Calif.) City Coll., 1965, Los Angeles City Coll., 1969, East Los Angeles Coll., 1971-72; lectr. dept. polit. sci. Calif. State U., Fullerton, 1970-71, Calif. State U., Long Beach, 1971-72; research asso. Inst. on Law and Urban Studies, Los Angeles, 1971-72; legis. asst. Congressman George E. Brown, Jr., 1973-74; staff dir. Joint Com. for Revision of Elections Code, Calif. Legislature, 1975-76; prin. cons. Com. on Elections and Reapportionment, Calif. State Assembly, Sacramento, 1977-79; dist. mgr. U.S. Census Bur., 1979-80; county clk.-recorder Nevada County (Calif.), Nevada City, 1980—. Mem. Los Angeles County Charter Revision Com., 1961; vice chmn. Los Angeles County Election Devices Com., 1966-68; mem. ethics and elections com. Nat. Conf. State Legislatures, 1978-79. Served with U.S. Army, 1962-64. Calif. Assembly fellow, 1960-61; Calif. State fellow, 1968-69. Mem. Am. Polit. Sci. Assn., Western Polit. Sci. Assn., County Clks. Assn., County Recorders Assn. Calif., Phi Beta Kappa, Pi Sigma Alpha. Home: 12704 Butterfly Dr Nevada City CA 95959 Office: County Courthouse Nevada City CA 95959

BOLINGER, TRUMAN, sculptor; b. Sheridan, Wyo., Dec. 3, 1944; s. Claude and Cora (Fowler) B.; m. Bonnie Beaucage, Oct. 31, 1966 (div. 1979); children—Kiki Cherie, Travis Justin; m. 2d, Sherrie Berry, June 4, 1983. Student Colo. Inst. Art, Denver, 1964-65, Art Students League, N.Y.C., 1968-69. One man shows: Washington, 1971, Wyo. State Art Gallery, 1971, Hammer Gallery, N.Y.C., 1975, 76, 79, 83, Seaport Village San Diego, 1981; group shows include: Northwestern Nat. Bank, Mpls., 1974, 75, Nat. Cowboy Hall of Fame, 1975; represented in permanent collections: Minn. Hist. Soc., Mpls., First Fed. Savs. Collection, Phoenix. Republican. Scientologist. Contbr. articles to profl. jours. Home: 8802 N 86th St Scottsdale AZ 85254

BOLKA, ARNOLD ROBERT, public relations executive, licensing consultant; b. Bronx, N.Y., Apr. 3, 1924; s. Max and Sylvia (Kollin) B.; m. Muriel Liebowitz, June 23, 1946; children—Sindy Ann Bolka Martin, Scott Ian, Matt Kollin. Student NYU. Pub. relations exec. W. Colston Leigh Inc., Cunard Line, Toy Guidance Council; owner, operator Arnold R. Bolka Pub. Relations Co., N.Y.C., 1963—; founder, pub. The Licensing Letter, 1977—, Ofcl. Register Lic. Products, 1983; founder, exec. dir. Lic. Industry Assn., 1979-82, Lic. Merchandisers' Assn., 1982—; lic. cons., speaker. Served with USAF, 1943-46. Office: 200 Park Ave Suite 303 E New York NY 10166

BOLLERT, JOE A., research biologist; b. Lansing, Mich., Jan. 14, 1943; s. Clare A. and Louise I. (King) B.; m. Bonnie J. Hines, Nov. 23, 1962; children—Joe A., Robert J. B.A., Kalamazoo Coll., 1965; M.S., Mich. State U., 1967, Ph.D., 1969. Instr., Sch. Human Medicine, Mich. State U., 1968; scientist The Upjohn Co., Kalamazoo, 1969-73, clin. research asso. 1973-76; exec. v.p. Inst. Biol. Research and Devel., Newport Beach, Calif., 1976—. Active Boy Scouts Am. Mem. Am. Group Practice Assn. Republican. Mem. South Coast Community Ch. Club: Sierra. Home: 908 Almond Pl Newport Beach CA 92660 Office: 901 Dove St 165 Newport Beach CA 92660

BOLLES, CHARLES AVERY, librarian; b. Pine Island, Minn., Aug. 10, 1940; s. Arthur Marston and Clarice Ione (Figy) B.; B.A., U. Minn., 1962, M.A. in Library Sci., 1963, M.A. in Am. Studies, 1969, Ph.D. in Library Sci., 1975; m. Marjorie Elaine Hancock, May 17, 1964; children—Jason Brice, Justin Brian. Catalog and serials librarian U. Iowa, Iowa City, 1964-67; asst. prof. Emporia (Kans.) State U., 1970-76; dir. library devel. div. Kans. State Library, 1976-78; dir. Sch. Library Sci., Emporia State U., 1978-80; state librarian State of Idaho, Boise, 1980—; computer services council Wash. Library Network; bd. dirs. Pacific N.W. Bibliog. Center. Mem. ALA, Pacific N.W. Library Assn., Idaho Library Assn. Office: 325 W State St Boise ID 83702

BOLLES, RICHARD NELSON, clergyman, author; b. Milw., Mar. 19, 1927; s. Donald Clinton and Frances Fethers (Fifield) B.; student M.I.T., 1946-48; B.A. cum laude, Harvard U., 1950; S.T.B., Gen. Sem., 1953, S.T.M., 1957; m. Janet Price, Dec. 30, 1949 (div. Feb. 1971); children—Stephen, Mark, Gary, Sharon. Ordained to ministry Protestant Episcopal Ch. as deacon, 1953, as priest, 1953; fellow, tutor Gen. Sem., N.Y.C., 1953-55; vicar St. James Ch., Ridgefield, N.J., 1955-58; rector St. John's Ch., Passaic, N.J., 1958-66; canon pastor Grace Cathedral, San Francisco, 1966-68; nat. staff mem. United Ministries in Higher Edn., Walnut Creek, Calif., 1968—, dir. Nat. Career Devel. Project, 1974—. Served with USNR, 1945-46. Fellow Coll. Preachers, Washington; mem. Am. Soc. Tng. and Devel., Mensa. Author: What Color Is Your Parachute? A Practical Guide for Job-Hunters and Career Changers, 1972, 83; Where Do I Go From Here With My Life, 1974, The Three Boxes of Life and How To Get Out of Them, 1978; creator Quick Job-Hunting Map; editor Newsletter about Life/Work Planning, 1974—. Address: PO Box 379 Walnut Creek CA 94597

BOLLING, CHERIE ROSEMARIE, video productionist, consumer advocate; b. Southgate, Calif., Dec. 13, 1939; d. Russell Alonzo and Violet Drucilla (Van Cleave) Drake; A.A., Santa Monica City Coll., 1959; B.S., UCLA, 1963; postgrad. Calif. State U., Northridge, 1979—; m. William Edward, July 1, 1960; children—William Edward, Dennis Keith, Richard Lee. Grievance chmn. Consumers United, Palo Alto, Calif., 1962-64, chmn. bd., 1974-76; pres. TV prodn. co., 1976—; pres. Mine, Yours and Ours, 1982—; lectr. consumer problems, 1962-76; mem. Santa Clara County Adv. Commn. on Consumer Affairs, 1974-76; radio commentator KZSU, Stanford, Calif., 1972-76; head prodn. Teleprompter cable TV studio, pub. access div., hostess weekly consumer affairs program Channel 6B, Milpitas, Calif., 1975-76. Dir. mil. dependents sch., Athens, Greece, 1962-63; interior designer, clothing designer Athens, 1962, Mannheim, also Heidelburg, Germany, 1963-65. Mem. Beta Sigma Phi. Home: 25142 Ericson Way Laguna Hills CA 92653

BOLLINGER, ORAN EDWARD ASA, clergyman; b. Fresno, Calif., Feb. 21, 1914; s. Archie A. and Edna (Hamilton) B.; B.A., Chapman Coll., 1939; M.Div., Coll. Bible, Lexington, Ky., 1951; Dr. Psychology, Sussex (Eng.) U., 1964; m. Christina Cattell, Apr. 14, 1961; children—Lynda Lou (Mrs. Dunn), Stephen Fred, David, Laura. Ordained ministry Christian Ch., 1939; minister Christian Ch., College City, Colusa, Visalia, Calif., 1939-45, Carrollton, Ky., 1948-51, Ukiah, Calif., 1954-60, Gridley, Calif., 1960-64; vocations counselor Calif. State Dept. Employment, 1961-64; dir. Merced County Welfare Dept., 1968-69; exec. dir. Kings County OEO, 1969-71; minister 1st Christian Ch., Turlock, Calif., 1970-79. Pres., Turlock Pastors Fellowship, 1975. Dir. Civil Def., Ukiah, 1955-60; dir. Nev. County Welfare, later dir. Imperial County Welfare Dept. Served from first lt. to capt. AUS, 1945-47, capt. to maj., 1951-54, lt. col. Res. Mem. Inst. Family Relations. Mason (32 deg.). Author: Meditations from the Pastor's Window, 1941; The French Franc Speaks, 1953; Penny Power Recipes, 1970. Home: 1010 Edwards Dr Turlock CA 95380

BOLLWINKEL, TED WALKER, architect; b. American Falls, Idaho, Nov. 30, 1936; s. John Murray and Erma B.; B.S., Idaho State U., 1965; postgrad. Utah State U., 1969-70; m. Billie Kay Bean, July 2, 1962; children—Tonja, Derek, Samuel, Kari, Lara. Project mgr. Cedric M. Allen, Pocatello, Idaho, 1965-69, Glen H. Lloyd, Salt Lake City, 1970-71, Brixen & Christopher, Salt Lake City, 1971-72 (all architects); mgr. real estate/architecture Mountain Bell Telephone Co., Salt Lake City, 1972—; prin. Studio 110, Architects and Planners, Salt Lake City, 1972—. Merit badge counselor Boy Scouts Am.; area supr. Republican Com. Served with USAF, 1954-58. Recipient grant Utah State U., 1969-70; Western Region Design award AT&T, 1976. Mem. AIA (nat. chmn. elect architects in industry com.), Am. Planning Assn., Nat. Rifle Assn. Mormon. Office: 3033 N 3d St Phoenix AZ 85021

BOLTHOUSE, FREDERICK JOHN, food company executive; b. Muskegon, Mich., Sept 7, 1935; s. Harold Alvin and Clara (DeKiep) B.; m. Nancy Lee Teunis, Dec. 28, 1954; children—Douglas Alan, Dale Eugene, Dawn Ilene, Karen Lee, Karla Lyn. B.S., Western Mich. U., 1959, M.B.A., 1965. With Gen. Foods Corp., various locations, 1959-73; sr. v.p. Lamb Weston, Amfac Foods, Inc., Portland, Oreg., 1973-80, pres. Pacific Pearl Seafoods div., Bellevue, Wash., 1980—. Served with USNR, 1954-56. Office: 1203 114th Ave SE Bellevue WA 98004

BOLY, JEFFREY ELWYN, lawyer; b. Portland, Oreg., Mar. 16, 1942; s. Elwyn and Frances Rolland (Hulse) B.; A.B., Georgetown U., 1964; J.D., U. Calif., San Francisco, 1967; m. Diane Edna Davis, Jan. 8, 1976; children—Jeffrey Elwyn, Teresa, Justin, Craig. Admitted to Calif. bar, 1967, Oreg. bar, 1971; trial atty. Office Chief Counsel to Commr. Internal Revenue, San Francisco, 1967-71; partner firm Wood, Tatum, Mosser, Brooke & Holden, Portland, Oreg., 1971—. Trustee, Portland Civic Theatre, 1975-81, pres. bd., 1979-80; bd. dirs. Oreg. Advocates for Arts, 1980—, pres. bd., 1981-82. Mem. Am. Bar Assn., Oreg. State Bar (officer taxation and estate planning sects.), Calif. State Bar Assn., Multnomah County Bar Assn., Georgetown U. Alumni Assn. (pres. Portland chpt. 1977). Democrat. Roman Catholic. Home: 2879 SW Champlain Dr Portland OR 97201 Office: Suite 1300 1001 SW 5th Ave Portland OR 97204

BOMBERGER, AUDREY SHELLEY, hospital educator, nurse, consultant; b. Lebanon, Pa., June 12, 1942; d. Allen A. and Ruth M. (Arnold) Shelley; m. Edward K. Bomberger, Sept. 29, 1963; children—Beth Ann, Gary Allen. R.N., Reading Med. Center, 1963; B.S. in Edn., Millersville State Coll., 1974; M.S. in Edn., Temple U., 1979; Ph.D. in Health Service Adminstrn., Columbia Pacific U., 1983. Cert. nursing adminstr. Staff nurse Hershey (Pa.) Hosp., 1963-64; charge nurse Good Samaritan Hosp., Lebanon, Pa., 1964-65, VA Med. Center, Lebanon, 1965-70, Lebanon Valley Gen. Hosp., 1970-75, dir. edn., 1975-79; dir. edn. St. Mary's Hosp., Reno, 1979—; cons. to nurse educators, Lebanon; lectr. on radiation U. Va., Med. Inst. Tech., Green Bay, Wis. Served to maj. USAR Nurse Corps, 1977—. Fellow Anglo-Am. Acad. (hon.); mem. Am. Nurses Assn., Nat. League of Nurses, Nev. Nurses Assn., Am. Soc. Health Edn. and Tng. of Am. Hosp. Assn. (cert. achievement 1982), Res. Officers Assn., Am. Heart Assn., Nat. Inst. Critical Care Edn. Author: Radiation: For Health Care Providers, 1984; contbr. articles to profl. jours. Home: 1590 Zolezzi Ln Reno NV 89511 Office: 235 W 6th St Reno NV 89502

BOMES, STEPHEN D., lawyer; b. Providence, Jan. 15, 1948; s. Edward and Lillian (Dick) B.; m. Michele Dawn Ross, Dec. 19, 1981. B.S. in Fin., Boston U., 1968; J.D., U. Calif.-Hastings Coll. Law, 1971; postgrad. Columbia U. Sch. Law, 1973; LL.M., NYU, 1975. Bar: Calif. 1972, D.C. 1973, N.Y., Fla. 1975. Instr. Hastings Coll. Law, 1971-73; adj. asst. prof. CUNY, 1973-74; instr. law NYU, 1973-75; assoc. Milbank, Tweed, Hadley & McCloy, N.Y.C., 1975-81; ptnr. Brobeck, Phleger & Harrison, San Francisco, 1981—. Mem. World Wildlife Fund, Mus. Soc. San Francisco. Mem. Bar Assn. City of N.Y., N.Y. State Bar Assn., Fla. Bar Assn., State Bar Calif., Bar Assn. San Francisco, D.C. Bar Assn., ABA. Clubs: NYU, Barcave of London, Commonwealth of San Francisco. Author: Real Estate Transfer, Development and Finance, 1975; The Dead Hand: The Last Grasp?, 1976. Home: San Francisco CA 94118 Office: 1 Market Plaza Spear St Tower 28th Floor San Francisco CA 94105

BOMMAREDDY, APPIREDDY, ophthalmologist; b. Pamarru, India, Mar. 1, 1943; came to U.S., 1972, naturalized, 1982; s. Gangireddy and Anasuya (Tamma) B.; m. Uma M. Tamma,; children—Padma Sailaja, Padma Sereesha, Kamala Sudheera. M.B.B.S., Andhra U., 1964, M.S., 1969; M.D., Wayne State U., 1977. Civil asst. surgeon Govt. Infectious Diseases Hosp. Guntur, A.P., India, 1964-66; postgrad. tng. ophthalmology Andhra (India) U., 1966-69; asst. prof. ophthalmology Andhra U., 1969-72; intern Mercy Hosp., Des Moines, Iowa, 1972-73; resident in gen. psychiatry U. Va., Richmond, 1974-75; resident in ophthalmology Wayne State U., Detroit, 1975-77; practice medicine specializing in ophthalmology, Merced, Calif., 1977—; pres. ARB Reddy M.D., Inc., 1977—; mem. staff Mercy Hosp., Community Hosp., Merced, 1977. Mem. Merced-Mariposa Med. Soc., Calif. Med. Assn., Calif. Assn. Ophthalmologists, AMA.

BONACINA, JOSEPH ANDREW, ret. lawyer, writer; b. Gravedona, Italy, Oct. 30, 1903; s. Antonio and Annunciata (Riella) B.; Ph.B., U. Santa Clara, 1927, J.D., 1931; postgrad. Humboldt State Coll., 1926; m. Clare M. Valle, Nov. 28, 1928 (dec. May 1981); m. Elien S. Stark, Dec. 5, 1981. Newspaper reporter San Jose (Calif.) Mercury Herald, San Jose News, San Francisco Examiner, 1923-36; dep. county clk., ct. clk. Santa Clara County, 1935-41; city atty. City of Sunnyvale (Calif.), 1942-48; practice, San Jose, 1951—; city atty. City of Campbell (Calif.), 1952-71, emeritus, 1971—; now writer. Clubs: Rinconada Country, KC (4 deg.). Home: 15215 Sobey Rd Saratoga CA 95070

BONADURER, GRACE LAURA, data processing consultant, computer science educator; b. Tacoma, Apr. 13, 1931; d. William Byron and Helen Clarabelle (Dean) Hipsley; m. Rex William Greer, July 1949; children—Dona, Helen, James, John; m. 2d. Robert Max Bonadurer, Aug. 15, 1969. B.A. in Edn., Osego State U., 1970, Ph.D., in Edn., 1972; M.A. in Bus. Adminstrn., Margaret Mears Meml. U., 1972. Cert. tchr., N.Y.; cert. data processor. Programmer/analyst Xerox Corp., Webster, N.Y., 1968-70; data processing tchr. pub. high sch., Wayne-Fingerlakes, Williamson, N.Y., 1970-72; mgmt. systems specialist Lockheed Calif. Corp., Burbank, 1973-80; programmer, instr. TRW Co., Redondo Beach, Calif., 1980-81; pvt. practice as computer instr., cons., L & B Co., Redondo Beach, Calif., 1981—; instr. UCLA, 1978-79. Mem. Calif. Hist. Soc., So. Calif. Hist. Soc., T.R. Wilcox Trainers Assn. So. Calif., Nat. Vocat. Tchrs. Assn. (life), Am. Aerospace Mgmt. Assn., Software/Hardware Assn. Related Engrs., Guild United IBM Indsl. Data Processing Engrs., Data Processing Mgmt. Assn. Redondo Beach C. of C. Democrat. Office: L & B Co PO Box 913 Redondo Beach CA 90277

BONADURER, ROBERT MAX, systems analyst, consultant; b. Portland, Oreg., Apr. 23, 1941; s. John Max and Magaline Mary (McClay) B.; m. G. Laura Hipsley Greer, Aug. 15, 1969; B.S. in Indsl. Tech., Calif. State U.-Long Beach, 1964; M.B.A., Calif. State U.-Fullerton, 1966. Cert. data processor. Programmer, McDonnell-Douglas Corp., Long Beach, Calif., 1967-69; systems analyst Xerox Corp.-BPG, Webster, N.Y., 1969-72; project leader, sr. analyst Am. Honda Motor Co., Gardena, Calif., 1972-79; cons. adminstrv. services data processing Airesearch Mfg. Co. div. Garrett Corp., Torrance, Calif., 1979—. Mem. (Nat. Mgmt. Assn. (v.p. 1968), Data Processing Mgmt. Assn., Assn. Systems Analysts, Calif. Hist. Soc., So. Calif. Hist. Soc., Alpha Gamma Sigma. Home: 218 N Prospect Ave Redondo Beach CA 90277

BONANT, MICHELE YVONNE, health educator; b. Pitts.; d. Joseph Michael and Catherine Joanne (Conti) B. B.S. summa cum laude, Calif State U., 1971, M.P.H., 1975, postgrad., 1976-78. Humanities reference asst. Calif. State U., 1973-80; coordinator patient and community edn. Saint John's Hosp. and Health Ctr., Santa Monica, Calif., 1980—. Granada Hills Bus. and Profl. Women's Club scholar, 1967-68. Mem. Am. Pub. Health Assn., Am. Soc. Healthcare Edn. and Tng., Soc. Pub. Health Edn., Phi Kappa Phi. Contbr. in field. Office: 1328 22d St Santa Monica CA 90404

BONAR, JOHN ROBERT, microelectronics company official, consultant; b. West Liberty, W.Va., May 23, 1937; s. John R. and Katherine L. (Harris) B. B.S., Fla. State U., 1961, M.S., 1966, Ph.D., 1972, postgrad., 1980-82. Research and devel. chemist U.S. Phosphoric Products Corp./Nitram Chems., Tampa, Fla., 1961-64; asst. dean edn., assoc. dean student affairs, asst. prof. higher edn., research assoc. Fla. State U., Tallahassee, 1964-77; sr. edn. and tng. cons., mgr. corp. edn. and tng. B.F. Goodrich Co., Akron, Ohio, 1977-80; mgr. tng. and devel. Medtronic/Micro-Rel, Tempe, Ariz., 1980—; cons. edn. and tng. Active Jr. Achievement, 4-H Club. Mem. Am. Soc. Tng. and Devel., Am. Soc. Personnel Adminstrn. (accredited personnel diplomate), Am. Mgmt. Assn., Phi Kappa Phi, Phi Theta Kappa, Kappa Delta Pi. Republican. Club: Elks. Contbr. articles profl. jours. Office: 2343 W 10th Pl Tempe AZ 85281

BONAR, ROLAND BIRT, ednl. adminstr.; b. El Paso, Tex., Jan. 24, 1932; s. Bernard E. and Dorothy L. (Birt) B.; student Calif. Inst. Tech., 1951-54, U. Tex. at El Paso, 1957-62; L.H.D., Lincoln Meml. U., 1968; Ph.D., Columbia U., 1972; children—Robert James, Marla Lynn, Michael G. Vice-pres., gen. mgr. Western GMC Truck Co., El Paso, 1955-60; tchr. Dale Carnegie courses N.Mex. and W. Tex., 1960-66; prin. Roland B. Bonar & Assos., presenting Dale Carnegie courses, Balt., 1966-73, Denver, 1973—; past pres. Dale Carnegie Internat. Sponsors Assn.; guest lectr. U. Md., 1968-74; chmn. bd. Explorex Oil Co., Houston, 1975—; chmn. First Savs. & Loan of Orland Park, Chgo.; dir. Transportes de Ref de Mex. S.A., Bombas Turbinas de Mex. S.A., B & M Oil Co., N.Mex. Vice-pres. Denver area Boy Scouts Am., 1973—; chmn. fin. Denver area council Cancer Soc., 1964—, fin. dir., 1974-75; mem. Pres. Johnson's Council on Mental Retardation, 1965-68; mem. cabinet Mile Hi United Way, 1978—; bd. dirs. Colo. Boys Ranch, 1976—, Balt. Cystic Fibrosis Found., 1966-70; trustee Lincoln Meml. U., 1969-80, Luth. Social Services Colo. Served with USAF, 1949-54; Korea. Decorated D.F.C., Air medal; named outstanding citizen Albuquerque, 1972; Group Pres.'s awardee Dale Carnegie & Assos., 1974-76. Mem. Am. Soc. Tng. Dirs., Am. Mgmt. Assn., U. Tex., Columbia, Lincoln Meml. U. alumni assns., Denver C. of C., Colo. Assn. Commerce and Industry (chmn. fin.), Civil War Round Table. Republican. Lutheran. Clubs: Rolling Hills Country; University (N.Y.C.);

Lawyers (Washington); Denver Rotary, Masons. Office: 210 University Blvd Suite 820 Denver CO 80206

BONATO, DOMINIC (DON) JOHN, investment adviser; b. Sopris, Colo., Jan. 30, 1906; s. Joseph Dominic and Martina (Menapace) B.; m. Lillian Florence Poletto, June 24, 1928; children—Robert Martin, Paul Alfred, Laura Ann. Barber, Oakland, Calif., 1926-34; buyer Stop N Shop Market, Oakland, 1934-42; pipefitter Shell Devel. Co., 1945-66; prin. Bonato Investments, Oakland, 1978—; pres. Bonato China Trading Corp.; ptnr. Baron & Bonato, Torino Pizza, Inc., Los Angeles. Republican. Roman Catholic. Clubs: Fratellanza (Oakland); Moose. Home and Office: 611 Jean St PO Box H080 Oakland CA 94611

BOND, BALF WELLINGTON, optometrist; b. Eugene, Oreg., May 30, 1923; s. Balf M. and Esther F. (Frisbee) B.; m. Doris A. Philpott, Oct. 26, 1942; children—Barbara Steiner, Richard, Lanni Aasen, Renee. B.S. in Biology, Pacific U., 1949, O.D., 1950. Lic., Oreg. Pvt. practice, Eugene, 1950—; assoc. adminstr. health and temperance dept. Gen. Conf. Seventh-day Adventists, 1982—. Lane County chmn. March of Dimes, 1960-67. Mem. Am. Optometric Assn., Am. Acad. Optometry, Oreg. Optometric Assn., Lane County Optometric Assn. and Optometric Extension. Seventh Day Adventist. Club: Cascade Lions (Eugene). Contbr. articles to profl. jours. Home: 612 Montara Way Eugene OR 97405 Office: 1730 Chambers St Eugene OR 97402

BOND, CHARLES LINDEN, personnel executive; b. N.Y.C., May 4, 1933; s. Paul and Evangeline (Rosendahl) B.; m. Cynthia Newton, Feb. 1, 1958; children—Timothy, Teri, Susan. B.S. in Bus. Adminstrn., UCLA, 1955. Placement dir. U. Calif.-Riverside, 1959-64; personnel prin. Coopers & Lybrand, Los Angeles, 1964-79; regional v.p. Contract Staffing of Am., Los Angeles, 1979-80; dist. services mgr. Career Research Systems, Los Angeles, 1980-82; dir. personnel Condit Appraisal Co., Corona Del Mar, Calif., 1982-83; Pacific zone coordinator Coll. Placement Council, Newport Beach, Calif., 1983—. Served with AUS, 1955-57. Mem. Coll. Placement Council (gov.), Western Coll. Placement Assn. (pres.), Calif. Ednl. Placement Assn. (pres.). Republican. Club: Toastmasters (Newport Beach). Contbr. articles to profl. jours. Home: 203 Garnet Ave Balboa Island CA 92662 Office: 2333 E Coast Hwy Suite F Newport Beach CA 92625

BOND, GEORGE CLINE, lawyer; b. Abingdon, Ill., May 30, 1920; s. George Clair and Bertha Rose (Cline) B.; m. Winifred Cammack, Dec. 27, 1942; children—Kathryn Elizabeth, Walter C., Margaret A., Bruce C. A.B., Swarthmore Coll., 1942; LL.B., Stanford U., 1949. Bar: Calif. 1949, D.C. 1954. Assoc. counsel Union Title Ins. and Trust Co., San Diego, 1949-51; asst. sec., staff atty. Consol. Vultee Aircraft Co., San Diego, 1951-55; sec., gen. counsel Pacific Airmotive Corp., Burbank, Calif., 1955—; mem. legal dept. Union Oil Co., Los Angeles, 1955-60, asst. chmn. bd., 1960-62, asst. counsel, 1963-69, asst. gen. counsel, 1969-73, v.p., gen. counsel, 1973—; adv. bd. Oil and Gas Ednl. Ctr., Internat. Comparative Law Ctr., Southwestern Legal Found. Served to lt. comdr. USNR, 1942-46. Mem. Am. Corp. Counsel Assn. (dir.), ABA, Calif. State Bar Assn., Los Angeles County Bar Assn. Republican. Presbyterian. Clubs: Chancery, Calif., Anandale Golf. Home: 1419 Wellington Ave Pasadena CA 91103 Office: 461 S Boylston Los Angeles CA 90017

BONDI, BERT ROGER, accountant, financial planner; b. Portland, Oreg., Oct. 2, 1945; s. Gene L. and Elizabeth (Poynter) B. B.B.A., U. Notre Dame, 1967. C.P.A., Colo., Calif., Wyo. Sr. tax acct. Price Waterhouse, Los Angeles, 1970-73; ptnr. Valentine Adducci & Bondi, Denver, 1973-76; sr. ptnr. Bondi & Co., Englewood, Colo., 1977 . Served with U.S. Army, 1968-70. Mem. C. of C., Community Assns. Inst., Mcpl. Fin. Officers Assn., Home Builders Assn., Am. Inst. C.P.A.s, Colo. Soc. C.P.A.s, Wyo. Soc. C.P.A.s. Roman Catholic. Clubs: Notre Dame, Metropolitan (Denver). Home: 6765 S Magnolia Ct Englewood CO 80112 Office: Bondi & Co 44 Inverness Dr E Bldg B Englewood CO 80112

BONDURANT, CECIL WILLIAM, emeritus educator; b. Grass Creek, Wyo., June 26, 1918; s. Perle Oscar and Mary Lucile (Williams) B.; B.S., Am. TV Inst. Tech., 1952; m. Doris Mac Box; children by previous marriage—Curtis Dean, Gary Michael, Laura Marie. TV engr. WENR-TV, Chgo., 1952; engring. supr. KBTV, Denver, 1953-60; engr. and instr. Washington State U., 1961; instr., dir. radio TV engring. U. Idaho, Moscow, 1962-81, emeritus, 1981—; learning lab cons. for sch. dists. in No. Idaho; vol. exec. Internat. Exec. Service Corps., Ecuador TV, 1981. Pres. Idaho chpt. Am. Junior Bowlers Congress, 1968-81. Served with AUS, USAF, 1939-47. Decorated Bronze Star medal. Mem. IEEE, Soc. Broadcast Engrs., Internat. Platform Assn., AAUP, Alpha Epsilon Rho. Mason. Moose. Mem. Order Eastern Star. Home: 3300 E Broadway #102 Mesa AZ 85204

BONE, LUCIEN ARMINT, JR., supermarket product management company executive; b. Los Angeles, Sept. 28, 1937; s. Lucien Armint and Rose Erma (Bernard) B.; m. Carol Leta Smale, June 20, 1969. A.A., Compton Jr. Coll., 1957; student Long Beach State Coll., (Calif.) 1957. Store mgr. Albertson's, Long Beach, 1961-66; Gardena, Calif., 1966-68; with PIA Merchandising Co., Los Angeles, 1969—, exec. v.p., chief operating officer, 1981-82, pres., 1983—; pres. In-Store Directory; pres. Pivotal Mktg. Services. Mem. East Los Angeles (Calif.) Library Com., 1982. Recipient award of appreciation Bd. Trustees North Orange County Regional Occupational Program and Calif. Dept. Edn., 1976. Mem. Sales and Mktg. Execs. Los Angeles (dir. 1982-83, Disting. sales award 1971, Merit award 1980, honor award 1983), Illuminators (com. chmn.), Calif. Grocers Assn. (assoc.). Republican. Clubs: Capitol (exec. com.) (Sacramento); Shriners, Masons. Office: 1731 Workman St Los Angeles CA 90031

BONFIELD, ANDREW JOSEPH, tax practitioner; b. London, Jan. 26, 1924; s. George William and Elizabeth Agnes B.; came to U.S., 1946, naturalized, 1954; m. Eleanor Ackerman, Oct. 16, 1955; children—Bruce Ian, Sandra Karen. Gen. mgr. Am. Cushion Co., Los Angeles, 1948-50, Monson Calif. Co., Redwood City, 1951-58; mfrs. mktg. rep., San Francisco, 1958-62; tax practitioner, bus. cons., Redwood City, San Jose, Los Gatos, Calif., 1963—. Past treas., dir. Northwood Park Improvement Assn.; mem. exec. bd. Santa Clara County council Boy Scouts Am., 1971—, past council pres., mem. Nat. council; mem. Santa Clara County Parks and Recreation Commn., 1975-81, 82—; mem. County Assessment Appeals Bd., 1978—. Served with Brit. Royal Navy, 1940-46. Decorated King George VI Silver Badge; recipient Silver Beaver award, Vigil honor award Boy Scouts Am. Mem. Nat. Soc. Public Accts., Nat. Assn. Enrolled Agts., Calif. Soc. Enrolled Agts., Royal Can. Legion (past state parliamentarian, past state 1st vice comdr.). Club: Rotary (pres. San Jose E. 1977-78). Home: 16140 Shannon Rd Los Gatos CA 95030

BONGAR, BRUCE MICHAEL, clinical and consulting psychologist, psychotherapist; b. Madison, Wis., Sept. 20, 1950; s. Larry and Elaine (Melnik) B. B.A. with distinction, U. Wis., 1972; M.S., U. So. Calif., 1975, Ph.D., 1977. Diplomate Am. Bd. Psychotherapy, Am. Acad. Behavioral Medicine; lic. psychologist, Calif., Mass., Conn., Ariz. Staff clin. psychologist Children's Hosp. Los Angeles, 1977-79, sr. psychologist, 1979-80; pvt. practice clin. and health psychology, Santa Monica, Calif., 1978—; cons. behavioral medicine, 1978—; oral commr. Bd. Behavioral Sci. Examiners Calif., 1981, Calif. Bd. Med. Quality Assurance Psychology Examining Com., 1982. Fellow Explorers Club; mem. Am. Psychol. Assn., Calif. State Psychol. Assn., Los Angeles County Pschol. Assn., Am. Soc. Clin. Hypnosis, Am. Coll. Sports Medicine, Biofeedback Soc. Am., Acad. Psychologists in Marital and Family Therapy, Soc. Behavioral Medicine (charter), Brit. Psychol. Soc. Author: (with Lyn Paul Taylor) Clinical Applications in Biofeedback Therapy, 1976. Office: 2700 Neilson Way 631 Santa Monica CA 90405

BONGIOVI, CARUSO JOSEPH, JR., safety engineer; b. Williamsport, Pa., Oct. 22, 1942; s. Caruso Joseph and Rachel Irene (Foresman) B.; m. Kathleen LaVern Craig, June 12, 1964; children—Harold J., Enrico C. B.A., Boise State Coll., 1969. Secondary sch. tchr., Kuna, Idaho, 1969-72; range tech. supr. Vale Dist. BLM, Vale, Oreg., 1976-78; forestry tech. supr. Sawtooth Nat. Forest, Twin Falls, Idaho, 1978-79; safety dir. DeLamar Silver Mine, Earth Resources Co. and MAPCO Minerals Corp., Jordan Valley, Oreg., 1980—. Chief Jordan Valley Vol. Fire Dept., 1980; CPR instr. Idaho and Oreg. Heart Assn.; mem. Jordan Valley Emergency Med. Technicians, 1980. Served with USAF, 1961-63. Mem. Am. Soc. Safety Engrs. Nat. Safety Council Exec. Com. (Mining Sect.). Episcopalian. Contbr. articles to profl. jour. Home: PO Box 574 Jordan Valley OR 97910 Office: PO Box 52 Jordan Valley OR 97910

BONHAM, CLIFFORD VERNON, social worker, educator; b. Paradise, Calif., July 11, 1921; s. Leon C. and Mary M. (Horn) B.; student San Francisco State U., 1948-49; B.A., U. Calif., Berkeley, 1951, M.S.W., 1953; m. Vesta H. Williamson, May 4, 1956; children—William Robert Rohde, Jr. (stepson), Larry Dean, Tami Marie. Parole agt. Calif. State Dept. Youth Authority, 1953-59, research interviewer, 1959-61, supervising parole agt., 1961-64; field instr. Grad. Sch. Social Work, Calif. State U., Fresno, 1964-67, asso. prof., 1967-74, prof., 1974—, field sequence coordinator, 1973-80; counselor Suicide Prevention Program, Fresno, Calif., 1964-70; cons. Fresno County Domestic Relations, 1967-70; commr. Fresno County Juvenile Justice Commn., 1971—; social work cons. various sanitariums and convalescent hosps., Fresno, 1971—. Bd. dirs. Piedmont Pines Assn., Oakland, Calif., 1960-64. Served with USN, 1940-46. Lic. clin. social worker, marriage and family counselor. Mem. Nat. Assn. Social Workers, Council on Social Work Edn., Calif. Probation and Parole Assn. (regional v.p. 1973-74), Acad. Cert. Social Workers (com. alt. housing for felons 1980). Democrat. Unitarian. Home: 49717 Meadowood Rd Oakhurst CA 93644 Office: 5241 N Maple St Fresno CA 93740

BONHAM, HAROLD FLORIAN, JR., geologist; b. Los Angeles, Sept. 1, 1928; s. Harold Florien and Viola Violet (Clopine) B.; A.A., U. Calif. at Berkeley, 1951; B.A., U. Calif. at Los Angeles, 1954; M.S., U. Nev., 1963; m. Sally Mae Reimer, Sept. 7, 1952; children—Cynthia Jean, Douglas Craig, Gary Stephen. Geologist, So. Pacific Co., 1955-61; grad. research asst. Nev. Bur. Mines, W. Nev., Reno, 1961-62, asst. mining geologist, 1963-67, asso. mining geologist, 1967-74; mining geologist, 1974—; also prof. geology. Vice pres., trustee Palamino Valley Gen. Improvement Dist. Served with USNR, 1946-49. Office Water Resources grantee, 1967-69. Fellow Geol. Soc. Am.; mem. Soc. Econ. Geologists. Home: 2100 Right Hand Canyon Rd Reno NV 89510 Office: Nev Bur Mines and Geology U Nev Reno NV 89507

BONIFACE, ROBERT LEE, electronics co. exec.; b. San Diego, Nov. 25, 1924; s. Frank L. and Alice M. (Wood) B.; A.A. in Bus. Mgmt., Los Angeles City Coll., 1948; m. Sue Alexander, Jan. 20, 1951; children—Christine McArthur, Craig. With Neely Enterprises, 1942-63, v.p., gen. mgr., 1952-63; gen. mgr. Hewlett-Packard Co., Palo Alto, Calif., 1963-70, v.p. mktg., 1970-74, v.p. corp. adminstrn., 1974-75, exec. v.p., 1975—, also dir. Served to capt., inf. AUS, 1943-46, U.S. Army, 1950-52. Decorated Silver Star medal, Bronze Star medal with oak leaf cluster, Purple Heart. Mem. Radio Pioneers, Electronic Reps. Assn. (past pres. So. Calif. chpt.), Horsemen's Quarter Horse Racing Assn. (pres., dir.), NAM (dir.). Home: 276 Atherton Ave Atherton CA 94025 Office: 1501 Page Mill Rd Palo Alto CA 94304

BONILLA, MANUEL GEORGE, geologist; b. Sacramento, July 19, 1920; s. Alfonso Guerrero and Mary Sebastiana (Perea) B.; A.A., Sacramento City Coll., 1941; A.B., U. Calif. at Berkeley, 1943; M.S., Stanford, 1960; m. Ruth Eleanor Raleigh, Mar. 12, 1949; children—Janice Leigh, Roger Bryce, Laurie Ann. Geologist, U.S. Bur. Reclamation, Sacramento, Visalia, Calif., 1946-47; geologist U.S. Geol. Survey, San Francisco, 1947-53, Menlo Park, Calif., 1953—. Served with AUS, 1943-46. Recipient two Spl. Act awards, U.S. Geol. Survey, 1965; Claire P. Holdredge award, Assn. Engring. Geologists, 1971, Meritorious Service award U.S. Dept. Interior, 1975. Fellow Geol. Soc. Am.; mem. Seismol. Soc. Am., Am. Geophys. Union, Assn. Engring. Geologists, Internat. Assn. Engring. Geology. Contbr. articles to profl. jours. Home: 4127 Wilkie Ct Palo Alto CA 94306 Office: 345 Middlefield Rd MS 77 Menlo Park CA 94025

BONK, JAMES RAYMOND, rehabilitation psychologist; b. Columbus, Nebr., July 15, 1953; s. Raymond Francis and Gloria Ann B.; m. June Elizabeth Dail, May 27, 1978. B.S. in Nursing cum laude, Creighton U., 1975; M.S. in Nursing, U. Ariz.-Tucson, 1977, postgrad., 1977—. Clin. specialist in adult psychiat. and mental health nursing; cert. alcoholism counselor. Psychiat. nurse human services ctr. St. Joseph's Hosp., Omaha, 1975-76, children's outpatient unit So. Ariz. Mental Health Ctr., Tucson, 1976-77; course chmn., instr. div. nursing Midland Coll., Fremont, Nebr., 1977-80; practicum student Westcenter, Tucson Gen. Hosp., 1980-81; grad. research and teaching assoc. Coll. Nursing, U. Ariz., Tucson, 1980-82; predoctoral intern alcohol treatment unit VA Med. Ctr., Tucson, 1982—; pvt. practice, Tucson, 1983—. Co-leader treatment group for children Alcoholism Council Tucson; guest speaker U. Ariz.; participant workshops on alcoholism Tucson Gen. Hosp. and Davis-Monthan AFB. Sect. capt. Creighton U. fund drive, 1980. Mem. Am. Nurses Assn., Ariz. Nurses Assn., ARC, Am. Personnel and Guidance Assn., Nat. League Nursing, Nat. Rehab. Assn., Am. Psychol. Assn. (student), Nat. Nurses Soc. on Alcoholism, Sigma Theta Tau, Kappa Delta Pi. Contbr. articles to profl. publs. Home: 3816 E Pima St Tucson AZ 85716

BONKER, DONALD LEROY, congressman; b. Denver, Mar. 7, 1937; s. Warren J. and Margaret (Collier) B.; A.A., Clark Coll., Vancouver, Wash., 1962; B.A., Lewis and Clark Coll., 1964; postgrad. Am. U., 1964-66; m. Carolyn Jo Ekern, July 10, 1971; children—Dawn Elyse, Jonathan Todd. Research asst. to U.S. Senator Maurine B. Neuberger, Oreg., 1964-66; auditor Clark County (Wash.), 1966-74; mem. 94th-98th Congresses from 3d Wash. Dist., chmn. export task force. Democratic candidate for sec. of state, Wash., 1972. Mem. World Affairs Council, Am. African Inst., Center for Strategic Studies. Office: 434 Cannon House Office Bldg Washington DC 20515*

BONN, ETHEL MAY, psychiatrist, educator; b. Cin., Oct. 14. 1925; d. Stanley Ervin and Ethel May (Cliffe) B.; B.A., U. Cin., 1947; M.D., U. Chgo., 1951. Intern, Strong Meml. Hosp., Rochester, N.Y., 1951-53; resident psychiatry VA Hosp. and Menninger Sch. Psychiatry, Topeka, 1953-55, asst. chief women's psychiat. sect., 1956-57, chief, 1957-61, chief N. psychiat. service, 1961-62; practice medicine specializing in psychiatry, Topeka, 1956-62, Denver, 1962-78; asst. hosp. dir. Ft. Logan Mental Health Center, Denver, 1962-67, dir., 1967-76; field rep. Joint Commn. Accreditation Hosps., 1976-78; quality assurance officer Brentwood VA Med. Center, Los Angeles, 1978-81; chief psychiatry service Albuquerque VA Med. Ctr., 1981—; assoc. prof. psychiatry U. N.Mex., Albuquerque, 1981—; cons. staff Fitzsimons Army Gen. Hosp., Denver, Ft. Lyons (Colo.) VA Hosp. Clin. instr. psychiatry U. Colo., 1964-76; adj. assoc. prof. psychiatry UCLA, 1978-81. Fellow Am. Coll. Psychiatrists, Am. Coll. Psychiat. Adminstrs. (founding), Am. Coll. Utilization Rev. Physicians, Am. Psychiat. Assn.; mem. Am. Coll. Hosp. Adminstrs., Am. Assn. Psychiat. Adminstrs., Assn. Mental Health Adminstrs., Am. Hosp. Assn. Club: Altrusa. Author numerous publs. Home: 4815 Vista Del Oso Ct NE Albuquerque NM 87109 Office: VA Med Ctr 2100 Ridgecrest Dr SE Albuquerque NM 87108

BONN, FRED, artist, publisher; b. Culver City, Calif., May 13, 1940; m. Linda Jeanne Anderson, Nov. 28, 1969; children—Anna Marie, Allison Lynn. Student Art. Ctr. Sch. Design, 1961-65. Comml. artist Lockheed Calif. Co., Burbank, 1965-70; art. dir. Headlines Ink Inc., Los Angeles, 1970—; pub.; artist; several one-man shows.

BONNELL, VICTORIA EILEEN, sociologist; b. N.Y.C., June 15, 1942; d. Samuel S. and Frances (Nassau) B.; m. Gregory Freidin, May 4, 1971. B.A. Brandeis U., 1964; M.A., Harvard U., 1966, Ph.D., 1975. Lectr. politics U. Calif.-Santa Cruz, 1972-73, 74-76; asst. prof. sociology U. Calif.-Berkeley, 1976-82, assoc. prof., 1982—. AAUW fellow, 1979; Regents Faculty fellow, 1978; Fulbright Hays faculty fellow, 1977; Internat. Research and Exchanges Bd. fellow, 1977; Stanford U. Hoover Instn. nat. fellow, 1973-74; grantee Am. Philos. Soc., 1979, Am. Council Learned Socs., 1976. Mem. Am. Sociol. Assn., Am. Assn. Advancement Slavic Studies. Author: Roots in Rebellion: Workers' Politics and Organizations in St. Petersburg and Moscow, 1900-1914, 1983; editor: The Russian Worker: Life and Labor under the Tsarist Regime, 1983; contbr. articles to profl. jours. Office: Dept Sociology U Calif Berkeley CA 94720

BONNEMORT, JANICE KAY, hospital official; b. Fairfield, Calif.; d. Hyrum Stewart and Alice (Watkins) B. B.S. cum laude, Weber State Coll., 1970; M.A., Brigham Young U., 1981. Jr. vol. coordinator St. Benedict's Hosp., Ogden, Utah, 1968-75, pub. relations asst., 1971-76, asst. supr. in-patient services, 1976—. Mem. Am. Soc. Tng. and Devel., AAUW (community chair). Mormon. Home: 5032 Doren Dr Ogden UT 84403 Office: 5475 S Adams Ave Ogden UT 84403

BONNER, JAMES FREDRICK, scientist, educator; b. Ansley, Nebr., Sept. 1, 1910; s. Walter Daniel and Grace (Gaylord) B.; m. Ingelore Silberbach, Nov. 1, 1947; children—Joey Sheehan, J. Jose, Pamela, Terry. A.B. in Chemistry and Math., U. Utah, 1931; Ph.D. in Genetics and Biochemistry, Calif. Inst. Tech., 1934. Instr. to prof. biology Calif. Inst. Tech., 1935-81; chmn. bd. Phytogen Corp., Pasadena, Calif., 1980—; mem. Malaysian Research and Devel. Bd., 1960—. Mem. Nat. Acad. Scis., Am. Chem. Soc., Sierra Club. Author: The Next 80 Years, 1977; The World's People and the World's Food Supply, 1979; contbr. numerous articles to profl. jours.

BONNETT, ALLEN DEAN, architect; b. Rawlins, Wyo., Nov. 26, 1951; s. David Lawerence and Doris Florince (Hansen) B.; student Casper Coll., 1970-72; B.A. in Arch., Mont. State U., 1977; m. Mary Jane Philo, May 27, 1972; children—Michelle Marie, Brandi Dawn, Allen David. Architect-in-tng. Dana, Larson, Roubal, Billings, Mont., 1977-78; owner, architect Design/Build Enterprises, Rawlins, 1980; project architect, office mgr. Banner & Assocs., Rawlins, 1980—. Recipient John Philip Sousa Band award, 1970; Casper Coll. scholar, 1970-71. Designer passive solar home for Robert Pappenheim, Rawlins, 1980. Address: 410 E Murray St Rawlins WY 82301

BONNEY, DONALD ROBERT, energy economist; b. Peoria, Ill., Apr. 22, 1943; s. Robert H. and Leona M. (Runion) B.; m. Sharon June Zimmerman, June 18, 1966. B.S. in Econs., U. Ill., 1965; M.A. in Econs., Northwestern U., 1966; Ph.D. in Econs., U. Iowa, 1978. Instr. econs. Luther Coll., Decorah, Iowa, 1969-72; asst. prof. econs. U. Tenn., Chattanooga, 1977-79; economist TVA, Chattanooga, 1979; energy forecast analyst Pacific Gas & Electric Co., San Francisco, 1979-82, sr. energy economist, 1982—. Mem. Am. Econ. Assn., Internat. Assn. Energy Economists, Western Econ. Assn. Home: 3332 Mildred Ln Lafayette CA 94549 Office: 77 Beale St San Francisco CA 94106

BONNEY, GEORGE WILLIAM, judge; b. Midwest, Wyo., Aug. 22, 1923; s. George William and Bertha Anne (Ormsby) B.; A.B., U. Wis., 1950, LL.B., 1952; m. Kerminette Schweers, Aug. 27, 1949; children—Susan Mary, George William III, Michael Kermit. Admitted to Calif. bar, 1952, since practiced in San Jose; ptnr. Rankin, Oneal, Luckhardt, Center, Ingram, Bonney, Marlais & Lund, 1967—; judge Santa Clara (Calif.) Mcpl. Ct., 1972-80, Santa Clara County Superior Ct., 1980—. Dist. chmn. Santa Clara County chpt. Boy Scouts Am., 1967—, mem. exec. bd., 1967—. Mem. Saratoga Parks and Recreation Commn., 1970—. Served as pilot USAAF, 1942-45. Mem. Conf. Calif. Judges, Am., Calif. (conf. dels.), Wis., Santa Clara County bar assns., U. Wis. Alumni Assn., Santa Clara County Trial Lawyers Assn. (pres. 1971), Santa Clara County Conf. Mcpl. Judges (pres. 1977), Sigma Phi Epsilon. Club: Rotary. Home: 12740 Carniel Ave Saratoga CA 95070 Office: 191 N 1st St San Jose CA 95113

BONNEY, JOHN DENNIS, oil company executive; b. Blackpool, Eng., Dec. 22, 1930; s. John P. and Isabel (Evans) B.; m. Ann Auriol Ross, Nov. 12, 1960; children—Peter, Ferelith, Vivian, Michael. B.A. in Law, Oxford U. (Eng.), 1954; LL.M., U. Calif., 1955. Atty., Eng., 1956-59; with Iraq Petroleum Co., London and Baghdad, 1959-60; assoc. analyst Eastern Hemisphere ops. Standard Oil Co. Calif., 1960-62, staff asst., 1962-66, sr. advisor fgn. adv. staff, 1966-67, asst. mgr. fgn. adv. staff, 1967-71, mgr. fgn. ops. staff, 1971-72, v.p., San Francisco, 1972—. Mem. World Affairs Council, Council Fgn. Relations. Club: Commonwealth of Calif. (San Francisco). Office: 225 Bush St 18th Floor San Francisco CA 94104

BONNY, MARY CLEINMARK, nurse; b. Bloomington, Ill., June 30, 1934; d. Robert William and Elizabeth Helen (Buckley) Cleinmark; m. William Ralph Bonny, Oct. 29, 1965; 1 son, Stephen Robert. R.N., Good Samaritan Hosp., Phoenix, 1960; B.S.N., Ariz. State U., 1964, M.C., 1971, M.S., 1983. Staff nurse Good Samaritan Hosp., Phoenix, 1960-62, Ariz. Crippled Children's Hosp., Phoenix, 1962-64; instr. St. Joseph's Hosp. Sch. Nursing, 1964-66; staff nurse and head nurse Drs. Hosp., Phoenix, 1967-68; instr. Good Samaritan Hosp. Sch. Nursing, Phoenix, 1968-73; mem. faculty nursing program Mesa Community Coll., 1973-75, chmn. nursing program, 1975-80, dir. nursing, 1980—; mem. Ariz. Statewide Council on Nursing. Mem. Nat. League Nursing (exec. com. council assoc. degree programs 1978-80), Ariz. League Nursing, Am. Assn. Women Community and Jr. Colls., Am. Vocat. Assn., Sigma Theta Tau. Democrat. Roman Catholic. Office: 1833 W Southern Ave Mesa AZ 85202

BONO, ANTHONY S(ALVITORE) E(MANUEL), II, systems analyst; b. N.Y.C., Nov. 24, 1946; s. Anthony S.E. and Lola M. (Riddle) B. B.A. in Polit. Sci., Hartwick Coll., 1969; postgrad. UCLA Ext., 1980—. Mgmt. trainee Mfrs. Hanover Trust Co., N.Y.C., 1973-74; with Johnson & Higgins of Calif., 1974—, supr. client services, mass coverages dept., 1975-77, account exec. comml. accounts, 1977-80, internal automation systems coordinator Los Angeles br., 1981—. Deacon Westwood Presbyterian Ch., Los Angeles. Served in USAF, 1969-73. Mem. Assn. Systems Mgmt. (chpt. dir. publicity and awards), San Bernardino C. of C. (Airman of Yr. 1970), Alpha Sigma Phi. Home: 400 S Gramercy Apt 208 Los Angeles CA 90020 Office: 2029 Century Park E Suite 2300 Los Angeles CA 90067

BONO, PHILIP, aerospace engr.; b. Bklyn., Jan. 13, 1921; s. Julius and Marianna (Culcasi) B.; B.E., U. So. Calif., 1947, postgrad., 1948-49; m. Gertrude Camille King, Dec. 15, 1950; children—Richard Philip, Patricia Marianna, Kathryn Camille. Research and systems analyst N.Am. Aviation, Inglewood, Calif., 1947; engring. design specialist Douglas Aircraft Co., Long Beach, Calif., 1948-49; preliminary design engr. Boeing Airplane Co., Seattle, 1950-59; dep. program mgr. Douglas Aircraft Co., Santa Monica, Calif., 1960-62, tech. asst. to dir. advanced launch vehicles and space stas., Huntington Beach, Calif., 1963-65, sr. engr., scientist, Long Beach, Calif., 1973—; br. mgr. advanced studies, sr. staff engr. advanced systems tech. integration McDonnell Douglas Astronautics Co., Huntington Beach, 1966-72; pres. Cal-Pro Photo Accessories, 1973—; lectr. seminars, univs. and insts. including Soviet Acad. Scis., 1965; instr. engring. Wash., Calif. Served with USNR, 1943-46. Recipient Golden Eagle award Council Internat. Nontheatrical Events, 1964, A.T. Colwell merit award Soc. Automotive Engrs., 1968, N.M. Golovine award Brit. Interplanetary Soc., named engr. of distinction Engrs. Joint Council, 1971. Fellow AAAS, Royal Aero. Soc., Brit. Interplanetary Soc. (editorial adv. bd.), AIAA (assoc.); sr. mem. Am. Astronautical Soc.; mem. N.Y. Acad. Scis., Internat. Acad. Astronautics, ASME, Soc. Automotive Engrs. (chmn. space vehicle com.). Author: Destination-Mars, 1961; (with K. Gatland) Frontiers of Space, 1969, translated into 6 fgn. langs. Contbr. articles to profl. jours., chpts. to books. Inventor recoverable single-stage space shuttle for NASA. Home: 1951 Sanderling Circle Costa Mesa CA 92626 Office: 3855 Lakewood Blvd Long Beach CA 90801

BONSER, QUENTIN, surgeon; b. Sedro Wooley, Wash., Nov. 1, 1920; s. George Wayne and Kathleen Imogene (Lynch) B.; B.A. in Zoology, U. Calif. at Los Angeles, 1943; M.D., U. Calif., San Francisco, 1947; m. Loellen Rocca, Oct. 20, 1945; children—Wayne, Gordon, Carol, Patricia Adams (Mrs. Terry Adams). Intern U. Calif. Hosp., San Francisco, 1947-49, resident gen. surgery, 1949-56; practice gen. surgery, Placerville, Calif., 1956—; vis. prof. surgery U. Calif., San Francisco, 1968. Served to capt. M.C., USAF, 1950-51. Vol. physician, tchr. surgery Vietnam, 1971, 72, 73. Diplomate Am. Bd. Surgery. Fellow A.C.S.; mem. H.C. Naffziger Surg. Soc. (pres. 1974-75). Home: 2590 Northridge Dr Placerville CA 95667 Office: 1108 Corker Dr Placerville CA 95667

BONY, JEAN VICTOR, art historian, educator, writer; b. Le Mans, France, Nov. 1, 1908; came to U.S., 1961; s. Leon Henri and Marie Elise (Normand) B.; m. Clotilde Roure, June 2, 1936; m. 2d, Elizabeth Mary England, July 1, 1953; 1 dau., Claire. Licencé, U. Paris, 1930, M.A., 1931, Agregation, 1933; M.A., Cambridge (Eng.) U., 1958. Cert. agregation d'histoire, French Ministry of Edn., 1933. Asst. master Eton Coll. (Eng.), 1937-39, 1945-46; lectr. French Inst., London, 1946-61; Slade prof. fine art Cambridge U., 1958-61; Matthews lectr. Columbia U., 1961; art history prof. U. Calif.-Berkeley, 1962-80, prof. emeritus; Wrightsman lectr. NYU, 1969; Kress prof. Nat. Gallery Art, Washington, 1982; Mellon prof. U. Pitts., 1983—. Served to lt. French inf., 1934, 39-44. Research fellow Centre National de la Recherche Scientifique, France, 1944-45; grantee Am. Philos. Soc., 1967, Samuel H. Kress Found., 1969; recipient Disting. Teaching award U. Calif.-Berkeley, 1975; Guggenheim fellow, 1981. Mem. Coll. Art Assn. Am., Soc. Archtl. Historians, Internat. Ctr. Medieval Art. Author: French Cathedrals, 1951; The English Decorated Style, 1979; French Gothic Architecture of the 12th and 13th Centuries, 1983; contbr. articles to profl. jours. Office: Dept History Art U Calif Berkeley CA 94720

BOOCHEVER, ROBERT, federal judge; b. N.Y.C., Oct. 2, 1917; s. Louis C. and Miriam (Cohen) B.; A.B., Cornell U., 1939, LL.B., 1941; m. Lois Colleen Maddox, Apr. 22, 1943; children—Barbara K., Linda Lou, Ann Paula, Miriam Deon. Admitted to N.Y. bar, 1944, Alaska bar, 1947; asst. U.S. atty., Juneau, 1946-47; partner firm Faulkner, Banfield, Boochever & Doogan, Juneau, 1947-72; asso. justice Alaska Supreme Ct., 1972-75, 78-80 chief justice, 1975-78; circuit judge U.S. Ct. Appeals, 9th Circuit, 1980—; chmn. Alaska Jud. Council, 1975-78; mem. appellate judges seminar N.Y. U. Sch. Law, 1975; mem. adv. bd. Nat. Bank of Alaska. Chmn., Juneau chpt. ARC, 1949-51, Juneau Planning Commn., 1956-61; mem. Alaska Devel. Bd., 1949-52, Alaska Jud. Qualification Commn., 1972-75; adv. bd. Juneau-Douglas Community Coll. Served to capt., inf., AUS, 1941-45. Named Juneau Man of Year, 1974. Fellow Am. Coll. Trial Attys.; mem. Am. Bar Assn., Alaska Bar Assn. (pres. 1961-62), Juneau Bar Assn. (pres. 1971-72), Am. Judicature Soc. (dir. 1970-74), Am. Law Inst., Conf. Chief Justices (vice chmn. 1979), Juneau C. of C. (pres. 1952, 55), Alaskans United (chmn. 1962), Explorers Club (chmn. Juneau br. 1972-78). Clubs: Rotary (pres. Juneau 1966-67), Juneau Racket; Wash. Athletic. Office: 311 Franklin St Juneau AK 99801

BOOHER, DAVID ELLIS, planning and policy consultant; b. Knoxville, Tenn., Jan. 19, 1946; s. Jacob O. and Sue Lenore (Ellis) B.; m. Carolynn Bishop, Sept. 22, 1968; 1 dau., Michelle Judith. B.S., U. Tenn., 1968, M.S.P., 1974. M.A. in Polit. Sci., Tulane U., 1971. Planner, Tenn. State Planning Office, Knoxville, 1971-74, prin. planner, 1974-75; cons. Calif. Research, Sacramento, 1976-77; v.p., gen. mgr. Geyer Assocs. Inc., Sacramento, 1978—. Bd. dirs. E. Tenn. Design Ctr., 1973-75; chmn. City of Davis Alternative Land Use Planning Com., 1981-82; mem. City of Davis Housing Task Force, 1982-83; mem. adv. coms. Calif. State Legislature on housing policy, 1980-82. Served to 1st lt. USAF, 1970-72. Mem. Am. Planning Assn. (dir.), Am. Inst. Cert. Planners (cert., commr.), Calif. Planning Round Table, Urban Land Inst., Am. Polit. Sci. Assn., Policy Studies Orgn., Am. Soc. Pub. Adminstrn., U. Tenn. Sch. Planning Alumni Assn. (pres. 1973-75). Democrat. Unitarian. Author numerous studies on planning and related topics. Home: 912 Valencia Ave Davis CA 95616 Office: 1029 K 33 Sacramento CA 95814

BOOKER, KAREN MCNEAL, accountant; b. Great Falls, Mont., Dec. 30, 1944; d. Clarence A. and Beulah G. (Brown) McNeal; m. Douglas Martin Booker, July 7, 1978; 1 dau., Mayje Merrea. B.S., Mont. State U., 1966, M.S., 1968, postgrad., 1969—. C.P.A., Mont., 1970. Acctg. instr. Mont. State U., Bozeman, 1968-71; staff acct. Rowland, Thomas and Co., Miles City, Mont., 1971-73; researcher Mont. State Dept. Revenue, Helena, 1973-74; planner, analyst Mont. Gov.'s Office, 1974-76, chief fiscal affairs bur. Dept. Instns., 1976-77; sr. acct. Kindred, Holland and Co., 1978-80, ptnr., 1981—. Mem. Mont. Merit System Council, 1982-87; instr. local colls. Active Big Bros. and Sisters, Inc. Mem. Am. Inst. C.P.A.s, Mont. Soc. C.P.A.s. Democrat. Methodist. Club: Montana (Helena). Home: 1973 Oro Fino Gulch Helena MT 59601 Office: Kindred Holland and Co 555 Fuller Ave PO Box 245 Helena MT 59624

BOOKMAN, JOHN TURNER, political science educator; b. Cin., Dec. 7, 1938; s. John F. and Helen M. (Turner) B. Children—Leah F., Jessica T., Rachel E. A.B., U. Cin., 1960, Ph.D., 1966. Asst. prof. polit. sci. U. No. Colo., Greeley, 1966-70, assoc. prof., 1970-77, prof., 1977—. Chmn. Nelo County chpt. ACLU, 1968-72; mem. credentials com. Colo. State Assembly, Democratics, 1972, mem. resolutions com., 1974. NDEA Title IV fellow, 1961-64; Ford Found. fellow, 1964-66. Mem. Am. Polit. Sci. Assn., Conf. Study of Polit. Thought. Contbr. articles to profl. jours. Home: 1850 12th Ave Greeley CO 80631 Office: Dept Polit Sci U No Colo Greeley CO 80639

BOOKMAN, PHILIP, newspaper editor; b. N.Y.C., July 11, 1936; s. Henry and Anne (Mandel) B.; m. Martha Rapaport, Nov. 4, 1962 (div.); children—Jonathan, Charles; m. 2d H. Mary (Bookman,) Oct. 25, 1975. B.A. in English Lit., U. Buffalo, 1957. Assoc. editor Lebhar-Friedman Publs., N.Y.C., 1959-63; regional editor Evening Press, Binghamton, N.Y., 1964-71; asst. mng. editor Sun-Bull., Binghamton, 1971-74; mng. editor Camden (N.J.) Courier-Post, 1975-80; exec. editor The Record, Stockton, Calif., 1980—. Served with U.S. Army, 1959, U.S. N.G., 1959-61. Mem. AP Mng. Editors Assn. (bd. dirs.), Calif. Freedom of Info. Com. (exec. com.), Sigma Delta Chi. Office: 530 E Market St Stockton CA 95201

BOONE, JAMES VIRGIL, engineering executive; b. Little Rock, Sept. 1, 1933; s. Virgil Bennett and Dorothy Bliss (Dorough) B.; m. Gloria Marjorie Giesler, June 5, 1955; children—Clifford B., Sandra J. Smyser, Steven B. B.S. in Elec. Engring., Tulane U., 1955; M.S.E.E., Air Force Inst. Tech., Ohio, 1959. Assoc. elec. engr. Martin Co., Balt., 1955; research and develop. engr. U.S. Air Force, 1955-62; electronics engr. Nat. Security Agy., Ft. Meade, Md., 1962-77, dep. dir. for research and engring., 1978-81; spl. asst. to gen. mgr. Mil. Electronics div. TRW, Inc., San Diego, 1981-83, asst. gen. mgr., 1983—. Served to capt. USAF, 1955-62. Recipient Nat. Security Agy. Exceptional Civilian Service award, 1975. Mem. IEEE (sr.), AIAA, AAAS. Republican. Presbyterian (elder). Contbr. articles to profl. jours. Home: 2811 Los Alisos Dr Fallbrook CA 92028 Office: 4045 Sorrento Valley Blvd San Diego CA 92121

BOONE, PATRICIA NEEF, educational administrator, educator; b. Houston, Mar. 7, 1952; d. William G. and Hazel Eve (Mouton) Neef; m. Ronald W. Boone, June 4, 1982; 1 stepdau., Amy Marie. B.A., U. Southwestern La., 1974, M.Ed. in Elem. Edn., 1977. Cert., tchr., La. Tchr., head prep. English Dept. Acad. of Sacred Heart, Grand Coteau, La., 1974-75; high sch. relations coordinator U. Southwestern La., Lafayette, 1975-80; tchr. academically gifted St. Mary Parish (La.) Sch. Bd., 1980-82; adminstrv. specialist Chapman Coll. Residence Edn. Center, Holloman Air Force Base, N.Mex., 1982, adminstrv. asst., 1982-83, dir., 1983—; instr. communications Chapman Coll.; instr. math. Park Coll. Residence Center. Mem. Assn. for Gifted, Talented Students (corr. sec. Acadiana chpt. 1978-80, pub. relations chmn. Atchafalaya chpt. 1980-82), Assn. Supervision and Curriculum Devel., NEA, Council for Exceptional Children, Great Books Found. (leader 1980—), Kappa Delta. Democrat. Roman Catholic.

BOONE, ROBERT EARL, civil engineer; b. Memphis, Apr. 30, 1927; s. Herman Elbert and Emma (May) B.; m. Shirley Mae Boone, Dec. 6, 1953; children—Kevin, Bryan, Patrick. B.C.E., U. Ark., 1951. Registered profl. engr., Calif., Mo. Civil engr. Black & Veatch, Kansas City, Mo., 1951-63, Wilsey, Ham & Blair, Foster City, Calif., 1963-66, McCandless Engrs., Palo Alto, Calif., 1966-72, McCandless, Boone & Cook, Palo Alto, 1973-82, Boone, Cook & Assocs., Palo Alto, 1982—. Served to 1st lt. C.E., U.S. Army, 1945-47. Mem. Am. Water Works Assn., Water Pollution Control Fedn., ASCE. Club: Elks (Milpitas). Home: 1723 Shenandoah Ave Milpitas CA 95035 Office: Boone Cook & Assocs 1020 Corporation Way Palo Alto CA 94303

BOONE, ROBERT KENNETH, civil engr.; b. Kansas City, Mo., Jan. 29, 1923; s. Forrest E. and Alice L. (Louthan) B.; student U. Wis., 1943-44; B.S. in Engring., U. Calif., Berkeley, 1948; m. Laurel Fraser, June 24, 1951; children—Kenneth, Marlene, Carol. Regional engr. for West Coast bldgs. div. Butler Mfg. Co., Visalia, Calif., 1949—. Served with U.S. Army, 1942-46. Decorated Bronze Star. Registered profl. engr., Alaska, Ariz., Calif., Mont., Nev., Oreg., Wash., Guam. Mem. ASCE, Structural Engrs. Assn. No. Calif. Baptist. Home: 3024 Mill Creek Dr Visalia CA 93291 Office: 7440 Doe Ave Visalia CA 93279

BOONE, TIMOTHY ALLEN, orgn. devel. cons.; b. Watsonville, Calif., June 14, 1945; s. Arthur M. and Lillian M. (Rudolph) B.; B.A. magna cum laude, Chapman Coll., 1975; M.A., Pepperdine U., 1976; Ph.D., U.S. Internat. U., 1981; m. Linda Lee Snyder, Jan. 11, 1975; children—Jennifer Susan, Conor Patrick. Commd. 2d. lt., U.S. Army, 1966, advanced through grades to capt., 1968, with 46th Spl. Forces Co., Thailand, 1967-68, with 82d Airborne div., Ft. Bragg, N.C., 1968-69, 5th Spl. Forces Group (Airborne), Vietnam, 1969-70; with Orgn. Effectiveness Tng. Center, Ft. Ord, Calif., 1971-76; resigned, 1976; gen. mgr. NTL/Learning Resources Corp., San Diego, 1976-78: v.p. ops., cons. Univ. Assocs., La Jolla, Calif., 1978-79; pres. T.A. Boone Assocs., Inc., San Diego, 1980—; sr. cons. Center for Leadership Studies, Escondido, Calif., 1980-81; ptnr. Keilty, Goldsmith & Boone, La Jolla, 1981—. Youth dir. Monterey Jaycees, 1973-74; mem. Community Goals Monitoring Com., Poway (Calif.) Sch. Dist., 1976-77. Served with U.S. Army, 1965-76. Decorated Bronze Star (2), Meritorious Service medal, Air Medal (3), Army Commendation medal (2), Purple Heart, Combat Infantryman's Badge, Sr. Parachutist Badge. Mem. Acad. of Mgmt., Am. Soc. Tng. and Devel., Orgn. Devel. Network. Office: 14531 Yukon St San Diego CA 92129

BOONSTRA, JOHN CHARLES, manuscript editor; b. Orange City, Iowa, June 2, 1949; s. Charles John and Olive Mae (Green) B.; m. Andrea Marie Malott, Jan. 4, 1982. B.A., Hope Coll., 1971; M.A., San Francisco Theol. Sem., 1973, M.Div., 1975; postgrad. Berkeley Theol. Union, 1975-78. Nat. staff organizer Joint Strategy and Action Com., N.Y.C., 1973; researcher, writer Reformed Ch. in Am., Chgo., 1975-77; north Am. regional sec. World Student Christian Fedn., Toronto, Can., 1977-80; contbg. editor Interreligious Task Force for Social Analysis, Oakland, Calif., 1978-79; editor Radical Religion Quarterly, Oakland, 1980-82; manuscript editor Frontier Internship in Mission Program, Geneva, 1982; manuscript editor Orbis Books, Maryknoll, N.Y., 1982—. Pres., Community for Religious Research and Edn., Inc., Berkeley, Calif., 1980—; mem. task force West Coast Chs. on Econ. Dislocation, Oakland and Seattle, 1983—. Office: 4534 1/2 University Way NE Suite 203 Seattle WA 98105

BOOP, JOHN MARTIN, hospital official; b. Indpls., Sept. 28, 1944; s. George Martin and Helen Elnora (Teal) B.; B.A. in Econs., Duke U., 1966; M.B.A. in Fin., U. Chgo., 1968. Asso. dir. devel. U. Chgo., 1970-74; dir. devel. and public relations Tulane Med. Center, New Orleans, 1974-76; dir. devel. Mary's Help Hosp., San Francisco, 1976-79; v.p. devel. and mktg. St. Joseph's Hosp., Tucson, 1979—. Bd. dirs. St. Gregory's High Sch., Tucson; nat. alumni fund bd. U. Chgo., 1974-76, 79-81, nat. alumni council, 1979-83, pres. Tucson chpt. alumni; pres. bd. Tucson Awareness House, CODAC, Parents United. Served with USMC, 1969; with USMCR, 1969-75. Mem. Nat. Assn. Hosp. Devel., Ariz. Hosp. Assn., Western Hosp. Assn., Health Systems Agy. So. Ariz., Tucson C. of C. Clubs: Kiwanis. Home: 6255 Camino Primera Alta Tucson AZ 85718 Office: St Josephs Hospital PO Box 12069 Tucson AZ 85732

BOOSTROM, RONALD LEE, criminologist; b. Alhambra, Calif., Feb. 29, 1936; s. Ralph Eugene and Nettie B.; student Whittier Coll., 1954-56; B.A. in Psychology, Long Beach State Coll., 1958; postgrad. U. So. Calif., 1962-63; M. Criminology, U. Calif., Berkely, 1971, D.Criminology, 1974; m. Mary Gonzales, Jan. 7, 1961; children—Deborah, Steven, Victoria (dec.). Personnel analyst, San Francisco, 1963-64; sr. dep. probation officer Contra Costa County (Calif.), 1964-70; asst. prof. pub. adminstrn. and urban studies San Diego State U., 1971-74, asso. prof., 1976—, dir. criminal justice adminstrn. program, 1975—; asso. prof. Center for Study Crime, Delinquency and Corrections, So. Ill. U., 1975-76; chmn. bd. New Entra Casa Corp.; cons. in field; project dir. Minority Internships in Criminal Justice. Mem. exec. bd. San Diego region ACLU. Served as officer USN, 1959-62. NIMH grantee, 1969-70; Charles Fish fellow, 1970-71; NIMH postdoctoral fellow, 1975-76; Pres.'s grantee, 1976-77. Mem. Am., Western (pres.) socs. criminology, Acad. Criminal Justice Scis., Nat. Council Crime and Delinquency, Pacific-N.W. Criminal Justice Educators Assn., Am. Acad. Polit. and Social Sci. Author: The Personalization of Evil, 1974; Victim-Witness Assistance: New Directions in Criminal Justice Administration, 1977; research on social origins of Am. criminology and criminologists. Home: 10163 Canyonridge Pl Spring Valley CA 92078 Office: Sch Pub Adminstrn and Urban Studies San Diego State U San Diego CA 92182

BOOTH, CHARLES BENNIE, computer systems executive, accountant; b. Memphis, Sept. 1, 1948; s. Elza Lathe and Mary Nadine (Johnson) B.; m. Sylvia Kay Pickett, June 10, 1967; children—Charles David, Dennis Wayne. Student Odessa Coll., 1966-68, Tex. Tech. U., 1968; B.S. in Acctg., Arizona State U., 1971. C.P.A., Ariz. Acct. various firms Odessa, Tex., Lubbock, Tex., Phoenix, 1965-73; ptnr. Raymond & Booth, C.P.A.s, Scottsdale, Ariz., 1973-76; ptnr. R & B Computer Systems, Tempe, Ariz., 1978-80, prin., 1981, pres., 1982-83; owner Profl. Mgmt. Info. Systems, Mesa, Ariz., 1983—. Mem. Am. Inst. C.P.A.s. Office: 2830 E Brown Rd Suite 16 Mesa AZ 85203

BOOTH, DONALD RICHARD, economist, educator; b. Marble, Minn., June 1, 1931; s. Floyd J. and Maude G. (Marquart) B.; m. Helen Louise Hitt, Aug. 22, 1953; 1 son, David. B.A., Whittier Coll., 1955; M.A., Claremont Grad. Sch., 1956; Ph.D., UCLA, 1970. Prof. econs. Chapman Coll., 1959—, dean Sch. Bus. and Mgmt., 1979-81, dean, 1977, exec. v.p., 1977-79; dir. United Am. Bank. Served with USMC, 1950-53. Grantee NSF, Ford Found., Danforth Found., Gen. Electric Found. Mem. Am. Econ. Assn., Western Econ. Assn. (Eliot Jones award 1959). Home: 18551 Via Bravo Villa Park CA 92667 Office: Dept Econs Chapman Coll Orange CA 92666

BOOTH, JAMES RONALD, oil company executive; b. Los Angeles, Dec. 5, 1942; s. Orville N. and Bettine Barbara (Wilson) B.; B.S., Lewis and Clark Coll., 1964; M.B.A., U. So. Calif., 1966; m. Sharon Lee McLean, Sept. 6, 1964; children—Colin, Kathleen, James. Transp. analyst Shell Oil Co., Los Angeles, 1966-69; research analyst So. Pacific Transp. Co., San Francisco, 1970-74; expediter Bechtel Corp., San Francisco, 1974; mgr. transp. Valley Nitrogen Producers, Inc., Fresno, Calif., 1974-79; transp. mgr. Husky Oil Co., Denver, 1979—. Advisor, Jr. Achievement, San Francisco, 1973-74. Mem. Fresno Transp. Club, Calif. Fertilizer Assn. (mem. transp. and distbn. com.), Agrl. Council Calif., Am. Petroleum Inst. (vice chmn. truck com.), Traffic Club of Denver, Delta Nu Alpha (v.p. 1974-77), Alpha Kappa Psi. Republican. Presbyterian. Contbr. articles in field to profl. jours. Home: 9466 W Geddes Pl Littleton CO 80123 Office: 6060 S Willow Dr Englewood CO 80111

BOOTH, JAMES THOMAS, clergyman; b. Needles, Calif., Sept. 24, 1921; s. James Thomas and Henrietta (Hirning) B.; student Holy Cross Coll., 1939-40; A.A., Los Angeles Coll., 1940-41; B.A., St. John Seminary, 1941-46; J.C.D. Pontifical Lateran U., Rome, Italy, 1949-52; LL.D., U. San Diego, 1966; m. Deborah Ann Dayhoff, Feb. 7, 1971 (div. 1980); 1 dau., Teresa Marie. Ordained priest Roman Catholic Ch., 1946; asst. priest St. Joseph Cathedral, San Diego, 1946-47, St. Vincent, 1947, Sacred Heart Ch., 1947; sec. Diocesan Matrimonial Tribunal, San Diego, 1947-48, chief justice, 1954; 1st resident chaplain Patton Mental Hosp., San Diego, 1953-54; vice-chancellor Diocese of San Diego, 1953-54, chancellor, 1954-68; pastor Mission San Diego de Alcala, 1954-71; mem. faculty Acad. of Our Lady of Peace, San Diego, 1954-68; chaplain Nazareth Orphanage, San Diego, 1953-71; pub. rep. Greenwood Cemetery, San Diego, 1971; assigned canon to St. James Episcopal Cathedral, Fresno, 1972-74, canon pastor, 1974—; rector St. John the Evangelist Ch., Stockton, 1974—; chaplain San Diego Navy League, 1959; founder Cus Angelus Enterprises, 1962, the Mission Art Room, 1964. Mem. adminstrv. council, pres.-dir. Indian missions Diocese of San Diego, 1964; mem. standing com. Diocese of San Joaquin, 1974-79, sec. standing com., 1974, chmn. diocesan canon law com., 1974—; diocesan rep. Episcopal Nat. Com. for Asians, 1974—, Nat. Catholic Welfare Conf.; San Diego Catholic dir. of resettlement of all refugees, mem. child abuse council Children's Home, Stockton, 1979; mem. Hispanic Commn., Diocese of San Joaquin, 1980. Bd. dirs. Diocesan Sch. Corp., ARC, Legal Aid, 1959 (all San Diego), Community Council Stockton, 1975—; dep. sheriff San Diego County, 1964; matrimonial advisor to dep. sheriff San Joaquin County, 1975—; bd. advisers Calif. Mental Health San Diego Daytime Center, 1960; trustee U. San Diego; bd. dirs. Congress History San Diego, 1968. Named Domestic Prelate, 1956; recipient Cus Angelus Mosaic Award, 1959. Mem. Propagation of Faith Soc., Union of Clergy, San Diego Tourist and Convention Assn., Assn. History Groups San Diego County (pres.). Democrat. Elk, Rotarian. Author: Church Educational Problems in the State of California, 1960; San Diego Mission, California's First Mission, 1962; Father Luis Jayme, California's First Martyr, 1964. Home: 313 Marc Ave Stockton CA 95207 Office: 117 E Miner Stockton CA 95202

BOOTH, WALLACE WRAY, business executive; b. Nashville, Sept. 30, 1922; s. Wallace W. and Josephine (England) B.; B.A., U. Chgo., 1948, M.B.A., 1948; m. Donna Cameron Voss, Mar. 22, 1947; children—Ann Conley Cox, John England. Various positions Ford Motor Co., Dearborn, Mich., 1948-59; v.p. finance, treas., dir. Ford Motor Co. of Can., Oakville, Ont., 1959-63; mng. dir., chief exec. officer Ford Motor Co. of Australia, Melbourne, 1963-67; v.p. corporate staffs and indsl. products Philco Ford Corp., Phila., 1967-68; sr. v.p. corporate staffs, dir. Rockwell Internat. Corp., El Segundo, Calif., 1968-75; pres., chief exec. officer United Brands Co., Boston, 1975-77, also dir.; chmn., pres., dir., chief exec. officer Ducommun Inc., Los Angeles, 1977—; dir. Litton Industries, Inc., Beverly Hills, Calif., Internat. Harvester Co., Chgo., Rohr Industries, San Diego, United Calif. Bank, Los Angeles. Past pres. Los Angeles United Way; trustee U. Chgo., also vice chmn. council Grad. Sch. Bus.; bd. councilors U. So. Calif. Sch. Bus. Adminstrn. Served to 1st lt. USAAF, 1943-46. Mem. Los Angeles C. of C. (vice-chmn.). Clubs: Calif. Los Angeles Country (Los Angeles). Office: 611 W 6th St Suite 2500 Los Angeles CA 90017

BORCHARDT, GLENN, soil mineralogist; b. Watertown, Wis., July 28, 1942; m. Marilyn Gerbig, June 12, 1965; children—Nina, Natalie. B.S. in Soil Sci., U. Wis.-Madison, 1964, M.S. in Soil Clay Mineralogy, 1966; Ph.D. in Soil Mineralogy, Oreg. State U., 1969. NRC postdoctoral research assoc. U.S. Geol. Survey, Denver, 1969-71; soil mineralogist Calif. Div. Mines and Geology, San Francisco, 1972—; tech. cons. and witness. Recipient Herfurth Efficiency award U. Wis., 1964; Louis Ware scholar, 1963-64. Mem. Soil Sci. Soc. Am., Clay Mineralogy Soc., Geol. Soc. Am. (assoc. editor 1972-82), Soc. Gen. Systems Research, AAAS, Philosophy of Sci. Assn., Sigma Xi, Alpha Zeta, Phi Kappa Phi. Author: Clay minerals sand slope stability, 1977; Fault features in soils of the Mehrten Formation, Auburn Damsite, California, 1980; Paleosols overlying the Foothills fault system near Auburn, California, 1980; contbr. numerous articles on soil mineralogy, geochemistry, geology to profl. jours.; co-developer of Instrumental Neutron Actiation Analysis method for correlating geologic materials; developer of SIMAN coefficient for use in similarity analysis. Office: Calif Div Mines and Geology Ferry Bldg San Francisco CA 94111

BORCHARDT, MARILYN, public relations director; b. Clintonville, Wis., Aug. 13. Student Berea Coll., 1962-64; B.S., U. Wis., 1964-66; M.S., Oreg. State U., 1969. Research asst. USDA, Oreg. State U., Corvallis, 1967-69; child welfare worker Jefferson County Welfare Dept., Golden, Colo., 1970-71; bd. dirs. JACKIE, San Francisco, 1972-76;

exec. sec., 1974-76, coordinating dir., 1976-80, exec. dir., 1981-82; writer, editor JACKIE Quar.; pub. relations cons.; guest expert TV talk shows. Founding mem., pres. Bay Area Action for Foster Children, 1976-78. Recipient award for service JACKIE, 1980; named Person of Yr., Foster Parents United of San Francisco, 1980. Home: 6035 Ocean View Dr Oakland CA 94618

BORCHERDT, WENDY HAWLEY, government official; b. Oakland, Calif., Apr. 12, 1936; d. Stuart Meek and Lois (Weinmann) Hawley; B.A., Stanford, 1958; m. Edward Rahr Borcherdt, Jr., July 12, 1958; children—Kimberley, Edward Rahr III. Tchr. leadership and mgmt. Teren & Co., 1976-77; pres. Tng. for Effective Mgmt., 1977—; spl. asst. for pub. liaison Pres. of U.S., Washington, 1981, assoc. dir. Presdl. personnel, White House, 1981; dep. undersec. for edn., 1982—. Div. chmn. Community Chest, Los Angeles, 1960-61; active various community drives; Blue Bird leader Camp Fire Girls, 1966-68. Bd. dirs. Jr. League of Los Angeles, rec. sec., 1965-66, treas., 1969-70, pres., 1972-73; area rep. Assn. Jr. Leagues, 1973-75; vice chmn. Citizens for Law Enforcement, 1975-78; mem. subcom. on indsl. and comml. firm retention City of Los Angeles Econ. Adv. Council, 1976; bd. dirs., pres. Symphonians, 1961-66. Jr. Philharmonic com., 1971—; bd. overseer Hoover Instn. War, Revolution and Peace, 1974-81; bd. dirs. Harvard Sch. Boys, 1975-78, Hancock Homes Owners Assn., 1975-77, Good Samaritan Hosp. Aux, 1975—, Pacific Legal Found., 1979-81; vice chmn. Ind. Colls. So. Calif., 1975-81; div. chmn. Nixon, 1960-62; area chmn. Goldwater, 1964, Reagan, 1966; asst. co-chmn. Women for Nixon, Los Angeles, 1968; area chmn. Samuel Yorty, 1969; campaign worker Ronald Reagan for Pres., 1975-76, regional fin. dir., 1979-80; vice chmn. Alcoholism Info. Center, Los Angeles, 1977-79; bd. dirs. Los Angeles chpt. Nat. Council on Alcoholism, 1977-79; mem. exec. com. Ed Davis for Gov., 1978. Episcopalian (tchr. Sunday Sch. 1977-81). Clubs: Los Angeles Country, Beach, Stanford Women's (dirs., pres. 1965-69) (Los Angeles); Larchmont Republican (dir., v.p. 1975-78). Home: 401 S June St Los Angeles CA 90020 also 2828 Wisconsin Ave NW 108 Washington DC 20007

BORCHERT, SUSAN DANZIGER, sociology educator; b. Columbus, Ohio, Mar. 2, 1947; d. Joseph M. and Janet (Goldberg) Schwartz; m. James Allan Borchert, Jan. 13, 1941. Ph.D., Ohio State U., 1979. Asst. dir. Associated Neighborhood Ctrs., Youngstown, Ohio, 1976-79; asst. prof. sociology Adrian (Mich.) Coll., 1979-82. Active Crisis Intervention Ctr., Adrian, Career Devel. Ctr. for Women, Youngstown. Nat. Endowment Humanities fellow, 1981. Mem. Am. Sociol. Assn., Mich. Acad. Sci. Arts Letters, ACLU, NOW. Home: 1925 46th Ave #94 Capitola CA 95010

BORDA, RICHARD JOSEPH, banker; b. San Francisco, Aug. 16, 1931; s. Joseph Clement and Ethel Cathleen (Donovan) B.; m. Judith Maxwell, Aug. 30, 1953; children—Michelle Borda Pahl, Stephen J. B.A. in Econs., Stanford U., 1953, M.B.A., 1957. Asst. cashier Wells Fargo Bank, Stanford, Calif., 1960; asst. mgr. Old Stanford Farm Office, 1962; asst. mgr. Stanford Indsl. Park Office, 1962-63; mgr. Mountain View Office, 1963-66; asst. v.p., mgr. Stanford Indsl. Park Office, 1966-67; v.p. Met. Div. Bus. Devel., 1967-68, v.p. personnel div., 1968-70; asst. sec. Air Force, Manpower and Res. Affairs, 1970-73; sr. v.p. Wells Fargo Bank, West Bay Div., 1974-75, sr. v.p. trust div. and investment advisors div., 1975-78; exec. v.p. So. Calif. Exec. Office, Los Angeles, 1978—, exec. v.p. domestic corr. banking, 1983—; dir. Nat. Life Ins. Co. Montpelier, Vt., Wells Fargo Realty Advisors, Wells Fargo Bus. Credit. Bd. dirs. Wells Fargo Found.; pres. Air Force Aid Soc.; bd. dirs. Hollywood Presbyn. Med. Ctr., Central City Assn. Los Angeles, So. Calif. Bldg. Funds, YMCA Met. Los Angeles; chmn. Stanford U. Athletic Bd.; vice chmn. Los Angeles chpt. ARC. Served to lt. col. USMCR, 1953-55. Recipient Dept. Air Force Exceptional Civilian Service award. Republican. Episcopalian. Clubs: Los Angeles Country, Calif., Army and Navy, Univ. (San Francisco); Beach. Home: 8050 Mulholland Dr Los Angeles CA 90046 Office: 4444 S Flower St 48th Floor Los Angeles CA 90017

BOREK, MARY BURNS, psychologist; b. Pitts. Sept. 6, 1916; s. Joseph Anthony and Myral (Anderson) Burns; m. Theodore Borek, Mar. 3, 1943; 1 son, Theodore Burns. A.B., West Liberty Coll., 1942, M.A., Columbia U., 1953; Ed.D., Ariz. State U., 1970. Lic. psychologist, Ariz. Instr. chemistry West Liberty (W.Va.) Coll., 1945-48; counselor Phoenix Union High Sch. Dist., 1953-75, psychologist, 1975-82; pvt. practice psychology, Phoenix, 1982—; co-dir. human relations workshops. Mem. Am. Psychol. Assn., Ariz. Psychol. Assn. Mem. United Ch. Christ. Author: Problem Solving, 1977. Address: 1526 W Avalon Dr Phoenix AZ 85015

BORELLI, BEULAH MAY, retired school psychologist; b. Madison, S.D., Sept. 19, 1918; d. Joseph Charles and Edna May (Van Nostrand) Westaby; student U. Wash., Seattle, 1937-39, Stockton Jr. Coll., 1959; B.A., U. Pacific, Stockton, Calif., 1962, M.A., 1967, postgrad., 1968-70; m. Frank M. Borelli, Feb. 14, 1954 (dec. Nov. 1976). Sec. county agrl. office, Port Orchard, Wash., 1941-42; s c. to dir. div., officer in charge Corr. div., Supply Dept., Puget Sound Navy Yard, Bremerton, Wash., 1942-44; adminstrv. sec. to dir. welfare services for ablebodied Southwestern Theatre, ARC, Manila, 1945-46, Far East Theatre, Tokyo, 1946-49, exec. dir. Seneca County chpt. ARC, Tiffin, Ohio, 1949-51, dir. home service San Joaquin County chpt., Stockton, 1951-57; tchr., Fillmore Elementary Sch., Stockton, 1962-63, Zackary Taylor Sch., Stockton, 1966-67; psychometrist Manteca (Calif.) Unified Sch. Dist., 1967-71, sch. psychologist, 1971-83. Mem. Internat. Sch. Psychology Assn., Nat. Assn. Sch. Psychologists, Calif. Assn. Sch. Psychologists and Psychometrists, Delta Area Assn. Sch. Psychologists (sec. 1975-78), San Joaquin County psychol. soc., Sacramento Area Sch. Psychologists Assn., AAUW. Mem. Disciples of Christ. Club: Zonta (pres. San Joaquin County 1965-66). Home: 40 E Mariposa Ave Stockton CA 95204

BORENSTEIN, DANIEL BERNARD, physician; b. Silver City, N.Mex., Mar. 31, 1935; s. Jack and Marjorie Elizabeth (Kerr) B.; B.Ch.E., MIT, 1957; M.D., U. Colo., 1962; m. Bonnie Denice Ulland, June 11, 1967; 1 son, Jay Brian. Intern, U. Hosp., U. Ky., 1962-63; resident psychiatry U. Colo. Med. Center, 1963-66, chief resident, instr. dept. psychiatry U. Colo. Sch. Medicine, 1965-66; instr. dept. psychiatry U. So. Calif. Sch. Medicine, 1966-67, asst. clin. prof. dept. psychiatry UCLA Sch. Medicine, 1972—, dir. mental health program for physicians in tng., 1980—; clin. asso. Los Angeles Psychoanalytic Soc. and Inst., 1967-71, pres. clin. assos., 1970-71, faculty, 1973—; pvt. practice medicine specializing in psychoanalysis and psychiatry, West Los Angeles, 1966—; mem. staff UCLA Hosp. Neuropsychiat. Inst., 1973—. Served to lt. AUS, 1957-58. Diplomate Am. Bd. Psychiatry and Neurology. Fellow Am. Psychiat. Assn. (council Area VI 1977-79, 81—, dep. rep. assembly of dist. brs. 1981-82, rep. 1982—, com. to rev. psychiat. news 1979-81, nominating com. 1982-83, assembly liaison to peer rev. com. 1982—); mem. So. Calif. Psychiat. Soc. (outstanding service citation 1975, chmn. peer rev. com. 1974-77, exec. council 1976—, mem. ethics com. 1977—, pres. 1978-79, chmn. fellowship com. 1979—, chmn. Commn. on Psychiatry and the Law 1980-81), Los Angeles County (chmn. Bay dist. mental health com. 1980—, dir. 1981—), Calif. (rep. for psychiatrists to Ho. of Dels., Calif. Med. Assn. 1979—, com. on mental health and mental disabilities 1979—) med. assns., Calif. Psychiat. Assn., Los Angeles Psychoanalytic Soc. and Inst. (co-chmn. extension div. 1973-74, chmn. peer rev. com. 1975-78, mem. curriculum com. 1980—), Am. (asso.), Internat. psychoanalytic assns. Contbr. articles to profl. publs. Office: 151 N Canyon View Dr Los Angeles CA 90049

BORGIA, CHARLES ANTHONY, orthopaedic surgeon; b. Rockford, Ill., Oct. 30, 1930; s. James F. and Camilla (Montanariello) B.; A.B., U. Calif. at Berkeley, 1952; M.D., U. Calif. at San Francisco, 1955; m. Patricia June Anderson, June 21, 1953; children—Scott, Ann Marie, Steven, Brian. Intern Santa Clara County Hosp., 1955-56; resident orthopaedic surgery Walter Reed Army Hosp., Washington, 1957-60, practice of medicine specializing in orthopaedic surgery, San Jose, Calif., 1964—; mem. staff Good Samaritan Hosp., San Jose, sec.-treas, med. staff, 1969-70, chmn. div. orthopedic surgery, 1972-73. Chmn. Santa Clara County Disaster and Emergency Com., 1969-70, Mass Casualty Com., 1972-73. Served to maj. USAF, 1956-64. Diplomate Am. Bd. Orthopaedic Surgeons. Mem. AMA, Calif., Santa Clara County med. socs., Western Orthopaedic Assn., Am. Acad. Orthopaedic Surgeons. Club: Santa Clara Valley Orthopaedic (sec.-treas. 1971, pres. 1974—). Office: 2505 Samaritan Dr San Jose CA 95124

BORGMANN, DMITRI ALFRED, research co. and loan brokerage firm exec., investment firm co. exec., ch. ofcl.; b. Berlin, Germany, Oct. 22, 1927; s. Hans and Lisa (Kalnitzkaya) B.; brought to U.S., 1936, naturalized, 1943; Ph.B., U. Chgo., 1946; D.D., Universal Life Ch., 1976; Ph.D., Sussex Coll. Tech. (Eng.), 1979; m. Iris Sandra Sterling, Oct. 27, 1962; 1 son, Keith Alan. Policy change supr. Central Standard Life Ins. Co., Chgo., 1946-61; actuarial asst. Harry S. Tressel & Assos., Chgo., 1961-65; ind. writer, columnist, researcher, Chgo., 1965-71; owner RC Research Co., also Jackpot Jubilee, Chgo., 1970-72, Dayton, Wash., 1972-75, Research Unltd., Dayton, 1975—, Intellex, Dayton, 1976—, Service Unltd., Dayton, 1976—; corporate identity cons., 1967—; co-owner Crossword Cash, 1970—; ordained minister Universal Life Ch., Modesto, Calif., 1976; founder, pres. Divine Immortality Ch., Dayton, 1978—; loan broker 1980—; pres. Myriagon, Inc., 1983—. Mem. Life Office Mgmt. Assn. Inst., Word Guild, Mensa, Nat. Puzzlers League. Author: Language on Vacation, 1965; Beyond Language, 1967; Curious Crosswords, 1970. Founding editor, contbr. Word Ways, 1968—; columnist Books, 1966, Puzzle Lovers Newspaper, 1968-71, Chgo. Tribune Mag., 1973-74, Games Mag., 1979-80. Home and Office: PO Box 120 Dayton WA 99328 Office: 410 S 2d St Dayton WA 99328

BORGSTROM, HAROLD E(DWARD) (NED), JR., accountant; b. Bellingham, Wash., Oct. 8, 1943; s. Harold Edward and Ruth Ingeborg (Hallgren) B.; m. Sue Cortelyou, July 11, 1970; 1 dau., Carrie. B.S. in Math., Stanford U., 1965, M.B.A., 1970; postgrad. Div. Sch. Yale U., 1965-66. C.P.A., Wash. Staff cons. Arthur Andersen & Co., San Francisco, 1970-73, audit mgr., Seattle, 1974-80, audit ptnr., Seattle, 1980—; clin. faculty Sch. Pub. Health and Community Medicine, U. Wash. Mem. Seattle Symphony Chorale. Served to 1st lt. USAR, 1966-68. Rockefeller fellow (Fund for Theol. Edn.), 1965-66. Mem. Am. Inst. C.P.A.s, Wash. Soc. C.P.A.s, Healthcare Fin. Mgmt. Assn. (v.p. Wash. chpt.). Republican. Methodist. Clubs: Bellevue Athletic, Harbor (Seattle). Office: 501 Norton Bldg Seattle WA 98104

BORHANI, NEMAT O., physician; b. Teheran, Iran, Apr. 28, 1926; B.A., Am. Coll. Teheran, 1945; M.D., U. Teheran, 1949; M.P.H., Johns Hopkins U., 1960; m. Patricia Hyde, June 29, 1956; children—Diane, Tracy, David. Intern, St. Mary's Long Beach (Calif.) Hosp., 1953-54, Kaiser Found. Hosp., Oakland, Calif., 1954-56, Bellevue Hosp., N.Y.C., 1956-58; acting head hypertension clinic, physician Johns Hopkins U. Hosp., Balt., 1958-60; head heart disease control program Bur. Chronic Diseases, Calif. Dept. Public Health, Berkeley, 1960-65, chief Bur. Chronic Diseases, 1965-67; mem. staff Pres.'s Commn. on Heart Disease, Cancer and Stroke, Washington, 1964; prof. medicine, prof. community health, chmn. dept. community health Sch. Medicine, U. Calif.-Davis, 1968—, vice-chmn. div. community and postgrad. medicine Sch. Medicine, 1968-78, prof. nutrition Coll. Agrl. and Environ. Scis., 1971—; vis. prof. medicine U. Santo Tomas, Manila, Philippines, 1975. Recipient Presdl. Citation, Pres. Philippines, 1975. Fellow Am. Coll. Cardiology (chmn. com. prevention cardiovascular diseases 1975-81, Theodore and Susan B. Cummings Humanitarian award 1976, 78), Am. Coll. Chest Physicians, Am. Coll. Angiology, Internat. Coll. Angiology, Am. Heart Assn. (chmn. council on epidemiology 1973-75, mem. exec. com. council on epidemiology 1968-82), Internat. Soc. Studies of Twins; mem. Am. Epidemiol. Soc., Soc. Epidemiologic Research, Internat. Epidemiol. Assn., N.Y. Acad. Scis., Johns Hopkins Med. and Surg. Assn. Editor-in-chief Jour. Community Health, 1982—. Contbr. numerous articles to nat. and internat. profl. jours. Office: Dept Community Health Sch Medicine U Calif David CA 95616

BORINGER, KAREN LINDA, communications consultant; b. Hastings, Nebr., Feb. 12, 1948; d. Berton Ozro and Bobbette Romona (model) Young; m. John Wayne Fox, Apr. 22, 1967; children—John Robert, Christopher Brian; m. Fred Edward Boringer, Dec. 31, 1974. B.A., U. Colo., 1977, M.A., 1983. Sec., data processing technician U. Minn.-Morris, 1969-74; accounts payable dept. head Schlumberger Well Services, Denver, 1975-77; pres., buyer Foxylady Creations Custom Jewelry, Minn. and Denver, 1975-78; owner, operator Communi Concepts, Denver, 1979—; ptnr. Communication Resources, Lakewood, Colo., 1979—. Founding pres. Women Bus. Owners Assn. Denver, 1979; sec. bd. dirs. Womanschool Network, 1982-83. Mem. Am. Soc. Tng. and Devel., Nat. Assn. Female Execs., Associated Photographers Internat. Club: Win/Win Forum of Denver. Home: 5713 Saulsbury St Arvada CO 80002 Office: 390 Union Blvd Suite 404 Lakewood CO 80228

BORISSOFF, ROBERT ALEXANDER, security company executive, educator; b. Vladivostok, Siberia, Russia, Nov. 4, 1927; came to U.S., 1947, naturalized, 1953; m. Gail V. Pochaeff, Feb. 15, 1952; children—Nicholas, Maria, Boris. B.A., Aurora U., Shanghai, China, 1947; A.A. in Criminology, City Coll. San Francisco, 1961; B.A., Diablo Coll., 1963; grad. Concord Police Acad., 1963. Adminstrv. asst. U.S. Purchasing and Fiscal Office for Calif., San Francisco, 1951-61; police officer Pacifica (Calif.) Police Dept., 1961-65; security cons. Citywide Investigations Co., San Francisco, 1965—; dir. Nor-Cal Security, San Francisco, 1965-81, Nor-Cal. Tng. Acad., San Francisco, 1981—, Master Alarm Co., 1981—; sr. instr. U.S. Army Res. Sch., San Francisco, 1970—; dir. Security Travel Internat., 1978—; hon. del. Am. Police Conf., 1980; cons. in field. Served with U.S. Army, 1945-48; with USAR, 1948—. Recipient commendation Gov. Reagan Calif., 1969, Internat. Security Conf., 1973, U.S. Army, 1981; Mem. Acad. Security Educators and Trainers (cert. security trainer), World Assn. Detectives, Calif. Assn. Lic. Investigators (gov. 1974-75), Nat. Assn. Federally Lic. Fire-Arms Dealers, Nat. Assn. Chiefs of Police. Club: Russian-Am. (master-at-arms San Francisco). Author publs. in field. Office: Nor-Cal Tng Acad 2016 Oakdale Ave San Francisco CA 94124

BORKON, BARNEY BERNARD, Realtor; b. Koenigsberg, Germany, Nov. 7, 1906; s. Sali and Martha (Mendelsohn) B.; came to U.S., 1951, naturalized, 1957; D.Dental Medicine, Albertus U., Koenigsberg, 1931; m. Ruth Mueller, Dec. 24, 1940; children—Michael Stephen, Monica Helen (Mrs. Hugh H. Bartlett). Dental surgeon, Germany, 1931-35, Birmingham, Eng., 1936-51; with Wiener & Assos., and predecessor, San Francisco, 1953—, v.p., 1963-80. Chmn. Birmingham Jewish Refugee Club, 1940-48; pres. Crestlake Property Owners Assn., 1972-73; hon. life mem. Calif. State PTA. Mem. San Francisco Real Estate Bd. (dir., exec. com. 1970-72, chmn. multiple sales com. 1974-75), Calif. Assn. Realtors (dir., dist. chmn. 1975-80). Mem. B'nai B'rith. Home: 15 Goleta Ave San Francisco CA 94132 Office: 2512 Noriega St San Francisco CA 94122

BORLAND, CAROL JOAN, editor; b. Camden, N.J., May 11, 1948; d. I. James and Doris M. (McGettigan) Smith; m. Ralph J. Borland, Sept. 14, 1967. Student Glassboro State Coll., 1971-76, Ariz. State U., 1981—. Adminstrv. asst. Bryant & Stratton Bus. Inst., Williamsville, N.Y., 1977-78; asst. editor Univ. Microfilms Internat., Ann Arbor, Mich., 1979; editor Jaques Cattell Press, Tempe, Ariz., 1980—. Democrat. Home: 9459 E Jenan Dr Scottsdale AZ 85260 Office: Jaques Cattell Press PO Box 25001 Tempe AZ 85282

BORLENGHI, ROBERT SERGE, real estate investor; b. Turin, Italy, Apr. 17, 1944; s. Lawrence H. and Carla (Sconfienza) B.; came to U.S., 1965, naturalized, 1977; B.Sc., U. So. Calif., 1967; M.Sc., U. Padua (Italy), 1969; m. Francesca d'Althan, Jan. 1, 1966 (separated Jan. 1982); children—Matthew, Lawrence, Edward. Partner, Borlenghi Gen. Bldg. Co., Milan, Italy, 1968-69; v.p. Immobiliare of Rome, Hollywood, Calif., 1970-74; pres., dir. Resdeco, real estate devel. corp., Beverly Hills, Calif., 1974—; pres. Bortex Corp., Dallas; dir. Fordesco, Inc.; partner Warmington Ventures, Red Mill Trading Co., Internat. Real Estate Assos. Bd. dirs. Marina Del Rey Assn. Los Angeles County; mem. dean's council Sch. Architecture, UCLA; founder Children's Mus., Los Angeles, Mus. Contemporary Art, Los Angeles; trustee Dallas Ballet. Recipient Owner's Design award Nat. Assn. Architects, 1972. Mem. Archimedes Circle, Nat. Home Builders Council, Bldg. Industry Assn., Nat. Real Estate Council, Newcomen Soc. N.Am., Confrerie de la Chaine des Rotisseurs. Republican. Roman Catholic. Club: Yacht. Home: 703 N Sierra Dr Beverly Hills CA 90210 Office: 9460 Wilshire Blvd Beverly Hills CA 90212

BORMAN, CHARLES EDWARD, artist, educator; b. Los Angeles, Aug. 20, 1930; s. Edward James and Nellie Marie B.; A.A., Los Angeles City Coll., 1951; B.A., Calif. State U., Los Angeles, 1953, M.A., 1959; postgrad. U. So. Calif., 1961-65; m. Thelma Esther Olsen, June 29, 1952; children—Craig Lewis, Lynn Carol. Tchr. pub. schs. Los Angeles, 1953-59; instr. art Los Angeles City Coll., 1965-70; prof. art Calif. State U., Los Angeles, 1960—, asso. chmn., 1976—; one-man shows include Bullock's Gallery, Los Angeles, 1961, Brand Art Center, Glendale, Calif., 1965, West Gallery, Studio City, Calif., 1977, Office of Chancellor, Long Beach, Calif., 1982; group shows Pasadena (Calif.) Art Mus., 1971, Brand Art Center, 1971, 72, 79, Mcpl. Art Gallery, Los Angeles, 1973, Crocker Gallery, Sacramento, 1973, West Gallery, 1976; represented in permanent collections; freelance designer, cons. Mem. adv. bd. So. Calif. Designer-Crafts, Inc., 1980—. Served with U.S. Army, 1955-57. Mem. Secondary Art Tchrs. Assn. (pres. Los Angeles 1958-60), So. Calif. Art Edn. Assn. (pres. 1966-68), Univ. and Coll. Designers Assn., Phi Delta Kappa. Home: 600 E Cypress St Glendale CA 91205 Office: Calif State U 5151 State University Dr Los Angeles CA 90032

BORN, ROBERT HEYWOOD, consulting engineer; b. Los Angeles, Nov. 7, 1925; s. Robert Bogle and Mignon Mary (Heywood) B.; student Stanford U., 1943; B.E., U. So. Calif., 1949, M.S., 1956; m. Marilyn Alice Simpson, Aug. 15, 1947; 1 dau., Stefanie. Assoc. hydraulic engr. Calif. Dept. Water Resources, Los Angeles, 1949-58; chief engr., county hydraulic engr. San Luis Obispo County Flood Control and Water Conservation Dist., 1958-70; exec. v.p. CDM Inc., subs. Camp Dresser & McKee, Inc., Pasadena, Calif., 1970-77, also dir., v.p. parent co., 1978; pres. Born, Barrett & Assocs., 1978—, vis. lectr. Calif. State Poly. U., Calif. State U., San Bernardino. Served with Infantry, U.S. Army, 1943-45; ETO. Decorated Bronze Star. Recipient certificate Outstanding Pub. Works Project, Am. Pub. Works Assn., 1969; diplomate Am. Assn. Environ. Engrs. Mem. ASCE, Nat. Soc. Profl. Engrs., Am. Water Works Assn., Am. Pub. Works Assn., Water Pollution Control Fedn., U.S. Com. on Large Dams, Chi Epsilon. Republican. Presbyterian. Home: 76 W Yale Loop Irvine CA 92714 Office: 1200 Quail St Suite 260 Newport Beach CA 92660

BORN, STEVEN MURRAY, podiatrist; b. Chgo., Sept. 29, 1947; s. Victor Harry and Selma (Teplitz) B., student Eureka Coll., 1970-73; B.S., D.P.M., Ill. Coll. Podiatric Medicine, 1977; m. Janice Rochelle Aronesti, July 11, 1971; children—Jamie, Jordan. Surg. resident Henrotin Hosp., Chgo., 1977-70, gen. practice podiatric medicine, Glendale, Ariz., 1978—. Served with U.S. Army, 1966-69. Recipient Cert. of Appreciation, Ill. Coll. Podiatric Medicine, 1977. Mem. Am. Podiatry Assn., Am. Assn. Hosp. Podiatrists, Acad. Ambulatory Surgery, Am. Public Health Assn., Ariz. Podiatry Assn., Glendale Jr. C. of C. Clubs: Pro, Optimists. Home: 8061 N 31st Ln Phoenix AZ 85021 Office: 5748 W Glendale Ave Glendale AZ 85301

BORNS, CHARLES ROBERT, educator, ret. army officer; b. Dayton, Ohio, Dec. 10, 1917; s. Joseph Bernard and Caroline (Fowler) B.; B.S. with honors in Bus. Adminstrn. U. Dayton, 1940; M.B.A. with distinction, Harvard U., 1950; grad. Army Command and Gen. Staff Coll., 1954, Armed Forces Staff Coll., 1961; m. Frances Magdalena Schnell, Jan. 21, 1942; children—Carolyn Ann (Mrs. Michael J. Cowell), Charles Joseph, Michael Oscar. Commd. 2d lt. U.S. Army, 1940, advanced through grades to lt. col., 1954, stationed at Ft. Knox, Ky., 1940-42, 1945-46, Gt. Britain, 1942, North Africa 1943, Italy, 1944, dep. q.m., Stuttgart, Germany, 1950-53, chief requirement br. G-4, USARPAC, Hawaii, 1958-61, logistics research officer logistics Mgmt. Center, Ft. Lee, Va., 1961-64, ret., 1964; prof. bus. adminstrn., chmn. dept. Chaminade Coll., Honolulu, 1964—, asst. to pres. for planning, 1965—, dean spl. sessions, 1969, assoc. dean for spl. programs, 1972, dean adult edn., 1973, v.p., 1974—; vis. prof. Xavier U., Cin., 1974, 75, 81; vis. prof. Hakuoh Women's Coll., Japan, 1977, 80; adj. prof. Alaska Pacific U., summer 1982. Mem. Hawaii Joint Council Econ. Edn., 1965—, exec. com., 1968—, treas., 1970, chmn., 1971. Mem. Cath. Diocesan Sch. Bd., Honolulu, 1965—; bd. advisers Cath. Social Service Hawaii, 1967—, treas., 1969, v.p., 1971. Decorated Legion of Merit, Commendation medal with oak leaf cluster; C.P.A., Hawaii. Mem. Western Assn. Schs. and Colls. (vis. com., 1965), Harvard Bus. Sch. Assn., Hawaii Mfrs. Assn., Soc. Coll. and U. Planning, Hawaii C. of C. (planning com.), Alpha Sigma Tau, Delta Mu Delta, Delta Epsilon Sigma. Contbr. articles on operations research and logistics, community relations, and higher edn. to publns. Home: 6614 Kalopa St Honolulu HI 96825

BOROFSKY, ARNOLD JACOB, quality engr.; b. Boston, Apr. 22, 1921; s. Israel Herman and Esther (Sallow) B.; B.S., Northeastern U., 1943; Ed.M., Boston U., 1949; m. Mariko Nagumo, July 24, 1974; 1 son, Evan I. McKee. Sr. project engr. Autonetics div. Rockwell Internat., Anaheim, Calif., 1962-68; dir. Fairchild Semicondr., Mountain View, Calif., 1968-70; cons. Borofsky Assos., Foster City, Calif., 1970-72; project engr. Aerospace Corp., El Segundo, Calif., 1972-82; staff engr. Lockheed Missile and Space Co., San Mateo, Calif., 1982—. Served with USNR, 1943-46. Registered profl. engr., Calif. Office: Box 191 San Mateo CA 94401

BORONKAY, ATTILA DENES, electronics engr.; b. Budapest, Hungary, Dec. 19, 1923; s. Aladar Jozsef and Krisztina (Erkeserui-Szilagyi) B.; came to U.S., 1959, naturalized, 1964; grad. engring. Hungarian Royal Mil. Acad., 1943; dip. engring. Budapest U. Tech., 1950; children—Laszlo, Susan. Design engr. EMG Electronic Instruments Co., Budapest, 1950-52; research fellow Physics Research Inst., Hungarian Acad. Scis., 1953-56; design engr. UNICAM Instruments Co., Cambridge, Eng., 1957-59; prin. electronics engr. Beckman Instruments Co., Fullerton, Calif., 1959-74, Irvine, Calif., 1975—. Served to lt. Hungarian Royal Air Force, 1943-45. Mem. IEEE, Soc. for Applied

Spectroscopy (regional chmn. 1979-81). Contbr. articles in field to profl. jours.; patentee in field. Office: PO Box C 19600 Irvine CA 92713

BOROS, JOHN, fire chief; b. Braddock, Pa., Dec. 19, 1936; s. Andrew and Mary (Matta) B.; student Boise State Univ., 1967-68, Nat. Fire Acad., 1981; m. LaUna Kay Helm, Aug. 24, 1957; children—Steven Andrew, Michael John. With Boise (Idaho) Fire Dept., 1962—, driver engr., 1965, lt. alarm maintenance, 1965, capt. maintenance, 1965-67, capt. fire insp., 1967-73, asst. fire marshal, 1973-76, fire marshal, 1976-78, fire chief, 1978—, mgr. Credit Union, 1965-76; instr. Idaho Vocat. Tng. Div. on Fire Prevention, 1969-75; mem. bd. Idaho Adv. Bd. for Fire Service Tng. Served with USAF, 1954-62. Recipient Mayor's Spl. Recognition award, 1970; Achievement award Am. Legion, 1976; Idaho Fire Prevention Safety award, 1976; named Idaho Fireman of Yr., 1975; Fireman of Yr. local 672 Internat. Assn. Firefighters, 1975. Mem. Fire Marshals Assn. N. Am., Nat. Fire Protection Assn., Internat. Assn. Arson Investigators, Idaho Conf. Fire Prevention Ofcls. (treas.), Idaho Fire Chief's Assn. (chmn. com.), Boise C. of C., Boise Fire Dept. Assn., Internat. Assn. Fire Chiefs, Ada County Fire Chiefs Assn. (pres.), Western Fire Chiefs Internat. Assn., DAV, Hon. Order Blue Goose. Clubs: Elk, Civitan (Boise). Office: Office of Fire Chief 520 Idaho St Boise ID 83702*

BOROUGH, HOWARD COLSON, physicist; b. Klamath Falls, Oreg., Mar. 28, 1930; s. Lionel Lincoln and Lorena Helen (Colson) B.; B.S., U. Wash., 1952, M.S., 1956; cert. Inst. Optics, U. Rochester, 1964, U. So. Calif. Image Processing Inst., 1974; children from previous marriage—David, Mark, Brita. Supr. optics group Boeing Aerospace, Seattle, 1956-67; mgr. optics research sect. IIT Research Inst., Chgo., 1967-69; sensor systems mgr. Mil. Spacecraft br. Boeing Aerospace Co., Seattle, 1969-73, mgr. spl. projects Info. Systems div., 1973-79, prin. engr. MX phys. security program, 1980-81, acting mgr. IR optics product devel., 1982—. cons., 1969—; freelance photographer, 1982—. Safety chmn. Wash. State Sports Diving Council. Mem. Am. Soc. Photogrammetry, Soc. Photo Optical Instrumentation Engrs., Discovery South (pres. 1982-83), Infrared Info. Symposium. Patentee in field; contbr. articles to profl. jours. Club: Wash. Council Skin Diving (past pres.). Home: 12715 Shorewood Dr SW Seattle WA 98146 Office: PO Box 3999 Seattle WA 98124

BOROUGH, LESLIE ANN, bank holding company official; b. South Bend, Ind., June 16, 1953; d. Paul LeRoy and Annese Eveline (Brown) B. B.A. in Tech. Journalism, Colo. State U., 1975. Graphic artist Leed Ltd., Denver, 1975-76; account exec. Aadvark Advt., Denver, 1976-77, Plain Brown Wrapper Co., Denver, 1977; art. dir. Ranck-Ross-Moore Advt. Agy., Denver, 1977; advt. dir. Am. Furniture Warehouse, Denver, 1977-78; advt. mgr. Affiliated Bankshares of Colo. Inc., Boulder, 1979—. Mem. Denver Advt. Fedn. Methodist. Home: 3100 Broadway Apt 309 Boulder CO 80302 Office: Affiliated Bankshares of Colo Inc 1101 Arapahoe Ave Boulder CO 80302

BORRELLI, JOHN, agrl. engring. educator; b. Florence, Colo., Mar. 20, 1941; s. John and Matilda (Yellico) B.; B.S. in Agrl. Engring., Colo. State U., 1965, M.S., 1967; Ph.D. in Civil Engring., Pa. State U., 1973; m. Trudy Mae Geyer, June 17, 1973; children—Jose, Josette. Marine engr. San Francisco Bay Naval Shipyard, Vallejo, Calif., 1967-68; asst. devel. engr. U. Calif., Davis, 1968-70; irrigation engr. U. Wis., Recife, Brazil, 1973-74; prof. agrl. engring. U. Wyo., Laramie, 1975—; research in field. Grantee EPA, Dept. Agr., Union Pacific R.R., Old West Regional Commn., Office of Water Research and Tech.; registered profl. engr., Colo. Mem. ASCE, Am. Soc. Agrl. Engrs., Internat. Commn. Irrigation and Drainage, Sigma Xi, Phi Kappa Phi, Gamma Sigma Delta. Lutheran. Contbr. articles to profl. publs. Home: 1472 N 22d Laramie WY 82070 Office: Univ Wyoming Laramie WY 82071

BORRUP, RONALD JAMES, mfg. engr.; b. New Brunswick, N.J., Apr. 19, 1920; s. John Jensen and Margaret Elizabeth Addison (Jack) B.; B.S., Worcester Poly. Inst., 1942; m. Margo Vivian Peterson, Aug. 25, 1979; children by previous marriage—David Hollister, Carol Elizabeth, Beth Tracy, John William. Test engr. Hamilton Standard div. United Aircraft Corp., 1946-48; chief design, devel. engr. Safeway Heat Elements Co., 1948-54; founder, pres., chmn. bd. Electro-Flex Heat Inc., 1954-63; founder, dir. Electro-Flex Calif., 1958-61; market devel. engr. Pratt & Whitney Aircraft div. United Aircraft Corp., 1963-67; project engr. Hamilton Standard div., Windsor Locks, Conn., 1967-70; sales mgr. Kaman Automation div. Kaman Aerospace Corp., Bloomfield, Conn., 1970-73; chief engr. Thermal Systems div. Sierracin Corp. (formerly Electroflex Corp. Calif.), Los Angeles, 1974-81; founder Rongo Co., South Pasadena, Calif., 1981—. Pres. congregation Congregational Ch., South Glastonbury, Conn., 1959-60. Served from ensign to lt. USNR, 1942-46. Mem. Lambda Chi Alpha. Republican. Patentee in field. Home: 1311 Lyndon St South Pasadena CA 91030 Office: PO Box 1472 South Pasadena CA 91030

BORT, JOSEPH PARKER, county official; b. Avalon, Calif., July 23, 1915; s. Milo C. and Mary (Parker) B.; m. Jacklyn Taylor, May 14, 1942; children—Samuel, Daniel, Margaret, Imrie. B.S., U. Calif.-Berkeley, 1939, LL.D., 1942. Bar: Calif. Practice law, Oakland, Calif.; mem. city council Berkeley, Calif., 1963-67; county supt. Alameda County, Calif., 1967—. Served to lt. USN. Mem. Calif. Bar Assn., Alameda County Bar Assn. Republican. Christian Scientist. Office: Office of the County Board 1221 Oak St Oakland CA 94612

BORTON, WILLIAM MONROE, mgmt. cons.; b. Cambridge, Ohio, Nov. 26, 1914; s. Grover Cleveland and Estella Corinne (Monroe) B.; B.Sc. with honors in Mktg., Ohio State U., Columbus, 1938, M.B.A., 1944; Ph.D. (grantee Sales Execs. Club Los Angeles), U. So. Calif., 1956. Advt. mgr., gen. mgr. J.G. Bair Co., Cambridge, 1939-44; market analyst, sales mgr. Van Tuyl Engring. Corp., Los Angeles, 1944-45; market analyst Lane-Wells Co., Los Angeles, 1945-46; market, product research mgr. Weber Showcase & Fixture Co., Los Angeles, 1946-47; mgmt. cons., Los Angeles, 1947—; instr. bus. Ohio State U., 1944, U. So. Calif., 1946-49, Calif. State U. at Los Angeles, 1949-51, UCLA, 1957-59, 77. Licensed psychologist, Calif. Mem. Am. Psychol. Assn., Am. Mktg. Assn., AAAS, Phi Delta Theta, Phi Eta Sigma, Beta Gamma Sigma. Club: Sports Connection. Contbg. editor So. Calif. Yachting News, 1968-69. Contbr. articles on bus., social sci. to profl. jours. Address: 8400 De Longpre Ave Suite 411 Los Angeles CA 90069

BORUM, ELIZABETH ANN, psychologist; b. Newman, Calif., May 4, 1930; d. John Allen and Helen Eliza (Sheedy) B.; m. Robert Arthur Arey, Jan. 27, 1951 (div.). B.A. in Psychology with honors, U. Calif.-Berkeley, 1951, M.A. in Psychology, 1953. Lic. psychologist, Calif. 1967. Research psychologist Inst. Child Welfare, U. Calif.-Berkeley, 1951-53; chief psychometrist and vocat. counselor Vocat. Service Ctr., YMCA, N.Y.C., 1953-57; grad. research psychologist Inst. Human Devel., U. Calif.-Berkeley, 1957-61; research psychometrist Inst. Med. Services, San Francisco, 1961-67; psychologist Contra Costa (Calif.) County Probation Dept. 1967—; affiliate staff Walnut Creek Hosp., 1978—. Mem. adv. com. San Francisco Mayor's Com. Celebration UN's 20th Anniversary; mem. Mayor's Bicentennial Com., City of Berkeley (Calif.); pres. East Bay chpt. People-to-People, 1975—; mem. Campaign for UN Reform. Recipient Fremont Poetry award, 1947; Anchor Poetry award, 1969, UNICEF Meritorious Service award, 1972; named Woman of Achievement Bay Valley Dist. Bus. and Profl. Women's Club, 1980. Mem. Am. Psychol Assn., Western Psychol. Assn. (past pres. Contra Costa County), No. Calif. Council of Psychol. Assn. (past sec., past treas. Bay Area Council), Calif. State Psychol. Assn., Am. Correctional Assn., Am. Acad. Polit. and Social Sci., AAAS, Soc. Psychol. Study Social Issues, Bay Area Fellowship Ethical Culture (past pres.), West Coast Council Ethical Culture (past chmn.), Bus. and Profl. Women's Club (past pres.), Internat. Platform Assn., ACLU, UN Assn. USA (treas. East Bay chpt. 1975—). Contbr. articles to profl. jours. Home: 1830 Lakeshore Apt 304 Oakland CA 94606 Office: 2525 Stanwell Psychol Clinic Concord CA 94520

BOS, RALPH JOHN, data processing exec.; b. Paterson, N.J., Feb. 14, 1931; s. John R. and Henrietta M. (Balfoort) B.; student Calvin Coll., 1948-50, Davenport Bus. Coll., 1950-52; B.B.A., U. Beverly Hills, 1980, M.B.A. in Fin., 1982; m. Margaret Mengers, Dec. 30, 1952; children—John R., David R., Patricia R., Peter R., Karen R. Bookkeeper, Jacobson Heating Co., Grand Rapids, Mich., 1952-60; acct. Bergen Brunswig Drug Co., Grand Rapids, Mich., 1960-66; gen. mgr. Bergen Brunswig Dataservice Co., Mich. and Carson, Calif., 1966-77, v.p. fin., Carson, 1977—. Served with AUS, 1954-56. Office: Bergen Brunswig Dataservice Co 22351 S Wilmington Ave Carson CA 90745

BOSCO, DOUGLAS H., congressman; b. N.Y.C., July 28, 1946. B.A., Willamette U., 1968, J.D., 1971. Formerly practiced law; mem. 98th Congress from Calif. Bd. dirs. Marin County Housing Authority, Marin County Consumer Protection Agy., Sonoma County Fair; fundraiser hosp. ship SS Hope; co-founder No. Calif. Emeritus Coll. Sr. Citizens; mem. Calif. Wildlife Conservation Bd.; elected to Calif. State Legislature, 1978. Democrat. Office: 1330 Longworth House Office Bldg Washington DC 20515*

BOSE, SAM C., aerospace engineer, system scientist; b. Calcutta, India, July 28, 1953; came to U.S., 1969; s. Amaresh Chandra and Renuka (Sen) B. B.S. summa cum laude in Elec. Engring., Poly Inst. of Bklyn., 1973, M.S., 1974; Ph.D. in Engring., UCLA, 1980. Mem. tech. staff Computer Scis. Corp., Mountain View, Calif., 1974-76; mem. tech. staff Litton Guidance and Control Systems, Woodland Hills, Calif., 1976-82; pres. and chief exec. officer Applied Sci. Analytics Inc., Canoga Park, Calif., 1982—; cons. and lectr. in field; chmn. sessions nat. and internat. confs. Rotary Internat. and Danforth Found. fellow; Oceanographic Inst. fellow; Polytech. Inst. of Bklyn. fellow. Mem. IEEE, AIAA, Inst. of Nav., Internat. Fedn. of Automatic Control, Am. Geophys. Union, Eta Kappa Nu, Tau Beta Pi, Sigma Xi. Contbr. articles in field to profl. jours. Home: 7101 Farralone Ave 156 Canoga Park CA 91303 Office: 7041 Owensmouth Ave Suite 101 Canoga Park CA 91303

BOSEKER, EDWARD HERBERT, orthopedic surgeon; b. Fort Wayne, Ind., Feb. 16, 1936; s. Herbert W. and Helen M. (Mueller) B.; B.S. with honors, U. Mich., 1958; M.D., Ind. U., 1962; M.S. in Orthopedic Surgery, 1967; m. Yvonne Jean Park, June 9, 1962; children—Andrea, Susan, Resa. Intern, Lutheran Hosp., Ft. Wayne, Ind., 1962-63; resident Mayo Clinic, Rochester, Minn., 1963-67; practice medicine, specializing in orthopedic surgery, Santa Ana, Calif., 1967—; asst. clin. prof. U. Calif., Irvine, 1970—. Pres. Tustin (Calif.) Unified Sch. Dist., 1981—. Diplomate Am. Bd. Orthopedic Surgeons. Fellow ACS; mem. Am. Acad. Orthopedic Surgeons. Office: 801 N Tustin Santa Ana CA 92705

BOSH, MARY ANNE, city official, computer consultant; b. Pocatello, Idaho, Nov. 12, 1950; d. Pharis Grant and Ruby (Johnson) Stewart; m. Michael Eugene Bosh, Apr. 24, 1970; children—Alan, Brady. Student Idaho State U., 1969; mgmt. courses Weber State U., 1980-81; IBM computer and programming workshops, 1977-82. Clk./steno, City of Pocatello (Idaho), 1970-73, data entry operator, 1973-76, programmer, 1976-77, systems operator, 1977-78, ops. mgr., 1978-80, mgr. data processing Systems/Ops., 1980—; cons. small IBM systems. Pres., bd. dirs. Citco Fed. Credit Union. Office: City of Pocatello 902 E Sherman Pocatello ID 83201

BOSKIND, CHRISTOPHER FRANKLIN, medical center executive; b. Malabar, Fla., May 4, 1942; s. Sidney Milton and Ethelwyn (Glatter) B.; m. Constance M. Boskind, June 9, 1964; children—Jeffrey, Dawne. B.A., Walla Walla Coll., 1964; M.B.A., Stetson U., 1970. Acct., treas. Forest Lake Acad., Maitland, Fla., 1966-69; treas., bus. mgr. Adelphian Acad., Holly, Mich., 1970-76; dir. reimbursement Loma Linda U. Med. Ctr., 1976-78, asst. v.p., 1978-79, v.p., 1979—. Mem. Hosp. Fin. Mgmt. Assn., Am. Hosp. Assn., Am. Coll. Hosp. Adminstrs. Adventist. Office: Loma Linda U Med Ctr Loma Linda CA 92354

BOSLEY, GARY OSCAR, stock broker; b. Oakland, Calif., Apr. 11, 1944; s. Allen Eugene and Eva Marie Bosley; A.B. in Econs., U. Calif., Berkeley, 1966. Agrl. specialist, analyst Merrill Lynch, Pierce, Fenner & Smith, Winnipeg, Man., Can., 1971-72, stockbroker, commodity broker, Houston, 1972-74; stockbroker, commodity broker Dean Witter & Co., Hayward, Calif., 1975—. Republican candidate for Calif. Assembly, 1976; mem. Alameda County Rep. Central Com., 1977-78; mem. Calif. State Rep. Central Com., 1977-78; past bd. dirs. Regional Citizens Forum, San Francisco Bay Area; past deacon, past mem. council, past moderator Broadmoor Congregational Ch., San Leandro, Calif. Served to capt. USAF, 1967-71. Decorated Commendation medal. Mem. Rep. Bus. and Profl. Club of Hayward (past pres.), Delta Tau Delta. Clubs: Commonwealth (San Francisco); Rotary (past dir.) (Castro Valley, Calif.); Execs. Assn. So. Alameda County. Address: 17887 Trenton Dr Castro Valley CA 94546

BOSLEY, LARRY LEE, dermatologist, surgeon; b. Lincoln, Nebr., Sept. 19, 1931; s. Clifford Lee and Alice Vera (Gerbeling) B.; m. Sandra Neubarth, Mar. 21, 1970; 1 son, John Lee. B.S., (Regents scholar), U. Nebr., 1952, M.D., 1956. Diplomate Am. Bd. Dermatology. Intern, Pierce County Hosp., Tacoma, Wash., 1956-57; resident in dermatology U. Oreg. Med. Ctr., Portland, 1960-62, U. Calif. Med. Ctr., San Francisco, 1962-63; practice medicine, Tacoma, 1959-60; practice medicine specializing in dermatology and hair transplantation, San Francisco, 1963-70; clin. instr. dermatology U. Calif. Med. Ctr., San Francisco, 1963-70; practice dermatology and cosmetic surgery, specializing in hair transplantation, Beverly Hills, Calif., 1973—; pres. Bosley Med. Group, Beverly Hills, 1974—; aviation med. examiner FAA, 1967; participant internat. dermatology confs., Switzerland, 1970-71; civilian cons. dermatology U.S. Navy Hosp., Rota, Spain, 1972-73. Served to capt. M.C., U.S. Army, 1957-63. Mem. Am. Acad. Dermatology, Pacific Dermatol. Assn., Internat. Acad. Cosmetic Surgery, AMA. Clubs: Los Angeles Tennis; Calif. Tennis (San Francisco); Hurlingham (London); Sunrise Country, Rancho Mirage (Palm Springs, Calif.). Contbr. article to med. jour. Office: Bosley Med Group 8447 Wilshire Blvd Suite 400 Beverly Hills CA 90211

BOSMAJIAN, HAIG ARAM, speech communication educator, author; b. Fresno, Calif., Mar. 26, 1928; s. Aram and Aurora (Keosheyan) B.; m. Hamida Just; 1 son, Harlan Aram. B.A., U. Calif.-Berkeley, 1949; M.A., U. Pacific, 1951; Ph.D., Stanford U., 1960. Instr. pub. speaking, parliamentary procedure, rhetoric U. Idaho, Moscow, 1959-61; asst. prof. rhetoric and pub. speech U. Conn., Storrs, 1961-65; assoc. prof. freedom of speech, rhetoric U. Wash., Seattle, 1965-73, prof., 1973—. Mem. Speech Communication Assn., Nat. Council Tchrs. English, Western Speech Communication Assn., AAUP. Author: The Rhetoric of the Civil Rights Movement, 1969; Dissent: Symbolic Behavior and Rhetorical Strategies, 1972, 2d edit., 1980; The Language of Oppression, 1974; Obscenity and Freedom of Expression, 1976; The Principles and Practice of Freedom of Speech, 2d edit., 1983; Censorship, Libraries and the Law, 1983. Office: Speech Communication Dept U Wash Seattle WA 98195

BOSNOS, CHARLES MARK, laser systems engineer; b. Tucson, May 8, 1951; s. Alfred G. and Sylvia (Sabbeth) B.; B.S.M.E., U. Ariz., 1977, postgrad., 1977; m. Mary Ann McPhee, Dec. 23, 1977. Self-employed auto/home repairs, Tucson, 1975-77; asso. reliability engr. AiResearch Mfg. Co. of Calif. div. Garrett Corp., Torrance, 1977-78, environ. control systems engr., 1979-80; project engr. Apollo Lasers Inc., div. Allied Corp., Chatsworth, Calif., 1980-82, systems devel. supr., 1982—. Mem. Laser Inst. Am. Vol., ARC, 1975-77. Home: 17701 Avalon Blvd No 24 Carson CA 90746 Office: 9201 Independence Ave Chatsworth CA 91311

BOSS, RUSSEL WAYNE, educator; b. Springfield, Mo., Jan. 6, 1943; s. Russel Herbert and Elizabeth (Thompson) B.; B.S., Brigham Young U., 1968, M.P.A., 1969; D.P.A., U. Ga., 1973; m. Margaret Elaine Kingston, Aug. 22, 1967; children—Scott Russel, Alan Dennis, Erin Camille, David Spencer. Govt. research analyst U. Ga., 1972-73; asst. prof. public affairs U. Colo., 1973-76, asso. prof., 1976-80, project dir. fed. grants, 1974-80, vis. prof. Coll. Medicine, Health Scis. Center, 1980-81, prof. bus. adminstrn., 1981—; cons. Mem. Internat. Assn. Applied Social Scientists (chmn. peer rev. panel 1976-79, trustee 1979—, cert orgn. devel. cons. 1975), Acad. Mgmt., Am. Soc. Public Adminstrn. Mormon. Contbr. numerous articles, chpts. to profl. publs.; cons. editor Jour. Applied Behavioral Scis., 1978—. Home: 1990 Vassar Dr Boulder CO 80303 Office: Grad Sch Bus Adminstrn 450 Business Bldg U Colo Boulder CO 80309

BOSSE, DEAN ALAN, educator; b. Belleville, Ill., Aug. 9, 1943; s. Melvin Joseph and Irma Cornellia B.; student Evansville Coll., 1961-63; B.A., So. Ill. U., 1969; M.A., St. Louis U., 1971; adminstrv. credential Calif. State U., Long Beach, 1976; m. Mary Alice Gatawakas, Sept. 28, 1964; children—Michael Joseph, Brian John, Benjamin Alan. Speech therapist Cahokia (Ill.) Sch. Dist., 1969-70, Kern County Supt. Schs., Bakersfield, Calif., 1971-72, Santa Ana (Calif.) Unified Sch. Dist., 1972-74; coordinator aphasia program Santa Ana United Sch. Dist., 1974-75; instr., learning specialist Orange Coast Coll., Costa Mesa, Calif., 1975-77, asso. prof. psychology, learning specialist, 1977—. Div. dir., mgr. Robinwood Little League Baseball, 1976-80; coach Huntington Beach N. Jr. All American Football, 1977-80. Mem. Western Coll. Reading assn., Calif. Assn. Post-Secondary Educators of the Disabled, Nat. Assn. Remedial/Developmental Studies in Post-Secondary Edn., Coast Community Tchrs. Guild. Democrat. Home: 16291 Mercier Ln Huntington Beach CA 92647 Office: 2701 Fairview Rd Costa Mesa CA 92626

BOSSERT, STEVEN THOMAS, educational researcher; b. San Diego, July 22, 1948; s. Thomas Richard and Evelyn Mae (Harris) B.; m. Linda Gay Gelvin, Oct. 20, 1978; 1 dau., Kathleen Ann. B.A. with high honors, U. Calif.-San Diego, 1970; Ph.D. (NDEA fellow), U. Chgo., 1975. Computer programmer, data analyst Space Scis. Lab., U. Calif.-San Diego, 1968-70; guest lectr. dept. sociology Purdue U., Calumet, Ind., 1972-74; lectr. dept. edn. U. Chgo., summer 1973; asst. prof. dept. sociology U. Mich., 1974-79; sr. research dir. programs on schooling Far West Lab. for Ednl. Research and Devel., San Francisco, 1980—, mem. seminar scholars, program adv. panel ecol. theory of teaching program, 1978—; mem. adv. panel for profl. level adminstrv. service credential Calif. Commn. on Tchr. Credentialing, 1981—; mem. panel on standards teaching credential Calif. Commn. for Tchr. Prepartion and Licensing, 1981; reviewer various grants competitions Nat. Inst. Edn., 1978—, NSF, 1982. Mem. Am. Sociol. Assn. (editorial bd. jour. 1982-84), Am. Ednl. Research Assn., Sociology of Edn. Assn. (dir. 1980-82). Author: Tasks and Social Relationships in Classrooms: A Study of Instructional Organization and Its Consequences, 1979. Contbr. chpts. to books, articles to profl. jours. Office: 1855 Folsom St San Francisco CA 94103

BOSTED, RICHARD JOHN, fire chief; b. Bklyn., May 11, 1931; s. John Reinholt and Helen Mary (DuMolin) B.; A.A., San Jose City Coll., 1969; m. Saundra Sue Payne, Oct. 10, 1957; Fire fighter, engr. Compton (Calif.) Fire Dept., 1955-69; tng. officer Campbell City (Calif.) Fire Dept., 1969-73; fire chief San Carlos (Calif.) Fire Dept., 1973-77, Riverside (Calif.) City Fire Dept., 1977—; fire sci. tchr. Santa Ana City Coll., San Jose Community Coll., Coll. San Mateo. Vice pres. We Turn in Pushers, Calif., 1978—. Served with U.S. Army, 1953-55. Recipient Gold award United Way Riverside, 1980; named Man of Year, We Turn In Pushers, 1979-80. Mem. Internat. Assn. Fire Chiefs, Citrus Belt Fire Chiefs (pres. 1983—), Calif. Fire Chiefs Assn. (dir., v.p. 1983—), Calif. Firemen's Assn., Riverside County Fire Chiefs Assn. (v.p. 1983—). Republican. Roman Catholic. Club: Exchange (pres. 1980). Contbr. articles to profl. jours. Home: 909 Le Conte St Riverside CA 92507 Office: 3900 Main St Riverside CA 92522

BOSTICK, SHEILA LIVINGSTON, telecommunications company executive; b. San Francisco, Nov. 9, 1935; d. Harvey Laurence and Florence (Kirchen) Livingston; m. Hoyt Alan Bostick, Dec. 16, 1955 (div.); children—Diana Gail, Alan Livingston. B.S. in Physics, U. Calif.-Berkeley, 1956. Tchr. physics Acton Boxborough Regional High Sch., Acton, Mass., 1967-70; tchr. math. Kwajalein (Marshall Islands) Jr.-Sr. High Sch., 1972-74; media specialist Ford Aerospace & Communications Co., Twentynine Palms, Calif., 1974-76; curriculum developer, instr. GTE Sylvania, Mountain View, Calif., 1976-78; mgr. software course devel. Rolm Corp., Santa Clara, Calif., 1979-80, mgr. publs. prodn., 1980-82, mgr. tng. ctrs., 1982—. Mem. Am. Soc. for Tng. and Devel. (v.p. fin. El Camino chpt.), Nat. Soc. for Performance and Instrn., Phi Beta Kappa. Republican. Methodist. Office: 4900 Old Ironsides MST440 Santa Clara CA 95050

BOSTWICK, RICHARD RAYMOND, lawyer; b. Billings, Mont., Mar. 17, 1918; s. Leslie H. and Maude (Worthington) B.; student U. Colo., 1937-38; A.B., U. Wyo., 1943, J.D., 1947; m. Margaret Florence Brooks, Jan. 17, 1944; children—Michael, Patricia, Ed, Dick. Admitted to Wyo. bar, 1947; claim atty. Hawkeye Casualty Co., Casper, Wyo., 1948-49; partner Murane & Bostwick, Casper, 1949—; dir. Banta Petroleum, Inc., UCOR, Inc. Lectr. U. Wyo. Coll. Law. Past trustee Casper YMCA; dep. dir. Civil Def., 1954-58; chmn. local SSS, 1952-70; mem. curriculum coordinating com. Natrona Co. Sch. Dist. 2, High Sch. Dist. Served to capt. AUS, 1943-46. Decorated Bronze Star medal; recipient Silver Merit awards Am. Legion. Mem. Am., Wyo. (pres. 1964-65), Natrona County (pres. 1956) bar assns., Am. Judicature Soc. (exec. com. 1973-75, sec. 1975-77), Internat. Assn. Ins. Counsel, Nat. Conf. Bar Pres. (exec. council 1970-72), Internat. Soc. of Barristers (dir. 1971-76, pres. 1975), Am. Legion (dir. 1951-58, post comdr. 1953-54), Wyo. Alumni Assn. (trustee 1955-57), Casper C. of C. (chmn. legislative com. 1955-57, dir. 1959-62, v.p.). Presbyn. Mason (Shriner, K.T.). Contbr. articles profl. jours. Home: 1137 Granada Ave Casper WY 82601 Office: 350 West A St Casper WY 82601

BOSWORTH, BRUCE LEIGHTON, educator, consultant; b. Buffalo, March 22, 1942; s. John Wayman and Alice Elizabeth Rodgers; children—David, Timothy, Paul, Reuben, Sheri. B.A., U. Denver, 1964; M.A., U. No. Colo., 1970; Ed.D., Walden U., 1984. Elem. tchr. Littleton (Colo.) Pub. Schs., 1964-67, 70-81; bldg. prin. East Smoky Sch. Div. 54, Valleyview, Alta., Can., 1967-70; pres., tchr. Chatfield Sch., Littleton, 1981—; adoption cons. hard-to-place children; ednl. cons. spl. needs children. Mem. Council Exceptional Children, Assn. Supervision and Curriculum Devel. Republican. Methodist. Clubs: Masons, Shriners.

Home: 6170 S Bemis St Littleton CO 80120 Office: Chatfield School PO Box 1039 Littleton CO 80160

BOSWORTH, CECILE MARY (MRS. HOBART VAN ZANDT BOSWORTH), civic leader; b. Phila., Oct. 16; d. Kenneth and Jane (Ploné) Kibre; student U. Calif. at Los Angeles, 1928-32, Art Students League N.Y., 1925; m. Hobart Bosworth, Dec. 22, 1920 (dec.); 1 son, George Hobart. Pres., Nat. Radio & TV Service, Washington, 1944-47; producer, dir. congl. forum Cong. on the Air, 1944-47, charter mem. U. Calif. at Los Angeles Alumni Assn., also life mem., dist. chmn. scholarship com., 1959—; life mem. Women's U. Club, Los Angeles, v.p., 1940-42, dir., 1939-42; alumnae pres. Delta Omicron, 1941; dir. women's div. Los Angeles C. of C., 1941, 43; dir. Antelope Valley chpt. Nat. Cath. Welfare Bur., 1956—, pres., 1965; dir. United Way, 1963—, pres., 1965; Pacific Coast regional chmn. Citizenship Ednl. Service, 1941; 1st vol. chmn., coordinator community resources and canteen United Service Orgns., Los Angeles, 1941; oblate Order St. Benedict; hon. mem. Sans Souci Celebrity Breakfast Club; pres. Internat. Humane Ednl. League; life mem. Schornsteinfer Club. Roman Catholic. Originator, instrumental in securing passage of bill in Cong. for Armed Services Honor Day 1943, observed as Armed Forces Day, 1949. Research in motion picture history. Address: Double C Ranch PO Box 115 Palmdale CA 93550

BOTTAINI, LEO JOHN, accountant; b. Portland, Oreg., June 21, 1930; s. Silvio and Amelia B.; m. Joanne T. Mayer, Sept. 13, 1958; 1 dau., Ann A. B.A., U. Portland, 1952. C.P.A., Oreg. Ptnr. Pope Loback & Co., C.P.A.s., Portland, 1954-74, Main LaFrentz & Co., Portland, 1974-79, Main Hurdman, Portland, 1979-81; mng. ptnr. Bottaini & Gallucci, Portland, 1981—. Past pres. Portland Met. Softball Assn.; chmn. taxation com. Portland C. of C. Served with Fin. Corps, U.S. Army, 1952-54. Mem. Am. Inst. C.P.A.s., Oreg. Soc. C.P.A.s. Democrat. Roman Catholic. Clubs: Multnomah Athletic; Kiwanis (lt. gov., chmn. Mt. Hood Kiwanis Camp). Home: 3210 SE Raymond Portland OR 97202 Office: 1500 SW 1st St Suite 270 Portland OR 97201

BOTTARI, MARIANNA TERESA, public relations executive, fund raiser, editor; b. Phila., Nov. 17, 1941; d. Guido Albert and Malvina Rose (Seccia) B.; m. James F. Derham, Feb. 3, 1973; m. 2d Marc Lee Rubin, Jan. 2, 1982. Student U. Pa., 1962-64, Charles Morris Price Sch. Journalism and Advt., 1964-66. News relations asst. Smith Kline & French Labs., Phila., 1962-64; pub. relations asst. St. Luke's and Children's Med. Ctr., Phila., 1964-66, Thomas Jefferson U. Hosp., Phila., 1969-71; pub. relations dir. Albert Einstein Med. Ctr., Phila., 1971-74, John Muir Meml. Hosp., Walnut Creek, Calif., 1974-77, Peralta Hosp., Oakland, Calif., 1977-80; community relations and devel. dir. Sequoia Hosp., Redwood City, Calif., 1980-82; pub. relations dir. Valley Meml. Hosp., Livermore, Calif., 1982—; cons. PR Woman & Co. Bd. dirs. Coop. Center Council, 1976-77; v.p. Sun Country Homeowners Assn., 1977-79. Served with USNR, 1979-81. Recipient MacEachern nat. award, 1973, MacEachern cert. of merit, 1976. Mem. Acad. Hosp. Pub. Relations, Hosp. Pub. Relations Assn. No. Calif., Internat. Assn. Bus. Communicators, Nat. Assn. Hosp. Devel., Nat. Assn. Female Execs. Home: 315 Gil Blas Rd Danville CA 94526 Office: 1111 E Stanley Blvd L Livermore CA 94550

BOTTI, RICHARD CHARLES, assn. exec.; b. Brockton, Mass., May 1, 1939; s. Alfred Benecchi and Elizabeth Savini; stepson Ernest Botti; student Pierce Jr. Coll., 1959, Orange Coast Coll., 1964; m. Gwen Botti; children—Randolph K., Douglas J., Richard II. Pres., Legis. Info. Services Hawaii, Inc., Honolulu, 1971—; exec. dir., profl. lobbyist Hawaii Food Industry Assn., Honolulu, Hawaii Automotive & Retail Gasoline Dealers Assn., Inc., Honolulu, Hawaii Bus. League, Retail Liquor Dealers Assn. Hawaii, Liquor Dispensers of Hawaii, Honolulu. Mem. Food Industry Assn. Execs., Am. Soc. Assn. Execs. Address: Legis Information Services 1177 Kapiolani Blvd Suite 201 Honolulu HI 96814

BOTTIGER, RUSSELL TED, lawyer, state senator; b. Tacoma, Nov. 8, 1932; s. Albert and Mabel Bottiger; J.D. with honors, U. Wash.; m. Darlene Naughton, June 25, 1955; children—Tedene, Terri. Admitted to Wash. bar; asst. atty. gen. State of Wash., 1960-64; mem. Wash. Ho. of Reps., 1964-71, asst. minority leader, mem. legis. council; mem. Wash Senate, Tacoma, 1972—, majority leader, 1982—, mem. ways and means, fin. instns. and rules coms., also past chmn. energy and utilities com. Active James Sales Grange, Parkland Youth Activities Council; past pres. Pierce County Young Democrats; past officer Wash. Young Dems. Recipient Golden Badge, Fire Dist. Commrs. Mem. Nat. Conf. State Legislators (energy com.), Western Conf. Council State Govts. (chmn. ad hoc com. for Pacific Northwest energy). Lutheran.

BOUCHARD, JOYCE PATRICIA, librarian; b. Sacred Heart, Minn., Mar. 9, 1929; d. Emile Arthur and Elizabeth (McMillan) B. Staff librarian Butte (Mont.) Free Pub. Library, 1951-57, asst. librarian, 1957-62, library dir., 1962-80; law librarian Silver Bow County Law Library, Butte, 1980—. Mem. Butte Drug Council, 1970-73. Mem. Mont. Library Assn. Presbyterian. Clubs: Soroptimist (past pres.), Shriners. Home: 1924 Adams Butte MT 59701 Office: Courthouse 155 W Granite Butte MT 59701

BOUCHER, GEORGE WADE, broadcast executive; b. Dyer, Tenn., Feb. 27, 1924; s. George Washington and Wilma Wade (Cunningham) B.; m. Ruthlea Eberhart, Feb. 23, 1946; children—Melinda Ruth, George Eugene. Broadcaster, Sta. WTMV, East St. Louis, Ill., 1945-46; small bus. owner, 1947-52; broadcaster Sta. KGDN, Seattle, 1954-57, Sta. KTW, 1957-60, Sta. KBLE, Seattle, 1960—, gen. mgr., 1965—. Recipient award for outstanding public service Seattle Fed. Exec. Bd., 1973. Mem. Nat. Assn. Broadcasters, Wash. Assn. Broadcasters, Tucker Automobile Club Am. Republican. Baptist. Club: Masons. Office: 114 Lakeside Ave Seattle WA 98122

BOUCHER, MAYO TERRY, lawyer, judge; b. Stephenville, Tex., July 15, 1918; s. Terry S. and Henryetta (Turley) B.; student Tex. Tech. Coll., 1937-41; LL.B., U. N.Mex., 1952, J.D., 1969; m. Mary Catherine Lake, July 31, 1942; children—Phillip Larry, Terri Sue. With A.T. & S.F. Ry., Belen, N.Mex., 1946-52; admitted to N.Mex. bar, 1952; practiced in Belen, 1952-80; dist. judge 13th Jud. Dist., 1980—. mem. N.Mex. House of Reps., 1957-64. Dir., v.p. Belen Broadcasting Co., 1963-64; dir. 1st Nat. Bank, City atty., Belen, N.Mex., 1956-57. Served with USNR, 1942-45. Mem. C. of C. (dir. 1954-57, pres. 1955), Pi Sigma Alpha. Baptist (deacon). Clubs: Masons (32 deg., past master), Order Eastern Star (past patron, grand sentinel 1982-83, asso. grand patron 1983-84), Rotary, (pres. 1961-62). Home: 1620 Velta Dr Belen NM 87002 Office: 700 Dalies Ave Belen NM 87002

BOUCKHOUT, RICHARD JOHN, air force officer; b. San Francisco, Aug. 24, 1937; s. Fred Godfrey and Medelice (Lafayette) B.; m. Bernadine Carolyn Viegas, Aug. 8, 1959. B.S. in Social Sci., San Jose State U., 1959; M.S. in Edn., Radford Coll., 1972; grad. Air War Coll., Montgomery, Ala., 1979. Commd. 2d lt. U.S. Air Force, 1959, advanced through grades to col., 1980; served in Calif., N. Africa, Tex., Korea, 1961-67; helicopter rescue aircraft comdr., Vietnam, 1968-69; instr. ROTC, asst. prof. human relations Va. Poly. Inst., Blacksburg, 1969-72; wing chief current ops. Kirtland AFB, N.Mex., 1972-78, dep. comdr. ops. 1550 aircrew tng. and test wing, 1980—; comdr. rescue detachment Fairchild AFB, Wash., 1978-80. Decorated D.F.C. (3), Air medal (13), Meritorious Service medal (2), Air Force Commendation medal (3). Mem. Albuquerque C. of C., Order Daedalians. Republican. Roman Catholic. Club: Rotary. Home: 7538 E Corrine Dr Scottsdale AZ 85260 Office: 1550 ATTW/DO Kirtland AFB NM 87117

BOUDREAU, KEITH EUGENE, financial executive; b. Slayton, Minn., Sept. 12, 1946; s. Eugene M. and Kathryn I. (Thraen) B.; m. Connie A. Grall, Aug. 31, 1968; children—Michelle, Kristopher. B.S. in Acctg., Calif. State U.-Long Beach, 1968. C.P.A., Calif., Idaho. Sr. acct. Peat, Marwick, Mitchell & Co., Los Angeles, 1968-72; asst. v.p., asst. controller Avco Fin. Services Inc., Newport Beach, Calif., 1972-78; asst. sec., v.p., treas. Pacific Empire Life Ins. Co., Boise, Idaho, 1978—. Served with USAR, 1968-74. Mem. Am. Inst. C.P.A.s, Idaho Soc. C.P.A.s. Republican. Roman Catholic. Office: PO Box 5538 Boise ID 83705

BOUGHTON, WILLIAM HARRISON, artist; b. Dubuque, Iowa, Feb. 19, 1915; s. Richard and Mayme (Pierce) B.; m. Cleta Margaret Olmstead, Dec. 30, 1950 (dec.); m. 2d, Leta Shelly, July 16, 1971. B.A., U. Iowa, 1943; M.A., U. Calif.-Berkeley, 1945, postgrad., 1945-46. Asst. prof. art Fla. State U., 1947-54; prof., head dept. art Lamar U., Beaumont, Tex., 1954-70, prof. art, 1970-77; 23 one man shows: numerous group shows including 3 traveling shows sponsored by U.S. State Dept.; works represented in pub. and pvt. collections. James Phelan fellow, 1945-47; recipient Silver medal Internat. Acad. Arts and Letters, Rome, Italy, 1972. Mem. Coll. Art Assn., AAUP, Taos Art assn., Taos C. of C., Delta Epsilon, Phi Kappa Pi. Contbr. articles to profl. jours. Address: PO Box 376 El Prado NM 87529

BOUGON, STEPHEN HENRY, pest control company executive; b. New Orleans, Oct. 5, 1949; s. Henry J. and Janet Josaphine (Warner) B.; m. Charlene C. Schwarz, Nov. 18, 1972; children—Chrystal, Connie, Stephen. A.A.S., Clark County Community Coll., 1981. Pres., Busy Bee Pest Control, Inc., Las Vegas, 1976—. Mem. Nev. Bd. Agr., 1981—. Served with USAF, 1968-77. Mem. Nat. Pest Control Assn. (state dir.), So. Nev. Execs. Council. Republican. Roman Catholic.

BOULIERIS, WILMA LOUISE, optometrist; b. Newport, Wash., Jan. 2, 1940; d. Francis Edmond and Elizabeth Jane (Penhallurick) Coy; m. Andrew Boulieris, Jan. 31, 1962 (div.); children—Helaina Yvonne, Elizabeth Theodora. Student Walla Walla Coll., 1956-59, Seattle Community Coll., 1969-70; B.S., Ill. Coll. Optometry, 1974, O.D., 1976. Gen. practice optometry, Moses Lake, Wash., 1976—. Mem. Am. Optometry Assn., Wash. Optometry Assn., Assn. Seventh Day Adventist Optometrists, Council on Visual Devel., Optometric Extension Program, Moses Lake C. of C. Republican. Seventh-day Adventist. Club: Soroptimist Internat. (Moses Lake). Office: 350 Penn Plaza Moses Lake WA 98837

BOULLION, BERTHA MITCHELL, educator, reading specialist; b. Springfield, Mo., Oct. 13, 1944; d. John Jerome and Opal (Weisenberger) Mitchell; m. Delmar Nicklas Boullion, June 12, 1971. B.A. in Edn., Seattle Pacific U., 1966; M. A., Calif. State Coll., 1979; postgrad. in ednl. adminstrn. Standard life teaching credential, Calif., 1973, reading specialist, 1979. Tchr. pub. schs. Highline Dist., Seattle, 1966-69, Greenfield Union Sch. Dist., Bakersfield, Calif., 1969-77; reading specialist Greenfield Dist., Bakersfield, 1977-82, spl. programs coordinator, 1982—. Mem. reading adv. com. Calif. State Coll., 1980—. Mem. Bakersfield Masterworks Chorale, 1969—, pres., 1980-82. Mem. Greenfield Educators Assn., Calif. Tchrs. Assn., Internat. Reading Assn. (Kern council), Assn. Supervision and Curriculum Devel. Republican. Office: Fairview Sch 425 E Fairview Rd Bakersfield CA 93307

BOULTON, SHAUNA DEE, educator; b. Salt Lake City, May 29, 1949; d. Melvin and Afton Lillie (Davidson) Boulton. B.S., U. Utah, 1971, M.Ed., 1981. Cert. elem., severely handicapped, spl. resource tchr., Utah. Tchr. Habilitation Ctr. for Multiple Handicapped, Salt Lake City, 1971-73, Hartvigsen Sch. for Multiple Handicapped, Salt Lake City, 1973-79, William Penn Elem. Sch., Salt Lake City, 1979—. Vol., Spl. Olympics. Mem. NEA, Utah Edn. Assn., Granite Edn. Assn., Assn. Supervision and Curriculum Devel. Home: 1516 Glen Arbor St Salt Lake City UT 84105 Office: William Penn Sch 1670 Siggard Dr Salt Lake City UT 84106

BOUQUET, FRANCIS LESTER, physicist; b. Enterprise, Oreg., Feb. 1, 1926; s. Francis Lester and Esther (Johnson) B.; m. Betty Davis Perry, Sept. 26, 1979; children—Tim, Jeffrey, Janet; stepchildren—John Perry Jr., Peggy Perry. A.A., U. Calif.-Berkeley, 1948, B.A., 1950; M.A., UCLA, 1953. Physicist, U.S. Radiol. Def. Lab., San Francisco, 1953-55; engr., mgr. Lockheed Aircraft Co., Burbank, Calif., 1955-74; physicist Jet Propulsion Lab., Pasadena, Calif., 1974—; cons. in field. Elder 1st Presbyn. Ch., Van Nuys, Calif., 1970-81. Served with U.S. Army, 1944-46, with Signal Corps U.S. Army, 1951-52; PTO. Recipient Eagle Scout award Boy Scouts Am., 1940, Performance commendation Lockheed Aircraft Co., 1964, Mgmt. Achievement Program award, 1973; named to Honor Roll of Inventors, 1966. Mem. N.Y. Acad. Sci., Nat. Soc. Profl. Engrs., IEEE (chmn. Los Angeles chpt. Nuclear and Plasma Scis. Soc. 1973-74), Am. Inst. Physics, AIAA, Nat. Mgmt. Assn., Air Force Assn., Lockheed Mgmt. Club. Republican. Author numerous govt. and industry reports; contbr. articles to sci. jours. Office: Mail Stop 157-515 Jet Propulsion Lab 4800 Oak Grove Dr Pasadena CA 91109

BOURGERIE, JAY GREGORY, management training firm executive, educator; b. Mpls., May 6, 1942; s. Robert J. and Dorothy L. (Hamlin) B. B.A. in Spanish and French, San Jose State U., 1965, postgrad., 1967-70; M.A. in Modern Langs., U. Santa Clara, 1973. Cert. standard life tchr., Calif. Tchr., Los Gatos (Calif.) Joint High Sch. Dist., 1969-80, dept. chmn. foreign langs., Saratoga High Sch., Saratoga, Caif., 1972; cons. Quality Control Circles, Inc., Los Gatos, 1980-82, sr. cons., 1983—; cons. internat. corps.; lectr. in field. Recipient Yearbook dedication Saratoga High Sch., 1980. Mem. Am. Soc. Tng. and Devel., Internat. Assn. Quality Circles, Calif. Tchrs. Assn. (NEA chpt.) pres. Saratoga 1972-73, negotiator 1976-80). Republican. Contbr. Proceedings Quality Control Circles Internat. meeting, 1981; translator (Spanish), editor company tng. materials. Home: PO Box 151 Los Gatos CA 95031 Office: Quality Control Circles Inc 400 Blossom Hill Rd Los Gatos CA 95030

BOURKE, THOMAS GILMOUR, banker, executive; b. Memphis, Oct. 13, 1919; s. Ernest Walter and Nettie (Gilmour) B. m. Virginia Bass, Dec. 20, 1948; children—Michael and Patricia. B.S., Stanford U., 1947. Nat. Bank examiner U.S. Treasury Dept., San Francisco, 1949-55; v.p. Pacific Nat. Bank, San Francisco, 1955-64; v.p. 1st Security Bank Idaho, Boise, 1968-70, sr. v.p., 1970-72, exec. v.p., 1972-75, pres., 1975—; dir. 1st Security Corp., Salt Lake City. Dir., past pres. Idaho Council Econs. Edn. Served with USN to lt. comdr., 1941-45. Pres. Idaho Bankers Assn., Boise C. of C. (pres.), Club: Rotary, Boise. Home: 520 Crestline Boise ID 83702 Office: 119 N Ninth Box 1069 Boise ID 83730

BOURKOFF, ETAN, electrical engineering educator, researcher; b. Tel-Aviv, Israel, Oct. 14, 1949; s. Eliezer and Theresia (Roth) B.; B.S., MIT, 1972, M.S., 1972; Ph.D., U. Calif.-Berkeley, 1979; m. Vivien Roumani, June 6, 1971; children—Aryeh, Dania, Natan. With research div. Raytheon Corp., Waltham, Mass., 1969-72; sr. engr. Western Devel. Labs., Ford Aerospace & Communications Corp., Palo Alto, Calif., 1972-76; research asst. elec. engring. U. Calif., Berkeley, 1976-79; mem. tech. staff Hewlett-Packard Labs., Palo Alto, 1979-81; asst. prof. elec. engring. and computer sci. Johns Hopkins U., Balt., 1981—. Mem. IEEE (sr.), Optical Soc. Am., Am. Phys. Soc., AAUP, Sigma Xi. Contbr. articles to profl. jours. Home: 2808 Laurelwood Ct Baltimore MD 21209 Office: Dept Elec Engring and Computer Sci Johns Hopkins U Baltimore MD 21218

BOURNE, LYLE EUGENE, JR., psychology educator; b. Boston, Apr. 12, 1932; s. Lyle E. and Blanche (White) B.; B.A., Brown U., 1953; M.S., U. Wis., 1955, Ph.D., 1956. Asst. prof. psychology U. Utah, 1956-61, assoc. prof., 1961-63; vis. assoc. prof. U. Calif., Berkeley, 1961-62, vis. prof., 1968-69; assoc. prof. psychology U. Colo., 1963-65, prof., 1965—, dir. Inst. of Cognitive Sci., 1979-83, chmn. dept. psychology, 1983—; clin. prof. psychiatry U. Kans. Med. Center, 1967—; vis. prof. U. Wis., 1966, U. Mont., 1967, U. Calif., Berkeley, 1968-69, U. Hawaii, 1969; cons. in exptl. psychology VA, 1965—. Recipient Research Scientist award NIMH, 1969, 74. Mem. Am. Psychol. Assn., (council editors 1975-80, chmn. early awards com. 1978-79), Psychonomic Soc. (governing bd. 1976-82, chmn. 1980-81), Sigma Xi. Author: Human Conceptual Behavior, 1966; Psychology of Thinking, 1971; Psychology: Its Principles and Meanings, 1973, rev. edits., 1977, 81; Cognitive Processes, 1979; acad. editor Basic Concept Series, Learning-Cognition Series, Scott, Foresman Pub. Co.; acad. editor Charles Merrill Co., 1980—; editor Jour. Exptl. Psychology: Human Learning and Memory, 1975-80; cons. editor Jour. Clin. Psychology, 1975—.

BOURQUE, PHILIP JOHN, business economist; b. Holyoke, Mass., Aug. 16, 1922; s. Oliver H. and Emma G. (Tremblay) B.; m. Dorothea A. Lohmann, June 18, 1949; children—Cynthia, Diane, Nancy, Alison, Constance. B.S., U. Mass., 1949; M.A. in Econs., U. Pa., 1950, Ph.D., 1956. Instr. econs., U. Pa., 1952-54; asst. prof. Muhlenberg Coll., Allentown, Pa., 1954-55; asst. prof. Lehigh U., 1955-57; prof. bus. econs. U. Wash., Seattle, 1957—; bd. govs. Council Econ. Advisors, State of Wash., 1978—. Served with USAF, 1943-46. Mem. Am. Econ. Assn., Regional Sci. Assn., Nat. Assn. Bus. Economists, Western Regional Sci. Assn. Contbr. numerous articles to econ. jours. Home: 19604 53d Ave NE Seattle WA 98155 Office: U Wash Grad Sch Bus Adminstrn Seattle WA 98195

BOUSFIELD, KENNETH HAROLD, civil engineer; b. Los Angeles, Nov. 14, 1946; s. William Harold and Shirley (Burgess) B.; m. Gail Nuttall, Sept. 2, 1970; children—TaraLee, Julie, Timothy Kenneth, Kelly Jean. B.E.S., Brigham Young U., 1971; postgrad. U. Utah, 1980. Registered profl. engr., Utah. Pub. health engr. Bur. Water Quality, Salt Lake City, 1971-72; engr. Nielsen, Maxwell & Wangsgard, Salt Lake City, 1973-76; pub. health engr. Bur. Pub. Water Supplies, Salt Lake City, 1976-78, chief engring. sect., 1978-80, asst. dir., 1980—, chief compliance sect., 1981—. Mem. Am. Water Works Assn. Republican. Mormon. Conbr. articles to profl. jours. Home: 11538 High Mountain Dr Sandy UT 84092 Office: Bur Pub Water Supplies 150 W North Temple St Salt Lake City UT 84110

BOUSMAN, WILLIAM GILES, aeronautical engineer; b. Scotia, N.Y., Mar. 2, 1941; s. Henry Woodford and Frieda Merrill (Goodenough) B.; m. Billie June Ruggles, Dec. 12, 1970; 1 son, Nicholas Sebastian. B.M.E., Cornell U., 1964; M.S., MIT, 1966. Aero. engr. U.S. Army Aviation Systems Command, St. Louis, 1966-70; research scientist U.S. Army Aeromechanics Lab., Moffett Field, Calif., 1970—. Served to 1st lt. U.S. Army, 1966-68. Mem. Am. Helicopter Soc., AIAA, Am. Ornithologists Union, Cooper Ornithol. Union. Club: Lower Peninsula Eating and Drinking Soc. (Sunnyvale, Calif.). Contbr. papers and reports to tech. jours.; patentee in field.

BOUTERIE, RONALD LEE, surgeon; b. New Orleans, Aug. 17, 1933; s. Victor J. and Marguerite Mary (Pecunia) B.; B.S., Loyola U., New Orleans, 1954; M.D., La. State U., 1957; m. Mary Alice Chauvin, Oct. 9, 1954; children—David, Kenneth, Rhonda, Brenda, Brian, Mark, Ronald Lee II. Commd. 1st lt. M.C., U.S. Navy, 1956, advanced through grades to capt., 1969, intern U.S. Naval Hosp., Oakland, 1957-58; gen. surg. resident U.S. Naval Hosp., Chelsca, Mass., 1959-64; asst. chief surgery U.S. Naval Hosp., Oakland, Calif., 1968-69, head surg. research, 1967-69, head surg. anatomy, 1967; practice medicine specializing in gen. and vascular surgery, San Diego, 1969—; dir. surgery Mercy Hosp., 1973-74; cons. Naval Hosp., San Diego, Am. Cancer Soc. Vice pres. Univ. High Sch. Sch. Bd., 1975—; bd. dirs. Confraternity Christians and Jews; sr. chmn. NCCJ, 1979-80; pres. Friends of Mercy, 1978-79. Decorated Navy D.S.M., Legion of Merit. Diplomate Am. Bd. Surgery. Mem. Am., Internat. colls. surgeons, Am., Calif. med. assns., Soc. Gen. Surgeons, Mil. Surgeons Assn., Pan Pacific Surg. Soc. Republican. Roman Catholic Club: San Diego Univ. (past dir.). Contbr. med. jours., books. Home: 6105 Pasatiempo Ave San Diego CA 95120 Office: 550 Washington St San Diego CA 92103

BOUWER, DENNIS RONALD, investment co. exec.; b. Republic of South Africa, Apr. 27, 1933; s. Jeremia J. and Catherine Elizabeth (DeBeer) B.; B.Sc. in Chemistry, Rhodes U., South Africa, 1954; M.A. (Rhodes scholar), Oxford (Eng.) U., 1960; M.B.A. (Knox fellow, Ford fellow), Harvard, 1963; m. Sara Margaret Holcroft, July 4, 1959; children—Consuelo Catherine, Richard J.A. Came to U.S., 1961, naturalized, 1966. Exec. trainee Bagshaw Gibaud & Co., Africa, 1951-54; math. master, asst. housemaster Kingswood Coll., South Africa, 1955; grad. chemist Am. Metal Climax, Zambia, 1955-57; mktg. mgr. trainee Unilever Ltd., London, Eng., 1960-61; tng. mgr. Ford Motor Co., South Africa, 1961; econs. analyst Mobil Oil Corp., N.Y.C., 1962; with E.I. duPont de Nemours & Co., Inc., Geneva, Switzerland and Wilmington, Del., 1963-67; asst. to pres. chem. plastics div. Gen Tire & Rubber Co., Akron, Ohio, 1967-68; asst. to chmn. Capital Research Co., Los Angeles, 1968—; asst. to chmn., v.p. Capital Strategic Services; v.p. Endowments, Inc., Bond Portofolio for Endowments, Inc. Former adviser Coloured Peoples Advancement Assn., Africa; mem. adv. bd., nat. bd. dirs. U.S.A. Exec. Council on Fgn. Diplomats. Served with RAF, 1957-61. Chartered fin. analyst, registered prin. Nat. Assn. Securities Dealers. Fellow Royal Commonwealth Soc. (life), Fin. Analysts Fedn. (nat. dir. U.S. and Can., chmn. resources com., nat. budget rev. com., program com.); mem. Royal Air Force Assn. (life), Oxford Union (life), Africa Soc. (founder, pres.), Los Angeles Soc. Fin. Analysts (gov., Most Outstanding Mem. award, pres. program and nominating coms.). Republican. Episcopalian. Clubs: Harvard (N.Y.C.); Harvard Bus. Sch. Soc. Calif. (gov.), Los Angeles Athletic; United Oxford and Cambridge Univs. (London). Internat. rugby player. Home: 15937 Temecula St Pacific Palisades CA 90272 Office: 333 S Hope St Los Angeles CA 90071

BOVA, V. ARTHUR, JR., lawyer, consultant; b. Pitts., Apr. 25, 1946; s. Vincent A. and Janie (Pope) B.; m. Breda Murphy, Mar. 20, 1971; 1 dau., Kate Murphy. B.A. in Bus. Adminstrn., Alma Coll., 1968; M.P.A., Ohio State U., 1972; J.D., Okla. City U., 1975. Bar: Okla. 1976, N.Mex. 1976, U.S. Dist. Ct. N.Mex. 1976, U.S. Tax Ct. 1976, U.S. Ct. Appeals (10th cir.) 1976, U.S. Supreme Ct. 1979. Mktg. and systems rep. computer systems div. RCA, Cin. and Dayton, Ohio, 1968-70; research analyst Research Atlanta, 1972-73; assoc. Threet, Threet, Glass, King & Maxwell, Albuquerque, 1976-78; ptnr. Lill & Bova, P.A., Albuquerque, 1978-81; sole practice, Albuquerque, 1981—. Asst. campaign mgr. for Republican and Democratic candidates for state rep. position, state assembly positions, mayorial elections, Presidential elections, Mich., Ohio, Ga., N.Mex., 1964—. Served with Air N.G., 1969-75. Recipient Pacesetters award Ohio State U., 1972. Mem. Assn. Trial Lawyers Am.

(advanced grad. Nat. Coll. Advocacy), Ct. Practice Inst. (advanced diplomate), ABA, N.Mex. Bar Assn. N.Mex. Trial Lawyers Assn., Internat. Assn., Fin. Planners, Nat. Orgn. Social Security Claimants Reps., Albuquerque Bar Assn., Phi Alpha Delta. Presbyterian. Clubs: Toastmasters, Bare Bulls, Ltd., Millionaires Tip. Home: 5604 Cresta Luna St NE Albuquerque NM 87111 Office: V Arthur Bova Jr Atty and Counselor at Law Albuquerque NM 87110

BOVEE, COURTLAND L., business communications and advertising educator; b. Red Bluff, Calif., Oct. 4, 1944; s. Courtney Van and Shirley Patricia (Safford) B. A.A., Shasta Coll., 1965; B.S., U. N.D., 1967; M.S., U. Tenn., 1968. Prof. Grossmont Coll., El Cajon, Calif., 1968—. Mem. Am. Bus. Communications Assn., Am. Acad. Advt. Author: Contemporary Advertising, 1982; Contemporary Business Communications, 1985. Office: 8800 Grossmont Coll Dr El Cajon CA 92020

BOVÉE, MICHAEL CHRISTOPHER, property manager, real estate broker; b. Los Angeles, July 15, 1943; s. John Lemuel Franklin and Margaret Keppler (Fowler) B.; A.A., Orange Coast Coll., 1965; B.S., U. East Fla., 1972; D. Comm. Sc., London Inst., 1973; m. Laura Mary Margaret Voegele, May 23, 1970; children—David Anthony, Jeffrey Michael, Marissa Ann. Owner, La Plage Enterprises, Newport Beach, Calif., 1964-71; dist. sales mgr. Valley Land Sales, Sherman Oaks, Calif., 1971; dir. property mgmt. Cal-Home Properties, Garden Grove, Calif., 1971-72; property mgr. Residential Leasing Corp., Garden Grove, Calif., 1972-73; dist. mgr. Grubb & Ellis Property Services, Inc., San Francisco, 1973-75; corporate broker, asst. sec., asst. dist. mgr. Property Mgmt. Systems, San Francisco, 1975-77; corporate broker, chmn. bd., pres. Pacific Property Services, Inc., Walnut Creek, Calif., 1977—; v.p. property mgmt. div. Grubb & Ellis Property Services, Inc., Oakland, Calif., 1979-81; corp. broker, chmn. bd., chief exec. officer MCB Assos., Inc., Pleasant Hill, Calif., 1981—. Bd. dirs. Culverdale Community Assn., 1971-74; cons. Homeowner Bd., Phase II, City of Irvine, 1972-73. Mem. Inst. Real Estate Mgmt., Internat. Inst. Valuers, Mcht. Brokers Exchange, Calif. Assn. Realtors (property mgmt. div.), Contra Costa County Bd. Realtors, Internat. Real Estate Fedn., Native Sons Golden West, Ancien Roseens. Home: 2205 Kenton Ct Walnut Creek CA 94596 Office: 620 Contra Costa Blvd 211 Pleasant Hill CA 94528 also 222 E Riverside 108 Austin TX 78704

BOW, PATRICIA SHEETZ, systems analyst; b. Washington, Mar. 23, 1949; d. John W. and Jane (Gowans) Sheetz; m. Douglas D. Bow, Aug. 2, 1975; children—Benjamin D., Sarah B. Student Lake Erie Coll., 1967-69; B.A. in Polit. Sci., Am. U., 1971. Coordinator asst. sch. nursing Mass. Gen. Hosp., Boston, 1972-75; coordinator, methods analyst methods and standards dept. Blue Cross, Cin. 1976-80; documentation specialist, bus. systems analyst Kaiser Health Plan, Honolulu, 1981—; instr. microcomputers. Mem. Assn. Systems Mgmt., Mayflower Soc. Methodist. Club: Kerry Blue Terrier (Honolulu). Home: 7218 Alakoko St Honolulu HI 96825 Office: Kaiser Health Plan 1697 Ala Moana Blvd Honolulu HI 96815

BOWDEN, DWIGHT RICHARD, realtor; b. Hope, Ark., Nov. 25, 1931; s. James Rister and Velma (Crews) B.; student Texarkana Coll., 1949-50, 52-53; m. Barbara Jean Orr, Dec. 9, 1953; children—Terry Michael, Scott Russell, Gary Raymond. With William Cameron Co., Texarkana, Tex., 1952-53, Nat. Cash Register Co., Anchorage, 1954-59, Communications Engring., Inc., Anchorage, 1960-62; asst. v.p., br. mgr. First Fed. Savs. & Loan Assn., Anchorage, 1963-68; salesman Action Realty, Inc., Anchorage, 1969-70; owner, broker Bowden Co., realtors, Anchorage, 1971—; chmn. bd. Home Fed. Savs. & Loan Assn., 1975-77. Bd. dirs. Realtors Multiple Listing Service, Anchorage, 1971-72, 78-79. Served with USMCR, 1950-52. Mem. Anchorage Bd. Realtors (pres. 1971, dir. 1972), Nat. (dir. 1974), Alaska (pres. 1974) assns. realtors, Anchorage C. of C., Landlord and Property Mgrs. Assn. Alaska (dir. 1972-78), Alaska Sports Car Club (pres. 1964). Methodist. Democrat. Elk. Home: 2101 Loussac Dr Anchorage AK 99503 Office: 2602 Seward Hwy Anchorage AK 99503

BOWDEN, SHARON ANN TODDY, psychologist; b. Beaumont, Tex., May 27, 1950; d. Robert Henry and Zoe (Brandau) Bowden; B.A., U. Tex., 1971, M.S. in Social Work (Criminal Justice scholar, NIMH scholar), 1974; Ph.D., Tex. A&M U., 1977; m. Larry P. Frazier, Feb. 1, 1978; children—Erin Bowden Frazier, Lara Ann Frazier. Psychiat. social worker, treatment supr. Mary Lee Sch., Austin, Tex., 1974-75; grad. asst., adminstrv. asst. Tex. A&M U., College Station, 1975-77; psychologist So. Highlands Mental Health Center, Princeton, W.Va., 1978; clin. supr. S.E. Tex. Mental Health Retardation Agy., Port Arthur, 1979-80; psychologist Student Counseling Service, U. Ariz., Tucson, 1981—; cons. Care Unit Alcoholism Program, Port Arthur, 1978-79, So. Ariz. Mental Health Center, 1980-81. Lic. psychologist, Tex.; cert. psychologist, Ariz. Mem. Am. psychol. Assn., Ariz. Psychol. Assn., So. Ariz. Psychol. Assn. Am. Assn. for Marriage and Family Therapy (clin. mem.). Contbr. articles to profl. jours. Home: 3833 W Sunny Shadows Pl Tucson AZ 85741 Office: Student Counseling Service U Ariz Old Main 200 W Tucson AZ 85721

BOWEN, BLAIR, interior designer, educator; b. Spanish Fork, Utah, July 22, 1920; s. David B. and Bertha (Swenson) B. B.A. with honors, Brigham Young U., 1942; cert. interior design, N.Y. Sch. Interior Design, 1944. Interior designer Dixon-Taylor-Russell Home Furnishings Co., Provo, Utah, 1944-55; interior designer Clark Leaming Residential/Comml. Interiors Co., Salt Lake City, 1955-62; interior designer Jacksons Residential Design Co., Oakland, Calif., 1962-63; owner, designer Blair S. Bowen Co., San Francisco, 1963—; instr. interior design San Francisco Acad. Art. Recipient Excellence in Interior Design award Utah chpt. AIA, 1953. Mem. Am. Soc. Interior Designers (pres. No. Calif. dist. chpt. 1976). Mormon. Contbr. articles to profl. jours. Office: 2101 Pacific Ave Suite 402 San Francisco CA 94115

BOWEN, CHARLES HUGH, JR., electronics engr., lawyer; b. Belle Ellen, Ala., Jan. 8, 1923; s. Charles Hugh and Lavada (Lawley) B.; student U. Ariz., 1939-40, 46, U. So. Calif., 1946-47; B.S. in Engring. Electronics, Naval Postgrad. Sch., 1953, M.S., 1954; grad. Naval War Coll., 1961; postgrad. Sch. Law U. Santa Clara, 1974-77; m. Nina Gwen Stevens, July 29, 1945 (div.); children—David Hugh, Charles Hugh III; m. 2d, Joan Steffens, Mar. 18, 1978. Commd. ensign U.S. Navy, 1943, advanced through grades to capt., 1965; flight tng., 1942-43; pilot and flight officer, PTO, 1944-45; flight instr. Aviation Tng. Unit 5, 1947-49; radar projects supr., VX-1 Key West, Fla., 1949-51; officer Attack Squadron 55, 1954-55; aviation electronics engring. officer, staff Comdr. Naval Air Force Pacific Fleet, 1956-58; assigned spl. studies sect. Spl. Projects Office, Bur. Weapons, 1958-60; student replace air tng. group Attack Squadron 122, 1961; comdg. officer Attack Squadron 115, 1962-63; navigator U.S.S. Kitty Hawk, 1963-64, exec. officer, 1964; tchr. elec. sci., head sci. dept. U.S. Naval Acad., 1965-67; command U.S.S. Vesuvius, 1967-68; advanced devel. engr. Sylvania Electronics Systems, Mountain View, Calif., 1968-74; individual practice law, Campbell, Calif., 1977-81; partner firm Finch, Tennant and Bowen, Campbell, 1981—. Decorated D.F.C. with gold star, Air medal with silver star. Mem. IEEE, Naval Inst., Internat. Platform Assn. Democrat. Home: 824 La Crosse Ct Sunnyvale CA 94087

BOWEN, CLOTILDE DENT, army officer, psychiatrist; b. Chgo., Mar. 20, 1923; d. William Marion Dent and Clotilde (Tynes) D.; m. William N. Bowen, Dec. 29, 1945 (dec.). B.A., Ohio State U., 1943, M.D., 1947. Intern, Harlem Hosp., N.Y.C., 1947-48; resident in psychiatry VA Hosp., Albany, N.Y., 1969-62; private practice, N.Y.C. 1950-55; chief pulmonary disease clinic, N.Y.C. 1950-55; chief psychiatry VA Hosp., Roseburg, Oreg., 1962-66, acting chief of staff, 1964-66; enlisted U.S. Army, 1967, advanced through ranks to col., 1968; neuropsychiat. cons. U.S. Army Vietnam, 1970-71; psychiatrist Tripler Gen. Hosp. Fitzsimons Army Med. Center, 1974-75, chief dept. primary care and community medicine, 1979-83; assoc. prof. psychiatry U. Colo. Med. Center, Denver, 1970-83. Decorated Legion of Merit, several other medals. Fellow Menniger Found. Fellow Am. Psychiat. Assn. Acad. Psychosomatic Medicine; mem. Nat. Med. Assn. Home: 1020 Tari Dr Colorado Springs CO 80908 Office: Dept Primary Care and Community Medicine Fitzsimons Army Med Center Aurora CO 80045

BOWEN, FRANCIS LEE, elec. engr.; b. Lincoln, Nebr., Jan. 17, 1932; s. Earl and Besse B.; B.E.E., U. Nebr., 1958; M.B.A., Calif. Luth. Coll., 1977; m. Bonnie Jean Yentes, June 5, 1951; children—Sandra Fern, Scott LeMar. With Pacific Missile Test Center, Point Mugu, Calif., 1958—, head communications engring. br., from 1970, now head inservice engring. div. Design and Fabrication Dept. Mem. Camarillo (Calif.) Planning Commn., 1970-82, chmn., 1971-75, 78-79; mem. Camarillo City Council, 1982—; trustee Camarillo Math. Ch., 1976-79, chmn., 1977. Served in USN, 1952-54. Republican. Clubs: Masons, Shriners, Order of DeMolay. Office: Code 3510 Point Mugu CA 93042

BOWEN, FRED WINBORNE, government official; b. Newport News, Va., March 7, 1942; s. Fred Winborne and Virginia Elizabeth (Arrington) B. B.S. in Physics, Coll. William and Mary, Williamsburg, Va., 1964, postgrad., 1964-67. Exec. asst. to assoc. adminstr. NASA Hdqrs., Washington, 1972-75; tech. mgr. for mgmt. ops. NASA Langley Research Ctr., Hampton, Va., 1975-79, acting dir. mgmt. ops., 1979-80; dir. adminstrn. Pres.'s Commn. Accident at Three Mile Island, Washington, 1979; mgr. NASA Resident Office, Jet Propulsion Lab., Pasadena, Calif., 1980—. Recipient Exceptional Service Medal, Pres.'s Commn. Accident at Three Mile Island, 1979. Mem. AIAA, Nat. Contract Mgmt. Assoc., Sigma Pi Sigma. Contbr. articles to profl. jours. Home: 1356 Journeys End Dr La Canada CA 91011 Office: 4800 Oak Grove Dr Stop 180-802 Pasadena CA 91109

BOWEN, GERARD THALES, music educator, composer; b. Zarephath, N.J., June 9, 1920; s. Thomas Cornelius and Frances Elizabeth (Borough) B.; m. Helen Ilene Brinkley, Nov. 21, 1944; 1 dau., Karen Lee. Student Los Angeles City Coll., 1940-42; B.A., Am. U., 1955. Head arranging staff, supr. bandmaster course U.S. Navy, U.S. Army, U.S. Marine Corps bandmasters, 1945-55; musical asst., bandmaster U.S. Delegation to UN, N.Y.C., 1964-67; semi-retired composer and tchr., San Diego, 1974—; tchr. U.S. Navy musicians seeking advancement; adjudicator band competitions. Served to lt. USN, 1942-73. Recipient John Philip Sousa Meml. March Writing Contest award ASCAP, 1955; selected by Pres. L.B. Johnson to record nat. anthems of Am. states to be presented to state reps. by Sec. of State Dean Rusk, 1963. Mem. Ret. Officer Assn., Fleet Res. Assn. Composer: White Hat March, 1955, Star Spangled Banner (ofcl. Dept. of Def. version), 1955; National Anthems of UN, 1953-55; author: Basic Music, 1956; Harmony, 1956. Home: 6690 Oakridge Rd San Diego CA 92120

BOWEN, JAMES ROSS, weapons design engr.; b. Wooster, Ohio, Feb. 20, 1935; s. James W.R. and Gayle L. (Altland) B.; B.S. in Elec. Engring., U. Ariz., 1958; m. Glada Roberts, Sept. 2, 1958; children—Michael D. (stepson), James R., Jason M. Project engr. guidance system for air-to-air missile Naval Weapons Center, China Lake, Calif., 1958-69, program mgr. weapon system, 1969-72, line supr. design groups, mgr. weapon systems, div. head, 1972-78, mgr. spl. facilities and equipment study, 1978-81, dep. support dir., 1981—. Safety dir. Ridgecrest (Calif.) Little League, 1975—; bldg. com. Calvary Assembly of God Ch., Ridgecrest, 1975—; pres. Indian Wells Valley chpt. Full Gospel Bus. Men's Fellowship Internat., 1978-81, field rep., 1980-83; v.p. Sierra Breeze Mobil Home Estates, 1980, pres., 1981. Mem. Nat. Contract Mgmt. Assn., Tech. Mktg. Soc. Am. Republican. Home: 5233 Ocotillo Ave Ridgecrest CA 93555 Office: Comdr (Code 02A) Naval Weapons Center China Lake CA 93555

BOWEN, PETER GEOFFREY, real estate investment advisor; b. Iowa City, Iowa, July 10, 1939; s. Howard Rothmann and Lois Berntine (Schilling) B.; m. Shirley Johns Carlson, Sept. 14, 1968; children—Douglas Howard, Leslie Johns. B.A. in Govt. and Econs., Lawrence Coll., 1960; postgrad. U. Wis., 1960-61, U. Denver, 1965. Dir. devel. Mobile Home Communities, Denver, 1969-71; v.p. Perry & Butler, Denver, 1972-73; exec. v.p., dir. Little & Co., Denver, 1973; pres. Builders Agy. Ltd., Denver, 1974-75; pres. The Investment Mgmt. Group Ltd., Denver, 1975—; lectr. on real estate syndications; ski sch. instr. Bd. dirs. Colo. Plan for Apportionment, 1966; mem. Greenwood Village, Colo. Planning and Zoning Commn.; bd. dirs. Lawrence U. Alumni Found. Contbr. articles to profl. publs. Home: 4950 S Beeler Greenwood Village Englewood CO 80111 Office: 1562 S Parker Rd Suite 208 Denver CO 80231

BOWEN, THOMAS GAYLE, air force officer; b. Tampa, Apr. 23, 1936; s. Reese and Maxine (Gayle) B.; B.S., USAF Acad., 1959; postgrad. U.S. Naval Test Pilot Sch., 1969-70; postgrad. U.S. Army Command and Gen. Staff Coll., 1972-73, Air War Coll., 1979-80; m. Sheilah Ann Niehouse, June 6, 1959; children—Deborah, Lynn, Kelly. Commd. 2d lt., USAF, 1959, advanced through grades to col., 1979; ops. staff officer 15th Air Force, 1964-66, 1968-69; helicopter pilot advisor Tan Son Nhut Air Base Vietnam, 1967; comdr. 6511th Support Squadron, El Centro, Calif., 1970-72; squadron operations officer, comdr. 11th Tacrical Drone Squadron, 1975-77; asst. dep. comdr. for ops. 432nd Tactical Drone Group, Davis-Monthan AFB, Ariz., 1977-79; operational test dir. Ground Launched Cruise Missile, Dugway Proving Ground, Utah, 1980—. Decorated D.F.C., Bronze Star, Meritorious Service medal (2), Air medal, Air Force Commendation medal; recipient Ops. award Assn. Unmanned Vehicle Systems, 1980. Roman Catholic. Home: 508 Peak Dugway UT 84022 Office: Ground Launched Cruise Missile 10T&E Test Team/TE Dugway Proving Ground UT 84022

BOWER, DONALD EDWARD, author; b. Lockport, N.Y., July 19, 1920; B.A., U. Nebr., 1942. Pres., D.E. Bower & Co., Inc., Denver, 1945-60; editor, pub. Arapahoe Tribune, 1960-62; editor Adams County Almanac, Adams County Dispatch, Jefferson County Herald, 1962-65; editor, pub. Buyer's Showcase mag. and FURN Club News 1965-66; exec. editor Colo. mag., 1966-69; editor-in-chief, v.p., dir. Am. West Pub. Co., editor Am. West mag., 1970-74; pres. Colo. Authors League, 1975—; dir. Nat. Writers Club, Denver, 1974—; dir. Asso. Bus. Writers Am., 1978—, also pres. assn. hdqrs., 1978—; editorial dir. Nat. Writers Press, 1982—; freelance staff writer Fawcett Publs., 1962-64; lit. cons., 1962-67. Mem. Soc. Authors and Journalists, Authors Guild Am., Denver Posse, The Westerners (dir. 1976), Outdoor Writers Assn. Am., Western Writers Assn. Am., Western Writers Am., Friends of Denver Pub. Library, Denver Press Club, Sigma Delta Chi. Author: Roaming the American West, 1970; Ghost Towns and Back Roads, 1972; intro. to The Magnificent Rockies, 1972; Fred Rosenstock: A Legend in Books and Art, 1976; also 4 paperback detective novels, 1960-64. Editor: Living Water, Living Earth, 1971; Anasazi: Ancient People of the Rock, 1973; The Great Southwest, 1972; Edge of a Continent, 1970; The Mighty Sierra, 1972; The Magnificent Rockies, 1972; The Great Northwest, 1973; Gold and Silver in the West, 1973; Steinbeck Country, 1973. Contbr. articles to mags. Address: 15087 E Radcliff Dr Aurora CO 80015

BOWER, DONALD L., petroleum company executive; b. 1923. B.S., Oreg. State U., 1947. With Standard Oil Co. of Calif., San Francisco, 1947—, pres. eastern div. Chevron Oil Co., 1963, corp. v.p. Standard Oil of Calif., 1967, pres. Chevron USA, 1977, vice chmn. Standard Oil Co. of Calif., also dir.; dir. Crocker Nat. Corp. Trustee Oreg. State Univ. Found. Office: Standard Oil Co of Calif Inc 225 Bush St Standard Oil Bldg San Francisco CA 94104*

BOWER, FAY LOUISE, nurse; b. San Francisco, Sept. 10, 1929; d. James Joseph and Emily Clare (Andrews) Saitta; B.S. with honors, San Jose State Coll., 1965; M.S.N., U. Calif., 1966, D.N.Sc., 1978; children—R. David, Carol Bower Tomei, Dennis James, Thomas John. Office nurse Dr. William Grannis, Palo Alto, Calif., 1950-55; staff nurse Stanford Hosp., 1964-72; asst. prof. San Jose State U., 1966-70, asso. prof., 1970-74, prof., 1974-82, coordinator grad. program in nursing, 1977-78, chairperson dept. nursing, 1978-82; dean U. San Francisco, 1982—; speaker; cons. univs.; vis. prof. Harding Coll., 1977, U. Miss., 1976; lectr. U. Calif., San Francisco, 1975. Cert. public health nurse, sch. nurse, Calif. Fellow Am. Acad. Nursing. Mem. Calif. Nurses Assn., Nurses Assn. Coll. Ob-Gyn, Calif. Tchrs. Assn., AAUP, Internat. Indsl. TV Assn., Santa Clara County Health Edn. Council, Public Health Assn. Calif., Santa Clara County PSRO, Health Edn. Media Assn., Nat. League Nursing, Western Gerontol. Assn., Sigma Theta Tau. Democrat. Roman Catholic. Club: Commonwealth (San Francisco). Author: (with Em O. Bevis) Fundamentals of Nursing Practice: Concepts, Roles and Functions, 1978; (with Margaret Jacobson) Community Health Nursing, 1978; The Process of Planning Nursing Care, 3d edit., 1982; Theoretical Foundations of Nursing I, II, and III, 1972; editor: Normal Development of Body Image, 1977; Distortions in Body Image in Illness and Disability, 1977; Foundations of Pharmacologic Therapy, 1977; Nursing Assessment, 1977. Home: 1820 Portola Rd Woodside CA 94062 Office: Sch Nursing U San Francisco San Francisco CA

BOWER, MICHAEL O'BANNON, communications exec.; b. Los Angeles, June 13, 1949; s. David F. and Barbara Jeanne (O'Bannon) B.; m. Jennifer Louise Robison, Aug. 23, 1975; children—Timothy, Jonathon. A.A., Cerritos Coll., 1970; B.A. in Communications, Calif. State U., 1972; M. Pub. Relations, U. So. Calif., 1979. Interscholastic press corr. Los Angeles Herald Examiner and Long Beach (Calif.) Press-Telegram, 1966-67; recreation and sports specialist S.E. Recreation and Parks dist., 1967-70; sports editor Daily S.E. News, Downey, Calif., 1969-71; asst. sports info. dir. Cerritos Coll., Norwalk, Calif., 1968-71; sports dir., show host —Sports Mike,— RETV, Laguna Hills, Calif., 1971; sports editor, Saddleback Valley News, Mission Viejo, Calif., Leisure World News, Laguna Hills, 1970-71; dir. pub. info. Orange County unit Am. Cancer Soc., 1972-73; pres. Sports Specialties, Norwalk, 1973; dir. pub. relations Orange County Youth Christ/Campus Life, 1973-74; dir. pub. info. Azusa Pacific Coll., 1973-74; info. specialist Norwalk-La Mirada Unified Sch. Dist., 1974-78; pres. chief exec. officer Bower Communications, Inc., Huntington Beach, Calif., 1981—; pres. Michael Bower and Assos., Dyna Graphics, Quill Pub. Co., Tellus Opinion Research, On-Stage Mgmt.; guest lectr., instr. area colls., univs. and adult edn. classes. Statistician state jr. coll. basketball playoffs, 1969; youth dir. Presbyn. Ch. Master, Mission Viejo, Calif., 1970; dir. youth ministries Presbyn. Ch. Covenant, Costa Mesa, Calif., 1971-74; dir. Orange County —Up with People—; mem. Combined Agys. Council, adv. com. S.E. Regional Occupation Program, bd. dirs. Los Angeles County Christian Endeavor Inc., Los Angeles Area Council communications com. Boy Scouts Am., La Mirada Fiesta de Artes Assn. Interscholastic Press Assn., scholar, 1967; Rotary scholar, 1967; recipient Freedoms Found. Schoolman medal, 1977, award of excellence internal communications, Jour. Ednl. Communication, 1977; 24 awards Pub. Relations Soc. Am. Mem. Orange County Press Club, Pub. Relations Soc. Am. Nat. Sch. Pub. Relations Assn., Publicity Club Los Angeles, Bldg. Industry Assn. (sales and mktg. council). Democrat. Club: Kiwanis (bd. dirs.). Contbr. articles to profl. jours. Office: 7400 Center Ave #208 Huntington Beach CA 92617

BOWER, ROBERT SHARON, JR., oceanographic institution administrator; b. Pocatello, Idaho, Aug. 21, 1937; s. Robert S. and Doris Elizabeth (Walton) B.; B.A., U. Redlands, 1959; J.D., Calif. Western U., 1964; m. Janet Esther Newlan, Nov. 23, 1968; children—Llance Clark, Esther Elizabeth. Sales Adminstr. in sales adminstrn. Solar div. Internat. Harvester, 1967-70; contracts mgr. Plessey Marine & Environ. Systems Co., 1970-71; mktg. adminstr. marketing Transp. Systems div., Rohr Corp., Chula Vista, Calif., 1971-72; program mgr. mktg. and contracts adminstrn. Lockheed Electronics Co., Los Angeles, 1972-73; asst. project mgr. Deep Sea Drilling Project Scripps Instn. Oceanography, U. Calif.-San Diego, La Jolla, 1973—. Served with U.S. Army, 1960. Episcopalian. Home: 9046 Terrace Dr La Mesa CA 92041 Office: Deep Sea Drilling Project Scripps Instn Oceanography A031 U Calif at San Diego LaJolla CA 92037

BOWERMAN, PRISCILLA VALESIO, educator, economist; b. N.Y.C. Dec. 7, 1944; d. Mario Joseph Valesio and Juliette (DeLodder) V.; m. Wendell James Bowerman, Aug. 5, 1967; children—Jude Paul, Luke Todd. A.B., Vassar Coll., 1966; M.Phil. in Econs., Yale U., 1971. Instr. Oreg. State U., Corvallis, 1971-73; mem. faculty Evergreen State Coll., Olympia, Wash., 1973—; cons. state agys. Woodrow Wilson fellow, 1966-67; NSF fellow, 1966-68; Danforth fellow, 1966-71. Mem. Am. Econ. Assn. Office: 1416 Library Evergreen State Coll Olympia WA 98505

BOWER-RAFTERY, BARBARA ANNE, museum director; b. Des Moines, Sept. 1, 1945; d. Robert Oral and Helen Anne (Potter) B.; B.A., U. Iowa, 1968; m. Thomas Lee Raftery, Oct. 17, 1980; 1 son, Patrick Lee. Dir. pub. relations State Hist. Mus., Des Moines, 1968-69; curator Hoover Presdl. Library and Mus., West Branch, Iowa, 1969-71; curator, dir. Fort Lewis Mil. Mus. (Wash.), 1971—. Mem. Am. Assn. Mus., Am. Assn. State and Local History, Daus. U.S. Army, DAR, Can. Mus. Assn., Wash. Mus. Assn. Office: Bldg 4320 Main St Fort Lewis WA 98433

BOWERS, ALBERT, pharmaceutical company executive; b. Manchester, Eng., July 16, 1930; s. Albert and Mary (Munn) B.; children—Anne, Karen, Deborah. B.Sc. in Chemistry, U. London, 1951; Ph.D. in Organic Chemistry, U. Manchester, 1954; Fulbright fellow, Wayne State U., Detroit, 1954-55. With Syntex Corp., Palo Alto, Calif., 1956—, beginning as group leader research, successively assoc. research dir., v.p. and dir., research Mex., v.p. research div., dir. Inst. Steroid Chemistry, v.p. Syntex Internat., v.p., 1956-81, chmn. bd., 1981—, chief exec. officer, 1980—, pres., 1976-82; listed co. adv. com. N.Y. Stock Exchange. Bd. dirs. Bay Area Council, Stanford Mid-Peninsula Urban Coalition, Bus. Higher Edn. Forum., Rockefeller U. Council; trustee Castilleja Sch., U. Calif.-San Francisco. Recipient Sci. prize Mex. Acad. Sci. Investigation, 1964. Mem. Pharm. Mfrs. Assn. (chmn., dir., Santa Clara County Mfg. Group (dir.). Contbr. articles on steroid research to sci. jours. Patentee in field. Developer new methods for selective fluorination of steroids, synthesis of new topical corticoid compounds for treatment of skin diseases, synthesis of norethindrone.

BOWERS, CHERYL OLSEN, educator, artist; b. Berkeley, Calif., Sept. 11, 1938. Student U. Calif.-Berkeley; M.F.A. with honors, San Francisco Art Inst. Group shows include: U. Calif.-Berkeley Mus., 1973, Nat. Drawing Exhbn., Potsdam, N.Y., 1973, Davidson (N.C.) Nat. Print and Drawing, 1973, Whitney Mus. Am. Art, N.Y.C., 1975, San Francisco Mus. Art, 1975, Los Angeles Inst. Contemporary Art, 1976,

Oakland (Calif.) Mus., 1976, U. Ky., 1977, Hamilton Gallery Contemporary Art, N.Y.C., 1979, Ruth Schaffner Gallery, Los Angeles, 1979; represented in permanent collections: U. Calif.-Berkeley Mus., Univ. Mus., Bellingham, Wash., Tamarind Lithographic Inst., Albuquerque; lectr. painting Calif. State Univ., Hayward, 1975; vis. lectr. painting U. Calif.-Berkeley, 1975-79; asst. prof. painting and drawing U. Calif.-Santa Barbara, 1979—. Tamarind Lithographic Inst. fellow, 1972; recipient SECA award Soc. Creative Arts, 1975; Tiffany award, 1980. Mem. Santa Barbara Contemporary Art Forum, New Mus. Office: University California Dept Art Santa Barbara CA 93106

BOWERS, ETHEL MAY, educator; b. Clifton Heights, Pa., Sept. 29, 1900; d. Frank and Jennie (Pyle) Bowers; A.B., Brenau Coll., 1924; student N.Y. U., 1927-29; m. Ben Solomon, Sept. 8, 1929. Chmn. dept. phys. edn. Brenau Coll., 1922-27; specialist Recreation for Girls and Women, Nat. Recreation Assn., 1928-45; mng. editor Youth Leaders Digest, 1945-68; mng. editor Leadership Library, Putnam Valley, N.Y., 1968-74; pres. Leadership Press, Claremont, Calif., 1980—; lectr., cons. recreation for girls and women. Mem. Nat. Recreation and Parks Assn., World Leisure and Recreation Assn., Am. Youth Hostel Assn. Author: Recreation for Girls and Women; (with Ben Solomon) You Can Be a Leader, 1981. Office: PO Box 1144 Claremont CA 91711

BOWERS, WILLIAM EUGENE, geologist; b. Big Run, Pa., Sept. 28, 1927; s. Arnold Goodrich and Mabel Lucille (Payne) B.; B.S., U. Wash., 1956; M.S., U. N.Mex., 1960. Geologist, U.S. Geol. Survey, Denver, 1961-82, Minerals Mgmt. Service, Denver, 1982-83. Served with USAAF (became USAF 1947), 1946-49; ETO. Mem. Geol. Soc. Am., Colo. Sci. Soc., N.Mex. Geol. Soc. Club: Appaloosa Horse Club (Moscow, Idaho). Research on geology So. Utah. Home: 1605 Iris St Lakewood CO 80215

BOWES, FLORENCE (MRS. WILLIAM DAVID BOWES), writer; b. Salt Lake City, Nov. 19, 1925; d. John Albreckt Elias and Alma Wilhelmina (Jonasson) Norborg; student U. Utah, 1941-42, Columbia, 1945-46, N.Y. U., 1954-55; grad. N.Y. TV Workshop, 1950; m. Samuel Ellis Levine, July 15, 1944 (dec. July 1953); 1 son, Alan Richard; m. 2d, William David Bowes, Mar. 15, 1958 (dec. 1976). Actress, writer Hearts Radio Network, WINS, N.Y.C., 1944-45; personnel and adminstrv. exec. Mut. Broadcasting System, N.Y.C., 1946-49, free-lance editor, writer, 1948-49; freelance writer NBC and ABC, 1949-53; script editor, writer Robert A. Monroe Prodns., N.Y.C., Hollywood, Calif., 1953-56; script and comml. dir. KUTV-TV, Salt Lake City, 1956-58; spl. editor, writer pub. relations dept. U. Utah, Salt Lake City, 1966-68, editor, writer U. Utah Rev., 1968-75; author: Web of Solitude, 1979; The MacOrvan Curse, 1980; Interlude in Venice, 1981; Beauchamp, 1983. Mem. Beta Sigma Phi. Home: 338-K St Salt Lake City UT 84103

BOWLAN, BUEL NATHAN, supt. schs.; b. Carlisle, Ark., Mar. 25, 1939; s. Buel Ferdinand and June Bell (Roberts) B.; B.S., Ariz. State Coll., 1962, M.A., 1963; Ed.S. (grad. fellow 1965), No. Ariz. U., 1965; Ph.D. (univ. grad. fellow 1970), U. Wis., Madison, 1971; m. Nancy Lynn Nowlen, Dec. 20, 1969; children—Ron, Sarah, Sandra, Michelle, John. Tchr., Chinle (Ariz.) public schs., 1962-65; instr. math. No. Ariz. U., 1965-66; dir. Headstart, Coconino County (Ariz.), 1966; supt. schs., Seligman, Ariz., 1966-70, Page (Ariz.) Unified Sch. Dist. 8, 1975—; dir. satellite tech. demonstration Ariz. Dept. Edn., 1971-75; mem. Ariz. Coordinated Community Child Care Com., 1975-80, Title XX Com., 1980—; mem. legis. council Ariz. Interscholastic Assn. Mem. Am. Assn. Sch. Adminstrs., Ariz. Sch. Adminstrs. Assn. (regional dir.), World Future Soc., Page C. of C., Phi Delta Kappa. Democrat. Roman Catholic. Club: Page Rotary. Home: Box 938 130 S Navajo St Page AZ 86040 Office: Box 1927 Page AZ 86040

BOWLER, GEORGE EDWARD, veterinarian; b. Manchester, Mich., July 2, 1908; s. John Edward and Alice (Lazell) B.; D.V.M., Mich. State U., 1930; M.P.H., U. Mich., 1960, M.Pub. Adminstrn., 1965; m. Gladys Louise Roberts, June 17, 1939 (div. Sept. 1970); children—Marjorie B. Bowler O'Neill, Constance Bowler Inboden), Elaine, Edith Bowler Lind; m. 2d, Virginia Pangman, Sept. 3, 1982. Gen. practice vet. medicine, Tecumseh, Mich., 1930-34, jr. veterinarian U.S. Dept. Agr., Chgo., 1934, Montgomery, Ala., 1935, N.Y.C., 1935-39; pub. health veterinarian City of Ann Arbor, Mich., 1939-66, dir. concentrated code enforcement, 1966-73, ret., 1973; contract veterinarian State of Mich., 1950-64. Diplomate Am. Bd. Vet. Pub. Health, Am. Coll. Vet. Preventive Medicine. Mem. AVMA (Honor Roll 1979), Am., Mich. (hon. life, treas. 1969-—) pub. health assns., Nat. Assn. Housing Redevel. Ofcls. (chpt. pres. 1971-72, mem. codes div. com.), Conf. Pub. Health Veterinarians, English Speaking Union (dir.). Republican. Presbyterian. Clubs: U. Mich. Alumni of Tucson (pres. 1977-79, 80-81), Masons, Kiwanis (gov. 1962). Home: 11 E Orange Grove Rd Apt 1711 Tucson AZ 85704

BOWLER, ORSON LLOYD, supt. schs.; b. Salt Lake City, Dec. 17, 1931; s. Orson Cutler and Sarah Helen (Lloyd) B.; B.S., U. Utah, 1959, Ed.D., 1966; M.S., U. Idaho, 1963; m. Janice Wilde, June 8, 1960; children—Suzanne, Janalyn, O. Paul, Matthew, David. Tchr. sci. and math. Soda Springs (Idaho) High Sch., 1959-62; research fellow U. Utah, 1963-64; supt. Teton County Sch. Dist., Driggs, Idaho, 1964-69, Preston (Idaho) Sch. Dist., 1969—; adv. com. Idaho Statewide Ednl. Planning and Reporting System, 1976—, chmn., 1978-79. Mem. bishopric Driggs 2d Ward, Mormon Ch., 1965-69, mem. high council Preston South stake, 1970-80, bishop Preston 8th Ward, 1980—. Served with M.C., AUS, 1953-56. Mem. Am. Assn. Sch. Adminstrs., NEA (life), Idaho Supts. Assn. (dist. pres. 1971-73), Phi Delta Kappa. Republican. Club: Lions (pres. Preston 1979-80). Contbg. author: School Organization and Administration for Utah Teachers, 1964. Home: 58 South 300 East Preston ID 83263 Office: 120 East 200 South Preston ID 83263

BOWLES, RICHARD JOSEPH, church administrator; b. Evanston, Ill., Mar. 2, 1944; s. Richard Joseph and Virginia (Minger) B.; m. Mary Ann Singer, July 16, 1966; children—Richard S., Brian E. A.B. with honors, Regis Coll., 1966; M.A., Cath. U. Am., 1970. Dir. religious edn. St. John's Parish, Clinton, Md., 1969-70; asst. prof. religious studies Regis Coll., Denver, 1970-75, assoc. dir. campus ministry, 1975-78; dir. liturgy Archdiocese of Denver, 1978—; deacon Basilica of the Immaculate Conception, Denver; archbishop's rep. Living the Good News. Mem. planning com. Holocaust Awareness Week, 1982-83; mem. Jewish-Cath. Dialogue, 1982—, Lutheran-Cath. Dialogue, 1975—; mem. planning com. Cath. Charities Run, 1982-83; mem. planning com. Denver Symphony Marathon. Recipient Faculty of Yr. award Regis Coll., 1974; Service award Denver Liturg. Commn., 1982. Mem. S.W. Liturg. Conf. Bd., Fedn. Diocesan Liturg. Commns., Alpha Sigma Nu. Office: Denver Archdiocese 200 Josephine St Suite 515 Denver CO 80206

BOWMAN, ALBERT SAMUEL, mgmt. cons.; b. Pitts., Mar. 29, 1935; s. Henry and Sara Helen (Rosenberg) B.; B.S., Mich. State U., 1957, M.S., 1966; postgrad. Eastern Ky. U., U. No. Colo., U. Colo.; m. Sarah Mendenhall Young, Sept. 26, 1959; children—J. Russell, Kathryn J. Patrolman, Dept. Pub. Safety, Mich. State U., 1957; cons. Pub. Adminstrn. Service, Chgo., 1965-67; asst. prof. criminal justice Eastern Ky. U., Richmond, 1966-68; dir. planning and research Gainesville (Fla.) Police Dept., 1968-69; dir. planning Central Fla. Region II, Gainesville, 1969-70; dir. research and planning, Lakewood, Colo., 1970; planner State of Colo., Denver, 1970-76; prin. Bowman & Assos., Lakewood, 1976-79; program mgr. Inst. Profl. Devel., 1979-82; pres. Bowman & Young Enterprises, Ltd., 1982—; staff Nat. Commn. Productivity and Quality of Working Life, 1973. Served to capt. U.S. Army, 1958-64. Mem. Am. Soc. Tng. and Devel., ACLU, Common Cause. Democrat. Reviewer articles Growth & Change; contbr., reviewer publs. of Internat. City Mgmt. Assn., U.S. GAO, Com. for Econ. Devel.

BOWMAN, JEAN LOUISE, civic worker; b. Albuquerque, Apr. 3, 1938; d. David Livingstone and Charlotte Louise (Smith) McArthur; student U. N.Mex., 1956-57, U. Pa., 1957-58, Rocky Mountain Coll., 1972-74; B.A. in Polit. Sci. with high honors, U. Mont., 1982, postgrad. Law Sch.; children—Carolyn Louise, Joan Emily, Amy Elizabeth, Eric Daniel. Dir. Christian edn. St. Luke's Episcopal Ch., 1979-80; dir. 1st Bank West; bd. trustees Rocky Mountain Coll., 1972-80; bd. dirs. Billings (Mont.) Area C. of C., 1977-80; mem. City-County Air Pollution Control Bd., 1969-74, chmn., 1970-71; del. Mont. State Constnl. Conv., 1971-72, sec. conv., 1971-72; chmn. County Local Govt. Study Commn., 1973-76; mem. Billings Sch. Dist. Long Range Planning Com., 1978-79; former pres. Billings LWV, Silver Run Ski Club. Named one of Billings' most influential citizens, Billings Gazette, 1977; Bertha Morton Scholar, 1982. Republican. Home: 1525 Gerald Ave Missoula MT 59801

BOWMAN, MICHAEL OREN, interior designer; b. Bluffton, Ind., Mar. 24, 1946; s. Daniel Booker and Hilda Marie (Steffen) B.; m. Rachel Valencia, Mar. 20, 1971; children—Catherine Maria, Rachel Anne. Grad. Parson's Sch. of Design, Paris, 1979. Interior designer Saxton's Furniture and Interiors, Tacoma, Wash., 1967—, retail mgr., 1977-79, designer, 1979—. Served with U.S. Army, 1967. Mem. Am. Soc. Interior Designers. Roman Catholic. Home: 4420 Elwood Dr Tacoma WA 98466 Office: Saxton's Inc 6030 South Tacoma Way Tacoma WA 98409

BOWMAN, RONALD RAY, physicist; b. Berea, Ky., Aug. 27, 1930; s. Willard Orlus and Jesse Maude (McDaniel) B.; B.S. in Engring. Physics, U. Colo., 1955, postgrad., 1956-58; m. Cherry M. Langstroth, Mar. 27, 1966 (div. Apr. 1975); 1 son Brian C. Physicist, U.S. Geol. Survey Radiation Lab., Denver Fed. Ctr., Denver, 1955-57; physicist Nat. Bur. Standards Electromagnetics div., Boulder, Colo., 1957-80, project leader, 1964-78; pres. Vitek Inc., 1977—; lectr. U. Calif. at Northridge, 1969, 71, 73, Ga. Tech. U., 1970, 72, U. Colo., 1974. Served with USAF, 1951-52. Recipient Disting. Authorship award Nat. Bur. Standards, 1963, Spl. Achievement award, 1974, Indsl. Research IR 100 award, 1973, 78. Mem. AAAS, Bioelectromagnetics Soc., Boulder Internat. Folkdancers (pres. 1963-64). Patentee in field. Home: 216 Sentinal Ln Jamestown Star Route Boulder CO 80302

BOWMAN, RONALD WILLIAM, chemical engineer; b. Hereford, Tex., Jan. 17, 1943; s. William Arthur and Hope Brunell (Adams) B.; B.S. in Chem. Engring., N.Mex. State U., 1965; M.S. (Exxon fellow), U. Mich., 1966; Ph.D., U. So. Calif.; m. Carol R. Walker, June 8, 1965; children—Shannon, Brittian and Brenden (twins). Engr., Shell Oil Co., Houston, 1965-71; sr. engr. Shell Devel., Houston, 1971-72; staff engr., sect. leader Shell Oil Co., Ventura, Calif., 1972-76; chief engr. Oilwell Research, Inc., 1977-78; pres., owner Case Engring. & Lab., Ventura, 1978—. Registered profl. engr., Tex., Calif.; lic. contractor. Mem. Nat. Assn. Corrosion Engrs., Soc. Petroleum Engrs., Soc. Profl. Engrs., Am. Inst. Chem. Engrs., Filtration Soc. Blue Key, Sigma Tau, Phi Kappa Phi. Republican . Baptist. Club: Toastmasters. Contbr. articles to profl. jours. Patentee steam bockage. Home: 4249 Case St Ventura CA 93003 Office: Lab Inc 5574 B Everglades St Ventura CA 93003

BOWMAN, WARREN DANIEL, JR., hematologist; b. Richmond, Va., Jan. 4, 1930; s. Warren Daniel and Olive Murann (Smith) B.; B.A., Bridgewater (Va.) Coll., 1950; M.D., U. Pa., 1954; m. Jean Louise McArthur, June 12, 1957 (div.); children—Carolyn Louise, Joan Emily, Amy Elizabeth, Eric Daniel; m. 2d, Viola Jean Fenton, June 5, 1980. Intern U. Mich. Hosp., Ann Arbor, 1954-55; resident intern medicine U. Pa., Phila., 1957-59; mem. staff dept. internal medicine Billings (Mont.) Clinic, 1960—; nat. med. adviser Nat. Ski Patrol System, 1970—; clin. asst. prof. medicine U. Wash. Med. Sch., Seattle, 1978—. Commnr., Western Interstate Commn. Higher Edn., 1970-74; exec. com. Gov. Mont. Council Phys. Fitness and Sports, 1972—. Served with USPHS, 1955-57. Fellow clin. hematology Jefferson Med. Coll., Phila., 1959-60. Diplomate Am. Bd. Internal Medicine, and Hematology. Fellow A.C.P., Internat. Soc. Hematology; mem. AMA, Am., Mont. (past pres.) socs. internal medicine, Am. Soc. Hematology. Republican. Episcopalian. Clubs: Am. Alpine, Beartooth Ski Patrol. Author, editor in field. Home: 2312 Pine St Billings MT 59101 Office: Billings Clinic PO Box 2555 Billings MT 59103

BOWYER, JAMES DON, investment banker; b. Abilene, Tex., June 21, 1939; s. John MacDonald and Wynona (Simmons) B.; student E. Tex. State U., 1959-62; m. Francesca Knittel, June 19, 1976; children—Nicole L., MacDonald J. West Coast partner H. Hentz & Co., Beverly Hills, Calif., 1970-73; nat. sales mgr. Roberts Scott & Co., San Diego, 1973-74; v.p., mgr. Loeb Rhoades & Co., Newport Beach, Calif., 1975-76; mng. dir. MacDonald, Krieger & Bowyer, Beverly Hills, Calif., 1974—. Founder, Los Angeles Music Center, 1978. Mem. Bond Club Los Angeles, Republican. Episcopalian. Clubs: Irvine Coast Country, Big Canyon Country, Balboa Bay, Bel Air Country. Office: 356 N Camden Dr Beverly Hills CA 92010

BOXER, BARBARA, congresswoman; b. Bklyn., Nov. 11, 1940; d. Ira and Sophie (Silvershein) Levy; m. Stewart Boxer, 1962; children—Doug, Nicole. B.A. in Econs., Bklyn. Coll., 1962. Stockbroker Merill Lynch, 1962-65; journalist, assoc. editor Pacific Sun Newspaper, 1972-74; congl. aide 5th Congl. Dist. Calif., 1974-76; supr. Marin County (Calif.) Bd. Suprs., 1976-82; mem. 98th Congress from 6th Calif. Dist. Pres. Democratic New Mems. Caucus, 1983—. Recipient Open Govt. award Common Cause, 1980. Mem. Marin Nat. Women's Polit. Caucus (founding), Marin Community Video (founding), Congl. Arts Caucus, Congl. Caucus for Women's Issues, Dem. Caucus at Congl. Space Caucus, Energy and Environment Study Conf. Jewish. Office: 1517 Longworth House Office Bldg Washington DC 20515

BOXER, JEROME HARVEY, accountant; b. Chgo., Nov. 27, 1930; s. Ben Avrum and Edith (Lyman) B.; A.A. magna cum laude, East Los Angeles Coll., 1952; A.B. with honors, Calif. State U., Los Angeles, 1954; m. Sandra Schaffner, June 17, 1980; children by previous marriage—Michael, Jodi. Lab. instr. Calif. State U., Los Angeles, 1953-54; staff accountant Dolman, Freeman & Buchalter, Los Angeles, 1955-57; sr. accountant Neiman, Sanger, Miller & Beress, Los Angeles, 1957-63; partner firm Glynn and Boxer, C.P.A.'s, Los Angeles, 1964-68; v.p., sec. Glynn, Boxer & Phillips Accountancy Corp., Los Angeles, 1968—; pres. Echo Data Services, Inc., 1978—; instr. data processing Los Angeles City Adult Schs.; tchr. lectr., cons. wines and wine-tasting. Mem. ops. bd. Everywoman's Village; co-founder, bd. dirs., officer Open Space Theatre. Recipient Youth Service award Mid-Valley YMCA, 1972-73; C.P.A., Calif. Mem. Am. Inst. C.P.A.'s, Calif. Soc. C.P.A.'s, Assn. for Systems Mgmt., Data Processing Mgmt. Assn., Am. Fedn. Musicians, Associated Photographers Internat., Friends of Photography, Los Angeles Photog. Ctr., Acad. Model Aeros., San Fernando Valley Silent Flyers, San Fernando Valley Radio Control Flyers, Associated Students Calif. State U., Los Angeles (hon. life), Acad. Magical Arts, Internal Brotherhood of Magicians, Soc. Preservation of Variety Arts, Les Amis du Vin, Knights of the Vine, Soc. Wine Educators, Soc. Bacchus Am., Blue Key, Alpha Phi Omega. Clubs: Kiwanis (pres. Sunset-Echo Park 1968), Braemar Country, Pacific Mariners Yacht, S.Coast Corinthian Yacht (Former dir., officer), B'nai B'rith. Cons., contbr. Wine World Mag., 1974—. Home: 15534 Morrison St Sherman Oaks CA 91403 Office: 1824 Sunset Blvd Los Angeles CA 90026

BOYCE, JAMES DANIEL, ophthalmologist; b. Rutland, Vt., Sept. 1, 1947; s. George Potter and Mary Emma (Bree) B.; B.A., Columbia U., 1969, M.D., 1973; m. Janet Muff, July 26, 1975. Intern, Los Angeles County-U. So. Calif. Med. Center, 1973-74; resident in ophthalmology Columbia-Presbyn. Med. Center, N.Y.C., 1974-77; practice medicine specializing in ophthalmology, Los Angeles, 1977-78, Garden Grove, Calif., 1978—; mem. staff Med. Center of Garden Grove, Western Med. Center; instr. U. So. Calif., Los Angeles, 1979—. Mem. AMA, Am. Acad. Ophthalmology, Orange County Ophthalmology Soc. Republican. Home: 202 Oaklawn Ave South Pasadena CA 91030 Office: 12665 Garden Grove Blvd Suite 606 Garden Grove CA 92643

BOYCE, RONALD REED, educator, mktg. location cons.; b. Los Angeles, Jan. 7, 1931; s. Reed S. and Martha Fern (Puzey) B.; B.S., U. Utah, 1955, M.S., 1956; Ph.D., U. Wash., 1961; m. Norma Rae Loraas, May 6, 1955; children—Renee, Susan. Instr., Western Wash. U., 1959; researcher Wash. U. Meramec Basin Research Project, 1960-61; asst. prof. community planning U. Ill., 1961-62; asso. prof. geography also Bur. Bus., U. Iowa, 1962-64; asso. prof. geography U. Wash., Seattle, 1964-76; prof. urban and regional studies Seattle Pacific U., 1976—, dir. Sch. Social and Behavioral Scis., 1976—; Am. Council on Edn. fellow and spl. asst. to pres. Baylor U., 1978-79; mktg. cons., Seattle, 1968—. Councilman, Woodway, Wash., 1969-74; pres. Allied Arts Symphony Orch., 1974-75, 77, Lynnwood Camp of Gideons, 1974-76. Served with AUS, 1953-54. Recipient guadrenniel award Congress S. African Geographers, 1981. Mem. Assn. Am. Geographers, Regional Sci. Assn., Am. Inst. Planners, Am. Geog. Soc., Gideons Internat. Author: Studies of the CBD and Urban Freeway Development, 1959; Regional Development and the Wabash Basin, 1964; The Bases of Economic Geography, 1978; Geographic Perspectives on Global Problems, 1981; editor: Geography as Spatial Interaction, 1980. Home: 23606 112th Pl W Edmonds WA 98020 Office: Seattle Pacific Univ Seattle WA 98119

BOYD, CHARLES GLENN, occupational safety and health adminstr.; b. Nevada, Mo., May 4, 1931; s. LeRoy Leonard and Alice Marie (Hall) B.; m. Angelina Reynoso, Jan. 24, 1960; children—Charles G., Alicia Maria. Grad. in indsl. mgmt. Non-Commd. Officers Acad., U.S. Air Force, Europe, 1965; grad. in programming Control Data Inst., 1975. Prodn. coordinator Automation Industries, Gardena, Calif., 1962-68; gen. foreman Filon Corp., Torrence, Calif., 1968-71; plant mgr. Fenton Corp., Gardena, 1971-78; safety and health dir. Teledyne Battery Products, Redlands, Calif., 1978—; cons. Served with USAF, 1947-55. Decorated Silver Star. Recipient Argonaut Ins. Safety award, 1982. Mem. Assn. Safety Engrs., Calif. Water Pollution Control Assn., Am. Legion. Republican. Episcopalian. Club: Kiwanis.

BOYD, CONSTANCE ANNE, financial advertising co. exec.; b. Evanston, Ill., Nov. 2, 1952; d. Richard Parker and Mary Lillian (Heberling) B.; A.A., Chaffey Coll., 1972; A.A., U. Calif., Riverside, 1973; student UCLA, 1979-81, U. Wis., 1978, Fin. Inst., Los Angeles. Asst. v.p. corp. communications USLIFE Savs. & Loan, Los Angeles, 1973-80; dir. corp. communications USLIFE Ins. Co., Pasadena, Calif., 1980-82; corp. advt. officer First Interstate Bank, Los Angeles, 1982—. Vol. cons. Ontario Pomona Assn. Retarded, Maryvale Orphanage, Hollywood Bowl Easter Sunrise Service, Rape Treatment Center at Med. Center of Santa Monica. Mem. Town Hall Los Angeles, Los Angeles Press Club, Internat. Assn. Bus. Communicators, Public Relations Soc. Am., Los Angeles Advt. Club, Los Angeles Publicity Club, Am. Mktg. Assn., Life Advertisers Assn., Internat. Meeting Planners Assn. Home: 145 S Reeves Dr Beverly Hills CA 90210 Office: 707 Wilshire Blvd Los Angeles CA 90017

BOYD, EDNA W., interior designer; b. Denver, Nov. 26, 1952; d. William Peterson and Margaret Agnes (Jordan) B. Student Huntington Community Coll., 1970-72; B.A. in Design, U. Colo., 1974. Interior designer Glasgow Interiors, Denver, 1974-76; mgr. design dept. Jacobson Better Design Co., Denver, 1976-78; head designer Werik Designs Inc., Tucson, 1978—; cons. in field. Instr. CPR, ARC, Tucson, 1980—. Mem. Am. Soc. Interior Designers, AAUW, Profl. Women's Network. Democrat. Presbyterian. Office: Werik Designs Inc 5399 E 29th St Tucson AZ 85711

BOYD, GERALD DALE, editor; b. Chester, Pa., Oct. 15, 1935; s. Richard Franklin and Elizabeth Margaret (Aurand) B.; m. Janet Mary Boyle, May 3, 1958; children—Kevin P., Mark G., Sean T. B.A. summa cum laude, Met. State Coll., Denver, 1979. Enlisted U.S. Air Force, 1953, advanced to master sgt., 1971; pub. info. technician; ret., 1976; free lance wine writer and educator, 1976-79; mng. editor The Wine Spectator, San Francisco, 1971-81, editor, 1981-83; educator, pub. speaker. Named Pride Man of Year, 437th Mil. Airlife Wing, Charleston AFB, S.C., 1971. Mem. Brotherhood Knights of the Vine (master knight), Soc. Wine Educators (instr.), Counseiller de le Grand Conseil l'Academie du Vin de Bordeaux. Co-author: Harvey's Pocket Guide to Wines, 1981; wine contbr. Americana Ency. Ann., 1982, Advt. Age mag.; wine columnist Rocky Mountain News and Denver mag. Office: Opera Plaza 601 Van Ness Ave Suite 2040 San Francisco CA 94102

BOYD, JAMES WILSON, real estate broker; b. Los Angeles, May 13, 1947; s. Gene and Lillian Ann B.; m. Deborah Julia Lindblad, Aug. 28, 1973; children—Julia Ann, Marshall Allen, Laura Elizabeth. B.S., San Diego State U., 1969; M.A., U. Calif.-Santa Barbara, 1972, Ph.D. in Econs., 1974. Lectr. econs. U. Calif.-Santa Barbara, 1973-74; research mgr., residential energy demand Electric Power Research Inst., Palo Alto, Calif., 1974-79; v.p. property acquisition and sales Essex Property Corp., Palo Alto, 1979; pres. Interstate Equities Corp., J.W. Boyd & Assocs., Menlo Park, Calif., 1979—. Mem. Am. Econs. Assn., Western Econs. Assn. Contbr. articles to profl. jours. Home: 12510 Minorca Ct Los Altos Hills CA 94022 Office: 3000 Sand Hill Rd #2-175 Menlo Park CA 94025

BOYD, JERRY LEE, mktg. exec.; b. Middletown, Ohio, Mar. 25, 1944; s. William Willett and Betty Elenor (Shockley) B.; B.S. in Chem. Engring., U. Cin., 1967; postgrad. U. Utah, 1976-78; m. Diane Elizabeth Lumpp, Sept. 17, 1966; children—Michelle Aubrey, Nicole Carolyn. Research engr. Eimco PMD, Salt Lake City, 1967-71, chief process application engr., 1971-72, dir. tech. services, 1972-75, mgr. parts mktg. and service, 1979, gen. mgr. parts services, 1979-80; v.p. parts services, 1981—; sr. mktg. specialist Eimco BSP, Salt Lake City, 1975-76, market mgr., 1976-77; mgr. sales tng. Envirotech Process Equip., Salt Lake City, 1977, mgr. sales devel., 1977-79. Mem. Water Pollution Control Fedn., Am. Inst. Chem. Engrs., AIME, Am. Mgmt. Assn., Nat. Rifle Assn. Republican. United Ch. of Christ. Contbr. articles in field to profl. jours. Home: 1825 Yarrow Circle Bountiful UT 84010 Office: 669 W 2d St S PO Box 300 Salt Lake City UT 84110

BOYD, KEITH EDWARD, mech. engr., educator; b. Salt Lake City, May 31, 1931; s. Alfred R. and Helen A. (Carlson) B.; B.S. in Mech. Engring., U. Utah, 1955, M.S., 1959; Ph.D., Ariz. State U., 1967; m. Patricia Daynes, Jan. 8, 1953; children—Kathleen, Keith Edward, Leslie Ann, Richard, Carol. Design engr. powerplant installations Lockheed Aircraft Corp., Burbank, Calif., 1955-56; devel. engr. control systems Marquardt Corp., Van Nuys, Calif., 1956-57; instr. mech. engring. U. Utah, Salt Lake City, 1957-59, asst. prof. mech. engring., 1959-62; cons. heat transfer Research Engring., Inc., Salt Lake City, 1959-62; sci. faculty fellow NSF, 1962-63; faculty asso. mech. engring. Ariz. State U., Tempe, 1963-64; engring. specialist AiResearch Mfg. Co. Ariz. div. Garrett Corp., Phoenix, 1964-67, sr. engring. specialist, 1967—; cons.

Utah Research and Devel., Salt Lake City, 1978—; faculty asso. dept. aerospace engring. Ariz. State U., Tempe, 1980—. Served with USAF, 1951-52. Registered profl. engr., Utah. Mem. ASME, Sigma Xi, Pi Tau Sigma. Mormon. Contbr. articles on mech. design and heat transfer to profl. publs. Home: 2065 E Kael Circle Mesa AZ 85203 Office: PO Box 5217 111 S 34th St Phoenix AZ 85034

BOYD, LEONA POTTER, former social worker; b. Creekside, Pa., Aug. 31, 1907; d. Joseph M. and Belle (McHenry) Johnston; grad. Ind. Normal Sch., 1927; student Las Vegas Normal U., summer 1933; postgrad. Carnegie Inst. Tech. Sch. Social Work, summer 1945, U. Pitts. Grad. Sch. Social Work, 1956-57; m. Edgar D. Potter, July 16, 1932 (div.); m. Harold Lee Boyd, Oct. 1972. Tchr. Creekside (Pa.) pub. schs., 1927-30, Papago Indian Reservation, Sells, Ariz., 1931-33; caseworker, supr. Indiana County (Pa.) Bd. Assistance, 1934-54, exec. dir., 1954-68, ret. Bd. dirs. Indiana County Tourist Promotion; cons. asso. Community Research Assos., Inc.; mem. Counseling Center Aux., Lake Havasu City, Ariz., 1978-80; mem. Western Welcome Club, Lake Havasu City. Recipient Jr. C. of C. Disting. Service award, 1965, Business and Profl. Women's Club award, 1965. Mem. Am. Assn. Ret. Persons, Daus. Am. Colonists, Indiana County, Sierra County hist. socs. Methodist. Club: Hot Springs Women's. Home: 507 N Foch St Truth or Consequences NM 87901

BOYD, MARY H. (MERRILL), assn. exec.; b. Winnetka, Ill., Sept. 11, 1929; d. Harold Gatton and Martha Emily (Lawson) Heberling; student Long Beach City Coll., 1956, UCLA, 1973; cert. in human services U. Calif.-Riverside, 1973-74; B.S., LaVerne U., 1982; children—Constance Anne Boyd, Richard Parker Boyd Jr. Exec. sec. Ontario-Pomona Assn. for Retarded Citizens, Montclair, Calif., 1962-65, exec. dir., 1965—; instr. Chaffey Coll., Alta Loma, Calif., 1972-76, coordinator classes for disabled, 1972-76; instr. weekend series LaVerne U., 1974, vis. lectr., 1969-74; vis. lectr. Mt. SanAntonio Coll., 1976, U. Calif. at Riverside, 1972, UCLA, 1981-82; trainer various subjects Kellogg Found.; lectr. in field. Founder, Mental Retardation Service Council of San Gabriel Valley, 1965; mem. Calif. Developmental Disabilities Area planning bd., Area 12, Inyo, Mono, Riverside, San Bernardino counties, 1970-76, chmn. profl. adv. counsel, 1977-80; mem. steering com. for development of Regional Centers Inland Counties, 1969-70, San Gabriel Valley, 1973; active Girl Scouts U.S.A., 1960-68; leader, advisor Tri-Hi-Y, 1968-71; bd. dirs. PTA, 1958-62; chmn. N.E. United Way Conf. Execs.; adv. bd. Mt. San Antonio Coll. Allied Health Adv. Bd., 1975—, Los Angeles United Way, 1966—, Calif. Inst. for Men, 1968-72, San Bernardino County Child Health and Disability Prevention, 1975-78, chmn., 1977-78; adv. bd. Chaffey Coll., 1972-78. Recipient Award of Merit, San Bernardino County Council of Community Services, 1966; Hon. Service award Ontario Montclair Sch. Dist., 1971: Humanitarian award, San Bernardino County, 1976; Chaffey Community Rep. Women Federated Recognition award, 1977; Community Service award U. LaVerne, 1982; HEW grantee, 1968, 69, 70, 72, 73, 74, 75, 76, 79; Calif. Community Found. grantee, 1968; Price Found. grantee, 1969, 72; Calif. Dept. Rehab. grantee, 1972, 73, 74, 75, 79, 81; Calif. Dept. Health grantee, 1976, 77. Mem. Assn. for Retarded-U.S., Assn. for Retarded-Calif. (v.p. 1979-81, pres. 1981-82), Conf. of Execs. of Assns. for Retarded U.S. (charter), Conf. Execs.-Calif. (chmn. 1982-83), Council Agy. Execs. Republican. Baptist. Author: (with J.Cook, J. Travers) Parents as Natural Helpers to Physicians at Time of Diagnosis of Developmental Disability, 1979. Home: 940 W 5th St Ontario CA 91762 Office: 9160 Monte Vista St Montclair CA 91763

BOYD, NANCY L(OUISE), garment manufacturing company controller, accountant; b. Ottumwa, Iowa, Aug. 3, 1945; d. Paul Judson and Dorothy Agnes (Pritchard) B.; m. James Mueller, Mar. 1969 (div. 1969). B.S. in Secondary Edn., N.W. Mo. State U., 1967; postgrad. U. Iowa, 1973, Los Angeles Valley Coll., 1978. Cert. tchr., Mo. Tchr. English, pub. high sch., 1967-69; adminstrv. sec. Legal Aid and Defender Soc., Kansas City, Mo., 1970; employment cons. Hallmark Personnel, Denver, 1971-72; in inventory control U. Iowa Press, Iowa City, 1972-73; accounts payable supr. Beren Corp., Denver, 1973-75; vocat. rehab. counselor Alcoholism Ctr. for Women, Los Angeles, 1976-77; office mgr., bookkeeper J.J. & Co., Los Angeles, 1977-79; bookkeeper, acct. Shirt Designs, Inc., Santa Monica, Calif., 1979, Marcal Sportswear, Los Angeles, 1979-80; controller, acct. Charles Towne Classics, Los Angeles, 1980-81; controller, acct. William Pearson, Inc., Los Angeles, 1981-83; controller, chief acct. The Field Co., Los Angeles, 1983—. Co-chmn. nat. task force NOW, 1975; bd. dirs. Van Ness Recovery House, Los Angeles, 1981—, treas., 1982—. Marcus Community High Sch. Tchrs.' scholar, 1963. Mem. Anti-Vivisection Soc., Couseteau Soc., Green Peace, Met. Museum Art, Smithsonian Assocs., Welsh Corgi League, Calif. Arboretum Found., Mensa, Kappa Delta Pi. Mem. Unity Ch. Author: Fractured Images, 1970; editor Tower yearbook, 1967.

BOYD, RICHARD DORR, construction company executive; b. San Mateo, Calif., Aug. 10, 1953; s. Milton Fletcher and Virginia Stewart (Dorr) B.; B.A. in Econs., U. Calif.-Davis, 1975; M.B.A., U. So. Calif., 1977; m. Linda June Waters, Sept. 17, 1978; 1 dau., Christy Margaret. Mgmt. trainee CBS Stores Inc., Emeryville, Calif., 1977-78, field supt., 1978-79; estimator, project mgr. Jack Horton Drywall Inc., Santa Clara, Calif., 1979-80; Nibbi Bros. Inc., San Francisco, 1980-81; project mgr. Nielsen, Vasko & Earl Inc., Sacramento, 1982—. Coach rugby team U.Calif.-Davis, 1981—. Republican. Presbyterian. Clubs: Bay Area Touring Side Rugby, No. Calif. Rugby Football Union Referees Soc., U. Calif. at Davis, Alumni, U. So. Calif. M.B.A. Alumni. Home: 5741 Classic Pl Carmichael CA 95608 Office: 320 N 10th St Sacramento CA 95813

BOYD, ROBERT GIDDINGS, JR., symphony executive; b. San Juan, P.R., Mar. 16, 1940; s. Robert Giddings and Laura Jean (Stephenson) B.; m. Amanda Gail McDonald, July 28, 1967; 1 dau., Stephanie Gail; m. 2d, Denise Ann, Dec. 10, 1978. B.A. in Sociology, Coll. of William and Mary, Williamsburg, Va.; postgrad. in bus. adminstrn. George Washington U., 1965-67. Supr. staff services Bellcomm, Inc., Washington, 1964-67; mgr. budget dept. Goodbody & Co., N.Y.C., 1968-70; bus. mgr. Westminster Sch., Simsbury, Conn., 1970-76; pres., gen. mgr. F & R Enterprises, Inc., Scottsdale, Ariz., 1976-78; bus. mgr. The Orme Sch., Mayer, Ariz., 1978-81; mng. dir. San Diego Symphony, 1981—. Served to 2d lt. U.S. Army, 1962-64. Mem. Am. Symphony Orch. League, Am. Mgmt. Assn., Am. Arts Alliance, Combined Arts and Edn. Council. Republican. Office: PO Box 3175 San Diego CA 92103

BOYD, WILLIAM ELKINS, lawyer; b. San Mateo, Calif., Oct. 13, 1947; s. William Sprott and Katherine (Elkins) Boyd; B.A., Stanford U., 1969; LL.B., J.D., Hastings Coll. of Law, 1974. Admitted to Calif. bar, 1975; partner firm Boyd and McKay, San Francisco, 1980—; v.p. Boyd Bros., investments, San Francisco, 1980—. Spl. asst. to chmn. Calif. Republican Com., 1968; bd. dirs. San Mateo County Planned Parenthood, 1971-73, Hastings Child Care Center, 1974-76. Mem. Am. Bar Assn., State Bar Calif. Assn. (bus. law sect.), Stanford U. Alumni Assn., Hastings Alumni Assn. Episcopalian. Clubs: Burlingame Country, Hastings 1066 Club. Home: 565 Tahos Rd Orinda CA 94563 Office: 601 Montgomery St Suite 1900 San Francisco CA 94111

BOYD, WILLIAM HARLAND, historian; b. Boise, Idaho, Jan. 7, 1912; s. Harland D. and Cordelia (Crumley) B.; A.B., U. Calif.-Berkeley, 1935, M.A., 1936, Ph.D., 1942; m. Mary Kathryn Drake, June 25, 1939; children—Barbara A. Boyd Voltmer, William Harland, Kathryn L. Tchr. Fall River High Sch., McArthur, Calif., 1937-38, Watsonville (Calif.) High Sch., 1941-42, San Mateo (Calif.) High Sch., 1942-44; prof. history Bakersfield Coll., 1946-73, chmn. social sci. dept., 1967-73. Pres., Kern County Hist. Soc., 1950-52; adv. com. Kern County Mus., 1955-60; chmn. Fort Tejon Restoration Com. Bakersfield, 1952-55, sec., 1955-60; mem. Kern County Hist. Records Commn., 1977—. Recipient Merit award Kern County Bd. Trade, 1960; commendation Kern County Bd. Suprs., 1952, 76, 78. Mem. Calif. Tchrs. Assn., Am. Hist. Assn., Phi Alpha Theta. Republican. Baptist. Author: Land of Havilah, 1952, (with G.J. Rogers) San Joaquin Vignettes, 1955, (with others) Spanish Trailblazers in the South San Joaquin, 1957; A Centennial Bibliography on the History Kern County, California, 1966; A California Middle Border, 1972; A Climb Through History, 1973; Bakerfield's First Baptist Church, 1975; Kern Country Wayfarers, 1977; Kern County Tall Tales, 1980; The Shasta Route, 1981; Stagecoach Heyday in the San Joaquin Valley, 1983. Contbr. to Ency. Brit. Home: 339 Cypress St Bakersfield CA 93304

BOYDSTUN, JOHN ERVIN, evaluation research exec., resort owner; b. Holdenville, Okla., July 18, 1933; s. Elza Timothy and Ethel Albertine (Sullivan) B.; A.A., Murray State Coll., 1953; B.A.with honors, Okla. State U., 1955; m. Lois Arlene Jones, Apr. 7, 1962; children—Stacy Lynn, Brett Alan, Beth Ann. With System Devel. Corp., Santa Monica, Calif., 1958-81, tng. advisor to Air Def. Command, 1958-59, control systems analyst to SAC, 1959-64, control cons. to Tactical Air Command, 1964-66, advisor to Japanese Air Self Def. Force, 1966-69, dir. evaluation research projects, 1969-81; owner Wayward Winds Lodge, Tucson; lectr. in field. Served to capt. USAF, 1955-57. Mem. Am. Acad. Polit. and Social Scis., Smithsonion Assos., Phi Kappa Phi, Phi Teta Kappa, Pi Gamma Mu. Republican. Research in field. Contbr. articles to profl. mags. Home: 707 W Miracle Mile Tucson AZ 85705

BOYER, DAVID MORGAN, civil engr.; b. Denver, May 21, 1951; s. Thomas V. and Donna J. (Wilson) B.; B.S. in Civil Engring., U. Nev., Reno, 1974; m. Rae Jean Collins Drew, Aug. 28, 1971. Jr. engr. Walters Engring., Reno, Nev., 1974-75; hydraulic engr. State of Nev. Div. Water Resources, Carson City, 1975-78; project engr. Spink Corp., Reno, 1978-80; project engr. Summit Engring., Reno, 1980-81, Omni-Means, Ltd., Reno, 1981—; water rights surveyor State of Nev. Advanced first aid instr. ARC, 1970—; CPR instr. ARC and Am. Heart Assn., 1974—; mem. CPR com. Am. Heart Assn., 1974-80, vice chmn., 1974-77; cert. mem. Nat. Ski Patrol System; mem. Far West Profl. Ski Patrol Assn.; mem. Citizens Adv. Com. on Housing. Registered profl. engr., Calif., Nev. Mem. Nat. Soc. Profl. Engrs., ASCE, Water Pollution Control Fedn. Republican. Presbyterian. Clubs: Sierra Yacht, Hobie Cat Fleet (treas. 1977-79). Home: 3334 Clan Alpine Dr Sparks NV 89431 Office: Omni-Means Ltd 777 W 2d St Reno NV 89503

BOYER, EDWARD CLAIR, coll. adminstr.; b. Rose Valley, Pa., Apr. 5, 1924; s. Albert Clinton and Mary Catherine (Rupp) B.; B.S., U. Wyo., 1971, M.Public Adminstrn., 1973; m. Patricia Ann Adams, May 25, 1968; children—Allen Clair, Charles Edward, Dennis Clyde. Various positions in industry, Pa., Wyo., 1942-67; coordinator petroleum tech. program Casper (Wyo.) Coll., 1974—; mem. mine maintenance adv. com. Sheridan (Wyo.) Coll., 1978. Natrona County del. Wyo. Gov.'s Conf. on Libraries, 1979. Served with USAAF, 1943-46. Mem. Am. Soc. Safety Engrs., Am. Petroleum Inst., Central Wyo. Indsl. Arts Assn. Lutheran. Club: Casper Lions. Home: 1505 Bonnie Brae St Casper WY 82601 Office: Casper Coll 125 College Dr Casper WY 82601

BOYER, GENE T., aerospace co. exec.; b. Akron, Ohio, July 24, 1929; s. George F. and Edna Marie (Monroe) B.; B.S., Ohio U., 1952; m. Cynthia Campbell, Feb. 28, 1964; children—Robin Lee, Curtis Christopher. Joined U.S. Army, 1952, advanced through grades to lt. col.; comdg. officer and sr. Presdl. helicopter pilot White House, 1964-75; dir. internat. mktg. Lockheed Aircraft Service Co., 1977-78; dir. sales Mid East, Hughes Helicopters, 1975-77; dir. internat. mktg. Mid-East and Africa Lockheed Calif. Co., Burbank, Calif., 1978—; pres. GRC Enterprises, Mid-East bus. cons., San Pedro, Calif., 1981—. Decorated Air medal (9), D.F.C. with oak leaf cluster, Bronze Star, Legion of Merit, Soldiers medal. Mem. Am. Helicopter Soc., Nat. Aviation Club, Nat. Pilots Assn. Republican. Home: 2246 Rue le Charlene Rancho Palos Verdes CA 90274 Office: Lockheed Calif Co PO Box 551 Burbank CA 91520

BOYER, MELVIN ALTON, data processing executive; b. Filmore, Calif., Apr. 22, 1938; s. Marvin Alfred and Lulu Marie (Hinkle) B.; m. Nancy Jean Walters, July 25, 1959; children—John Michael, Mark Allen. Unit record operator Boeing Airplane Co., Seattle, 1960-62; programmer Tektronix Inc., Beaverton, Oreg., 1962-65; sr. programmer, analyst Longview Fibre Co. (Wash.), 1965-78; dir. data processing La. Pacific Corp., Portland, Oreg., 1978—. Served with USMC, 1956-58. Mem. Soc. Info. Mgmt., Assn. System Mgmt., Beaverton Area C. of C. Republican. Roman Catholic. Club: K.C. Home: 1875 NE Lincoln St Hillsboro OR 97123 Office: 111 SW 5th Ave Portland OR 97204

BOYKAN, MITCH PAUL, counselor; b. Springfield, Mass., Sept. 10, 1952; s. Irving and Esther Florence B.; m. Toby Jean Clayman, July 26, 1980. B.S., Syracuse U., 1974; M.Counseling, Ariz. State U., 1977; A.A.S. in Bus. Data Processing, Phoenix Coll., 1982. Cert. alcohol counselor, Ariz. Psychiat. aide Inst. of Living, Hartford, Conn., 1974-75; alcoholism counselor intern, alcohol treatment program VA Hosp., Phoenix, 1975-76; counselor trainee Ariz. State U. Counselor Tng. Ctr., Tempe, 1976-77; work-study counselor Tri-City Mental Health Ctr., Mesa, Ariz., 1977; mental health technician Adobe Mountain Sch., Phoenix, 1978-79; therapist Phoenix South Community Mental Health Ctr., 1979-81, alcoholism therapist, 1981—, clin. supr., 1982—. Syracuse U. scholar, 1970-74; Ariz. State U. scholar, 1975; Data Processing Mgmt. Assn. scholar, 1979. Mem. Am. Personnel and Guidance Assn., Assn. Specialists in Group Work, YMCA, Phi Beta Kappa. Jewish. Office: 1424 S 7th Ave Phoenix AZ 85007

BOYKIN, BENJAMIN MATTHEWS, aerospace company executive; b. Clarendon, Tex., Mar. 3, 1930; s. Garland Lester and Edna (Matthews) B.; m. Gwen Royal, May 10, 1968; children—Scott Alan, Brian Matthews, Kimberly Mechelle. B.S.E.E., N.Mex. State U., 1953. Registered profl. engr. Project engr. Navajo and Hound Dog Weapon Systems, Rockwell Internat., 1957-64; project engr./site mgr. Apollo Environ. Test Ops., Houston, 1965-68, mgr. Apollo vehicle and GSE projects, 1969-73, mgr. shuttle project engring., 1973-74, dir. shuttle engring. and test ops., field ops., Houston, 1974—. Pres., Clear Lake City Water Authority, 1980—; bd. dirs. Brook Forest Community Assn.; vol. firefighter Brooks Fire Dept. Served to maj. USAF, 1953-57. Recipient Apollo Group Achievement award NASA, 1960. Mem. Nat. Mgmt. Assn., AIAA. Democrat. Methodist. Home: 308 E Purdy Ave Placentia CA 92670 Office: 1840 NASA Rd 1 Suite 102 Houston TX 77059

BOYKIN, JAMES LESTER, aerospace company engineer, consultant; b. Clarendon, Tex., Jan. 6, 1928; s. Garland Lester and Lucy Edna (Matthews) B.; m. Dulcie Mildred Ligon, Sept. 2, 1958; children—Tracy Lynette, Leslie Dee, James Russell, Robin Elisa. B.S.M.E., N.Mex. State U., 1951, B.S.E.E., 1959. Comml. pilot rating. With Hughes Aircraft Co., 1951-54; fighter pilot U. S. Air Force, 1954-58; flight test engr., test ops. supr. N.Am. Aviation div. Rockwell Internat., Los Angeles, 1959-63, Las Cruces, N.Mex., 1963-69; test ops. supr. LTV (Ling Timco Vaught), Las Cruces, 1969-71, Dynalectron Corp., Las Cruces, 1971-74; with Rockwell Internat., Las Cruces, 1974—, ops. supr., 1978—, project engr., 1983—, sr. project engr., 1983—; cons.; charter flying. Served to capt. USAF, 1946-48, 54-58; with USAFR, 1969. (ret.). Mem. Nat. Rifle Assn. (life), Air Force Assn., Res. Officers Assn. Democrat. Methodist. Club: Lions (pres. 1975-76) (Las Cruces). Home: 2390 Rosedale Dr Las Cruces NM 88005

BOYLAN, TIMOTHY LEE, psychologist; b. Canton, Ohio, Apr. 2, 1950; s. Robert E. and Irene (Tolin) B.; m. Sharon L. Beck, Apr. 4, 1970; children—Eric Richard, Jeffrey Timothy. B.S. in Edn., Kent State U., 1972; M.A. in Clin. Psychology, Akron U., 1977. Tchr. life sci. Coshocton (Ohio) City Schs., 1973-74; tchr. high sch. biology Canton City Schs., 1974-78; biofeedback technician Las Vegas Headache and Stress Clinic, 1979-81; psychologist, program coordinator Clark County Juvenile Ct., Las Vegas, 1981—; instr. Nellis AFB br. Park Coll., part-time 1979—. Coach youth soccer, 1981—; mgr. Little League, 1980—. Mem. Am. Psychol. Assn., Am. Assn. Correctional Psychologists, Nev. Psychol. Assn. Democrat. Roman Catholic. Club: K.C. Home: 5892 Arandas Ct Las Vegas NV 89103 Office: 3401 E Bonanza Rd Las Vegas NV 89101

BOYLE, BETTY GRACE, educator; b. Laramie, Wyo., May 17, 1933; d. Earl Edward and Rosielee (Knight) Smith; B.A. in Edn. (honor scholar), U. Wyo., 1954; M.S. in Ednl. Adminstrn. and Supervision, Pepperdine U., 1980; m. Daniel Wayne Boyle, Dec. 22, 1954; children—Gary E., Jerry M., Cary S. Elem. tchr. Laramie Public Schs., 1954; substitute tchr., Richmond, Calif., 1957-58; substitute tchr. Pinole-Hercules Sch., Pinole, Calif., 1958-63, home tchr., 1963-64; tchr. Adult Basic Edn., Richmond, 1965-66; tchr. Richmond Unified Schs., 1966—, tchr. kindergarten/first grade, 1968—, also mem. curriculum com.; liaison Contra Costa-Alameda Resource Center; sec. Sch. Adv. Council for Grant Sch. Mem. United Tchrs. Richmond, Calif. Tchrs. Assn., NEA, Assn. Supervision and Curriculum Devel., U. Wyo. Alumni Assn. Club: Women of Moose (San Pablo, Calif.). Home: 2534 Doidge Ave Pinole CA 94564 Office: 2400 Downer St Richmond CA 94804

BOYLE, BRUCE JAMES, publisher; b. Mpls., Aug. 31, 1931; s. Lorille James and Norma Elizabeth (Blish) B.; B.J., U. Mo., 1958; m. Betty Jean Tucker, May 28, 1960; children—Katherine Ann, Julia Caroline, Amy Elizabeth. Copywriter, Sta. KFRU, Columbia, Mo., 1958; continuity dir. KOMO-TV, Columbia, 1959; advt. salesman Better Homes & Gardens mag., 1960; advt. dir. Successful Farming mag., Des Moines, 1969-73, pub., 1973-80; pub. Meredith Pub. Services, 1976-78; pub. Meredith Video Pub., 1981—. Served with U.S. Navy, 1951-54. Mem. Nat. Agri-Mktg. Assn. (pres. 1973-74), Farm and Indsl. Equipment Inst., Farm Equipment Mfrs. Assn. (chmn. bd. govs. 1971-72), Alpha Delta Sigma. Clubs: Okoboji Yacht, Des Moines, Des Moines Golf and Country. Home: 718 55th St Des Moines IA 50312 Office: Meredith Corp 1716 Locust St Des Moines IA 50336*

BOYLE, CHARLES ALFRED, bus. exec.; b. Phila., July 6, 1916; s. John G. and Mae (Peterson) B.; student U. Pa., 1937-38, Brookings Instn., 1960, Ariz. State U., 1962-65, Indsl. Coll. of Armed Forces studies, 1955; m. Edith Christy, Sept., 1942. Manpower specialist Ariz. Govt. Service, Tucson, 1945-50, field supr. Ariz. Employment Service, 1951-54, chief, field operations, 1955-62, dep. adminstr., 1963, employment service adminstr., 1964-72; dir. unemployment ins., tech. assistance project, govt. edn. div. C & S Services Inc. div. Cordura Corp. (formerly Computing & Software, Inc.), Sacramento, 1972-75; now pres. Charles A. Boyle & Assos. Chmn. bd. Ariz. Bus.-Industry Edn. Council. Bd. dirs. Samuel Gompers Meml. Rehab. Center, Phoenix. Served with USAAF, 1940-45. Mem. Am. Acad. Polit. Sci., Internat. Platform Assn., Am. Legion, V.F.W., D.A.V., Urban League, Internat. Assn. Personnel in Employment Security, Ariz. Acad. Club: Rotary. Home: 9747 Augusta Dr Sun City AZ 85351 Office: 3747 Augusta Dr Sun City AZ 85351

BOYLE, CHARLES KEITH, educator, artist; b. Defiance, Ohio, Feb. 15, 1930. Student Ringling Sch. Art; B.F.A., U. Iowa. Group shows include Stanford U. Mus., 1964, San Francisco Mus. Art, 1965, Ann Arbor, Mich., 1965, Joslyn Art Mus., Omaha, 1970, San Jose Mus. Art, Calif., 1978; represented in permanent collections: San Francisco Mus. Art, Stanford U. Mus., Mead Paper Corp., Atlanta, Nat. Fine Arts Collection, Washington, Oakland Mus., Continental Bank, Chgo.; prof. painting and drawing Stanford U., 1962—. Nat. Endowment Arts grantee, 1981-82. Office: Stanford University Dept Art Cummings Art Bldg 115 Stanford CA 94305

BOYLE, DANIEL EDWARD, JR., real estate and oil investor; b. Pueblo, Colo., Feb. 11, 1931; s. Daniel Edward and Claire M. Boyle; B.A. in English, N.Mex. Mil. Inst., Roswell, 1953; m. Patricia Ann Bellamah, Jan. 9, 1954; children—Daniel Edward, III, Patricia Elaine Boyle Wilken, Cynthia Kay. With Dale J. Bellamah Corp., Albuquerque, 1956-73, pres., 1970-73, chmn. bd., 1972-73; pres., chmn. bd. Dale Bellamah Corp., 1973-78, Bellamah Corp., 1973-80; chmn. bd. D.B. Holding Co., 1978-81, Bellamah Group, Inc., 1980-81; pvt. investor, 1981—; dir. First Interstate Bank Albuquerque, S.W. Distbg. Co., Oilsearch Corp. Mem. bus. sch. adv. council N.Mex. State U., Las Cruces. Bd. dirs. Southwest Community Health Services, Albuquerque. Served as officer AUS, 1953-56. Methodist. Clubs: Four Hills Country, Tanoan Country. Office: 6121 Indian School Rd NE Suite 141 Albuquerque NM 87110

BOYLE, EDWARD LOUIS, III, electronics company executive; b. Pitts., Aug. 13, 1940; s. Edward Louis and Helen Mar (Shoop) B. B.S. in Econs., Ariz. State U., 1964. Logistics analyst Motorola, Inc., Scottsdale, Ariz., 1965-74, configuration and data specialist, 1974-76, mgr. classification rev., 1976-81, mgr. configuration and data mgmt., 1981—; cons. mil. provisioning. Adviser Jr. Achievement. Mem. Nat. Classification Mgmt. Soc., Soc. Logistics Engrs. Republican. Roman Catholic. Home: 7013 E Culver St Scottsdale AZ 85257 Office: Motorola Inc 8201 E McDowell Rd Scottsdale AZ 85252

BOYLE, JUNE, state senator; b. Greeley, Colo., Sept. 30, 1917; d. Walter J. and Millicent W. Ott; m. James M. Boyle; children—Kathleen Boyle Champain, Michael J. B.F.A., U. Colo. Dem. nat. committeewoman from Wyo.; del. Dem. Nat. Conv., 1968, 72; mem. Wyo. Commn. Status of Women from 1966; former mem. Wyo. Ho. of Reps., mem. Wyo. State Senate, 1972—. Chmn. Albany County Democratic Party. Named Legislator of Yr., Wyo. chpt. Nat. Assn. Social Workers, 1979, 80; Mem. S.E. Wyo. Mental Health Ctr., Laramie United Fund, LWV, Delta Phi Delta, Alpha Phi. Roman Catholic. Clubs: Laramie Woman's, U. Wyo. Faculty Women's. Home: 706 S 14th St Laramie WY 82070 Office: Wyoming State Senate Cheyenne WY 82002*

BOYLE, WILLIAM THOMAS, interior designer; b. Detroit, May 16, 1920; s. William Thomas and Sarah Ann (Sullivan) B.; m. Irene R. Boyle, Jan. 30, 1955. Student U. Detroit, 1944-45. Cert. Kitchen designer. Owner, v.p., interior designer St. Charles Co. of So. Calif., Los Angeles; cons. Served with U.S. Army, ETO. Mem. Am. Soc. Interior Designers (cert.), Am. Soc. Interior Designers. Democrat. Roman Catholic. Contbr. articles in field to publs. Office: 8660 Sunset Blvd Los Angeles CA 90069

BOYNTON, BUCK WILLIAM, physician; b. Houston, Feb. 27, 1920; s. George Wesley and Mabel (Palmer) B.; B.A., U. Tex., 1950, M.D., 1954; m. Maryanna Craig, Sept. 3, 1947 (div. Jan., 1965); children—Buck William, Suzanne; m. 2d, Donna Carlisle, Apr. 22, 1978. Intern,

Riverside County Gen. Hosp., 1954-55, resident, 1955-56; gen. practice of medicine, Riverside, Calif., 1954-82; physician Riverside County Jail, 1971-83; staff physician and surgeon Folsom State Prison, Represa, Calif., 1983—. Served with USNR, 1942-45. Clubs: Masons, Shriners. Home: Folsom Prison PO Box 42 Represa CA 95671

BOYNTON, DONALD ARTHUR, title ins. co. exec.; b. Culver City, Calif., Sept. 6, 1940; s. A.A. and Margaret Lena (Slocum) B.; student El Camino Jr. Coll., 1960-62, Antelope Valley Jr. Coll., 1963-64, Orange Coast Coll., 1969-72; B.A., Bradford U., 1977; m. Jean Carolyn Ferrulli, Nov. 10, 1962; children—Donna Jean Boynton, Michael Arthur. With Title Ins. & Trust Co., 1958-63; dep. sheriff County of Los Angeles, 1963-65; with Transamerica Title Ins. Co., Los Angeles, 1965-69; sr. title officer Calif. Land Title Co., Los Angeles, 1969-72; asst. sec. Lawyers Title Ins. Corp., 1972-77; analyst Am. Title Co., Santa Ana, Calif., 1977-79; v.p., mgr. Orange County ops. Chgo. Title Ins. Co., Tustin, Calif., 1979-80; state coordinator Transamerica Title Ins. Co., Los Angeles, 1981—. Mem. Orange County Escrow Assn. Republican. Clubs: Optimist (sec. treas.), Elks (chaplain, life), Rotary. Home: 625-A Hartford Ave Huntington Beach CA 92648 Office: 22691 Lambert St Lake Forest CA 92630

BOYNTON, EVERETT DOUGLAS, entertainment production company executive, consultant; b. Torrance, Calif., July 20, 1951; s. Everett Deming and Jacquelene (Corbin) B.; m. Moira Jeanne Gunnon, Apr. 7, 1979. B.A. in Polit. Sci., Calif. State U.-Fullerton, 1977. Attractions host, Walt Disney Prodns., 1970-79; employment interviewer WED Enterprises, Glendale, Calif., 1980, profl. staffing rep., 1981, rep. sr. tng. and devel., 1982—; cons. Deacon 1st Presbyterian Ch., Orange, Calif. Served with U.S. Army, 1971-73. Mem. Am. Soc. Tng. and Devel. Republican. Home: 6205 West View Dr Orange CA 92669 Office: Walt Disney Prodns 1401 S Flower St Glendale CA 92807

BOYNTON, WILLIAM LEWIS, electronic mfg. co. ofcl.; b. Kalamazoo, May 31, 1928; s. James Woodbury and Cyretta (Gunther) B.; ed. pub. schs.; m. Kei Ouchi, Oct. 8, 1953. Asst. mgr. Speigel J & R, Kalamazoo, 1947-48; served with U.S. Army, 1948-74, ret., 1974; with Rockwell/Collins div., Newport Beach, Calif., 1974—, supr. materiel, 1978-81, coordinator, 1981—; mem. faculty Western Mich. U., 1955-58. Trustee Orange County Vector Control Dist., 1980—; mem. adv. panel for bus./econ. devel. Calif. State Legislature, 1979—. Decorated Bronze Star. Mem. Assn. U.S. Army, Air Force Assn., Assn. U.S. Army, Non-Commd. Officers Assn., Nat. Mgmt. Assn., Nat. Geog. Soc., Smithsonian Inst. (asso.). Republican. Roman Catholic. Home: 5314 Lucky Way Santa Ana CA 92704 Office: PO Box 11963 Santa Ana CA 92711

BOZAJIAN, JOHN MARTIN, aerospace engineer; b. Los Angeles, Apr. 8, 1927; s. John Hrant and Rose (Najarian) B.; B.S., U. Calif.-Berkeley, 1950; M.S., Calif. Inst. Tech., 1951; m. Alice Rachel Boghosian, July 8, 1950; children—John Philip, Steven Haig, Mark David. With Hughes Aircraft Co., El Segundo, Calif., 1951—, dept. mgr., sr. project engr., 1960-66, mgr. Engring. Mechanics Lab., 1966-72, asso. program mgr. Pioneer Venus program, 1972-77, mgr. Space Vehicles Labs., 1977—, asst. mgr. Tech. Div., Space and Communications Group, 1978—. Served with U.S. Army, 1945-46. Named Master Designer in Aerospace Design, Product Engring. Mag., 1969; recipient NASA Disting. Public Service medal for design contbns. to Pioneer Venus Orbiter and Multiprobe spacecraft systems, 1980. Mem. Am. Inst. Aeros. and Astronautics, Tau Beta Pi, Pi Tau Sigma. Mem. Armenian Ch. N.Am. Club: Marina City. Contbr. articles in field to profl. jours. Patentee thermal switch used in thermal control Surveyor spacecraft. Home: 5535 W 64th St Los Angeles CA 90056 Office: 909 N Sepulveda Blvd El Segundo CA 90245

BOZEK, MARK PHILLIP, optometrist; b. Los Alamos, Nov. 3, 1950; s. Edward A. and Mary L. (Morrison) B.; m. Cathy Elaine Steller, Dec. 15, 1973; children—Jamie A., Andrew E. A.A. in Biology, Mt. San Antonio Jr. Coll., 1974; B.A. in Biology, Long Beach State U., 1976; O.D., Ill. Coll. Optometry, 1980. Lic. optometrist, Calif. Intern in visual therapy Dr. James Sanderson, Orland Park, Ill., 1979-80; assoc. Dr. A. I. Stolper, Oxnard, Calif., 1980-81; practice optometry specializing in family vision care, infant and children's vision, Ventura, Calif., 1981—; cons. Vision Care-Easter Seals Infant Stimulation Program, Ventura. Vice pres. individual devel. Ventura Jaycees, 1981—. Served with U.S. Army, 1969-70. Decorated Purple Heart; recipient Project of Yr. award Calif. Jaycees, 1982. Mem. Tri Counties Optometric Assn. (chmn. pub. health screenings), Calif. Optometric Assn., Am. Optometric Assn., Ill. Vol. Optometric Services for Humanity, Gold Key. Roman Catholic. Club: Order Purple Heart. Developing infant vision exam. techniques. Office: 9284 Telephone Rd Ventura CA 93004

BOZICH, ANTHONY THOMAS, motor freight co. exec.; b. Republic, Pa., July 31, 1924; s. Anthony Thomas and Johanna (Sternal) B.; student Duquesne U., 1942-43; A.M.P., Harvard U., 1972; postgrad. U. Calif. at Berkeley Extension Div., 1954-58; m. Gloria Fallentine, Apr. 9, 1944; children—Anthony Thomas, III, Craig A., Carol K., Gail F., Greta O., Eric D. Div. mgr. Pacific Intermountain Express Co., Denver, 1946-65; exec. v.p. ops. IML Freight, Inc., Salt Lake City, 1965-74, pres., 1974-77; pres., prin. Clark Tanklines Co., Salt Lake City. Served with USAAF, 1943-45. Decorated Purple Heart. Mem. Am. Trucking Assn. (v.p., gov., exec. com., mem. found., chmn. taxation and reciprocity com.), Western Hwy. Inst. (intermountain v.p., mem. exec. com.), Nat. Alliance of Businessmen (metro chmn.). Republican. Mormon. Clubs: Bonneville Exchange, Salt Lake Country, Alta. Home: 3608 Brighton Point Dr Salt Lake City UT 84121 Office: 1450 N Beck St Salt Lake UT 84110

BOZNER, JOHN CYRIL, geologist; b. Rock Springs, Wyo., Nov. 19, 1952; s. John C. and Evelyn (Parre) B.; Geol. Engr., Colo. Sch. Mines, 1975. Geologist, W.R. Grace & Co., Craig, Colo., 1975-76, Monsanto Co., Soda Springs, Idaho, 1976-79, Geokinetics, Vernal, Utah, 1979-81, Bennet Carder & Assos., Inc., Rock Springs, Wyo., 1981—. Mem. Am. Inst. Mining Engrs., Am. Assn. Petroleum Geologists, Wyo. Geol. Assn. Democrat. Roman Catholic. Clubs: Am. Kennel, Order of Eagles. Home: 616 4th Ave W Rock Springs WY 82901

BRAASCH, CATHERINE IRENE HOPKINS, hosp. ofcl.; b. Palo Alto, Calif., Aug. 15, 1948; d. Robert Hanchett Hopkins and Donna Ethel (Anderson) Hopkins Deebach; A.A. with honors, Cabrillo Coll., 1969; B.S.Ed. summa cum laude in Journalism, U. Wis., Whitewater, 1974; m. Leroy Raymond Thomas Braasch, Dec. 16, 1966; 1 dau., Sara Jill. Pres relations writer, Mont. Coll. Mineral Sci. and Tech., Butte, 1974-78; community relations dir. St. James Community Hosp., Butte, 1978-81; asst. adminstr. public affairs Holy Rosary Hosp., Ontario, Oreg., 1981—; lectr. workshops and classes in field; pres. Butte Press Club, 1978-79; cert. facilitator Emerging Woman in Mgmt. Workshop. Asso./cons. for media relations Mont. (Gov's.) Adv. Council Children and Youth, 1976-77; bd. dirs. Montanans for Children, Youth and Families, Inc., 1977-78, media cons., 1978—1978-81; dist. bd. edn. Luth. Ch.-Mo. Synod, 1978-81, Congregation Bd. of Stewardship and Ch. Properties, 1979-81, lay voting del. to Mont. Dist. Convs., 1976-78, to Internat. Synodical Conv., St. Louis, 1979; mem. council St. Paul Luth. Ch., 1983—. Recipient nat. awards for excellence in football programs Nat. Assn. Intercollegiate Athletics, 1974-76; named Montana's Outstanding Young Woman of 1978. Mem. Am. Soc. Hosp. Public Relations, Nat. Assn. Hosp. Devel. (membership chmn. Mont. 1978-81), Sigma Delta Chi, Phi Kappa Phi. Home: Route 1 Box 127A Payette ID 83661 Office: Holy Rosary Hospital 351 SW 9th St Ontario OR 97914

BRACE, CLAYTON HENRY, broadcasting co. exec.; b. Topeka, Aug. 8, 1923; s. Clayton Henry and Gladys (Hawley) B.; B.; student U. Denver, 1940-41, U. Colo., 1941; m. Jeanne Haney, Sept. 10, 1947 children—Kimball William, Dianne, Lynne, Kerry. With KLZ Radio, Denver, 1941-50, prodn. mgr., 1950-53; dir. TV research, program dir. KLZ-TV, 1953-57; asst. to pres. Time-Life Broadcast, Inc., Denver, 1957-61, v.p., gen. mgr. KOGO-TV-AM-FM, San Diego, 1963-72; ops. mgr. Compagnie Lebanaise de TV, Beirut, 1961-63; v.p. McGraw-Hill Broadcasting Co., Inc., KGTV 10, San Diego, 1972—. Bd. dirs. Donald N. Sharp Meml. Community Hosp., World Affairs Council; mem. nat. adv. com. Mexican-Am. Edn., 1967-69; chmn. adv. com. San Diego State U.; chmn. San Diego United Way Campaign, 1978; mem. San Diego Crime Commn., 1980. Served with Signal Corps, AUS, 1943-45. Recipient Try San Diego First award 1964. Mem. Nat. Assn. Broadcasters (bd. dirs. Code Authority, chmn. TV Code 1981-83), Calif. Broadcasters Assn. (chmn. bd. 1969-70), Broadcast Edn. Assn. (adv. bd. leadership devel. program), ABC-TV Affiliates Assn. (bd. govs.), U. Calif.-San Diego Chancellor's Assocs. (chmn. 1982-83), San Diego C. of C. (pres. 1969-70), Sigma Delta Chi. Clubs: Rotary (pres. San Diego 1970-71). Home: 5970 Madra Way San Diego CA 92120 Office: Box 85347 San Diego CA 92138

BRACE, KATHLEEN JACKSON, banker; b. Ogden, Utah, Nov. 7, 1947; d. Glen H. and Elta T. Jackson; m. Leon C. Brace, Sept. 1, 1967 (div.); children—Stephen, David. Student Weber State Coll., U. Utah, 1965-69. Supr. loan servicing Western Mortgage Loan Corp., 1969-76; mgr. loan servicing Mountain West Savs. & Loan Assn., Ogden, 1976—, asst. v.p., 1979-83, v.p., 1983—. Commr., organizer Weber County Women's Soccer, 1979—; mem. Kanesville Planning Commn., 1979-80; mem. Kanesville Community Council, 1979-80. Mem. Nat. Assn. Profl. Mortgage Women (Utah div. dir., past pres. Ogden br.), Nat. Assn. Female Execs., Mensa, Ogden Assn. Profl. Mortgage Women. Republican.

BRACHTENBACH, ROBERT F., state justice; b. Sidney, Nebr., Jan. 28, 1931; s. Henry W. and Elizabeth A. (Morfeld) B.; B.S., U. Wash., 1953, LL.B., 1954; m. Marilyn; children—Rick, Jeff, Randal, Curtis, David. Instr., U. Calif. Sch. Law, Berkeley, 1954-55; admitted to Wash. bar, 1954; practiced in Selah, Wash., 1955-72; justice Wash. Supreme Ct., 1972—, chief justice, until 1983. Mem. Selah Sch. Bd., 1960-72; mem. Wash. State Ho. of Reps., 1963-67; trustee Eastern Wash. State Coll. Contbr. articles to law revs. Office: Wash Supreme Ct Temple of Justice Olympia WA 98504*

BRACK, O M, JR., English language educator; b. Houston, Nov. 30, 1938; s. O.M. and Olivia Mae (Rice) B.; m. Christine Yvonne Ferdinand, July 5, 1983. Student U. Houston, 1956-57; B.A., Baylor U., 1960, M.A., 1961; Ph.D., U. Tex., Austin, 1965. Asst. prof. William Woods Coll., 1964-65; asst. prof. English lit. U. Iowa, Iowa City, 1965-68, assoc. prof., 1968-73, dir. center textual studies, 1967-73; prof. English lit. Ariz. State U., Tempe, 1973—, chmn. 18th-Century Short Title Catalogue com., 1970-73; pres. Arete Publs., Ltd., 1976-81. Albert H. Smith Meml. lectr. bibliography Birmingham (Eng.) Bibliog. Soc., 1983. Am. Philos. Soc. grantee, 1967; Huntington Library fellow, 1978, Am. Council Learned Socs. fellow, 1979-80; Phi Kappa Phi Disting. scholar, 1975; Newberry Library fellow, 1982; recipient Grad. Coll. Disting. Research award 1981-82. Mem. Am. Soc. 18th Century Studies, MLA, South Central 18th Century Soc. (pres. 1982-83), Bibliog. Soc. Am., Bibliog. Soc. U. Va., Bibliog. Soc. (London), Printing Hist. Soc., Am. Printing History Assn., Nat. Council Tchrs. English. Roman Catholic. Club: The Johnsonians. Author: Bibliography and Textual Criticism, 1969; Samuel Johnson's Early Biographers, 1971; Hoole's Death of Johnson, 1972, Henry Fielding's Pasquin, 1973; A Catalogue of the Leigh Hunt Manuscripts, 1973; The Early Biographies of Samuel Johnson, 1974; American Humor, 1977. Textual editor Works of Tobias Smollett, 1966—, gen. editor, 1973—; editor English Literature in Transition, 1981-82, mem. editorial com., 1982—; editor Studies in Eighteenth-Century Culture, 1981—, mem. editorial com. Rocky Mountain Rev. Lang. and Lit., 1980—; mem. editorial com. Yale edit. Works of Samuel Johnson, 1977—; editorial cons. Scott, Foresman & Co., 1977-79; asst. editor Eighteenth-Century Bibliography, 1964-73, Books at Iowa, 1966-73. Office: Dept English Ariz State U Tempe AZ 85287

BRACKEN, JAMES LUCAS, ret. editor; b. Greensburg, Kans., Nov. 20, 1913; s. John Newton and Mary Grace (Lucas) B.; m. Frances Cadzow, Mar. 24, 1943; children—Thomas Robert James, Dorothy Cadzow, Frances Bracken Huessy. Corr., Brit. newspaper syndicates, writer agrl. publs., 1933-37; field editor, later exec. editor Pacific N.W. Farm Trio, Spokane, 1937-42; mng. editor Western Metals mag., Los Angeles, 1946; editorial writer, asst. to mng. editor The Spokesman Review, Spokane, 1947-49, mng. editor, 1949-78, editor, 1978. Mem. State Health Coordinating Council of Wash. Served to capt. AUS, 1942-46. Home: 1417 Pinecrest Rd Spokane WA 99203

BRACKEN, THOMAS ROBERT JAMES, real estate developer; b. Spokane, Wash., Jan. 1, 1950; s. James Lucas and Frances (Cadzow) B.; m. Linda Diane Jacobson, Sept. 9, 1972; children—Karl Forrest, David Erskine. B.A. with departmental honors, Yale U., 1971; M.B.A., Columbia U., 1972. Sr. appraiser Prudential Ins. Co., N.Y.C. area, 1972-74, mgr. real estate investments, N.Y.C. and Newark, 1974-77; investment mgr. real estate investments, Seattle, 1977-78; v.p. First City Investments, Inc., Seattle, 1978-80; pres. Fenix, Inc., Kirkland, Wash., 1980—; v.p. Wash. Mortgage Corp., Seattle, 1982—; guest lectr. U. Pa., N.Y. U. Mem. Nat. Assn. Indsl. and Office Parks (officer Seattle chpt.), Internat. Conf. Shopping Centers. Presbyterian. Home: 4548 144th Ave SE Bellevue WA 98006 Office: PO Box 2363 Kirkland WA 98033

BRACY, DENNIS PATRICK, public affairs manager; b. St. Louis, Apr. 9, 1949; s. Webb B. and Jane T. (Blakeslee) B.; m. Tinsley Lauren Deibel, Aug. 13, 1977. B.A., U. Madrid, St. Louis U., 1971; postgrad. U. Puget Sound. Press sec. Watergate Trials, Washington, 1972-75; nat. fundraising dir. Udall for Pres., Washington, 1975-76; asst. regional adminstr. Gen. Services Adminstrn., Seattle, 1977-81; pub. affairs mgr. N.W. Region, Kaiser Aluminum & Chem. Corp., Spokane, Wash., 1981—; chmn. pub. affairs com. Western Aluminum Producers. Chmn. Heart Assn. Bus. Drive, 1982; bd. dirs. Sta. KSPS-TV, Interplayers, Century 2, Leadership Spokane. Recipient Max award Spokane Ad Fedn., 1982. Mem. Pub. Relations Soc. Am. (Totem award 1981). Clubs: Spokane, Washington Athletic. Office: 303 Washington Mutual Bldg Spokane WA 99201

BRACY, LESLIE RUTH, social worker; b. Quincy, Ill., Aug. 24, 1956; d. John Carr and Catherine Elizabeth (Schachtseik) B. B.S. in Psychology and Sociology, Eastern Mont. Coll., 1980. Dir. activities Yellowstone County Council on Aging, Billings, Mont., 1978-79; fin. dir. Ramirez for Gov. Com., Billings, 1980; clk. Mountain Bell Telephone Co., Billings, 1980-81; dir. Tumbleweed Runaway Program, Billings, 1981—. Mem. youth exec. com. United Way, Billings; bd. dirs. Southcentral Mental Health Bd.; fin. dir. MacKay for County Commr. Com., Billings. Mem. Am. Personnel and Guidance Assn., Mont. Pro-Rodeo Cir., Women's Profl. Rodeo Assn. Republican. Christian Scientist. Home: 1056 Wiloma St Billings MT 59105 Office: Tumbleweed Runaway Program 505 N 27th St Billings MT 59101

BRADBURY, ELLEN ADELE, museum director, curator, registrar; b. Louisville, Ky., Feb. 26, 1940; d. Edward and Dulcinea S. Wilder; children—John Wymond, Katharine D. B.A. U. N.Mex., 1963, M.A., 1967; postgrad. Yale U., 1968. Asst. registrar Mpls. Inst. of Arts, 1970-73, registrar, 1973-75, curator primitive art, 1975-78; dir. Mus. Fine Arts, Santa Fe, 1979-82; dir. Santa Fe Festival of the Arts, 1983—; cons. Arts in Architecture Western Panel, Nat. Endowment Arts; guest curator Landmark Ctr., St. Paul, 1978. Mem. Coll. Art Assn., Am. Assn. Mus. (regional rep.), N.Mex. Assn. Mus. (v.p.), Art Mus. Assn. Democrat. Episcopalian. Mailing Address: Santa Fe Festival of Arts 227 E Palace Santa Fe NM 87503

BRADBURY, JOHN FREDERICK, utility exec.; b. Boise, Idaho, Sept. 10, 1929; s. Frederick Carroll and Jeannette Frances (Plunkett) B.; student pub. schs., Oreg.; m. Thelma Ruth Jenson, Sept. 26, 1978; children—Roberta, Darrell, Kim, Raymond, Carol, Ross. Salesman, Bradbury Motor Co., Astoria, Oreg., 1955-58; clk. E.W. Hendrickson Inc., Warrenton, Oreg., 1959-60; with Pacific Power & Light Co., 1960, sales and mktg. exec., Riverton, Wyo., 1970-77, mgr. Arlington (Oreg.) office, 1977-82, Seaside, Oreg., 1982—. Dist. chmn. Freemont County council Boy Scouts Am., 1972. Served with USAF, 1951-55. Mem. Nat. Rifle Assn. (life), Ducks Unltd. Republican. Clubs: Lions, Elks, Shriners (past pres. Riverton). Home: 1227 Ave D Seaside OR 97138 Office: 910 Broadway Seaside OR 97138

BRADEN, VERLON PATRICK, automotive writer, producer, photographer; b. Flint, Mich., July 8, 1934; s. Verlon Lee and Mary Virginia (Presson) B.; m. Marie Elsie Kobrehel, June 30, 1956 (dec.); children—Mark Patrick, Leslie Marie; m. 2d, Cheryl Marie Olson, Oct. 5, 1980; 1 dau., Mary Kathryn. B.A., Western Mich. U., 1956; M.A., U. Mich., 1957; postgrad. U. Iowa, 1959. Cert. secondary tchr., Mich. Tchr., prison social worker, probation officer State of Mich., 1959-67; writer Bill Sandy Co., Communico, and Maritz Communications, Fullerton, Calif., 1969—; editor The Alfa Owner. Mem. Am. Soc. Tng. and Devel., Am. Alfa Romeo Owners Club, Am. Abarth Register. Author: The 365 GTB/4 Daytona Ferrari, 1982; Abarth, 1983. Office: 1440 N Harbor Blvd Suite 225 Fullerton CA 92635

BRADFORD, ROBERT SPENCER, JR., laser physicist; b. Chamblee, Ga., Nov. 6, 1945; s. Robert Spencer and Bernice Marilyn (Johnson) B.; B.A. in Physics, U. Calif., Santa Barbara, 1967, M.A., 1969, Ph.D., 1974; m. Marilyn Claire, June 21, 1969; children—Kirsten Marie, Mark David, Stephen Daniel. Instrument designer North American Weather, Santa Barbara, 1974-75; laser physicist Northrop Research & Technology Center, Hawthorne, 1975-77; prin. research scientist in laser physics Xonics/Hadron, Santa Monica, Calif., 1977-79; project mgr. repetitively pulsed chem. laser TRW Space and Tech. Group, Redondo Beach, Calif., 1979—; tchr., research asst. U. Calif., 1967-69. Served to lt. U.S. Army, 1969-71. Mem. IEEE, Am. Phys. Soc., Optical Soc. Am., Sigma Xi, Sigma Pi Sigma. Active in laser research. Home: 6376 W 84th St Los Angeles CA 90045 Office: One Space Park Redondo Beach CA 90278

BRADFUTE, RICHARD WELLS, store exec.; b. Albuquerque, May 26, 1943; s. Richard Washington and Lovilla (Winn) B.; B.A. cum laude, Eastern N.Mex. U., 1965, M.A., 1966; Ph.D., U. Colo., 1973; m. Zorita Danforth, Aug. 7, 1966; children—Richard Edward, David William, Steven Blake. Grad. asst. Eastern N.Mex. U., 1965-66, instr. history, 1975-76; teaching asst. U. Colo., 1966-68, teaching asso., 1967-69; instr. history Lamar Community Coll., 1969-74; inventory control clk. Safeway, Portales, N.Mex., 1974-75, head food clk., 1975-76, asst. mgr., 1976—. Recipient Compton Meml. History award, 1965. Mem. Am. Hist. Assn., Nat. Hist. Soc. Democrat. Author: The Court of Private Land Claims, 1975. Home: 112 N Houston St Portales NM 88130 Office: 501 W 18th St Portales NM 88130

BRADLEY, CHARLES WILLIAM, podiatrist; b. Fife, Tex., July 23, 1923; s. Tom and Mary Ada (Cheatham) B.; student Tex. Tech., 1940-42; D. Podiatry, Calif. Podiatry Coll., 1949; D.Sc. (hon.), Calif. Coll. Podiatric Medicine; m. Marilyn A. Brown, Apr. 3, 1948 (dec. Mar. 1973); children—Steven, Gregory, Jeffrey, Elizabeth, Gerald. Practice podiatry, Beaumont, Tex., 1950-51, Brownwood, Tex., 1951-52, San Francisco, San Bruno, Calif., 1952—; chief of staff Calif. Podiatry Hosp., San Francisco; mem. surg. staff Sequoia Hosp., Redwood City, Calif.; mem. podiatry staff Peninsula Hosp., Burlingame, Calif.; chief podiatry staff St. Luke's Hosp., San Francisco; v.p. Podiatry Ins. Co. Am. Mem. San Francisco Symphony Found.; mem. adv. com. Health Policy Agenda for the Am. People, AMA. Chmn. trustees Calif. Coll. Podiatric Medicine, Calif. Podiatry Coll., Calif. Podiatry Hosp. Mem. Am. Podiatry Assn. (trustee, pres. 1983), Calif. Podiatry Assn. (pres. No. div. 1964-66, state bd. dirs., pres. 1975-76, Podiatrist of Yr. award 1983), Nat. Council Edn. (vice chmn.), Nat. Acads. Practice, Am. Legion, San Bruno C. of C. (dir. 1978—). Clubs: Elks, Lions, Commonwealth of Calif. Served with USNR, 1942-45. podiatrist; b. Fife, Tex., July 23, 1923; s. Tom and Mary Ada (Cheatham) B.; student Tex. Tech., 1940-42; D. Podiatry, Calif. Podiatry Coll., 1949; D.Sc. (hon.), Calif. Coll. Podiatric Medicine; m. Marilyn A. Brown, Apr. 3, 1948 (dec. Mar. 1973); children—Steven, Gregory, Jeffrey, Elizabeth, Gerald. Practice podiatry, Beaumont, Tex., 1950-51, Brownwood, Tex., 1951-52, San Francisco, San Bruno, Calif., 1952—; chief of staff Calif. Podiatry Hosp., San Francisco; mem. surg. staff Sequoia Hosp., Redwood City, Calif.; mem. podiatry staff Peninsula Hosp., Burlingame, Calif.; chief podiatry staff St. Luke's Hosp., San Francisco; v.p. Podiatry Ins. Co. Am. Mem. San Francisco Symphony Found.; mem. adv. com. Health Policy Agenda for the Am. People, AMA. Chmn. trustees Calif. Coll. Podiatric Medicine, Calif. Podiatry Coll., Calif. Podiatry Hosp. Mem. Am. Podiatry Assn. (trustee, pres. 1983), Calif. Podiatry Assn. (pres. No. div. 1964-66, state bd. dirs., pres. 1975-76, Podiatrist of Yr. award 1983), Nat. Council Edn. (vice chmn.), Nat. Acads. Practice, Am. Legion, San Bruno C. of C. (dir. 1978—). Clubs: Elks, Lions, Commonwealth of Calif. Served with USNR, 1942-45. Home: 2965 Trousdale Dr Burlingame CA 94010 Office: 560 Jenevein Ave San Bruno CA 94066 also 2469 Mission St San Francisco CA 94110

BRADLEY, HASSELL GRIMES, writer, journalist; b. Paris, Tex., June 29, 1930; d. William Frank and Kathryn Lynn (Ellis) Grimes; m. Joe Allen Bradley, July 8, 1951; children—William Stanton, Margaret Lynn. B.A. in Journalism, U. Okla., 1951. Writer newspapers, Okla., Tex., R.I., Kans., 1949-77; editor Univ. Park News, Denver, Colo., 1969-71; food editor Sentinel Newspapers, Denver, 1971-77; freelance writer, 1977—; food personality Sta. KAO-TV, Denver, 1973; corr. Fairchild Publs., N.Y.; instr. foods, writing Arapahoe Community Coll., Littleton, Colo.; reviewer Denver area restaurants. Mem. planning com. Denver Consumer Forum, 1976; Mem. Nat. Consumer Adv. Council, U.S. Dept. Agr., 1979; bd. dirs. Corp. for Hosp. Alt. Plan, Bethesda Community Mental Health Ctr.; judge Littleton Creative Writing Contest; mem. planning com. ann. Rocky Mountain Food Safety Conf.; mem. adv. com. Nat. Sheep Producers Council. Recipient various press assns. awards; Headliner award Denver Chpt. Women in Communications, 1974. Mem. Nat. Press Women, Colo. Press Women (Woman of Achievement award 1976), Home Economists in Bus., Am. Home Econs. Assn., Colo. Home Econs. Assn., Denver Women's Press Club, Nat. Writers Club, Authors League Am., Alpha Chi Omega. Republican. Episcopalian. Club: Colo. Mountain. Author: (with Carole Sundberg) Keeping Food Safe, 1975; The Complete Fireplace Cookbook, 1982. Office: 1551 Larimer St Apt 804 Denver CO 80202

BRADLEY, MARION ZIMMER, novelist; b. Albany, N.Y., June 3, 1930; d. Leslie Raymond and Evelyn Parkhurst (Conklin) Zimmer; m. Robert Alden Bradley, Oct. 20, 1949; 1 son, David R.; m. 2d, Walter H. Breen, Feb. 1964; children—Patrick, Dorothy. Student N.Y. State Tchrs. Coll., 1946-48; B.A., Hardin-Simmons U., 1964; postgrad. U. Calif.-Berkeley, 1967. Author novels, including: Planet Savers, 1962; The Sword of Aldones (Hugo nominee), 1962; The Bloody Sun, 1964, rewritten, 1979; Star of Danger, 1966; The Winds of Darkover, 1970; The World Wreckers, 1971; Darkover Landfall, 1972; The Spell Sword, 1972; The Heritage of Hastur (Hugo nominee), 1975; The Shattered Chain, 1976; The Forbidden Tower (Hugo nominee), 1977; Stormqueen, 1978; The Catch Trap, 1979; House Between the Worlds, 1980; Two to Conquer, 1980; The Keeper's Price, 1980; Sharra's Exile, 1981; Sword of Chaos, 1982; Hawkmistress, 1982; Children of Hastur, 1982; Mists of Avalon, 1983; contbr. short stories to numerous mags., 1952-75. Founder Ctr. Non-traditional Religion, Berkeley, 1979. Mem. Sci. Fiction Writers Am. (v.p. 1976, mem. grievance com. 1976-79), Authors Guild, Mystery Writers Am., Poets and Writers Inc. Clubs: Darkmoon Circle, Covenant of Goddess. Features editor Sybil Leek's Astrology Mag., 1971-72. Office: Marion Zimmer Bradley PO Box 352 Berkeley CA 94701

BRADLEY, MYRA JAMES, hospital administrator; b. Cin., Feb. 1, 1924; d. John Joseph and Mary (McMannus) Bradley. B.S. in Edn., Atheneum of Ohio, 1950; R.N., Good Samaritan Hosp., Dayton, Ohio, 1954; B.S. in Nursing, Mt. St. Joseph Hosp. (Ohio), 1954; M.H.A., St. Louis U., 1959. Joined Sisters of Charity, Roman Catholic Ch., 1942; mem. faculty Good Samaritan Hosp., Dayton, 1955-57; asst. adminstr. St. Mary Corwin Hosp., Pueblo, Colo., 1960; adminstr. St. Joseph Hosp., Mt. Clemens, Mich., 1960-65; pres. Penrose Hosp., Colorado Springs, Colo., 1965—. Trustee, Mercy Hosp. Recipient Disting. Service award U. Colo., 1983. Mem. Am. Hosp. Assn., Catholic Hosp. Assn., Am. Coll. Hosp. Adminstrs., Sisters of Charity Health Care Systems. Home: 2417 N Cascade Colorado Springs CO 80907 Office: PO Box 7021 Colorado Springs CO 80933

BRADLEY, ORVAL LINCOLN, educator; b. Carthage, Mo., Mar. 10, 1933; s. Jack M. and Fleta C. (Box) B.; m. Rita J. Todhunter, Oct. 3, 1952; children—Alan, Vicky, Scott. A.A., Joplin Jr. Coll., 1959; B.S., Kans. State Coll. Pitts., 1961, M.S., 1963; Ed.D., U. Idaho, 1982. Tchr., adminstr. Connors State Coll., Warner, Okla., 1963-67; dean vocat.-tech. programs Coll. So. Idaho, Twin Falls, 1967—; ednl. cons. Mem. Area IV Private Industry Council. Served with U.S. Army, 1951-53. Mem. Am. Vocat. Assn., Idaho Vocat. Assn., Council Occupational Edn., Twin Falls Area C. of C. Baptist. Club: Lions. Office: Coll So Idaho 101 Vocat-Tech Ctr Twin Falls ID 83301

BRADLEY, RICHARD CRANE, educator; b. Chgo., May 14, 1922; s. Harold Cornelius and Mary Josephine (Crane) B.; A.B., Dartmouth Coll., 1943; Ph.D. U. Cal. at Berkeley, 1953; m. Dorothy Alice Holden, June 7, 1947; children—Richard, Helen (Mrs. Alan Williams), Josephine (Mrs. Laurence Lopez), David. Research asso. Cornell U., Ithaca, N.Y., 1953-56, instr. 1956-57, asst. prof., 1957-61, asso. prof., 1961; mem. faculty Colo. Coll., Colorado Springs, 1961—, prof. physics, 1965—, dean, 1973-79. Pres., Springs Area Beautiful Assn., 1971-73; treas. Citizens Lobby for Sensible Growth, 1972-73. Trustee Nat. Parks and Conservation Assn., 1965-77. Served with USNR, 1944-46. Recipient Conservation Service award Colo. Mountain Club, 1966. Fellow Am. Physics Soc.; mem. AAAS, Colo-Wyo. Acad. Scis. (pres., 1970-71), Am. Physics Tchrs. Contbr. to profl. and conservation mags. Home: 1035 Broadview Pl Colorado Springs CO 80904 Office: Colorado Coll Colorado Springs CO 80903

BRADLEY, ROSALEE, psychologist, horse breeder and trainer; b. Calhoun, Mo., Sept. 20, 1939; d. Wayne Beecher and Alice Maureen (Shrout) B. B.S., U. Kansas City, 1961; M.A., Hollins Coll., 1963; Ph.D., Wash. State U., 1969. Lic. psychologist, Calif., Wash. Staff psychologist No. State Hosp., Sedro-Woolley, Wash., 1968-74; staff psychologist Calif. Correctional Ctr., Susanville, Calif., 1974-78, adminstrv. asst. to supt., 1975-78, EEO officer, 1975-78, women's liaison rep., 1975-78; pvt. practice clin. psychology, Susanville, 1978—; cons. Right Way Homes, boy's ranch; tchr. in field; horse breeder, trainer, 19—. Mem. Lassen County Women Democrats. Recipient numerous awards in horse show circuit, 1981, 82. Mem. Am. Psychol. Assn., Mortar Bd., Psi Chi. Democrat. Clubs: Appaloosa Horse, Honey Lake Valley Riders. Exhibited photography: Lassen Community Coll. (Merit award), 1982, Lassen County Fair (2 First place awards and 2d place award), 1981. Home: PO Box 88 Janesville CA 96114 Office: 617 Main Suite 204 Susanville CA 96130

BRADLEY, THOMAS, mayor of Los Angeles; b. Calvert, Tex., Dec, 29, 1917; s. Lee and Crenner (Hawkins) B.; student U. Calif. at Los Angeles, 1937-40, Loyola U. at Los Angeles, 1954; LL.B., Southwestern U., 1956; m. Ethel Arnold, May 4, 1941; children—Lorraine, Phyllis. With Los Angeles Police Dept., 1940-61, lt., 1959-61; admitted to Calif. bar, 1956; individual practice law, Los Angeles, 1961-63; mem. Los Angeles City Council, 1963-73; mayor, Los Angeles, 1973—. Founder Bank of Finance, Los Angeles. Vice pres. Friendship Day Camp; chmn. Western region adv. council Joint Center Polit. Studies; mem. men's adv. com. Los Angeles County-U. So. Calif. Med. Center Aux. Adv. bd. Cal. Tomorrow, McCobb Homes for Boys, Salesian High Sch.; adv. bd. dirs. So. Calif. Conf. Community Relations; bd. dirs. Greater Los Angeles Urban Coalition, Housing Assistance Council, Inc., Indian Culture and Edn., South-Central Improvement Action Council, numerous others. Recipient numerous awards including award League Calif. Cities, 1968-69, achievement award Kappa Alpha Psi, 1969, Los Angeles Brotherhood Crusade, 1970-71, service award Neighborhood Adult Participation, 1971. Mem. Nat. League Cities (pres. 1973), League Calif. Cities (pres. Los Angeles County div. 1968-69), Nat. Assn. Regional Councils (pres. 1969-71), So. Calif. Assn. Govts. (pres. 1968-69), State Bar Calif., Am., Los Angeles County (mem. legislation com.) bar assns., Langston Law Club, N.A.A.C.P., Urban League (dir.). UN Assn. U.S.A. (local dir.), Loyola Human Relations Alumni, Assn. for Profl. Law Enforcement, Nat. Conf. Mayors, Soc. Order Blue Shield, Kappa Alpha Psi (nat. pres. 1964-67). Methodist. Office: Office of Mayor City Hall Los Angeles CA 90012*

BRADLEY, THOMAS DONALD, certified public accountant; b. Medford, Oreg., Dec. 13, 1950; s. Donald and Maxine (Riemer) B.; m. Melody J. Merriman, Dec. 27, 1969; children—Jason, Francis, Andrew, Thomas D. B.S. magna cum laude in Bus., So. Oreg. Coll., 1974. C.P.A., Oreg., Wash. Mgmt. trainee U.S. Nat. Bank Oreg., Medford, 1969-74; staff acct. Yergen and Meyer, C.P.A.s, Coos Bay, Oreg., 1974-79, ptnr., 1979—. Treas. Lewis County 4th July Assn., Chehalis Soccer Club, Inc. Mem. Am. Inst. C.P.A.s, Oreg. Soc. C.P.A.s, Wash. Soc. C.P.A.s, Chehalis C. of C. (dir.). Clubs: Classic Thunderbird, Internat., Lions (Chehalis). Home: 1764 SW Snively Chehalis WA 98532 Office: Yergen and Meyer 550 N Market Blvd PO Box 957 Chehalis WA 98532

BRADLEY, VIRGINIA ANNE, author; b. Omaha, Dec. 2, 1912; d. Stephen Pabulus and Anne Gertrude (Healy) Jonas; B.F.A., U. Nebr., 1933; m. Gerald Dwight Bradley, June 8, 1940; children—Stephen, Michael, Betty, Patricia. Mem. classified advt. staff Omaha World Herald, 1937-38; dir. creative writing workshop, adult div. Los Angeles schs., 1963-78, So. Calif. Women's Press Club, 1974—, Santa Monica (Calif.) Emeritus Coll., 1975—; author: Is There An Actor In The House?, 1975; Stage Eight, 1977; Bend to the Willow, 1979; Holidays on Stage, 1981; contbr. fiction and non-fiction to periodicals; speaker, cons. in field. Mem. Soc. Children's Book Writers, PEN, So. Calif. Ednl. Theatre Assn., Am. Film Tchrs. Assn., Profl. Writers League Los Angeles, Santa Monica Writers Club (pres. 1954-55), Chi Omega. Address: 425 15th St Santa Monica CA 90402

BRADLEY, WILLIAM MARVIN (BILL SILBERT), radio station executive; b. Detroit, Jan. 1, 1921; s. Louis and Helen (Krause) Silbert; B.S., U. Detroit, 1936; postgrad. So. Meth. U., 1945; M.S., N.Y. U., 1953; 1 son, William N. Silbert. Disc jockey, emcee numerous radio-TV shows, Detroit, 1947-52; panelist Songs for Sales, CBS-TV, 1952; emcee Bill Silbert Show, Let's Go Bowling, WABD-DuMont TV, 1952-53, Bill Silbert Show, WMGM radio; announcer Red Buttons Show, NBC-TV, Philco Phonorama Time, Mut.; emcee Nat. Radio Fan Club, NBC, Mag. of Air, Mut., KLAC, Hollywood, Bill Bradley Show, KTLA, Hollywood, Crime Story, Greet the People, Ad Lib, Hollywood Diary; sales mgr. Radio Sta. KLOS-FM (ABC), Los Angeles, 1969—; appeared in motion pictures Bundle of Joy, Thunderjets, Alligator People, Young Jesse James, Lost Missile, Breakfast at Tiffanys, Return to Peyton Place; appeared on TV shows Bronco, 77 Sunset Strip, Hawaiian Eye, Sugarfoot, Combat, Adventures in Paradise, Police Sta., Michael Shayne, Roaring 20's, Outlaws; numerous commls. Served to 1st lt. USAAF, 1944-46. Damon Runyon Meml. Fund fellow Nat. Assn. Mental Health, 1970-74. Mem. Screen Actors Guild, A.F.T.R.A., Variety Clubs Internat., Nat. Acad. Television Arts and Scis., So. Calif. Broadcasters Assn., VFW (certificate of appreciation 1958). Home: 13802 Northwest Passage Marina Del Rey CA 90292 Office: 3321 S La Cienega Los Angeles CA 90016

BRADSHAW, DAVID E., lawyer, business executive, real estate developer; b. Chgo., May 5, 1927; s. Enoch D. and Angela Mary (Hogan) B.; J.D., John Marshall Law Sch., Chgo., 1952; m. Joan Elizabeth Odell, Aug. 14, 1981; children—Marie, Barbara, Scott. Bar: Ill. 1952, D.C. 1977. Sr. ptnr. firm Bradshaw and Odell, 1952-79; gen. counsel, exec. v.p., dir. Beckett & Bean Ins. Co., Chgo., 1964-67; pres., dir. B & B Enterprises, Chgo., 1970-76; chmn. bd. dirs. Trans-Am. Video, Inc., Los Angeles, 1971-74; pres. Sunbelt Devel. Co., Tucson, 1979—; mng. ptnr. David E. Bradshaw and Assocs., Tucson, 1979—; exec. producer New Zoo Revue, Los Angeles, 1971-73; mem. Chgo. Bd. Trade; dir., founding mem. Chgo. Bd. Options Exchange; dir. United of Am. Bank, Chgo.; spl. asst. Atty. Gen. Ill., 1960-78. Mem. Ill. Crime Investigating Commn., 1963-69; bd. dirs. United Cerebral Palsy, Chgo., Chgo. Boys Club; trustee LaRabida Hosp., Chgo., Served with USMC, World War II. Mem. ABA, Fed. Bar Assn., Pima County Bar Assn., Internat. Bar Assn., Ill. State Bar Assn. (bd. govs.), Ill. Assn. Plaintiff Lawyers (bd. govs.), So. Ariz. Home Builders Assn., Chgo. Bar Assn., D.C. Bar Assn., Tucson C. of C. Clubs: Skyline Country, Tucson National; Mid-Am., Tavern, Internat. (Chgo.). Home: 6931 N Catalina Ave Tucson AZ 85718 Office: 252 N Ina Rd Tucson AZ 85704

BRADSHAW, JAMES RULON, educator; b. Beaver, Utah, Oct. 26, 1938; s. Lafey LaVel and Llynn (Christensen) B.; B.S., Coll. So. Utah, 1968; M.S., Utah State U., 1969; Ed.D., Brigham Young Young, Provo, Utah, 1974; m. Bok Dong Jeanie Chung, Sept. 4, 1964; children—Scott, Lisa, Jonathan, Mibi. Dist. supr. Mormon Ch. Mission, Korea and Japan, 1958-61; asst. prof. bus. Church Coll., Laie, Hawaii, 1969-73; grad. asst., spl. instr. Utah Tech. Coll., Provo, 1973-74; assoc. prof. bus. Brigham Young U., Hawaii, 1974-82, prof., 1982—, chmn. bus. div., 1975—; vis. prof. Chaminade U., Honolulu, 1976—; cons. Polynesian Cultural Ctr. First v.p. Kahuku Parent, Tchr. and Student Assn., 1980-81. Served with AIS, 1961-64. Decorated Army Commendation medal; NDEA fellow, 1968-69. Mem. Nat., Western (exec. bd. 1981—), Hawaii (pres. 1981-82; Disting. Service award 1981) bus. edn. assns., Am. Bus. Communication Assn., Delta Phi Epsilon, Author articles. Office: Box 108 Brigham Young Univ Hawaii Laie HI 96762

BRADSHAW, JOAN ELIZABETH ODELL, lawyer; b. Jo Davies County, Ill., May 3, 1932; d. Peter Emerson and Olive Isabelle (Bonnet) Odell; A.B. cum laude, U. Miami, 1956, J.D., 1958; m. David E. Bradshaw, Aug. 14, 1981; children—Dominique Rosalyn, Nicole Laurienne. Admitted to Fla. bar, 1958, D.C. bar, 1974, Ill. bar, 1977; trial atty. U.S. SEC, 1959-60; asst. state atty. Dade County, Fla., 1960-64; asst. county atty. Dade County, 1964-70; county atty. Palm Beach County, Fla., 1970-71; regional counsel U.S. EPA, Regional IV, Atlanta, 1971-73; asso. gen. counsel U.S. Environmental Protection Agy., Washington, 1973-77; partner David E. Bradshaw & Assos.; v.p. Angel Mining, Inc.; exec. v.p. Sunbelt Devel. Co.; pres. S.W. Land Investments, Inc., Tucson. Bd. dirs. Mental Health Assn. Palm Beach County. Named Among Outstanding Young Women in Am., 1965. Mem. Fed., Fla., Dade County, D.C., Am., bar assns., Nat. Assn. County Civil Attys. (sec.-treas.), Fla. Assn. County Attys. (dir.), AAUW, LWV, U. Ariz. Bus. and Profl. Women's Club. Home: 6352 N Barcelona Ln Tucson AZ 85704 Office: 252 W Ina Rd Tucson AZ 85704

BRADSHAW, ROBERT V., police chief, educator; b. Upland, Calif., Apr. 17, 1938; s. Charles B. and Alys P. (Dickinson) B.; m. Dixie L. Bradshaw, Aug. 16, 1960; children—Deborah A., Kelly L., Kimberly D. A.A. in Bus., Pasadena City Coll., 1959; B.A. in Criminal Justice, San Jose State Coll., 1964; M.P.A., Golden Gate U., 1980. Cert. secondary tchr., Calif. Successively police officer, sgt., lt., capt., dep. chief, asst. chief of police San Jose (Calif.) Police Dept., 1960-80; police chief Reno (Nev.) Police Dept., 1981—; instr. police adminstrn. Truckee Meadows Community Coll., Reno. Served with USAR. Mem. Internat. Assn. Chiefs of Police, Police Exec. Research Forum. Republican. Club: Rotary (Reno). Office: PO Box 1900 Reno NC 89505

BRADSHAW, WILLIAM NEWMAN, engineering and construction services company manager; b. Louisville, Nov. 2, 1928; s. Hugh Elmer and Rachel Elizabeth (Lundy) B.; m. Joyce Elaine Austin, Sept. 14, 1956; children—David N., Kathryn E. B.A., Austin Coll., 1951; M.A., U. Tex.-Austin, 1956; Ph.D., 1962. Asst. prof. dept. biology McMurray Coll., Abilene, Tex., 1956-61; lectr. dept. zoology U. Tex.-Austin, 1961; asst. prof. dept. biology W.Va. U., Morgantown, 1962-67, assoc. prof., 1967-73, prof., 1973-76; vis. assoc. prof. dept. cell biology M.D. Anderson Hosp., Tumor Inst., Houston, 1970-71; dir., sec.-treas. Acad. Assocs. Inc., Morgantown, 1973-76; environ. scientist, project mgr. Stearns-Roger Services Inc., Denver, 1976—. Served to capt. USMC, 1952-54. So. Fellowship Fund fellow, 1961-62; NSF grantee, 1968, 1974; NIH grantee, 1970-71. Mem. AAAS, Amer. Inst. Biol. Scis., Ecol. Soc. Am., Am. Soc. Mammalists, Southwestern Assn. Naturalists, Sigma Xi. Republican. Presbyterian. Club: Rotary. Contbr. articles to profl. jours. Home: 6175 Ponderosa Way Parker CO 80134 Office: 4500 Cherry Creek Dr PO Box 5888 Denver CO 80217

BRADSHER, JOHN WAYNE, steel manufacturing company executive; b. Wichita, Kans., Aug. 21, 1935; s. William Oliver and Gladys Marie (Charlton) B.; div.; children—Charlton Frederick, Nancy Marie, Sarah Elizabeth. Student Central Meth. Coll., 1952-54; A.B., U. Mo.-Columbia, 1956. Group field underwriter, sales rep. The Travelers Ins. Cos., Hartford, Conn., also Chgo., 1956-58; supr. group ins. acctg. Gen. Am. Life Ins. Co., St. Louis, 1960-61; asst. to corp. v.p. personnel McDonnell Douglas Corp., St. Louis, 1961-72, asst. corp. dir. personnel ops.-west, Santa Monica, Calif., 1972-74, corp. dir. personnel services-west, Long Beach, Calif., 1974-76, dir. personnel ops. McDonnell Douglas Astronautics Corp., Huntington Beach, Calif., 1974-76; exec. v.p. Four Seasons Marketers, Inc., Los Angeles, 1976, pres., 1977; dir. employee relations Soulé Steel Co., Los Angeles, 1978-81, v.p. personnel, asst. sec. dir., 1981—. Mem. adminstv. bd. dirs., chmn., personnel com. Arlington Meth. Ch., 1968-70; treas. St. Louis Boy Scouts Am., 1969-70; bd. dirs. Acad. Hill Homeowners Assn., Palos Verdes, 1975; trustee mem. planning com., nominating com., pub. relations com. Roessler-Chadwick Found., 1976-81. Served with U.S. Army, 1958-60. Mem. Am. Chem. Soc., Calif. Mfrs. Assn. (indsl. relations steering com. 1975-76), Long Beach C. of C. (com. of 300). Republican. Club: Jonathan (Los Angeles). Home: Palos Verdes CA 90274 Office: Soulé Steel Co 2160 E Dominguez St Carson CA 90749

BRADWAY, KATHERINE PRESTON, psychologist; b. Milw., Nov. 17, 1910; d. Charles Herbert and Ruth Louise (Peirce) Preston; B.A., U. Minn., 1931, M.A., 1933; Ph.D., Stanford U., 1942; m. Firman Bradway, Sept. 18, 1935. Research asst. Vineland (N.J.) Training Sch., 1934-37; supervisory clin. psychologist Inst. Pa. Hosps., Phila., 1937-39; clin. psychologist San Francisco City Clinic, 1943-44, 45-46, Alexander Sanitarium, Belmont, Calif., 1944-45; chief Child Guidance Clinic, Pub. Health and Welfare Dept. San Mateo County, Calif., 1944-45; chief psychologist Stanford (Calif.) U. Hosp., 1947-54; acting asso. prof. Stanford (Calif.) U., 1947-54, asso. clin. prof., 1954-69; pvt. practice clin. psychology, San Francisco, Mill Valley, Calif., 1945—; cons. to San Mateo Soc. Crippled Children and Adults, 1948-58, Convent of the Good Shepherd, San Francisco, 1950-55, Letterman Army Hosp., 1956-59, VA, 1948-81, Kaiser Found. Hosp., 1969—, Pacific Med. Center, San Francisco, 1962-77, Calif. Sch. Profl. Psychology, 1974—. NIMH grantee, 1956-58; Ernst and Eleanor van Loben Sels scholar, 1974-76. Mem. Am., Calif., San Francisco Bay Area psychol. assns., Soc. of Jungian Analysts of No. Calif. (founding mem., pres. 1960-62), C.G. Jung Inst. of San Francisco, Internat. Assn. Analytical Psychology. Author: The Villa of Mysteries: Pompeii Initiation Rites of Women, 1982; Co-author: Sandplay Studies: Origins, Theory and Practice, 1981; contbg. author: Jungian Analysis, 1982; contbr. articles in field to profl. jours. Home: 41 Monte Mar Dr Sausalito CA 94965 Office: 10 Millwood St Mill Valley CA 94941

BRADY, BRIAN JAMES, civil engr.; b. Pawtucket, R.I., Sept. 5, 1948; s. Paul Frances and Ethel (Hadfield) B.; B.C.E., Loyola U., Los Angeles, 1971; M.B.A., U. So. Calif., 1976; m. Janis Ann Alford, Apr. 19, 1969; children—Matthew Brian, Elizabeth Alford. With So. Calif. Edison Co., Rosemead, 1971—, lead environ. engr., tech. liaison with EPA, 1971-76, supervising valuation engr., 1977-78, valuation mgr., 1978-80, mgr. investor relations, 1981, mgr. property acctg., 1982—; gen. partner BJB Enterprises; mem. nat. tech. adv. com. Utility Water Act Group to EPA, 1972-76; staff instr. Calif. Inst. Tech.; civil engring. cons. Registered profl. engr., Calif. Mem. Nat., Calif. socs. profl. engrs., Pacific Coast Elec. Assn., Los Angeles C. of C. Republican. Roman Catholic. Research and publs. in field. Home: 1431 Calle Linda San Dimas CA 91773 Office: 2244 Walnut Grove Ave Rosemead CA 91770

BRADY, DANIEL WILLIAM, accountant, educator; b. Tacoma, Wash., Dec. 11, 1945; s. William C. and Helen E. B.; m. Barbara E. Jones, 1981; children—Daniel, Curtiss, Sean, Seth. B.A. in Fin., U. Wash., 1968, M.B.A., 1970. C.P.A., Wash. Auditing, acctg. and data processing positions Gen. Telephone, Everett, Wash., 1968-75; pvt. practice acctg., Edmonds, Wash., 1975—; mem. faculty City U., Seattle, 1975—; speaker convs. and confs. Mem. City Planning Commn., 1979-81; mem. City Council, 1981—. Mem. Am. Inst. C.P.A.s, Wash. Soc. C.P.A.s. Office: 8326 196th St SW Edmonds WA 98020

BRADY, JOHN ARTHUR, communications exec.; b. Bakersfield, Calif., May 25, 1944; s. Frank M. and Leota M. Brady; A.A., Bakersfield Coll., 1964; B.S., Calif. State Poly. U., 1971; M.B.A., Pacific Western U., 1981, Ph.D., 1981; m. Sharon Ardean Tallman, Nov. 19, 1966; children—Lara Heather, Heidi Lynn, Holly Allison, Sean Kelly. Communications cons. Pacific Tel. & Tel. Co., Calif., 1966-72, engr. customer facilities, 1972-75, mgmt. supr. installation force, 1975-76, complex installation and repair supr., 1976-77, account exec., 1977-80, account exec., industry cons., 1980-82; account exec., industry cons. Am. Bell, Inc., N.J., 1982—; assoc. prof. engring. and tech. dept. Calif. State Poly. U. Extension, San Luis Obispo, 1977-80. Active, Santa Lucia area council Boy Scouts Am., 1966—; v.p. PTA, San Luis Obispo, 1977-79; jail social service vol. San Luis Obispo County Sheriff, 1979—; mem. oral rev. bd. San Luis Obispo Police Dept., 1979—; commr. San Luis Obispo Local Area Formation Commn., 1982—; bishop Ch. of Jesus Christ of Latter-day Saints, 1978—, home tchr., 1966—. Served to sgt. USMC, 1964-66. Recipient Public Speaking award Pacific Tel. & Tel., 1975-81, Outstanding Achievement award, 1977, President's Outstanding Achievement award, 1979, 80, 81; Achievement award PTA, 1979. Mem. Am. Mgmt. Assn., Am. Public Works Assn., Calif. Public Safety Radio Assn., Associated Public Safety Communications Officers. Republican. Contbr. articles on communications adminstrn., bus. and public adminstrn. to profl. publs. Office: 3250 S Higuera Suite B San Luis Obispo CA 93401

BRADY, JOHN PATRICK, JR., university dean, electronics educator, consultant; b. Newark, Mar. 20, 1929; s. John Patrick and Madeleine Mary (Atno) B.; m. Mary Coop, May 1, 1954; children—Peter, John P., Madeleine, Dennis, Mary G. B.S. in E.E., MIT, 1952, M.S. in E.E., 1953. Registered profl. engr., Mass. Sect. mgr. Hewlett-Packard Co., Waltham, Mass., 1956-67; v.p. engring. John Fluke Mfg. Co., Inc., Mountlake Terrace, Wash., 1967-73; v.p. engring. Dana Labs., Irvine, Calif., 1973-77; engring. mgr., tech. advisor to gen. mgr. Metron Corp., Upland, Calif., 1977-78; ptnr. Resource Assocs., Newport Beach, Calif., 1978—; assoc. prof. electronics Orange Coast Coll., Costa Mesa, Calif., 1977-83, dean technology, 1983—; instr. computers and electrinc engring. Calif. State U., Long Beach, 1982—. Served with USN, 1946-48. Mem. Measurement Sci. Conf. (dir. 1982-83). Club: MIT (Los Angeles). Contbr. articles in field to profl. jours. Office: Orange Coast College Costa Mesa CA 92626

BRADY, LAUREN JEAN, editor; b. Youngstown, Ohio, Oct. 12, 1951; d. Charles Henry Joachim and Maryon Ellen (Johnson) J.; m. Paul Matthew Brady, June 21, 1975. B.A. with honors, Calif. Poly. State U., 1973. Pub. affairs asst. Standard Oil Co. Calif., 1973-77, audio visual prodns. asst., 1977-79; pub. affairs asst., staff writer Chevron Chem. Co., San Francisco, 1979-80; editor The Catalyst, San Francisco, 1980—. Recipient Pub. Relations Soc. Am. award merit 1983. Mem. Internat. Assn. Bus. Communicators (Internat. Gold Quill award merit 1982, Silver Six award 1982, Gold Quill commendation 1983). Home: 1454 45th Ave San Francisco CA 94122 Office: 575 Martex St #3448 San Francisco CA 94105

BRAGDON, PAUL ERROL, college president; b. Portland, Maine, Apr. 19, 1927; s. Errol F. and Edith (Somerville) B.; B.A., Amherst Coll., 1950, D.H.L. (hon.), 1980; J.D., Yale U., 1953; m. Nancy Ellen Horton, Aug. 14, 1954; children—David Lincoln, Susan Horton, Peter Jefferson. Bar: N.Y. 1954 Assoc., Dewey, Ballantine, Bushby, Palmer & Wood, N.Y.C., 1954-67; various staff positions N.Y.C. govt., 1964-67; v.p. pub. affairs NYU, 1967-71; pres. Reed Coll., Portland, Oreg., 1971—; dir. Evans Products, Tektronix, Inc. Dir., dir. Pres.'s Task Force on Priorities in Higher Edn., 1969-70. Mem. N.Y. Commn. on Powers of Local Govt., 1970-71, Oreg. Gov.'s Select Com. on Conflict of Interest, 1973-74, Oreg. Environ. Quality Commn., 1973; trustee Amherst Coll., 1972-78. Served with USMC, 1945-46. Mem. Nat. Assn. Ind. Colls. and Univs., Yale Law Sch. Alumni Assn. (exec. com.), N.Y.C. Bar Assn., ABA. Clubs: Univ., Century Assn. (N.Y.C.); Univ. (Portland), Portland

Downtown Rotary, Portland City (gov.). Office: Reed College 3203 SE Woodstock St Portland OR 97202

BRAGG, CLARENCE CORDER, elec. products mfg. co. exec.; b. Duffy, W.Va., Apr. 13, 1915; s. George William and Arcelia Mitilda (Pickens) B.; B.S. in Elec. Engring., W.Va. U., 1947; m. Mary Barbara McLain, July 1, 1938; children—Douglas M., Michael J., Steven M. With Westinghouse Electric Corp., 1936-39, 42-46, gen. foreman, Emeryville, Calif., 1945-46; gen. mgr. Indsl. Electric Co., Clarksburg, W.Va., 1947-51; prodn. supt. Lear, Inc., Grand Rapids, Mich., 1951-52; dept. supt. top secret security clearance Dow Chem. Co., Denver, 1952-53; mgr. mfg. Schwager-Wood Corp., Portland, Oreg., 1953-60; founder, dir., v.p. mfg. Powerdyne, Inc., Lake Oswego, Oreg., 1960-65; exec. v.p., gen. mgr. Portland Chain Co. (Oreg.), 1965-67; gen. mgr., dir. Williams Air Control, Portland, 1967-68; pres., chief exec. officer, chmn. bd. Eltec, Inc., Portland, 1968-76; regional mgr. elec. sales Willamina Lumber Co., Portland, 1974-81; pres., owner Gus Gragg & Assos., 1981—. Dist. advancement chmn. Pioneer Dist., Portland Area council Boy Scouts Am. Mem. citizens budget com. Lake Oswego Pub. Schs. Recipient Golden Hammer award Mechanix Illus. Registered profl. engr., W.Va., Oreg. Mem. IEEE (life), Eta Kappa Nu, Kappa Mu Alpha, Phi Sigma Kappa. Methodist (trustee). Mason (Shriner). Patentee garage door operator. Home and office: 1235 Andrews Rd Lake Oswego OR 97034

BRAIN, GEORGE BERNARD, univ. dean; b. Thorp, Wash., Apr. 25, 1920; s. George and Alice Pearl (Ellison) B.; B.A., Central Wash. U., Ellensburg, 1946, M.A., 1949; Ed.D., Columbia Tchrs. Coll., 1957; postgrad. U. Wash., Wash. State U., Harvard, U. Colo., Stanford; m. Harriet Gardinier, Sept. 28, 1940; children—George Calvin, Marylou. Tchr. math. and sci. Yakima (Wash.) secondary schs., 1946-49; instr. Central Wash. State Coll., 1949-50; elementary sch. prin., Ellensburg, 1950-51; successively elementary sch. prin., asst. supt. schs., supt., schs., Bellevue, Wash., 1951-59; vis. prof. Central Wash. State Coll., 1953, Wash. State U., 1959, U. Md., 1964; supt. schs., Balt., 1960-65; dean Coll. Edn., also dir. summer schs., Wash. State U., Pullman, 1965—. Lectr. Columbia, U. Conn., Harvard, U. Ga., U. Del., Johns Hopkins, Morgan U., U. Okla., Towson State Coll., Stanford, Wash. U. Chmn. Fulbright Group Western European Seminar Comparative Edn., 1959; chmn. ednl. policies commn. N.E.A.; ednl. cons. Office Edn., 1962—; cons. Ednl. Testing Service, Princeton, N.J., 1964-67. Bd. dirs. Md. Acad. Sci., 1960-65, Nat. Edn. Found., Field Enterprises Ednl. Corp., 1970—. Served with USNR, 1941-42, USMCR, 1942-46; maj. Res. Recipient Distinguished Service award Wash. State Jr. Assn. Commerce, 1956; named Man of Year, Met. Civic Assn. Balt., 1962; Distinguished Service award in edn. Nat. Conf. Christians and Jews, 1963. Fulbright scholar, 1959. Life mem. Am. Assn. Sch. Adminstrs. (exec. com. 1964-66, pres. 1965), N.E.A.; hon. life mem. Wash. State Assn. Sch. Adminstrs. (pres. 1959), Md. Assn. Sch. Adminstrs., Nat. Congress P.T.A.; mem. Wash. Edn. Assn. (pres. dept. adminstrn. and supervision 1957), A.A.A.S. (exec. com. commn. elementary and secondary sci. 1963-66), Assn. Supervision and Curriculum Devel., Univ. Council Ednl. Adminstrn. Nat. Joint Council Econ. Edn. (exec. com. 1963—), Nat. Conf. Profs. Ednl. Adminstrn., Am. Assn. U. Profs., Internat. Platform Assn., Nat. Council for Edn. in Health Professions, Nat. Acad. Sch. Execs., Nat. Council Fgn. Study League, Exec. Hall Fame, Phi Delta Kappa, Kappa Delta Pi. Presbyn. Rotarian (dir. Balt. 1964-65). Mem. editorial adv. bd. Scholastics Publs., 1963—, Am. Sch. and Univ., 1960-64, Education, USA, 1964-71; mem. editorial bd. World Book, 1966—, Jour. Tchr. Edn., 1966—. Home: 640 SE Spring St Pullman WA 99163 Office: Coll Edn Wash State U Pullman WA 99164

BRAINARD, EDWARD AXDAL, educational administrator; b. St. Cloud, Minn., Apr. 25, 1931; s. Dudley Shattuck and Merl Virginia (Anderson) B.; B.S., St. Cloud State U., 1953; M.A., U. No. Colo., 1957, Ed.D., 1961; m. Muriel Sandra Swanson, Feb. 13, 1954; children—Ann F., Thomas E. Tchr., Billings (Mont.) Jr. High Sch., 1955-57; prin., Lakewood (Colo.) Jr. High Sch., 1958-62; asst. prof. Kans. State U., Manhattan, 1962-63; dir. research Jefferson County Sch. Dist., Lakewood, Colo., 1963-66; dir. ednl. grants div. Charles F. Kettering Found., Dayton, Ohio, 1966-67; pres., CFK Ltd., Englewood, Colo., 1967-74; dir. leadership devel. Colo. Dept. Edn., Denver, 1974-76; prof. U. No. Colo., Greeley, 1976-81; asst. supt. Aurora (Colo.) Pub. Schs., 1981—. Chmn. citizens adv. com. Red Rocks Campus, Community Coll. Denver, 1971-73. Served with AUS, 1953-55. Recipient Distinguished Alumni award St. Cloud State U., 1971. Mem. NEA, Am. Assn. Sch. Adminstrs., Nat. Assn. Secondary Sch. Prins., Colo. North Central Assn. (chmn. 1976-81), Phi Delta Kappa. Co-author: School Climate Improvement; How School Administrators Make Things Happen. Contbr. articles to profl. jours. Home: 2527 S Allison St Denver CO 80227 Office: Aurora Public Schs Aurora CO 80011

BRAINARD, MARYTHELMA, counselor, educator; b. Quiriqua, Guatemala, July 31, 1933; came to U.S., 1937, naturalized, 1954; d. Cecil Rhodes and Margaret Rebecca (Miller) Bryant; children—Margaret Renee Brainard-Gentz, Robert Lyle, James Edward. B.A. in English, San Jose State U., 1966; M.A. in Counseling Psychology, U. Santa Clara, 1976; postgrad. in guidance and counseling U. N.Mex., 1977—. Tchr. English, Sonora (Calif.) Union High Sch., 1966-68; Title I reading specialist Live Oak Sch. Dist., Santa Cruz, Calif., 1968-72, Title I coordinator, 1972-75, staff devel. specialist/counselor, 1975-76; coordinator-counselor Albuquerque Transactional Analysis Assn., 1976-77; instr. N. Mex. State U.-Grants, 1977-79; cons. counselor Laguna (N. Mex.) Indian Services Ctr., 1977-82; pvt. practice counseling, Albuquerque, 1977—; tchr. transactional analysis seminars; condr. workshops in field; moderator Multi-ethnic Conf.; condr. tng. programs for vols. in reading instrn.; vol. asst. instr. U. Calif.-Santa Cruz, 1974; vol. instr. on group process U. N.Mex., Albuquerque; vol. trainer Hogares staff, Albuquerque, 1979. Named Outstanding Sophomore Woman, U. N. Mex., 1952-53. Mem. Internat. Transactional Analysis Assn., Nat. Acad. Cert. Clin. Mental Health Counselors, Am. Psychol. Assn., Mortar Bd. Republican. Home: PO Box 1021 Corrales NM 87048 Office: 617 San Mateo NE Albuquerque NM 87108

BRAITHWATIE, CHARLES HENRY, JR., chemist; b. Chgo., Dec. 16, 1920; s. Charles Henry and Wilhemina (Hoth) B.; m. Bernice Hyde, Apr. 29, 1949; children—Charles Henry III, Betty Susan. A.B., UCLA, 1941; B.S.E., U. Mich., 1943; M.S., Carnegie Inst. Tech., 1948, D.Sc., 1949. With Westinghouse Electric Co., East Pittsburgh, Pa., 1943-46, Shell Oil Co., Woodriver, Ill., 1949-51, Chlor-Alkali div. FMC, South Charleston, W.Va., 1951-57, Productol Co., Santa Fe Springs, Calif., 1957-59; pres. Cal Colonial Chemsolve Co., La Habra, Calif., 1959—; pres. Jack-Sons Products Co., 1970—; corp. bd. dirs. Nat. Testing Standards Pib-3 Corp. Mem. Am. Chem. Soc., Am. Inst. Chem. Engrs., Soc. Plastics Engrs., AAAS. Home: 11232 Tigrina St Whittier CA 90603 Office: Cal Colonial Chemsolve Co 871 E Lambert Rd La Habra CA 90631

BRAITO, RITA MURPHY, sociologist, nurse, educator; b. Winnemucca, Nev., Mar. 6, 1930; d. Frederick Enrico Braito and Glennie Ruthaperd Murphy. R.N., St. Vincent's Coll. Nursing, 1952; B.S. in Nursing, San Jose State U., 1955; M.S. in Nursing, U. Colo., 1958; M.A., U. Wash., 1967, Ph.D., U. Minn., 1970. Instr. U. Colo. Sch. Nursing, Denver, 1958-60, UCLA Sch. Nursing, 1960-62; asst. prof. Iowa State U., Ames, 1970-73; asst. to assoc. prof. dept. sociology U. Denver, 1973—; mem. bd. Hospice Metro Denver. Contbr. numerous articles to profl. publs. NIMH fellow, 1963-65. Mem. AAUP, Am. Sociol. Soc., Soc. Study Social Prolems, Soc. Study Symbolic Interaction, Sociologists for Women in Society, Midwest Sociol. Soc., Pacific Sociol. Soc. Democrat. Home: 1043 S Clarkson St Denver CO 80209 Office: GCB Bldg Room 424 Dept Sociology U Denver Denver CO 80208

BRAKKE, JAMES GLENN, insurance executive; b. Pomona, Calif., Apr. 16, 1942; s. Glenn Walden and Dessie Irene B.; A.A., San Jose City Coll., 1962; B.S., Colo. State U., 1964; Cert. Ins. Cons., Orange Coast City Coll., 1975; m. Glenys E. Heaney, June 19, 1965; children—Tifani E., Xanne M., Richard S. Account exec. comml. ins. sales Sentry Ins., Whittier, Calif., 1966-69; v.p. sales Fenley & Assocs., Inc., Orange, Calif., 1970-71; pres. Brakke-Schafnitz & Assocs., Inc., comml. ins. and cons. firm, Irvine, Calif., 1971—; founding dir., corp. sec. Westwood Nat. Ins. Co.; dir. Pacific Nat. Bank, Newport Beach. Chmn. local dist. assembly race, 1977-78; mem. Orange County Sheriff's Adv. Council. Named Jaycee of Yr., 1966; Profl. Adjuster of Yr., Sentry Ins., 1967; Outstanding Salesman INA Life Ins., 1975-76, La. & So. Life, 1976, Pan Am. Life, 1978, Travelers Ins., 1975. Mem. Ins. Agts. Adv. Council (chmn.), Colo. State U. Alumni Assn., Gamma Iota Sigma (pres. 1973). Republican. Methodist. Clubs: Roosters of Chanteclair, Ritz Brothers. Home: 26531 Broken Bit Laguna Hills CA 92653 Office: 17911 Fitch Ave Irvine CA 92714

BRAMBLE, JOHN MYLES, city manager; b. Vancouver, Wash., May 3, 1946; s. Paul Eugene and Beulah Elizabeth (Henderson) B.; B.S., Oreg. State U., 1969; M.P.A., U. Nev., Las Vegas, 1979; m. JoAnn Tolle, May 2, 1980; 1 son, Scott Byron. Adminstrv. asst. City of Salem (Oreg.), 1969-73; research analyst Abt Assocs., Inc., Cambridge, Mass., 1973-74; dir. budget and mgmt. City of Las Vegas (Nev.), 1975-79; asst. city mgr., fin. dir. City of Belmont (Calif.), 1979-81; city mgr. City of Commerce City (Colo.), 1981—. Vice pres. Commerce City Child Care Bd.; mem. exec. bd. Colo. Mcpl. League. Mem. Internat. City Mgmt. Assn., Mcpl. Fin. Officers Am., Denver Met. Mgrs. Assn. (chmn.). Club: Rotary (Commerce City). Home: 7040 Poplar St Commerce City CO 80022 Office: 5291 60th Ave Commerce City CO 80022

BRAME, ARDEN HOWELL, JR. II, herpetologist, genealogist; b. Los Angeles, Mar. 19, 1934; s. Arden Howe and Marguerite Lucile (Adams) B.; B.A., U. So. Calif., 1957, M.S., 1967; student UCLA, 1956-57; m. Susan Diane Bronn, Aug. 23, 1964 (div. June 1969); m. 2d, Patricia Louise Verret Reinholtz, Apr. 19, 1970. Grad. teaching asst. U. So. Calif., Los Angeles, 1959-65, also student profl. worker in ichthyology-herpetology and vertebrate paleontology Los Angeles County Mus., 1959-65, later research asst. in herpetology; supr. Eaton Canyon Nature Center, 1965-68, 70-78; asst. curator sect. herpetology Los Angeles County Museum of Natural History, 1968-70; instr. genealogy Pasadena (Calif.) City Coll., also Calif. State U. Northridge, 1977—; assoc. pub. TV Facts of Pasadena and Altadena, 1978-79; mem. citizen nongame adv. com. Calif. Dept. Fish and Game, 1975-79; herpetol. group adviser Survival Service Commn., Internat. Union for Conservation Nature and Natural Resources, Morges, Switzerland, 1974-82. Served with AUS, 1958. Fellow Herpetologists' League, Augustan Soc. (pres. 1980-81), mem. Soc. Study Amphibians and Reptiles (dir. 1967-70, chmn. 1973), Southwestern Herpetologists Soc. (pres. 1971-74) Am. Soc. Ichthyologists and Herpetologists, Brit., Phila., N.Y., Ariz., N.Mex., Conn., Chgo. herpetol. socs., Soc. Study of Evolution, Soc. Systematic Zoologists, Ecol. Soc. Am., Western Soc. Naturalists, Biol. Soc. Wash., So. Calif. Acad. Scis., Soc. Tropical Biologists, Pasadena Audubon Soc. (pres. 1971-76), SAR (pres. Pasadena chpt. 1977-83, genealogist Calif. Soc.), S.R., SCV (camp comdr. 1979-83), Gen. Soc. War of 1812, Soc. Colonial Wars (Calif. genealogist), Soc. Sons and Daus. of Pilgrims (Calif. registrar), First Families of Ohio, Sons Am. Colonists, Order Crown of Charlemagne in U.S.A., Baronial Order Magna Charta, Vet. Corps of Arty., Mil. Soc. War of 1812, Plantagenet Soc., Sovereign Colonial Soc. Ams. Royal Descent, Soc. Descs. Knights of the Garter, Colonial Order of Crown, Magna Charta Barons, Order of Washington, Sons of Union Vets of Civil War, Mil. Order Loyal Legion of U.S., Mil. Order of Stars and Bars (comdr. Calif. chpt.), Dames of Guild of St. Margaret of Scotland (protector), Order of Augustan Eagle, Order of Armigerous Augustans, Hospitaller Order of St. John of Jerusalem (companion of honor), Noble Co. of Rose, Jamestowne Soc., St. John's Vol. Corps, Sigma Xi, Phi Sigma. Author: (with Dr. D. B. Wake) The Salamanders of South America, 1963; Systematics and Evolution of the Mesoamerican Salamander Genus Oedipina, 1968. Contbr. articles to profl. jours. Research in systematics, classification and evolution of living and fossil salamanders. Home: 9545 E Guess St Rosemead CA 91770

BRAMMER, LAWRENCE MARTIN, psychologist; b. Crookston, Minn., Aug. 20, 1922; s. Martin G. and Edna L. (Thiesen) B.; B.S., St. Cloud (Minn.) State U., 1943; M.A., Stanford U., 1948, Ph.D., 1950; m. Marian S. Sjolin, Feb. 11, 1945; children—Karin Marie, Kristen Lenore. Psychologist, Stanford Counseling and Testing Center, 1948-75; asso. dean students Sacramento State Coll., 1950-64; prof. psychology U. Wash., Seattle, 1964—. Served to lt. M.C., AUS, 1944-46. Fulbright fellow, 1961-62, 64, 77; diplomate Am. Bd. Profl. Psychology. Fellow Am. Psychol. Assn.; mem. Am. Personnel and Guidance Assn., Assn. Humanistic Psychology. Democrat. Lutheran. Club: Queen City Yacht. Author: Therapeutic Psychology, 4th edit., 1982; Helping Relationship, 2d edit., 1979; Joys and Challenges of Middle Age, 1982. Home: 7714 56th Pl NE Seattle WA 98115 Office: University of Washington Miller DQ 12 Seattle WA 98195

BRAMSEN, CHERYL ANN, credit bureau manager, seminar speaker; b. Roswell, N.Mex., Oct. 1, 1953; d. Donald L. and BettyJean Ebbutt; m. Calvin C. Bramsen, July 15, 1972; 1 dau., Amy Dawn. Student U. Mont., 1971-72. Cert. collector, Mont., Wyo. Accounts rep. St. Patrick Hosp., Missoula, Mont., 1971-76; collector Credit Bur., Missoula, 1976-81; mgr. Credit Bur., Sheridan, Wyo., 1981-83, mgr. in charge all ops., 1981—; seminar speaker on credit and collecting. Mem. Credit Women Internat. (1st v.p.), Bus. and Profl. Women, Am. Bus. Women Assn. Libertarian. Methodist. Club: Cloud Peak Lanes. Office: Credit Bur 35 W Brundage Sheridan WY 82801

BRAMSON, GENE, designer, educator; b. Los Angeles, Aug. 23, 1950; s. Bernard and Shirley (Feyer) B.; m. Louise Rhonda Makowsky, June 23, 1979. Student Los Angeles City Coll., Art Ctr. Coll. Design, 1970-72. Pres., chief exec. officer Bramson & Assocs., Los Angeles, 1970—; tchr. design Art Ctr. Coll. Design, Pasadena, Calif. Active historic preservation Hollywood Heritage, Natl. Trust for Hist Preservation. Recipient Belding, ANDY awards, Art Dirs. Club of Los Angeles, 1982. Developer computerized video vending concept, interior furnishing systems restoration. Office: Bramson & Assocs 7400 Beverly Blvd Los Angeles CA 90036

BRANCH, TURNER WILLIAMSON, lawyer; b. Houston, Aug. 22, 1938; s. James Alexander and Juanita (Wilson) B.; B.A., U. N.Mex., 1960; J.D., Baylor U., 1965; children—Brian Kern, Rebecca Claire. Admitted to N.Mex. bar, 1966, U.S. Dist. Cts. of N.Mex., 1966, 10th Circuit Ct. of Appeals, 1966, 5th Circuit Ct. of Appeals, 1966, U.S. Supreme Ct., 1971; sr. partner firm Branch, Eaton & Krehbiel (and predecessors), Albuquerque, 1966—, sr. partner, 1974—. Dir., N.Mex. Alcoholic Beverage Control, 1966-68; mem. N.Mex. Ho. of Reps., 1968-74; bd. dirs. Albuquerque Little Theater, 1970-78; adv. bd. Am. Arbitration Assn., 1968—. Served to 1st lt. USMC, 1960-63. Recipient T.R. McDonald award, Baylor Coll. Law, 1965. Mem. N.Mex. Trial Lawyers Assn., Tex. Trial Lawyers Assn., Am. Soc. Law and Medicine, Am. Bar Assn., Assn. Trial Lawyers of Am., Am. Bd. Trial Advocates, C. of C., Calif. Trial Lawyers, Western Trial Lawyers of Am., Ariz. Trial Lawyers, Am. Arbitration Assn. Republican. Presbyterian. Clubs: Kiwanis, Albuquerque Country, Elks, Masons (Shriner). Contbr. articles to profl. jours. Home: 3820 Palacio del Rio Grande NW Albuquerque NM 87107 Office: Newport West 2501 Yale Blvd SE Albuquerque NM 87106

BRANCHFLOWER, JOHN WALTER, accountant; b. Los Angeles, May 17, 1946; s. Dale R. and Margaret (Burnham) B.; m. Yvonne C. Jennings, July 2, 1967; B.Music, U. Redlands, 1968; postgrad. in Bus. Adminstrn., Calif. State Coll.-San Bernardino, 1975-79. C.P.A., Calif. Staff acct. Eadie & Payne, San Bernardino, Calif., 1979-80; sr. acct. Cox & Battey, Hemet, Calif., 1980-81; prin. John W. Branchflower, C.P.A., Beaumont, Calif., 1981—. Dir. Community Legal Services, Riverside County, 1973-75; treas. Cherry Festival Assn., Beaumont, Calif., 1981-83; pres. Pass Crisis Ctr., Beaumont, 1972-76; dir. Hospital Citizens com. Banning, Calif., 1972-83, pres., 1976-80. Mem. Calif. State Soc. C.P.A.s. Club: Beaumont Rotary (pres. 1977-78, treas. 1978-79, 82-83). Office: PO Box 3035 Beaumont CA 92223

BRANCHFLOWER, LYLE WILLIAMS, business exec.; b. Seattle, Sept. 25, 1940; s. Norman H. and Edith R. (Williams) B.; B.A., U. Pa., 1962, M.B.A., 1968; m. Nancy Wildermuth; children—Hillary, Christine. Cost analyst Kimberly-Clark Corp., Anderson, Calif., 1969-70; mergers and acquisitions Pacific Lighting Corp., Los Angeles, 1970-73; pres. R G Mfg. Co., San Pedro, Calif., 1973-75, dir., 1973-77; project mgr. TRW, Redondo Beach, Calif., 1976-77; spl. cons. TCA Films, Palos Verdes Estates, Calif., 1976—; joint owner Conley-Branchflower Stables, 1980-81; pres. Branchflower Investment Co., 1980—; v.p. H.E.S., Inc., 1981; partner Branchflower-Carr Prodns., 1982—, B.F. Leasing, 1982—; instr. Fed. Correctional Inst., Terminal Island, 1975; cons. Spl. Offender Center, Wash. State Reformatory. Assoc. vestryman St. Peter's Episcopal Ch., San Pedro, Calif., 1975-76; adv. bd. Salvation Army, San Pedro, 1975-78; active fund raising YMCA, San Pedro, 1976-78; vestryman St. Aidan's Episcopal Ch., Camano Island, Wash., 1980. Served to lt. USN, 1961-65. Republican. Clubs: Seattle Tennis, Kiwanis; Wharton M.B.A. Contbr. articles to profl. jours.; patentee in mechanics. Home: 13614 56th Ave NE Marysville WA 98270

BRANDIN, ALF ELVIN, mining and shipping co. exec.; b. Newton, Kans., July 1, 1912; s. Oscar E. and Agnes (Larsen) B.; A.B., Stanford U., 1936; m. Marie Eck, June 15, 1936; children—Alf R., Jon, Erik, Mark. With Standard Accident of Detroit, 1936-42; bus. mgr. Stanford (Calif.) U., 1946-52, bus. mgr., exec. officer for land devel., 1952-59, v.p. for bus. affairs, 1959-70; sr. v.p. Utah Internat. Inc., San Francisco, 1970—, also dir., mem. exec. com.; pres. Richardson-Brandin; dir. Saga Corp., Hershey Oil Co. Bd. govs. San Francisco Bay Area Council; trustee Reclamation Dist. 2087, Alameda, Calif.; bd. overseers Hoover Instn. on War, Revolution and Peace, Stanford. Mem. VIII Olympic Winter Games Organizing Com., 1960. Served as comdr. USNR, 1942-46. Mem. Zeta Psi. Elk. Clubs: Stanford Golf; Bohemian; Pauma Valley Country; Silverado Country; Bankers (San Francisco); Royal Lahaina; San Francisco Golf. Home: 668 Salvatierra St Stanford CA 94305 Office: 550 California St San Francisco CA 94104

BRANDIN, JILL FELDMAN, banker; b. Angola, Ind., Mar. 16, 1951; d. Howard Earl and Mary Anson (Hunt) Feldmann. B.A. with honors, Mt. Holyoke Coll., 1973; M.B.A., U. Chgo., 1976. Loan officer, aerospace First Nat. Bank of Chgo., 1975-77; v.p., group head leveraged lease mktg. Bank of Am., San Francisco, 1977-82; mng. dir. Argent Group Ltd., San Francisco, 1982—. First Nat. Bank of Chgo. scholar, 1973-75. Office: Argent Group Ltd 3 Embarcadero Ctr Suite 1665 San Francisco CA 94111

BRANDNER, MARGARET ANNE SHAW, polygraph examiner; b. Denver, Sept. 4, 1937; d. Bertram James and Bessie (Syme) Shaw; B.A. in Elem. Edn., Loretto Heights Coll., 1959; A.A.S. in Polygraph Tech., Pike's Peak Community Coll., 1982; polygraph examiner Rocky Mountain Security Inst., 1978; grad. Inst. Forensic and Investigative Hypnosis, 1980; A.A.S. in Polygraph Tech., Pike's Peak Community Coll., 1982, m. Kenneth LeRoy Brandner, Dec. 26, 1970. Acct., Denver Children's Home, 1970; acct. Keny's Rentals, Keny's Equip., Inc., Green River, Wyo., 1971-78; polygraph examiner, sec.-treas. The Brandner Corp., Green River, Wyo., 1978—. Mem. Green River Planning Commn., 1971-79; bd. dirs. Green River Co-op Pre-Sch., Inc., 1977-79. Mem. Am. Acad. Forensic Hypnotists, Am. Mensa Ltd., Am. Polygraph Assn., Nat. Assn. Lady Polygraphists, Colo. Assn. Polygraph Examiners, Utah Polygraph Assn., World Congress Profl. Hypnotists. Roman Catholic. Home: 60 W Railroad Ave Green River WY 82935 Office: PO Box 1147 Green River WY 82935

BRANDON, DALE EDWARD, oceanographer; b. Canonsburg, Pa., Sept. 22, 1938; s. George Edward and Mabel Elizabeth (Pugh) B.; B.S. in Geology, Wayne State U., 1965; M.S., Ph.C. in Oceanography, U. Mich., 1967, Ph.D. in Phys. Oceanography, 1970; postgrad. (Fulbright fellow) U. Sydney (Australia), 1967-69. Sr. research oceanographer Esso Production Research Co., Houston, 1970-73; environ. adminstr. Alyeska Pipeline Service Co., Anchorage, 1973-76; environ. coordinator Exxon Minerals Co., Houston, 1976-78; sr. program mgr. Environ. Research & Tech., Houston, 1978-80; dir. ocean sci. dept. Interstate Electronics Corp., Anaheim, Calif., 1980-82; West Coast regional mgr. E.G.&G. Environ. Consultants, Long Beach, Calif., 1983—. Served with USN, 1955-59. NSF fellow, 1965, 66, 67, 69, 70. Mem. AAAS, Am. Geophys. Union, Soc. Econ. Paleontologists and Mineralogists, Sigma Xi. Home: 1518 Anna Ln Huntington Beach CA 92648 Office: 400 Oceangate Suite 333 Long Beach CA 90802

BRANDON, JAMES L., state senator, rancher; b. Onalaska, Colo., Mar. 20, 1942; s. Clifford and Veda Brandon. B.A., U. No. Colo., 1964. Mgmt. cons. farming and ranching, Akron, Colo.; with Brandon Bros., Akron; mem. Colo. Senate, 1982—. Active Farm Bur.; vice chmn. Washington County GOP. Served with USAF, 1964-68. Mem. Colo. Cattlemen's Assn., VFW, Am. Legion. Republican. Club: Elks. Office: State Capitol Denver CO 80203*

BRANDON, KATHRYN ELIZABETH BECK, pediatrician; b. Salt Lake City, Sept. 10, 1916; d. Clarence M. and Hazel A. (Cutler) Beck; M.D., U. Chgo., 1941; B.A., U. Utah, 1937; M.P.H., U. Calif., Berkeley, 1967; children—John William, Kathleen Brandon McEnulty, Karen. Intern, Grace Hosp., Detroit, 1941-42; resident Children's Hosp. Med. Center No. Calif., Oakland, 1953-55, Children's Hosp., Los Angeles, 1951-53; practice medicine, specializing in pediatrics, La Crescentia, Calif., 1946-51, Salt Lake City, 1960-65; med. dir. Salt Lake City public schs., 1957-60; dir. Ogden City-Weber County (Utah) Health Dept., 1965-67; pediatrician Fitzsimmons Army Hosp., 1967-68; coll. health physician U. Colo., Boulder, 1968-71; student health physician U. Utah, Salt Lake City, 1971-81; occupational health physician Hill AFB, Utah, 1981—; child health physician Salt Lake City-County Health Dept., 1971—; cons. in field; clin. asst. U. Utah Coll. Medicine, Salt Lake City, 1958-64; clin. asst. pediatrics U. Colo. Coll. Medicine, Denver, 1958-72; active staff Primary Children's Hosp., Latter Day Saints Hosp., and Cottonwood Hosp., 1960-67. Diplomate Am. Bd. Pediatrics. Fellow Am. Pediatric Acad., Am. Pediatric Health Assn., Am. Sch. Health Assn.; mem. Utah Coll. Health Assn. (pres. 1978-80), Pacific Coast Coll. Health Assn., AMA, Utah Med. Assn., Salt Lake County Med. Soc., Utah Public Health Assn. (sec.-treas. 1960-66), Intermountain Pediatric

Soc. Home: 61 University St Salt Lake City UT 84102 Office: Foothill PO Box 8482 Salt Lake City UT 84108

BRANDON, REGINALD FRANCIS, aerospace corporation executive; b. Balt., May 7, 1922; s. Reginald Francis and Bertha Mae (Langley) B.; student Howard U., 1941, George Washington U., 1957-60; m. Mary Jane Kaus, Sept. 22, 1979; children by previous marriage—Reginald, Christine, Jon, Keith, Laurin. Sr. prin. research engr. Amecom div. Litton Systems Corp., 1957-67, with mgmt., 1965-67; research engr. Boeing Co., Seattle, 1967-75, mgr. Navy avionics programs, 1975-79, mgr. preliminary design for all electric airplane projects, 1980-82; pres. Am. Energy Products, Inc., Seattle, 1981—, Brandon Enterprises, Seattle, 1981—. Served with U.S. Maritime Service, USNR, 1942-45. Recipient Performance Excellence award Boeing Aerospace Co., 1977; lic. pilot. Mem. Am. Def. Preparedness Assn., AIAA, Boeing Mgmt. Assn. Developer various aerospace technologies. Home: PO Box 80924 Seattle WA 98108

BRANDT, CARL CONRAD, JR., union offical, business representative; b. Eureka, Calif., Nov. 23, 1945; s. Carl Conrad and Laura May (Blachly) B.; m. Debra Verlaine Brandt, Feb. 5, 1978; children—Janice, Timothy, Carl, Bryan. Student Humboldt State Coll., 1964, Coll. of the Redwoods, 1964-79. Grocery clk. Calif. Fruit Market, Eureka, Calif., 1962-64; millworker Simpson Redwood Co., Fairhaven, Calif., 1965-81; bus. rep., fin. sec., Plywood Workers Local 2931, Eureka, 1981—; advocate Redwood Employees Protection Plan, Eureka First Congregational Ch. Unemployment Project, 1982—; mem. exec. bd., steering com. Displaced Workers Center, Eureka, 1981—; jr. engring. technician dept. transp. Cal-Trans. Served with USN, 1965-70. Democrat. Club: Moose. Home: 2125 Forbes Ave Eureka CA 95501 Office: PO Box 1091 Eureka CA 95501

BRANDT, KEITH DELANO, welding electrode mfg. co. exec.; b. Lincoln, Nebr., May 22, 1934; s. John Henry and Martha Margaret (Mueller) B.; B.S., U. So. Calif., 1956, M.B.A., 1965; m. Mary Fay Mathes, Nov. 23, 1957; children—Stephen, Christopher, Patrick. Systems engr. IBM, 1959-62; mgr. electronic acctg. Specialty Engrs., 1963-65; dir. data processing Coca Cola Bottling Co., Los Angeles, 1965-70; mgr. mgmt. cons. services Coopers & Lybrand, Los Angeles, 1970-76; v.p. fin. sec. Stoody Co., Industry, Calif., 1976—; dir. Stoody Asean Sdn. (Malaysia) Berhad. C.P.A., Calif. Mem. Am. Inst. C.P.A.'s, Fin. Execs. Inst., Nat. Mgmt. Assn., Calif. Soc. C.P.A.'s, Commerce Assos. U. So. Calif., Navy League, Los Angeles World Affairs Council, Pasadena Men's Com. for Arts, Beta Gamma Sigma. Republican. Home: 2037 San Pasqual St Pasadena CA 91107 Office: 16425 Gale Ave Industry CA 91749

BRANN, ALTON JOSEPH, aerospace executive; b. Portland Maine, Dec. 23, 1941; s. Donald Edward and Marjorie Margaret (Curran) B.; m. Dorothy Marie Mazeika, 1963; children—Katherine Gregory, Alton; m. 2d, Anna Jeanine Beaudoin, June 10, 1977. B.A., U. Mass., 1969. Mgr. advanced programs Dynamics Research Corp., Wilmington, Mass., 1969-74; dir. engring. Litton Guidance and Control Systems, Los Angeles, 1973-79, dir. program mgmt., 1979-81, v.p. engring., 1981-83, pres., 1983—. Mem. IEEE (sr.), Inst. Nav., Air Force Assn., Optical Soc. Am. Home: 23634 Justice St Canoga Park CA 91304 Office: 5500 Canoga Ave Woodland Hills CA 91364

BRANNON, ERNEST LEROY, educator; b. Port Angeles, Wash., Oct. 16, 1936; s. Ernest Madison and Helen Mae (Graham) B.; m. Charlene S. Brannon, June 6, 1980; children by a previous marriage—Nathan, Heidi, Mary. B.S., U. Wash., 1959, Ph.D., 1972. Field mgmt. staff Internat. Pacific Salmon Fisheries Commn., New Westminster, B.C., Can., 1953-59, research biologist, artificial propagation, 1959-69, supr. sockeye research, 1969-71, chief biologist, 1972-73; asst. prof. fisheries U. Wash., Seattle, 1973-75, assoc. prof., 1975—, dir. finfish aquaculture program, 1975—. Mem. Carkeek Park Watershed Com., Fisheries Com. for the Makah Fish Hatchery, Inst. for Island Research and Assistance, Olympic Peninsula Fisheries Com., Port Angeles, Wash., Game Fish Planning Com. for Lake Washington, Seattle, Lake Washington Fisheries Mgmt. Team. Served to capt. U.S. Army. Mem. Am. Fisheries Soc., Am. Inst. Fishery Research Biologists, Sigma Xi. Contbr. articles to profl. jours. Office: U Wash Coll Fisheries Seattle WA 98195

BRANSON, DEBRA LEE, public relations consultant; b. Spokane, Wash., Mar. 6, 1952; d. Al E. and Patricia A. (Dahl) Strohmaier; m. Scott Jerry Branson, Dec. 19, 1970; children—Amy Katherine, Adam Michael. B.A. in Communications and Pub. Relations, Wash. State U., 1981. Promotion asst. Sta. KWSU-TV, Pullman, Wash., 1981; freelance writer, pub. relations cons., Waitsburg, Wash., 1981-82; office asst. Whitman Coll., Walla Walla, Wash., 1982-83; pub. relations cons., copywriter Coffey Assocs., Walla Walla, 1983—. Exec. dir. Dayton-Waitsburg council Camp Fire Girls, 1978—; treas. Koinonia Club, Waitsburg, 1977-80. Coop. Editorial Assn. scholar, 1981. Mem. Pub. Relations Soc. Am., Phi Beta Kappa. Editor: Walla Walla Gardener's Association Sweet Onion Cookbook, rev. edit., 1982. Office: Coffey Assocs 2330 Eastgate N Walla Walla WA 99362

BRANSON, FARREL ALLEN, research botanist, consultant, educator; b. Coats, Kans., May 3, 1919; s. Samuel Joseph and Kathryn James (Layne) B.; m. Lydia Constance Tuttle, Aug. 9, 1947; children—Steven Arthur, Kirk Allen. B.S., Fort Hays (Kans.) State Coll., 1942, M.S., 1946; Ph.D., U. Nebr., 1952. Instr. Ft. Hays State Coll., 1947; asst. prof. Mont. State U., Bozeman, 1951-57; research botanist U.S. Geol. Survey, Denver, 1957—; cons. Bur. Land Mgmt., 1957—, Denver Regional Transp. Dist., 1971-72, Office Tech. Assessment, U.S. Congress, 1981-82. Served with USNR, 1942-46. Recipient U.S. Dept. Interior Superior Service award, 1981. Fellow AAAS; mem. Ecol. Soc. Am., Am. Inst. Biol. Scis., Soc. Range Mgmt., AAAS, Sigma Xi. Democrat. Unitarian. Sr. author: Rangeland Hydrology, 1981; contbr. articles to profl. jours. Home: 906 24th St Golden CO 80401 Office: Box 25046 Fed Ctr Mail Stop 420 Denver CO 80225

BRANSTROM, DONALD FREDERICK, engr.; b. Warren, Pa., May 28, 1923; s. Edwin F. and Arlene E. (Enos) B.; student Yale U., 1943-44; B.S.E., U. Mich., 1949; M.B.A., Pepperdine U., 1973; m. Phyllis Elaine Lindell, Feb. 6, 1946; children—Candice, Darlene, Donna, Paul. Engr., The Boeing Co., Seattle, 1949-55, Gen. Electric Co., Cin., 1955-59, United Tech., Sunnyvale, Calif., 1960-65, Aeronutronic div. Philco-Ford, Newport Beach, Calif., 1965-67, U.S. Navy Naval Ship Weapons Systems Engring. Sta., Port Hueneme, Calif., 1967—; prin. D.F. Branstrom, Cons. Engr., Oxnard, Calif., 1968—; instr. bus. mgmt. Ventura (Calif.) Community Coll., 1974—. Mem. Ventura County Air Pollution Adv. Bd., 1974-77. Served with U.S. Army, 1943-45. Decorated Purple Heart with oak leaf cluster; registered profl. engr., Calif. Mem. Navy League U.S., Am. Soc. Safety Engrs., AIAA. Presbyterian. Club: Channel Island Yacht. Patentee propulsion apparatus for water cycle. Home: 855 Portola Way Oxnard CA 93033

BRANT, JOHN GETTY, lawyer; b. Great Bend, Kans., Apr. 13, 1946; s. Vane M. and Virginia S. (Getty) B.; m. Barbara Spencer Harris, Aug. 25, 1968; children—John Getty, Charles Spencer. B.B.A., U. Okla, 1968; J.D., U. Tex., 1972. Bar: Tex. 1972, Colo. 1974, U.S. Tax Ct. 1974, U.S. Dist. Ct. Colo. 1974. Lawyer, IRS, Houston, 1972-74; ptnr. Bradley, Campbell & Carney, Golden, Colo., 1975-83, Doussard and Brant, Lakewood, Colo., 1983—. Past pres. Centennial Estate Planning Council, 1977-78; active Denver Estate Planning Council. Office: Doussard and Brant 143 Union Blvd Suite 660 Lakewood CO 80228

BRANTMAN, WILLIAM T., investment counselor; b. N.Y.C., July 9, 1916; s. John William and Blanche Edith (Turkus) B. B.S., U. Ala., 1938; registered investment counselor SEC. Pres. Allied We. Distbrs., 1947-64; investment counselor, Tiburon, Calif., 1966—; pres., dir. Brantman Capital, 1973—; dir. several investee cos. Served to lt. comdr., USNR, 1942-46; PTO. Republican. Clubs: World Trade (San Francisco), Marin Country (Novato, Calif.).

BRASELL, HAROLD KEARY, educator; b. Fort Sumner, N.Mex., Mar. 1, 1922; s. Hugh T. and Dora (Keary) B.; B.A., Eastern N.Mex. U., 1947; M.A., U. Denver, 1952, Ph.D., 1956; children—Sherrie Lou, Meriam Lynette, Hugh Keary. Sci. and lang. arts remedial tchr. Tatum (N.Mex) Pub. Schs., 1949-51; exec. asst. dir., class demonstration tchr. U. Denver Children's Speech Clinic, 1951-53; spl. edn. dir.-speech therapist Odessa (Tex.) Pub. Schs., 1954-56; coordinator psychology, speech and hearing U. Denver Clin. Services, 1956-60; sch. psychologist Ch. Study Services, Phoenix, 1968-69; dir., prin. spl. edn. Jefferson County Schs., Lakewood, Colo., 1960-62; instr., asst. prof. spl. edn. U. Denver, 1953-54, 1956-60; asso. prof. spl. edn. Ariz. U., 1961-68; asso. prof. Eastern N.Mex. U., Portales, 1969—, chmn. spl. edn. dept., 1969-77. Diagnostic cons. Navajo Nation. Served with USMC, 1944-45; PTO. Decorated Bronze Star medal, Purple Heart medal. Recipient certificates of Commendation, Gov. Ariz. for Outstanding Services to Handicapped, 1964, 65. Mem. N.E.A., Council for Exceptional Children, Am. Assn. for Mentally Retarded. Mason, Elk. Home: 213 W 3d St Portales NM 88130

BRASHEAR, WANDA SUE, nurse; b. Prairie Grove, Ark., June 19, 1939; d. Virgil and Walsie (Cone) Brashear. R.N., Hillcrest Med. Ctr., Tulsa, 1960; B.S., Coll. St. Francis, 1982. R.N., Colo., Okla. Pediatric staff nurse Hillcrest Med. Ctr., Tulsa, 1960-62; supr., asst. dir., dir. nursing service St. Anthony Hosp., Oklahoma City, 1962-67; staff nurse surgery St. Anthony Hosp., Denver, 1967-72, supr. surgery, 1972—. Mem. Assn. Operating Room Nurses. Republican. Home: 8025 W Calhoun Pl Littleton CO 80123 Office: 4231 W 16th St Denver CO 80204

BRASSELL, ROSELYN STRAUSS, lawyer; b. Shreveport, La., Feb. 19, 1930; d. Herman Carl and Etelka (McMullan) Strauss; B.A., La. State U., 1949; J.D., UCLA, 1962. Legal sec. Welton P. Mouton, Lafayette, La., 1949-50; office sec. Leake, Henry, Golden & Burrow, Dallas, 1950-57; admitted to Calif. bar, 1963; atty. CBS, Los Angeles, 1962-68, sr. atty., 1968-76, asst. gen. atty., 1976—. Named Angel of Distinction Los Angeles Central City Assn., 1975. Mem. Calif., Los Angeles County (exec. com. 1970—, sect. chmn. 1980-81), Beverly Hills bar assns., Los Angeles Copyright Soc. (treas. 1977-78, sec. 1978-79, pres. 1981-82), Am. Women in Radio and TV (nat. dir.-at-large 1971-73, nat. pub. affairs chmn. 1977-78), Nat. Acad. Television Arts and Scis., Los Angeles World Affairs Council, U. Calif. Law Alumni Assn. (dir. 1971-74), Order of Coif, Alpha Xi Delta, Phi Alpha Delta. Republican. Bd. editors: U. Calif. Law Rev., 1960-62. Home: 631 N Wilcox Ave Los Angeles CA 90004 Office: 7800 Beverly Blvd Los Angeles CA 90036

BRASSINGTON, MICHAEL JOHN, edn. assn. exec.; b. Tacoma, Wash., May 31, 1939; s. John Victor and Pearl Ardoth (Clinton) B.; student Central Wash. State Coll., 1958-60; A.B. in Bus. Adminstrn., U. Puget Sound, 1962; postgrad. John F. Kennedy U., Orinda, Calif., 1974-76. Ops. supr. Puget Sound Nat. Bank, Tacoma, 1957-62; workmen's compensation ins. underwriter Calif. Inspection Rating Bur., San Francisco, 1963-66; asst. exec. dir. Commonwealth Club of Calif., San Francisco, 1966-73, assoc. exec. dir., 1973-76, exec. dir., 1976—. Vice chmn. Devel. Com. for City of Pleasant Hill, Calif., 1972-74; bd. dirs. San Francisco Bay council Girl Scouts, 1978-81; mem. citizen's adv. com. East Bay Mcpl. Utility Dist. Served with U.S. Army, 1962-64. Recipient award of appreciation City of Pleasant Hill (Calif.), 1974. Mem. No. Calif., Am. socs. assn. execs., Western Govtl. Research Assn., Mechanics Inst., World Affairs Council No. Calif. (com. on fgn. relations San Francisco). Theta Chi. Clubs: Commonwealth of Calif., Town Hall. Asst. editor: The Commonwealth, 1966-70, mng. editor, 1970-76; researched, editor studies on Calif. State Ballot Measures, 1968, 70, 72, 74, 76, 78. Home: 343 Strand Ave Pleasant Hill CA 94523 Office: 681 Market St San Francisco CA 94105

BRATNOBER, JOHN POWERS, marketing manager; b. St. Paul, May 23, 1951; s. Harry Lewis Jr. and Patricia G. (Ray) B.; m. Margarita Ramos; 1 son, Tomas A. B.F.A., R.I. Sch. Design, 1974, M.F.A., 1976; M.A., U. Pa., 1982. Mktg. rep. Yearbook Med. Pub., Chgo., 1979-81; mktg. mgr. Med./Nursing div. Addison-Wesley Pub. Co., Menlo Park, Calif., 1982—. Mem. Med. Mktg. Assn., Bus./Profl. Advt. Assn. Office: Addison-Wesley Pub Co Med Nursing Div 2727 Sand Hill Rd Menlo Park CA 94025

BRATTAIN, WALTER HOUSER, physicist; b. Amoy, China, Feb. 10, 1902 (parents Am. citizens); s. Ross R. and Ottille (Houser) B.; B.S., Whitman Coll., 1924, D.Sc., 1955; M.A., U. Oreg., 1926; Ph.D., U. Minn., 1929; D.Sc., U. Portland, 1952, Union Coll., 1955, U. Minn., 1957, Gustavus Adolphus Coll., 1963; L.H.D., Hartwick Coll. 1964; m. Keren Gilmore, July 5, 1935 (dec. Apr. 1957); 1 son, William G.; m. 2d, Emma Jane Miller, May 10, 1958. With radio sect. Bur. Standards, 1928-29; research physicist Bell Telephone Labs., Murray Hill, N.J., 1929-67; with div. war research Columbia, 1942-43; vis. lectr. Harvard, 1952-53; part-time prof. Whitman Coll., Walla Walla, Wash., 1962-72, overseer emeritus, 1972-; specialized in study of semiconductors. Recipient Stuart Ballantine medal Franklin Inst., 1952, John Scott award City of Phila., 1955; (with William Shockley and John Bardeen) Nobel prize in Physics, 1956; named to Nat. Inventors Hall Fame, 1974. Fellow Am. Phys. Soc., AAAS, Explorers Club, Am. Acad. Arts and Scis.; mem. Franklin Inst., Nat. Acad. Scis., IEEE (hon.), Phi Beta Kappa, Sigma Xi. Co-inventor of transistor. Address: Whitman Coll Walla Walla WA 99362

BRATTEN, KENNARD CHARLES, govt. ofcl.; b. New England, N.D., June 24, 1916; s. Knute and Alma Clara (Ballweber) B.; student pub. schs.; m. Katherine Taft, Apr. 9, 1944 (dec. Dec. 1977); 1 son, Dan L. Owner, operator ranch, Slope County, N.D., 1933-41, Stanislaus County, Denair, Calif., 1945-70; dep. county auditor, Amidon, N.D., 1939-41; paymaster Grange Co., Modesto, Calif., 1947-62; postmaster, Denair, 1962-79; now rep. World Book Ency., Amway Quality Products; weather observer, Denair sta. Master, Gratton Grange 528, 1970-71; treas. Stanislaus Democratic Central Com., 1960-62. Served with AUS, 1941-45. Mem. Nat. Assn. Postmasters U.S. (past chpt. pres.), Nat. League Postmaster U.S., Denair C. of C. (past sec.), VFW (life), Am. Legion (life), DAV (life). Presbyterian. Clubs: Lions, Shriners, Masons, Scottish Rite. Address: 11249 E Grayson Rd Denair CA 95316

BRATTON, HOWARD CALVIN, fed. judge; b. Clovis, N.Mex., Feb. 4, 1922; s. Sam Gilbert and Vivian (Rogers) B.; B.A., U. N.Mex., 1941, LL.D. (hon.), 1971; LL.B., Yale U., 1947. Admitted to N.Mex. bar, 1948; law clk. U.S. Ct. Appeals, 1948; mem. firm Grantham & Bratton, Albuquerque, 1949-52; spl. asst. U.S. atty. charge litigation OPS, 1951-52; asso., then partner firm Hervey, Dow & Hinkle, Roswell, N.Mex., 1952-64; U.S. dist. judge Dist. N.Mex., 1964—, chief judge, 1978—. Chmn. pub. lands com. Interstate Oil Compact Commn., 1963-64. Mem. N.Mex. Commn. Higher Edn., 1962-64; bd. regents U. N.Mex., 1958-68, pres., 1963-64; mem. com. on operation of jury Jud. Conf. U.S., 1966-72, 79-82. Served to capt. AUS, 1942-45. Mem. N.Mex. Jr. (chmn. 1952), Chaves County (pres. 1962) bar assns., Trial Judges Assn. 10th Circuit (pres. 1976-78), N.Mex. Oil and Gas Assn. (chmn. pub. lands com. 1961-64). Office: US Courthouse Albuquerque NM 87103

BRATTSTROM, BAYARD HOLMES, educator; b. Chgo., July 3, 1929; s. Wilber LeRoy and Violet (Holmes) B.; B.S., San Diego State Coll., 1951; M.A., U. Calif. at Los Angeles, 1953, Ph.D., 1959; m. Cecile D. Funk, June 15, 1952; (div. May 1975); children—Theodore Allen, David Arthur; m. Martha A. Isaacs, July 8, 1982. Dir. edn. Natural History Mus., San Diego, 1949-51, asst. curator herpetology, 1951-56; asso. zoology UCLA, 1954-56; research fellow paleo ecology Calif. Inst. Tech., Pasadena, 1955; instr. biology Adelphi U., Garden City, N.Y., 1956-60; asst. prof. Calif. State U., Fullerton, 1960-61, asso. prof., 1961-66, prof., 1966—; asso. prof. zoology UCLA, summers 1962-63; hon. research asso. herpetology, vertebrate paleontology Los Angeles County Mus., 1961—. Pres. Fullerton Youth Mus. and Natural Sci. Center, 1962-64, dir., 1962-66. Recipient Disting. Teaching award, Calif. State U., 1968; Am. Philos. Soc. research grantee, Mexico, Panama, 1959; NSF grantee, 1964-66; NSF sr. postdoctoral fellow, Monash U., Australia, 1966-67. Fellow AAAS (mem. council 1965—), Herpetological League; mem. Am. Soc. Ichthyologists and Herpetologists (bd. govs. 1962-66, v.p. Western div. 1965), Orange County Zool. Soc. (bd. dirs. 1962-65, pres. 1962-64), So. Calif. Acad. Sci. (dir. 1964-67), Ecol. Soc. Am., Soc. for Study of Evolution, Soc. Systematic Zoology, San Diego Soc. Natural History, Soc. Vertebrate Paleontology, Am. Soc. Mammalogists, Cooper, Am. Ornithol. socs., Am. Soc. Zoologists, Sigma Xi. Author: The Talon Digs Deeply Into My Heart, 1974 (poetry); contbr. chpts. to books; contbr. articles in field to profl. jours. Office: Dept Biology Calif State Univ Fullerton CA 92634

BRAUN, BARBARA ILENE, advertising executive; b. Charleston, W.Va., May 8, 1944; d. Arthur Goodman and Charlotte C. Braun; B.S., Northwestern U., 1966; M.B.A., Pepperdine U., 1982. Supr., Leo Burnett Advt., Chgo., 1966-67; account coordinator Lake Public Relations, London, Eng., 1967-68; account exec. Beneficial Standard Corp., Los Angeles, 1968-70; asso. Argosy Group, Los Angeles, 1970-73; owner Braun & Assos., Los Angeles, 1973—; lectr., cons. in field. Mem. Nat. Assn. Female Execs. Phi Beta. Democrat. Office: 1460 4th St Santa Monica CA 90401

BRAUN, DAVID A., lawyer; b. N.Y.C., Apr. 23, 1931; s. Morris and Betty Braunstein; A.B., Columbia U., 1952, LL.B., 1954; m. Merna Feldman, Dec. 18, 1955; children—Lloyd, Kenneth, Evan. Admitted to N.Y. State bar, 1955, Calif. bar, 1974; asso. firm Ellis, Ellis & Ellis, N.Y.C., 1954-56, Davis & Gilbert, 1956-57; mem. firm Pryor, Cashman, Sherman & Flynn, N.Y.C., 1957-73; partner firm Hardee Barovick Konecky & Braun, N.Y.C., 1973, sr. partner Calif. office Los Angeles, 1974-80; pres., chief exec. officer Polygram Records, Inc., N.Y.C., 1980-81; ptnr. Wyman, Bautzer, Rothman, Kuchel & Silbert, 1982—. Mem. Nat. Acad. TV Arts and Scis. (past pres. N.Y. chpt.), Am. Arbitration Assn., Beverly Hills, Los Angeles County bar assns., Bar Assn. City N.Y. Home: 716 N Elm Dr Beverly Hills CA 90210 Office: 810 7th Ave New York NY 10019

BRAUN, GERALD CURTIS, psychologist; b. Red Wing, Minn., Aug. 24, 1946; s. Quentin Vernon and Marian Lucille (Stumpf) B.; B.A. with honors, St. Cloud State U., 1968, M.S., 1971; Ed.D., in counseling and personnel services U. Nev., Reno, 1981; m. Donna Susan Gustafson, Nov. 7, 1970; children—Eric, Kirsten, Rebecca, Joanna. Vocat. rehab. counselor Minn. Services for Blind, St. Paul, 1971-72; vocat. rehab. specialist VA, St. Paul, 1972-74, counseling psychologist, 1975-77; counseling psychologist trainee VA, Chgo., 1974-75; counseling psychologist, tech. supr. Nev. VA Regional Office Vocat. Rehab. and Counseling Activities, Reno., 1977—; instr. introduction to vocat. rehab. U. Nev., 1979—; pres. Vocat. Planning Service, Inc., Reno, Nev., 1982—. Served with U.S. Army, 1968-70. Decorated Army Commendation medal; cert. rehab. counselor Nat. Commn. Rehab. Counselor Certification. Mem. Am. Personnel and Guidance Assn., Am. Rehab. Counselor Assn. Democrat. Lutheran. Club: Elks (Reno). Office: VA Regional Office 245 E Liberty St Reno NV 89520

BRAUN, STEPHEN HUGHES, cons. psychologist; b. St. Louis, Nov. 20, 1942; s. William Lafon and Jane Louise B.; B.A., Washington U., St. Louis, 1964, M.A., 1965; Ph.D. (USPHS fellow in Clin. Psychology), U. Mo., Columbia, 1970; m. Penny Lee Prada, Aug. 28, 1965; 1 son, Damian Hughes. Asst. prof. psychology Calif. State U., Chico, 1970-71; dir. social learning div. Ariz. State Hosp., Phoenix, 1971-74; chief bur. planning and evaluation Ariz. Dept. Health Services, Phoenix, 1974-79; pres. Braun and Assocs., human service program cons.'s, Scottsdale, Ariz., 1979—; asst. prof. psychology Ariz. State U., 1971-79, vis. asst. prof. Ctr. of Criminal Justice, 1974-79, Ctr. for Public Affairs, 1979-81; cons. Law Enforcement Assistance Adminstrn., NIMH, Alcohol, Drug Abuse, and Mental Health Adminstrn., Ariz. Dept. Health Services, Ariz. Dept. Corrections, Ariz. Dept. Econ. Security, local and regional human service agys. NIMH research grantee, 1971-74; State of Calif. research grantee, 1971; cert. clin. psychologist, Ariz. Mem. Am. Psychol. Assn., Sigma Xi. Editorial cons.; contbr. articles to profl. publs. Home: 6122 E Calle Tuberia Scottsdale AZ 85251 Office: 7125 E Second St Scottsdale AZ 85251

BRAUNSTEIN, HERBERT, pathologist; b. N.Y.C., Jan. 10, 1926; s. Max and Ida (Meyerson) B.; B.S., CCNY and City U. N.Y., 1944; M.D., Hahnemann Med. Coll., 1950; m. Frances Toomey, Aug. 1, 1954; children—Sheila, Mary, John, Anne. Intern, Montefiore Hosp., N.Y.C., 1950-51; resident in pathology U. Mich., 1951-52, U. Cin., 1952-55; asst. prof. to asso. prof. pathology U. Cin., 1956-64; chmn. dept. pathology Michael Reese Hosp., also prof. pathology Chgo. Med. Sch., 1964-65; asso. prof. to prof. pathology U. Ky., 1965-70; chmn. dept. labs. San Bernardino County Med. Center, 1970-80; clin. prof. pathology Loma Linda U., 1980—, UCLA, 1980-83; prof. in residence biomed. scis. U. Calif., Riverside, 1979—; dir. sch. med. tech. San Bernardino County Med. Center, San Bernardino, Calif. Served with USNR, 1944-46; PTO. Recipient numerous research grants including Career Devel. award USPHS, 1958-64. Mem. AMA, Calif. Med. Assn., San Bernardino County Med. Soc., Am. Soc. Clin. Pathologists, Coll. Am. Pathologists, Internat. Acad. Pathology, Am. Assn. Pathologists, Histochem. Soc., Phi Beta Kappa, Sigma Xi, Alpha Omega Alpha. Republican. Contbr. articles to sci. jours., chpts. to books. Home: 30524 Los Altos Dr Redlands CA 92373 Office: 780 E Gilbert St San Bernardino CA 92404

BRAVERMAN-PAGE, MILLICENT LENORE, advertising executive, critic; b. N.Y.C.; d. Joseph Van and Rose (Alpert) Glub; m. Irving D. Braveran, Dec. 28, 1945 (div.); children—Kate, Harry A.; m. 2d, Earl Page, Sept. 18, 1981. Pres., Braverman-Mirisch Inc. advt. agy., Los Angeles, 1962—; critic daily radio program —A Word on Books—KFAC AM & FM, Los Angeles; lectr., cons. to publishers. Mem. adv. bd. UCLA, Am. Friends Hebrew U. Mem. Nat. Book Critics Circle, Western States Advt. Agys. Assn. (gold award pub. service, 1968). Office: 9255 Sunset Blvd Los Angeles 90069

BRAVO, LEONORE MCCRYSTLE, biologist, psychologist, conservationist; b. Vallejo, Calif., July 14, 1914; d. Arthur Bernard and Geraldine Marie (Winslow) McCrystle; B.A., San Francisco State U., 1934; M.A., U. Calif., Berkeley, 1947; m. Ignacio Bravo-Caro, Aug. 2, 1939; children—Nacho E., Michael A. Tchr. Indian schs. in Nev. and

Calif., 1937-40; tchr., adminstr. schs. in Calif., 1940-47; head psychologist Scramento Ccounty schs., 1948-51; tchr. San Francisco secondary schs., 1953-62; asst. prin. Indio (Calif.) High Sch., 1962-63; psychologist Oakland (Calif.) pub. schs., 1963-72, cons., 1972—; lectr. San Francisco Community Coll. Dist., 1975—; exec. sec. Tamalpais Conservation Club, 1974-77, bd. dirs., 1974—; pub. mem. Calif. Cling Peach Processors Adv. Bd., 1975-79. NSF fellow, 1957, 59-62; scholar intergroup relations Stanford U. NCCJ, 1959; fellow OAS, 1970. Mem. Am., Interam., Calif psychol. assns., Calif. Tchrs. Assn., Calif. Acad. Scis., Calif. Sch. Psychologists Assn., Western Apicultural Soc. (charter), People for Preservation of the Natural and Wild in Bay Area Open Space (founder, pres. 1977), San Francisco Beekeepers Assn. (founder 1976, pres. 1978, exec. sec. 1977-79), Women's Internat. League Peace and Freedom, Common Cause, Amnesty Internat., Calif. Wilderness Coalition, Internat. Platform Assn., San Francisco Democratic Women's Forum (dir. 1978-81, v.p. 1979), San Francisco Women for Peace, ACLU, Am. Friends Service Com., Friends of Earth, UN Assn., Wilderness Soc., U. Calif. Alumni Assn. (life), Consumers Coop. Berkeley. Author articles. Address: 47 Levant St San Francisco CA 94114

BRAY, ABSALOM FRANCIS, JR., lawyer; b. San Francisco, Nov. 24, 1918; s. A. F. and Leila (Veale) B.; A.B., Stanford, 1940; J.D., U. So. Calif., 1949; m. Lorraine Cerena Paule, June 25, 1949; children—Oliver W., Brian K., Margot E. Legal department Iowa Ordnance Plant, Burlington, 1940-42; admitted to Calif. bar, 1949, since practiced in Martinez; atty. Housing Authority of County of Contra Costa, Mt. Diablo Hosp. Dist.; past mem. adv. bd. Bank Am. Chmn. nat. bd. dirs. Camp Fire Girls; active Boy Scouts Am., Salvation Army; chmn. recreation commn. City of Martinez, 1949-54. Served as lt. USNR, 1942-46. Decorated Navy Commendation Ribbon, Navy Unit Citation. Mem. State Bar Calif. (chmn. adoption com. 1966), Contra Costa County Bar Assn. (pres. 1964), Navy League U.S. (pres. Contra Costa council 1981-83), Contra Costa County Devel. Assn. (pres. 1959-60), Am. Legion (comdr. 1955), V.F.W. (comdr. 1952), Soc. Calif. Pioneers, Contra Costa Hist. Soc., E. Clampus Vitus. Republican. Clubs: Rotary (pres. Martinez club 1970-71), Masons, Elks. Home: 600 Flora St Martinez CA 94553 Office: Ward and Ferry Sts Martinez CA 94553

BRAY, HAROLD VINCENT, JR., psychologist; b. Independence, Mo., Aug. 28, 1946; s. Harold Vincent and Marie Lucille B.; m. Suzanne Joy Couch, June 21, 1980. A.B., Westminster Coll., 1971; M.Ed., U. Mo., 1973; postgrad. U. Kans., 1974-75, Chapman Coll., 1977, U. Calif.-Berkeley, 1978; Ph.D., U.S. Internat. U., 1981; postgrad. McGeorge Sch. Law, U. Pacific, 1981, Harvard Med. Sch., 1983. Recreation dir./counselor Midwest Children's Ctr., 1970; clin. caseworker Mo. Dept. Mental Health, 1973-74; counselor Job Corps Tng. Ctr., Excelsior Springs, Mo., 1975; vocat. rehab. specialist VA, San Francisco, 1975-78; counselor Alcohol and Drug Abuse Div., Fort Ord, Calif., 1980; counseling psychologist VA, San Francisco, 1980-82, regional chmn. vocat. rehab. bd., 1981-82; clin. dir. U.S. Mil. Clinic, W.Ger., 1982—; instr. U. Md.-Europe, 1983—. Legis. asst. Mo. State Legislature, 1970-72; active Archtl. and Heritage Found., Vallejo, Calif.; mem. Republican Presdl. Task Force, 1981-83; mem. U.S. Congl. Adv. Bd., 1983—; mem. Rep. Senatorial Com., 1983—. Served with U.S. Army, 1966-68. Recipient Award for Research, Midwest Sociol. Soc., 1971, Mo. Soc. Sociology and Anthropology, 1970. Mem. ABA, Am. Psychol. Assn., AAAS, Psi Chi, Phi Alpha Delta. Republican. Presbyterian. Home: 89 D St Vallejo CA 94590 Office: USMCA HHQ CCC APO NY 09026

BRAY, JAMES OSCAR, economist; b. Monrovia, Ind., Dec. 31, 1920; s. Homer H. and Elizabeth (Shannon) B.; m. Marcile Seneff, Mar. 2, 1947; children—James H., Diane L., Carol A. B.S., Purdue U., 1943, M.S., 1948; A.M., U. Chgo., 1951, Ph.D., 1955; postdoctoral student Balliol Coll., Oxford, Eng., 1954. Asst. prof. agrl. econs. Kans. State U., 1951-56, assoc. prof., 1956; assoc. prof. econs. U. Chgo., Santiago, Chile, 1956-61; research assoc. Food Research Inst., Stanford, Calif., 1961-65, sr. economist SRI Internat., Menlo Park, Calif., 1965-78; pres. K & B Info. Systems, Los Altos Hills, Calif., 1972—; pres. Basic Bus. Computers, Los Altos Hills, 1979—; cons. World Bank, Argentina, Paraguay. Served with USAF, 1943-45. Mem. Am. Econs. Assn., Am. Agrl. Econ. Assn. Address: 27870 Altamont Circle Los Altos Hills CA 94022

BRAYER, HERBERT OLIVER, former ednl. adminstr.; b. Montreal, Que., Can., June 1, 1913 (parents Am. citizens); s. David Harold and Bertha Estelle (Boyland) B.; B.A., U. So. Calif., 1935; M.A., U. N.Mex., 1936; postgrad. (Panama-Pacific Golden Gate fellow), U. Calif. at Berkeley, 1937-38, Claremont Grad. Sch., 1964, U.S.I.U., 1968-69; H.H.D., U. London, 1973; m. Garnet Madeleine Kelly, Dec. 13, 1934 (dec. 1980); children—Kathleen (Mrs. John McCoy), Penelope Ann (Mrs. John Klipfel), Herbert Oliver, Michael Alan. Dir., Coronado Cuarto Centennial, N.M., 1939-40; archivist Denver & Rio Grande W. R.R. Co., 1941-43; state archivist, Colo., 1943-49; asst. prof. bus. history Northwestern U., 1949-53; asso. editor Am. Bus. Mag., 1954-56; prof. office automation Loyola U., Chgo., 1956-61; med. economist, exec. sec. Riverside County Med. Assn., Riverside, Calif., 1961-65; chmn. social sci. dept. Moreno Valley High Sch., Sunnymead, Calif., 1963-68; coordinator Title III, Coronado (Calif.) Unified Sch. Dist., 1968-70; asso. supt. edn. State of Ariz., Phoenix, 1970-71; coordinator Orange County Dept. Edn., Santa Ana, Calif., 1971-78; chmn. bd. Timeo Found., 1977—. Bd. dirs. Children's Home Soc., Vis. Nurses Assn. Social Sci. Research Council fellow, 1942-43. Fellow N. Mex. Hist. Assn.; mem. Soc. Am. Archivists (past nat. v.p.), Westerners (past pres.). Lion (dir. 1969-71). Author numerous books including: William Blackmore: The Spanish-Mexican Land Grants of New Mexico and Colorado 1863-1878, 2 vols., 1949, Pueblo Indian Land Grants of New Mexico, 1950, Pikes Peak-or Busted, 1954, Teenage Drug Abuse, an Innovative Solution, 1969; Valuing in the Family, 1973; Youth Involvement: A Teen-Preteen Student Counseling Leadership Manual, 1977; also monographs, pageants, scripts. Contbr. numerous articles to publs. Home: 31801 Westwood Dr Fort Bragg CA 95437

BRAYFIELD, FRANCES MCEACHERN, ednl. adminstr.; b. Jacksonville, Fla., Jan. 8, 1933; d. Don and Mayhoward (Austin) McEachern; B.A., U. Fla., 1956; M.A., Vanderbilt U., 1960; m. Arthur Hills Brayfield, July 28, 1968; stepchildren—Ann, Douglas, Don, Jean. Psychometrist spl. edn. dept. Tenn. Dept. Edn., 1958-59; cons., 1959-60; psychol. examiner Clover Bottom State Sch. & Hosp., Nashville, 1960; research psychologist Child Guidance Clinic, Children's Meml. Hosp., Chgo., 1961-63; adminstrv. asso. Am. Psychol. Assn., Washington, 1964-65; research asso., field dir. heart project. Med. Center, Vanderbilt U., Nashville, 1965-68; dir. career planning office Scripps Coll., Claremont, Calif., 1973-82, cons., 1982—. Mem. Am. Psychol. Assn., Am. Personnel and Guidance Assn., Claremont Civic Assn. Democrat. Author; (with Jerome Schulman and Joseph Kaspar) Brain Damage and Behavior, 1965; (with Rue Cromwell, Earl Butterfield, John Curry) Acute Myocardial Infarction: Nursing Care and Recovery, 1977. Contbg. author Progress in clinical Psychology, Vol. VII, 1966. Editor (with Robert Lockman) Preconference Materials Prepared for the Conference on the Professional Preparation of Clinical Psychologists, 1965. Home: 1030 Alamosa Dr Claremont CA 91711 Office: Career Planning Office Scripps Coll Claremont CA 91711

BRAYFIELD-CAVE, SUSAN ELAINE, psychologist; b. Dallas, Oct. 3, 1948; d. James Daniel and Polly Anne (Sanders) Rden; m. Robert Lyle Cave, Oct. 7, 1966; m. 2d, Donald Arthur Brayfield, Aug. 25, 1980; children—Ryan Arthur, Jessica Annemarie. B.A., Calif. State U., 1970; M.A., U. N.Mex., 1977, Ph.D., 1979. Lic. psychologist, N.Mex. Grad. asst. dept. psychology U. N.Mex., Albuquerque, 1971-73; counselor N.Mex. Dept. Corrections, Santa Fe, and psychology counselor, trainer N.Mex. Girls Sch., 1973-75; dir. clin. services health and environ. dept., Forensic Hosp., Las Vegas, 1976-79; pres., treas. S.W. Psychol. Services, Inc., Santa Fe, 1979—; exec. dir. N.E. Forensic Team and Sex Offenders Treatment Program, Santa Fe, 1981—; cons. in field. Mem. S.W. Extraterritorial Neighborhood Assn., 1981—. Mem. Am. Psychol. Assn., N.Mex. Psychol. Assn., Phi Kappa Phi. Democrat. Contbr. articles to profl. jours. Office: 839 Paseo Dr Peralta Suite D Santa Fe NM 87501

BRAYTON, DONALD FORREST, medical center administrator; b. Salt Lake City, Aug. 4, 1912; s. Dean Fleming and Aileen Mariner (Maclean) B.; A.B., Stanford U., 1934; M.D. cum laude, Harvard U., 1939; m. Virginia Esther Mayo, June 14, 1940; children—John Hamilton, Deborah Mayo Brayton Berger; m. 2d, Sarah Irene Conley, Sept. 9, 1961. Intern, then resident in gen. surgery St. Luke's Hosp., N.Y.C., 1939-41, 45-47; practice medicine specializing in pediatric and gen. surgery, Los Angeles, 1947-65; assoc. dean postgrad. edn. and community med. program UCLA, also dir. continuing edn. in health scis., project dir. med. media network, 1965-76, dir. UCLA regional med. program, coordinator Calif. Regional Med. Programs, 1967-73; med. dir. Kern Med. Center, Bakersfield, Calif., 1975-82; dir. profl. edn. UCLA Jonsson Comprehensive Cancer Center, 1982—; cons. surgeon Harbor Gen. Hosp., Torrance, Calif., Children's Hosp., Los Angeles; adv. com. Nat. Legal Program Health Problems Poor, OEO, 1969-73. Served to maj. M.C., AUS, 1942-45. Fellow ACS (gov. 1969-74, pres. So. Calif. br. 1967); mem. Los Angeles Surg. Soc. (pres. 1961), Pacific Coast Surg. Assn., Western Surg. Assn., Los Angeles Acad. Medicine. Contbr. articles med. jours. Home: 11687 Montana Ave Apt 107 Los Angeles CA 90049 Office: UCLA Jonsson Comprehensive Cancer Center 10920 Wilshire Blvd Suite 1106 Los Angeles CA 90024

BRAYTON, SANDRA KING, advertising agency executive; b. Torrance, Calif. Mar. 6, 1944; d. Walter Raymond and Eleanor Christina (Mehlhoff) King; m. George Brayton, Dec. 31, 1974 (div.); 1 son, Beau King. B.B.A., U. Miami, 1966. Sales rep. Chart Pak, N.Y.C., 1966-67; mem. acctg. staff Air Calif., Newport Beach, 1967-69; mktg. rep. U.S. Fin., Sandiego and Santa Ana, Calif., 1969-70, dir. advt. and pub. relations, 1970-72, regional sales mgr., 1972-73; account exec. Hubbert Advt., Tustin, Calif., 1973-74; pres. King Advt. and Pub. Relations, Inc., Newport Beach, Calif., 1974—; lectr. career counseling, advt. Vol. worker Orangewood Home of Dependent Children, Arthritis Telethon. Recipient 5 Mame awards Bldg. Industry Assn. Orange County Advt. Fedn., Indsl. League Orange County, Sales and Mktg. Council, Bldg. Industry Assn., Home Builders Council. Republican.

BRAZELTON, EUGENIA LOUISE, interior designer; b. Groesbeck, Tex., Sept. 4, 1919; d. Richard Oliver and Mary Elsie (Kierbow) B. A.A., Pasadena City Coll., 1941; student N.Y. Sch. Interior Design, 1944, UCLA, 1945-46. Freelance designer Los Angeles, 1945-47; staff designer, Barker Bros. Co., Los Angeles, 1948-58; owner, designer Interiors By Louise, Newport Beach, Calif., 1960-62; designer with several firms in Orange County, 1962-82; cons.; freelance travel writer; instr. Glendale Jr. Coll., 1953-55, Orange Coast Coll., 1960-66. Founding mem. Women's Div., Newport Harbor C. of C., 1960. Recipient award Orange County Builders Assn., 1965. Mem. Am. Soc. Interior Designers (cert.). Republican. Author various publs. on travel. Home and Office: 512 Tustin Ave Newport Beach CA 92663

BRAZELTON, FRANK ALEXANDER, optometry educator; b. Chgo., May 22, 1926; s. Frank Alexander and Katharine (Keating) B.; m. Margaret Shean, Aug. 14, 1948 (div.); m. Dorothy Mellem, Dec. 20, 1971 (div.); children—Stephen, Martin, Claire, Kathleen. Student Loyola U., Los Angeles, 1946-48; O.D., So. Calif. Coll. Optometry, 1951; M.S.Ed., U. So. Calif., 1975. Lic. optometrist, Calif. Instr. optometry, So. Calif. Coll. Optometry, Fullerton, 1952-55, asst. prof., 1955-58, assoc. prof., 1958-65, prof., 1965—, dir. low vision ctr., 1968-73, dir. clin. tng., 1973-77, chmn. dept. profl. studies, 1977-82. Served with USNR, 1944-46; PTO. Mem. Am. Acad. Optometry (exec. council 1976—, sec.-treas. 1982—), Nat. Bd. Examiners Optometry (pres. 1978-80), Council Optometric Edn., Am. Optometric Assn., AAAS, AAUP. Democrat. Roman Catholic. Contbr. to numerous textbooks. Home: 1505 Sherwood Village Circle Placentia CA 92670 Office: 2001 Associated Rd Fullerton CA 92631

BRAZER, WYNONA MARIE, association executive, accountant; b. Seattle, Mar. 6, 1937; d. Perry Henry and Katherine Emma (Bjordal) Moler; m. Henry Brazer, Dec. 1, 1955 (div.); children—Ronald, Kenneth, Gregory, Jeffory, Samuel, Nancy. A.A., Olympic Community Coll., 1971. Gen. clk. GN and NP Laureland, Billings, Mont., 1955-63; office mgr. Denny's Music Co., Portland, Oreg., 1971-72; bookkeeper GAM Distbg. Co., Portland, 1972; Acme Signs Inc., Portland, 1972-73; acct. Old Spaghetti Factory Inc., Portland, 1973-74; close-down mgr., lead acct. Portland Met. Steering Com., 1973-78; asst. controller Harsh Investment Inc., Portland, 1979; acctg. mgr. United Cerebral Palsy Assn., Portland, 1980-83; budget dir. Am. Cancer Soc., Oakland, Calif., 1983—. Mem. Am. Bus. Women Assn., Nat. Assn. Female Execs., Nat. C. of C. for Women. Democrat. Roman Catholic. Home: 240 Dolores St Apt 236 San Francisco CA 94103

BRAZINSKI, JOHN ARTHUR, lawyer; b. Elizabeth, N.J., May 28, 1946; s. Adolph Bartholomew and Anne Marie (Hamley) B.; m. Valerie Kaminski (div.). B.A. Coll. of Holy Cross, 1968; LL.D., Georgetown U., 1971. Bar: Wyo. 1980. Sole practice Jackson Hole, Wyo., 1980—. Co-chmn. Jackson Hole Jr. Miss Pageant, 1983; co-chmn. Dagan Lustfield Fund. Mem. Teton County Bar Assn., ABA (sect. taxation), Practising Law Inst. Democrat. Roman Catholic. Club: Jackson Hole Lions (sgt. at arms 1982, sec. 1982-83). Office: Hansen Office Bldg 290 E Broadway Jackson WY 83001

BRECHBILL, SUSAN REYNOLDS, govt. ofcl.; b. Washington, Aug. 22, 1943; d. Irving and Isabell Doyle (Reynolds) Levine; B.A., Coll. William and Mary, 1965; J.D., Marshall-Wythe Sch. Law, 1968; m. Raymond A. Brechbill, June 29, 1973; children—Jennifer Rae, Heather Lea. Admitted to Va. bar, 1969, Fed. bar, 1970; atty. AEC, Berkeley, Calif., 1968-73, indsl. relations specialist AEC, Las Vegas, 1974-75; atty. ERDA, Oakland, Calif., 1976-77; atty. Dept. Energy, Oakland, 1977-78, dir. procurement div. San Francisco Ops. Office, 1978—; mem. faculty U. Calif. Extension; speaker Nat. Contract Mgmt. Assn. Ann. Symposiums, 1980, 81; speaker on doing bus. with govt. Leader Girl Scouts U.S.A., Los Angeles area. Named Outstanding Young Woman Nev., 1974. Mem. Va. State Bar Assn., Fed. Bar Assn., Nat. Contract Mgmt. Assn., Nat. Assn. Female Execs. Republican. Christian Scientist. Contbr. articles to profl. jours. Home: 67 Scenic Dr Orinda CA 94563 Office: 1333 Broadway Oakland CA 94612

BRECK, ALLEN DUPONT, educator; b. Denver, May 21, 1914; s. Chesney Yales and Isabel Estelle (Lee) B.; B.A., U. Denver, 1936, L.H.D. (hon.), 1973; M.A., U. Colo., 1939, Ph.D., 1950; D.Litt. (hon.) Regis Coll., 1974; m. Alice Rose Wolfe, Sept. 7, 1944 (dec. June 1973); 1 dau., Anne Rose Breck Peterson; m. 2d, Salome Ripley Hansen, Dec. 19, 1974. Tchr. pub. schs., Denver, 1936-42, prof. history U. Denver, 1946—; Danforth lectr., 1949-61; mem. commn. on coll. student Am. Council on Edn., 1958-61. Mem. Colo. Commn. on Ednl. Standards, 1962-65; v.p. Colo. Commn. on Social Studies, 1964-68; regional program chmn. Danforth Found., 1960-63. Served with Field Artillery, U.S. Army, 1942-46. Danforth Asso., 1946—. Fellow Royal Hist. Soc. Gt. Britain; mem. Am. Hist. Assn., Medieval Acad. Am., Rocky Mounta Renaissance and Medieval Assn. (pres. 1968—), Far Western Slavic Conv., Western Social Sci. Assn., Western History Assn., Phi Beta Kappa, Lambda Chi Alpha, Phi Alpha Theta, Omicron Delta Kappa. Republican. Episcopalian. Author: A Centennial History of the Jews of Colorado, 1960; Johannis Wyclyf Tractatus de Trinitate, 1962; Episcopal Church in Colorado, 1860-1963, 1963; William Gray Evans, Western Business Executive, 1964; John Evans of Denver, 1971; Episcopal Church in Colorado, 1960-78, 1978; editor: Internat. Colloquim I: Physical Science, History, Philosophy, 1968, II: Biological Science, History, Natural Philsophy, 1971; III: Cosmology, History Theology, 1975; The West in America series, 1960—: Colorado Ethnic History series, 1977—; contbr. articles to profl. jours. Home: 2060 S St Paul St Denver CO 80210 Office: Dept History U Denver Denver CO 80208

BRECKENRIDGE, ROBERT ARTHUR, civil engineer; b. Los Angeles, Mar. 29, 1924; s. Chester Arthur and Helen (Twomey) B.; B.Engring., U. So. Calif., 1950, M.S., 1953; divorced; children—Sharon J. Breckenridge Trusty, John A.; m. 2d Elena Maluchin. With U.S. Navy Civil Engring. Lab., Port Hueneme, Calif., 1950-79, mgr. ocean engring. program, 1968-73, dir. found. engring. div., 1973-79; cons. civil engr. in pvt. practice, Los Angeles, 1979—. Served with AUS, 1942-45. Decorated Purple Heart with oak leaf cluster; registered profl. engr., Calif. Fellow ASCE; mem. Sci. Research Soc. Am. (past chpt. pres.), Calif. Soc. Profl. Engrs. (past chpt. pres.), Marine Tech. Soc., Am. Concrete Inst., Chi Epsilon, Phi Eta Sigma. Republican. Author tech. reports, papers in field. Patentee blast activated ventilator valve. Home and Office: 17132 Lynn St Apt A Huntington Beach CA 92649

BREDEMEIER, LORENZ FRIEDRICH, conservationist, consultant; b. Mayberry, Nebr., Apr. 2, 1911; s. Friedrich Wilhelm and Louisa (Gottula) B.; m. Audrey White, June 23, 1938; children—Linda Kay Bredemeier Holloway, Lana Loumeda Bredemeier McWilliams, Brenda Jean Bredemeier Kuehner. B.S., U. Nebr., 1934, M.S., 1938. Asst. agr. agt. Nebr. Agr. Extension, Lincoln, 1934-36, adminstrv. asst., 1936-38; jr agronomist Soil Conservation Service, U.S. Dept. Agr., Centerville, Iowa, 1938-39, Corydon, Iowa, 1939-41, soil conservationist, Auburn, Nebr., 1941-42, dist. conservationist, Hebron, Nebr., 1942-44, O'Neill, Nebr., 1944-48, Valentine, Nebr., 1948-49, area conservationist, Valentine, 1949-51, range conservationist, Valentine, 1951-52, North Platte, Nebr., 1952-63, Milw., 1963-64, resource devel. specialist, Madison, 1964-69, range conservationist, Ft. Worth, 1969-73; agrl. research officer, Maseru, Lesotho, 1974-78; cons. in range mgmt., resource conservation, land and resource use, 1978—; cons. in field. Recipient Superior Accomplishment award U.S. Dept. Agr., 1948, Outstanding Performance award, 1962; Nebr. Range Mgmt. award, 1965; Nebr. Centennial Grassland Mgmt. award, 1966. Mem. Am. Inst. Biol. Sci., AAAS, Ecol. Soc. Am., Soc. Range Mgmt., Soil Conservation Soc. Am., Tech. and Sci. Soc. Range Mgmt. (pres. 1971), Alpha Zeta, Gamma Sigma Delta, Alpha Gamma Rho. Methodist. Clubs: Masons, Shriners, Lions, Toastmaster. Contbr. articles to profl. jours. Home and office: 6507 S Pike Dr Larkspur CO 80118

BREDLOW, THOMAS GAYLE, designer, metalworker; b. Pontiac, Mich., Oct. 18, 1938; s. Warren Kenneth and Elizabeth (La Ponsa) B.; B.A. in Math., Tex. A&M Coll., 1960; postgrad. U. Ariz., 1960-61. Machinist, phys. dept. Tex. A&M Coll., 1958-60, U. Ariz., 1960-62; owner, sole metalworker, Tom Bredlow's Blacksmith Shop, Tucson, Ariz., 1964—; guest speaker Sch. of Architecture, Sch. of Anthropology, U. Ariz., 1965—; acting pres., dir. Artist-Blacksmith Assn., 1978-80; lectr.-demonstrator, metal work confs. throughout U.S., 1976—; chmn. Internat. Blacksmithing Conf., 1980. Served to lt. U.S. Army, 1962-64. Decorated Army Commendation Medal. Clubs: Mountain Oyster (hon. artist life mem.) (Tucson). Commd. works include: gates, railings, flower stands, candle stick, Church of Sts. Peter and Paul, The Nat. Cathedral, Washington, 1968—, gates, railings, grilles, handrails, downspouts, Barrio Historico, Tucson, 1970-75; gates, lighting fixtures, furniture, door hardware, sculpture, grilles, placques, wall decoration, tool making and dressing, restoration work, general blacksmithing to general public, 1960—. Contbr. articles to profl. jours. Home: 3524 N Olive Rd Tucson AZ 85719 Office: 1827 E Limberlost Tucson AZ 85719

BREECE, JENANNE NELSON, lawyer; b. Evanston, Ill., Dec. 30, 1941; d. Oscar William and Anne L. (Moll) Nelson. B.S. magna cum laude, U. So. Calif., 1967, J.D., 1976; M.B.A., NYU, 1972. Admitted to D.C. bar, 1977, Calif. bar, 1983; sec., corp. officer Sta. KUPD-AM-FM, Phoenix, 1959-61; media dir. West, Weir & Bartel, Los Angeles, 1962-65; asso. media dir. Eisaman, Johns & Laws, Los Angeles, 1966-68; media supr. Ogilvy & Mathers, N.Y.C., 1968-69; v.p. media and mktg. services Smith-Gent Advt. Co., N.Y.C., 1969-71; media supr. The Media Dept., N.Y.C., 1971-72; v.p. media Perkal Advt. Co., Los Angeles, 1972-74; research asst. U. So. Calif. Law Center, 1975-76; atty. advisor Complaints and Compliance div. Broadcast Bur. FCC, Washington, 1977-80; gen. atty. Nev. Ops. Office, Office Chief Counsel, U.S. Dept. Energy, Las Vegas, 1980—. Mem. ABA, Calif. Bar Assn., D.C. Bar, Fed. Bar Assn., Los Angeles Advt. Women, U. So. Calif. Alumni, Phi Beta Kappa, Beta Gamma Sigma. Democrat. Presbyterian. Clubs: Mensa, Cactus & Succulent Soc., Sierra, North Shore Animal League. Office: US Dept Energy Office Chief Counsel PO Box 14100 Las Vegas NV 89114

BREED, WILLIAM JOSEPH, geologist, tour leader, author; b. Massillon, Ohio, Aug. 3, 1928; s. Earl Fremont and Grace Amelia (Snyder) B.; B.A., Denison U., 1952; B.S., U. Ariz., 1955, M.S., 1960; Fulbright scholar Canterbury Coll., Christchurch, N.Z., 1957-58; m. Carol Sameth Carter, Dec. 12, 1965; 1 dau., Amelia Frances. Instr., Yavapai Coll., Clarkdale, Ariz., 1976-78; naturalist, tour guide to Alaska, N.Z., Galapagos Islands, Nature Expdns. Internat., Palo Alto, Calif., 1978—; head geology dept. Mus. No. Ariz., Flagstaff, 1978-80; mem. U.S. geodynamics com. NRC-Nat. Acad. Scis., 1970—; geology curator Mus. No. Ariz., 1960-78; mem. NSF expdn. to Antaractica, 1969-70; mem. Ariz. Atomic Energy Commn., 1979-80, Ariz. Bd. Pesticide Control, 1976-79, Radiation Regulatory Hearing Bd., 1981—; mem. dose assessment adv. council Dept. Energy, 1980—; co-investigator NSF and NASA grants; guest lectr. Soc. Expdns. to Antartica, 1983. Served with AUS, 1947-48. Recipient Antarctic Service medal NSF, 1977. Fellow Geol. Soc. Am. (Gladys M. Cole award 1982), AAAS; mem. Soc. Econ. Paleontologists and Mineralogists, Soc. Vertebrate Paleontologists, Antarctican Soc., Ariz. Acad. Sci. (pres. 1974-75), Grand Canyon Natural History Assn. (dir. 1975-80), Four Corners Geol. Soc., N.Mex. Geol. Soc., N.Z. Geol. Soc., Ariz. Geol. Soc., Sigma Xi. Co-author: Geologic Map of Grand Canyon, 1976; Geologic Map of Canyonlands; editor: Geology of Grand Canyon, 1974; contbr. articles to Nat. Geog., Natural History mag., Ariz. Hwys. and profl. jours. Home: 1456 Meade Ln Flagstaff AZ 86001 Office: Box 1424 Flagstaff AZ 86001

BREEDEN, CAROLYN SULLIVAN, curriculum coordinator, educator, designer, consultant; b. Great Bend, Kans., Apr. 6, 1943; d. T.R. and Lillian Oleta (Weaver) Sullivan; m. Ronald Gene Breeden, Dec. 23, 1961; children—Ronald Gene, Jon Charles. B.A. in Home Econs., Kans. State U., 1966; M.A. in Textile Sci. and Design (Outstanding Designer award), Calif. State U.-Long Beach, 1976; postgrad. U. So. Calif., 1984—. Instr., dept. chmn. Anaheim Union High Sch. Dist., 1966-73; instr. pub. relations Southwestern Bell Telephone, Hays, Kans., 1965-66; instr., dept. chmn. family and consumer studies Santa Ana (Calif.) Community Coll., 1974-82, curriculum coordinator, instr., 1982—. Recipient Rotary Club Outstanding Citizen award 1965; Women in Community Coll. Adminstrn. Leaders of 80s award 1981. Mem. Am. Vocat. Assn., Am. Assn. Research Postsecondary Edn., Am. Assn. Women Community and Jr. Colls., Am. Home Econs. Assn., Calif. Home Econs. Assn., Assn. Coll. Profs. Textiles and Clothing, Inst. Bus. Designers, Interior Design Edn. Council, Am. Soc. Interior Designers, Kappa Omicron Phi. Author: Designing Home Interiors: A Study Guide for Telecourses, 1979; A Matter of Taste, 1980; Light Cuisine, 1981. Home: 2535 Juanita Way Laguna Beach CA 92651 Office: 17th at Bristol Sts Santa Ana CA 92706

BREEN, MARVIN GOLDEN, securities co. exec.; b. New Orleans, Aug. 11, 1930; s. Nathaniel and Bluma (Teles) B.; B.S., La. State U., 1955; m. Carole Rambach, Dec. 23, 1956; children—Robin, Neff. Trainee Merrill Lynch Pierce Fenner & Smith, New Orleans, 1955, account exec., 1956-69, mgmt. staff, N.Y.C., 1969-70, partner, 1965, v.p., 1971—, br. mgr., Clayton, Mo., 1970-75; mem. Chgo. Bd. Options Exchange, 1975—; mem. Pacific Stock Exchange, 1976—, mem. options governing com., 1977-80. Bd. dirs. numerous civic orgns. Served to capt. AUS, 1950-53. Home: 18 Noche Vista Ln Tiburon CA 94920 Office: Merrill Lynch Pierce Fenner & Smith Pacific Stock Exchange 301 Pine St San Francisco CA 94104

BREIDENBACH, STEVEN THEODORE, research psychologist; b. Oakes, N.D., June 30, 1953; s. Theodore Michael and Elizabeth Catherine (Ackerman) B.; m. Cherie Elizabeth Johnson, Aug. 9, 1975. B.A., U. S.D., 1975, M.A. in Human Factors/Applied Exptl. Psychology, 1977, Ph.D., 1979. Research asst. Human Factors Lab., U. S.D., 1975-77, 78-79; personnel mgmt. specialist State of Wyo., 1977-78; assoc. scientist Dunlap and Assocs., Inc., La Jolla, Calif., 1979-83; research psychologist U.S. Navy Personnel Research and Devel. Center, San Diego, 1983—; tech. adv. Tng. Tech. Jour. Mem. Am. Psychol. Assn., Human Factors Soc., Soc. Applied Learning Tech., Soc. Engring. Psychologists, Alpha Tau Omega. Republican. Roman Catholic. Contbr. articles to profl. jours. Home: 5560 Caminito Jose San Diego CA 92111 Office: US Navy Personnel Research and Devel Center San Diego CA 92152

BREINER, SHELDON, business executive, geophysics educator; b. Milw., Oct. 23, 1936; s. James and Fannie (Apple) B.; m. Phyllis Farrington, Feb. 4, 1962; children—David, Michelle. B.S., Stanford U., 1959, M.S., 1962, Ph.D. in Geophysics, 1967. Registered geophysicst, geologist, Calif. Product mgr. Varian Assocs., 1961-68; founder, chmn. Geometrics, 1969—; chmn. Syntelligence, Inc.; dir. Cadtec Corp., OSI, Inc.; pres. Paramagnetic Logging, Inc.; chmn. Fracture Tech.; pres. Foothill Assocs.; cons. prof., lectr. geophysics Stanford U.; lectr. Stanford Grad. Sch. Bus.; cons. archaeol. exploration problems and search for buried objects. Trustee Peninsula Open Space Trust; vice chmn. Resource Ctr. for Women; maj. gifts com. Stanford U. Served with U.S. Army, 1960. Honors scholar, 1955-56; NSF grantee for earthquake research, 1965. Fellow Explorers Club; mem. Soc. Exploration Geophysicists, Am. Geophys. Union, European Assn. Exploration Geophysicists. Democrat. Jewish. Author: Applications Manual for Portable Magnetometers, 1973; contbr. articles profl. jours. Patentee in oil exploration; inventor gun detector in use at all airports; runner Boston Marathon. Home: 45 Buckeye St Portola Valley CA 94025 Office: 395 Java Dr Sunnyvale CA 94086

BREITBARD, ROBERT, sports exec.; grad. San Diego State Coll., U. So. Calif.; m. Lillie Breitbard; children—Denise, Gayle. Pres. San Diego Sports Enterprises, San Diego Gulls Hockey Club; founder Breitbard Athletic Found.; pres. Calif. Linen & Indsl. Supply. Founder San Diego Hall of Champions. Office: 101 16th St San Diego CA 92101 Mailing Address: Calif Linen and Indsl Supply PO Box 28 San Diego CA 92112

BREJCHA, ALBERT GEORGE, JR., electronics engineer; b. Chgo., Dec. 23, 1939; s. Albert George and Frances (Sedlak) B.; m. Lucille Genevieve Bujak, Aug. 8, 1964; children—Dawn Marie, Lisa Louise. A.A., Morton Jr. Coll., 1960; B.S. in Elec. Engring., U. Ill., 1963, M.S. in Elec. Engring., 1964, M.B.A., Calif. State Poly. U., 1976. With Jet Propulsion Lab., Pasadena, Calif., 1964—, engr. spacecraft antenna research, 1964-66, cognizant engr. Mariner Mars antenna subsystem, 1966-68, tech. mgr., 1968-70, tech. mgr. Mariner-Venus-Mercury and Viking Orbiter spacecraft antenna subsystems, 1970-81, group supr. spacecraft antenna group, 1972-82, product requirements and assurance mgr. def. programs, 1982—. Recipient Sci. Recognition award for devel. low loss coaxial connector NASA, 1971, Mariner-Mars group achievement award, 1970, Apollo achievement award, 1970, Mariner-Venus-Mercury group achievement award, 1974, Viking group achievement award, 1978, Seasat group achievement award, 1979, Shuttle Imaging Radar group achievement award, 1982, others. Mem. IEEE. Roman Catholic. Patentee in field. Office: Jet Propulsion Lab 4800 Oak Grove Dr Pasadena CA 91103

BREMER, RONALD ALLAN, genealogist, editor; b. South Gate, Calif., May 2, 1937; s. Carl Leonard and Lena Evelyn (Jury) B.; m. Joan Ellen Brenner, Apr. 30, 1967 (div.); children—Elizabeth, Hans, Adam, Rachel. Student Los Angeles Trade Tech., Cerritos Coll., Am. U., Brigham Young U. Research specialist Geneal. Soc., Salt Lake City, 1969-72; profl. lectr. on genealogy, Salt Lake City, 1973-83; editor Genealogy Digest mag., Salt Lake City, 1983—; lectr. in field. Mem. German Harmony Choir. Mem. Fedn. Geneal. Socs. (founder), Wholistic Soc. (founder), Assn. Geneal. Editors (founder). Republican. Mormon. Author: World's Funniest Epitaphs, 1982; Ron Bremer's Genealogy Handbook, 1983. Office: PO Box 16422 Salt Lake City UT 84115

BREMER, WILLIAM RICHARD, lawyer; b. San Francisco, Jan. 5, 1930; s. Milton Arthur and Alice (Herring) B.; B.S., Menlo Coll., 1952; J.D., U. San Francisco, 1958; m. Margaret C. Herrington; children—Mark Richard, Karen Elizabeth, William Richard. Admitted to Calif. bar, 1959, Dist. Ct. bar, 1959, Circuit Ct. Appeals bar, 1959, U.S. Supreme Ct. bar, 1965, U.S. Ct. Mil. Appeals bar, 1973; gen. trial practice civil and criminal law, San Francisco, 1959—; arbitrator San Francisco and Marin County Superior Ct., 1977—; guest lectr. Menlo Coll., 1978. City councilman, Tiburon, Calif., 1966-70; mayor of Tiburon, 1968-69. Bd. dirs. Tiburon Peninsula Found., v.p. and gen. counsel, 1970—; bd. dirs. Bay Area USO, 1980—. Served with USMC, 1952-54; col. Res. Mem. Am., Marin County, San Francisco bar assns., Am., Calif. (dir. San Francisco chpt. 1969-73) trial lawyers assns., Marine Corps Res. Officers Assn. (pres. San Francisco council 1978-79), Navy League U.S. (pres. San Francisco Council 1978-80, nat. dir. 1978—, regional v.p. 1980, state pres. Calif. (North) 1981), Naval Order U.S. (pres. San Francisco commandery 1982—), Res. Officers Assn., Am Arbitration Assn. (panel arbitrator 1965—), Tiburon Landmarks Soc., Marin Conservation League, San Francisco Mus. Soc., Far East Soc., Royal Brit. Legion, Am. Philatelic Soc. Phi Alpha Delta. Clubs: Commonwealth of Calif., Marine Meml., Queens, Montgomery St. Motorcycle (pres. 1974, dir.), San Francisco Press, Kiwanis (bd. dirs. 1981—), Corinthian Yacht (bd. dirs. 1982—). Home: 120 Taylor Rd Tiburon CA 94920 Office: 595 Golden Gate Ave San Francisco CA 94102

BREMNER, JAMES DOUGLAS, psychiatrist; b. Lynden, Wash., Aug. 9, 1932; s. George Adelbert and Marian Alice (Bay) B.; student U. Puget Sound, 1949-52; M.D., U. Wash., 1956; m. Linnea Marie Leonardson, June 4, 1966; children—Steven, Lynn, Anne, James Douglas. Intern, USPHS Hosp., N.Y.C., 1956-57; resident Menninger Sch. Psychiatry and Topeka VA Hosp., 1959-62; practice medicine specializing in psychiatry, Olympia, Wash., 1962—; clin. asso. prof. psychiatry U. Wash., 1968—; pharm. research Hoechst-Roussel, Hoffman-LaRoche, Eli Lilly, Sandoz, Shering; staff mem. St. Peter Hosp.; cons. Madigan Army Hosp. Chmn. bd. Thurston County Guidance Assn., 1965-66; bd. dirs. Wash. Capital Hist. Assn., 1963-64. Served with USPHS, 1956-59. Fellow Am. Psychiat. Assn. (pres. Tacoma chpt. 1968-69, pres. N. Pacific br. 1972-73); mem. Am., Wash. med. assns., Fellows Assn. Menninger Sch. Psychiatry (past pres.), Thurston-Mason Med. Soc. (pres. 1972), PSRO (mem. state bd.). Home: 3422 Country Club Dr NW Olympia WA 98502 Office: 1021 W 4th St Olympia WA 98502

BRENDLER, ROBERT ANTON, farm advisor; b. Modesto, Calif., Apr. 11, 1916; s. Edward R. and Harriet (Park) B.; m. Rose Anne Wilson, Aug. 5, 1951; children—Edwards Hans, Anna Christina, Sarah Jane, Mary Catherine. B.S. in Agronomy, U. Calif.-Davis. Farmer, 1941-43; farm advisor U. Calif. Coop. Extension, Ventura, 1946—. Served to lt. USNR, 1943-45. Mem. Am. Soc. Hort. Sci., Soil Conservation Soc. Am. (sec. South Coast sect. Calif. chpt.), Soc. for Range Mgmt., Am. Inst. Biol. Scis. Republican. Contbr. articles on vegetable crops, irrigation, farm mgmt. to profl. jours., farm mags. Home: 4657 Varsity St Ventura CA 93003 Office: 800 N Victoria Ave Ventura CA 93009

BRENIMAN, GEORGE WILLIAM, animal nutritionist; b. Windsor, Colo., June 19, 1927; s. Carl Frederick and Dorothy Delphine (Henderson) B.; B.S. in Animal Husbandry, Colo. State U., 1949; M.S. in Animal Nutrition, Colo. State U., 1959, Ph.D. in Animal Sci., U. Ill., 1962; m. Alice Eliza Timpe, Oct. 4, 1958; 1 son, Eric Carl. Instr. on-farm tng., Wiggins, Colo., 1950-51, Ft. Collins, Colo., 1955-56; instr. agr. Fort Lewis Coll., Durango, Colo., 1961-63; owner, operator Western Feed Analysis, Windsor, Colo., 1964-65; animal nutritionist, feed analyst Agrl. Cons., Brighton, Colo., 1966-75; pvt. animal nutrition cons., Brighton, 1975—; animal nutritionist, feed analyst Weld County Agrl. Lab., Greeley, Colo., 1980—. Served with M.C., U.S. Army, 1951-53. Mem. Am. Soc. Animal Sci. (cert. animal scientist with spl. competence in animal nutrition, animal prodn. and beef cattle), Colo. Cattle Feeders' Assn., Alpha Zeta. Mem. Christian Ch. Home: 141 S 15th Ave Dr Brighton CO 80601 Office: 714 1/2 6th St Greeley CO 80631

BRENNAN, JAMES THOMAS, school administrator, educator; b. Evergreen Park, Ill., Apr. 30, 1947; s. Thomas J. and Sheila Ann (McFee) B. A.A., St. Bede Jr. Coll., 1967; B.A., Loras Coll., 1969; M.S. in Edn., Chgo. State U., 1977; Ed.D., U. San Francisco, 1983. Credentials community coll. service, community coll. chief exec. officer, community coll. counselor, tchr. K-12 social scis., pupil personnel services K-12, Calif. Tchr., Chgo. parochial schs., 1969-74, St. Mary's Sch., Lake Forest, Ill., 1974-75; prin. St. Joseph's Sch., Libertyville, Ill., 1975-79; prin. St. Paul's Sch., San Pablo, Calif., 1979-83; adminstr. Salesian High Sch., 1983—; adj. prof. dept. grad. edn. St. Mary's Coll., 1982—; instr. dept. mgmt. and supervision Contra Costra Community Coll., 1980—; assoc. dir. student leadership program Diocese of Oakland, 1981—; mem. Diocese Oakland Sch. Bd. Mem. Nat. Catholic Edn. Assn. (assoc. dir. vision and value leadership tng. program), Assn. Supervision and Curriculum Devel., Nat. Assn. Elem. Sch. Prins. Democrat. Roman Catholic. Club: K.C. (San Pablo). Editor Chgo. Archiocesan Tchrs. Assn. Monthly, 1970-74. Home: 5290 San Pablo Dam Rd W El Sobrante CA 94803 Office: 2851 Salesian Ave Richmond CA 94804

BRENNAN, JERRY MICHAEL, economics educator, statistician, researcher; b. Grosse Pointe, Mich., July 17, 1944; s. Walter X. and Aretta May (Gempler) B. Student Kalamazoo (Mich.) Coll., 1962-64, Pasadena (Calif.) City Coll., 1966-67; B.A., UCLA, 1969; M.A., U. Hawaii, 1973, Ph.D., 1978. Researcher, UCLA, 1968-69; researcher U. Hawaii, 1972, 74-78, cons., 1975, 77, 78, data analyst and statis. cons., 1979-80, lectr., 1976-80, asst. prof. econs., 1980—; cons. WHO; v.p. Hawaii Sch. Profl. Psychology. Light scholar, 1964-66. Mem. Am. Psychol. Assn., Soc. Multivariate Exptl. Psychology, Psychometric Soc., Western Psychol. Assn., AAUP, Hawaii Ednl. Research Assn. Contbr. psychol. articles to profl. jours. Address: U Hawaii 2430 Campus Rd Honolulu HI 96822

BRENNAN, JOHN JOSEPH, JR., demographer, consultant; b. Balt., Nov. 24, 1948; s. John Joseph and Anna May (Tierney) B.; B.S., Towson State Coll., 1971; M.A., Georgetown U., 1975; Ph.D., U. So. Calif., 1982. Tchr. Balt. pub. schs., 1972-73; intern U.S. Bur. Census, Washington, 1974-75; NIMH trainee Population Research Lab., U. So. Calif., Los Angeles, 1975-78, research asst. Social Sci. Research Inst., 1978-82; market analyst So. Calif. Edison Co., Rosemead, Calif., 1982—; cons. in field, 1981—. Mem. Population Assn. Am., Am. Sociol. Assn., Assn. Computing Machinery, Valley Computer Club. Home: 12465 Walsh Ave Los Angeles CA 90066 Office: So Calif Edison Co PO Box 2244 Walnut Grove Ave Rosemead CA 91770

BRENNAN, MARTHA REDMON, educational administrator; b. Kansas City, Mo., Oct. 26, 1926; d. Theron Alfred and Bertha Little (Jackson) Redmon; grad. nurse Kansas City Gen. Hosp., 1948; B.S. in Nursing, U. Nebr., 1963; M.A., Ariz. State U., 1970, Ed.D., 1974; m. John J. Brennan, July 19, 1980; 1 son, Jonathan D. Newby. Psychiat. nurse, Omaha, 1963-68; dir. nursing Valley of Sun Sch. for Retarded Children, Phoenix, 1970-73; coordinator continuing edn. for allied health profls. Maricopa County Community Coll. Dist., Phoenix, 1973-78; dir. edn. Walter O. Boswell Meml. Hosp., Sun City, Ariz., 1978-81; coordinator parent edn. Sun City Orthopaedic Surgeons Ltd., 1982—. Mem. Adult Edn. Assn. U.S.A., Mountain Plains Adult Edn. Assn., Ariz. Adult Edn. Assn. (pres. 1971, 72). Club: Order Eastern Star. Home: 13822 Lake Shore Point Sun City AZ 85351 Office: 13200 N 103d Ave Suite 11 Sun City AZ 85351

BRENNER, BARRY EVAN, physician; b. N.Y.C., Dec. 26, 1949; s. Frederic Howard and Irma Yvonne B.; student Hamilton Coll., 1967-69; B.A., Bard Coll., 1971; M.D., Med. Coll. Va., 1974, Ph.D. in Microbiology, 1976; m. Dianne Shula, Aug. 14, 1981; 1 dau., Rachel. Intern, Univ. Hosp., Cleve., 1976-77; resident in internal medicine Univ. Hosp., Cleve., Case Western Reserve U., 1977-78; resident in emergency medicine U. Chgo. Hosps. and Clinics, 1978-80; gen. practice medicine, Richmond, Va., 1974-76, asst. dir. emergency med. services and asst. prof. medicine UCLA Hosps. and Clinics, 1980—. A.D. William fellow, 1972; Life of Va. fellow, 1972-76. Diplomate Am. Bd. Internal Medicine, Am. Bd. Emergency Medicine. Fellow ACP, Am. Coll. Chest Physicians, Am. Coll. Emergency Physicians; mem. Sigma Xi, Alpha Omega Alpha. Office: UCLA Hosp Emergency Med Center 10833 LeConte Ave Los Angeles CA 90024

BRENNER, DENNIS MAYNARD, accountant; b. Oak Hill, Kans., Nov. 13, 1924; s. Herman A. and Emma M. (Macy) B.; m. Magdalene Rae Jackman, Mar. 30, 1947 (dec.); children—David, Rebecca Brenner Stauber. Student Merritt Davis Sch. Commerce, 1944-45. C.P.A. Co-founder, ptnr. Brenner & Co., Salem, Oreg., 1946—, also Woodburn, Oreg., mng. ptnr., 1968-81. Past officer Salem Jr. C. of C.; past chmn. bd. Salem Acad.; past mem. gen. bd. adminstrn. Wesleyan Ch. (formerly Wesleyan Methodist Ch. Am.), mem. bd. adminstrn. Northwest Dist. Wesleyan Ch. Mem. Am. Inst. C.P.A.s, Oreg. Soc. C.P.A.s, Salem C. of C. Republican. Home: 412 Rural St S Salem OR 97302 Office: 245 Court St NE Salem OR 97301

BRENNER, THOMAS M(ELVIN), optometrist; b. Los Angeles, Aug. 5, 1946; s. Melvin A. and Ilene M. (Ashley) B.; m. Aug. 26, 1972; 1 dau., Laurie Ashley. Student Pierce Coll., 1964-66, Calif. Western U., 1966-68; B.A., So. Calif. Coll. Optometry, 1970, O.D., 1972. Practice optometry, Yorba Linda, Calif., 1972-78, Auburn, Calif., 1979—; clinic instr. So. Calif. Coll. Optometry, 1972-76, asst. prof., 1976. Fellow Am. Acad Optometry mem. Calif. Optometric Assn., Am. Optometric Assn. Club: Lions (Auburn). Office: 1214 High St Auburn CA 95603

BRENT, JASON G., lawyer, accountant, engineer; b. N.Y.C., Apr. 9, 1936; s. George A. and Jean (Heitel) Berkowitz; m. Linda R. Polinger, May 7, 1957; children—Lorri Jill, Tracy. B.S. in Indsl. Engring, Lehigh U., 1956; M.S. in Bus., Columbia U., 1957, J.D., 1960. C.P.A., N.Y., Calif. Bar: N.Y. 1960, Calif. 1971. Cons. Touche Ross & Co., N.Y.C., 1960-62; chief fin. officer features div. Paramount Pictures, Hollywood, Calif., 1962-70; sole practice law and acctg., Los Angeles, 1970-74; v.p. Donnenfeld & Brent, A Law Corp., Los Angeles, 1974—. Club: Knights of Pythias. Office: Suite 1117 1888 Century Park E Los Angeles CA 90067

BRENT, PAUL LESLIE, educator; b. Douglass, Okla., July 3, 1916; s. Paul Leslie and Ruth (McKee) B.; B.S., Central State U., 1938; M.Ed., U. Okla., 1949, Ed.D., 1959; m. Aledo Render, May 29, 1938; children—Carolyn J., Paul Richard; m. Josephine R. Montilepre, July 15, 1979. Tchr. math. and sci. public schs., Adair, Okla., 1938-40; prin. Alden Public Schs., Carnegie, Okla., 1940-43, supt., 1950-58; tchr. public schs., Cooperton, Okla., 1946-47; prin. high sch. public schs., Washita, Okla., 1947-48, supt., 1948-50; asst. prof. Calif. State U., Long Beach, 1959-63, asso. prof. edn., 1963-72, asst. to chmn. div. of edn., 1961-67, prof. instructional media, 1972—. Mem. Baptist Edn. Study Task, 1966-67; trustee Calif. Baptist Coll., 1969-74. Served with USNR, 1943-46. Mem. Calif. Coll. and Univ. Faculty Assn. (pres.-elect), NEA, Calif. Media and Library Educators Assn., Am. Assn. Sch. Adminstrs., Congress of Faculty Assns., Phi Delta Kappa, Kappa Delta Pi, Phi Kappa Phi. Democrat. Baptist. Home: 11112 Bos Pl Cerritos CA 90701 Office: 1250 Bellflower Blvd Long Beach CA 90840

BRESNOCK, ANNE ELIZABETH, economics educator; b. Belfonte, Pa., Mar. 22, 1951; d. Edward and Dorothy Catherine Ann (Geffert) B. B.A. in Econs., Russell Sage Coll., 1973, M.A. in Econs., U. Colo., Boulder, 1976, Ph.D., 1981. Research asst. Econs. Inst., Boulder, 1974; research asst. Ctr. for Energy and Econ. Devel., 1974-76; teaching asst. dept. econs. U. Colo., 1976-77, research asst. Bur. Econ. Research, 1977-78, instr. dept. econs., 1978-79; asst. prof. San Diego State U., 1979-83; lectr. Sch. Bus., U. San Diego, 1980-83; asst. prof. econs. U. Redlands, 1983—. Mem. Am. Econ. Assn., Am. Environ. and Resource Econs. Assn., Com. on Status of Women in Econs., Acad. Ind. Scholars. Democrat. Roman Catholic. Club: Sierra. Office: Dept Econs U Redlands Redlands CA 92373

BRESS, ARTHUR GERALD, pilot, aero. engr.; b. Chgo., Mar. 24, 1947; s. Moe and Anne B.; student Northwestern U., 1967, Foothill Coll., 1974—. With air freight dept. Am. Airlines, Chgo., 1967-68, United Airlines, 1968-70; tng. pilot Lease-A-Plane Internat., Alaska, Fla., Mexico, Europe, Africa, 1967-72; flight ops. specialist NASA Ames Research Center, Moffett Field, Calif., 1977-78, research asst., 1983—; pilot Hancock Investments Inc., Los Altos, Calif., 1979—. Mem. Center Study Presidency, 1977, mem. Republican Congl. Com.; sustaining mem. Rep. Nat. Com. Served with AUS, 1964-67. Mem. Flying Doctors of San Francisco Bay Area. Home: 414 Wilshire Dr E Wilmette IL 60091 Office: PO Box 218 Menlo Park CA 94025

BRESSETT, KENNETH EDWARD, numismatist, authentication consultant; b. Kenne, N.H., Oct. 5, 1928; s. George Edward and Florence Elizabeth (Forkey) B.; m. Bertha Britton, Oct. 7, 1950; children—Philip Edward, Richard Joseph, Mary Elizabeth. Student Dresser Bus. Sch., 1948. Sr. numismatic editor Western Pub. Co., Inc., Racine, Wis., 1959-69, mgr. publs., 1969-80; v.p. Kagin's Numismatic Investment Corp., Des Moines, 1980-81; dir. certification services Am. Numis. Assn., Colorado Springs, Colo., 1982—; mem. U.S. Assay Commn., 1966; cons., lectr in field. Fellow Am. Numis. Assn., Can. Numis. Assn. Roman Catholic. Editor: A Guide Book of U.S. Coins, 1960—; contbr. articles to profl. jours. Home: PO Box 2366 Colorado Springs CO 80901 Office: 818 N Cascade Colorado Springs CO 80903

BRESSLER, RICHARD MAIN, railroad executive; b. Wayne, Nebr., Oct. 8, 1930; s. John T. and Helen (Main) B.; B.A., Dartmouth Coll., 1952; m. Dianne G. Pearson, Apr. 17, 1981; children—Kristin M., Alan L. With Gen. Electric Co., 1952-68; v.p., treas. Am. Airlines Inc., 1968-72, sr. v.p., 1972-73; v.p. finance Atlantic Richfield Co., Los Angeles, 1973-75, sr. v.p. fin., 1975-77; pres. Arco Chem. Co., 1977-78, exec. v.p., 1978-80; pres., chief exec. officer, dir. Burlington No., Inc., Seattle, 1980—, chmn., 1982—; dir. Federated Dept. Stores, Inc., First Bank System, Inc., Honeywell Inc.; trustee Penn Mut. Life Ins. Co. Office: Burlington Northern Inc 1111 3d Ave Seattle WA 98101

BRETOI, REMUS NICOLAE, aero. engr.; b. St. Paul, Apr. 9, 1925; s. Nicolae and Elena (Puscas) B.; B.Aero.Engring., U. Minn., 1945, M.S., 1946; M.B.A., Golden Gate U., 1979; m. Yvonne Glendinning Zumbusch, Dec. 28, 1953; children—Christopher Lee, Stephen Nicolae, Kim Ferdinand, Anita Elena. Research analyst aerophysics lab. N.Am. Aviation, Inc., Inglewood, Calif., 1946-48; research engr., research supr., staff engr. mil. products planning group Honeywell, Inc., Mpls., 1948-61, mgr. research and devel., Honeywell GmbH, Doernigheim, W. Ger., 1961-63, sect. head guidance and control, systems and research center, Mpls., 1963-66; chief control lab., chief spl. project office Electronics Research Center, NASA, Cambridge, Mass., 1967-70, chief STOL expts. office, chief avionics research br., Ames Research Center, Moffett Field, Calif., 1970-72, staff asst. for programs, 1972—. Past bd. dirs. Internat. Inst. Minn.; founder Casa Romana and Capella, Oakland, Calif., 1979. Recipient cert. accomplishment Golden Gate U., 1979; named Boss of Year, Palo Alto (Calif.) chpt. Am. Bus. Women's Assn., 1972; registered profl. engr., Minn., Calif. Mem. AIAA, Nat. Soc. Profl. Engrs., Calif. Soc. Profl. Engrs., Minn. Soc. Profl. Engrs., U. Minn. Inst. Tech. Alumni Assn. (past exec. com.), Tau Omega, Theta Tau. Club: Companions of Trail. Home: 1095 McGregor Way Palo Alto CA 94306 Office: NASA Ames Research Center Moffett Field CA 94035

BRETT, PETER DAVID, writer; b. Jackson, Mich., Apr. 23, 1943; s. Benjamin Thomas and Fanchon (Hillsburg) B.; B.S. in Microbiology, Wayne State U., 1965; postgrad. U. Mich., 1969-70; m. Hazel Zeldes; 1 dau., Rebecca. Free-lance writer, 1970—; books include: Crossing Paradise, 1970, Ghost Rhythms, 1976, Gallery, 1978, Borrowing the Sky, 1978; contbr. stories and poems to numerous jours., quarterlies, mags. and anthologies; pvt. tchr. writing, Marin County, Calif., 1976—; cons. on writing and pub. writing to various corps., univs., govt. agys., assn., 1970—; teaching fellow U. Colo. Writer's Conf., 1969-70; lectr. U. Calif., San Diego, 1978—. Recipient Hopwood award U. Mich., 1970; Calif. Arts Council fellow, 1978-79. Mem. Poets and Writers, Artists Writers and Editors (pres. 1977-78). Home: 23 Porteous St Fairfax CA 94930 Office: PO Box 697 Ross CA 94957

BRETTSCHNEIDER, EDMUND ALBERT, journalist; b. Buenos Aires, Argentina, July 4, 1936; came to U.S., 1971; s. Johannes and Lydia

(Knuth) B.; m. Kiki Kachrimani, Aug. 28, 1969; 1 dau., Nadja. Law diplom Humboldt-U., Berlin, 1961. Assoc. editor Radio Deutsche Welle, Cologne, Germany, 1966-68; fgn. affairs editor Stern mag., Hamburg, Germany, 1967-69; news editor Bauer Publs., Hamburg, 1969-71; U.S.A. corr. Bauer Pub. Co., Hamburg, 1971—. Mem. Fgn. Press Center USIA, Hollywood Fgn. Press Assn. Social Democrat.

BRETZING, BURKE HARPER, psychologist; b. Indpls., July 15, 1953; s. Walter John and Maribeth (Harper) B.; A.B. summa cum laude in Psychology, U. Calif., 1975; M.A., Ariz. State U., 1977, Ph.D., 1980. Grad. assoc. Ariz. State U., Tempe 1976-79; psychologist intern Kyrene Sch. Dist., Tempe, 1979-80; psychologist Wash. Sch. Dist., Phoenix, 1980—; pvt. practice, 1980—. Recipient research excellence award Ariz. State U., 1980-81. Mem. Am. Psychol. Assn. (1st prize student paper competition 1977), Nat. Assn. Sch. Psychologists, Ariz. State Assn. Sch. Psychologists (regional dir.), Phi Delta Kappa (research award, 1979). Methodist. Contbr. chpts. to books, articles to profl. jours.; mem. editorial bd. Sch. Psychology Rev. Office: Psychology Dept 8610 N 19 Ave Phoenix AZ 85021

BREUER, STEPHEN ERNEST, ednl. adminstr.; b. Vienna, Austria, July 14, 1936; s. John Howard and Olga Marion (Haar) B.; came to U.S., 1938, naturalized, 1945; B.A. cum laude, UCLA, 1959, gen. secondary credential, 1960; m. Gail Fern Breitbart, Sept. 4, 1960; children—Jared Noah, Rachel Elise. Tchr. pub. high schs., Los Angeles, 1960-62; dir. Wilshire Blvd. Temple Camps, Los Angeles, 1962—; adminstr. Wilshire Blvd. Temple, 1980—; dir. Edgar F. Magnin Religious Sch., Los Angeles, 1970-80. Instr. edn. Hebrew Union Coll., Los Angeles, 1965-76; field instr. San Francisco State U., 1970-80, Calif. State U., San Diego, Hebrew Union Coll., 1977-81. Vice pres. Los Angeles Youth Programs Inc., 1967-77; youth adviser Los Angeles County Commn. Human Relations, 1969-72. Bd. dirs. Community Relations Conf. So. Calif., 1965—; active United Way. Recipient Service awards Los Angeles YWCA, 1974, Los Angeles County Bd. Suprs., 1982, Ventura County Bd. Suprs., 1982. Mem. So. Calif. Camping Assn. (dir. 1964—), Nat. Assn. Temple Adminstrs., Nat. Assn. Temple Educators, Los Angeles Assn. Jewish Edn. (dir.), Assn. Supervision and Curriculum Devel., Am. Mgmt. Assn., So. Calif. Conf. Jewish Communal Workers, Amnesty Internat., Jewish Resident Camping Assn. (pres. 1976-82), UCLA Alumni Assn., Wilderness Soc., Center for Environ. Edn., Wildlife Fedn., Los Angeles County Art Mus., People for the Am. Way, Assn. Reform Zionists Am. Jewish. Home: 9318 Olympic Blvd Beverly Hills CA 90212 Office: 3663 Wilshire Blvd Los Angeles CA 90010

BREUNIG, ROBERT HENRY, management and fund raising executive, consultant; b. Phila., May 12, 1926; s. Robert Henry and Gertrude Florence (Burke) B.; student Princeton U., 1943, Hunter Coll., 1946; B.A., Ind. U., 1950; M.A., Goddard Coll., 1975; Ph.D., Union Grad. Sch., 1980; m. Ruth Carolyn Cole, Aug. 30, 1947; children—Lynn Carol, Mark Robert, Eric Martin, Christopher John. City hall reporter Atlantic City Press-Union, 1950; dir. info. services U. Md., 1954-66; dir. public affairs Planning Research Corp., Washington, 1966-68; sr. staff scientist URS Systems Corp., Washington, 1969-70; asst. to pres. Capital U., Columbus, Ohio, 1971-72; dir. advt. Am. Petroleum Inst., Washington, 1973-74; dir. devel. Antioch Coll. Ohio, 1974; dir. public affairs Calif. State U., Long Beach, 1974-82; asst. to pres. Sonoma State U., Rohnert Park, Calif., 1982-83; pres. pres. Breunig and Sons Internat. Traders. Served with AUS, 1943-45. Decorated Bronze Star. Mem. Council for Advancement and Support Edn., Am. Assn. Higher Edn., Public Relations Soc. Am., Am. Assn. Univ. Adminstrs. Episcopalian. Clubs: Pacific Coast Press, Greater Los Angeles Press. Author: Tuition Guide to American Colleges and Universities, 1970. Contbr. articles on nat. and Calif. public affairs to newspapers and profl. jours.; contbg. editor Calif. Higher Edn. mag. Home: 3372 Cortese Dr Los Alamitos CA 90720

BREWER, DON DELANO, children's home administrator; b. Blackwell, Okla., July 18, 1935; s. George William and Alice Annettie (Rounds) B.; B.A., Phillips U., 1960, D.Hum., 1981; M.S.W., U. Okla., 1962; m. Shirley Ann Shiflett, Dec. 22, 1958; children—Don Delano II, Deidre Diane. Caseworker, Dept. Pub. Welfare, Oklahoma City, 1960-61; summer intern Okla. Christian Home for Aging, Edmond, 1961; caseworker Central State Hosp., Norman, Okla., 1961-62, Family and Children's Services of Greater St. Louis, 1962-65; adminstr. Child Saving Inst., Omaha, 1965-70; exec. dir. Colo. Christian Home, Denver, 1970—; lectr. psychology dept. Met. State Coll., Denver, 1975-76. Asst. survey cons. Child Welfare League of Am., N.Y.C., 1968, survey cons., 1978, chmn. S.W. regional conf., Denver, 1980, mem. Adv. Council of Execs., 1980-82; deacon Central Christian Ch., Denver, 1972-77, elder, 1981—; mem. Gov.'s Adv. Com. on Licensing of Child Care Facilities, 1983—. Mem. Nat. Assn. Social Workers, Acad. Cert. Social Workers, Nat. Benevolent Assn. (chmn. child care adminstrs. group 1971-76, cons. child care and family services 1976-77). Home: 1920 Alkire Golden CO 80401 Office: 4325 W 29th Ave PO Box 12295 Denver CO 80212

BREWER, JESSE WAYNE, zoologist, educator; b. Rives, Mo., Oct. 10, 1940; s. Jesse James and Hazel Faye (Loveless) B.; B.S., Central Mich. U., 1963, M.A., 1965; Ph.D., Purdue U., 1968; m. Jane Lynn Whitcomb, Dec. 26, 1964; children—Laura Elizabeth, Matthew Whitcomb. Prof. zoology and entomology Colo. State U., Fort Collins, 1968—; vice-pres. Biol. Research Assn., Inc., environmental cons. agy., Fort Collins, 1972—. Mem. Colo. Apiary Adv. Bd., 1969—; mem. Dutch Elm Disease Planning Com., State of Colo., 1970—. Mem. Entomol. Soc. Am., Canadian Entomol. Soc., Midwest Benthological Soc., Sigma Xi, Gamma Sigma Delta. Editor: Readings in Insect-Plant Disease Relationships, 1973. Contbr. articles to profl. jours. Home: 1013 Boltz Dr Fort Collins CO 80525

BREWER, RANDALL KEITH, rancher; b. Buhl, Idaho, Aug. 13, 1942; s. Claude Edward and Myrtle Alice (Crisp) B.; m. Bethene Patrick, May 24, 1963; children—Shana Daun, Shellie Renae, Derek Karl. Student Idaho State U., 1960-61, Boise State U., 1961-62. With Nev. Bank of Commerce, 1964-66; co-owner, mgr. Devil Creek Ranch, Rogerson, Idaho, 1966—; Idaho del. Nat. Young Cattlemen's Traveling Leadership Conf., 1982. Mem. Three Creek Sch. Bd., 1972-78, chmn., 1972-74, clk., 1974-78. Mem. Nat. Cattlemen's Assn., Idaho Cattlemen's Assn. (dir., dist. v.p., membership chmn.), Magic Valley Cattlemen's Assn. (pres.), 71 Livestock Assn. (v.p.). Methodist. Club: Masons.

BREWER, ROSS KELVIN, coll. ofcl.; b. American Fork, Utah, Sept. 8, 1930; s. Daniel William and Alice Luretta (Nielsen) B.; B.S., Brigham Young U., 1956, Ed.D., 1978; M.Ed., U. Oreg., 1962; m. Albrea Jayne Knowlton, Aug. 27, 1952; children—Kelvin Knowlton, Cynthia, Michael Clark, Kathy Jayne, Bruce Nielsen. Ordained missionary Ch. of Jesus Christ of Latter-day Saints, 1950-52; social sci. instr. Portland (Oreg.) Public Schs., 1956-69; dir. continuing edn. Clark Coll., Vancouver, Wash., 1969-80, personnel dir., 1979-81, dean adminstrv. services, 1981—. Treas., Clark County Econ. Opportunity Com., 1971—; stake patriarch Ch. Jesus Christ of Latter-day Saints, 1979—. Named Person of Year, Region X, Nat. Council on Community Service and Continuing Edn., Am. Assn. Community and Jr. Colls., 1978-79; NSF scholar, 1968. Mem. N.W. Adult Edn. Assn. (pres., pres.-elect 1979-80), Wash. Continuing Edn. Assn. (pres., pres.-elect 1971-73), Nat. Assn. Public Continuing and Adult Edn., Nat. Community Edn. Assn., N.W. Coll. and Univ. Personnel Assn., Clark County Personnel Assn. Republican. Home: 11912 NW 36th Ave Vancouver WA 98665 Office: Clark Coll 1800 E McLoughlin Blvd Vancouver WA 98663

BREWER, ROY EDWARD, regional and urban planner; b. Atlanta, Ga., Dec. 22, 1949; s. Roy M. and Martha JoAnn (Still) B.; B.A. in Polit. Sci., U. Fla., 1971, M.A. in Public Adminstrn., 1973; J.D., McGeorge Sch. Law, Sacramento, 1982; m. Catherine Elizabeth Schindler, May 5, 1979. Sr. planner N. Central Fla. Regional Planning Council, Gainesville, 1973-78; mgr. met. devel. Sacramento Met. C. of C., 1978-79; dir. community and environ. planning Raymond Vail & Assos., Sacramento, 1980—. Co-founder, Fla. Rugby Union, Inc., Orlando, 1973-74, acting dir., 1973-74, sec.-treas., 1974-76, sec., 1976-78; mem. tours and tournaments com. U.S.A. Rugby Union, 1976-78; bd. dirs. Eastern Rugby Union Am., 1978. Mem. Am. Inst. Cert. Planners, Assn. Environ. Profls., Phi Gamma Delta. Editor Fla. Planner newsletter Am. Inst. Planners, 1976-78. Home: 3640 Parrett Ave Napa CA 94558 Office: 1410 Ethan Way Sacramento CA 95825

BREWSTER, DAVID CLARK, publishing company executive; b. Newark, Sept. 26, 1939; s. Gaylord Clark and Marjorie Jane (Anderson) B.; m. Joyce Skaggs, May 14, 1939; children—Kate Eliza, Anne Olivia. B.A. with honors, Yale U., 1961, M.A., 1963. Asst. prof. English, U. Wash., Seattle, 1965-68; assoc. editor Seattle Mag., 1969-70; assignment editor KING-TV News, 1971; mng. editor The Argus, 1972-75; founder, pub., editor The Weekly, 1976—; pres. Sasquatch Pub. Co., Inc., 1976—. Pres. English Pub. Assoc., Inc., 1982—. Bd. dirs. Seattle Symphony Orch., 1980—, Seattle Chamber Music Festival, 1982—. Mem. Phi Beta Kappa. Author: Best Places Guidebooks, 1975, 77, 79, 81; The Seattle Book, 1978; Seattle Best Places, 1983. Home: 1415 35th Ave Seattle WA 98122 Office: The Seattle Weekly 1932 1st Ave Suite 605 Seattle WA 98101

BREWSTER, F. MICHAEL, physician; b. Berlin, Nov. 16, 1924; came to U.S., 1959, naturalized, 1962; s. Erwin and Gertrude A. (Hecht) Berger; m. Leona B. Flood (div.); 1 dau., Iris M. Brewster. M.D., Eberhard Karl's U., Tubingen, 1949; Dr. in Med. Scis., Central U., Ecudaor, 1955; diploma in cardiology Harvard U., 1961. Intern, St. Francis Hosp., Honolulu, 1959-60; resident San Joaquin Gen. Hosp., Stockton, Calif., 1961-63; practice family medicine, Concord, Calif., 1968—; chmn. dept. family practice Mt. Diablo Hosp., Concord, 1979-80. Served with German Navy, 1942-44. Diplomate Am. Bd. Family Practice. Mem. AMA, Alameda Contra Costa County Med. Soc. Republican. Clubs: Bohemian, Bachelors, Orinda Country. Home: 65 Singingwood Ln Orinda CA 94563 Office: 3301 Clayton Rd Concord CA 94520

BREWSTER, HENRY HODGE, psychiatrist; b. Boston, Oct. 20, 1912; s. George W.W. and Ellen (Hodge) B.; M.D., Harvard U., 1938; children by previous marriage—Rodman Peabody, Ellen Hodge, Henry Hodge; m. 3d, Judy M. Jacobsen, Aug. 29, 1970; stepchildren—Penny Robben, Daryl Ray Jacobsen. Intern, Mass. Gen. Hosp., Boston, 1938-40; resident in medicine Boston City Hosp., 1940-42; practice medicine specializing in psychiatry and psychoanalysis; asst. prof. psychiatry Western Res. Sch. Medicine, Cleve., 1954-60, Harvard U. Med. Sch., 1962-65; assoc. prof. psychiatry Colo. Med. Center, Denver, 1960-62; chief profl. edn. Stockton (Calif.) State Hosp., 1967-78; asst. clin. prof. psychiatry U. Calif. at Davis, 1968-73, assoc. clin. prof., 1973-83. Bd. dirs. Stockton Symphony Assn. Served with M.C., U.S. Army, 1942-45; ETO. Mem. AMA, San Francisco, Am. psychoanalytic assns., Am. Psychiat. Assn., Calif. Med. Assn., San Joaquin County Med. Soc., Soc. Mayflower Desc. Republican. Episcopalian. Clubs: Delphic (Harvard); Masons, Stockton Golf and Country, N. Stockton Rotary. Contbr. chpt. Psychiatry and Religion, 1948. Home: 3414 Quail Lakes Dr Stockton CA 95207 Office: 510 E Magnolia St Stockton CA 95202

BREWSTER, LEONARD LYMAN, dentist; b. Phoenix, July 24, 1934; s. Harold Lyman and Else Mae (Leonard) B.; m. E. Jane Miller, June 8, 1958; children—Diane Elizabeth, Laura Kay, Susan Gay. A.A., Phoenix Coll., 1954; student Ariz. State U., 1954-55; D.D.S., Baylor U., 1959. Practice dentistry, Tucson, 1962—; mem. staff Tucson Med. Ctr.; dir. Ariz. Delta Dental Ins. Co.; pres. Delta Dental Plans, 1980-82. Served with Dental Corps, USAF, 1959-62. Fellow Internat. Coll. Dentists, Internat. Coll. Applied Nutrition; mem. Ariz. State Dental Assn. (pres. 1972-73), Psi Omega. Methodist. Dental art work. Office: 5709 E 5th St Tucson AZ 85711

BREWSTER, MICHAEL LESLIE, sculptor, art educator; b. Eugene, Oreg., Aug. 15, 1946; s. Richard Leslie and Marian (Burt) B.; divorced; 1 dau., Lily. B.A., Pomona (Calif.) Coll., 1968; M.F.A., Claremont. (Calif.) Grad. Sch., 1970. Instr. sculpture Bradley U., Peoria, Ill., 1970-71, Pomona Coll., 1971-73; vis. artist Claremont Grad. Sch., 1973—, assoc. prof. art, 1981—; exhbns. acoustic sculptures, 1972—, latest being Whitney Mus. Am. Art, N.Y.C., 1981, Los Angeles County Mus. Art, 1981, Neuberg Mus., Purchase, N.Y., 1981-82, Mus. Art, R.I. Sch. Design, 1982, U. Mass. Gallery, Amherst, 1982. Nat. Endowment Arts fellow, 1976, 78. Mem. AAUP, Los Angeles Inst. Contemporary Art. Home: 11 Navy St Venice CA 90291 Office: Dept Fine Art Claremont Grad Sch Claremont CA 91711

BREWSTER, PATRICIA KORMANSKI, marketing consultant; b. Nyack, N.Y., July 11, 1951; d. Michael John and Marianne (Gillelan) Kormanski; m. James Langdon Taylor, Aug. 4, 1974; m. Robert Burnett Brewster, Apr. 22, 1981; 1 son, Jonathan Hundley. B.A., Muhlenberg Coll., 1973; postgrad. U. Calif.-Berkeley, 1975. Secondary edn. teaching cert., N.Y., Calif., Pa. Asst. mgr. advt. sales promotion Pfizer Med. Systems, N.Y.C., 1976-80; med. account mgr. Muir, Cornelius, Moore Advt., N.Y.C., 1980-81; advt. mgr. Am. Edwards Labs., Irvine, Calif., 1981; cons. mktg. communications healthcare industry, Palos Verdes Estates, Calif., 1980—. Recipient Mktg. Presentation award Pfizer Med. Systems, 1979. Home and Office: 3124 Via La Selva Palos Verdes Estates CA 90274

BRICKEN, GORDON L., acoustical engr., mayor; b. Louisville, Nov. 1, 1936; B.S. in Elec. Engring., Loyola U., Los Angeles, 1960; M.S., UCLA, 1961; cert. in urban planning U. Calif., Irvine; m. Maureen Mulligan, 1963; children—Barbara, Mary, Patricia, Victoria. Former mem. tech. staff Hughes Aircraft, Fullerton, Calif.; formerly with Northrup Corp.; pres. Gordon Bricken & Assocs., Inc., Santa Ana, Calif., mayor City of Santa Ana, mem. city council, 1975-81. Mem. Santa Ana Planning Commn., 1963-73, Santa Ana Redevel. Commn., 1973-75. Clubs: Rotary, Elks. Office: 1621 E 17th St Santa Ana CA 92701

BRICKER, RONALD HAROLD, psychologist; b. Vincennes, Ind., Dec. 23, 1942; s. Harold E. and Edna P. Bricker; m. Anna Marie Ryan, Dec. 28, 1968; 1 son, Stuart Ryan. M.S. in Psychology, Ind. U., 1968; Ed.D. in Psychology, No. Ill. U., 1973. Lic. clin. psychologist, Ariz. Dir. spl. edn. Sch. Dist. 89, Glen Ellyn, Ill., 1971-78; clin. psychologist Verde Valley Community Guidance Clinic, Cottonwood, Ariz., 1978-81, exec. dir., 1981—. Regional commr. Am. Youth Soccer Orgn., 1981—. Mem. Am. Psychol. Assn., Phi Delta Kappa. Home: PO Box 3955 West Sedona AZ 86340

BRICKER, RUTH, national foundation administrator, real estate developer; b. Oak Park, Ill., Mar. 23, 1930; m. Neal S. Bricker; children—Daniel Baker, Cary, Dusty, Suzanne. B.A. in Urban Planning, Antioch U. Staff writer Artforum Mag., Los Angeles, 1966-69; western dir. Expts. in Art and Tech., Los Angeles, 1969-75; owner Empire Real Estate and Property Mgmt., Los Angeles, 1975—; designer Trade-Off, a computer simulation for use in urban planning; developed programs in art and technology for Calif. State Coll.-Long Beach, U. So. Calif., UCLA; designer laser light wall Calif. Inst. Tech.; lectr. and cons. in field. Mem. Mayor's Housing Task Force, Los Angeles; bd. councillors Internat. Inst. Kidney Diseases UCLA, mem. exec. com. Savings and Preserving Archtl. and Cultural Environ.; mem. Am. Found. for Pompidou Mus., Paris. Author: Getting Rich-Investing in Real Estate Partnerships, 1982; editor, contbg. author: Experiments in Art and Technology/Los Angeles jour., 1974-79.

BRICKLEY, MICHAEL WAYNE, mortgage banker; b. Schenectady, Mar. 8, 1948; s. Walter William and Edith Lillian (Murphy) B.; B.A., Bates Coll., Lewiston, Maine, 1970; M.B.A., Rutgers U., 1971; m. Catherine Jayne Eldridge, May 22, 1971; children—Matthew, Lisa. Staff acct. Arthur Anderson & Co., C.P.A.'s, Boston and San Jose, Calif., 1970-72; pres. Westward Distbrs., Inc., San Jose, 1973-77, Unified Mortgage Co., Santa Clara, Calif., 1977—. C.P.A., Calif. Mem. Am. Inst. C.P.A.'s, Mortgage Bankers Assn. Am., Nat. Assn. Home Builders, Calif. Soc. C.P.A.'s, Calif. Mortgage Bankers Assn. Republican. Roman Catholic. Office: 1850 Warburton Ave Santa Clara CA 95055

BRIDGE, HERBERT MARVIN, jewelry exec.; b. Seattle, Mar. 14, 1925; s. Ben and Sally (Silverman) B.; m. Shirley Selesnick, Jan. 25, 1948; children—Jonathan J., Daniel E. B.A. in Polit. Sci., U. Wash., 1947. Pres. Ben Bridge Jeweler Inc., Seattle, 1955-57, chmn., 1977—; dir. Wash. Mut. Savs. Bank. Past pres. Downtown Seattle Assn., Am. Jewish Com.; bd. dirs. March of Dimes, Naval Acad. Found. Served to rear adm. USNR, 1942-83; World War II, Korea. Decorated Legion of Merit with Gold Star; recipient Israel Bonds Masada award, 1974; Am. Jewish Com. human relations award, 1976; NCCJ brotherhood award, 1978; Navy League scroll honor, 1980. Mem. Pacific N.W. Jewelers (past pres.), Seattle C. of C. (past pres., mem. pres. club), Naval Res. Assn. (past pres.), Assn. Wash. Bus. Democrat. Clubs: Wash. Athletic (dir.), City (dir.), Rotary (dir. found.), Shriners. Home: 2125 1st Ave Seattle WA 98121 Office: Box 1908 Seattle WA 98111

BRIDGE, MARVIN EUGENE, accountant; b. Ainsworth, Nebr., Aug. 16, 1940; s. Dale Eugene and Mildred Cristel (Kaplan) B.; m. Constance Meyer, Nov. 29, 1974; m. Elizabeth Helen Kring, Jan. 5, 1977. B.S. in Bus. Adminstrn., Oreg. State U., 1973. Lic. tax cons., Oreg.; enrolled to practice before IRS, 1974. Owner, Bridge & Assocs., Ltd., Tax Cons., Portland, Oreg., 1976—. Served with USAF, 1959-63. Mem. Oreg. Assn. Pub. Accts., Nat. Assn. Tax Cons. Democrat. Methodist. Club: S.E. Portland Lions.

BRIDGEMAN, BRUCE, psychologist, educator, writer; b. Bloomfield, N.J., Sept. 17, 1944; s. Jack and Elsie (Knorr) B.; m. Diane Laura Turchiarelli, Dec. 12, 1970; children—Natalie, Theresa. B.A. cum laude in psychology, Cornell U., 1967; Ph.D. in Physiol. Psychology, Stanford U., 1971. Asst. prof. psychology and psychobiology U. Calif.-Santa Cruz, 1973-78, assoc. prof., 1979—. Palmer scholar, 1962-67; Humboldt fellow, 1971-72; NIH postdoctoral fellow 1972-73, travel fellow, 1974; NIH research grantee, 1975, 82; NSF research grantee, 1979; Mem. Soc. Neuroscis, Psychonomic Soc., Am. Psychol. Assn., AAAS, Assn. Research Vision and Ophthalmology. Democrat. Editor: (with D. Bridgeman and M. Baer) Readings on Fundamental Issues In Learning and Memory, 1977; translator, editor (with L. Stark); Theory of Binocular Vision, 1977; contbr. articles to sci. jours.

BRIDGES, ROBERT MCSTEEN, mechanical engineer; b. Oakland, Calif., Apr. 17, 1914; s. Robert and Josephine (Hite) B.; B.S. cum laude in Mech. Engring., U. So. Calif., 1940; postgrad. UCLA; m. Edith Brownwood, Oct. 26, 1945; children—Ann, Lawrence, Robert. Engr. Nat. Supply Co., Torrance, Calif., 1940-41; design engr. landing gear and hydraulics Lockheed Aircraft Corp., Burbank, Calif., 1941-46; missile hydraulic controls design engr. Convair, San Diego, 1946-48; sr. staff engr. oceanic systems mech. design Bendix Corp., Sylmar, Calif., 1948—, adv. ocean engring. U.S. Congress. Com. chmn. Boy Scouts Am., 1961. Recipient award of Service Am. Inst. Aero. Engrs., 1965. Mem. Marine Tech. Soc. (charter; com. cables, connectors 1969), Tau Beta Pi. Republican. Patentee in field of undersea devices (14), including deep ocean rubber band moor; inventor U.S. Navy sonobuoy rotochute; contbr. articles to profl. jours. and confs. Home: 10314 Vanalden Ave Northridge CA 91326 Office: 15825 Roxford St Sylmar CA 91342

BRIDGFORTH, ROBERT MOORE, JR., research specialist; b. Lexington, Miss., Oct. 21, 1918; s. Robert Moore and Theresa (Holder) B.; student Miss. State Coll., 1935-37; B.S., Iowa State Coll., 1940; M.S., M.I.T., 1948; postgrad. Harvard U., 1949; m. Florence Jarnberg, November 7, 1943; children—Robert Moore, Alice Theresa. Asst. engr. Standard Oil Co., of Ohio, 1940; teaching fellow M.I.T., 1940-41, instr. chemistry, 1941-43, research asst., 1943-44, mem. staff div. indsl. cooperation, 1944-47; asso. prof. physics and chemistry Emory and Henry Coll., 1949-51; research engr. Boeing Airplane Co., Seattle, 1951-54, research specialist 1954-55, sr. group engr., 1955-58, chief propulsion systems sect. Systems Mgmt. Office, 1958-59, chief propulsion research unit, 1959-60; chmn. bd. Rocket Research Corp. (name now Rockcor, Inc.), 1960-69, Explosives Corp. Am., 1966-69. Fellow Brit. Interplanetary Soc., AIAA (asso.), Am. Inst. Chemists; mem. Am. Astronautical Soc. (dir.), AAAS, Am. Chem. Soc., Am. Rocket Soc. (pres. Pacific NW 1955), Am. Ordnance Assn., Am. Inst. Physics, Am. Assn. Physics Tchrs., Tissue Culture Assn., Reticuloendothelial Soc., N.Y. Acad. Scis., Combustion Inst., Sigma Xi. Home: 4325 87th Ave SE Mercer Island WA 98040

BRIDGWATER, CAROL AUSTIN, psychologist; b. Boston, Apr. 16, 1954; d. Alfred and Grace B.; B.A. in Econs., Stanford U., 1976; M.A. (NIMH fellow), U. Mont., 1980, Ph.D. in Psychology, 1981. Research asst. U. Oxford (Eng.), 1976-77; teaching asst. dept. psychology U. Mont., Missoula, 1979-80, sr. research assoc., 1980-81; sr. research analyst Wells Fargo Bank, San Francisco, 1981—. Bertha Mortan scholar, 1979. Mem. Am. Psychol. Assn., Am. Mktg. Assn., Sigma Xi. Democrat. Presbyterian. Contbr. numerous articles to profl. jours.

BRIED, HENRY WILLIAM, elec. mfg. co. exec., mech. engr.; b. Teaneck, N.J., June 17, 1933; s. Henry F. and Rose M. Bried; M.E., Stevens Inst. Tech., 1955; M.B.A., Drexel U., 1965; m. Patricia J; children by previous marriage—Kathleen, James, Henry William, Stephen. Tech. planning engr. Gen. Electric Co., Phila., 1958-60, product design engr., Valley Forge, Pa., 1961-63, mgr. payload integration, 1963-65, mgr. mil. aerospace systems, Washington, 1965-68; mgr. WWMCCS Program, Honeywell Info. Systems, Phoenix, Ariz., 1968-71, mgr. production programs, 1968-74; mgr. info. systems Motorola, Inc., Phoenix, 1974-76, mgr. participative mgmt. program, 1976-80, corp. dir. participative mgmt. program, 1980—. Coach, Wheaton Boys Club, 1961-68; pres. Layhill Rd. Citizens Assn., 1965-68; pres. Kiva-Kaibab Little League, 1972-74, coach, 1969-76; bd. dirs. Ariz. Boys Community, 1976—; adv. bd. prisoner rehab. program Ariz. State Prison. Served to 1st lt., Ordnance Corps, U.S. Army, 1955-58. Mem. Am. Mgmt. Assn., ASME, Air Force Assn., U.S. Navy League. Republican. Roman Catholic. elec. mfg. co. exec., mech. engr.; b. Teaneck, N.J., June 17, 1933; s. Henry F. and Rose M. Bried; M.E., Stevens Inst. Tech., 1955; M.B.A., Drexel U., 1965; m. Patricia J; children by previous marriage—Kathleen, James, Henry William, Stephen. Tech. planning engr. Gen. Electric Co., Phila., 1958-60, product design engr., Valley Forge, Pa., 1961-63, mgr. payload integration, 1963-65, mgr. mil. aerospace systems, Washington, 1965-68; mgr. WWMCCS Program, Honeywell Info. Systems, Phoenix, Ariz., 1968-71, mgr. production programs, 1968-74; mgr. info. systems Motorola, Inc., Phoenix, 1974-76, mgr. participative mgmt. program, 1976-80, corp. dir. participative mgmt. program, 1980—. Coach, Wheaton Boys Club, 1961-68; pres. Layhill Rd. Citizens Assn., 1965-68; pres. Kiva-Kaibab Little League, 1972-74, coach, 1969-76; bd. dirs. Ariz. Boys Community, 1976—; adv. bd. prisoner rehab. program Ariz. State Prison. Served to 1st lt., Ordnance Corps, U.S. Army, 1955-58. Mem. Am. Mgmt. Assn., ASME, Air Force Assn., U.S. Navy League. Republican. Roman Catholic. Home: 8501 E Cholla St Scottsdale AZ 85260 Office: 8201 E McDowell Rd PO Box 1417 Scottsdale AZ 85252

BRIEGER, STEPHEN GUSTAVE, mfg. co. ofcl.; b. Marburg, Ger., Sept. 7, 1935; came to U.S., naturalized, 1945; s. Heinrich and Kate L. (Steitz) B.; B.Sc., Springfield (Mass.) Coll., 1955; M.S., Fla. State U., 1970, Ph.D., 1972; m. Karen L. Jentes, Nov. 27, 1968; 1 dau., Jennifer B. Tchr., Calif. schs., 1954-69; indsl. cons. mgmt. tng., 1960-70; mgmt. cons. Nebr. Criminal Justice System, 1972; research criminologist Stanford Research Inst., 1972-74; evaluation cons. Office Gov. Calif., 1974-76; mgmt. devel. assoc. Am. Electronics Assn., 1976-80; mgr. employee and mgmt. devel. ISS Sperry Univac, Santa Clara, Calif., 1980-83; mgmt. and organizational devel. Osborne Computer Corp., 1983—; mem. faculty U.S. Internat. U., St. Mary's Coll., U. San Francisco. Mem. Am. Soc. Tng. and Devel., Am. Mgmt. Assn., Am. Electronics Assn. Author studies, reports in field. Home: 1665 Fairorchard Ave San Jose CA 95125 Office: 3333 Scott Blvd Santa Clara CA 95051

BRIERLEY, JAMES ALAN, microbiology educator; b. Denver, Dec. 22, 1938; s. Everette and Carrie (Berg) B.; m. Corale Louise Beer, Dec. 21, 1965. B.S. in Bacteriology, Colo. State U., 1961; M.S. in Microbiology, Mont. State U., 1966. Asst. prof. Biology N.Mex. Inst. Mining and Tech., Socorro, 1966-68; research scientist Martin Marietta Corp., Denver, 1968-69; successively asst. prof., assoc. prof., prof., chmn. dept. biology N.Mex. Inst. Mining and Tech., 1969—. Served to staff sgt. Air N.G., 1956-61. Recipient 28 research grants. Mem. Am. Soc. Microbiology, Soc. Gen. Microbiology, AAAS, N.Mex., Socorro C. of C., Sigma Xi. Contbr. numerous articles in field to profl. jours. Patentee bacterial metal leaching process. Home: 1103 Bullock Socorro NM 87801 Office: Dept Biology N Mex Inst Mining and Tech Socorro NM 87801

BRIERLY, KEPPEL, investment exec.; b. Denver, Mar. 9, 1909; s. Justin Keppel and Pearl A. (Walters) B.; grad. Colo. Sch. Mines, 1934; student, Denver U., 1936-37, U. Colo., 1939-41; m. Ruth E. Davis, Nov. 4, 1934; 1 dau., Barbara Brierly Brann. Engr., Pub. Service Co. of Colo., Denver, 1930-38; coordinator, tchr. Denver pub. schs., 1938-41; pres. J & K Constrn. Co., Denver, 1945-68; investment exec. Am. Trustee, mayor pro tem Town Bow Mar.; pres. Denver Lions Found., 1967-68; bd. dirs. Colo. Leukemia Soc. Served to lt. col. AUS, 1941-45; lt. col. Res. ret. Decorated Bronze Star Medal; also VI Haakon (Norway); award (France). Registered profl. engr., Colo.; real estate license, Colo. Mem. Denver Assn. Home Builders (pres. 1949, hon. life mem.), Asso. Bldg. Contractors Colo. (pres. 1956-57, Asso. Gen. Contractors Am. (dir. 1956-65), hon. life mem.), Am. Arbitration Assn., Theta Tau, Kappa Sigma, Blue Key. Presbyterian. Clubs: Denver Press (life), Denver Athletic (life), Pinehurst Country (life), Mount Vernon Country, Lions (pres. 1963-64), Masons, Shriners, Royal Order Jesters. Home: 5151 Juniper Rd Bow Mar Littleton CO 80123 Office: Suite 206 601 Broadway Denver CO 80203

BRIËT, RICHARD, electrical engineer; b. Temanggoeng, Indonesia, June 18, 1942; s. Fernand A. and Amelia B. (Hofdijk) B.; B.S. in Physics, Math. (Long Beach scholar), Calif. State U., 1968; Ph.D. in Physics, U. Utah, 1974; children—Rosewita, Paul, Pierre. Research specialist, cons. Asso. Food Stores, Mchts., Inc., Salt Lake City, 1974-77; sr. engr. nuclear survivalbility and vulnerability Boeing Wichita Co. (Kans.), 1977-79; design specialist electromagnetic and nuclear radiation effects Gen. Dynamics, San Diego, 1979-81; staff engr. TRW, Redondo Beach, Calif., 1981—. NDEA fellow, 1972. Mem. IEEE. Club: Toastmasters. Office: TRW Space and Tech Group One Space Park Redondo Beach CA 90278

BRIGANTE, THOMAS ROBERT, psychologist; b. Buffalo, May 31, 1930; s. Michael Harry and Beatrice Rita (Steinwachs) B.; B.A., SUNY-Buffalo, 1951; M.A., Boston U., 1953, Ph.D., 1956; S.M. in Hygiene (NIH fellow), Sch. Pub. Health, Harvard U., 1961; m. Mary Ellen Chasey, Aug. 29, 1951; children—Beth Ellen, David Michael. Staff psychologist Brockton (Mass.) VA Hosp., 1956-60; research assoc. Sch. Pub. Health, Harvard U., 1961-62; dir. mental health services The Claremont (Calif.) Colls., 1962-67; assoc. prof. psychology Claremont Grad. Sch., 1967-68; pvt. practice Claremont Psychol. Assocs, 1967—. Served with U.S. Army, 1949-50. Mem. Am. Psychol. Assn., Calif. State Psychol. Assn., Common Cause. Contbr. article to profl. jours. Home: 481 University St Claremont CA 91711 Office: 219 N Indian Hill Blvd Suite 204 Claremont CA 91711

BRIGGS, ARLENE LOUISE MORGAN, educator; b. Yakima, Wash.; d. Leslie V. and Mabel (Steele) Morgan; student Yakima Jr. Coll., 1940-42; B.A., U. Wash., 1944; M.Ed., Calif. State U., Los Angeles, 1969; m. Richard A. Briggs, 1945 (div. 1967); children—Joan York, Janis Morgan, Brian Kent. Tchr., Rosemead (Calif.) Sch. Dist., 1963—. Vol., Arcadia (Calif.) Meth. Hosp., 1978, 79, 80; bd. dirs. Savannah Sch. PTA, 1979-80; mem. worship work com. United Meth. Ch. of Good Shepherd, Arcadia, 1979-81. Mem. Rosemead Tchrs. Assn. (sec. 1968-69, 74-75), Delta Phi Upsilon (chpt. sec. 1963-64), Pi Lambda Theta (rec. sec. 1963-65, corr. sec. 1967-69, historian 1973-74, v.p. 1971-72; treas. So. Calif. council 1971-73), Delta Kappa Gamma (chpt. pres. 1974-76, parliamentarian 1976-78; So. Calif. legis. chmn. 1977-81, membership chmn. 1980-82). Home: PO Box 1253 1161 W Duarte Rd Arcadia CA 91006 Office: 3720 Rio Hondo Rosemead CA 91770

BRIGGS, DAVID MARSHALL, accountant; b. San Bernardino, Calif., Apr. 23, 1942; s. Joseph Fritz and Thelma Julia (Smith) B.; B.A., San Francisco State Coll., 1965; m. Barbara Ann Wallis, June 15, 1963 (dec. Feb. 1981); children—John David, Joseph Richard; m. 2d, Patricia Ann Coffey, Dec. 19, 1981; 1 son, Dennis Michael. Staff acct. Smith, Rohmiller, Swenson & Clark, Bakersfield, Calif., 1966-68; partner Swenson, Clark & Co., Los Angeles, 1968-75; pvt. practice acctg., San Fernando, Calif., 1975-80; partner Briggs & Martin, San Fernando, 1981—. Mem. Am. Inst. C.P.A.s, Calif. Soc. C.P.A.s. Republican. Club: Porter Valley Country. Office: 566 S Brand Blvd San Fernando CA 91340

BRIGGS, DONALD CLIFFORD, mech. engr., motor mfg. co. exec.; b. Los Angeles, Sept. 19, 1932; s. Clifford R. and Mildred Louise (Wainscott) B.; B.S. in Mech. Engring., Stanford U., 1957, M.S., 1958; M.B.A., U. Santa Clara, 1965, M.S. in Elec. Engring., 1973; m. Sonja Louise Schwab, May 11, 1963; children—Robin, Tammie, Linda. Design engr. Airesearch Mfg. Co., Los Angeles, 1959-61; sr. engr. Itek Corp., Palo Alto, Calif., 1961-65; space power systems mgr. Ford Motor Co., Palo Alto, 1965-80, staff engring. splty. mgr., 1980—. Cub scout leader Stanford council, 1965-68, leader Boy Scouts, 1968-72. Served with USN, 1953-55. Trane research fellow, 1957-58; registered profl. engr., Calif. Mem. AIAA, Sigma Xi, Tau Beta Pi, Beta Gamma Sigma. Republican. Clubs: Elks, Masons. Contbr. articles on aerospace elec. [illegible]tems to profl. publs.; patentee electrochem. cells. Home: 2713 [illegible]ton Sq Mt View CA 94040 Office: 3939 Fabian Way Palo Alto CA

BRIGGS, PETER ALAN, industrial relations specialist; b. Ann Arbor, Mich., Feb. 20, 1937; s. Robert Peter and Maxine (Corliss) B.; B.B.A., U. Mich., 1962, M.B.A., 1965; 1 dau., Rebecca Anne. Indsl. relations analyst Ford Motor Co., Dearborn, Mich., 1962-67; mgr. personnel and indsl. relations Western U.S., Packaging Co. Am., Denver and Evanston, Ill., 1967-74; dir. indsl. and employee relations Ball Corp. Metal Container Group, Lakewood, Colo., 1974-76; dir. personnel and indsl. relations Nekoosa Envelopes, Inc., Denver, 1976—, Butler Paper Co., 1980—; cons. in field. Vol. funds campaigner U. Denver, 1975. Served with AUS, 1956-57. Mem. Am. (accredited), Colo. socs. personnel adminstrn., U. Mich. Alumni Assn. (life). Republican. Episcopalian. Home: 565 Mohawk Dr Boulder CO 80303 Office: 23 Inverness Way E Englewood CO 80112

BRIGGS, REID RICHMOND, lawyer; b. Evanston, Ill., Aug. 25, 1911; s. Henry B. R. and Mary Florence (Dennis) B.; A.B., Stanford U., 1932; J.D., George Washington U., 1938; m. Elizabeth Olwen Hughes, Aug. 23, 1935. Reporter, Los Angeles Record, 1932; clk. to U.S. Senator William Gibbs McAdoo, 1933-38; admitted to Calif. bar, 1938, D.C. bar, 1938, U.S. Supreme Ct. bar, 1945; with firm Lillick McHose & Charles, Los Angeles, 1939-76, partner, 1950-76. Asso. founder Los Angeles Music Center; counsel Japanese Philharm. Orch., Los Angeles, 1970-81. Served to lt., USNR, 1942-46; lt. comdr. res., 1946-54. Recipient Gold Spike award Stanford U., 1976; Disting. Profl. Achievement award George Washington U. Law Assn., 1979. Mem. Los Angeles Bar Assn., Am. Judicature Soc., Stanford Assos. (bd. govs. 1961-69, v.p. 1964-65), Order of Coif. Methodist. Clubs: UCLA (pres. 1959-60), Chancery. Home: 3901 E California Blvd Pasadena CA 91107

BRIGGS, ROBERT ALVIN, JR., real estate investor; b. Greeley, Colo., Dec. 24, 1937; s. Robert Alvin and Leta Zora (Edison) B.; B.S., Colo. State U., 1959, M.S., 1961; m. Shirley Christine Abbott, Sept. 8, 1957; children—Robert Reuben, Christy Lynn. Pres., Briggs Flower Shop & Garden Center, Westminster, Colo., 1961-80; commr. Adams County, Denver, 1979-83; pres. Fin. Devel. Group, 1983—; engaged in real estate investments, 1983—. Dist. chmn. Valley dist. Boy Scouts Am., 1980-82, mem. exec. bd. Denver Area council, 1980-84. Recipient Disting. Service award Westminster Jaycees, 1965, 70, Ortho Co., 1977, Colo. Flowers Growers Assn., 1971; Silver Beaver award Boy Scouts Am., 1982; named Outstanding Elected Ofcl. Adams County, 1982. Mem. Colo. Flower Growers Assn. (pres. 1969-71), Colo. Bedding and Pot Plant Assn. (pres. 1979), Westminster C. of C. (pres. 1968), Adams County C. of C. (dir. 1980-82), Metro North C. of C. (dir. 1980-82), Am. Carnation Soc., Soc. Am. Florists, Am. Nurseryman Assn., Am. Hort. Assn., Colo. Nurserymen Assn., Denver Bot. Gardens, Colo. Counties, Inc., Nat. Assn. Counties, North Suburban Bd. Realtors (vice chmn. exec. bd.), Denver Regional Council Govts. (exec. bd.). Republican. Presbyterian. Clubs: Mt. Vernon Country, Masons, Elks, Shriners. Office: 7970 Sheridan Blvd Westminster CO 80003

BRIGGS, WINSLOW RUSSELL, biologist; b. St. Paul, Apr. 29, 1928; s. John Dequedville B.; B.A., Harvard U., 1951, M.A., 1952, Ph.D., 1956; m. Ann Morrill, June 30, 1951; children—Caroline, Lucia Russell, Marion Stephen. Mem. faculty Stanford (Calif.) U., 1955-67, prof. biology, 1966-67; prof. biology Harvard U., 1967-73; dir. dept. plant biology Carnegie Instn. Wash., Stanford, Calif., 1973—. Guggenheim fellow, 1973-74. Mem. Am. Soc. Plant Physiologists (pres. 1975-76), Calif. Bot. Soc. (pres. 1977-78), Am. Inst. Biol. Scis. (pres. 1980-81), Nat. Acad. Scis., Am. Acad. Arts and Scis., AAAS, Bot. Soc. Am., Am. Soc. Photobiology. Author: (with others) Life on Earth, 1978; contbr. articles to profl. jours. Office: 290 Panama St Stanford CA 94305

BRIGHAM, THOMAS GLEN, advertising agency executive; b. Elkhorn, Wis., Apr. 11, 1947; s. Glen Allan and Harriet Coletta (Cummings) B.; m. Beatrice Elliot Rogers, May 8, 1976; children—Kristina, Jennifer, Justine; B.A. in Journalism and Advt., U. Wis.-Madison, 1970. Continuity dir., head copywriter, WKOW-TV, Madison, 1968-70; advt., pub. relations mgr. Hewlett-Packard, Calculator Products Div., Loveland, Colo., 1970-71; dir. communications, Compucorp, Los Angeles, 1971-74; pres. Brigham/Scully, Inc., Los Angeles, 1974—; ptnr. Greystone Mktg., 1982—; dir. Santa Monica Bay Printing & Pub. Co. Bd. advs. UCLA Hosps. and Clinics, 1980-82; bd. dirs. UCLA Med. Ctr. Aux., 1975-81, mem. adv. bd., 1981—), bd. dirs. Pacific Palisades Boys Football Assn., 1976-78; founder Karen Brigham Fund for Pediatric Cancer Research, UCLA, pres., 1974—. bd. dirs. Bus./Profl. Advt. Assn., 1981-83, pres., 1982. Republican. Office: 1122 S Robertson #9 Los Angeles CA 90035

BRIGHT, DARRIS J., electronics corp. ofcl.; b. Teton City, Idaho, Apr. 17, 1939; s. Charles Artell and Edna Leila (Hollist) B.; B.S. in Indsl. Mgmt., Brigham Young U., 1961; M.B.A., U. Idaho, 1971; m. Paulette A. McMurray, Sept. 21, 1975; children—Darrin M., Kevin A., Jason Darris, Daniel Mark Denney. Material planner Hercules Inc., Salt Lake City, 1961-67, indsl. engr., 1967-68; reactor modification scheduler Argonne Nat. Lab. (Ill.), 1968-71; scheduling supr., dept. supr., prodn. control mgr. Am. Microsystems, Inc., 1971-80, mgr. inventory control and indsl. engring., 1980-81, mgr. indsl. engring., project mgr./facilitator for qualitivity program, 1981—. Vice commr. Pocatello Little League Football, 1976-79; officer Pocatello Slow Pitch Assn., 1978; coach Little League Basketball, 1976-77; parks commr. Little League Baseball, 1974-75; city volleyball coordinator, 1978-79; scoutmaster Tendoy council Boy Scouts Am., 1980. Mem. Am. Inst. Indsl. Engrs., Am. Soc. Tng. and Devel. (chpt. v.p., 1979). Mormon. Home: 169 Valleyview Pocatello ID 83201 Office: 2300 Buckskin Rd Pocatello ID 83201

BRIGHT, HAZEL MABEL, speech therapist; b. Kimberly, Minn., Dec. 19, 1919; d. Edward Mac and Viva C. (Drone) Bright; B.S. in Edn., Moorhead State Tchrs. Coll., 1941; M.S. in Spl. Edn., St. Cloud State Coll., 1970; postgrad. in Speech Pathology, U. Minn., 1948-50, Calif. Poly. Coll., St. Cloud State Coll., 1971-75. Tchr., LaPorte (Minn.) Pub. Schs., 1941-42; tchr., prin. Lake Park (Minn.) Jr. High Sch., 1942-48; teaching fellow U. Minn., Mpls., 1948-49; speech therapist, audiometrist San Luis Obispo (Calif.) City Schs., 1948-82; owner Redwood Pub. Co. Clinician speech clinic Coll. of Pacific, Stockton, Calif., summer 1947; guest speaker Central Regional Speech Conf., Omaha, 1949, Western Regional Speech Conf., Salt Lake City, 1959, Calif. State Conf., 1973; dir., founder SLO Hearing Project. Youth leader 4-H Club, Kimberly, Minn., 1942-45. Bd. dirs. San Luis Obispo County Crippled Children and Adults Soc. Named Spl. Edn. Tchr. of Year, San Luis Obispo County. Mem. Am. Speech and Hearing Assn. (clin. mem.), NEA, Calif. Tchrs. Assn., Bus. and Profl. Women's Club (sec. 1955-56, pres. 1958-59), Delta Kappa Gamma (treas. 1958-62), Tau Kappa Alpha, Alpha Psi Omega. Clubs: Classroom Teachers (treas. San Luis Obispo 1955-56, pres. 1956-57), Soroptimist (San Luis Obispo). Author: Boehm Test Remediation, Books I-II, 1973; Out in the Back 40, 1978; contbr. articles to profl. jours. Home: 3860 S Higuera St #105 San Luis Obispo CA 93401 Office: City Schs 1499 San Luis Dr San Luis Obispo CA 93401

BRIGHT, LYN EDWARD, packaging machinery mfg. co. exec.; b. Sacramento, Apr. 7, 1947; s. Calvin Edward and Marjorie O. (Hensley) B.; B.S., Brigham Young U., 1969; M.B.A., U. So. Calif., 1971; m. Cheryl Ann Varone, Aug. 22, 1974; children—Parker Hensley, Lindsay Varone. Prodn. asst. Bright Foods, Inc., Turlock, Calif., 1963-69; project mgr. F.M. Stamper Co., Turlock, 1969-70; with Wilson & Co., Buenos Aires, Argentina, 1968; asst. to pres., dir. A G I, Modesto, Calif., 1971-72; gen. mgr., cons. Woodside Properties, Turlock, 1972-75; gen. mgr., dir. B & H Mfg., Ceres, Calif., 1975—; dir. Valley Sales, Inc.; cons. CLS Investment. Republican. Mormon. Home: 3625 Lockwood Rd Ceres CA 95307 Office: 3461 Rording Ave Ceres CA 95307

BRIGHT, PETER BOWMAN, aerospace scientist, engineer, consultant; b. Galipolis, Ohio, Dec. 27, 1937; s. Warren Harris and Elizabeth (Bowman) B.; m. Edris Brown, Apr. 21, 1938 (div.); children—Alicia Laurel, Debra Elaine, Michael Murray. B.S. in Math., Antioch Coll., 1960; Ph.D. in Math. Biology, U. Chgo., 1966. Asst. prof. biophysics U. Tex., Dallas, 1969-73; asst. research biomathematician UCLA, 1973-75; cons. Aerospace Corp., Los Angeles, 1975-78, mem. tech. staff, 1980—; asst. prof. math. Calif. State U.-Northridge, 1977-79; project dir. U. So. Calif., 1979-80; cons. Mem. IEEE, Assn. Computing Machinery, AIAA, Sigma Xi. Unitarian. Contbr. articles and abstracts to profl. jours., chpt. in book. Home: 12861 Winthrop Ave Granada Hills CA 91344 Office: 2350 E El Segundo Blvd M1 114 El Segundo CA 90245

BRIGHTBILL, THOMAS EUGENE, management consultant; b. Mansfield, Ohio, Dec. 4, 1940; s. Mark and Clara M. (Shultz) B.; B.S. in Chemistry, Case Inst. Tech., 1962; M.B.A., Case Western Res. U., 1965; m. Maureen E. Topping, Apr. 4, 1962. Systems analyst Cleve. Electric Illuminating Co., 1962-66; research cons. Spindletop Research, Inc., Lexington, Ky., 1966-69; cons. Arthur Young & Co., Sacramento, 1969-70, 1970—, prin., office dir., 1976-81, dir. (partner equivalent), Honolulu, 1981-82; prin. Main Hurdman, San Francisco, 1982—. Mem. Hawaii state adv. council ARC, 1979-81; chmn. bd. trustees Hawaii Bound, 1981. Mem. Hawaii Soc. Corporate Planners (dir. 1975-78), Ops. Research Soc. Am., Inst. Mgmt. Sci., Data Processing Mgmt. Assn. Clubs: World Trade, Honolulu (founding dir.). Home: 1980 Washington St Apt 204 San Francisco CA 94109 Office: 2500 Two Embarcadero Center San Francisco CA 94111

BRIGHTWELL, BETTY L., savings and loan executive; b. Huntington, W.Va., Jan. 10, 1926; d. James L. and Grace M. (Huddleston) B.; student Marshall U., 1943-46; B.A., U. Colo., 1970. Personnel and labor relations ofcl. C. & O. R.R., Richmond, Va., 1945-57; mgr. processing closing shipping Kassler & Co., Denver, 1957-63; mgr. closing dept. Ft. Wayne Mortgage Co., Denver, 1963-68; asst. v.p. Security Pacific Mortgage Co., Denver, 1968-78; v.p. Majestic Investment Co., Denver, 1978-82, World Savs. & Loan Assn., 1982—. Mem. Colo. Mortgage Bankers Assn., Mortgage Bankers Assn. Am. Club: Photography. Office: World Savings and Loan Assn 2460 W 26th Ave Denver CO 80211

BRILLIANT, ASHLEIGH ELLWOOD, writer, cartoonist, publisher, educator; b. London, Dec. 9, 1933; s. Victor and Amelia (Adler) B.; came to U.S., 1956, naturalized, 1969; B.A. with honors, Univ. Coll., London, 1955; M.A. in Edn., Claremont Grad. Sch., 1957; Ph.D. in Am. History, U. Calif., Berkeley, 1964; m. Dorothy Low Tucker, June 28, 1968. Tchr. English, Hollywood High Sch., Los Angeles, 1956-57; teaching asst., reader in history U. Calif., Berkeley, 1960-63; asst. prof. history Central Oreg. Coll., Bend, 1964-65, Floating Campus div. Chapman Coll., Orange, Calif., 1965-67; entertainer in coffeehouses, outdoor speaker San Francisco, 1967-68; syndicated cartoonist, dir. Brilliant Enterprises, pub. and licensing, San Francisco, also Santa Barbara, Calif., 1967—; creator Pot-Shots postcards, T-shirts, cocktail napkins, tote-bags, other items; mem. faculty Sonoma State U., Santa Barbara City Coll. Claremont Grad. Sch. scholar, 1956, Haynes fellow, 1962, Panama-Pacific fellow, 1963. Mem. Newspaper Comics Council, No. Calif. Cartoonists Assn., Mensa. Jewish. Author: I May Not Be Totally Perfect, But Parts of Me Are Excellent, And Other Brilliant Thoughts, 1979; I Have Abandoned My Search for Truth and Am Now Looking for a Good Fantasy, 1980; Appreciate Me Now and Avoid the Rush, 1981. Home and office: 117 W Valerio St Santa Barbara CA 93101

BRILLIANT, ELLIOTT HIRSCH, accountant; b. St. Louis, Sept. 9, 1938; s. David and Anna (Stein) B.; B.S. in Bus. Adminstrn., Washington U., St. Louis, 1960; J.D., Yale U., 1963; m. Robin Kling, Aug. 9, 1975. Admitted to Mo. bar, 1963; acct. Ernst & Whinney, St. Louis, 1963-67, partner charge of tax, Honolulu office, 1967-81, Century City (Calif.) office, 1982—; vis. prof. law U. Hawaii, 1975-78. Treas., Hawaii div. Am. Cancer Soc., 1971-74, v.p., 1974-75; pres. Honolulu Symphony Soc., 1975-78, chmn. bd., 1978-80; bd. dirs. Los Angeles Chamber Orch., 1983—; trustee Tax Found. Hawaii, 1979-82. C.P.A., Hawaii. Mem. Am. Inst. C.P.A.s, Hawaii Soc. C.P.A.s, Am. Bar Assn., Mo. Bar Assn., Hawaii C. of C. (chmn. subcom. on taxation 1977-82, dir. 1979-82). Clubs: Pacific; Outrigger Canoe; Waialae Country; Yale. Co-author: Taxes of Hawaii, 1975-83 edits. Office: 1875 Century Park E Suite 2200 Los Angeles Ca 90067

BRIM, ERMA L., nurse; b. Birmingham, Ala.; d. Norman and Gladys Hill; student Galileo Vocat. Nursing Sch., 1954; cert. in English, U. Calif. Extension, 1960, in Social Service, 1961; A.A. in Nursing, Community Coll. San Francisco, 1974; children—Emelda J. Atkins, Jon Brim Yasin. R.N. Lic. vocat. nurse Mt. Zion Hosp., San Francisco, 1954, San Francisco Gen. Hosp., 1954-70, R.N., 1970-77; nurse venereal disease clinic Dept. Public Health, San Francisco, 1977-82, Dept. Pub. Health Ctr. V, 1982—; mem. Council on Continuing Edn. for Health Occupations, State of Calif., 1974, State Council on Developmental Disabilities, 1982. Rec. sec. Nat. Council Negro Women, San Francisco, 1963; mem. Rep. county and state central com., 1960-69; active parent aux. Recreation Center for Handicapped, nursing and health services ARC, Council of Rep. Women, PTA, NAACP; trustee Aid to Retarded Citizens; mem. spl. edn. council San Francisco Unified Sch. Dist.; rec. sec. Woman's Soc. Christian Service, Jones Meth. Ch., 1965, Commn. on Christian Social Concerns, 1961-68, chmn., 1978, active Black Meth. Ch. Renewal, 1972. Recipient Disting. Citizens Service Citation, State of Calif., 1974. Mem. West Bay Health Systems Agy., Lic. Vocat. Nurses League, Civil Service Assn., Health Care Coordinating Council, Devel. Disabilities Council of San Francisco, Coalition of Black Trade Unionists, Service Employees Internat. Union (locals 250 and 400), Black Am. Polit. Assn., Black Women Organized for Action, Black Women Organized for Polit. Action Bay Area, Nat. Fedn. Rep. Women (San Francisco council), LWV. Address: 635 Spruce St San Francisco CA 94118

BRIMHALL, GRANT R., city mgr.; b. Taylor, Ariz., Aug. 14, 1937; s. Logan and Mary (Hatch) B.; m. Avis Marie Ardian, Sept. 6, 1962; children—Tamara Hyer, Michelle, Brett, Rebecca, Dana, Lindy. B.S., Brigham Young U., 1960, M.S., 1963; M.P.A., U. So. Calif., 1977, D.P.A., 1979. Asst. mgr., fin. dir. City of Claremont (Calif.), 1964-69; city mgr. City of Glendora (Calif.), 1969-78, City of Thousand Oaks (Calif.), 1978—. Mem. Am. Soc. Pub. Adminstrn. (Scoville award for Outstanding Young Adminstr. 1969), Internat. City Mgmt. Assn. Mormon.

BRIMHALL, JOHN CLARK, editor, composer, arranger; b. Huntington Park, Calif., Nov. 22, 1928; s. John Clark and Nora Louise (Baffa) B.; m. Virgin Mae Ravain, Apr. 1, 1951; children—James, Mary, Anthony. Mus.B. cum laude, Loyola U., 1950; M.A., Calif. State U.-San Francisco, 1952. Tchr., Corcoran (Calif.) High Sch., 1953-55; supr.

music Corcoran Union Sch. Dists., 1955-56; instr. Porterville (Calif.) Coll., 1956-59, Orange Coast Coll., Costa Mesa, Calif., 1959-61; chief editor Hansen Publs., Inc., Miami Beach, Fla., from 1962; now pres. Brimhall Publs., Inc., Las Vegas; composer, arranger, numerous books, sheet music; composer primary series John Brimhall Piano Method, John Brimhall Organ Method. Recipient La Croix de Commandeur, Merite et Devouement Francais (France), 1973. Mem. ASCAP, Am. Fedn. Musicians, Music Educators Nat. Conf. Clubs: Palm Bay (Miami, Fla.). Home: 3111 Bel Air Dr Las Vegas NV 89109 Office: 900 E Karen Ave Suite H 220 Las Vegas NV 89109 also 1860 West Ave Miami Beach FL 33139

BRIMMER, CLARENCE ADDISON, judge, former atty. gen. Wyo.; b. Rawlins, Wyo., July 11, 1922; s. Clarence A. and Geraldine (Zingsheim) B.; student U. Wyo., 1942; B.A., U. Mich., 1944, J.D., 1947; m. Emily O. Docken, Aug. 2, 1953; children—Geraldine, Philip, Andrew, Elizabeth. Admitted to Wyo. bar, 1948, practiced in Rawlins; mem. firms Brimmer & Brimmer 1948-63, Brimmer & MacPherson, 1968-71; atty. gen., Wyo., 1971-74; U.S. atty., 1975; U.S. dist. judge, 1975—; dir. 1st Nat. Bank, Rawlins, 1963-75. Sec. Rawlins Bd. Pub. Utilities, 1954-66; mem. Gov.'s Water Com., 1955-56. Chmn. Republican State Com., 1967-71; municipal judge, Rawlins, 1948-54. Trustee, Rocky Mountain Mineral Law, 1968-75. Served with USAAF, 1945-46. Mem. Am., Wyo. bar assns., Sigma Delta Chi, Sigma Phi Epsilon, Phi Delta Phi. Clubs: Masons, Rotary. Office: O'Mahoney Fed Center Cheyenne WY 82001

BRIMMER, WILLIAM NICHOLSON, petroleum co. exec.; b. Rawlins, Wyo., July 23, 1917; s. George Edric and Anna N. (Gould) B.; B.A., U. Wyo., 1938, D.J., 1941; m. Marian V. Hall, Dec. 22, 1960; children—Patricia Anne, April D. Admitted to Wyo. bar, 1941; gen. practice, Rawlins, 1945-59; county pros. atty. Carbon County, Wyo., 1950-54, city atty., Rawlins, 1955-56; atty. Bd. Pub. Utilities, Rawlins, 1955-59; pres. Ft. Collins Consol. Royalties, Inc., 1959—, Lance Creek Royalties Co., 1968—. Served with AUS, 1941-45; PTO. Decorated Bronze Star medal; recipient Disting. Service award Rawlins, 1948. Mem. Rocky Mountain Oil and Gas Assn., ABA, Wyo. State Bar, Wyo. Pioneer Assn., Wyo. Hist. Soc., Wyo. Jaycees (past pres.), Rawlins Jaycees (past pres.), VFW, Am. Legion. Clubs: Masons (past master Rawlins), Elks, Rotary (past pres. Rawlins). Address: PO Box 1363 Cheyenne WY 82003

BRINCKERHOFF, SIDNEY BURR, historian; b. N.Y.C., Sept. 27, 1933; s. William Weeks and Marguerite (Hall) B.; B.A. Princeton U., 1956; postgrad. U. Ariz., 1963-65; children—William, Laura. Pres., Ariz. Publicity Assocs., 1959-62; mus. curator Ariz. Hist. Soc., Tucson, 1962-64, asst. dir. for mus., 1964-68, dir., 1968-80, exec. dir., 1980—; chmn. Ariz. Hist. Adv. Commn., 1969-71; chmn. State Landmarks Com., 1979—; mem. Ariz. Bicentennial Commn.; mem. Ariz. Hist. Records Adv. Commn., 1976—; cons. Ariz. Edn. Dept. Chmn. Historic Preservation Task Force, Tucson Tomorrow, 1980; mem. adv. bd. Primavera Sch., 1972-78; bd. govs. Co. of Military Historians, 1976-79. Served with U.S. Army, 1956-59. Mem. Assn. State and Local History, Western History Assn., Am. Assn. Museums, Ariz.-Sonora Desert Mus., Council Abandoned Military Posts, Adobe Corral, The Westerners. Club: Old Pueblo, Tucson Racquet. Author: Lancers for the King, 1965, Spanish Military Weapons on Colonial America, 1972; Life on the American Nile, 1976; editor: Richard C. McCormick, Arizona: Its Resources and Prospects, 1967. Office: 949 E 2d St Tucson AZ 85719

BRINEY, KENNETH LAUREN, educator; b. Bradshaw, Nebr., July 26, 1930; s. Orville James and Irene Marie (Butler) B.; B.S., U. Calif., Berkeley, 1952, M.P.H., 1956, M.A., 1958, Ph.D., 1964; m. Donna Mae Lindley, Nov. 30, 1949; children—Susan Lauren, David Lindley. Exec. dir. Am. Cancer Soc., Alameda County br., Oakland, Calif., 1938-39, Alameda County Heart Assn., Oakland, Calif., 1959-64; dir. sch. health and health careers Am. Heart Assn., N.Y.C., 1964-68; exec. dir. Health Manpower Council of Calif., Orinda, 1968-74; prof. dept. health edn. San Francisco State U., 1974—; cons. in field. Mem. Lafayette-Moraga Trail citizens adv. com. East Bay Regional Parks, 1977—. Served with Med. Service Corps, U.S. Army, 1953-55. Fellow Am. Pub. Health Assn. (life fellow); mem. Am. Soc. Allied Health Professions, Am. Sch. Health Assn., Calif. Pub. Health Assn., Calif. Horsemen's Assn., Moraga Horsemen's Assn. (pres. 1978-79), Phi Delta Kappa (life). Author: Cardiovascular Diseases: A Matter of Prevention, 1970. Home: 99 Shuey Dr Moraga CA 94556 Office: San Francisco State U 1600 Holloway Ave San Francisco CA 94132

BRINGI, VISWANATHAN NAGANATHAN, electrical engr., educator; b. Bombay, India, July 17, 1949, came to U.S., 1971; s. Naganath Viswanath and Lakshmi B.; B.Tech., Indian Inst. Tech., Bombay, 1971; M.S., Ohio State U., 1973, Ph.D., 1976; m. Sreedevi K. Bringi, Aug. 27, 1976; 1 child, Vinayak. Sr. research assoc. Ohio State U., 1977-81; assoc. prof. dept. elec. engring. Colo. State U., Ft. Collins, 1981—. Univ. Corp. for Atmospheric Research fellow, 1974-76. Mem. IEEE, Am. Meteorol. Soc. Hindu. Contbr. articles to profl. jours. Office: Dept Elec Engring Colo State U Fort Collins CO 80523

BRINING, DENNIS LEE, aircraft company executive; b. Gary, Ind., Aug. 15, 1946; s. George Lee and Mary May (Popoff) B.; m. Linda L. Shaw, Sept. 7, 1968; children—Eric Lee, Tamara Suzanne. B.S. in Biology, San Diego State U., 1967, M.S. in Biology, 1969. Sr. scientist, mgr. new bus. devel. Lockheed Aircraft Service Co., Carlsbad, Calif., 1969-80; mgr. new bus. devel., mgr. Ocean Sci. Labs. Lockheed Missiles and Space Co., Carlsbad, 1980—; environ. cons., tchr. in 3rd world countries. Mem. marine activities adv. com. Saddleback Coll., Orange County, Calif.; mem. marine activities adv. com. Fullerton (Calif.) Coll. Mem. Marine Tech. Soc., Am. Water Works Assn., Internat. Desalination and Environ. Assn. Republican. Roman Catholic. Writer numerous publications, reports in marine research.

BRINK, THOMAS JAMES, safety engineer; b. Crookston, Minn., Sept. 22, 1947; s. Allen Leroy and Betty Erline (Bunch) B.; m. Marge White, Apr. 25, 1981. A.A., Foothills Jr. Coll., 1975; B.S., St. Cloud State U., 1977. Cert. assoc. safety profl. Served with U.S. Navy, 1965-75; risk mgmt. services rep. St. Paul Fire & Marine Ins., San Francisco, 1978—. Mem. Nat. Rifle Assn., Am. Soc. Safety Engrs. Republican. Club: Lions. Office: 201 3d St San Francisco CA 94103

BRINKMAN, MADELINE MARY, ins. agt., tax cons.; b. Dardanelle, Ark., Dec. 17, 1920; d. Robert Lee and Eula Ada (Robinson) Garner; student Lane Community Coll., 1971-72; m. Donald Emil Brinkman, Sept. 15, 1976; children—Richard Arlan Howard, Donald LeRoy Howard. Tax preparer H&R Block, 1968-70; owner, mgr. Brinks Enterprises Ltd., Eugene, Oreg., 1970-80; tax preparer Tax Corp. Am., Eugene, 1970—; ins. agt. Am. Bankers Ins. Co., Eugene, 1978—; mem. RAND Group Real Estate. Mem. Assn. Tax Consultants, Rental Owner Assn. Home: 2237 Wisconsin St Eugene OR 97402

BRINKMAN, THOMAS CHRISTOPHER, real estate broker; b. South Bend, Ind., Feb. 10, 1942; s. John Fredrick and Phyllis G. (Trout) B.; 1 dau., Lessley Ann. Gen. mgr. restaurant Villa Roma, Concord, Calif., 1972-73; real estate salesman Transcentury Properties, Bodega Bay, Calif., 1973-77; owner, broker Brinkman Realty, San Leandro, 1977—; pres. T&L Properties, Inc., San Leandro, Calif., 1979—; v.p. Wildwood, Inc., Sierra High, Inc., Hidden Valley, Inc., Concepts in Time Inc.; vacation sales mgr. Camper Resorts Am. Chmn., Boot Jack Golf Tournament, Easter Seal Soc., 1972-75. Served with USMC, 1959-63. Mem. No. Calif. Thoroughbred Assn. Republican. Roman Catholic. Club: Spring Valley Lake Country. Home: 585 Ocean View Grover City CA 93433 Office: 15287 Hesperian Blvd San Leandro CA 94578

BRINSON, KAREN RAE, clin. lab. technologist; b. Bakersfield, Calif., Feb. 6, 1944; d. Doni Winfred and Mildred Ethel (Purdy) Shophire; B.S., Calif. State Poly. U., San Luis Obispo, 1967; M.S., Calif. State Poly. U., Pomona, 1972; m. Michael James Brinson, Jan. 1, 1965; 1 dau., Katerina Lynn. Clin. lab. technologist Little Company Mary Hosp., Torrence, Calif., 1968-69; clin. lab. technologist Kaiser Hosp., Fontana, Calif., 1969-79, asst. lab. supr., 1979—; research technologist Calif. State Poly. U., Pomona, 1970-72. Mem. Am. Soc. Microbiology, Am. Inst. Biol. Scis. Democrat. Office: Kaiser Hosp 9961 Sierra Ave Fontana CA 92335

BRINTON, ROBERT WAYNE, hotel marketing director; b. Mesa, Ariz., Oct. 15, 1951; s. Dilworth Carlos and Pearl (Randall) B.; m. Nanette Maree Phelps, May 22, 1975; children—Kylie, Robert Wayne, Matthew, Staci. B.S., Ariz. State U., 1977. With Ramada Inns Inc., Phoenix, 1977—, mgmt. tng. dir., 1982—; dir. mktg. services Ramada Renaissance Hotels, 1982—. Bd. dirs. Ramada Employees Credit Union; mktg. and advt. cons. Active Boy Scouts Am.; fundraiser United Way, Ramada co-chmn., 1978-79; Easter Seals, 1980—. Mem. Am. Mktg. Assn., Hotel Sales Mgmt. Assn., Nat. Restaurant Assn. Republican. Mormon. Office: Ramada Inns Inc PO Box 590 Phoenix AZ 85001

BRISCOE, JAMES AUSTIN, geol. exploration co. exec.; b. Tucson, July 30, 1941; s. James Watkins and Lura (Austin) B.; B.S., U. Ariz., Tucson, 1964, M.S., 1967; children—Lura Kirsten, James Austin, Maribeth. Exploration geologist Am. Smelting and Refining Co., 1965-69; chief geologist Geodata, Inc., Orange, Calif., 1969-71; v.p., chief geologist Sierra Mineral Mgmt. Co., Tucson, 1971-73; pres., founder Southwestern Exploration Assocs., Inc., Tucson, 1973-81; prin. J.A. Briscoe & Assocs., Inc., 1981—. Registered profl. geologist, Ariz., Calif. Mem. AAAS, Am. Inst. Mining and Metall. Engrs., Ariz. Geol. Soc., N.Mex. Geol. Soc., Sigma Xi, Sigma Gamma Epsilon. Republican. Episcopalian. Author reports. Address: 5701 E Glenn St Suite 120 Tucson AZ 85712

BRISCOE, JERRY BOWLES, political science educator; b. Wellington, Kans., Dec. 10, 1927; s. Jesse Bowles and Lena Moselle (Gilbert) B.; m. Elizabeth Joan Briscoe, 1955; children—Sandra Michelle, Steven Eliot. B.S., Northwestern U., 1948; M.A. in Internat. Relations, U. Chgo., 1949, Ph.D., 1954; postgrad. Univ. Coll., London, 1949-50, Boston U., 1956-59. Asst prof. Amarillo (Tex.) Coll., 1959-62; assoc. prof. World Affairs Council No. Calif., San Francisco, 1962-64; prof. polit. sci. U. of the Pacific, Stockton, Calif., 1964—; dir. five Robert A. Taft Insts. for Tchrs., U. Pacific. Served with U.S. Army, 1954-56. Rotary Found. fellow for Study Abroad, 1949-50. Mem. AAUP, No. Calif. Polit. Sci. Assn. (past pres.), Common Cause, UN Assn., World Affairs Council No. Calif., Community Forward of Stockton. Democrat. Unitarian. Home: 2635 Westminster Stockton CA 95204 Office: Dept Political Science Wendell Phillips Ctr University of the Pacific Stockton CA 95204

BRISKIN, BERNARD, business executive; b. N.Y.C., May 21, 1924; s. Samuel Jacob and Sara (Meyers) B.; B.A., UCLA, 1949; m. Judith Esther Friedman, Apr. 30, 1972; children—Jeffrey, Deborah, Julie; stepchildren—Rex Wilder, Cam Wilder. Staff asst. Norton Simon, Inc., 1950-60; self-employed, 1960-63; pres. Telautograph Corp., 1963-78; pres. chief exec. officer Arden Group, Inc., Los Angeles, 1978— . Served with USMC, 1943-45. Office: Arden Group Inc PO Box 2256 Terminal Annex Los Angeles CA 90051*

BRISTOL, THOMAS WHITMORE, elec. engr.; b. Ilion, N.Y., Nov. 17, 1937; s. Thomas Patrick and Agnes Marie (Bucek) B.; B.M.E., Gen. Motors Inst., 1960; M.S. in Elec. Engring., U. Mich., 1963, Ph.D. in Elec. Engring., Syracuse U., 1968; m. Patricia Sue Middlesworth, Aug. 24, 1963; children—Thomas Whitmore, Jr., Margaret Kay, Scott David. Instr. elec. engring. Syracuse U., 1963-67; mem. tech. staff North Am. Rockwell, Anaheim, Calif., 1967-71; dept. mgr. Hughes Aircraft, Fullerton, Calif., 1971—. Recipient Hyland patent award Hughes Aircraft, 1975. Mem. I.E.E.E., Sigma Xi, Tau Beta Pi, Eta Kappa Nu, Phi Sigma Phi. Roman Catholic. Home: 526 E Meadowbrook Ave Orange CA 92665

BRISTOL, WANDA (JUNE) MASON, nurse, therapist; b. Ft. Cobb, Okla., Jan. 26, 1931; d. Alva Albert and Clara Belle (Bowman) Mason; A.A. diploma of nursing San Bernardino Valley Coll., 1951; B.S. (Polio Fund scholar), Calif. State U., Los Angeles, 1961, M.A., 1968; M.S. (USPHS grantee), Loma Linda U., 1964; M.S.Ed., U. So. Calif., 1976, postgrad., 1976—; m. Carl Eugene Bristol, Nov. 18, 1951 (div.); children—Bruce Edward, Brian Keith, Barry Lee. Staff nurse San Bernardino County Hosp., 1951-52, head nurse, 1952-59; staff nurse San Bernardino Community Hosp., 1954; spl. staff nurse Riverside (Calif.) Health Nurse, 1959-60; instr. Mt. San Antonio Coll., 1961-62; sch. nurse Bloomington (Calif.) Sch. Dist. unified with Colton Joint Unified Sch. Dist., 1963—; pvt. practice marriage, family, and child counseling, Rialto, Calif., 1979—; also pvt. practice hypnotherapy; psychodrama practitioner; vol. counselor. Health chmn. Bloomington Community Services Council, including establishment dental clinic, 1964-67; mem. Colton Children's Services Council, 1967—; mem. mental health task force Los Angeles chpt. Calif. NOW. Mem. Am. Nurses Assn., Calif. Nurses Assn., Calif. Assn. Marriage and Family Therapists, Colton Educators, Calif. Tchrs. Assn., Nat. Tchrs. Assn., Am. Assn. Marriage and Family Therapists, Calif. Assn. Marriage and Family Therapists, Am. Psychol. Assn., Calif. State Psychol. Assn., Inland Psychol. Assn., San Bernardino Mental Health Assn., Am. Soc. Group Psychotherapy and Psychodrama. Republican. Methodist. Contbr. articles to profl. jours. Home and office: 1485 N Mulberry Rialto CA 92376

BRISTOW, ARTHUR ALBERT, retired tractor company executive; b. Meridian, Calif., Dec. 20, 1919; s. Jessie and Myrtle Grace (Snyder) B.; A.A., Yuba Jr. Coll., 1940; m. Nancy M. VanArsdale, Feb. 23, 1946; children—Harry E., Mary Ann., Steve A. With the Tenco Tractor, Inc., Pleasant Grove, Calif., 1935—, service mgr., 1946-48, gen. sales mgr., 1948-52, dir. sales, 1952-70, v.p. sales, 1970-83, spl. cons., 1983—. Pres. Lincoln Elementary Sch., 1956-65. Bd. dirs. Fremont Hosp., Yuba City, Calif., 1972—, pres., 1982-83; sec. United Communities Med. Service Bd.; bd. dirs. Buttes area council Boy Scouts Am.; trustee Lincoln Sch. Served with USAF, 1941-45; PTO. Recipient Silver Beaver award Boy Scouts Am. Republican. Methodist. Mason (Shriner), Rotarian (pres. 1960-61, Paul Harris fellow 1983), Royal Order Jesters Ct., Elk. Home: 2339 Franklin Rd Yuba City CA 95991 Office: PO Box X Sacramento CA 95813

BRITT, MICHAEL ROY, personnel adminstrator; b. Oakland, Calif., Nov. 13, 1953; grandson Willie and Theresa (Clark) Gray. B.A. in Music, Calif. State U.-Hayward, 1974; M.A. in Mus. Edn., Stanford U., 1975, Ed.D., 1980. Cert. personnel worker, supr., music instr., Calif. Tchr. Palo Alto (Calif.) Unified Schs., 1974-80; employment coordinator Stanford (Calif.) U., 1981—; pvt. music instr.; mus. cons., guest condr., performing artist. Vol. fund raiser Stanford U. Devel. Office; campaign worker Bradley for Gov. Oakland Model Cities scholar, 1971-75; Stanford U. scholar, 1974; Calif. State grad. fellow, 1977-80; recipient Outstanding Tchr. award, Palo Alto Unified Schs., 1977. Mem. Am. Soc. Tng. and Devel., Peninsula Assn. Black Personnel Adminstrs., Phi Delta Kappa. Democrat. Baptist. Club: Jubilee Investment Group (Stanford). Office: Personnel Dept Old Pavilion Stanford U Stanford CA 94305

BRITT, RONALD JOSEPH, lawyer; b. Colusa, Calif., Oct. 6, 1949; s. Henry Grover and Helen Elaine (Ferreria) B.; B.A. in Econs., Calif. State U., Sacramento, 1967-71; J.D., U. Pacific, 1974; m. Elaine Elizabeth Cavaco, Feb. 14, 1970; children—Lucas Henry, Logan Sebastian, Lance Joseph. Admitted to Calif. bar, 1974; research asst. Calif. Dept. Benefit Payments, Sacramento, 1974-75; partner firm Waits & Britt, Sacramento, 1975-77, Waits & Britt, A Law Corp., Sacramento, 1977—; legal counsel Sacramento Jr. C. of C., Div. 7 of Calif.-Nev.-Hawaii dist. Kiwanis Internat. Mem. Am., Calif. State, Sacramento County bar assns., Calif. Trial Lawyers Assn., Capitol City Trial Lawyers Assn., Sacramento Young Lawyers Assn., Sacramento Jr. C. of C. (dir. 1980-81). Democrat. Episcopalian. Clubs: Kiwanis (disting. past pres. Elk Grove-Florin club 1981-82); Masons (Sacramento). Office: 5240 Fruitridge Rd Sacramento CA 95820

BRITTAIN, JERRY LEE, clinical psychologist, naval officer; b. Bossier City, La., Aug. 4, 1947; s. Melvin Houston and Reba Cleo (Eaves) B.; m. Marion Frances Szewczyk; B.A. in Psychology, Villanova U., 1972; B.S. in Biology, Centenary Meth. Coll., 1974; M.A. in Counseling Psychology, La. Tech., 1975; Ph.D. in Clin. Psychology, Calif. Sch. Profl. Psychology, 1978; lic. clin. psychologist, Calif. Psychologist, medic U.S. Army, Valley Forge, Pa., 1969-72; med. intern Mental Health Ctr., Shreveport, La., 1975; pre-doctoral intern Calif. Mens Colony, San Luis Obispo, 1975-76; doctoral intern Visalia (Calif.) Community Counseling Ctr., 1976-77, Fresno County (Calif.) Mental Health Ctr., 1977-78; commd. lt. U.S. Navy, 1979; chief psychologist Naval Drug Rehab. Ctr., San Diego, 1979-83, Naval Hosp., Naples, Italy, 1983—; instr., pvt. practice psychology, San Diego. Mem. Am. Psychol. Assn. Republican. Mem. Ch. of Nazarene. Contbr. articles to profl. jours.

BRITTAIN, STEVEN WAYNE, probation officer, counselor; b. Travis AFB, Calif., Nov. 8, 1953; s. Harland James and Sharon Lavoyce (Wood) B.; m. Mary Jeanne Krul, June 10, 1978; children—Danika Elizabeth, Eric Steven. B.A. in Psychology, Ft. Lewis Coll., 1979; M.A. in Counseling and Guidance, U. No. Colo., 1981. Cert. alcoholism counselor and probation officer, Colo. Family therapist Daybreak, Farmington, N.Mex., 1979-80; probation officer 6th Jud. Dist., Durango, Colo., 1980—; cons. Ednl. Concepts, Durango, 1982—. Centennial Savs. and Loan scholar, 1978. Mem. Am. Psychol. Guidance Assn. (child protection team), S.W. Colo. Community Corrections Rape Intervention Team. Club: Elks (Durango). Home: 2036 Delwood St Durango CO 81301 Office: 6th Jud Dist PO Box 41 Durango CO 81301

BRITTON, B. ELIZABETH, university administrator, nurse, counselor; b. Gary, Ind., July 18, 1930; children—Darryl, Tamara, John, Lisa, Anthony, Alycyn. Diploma Chgo. Coll. Lab. and X-ray Technique, 1953; student DePaul U., 1965-67; A.A. in Nursing, Mayfair Chgo. City Coll., 1969; B.S.N., Purdue U., 1974, M.S. in Counseling, Portland State U., 1982. Profl. registered nurse, Oreg., Ill. Various nursing positions, Chgo., Evergreen, Ill., 1970-73; nurse practitioner preceptorship Carolyn M. Rawlings, M.D., Hammond, Ind., 1974; instr. maternity nursing U. Oreg. Health Scis. Ctr., Portland, 1976-77, assoc. project dir. acad. devel. and recruitment, 1979-81; mgr. mass immunization program Multi-Service Ctr. Multnomah County Health Dept., Portland, 1978; asst. dir. Office Minority Student Affairs Oreg. Health Scis. U., Portland, 1981—. Co-chmn. Task Force; Health Careers for Minorities, N.W., vol. Am. Indian Ctr., Chgo., 1972-73, Beverly Learning Ctr., Chgo., 1972-74, N.W. Ind. Home Health Agy., 1973; mem. adv. bd. Women's Resource Ctr., YMCA, Portland, Urban League, mem. auditing, found. coms. Jack and Jill Am., pres. Lake Oswego Welcome Wagon Club, 1976; mem. Howe Assn. Retarded Citizens, Tinley Park, Ill.; chmn. Willamette Valley Racial Minorities Consortium, 1983. Mem. Ethnic Nurses for Advancement Health Care, Am. Personnel and Guidance Assn., Assn. Non-White Concerns, Nat. League Nursing, Oreg. Citizens League Nursing (scholarship com.), Sigma Theta Tau, Alpha Kappa Alpha. Office: Oreg Health Scis U Portland OR 97201

BRITTON, DAVID CARL, hotel manager; b. Dallas, Oreg., Aug. 7, 1946; s. Robert Elwin and Corinne Ana (Applequist) B.; m. Rosalind Kathryn Thomas, Nov. 30, 1947; 1 dau., Tina Marie. Student San Diego State U., 1964-65. Cert. hotel adminstr. Asst. mgr. Las Vegas Marina Hotel, Fred Harvey, Inc., 1974-75; gen. mgr. The Inn at the Park, Wrather Hotels div., Anaheim, Calif., 1975-80, v.p. hotel ops. RMS Queen Mary, Long Beach, Calif., 1980-81; gen. mgr. Ramada Hotel, Beverly Hills, Calif., 1981-82; resort and club mgr. Coto de Caza Resort, Tracubo Canyon, Calif., 1982—. Mem. Soc. Preservation of Variety Arts; mem. Cousteau Soc. Served with USAF, 1965-68. Mem. ASTD, Am. Hotel and Motel Assn. (mktg. com.), So. Calif. Soc. Assn. Execs., Hotel Sales Mgmt. Assn. (past territorial dir. internat.). Democrat. Office: PO Box 438 22000 Plano Trabuco Trabuco Canyon CA 92687

BRITTON, DAVID L(ESTER), psychotherapist; b. Austin, Tex., Apr. 14, 1952; s. Howard Arthur and June Elaine (Madowsky) B.; m. Roberta Lester, Oct. 5, 1980. B.A., U. Tex., 1974; M.A., Pepperdine U., 1977. Lic. marriage, family and child counselor, Calif. Founder, prin. Family Supportive Services, Santa Monica, Calif., 1977-79; staff therapist South Bay Therapeutic Clinic, Hawthorne, Calif., 1977-80; sr. staff therapist Helpline Youth Counseling, Bellflower, Calif., 1979-80; pvt. practice psychotherapy, Hermosa Beach, Calif., 1978—; asst. clin. dir. South Bay Free Clinic, Hermosa Beach; tchr. Mem. Calif. Assn. Marriage and Family Therapists, Am. Acad. Psychotherapists. Office: 200 Pier Ave Suite 25 Hermosa Beach CA 90254

BRITTON, THOMAS WARREN, JR., mgmt. cons.; b. Pawhuska, Okla., June 16, 1944; s. Thomas Warren and Helen Viola (Haynes) B.; B.S. in Mech. Engring., Okla. State U., 1966, M.S. in Indsl. Engring. and Mgmt., 1968; m. Deborah Ann Mansour, Oct. 20, 1973; children—Natalie Dawn, Kimberly Ann. Cons., Arthur Young & Co., Los Angeles, 1968-72, mgr., 1972-76, prin., 1976-79, partner, 1979—, office dir. mgmt. services dept., Orange County, Calif., 1980—; lectr. in field. Mem. City of San Dimas Creative Growth Bd., 1976-77, chmn. planning commn., 1977-83; trustee World Affairs Council of Orange County, 1980; benefactor, founders com., trustee South Coast Repertory Theater. Served to capt. USAR, 1971—. Cert. mgmt. cons. Mem. Los Angeles Inst. C.P.A.s, Mgmt. Adv. Services Com., Pacific Coast Electric Assn., Pacific Coast Gas Assn., Am. Inst. Indsl. Engrs., Greater Irvine Indsl. League, Okla. State Alumni Assn. Clubs: Univ. of Los Angeles, Via Verde Country, Jonathan. Home: 18982 Wildwood Circle Villa Park CA Office: 3200 Park Center Dr Costa Mesa CA 92626

BRITTON-SIMMONS, GEARY MICHAEL, rehab. workshop adminstr.; b. Oak Park, Ill., Dec. 7, 1939; s. Howard Alexander and Irene Veronica (Moeller) S.; M.S., So. Ill. U., 1970; m. Mary Susan Britton, Aug. 23, 1968; children—Kevin, Todd, Brian. Dir. migrant program Community Action Group, Altus, Okla., 1969-71; urban planner model cities City Carbondale (Ill.), 1971-73; dir. unified social services Attucks

Community Service Bd, Carbondale, Ill., 1973-76; exec. dir. Conbela Assn. psychiat. rehab. workshop, Seattle, 1976—. Bd. dirs. Center for Addiction Services, Seattle, 1978; youth coach Lake Hills Soccer Club, 1978-82. Mem. Am. Mgmt. Assn., Wash. Assn. Rehab. Facilities (v.p., dir. 1981-83). Home: 16607 NE 32d St Bellevue WA 98008 Office: 945 Elliott Ave W Seattle WA 98119

BRIX, JAMES ALEXANDER, accountant; b. Seattle, Aug. 30, 1913; s. James S. and Edith (Seedorff) B.; B.A. in Bus. Adminstrn. magna cum laude, U. Wash., 1954; m. Sigrid Lena Forsberg, Feb. 13, 1935; children—Joan Lenea Carter, James Alexander, Julee Karen (Mrs. George E. Barber). Asst. personnel supr. Dept. Lighting, Seattle, 1937-41, 44-49, accountant Haskins and Sells, C.P.A.s, 1954-56; partner Brix and Shank, C.P.A.s, Poulsbo, Wash., 1956-58, pvt. practice pub. accountant, 1958—; gen. partner BHLW & Co.; v.p., dir. Fairview Estates, Inc.; dir. Jensen, Richards and Olhava, Inc., Alpine Evergreen Co., Inc. Served to capt., AUS, 1940-44. President's medalist U. Wash., 1954. Mem. Am. Inst. C.P.A.'s, Wash. Soc. C.P.A.s, Am. Legion, Disabled Officers World Wars, Ret. Officers Assn., C. of C. (past treas.), Phi Beta Kappa, Beta Gamma Sigma, Beta Alpha Psi, Alpha Kappa Psi. Mason. Lutheran (past treas.). Clubs: Collins Lake Community (past v.p., dir.); Emerald Lake Community (past pres., dir.); Poulsbo Yacht (past treas.). Home: PO Box 823 Poulsbo WA 98370

BROAD, ELI, housing and insurance company executive; b. N.Y.C., June 6, 1933; m. Edythe L. Lawson, Dec. 19, 1954; children—Jeffrey Alan, Gary Steven. B.A. cum laude, Mich. State U., 1954. Pvt. acctg practice, 1954-56; asst. prof. Detroit Inst. Tech., 1956; co-founder, pres., chmn. Kaufman and Broad, Inc., Los Angeles, 1957-72, chmn, 1973-75, chmn., chief exec. officer, 1976—; chmn. Sun Life Ins. Co. of Am., Baltimore, 1976-79, Sun Life Group Am., Inc., Atlanta, 1978—; mem. real estate adv. bd. Citibank, N.Y.C., 1976-81; dir. Biscayne Fed. Savs. & Loan Assn., 1981; dir. mem. exec. and audit com. Verex Corp., Wis., 1973-80. Trustee Calif. State U., 1978-82, chmn. bd., 1979-80, trustee emeritus, 1982—; trustee, Pitzer Coll., Claremont, Calif., 1972—, chmn, 1972-79; bd. dirs. Nat. Energy Found., 1979—; chmn. bd. trustee, Mus. of Contemporary Art., Los Angeles, 1980—; mem. adv. bd., bd. dirs. Gt. Western Council Boy Scouts Am., 1982—; bd. dirs. YMCA, Los Angeles, 1975-78; mem. campaign com. Am. Heart Assn., Los Angeles, 1974-76; bd. dirs. United Way, Los Angeles, 1972-74, chmn. loaned exec. campaign, 1980-81; del., speaker State Economic Summit Conf., 1974, Fed. Econ. Conf., 1974; chmn. Mayor's Housing Policy Com., 1974-75; chmn. Alan Cranston for U.S. Senate Campaign Com., 1970, co-chmn, 1982; del. Democratic Nat. Conv., 1968; active in campaigns for Pres. Carter, Gov. Brown, Mayor Bradley; active Eli and Edythe L. Broad Found., Eli Broad Family Found; founder Music Ctr., Los Angeles; active United Jewish Welfare. Recipient NAACP award, 1982; Labor's Award for Services in the Arts, AFL-CIO, 1982; Housing Man of Yr. award Nat. Housing Conf., 1979; Humanitarian award NCCJ, 1977; Disting. Alumni award Mich State U., 1968; Man of Yr. award City of Hope, 1967. Mem. Los Angeles C. of C. (dir. 1978-79). Clubs: Hillcrest Country, Regency. Home: 1 Oakmont Dr Los Angeles CA 90049 Office: 10801 National Blvd Los Angeles CA 90064

BROADBENT, DENNIS ELTON, psychologist, counseling services adminstr.; b. Price, Utah, Feb. 6, 1945; s. Cecil and Edna I. (Johnson) B.; B.S. magna cum laude, Brigham Young U., 1972; M.S. in Ednl. Psychology, Fla. State U., 1973, Ph.D., 1980; m. Helen Louise McRae, Dec. 10, 1974; children—Adrienne, Alexander (Alex), Stephanie, Heather. Religious tchr. and missionary Ch. of Jesus Christ of Latter-day Saints, Zurich, Switzerland, 1964-65, Florence, Italy, 1965-67; tchr. devel. seminars Ch. of Jesus Christ of Latter-day Saints, Tallahassee, Fla., 1971-72; program and tng. psychologist Fed. Correctional Instn., Tallahassee, 1971-72; sch. psychologist Wakulla County (Fla.) public schs., 1972-73, instr. tchr. tng. program, 1972-73; adjustment psychologist Easter Seal Rehab. Center, Tallahassee, 1974-75; exec. sec. Psycho-Ednl. Cons., Inc., Tallahassee, 1972-76; cons. clin. and ednl. psychologist, Tallahassee, 1972-75; clin. and cons. psychologist Dept. of Retardation, Sunland Tng. Center, Marianna, Fla., 1975-76; asst. instr. Fla. State U., Tallahassee, 1976; sch. psychologist Scottsdale (Ariz.) and Deer Valley sch. dists., Maricopa County, Ariz., 1977-79; clin. dir. Psychological and Family Health Associates, Phoenix, 1980—; pres. Family Devel. Resources, Inc., Phoenix, 1980—; instr. Glendale (Ariz.) Community Coll., 1981—. Exec. sec. Tallahassee Ward, Ch. of Jesus Christ of Latter-day Saints, Tallahassee, 1974-76, counselor to br. pres., Vung Tau, Vietnam, 1968-69, asso. chmn. Stake Public Relations Com., Tallahassee, Fla., 1975-77. Served with M.C., U.S. Army, 1967-71; Vietnam. Recipient Religious Service award Ch. of Jesus Christ of Latter-day Saints, 1972, Duty to God award Boy Scouts Am., 1964; cert. psychologist, Ariz. Mem. Am. Psychol. Assn., Western Psychol. Assn., Internat. Platform Assn., Nat. Council on Family Relations, Assn. for Advancement Behavior Therapy, Assn. Mormon Counselors and Psychotherapists. Republican. Club: Sertoma. Office: 2302 W Greenway Rd Phoenix AZ 85023

BROADHEAD, EDWARD HALL, former librarian; b. Jamestown, N.Y., Apr. 5, 1910; s. Wright D. and Katherine (Clapsadel) B.; A.B., Denison U. 1931; M.A., Duke, 1933; Mus.M., U. Mich., 1939; B.S. in L.S., Columbia, 1948; m. Helen Reeder Cross, June 5, 1936; children—David Edward, Cynthia (Mrs. Philip Joseph). Organist, instr. Duke, 1933-44; librarian, chmn. dept. organ and ch. music Hartt Coll. Music, Hartford, Conn., 1946-60; librarian Fairleigh Dickinson U., Madison, N.J., 1960-65; librarian So. Colo. State Coll., Pueblo, 1965-75. Organist, choir dir. 1st Congl. Ch., Meriden, Conn., 1945-47, Asylum Hill Congl. Ch., Hartford, 1947-56, Temple Beth Israel, Hartford, 1951-53; librarian U. Hartford, 1957-60. Bd. dirs. Pueblo Met. Mus. Assn., 1968-72, pres., 1970-71; mem. vocat. adv. council Pueblo Community Coll., 1983—. Mem. Colo. Council Acad. Librarians (chmn. 1970-72), ALA, Colo. Library Assn., Am. Guild Organists (dean Hartford chpt. 1950-51), Pueblo County Hist. Soc. (pres. 1977—), Am. Assn. Ret. Persons, Nat. Ret. Tchrs. Assn. (pres. Pueblo 1979-81), Pueblo C. of C. (com. on aging 1976-77), Phi Beta Kappa, Phi Mu Alpha. Home: 33550 Hwy 96E Sp 190 Pueblo CO 81001

BROADWAY, MONROE JACKSON, clergyman; b. Killeen, Tex., Aug. 19, 1937; s. George William and Hazel (Barnett) B.; B.A., Calif. Bapt. Coll., 1967; M.Div., Southwestern Bapt. Theol. Sem., 1970; Ph.D., Calif. Grad. Sch., 1975; m. Jacquelyn Jean Peugh, June 6, 1959; children—Michael Ray, Sharon Kay, Carol Annette. Ordained to ministry Baptist Ch., 1964; pastor First Bapt. Ch., Goree, Tex., 1970-72, First So. Bapt. Ch., Payson, Ariz., 1972-75, First Bapt. Ch., Rialto, Calif., 1975-78, First So. Bapt. Ch., Redding, Calif., 1978—; chaplain CAP, 1976-78, Redding Police Dept., 1978—; vice-coordinator Redding Police Chaplains Corps, 1978-80, coordinator, 1981, 82, coordinator exec. bd. Shasta County Chaplains Corps; mem. adv. bd. Today and Tomorrow's News, Redding, 1981. Trustee, Calif. Bapt. Coll., 1980-84; v.p. Payson Little League, 1974-78, coach, 1970-78; bd. dirs. Meml. Hosp., Redding, 1981—; mem. pastoral care com. Mercy Hosp., 1983—. Served with USAF, 1955-60. Recipient Letters of Appreciation, C. of C., 1975, Redding Police Dept., 1980. Mem. Shasta County Evang. Ministers Assn., Shasta Bapt. Assn., Southwestern Alumni Assn. Clubs: Lions, Internat. Order Foresters. Author: Religion in the Public Schools, 1975; Children's Seminar on Prayer, 1982. Home: 1205 Lorraine Dr Redding CA 96002 Office: 916 E Cypress Ave Redding CA 96002

BROCA, LAURENT ANTOINE, aerospace scientist; b. Arthez-de-Bearn, France, Nov. 30, 1928; came to U.S., 1957, naturalized, 1963; s. Paul L. and Paule Jeanne (Ferrand) B.; B.S. in Math., U. Bordeaux, France, 1949; Lic. es Scis. in Math. and Physics, U. Toulouse (France), 1957; grad. Inst. Technique Professionnel, France, 1960; Ph.D. in Elec. Engring., Calif. Western U., 1979; postgrad. Boston U., 1958, MIT, 1961, Harvard U., 1961; m. Leticia Garcia Guerra, Dec. 18, 1962; 1 dau., Marie-There Yvonne. Teaching fellow physics dept. Boston U., 1957-58; spl. instr. dept. physics N.J. Inst. Tech., Newark, 1959-60; sr. staff engr. advanced research group ITT, Nutley, N.J., 1959-60; examiner math. and phys. scis. univs. Paris (France) and Caen, Exam. Center, N.Y.C., 1959-69; sr. engr. surface radar div. Raytheon Co., Waltham, Mass., 1960-62, Hughes Aircraft Co., Culver City, Calif., 1962-64; asst. prof. math. Calif. State U., Northridge, 1963-64; prin. engr. astrionics lab. NASA, Huntsville, Ala., 1964-65; fellow engr. Def. and Space Center, Westinghouse Electric Corp., Balt., 1965-69; cons. and sci. adv. electronics, phys. scis. and math. to indsl. firms and broadcasting stations, 1969-80; head engring. dept. Videocraft Mfg. Co., Laredo, Tex., 1974-75; asst. prof. math. Laredo State U., summer, 1975; engring. specialist dept. systems performance analysis ITT Fed. Electric Corp., Vandenberg AFB, Calif., 1980-82; engring. mgr. Ford Aerospace and Communications Corp., Nellis AFB, Nev., 1982—. Served with French Army, 1951-52. Recipient Published Paper award Hughes Aircraft Co., 1966; Fulbright scholar, 1957. Mem. IEEE, Am. Nuclear Soc. (vice chmn. Nev. sect. 1982-83, chmn. 1983-84), Am. Def. Preparedness Assn. Home: 5009 Lancaster Dr Las Vegas NV 89120 Office: Ford Aerospace and Communications Corp Nellis AFB 89191

BROCCOLI, ALBERT ROMOLO, motion picture producer; b. N.Y.C., Apr. 5, 1909; s. Giovanni and Cristina (Vence) B.; student pub. schs., N.Y.C.; m. Dana Natol Wilson, June 21, 1959; children—Michael Wilson, Anthony, Christina, Barbara. Asst. dir. 20th Century Fox, 1941-42, RKO under Howard Hughes, 1947-48; theatrical agt. Charles Feldman, 1948-51; producer Warwick Films, 1951-60, Eon Prodns., Inc., 1960—. Served to lt. (j.g.) USN, 1942-47; PTO. Decorated grand officer Order of Crown (Italy), Order St. Constantine (Italy); recipient Man of Year award Bd. Dirs. Boys Club of Queens, Inc., 1968, Irving G. Thalberg Meml. award, 1982. Mem. Producers Guild, Am. Film Inst. Roman Catholic. Club: Metropolitan (N.Y.C.). Producer: Red Beret, 1952, Hell Below Zero, 1953, Black Knight, 1954, Prize of Gold, 1955, Cockleshell Heroes, 1956, Safari, 1956, April in Portugal, 1956, Fire Down Below, 1956, Odongo, 1956, Pickup Alley, 1957, Arrivederci Roma, 1957, Interpol, 1957, How to Murder a Rich Uncle, 1957. High Flight, 1958, No Time to Die, 1958, The Man Inside, 1958, Killers of Kilimanjaro, 1958, Bandit of Zhobe, 1958, In The Nick, 1959, Jazz Boat, 1960, Let's Get Married, 1960, The Trials of Oscar Wilde, 1960, Idol on Parade, 1960, Johnny Nobody, 1961, Call Me Bwana, 1963, Chitty Chitty Bang Bang (Family Film award So. Calif. Motion Picture Council 1968), 1967; (James Bond films) Dr. No, 1962, From Russia With Love (Screen Producers Guild certificate of nomination as best picture 1964), 1963, Goldfinger (Screen Producers Guild certificate of nomination as best picture 1964), 1963, Thunderball (Mkkin Kogyo Tsushin certificate of award 1966), 1964, You Only Live Twice (Mkkin Kogyo Tsushin certificate of award 1967), 1966, On Her Majesty's Secret Service, 1969, Diamonds Are Forever, 1971, Live and Let Die, 1972, The Man With the Golden Gun, 1974, The Spy Who Loved Me, 1977, Moonraker, 1979, For Your Eyes Only, 1981, Octopussy, 1983. Office: 1801 Century Park E Suite 1850 Los Angeles CA 90067

BROCK, DENNIS GLEN, wood products company official; b. Nampa, Idaho, Feb. 21, 1942; s. Glen Gordon and Wilma Bernice (Bryant) B.; m. Caroline Anne Jones, Feb. 2, 1962; children—Dennis Leon, Quintin Neal, Marie Danielle. B.A. in Secondary Edn., Northwest Nazarene Coll., 1968. With employee relations dept. Meridian Wood Products Co., Nampa, 1968-73, safety, trng. coordinator, 1973-77, personnel, safety dir., 1977-83; gen. mgr. Baker div., Baker, Oreg., 1983—. Mem. safety com. Timber Products Mfrs. First aid instr. ARC; adv. CETA. Republican. Office: Meridian Wood Products PO Box 558 Nampa ID 83651

BROCK, DONALD EDWARD, agrl. prodn. co. exec.; b. El Centro, Calif., Dec. 30, 1941; s. Warren H. and Jean (Malan) B.; B.S., U. Calif.-Davis, 1964; m. Melinda Woods, May 11, 1968; children—Julie, Kristina, Matthew. Dist. mgr. Brock Ranches, Inc., El Centro, 1966-69; exec. asst. to U.S. Sec. Agr., Washington, 1969-75; owner, mgr. Signal Produce Co., El Centro, 1975—. Nat. pres. Alpha Gamma Rho Fraternity Found.; Calif. chmn. Farmers for Ford, 1976; mem. Calif. Republican Central Com., U. Calif. Agrl. Adv. Council; active Boy Scouts Am. Served with AUS, 1964-66. Mem. Am. Legion, Am. Agrl. Econs. Assn. Republican. Methodist. Clubs: Rotary, Commonwealth. Address: PO Box 2190 El Centro CA 92244

BROCK, JAMES MELMUTH, engring. co. exec.; b. Brockton, Mass., Jan. 12, 1944; s. James Melmuth and Ruth Eleanor (Copeland) B.; student U. Hawaii, 1964-65, Taiwan Normal U., 1969; m. Mary Soong, June 24, 1964; 1 dau., Cynthia. Survey apprentice Malcolm Shaw, Hanson, Mass., 1959-62; with Peace Corps, N. Borneo, 1962-64; engr. Austin, Smith & Assos., Honolulu, 1964-65, Trans-Asia Engrs., Vietnam, 1965-67; ops. mgr. Teledyne, Bangkok, Thailand, 1967-69; chief surveys Norman Saito Engrs. Hawaii, 1970-73; sr. prin. Brock and Assos., Maui, Hawaii, 1973—; dir. Pitt Engring. Inc., Brock Realty Ltd.; del. White House Conf. Small Bus., 1980. Registered land surveyor, Hawaii. Mem. Am. Congress Surveying and Mapping, Am. Water Works Assn., Profl. Services Mgmt. Assn., Hawaii Soc. Profl. Engrs. Democrat. Congregationalist. Home: 766 Kupulau Dr Kihei Maui HI 96752 Office: 48 Market St Wailuku Maui HI 96793

BROCK, LESLIE VAN HORN, former educator; b. Pitts., Sept. 27, 1903; s. Lem Strosnider and Rachel (Van Horn) B.; B.S. summa cum laude, Waynesburg Coll., 1928; M.A., U. Mich., 1932, Ph.D., 1941; LL.D., Waynesburg Coll., 1968; m. Frances Sutherland, Dec. 24, 1938; 1 dau., Susan Frances. Instr., asst. prof., asso. prof. Waynesburg Coll., 1928-39, prof. history, econs., govt., 1939-47; prof. history, head dept. Coll. of Idaho, Caldwell, 1947-69, John Philip Weyerhaeuser, Jr., prof. of history, 1966-69, emeritus, 1969—; vis. asst. prof. U. Mich. summers 1942, 46. Mem. Am. Hist. Assn., Orgn. Am. Historians, Idaho Hist. Soc., Am. Econ. Assn., Delta Sigma Phi, Tau Kappa Alpha, Phi Kappa Phi, Phi Alpha Theta. Author: The Currency of the American Colonies, 1700-1764: A Study in Colonial Finance and Imperial Relations, 1975. Home: 1801 Dearborn St Caldwell ID 83605

BROCK, LINDA VOSS, retail executive; b. Austin, Tex., Mar. 14, 1942; d. William Bruce and Sara Louise V.; student U. Tex., Austin, 1959-62; B.S., Oklahoma City U., 1963, postgrad. 1964-66; M.C., Ariz. State U., 1975; children by previous marriage—Catherine Louise, Deborah Elizabeth, Stephen Lawrence, Richard Keith. Dispatcher, Xerox Corp., Oklahoma City, 1963-64; acct., bookkeeper Star Constrn. Co., Oklahoma City, 1964-66; counselor, tchr., lectr., retreatmaster Franciscan Renewal Center, Scottsdale, 1975—; v.p. Linda Brock BMW-Volkswagen, Scottsdale, 1969-79, owner, pres., gen. mgr., 1979— Pres., Lucky 13 Ednl. Center, 1977-79; sec. council St. Maria Goretti Catholic Ch., 1978-79; bd. dirs., v.p. pub. relations Ariz. Bus. and Industry Edn. Council, 1982-82; bd. dirs. Nat. Council on Alcoholism; pres. Brock Haus. Mem. Scottsdale Auto Dealers Assn. (pres. 1980—), Ariz. Auto Dealers Assn., Nat. Auto Dealers Assn., Scottsdale C. of C., Ariz. C. of C., Ariz. Safety Assn. (bd. dirs. 1981—), Scottsdale Exec. Club. Republican. Office: 3230 N Scottsdale Rd Scottsdale AZ 85252

BROCK, PHILIP LESLIE, jeweler, educator; b. Santa Monica, Calif., Dec. 25, 1953; s. Elrie L. and Beverly R. B.; m. Kesmat Kereim, Sept. 15, 1979 (div.). A.A., Santa Monica Coll., 19; B.A., UCLA, 1978; M.A. in Ednl. Adminstrn., Loyola Marymount Coll., 1979. Cert. secondary tchr., athletic dir., adminstr, Calif. Athletic dir. Boys Clubs Am., 1973-75, Jonathan Club, Los Angeles, 1976; athletic dir., dean of students, tchr. history and psychology Los Angeles Unified Schs., 1979-82; v.p. Brock Property and Real Estate Investment, 1977—; pres. Hamlet Jewelers, Inc., Los Angeles, 1980—; pres. Seaside Studio Gallery, Inc., 1980—. Mem. Santa Monica C. of C., Century City C. of C. Mem. Jewelers of Am., Calif. Jewelers Assn., Calif. Coaches Assn., So. Calif. Basketball Ofcls. Assn., Jewelers Security Alliance. Republican. Lutheran. Office: Seaside Studio Gallery 2818 Main St Santa Monica CA 90405

BROCK, ROBERT MAHLON, town owner; b. Indpls., Feb. 9, 1943; s. Daniel A. and Virginia M. (Wright) B.; A.B. in Econs., Ind. U., 1973; children—Roxanna Marie, Theodor Christian. Aircraft salesman, Sky Harbor Inc., Indpls., 1968-75, Sawyer Aviation, Phoenix, 1976-80; owner Tortilla Flat., Ariz., including saloon, restaurant, gen. store, motel, post office, souvenir shop, riding stable, 1980—; sole propr. Jojoba Super-Seed Co.; partner Ironwood Imports, importer Seri Indian ironwood carvings; Co-founder, internal v.p. Danville, Ind., Jaycees, 1967-68. Served with USNR, 1961-67. Address: PO Box 34 Tortilla Flat AZ 85290

BROCK, THERESA JEAN, educator; b. Ft. Worth, Aug. 30, 1929; d. Theodore Roosevelt and Naomi (Jones) Roberson; B.A., San Francisco State Coll., 1951; M.A., Mills Coll., Oakland, Calif., 1981; m. Buddy LeRoy Brock, Apr. 6, 1952; children—Angela Lynn, Richard LeRoy. Classroom tchr. Oakland Public Schs., 1969—, tchr. Crocker Highlands Elem. Sch., 1974-82; master tchr. San Francisco State U. and Mills Coll., 1970—; presenter tchr. workshops; cons. Piaget Conf., Stanford U., 1977; tchr. cons. Bay Area Writing Project, U. Calif.-Berkeley; facilitator Project Learning Tree, 1981-82; writer social sci. curriculum Calif. Dept. Edn., 1981; mem. policy bd. Alameda/Contra Costa County Tchr. Edn. and Computer Center. Active Crocker Highlands Parent-Tchr.-Student Assn. Teaching activities filmed by Fuji Telecasting Co., Ltd., Tokyo, 1978; recipient Service award Calif. Congress Parents and Tchrs., 1978; Oakland Tchr. of Yr. award, 1981; Alameda County Tchr. of Yr. award, 1981. Mem. Assn. Childhood Edn. Internat., Calif. Council Social Studies, East Bay Council Social Studies, Nat. Council Tchrs. of English, Assn. Supervision and Curriculum Devel., Nat. Council Tchrs. of Math., Calif. Math. Council, Alameda-Contra Costa Counties Math. Educators, NEA, Calif. Tchrs. Assn., Oakland Edn. Assn., NAACP, Nat. Council Negro Women, LWV (adminstrv. v.p. Oakland 1967-69), Delta Sigma Theta, Phi Delta Upsilon. Methodist. Home: 38 Drake Ln Oakland CA 94611 Office: 525 Midcrest Rd Oakland CA 94610

BROCKENBROUGH, EDWIN CHAMBERLAYNE, surgeon; b. Balt., July 24, 1930; s. Edwin C. and Martha (Coale) B.; B.S., Coll. of William and Mary, 1952; M.D., Johns Hopkins U., 1956; m. Jean Isabelle McClure, May 4, 1968; children—John, Martha, Andrew, Ann, Susan. Resident in surgery Johns Hopkins Hosp., Balt., 1956-59; sr. asst. surgeon Nat. Heart Inst., Bethesda, Md., 1959-61; asst. in surgery U. Wash., Seattle, 1961-64, asso. prof. surgery, 1964-75, clin. asso. prof. surgery, 1975—; practice medicine specializing in vascular and thoracic surgery, Seattle, 1975—; staff Northwest, Swedish, Providence, Ballard and Children's hosps. (all Seattle). Adv. council Bellevue Art Mus., 1976-78. Served with USPHS, 1959-61. Mem. ACS, Am. Heart Assn., AMA, Assn. for Acad. Surgery, Johns Hopkins Med. and Surg. Soc., King County Med. Soc., N. Pacific Surg. Assn., Pacific Coast Surg Assn., Seattle Surg. Soc., Am. Rhododendron Soc. (nat. pres. 1977-79). Republican. Episcopalian. Clubs: Bellevue Athletic, Overlake Golf and Country. Contbr. articles to profl. jours.; researcher cardiovascular diagnostic techniques. Home: 3630 Hunts Point Rd Bellevue WA 98004 Office: 1221 Madison St Seattle WA 98104

BROCKHAUS, WILLIAM DILLON, food service company executive; b. La Junta, Colo., Oct. 6, 1945; s. Clayton William and MaryJo (Dillon) B.; m. Debra Anne Handley; 1 son, Matthew Dillon. B.A., U. Oreg., 1967; M.A., U. Ky., 1974; postgrad. Portland State U., 1971, U. Istanbul (Turkey), 1971-72. Tchr. English as fgn. lang. U.S. Peace Corps, Turkey, 1967-69; teaching asst. English, instr. U.S. AID-TEFL program U. Ky., Lexington, 1969-74; mgmt. trainee M. Loeb Corp., Elk Grove Village, Ill., 1974-75; regional sales mgr. Everpure, Inc., Westmont, Ill., 1975—, now sales mgr. western food service markets, Santa Ana, Calif. Pres. bd. dirs. Homeowners Assn., San Clemente, Calif. NDEA grantee, 1971; Fulbright-Hayes grantee, 1971-72. Mem. Nat. Automatic Merchandisers Assn., Nat. Restaurant Assn. Methodist.

BROCKMAN, SUSAN KATHLEEN, advertising manager; b. Portland, Oreg.; d. Chester and Dorothy Marie (McEachin) Winn; m. Jerrold Alan Brockman, Nov. 30, 1973; 1 dau., Tracy Claire. B.A. in Communications, U. Wash., 1972. Advt. asst. REI Coop, 1972-75, retail advt. adminstr., 1975-79, advt. mgr., 1979—. Mem. Am. Advt. Fedn., Women in Communications, Theta Sigma Phi, Delta Delta Delta. Roman Catholic. Club: Gallery Court and Racquet (Seattle). Office: REI Coop 18200 Segale Park Dr B Tukwila WA 98188

BRODEN, CARL VICTOR, dentist; b. Turlock, Calif., May 15, 1943; s. Claud Victor and Florence Mary (Finley) B.; D.D.S., U. Pacific, 1973; m. Susan Gail Fischer, July 29, 1972; 1 son, Jason Carl. Gen. practice dentistry, Rio Linda, Calif., 1974-79; owner, pres. Eco-Dent Co., dental products firm, 1980—. Served with AUS, 1962-65. Mem. Sacramento Dist. Dental Soc., Calif. Dental Soc., Am. Dental Assn. Democrat. Inventor silver saving device for dentistry. Home: 5080 Keane Dr Carmichael CA 95608 Office: 958 Oak Ln Rio Linda CA 95673

BRODERICK, CARLFRED BARTHOLOMEW, educator; b. Salt Lake City, Apr. 7, 1932; s. Frederick Anthony and Napina (Bartholomew) B.; A.B. magna cum laude, Harvard U., 1953; Ph.D., Cornell U., 1956; postgrad. U. Minn., 1966-67; m. Kathleen Adelle State, July 3, 1952; children—Katherine, Carlfred Bartholomew, Victor, Wendi, Jenifer, Frank, Beverly, Benjamin. Assoc. prof. family devel. U. Ga., 1956-60; assoc. prof. family relations Pa. State U., 1960-69, prof., 1969-71; prof. sociology, dir. Marriage and Family Therapy Program, U. So. Calif., Los Angeles, 1971—. Pres. Cerritos (Calif.) Stake Ch. Jesus Christ of Latter-day Saints, 1976-82. Fellow Am. Assn. Marriage and Family Therapy, Am. Sociol. Assn.; mem. Internat. Sociol. Assn., Nat. Council Family Relations (pres. 1975-76), So. Calif. Assn. Marriage and Family Counselors (pres. 1974), Assn. Mormon Counselors and Psychotherapists (pres. 1982-83). Author: Sexuelle Entwickland in Kindheit und Jungend, 1970; editor: (with Jessie Bernard) The Individual, Sex and Society, 1969; A Decade of Research and Action on the Family, 1971; author: Marriage and the Family, 1979, 2d edit., 1984; Couples: How to Confront Problems and Maintain Loving Relationships, 1979; The Therapeutic Triangle, 1983; Jour. Marriage and the Family, 1970-75; contbr. articles to profl. jours. Home: 18902 Alfred Ave Cerritos CA 90701 Office: Dept Sociology U So Calif University Park Los Angeles CA 90089

BRODERICK, DAVID EDWARD, real estate exec.; b. Norwood, Mass., Apr. 21, 1942; s. Michael Francis and Margaret Ellen (Doyle) B.; B.S. in Edn., No. Ill. U., DeKalb, 1966; m. Dorothy Donovan, Dec. 20, 1973. Pres., owner United Am. Realty, Ltd., Los Angeles, 1976—. Mem. Am. Land Devel. Assn. (chmn. recreational vehicle park and camp resort council 1982-83). Republican. Roman Catholic. Clubs: Riviera Tennis, Safari Internat. Author articles in field of resort real estate. Office: 1888 Century Park E Suite 708 Los Angeles CA 90067

BRODERICK, HAROLD CHRISTIAN, interior designer; b. Oakland, Calif., Apr. 8, 1925; s. Harold Christian and Laura Jane (Lloyd) B. B.A., U. Tex., 1947. A founder Arthur Elrod Assos., Inc., Palm Springs, Calif., 1954, now pres. Mem. Planning Commn., City of Palm Springs, 1972-74; trust Palm Springs Desert Mus.; bd. dirs. Easter Seal Soc. Riverside County (Calif.). Mem. Am. Soc. Interior Designers. Republican. Club: Racquet (Palm Springs). Office: Arthur Elrod Associates Inc 850 N Palm Canyon Dr Palm Springs CA 92262

BRODERICK, JAMES LIVELY, psychologist; b. Vallejo, Calif., June 5, 1950; s. James L. and Marguerite K. (Gregory) B.; B.A., U. San Francisco, 1972; M.A., Calif. Sch. Profl. Psychology, 1974, Ph.D., 1976. Intern clin. and community psychology Linda Vista Health Care Center, San Diego, 1972-73; intern organizational and clin. psychology Allied Home Health Assn., San Diego, 1973-74; intern clin. psychology Western Inst. Human Resources, San Diego, 1974, U. Calif., San Diego, 1975, Mercy Hosp. and Med. Center, San Diego, 1975-77; clin. psychologist and adolescent therapist Shasta County Mental Health, Redding, Calif., 1978—, chief of psychology and dir. tng., 1979—; clin. instr. dept. family practice Sch. Medicine, U. Calif., Davis, 1980—; instr. Shasta Coll., 1978—, Chapman Coll., Redding, 1982. Bd. dirs. Group Foster Home Inc., 1978-79, Shasta County Women's Refuge, 1979—. Mem. Am. Psychol. Assn., Calif. Psychol. Assn., Assn. Advancement of Psychology, Assn. Asian Studies. Home: 8000 Calle de Gato Redding CA 96001 Office: 2750 Eureka Way Redding CA 96001

BRODERICK, RICHARD FRANCIS, electronics engineer; b. Waltham, Mass., Dec. 6, 1932; s. John William and Alice Josephine (Fitzpatrick) B.; B.S. in Elec. Engring., Northeastern U., 1956; M.S., U. Houston, 1964, Ph.D., 1968; m. Cecily Anne Mayhew, June 30, 1962. Sr. engr. Raytheon, Bedford, Mass., 1957-60; sect. head Dresser, Houston, 1960-62; with NASA, Houston, 1963-69; staff engr. electronics dept. Martin Marietta Aerospace, Denver, 1969—. Served to 1st lt., Signal Corps, U.S. Army, 1956-57. Registered profl. engr., Tex. NASA grantee, 1967-68. Mem. N.Y. Acad. Sci, Sigma Xi. Club: Toastmasters. Contbr. articles to profl. jours. Patentee in field. Home: 5150 S Flower St Littleton CO 80123 Office: Martin Marietta Aerospace PO Box 179 Denver CO 80201

BRODERSEN, HENRY ELMER, Realtor; b. Okla., Mar. 14, 1913; s. Henry Edward and Jennie Sabrina (Hansen) B.; B.S. in Civil Engring., U. Okla., 1935; m. Juanita Garner Longmire, Aug. 5, 1935; children—Betty Jean Brodersen Davis, Martha Jane, Linda Joan Brodersen Tonn, Nan Brodersen Jackson. With U.S. Soil Conservation Service, Okla., 1935, E.H. Moore Oil Co., Inc., Ada, Okla., 1935-36; staff Internat. Boundary Commn., McAllen, Tex., 1938-41; real estate salesman, Phoenix, 1946-48; real estate broker, owner Brodersen Realty, Phoenix, 1949—; chmn. bd. Stewart Title & Trust Co. of Phoenix, Inc., 1962—; dir. Citizens Title & Trust, Yuma; pres. Phoenix Real Estate Bd., 1958. Mem. Phoenix City Council, 1970-74; vice mayor, Phoenix, 1973; mem. Maricopa County (Ariz.) Flood Control Dist. Citizens' Adv. Bd., 1974-79, chmn., 1977; adv. panel YWCA, Maricopa County, 1974-76. Served with AUS, 1941-46; col. Res. (ret.). Decorated Bronze Star. Mem. Ariz. Assn. Realtors (pres. 1963-64), Res. Officers Assn. U.S., Mil. Order World Wars. Republican. Methodist. Club: Trunk and Tusk. Home: 2225 E Solano Dr Phoenix AZ 85016 Office: 4516 N 16th St Suite 2 Phoenix AZ 85016

BRODIE, MICHAEL JAMES, computer service company executive; b. Los Angeles, Sept. 23, 1954; s. James T. and Florence Maire (Witkowski) B. B.A., Pepperdine U., 1976; B.A., UCLA, 1976. Art dir. Creative Age Pubs., North Hollywood, Calif., 1974-75, prodn. mgr., 1975-76; mng. dir. Internat. Computer Group, North Hollywood, 1976—. Republican. Roman Catholic. Home: 15059 St Van Nuys CA 91411 Office: 5233 Bakman Ave North Hollywood CA 91601

BRODWIN, MARTIN GEORGE, rehabilitation services administrator/counselor; b. N.Y.C., June 1, 1944; s. Allen Leonard and Dorothy Elaine (Wallman) B.; A.B., UCLA, 1966; M.S. (HEW fellow), Calif. State U.-Los Angeles, 1969; Ph.D. (HEW fellow), Mich. State U., 1973. Teaching asst. Calif. State U.-Los Angeles, 1968-69; research asst. Mich. State U., East Lansing, 1971-73; coordinator research-vocat. services Rancho Los Amigos Hosp., Downey, Calif., 1973-74; dir. Clin. Rehab. Services, Los Angeles, 1974-79; co-owner, counselor, adminstr. Image Devel., Los Angeles, 1979—; vocat. expert Bur. Hearings and Appeals, Social Security Adminstrn. Cert. rehab. counselor. Mem. Am., Western, Rocky Mountain psychol. assns., Am. Personnel and Guidance Assn., Am. Rehab. Counseling Assn., Nat. Rehab. Assn., Calif. Assn. Rehab. Profls. (founding bd. mem.; v.p. 1975, pres. 1976, treas. 1977, 78). Co-author: Medical Aspects of Disability: A Casebook, 1969; Workshops for the Handicapped: An Annotated Bibliography, 1969; contbr. articles to profl. jours., papers to symposia and profl. confs. Home: 4040 Via Marisol #125 Los Angeles CA 90042 Office: 5410 Wilshire Blvd Suite 500 Los Angeles CA 90036

BRODY, ARTHUR WILLIAM, art educator; b. N.Y.C., Mar. 2, 1943; s. Joshua and Evelyn Charlotte (Edelburg) B.; m. Anne Loring Sullivan, Sept. 15, 1964; m. 2d, Bonnie Ann Mechlowe, June 22, 1969; children—Anna Laura, Darva Sarette, Sol Isaiah. B.S., Harvey Mudd Coll; M.F.A. Claremont Grad. Sch., 1967. Instr. U. Alaska, Fairbanks, 1967-69, asst. prof., 1977-80, assoc. prof., 1980—; instr. Ripon (Wis.) Coll., 1970-73, asst. prof., 1973-75; work represented in numerous permanent collections; evaluator Visual Arts Center Alaska. Road commnr. Chena Spur Service Dist., asst coach youth soccer team; judge Tanana Valley State Fair. Recipient Best-in-Show award Wis. Art Ann., 1974, Print award All Alaska Juried Show, 1979. Mem. Coll. Art Assn., World Print Council, N.W. Printmakers, The Print Club. Democrat. Jewish. Club: Running North. Home: SR10276 Fairbanks AK 99701 Office: Fine Arts Complex U Alaska Fairbanks AK 99701

BRODY, JACOB JEROME, educator, mus. adminstr.; b. Bklyn., Apr. 24, 1929; s. Aladar and Esther (Kraiman) B.; B.A., U. N.Mex., 1956, M.A., 1965, Ph.D., 1970; m. Jean Lindsey, Feb. 13, 1956; children—Jefferson, Jonathan, Allison. Curator art Everhart Mus., Scranton, Pa., 1957-58; curator collections Isaac Delgado Mus. Art, New Orleans, 1958-60, Mus. Internat. Folk Art, Santa Fe, 1961-62; curator Mus. Anthropology, U. N.Mex., Albuquerque, 1962-72, dir., 1972—; mem. faculty U. N.Mex., Albuquerque, 1965—, prof. anthropology and art, 1965—; mem. policy adv. com. N.Mex. Mus. Natural History, 1980—; trustee N.Mex. Archaeol. Soc., 1981—. Served with U.S. Army, 1952-54. Recipient Art Book award Border Regional Library Assn., 1978; fellow Schs. Am. Research, 1980-81. Mem. Am. Assn. Museums, Internat. Commn. Museums, Mountain-Plains Mus. Assn., N.Mex. Museums Assn., Council Mus. Anthropology, Soc. Am. Archaeology. Author: Indian Painters and White Patrons, 1971; Mibres Painted Pottery, 1978; Between Traditions, 1976. Contbr. articles to various publs. Office: Maxwell Museum U New Mexico

BRODY, RICHARD ALAN, political scientist, educator; b. N.Y.C., March 2, 1930; s. Lee and Felice (Auslander) B; m. Marjorie Jean Levy, Aug. 23, 1964; children—Gordon C. Zink-Brody, David E. Zink-Brody, Aaron J. Brody. B.A., San Francisco State U., 1958; M.A., Northwestern U., 1958, Ph.D., 1963. Asst. prof. Stanford (Calif.) U., 1962-66, assoc. prof., 1966-70, prof. polit. sci., 1970—. Served in U.S. Army, 1948-52. Ctr. Advanced Study in Behavioral Sci. fellow, 1967; Fulbright prof., 1970; NSF grantee, 1968. Mem. Am. Polit. Sci. Assn., Midwest Polit. Sci. Assn. Co-author: Simulation in Internat. Relations, 1963; Cubans in Exile: Revolution and Disaffection, 1968; International Events Interaction Analysis, 1972; contbr. articles to profl. jours. Office: Dept Polit Sci Stanford U Stanford CA 94305

BRODY, STEVE, psychologist; b. Bklyn., Apr. 6, 1947; s. Walter and Roslyn (Fabian) B.; student Reed Coll., 1965-68; B.A., U. Calif.-Irvine, 1971; M.A., Calif. Sch. Profl. Psychology, 1976, Ph.D., 1978; m. Cathy Stanley, July 15, 1971; children—Justin Stanley, Matthew Randall. Founder, exec. dir. The Nurtury, Sherman Oaks, Calif., 1975-78; pvt. practice clin. psychology, San Luis Obispo Calif., 1979—; media psychologist with TV show and syndicated newspaper column. Mem. Am. Psychol. Assn., Calif. Psychol. Assn., Psychologists for Social Responsibility (mid-state coordinator). Office: 1461 Higuera St San Luis Obispo CA 93401

BROER, ROGER L., painter, sculptor; b. Omaha, Nov. 9, 1945; s. Ludwig F. and Frieda A. (Lienemann) B.; m. Merlene Julie Good, May 31, 1970; children—Juli Jyll, Zame Stockton. B.A. in Extended Fine Arts, Eastern Mont. Coll., 1974; postgrad. in fine arts Central Wash. U., 1975. One-man shows: Hukahee Fine Arts, Scottsdale, Ariz., 1979, Mus. Native Am. Cultures, Spokane, Wash., 1979, Magic Mushroom, Missoula, Mont., 1979, Louise Matzke Gallery, Seattle, 1981, Rendezvous Gallery, Anchorage, 1982; group shows: Am. Indian and Cowboy Artists, San Dimas, Calif., 1979, 80, 81, 82, Frye Art Mus., Seattle, 1980, 81, Red Cloud Indian Art, Pine Ridge, S.D., 1980, Indian Market, Santa Fe, 1982; work represented in numerous collections including: Dept. Interior, Washington D.C., Pierre Cardin, Paris. Recipient Best-of-Show award Yellowstone Art Ctr., Billings, Mont., 1978, Yakima Valley (Wash.) Ann., 1978, Rapid City Boys' Club Art Show, 1981, 82, Am. Indian and Cowboy Artists Show, 1979, 81. Served with USAF, 1964-68. Mem. Puget Sound Group of N.W. Painters, Am. Indian and Cowboy Artists, Nat. Wildlife Fedn. Presbyterian. Address: 10819 S E 231 St Kent WA 98031

BROGLIATTI, BARBARA SPENCER, television and motion picture executive; b. Los Angeles, Jan. 8, 1946; d. Robert and Lottie (Goldstein) Spencer; m. Raymond Haley Brogliatti, Sept. 19, 1970. B.A. in Social Scis. and English, UCLA, 1968. Asst. press. info. dept. CBS TV, 1968-69, sr. publicist, 1969-74; dir. publicity Tandem Prodns. and T.A.T. Communications (now Embassy Communications), 1974-76, corp. v.p., 1977-82, sr. v.p. worldwide publicity, promotion and advt. Embassy Communications, 1982—. Mem. Dirs. Guild Am., Publicists Guild, Nat. Acad. TV Arts and Scis. Office: 100 Universal City Plaza Room 4 Universal City CA 91608

BROKENBOUGH, WILLA MAE, caterer; b. Clio, S.C., Dec. 5, 1921; d. Joseph and Rebecca (Ales) Burch; student Va. State U., 1940-41; m. John Robert Brokenbough, Feb. 4, 1942; children—Jack, Russell Allen, Diane Elaine Brokenbough Brown. Caterer, Elk's Lodge, Vineland, N.J., 1939-40; cafeteria mgr. Gen. Floor Co., Los Angeles, 1960-63, Schick Safety Razar Co., Culver City, Calif., 1963-66; owner, pres. Willa Brokenbough Parties, Los Angeles, 1963—. Recipient award SBA, 1978, 79. Mem. Calif. Restaurant Assn., Internat. Food Service Execs. Assn. Lutheran. Clubs: Eastern Star, Heroines of Jericho. Office: 4853 Crenshaw Blvd Los Angeles CA 90042

BROM, LIBOR, educator; b. Ostrava, Czechoslovakia, Dec. 17, 1923; s. Ladislav and Bozena (Bromova) B.; came to U.S., 1958, naturalized, 1964; student Czech Inst. Tech., 1945-48; Ing., Charles U. Prague, 1951; postgrad. San Francisco State Coll.; M.A., U. Colo., 1962, Ph.D., 1970; m. Gloria S. Mena, Aug. 31, 1961; 1 son, Rafael. Vice pres. Brom, Inc., Ostrava, Czechoslovakia, 1942-48; economist Slovak Magnesite Works, Prague, Czechoslovakia, 1948-49, economist, chief planner Vodostavba, Navika, Prague, Czechoslovakia, 1951-56; tchr. Jefferson County Schs., Colo., 1958-67; prof., coordinator Russian Area Studies Program, U. Denver, 1967—. Pres., Colo. Nationalities Council, 1970-72; comptroller Exec. Bd. Nat. Heritage Groups Council, 1970-72; v.p., Colo. Citizenship Day, 1968-69; v.p. Comenius World Council, 1976—; v.p. World Representation of Czechoslovak Exile, 1976—; co-chmn. human rights com. Nat. Republican Nationalities Council, 1980-82; adv. bd. Nat. Security Council. Recipient Americanism medal D.A.R., 1969; Am. by Choice, Distinguished Service award, 1968; named Tchr. with Superlative Performance, Modern Lang. Assn., 1961, Outstanding Faculty Mem., Omicron Delta Kappa, 1972. Mem. Econ. Inst. for Research and Edn., Am. Assn. Tchrs. Slavic and Eastern European Langs. (v.p. 1973-75), Am. Assn. Advancement Slavic Studies, Intercollegiate Studies Inst., Lincoln Ednl. Assn., Western Social Sci. Assn., Rocky Mountain Assn. Slavic Studies (sec.-treas. 1975—, pres.-elect 1981-82, pres. 1982-83), Czechoslovak Nat. Council of Am., Republican Movement of Czechoslovakia (acting gen. sec.), U.K. Com. of Unjustly Prosecuted, Czechoslovak Christian Dem. Com., Dobro Slovo, Aleksandr Solzhenitsyn Soc. Republican. Roman Catholic. Author: Ivan Bunin's Proteges. Leonid Zurov, 1973; (in Czech) In the Windstorms of Anger, 1976, On Restoring the Moral Order, 1980; Time and Duty, 1981; The Teacher of Nations and Our Times, 1982; On the Way of Light, 1982; On the Attack, 1983; permanent mem. editorial staff Denni Hlasatel, Chgo. Home: 39 Hillside Dr Wheat Ridge CO 80215 Office: U Denver Denver CO 80208

BROMMER, GERALD FREDERICK, artist, author; b. Berkeley, Calif., Jan. 8, 1927; s. Edgar C. and Helen (Wall) B.; m. Georgia Elizabeth Pratt, Dec. 19, 1948. B.S. Ed., Concordia Coll., Nebr., 1948; M.A., U. Nebr., 1955; postgrad. UCLA, U. So. Calif., Otis Art Inst., Chouinard Art Inst. Instr., St. Paul's Sch., North Hollywood, Calif., 1948-55, Lutheran High Sch., Los Angeles, 1955-76; one-person shows throughout country; exhibited in numerous group shows including Am. Watercolor Soc., NAD, Royal Watercolor Soc., London; represented in permanent collections Claremont Colls. (Calif.), Cola Cola Co., Ky., Concordia Coll., Nebr., Ill., Mo., Utah State U., Provo; books include: Discovering Art History, 1981; The Art of Collage, 1978; Drawing, 1978; Landscapes, 1977; Art in your World, 1977; Art: Your Visual Environment, 1977; Movement and Rhythm, 1975; Space, 1974; Transparent Watercolor, 1973; Relief Printmaking, 1970; Wire Sculpture, 1968; and others; editor: The Design Concept Series, 10 vols., 1974-75, Insights to Art series, 1977—; various texts; assoc. Hewitt Painting Workshops. Recipient prizes Am. Watercolor Soc., 1965, 68, 71, Watercolor U.S.A., 1970, 73, Los Angeles City Art Festival, 1970, 75, Calif. State Fair, 1975. Mem. Nat. Watercolor Soc. (treas., v.p., pres., awards 1972, 74, 78, 80), West Coast Watercolor Soc., Nat. Arts Club, Rocky Mountain Nat. Watermedia Soc., Artists for Econ. Action, Artists Equity, Nat. Art Edn. Assn. Republican. Lutheran. Club: Nat. Arts (N.Y.C.). Address: 11252 Valley Spring Ln North Hollywood CA 91602

BRONG, GERALD RUSSELL, educational technologist; b. Tacoma, Wash., July 20, 1939; s. Gordon Allen and Helen L. (Blatt) B.; m. Marlene A., Sept. 18, 1960; children—Christopher S., Richard C. B.A. in Edn., Central Wash. U., 1961, M.Ed., 1965; Ed.D., Wash. State U., 1973. Elem. tchr. Tacoma Pub. Schs., 1961-65; dir. instructional services Instructional Media Services, Wash. State U., 1965-82; pres. chief operating officer Community Computer Ctrs., Pullman, Wash., 1982—; dir. Library Futures Planning Task Force, Wash. State Library, 1972-74; cons., vis. lectr., writer, Mem. Pullman City Council, 1982—. Del. leader to Australia People-to-People, 1981. Mem. Assn. Ednl. Communication and Tech. (Scholar 1970, Wash. pres. 1973-74, Profl. Service award 1980), ALA, Library Info. Tech. Assn. Club: Rotary (pres. 1983-84) (Pullman). Editorial cons. Mult-Media Revs. Index, 1970-78; mem. editorial adv. bd. Audio-Visual Instrn., 1970-71; book reviewer Jour. Library Automation.

BRONSKI, EUGENE WILLIAM, multi-national corporation executive; b. Detroit, Apr. 12, 1936; s. Eugene and Frances (Maehler) B.; m. Mary Kathren Bronski, July 5, 1958, children—Donna Marie, Karen Lynn, Michael John. B.S., Wayne State U., 1958, J.D., 1961. Bar: Mich. 1962. Staff atty. Detroit Edison Co., 1963-68; gen. counsel Greyhound Food Mgmt., Inc., Detroit, 1968-74, v.p. indsl. relations, 1974-76, v.p. corp. counsel, 1976-81; sr. v.p. Greyhound Corp., Phoenix, 1981—; dir. Restaura, S.A., Restauration Roger Lorent, S.A. Mem. State Bar Mich., Nat. Restaurant Assn., Foodservice and Lodging Inst. (pres. 1980), Am. Arbitration Assn. (mem. panel arbitrators 1972—). Club: Arizona (Phoenix). Office: Greyhound Tower 1933 Phoenix AZ 85077

BRONSON, SHIRLEY GERENE, govt. agy. ofcl.; b. Grape Vine, Ark., Oct. 15, 1936; d. Dee Lawrence and Velma Geneva (Smith) Green; B.A. in Mgmt. cum laude, Golden Gate U., 1975, M.B.A., 1977; m. Bobby Ed Bronson, Sept. 29, 1953; children—Richard Ed, David Dee, Daniel Lee, Robert Edward. Fed. women's program mgr. Air Force Flight Test Center, Edwards, Calif., 1973-74, budget/acct. asst., 1973-74, asst. to comptroller, 1974-76, records mgmt. officer, 1976-77, program/budget analyst, 1977—; fed. women's program mgr. Air Force Space Div., Los Angeles, 1979—; contract tchr. Pacific Christian Coll. Calif. del. Nat. Women's Conf., 1977; mem. Fed. Task Force UN Decade for Women, 1977-79. Recipient cert. merit Air Force Systems Command, 1972, Outstanding Performance award, 1971, 72, 75, 76; Sustained Superior Performance award Dept. Air Force, 1971, 76, 82, cert. appreciation, 1976, Spl. Achievement award, 1971, 76; Spl. Recognition award Air Force Flight Test Center Fed. Women's Program, 1976; named Air Force Systems Command Fed. Women's Program Mgr. of Yr., 1979, 80, 81, 82, Dept. Air Force Fed. Women's Program Mgr. of Yr., 1980; Disting. EEO awards Hdqrs. Space Div., 1979-82; Disting. Public Service award Fed. Exec. Bd., 1981. Mem. Nat. Assn. Female Execs., Am. Soc. Mil. Comptrollers, Federally Employed Women, Fed. Women's Program Com., Los Angeles Fed. Exec. Bd., Air Force Assn. Office: SD/ACB PO Box 92960 Worldway Postal Center Los Angeles CA 90009

BRONSTEIN, GERALD M., real estate executive, accountant; b. N.Y.C., Jan. 16, 1927; s. Jay and Dorothy (Meyers) B.; m. Carolyn Zena Falitz, July 12, 1953; children—Nancy, John, William, Robert. B.S., UCLA, 1947. C.P.A., Calif. Acct., Rashba Pokart & Greene, 1947-52; builder, ptnr. Bronley Bldg. Co., Los Angeles, 1952-67; real estate developer, pres. United Continental Devel. Corp., Los Angeles, 1967-69; pres. Bomaine Corp., Santa Monica, Calif., 1969—. Served with USNR, 1945-46. Home: 7102 Crest Rd Rancho Palo Verdes CA 90274 Office: 2716 Ocean Park Blvd Suite 1030 Santa Monica CA 90405

BRONTE, CHERYL LYNN, assn. exec.; b. Cleve., May 31, 1948; d. Jack and Peggy Jean Cohen; student UCLA, 1972-74, Calif. State U., Los Angeles, 1966-69; B.A. in Psychology, M.A. in Organizational Devel., both Columbia Pacific U. Teen dir., dance instr., program dir. Girls Clubs of Pasadena (Calif.), 1966-73, assoc. dir., 1973—. Mem. youth adv. bd. ARC, 1970-78; mem. juvenile justice tng. team Law Enforcement Assistance Adminstrn., 1978; chmn. Council of Juvenile Diversion Agys.; chmn., co-founder Youth Agys. Consortium, Pasadena; bd. dirs. Sierra Madre council Girl Scouts U.S.A., 1976-77. Nat. Youth Worker Edn. Project scholar, 1977. Mem. Am. Soc. Tng. and Devel., Calif. Assn. Diversion and Youth Service Counselors, Youth Agys. Consortium. Co-producer tng. films. Office: 3160 E Del Mar Blvd Pasadena CA 91107

BROOK, BENJAMIN NATHAN, social worker, orgn. adminstr.; b. N.Y.C., Jan. 31, 1913; s. Hyman and Dora (Berenson) B.; A.B., N.Y. U., 1934; M.S.W., Columbia, 1949; Ed.D., U. Ariz., 1972; m. Elizabeth, Dec. 31, 1938; children—Robert, Mark. Caseworker Dept. Welfare, N.Y.C., 1938-41; field dir. ARC, North Africa and Italy, 1942-49; country dir. for Italy, regional rep. for Middle Atlantic states Joint Distbn. Com., 1944-49; exec. v.p. Tucson Jewish Community Council, 1949—; lectr. in pub. adminstrn. Sch. Edn., U. Ariz., Tucson 1965—; referee Pima County Juvenile Ct., Ariz., 1959—; pres. Ariz. Conf. Social Welfare, 1965-67; asst. prof. sociology Calif. State U., Los Angeles, 1968-70. Decorated commendatore Italian Govt., 1947; recipient Outstanding Citizen award Office of Mayor Tucson, 1969, 75, Spl. award Tucson Jewish Community Council, 1969. Mem. Acad. Certified Social Workers, Council on Social Work Edn., Acad. Polit. Sci., Nat. Assn. Social Workers, United Way Execs. Assn. Jewish. Home: 2542 Ave San Ville Tucson AZ 85715 Office: 102 N Plumer Tucson AZ 85719

BROOK, CHARLES ALBERT, geologist; b. Sanger, Calif., Mar. 20, 1947; s. Lester Raymond and Delphia May (Saltenberger) B.; A.A., Reedley Coll., 1967; B.A. summa cum laude, Calif. State U.-Fresno, 1970, M.A., 1973; postgrad. U. Calif.-Santa Barbara, 1972-74. Geologist, U.S. Geol. Survey, Menlo Park, Calif., 1974-82; geologist Minerals Mgmt. Service, Menlo Park, Calif., 1982-83, Lakewood, Colo., 1983—. Recipient Outstanding Grad. Student award Calif. State U., Fresno, 1971. Mem. Geol. Soc. Am., No. Calif. Geol. Soc., Soc. Econ. Paleontologists and Mineralogists (Pacific sect.), Peninsula Geol. Soc., Geothermal Resources Council, Am. Assn. Petroleum Geologists, Phi Kappa Phi, Alpha Gamma Sigma. Baptist. Home: 242 Allen St Golden CO 80401 Office: PO Box 25165 Lakewood CO 80225

BROOKE, EDNA MAE, educator; b. Las Vegas, Feb. 10, 1923; d. Alma Lyman and Leah Mae (Ketcham) Shurtliff; B.S. in Acctg., Ariz. State U., 1965; M.A., Edn., 1967, Ed. D., 1975; m. Bill T. Brooke, Dec. 22, 1949; 1 son, John C. Brooke. Instr. bus. Phoenix Coll., 1966-68; grad. teaching asst. Ariz. State U., Tempe, 1968-69; prof. bus. Maricopa Tech. Coll., Phoenix, 1967-72, asso. dean instl. services, 1972-74; prof. bus. and acctg. Scottsdale (Ariz.) Community Coll., 1974—; con. in field. Mem. Nat. Bus. Edn. Assn., Western, Ariz. bus. edn. assns., Am. Acctg. Assn., Delta Pi Epsilon. Author: The Effectiveness of Three Techniques used in Teaching First Semester Accounting Principles to Tech. Jr. Coll. Students, 1974. Home: 2139 E Solano Dr Phoenix AZ 85016 Office: 9000 E Chaparral Scottsdale AZ 85252

BROOKER, ALAN EDWARD, psychologist, air force officer; b. Madison, Wis., Jan. 26, 1949; s. Russell Alan and Margaret Gorman (Simpson) B.; m. Mary Naglee, Apr. 15, 1972; children—Jeffrey Alan, Jarrod Russell. B.A. in Psychology, Chapman Coll., Orange, Calif., 1971; M.S. in Rehab. Counseling, Calif. State U., Sacramento, 1975; Ph.D. in Psychology, Kans. State U., Manhattan, 1977. Diplomate in profl. psychotherapy Internat. Acad. Profl. Counseling and Psychotherapy; diplomate Am. Bd. Profl. Neuropsychology; cert. rehab. counselor. Rehab. counselor Auburn office State of Calif., 1973-75; commd. 2d lt. U.S. Air Force, 1968; advanced through grades to capt., 1973; intern clin. psychology Wright-Patterson AFB Med. Ctr., Ohio, 1977-78; clin. psychologist, chief psychol. testing USAF Hosp., Wiesbaden, W. Ger.,

1978-81; resident in med. psychology specializing in neuropsychology U. Oreg. Med. Sch., Oreg. Health Scis. U., Portland, 1981-82; chief psychology service dept. mental health services Travis AFB, Calif., 1982—; vocat. expert Bur. Hearings and Appeals, Social Security Adminstrn.; cons. Surgeon Gen. USAF. Vice pres. Central Sierra chpt. Calif. Human Services Orgn., 1974-75; v.p. Voluntary Action Ctr., South Lake Tahoe, Calif., 1976-77. Decorated Meritorious Service medal, Humanitarian Service medal, Air Force Achievement medal. Fellow Am. Psychol. Assn. (Div. 19 mil. psychology award, 1981); mem. Assn. Advancement Psychology; Assn. Advancement Behavior Therapy; Internat. Neuropsychol. Soc., Air Force Soc. Clin. Psychologists (Europe rep.). Democrat. Roman Catholic. Club: Wiesbaden-Am. Ski. Contbr. articles to profl. jours. Home: PSC 4 Box 9786 Travis AFB CA 94535 Office: David Grant USAF Med Ctr SGHAC Travis AFB CA 94535

BROOKES, CRITTENDEN EDWARDS, psychiatrist; b. Oakland, Calif., May 8, 1931; s. Arthur Blayne and Ruth Delilah (Crittenden) B.; m. Mauna Berkov; children—Lisa, Aaron, Jedidiah, Jesse. A.B., Calif. State U.-Chico, 1952; M.A., Stanford U., 1953, Ph.D., 1956, M.D. (J. Kaiser Family, USPHS, John D. Nappert scholars, USPHS, Univ., Russell Sage Found. fellows), 1960. Diplomate Am. Bd. Psychiatry and Neurology. Psychoanalytical tng. C.G. Jung Inst., San Francisco; intern, USPHS Hosp., S.I., N.Y., 1960-61; resident U. Calif., San Francisco, 1961-63, clin. instr., 1964-67, asst. clin. prof., 1967-75, assoc. clin. prof., 1979—; resident Mt. Zion Hosp., San Francisco, 1963-64, asst. clin. prof. psychology, 1964-67, adj. prof., and supr., 1967—, asst. chief, 1966—; cons. Letterman Gen. Hosp., San Francisco, 1976—, Family Service Agy., San Francisco, 1979—; pvt. practice psychiatry, 1964—. Served with USPHS, 1960-64. Fellow Am. Psychiat. Assn., Am. Acad. Psychoanalysis; mem. Am. Psychol. Assn., AMA, No. Calif. Psychiat. Soc. Contbr. articles to profl. lit. Office: 407 Locust St San Francisco CA 94118

BROOKES, VALENTINE, lawyer; b. Red Bluff, Calif., May 30, 1913; s. Langley and Ethel (Valentine) B.; A.B., U. Calif., 1934, J.D., 1937; m. Virginia Stovall Cunningham, Feb. 11, 1939; children—Langley Brookes Phillips, Lawrence Valentine, Alan Cunningham. Admitted to Calif. bar, 1937; asst. tax counsel Calif. Franchise Tax Commr., 1937-40; dep. atty. gen. Calif., 1940-42; spl. asst. to atty. gen. U.S., asst. to Solicitor-Gen., 1942-44; partner Brookes & Brookes, and predecessor firms, San Francisco, 1944—, Lee, Toomey & Kent, Washington, 1950-79; part-time instr. Hastings Coll. Law, U. Calif., 1942-46; vis. lectr. U. Calif. Sch. Law, 1946-72. Bd. regents St. Mary's Coll. (Calif.), pres., 1970-72. Fellow Am. Bar Found.; mem. Am. Coll. Tax Lawyers, State Bar Calif. (com. on taxation 1946-52, chmn. 1950-52, 60-61), Am. Law Inst., Am. Bar Assn. (past mem. council sect. taxation), Soc. Calif. Pioneers (v.p.), Phi Kappa Sigma, Phi Delta Phi. Clubs: World Trade, Pacific Union (San Francisco); Orinda (Calif.) Country. Author: The Continuity of Interest Test in Reorganizations, 1946; The Partnership Under the Income Tax Laws, 1949; The Tax Consequences of Widows' Elections in Community Property States, 1951. Corporate Transactions Involving Its Own Stock, 1954; Litigation Expenses and the Income Tax, 1957; Recent Developments in Tax Aspects of Corporate Liquidations, 1959. Home: 7 Sycamore Rd Orinda CA 94563 Office: Suite 1902 601 California St San Francisco CA 94108

BROOKHART, GEORGE CLINTON, JR., mfg. co. exec.; b. Balt., Apr. 30, 1940; s. George Clinton and Dorothy Marie (Roop) B.; B.C.E., Cornell U., 1962; M.S., U. Wash., SEattle, 1966; m. Marilyn Jane Hughes, Aug. 3, 1963; children—Erica, Tyler, Ramsey. Research engr. U. Wash., 1966; dir. computer Sci. Cal Com Center, Harrisburg, Pa., 1967-70; pres. Mountain Modular Mfg., Inc., Eagle, Colo., 1972-76; v.p. planning and devel. Amcor, Inc., Ogden, Utah, 1978-80; v.p. Carder Concrete Products Co., Denver, 1980—. Registered profl. engr., Pa., Colo. Mem. ASCE, Am. Concrete Inst., Prestressed Concrete Inst. Home: 1557 W Briarwood Littleton CO 80120 Office: 8311 W Carder St Littleton CO 80125

BROOKIE, DEAN ROBERT, architect; b. Bozeman, Mont., June 3, 1953; s. Robert Hill and Edna Clara (Bryant) B. B.Environ. Design, U. Colo., 1975, M.Arch., 1977. Designer, Key-Fletemeyer, Landscape Architects, Boulder, Colo., 1975-77; project architect, designer Everett, Zeigel, Tumpes and Hand, Architects, Boulder, 1977-80; prin., owner Brookie Architecture and Planning, Durango, Colo., 1980—; dir. Rocky Mountain Passive Solar Structures, Inc.; instr. U. Colo. Grad. Sch. Planning and Community Devel., 1980-81; designer urban housing complexes. Mem. design com. Downtown Durango Devel. Mem. Colo. Soc. Architects (bd. dirs. 1975-76), Architects and Planners of Boulder (dir.), AIA, Nat. Trust Historic Preservation. Democrat. Methodist. Club: Durango Artists. Office: 105 W 9th St PO Box 714 Durango CO 81301

BROOKINS, DOUGLAS GRIDLEY, geochemist, educator; b. Healdsburg, Calif., Sept. 27, 1936; s. Rex McKain and Ellyn Caroline (Hitt) B.; A.A., Santa Rosa Jr. Coll., 1956; A.B., U. Calif., Berkeley, 1958; Ph.D., Mass. Inst. Tech., 1963; m. Barbara Flashman, Sept. 16, 1961; children—Laura Beth, Rachel Sarah. Geologist, Bear Breek Co., San Francisco, 1957-59; research asst. Mass. Inst. Tech., Cambridge, 1958-63, cons., 1963; physicist Avco Corp., Wilmington, Mass., 1961; asst. prof. geology Kans. State U., Manhattan, 1963-65, asso. prof., 1965-70; prof. geology U. N.Mex., Albuquerque, 1971—, acting chmn., 1972, chmn., 1976-79. Bd. dirs. Jewish Community Council of Albuquerque, 1974; trustee Congregation Albert, 1975—. Named Researcher-Tchr. of Year, 1971. Fellow Geol. Soc. Am., Am. Inst. Chemists, Meteoritical Soc., Explorers Club, Mineral. Soc. Am.; mem. Geochem. Soc., Am. Geophys. Union, N.Y. Acad. Sci., AAAS, AAUP, Albuquerque Geol. Soc. (pres. 1973), N.Mex. Geol. Soc., N.Mex. Inst. Chemists (councillor 1974-75), Am. Assn. Petroleum Geologists, Soc. Econ. Paleontologists and Minerologists, Internat. Assn. Geochemistry and Cosmochemistry, Materials Research Soc., Am. Chem. Soc., Am. Nuclear Soc., Soc. Geology Applied to Ore Deposits, Am. Inst. Mining Engrs., Soc. Exploration Geochemists, Clay Minerals Soc., Soc. Econ. Geology, Minn. Soc. Am., Smithsonian Assos., Phi Beta Kappa (pres. Alpha Assn. Kans. 1967-68), Sigma Xi. Mem. B'nai B'rith (financial sec. 1974-75). Author 2 books in field; contbr. articles to profl. jours. Address: Dept Geology U NMex Albuquerque NM 87131

BROOKINS, JACOB BODEN, artist, sculptor, art consultant; b. Princeton, Mo., Aug. 28, 1935; s. Eugene Clements and Alice Jeno (Young) B.; m. Delores Darlene Miller, June 9, 1954 (div.); children—Cynthia, Robert, Natalie, Andrea; m. 2d, Jean Carol Libby, May 26, 1971; children—Scott, Colin. Student Boise State U., 1960; B.S. U. Oreg., 1962, M.F.A. in Design, 1968, M.F.A. in Sculpture, 1969. Design cons. Tri State Elec. Co., Boise, Idaho, 1962-65; instr. applied design U. Oreg., Eugene, 1967-68; studio asst. to sculptor Jan Zach, Elmira, Oreg., 1967-69; instr., asst. prof. studio arts No. Ariz. U., Flagstaff, 1969-75; dir. Art Inst. Mus. No. Ariz., Flagstaff, 1975-78; dir. Cosnino Studios, Flagstaff, 1978—. Exec. dir. Cosnino Research Ctr., 1979—; exec. officer Doney Park (Ariz.) Fire Dist. Fire Sci. Inst., 1980—; chmn. Coconino County Arts Commn. Served with USN, 1954-56. Mem. World Crafts Council, Am. Craft Council, Internat. Sculpture Soc., AAUP, S.W. Artist Blacksmiths Assn., Ariz. Artist Blacksmiths Assn. Republican. Home and office: 431 Cosnino Rd Flagstaff AZ 86001

BROOKLER, HARRY AARON, anesthesiologist; b. Winnipeg, Man., Can., Jan. 16, 1915; came to U.S., 1954, naturalized, 1959; s. Samuel David and Rachel (Farbstein) B.; M.D. (Isbister Scholar), U. Man., 1938; m. Gertrude Mandel, Jan. 1, 1941; children—Jerome Leon, Rickey Evelyn, Jacqueline Brenda, Resa Shanee, Maxwell Myer. Intern, Winnipeg Gen. Hosp., 1937-38, resident in surgery, 1938-39; gen. practice medicine, Bienfait, Sask., 1939-40, Lemberg, Sask., 1940, Weyburn, Sask., 1941-54, San Diego, 1954-59; resident in anesthesia Harbor Gen. Hosp., Torrance, Calif., 1959-61; practice medicine specializing in anesthesiology, San Diego, 1961—; mem. staff Doctors Hosp., 1961—, chief of staff, 1973-74; mem. staffs Paradise Valley Hosp., Mission Bay Hosp., Community Hosp.; med. dir. Care Enterprises, 1976—. Bd. dirs. Jewish Family Service, San Diego, 1965-70; bd. dirs. Jewish Bd. Edn., San Diego, 1970—, pres., 1977-79. Licentiate Med. Council Can.; diplomate Am. Bd. Anesthesiology. Fellow Am. Coll. Anesthesiologists; mem. Internat. Anesthesia Research Assn., Calif. Med. Assn., Calif. Assn. Med. Dirs., San Diego County Med. Assn. Club: Masons (past worshipful master). Home and Office: 5310 Prosperity Ln San Diego CA 92115

BROOKMAN, ANTHONY RAYMOND, SR., lawyer; b. Chgo., Mar. 23, 1922; s. Raymond Charles and Marie (Alberg) B.; student Ripon Coll., 1940-41; B.S., Northwestern U., 1947; LL.B., J.D., U. Calif., Hastings Coll. Law, 1953; children—Meribeth Logan, Anthony Raymond, Lindsay Logan. Bar: Calif. 1953. Law sec. Justice Jesse W. Carter, Calif. Supreme Ct., 1953-54; now pres. Brookman & Hoffman, Inc., P.C., specializing in trial of cases in state and fed. cts., Oakland, Sacramento and Walnut Creek. Pres. Young Reps. of Calif., San Mateo County, 1953-54. Served with USAF, 1943-46, PTO; 1st lt. res. Mem. ABA, Alameda County Bar Assn., Contra Costa County Bar Assn., State Bar Calif., Calif. Trial Lawyers Assn., Lawyers Club Alameda County, Oakland Mus. Assn., Thurston Soc., Am. Trial Lawyers Assn., Beta Theta Pi, Phi Alpha Delta. Elk. Clubs: Athenian Nile, Crow Canyon Country. Home: 134 Rudgear Dr Walnut Creek CA 94598 Office: Walnut Creek Plaza Bldg Walnut Creek CA 94596 also Court Plaza Bldg Sacramento CA 95814

BROOKS, ANN LOUISE, property manager; b. Flagler, Colo., Oct. 11, 1951; d. Orville Lawrence and Joan Loretta (Asheman) Thisius; m. Richard Ford Brooks, Mar. 11, 1978. A.A., Diablo Valley Jr. Coll., 1972; B.A., Ryan teaching credential Sacramento State U., 1975; postgrad. San Francisco State U., 1977-81. Realtor assoc., 1979-82; tchr. jr. high sch. math. and sci. Mt. Diablo Unified Sch. Dist., Concord, Calif., 1975-78; sales rep. Coldwell Banker Residential Real Estate, 1978-79; sales rep. Valley of Calif. Residential Real Estate, 1979-81; property mgmt. tenant adminstr. Milton Meyer & Co., 1981-82; adminstrv. sec. Coldwell Banker Real Estate Mgmt. Services, San Francisco, 1982—; property mgr., leasing agt. Duffel Fin. & Constrn. Co., Lafayette, Calif., 1983—. Named Rookie of Yr., Star Contbr., Valley of Calif., Pleasant Hill, 1980-81. Republican. Roman Catholic. Club: Contra Costa Ballet Studio. Choreographer, Gymnast Club, Walnut Creek Gymnastics, 1981-82.

BROOKS, BARRY DAVID, advertising company official; b. Los Angeles, Jan. 1, 1939; s. Harry David and Dorothy (Kaplan) B.; m. Rachel Miriam Fishbein, Jan. 22, 1966; children—Dena, Greg. B.A., UCLA, 1962. With Bowes Co., Los Angeles, 1963-65, Erwin Wasey Co., Los Angeles, 1965-67, Davis Johnson Columbatto, Los Angeles, 19-; dir. print prodn. Doyle Dane Bernbach, Inc., Los Angeles, instr. Advt. Ctr., Los Angeles, 1975—. Served with Air N.G., 1957-63. Mem. Advt. Prodn. Assn. So. Calif. (Man of Yr. 1980). Office: Doyle Dane Bernbach Inc 5900 Wilshire Blvd Los Angeles CA 90036

BROOKS, CHARISSE LIANE (MRS. GORDON BROOKS), architectural and interior designer; b. Long Beach, Calif., Aug. 28, 1950; d. Charles Elwood and Betty Louise (Atkinson) Hain; m. Gordon Winslow Brooks, June 30, 1978 (dec.). A.A., Long Beach City Coll., 1970; B.A. in Home Econs., Housing and Interior Design, Calif. State U., Long Beach, 1976. Draftsman The Alamo Constrn. Co., Norwalk, Calif., 1977; freelance designer Long Beach, 1977-78; designer Moorewood Constrn. Co., West Covina, Calif., 1977-78, Associated Builders Constrn. Co., Downey, Calif., 1979, Brooks Drafting and Design, Anchorage, 1980—. Mem. corrections com. Anchorage Crime Commn. Mem. Am. Soc. Interior Designers, Assn. Vol. Adminstrs., Jaycees, Delta Gamma. Republican. Lutheran. Home and Office: 7521 Trenton Lane Anchorage AK 99502

BROOKS, FILOMENA MATIA, early childhood educator; b. N.Y.C., June 3, 1940; d. Albert and Frances Bena Jurlin; m. Roger W. Brooks, Nov. 23, 1963; children—Andrew, Jason, Stephanie. B.A., U. Ariz., 1962, M.Ed., 1966. Cert. tchr., Ariz. Tchr. primary grades Wheeler Elem. Sch. and Erickson Elem. Sch., 1962-71; owner Young Explorers, Tucson, 1971—, developer new sch., 1976, ednl. dir. 2 locations Young Explorers, 1983—; chmn. Gov.'s Day Care Adv. Bd. Mem. Tucson Assn. Edn. Young Children (v.p.), Nat. Assn. Edn. Young Children, Ariz. Assn. Child Devel. Edn. (v.p.), Alpha Delta Kappa. Democrat. Methodist. Contbr. article to publ. in field. Office: 607 E Bellevue Tucson AZ 85712

BROOKS, FRANK C., manufacturing executive; b. Mpls., June 14, 1919; s. Frank and Frances (Carver) B.; m. Nancy Gray, May 18, 1942; children—Carol Johnstone, Mary Ferlin. B.A., U. Wash., 1941. Pres. Frank Brooks Mfg. Co., Bellingham, Wash., 1945—; v.p. Valley Ford Sales, Yakima, Wash., 1958—; pres. Millbrook Equipment Co. (John Deere Indsl.), Mt. Vernon, 1976—; chmn. Assn. Wash. Bus., 1974-75. Active Mt. Baker council Boy Scouts Am., 1967—; campaign chmn. United Way, Whatcom County, 1969; pres. Whatcom County Devel. Council, 1964-65; mem. Whatcom County Alcoholism Administrv. Bd., 1968—; pres. Nat. Council on Alcoholism, 1981-82, chmn. adv. council Div. Alcoholism, Dept. Social and Health Services. Served to lt., USNR, 1941-45. Republican. Protestant. Clubs: Rotary, Wash. Athletic, Ranier. Home: 306 Briar Rd Bellingham WA 98225 Office: PO Box 7 Bellingham WA 98227

BROOKS, HARRY WILLIAM, JR., former army officer, business executive; b. Indpls., May 17, 1928; s. Harry William and Nora Elaine (Bailey) B.; B.S., U. Omaha, 1962; M.A., U. Okla., 1973; m. Doris Green, Oct. 8, 1948 (dec. Oct. 1979); children—Harry W. III, Wayne L., Craig L. Commd. 2d lt. U.S. Army, 1949, advanced through grades to maj. gen., 1974; student officer Command and Gen. Staff Coll., Fort Leavenworth, Kans., 1965-66; bn. comdr., Ft. Benning, Ga., 1966, Vietnam, 1966-67; staff officer Office of Asst. Chief of Staff, Washington, 1967-69; student officer Army War Coll., Carlisle, Pa., 1969-70; comdr. arty. group, Wertheim, Germany, 1970-72; army dir. of equal opportunity programs Pentagon, Washington, 1972; asst. div. comdr., Korea, 1973; comdg. gen. 25th Inf. div., Hawaii, 1974-76, ret., 1976; v.p. pub. affairs Amfac Inc., Honolulu, 1976-78, sr. v.p., 1978-81, exec. v.p., 1981—. Hon. chmn. Hawaii Spl. Olympics, 1975; mem. exec. com. Boy Scouts Am., Hawaii, 1974-81; chmn. Hawaii Citizenship Day, 1974; bd. dirs. Bay Area Urban League; mem. adv. bd. Nat. Armed Forces Mus. Decorated D.S.M., Legion of Merit with 1 oak leaf cluster, Bronze Star with 1 oak leaf cluster, Air medal with 6 oak leaf clusters, others. Recipient Freedom award Hawaiian chpt. NAACP, 1975, Top Hat award Pitts. Courier, 1973, named NAACP Meritorious Service award, 1978; named Disting. Hoosier, State of Ind., 1972. Mem. Hawaii C. of C. (dir. 1977-81). Clubs: Masons (33 deg.), Shriners, Rotary. Home: 14 Antique Forest Ln Belmont CA 94002 Office: Amfac Inc Horticulture Group 1601 Bayshore Hwy Suite 323 Burlingame CA 94010

BROOKS, HARVEY C., sociologist, educator; b. Macon, Ga., Mar. 12, 1942; s. Clarence and Evelyn (Bray) S.; B.A., La Salle Coll., 1974; M.A. in Sociology, Wash. State U., 1978, Ph.D. candidate, 1979; postgrad. U. Idaho Law Sch., 1979-80; m. A. Jean Hill, Oct. 6, 1978; children—Tracy W., Harvey C., III, Clifford Hill. Plainclothes investigator The Phila. Police Dept., 1968-73; adminstrv. asst. Ams. United Against Crime, Phila., 1973-74; census interviewer, 1974; youth supr. Phila. Youth Detention Center, 1974-75; dep. sheriff Latah County, Idaho, 1978-79; mem. faculty Wash. State U., Pullman, 1979—, prof. sociology; lead caseworker Dept. Human Services, State of Wash., 1981—. Parks and recreation commr. City of Pullman (Wash.), 1979-80; council-person-at large Inland Empire Assn., 1975-80; pres. Pullman P.T.A. Council, 1978; founder, v.p. coach Pullman Comet Trace Team, 1975-80; nat. del. 1978 Dem. Conv.; state del. 1980 Dem. Conv.; del. King County Labor Council. Served with USAF, 1960-68. Mem. Pacific Sociol. Assn., Wash. Fedn. State Employees (mem. exec. bd., polit. action coordinator Local 843). Roman Catholic. Clubs: Rotary; University Place Boxing (dir.). Contbr. articles to profl. jours. Home: 4230 Beacon Ridge Dr W Tacoma WA 98466

BROOKS, JAMES SPRAGUE, national guard officer; b. Los Angeles, Feb. 16, 1925; s. Julian Chesney and Louise Heegaard (Sprague) B.; B.C.E., Oreg. State Coll., 1951; m. Loa Marie Woolf, June 17, 1947; children—Georgia Lee (stepdau.), Kerri Louise, James Patrick. Served with USAAF, 1943-46; commd. lt. Idaho N.G., 1947, advanced through grades to maj. gen., 1975; engrig. staff officer Idaho Mil. Dept., Boise, 1951-64, engr. Budget and Property Office, 1953-64, chief of staff, 1965-74, adj. gen., chief Bur. Disaster Services, 1975—; chmn. army res. forces policy com. Dept. Army, 1979. Mem. Boise Municipal Airport Commn., 1963—, Idaho Law Enforcement Planning Commn., 1975, Boise Metro Plan Steering Com., 1976. Decorated Legion of Merit; recipient Idaho Safe Pilot award, 1974; named Distinguished Citizen, Idaho Statesman, 1977. Mem. N.G. Assn. U.S., Army Aviation Assn. Am., U.S. Civil Def. Council, Tau Beta Pi, Sigma Tau. Contbr. articles to Aviation Digest, 1968-73. Office: Adj General Office PO Box 45 Boise ID 83707

BROOKS, JOHN STUART, statistician; b. Furstenfeldbruck AFB, Germany, June 19, 1954 (parents Am. citizens); s. Allison Cochran and Geraldine (Nordell) B.; m. Elaine Marie Emery, Mar. 19, 1977; children—Emily Renee, David Michael. B.A. summa cum laude in Health Edn., U. Wash., 1977, M.S. in Biostats., 1979. Research assoc., dept. health services U. Wash., Seattle, 1979-82; statistician, systems analyst Boeing Computer Services, Tukwila, Wash., 1982—. Mem. Am. Statis. Assn., Phi Beta Kappa. Office: BoeingComputer Services MS: 9C-01 565 Andover Park W Tukwilla WA 98188

BROOKS, JUDITH ANN MARIE, association executive; b. Portland, Maine, July 14, 1940; d. Ralph D. and Jacqueline (Lucas) B. B.A., U. Maine-Orono, 1958; cert. teaching English as a fgn. lang. U. Mich., 1964. Cert. Armed Forces Recreation Soc., 1980. Vol., Peace Corps, 1964-66; sr. counsel, resident leader Poland Spring (Maine) Job Corps Center, 1966-67; with USO, 1967—, exec. dir., Thailand, 1967-85; dir. Airport USO Lounge, San Francisco Internat. Airport, 1975-76, exec. dir., Wiesbaden, Germany, 1977-78, exec. dir., Naples, Italy, 1978-79, Pacific Area exec., 1979—. Recipient civilian patriotic citation U.S. Army, 1978, placques of recognition U.S. Air Forcas, Thailand, 1972, 75. Mem. Nat. Parks and Recreation Assn. Republican. Episcopalian. Office: USO PAO Box 743 FPO Seattle WA 98773

BROOKS, MICHAEL BLAINE, control systems engineer; b. Oceanside, Calif., July 9, 1957; s. J.B. and Shirley Ann (Sexton) B.; B.S. cum laude in Engring., UCLA, 1979, M.S. in Engring., 1981; m. Janet Leigh Pink, June 23, 1979; 1 dau., Marilyn DeeAnne. Control systems engr. Hughes Aircraft Co., Los Angeles, 1979, 80—; teaching asst. UCLA Sch. Engring., Los Angeles, 1979-80, teaching assoc., 1980-83, Hughes doctoral fellow, 1983—. Mem. IEEE, Nat. Soc. Profl. Engrs., Calif. Soc. Profl. Engrs., AIAA, AAAS. Office: 8433 Fallbrook Ave Canoga Park CA 91304

BROOKS, RICHARD M., business executive; b. 1928; B.S., Yale U.; M.B.A., U. Calif.-Berkeley; C.L.U.; married. With Mut. of N.Y., to 1957; with Calif. and Hawaiian Sugar Co., 1957-79, sr. v.p. fin. and adminstrn., 1973-79; sr. v.p. fin. Amfac, Inc., San Francisco, 1979—. Past pres. Piedmont council Boy Scouts Am., trustee Golden Gate council; trustee Coll. Prep. Sch. Mem. Oakland Mus. Assn. (dir., officer). Address: 50 O'Farrell St PO Box 7813 San Francisco CA 94120

BROOKS, ROGER BURTON, management consultant, educator; b. Salem, Oreg., Dec. 11, 1943; s. Joseph William and Louise Caroline (Erb) B.; m. Linda Ellen Gill, Dec. 30, 1965; children—Wade T., Jason W. Student U.S. Air Force Acad., 1962-64; B.A. in Physics, Willamette U., 1966; M.S.I.E., Columbia U., 1970. Engr., Hyster Co., Portland, Oreg., 1966, served as prodn. foreman, mgr. assembley dept., mgr. indsl. engring., mgr. mfg. engring., Danville, Ill., 1970-74, capacity and material planning mgr., Portland, 1974-78; pres. Roger Brooks Inc., specialist in MRP edn. and cons., Beaverton, Oreg., 1978—; assoc. Oliver Wight Edn. Assocs., Newbury, N.H., 1979—; exec. v.p. Oliver Wight Inc., Newbury, 1983—. Mem. Am. Prodn. and Inventory Control Soc. (cert.), Alpha Pi Mu. Republican. Methodist. Club: Masons. Contbr. to Master Production Scheduling Principles and Practice, 1979. Home: 13520 SW Fircrest Ct Beaverton OR 97005 Office: PO Box 949 Beaverton OR 97075

BROOKS, STEVEN WESLEY, safety supervisor; b. Spokane, Wash., Aug. 22, 1946; s. Jess Severian and Edith Irene (Benson) B.; A.A. in Police Sci. and Adminstrn., Spokane Community Coll., 1972, A.A. in Lab. Sci., 1973; B.A. in Gen. Studies, B.S. in Occupational Safety and Health, 1977; m. Doris Nancy Strom, June 19, 1971; children—Jody Ann, John Severian Bradford. Personnel dir., safety officer Hygrade Food Product Corp., Spokane, 1977-78, safety dir., asst. personnel dir., Tacoma, 1978-79; safety edn. rep. II Eastern Wash., Wash. State Dept. Social and Health Services, Spokane, 1979—; mem. panel Gov.'s Safety Conf. Food and Beverage Industries, 1977-79. Served with U.S. Army, 1967-70. Mem. Am. Soc. Safety Engrs., Nat. Fire Protection Assn. Methodist. Clubs: Kiwanis, Eagles, DeMolay. Home: 3022 N Girard St Spokane WA 99206 Office: S 121 Arthur Suite A Spokane WA 99202

BROOKS, THURSTON LEONDUS, III, research engineer; b. Lakeland, Fla., Apr. 9, 1950; s. Thurston Leondus and Rosemary Anne (Purcell) B.; B.S. in Mech. Engring., U. Fla., 1977; M.S. in Mech. Engring., MIT, 1979; m. Mudah Elaine Wolfe, July 19, 1973. Research asst. MIT, 1977-79, Woods Hole Oceanographic Inst., 1977-79; research engr. Jet Propulsion Lab., Pasadena, Calif., 1979—. Served with USAF, 1968-73. Mem. ASME (mem. tech. com. on robotics and manipulators), Human Factors Soc., Pi Tau Sigma, Tau Beta Pi, Phi Kappa Phi. Office: T 1201 Jet Propulsion Lab 4800 Oak Grove Dr Pasadena CA 91103

BROOKS, TONEY, broadcasting exec.; b. Tuscaloosa, Ala., July 15, 1943; s. Ralph Stone and Mary London (Pou) B.; B.B.A., U. Ala., 1965; m. Mary K. Eppler, June 21, 1969; children—Maxwell M., Mary B., Catherine K. Mgr. Sta. KLAW, Lawton, Okla., 1971-74; gen. sales mgr. Sta. KBPI, Denver, 1974-79; v.p. KBPI Radio, Denver, 1979-81; pres. Sandusky Newspapers Radio Div., Denver, 1981—. Served with U.S. Army, 1966-69. Decorated Bronze Star. Republican. Episcopalian. Club: Rotary (pres. 1972). Home: 545 S Nelson St Denver CO 80226 Office: 11340 W Olympic St Suite 207 Los Angeles CA 90064

BROOKS, WILLIAM CLIFFORD, VI, social worker; b. Mpls., Feb. 10, 1944; s. William Clifford and Rosalie Therese (Karbo) B. Student Tex. A&M U., 1962-63, Abilene Christian Coll., 1963, U. Calif., San Diego, 1963-64, Mesa Jr. Coll., 1964-67; A.B., San Diego State U., 1969, M.S.W., 1975. Counselor, Ednl. Opportunities Program, San Diego State U., 1967-68; dialogue program dir. USO, Biloxi, Miss., 1969-70; counselor Narcotics Prevention & Edn. Systems, Inc., San Diego, 1971-72; project Can Do group leader Econ. Opportunity Commn., San Diego, 1972; outreach worker Copley YMCA, San Diego, 1972-73; spl. projects coordinator Jewish Community Center, San Diego, 1972-76; juvenile probation officer San Diego County, Calif., 1973-76; dir. evaluation and planning Abilene (Tex.) Regional Mental Health, Mental Retardation Center, 1976-79; research and statis. analyst, div. behavioral health services Bur. Planning and Evaluation State of Ariz., Phoenix, 1979-81; dep. dir. ops. Community Services Dept. County of San Bernardino (Calif.), 1981-82; div. social services Vista Pacific In-Patient Psychiat., Riverside, Calif., 1982; adminstrv. analyst County Adminstrv. Center, Riverside, 1982—; founder Tex. Evaluation Network. Mem. Nat. Assn. Social Workers, Evaluation Research Soc. Democrat. Contbr. articles to profl. jours.; editorial bd. Ariz. Evaluators Network; editor Introspections Jour. Home: 1415 E Orchid Dr San Bernardino CA 92404 Office: 4080 Lemon St 12th Floor Riverside CA 92501

BROOKS, WILLIAM MATHEWS, lawyer, real estate broker; b. Oakland, Calif., June 26, 1951; s. John, Sr., and Barbara (Mathews) B.; B.A., U. Santa Clara, 1974; J.D., Hastings Coll. of Law, 1976. Admitted to Calif. bar, 1977; chmn. Wm. Mathews, Inc., San Leandro, Calif., 1979—; gen. counsel Fremont Bank; sr. mem. firm Brooks & Hughes. Active, Democratic Party. Recipient various scholarship awards, various real estate industry awards. Mem. C. of C. (dir.). Roman Catholic. Clubs: St. Francis Yacht, Commonwealth. Office: PO Box 855 William Mathews Bldg 2450 Washington Ave San Leandro CA 94577

BROOME, MELODY, health research and education administrator; b. Calif., Nov. 22, 1947; d. Thomas A. and Henrietta E. Dunham; student UCLA, 1965-66; m. Edward C. Broome, Dec. 4, 1976; stepchildren—Curtis, Tanyen, Deanna. Sec., U.S. Air Force and U.S. Army at Hughes Aircraft Co., Culver City, Calif., 1966-68; sec. Control Data Corp., Los Angeles, 1968-69; office mgr. Stender & Lapides, law firm, San Francisco, 1969-73; fiscal dir. Sickle Cell Anemia Research & Edn. Inc., Oakland, Calif., 1973—; mem. community adv. bd. No. Calif. Comprehensive Sickle Cell Center, 1978-83 Oakland (Calif.) Concours D'Elegance Steering Com., 1979—; mem. allocations panel United Way Bay Area, 1979-80; mem. speakers bur., 1976; mem. Mem. No. Calif. coordinator Maureen Reagan for U.S. Senate, 1982; mem. Oakland Mayor's Summer Jobs Program Com., 1982—. Recipient commendation King Football Conf., Los Angeles, 1967, Service award Oakland Public Schs., 1978; cert. in sickle cell edn. and counseling, Calif. Mem. NOW. Mem. Christian Ch. Co-editor: Sickle Cell Patient-Perceived Needs Assessment, 1980. Office: 330 41st St Oakland CA 94609

BROOMFIELD, ANN LOUISE, heavy construction company executive; b. Portland, Oreg., June 2, 1943; d. Harold Eugene and Betty Anne (Applegate) Sanders; m. Robert William Broomfield, July 1, 1978; 1 dau., Mary Louise. A.A., Pima Coll., Tucson, 1978, postgrad., 1978—. Civil engring. technician, maintenance analyst Ariz. Dept. Transp., 1975-82; office mgr., comptroller Borderland Constrn. Co., Inc., 1982—. Bd. dirs. Big Bros./Big Sisters; active girl Scouts U.S., United Way. Mem. Nat. Assn. Women in Constrn. (pres.-elect 1983—), Profl. Secs. Internat., Nat. Rifle Assn., Nat. Wildlife Fedn. (life), Phi Theta Kappa. Republican. Episcopalian. Office: PO Box 30473 Tucson AZ 85751

BROSS, DONALD CECIL, legal educator, association executive; b. Oklahoma City, Mar. 29, 1942; s. Ervyl E. and Letty Fay (Cotner) B.; m. Mary Jo Stennette, Jan. 4, 1969; 1 son, John J. B.A. with high distinction, Dartmouth Coll., 1964; M.S., U. Wis., 1971, Ph.D., 1979; J.D., U. Colo., 1975. Bar: Colo. 1975. From asst. to assoc. univ. counsel U. Colo. Health Scis. Ctr., Denver, also cons. Colo. Health Dept., 1975-76; legal counsel Kempe Nat. Ctr. Prevention and Treatment of Child Abuse and Neglect, dept. pediatrics U. Colo., also dir. Regional Child Abuse and Neglect Resource Ctr., 1976—; instr. pediatrics U. Colo., 1976-79, asst. prof. family law, 1979—; co-founder, pres., exec. dir. Nat. Assn. Counsel for Children, 1979—; conf. organizer; mem. adv. com. child welfare Am. Indian Lawyers Tng. Ctr. Served to lt. USN, 1964-69. Naval ROTC scholar, 1960-64; NIMH trainee U. Wis., 1969-72. Mem. AAAS, Am. Sociol. Assn., ABA, Colo. Bar Assn., Denver Bar Assn., Hastings Inst. Soc., Ethics and Life Scis., Internat. Soc. Prevention of Child Abuse and Neglect, Nat. Com. Prevention of Child Abuse, Nat. Assn. Counsel for Children, Nat. Health Lawyers Assn., Dartmouth Assn. Gt. Divide. Editor: Legal Representation of the Maltreated Child, 1979; Advocacy for the Legal Interests of Children, 1980; (with Roger G. Sanger) Implications of Child Abuse and Neglect, 1983; contbr. articles to profl. jours., chpts. to books. Home: 4775 Hancock Dr Boulder CO 80303 Office: 1205 Oneida St Denver CO 80220

BROSTER, JOHN BERTRAM, archaeologist; b. Tallahassee, May 17, 1945; s. Roy Bertram and Mary Anne (Hardison) B.; m. Diane E. Gusky. B.A., George Peabody Coll., Nashville, 1968; M.A., U. N.Mex., 1971. Regional archaeologist div. archaeology Tenn. Dept. Conservation, Nashville, 1973-75; research archaeologist Office Contract Archaeology, U. N.Mex., 1975-77; pres., prin. investigator Cumberland Archaeology Cons., Albuquerque, 1977—; supervisory archaeologist forestry archaeol. program Bur. Indian Affairs, Albuquerque, 1978—. Grantee Nat. Park Service, 1975. Mem. Soc. Profl. Archaeologists, Soc. Am. Archaeology, Soc. Hist. Archaeology, N.Mex. Archaeol. Council, Table Ind. Scholars, Sigma Xi. Democrat. Co-author: The Middle Cumberland Culture, 1972, Archaeological Investigations at Pinson Mounds State Archaeological Area, 1980; co-editor: Pinson Mounds Archaeological Project: Excavations of 1974-75, 1975; contbr. articles to profl. jours. Home: 1212 Vassar Dr NE Albuquerque NM 87106 Office: 500 Gold Ave Albuquerque NM 87103

BROTCHNER, DOROTHY GOLDBLUM (MRS. ROBERT BROTCHNER), civic worker; b. Mpls.; d. Hal and Emma (Shapere) Goldblum; student Macalester Coll., 1935-36, U. Minn., 1936-38; m. Robert Brotchner, Apr. 3, 1943; children—Richard Raymond, Leslie Alison Zentner. Mem. bd. Ramsey County (Minn.) Med. Aux., 1947-51, rec. sec., 1950-51; mem. bd. Rheumatic Diagnostic Clinic, St. Paul, 1949-51; unit chmn. LWV, St. Paul, 1950; mem. U. Minn. Faculty Wives' Club, 1949-51; mem. bd. univ. sect. Newcomers, 1949-51; mem. various local and council bds. Calif. PTA, 1951-64, hon. life mem., 1956—; mem. aux. bd. Queen of Angels Hosp., Los Angeles, 1953-62; den mother Cub Scouts, Los Angeles, 1952-54; patrol sponsor Boy Scouts Am., Los Angeles, 1954-55; Brownie leader Girl Scouts U.S.A., Los Angeles, 1954-58, troop leader, 1959; mem. U. So. Calif. Med. Faculty Wives' Club, 1960—; bd. dirs. met. sect. Los Angeles County Med. Aux., 1960, mem. bd. West Valley sect., 1969-70; pres. Gamma Phi Beta Mothers' Club, 1963-64, assoc., 1969-75; bd. dirs. bd. UCLA Intersorority Mothers' Club, 1964-69; vol. Los Angeles Youth Employment Service, 1962; mem. The Affiliates of UCLA, 1970—, life mem., 1971—, bd. dirs., 1973—, pres., 1974-75; mem. Arts Council, UCLA, 1974—, Valley Heart Guild of Children's Hosp.; mem. exec. bd. Alumni Council, UCLA, 1973-74; mem. counterpoint com. Partners for Los Angeles Music Center; bd. dirs. Design for Sharing, UCLA, 1982-84; mem. Encino (Calif.) Republican Women's Club, 1965—, bd. dirs., 1969-70. Recipient certificate for Outstanding Pub. Service, Civil Def. and Disaster Corps. Mem. Town Hall of Calif., Town and Gown (U. So. Calif.) (life), Los Angeles Mus. Art, Los Angeles Natural History Mus., Los Angeles World Affairs Council, Assistance League of So. Calif. (life), Calif. Museum Found. (The Muses), Friends of Robinson Gardens. Clubs: Westwood Women's Bruin (dir. 1969—, pres. 1972-74, 78-79), Westside Trojan, Westside Bruin, Braemar Country, Riviera Country, Club 100 of Music Center. Home: 15604 Royal Woods Pl Sherman Oaks CA 91403

BROTCHNER, ROBERT JACOB, cardiologist; b. St. Paul, Apr. 3, 1912; s. Harry M. and Henrietta B. (Birnberg) B.; B.S., U. Minn., 1935, M.B., 1935, M.D., 1936, M.S., 1939; m. Dorothy Goldblum, Apr. 3, 1943; children—Richard Raymond, Leslie Alison Zentner. Intern, fellow Hennepin County Hosp., U. Minn., 1935-40; pvt. practice specializing in internal medicine, St. Paul, 1947-52, Los Angeles, 1952—; chmn. dept. medicine Ross-Loos Hosp., Los Angeles, 1974-76; mem. staff Good Hope Found., 1952—; chmn. dept. medicine, partner Ross-Loos Med. Group, 1956-77, emeritus chmn. dept. medicine, 1978—; chief of cardiology, 1954-72; chmn. dept. medicine Queen of Angeles Hosp., Los Angeles, 1957-58, 64, mem. active staff, from 1952; emeritus clin. asst. prof. medicine U. So. Calif., also mem. Edmondson Health Sci. Faculty Ctr. Served to lt. col. M.C., AUS, 1940-47; PTO. Diplomate Am. Bd. Internal Medicine. Fellow ACP, Am. Coll. Chest Physicians, Am. Coll. Cardiology; mem. AMA, Los Angeles County Med. Assn., Am. Heart Assn., Calif. Med. Golfers Assn. (pres. 1966), U. Minn., U. Minn. Med. alumni assns., Los Angeles World Affairs Council, Affiliates UCLA, Sigma Xi, Alpha Omega Alpha. Clubs: Riviera Country (Pacific Palisades); Braemar Country (Tarzana); Westwood Kiwanis; Westside Bruin. Contbr. articles profl. jours. Home: 15604 Royal Woods Pl Sherman Oaks CA 91403 Office: 1711 W Temple St Los Angeles CA 90026

BROTHERS, JUNE D'ESTERNAUX SCOTT, state ofcl.; b. Bend, Oreg., June 4, 1936; d. Frank Aaron and Blanche Angeline (D'Esternaux) Scott; student Central Oreg. Community Coll., 1953-55; B.S., U. Oreg., 1957; postgrad. Atlanta U., 1968, Willamette U., 1980—; m. Charles Paskel Brothers, June 22, 1957; children—Charles Paskel, Theodore Edwin, Sandra Zoe, Lorna Scott. News editor The Redmond (Oreg.) Spokesman, 1966-67; staff writer The Sumter Daily News, Sumter, S.C., 1967-68; community centers dir. Sumter County (S.C.) Econ. Opportunity Corp., 1968-70; editor The Redmond Spokesman, 1970-75; asst. adminstrn. accident prevention div. Oreg. Dept. Workers Compensation, Salem, 1975—; guest lectr. Pres., PTA, Commerce City, Colo., 1965-66; den mother Modoc Area council Boy Scouts Am., Bend, Oreg.; bd. dirs. Sumter County Mental Health Assn., 1969-70; trustee Central Oreg. Community Coll. Found., 1974-78, chmn. fund dr.; leader Camp Fire, Inc., Bend, 1978-79; bd. govs. Theatre of the Cascades, Bend. Recipient Outstanding Achievement award Nat. Fedn. Press Women, 1974; Outstanding Soil Conservation Service Communications award, 1973; Outstanding Citizen award Redmond C. of C., 1973; Outstanding Sr. Citizen award Redmond Jaycees, 1974. Mem. Am. Soc. Safety Engrs. Democrat. Home: 3257 Jay Ct NW Salem OR 97304 Office: Labor and Industries Bldg Salem OR 97310

BROTHERS, LEE HESTER, nurse, educator; b. Earle, Ark., Aug. 18, 1936; d. James and Lubertha (Knox) Woodson; R.N., Meth. Hosp. Sch. Nursing, 1957; B.Vocat. Edn., Calif. State U., 1980, M.A., 1981; m. John Warren Brothers, July 22, 1970; 1 dau., Tamara Jovita. Head nurse Meth. Hosp., Gary, Ind., 1957-61; office nurse, Gary, 1961-66; public health nurse, Gary, 1966-68; supr. med. audit/rev. Blue Cross of So. Calif., Los Angeles, 1968-70; dir. nurses Century Convalescent Hosp., Los Angeles, 1970-71; staff nurse U.S. Naval Hosp., Naples, Italy, 1971-75; dir. nursing Country Villa, Los Angeles, 1976-78, Royal Wood, Los Angeles, 1978-79; tchr. Los Angeles Unified Sch. Dist., 1979—, asst. dir. vocat. nursing, 1981—. Vol., Easter Seal Fund, Am. Heart Assn., Sickle Cell; coordinator South Central Dist. Bloodmobile drive for ARC, 1979—. Recipient Letters of Appreciation for participation in Heart-A-Thon, 1980, Am. Heart Assn., ARC, 1980, Easter Seal Soc., 1980. Mem. Calif. State Bd. Nurses, Am. Vocat. Assn., Calif. Assn. Vocat. Edn., Calif. Tchrs. Assn., NEA, Calif. Assn. Health Careers Educators, Kappa Delta Pi. Baptist. Contbr. articles to profl. jours. Home: 6125 Canterbury Dr Apt 105 Culver City CA 90230 Office: 1320 W 3d St Room 214 Los Angeles CA 90017

BROTHERS, LYMAN RIDDICK, III, urologist; b. Charlottesville, Va., May 29, 1946; s. Lyman Riddick and Sudie (Dunton) B.; B.S., Va. Mil. Inst., 1968; M.D., Med. Coll. Va., 1972; m. Jane Greif, Dec. 27, 1968; children—Michael D., Evelyn A., Jennifer A. Commd. 1st lt. M.C., U.S. Air Force, 1971, advanced through grades to lt. col., 1980; intern in gen. surgery David Grant USAF Med. Center, Travis AFB, Calif., 1972-73; resident in urology Wilford Hall Med. Center, San Antonio, 1973-77; practice medicine specializing in urology; mem. staffs Ivinson Meml. Hosp., Laramie, Wyo. Diplomate Am. Bd. Urology. Mem. AMA. Republican. Home: Laramie WY Office: Urology Clinic PC 204 McCollum St Laramie WY 82070

BROTMAN, RICHARD DENNIS, marriage, family and child counselor; Detroit, Nov. 2, 1952; s. Alfred David and Dorothy G. (Mansfield) B.; m. Debra Louise Hobold, Sept. 9, 1979. A.A., E. Los Angeles Jr. Coll., 1972; A.B., U. So. Calif., 1974, M.S., 1976. Instructional media coordinator Audio-Visual Div., Pub. Library, City of Alhambra, Calif., 1971-78; clin. supr. Hollywood-Sunset Free Clinic, Los Angeles, 1976—; client program coordinator N. Los Angeles County Regional Center for Developmentally Disabled, 1978-81; resdl. program Coordinator Eastern Los Angeles Regional Ctr. for Developmentally Disabled, 1981—; intern U. So. Calif. Student Affairs Div., 1976. Corp. dir. San Gabriel Mission Players, 1973-75. Lic. marriage, family and child counselor, Calif.; cert. counselor Calif. Community Coll. Bd. Mem. Calif. Personnel and Guidance Assn. (conv. participant, 1976, 77, 79), Calif. Rehab. Counselors Assn. (officer), San Fernando Valley Consortium of Agys. Serving Developmentally Disabled Citizens (chmn. recreation subcom.), Los Angeles Aquarium Soc. Democrat. Home: 3515 Brandon St Pasadena CA 91107 Office: 801 S Garfield St Alhambra CA 91801

BROUGH, ROBERT CLAYTON, climatologist; b. Los Angeles, May 29, 1950; s. Robert Marshall and Utahna Clayton (Peterson) B.; m. Ethel Mickelson, Aug. 22, 1973; children—Alison, Richard, Michael, Adam. B.S., Brigham Young U., 1974, M.S., 1975. Cert. secondary tchr. Utah. Phys. sci. instr. Springville (Utah) Jr. High Sch., 1975-78; dir. research WeatherBank Inc., Salt Lake City, 1978-80; pres. Atmospheric Research Inc., West Valley City, Utah, 1980—; weathercaster KTVX-TV, Salt Lake City; cons. in field. Mem. Soc. Applied Climatology (trustee), Gamma Theta Upsilon. Republican. Mormon. Author: Mosida, Utah; Past, Present and Future, 1974; Utah Weather, 1979; contbr. articles to tech. jours. Home and office: 4329 S Stafford Way West Valley City UT 84119

BROUGH, THEODORE GORDON, statistician; b. Congress Park, Ill., Mar. 4, 1924; s. John Capen and Helen Merle (McFadden) B.; student Lyons Town Jr. Coll., 1945-46; A.B., UCLA, 1953; M.A., N.Mex. State U., 1966, Ph.D., 1974; m. Martha W. Johnson, July 4, 1964. Asst. to curator reptiles and invertebrates Brookfield Zoo, Chgo., 1947-48; lit. editor Inland Journalist, Congress Park, 1949-51; editor Sears Catalog, Chgo., 1950-52; sci. editor U.S. Naval Radiol. Def. Lab., San Francisco, 1953-59, publ. br. head, 1955-59, research physicist, 1959-61, sr. physicist, 1961-65; teaching asst. English dept. N.Mex. State U., Las Cruces, 1966, ednl. research tng. fellow Office of Edn., 1966-69; research specialist Western Nev. Regional Edn. Center, Lovelock, 1969-71; project supr. Pupil Personnel Center, Fallon, Nev., 1971-72; dir. Western Research and Evaluation Center, Las Cruces, 1972—; environ. scientist in radiation N.Mex. Environ. Improvement Div., Milan, 1977—; cons. Bi-Lingual Migrant Student Project, Pasco, Wash., 1975-76. Co-dir., co-founder Mt. Taylor Wilderness Forum, Grants, N.Mex., 1978. Served with USNR, 1942-46. Recipient award for outstanding research in Nev., Office of Edn., 1970, HEW award for outstanding bilingual project, 1976. Mem. Am. Phys. Soc., Health Physics Soc., AAAS, Sigma Xi, Phi Delta Kappa, Beta Beta Beta, Sigma Pi Sigma, Psi Chi. Methodist. Club: Lions. Editor: Principles of Radiation Contamination and Control, 3 vols., 1959; contbr. chpt. to book, Effects of Nuclear Weapons, 1962, articles to sci. and edn. publs. Home: 744 Cibola Ct Grants NM 87020 Office: 708 Uranium Ave PO Box 2536 Milan NM 87021

BROUGHAM, WILLIAM POWERS, land mgmt. exec.; b. Joilet, Ill., Jan. 16, 1942; s. Erwin Roy and Ann (Powers) B.; B.S. in Community Recreation and Bus. Mgmt., So. Ill. U., 1966; M.S., Ind. U., 1968; m. Sandra Elaine Schechter, Nov. 30, 1968 (div. 1974); children—Calburn Powers, Brandy Ayn. Asst. dir. parks and recreation Village of Park Forest (Ill.), 1966-67; teaching asso. Ind. U., Bloomington, 1967-68; regional parks mgr. Colo. Div. Games, Fish & Parks, S.E. region, 1968-72; met. regional mgr. Colo. Div. Parks and Outdoor Recreation, Denver, 1972-78; founder, pres. Colo. Gold Consulting, Inc., Denver, 1978—; recreation land and property specialist, broker-assoc. Del Webb Realty & Mgmt., Inc., real estate, 1978—; registered lobbyist Colo. Legislature, 1978—; cons. on park devel. and recreation programming; cons. on environ. ecology Pikes Peak Area Council of Govts., also Denver Regional Council Govts.; guest lectr. U. Colo., Met. State Coll. Chmn. bd. Colo. State Park Found. Named to Hall of Fame, Denver Post Newspaper, 1976; named Man of Yr., Colo. Div. Parks and Outdoor Recreation, 1976. Mem. Nat. Recreation and Park Assn. (nat. membership chmn. 1974-78), Nat. Soc. for Park Resources (dir.), Colo. Park and Recreation Soc. (dir.), Colo. Regional Park Assn., Denver Bd. Realtors, Colo. Assn. Realtors, Nat. Assn. Realtors, Farm and Land Inst., Time-Off, Inc. (dir.), Alumni Tau Kappa Epsilon. Home: 4517 S Lowell Blvd Denver CO 80236 Office: 1050 17th St Suite 212 Denver CO 80265

BROUGHTON, RAY MONROE, banker; b. Seattle, Mar. 2, 1922; s. Arthur Charles and Elizabeth C. (Young) B.; B.A., U. Wash., 1947, M.B.A., 1960; m. Margret Ellen Ryno, July 10, 1944 (dec.); children—Linda (Mrs. Marc E. Hellenthal), Mary Catherine (Mrs. Tomas Boutin); m. 2d, Carole Jean Chrisman, Nov. 8, 1980. Partner, Chinook Press, Seattle, 1946-48; mgr. communications and managerial devel. Gen. Electric Co., Richland, Wash., 1948-59; mgr. mktg., asst. to pres. Smyth Enterprises, Seattle, 1960-62; dir. research Seattle Area Indsl. Council, 1962-65; mgr. econ. research dept. First Interstate Bank of Oreg. (formerly First Nat. Bank of Oreg.), Portland, 1965—. Instr. bus. communications, U. Wash., Richland, 1955-56; instr. typography U. Wash., 1947. Mem. Mayor's Revenue Adv. Com., Portland, 1974-75; chmn. Econ. Adv. Com. State Econ. Devel. Commn., 1974-76; chmn. bd. dirs. Oreg. chpt. Am. Heart Assn., 1980-81, bd. dirs., 1980—. Served to 1st lt. AUS, 1943-46. Mem. Am. Bankers Assn. (econ. adv. com. 1980—), Western Econ. Assn., Am. Mktg. Assn. (chpt. pres. 1971-72), Pacific Northwest Regional Econ. Conf. (bd. dirs. 1967—), Nat. Assn. Bus. Economists (chpt. co-founder 1971), Gov.'s Council Econ. Advs., Portland C. of C., Alpha Delta Sigma. Episcopalian. (dean's com. 1970-73). Contbg. editor Pacific Banker and Business mag., 1971-80. Home: 3008 SW Wilbard St Portland OR 97219 Office: PO Box 3131 Portland OR 97208

BROUGHTON, RUSTY EVELYN, personal and management counselor; b. Holdrege, Nebr., Apr. 22, 1944; s. Mitchell Woodrow and Aline G. McCain; m. James Michael Broughton, Nov. 13, 1970 (div.); children—Stephen Edward, Eric Sean, Kirsten Lee. A.A., Northeastern Colo. Coll., 1964; B.A., Western Colo. Coll., 1966; postgrad. Tulane U., 1968; M.A., Idaho State U., 1977. Supr. in child protection Colo. Dept. Health and Welfare, 1968-70; coordinator aftercare Boise (Idaho) Mental Health, 1970-73; coordinator, psychologist, mgr. mental health services Idaho Falls (Idaho) Dept. Health and Welfare, 1973-77; initiator, mgr., indsl. psychologist Idaho Nat. Engring. Lab., Employee Assistance Program Idaho, Idaho Falls, 1977-81; sr. facilitator, dir. Learning Dynamics, Inc., Boston and Idaho Falls, 1980—, cons., 1983—; pres. Interpersonal Dynamics, Inc., Idaho Falls, 1980. Bd. dirs. YMCA; bd. dirs., assoc. campaign chmn. United way. Recipient Outstanding Achievement award United Way; Idaho Gov.'s Outstanding Achievement award; appreciation awards from various local orgns.; Northeastern Colo. Coll. scholar; Western Colo. Coll. scholar; Tulane U. scholar. Mem. Am. Soc. for Tng. and Devel., Am. Soc. for Personnel Adminstrn., San Diego C. of C., Idaho Falls C. of C. Office: 3680 S Ross St Idaho Falls ID 83401

BROUILLET, FRANK B., state ofcl., ednl. adminstr.; b. Puyallup, Wash., May 18, 1928; s. Vern and Doris B.; B.A., in Econs., U. Puget Sound, 1951, B.E., 1953, M.A., 1953; Ed.D., U. Wash., 1968; m. Marge Sarsten, June 8, 1955; children—Marc, Blair. Fellow, dept. econs. U. Mont., Missoula, 1952; tchr., coach Puyallup (Wash.) Jr.-Sr. High Sch., 1955-58; mem. Wash. Ho. of Reps., 1956-72, head of edn. com. and Democratic Caucus, chmn. Joint House-Senate Edn. com.; tchr. counselor Wilson High Sch., Tacoma, Wash., 1959-63; instr. edn., counselor, adminstr. U. Wash., Seattle, 1963-67; asst. to pres. Highline Community Coll., Seattle, Wash., 1967-72; supt. of pub. instrn. State of Wash., Olympia, 1972—; commr. Interstate Compact for Edn., Washington; mem. Nat. Legis. Leaders Conf.; mem. Wash. Council Higher Edn.; vice chmn. Wash. Spl. Levy Study Commn.; mem. Council Chief State Sch. Officers; pres. Wash. Bd. Edn.; chmn. Wash. Library Commn. Served with AUS, 1953-55, Alaska. Contbr. articles to edn. jours. Home: 619 7th Ave SW Puyallup WA 98371 Office: Washington Superintendant Public Instruction Old Capitol Bldg Olympia WA 98504

BROWDY, BETH ROBIN, optometrist; b. N.Y.C., Nov. 13, 1955; d. Joseph Michael and Gertrude Sandra (Kreiser) B. B.S. summa cum laude, SUNY-Albany, 1975; O.D., SUNY-N.Y.C., 1980. Lic. optometrist. Ptnr., Drs. Mann, Mann, and Browdy, San Carlos, Calif., 1980—; vision cons., adminstr. Learning Disability Clinic, Fremont, Calif., 1980-82. Mem. Am. Optometric Assn., Calif. Optometric Assn., Coll. Optometrists in Vision Devel., Optometric Extension Program, Phi Beta Kappa. Club: Soroptimists (Belmont). Home: 801 Foster City Blvd Apt 305 Foster City CA 94404 Office: 1234 Cherry St San Carlos CA 94070

BROWER, DAVID ROSS, conservationist; b. Berkeley, Calif. July 1, 1912; s. Ross J. and Mary Grace (Barlow) B.; student U. Calif., 1930-31; D.Sc., Hobart and William Smith Colls., 1967; D.H.L., Claremont Colls. Grad. Sch., 1971, Starr King Sch. for Ministry, 1971, U. Md., 1973; Ph.D. in Ecology, U. San Francisco, 1973, Colo. Coll., 1977; m. Anne Hus, May 1, 1943; children—Kenneth David, Robert Irish, Barbara Anne, John Stewart. Editor, U. Calif. Press, 1941-52; exec. dir. Sierra Club, 1952-69, hon. v.p., 1971—; dir. John Muir Inst. Environ. Studies, 1969-71, v.p., 1968-72; founder, pres. Friends of the Earth, 1969-79, chmn., 1979—; founder, pres. Friends of the Earth Found., 1972-79, chmn., 1979—; pres. Friends of the Earth Internat., 1973—; prin. activist in conservation campaigns: saving Dinosaur Nat. Monument, 1952-56; initiating Nat. Outdoor Recreation Resources Rev., 1956-58; Wilderness Act, 1952-64; North Cascades Nat. Park, 1955-68; Redwood Nat. Park, 1963-68; saving Grand Canyon from dams, 1952-68; opposing nuclear proliferation, 1969—; conservation lectr., U.S., 1939—, Finland, 1971, Sweden, 1972, Kenya, 1972, 74, Italy, 1972, 74, 79, N.Z., 1974, Japan, 1976, 78; founder Trustees for Conservation, 1954, sec., 1960-61, 64-65, past v.p., trustee; founder Sierra Club Found., 1960; bd. dirs. Citizens Com. Natural Resources, 1955-78; mem. Natural Resources Council Am., chmn., 1955-57; bd. dirs. North Cascades Conservation Council, 1957--; bd. dirs. Rachel Carson Trust for Living Environment, 1966-72, cons. expert, 1973—; founder, steering com. League Conservation Voters, 1969—; founder Les Amis de la Terre, 1970; guarantor Friends of the Earth U.K., 1970—; chmn. Earth Island Ltd., London, 1971-74; bd. dirs. Environ. Liaison Center, Nairobi, 1975—, Spirit of Stockholm Found., 1977; mem. Com. on Nat. Security, 1980—. Served as 1st lt. with 10th Mountain div. Inf., AUS, 1943-45; maj. Inf.-Res. ret. Decorated Bronze Star; recipient awards Calif. Conservation Council, 1953, Nat. Parks Assn., 1956, Carey-Thomas award, 1964, Paul Bartsch award, Audubon Naturalist Soc. of Central Atlantic States, 1967. Mem. Nat. Parks Assn. (hon.), The Mountaineers (hon.), Appalachian Mountain Club (hon.), Sierra Club (editorial bd. 1935-69, dir. 1941-43, 46-53; John Muir award 1977). Initiator, designer, gen. editor Sierra Club Exhibit Format Series, 20 vols., 1960-68, Friends of the Earth series The Earth's Wild Places, 10 vols., 1970-79, Celebrating the Earth series, 1972-73, numerous other films and books, 1939—. contbr. articles to nat. mags., profl. publs., others; contbr. to U.S. Army mountain manuals, instruction, 1943-45. 1st ascent, Shiprock, N.Mex., 1939; many first ascents, Sierra Nevada, 1933-41. Office: 1045 Sansome St San Francisco CA 94111*

BROWER, GERALD GRANT, architect; b. Pocatello, Idaho, July 4, 1945; s. Grant Crapo and Doris Ellen (Bayly) B.; B.A., U. Utah, 1977; m. Annette Kathleen LaMothe, Aug. 23, 1967; children—Scott Andrew, Kelly Dae, Richard Grant, Devin G. Partner, Bowen & Brower, Architects & Planners, Pleasant Grove, Utah, 1978, v.p., sec., 1978-79; prin., owner Gerald Grant Brower & Assos., Pleasant Grove, 1979—. Chmn. troop com. Boy Scouts Am., 1973-74; chmn. voting dist., 1976. Mem. AIA (pres. 1979-80), Constrn. Specification Inst., Phi Kappa Phi. Republican. Mem. Ch. Jesus Christ Latter-day Saints. Club: Rotary. Home: 1584 N 1040 W Orem UT 84057 Office: 140 S Main St Suite 3 Pleasant Grove UT 84062

BROWER, JIMMIE PAUL, chiropractor, health lectr.; b. Burlington, Iowa, May 13, 1941; s. Frank Zelton and Reva Minnie (Jones) B.; student Monmouth Coll., 1959-61, Western Ill. U., 1964-65, Pasadena City Coll., 1966-70, Calif. State U., Los Angeles, 1970-71; D.C., Cleveland Chiropractic Coll., Los Angeles, 1975. Chemist, aerospace industry, 1966-69, Paper Mate Pen Co., Santa Monica, Calif., 1971-75; practice chiropractic, Pasadena, Calif., 1975-81, Bakersfield, Calif., 1981—; mem. faculty Cleveland Chiropractic Coll., 1975-81, asst. clinic dir., 1978-81; asst. clinic dir. Pasadena U. Chiropractic, 1976. Active Boy Scouts Am., recipient appreciation award, 1978. Served with USMC, 1961-64. Recipient Outstanding Service award, student body Cleveland Chiropractic Coll., 1976. Fellow Internat. Coll. Applied Nutrition; mem. AAAS, Nat. Health Fedn., Nat. Geog. Soc., Smithsonian Assos., Franklin Mint Collectors Soc., Nat. Rifle Assn. Libertarian. Mem. Ch. Religious Sci. Office: 322 S Chester Bakersfield CA 93304

BROWN, ALBERT C., JR., mayor, automotive company executive; b. Los Angeles, Oct. 25, 1918; s. Albert C. and Wanda (Albright) B.; m. Virginia Little, 1941; children—Cheryl Brown Kinsman, Susan Brown Baltagi, Becky Brown Westerdahl. A.A., Riverside City Coll. Owner Brown's Engine Rebldg., Riverside, Calif.; mayor City of Riverside. Trustee Riverside City Coll., 1964-78. Served with USN, 1940-45. Named Alumnus of Yr., Riverside City Coll., 1977; recipient recognition award Catholic Athletic League. Republican. Office: 3900 Main St Riverside CA 92522

BROWN, ALBERTA MAE, respiratory clinician; b. Columbus, Ohio, Nov. 11, 1932; d. Sylvester Clarence and Malinda (Mason) Angel; grad. Antelope Valley Coll., 1961; A.A., Los Angeles Valley Coll., 1975; B.S., Calif. State U., Dominguez Hills, 1981; m. Norman Brown, Dec. 29, 1967; children—Charon, Stevan, Carole. Nurses aid, vocat. nurse, respiratory therapist St. Bernardines Hosp., 1965-69, Good Samaritan Hosp., Los Angeles, 1969-70, Midway Hosp., Los Angeles, 1973-81; allergy nurse, instr. respiratory therapy VA Hosp., Los Angeles, 1970—, also acting dept. head; instr. Los Angeles Valley Med. Technologists Sch., Compton Coll. seminar instr., 1979. Active Arrowhead Allied Arts Council of San Bernardino; CPR instr. Am. Heart Assn. Lic. vocat. nurse; R.N. Mem. Am. Assn. Respiratory Therapy, Nat. Honor Soc., Eta Phi Beta. Democrat. Baptist. Clubs: Social-Lites, Inc. of San Bernardino, (pres.) Order Eastern Star. Patentee disposable/replaceable tubing for stethoscope. also 1545 N Hancock St Orangewood Estates San Bernardino CA 92411 Office: VA Hospital Wilshire and Sawtelle Blvd Los Angeles CA 90073

BROWN, ANTHONY B, aerospace executive; b. Mpls., Apr. 5, 1922; s. Wayland Hoyt and Adele (Birdsall) B.; B.S., Rutgers U., 1949; postgrad. U. So. Calif., 1968-69; Sc.D., London Inst., 1975; m. Mary Alice Ann Anderson, July 28, 1956. Sr. system analyst Thrifty Corp., Los Angeles, 1957-69; system engr. teaching of MARK IV computer software system through U.S., Can. Informatics, Inc., Los Angeles, 1969-73; sr. system engr. Jet Propulsion Lab., La Canada, Calif., 1974-76; sr. system engr. Informatics, Inc., Anchorage, Los Angeles, Washington, 1976-78; supr. project control Hughes Aircraft Co., Los Angeles, 1978-81; mgr. fin. Space Communications Co., Hawthorne, Calif., 1981—. Chmn. bd. govs. La Brea Vista Townhouses, 1967-68. Served with Finance Corps, U.S. Army, 1951-57. Decorated Bronze Star; certified CDP. Fellow Brit. Interplanetary Soc.; mem. Nature Conservancy, Assn. Computer Machinery (chpt. sec. 1973-74), Assn. Systems Mgmt., Data Processing Mgmt. Assn., Mensa, Am. Soc. Profl. Cons., Am. Def. Preparedness Assn., AAAS, Washington Legal Found., Nat. Adv. Council, Am. Security Council (mem. nat. adv. bd.), Calif. Soc., SAR, Mil. Order World Wars, Aircraft Owners and Pilots Assn. Club: Mason (Shriner). Home: 4333 Redwood Ave Marina del Rey CA 90292 Office: Space Communications Co 5155 Rosecrans Ave Hawthorne CA 90250

BROWN, ARNOLD SMITH, sociology educator, researcher in aging; b. Havre, Mont., Mar. 30, 1927; s. Loren and Carrie Ellen (Camp) B.; m. Harriet Ruth Crisp, June 7, 1954; children—Craig Michael, Rita Kay. B.A. in History, Sioux Falls Coll., 1954; B.D. in Theology, Berkeley Bapt. Div. Sch., 1957; M.S. in Sociology, Mont. State U., 1968; Ph.D. in Sociology, U. Mont., 1972. Active new church devel. Am. Bapt. Chs., Calif. and Mont., 1957-66; faculty Rocky Mountain Coll., Billings, Mont., 1973-76; assoc. prof. sociology No. Ariz. U., Flagstaff, 1976—, curriculum and research program devel. in aging; vol. cons. with Aging Network, Ariz. Served with U.S. Army, 1945-46. Mem. Am. Sociol. Assn., Gerontol. Soc., Western Gerontol. Soc., Soc. for Study of Symbolic Interaction, Phi Delta Kappa. Democrat. Baptist. Contbr. articles and reports to publs. in fields.

BROWN, AUDREY MAE, educator; b. Belleville, Ill., July 17, 1930; d. Arthur A. and Olivia K. (Langsdorf) Keim; m. Donald N. Runge, July 10, 1951; 1 son, Kent R.; m. 2d, Edgar R. Brown, July 16, 1979. B.S., So. Ill. U., 1953; M.Ed., U. Ill., 1959. Life credential gen. secondary teaching. Tchr., Pub. Schs. Harrisville (Mich.), 1953-55, St. Joseph (Ill.), 1955-59; tchr. Walker Jr. High, Union High Sch. Dist., Anaheim, Calif., 1962-64, tchr. home econs. Loara High Sch., 1964—. Named Mason Tchr. of Yr., 1974. Hon. life mem. PTA. Office: Loara High Sch 1765 W Cerritos St Anaheim CA 92804

BROWN, BETTE DRUMMOND, educator, consultant; b. Rye, N.Y., Mar. 9, 1926; d. Arthur and Minnie (Ryder) Drummond; m. Donald George Brown, Oct. 30, 1946; m. 2d Robert James S. Brown, Aug. 12, 1961; children—Erich, Dirk, Eleanor, Sidford, Kurt. B.A., Chapman Coll., 1958; M.A., Pacific Oak Coll., 1983. Cert. tchr., adminstr., Calif. Cons., Office of Pvt. Postsecondary Edn., Calif. Dept. Edn., Los Angeles, 1978—, spl. asst. to dir. Office of Child Devel., 1974-78; tchr., devel. examiner Fullerton (Calif.) City Schs., 1965-73; tchr., co-dir. Child Study Ctr., Long Beach (Calif.) City Coll., 1978-81. Mem. Human Relations Commn. Fullerton. Mem. Calif. Assn. Marriage and Family Therapists, LWV, NOW, Phi Delta Kappa. Home: 916 W Fern Dr Fullerton CA 92633

BROWN, BRENT W., company executive, engineer; b. Ogden, Utah, Feb. 6, 1942; s. Willard K. and Vonda (Barber) B.; m. Geraldine Krebs, June 25, 1965; children—Laurie, Lisa, Clifford, Jennifer. B.A. in Math., Weber State Coll., 1968. Math Instr. Thiokol Chem. Corp., Clearfield, Utah, 1969; owner Keith Jorgensen's Magnavox Service Ctr., Logan, Utah, 1969-73; engr., chief-exec.-officer, co-founder Integrated Systems Engring., Inc., Logan, Utah, 1973—. Active Rotary Internat.; mem. panel Nat. Fire Protection Assn., Nat. Electric Code. Republican. Mormon. Patentee in field. Home: 610 E 3d S Smithfield UT 84335 Office: 1850 N 600 W Logan UT 84321

BROWN, CHARLES ALFRED, advertising executive; b. Ashland, Wis., Dec. 30, 1926; s. Frank E. and Lavina M. (Taylor) B.; m. Kathryn F. Stein, Dec. 20, 1970. B.S. in English, U. Wis., 1948. Copywriter Leo Burnett, Chgo., 1954-59; creative dir. Honig-Cooper, Los Angeles, 1959-65, Compton Advt., Los Angeles, 1966-69; creative dir. Brown, Keefe, Marine/Bowes (now Brown, Keefe, Marine), Los Angeles, 1969—. Served with USN, 1944-46. Recipient Best in the West awards, 1973, 76, 79, 80. Mem. advt. Club Los Angeles, Western States Advt. Agys. Assn. Republican. Office: 3435 Wilshire Blvd Suite 2200 Los Angeles CA 90010

BROWN, CHARLES ARNOLD, environmental engineer, educator; b. Fairchild AFB, Wash., Feb. 14, 1951; s. Joseph Arnold and Martha Marie (Rudlof) B.; m. Susan Ida Culler, Sept. 9, 1972; children—Vanessa Mikael, Kevin Charles. B.S. in Chem. Engring. with distinction, Wash. State U.-Pullman, 1973; M.S. in Engring., U. Wash.-Seattle, 1982. Registered profl. engr., Wash., Calif. Engr., Gen. Atomic Co., San Diego, Calif., 1973-76; sr. engr. Kaiser Aluminum and Chem. Corp., Spokane, 1976-80; prin. engr. Brown Fluid Systems, Spokane, 1982—; cons. and lectr. in field. Commr. Inland Empire Soccer Assn., Spokane, 1979-80. Recipient numerous scholarships. Mem. Am. Inst. Chem. Engrs., Air Pollution Control Assn., Water Pollution Control Fedn., Am. Water Works Assn., Nat. Soc. Profl. Engrs. Roman Catholic. Club: Eagles. Home and Office: W 1024 Banbury Dr Spokane WA 99218

BROWN, CHARLES FRANCIS, optometrist; b. San Francisco, Nov. 2, 1922; s. Joseph R. and Molly (Rose) B.; student San Jose State Coll., 1939-42, Vanderbilt U., 1944, Ga. Tech. U., 1944; O.D., U. Calif. Sch. Optometry, 1947; m. Elaine B. Bloom, June 14, 1953; children—Diane, Beth Ann. Pvt. practice optometry, San Jose, Calif., 1947—, optometric cons. Plan Vision Care. Optometry chmn. Santa Clara County United Fund, San Jose, 1964-65. Chmn. Adv. Bd. Health City of San Jose. Bd. dirs. Mexican-Am. Scholarship Fund Santa Clara County, Pub. Vision League, San Jose chpt. Calif. Optometric Care Found.: mem. San Jose Library Commn., 1982—. Served with Signal Corps, AUS, 1942-46. Mem. Am. (com. on pub. health), Calif. (trustee, pres. 1972-73) optometric assns., Calif. Vision Services (past dir.), Nat. Assn. Optometrists (pres. 1952-58), San Jose Jr. C. of C. (v.p., state bd. dirs. 1950-52). Rotarian (pres. San Jose Endowment), Optimist, Elk; mem. B'nai B'rith (past pres.). Home: 1803 Comstock Ln San Jose CA 92515 Office: 1817 Hamilton Ave San Jose CA 95125

BROWN, CHESTER ARTHUR, JR., marketing executive; b. Boston, Oct. 14, 1938; s. Chester Arthur and Anna Hilda (Smith) B.; divorced; children—Patricia, Lind, Stephen, Christopher, Laura, Edward. B.A. in Chemistry, Boston U., 1960; M.B.A. in Mktg., Northeastern U., 1962. Vice pres., sales and mktg. High Voltage Engring. Corp., Burlington, Calif., 1961-72; founder/ptnr. Ferro Fluidics Corp., Burlington, 1972-75; mgr. West Coast Office, Alpha Industries, San Jose, Calif., 1976-78; internat. sales mgr. Network Products Operation, Beckman Instruments, Fullerton, Calif., 78-80; dir. mktg. Western Digital Corp., Irvine, Calif., 1980—. Mem. IEEE, Am. Mgmt. Assn., Assn. Old Crows. Republican. Recipient Assn. Indsl. Advertisers award, 1967; Bus. Press Assn. awards; patentee in field. Office: 2445 McCabe Way Irvine CA 92714

BROWN, CONNIE DEAN, jewelry manufacturing company official, accountant; b. Lovington, N.Mex., Dec. 31, 1934; d. Robert Harold and Sally Ruth (Lumpkin) Dean; m. Jack Lewis Brown, Aug. 22, 1952 (div.); children—Gary Jack, Marsha Colleen. Student Tech. Vocat. Inst., Albuquerque, 1977-78. Bookkeeper Melva's Bookkeeping & Tax Service, Belen, N.Mex., 1968-69; bookkeeping clk. Becker Dalies Dept. Store, Belen, 1969-70; bookkeeper, dental asst. to pvt. practice dentist, Belen, 1971-72; bookkeeper N.Mex. Health Care Corp., Albuquerque, 1977-78; prodn. mgr. Coleman Co., Inc., Albuquerque, 1978, bookkeeper, 1979, asst. mgr., 1980—; income tax acct. Mem. Ch. of Christ. Office: 4108 Alcazar NE Albuquerque NM 87109

BROWN, DALE LEWIS, ins. and real estate exec.; b. Hannibal, Mo., Nov. 2, 1915; s. Lewis Frank and Grace Elizabeth (Walton) B.; student public schs.; m. Catherine L. Lauver, Feb. 28, 1937; 1 dau., Sondra S. Engaged in life ins. sales, 1938—; agt., sales mgr., Solvang, Calif., 1970—; real estate broker Dale Brown Real Estate and Ins., Solvang, 1976—. Served with USAAF, 1942-45, USAF, 1950-54. Mem. Nat. Assn. Realtors, Calif. Realtors Assn., Santa Ynez Valley Bd. Realtors, Ret. Officers Assn., Channel City Airmen, Airplane Owners and Pilots Assn. Republican. Mem. Unity Ch. Clubs: Masons, Santa Ynez Valley Aero, Rotary. Home: PO Box 294 Figueroa Mountain Rd Los Olivos CA 93441 Office: 1120 Edison St Santa Ynez CA 93460

BROWN, DAVID MICHAEL, construction company executive, educator; b. East Liverpool, Ohio, Apr. 13, 1933; s. Alexander Jack and Delores (Allison) B.; m. Rosemary Gail Armstrong, Sept. 13, 1962; children—Lisa, Michael, David, Michele. B.A. in Polit Sci., Mt. Union Coll., 1954; M.A. in Pub. Adminstrn., Western Res. U., 1958; postgrad. U. Minn., 1958-59. Mem. exec. devel. program Los Angeles County, Los Angeles, 1959-60; asst. dir., cons. Bur. Mcpl. Research, U. Oreg., Eugene, 1960-61; asst. city mgr. City of Arcadia (Calif.), 1961-63; city mgr., pub. works dir. City of South El Monte (Calif.), 1963-67; city mgr. City of Escondido (Calif.), 1967-69; gen. mgr., cons. Gr. SW Corp., Newport and Red Bluff, Calif., 1969-71; regional mgr. Ervin Co., Atlanta, 1971-72; pres. Kaufman & Broad Homes, Chgo., 1972-74; pres., chief exec. officer Grant Corp., Newport Beach, Calif., 1974-76, also dir.; chmn. bd., chief exec. officer Homes by Dave Brown, Phoenix, 1976—; mem. faculty Bus. Sch., Ariz. State U., 1981—; lectr. in field. Bd. dirs., campaign chmn. Arcadia Am. Red Cross, 1963; bd. dirs. El Monte Coordinating Council, 1963, Los Angeles County Probation dept., 1965-69, Biltmore Homeowners, 1982, Xavier High Sch., Phoenix, 1982—; bd. dirs., indsl. campaign chmn. El Monte United Fund, 1964; mem. adv. bd. Grad. Sch., U. Calif.-Irvine, 1975-77; trustee Whittier (Calif.) Coll., 1979-82; mem. adv. council Coll. Bus. Adminstrn., Ariz. Real Estate Inst., Ariz. State U., 1982—; dir. City of Phoenix Housing Fin. Corp., 1982-83. Named Man of Yr., El Monte C. of C., 1963; recipient Real Estate Profl. of Yr. award Ariz. State U., 1981. Office: Homes by Dave Brown 8433 N Black Canyon Hwy Suite 110 Phoenix AZ 85021

BROWN, DENNIS EDWARD, educator; b. Marshalltown, Iowa, Feb. 4, 1933; s. Theodore Thomas and Pauline Evangeline (Bootjer) B.; A.B. magna cum laude (Coll. scholar), Harvard, 1955; postgrad. (Rockefeller Theol. fellow), Union Theol. Seminary, 1955-56; M.A., U. Iowa, 1961; Ph.D. (U.S. Steel Found. fellow), U. Mo., 1970; m. Maureen Ann Cavanaugh, Sept. 7, 1963; children—Katherine Ann, Douglas Edward, Laura Elizabeth. Reporter Des Moines Register, 1959-60; editor-writer Office Pub. Information, U. Iowa, Iowa City, 1960-65; asso. dir. Office Pub. Information, U. Mo. at Columbia, 1966-67; asst. dir. Freedom of Info. Center, 1967-68; mem. faculty dept. journalism and mass communications San Jose State U., 1968—, prof. journalism, 1971—, chmn. dept., 1970—. Served to 2nd lt., AUS, 1957-58. Mem. Am. Soc. Journalism Sch. Adminstrs., Assn. Schs. Journalism, Assn. Edn. Journalism and Mass Communications, Sigma Delta Chi, Kappa Tau Alpha. Editorial bd. Harvard Crimson, 1954-55. Contbr. articles. to profl. jours. Home: 7008 Elmsdale Dr San Jose CA 95120

BROWN, DENNIS MAYER, cancer biologist; b. Detroit, May 12, 1949; s. Henry and Harriet (Stone) B.; m. Kay Ann Yoffee, June 17, 1973; 1 dau., Berry Lauren. B.A., NYU, 1971, M.S., 1976, Ph.D., 1979. Research asst. Cancer and Radiol. Research Lab., Inst. Cancer Research, Columbia U., 1975-77; research assoc. Anna Goldfeder Lab. Cancer and Radiol. Research, NYU, 1977-79; research assoc. dept. radiology Stanford U., 1979—. Recipient Jr. Investigator award Com. on Radiation Oncology Studies Conf., 1981; Young Investigator award Seventh Internat. Congress Radiation Research, 1983, Am. Cancer Soc. fellow, 1979. Mem. Radiation Research Soc., N.Y. Acad. Sci., AAAS. Contbr. articles to profl jours. Office: Dept Radiol Stanford Univ Med Ctr Stanford CA 94305

BROWN, DERWIN LOU (DUD), occupational information specialist; b. Missoula, Mont., Aug. 9, 1937; s. William T. and Alma J. (Thompson) B.; m. Sharon J. Morris (div.); m. Mary Ann Fox; children—Mark T., Todd E., Shauna J. Student U. Okla., 1956-57, Mont. State U., 1958. Cert. vocat. tchr., occupational info. specialist, Wash. Fire fighter, officer City of Helena (Mont.), 1960-69; fire instr. L.H. Bates Vocat.-Tech. Inst., Tacoma, 1969-78, occupational info. specialist, 1978; vocat. adminstrv. intern State of Wash. Supt. Pub. Instrn., Olympia, 1982—. State lobbyist for firefighters, Mont. Served with USN, 1955-58. Mem. Bates Local Union 4184, (dir.), Firefighters Union 448. Office: 1101 S Yakima Ave Tacoma WA 98405

BROWN, DONALD D., educator; b. Keithsburg, Ill., Sept. 18, 1931; s. Daniel Lawrence and Ona Fay (Frazee) B.; student Shurtleff Coll., 1949-50; B.S., So. Ill. U., 1953, M.F.A., 1954; m. Phyllis Marguerite Jordan, Nov. 24, 1955; 1 son, Paul Martin. Prof. art Idaho State U., Pocatello, 1956—; exhibited in numerous one man, group shows at regional, nat. and internat. levels. Recipient numerous commns. for art in pub. bldgs., sculptures, mosaics and murals. Mem. Am. Craftmen's Council, Idaho Art Assn., Am. Sculpture Soc., Nat. Wildlife Fedn., Nat. Audubon Soc., Internat. Wildlife Fedn., Nature Conservancy. Home: 4285 Bannock Hwy Pocatello ID 83204

BROWN, DONALD WILLIAM, educator; b. Santa Ana, Calif., Mar. 27, 1930; s. Donald and Blanche (Barnes) B.; student Orange Coast Coll., 1948-49, Occidental Coll., 1949-50; B.A. in Journalism, U. So. Calif., 1952, postgrad. 1952-53; gen. secondary teaching credential San Jose State Coll., 1956; M.A. in Edn. Adminstrn., Long Beach State Coll., 1961; m. Andrea Dianne Williams, Aug. 6, 1954; children—Donald Evan, Joanna Dianne, David William. News editor East Los Angeles Tribune, 1950-52; city editor Orange (Calif.) Daily News 1952; editor-in-chief Monterey Park (Calif.) Californian, 1952-53; dir. pub. relations Orange (Calif.) Unified Sch. Dist., 1955-58; journalism instr. Fullerton (Calif.) Union High Sch. Dist., 1958-61; prof. photo-journalism El Camino (Calif.) Coll., 1961-65, coordinator pub. info., 1965-73, dean div. communications, 1974-75, asso. dean pub. info., 1976-77, prof. journalism and photography, 1977—. Mem. youth adv. com. San Pedro-Penninsula YMCA, 1970. Bd. dirs. Orange YMCA, 1956-60; pres. citizens adv. com. Weymouth Sci Center, 1970-72; mem. Citizens' Adv. Com. Los Angeles City Schs., 1974-76; 4-H community leader, 1979-82. Served with USNR, 1953-55; PTO; lt. Res. ret. Mem. Am. Coll. Pub. Relations Assn., Nat. Sch. Pub. Relations Assn., Journalism Assn. Jr. Colls. (pres. 1962-63), Beta Phi Gamma (pres. 1964-66), nat. exec. sec. 1967-77), Sigma Delta Chi. Presbyterian (elder). Republican. Home: San Pedro CA Office: El Camino College El Camino CA 90506

BROWN, DOUGLAS MINGE, banker: b. Oakland, Calif., Jan. 15, 1938; s. Robert Minge and Gloria Francis (Gillingham) B.; A.B., Stanford U., 1959, M.B.A., 1961; m. Sarah Belle Elliott, July 15, 1972; children—Rebecca, Kenneth, Elliott, Joseph. With Wells Fargo Bank, 1961—, asst. v.p., mgr. Pasadena (Calif.) office, 1969-71, v.p. corp. devel., 1972-74, v.p., mgr. WellService dept., 1974-76, v.p., mgr. retail group staff, 1976-79, v.p., mgr. San Francisco main office, 1978-80, sr. v.p. and mktg. dir., 1980-83; exec. v.p., gen. mgr. WESTNET Group Inc., 1983—. Nat. chmn. Stanford Ann. Fund; chmn. Stanford Bus. Sch. Trust; bd. dirs. Stanford Athletic Bd., Hillsborough Found. trustee Exploratorium Mus. Served with AUS, 1958-59. Recipient Outstanding Soldier award U.S. Army, Ft. Meade, Md., 1959. Mem. Stanford Assos. Club: Bohemian. Office: 150 4th St San Francisco CA 94103

BROWN, ELLEN MABEL EDWARDS (MRS. CHARLES WESLEY BROWN), editor, publisher; b. Golden, Colo., Jan. 19, 1914; d. Robert Ogden and Jessie (Fry) Edwards; student U. Wyo., U. Nebr.; m. Charles Wesley Brown, Dec. 14, 1931; children—Jean Loray Brown Martin, Martha Marie Brown Allender. Corr., News Letter Jour., Newcastle, Wyo., 1954—, Rapid City (S.D.) Daily Jour., 1959-81, Sheridan (Wyo.) Press, Wyo. Stockman Farmer, Cheyenne, 1959—, Mont. Farmer Stockman, Helena, 1960-64; now spl. corr. Rapid City Daily Jour.; photographer, writer articles pub. in Denver Post, Cheyenne Eagle & Tribune, Washington Post, others; public info. and public relations Newcastle Schs., 1969-77; dir. Anna Miller Mus., 1977—, trustee, 1965—; editor, pub. hist. mag. Bits and Pieces, Newcastle, 1965—; field historian Black Hills State Coll., Spearfish, S.D., 1976—; instr. adult edn., 1980—. Organizer, adviser Jr. Leaders Council; leader 4-H Clubs, 1953-64; nature cons. Girl Scouts U.S.A., 1956—; mem. Wyo. Am. Revolution Bicentennial Commn., 1972-77; trustee Newcastle Community Concert Assn. (publicity chmn.); mem. Wyo. Cons. Com. Historic Sites and Markers, 1978-79, Wyo. State Hist. Found., 1978—. Recipient awards Wyo. Hist. Soc., 1979, 81, 82, Outstanding Woman of Wyo. award, 1974, Bicentennial First Lady, 1976; 4-H Burlington award, 1956, 58; Leader of Year award Agrl. Extension Service, 1959, service award, 1962; press and hist. awards, 1966-74, Nat. Press award, 1974; State Sch. Bell award Wyo. Edn. Assn., 1970; Community Service award Jaycees, 1977, also Newcastle C. of C.; Golden Apple award Newcastle Elem. Tchrs., 1981; named Mother of Year, Weston County, 1959; Hon. Wyo. Native, Gov. Wyo., 1983; others. Mem. Am. Assn. State and Local History, Western History Assn., Wyo. Press Women (sec. 1968—, historian 1970—), Weston County (v.p. 1959, 65, pres. 1960, 67, 2d v.p. 1971, dir. 1978-81), Mont., Wyo. (life; pres. 1978-79), S.D., Nebr. (life) hist. socs., Colo.-Wyo. Assn. Mus., Internat. Platform Assn., Future Farmers Am. (hon.), Weston County Cowbelles, Wyo.

Writers, Western Writers, Nat. Outlaw and Lawmen Assn., Wyo. Pioneer Assn. (dir. 1979—), PEO (chaplain, publicity chmn., treas., rec. sec., v.p., pres.), Delta Kappa Gamma (hon.). Club: Newcastle Women's. Methodist. Co-author: and then there was one, 1962; Jubilee Memories, 1963. Address: PO Box 746 10 West Hill St Newcastle WY 82701

BROWN, FREDERICK WILLIAM, real estate exec.; b. N.Y.C., July 29, 1914; s. Frederick William and Rose Katherine (Hartel) B.; B.S., U.S. Naval Acad., 1948; J.D., George Washington U., 1954; m. Evelyn Magdelene Walther, July 11, 1940; children—Bruce Frederick, Bonnie Beth Brown Schuman, Laurie Anne. Commd. ensign U.S. Navy, 1938, advanced through grades to capt., aviator, 1958; service in Brazil, Panama, U.S.S. Enterprise; ret., 1963; social worker San Diego County Welfare Dept., 1965-73; exec. dir. several non-profit corps., 1973-75; realtor asso. J.D. Kelleher & Assos., Realtors, San Diego, 1978-82; Art Leitch Assocs., 1982—. Bd. dirs. San Diego County Assn. Mentally Retarded, 1968-70. Mem. San Diego County Bd. Realtors, Navy Inst., Am. Security Council, Coalition for Peace Through Strength, Am. Soc. Internat. Law, Am. Acad. Polit. and Social Sci., Navy League, Ret. Officers Assn., Mil. Order World Wars, Naval Aviation Assn., Marine Meml. Assn., Friends of Handicapped. Home: 2640 Tokalon St San Diego CA 92110 Office: 2351 Morena Blvd Garnet Ave San Diego CA 92170

BROWN, GARY ROSS, lawyer, U.S. magistrate; b. Denver, Nov. 11, 1949; s. F. Ross and Leona Ruth (Temple) R.; m. Kelly Ann Simms, May 31, 1969; children—Julie Marie, Phillip Ross. B.A., Lewis and Clark Coll., Portland, 1969; J.D., U. Denver, 1973. Bar: Colo. 1973, U.S. Dist. Ct. (Colo.), 1973. Assoc., Clarence O. Bartholic, Denver, 1973-76; sole practice, Denver and Estes Park, Colo., 1976—; U.S. Magistrate Dist. Colo. jurisdiction Rocky Mountain Nat. Park, 1980—. Served with NG U.S. Army, 1969—. Mem. ABA, Colo. Bar Assn., Denver County Bar Assn., Larimer County Bar Assn. Presbyterian. Club: Mason (presiding officer Rocky Mt. consistory). Home: 415 Wonderview St PO Box 778 Estes Park CO 80517 Office: 205 Park Ln PO Box 778 Estes Park CO 80517

BROWN, GENEVIE EEARLIS, educator; b. Blockton, Iowa, June 23, 1928; d. William Earl and Clara Goldie (Fulwider) Wintermute; m. William Kenneth Brown, June 10, 1951; children—Debra, David, Kevin. B.S., Fla. State U., 1950; postgrad. Calif. State Coll.-San Bernardino, 1972-73., Calif. State Poly. U., 1974-75, Calif. State U.-Long Beach, 1976-77. Payroll clk. Armed Forces Inst. Pathology, Washington, 1950-51; bookkeeper Pomona Valley Creamery, 1951-75; substitute tchr. Claremont (Calif.) Unified Sch. Dist., 1967-73; tchr. bus. dept. Claremont High Sch., 1973-74, coordinator work experience program, 1974—, co-chmn. Adopt a Sch. program., 1983, acting chmn. work experience adv. com., 1983. Central council chmn. Parent Faculty Assn., staff membership chmn. Claremont High Sch., 1st v.p., membership chmn. intermediate sch., pres., 1st v.p., 2d v.p., treas., chmn. nominating com. elem. sch.; co-dir. high sch. dept. First Bapt. Ch. Mem. NEA, Calif. Assn. Work Experience Educators (pres.-elect 1982-83), Calif. Assn. Vocat. Edn. (conf. coordinator state conf. 1983, mem. sch. improvement program com. 1982-84), Calif. Bus. Edn. Assn., Calif. Tchrs. Assn., Foothill Industry Edn. Council (student awards com. 1983). Baptist.

BROWN, GEORGE EDWARD, JR., congressman; b. Holtville, Calif., Mar. 6, 1920; s. George Edward and Bird Alma (Kilgore) B.; B.A., U. Calif. at Los Angeles, 1946; m. Rowena Somerindyke; children—David, Dale, Howard, Bonnie (dec.), Paul. Mgmt. cons., Calif., 1957-61; v.p. Monarch Savs. & Loan Assn., Los Angeles, 1960-68; mem. Calif. Assembly 45th Dist., 1959-62; mem. 88th to 91st Congresses from 29th Dist., 93d Congress from 38th Calif. Dist., 94th-96th Congresses from 36th Calif. Dist., mem. sci. and tech. com.; mem. agr. com., chmn. subcom. on dept. ops., research and fgn. agriculture; bd. dirs. Office Tech. Assessment. Councilman, Monterey Park, Calif., 1954-58, mayor, 1955-56. Served to 2d lt., inf. AUS, 1944-46. Study grantee Fund for Adult Edn., 1954. Mem. Ams. for Dem. Action, Am. Legion, Colton C. of C., Internat. Brotherhood Elec. Workers, NAACP, Council Mexican-Am. Affairs. Methodist. Democrat. Kiwanian. Office: 2342 Rayburn House Office Bldg Washington DC 20515 also 657 LaCadena Ave Colton CA 92324

BROWN, GEORGE FRANCIS, physician; b. Many, La., June 3, 1943; s. Eugene I. and Helen (Thompson) B.; B.A., U. Mo., 1965, M.D., 1970. Resident in family practice Good Samaritan Hosp., Phoenix, 1970-71; practice medicine specializing in family practice, Glendale, Ariz., 1974—; mem. staff Phoenix Baptist Hosp., also teaching faculty family practice residency program, vice chmn. dept. family practice, 1982-83; mem. staff John C. Lincoln Hosp., Phoenix; TV panelist public edn. programs Ariz. Med. Assn., 1977-78; flight surgeon Superchicken I, II and III trans-Am. helium balloon flights, 1980, 81. Served to lt. comdr. USN, 1966-69, M.C., 71-73; Vietnam. Decorated Cross of Gallantry (Vietnam); diplomate Am. Bd. Family Practice; lic. comml. pilot. Mem. AMA, Ariz. Med. Assn. (news release editor 1977-80, alt. del. 1981, 82), Maricopa County Med. Soc., Am. Acad. Family Physicians, Am. Legion, Phoenix Men's Arts Council, Beta Theta Pi. Methodist. Club: Masons. Office: 5422 W Thunderbird Rd Glendale AZ 85306

BROWN, GEORGIA LYNN, govt. adminstr.; b. Gunnison, Colo., Oct. 18, 1940; d. George Scott and Florence Josephine (Lewis) Gorsuch; B.A., U. Colo., 1968; M.P.A., U. So. Calif., 1977; 1 dau., Wendy Roma. Intelligence specialist U.S. Dept. Army, Washington, 1968-69; personnel specialist, Washington, 1969, Corpus Christi, 1969-70; urban intern HUD, Denver, 1970-71, equal opportunity specialist, 1971-75, housing specialist, 1975-77; regional adminstr. Women's Bur., U.S. Dept. Labor, Denver, 1977-83; exec. dir. Met. Denver YWCA, 1983—; mem. Colo. State Personnel Affirmative Action Adv. Bd.; gov.'s appointee Colo. Commn. on Status of Women, Colo. Civil Rights Commn. Recipient Cert. of Achievement, HUD, 1977; Assn. Fed. Profl. and Adminstrv. Women Upward Mobility award, 1974. Mem. Am. Soc. Public Adminstrn., World Future Soc., Women's Polit. Caucus, Women's Forum, NOW (sec. Colo. orgn. 1974, pres. Denver chpt. 1975), Federally Employed Women. Office: 1038 Bannock St Denver CO 80204

BROWN, GERALD DEAN, conservationist; b. San Saba, Tex., July 20, 1948; s. James O. and Vada B. (Churchwell) B.; A.A., Tex. S.M. Coll., 1968; B.A., U. Nebr., Omaha, 1970; M.S. (Ceaser Kleberg fellow), Tex. Agrl. and Indsl. U., 1975; m. Karen Ann Fox, Dec. 23, 1971; 1 son, Jeffrey Lloyd. Teaching asst. U. Nebr., Omaha, 1970-71, Tex. Agrl. and Indsl. U., Kingsville, 1971-72; range conservationist Pine Ridge (S.D.) Reservation, Bur. Indian Affairs, 1976-77, range conservationist Ft. Peck Agency, Poplar, Mont., 1977-82; field rep. Sheehan Exploration, 1980—; instr. biology Pine Ridge Community Coll., 1976-77. Deacon St. John's Lutheran Ch., 1977-78. Recipient Spl. Achievement award Bur. Indian Affairs, 1978. Mem. Soc. for Range Mgmt., Wildlife Soc., Poplar Jr. C. of C. (treas. 1977-78). Home: PO Box 1185 Poplar MT 59255 Office: PO Box 637 Poplar MT 59255

BROWN, GERARD DOUGLAS, JR., oral surgeon; b. Richmond, Va., Dec. 8, 1921; s. Gerard and Viola (Dorsey) B.; B.S., Va. Union U., 1942; D.D.S., Howard U., 1947; children by previous marriage—Gerard Douglas III, Shelly Dee Brown Land and Carola Brown Newson (twins), Melanie R., Dexter Caffee, Corliss Caffee; m. 2d, Mattie Moss Mitchell Jan. 21, 1971. Instr., Howard U. Dental Sch., 1948-51; practice oral surgery, Washington, 1949-51; commd. 1st lt. USAF, 1951, advanced through grades to lt. col., 1968; chief dental services various bases, 1961-71, ret., 1971; practiced oral surgery, Victorville, Calif., 1971—; mem. staff St. Mary, Victor Valley (dir.), San Bernardino County Gen. hosps. Mem. sch. bd. Victor Valley Joint Univ. High Sch. Dist., 1978—. Mem. Am. Assn. Endodontists, ADA, Am. Soc. Oral Surgeons, Am. Soc. Endodontists, Am. Acad. Implantology, Howard U. Alumni Assn., NAACP, Alpha Phi Alpha. Democrat. Presbyterian. Club: Rotary. Home: HSR 503 Victorville CA 92392 Office: 15247 11th St Victorville CA 92392

BROWN, GILES TYLER, univ. adminstr.; b. Marshall, Mich., Apr. 21, 1916; s. A. Watson and Ettroile (Kent) B.; A.B., San Diego State Coll., 1937; M.A., U. Calif. at Berkeley, 1941; Ph.D., Claremont Grad. Sch., 1948; postdoctoral seminar U. Edinburgh, Scotland, 1949; m. Crysta Beth Cosner, Nov. 21, 1951. Tchr., counselor, Binet intelligence tester San Diego city schs., 1937-46; dir. social sci. project, chmn. social sci. div. Orange Coast Coll., Newport Beach, Calif., 1948-60; prof. history, chmn. social sci. div. Calif. State U., Fullerton, 1961-66, also chmn. history dept., dean grad. studies, 1967—, asso. v.p. for acad. programs, 1979—; public lectr. nat., internat. affairs, 1951—; mem. task force assessment quality master's degree program Council Grad. Schs.; also cons. gerontology; moderator weekly Behind the Headlines forum Orange Coast Coll.; invited participant Wilton Park Conf., Eng., 1976. Mem. joint grad. bd. Calif. Postsecondary Edn. Commn., 1978—; mem. Acad. Planning Council, Calif. State Univs. and Colls.; mem. grad. fellowship adv. com. State of Calif., 1980; past pres. U. Calif. at Irvine Friends of Library; past pres. World Affairs Council Orange County; mem. adv. bd. Pacific Chamber Orch.; bd. dirs. Pacific Symphony Orch. Served ensign to lt., USNR, 1942-46. Recipient Pacific History award Pacific Coast br. Am. Hist. Assn., 1950, Honor medal Nat. Soc. D.A.R., 1977. named Outstanding Prof., Calif. State U., 1966; Honored Citizen, Orange County Bd. Suprs., 1970. Mem. AAAS, Internat. Platform Assn. (past pres. Western Region; nat. bd. dirs.), S.A.R., Phi Beta Kappa, Phi Delta Kappa, Phi Alpha Theta, Kappa Delta Pi. Baptist. Clubs: Travelers Century (nat. pres., dir.), Explorers, Masons. Author: Ships That Sail No More, 1966; also author numerous articles on hist., internat. relations subjects pub. in ednl., profl., mags.; also book reviews in profl. jours. Contbr. to: Help in Troubled Times, 1962; field studies in areas including Mongolia and Gobi Desert, Western New Guinea, Gilgit-Hunza region along Pakistani-Chinese border. Home: 413 Catalina Dr Newport Beach CA 92663 Office: Calif State U Fullerton CA 92634

BROWN, GORDON VALLANCE, architect; b. Chgo., Jan. 22, 1929; s. Arthur Thomas and Margaret Caroline (Munn) B.; B.Ed., U. Ariz., 1951; B.Arch., Ohio State U., 1960; student Indsl. Coll. Armed Forces, 1968, 69, Naval War Coll., 1970, 73, 75, 82, Nat. Def. U., 1978; m. Frances Russell, July 7, 1956; children—Jeffrey Russell, James Gordon, Steven Arthur, Kathrine Lynn. Archtl. project mgr. Arthur T. Brown, architect, Tucson, Ariz., 1960-70; partner Brown & Brown, architects, Tucson, 1970—. Prospective archtl.-engrng. employee evaluator Tucson Civil Service Commn., 1971; mem. Tucson Community Improvements Com., 1965; mem. St. Joseph's Hosp. Com. of 100, 1975-79; troop committeeman Catalina council Boy Scouts Am., 1969-78. Served to lt. (j.g.) USNR, 1951-55; capt. Res. Mem. AIA (past dir., treas. and sec. So. Ariz. chpt.), Constrn. Specifications Inst., Navy League (nat. dir. 1977-78, Ariz. pres. 1976-78, Tucson pres. 1974-76), U.S. Naval Inst. (life), Naval Res. Assn. (pres. Tucson chpt. 1967-68) (life), Res. Officers Assn., Tucson C. of C. (mil. affairs com. 1971—), Mil. Order World Wars, Nat. Eagle Scout Assn., Alpha Phi Omega. Republican. Presbyterian (elder 1959, deacon 1956-58, 65-70). Rotarian. Prin. archtl. works include Baboquivari and Patagonia High Schs., Tucson Fire Tng. Center, Stage Stop Motel, Flower Sq. Nursing Home, Prototype grant Dept. Energy solar water heater, 1980. Office: 726 N Country Club Tucson AZ 85716

BROWN, HANK, congressman; b. Denver, Feb. 12, 1940; s. Harry W. and Anna M. (Hanks) B.; m. Nana Morrison, Aug. 27, 1967; children—Harry, Christy, Lori. B.S., U. Colo., 1961; J.D., 1969. Bar: Colo. 1969. Tax acct. Arthur Anderson Co., Denver, 1968-69; with Monfort of Colo., Greeley, 1969-80, v.p. corp. devel., 1973-75, v.p. internat. ops., 1976-78, v.p. Lamb div., 1979-80; mem. 97th-98th Congresses from 4th Colo. Dist., 1981—; asst. majority leader Colo. State Senate, 1972-76. Served to lt. USN, 1962-66; Vietnam. Decorated Air medal. Mem. Colo. Bar Assn. Republican. Congregationalist. Office: 1510 Longworth House Office Bldg Washington DC 20515

BROWN, HAROLD EUGENE, educator; b. Springfield, Ohio, Sept. 27, 1934; s. Timothy Leroy and Ruby Marie (Standley) B.; m. Rose Marie Cusimano, May 20, 1967; children—Susan, Anna, Timothy, Gena, Jeffrey. B.A., Park Coll., 1970; M.Ed., Colo. State U., 1982. With Johnson Mfg. Co., Urbana, Ohio, 1953-54; enlisted U.S. Air Force, 1954; electronics and instrumentation technician, instr.; ret., 1977; instr. Denver Inst. Tech., 1977-79; chmn. dept. electronics Boulder (Colo.) Valley Area Vocat.-Tech. Center, 1979—. Chmn. local council Cub Scouts, Boy Scouts Am., 1978-81. Decorated Commendation medal (2). Mem. Am. Vocat. Assn., Am. Tech. Edn. Assn. Colo. Vocat. Assn. (pres. Tech. Edn. div.), Colo. Edn. Assn., NEA, Internat. Platform Assn., Boulder Valley Edn. Assn., Iota Lambda Sigma. Club: Toastmasters (past pres. Pioneer chpt.). Home: 6808 Newman St Arvada CO 80004 Office: 6600 E Arapahoe Rd Boulder CO 80303

BROWN, HAROLD ZELIG, physician; b. Bklyn., Aug. 7, 1924; s. Nathan and Sylvia (Apeloig) B.; B.S., U. Chgo., 1943, M.D., 1946; m. Amy Elsie Ziegler, May 2, 1948; children—Charles, Kenneth, Theodore. Intern, resident in pediatrics Michael Reese Hosp., Chgo., 1946-52; practice medicine specializing in pediatrics, Los Angeles and Beverly Hills, 1952—; clin. chief pediatrics Cedars Sinai Med. Center; clin. prof. pediatrics U. So. Calif; mem. exec. council, staff treas. Cedars Sinai Med. Center. Pres. Los Angeles Docters Symphony Orch., 1962-64, 79-80, now concertmaster. Served to capt. AUS, 1947-49. Diplomate Am. Bd. Pediatrics. Fellow Am. Acad. Pediatrics; mem. Los Angeles County Med. Assn., Calif. Med. Assn., Beverly Hills Med. Soc., Los Angeles Pediatric Soc., AMA. Jewish. Home: 2669 Hutton Dr Beverly Hills CA 90210 Office: 9735 Wilshire Blvd Beverly Hills CA 90212

BROWN, HOLLACE ANN, video executive; b. N.Y.C., June 1, 1946; d. Sydney H. and Muriel (Smukler) Brown; m. Lewis M. Wallensky, June 26, 1982. B.S., Boston U., 1968; M.A. candidate Hunter Coll., 1970-72. Publicity asst. Vidal Sassoon Co., N.Y.C., 1970-71; sec., statis. researcher Roth, Gerard and Co., N.Y.C., 1971-73; publicity asst. MGM Records, Hollywood, Calif., 1974-75, publicity dir., 1975; mgr. sales communications Max Factor and Co., Hollywood, 1975-80; v.p. advt. and sales promotion Paramount Home Video, Hollywood, 1980—. Mem. Women in Bus., Advt. Club Los Angeles. Office: Paramount Home Video 5555 Melrose Ave Hollywood CA 90038

BROWN, JAMES ARTHUS, architect, engr.; b. LaHabra, Calif., Dec. 22, 1931; s. Joel Ray and Bea Anna (Longacre) B.; B.S., Walla Walla Coll., 1954; m. Rosemary Juliette Roberts, Nov. 2, 1979; children by previous marriage—David Owen, Donald Allen; stepchildren—Thomas Edwin Cress, Donald Louis Cress. Foreman, West Wood Homes, Beaverton, Oreg., 1954-55; structural engr. C.E., Portland, Oreg., 1956-57, 58-75, architect. Santa Rosa, Calif., 1975-76, architect, engr., negotiator, San Francisco, 1976-80, program mgr., Norton AFB, Calif., 1980—; founding dir. Adventist Engrs. & Architects, 1974—. Registered profl. engr., architect, Oreg., Calif. Mem. Nat. Soc. Profl. Engrs., ASCE. Republican. Home: 1326 Citrus Ave Redlands CA 92373 Office: Corps of Engineers Norton AFB CA 92409

BROWN, JAMES DUNLEVY, life insurance company exec.; b. Mpls., May 26, 1934; s. Rollo B. and Catherine Mary (Dunlevy) B.; B.S., UCLA, 1956; m. Merrilyn Jean Williams, June 23, 1956; children—Kenneth, Karen, Kristopher, Kevin, Kathryn. Mgmt. devel. positions Conn. Gen. Life Ins. Co., Los Angeles, 1958-66; pres. FM Fin., FM Investors, FM Realty, FM Fin. Services, Los Angeles, 1966—. Served with U.S. Army, 1956-57. Mem. UCLA Alumni Assn. Republican. Roman Catholic. Club: Ironwood Country. Office: Suite 300 1800 Century Park E Los Angeles CA 90067

BROWN, JAMES ELMER, aerospace executive, banker; b. Falconer, N.Y., Sept. 22, 1927; s. Joseph Sandford and Chrity (Joyce) B.; m. Gloria Gayle Gay, Mar. 29, 1957; children—Richard, David, Jennifer, Christopher, Kimberly. J.D., U. Maine, 1954. Spl. agt. FBI, 1954-59; legal asst. to pres. Thiokol Chem. Corp., Tremonton, Utah, 1959-61; spl. ambassador to Nepal, 1975; mgr. bus. affairs Morton Thiokol, Inc., Brigham City, Utah, 1983—; dir. Tracy Collins Bank & Trust Co., Salt Lake City; chmn. bd., chief exec. officer Golden Spike State Bank. Mem. institutional council Utah State U.; chmn. bd. visitors USAF Acad., Colorado Springs, 1974-76; treas. Utah Republican State Com.; mem. Nat. Ford Re-election Com. Served with USN, 1945-46. Mem. Soc. Former Agts. FBI, Air Force Assn. Mormon. Clubs: Weber, Masons. Contbr. articles to tech. and outdoor mags. Home: 221 E 5th N Tremonton UT 84337 Office: PO Box 524 Brigham City UT 84302

BROWN, JAY DEAN, savs. and loan assn. exec.; b. Payson, Utah, Oct. 15, 1936; s. Darrel and Nadine Jane (Fowler) B.; B.S. in Accounting, Brigham Young U.; m. Avon Alleen Freudiger, Nov. 30, 1973; children—Steven Jay, Tamara, Linda Lee, Jay Darrel, Kelly Avon, Shauntelle Alleen, Brian Aaron, Shane Jason. Semi-sr. auditor Haskins & Sells, C.P.A.'s, Los Angeles, 1962-65; asst. treas. Pacific Savs. and Loan Assn., Los Angeles, 1965-67; financial v.p. Investors Savs. and Loan Assn., Pasadena, Calif., 1967-68, Sterling Savs. and Loan Assn., Riverside, Calif., 1968-69; adminstrv. v.p. Mercury Savs. and Loan Assn., Huntington Beach, Calif., 1969-76; sr. v.p., treas. Great Northwest Fed. Savs. and Loan Assn., Bremerton, Wash., 1976-79; pres. Arrowhead Savs. & Loan Assn., 1979-82; pres. County Savs. and Loan Assn., Santa Barbara, Calif., 1982—. Rep. to Utah Boys State, 1954; account exec. United Crusade, 1972, 73; chmn. finance com. Pacifica dist. Boy Scouts Am., 1973; bd. dirs. Kitsap County chpt. ARC, 1977-79; bd. dirs. Mountains Community Hosp., Lake Arrowhead, Calif., 1981—. Mormon (bishop 1966-71). Club: Lake Arrowhead Rotary (officer, dir. 1979—). Home: 3938 Laguna Blanca Dr Santa Barbara CA 93110 Office: 1200 State St Santa Barbara CA 93101

BROWN, JEAN HOWARD, civic worker; b. Fresno, Calif., Feb. 14, 1944; d. Hans Peter Einar and Marion Edith (Roughton) Cook; m. Richard Lee Dahlgren, June 19, 1965; 1 son, Robert Todd; m. 2d, Phillip Jackson Brown, Nov. 18, 1972; 1 dau., Marni Allison. B.A. in Elem. Edn. cum laude, Calif. State U.-Fresno, 1965; B.A. in Home Econs. and Interior Design, San Francisco State U., 1980. Tchr., Evergreen Sch. Dist., 1965-67, Madera Unified Sch. Dist., 1967-72; asst. Pern K. Interiors Novato, Calif., 1980; asst. designer, asst. Thomas Erwin Collection, San Anselmo, Calif., 1981-82. Br. co-chmn. Am. Cancer Soc., 1981-82, field rep. Marin unit, 1982—, bd. dirs. Marin Unit, 1982—; mem. exec. council Calif. State div. AAUW, 1979-81, bd. dirs. Novato AAUW, 1975—; bd. dirs. Novato Hist. Guild, 1982. Mem. Am. Soc. Interior Designers (assoc.). Methodist. Address: 16 Ramona Way Novato CA 94947

BROWN, JERRY LEONARD, law office administrator; b. Provo, Utah, Feb. 6, 1937; s. Leonard W. and Helen Brown; m. Jane Terry, Aug. 19, 1961. children—Steven, Anthony. B.S., U. Utah, 1959. C.P.A., Utah. Acct., Frontier Refining Co., Salt Lake City, 1961-63, internal auditor, Denver, 1963-65; staff acct. Fox & Co., Salt Lake City, 1965-67; bus. mgr. Van Cott Bagley, Cornwall & McCarthy, Salt Lake City, 1967—. Mem. Assn. Legal Adminstr. (regional v.p. 1980-82, chmn., dirs. of adminstrn. sect. 1982-83), Am. Inst. C.P.A.s, Utah Assn. C.P.A.s, ABA (assoc.). Home: 2114 Scenic Dr Salt Lake City UT 84109 Office: 50 S Main St Suite 1600 Salt Lake City UT 84144

BROWN, JOHN DAVID, government official; b. Durango, Colo., Oct. 13, 1935; s. Percy High and Maude Katherine (Fager) B.; student Ft. Lewis Coll., 1953-56; B.S., Colo. State U., 1960; postgrad. U. Nev., 1976; m. Eileen Rose Haffey, Aug. 20, 1960; children—Charles P., Elizabeth Ann, Patrick Earl, David Edward. With Water & Power Resources Services, 1960—, chief designs and estimate br., Durango, 1960-64, with power ops. Colorado River Storage Project, Montrose, 1964-67, Lower Colo. River Power Ops., Boulder City, Nev., 1967-73, mgr. devel. tng. program, Denver, Sacramento, Washington, 1973-74, with planning div., Boulder City, 1974-78, chief environ. coordination and phys. sci. br., Boulder City, 1978-79, projects mgr. Durango Projects Office, 1979—. Mem. Montrose Planning Commn., 1966; chmn. Boulder City Parks and Recreation Commn,, 1971; pres. bd. trustees Boulder City Cultural Center, 1971. Recipient Boulder City Disting. Service award, 1970. Mem. ASCE, Am. Public Works Assn., Colo. State U.-Durango Alumni Assn. (pres. 1961), Boulder City C. of C. (pres. 1971). Clubs: Elks, K.C., Rotary. Home: 1715 Mariposa Way Boulder City NV 89005

BROWN, JOHN PAIRMAN, disarmament worker, church executive, writer; b. Hanover, N.H., May 16, 1923; s. Bancroft Huntington and Eleanor (Pairman) B.; m. Dorothy Emily Waymouth, June 26, 1954; children—George Waymouth, Felicity Emily Brown McCarthy, Maryam Eleanor Brown Beros, David Pairman. B.A. summa cum laude, Dartmouth Coll., 1944; jr. fellow Harvard U., 1946-49; S.T.B., Gen. Theol. Sem., N.Y.C., 1952; Th.D., Union Theol. Sem., N.Y.C., 1958. Ordained priest Episcopal Ch., 1953; joint ministerial standing Christian Ch. (Disciples of Christ). Curate, Grace Ch., Newark, 1952-54; tutor Gen. Theol. Sem., N.Y.C., 1954-56; instr. Hobart Coll., Geneva, N.Y., 1956-58; assoc. prof. classics and ancient history, Am. U., Beirut, Lebanon, 1958-65; prof. New Testament, Ch. Divinity Sch. of the Pacific, 1965-68; editorial staff U. Calif. Press, 1968-70; staff Ecumenical Peace Inst., San Francisco, 1971-76; exec. dir. No. Calif. Ecumenical Council, San Francisco, 1976—; rep. U.S. churches and peace movement confs. Hanoi, 1967, Santiago, 1976, Belfast, 1976; non-govtl. orgn. rep. Conf. Geneva and UN Spl. Session, 1982, Uppsala Ch. World Conf. and Moscow, 1983. Active opposition to conscription during Viet Nam War, to building B-1 Bomber, to Livermore Nuclear Weapons Lab. Served with USAAF, 1944-46. Mem. Soc. Bibl. Lit., Nat. Assn. Ecumenical Staff. Editor: The Witness, 1955-58, Sequoia, 1980—; author: The Displaced Person's Almanac, 1961: The Lebanon and Phoenicia: Ancient Texts ... The Forest, 1969; The Liberated Zone, 1969; Planet on Strike, 1970; To a Sister on Laurel Drive, 1972; contbr. articles to publs. in field. Address: 1630 Arch St Berkeley CA 94709

BROWN, JOHN WEBSTER, civil engr.; b. Reno, July 17, 1926; s. Ernest S. and Edna Louise (Bonner) B.; B.S. in Civil Engring., U. Nev., 1950; m. Estella Marie Hicks, Dec. 23, 1949; children—Ernest C., Curtis Webster, Denise Gail. Bridge design engr. Nev. Dept. Hwys., 1950-51; civil engr. Kaiser Engrs. Corp., Oakland, Calif., 1951-53; structural designer H.M. O'Neil Co., Oakland, 1953; pres. John Webster Brown Civil and Structural Engrs., Inc., Reno, 1953—. Mem. Washoe County (Nev.) Pub. Works Commn., 1961-66; mem. Gov.'s Hwy. Safety Com., 1968-70; mem. cub pack com. Reno council Boy Scouts Am., 1967-68, chmn. activities troop com. 1967-74; mem. SSS, Nev. State Appeals Bd., 1969-76. Served with USNR, 1944-46. Registered profl. engr., Nev., Calif., Idaho. Mem. Nev. Soc. Profl. Engrs. (univ. com. 1957-60; Engr. of the Year award 1969; state pres. 1960-61), Nat. Soc. Profl. Engrs. (awards com. 1970-71), ASCE (pres. Nev. br. 1961-62, bldg. code com. 1963-65), Structural Engrs. Assn. of Calif., Am. Assn. Engring. Socs., Sigma Tau, Tau Beta Pi. Home: 387 Chevy Chase Dr Reno NV 89509 Office: 642 N Sierra St Reno NV 89503

BROWN, JOY ALICE, social service adminstr.; b. Redmesa, Colo., Mar. 19, 1917; d. Ezra E. and Alice M. (Pinkerton) Walker; B.A., Highlands U., 1958; M.A., U. No. Colo., 1967, Ed.D., 1970; m. Clayton Henry Brown, Apr. 9, 1941; children—Kimleigh Clayton, Loraleigh Joy. Tchr., La Plata County, Colo., 1936-41; prin. Bayfield (Colo.) pub. schs., 1942-46; tchr. Aztec (N.Mex.) pub. schs., 1946-63; spl. edn. coordinator primary schs., Palmer, Alaska, 1963-67; lab. sch. supr. U. No. Colo., 1967-70; asso. prof. edn. N.Mex. State U., 1970-75; dir. Open Door Center, Las Cruces, N.Mex., 1975—; cons. Tex. Edn. Service Center, Roswell (N.Mex.) schs.; sec. Dona Ana Human Services Consortium, 1977. Recipient Community Service award Las Cruces Eastside Center, 1972. Outstanding Contribution award N.Mex. Council of Exceptional Children, 1977. Mem. NEA, Council for Exceptional Children, Nat. Assn. Retarded Citizens, Phi Delta Kappa. Contbr. articles on edn. to profl. jours. Home: 1232 Barker Rd Las Cruces NM 88001 Office: 2325 E Nevada Las Cruces NM 88001

BROWN, JUDY R., computer software company executive; b. Axtell, Kans., Nov. 25, 1948; d. Herman J. and Lucille E. (Kuckelman) Preston. Student Donnelly Jr. Coll., 1966 68, Emporia State Coll., 1967-68, Penn Valley Jr. Coll., 1968-69, U. Mo.-Kansas City, 1969-70. Programmer, Hallmark Cards, Kansas City, Mo., 1968-74; systems analyst Champion Petroleum, Ft. Worth, 1974-76; product mgr. Nat. CSS, Wilton, Conn., 1976-70; v.p. ops. World Research Systems, Los Angeles, 1980—. Chmn. pre-sch. religious edn. St. Mark's Ch., Venice, Calif. Mem. Am. Mktg. Assn. Roman Catholic. Club: St. Mark's Singles. Office: World Research Systems 3007 Washington Blvd Suite 115 Marina del Rey CA 90291

BROWN, KENNETH BRYSON, city ofcl.; b. Plainview, Tex., May 3, 1934; s. George Bryson and Pauline Amelia (Thornhill) B.; student Sacramento State U., 1970-71, U. Calif., Berkeley, 1971-72; children—Bradford E., Barrett S., Bonnie G. Safety engr. Nelson Spity. Corp., San Leandro, Calif., 1954-59; safety dir. Judson Steel, Emmeryville, Calif., 1959-60; safety engr. Indsl. Indemnity Co., Sacramento, 1960-64; pres. Sacramento Safety Council, Inc., 1964—. Registered profl. engr., Calif.; cert. hazard control mgr.; cert. assn. exec. Mem. Am. Soc. Assn. Execs., Am. Soc. Safety Engrs. (pres. 1965-66), Sacramento Soc. Assn. Execs. (founder, pres. 1979-80), Vets. of Safety (pres. 1973-74), World Safety Orgn. Republican. Office: Sacramento Safety Council Inc 3909 Bradshaw Rd Sacramento CA 95827

BROWN, KENNETH RAY, environmental engineer; b. Spokane, Wash., Sept. 23, 1943; s. Harold James and Senna Katherine (Garcea) B.; m. Barbara Ann Nicholson, Sept. 12, 1964. B.S. in Chem. Engring., Wash. State U., 1966; M.S. in Environ. Engring., U. Tex., 1974. Process engr. Shell Oil Co. Anacortes Refinery (Wash.), 1966-70; process design engr. Continental Oil Co., Ponca City, Okla., 1970-71; spur. air and water conservation Texaco USA Puget Sound Refinery, Anacortes, 1972—; facilitator for new age thinking Pacific Inst. USPHS grantee, 1971. Mem. Western Oil and Gas Assn. (chmn. N.W. tech. subcom.). Roman Catholic. Club: Bellingham (Wash.) Tennis. Office: PO Box 622 Marchs Point Anacortes WA 98221

BROWN, LARRY FRANK, mining ecologist; b. Denver, Nov. 30, 1940; s. Wendell Wilson and Florence Rebecca (Bruce) B.; m. Anne Loomis Morgan, Jan. 25, 1969; children—Heidi, Molly. B.S. in Phys. Sci., Colo. State U., 1962, Ph.D. in Range Ecophysiology, 1974. Peace Corps vol. beekeeping research and extension, India, 1963-65; sci. tchr., coach Clear Creek Secondary Sch., Idaho Springs, Colo., 1966-70; successively teaching asst., research asst., research assoc. Colo. State U., Ft. Collins, 1971-74; environ. control engr. Urad and Henderson mines, Climax Molybdenum Co., Empire, Colo., 1974-79; dep. dir. environ. control AMAX Molybdenum Div., Golden, Colo., 1979—; instr. Colo. Outward Bound schs., summers 1968, 69; mem. adv. com. Colo. Mountain Coll. environ. protection tech., 1975-79; chmn. Com. High-Altitude Revegetation; mem. Mineral Waste Stblzn. com.; gov.'s appointee industry rep. Colo. Mined Land Reclamation Bd.; chmn. 208 Water Quality Policy Adv. Group, Clear Creek, Gilpin, Park counties; guest lectr., chmn. workshops, instr. in field, of ecology. Mem. Clear Creek County Sch. Bd., 1975—, U.S. Forest Service Arapahoe and Roosevelt Nat. Forests Idaho Springs dist. involvement group, 1978-79. Mem. Idaho Springs Hist. Soc. (bd. dirs., 1974-77), Sigma Xi. Contbr. articles to ecol. publs. Home: PO Box 698 Idaho Springs CO 80452 Office: 1707 Cole Blvd Golden CO 80401

BROWN, LAURA SUSAN, psychology educator, psychotherapist; b. Oak Park, Mich., Dec. 24, 1952; d. Sanford and Shirley Zelda (Schwartzberg) B. B.A. cum laude, Case Western Res. U., 1972; M.A., So. Ill. U., Carbondale, 1975, Ph.D. (USPHS fellow), 1977. Lic. psychologist, Wash. State. Asst. prof. psychology So. Ill. U., 1977-78; asst. prof. U. Wash., 1978-80, clin. asst. prof., 1980—; pvt. practice psychotherapy, Seattle, 1979—; pub. WSE Rev., 1980—; host call-in talk therapy show Sta. KVI-AM, Seattle, 1980-82; bd. dirs. Women's Skills Exchange, Seattle; conf. presentations. Mem. NOW, Nat. Gay Task Force. Mem. Am. Psychol. Assn., Assn. Women in Psychology (nat. conf. coordinator), Assn. Media Psychologists, Soc. Psychol. Study Social Issues. Jewish. Contbr. chpts., articles to profl. publs. Office: PO Box 20366 Broadway Sta Seattle WA 98102

BROWN, LES, ins. agt.; b. Bklyn., Apr. 25, 1926; s. Robert and Rose B.; student U. N.C., 1946-48; m. Doris Goldstein, Dec. 25, 1949; children—Sandra E., Joan S., Gilbert W. Sales mgr. Armour & Co., 1950-53; announcer various radio stas., 1945-49; pres. trucking firm, Rockville Centre, N.Y., 1953-63; sales agt. Conn. Gen. Life, Queens, N.Y., 1963-75; sales trainer, estate planner Lincoln Nat. Life Ins. Co., Albuquerque and Phoenix, 1975—, also pres. cabinet; dir. Money Mgmt. Inc., Phoenix. Pres., founder Fairview Jewish Meml. Cemetery, Albuquerque; lectr. Community Relations Council of Jewish Fedn. Served with U.S. Mcht. Marines, 1943-45, U.S. Army, 1945-46. Mem. N.Mex. Estate Planning Council, Estate Planning Council Ariz. Republican. Club: Knights of Pythias (past chancellor, founder Valley Shalom lodge, Phoenix 1979). Office: 2602 N 44th St Suite 104 Phoenix AZ 85008

BROWN, LOWELL KENT, research manufacturing executive; b. Roosevelt, Utah; June 5, 1939; s. Rulon Richard and Revoe (Allen) B; m. Katherine Bee Moon, Aug. 28, 1964; children—Erik, Julie, Kirk. A.B. in Sci., Coll. So. Utah, Cedar City, 1959; B.S.E.E., U. Utah, Salt Lake City, 1967. Quality engr. Electronic Memories and Magnetics, Hawthorne, Calif., 1967-69; design engr. Edo Western Corp., Salt Lake City, 1969-70; v.p. engring. Utah Research and Devel. Corp., Salt Lake City, 1973-76, v.p. mktg., 1976-79, exec. v.p., 1979—. Bd. dirs. Mormon. Patentee battery charger. Office: Utah Research and Devel Corp 1820 Industrial Rd Salt Lake City UT 84104 Home: 208 Marla Way Midvale UT 84047

BROWN, MARTHA E(DNA), communications company official; b. Los Angeles, Nov. 23, 1941; d. Joe and Celia (Aduna) Oliva; m. Jack D. Corrales, Nov. 26, 1960; children—Jack Joseph, Tyla Maria Corrales Cox, Mia Christine; m. 2d Lawrence D. Brown, July 3, 1982. Student Valley Coll., Moorpark Coll., UCLA Extension. With Storer Cable Communications, 1967—, receptionist, clk., Thousand Oaks, Calif., 1967, cash receipts coordinator western region office, Thousand Oaks, 1969, adminstrv. asst., 1970-73, exec. sec., 1973-76, exec. sec. and office mgr., 1976-77, service rep. Thousand Oaks system, 1977-79, mktg. and customer service mgr., 1979-80, asst. mgr., 1980-81, system gen. mgr., 1981-83, community services dir. Laguna Beach system, 1983—; lobbyist; participant seminars in field. Mem. Women in Cable (treas. 1981), So. Calif. Cable Club (edn. com.), Calif. Cable TV Assn. (lobbyist; govt. relations com.), Nat. Assn. Female Execs. Democrat. Clubs: Toastmistress (treas. 1981). Soroptomists. Home: 106 Galsworthy St Thousand Oaks CA 91360

BROWN, MARY ALICE BUNYARD, community services executive officer, consultant, author; b. Chgo., Aug. 3, 1945; d. Prince William and Stella D. (Broderson) Bunyard; m. Ira Leslie Brown, Jan. 29, 1970 (div.). B.A. in Design, U. Ill.-Chgo., 1969; M.S. in Counseling Psychology, U. Oreg., 1974. Research asst. Batten, Barton, Durstine & Osborn, Chgo., 1965-66; counselor Pritzker Ctr. and Hosp., Chgo., 1967-68; writer Coronet Instructional Films, Chgo., 1970-71; student adviser Community Services and Pub. Affairs, U. Oreg., Eugene, 1972-74, grad. teaching fellow, 1974-75; exec. dir. Community Services of Lane County, Inc., Eugene, 1975—; cons. in field. Mem. planning com. United Way of Lane County, 1981-82; mem. Gov.'s Task Force on Mental Health, 1980-81; mem. United Way Agy. Dirs.' Orgn., 1978—, pres., 1981; mem. Lane County Employment and Tng. Council, 1979-81, Mental Health Assn., 1976—, pres., 1976. Research grantee Boston U., 1982-83; Ind. Living Program grantee Oreg. Vocat. Rehab. Div., 1981-83. Mem. Nat. Rehab. Assn., Nat. Assn. Female Execs. Author: Training Manual for the Development of Community Centers and Work Programs for the Psychiatrically Disabled, 1981, rev., 1982, 83. Home: 33481 Bloomberg Rd Eugene OR 97405 Office: 2621 Augusta St Eugene OR 97403

BROWN, MARY EDITHA, educational administrator, nun; b. Dubuque, Iowa, Mar. 28, 1923; d. William Henry and Mary Ethel (Rowan) B. B.A., Clarke Coll., 1962; M.A., U. Notre Dame, 1969; M.A. equivalency, Gregorian U., Rome. Tchr. schs. in Iowa, Mo., Ill., Calif., 1945-55; adminstr., Washington, Iowa, 1955-61, Rock Island, Ill., 1966-75; supt. schs. Diocese of Great Falls-Billings (Mont.), 1977—; cons. bds. edn., parish councils; conductor inservice of tchrs. Past pres. bd. dirs. Great Falls Crisis Ctr., 1982-84. Recipient Service award Great Falls Crisis Ctr., Speakers Club, Kiwanis, Rotarians. Mem. Nat. Cath. Ednl. Assn., Mont. Cath. Conf. (chmn. edn. com.), Assn. Non-pub. Schs. Mont., Notre Dame Alumni Assn.

BROWN, MELVIN JONATHAN, soil scientist, farmer; b. Buhl, Idaho, Mar. 10, 1932; s. Ernest and Ava (Hunt) B.; m. Norma Lynn Francis, June 2, 1954; children—David Jonathan, Julie Lynn Brown Watson, Lori Ann Brown Wood, Gary Francis. M.S. in Soil Sci., U. Calif.-Riverside, 1964. Student trainee soil scientist Agr. Research Service U.S. Dept. Agr., Logan, 1958-60, soil scientist Citrus Experiment Sta., Riverside, 1960-65, Snake River Conservation Research Ctr., Kimberly, Idaho, 1965—. Served with U.S. Navy, 1951-55. Recipient Superior Service award U.S. Dept. Agr., 1968. Mem. Soil Sci. Soc. Am., Am. Soc. Agronomy, Western Soc. Soil Sci., Sigma Xi. Mormon. Contbr. articles to profl. jours. Home: Route 1 Box 287 Wendell ID 83355 Office: Route 1 Box 186 Snake River Conservation Research Center Kimberly ID 83341

BROWN, MICHAEL JAMES, radio broadcaster, auto dealer; b. Los Angeles, Nov. 24, 1932; s. Willet Henry and Stella Edith (Huggins) B.; m. Nancy Kent, Aug. 11, 1954; children—Kent Edwin, Gretchen Huggins, Stephanie Doyle. B.A. in Econs., Claremont Mens Coll., 1954; postgrad. Gen. Motors Inst., 1957. Vice-pres., gen. mgr., part owner Hillcrest Motor Co., Cadillac dealership, Beverly Hills, Calif., 1957—; v.p., stockholder Sta. KGB and KCNN, San Diego, 1962—, Sta. KXOA, Sacramento, 1971—. Pres. Beverly Hills Jr. C. of C., 1961-62; mem. Catalina Island Conservancy, 1981—; bd. dirs. Beverly Hills Men's Club, 1963-65. Served to 1st lt. U.S. Army, 1954-56. Mem. Nat. Auto Dealers Assn., Nat. Radio Broadcasters Assn. Clubs: Los Angeles Country, Vikings of Scandia (bd. dirs.). Home: 432 N McCadden Pl Los Angeles CA 90004 Office: 9230 Wilshire Blvd Beverly Hills CA 90212

BROWN, OGDEN, JR., human resources educator; b. Evanston, Ill., Apr. 1, 1927; s. Ogden and Frances Louise (Falck) B.; A.B., Am. U., 1950, M.A., 1951; Ph.D., Purdue U., 1965; m. Alyce Marie Whitesides, May 1, 1953; children—Marsha Marie Brown Akse, Lynda Lou Brown Dunne, Ogden III, Tarleton II. Psychometrician, U.S. Employment Service, Washington, 1950-51; commd. 2d lt. USAF, 1951, advanced through grades to col., 1971; from instr. to assoc. prof. U.S. Air Force Acad., 1961-68; asst. for edn. and tng. Office of Sec. of Air Force, Washington, 1968-71; comdr. 3415 Spl. Tng. Group, Lowry AFB, Colo., 1971-73; ret., 1973; exec. v.p. Am. West Enterprises, Colorado Springs, Colo., 1973-78; from asst. prof. to assoc. prof. human factors Inst. Safety and Systems Mgmt., U. So. Calif., Los Angeles, 1978—; pres. Mgmt. Devel. Assocs., Colorado Springs, 1973—. Decorated Legion of Merit, Meritorious Service medal, Commendation medal. Mem. Acad. of Mgmt., Am. Psychol. Assn., Human Factors Soc., Midwestern Psychol. Assn., Rocky Mountain Psychol. Assn., Sigma Xi, Psi Chi, Omicron Delta Kappa, Delta Phi Alpha. Republican. Episcopalian. Club: Elks, Contbr. articles to profl. jours. Home: 17 Sanford Rd Colorado Springs CO 80906 Office: Human Factors Dept ISSM U So Calif Los Angeles CA 90089

BROWN, PATRICIA BUFORD, association executive; b. Jacksonville, Fla., May 3, 1938; d. Herman and Mildred Wainwright (Newsome) Buford; B.A., Nat. U., San Diego, 1976, M.B.A., 1978; divorced; children—Andrew James, Allison Paige. Mem. Faculty Foothill Community Coll., San Diego, 1978-79; dir. admissions and records, registrar Western State U. Coll. Law, San Diego, 1969-79; dist. mgr. Victor Temp. Services, San Jose, Calif., 1979-81; v.p. sales Freedom Travel Service, San Jose, 1981-83; exec. dir. Am. C. of C. in Egypt, Cairo, 1983—. Mem. Peninsula Profl. Women's Network, Women in Bus. (chmn. 1981), San Jose C. of C. (dir.). Address: Am C of C in Egypt Marriott Hotel Suite 1537 PO Box 33 Zamalek Cairo Egypt

BROWN, PATRICIA CARLEEN, employment agency owner; b. Honolulu, May 12, 1939; d. Vernon N. and Eleanor M. (Gomes) Andrade; m. Edward Tate Harrison, Jr., July 19, 1958; children—Edward Harrison, Mark; m. 2d Percy Brown, Jr., Dec. 6, 1968; 1 son, Brady. Student pub. schs., Honolulu. Traffic mgr. KGU, Radio, Honolulu, 1959-60, KGMB-TV, Honolulu, 1966-67; mgr. Adams & Assocs., 1977-79; owner Employment Specialists and Career Opportunities, Honolulu, 1979—. Mem. Hawaii Assn. Personnel Cons. (sec. 1977-79), Nat. Assn. Personnel Cons., Hawaii Bus. League.

BROWN, PATRICIA CHARLES, educator; b. Jersey City, N.J., Feb. 17, 1927; d. Perry Marshall and Virginia Marie (Marr) Charles; 1 dau., Candace Marie. B.A., Calif. State U.-Northridge, 1970, M.A., 1971. Publicist, Desilu Studios, Hollywood, Calif., 1956-60; casting dir. Standard Sch. Broadcast, Los Angeles, 1962-65; tchr. Pierce Coll., 1971-82, Calif. State U., 1973-74; tchr. Crespi Carmelite High Sch., Encino, Calif., 1974—, chmn. English dept., 1976—; reader book tapes for blind Library of Congress, 1964-65; freelance columnist, Los Angeles Daily News, 1983—. Mem. NEA, Calif. Tchrs. Assn., Nat. Council Tchrs. English. Roman Catholic. Co-author: Textbook on Individual English Instruction, 1973. Home: 8425 Amigo Ave Apt 6 Northridge CA 91324 Office: 5031 Alonzo Ave Encino CA 91316

BROWN, PAUL FREMONT, aerospace engineer, educator; b. Osage, Iowa, Mar. 10, 1921; s. Charles Fremont and Florence Alma (Olson) B.; m. Alice Marie Culver, Dec. 5, 1943; children—Diane, Darrell, Judith, Jana. B.A. in Edn. and Natural Sci., Dickinson State Coll., 1942; B.S. in Mech. Engring., U. Wash., 1948; M.S. in Cybernetic Systems, San Jose State U., 1971. Profl. quality engr., Calif., 1978; cert. reliability engr., Am. Soc. Quality Control, 1976. Test engr., supr. Boeing Aircraft Corp., Seattle, 1948-56; design specialist, propulsion systems, Lockheed Missiles and Space Co., Sunnyvale, Calif., 1956-59; supr. system effectiveness, 1959-66, staff engr., 1966-76, mgr. product assurance, 1976—; v.p. research, devel. Gen. Agriponics Inc. of Hawaii, 1971-76; coll. instr., lectr., San Jose State U. Active in United Presbyn. Ch., 1965—; scoutmaster, Boy Scouts Am., 1963-65. Served to 1st lt., USAF, 1943-46. Recipient awards for tech. papers, Lockheed Missiles and Space Co., 1973-75. Mem. Am. Soc. Quality Control, AIAA. Clubs: Toastmasters (Sunnyvale, Calif.). Contbr. articles to profl. jours. Home: 19608 Braemar Dr Saratoga CA 95070 Office: 1111 Lockheed Way Bldg 579 Sunnyvale CA

BROWN, RAYMOND DUTSON, state agy. adminstr.; b. Phila., Feb. 3, 1933; s. Allen Webster and Helen Ruth (Belshaw) B.; B.A., Brown U., 1959; M.Div., Sch., 1962; m. Joyce Marie Foor, Feb. 10, 1978; children by previous marriage—Raymond D., Timothy R., Katherine E., Lura A. Ordained to ministry Episcopal Ch., 1962; curate, Schenectady, 1962-63; vicar Whitefish (Mont.) Mission field, 1963-66; dean St. Peter's Cathedral, Helena, Mont., 1966-75; adminstr. Mont. Human Rights Div., Helena, 1975—; chaplain Mont. Ho. of Reps., 1967, 69. Mem. Helena Sch. Bd., 1973-76; pres. Lewis and Clark Search & Rescue, 1973-77; bd. dirs. St. Peter's Hosp., United Way. Served to s/sgt. USMC, 1951-54. Mem. Nat. Assn. Human Right Workers, Internat. Assn. Ofcl. Human Rights Agys., Mont. Assn. Chs. (pres. 1973-74), Mont. Council Chs. (chmn. Indian task force 1968-70). Democrat. Office: Cogswell Bldg Room C-317 Helena MT 59620

BROWN, ROBERT EARL, educator, photographer; b. Gouverneur, N.Y., Jan. 26, 1937. A.A.S., Rochester Inst. Tech., 1957, B.F.A., 1959; M.A., San Francisco State U., 1967; M.F.A., San Francisco Art Inst., 1972. One-man shows: George Eastman House, Rochester, N.Y., 1968, 72, Los Angeles Inst. Contemporary Art, 1981, San Francisco Art Mus., 1969, Mus. Modern Art, N.Y.C., 1970, Calif. State U.-Fullerton, 1979, European tour U.S. Internat. Community Agy., 1981-82; group shows include: Hayden Art Gallery, MIT, 1969; represented in permanent collections George Eastman House, MIT, Oakland (Calif.) Mus.; asst. prof. art Calif. State U.-Northridge, 1967-70; assoc. prof. art U. Nev., Las Vegas, 1976—. Nat. Endowment for Arts photog. fellow, 1975. Mem. Soc. Photog. Edn. Office: University Nevada Dept Art 4505 Maryland Pkwy Las Vegas NV 89154

BROWN, ROBERT JOSEPH, psychologist; b. Hollywood, Fla., Apr. 21, 1943; s. Harold LaRue and Margaret Rose (Perin) B.; m. Virginia E., Jan. 22, 1966; children—Shawn, Julie. B.A. in Psychology, SUNY-Cortland, 1966; postgrad. U.S. Internat. U., Elliott Campus, San Diego, 1970-71; Ph.D. in Counselor Edn., Ohio U., 1972; also various spl. tng. courses. Lic. psychologist, S.C., Calif. Residential counselor Susquehanna Valley Home for Children, Binghamton, N.Y., 1966-67; computer programmer Fed. div. IBM, Oswego, N.Y., 1966-67; software programmer NCR, Hawthorne, Calif., 1967-68; research cons., computer programmer asst. Ohio U., 1968-70; head resident and counselor U.S. Internat. U., Calif. Western Campus, 1970; intern Project Oz, San Diego, 1970-71; staff clin. psychologist Children's Psychiat. Ctr., Eatontown, N.J., 1971-72; exec. dir. Pre-Trial Intervention Project, Columbia, S.C., 1972-73; staff clin. psychologist II, mental health services Shasta Gen. Hosp., Redding, Calif., 1973-76; prin. Psychology and Counseling Services, Redding, 1976—; workshop, seminar and meeting presentations; mem. adv. bd. S.C. Assn. Improved Justice, Columbia, 1972; pres. Shasta County (Calif.) Council for Crime and Delinquency, 1978; mem. Shasta County Mental Health Adv. Bd., 1982-84. Fellow Am. Orthopsychiat. Assn.; mem. Calif. State Psychol. Assn., Am. Psychol. Assn. Home: 3441 Pioneer Ln Redding CA 96001 Office: 620 Azalia Ave Redding CA 96002

BROWN, ROBERT MAFFETT, criminologist; b. Williamsport, Pa., Nov. 19, 1942; s. Robert Maffett and Martha Jane (Rohe) B.; B.S., Calif. State U. at Long Beach, 1968; M.Pub. Adminstrn., U. So. Calif., 1970; children—Andrew, Rohe, Daniel Robert. Program coordinator Delinquency Control Inst., U. So. Calif., Los Angeles, 1968-70; cons. Bd. of Corrections, State of Calif., Sacramento, 1970-71; asst. project supr. Atty. Gen's Adv. Commn. on community-police relations, Los Angeles, 1971-73; cons. Nat. Standards and Goals, Law Enforcement Adminstrn., 1972; cons. Calif. Youth Authority, 1968—; asst. dir., trainer Nat. Inst. Corrections, Long Beach, 1972-73; dir. Correctional Adminstrn. Inst., 1973-76, also interim dir. Jud. Adminstrn. Inst., U. So. Calif., 1974-75, dir. ednl. programs in corrections Coll. Continuing Edn., 1976-79, exec. dir. public sector programs, 1979—. Policy com. mem. U. So. Calif. Sch. Pub. Adminstrn., 1969-70. Trustee for John D. Gerletti Scholarship U. So. Calif., 1970—. Served with USAF, 1960-64. Mem. Nat. Soc. for Study of Edn., Am. Soc. Pub. Adminstrn., Am. Acad. for Polit. and Soc. Sci., Am. Correctional Assn., Calif. Juvenile Officers Assn., So. Calif. Advancement Pub. Adminstrs., Praetors of U. So. Calif., Common Cause. Home: 9176 Sara River Circle Fountain Valley CA 92708 Office: 3535 S Figueroa CES 212 Los Angeles CA 90089

BROWN, R(OBERT) MICHAEL, psychology educator; b. Seattle, Jan. 17, 1945; s. Robert Bruce and Katherine Elizabeth (Schneider) B.; m. Norma Lynn Andersen, Nov. 12, 1966; children—Stephanie Lynn, Michelle Terese. B.A., Seattle U., 1967; M.Sc., U. Calgary, Can., 1972; Ph.D., U. N.C., 1974. Teaching fellow U. N.C.-Chapel Hill, 1972-73; asst. prof. dept. psychology Seattle U., 1974-77, No. Mich. U., Marquette, 1977-78, U. Wash., Seattle, 1978-82, Pacific Lutheran U., Tacoma, 1982—; cons. to tchrs., parents. Active Catholic Youth Orgn., 1962-67, Norwalk (Conn.) Jaycees, 1973-74. Research grantee Seattle U., 1976, U. Wash., 1979, 80, Pacific Luth. U., 1982. Mem. AAUP, Am. Psychol. Assn., Soc. Research in Child Devel. Internat. editorial bd. Cognitive Development Abstracts; cons. reviewer Prentice-Hall, Dorsey Press, Little Brown, also psychology jours.; contbr. articles to profl. publs.

BROWN, RONALD PRESTON, advertising executive; b. Staton, Oreg., July 26, 1953; s. Maxwell Allen and Alta May (Siegmund) B. m. Deanna Lynn Medvin, July 2, 1955; 1 dau., Linsey. B.A. in Advt., San Jose State U., 1976, M.B.A., 1978. Account exec. Bozell & Jacobs, Palo Alto, Calif., 1980-81, Allen & Dorward, San Francisco, 1981-83; account rep. J. Walter Thompson, San Francisco, 1983—. Office: J Walter Thompson Four Embarcadero Ctr San Francisco CA 94111

BROWN, RONALD RAY, accountant; b. Loma Linda, Calif., May 11, 1947; s. Perry and Dorothea Lucille (Burgeron) B.; B.S. in Bus. Adminstrn. with high honors, Calif. State U., Los Angeles, 1974; m. Bonnie Jean McGuire, Jan. 16, 1971; 1 dau., Rhonda Rae. Sr. accountant Haskins & Sells, Santa Ana, Calif., 1974-77; partner Brown, Stuetz & Co., C.P.A.s, San Juan Capistrano, Calif., 1977-79; owner, prin. Ronald R. Brown, C.P.A., San Juan Capistrano, 1979-83; sr. assoc. TMS Fin. Group, Inc., El Toro, Calif., 1983—; mem. adv. bd. Capistrano Nat.

Bank. Mem. San Juan Capistrano Traffic and Transp. Commn. Served with U.S. Army, 1967-70; Viet Nam. Decorated Air Medal, Bronze Star; cert. San Juan Capistrano city Council, 1982. C.P.A., Calif. Mem. Am. Inst. C.P.A.s, Calif. Soc. C.P.A.s, San Juan Capistrano Hist. Soc. (dir., treas.), San Juan Capistrano C. of C. (dir.), San Juan Capistrano Fiesta Assn., South Coast Jaycees, Beta Alpha Psi, Beta Gamma Sigma. Democrat. Club: Kiwanis (dir.). Office: 23705 Birtcher Dr El Toro CA 92630

BROWN, SHARON ELISE, college counselor, therapist; b. Flint, Mich., Sept. 4, 1948; d. Jack and Edith Frances (Smith) Swick; m. Timothy Lee Brown, Aug. 26, 1969; children—Joshua Benjamin, Nathan Thomas. B.A. with high honors, Mich. State U., 1970, M.A., 1972. Resident adv. Mich. State U., East Lansing, 1970-78; dir. resident camps Freedom Valley Council, GSA, Valley Forge, Pa., 1972-73; counselor Lansing (Mich.) Community Coll., 1971-74; assoc. student affairs Whitman Coll., Walla Walla, Wash., 1974-78, counselor, spl. programs coordinator, 1978—; student personnel cons. therapist. Bd. dirs. Planned Parenthood, 1982—, chmn. bd. devel. 1983—, conf. del., 1982. Mem. Northwest Coll. Personnel Assn. (treas. 1967-68, pres. 1981, conf. chmn 1980), Am. Coll. Personnel Assn., Am. Personnel and Guidance Assn. Democrat. Presbyterian. Home: Route 4 Box 425 Mill Creek Glen Walla Walla WA 99362 Office: Counseling Ctr Whitman College Walla Walla WA 99362

BROWN, SHARON SHELTON, government official; b. Washington, Oct. 10, 1948; d. James William and Shirley (Herrity) Shelton. B.S., U. Md., 1978. Pub. service dir. Sta. WPGC/AM/FM, Washington, 1969-71; office mgr. Sta. KJAZ/FM, Alameda, Calif., 1972; asst. ops. mgr. Sta. KPIX-TV, San Francisco, 1972-73; copywriter William D. Murdock Advt., Alexandria, Va., 1973-75; dir. pub. affairs Naval Security Group Activity, Fort Meade, Md., 1976-78; photojournalist NAS Alameda Pub. Affairs Office, 1978-79; asst. public affairs officer Mil. Sealift Comand, Pacific, Oakland, Calif., 1979-81, dir. legis. and public affairs, 1981-83; dir. pub. affairs Mil. Traffic Mgmt. Command, Western Area, Oakland, 1983—. Recipient Outstanding Performance awards Dept. Navy. Mem. Pub. Relations Soc. Am., East Bay Press CLub, Am. Film Inst., NOW, Oakland C. of C. Contbr. stories, photos to Navy publs. Office: Mil Traffic Mgmt Command Oakland Army Base Oakland CA 94626

BROWN, STEPHEN DADCOCK, advertising executive; b. N.Y.C., Feb. 7, 1943; s. Donald Winchester and Prudence Heath (Bredt) B.; m. Elizabeth McGrath, Apr. 17, 1970; children—Flemming, Winchester. B.A., M.B.A., U. Pa., 1966. Account supr. Compton Advt., N.Y.C., 1968-72; v.p., mgmt. supr. McCann-Erickson, N.Y.C. and Tokyo, 1973-78; v.p., mgmt. supr. S.S.C.&B., Los Angeles, 1978-80; sr. v.p., mgmt. supr. Dailey & Assocs., Los Angeles, 1980—. Served with U.S. Army, 1966-68. Episcopalian. Club: Union (N.Y.C.). Office: Dailey & Assoc 3055 Wilshire Blvd Los Angeles CA 90010

BROWN, STEPHEN WOODY, clin. and research psychologist; b. Cleve., Aug. 3, 1939; s. Joe and Enid G. (Hersch) B.; B.A. in Psychology with honors, Calif. State U., Los Angeles, 1962; Ph.D. in Psychology, U. So. Calif., 1966; m. Malinda Marie Slugocki, July 27, 1975; children—Kimberly Michelle, David Michael. Research psychologist U. So. Calif., 1962-66; asst. prof. Calif. State U., Dominquez Hills, 1966-68; postdoctoral fellow U. So. Calif., 1968-69; dir. dept. edn. Med. Media Network, UCLA Sch. Medicine, 1969-71; dir. counseling services Nat. Family Planning Council, 1970-71; staff psychologist to program dir. Camarillo State Hosp., 1971-74; asst. prof. U. So. Calif., 1974-75; sr. instructional developer Charles R. Drew Med. Sch., 1975-76; clin. psychologist, prof. Calif. Sch. Profl. Psychology, Fresno, 1976-81; asso. prof. psychology Pepperdine U., Los Angeles, 1981—, clin. psychologist Fresno Community Hosp., 1979-80; tchr. Fresno City Coll.; commr. Calif. State Psychology Exam. Com. Active Fresno County Mental Health Assn. USPHS postdoctoral fellow, 1969-70. Fellow Am. Geriatrics Soc.; mem. Calif. Psychol. Assn., Am. Psychol. Assn., San Joaquin Psychol. Assn., Blue Key, Sigma Xi, Psi Chi. Contbr. articles to profl. jours. Home: 23391 Devonshire St El Toro CA 92630

BROWN, STEVEN EUGENE, lawyer; b. N.Y.C., May 25, 1946; s. Harold Eugene and Mary Gertrude (Lynch) B.; A.B., Columbia U., 1968; J.D., U. So. Calif., 1972; m. Janelle Prosser; 1 son, Michael. Admitted to Calif. bar, 1973; atty., Legal Aid Found. Los Angeles, 1973-74; practiced in Los Angeles, 1975—. Mem. Am. Bar Assn., Calif. Bar Assn., Los Angeles County Bar Assn., Ventura County Bar Assn. Office: 650 Westlake Blvd Suite 204 Westlake CA 91362

BROWN, STEVEN HAROLD, counselor, educator; b. Chester, Pa., Apr. 20, 1954; s. Harold and Elizabeth (Brown) B. A.A., Mesa Community Coll., 1974; B.S. magna cum laude, Ariz. State U., 1976; M.A., No. Ariz. U., 1977. Cert. coll. instr., Ariz. Life skills instr. Tempe (Ariz.) Ctr. Handicapped, 1976; asst. coordinator student services N.Mex. State U., Grants, 1977; student services counselor Ariz. State U., Tempe, 1979-80; dir. counseling Low Cost Weightless Ctrs., Phoenix, 1979-82; dir. counseling, asst. prof. DeVry Inst. Tech., Phoenix, 1981—; psychology instr. Mesa Community Coll., 1978—. Mem. Am. Personnel and Guidance Assn., Am. Coll. Personnel Assn., Am. Soc. Tng. and Devel., N.Am. Soc. Psychology of Sports and Phys. Activities. Developed study skills workshops. Home: 326 La Jolla Dr Tempe AZ 85282 Office: DeVry Institute 4702 N 24th St Phoenix AZ 85016

BROWN, STEVEN MICHAEL, educational administrator, computer consultant; b. Los Angeles, Aug. 5, 1947; s. Harold and Roslyn (Bigman) B.; B.S., U. Fla., 1969; M.A., U. South Fla., 1973; Ph.D., Iowa State U., 1977; m. Deborah Levine, Aug. 15, 1971. Lang. arts instr., media dir. Hillsborough County Schs., Tampa, Fla., 1970-75; instr. coll. of edn. Iowa State U., Ames, 1975-77; high sch. prin. North Hills Schs., Pitts., 1977-78; high sch. asst. prin. for curriculum, Sierra Vista (Ariz.) Public Schs., 1978-80; high sch. asst. prin. for student services Scottsdale (Ariz.) Public Schs., 1980-81; dir. funded and enrichment programs Madison Public Schs., Phoenix, 1981-83; exec. dir. Ednl. Horizons Unltd., 1983—; cons. Vice pres. Young Democrats, Tampa, 1973; com. chmn. troop 423, Cochise County council Boy Scouts Am., Sierra Vista, 1979—. Served with USAR, 1970-76. Recipient PACE award Iowa State U., 1976-77; named Outstanding Young Educator, Cochise County, Ariz., 1979-80. Mem. Nat. Assn. Secondary Sch. Prins., Assn. Supervision and Curriculum Devel., Ariz. Assn. for Gifted and Talented (dir. 1982-84), Am. Assn. Sch. Adminstrs., Scottsdale Affiliated Adminstrs., Phi Delta Kappa (pres. Cochise County chpt. 1979—, state coordinator 1982-84, named to Ten Outstanding Young Educators Ariz. 1979-80). Democrat. Contbr. articles to profl. publs. Home: 1239 N Nevada Way Mesa AZ 85203 Office: 1059 S Country Club Suite 60 Mesa AZ 85202

BROWN, SUSAN KAY STOECKIG, educator; b. Dickinson, N.D., June 16, 1953; d. Edward Warren and Margie L. (Carroll) Stoeckig; m. Robert Joseph Brown, Sept. 20, 1975. B.S. in Edn., Eastern Mont Coll., 1975; postgrad., U. Utah, 1975-76; M.A. in Interpersonal Communication, U. Mont., 1982. Tchr., head speech coach, Flathead High Sch., Kalispell, Mont., 1977—; leadership trainer, Mont. Girls' State, 1979-82; organizer, instr., speech camp., Coll. of Great Falls, Mont., 1979-80. Div. chmn., ERA, 1978-80, div. parliamentarian, 1980-82. Recipient Inspirational Tchr. award, Mont State U., 1983; named AA Speech Coach of Yr., Mont., 1982; named an Outstanding Young Woman of Am., Jaycees, 1980. Mem. Am. Forensic Assn., Nat. Forensic League, Speech Communication Assn., Mont. Forensic Educators' Assn., Nat. Council Tchrs. English, Kalispell Edn. Assn. Republican. Roman Catholic. Home: 333 Cougar Trail Whitefish MT 59937 Office: Flathead High Sch 644 4th Ave W Kalispell MT 59901

BROWN, SUZANNE GOLDMAN, art historian, gallery owner; b. N.Y.C., Sept. 8, 1929; d. Maurice Elwell and Agnes (Wilson) Goldman; B.A. cum laude, Radcliffe Coll., 1951; postgrad. Harvard U. Sch. Law, Tufts U., Ariz. State U.; m. Jack Edward Brown, Aug. 27, 1950; children—Charles, Abigail, James, Amanda. Owner, operator Suzanne Brown Gallery and Suzanne Brown Collection, Scottsdale, Ariz., 1963—; lectr. art history various univs., museums, pvt. orgns. Bd. dirs. Ariz. Women's Caucus, Crisis Nursery for Prevention of Child Abuse, Seven Coll. Conf., Ariz. Theatre Co. Mem. Main St. Art Assn., Ariz. Acad. Home: 6645 N Central St Phoenix AZ 85012 Office: 7156 Main St Scottsdale AZ 85251

BROWN, TERENCE DANIEL, wood scientist; b. Albuquerque, Jan. 14, 1948; s. Kenneth Lee and Pauline Priscilla B.; B.S., Colo. State U., 1970, Ph.D., 1975; B.S., U. Utah, 1971; m. Patricia Ann Hoglund, Aug. 12, 1967; children—Cheri Lyn, Christine Michelle. Asso. prof., forest products extension specialist Oreg. State U., Corvallis, 1975—; cons. forest products industry. Asst. scoutmaster Boy Scouts Am., 1972-78; instr. 1st aid ARC, 1976—; v.p. Jefferson PTA, 1978; mem. Christian edn. com. 1st United Presbyterian Ch., 1974-75. Served to capt. USAFR, 1970—. Mem. Forest Products Research Soc., Oreg. Extension Assn., Soc. Wood Sci. and Tech., Sigma Xi, Xi Sigma Pi, Phi Kappa Phi. Republican. Methodist. Author: Quality Control in Lumber Manufacturing. Home: 2220 NW 27th St Corvallis OR 97330 Office: Dept Forest Products Oreg State U Corvallis OR 97331

BROWN, THOMAS JAMES, transportation company executive; b. Fullerton, Calif., Apr. 13, 1948; s. James L. and Beulah J. B.; m. LaVonne Marie Smith, June 27, 1970; children—Eric James, Angela Marie, Julia Diane. A.A. in Phys. Distbn. and Traffic Mgmt., Chabot Coll., 1974; B.S.B.A., Central Wash. U., 1981. Intermodal ops. coordinator BN Transport Co., Seattle, 1976-78; regional intermodal ops. mgr. Pacific N.W. region Am. Pres. Lines, Seattle, 1978-83; ops. supt. Port of Tacoma, 1983—. Served with USN, 1969-72; Vietnam. Republican. Home: 4221 S 297th Pl Auburn WA 98002 Office: One Sitcum Plaza PO Box 1837 Tacoma WA 98401

BROWN, THOMAS PAUL, oil co. exec.; b. Miles City, Mont., Aug. 5, 1927; s. Thomas Ambrose and Eleanor Ann (Boyce) B.; m. Virginia Sue Sayers, June 2, 1961; children—Dana, Tina, Nelson, Paul, Susan, Diane, David. With mktg. dept. Carter Oil Co., Billings, Mont., 1946-53; v.p. Modern Oil Co., Shelby, Mont., 1953-55, N.W. Oil & Refining, Billings, 1955-58, Berry Refining Co., Chgo., 1958-64, Pana Refining (Ill.), 1964-68; pres., chmn. bd. Synthetic Crude Devel. Co., Santa Barbara, Calif., 1980—; cons. Tosco Corp., Los Angeles, 1968-70, v.p., 1973-78, exec. v.p., 1978-80, also dir.; pres. Tosco Petro, 1970-73. Served with USAAC Res., 1944-45. Republican. Roman Catholic. Clubs: Los Angeles Petroleum, Calif., Jonathan, Los Angeles Athletic. Home: 4235 Cresta Ave Santa Barbara CA 93110 Office: 3892 State St Santa Barbara CA 93105

BROWN, THOMAS ROPER, market researcher and consultant; b. Toledo, July 30, 1944; s. Willis McMikken and Ruth Lillian (Roper) B.; m. Ann Sterling Dusseau, Feb. 26, 1945 (div.); children—Vaughn, Carl, Elizabeth. Student Drew U., 1965; B.A. in Econs., U. Redlands, 1966; M.B.A., U. Calif.-Berkeley, 1971. Marketing specialist Boise Cascade Corp., Los Angeles, 1970-71; mktg. mgr. Am. Western Corp., Phoenix, Ariz., and Boise, Idaho, 1971-72; chmn. Gametree Corp., Boise, 1978-82; pres. Marcept Consulting and Research, Boise, 1973—; mktg. cons. to nat. ARC Blood Services; lectr. seminar. Chmn. Snake River regional blood program, 1979-82; advisor Junior League Inc.; cons. Planned Parenthood, Idaho. Served to lt. U.S. Army, 1966-69. Mem. Nat. Mktg. Com., Am. Statis. Assn., Am. Mktg. Assn., Council of Survey Research Orgns., Republican. Club: Rotary (Boise). Holder several copyrights for computer programs for mktg. analysis and forecasting. Office: 815 Park Blvd Ste 200 Boise ID 83706

BROWN, THOMAS TOWNSEND, research co. exec.; b. Zanesville, Ohio, Mar. 18, 1905; s. Lewis K. and Mary (Townsend) B.; student Calif. Inst. Tech., 1922-23, Kenyon Coll., 1923-24, Denison U., 1924-25, Bowdoin Coll., 1941; m. Josephine Alberta Beale, Sept. 8, 1927; children—Joseph Townsend, Linda Ann. Lab. asst. electronics research dept. physics Denison U., Granville, Ohio, 1924-25; mem. staff astrophysics research lab. Swazey Obs., Granville, 1926-30; jr. physicist radiation and spectroscopy Naval Research Lab., Washington, 1930-33; state erosion engr. Fed. Emergency Relief Adminstrn., Columbus, Ohio, 1934; asst. adminstr. relief Ohio, dir. fed. student aid, dir. selection CCC, Ohio, 1934-35; research cosmic radiation observations Townsend Brown Found., Zanesville, Ohio, Laguna Beach, Calif., 1936-37; material and process engr. Glenn L. Martin Co., Balt., 1939-40; officer in charge magnetic and acoustic minesweeping research and devel. Bur. Ships, Navy Dept., Washington, 1940-41; radar cons. advanced design sect. Lockheed Aircraft Corp., Burbank, Calif., 1944-45; individual research biophysics, plant growth Island Kauai, Hawaii, 1948-52; cons. physicist Société Nationale Construction Aeronautique, Paris, France, 1955-56; chief cons. research and devel. Whitehall-Rand project Bahnson Co., Winston-Salem, N.C., 1957-58; pres. RAND Internat., Ltd., Nassau, Bahamas, 1958-74, Energy Resources Group, Ltd., Honolulu, 1974-82. Staff physicist Navy-Princeton Gravity Expdn., W.I., Navy Dept., 1932; physicist Johnson-Smithsonian deep sea expdn., Smithsonian 1933; cons. physicist Pearl Harbor Navy Yard, Honolulu, 1950; cons. Clevite-Brush Electronics Co., Cleve., 1954. Served to lt. comdr. USNR, 1933-43. Fellow AAAS; mem. Soc. Naval Engrs., Physics Soc., Astron. Soc. of Pacific, Geophys. Union. Home: PO Box 1565 Avalon CA 90704

BROWN, VALARIE LYNN, public relations executive; b. Houston, July 30, 1954; d. Mario A. and Berneice Saladino; m. Calvin Brown, Nov. 4, 1972 (div.). B.A., U. Houston, 1976. Youth cons. Harris County Juvenile Probation Dept., Houston, 1972-76; adminstrv. asst. Intercoastal Operating Co., Houston, 1976-77; account exec. Hill & Knowlton, Inc., Houston, 1977-81; public relations coordinator Drilco div. Smith Internat., Houston, 1981-82; public relations account mgr. Broyles, Allebaugh & Davis, Englewood, Colo., 1982—. Mem. Public Relations Soc. Am., Internat. Assn. Bus. Communicators. Lutheran. Home: 8330 E Quincy H-308 Denver CO 80237 Office: Broyles Allebaugh and Davis 8231 E Prentice St Englewood CO 80111

BROWN, VICTOR LEE, clergyman; b. Cardston, Alta., Can., July 31, 1914; s. Gerald Stephen and Maggie (Lee) B.; student U. Utah, Latter-day Saints Bus. Coll., U. Calif., Berkeley; m. Lois Kjar, Nov. 13, 1936; children—Victor Lee, Jr., Gerald E., Joanne K., Patricia L., Stephen M. Came to U.S., 1931, naturalized, 1942. Reservations mgr. United Airlines, Washington, 1940-47, Denver, 1948-56, mgr. space control, chief space control Denver, 1956-60, asst. to dir. reservations, Chgo., 1960-61; 2nd. counselor in presiding bishopric Ch. of Jesus Christ of Latter-day Saints, 1961-72, presiding bishop, Salt Lake City, 1972—; pres., chmn. bd. Utah Hotel Co., Salt Lake City, 1972—; dir. Western Airlines, Los Angeles. Bd. dirs. Utah Symphony, Salt Lake City, 1962—; mem. ch. bd. edn., Brigham Young U., Provo, 1972—; chmn. festival com. Utah Bicentennial Commn., Salt Lake City, 1975-77; mem. Pioneer State Theatre Found., 1974—. Mem. Am. Mgmt. Assn., Beta Gamma Sigma. Home: 1653 Orchard Dr Salt Lake City UT 84106 Office: 50 E North Temple Suite 1815 Salt Lake City UT 84150

BROWN, WALTER FREDERICK, state senator, library educator; b. Los Angeles, July 28, 1926; s. Walter Andrew and Emily Anna (Weber) B.; m. Barbara Mae Porter Stahmann, 1950; children—Jeffrey David, Kendall Paul, David Walter. A.B. cum laude, U. So. Calif., 1949, J.D., 1952; postgrad. Harvard U., 1957; M.A. in Govt., Boston U., 1961; postgrad. U. Oreg., summers 1972, 73, 75. Assoc. prof., librarian Lewis and Clark Coll., 1970—; mem. Oreg. State Senate from Dist. 13, 1975—, vice chmn. judiciary com., mem. human resources, environ. energy coms. Mem. 1st Congl. Dist. Democratic Com., 1972-74; precinct committeeman Clackamas County Dem. Party, 1972—; mem. Multnomah County Pub. Safety Retirement Bd., 1972—. Served to comdr. JAGC, U.S. Navy, 1944-70; PTO. Mem. ABA, Fed. Bar Assn., VFW, Oreg. Consumer League, Phi Beta Kappa, Phi Eta Sigma, Blue Key, Phi Kappa Phi, Delta Theta Phi, Kappa Sigma. Unitarian. Office: Northwestern School of Law Lewis and Clark College Portland OR 97219 also Oregon State Senate Salem OR 97310*

BROWN, WALTON EDWARD, publisher; b. Los Angeles, July 17, 1925; s. Frederick Walton and Mary (Clark) B.; children—Walton E. Jr., Christopher Mauldin. B.A. in Journalism, Stanford U., 1949. Advt. mgr. Northrop Aircraft, 1952-56; nat. sales mgr. Missiles and Rockets Mag., 1956-60; Western region sales mgr. Sci. and Tech. Mag., 1961-65; pub. designers West Mag., 1965—. Served to staff sgt. Inf., U.S. Army 1944-46. Decorated Purple Heart, Bronze Star, Presdl. Citation with oak leaf cluster. Mem. Western Publs. Assn. (pres., 1982-83, gov. Ednl. Found.), Nat. Home Fashions League, Fashion Inst. Design and Merchandising (adv. bd.), Am. Soc. Interior Designers (press affiliate). Home: 8530 Holloway Los Angeles CA 90069 Office: Designers West Mag 8564 Melrose Ave Los Angeles CA 90069

BROWN, WARREN EVERETT, personnel exec.; b. Ventura, Calif., Dec. 25, 1938; s. Everett F. and Ama M. (Morss) B.; A.A., Mt. San Antonio Coll., 1961; B.A. in Psychology, Long Beach State Coll., 1964; M.S. in Interdisciplinary Studies, So. Oreg. State Coll., 1980; m. Joanne L. Reynolds, Jan. 24, 1959; children—Gregory W., Michael W., Karyn M. Engrng. planner in engrng. dept. McDonnel Douglas Corp., Douglas Aircraft Co., Long Beach, Calif., 1965-67, employment rep., 1967, coordinator spl. employment ops. sect., 1968, manpower utilization and planning adminstr., 1968-70, compensation rep., 1970-71, br. mgr. of engrng. personnel ops., 1971-73; personnel dir. Sacred Heart Gen. Hosp., Eugene, Oreg., 1973-75; indsl. relations mgr. so. Oreg. region Boise Cascade Corp., 1975-77; personnel dir. Providence Hosp., Medford, Oreg., 1977—; instr evening sch. Rogue Community Coll. Bd. dirs. United Way of Jackson County (Oreg.), 1976-78; mem. So. Oreg. State Coll. Regional Adv. Bd., 1978-82; adv. council Area Agy. on Aging, 1982—, Rogue Valley Inst., 1982—. Served with USMC, 1956-59. Mem. Pacific Northwest Personnel Mgmt. Assn. (Rogue Valley chpt. pres. 1975-76). Home: 2433 Greenbrook Dr Medford OR 97501 Office: Providence Hosp 1111 Crater Lake Ave Medford OR 97501

BROWN, WILL GENE, superintendent schools; b. Pickardville, N.D., July 23, 1931; s. Harold Francis and Vergil Jane B.; 1 son, Vance Lee. B.S., U. Idaho-Moscow, 1960, M.Ed., 1960, Ed.S., 1979; Ph.D., Lawrence U., 1981. Tchr., Oxford (Calif.) Sch. Dist., 1964-65; curriculum and testing, prin. Oakley (Calif.) Union Sch. Dist., 1965-69; dir. spl. services Humboldt County Sch. Dist., Winnemucca, Nev., 1969-73; prin. Weiser (Idaho) Sch. Dist., 1973-78; supt. Wilder (Idaho) Sch. Dist., 1978—. Commr., Wilder Housing Authority, 1978—. Served with U.S. Army, 1953-55. Mem. Assn. Supervision and Curriculum Devel., Am. Assn. Sch. Adminstrs., Idaho Assn. Sch. Supts., Phi Delta Kappa Clubs: Toastmasters (ednl. v.p. 1983-84) (Caldwell, Idaho); Lions. Home: Box 266 Wilder ID 83676 Office: Box 488 Wilder ID 83676

BROWN, WILLIAM REYNOLD, artist, illustrator; b. Los Angeles, Oct. 18, 1917; s. William Reynold and Ada (Fairley) B.; m. Mary Louise Tajeda, 1921; children—Marie, Reynold, Franz, Elisa, Cristina, Regina, Marta, Marianne. Student Otis Art Sch., 1935-36. Illustrator for Tailspin Tommy and Four Aces for syndicated newspapers, 1934-40; illustrator N.Am. Aviation Flying Mag., created inboard drawings of airplanes, 1940-46; illustrator mags. including Outdoor Life, True, Argosy, Boy's Life; artist covers for paperback books, 1946-50; illustrator billboards, lobby posters for 250 motion pictures including Dr. Zhivago, How the West Was Won, Four Horsemen of Apocalypse, The Alamo (illustration now at mus. in San Antonio); artist several U.S. Air Force paintings now hanging on permanent display in Pentagon; portrait painter; Western genre; represented by Trailside Galleries, Scottsdale, Ariz. and Jackson, Wyo., Mollring Gallery, Houston; presently involved in the impressionist painting. Mem. Soc. Illustrators (New York, Los Angeles). Home and Office: 4840 N Live Oak Canyon Rd La Verne CA 91750

BROWN, WILLIE LEWIS, JR., state assemblyman, lawyer; b. Mineola, Tex., Mar. 20, 1934; s. Willie Lewis and Minnie (Collins) B.; m. Blanche Vitero, 1957; children—Susan Elizabeth, Robin Elaine, Michael Elliott. A.B., San Francisco State Coll., 1955; J.D., U. Calif.-Berkeley, 1958. Mem. Calif. State Assembly, 1965—, speaker from 1980. Mem. County Democratic Com., 1960-62; mem. Calif. Dem. State Central Com.; del. Dem. Nat. Conv., 1968, del., chmn. Calif. delegation, 1972—, del., 1976, co-chmn. Calif. delegation, 1980; del. Dem. Nat. Mid-Term Conf., 1974. Served with USNG. Fellow Crown Coll. of U. Calif.-Santa Cruz. Mem. Black Am. Polit. Assn. Calif. (founder, past chmn.), Phi Alpha Delta, Alpha Phi Alpha. Home: 540 Van Ness Ave San Francisco CA 94102 Office: Office of the Speaker State Captiol Sacramento CA 95814*

BROWNE, ALAN KINGSTON, bank cons.; b. Alameda, Calif., Nov. 12, 1909; s. Ralph Stuart and Etta E. (Bouve) B.; student U. Calif., 1929; m. Elisabeth Leone Henrotte, Feb. 7, 1942. With Bank-Am. Co. (successor to securities div. Nat. Bankitaly Co.), 1929-41, successively clk., mgr. municipal bond dept., asst. v.p.; with Bank of Am. N.T. & S.A., 1941-71, asst. cashier, 1941-42, asst. v.p., mgr. mcpl. bond dept., 1946-52, v.p., 1952-65, head of investments, 1964-71, sr. v.p., 1965-71, cons., 1971-72; sr. v.p., dir. Drexel Firestone, Inc., N.Y.C., 1972-73; cons., dir. Drexel Burnham Co., Inc., 1973, cons., 1974—. Past pres. and bd. dirs. San Francisco Stadium, Inc.; past chmn. bd., past pres. Friends San Francisco Pub. Library; former mem. Presdl. Adv. Com. on Fed. Debt Mgmt.; bd. dirs. dist. adminstrv. bldg. corp., chmn. adv. bd. on Financing San Francisco Bay Area Rapid Transit Dist.; chmn. San Francisco Bay Area Rapid Transit Com.; bd. dirs. Golden Rain Found. Served from pvt. to maj., AUS, 1942-46. Recipient Disting. Citizens award Nat. Mcpl. League, 1964. Mem. Securities Industry Assn. (past v.p. mcpl. fin., mem. exec. com., bd. govs., chmn. mcpl. div. council, chmn. mcpl. securities com.), Air Force Assn., Assn. U.S. Army, Calif. Geneal. Soc., U. Calif. Alumni Assn. (life), Navy League U.S., Calif. Hist. Soc., Mus. Soc., San Francisco Mcpl. Forum, Mcpl. Forum N.Y., Mcpl. Fin. Forum Washington, SAR, Phi Kappa Sigma. Clubs: Rotary; Mcpl. Bond, San Francisco Bond (past pres.; trophy Outstanding Investment Banker of Year 1958), Olympic, Merchants Exchange, Stock Exchange (San Francisco); Faculty (Berkeley). Contbr. articles to profl. jours. Home: 1113 Singing Wood Ct Apt 6 Walnut Creek CA 94595

BROWNE, CHARLES IDOL, radiochemist; b. Atlanta, Feb. 8, 1922; s. Charles Idol and Lillie Aurelia (Thweatt) B.; A.B., Drew U., 1941; M.S., U. Tex., 1942; M.S., Calif. Inst. Tech., 1948; Ph.D., U. Calif., Berkeley, 1952; m. Nancy Elizabeth Brown, Aug. 9, 1942; 1 son, Carter T. With Los Alamos Sci. Lab., 1955—, asso. div. leader, 1965-72, div. leader, 1972-74, assoc. dir., 1974-83; sci. advisor AEC, 1965-74. Served with USAF, 1943-55. Fellow Am. Phys. Soc., Am. Inst. Chemists; mem. Sigma Xi. Republican. Home: 428 Estante Way Los Alamos NM 87544 Office: PO Box 1663 Los Alamos NM 87545

BROWNE, JOSEPH PETER, librarian; b. Detroit, June 12, 1929; s. George and Mary Bridget (Fahy) B.; A.B., U. Notre Dame, 1951; S.T.L., Pontificium Athenaeum Angelicum, Rome, 1957, S.T.D., 1960; M.S. in L.S., Cath. U. Am., 1965. Joined Congregation of Holy Cross, Roman Cath. Ch., 1947, ordained priest, 1955; asst. pastor Holy Cross Ch., South Bend, Ind., 1955-56; librarian, prof. moral theology Holy Cross Coll., Washington, 1959-64; mem. faculty U. Portland (Oreg.), 1964-73, 75—, dir. library, 1966-70, 76—, dean Coll. Arts and Scis., 1970-73, asso. prof. library sci. 1967—, regent, 1969-70, 77-81; prof., head dept. library sci. Our Lady of Lake Coll., San Antonio, 1973-75; chmn. Interstate Library Planning Council, 1977-79. Mem. Greater Oreg. chpt. Com. to Combat Huntington's Disease, 1975—, pres., 1979-82. Recipient Culligan award U. Portland, 1979. Mem. Cath. Library Assn. (pres. 1971-73), ALA, Cath. Theol. Soc. Am., Pacific N.W. Library Assn., Oreg. Library Assn. (pres. 1967-68), Nat. Assn. Parliamentarians, Mensa Internat., All-Ireland Cultural Soc. Oreg. Democrat. Club: KC. Home: 5410 N Strong St Apt 8 Portland OR 97203 Office: 5000 N Willamette Blvd Portland OR 97203

BROWNE, THEODORE DAVID, fin. cons. and research co. exec.; b. New Kensington, Pa., Dec. 2, 1932; s. Gordon Scott and Florence Llewllyn B.; B.S., Pa. State U., 1954; M.S. in Fin., U. Colo., 1957; m. Kathryn Vermillion, Nov. 28, 1959; children—Tamra D., Kristin A. Personnel specialist Martin Co., Denver, 1958-64; research economist U. Denver Research Inst., 1964-70; pres. Bickert, Browne, Coddington & Assos., Inc., Denver, 1970—; mng. partner Browne, Bortz & Coddington, Denver, 1979—; chmn., pres. Gunnison Indsl. Bank, Delta Indsl. Bank. Served to lt. col. USMCR, 1954-56; ret. Res., 1977. Mem. Nat. Assn. Bus. Economists, Phi Gamma Delta. Republican. Home: 5525 Pemberton Dr Littleton CO 80121 Office: 155 S Madison St Denver CO 80209

BROWNELL, GORDON STEWART, lawyer; b. Washington, Feb. 24, 1944; s. John C. and Margaret E. (Slocum) B.; B.A., Colgate U., 1966; J.D. (Arthur M. Laufer Meml. scholar, 1968-69), Fordham U., 1969; m. Sandra Lee Kutik, Aug. 21, 1976. Adminstrv. asst. to spl. counsel to Pres., White House staff, Washington, 1969-70; asst. to chmn. Com. to Re-Elect Gov. Reagan, 1970; v.p. Am. Polit. Research Corp., Bethesda, Md., 1971-72; asso. editor Am. Polit. Report, Bethesda, 1971-72; dir. govt. relations Amorphia, Inc., San Francisco, 1972-73, pres., 1973-74; West Coast dir. Nat. Orgn. for Reform of Marijuana Laws, San Francisco, 1974-80, bd. dirs., 1975—, chmn. bd. dirs., 1981-82, acting nat. dir., 1980, chmn. exec. com., 1981—. Bd. dirs. Youth Projects, Inc., Haight-Ashbury Free Med. Clinic, 1978—, ACLU of No. Calif., 1981—; mem. Citizens for Justice, 1974-79, chmn., 1976; asso. mem. Rep. State Central Com. of Calif., 1973-74; statewide polit. coordinator Calif. Marijuana Initiative (Proposition 19), 1972; mem. ACLU, Amnesty Internat., Sierra Club, San Francisco Tomorrow, Nat. Geog. Soc., Internat. Oceanographic Found., San Francisco Mus. Soc., Internat. Giraffe Appreciation Soc. Served with Army N.G., 1969-75. Recipient cert. of honor San Francisco Bd. Suprs., 1981. Mem. Am. Bar Assn., State Bar Calif., Bar Assn. San Francisco, Sigma Chi. Democrat. Office: 26 O'Farrell St Suite 600 San Francisco CA 94108

BROWNEWELL, ELIZABETH CECIL, home economics educator; b. Enid, Okla., Dec. 22, 1919; d. Lawrence Keith and Jennie Louise (Anderson) Cecil; m. John Landrum Brownewell, Sept. 9, 1939; children—Ann Payne, Margaret E. Baker, Karen L. Schmick, Barbara B. Kerlick. B.S., U. Ariz., 1968, M.S., 1971. Cert. tchr., Calif. Tchr. home econs. Santa Maria (Calif.) Joint Union High Sch., 1968—; cons., speaker in field. Juliette Lowe fellow Internat. Workshop Girl Scouts Am., 1961. Mem. NEA, Calif. Tchrs. Assn., Santa Maria Joint Union High Sch. Tchrs. Assn., Omicron Nu, Kappa Delta Pi, Pi Lambda Theta. Republican. Congregationalist. Club: Santa Maria Country. Home: 1033 E Orange St Santa Maria CA 93454 Office: 901 S Broadway Santa Maria CA 93454

BROWNFIELD, SHELBY HAROLD, soil scientist; b. Ava, Ill., June 12, 1931; s. William Edward and Mabel (Ditzler) B.; B.S., U. Ill., 1954; postgrad. Iowa State U., 1968; m. Lois Marie Landreth, Apr. 27, 1952; children—Susan, Nancy, David, Judy, Lori. Lab. technician Agr. Research Service, Champaign, Ill., 1952-54; soil conservation tech. Agrl. Research Service, U.S. Dept. Agr., Joliet, Ill., 1954-55; field rep. Swift & Co., Watseka, Ill., 1955-56; soil scientist-mapper Soil Conservation Service, Greencastle, Ind., 1956-67, SCS, Spencer, Ind., 1957-60, soil scientist/soil survey party leader Franklin, Ind., 1960-67, party leader, N. Vernon, Ind., 1967-72, Kendelville, Ind., 1972, correlator, Bozeman, Mont., 1972-77, state soil scientist, Boise, Idaho, 1977—; tech. dir. Idaho Soil Survey, 1977—. Recipient Performance award U.S. Dept. Agr. Soil Conservation Service, 1969, 72, Cert. of Merit, 1979. Mem. Am. Soc. Agronomy, Soil Sci. Soc. Am., Soil Sci. Assn. Ida., Soil Conservation Soc. Am. Baptist. Clubs: Masons, Elks. Contbr. articles to profl. jours. Home: 7689 Stirrup St Boise ID 83709 Office: 304 N 8th St Boise ID 83702

BROWNING, BOB DEAN, business executive, former air force officer; b. West Frankfort, Ill., Apr. 16, 1933; s. Burles and Pearl M. (Butler) B.; m. Lynn D. Howard, Nov. 26, 1977; children—Robert, Michael, Alison. B.S. in Aero. Engring., St. Louis U., 1953; M.S. in Aero. Engring., Air Force Inst. Tech., 1961. Commd. 2d lt. U.S. Air Force, 1954, advanced through grades to col., 1974; project engr. aircraft and space programs, 1954-66; staff officer Hdqrs. USAF, 1966-69; career devel. officer Mil. Personnel Ctr., 1969-72; dir. personnel plans Hdqrs. Air Force Systems command, 1972-74; program dir. shuttle and ELMS and NATO satellite programs, dir. advanced planning Air Force Space Div., 1974-80; ret., 1980; dir. mission analysis N.Am. space ops. Rockwell Internat., El Segundo, Calif., 1980—. Decorated Legion of Merit. Mem. AIAA, Air Force Assn., Nat. Aero. Assn., Assn. U.S. Army. Office: 2230 E Imperial Hwy El Segundo CA 90245

BROWNING, EDMOND LEE, bishop; b. Corpus Christi, Tex., Mar. 11; s. Edmond Lucian and Cora Mae (Lee) B.; B.A., U. of South, 1952, B.D., 1954, D.D., 1970; m. Patricia Sparks, Sept. 10, 1953; children—Robert Mark, Patricia Paige, Philip Myles, Peter Sparks, John Charles. Ordained priest Episcopal Ch., 1954, named bishop, 1968; curate Ch. of the Good Shepherd, Corpus Christi, 1954-56; rector Redeemer Ch., Eagle Pass, Tex., 1956-59, All Souls Ch., Okinawa, 1959-63, St. Matthews Ch., Okinawa, 1965-67; archdeacon Okinawa Episc. Ch., 1965-67, 1st missionary bishop of Okinawa, 1968-71; bishop of convocation Episc. Chs. in Europe, 1971-74; exec. Nat. and World Mission Exec. Council, N.Y.C., 1974-76; bishop of Hawaii, 1976—. Bd. dirs. Anglican Center, Rome, 1971-74, St. Stephens Sch., Rome, 1971-74. Named hon. canon St. Michaels Cathedral, Kobe, Japan. Address: Queen Emma Sq Honolulu HI 96813

BROWNING, HERB HADDON, state wildlife manager; b. Armel, Colo., Feb. 1, 1930; s. Charley Alden and Marie Elizabeth (Davidson) B.; m. Iona May Reitmeyer, Mar. 28, 1948; children—Penny Planeta, Cindy Wood. Cert. peace officer Colo. Fish culturist Colo. Div. Wildlife, Chimney Rock, 1952-56, supt. fish hatchery, 1956-62, dist. wildlife officer, 1962-78, dist. wildlife mgr., 1978—; lectr. in field. Mem. bd. cooperative services Pagosa Springs Sch. Bd.; dep. coroner, dep. sheriff Archulata County; U.S. game warden, Pagosa Springs, Colo.; chmn. Chimney Rock Boy Scout Council; chmn. adminstrv. bd. Pagosa Springs Community United Meth. Ch. Mem. Colo. Wildlife Soc., Colo. Assn. Pub. Employees, Employees Protective Assn. Republican. Home and Office: PO Box 76 Chimney Rock CO 81127

BROWNING, JAMES ROBERT, federal judge; b. Great Falls, Mont., Oct. 1, 1918; s. Nicholas Henry and Minnie Sally (Foley) B.; LL.B. with honors, Mont. State U., 1941; LL.D. (hon.), U. Mont., 1978; m. Marie Rose Chapell. Admitted to Mont. bar, 1941, D.C. bar, 1952; with antitrust div. Justice Dept., 1941-51 chief N.W. Regional Antitrust Office, 1948-51, 1st asst. civil div., 1951-52; exec. asst. to atty. gen. of U.S., 1952-53; chief Exec. Office for U.S. Attys., 1953; partner Perlman, Baldridge, Lyons & Browning, Washington, 1953-58; clk. Supreme Ct. of U.S., 1958-61; judge U.S. Ct. Appeals, Ninth Circuit, San Francisco, 1961—, now chief judge. Lectr. fed. antitrust law N.Y. U. Sch. Law, 1953, Georgetown U. Law Center, 1958-58. Served with AUS, 1943-46. Decorated Bronze Star. Mem. Am. Law Inst., Am., Fed. (nat. bd. govs. 1952-61) bar assns., Am. Judicature Soc., Inst. Jud. Adminstrn., Am. Soc. Legal History. Office: PO Box 547 San Francisco CA 94101

BROWNING, RODERICK HANSON, banker; b. Salt Lake City, Oct. 9, 1925; s. Frank M. and Eugenia H. B.; A.B., Stanford U., 1948; m. Mary Wadsworth, Mar. 7, 1956; children—Patricia Ann, Jonathan Wadsworth, Frank Wadsworth, Anthony Stuart, Carolyn Rae. Vice pres. Bank of Utah, Ogden, 1954-59, chmn. bd., pres., 1959—; chmn. bd., pres. Bank of Brigham City (Utah), 1973—; chmn. bd. Bank No. Utah, Clearfield, 1971—; dir. Salt Lake City br. Fed. Res. Bank San Francisco, 1969-74. Bd. dirs., treas. Ogden Indsl. Devel. Corp.; dir., treas. Weber County (Utah) Indsl. Devel. Bur.; adv. bd. St. Benedicts Hosp.; bd. dirs. Weber State Coll., Ogden; former pres. United Fund No. Utah. Served with U.S. Army, 1948-53. Mem. Am., Utah, (former mem. exec. com.), Western Independent bankers assns., Am. Legion. Clubs: Rotary (Ogden), Weber, Alta, Ogden Golf and Country. Office: Box 231 Ogden UT 84402

BROWNING, RUFUS PUTNAM, political science educator, researcher; b. Cleve., Mar. 16, 1934; s. Robert Hamilton and Lucy (Beckett) B.; m. Patricia Jean Parker, Apr. 28, 1956 (div.); children—Marla, Ross Parker, Charles Mentzer, Mark Woods; m. Elizabeth Barkin, Mar. 20, 1982. A.B., Oberlin Coll., 1954; Ph.D., Yale U., 1961. Asst. prof. polit. sci. U. Wis., 1961-67; assoc. prof. polit. sci. Mich. State U., 1967-73; prof. polit. sci. San Francisco State U., 1974—, chmn. dept., 1974-77; sr. research polit. scientist Inst. Govt. Studies, U. Calif.-Berkeley, 1976-81. Served in U.S. Army, 1955-57. Yale U. fellow, 1954-55; Ford Found. fellow, 1959-60; Social Sci. Research Council fellow, 1960-61; NSF grantee, 1965-67, 76-81; Am. Council Learned Socs. grantee, 1968, 72. Mem. Am. Polit. Sci. Assn., Am. Soc. Pub. Adminstrn., Policy Studies Orgn. Contbr. numerous articles to profl. jours. Office: Dept Polit Sci San Francisco State U San Francisco CA 94132

BROWN-MYERS, STEPHANIE ELLIS, speech/language pathologist; b. Pittsburg, Calif., Dec. 1, 1951; d. Clyde Ellis and Vera Frances (Achord) B.; B.A., U. Calif., Santa Barbara, 1973; M.A., Calif. State U., Chico, 1974; admnstrv. credentials, Calif. State U., Hayward, 1979; m. David Pettygrove Myers, June 23, 1979. Speech, hearing, lang. therapist San Ramon (Calif.) Valley Unified Sch. Dist., 1975—; pvt. practice Danville (Calif.) Speech and Lang. Center. Mem. Calif., Am. speech and hearing assns. Contbr. research in field. Office: 699 Old Orchard Rd Danville CA 94526

BROWNSMITH, CYNTHIA LYNNE, psychologist, educator; b. Dallas, Mar. 23, 1947; d. Harvey Chester and Billie Jo (Smith) Smith; m. R. Keith Brownsmith, Dec. 14, 1974; 1 dau., Ariel Elizabeth Dehaven. B.A., Tex. Tech. U., 1968, M.A., 1970; A.B.D., U. Louisville, 1972; Ph.D., Ind. U.-Bloomington, 1976; lic. psychologist, Ind., Idaho. Intern in clin. psychology South Plains Mental Health Ctr., Lubbock, Tex., 1969-70; staff psychologist River Region Mental Health Services, Louisville, 1972-73; asst. prof., research assoc. Ind. U., 1976-78; assoc. prof. Boise State U.; pvt. practice clin. psychology, Boise; cons., speaker in field; trainer family practice med. residents. Bd. dirs. YWCA, Boise; mem. Democratic State Com. to Elect Gail Bray; established Fund for Leukemic Child, Boise. Named Outstanding Young Woman in Am., U.S. Jaycees, 1981; Dept. Edn.-HEW grantee, 1976-79. Mem. Am. Psychol. Assn., Assn. Advancement Behavior Therapy, Am. Orthopsychiat. Assn., Council for Exceptional Children. Episcopalian. Author videotape and print materials on treatment emotionally disturbed adolescents and self-mgmt. tng. for counselors, tchrs. emotionally disturbed adolescents. Home: 1006 Bergeson St Boise ID 83706 Office: Dept Psychology Boise State U Boise ID 83725

BROWNSTONE, LOUIS H., III, retailer; b. San Francisco, June 25, 1938; s. Louis H. and Lillian (Goldstein) B.; m. Patricia S., July 11, 1963 (div.); m. 2d, Caroline T., Feb. 7, 1975; children—Harold L., Kimberly F., Lawrence H., John H., Stephanie T., Louis H. IV. B.A., Stanford U.; postgrad. U. Calif.-Berkeley, San Francisco State U. Exec. tng. squad Macy's, Calif., 1963-65; asst. to mdse. mgr. Grodins of Calif., San Lorenzo, 1965-68, tng. dir., 1970-72, basic stock adminstrn., 1968-70, mdse. mgr., corp. dir., 1970—, mgr. mdse. stats., 1972—. Active San Francisco Symphony Assn., San Francisco Ballet Assn., World Affairs Council. Office: 2225 Grant San Lorenzo CA 94580

BROZ, THOMAS ANTHONY, structural engr.; b. Chgo., June 30, 1950; s. Anton Joseph and Bessie Francis (Machala) B.; B.S.C.E., U. Notre Dame, 1972; M.S.C.E., U. Ill., 1973; m. Colleen Monahan, Dec. 30, 1972. Engring. group supr. Bechtel Power Co., Norwalk, Calif., 1973—. Registered profl. engr., Ill., Ind., Calif. Mem. ASCE. Home: 6306 E Bryce Orange CA 92667 Office: 12400 E Imperial Hwy Norwalk CA 90650

BROZOVICH, STANLEY M., clinical psychologist; b. Cle Elum, Wash., Nov. 22, 1921; s. Stanley and Agatha (Matkovich) B.; m. Margaret F. Paulson, June 24, 1944; 1 dau., Margaret Agatha. M.A., Occidental Coll., Los Angeles, 1951; postgrad. Claremont Grad. Sch., 1949-51. Lic. psychologist, Calif. Psychologist Ingleside Mental Health Ctr., South San Gabriel, Calif.; cons. psychology, Whittier Area Spl. Edn. Program (9 sch. dists.), 1955-65; staff psychologist Whittier Human Relations Ctr., 1965-70; pvt. practice S.M. Brozovich Psychol. Corp., Whittier, 1970—; instr. UCLA extension, 1960-61; cons. in field. Served with U.S. Air Force, 1943-46. Muzzle loading pistol champion, Calif. and Southwestern states, 1970. Mem. Am. Psychol. Assn., Calif. Psychol. Assn., Pasadena Psychol. Assn., Soc. for Personality Assessment. Home: 449 E Pine St Altadena CA 91001 Office: 12468 Washington Blvd Whittier CA 90602

BRUBAKER, MARIA MICHELE HUGHES, educator; b. Bisbee, Ariz., Jan. 24, 1947; d. Dale Adams and Artemisa (Gomez) H.; B.A. in Edn., U. Ariz., 1969; 1 dau., Rina Michele. Tchr. Loretto Sch., Douglas, Ariz., 1969-70, Our Mother of Sorrows, Tucson, 1970-71, Salpointe Cath. High Sch., Tucson, 1974—, chmn. English dept., 1979—. Corr. sec. Tucson Area Reading Council, 1977-78, treas., 1978-79, v.p., 1979-80, pres., 1980-81. Mem. Internat. Reading Assn. (nat. com. on reading and arts), Tucson Area Reading Council, Ariz. State Reading Council, Nat. Council Tchrs. English (mem. task force on racism and bias). Roman Catholic. Writer column in Tucson Reading Council Newsletter, The Reading/Writing Connection, 1980-81; contbr. poem to anthology; editorial bd. Jour. Reading, 1982—. Office: 1545 E Copper St Tucson AZ 85719

BRUBAKER, MARY FURGERSON, accountant; b. Searcy, Ark., July 30, 1935; d. John Henry and Opal Mae (Winnett) Furgerson; m. Arlon Robert Brubaker, July 9, 1957; children—Karen, Kurtis. B.A., Pomona Coll., 1957. C.P.A., Calif. Staff acct. Guill, Blankenbaker & Co., Pasadena, Calif., 1957-63; practice acctg., Arcadia, Calif., 1963-76; ptnr. Brubaker & Bohannon, C.P.A.s, San Marino, Calif., 1976-83; sole practice, San Marino, Calif., 1983—. Mem. Estate Planning Council San Gabriel Valley, 1982; treas. United Methodist Ch. of Good Shepherd, 1969-82; bd. dirs. Meth. Hosp. of So. Calif., 1977—, treas., 1979—. Mem. San Marino C. of C., Pasadena C. of C., Am. Inst. C.P.A.s, Calif. Soc. C.P.A.s. Home: 1201 Oakglen Ave Arcadia CA 91006 Office: 2100 Huntington Dr Suite 8 San Marino CA 91108

BRUBAKKEN, DAVID MELVIN, clin. psychologist; b. Grafton, N.D., June 24, 1946; s. Melvin Oliver and Bernice Alberta (Schrank) B.; B.S. with honors, U. N.D., 1968; Ph.D., Wash. State U., 1972, M.S., 1970. Dir. project for psychotic and neurologically impaired children Mendota Mental Health Inst., Madison, 1972-76; asst. clin. instr. dept. psychiatry U. Wis. Med. Sch., Madison, 1973-76, dir. child/adolescent programs, 1976-79, dir. psychology internship program, 1978, asst. clin. prof. dept. psychiatry, 1976-79; clin. psychologist Group Health Coop. of Puget Sound, Seattle, 1979—; cons. Internat. Office of Am. Fedn. of State, County and Mcpl. Employees, Washington, 1975-76, Minn. Dept. Public Welfare, 1976-79, Clin. Psychology Tng. Program, U. Wis., Madison, 1976-79, Autism Public Awareness Project, 1977-79. Mem. tech. adv. com. Mental Health Planning Council of Milw. County, 1976-77; pres. Madison Area Soc. Autistic Children, 1977. Recipient Outstanding Performance award State of Wis., Dept. Health and Social Services, 1976, 78, 79; lic. psychologist, Wis., Wash. Mem. Nat. Registry Health Care Providers in Psychology, Am. Psychol. Assn., Nat. Soc. Autistic Children, Assn. Advancement of Behavior Therapy, Soc. Behavioral Medicine, Phi Beta Kappa, Sigma Xi, Psi Chi. Contbr. articles to profl. jours.; sr. author: Contemporary Issues in the Treatment of Psychotic and Neurologically Impaired Children: A Systems Approach, 1980. Home: 3214 E Madison St Seattle WA 98112 Office: 200 15th Ave E Seattle WA 98112

BRUCE, CHERYL LYNN, optometric technician, educator; b. Spokane, Wash., Feb. 17, 1954; d. Ralph Eugene and Margaret Louise (Berrong) B.; m. M. Gibson, Mar. 10, 1977 (div.); 1 dau., Megan Christan. A.A., So. Calif. Coll. Optometry, 1975; A.A., Spokane Falls Community Coll., 1976. Cert. vocat. tchr., Wash. Optometric asst., office mgr. Dr. Ralph E. Bruce, Spokane, Wash., 1969-73; optometric technician Dr. Robert Kettenhofen, Pomona, Calif., 1975-76; optician Lund Optical, Provo, Utah, 1976-77; program coordinator, instr., optometric technician Spokane Community Coll., 1978—. Mem. Am. Optometric Assn., Assn. Higher Edn., Wash. Edn. Assn., Assn. Paraoptometric Edn. Programs, Optometric Extension Program. Home: 3613 N Harvard Rd Apt A Otis Orchards WA 99027 Office: Spokane Community Coll 1810 N Greene St Health Sci Bldg 9 Spokane WA 99207

BRUCE, GAYE FISK, nurse; b. Hamilton, Mont., Apr. 10, 1937; s. William James and Carrol Bethany (Grafton) Fisk; m. Allen Sevoy Bruce, Nov. 21, 1959 (div.); children—Stephen Sevoy, Jeffrey Bryan, Scott William. Student U. Calif.-Berkeley, 1955-56; grad. O'Connor Hosp. Sch. Nursing, 1959; postgrad. in hosp. adminstrn. UCLA, 1960; postgrad. Coll. Notre Dame, 1982—. R.N., Calif. Staff nurse Stanford U. Hosp., 1959, psychiat. nurse, clin. supr., 1960-67; nurse researcher Stanford (Calif.) U. Med. Sch., 1972-75, co-dir. Couple/Family Clinic, 1976-78, asst. clin. prof. dept. psychiatry and behavioral scis., 1977—; coordinator mktg. and nurse recruiting Stanford U. Hosp., 1979—. Past pres. So. Peninsula San Francisco Opera Action; past chmn. publicity and pub. relations Palo Alto aux. Stanford Children's Hosp. Mem. Nat. Assn. Nurse Recruiters, Clin. Faculty Assn. Stanford U. Med. Sch., PEO. Republican. Home: 1875 Oakdell Dr Menlo Park CA 94025 Office: Stanford Univ Hosp 300 Pasteur Dr Stanford CA 94305

BRUCE, GREGORY ALAN, human resource development specialist; b. Greeley, Colo., Jan. 14, 1956; s. Carroll Edwin and Anna Mae (Snider) B.; m. Laura Christine Ochoa, July 14, 1979. B.A. in Psychology, U. Calif.-Santa Barbara, 1978; M.S. in Adminstrn., Calif. State U.-Dominguez Hills, 1983. Adminstr. mgmt. devel. and program design Hartfield-Zodys Corp., Los Angeles, 1980-81; mgmt. devel. specialist Rockwell Internat., Los Angeles, 1981-82; tng. adminstr. Bergen Brunswig Corp., Carson, Calif., 1982—; cons., tchr. in field; program dir., trainer Devel. Dimensions Internat. Interaction Mgmt. Mem. Am. Soc. Tng. and Devel. Author, narrator Effective Business Writing (video tape), 1982. Home: 1639 10th St Manhattan Beach CA 90266 Office: 22351 S Wilmington Ave Carson CA 90745

BRUCE, JOHN CLAYTON, JR., educator, clergyman; b. Warrensburg, Mo., Mar. 31, 1918; s. John Clayton and Maybelle (Warnick) B.; B.S., Central Mo. State Coll., Warrensburg, 1939; B.Div., San Francisco Theol. Sem., San Anselmo, Calif., 1950, M.Div., 1971; M.A., San Francisco State U., 1962; postgrad. State U. Iowa, Iowa City, 1940-41, U. Calif., Berkeley, 1962-63, Sonoma State Coll., Cotati, Calif., 1972-73; m. Eleanor Mortensen, May 25, 1941. Tchr. bus. and English, Alma (Mo.) High Sch., 1939-41; tchr. bus. Naperville (Ill.) High Sch., 1941-46; psychologist VA Regional Office, Kansas City, Mo., 1946-47; ordained to ministry Presbyn. Ch., 1950; minister St. Marks Presbyn. Ch., Van Nuys, Calif., 1950-54, Sleepy Hollow Presbyn. Ch., San Anselmo, Calif., 1954-61; prof. bus. and econs. dept. Coll. of Marin, Kentfield, Calif., 1961—; chmn. candidates com. Presbytery of Redwoods, United Presbyn. Ch. in U.S.A., 1958-63; elder First Presbyn. Ch., San Anselmo, 1971-74. Served with AUS, 1942-46. Recipient Hon. plaque for 25th Anniversary, St. Marks Presbyn. Ch., 1976. Mem. Kappa Delta Pi, Phi Sigma Pi. Contbr. articles to religious publs. Home: 9 Bay Tree Ln San Anselmo CA 94960 Office: Dept of Bus and Econs Coll of Marin Arcade Bldg Kentfield CA 94904

BRUCE, RAYMON RENE, management consultant; b. Denver, Sept. 18, 1934; s. William Rene and Eugenia Alice (Thomas) B.; student Rupert-Karl-Universitat, Heidelberg, Germany, 1958-59; B.A. with with honors, U. Mont., 1962, M.A., 1965; M.S. in Orgn. Devel., Pepperdine U., 1980; m. Sharon Esther Dudley, June 27, 1976; 1 dau., Esther; stepchildren—Joshua Dudley, Jessie Dudley. Asst. to producer Metro-Goldwyn-Mayer, Inc., Culver City, Calif., 1965-66; theatre producer New World Theatre, San Francisco, 1966-67; orgn. devel. adv., mgmt. analyst State Comp. Ins. Fund, San Francisco, 1967—; pres. Universe Survey, Inc., San Francisco, 1972-78; orgn. devel. cons. Valley Med. Center, Santa Clara County, 1976-78; mgmt. services officer U.S. Trust Ters. of Pacific, 1980; spl. cons. to pres. Republic of Palau, 1981; instr. Golden Gate U., 1979. Served with U.S. Army, 1954-56. Recipient German Consul award, 1962, Best Play award U. Mont., 1962, 65, Best One Act Play award Immaculate Heart Acad., Los Angeles, 1964. Mem. Corp. Planners Assn., Orgn. Devel. Network, N. Am. Soc. Corp. Planners, Dramatist Guild, Inc., Author numerous plays; contbr. poems to lit. jours., articles to bus. and profl. jours.; editor New Albion Press, 1972-79. Office: 691 Dolores St San Francisco CA 94110

BRUCE, RICHARD ALAN, engineer; b. Salina, Pa., Apr. 1, 1932; s. Earl Jerome and Mary Caroline (Whitesell) B.; m. Barbara Collins White, Oct. 6, 1958; m. 2d, Ellen Alexandria Burgin, Dec. 24, 1969; children—Laura Jane, Stewart Cameron. B.S. in Aero. Engring., Pa. State U., 1954; M.S. in Systems Engring., Air Force Inst. Tech., 1964. Engr., Republic Aviation, Farmingdale, N.Y., 1954-55; asst. chief engr.

Douglas Aircraft Co., Culver City, Calif., 1965-68; mgr. systems analysis and reliability Douglas United Nuclear Corp., Richland, Wash., 1969-70; systems design analyst, McDonnell Douglas Astronautics Co., Huntington Beach, Calif., 1971-80; work package mgr. TRW Def. Systems Group, Redondo Beach, Calif., 1980—. Chmn. Air and Water Pollution Control Com., Tri-Cities C. of C., 1969-70. Served to capt. USAF, 1955-65. Mem. AIAA, Air Force Assn., IEEE, Am. Nuclear Soc., Los Angeles Maintainability Assn. (co-founder, sec.), Sigma Nu. Republican. Clubs: Palos Verdes Golf. Contbr. articles to profl. jours. Office: 3535 Lomita Blvd Torrance CA 90505

BRUCE, WILLIAM JOHN, mktg. exec.; b. Queens, N.Y., Oct. 31, 1940; s. John Norman and Genevieve (Trent) B.; A.A., Chabot Coll., 1964; B.S.M.E., San Jose State U., 1970, M.S.M.E., 1974; m. Janet Luella Turner, Aug. 5, 1962; children—Jennifer M., Penelope E. Engring. asst., design engr., nuclear engr. Gen. Elec. Co., San Jose, Calif., 1965-74, program mgr., 1976-77; chief engr., quality assurance mgr. MBC Engring., Santa Clara, Calif., 1974-76; mgr. equipment devel. engring., program mgr., mktg. mgr., product planning mgr., maj. accounts mgr. Memorex Corp., Santa Clara, 1977—. Pres., No. Calif. Highland Dance Assn., 1981-82. Served with U.S. Army, 1958-61. Life cert. instr. community colls., Calif.; registered profl. engr., Calif. Mem. Am. Nuclear Soc., ASME, Am. Soc. Quality Control, Nat. Soc. Profl. Engrs., Calif. Soc. Profl. Engrs. Home: 1528 Shasta Ave San Jose CA 95126 Office: Memorex Corp San Tomas at Central Expressway Santa Clara CA 95052

BRUCH, CAROL SOPHIE, lawyer, educator; b. Rockford, Ill., June 11, 1941; d. Ernest and Margarete (Willstätter) B.; A.B., Shimer Coll., 1960; J.D. (Bartley Cavanaugh Crum scholar), U. Calif., Berkeley, 1972; m. Jack E. Myers, 1960 (div. 1973); children—Margarete Louise Myers, Kurt Randall Myers. Bar: Calif. 1973, U.S. Supreme Ct. 1980. Mem. profl. staff San Francisco council Girl Scouts U.S.A., 1960-62, summers 1963, 64; substitute tchr. elem. sch. Oakland (Calif.) Pub. Schs., 1966-67; tchr. primary grades Dependents' Sch., Bendix Field Engring. Corp., Madagascar, 1967-68; law clk. to Assoc. Justice William O. Douglas, U.S. Sup. Ct. 1972-73; acting prof. law U. Calif., Davis, 1973-78, prof., 1978—; vis. prof. U. Calif.-Berkeley, 1983; cons. to Ctr. for Family in Transition, 1981—, Calif. Law Revision Commn., 1979-82, NOW Legal Def. and Edn. Fund, 1980-81. Mem. adv. com. child support and child custody Calif. Commn. on Status of Women, 1981—; host parent Am. Field Service, Davis, 1977-78. Max Rheinstein sr. research fellow Alexander von Humboldt Found., W.Ger., 1978-79. Mem. ABA, Calif. State Bar, Am. Law Inst., Order of Coif. Contbr. articles to legal jours.; editor Calif. Law Rev., 1971; editorial bd. Family Law Quar., 1980—. Democrat. Jewish. Office: Sch Law U Calif Davis CA 95616

BRUCH, RUSSELL ADRIAN, career consultant; b. Charles Robert and Ruby Ferne (McKeever) B.; m. Donna Lee Stimely, May 9, 1964; m. Gwyneth Cary, June 30, 1973; children—Michael Robert, Kristine Renee. B.S. in Math., Ball State U., 1962; M.S. in Higher Edn., So. Ill. U., 1964. Tchr. math. C.K. McClatchy High Sch., Sacramento, 1964-65; asst. dir. housing S.D. State U., Brookings, 1965-66; grad. asst. N.Mex. State U., Las Cruces, 1966-67; career counselor U. Calif.-Davis, 1967-68, dir. career planning and placement, 1968-69, dir. Life Career Devel., Davis, 1969—; workshop staff coordinator Nat. Career Devel. Project, Walnut Creek, Calif., 1974—; lectrs. to various civic, bus. and profl. orgns. Pres. bd. dirs. Davis Art Center, 1974; pres. Davis Players, 1976-78, treas., 1979, 81. Recipient cert. of appreciation U. Calif., 1969. Mem. Am. Soc. Tng. and Devel. (cert. of appreciation 1981, 82, 83), Nat. Speakers Assn. Democrat. Episcopalian.

BRUCK, HENRY WOLFGANG, policy and strategic analyst, writer; b. Berlin, Sept. 1, 1926; s. Ernst Alfred and Beatrice (Asarch) B.; m. Eugenie Tourison, Dec. 31, 1951. A.B., UCLA, 1948; A.M., Princeton U., 1952. Dir. regional planning Penn Jersey Transp. Study, Phila., 1959-64, Northeast Corridor Transp. Study, U.S. depts. Commerce and Transp., Washington, 1964-67; lectr. dept. civil engring., assoc. dir. Urban Systems Lab., MIT, Cambridge, 1967-74; research planner Univ. Calif.-Berkeley, 1974-82; free-lance writer, 1982—; cons. Served with U.S. Army, 1944-46. Mem. AAAS, Am. Sociol. Assn., World Future Soc. Co-author: Foreign Policy Decision-Making, 1962; Getting It Off the Shelf, 1977; contbr. numerous articles to jours. Home: 600 Cragmont Ave Berkeley CA 94708

BRUCKNER, JOANNE OLDS, psychotherapist; b. Lima, Ohio, Aug. 9, 1919; d. Loyd Warner and Rose (Armstrong) Olds; m. Leslie C. Bruckner, June 27, 1941; children—Douglas, Gregory. B.A., Eastern Mich. U., 1941; M.A., Azusa Pacific Coll., 1976; postgrad. UCLA, 1970, Calif. State U.-Northridge, 1979. Lic. community coll. tchr., Calif. Owner, dir. Sch. of Charm, Los Angeles, 1968-73; tchr. community coll. adult program, Glendale, Calif., 1974-76; tchr. occupational skills pilot program, Los Angeles, 1975-78; counselor alcoholism/addictions, Glendale (Calif.) Seventist Hosp., 1976-77; pvt. practice psychotherapy, Glendale, 1976—; pvt. practice hypnotherapy, Glendale, 1978—; dir., therapist Terrap Assocs., Glendale, 1976—; counselor Glendale Adventist Hosp., 1975. Mem. Am. Assn. Marriage and Family Therapists, Am. Guild Hypnotists, Counselors for Alcohol and Addiction Related Disorders, Calif. Family Study Ctr. Alumni Group. Republican. Club: Zonta. Home: 427 E Orange Grove Apt 203 Burbank CA 91501 Office: 2505 Canada Blvd Suite 1C Glendale CA 91208

BRUCKNER, WALTER SHERMAN, floor covering exec.; b. Bronx, N.Y., June 5, 1935; s. Samuel Isaac and Marie (Blaustein) B.; B.A., L.I. U., 1956; M.B.A., U. Pa., 1958; m. Lenore Joan Miller, Nov. 20, 1971. Market research supr. RCA Record Div., N.Y.C., 1962-67; mgr. marketing sales analysis ITT Continental Baking Co., Rye, N.Y., 1967-69; mgr. fin. planning Capitol Records, Hollywood, Calif., 1969-70; mgr. mktg. services Roberts Consol. Industries, Industry, Calif., 1970-74; mgr. mktg. planning and internat. mktg. Taylor Industries, Industry, 1974-76; pres. Walter S. Bruckner & Assos., 1977-79; v.p., dir. mktg. Adhesive Industries Mfg. Corp., Cerritos, Calif., 1979—. Active Big Bros. Assn. Served to 2nd lt. AUS, 1958-60. Mem. Am. Mktg. Assn., Mfrs. Agts. Nat. Assn., Assn. M.B.A. Execs. Clubs: Internat. Health (Los Angeles). Home: 5319 Vista Montana Yorba Linda CA 92686 Office: 13927 E 166th St Cerritos CA 90701

BRUDI, RONALD ADAIR, manufacturing executive; b. E. Leroy, Mich., May 1, 1927; s. Carl Ernest and Gertrude Mae (Spencer) B.; m. Lois Jeanne Payne, Mar. 4, 1950; children—Jeanne Adair Nortness, Lisa Ann, Eric Carl. Student pub. schs., Battle Creek, Mich., 1933-46. With Clark Equipment Co., Battle Creek, 1953-60; chief engr. Swingshift Mfg. Co., Longview, Wash., 1966-67; pres. Bundi Equipment Co., Kelso, Wash., 1967—. Served to ssgt. USAF, 1946-48, 51-52. Baptist. Club: Elks. Home: 205 E Cedar Ln Longview WA 98632 Office: 2401 Talley Way Kelso WA 98626

BRUE, STANLEY LEONARD, economist educator; b. Sioux Falls, S.D., Feb. 3, 1945; s. Everett R. and Esther A. (Ekberg) B.; m. Terryl Lea Buzek, Apr. 11, 1970; 1 son, Craig R. B.A., Augustina Coll., S.D., 1967; Ph.D. in Econs. (Johnson Fellow), U. Nebr.-Lincoln, 1971. Asst. prof. econs. Pacific Luth. U., Tacoma, Wash., 1971-76, assoc. prof., 1976-81, prof., 1982—. Mem. Am. Econ. Assn., Western Internat. Econ. Assn. Author: Local Economic Impacts of Corporate Mergers, 1972; Economic Scenes: Theory In Today's World, 2d edit., 1980; The American Poor, 1982; contbr. articles to profl. jours. Office: Dept Econs Pacific Luth U Tacoma WA 98447

BRUINGTON, NEIL ELWIN, graphic communications executive; b. Upland, Calif., June 25, 1945; s. Dean J. and Lillian; m. Christine E. Trankla; children—Ryan, Dana. B.A., San Diego State U., 1968, M.A., 1974; postgrad. UCLA, 1974. Lectr. graphic arts dept. San Diego State U., 1969; tchr. Orange (Calif.) Unified Sch. Dist., 1970-73, San Diego City Schs., 1973-76, San Diego High Sch. Dist., 1976-78; dir. graphic communications Palomar Coll., San Marcos, Calif., 1978—, inplant mgr.; v.p. Calif. graphic Arts Instrs. Community Colls. Pres. Cardiff Soccer Club. Graphic Art Tech. Found. grantee 1979, 82; recipient San Diego County Tchr. of Yr. award 1977. Mem. Am. Vocat. Assn., Graphic Arts Tech. Assoc., Calif. Indsl. Edn. Assn., Graphic Arts Assn. Community Colls. Instrs., Nat. Assn. Printers Lithographers, Printing Industries Am., Printing Industries San Diego, Internat. Graphic Arts Assn., Nat. Typographical Assn., Calif. Assn. Vocat. Edn. Club: Rolf Soccer, Cardiff Courts Tennis. Contbr. articles to profl. jours. Office: 1140 W Mission Rd San Marcos CA 92069

BRUMBAUGH, JEANNE MALOTT, educator; b. Indianapolis, July 18, 1926; d. Burton Joseph and Ruth Irene (Boyd) Malott; m. Paul Baker Brumbaugh, Nov. 26, 1950; children—Stephen Paul, James Burton. B.A. magna cum laude, Butler U., 1948; M.A. in Sci., U. Wis., 1950; M.A. in Edn. and Sch. Adminstrn., Calif. Luth. Coll., 1982. Cert. tchr., Mich., 1969. Tchr. English and French, Evart (Mich.) High Sch., 1961-63, Big Rapids (Mich.) High Sch., 1963-69; tchr. langs. Bais Yaakov and Elem. Yeshiva Torath Emeth Acad., Los Angeles, 1969-76, prin. gen. studies, 1976—; tutor, counselor. NDEA fellow, 1965; PEO grantee, 1981. Mem. Calif. Assn. Pvt. Schs., Yeshiva Gen. Studies Prins. Council Los Angeles (sec.), Am. Soc. Curriculum Devel., Parents for Torah for All Children, Phi Kappa Phi, Delta Kappa Gamma. Republican. Presbyterian. Club: PEO (v.p.).

BRUMBAUGH, TEDD STEPHENS, educational administrator; b. Denver, Apr. 29, 1942; s. David Earle and Coral Della (Stephens) B.; m. Shirley Marie Fasnacht, May 29, 1965; children—Aaron David, Stephen Todd, Matthew Brian. A.A., Mesa Jr. Coll., 1962; B.A., McPherson Coll., 1964; M.S., Western Colo. State Coll., 1967. Cert. tchr. and adminstr., Colo., 1967. Tchr. social studies Golden State Jr. High Sch., Bakersfield, Calif., 1967-68; program writer and evaluator Bakersfield City Schs., 1968-70; coordinator R&D, Mesa County Valley Sch. Dist. #51, Grand Junction, Colo., 1970-72, dir. fed. programs, 1972-78, asst. dir. personnel, 1978-80, dir. resources, R&D, 1980—; cons. Mem. Colo. Assn. Sch. Execs., Assn. Supervision and Curriculum Devel., Nat. Assn. Adminstrs. State and Fed. Edn. Programs, Assn. Ednl. Data Systems. Democrat. Mem. Ch. of the Brethren. Clubs: Rotary. Home: 621 Fort Uncompahgre Grand Junction CO 81504 Office: 2115 Grand Ave Grand Junction CO 81501

BRUMER, SUZANNE, psychologist, university dean; b. Paris, June 15, 1947; came to U.S., 1952, naturalized, 1957; d. Oscar and Rose Rachel (Laufer) B. B.S. in Math., (N.Y. State Regents scholar), Bklyn. Coll., 1969; M.A. in Math., U. Mich., 1971, Ph.D. in Psychology (NIMH trainee), 1974. Lic. psychologist, Calif. Research assoc. Mental Health Research Inst., U. Mich., 1974-76; intern and research fellow Mt. Zion Hosp., San Francisco, 1976-78; instr. Calif. Sch. Profl. Psychology, Berkeley, 1977-78; mem. faculty Pacific Grad. Sch. Psychology, Palo Alto, Calif., 1978-79, asst. dean research, 1979-81, dean acad. affairs, 1981—; pvt. practice psychology, San Francisco, 1978—; asst. research psychologist U. Calif. Med. Ctr., San Francisco Sch. Dentistry; cons. Behaviordyne Psychol. Corp. Bd. dirs. Generation to Generation, 1980—. Rackham grantee, 1973-74; NIH grantee, 1969-74. Mem. Am. Psychol. Assn., Soc. Psychol. Study Social Issues, San Francisco Bay Area Psychol. Assn. Office: 2504 Clay St San Francisco CA 94115

BRUMFIELD, NANCY LEE, public relations executive; b. Lexington, Ky., Apr. 10, 1954; d. Clyde B. and Margaret Ann (Stallsworth) B.; m. Francis Daniel Heckler, Mar. 19, 1977 (div.). B.A. with honors in Journalism, U. Ky., 1976; M.B.A., U. Hawaii, 1985. Communications asst. First Security Nat. Bank, Lexington, 1973-76, pub. relations dir. Louisville (Ky.) Bank for Co-ops., 1976-78, Hawaii Heart Assn., Honolulu, 1978—. Active pub. relations projects Honolulu Marathon Assn. Mem. Pub. Relations Soc. Am., Internat. Assn. Bus. communicators (best feature story award Ky. chpt. 1976), Soc. Heart Assn. Profl. Staff (chmn. southwest region), Phi Beta Kappa. Clubs: Honolulu, Jr. League (Honolulu). Contbr. articles to newspapers and mags. Office: Hawaii Heart Assn 245 N Kukui St Honolulu HI 96817

BRUMGARDT, JOHN RAYMOND, museum director; b. Riverside, Calif., Feb. 3, 1946; s. Reuben R. and Grace G. (Taylor) B.; B.A. in History, U. Calif., Riverside, 1967, M.A., 1968, Ph.D., 1974; mgmt. devel. cert. U. Colo., 1981; m. Doris Ann Tarasko, Dec. 20, 1969; children—Jennifer Rae, Thomas Alexander. Teaching asst. U. Calif., 1969, 72-74; Riverside County historian Riverside Mcpl. Mus., 1974-76; head history div. Riverside County Parks Dept., 1976-78; dir. Mus. of Western Colo., Grand Junction, 1978—; instr. history Chapman Coll., Orange, Calif., 1973-79; lectr. in field; dir. Conf. Calif. Hist. Socs., 1978. Chmn., Riverside County Bicentennial Commn., 1975-76; mem. adv. bd. Nat. Bus. Inst., Riverside, 1975-78; vice chmn. state com. Colo. Humanities Program. Served with U.S. Army, 1970-72. NDEA fellow, 1967; Haynes Found. fellow, 1969; grantee in field. Mem. Am. Assn. Mus. (vis. com. accreditation com., surveyor mus. assessment program), Colo.-Wyo. Assn. Museums (bd. dirs.). Lutheran. Author: Civil War Nurse: The Diary and Letters of Hannah Ropes, 1980; People of the Magic Waters: The Cahuilla Indians of Palm Springs, 1981; also 5 local history books; contbr. articles and book revs. to profl. publs. Office: Museum Western Colo 248 S 4th St Grand Junction CO 81501

BRUMMEL, STEVEN WILLIAM, business exec.; b. Los Angeles, Feb. 17, 1946; s. Henry William and Claudia (Borja) B.; stepson Netha Olive (Barlow) B.; B.A. in Govt. and Journalism with honors, Calif. State U., Sacramento, 1972, M.A. in Govt., 1975. Newsman, Sta. KNTV-TV, San Jose, Calif., 1969-71, Sta. KCRA-TV, Sacramento, 1971-73; cons. Calif. Assembly, 1973; dist. rep. U.S. Congressman Leo J. Ryan, 1973-75; pres. Pacific Cons., San Francisco, 1975, ELS, Inc., Santa Cruz, Calif., 1975—; tchr., counselor Operation SHARE, 1970-71. Pres., Elvirita Lewis Found. Geriatric Health and Nutrition, Santa Cruz, 1976—; v.p. San Jose Ecology Action, 1970-71; publicity chmn. Santa Clara County Easter Seals, 1970-71; mem. Republican Nat. Com.; mem. Santa Cruz County Housing Adv. Commn., 1976-81. Served with USN, 1964-67; Vietnam. Mem. Am. Acad. Polit. and Social Scientists, Nat. Council on Aging, Western Gerontol. Soc., World Affairs Council San Francisco, Calif. Council on Internat. Trade, Calif. Farm Bur., Export Mgrs. Assn., Nat. Rifle Assn., Internat. Platform Assn., Acad. Polit. Sci., Smithsonian Instn., Am. Mus. Natural History, Gerontol. Soc. Sigma Delta Chi (Journalism award 1972, 73), Pi Sigma Alpha. Clubs: Commonwealth (San Francisco); Los Angeles; Seascape Swim and Racquet (Aptos). Home: 132 Don Lorenzo Ct Aptos CA 95003 Office: Latin Lady Ranch 84-525 Ave 66 Thermal CA 92274

BRUNACINI, ALAN VINCENT, fire chief; b. Jamestown, N.Y., Apr. 18, 1937; s. John N. and Mary T. Brunacini; B.S., Ariz. State U., 1970, M.P.A., 1975; m. Rita McDaugh, Feb. 14, 1959; children—Robert Nicholas, John Nicholas, Mary Candice. Mem. Phoenix Fire Dept., 1959—, bn. chief, then asst. fire chief, 1971-78, fire chief, 1978—; condr. nat. seminar on fire dept. mgmt., 1970—. Redford scholar, 1968. Mem. Am. Soc. Public Adminstrn. (Superior Service award 1980), Nat. Fire Protection Assn. (chmn. fire service sect. 1974-78, dir. 1978), Internat. Assn. Fire Chiefs, Soc. Fire Service Instrs. Author: Fireground Command; also articles in field. Office: Office of Fire Chief 620 W Washington Ave Phoenix AZ 85003*

BRUNDAGE, ARTHUR LAIN, animal science educator; b. Wallkill, N.Y., Dec. 19, 1927; s. David E. and Caroline M. Brundage; m. Helen E. Harvey, June 23, 1951; children—William H., Caroline E. (dec.), Richard T., Rodney A. B.S. with distinction, Cornell U., 1950; M.S., U. Minn., 1952, Ph.D., 1955. Research dairy husbandman Alaska Agrl. Expt. Sta., U.S. Dept. Agr., Palmer, 1952-68; prof. animal sci. U. Alaska, 1968—; vis. prof. Iowa State U., 1977-78, U. Ill., spring 1980; NSF travel grantee 8th Internat. Grassland Congress, 1960. Coach, mgr., umpire Little League Baseball; active Boy Scouts Am.; tchr., supt. United Protestant Presbyn. Ch. Fellow AAAS; mem. Am. Dairy Sci. Assn., Am. Soc. Animal Sci., Am. Statis. Assn., Brit. Grassland Soc., Am. Registry Cert. Animal Scientists, AAUP, Alaska Congress Parents and Tchrs. (hon. life), Biometric Soc., Am. Inst. Biol. Scis., Sigma Xi, Gamma Sigma Delta. Club: Dairy Shrine. Contbr. articles to profl. jours. Home: PO Box 616 Palmer AK 99645 Office: U Alaska Agrl Expt Sta PO Box AE Palmer AK 99645

BRUNDAGE, JANICE KAY, mental health therapist, consultant; b. Ann Arbor, Mich., Apr. 9, 1952; d. Leon Carlton and Annette (Palmquist) B.; m. Marshall Humphrey, III, Aug. 1, 1975. B.A., U. Mich., 1974; M.Ed. in Counseling, W. Ariz., 1980; postgrad. in counseling psychology U. Ariz., 1983—. Program supr. Pima County Socialization and Nutrition, Tucson, 1975-77, coordinator Pima County Spl. Olympics, 1977-78, recreation program coordinator, 1977-79, aquatic therapist Pima County Parks and Recreation Dept., 1977-80; social problem-solving project specialist So. Ariz. Mental Health Ctr., Tucson, 1979-80; mental health therapist St. Mary's Hosp. and Mental Ctr., Tucson, 1980; counselor U. Ariz., Tucson, 1980; social worker patient and family counseling dept. Tucson Med. Ctr., 1980-81, dir., 1981—; cons. Active Govs. Task Force on Aging; Am. Cancer Soc., 1982-83; coordinator Pima County Spl. Olympics, 1977-78. Mem. Am. Personnel and Guidance Assn., Ariz. Hosp. Assn., Ariz. Hosp. Social Work Dirs. Assn., Ariz. Parks and Recreation Assn., Western Gerentol. Assn., Nat. Assn. Hosp. Social Work Dirs. Assn. Office: 5301 E Grant Rd Tucson AZ 85733

BRUNE, JAMES NEIL, geophysics educator; b. Modesto, Calif., Nov. 23, 1934; s. Alphonse Frank and Margie Jean (Whitmore) B.; m. Karla Sue Whitney, June 5, 1957. B.Sc., U. Nev., 1956; Ph.D., Columbia U., 1961. Exploration in geophysics and research Chevron Oil Co., Calif. and Tex., 1956-57; research scientist Columbia U., N.Y.C., 1958-63; adj. prof. geology Columbia U., N.Y.C., 1964; assoc. prof. geophysics Calif. Inst. Tech., Pasadena, 1965-69; prof. U. Calif.-San Diego, La Jolla, 1969—. Fellow Seismological Soc. Am., Geol. Soc., Am. Geophys. Union. Quaker. Office: University of California-San Diego Scripps Institute of Oceanography A-025 La Jolla CA 92093

BRUNELLE, HERTHA-EDELGARD ADA, gallery curator, educator; b. Sangerhausen, E.Ger., Mar. 1, 1938; d. Walter Schulte-Victing and Hertha (von Luettichau); m. Richard Munson Brunelle, Aug. 29, 1964; children—Stephan, Paul, Martin. Ph.D., Johann Wolfgang Goethe U., 1973. Cert. secondary tchr., Calif.; cert. community coll. tchr., Calif. Lectr. in art history and humanities U. Calif., Davis, and U. Calif., Davis Extension, 1973, 74, 77; curator Pence Gallery, Davis, 1979—; lectr. in 20th century art and women in art Woodland Ctr., Yuba Coll., Marysville, Calif., 1980—; appraiser fine arts. Mem. Civic Arts Commn., Davis, 1981—; bd. dirs. Davis Sch. Arts Found., 1981—. Mem. Am. Soc. Appraisers (asso.). Author: The Portraits of the Ptolemaic Queens, 1975; contbg. author: Handbook of the Crocker Art Mus., 1980. Home: 217 E 8th St Davis CA 95616 Office: 212 D St Davis CA 95616

BRUNER, JACK GENE, plastic and reconstructive surgeon; b. Evansville, Ind., Dec. 5, 1935; s. Chales Emerson and Dorothy Jeanette (Fulton) B.; B.S., U. Calif. at Los Angeles, 1959; M.D., U. Calif. at Irvine, 1963; m. Anne-Marie Hjort, Apr. 28, 1969; children—Paul, Susanne. Intern, Los Angeles County Hosp., 1963-64, resident gen. surgery Fresno (Calif.) Gen. Hosp., 1964-67; resident plastic surgery Downstate Med. Center, King's County Hosp., Bklyn., 1967-68, St. Vincent's Hosp., Toledo, 1968-69; practice medicine, specializing in plastic surgery, Sacramento, 1969—; mem. staff Mercy Gen. Hosp., Sutter Community Hosps., Am. River Hosp., Sacramento Med. Center, all 1975—; asso. clin. prof. plastic surgery U. Calif. at Davis Med. Sch., 1973—. Served with M.C., AUS, 1954-56. Diplomate Am. Bd. Plastic and Reconstructive Surgery, Nat. Bd. Med. Examiners. Fellow A.C.S.; mem. Am. Soc. Plastic and Reconstructive Surgeons, Am. Soc. Aesthetic Plastic Surgeons, Am. Burn Assn., Am. Cleft Palate Assn., Am., Calif. med. assns., Calif. Plastic Surgery Soc., Sacramento County Med. Soc. Home: 3741 Random Ln Sacramento CA 95825 Office: 95 Scripps Dr Sacramento CA 95825

BRUNETZ, NICKOLAS, chemist, chem. engr.; b. Szombathely, Hungary, Aug. 30, 1922; s. Viktor and Margit (Koloszar) B.; grad. Count Szecheny Polytech., 1941; D.Chem. Engr., Josef Duke Polytech. Budapest, Hungary, 1943; postgrad Long Beach State Coll., U. So. Calif.; m. Maria Boros, Dec. 8, 1944; children—Maria (Mrs. Richard R. Lussier), Sylvia Susanne (Mrs. Ronald J. Ferrieri). Came to U.S., 1949, naturalized, 1955. Tech. interpreter, asst. to French High Commr. Austria, 1945-49; chem. asst. plant maintenance Kelite Corp., Los Angeles, 1949-55; air pollution engr. Air Pollution control Dist., County of Los Angeles, Calif., 1955-60; chemistry specialist Aerojet Gen. Corp., Downey, Calif., 1960-75; sr. air quality scientist Aerovironment Inc., Pasadena, Calif., 1975-76, KVB Inc., Irvine, Calif., 1976—. Served as 2d lt. Hungarian Army, 1944. Mem. ASTM, AAAS. Patentee in field. Contbr. articles to profl. jours. Research in fields of energy conversion and air pollution. Home: 14009 El Espejo Rd La Mirada CA 90638

BRUNS, PHYLLIS ANN, coll. dean; b. Boston; d. Harold Joseph and Antoinette Frances (Bianco) McQuin; B.Vocat. Edn., Calif. State U., Long Beach, 1977, M.A., 1978; children—Gary Paul, Bruce O'Neill, John Brian, Pamela Frances. Various secretarial positions, 1961-73; mem. adminstrv. staff Orange Coast Coll., Costa Mesa, Calif., 1970—, assoc. dean, dir. coop. work experience edn., 1978-82, assoc. dean Office Ednl. Affairs, 1982-83; mem. Orange County Industry Edn. Council; bd. dirs. commn. women Calif. Community and Jr. Colls. Assn.; cons. Mem. Council Advancement Exptl. Learning Coop. Edn. Assn., Calif. Coop. Edn. Assn., Calif. Community Coll. Placement Assn., Calif. Assn. Work Experience Educators. Republican. Roman Catholic. Club: Fountain Valley Racquet. Author handbooks, guides in field. Home: 36 Silverwood St Irvine CA 92714 Office: 2701 Fairview Rd Costa Mesa CA 92626

BRUNS, TONU, aerospace engr.; b. Johvi, Estonia, Mar. 13, 1941; came to U.S., 1949, naturalized, 1959; s. Paul and Maimu Elise (Uustalu) B.; B.S., Va. Poly. Inst. and State U., 1964; M.S., U. So. Calif., 1976; m. Nancy Eileen Clayton, July 24, 1965; children—Christopher Clayton, Michael Paul. Chief mech. and fluids sect. Payload Ops. Dept., Martin Marietta Corp., Vandenberg AFB, Calif., from 1976, now chief payload program Interfaces, Mission and Payload Dept. Leader, Boy Scouts Am., Santa Maria, Calif., 1980—, mem. troop com., 1980; head rules and regulations com. Santa Maria Valley Youth Soccer Assn., 1979—, referee, 1980—. Served with USAF, 1965-76. Decorated Air Force Commendation medal, Air Force Meritorious Service medal. Mem. Nat. Mgmt. Assn. Office: PO Box 1681 Vandenberg AFB CA 93437

BRUSH, RAY WILLIAM, II, electrical engineer; b. Billings, Mont., Mar. 31, 1950; s. Ray William and Naomi (Schneidmiller) B.; m. Bette Jeanne Burditt, Sept. 9, 1972; children—Niles Everett, Edward Nelson. B.S.E.E., Mont. State U., 1972, M.S.E.E., 1982. Registered profl. engr., Mont. Planning engr. Mont. Power Co., Butte, 1976-80; sr. engr. power ops. dept., 1981—. Mem. Citizens for Responsible Govt. Served to lt. U.S. Army, 1973-76. Mem. IEEE, Nat. Soc. Profl. Engrs.

BRUSH, SUE ANN, public relations director; b. Toledo, Sept. 20, 1949; d. Darel Marcus and Ruth Pearl (Marshall) Austermiller; m. Kenneth L. Brush, July 8, 1972; 1 son, Kevin Matthew. B.S. in Elem. Edn., Bowling Green State U., 1971; M.B.A., U. Puget Sound, 1981. Accredited, Pub. Relations Soc. Am. Sec./bookkeeper, Strachan Co., 1972-74; jr. account exec. Kelly/Nason Inc. Advt., Seattle, 1974-75; pub. relations dir. Olympic Hotel, Seattle, 1975-80, Westin Hotel, Seattle, 1980—; cert. instr. Devel. Dimensions Inc. Recipient Gold Key Pub. Relations award Hotel and Motel Assn., 1980, hotel sales and mgmt. awards, 1980, 81. Mem. Pub. Relations Soc. Am., Seattle Advt. Fedn. Republican. Methodist. Home: 4524 W Ruffner St Seattle WA 98199 Office: Westin Hotel 1900 5th Ave Seattle WA 98101

BRUST, DAVID, physicist; b. Chgo., Aug. 24, 1935; s. Clifford and Ruth (Klapman) B.; B.S., Calif. Inst. Tech., 1957; M.S., U. Chgo., 1958, Ph.D., 1964. Research asso. Purdue U., Lafayette, Ind., 1963-64; research asso. Northwestern U., Evanston, Ill., 1964-65, asst. prof. physics, 1965-68; theoretical research physicist U. Calif., Lawrence Radiation Lab., Livermore, Calif., 1968-73; pres. Material System Analysts, Oakland, Calif., 1973—; cons. Bell Telephone Lab., Murray Hill, N.J., 1966. Campaign co-ordinator No. Calif. Scientists and Engrs. for McGovern, 1972. NSF travel grantee, 1964; NSF research grantee, 1966-68. Mem. Am. Phys. Soc., Am. Assn. Coll. Profs., Internat. Solar Energy Soc., Pacific Assn. of AAU, Sierra Club, Sigma Xi. Office: PO Box 13130 Oakland CA 94661

BRUSTAD, WESLEY O., symphony executive, theater and film director; b. Fergus Falls, Minn., Aug. 16, 1943; s. Otto Waldemar and Doris Mina (Holoien) B.; m. Sharon D. Culbertson, Aug., 1963; m. Karla Kay Stratford, Dec. 23, 1970; children—Robert W., Jason M., Stephanie B., Jessica A. B.A., Sch. of Drama, U. Wash., 1965, M.A., 1970. Asst. dir. Ohio Arts Council, Columbus, 1970-71; exec. dir. S.C. Arts Commn., Columbia, 1971-73; v.p. Guthrie Theater, Mpls., 1974-75; mng. dir. Tenn. Performing Arts Ctr., 1975-77; artistic dir., producer Advent Theater, Nashville, 1978-79; exec. producer Creative Factory, Deer Park, Wash., 1979-80; exec. dir., gen. mgr. Spokane (Wash.) Symphony Orch., 1980—; founder, pres. Phoenix Entertainment, 1974-80; producer records, TV spls., films; theater director; cons. in field. Bd. dirs. Friends of Seven/KSPS-TV, 1982—, Deer Park Community Ch., 1982—, Wash. Arts Alliance, 1981—. Served to capt. USAF, 1965-69. NSF scholar, 1960; Alcoa Aluminum scholar, 1961-65. Mem. Am. Symphony Orch. League. Author play, TV spl.: Fat Tuesday (And All That Jazz!), 1977; author: Reason for Being, 1972.

BRUTOCAO, RICARDO GAETANO, data processing systems company executive; b. Toronto, Ont., Can., Dec. 16, 1944; came to U.S., 1951, naturalized, 1956; s. Louis and Dorina (Pacini) B.; B.S. in Elec. Engring., U. Santa Clara (Calif.), 1966; M.B.A. with honors, Calif. State U.-Los Angeles, 1972; m. Michelle Joans, Sept. 3, 1966; children—Louis, Andrew, Christina, Phillip, Nicholas. From project mgr. to mgr. prodn. engring. Burroughs Corp., 1969-72; from v.p. Riva Yacht subs. to dir. internat. ops. Whittaker Corp., 1972-76; pres., chief exec. officer LDM, Inc., Covina, Calif., 1976—. Mem. personnel adv. bd. City of Covina. Served with USAR, 1967-69; Vietnam. Decorated Bronze Star. Mem. Covina C. of C. (dir.), U. Santa Clara President's Club, Alumni Assn. Calif. State U. Los Angeles, So. Calif. Tech. Exec. Network (vice-chmn.), Beta Gamma Sigma. Republican. Roman Catholic. Club: South Hills Country. Office: 529 S 2d Ave Covina CA 91723

BRUYN, HENRY BICKER, pediatrician; b. Bklyn., Jan. 24, 1918; s. Henry B. and Mary J. (Retter) B.; B.A., Amherst Coll., 1940; M.D., Yale U., 1943; m. Harriet Hall Brainerd, Apr. 22, 1973; children by previous marriage—Martha Elizabeth, Barbara Jane, Charles DeWitt, Jonathan Henry. Intern in pediatrics New Haven Hosp., 1943-44; asst. resident in pediatrics Buffalo Children's Hosp., 1944, resident, 1945; fellow in infectious diseases U. Calif. Med. Sch., San Francisco, 1946-47; practice medicine specializing in pediatrics Berkeley, Calif., 1947-59; chief of isolation service San Francisco Hosp., 1950-59; attending physician Child Health Center, San Francisco, 1950—; dir. student health service U. Calif., Berkeley, 1959-72; instr. pediatrics U. Calif. Med. Sch., San Francisco, 1948-50, asst. prof., 1950-54, asso. prof., 1954-59, clin. prof. medicine and pediatrics, 1959—; lectr. Sch. Public Health, U. Calif., Berkeley, 1960—; asst. clin. prof. pediatrics Stanford (Calif.) U. Med. Sch., 1949-59; dir. Child Health and Disability Prevention Program, San Francisco, 1974—; cons. Comprehensive Health Service Inc., 1972-74, various community and vol. orgns., 1948—; mem. Head Start Med. Adv. Bd., San Francisco, 1974—; mem. adv. bd. East Bay Health Testing Center, Berkeley, 1965-77; cons. U.S. Navy Biol. Lab., Oakland, Calif., 1966-72; cons. infectious diseases U.S. Army Letterman Gen. Hosp., 1950—, Naval Hosp., Oakland, 1948—, chief pediatrics, 1945-46. Mem. adv. com. on drug abuse Calif. Council on Criminal Justice, 1968; bd. dirs. Berkeley Med. Instrument Co., 1960-69, chmn., 1960-66; bd. dirs. Ronoh Sch., 1967-72, Clausen House, 1975-76; bd. dirs. Goodwill Industries, 1975—, pres., 1981—; bd. dirs. New Bridge Found., 1968—, chmn., 1970—; bd. dirs. Jack B. Goldberg Found., 1978—, Carmel Valley Manor Retirement Community, 1969—, Alameda County Drug Coalition, 1971-75; bd. dirs. Arlington Community Ch., 1954-70, chmn. ch. council, 1964-68. Served with M.C., USN, 1945-46, 53-54. Diplomate Am. Bd. Pediatrics. Mem. Am. Acad. Pediatrics (chmn. com. on public health dist. IX 1960-68, 80—), Am. Coll. Health Assn. (pres. 1965-66), Am. Public Health Assn., Calif. Acad. Medicine, Pacific Coast Coll. Health Assn. (pres. 1968-69), Am. Fedn. for Clin. Research, Western Soc. Clin. Research, Calif. Med. Assn. (mem. com. on sch. and coll. health 1966-72), AMA (Disting. Physician award 1977), Calif. Sch. Health Assn., Royal Soc. Health. Contbg. author: Handbook of Pediatrics, 1954-83); Parents Guide to Child Raising, 1978; contbr. articles on pediatric therapy and diagnosis, pub. health to med. jours. Home: 432 Woodland Rd Kentfield CA 94904 Office: 101 Grove St San Francisco CA 94102

BRUZEWSKI, JAMES ROBERT, vocational rehabilitation counselor; b. Dubuque, Iowa, Sept. 20, 1946; s. Robert F. and Ann M. (McGovern) B. B.A. U. Mo., 1969, postgrad., 1972-77; M.S. Okla. State U., 1979. Cert. rehab. counselor, 1979. Vocat. rehab. counselor State of Ariz., Mesa, 1979-83. Chmn. housing accessibility com. Mesa Community Council, Mesa Mayor's Handicap Awareness Com.; active Gov.'s Com. on Employment of Handicapped. Served to 1st lt. USAF, 1969-74. Decorated Silver Star, DFC, Bronze Star, Air medal. Mem. Nat. Rehab. Assn. Am. Personnel and Guidance Assn., Nat. Rehab. Counselors Assn., Ariz. Rehab. Assn., Am. Rehab. Counselors Assn.

BRYAN, DAVID BARCLAY, lawyer; b. Los Angeles, Aug. 30, 1933; s. Frederick Conger and Florence Evelyn (Hamburger) B.; m. Jeanne Yvonne Wo, May 17, 1959; children—Michael David, Jon Frederic. B.A., Duke U., 1955; J.D., U. Calif.-Berkeley, 1958. Bar: Hawaii 1964, U.S. Supreme Ct. 1968. Labor relations mgr. Hawaiian Airlines, Honolulu, 1960-61; dir. personnel Civil Air Transport, Air Asia and Air Am., Taipei, Taiwan, 1961-63; employment and tng. mgr. Hawaiian Electric Co., Honolulu, 1963-65; dep. pros. atty. City and County of Honolulu, 1965-68; ptnr. Kai & Dodge, and predecessor firms, Honolulu, 1968-79; sole practice, Honolulu, 1979—. Active Muscular Dystrophy Assn., Honolulu, pres., 1980-82; bd. dirs., trustee Alliance Francaise, Honolulu; bd. dirs. Iaorana Tahiti, Young Republicans. Recipient awards from civic organizations. Mem. Am. Assn. Trial Lawyers, Assn. Imigration Lawyers Am., ABA, Hawaii Bar Assn., Am. Tng. Dirs. Assn., Indsl. Relations Assn. Hawaii. Episcopalian. Clubs: Honolulu, Outrigger Canoe (Honolulu). Office: Financial Plaza of the Pacific Suite 1808 Honolulu HI 96813

BRYAN, GERALD OREN, educator; b. Greeley, Colo., Aug. 17, 1935; s. Oren and Bertha Elizabeth (Ward) B.; B.A., U. No. Colo., 1960, M.A., 1964; D.B.A., Ariz. State U., 1973; m. Patricia Karen Grossnickle, July 9, 1961; children—Linda Lee, Richard Alan. Tchr.-coordinator distributive edn. Santa Fe, N.Mex., 1960-61, Des Moines, 1961-64, Tucson, 1964-67; vis. instr. extension div. U. Ariz. also Adult Evening Sch., Tucson Pub. Schs., 1964-67; asso. exec. programs Center for Exec. Devel., Coll. Bus. Adminstrn., Ariz. State U., Tempe, 1967-73; dir. Bur. Bus. Research and Services, Calif. State U., Fresno, 1973-77, acting dir. Sch. Bus. Grad. Program, 1982, prof. mgmt., 1973—. Mem. sales and receiving operations Sears, Roebuck & Co., Tucson, 1967; tng. dir. Iowa Retail Hardware Assn., Des Moines, 1962-63; cons. div. vocat. edn. Ariz. Dept. Edn., State Compensation Fund Ariz., Sales and Mktg. Execs. Phoenix, N.Mex State Hwy. Dept., Sierra Nat. Forest, SBA; pres. Ariz. Vocat. Assn., 1969. Served with AUS, 1955-57. Mem. Ariz. Distributive Edn. Clubs Am., Am. Soc. Tng. and Devel. (chpt. pres. 1975), Sigma Iota Epsilon, Beta Gamma Sigma (chpt. pres. 1974), Delta Pi Epsilon. Editor: The Manager's Key Jour., 1969. Project dir., editor: Ariz. Cooperative Education, 1971. Contbr. articles to profl. jours. Home: 6599 N Barton St Fresno CA 93710

BRYAN, JACK YEAMAN, author, photographer; b. Peoria, Ill., Sept. 24, 1907; s. James Yeaman and Regina (Gibson) B.; student U. Chgo., 1925-27; fellow philosophy Duke, 1933-35; B.A. with high distinction, U. Ariz., 1932, M.A., 1933; Ph.D., U. Iowa, 1939; m. Margaret Gardner, June 21, 1934; children—Joel Yeaman, Guy Kelsey, Donna Gardner, Kirsten Stuart Winkle-Bryan. Research analyst Fed. Emergency Relief Adminstr., Washington, 1935-36; from instr. English to prof., head dept. journalism, U. Md., 1936-48; pub. relations adviser OCD, 1942-43; dir. pub. relations Welfare Fedn. Cleve., 1943-45; pub. information officer UNRRA, 1945-46; cultural attache embassy, Manila, P.I., 1948-51; chief program planning Internat. Exchange Service, State Dept., 1951-53; pub. affairs officer USIS, Bombay, India, 1953-54, Bangalore, India, 1954-55; cultural affairs officer embassy, Cairo, Egypt, 1956, Tehran, Iran, 1956-58; cultural attache, chief cultural affairs officer embassy, Karachi, Pakistan, 1958-63; area personnel officer USIA, 1964-65; officer-in-charge, project Am. Idea Men for Service Abroad, State Dept., Washington, 1965-67, chief cultural affairs adviser USIA, 1968; retired, 1968; lectr. in creative photography U. Calif., Riverside, 1968-81. Chmn. publs. bd. U. Md., 1946-48; chmn. bd. dirs. U.S. Ednl. Found., Philippines, 1949-51, U.S. Ednl. Found., Pakistan, 1958-63; exec. dir. Iran-Am. Soc. in Tehran, 1956-58; founder, exec. dir. Pakistan-Am. Cultural Center, 1959-60, 1962-63. Mem. Am. Soc. Mag. Photographers, Internat. Photography Soc., Tex. Hist. Assn., Tex. Inst. Letters (award for best short story of 1974), Am. Mus. Natural History, Sierra Club, Arts Council Riverside, Nat. Wildlife Fedn., Nature Conservancy, Audubon Soc., Phi Delta Theta, Delta Sigma Rho. Author: (novel) Come to the Bower (Best Fiction award Tex. Inst. Letters 1964, Summerfield Roberts award Sons of Republic of Tex. 1964), 1963. Contbr. stories, photographs, articles to various mags.; contbr. photographs of Mexico and California Coast to Sunset books. Exhibited one-man photo shows, India, 1955, Pakistan, 1961-62, Perspectives Eastward, on tour U.S., 1968-76. Home: 3594 Ramona Dr Riverside CA 92506

BRYAN, ROBERT EDWARD, JR., computer dealer and lessor; b. Peoria, Ill., June 11, 1929; s. Robert Edward and Jenny Alnore (Lawton) B.; B.A. in Gen. Sci., U. Iowa, 1951; M.S. in Mgmt. (Sloan fellow), M.I.T., 1969; m. Ann Shouvlin, June 6, 1959; children—Elizabeth, Amy, Molly. Asst. program contracts mgr., contracts mgr. The Glenn L. Martin Co., Balt., 1953-57, program sales mgr., 1958-59, European sales mgr., 1959-61; mgr., dir. contracts Martin Marietta Corp., Denver, 1961-68; exec. dir. Martin Marietta Data Systems, Denver, 1969-72, v.p., 1972-75; pres. Econ. Data Corp., Denver, 1975—. Served with USAF, 1951-53. Mem. Computer Dealers and Lessors Assn., Nat. Contracts Mgmt. Assn. (dir. 1966-68). Club: University (Denver). Home: 4601 S Franklin St Englewood CO 80110 Office: 650 S Cherry St Suite 506 Denver CO 80222

BRYANT, BETTY JEAN, bank executive; b. Mountain Grove, Mo., Oct. 9, 1940; d. James A. and Joyce D. (Cramer) B.; m. Fernando Guzman, Apr. 1, 1981. J.D., Whittier Coll., 1968. Bar: Calif., U.S. Dist. Court (cen. dist.) Calif. 1969. Clk., Los Angeles County Clk's Office, 1963-69; assoc. trust counsel Security Pacific Nat. Bank, Los Angeles, 1969-73; assoc. counsel Union Bank, Los Angeles, 1973-77; asst. sec., gen. counsel Calif. Bus. and Transp. Agy., Sacramento, 1977-78; dir. Calif. Dept. Econ. and Bus. Devel., Sacramento, 1978-80; sr. v.p., dir. Am. City Bank, Los Angeles, 1980—. Mem. Mayor of Los Angeles Adv. Com. on Revenue, 1975; mem. Calif. Atty. Gen.'s Task Force on Women's Rights, 1974, 1975; mem. Los Angeles County Econ. Devel. Council, Calif. Job Creation Bd.; mem. adv. council Los Angeles County Dist. Atty.; pres. Central Adv. Council Los Angeles City Sch. Dist. for Girl's Week. Recipient Outstanding Career Woman award, 1973; Outstanding Voluntary Service to Community award, 1976; Ernestine Stahlhut award, 1978; Whittier Coll. Alumnus of Yr. award, 1978. Mem. Los Angeles County Bar Assn. (trustee 1975-77), Calif. State Bar (joint com. on structures of judiciary), Nat. Bus. and Profl. Women Los Angeles (past pres., named woman of achievement 1978), Calif. C. of C., Women's Assn., Calif. Women Lawyers, Women Lawyers' Assn. Los Angeles (past pres.), ABA, Am. Inst. Banking, Calif. Bankers' Assn. Clubs: Los Angeles Breakfast. Address: 10126 Empyrean Way Los Angeles CA 90067

BRYANT, EDWARD ALBERT, art gallery executive; b. Lenoir, N.C., July 23, 1928; s. Edmond Henry and Shelton Emmaline (Robbins) B.; A.B., U. N.C., 1950, M.A., 1955; postgrad. U. Italiana per Stranieri, Perugia, 1954, U. di Pisa (Italy), 1954-55, U. di Ravenna (Italy), 1955, N.C. State Coll., 1956, Columbia U., 1958; m. Tamara Thompson, May 28, 1965; children—Adam Edmond, Mary Emmaline. Fellow, Bklyn. Mus., 1957-58; European study grant for research contemporary Italian drawings, 1958-59; gen. curator Wadsworth Atheneum, Hartford, Conn., 1959-61; asso. curator Whitney Mus. Am. Art, N.Y.C., 1961-65; dir. U. Ky. Art Gallery, Lexington, 1965-68; dir. Picker Gallery; asso. prof. Colgate U., 1968-80, prof. art, 1980; chmn. dept. fine arts, 1976-77; prof. art, dir. Art Mus., U. N.Mex., Albuquerque, 1980—; exhbns. include African sculpture Bklyn. Mus., 1958, contemporary Italian drawings and collage Am. Fedn. Arts, 1959; Jack Tworkov Retrospective Exhbn., Whitney Mus., 1964; A Decade of New Talent, Am. Fedn. Arts, 1964; Graphics 1968; U. Ky., 1969; Larry Zox, Jason Seley, Alex Katz, John Koch, Sidney Tillim, Nell Blaine, Tom Doyle, Leon Golub, Nancy Spero, Victor Burgin, Viewpoint exhbn. series, Colgate U.; Images of N.Mex., U. N.Mex.; cons. Ky. Arts Commn., 1967-68. Pres., Poolville (N.Y.) Vol. Fire Dept., 1972-73; Cub master Boy Scouts Am., Earlville, N.Y., 1975-76, treas. 1976-77; mem. adv. panel Inst. Architecture and Urban Studies, N.Y.C., 1976-79; mem. sculpture panel NEA Art in Pub. Places, Albuquerque Arts Bd., 1980; mem. visual arts fellowship panel Ariz. Commn. on Arts, Phoenix, 1981. Fulbright fellow, 1954-55; spl. research grant Colgate U., 1969-70, 76, Nat. Endowment for the Arts grantee, 1974-75. Author: Painting, 1958; Jack Tworkov, 1964; 32 Drawings by Robert Broderson, 1964; Jason Seley, 1980; Joseph Pennell's New York City, 1980. Co-author: African Sculpture, 1958; Forty Artists Under Forty (with Lloyd Goodrich), 1962. Home: 1400 Marron Circle NE Albuquerque NM 87112 Office: Room 320 Art Bldg U NMex Albuquerque NM 87131

BRYANT, FRANK RICHARD, insurance agency owner; b. Las Animas, Colo., June 29, 1935; s. C.P. and Mary Charlotte (Morley) B.; B.S., U. Wyo., 1958; m. Patricia Elizabeth Hoben, July 22, 1967; children—Deborah, Michael. Mgmt. trainee J.C. Penney Co., Denver, 1958-59, mgr., 1961-63; co-mgr. Plains Furniture Co., Riverton, Wyo., 1963-64; mgr. Retail Credit, Riverton, Wyo., 1964-65; owner Bryant Agy. and Bryant-Vandiver Agy., Las Animas, 1965—. Real estate instr. U. Colo., Colorado Springs, 1971-72. Pres., Bent County Combined Fund, 1970; mem. Bent County Econ. Devel. Council, 1967—, Bent County Welfare Adv. Com., 1967—; sec. Bent County Republican Central Com., 1968; chmn. bd. govs. Bent County Meml. Hosp. and Nursing Home, 1977-79. Served to 1st lt. AUS, 1959-61. Mem. Colo. Small Bus. Council, Colo. Insurors, Las Animas-Bent County C. of C. (v.p. 1967, dir. 1979—), Sigma Nu. Presbyterian (ruling elder 1973-76, 81). Clubs: Valley Knife and Fork (pres. La Junta, Colo. 1974-75, internat. staff club visitor 1976—), Kiwanis (pres. Las Animas 1968) Men's Thursday Evening Study (pres. 1980-82), Masons. Home: 1654 W 6th St Las Animas CO 81054 Office: PO Box 506 Las Animas CO 81054

BRYANT, JAN DAVID, controller; b. Danville, Ky., Sept. 6, 1946; B.S., U. Ky., 1975; m. Susan Hudson, Mar. 6, 1969; 1 dau., Penelope. Payroll acct. Hills Bros. Coffee, Inc., San Francisco, 1975-76, tax acct., 1976-80, tax mgr., 1980-82; asst. controller Calif. Pacific Ins. Services, 1982—. Served with USNR, 1967-71. Mem. Am. Mgmt. Assn., Tax Execs. Inst. Office: Calif Pacific Ins Services 555 Northgate Dr San Rafael CA 94903

BRYANT, ORVIS S., interior designer; b. Oklahoma City, Feb. 3, 1927; s. Carter H. and Grace L. (Orvis) B. B.A. U. Colo., 1949. Asst. buyer, dir. display Sterling Furniture Co., San Francisco, 1941-61; interior designer Webers Interiors Co., Richmond, Calif., 1961-63; ptnr., v.p. Bryant-Forney Assocs., San Francisco, 1963—; instr. Nat. Home Furnishings Assn. Mem. Am. Soc. Interior Designers (cert.), Interior Design Soc., Internat. Home Furnishings Reps. Assn. Contbr. articles to publs. in field. Republican. Office: Bryant-Forney Assocs 2005 16th St San Francisco CA 94103

BRYANT, ROGER ALLEN, psychotherapist; b. Medicine Lodge, Kans., Aug. 7, 1954; s. Ronald Lee and Naomi Corine (Nuckolls) B.; m. Cathy Diane Doughty, June 18, 1977; 1 son, Aaron Christopher. B.A. in Zoology, U. No. Colo., 1976, cert. tchr. biology, 1977; M.A. in Counseling Psychology, Trinity Evang. Div. Sch., Deerfield, Ill., 1980. Tutor/counselor Central Baptist Family Services, Lake Villa, Ill., 1978-79; tchr. aide/counselor Glenbrook North High Sch., Northbrook, Ill., 1979; counselor-intern Concern Counseling Ctr., Waukegan, Ill., 1980; counselor Christian Counseling Ministries, Buena Vista, Colo., 1980—; conf. and seminar speaker; testing diagnostician for vocat. rehab. Dept. Colo. Social Services. Pres. Buena Vista Ministerial Assn., 1982-83. Mem. Nat. Assn. Social Workers, Am. Personnel and Guidance Assn., Am. Mental Health Counselors Assn., Mental Health Assn. Colo., Buena Vista C. of C. Mem. Evangelical Free Ch. Clubs: Kiwanis, Optimists (Buena Vista). Home: 113 Surrey PO Box 1873 Buena Vista CO 81211 Office: Mt Princeton Counseling and Family Services 111 E Sterling St PO Box 789 Buena Vista CO 81211

BRYANT, TANYA MIFSUD (MRS. GLENDELL W. DOBBS), real estate exec.; b. Shema, Island of Malta, May 15, 1920; d. Jose Louis and Vera (Jarmonkine) Mifsud; student pvt. schs.; m. Arthur J.W. Pitt, Nov. 17, 1937 (div. Feb. 1952); children—Natasha, Valerie Bryant Deeds, F. David, Micheline Bryant Magdaleno; m. 2d, William Cullen Bryant, Dec. 29, 1959 (div. June 1960); m. 3d, Jack F. Cutler, May 4, 1963 (div. 1969); m. 4th, Glendell W. Dobbs, 1969; came to U.S., 1949, naturalized, 1957. Imported model Jacques Heim, Paris, 1949-50; Conover model all maj. fashion shows and TV shows U.S., 1950-52; sportswear-buyer, exec. trainee Neiman Marcus, Dallas, 1952-54; mgr. ladies wear Broadway Dept. Store, Panorama City, Calif., 1954-56; owner, buyer Brides and Besides shops, Los Angeles, Bakersfield, Westwood, Calif., 1956-60; owner Tanya Bryant, Realtor, Canoga Park, Calif., 1957—. Originator, dir. Pamper House, Rockefeller Center, 1952. Staff asst. ARC, London, 1942-45; gray lady, Los Angeles, 1957-60; bd. dirs. Better Bus. Bur., 1976—. Mem. Women's Council Nat. Assn. Real Estate Bds. (chpt. pres. 1966-69), San Fernando Valley Bd. Realtors (dir. 1966), C. of C. (dir. 1966), Calif. Real Estate Assn. (dir. 1966-67, 70-73, chmn. public relations com. 1969—), San Jose Real Estate Bd. (dir. 1970—), Lodi Bd. Realtors (dir. 1982—), Internat. Inst. Valuers (sr. cert.), Internat. Platform Assn., Internat.-Traders Club. Contbr. articles to profl. jours. Home: 2621 W Hiway 12 Lodi CA 95240 Office: 107 W Lockeford Lodi CA 95240

BRYCE, MURRAY DAVIDSON, real estate development and management corp. exec.; b. Keeler, Sask, Can., Sept. 25, 1917; s. David Henry and Evelyn Margaret (Morgan) B.; m. Anna-Maria Sophia De la Cour, May 15, 1975; children by previous marriage—Karen L. Bryce Funt, Lisa K. B.A., U. B.C., 1949; M.A., Am. U., 1956. Ops. officer World Bank, Washington, 1951-57; sr. internat. economist A.D. Little Inc., Cambridge, Mass., 1959-64; pres. Projects Internat. Inc., Winchester, Mass., 1964-68, Can. Projects Ltd., Vancouver, B.C., Can., 1968—; vis. prof. U. B.C., Vancouver, 1974-75. Chmn. edn. com. Bd. of Trade, Vancouver, 1971-72. Served with RCAF, 1940-45. Mem. Soc. for Internat. Devel. Author: Industrial Development, 1960, Policies and Methods for Industrial Development, 1965. Address: Apt 701 845 Chilco St Vancouver BC V6G 2R2 Canada

BRYDEN, JAMES NICKOLAUS, aerospace engineer; b. Bern, Switzerland, July 7, 1930; came to U.S., 1941, naturalized, 1944; s. Eugene and Sonja (Chacham) B.; B.S. in Physics, UCLA, 1959, postgrad., 1958-63, 77; m. Janice Peron, Dec. 25, 1959; children—Nina, Philip. Physicist, mem. tech. staff Atomics Internat., Canoga Park, Calif., 1957-58; mem. tech. staff Hughes Aircraft, Culver City, Calif., 1958-60; sr. engr., group supr., sect. mgr. Jet Propulsion Lab., Calif. Inst. Tech., Pasadena, 1960-68, sr. tech. mgr., sr. staff, mgr. def. tech. program, 1970-83; chief engr. electronics Bendix Electrodynamics Div., Sylmar, Calif., 1968-70; mem. tech. staff Research & Devel. Assocs., Marina Del Rey, Calif., 1983—; math. instr. Santa Monica, Calif., 1960-63. Bd. dirs. Campfire Girls, Glendale, Calif., 1968-69. Served with USAF, 1951-54. Decorated Air medal with two oak leaf clusters, D.F.C.; recipient NASA Apollo achievement award; NASA Surveyor achievement award; NASA Exceptional Service medal; engring. mgmt. cert. UCLA. Assn. fellow AIAA; mem. IEEE (sr.), Am. Def. Preparedness Assn., Assn. Unmanned Vehicles, UCLA Alumni Assn. Home: 562 Woodbury Rd Glendale CA 91206

BRYDEN, VICKI ANNE, retail merchant; b. Tacoma, Wash., July 24, 1945; d. Elmer Clyde Delaney, Jr., and Edith May (Nelsen) Delaney Ingram; m. Bruce Douglas Bryden, Dec. 23, 1967; children—Amy Annette, Andrew Douglas. Student Oreg. State U., 1963-64; B.S. in Edn., So. Oreg. Coll., 1967. Elementary tchr. Puyallup (Wash.) Public Schs., 1967-69, Medford (Oreg.) Sch. Dist. 549c, 1969-70; owner Bryden's Store, Medford, 1974—. Active mayor's Downtown Revitalization Com., Medford, 1977-80; mem. Medford Citizens Planning Adv. Com., 1982—; bd. dirs. Jackson County Community Concert Assn., 1975-79; participant polit. activities. Recipient Outstanding Woman of Medford award, Medford Jayceettes, 1979. Mem. AAUW (name grant award, Medford Br., 1980), Nat. Fedn. Ind. Businesses, Oreg. Retail Council, Greater Medford C. of C., Medford Downtown Merchants Assn. (bd. dirs., 1977-79, pres., 1980), So. Oreg. Hist. Soc. (trustee 1983—). Democrat. Lutheran. Club: Medford Jr. Women's (clubwoman of year, 1977, 78). Active in registration of first Medford Hist. Dist. with Nat. Trust of Hist. Places, 1978. Home: 1009 S Oakdale Medford OR 97501 Office: 217 E Main St Medford OR 97501

BRYDON, HAROLD WESLEY, entomologist; b. Hayward, Calif., Dec. 6, 1923; s. Thomas Wesley and Hermione (McHenry) B.; A.B., San Jose State Coll., 1948; M.A., Stanford, 1950; m. Ruth Bacon Vickery, Mar. 28, 1951; children—Carol Ruth, Marilyn Jeanette, Kenneth Wesley. Insecticide sales Calif. Spray Chem. Corp., San Jose, 1951-52; entomologist, fieldman, buyer Beech-Nut Packing Co., 1952-53; mgr., entomologist Lake County Mosquito Abatement Dist., Lakeport, Calif., 1954-58; entomologist, adviser Malaria Eradication Programs ICA (name changed to AID), Kathmandu, Nepal, 1958-61, Washington, 1961-62, Port-au-Prince, Haiti, 1962-63; dir. fly control research Orange County Health Dept. Santa Ana, Calif., 1963-66; free-lance writer in field, 1966—; research entomologist U. N.D. Sch. Medicine, 1968; developer, owner Casierra Resort, Lake Almanor, Calif., 1975-79; owner Westwood (Calif.) Sport Shop, 1979—; instr. Lassen Community Coll., Susanville, Calif., 1975—. Served with USNR, 1943-46. Recipient Meritorious Honor award for work in Nepal, AID, U.S. Dept. State, 1972. Mem. Entomol. Soc. Am., Am. Mosquito Control Assn., Pacific Coast Entomol. Soc., Am. Legion. Republican. Methodist. Mason. Club: Commonwealth of California. Research and publs. on insecticides, mech. methods for dispersing insecticides for control of aquatic forms of gnats and mosquitoes, biol. control parasites of houseflies. Home: PO Box 312 Westwood CA 96137

BRYDON, RUTH VICKERY, educator; b. San Jose, Calif., June 2, 1930; d. Robert Kingston and Ruth (Bacon) Vickery; m. Harold Wesley Brydon, Mar. 28, 1951 (div.); children—Carol Ruth Brydon Koford, Marilyn Jeanette, Kenneth Wesley. B.A., Stanford U., 1952; student San Jose State Coll., 1964-65, Calif. State Coll.-Chico, 1979—. Cert. tchr., Calif. Tchr., Lincoln Sch., Kathmandu, Nepal, 1959-60; tchr. Am. Sch., Port-au-Prince, Haiti, 1962-63; tchr. social studies Norte Vista High Sch., Riverside, Calif., 1965-67, chmn. social studies dept., 1966-67; tchr. home econs. Westwood (Calif.) High Sch., 1967—, coordinator Lassen Coll. Extended Day Classes, 1977—. Co-chairperson Almanor Art Show, 1980—. NDEA grantee, 1967. Mem. Nat. Council Social Studies, Am. Home Econs. Assn., Calif. Home Econs. Assn., Home Econs. Tchrs. Assn. Calif., NEA, Calif. Edn. Assn. United Methodist. Club: Commonwealth of Calif. Home: 3454 Hill Crest Dr Hamilton Br Lake Almanor CA 96137 Office: Westwood High Sch PO Box H Westwood CA 96137

BRYND, SCOTT RICHARD, ballet company executive, producer; b. Chgo., Oct. 29, 1954; s. Ricchard J. and Betty L. (Schluraff) B. B.F.A. in Communications, Pacific Lutheran U.; M.F.A. in Theatre Mgmt., UCLA. Formerly pres. Am. Theatrical Prodns., Los Angeles, fin. v.p. Hollywood's New View (Calif.), producing mgr. UCLA's Resident Theatre Co.; currently mng. dir. Los Angeles Ballet; actor, dir., theatrical producer. Recipient Amoco Oil award of Excellence, John F. Kennedy Ctr. Mem. Wilshire C. of C. Republican. Lutheran. Office: 1035 N McCadden Pl Los Angeles CA 90038

BRYNGELSON, JAMES DAVID, ednl. adminstr.; b. Billings, Mont., Mar. 8, 1941; s. Ivan Carl and Claire Elizabeth (Ellingwood) B.; B.S., U. Mont., 1963; edn. cert. Eastern Mont. Coll. Edn., 1964; M.S. in Counseling, Purdue U., 1967; ednl. specialist degree in sch. psychology U. No. Colo., 1974, Ed.D., 1976; m. Judy Bryngelson, June 27, 1969; children—Joy, Nick. Jr. high sch. tchr. Littleton (Colo.) Public Schs., 1964-66, jr. high sch. counselor, 1967-73, sch. psychologist, 1974-75; coordinator spl. edn. inservice adminstrn. Steamboat Springs (Colo.) Pub. Schs., 1975-78; dir. edn. Sch. Dist. 58, Yellowstone Boys and Girls Ranch Sch., Billings, 1978—; bd. dirs. Foster parent Tumbleweed Foster Homes; mem. youth adv. council, mem. ch. council Am. Luth. Ch.; bd. dirs. Billings Mental Health Assn. Mem. Council Exceptional Children, Council Children with Behavior Disorders, Acad. Fellows of Charles F. Kettering Found., Assn. Supervision and Curriculum Devel., Nat. Assn. Elem. and Secondary Sch. Prins., Nat. Assn. Sch. Psychologists, Mont. Assn. Sch. Psychologists, Self Esteem Assocs., Mont. Educators of Emotionally Disturbed (bd. dirs., charter), Sigma Chi, Phi Delta Kappa (v.p.). Democrat. Clubs: Toastmasters, Exchange. Home: 1144 Henry Rd Billings MT 59102 Office: Sch Dist 58 Route 1 Box 212 Billings MT 59102

BRYNJESTAD, ULF AKE GUNNAR, aeronautical engineer, management consultant; b. Goteborg, Sweden, Sept. 29, 1940; s. Ake Fridolf and Alida Charlotta (Berndtson) B.; m. Jo Anne Spear, July 4, 1964; children—Michael Lee, Katherine Ann-Marie. B.S.A.E., NKI Inst. Tech., Stockholm, 1963; M.S.A.E., U. So. Calif., 1969, M.S.S.M., 1971; Ph.D., LaJolla U., 1981. Design engr. A.B. Volvo, Goteborg, Sweden, 1960-64; research engr. Northrop Corp., Hawthorne, Calif., 1964-77; program mgr. Gen. Dynamics/Convair, San Diego, 1977—; mgmt. cons., systems forecaster. Dist. master, Pacific SW Dist. Served to 1st lt., Royal Swedish Army Res., 1957-67. Mem. AIAA, ops. Research Soc. Am., Tech. Aerospace Soc. Am. Republican. Lutheran. Club: Los Angeles Swedish (dir. 1974-77). Patentee in field of fluid control system for operation of aircraft high-lift devices; non-tracking solar energy concentrator. Home: 1926 Rancho Andrew Alpine CA 92001

BRYSON, JEFF BELL, psychologist; b. Corpus Christi, Tex., June 26, 1943; s. James Gordon and Martha Louise (Bell) B.; m. Rebecca Blount, Aug. 13, 1966 (div.); 1 son, Jeffrey. B.A., U. Tex.-Austin, 1965; M.S., Purdue U., 1968, Ph.D., 1970. Research assoc. Psychonometrics Lab., U. Ga., 1969-70; project dir. U.S. Naval Personnel Research Lab., San Diego, 1970-71; asst. prof. psychology San Diego State U., 1971-73, assoc. prof., 1973-76, prof., 1976—. Mem. Am. Psychol. Assn., Western Psychol. Assn., Soc. Exptl. Social Psychology, AAAS, Sigma Xi. Office: Dept Psychology San Diego State U San Diego CA 92182

BRYSON, MARION RITCHIE, federal agency administrator; b. Centralia, Mo., June 22, 1947; s. Thomas Raymond and Helen Price (Pool) B.; m. Lenora Jane Kalips; children—Rosalyn Irby, Nina Harmon, Kevin, Richard. B.S. in Edn., U. Mo., 1949, M.A., 1950; Ph.D., Iowa State U., 1958. Cons. Army Research Office, Durham, N.C., 1958-68; assoc. prof. math., community health services, dir. spl. research stats., Duke U., Durham, 1958-68; tech. dir. Systems Analysis Group, U.S. Army Combat Devels. Command, Ft. Belvoir, Va., 1968-73, sci. advisor combat devels. Experimentation Command, 1973-83, dir. Experimentation Ctr., 1983—; author, lectr., sci. advisor. Vice pres. Am. Cancer Soc., Durham, 1965-68. Served with AUS, 1946-47. Recipient Meritorious Civilian Service award U.S. Army, 1977. Mem. Sr. Exec. Service U.S.A. (charter), Am. Statis. Assn., Inst. Math. Stats., Ops. Research Soc. Am., Mil. Ops. Research Soc. (bd. dirs. 1970-77, nat. pres. 1976). Club: Toastmasters (div. gov. 1967). Home: 25820 Tierra Grande Carmel CA 93923 Office: US Army Combat Developments Experimentation Center Fort Ord CA 93941

BRYSON, MAURICE CONREY, statistician; b. El Paso, Tex., Apr. 19, 1936; s. (Melvin) Conrey and Pearl Melvina (Hale) B.; m. (Paula) Joan Mumper, Aug. 28, 1976. B.A., Harvard U., 1957; M.S., Colo. State U., 1966, Ph.D., 1968. Aerospace systems engr. Douglas Aircraft, 1957-64; br. mgr. for systems analysis McDonnell-Douglas Astro., 1968-69; assoc. prof. stats. Colo. State U., Ft. Collins, 1969-81; stats. group leader Los Alamos Nat. Lab., 1981—. Harvard nat. scholar, 1953-57; NSF grad. fellow, 1965-67. Mem. AAAS, Am. Mgmt. Assn., Am. Soc. Quality Control, Am. Statis. Assn., IEEE, Assn. Energy Engrs., Phi Beta Kappa. Co-author: Basic Statistical Inference, 1981; contbr. articles to tech. jours. Home: PO Box 983 Los Alamos NM 87544 Office: Mailstop F600 Los Alamos Nat Lab Los Alamos NM 87545

BRYSON, NATALIE ELIZABETH, antique dealer, consultant; b. Weymouth, Mass., Feb. 20, 1931; d. Harry Follett and Amy Louise (Hill) Duncan; student public schs.; children—Elizabeth Alice, Muriel Anne, William MacLean, Rebecca Jane, David Duncan, James Hill. Owner, Antiques and Epicure, Silverdale, Wash., 1972—; instr. gourmet cooking and antiques Olympic Coll., Bremerton, Wash., 1971—, lectr. on China, 1979—; tour guide trip to China, 1982, 83; cons., mem. Mus. History and Industry, Seattle; rep. Wash. Art Commn. Pres. Olympic View Community, 1978; bd. dirs. March of Dimes, 1983-84, Wing Luke Mus., Seattle. Recipient Golden Acorn award Wash. PTA, 1970, Outstanding Achievement award Lockheed Mgmt. Assn., 1979; flag officer Keechong Soc., Mus. Am. China Trade, Milton, Mass., 1979—. Mem. Oriental Ceramic Soc. (London and Hong Kong), Nat. Assn. Female Execs., Nat. Assn. Dealers Antiques, Victorian Soc. Am., Kitsap County Hist. Soc., Seattle Antique Study Group, Decorative Arts Council, Seattle Art Mus., U.S.-China Friendship Assn. (bd. dirs.), Asian Arts Council (bd. dirs.), U.S. C. of C., Central Kitsap C. of C. Home: 15251 Olympic View NW Silverdale WA 98383 Office: 4 Bogard Bldg PO Box 87 Silverdale WA 98383

BRYSON, VERN ELRICK, nuclear engr.; b. Woodruff, Utah, May 28, 1920; s. David Hyrum and Luella May (Eastman) B.; student Brigham Young U., 1938-41; grad. Center for Safety Edn. N.Y. U., 1948; grad. in Electronic Engring., Air Force Inst. Tech., 1950, M.S., in Nuclear Engring., 1959; m. Esther Sybil de St. Jeor, Oct. 14, 1942; children—Britt William, Forrest Lee, Craig Lewis, Nadine, Elaine. Commd. 2d lt., USAAF, 1941, advanced through grades to lt. col. USAF, 1960, ret., 1961; pilot, safety engr., civil engr., electronic engr., nuclear engr.; chief Aircraft Nuclear Propulsion Program Office, Aeronatucial Systems div., Wright-Patterson AFB, Ohio, 1960-61; chief Boeing Radiation Effects Lab., also chief radiation effects group Boeing Airplane Co., Seattle, 1961-65; nuclear engr. Aerospace Corp., San Bernardino, Calif., 1965-68; service engr., also head instrumentation lab. Sacramento Air Logistic Center, USAF, McClellan AFB, Calif., 1968-77; owner, mgr. Sylvern Valley Ranch. Mem. Transient Radiation Effects on Electronics panel Weapons Effects Bd., 1959-61. Decorated D.F.C. with oak leaf cluster, Air medal with 12 oak leaf clusters. Mem. IEEE. Mem. Ch. of Jesus Christ of Latter-Day Saints. Research and publ. in radiation problems. Home: 1426 Caperton Ct Penryn CA 95663

BRZEINSKI, JOSEPH EDWARD, superintendent schools; b. Denver, Jan. 1, 1926; s. Lad H. and Jennie L. (Schutte) B.; A.B., U. Denver, 1949, M.A., 1951; Ed.D. (Macmillan fellow), Columbia U., 1956; m. Willow Hasse, Sept. 4, 1948; children—John, Judith, Betsy. With Denver Public Schs., 1949—, asst. supt. for adminstrv. services, 1973-75, assoc. supt. for sch. and bus. services, 1975-77, supt., 1977—; cons. in field; mem. Research Steering Com. of Gt. City Schs.; mem. adv. com. for research and devel. Colo. Dept. Edn.; project evaluator Nat. Inst. Edn. Served with inf. U.S. Army, 1944-46. Mem. Am. Assn. Sch. Adminstrs., Assn. Childhood Edn., Assn. Supervision and Curriculum Devel., Internat. Reading Assn. (pres. Denver br. 1962-63), Council Gt. City Schs. (exec. bd. 1977-81), Rocky Mountain Sch. Study Council (pres. 1980-81). Contbr. articles to profl. publs.; author tests; research abstractor Phi Delta Kappa. Office: 900 Grant St Denver CO 80203

BUBB, HARRY GEIPLE, insurance company executive; b. Trinidad, Colo., Dec. 16, 1924; s. Harry H. and Grace Allcine (Geiple) B.; B.A. in Econs., Stanford U., 1946; M.B.A., 1949; grad. Advanced Mgmt. Program, Harvard U., 1973; m. June 9, 1951; children—Melinda, Howard, Susan, John, Mary. With Pacific Mut. Life Ins. Co., 1949—, asst. v.p., 1966-68, then v.p., 1968-72, sr. v.p. group ins., 1972-75, pres., 1975—. Mem. Orange County dv. bd. Town Hall of Calif.; bd. dirs. Orange County Bus. Com. for Arts, United Way Orange County; trustee Calif. Mus. Found., Newport Harbor Art Mus., U.S. Acad. Decathlon. Served as pilot USNR, World War II. Mem. World Affairs Council Orange County, Health Ins. Assn. Am. (bd. dirs.), Los Angeles Area C. of C. (dir.). Clubs: Lincoln of Orange County, Balboa Yacht. Home: 27 Beacon Bay Newport Beach CA 92660 Office: 700 Newport Center Dr Newport Beach CA 92660

BUBENIK, PATRICIA JEAN HADLE, sch. prin.; b. Denver, Jan. 12, 1947; d. H. Paul and Allie Hadle; B.A., Colo. State U., 1969; M.A., U. Calif., Santa Cruz, 1970; Ed.D., U. San Francisco, 1981; m. David M. Bubenik, June 21, 1969. Tchr. Madrone Sch., Sunnyvale Sch. Dist. (Calif.), 1970-77; tchr. Demonstration Sch. for Gifted, San Jose State U., 1977; lang. arts specialist Sunnyvale Sch. Dist., 1977-78, vice prin., Madrone Sch., 1978-79, prin. summer sch., 1979, prin. Lakewood Sch., 1979-82; prin. Columbia Community Sch., Sunnyvale, 1982—; ednl. cons., Calif., 1977—. Bd. dirs. Calif. Young People's Theatre, Noetics Found. Fellow, Bay Area Writing Project, U. Calif., Berkeley, 1978. Mem. Assn. Calif. Adminstrs., Assn. Curriculum and Supervision Devel., Santa Clara Reading Council (exec. bd.), Calif. Reading Assn., Nat. Council Tchrs. English, Calif. Assn. Gifted, Calif. Assn. Tchrs. English, Internat. Reading Assn., Phi Delta Kappa, Phi Beta Kappa, Phi Kappa Phi. Club: Women Leaders in Edn. Author: A New Direction: Focusing on the Whole Person Through the Affective Domain, 1977. Office: 739 Morse Ave Sunnyvale CA 94086

BUCEY, CONSTANCE VIRGINIA RUSSELL, educator; b. Miami, Fla., Aug. 22, 1936; d. Mose and Lillian (Jones) Russell; B.S., Va. State Coll., 1959; postgrad. U. Miami, Fla., 1961-63, UCLA, 1970-71; M.A., Pepperdine U., 1976; m. Henry Lee Bucey, Oct. 21, 1966. Tchr., Lee Elem. Sch., South Miami, Fla., 1959-67; tchr. Duff Elem. Sch., Rosemead, Calif., 1967-74, reading specialist, 1974—. Pres., Calif. Tchrs. Fed. Credit Union, 1977—. Mem. NEA, Nat. Assn. Credit Union Presidents, Nat. Credit Union Assn., Calif. Tchrs. Assn., Garvey Tchrs. Assn., Reading Specialist Calif., AAUW, Bus. and Profl. Women's Club. Episcopalian. Home: 871 Ashiya Rd Montebello CA 90640 Office: Duff Elementary School 7830 Dorothy St Rosemead CA 91770

BUCHALTER, DANIEL DAVID, lawyer; b. Lynwood, Calif., Apr. 12, 1953; s. Oscar and Ada Fay (Osser) B. B.A. cum laude, U. Calif.-Irvine, 1975; J.D., U. Calif.-San Francisco, 1978. Bar: Calif., 1978. Sole practice, San Francisco, 1978-79, assoc. David B. Green, 1979; lectr. landlord-tenant law. Mem. Calif. Bar Assn., Lawyers Club San Francisco. Democrat. Jewish. Office: 2370 Market St Suite 2000 San Francisco CA 94114

BUCHANAN, BEN F(RANKLIN), food science and technology consultant; b. Fontana, Kans., Aug. 12, 1908; s. William Johnson and Margaret Irene (Erps) B.; m. Edith Cornelia Ross, Sept. 9, 1934; children—Fredrick Earl, Margaret Lynn. A.B., U. Kans., 1933; Ph.D., Iowa State U., 1938. Dir. tech. service lab. Am. Maize Products Co., N.Y.C., 1938-45, dir. research, 1945-46; dir. tech. service, mgr. pharm. dept. Internat. Mineral & Chem. Corp., Chgo., 1946-57; dir. product devel. and engring. research Gen. Foods Corp., Tarrytown, N.Y., 1957-60, dir. tech. applications, 1960-73; cons. food sci. and tech., Santa Rosa, Calif., 1973—; dir. APPL, Inc., Fresno, Calif. Mem. Inst. Food Technologists (pres. 1972-73), Am. Chem. Soc., Am. Assn. Cereal Chemists, N.Y. Acad. Scis., AAAS. Club: Chemists of N.Y. Author profl. publs. and patentee in food formulations and processing concerning starches, surgars, proteins, monosodium glutamate, sodium lactate, and meat and poultry processing. Home: 7326 Oakleaf Dr Santa Rosa CA 95405

BUCHANAN, DANA PATRICK, correctional educator; b. Pasadena, Calif., Mar. 17, 1939; s. Patrick Henry and Josephine (Becker) B.; m. Mariluz Castro, June 26, 1965. B.A., U. Calif.-Berkeley, 1961; M.A., Calif. State U.-Sacramento, 1970; Ph.D., U. Madrid, 1980. Entertainer, Spanish Nat. Radio, 1962-65; Spanish educator Sierra Coll., Rocklin, Calif., 1972-78; correctional tchr. Calif. Youth Authority, Ione, 1969—. Served with AUS, 1962-64. Mem. Am. Soc. Tng. and Devel. Republican. Methodist. Club: Circulo Hispano de Sacramento (pres. 1975-76). Office: PO Box 27 Martell CA 95654

BUCHANAN, JERRY MAJOR, educator, publisher; b. Seattle, Dec. 10, 1923; s. Herbert Henry and Doris Kathryn (De Nully) B.; student pub. schs., Seattle. Mechanic, Boeing Airplane Co., 1946-50; ednl. salesman, 1950-57; mem. original staff Sales Tng., Inc., sales sch., Seattle, 1957, owner Sales Tng., Inc., Los Angeles, 1958-60; publisher, owner TOWERS Club, USA Newsletter, Vancouver, Wash., 1974—. Served with USMCR, 1942-46. Mem. Direct Mail Mktg. Guild, Nat. Geog. Soc. Author: Poems to an Unmet Friend, 1971; Looking Back at Country, 1973; Writer's Utopia Formula Report, 1974. Home: 3601 E 11th St 1 Nob Hill Dr Vancouver WA 98661 Office: PO Box 2038 Vancouver WA 98668

BUCHEN, CHARLOTTE, public relations cons.; b. Canton, Ill., Jan. 11, 1927; d. Bert and Edith (Melgreen) Buchen; profl. journalism fellow Stanford U., 1966-67. Editor house organ Cuneo Press, Inc., Chgo., 1949-51; mag. prodn. coordinator Internat. Harvester Co., Chgo., 1951-52; reporter, writer Canton Daily Ledger, 1953-56, The Arizona Republic, Phoenix, 1956-69; dir. urban affairs Nat. Housing Industries, Inc., Phoenix, 1969-72, dir. communications, 1971-73; asst. to pres. Samaritan Health Service, Phoenix, 1973-79; prin. Charlotte Buchen Communications, Phoenix, 1979-80; partner Buchen, Snell & Co., Inc., Phoenix, 1980-83, pres., chmn. bd., 1983—. Editorial cons. Ariz. Welfare Study, Ariz. State U., 1970; mem. rate rev. com. Comprehensive Health Planning Council Maricopa County, 1972-74; mem. Blue Ribbon Task Force on Tchr. Cert., Ariz. Dept. Edn., 1978; bd. dirs. Phoenix Opportunities Industrialization Center, 1970-71. Mem. Ariz. Hosp. Assn., Phoenix Press Club (past dir.), Women in Communications (named Woman of Achievement, Phoenix chpt. 1982). Clubs: Kiva; Mountain Shadows Country. Home: 5301 N 45th St Phoenix AZ 85018 Office: 1002 E Missouri St Phoenix AZ 85014

BUCHER, CHARLES AUGUSTUS, educator; b. Conesus, N.Y., Oct. 2, 1912; s. Grover C. and Elizabeth (Barr) B.; B.A., Ohio Wesleyan U., 1937; M.A., Columbia, 1941; Ed.D., N.Y. U., 1948; postgrad. Yale, 1948-49; m. Jacqueline N. Dubois, Aug. 24, 1941; children—Diana, Richard, Nancy, Gerald. Tchr. pub. schs. N.Y., 1937-41; asst. prof. New Haven State Coll., 1946-50; prof. edn. NYU, N.Y.C., 1950-80; prof. U. Nev., Las Vegas, 1980—, dir. Sch. Phys. Edn., Health, Recreation and Dance, 1981—; editor Appleton-Century-Croft, N.Y.C.; Am. specialist U.S. Dept. State, 1962; del. Pres. Eisenhower's White House Conf. on Youth Fitness, 1956; cons. Pres.'s Council on Phys. Fitness and Sports, 1972—. Trustee, chmn. scholarship com. Coll. Scholarship Plan, Inc., 1959—. Recipient Sch. Bell award, 1960, Healthy Am. Fitness leader award U.S. Jaycees, 1982. Served to capt., USAAF, 1941-46. Fellow AAHPER, Am. Coll. Sports Medicine, Am. Sch. Health Assn.; mem. NEA, Higher Edn. Assn. Author: Foundations of Physical Education, 1952, rev., 1983; Methods and Materials in Physical Education and Recreation, 1934, Methods and Materials in Secondary School Physical Education, 1961, rev. edit., 1983; Administration of School Health and Physical Education Programs, 1954, rev. 1983; Physical Education in Modern Elementary School, 1958, rev., 1971; College Ahead, 1958, rev. 1961; Athletics in Schools and Colleges, 1965; Foundations of Modern Health, 1976; Guiding Your Child Toward College, 1967; Physical Education for Life, 1969. Editor: Dimensions of Physical Education, 1969, rev., 1974; Administrative Dimensions of Health and Physical Education Programs, 1971; Recreation for Today's Society, 1974, rev. edit., 1983; Physical Education for Children: Movement Foundations and Experiences, 1979; Health, 1981; Physical Education and Sport: Change and Challenge, 1981; contbr. numerous articles to profl. jours. Home: 4239 Pinecrest Circle W Las Vegas NV 89121 Office: U Nev Las Vegas NV 89154

BUCHNER, JAMES, real estate and econ. devel. exec.; b. Middletown, Conn., Aug. 9, 1932; s. Frank D. and Anna R. (Augeri) B.; A.A., Compton Coll., 1956; B.A., Whittier Coll., 1958; B.S. in Mech. Engring., West Coast U., 1969, M.S. in Mgmt. Fin., 1972; m. Dora Guerrero, Dec. 26, 1964; 1 son, Donald. Sales rep. Los Angeles Dept. Water and Power, 1960-61, comml. lighting specialist, 1961-62, govtl. sales cons., 1962-64, power sales cons., 1964-68, promotional planner, 1968, power sales engring. asso., 1968-69, supr. market research, 1969-72; devel. dir. City Placentia, Calif., 1972-77; pres. Real Estate Consultants & Assos., Whittier, Calif., 1977—; pres., chief exec. officer Econ. Devel. Corp. Orange County, Orange, Calif., 1977—; dir. Unisen Inc. Mem. Calif. Econ. Devel. Com., 1972-82; mem. exec. com. So. Calif. Econ. and Job Devel. Council, 1977-82; bd. dirs. Los Angeles Dept. Water and Power Employees Credit Union, 1970-72, asst. treas., 1971, treas., 1972; bd. dirs. Orange County Family Service Assn.; community chmn. March of Dimes, 1976-77; chmn. Orange County Task Force on Pvt. Sector Employment Incentives. Served with USN, 1953-55. Cert. indsl. developer; lic. real estate broker. Mem. Illuminating Engring. Soc., Fallbrook Citrus Assn., Western Govtl. Research Assn., Am. Econ. Devel. Council, Indsl. Devel. Execs. Assn. Club: Anchor (Los Angeles). Home: 5536 Adele Ave Whittier CA 90601 Office: 1 City Blvd W Suite 705 Orange CA 92668

BUCHTA, RICHARD MICHAEL, physician; b. Binghamton, N.Y., Feb. 8, 1941; s. Martin Joseph and Pauline (Perchinsky) B.; m. Diane Zirilli, June 1, 1963; children—Richard Michael, Daniel, Kymberly. B.S., LeMoyne Coll., 1963; M.D. cum laude, Stritch-Loyola U., Chgo., 1957. Rotating intern Naval Hosp., San Diego, 1967-68, resident in pediatrics, 1968-70; fellow in adolescent medicine Children's Hosp. Los Angeles, 1973-74; pediatric cons. Oceanside Community Hosp., 1971-73; dir. med. edn. of pediatrics Naval Hosp., Camp Pendleton, 1971-73; clin. instr. pediatrics U. Calif., San Diego, 1972-74, asst. clin. prof. pediatrics, 1975-79, assoc. clin. prof. pediatrics, 1979—; supr. pediatric services Hillcrest Receiving Home, 1975—; supr. pediatric service Loma Portal, 1980—; mem. staff Scripps Meml. Hosp., Mercy Hosp., Children's Hosp., Univ. Hosp., Sharp Hosp., Mesa Vista Hosp., Scripps Clinic and Research Found.; preceptor pediatric nurse practitioner program San Diego State U., U. Calif., San Diego, 1977—; practice medicine specializing in pediatrics and adolescent medicine, La Jolla, Calif., 1974—. Vice pres., P.T.A., Oceanside, Calif., 1971-72. Served to comdr. USNR, 1966-73. Recipient Physician's Recognition award AMA, 1969-72, 72-75, 75-78, Letter of Commendation USN, 1973. Diplomate Am. Bd. Pediatrics. Mem. Am. Acad. Pediatrics (chmn. com. on youth chpt. III 1974-75, 81—), Soc. Adolescent Medicine, AMA. Roman Catholic. Contbr. articles in field to med. jours. Home: 2752 Caminito Prado La Jolla CA 92037 Office: 6529 La Jolla Blvd La Jolla CA 92037

BUCK, BRENTON OTIS, engring. co. exec.; b. Sawyer, Kans., July 26, 1920; s. Bert Brenton and Emma Frances (Banker) B.; student Pratt (Kans.) Jr. Coll., 1938-40; student Wichita U., 1941-42; B.S. in Mech. Engring., U. Calif.-Berkeley, 1945-48; postgrad. Okla. State U., 1955-56; m. Mary Lou Ralston, June 27, 1945; children—Andrew Brenton, Barbara Nell, Brenda Gale. Prodn. chemist Cutter Labs., 1945-46; engr. Cities Service Oil Co., 1941-42, 48-56; v.p. Petrocon Engring. Co., 1956-58; chmn. bd. Mustang Engring. Co., Santa Fe Springs, Calif., 1959—; partner Sawyer Equipment Co., Gas Research Labs. Active Equestrian Trails, Inc. Served with AUS, 1940-41; with USNR, 1942-45. Registered profl. engr., Okla., Calif. Mem. ASME, Am. Inst. Chem. Engrs., Pacific Energy Assn., Natural Gas Processers Supply Assn. Club: Candlewood Country (Whittier). Contbr. articles on carbon dioxide extraction from natural gas, gas treating, perforated trays. Home: 12928 Ocaso Ave La Mirada CA 90638 Office: 13230 Cambridge St Santa Fe Springs CA 90670

BUCK, CAROLYN BURRELL, learning skills administrator, counselor; b. Benham, Ky., Oct. 12, 1948; d. Rumiller and Ola Mae (Norwood) Burrell; children—Patricia Ayodele, Roland Ade Kule. B.S., Bennett Coll., 1971, M.S. in Counselor Edn., 1976; postgrad. N.C. Agrl. and Tech. State U., 1977. Cert. Class A tchr., counselor, N.C.; pupil personnel service, Calif. Resident counselor N.C. Sch. Arts, Winston-Salem, 1973-76; asst. dir., tchr. United Day Care Services, Greensboro, N.C., 1972-77; counseling intern Greensboro City Schs., 1976; residence hall dir. SUNY-Stony Brook, 1977-79; asst. coordinator acad. success program Office Acad. Support and Instructional Services U. Calif.-San Diego, 1980-81, coordinator Acad. Success and Summer Bridge programs, 1981—, group facilitator orientation and student devel. impacting students of color, 1979-80, facilitator/trainer peer cong. and personal growth and develop. workshops, 1981—. Strongly Oriented for Action Community Ctr., La Jolla, Calif., 1983-86; 2d v.p. Albirda Green Missionary Soc., 1982—. Mem. Am. Personnel and Guidance Assn., Calif. Personnel and Guidance Assn., Nat. Assn. Employment Counselors, Assn. Non-White Concerns, Bennett Coll. Alumni Assn. (bus. mgr., co-chmn. recruitment com. 1978-79, pres. chpt. 1979-80). Club: Order Eastern Star. Office: B-005 OASIS Student Ctr B U Calif San Diego La Jolla CA 92093

BUCK, CHRISTIAN BREVOORT ZABRISKIE, ind. oil operator; b. San Francisco, Oct. 18, 1914; s. Frank Henry and Zayda Justine (Zabriskie) B.; student U. Calif., Berkeley, 1931-33; m. Natalie Leontine Smith, Sept. 12, 1948; children—Warren Zabriskie, Barbara Anne. Mem. engring. dept. U.S. Potash Co., Carlsbad, N.Mex., 1933-39; ind. oil operator, producer, Calif., 1939-79, N.Mex., 1939—; owner, operator farm, ranch, Eddy County, N.Mex., 1951-79; dir. Belridge Oil Co. until 1979; dir. Buck Ranch Co. (Calif.). Served with RAF, 1942-45. Democrat. Episcopalian. Club: Riverside Country (Carlsbad). Home: 108 W Alicante Rd Santa Fe NM 87501 Office: PO Box 2183 Santa Fe NM 87504

BUCK, LINDA DEE, exec. recruiting company executive; b. San Francisco, Nov. 8, 1946; d. Sol and Shirley D. (Setterberg) Press; student Coll. San Mateo (Calif.), 1969-70; divorced. Head hearing and appeals br. Dept. Navy Employee Relations Service, Philippines, 1974-75; dir. personnel Homestead Savs. & Loan Assn., Burlingame, Calif., 1976-77; mgr. fin. placement VIP Agy., Inc., Palo Alto, Calif., 1977-78; exec. v.p., dir. Sequent Personnel Services, Inc., Mountain View, Calif., 1978-83; Founder, pres. Buck & Co., San Mateo, 1983—. Publicity mgr. for No. Calif., Osteogenesis Imperfecta Found., 1970-72; cons. Am. Brittle Bone Soc., 1979—. Mem. Nat. Assn. Personnel Cons., Calif. Assn. Personnel Cons. Jewish. Home: San Mateo CA Office: Mills Sq Tower 9th Floor 100 S Ellsworth Ave San Mateo CA 94401

BUCK, NATALIE SMITH, former state ofcl.; b. Carlsbad, N.Mex., Jan. 10, 1923; d. Milton R. and Rosa Adele (Binford) Smith; student Coll. William and Mary, 1940-41; B.S., U. Colo., 1943; postgrad. U. Tex., 1945-46; m. C. B. Buck, Sept. 12, 1948; children—Warren Z., Barbara Anne. Chief clk., State Senate, N.Mex., 1951-53; sec. of state, N.Mex., 1955-59; chief personnel adminstr. N.Mex. Health and Social Services Dept., 1959-73. Democrat. Home: 108 W Alicante Rd Santa Fe NM 87501

BUCKELEW, DEBORAH LYNN, civic association executive; b. Memphis, Dec. 10, 1951; d. Clyde Truman and Helen Jean (Jackson) B. B.A., Calif. State U.-Los Angeles, 1976. Editor, Discover monthly theme supplement, Los Angeles Civic Ctr. Newspapers, 1977-79; promotion mgr. Los Angeles Knapp Communications, 1979-81; mem. corp. pub. relations staff Vidal Sassoon, Century City, Calif., 1981; dir. pub. relations ARC Santa Ana, 1981—, dir. nat. disasters, 1982-83. KNBC scholar, 1975. Mem. Pub. Relations Soc. Am., Orange County Press Club, Internat. Assn. Bus. Communicators, United Way Communications Com. Club: Zonta. Editor: Bon Appetit Social Planner, 1980, 81, Wine Jour., 1980, Archtl. Digest Engagement Calendar, 1980, 81, Metalsource Directory, 1981. Office: 601 N Golden Circle Dr Santa Ana CA 92711

BUCKLAND, GARY MITCHELL, marketing executive; b. N.Y.C., Mar. 27, 1952; s. Charles F. and Doris A. Buckland; m. Lyne Arlene Campbell, Feb. 26, 1960. B.B.A., U. Mich., 1973, M.B.A., 1975. Account exec. Leo Bernett Co., Chgo., 1975-77; mktg. mgr. Armour Dial Inc., Phoenix, 1978—. Office: Armour Dial Greyhound Tower Phoenix AZ 85077

BUCKLEW, NEIL S., university president; b. Morgantown, W.Va., Oct. 23, 1940; s. Douglas Earl and Lanah L. (Martin) B.; A.B., U. Mo.; M.S., U. N.C.; Ph.D. (grad. fellow), U. Wis.; m. JoAnn M. Krudwig, June 9, 1962; children—Elizabeth, Jennifer, Jeffrey. Dir. personnel Duke U., 1964-66; dir. employee relations U. Wis., 1966-70; prof., v.p. Central Mich. U., Mt. Pleasant, 1970-76; prof., provost Ohio U., Athens, 1976-80; pres. U. Mont., Missoula, 1981—; vis. research fellow Pa. State U. Arbitrator, State of Wis. Mem. Am. Assn. Higher Edn., Acad. for Academic Personnel Adminstrn. Author: Academic Collective Bargaining, 1976. Office: Main Hall Univ Montana Missoula MT 59801

BUCKLEY, JAMES WHITNEY, librarian; b. Los Angeles, Aug. 16, 1933; s. George W. and Alta L. (Hale) B.; A.A., Los Angeles Harbor Coll., 1953; B.A., Calif. State U., Long Beach, 1960; M.L.S., U. So. Calif., 1961, M.P.A., 1974; m. Margaret Ann Wall, Aug. 7, 1965; children—Kathleen Ann, James William, John Whitney. Librarian, Los Angeles County Public Library, West Gardena br., 1961-62, Carson br., 1962-63, Montebello Regional Library, 1963-68; regional librarian Orange County (Calif.) Public Library, 1968, dir. public services, 1969-74; county librarian San Mateo County (Calif.) Library, 1974-77, Marin County (Calif.) Library, 1978; city librarian Torrance (Calif.) Pub. Library, 1979—; exec. dir. Calif. Nat. Library Week, 1970; tchr. public service Coll. San Mateo, 1975. Served with U.S. Army, 1955-57. Cert. tchr., Calif. Mem. ALA, Am. Soc. Public Adminstrn., Calif. Library Assn., Public Library Execs. of So. Calif. Club: Rotary. Office: 3301 Torrance Blvd Torrance CA 90503

BUCKLEY, JOHN THOMAS, quality assurance executive; b. Milton, Mass., Jan. 16, 1930; s. Arthur John and Emily Mary (Walker) B.; m. Maureen Finn, Nov. 8, 1952 (div. Apr. 1968); children—Kathleen Westbay, Judith Ann Harrison; m. 2d, Lydia Maranan Del Mundo, Sept. 20, 1969; 1 dau., Denise Pamela. B.A., SUNY, 1979; postgrad. U. San Francisco, 1979-80; Ph.D., Century U., 1983. Commd. ensign USN, advanced through grades to comdr., 1978; assignments in Mediterranean, Vietnam, Philippines; ret., 1979; dir. quality assurance CTS Printex, Inc., Mountain View, Calif., 1979—. Decorated Bronze Star medal. Mem. Am. Soc. Quality Control, Ret. Officers Assn., U.S. Naval Inst. Procs. Alumni, VFW. Roman Catholic.

BUCKLEY, NANCY KAY, psychologist; b. Cottage Grove, Oreg.; d. Rex W. and Mabel J. (Robertson) Wakefield; m. John S. Buckley, Dec. 20, 1964; children—Jennifer K., Kimberly J. B.S., U. Oreg., 1966, M.S. with honors, 1967. Cert. sch. psychologist. Psychologist, U. Oreg., Eugene, 1967-70; psychologist Spanish Peaks Mental Health Ctr., Pueblo, Colo., 1970-76, dir. child and adolescent services, 1977-82; dir. McClelland Ctr. for Child Study, Pueblo, 1982—; cons. schs. Author: Modifying Classroom Behavior, 1979, Classroom Applications for the Hard-To-Teach Child, 1974, also articles.

BUCKLEY, ROBERT, business executive; b. N.Y.C., July 15, 1928; s. Irving Herbert and Bertha (Goldberg) B.; m. Marilyn Carole Epsteen, Aug. 29, 1954; children—Brian, Illece, Elizabeth. B.S., U. So. Calif., 1954. Mktg. dir. Litton Industries, Los Angeles, 1954-63; pres., chief exec. officer Nat. Printing Converters, Inc., Van Nuys, Calif., 1963—; dir. Transworld Bank, COM Systems Inc., So. Calif. Signal Industries, Corp. Creative Service, inc. Mem. Valley Polit. Action Com. Served in U.S. Army, 1946-48. Democrat. Jewish. Patentee label tab cleaner. Office: 7722 Densmore Ave Van Nuys CA 91406

BUCKNER, KAY LAMOREUX, painter; b. Seattle, Dec. 26, 1935; d. Harvey DeWitt and Mary Eunice (Coble) Lamoreux; B.A. in Fine Art, U. Wash., Seattle, 1958; M.F.A. in Painting, Claremont (Calif.) Grad. Sch., 1961; m. Paul Eugene Buckner, Aug. 15, 1959; children—Matthew, Nathan. Profl. artist, 1961—; one-woman exhbns. include: Phoenix Gallery, Seattle, 1963, 12th Ave. Gallery, Eugene, Oreg., 1966, Gallery West, Portland, Oreg., 1973, 75, 77, 80, U. Idaho Gallery of Fine Art, Moscow, 1978, Kerns Art Center, Eugene, 1978, Frye Art Mus., Seattle, 1979; Oreg. Mus. Art, Eugene, 1981; group exhbns. include: Exhbn. NW Artists, Seattle, 1963, Am. Drawings '66, Mercyhurst (Pa.) Coll., 1966, Mainstreams '74, 76, Internat. Exhbn., Marietta, Ohio, 1974, 76, Greater Fall River (Mass.) Nat., 1976, 80, New Orleans Internat., 1978, 80, Nat. Small Painting Exhbn., Los Angeles, 1980, Nat. Landscape in Art Exhbn., Springfield, Ill., 1982; vis. lectr. fine art U. Oreg., Eugene, 1976-79. Recipient 1st prize Wash. Drawing Exhbn., 1957, 58, Puget Sound painter's award, 1959, 1st prize figure exhbn. Woessner Gallery, Seattle, 1962, spl. jury commendation Salem (Oreg.) Civic Center, 1976, 1st prize Greater Fall River Nat. Exhbn., 1976, 1st prize N.Mex. Internat., 1981; Avery fellow, 1960-61. Address: 2332 Rockwood Ave Eugene OR 97405

BUCKNER, PAUL EUGENE, sculptor; b. Seattle, June 16, 1933; s. Martin Monroe and Edna Laurel (Olson) B.; B.A., U. Wash., 1959; M.F.A., Claremont Grad. Sch., 1961; postgrad Slade Sch., Univ. Coll. London, 1961-62; m. Kay Lamoreux, Aug. 15, 1959; children—Matthew, Nathan. Studio asst., sculptor Albert Stewart, Claremont, 1959-61; one man shows Oreg. Mus. Art, Eugene, 1964; Gallery West, Portland, Oreg., 1977; Frye Art Mus., Seattle, 1979; exhibited in group shows Seattle Art Mus., 1964, 67; Oreg. Sculpture, Portland, 1968; Mainstreams Internat. Exhbns., Marietta, Ohio, 1971, 76, 77; Portland Art Mus., 1976; represented in permanent collections Salem (Oreg.) Civic Center, Olympic Coll., Bremerton, Wash., St. Paul's Cath. Ch., Silverton, Oreg., St. Mary's Cath. Ch., Hood River, Oreg., Leighton Pool, U. Oreg., Eugene, Sacred Heart Gen. Hosp., Eugene, Multnoma Athletic Club, Portland, United Ch. of Christ, Forest Grove, Oreg.; instr. Sculpture U. Wash., Seattle, summer 1959, 62, San Bernardino Valley Coll., 1961; mem. faculty Oreg., 1962—, prof., 1972—. Served with USCG, 1953-57. Avery fellow, 1959-61; Fulbright grantee, 1961-62; Oreg. U. faculty grantee, 1965; recipient prize Nat. Sculpture Rev., N.Y.C., 1977. Home: 2332 Rockwood Ave Eugene OR 97405 Office: Sch Architecture and Applied Arts U Oreg Eugene OR 97403

BUCKNER, PAULA JEAN, speech and lang. specialist: b. Pryor, Okla., Feb. 4, 1948; d. Elmer D. and Pauline M. Buckner. B.A., Calif. State U., San Jose, 1970, M.A., 1973. Tng. program speech and lang. VA Hosp., Palo Alto, Calif., 1970-71; speech and lang. specialist Hayward (Calif.) Unified Sch. Dist., 1972-73, Fremont (Calif.) Unified Sch. Dist., 1973-79, tchr. severely lang. handicapped, 1979—. Lic. speech pathologist, Calif. Mem. Am. (cert. clin. competence), Calif. speech and hearing assns. Home: 3329 Canongate Ct San Jose CA 95121

BUCKOVETZ, KATHERINE JOSEPHINE, social psychologist, consultant; b. Munich, Germany, Aug. 26, 1947; d. Martin Joseph and Monika (Huebler) B. A.A., Am. River Coll., 1966; B.A., U. Calif.-Berkeley, 1968; M.S., Calif. State U., 1970; Ed.D., U. San Francisco, 1984. Cert. community coll. counselor and instr., sch. psychologist, secondary tchr., Calif. Lab. technician Inst. Human Learning, Berkeley, 1967; asst. dir. Suicide Prevention Ctr., Hayward, Calif., 1969-71; state guidance dir. Peace Corps, Jamaica, 1971-73; counselor, spl. edn. supr. Shasta Unified Sch. Dist., Redding, Calif., 1973-78; rehab. specialist Comprehensive Rehab. Services, Fresno, Calif., 1978-79; psychol. services sect. supr. City of Stockton, (Calif.), 1979-83; dir. Contemporary Systems Inst., Stockton, Calif., 1983—; cons. organizational devel., employment of handicapped and economically disadvantaged; rape and child abuse counselor. Pres. ARC, 1965-66; mem. Women's Polit. Caucus; pres. Women in Mgmt., 1981; bd. dirs. Female Mgrs. Network, 1982; mem. Mayor's Com. Employing Handicapped. Recipient Action award of appreciation Peace Corps, 1973; VITAS cert. of award Jewish Employment and Vocat. Service, 1981; award for outstanding contbns. ARC, 1965. Mem. Am. Psychol. Assn., Calif. Psychol. Assn., Am. Personnel and Guidance Assn., Nat. Assn. Female Execs., AAUW. Democrat. Roman Catholic. Author: Creativity and Schizophrenia, 1970; Family Life Curriculum, 1972; Communication Skills Manual, 1969; The Deaf and the Law, 1979; Student College Prep Handbook, 1979; Handbook for Parents of EMR Students, 1979; Manuals on developing affirmative action program, needs, assessment and tng. program, 1981; Culture and the Urban Environment, 1982; Employing Economically Disadvantaged and Handicapped, 1982. Home: 3112 Kelley Ct Stockton CA 95207 Office: 300 N Harrison St Stockton CA 95203

BUDAGHER, JOHN A., state senator, lawyer; Albuquerque, June 13, 1946; s. John and Frances Dolores (Ramirez) B.; m. Sandra Kay C'Debaca, July 28, 1979; 1 son, John A. Grad. U. N.Mex.; J.D., U. Tulsa; M. in Law Estate Planning, U. Miami. Bar: N.Mex. 1974. Mem. Firm Johnson, Poulantis & Lanphere, N.Mex., 1974-75; asst. dist. atty. Santa Fe, 1975-76; sole practice, 1976—; mem. N.Mex. Senate, 1980—. Served with USAF, 1968-74. Mem. N.Mex. Bar Assn., VFW, DAV. Republican. Roman Catholic. Club: Elks. Office: 1115 3d St NW Albuquerque NM 87102

BUDD, HAROLD MONTGOMERY, composer; b. Los Angeles, May 24, 1936; s. Harold Montgomery and Dorothy Quentan (McNeill) B.; student Los Angeles City Coll., 1957-59; B.A., Calif. State U. at Northridge, 1963; Mus.M., U. So. Calif., 1966; m. Paula Bethsebe Katzman, June 27, 1960; children—Matthew Montgomery, Terrence Darian. Mem. faculty Calif. Inst. Arts, Valencia, 1969-76. Served with AUS, 1959-61. Nat. Endowment for Arts fellow, 1974, 79-80. Composer: The Candy-Apple Revision, 1970; The Pavilion of Dreams, 1972-76; recs. include The Pavilion of Dreams, 1978, The Plateaux of Mirror, 1980, The Serpent (In Quicksilver), 1981. Office: EG Records Inc 161 W 54th St New York NY 10019

BUDDE, DALE GENE, medical center executive; b. Parker, S.D., Jan. 19, 1939; s. Ervin D. and Mae E. (Nowstrup) B.; B.S., No. State Coll., S.D., 1965; M.S. in Health Care Adminstrn., Trinity U., 1970; m. Barbara S. Baldwin, Aug. 14, 1965; children—Jennifer M., Catherine M., Suzanne M., Theresa M., John D Andrew. Adminstr., Marshall County Hosp., Britton, S.D., 1966-68, Coteau des Prairies Hosp., Sisseton, S.D., 1968-69; adminstrv. resident Mercy Hosp., Denver, 1970; adminstr. St. James Hosp., Pontiac, Ill., 1971-73; pres. Mercy Med. Center, Denver, 1973—; mem. fin. com. Health Systems of Mercy, 1979-80, mem. human resource com., 1980-81; mem. liaison adv. bd. Dept. Health Affairs, Archdiocese of Denver, 1975—; chmn. Wellness Com., Cath. Health Care Corp., 1981—. Trustee Colo. Hosp. Shared Services Corp., 1975, chmn. 1976-77; trustee Snake River Family Health Center, Keystone, Colo., 1978—, Mountain States Hosp. Shared Services Corp., 1979—, Colo. Found. for Med. Care, 1980—. Served with USNG, 1962-69. Mem. Am. Hosp. Assn., Colo. Hosp. Assn. (trustee 1974—, sec. 1981-82, chmn. bd. dirs. 1983), Denver Met. Hosp. Council, Trinity U. Health Care Assn., Am. Coll. Hosp. Adminstrs., S.D. Hosp. Assn., Midtown Hosp. Assn. (chmn. bd. trustee 1976-78), Sigma Iota Epsilon. Republican. Roman Catholic. Home: 4955 Larkspur Dr Littleton CO 80123 Office: Mercy Medical Center 16th and Milwaukee St Denver CO 80206

BUDGE, REED WILLIAM, state senator; B.S., Utah State U.; m. Gwen Budge; 5 children. Mem. Idaho Senate from 32d dist., 1967—, pres. pro tempore, 1979 for 45th Legislature, vice chmn. Legis. Council. Past commr. of Caribou County. Served with U.S. Army, World War II. Decorated Silver Star, Purple Heart. Mem. Idaho Cattlemen's Assn., Am. Assn. Motor Vehicle Adminstrs., Council State Govts. (past chmn. Western Conf. com. on transp.). Republican. Club: Kiwanis. Office: PO Box 804 Soda Springs ID 83276*

BUDINGER, FRED CHARLES, geotech. engr.; b. Chgo., June 13, 1936; s. Charles Edward and Gertrude Rose (Brost) B.; B.A. in Math. and Physics, Ariz. State U., 1959; postgrad. Calif. State U., Los Angeles, 1972-73, in civil engring. Internat. Corr. Sch., 1969-72; m. Shirley Marie Watson, Aug. 5, 1961; children—Theresa, Elizabeth, Vincent, Jesse, Bernadete, Robert, Stephen, Clare, Martin. Tchr. math. Scottsdale (Ariz.) High Sch., 1959-60; tchr. sci. Central Cath. High Sch., Portland, Oreg., 1960-61; field engr. Warne Sergent & Hauskins Engrs., Phoenix, 1961-67; soil engr. S/G Testing Labs., Lompoc, Calif., 1967-72; br. mgr. Braun Skaggs & Kevorkian, Bakersfield, Calif., 1971-76; prin. Budinger & Assocs., Geotech. & Material Engrs., Spokane, Wash., 1976—. Registered civil engr., Calif., Oreg., Wash., Idaho, Mont. Mem. Internat. Soc. Soil Mechs. and Found. Engrs., ASCE (sect. pres. 1981-82), Assn. Soil and Found. Engrs., Structural Engrs. Assn. Wash., Wash. Soc. Profl. Engrs. (state trustee 1978-79), ASTM. Republican. Roman Catholic. Club: Rotary (club dir. 1975-76). Home: E 11116 21st St Spokane WA 99206 Office: N 920 Lake Spokane WA 99206

BUDKE, GORDON E., accountant; b. Aberdeen, Wash., Oct. 20, 1941; s. Clarence H. and Viola (Boerner) B.; m. Rhoda M. Paulson, Sept. 17, 1961; children—David, Jeffrey, Matthew. B.A., Eastern Wash. U., 1963. C.P.A., Wash. Staff acct. Randall, Emery, Campbell & Parker, Spokane, 1963-71, ptnr., 1971-73; ptnr. Coopers & Lybrand, Spokane, 1973-81, mng. ptnr., 1981—. Bd. dirs. Spokane Area Economic Devel. Council. Mem. Wash. Soc. C.P.A.s, Am. Inst. C.P.A.s. Clubs: Empire, Spokane. Contbg. author: The Emerging Business-Managing for Growth, 1983. Office: 1600 Seafirst Fin Center Spokane WA 99201

BUDLONG, THEODORE WARREN, insurance company executive; b. N.Y.C., Mar. 16, 1946; s. Theodore W. and Ware (Torrey) B.; B.A., Amherst Coll., 1968; M.A., Cornell U., 1971, Ph.D., 1973. Asst. prof. Purdue U., 1972-76; underwriting mgr. Workmen's Auto Ins. Co., Los Angeles, 1976-78; facultative underwriter Gen. Reins. Corp., San Francisco, 1978-79; v.p. underwriting Workmen's Auto Ins. Co., Los Angeles, 1979-82; regional acctg. mgr. CNA Ins., Los Angeles, 1983—. Contbr. articles to profl. jours. Home: 1262 1/2 Ozeta Terr Los Angeles CA 90069 Office: 600 S Commonwealth Ave Los Angeles CA 90005

BUDZINSKI, JAMES EDWARD, interior designer; b. Gary, Ind., Jan. 4, 1953; s. Edward Michael and Virginia (Caliman) B.; student U. Cin., 1971-76. Mem. design staff Perkins & Wills Architects, Inc., Chgo., 1973-75, Med. Architectonics, Inc., Chgo., 1975-76; v.p. interior design Interior Environs., Inc., Chgo., 1976-78; pres. Jim Budzinski Design, Inc., Chgo., 1978-80; asso. Robinson, Mills & Williams, San Francisco, 1980—; instr. design Harrington Inst. Design, Chgo.; cons. Chgo. Art Inst., Storwal Internat., Inc. Designs include 1st Chgo. Corp. Pvt. Banking Center, 1st Nat. Bank Chgo. Monroe and Wabash Banking Center, 1978, IBM Corp., San Jose, Deutsch Bank, Frankfort, Crowley Maritime Corp., San Francisco, offices for Brobeck, Phleger and Harrison, offices for chmn. bd. Fireman's Fund Ins. Cos. Office: Robinson Mills & Williams 153 Kearny St San Francisco CA 94108

BUECHEL, DONALD ROBERT, anesthesiologist, educator; b. Wichita, Kans., Sept. 29, 1924; s. Donald William and Bonnie Sue (Priddy) B.; A.B., U. Kans., 1947, M.D., 1949; m. Barbara Joan Bissett, Nov. 28, 1952; children—Jane, Sally, Donald Robert, Rebecca. Commd. lt. (j.g.), M.C., U.S. Navy, 1949, advanced through grades to capt., 1966; intern U.S. Naval Hosp., Charleston, S.C., 1949-50; resident in anesthesiology U.S. Naval Hosp., Bethesda, Md., 1951-53; chief anesthesia U.S. Naval Hosp., Camp Pendleton, Calif., 1953-57, Chelsea, Mass., 1957-61, Oakland, Calif., 1961-66, San Diego, 1966-70; dep. surgeon U.S. Mil. Assistance Command, Vietnam, 1971; comdg. officer U.S. Naval Hosp., Roosevelt Roads, P.R., 1972-75; ret., 1975; prof. clin. anesthesia Stanford U., 1975—; asst. clin. prof. U. Calif., San Francisco, 1961-67; asso. clin. prof. U. Calif., San Diego, 1970-72; sec. Arthur E. Guedel Meml. Anesthesia Center, San Francisco, 1979-80, pres., 1980—. Decorated Legion of Merit, Joint Services Commendation medal. Diplomate Am. Bd. Anesthesiology. Mem. Am. Soc. Anesthesiologists, AMA, Assn. Anesthetists Gt. Britain and Ireland, Fed. Health Care Execs. Office: 751 S Bascom Ave San Jose CA 95128

BUEHL, CYNTHIA R., youth facility administrator; b. Abington, Pa., May 18, 1954; d. Ernest H. Jr. and Helen F. (Wagner) B. B.A., Hood Coll., 1976. Teaching parent Yellowstone Boys Ranch, Billings, Mont., 1976-78, clin. supr., 1978-80; dir. Billings Youth Home, 1980—. Bd. dirs. St. Stephen's New Child Montessori Sch. Mem. Am. Personnel and Guidance Assn., Mont. Group Home Assn., Mont. Council Pvt. Child Care Agys., Mont. Residential Child Care Assn. Clubs: Toastmasters. Home: 637 Lewis St Billings MT 59101 Office: PO Box 20234 Billings MT 59104

BUEHLER, JOANNE MARGARET, engineering company executive; b. Utica, N.Y., Apr. 8, 1951; d. Jerome John and Adree Phyllis (Clark) Buehler. B.S. in Biology, SUNY, 1973; M.A., Mich. State U., 1975; postgrad. Boston U. Grad. asst. Mich. State U., East Lansing, 1975; tchr. chemistry Maple Shade (N.J.) High Sch., 1975-76; energy lectr./demonstrator Oak Ridge Assoc. Univs., 1976-77; plant communications coordinator Vt. Yankee Nuclear Power Corp., Vernon/Rutland, 1977-78; program coordinator Pub. Service Co. N.Y., Seabrook Sta.

Edn. Center, 1978-80, program devel. coordinator, 1980; mgr. pub. affairs West Coast, U.S. Ecology, Inc., Bellevue, Wash., 1980—. N.Y. Regents' scholar, 1969. Mem. AAAS, Pub. Relations Soc. Am., Am. Nuclear Soc., Women's Energy Forum, Energy Women's Round Table, Nuclear Energy Women (chmn. region 1979-80). Club: Evergreen Afghan Hound (past dir.). Contbr. articles to profl. jours. Office: 600 108th Ave NE Suite 530 Bellevue WA 98004

BUEHLER, SALLY SALMEN, clin. social worker; b. Newton, Mass., July 31, 1938; d. Stanley C. and Margaret (Green) Salmen; B.A., U. N.H., 1960; M.S.W., U. Calif., 1963; m. John Arthur Buehler, Aug. 24, 1971; 1 son, Daniel Lawrence. Psychiat. social worker, supr. Child Guidance Clinic, Children's Hosp., San Francisco, 1956-69, Family Service Agy., Pittsfield, Mass., 1970; pvt. practice psychiat. social work, Kentfield, Calif., 1970—. Fellow Soc. for Clin. Social Work; mem. Nat. Assn. Social Workers, Acad. Certified Social Workers. Home: 18 Turnagain Rd Kentfield CA 94904 Office: 1125 Sir Francis Drake Blvd Kentfield CA 94904

BUEKER, ROBERT ARTHUR, aeronautical engineer; b. Ft. Wayne, Ind., July 8, 1928; s. Chester Clemmens and Nellie Louise (Dardine) B.; B.S. in Aero. Engring., Purdue U., 1951; M.B.A., UCLA, 1964; m. Patricia June Huyser, Dec. 12, 1953; children—Robert Allen, Cynthia Diane, Design engr. Douglas Aircraft, Santa Monica, Calif., 1951-60; mem. tech. staff Aerospace Corp., El Segundo, Calif., 1960-66; mem. tech. staff TRW, Inc., Redondo Beach, Calif., 1966-78; project engr. Hughes Aircraft, Torrance, Calif., 1978—; dir. Destro Inc., Torrance. Mem. AIAA. Home: 7233 Columbus Dr Anaheim Hills CA 92807 Office: Hughes Aircraft 3060 W Lomita Blvd Torrance CA 90509

BUELL, EDWARD RICK, II, lawyer; b. Des Moines, Jan. 28, 1948; s. Edward Rick and Betty-Jo (Heffron) B.; B.S. with high honors, Mich. State U., 1969; J.D. magna cum laude, U. Mich., 1972; children—Erica Colleen, Edward Rick III. Bar: D.C. 1973, Calif. 1975; cert. specialist in taxation law, Calif. Assoc. firm Arent, Fox, Kintner, Plotkin & Kahn, Washington, 1972-74, Brobeck, Phlegher & Harrison, San Francisco, 1974-77; ptnr. Winokur, Schoenberg, Maier & Zang, San Francisco, 1977-81; ptnr. Knudsen, Buell & Berner, San Francisco, 1981—. Mem. ABA, San Francisco Bar Assn., Order of Coif. Contbr. articles to legal jours. Home: 50 Stewart Dr Tiburon CA 94920 Office: 4 Embarcadero Ctr Suite 2140 San Francisco CA 94111

BUERGER, JULIUS ALBERT, JR., real estate executive; b. Denver, Dec. 26, 1932; s. Julius Albert and Roberta Carolyn (Cresap) B.; B.S. in Bus. Adminstrn., U. Denver, 1956; student U. Colo., 1954-55; m. Joanne Rae Ainsworth, Sept. 9, 1955 (div. July 1975); children—Julius II, Raymond, Holly, Matthew; m. 2d, Greta E. Jonas, May 29, 1982. Sec.-treas. Buerger Bros. Supply Co., Denver, 1956-63; real estate mgmt. Van Schaack & Co., Denver, 1964-69; sales and devel. Perry & Butler, Denver, 1970-73; v.p. Lincoln Co. real estate, 1973-75, Moore Realty, Denver, 1975-80; with Property Brokers, Denver, 1980-82; pres. Buerger Realty Co., 1982—. Tchr. piano and organ. Bd. dirs. East Belleview Water and Sanitation Dist., 1967-74, treas., 1970-74; Republican precinct committeeman, 1968—, state and county del., 1968, 72, 74; bd. dirs. Denver br. Mental Health Assn. Colo., sec., 1977, 1st v.p., 1978-79; bd. dirs. Denver Mental Health Center, 1980—. Cert. property mgr. Mem. Timberline Toastmasters Internat. (pres. 1976, 79), Denver Round Table, Denver Musicians Assn., Beta Theta Pi. Home: 4351 W Ponds Circle Littleton CO 80123 Office: 5031 S Ulster Pkwy Suite 200 Denver CO 80237

BUERK, ARTHUR WISER, real estate development company executive; b. Seattle, Mar. 17, 1936; s. Arthur Wiser and Janet Stark (Main) B.; B.A. cum laude in Fin., U. Wash., 1958; M.B.A. in Mktg., Harvard U., 1963; m. Charlene Marie Weaver, Dec. 23, 1975; children—Teresa Marie Vall-Spinosa, Mark Mitchell, Rebecca Lynn Vall-Spinosa. Vice pres. 1812 Distbg. Co., Los Angeles, 1964-67; asst. to pres. Pacific Food Products Co., Seattle, 1967-68; dir. devel. U. Wash., Seattle, 1968-77, prof. personal fin., 1976—, dir. Devel. Council, 1977—; pres. Shurgard Capital Group, Olympia, Wash., 1977—; Mem. council Harvard U. Bus. Sch., 1979-83; v.p. Seattle Ctr. Found., 1980; chmn. Wash. State Republican Fin. Com., 1981-82. Served with Supply Corps, USN, 1958-60. Mem. Internat. Assn. Fin. Planners (pres. Puget Sound 1982-83), Self Service Storage Assn. (nat. treas., dir.), U. Wash. Alumni Assn., Harvard U. Bus. Sch. Assn. (pres., class sec.). Republican. Clubs: Seattle Tennis, Rainier, Wash. Athletic, Harvard Bus. Sch. Western Wash. (pres. 1971-72). Home: 3831 49th St NE Seattle WA 98105 Office: PO Box 187 Olympia WA 98507

BUETTNER, GEORGE ARTHUR, clergyman, counselor; b. Stockton, Calif., Nov. 10, 1938; s. George Rex and Doris Isabel (Allenberg) B.; m. Judy Mae Fuller, Sept. 3, 1960; children—Philip, Mark, Dee Ann. Grad. Eugene Bible Coll., 1959; B.A., Portland State U., 1972, M.A., 1981; M.A., Western Conservative Bapt. sem. 1978. Cert. counselor, sch. adminstr. Oreg. Ordained minister Assemblies of God Ch., 1961; minister, educator counselor Neighborhood Ch., Portland, Oreg., 1972-80, Grace Community Ch., Portland, 1980-82; pvt. practice in counseling; counselor North Clackamas Sch. Dist. 12, Milwaukie, Oreg.; instr. Portland State U. Mem. Am. Personnel and Guidance Assn., Evang. Theol. Soc. Democrat.

BUETTNER, MARK ROLAND, agronomist, educator; b. Cottonwood, Idaho, Sept. 9, 1949; s. Roland and Dorothea (Ruhoff) B.; m. Carol Ann Smith, Dec. 20, 1949; children—Heather, Jeffrey, Lisa. B.S., U. Idaho, 1972, M.S., 1974; Ph.D., Purdue U., 1978. Asst. prof. Colo. State U., Denver, 1978-79, Oreg. State U., Klamath Falls, 1979—. Mem. Am. Soc. Agronomy, Animal Sci. Soc. Am., Forage and Grassland Council. Office: PO Box 399 Klamath Falls OR 97601

BUFFINGTON, FORREST GRANT, assistant district attorney; b. Ventura, Calif., Oct. 25, 1954; s. David Lee and Lyn B.; B.A., Baylor U., 1976, J.D., 1978. Bar: Ariz. 1979, N.Mex. 1982. Sole practice law, Flagstaff, Ariz., 1980-81; staff atty. Navajo Legal Aid and Defender Service, Window Rock, Ariz., 1981, acting dir., 1981-82; asst. dist. atty. McKinley County (N.Mex.), 1982—. Mem. Ariz. Bar Assn., Hopi Bar Assn., Navajo Bar Assn. Home: PO Box 3072 Gallup NM 87301 Office: McKinley County Courthouse Gallup NM 87301

BUFFINGTON, LINDA BRICE, interior designer; b. Long Beach, Calif., June 21, 1936; d. Harry Bryce and Marguerite Leonora (Tucciarone) Van Bellehem; student El Camino Jr. Coll., 1955-58, U. Calif., Irvine, 1973—; children—Lisa Ann, Phillip Lynn. with Public Finance, Torrance, Calif., 1954-55, Beneficial Finance, Torrance and Hollywood, Calif., 1955-61; interior designer Vee Nisley Interiors, Newport Beach, Calif., 1964-65, Leon's Interiors, Newport Beach, 1965-69; partner Marlind Interiors, Tustin, Calif., 1969-70; owner, designer Linda Buffington Interiors, Villa Park, Calif., 1970—; cons. builders, housing developments. Mem. Bldg. Industry Assn., Sales and Mktg. Council, Home Builders Council, Nat. Assn. Home Builders. Republican. Club: POCA. Office: 17767 Santiago Blvd Villa Park CA 92667

BUFFORD, RODGER KEITH, psychologist, educator; b. Santa Rosa, Calif., Dec. 23, 1944; s. John Samuel and Evelyn A. (Rude) B.; m. Kathleen A. Parson; children—Heather, Brett. B.A., King's Coll., 1966; M.A., U. Ill., 1970; Ph.D., 1971. Lic. psychologist, Ga., Oreg., Va. Psychologist, Adolph Meyer Zone Ctr., Decatur, Ill., 1969-70; asst. prof. psychology Am. U., Washington, 1971-76; asst. prof., chmn. dept. psychology Huntington (Ind.) Coll., 1976-77; assoc. prof. Psychol. Studies Inst., Atlanta, 1977-81; psychologist Atlanta Counseling Ctr., 1980-82; assoc. prof., chmn. dept. psychology Western Baptist Sem., Portland, Oreg., 1982—; pvt. practice psychology, 1973—; dir. Mental Health Assn., Huntington, Ind., 1976-77. Elder, Chapel Woods Presbyterian Ch., 1983. USPHS trainee, 1967-68, 70-71; Am. U. Faculty Research grantee, 1972. Mem. Am. Psychol. Assn., Midwestern Psychol. Assn., Southeastern Psychol. Assn., Western Psychol. Assn., Christian Assn. Psychol. Studies, Am. Sci. Affiliates, Ga. Psychol. Assn. Author: The Human Reflex: Behavioral Psychology in Biblical Perspective, 1981; contbr. chpts. to texts, numerous articles to profl. jours. Home: 19504 Hidden Springs Rd West Linn OR 97068 Office: 5511 SE Hawthorne Blvd Portland OR 97215

BUFFUM, NANCY KAY, interior designer; b. Portland, Oreg., Aug. 10, 1941; d. William Cheely and Wanda (Camblin) Whitman; student Shasta Coll., 1959-60, U. Calif.-Berkeley, 1960-63; m. Jack Erwin Buffum, Mar. 24, 1961 (div. 1981); children—Andrew Lewis, Airenne. Exec. sec. Pacific Mut. Life Ins. Co., San Francisco, 1961-63; gen. cashier N.Am. Brokers, San Francisco, 1963-64; mgr. So. area office Lindsey & Co., Sacramento, 1964-65; escrow office, sales rep. Kennicott Constrn. Co., Redding, Calif., 1967-69; office mgr., gen. ptnr. Buffum & Assocs., Redding, 1969-72; asst. designer Penthouse Interiors, Redding, 1973-75; owner, designer The Design Works, Redding, 1976—; lectr. on design and antiques to community groups. Pres., Shasta County Easter Seal Soc., 1971-72, Redding Elem. Sch. PTA, 1973-77, trustee, adv. com., 1975-78; bd. dirs. Redding Mus.; adv. KIXE Pub. TV Sta.; mem. Redding Planning Commn.; mem. adv. bd. Pvt. Industry Council. Recipient award for pub. service Rotary Internat., 1976. Mem. Nat. Home Furnishing Assn., Am. Soc. Interior Designers (assoc.), Inst. Bldg. Designers, DAR (hon. pub. service award), Redding C. of C. (dir. 1981). Republican. Club: Soroptimist. Office: 1600 California St Redding CA 96001

BUFORD, CARMEN, univ. ofcl., ednl. cons.; b. Los Angeles, May 31, 1932; d. George and Gladys (Edgenton) Buford; student Oberlin Coll., 1950-51; B.A. in Music with distinction, Calif. State U., Dominguez Hills, 1975, M.A. in Humanities, 1978; doctoral candidate UCLA; children—Laurine Towler, Jocelyn Towler, Michael Towler, Virginia Towler, Carolyn Towler, Stephanie Towler. Clerical worker in public sector and pvt. industry, 1952-73; job devel. specialist Compton Community Coll., 1976-77; tchr.-discussion leader Project INFO, Whittier, Calif., 1976-79; adminstrv. asst. Calif. State U., Dominguez Hills, Carson, 1977-80, acting coordinator Women's Center, 1979-80, asst. to dean Univ. Coll., 1980-83, asst. dean, 1983—; cons. on vocat. and ednl. equity State of Calif., 1981—; mem. steering com. for Aequus III Model Program for Sex Equity in Ednl. Policy and Adminstrn.; condr. workshops, tchr., lectr. in field; recitalist, organist and music tchr. St. Anselm's Cath. Ch., Los Angeles, Calvary Meth. Ch., Los Angeles. Los Angeles area coordinator Black Caucus, 1978. Named South Bay Woman of Yr. in Edn., 1980. Mem. Calif. Personnel and Guidance Assn. (chairperson women's caucus 1980), Am. Personnel and Guidance Assn., Nat. Assn. Student Personnel Adminstrs., Nat. Assn. Women Deans, Adminstrs. and Counselors, Nat. Assn. Negro Musicians, Am. Guild Organists, Music Tchrs. Assn. Calif., AAUW, Assn. Black Women Historians, Assn. for Study Afro-Am. Life and History, Am. Coll. Personnel Assn., Calif. Coll. Personnel Assn., Assn. Afro Am. Studies, Calif. Concerns, Coll. English Assn., Natl. Women's Studies Assn., Western Assn. Historians, Third World Counselors Assn., Black Women's Ednl. Policy and Research Network, Phi Delta Kappa. Democrat. Mem. African Methodist Episcopal Zion Ch. Office: 1000 E Victoria St Carson CA 90747

BUFORD, WILLIAM HOLMES, JR., computer systems co. exec.; b. Ruston, La., June 15, 1934; s. William Holmes and Virginia (Holloway) B.; B.S. in Physics, La. State U., 1956; postgrad. U. So. Calif., 1958-61; m. Catherine de Montmeja, Mar. 17, 1979; children—William Holmes III, Deryl Louise, Elodie de Montmeja. Dir. advanced systems Marquardt Corp., Van Nuys, Calif., 1958-69; v.p. advanced studies Satellite Positioning Corp., Encino, Calif., 1969-70; v.p. Seismark Internat.-System Engring., Reseda, Calif., 1970-71; pres. Codevintec Pacific, Inc., Woodland Hills, Calif., 1971-79, Electronic Frontiers Inc., Woodland Hills, 1979—; dir. Seismark Internat., Inc., Reseda. Served to 1st lt. USAF, 1956-58. Patentee nuclear tech., sonar navigation. Home: 19407 Shenango Dr Tarzana CA 91356 Office: 357 N Canon Dr Beverly Hills CA 90218

BUGE, EDWARD WILLIAM, accountant; b. Chgo., Nov. 9, 1911; s. William Dwight and Clarice (Nicholson) B.; B.A., U. Ill., 1933; B.A. in Accounting, Walton Sch. Commerce, 1934; m. Margaret Louise Terhune, June 25, 1938; 1 son, David Edward. Accountant, Lybrand, Ross Bros. and Montgomery, Chgo., 1934-44; with S. C. Johnson, Racine, Wis., 1944-46, Marathon Corp., Menasha, Wis., 1946-47, Stewart Motor Sales, Indpls., 1947-49; with Bernardin, Inc., Evansville, Ind., 1949-68, controller, mem. exec. com., 1960-68; v.p. Bernardin Can., Ltd., Toronto, Ont., 1960-68, dir., 1960-68; treas. Neptune, Inc., Evansville, 1963—; prin. E. W. Buge C.P.A., Tucson, 1968—; pres. Tucson Ornamental Iron, 1972-74; pres. Task Analysis Center, Inc., Tucson, 1974—; dir. Carol Lighting, Inc., Tucson. Chmn. Tax Adjustment Bd., Evansville, 1959-61. C.P.A., Ill., Ind., Wis., Ariz. Mem. Nat. Assn. Accountants (pres. Tucson chpt. 1971-72), Fin. Execs. Inst., Am. Inst. C.P.A.'s, Budget Execs. Inst., Nat. Assn. Credit Mem. (pres. 1962-63), Ind. Mfrs. Assn. (taxation com. 1961-66), C. of C. (taxation com. 1964-68). Author: How to Get More Net From The Gross Sales Dollar, 1963; Administering the Financial Function of a Business, 1977; Business Financing Handbook, 1981. Contbr. articles to profl. jours. Home and Office: 4444 E Whitman St Tucson AZ 85711

BUHISAN, ANGELITO TAGANILE, JR., lawyer; b. Manila, Sept. 4, 1946; s. Angelito T. and Rosalia L. (Llepun) B.; came to U.S., 1952, naturalized, 1956; B.A. (Univ. Scholar), U. Kans., 1969; J.D., (Univ. Scholar), U. Calif., Davis, 1975; postgrad. San Francisco State U., 1976-77, City Coll. San Francisco, 1978; student Command and Gen. Staff Coll., 1980—. Coordinator vocat. edn. San Jose City Coll., 1972; comdr. U.S. Army Res. Army Hosp., Sacramento, 1972-73; legal clk. dist. atty.'s office Sacramento, 1974-75; legis intern to Senator Moscone, Sacramento, 1974-75; atty. Community Action for Legal Services, N.Y.C., 1978—; instr., lectr. U. Calif., Davis, 1974-75. Served as officer U.S. Army, 1969-71, to maj. Res. Mem. U. Calif. Sch. Law Alumni Assn., Internat. Union Security Officers, U. Kans. Alumni Assn., Pershing Rifles, Scabbard and Blades. Poetry pub. in anthologies; copyrighted and recorded numerous works. Democrat. Home: 6254 Blossom Ave San Jose CA 95123 also 80 Bruce Ave San Francisco CA 94112

BUHLER, WILLIAM IVES, lawyer; b. St. Paul, Jan. 31, 1930; s. Ernest O. and Harriet (Ives) B.; B.S., U. Minn., 1952; J.D., U. N.Mex., 1956; m. Betty Ann Buhler, Sept. 4, 1952; children—Susan Elizabeth, William Ives II, Wendy Lee. Admitted to N.Mex. bar, 1957, since practiced in Truth or Consequences; chmn. bd. First Sierra Nat. Bank, 1974-76. City commr., Truth or Consequences, 1961-65; chmn. Sierra County Democrats, 1967-69. Bd. dirs. Carrie Tingley Crippled Children Hosp. Found. Served with USN, 1952-54 to lt. comdr. Res., 1954-67. Mem. C. of C. (pres. 1958-59), Sierra County Hist. Soc. (pres. 1971-81). Democrat. Episcopalian (lay reader, sr. warden). Club: Rotary (pres. 1979-80). Home: 1800 Riverside Dr Truth or Consequences NM 87901 Office: 418 Main St Truth or Consequences NM 87901

BUKOFSKY, WARD MARKS, accountant; b. Mpls., Aug. 12, 1952; s. Milton G. and Ethel Jean (Abrahams) B.; m. Mari Pernice Shone, Aug. 7, 1976; 1 dau., Jessica Dyan. B.A. cum laude, UCLA, 1974. C.P.A., Calif. Staff acct. Braverman, Codron & Co., Beverly Hills, Calif., 1974-80, ptnr., 1981—, mng. ptnr. Newport Beach Office, 1982—. Mem. Am. Inst. C.P.A.s, Calif. Soc. C.P.A.s. Home: Fox Hills CA Office: 233 S Beverly Dr Beverly Hills CA 90212 also 19752 MacArthur Blvd Suite 150 Irvine CA 92715

BUKTENICA, DWANE HAROLD, engineer; b. Chgo., May 28, 1947; s. Harold Joseph and Ly Doll Helen (Murray) B.; A.A. in Bus. Mgmt., Mt. San Antonio Coll., 1979, A.S. in Real Estate, 1980; m. Nancy Louise Goble, Aug. 31, 1968; children—Alicia Michelle, Jennifer Monique, Amanda Mellissa, Jason Douglas. Asst. schedule engr. Fluor Engrs. and Constructors, Los Angeles, 1969-72; assoc. schedule engr. Fluor Metals and Mining, San Mateo, Calif., 1972-75; sr. schedule engr. Ralph M. Parsons Co., Pasadena, Calif., 1975; supr. project controls Holmes & Narver, Inc., Orange, Calif., 1975-81; mgr. Cost and Scheduling Occidental Engring. Co., Irvine, Calif., 1981-82; project controls mgr. SF/Braun, Orange, Calif., 1982—. Served with USN, 1966-69. Mem. Am. Assn. Cost Engrs., North Orange County Bd. Realtors, Calif. Assn. Realtors, Nat. Assn. Realtors. Republican. Roman Catholic. Home: 20925 Gold Run Dr Diamond Bar CA 91765 Office: 505 S Main St Orange CA 92668

BULGIN, RICHARD GREGORY, JR., nuclear cons.; b. Ft. Smith, Ark., Apr. 7, 1919; s. Richard Gregory and Grace Andrea (Dobyns) B.; m. Marion Adele Kunz, July 11, 1942; children—Ann Bulkley, Richard Gregory. Student, U. Ark., 1937-40; grad. Army War Coll., 1957, Indsl. Coll., 1962. Commd. cadet U.S. Army Air Corps, 1940, advanced through grades to brig. gen., 1968; dir. ops. and logistics, indsl. systems designs, 1940-60, dir. strategic plans, policies, 1960-70; ret., 1970; v.p. Energy Equities, Inc., Albuquerque, 1970-75; founder, exec. dir. Associated Nuclear Cons. of Am. Ltd., Albuquerque, 1975—; lectr. in field. Sustaining mem. Republican Nat. Com., 1981, county com., 1982, ward chmn., 1982; adv. com. Kirtland AFB, 1970-79. Mem. Lambda Chi Alpha. Clubs: Town, Petroleum, Blue and Silver, Masons. Contbr. articles to profl. jours. Home: 504 Aliso Dr SE Albuquerque NM 87108 Office: 8521 Central Ave NE Albuquerque NM 87108

BULL, BRENDA LEE, air force officer; b. Kendallville, Ind., Dec. 21, 1942; d. Howard Paul and Marjorie Ellen (Trowbridge) Frick. B.S. in Med. Technology, Mich. State U., 1966; M.A. in Vocat. Rehab. Counseling, 1967. Commd. 2d lt., USAF, 1968; advanced through grades to maj., 1980; personnel officer McConnell AFB, Kans., 1968-71, HQ USAF, Pentagon, 1971-72, Wiesbaden AB, Germany, 1972-74, Lindsey AS, Germany, 1974-76, Andrews AFB, Md., 1976-80, chief Consol. Base Personnel Office, Castle, Calif., 1980—. Mem. Air Force Assn., Atwater Bus. and Profl. Women's Club (corresponding sec. 1982-83). Presbyterian.

BULL, BRIAN STANLEY, physician, educator; b. Watford, Hertfordshire, Eng., Sept. 14, 1937; s. Stanley and Agnes Mary (Murdoch) B.; came to U.S., 1954, naturalized, 1961; B.S. in Zoology, Walla Walla Coll., 1957; M.D., Loma Linda (Calif.) U., 1961; m. Maureen Hannah Huse, June 3, 1963; children—Beverly Velda, Beryl Heather. Intern, Yale U., 1961-62, resident in anat. pathology, 1962-63; resident in clin. pathology NIH, Bethesda, Md., 1963-65, fellow in hematology and electron microscopy, 1965-66, staff hematologist, 1966-67, research asst. dept. anatomy Loma Linda U., 1958, dept. microbiology, 1959, asst. prof. pathology, 1968-71, assoc. prof., 1971-73, prof., chmn. dept. pathology, 1973—, cons. pathologist Med. Center, 1968—; vis. prof. Institut de Pathologie Cellulaire, Paris, 1972, 74, Royal Postgrad. Med. Sch., London, 1972, U. Wis.-Madison, 1973, U. Ohio, Columbus, 1974, U. Minn., Mpls., 1979, U. Hawaii, 1981; vis. fellow Wolfson Coll., Cambridge, Eng., 1981. Served with USPHS, 1963-67. Nat. Inst. Arthritis and Metabolic Diseases fellow, 1967-68; recipient Daniel D. Comstock Meml. award Loma Linda U., 1961, Merck Manual award, 1961, Mosby Scholarship Book award, 1961; Ernest B. Cotlove Meml. lectr. Acad. Clin. Lab. Physicians and Scientists, 1972. Diplomate Am. Bd. Pathology. Fellow Am. Soc. Clin. Pathologists, Am. Soc. Hematology, Coll. Am. Pathologists, N.Y. Acad. Scis.; mem. AMA, Assn. Pathology Chmn., Calif. Soc. Pathologists, San Bernardino County Med. Soc., Acad. Clin. Lab. Physicians and Scientists, Am. Soc. Exptl. Pathology, Sigma Xi, Alpha Omega Alpha. Seventh-day Adventist. Contbr. chpts. to books and numerous articles to med. jours. Patentee in field. Home: 24489 Barton Rd Loma Linda CA 92354 Office: Dept Pathology and Lab Medicine Loma Linda U Sch Medicine Loma Linda CA 92354

BULLARD, GILDA, state govt. ofcl.; b. Chicago Heights, Ill., Dec. 12, 1927; d. Pietro Antonio and Philomena D'Antonoli; B.S., Calif. State U., Sacramento, 1967, M.B.A., 1973; 1 son, David L. Gard. With Pacific Telephone Co., 1945-61; with State of Calif., 1961—, fiscal specialist in state welfare programs, 1966-74, staff mgr. licensing div., Sacramento, 1974-76, San Jose, 1975, citation hearing officer on appeals by nursing homes Dept. Health, Berkeley, 1976-78, mgr., fed.-audits specialist, audits and investigations div. Dept. Health Services, 1978—; part-time instr. Am. River Coll., 1976-77, Consumnes River Coll., 1980-83. Mem. Nat. Assn. Accts. (asst. treas. 1971, editor 1971), AAUW, Calif. State Employees Assn. (editor 1971, 72, chpt. pres. 1977, 81, 82, 83). Presbyterian. Home: 423 Alvarado Ave Davis CA 95616 Office: 714 P St Sacramento CA 95814

BULLEN, ROBERT BUDGE, real estate broker; b. Salt Lake City, Apr. 5, 1926; s. Roy and Annie (Nibley) B.; B.S., U. Utah, 1947; m. Janice Squires, Dec. 28, 1955; children—Robert Squires, Joan, Rebecca. Spl. agt. Fidelity and Deposit Co. Md., Salt Lake City and Portland, Oreg., 1947-52; with Merrill Lynch, Pierce Fenner & Smith, Inc., Salt Lake City, 1953-55; account exec. Schwabacher & Co., Salt Lake City, 1955-66, mem. corporate finance dept., San Francisco, 1967-68; mgr. corporate finance dept. Goodbody & Co., San Francisco, 1968-71; instl. account exec. Equitable Securities, Morton & Co., Inc., San Francisco, 1971-72; instl. account exec. R.W. Pressprich & Co., Inc., San Francisco, 1972-73; pvt. investment mgr., San Francisco, 1973-76, realtor asso. Mason-McDuffie Co., Walnut Creek, Calif., 1976-81; asso. broker Security Pacific Real Estate Brokerage Co., Walnut Creek, 1981—. Del. Republican party state conv. Utah, 1960, 62, voting dist. chmn., 1964. Fellow Fin. Analysts Fedn.; mem. Utah Securities Dealers Assn. (pres. 1962-63), Security Analysts San Francisco, Contra Costa Bd. Realtors, Solano Bd. Realtors, Scottsdale Assn., Inc. (treas., dir. 1978-79), Sigma Chi Alumni Assn. San Francisco. Mem. Ch. Jesus Christ of Latter-day Saints (ordained elder 1945, Sunday sch. pres. 1965-74). Home: 342 El Divisadero Ave Walnut Creek CA 94598 Office: 587 Ygnacio Valley Rd Walnut Creek CA 94596

BULLER, ELAINE EVELYN, executive secretary, real estate agent; b. Jacksonville, Oreg., May 2, 1929; d. Horace A. and Evelyn Jenkins; m. Glenn R. Buller; children—Bob, Donald, Linda, Kathy. Student Pacific Union Coll. Lic. real est. agt., Calif. Exec. sec. St. Helena (Calif.) C. of C., 1948—; real est. agt., mgr. small rest home. Mem. Nat. Assn. Realtors, Calif. Assn. Realtors, Napa County Bd. Realtors. Republican. Seventh Day Adventist. Office: 1508 Main St St Helena CA 94574

BULLIN, CHRISTINE NEVA, arts administrator; b. New Plymouth, N.Z., Apr. 13, 1948; d. Kenneth and Hazel Iris B. B.A., Wellesley Coll., 1969; M.L.A., Simmons Coll., 1973. Dir., Opera New England, Boston, 1974-78; with San Francisco Opera, 1978-81; mgr. San Francisco Opera Ctr., 1981—. Office: War Memorial Opera House San Francisco CA 94102

BULLIS, DAVID JAMES, clinical and counseling psychologist; b. Plattsburgh, N.Y., Dec. 9, 1947; s. Frank James and Delphine Marie (Ryer) B. m. Betty Marie Merchant, June 7, 1969; children—Damon, Danica. Ph.D., Harvard U., 1976. Lic. psychologist, Colo., N.Mex. Sch. psychologist Shiprock (N.Mex.) Boarding Sch., 1970-72; behavior specialist Borrego Pass (N.Mex.) Sch., 1974-76; pvt. practice psychology, Durango, Colo., 1976—; mem. staff dept. psychology Ft. Lewis Coll., Durango, 1980—; cons. Children's Devel. Evaluative Clinic, Tri-County Head Start Program, others. Served with Air N.G., 1970-76. Recipient Faculty Devel. award Ft. Lewis Coll., 1982. Mem. Am. Psychol. Assn., Am. Orthopsychiat. Assn., Soc. for Research and Child Devel. Home: 30 Moenkopi Dr Durango CO 81301 Office: 1474 Main Ave Suite 203 Durango CO 81301

BULLOCK, BRUCE LEWIS, computer scientist; b. Bartlesville, Okla., July 28, 1947; s. Oakle Porter and Jane Katherine (Livingston) B.; B.S. in Physics, U. Calif., Riverside, 1970, B.S. in Mathematics, 1970; m. Cheryl Kea Williams, Sept. 6, 1969; children—Amy Elizabeth, Chad Michael. Sr. staff computer scientist, head Intelligent Systems Group, Hughes Research Lab., Malibu, Calif., 1970-83; v.p. Fed. Systems Teknowledge Inc., Westlake, Calif., 1983—. Air Force Office Sci. Research grantee, 1973—; Howard Hughes doctoral fellow, 1975—. Mem. Assn. for Computing Machinery, Pattern Recognition Soc., Am. Assn. for Artificial Intelligence. Contbr. articles in field. to profl. jours.; researcher artificial intelligence, Image processing and robotics. Office: 2659 Towngate Rd Suite 100 Westlake CA 91361

BULLOCK, DOROTHY DODSON, educator, counselor, clergyman; b. Hannibal, Mo., Aug. 19, 1928; d. Walter E. and Emma R. (Seeger) Dodson; B.S. in Home Econs., U. Ariz., 1951; postgrad. U. Utah, 1952; M.A. in Counseling, Ariz. State U., 1969, postgrad. 1969-74; Ph.D. in Edn., 1977, M.A. in Theology, 1980, Ph.D. in Theology, 1981; 1 dau. by previous marriage, Pamela Jean. Tchr. home econs., secondary schs., Phoenix, Thatcher, Ariz., 1951-54; tchr. primary sch., Anne Arundel County, Md., Tokyo, 1955-59; tchr. primary level pub. schs., Prince Georges County, Md., 1960-65, Brownsville, Tex., 1966-67, Madison Sch. Dist., Ariz., 1967-70; tchr. emotionally and educationally handicapped, Phoenix, 1971-74; spl. edn. cons. Cartwright Sch. Dist., 1974-80; mem. faculty Ariz. State U., 1976-77; ret., 1980; cons. in field, 1980—; ordained minister Univ. of Healing, 1977. Bd. dirs. Goodly Renewal Found. Mem. Am. Personnel and Guidance Assn., Nat. Assn. of Sch. Psychologists, Nat., Ariz. assns. for children with learning disabilities, Council for Exceptional Children, Nat. Audistic Soc., Delta Kappa Gamma. Clubs: Am. Appaloosa. Author: A Simplified Phonetic Approach, 1974; Give Your Child Permission to Unfold, 1980. Home and office: Box 150 Route 11 Silver City NM 88061

BULLPITT, DORNA ELIZABETH, educator; b. San Francisco, July 21, 1934; d. George Berry and Anna W. (Stevens) Martin; m. Darrell D. Slone, June 17, 1956; children—Dori Ayers, Linda, Julie; m. 2d, Howard Bullpitt, June 5, 1976. B.S. in Bus. Adminstrn., Lewis and Clark Coll., Portland, Oreg., 1956; M.S. in Occupational Edn., Central Wash. U., Ellensburg, 1983. Librarian, instr. Olympia (Wash.) Tech. Community Coll., part-time 1971-75, instr., 1975-81, dir. placement and coop. edn. programs, 1981—. Wash. Bd. for Community Coll. Edn. grantee, 1980. Mem. Am. Vocat. Assn., Wash. Vocat. Assn., Am. Assn. Women in Community and Jr. Colls., Northwest Placement Assn., Western Assn. Student Employment Adminstrs., Wash. Assn. Student Employment Adminstrs., Wash. Coop. Edn. Consortium. Office: 2011 Mottman Rd SW Olympia WA 98502

BULTMANN, PHYLLIS WETHERELL, journalist; b. Ottumwa, Iowa, Aug. 21, 1923; d. Harry Gillette and Venice B. (Lewis) Wetherell; B.A., UCLA, 1944, M.A., 1945, Ph.D., 1950; m. William Arnold Bultmann, Dec. 28, 1949; 1 dau., Janice. Instr. Ark. State U., Conway, 1950-58, Ohio Wesleyan U., Delaware, 1958-64, Western Wash. U., Bellingham, 1966-71, 80—; profl. writer columnist SEA Mag., Newport Beach, Calif., 1973—; columnist Everett (Wash.) Herald, 1981—; public relations officer Press Boat, PITCH Regatta, Bellingham, 1976-78; sr. Fulbright lectr., East Pakistan, 1960-61; dir. Maritime Heritage Found., Bellingham, 1980—. Mem. Conf. Brit. Studies. Episcopalian. Clubs: Bellingham Yacht; Squalicum Yacht (commodore 1981-82). Author: Two Burners and An Ice Chest, 1977; (with Bill Bultmann) Border Boating, 1979; Editor: (with W.A. Bultmann) Current Research in British Studies, 1975; (with Leroy Dresbeck) British Studies Intelligencer, 1972-77. Home and office: 447 14th St Bellingham WA 98225

BULTMANN, WILLIAM ARNOLD, historian; b. Monrovia, Calif., Apr. 10, 1922; s. Paul Gerhardt and Elsa (Johnson) B.; A.B., U. Calif. at Los Angeles, 1943, Ph.D., 1950; m. Phyllis Jane Wetherell, Dec. 28, 1949; 1 dau., Janice Jane. Asso. prof. history Central Ark. U., Conway, 1949-52, prof., 1954-57; asso. prof. Ohio Wesleyan U., Delaware, 1957-61, prof., 1961-65; prof. Western Wash. U., Bellingham, 1965—, chmn. dept., 1968-70, dean arts and scis., 1970-72, provost, 1971-73; vis. asso. prof. U. Tex., Austin, 1952-53; vis. prof. U. N.H., summers 1965, 66; acad. cons. Wash. Commn. for Humanities, 1973—, Nat. Endowment for Humanities, 1976—; reader Ednl. Testing Service Princeton, 1973—. Bd. dirs. Bellingham Maritime Heritage Found., 1980—; adminstrv. officer Bellingham Power Squadron, 1981-82, comdr., 1982—. Fulbight sr. lectr. Dacca (Bangladesh) U., 1960-61; Ohio Wesleyan U. research fellow, 1964; Fund for Advancement Edn. fellow for fgn. study, 1953-54; recipient research award Social Sci. Research Council, 1957. Mem. Am. Hist. Assn., Ch. Hist. Soc., Conf. Brit. Studies, Pacific, Pacific N.W. confs. Brit. studies, AAUP, Phi Beta Kappa, Phi Delta Kappa, Pi Gamma Mu. Episcopalian. Clubs: Park Athletic Recreation, Bellingham Yacht (chmn. public relations com. 1981—), Squalicum Yacht (trustee 1979-82), Birch Bay Yacht, Co-author: Border Boating, 1978; co-founder, mem. editorial bd. Albion, 1968—; mng. editor Brit. Studies Intelligencer, 1973-80; co-editor Current Research in British Studies, 1975; feature writer, columnist Sea mag., 1974—; feature writer Venture mag., 1981—. Home: 447 14th St Bellingham WA 98225 Office: Dept History Western Wash U Bellingham WA 98225

BUMB, MICHAEL JOHN, advertising representative; b. Los Angeles, Sept. 22, 1956; s. August Joseph and Ilene (Wolverton) B.; m. Marcia Lynn Lance, July 27, 1980. B.S. in Communications, Lewis and Clark Coll., 1979. Staff, Bus. Success mag., Portland, Oreg., 1979-80; advt. mgr. People Potential mag., Portland, 1980; circulation dir. Travel Oregon mag., Portland, 1980-81; coop. advt. dir. Sta. KMJK, Portland, 1981-82; advt. mgr. Sta. KXL, Portland, 1982—; freelance announcer. Mem. Portland Ad 2 Club. Democrat. Clubs: Wilamette Athletic (Portland); Lake Sports and Fitness (Lake Oswego, Oreg.). Home: 2120 SW Vermont St Portland OR 97219 Office: Sta KXL 1415 Ankeny St Portland OR 97214

BUMGARNER, MARLENE ANNE, author, educator; b. Yorkshire, Eng., Nov. 6, 1947; came to U.S., 1949, naturalized, 1965; d. Rowland and May (Whittaker) Skirrow; A.A., Coll. San Mateo, 1967; B.A., San Diego State Coll., 1970; M.A., San Jose State U., 1982; m. John Owen Bumgarner, June 17, 1967 (div. 1982); children—Doña Ana, John Rowland; m. 2d, Robert John Eltgroth, Feb. 19, 1983. Tech. editor electronics firms, 1967-70; coordinator Peer Counseling Center, Las Cruces, N.Mex., 1970-72; tchr. elem. sch., 1974-76; owner, mgr. Morgan Hill Trading Post, natural food store, Morgan Hill, Calif., 1976-78; editor Natural Living Newsline, Morgan Hill, 1979-81; mgr. Natural Living Assocs., 1979—; dir. Country Living Day Sch., 1980—; instr. Gavilan Community Coll., Gilroy, Calif., 1980—; sr. tech. writer Book & Babbage Inc., 1982—. Leader, founder La Leche League of Morgan Hill, 1977—; Sunday Sch. supt. St. John's Episcopal Ch., Morgan Hill, 1982—; coordinator Morgan Hill Community Ctr., 1983—. Mem. Soc. Children's Book Writers, Nat. Newspaper Food Writers and Editors Assn., Calif. Press Women, Soc. for Tech. Communication. Author: Book of Whole Grains, 1976; Organic Cooking for Not So Organic Mothers, 1980; contbg. author: People's Cookbook, 1977; Real Food Places, 1981; columnist San Jose (Calif.) Mercury, 1977-80; contbg. editor Mothering Mag., 1980—. Office: PO Box 1326 Morgan Hill CA 95037

BUNCE, RICHARD SMITHDEAL, sociologist; b. Washington, June 8, 1945; s. Edward Donald and Betty Francis (Smithdeal) B.; m. Deane Calhoun, Aug. 26, 1967; children—Noah Yarrow, Cody Webster. B.A., Coll. Wooster, 1967; M.S., U. Wis., 1969. Project dir. Nat. Citizens Com. Broadcasting, N.Y.C., 1972; fieldwork coordinator U. Calif.-Berkeley Survey Research Ctr., 1973-74, research specialist Social Research Group, Sch. Pub. Health, 1974-81; treas. Ctr. Social Research and Edn., mng. editor Socialist Rev., Oakland, Calif., 1981—; cons. Nat. Acad. Scis.; mem. com. substance abuse Nat. Inst. Alcohol Abuse and Alcoholism. Cons., advisor Nat. Task Force Pub. Broadcasting and Com. to Save KQED; mem. Berkeley Citizens Action. Nat. Inst. Alcoholism and Alchol Abuse research grantee, 1976-80. Mem. Am. Sociol. Assn., Media Alliance, Friends of Earth, Sierra Club. Books: Television in the Corporate Interest, 1976; (with orthers) Alcohol, Society and the State, Vols. I and II, 1981; contbr. numerous articles to profl. jours. Office: 3202 Adeline St Berkeley CA 94703

BUNDESEN, FAYE STIMERS, educator, investment/management company owner; b. Cedarville, Calif., Sept. 16, 1932; d. Floyd Walker and Ermina Elizabeth (Roberts) Stimers; m. Allen Eugene Bundesen, Dec. 27, 1972; children—William, David, Edward Silvius; Ted, Eric Bundesen. B.A., Calif. State U.-Sacramento, 1955; M.A., Calif. State U.-San Jose, 1972. Elem. sch. tchr. San Francisco Pub. Schs., 1955-60; elem. and jr. high sch. tchr., lang. arts specialist Sunnyvale (Calif.) Schs., 1978—; v.p. Bundesen Enterprises, San Jose, Calif., 1975-81, pres., 1981—; cons., seminar leader. Bd. dirs. Sunnyvale Sch. Empolyees' Credit Union, 1983—, mem. Med. Aux. Service, 1958-66. Mem. Calif. Tchrs. Assn., NEA, Internat. Reading Assn., Santa Clara County Reading Assn., Nat. Council Tchrs. English, Calif. Assn. Tchrs. English, Assn. Supervision and Curriculum Devel., Calif. Personnel and Guidance Assn., Tri-County Apt. Assn., Calif. Scholarship Fedn. (life), AAUW. Presbyterian. Author, editor numerous dist. publs. Home: 1334 Randol Ave San Jose CA 95126 Office: 830 McKinley Ave Sunnyvale CA 94088

BUNDRANT, JOHN PATTON, electric utility ofcl.; b. Rogersville, Tenn., Mar. 15, 1932; s. George Jarvis and Effie (Sizemore) B.; B.S. in Elec. Engring., U. N.Mex., 1960; m. Martha Ann Hewes, May 21, 1955; children—Sandra, Chuck, Kristi. Field engr. Pub. Service Co. N.Mex., Albuquerque, 1960-64; sales mgr. Santa Fe div. Pub. Service Co. N.Mex., 1964-68, mgr. Deming (N.Mex.) div., 1968-71, v.p. Albuquerque div., 1971-75, v.p. div. elec. ops., 1975-76, v.p. div. ops., 1976-81, v.p. demand sector, 1981—, dir., 1983—, mem. exec. com. Pres. Santa Fe Jaycees, 1967-68, Deming-Luna County C. of C., 1968-69; trustee, bd. advisors, mem. tech. bd. Lovelace Med. Found. Served with AUS, 1953-55. Mem. Greater Albuquerque C. of C. (dir. 1971-75, pres. Metro 70's 1975-76). Methodist. Mason. Clubs: Albuquerque Petroleum, Four Hills Country (both in Albuquerque. Home: 1012 Cuatro Cerros Trail SE Albuquerque NM 87123 Office: Public Service Co of New Mexico Alvarado Sq Albuquerque NM 87103

BUNDY, DOROTHY MARIE, marketing director, interior designer; b. Olympia, Wash., Jan. 18, 1939; d. Roy Peter and Hazel E. (Norman) Bergh; children—William Paul, Richard Larry. Student Wash. State U., 1957-60; grad. in Home Econs., Central Wash. State U., 1961; postgrad. U. Utah, 1962-63. Pvt. practice interior design, Olympia, Wash., 1971-78; spl. edn. tchr.'s aide, Olympia, 1975-78; mktg. dir. Capital Mall, E. W. Hahn, Inc., Olympia, 1978—; speaker in field. Mem. mktg. adv. bd. Olympia Tech. Community Coll., 1978—; mem. Tri-City Distributive Edn. Bd., 1978—, Youth Employment Services Bd., 1978-80; bd. dirs. Olympia Visitors and Conv. Bur.; pres. PTA, 1972. Recipient Ernest W. Hahn Highlight award, 1981; FAME award, 1982, 83; Olympia Tech. Community Coll. Citizen of Yr. award, 1982. Mem. Northwestern States Shopping Ctrs. Mktg. and Mgmt. Assn. (pres. 1980-81), Internat. Council Shopping Ctrs., Women in Communications. Club: Olympia Antique Glass. West Coast editor Shopping Center Network. Home: 1860 Yantis Pl Olympia WA 98502 Office: 324 Capital Mall Olympia WA 98502

BUNDY, STEPHEN ALLEN, artist, chef; b. Denver, Apr. 10, 1942; s. Kenneth Alvin and Virginia Lee (Carr) B.; B.A., U. Colo., 1964; M.A., 1967, M.F.A., 1972; m. Sally Louise Vandegrift, Jan. 26, 1972; children—Ryder Dale, Wade Carr. Engr., Avco Corp., Boston, 1967-68; research scientist Lab. Atmospheric & Space Physics, U. Colo., Boulder, 1968-70; asst. prof. art U. Iowa, Iowa City, 1973-79, fellow Center for New Performing Art, 1974-77, co-founder Corroboree Gallery, 1977—; head, 4-D studies Hornsey Coll. Art, Middlesex Poly., London, 1977-78; owner, chef The Fine Art Restaurant, Telluride, Colo., 1980-81; chef. Flatirons Country Club, Boulder, 1981-82; exec. chef Valley Country Club, Denver, 1982—; one man shows: N.A.M.E. Gallery, Chgo., 1974, Nancy Laurie Gallery, Chgo., 1977, O.K. Harris, N.Y.C., 1977, Walker Street Gallery, N.Y.C., 1975, Jordan Gallery, London, 1978. Mem. Telluride Council for Arts and Humanities, 1979-80. Mem. Coll. Art Assn., Chefs de Cuisine, Am. Culinary Fedn., Sigma Pi Sigma.

BUNJE, RALPH BERNHARD, agrl. marketing cons.; b. Uplands, Calif., July 5, 1911; s. Bernhard D. and Freida (Bischoff) B.; ed. spl. courses U. So. Calif., Am. Inst. Banking; m. Elizabeth G. Paull, June 20, 1935; children—Ralph B., Robert P. Supr. The Texas Co., 1934-43; program dir. radio sta. KARM, 1943-44; mgr. Agrl. Labor Bur. of San Joaquin Valley, 1945-49; legis. rep. Western Cotton Growers Assn., 1948-49; pres. Calif. Canning Peach Assn., San Francisco, 1950-74; agrl. mktg. cons., 1974—; partner Agribus. Group, Fresno, Calif. Clubs: Peninsula Golf and Country (San Mateo); World Trade. Home: 2135 Geri Ln Hillsborough CA 94010

BUNKER, JAMES EDWARD, communications counselor; b. Sacramento, Nov. 28, 1942; s. Lloyd Edward and Vivian (Rablin) B.; B.A. in History, U. Santa Clara, 1965; M.P.A., Calif. State U., Hayward, 1981; m. Gail Ann Fazackerley, Feb. 25, 1968; children—Michele Viviene, Brian Christian, Keirsten Jeanine. Asst. supr. publs. Kaiser Steel Corp., Oakland, Calif., 1966-68; dir. communications Saga Corp., Menlo Park, Calif., 1968-70; communications coordinator U.S. Natural Resources, Inc., Menlo Park, 1970-71; public relaticns counsel Qantel Corp., Hayward, Calif., 1972-76; cons. Ravenswood City Sch. dist., East Palo Alto, Calif., 1970-72, Woodland (Calif.) Joint Unified Sch. Dist., 1972-74, Copico, Burlingame, Calif., 1972-74, DJMC Advt., San Francisco, 1976-81, J. Bunker & Assos., Hayward, 1981—. Corp. liaison United Bay Area Crusade, 1966-75; mem. Hayward Parks Commn., 1974-75; nat. conv. chmn. 7th Step Found., 1975; founding chmn., mem. Hayward Environ. Quality Commn., 1975—; bd. dirs. Social Service Bur. of East Bay, 1976-81, Children's Hosp. at Stanford Family Center, 1978—, San Francisco Bay Area chpt. March of Dimes Found., 1980—. Democrat. Catholic. Home: 30596 Treeview St Hayward CA 94544 Office: PO Box 28 Mount Eden CA 94557

BUNKER, RICHARD DEAN, photographic manufacturing company executive; b. Fillmore, Utah, Oct. 10, 1933; s. Owen Woodruf and Ruth (Robison) B.; student U. Utah, 1952-55; m. Edith Scott, Aug. 28, 1959. Pres., Panama Supply Co., Salt Lake City, 1957-61; founder-owner Mont. Stamp & Die Co., Missoula, 1961-64; founder Deseret Ribbon Mfg. Co., Salt Lake City, 1965-71; founder, exec. corp. officer Prudential Carbon & Ribbon Corp., Salt Lake City, 1966-68; v.p. Dyna-Flex Corp., Salt Lake City, 1968-74; pres. Dyna-Flex Internat. Corp., 1974-76, Warm Springs Ranches, Inc., Gandy, Utah, 1971-82; v.p. Micro Investment Corp., Salt Lake City, 1971-75; pres. Richard D. Bunker, Inc., Research, Inventions & Cons., Salt Lake City, 1973-82; founder Bunker Techs., 1970-83, Micro Hydro Power, Inc., 1980-83; founder, pres. Bunker/Dyna-Flex Corp., 1982—. Mem. Airplane Owners and Pilots Assn. Inventor Dyna-flex printing system, Helio-graph printing plate and system. Home: 5238 S 2030 W Salt Lake City UT 84118 Office: 2300 S 3600 W Salt Lake City UT 84119 Mailing Address: PO Box 20623 Salt Lake City UT 84120

BUNKER, WILLIAM ROBISON, insurance executive; b. Filmore, Utah, Jan. 25, 1927; s. Owen W. and Ruth (Robison) B.; m. Mary Jean, Aug. 1, 1962; children—Miachel, Daniel, Todd. Student U. Utah, 1947-48. Ins. agent Salt Lake City, 1949-60; prin. Gen. Agy., 1960-74; pres. Consumers Ins. Co., Spokane, Wash., 1975—. Served with USN, 1945-47. Republican. Mormon. Club: Order of Blue Goose (Most Loyal Gander). Home: S 1830 Upper Terrace Rd Spokane WA 89203 Office: W 921 Sprague Ave Spokane WA 99210

BUNN, BEVERLY, lawyer; b. Sacramento, Sept. 2; d. Guy Alvis and Violet (Pelzel) B.; 1 son, Jeffery Cramer. Student Portland State U., U. Portland; J.D., Pepperdine U., 1969. Bar: Calif. 1971. Stewardess, United Air Lines, N.Y.C. and Los Angeles, 1964, stewardess recruiter, 1964; dir. Airline Stewardess Tng. Sch., Viva Modeling Sch., Riverside, Calif., 1965; social worker Calif. State Dept. Social Welfare, Riverside and Orange counties, 1965-70; practice law, Orange County, Calif., 1971-76; overseas project mgr. econ. devel., project mgr. emergency assistance to war victims and refugees Cath. Relief Services, Yemen Arab Republic, 1976-79, econ. devel., Tunis, Tunisia, 1980-81; supervising atty. NANA region Alaska Legal Services Corp., Kotzebue, 1982—. Legal counsel Anaheim Young Republicans, 1971; gen. counsel Calif. Young Reps., 1972-73; lectr. U. Calif.-Irvine, 1973; vice-chmn. Calif. Citizens Com. Welfare Reform, 1971. Sec., Orange County Young Reps., 1972-73. Mem. ABA, Internat. Bar Assn. (London), Am. Soc. Internat. Law, Assn. Immigration and Nationality Lawyers, United Air Lines Stewardess Alumni Assn., Calif. Bar Assn., N.W. Arctic Area Bar Assn. (pres. 1982—), Santa Ana C. of C. (ambassador). Editor Clipped Wings, 1964-65, The Double Tau, 1967-69. Home: 864 49th St Sacramento CA 95819 Office: PO Box 316 Kotzebue AK 99752

BUNN, CHARLES NIXON, strategic bus. planning cons.; b. Springfield, Ill., Feb. 8, 1926; s. Joseph Forman and Helen Anna Frieda (Link) B.; student U. Ill., 1943-44; B.S. in Engring., U.S. Mil. Acad., 1949; M.B.A., Xavier U., Cin., 1958; m. Cecine Elizabeth Cole, Dec. 26, 1951; children—Sisene, Charles. Flight test engr. Gen. Electric Co., Cin., also Edwards AFB, Calif., 1953-59; sr. missile test engr., space systems div. Lockheed Aircraft Corp., USAF Satellite Test Center, Sunnyvale, Calif., 1959-60, 63-70, economist, advanced planning dept., 1961-63; economic and long-range planning cons., Los Altos, Calif., 1970-73; head systems planning, economist, strategic bus. planning, Western Regional hdqrs. U.S. Postal Service, San Bruno, Calif., 1973-78; strategic bus. planning cons., investment analysis cons., 1978-79; strategic bus. planning Advanced Reactor Systems dept. Gen. Electric Co., Sunnyvale, Calif., 1979—. Served with inf. paratroops U.S. Army, 1944-45, with inf. and rangers, 1949-53; Korea. Decorated Battle Star (5). Mem. Nat. Assn. Bus. Economists, World Future Soc., Sigma Nu. Episcopalian. Home: 870 E El Camino Real 143 Mountain View CA 94040 Office: 955 Arques Ave Sunnyvale CA 94086

BUNN, WILEY DOUGLAS, lawyer, broadcasting co. exec.; b. Los Angeles, July 22, 1929; s. Thomas S. and Ellen (Douglas) B.; student Wheaton Coll., 1948-49; B.A., U. So. Calif., 1950, J.D., 1953; m. Marilyn Granger, June 19, 1951; children—Barbara, Douglas, David, Carolyn. Admitted to Calif. bar, 1953; practiced in Los Angeles, 1953-72; partner firm Bunn and Peterson, Pasadena, 1973—; pres. Coast TV Broadcasting Corp. Channel 22 KWHY-TV, Los Angeles, 1970-82; sec. bd. Far East Broadcasting Co., 1964-81, chmn. bd., 1981—. Mem. Am., Los Angeles County bar assns., State Bar Calif., Phi Beta Kappa. Home: 4839 Gould Ave LaCanada CA 91011 Office: 283 S Lake Ave Pasadena CA 91101

BUNNING, RICHARD LESLIE, hospital administrator; b. Buffalo, Wyo., Apr. 22, 1945; s. Harold W. and Jean M. (Eder) B.; m. Kathleen E. Powers, Jan. 28, 1970; m. 2d, Eileen Hallamek, June 27, 1981; children—Bridget K., Dawn K., Melinda C. B.A., U. Wyo., 1967, M.A., 1970; Ph.D., Ariz. State U., 1976. Dir. adult edn. Morgan Community Coll., Ft. Morgan, Colo., 1970-73; dir. orgn. devel. Samaritan Health Service, Phoenix, 1974-79, dir. project coordination, 1981-82; exec. dir. Ariz. Consortium for Edn. in the Social Service, Tempe, 1979-81; spl. asst. to v.p./chief exec. officer Good Samaritan Med. Ctr., Phoenix, 1982—; mem. adj. faculty Ariz. State U. Served with U.S. Army, 1967-69. Named Outstanding Young Educator, Ft. Morgan (Colo.) Jaycees, 1972. Mem. Am. Soc. Tng. and Devel., Mountain Plains Adult Edn. Assn., Ariz. Adult Edn. Assn. Democrat. Roman Catholic. Contbr. articles to various publs.

BUNTING, DAVID RABE, real estate broker, civil engineer, land surveyor; b. Quincy, Ill., Nov. 3, 1938; s. Robert Russell and Lydia Frederika (Rabe) B.; m. Gloria May Poole, June 2, 1976. Student U. Ill., 1956-59, U. Wash., 1960-63. Registered profl. land surveyor, Wash., Oreg.; registered profl. engr., Wash. Oreg.; lic. real estate broker, Wash. Project engr. U.S. Forest Service, Gifford Pinchot Nat. Forest, Packwood and Randle, Wash., 1959-72; designated broker Ethel White Real Estate, Packwood, 1973—; owner and prin. engr. and surveyor D. R. Bunting & Assocs., Cons. Engrs. & Land Surveyors, Packwood, 1969—. Mem. Wash. Senate ad hoc com. on geologic hazards in State of Wash., 1974; past pres., sec., treas., and chmn. bd. Packwood Improvement Club; past chmn. Lewis County Planning Com. Served with Army N.G., 1962-64. Mem. Land Surveyors Assn. of Wash., Sigma Phi Delta. Republican. Presbyterian elder. Office: PO Box 435 13053 US Hwy 12 Packwood WA 98361

BUNZEL, JOHN HARVEY, political science educator, researcher; b. N.Y.C., Apr. 15, 1924; s. Ernest Everett and Harriett (Harvey) B.; m. Barbara Bovyer, May 11, 1963; children—Cameron, Reed. A.B.,

Princeton U., 1948; M.A., Columbia U., 1949; Ph.D., U. Calif.-Berkeley, 1954; LL.D., U. Santa Clara, 1976. Mem. faculty San Francisco State U., 1953-56, 63-70, vis. scholar Ctr. Advanced Study in Behavioral Scis., 1969-70; mem. faculty Mich. State U., East Lansing, 1956-57, Stanford (Calif.) U., 1957-63; pres. San Jose State U., Calif., 1970-78; sr. research fellow Hoover Inst., Stanford U., Calif., 1978—; trustee Monterey Inst. Internat. Studies, Calif. Bd. dirs. No. Calif. Citizenship Clearing House, 1959-61; mem. Calif. Atty. Gen.'s Adv. com., 1960-61; mem. Calif. Democratic del., 1968; del. Dem. Nat. Conv., 1968. Recipient Presdl. award No. Calif. Polit. Sci. Assn., 1969; Cert. of Honor, San Francisco Bd Suprs., 1974; Ford Found. grantee; Rockefeller Found. grantee; Rabinowitz Found. grantee. Mem. Am. Polit. Sci. Assn. Author: The American Small Businessman, 1962; Anti-Politics in America, 1967; Issues of American Public Policy, 1968; New Force on the Left, 1983; contbr. articles to profl. jours., popular mags., newspapers; weekly columnist San Jose Mercury-News. Home: 1519 Escondido Way Belmont CA 94002 Office: Hoover Inst Stanford U Stanford CA 94305

BURBIDGE, GEOFFREY, astrophysicist; b. Chipping Norton, Oxon, Eng., Sept. 24, 1925; s. Leslie and Eveline Burbidge; B.Sc. with spl. honors in Physics, Bristol U., 1946; Ph.D., U. Coll., London, 1951; m. Margaret Peachey, 1948; 1 dau. Asst. lectr. U. Coll., London, 1950-51; Agassiz fellow Harvard U., 1951-52; research fellow U. Chgo., 1952-53, Cavendish Lab., Cambridge, Eng., 1953-55; Carnegie fellow Mt. Wilson and Palomar Obs., Calif. Inst. Tech., 1955-57; asst. prof. dept. astronomy U. Chgo., 1957-58, asso. prof., 1958-62; assoc. prof. U. Calif. at San Diego, La Jolla, 1962-63, prof. physics, 1963-78; dir. Kitt Peak Nat. Obs., Tucson, 1978—; Phillips vis. prof. Harvard U., 1968; bd. dirs. Assoc. Univs. Research in Astronomy, 1971-74; trustee Assoc. Univs., Inc., 1973-82. Fellow Royal Soc. London, Am. Acad. Arts and Scis., Royal Astron. Soc.; mem. Am. Phys. Soc., Am. Astron. Soc., Internat. Astron. Union, Astron. Soc. of Pacific (pres. 1974-76). Author (with Margaret Burbidge) Quasi-Stellar Objects, 1967. Contbr. articles to sci. jours. Office: Kitt Peak Nat Obs PO Box 26732 Tucson AZ 85726

BURCAW, GEORGE ELLIS, museum director, educator; b. Houston, July 13, 1921; s. George Henry and Mary Elizabeth (Ellis) B.; m. Susan Straight, June 24, 1961 (div.); children—Geordi Elizabeth, Geoffrey George; B.A., Maryville Coll., 1943; M.A., U. Idaho, 1973; postgrad. U. Chgo., 1946-48, U. Ariz., 1949-50, U. Paris, 1951-52, U. Wis., 1956—, U. Pa., 1960—. Mus. dir. Neville Pub. Mus., Green Bay, Wis., 1952-58; chief curator Comml. Mus., Phila., 1958-62; curator State Museums Colo., Denver, 1962-66; dir. mus., chmn. mus. studies, prof. museology, prof. anthropology U. Idaho, Moscow, 1966—; archaeologist Smithsonian Instn., 1950, Am. Found. Study of Man, 1950-51, New World Archaeol. Found., 1956. Bd. dirs. Appaloosa Horse Club Mus., 1979—. Served to 1st lt. USMC, 1942-46. Mem. Internat. Council Mus. (mus. tng. com.), Am. Assn. Mus. (sr. examiner accreditation commn.), Am. Assn. State and Local History, Western Museums Conf., Sigma Xi, Phi Alpha Theta, Beta Theta Pi, Phi Kappa Phi. Author: Directory of Museum Training, 1971; Introduction to Museum Work, 1975; The Saxon House: A Cultural Index in European Ethnography, 1979; mem. editorial bd. Mus. Studies Jour., 1982—; contbr. articles in field to mus. jours. Office: U Idaho Mus Moscow ID 83843

BURCH, DIANNE KAYE, educator; b. Los Angeles, Mar. 13, 1944; d. Glen E. and Alpha J. (Campbell) Finkenbinder; m. Carroll Lee Downs; m. 2d Thomas Lee Burch; 1 stepdau., Jennifer Carrie Burch. A.A., Cerritos Coll., 1972; B.A. in Home Econs., Calif. State U.-Los Angeles, 1976; postgrad. Mt. Saint Mary's Coll., 1982—. Tchr. children's ctr. Bellflower (Calif.) Unified Sch. Dist., 1968-77; tchr. Bell High Sch. Los Angeles Unified Sch. Dist., 1981—, chmn. home econs. dept., 1982—; sponsor Key Club. Mem. Am. Home Econs. Assn., Calif. Home Econs. Assn., Phi Upsilon Omicron (service award 1977, leadership award 1978, named outstanding mem. 1979). Democrat. Lutheran.

BURCH, KARL DOUGLAS, management skills trainer; b. Lorain, Ohio, Nov. 28, 1948; s. Kenneth Edward and Gloria Lorraine (Wilson) B.; m. Marilyn Cleary, June 23, 1972; children—Merideth, Jessica. B.S. cum laude, Ohio State U., 1974, M.S., 1976; student Bowling Green State U., 1967-70. Researcher Ohio Biol. Survey, Columbus 1975-76; county extension agt. Coop. Extension Service, Canton, Ohio, 1976-79; community relations mgr. Weyerhaeuser Co., Chehalis, Wash., 1979-82, region tng. cons., Federal Way, 1982—. Campaign co-chmn., v.p. United Way Lewis County, 1980-82. Recipient Leadership award United Way, 1980, 81, 4-H, 1978; grantee Ohio Biol. Survey, 1975; Outstanding Hawaii Outrigger Canoe paddler, 1971. Mem. Am. Soc. Tng. and Devel., Chehalis C. of C. (dir. 1981-82). Club: Rotary. Home: 3207 Laurel Ln Centralia WA 98531 Office: 1100 Sylvenus St Chehalis WA 98532

BURCH, STEVEN LEE, soil scientist; b. San Bernardino, Calif., Apr. 28, 1950; s. Richard C. and Shirley B. (Thomas) B.; B.S. in Soil Sci. (Soil Conservation Soc. Am. scholar), Calif. Poly. State U., San Luis Obispo, 1974; m. Virginia Susan Burnell, Sept. 18, 1971; children—Karen Leann, Brent Cameron. Agrl. chems. sales rep. Ciba Geigy Corp., Phoenix, 1974-76; soil technologist Agrl. Tech. Co., Tempe, Ariz., 1976-79; mgr. agrl. cons. services div., soil scientist Western Farm Mgmt. Co., Visalia, Calif., 1979-81; owner Burch Agrl. Services, 1981—. Home and Office: 3807 W Feemster Visalia CA 93277

BURCHAM, LEVI TURNER, ecologist, geographer; b. Ronda, N.C., May 30, 1912; s. James Avery and Della (Smoot) B.; B.S., U. Calif. at Berkeley, 1941, Ph.D., 1956; M.S., U. Nebr. at Lincoln, 1950; m. Miriam Lee Parsons, Jan. 7, 1942; children—Arthur Forrest, Charles Lee. Range examiner U.S. Dept. Interior, Reno, Nev., 1941-42; forester Calif. Div. Forestry, Fresno, Calif., 1947-48, Sacramento, 1948-56, asst. dept. forester, 1956-64, 66-75; cons. forestry, ecology and geography, 1976—; environ. scis. adviser Office of Sec. Def., Advanced Research Projects Agy., Washington, 1964-66; cons., lectr. in field. Served with USMC, 1933-37, to capt. USMCR, 1942-46. Mem. AAAS, Am. Geog. Soc., Calif. Acad. Scis. (life), Ecol. Soc. Am., Soc. Am. Foresters, Soc. Range Mgmt. (life), Wildlife Soc. Contbr. articles to profl. publs. Home: 4701 Crestwood Way Sacramento CA 95822

BURCHETT, ALAN EDWARD, lawyer; b. Chico, Calif., May 18, 1943; s. Clyde Edward and Vivian (Roberts) B.; m. Brenda Hope Cook, Jan. 10, 1970; children—Andrew E., Wendy E. B.S., U. Calif.-Berkeley, 1965; J.D., U. Calif. Hastings Coll. Law, 1968. Bar: Calif. 1969. Assoc. firm Dinkelspiel & Dinkelspiel, San Francisco, 1969-70; staff counsel Occidental Petroleum Corp., Los Angeles, 1970-72; dep. county counsel Butte County, Oroville, Calif., 1972-73; assoc. Goldstein, Barceloux & Goldstein, Chico, 1974-79; ptnr. Stewart, Craig, Humpherys, Burchett & Patrick, Chico, 1979—; town atty. Town of Paradise, Calif., 1979-82. Bd. dirs. Am. Lung Assn., Superior, Calif., 1978-79. Named to Thurston Soc., Hastings Coll. Law, 1967-68. Mem. ABA, Butte County Bar Assn., Greater Chico C. of C. (dir. 1981—). Republican. Contbr. articles to profl. jours. Home: 1388 Keri Ln Chico CA 95926 Office: PO Box 658 Chico CA 95927

BURCHETT, LADEANA LYNN, educational administrator; b. Orange, Calif., Jan. 29, 1953; d. Robert Dean and Lovena Aleen (Friend) B. B.S. in Human Services, Calif. State U., 1978; A.A. in Edn., Orange Coast Coll., 1975. Teaching credential, Calif. Pvt. practice piano tchr., Costa Mesa, Calif., 1973-74; tchr., asst. dir. Costa Mesa Christian Sch., 1974-75; dir. LaPalma (Calif.) Christian Sch., 1975-77; dir. Children's House Christian Sch., Orange, 1977—. Mem. Orange County Reading Assn., So. Calif. Assn. Edn. Young Children, Assn. Supervision and Curriculum Devel., Ednl. Leadership. Republican. Mem. Evangelical Free Ch. Club: Toastmasters (Orange). Home: 221 Kodiak Anaheim CA 92807 Office: 1400 E Taft Orange CA 92665

BURCHETT, THERESA ANN, counselor; b. Nashville, Sept. 4, 1947; d. Clyde Rolen and Dorothy (Armstrong) B.; B.A., Wichita State U., 1970; M.S., U. Ariz., 1975. Counselor, supr. Contact Program, So. Ariz. Valley Nat. Bank, Tucson, 1975-78; client services coordinator Pima Alcoholism Consortium, Tucson, 1978-81; mgmt. devel. coordinator Tucson Med. Ctr., 1981—; counselor, trainer, cons. clin. and mgmt. problems. Bd. dirs. Women's Retreat Shelter, 1975-77; mem. adv. bd. Terros Inc., drug treatment, 1976. Mem. Am. Rehab. Counseling Assn., Am. Personnel and Guidance Assn., Am. Soc. Tng. and Devel. Home: 1612 N Treat Tucson AZ 85716 Office: PO Box 42195 Tucson AZ 85733

BURCHFIELD, SUSAN RENEE, psychologist, nurse; b. Columbus, Ohio, Nov. 16, 1951; s. James Ralph and Dorothy Alice (Underwood) B.; m. William Chapman Holliday, May 30, 1980. B.S. in Nursing, Ohio State U., 1974; Ph.D., U. Wash., Seattle, 1978. Lic. psychologist, Ky., 1980. Nurse Harborview Med. Ctr., Seattle, 1974-79; asst. prof. psychology U. Ky., Lexington, 1979-81; nurse Univ. Hosp., Seattle, 1982—; research assoc. dept. psychology U. Wash., Seattle, 1981—, postdoctoral fellow, 1982—. NIMH grantee, 1981-82. Mem. Am. Psychol. Assn., Neuroscis. Soc., Am. Psychosomatic Soc., Sigma Theta Tau. Contbr. articles to profl. jours. Office: Psychology Dept N1-25 U Wash Seattle WA 98195

BURD, MICHAEL SEDGWICK, investment banker; b. Berkeley, Calif., Dec. 28, 1952; s. John Sedgwick, Jr. and Patricia (Lennon) B.; A.B. in History, Stanford U., 1974; M.B.A., Harvard U., 1976; m. Janet Carolyn Ramsay, Sept. 13, 1980. Corp. fin. officer Crocker Nat. Bank, Los Angeles, 1976-78; asst. v.p. Warburg Paribas Becker Inc., Los Angeles, 1978-80; v.p. E.F. Hutton & Co. Inc., Los Angeles, 1980—. Mem. Harvard Bus. Sch. Assn. So. Calif. (group v.p. 1980-82), Sigma Chi. Republican. Club: Calif. (Los Angeles). Home: 8835 Gerald Ave Sepulveda CA 91343 Office: 888 W 6th St Los Angeles CA 90017

BURDEN, JAMES EWERS, lawyer; b. Sacramento, Oct. 24, 1939; s. Herbert Spencer and Ida Elizabeth (Brosemer) B.; B.S., U. Calif., Berkeley, 1961, J.D., U. Calif., San Francisco, 1964; postgrad. U. So. Calif., 1964-65; m. Kathryn Lee Gardner, Aug. 21, 1965; children—Kara Elizabeth, Justin Gardner. Admitted to Calif. bar, 1965; asso. firm Elliott and Aune, Santa Ana, Calif., 1964-65, White, Harber, Fort & Schei, Sacramento, 1965-68; mem. firm Miller, Starr & Regalia, Oakland, 1968-73, partner, 1970-73; individual practice, 1973; partner firm Burden, Aiken & Mansuy, and predecessors, San Francisco, 1974-82, James E. Burden, Inc., P.C., 1982—; instr. real estate law and taxation U. Calif. Extension, Berkeley, 1971-78, Merritt Coll., Oakland, 1969-71. Mem. Am., San Francisco, Alameda bar assns., Am. Inst. Continuing Edn., Phi Delta Phi. Contbr. articles to profl. jours. Home: Piedmont CA Office: 451 Jackson St San Francisco CA 94111

BURDETT, CUILLY, interior designer, educator; b. Stillwater, Okla. Apr. 25, 1931; d. Donald H. and Caralu Woodyard; divorced. Grad. U. Okla., 1955; grad. McDowell Sch. Design, N.Y.C., 1956, Prin. interior design firm Barker Bros. Studio Interior Design, La Jolla, Calif., 1957-59; dir. W. & J. Sloane, Inc., La Jolla, 1959-61; guest lectr. dept. design San Diego State U., 1966-78, adj. prof., 1982—; lectr. U. Calif.-San Diego, 1970-74. Bd. dirs. San Diego Ballet Assn., San Diego Symphony. Mem. Am. Soc. Interior Designers (bd. dirs., chmn. public relations and spl. events, nat. bd. dirs. 1979-81), San Diego Zool. Soc., La Jolla Mus. Contemporary Art, San Diego Mus. Art, Sigma Chi. Republican. Presbyterian. Clubs: La Jolla Beach and Tennis. Office: PO Box 2369 La Jolla CA 92038

BURDGE, ROBERT EUGENE, savings and loan executive; b. Omaha, Feb. 4, 1942; s. Lloyd Richard and Betty Trier (Rettenmayer) B.; m. Cheryl Lynn Beckman, June 26, 1971; 1 dau., Christina Lynn. B.A. in Speech, U. Nebr.-Omaha, 1964. Mgr. sales promotion dept. Mut. of Omaha, 1969-80; asst. v.p., advt. pub. relations mgr. Comml. Fed. Savs. & Loan, Omaha, 1980—. Served to capt. USAF, 1965-69. Recipient Commendation award Nat. Premium Sales Execs., Inc., 1982. Mem. Sales and Mktg. Execs. of Midlands (dir.), Savs. Instn. Mktg. Soc. Am., Pub. Relations Soc. Am. Republican. Presbyterian. Home: 11435 Taylor St Omaha NE 68164 Office: 2120 S 72d St Omaha NE 68124

BURESON, MAUREEN, grantsmanship consultant; b. Butte, Mont., Aug. 19, 1947; d. Wayne George and Mary Elizabeth (Duffy) B. B.S. in Edn., Eastern Mont. Coll., 1969; student Western Wash. State Coll., 1970, 71, U. Minn., 1974; M.Ed., U. Idaho, 1976. Tchr. social sci. Moses Lake (Wash.) High Sch., 1969-72; coordinator Upward Bound program Idaho State U., Pocatello, 1972-75; planning cons. Mont. Office Pub. Instrn., Helena, 1977; novice Sisters of Providence, Spokane, Wash., 1978; vocat. spl. needs cons. Great Falls (Mont.) Pub. Schs., 1979; dir. Human Growth Ctr., Great Falls, 1979; planning dir. Opportunities, Inc., Great Falls, 1980-82; pres. Bureson Cons., Inc., Great Falls, 1982—. Bd. dirs. Human Growth Ctr., 1981; bd. dirs., v.p. Wesley Community Ctr., 1979-81; mem. Great Falls Citizens Adv. Com. for Community Devel. Grant, 1980-81, Great Falls Econ. Growth Council, 1981-82, Cath. Diocese Long Range Planning Task Force, 1982-83; co-chairperson Community Found. Task Force, 1983; facilitator Community Forum, 1983; founder Providence Lay Assocs., Great Falls. Mem. Nat. Assn. Vocat. Spl. Needs Personnel (cert. of appreciation 1976), AAUW. Democrat. Roman Catholic. Home and Office: 706 8th Ave S Great Falls MT 59405

BURG, GERALD WILLIAM, management and financial consultant; b. Pitts., Oct. 16, 1923; s. Julius Samuel and Anna (Shapiro) B.; student Walsh Inst., 1940-43; m. Flavia Kafton, Aug. 12, 1945; children—Cindy, Melinda, Andrew. Engring. rep. U.S. Rubber Co., 1943-45; adminstr. Beverly Hills (Calif.) B'nai B'rith, 1945-52, Univ. Synagogue, Brentwood, 1952-55; exec. dir. Wilshire Blvd. Temple, Los Angeles, 1956-80; mgmt. and fin. cons., 1980—. Mem. Jewish relations com. Los Angeles council Boy Scouts Am., 1959—; mem. Mayor's Adv. Com. on Community Activities, Los Angeles, 1963-73; chmn. Crime Prevention Fifth Councilmanic Dist., Los Angeles, 1968-73. Bd. dirs. McCobb Home for Boys, Los Angeles Psychiat. Service, Maple Center for Crises Intervention; bd. dirs. Didi Hirsch Community Mental Health Services, pres., 1975-77; bd. dirs., chmn. finances, chmn. adminstrv. com. Community Care and Devel. Services, 1975—. Mem. Nat. (bd. dir., pres. 1975-77), Western (pres. 1969-71, bd. dirs.), So. Calif. (pres. 1958-60) assns. temple adminstrs., NCCJ (bd. dirs. brotherhood anytown 1966-82), Los Angeles Jewish Communal Execs. (dir.). Mem. B'nai B'rith (youth dir. 1945-82, Akiba award 1950, Beverly Hills pres. 1953-54). Club: Sertoma (v.p. 1973-82). Home: 141 N La Peer Dr Beverly Hills CA 90211 Office: 427 N Canon Dr Beverly Hills CA 90210

BURGEI, THOMAS JOHN, school administrator; b. Kendallville, Ind., Dec. 26, 1947; s. John Joseph and Mildred Mary (Pfefferkorn) B.; m. Nancy Jean Noble, Sept. 6, 1969; children—Sarah Elizabeth, Rachel Alyssa. B.A., Ind. U., 1970; M.A., Calif. State U.-San Jose, 1977. Speech therapist Oak Grove Sch. Dist., San Jose, Calif., 1970-78, resource tchr., 1978-80, elem. sch. prin., 1980—, summer sch. prin., 1973-77, summer sch. administr., 1978. Tchr., leader San Jose Parks and Recreation. Mem. Assn. Supervision and Curriculum Devel., Assn. Calif. Sch. Adminstrs., Oak Grove Mgmt. Assn. (v.p.), Calif. Tchrs. Assn., NEA, Assn. Calif. Sch. Adminstrs., Am. Speech and Hearing Assn. (cert.). Democrat. Home: 2439 Dolphin Dr San Jose CA 95124 Office: 280 Martinvale Ln San Jose CA 95119

BURGER, OTHMAR JOSEPH, agronomist, educator; b. Jasper, Ind., May 23, 1921; s. August and Katherine (Lechner) B.; m. Elizabeth Ann Evans, Aug. 21, 1943; children—Thomas Glen, Robert Howard, David William. B.S., Purdue U., 1943, M.S., 1947, Ph.D., 1950. Prof. agronomy W.Va. U., 1950-57, asst. dean agr., 1959-68, asst. to provost for instrn., 1968-69; prof. agronomy Iowa State U., 1957-59; dean Sch. Agr. and Home Econs., Calif. State U.-Fresno, 1969—, also prof. agronomy. Cubmaster local council Boy Scouts Am., 1956-58. Bd. dirs. United Fund, Morgantown, W.Va., 1953-55. Served with USMCR, 1943-46. Decorated Bronze Star, Purple Heart. Fellow Am. Soc. Agronomy; mem. Nat. Assn. Colls. and Tchrs. Agr. (pres. 1978-79; Disting. Educator award 1982), Gamma Sigma Delta, Phi Lambda Upsilon, Alpha Zeta. Club: Kiwanis. Home: 2689 San Carlos Ave Fresno CA 93711 Office: Cedar at Shaw Ave Fresno CA 93740

BURGER-BROWN, MADELEINE JOAN, home economics adminstr., writer; b. San Bernardino, Calif., Feb. 10, 1937; d. Edward Jacob and Gladys Elizabeth (Williams) Burger; m. William Garth Brown, June 4, 1960 (div.); 1 dau., Traci Elizabeth. A.A. in Home Econs., San Bernardino Valley Coll., 1956; B.A. in Home Econs., Art and Edn., U. Redlands, 1959. Home economist Southern Calif. Gas Co., Los Angeles and San Bernardino, 1959-63; dir. home econs. Thermador Waste King Co., Los Angeles, 1968—. Mem. Am. Home Econs. Assn., Calif. Home Econs. Assn., Los Angeles Home Economists in Bus., Elec. Women's Round Table, Alpha Theta Phi. Clubs: DeMolay, Rainbow Girls, White Shrine of Jerusalem, Eastern Star. Author Theramador Micro-Convection Cooking Guide, Micro-Thermal Cookbook. Home: 2075 Rialto Ave Apt 71 San Bernardino CA 92410 Office: 5119 District Blvd Los Angeles CA 90040

BURGESON, NICHOLAS RUDOLPH, business consultant; b. Portland, Oreg., July 4, 1943; s. Rudolph and Grace (Nimlos) B.; A.S. in Nursing, Pacific Union Coll., 1964; B.S., Golden Gate U., 1977; M.B.A., U. Beverly Hills, 1980; m. Donna Irene MacGlashan, Oct. 18, 1964; children—Tina Lynn, Robert Gene. Staff nurse Napa (Calif.) State Hosp., 1964-66, nursing coordinator adolescent program, 1968-70, asst. to med. dir., 1970-71; nursing supr. Sibly Meml. Hosp., Washington, part-time 1967-68; asst. chief hosp. services sect. Calif. Dept. Health, Sacramento, 1971-77; adminstr. Met. State Hosp., Norwalk, Calif., 1977-81; pres. Hosp. Canteen Corp., Norwalk, 1977-81; assoc. adminstr. Loma Linda (Calif.) Community Hosp., 1981-82; pres. Redlands Mgmt. Specialists (Calif.), 1982—. Campaign dir. United Way, 1970, 73; mem. North Bay Area Youth Council, 1968-70. Served in Nurse Corps, U.S. Army, 1966-68. Lic. nursing home adminstr. Mem. Calif. Assn. Mgmt. (charter mem.; pres. 1976-77, sec. 1975), Health Care Execs. of So. Calif. Club: Kiwanis. Adv. bd. Calif. Health Rev. Home and Office: 11843 Eton Dr Grand Terrace CA 92324

BURGESS, ARTHUR LEE, mechanical design engineer; b. Aberdeen, Wash., Apr. 10, 1937; s. Arthur Chester and Josephine F. (Griffin) B.; m. Diane Jeanine Deschler (div.), Aug. 11, 1965; children—Arthur Blaine, Scott Reid. B.A. in Edn., Eastern Wash. State Coll., 1965. Cert. tchr. Wash. Tchr., Ocean Falls Sch. Dist., B.C., Can., 1964-65; tchr. Mead Sch. Dist., Wash., 1965-66; project engr. Eldec Corp., Lynnwood, Wash., 1967-79; mech. design engr., Teltone Corp., Kirkland, Wash., 1979—; cons.; instr. Served with U.S. Army, 1962-64. Mem. Nat. Assn. Watch and Clock Collectors, Elec. Horology Soc., Wash. Watch Makers Assn., Apple Puget Sound Library Exchange, Nat. Rifle Assn. (life). Office: 10801 120th Ave NE Kirkland WA 98033

BURGESS, DONNIE WILLIAM, data processing exec.; b. Pocatello, Idaho, Feb. 16, 1939; s. William John and Frankie (Roberts) B.; student Idaho State U., 1956-58; B.S. in Computer Sci., Colo. State U., 1969; M.A., U. Nebr., 1977; m. VaNeal Elizabeth Ellis, May 29, 1959; children—Carl Dawn, Lori VaNeal, Nathan Ellis, Becky Jean. Commd. 2d lt. U.S. Air Force, 1958, advanced through grades to lt. col., 1975, ret., 1979; data processing mgr. Looart Press, Inc., Colorado Springs, Colo., 1978—; lectr. in field. Explorer Post adv. Boy Scouts Am., Bellevue, Nebr., 1975-77, dist. commr., Colorado Springs, 1979—; Webelo den leader, 1979-81, asst. scout-master, 1982—; adv. Young Men's Mut. Improvement Assn., Bellevue, 1977-78; bd. dirs. Athletic Assn. of Black Forest, 1979—; youth soccer coach, 1978—; youth basketball coach, 1981—; chmn. voter edn. com. Looart Citizen Action Program, 1979-80; mem. Looart polit. action contbns. subcom., 1979-80; pres. Wolford Elem. Sch. PTA, Colorado Springs, 1982-83. Decorated Air medal with 5 oak leaf clusters, D.F.C. Mem. Data Processing Mgrs. Assn., Am. Mgmt. Assn., Colo. Honeywell Users Group (pres. 1982), Honeywell Large Systems User Group, Assn. Time-Sharing Users, Internat. Assn. Approved Basketball Ofcls., Colorado Springs Basketball Ofcls. Assn., Beta Gamma Sigma. Mormon. Home: 9755 Shoup Rd Colorado Springs CO 80908 Office: 3525 N Stone St Colorado Springs CO 80907

BURGESS, JOSEPH JAMES, JR., artist educator; b. Albany, N.Y., July 13, 1924; s. Joseph James and Marie (Southwell) B.; A.B., Hamilton Coll., 1947; M.A., Yale U., 1948; postgrad. Pratt Inst., 1950-52; M.F.A., Cranbrook Acad. Art, 1954; m. Anna Kang, Aug. 25, 1959; children—Ian Tai Kyung, Dana Tai Soon. Asst. prof. fine arts, head dept. St. Lawrence U., Canton, N.Y., 1954-55; instr. art, chmn. dept. Flint Community Jr. Coll., 1956-65, dir. DeWaters Art Ctr., 1956-65; asst. prof. design Ariz. State U., Tempe, 1965-66; instr. dept. continuing edn. Coll. of Santa Fe, 1977-82; lectr. audio-visual dept. Santa Fe Pub. Library, 1981-82; owner design studio and retail store Origins, 1966-75; dir. Blair Galleries, 1976-80; one or two-man shows: Albany Inst. History and Art, 1958, Ball State Tchrs. Coll., 1958, Palace of Legion of Honor, San Francisco, 1959, DeWaters Art Ctr., 1964, Pasadena Art Mus., 1968, Santa Fe Festival of Arts, 1979, 80; group shows: Detroit Inst. Arts. 1956, Mus. Modern Art, N.Y.C., 1956, Flint Inst. Arts, 1956-65, Albany Inst. of History and Art, 1957. Served with USN, 1943-46. Mem. Phi Beta Kappa. Author: Three Chinese Poems, 1962; Four Chinese Poems, 1961; A Random Poem, 1973; A Shining Legend, 1974; Asia's First Iron-Clad Warship, 1975; contbr. articles to various periodicals. Address: PO Box 2151 Santa Fe NM 87501

BURGESS, JOSEPH WESLEY, metall. engr., photographer; b. St. Louis, Nov. 27, 1910; s. Joseph Francis and Amanda (Woodrome) B.; B.S. in Civil Engring., Washington U., St. Louis, 1932; m. Dorothea Ines Nelson, Mar. 5, 1941; children—Joseph Wesley, Sarah Jane. Trainee, Shell Pipe Line Corp., Kilgore, Tex., 1933-35, asst. div. supt., Tex., N.Mex., St. Louis, 1935-39; mgr. products pipe line dept. Shell Oil Co., N.Y.C., 1939-41; chief engr., gen. supt. Am. Zinc Co. of Ill., Dumas, Tex., 1941-59; gen. mgr. constrn. Uranium Reduction Co., Salt Lake City, Moab, Utah, 1955-59; chief engr. Am. Zinc Co., St. Louis, 1959-71; mgr. project engring. Fluor Utah, Inc., San Mateo, Calif. 1971-73, v.p. engring., 1973, v.p. project mgmt., 1974-76; ret., 1976; cons., 1976—, photographer, 1977—; photographs exhibited in one-man shows including: San Jose (Calif.) Mus. Art, 1980, Stanford U. Faculty Club, Palo Alto, Calif., 1981; group shows include: Olive Hyde Art Gallery, Fremont, Calif., 1977, Atkinson Art Gallery, Santa Barbara, Calif., 1978, Tower Art Gallery, Berkeley, Calif., 1979, Internat. Exhbn. of Photography, Adelaide, Australia, 1980, Arts Nat. Photog. Exhbn., Los Angeles, 1980, others. Registered profl. engr., Tex. Mem. Am. Inst. Mining, Metall. and Petroleum Engrs., Nat., Calif. socs. profl. engrs., Mo. Hist. Soc., Calif. Hist. Soc., Am. Rose Soc., Sigma Xi, Tau Beta Pi.

Co-author: European Zinc Smelters, 1964; contbr. articles to profl. jours. Home: 1178 Hamilton Ave Palo Alto CA 94301

BURGESS, JOY BELLE, city govt. ofcl.; b. Portland, Oreg., Sept. 20, 1928; d. Claude Sanford and Beulah Essia (Evans) McCoy; student Lewis and Clark Coll., Portland, 1946-47; m. John Alford Burgess, Dec. 17, 1948; children—Cathy, Jeffrey, David, Julie, Jeannie, Randy. Various secretarial positions, 1948-51; poet, contbr. Ideals Publishing Co., 1970—; mem. city council City of Milwaukie (Oreg.), 1972-80; mayor City of Milwaukie, 1981—; chmn. Milwaukie Parks and Beautification Com., 1971-72; chmn. local ofcl. adv. com. Met. Regional Govt., Portland, 1979-80; mem. citizens policy bd. Clackamas County Coop. Library Services, 1978-80; alt. del. White House Conf. on Libraries, 1979. Recipient Milwaukie Kiwanis Bullfrog award, 1972. Mem. LWV, Oreg. Fair Share, Milwaukie Hist. Soc. Home: 12208 SE 22d Ave Milwaukie OR 97222 Office: City Hall 10722 SE Main St Milwaukie OR 97222

BURGESS, LEONARD RANDOLPH, educator, writer; b. Washington, Mar. 8, 1919; s. W. Randolph and May Ayres B.; B.A., Brown U., 1942; M.B.A., Harvard U., 1947; Ph.D., Columbia U., 1961; m. Virginia Frost, May 26, 1946 (dec. Feb. 1978); m. 2d, Marga Minnick, Dec. 26, 1979 (div. 1983). Chief statistician W.Va. Pulp and Paper Co., N.Y.C., 1947-52; sr. staff assoc. Nat. Indsl. Conf. Bd., N.Y.C., 1952-57; lectr., instr. CCNY, N.Y.C., 1958-59; asst. prof. N. Tex. State U., Denton, 1961-64; assoc. prof. Tex. A&M U., College Station, 1964-68, prof., 1968-73, Temple U., Phila., 1973-74, U. Del., Wilmington, 1974-75; lectr. San Francisco State U., 1975-78; prof. Lincoln U., San Francisco, 1978—, head dept. bus. adminstrn. and econs., 1981—; mem. Lang. Research Inc., Cambridge, Mass., 1961-76. Staff asst. Brazos County (Tex.) Community Action Com., 1966-72, Brazos Valley Community Action Program, 1972-73. Served with AUS, 1941-45; lt. col. Res. Decorated Purple Heart. Mem. Acad. Mgmt., Acad. Polit. Sci., AAUP, Am. Compensation Assn., Harvard Bus. Sch. Assn. No. Calif., Delta Upsilon. Club: Presidio Officers. Author: (with Malcolm C. Neuhoff) Managing Company Airplanes, 1954, Top Executive Pay Package, 1963, Wage and Salary Adminstration in a Dynamic Economy, 1968; Wage and Salary Administration: Pay and Benefits, 1984; contbr. articles profl. jours. Home: 899 Crestview Dr San Carlos CA 94070 Office: Coll of Grad and Undergrad Studies Lincoln U 281 Masonic Ave San Francisco CA 94118

BURGESS, MARTHA AMES, museum official; b. Washington, Nov. 27, 1945; d. Robert Hyde and Virginia Dunbar (Wade) Ames; B.A. in Geology, Pembroke Coll., Brown U., Providence, 1967; M.S. in Geochronology, U. Ariz.-Tucson, 1972; m. Tony Lambard Burgess, Aug. 4, 1979. Dendrochronologist, Lab. Tree Ring Research, Tucson, 1972-76; research cons. plant dept. Ariz.-Sonora Desert Mus., Tucson, 1976-77, expdn. leader, coordinator spl. events and interpretation and edn. dept., 1977—. Mem. Am. Quaternary Assn., Tree Ring Soc., Am. Mus. Natural History, Tucson Mus. Assn., No. Ariz. Soc. Sci. and Art, Ariz. Native Plant Soc. (bd. dirs.), S.W. Mission Research Center, Oceanic Soc., Internat. Zoo Educators Assn., Sigma Xi. Republican. Episcopalian. Author: (with E. DeWitt) Tree-Ring Chronologies in Eastern North America; contbr. articles in field. Home: 812 S 5th Ave Tucson AZ 85701 Office: Ariz-Sonora Desert Museum Route 9 Box 900 Tucson AZ 85743

BURGESS, WILLIAM HENRY, financier, entrepreneur; b. Mpls., June 30, 1917; s. Gerald H. and Louise (Bailey) B.; m. Clara Ethel Woodward, June 21, 1941; children—Sarah Louise, Molly. B.B.A., U. Minn., 1939; M.B.A., Harvard U., 1941. Field rep. Panama Carbon Co., summer 1935, Burroughs Co., summer 1936, Northrup-King & Co., summers 1937-38; indls. engr. R.R. Donnelley & Sons, 1941-42; mgmt. engr. Hollister & Evans, 1945-46; founder, chmn. bd. Shavex Corp., 1949-56, Electornic Splty. Co., 1949-68; chmn. bd. Hydro-Jet Corp., 1971-74, Continental Controls Corp., 1972-77, RHG Corp., El Monte, Calif., 1976—, TimeLapse Corp., Mountain View, Calif., 1976—, Internat. Controls Corp., Boca Raton, Fla., 1978—; prin. assoc. Century Indsl. Assocs., 1976-77; dir. Titech Corp., Ponoma, Calif., 1976—, Early Calif. Industries, Los Angeles, 1976—; mem. panel arbitrators N.Y. Stock Exchange, 1973—. Trustee Pasadena (Calif.) Mus. Modern Art, 1956-74, L.S.B. Leakey Found., 1969-79, Palm Springs Desert Mus., 1977-79; dir. Huntington Meml. Tumor Clinic, 1958-60, So. Calif. council Inst. Internat. Edn., 1970-72, Palm Springs Friends of Philharm., 1974-79, Palm Springs World Affairs Council, 1974—; mem. adv. bd. YWCA, 1958-60; mem. adv. council Internat. Mktg. Inst., 1959-63; bd. dirs. Los Angeles World Affairs Council, 1962-80, treas., v.p., 1966-68; mem. hon. bd. Pasadena Foothill Tennis Patrons Assn., 1964-68; bd. overseers, mem. vis. com. Harvard U., 1964-70; dir., co-founder Los Angeles Music Ctr., 1967-71; bd. govs. Tennis Patrons Assn. So. Calif., 1966; trustee Otis Art Inst., 1967-74; mem. hon. adv. bd. Internat. Profl. Tennis Assn., 1967-68; trustee San Gabriel Valley Scout Found., Boy Scouts Am., 1968-69, Space Age Hall Sci., 1973-76; vice chmn. commerce and industry United Crusade, 1968; mem. pres.'s council Calif. Inst. Tech., 1968-71; world ambassador UCLA Internat. Student Ctr., 1970-71; mem. pres.'s adv. council U. Redlands, 1971-78; mem. curriculum adv. com. U. So. Calif. Bus. Sch., 1972-74; mem. Atty. Gen.'s Vol. Adv. Com., 1971-76; mem. orthopaedic council Los Angeles Orthopaedic Hosp., 1972-76. Served to lt. USNR, 1941-45. Recipient So. Calif. Bus. Achievement award Harvard Bus. Sch. Club, 1963; citation disting. service DAV, 1963; Outstanding Achievement award U. Minn., 1964. Mem. Nat. Inst. Social Sci., U. Minn. Alumni Assn., Am. Security Council (nat. adv. bd. 1971—), Phi Delta Theta. Republican. Presbyterian. Clubs: River (N.Y.C.); Harvard, California, Harvard Bus. Sch., Lincoln (Los Angeles); Valley Hunt (Pasadena); Eldorado Country, Palm Springs Racquet, Palm Springs Tennis, Desert Dinner Vintage Country (Palm Springs); Super Sr. Tennis Assn. Home and office: 550 Palisades Dr Palm Springs CA 92262

BURGETT, MICHAEL JOSEPH, safety coordinator; b. Oklahoma City, May 13, 1956; s. Joseph Wayne and Claudette Mary (Weller) B.; m. Paula Ann Medill, Feb. 12, 1977; children—Katie, Harlen, Clayton. Student Colo. Mountain Coll., Leadville, 1975-76, Brigham Young U., Provo, Utah, 1978-79. Miner 1st class AMAX, Climax Molybdeum Mine, Colo., 1975-77; blasting supt. Horner Coal Co., Agiliar, Colo., 1977-78; safety coordinator Anaconda Minerals Co., Carr Fork Mine, Tooele, Utah, 1980—. Mem. Am. Soc. Safety Engrs., AIME. Republican. Mormon. Home: 27 Park Ave Tooele UT 84074 Office: Anaconda Carr Fork Rt 1 Box 79 Tooele UT 84074

BURGHARD, RONALD ALBERT, elec. engr.; b. Spokane, Mar. 11, 1946; s. Fred Albert and Gladys Irene (Whitman) B.; B.S.E.E., Mont. State U., 1968; M.S.E.E., Stanford U., 1969; Ph.D. in Physics, Mont. State U., 1977; m. Sharon Louise Laws, June 24, 1967; children—John Albert, Melody Ruth. Engr., Sandia Labs., Albuquerque, 1968-74; engr. Tektronix, Inc., Beaverton, Oreg., 1977-79; engr. Intel Corp., Aloha, Oreg., 1979—. Mem. IEEE. Home: 20530 SW Wyngate Aloha OR 97007 Office: 3585 SW 198th Aloha OR 97007

BURGIN, ROBERT AUGUSTUS, transportation company executive; b. Rolling Fork, Miss., July 20, 1924; s. Robert Augustus and Jane (Sullivan) B.; m. Sara Porter Shofner, Dec. 4, 1948 (dec.); children—Sally Burgin Margolis, Robert Augustus III, Christopher. B.S., U. Tenn., 1949. With Oak Ridge Inst. Nuclear Studies, 1949-51; br. chief Dept. Def., Washington and Albuquerque, 1951-56; cons. Stanford Research Inst., 1956-57; with TRW, 1956-78, v.p., asst. to chmn. bd. TRW Systems, 1965-67, v.p., gen. mgr. TRW Automotive Internat., 1967-71, v.p. planning and devel. Automotive Worldwide, 1972-73, v.p., gen. mgr. telecommunications, 1974-78, v.p. planning and devel. TRW Electronics, 1973-78; chmn., chief exec. officer Leaseway Transp. Co., Cleve., 1978-82, now dir.; dir. E.F. Johnson Co., Waseca, Minns., Storage Corp., Louisville, Colo., Provident Life and Accident Co., Chattanooga, CFS Continental Inc., Chgo., Western Union, N.Y.C., Telenova, San Jose, Calif. Mem. exec. bd. Greater Cleve. council Boy Scouts Am., 1979; mem. exec. com. Hugh O'Brian Youth Found., 1977-79; bd. dirs. Greater Cleve. Growth Assn., 1979; trustee Fuller Theol. Sem., Pasadena, Calif., 1978, Calif., 1978; mem. Served to capt. USAAF, 1943-45, 51-52. Mem. Sigma Phi Epsilon. Clubs: Union, Sunrise Country, Desert Horizons Country. Home and Office: 2505 Ardath Rd La Jolla CA 92037

BURHANS, FRANK MALCOLM, mechanical engineer; b. Hagerstown, Md., Dec. 11, 1920; s. William Humphrey Sr. and Ethel Adele (Forthman) B.; m. Jean Maria Dermott, Oct. 10, 1943; children—Stephen William, Douglas Allan, Jeffrey Malcolm. B.E. in Mech. Engring., Johns Hopkins U., 1942; postgrad. U. Conn., 1942-43. Registered profl. engr., Wash. Design engr. Pratt & Whitney, East Hartford, Conn., 1942-55, Ford Motor Co., Dearborn, Mich., 1955-58; sr. design engr. Fairchild Engine Div., Deer Park, N.Y., 1958-59; sr. specialist engr. Turbine Div. Boeing Co., Seattle, 1959-66, prin. engr. Boeing Aircraft Engine Installations, 1967—. Active Boy Scouts Am. Served with AC, U.S. Army, 1945-47. Recipient Silver Beaver award Boy Scouts Am. Mem. AIAA, ASME. Presbyterian. Club: Masons (past master) (Bellevue). Designer products and devices related to gas turbines. Office: PO Box 3707 Seattle WA 98124

BURIMA-SIPERKO, GLORIA M., psychology educator, developmental specialist; b. Saskatoon, Sask., Can., Feb. 11, 1945; d. Paul A. and Nina (Postnikoff) Burima; m. Eric A. Siperko, Sept. 5, 1965; children—Keesa, Kelee, Kai. B.A. in Sociology and Psychology, U. Alta., 1967, M.A. in Sociology, 1970, Ph.D. in Devel. Psychology, 1976. Research asst. Dept. of Youth, 1970-71; reviewer grants in aid Human Resources Research Council, 1971; research officer planning and devel. br. Alta. Culture, Youth and Recreation, 1971-74, dir. ECS coordination br., 1974-75; planning cons. research and systems Dept. Recreation, Parks and Wildlife, 1975-76; assoc. prof. psychology Pacific Union Coll., Angwin, Calif., 1976—; pvt. practice clin. psychology, 1982—; dir. Grandview Children's Ranch, 1982—. Mem. Am. Psychol. Assn., Western Psychol. Assn., Internat. Council Psychologists. Seventh-day Adventist. Home and Office: 955 Friesen Dr Angwin CA 94508

BURK, JACK ANDREW, investment co. exec.; b. Springfield, Tenn., Mar. 19, 1935; s. Andrew Jackson and Elizabeth Ethelyne (Revels) B.; student Central Bible Inst., Springfield, Mo., 1953-54, So. Calif. Coll., Costa Mesa, 1955; student San Fernando Valley Coll., 1956; m. Alice Jean Jackson, Apr. 24, 1965; children—Teresa Lynn, Cheryl Ninette, Loren Dwayne. With Rocketdyne div. N. Am. Aviation Santa Susana Rocket Test sect., 1959-65; with Equity Funding Corp., 1965-73, area. v.p. So. Calif., Century City, 1970-71, v.p., resident mgr., Tarzana, Calif., 1972-73; founder, pres. Preferred Exec. Programs Inc., Woodland Hills, Calif., 1973-76; mem. adv. com. Am. Pacific Life Ins. Co., San Rafael, Calif., 1973-77; dir. bus. affairs Peoples Found., Fresno, Calif., 1977—; gen. mgr. PF Communications Inc., Fresno, 1979—. Mem. Nat. Assn. Securities Dealers, Nat. Assn. Life Underwriters, Internat. Assn. Fin. Planners. Republican. Home: 9391 E Ellery Clovis CA 93612 Office: 2727 N Grove Industrial Dr Fresno CA 93727

BURK, JERRY LEONARD, aluminum company executive; b. Sulphur, Okla., Nov. 18, 1945; s. Cecil Leonard and Mildred Oleta (Trent) B.; m. Sharon Diane Peterson, Dec. 18, 1964; children—Jerry Carl, Christopher Troy. A.A., Bakersfield Coll., 1966; B.A., Fresno State Coll., 1967; M.A., U. Mont., 1969; Ph.D., U. Okla., 1973. Mem. faculty Phillips U., Enid, Okla., 1968-71, U. Detroit, 1973-75, Boise (Idaho) State U., 1975-77; dir. Process Cons. Assocs., Boise, 1977-78; dir. research Morrison Knudsen Inc., Boise, 1978-80; mgr. tng. and devel. Martin Marietta aluminum Co., Goldendale, Wash., 1980—. Mem. Am. Soc. for Tng. and Devel. (sec.-treas. Valley chpt. 1979-80). Democrat. Club: Kiwanis (pres. 1982, 83) (Goldendale). Contbr. to publs. in field. Home: 417 Brashear Way Goldendale WA 98620 Office: PO Box 46 Star Route 677 Goldendale WA 98620

BURKE, ARTHUR THOMAS, engineering consultant; b. Pueblo, Colo., Nov. 26, 1919; s. Daniel Michael and Naomi Edith (Brashear) B.; B.S., U.S. Naval Acad., 1941; postgrad. UCLA; m. Regina Ahlgren Malone, June 15, 1972; children—Arthur Thomas, Craig Timothy, Laura Ahlgren, Scott Ahlgren. With USN Electronics Lab. Center, San Diego, 1947-72, sr. satellite communications cons., 1964-72, satellite communications engring. cons., 1974—. Judge, San Diego Sci. Fair, 1960—. Served with USN, 1938-46; comdr. Res., ret. Recipient Superior Performance award USN Electronics Lab. Center, 1967. Mem. IEEE (mem. San Diego membership com. 1958-68), AAAS, San Diego Astronomy Assn., San Diego Computer Assn., Am. Radio Relay League. Patentee electronic bathythermograph. Home and Office: 4011 College Ave San Diego CA 92115

BURKE, BEVERLY A., psychologist; b. Pulaski, Va.; d. Jack Edward and Mary Elizabeth (Brewer) B. B.A. cum laude in Psychology, Lipscomb Coll., Nashville, 1965; M.Ed. summa cum laude in Spl. Edn., Central State U., Edmond, Okla., 1969; Ph.D. cum laude in Psychology, Okla. U.-Norman, 1977. Lic. psychologist, Okla. Tchr. Nashville Pub. Schs., 1965-66; instr. dept. edn. and psychology Central State U., Edmond, Okla., 1969-71; mem. psychol. staff and asst. dir. S.W. Guidance Ctr., Wheatland, Okla., 1974-78; psychologist and dir. Canadian County Guidance Ctr., El Reno, Okla., 1978-80; children's mental health specialist Seattle Indian Health Bd., 1981—; cons. to Nat. Inst. on Drug Abuse, Concho Indian Sch., Jones Acad. Mem. bd. dirs. Okla. Indian Edn. Assn.; mem. Okla. City Cherokee Community Orgn.; Mem. Cherokee Tribe of Okla. Mem. Am. Psychol. Assn., Nat. Indian Edn. Assn., Okla. Psychol. Assn., Wash. State Psychol. Assn., S.W. Psychol. Assn., Soc. of Indian Psychologists. Office: Box 98311 Seattle WA 98188

BURKE, DANIEL MARTIN, lawyer; b. Casper, Wyo., Sept. 9, 1946; s. Michael Joseph and Mary Josephine (Sirridge) B.; B.A., U. Wyo., 1968, J.D., 1970; m. Ellen Arden, July 3, 1970; children—Daniel Martin III, Kathleen Ellen, Brendan Arden, Anne Mary, Susan Theresa. Bar: Wyo. 1970. Law clk. to judge U.S. 10th Cir. Ct. Appeals (10th cir.), Cheyenne, Wyo., 1970; spl. asst. atty. gen. State of Wyo., Cheyenne, 1970-71; instr. Casper Coll., 1971-75; county and pros. atty. Natrona County, Casper, 1975-79; mem. Burke, Horn & Lewis, Casper, 1975-79; pres. Burke & Horn, P.C., Casper, 1979-82, Burke & Brown, P.C., Casper, 1983—; chmn. bd., pres. Rocky Mountain Communications Network, Inc., 1982—; v.p., dir. Evco, Inc., 1982—; dir. Guarantee Fed. Bank, First Nat. Bank Evanston (Wyo.), Wyo. Fin. Services, Inc.; gen. partner Bantry Bay Co.; pres. The Chrysostom Corp.; sec. Shamrock Ranch Co., Casper, 1969—; asst. city atty. City of Casper, 1971-74. Mem. council St. Anthony Parish; mem. St. Anthony Parochial Sch. Bd.; bd. arbitrators Am. Arbitration Assn., Mem. ABA, Wyo. State Bar (sec. 1973-75), Natrona County bar assns., Am. Judicature Soc., Nat. Assn. Dist. Attys. (dir. 1977-78), Wyo. Assn. County Attys. (pres. 1977-78), Caper C. of C. Republican. Roman Catholic. Clubs: Casper Country, KC. Home: 1008 S Wolcott St Casper WY 82601 Office: 111 S Durbin St Casper WY 82601

BURKE, DAVID PATRICK, educational administrator, political scientist; b. Washington, Apr. 8, 1934; s. William P. and Dolores A. (Keffler) B.; m. Anna Frances Donovan, Mar. 7, 1959; children—Maureen, Sean, Kevin, Michael. B.A., U. Calif., 1956; M.A., San Francisco State U., 1963; M.P.A., Harvard U., 1969, Ph.D., 1975. Commd. 2d lt. U.S. Air Force, 1956, advanced through grades to lt. col., 1980; intelligence officer, Japan, 1958-61; staff officer hdqrs. SAC, 1962-65; instr. polit. sci. U.S. Air Force Acad., 1965-67; adv. to dean Vietnamese Nat. Mil. Acad., 1970-71; staff officer Orgn. Joint Chiefs of Staff, 1971-75; asst. prof. polit. sci. Naval Postgrad. Sch., Monterey, Calif., 1976-80; dir. Ft. Ord Campus Monterey Peninsula Coll., Monterey, 1980—; adj. prof. nat. security affairs Naval Postgrad. Sch., Monterey, 1980—. Decorated Bronze Star, Honor medal 1st class (Vietnam); Air Force Inst. Tech. grantee, 1968-69; Naval Postgrad. Sch. Found. grantee, 1977, 78. Fellow Inter-Univ. Seminar on Armed Forces and Soc.; mem. Internat. Inst. Strategic Studies, Am. Polit. Sci. Assn., Assn. Can. Studies in U.S., Phi Beta Kappa. Democrat. Roman Catholic. Co-editor: Eurocommunism between East and West, 1980; contbr. articles and revs. to profl. jours., chpts. to books on comparative def. policy, Can. and Romanian studies, mil. history. Home: 18 Wyndemere Rise Monterey CA 93940 Office: Monterey Peninsula Coll 980 Fremont Blvd Monterey CA 93940

BURKE, EDMOND WAYNE, judge; b. Ukiah, Calif., Sept. 7, 1935; s. Wayne P. and Opal K. B.; A.B., Humboldt State Coll., 1957, M.A., 1958; J.D., U. Calif., 1964; m. Sharon E. Halverson, Jan. 25, 1977; children—Kathleen R., Jennifer E. Admitted to Calif. bar, Alaska bar; individual practice law, Calif. and Alaska, 1965-67; asst. atty. gen. State of Alaska, 1967; asst. dist. atty., Anchorage, 1968-69; judge Superior Ct., Alaska, 1970-75; justice Supreme Ct. State of Alaska, Anchorage, 1975—. Mem. Alaska Bar Assn., Am. Judicature Soc. Republican. Presbyterian. Office: 303 K St Anchorage AK 99501*

BURKE, EDMUND ROBERT, physical fitness association executive, consultant; b. N.Y.C., Aug. 23, 1949; s. Michael and Mary (Burke) B. B.S. Ball State U., 1971; M.A., 1976; Ph.D., Ohio State U., 1979. Postdoctoral fellow U. Iowa Hosps., Iowa City, 1979-81, research scientist, 1981-82; tech. dir. U.S. Cycling Fedn., Colorado Springs, Colo., 1982—; research scientist Karolinska Inst., Stockholm, 1981. Fellow Am. Coll. Sport Medicine; mem. Am. Alliance Health and Phys. Edn., Am. Physiol. Soc. Roman Catholic. Researcher in biomechanics, physiology, pathomechanics, aerodynamics of competitive cycling. Office: US Cycling Fedn 1750 E Boulder St Colorado Springs CO 80909

BURKE, JAMES EDWARD, accountant; b. Wilkes-Barre, Pa., Jan. 22, 1951; m. Lisa Mann, Dec. 1, 1973; children—Joshua, Zachary. A.B., Bowdoin Coll., 1972; M.L.S., Simmons Coll., 1975. C.P.A., N.Mex. Staff acct. Konowitz, Kahn, Rashba, Leibowitz, P.C., New Haven, 1979-81; mem. staff Pulakos & Alongi, Ltd., Albuquerque, 1981-82; ptnr. Lees & Burke, C.P.A.s, Albuquerque, 1982—; treas. La Puerta De Los Ninos, Albuquerque. Mem. Am. Inst. C.P.A.s, N.Mex. Soc. C.P.A.s. Office: 12800 Lomas Blvd NE Albuquerque NM 87123

BURKE, JANICE MARIE, supt. schs.; b. Wenatchee, Wash., Feb. 22, 1934; d. Bernard Keigher and Anne Margaret (Mertens) B.; B.S. in Edn., Marylhurst Coll., 1959; M.A.T. in Sci. and Math., Oreg. Coll. Edn., 1971; cert. in religious edn., Seattle U., 1960; postgrad. San Jose State Coll., 1965, Western Wash. State Coll., 1975, U. San Francisco, 1978, U. Oreg., 1978, Portland State U., 1978. Joined Sisters of the Holy Names, 1952; tchr. St. Mary's, St. Anne's and St. Patrick's elem. schs., Seattle, also St. Vincent's Sch., Salem, Oreg., St. Peter's Sch., Newberg, Oreg. and St. Peter's Sch., Portland, Oreg., 1955-66; elem. prin. Madeleine Sch., Portland, 1966-72; adminstrv. asst. dept. edn. Marylhurst Coll., Oreg., 1972-74; elem. prin. St. Joseph's Sch., Vancouver, Wash., 1974-77; asso. dir. elem. edn. Archdiocesan Office of Edn., Portland, 1977-80; supt. schs. Archdiocesan Office of Edn., Portland, 1978-80, Diocese of Yakima, Wash., 1980—; ednl. cons. schs., bus., chs.; exec. sec. Sisters of the Holy Names, 1972-74, vice chmn., 1974-75, chmn., 1975-76. NSF grantee, 1965. Mem. Nat. Cath. Edn. Assn., Chief Adminstrs. Cath. Edn., Assn. Curriculum Devel. and Supervision, Am. Assn. Sch. Adminstrs., Wash. Assn. Sch. Adminstrs. (sec. region, pres.-elect region), Wash. Fedn. Ind. Schs., Nat. Assn. Elem. Prins. Democrat. Home: 924 S 20th Ave Yakima WA 98902 Office: PO Box 2834 Yakima WA 98907

BURKE, ROBERT EUGENE, historian, educator; b. Chico, Calif., July 22, 1921; s. Ralph Ambrose and Frieda (Rupp) B.; A.B., Chico State Coll., 1946; M.A., U. Calif.-Berkeley, 1947, Ph.D., 1950; 1 dau., Elizabeth Anne. Teaching fellow U. Calif. at Berkeley, 1948-50; dir. Bancroft Library Research Program. Eng., 1950-51; head manuscripts div. Bancroft Library, U. Calif. at Berkeley, 1951-56; asst. prof. history U. Hawaii, 1956-57; asst. prof. history U. Wash., Seattle, 1957-60, asso. prof., 1960-65, prof., 1965—, chmn. dept., 1962-67. Mem. Nat. Hist. Publs. and Records Commn., 1977-80. Served with AUS, 1942-45; PTO. Mem. Am. Hist. Assn., Am. Assn. for State and Local History, Western History Assn., Orgn. Am. Historians. Author: Olson's New Deal for California, 1953. Co-author: The American Nation, 1963, 4th edit., 1971; The Federal Union, 1964, 4th edit., 1970; A History of Am. Democracy, 4th edit., 1970; The New Era and The New Deal, 1920-1940, 1981. Mng. editor: Pacific Northwest Quar.; gen. editor Americana Library. Home: 7336 19th Ave NE Seattle WA 98115

BURKE, ROGER WILLIAM, accountant; b. Portland, Oreg., Feb. 15, 1947; s. Robert Julius and Laura Marie (Rowley) B.; m. Linda Eleanor Lippert, Sept. 9, 1966; children—Scott, Steven, Katherine. B.S., Portland State U., 1973. C.P.A., Oreg. Acct. Maier & Chatterton, Portland, 1973-74, Main, Hurdman & Cranstoun, Portland, 1974-76, Pihas, Schmidt & Westerdahl Co., 1976-79; self-employed CPA, Portland, 1979—. Chmn. Oreg. Legislators Tax Guide, 1980; chmn. bd. Parent Child Services, 1979; bd. dirs. Am. Lung Assn., 1979-81; bd. dirs., chmn. fin. com., Oreg. Lung Assn.; trustee Sadie Dunbar Trust. Served with U.S. Army, 1966-69. Mem. Am. Inst. C.P.A.s, Oreg. Soc. C.P.A.s. Republican. Lutheran. Columnist Daily Jour. Commerce, other publs. Office: 811 E Burnside St Suite 224 Portland OR 97214

BURKE, YVONNE BRATHWAITE (MRS. WILLIAM BURKE), lawyer; b. Los Angeles; d. James T. and Lola (Moore) Watson; B.A. in Polit. Sci., UCLA; J.D., U. So. Calif., 1956; m. William Burke, June 14, 1972; 1 dau., Autumn. Admitted to Calif. bar, 1956; practiced in Los Angeles, 1956-66; mem. Calif. Ho. of Reps., 1966-72; mem. 93d Congress from 37th Dist. Calif., 94th-95th Congresses from 28th Dist. Calif.; former supr. Los Angeles County; of counsel Fine Perzik & Friedman, Los Angeles. Bd. regents U. Calif., 1979—; mem. exec. com. Los Angeles Olympic Organizing Com., 1979—. Fellow Inst. Politics, Harvard. Recipient Loren Miller award for outstanding contbn. to Calif. legal system NAACP, Sojourner Truth award Negro Bus. and Profl. Women's Clubs; named Woman of Year, Iota Phi Lambda, Zeta Phi Beta, One of 100 Outstanding women opinion-makers Harpers Bazaar; also numerous awards from Los Angeles City Council, Los Angeles Bd. Suprs., numerous ch. and lay orgns. lawyer; b. Los Angeles; d. James T. and Lola (Moore) Watson; B.A. in Polit. Sci., UCLA; J.D., U. So. Calif., 1956; m. William Burke, June 14, 1972; 1 dau., Autumn. Admitted to Calif. bar, 1956; practiced in Los Angeles, 1956-66; mem. Calif. Ho. of Reps., 1966-72; mem. 93d Congress from 37th Dist. Calif., 94th-95th Congresses from 28th Dist. Calif.; former supr. Los Angeles County; of counsel Fine Perzik & Friedman, Los Angeles. Bd. regents U. Calif., 1979—; mem. exec. com. Los Angeles Olympic Organizing Com., 1979—. Fellow Inst. Politics, Harvard. Recipient Loren Miller award for outstanding contbn. to Calif. legal system NAACP, Sojourner Truth award Negro Bus. and Profl. Women's Clubs; named Woman of Year, Iota Phi Lambda, Zeta Phi Beta, One of 100 Outstanding women opinion-makers Harpers Bazaar; also numerous awards from Los Angeles City Council, Los Angeles Bd. Suprs., numerous ch. and lay orgns. Office: Suite 1400 600 Wilshire Blvd Los Angeles CA 90017

BURKEE, IRVIN, artist; b. Kenosha, Wis., Feb. 6, 1918; s. Omar Lars and Emily (Quardokas) B.; diploma Sch. of Art Inst. Chgo., 1945; m. Bonnie May Ness, Apr. 12, 1945; children—Brynn, Jill, Peter (dec.), Ian. Owner, silversmith, goldsmith Burkee Jewelry, Blackhawk, Colo., 1950-57; painter, sculptor, Aspen, Colo., 1957-78, Cottonwood, Ariz., Pietrasanta, Italy, 1978—; instr. art U. Colo., 1946, 50-53, Stephens Coll., Columbia, Mo., 1947-49. John Quincy Adams travel fellow, Mex., 1945. Executed copper mural of human history of Colo. for First Nat. Bank, Englewood, Colo., 1970, copper mural of wild birds of Kans. for Ranchmart State Bank, Overland Park, Kans., 1974; exhibited Art Inst. Chgo., Smithsonian Instn., Milw. Art Inst., Krannert Mus., William Rockhill Nelson Gallery, St. Louis Art Mus., Denver Art Mus.; represented in permanent collections several southwestern galleries, also pvt. collections throughout U.S.; work illustrated in books Design and Creation of Jewelry, Design through Discovery, Walls. Address: Box 2071 Rio Verde Acres Cottonwood AZ 86326

BURKHALTER, THOMAS HERBERT, ret. army officer; b. Iron Mountain, Mich., Jan. 13, 1930; s. Herbert Walter and Mildred Eva (Thomas) B.; m. Lieu Thi Luong, July 11, 1972; 1 child, Kim Van. B.S., U. Wis., 1952; M.A., Ohio State U., 1956; postgrad. Army Command and Gen. Staff Coll., 1963-64, Armed Forces Staff Coll., 1966, Indsl. Coll. of Armed Forces, 1971. Commd. 2d lt. U.S. Army, 1952, advanced through grades to col., 1972; served with inf. Korean War, petroleum terminal and pipeline, France; bn. comdr. Vietnam; dir. depot storage, dep. comdr. inventory control center; army staff force devel.; dep. chief of staff Logistics, Thailand; V Corps, W. Ger.; dep. chief of staff Logistics, 6th U.S. Army, Presidio, San Francisco, 1980-82, ret., 1982; ops. mgr. Curley-Bates Co., Burlingame, Calif., 1982—; pres. German-Am. Logistic Soc., 1979-80. Decorated Legion of Merit with 3 oak leaf clusters, Bronze Star, Purple Heart. Mem. Am. Psychol. Assn., Assn. U.S. Army. Methodist. Clubs: Masons, Scottish Rite, Royal Arch, Sojourners. Home: 1821 Canyon Oak Ct San Mateo CA 94402 Office: 860 Stanton Rd Burlingame CA 94010

BURKHAMMER, STEWART CURTIS, constrn. and engring. co. exec.; b. Long Beach, Calif., Dec. 27, 1943; s. Henry Bland and Edith Marie (Jones) B.; student U. Wis., Whitewater, 1962-65; cert. in Safety Engring., U. Wis., 1967; m. Cheryl Ernestine Fisher, June 28, 1969; children—S. Christopher, Wendy Lynette. With Bechtel Power Corp., 1966—, regional safety mgr. San Francisco, 1977—. Registered safety engr., Calif.; cert. safety profl. Mem. Am. Soc. Safety Engrs. (profl.) Republican. Baptist. Clubs: Las Positas Men's Golf, Elks. Home: 837 Orion Way Livermore CA 94550 Office: 50 Beale St San Francisco CA 94119

BURKHART, DONALD EDGAR, JR., safety director; b. Red Bank, N.J., Sept. 4, 1948; s. Donald Edgar and Mary (DeStefano) B.; m. Mary Roberta Ott, June 27, 1970; children—Matthew Donald, Andrew Robert, Catherine Marie. B.S. in Physics, John Carroll U., Cleveland, 1970. Cert. safety profl. Sr. loss prevention rep. Liberty Mut. Ins. Co., Pitts., 1970-74; underwriting surveyor Chubb & Son, Inc., Cin., 1974-75; product safety engr. FMC Corp., Fairmont, W.Va., 1975-79; sr. safety engr. Reynolds Elec. & Engring. Co., Las Vegas, 1979-80; safety dir. Arch Mineral Corp., Hanna, Wyo., 1980-82, NERCO Antelope Coal Co., Douglas Wyo., 1982—. Mem. Civic Water Improvement Group, Nat. Fire Protection Assn., Am. Soc. of Safety Engrs. Roman Catholic. Clubs: White Oak Rod and Gun (North Huntingdon, Pa.). Office: PO Drawer 1450 Douglas WY 82633

BURKHART, JOE EARL, mortgage company executive, banker; b. Atchison, Kans., July 11, 1924; s. Earl Charles and Blanche Anna (Scheib) B.; m. Rita Yvonne Hipner, Feb. 19, 1949; children—Barbara, Cathleen, Nancy. Student Phoenix Coll., 1942-43; B.S. in Bus. Adminstrn., U. Ariz., 1948. With FHA, Phoenix, 1950-59, chief appraiser, 1956-59, asst. chief underwriter, 1958-59; with Valley Nat. Bank Ariz., Phoenix, 1959—, asst. v.p., chief appraiser, 1962-67, v.p., asst. mgr. real estate loan div., 1967-74, v.p., mgr. real estate loan div., 1974-80; v.p., gen. mgr. Valley Nat. Mortgage Co. subs. Valley Nat. Bank Ariz., Phoenix, 1980—; bd. regents Nat. Sch. Real Estate Fin.; thesis examiner Stonier Grad. Sch. Banking, Am. Bankers, 1980-83. Mem. adv. bd. Salvation Army, Phoenix, 1964—, chmn., 1967, treas., 1975; chmn. Phoenix Housing Commn., 1976-77; bd. dirs. Neighborhood Housing Services, Phoenix, 1976—, Med. Ctr. Redevel. Corp., 1981—; mem. steering com. City of Phoenix Community Devel. Block Grant, 1977-80; elder Camelback United Presbyn. Ch., Paradise Valley, Ariz., 1982—. Served with U.S. Army 1943-45; to capt. USAF, 1950-52. Recipient Sally award Salvation Army, 1979. Mem. Am. Bankers Assn. (exec. com. housing and real estate fin. div. 1977-80), Phoenix Bd. Realtors (judge ct. ethics 1964-75), Am. Inst. Real Estate Appraisers (pres. Ariz. chpt. 1963), Soc. Real Estate Appraisers (pres. Phoenix chpt. 1963), Robert Morris Assn. (nat. real estate fin. com. 1980-81). Clubs: Phoenix Country, Kiwanis of Sky Harbor (pres. 1972) (Phoenix).

BURKHART, WILLIAM EDWARD, advertising sales director; b. Elizabeth, N.J., July 27, 1933; s. William E. and Isabelle (Duck) B.; m. Deborah Ann Davidson, May 29, 1966; children—Kirsten Ann, Brandy Nicole. B.A., Sayracuse U., 1959. New Eng. sales mgr. Field & Stream, 1970-77; so. advt. mgr. Sea mag., 1977-79; advt. sales mgr. New Fla. mag., 1980-81; advt. sales dir. Soldier of Fortune mag., Boulder, Colo., 1982—. Served with U.S. Army, 1956-58. Club: Advt. Sportsman's of N.Y. (past pres.). Address: PO Box 693 Boulder CO 80306

BURKHOLDER, JAMES ALFRED, JR., air force officer; b. Bonners Ferry, Idaho, June 23, 1944; s. James Alfred and Valdie Virginia (White) B.; m. Karen Ann Simmons, May 30, 1968 (div.); 1 son, James Alfred III. B.S. in English, Speech and Secondary Edn., U. Idaho, 1967; M.A. in Bus. Adminstrn., Boise State U., 1977. Commd. 2d lt U.S. Air Force, 1967; advanced through grades to lt. col., 1983; pilot Vance AFB, Okla, 1967-68, Vietnam, 1969, Holloman AFB, N.Mex., 1969-71; chief Standarization and Evaluation Div., Shaw AFB, S.C., 1971-74; chief Tng. Support Div., Mountain Home AFB, Idaho, 1974-77; chief ops. and tng., Lakenheath, Eng., 1977-79, Air Command and Staff Coll., Maxwell AFB, Alaska, 1979-80; Cadet Squadron comdr. U.S. Air Force Acad., 1980-82, chief mil. tng., 1982—; mem. base Speakers Bur. Decorated D.F.C., 13, Air medals, 2 Meritorious Service medals, Air Force Commendation medal; Vietnam Campaign medal with 4 Bronze Stars, Vietnam Cross of Gallantry. Mem. Air Froce Assn., Am. Soc. Tng. and Devel., Orders and Medals Soc. Am., Orders and Medals Soc. Eng., Am. Soc. Mil. Insignia Collectors, Am. Legion, Theta Chi. Methodist. Author: Concepts of Airforce Leadership, 1983; contbr. articles to profl. publs. Home: 5620 Old Farm Terr Colorado Springs CO 80917 Office: Military Training Div US Air Force Academy CO 80840

BURKHOLDER, SHIRLEY JEAN, publishing company executive; b. Metropolis, Ill. July 21, 1937; d. James H. and Helen Patlijo (O'Brien) Gray; m. Harold Richard Burkholder, June 27, 1968; 1 son, Richard Jonathan. Student Bapt. Coll., Springfield, Mo., 1956-59. Audit supr. Sears Roebuck & Co., Kansas City, Kans., also Denver, 1966-75; personal lines supr. SafeCo Ins. Co., Denver, 1975-76; gen. mgr. Central Bapt. Temple, Huntington Beach, Calif., 1976-77; v.p. Gick Pub., Inc., Irvine, Calif., 1977—; v.p. Western Nursery Supply, 1982—. Mem. Nat. Fedn. Ind. Bus., Hobby Industry Am., Am. Home Sew Assn. Republican. Baptist. Office: 9 Studebaker Dr Irvine CA 92714

BURKS, MICHAEL E., television sports producer; b. Mineral Wells, Tex., Aug. 20, 1952; s. Chester A. and Mary D. (Doheny) B. B.A., Ind. U., 1975. With various local TV stas., Boston, Indpls., 1971-75; with CBS, Los Angeles, 1975, 77—, unit mgr. CBS Sports, 1977-79, assoc. producer/dir., 1979—. Recipient nat. Emmy award, 1982. Mem. Dirs. Guild Am., Nat. Acad. TV Arts and Scis., Sigma Delta Chi. Office: CBS 7800 Beverly Blvd Los Angeles CA 90036

BURKS, WILLIAM FENTON, savings and loan association executive; b. Springfield, Mo., June 13, 1930; s. Theron T. and Ethyl (Frieze) B.; A.B. in Econs., U. Mo., 1952; m. Susanne Martin, Sept. 27, 1964; children—William Randolph, Julie Ann. Mgr. loan dept. Farm & Home Savs. Assn., Kansas City, Mo., 1954-61; v.p. People's Savs. Assn., Toledo, 1961-64; exec. v.p., mng. officer Home Savs. & Loan Assn., Albuquerque, 1964-67; pres., dir. Am. Savs. & Loan Assn., Albuquerque, 1967-82; vice chmn., dir. Am. Fed. Savs. & Loan, Albuquerque, 1982—; mem. adv. council Fed. Home Loan Bank, 1979-81, past pres. League Insured Savs. and Loan Assns. N. Mex., 1971-72; vice chmn. bd. dirs. Fed Home Loan Bank of Little Rock 9th Dist., 1976-78, dir., 1973-78. Vice chmn. N. Mex. State Fair Commn., 1979—; treas., bd. dirs. Albuquerque Little Theatre, 1973-77. Served to col. USMCR, 1952-82. Mem. U.S. League Savs. Assns., Albuquerque C. of C., Albuquerque Mortgage Bankers Assn., Am. Rose Soc., Bldg. Contractors Assn. N.Mex., Exec. Assn. Greater Albuquerque (past pres.), Friends of Vista Sandia Hosp., Internat. Connoisseurs of Green and Red Chili, Marine Corps Res. Officers Assn., Navy League, Res. Officers Assn., Albuquerque Home Builders Assn. (assoc.), Soc. Real Estate Appraisers (assoc.) Execs. Assn. Greater Albuquerque (past pres.). Clubs: Albuquerque Press, Masons, U. N.Mex. Lobo (past v.p. and dir.). Home: 6901 Seminole Rd NE Albuquerque NM 87110 Office: 2400 Louisiana Blvd NE Albuquerque NM 87110

BURLEIGH, ALLISON CURTIS, psychologist; b. Portland, Oreg., Apr. 12, 1920; d. Francis Day and Edith (Clements) C.; m. Charles LeMoyne Burleigh, June 19, 1940; children—Charles LeMoyne, Catherine Burleigh Rickert. B.A. with distinction, U. Mich., 1954; M.A.Ed., UCLA, 1969. Ednl. psychologist Gateways Hosp. Ctr. of Hyperkinetic Children, Los Angeles, 1969-73; program analyst, health systems planner, health systems specialist VA Med. Ctr., Brentwood, Los Angeles, 1973-82; EEO specialist VA Med. Ctr., Wadsworth, Los Angeles, 1982—; Fed. women's program mgr., Brentwood, 1979-81; chmn. VA Med. Dist. #26 Com. for Study of Violence and Suicide, 1976-79; condr. workshops, cons. in field. Recipient Teaching Faculty award, VA Med. Ctr. Brentwood, 1976; Fed. Women's Program Mgr. of Yr. award Los Angeles Fed. Exec. Bd., 1981; Superior Performance award, VA Med. Ctr. Wadsworth, 1982. Mem. Am. Assn. Tng. and Devel., Am. Psychol. Assn., Calif. Assn. Program Evaluators, Calif. Psychol. Assn., NOW, Researchers for Action, Western Psychol. Assn. Contbr. articles to profl. jours. Home: 15907 Asilomar Blvd Pacific Palisades CA 90272 Office: VA Med Ctr Wadsworth (691-05F) Wilshire and Sawtelle Blvds Los Angeles CA 90073

BURLESON, LOU RUFUS, JR., educator; b. Douglas, Ariz., Sept. 24, 1941; s. Louis Rufus and Nellie Frances (Myers) B.; B.S., U. Ariz., 1963, M.Agr. Edn., 1970; m. Bonnie Lou Neal, July 6, 1963; children—Kelly Elizabeth, Brady William. Tchr. vocational agr. Parker (Ariz.) High Sch., 1963-64, Benson (Ariz.) Union High Sch., 1964—; part-time agr. instr. Cochise Coll., Douglas. Leader 4-H; coach Little League. Mem. Nat. Vocat. Agr. Tchrs. Assn., Am. Vocat. Assn., NEA, Ariz. Vocat. Agr. Tchrs. Assn., Ariz. State Vocat. Assn., Ariz. Edn. Assn., Benson Edn. Assn., Phi Delta Kappa. Republican. Presbyterian. Office: PO Drawer B Benson AZ 85602

BURLEY-ALLEN, MADELYN ANNE, profl. devel. cons., author; b. Fond du Lac, Wis., d. Albert John and Doris Anne (Hoffman) Fries; B.A., San Francisco State U., 1975, M.A., 1978; children—Kathleen Burley Livingston, Janniece Burley Tarp, Arlene Burley Blackton. Owner, Dinks Sportswear, San Carlos, Calif., 1961-64; office mgr. Bay Area Carpet Co., San Carlos, 1964-68; v.p. mktg. Vestor Fin. Corp., San Mateo, Calif., 1968-70; founder, pres. Dynamics of Human Behavior, San Mateo, 1970—; cons. in field. Fellow Am. Biog. Inst. Research Assn. (life); mem. Internat. Transactional Analysis Assn. (mem. ethics com. 1979-81), Am. Soc. Tng. and Devel., Internat. Platform Assn. Republican. Home: 34 10th Ave San Mateo CA 94402

BURLINGAME, ROBERT MARTIN, mgmt. cons.; b. Chgo., Mar. 2, 1928; s. Charles Martin and Gladys (Dennis) B.; B.S. with honors, U. Tenn., 1948; M.B.A., Harvard U., 1950; m. Sandra A. Wolkersdorfer, May 24, 1964; children—Martin Robert, Dennis Alexander. Sec.-treas. George F. Fry & Assos., Chgo., 1950-65; controller Kimberly-Clark Corp., Neenah, Wis., 1965-71; pres. Hanson France, Paris, 1971-79; v.p. Barry and Co., Los Angeles, 1979—; mem. faculty Center Nonprofit Mgmt.; lectr. in field. Served with AUS, World War II. C.P.A., Ill., Calif.; cert. purchasing mgr. Mem. Am. Inst. C.P.A.'s, Assn. Purchasing Mgrs., Systems and Procedures Soc., Explorers Club. Clubs: Adventurers (Chgo., Los Angeles); City (San Marino, Calif.); Royal Sydney (Australia) Yacht Squadron (hon.); Harvard. Office: 900 Wilshire Blvd Suite 900 Los Angeles CA 90017

BURMAN, ALDEN HAYWARD, nursing home exec.; b. Bellingham, Wash., Nov. 18, 1919; s. John A. and Winifred C. (Larson) B.; student health care adminstrn. U. Wash., 1967-68; m. Winifred L. Hartman, Mar. 16, 1951 (dec.); children—Ronald Alden, Richard, James David, Shirley Ann. Pres., Federal Way Convalescent Center, Inc., 1968—; pres., Parklane Convalescent Center, Inc., Aberdeen, Wash., 1969—; owner The Gallery gift and antique store, Ocean Shores, Wash., 1962—; owner AFCO Personnel Services, Buffalo and Seattle, 1973—; v.p. Western Farms, Inc., Moses Lake, Wash., 1974—; Fellow Am. Coll. Nursing Home Adminstrs., Internat. Biog. Assn. (life); mem. Wash. Health Facilities Assn. (state pres. 1962, bd. govs. 1961-65), Am. Health Care Assn. (bd. govs. 1962), Nat. Employment Assn. Home: 424 N D St Tacoma WA 98403 Office: PO Box 3260 Federal Way WA 98003

BURNASH, ROBERT JOHN CHARLES, hydrologist; b. Bklyn., Aug. 17, 1931; s. James Francis and Marion Josephine (Olifiers) B.; B.S., Bucknell U., 1953; postgrad. Naval Postgrad. Sch., 1954; m. Jeanne Carolyn Mack, July 11, 1953; children—Charles, Kathleen, Mary, Elizabeth, David, Daniel. Hydrologist, Nat. Weather Service River Forecast Center, Cin., 1957-62, prin. asst., Sacramento River Forecast Center, 1963-71, hydrologist in charge Calif.-Nev. River Forecast Center, 1972—; prin. organizer Internat. Tech. Conf. on Mitigation of Natural Hazards through Real-Time Data Collection and Hydrological Forecasting, World Meteorol. Orgn., Sacramento, 1983. Served with USNR, 1953-56. Recipient Bronze medal Dept. Commerce, 1970, Silver medal, 1975, Gold medal, 1980; Outstanding Public Service award NOAA, 1978. Fellow Am. Meteorol. Soc. (Outstanding Forecaster award 1979, Robert E. Horton meml. lectr. 1983); mem. Am. Geophys. Union, AAAS, Western Snow Conf., Delta Mu Delta, Phi Lambda Theta. Author: (with others) The Sacramento Model. Contbr. articles to profl. jours. Originator real time event reporting telemetering systems and ALERT flood warning system. Home: 3539 Ridgeview Dr El Dorado Hills CA 95630 Office: 1641 Resources Bldg 1416 9th St Sacramento CA 95814

BURNER, LAVERNE CAROLYN, nursing adminstr.; b. St. Louis, Apr. 15, 1923; d. Herman Frank and Caroline Mary (Spreckelmier) B.; R.N., DePaul Hosp. Sch. Nursing, 1948; B.S.N. (scholar 1948, 50), St. Louis U., 1952; M.S. in Hosp. Adminstrn., Northwestern U., 1957; postgrad. No. Ill. U., 1973. Instr., DePaul Hosp. Sch. Nursing, St. Louis, 1950-52; clin. coordinator St. Francis Sch. Nursing, Evanston, Ill., 1952-56; adminstr. Sandwich (Ill.) Community Hosp., 1957-61; bus. mgr. Victory Meml. Hosp., Waukegan, Ill., 1961-65; asst. adminstr. Rockford (Ill.) Meml. Hosp., 1966-74; v.p. Bergan-Mercy Hosp., Omaha, 1974-77; asst. adminstr. patient services St. Joseph's Hosp., Tucson, 1978—; faculty No. Ill. U., DeKalb, 1972-74; clin. asso. U. Nebr., Omaha, 1974-77; guest lectr. U. Ariz., Tucson, 1979-81. Mem. task force Rockford Sch. Medicine, 1972-74, task force on nursing State of Ariz., 1980-82; steering com. Crusader's Clinic, Rockford, 1971-73; pres. Hidden Valley Townhomes Assn., 1980. Recipient award for acad. and clin. performance Class of '48, DePaul Hosp., 1948. Mem. Nat. League Nursing, Nat. Forum Nursing Adminstrs., Ariz. Hosp. Assn., Ariz. Soc. Nursing Adminstrs. (treas. 1978-80, dir. 1981, pres.-elect 1982, pres. 1983), Am. Hosp. Assn. Democrat. Roman Catholic. Office: 350 N Wilmot Rd Tucson AZ 85711

BURNETT, BEVERLY JOAN, car rental company executive; b. Mpls., July 12, 1929; d. Archie Engles and Evelyn Mildred (Day) Iverson; m. Guy Owen Foss, Aug. 29, 1946; children—Guy Owen, Evelyn Gwen Satterlee, Eric Nels; m. 2d, Donald Fred Burnett, Feb. 8, 1980. Student pub. schs., Seattle. Owner B&G Constrn. Co., Seattle, 1961-64, Rentit Rent-A-Car, Seattle, 1972—. Mem. Wash. State Legislature Com. Hwy. Safety. Mem. Women Hwy. Safety Leaders, Shoreline Safety Council (past com. mem.), Am. Car Rental Assn. Lutheran. Clubs: Catrala of Seattle, Elks, Moose. Home: Apt 301 337 3d St S Edmonds WA 98020 Office: 15225 Aurora St N Seattle WA 98133

BURNETT, BRENDA BULLOCK, govt. ofcl.; b. Red Mountain, Calif., Apr. 12, 1941; d. Miles Wallace and Harriet Jane (Wittmeyer) Bullock; student U. Redlands, 1959-60, 61-62; B.A., U. Md., 1967; m. Daniel George Burnett, Oct. 3, 1970. With U.S. Navy, various locations, 1969—, asso. head budget div. Naval Weapons Center Office Fin. and Mgmt., China Lake, Calif., 1975-77, head reports and analysis br., 1977-78, head fin. mgmt. Br. A, 1978-81, mem. staff Hdqrs. Dept. Def. Schs. Ger., 1982—. Mem. Ridgecrest City Council, 1980-81; instr. Stop Smoking Clinic, Am. Cancer Soc.; founding mem. Maturango Mus., Ridgecrest. Mem. Am. Soc. Public Adminstrn., Am. Soc. Mil. Comptrollers, Naval Aviation Exec. Inst., NAACP. Democrat. Baptist. Club: Altrusa. Home: 521 N Randall St Ridgecrest CA 93555 Office: Code 0832 Naval Weapons Center China Lake CA 93555

BURNETT, ERIC STEPHEN, environmental engineer; b. Manchester, Eng., Apr. 15, 1924; s. William Louis and Edith Winifred (Gates) B.; came to U.S., 1963; naturalized, 1974; B.Sc. in Physics (with honors), London U., 1954; M.S. in Environ. Studies, Calif. State, Dominguez Hills, 1976; Ph.D. in Environ. Engring., Calif. Western U., 1982; m. Kathryn Nelson Bunyan, May 1, 1975 (dec. 1982); children—Diana, Ian, Brenda, Keith. Program mgr. Brit. Aircraft Corp., Stevenage, Eng., 1953-63; sr. systems engr. RCA, Princeton, N.J., 1963-66; project mgr. Gen. Electric Co., Valley Forge, Pa., 1966-67; dept. head TRW systems Group, Redondo Beach, Calif., 1967-72; dir. energy and pollution control ARATEX Services, Inc., Calif., 1974-81, dir. tech. devel., 1981—; cons., lectr. in field. Served with Royal Air Force, 1942-47. Asso. fellow AIAA; mem. Water Pollution Control Fedn., Air Pollution Control Assn., So. Calif. Safety Soc., AAAS, Inst. Environ. Scis. (sr.). Contbr. articles in field to profl. jours. Home: 22901 Leadwell Ave Canoga Park CA 91307 Office: PO Box 3000 Encino CA 91316

BURNETT, LOWELL JAY, physicist, educator; b. Portland, Oreg., June 15, 1941; s. Jay Duffy and Barbara Montana (Blair) B.; B.S., Portland State U., 1964; Ph.D. (NSF predoctoral trainee), U. Wyo., 1970; m. Joan Susan Merk, June 17, 1961; children—David Alan, Craig Michael. Instr. physics U. Wyo., Laramie, 1970; presdl. fellow, chemistry div. Los Alamos (N.Mex.) Sci. Lab., 1971-72; prof. physics San Diego State U., 1972—, chmn. physics dept., 1979—. Asso. Western Univs. faculty fellow, 1973-74; cons., USN, UOP Inc., Gillette Corp., IRT Corp., SAI Inc., Control Data Corp., Los Alamos Sci. Lab., energy conservation utilization, environ monitoring and control, sci. instrumentation design; mem. internat. advisory panel, Electronics, McGraw-Hill, Quarter Century Wireless Assn. Am. Chem. Soc. petroleum research grantee, 1974—; Research Corp. grantee, 1975. Contbr. articles to sci. jours.; co-developer membrane for oxygen enrichment of air. Home: 8696 Jackie Dr San Diego CA 92119

BURNETT, MARK WAYNE, university official; b. Seattle, Mar. 19, 1951; s. Wayne O. and Rosanne G. (Forler) B. B.A. in Communications, U. Wash., 1973; M.Pub. Adminstrn., Seattle U., 1983. Publs. coordinator Outdoor Empire Pub., Inc., Seattle, 1973-76; pub. relations mgr. Am. Plywood Assn., Tacoma, 1976-77; media relations specialist Municipality of Met. Seattle, 1977-80; dir. communications Seattle U., 1980—. Bd. dirs. Sta. KCTS, Seattle. Mem. Pub. Relations Soc. Am., Council for Advancement Secondary Edn. Office: Communications Dept Seattle U Seattle WA 98122

BURNETTE, JANIECE LEOLA, artist; b. Los Angeles, May 14, 1926; d. Walter William and Betty Olga (Lester) Burnette; B.S., U. So. Calif., 1950, M.S. in L.S., 1964, M.S. in Instructional Tech., 1970; student art Sorbonne, U. Munich (W. Ger.). Tchr., artist Los Angeles public schs., 1955—; pres. Ars Aristos, art design, Huntington Beach, Calif., 1972—, head designer stained glass mosaics, 1972—; prin. works include Angel and Saint, 1955, Fleeing Angel, 1967, Angel at the Organ, 1967, goblet with 2 lemons, 1978, Angels in Flight, 1980, Princess Balna, 1979, others. Mem. Gifts and Decorative Accessories Assn., Newport Harbor Art Mus. Republican. Address: 9571 Bay Meadow Dr Huntington Beach CA 92646

BURNHAM, STANLEY, univ. adminstr.; b. Goldthwaite, Tex., July 5, 1924; s. Leslie Dee and Myrtle Lane B.; B.S., Daniel Baker Coll. of Southwestern U., 1949; M.Ed., U. Tex., 1950, Ed.D., 1965; m. Mildred Edith Mendenhall, July 9, 1948; children—Ronald K., Diana L., Patricia A. Tchr., coach, public schs., Tex., 1950-54; coach, athletic dir. Ranger Coll., 1954-56; asso. prof. biology, chmn. dept. biology, head basketball coach McMurry Coll., 1956-59; instr. U. Tex., Austin, 1960-65, asst. prof. health edn., 1965-67, asso. prof., 1967-69, prof., 1969-75, chmn. dept. phys. instrn., 1969-75, asso. to provost in health, dir. athletic medicine, 1966-75; dir. regional med. program U. Tex. System, 1970-74; dean Coll. Applied Arts and Scis., San Jose State U., 1975-79; v.p. for acad. affairs No. Mont. Coll., 1979-81; pres. Calif. Coll. Podiatric Medicine, San Francisco, 1981—. dir. public health programs; cons. health planning, health edn; chmn. Tex. Gov.'s Commn. Phys. Fitness, 1971-75; vice chmn. Austin Health Adv. Council, 1974-75, chmn., 1975; mem. exec. bd. Health Service Edn. Council—Bay Area San Francisco, 1976-78; vice chmn. bd. dirs. San Jose Hosp. and Health Center, 1977-79; vice chmn. Adv. Commn. on Health of San Jose, 1978-79. Mem. San Jose Commn. on Parking and Traffic, 1976-78; guest of honor Ministry of Edn., Republic of China, 1978. Served with M.C., USN, 1942-46. HEW grantee, 1971, 72; Office Edn. grantee, 1978. Fellow Am. Coll. Sports Medicine; mem. Am. Congress Rehab. Medicine, Am. soc. Public Health, Am. Soc. Allied Health Professions,

Am. Sch. Health Assn., Calif. Public Health Assn., Am. Assn. Higher Edn., Nat. League Nursing, Am. Occupational Therapy Assn., Am. Public Health Assn., Nat. Coll. Phys. Edn. Assn. Republican. Methodist. Club: Rotary. Contbr. numerous articles to profl. jours. Office: Calif College Podiatric Medicine 1210 Scott St San Francisco CA 94115

BURNISON, BOYD EDWARD, lawyer; b. Arnolds Park, Iowa, Dec. 12, 1934; s. Boyd William and Lucile (Harnden) B.; B.S., Iowa State U., 1957; J.D., U. Calif. at Berkeley, 1961; m. Mari Amaral; children—Erica Lafore, Alison Katherine. Admitted to Calif. bar, 1962, U.S. Supreme Ct. bar, 1971, U.S. Dist. Ct. for No. Dist. Calif., 1962, Eastern Dist. Calif., 1970, U.S. Ct. Appeals for 9th Circuit, 1962; dep. county counsel, Yolo County, Calif., 1962-65; counsel Davis and Woodland (Calif.) Unified Sch. Dists., 1962-65; asso. firm Steel & Arostegui, Marysville, Calif., 1965-66, St. Sure, Moore, Hoyt, Oakland, 1966-70; partner St. Sure, Moore & Hoyt & Sizoo, Oakland, and San Francisco, 1970-75; v.p., dir. firm Crosby, Heafey, Roach & May, profl. corp., Oakland, 1975—. Adviser, Berkeley YMCA, 1971—, Yolo County YMCA, 1962-65. Bd. dirs. Easter Seal Soc. Crippled Children and Adults of Alameda County, 1972-75, Yolo County YMCA, 1965, Moot Ct. Bd., U. Calif., 1960-61; trustee, sec., legal counsel Easter Seal Found. Alameda County, 1974-79, hon. trustee, 1979—. Mem. Am. (labor relations law sect. 1966—, equal employment opportunity law com. 1972—), Alameda County (mem. fee arbitration com. 1972-81; mem. memberships com. 1972-81, chmn. 1973-74, 80; law office econs. com. 1972-78, chmn. 1975-77; mem. nominating com. 1974—, vice chmn. bank-bar liaison com. 1983, chmn. 1984; client relations com. 1979—, assn. dir. 1981—, pres.-elect 1983, pres. 1984), Yolo County (sec. 1965), Yuba Sutter bar assns., State Bar Calif. (labor and employment law sect. 1982—, spl. labor counsel 1981—), Bar Assn. San Francisco (labor relations law sect. 1970—), Counsellor's Table of Boalt Hall Law Sch., U. Calif. at Berkeley, Iowa State U. alumni assns., Order of Knoll, Pi Kappa Alpha, Phi Delta Phi. Democrat. Clubs: Oakland Athletic, Rotary. Home: 2500 Caballo Ranchero Dr PO Box 743 Diablo CA 94528 Office: 900 Park Plaza Bldg 1939 Harrison St Oakland CA 94612

BURNS, DAN W., mfg. co. exec.; b. Auburn, Calif., Sept. 10, 1925; s. William and Edith Lynn (Johnson) B.; 1 son, Dan. Dir. materials Menasco Mfg. Co., 1951-56; v.p., gen. mgr. Hufford Corp., 1956-58; pres. Hufford div. Siegler Corp., 1958-61; v.p. Siegler Corp., 1961-62, Lear Siegler, Inc., 1962-64; pres., dir. Electrada Corp., Culver City, Calif., 1964; now pres., chief exec. officer, dir. Sargent Industries and related cos.; chmn., chief exec. officer Arlington Industries Inc.; dir. Data Design Corp. Served to capt. U.S. Army, 1941-47; P.O.W.; counter-intelligence officer; asst. mil. attache to China, 1946; a.d.c. to Gen. George C. Marshall, 1946-47. Clubs: California, Los Angeles Country (Los Angeles); Garden of the Gods Country (Colorado Springs, Colo.); St. Francis Yacht (San Francisco). Home: 10851 Chalon Rd Los Angeles CA 90077 Office: Sargent Industries 1901 Bldg #1251 Los Angeles CA 90067

BURNS, DONALD IRWIN, bank executive; b. Chgo., Oct. 13, 1928; s. David and Marcia (Leibo) B.; m. Katherine Rose Heitz, July 4, 1953; children—Karen Lee, Cynthia Alison. B.S., U. Ill., 1950. Advt. dir. Standard Safety Equipment Co., Palatine, Ill., 1952-54; sales promotion dir. Diversey Corp., Chgo., 1954-56; account exec. Roche, Rickerd & Cleary, Advt. Agy., Chgo., 1956-58; pres. Don Burns Advt., Phoenix, 1959-63; exec. v.p. Nat. Producers Life, Phoenix, 1963-68; pres. Western Eagle Advt. Agy., Phoenix, 1969-75; sr. v.p. Southwest Savs. & Loan Assn., Phoenix, 1971-75, Surety Savs. & Loan Assn., Phoenix, 1976-80; exec. v.p. Century Bank, Phoenix, 1981—. Served with U.S. Army, 1950-52. Office: 3225 N Central Ave Phoenix AZ 85012

BURNS, DOROTHY MCARTOR, ednl. adminstr.; b. Burns City, Ind., Dec. 11, 1920; d. Edgar and Sarah J. (Bays) McArtor; B.A., Ind. State Tchrs. Coll., 1942; B.S., U. Ill., 1944; M.A., San Diego State Coll., 1962; D.Ed., U. Oreg., 1964; m. Robert Burns, July 17, 1945; children—Mariana Burns Rochman, Robert. Dir. Women's Job Corps Center, prof. edn. U. Oreg., Eugene, 1967-71; asst. regional manpower adminstr. Job Corps, Dept. Labor, Seattle, 1971-72; dean acad. affairs, prof. edn. Castleton (Vt.) State Coll., 1972-75, interim pres., 1975-76; vice chancellor ednl. services San Jose (Calif.) Community Coll. Dist., 1976-79, interim supt., 1979-80; asst. supr. Santa Clara County (Calif.) Office Edn., 1980—; formerly mem. Oreg. Gov.'s Conf. Youth and Drug Abuse; cons. Ford Found.; adv. com. Nat. Acad. Scis. Formerly mem. Oreg. Republican Task Force on Problems of Poverty. Recipient Golden Torch award Oreg. Bus. and Profl. Women; Outstanding Educator award, 1975. Home: 8412 Chenin Blanc Ln San Jose CA 95135 Office: 101 Skyport Dr San Jose CA 95112

BURNS, JAMES M., judge; b. 1924; B.A., U. Portland; J.D., Loyola U., Chgo. Admitted to bar, 1950; chief judge U.S. Dist. Ct., Portland. Office: US Dist Ct 702 US Courthouse Portland OR 97205

BURNS, JAMES MARTIN, hosp. supply ofcl.; b. Troy, N.Y., Sept. 19, 1949; s. James Joseph and Margaret Loretta B. B.A. in Psychology, U. Conn., 1971; postgrad. Northeastern U., 1975; postgrad. in Public Adminstrn., Golden Gate U., 1980-83. Unit mgr. Univ. Hosp., Boston, 1973-76, employment specialist, 1976-77; mgr. central supply Marshal Hale Meml. Hosp., San Francisco, 1977—. Mem. Am. Soc. Hosp. Central Supply Personnel, Golden Gate Assn. Hosp Central Service Personnel (pres.), U. Conn. Alumni Assn.

BURNS, JOHN CHARLES, civil engr.; b. Jersey City, Feb. 14, 1947; s. Michael and Serena (Mould) B.; B.S. in Geol. Engring., U. Ariz., 1969; m. Anne Elizabeth Grisafe, Aug. 3, 1968; 1 son, David Anthony. Materials research engr. Ariz. Dept. Transp., Phoenix, 1969-75, sr. pavement performance engr., 1975-79; v.p. Novak, Dempsey and Assocs., Inc., Tempe, Ariz., 1979-81, Testing Engrs.-San Diego, 1981—; cons. engr. in pavement evaluation, skid resistance, pavement safety and hwy. engring., 1973—; continuing lectr. Vehicle Accident Investigation and Reconstrn. Sch., Ariz. State U., 1977—; mem., coordinator Tri-State Mu-Meter Calibration Com., 1974—; mem. Mu-Meter Tech. Com., 1974—. Vice pres. Park Priemere Town House Assn., 1975-76. Recipient K. B. Woods award Transp. Research Bd., Nat. Acad. Sci., 1977; registered profl. engr., Ariz., Fla., Calif. Mem. Nat. Soc. Profl. Engrs. (Young Engr. of Yr. award Papago chpt. 1976), ASCE, ASTM, Ariz. Soc. Profl. Engrs. (Young Engr. of Yr. award 1976, dir. Papago chpt. 1977—), Am. Public Works Assn. (guest lectr. nat. edn. workshops 1979-80, 82-83, San Diego chpt. 1982—), Soc. Am. Mil. Engrs. Democrat. Roman Catholic. Author: numerous publs. on pavement evaluation and safety. Home: 12850 Abra Pl San Diego CA 92128 Office: Testing Engrs-San Diego 3467 Kurtz St San Diego CA 92138

BURNS, MARCELLINE MOORE, research psychologist; b. Pine Bluff, Ark., Jan. 2, 1928; d. Mark and Johnnie Leslie (Stark) Moore; B.A., San Diego State U., 1955; M.A., Calif. State U. Los Angeles, 1969; Ph.D., U. Calif. at Irvine, 1972; m. William L. Burns, Aug. 24, 1945; children—Mark W., Paul. Research psychologist UCLA, 1972—; research psychologist, also sec.-treas. So. Calif. Research Inst., Los Angeles, 1973—; cons. in field; tchr. adult edn. Los Angeles City Schs., 1962-65. Mem. Am., Western psychol. assns., Internat. Assn. Applied Psychology, Human Factors Soc. Contbr. articles to profl. publs. Home: 837 Appelby St Venice CA 90291 Office: 11912 W Washington Blvd Los Angeles CA 90066

BURNS, MARETTA JO, accountant; b. San Antonio, Nov. 7, 1941; d. Joseph Wallis and Mary Vesta (Shepard) B.; B.B.A., Baylor U., 1962. Supervisory cost acct. asst. Pueblo (Colo.) Army Depot, 1962-65; employment security adv. U.S. Dept. Labor, Denver, 1965-68, Seattle, 1968-70, budget and acctg. officer, Denver, 1970—; mem. Cost Acctg. Task Force, 1969-70, Regional Automated System Redesign Task Force, 1979-80. Recipient profl. awards. Mem. Nat. Assn. Female Execs., Am. Mgmt. Assn., Digital Equipment Users Soc., Baylor Alumni Club, Phi Gamma Nu, Beta Alpha Psi, Beta Gamma Sigma; fellow Internat. Biog. Assn., Am. Biog. Assn. (life). Baptist. Home: 3784 S Quince St Denver CO 80237 Office: 1961 Stout St Denver CO 80294

BURNS, MARILYN MARIE, home economics, educator; b. Colorado Springs, Colo., July 24, 1931; d. Preston Wallace and Sarah Eloise (Mitchell) Johnson; m. Gerald Neil Burns, Dec. 28, 1951; children—Michael Reid, Kevin Neil, Erin Eileen. B.S., Colo. U., 1955; M.A., U. No. Colo., 1961; Ph.D., Okla. State U., 1982. Assoc. prof. home econs. U. No. Colo., Greeley, 1962-76, chmn. dept., 1976-82; assoc. prof. Okla. State U., Stillwater, 1982—. Fulbright Hays grantee, 1970-71. Mem. Am. Home Econs. Assn., Assn. Coll. Profs. Textiles/Clothing, Costume Soc. London, Am. Costume Soc., AAUW. Home: 1101 Oak Ridge Dr Stillwater OK 74074 Office: Coll Home Econs Okla State U Stillwater OK 74078

BURNS, RICHARD LELAND, marketing executive; b. Oakland, Calif., Sept. 22, 1930; s. Leland S. and Rachel (Borncamp) B.; A.B., Stanford U., 1952; m. Nancy Belle Clark, Apr. 2, 1955; children—Lisa Anne, Shelley Kristine, Richard Clark. Sales service dir., traffic dir., promotion and research dir., nat. sales coordinator, account exec. Westinghouse Broadcasting, Inc., KPIX, San Francisco, 1954-61; gen. mgr. Amerco Advt., Inc., Oakland, 1961-64; dir. advt. DeLuxe Reading Corp., Elizabeth, N.J., 1964-65; partner, v.p. Edward S. Kellogg Co., San Francisco 1965-68; v.p. Gross, Pera and Rockey, San Francisco, 1968-69; pres. Burns Communications, Inc., Oakland, 1969-71; v.p., pres., dir. Latham Found., Oakland, 1971-78; pres. Mktg. Assos., Oakland, 1978—. Regional chmn. Stanford U. Quad; area chmn. Stanford U. Parents Fund; chmn. Stanford U. East Bay Region Cabinet; mem. nat. adv. com. Am. Humane Assn., Denver; past mem. exec. com. and pub. relations adviser Cerebral Palsy Assn., Alameda County, Calif.; communications chmn. Piedmont council Boy Scouts Am. Served with U.S. Army, 1952-54. Mem. Am. Mktg. Assn., Advt. Assn. West, Pearl S. Buck Found., Council on Founds., Piedmont and Alameda County Jaycees (past pres., county exec.), Stanford Assos., Phi Sigma Kappa. Republican. Presbyterian. Clubs: Univ., Commonwealth, Stanford Men's (pres.). Address: 6 Pacific Ave Piedmont CA 94611

BURNS, SHARON JEAN, business products company executive; b. Pomona, Calif., June 23, 1949; d. Alfred George and Helen Elizabeth (Brewer) Lepore; m. Walter Alvin Burns, June 3, 1965 (div.); 1 son, James Forrest. Student pub. schs., Pomona, Calif. Clk. shipping and receiving Xerox Corp., Pomona, Calif., 1967-69, clk. material control, 1969-72, purchasing expediter, 1972-74, assoc. buyer II, 1974-79, buyer, 1979—. Worker Muscular Dystrophy Telethon, 1980; sec. Bonita High Sch. Band Boosters, 1981-83. Mem. Nat. Assn. Female Execs. Office: Xerox Corp 800 E Bonita Ave Pomona CA 91767

BURNS, THOMAS STEPHEN, international management consulting company executive; b. Holyoke, Mass., Jan. 7, 1927; s. Thomas Raymond and Ann Agatha (Bush) B.; m. Eleanor Hartigan, June 7, 1931; children—Brian, Erin Burns Griffin, George, Mary, James, Braeden. B.S., U.S. Naval Acad., 1951; M.B.A., U. Mass., 1958; M.S.E.E., 1958 grad. Advanced Mgmt. Program, Harvard U., 1967; A.S.R.E., Southwestern Coll., 1978. Registered profl. engr., Mich., N.H. Dist. mgr. Gen. Electric Co., 1955-60; regional mgr. Hughes Aircraft Co., 1960-62; v.p. Simplex Corp., Boston, 1962-70; v.p. IT&T, N.Y.C., 1970-72; pres. Nat. Tech. Assocs., Los Angeles and San Francisco, 1972—; lectr. Grad. Sch. Systems Mgmt., U. So. Calif. Bd. dirs. Regional Planning Commn., Portsmouth, N.H.; mem. Hydrospace Commn., Boston; dir. Port Authority, Nashua, N.H. Served as lt. USN, 1951-55; Korea. Recipient Outstanding exec. award Simplex Corp., 1968; Mark Twain award Mark Twain Soc., 1974. Mem. IEEE, IEEE Computer Soc., Assn. Aeros. and Astronautics Engring. Soc. Detroit, Naval Acad. Alumni Assn., Harvard Bus. Sch. Assn. Democrat. Roman Catholic. Author: Tales of ITT, 1974; The Secret War for the Ocean Depths, 1976; Personal Computers-Strategics for Success, 1981; A Silence Like Cheers, 1982; editor Spectator, 1962-70. Office: PO Box 7400 280 Bernardo Ave Mountain View CA 94039

BURNSIDE, HOUSTON MARVIN, educator; b. South Gate, Calif., June 22, 1930; s. Houston Augustus and Anna Ruth (Gregg) Burnside; m. Patricia Marie Gee, Feb. 24, 1950; children—Houston Marvin, Stephen Edward, Susan Marie. Ministerial diploma, Life Bible Coll., 1952; B.S. in Edn., Kent State U., 1960; M.A., Claremont Grad. Sch., 1963, Ph.D., 1970. Ordained to ministry, Am. Baptist Chs. U.S., 1963; cert. Tchr., Calif. Tchr., Canton (Ohio) City Schs., 1959-60, Pomona (Calif.) City Schs., 1960-63; minister pastoral care, prin. day sch. First Bapt. Ch., Pomona, Calif., 1963-66; pastor Alvarado Bapt. Ch., San Diego, 1966-68; prof. elem. edn. San Diego State U., 1968—. Mem. San Diego County Council Chs., 1966-68. Served with USMC, 1945-49. Mem. Nat. Council Social Studies, Nat. Council Tchrs. Math., Coalition for Law-Related Edn., Congress Faculty Assns., Ministers Council Am. Bapt. Chs., Calif. Articulation Council (liaison com. on early childhood edn. and child devel.), Kappa Delta Pi, Phi Delta Kappa. Republican. Author: (with C.M. Charles, D.K. Gast, R.E. Servey) Schooling, Teaching and Learning: American Education, 1978; contbr. articles to profl. jours., newspapers. Office: Coll Edn San Diego State U San Diego CA 92182

BURNSIDE, WALDO HOWARD, department store executive; b. Washington, Nov. 5, 1928; s. Waldo and Eleanor (Tavenner) B.; m. Jean Mae Culbert, June 24, 1950; children—Diane Louise, Leslie Ann, Arlene Kay, William Howard. B.S., U. Md., 1949. With Woodward & Lothrop, Washington, 1949-80; divisional mdse. mgr., 1957-65, v.p., gen. mdse. mgr., 1965-74, exec. v.p., 1974-78, pres., 1978-80, also dir; vice chmn., chief operating officer Carter Hawley Hale Stores, Inc., Los Angeles, 1980—; dir. Assoc. Mdse. Corp., Washington Blue Cross, 1974-77. Bd. dirs. Washington Better Bus. Bur., 1973-77, pres., 1976-77; trustee, past chmn. U. Md. Alumni Internat.; trustee Md. Ednl. Found., St. John's Hosp. and Health Ctr. Found. Mem. Automobile Club So. Calif. (dir.), Los Angeles Area C. of C., Ind. Colls. So. Calif., Sigma Chi, Phi Kappa Phi. Episcopalian. Clubs: U. Md. Terrapin (past pres.); California; N.Y. Athletic; University, Columbia Country (Washington). Office: Carter Hawley Hale Stores 550 S Flower St Los Angeles CA 90071

BURNWORTH, RANDY JAMES, video company executive; b. Portland, Oreg., Aug. 1, 1949; s. Art Clifton and Virginia May (Bobbit) B.; m. Carolyn Ruth Bowers, Apr. 18, 1967; children—James Randy, Deanna Michelle, Darrin Daniel. A.A., Bates Coll., 1969; postgrad. Pierce Coll., 1974. Chief exec. officer Video Ventures, Inc. and Showtime Video Ventures, Tillamook Oreg., 1978—. Elder Mormon Ch.; mem. Republican Presdl. Task Force. Recipient Merit medal Rep. Presdl. Task Force, 1982; named Man of Decade, Audio Video Digest, 1982; Entrepreneur of Yr., Video Entertainment, 1982; Best Products of Yr. awards, 1980, 81, 82, Video Rev., 1982. Clubs: U.S. Senatorial, Elks. Inventor; contbr. tech. articles to profl. jours. Office: 2715 5th St Tillamook OR 97141

BURQUEST, BRET, psychiatrist, educator; b. Sarasota, Fla., June 26, 1935; s. Weston and Bonnie (Glisson) B. B.A., Duke, 1957; M.D., U. Miami (Fla.), 1961. Intern, Phila. Gen. Hosp., 1961-62; resident UCLA Hosp., 1962-65; head physician psychiat. day-treatment service Harbor Gen. Hosp., Los Angeles, 1965-67; cons. Las Palmas Sch. Girls, Los Angeles, 1970-78; asst. clin. prof. psychiatry UCLA, 1970-81, Baylor Coll. Medicine, Houston, 1981—; pres. med. staff Westwood Hosp., 1978-79; med. dir. West Oaks, The Psychiat. Inst. of Houston, 1981—. Served to capt. AUS, 1967-68. Diplomate Am. Bd. Psychiatry and Neurology. Fellow Am. Psychiat. Assn., Am. Soc. Adolescent Psychiatry (editor newsletter 1976-79, editorial bd. annals 1975-81, v.p. 1979-81, pres.-elect 1981-82, pres. 1982-83); mem. Am., Tex., Harris County County med. assns., So. Calif. Soc. Adolescent Psychiatry (treas. 1972-73, pres. 1973-75), So. Calif. Psychiat. Soc. (treas. 1975-76). Contbr. chpt. to Adolescent Psychiatry, Vol. VII, Adolescence, Vol. XVI. Office: Medical Director West Oaks Hosp 6500 Hornwood Houston TX 77074

BURR, BEVERLY HERALD, clinical psychologist, researcher; b. Cadillac, Mich.; d. Claude and Lucille Marian (Antrup) Herald; m. Lawrence Burr; children—Terry L., Brooks M. Woodrow S., Montgomery H., Michelle J. A.S., Spring Arbor Coll., 1953; B.A., Calif. State U., Los Angeles, 1970; Ph.D. in Psychology, Fla. Inst. Tech., 1981. Cert. psychologist asst. Calif. Counselor Ventura Girls Club, Calif., 1974-76; research asst. Temporomandibular Research Found., La Cresenta, Calif., 1975-77; pvt. practice clin. psychology. Recipient joint appreciation award Temporomandibular Research Found. and Otolaryngology Found., 1975. Mem. Am. Psychol. Assn., Western Psychol. Assn., Calif. State Psychol. Assn. Contbr. book chpt. Diseases of the Temporomandibular Apparatus: A Multi-Disciplinary Approach, 1977. Office: Van Nuys Multi Specialty Group 14547 Victory Blvd Van Nuys CA 91411

BURR, EDWARD BENJAMIN, life insurance company executive; b. Worcester, Mass., Dec. 19, 1923; s. Guy Weatherbee and Bertha Mary (Clark) B.; A.B. cum laude, Bowdoin Coll., 1945; M.B.A., Wharton Sch. U. Pa., 1948; C.L.U., 1951; m. Mary Elizabeth Hayes, Sept. 2, 1944 (div.); children—Susan Jean, Nancy Carol; m. 2d, Kay F. Hanten, Nov. 1, 1970; children—Kristine Kay, Kelly Anne. Ednl. dir. Inst. Life Ins., N.Y.C., 1948-54; dir. pub. information Nat. Assn. Investment Cos., 1954-55, exec. dir., 1955-58; bd. govs., 1958-61; exec. v.p., dir. One William St. Fund, Inc., N.Y.C., 1958-62; pres., dir. William St. Sales, Inc., N.Y.C., 1958-62; chmn. bd. Hugh W. Long & Co., 1962-65; chmn. Fundamental Investors, Inc., Diversified Investment Fund, Inc., Diversified Growth Stock Fund, Inc., Westminster Fund, Inc., 1964-78, Anchor Corp., Anchor Growth Fund, Inc.; pres. Anchor Corp., Inc., 1964-78; chmn. Anchor Nat. Life Ins. Co., Phoenix, 1962— dir. United Bancorp. Ariz. Served with Inf. AUS, 1943-46. Decorated Silver Star medal, Bronze Star medal (2). Mem. Am. Soc. C.L.U.s, Nat. Assn. Life Underwriters, Phoenix Met. C. of C. (dir. 1982—), Kappa Sigma. Clubs: Wall Street (N.Y.C.); Kiva, Plaza (Phoenix). Office: 2202 E Camelback Rd Phoenix AZ 85016

BURR, IRVING WINGATE, statistician, educator; b. Fallon, Nev., Apr. 9, 1908; s. Eugene Wyllys and Mary Hopper (Jennings) B.; B.S., Antioch Coll., 1930; M.S., U. Chgo., 1935; Ph.D., U. Mich., 1941; m. Elsie Darrington Haney, Mar. 26, 1966; children by previous marriage—John T., Mary Kate, Peter S.; 1 stepson, John D. Haney. Asso. prof. math., chmn. dept. Antioch Coll., Yellow Springs, Ohio, 1930-41; faculty statistics Purdue U., West Lafayette, Ind., 1941-74, prof., 1949—, head dept. statistics, 1962-64; cons. Ocean Park, Wash., 1974—. Fellow Am. Statis. Assn., Am. Soc. Quality Control (Shewhart medal, 1959, Brumbaugh award 1950, Edward J. Oakley citation 1971), Ind. Acad. Sci.; mem. Am. Math. Soc., Math. Assn. Am., Biometric Soc., Inst. Math. Statistics. Author: Engineering Statistics and Quality Control, 1953; Applied Statistical Methods, 1974; Statistical Quality Control Methods, 1976; Elementary Statistical Quality Control, 1979. Editor Industrial Quality Control, 1961-65. Address: PO Box 527 Ocean Park WA 98640

BURR, JOHN CLARENCE, physician; b. Tonkawa, Okla., Jan. 27, 1931; s. Clarence E. and Gladys (Jones) B.; student No. Okla. Jr. Coll., 1949-50; B.S., Tulsa U., 1953; M.D., U. Okla., 1957; m. Mary Patricia Casey, May 29, 1956; children—Andrea, John David. Intern, St. Lukes and Denver Gen. hosps., 1957-58; resident U. Okla. Med. Center, 1958-61; practice medicine, specializing in gen., adolescent, diagnostic and forensic psychiatry, Denver, 1963-83; now clin. med. dir. Forensic Div., N.Mex. State Hosp., Las Vegas; med. dir. Mt. Airy Hosp., 1967-68, youth dir., 1969; mem. staff St. Lukes Hosp., Mount Airy Psychiat. Center, Bethesda Hosp., St. Joseph Hosp. Chmn. bd., mng. dir. Gallery of Fine Art Ltd., 1973-74. Pres. bd. trustees, chmn. bd. dirs. Colo. Orgn. for Drug Abuse Control, 1970-71. Past prin., past chmn. bd. trustees St. Anne's Episcopal Sch.; trustee Mount Airy Found., 1967-83, trustee emeritus, 1983—, past mem. exec. com., chmn. staff edn. program, 1972-74. Served to capt. AUS, 1961-63. Mem. Am., Colo. psychiat. assns., Colo., Denver med. socs., Central Neuropsychiat. Assn., Phi Beta Pi, Sigma Chi. Republican. Episcopalian. Home: Box 6418 Santa Fe NM 87502 Office: Forensic Div NMex State Hosp Las Vegas NM 87701

BURR, LOIS GOODELL, employment counselor, genealogical researcher; b. Fort Collins, Colo., May 22, 1923; d. Francis Clark and Frances Adele (Hollinshead) Goodell; m. Morrison William Burr, Mar. 23, 1940 (dec. Mar., 1956); children—Joyce Ann Hostetter, Harlan Don, Frances Kaye. B.S. in Psychology, Colo. State U., 1964; M.A. in Spl. Edn. and Rehab. Counseling, U. Northern Colo., 1973. Cert. Colo. Employment Service, 1966. Career counselor Southwest Youth Opportunity Ctr., Colo. Employment and Tng. Div., 1965-75, counselor to handicapped and disavantaged Aurora Job Service, 1975-78; counselor to ex-offenders and parolees Employ-Ex, Denver, 1978—. Named State Employee of Month, Colo. Gov., Oct. 1980; Hon. Ex-Offender, 1980. Mem. Am. Personnel and Guidance Assn., Nat. Employment Counselors Assn., Nat. Pub. Offender Counselors Assn., Colo. Personnel and Guidance Assn. (exec. bd.; Outstanding Service award 1981, 82), Colo. Employment Counselors Assn. (past treas.), Colo. Pub. Offender Counselors Assn. (past pres., past treas.), Internat. Assn. Personnel in Employment Security, N.Y. Geneal. Soc., R.I. Geneal. Soc., Conn. Geneal. Soc. Democrat.

BURRELL, RANDIE BLANE, real estate investment company executive, accountant; b. San Diego, Nov. 20, 1947; s. Miles Loren and Letha Grace (Larson) b.; m. Marsha Orton, June 5, 1970; children—Tanya, Christian. B.S. in Acctg., Brigham Young U., 1972. C.P.A., Calif., 1974. Acct., Touch Ross, C.P.A., San Diego, 1972-73; tax specialist Deloitte Haskins & Sells, San Diego, 1973-77; v.p. fin. Black Mountain Corp., San Diego, 1977—. Mem. Calif. Soc. C.P.A.s, Am. Inst. C.P.A.s. Mormon. Office: Black Mountain Corp 9393 Activity Rd Suite I San Diego CA 92126

BURRESS, DONALD ALLEN, ophthalmologist; b. Milw., Feb. 18, 1932; s. Thomas Allen and Angeline (Doll) B.; A.B., Ripon Coll., 1955; B.S., Mass. Inst. Tech., 1955, M.S., 1956, Ph.D., 1966; M.D., Columbia, 1962; m. Betty Jean Hammons, Apr. 25, 1970. Intern, Presbyn. Hosp., N.Y.C., 1962-63; resident ophthalmology U. Oreg. Med. Sch., 1966-69; practice medicine specializing in ophthalmology, Gresham, Oreg., 1969—; mem. staff Gresham Community Hosp., Woodland Park Hosp., Portland. Served with AUS, 1956. NIH fellow, 1964-69. Diplomate Am. Bd. Ophthalmology. Mem. Am., Oreg. med. assns., Multnomah County Med. Soc., Am. Assn. Ophthalmology, Am. Acad.

Ophthalmology, Contact Lens Assn. Ophthalmologists, Oreg. Acad. Ophthalmology. Home: 23753 NE Shamrock Dr Troutdale OR 97060 Office: 711 NE Hood Ave Gresham OR 97030

BURRILL, MELINDA JANE, geneticist; b. Washington, Mar. 31, 1947; d. Richard William and Virginia (Jones) B.; B.S., U. Ariz., 1969; Ph.D. (NDEA fellow 1970-71), Oreg. State U., 1974. With Indsl. Bio-Test, Inc., Northbrook, Ill., 1969; research fellow U. Minn., St. Paul, 1975-76; faculty Calif. State Poly. U., Pomona, 1976—, assoc. prof. dept. animal sci. 1980—. Kellogg Found. grantee, 1980; French Ministry of Sci. CIES grantee, 1980. Mem. Am. Soc. Animal Sci., Internat. Soc. Gen. Semantics, Brit. Soc. Animal Prodn., Can. Soc. Animal Sci., Am. Assn. Lab. Animal Sci., Am. Genetics Assn., Sigma Xi (bd. dirs. 1979-81, 83-86), Phi Beta Kappa, Phi Kappa Phi, Alpha Lambda Delta, Gamma Sigma Delta, Sigma Delta Epsilon, Beta Beta Beta, Alpha Omicron Pi. Methodist. Contbr. articles in field to profl. jours. Home: 149 Stillman Way Upland CA 91786 Office: Calif Poly State U Dept Animal Science Pomona CA 91768

BURRISS, RICHARD CLARK, computer scientist; b. Smithfield, Ohio, Apr. 23, 1922; s. Virgil Elton and Grace Eldora (Dorrance) B.; B.S., Kent State U., 1947; M.S., Fla. State U., 1954; m. Ann Kotsch, Nov. 22, 1945; 1 dau., Deborah. Joined U.S. Air Force, 1943, advanced through grades to col., 1963, ret., 1966; sr. research scientist Kaman Scis. Corp., Colorado Springs, Colo., 1966—; faculty computer programming U. Colo., 1967-69; cons. U.S. Air Force Acad. Architects, 1955-56. Home: 734 Crown Ridge Dr Colorado Springs CO 80904 Office: 1500 Garden of Gods Rd Colorado Springs CO 80907

BURROUGHS, JEAN JAMES, jewelery wholesale, retail and mfg. co. exec.; b. Ft. Peck, Mont., May 27, 1938; s. Donald and Ruth June (Griner) B.; student pub. schs., Maple Valley, Wash.; div.; children—Mark, Robert, David, James, Jeffrey. Constrn. laborer, aircraft tooling insp. Boeing Aircraft Co., Seattle, 1959-65; sr. journeyman grocery co., Maple Valley, 1965-71; owner, mgr. Yoho Downieville Gold Sales, Downieville, Calif., 1972—; pres., gen. mgr. No. Mining Council, Inc., 1979—. Sponsor ann. Easter egg hunt. Downieville; founder ann. Miners Downieville Days Celebration. Served with USAR, 1956-64. Recipient Citizen of Yr. award Goodyears Dist. Community Club, 1980; donor land for Am. Legion Park, Downieville. Mem. Nat. Fedn. Ind. Bus., Jewelers Bd. Trade, Sierra County C. of C. (dir.), Sierra County Hist. Soc. Club: Downieville Lions. Home and Office: PO Box 431 Downieville CA 95936

BURROUGHS, WALTER LAUGHLIN, journalist, editor; b. Bridgewater, S.D., Aug. 21, 1901; s. William S. and Bertha (Laughlin) B.; B.A., U. Wash., 1924; postgrad. U. Calif. at Berkeley, 1925-28; m. Hazel Georgia Sexsmith, June 1, 1925 (dec. Oct. 1970); 1 dau., Toni (Mrs. Philip Schuyler Doane); m. 2d, Lucy Bell, Feb. 28, 1972. Dir. publs. U. Calif. at Berkeley, 1925-28; gen. mgr. North Pacific Gravure Co., Seattle, 1928-30; gen. mgr. Crocker Union Lithograph and Publishing Co., Los Angeles, 1930-41; co-founder Bantam Books, Los Angeles, 1938; ind. book pub. with Merle Armitage, 1938-42; Pacific coast rep. H.W. Kaster & Sons, advt. agy., Los Angeles, 1941-42; exec. v.p. Eldon Industries Los Angeles, 1946-62; corp. pres., pub. Orange Coast Daily Pilot, Newport Beach, Costa Mesa, Huntington Beach, Calif., 1948-65, chmn. bd., 1965-68; pres. Orion Mgmt. Corp. Chmn. bd. dirs. emeritus Children's Hosp. Orange County; mem. exec. com., trustee Children's Hosp. Orange County Found.; trustee Jefferson Trust, Western World Med. Found., Irvine, Calif. Served to col. U.S. Army, 1942-45. Honored (with late E.J. Power) for role in bringing U. Calif. to Irvine with dedication of Founders Ct. on campus, 1978. Mem. Sigma Delta Chi (nat. pres.). Clubs: Bohemian (San Francisco); Jonathan (Los Angeles); Newport Harbor Yacht, Irvine Coast Country, Rotary. Home: 260 Cagney Ln Apt 313 Newport Beach CA 92663 Office: 1670 Westminster Ave Costa Mesa CA 92627

BURROW, FREDERIC HENDERSON, advertising executive; b. Colorado Springs, Colo., Aug. 16, 1935; s. Fred Henderson and Ruth (McKenzie) B.; m. Eleanor JoAnne Minning, Dec. 30, 1954; children—Amy Ruth, Betsy Ann, Frederic Christopher. B.S. in Business U. Idaho, 1957; postgrad Pacific Coast Banking Sch., 1967. Exec. trainee to sr. v.p., adminstrv. br., First Interstate Bank of Oreg., 1959-74, exec. v.p., banking, 1974-76; pres., dir. First Interstate Bank of Wash., 1976-80, pres., dir., mktg., advt., public relations exec., Ehrig & Assocs., Seattle, 1981—; dir. Seattle Fur Exchange, Bekins Van Lines, Seattle, Wash. Bd. dirs. Community Devel. Corp.; v.p., bd. dirs. Wash. State Internat. Trade Fair; bd. dirs. Seattle Seafair, Forest Industries Mus., Seattle-King County Conv. Bur., Seattle Ctr. Found.; regent Gonzaga U.; chmn. Interaction/Transition Social Service Agy. Served to capt. U.S. Army Res., 1957-62. Mem. Am. Advt. Assn. Republican. Methodist. Clubs: Wash. Athletic (dir.), Seattle Golf, Seattle Rotary, Rainier. Home: 5216 W Mercer Way Mercer Island WA 98040 Office: 4th and Vine Bldg 8th Floor Seattle WA 98121

BURROW, HAROLD, gas company executive; b. Navasota, Tex., Dec. 1, 1914; s. Benjamin Donald and Minnie (Weaver) B.; grad. Advanced Mgmt. Program, Harvard U.; m. Vassa Woodley; children—Larry W., Harry W., Janice K. With Tenneco, Inc., Houston, 1943-66, pres., 1960-66; chmn. bd., chief exec. officer Colo. Interstate Gas Co., Colorado Springs, 1974—; vice chmn. bd. Coastal States Gas Corp., Houston, from 1974, also mem. exec. com. Mem. Petroleum Club Houston. Methodist. Club: Ramada (Houston). Office: Colo Interstate Gas Co Box 1087 Colorado Springs CO 80944*

BURSON, THOMAS DANIEL, electronics co. exec.; b. Hartselle, Ala., Jan. 7, 1936; s. Daniel Webster and Ardia (Starks) B.; B.M.E. with high honor, Auburn U., 1958; M.B.A., U. So. Calif., 1969; m. Mary Frances Wilson, June 7, 1958; children—Kelly Frances, Robyn Elizabeth, Thomas Scott. Asst. mgr. contract adminstrn. Hycon Co., Monrovia, Calif., 1961-63, mgr. customer contracts, 1963-66, asst. to pres., 1966-67, dir. mktg. 1967-71, v.p., 1969-71; dir. product and bus. planning Actron div. McDonnell Douglas Corp., Monrovia, Calif., 1971, dir. contracts and pricing, 1971-76, v.p. fiscal mgmt., 1976-78, v.p. indsl. control products McDonnell Douglas Astronautics Co., 1978—. Served with USNR, 1958-61. Mem. ASME, Am. Inst. Aeros. and Astronautics, Nat. Contract Mgmt. Assn., Phi Kappa Phi, Tau Beta Pi, Pi Tau Sigma, Beta Gamma Sigma, Kappa Alpha. Democrat. Club: Glendora (Calif.) Country. Home: 1129 E Sierra Madre Ave Glendora CA 91740 Office: 700 Royal Oaks Dr Monrovia CA 91016

BURSTEN, LYNN KELVIN, organization development consultant; b. Mt. Vernon, N.Y., Sept. 3, 1946; d. David I. and Marjorie White (Kelvin) B.; m. Clifford Donald Stirba, Oct. 16, 1970 (div.). B.A. in Math., U. Pa., 1967; postgrad. So. Ill. U. Orgn. devel. facilitator Weyerhaeuser Co., Tacoma, Wash., 1981—; info. systems cons. Am. Airlines, N.Y.C., 1968-78; pres. Office Tech. Assn., Palm Beach, Fla., 1978-79; office automation cons. United Techs. Corp., West Palm Beach, Fla., 1979-81; speaker on office automation; bus. cons. to arts orgns., Seattle. Mem. Am. Mgmt. Assn., Internat. Info. Word Processing Assn., Assn. Records Mgrs. and Adminstrs., Beta Gamma Sigma. Office: Weyerhaeuser Co Tacoma WA 98477

BURTNETT, STEVEN CHARLES, judge; b. Hollywood, Calif., July 29, 1942; s. Joseph Mark and Mildred (Walker) B.; B.S., Iowa State U., 1964; J.D., U. Calif.-San Francisco, 1967; grad. Calif. Center Jud. Edn. and Research, Berkeley, 1975; m. Judith Jean Lambert, June 29, 1968; 1 son, Steven Christian. Bar: Calif. 1967. Intern in pub. affairs Coro Found., Los Angeles, 1967-68; dep. dist. atty. Los Angeles County, also dep.-in-charge juvenile br. Norwalk Superior Ct., 1972-74; commr., judge pro tem Los Cerritos Mcpl. Ct., Bellflower, Calif., 1974—; instr. Calif. State U. at Long Beach, 1972—. Field dep. Joe Blatchford for Congress campaign, 1968; mem. steering com. Mike Donaldson for Congress campaign, 1970; chmn. bd. mgrs. Los Cerritos YMCA, 1979-82; mem. Speakers Bur., Gov. campaign, 1982. Served with USMC, 1968. Mem. ABA, Los Angeles County, S.E. Dist. bar assns., State Bar Calif., Nat. Dist. Attys. Assn. (Los Angeles County del. to nat. conv., 1971), Am. Judicature Soc., Calif. Ct. Commrs. Assn. (founding, v.p.), Am. Judges Assn., Calif. Judges Assn., SAR, Sons Union Vets. of Civil War, Hastings Alumni Assn (v.p., bd. govs.), Sigma Alpha Epsilon, Phi Delta Phi. Clubs: Commonwealth, Rotary. Republican. Methodist. Editor-in-chief Voir Dire, Hastings Coll. Law, U. Calif., 1967-68. Home: 16911 Coral Cay Huntington Beach CA 92649 Office: 10025 E Flower St Bellflower CA 90706

BURTON, AL, producer, director, writer; b. Chgo., Apr. 9, 1928; s. D. Chester and Isabelle (Olenick) G.; B.S. cum laude, Northwestern U., 1948; m. Sally Lou Lewis, Jan. 8, 1956; 1 dau., Jennifer. Producer various youth-oriented TV series, 1949-52; producer Johnny Mercer's Mus. Chairs, 1952-55, Oscar Levant Show, 1955-61; creative producer Teen-Age Fair, 1962-72; exec. v.p. creative affairs Norman Lear-Embassy Communications, Inc., 1973-83, creative supr. Mary Hartman, Mary Hartman, composer/lyricist Facts of Life, Diff'rent Strokes, prodn. supr. One Day At A Time, Diff'rent Strokes, Silver Spoons, Gloria, The Jeffersons, Square Pegs, Facts of Life; exec. producer, cons. Universal TV, 1983—; cons. Domestic Life, CBS-TV, 1983-84; dir. 42 Products Ltd. Inc. Media cons. Democratic Congl. Com., Calif. Dem. State Com. Trustee Oakwood Sch. Recipient Emmy award nomination for Oscar Levant Show, 1961; Emmy honors for outstanding comedy series (All in the Family), 1979. Mem. Caucus for Producers, Writers and Dirs., Dirs. Guild Am., Writers Guild Am., AFTRA, Acad. of TV Arts and Scis., Acad. of Magical Arts. Office: 100 Universal City Plaza Universal City CA 91608

BURTON, ARTHUR GRANT, marine biologist; b. Concord, Calif., July 31, 1945; s. Grant Arthur and Isabel Mary (Byrne) B.; m. Kathleen Keane, Dec. 14, 1968; children—Shannon, Rebecca, Bridget. B.A., Stanford U., 1970; M.A., San Francisco State U., 1972. Supervising biologist Kennedy/Jenks Engrs., San Francisco, 1972-77; pres. Sequoia Analytical Lab., Redwood City, Calif., 1977—. Served with USN, 1965-68. Mem. Water Pollution Control Fedn., Am. Water Works Assn., Am. Chem. Soc. Office: Sequoia Analytical Lab 2549 Middlefield Rd Redwood City CA 94063

BURTON, CATE, telecommunications adminstr.; b. Chgo., Sept. 6, 1952; d. John Louis and Nancy Virginia (Stine) Burton. Student Ithaca Coll., 1970-72, Golden Gate U., 1982—. PBX supr. U. Chgo. and U. Chgo. Hosps., 1972-74, St. Francis Meml. Hosp., San Francisco, 1974-78; mgr. telecommunications Presbyterian Hosp. of Pacific Med. Ctr., San Francisco, 1978—. Mem. Am. Soc. Hosp. Engring., Hosp. Telecommunications Mgmt. Assn. (founder, dir.). Democrat. Office: 2333 Buchanan P-1311 San Francisco CA 94115

BURTON, GWENDOLYN RAYE WILSON, biology educator; b. Norman, Okla., May 4, 1925; d. Clarence Dewey and Clara Mae (Glenn) Wilson; B.S., Colo. State U., 1947; M.S., U. Denver, 1967, Ph.D., 1975; m. Lynn Ross Burton, June 15, 1946; children—Cynthia A. Sluyter, Gary Lynn, Alan Dale, Earl Wilson. Research technician Denver Research Inst., 1962-64; instr. biology and microbiology U. Denver, 1968-71; prof. biology and microbiology, coordinator biology Community Coll. of Denver, 1971—; Colo. State Sci. Fair judge, 1972 ; Internat. Sci. Fair judge, 1976; People to People del. to China, 1983; lectr. in field. Mem. Am. Soc. Microbiology, AAAS, Nat. Sci. Tchrs. Assn., Nat. Assn. Biology Tchrs., Phi Sigma, Alpha Epsilon Delta. Mem. Order of Faster Star. Contbr. articles in field to profl. jours.; author: Microbiology for Health Sciences, 1979, 2d edit., 1983. Home: 7155 S Poplar Way Englewood CO 80112 Office: 3645 W 112th Ave Westminster CO 80030

BURTON, LYNDLE RIEKE, industrial hygienist; b. Quincy, Ill., Aug. 3, 1955; s. Lyle Allen and Chrystal Auretta (Janssen) B.; B.S., Baker U., 1978; M.S., Central Mo. State U., 1979, m. Linda Faye Townsend, Dec. 3, 1977; 2 daus., Heidi Christine, Jennifer Lynn. Loss control rep. Hewitt, Coleman & Assocs., Louisville, 1979-81. Served to lt. Med. Service Corps, USNR, 1981—. Mem. Am. Indsl. Hygiene Assn., Nat. Safety Council Am. Soc. Safety Engrs., Kappa Sigma. Democrat. Methodist. Office: Naval Environmental Preventive Medicine Unit 6 Box 112 Pearl Harbor HI 96860

BURTON, NELSINE, accountant; b. Wilbur, Wash., Oct. 20, 1926; d. Chris Henrik and Kathrine Marie (Hansen) Mikkelsen; m. Keith Laverne Burton, Feb. 2, 1947; 1 son, Jeffrey Keith. Student Whitman Coll., 1944-46. C.P.A., Oreg. Acct., Yergen and Meyer, Coos Bay, Oreg., 1965-76; fin. dir., asst. bus. mgr. Southwestern Oreg. Community Coll., 1975-80; sr. staff acct. Scoville & Franklin P.C., C.P.A.s, Coos Bay, 1980—. Mem. adv. bd. Goodwill Industries; bd. dirs. Coos County Heart Fund. Mem. Am. Inst. C.P.A.s, Oreg. Soc. C.P.A.s. Club: Zonta (Coos Bay). Office: Scoville & Franklin PC 391 N 2d St Coos Bay OR 97420

BURTON, PAUL FLOYD, social worker; b. Seattle, May 24, 1939; s. Floyd James and Mary Teresa (Chovanak) B.; B.A., U. Wash., 1961, M.S.W., 1967; m. Roxanne Maude Johnson, July 21, 1961; children—Russell Floyd, Joan Teresa. Juvenile parole counselor Div. Juvenile Rehab. State of Wash., 1961-66; social worker VA, Seattle, 1967-72, social worker, cons. Work Release program King County, Wash., 1967-72; supr., chief psychiatry sect. Social Work Service VA, Topeka, Kans., 1972-73; pvt. practice social work, Topeka and Los Angeles, 1972—; chief social work service VA, Sepulveda, Calif., 1974—, Equal Employment Opportunity coordinator Med. center, 1974-77. Mem. Nat. Assn. Social Workers (newsletter editor Puget Sound chpt. 1970-71), Acad. Cert. Social Workers, Am. Group Psychotherapy Assn., Internat. Transactional Analysis Assn., Center for Studies in Social Functioning, Am. Sociol. Assn., Am. Public Health Assn., Am. Hosp. Assn., Soc. Hosp. Social Work Dirs., Assn. VA Social Work Chiefs (founder 1979, charter mem. and pres. 1980-81, newsletter editor 1982-83), Am. Assn. Sex Educators, Counselors, and Therapists. Home: 14063 Remington St Arleta CA 91331 Office: 16111 Plummer St Sepulveda CA 91343

BURTON, RICHARD ROGHAAR, architect; b. Ogden, Utah, Dec. 17, 1941; s. Laurence S. and Marguerite (Roghaar) B.; B.Arch., U. Utah, 1968; m. Linda Moore, Dec. 28, 1959; children—Deborah Lynn, Kathleen Ann, Colleen Elizabeth. Draftsman, Ashton, Brazier, Montmorency Architects, Salt Lake City, 1967-68; architect intern John L. Piers & Assos. Architects, Ogden, 1968-72; asso. architect Mascarella/Merry & Assos. Architects, Tucson, 1972-76; chief architect, pres. Burton & Assocs., Architects, Tucson, 1976—; dir. Arc 5 Devel. Co.; partner, v.p. E.R.A. Huff Realty. Mem. Tucson City Sign Code Com.; mem. Tucson north stake presidency Ch. Jesus Christ of Latter-day Saints. v.p., bd. dirs. Tucson Boys' Clubs; scoutmaster Bonneville council Boy Scouts Am., mem. exec. bd. Catalina council; mem. Tucson Tomorrow. Registered architect, Ariz., N.Mex., Utah. Mem. AIA, Nat. Council Archtl. Registration Bds. Republican. Club: Optimists (pres. Uptown club, lt. gov. and gov. Ariz. dist.; Service award 1979). Designer Bell/Clock Tower at Weber State Coll., 1970; designer numerous schs., chs., office bldgs., residences. architect; b. Ogden, Utah, Dec. 17, 1941; s. Laurence S. and Marguerite (Roghaar) B.; B.Arch., U. Utah, 1968; m. Linda Moore, Dec. 28, 1959; children—Deborah Lynn, Kathleen Ann, Colleen Elizabeth. Draftsman, Ashton, Brazier, Montmorency Architects, Salt Lake City, 1967-68; architect intern John L. Piers & Assos. Architects, Ogden, 1968-72; asso. architect Mascarella/Merry & Assos. Architects, Tucson, 1972-76; chief architect, pres. Burton & Assocs., Architects, Tucson, 1976—; dir. Arc 5 Devel. Co.; partner, v.p. E.R.A. Huff Realty. Mem. Tucson City Sign Code Com.; mem. Tucson north stake presidency Ch. Jesus Christ of Latter-day Saints. v.p., bd. dirs. Tucson Boys' Clubs; scoutmaster Bonneville council Boy Scouts Am., mem. exec. bd. Catalina council; mem. Tucson Tomorrow. Registered architect, Ariz., N.Mex., Utah. Mem. AIA, Nat. Council Archtl. Registration Bds. Republican. Club: Optimists (pres. Uptown club, lt. gov. and gov. Ariz. dist.; Service award 1979). Designer Bell/Clock Tower at Weber State Coll., 1970; designer numerous schs., chs., office bldgs., residences. Home: 4205 E Presidio Rd Tucson AZ 85712 Office: 4400 E Broadway Suite 805 Tucson AZ 85711

BURTON, ROBERT ELLIOTT, life ins. co. exec.; b. N.Y.C., Sept. 14, 1930; s. Frederick Arthur and Carol Edith (King) B.; B.S. in Econs., Yale, 1952; LL.B., Columbia Univ. Law Sch., 1955; m. Elza Mirsky, July 1, 1956; children—Kenneth Michael, Abigail Ann. Admitted to N.Y. bar, 1955, Calif. bar, 1968; asso. Hetkin, Jervis & Hetkin, N.Y.C., 1955-56, Skutch & Burton, N.Y.C., 1956-59, McGuigan & Kilcullen, N.Y.C., 1959-64; advanced underwriting cons. N.Y. Life Ins. Co., N.Y.C., 1964-65, San Francisco, 1966—, sr. cons., 1974—. Chmn., Mill Valley Planning Commn., 1970-72, commr., 1967-72; councilman City of Mill Valley, 1972-76, mayor, 1974-76; bd. dirs. Marin County Transit Dist., 1974-76; mem. adv. bd. dirs. Marin County Flood Control Zone #3, 1974—; commr. Marin County Transit Commn., 1977—, chmn., 1977-79. C.L.U. Mem. San Francisco Life Underwriters Assn., San Francisco Estate Planning Council (dir., v.p.), Am. Soc. C.L.U.s (chpt. dir., v.p.). Clubs: Scott Valley Swimming and Tennis; Yale (San Francisco). Contbr. articles to various publs. Home: 114 Hazel Ave Mill Valley CA 94941 Office: 44 Montgomery St San Francisco CA 94104

BURTON, THOMAS WHITTIER, lawyer; b. Cleve., Aug. 14, 1946; s. Kenneth Lewis and Caroline (Smith) B. B.A. in Econs. and Acctg., Claremont (Calif.) Men's Coll., 1968; J.D., U. San Diego, 1971. Bar: Calif. 1973, D.C. bar 1973. Ptnr. Burton, Englebrecht & Andrade, Newport Beach, Calif., 1973—; developer Newport Law Center Condominium Offices; pres., chmn. bd. W. Bert Knight Co., Newport Beach, 1975-77; mem. exec. adv. com., instr. Orange County Legal Edn. Program, 1977-80. Trustee, ABC Scholarship, Claremont Mc Kenna Coll., 1970—; pres., bd. dirs. Newport Harbor Kiwanis Found., 1975—; trustee Yoga Center and Spiritual World Soc., 1976—. Served to 1st lt. C.E., U.S. Army, 1971-73. Mem. ABA, Los Angeles County, Orange County, D.C. bar assns. Office: 500 Newport Blvd Suite 100 Newport Beach CA 92663

BURTT, GEORGE WOOLSON, clergyman; b. Vancouver, B.C., Can., May 18, 1914; s. George Keyes and Josephine Cutter (Woolson) B.; student pub. schs.; m. Dorothy Smith, Sept. 28, 1937; children—Gregory, Marcia, Jonathan and Portia (twins); m. 2d, Marian Zametkin, June 3, 1950; 1 dau., Jennifer; m. 3d, Marian Simpson, Jan. 29, 1977. Advt. designer, writer Washington Times, 1935-44; account exec. Kal Advt., Washington, 1945; art dir. Courtland D. Ferguson, Inc., Advt., Washington, 1946-48; advt. mgr. Western Stove Co., Los Angeles, 1949-52; exec. dir. Hollywood (Calif.) Advt. Club, 1952-58; creative dir. Enyart & Rose Advt., Los Angeles, 1958-69; ordained to ministry, Vector Ch., 1966; founder, minister Vector Community Ch., Los Angeles, 1967-68. Mem. Author's Guild, Hollywood Radio and TV Soc., Pacific Pioneer Broadcasters, Mensa. Author: Vector Handbook, 1969; Putting Yourself Across with the Art of Graphic Persuasion, 1972; Psychographics in Personal Growth, 1972; Stop Crying at Your Own Movies, 1975; The Explicated Tao, 1978; The Barter Way to Beat Inflation, 1980. Address: Box 1271 Mount Vernon WA 98273

BURWEN, MICHAEL P., computer industry executive, consultant; b. Winthrop, Mass., Mar. 15, 1938; s. Charles D. and Charlotte (Freedman) D., children—Marcy, Jill; m. 2d, Margaret March Ross, Nov. 8, 1976; 1 son, Ross. B.A.E., Rensselaer Poly. Inst., 1959; M.S.E., UCLA, 1964. With Gen. Dynamics, Pomona, Calif., 1959-63; mgr. Electronic Assocs., Palo Alto, Calif., 1963-68; pres. Basic Computing Arts, Mountain View, Calif., 1968-70; sr. v.p. Quantum Sci. Corp., Palo Alto, 1970-75; pres. Mackintosh Research, 1975-77; pres., dir. Input, Palo Alto, 1977-81; founder, pres. Palo Alto Mgmt. Group, 1981—; lectr. Home: 611 Teresi Ln Los Altos CA 94022 Office: 2685 Marine Way Suite 1212 Mountain View CA 94043

BURY, JAMES KENNEDY, personnel executive; b. Madison, Wis., Mar. 7, 1934; s. Waldemar John and Lydia (Reed) B.; B.B.A., Calif. Western U., 1961; m. Joan Kelch, Dec. 22, 1962; children—Scott, Steven, Douglas. Personnel mgr. Electrolab., Encinitas, Calif., 1961-62; employment and personnel mgr. Univac-Sperry Rand Corp., San Diego, 1962-65, Washington, 1966, Phila., 1966-68, Los Angeles, 1968; indsl. realtions dir. Maxwell Labs., Inc., San Diego, 1968-77, Lamco Industries, Inc., El Cajon, Calif., 1977-78; regional personnel mgr. Raytheon Data Systems Co., Irvine, Calif., 1978-81; dir. personnel Automatic Data Processing, El Toro, Calif., 1981-82, dir. recruiting and profl. employment, La Palma, Calif., 1982—; cons. in field. Pres., State of Calif. Adv. Bd., 1976—. Served with USNR, 1954-58. Mem. Am. Soc. Personnel Adminstrn. (exec. in personnel accreditation 1976—), Personnel and Indsl. Relations Assn. Orange County, Employment Mgmt. Assn. Home: 26562 Tampico Pl Mission Viejo CA 92691 Office: 5355 Orangethorpe Ave La Palma CA 90623

BURY, THOMAS LINCOLN, constrn. co. exec.; b. Gowanda, N.Y., Dec. 1, 1942; s. Burt John and Ruth (Lincoln) B.; B.S. in Bus. Adminstrn., Bowling Green (Ohio) State U., 1965; M.B.A., Syracuse (N.Y.) U., 1969; m. Rene Priemazon, Aug. 29, 1970; children—Matthew Lincoln, Sarah Elizabeth. Corp. acct. Samsonite Corp., Denver, 1969-70; controller Electronic Processors Inc., Englewood, Colo., 1970-72; controller Natkin & Co., Englewood, 1972-77, sec.-treas., 1977—, also dir.; dir. Natkin Service Co. Served with USAR, 1965-67. Mem. Fin. Execs. Inst., Nat. Assn. Accts. Club: Masons. Home: 5049 W Maplewood Pl Littleton CO 80123 Office: PO Box 1258 Englewood CO 80150

BUSCEMI, PHILIP AUGUSTUS, biology educator; b. Mt. Pleasant, Iowa, Mar. 1, 1926; s. Philip Andrew and Hazel (Cain) B.; student Ill. State U., Normal, 1944-46, U. Tenn., Knoxville, 1947-48; B.A., U. Colo., Boulder, 1950, M.A., 1952, Ph.D., 1957; postgrad. Eastern N.Mex. U., 1966; m. Margaret Louise Miller, Aug. 19, 1950; children—Stephen, Cynthia, Lisa. Instr. invertebrate zoology and gen. biology labs. U. Colo., Boulder, 1950-53; non-resident instr. biology U. Colo. Med. Center, Denver, 1955-56; instr. zoology U. Idaho, 1956-59, asst. prof., 1959-65; asso. prof. Okla. State U., 1966, asst. prof. zoology, 1965-66; assoc. prof. biology Eastern N.Mex. U., Portales, 1966-71, prof. biology, 1971—, chmn. dept. biol. sci., 1966-75, prof. biology div. natural sci., 1976—; vis. prof. invertebrate zoology Wash. State U., NSF Summer Inst. High Sch. Biology Tchrs., 1962; vis. lectr. U. Colo., 1961, 63, 64, 65; vis. prof. zoology Flathead Lake Biol. Sta., U. Mont., 1973; com. chmn. N.Mex. State Sci. Fair, Socorro, 1973—; vis. scientist lectr. N.Mex. Acad. Sci., 1967—; chmn. Interdisciplinary Environ. Inst., Eastern N.Mex. U., 1971-75; mem. Lawrence Livermore Lab. Summer Inst. Biology Medicine, 1970. Recipient Stipend, NSF, 1958, Resear award Colo.-Wyo. Acad. Sci., 1955; U. Colo. Grad. Sch. fellow and scholar, 1952, 53, 54. Fellow AAAS; mem. Internat. Platform Assn., Am. Soc. Zoologists, Am. Inst. Biol. Sci., Internat. Assn. Theoretical and Applied Limnology, Am. Soc. Limnology and Oceanography (travel award 1959), Explorers Club, N.Mex. Acad. Sci. (pres.-elect 1979-80, pres. 1980-81), Beta Beta Beta, Alpha Epsilon Delta, Phi Sigma, Biologia, Gamma Theta Epsilon, Sigma Xi. Contbr. articles to profl. jours. Home: PO Box 2014 Portales NM 88130 Office: Division Natural Sci Eastern NMex U Portales NM 88130

BUSCH, JOSEPH SHERMAN, chem. engr.; b. Chgo., Feb. 20, 1927; s. Max Louis and Emma Elizabeth (Garland) B.; B.S. in Zoology with honors, Northwestern U., 1946, B.S. in Chem. Engring., 1949; M.S., Johns Hopkins, 1953; Ph.D., Carnegie-Mellon U., 1960; m. Barbara Joy Ehrman, Aug. 12, 1951; children—David Bruce, Jethro Sanford. Civilian with U.S. Army Chem. Corps, 1949-51; research fellow Columbia, 1951-53; engr. nuclear projects Westinghouse Electric Co., 1953-60; head nuclear reactor design and test sect. Atomic Power Devel. Assos., Detroit, 1960-62; project mgr. Kaiser Engrs., Oakland, Calif., 1962—. Instr. mech. engring. Carnegie-Mellon U., 1959. Treas., Lafayette Houses, Detroit, 1961-62; mem. Berkeley (Calif.) Police Res., 1971-74. Registered profl. engr., N.Y., Pa., Mich., Miss. Mem. Am. Inst. Chem. Engrs., Sigma Xi. Clubs: Berkeley City; Briard of Am. Contbr. papers to profl. lit. Home: 1598 Hawthorne Terr Berkeley CA 94708 Office: 300 Lakeside Dr PO Box 23210 Oakland CA 94623

BUSCH-ROSSNAGEL, NANCY ANN, family studies educator; b. Denver, May 29, 1951; d. Edwin J. and Eleanor (Edison) Busch; m. Stephen Mark Rossnagel, Aug. 24, 1978; B.A., Scripps Coll., 1972; M.A., Wayne State U., 1973; postgrad. Merrill-Palmer Inst., 1972-73; Ph.D., Pa. State U., 1979. Lectr. child studies U. Guelph (Ont.), 1973-77; trainee Bur. Edn. for Handicapped, 1976-79; asst. prof. human devel. and family studies Colo. State U., Ft. Collins., 1979—; evaluator Office Mental Retardation, Pa., 1979. Sr. high fellowship sponsor First United Presbyn. Ch., 1981—, rep. youth subcom., 1981—. Pa. State U. grad. sch. fellow, 1978-79, Merrill-Palmer Inst. scholar, 1972, Colo. State U. grantee, 1979-82, Bur. Edn. Handicapped grantee, 1978-79, U. Guelph grantee, 1975-76, Canadian Book Pubs. Council grantee, 1974. Mem. Am. Assn. Marriage and Family Therapy, Am. Psychol. Assn., Nat. Council Family Relations, Soc. Research Child Devel., Rocky Mountain Council on Family Relations (mem. exec. bd., conf. chmn.), Omicron Nu. Presbyterian. Author: Instructor's Manual for Families, 1980; Student Guide and Instructor's Manual for Children, 1982; editor: (with Richard M. Lerner) Individuals as producers of their Development: A Life-Span Perspective, 1981; reviewer Child Care Quar., 1978—, Macmillan Pub. Co., 1980—; contbr. articles to profl. jours. Office: 106 Gifford Bldg Colo State U Fort Collins CO 80523

BUSE, LUCILLE JEAN (SALLY), safety engineer; b. Milw., Dec. 13, 1928; d. Edwin Arthur and Margaret Mamie (Bentz) Hellmich; children—Larry Scott Miller, Randy Jay Miller, Lauri Jo Miller. B.A., U. Puget Sound, 1962; M.S.T., 1965, M.A. Wash. State U., 1976, postgrad., 1976—. Cert. safety profl. Tchr. jr. high sch., Tacoma, 1965-68; counselor, tchr. sr. high sch., Newport, Oreg., 1968-71; tchr.-demonstrator Trojan Nuclear Power Plant, 1977; plant cost analyst Portland Gen. Electric, 1977-78; apprentice, surveyor Operating Engrs. Local 701, 1979; loss control tech. Fireman's Fund Ins. Co., Portland, Oreg., 1979—; mem. 5 county safety services bd. ARC; mem. steering com. 1983 Gov.'s Conf. on Health and Safety, also chmn. pub. relations com. Mem. Am. Soc. Safety Engrs. Clubs: Toastmasters. Home: 2998 SE Creek Ct Hillsboro OR 97123 Office: PO Box 3825 Portland OR 97208

BUSH, ALFRED LERNER, econ. geologist; b. Rochester, N.Y., Dec. 21, 1919; s. Arthur Hyman and Eleanor Hermione (Lerner) B.; B.A., U. Rochester, 1941, M.Sc. in Econ. Geology, 1946; m. Caroline Antoinette Wiener, Oct. 21, 1942; children—Caroline L., John E., James A., Margaret A., Martha E., Amy E.; m. 2d, Jo Ann Gilstrap Heath, Jan. 22, 1965; stepchildren—David, Diane. Jr. geologist to sr. research geologist U.S. Geol. Survey, Denver, 1946—; sci. sec. mineral resources U.S. del. UN Conf. on Sci. and Tech. for Less Developed Nations, 1963. Served with USNR, 1942-45; PTO. Fellow Geol. Soc. Am.; mem. Soc. Econ. Geologists, Soc. Mining Engrs., AIME, Geol. Soc. Wash., Colo. Sci. Soc., Internat. Assn. Genesis of Ore Deposits. Contbr. articles to sci. jours. Home: 10445 W Kentucky Dr Lakewood CO 80226 Office: US Geological Survey MS 941 Box 25046 Federal Center Denver CO 80225

BUSH, DRAKE, editor; b. Cin., Sept. 22, 1937; s. George Baber and Mary Louise (Foster) B.; m. Mary Major Normand, June 1, 1956; children—Mary Lou, Kelly Ann. A.B., U. Tenn., 1963, M.A. in English, 1965. Asst. comml. mgr. WCPO-TV, Cin., 1959-61; English instr. U. Tenn., Knoxville, 1965-68; coll. book salesman Harcourt Brace Jovanovich, Denton, Tex., 1969-70, sales mgr., Atlanta, 1970-77, English editor, N.Y.C., 1977-80, history and polit. sci. editor, San Diego, 1981—. Mem. Am. Polit. Sci. Assn., Am. Hist. Assn., Orgn. Am. Historians. Democrat. Home: 2301 Plum St San Diego CA 92106 Office: 1250 6th Ave San Diego CA 92101

BUSH, ELMER W., mfg. co. exec.; b. Sacramento, Nov. 26, 1923; s. Charles J. and Alice E. (Pittman) B.; ed. public schs.; m. Felomena T. Cimaroli, Nov. 26, 1973; 1 son, Michael M. Pres., Pal-Pen Chem. Corp., Sacramento, 1956—; chief engr., pres., inventor Condensator Inc., Sacramento, 1975—, also dir. internat. sales. Served with USAAF, 1943-46. Patentee in field.

BUSH, JOHN CLIFFORD, JR., psychologist, educator; b. Peoria, Ill., June 11, 1938; s. John Clifford and Clara Elizabeth (Siepel) B.; B.S., Western Ill. U., 1960, M.S., 1967; Ed.D., Wash. State U., 1970; m. Mary Lee Petersen, Jan. 7, 1959; children—Sherri, Julie, Michael, Patrick. Bus. tchr., coach Arlington High Sch., Arlington Heights, Ill., 1963-68; counseling asst. Wash. State U., Pullman, 1968-69; counselor Green River Community Coll., Auburn, Wash., 1969-71, chmn. counseling div., 1971—; also psychologist in pvt. practice, Kent, Wash. Chmn. Task Force V, Wash. Assn. Community Coll. Info. Systems Commn., 1974-75; bd. dirs. Kent Valley Youth Services. Lic. psychologist, Wash. Mem. Am., Wash. psychol. assns., Am. Personnel and Guidance Assn., Internat. Assn. Counseling Services (chmn. accrediation bd. for community colls. 1974-79, v.p.), Counseling and Guidance Dirs. Assn. Wash. State Community Coll. (pres. 1972-74), Acad. Affairs Adminstrs. Assn. (treas. 1970-76), Am. Arbitration Assn. (family dispute services panel 1979), Am. Assn. Sex Educators, Counselors and Therapists (chmn. Wash. sect. 1981—), Phi Delta Kappa, Psi Chi. Contbr. articles to profl. jours. Home: 22346 10th Ave S Des Moines WA 98188 Office: 12401 SE 320th St Auburn WA 98002 also 1819 S Central Ave Suite 111 Kent WA 98031

BUSH, ROBERT D(ONALD), museum director, educator; b. Marshaltown, Iowa, Apr. 9, 1939; s. Donald Dudley and Ruth Eleanor (Lorimer) B.; m. Bonnie Ruth Thielges, May 29, 1962; children—Sarah Beth, Susan Lynn, Carolyn Ruth, Jennifer Ann, David Alan. B.A., U. Dubuque, 1962; M.A., U. Richmond, 1963, Ph.D., U. Kans., 1969. Cert. of study Art Security Inst., U. Minn., 1980. Social studies tchr. Oak Lawn, Ill., 1963-65; asst. instr. in history, U. Kans., Lawrence, 1965-68; asst. prof. [illegible]ry Nebr. Wesleyan U., Lincoln, 1968-74; asst. dir. Hist. New [illegible] Collection, 1974-82; dir. Wyo. State Archives, Mus. and Hist. [illegible]enne, 1982—; cons. in field. Sec.-treas. La. Assn. Mus., [illegible] grad. fellow, U. Richmond, 1963; Kans. Regents fellow, [illegible]llow Nebr. Wesleyan U., 1968-69; recipient Pres.' award, 1971. Mem. Am. Assn. State and Local History, Am. Assn. Mus.-Internat. Council Mus., Wyo. Hist. Soc. (exec. sec. 1982—). Presbyterian. Gen. editor Historic New Orleans Collection Monograph Series, 1975-79; contbr. articles to publs. in field including Louisiana History, Louisiana Rev., McNeese Rev., Jour. of Southern History. Northwest Rev., Revue de Etude Napoleon. Office: Barrett Bldg Wyoming State Museum Cheyenne WY 82002

BUSHMAN, EDWIN FRANCIS ARTHUR, engr., plastics cons., rancher; b. Aurora, Ill., Mar. 16, 1919; s. George J. and Emma (Gengler) B.; B.S., U. Ill., 1941, postgrad., 1941-42, Calif. Inst. Tech., 1941; m. Louise Kathryn Peterson, Jan. 3, 1946; children—Bruce Edwin, Gary Robert, Joan Louise, Karen Rose, Mary Elisabeth, Paul George. Jr. engr, Gulf Refining Co. Gulf Oil Corp., Mattoon, Ill., 1940-41; engr. radio and sound lab. war research, div. U. Calif. at Navy Electronics Lab., Pt. Loma, San Diego, 1942-45; project engr. Bell and Howell Co., Lincolnwood, Ill., 1945-46; research cons., Scholl Mfg. Co., Inc., Chgo., 1946-48; project engr. deepfreeze div. Motor Products Corp., North Chicago, Ill., 1948-50; research and product design engr. Bushman Co., Aurora, Ill. also Mundelein, Ill., 1946-55; with Plastics div. Gen. Am. Transp. Corp., Chgo., 1950-68, tech. dir., 1950-55, mgr. sales and sales engring. Western states, Compton, Calif., 1955-68, sales and sales engring. research and devel. div., 1962-64; with USS Chems., 1968-70; plastics cons. E.F. Bushman Co., 1970—, Tech. Conf. Assos., 1974—. Program mgr. Agriplastics Symposium Nat. Agrl. Plastics Conf., 1966; program mgr. Plastics in Hydrospace, 1967; originator Huisman Plastics awards, 1970, Un-Carbon Polymer prize and Polymer Pool Preserve Plan, 1975, Polymer Independence award, 1977, 78. Bd. dirs. Coastal Area Protective League, 1958-66, Lagunita Community Assn., 1959-66 (pres. 1964-65), Calif. Marine Parks and Harbors Assn., 1959-69. Recipient Western Plastics Man of Yr. award, 1972. Mem. Soc. Plastics Industry Inc. (chpt. pres. 1971-72), Soc. Plastic Engrs. (Lundberg award 1981), Western Plastics Engrs., ASTM, Sunkist Growers, Calif. Avocado Soc., Cal. Citrus Nurserymen's Soc., Calif. Farm Bur. Fedn. U. Ill. Alumni Assn., Lemon Men's Club, Soc. for Advancement Materials and Process Engring., Geopolymers Inst. Roman Catholic. Moose. Author various profl. and strategic resource papers. Patentee in field of plastics, carbon and colored glass fibers, process, and applications. Home: 19 Lagunita Laguna Beach CA 92651 Office: PO Box 581 Laguna Beach CA 92652

BUSHMAN, WILLARD MARTIN, lawyer, ednl. adminstr.; b. Portland, Oreg., Feb. 22, 1937; s. Ted and Dorothy (Lyman) B.; B.A., Stanford, 1960; J.D., U. Calif. at Berkeley, 1964; postgrad. (Ford Found. fellow) U. Munich (Germany), 1964-65; children by previous marriage—Jeffrey, Meg, Kathryn; m. 2d, Pamela Jeanne Bushman; children—Heidi, Christopher, Joseph, Joshua. Admitted to Oreg. bar, 1966, U.S. Supreme Ct. bar, 1973, Calif. bar, 1975; practiced in Portland, 1966-67; dir. edn. Oreg. State Bar, Portland, 1967-73; chief tng. Nat. Center State Cts., Denver, 1973; asso. dir. Calif. Center for Judicial Edn. and Research, Berkeley, 1973—. Served with AUS, 1961. Mem. Assn. Continuing Legal Edn. Adminstrs. (pres. 1973-75), Ore. State Bar, State Bar Calif., Am. Judicature Soc. Mormon. Editor: The Continuing Legal Education Administrators Handbook, 1970. Home: 3549 Tabora Dr Antioch CA 94509 Office: 1947 Center St Berkeley CA 94704

BUSHNELL, GEORGE ELMORE, JR., business executive; b. Los Angeles, Aug. 30, 1915; s. George Elmore and Edith Marguerita (Vincent) B.; student Santa Monica Jr. Coll., 1934-35; B.A., UCLA, 1937; m. Winifred Louise Kiehl, Dec. 9, 1943; 1 son, George Elmore. With Standard Oil Calif., Los Angeles, 1937-38, Equitable Life, Los Angeles, 1938-40, Lockheed Aircraft, Burbank, Calif., 1940-42, Marwood, Ltd., Honolulu, 1946-58; pres. Oceanic Agencies, Ltd., Honolulu, 1958-77, v.p. S & K sales, 1977-80; pres. Ruthwin, Inc., Honolulu, 1971-73. Served with USNR, 1942-46, 50-52; capt. Res. (ret.). Mem. Navy League (pres. Windward 1983-84). Lodges: Masons, Shriners. Club: Oahu Country. Home: 84 Laiki Pl Kailua HI 96734 Office: 97-731 Kam Hwy Pearl City HI 96782

BUSHNELL, JIM L., agronomist, consultant; b. Fillmore, Utah, Apr. 7, 1946; s. Leland Mainwaring and Lola (Duncan) B.; m. Carolyn Sue Memmott, May 15, 1969; children—Sheree, Michelle, Staci, James Lee, Susan, Mark Ralph. B.S., Brigham Young U., 1970; M.S. in Botany/Biochemistry, Ph.D., Ohio State U., 1976. Research specialist Chevron Chem. Co., 1976-78; county agt. Utah State U., Millard County, 1978-80, state extension agronomist, 1980-82, tchr. extension agronomist, 1982—. Served to capt. U.S. Army, 1972-78. Mem. Crop Sci. Soc. Am., Western Soc. Crop Sci., Nat. Alfalfa Improvement Conf., Western Alfalfa Improvement Conf. Mormon. Home: 2060 N 1400 E Logan UT 84321 Office: 326 Agriculture Science UMC 49 Utah State U Logan UT 84322

BUSHNELL, JOSEPH MERRILL, manufacturing company executive; b. Meadow, Utah, June 19, 1920; s. Daniel Deardon and Melba Ellen (Stott) B.; m. Lillian Lucille Booth, June 5, 1946; children—Bruce, Ned, Pamela. B.A., Brigham Young U., 1947; M.B.A., Stanford U., 1949. Indsl. engr. Pacific States Cast Iron Co., Provo, Utah, 1949-54, purchasing agt., 1954-62, asst. gen. mgr., 1962-67, v.p., gen. mgr., 1967—; spl. instr., guest lectr. prodn. mgmt. Brigham Young U., 1954-62, mem. nat. adv. council Sch. Mgmt.; bd. advisors Mountain Bell Utah; dir. Mountain Bell, Denver. Exec. bd. Utah Nat. Parks council Boy Scouts Am.; founding mem., bd. dirs. Eyering Research Inst., Provo. Served with USAAF, World War II. Recipient Disting. Alumni award Brigham Young U., 1980, Bus. and Industry Service award, 1982. Mem. Utah Mfrs. Assn. (Utah Businessman of Yr. 1982; pres. 1975), Utah Indsl. Relations Council (dir.), Am. Water Works Assn., Ductile Iron Research Assn. Republican. Mormon. Clubs: Riverside Country, Kiwanis (Provo). Home: 2005 N 1450 E St Provo UT 84604 Office: Pacific States Cast Iron Pipe Co PO Box 1219 Provo UT 84601

BUSHNELL, WILLET RAY, accountant; b. Rapid City, S.D., Nov. 16, 1948; s. Vernon Edwin and Elsie Geneva (Wright) B.; m. Carol Jean Coykendall, May 20, 1967; 1 son, Eric M.; m. 2d, Ida Marie Hjellen McMahon, Jan. 1, 1980. Student Fullerton Jr. Coll., 1966-68; B.A. in Bus. Adminstrn., Calif. State U.-Fullerton, 1971. C.P.A., Calif., Alaska. Acct. Thomas Byrne & Smith, C.P.A.s, Riverside, Calif., 1971-73; sr. acct. Thomas, Head, & Greisen, C.P.A.s, Anchorage, Alaska, 1973-76; mgr. Burnett & Meyer, C.P.A.s, Anchorage, 1976-80; prin. Willet R. Bushnell, C.P.A., Wasilla, Alaska, 1980-82; ptnr. Bushnell & McMahon, C.P.A.s, Wasilla, 1982—. Mem. budget com. Concerned Parents Wasilla High Sch.; mem. computer com. City of Wasilla. Mem. Am. Inst. C.P.A.s (mem. mktg., distbn. subcom. 1980—), Alaska Soc. C.P.A.s (bd. dirs. 1979-81, chmn. conf. com. 1982-83, mem. other coms.), Calif. Soc. C.P.A.s, Anchorage Estate Planning Council, Wasilla C. of C. (bd. dirs. 1983), Democrat. Presbyterian. Home and Office: PO Box 971684 Wasilla AK 99687

BUSK, PATRICIA LYNN, statistics educator; b. Southampton, N.Y., Nov. 25, 1944; d. Andrew Stanley and Julia (Maziarz) Zuczek; m. Michael Christopher Busk, June 7, 1969. B.A., Trenton State Coll., 1966; M.A., Catholic U. Am., 1969; Ph.D., U. Wis., 1976. Statistician, asst. dir., dir. research projects Children's Meml. Hosp., Chgo., 1969-73; asst. prof. ednl. psychology Mich. State U., East Lansing, 1976-78; statistician research projects Inst. Research on Pvt. Edn., U. San Francisco, 1978-80, asst. prof. ednl. psychology, counseling, 1980—; vis. lectr. ednl. psychology U. Calif.-Berkeley, 1979—. NIMH fellow, 1967-69. Mem. Am. Ednl. Research Assn., Am. Statis. Assn., Nat. Council Measurement Edn., Psychometric Soc. Democrat. Roman Catholic. Office: Sch Edn U San Francisco Lone Mountain Campus San Francisco CA 94117

BUSKIRK, RICHARD HOBART, educator; b. Bloomington, Ind., Jan. 24, 1927; s. Cyrus Hobart and Amiee Ruth (Borland) B.; B. in Bus. with distinction, Ind. U., 1948, M.B.A., 1949; Ph.D., U. Wash., 1955; m. Barbara Jean Lusk, June 14, 1947; children—Bruce David, Carol Ann. Instr. mktg. U. Kans., 1949-53, U. Wash., 1953-55; asst. prof. mktg. U. Okla., 1955-57; prof. mktg. U. Colo., Boulder, 1957-70, Calif. State U., Fullerton, 1970-73; prof. bus. adminstrn. U. So. Calif., Los Angeles, 1973-74; Herman W. Lay chair mktg. So. Meth. U., Dallas, 1974-80; prof. mktg. and dir. entrepreneur program U. So. Calif., Los Angeles, 1980—; dir. Regiment Shops Colo., Boulder, 1963-70, A.R.F. Products, Inc., Raton, N.Mex., 1960-70, Health Wheels, Inc., 1970-74; cons. Delta Drilling Co., Tyler, Tex., 1978-79, Weyerhaeuser Co., Tacoma, 1962-64. Mem. Minority Bus. Opportunity Com. of Fed. Exec. Bd. Served with USN, 1944-46. Mem. Assn. Bus. Simulation and Exptl. Learning (past pres.), Am. Mktg. Assn. Methodist. Club: Palos Verdes. Author: Cases in Marketing, 1970, 74; Concepts of Business, 1970; Business and Administrative Policy, 1970; Retail Selling, 1974; Machivelli and Modern Management, 1974; Your Career, 1975; Principles of Marketing, 4th edit., 1975; Handbook of Managerial Tactics, 1975; Retailing, 1979; Management of the Sales Force, 6th edit., 1982; Textbook of Salesmanship 11th edit., 1982; How to Beat Men at Their Own Game, 1980. Home: 180 Madrid Palm Desert CA 92260 Office: Sch Bus U So Calif Los Angeles CA 90007

BUSS, JERRY HATTEN, real estate co. exec., sports team owner; b. Kemmerer, Wyo., Jan 27, 1933; m. Joann Buss (div.); children—John, Jim, Jeanie, Janie. B.S. in Chemistry, U. Wyo., M.S., Ph.D. in Chemistry, U. So. Calif., 1957. Chemist, Bur. Mines; past mem. faculty dept. chemistry U. So. Calif.; mem. missile div. McDonnell Douglas, Los Angeles; partner Mariani-Buss Assos.; former owner Los Angeles Strings; chmn. bd., owner Los Angeles Lakers, 1979—, Nat. Basketball Assn.; owner Los Angeles Kings, Nat. Hockey League. Office: care Los Angeles Lakers PO Box 10 The Forum Ingelwood CA 90306*

BUSSIERE, BARRY, real estate executive; b. Santa Monica, Calif., Apr. 10, 1947; s. George A. and Geraldine M. (Ackerman) B.; B.A. in Zoology, UCLA, 1969; B.S. in Bus. magna cum laude, Calif. State U., Northridge, 1973. Real estate sales rep. Great Western Cities, Inc., 1969, 72; asst. mgr. Security Pacific Nat. Bank, Orange County, Calif., 1973-76; property mgr. R & B Devel. Co., Los Angeles, 1976-77; mgr. Fredericks Devel. Co., 1977-78; pres. Touchstone Realty, Inc., Huntington Beach, Calif., 1978-83, Real Estate by McVay, 1983—; tchr. real estate adv. com. Coastline Community Coll. Mem. citizens adv. bd. City of Huntington Beach, 1980. Recipient various awards Huntington Beach/Fountain Valley Bd. Realtors. Mem. Calif. Assn. Realtors (state dir. 1979-83, Pres.'s com. 1982, long range planning com. 1983; housing and community devel. com. 1983), Nat. Assn. Realtors, Calif. Assn. Real Estate Tchrs., Home Builders Council, Bldg. Industry Assn., Sales and Mktg. Council, Huntington Beach/Fountain Valley Bd. Realtors (treas. 1979-80, broker/dir. 1981, Realtor of Yr. 1980, pres. 1982, dir. 1983), Huntington Beach C. of C. (dir., ambassador 1982—). Office: 20951 Brookhurst Huntington Beach CA 92646

BUSWELL, ARTHUR WILCOX, physician, surgeon; b. Oklahoma City, Jan. 6, 1926; s. Albert Currier and Enid May (Scott) B.; B.Sc., U. Okla., 1950, M.D., 1952; m. Loleta JoAnn Sherrill, June 11, 1950; children—Arthur Lee, Robert Joseph, Barbara JoAnn, Brian A., Gayla, Richard; m. 2d, Jane Marie Fuksa, Mar. 1, 1969. Intern. Fitzsimons Army Hosp. Aurora, Colo., 1952-53; surg. resident Wesley Hosp., Oklahoma City, 1954-55; practice medicine and surgery, Hennessey, Okla., 1955-63; dep. surgeon, Fort Wainwright and Yukon Command, 1963-65; chief staff Kingfisher (Okla.) Community Hosp., 1956-57; supt. health Kingfisher County, 1960-61; chief profl. service Bassett Army Hosp., 1963-65; div. surgeon 1st Armored Div., Ft. Hood, Tex., 1965-67, 1st Inf. Div., 1967-68; med. project officer U.S. Army Combat Devels. Command, Experimentation Command, Ft. Ord, Calif., 1968-72, also chief human factors div. and chief experimentation div. of experimentation command; chief profl. services Reynolds Army Hosp., Ft. Sill, Okla., 1972-73; comdr. med. dept. activities Ft. Stewart, Ga., 1973-77; chief profl. services Kenner Army Hosp., Ft. Lee, Va., 1977-78; comdr. med. dept. activities, Alaska, 1979-83; adj. asst. prof. med. scis. Baylor U., 1973—. Pres., Ft. Stewart Sch. Bd., 1977; bd. dirs. Ft. Stewart Fed. Credit Union, 1977. Served with AUS, 1944-46, 1st lt. U.S. Army, 1952-54, maj. to col., 1961-83. Decorated Legion of Merit with 2 oak leaf cluster, Soldier's medal, Bronze Star for Valor with oak leaf cluster, Meritorious Service medal, Air medal with 3 oak leaf clusters, Army Commendation medal; Gallantry cross with palm, Honor medal 1st class (both Vietnam). Fellow Royal Soc. Health; mem. Am., Okla. State (mem. no. dels.), Aerospace, Army Aviation (charter) med. assns., Assn. Mil. Surgeons U.S., Garfield-Kingfisher County Med. Soc. Home: Rt 2 Box 64 Kingfisher OK 73750

BUTCHER, JOHN E., animal science educator; b. Belle Fourche, S.D., Aug. 4, 1923; s. James E. and Eva L. (Kirk) B.; m. Virginia O'Connell, April 28, 1951; children—Joan, Jean, James. B.S., Mont. State U., 1950, M.S., 1952; Ph.D., Utah State U., 1956. Ranch mgr. Mont. State U., Bozeman, 1950-51, mem. staff Coop. Extension, 1952-53; mem. staff Utah State U., Logan, 1955—; cons. Office Internat. Cooperation and Devel. Mem. Nat. Pub. Land Adv. Council, 1982—. Served with AUS, 1946-47. Recipient Utah Citizen of Yr. award, 1982. Fellow Am. Soc. Animal Sci., AAAS; mem. Am. Registry Cert. Animal Scientists, 1972, Soc. Range Mgmt., Am. Inst. Biol. Scis., Council Agrl. Sci. and Tech. Presbyterian. Club: Masons. Contrb. articles to profl. jours. Home: 1703 E 1030 N Logan UT 84321 Office: Animal Sci Dept UMC 48 Logan UT 84322

BUTKI, ARNOLD, steel co. exec., educator; b. Detroit, Apr. 25, 1935; s. Julius Joseph and Clara Tillie (Sadowski) B.; B.S., U. Mich., 1960; M.B.A., Claremont Grad. Sch., 1968; m. Joanne Ruth Schumacher, July 22, 1961; children—Jay Michael, Ellen Kay, Scott Andrew. With Kaiser Steel Corp., Fontana, Calif., 1960—, supr. indsl. engring., 1968-70, div. indsl. engr., 1970—, div. supr. operating practices, 1976—; prof. mgmt. Calif. State U., Los Angeles, 1968—. Bd. dirs. YMCA Trail Blazers, 1976-82, dir., chief, 1968-71, 73-76. Served with U.S. Army, 1954-56. Registered profl. engr. Mem. Am. Iron and Steel Engrs., Am. Inst. Indsl. Engrs., Iron and Steel Soc. Am. Inst. Mining and Metall. Engrs., Nat. Soc. Profl. Engrs., Calif. Profl. Engrs., Claremont Grad. Sch. Alumni Assn. (fin. v.p. council 1969-73, pres. 1974-76). Republican. Roman Catholic. Club: Riverside Running (treas., dir. 1979-82). Contbr. articles to profl. jours. Home: 2180 Buckskin Pl Riverside CA 92506 Office: PO Box 217 Fontana CA 92336

BUTLER, BYRON CLINTON, physician; b. Carroll, Iowa, Aug. 10, 1918; s. Clinton John and Blance (Prall) B.; M.D., Columbia Coll. Phys. and Surg., 1943; D.Med.Sci., Columbia, 1953; m. Jo Ann Nicolls; children—Marilyn, John Byron, Barbara, Denise. Intern Columbia Presbyn. Med. Center; resident Sloane Hosp. for Women; instr. Columbia Coll. Phys. and Surg. 1950-53; dir. Butler Research Found., Phoenix, 1953-79, pres., 1970—; pres. Art Cons., Ltd., dealer in art, gemstones, gold and silver, Phoenix, 1970; pres. G.S.G., Inc., appraisal and sale diamonds and gems, 1979—; practice medicine specializing in gynecology and cancer, Phoenix; mem. staff St. Luke's, St. Joseph's and Drs. Hosps. Bd. dirs. Heard Mus., Phoenix, 1965-74. Served to capt. M.C. AUS, 1944-46. Am. Cancer Soc. grantee, 1946-50, NIH grantee,

1946-50. Fellow AAAS, Gemological Inst. Am. Home: 6302 N 38th St Paradise Valley AZ 85253 Office: 550 W Thomas Rd Phoenix AZ 85013

BUTLER, CHARLES WILLIAM, chemist, metallurgist; b. Amsterdam, N.Y., Nov. 24, 1923; s. Charles V. and Catherine C. (Johnston) B.; student Union Coll., 1949, Marshall Coll., Huntington, W.Va., 1950; B.A., Russell Sage Coll., 1951; m. Yvonne L. Jackson, Feb. 9, 1958; children—Charles W., Christopher Balfour, Yvonne Catherine Rose, Amber Charese. With Menasco Mfg. Co., Burbank, Calif., 1953-56; engr. Petroleum Co., Los Angeles, 1956-58; with Lockheed Missiles & Space Co., Sunnyvale, Calif., 1959; chemist, metallurgist Sylvania Electronics Systems, Santa Cruz, Calif., 1959-66, Applied Tech., Palo Alto, Calif., 1966-70; pres. Butler Chem. & Metall. Products, Inc., Santa Clara, Calif., 1970—. Pres., Huckleberry Water Co., Boulder Creek, Calif., 1965—, San Lorenzo Valley (Calif.) Property Owners' Assn., 1978. Served with AUS, 1943-44. Mem. Soc. Aerospace Material and Process Engrs. (chmn. No. Calif. chpt. 1963-64), Calif. Circuits Assn. Club: Kiwanis (pres. San Lorenzo Valley chpt. 1978-79, dist. lt. gov. 1983-84). Home: PO Box 595 Boulder Creek CA 95006 Office: 2075 Bering Dr San Jose CA 95131

BUTLER, DONALD, cattle mgmt. co. exec.; b. Evanston, Ill., Dec. 1, 1925; s. Donald and Katharine (Harper) B.; B.S. in Agr., U. Ariz., 1951; m. Palmer Mary Brooks, Nov. 1, 1952; children—Sarah H., Donald II, Nora C., Marne B., John S., Robert P. Buyer, Producers Livestock Marketing Assn., Phoenix, 1951-53, Yuma, Ariz., 1960-64; agr. loan specialist So. Ariz. Bank & Trust Co., Tucson, 1953-56; asst. cashier crop and livestock loans First Nat. Bank of Ariz., Yuma, 1956-60; v.p., mgr. Investment Research of Southwest, Inc., Yuma, 1964-70; v.p. Coronado Cattle Co., Inc., Tucson, 1970-72, pres., 1972—; past dir. Am. Red Brangus Assn., Austin, Tex.; dir., chmn. U.S. Meat Export Fedn. Mem. bd. Desert Trails council Boy Scouts Am., 1967-70; pres. Yuma County Fair Commn., 1962-63, Southwestern Fair Commn., Tucson, 1974—; trustee Ariz. 4-H Youth Found. Chmn. Ariz. Racing Commn., 1966-68; mem. governing bd. Ariz. Western Coll., Yuma, pres., 1966-67, 69-70. Treas., Ariz. Young Republicans, 1952. Served with USAAF, 1943-46. Mem. Nat. Cattlemen's Assn. (dir.), Ariz. Cattle Growers Assn., Ariz. Cattle Feeders Assn. (past pres.), U. Ariz. Alumni Assn. (dir., pres.). Club: Mountain Oyster (pres.). Home: 1730 N Tanque Verde Loop Rd Tucson AZ 85749 Office: 376 S Stone Ave Tucson AZ 85701

BUTLER, ELAINE RUTH MARJORIE MALLORY (MRS. HAROLD ARTHUR BUTLER), civic worker, author; b. North Bergen, N.J., July 2; d. Eugene Lester and Adele May (Reeder) Mallory; A.B., Barnard Coll., 1930; postgrad. Montclair Coll., 1932; M.S., N.Y. Sch. Social Work, 1935; postgrad. Seton Hall U., 1939, 53; M.S., Newark State Coll., 1959; postgrad. U. San German (P.R.), 1959, No. Ariz. U., 1978, Scottsdale Community Coll., 1979; Ph.D. (hon.), Hamilton U., 1974; m. Harold Arthur Butler, Feb. 17, 1928; 1 dau., Dellamay Dorothy Butler Seibold. Tchr. Horace Mann Sch., Tchrs. Coll., N.Y.C., 1926; statistician, confidential sec. Boy Scouts Am., N.Y.C., 1926-30; investigator Tenement Housing Authority, N.Y. Assembly, 1927; tchr., asst. to prof. Montclair (N.J.) Coll., 1932-37; social worker Dept. Instns. and Agys., Trenton, N.J., 1937-48; adminstrv. sec. N.J. Heart Assn., Newark, 1948-51; tchr. specialist Montclair Pub. Schs., 1953-64; free lance writer, artist, 1964—. Worker, Gompers Rehab. Inst., Phoenix, 1966; mem. aux. Goodwill Industries, Phoenix, 1968—; chmn. Fun for Funds and Bridge Builders, Phoenix, 1966—, active Community Orgn. for Drug Abuse Control, Phoenix, 1969—; corp. sec. 7th Step Found., 1974-75, 79—, bd. dirs., 1974—; bd. dirs. Ariz. Corrections Project; v.p. Ariz. Citizens' Com. Self Help Now; adv. bd. Save-A-Child League, Loretta Young Youth Project. Sec., Democratic Club, New Brunswick, N.J., 1939; campaign mgr. South Orange Village Council, 1955; treas. Northwood Inst., Midland, Mich., 1983—. Recipient numerous awards latest including Ariz. Dept. Corrections for Vol. Work, cert. honor Bd. Edn., Montclair, N.J. Fellow Internat. Biog. Assn.; mem. AAUW (chmn. Scottsdale br. 1977), Nat. Assn. Ret. Fed. Employees (sec. Phoenix 1965-69, sec.-treas. Ariz. Fedn. 1969-71, charter mem. Scottsdale 1972—, sec.-treas. 1972-73, news editor 1979—, nat. 2d v.p. 1981—), Seven Coll. Conf., Nat., N.J., Montclair edn. assn., Franklin Mint Soc. (charter), Friends of Mexican Art, Friends for Terros Aux. (charter), Internat. Platform Assn., Scottsdale YWCA Triangles Aux., Valley Artists League, Ariz. Poets, Musicians and Artists Assn., Ariz. Women in Transition (charter, treas.), Scottsdale Artists League, Nat. Bus. and Profl. Women, Barnard Coll. Bus. and Profl. Women, AAUW, Phoenix Art Mus., Heard Mus. Presbyterian (fellowship chmn. 1965-66, coordinator for Involvement in Action 1966-68). Clubs: Orange Lawn Tennis (South Orange, N.J.), Scottsdale College; College of the Oranges (West Orange, N.J.). Home: 4015 E Sierra Vista Dr Scottsdale AZ 85253 also Las Conchas Puerto Penasco Sonora Mexico

BUTLER, JACKIE DEAN, horticulture educator, consultant; b. Raleigh, Ill., Mar. 1, 1931; s. Gilbert Lowry and Winnie Ellen B.; m. Dianne Mathis, June 9, 1957; children—Lisa Mathis, John Eric. B.S., U. Ill.-Urbana, 1957. M.S., 1959, Ph.D., 1966. Asst. farm advisor U. Ill.-Jersey County, Jerseyville, 1957-58; research asst. U. Ill.-Urbana, 1958-63, asst. prof. horticulture, 1963-70, assoc. prof., 1970-71; assoc. prof. Colo. State U., Ft. Collins, 1971-76, prof., 1976—; cons. Served with USN, 1950-54. Recipient Disting. Service awards Midwest, Central, Northwest Ill. and Chgo. Golf Course Supts. Assns., 1971; Rocky Mountain Dist. Turf award Jack D. Butler Found., 1982. Mem. Am. Soc. Hort. Sci., Am. Soc. Agronomy, Internat. Turfgrass Soc. (Outstanding Contbn. award Found. 1969). Presbyterian. Contbr. numerous articles to profl. jours. Home: 220 S County Rd 5 Fort Collins CO 80524 Office: Dept Horticulture Colo State U Fort Collins CO 80523

BUTLER, JAMES H., educator; b. Cathlament, Wash., Dec. 16, 1908; s. Don Carlos and Maude (Kimball) B.; A.B., Western Wash. Coll. Edn., 1937; A.M., U. So. Calif., 1939, Ph.D., 1948; m. E. Willena Barnhart, June 5, 1937. Tchr. pub. schs., Kelso, Wash., 1934-38, Tulare (Calif.) Union High Sch., 1939-40; asst. prof. speech W. Tex. State Coll., Canyon, 1940-42, 43-44; asst. prof. speech San Jose (Calif.) State Coll., 1945-46; asst. prof. drama U. So. Calif., 1946-57; prof. drama, 1957-74, head dept. drama, 1953-70, DeMille prof. drama, 1953-74, emeritus, 1974—. Served as pvt. AUS, 1942-43. Recipient Service Award to Ednl. Theatre, Am. Theatre Assn., 1973, Award of Excellence, Am. Coll. Theatre Festival, 1972. Mem. Am. Legion, Nat. Coll. Players (past pres.), Am. Ednl. Theater Assn. (pres. 1968), Nat., Western speech assns., Blue Key, Phi Beta Kappa, Phi Kappa Phi, Phi Delta Kappa. Author: The Theatre and Drama of Greece and Rome, 1972. Author numerous filmstrips on history of theater; contbr. articles to theater jours. Home: 5030 W Slauson Los Angeles CA 90056

BUTLER, JAMES HERMAN, safety engr.; b. Lufkin, Tex., Feb. 22, 1916; s. James Hansford and Ollie Edna (Hicks) B.; student Saterwhite Bus. Coll., Lufkin, Tex. A&M U.; m. Laura Ross, Apr. 9, 1939; children—Charline, Charles F. With Tex. Foundries, Lufkin, 1950-60; safety officer U.S. Bur. Reclamation, 1961-72, Met. Water Dist. So. Calif., Los Angeles, 1972-77; safety engr. Christie Co., Sacramento, 1977-78, Continental Heller, Swinerton & Wallberg Co., Sacramento and San Francisco, 1978-81, Butler Enterprises, 1981-82, also D.C. Christie and Assos., Inc., to 1981, Carmichael, Calif. Registered safety engr., Calif. Mem. Am. Soc. Profl. Engrs., Vets. of Safety. Democrat. Baptist. Clubs: Lions (past pres.), Masons, Shriners. Home and Office: 5266 Rimwood Dr Fair Oaks CA 95628

BUTLER, JEFFREY SHERIDAN, publisher; b. Christopher, Ill., June 19, 1939; s. Jefferson Macklin and Veneita May (Slinger) B.; B.S. in Mktg., U. Ill., 1961; m. Erin Clarke; children— Drew Sheridan, Emily Louise. With UARCO Bus. Systems Sales, Chgo., 1961-62; dir. public relations Pacific S.W. Airlines, San Diego, 1965-68; chmn. bd., chief exec. officer, founder, pub. East/West Network Inc., Los Angeles, 1968—; pub. mags. Pan Am. Airlines, United Airlines, Continental Airlines, Ozark Airlines, Republic Airlines, Eastern Airlines, Western Airlines, USAir, Amtrak. Bd. dirs. So. Calif. Visitors Council. Served with M.C., AUS, 1962-65. Mem. Sigma Nu. Club: Regency (Los Angeles). Office: 5900 Wilshire Blvd 8th Floor Los Angeles CA 90036

BUTLER, MATILDA LOU, psychologist, educator; b. Oklahoma City, Feb. 5, 1942; d. Edward Ainsworth and Flossie Jewel (Calderhead) Butler; student U. Okla., 1960-62; B.S. magna cum laude, Boston U., 1964; M.A., Stanford, 1966; Ph.D., Northwestern U., 1970; m. William John Paisley, Oct. 16, 1970; children—Kenneth Earl, Edward Ainsworth, William John. Research asso. psychology dept. Stanford, 1970, lectr., research asso. Inst. for Communication Research, 1971-77; research asso. U. Calif. at Berkeley Grad. Sch. Pub. Policy, 1971; co-founder, v.p. Applied Communications Research, Inc., 1974-77; dir. Women and Minorities Mgmt. Tng. Program, 1978-79; dir. Women's Ednl. Equity Communications Network, 1977-80, chmn. ednl. tech. and communication dept., 1980-82, dir. Far West Research and Devel. div., 1982; pres. Edupro, 1982—; cons. Coll. Bds., Lockheed-Technicon Info. Systems, Palo Alto Unified Sch. Dist. NIMH trainee. Mem. Am. Psychol. Assn., Am. Assn. Pub. Opinion Research (program chmn. Pacific chpt. 1972, mem. council 1976), Assn. for Edn. in Journalism (co-chmn. com. on status women), Internat. Communication Assn. (co-chmn. com. on status women in communication), Am. Soc. Info. Sci. (council rep. Info. Services for Edn.), Am. Ednl. Research Assn. Author: (with William Paisley) Women and the Mass Media: Sourcebook for Research and Action, 1980. Editor: (with William Paisley) Knowledge Utilization in Education: Dissemination, Technical Assistance, and Networking, 1983. Home: 717 Charleston Ct Palo Alto CA 94303 Office: Edupro PO Box 51346 Palo Alto CA 94303

BUTLER, PARLEY NARVIN, metal products manufacturing company executive; b. Ogden, Utah, Dec. 22, 1928; s. Parley A. and Louisa Ardelia (Thompson) B.; grad. Weber Coll., 1950; grad. indsl. engr., 1958; m. Wilma Johansen, Sept. 11, 1950; children—Susan, Curtis, Paul, Julie, Mary. Crew foreman Ogden Union Ry. & Depot Co. (Utah), 1944-50; office mgr. Quaker Oats Co., Ogden, 1950-55, office mgr. pet foods mfg. plant, Joplin, Mo., 1955-59, office mgr. pet foods mfg. plant, Marion, Ohio, 1959-62, office mgr., Chattanooga, Tenn., 1962-65, office mgr., St. Joseph, Mo., 1965-73; controller Magic Pan Inc., subs. of Quaker Oats Co., San Francisco, 1973-74; asst. gen. mgr., controller Powder River Enterprises, Provo, Utah, 1974-81; asst. sec., treas. Powder River Enterprises, Inc., Provo, 1975—; v.p. Provo Aviation, 1978-80, Am. West Advt., 1978-82; sec. Powder River Motor Transport, Inc., 1977—; pres. Quaker Oats Employees Credit Union, St. Joseph, 1971-73. Served with U.S. Army, 1946-48. Mem. Nat. Assn. Accountants (v.p. 1972-73), Adminstrv. Mgmt. Assn. (v.p. 1964-65). Republican. Mormon. Club: Lions (past pres. 1971-72). Home: 625 E 60 N Circle St Orem UT 84057 Office: PO Box 758 Provo UT 84601

BUTLER, ROBERT HENRY, physician; b. Broken Bow, Nebr., Oct. 19, 1920; s. John H. and Elizabeth M. (Ernst) B.; B.S., Wayne State, 1942; M.D., U. Nebr., 1949, M.S., 1950; m. Mary Louise Grote, Dec. 19, 1942; children—Robert Brian, Lynne Ann, Pamela Jean. Intern, Univ. Hosp., Omaha, 1949-50; resident in radiology and fellow Am. Cancer Soc. U. Hosp., Omaha, 1950-53; gen. practice radiology, Santa Rosa, Calif., 1953—; attending radiologist Sonoma Community, Warrack Gen., Healdsburg (Calif.) Gen., Petaluma Valley, Petaluma (Calif.) Gen. hosps., Palm Dr. Hosp., Sebastopol, Calif.; asso. prof. clin. and ambulatory medicine U. Calif. Coll. Medicine. Served with AUS, 1942-43. Fellow Am. Coll. Radiology; mem. Am. Coll. Nuclear Medicine (charter), Am. Coll. Nuclear Physicians (charter), Sonoma County Med. Soc., Pan Am., Calif. med. assns., A.M.A., Redwood Empire, Calif. radiol. socs., Nuclear Soc. Am., Radiol. Soc. N.Am., Calif. State Horseman's Assn., Sigma Xi, Alpha Omega Alpha. Republican. Roman Catholic. Clubs: Commonwealth of San Francisco, Sonoma County Trailblazers. Home: 1928 Hidden Valley Dr Santa Rosa CA 95404 Office: 121 Sotoyome St Santa Rosa CA 95404

BUTLER-MILLER, LESLIE ANN, advertising copywriter; b. Salem, Oreg., Nov. 19, 1945; d. Marlow Dole and Lala Ann (Erlandson) Butler; m. Richard Wilson Butler-Miller, May 12, 1978. Student Lewis and Clark Coll., 1963-64; B.S., U. Oreg., 1969; postgrad. Portland State U. 1972-73. Creative trainee Botsford Ketchum San Francisco, 1970-71; asst. advt. dir. Marketing Systems, Inc., Portland, Oreg., 1971-74; prodn. mgr., art dir., copywriter Finzer-Smith Co., Portland, 1974-76; copywriter Gerber Advt. Co., Portland, 1976-78; freelance copywriter, Portland, 1978-80, 83—; copywriter McCann-Erickson Co., Portland, 1980-81; copy chief Brookstone Co., Peterborough, N.H., 1981-83. Co-founder Harmony Works, Inc., 1979; co-founder, v.p., newsletter editor Animal Rescue and Care Fund, 1972-81. Recipient award for energy savings Pub. Utilities Commn., 1977. Mem. Portland Advt. Fedn. Address: 6005 SE 21st Ave Portland OR 97202

BUTT, THOMAS KING, architect, real estate broker; b. Albuquerque, Mar. 23, 1944; s. Thomas Franklin and Cecilia (King) B.; B.A., B.Arch., U. Ark., 1967; M.Arch., UCLA, 1973; m. Shirley Ann Ryland, Nov. 26, 1971; children—Andrew Martin, Daniel Ryland. Architect, Edward Durrell Stone, Inc., N.Y.C. and Palo Alto, Calif., 1968-69, 70; design architect Mayhew & Thiederman, Architects, San Francisco, 1971; founder, pres. Interactive Resources, Inc., Richmond, Calif., 1973—; pres. Soleil Realty, Inc., Richmond, 1978—, Mariner Devel. Corp., Richmond, 1979—; lectr. in field. Pres., East Bro. Light Sta., Inc., San Francisco, 1979-81; adv. bd. East Bay Center for Performing Arts, Richmond, 1980—; former rep. Richmond Community Devel. Commn.; mem. CETA adv. com., 1975-77; pres. PTA, 1982-83. Served with C.E., U.S. Army, 1968-70. Decorated Bronze Star, Army Commendation medal; recipient Pres.'s Cert. for Outstanding Community Achievement of Vietnam-Era Vets., 1979; Pub. Service award U.S. Coast Guard, 1982; registered architect, Calif., Nev., Tex., Wis.; lic. real estate broker, Calif.; lic. gen. contractor, Calif. Mem. AIA, Nat. Assn. Realtors, Am. Arbitration Inst., Constrn. Specifications Inst., Richmond C. of C. (bd. dirs. 1983), Nat. Trust for Historic Preservation (honor award 1982), Sigma Nu. Club: Rotary. Contbr. articles to profl. jours. Office: 117 Park Pl Richmond CA 94801

BUTTERFIELD, LINDA, bank official; b. Mpls., Dec. 7, 1943; d. Kenneth J. and June (Warren) B. A.A., Coll. Marin, 1964; B.A., San Francisco State U., 1967. Programmer, analyst, project leader United Airlines, San Francisco, 1967-75; sr. EDP auditor Levi Strauss & Co., San Francisco, 1975-76; data processing rep., product mgr. ops. planning Bank of Am., San Francisco, 1976-82, mgr. item processing quality assurance, 1979-81, group product mgr. cash mgmt. world banking div., 1981-82, group product mgr. fin. acctg. cashiers div., 1982—. Home: 2001 Marylyn Circle Petaluma CA 94952 Office: Dept 3165 PO Box 37000 San Francisco CA 94137

BUTTERFIELD, OSSIAN RUFUS, civil engineer; b. Leominster, Mass., May 12, 1927; s. Ossian Rufus and Helen Agatha (Perry) B.; m. Ann Kathryn Churchill, Dec. 9, 1926; children—Marcia Ann, Ossian Brian. Sc.B. in Engring., Brown U., 1947; B.C.E., Rensselaer Poly. Inst., 1956; M.S. in Petroleum Engring., U. Tex., 1964. Registered profl. engr., Calif., Nev., Va., NY., Tex. Commd. capt. C.E., U.S. Navy, 1972, advanced through grades to capt., 1968; ret., 1972; gen. mgr., chief engr. Advanced Wastewater Treatment Plant, Tahoe-Truckee Sanitation Agy., Truckee, Calif., 1972—; cons. constrn. mgmt. engring. Mem. ASCE, Am. Pub. Works Assn., Water Pollution Control Fedn., Tau Beta Pi, Chi Epsilon, Pi Epsilon Tau. Republican. Episcopalian. Clubs: Rotary, Masons. Home: PO Box 370 111 Edgewood Dr Tahoe City CA 95730 Office: PO Drawer B Martis Creek Rd Truckee CA 95734

BUTTERFIELD, PAUL GORDON, educator; b. Murray, Utah, Nov. 3, 1928; s. Mahonri and Hazel (Bills) B.; B.S., (Sears Roebuck fellow), Utah State U., 1951; M.Ed., Colo. State U., 1960; Ph.D. (NDEA fellow), U. Wis., 1965; m. Beth Macfarlane, Apr. 10, 1976; children—Paula, Gregory, Carol Sue, Lynn, David, Tammy. Tchr. agr. Akron (Colo.) High Sch., 1951-55, Windsor (Colo.) High Sch., 1957-59; young farmer advisor Weber State Coll., Ogden, Utah, 1959-62, dean continuing edn., 1965-73, dir. vocat. and tech. edn., 1975—; cons. U.S. Office Edn., 1976—; mem. Utah Planning Com. for Adult Edn., 1974, Utah Apprenticeship Council, 1981-82. Chmn. Community Action, 1967, Utah Manpower Planning Council, 1975; active Boy Scouts Am. Served to 1st lt. USAF, 1955-57. Recipient Outstanding Service award Skills Ctr., 1975, Social Services Council, 1975. Mem. Nat. Adult Edn. Assn., Utah Adult Edn. Assn. (Outstanding Service award 1980), Nat. Assn. Vocat. Edn., Utah Assn. Vocat. Edn., NEA, Nat. Univ. Extension Assn., Western Deans Summer Sessions, Phi Delta Kappa. Republican. Mormon. Club: Lions (pres. 1973). Home: 3825 N Westwood Dr Ogden UT 84404 Office: Weber State College Ogden UT 84408

BUTTERWORTH, JOHN ALLAN, hosp. adminstr.; b. Los Angeles, Oct. 11, 1944; s. John Joseph and Jessie Lee (Stewart) B.; student Divine Word Sem. Coll., Mass., 1962-64; B.A., Calif. State U., Long Beach, 1977. With Fairview State Hosp., Costa Mesa, Calif., 1964-73, shift charge, 1968-70, unit supr., 1970-73, nursing coordinator Fairview State Hosp. Adult Social Devel. Program, 1974-79, program asst., 1979-80; dir. behavior adjustment program Lanterman State Hosp. and Devel. Center, Pomona, Calif., 1980—. Served with AUS, 1966-68. Mem. Am. Assn. Mental Deficiency, Am. Soc. Public Adminstrn., Am. Legion. Home: 4286 Fauna St Montclair CA 91763 Office: PO Box 100 Pomona CA

BUTTERWORTH, ROBERT R., psychologist, psychoanalytic psychotherapist; b. Pittsfield, Mass., June 24, 1946; s. John Leon and Martha Helen (Roman) B. B.A., SUNY, 1972; M.A., Marist Coll., 1975; Ph.D. in Clin. Psychology, Calif. Grad. Inst., 1983; postgrad. Am. Inst. for Psychotherapy and Psychoanalysis, 1978. Counselor intern Community Mental Health Center, Albany, N.Y., 1971, SUNY Coll., New Paltz, 1974-75; asst. clin. psychologist N.Y. State Dept. Mental Hygiene, Wassaic, 1972-75; pvt. practice clin. psychology, Encino and Westwood, Calif., 1976—; psychometrist SAFA Med. Center, Hollywood, Calif., 1976-77; staff counselor Friends of the Family Counseling Center, Van Nuys, Calif., 1977-78; dir. clin. alcohol services Los Angeles County Dept. Health Services, 1977-78; psychologist Acad. Guidance Services, Los Angeles, 1977-78; psychol. cons., Los Angeles, 1977-78, dir. Family Service Agy., 1981-82; clin. psychologist Sir Thomas More Clinic, 1982—; staff clinician San Bernardino County Dept. Mental Health, 1983—. Mem. Los Angeles County Drug Commn. Served with USAF, 1965-69. Mem. Am. Personnel and Guidance Assn., Am. Psychol. Assn., Calif. State Psychol. Assn., Am. Assn. Marriage and Family Counselors, Assn. Humanistic Psychology, Nat. Accreditation Assn. of Psychoanalysis. Office: 444 S Kingsley Dr Suite 225 Los Angeles CA 90020

BUTTERWORTH, STANLEY ROBERT, state agency executive; b. Syracuse, N.Y., Dec. 4, 1929; s. Glenn Taylor, Sr., and Marjorie Laura (Barnard) B.; A.A., Phoenix Coll., 1961; B.A., Ariz. State U., 1970; m. Lavonne Betty Hurley, May 27, 1978; children by previous marriages—James, Richard, David, Lorrie, Carrie. Ops. analyst, supr. statis. officer FHA, 1965-67; sales engr. Honeywell EDP, Inc., 1967-68; sr. systems analyst, chief data processing Ariz. Dept. Public Welfare, also Ariz. Dept. Econ. Security, Phoenix, 1968-80; exec. dir. Ariz. Occupational Info. Coordinating Com., Phoenix, 1980—. Commr., Boy Scouts Am., 1970-71; founding com. Alaska Methodist U. Served with USAF, 1948-59. Found. Econ. Edn. fellow, 1971, 73; recipient public service award Phoenix United Way, 1973. Mem. Assn. for Systems Mgmt. (Systems Man of Yr. 1971, Achievement award 1974, Disting. Service award 1977, nominee internat. v.p. 1979), Soc. Advancement of Mgmt., Am. Soc. Pub. Adminstrn., Ariz. Adminstrs. Assn., Internat. Platform Assn., Ariz. State U. Alumni Assn. (life), DAV, Nat. Bus. Edn. Assn., Nat. Geog. Soc., Iota Sigma Alpha, Phi Theta Kappa. Republican. Methodist. Contbr. articles to Ariz. Profl. Engr., Jour. Systems Mgmt. Home: 4551 W McLellan Glendale AZ 85301 Office: 1535 W Jefferson St Phoenix AZ 85007

BUTTON, A(LBERT) RONALD, lawyer; b. Plainview, Nebr., Aug. 29, 1903; s. Albert L. and Sue E. (Bridwell) B.; A.B., Stanford, 1925, J.D., 1928; Harvard Law Sch., 1925-26; m. Jeannette C. Cushman, 1921 (div. 1930); 1 son, Richard Ronald; m. 2d, Gladys McConnell, Aug. 29, 1931 (div. 1973); children—Albert Ronald II, Mary Barbara; m. 3d, Dorothy A. Shelton, Sept. 30, 1974. Admitted to Calif. bar, 1928, Ariz. bar, 1940, Nev. bar, 1934, U.S. Supreme Ct., 1935; specializing in corp., bus., real estate law, Hollywood, 1928—; pres., dir. Gen. Investment Corp., Placer County Land Co., Desert Sky Devel. Corp., Rancho Mirage Realty Co., Desert Sky Realty Co.; treas. State of Calif., 1956-59. Mem. Martin Luther King Hosp. Commn., 1973—. Treas. Calif. State Republican Central Com., 1950-53; chmn. Calif. State Central Com., 1952-53; chmn. rules com. Rep. nat. conv., Chgo., 1952; state campaign coordinator in Calif. delegation campaign 1952; vice chmn. Eisenhower campaign So. Calif., 1952; state pres. Calif. Republican assembly 1951-52; treas. Rep. Western Conf., 1955—; Rep. nat. committeeman, 1953-56, exec. com., 1954-56; host nat. committeeman Rep. Nat. Conv., 1956. Trustee, mem. investment and finance com. U. Redlands, 1972—; trustee Rotary Found., 1970-72. Served as maj. Signal Corps, AUS, 1942-45. Mem. Am., Los Angeles, Ariz., Calif., Nev., Hollywood (pres. 1931-32) bar assns., Am. Legion, Amvets World War II (Calif. comdr. 1946), Hollywood C. of C. (v.p. 1968-69, pres. 1969-73, dir. 1968—), Fin. Officers Assn. U.S. and Can., Delta Upsilon, Phi Alpha Delta, Delta Sigma Rho. Mason (32 deg., K.T., Shriner). Clubs: Bohemian (San Francisco); Los Angeles Country, California (Los Angeles); Harvard Southern Cal.; Thunderbird Golf and Country (Rancho Mirage); Rotary (local pres. 1966-67, dist. gov. 1968-69, trustee internat. found. 1970-72, mem. internat. finance com. 1972-74, chmn. 1973-74, cons. group 1975-76). Home: Apt 3D 10375 Wilshire Blvd Los Angeles CA 90024 Office: 10375 Wilshire Blvd Suite 9K Los Angeles CA 90024

BUTTORFF, MERCY LYNNE, home economist, educator, entrepreneur; b. Malden, Mo., Apr. 12, 1944; d. Fay Hatch and Mercy (Sargent) Johnson; B.S. in Home Econs., U. Utah, 1967; postgrad. Utah State U., 1970-77; m. Roy John Buttorff, Aug. 29, 1967; children—Mercy Anne, Jefferson Lee, Braxton John. Tchr., curriculum writer Granite Sch. Dist., Salt Lake City, 1967—, Young Mothers Programs, 1970-75, Kearns High Sch., 1970; free-lance home economist educator,

Salt Lake City, 1975—; career tchr. Granger High Sch., 1978—; pres. Buttorff & Johnson Enterprises Inc., 1981-82; cons. Utah Bd. Edn.; conv. speaker on vocat. edn.; commd. curriculum writer; cons. Festival of the Arts; tchr. Utah Girls' Village for delinquent teenage girls; tchr. sr. citizens, low income mothers; author plays and musicals for schs. and religious groups. Active Internat. Women's Year. Named Nat. Home Econs. Tchr. of Year, 1974, Utah Home Econs. Tchr. of Year, 1974, by Am. Home Econs. Assn. and Family Circle Mag. Lic. real estate agt. Mem. Am. Home Econs. Assn., Utah Vocat. Assn., Delta Kappa Gamma. Mormon. Author: Being On Your Own; The First Six Months of Life; The Fascinating World of Home Economics Careers. Home and Office: 6902 S 2510 E Salt Lake City UT 84121

BUXBAUM, JAMES MONROE, educator; b. Jamaica, N.Y., Mar. 8, 1928; s. Edward J. and Theresa (Gross) B.; B.A. cum laude, Harvard U., 1949; J.D., Columbia U., 1955; Ph.D., Claremont (Calif.) Grad. Sch., 1978. Admitted to Calif. bar, 1959; story editor, asso. producer Seahunt and Aquanauts TV programs, 1957-60; atty. firm William Morris Agy., Beverly Hills, Calif., 1960-62; TV writer, v.p. Ivan Tors Enterprises, Inc., Culver City, Calif., 1962-65; producer TV series Flipper, 1965-67; exec. v.p., dir. Ivan Tors Films, Inc., Hollywood, 1968-69; gen. mgr. Am. Film Inst., Center Advanced Film Studies, Beverly Hills, 1969-70; asso. prof. bus. adminstrn. Sch. Bus., Calif. Poly. State U., San Luis Obispo, 1978—. Mem. Calif. Bar Assn., Pilgrims U.S., Am. Mgmt. Assn., Delta Psi, Phi Delta Phi. Author: The Corporate Politeia-A Conceptual Approach to Business, Government and Society, 1981. Office: Sch Business Calif Poly State Univ San Luis Obispo CA 93407

BUXTON, AMITY PIERCE, ednl. adminstr.; b. Medford, Mass., Feb. 20, 1929; d. Alfred and Nancy Mary (Walsh) Pierce; student Conn. Coll. Women, 1947-49; B.A. cum laude, Marymount Coll., 1951; M.A., Columbia U., 1952, Ph.D., 1962; m. John William Buxton, June 27, 1958; children—Pierce Alfred, Felicity Loring. Tchr. English, Grosse Pointe (Mich.) High Sch., 1952-54; lang. arts instr. San Francisco State Coll., 1954-56; curriculum developer, tchr. elem. schs., N.Y.C., and Bronxville, N.Y., 1956-57; tchr. English, Scarsdale (N.Y.) High Sch., 1957-58; chmn. Community Pre-School Program, San Francisco, 1964-66; curriculum coordinator, pre-service, in-service tchr. edn. urban schs., San Francisco State Coll., 1966-71; dir. Tchrs.' Active Learning Center/Tchr. Shelter, San Francisco/Oakland, 1971-80; staff devel. specialist Oakland United Sch. Dist., 1980—; tchr. communication arts Tchrs. Coll., Columbia U., 1955, curriculum development, creative arts San Francisco State Coll., 1964; tchr. elem. sch. French, Mill Valley, Calif., 1968-69; cons. tchr. centers, 1971-79; instr. and active learning and interdisciplinary curriculum, nat. and state confs.; coll./univ. extension instr. U. Calif. at San Diego, Holy Names Coll., Oakland, Calif., Calif. State U. at Hayward, 1973—; mem. N.D. Study Group on Evaluation, 1974—, Nat. Consortium on Testing, 1979—. Mem. budget study com. United Community Fund, San Francisco, 1963-65; mem. steering com. adv. bd. service com. pub. edn., San Francisco, 1964-70; mem. Com. of 100, Sausalito (Calif.) Sch. Dist., 1966-67; bd. dirs., exec. com. Marin Child Devel. Center, Tiburon, Calif., 1968-74; bd. dirs. French-Am. Bilingual Sch., San Francisco, 1971-72. Mem. Nat. Council Tchrs. English, AAUP, Mus. Soc. San Francisco, Calif. Hist. Soc., Jr. League San Francisco, Inc. (chmn. edn. and community research), Nat. Assn. Elem. Prins., L'Ecole Française (bd. dirs. 1970-74), Pocket Opera Guild (exec. com.). Contbr. articles on internat. research, tchr. centers, staff devel., lang. devel. to profl. publs., research on lang. devel., tchrs.' centers, Eng., France, Japan, 1972-79. Home: 18 Vasco Dr Mill Valley CA 94941 Office: care Oakland Public Schs 1025 2d Ave Oakland CA 94606

BUXTON, WARREN FREDERICK, computer scientist; b. Arlington, Mass., Oct. 7, 1929; s. Frank Everett and Gertrude Marie (Arendt) B.; B.S. in Math., U. Mo., Kansas City, 1961, M.A. in Bus. and Ednl. Adminstrn., 1963; Ph.D. in Adminstrn. of Higher Edn., Ariz. State U., 1972; m. Josephine Rubin, Jan. 23, 1954. Meteorologist, TWA, 1956-59; dir. data processing U. Mo., Kansas City, 1961-63; instr. data processing Phoenix Coll., 1963-68; dir. ednl. data processing Maricopa County Community Coll. Dist., 1968-72; prof., chmn. dept. computer tech. Maricopa Tech. Community Coll., Phoenix, 1968—; cons. data processing, computer tech. curriculum design. Served with USAF, 1948-56. Cert. data processor. Mem. Am. Meteor. Soc., Nat. Rifle Assn., Ariz. Hist. Soc., Data Processing Mgmt. Assn. (pres. Phoenix 1968, 78, now dir.; Gold medal 1979), Omicron Delta Kappa. Home: PO Box 2179 Carefree AZ 85377 Office: 108 N 40th St Phoenix AZ 85034

BUYERS, JOHN WILLIAM AMERMAN, agribusiness company executive; b. Coatesville, Pa., July 17, 1928; s. William Buchanan and Rebecca (Watson) B.; m. Elsie Palmer Parkhurst, Apr. 11, 1953; children—Elsie Buyers Viehman, Rebecca Watson Buyers-Basso, Jane Palmer Buyers-Russo. B.A. in History cum laude, Princeton U., 1952; M.S. in Indsl. Mgmt., M.I.T., 1963. Salesman, Proctor and Gamble, 1952; various positions Bell Telephone Co. Pa., 1953-64, div. ops. mgr., 1964-66; dir. ops. and personnel communications services div. Gen. Waterworks Corp., 1966-68, pres., chief exec. officer, 1971-75; v.p. adminstrn. Internat. Utilities Corp., Phila., 1968-71; pres., chief exec. officer C. Brewer and Co. Ltd., Honolulu, 1975-82, chmn. bd., 1982—, also dir.; chmn. bd. Calif. and Hawaiian Sugar Co., 1983—, also dir.; dir. IU Investment Corp., 1st Hawaiian Bank. Bd. dirs. Research Corp. U. Hawaii; trustee U. Hawaii Found., pres., 1982-83, chmn. Pres.'s Club, 1981-82; trustee First Presbyn Ch., Honolulu; mem. civilian adv. group U.S. Army; mem. Japan-Hawaii Econ. Council, Hawaii Joint Council on Econ. Edn., Aloha council Boy Scouts Am., Commn. on Judicial Discipline, Goals for Hawaii, Gov.'s Adv. Council on China Affairs, Gov.'s Adv. Council on Fgn. Lang. and Internat. Studies; mem. Council of Distinguished Friends, U. Hawaii, also Disting. Bd. Coll. Bus. Adminstrn. Served with USMC, 1946-48. Mem. C. of C. of Hawaii (chmn. 1981-82), Nat. Alliance Businessmen (chmn. Hawaii Pacific Metro chpt. 1978), Calif. Sugar Planters Assn. (chmn. 1981-83), S.R., Pa. Soc., Newcomen Soc. N. Am. Clubs: Cap and Gown (Princeton); Honolulu Internat. Country (gov.), Waialae Country, Oahu Country, Pacific, Plaza (Honolulu); Hilo Yacht; Waynesborough Country (Paoli, Pa.); Racquet (Phila); Prouts Neck (Maine) Country. Author: Wings of the Morning, 1963. Office: 827 Fort St Honolulu HI 96813

BUYS, ARCHIE DALE, pharmacist, drug co. exec.; b. Heber City, Utah, Jan. 14, 1921; s. Archie DeVere and Florence Edna (Bonner) B.; educated Brigham Young U., 1939-41, 46; A.R., U. Tenn., 1943; A.M., Shrivenham Am. U., England, 1945; B.S., B.Ph., Wash. State U., 1950; m. Geniel V. Epperson, Aug. 3, 1946; children—Linda, Susan, Kathy, Dale K. Pharmacist, Pomeroy Pharmacy (Wash.), 1950; pharmacist, asst. mgr. Namor's Drug Co., Lewiston, Ida., 1950-54, Thrifty Drug Co., Lewiston, 1954-56; mgr. Pay Less Drug Co., The Dalles, Oreg., 1956-59, Yakima, Wash., 1959-69, Beaverton, Ore., 1969-77, chain price coordinator, 1977-80, mgr. chain pricing and inventory control, 1980—. Mem. advisory com. Ind. New. Mem. Mayor's Action com., Yakima. Pres. dir. Camerata Male Chorus; participant Ambassadors Male Quartet, Yakima. Mem. Troop com. Beaverton (Ore.) council Boy Scouts Am. Active U.S. Power Sqdrn., Beaverton, Portland. Served with U.S. Army, 1942-46. Mem. Yakima C. of C. (bd. dirs.), Am. Pharm. Assn., Retail Merchants Assn. (pres. dir.). Republican. Mormon. Clubs: Lions. Elks. Home: 7490 Downs Post Rd Wilsonville OR 97070 Office: 9275 SW Peyton Ln Wilsonville OR 97070

BUZBEE, BILLY LEWIS, mathematician; b. Gorman, Tex., Sept. 12, 1936; s. Elzie Lewis and Willie Mae (Chandler) B.; B.A., U. Tex., Austin, 1961, M.A., 1962; Ph.D., U. N.Mex., 1972; m. Glenda Ann Calvert, June 2, 1962; children—William Andrew, Douglas Calvert, Leslie Diane. With Texaco Research, 1961, ESSO Prodn. Research, 1967-68; with Los Alamos Sci. Lab., 1962-67, 68—, asst. div. leader computing div., 1979—, on leave with Chalmers Inst. Tech., Gothenburg, Sweden, 1973-74. Coach Little League, Young Am. Football League. Served with USAF, 1955-58. Mem. Assn. Computing Machinery, Sigma Xi. Republican. Mem. Ch. of Christ. Research on devel. of fast Poisson solvers, devel. capacitance methods, solution of parabolic problems for preceeding times, vector and parallel computation; contbr. articles to profl. jours. Home: 700 Meadow Ln Los Alamos NM 87544 Office: MS 260 Los Alamos Sci Lab Los Alamos NM 87545

BUZOGANY, BRUCE LEWIS, broadcasting co. exec.; b. Alliance, Ohio, Nov. 14, 1949; s. Michael and Irene (Fodor) B. B.S., Bowling Green State U., 1971, M.A., 1974. Prodn. mgr. Joy Hamann Advt., Las Vegas, 1974-76; writer/news producer Sta. KTVU, Oakland, Calif., 1976-78; media cons. Bob Rose for Gov., Las Vegas, 1978; promotion mgr. Sta. WKBS, Phila., 1979-80; dir. advt. and promotion Sta. KTLA, Los Angeles, 1980—; sales cons. Los Angeles Studios, 1982—. Mem. Am. Film Inst., Broadcast Promotion Assn. Democrat. Presbyterian. Office: Station KTLA 5800 Sunset Blvd Bldg 16 Los Angeles CA 90028

BUZZARD, CHARLES EUGENE, communications educator, broadcasting mgmt. cons.; b. Normal, Ill., Oct. 11, 1927; s. Robert Guy and Irene (Couchman) B.; B.A., State U. Iowa, 1950; M.A., U. So. Calif., 1955, M.Ed., 1964, M.S., 1965; 1 son, Thomas Guy. With NBC, Hollywood, Calif., 1954-58; TV producer, dir. Hollywood, 1958-60; faculty Muskingum Coll., New Concord, Ohio, 1960-61; gen. mgr. WMCO-FM, New Concord, 1960-61; gen. mgr. KTXT-FM, Lubbock, Tex., 1961-64; faculty Tex. Technol. Coll., Lubbock, 1961-64; cons. U. So. Calif., Los Angeles, 1964-65; faculty Phoenix Coll., 1965-71; with KFCA-FM, Phoenix, 1965-70; gen. mgr. KMCR-FM, Phoenix, 1970-78; chmn. mass communications dept. Phoenix Coll., 1978—; broadcast mgmt. cons., 1978—; vis. prof. Ariz. State U., 1970; cons. various high schs., colls., 1969—. Bd. dirs. Park Riviera Townhouses, 1972, 77, Community Orgn. for Drug Control, 1976-77; pres. Buzzard Enterprises, 1976—. Served to condr. USNR, 1950-54. Mem. Ariz. Soc. Broadcast Engrs. (pres. 1969), Ariz. Assn. Children with Learning Disabilities (mem. state adv. bd. 1970-74), Ariz. Assn. Broadcasters, Phoenix Met. Broadcasters, Nat. Assn. Ednl. Broadcasters, Acacia, Phi Delta Kappa, Theta Alpha Phi, Tau Alpha Sigma, Alpha Epsilon, Rho Alpha Omega. Home: 1401 E Malibu Dr Tempe AZ 85282 Office: 1202 W Thomas Phoenix AZ 85013

BUZZATTO, JOHN LEONARD, air force officer; b. Carengie, Penn., Sept. 1, 1949; s. John Vanzo and Mary (Popichak) B.; m. Miao-Ying Chang, Nov. 13, 1974. B.S., U. Pitts., 1971; M.S., U. Ark., 1978. Commd. capt. U.S. Air Force, 1972; instructor pilot Little Rock AFB, 1975-78; program mgr. Los Angeles AFB, 1979—; chief Western Space and Missile Center Programs, 1979—. Mem. AIAA, Air Force Assn., Aircraft Owners and Pilots Assn. Home: 15611 Poinsettian Way Westminster CA 92683 Office: 2400 El Segundo Blvd El Segundo CA 90009

BUZZO, MARGARET MINNIE WALKER (MARGE), artist; b. San Diego, Nov. 28, 1927; d. Harold Styles and Mollie (Whittman) Walker; m. Frank Ross Buzzo, Mar. 4, 1946; children—Yvonne, Marie, Wayne Bennette. A.A., Long Beach City Coll., 1952; postgrad. Los Angeles Art Ctr. Sch. Design, 1956-58. Artist, owner Marge Buzzo Art Service, Canoga Park, Calif., 1972—; owner Margie Ditto Creations; lectr. in field. Recipient Flier Prodns. Desi award, 1980. Roman Catholic. Illustrator children's books. Home: 4620 Santa Lucia Dr Woodland Hills CA 91364 Office: 21500 Wyandotte St Suite 101 Canoga Park CA 91303

BYARD, RICHARD GEORGE, school administrator; b. Bklyn., Dec. 20, 1953; s. George Warren and Gertrude Isabel (Bart) B.; m. Lucile Marie Merin, June 21, 1980. B.A. in Psychology, Cornell U., 1976; M.S. in Ednl. Psychology, U. Utah, 1981. Counselor Allendale Sch. for Boys, Lake Villa, Ill., 1976-77; career workshop coordinator Upward Bound Projects, Salt Lake City, 1978; instructional assoc. Granite Sch. Dist., Salt Lake City, 1978-79; vocat. evaluator/evaluation supr. Career Guidance Center, Salt Lake City, 1979-82; dir. Mountainwest Computer Schs., Salt Lake City, 1982—; cons. resume devel. Mem. edn. com. Salt Lake Area C. of C. Mem. Am. Personnel and Guidance Assn., Am. Soc. Tng. and Devel. Home: 358 Westminster Ave Salt Lake City UT 84115 Office: 220 E 3900 S Suite 16 Salt Lake City UT 84107

BYE, RAYMOND SIGURD, marketing executive; b. Mpls., May 30, 1919; s. Sigurd Hjalmer and Alice Marie (Johansen) B.; student Hamline U., 1940-42, U. Minn., 1944-46; m. Mary Clarissa Edwards, July 7, 1944; children—Monte R., Marianne, Joseph, Christine, Virginia. Packaging engr. 3M Co., Mpls. and St. Paul, 1945-65; regional dir. Saturday Evening Post, Curtis Pub. Co., Atlanta, Washington and Louisville, 1949-67; asst. to v.p., loan officer Monroe Mortgage Corp., Vienna, Va., 1968-72; v.p. Travel Host of Utah, Salt Lake City, 1973-78; v.p. Mgmt. Corp. Unltd., Bountiful, Utah, 1973-78; nat. sales dir. Direct Line Communications Corp. and ins. exec. A.I.M., Salt Lake City, 1978—; mktg. v.p. Travelhost Mag. of Utah, Salt Lake City, 1976—; mgmt. cons. Mayor, Town of South Arlington (Va.), 1962-63; mem. Atlanta Stake presidency Ch. of Jesus Christ of Latter-day Saints, 1955-60. Served with USAAF, 1939-43. Patentee packing list inserter; Scotchlite fabric. Home: 7596 Silver Fork Dr Salt Lake City UT 84121

BYE, ROSEANNE MARIE, mktg. profl.; b. Chgo., Nov. 27, 1946; d. Paul David and Gwendalynn Luciell (Hipp) Forrester; B.S. in Foods and Nutrition, Western Ill. U., 1969; m. Richard Wayne Bye, June 14, 1969. Banquet mgr. Western Ill. U., 1967-69; new product home economist Hunt/Wesson Foods, Fullerton, Calif., 1969-73; retail and restaurant home economist Lawry's Foods, Los Angeles, 1973-74; mgr. product devel. Carl Karcher Enterprises, Anaheim, Calif., 1974-81; dir. research and devel. Denny's Restaurants, La Mirada, Calif., 1981—; mem. speakers bur. mktg. fast food Industry/Edn. Council. Mem. adv. com. Santa Ana Jr. Coll., Garden Grove Sch. Dist. Recipient Nat. Mktg. award for devel. of Charbroiler Steak Sandwich, 1975-76, serve-yourself salad bar, 1978-79. Mem. Am. Home Econs. Assn., Calif. Home Econs. Assn. (Outstanding Economist in Bus. 1977, 79, pres. 1977-79), Home Economists in Bus. (award of excellence, Western regional adv. 1976-78), Women in Mgmt., Nat. Restaurant Assn. (chmn. mktg. research div.), NOW, Anaheim C. of C. (publicity chmn. 1977-78), Soc. Advancement Food Service Research, Internat. Food Service Editorial Council, Internat. Platform Assn. Republican. Presbyterian. Clubs: Tennis and Swim; Literary Guild, Newport Harbor Art Mus. Office: Carl Karcher Enterprises 1200 N Harbor Blvd Anaheim CA 92803

BYERS, EDWARD W., library director; b. Pitts., Jan. 2, 1948. B.A. in History, Lawrence U., 1971; M.A.L.S., U. Denver, 1972. Sci. ref. librarian Pub. Library of Cin. and Hamilton County, 1972-73; head of reference Warder Pub. Library, Springfield, Ohio, 1973, head main library, 1974-77; dir. Laramie County Library System, Cheyenne, Wyo., 1977—. Mem. Wyo. Library Assn. (exec. bd.), ALA (mem. council), PLA, LAMA, Mountain Plains Library Assn., Am. Mgmt. Assn. Bd. editors Miami Valley List of University Serials, 1973-77. Office: Laramie County Library System 2800 Central Ave Cheyenne WY 82001*

BYERS, HELEN JEAN, hosp. adminstr.; b. Tillamook, Oreg., Dec. 22, 1926; d. Vern C. and Helen B. (Hansen) B.; diploma St. Mary's Hosp. Sch. Nursing, Astoria, Oreg., 1946; B.S. in Nursing, Incarnate Word Coll., San Antonio, 1967; M.S. in Nursing, Cath. U. Am., Washington, 1970. Staff nurse VA Hosp., Vancouver, Wash., 1947-48; asst. supr. operating room Dalles (Oreg.) Gen. Hosp., 1948-49; staff nurse Nix Meml. Hosp., San Antonio, 1952-53; supr. surg. services Bexar County Hosp. Dist., San Antonio, 1953-63; supr. operating rm., recovery rm., surg. intensive care unit and central supply SW Tex. Meth. Hosp., San Antonio, 1963-65; asst. dir. nursing, surg. services Children's Hosp., Washington, 1967-69; asst. adminstr., dir. nursing Sibley Meml. Hosp., Washington, 1970-74; asso. exec. dir., dir. nursing Swedish Hosp. Med. Center, Seattle, 1974—; clin. asst. prof. U. Wash., 1975—, Seattle U., 1977—. Mem. Am. Nurses Assn., Am. Soc. Nursing Service Adminstrs., Nat. League Nursing, Nat. Forum Adminstrs. of Nursing Services, Sigma Theta Tau. Home: 14825 39th St NE Seattle WA 98155 Office: 747 Summit Ave Seattle WA 98104

BYINGTON, CHARLES HAROLD, data processing exec.; b. N.Y.C., Oct. 29, 1941; s. Alfred Hall and Dorothy Clare (Krauss) B.; m. Gale Crotty, Sept. 12, 1964; children—Katherine, Craig. B.E.E., Rensselaer Poly. Inst., 1963, M.E.E., 1966; M.B.A., Temple U., 1974. Asst. adminstr. Yale-New Haven Hosp., Conn., 1974-78; v.p. Shared Health Info. Systems, Cleve., 1978-80; v.p. Info. Services, Crowley Maritime Corp., San Francisco, 1980—; instr. Yale U., 1974-78. Served to capt. U.S. Army, 1966-68. Mem. Data Processing Mgmt. Assn. Contbr. articles to jours. in field. Office: 500 Howard St San Francisco CA 94105

BYRD, RUSSELL AARON, assn. exec., b. Little Rock, Aug. 1, 1904; s. Erasmus Aaron and Clara Isabel (Alsbury) B.; student Leland Stanford Jr. U., 1931-32; m. Lillie Mae Hill, Jan. 27, 1949; children—Wesley Oliver, Jeannette (Mrs. Dave Dahle), Evelyn Ray. With Greyhound Lines, 1929-31, Columbia Pacific Nite Coach Lines, Inc., 1932-35, Santa Fe Transp. Co., 1935-68, Calif. Sightseeing Co., 1968-73, Las Vegas Travel Club, 1973-74; asst. to pres. Douglas Bus Lines, Inc., operating as Commuter Bus Lines, Long Beach, Calif., 1974-79; with Gray Line Tours Co., Inc., Bakersfield, 1979—; exec., dir. Nat. Drivers Assn. Prevention of Traffic Accidents, Inc., Bakersfield, Calif., 1958—; dir. Space Parking, Inc.; pres. Green-Byrd Assos., Inc. Named admiral of Am. hwys., Bakersfield Jr. C. of C., 1956; recipient cert. of recognition Dept. Transp., 1979. Mem. Brotherhood R.R. Trainmen (past local pres.), United Transportation Union Lodge 1812. Democrat. Methodist. Mason. Club: Stanford Alumni (Bakersfield). Author: Russ's Bus, 1945; Driving to Live, 1948; Americanism, 1934; Highway Killers, 1978. Address: 2601 17th St Bakersfield CA 93301

BYRNE, BARBARA, lawyer; b. Abington, Pa., May 27, 1953; d. Patrick Joseph and Marie Adele (Day) Byrne. B.A. cum laude, Franklin and Marshall Coll., Lancaster, Pa., 1975; J.D., Boston U., 1978. Bar: Mass. 1978, Nev. 1980, U.S. Dist. Ct. Nev. 1982. Dep. dist. atty. Elko County, Nev., 1980-81; dep. pub. defender, Carson City, Nev., 1981-82; sole practice, Reno, 1982; pub. defender, Elko, Nev., 1983—; sole practice, Elko., 1983—. Mem. State Nev. Bar Assn., Mass. Bar Assn. Democrat. Office: Suite 210 Blohm Bldg Elko NV 89801

BYRNE, EDWARD JOSEPH, mechanical engineer; b. N.Y.C., Mar. 2, 1934; s. Edward and Ellen (Hawkins) B.; m. Marilyn Joan Drake, Feb. 8, 1964; children—Margaret Ann, Edward Anthony, Jean Marie. B.S. in Mech. Engring., Ind. Inst. Tech., 1961. Mech. engr. Calif. Dept. Water Resources, 1961-63; mem. tech. staff Rockwell Internat., Downey, Calif., 1963-80, supr. fluid and environ. systems labs., 1980—. Mem. La Palma City Council, 1971—, mayor, 1972-76, 83-84. Served with USAF, 1954-58. Mem. AIAA (Nat. Working Group on Space Simulation), Nat. Mgmt. Assn., Calif. League of Cities. Roman Catholic. Contbr. articles to profl. jours. Home: 5052 Malaga Dr La Palma CA 90623 Office: 12214 S Lakewood Blvd Downey CA 90241

BYRNE, GEORGE MELVIN, physician; b. San Francisco, Aug. 1, 1933; s. Carlton and Esther (Smith) B.; B.A., Occidental Coll., 1958; M.D., U. So. Calif., 1962; m. Joan Stecher, July 14, 1956; children—Kathryne, Michael, David; m. 2d, Margaret C. Smith, Dec. 18, 1982. Intern, Huntington Meml. Hosp., Pasadena, Calif., 1962-63, resident, 1963-64; family practice So. Calif. Permanente Med. Group, 1964-82, physician-in-charge Pasadena Clinic, 1966-81; asst. dir. Family Practice residency Kaiser Found. Hosp., Los Angeles, 1971-73; clin. instr. emergency medicine Sch. Medicine, U. So. Calif., 1973-80; v.p. East Ridge Co., 1983—; dir. Alan Johnson Porsche Audi, Inc., 1974-82, sec., 1974-77, v.p., 1978-82. Bd. dirs. Kaiser-Permante Mgmt. Assn., 1976-77; mem. regional mgmt. com. So. Calif. Lung Assn., 1976-77. Diplomate Am. Bd. Family Practice. Fellow Am. Acad. Family Physicians (charter); mem. Am., Calif., Los Angeles County med. assns., Calif. Acad. Family Physicians, Los Angeles Drs. Symphony Orch., Nat. Rifle Assn. (life), Am. Radio Relay League (Pub. Service award). Clubs: Sierra (life mem.), Porsche Owners (dir. 1974-75), Porsche of Am. physician; b. San Francisco, Aug. 1, 1933; s. Carlton and Esther (Smith) B.; B.A., Occidental Coll., 1958; M.D., U. So. Calif., 1962; m. Joan Stecher, July 14, 1956; children—Kathryne, Michael, David; m. 2d, Margaret C. Smith, Dec. 18, 1982. Intern, Huntington Meml. Hosp., Pasadena, Calif., 1962-63, resident, 1963-64; family practice So. Calif. Permanente Med. Group, 1964-82, physician-in-charge Pasadena Clinic, 1966-81; asst. dir. Family Practice residency Kaiser Found. Hosp., Los Angeles, 1971-73; clin. instr. emergency medicine Sch. Medicine, U. So. Calif., 1973-80; v.p. East Ridge Co., 1983—; dir. Alan Johnson Porsche Audi, Inc., 1974-82, sec., 1974-77, v.p., 1978-82. Bd. dirs. Kaiser-Permante Mgmt. Assn., 1976-77; mem. regional mgmt. com. So. Calif. Lung Assn., 1976-77. Diplomate Am. Bd. Family Practice. Fellow Am. Acad. Family Physicians (charter); mem. Am., Calif., Los Angeles County med. assns., Calif. Acad. Family Physicians, Los Angeles Drs. Symphony Orch., Nat. Rifle Assn. (life), Am. Radio Relay League (Pub. Service award). Clubs: Sierra (life mem.), Porsche Owners (dir. 1974-75), Porsche of Am. Home: 528 Meadowview Dr La Cañada Flintridge CA 91011

BYRNE, JOHN PATRICK, physician; b. Montrose, S.D., Mar. 26, 1926; s. James Henry and Genevieve Alice (Smith) B.; m. Emma Nash McDermott, June 6, 1953; children—Kathryn, Patrick, Teresa, Barbara, Michael, Shelia, Elizabeth, Thomas. Student Creighton U., 1947-50, M.D., 1954, M.S. in Medicine, 1960. Diplomate Am. Bd. Internal Medicine. Intern, St. Joseph's Hosp., Omaha, 1954-55; hematology fellow, 1956-59; gen. practice medicine, Anamosa, Iowa, 1955-56; mem. staff Omaha VA Med. Ctr., 1960-67; mem. staff Phoenix VA Med. Ctr., 1967-75, assoc. chief staff amulatory care, 1975—; instr. medicine Creighton U., 1960-67; instr. medicine Nebr. Med. Coll., 1960-66, asst. prof. medicine, 1966-67; mem. adv. com. Ariz. Tumor registry, 1981—. Mem. Exec. Com. Boy Scouts Am., 1969-74, instl. rep., 1969-72. Served with U.S. Army, 1944-47. Decorated Purple Heart; recipient Dir.'s. Commendation, Phoenix VA, 1977, 78. Fellow ACP; mem. Am. Geriatrics Soc., Assn. Mil. Surgeons, U.S., Phi Rho Sigma. Democrat. Roman Catholic. Office: VA Med Ctr 11c Phoenix AZ 85012

BYRNE, JOHN PATRICK, state ofcl., ret. army officer; b. Detroit, May 25, 1929; s. George Arnold and Opal Vere (Cooper) B.; B.S., Johns

Hopkins U., 1958; M.B.A. with high distinction, U. Mich., 1961; m. Dolores Ann Meyer, Aug. 11, 1951; children—John Patrick, David Michael, Richard Terrence, Kevin Francis. Commd. 2d lt. Chem. Corps, U.S. Army, 1950, advanced through grades to col., 1970; served with Far East Command in Japan, 1951-54; various logistic assignments Army Chem. Center, Md., 1954-58; assigned to Chem. Corps Hdqrs. and Dept. of Army, The Pentagon, Washington, 1961-65; U.S. Army exchange officer to Brit. Army, Eng., 1965-68; comdr. 2d chem. bn. Ft. McClellan, Ala., 1968-70; chief of staff Cam Ranh Support Command in Vietnam, 1970-71, dep. comdr., 1971-72; dep. comdr. Bayern Support Dist., Germany, 1972-73, exec. to comdg. gen. of Theater Army Support Command, 1973-74, dep. comdr. of 1st. Support Brigade, 1974-75; comdr. Rocky Mountain Arsenal, Denver, 1975-78; dir. emergency preparedness Denver County, 1978-79; dir. disaster emergency services State of Colo., Golden, 1979—; dir. St. Vincent DePaul Stores, Denver, 1979—. Pres. Brookland Estates Citizens Assn., Alexandria, Va., 1963-65. Decorated Legion of Merit, Bronze Star; Vietnam Cross of Gallantry with palm. Mem. Nat. Emergency Mgmt. Assn. (pres. 1983—), Assn. of U.S. Army (sec. Gallant Pelham chpt. 1969-70), Nat. Def. Preparedness Assn., Nat. Emergency Mgmt. Assn. (pres. 1983), Ret. Officers Assn., Denver C. of C. (mil. affairs com. 1975—), Colo. CD Assn. (sec.-treas. 1978-80), Emergency Med. Technicians Assn. of Colo. (adv. 1980—), Beta Gamma Sigma, Delta Sigma Pi, Phi Kappa Phi. Roman Catholic. Clubs: Rotary, Denver Execs. Home: 7679 Waverly Mountain Littleton CO 80127 Office: Division of Disaster Emergency Services State of Colo Camp George W Golden CO 80401

BYRNE, JOSEPH, oil co. exec.; b. Santa Fe, June 21, 1923; s. Joseph and Nelle Dix (Laird) B.; m. Nancy J. Jennings, Apr. 23, 1955; children—Nelle, Elizabeth, John. B.A. in Chem. Engring., Stanford U., 1944; S.M., MIT, 1948, Sc.D., 1950. Asst. prof. MIT, 1950-53; engr. Union Oil Co., Los Angeles, 1953-62, mgr. refining planning, 1962-68, mgr. mktg. and refining planning, 1968, mktg. v.p. 13 western states, 1968-77, v.p. nat. mktg. and ops. coordination, 1977-81, v.p. corp. human resources, 1981—. Served with USNR, World War II. Mem. Am. Inst. Chem. Engrs., Am. Petroleum Inst., AAAS. Republican. Congregationalist. Club: Los Angeles Athletic. Office: 461 S Boylston St Los Angeles CA 90017

BYRNE, NOEL THOMAS, sociology educator; b. San Francisco, May 11, 1943; s. Joseph Joshua and Naomi Pearl (Denison) B.; m. Elizabeth Carla Rowlin, Nov. 5, 1966 (div.); 1 dau., Ginger Butler. Instr. sociology Douglass Coll., Rutgers U., New Brunswick, N.J., 1974-76, Hartnell Coll., Salinas, Calif., 1977-78; lectr. depts. sociology and mgmt. Sonoma State U., Rohnert Park, Calif., 1978—. Recipient Dell Pub. award Rutgers U. Grad. Sociology Program, 1976; Louis Bevier fellow, 1977-78. Mem. Am. Sociol. Assn., Pacific Sociol. Assn., AAAS, Soc. for Study Symbolic Interaction (rev. editor Jour. 1980—), Soc. for Study Social Problems. Democrat. Contbr. sects. to books, articles to profl. lit. Home: 330 W Sierra Ave Cotati CA 94928 Office: Dept Mgmt Studies Sonoma State U Rohnert Park CA 94928

BYRNE, THERESA MARY, parochial sch. prin.; b. N.Y.C., Jan. 18, 1926; d. Frank and Christina Mary (Punch) McDaniel; B.A., Manhattan Coll., 1953; M.A., Fordham U., 1963; postgrad. Richmond Coll., 1967-69, St. John's U., 1975-77; m. Francis X. Byrne, June 30, 1973. Tchr., prin. St. Gregory's Sch., N.Y.C., 1947-67; tchr. St. Christopher's Sch., 1967-70; supr. Continental Nat. Assurance Co., N.Y.C., 1970-74; tchr. St. Ann's Sch., 1974-78; prin. St. Joseph's Sch., Tucson, 1978—. Mem. Nat. Cath. Edn. Assn., Assn. Supervision and Curriculum Devel., Ariz. Assn. Supervision and Curriculum Devel. Roman Catholic. Office: 215 S Craycroft Rd Tucson AZ 85711

BYRON, REBECCA ANN, office manager; b. Longview, Tex., Nov. 5, 1952; d. Robert Owen and Eileen Mary (Goodall) Byron. A.A. in Secretarial Sci., Casper Coll., 1973. Bookkeeper, office mgr. E.K. Williams Co., Casper, Wyo., 1972-73; computer operator First Western Securities, Casper, 1974; office mgr. Greiner Ford Co., Casper, 1974—. Mem. Casper Credit Women, Internat. Consumer Credit Assn. Office: PO Box 2460 Casper WY 82602

BYRTUS, JOE ROBERT, aviation company executive; former air force officer; b. Sheridan, Wyo., Dec. 27, 1914; s. Paul and Anna (Ruski) B.; B.S., Nebr. State Coll., 1937; M.S., Ohio Inst. Tech., 1952; m. Harriet E. Taggart, Jan. 2, 1946; children—Robert T., Jesse J., Anna T. Sci. tchr., Cody, Wyo., 1938-41; commd. 2d lt. USAF, 1942, advanced through grades to lt. col., 1950; navigator W.W.II, 1942-46; sec. Aero Bd. HQ AAF, 1946-49; group nava-bomber-radar Korean War, 1950-51; proc. HQ AMC, 1952-55; acting dir. for single mgr. HQUSAF, 1956-59; chief Air Proc. HQ AFFC., 1960-62; ret., 1962; exec. v.p. Stanley Aviation, Denver, 1962-64; sci. tchr., Sheridan, Wyo., 1965-77. Republican precinct chmn., 1966-79, state committeeman, 1968-79; chmn. bldg. com. Forest Glen Assn., 1981-83; sec., 1983—. Recipient cert. of Merit, Pres.'s Missile Sites Labor Com., 1961. Mem. Sheridan Translators Assn. (pres. 1975-79), Wyo. Sr. Golfers Assn. (sec.-treas. 1974-78), Nat. Ret. Tchrs. Assn., Air Force Assn., Am. Legion, Utah Golf Assn., Western Sr. Amateur Assn. Clubs: Elks (life); Kendrick Golf (pres. 1976-78). Roman Catholic. Home: 2592 Elizabeth St Salt Lake City UT 84106

BYSINGER, WALLACE GEORGE (BILL), JR., data processing company executive; b. Moline, Ill., Mar. 27, 1946; s. Wallace George and Catherine May (Gross) B.; m. Carol Lynn Schultz, July 27, 1969; children—John, Amber. B.B.A., U. Mo.-Kansas City, 1976, M.B.A., 1979. With Hallmark Cards, Inc., Kansas City, Mo., 1970-79, corp. fin. analyst, 1975-77, corp. systems engr., 1977-79; v.p. mktg. and fin. Roll-Core Internat., Inc., Merriam, Kans., 1979-80; v.p., gen. mgr. Unicomp Corp., Seattle, 1980—; advisor data processing City U., Seattle, Seattle Country Day Sch.; lectr. Served in U.S. Army, 1967-70. Mem. Digital Equipment Users Soc. (chmn. Seattle group), Data Processing Mgmt. Assn., Assn. Systems Mgmt. Lutheran. Office: Unicomp Corp 500 4th & Battery Bldg Seattle WA 98121

BYWATER, MURRAY ALSTON, airport dir.; b. Salt Lake City, Feb. 7, 1915; s. Murry Mowry and Annie (Alston) B.; B.S. in Bus. Adminstrn., U. Utah, 1936; postgrad. George Washington U.; m. Frankie Lale Galloway, July 2, 1941; 1 dau., Teresa Kaye. Commd. 2d lt. USAAF, 1937, advanced through grades to brig. gen. USAF, 1960; service in Europe, Africa, Pacific, Philippines; ret., 1968; mgr. Salt Lake City Internat. Airport, 1969-76; dir. Riverside (Calif.) Mcpl. Airport, 1979—. Decorated Legion of Merit with 2 oak leaf clusters, D.F.C., Air medal with 3 oak leaf clusters, Purple Heart; accredited airport exec. Mem. U.S. Congl. Adv. Bd., Am. Security Council, Armed Services Mut. Benefit Assn. (advisor), Fifteenth Air Force Assn. (pres.), Am. Theatre Organ Soc. Mem. Ch. of Jesus Christ of Latter-day Saints. Author: Island Hopping to Kyushu, Airport Report. Office: 6951 Flight Rd Riverside CA 92504

CABAT, ERNEST, artist, craftsman, advertising agency executive; b. N.Y.C., July 7, 1914; s. Harry and Anna Cabat; m. Rose Cabat, 1936. Grad. Cooper Union Inst., 1936; postgrad. CCNY, 1940-41, U. Ariz., 1944-45. Formerly with J. Walter Thompson, Benton & Bowles, Young & Rubicam, also others, N.Y.C.; owner, pres. Cabat-Gill Advt. Agy., Tucson, 1945—; owner Cabat Studio, Tucson; tchr. creativity USIS, Brazil, 1972, Peru, 1975; tchr. Internat. Exec. Service Corps, Iran, 1972; lectr. on creative art programs to painting orgns.; condr. creativity workshops in U.S., Brazil, Peru, Iran; painter; tchr. Recipient numerous awards and prizes in advt., craft and painting competitions. Mem. World Crafts Council, Am. Crafts Council, Ariz. Designer Craftsmen, Tucson Craft Guild, Tucson Mus. Art, So. Ariz. Watercolor Guild, Ariz. Watercolor Assn., Ariz. Artists Guild, Palette and Brush Club, Tucson Advt. Club, Advt. Assn. West, Am. Fedn. Advt., Ariz. Philatelic Rangers, Tucson Stamp Club, Alpha Delta Sigma. Author, illustrator: Kino Missions, Book I, 1982. Home: 3204 E Blacklidge Dr Tucson AZ 85716 Studio: 627 N 4th Ave Tucson AZ 85705

CABIRAC, HENRY ANTHONY, JR., municipal administrator; b. New Orleans, Sept. 20, 1924; s. Henry Anthony and Ida (Jewell) C.; m. Odile Marie Jaubert, Sept. 23, 1930; children—Henry Anthony III, Gary Francis, Michael Andrew. B.A. in Bus. Adminstrn., Tulane U., 1947; M.A. in Pub. Adminstrn., Ariz. State U., 1973. Vice-pres. Cabirac Mech. Contractors, New Orleans, 1948-60; exec. dir. New Orleans Cath. Council Human Relations and So. Field Service for Nat. Cath. Conf. Interracial Justice, 1961-64; adminstr. City of Phoenix Human Relations Div. Commn., 1964—; lectr. univ., coll. courses. Served with USN, 1944-46. Mem. Am. Soc. Pub. Adminstrn. (past pres. Ariz. chpt.), Nat. Assn. Human Rights Workers (bd. dirs., regional chmn., chmn. nominating com. 1973).

CABOT, HUGH, III, painter-sculptor; b. Boston, Mar. 22, 1930; s. Hugh and Louise (Melanson) C.; m. Olivia P. Taylor, Sept. 8, 1967; student Boston Museum, 1948, Ashmolean Mus., Oxford, Eng., 1960, Coll. Ams., Mexico City, 1956, San Carlos Acad., Mexico City. Portrait, landscape painter; sculptor in bronze; one-man shows: U.S. Navy Hist. and Recreation Dept., U.S. Navy Art Gallery, The Pentagon, Nat. War Mus., Washington, La Muse de la Marine, Paris; group shows include: Tex. Tri-state, 1969 (1st, 2d, 3d prizes). Served as ofcl. artist USN, Korean War. Named Artist of Yr., Scottsdale, Ariz., 1978. Clubs: Valley Country (Tubac); Salmagundi (N.Y.C.). Illustrator: Mountain of Gold (Berg), 1965. Office: Hugh Cabot Studios-Gallery Casa de Anza Tubac AZ 85640

CABRAL, LESTER PUMEHANA, education counselor; b. Honolulu Oct. 19, 1946; s. Manuel Pina and Miriam Kaloaaole (Voeller) C.; m. Sheryl Lynn West, Sept. 5, 1981. B.M.Ed., Morehead State U., 1970; M.S.Ed., U. So. Calif., 1974, postgrad. U. So. Calif. Hawaii Ctr., 1982—. Prep. high sch. tchr., guidance counselor, 1974-75; profl. musician, music tchr. Kamehameha Schs., Hawaii, 1976-79; tour coordinator Hawaiian Adventure Co., 1979-80; employment and tng. specialist Hawaii Office of Human Resources, 1980-81; job developer Oahu Pvt. Industry Council, Hawaii, 1981; edn. counselor USAF Civilian Dept. Def., 1981—. Choirmaster, United Ch. of Christ. Served to Capt. USAR, 1973—. Mem. ASCAP, Am. Personnel and Guidance Assn., Hawaiia Personnel and Guidance Assn., Am. Choral Dirs. Assn., Hawaiia Profl. Songwriters Soc. Office: Education Services 15th ABW DPE Hickam AFB HI 96853

CADOW, BARBARA ANN, psychology educator; b. Dover, N.J., Apr. 30, 1952; d. Edward Percival and Ruth Shirley (McDougall) C. B.A. with highest honors, U. Fla., Gainesville, 1974; M.S. in Clin. Psychology, Fla. State U., Tallahassee, 1976, Ph.D., 1979. Lic. clin. psychologist, Calif. Postdoctoral fellow San Fernando Valley Child Guidance, Northridge, Calif., 1978-79; staff psychologist Los Angeles County/U. So. Calif. Med. Ctr., 1979-81, asst. clin. prof. psychiatry, med. sch., 1979—; clin. assoc. dept. psychology dir. tng. student counseling services, 1981—; pvt. practice Los Angeles, 1980—; cons. in field. Mem. San Fernando Valley Juvenile Justice Com., 1978-79. VA trainee, 1974-75; USPHS fellow, 1975-77. Mem. Am. Psychol. Assn., Western Psychol. Assn., Calif. State Psychol. Assn., ACLU, NOW, Mortar Bd., Phi Beta Kappa, Psi Chi, Alpha Lambda Delta. Contbr. articles to profl. jours. Office: 857 W 36th Pl Suite YWC 200 Los Angeles CA 90089

CADY, CLARICE ELAINE, accounting firm executive; b. Platte, S.D., Aug. 14, 1943; d. Clarence F. and Johanna (DeJong) Wynia; m. Albert E. Hockett, Aug. 26, 1977; children—Susan, Jason. B.A., Colo. State U., 1970, C.P.A., Colo. Prin., pres. Clarice Cady & Co., P.C., Ft. Collins and Loveland, Colo., 1973—; mem. exam critique com. Nat. Assn. State Bd Accountancy; mem. No. Colo. Estate Planning Council. Bd. dirs. United Way Ft. Collins, Inc. Mem. Am. Inst. C.P.A.s, Colo. Soc. C.P.A.s, Colo. State Bd. Accountancy (past sec.), Nat. Fedn. Ind. Bus., Colo. State U. Alumni Assn., AAUW, Ft. Collins C. of C. Home: 2816 Harvard St Ft Collins CO 80525 Office: Clarice Cady & Co PC 2801 Remington St Ft Collins CO 80525

CAESAR, RICHARD CORNELIUS, dentist; b. Lake Village, Ark., Apr. 12, 1918, s. Robert C. and Lenora (Campbell) C.; B.S., Morehouse Coll., 1940; postgrad. Atlanta U., 1946-47; D.D.S., Meharry Med. Coll., 1951; m. Lois Towles, June 6, 1956. Pvt. practice dentistry, San Francisco, 1951—. Pres. bd. dirs. San Francisco YMCA, 1978-80; v.p. Pacific region bd. Nat. Council YMCA, 1974-77; trustee United Way Bay Area, 1973-77; chmn. San Francisco Subarea Adv. Council, West Bay Health System Agy., 1977-78. Served to lt. col. USAF, 1941-46. Fellow Am. Coll. Dentistry, Acad. Dentistry Internat. (trustee, pres. Pacific Coast area); mem. Am. Dental Assn. (alternate del. 1970-74), Calif. Dental Assn. (del. house 1970-77, state council for membership 1975—), Acad. Gen. Dentistry, Pierre Fauchar Acad. (chmn. No. Calif. sect.), San Francisco Dental Soc. (pres. 1974-75), NAACP, Kappa Alpha Psi (Life). Republican. Episcopalian. Home: 150 Topeka Ave San Francisco CA 94124 Office: 2340 Sutter St Suite 208 San Francisco CA 94115

CAESAR, SHARLYN ALICIA CHALON, art and designing company executive; b. Los Angeles, Apr. 6, 1947; d. Johnnie and Lillie Mae (Marshall) Boyd; A.A., Lagos, Nigeria, 1969; B.A., U. Dallas, 1973; m. Norman Henry Caesar, Jr., Feb. 28, 1966; children—Alicia LaVonn, Debraux Marie, Norman Anthony, Christopher Garfield, Konstance Bavia. Customer rep. Pan Asia Internat., Ltd., Los Angeles, 1968-71; sales mgr. Johnnie Boyd. Constrn. Co., Los Angeles, 1972-74; owner, designer Chalon Ltd., Los Angeles, 1974—; design cons. Kuba Galleria Ltd. Corp., Los Angeles, 1971—; pres. April Six Prodns., Inc., Los Angeles subs. Candsk Corp., Del.; asst. mgr. Hartfields-Zodys, Santa Monica, Calif. Mem. Nat. Small Bus. Assn. Home: 4427 Morgan Ave Los Angeles CA 90011 Office: 4375 Ascot Ave Los Angeles CA 90011

CAETANO, DONALD FRED, sociology educator, research analyst; b. Bakersfield, Calif., Nov. 22, 1940; s. Frank and Eda Marie (Sandrini) C.; m. Suzan Fortier, Sept. 19, 1966. B.A., U. Calif.-Santa Barbara, 1965, M.A., 1968, Ph.D., 1971. Teaching and research asst. U. Calif.-Santa Barbara, 1966-69; lectr. Calif. State U., Northridge and San Luis Obispo, 1970-71; asst. prof. sociology U. Iowa, Iowa City, 1972-73; asst. prof., co-dir. fac. devel. Calif. State Coll.-San Bernardino, 1974-78; lectr., researcher U. Calif. Extension and Laverne Coll., Ventura, 1979-83; researcher on effects of civil litigation on Calif. Workers Compensation System. Served with U.S. Army, 1959-62. Regents scholar, 1974-77; NSF grantee, 1974-77. Mem. Am. Sociol. Assn. Republican. Roman Catholic. Contbr. articles to profl. jours. Home: 2507-4 Harbor Blvd Ventura CA 93001 Office: PO Box S Ventura CA 93002

CAFFERATA, PATRICIA DILLON, state treasurer; b. Albany, N.Y., Nov. 24, 1940; d. Kenneth P. and Barbara Vucanovich (Farrell) Dillon; m. H. Treat Cafferata, June 17, 1961; children—Elisa, Janet, Reynolds. Student Mills Coll., 1958-61; B.A., Lewis and Clark Coll., 1963. Mem. Nev. Assembly, 1980-82; treas. state of Nev., Carson City, 1982—. Mem. Nev. Republican Central Com.; past pres. Doctor's Wives Washoe County, St. Mary's Hosp. Guild. Named outstanding freshman legislator Nev. State Med. Assn., 1981. Mem. Nat. Assn. State Auditors, Controllers and Treasurers, Western State Treasurers, Carson City C. of C. Episcopalian. Office: Capitol Complex Carson City NV 89710

CAGE, RICHARD HOWARD, statistician; b. May, Tex., May 22, 1933; s. Horace Hamilton and Ima Dee (Petty) C. B.S., SUNY-Albany, 1957. Math. statistician various govt. agys., 1967-81; pres. Evergreen Decision Inst. (Colo.), 1983—. Served with USAF, 1950-53. Mem. Am. Soc. Quality Control (quality control engr.; pub. relations award 1975, teaching statis. methods of quality control award 1975), Long Range Planning Soc., Am. Statis. Assn., European Orgn. Quality Control, Delta Sigma Phi. Republican. Baptist. Clubs: Evergreen Artists, Evergreen Photography. Home: 4927 Evergreen Trail Evergreen CO 80439 Office: Evergreen Decision Inst 4898 Indian Trail Evergreen CO 80439

CAHILL, GINGER LEE, medical centers administrator; b. Northampton, Pa., Oct. 24, 1946; d. Clarence Edward and Anna Irene (Kilpatrick) Gogle; m. Franklin Timothy Cahill, June 6, 1971. B.A. in Polit. Sci., Chapman Coll., 1969. Claims examiner Aetna Life & Casualty, Long Beach, Calif., 1969-71; claims examiner 3/33 Adminstrn. Co., Santa Ana, Calif., 1971-73; claims mgr. Universal Welfare Adminstrn. Co., Santa Ana, 1973-80; mgr. systems and procedures Far West Adminstrn. Co., Santa Ana, 1980-81; dir. med. claims Gen. Med. Ctrs., Anaheim, Calif., 1982—. Mem. Nat. Assn. Female Execs., Women in Mgmt. Mem. United Ch. of Christ. Club: Orange County World Affairs Council. Home: 3929 W 5th St Apt 66 Santa Ana CA 92703 Office: 2121 Towne Centre Pl Anaheim CA 92806

CAHOON, JOE SULLIVAN, soil scientist; b. Muskogee, Okla., June 6, 1924; s. Robert Henry and Ora Esther (Sullivan) C.; B.S., Okla. State U., 1946, postgrad. (teaching fellow), 1947-48; postgrad. Iowa State U., 1966; m. Tallia Margaret Pfrimmer, Sept. 26, 1953; children—Joe Robert, John Warren. Soil scientist Bur. Indian Affairs, Shiprock, N.Mex., 1948, supervising soil scientist Klamath Indian Reservation, 1956-58; soil scientist Soil Conservation Service, Farmington and Silver City, N.Mex., 1949-53, Muskogee, 1953-56, Lakeview and Klamath Falls, Oreg., 1958-77, Pendleton, Oreg., 1978; state soil correlator Bur. Land Mgmt., Portland, Oreg., 1978-81; ret., 1981; soil scientist cons., Tucson, 1981—. Co-organizer, pres. Lake County Jaycees, 1958-60. Recipient Superior Service award Bur. Indian Affairs, 1958; Outstanding Performance award Soil Conservation Service, 1960. Mem. Am. Soc. Agronomy, Soil Sci. Soc. Am., Soil Conservation Soc. Am., Phi Sigma. Author: Soil Survey of the Hart Mountain National Antelope Refuge, 1970; Soils of the Klamath Indian Reservation, 1958; General Soil Map Report with Irrigable Areas, Klamath Drainage Basin, 1969; Soil Survey of the Klamath County Area, Southern Part, 1977. Pvt. pilot. Home and office: 2812 W Jacinto Tucson AZ 85745

CAHOUET, FRANK VONDELL, banker; b. Cohasset, Mass., May 25, 1932; s. Ralph Hubert and Mary Claire (Jordan) C.; m. Ann Pleasonton Walsh, July 14, 1956; children—Ann P., Mary G., Frank V., David R. B.A., Harvard U., 1954; M.B.A., U. Pa., 1956. Comml. loan asst. Security Pacific Nat. Bank, Los Angeles, 1960-61, asst. v.p., 1961-66, v.p., 1966-69, v.p. London and Africa, 1969-73; exec. v.p. Security Pacific Corp., 1973-78; exec. v.p. Security Pacific Corp./Security Pacific Nat. Bank, 1978-80, vice chmn. bd., 1980-81, vice chmn., chief fin. officer, 1981—; dir. Avery Internat. Mem. Los Angeles World Affairs Council; trustee Scripps Coll., Della Martin Found. Served to 1st lt. U.S. Army, 1954-56. Mem. Fin. Execs. Inst., Calif. Bankers Assn. Clubs: Calif. (Los Angeles); Valley Hunt (Pasadena); Harvard of So. Calif., Wharton Alumni So. Calif. Office: 333 S Hope St Los Angeles CA 90071

CAHOW, DALE LEE, safety analysis engr.; b. Denver, Apr. 2, 1943; s. Val Ray and Frances Marie (Ellar) C.; B.S. in Chemistry, Colo. State U., 1970; M.B.A., Nova U., 1983; m. Elizabeth Ann Brunner, Jan. 18, 1974; children—Heather Marie, Holly Celeste. Analytical chemist, process liaison, lab. mgr. Atlantic Richfield, Hanford Ops., Richland, Wash., 1971-76, safety analysis engr. Rockwell Hanford Ops., Richland, 1976—, past pres. Cumulus Inc. Mem. Columbia Basin Apt. Owners Assn. Served with U.S. Army, 1961-64. Mem. Am. Chem. Soc., Am. Nuclear Soc., Nat. Locksmith Assn., Wash. Pilots Assn., Nat. Rifle Assn. (life). Republican. Author numerous safety analysis reports on reprocessing, packaging and shipment of radioactive materials. Home: 6520 W Victoria Kennewick WA 99336 Office: 2750-E 200-E Richland WA 99352

CAIN, DAVID FRED, accountant, tax advisor; b. Mt. Vernon, Wash., May 12, 1954; s. Victor W. and Erdice G. (Rhoades) C. B.A., Western Wash. U., 1978. C.P.A., Wash. Ptnr. Peters & Cain, C.P.A.s., Mt. Vernon, Wash., 1981—. Mem. Wash. Soc. C.P.A.s., Am. Inst. C.P.A.s. Office: 314 Myrtle St Mount Vernon WA 98273

CAIN, DAVID JOHN, clinical psychologist; b. Albany, N.Y., Dec. 27, 1944; s. Marvin Russell and Esther Victoria (Scicchitano) C.; married Feb. 10, 1979. B.A. in Psychology, U. Richmond (Va.), 1966; M.S. in Clin. Psychology, Va. Commonwealth U., 1968; Ph.D., U. Wyo., 1972. Diplomate Am. Bd. Profl. Psychology. Clin. child psychologist Clifford W. Beers Guidance Clinic, New Haven, 1972-80; clin. psychologist Counseling Ctr., Calif. Poly. State U., San Luis Obispo, 1980—; founder Client-Centered Therapy Network; pvt. practice clin. psychology, Atascadero, Calif., 1973—. Mem. Am. Psychol. Assn., Am. Orthopsychiat. Assn., Am. Personnel and Guidance Assn., Assn. Humanistic Psychology, San Luis Obispo County Psychol. Assn., Atascadero C. of C. Democrat. Contbr. book revs. to profl. jours. Office: Counseling Ctr Calif Poly State U San Luis Obispo CA 93407

CAIN, JAMES DOUGLAS, JR., government official; b. Oakland, Calif., July 4, 1946; s. James Douglas and Daisy Doris (DeBerry) C.; m. Joyce Mae Dilworth, Aug. 12, 1967. B.S., SUNY-Albany, 1980; postgrad. Troy State U., 1980-81; B.A. in History cum laude, U. Md., 1982. Fgn. service staff officer Office Def. Attache, Saigon, Vietnam, 1973-74; counter-intelligence ops. specialist Dept. Army, various locations, 1974—. Active Minn. Chippewa Tribe, Nat. Congress Am. Indians. Served from 2d lt. to capt., M.I., U.S. Army, 1967-73. Mem. Internat. Polit. Sci. Assn., Am. Econs. Assn., Nat. Geog. Soc., Middle East Inst., VFW, Vietnam Vets. Am., Alpha Sigma Lambda, Pi Alpha Theta, Pi Sigma Alpha. Democrat. Club: Masons. Office: PO Box 1702 APO New York NY 09021

CAINE, PHILIP DAVID, air force officer; b. Chadron, Neb., July 3, 1933; s. Clifford M. and Eulah A. (Robertson) C.; m. Doris E. Johnson, Aug. 1, 1954; children—Barbara Wagenfuhr, Virginia Tonneson, Jennifer. B.A., U. Denver, 1955; M.A. Stanford U., 1963, Ph.D., 1966; grad. Air War Coll., 1975, Nat. War Coll., 1978. Commd. U.S. Air Force; advanced through grades to col., 1955; pilot, 1955-61; history instr. U.S. Air Force Acad., Colo., 1964-66, asst. history prof., 1966-69, dep. dept. head, head dept. history, 1977-78, dep. head, 1980-82, dep. commandant for mil. instrn., 1982—; chief Project Contemporary Hist. Exam. Combat Ops., Republic of Vietnam, 1969-70; prof. internat. studies Nat. War Coll., 1977-78. Mem. Woodmoor Improvement Assn., dir., 1976-78; bd. mgrs. Rocky Mountain AAU, 1974-78; mem. parish council Ch. of Woodmoor, 1974-75. Decorated Bronze Star. Mem. Air Force Assn., Soc. Historians Am. Fgn. Relations, Am. Assn. Tng. and Devel. Club: Order Daedalins. Contbr. articles to mil. jours. Home: 19060 Pebble Beach Monument CO 80132 Office: CWI USAF Acad CO 80840

CAINE, STEPHEN HOWARD, computer software co. exec.; b. Washington, Feb. 11, 1941; s. Walter E. and Jeanette (Wenborne) C.; student Calif. Inst. Tech., 1958-62. Sr. programmer Calif. Inst. Tech., Pasadena, 1962-65, mgr. systems programming, 1965-69, mgr. programming, 1969-70; pres. Caine, Farber & Gordon, Inc., Pasadena, 1970—; lectr. applied sci. Calif. Inst. Tech., Pasadena, 1965-71, vis. asso. elec. engring., 1976, vis. asso. computer sci., 1976—. Mem. Pasadena Tournament of Roses Assn., 1976—. Mem. Assn. Computing Machinery, Nat. Assn. Corrosion Engrs., AAAS, Am. Ordnance Assn. Clubs: Athenaeum (Pasadena); Engrs. (N.Y.C.). Home: 77 Patrician Way Pasadena CA 91105 Office: 750 E Green St Pasadena CA 91101

CAINES, KENNETH LESLIE DORE, management consulting company executive; b. N.Y.C., Sept. 22, 1926; s. Clarence Leslie and Monica Isabel (Doré) C.; B.S. in Psychology and Sociology, N.Y. U., 1954; postgrad. Calif. State Coll., 1961-63, U. Calif. at Los Angeles, 1965-67; m. Josephine A. Robinson, July 17, 1950; children—Ken Christopher, Clarke Arthur, Leslie Jo. Human factors scientist Planning Research Corp., Los Angeles, 1963-67; mktg. mgr. Serendipity Assos., Chatsworth, Calif., 1967-68; dir. Joken Human Factors Assos., Orange, Calif., 1968-74; pres. People Oriented Systems, Santa Ana, Calif., 1969—; lectr. civil and social systems U. Calif. at Irvine, 1970-71. Vice pres. tech. adv. com. on testing Cal. Fair Employment Practices Commn., 1967-71; chmn. family and children's service com. Orange County Dept. Welfare, 1970-72; mem. U. Calif. at Irvine-Project 21 Com. on Population Growth, 1971-72; pres. Orange YMCA, 1973; mem. adv. bd. Orange County council Boy Scouts Am., 1970—; mem. Orange County Grand Jury, 1980-81. Mem. Orange Planning Commn., 1973-76. Bd. dirs. Orange County United Way, 1971-73. Served with USAAF, 1944-46. Recipient N.Y. State War Service scholarship, 1955; named Citizen of Year Orange YMCA, 1972. Mem. IEEE, Am. Mgmt. Assn., Human Factors Soc. Orange County (bd. dirs.), Assn. Profl. Cons. (bd. dirs. 1982-83). Office: 1720 N Broadway Santa Ana CA 92706

CAIRES, PATRICK VALENTINE, cemetery exec.; b. Honolulu, Feb. 15, 1929; s. Abraham Frietas and Clara (Picansa) C.; children—Donna, Mark, Celeste, Patrick, Carl. Engaged in mortuary and cemetery bus., Hawaii, 1960—; founder, owner, operator Maui Meml. Park, Wailuku, 1964—, exec. v.p., 1976—; exec. v.p. Hualalai Meml. Park, 1975—; v.p. Longview Meml. Park (Wash.), 1971—; gen. mgr., sec. Maui Funeral Plan, 1967—; pres. Polynesian Mktg. Assos., 1976—; trustee Maui Funeral Trust, Maui Meml. Perpetual Care Trust, Maui Meml. Park Contract Service Trust; chmn. Hawaii Cemetery Bd., 1967—. Chmn. fund raising St. Anthony Sch., Aailuku, 1967—; chmn. Wailuku Planning Commn., 1980—. Mem. Am. Cemetery Assn. (dir. 1974—, sec. 1979-80, v.p. 1980—), Hawaii Interment Assn. (pres. 1967—), Hawaii Alied Meml. Council (pres. 1971—), St. Anthony Alumni Assn. (v.p. 1973—). Democrat. Roman Catholic. Office: 485 Waiale Dr PO Box M Wailuku Maui HI 96793

CAIRNS, SHIRLEY ANNE, financial planner; b. Hundred, W.Va., Sept. 26, 1937; d. John Martin and Thelma Irene Stiles; B.S., W.Va. U., 1959, M.A., 1964; children—John Michael, Lyle Dennis, Glynis Ann. Tchr. public schs., Alliance, Ohio, 1958-60, Morgantown, W.Va., 1960-61; receptionist Strand Realty, Coronado, Calif., 1962-63; tchr., head bus. edn. dept. Sutherlin (Oreg.) High Sch., from 1964; now registered rep. IDS. Mem. Democratic Central Com., bd. dirs. Oreg. Dem. Platform Com.; sec. Calapoola Rural Fire Dist. Mem. Nat. Women's Polit. Caucus, Oreg. Women's Polit. Caucus, Nat. Assn. Female Execs., Am. Mgmt. Assn., Internat. Assn. Fin. Planning, Inst. Cert. Fin. Planners, Nat. Assn. Profl. Saleswomen, Am. Bus. Women's Assn. (edn. chmn.), Life Underwriters Assn. (1st v.p.), Sutherlin C. of C. (dir.), AAUW, LWV. Club: Toastmistresses. Home: Umpqua Route Box 209 Oakland OR 97462 Office: 1273 W Central St Sutherlin OR 97479

CALABRESE, MARILYN BROWN, hotel executive; b. San Francisco, Oct. 22, 1948; d. Ernest Mark and Vivian (Schwartz) Cohan. Student U. Colo., 1968-70; B.F.A., UCLA, 1972, postgrad., 1972—. Lic. real estate sales, Calif. Supr. flight service personnel Pan Am. Airways, 1972-74; with real estate sales Raleigh Enterprises, Los Angeles, 1972-78, sales mgr. Westwood Marquis Hotel, Los Angeles, 1978, dir. sales, 1979-81, dir. pub. relations, 1981-83, corp. dir. Raleigh Enterprises, 1983—; cons. Mem. Visitors, Conv. Bur., Beverly Hills, Calif. Mem. Travel and Tourism, Research Assn., Women in Bus., Royce 270 (UCLA), Western La Regional C. of C., French-Am. C. of C., Brit. C. of C. Club: Publicity (Los Angeles).

CALABRO, ANTHONY DOMINIC, educational administrator, consultant; b. Denver, Aug. 21, 1938; s. Anthony F. and Amelia (Molaske) C.; m. Claudia Ann Persichette, July 12, 1958; children—Michael E. and Melissa A. B.A. U. Colo., 1961; M.A., U. No. Colo., 1966; Ed.D., 1973. Tchr. social sci. Arvada (Colo.) High Sch., 1961-65; counselor Golden (Colo.) High Sch., 1965-68; mgr. Manpower Skill Ctr. Community Coll. Denver, 1968-72; dir. spl. programs, 1972-75; adminstrv. asst. to pres. Community Coll. Div., U. Nev. System, Reno, 1975-77; assoc. dean ednl. and instructional services Western Nev. Community Coll., Carson City, 1977-78, asst. to pres. institutional studies and planning, 1978-79; asst. pres. Truckee Meadows Community Coll., Reno, 1979-83; pres. Western Nev. Community Coll., Carson City, 1983—; instr. U. Nev.-Reno, Community Coll.; ednl. cons. in community coll. curriculum, textbooks, adminstrv. orgn. Vice pres. S. Hills Homeowners Assn.; mem. adv. council vocat. edn. Washoe County Sch. Dist., 1980; chmn. bd. selective service appeals State of Nev. Served to capt. Air Force N.G., 1961-68. Mem. Am. Vocat. Assn., Nev. Vocat. Assn., Nat. Council Resource Devel., Nat. Council Local Adminstrs. Vocat. Edn. Club: Kiwanis (North Reno). Office: Western Nev Community Coll 2201 W Nye Ln Carson City NV 89701

CALDER, ROBERT MAC, aerospace engineer; b. Vernal, Utah, Oct. 16, 1932; s. Edwin Harold and Sydney (Goodrich) C.; m. Yoshiko Iemura, Feb. 14, 1959; children—Suzanne, Alex, Irene, John. B.S. in Chem. Engring., U. Utah, 1956, M.S. in Math. and Geology (NSF grantee), 1967; postgrad. U. Wash., 1964, Utah State U., 1965, U. Iowa, 1966. Cert. secondary tchr., Utah. Tchr. Utah Pub. Schs., 1958-82; v.p. Sydney Corp., Bountiful, Utah, 1958-82; sr. engr. aero. div., Hercules Inc., Magna, Utah, 1979—; cons. in field, 1960—. Active Boy Scouts Am., 1960-75, instr., Philmont Scout Ranch, 1972, asst. scoutmaster Nat. Jamboree Troop, 1973; instr. hunter safety and survival, Utah Dept. Fish and Game, 1964-74; state advisor U.S. Congl. Adv. Bd., 1982-83. Served to capt. USAF, 1956-70. Mem. AIAA, Nat. Rifle Assn. (life). Republican. Mormon. Club: Hercules Toastmasters (treas. 1980, v.p. edn. 1981, pres. 1982). Office: PO Box 98 Magna UT 84044

CALDERÓN, MARGARITA ESPINO, educational administrator; b. Juarez, Mexico, Nov. 2, 1944; came to U.S., 1969; d. Ruben R. and Alexandrina R. (Ramirez) Espino; B.A. in English, French and Edn., U. Tex., 1966, M.A. in Linguistics, 1972; postgrad. N.Mex. State U., 1975-77; Ph.D., Claremont (Calif.) Grad. Sch., 1983; m. Eduardo Calderón, July 9, 1972; 1 son. Translator Am. Embassy, Mexico City, 1966-68; tchr. Lydia Patterson Inst., El Paso, 1968-73, 74-75; English instr. Normal Superior de Chihuahua, Mexico, summer 1970; adj. instr. linguistics U. Tex., El Paso, summer 1974; instr. Spanish, El Paso Community Coll., 1972-73; elem. head bilingual tchr. Fabens Sch. Dist., Tex., 1973-74; info. specialist N.Mex. State U., 1975-77; coordinator Desert Sands Unified Sch. Dist., Calif., 1977-78; profl. devel. coordinator Bilingual Edn. Service Center, San Diego State U., 1978—; instr. bilingual edn. Claremont Grad. Sch., summer 1980; cons. to sch. dists., univs. and govt. agys., 1976—; co-chmn. lang. com. Calif. Edn. Research Consortium, 1979-80. Recipient Best of Show award Sun Country Camera Club, 1976; U.S. Dept. Edn. fellow, 1979-82. Mem. Tchrs. of English as Second Lang., Am. Edn. Research Assn., Am. Mgmt. Assn., Bus. and Profl. Women's Assn., Nat. Assn. for Bilingual Edn., N.Mex. Press Women (pres. 1975-76), Lydia Patterson Inst. Alumni Assn. (pres. 1974-75), Sun Country Camera Club (dir. 1974-76). Author: Communicative Competence series, Multidistrict Teacher Trainers Institute series; contbr. articles on bilingual edn. to profl. publs. Home: 3060 Chavez Rd San Diego CA 92154 Office: 6363 Alvarado Ct San Diego CA 92120

CALDERWOOD, WILLIAM ARTHUR, physician; b. Wichita, Kans., Feb. 3, 1941; s. Ralph Bailey and Janet Denise (Christ) C.; M.D., U. Kans., 1968; m. Nancy Jo Crawford, Mar. 31, 1979; children—Lisa Beth, William Arthur, Christopher Robert. Intern, Wesley Med. Ctr., Wichita, 1968-69; gen. practice family medicine, Salina, Kans., 1972-80, Peoria, Ariz., 1980—; pres. staff St. Johns Hosp., Salina, 1976; dist. coroner, Salina, 1973-80; clin. instr. U. Kans., Wichita, 1978-80. Served to lt., M.C., USN, 1969-70. Diplomate Am. Bd. Family Practice. Fellow Am. Acad. Family Physicians; mem. AMA, Ariz. Med. Soc., Maricopa County Med. Soc. Club: Shriners. Home: 7015 W Calavar Peoria AZ 85345 Office: 13660 N 94th Dr Peoria AZ 85345

CALDWELL, ALEXANDER BRYAN, psychologist, educator; b. Winston-Salem, N.C., Oct. 5, 1929; s. Alexander Bryan and Jessie Mae (Houts) C.; children—Byran, Kris, Douglas. B.A., U. Minn., 1951, M.A., 1956, Ph.D., 1958. Lic. psychologist, Calif. Instr. dept. psychiatry U. Minn., 1956-59; asst. prof. psychiatry UCLA, 1959-63, assoc. prof., 1963-69, adj. assoc. prof., 1969-81, clin. assoc. prof., 1981—; pres. Caldwell Report, Santa Monica, Calif., 1969—; cons. VA. Mem. Am. Psychol. Assn., Western Psychol. Assn., Calif. Psychol. Assn., AAAS. Democrat. Contbr. articles to psychol. med., legal jours. Home: #8 23d Ave Apt 203 Venice CA 90291 Office: 3122 Santa Monica Blvd Santa Monica CA 90404

CALDWELL, ERSKINE, author; b. Moreland, Ga., Dec. 17, 1903; s. Ira Sylvester and Caroline Preston (Bell) C.; student Erskine Coll., S.C., 1920, 21, U. Va., 1922, 25, 26, U. Pa., 1924; m. Helen Lannigan, Mar. 3, 1925; children—Erskine Preston, Dabney Withers, Janet; m. 2d, Margaret Bourke-White, Feb. 27, 1939; m. 3d, June Johnson, Dec. 21, 1942; 1 son, Jay Erskine; m. 4th, Virginia Moffett Fletcher, Jan. 1, 1957. Newspaper writer, 1925; cotton picker, stage hand, profl. football player, book reviewer, lectr., editor; motion picture screen writer, Hollywood, Calif., 1933-34, 42-43; corr., Mexico, Spain, Czechoslovakia, 1938-39, China, Mongolia, Turkestan, 1940; editor Am. Folkways, 1940-55; war corr. Life mag., PM, CBS, Russia, 1941. Recipient Yale Rev. $1,000 award for fiction, 1933. Mem. Authors League Am., Am. Acad. and Inst. Arts and Letters, Internat. P.E.N., Euphemian Lit. Soc., Raven Soc. Clubs: Phoenix Press; San Francisco Press. Author: The Bastard, 1929; Poor Fool, 1930; American Earth, 1931; Tobacco Road, 1932; God's Little Acre, 1933; We Are The Living, 1933; Journeyman, 1935; Kneel to the Rising Sun, 1935; Some American People, 1935; (with Margaret Bourke-White), You Have Seen Their Faces, 1937; Southways, 1938; (with Margaret Bourke- White) North of the Danube, 1939; Trouble in July, 1940; Jackpot, 1940; (with Margaret Bourke-White) Say, Is This the U.S.A.?, 1941; All-Out on the Road to Smolensk, 1942; Moscow Under Fire, 1942; All Night Long, 1942; Georgia Boy, 1943; Stories, 1944; Tragic Ground, 1944; A House in the Uplands, 1946; The Sure Hand of God, 1947; This Very Earth, 1948; Place Called Estherville, 1949; Episode in Palmetto, 1950; Call It Experience, 1951; The Courting of Susie Brown, 1952; A Lamp for Nightfall, 1952; The Complete Stories of Erskine Caldwell, 1953; Love and Money, 1954; Gretta, 1955; Erskine Caldwell's Gulf Coast Stories, 1956; Certain Women, 1957; Molly Cottontail, 1958; Claudelle Inglish, 1959; When You Think of Me, 1959; Jenny by Nature, 1961; Close to Home, 1962; The Last Night of Summer, 1963; (with Virginia M. Caldwell) Around About America, 1964; In Search of Bisco, 1965; The Deer at Our House, 1966; In The Shadow of The Steeple, 1966; Writing in America, 1966; Miss Mamma Aimee, 1967; Deep South, 1968; Summertime Island, 1968; The Weather Shelter, 1969; The Earnshaw Neighborhood, 1971; Annette, 1973; (with Alexander Calder) The Sacrilege of Alan Kent, 1976; (with Virginia M. Caldwell) Afternoons in Mid-America, 1976; Stories of Life, 1983; contbr. to mags. Home: PO Box 4550 Hopi Station Scottsdale AZ 85258 Office: Scare McIntosh & Otis Inc 475 Fifth Ave New York NY 10017

CALDWELL, JAMES DAHL, pig farmer; b. Cardston, Alta., Can., June 25, 1928; came to U.S., 1953, naturalized, 1962; s. Edward Dahl and Una M. (Jensen) C.; B.S. Brigham Young U., Provo, Utah, 1957; M.S., U. Nebr., 1960; m. Dixie V. Flake, Dec. 20, 1954; children—Clay, Mark, Jill, Jackie, Bret, Janet, Julie, Ben, Tom. Fieldman, U. Nebr., 1957-60, Jackson & Krautman, Chillicothe, Mo., 1960-62; animal researcher U. Nev., Reno, 1962-64; pres., owner Snowflake Pig Farms, Inc. (Ariz.), 1964—; mem. Ariz. Livestock and San. Bd.; lectr. pig raising. Named Ariz. Farm Family of Yr., USDA, 1973. Mem. Ariz. Pork Producers Assn. Republican. Mormon. Contbr. articles to Jour. AVMA. Home and Office: PO Box AF Snowflake AZ 85937

CALDWELL, MARK DONALD, magazine sales manager; b. N.Y.C., Nov. 23, 1954; s. Roy Arthur and Beverly Jean (Kline) C.; m. Patricia Little, July 16, 1977. A.A.S., SUNY, 1974, B.A., 1976. Wine mcht. Wine Mchts. Ltd., Syracuse, N.Y., 1977-78; sales rep. Time Inc., Houston and N.Y.C., 1978-81, circulation sales mgr. So. Calif. Laguna Hills, 1981—. Mem. Thistle Class Assn., Newport Beach Runners Assn. Office: Time Inc 23177 La Cadena St Suite 104 Laguna Hills CA 92653

CALDWELL, ROBERT DONALD, computer systems company executive; b. San Diego, Sept. 17, 1951; s. Albert Donald and Ruby Marie (Gettman) C. B.A., U. Calif., 1975, M.S. in Physics, 1978. Researcher, Inst. for Pure and Applied Physics, 1976-77; systems analyst Computer Center U. Calif., San Diego, 1977-78; software mgr. Environ. Mgmt. Systems, San Diego, 1978-79; pres. Scientific/Humanistic Interfaces, San Diego, 1979-81; v.p. Internetwork, Inc., San Diego, 1979-81; pres. Centaurus Software, Inc., San Diego, 1980—; assoc. lectr. dept. physics U. Calif.-San Diego. Chmn. San Diego-Imperial chpt. Nat. Found. March of Dimes, 1975-80. Recipient March of Dimes Nat. Service award, 1978. Mem. AAAS, Am. Astron. Soc., Assn. Computing Machinery, Sigma Xi. Club: Nat. Exchange. Office: 4425 Cass St San Diego CA 92109

CALDWELL, ROBERT JOHN, newspaper publisher; b. LaGrande, Oreg., Feb. 28, 1949; s. Donald John and Barbara Cecelia (Joyce) C.; m. Vicki Jane Meierjurgen, June 12, 1971; 1 dau., Elizabeth Anne; m. 2d, Lora Beth Cuykendall, Jan. 1, 1980; 1 dau., Katherine Marie. Student Eastern Oreg. U., 1967-69; B.S. in Journalism, U. Oreg., 1971. Reporter, LaGrande Observer, 1968-69, Eugene (Oreg.) Register Guard, 1969-71; reporter Albany Democrat-Herald, 1971-73, assoc. editor, 1973-76, mng. editor, 1976-79; mng. editor Fournier Newspapers, Kent, Wash., 1979; editor Springfield (Oreg.) News, 1979-81; pub. Gresham (Oreg.) Outlook, 1981—. Mem. Soc. Profl. Journalists (pres. Williamette Valley chpt. 1978-79), Nat. Conf. Editorial Writers, Oreg. Newspaper Pubs. Assn., Democrat. Club: Gresham Rotary. Office: Gresham Outlook PO Box 880 Gresham OR 97030

CALDWELL, WILLIAM MACKAY, IV, furniture manufacturing company exec.; b. Boston, July 23, 1947; s. William M. and Mary Louise C.; m. Kathleen Fogwell, Mar. 19, 1977; 2 sons, William M. V., Blake Harrison. B.A., U. So. Calif., 1969; M.B.A., Wharton Grad. Sch., 1973. Multi-Nat. Enterprise fellow Christ Coll., Cambridge, Eng., 1969-70; mktg. adminstr. Sepulveda Properties, Inc., Standard Oil of Calif., 1970-71; sr. assoc. Booz, Allen & Hamilton, Washington, 1973-75; v.p. mktg. Flying Tiger Line, Los Angeles, 1975-80; sr. v.p. fin. and adminstrn. Van Vorst Industries, Pasadena, Calif., 1980—. Team leader United Way, 1981. Mem. Am. Mgmt. Assn., Newcomen Soc., Town Hall. Presbyterian. Clubs: California, Bel Air Bay, Jonathan. Home: Marina del Rey CA Office: Pasadena CA 91102

CALDWELL, WILLIAM STUART, journalist, educator; b. Alexandria, S.D., Feb. 4, 1921; s. Leslie Omar and Margaret (Macauley) C.; B.A., U. Minn., 1943, M.A. (Regent's scholar), 1954, Ph.D., 1960; m. Marjorie Louise Searing, Jan. 31, 1944 (div. June 1968); children—Linda M. Caldwell Hanna, Bonnie J. Caldwell Stroock, Angela M., Ralph W., Stephen L.; m. 2d, Therezinha A. Leony, May 29, 1970 (div. July 1974); 1 son, William Stuart; m. 3d, Mildred L. Murry, Apr. 21, 1979 (div. June 1983). Fgn. service officer, Rome and Palermo, Italy, 1946-49; pub. relations dir. U. Minn., Duluth, 1949-50; journalist Mpls. Star and Tribune, 1950-55, 58-60; mem. faculties U. N.C., 1955-58, U. Calif. at Los Angeles, 1960-62; asso. prof., head pub. relations sequence U. So. Calif. Sch. Journalism, Los Angeles, 1962-73; asso. prof. Ball State U., Muncie, Ind., 1973-75; sr. lectr. Calif. Poly. U., Pomona, 1977—; v.p. pub. relations AMSTRO Enterprises and Dudley Prodns. Ltd., Los Angeles, 1975—; cons. edn. Los Angeles Times, 1961, Los Angeles Unified Sch. Dist., 1979, Orange County Acad. Decathlon, 1981—; cons. on communication Calif. and Ind. agys., 1970—. Mem. Los Angeles Mayor's Com. on Internat. Visitors and Sister Cities, 1966-73, 75—; vice chmn. Los Angeles Sister City Exec. Com., 1977-82; mem. adv. bd. Intercultural Found. Beverly Hills, 1982—; mem. assembly Orange County Health Planning Council, 1980-83; mem. pub. info. com. Breast Inst. Anaheim, 1983—; Calif. state rep. Sister Cities Internat., 1977-1979; So. Calif. chmn. Educators for Ford, 1976. Served to lt. AUS, 1943-46. Recipient honors St. Andrews U., Scotland, 1981; Nat. Endowment for Humanities fellow. Fellow Pub. Relations Soc. Am.; mem. Assn. Edn. in Journalism (nat. chmn. pub. relations div. 1969-71, mem. nat. com. affiliates 1976-78), Pub. Relations Student Soc. Am. (founder U. So. Calif. chpt.), Travel Research Assn., Am. Polit. Sci. Assn., AAUP, Los Angeles World Affairs Council, Kappa Tau Alpha, Theta Chi, Sigma Delta Chi, Alpha Delta Sigma. Clubs: Palm Springs Tennis; Presidents Circle (U. Calif.); Publicity (Los Angeles); Advt. (Muncie). Contbr. articles to profl. publs., chpts. to books. Home: PO Box 5167 Balboa Island CA 92662 Office: Dept Social Scis Calif Poly U Pomona CA 91768

CALE, CHARLES GRIFFIN, lawyer; b. St. Louis, Aug. 19, 1940; s. Julian Dutro and Judith Hadley (Griffin) C.; B.A., Principia Coll., Elsah, Ill., 1961; LL.B., Stanford U., 1964; LL.M., U. So. Calif., 1966; m. Jessie Leete Rawn, Dec. 30, 1978; children—Whitney Rawn, Walter Griffin. Bar: Calif. 1965. Practice law, Los Angeles, 1965—; ptnr. firm Adams, Duque & Hazeltine, 1970-81, firm Morgan, Lewis & Bockius, Los Angeles, 1981—. Bd. dirs. Hallum Prevention Child Abuse Fund, Los Angeles; v.p. sports Los Angeles Olympic Organizing Com., 1982—; bd. dirs. Big Bros. of Greater Los Angeles. Mem. ABA, State Bar Calif., Calif. Thoroughbred Breeders Assn. Clubs: California, Los Angeles Country.

CALE, LETTIE BEASLEY, education program specialist; b. Lyon County, Minn., May 7, 1935; d. William Leonard and Emma Ingeborg (Anderson) Beasley; m. Robert C. Noe, Jan. 22, 1955; m. 2d, Charles Ellison Cale, Oct. 24, 1971. B.S., Ariz. State U., 1957; M.S. in Home Econs. Edn., U. Ariz., 1969. Cert. standard vocat. tchr., Ariz. Tchr. pub. schs., Ariz., 1957-61; kindergarten tchr., Tucson, 1962-63; tchr. home econs., biology, phys. edn. Pinetop-Lakeside High Sch., Lakeside, Ariz., 1963-67; asst. supr. home econs. edn. and state adviser Future Homemakers Am., Ariz. Dept. Edn. Phoenix, 1968-77, specialist adult vocat., community edn., 1977—. Recipient Nat. Disting. Service award Future Homemakers Am.; speech contest winner Toastmasters Internat., 1978, 82; Disting. Service award State Toastmasters, 1983; Ariz. Community Educator of Yr. award, 1983. Mem. Future Homemakers Am. (chmn. bd. dirs.), Ariz. Assn. Supervision and Curriculum Devel., Ariz. Community Edn. Assn., Ariz. Sch. Adminstrs. Inc., Am. Vocat. Assn., Ariz. Vocat. Assn., Nat. Community Edn. Assn., Ariz. Adult Edn. Assn., Nat. Council State Edn. Agy. Community Educators. Clubs: Toastmasters Internat., Norseman's Forbundet. Author: Guidelines for Training Volunteers in Community Education, 1980; Reaching the Hard-to-Reach Parent, 1981; Administrative Perspectives, 1981; Directory of Educational Resources, 1982; editor: Displaced Workers Program: Guidelines for Instruction and Operation, 1983. Home: 1924 W Ashland Phoenix AZ 85009 Ariz Dept Edn 1535 W Jefferson Phoenix AZ 85007

CALFEE, DAVID W., lawyer, retired judge; b. Richmond, Calif., Sept. 23, 1921; s. Tsar N. and Leona (Jones) C.; m. Mary Helen Bergman, May 15, 1943; children—David W. III, Kent Neville, Shirley, Laura. A.B., Stanford U., 1942; J.D., U. Calif-Hastings Coll. Law, 1949. Assoc. firm Califee, Gregg, Moses & Calfee, Richmond, 1950-58; judge Bay Municipal Ct., Contra Costa County, Calif., 1959-81, assoc. firm Whiting, Rubenstein & Swager, Richmond, 1982—. Served to maj. USMCR, 1943-46. Decorated D.F.C.; recipient Silver Beaver award Boy Scouts Am.; named Richmond Man of Year Richmond Jaycees, 1965, Paul Harris fellow. Mem. State Bar Calif., Contra Costa Bar Assn., Calif. Judges Assn., Order of Coif. Republican. Methodist. Clubs: Rotary (Richmond), Elks, Eagles. Home: 5372 Zara Ave Richmond CA 94805 Office: Whiting Rubenstein & Swager 3220 Blume Dr 260 Hilltop Office Pk Richmond CA 94805

CALFEE, ROBERT CHILTON, education and psychology educator; b. Lexington, Ky., Jan. 26, 1933; s. Robert Klair and Nancy Bernice (Stipp) C.; children by previous marriage—Adele, Robert, Elise; m. 2d, Kathryn Hoover, Dec. 26, 1975; stepchildren—LeeAnn Hoover, Janet Hoover, Jeffrey Hoover. B.A., UCLA, 1959, M.A., 1960, Ph.D., 1963. Asst. prof. Stanford (Calif.) U., 1969-71, prof. edn. and psychology, 1971—, assoc. dean research and devel. Sch. Edn., 1976-80; assoc. prof. U. Wis., Madison, 1966-69. Served with USAF, 1953-57. Guggenheim fellow, 1972; Center Advanced Study Behavioral Scis. fellow, 1981-82. Mem. AAAS, Am. Ednl. Research Assn., Am. Psychol. Assn., Internat. Reading Assn., Nat. Conf. Research English, Nat. Council Measurement Edn., Nat. Council Tchrs. English, Nat. Soc. Study Edn., Orton Soc., Psychonomics, Soc. Research Child Devel. Author: Human Experimental Psychology, 1975; contbr. articles to profl. jours. Home: 995 Wing Pl Stanford CA 94305 Office: Stanford U Sch Edn Stanford CA 94305

CALHOUN, ROBERT MILTON, real estate developer; b. Bakersfield, Calif., Nov. 25, 1918; s. David and Miriam (Kamp) C.; student UCLA, 1937-41; Ph.D. (hon.), Los Angeles U. Arts and Scis., 1944; m. Elaine Zazueta, Nov. 20, 1971; 1 dau., Heather June. Real estate developer and investor, Beverly Hills, Calif., 1946—. West Coast chmn. Nat. Audience Bd.; bd. govs. Women's Aux. Internat. Fedn.; chmn. Calif. Rehab. Center of Kaiser Found. Served with USN, 1942-45. Mem. Ind. Consultants Am., Am. Mgmt. Assn., Nat. Inst. Fin. Planners. Episcopalian. Clubs: Beverly Hills Tennis, The Cellar, Beverly Hills Health, Rotary. Author: The Power Profane, 1979. Home: 818 N Doheny Dr

Los Angeles CA 90069 Office: 9701 Wilshire Blvd Beverly Hills CA 90212

CALIGIURI, JOSEPH FRANK, engineering executive; b. Columbus, Ohio, Feb. 13, 1928; s. Frank and Angeline Josephine (Gentile) C.; m. Barbara Jane Delaney, June 15, 1948; children—Mark, Timothy, Jeffrey, Andrew. B.S.E.E., Ohio State U., 1949, M.S.E.E., 1951. Chief engr. Sperry Gyroscope Co., Great Neck, N.Y., 1966-69; v.p. engring. Guidance and Control Systems div. Litton Industries, Inc., Woodland Hills, Calif., 1969-71, pres., 1971-77; v.p. Litton Industries, Inc., Woodland Hills, 1974-77 sr. v.p., group head, Beverly Hills, 1977-81, exec. v.p., advanced electronics group head, 1981—. Mem. Assn. U.S. Army (Los Angeles chpt.), Nat. Security Indsl. Assn. (dir., pres.), Am. Def. Preparedness Assn. (trustee), IEEE (dir.), Inst. Navigation, AIAA. Republican. Home: 1353 Oakgrove Pl Westlake Village CA 91361 Office: 360 N Crescent Dr Beverly Hills CA 90210

CALL, CHARLES HARVEY, JR., civil engineer; b. Dublam, Chihuahua, Mex., June 26, 1950; s. Charles Harvey and Jane Kaye (Morrill) C.; m. Robin Jean Esplin, June 8, 1970; children—Kimberley, Kenra, Kenton, Kaleb. B.S., Brigham Young U., 1973, M.S., 1974. Registered profl. engr., Utah, Colo., Wyo., Ariz.; Registered land surveyor, Utah. Vice-pres., mgr. engring. ops. Patterson and Assocs., Salt Lake City, 1980, pres., mgr. engring. ops., 1980-81; engr. Salt Lake City Corp., 1981—; pres., mgr. engring. ops. Call Cons., 1981—. Mem. ASCE (pres. Utah 1982-83), Am. Water Works Assn., Am. Water Resources Assn., Am. Concrete Inst. Mormon. Home: 158 S 200 E Provo UT 84601 Office: Salt Lake City Corp Room 401 City & County Bldg Salt Lake City UT 84111

CALL, DWIGHT VINCENT, accountant, educator; b. Chgo., Mar. 19, 1934; s. Jerome V. and Ruth E. (Wright) C.; m. Claudia Louise Hand, July 13, 1956; children—Jeanene Lee, Victoria Irene, Doreen Ann, Carrie Leann, Dwayne Vincent. m. Christine Gail Fox, Dec. 30, 1976. B.S., UCLA, 1957, M.B.A., 1959, Ph.D., 1966. C.P.A., Calif. Prof. acctg. Calif. State U.-Northridge, 1959—; staff acct. Anderson, Gursky & Maccallum, Los Angeles, 1959-62; ptnr. Call & Call, Sherman Oaks Calif., 1962-76; owner Dwight V. Call, C.P.A., Sherman Oaks, 1976-81; ptnr. Call & Trapani, Van Nuys, Calif., 1981—; instr. UCLA, 1964-69; lectr. in field. Recipient Outstanding Prof. award from acctg. students Calif. State U., 1968. Mem. Nat. Assn. Accts., Calif. Soc. C.P.A.s, Am. Inst. C.P.A.s, Beta Gamma Sigma. Clubs: Lakeside Golf, Desert Island Country. Office: 5900 Sepulveda Blvd Suite 431 Van Nuys CA 91411

CALL, EUGENE HENRY, airline transport pilot; b. Boston, Feb. 8, 1940; s. Kenneth Lyman and Theresa Mildred (Tracy) C.; B.A., U. N.H., 1963; m. Michaele Darleen Powell, Dec. 31, 1972; children—Justin Michael, Christopher Patrick Kenneth. Airline pilot TWA, San Francisco, 1969-83; lt. col. command pilot Calif. Air N.G., 1970—; flight comdr. 129th Aerospace Rescue and Recovery Squadron; cons. CAP, 1979—. Served with USAF, 1963-69. Decorated Air medal with 8 clusters; Air Force Commendation medal; recipient Outstanding Pilot Grad. award USAF, 1964. Mem. USNG Assn., Airline Pilots Assn., Calif. Air N.G. Assn. Republican. Episcopalian. Club: Meadow Swim and Tennis. Home: 87 Bates Blvd Orinda CA 94563

CALL, JOSEPH RUDD, accountant; b. Pensacola, Fla., Oct. 18, 1950; s. Melvin Eliason and Doris Mae (Rudd) C.; m. Nola Jean Pack, Jan. 29, 1953; children—Benjamin, Jeremy, Joshua, Rebecca. B.S., Brigham Young U., 1974. C.P.A., Calif., Idaho. Small bus. specialist Deloitte, Haskins & Sells, Los Angeles, 1974-78; audit mgr. Rudd, DaBell & Hill, Rexburg, Idaho, 1978-80, audit ptnr. Rudd, DaBell, Hill & Call, 1980-82, ptnr. in charge Idaho Falls, office; 1982—. Task force mem. Small Bus. High Tech. Devel. State of Idaho, 1983. Mem. Am. Inst. C.P.A.s, Calif. Soc. C.P.A.s, Idaho Soc. C.P.A.s, Internat. Assn. Fin. Planners Mcpl. Fin. Officers Assn., Healthcare Fin. Mgmt. Assn., Rexburg C. of C. (dir. 1981-82), MENSA, Eastern Idaho Sailing Assn. Mormon. Office: Rudd DaBell Hill & Call 1820 E 17th St Suite 310 Idaho Falls ID 83401

CALL, LOWELL ELIASON, educator; b. Bancroft, Bannock, Idaho, Feb. 18, 1922; s. Joseph Clarence and Myrtle Elizabeth (Eliason) C.; m. Carolyn Johnson, Oct. 11, 1922; children—Janene, Scott J., Marlae, Clair J., L. Monte, Val J., Jacquelyn, Lori. Student, Ricks Coll., 1940-41, Los Angeles City Coll., 1941, Fletcher Aircraft Sch., 1941, Mont. State U., 1943; B.S., Brigham Young U., 1947, M.S., 1955. With Lockheed Aircraft, Burbank, Calif., 1941-42; flight instr. Provo (Utah) Flying Service, 1946-49; commd. 2d lt. U.S. Air Force, 1949, advanced through grades to lt. col., 1968, ret., 1970; tchr. aerospace edn. Orem (Utah) High Sch., 1972—. Dist. pres. Ch. of Jesus Christ of Latter-day Saints, 1950, high counselor, 1955, br. pres., 1968, 1st counselor, Bishopric of Orem, 72d Ward, 1981-83. Served with USAAF, 1942-45. Decorated Air medal with 1 oak leaf cluster, Bronze Star with 1 oak leaf cluster; recipient Outstanding Pilot award, Western Flying Tng. Command, Stockton Army Air Field, 1944, 45. Mem. NEA, Utah Edn. Assn., Alpine Edn. Assn., Utah Aerospace Edn. Assn., Nat. Aerospace Edn. Assn. Co-compiler 3 vols. History of the Descendents of Ira Call, 1973. Address: 432 E 1200 N St Orem UT 84057

CALL, OSBORNE JAY, petroleum products company executive; b. Afton, Wyo., June 4, 1941; s. Osborne and Janice Call; student Ricks Coll., Rexburg, Idaho, Brigham Young U., Provo, Utah; m. Tamra Compton, Dec. 16, 1977; children—Tad, Crystal. Engaged in petroleum mktg., 1960-68; v.p. Caribou Four Corners, Afton, 1964-68; pres. Flying J Inc., Brigham City, Utah, 1968—; dir. No. div. First Security Bank, Brigham City. Mormon. Address: Flying J Inc 770 W 2250 S Perry Brigham City UT 84302

CALL, STEVEN TAYLOR, economist, educator; b. Ely, Nev., Aug. 1, 1940; s. Ivan and Marietta (Taylor) C.; m. Janean Moore, Aug. 1, 1963; children—Mark, David, Stephanie, Michelle, Daniel, Heather. B.S., Brigham Young U., 1966; M.A., Ind. U., 1968, Ph.D., 1977. Asst. prof. U. Wis., Milw., 1970-79; assoc. prof. Met. State Coll., Denver, 1979—; assoc. prof. U. Colo., Denver, 1980—; cons. Mem. Am. Econ. Assn., Midwest Econ. Assn. Mormon. Author: (with W. L. Holahan) Microeconomics, 2nd edit., 1983; Managerial Economics, 1983. Home: 7512 Braun St Arvada CO 80005 Office: Econs Dept Met State Coll 1006 11th St Denver CO 80005

CALL, WILSON, architect; b. Bakersfield, Calif., July 20, 1916; s. Urban Wilson and Alva I. (Trout) S.; cert. arch. Internat. Corr. Schs., 1958; m. Willie Steele, Aug. 3, 1963. With Shell Oil Co., 1937-39, 40-42, Kern County (Calif.), 1939-40; bldg. designer, 1945-57; architect, Bakersfield, 1963—; mem. housing adv. panel McGraw-Hill Book Co.; prin. works include: Barstow (Calif.) City Hall and Jail, 1966, Bakersfield Mennonite Ch., 1966, Bakersfield Hillcrest Meml. Park & Mortuary, 1967, Bank of Am., Lamont, Calif., 1978, 9 U.S. Post Office bldgs.; builder, owner, operator Oildale Frosted Food Locker Co., 1945-57, Marinello Beauty Sch., 1964-75; owner, operator Dusty's Drive-In Restaurant, 1939; author booklet: Are There Too Many of Us/Universal Birth Control Chart, 1959; founder Modern-Aire Homes, Inc., Olympic Record Co., Call-Pascoe Pub. Co.; record producer. Served in USAAF, 1942-45. Recipient Architects and Engrs. Forum award for D. M. Steele Bldg., Delano, Calif., 1969. Mem. AIA. Democrat. Clubs: Cortez Viajeros, Elks. Patentee chain binder, cotton spindle. Home: 3014 Panorama Dr Bakersfield CA 93306 Office: 2200 F St Bakersfield CA 93301

CALLAGHAN, TERENCE JOSEPH, accountant, educator; b. Seattle, July 26, 1940; s. John Joseph and Katherine Clara (Emard) C.; m. Ardell Anne Foeltz, Mar. 2, 1968; children—Christopher, Michelle. B.A. with honors, Seattle U., 1962; M.A., U. Wash., 1964. C.P.A., Calif. Audit sr. Price Waterhouse & Co., San Francisco, 1965-72; mgr. Wallace, Meyer & Co., Oakland, Calif., 1973-77; ptnr. John R. McKean, Accts., P.C., San Francisco, 1978—; adj. prof. Grad. Sch. Acctg. Golden Gate U., San Francisco; lectr. in field. Served with USAR, 1964-70. Mem. Am. Inst. C.P.A.s, Calif. Soc. C.P.A.s, AAUP, Alpha Sigma Nu, Beta Alpha Psi. Club: Berkeley Camera. Office: One California St San Francisco CA 94111

CALLAGY, FLORENCE MAE, accounting executive; b. Canton, Ohio, May 6, 1920; d. Charles J. and Pearl M. (Sadler) Brown; m. Francis Henry Callagy, Sept. 14, 1940 (dec.), children—Larry Francis, Richard Michael. Student San Diego State Coll., 1937-39; U. Calif.-San Diego, 1951, 1966-67. Jr. acct. Kramer and Zucker C.P.A.s, San Diego, 1951-53; office mgr., auditor, Town and Country Devel. Inc., San Diego, 1953-59, sec., treas., 1953-68; sec., treas., comptroller, Atlas Hotels, Inc., San Diego, 1959-70, dir., 1959—, cons., 1981—; ptnr. Callagy Snyder and Assocs., San Diego, 1971-81; owner, mgr. FMC Cons., San Diego, 1981—; sec., dir. Electra Corp., Crest Advt., Inc., Mut. Hotel Supply Co., OmniVideo, Inc., Mission Valley Inn, Inc., Mission Valley Devel., Inc. Sustaining mem., capital fund com. YMCA, 1978-79; active United Community Services; bd. dirs. San Diego Pres. Council, 1982-83, Freedom Found. Mem. Nat. Hotel Accts. (dir. 1972-73), San Diego Advt. Club, San Diego Assn. Advt. Agys., Nat. Mgmt. Assn. (past dir. San Diego chpt.), La Mesa C. of C., San Diego C. of C. Clubs: Altrusa (holder numerous offices, dist. gov. 1983—); Toastmistress, Calif. Staters. Home: 6349-1 Rancho Mission Rd San Diego CA 92108

CALLAHAN, DENNIS WILLIAM, lawyer; b. San Francisco, Oct. 29, 1947; s. William James and Dorothy Marie Callahan; B.S., Dresno State Coll., 1969; J.D., U. Pacific, 1972. Bar: Calif. 1973. Gen. practice law, Atwater, 1973—. Mem. ABA, Calif. Bar Assn., Merced County Bar Assn., Atwater C. of C. Roman Catholic. Club: K.C. Home: 2792 Glen Ave Merced CA 95340 Office: 800 Bellevue Rd Atwater CA 95301

CALLAHAN, JOSEPH PAUL, college administrator; b. Carbondale, Pa., Dec. 22, 1948; s. Joseph Paul and Margaret E. (Kennedy) C.; B.S., East Stroudsburg State Coll., 1970, M.Ed., 1973; Ed.D., U. Mont., 1979; m. Kim Bauer, Dec. 30, 1978; 1 son, Joseph Paul. Mem. faculty East Stroudsburg (Pa.) State Coll., 1970-73, No. Mont. Coll., Havre, 1973-75, asst. to v.p., dean continuing edn., 1977—; research asst. U. Mont., 1975-77. Mem. tuition-policy com. Nat. Elderhostel, 1979. Mem. Evaluation Research Soc., Aml Ednl. Research Assn., Nat. Council Measurement in Edn., Assn. Supervision and Curriculum Devel., Phi Delta Kappa. Roman Catholic. Home: 612 16th St Havre MT 59501 Office: No Mont Coll Havre MT 59501

CALLAN, JOHN GARLING, air transportation executive; b. N.Y.C., Oct. 12, 1946; s. Andrew Thomas and Virginia Garling (Wheatley) C.; m. Linda Ferguson Adkinson, Aug. 28, 1978. B.A. in Russian Lang., U. N.C., 1969. Pres., Alex Nichols Agy., Inc., Los Angeles, 1971-73; pres., founder Calico Air Courier Service, Los Angeles, 1973-79; v.p. mktg. DHL Corp., Burlingame, Calif., 1979-82; pres. IPEC Courier/Skypak Internat., Inc., Burlingame, 1982—. Morehead scholar, 1969. Mem. Air Courier Conf. Am., Inc. (sec., dir.).

CALLAN, PATRICK M., state higher edn. commn. adminstr.; b. Tacoma, Oct. 7, 1942; s. Marc and Mary (Harrison) C.; B.A., U. Santa Clara, 1964, M.A., 1965; postgrad. UCLA, 1968, U. Calif., Irvine, 1969-71. Staff dir. Joint Com. on Master Plan for Higher Edn., Calif. State Legislature, 1971-73; dir. Mont. Commn. on Postsecondary Edn., 1973-74; dir. Wash. State Council for Postsecondary Edn., 1975-78; dir. Calif. Postsecondary Edn. Commn., Sacramento, 1978—, nat. bd. Fund for Improvement of Postsecondary Edn., U.S. Dept. Edn., 1979-82, mem. State of Calif. Student Fin. Aid Policy Study Group, 1979-80; commr., vice chmn. Western Interstate Commn. for Higher Edn.; mem. nat. adv. panel Carnegie Found. Study of Governance and Control of Higher Edn., 1981-82, faculty Inst. for Ednl. Mgmt., Harvard U., 1982-83; commr. Edn. Commn. of the States, 1975-78; mem. adv. council Area of Higher Edn., U. Wash., 1976-78; bd. dirs. Nat. Center for Higher Edn. Mgmt. Systems, 1976-77; cons. State of Oreg., 1975, Ill., 1978, N.Mex., 1982, Idaho, 1982-83, So. Regional Edn. Bd., 1980-82. Mem. Calif. Public Broadcast Commn., 1978—; mem. Western Tech. Manpower Council; mem. adv. council of presidents Assn. for Gov. Bds. bd. dirs. Eleanor McClatchy Ctr. for Performing Arts, 1980—. Served with U.S. Army, 1966-67. Mem. State Higher Edn. Officers Assn. (pres.-elect), Am. Assn. Higher Edn. (past pres.). Contbr. articles to profl. jours. Office: Calif Postsecondary Edn Commn 1020 12th St Sacramento CA 95814

CALLANAN, RITA, educator; b. Los Angeles, June 13, 1938; d. Joseph John and Rita Marie (Burke) C.; B.A., Mt. St. Mary's Coll., 1960, M.S., 1980. Joined Sisters of the Immaculate Heart, Roman Cath. Ch., 1968; tchr. schs., Monterey-Fresno Cath. Diocese, 1965-69, Los Angeles Cath. Archdiocese, 1969—, religion coordinator. Mem. Calif. adv. bd. Inst. Cultural Affairs. Mem. Nat. Cath. Edn. Assn., Assn. Supervision and Curriculum Devel., Action for Children's TV. Republican. Home: 5001 White Oak Ave Encino CA 91316

CALLAO, MAXIMO JOSE, psychologist, educator; b. San Jose, Calif., Feb. 18, 1941; s. Juan Alfonso and Marta (Pinaroc) C.; m. Denise Naomi Inafuku, Mar. 29, 1969; children—Aaron Mark, Jenny Alia. B.A. in Psychology, San Jose State Coll., 1962; Ph.D. in Counseling Psychology, Purdue U., 1971. Lic., psychologist, Idaho. Tchr., U.S. Peace Corps, Philippines, 1962-64; tchr. Baker Sch., San Jose, Calif., 1965-66; counselor Maili Sch., Waianae, Hawaii, 1967-69; adminstrv. intern State of Hawaii Dept. Educ., 1969; counselor Psychol. Services Clinic Purdue U., Lafayette, Ind., 1969-71; counseling psychologist, prof. psychology Boise State U., Idaho, 1971—, also dir. Counseling and Testing Center. Mem. Am. Mental Health Counselors Assn., Idaho Psychol. Assn., Assn. Asian-Am. Psychologists. Democrat. Presbyterian. Clubs: Highlanders Bagpipe Band (Boise), Boise State U. Fencing Assn. Home: 5680 Kriscliffe Ct Boise ID 83704 Office: Boise State U 1910 University Dr Boise ID 83725

CALLAWAY, JAMES ALBERT, dentist; b. Las Vegas, Apr. 24, 1947; s. Albert Moore and Kathlyn Lilythe (Peck) C.; B.S., U. Nev., 1969; D.D.S., U. Detroit, 1972; m. Pamela Maria Luczynski, Oct. 27, 1972; children—Casey James, Bonnie Rebecca, Daniel Albert. Gen. practice dentistry, Troy, Mich., 1973, Las Vegas, Nev., 1973—; owner Griffith Callaway Gallery, Las Vegas, 1978—. Mem. Am. Orthodontic Assn., Am. Endodontic Soc., ADA, Nev. Dental Assn., Acupuncture Research Inst., Freeman Inst., Portrait Inst., Am. Portrait Soc., Clark County Dental Soc. Democrat. Mormon. Clubs: Las Vegas Gem, Lions. Exhibitor Las Vegas Art Mus. Home: 6225 Shadywood Las Vegas NV 89102 Office: 3100 W Sahara St Las Vegas NV 89102

CALLEN, LON EDWARD, county ofcl.; b. Kingman, Kans., Mar. 31, 1929; s. Cleo Paul and Josephine Nell (Mease) C.; B.A. in Math. and Physics, U. Wichita (Kans.), 1951; m. Barbara Jean Sallee, Oct. 12, 1954; children—Lon Edward, Lynnette J. Commd. 2d lt. USAF, 1951, advanced through grades to lt. col., 1968; comdr. Tuslog Detachment 93, Erhac, Turkey, 1966-67; sr. scientist Def. Atomic Support Agy., Washington, 1967-71; ret., 1971; dir. emergency preparedness City-County of Boulder, Colo., 1976—; bd. dirs. Boulder County Emergency Med. Services Council, 1977, Boulder County Amateur Radio Emergency Services, 1978—. Mem. hon. awards com. Nat. Capital Area council Boy Scouts Am., 1971; chmn. Boulder County United Fund, 1976-82; mem. asst. staff Indian Princesses and Trailblazer programs Boulder YMCA, 1974-78. Decorated Joint Service Commendation medal; recipient cert. achievement Def. Atomic Support Agy., 1970. Mem. AAAS, Am. Ordnance Soc., Am. Soc. Cybernetics, Planetary Soc., Math. Assn. Am., N.Y. Acad. Scis., Fedn. Am. Scientists, U.S. Civil Def. Council, Nat. Assn. Atomic Vets., Union Concerned Scientists, Colo. Civil Def. Assn., Boulder County Fire Fighters Assn., Ret. Officers Assn., Colo. Front Range Protective Assn., Mensa, Sigma Xi, Pi Alpha Pi. Clubs: Boulder Knife and Fork, Boulder Gunbarrel Optimists, Denver Matrix, U. Colo. Ski, U. Wichita. Author articles in field. Home: 4739 Berkshire Ct Boulder CO 80301 Office: Box 471 County Courthouse Boulder CO 80306

CALLIHAN, C. MICHAEL, state senator, broadcaster; b. Spokane, Wash., Aug. 7, 1947; s. Cal and Dorothy C.; m. Ann L. Duckett, 1973. B.A., Western State Coll., 1973; postgrad. Colo. U. Owner, Callihan Broadcasting Group; county assessor, 1975-78; mem. Colo. Ho. of Reps., 1979; mem. Colo. Senate, 1982—. Served with USN. Mem. Am. Legion. Democrat. Club: Lions. Office: State Capitol Denver CO 80203*

CALLISON, NANCY FOWLER, nurse; b. Milw., July 16, 1931; d. George Fenwick and Irma Esther (Wenzel) Fowler; diploma Evanston (Ill.) Hosp. Sch. of Nursing, 1952; B.S., Northwestern U., 1954; m. B.G. Callison, Sept. 25, 1954 (dec. Feb. 1964); children—Robert, Leslie, Linda. Staff nurse, psychiat. dept. Downey VA Hosp., 1954-55; staff nurse Camp Lejeune Naval Hosp., 1955, 59-61; obstetrical supr. Tri-City Hosp., Oceanside, Cal Calif., 1961-62; pub. health nurse San Diego County, 1962-66; sch. nurse Rich-Mar Union Sch. Dist., San Marcos, Calif., 1966-68; head nurse San Diego County Community Mental Health, 1968-73; dir. patient care services Southwood Mental Health Ctr., Chula Vista, Calif., 1973-75; program cons. Comprehensive Care Corp., Newport Beach, Calif., 1975-79; dir. Manpower Health Care, Culver City, Calif., 1979-80; dir. nursing services Peninsula Rehab. Ctr., Lomita, Calif., 1980-81; clinic supr., coordinator utilization and authorizations, acting dir. provider relations Hawthorne (Calif.) Community Med. Group, 1981—; clinic coordinator, translator Flying Samaritans, 1965—, mem. internat. bd. dirs., 1975-77, 79—, pres. South Bay chpt., 1975-81. Registered nurse, Calif. Mem. Am. Nurses Assn., Nat. Assn. Female Execs., Aircraft Owners and Pilots Assn. Office: 11616 Hawthorne Blvd Hawthorne CA 90205

CALLISTER, LOUIS HENRY, JR., lawyer; b. Salt Lake City, Aug. 11, 1935; s. Louis Henry and Isabel (Barton) C.; B.S., U. Utah, 1958, J.D., 1961; m. Ellen Gunnell, Nov. 27, 1957; children—Mark, Isabel, Jane, Edward, David, John Andrew, Ann. Admitted to Utah bar, 1961; asst. atty. gen. Utah, 1961; sr. partner Greene, Callister & Nebeker, Salt Lake City, 1961—; pres. Callister Devel. Corp.; dir. Premium Oil Co., Salt Lake City. Vice chmn. Salt Lake City Zoning Bd. Adjustment, 1979—; bd. govs. Latter Day Saints Hosp., 1983—; treas. exec. com. Utah Republican Com., 1965-69; chmn. Utah chpt. Rockefeller for Pres. Com., 1964-68; sec., trustee Salt Lake City Police Hon. Cols., 1982—. Mormon. Home: 1454 Tomahawk Dr Salt Lake City UT 84103 Office: 800 Kennecott Bldg Salt Lake City UT 84133

CALLISTER, MARION JONES, judge; b. Moreland, Idaho, June 6, 1921, m. Nina Lynn Hayes, June 7, 1946; children—Nona Lynn Callister Haddock, Lana Sue Callister Meredith, Jerry Ann Callister Thomas, Tamara Callister Banks, Idonna Ruth Callister Anderson, Betty Patricia Callister Jacobs, Deborah Jean, Mary Clarice, David Marion, Nancy Irene, Michelle, Kimberly Jane. Ed. Utah State U. (formerly Utah State Agrl. Coll.), 1940-41; B.S.L., U. Utah, 1951, J.D., 1951. Bar: Idaho, 1951. Dep. pros. atty. Bingham County (Utah), beginning 1951; judge Idaho Dist. Ct. Third Jud. Dist., 1970-75, U.S. Dist. Ct. Idaho, Boise, 1976—. Served with U.S. Army, 1944-46. Mem. Am. Judicature Soc., Fourth Jud. Dist. Bar Assn., Idaho State Bar. Republican. Mormon. Office: US Courthouse PO Box 040 550 W Fort St Boise ID 83724*

CALLOW, KEITH MCLEAN, judge; b. Seattle, Jan. 11, 1925; s. Russell and Dollie (McLean) C.; student Alfred U., 1943, Coll. City N.Y., 1944, Biarritz Am. U., 1945, Nat. Coll. State Judiciary, 1970; B.A., U. Wash., 1949, J.D., 1952; m. Evelyn Case, July 9, 1949; children—Andrea, Douglas, Kerry. Admitted to Wash. bar, 1952; asst. atty. gen. Wash., 1952; law clk. Wash. Supreme Ct., 1953; dep. pros. atty. King County, 1954-56; pvt. practice, 1956-69; judge King County Superior Ct., 1969-71; judge Wash. State Ct. of Appeals, 1972—, chief judge Div. 1, 1979, presiding chief judge 1980—; lectr. bus. law U. Wash., 1956-62; lectr. med. malpractice, panelist C.L.E. on uniform comml. code, trial and appellate practice, products liability; mem. faculty Nat. Jud. Coll., 1980; mcpl. judge pro-tem Seattle, 1960-64; chmn. legis. com. Superior Ct. Judges Assn., 1970-71; co-organizer, sec. Council of Chief Judges of Cts. of Appeal, 1980. Pres. Young Mens Republican Club, 1957. Bd. dirs. Evergreen Safety Council. Served with AUS, 1943-46. Recipient Brandeis award, 1981. Mem. Am., D.C., Wash., Seattle-King County (chmn. local adminstrv. com. King County 1967-69) bar assns., Estate Planning Council, Navy League (dir. Seattle chpt.) Psi Upsilon (state pres. 1976-79), Phi Delta Phi. Clubs: Rainier (sec. 1979), Forty Nine (pres. 1974) (Seattle). Lodge: Rotary. Editor: Pattern Jury Instructions; mem. Wash. Law Rev. Home: 4560 52d NE Seattle WA 98105 Office: 1 Union Sq 600 University St Seattle WA 98101

CALOF, DAVID LORNE, hypnotherapist; b. Seattle, Dec. 12, 1949; s. Jacob and Thea (Golden) C.; m. Cindy Salazar, Nov. 14, 1974 (div.). Cert. hypnotherapist Wash. Coordinator Office Coop. Edn., spl. asst. to Dean Devel. Services, Evergreen State Coll., 1971-72; dir. mgmt. services, mgr. personnel staff devel. Seattle Opportunities Industrialization Center, 1974-77; family hypnotherapist, co-founder Seattle Family Inst., pvt. practice specializing in hypnotherapy and treatment of multiple personality, 1977—. Mem. Wash. Gov.'s Youth Commn., state chmn. Wash. Assn. Student Govts., 1970-71; exec. dir. Citizens Conf. on Wash. State Legislature, 1972-73. Mem. Am. Mental Health Counselors Assn., Am. Personnel and Guidance Assn., Assn. Advancement Ethical Hypnosis, Am. Hypnosis Assn., Northwest Family Tng. Inst. Contbr. to tech. publs.; spl. cons. Wash. State Council Higher Edn. —State Report on Campus Unrest.— Office: 2722 Eastlake Ave E Suite 210 Seattle WA 98102

CALT, JAMES MICHAEL, retail executive; b. Chgo., Aug. 23, 1942; s. Owen Francis and Mary (O'Hallerian) C.; m. Judy Marie Larsen, Oct. 1, 1977; children—Shannon, Shayne, Shawna. Student LaSalle Inst., 1956-60, U. Md., 1966-69, U. Alaska, 1974-75. With Teamco, Inc., Anchorage, Alaska, 1970—, pres., 1976—; dir. Arctic Sounds, Inc., Co-Op Records, J.C. Advt., The Shop, Inc., J.M. Leasco.

CALVERT, DONALD JOSEPH, entomologist, researcher, consultant; b. Granada, Nicaragua, July 25, 1939; s. Thomas Leslie and Dora Carmen (Trana) C.; m. Rosa Argentina Vargas, Oct. 5, 1968. B.S., U. Calif.-Berkeley, 1965, Ph.D., 1970. Tchr., research asst. dept. entomology U. Calif.-Berkeley, 1965-69; asst. research entomologist, 1974—, crop protection specialist, 1975—; asst. research entomologist U. Calif., Parlier, 1970-72; agrl. officer FAO, Costa Rica, 1973-74; cons. FAO, 1972—, AID, 1975—. Served with AUS, 1961-64. Mem. AAAS, Am. Inst. Biol. Scis., Entomol. Soc. Am., Internat. Orgn. Biol. Control, Sociedad Entomológica del Perö. Republican. Roman Catholic. Contbr.

articles to profl. jours. Home: 1246 Greenway Dr Richmond CA 94803 Office: 2288 Fulton St Suite 310 Berkeley CA 94704

CALVERT, EARL WALTER, historian, theatre owner; b. San Jose, Calif., Sept. 25, 1905; s. Walter Albert and Nellie Bell (Richardson) C.; m. Annie Josephine Scolari, June 16, 1929; children—Erlan Joseph, Kenneth Francis. Student U. Calif.-Berkeley. Pres. Lompoc Valley (Calif.) Hist. Soc. Inc., 1964—; owner theatres, Lompoc, Calif., 1930—; v.p. Integrated Industries, Inc. Vice-pres. Community Concert Assn., past pres.; mem. exec. bd. Conf. Calif. Hist. Socs., pres. 1970-71, chmn. trust fund com.; mem. task force Republican Party; active Boy Scouts Am.; mem. Santa Barbara County Landmark Com., 1965—; chmn. Lompoc adv. Landmark Com.; adv. La Purisima Mission; dir. Farm Bur.; assoc. Lompoc Mus. Recipient U.S. Treasury Dept. silver medal award, 1941-45; Silver Beaver award Boy Scouts Am., 1960. Mem. Calif. Hist. Soc., Pioneer Soc., C. of C. Methodist. Clubs: Rotary (Lompoc), Village Country, Methodist Men; Masons, Shriners, K.P. Home: 780 Purisima Rd PO Box 398 Lompoc CA 93438 Office: Lompoc Theatre Bldg Suite 7 114 1/2 North H PO Box 398 Lompoc CA 93438

CALVERT, MARSHALL ALAN, financial services manager, substance abuse counselor; b. Kansas City, Mo., Aug. 15, 1952; s. Wesley Dale and Maxine Leona C.; m. Darcy Lou Berline, Dec. 28, 1974; 1 dau., Cara Lynne. Grad. in Geology, Wichita State U., 1974. Cert. substance abuse counselor, Alaska. Dept. mgr. Gibson Discount Ctr., Wellington, Kans., 1972-74; commd. 2d lt. U.S. Air Force, 1974, advanced through grades to capt., 1978; assignments in Tex., Calif., Kans., Ala., Alaska, 1974-82; exec. dir. Alaska Native Tng. Inst., Anchorage, 1982; coordinator Brother Francis Shelter, Anchorage, 1982—; mgr. A.L. Williams Corp., Anchorage, 1983—; pvt. practice counseling; contract prospector; mineral evaluator; comml./instrument pilot Gen. Aviation Aircraft. Pres. bd. dirs. Alaska Council for Prevention of Alcohol and Drug Abuse. Served with Air N.G., 1983. Recipient God and Country award First Christian Ch., Wellington, Kans., 1964; Eagle Scout award Boy Scouts Am., Wellington, 1966; Nat. Exploration award Explorers Club, N.Y.C., 1970; Tasch geology scholar, 1972. Mem. AIME, Soc. Petroleum Engrs., Alaska Miners Assn., Alaska Geol. Soc., Res. Officers Assn., Air Force Assn., Am. Personnel and Guidance Assn., Soc. for Specialists in Group Work, Alaska Airmen's Assn., Wellington Gem and Mineral Soc., Aircraft Owners and Pilots Assn. Clubs: Elmendorf AFB Aero, Nat. Rifle Assn. Office: 3400 Spenard Rd Suite 7 Anchorage AK 99503

CALVIN, ALLEN DAVID, psychologist; b. St. Paul, Feb. 17, 1928; s. Carl and Zelda (Engelson) C.; B.A. in Psychology cum laude, U. Minn., 1950; M.A. in Psychology, U. Tex., 1951, Ph.D. in Exptl. Psychology, 1953; m. Dorothy VerStrate, Oct. 5, 1953; children—Jamie Louise, Kris Ellen, David, Scott. Instr. Mich. State U., East Lansing, 1953-55; asst. prof. Hollins Coll., 1955-59, asso. prof., 1959-61; dir. Britannica Center for Studies in Learning and Motivation, Menlo Park, Calif., 1961; prin. investigator Carnegie Found. grant for automated teaching fgn. langs., 1960, USPHS grantee, 1960; pres. Behavioral Research Labs., 1962-74; prof., dean Sch. Edn., U. San Francisco, 1974—, Henry Clay Hall prof. orgn. and leadership, 1978—. Served with USNR, 1946-47. Mem. Am. Psychol. Assn., AAAS, Sigma Xi, Psi Chi. Author textbooks. Home: 1645 15th Ave San Francisco CA 94122 Office: U San Francisco San Francisco CA 94117

CALVIN, MELVIN, chemist, educator; b. St. Paul, Apr. 8, 1911; s. Elias and Rose I. (Hervitz) C.; B.S., Mich. Coll. Mining and Tech., 1931, D.Sc., 1955; Ph.D., U. Minn., 1935, D.Sc., 1969; hon. research fellow U. Manchester (Eng.), 1935-37; Guggenheim fellow, 1944; D.Sc., Nottingham U., 1958, Oxford (Eng.) U., 1959, Northwestern U., 1961, Wayne State U., 1962, Gustavus Adolphus Coll., 1963, Poly. Inst. Bklyn., 1962, Notre Dame, 1965, U. Ghent (Belgium), 1970, Whittier Coll., 1971, Columbia U., 1979; m. Marie G. Jemtegaard, 1942; children—Elin, Karole, Noel. With U. Calif. at Berkeley, 1937—, successively instr. chemistry, asst. prof., prof., Univ. prof., dir. Lab. Chem. Biodynamics, 1963-80, asso. dir. Lawrence Radiation Lab., 1967-80; Peter Reilly lectr. U. Notre Dame, 1949; Harvey lectr. N.Y. Acad. Medicine, 1951; Harrison Howe lectr. Rochester sect. Am. Chem. Soc., 1954; Falk-Plaut lectr. Columbia U., 1954; Edgar Fahs Smith Meml. lectr. U. Pa. and Phila. sect. Am. Chem. Soc., 1955; Donegani Found. lectr. Italian Nat. Acad. Sci., 1955; Max Tishler lectr. Harvard U., 1956; Karl Folkers lectr. U. Wis., 1956; London lectr., 1961; Eastman prof. Oxford (Eng.) U., 1967-68. Recipient prize Sugar Research Found., 1950; Flintoff medal prize Brit. Chem. Soc., 1953; Stephen Hales award Am. Soc. Plant Physiologists, 1956; Nobel prize in chemistry, 1961; Davy medal Royal Soc., 1964; Virtanen medal, 1975; Priestley award Dickenson Coll., 1979; Gold Medal award Am. Inst. Chemists, 1979; Feodor Lynen medal, 1983. Mem. Royal Soc. (London) (fgn. mem.), Am. Chem. Soc. (Richards medal N.E. sect. 1956, Nichols medal N.Y. sect. 1958, Gibbs medal Chgo. sect. 1977, Priestley medal 1978, Oesper award Cin. sect. 1981, Sterling B. Hendricks medal div. agr. and food chemistry 1983; pres. 1971), Am. Acad. Arts and Scis., Nat. Acad. Scis., Royal Dutch Acad. Scis., Japan Acad., Am. Philos. Soc., Sigma Xi, Tau Beta Pi, Phi Lambda Upsilon. Author: The Theory of Organic Chemistry (with G. E. K. branch), 1940; Isotopic Carbon (with others), 1949; Chemistry of Metal Chelatated Compounds (with Martell), 1952; (with Bassham) Path of Carbon in Photosynthesis, 1957, Photosynthesis of Carbon Compounds, 1962; Chemical Evolution, 1969. Contbr. articles to chem. and sci. jours. Home: 2683 Buena Vista Berkeley CA 94708

CAMACHO, LUIS GUILLERMO, physician; b. Bolivia, Nov. 6, 1939; came to U.S., 1965, naturalized, 1969; s. Juan J. and Angela M. (Parrilla) C.; M.D., Nat. U. Cordoba (Argentina), 1963; m. Nov. 7, 1970; children—William Andrew, Ana Maria. Intern, Christ Community Hosp., Oaklawn, Ill., 1967-68; resident Mayo Clinic, Rochester, Minn., 1968-72, chief resident, 1972; cons. Riverside Clinic, Menasha, Wis., 1973-74; pvt. practice medicine, specializing in gen. and vascular surgery, Concord, Calif., 1974—; pres. Luis G. Camacho MD, Inc, Concord, 1974—; mem. staff Mt. Diablo Med. Center, John Muir Meml. Hosp., Walnut Creek Calif., Los Medanos Hosp., Pittsburg, Calif. Mem. AMA (Physician Recognition award 1972-83), A.C.S., Royal Soc. Health (London), Am. Coll. Angiology, Internat. Acad. Proctology, Inter-Am. Coll. Physicians and Surgeons, Priestley Soc., Am. Soc. Abdominal Surgeons, Mayo Clinic Alumni Assn. Office: 2211 East St Concord CA 94520 also 2260 Gladstone Dr Pittsburg CA 94565

CAMBLIN, ROY WILLIAM, III, mgmt. info. systems exec.; b. San Antonio, Jan. 5, 1947; B.S.B.A., Fla. State U., 1969; M.S. in Systems Mgmt., U. So. Calif., 1977; cert. Air Command and Staff Coll., 1978; postgrad. U. Hawaii, 1978-79; m. Jane Anne Day, Apr. 20, 1981; 1 son. Commd. 2d lt. U.S. Air Force, 1969, advanced through grades to maj., 1980; supply ops. officer, 1969-71; instr., pilot, flight examiner, 1972-81, ops. planner, analyst, 1976-78; maj. fiscal policy adminstr., 1978-81, resigned, 1981; dir., designer mgmt. info. systems, 1981—; also pub. speaker. Cert. airline transport pilot. Mem. Hawaii C. of C., Order of Daedalians, Hawaii World Trade Assn., Small Bus. Assn. Address: PO Box 2048 San Francisco CA 94126

CAMENZIND, HANS R. (JOHN PENTER), author; b. Zurich, Switzerland, June 29, 1934; came to U.S., 1960, naturalized, 1965; B.S. in E.E., Inst. Juventus, Zurich, Switzerland, 1959; M.S. in E.E., Northwestern U., 1967; M.B.A., U. Santa Clara, 1971; m. Pia M. Brodmann, Apr. 21, 1959; children—Robert, Susan, Peter, Tim. Design engr. P. R. Mallery Co., Burlington, Mass., 1960-68; design mgr. Signetics Corp., Sunnyvale, Calif., 1968-70; pres., chmn. Interdesign, Inc., Sunnyvale, 1970-77; lectr. U. Santa Clara Grad. Sch., 1968-76; dir. Universal Semiconductor Inc., San Jose, Calif.; San Jose Capital Corp.; author: Cir. design Integrated Electronics, 1968; Electronic Integrated Systems Design, 1972; Circumstantial Evidence, 1981. Address: 166 Hawthorn Ave Los Altos CA 94022

CAMERON, COLIN CAMPBELL, pineapple company and land development executive; b. Paia, Maui, Hawaii, Feb. 2, 1927; s. J. Walter and Frances (Baldwin) C.; A.B., Harvard, 1950, M.B.A., 1953; m. Margaret Hartley, Aug. 25, 1951; children—Douglas, Richard, Margaret, Frances. Chmn., pres. Maui Land & Pineapple Co., Inc., 1969—; chmn., Kapalua Land Co., Ltd., 1974—, Maui Pineapple Co. Ltd.; v.p., dir. Haleakala Ranch Co., Ltd.; pres., dir. Maui Pub. Co. Ltd., publishers Maui News, dir. Bank of Hawaii, Hawaiian Electric Co., Inc., Maui Electric Co., Ltd. Vice pres., chmn. long-range planning com. J. Walter Cameron Center; bd. dirs., pres. Lahaina Restoration Found., bd. dirs. Hawaii Resort Developers Conf.; chmn. Maui Econ. Devel. Bd.; mem. Pa Basin Econ. Council; mem. vis. com. Dept. E. Asian Studies, Harvard U.; bd. visitors Fletcher Sch. Law and Diplomacy; mem. adv. bd. Travel Industry Mgmt. Sch. and Sch. Architecture, both U. Hawaii. Served with USNR, 1945-46. Mem. Japan-Calif. Assn., Hawaii Bus. Roundtable. Clubs: Pacific, Plaza. Office: PO Box 187 Kahului HI 96732

CAMERON, DUNCAN FERGUSON, museum director; b. Toronto, Ont., Can., Feb. 1, 1930; s. Charles Gordon and Winnifred Petrie (Pepperdeane) C.; m. Nancy Tousley, Apr. 24, 1975. Chief info. services Royal Ont. Mus., Toronto, 1956-61; pres. Janus Ltd., Toronto, 1961-70; nat. dir. Can. Conf. Arts, Toronto, 1968-70; dir. Bklyn. Mus., 1971-73; prin. P. S. Ross & Partners, Toronto, 1974-77; dir. Glenbow-Alta. Inst., Calgary, 1977—. Mem. Internat. Council Museums, Museums Assn., Am. Assn. Museums, Can. Museums Assn., Can. Art Mus. Dirs. Orgn., Commonwealth Assn. Museums. Anglican. Clubs: Royal Can. Mil. Inst. (Toronto); Masons. Contbr. articles to various publs. Home: #8 927 19th Ave SW Calgary AB T2T 0H8 Canada Office: 130 9th Ave SE Calgary AB T2G 0P3 Canada

CAMERON, JAMES DUKE, justice Ariz. Supreme Court; b. Richmond, Calif., Mar. 25, 1925; s. Charles Lee and Ruth (Mabry) C.; A.B. in Polit. Sci. and History, U. Calif.-Berkeley, 1950; J.D., U. Ariz., 1954; LL.M., U. Va., 1982; m. Suzanne Jane Pratt, Aug. 16, 1952 (div. 1982); children—Alison Valerie, Craig Charles, Jennifer Elaine. Bar: Ariz. 1954. Practiced in Yuma, 1954-60; ptnr. firm Cameron & Varga, 1961-65; judge Superior Ct. Yuma County, 1960-61; chmn. Ariz. Bd. Pub. Welfare, 1961-64; judge Ariz. Ct. Appeals, 1965-70, chief judge, 1968-70; justice Ariz. Supreme Ct., 1971—, vice chief justice, 1972-75, chief justice, 1975-80, presiding justice, 1980—; mem. faculty appellate judges seminar Inst. Jud. Adminstrn., NYU, 1968—. Alt. del. Republican Nat. Conv., 1952; chmn. Pima County Young Rep. Club, 1952-54. Trustee Yuma City-County Library, 1957-68; bd. visitors U. Ariz. Coll. Law, 1972—. Served with AUS, World War II. Mem. Am. Law Inst., Am. Judicature Soc., Inst. Jud. Adminstrn., Am. (appellate judges conf. 1966), Ariz., Yuma County bar assns., Newcomen Soc., Ariz. Acad. Mason (Shriner). Author: Arizona Appellate Forms and Procedures, 1968; also articles. Office: State Capitol Bldg Phoenix AZ 85007

CAMIEN, MERRILL NELSON, biochemist; b. Redlands, Calif., Dec. 10, 1920; s. Gus Antone and Kathryn Violet (Nelson) C.; B.A., U.C.L.A., 1943, M.A., 1945, Ph.D., 1948; m. Teresa Ulysse Apfel, July 16, 1944; children—Juliette Catharine, Andrew Nelson. Research asso. UCLA, 1948-50, asso. research chemist, 1951-62; research chemist VA Hosp., Los Angeles, 1962-64; sr. research biochemist Cedars-Sinai Med. Research Inst., 1964-67; research physiologist U. Calif. Med. Center, Los Angeles, 1967-68; head dept. neuropharmacology ICN Nucleic Acid Research Inst., Irvine, Calif., 1968-73; research asso. U. Calif., Irvine, 1973-76, asst. research biochemist, 1976—. Fulbright scholar Universite de Liege, Belgium, 1950-51. Mem. Am. Soc. Biol. Chemists, Am. Chem. Soc., N.Y. Acad. Scis., AAAS, Am. Soc. Microbiology, Soc. Exptl. Biol. Medicine, Sigma Xi. Unitarian. Contbr. articles to profl. jours. Home: 1606 Warwick Ln Newport Beach CA 92660 Office: Dept Molecular Biology and Biochemistry U Calif Irvine CA 92717

CAMIN, BERNIE (BERNIE CAMINKER), business executive, industrial designer; b. Los Angeles, Aug. 18, 1930; s. Elleck and Anna (Shevelenco) C.; B.A., UCLA, 1956, postgrad. in engring. and indsl. design, 1956-60; student U. Calif.-Berkeley, 1950-52; m. Irma Judith Abramson, Aug. 22, 1954 (div.); children—Lisa Ellen, Evan Howard. Indsl. designer Henry Dreyfuss Indsl. Design, Pasadena, Calif., 1956-57; ptnr. Powell-Caminker Indsl. Design, Los Angeles, 1957-63; mgr. indsl. design, project mgr. Computer div. Packard Bell Electronics, Los Angeles, Santa Ana, Calif., 1959-64; chief, mech. engring. and devel. Eldorado Electronics, Walnut Creek, Calif., 1964-65; staff engr., head, systems design group Hughes Aircraft Co., Fullerton, Calif., 1965-73; pres. Apex Diamond Tool Co., Santa Ana, 1974—; owner The Camin Design Group, Santa Ana, Calif., 1978—; design, engring., graphics, archtl. cons. Served with Signal Corps, AUS, 1952-54. Recipient 3 Design awards Western Electronics shows and convs. Patentee in field; responsible for implementation of automatic checkout systems for Saturn space booster, 1961, USAF 407L field mobile ops. centers, 1964-69. Home: 2184 Canyon Dr No N Costa Mesa CA 92627 Office: 1426 E Borchard Ave Santa Ana CA 92705

CAMMALLERI, JOSEPH ANTHONY, university program representative, retired air force officer; b. Bronx, N.Y., Feb. 2, 1935; s. Leo Anthony and Angela Marie (Mirandi) C.; B.S., Manhattan Coll., 1956; M.S., Okla. State U., 1966; postgrad. Golden Gate U., 1974—; m. Virginia Mary Towle, Oct. 10, 1970; children—Anthony R., Aaron L., Thomas K., Jeffrey A. Commd. 2d lt. USAF, 1956, advanced through grades to lt. col., 1973; trainee flight crew, 1956-58; crew mem. B-52, 1958-64; behavioral scientist Aerospace Med. Research Labs., Wright-Patterson AFB, Ohio, 1966-68; EB-66 crew mem. Tahkli AFB, Thailand, 1968-69; faculty mem. dept. life and behavioral scis. USAF Acad. (Colo.), 1969-74, asso. prof., dir. operational psychology div., 1972-74, B-1 human factors engring. mgr. Air Force Flight Test Center, Edwards AFB, Calif., 1974-76, chief handbook devel., 1976-77; ret., 1977; account exec. Merril Lynch, Pierce, Fenner & Smith, Sherman Oaks, Calif., 1977-80; acad. program rep. U. Redlands (Calif.), 1980—, mem. faculty, 1979—; faculty Golden Gate U., 1975-80. Decorated D.F.C., Air medal (5), Meritorious Service medal. Mem. Nat. Ry. Hist. Soc., Ry. and Locomotive Hist. Soc., Rocky Mountain R.R. Club, Los Angeles Live Steamers, Nat. Model R.R. Assn., Colo. R.R. Hist. Found. (life), Santa Fe Ry. Hist. Soc., USAF Acad. Athletic Assn. (life), Psi Chi. Home: 3093 Charlotte St Newbury Park CA 91320 Office: U Redlands Redlands CA 92373

CAMP, JOAN CAROLYN, extension agent, home economist; b. Greeley, Colo., May 4, 1945; d. Melvin James and Ruth Carol (Bowman) C. B.A. in Home Econs. Edn. (award), U. No. Colo., 1969; M.A. in Adult Edn., Colo. State U., 1976. Home econs. tchr., Walsenburg, Colo., 1969-70, Lamar, Colo., 1971-73; extension agt., Lamar Colo., Prowers County, 1973—; internat. 4-H youth exchange del. to Ireland, Colo. State U., 1970. Active Zonta Internat. (treas. Boulder County), PEO Sisterhood. Mem. Am. Home Econs. Assn., Nat. Assn. Extension Home Economists, Nat. Assn. Extension 4-H Youth Agts., Adult Edn. Assn. Republican. Methodist. Office: 9595 Nelson Rd Box B Longmont CO 80501

CAMP, LOUISE PHIFER (MRS. WOFFORD BENJAMIN CAMP), farmer, musician; b. Winston-Salem, N.C., Mar. 22, 1912; d. Charles McKnight and Louisa (Williams) Phifer; B.A. in Mus., Limestone Coll., 1933, H.H.D. (hon.), 1977; postgrad. in music Converse Coll., 1933-34; m. George William Wise, June 7, 1934 (dec. 1945); children—Addie Louise, George William, Sarah Emily; m. 2d, Wofford Benjamin Camp, Jan. 18, 1956. Minister of music Baptist evang. meetings in N.C., S.C., Ga., summers 1930-34; tchr. voice Limestone Coll., Gaffney, S.C., summer 1932, trustee, 1960—; tchr. elementary sch., Gaffney, 1933-34; farmer, Edgefield County, S.C., 1945-77; dir. Bank of Trenton (S.C.), 1945-78; dir., sec. W.B. Camp, Inc., Bakersfield, Calif., 1956—. Organizer, dir. numerous choral groups, N.C., S.C., Ga., 1935-55; soloist St. John's Methodist Ch., Augusta, Ga., 1953-55; soloist Presbyn. Ch., Trenton, S.C., 1934-55, organist, 1946-53. Co-founder Trenton Devel. Corp., 1950; pres. Pro-Am., Bakersfield, 1958-59; dir. Kern County (Calif.) Music Assn., 1957-59, program chmn., 1958-59; co-founder Louise Phifer Camp Found., Limestone Coll., 1957; mem. Bakersfield Woman's Club, Bakersfield Garden Club, Farm Bur.; co-founder, dir. Kern County Free Enterprise Assn., 1960; mem. hospitality com. Philharmonic Assn., Bakersfield, 1958-61; organizer, pres. Kern County Women's chpt. Freedom's Found. at Valley Forge, 1969; pres. Symphony Assos. of Kern County, 1972-73, life mem. bd. trustees Limestone Coll., 1973—, chmn. bd. trustees, 1973-83. Trustee Freedoms Found. at Valley Forge; bd. dirs. John and Beverly Stauffer Found.; mem. exec. bd., nat. treas. Religious Heritage Am.; mem. nat. exec. bd. Gospel Music Assn., 1978—, nat. campaign chmn. Gospel Music Hall of Fame Research Library and Mus. Recipient award as outstanding cotton grower S.C., S.C. Agrl. Extension Service, 1954, Outstanding Alumna award Limestone Coll., 1956, Freedom Founds. award, 1973. Mem. D.A.R., UDC, AAUW, P.E.O. Democrat. Presbyn. Home: 701 Oleander Ave Bakersfield CA 93304

CAMPANELLA, YVETTE LYNN, cosmetics co. ofcl.; b. Rockland County, N.Y., May 31, 1952; d. John Alfred and Marie Christine (Hill) Johnson; B.A. in Psychology, Vassar Coll., 1974; m. John Deloach Campanella, Sept. 22, 1978; 1 son, Jon Thomas. Operational analyses and controls sr. analyst Met. Life Ins. Co., N.Y.C., 1975-78; indsl. engr. Security Pacific Bank, Los Angeles, 1979; dir. new product introduction system Max Factor & Co., Hollywood, Calif., 1979—. Mem. Nat. Assn. Female Execs., Am. Inst. Indsl. Engrs., Am. Mgmt. Assn. Congregationalist. Home: 3212 Oakhurst Ave Cheviot Hills CA 90034 Office: 1655 N McCadden Pl Hollywood CA 90028

CAMPBELL, ALICE LOUISE, state employment counselor; b. Champaign, Ill., Nov. 13, 1950; d. Robert Harry and Anna Louise (Nelson) Eagleton; m. Rodney Dennis Campbell, July 14, 1975; 1 dau., Jessie Louise. B.A. in Anthropology, U. Mo., 1972, M.Ed. in Counseling, 1975. Loan closer 1st Nat. Bank of Anchorage, 1977-79; employment counselor II Alaska Dept. Labor Fairbanks Job Service, 1980—. Mem. Am. Personnel and Guidance Assn., Am. Soc. Tng. and Devel., Nat. Employment Counselors Assn. Office: PO Box 1010 Fairbanks AK 99701

CAMPBELL, ANDREW GREGVER, health care exec.; b. Kansas City, Mo., Sept. 25, 1944; s. William Thaddeus and Ruth Logan (Coursault) C.; B.S., Cornell U., 1966; M.B.A., U. So. Calif., 1969. Sr. auditor, cons. Harris, Kerr, Forster & Co., C.P.A.'s, Los Angeles, 1967-74; acctg. mgr. First Travel Corp., Encino, Calif., 1974-75; v.p. fin. Family Health Program, Fountain Valley, Calif., 1975—; exec. v.p. Cost Care, Inc., Huntington Beach, Calif., 1983—; health care cons., acct., 1981-83; dir. Health Maintenance Life Ins. Co., Providers & Consumers, Inc., Providers Protective Ins. Co.; mem. health maintenance orgn. adv. com. Calif. Corps. Commn.; bd. dirs., past pres. Health Services Polit. Action Com. Served with USAR, 1969-71. C.P.A., Calif. Mem. Am. Inst. C.P.A.'s, Group Health Assn. Am., Am. Mgmt. Assn., Calif. Soc. C.P.A.'s, Cornell U. Hotelmen's Soc., Internat. Food and Wine Soc., Les Amus Du Vin. Home: 425 Longfellow Ave Hermosa Beach CA 90254 Office: 18652 Florida St Huntington Beach CA 92648

CAMPBELL, CAROLINE KRAUSE, retail drug co. exec.; b. Praha, Tex., May 5, 1926; d. Charles Joseph and Mary Victoria (Havrde) Krause; student U. N.Mex.; diploma Alexander Hamilton Inst., N.Y.C., 1969; widow; children—Richard Elton, Don Michael, Scott Gary, Jonathan Miles, Candace Kay. Various secretarial positions, 1945-49; survey researcher Winona Research Co., Mpls., 1953-54; merchandiser, buyer Campbell Drug, Inc., Albuquerque, 1961-77, gen. mgr., 1978—, pres., 1978—, also dir. Mem. Nat. Fedn. Ind. Bus., Nat. Assn. Retail Druggists, N.Mex. Pharm. Assn., Internat. Platform Assn., Albuquerque Symphony Women's Assn., Albuquerque C. of C., N.Mex. Assn. Commerce and Industry, Albuquerque Rose Soc. Republican. Clubs: Italian Cultural, Elks. Office: 8252 Menaul Blvd NE Albuquerque NM 87110

CAMPBELL, CHARLES WILLIAM, JR., printer, publisher, editor, educator; b. Great Falls, Mont., Nov. 12, 1916; s. Charles William and Mabel Prudence (Rorabeck) C.; m. Marjorie Thomson Cook, Sept. 26, 1936; children—Lynnette A. Campbell Finch, Nancie L. Campbell Crowley. Student San Diego State U., 1934-35. Tchr. printing and newspaper make-up San Diego High Sch., 1937-42; owner, operator, Campbell Printing Co., 1943-45; linotype operator Union/Tribune, San Diego, 1946-50; foreman composing room Coronado (Calif.) Jour., 1950-70, editor-publisher, 1970—; dir. Bank Coronado; Served with U.S. Army, 1945-46. Recipient Spl. Teaching Credential Quill & Scroll, 1934; Optimists Club Appreciation award, 1980; John Swett award Calif. Tchrs. Assn., 1982; Mem. Internat. Quill and Scroll (hon.), Internat. Typographical Union, Coronado C. of C. (dir.). Democrat. Clubs: Rotary (Appreciation award 1981), San Diego Water Ski and Power Boat (commodore 1960). Office: Coronado Jour 1125 Loma Ave Coronado CA 92118

CAMPBELL, COLIN HERALD, mayor, former management consultant; b. Winnipeg, Man., Can., Jan. 18, 1911; s. Colin Charles and Aimee Florence (Herald) C.; B.A., Reed Coll., 1933; m. Virginia Paris, July 20, 1935; children—Susanna Herald, Corinna Buford, Virginia Wallace. Exec. sec. City Club of Portland, 1934-39; alumni sec., dir. endowment adminstrn. Reed Coll., 1939-42, exec. sec. N.W. Inst. Internat. Relations. 1940-42, instr. photography, 1941-42; contract engr. Kaiser Co., Inc., 1942-45; asst. personnel dir. Portland Gas & Coke Co., 1945-48; dir. indsl. relations Pacific Power & Light Co., Portland, 1948-76. Mem. Oreg. Advisory Com. on Fair Employment Practices Act, 1949-55; trustee, chmn., pres. Portland Symphonic Choir, 1950-54; trustee Portland Civic Theater, 1951-54; bd. dirs. Portland Symphony Soc., 1957-60, Community Child Guidance Clinic, 1966-68; active United Way, 1945-75; bd. dirs. Contemporary Crafts Assn., 1972—, treas., 1975-76; bd. dirs. Lake Oswego Corp., 1961-65, 71-73, 74-76, corporate sec., 1964, pres., 1973-74, treas., 1975-76; mem. Com. on Citizen Involvement, City of Lake Oswego, 1975-77; chmn. Bicentennial Com., Lake Oswego; sec.-treas. Met. Area Communications Commn., 1980—; treas. Clackamas County Community Action Agy., 1980-82, chmn., 1982—; mem. fin. adv. com. W. Clackamas County LWV, 1974-76, 78-80; councilman City of Lake Oswego, 1977-78, mayor, 1979—. Mem. Edison Electric Inst. (exec. com.), NW Electric Light and Power Assn., Lake Oswego C. of C., Portland Art Assn., Pacific NW Personnel Mgmt. Assn. (past regional v.p.), St. Andrews Soc., Oreg. Hist. Soc. Republican. Presbyterian. Clubs: Rotary, University (Portland). Home: 1219 Maple St Lake Oswego OR 97034

CAMPBELL, DAVID ELLIOTT, psychology educator; b. Evanston, Ill., Apr. 2, 1945; s. James Alan and Frances Holliday (Hurlburt) C.; m. Toni Ann Doke, June 5, 1946; 1 son, John Elliott. B.A., U. Calif.-Berkeley, 1966; M.S. in Psychology, San Francisco State U., 1970; Ph.D. in Psychology, U. Houston, 1974. Assoc. dir. behavioral ecology project Tex. Inst. Rehab. and Research, 1974-75; asst. prof. dept. psychology U. Kans., 1975-81; assoc. prof. dept. psychology Humboldt State U., Arcata, Calif., 1981—. Mem. Am. Psychol. Assn., Environ. Design Research Assn. Contbr. numerous articles to profl. jours. Home: 1547 S Street Eureka CA 95501 Office: Dept Psychology Humboldt State U Arcata CA 95521

CAMPBELL, DAVID PETER, pediatric surgeon; b. Schenectady, N.Y., Apr. 3, 1936; s. Peter H. and Elizabeth J. (Schiels) C.; B.S., Union Coll., 1959; M.D., U. Rochester, 1964; m. Marjorie E. Jewett, Aug. 29, 1959; children—Susan, Elizabeth, Rebecca, Jennifer. Intern, Yale-New Haven Hosp., New Haven, Conn., 1964-65; resident, 1965-66, 68-70; resident Children's Meml. Hosp., Chgo., 1970-72; practice medicine specializing in pediatric surgery, Oklahoma City, 1972-76, Hilo, Hawaii, 1976-78, Tucson, Ariz., 1978—; asso. prof. surgery and pediatrics U. Okla., Health Scis. Center, Oklahoma City, 1972-76, chief of pediatric surgery, 1974-76; chief of surgery Hilo (Hawaii) Hosp., 1976-78; adj. asso. prof. surgery U. Ariz. Med. Center, Tucson, 1978—. Served with M.C., USAF, 1966-68. Diplomate Am. Bd. Surgery. Fellow A.C.S., Am. Acad. Pediatrics; mem. Am. Pediatric Surg. Assn., AMA. Contbr. chpts. in field to med. texts; contbr. articles on pediatric surgery to profl. jours. Home: 4130 N Cerro De Falcon Tucson AZ 85718 Office: 5402 E Grant Rd Bldg K Tucson AZ 85712

CAMPBELL, DONALD MILLER, leasing company executive; b. Lincoln, Nebr., Oct. 18, 1939; s. John Miller and Doris Andrews C.; student Doane Coll., 1957-59; m. Virginia Schilling, Aug. 13, 1960; children—Jeffrey Erle, Brian Scott. B.S. in Engring., U. Nebr., 1962; M.B.A., Stanford U., 1965. Planning coordinator Boise Cascade Corp., Idaho, 1965-67; prodn. mgr. Finnigan Corp., Palo Alto, Calif., 1967-68; treas. Memorex Corp., Santa Clara, Calif., 1968-76; v.p. fin. ICD Leasing Group, Inc., Palo Alto, 1976-78; pres. Sequoia Capital Corp., Palo Alto, 1978-79, 80—; v.p., treas. Memorex Fin. Co., Sunnyvale, Calif., 1979-80; sr. v.p., chief fin. officer Magnuson Computer Systems, Inc., 1982-83. Mem. Fin. Execs. Inst., Am. Assn. Equipment Lessors. Office: 5 Palo Alto Sq Suite 1022 Palo Alto CA 94304

CAMPBELL, ETTA ELAINE, accountant; b. Lake Thelma, Alta., Can., Mar. 11, 1914; d. Roderick and Minnie (Ricketts) McGregor; m. Norman Campbell, Oct. 12, 1944; 1 son, Roderick Bruce. Student Alta. Coll., 1936, Pasadena City Coll., 1963, LaSalle U., 1957-59. C.P.A., Calif. Staff acct. Robert J. Gress, South El Monte, Calif., 1962-66; asst. to controller San Diego Sports Arena and San Diego Gulls, 1966-68; acct. Robert McCulloch C.P.A., Palm Springs, Calif., 1968-69; acct., prin., treas. Maryanov Madsen Gordon Campbell P.C., Palm Springs, Calif., 1969—. Bd. dirs., treas. Palm Springs Desert Mus. Mem. Calif. Soc. C.P.A.s, Am. Inst. C.P.A.s, Nat. Assn. Estate Planning Councils. Republican. Presbyterian. Clubs: Soroptimist (dir.), Order Eastern Star. Home: 74072 Mercury Circle W Palm Desert CA 92260 Office: 801 E Tahquitz St McCallum Palm Springs CA 92262

CAMPBELL, FREDERICK HOLLISTER, lawyer; b. Somerville, Mass., June 14, 1923; s. George Murray and Irene Ivers (Smith) C.; A.B., Dartmouth, 1944, J.D., Northwestern U., 1949; postgrad. Indsl. Coll. Armed Forces, 1961-62, m. Amy Holding Strohm, Apr. 14, 1951; 1 dau., Susan Hollister. Served with USMCR, 1944-46; joined USMC, 1950, advanced through grades to lt. col., 1962; admitted to Ill. bar, 1950, U.S. Supreme Ct. bar, 1967, Colo. bar, 1968; judge adv. USMC, Camp Lejeune, N.C., Korea, Parris Island, S.C., El Toro, Calif., Vietnam, Washington, 1950-67; asso. editor Callaghan and Co., Chgo., 1949-50; practice law, Colorado Springs, Colo., 1968—, partner firm Gibson, Gerdes and Campbell, 1969-79, Frederick H. Campbell, P.C., 1980—. Mem. Estate Planning Council, Colorado Springs, 1971—, v.p., 1977-78. Republican precinct committeeman, 1971—; del. Colo. Rep. State Conv., 1972, 74, 76, 80, alt., 1978; trustee Frontier Village Found., 1971-77; bd. dirs. Rocky Mountain Nature Assn., 1975—, pres., 1979—. Mem. Colo. (statutory revision and forms standardization coms. 1972-75, fee arbitration com. 1976-79), El Paso County (legis. com. 1971-73, membership com. 1973, fee arbitration com. 1976-79) bar assns., Internat. Soc. for Japanese Philately (dir. 1966—), Am. Arbitration Assn., Phi Alpha Theta. Congregationalist. Club: Kiwanis (lt. gov. Rocky Mountain Dist. 1973-74, pres. Rampart Range Club 1970-71), Author: John's American Notary and Commissioner of Deeds Manual, 1950. Contbr. articles to profl. jours. Home: 2707 Holiday Ln Colorado Springs CO 80909 Office: Mining Exchange Bldg Colorado Springs CO 80903

CAMPBELL, FREMONT LEE, lawyer; b. Tacoma, Aug. 24, 1923; s. Fremont C. and Dora B. (Payn) C.; m. Helen Veatch, July 28, 1950; children—Susan L., Scott F., David P. Bar: Wash., 1950. Atty. Md. Casualty Co., Seattle, 1950-51; ptnr. Karr, Tuttle, Koch, Campbell, Mawer and Morrow, Seattle, 1951—, pres., mng. dir., 1973—; chmn. Wash. State Jud. Qualifications Commn., 1981-82. Active in local politics, Clyde Hill, Wash., 1951-73. Served to 1st lt. U.S. Army, 1943-46. Mem. ABA, Wash. State Bar Assn. (award of merit, 1980, bd. govs. 1979-82), Seattle-King County Bar Assn. (pres. 1977-78), Am. Coll. Trial Lawyers, Internat. Acad. Trial Lawyers. Republican. Clubs: Rainier (Seattle), Overlake Golf and Country (Bellevue, Wash.) Author: Annotated Aviation Policy, 1972. Home: 7871 NE 21st St Bellevue WA 98004 Office: Karr Tuttle Koch Campbell Mawer and Morrow 1111 3d Ave Suite 2500 Seattle WA 98101

CAMPBELL, JAMES WILLIAM, dairy farmer, management consultant; b. Rupert, Idaho, Feb. 26, 1944; s. Frank S. and Lula H. C.; m. Carol Moffitt; children—James Andrew, Sean William, Victoria. B.A. in Edn., Ariz. State U. Real estate salesman, v.p. C & A Investment Co., 1967-72; exec. v.p., 1976-80; pres. United Phoenix Co.; owner, mgr. dairy farm, Gilbert, Ariz. Dist. chmn. Tempe Dist. Boy Scouts Am., mem. Theodore Roosevelt Council; mem. council bd., sectional bus. adv. bd. Republican Presdl. Task Force. Mormon. Office: PO Box 1300 Gilbert AZ 85234

CAMPBELL, JOHN OWEN, physicist, electronics engr.; b. Louisville, July 19, 1919; s. Morton Reck and Lillian Mary (Wood) C.; B.S., Ga. Inst. Tech., 1941; postgrad. U. Calif., 1945-47, Georgetown U., 1948-49; m. Virginia Ann Maier, June 27, 1959; children—John Owen, Virginia, James, Randolph, Stephen, Mary. Test engr. Gen. Electric Co., Schenectady, 1941-42; with Bur. Ships, USN, 1942-43, Bell Aircraft Corp., Marietta, Ga., 1943-44, Tenn. Eastman Corp., Oak Ridge, 1944-45; research engr. Hughes Aircraft Co., Culver City, Calif., 1949-52; project engr. Bendix Aviation Corp., North Hollywood, Calif., 1952-54; research scientist Lockheed Missiles & Space Div., Van Nuys, Calif., 1954-56; exec. v.p. Aerosystronics Corp., Los Angeles, 1956-59; sr. project engr. TRW Systems, Inc., Redondo Beach, Calif., 1959-63; ind. sci. and engring. cons., Los Angeles, 1963—. Served with USMCR, 1943. Mem. N.Y. Acad. Scis. Patentee in field. Contbr. articles to profl. publs. Address: 15955 Community St Sepulveda CA 91343

CAMPBELL, KATHLEEN QUINN, psychotherapist; b. Scottsbluff, Nebr., Aug. 31, 1949; d. Dale H. and Marabelle (Woodring) Quinn; m. Michael C. Campbell, Mar. 22, 1969; children—Joshua, Sarah. B.S., Colo. State U., 1971; M.A., Western State Coll., 1977. Dir. Vol. Counseling Services Inc., Gunnison, Colo., 1975-76; asst. adminstr. Yellowstone Boys and Girls Ranch, Billings, Mont., 1978-82; self-employed psychotherapist, Billings, 1982—. Bd. dirs. Community Day Care, Mont. Criminal Justice Coalition. Mem. Am. Personnel and Guidance Assn., Nat. Assn. Social Workers. Home: 2925 Cactus Dr Billings MT 59102 Office: 2520 17th St W Billings MT 59102

CAMPBELL, LORENE ANN, paper co. exec.; b. Glendale, Calif., Nov. 5, 1946; d. Clarence Clarke and Eleanor Elizabeth (Starr) Campbell; A.A., Los Angeles Valley Coll., 1967; student Loyola Marymount U., Los Angeles, 1976-78; m. Bronson Halstead Purdy, Jr., Sept. 9, 1979. Editor employee pubs. Xerox Data Systems, El Segundo, Calif., 1967-70; staff interface M/D Systems, Los Angeles, 1970-71; publ. services mgr. HMO Internat., Los Angeles, 1972-75; communications specialist Title Ins. & Trust Co., Los Angeles, 1975-77; owner MCG Communications, Los Angeles, 1977-81; pres., owner Tewkesbury Paper Co., Inc., Rolling Hills Estates, Calif., 1981—. Vol., Los Angeles Inst. Contemporary Art, 1974-75; Recs. for the Blind, 1975-76. Office: Tewkesbury Paper Co Inc 550 Deep Valley Dr Rolling Hills Estates CA 90274

CAMPBELL, MAYNARD THOMAS, former counselor; b. Atlanta, Ohio, Mar. 23, 1917; s. James Wiley and Florence (Thomas) C.; cert. Capital U., 1937; B.S., Ohio State U., 1942; M. Ed., U. Ariz. at Tucson, 1952, Ed.D., 1967; m. Shirley I. Hare, July 14, 1960; stepchildren—Michael R. Hare, Kathleen D. Rogers, Kevin S. Hare. Tchr., Salt Creek Twp. Schs., Pickaway County, Ohio, 1937-40; tchr.-prin. Venice (Ohio) Elem. Sch., 1942-44, Sasebo (Japan) Dependents Sch., 1954-55, Upper Secondary Comml. Japanese High Sch., Sasebo, 1954-55; tchr. counselor Tucson Pub. Schs., 1944-81. Mem. NEA (life), Ariz. Edn. Assn., Tucson Edn. Assn., Am. Personnel and Guidance Assn., Ariz. Counselors Assn., George Washington Masonic Nat. Meml. Assn. (life), Pickaway County (Ohio) Hist. Soc., So. Ariz. Polit. Action Com., Phi Delta Kappa (life, pres. chpt. 1965-66). Unitarian Universalist. Club: Masons. Author: Role Concept and Functions of Counselors in Arizona, 1968; Campbell, Evans, Hosler and Thomas Family Trees of Ohio, 1973. Home: 1310 Avenida Sirio Tucson AZ 85710

CAMPBELL, MILDRED WASSON, health care exec.; b. Muskogee, Okla., May 1, 1926; d. Clement W. and Goldie Sybil (Jones) Wasson; student Northeastern State U., Tahlequah, Okla., 1944-46; m. Bruce L. Campbell, Mar. 24, 1973; children—Linda A. Trujillo, Carl W. Lagoni. Gen. mgr. claims dept. Blue Shield Calif., 1970-73; exec. sec. inservice dept. and infection control dept. Bannock Meml. Hosp., Pocatello, Idaho, 1975-77; profl. relations rep., mktg. rep., officer mgr. Southeastern Idaho region Blue Shield Idaho, Pocatello, 1977—; lectr. S. Idaho Coll.; owner Serenity Studio; mem. orientation staff Idaho State U., other Idaho State facilities. Mem. Bus. and Profl. Women (treas.), Nat. Assn. Female Execs., Profl. Women's Network, Twin Falls Networking, Aircraft Owners and Pilots Assn., Greater Pocatello C. of C., Ninety-Nines (membership chmn.). Seventh-day Adventist. Author Grandma Puddin children's books. Home: Route 1 Box 340 McCammon ID 83250 Office: PO Box 2334 Blue Shield Idaho Pocatello ID 83201

CAMPBELL, ROBERT ALLEN, computer scientist, consultant; b. Afton, Lincoln, Wyo., Dec. 27, 1942; s. Allen Ernest and Ellen (Pearson) C.; m. Susan Vanilleer Shafer, Jan. 27, 1967; children—Cristine, Robert Glen, Cindalee, Scott O'Brian, Dustin Troy. B.S. in Stats., Brigham Young U., 1968, M.S. in Stats., 1970; Ph.D. in Stats. and Computer Sci., Kans. State U., 1973. Cert. computer programmer Inst. Cert. Computer Profls. Actuarial programmer Pacific Mut. Life, Los Angeles, 1968; statistician Hill AFB, Utah, 1969; environ. data analyst Kennecott Copper Corp., Salt Lake City, 1970; programmer Great Western Sugar, Longmont, Colo., 1971; asst. prof. computer sci., Kearney (Nebr.) State Coll., 1973-75; asst. prof. stats., No. Ariz. U., Flagstaff, 1975-81; software engr. Abacus Programming Corp., Los Angeles, 1981; assoc. prof. computer sci. Montana State U., Bozeman, 1981-83; assoc. prof. computer sci. Utah State U., Logan, 1983—; pres. Computer Software Cons., cons. Superior Info. Services, Idaho Falls, Idaho, NSF grantee, 1978. Mem. Mont. Acad. Sci. (sect. v.p.), Statis. Assn. (com. on coms. 1980-83) Assn. Computing Machinery, Assn., Sunstone Found., B.H. Roberts Soc., Sigma Xi. Republican. Mormon. Author numerous manuals on computer use and data analysis. Office: Dept Computer Sci Utah State U Logan UT 84322

CAMPBELL, ROBERT BRAUN, management systems analyst; b. Battle Creek, Mich., July 15, 1917; s. Thomas Dewitt and Maria Sophia (Braun) C.; student Ventura Coll., 1959-60, Orange Coast Coll., 1972-73, U. Calif.-Fullerton, 1975; m. Beulah Mae Landis, June 25, 1937 (dec.); children—David Rolland, Susan Marie, Bruce Allan; m. 2d, Jane Ann Boulware, Oct. 10, 1963. Material mgmt. analyst and tng. supr. Ford Motor Co., Dearborn, Mich., 1937-48; mem. staff to exec. mgmt. McCulloch Corp., Los Angeles, 1949-55; ordained to ministry Methodist Ch., 1958; minister edn., Santa Paula, pastor Shandon and San Miguel, Calif. in the So. Calif., Nev. Conf., 1958-62; nat. mgmt. systems coordinator R.J. Reynolds, Inc., N.Y.C., 1964-70; methods engring. analyst nuclear ops. So. Calif. Edison Co., Los Angeles, 1971-77, research and devel. methods analyst, 1977-79, sr. staff analyst/coordinator advanced engring., 1980—; cons., speaker indsl. cos., univs., profl. assns.; condr. tng. courses. Commr. Boy Scouts Am., Detroit, 1942-48; chaplain Ventura County (Calif.) Fire Dept., 1958-59, San Luis Obispo County (Calif.) Fire Dept., 1961-62. Served with U.S. Army, 1945-46. Mem. Assn. for Systems Mgmt. (pres. Orange County chpt. 1967, dir. western systems conf. 1968, 69, div. dir. 1970, 71, 72, gen. chmn. western systems conf. 1971, internat. committeeman 1970, 73; merit award 1971, achievement award 1973, Disting. Service award as Man of Year, Atlanta 1978). Author: The Secretary's Handbook, 1974; The Forms Control Function, 1975; Analyzing Systems Analysts, 1976; Standardizing Procedure Documentation, 1976. Home: 453 Baywood Dr Newport Beach CA 92660 Office: PO Box 800 Room 405 Rosemead CA 91770

CAMPBELL, SARAH ANN, data processing manager; b. Pomona, Calif., Nov. 16, 1949; d. Richard Sewall and Dorothy Jean (Thomason) Campbell; m. Howard Archie McDaniel, May 8, 1976 (div.). Student Colo. State U., 1967-68; B.A. in Applied Physics and Info. Scis., U. Calif.-San Diego, 1972; postgrad. Pepperdine U., 1982—. Sr. sci. programmer, Sperry Univac, San Diego, also Blue Bell, Pa., 1973-75, sr. systems analyst, 1975-77, sci. programmer, 1977-80; tng. specialist, sr. systems analyst Datagraphix, Inc., San Diego, 1980-81; instr. U. Calif. extension, San Diego, 1980-81; mgr. systems and programming Pepperdine U., Malibu, Calif., 1981—; cons. Computer Software Services; instr. microcomputer usage Pepperdine U. Nat. Summer Computer Literacy Inst. Speaker San Diego Woman's Opportunity Week, 1980-81. Mem. Am. Mgmt. Assn., Assn. for Computing Machinery, Data Processing Mgmt. Assn., IEEE, Mensa. Office: Pepperdine Univ Systems and Planning 24255 Pacific Coast Hwy Malibu CA 90265

CAMPBELL, SHELLEY N., interior designer; b. Nelson, B.C., Can., Mar. 29, 1953; d. Douglas Jean O. (Young) C. B.S. in Environ. Design, U. Calif.-Davis, 1975. Showroom mgr. Design-Tex, San Francisco, 1975-76; design supr. Inside Story, San Francisco, 1976-77; v.p. design and mktg. Southwest Bus. Interiors, San Diego, 1977—. Mem. Am. Soc. Interior Designers (pub. relations chmn.), Inst. Bus. Designers (pres.), Young Friends of Symphony. Office: 7480 Convoy Court San Diego CA 92111

CAMPBELL, STEPHANIE MARYLIN, computer consulting company executive; b. Sheffield, Eng., Jan. 28, 1950; came to U.S., 1964, naturalized, 1970; d. Bernard and Denise Rachel (Cowen) Roseby; m. Stephen Douglas Campbell, July 3, 1971, (div. 1973); m. 2d, Richard Randolph Gillock, Oct. 9, 1982. B.A., U. Wash., 1971; M.B.A., Calif. State U.-Fullerton, 1980. Computer analyst Alfred Gobar Assocs., Brea, Calif., 1977-80; systems analyst Real Estate Analysts of Newport, Newport Beach, Calif., 1980-82; owner, mgr. Fin. Computer Services, Mission Viejo, Calif., 1982—. Mem. IEEE Computer Soc., Real Estate Analysts User Group, Assn. Computer Users, LWV. Democrat. Jewish. Contbr. to REANUG. Office: PO Box 3647 Mission Viejo CA 92690

CAMPBELL, WESLEY GLENN, economist, educator; b. Komoka, Ont., Can., Apr. 29, 1924; s. Alfred E. and Delia (O'Brien) C.; B.A., U. Western Ont., 1944; M.A., Harvard U., 1946, Ph.D., 1948; m. Rita Ricardo, Sept. 15, 1946; children—Barbara Campbell Bizewski, Diane Campbell Porter, Nancy. Instr. econs. Harvard U., 1948-51; research economist U.S. C. of C., 1951-54; dir. research Am. Enterprise Assn., 1954-60; dir. Hoover Instn. War, Revolution and Peace, Stanford U., 1960—; program adv. Am. Enterprise Inst. Pub. Policy Research, Washington, 1960—. Co-dir. project on Am. competitive enterprise, fgn. econ. devel. and aid program, spl. com. to study fgn. aid program U.S. Senate, 1956-57; mem. Pres.'s Commn. on White House Fellows, 1969-74, Pres.'s Com. on Sci. and Tech., 1976; mem. Personnel Adv. Com. to Pres., 1980-81; chmn. Pres.'s Intelligence Oversight Bd., 1981—; mem. Pres.'s Fgn. Intelligence Adv. Bd., 1981—; chmn. Am. panel Joint Com. Japan-U.S. Cultural and Ednl. Cooperation, 1983—; chmn. Japan-U.S. Friendship Commn., 1983—; mem. adv. bd. Ctr. for Strategic and Internat. Studies, 1980—; bd. dirs. Hutchins Ctr. Study Democratic Instns., 1981—, Com. on Present Danger, 1976—, NSF, 1972-78; bd. regents U. Calif., 1968—, vice chmn., 1981-82, chmn., 1982-83; trustee Herbert Hoover Presdl. Library Assn.; bd. visitors Bernice P. Bishop Mus. Fellow Royal Econ. Soc.; mem. Am. Econ. Assn., Phila. Soc. (pres. 1965-67), Mont Pelerin Soc. Clubs: Bohemian, Cosmos, Commonwealth (Calif.). Co-author: The American Competitive Enterprise Economy, 1952; editor, prin. author: The Economics of Mobilization and War, 1952; contbr. articles to profl. jours. Office: Hoover Instn Stanford U Stanford CA 94305

CAMPBELL, WILLIS PRESTON, JR., photographer, artist; rental mgr.; b. Portsmouth, Va., May 16, 1945; s. Willis Preston and Dorothy Lee (Eshman) C.; m. Sherelyn Louise Douglas, Dec. 13, 1975; 2 sons, Jonathan, Paul. Student Santa Rosa Jr. Coll., 1963-64; B.A., Westmont Coll., Santa Barbara, Calif., 1967; M.A.U. Calif.-Santa Barbara, 1971. Staff photographer, Westmont Coll., Santa Barbara, 1971-77; owner, photographer, Campbell Photography, Santa Cruz, Calif., 1977—. Mem. Profl. Photographers Assn. Am. (cert. profl. photography), Profl. Photographers Calif., Profl. Photographers Santa Clara Valley and Monterey Bay Area. Republican. Baptist. Contbr. articles to profl. jours. Home: 354 Lee St Santa Cruz CA 95060 Office: 1015 Cedar St Santa Cruz CA 95060

CAMPER, JOHN SAXTON, public relations and marketing executive, consultant; b. Trenton, N.J., Apr. 24, 1929; s. Thomas Emory and Mildred Ruth (Burke) C.; m. Ferne Arlene Clanton; children—Susan Jennifer, John Saxton III. B.S. in History and Econs., U. Nebr., 1968. Enlisted U.S. Army, 1948, commd. to 1st lt., advanced through ranks to maj., 1972, ret., 1972; regional mktg. officer First Bank System, Mont., 1982—; mng. dir. R.A. Howard and Assoc., Helena, Mont., 1983; lectr., instr. mktg. and advt., pub. relations. Decorated Legion of Merit. Mem. Helena Advt. Fedn. (1st pres., founder). Republican. Methodist. Club: Rotary Internat.

CAMPHAUSEN, FRED HOWARD, physicist; b. Los Angeles, Aug. 23, 1933; s. Fred Henry and Eloise (Ingebretsen) C.; B.A. in Physics, U. Calif., 1961; m. Martina Simon, Apr. 2, 1956 (div.); children—Raymond Thomas, Karin Maria; m. 2d, Marianna P. Dembinski, Aug. 2, 1980. With Naval Weapons Center, China Lake, Calif., 1961—, physicist, project mgr., 1980—; owner, mgr. Sierra Desert Guides (Mountain High, Ltd.), 1980—. Chmn. br. instrs. com. China Lake Mountain Rescue Group, ARC, 1970—. Served with U.S. Army, 1953-56. Mem. Naval Aviation Execs. Inst., Am. Alpine Club, Sierra Club. Republican. Roman Catholic. Club: Vägmarken. Contbr. tech. writings to publs. Home: 824 W Graaf Ridgecrest CA 93555 Office: Naval Weapons Center China Lake CA 93555

CAMPION, ROBERT THOMAS, mfg. co. exec.; b. Mpls., June 23, 1921; s. Leo P. and Naomi (Revord) C.; student Loyola U., Chgo., 1939-41, 46-48; m. Wilhelmina Knapp, June 8, 1946; 1 son, Michael. With Alexander Grant & Co., Chgo., 1946-57, partner, 1954-57; with Lear Siegler, Inc., Santa Monica, Calif., 1957—, pres. chief exec. officer, dir., 1971—, chmn., 1974—. Served with AUS, 1942-46. C.P.A., Ill. Mem. Am. Inst. C.P.A.'s, Ill. Soc. C.P.A.'s. Republican. Clubs: Bel Air (Cal.) Country; Metropolitan (N.Y.C.); Jonathan (Los Angeles); Burning Tree (Md.). Home: 4188 High Valley Rd Encino CA 91316 Office: 2850 Ocean Park Dr Santa Monica CA 90406

CAMPO, FRANK PHILIP, composer, educator; b. N.Y.C., Feb. 4, 1927; s. Philip and Charlotte (Rothe) C.; Mus.B., U. So. Calif., 1950, Mus.M., 1953, D. Mus. Arts, 1968; m. Leda LaPeyre, July 10, 1955; 1 son, Darius. Arranger, performer clarinet, 1943—; mem. faculty U. So. Calif., Los Angeles, 1966-68, mem. faculty Calif. State U., Fullerton, 1967-68, prof. composition, chmn. composition-theory dept., 1968—. Served with AUS, 1945-47. Recipient Composers award Broadcast Music Inc., 1958, Screen Composers Assn. award, 1966. Fulbright scholar, 1957. Mem. Internat. Soc. Contemporary Music, Nat. Assn. Am. Composers and Condrs., A.S.C.A.P., Pi Kappa Lambda. Composer: Bassoon Concerto, 1966; Madrigals for Brass Quintet, 1970; Dialogues II for Orchestra, 1971; Cantata No. 3, 1972; Sinfonia Sacra, 1974. Home: 12336 Milbank St Studio City CA 91604 Office: Dept Music Calif State U 18111 Nordhoff St Northridge CA 91324

CAMPUS, ROGER ARTHUR, electronics company executive; b. Houston, Mar. 3, 1946; s. Arthur Roger and Marian (Lang) C. B.A., U. Calif.-Santa Barbara, 1969; J.D., U.S. Internat. U., 1972. Atty., USDA, Washington, 1972; div. legal counsel Cost of Living Council, Washington, 1973; mgmt. assoc. Office Mgmt. and Budget, 1973-77; spl. asst. to asst. dir. for policy, planning and evaluation Community Services Adminstrn., Washington, 1977; pres. Campos Foods, Inc., Modesto, Calif., 1977-79; pres. Roger A. Campos & Assocs., Modesto, Calif., 1979-81; pres. Pacific Internat. Commerce & Planning Co., Modesto, Calif., 1981-82; pres., chmn. bd. Premier Electronics Inc., Phoenix, 1982—. Office: 2917 N 33d Ave Phoenix AZ 85017

CANADY, DARRYL EUGENE, advertising executive; b. Pasadena, Calif., Jan. 1, 1935; s. John E. and Blanche A. (Albright) C.; m. Jody Sue Nielsen; children—Brad E., Cyndia A. A.A., Riverside Coll., 1974. Pres. Darryl Canady & Assocs. Inc., Seattle. Served with USN. Mem. Nat. Yellow Pages Pubs. Assn., Sales Mktg. Execs. Clubs: Seattle Yacht, Lions (Queen Anne-Magnolia). Office: 3520 27th Pl W Suite 423 Seattle WA 98199

CANCIAN, FRANCESCA MICAELA, sociology educator; b. N.Y.C., Oct. 31, 1937; d. Pierre Rudolf and Natascha Rose (Hirschberg) Wendel; m. Frank Cancian, Oct. 30, 1959; m. Maria Michele, Steven Alexander. Student Reed Coll., 1955-58; Ph.D., Harvard U., 1963. Lectr. social relations Harvard U., 1963-64; research assoc. Stanford (Calif.) U., 1964-65; asst. prof. child devel. and family relations Cornell U., Ithaca, N.Y., 1966-69; asst. prof. sociology Stanford (Calif.) U., 1969-76; prof. U. Calif.-Irvine, 1976—; cons. Stanford Research Inst., Prentice-Hall

Co. NIMH fellow, 1959-63, 64-66; NSF grantee, 1966-70; fellow Ctr. Advanced Study Behavioral Scis., 1970-71. Mem. Women's Equity Action League, NOW, Sociologists for Women in Soc. (pres. chpt. 1975-76), Phi Beta Kappa. Author: What are Norms? A Study of Beliefs and Action in a Maya Community, 1975. Home: 2327 Port Lerwick Pl Newport Beach CA 92660 Office: Sch Social Scis Univ Calif Irvine CA 92717

CANCIAN, FRANCIS ALEXANDER, anthropology educator; b. Stafford Springs, Conn., Aug. 14, 1934. A.B., Wesleyan U., 1956; Ph.D. in Social Anthropology, Harvard U., 1963. Reporter, photographer Providence Jour. Co., 1957-58; instr. social anthropology, dept. social relations Harvard U., Cambridge, Mass., 1963-64; asst. prof. anthropology Stanford (Calif.) U., 1964-66, prof., 1969-76, chmn. dept., 1974-76; assoc. prof. anthropology Cornell U., Ithaca, N.Y., 1966-69; prof. anthropology U. Calif.-Irvine, 1976—, chmn. social relations program, 1979-81, mem. numerous univ. coms.; lectr. and cons. in field. Fulbright fellow, Italy, 1956-57; Fgn. Area fellow Latin Am. Studies, 1966-68; Ctr. Advanced Study Behavioral Scis. fellow, 1970-71; NIMH grantee, 1963-64; Wenner-Gren Found. grantee, 1971, 1981; Ford Found. grantee, 1975-77; Rockefeller Found. grantee, 1976-78. Fellow Am. Anthrop. Assn., Soc. Applied Anthropology; mem. AAAS, Am. Ethnol. Soc., Culture and Agr., Pacific Coast Council Latin Am. Studies, Rural Sociol. Soc., Soc. Econ. Anthropology (dir.; program com. 1982-83). Author: Economics and Prestige in a Maya Community: The Religious Cargo System in Zinacantan, 1965; Change and Uncertainty in a Peasant Economy: The Maya Corn Farmers of Zinacantan, 1972; Another Place: Photographs of a Maya Community, 1974; The Innovator's Situation: Upper Middle Class Conservatism in Agricultural Communities, 1979; editorial bd. Reviews in Anthropology, 1973-78; contbr. numerous articles to profl. jours. Home: 2327 Port Lerwick Pl Newport Beach CA 92660 Office: Sch Social Sciences U Calif-Irvine CA 92717

CANDELARIA, J. E., bank exec.; b. Colo., Dec. 5, 1931; m. Julie E. Candelaria, Aug. 18, 1956; children—Erin, Eric, Karla. Grad., Sch. Banking, Stanford U. Distr. br. mgr., Pacific Fin. Corp., 1954-66; sr. loan, credit officer Union Bank, 1966-75; v.p. sr. credit officer, Commonwealth Bank, Hawthorne, Calif., 1975-78, exec. v.p., 1978-79, pres., chief exec. officer, dir., 1979-81; vice chmn. bd. Commonwealth Thrift & Loan, Torrance, Calif., 1981—. Bd. dirs. East Los Angeles Community Union; active Community Devel. Corp. Served with U.S. Army, 1952-54. Republican. Presbyterian. Office: 3425 Carson St Hawthorne CA 90503

CANEER, WILLIAM THOMAS, geologist; b. Senath, Mo., Mar. 22, 1928; s. William Thomas and Bertha Christina (Weaver) C.; B.S. in Geology, U. Mo., 1952, M.S. (A.P. Green fellow), 1956; m. Carolynn Jo Davis, May 10, 1952; children—Mary Kathleen, Cheryl Lynn. Geologist, Gulf Research and Devel. Co., Pitts., 1956-61; lab. mgr. A.P. Green Refractories, Mexico, Mo., 1961-67; asst. mgr. mining Colo. Sch. Mines Research Inst., Golden, 1967-75, mgr. bus. devel., 1975—. Served with AUS, 1946-47. Mem. AIME, Soc. Mktg. Profl. Services, Rocky Mountain Assn. Geologists, Am. Assn. Petroleum Geologists, Colo. Mining Assn. Republican. Author papers in field. Home: 307 Lookout View Ct Golden CO 80401 Office: PO Box 112 Golden CO 80402

CANEPA, CARLOS YORI, architect, interior designer; b. Lima, Peru, Oct. 5, 1945; s. Hector Alfredo Campodonico and Isabel Ringold (Yori) C. B. Arch., Universidad Nacional De Ingeniería, Lima, Peru, 1969. Freelance architect, Lima, Peru, Caracas, Venezuela, Riyadh, Saudi Arabia, until 1979; interior designer architect Ciurlizza Maurer Co., Lima, until 1982; interior designer, architect Kasdens Interiors, Torrance, until Calif., 1980, Recipient award Design Hogar SA, Lima. Mem. Peruvian Soc. Architects, Colegio De Arquitectos Del Perú, Am. So. Interior Designers (assoc.). Author: History of Architecture in Lima, 1900-1930, 1970; Interior Design in Lima, Peru, 1968-1980. Home: 2105 Rockefeller Ln 7 Redondo Beach CA 91278 also 300 The Village Suite 215 Redondo Beach CA 90278

CANFIELD, GRANT WELLINGTON, JR., orgn. exec.; b. Los Angeles, Nov. 28, 1923; s. Grant Wellington and Phyllis Marie (Westland) C.; B.S., U. So. Calif., 1949, M.B.A., 1958; m. Virginia Louise Bellinger, June 17, 1945; 1 dau., Julie Marie. Personnel and indsl. relations exec., Los Angeles area, 1949-55; employee relations cons., regional mgr. Mchts. and Mfrs. Assn. Los Angeles, 1955-60; v.p., orgnl. devel. cons. Hawaii Employers Council, Honolulu, 1960-75; pres., dir. Hawaiian Ednl. Council, 1969—; exec. v.p. Hawaii Garment Mfrs. Assn., 1965-75, Assn. Hawaii Restaurant Employers, 1966-75; exec. dir. Hawaii League Savs. Assns., 1971-78; exec. dir. Pan-Pacific Surg. Assn., 1980-81, exec. v.p., 1982-83; lectr. orgn. devel. and human resources mgmt. Bd. dirs. Hawaii Restaurant Assn., 1974-76, bd. dirs. Hawaii chpt. Nat. Assn. Accountants, 1963-67, nat. dir., 1965-66; bd. dirs. Vol. Service Bur. Honolulu, 1965-66, pres., 1966-68; bd. dirs. Vol. Info. and Referral Service Honolulu, 1972-75, Goodwill Vocat. Tng. Centers of Hawaii, 1973-81, Girl Scout council Pacific, 1961-65, 71-72; bd. dirs. Hawaii Com. Alcoholism, 1962-71, co-chmn., 1964-68; pres., dir. Friends of Punahou Sch., 1972-75; mem. community adv. bd. Jr. League Hawaii, 1968-70; exec. bd. Aloha council Boys Scouts Am., 1962-65; bd. regents Chaminade U., 1982—. Served to 1st lt., inf. AUS, 1943-46. Decorated Purple Heart, Combat Inf. badge. Mem. Am. Soc. Assn. Execs. (cert. assn. exec.), Am. Soc. Tng. and Devel., Internat. Assn. Agrl. Economists, Am. Agrl. Econs. Assn., Am. Soc. Personnel Adminstrn., Rotarian, Mason. Clubs: Pacific (Honolulu) Kaneohe Yacht; Plaza (Honolulu). Co-author: Resource Manual for Public Collective Bargaining, 1973. Home: 1605 Mokulua Dr Kailua HI 96734 Office: 1164 Bishop St Honolulu HI 96813

CANFIELD, JACK, motivational educator; b. Fort Worth, Tex., Aug. 19, 1944; s. Elmer Elwyn Canfield and Ellen (Taylor) Angelis; m. Judy Sue Ohlbaum, July 1, 1973; m. 2d, Georgia Lee Noble, Sept. 9, 1978; children—Oran David, Kyle Dania. B.A., Harvard U., 1966; M.Ed., U. Mass., 1973; Ph.D., Koh-e-nor U., 1981. Dir. tchr. tng. program Job Corps Ctr., Clinton, Iowa, 1968-69; assoc. dir. achievement motivation programs W. Clement & Jessie V. Stone Found., Chgo., 1969-70; assoc. dir. Combined Motivation Edn. Systems, Chgo., 1970; founder, dir. New Eng. Ctr., Amherst, Mass., 1971-77; dir. Inst. Wholistic Edn., Amherst, 1977-81; co-dir. Ctr. Whole Being, Amherst, 1977-79; dir. ednl. services Insight Transformational Seminars, Santa Monica, Calif., 1981—; bd. advs. Nat. Humanistic Edn. Ctr., Ky. Ctr. Psychosynthesis, Holistic Edn. Network, Kripalu Ctr. Hollstic Health, Kapp Ctr. Continuing Edn., Children's Media Workshop. Mem. Calif. Democratic party ednl. platform com. Recipient U.S. Jaycees Outstanding Young Men of Am. award, 1978. Mem. Assn. Humanistic Edn. (pres. 1978-79), Assn. Humanistic Psychology, Assn. Transpersonal Psychology, Am. Assn. for Study Mental Imagery, Ednl. Leadership Council of Am., Internat. Imagery Assn., Nat. Speakers Assn., Confluent Edn. Devel. and Research Ctr. Author: About Me, 1970; (with Harold Wells) 100 Ways to Enhance Self-Concept in the Classroom 1976; A Guide to Resources in Humanistic and Transpersonal Education, 1977; contbr. to Yearbook in Humanistic and Transpersonal Education, 1977; editorial bd. Jour. Humanistic Edn., Psychosynthesis Digest, Holistic Edn. Network newsletter. Home: 17156 Palisades Circle Pacific Palisades CA 90272 Office: 2101 Wilshire Blvd Santa Monica CA 90403

CANNALTE, DONALD CHARLES, university public relations administrator, consultant; b. Chgo., Apr. 13, 1931; s. Santrew C. and Dagny (Miller) C.; m. Bonnie June Young, June 6, 1957 (dec.); children—Douglas, Mark, Ross; m. 2d, Gwinavere A. Johnston, Apr. 4, 1981; stepchildren—G. G., Gabriel. B.A. in History, Beloit Coll., 1953. Reporter, Beloit (Wis.) Daily News, 1953; Alhambra (Calif.) Post Advocate, 1956-57; picture editor Pacific Stars & Stripes, Tokyo, 1957-60; pub. relations rep. United Airlines, Los Angeles, 1960-62, regional mgr. pub. relations, Denver, 1962-81; dir. pub. relations U. Colo., Boulder, 1981—; cons. in pub. relations; dir. The Johnston Group, Denver. Served to cpl. U.S. Army, 1953-56. Recipient Wright Bros. award Colo. Aviation Hist. Soc., 1980. Mem. Pub. Relations Soc. Am. (chmn. Colo. Eligibility com., exec. bd. ednl. inst. sect.), Colo. Press Assn., Council for Advancement and Support Edn., Boulder C. of C. (univ. relations com.), Denver C. of C., Denver Press Club. Republican. Club: Internat. Athletic. Home: 717 Monaco Pkwy Denver CO 80220 Office: Office of Pub Relations U Colo 914 Broadway St Campus Box 16 Boulder CO 80309

CANNELL, STEPHEN JOSEPH, TV producer; b. Los Angeles, Feb. 5, 1943; s. Joseph Knapp and Carolyn (Baker) C.; B.A., U. Oreg., 1964; m. Marcia C. Finch, Aug. 8, 1964; children—Chelsea, Tawnia. Creator, producer Baa Baa Blacksheep, Stone, Richie Brockelman, The Duke; creator Baretta; creator, writer, producer Rockford Files, Universal Studios; creator, writer, exec. producer Tenspeed and Brownshoe, The Greatest American Hero, The A-Team; now chief exec. officer Stephen J. Cannell Prodns., Los Angeles. Recipient Emmy award; Mystery Writers award; Writers Guild awards. Mem. Producers Guild, Dirs. Guild, Writers Guild. Episcopalian. Office: 5555 Melrose Ave Los Angeles CA 90038

CANNISTRACI, DIANE FRANCES, sales manager; b. Bronx, N.Y., Jan. 9, 1950; s. John Albert and Dorothy Cannistraci; m. Stephen William Burton, June 12, 1971 (div.). Student Orlando Jr. Coll., 1968-70. Bookkeeper, Barnett Bank of Winter Park (Fla.), 1970-73; adminstrv. asst. United Horticulture, Apopka, Fla., 1973-75; mgr. U.S. Life and Credit Co., Orlando, Fla., 1975-77; sales rep. Victor Office Machines, Orlando, 1977-80; eastern sales mgr. Airline Supply/Internat., Wallingford, Conn., 1980—. Republican committeewoman, Huntington, N.Y. Serves with Air N.G., 1981—. Recipient Gold Key award Suffolk County Women Athletic Assn., 1968; All Around Womanhood award PTA, Huntington Station, N.Y., 1968. Mem. Airline Transp. Assn., Electronic Connector Study Group, Italian-Am. Arts and Assistance Council (charter; sec. Huntington Station). Roman Catholic. Home: 581 Crown St Bldg 1 Unit 21 Meriden CT 06450 also 2301 E Del Amo Blvd Compton CA 90220 Office: 165 N Plains Industrial Rd Wallingford CT 06492

CANNON, BARBARA E. M., educational administrator; b. Big Sandy, Tex., Jan. 17, 1936; d. Archie and Jimmie (Jones) C.; m. Rev. Booker T. Anderson, Jr., May 8, 1982 (dec.). B.A. (Theodore Presser Found. scholar), San Francisco State U., 1957, M.A., 1965; M.A., Stanford U., 1975, Ed.D. (Inst. Ednl. Leadership fellow), 1977. Cert. spl. secondary sch. tchr., adminstr., Calif. Tchr., adminstr., staff devel. assoc. Berkeley (Calif.) Pub. Schs., 1958-74; research asst. Stanford Ctr. Research and Devel. in Teaching, Palo Alto, Calif., 1976-77; research assoc. Ctr. Ednl. Research Stanford U., 1977-78; asst. dean fine, applied and lang. arts div. Coll. Alameda (Calif.), 1978-82, asst. dean student services, 1982—; mem. Calif. Community and Jr. Coll. Commn. on Instrn., 1979-81. Bd. dirs. Mozart Festival of Alameda, v.p., 1981; mem. Black Women Organized for Polit. Action, 1981—; mem. Progressive Black Bus. and Profl. Women. Mem. Assn. Calif. Community Coll. Adminstrs., Phi Delta Kappa, Pi Lambda Theta. Methodist. Office: Coll of Alameda 555 Atlantic Ave Alameda CA 94501

CANNON, EARL NELSON, lawyer; b. Delavan, Wis., Jan. 20, 1900; s. Dan E. and Lenora (Nelson) C.; B.S., U. Wis., 1924, LL.B., 1927, J.D., 1966; m. Helen Gibson, July 23, 1926. Atty., law firm Stephens, Cannon & Cooper (now Stephens, Cannon, Bieberstein & Cooper), 1928-53; pres. Yellow Truck Lines, Inc., 1930-45; exec. dir., legal counsel Central States Area Employers Assn., 1940-53; labor counsel Central Motor Freight Assn., 1940-53; v.p. charge personnel and labor relations Greyhound Corp., Chgo., 1952-65. Pres. Idyllwild Property Owners Assn.; dir. Idyllwild County Water Dist. Industry mem. War Labor Bd., 1944-45; industry mem. Nat. WSB, 1946; v.p. Am. Trucking Assn., 1936-46 commr. Riverside County Flood Control and Water Conservation Dist.; mem. adv. com. Hemet-San Jacinto YMCA; bd. dirs. Idyllwild (Calif.) Arts Found., Hemet-San Jacinto YMCA. Mem. Theta Chi, Phi Alpha Delta. Clubs: Executive, Union League (Chgo.); Madison; Indian Wells Country (Palm Desert, Calif.); Palm Springs Country, Tennis (Palm Springs, Calif.); Idyllwild Lions (pres.); Ojai (Calif.) Country; San Jacinto Lions (Zone A chmn.), Sobobe Springs Country Soboba Springs Mens (chmn. membership com.) (San Jacinto, Calif.). Home: 42701 Main St #116 San Jacinto CA 92383 Office: Greyhound Towers Phoenix AZ

CANNON, ELAINE WINIFRED ANDERSON, author, lectr.; b. Salt Lake City, Apr. 9, 1922; d. Aldon Joseph and Minnie (Egan) Anderson; B.S., U. Utah, 1943; m. Donald James Cannon, Mar. 25, 1943; children—James Quayle, Carla, Christine (Mrs. Heber Jacobsen), Su (Mrs. Bryant McOmber), Holly (Mrs. Richard Metcalf), Anthony Joseph. With Deseret News, Salt Lake City, 1943-69, feature writer, columnist, 1944-47, editor teen dept., 1947-69; asso. editor New Era mag., Salt Lake City, 1970-73; asso. editor Era of Youth mag., 1960-70; moderator It's a Date, Sta. KSL-TV, Salt Lake City, 1952-55, Focus on Youth, Sta. KUTV, 1961-65, 67-69, Public Pulse for Youth, Sta. KSL, 1966-67. Instr. continuing edn. Brigham Young U., Provo, Utah, 1958—, U. Utah, Salt Lake City, 1964, Utah State U., Logan, 1968-70. Del. White House Conf. on Children and Youth, 1950-51; mem. adv. bd. Juvenile Ct., Salt Lake City, 1970-71, Boy's Ranch Utah, Salt Lake City, 1966—; mem. spl. program com. Am. Cancer Soc., Salt Lake City, 1965-66. Bd. dirs. Women Unlimited Conv. Program Bur., Salt Lake City; internat. pres. Young Women Ch. Jesus Christ of Latter-day Saints, also mem. coordinating council; bd. dirs. Deseret Gymnasium, Promised Valley Theatre. Recipient 1st prize writing youth div. Nat. Press Women Assn., 1958, service to youth citation Seventeen mag., 1955; named Woman Year, Ricks Coll., 1965, Weber State Coll., 1971, Idaho State U., 1972. Mem. Authors Club, Am. Press Women Assn., Nat. Council Women of U.S.A. (exec. bd. 1979—, v.p.), Mortar Bd., Internat. Platform Assn., Alpha Lambda Delta, Chi Omega. Republican. Mem. Ch. Jesus Christ Latter-day Saints (All-Ch. Honored Woman 1967). Author: Time of Your Life, 1954; Corner on Youth, 1963; Teens and Their Times, 1964; How Glorious is Youth, 1969; A Time for Living; After the Manner of Happiness; It's A Great Idea; Woman, Her Hope and Her Heritage, 1975; Summer of My Content, 1976; The Mighty Change, 1981; Putting Life in Your Life Story, 1981; The Seasoning, 1981. Weekly radio show You and Your World. Home: 1283 E South Temple Salt Lake City UT 84102 Office: 50 E N Temple Salt Lake City UT 84150

CANNON, GEORGE RICHARDS, JR., business executive; b. Pasadena, Calif. Nov. 2, 1942; s. George Richards and Lois Minnie (Eriksson) C.; B.S., Calif. Inst. Tech., 1964; M.S., U. So. Calif., 1974; Candidate in Philosophy, U. Calif., Santa Barbara, 1981; m. Tanja Virginia Larson, Dec. 20, 1969; children—Cynthia Suzanne, Carrie Margaret. Staff systems programmer Fed. Systems div. IBM, Los Angeles, 1966-68, Thailand, 1968-70, Atlantic City, 1970-72, Vandenberg AFB, Calif., 1972-73; program mgr. Logicon Inc., Lompoc, Calif., 1974-79, software tools mgr. strategic and info. systems div., 1979-83; exec. v.p. Utah Computer Industries Inc., St. George, 1983—; tchr., cons. in field. Missionary, Ch. Jesus Christ of Latter-day Saints, Chile, 1964-66, dir. ch. Boy Scout program, 1965-66. Mem. Assn. Computing Machinery, IEEE, Calif. Inst. Tech. Alumni Assn., U. So. Calif. Alumni Assn. Home and Office: 42 Aldebaran Ave Lompoc CA 93436

CANNON, ROSS WARREN, lawyer; b. Butte, Mont., May 1, 1929; s. Paul and Caroline (Duffes) C.; children—Stephanie Suzanne, David Scott, Stacy Michelle. B.A., U. Mont., 1952, LL.B., 1957; LL.M., George Wash. U., 1959. Atty., advisor ICC, Washington, 1957-59; sole practice, Helena, Mont., 1959—. Served to col. USAFR, 1953—. Mem. ABA, Mont. Bar Assn., Assn. Trial Lawyers Am., First Dist. Bar Assn. (Helena, Mont.), Mont. Trial Lawyers Assn. Clubs: Montana, Green Meadow Country (Helena). Home: 705 Touchstone Dr Helena MT 59601 Office: 2031 Eleventh Ave Helena MT 59601

CANNON, SHARON LEE, accountant; b. Vermillion, S.D., Feb. 1, 1947; d. Archie Lorrel and Lillian (Hustrulid) Powell; m. Robert Eugene Cannon, May 12, 1969 (div.). B.S. in Mktg., U. Ariz., 1971, C.P.A., Ariz. 1975. Data processing mgr. Tucson Ariz. Bank, 1971-73; budget analyst Pima County Fin. Dept., Tucson, 1973-76; staff, mgr. Good & Fowler C.P.A.s, San Francisco, 1979-82, ptnr., 1982—. Mem. Am. Inst. C.P.A.s, Calif. State Soc. C.P.A.s, San Francisco C. of C.

CANNON, VANCE CHIPMAN, office equipment co. exec.; b. Los Angeles, Apr. 2, 1939; s. George Quayle and Irene Florence (Chipman) C.; m. Donna Aschenbrenner, July 1, 1961; children—Deborah, Ginni. Student Brigham Young U., Hawaii, 1958-59. Sales rep. Koss Sherry Ltd., Honolulu, 1961-63; sales mgr., 1963-65, pres., 1965-70; pres. Olivetti of Hawaii, Inc., Honolulu, 1970-71; pres. Office Things, Inc., Honolulu, 1970—; dir. Electronic Measurements Corp. Commr., Hawaii Housing Authority, 1981-82; dir. Pacific Fleet Submarine Meml., 1979—; dir., dist. chmn. Aloha council Boy Scouts Am., 1978—. Recipient Silver Beaver award Boy Scouts Am., 1978, Dist. Award of Merit, 1981; Brigham Young U. Alumni Disting. Service award, 1980. Mem. Hawaii Office Machine Dealers Assn., Nat. Office Products Assn., Nat. Office Machine Dealers Assn. Mormon. Clubs: Rotary Club of Honolulu, Oahu Country Club. Home: 1705 Palaau St Honolulu HI 96821 Office: 2340 Kam Hwy Honolulu HI 96819

CANNON, WILLIAM WAREING, mfg. co. exec.; b. Salt Lake City, Apr. 10, 1925; s. Edwin Quayle and Luella (Wareing) C.; m. Margery Sorensen, Sept. 13, 1946; children—Michael, David, Layne, Wendy, Robert, Merilee, Christian, Matthew. B.S.C.E., Ill. Inst. Tech., 1946; M.S., U. Utah, 1950. Instr., U. Utah, 1946-47, 49-51; missionary Ch. of Jesus Christ of Latter-day Saints Ch., Hawaii, 1947-49, pres. Hawaii-Honolulu Mission, 1975-78 (on leave); sec.-treas. Salt Lake Stamp Co., 1951-71, pres., 1971—; v.p. Wram Corp., Salt Lake City, 1980—; dir. S.E. Furniture Co. Mem. Salt Lake City Bd. Edn., 1969-72, v.p., 1971-72; mem. Utah Bd. Edn., 1973-74. Served to ensign USNR, 1943-46; lt. Res. (ret.). Mem. Marking Device Assn. Republican. Clubs: Salt Lake Rotary, Timpanogos (Salt Lake City). Office: 380 West 2d South Salt Lake City UT 84101

CANTAFIO, LEOPOLD JOSEPH, aerospace co. exec.; b. Bklyn., Oct. 23, 1927; s. William Joseph and Anna (D'Auria) C.; student Bklyn. Coll., 1947-48; B.S. in Elec. Engring., U. Ala., 1952; postgrad. U. Pa., 1952-60; M.S. in Systems Mgmt., U. So. Calif., 1971; m. Norma B. Trapani, June 5, 1949; children—Leigh Joseph, Lisa Joan, Alex William. Class A. Engr., RCA, Moorestown, N.J., 1952-60; prin. scientist Raytheon Co., Bedford, Mass., 1960-65; tech. staff Aerospace Corp., El Segundo, Calif., 1965—; lectr., cons. in field. Vice-pres. Acad. Hill Homeowners Assn., 1972—. Served with USNR, 1945-47. Mem. IEEE (sr.), Air Force Assn., U.S. Chess Fedn. (life), Theta Tau. Contbr. author Range Instrumentation, 1967. Inventor in field. Home: 4226 Cartesian Circle Palos Verdes Peninsula CA 90274 Office: TRW One Space Park Redondo Beach CA 90278

CANTERBURY, PATRICIA EZELL, state official; b. Sacramento, Aug. 6, 1939; d. Edmund and Elaine Hope (Ballon) Patterson; m. Richard Allen Canterbury, Dec. 27, 1972. A.A., Sacramento City Coll., 1959; B.A., Sacramento State U., 1960, M.A., 1962, cert. in public and labor mgmt. relations U. Calif.-Davis, 1978. Mktg. statistician Crown Zellerbach, 1969-72; mgmt. analyst State of Calif., Sacramento, 1973-74, legis. analyst and first state murals mgr., 1974-76, program mgr. and first state rehab. ombudsman, 1976-78, first dep. sec. personnel and human services Bus. Transp. and Housing Agy., mem. Gov.'s Cabinet, 1978—; bd. dirs. State Women's Program. No. Calif. affirmative action coordinator Democratic Party, 1981-82; chairperson 4th dist. Arts and Culture Issues Conf., Sacramento; 3d dist. co-chairperson Issues Memphis Mid-Conv., 1980. Recipient Return to the Source award Calif. Assn. Black Sch. Educators, 1981, Outstanding Service to Community award Black Advs. in State Service, 1978, 79. Mem. Black Women's Forum, Black Women's Organized for Polit. Action, Women's Communication Corp., Nat. Women's Polit. Caucus (nat. del. 1979, 81), Sacramento Women's Network, Women's Justice Service, Women in Politics, Sierra Curtis Neighborhood Assn., Sacramento C. of C. (Community Service award 1979), Calif. Coalition for Women in State Service (founder 1975, v.p. 1976-79). Unitarian. Clubs: Zonta, Bus. and Profl. Women's, Comstock. Author books of poetry: S'Hertogenbosch and other Places, 1979, Ragged Wind and Painted Paper Kites, 1983; weaving donated to Sacramento Conv. Center for Adminstrv. Bd. Room. Office: 2570 24th St Sacramento CA 95818 Mailing Address: PO Box 160127 Sacramento CA 95816

CANTILLON, WILLIAM HOUCK, transp. co. exec.; b. Cleve., Sept. 17, 1943; s. Daniel James and Genevieve (Houck) C.; B.S., Case Inst. Tech., 1965; M.B.A., Butler U., 1968; divorced; children—Denice Renee, William Houck II. Coordinator planning parts div. Gen. Motors Corp., Flint, Mich., 1966-72; gen. mgr. Nat. Distbn. Service, Inc., Atlanta, 1972-75, Carson, Calif., 1976; div. mgr. Lyon Moving & Storage Co. subs. Transam. Corp., Los Angeles, 1976-80; gen. mgr. Yowell Transport, Inc., Dayton, Ohio, 1980—. Mem. Am. Mktg. Assn., Nat. Council Phys. Distbn. Mgmt. Republican. Roman Catholic. Club: Rotary. Home: 18681 San Marcos St Fountain Valley CA 92708 Office: 1840 Cardington Rd Dayton OH 45409

CANTIN, ROBERT LEE, manufacturing company communications director; b. Davenport, Iowa, Apr. 22, 1940; s. Adolph Herbert and Lillian (Pue) C.; m. Marsha Anne Reece, Apr. 24, 1965; children—Kimberly Lynne, Jeffrey Robert. B.S. in Journalism, Lewis and Clark Coll., 1962. News rep. Pacific Power & Light Co., Portland, Oreg., 1964-69, news dir., 1970-71, communication services dir., 1972-79; v.p. MARCO-Ideas Unltd., Portland, 1971-72; dir. communications Karsten Mfg. Corp., Phoenix, 1979—; Bd. dirs. Tournament Golf Inc., Portland, 1972—, Phoenix Press Box Assn., 1979—. Served with USN, 1962-64. Recipient Gold Pyramid award Specialty Advt. Assn. Internat., 1973, 1974. Mem. Indsl. Communications Council. Republican. Episcopalian. Club: Moon Valley Country (Phoenix). Home: 418 E Brook Hollow Dr Phoenix AZ 85022 Office: Karsten Mfg Corp PO Box 9990 Phoenix AZ 85068

CANTRELL, WILLIAM KEY, sales and mgmt. tng. co. exec.; b. Amarillo, Tex., Aug. 11, 1944; s. George Anthony and Esther Lois (Key) C.; grad. pub. schs.; m. Nancy Jean Wildow, Feb. 13, 1964 (div.); children—David Key, Anthony Ernest; m. 2d, Jacqueline Yu Sau-Hung, July 5, 1981. Designer, Lockheed Missile and Space Co., Sunnyvale,

Calif., 1966-67, Boeing Airplane Co., Seattle, 1967-69; engr. Ted Smith Aircraft Co., Van Nuys, Calif., 1969-70; sales rep., trainer Monroe Calculator Co., Van Nuys, 1970-71; v.p. The Parent Corp., North Hollywood, Calif., 1971-73; v.p., owner Synergy Mgmt. Co., Van Nuys, 1973-75; dir. tng. Lincoln Ins. Mktg., Encino, Calif., 1975-77; pres. Cantrell & Assos., Van Nuys, 1975—; asst. v.p. Valley Fed. Savs. & Loan Assn., Van Nuys, 1977-80. Mem. adv. com. Mgmt. Devel. Inst. Mem. Calif. Democratic State Com. Mem. Sales and Mktg. Execs. Internat., Sales and Mktg. Execs. Los Angeles, Am. Soc. Tng. and Devel. Democrat. Home: 21736 Roscoe Blvd Apt 37 Canoga Park CA 91304

CANTU, VIRGINIA, educational coordinator; b. Mesa, Ariz., Sept. 22, 1946; d. Francisco and Maria Luisa Valenzuela.; m. Reynaldo S. Cantu, Apr. 16, 1967; 1 dau., Anna Lisa. A.A. with distinction, Mesa Community Coll., 1981; student Ariz. State U., 1983—. Adminstrv. sec., mgr. peer tutoring program, Ariz. State U., Tempe, 1974; adminstrv. sec. Mesa (Ariz.) Community Coll., 1980-81, coordinator Ltd. English Speaking Program, 1980—; researcher in bilingual edn., conf. coordinator for ltd. English speaking adults in vocat. edn., 1982-83. Mem. Am. Vocat. Assn., Coll. Adv. com. (spl. needs population), Sister City Assn. Youth and Edn. Com., Nat. Assn. Bilingual Edn., Bilingual Tchr. Aide Adv. Com., Women in Higher Edn. in Ariz., Ariz. Assn. Chicanos for Higher Edn. Author: 2 resource manuals for ltd. English speaking adults; contbr. articles to profl. jours. Home: 643 E Buffalo Chandler AZ 85224 Office: Mesa Community Coll 1833 W Southern Ave Mesa AZ 85202

CANZONIERI, LOIS KNIGHT, editor; b. Pitts., Apr. 19, 1947; d. R. Gordon and Jean (Gleason) Knight; 1 dau., Lisa Jean. Student Pa. State U., 1965-66; B.S., George Mason U., 1974. Prodn. mgr. Carver Photocomposition, Arlington, Va., 1974-78; with Colo. Daily Corp., Boulder, 1978—, prodn. mgr. New Morning Composition, 1978-79, mng. editor Audience Mag., 1979—, also pres. corp. bd. dirs.; pres. Audience, Inc. Pub. relations chmn. Nancy Spanier Dance Theatre, Kinetic Conveyance Contest. Mem. Boulder C. of C., Denver Advt. Fedn. Democrat.

CAPE, ROBERT LEE, plastics design engineer; b. Desloge, Mo., Apr. 8, 1943; s. Farrel Woodrow and Mildred Eloise Smith; m. Elizabeth Florence Grimm, Apr. 20, 1963 (div.); 1 son, Matthew Kenyon. Student, U. Colo., 1960-61, Washington U., St. Louis, 1963-71, evening colls. NYU. Various design positions 1963-72; prin. project engr. Gen-Tire Automotive Plastics, Detroit, 1972-74; process devel. engr. Raychem Corp., Calif., 1974-76; project engr. Injection Molded B.M.C., Cleve., 1976-79; sr. prodn. engr., design engr. computers TRIAD, Sunnyvale, Calif., 1979—; lectr. indsl. design program San Jose State U. Served with USN, 1961-62. Mem. Soc. Plastics Engrs., Am. Soc. Cert. Engring. Technicians. Home: 1681 Peachwood Dr San Jose CA 95132 Office: 1252 Orleans Dr Sunnyvale CA 94086

CAPENER, RONALD L(EGRAND), advertising executive; b. Salt Lake City, Apr. 20, 1927; s. Daniel LeGrand and Christine Helensworth (Wach) C.; m. Rosalie Randal, Feb. 17, 1968; children—Michael, Cole, Jennifer, Don, Cori, Bob, Merrilee. B.S., U. Utah, 1948. With David W. Evans Inc., Salt Lake City, 1948-55, sr. v.p., northwest mgr., Seattle, 1955-72, pres. David W. Evans/Calif. Inc., San Francisco, 1972-77; owner The Capener Co., Inc., Seattle, San Francisco and Del Mar, Calif., 1977—. Home: 2114 De Mayo Rd Del Mar CA 92014 Office: 110 15th St Del Mar CA 92014

CAPIAUX, RAYMOND, aerospace company executive; b. Lille, France, Aug. 19, 1927; came to U.S., 1953, naturalized, 1959; s. Lucien and Aimee (Maucourt) C.; children—Claude, Frank, Philip, Corinne, Sean. B.S. in Aero. Engring., Swiss Inst. Tech., Zurich, 1949, M.S. in Aero. Engring., 1950. Research engr. Sulzer Bros., Winterthur, Switzerland, 1950-53; sr. propulsion-aerodynamics engr. Convair/Ft. Worth, 1953-56; supr. aerodynamic design Curtiss-Wright Corp., 1956-57, staff engr. Fairchild Engine and Airplant Corp., 1957-58; with Lockheed Missile and Space Co., Inc., Palo Alto, Calif., 1958—, mgr. aerospace scis. lab., 1966-70, dir. engring. scis., 1970, asst. gen. dur., dir. research Lockheed Palo Alto Research Lab., 1970-75, v.p. research and devel., advanced systems div., 1975—. Mem. AIAA, Assn. U.S. Army, Am. Def. Preparedness Assn. Patentee optimum method of clustering turbojet engines. Home: 12610 Via Ventana Los Altos Hills CA 94022 Office: Lockheed Missile and Space Company Inc 3251 Hanover St Palo Alto CA 94304

CAPIZZI, MICHAEL THOMAS, marketing information consulting firm executive; b. Niagara Falls, N.Y., Apr. 29, 1952; s. Salvatore Michael and Irene (Cornacchia) C.; m. Martha Ann Seitz, May 27, 1978. B.B.A., U. Cin., 1975; M.A., NYU, 1979. Field mgr. Burgoyne, Inc., Cin., 1972-76, account exec., N.Y.C., 1976-79, gen. mgr. western client services, San Francisco, 1980-82, v.p., 1982—. Mem. Am. Mktg. Assn., Beta Gamma Sigma. Democrat. Roman Catholic. Office: Burgoyne Inc Suite 1078 870 Market St San Francisco CA 94102

CAPKO, JUDITH LEA, management consultant; b. Ravenna, Ohio, May 17, 1942; d. Charles Vernon and Mildred Kathryn (Cady) Bentz; m. C. J. Capko, Sept. 15, 1962; children—Joseph, Christopher, Cheryl. Student Moorpark (Calif.) Coll. Cert. med. transcriptionist, Calif. With Robinson Meml. Hosp., Ravenna, 1962-63, Med. Group, Oakland, Calif., 1964-66, Lowry Smith, M.D., Camarillo, Calif., 1968-75, Arthritis Ctr. of Thousand Oaks (Calif.), 1977-79; founder Physicians Mgmt. Cons., Newbury Park, Calif., 1979—; cons., lectr. in field. Mem. Manzanita Sch. PTA, Newbury Park, 1982—; active Girl Scouts Am.; v.p. Soroptimist Internat. of Conejo; mem. pub. relations com. Childcare project Ventura County Commn. for Women, 1982. Mem. Ventura Co. Profl. Womens Network, Nat. Assn. Female Exec., Am. Assn. Med. Transcriptionists. Roman Catholic. Office: 7 Albion Pl Newbury Park CA 91320

CAPLAN, BARRY PAUL, lawyer; b. Portland, Oreg., Dec. 4, 1940; s. Philip and Tillie (Burke) C.; B.A., U. Wash., 1962; LL.B., U. Calif. at Berkeley, 1965; m. Barbara Sue Friedman, Aug. 5, 1962; children—Jonathan Burke, Lisa Anne. Admitted to Oreg. bar, 1965; dep. dist. atty. Multnomah County, Portland, 1965-68; asso. firm Sussman, Shank, Wapnick, Caplan & Stiles, 1968-71, partner, 1971—; instr. tng. class social workers Oreg. State Bar, 1972, mem. Bd. Bar Examiners, 1977-80, chmn., 1980. Mem. community relations com. Jewish Welfare Fedn., 1968-73, allocations com., 1973-78; chmn. community relations com. Soviet Jewry Task Force, 1972-74. Bd. dirs. B'nai B'rith Camp. Mem. Am. (active various coms.), Multnomah County bar assns., Oreg. State Bar (active various coms.), Comml. Law League Am. (exec. bd.-western region 1977—), Anti Defamation League (mem. regional bd. 1970-76). Jewish (trustee Congregation 1971-77, 2d v.p. 1976-77). Club: City (Portland). Contbr. chpts. to legal pubs. Home: 7895 SW Broadmoor Terrace Portland OR 97225 Office: 1001 SW 5th Ave Portland OR 97204

CAPLAN, EDWIN HARVEY, university dean, accounting educator; b. Boston, Aug. 24, 1926; s. Henry and Dorothy (Nathanson) C.; m. Ramona Hootner, June 20, 1948; children—Gary, Dennis, Jeffrey, Nancy. B.B.A., U. Mich. 1950, M.B.A., 1952, Ph.D., U. Calif., 1965. C.P.A. Calif., Mich. Ptnr., J.J. Gotlieb & Co., C.P.A.s, Detroit 1953-56; prof. acctg. Humboldt State U. 1956-61; prof. acctg. U. Oreg. 1964-67; prof. U. N.Mex. 1967—, assoc. dean Sch. Mgmt. 1982—; cons. in field. Served to 1st lt. U.S. Army 1944-46. Mem. Am. Acctg. Assn., Am. Inst. C.P.A.s, Nat. Assn. Accts., Am. Econs. Assn. Contbr. articles to profl. jours. Home: 8201 Harwood Ave NE Albuquerque NM 87110 Office: Anderson Sch Mgmt Univ NMex Albuquerque NM 87131

CAPLAN, GAIL RISLEY, public sch. ofcl.; b. Hartford, Conn., Jan. 15, 1941; d. Ludlum Leroy and Doris Risley (Finlay) Keyes; B.S. with honors (West Hartford Future Tchrs. Am. scholar), Central Conn. State Coll., 1963, postgrad. in reading, 1963-66; M.A. in Ednl. Adminstrn., Calif. State U., Dominguez Hills, 1983; m. David J. Caplan, Aug. 22, 1971; 1 dau., Mollie Beth Risley. Elem. tchr., West Hartford, Conn., 1963-67, Roosevelt Rds. Naval Sta., HEW, P.R., 1967-69, Paramount (Calif.) Unified Sch. Dist., 1969-70; elem. tchr. Long Beach (Calif.) Unified Sch. Dist., 1970-74, reading specialist, 1974-79, program facilitator, 1979—. Recipient cert. of appreciation Long Beach Community Coll.; cert. tchr. and adminstr., Calif. Mem. Internat. Reading Assn., Orange County Reading Assn., Nat. Council Tchrs. of English, Assn. Supervision and Curriculum Devel., Delta Kappa Gamma (chpt. treas. 1982-84), Phi Delta Kappa, Kappa Delta Pi.

CAPLINGER, AUDREY LYDIA, tour and travel agy. exec.; b. Birmingham, Eng., Apr. 2, 1937; came to U.S., 1958; d. Charles Edward and Phyllis May (Clifford) Horton; divorced; children—Debra L. Stotler, Charles L. Caplinger. Rental agt., supr. Avis Rent A Car, Columbus, Ohio, 1966-69; nat. personnel dir. Lincoln Mercury div. Ford Motor Co., Dearborn, Mich., 1969-71; mgr., sales rep. Graham Ford, Inc., Columbus, 1971-78; v.p., sales dir. Pacific Car Rental, San Diego, 1978-79; dir. mktg. Am. Internat. Rent-A-Car, San Diego, 1979-81; pres. Tour and Leisure Concepts, Inc., San Diego, 1982—; cons. Graham Ford Inc., Columbus. Mem. Exploratory com. San Diego World Fair, 1982-83. Mem. Am. Soc. Assn. Execs., Meeting Planners Internat., Hotel Sales Mgrs. Assn., Nat. Assn. Female Execs., San Diego Conv. and Visitors Bur. Address: 727 Sapphire St Suite 205 San Diego CA 92109

CAPLINGER, KENNETH TRAVERS, appraisal co. exec.; b. Advance, Ind., June 16, 1912; s. James Sylvester and Buelah E. (Dale) C.; student LaSalle Extension U., 1936-39, Edison Tech. Sch., 1955-57, Am. Soc. Appraisers, 1959-60; m. Jessie Mary Edrington, Nov. 30, 1933; children—Paul Jay, Ronald Dale, Janet Gail. Pres., Caplinger & Co., Seattle, 1945-50; indsl. specialist U.S. Def. Prodn. Adminstn., Washington, 1951-52; chief regional appraiser for State of Washington, U.S. Small Bus. Adminstrn., Seattle, 1953-72; owner, mgr. Equitable Appraisal Co., Seattle, 1972—. Cons. bus. mgmt.; lectr., instr. property valuation seminars, Seattle, 1953-72; mem. Wash. State Gov.'s Bd. Econ. Advisors, 1978—. Founder, pres. Stevens Meml. Hosp., Edmonds, Wash., 1958, dir., 1959—; pres., founder Hillwood Park Community Club, Lynnwood, Wash., 1956. Pres. Young Democratic Clubs, King County, Wash., 1939. Served with AUS, 1944. Mem. Am. Soc. Appraisers (sr. mem., award outstanding achievement as regional gov. 1964), Am. Arbitration Assn. (mem. panel). Am. Legion. Congregationalist. Mason (32 deg., Shriner). Address: 3424 Magnolia Blvd W Seattle WA 98199

CAPOBIANCO, TITO, opera dir.; b. La Plata, Argentina, Aug. 28, 1931; student pub. schs., La Plata; m. Elena Denda; 2 children. Operatic debut in Aida, Teatro Argentino, La Plata, 1953; theatre debut State Co., Buenos Aires, 1954; prof. U. Chile, 1954-56; art dir. Cin. Opera, 1962-65; artistic dir. Cin. Opera Festival, 1961-65; tech. dir. Teatro Colon, 1958-62; gen. dir. Chile Opera Co., 1967-70, La Plata, 1959-61, San Diego Opera, 1975—; founder San Diego Opera Center, 1977, Verdi Opera Festival, San Diego, 1978; dir., producer maj. opera cos. in Argentina, Australia, France, Germany, Holland, Italy, Mexico, Spain and U.S., including N.Y.C., Phila., Houston, San Francisco, Washington, Met. Opera; prof. acting and interpretation Acad. Vocal Arts, Phila., 1962-68; founder, gen. dir. Juilliard Sch. Music, N.Y.C., Am. Opera Center, 1967-69; dir. Council of Arts, Argentina, 1959-61. Named One of Ten Best Talents in Argentina, 1968, Hon. citizen Balt., New Orleans and Miami; recipient Cavaliere award (Italy). Office: PO Box 988 San Diego CA 92112*

CAPOLUNGO, BARBARA ANN, customs officer; b. Mpls., Jan. 27, 1933; d. George Charles and Signa Amanda (Sherve) Larsen; B.A. magna cum laude, U. Calif., San Diego, 1973; M.S.W., U. Calif., Berkeley, 1977; children—Ronald G. Burghall, Brandt E. Burghall, Dirk F. Burghall. Social worker Ct. Dependency div. Dept. of Public Social Services, County of Riverside, Riverside, Calif., 1978; community devel. intern City of Oakland, Calif., 1976-77, planning cons., 1977, mgmt. and budget analyst, 1977-78; inspection and control officer U.S. Customs Service, San Ysidro, Calif., 1978-80, San Francisco, 1980—. Bd. dirs. San Diego Interfaith Housing Found., 1979 80; allocations com. panel United Way of San Diego County, 1978-80; mem. exec. com. Alameda County Supr., Oakland, 1977-78; legis. com. Alameda County chpt. Nat. Assn. Social Workers, 1977-78. Recipient Fellowship U. B.C., Vancouver, Can., 1975; Adminstrn. on Aging grantee U. Calif., Berkeley, 1975; Outstanding Service award Oakland Econ. Devel. Council, 1970. Mem. Federally Employed Women, Nat. Assn. Social Workers, Internat. Police Officers Assn. Democrat. Mem. United Ch. of Christ. Home: 4 Admiral Dr 233 Emeryville CA 94608 Office: US Customs Service San Francisco Dist 555 Battery St San Francisco CA 94104

CAPORASO, JAMES ALBERT, international relations educator; b. Sayre, Pa., Sept. 2, 1941; s. James D. and Mildred (Liberto) C.; Jean E. Mellon, children—Jeanice Gail, Jody M. B.A., Pa. State U., 1963; M.A. in Polit. Sci., Villanova U., 1965; Ph.D., U. Pa., 1968; postgrad. Inter-U. Consortium Polit. Research, U. Mich., 1965. Mem. faculty dept. polit. sci. Northwestern U., Chgo., 1968-78; mem. faculty dept. Grad. Sch. Internat. Studies, U. Denver, 1978—, Andrew W. Mellon prof. internat. relations, 1978—; mem. polit. sci. panel NSF, 1981—; lectr. numerous countries. Rockefeller Found. fellow, 1974-75; recipient Most Outstanding Grad. award Villanova U., 1982. Mem. Am. Polit. Sci. Assn., Internat. Studies Assn., Peace Research Soc. Author: Quasi-Experimental Approaches, 1973; The Structure and Function of European Intergration, 1978; contbr. articles to profl. jours. Home: 2250 S Madison St Denver CO 80210 Office: Sch Internat Relations U Denver 2201 S Gaylord St Room 325 Denver CO 80208

CAPOSSELA, FREDERICK LOUIS, educator; b. N.Y.C., Sept. 15, 1937; s. Fred Louis and Frances Kathryn (Lawler) C.; m. Ava Kathryn Sprague, Aug. 21, 1976; children—Ava Kathryn, Thomas Jordan. B.S., Fordham U., 1959; M.B.A., Calif. Poly. U., 1974. Producer, CBS News, N.Y.C., 1962-66; creative dir. PH&B, N.Y.C., 1966-68; creative supr. BBDO Advt., N.Y.C. and Los Angeles, 1968-79; lectr. mktg. mgmt. Calif. State Poly. U., Pomona, 1979—. Served to 1st lt. U.S. Army, 1959-62. Mem. Am. Mktg. Assn. Republican. Episcopalian. Clubs: Copy, Advt. of Los Angeles. Office: California State Polytechnic University Marketing Management Dept 3801 W Temple Ave Pomona CA 91768

CAPOZZI, PAULA CONSTANCE, telephone company manager; b. Laupehoehoe, Hawaii, Aug. 27, 1950; d. Paul Merton and Volga Geneva (James) Condon; m. Anthony Patrick Capozzi, Apr. 22, 1978; 1 son, Nicholas. B.A. in Journalism, Calif. State U.-Sacramento, 1972. Operator, Pacific Telephone Co., Fresno, Calif., 1968-73, asst. mgr. pub. relations, 1973-75, staff mgr. news and employee info., 1975—; cons. press relations, polit. campaigns. Mem. Fresno Press Club, Kern County Press Club, Tri-County Media Club. Democrat. Presybterian. Club: Four Walls West (Fresno). Home: 7560 N Valentine Ave Fresno CA 93711 Office: Pacific Telephone Co 1925 E Dakota Ave Room 122 Fresno CA 93762

CAPPELLO, EVE, behavioral cons.; b. Sydney, Australia, Dec. 4, 1922; d. Nem and Ethel Shapira; came to U.S., 1940, naturalized, 1944; A.A., Santa Monica City Coll., 1972; B.A., Calif. State U., 1974; M.A., Pacific Western U., 1977, Ph.D., 1978; children—Frances Soskins, Alan Kazdin. Singer, pianist, Los Angeles, 1958-78; pvt. practice behavior and bus. cons., Los Angeles, 1976—; asst. prof. Calif. State U. Extension, Dominguez Hills, 1977—; prof. Mt. St. Mary's Coll., U. of Judaism, U. So. Calif.; founder, dir. A-C-T Inst.; co-exec. dir. Total One Devel. Ctr. of Marina Del Rey. Mem. Calif. State U. Alumni Assn., Assn. Advancement Behavior Therapy, Assn. Behavioral Analysis, Orgnl. Bus. Mgmt. Assn., Wilshire Bus. and Profl. Women's Orgn., Marina Del Rey C. of C., Alpha Gamma. Author: Let's Get Growing, 1979; The Professional Touch, 1983; newspaper columnist, 1976-79; contbr. articles to profl. jours. Office: PO Box 10578 Marina Del Rey CA 90291

CAPPS, ANTHONY THOMAS (CAPOZZOLO), internat. pub. relations exec.; b. Pueblo, Colo.; s. Nicolo and Anna (Solomone) Capozzolo; student Los Angeles Bus. Coll., Pueblo (Colo.) Bus. Coll., 1929-33; ed. pvt. tutor, arts and music; m. Theresa Cecelia Harmon, Nov. 12, 1945. Dance dir., choreographer, producer motion pictures, TV and radio; featured profl. dance team Biltmore Bowl, Cocoanut Grove, Los Angeles, St. Catherine Hotel, Catalina, 1939-42; dance dir., producer NBC, ABC, KCOP-TV, Columbia Pictures, 20th Century Fox and Calif. Studios, 1940-60; numerous TV interviews on religion and politics, history of ballet and opera of last 500 yrs.; exec. dir. Lockheed and Vega Aircraft Co. activities, various locations, 1942-44; columnist Desert Sun Newspapers, 1959—; internat. pub. relations dir. Howard Manor, Palm Springs Key Club, 1960—, Country Club Hotel, Palm Springs Ranch Club, 1970-71, Kedes Radio, Cameron Center, 1971-73, Cameron Enterprises, Murietta Hot Springs Hotel, Health and Beauty Spa, 1972-73; founder, pres., dir. Tony Capps Enterprises, Inc., Palm Springs, Calif., 1959—, chmn., exec. dir. golf and tennis tournaments, benefit dinners, govt. ofcls., various fund-raising events; founder, co-chmn. Nat. Football Found. and Hall of Fame Golf Classic, Palm Springs; founder, pres. Capps-Capozzolo Art Gallery, City of Hope, Duarte, Calif. Chmn., exec. dir. Alan Cranston for Senator Dinner, 1963; Edmund G. (Pat) Brown Testimonial Dinner, 1964; Progressive Jet Set Party - Nat. Cystic Fibrosis Research Found. fund raising, 1968; United Fund Gala Premier Camelot Theatre Opening, 1967; United Fund Desert Circus Big Top Ball, 1971. Mem. Assistance League Palm Springs Desert Area, Desert Hosp., Palm Springs Desert Mus., Desert Art Center of Coachella Valley, Mary and Joseph League, Eisenhower Med. Center (charter), Women's Aux. Internat. Found., City of Hope Duarte (founder, pres.), Nat. Artists and Art Patrons Soc., Am. Film Inst., Nat. Cystic Fibrosis Assn., AFTRA, Am. Security Council, Pathfinders, Nat. Football Found. and Hall of Fame in Calif. (founder, pres. Tri-County chpt., founder, co-chmn. golf classic at Palm Springs), Internat. Platform Assn., Nat. Hist. Soc. Gettysburg, Nat. Trust for Historic Preservation, Smithsonian Instn., Jacques Cousteau Soc., Palm Springs Pathfinders (life). Clubs: Balboa Bay, Newport Beach, Internationale Philanthropique Societe de Gourmet (founder). Home: 2715 Junipero Ave Palm Springs CA 92262

CAPPS, BARBARA LOUISE, respiratory therapist; b. Fresno, Calif., Dec. 11, 1933; d. Eugene Victor and Ruth (Lankford) Thalman; med. asst. diploma Fresno Tech. Coll., 1965; m. Ronald Dean Capps, Aug. 9, 1968; children—Rochelle Ruth Pope, Jeffra Lynn Busby, Karen Kay Pope, Jeannie Louise Briggs, Jay Eugene Pope, Ronald Lee Pope, Lisa Dianne Capps. From nurses aide to shift leader respiratory therapy Fresno Community Hosp., 1965-70; staff technician, then shift leader St. Agnes Hosp., Fresno, 1970-71; coordinator Hosp. Pulmonary Services, Modesto, Calif., 1972-73, regional mgr., 1973—; instr., trainer Am. Heart Assn. Mem. Am. Assn. Respiratory Therapy, Calif. Soc. Respiratory Therapy (chpt. membership chmn. 1972-73). Democrat. Office: 1400 Lone Palm Dr Modesto CA 95353

CAPPS, TERI ANNE ROTH, educator; b. Denver, Oct. 9, 1952; d. Herman and Florence Luella (Fritz) Roth; A.A.S., Mesa Coll., 1972; B.A., U. No. Colo., 1977; m. Jerrel Waller Capps, Apr. 2, 1977. Head tchr. kindergarten and pre school Naval Communication Sta., Guam, 1972-75; tchr. kindergarten Jaycee Nursery, Grand Junction, Colo., 1977-78; pre-sch. tchr. and coordinator Grand Junction, Regional Ctr., 1978—. Pub. relations coordinator Childfind, 1982-83, interagy. council chair, 1983-84, developmental tester, 1979—. Mem. Am. Assn. Mental Deficiency, Library Spl. Edn., Nat. Assn. Edn. of Young Children, Colo. Assn. Edn. of Young Children, Western Slope Assn. Edn. of Young Children. Democrat. Lutheran. Home: 485 31 1/4 Rd Grand Junction CO 81504 Office: 2800 D Rd Grand Junction CO 81501

CARAS, ALAN MEYER, personnel cons.; b. Lawrence, Mass., Apr. 18, 1939; s. Mitchell Ralph and Gertrude (Zuckerman) C.; B.S. in Bus. Adminstrn., Suffolk U., Boston, 1961; m. Selma Sattin, Apr. 12, 1964; children—Daani-Ruth, Samuel, Benjamin. Mgmt. trainee Merrimack Valley Nat. Bank, Andover, Mass., 1962; budget mgr. J.M. Fields, Inc., Boston, 1962-65; acctg. mgr. Zayre Corp., Framingham, Mass., 1965-66; budget mgr. Rust Craft Greeting Cards, Dedham, Mass., 1966-67; controller Caceres Johnson Corp., Hato Rey, P.R., 1967-68; div. controller Computing & Software, Inc., Los Angeles, 1968-70; ind. cons. mktg. search, 1970-71; acctg. mgr. Jewish Fedn. Council Los Angeles, 1971-73; owner, operator Corp. Dimensions, Inc., Los Angeles, 1973—; dir. Denver Group. speaker in field. Served with U.S. Army, 1961-62. Mem. Culver City C. of C. Office: 8599 Venice Blvd Los Angeles CA 90034

CARAU, FRANK PAUL, SR., electronics co. ofcl.; b. Washington, Oct. 29, 1948; s. Frank Louis and Gladys Elizabeth (Persons) C.; B.S.E.E. with honors, Va. Poly. Inst. and State U., 1971; postgrad. Colo. State U., 1975—; m. Linda Lou Hepler, Sept. 6, 1969; children—Frank Paul, Christen Elizabeth, Cynthia Gayle. With coop. edn. program CIA, Washington, 1967-70, staff engr., 1970-74; design engr. Desktop Computer div. Hewlett-Packard, Loveland and Ft. Collins, Colo., 1974-78, engring. project mgr., Ft. Collins, 1978-80, product mktg. mgr. Greeley div., Ft. Collins, 1980—; pres., dir. Brown Caru Assos., Inc., 1977-78. Mem. Phi Kappa Phi, Tau Beta Pi, Eta Kappa Nu. Libertarian. Lutheran. Patentee in field. Home: 2719 Greenland Dr Loveland CO 80537 Office: 3404 E Harmony Rd Fort Collins CO 80525

CARD, JOSEFINA JAYME, research psychologist; b. Manila, Apr. 27, 1946; came to U.S., 1967, naturalized, 1978; d. Fortunato Rabadilla and Josefina Ungson (Bulatao) Jayme; A.B. in Math. summa cum laude, Maryknoll Coll., Manila, 1966; M.S. in Social Psychology (Fulbright-Hays scholar in Psychology, 1967-71), Carnegie-Mellon U., 1969, Ph.D., 1971; m. Stuart K. Card, Jan. 26, 1972; children—Gwyneth Megan, Tiffany Heather. Sr. asst. computer cons. group Sycip, Gorres, Velayo & Co., Manila, 1966-67; asst. prof. dept. psychology Ateneo de Manila U., 1971; research psychologist suicide prevention research program, Pitts., 1972-73; prin. research scientist Am. Insts. for Research, Palo Alto, Calif., 1973—; cons. Psychol. Service of Pitts., Pitts. Plate Glass, Sch. Urban and Public Affairs Carnegie-Mellon U., Group Developers and Financiers, Inc. Recipient Asian student leader award, 1966. Mem. Am Sociol. Assn., Population Assn. Am., Am. Psychol. Assn. Author: Development of a ROTC/Army Career Commitment Model, 1975; Antecedents and Consequences of the Motivation for Fertility Control: A Cross-Cultural Study of Filipino Migrants and Caucasian Controls,

1977; Consequences of Adolescent Childbearing for the Young Parent's Future Personal and Professional Life, 1977; Long-term Consequences for Children Born to Adolescent Parents, 1978; Lives after Vietnam: The Personal Impact of Military Service, 1983. Home: 3191 Cowper St Palo Alto CA 94306 Office: AIR 1791 Arastradero Palo Alto CA 94302

CARDELLA, KENNETH CHARLES, airline exec.; b. Los Angeles, Jan. 3, 1932; s. Ben and Lucy (Colletta) C.; B.S. in Indsl. Mgmt., U. Ariz., 1955; m. Sharon Townsdin, Aug. 24, 1963; children—Kynn, Kenneth Charles, Marisa. Mgmt. trainee Union Oil Calif., 1955; pilot Am. Airlines, N.Y.C., 1959-60; mgr. Bankers Life Iowa, Tucson, 1964-67; mem. Ariz. Senate, 1967-71; founder, pres., chief exec. officer Cochise Airlines, Inc., Tucson, 1971—. Served with USAF, 1955-59. Recipient Disting. Citizen award Alumni Assn. U. Ariz., 1978. Office: 7120 N Oracle Rd Suite F Tucson AZ 85704

CARDELLI, GIOIA CECILIA, home bldg. co. ofcl.; b. Chgo., Mar. 28, 1942; d. Giovanni and Jacqueline (Stewart) C.; m. Woodruff Price, Oct. 28, 1961 (div.); 1 son, Ian Price. With Levitt & Sons, Inc., Lebanon, N.H., Denver, 1973-75; mktg. coordinator Wood Bros. Homes, Denver, 1975-79, mktg. mgr., 1980—; merchandising mgr. Medema Homes, Denver, 1979-80. Mem. Home Builders Assn. Met. Denver, Denver Advt. Fedn. Office: Bldg 12 Lakeside Ln Denver CO 80212

CARDEN, ROBERT CLINTON, III, electrical engineer; b. Phila., Mar. 26, 1933; s. Robert Clinton and Mary Alice (Blanton) C.; B.E.E., Ga. Inst. Tech., 1955, M.S. in Elec. Engring. (grantee), 1959; postgrad. UCLA, 1961-74, U. Calif.-Irvine, 1980-81; m. Mary Eleanore Clapp, Aug. 15, 1959; children—Robert Clinton IV, Linda Warren. Project engr. Bendix Radio div. Bendix Aviation, Towson, Md., 1950-57; mem. tech. staff Space Tech. Labs. TRW, 1959-62, El Segundo, Calif.; mem. tech. staff Marshall Labs., Torrance, Calif., 1962-68; founder, dir. Time Zero Corp., Torrance, 1968-71; founder, dir., mgr. engring. Comtec Data Systems div. Am. Micro Systems, Cupertino, Calif., 1971-75; engring. mgr., prin. engr. Ball Corp., Gardena, Calif., 1975-80, staff cons. Ball Corp., Huntington Beach, Calif., 1980-83; sr. staff engr. TRW Inc., Redondo Beach, Calif., 1983—; cons. engr. digital systems, 1980—; instr. in field. Served with AUS, 1957. Mem. Am. Rocket Soc., IEEE, Computer Soc., Ga. Tech. Alumni Assn., Tau Beta Pi, Eta Kappa Nu, Scabbard and Blade, Chi Phi. Republican. Presbyterian. Research in digital space systems. Author, producer: Space for the Everday Man, 1978; contbr. articles to profl. jours. Home: 1217 N Kennymead St Orange CA 92669 Office: TRW Inc 1 Space Park Redondo Beach CA 90278

CÁRDENAS, RENÉ, television executive, demographer; b. San Francisco, Feb. 13, 1923; s. Lauro and Maria (Ball) C.; m. Doris F. Marino, June 7, 1952; children—Rene, Kevin, Gregory. Ph.D. in Cultural Anthropology, Stanford U., 1970. Producer, writer Villa Alegre, Oakland, Calif., 1970-81; mgr. Kingston Trio, 1959-69; with Stanford Research, Inc., 1956, Ampex Corp., San Juan, P.R., 1957-59; pres. BCTV, San Leandro, Calif., 1969—; cons. U.S. Office Edn., 1971-72, Office Mgmt. and Budget, 1972-73, White House, 1974-75, also fed. govt. agys. Served with USNR, 1941-45. Grantee Exxon USA Found., 1973-76, Ford Found., 1972, Lilly Endowment Found., 1975-76, HUD, 1978, Dept. Labor, 1972-73, Levi Strauss Corp., 1975; named Hon. Col. N.Mex.; Hon. Citizen Okla.; recipient Tex. Silver Spur award, 1975; NEA Humanitarian award, 1974; recognition Calif. State Legislature for outstanding ednl. achievement in broadcasting; 4 Emmys, 1977, 79, 80, 81. Mem. Nat. Acad. TV Arts and Scis. Democrat. Club: Oakland Athletic. Author: Parenting in a Multi Cultural Society, 1980; contbr. numerous articles on edn. of culturally disadvantaged child to profl. jours. Home: 4265 Bemis St Oakland CA 94605 Office: BCTV 155 Callan Ave San Leandro CA 94577

CARDINAL, ROGER JOSEPH, ednl. adminstr.; b. Chippewa Falls, Wis., Sept. 26, 1948; s. Robert E. and Mary L. (Nunke) C.; B.S. in Bus. Adminstrn., Oreg. State U., 1970; m. Kay M. Wynn, Apr. 20, 1974; 1 son, Logan J. Dist. exec. Oreg. Trail council Boy Scouts Am., Corvallis, Oreg., 1972-76; mgr. bus. services Oreg. Inst. Tech., Klamath Falls, 1976-79; asst. budget officer U. Oreg., Eugene, 1979-81; dir. purchasing Lane Community Coll., Eugene, 1981—. Served with U.S. Army, 1970-72. Mem. Purchasing Mgmt. Assn. Oreg., Oreg. Pub. Purchasing Assn. Roman Catholic.

CARETTO, LAURENCE STEPHEN, engr.; b. Los Angeles, Oct. 5, 1939; s. Bert and Katherine (Gaudino) C.; B.S. in Engring., UCLA, 1960, M.S., 1963, Ph.D., 1965; m. Barbara Caretto, Feb. 16, 1980. Technologist, Shell Chem. Co., 1960-61; asst. prof. U. Calif., Berkeley, 1965-70; sr. vis. fellow Imperial Coll. Sci. and Tech., London, 1970; mem. faculty Calif. State U., Northridge, 1971—, prof. engring., 1974—, chmn. dept. mech. and chem. engring., 1974-79; mem. Calif. Air Resources Bd., 1978—; cons. air pollution, combustion and energy. Mem. Air Pollution Control Assn., Soc. Automotive Engrs., AAAS, Am. Chem. Soc., Combustion Inst. Author articles in field. Office: Dept Mech and Chem Engring Calif State U Northridge CA 91330

CAREY, CHARLES HOWARD, city official; b. Cheyenne, Wyo., Oct. 21, 1938; s. Albyn Leslie and Amelia Regina (Zeller) G.; m. Mary Frances Hensley, Dec. 30, 1942 (div.); children—Terry Don, Deborah Ann. Student pub. schs., Cheyenne. Firefighter, Cheyenne Fire Dept., 1962-78, fire chief, 1978—. Served with USN, 1956-59. Mem. Internat. Assn. Fire Chiefs, VFW. Lodge: Elks. Office: 2101 O'Neil Hwy Cheyenne WY 82001

CAREY, KATHRYN ANN, automotive company advertising executive, consultant; b. Los Angeles, Oct. 18, 1949; d. Frank Randall and Evelyn Mae (Walmsley) C.; m. Richard Kenneth Sundt, Dec. 28, 1980. B.A. in Am. Studies with honors, Calif. State U.-Los Angeles, 1971. Tutor Calif. Dept. Vocat. Rehab., Los Angeles, 1970; teaching asst. U. So. Calif., 1974-75, UCLA, 1974-75; claims adjuster Auto Club So. Calif., San Gabriel, 1971-73; corp. pub. relations cons. Carnation Co., Los Angeles, 1973-78; pub. relations cons. Vivitar Corp., Santa Monica, Calif., 1978; sr. advt. asst. Am. Honda Motor Co., Gardena, Calif., 1978—; cons. advt., pub. relations, promotions. Calif. Life Scholarship Found. scholar, 1967. Mem. Advt. Club Los Angeles, Pub. Relations Soc. Am., Los Angeles Soc. for Prevention Cruelty to Animals, Green Peace, German Shepherd Dog Club Am., Am. Humane Assn., Elsa Wild Animal Appeal. Democrat. Methodist. Editor: Honda Views, 1978—. Office: 100 W Alondra Blvd Gardena CA 90247

CAREY, LYNNE MARIE, interior designer; b. Sarasota, Fla., June 29, 1951; d. William Pershing and Edna Grace (Hansen) C.; m. Randolph John Meadors, May 23, 1983. B.S. in Interior Design, Fla. State U., 1973. Interior designer Neil Mitchell Cowan, Los Angeles, 1976-78, Milton I. Swimmer, Beverly Hills, 1978-79; project designer, assoc. Environ. Planning and Research, San Francisco, 1979-82; owner, design prin. Lynne Carey Assocs., San Francisco, 1982—. Designs include: Visa Internat. Hdqrs., Matson Nav. Corp. Hdqrs., Guy Carpenter and Co., Brown, Wood, Ivey, Mitchell & Petty (all San Francisco).

CAREY, THOMAS ROBERT, psychologist; b. Cin., Jan. 23, 1945; s. Thomas Richard and Beatrice (McKnight) C.; B.S. in Psychology, Eastern Ky. U., 1968, M.A. in Counseling, 1970; Ph.D., U. N.Mex., 1975; m. Linda K. Moore, Aug. 28, 1968; 1 dau., Shelby Lynn. Teaching asst. Eastern Ky. U., 1968-69; supr. practicum students U. N.Mex., Albuquerque, 1970-71, teaching asst., 1971-72; dir. adolescent services Vista Sandia Hosp., Albuquerque, 1970-77; adolescent, family and group therapist A.A. Hovda, M.D., P.C., Albuquerque, 1975-80, corp. practice/therapist 1980—; cons. Albuquerque Public Schs., 1978-80. Vice pres. Albuquerque Learning Disability Assn., 1980-81. Served with USMC, 1963-64. Named Albuquerque Bus. Women's Boss of Yr., 1975. Mem. Am. Psychol. Assn., Am. Group Psychotherapy Assn., Am. Assn. for Marital and Family Therapists, Psi Chi. Democrat. Roman Catholic. Office: 344 Winrock Med Plaza NE Albuquerque NM 87110

CARGILE, PATSY KAYE, ins. corp. exec.; b. Hobbs, N.Mex., Aug. 31, 1938; d. Ralph Eugene and Virgie Augusta (Denton) Beard; student U. N.Mex., 1956-57; m. Hulin Woodrow Cargile, Sept. 21, 1957; children—Zane Edward, Colleen Elaine, Melissa Evelyn. Sec. with Daniels Ins., Inc., Hobbs, N.Mex., 1957-59, 61—, office mgr., 1971-79, mktg. mgr., 1979—, also sr. v.p., corp. sec., dir.; catalog sales clk. Montgomery Ward, Casper, Wyo., 1960-61. Bd. dirs. Child Devel. Center, 1973-77; adv. bd. secretarial dept. N.Mex. Jr. Coll., 1977—, chairperson, 1981—; bd. dirs. United Fund, 1981—. Cert. ins. counselor, profl. ins. woman. Mem. Ins. Women Lea County (pres. 1978—), Lea County Insurors. Democrat. Methodist. Club: Altrusa of Hobbs (pres. 1966-67). Home: 1909 N McKinley St Hobbs NM 88240 Office: 300 N Linam St Hobbs NM 88240

CARGILL, MARTHA, publishing co. ofcl.; b. Munich, W. Ger., Jan. 2, 1954 (parents Am. citizens); d. Everett Leslie and Elizabeth Cecelia (Vercuski) C.; m. David Hal Schwartz, 1981. B.S. in Anthropology, Ariz. State U., 1978. Proofencoder, Valley Nat. Bank Mesa (Ariz.) Ops. Center, 1972-74; reconciler Continental Bank Ops. Center, Phoenix, 1974-75; records clk. Admissions Office, Ariz. State U., Tempe, 1977-79; editorial asst. Jaques Cattell Press, Tempe, Ariz., 1980, asst. editor, 1981, editor Biog. div., 1981—. Active Scottsdale Center for Arts Assn. Mem. Jersey Wildlife Assn., Valley Shakespeare Assn. Home: 8108 E Buena Terra Way Scottsdale AZ 85253 Office: 2216 S Industrial Park Tempe AZ 85282

CARHART, NANCY KATHLEEN, hotel mgr.; b. Phoenix, Aug. 25, 1931; d. Floyd Donald and Martha Kathleen (White) King; B.S. in Psychology with distinction, Ariz. State U., 1956; student U. Ariz., 1951-53, U. Hawaii, 1953-55, Phoenix Coll., 1949-50; grad. Delinquency Control Inst., 1955; m. Roger A. Carhart, Mar. 23, 1961 (dec.); children—Karen Kathleen, Todd Albert. Clk., Walsh Bros., Phoenix, 1950-51; bookkeeper Penn Mut. Life Ins. Co., Phoenix, 1951-52; office mgr. Spearling Engring. Co., 1952-53; interior decorator Ruth Carroll Interiors, Phoenix, 1960; bookkeeper Kathleen Flowers, Phoenix, 1966-69; sales dir. Exec. House, 1969-72, Carefree (Ariz.) Inn, 1972-76, Arz. Resorts, Scottsdale, 1976-81; mgr. travel indsl. sales Ramada Inn, Inc., Phoenix, 1976-80, dir. travel indsl. sales, 1983—; dir. travel indsl. sales Ramada Renaissance Hotels, 1980-83; mem. Gov.s' State Council on Tourism, 1973-74; recipient award of merit. Recipient golf awards, state sewing achievement award Women's Club of Ariz., 1953. Mem. Meeting Planners Internat., Am. Soc. Tng. and Devel., Jr. League Phoenix. Republican. Clubs: Paradise Valley Country (pres.'s cup 1966), Jr. Women's, Kiva. Home: 8049 Via Palma Scottsdale AZ 85258 Office: 3838 E Van Buren St Phoenix AZ 85008

CARL, JOAN STRAUSS, sculptor, painter, designer, consultant; b. Cleve., Mar. 20, 1926; d. Abraham and Marion R. (Halle) Strauss; m. Elwood Stanley Carl, Dec. 24, 1944; children—Barry Strauss, Michael Strauss. Student Cleve. Sch. Art, 1943, Chgo. Art Inst. Chgo., 1944-45, Mill. Coll., 1944, New Sch. Art, 1952-54; pvt. study with Bill Givler, 1950, Carl Morris, 1951, Ted Gillian, 1955. Apprenticehip with Sherry Petticolas, 1956-57, with Albert Wein, 1962-63; one-man shows Paideia Gallery, Los Angeles, 1964-69, Fresno Art Ctr. Mus. (Calif.), 1971, Courtney-Collins Gallery, Raleigh, N.C., 1972, Linden-Kicklighter Gallery, Cleve., Muskegon Community Coll. (Mich.), Bakersfield Coll. (Calif.), also others; exhibited in group shows including Los Angeles Art Assn., 1958-62, AIA Design Ctr., Los Angeles, 1969, Laguna Art Mus., 1969, So. Calif. Expn., 1970, Santa Cruz Art Show (Calif.), 1973, Fresno Art Ctr. Mus., 1973, Oborn Gallery, Kansas City, Mo., 1973, Santa Barbara Small Image Show, 1975, also Cerritos Coll., Harbor Coll., Los Angeles, West End Gallery, N.Y.C., Stuart Kingston Galleries, Naples, Fla., Mint Mus., Charlotte, N.C., Paideia Gallery; represented in permanent collections Magnes Mus., Berkeley, Calif., Raleigh Mus. (N.C.), also pvt. collections throughout U.S. and Israel; recipient numerous commns. for sculpture. Recipient design award Ceramic Tile Inst., 1975; award Madonna Festival Competition, Los Angeles, Nat. Orange Show, San Bernardino, Calif., Calif. State Fari, Sacramento. Home and studio: 4808 Mary Ellen Ave Sherman Oaks CA 91423

CARL, RICHARD ALAN, computer cons. co. exec.; b. Little Rock, Oct. 23, 1945; s. Richard Charles and Catherine Ann (Lee) C.; m. Bonnie Sue Mandel, Nov. 28, 1982. A.B., Columbia U., 1967; A.M., U. Chgo., 1969, M.B.A., 1972. Statis. program advisor U. Chgo., 1967-69; instr. computer sci. U. Ill., Chgo., 1969-72; research analyst First Nat. Bank of Chgo., 1970-72; asst. v.p., economist Wells Fargo Bank, NA, San Francisco, 1972-76; founder, pres. Automation Cons., Menlo Park, Calif., 1976—. Mem. Nat. Assn. Bus. Economists (v.p. San Francisco Bay Area Chpt. 1974-75, pres. 1975-76), Columbia U. Alumni Assn. No. Calif. (pres. 1974-76), Assn. Computer Programmers and Analysts, Data Processing Mgmt. Assn., Profl. and Tech. Cons. Assn., Ind. Computer Cons. Assn. Home: 350 Sharon Park Dr Apt M-3 Menlo Park CA 94025 Office: 610 Santa Cruz Ave Suite 204 Menlo Park CA 94025

CARLAND, JAMES FRANK, III, pediatrician; b. St. Louis, Mar. 24, 1941; s. James Frank and Winifred (Miller) C.; B.A. cum laude in Psychology, U. Colo., 1963, M.D. cum laude 1967; m. Jane Hopp, Sept. 23, 1978; children—Patrick N., Liesl R., Jill M. Intern in pediatrics, U. Colo Sch. Medicine, Colo. Gen. Hosp., 1967-68; resident in pediatrics, U. Wash., Children's Orthopedic Hosp., Seattle, 1968-69, chief resident, 1969-70; fellow in pediatric respiratory disease, 1969-70; pediatrician, Mesa Pediatrics Profl. Assn., Mesa, Ariz., 1970-72; practice medicine specializing in pediatrics, Mesa, 1972—; chmn. pediatrics, Southside Dist. Hosp., 1972-73; chmn. pediatrics Mesa Luth. Hosp., 1974-75, sec. med. staff, 1976; chmn. pediatrics Desert Samaritan Hosp., 1978—, chmn. pediatric critical care, 1979—; cons. in field. Pres., Yesterday's Wings, Ltd., Mesa, 1976—. Served with USNR, 1967-73. Recipient A. Gordon Meml. award, 1965; F.E. Gengenbach award, 1966; W.A. Robb award, 1967; Gottesfield Meml. Prize, 1965, 67 (all from U. Colo. Sch. Medicine), U.S. Pub. Health Service grantee. Mem. Am. Acad. Pediatrics (sec. Ariz. chpt.), Maricopa County (exec. com.), Ariz. pediatric socs., AMA, Maricopa County, Ariz. med. socs., Flying Physician's Assn., Alpha Omega Alpha, Waring Soc. Contbr. articles in field to profl. jours. Patentee in field. Home: 2434 S Catarina St Mesa AZ 85202 Office: 2600 E Southern Mesa AZ 85282

CARLBERG, DUANE ALLEN, hospital administrator; b. Los Angeles, Feb. 10, 1948; s. Charles Duane and Flora Millie (Seals) C.; m. Barbara Lynn Chapluk, Oct. 31, 1970; children—Kristina Michele, Kara Maureen, Kevin Michael John. B.A., Calif. State U., Fullerton, 1971; M.P.A. in Health Services Adminstrn., U. So. Calif., 1979. Various health care mgmt. positions, 1970-76; adminstr. Lincoln Community Hosp., Buena Park, Calif., 1976-78; exec. v.p., dir. Inter-Community Hosp., Covina, Calif., 1978—; preceptor Health Services Adminstrn. Residency Program, U. So. Calif. Mem. Bd. Orgn. for After-Stroke Resocialization; mem. emergency care task force Orange County Health Planning Council, 1977-78; bd. dirs. East San Gabriel Valley Vis. Nurses Assn. Mem. Am. Coll. Hosp. Adminstrs., Hosp. Fin. Mgmt. Assn. (advanced), Am. Pub. Health Assn., Am. Soc. Law and Medicine, U. So. Calif. Health Services Adminstrn. Alumni Assn. (pres. 1981-82), Pi Sigma Alpha. Office: 303 N 3d St Covina CA 91723

CARLE, HARRY LLOYD, social worker, career devel. specialist; b. Chgo., Oct. 26, 1927; s. Lloyd Benjamin and Clara Bell (Lee) C.; B.S.S., Seattle U., 1952; M.S.W., U. Wash., 1966; m. Karlen Elizabeth Howe, Oct. 14, 1967; children—Kristen Elizabeth and Sylvia Ann (twins), Eric Lloyd. Indsl. placement and employer relations rep. State of Wash., Seattle, 1955-57, parole and probation officer, Seattle and Tacoma, 1957-61, parole employment specialist, 1961-63, vocat. rehab. officer, 1963-64; clin. social worker Western State Hosp., Ft. Steilacoom, Washington and U.S. Penitentiary, McNeil Island, Wash., 1964-66; exec. dir. Community Action Council/Social Planning Council, Everett, Wash., 1966-77; career devel. counselor, 1962—; employment and edn. counselor Pierce County Jail Social Services, Tacoma, 1979-81; dir. employment devel. clinic North Rehab. Facility, King County Div. Alcoholism and Substance Abuse, Seattle, 1981—; community orgn./agy. problems mgmt. cons., 1968—; mem. social service project staff Pacific Luth. U., Tacoma, 1979-81. Cons. to pres. Geneal. Inst., Salt Lake City, 1974-78. Served with USN, 1944-46. U.S. Office Vocat. Rehab. scholar, 1965-66. Mem. Seattle Geneal. Soc. (pres. 1974-76), Soc. Advancement Mgmt. (chpt. exec. v.p. 1970-71), Acad. Cert. Social Workers, Nat. Assn. Social Workers, Pa. German Soc., Henckel Family Nat. Assn., various hist. and geneal. socs. in Cumberland, Perry and Lancaster counties, Pa., Peoria and Fulton Counties, Ill., Seattle. Roman Catholic. Home: 1425 10th Pl N Edmonds WA 98020 Office: North Rehab Facility 2002 NE 150th St Seattle WA 98155

CARLEONE, JOSEPH, administrative mechanical engineer; b. Phila., Jan. 30, 1946; s. Frank Anthony and Amelia (Ciaccia) C.; m. Shirley Elizabeth Atwell, June 29, 1968; children—Gia Maria, Joan Marie. B.S., Drexel U., 1968, M.S., 1970, Ph.D., 1972. Civilian engring. trainee, mech. engr. Phila. Naval Shipyard, 1963-68; grad. asst. in applied mechanics Drexel U., Phila., 1968-72, postdoctoral research assoc., 1972-73, NDEA fellow, 1968-71, adj. prof. mechanics, 1974-75, 77—; chief research engr. Dyna East Corp., Phila., 1973-82; chief scientist warhead tech. Aerojet Ordnance Co., Downey, Calif., 1982—. Mem. ASME, Sigma Xi, Tau Beta Pi, Pi Tau Sigma, Phi Kappa Phi. Contbr. articles to profl. jours.; researcher explosive and metal interaction, ballistcis, projectile penetration, impact of plates. Home: 19741 Marsala Dr Yorba Linda CA 92686 Office: 9236 E Hall Rd Downey CA 90241

CARLINE, JAN DANA, educational evaluator; b. Pontiac, Mich., Sept. 3, 1948; s. Stanley E. and Marjorie Jacquelyn (Walsh) C.; m. Carol Sue Ivory, Aug. 17, 1970. B.A., U. Mich., 1970; M.Ed., U. Wash., 1976, Ph.D., 1979. Asst. research prof. div. research in med. edn. U. Wash., Seattle, 1981—. Vol. coordinator Seattle Art Mus.; safety chmn. Mountaineers. Recipient Alumni award U. Mich., 1967. Mem. Am. Ednl. Research Assn., Am. Psychol. Assn., Pi Lambda Theta. Contbr. articles to profl. jours. Office: WAMI SM-22 U Wash Seattle WA 98195

CARLING, RICHARD JUNIUS, lawyer, state senator; b. Salt Lake City, Dec. 6, 1937; s. Jacob Junius and Reba (Olsen) C.; B.S. in Polit. Sci., U. Utah, 1962, J.D., 1965; m. Barbara Diane Saxey, June 8, 1961; children—Angela, Cynthia, Teresa, Douglas Richard. Compiler water rights sect. Utah State Engrs. Office, Salt Lake City, 1960-62; admitted to Utah bar, 1965, since practiced in Salt Lake City; mem. Utah Ho. of Reps., 1967-73, chmn. bus. and commerce, 1969-73; mem. Utah Senate, 1974—, chmn. bus., labor and econ. devel. com. and higher edn. appropriations com., 1979—, mem. judiciary com., 1981—; partner firm Shearer, Carling & Dangerfield. Del. NATO Conf., Am. Council Young Polit. Leaders, Europe, 1967, chmn. policy adv. com. Salt Lake Project Head Start, 1967-68; dir. Salt Lake County Assn. Retarded Children, Travelers Aid; chmn. Indian Hills Sch. Community Council; mem. Utah Gen. Aviation Council, 1967-70; mem. adv. com. 2d Dist. Juvenile Ct. Mem. Salt Lake County and Utah Republican Exec. Com. Trustee, Salt Lake Community Services Council, 1975—; mem. Salt Lake City Track Club, 1978—; bd. dirs. Beehive Track Club, 1978; mem. Utah Non-Game Adv. Council, 1980—. Mem. Utah (legis. com., tax sect. 1965—), Salt Lake County bars, Phi Delta Phi. Mem. Ch. of Jesus Christ of Latter-day Saints. Club: Bonneville Knife and Fork. Home: 1075 Alton Way Salt Lake City UT 84108 Office: Continental Bank Bldg Salt Lake City UT 84101

CARLINGTON, GARY ALLEN, accountant; b. Puyallup, Wash., Feb. 25, 1947; s. Harry Arthur and Frances Lucille (Rosin) C.; B.A., U. Puget Sound, 1969; M.S. in Taxation, Golden Gate U., 1978; m. Sara Ann Martinson, Dec. 4, 1976; children—Rachel Amber and Courtney Ann (twins). Acct., Knight, Vale & Gregory, C.P.A.s, Tacoma, 1969-76, Moreland, Phillips, Carlington & McCutcheon, C.P.A.s, Tacoma, 1976-78; acct., v.p., mng. dir. Phillips, Carlington & Co., C.P.A.s, Tacoma, 1978-83; owner Gary A. Carlington, C.P.A., Puyallup, Wash., 1983—. C.P.A., Wash. Mem. Am. Inst. C.P.A.s, Wash. Soc. C.P.A.s, Tacoma Estate Planning Council. Republican. Lutheran. Home: 1122 W Main Ave Puyallup WA 98371 Office: 315 S Meridian St Puyallup WA 98371

CARLISLE, JAMES HENRY, IV, surgeon; b. Manila, Philippine Islands, Nov. 15, 1935 (parents Am. citizens); s. James Henry III and Virginia (Anderson) C.; B.S., U. Wyo., 1957; M.D., U. Colo. Sch. Medicine, 1964; m. Gisela Mannhardt, Mar. 13, 1959; children—George, Julia, David. Intern, U. Colo. Med. Center, Denver, 1964-65, resident in gen. surgery, 1965-69; resident in thoracic surgery U. Calif. Med. Center, Sacramento, 1969-70; practice medicine specializing in gen., vascular surgery, Phoenix, 1973—; mem. staff Phoenix Bapt. Hosp., John C. Lincoln Hosp., Phoenix. Served with M.S.C. U.S. Army, 1957-60. Diplomate Am. Bd. Surgery. Fellow A.C.S.; mem. Denver Acad. Surgery, Phoenix Surg. Soc. Democrat. Methodist. Office: 6036 N 19th Ave Phoenix AZ 85015

CARLISLE, WAYNE JOSEPH, geologist; b. Kemmerer, Wyo., Mar. 23, 1948; s. Wayne Harlan and Charlotte Marion (Duthie) C.; B.S., Weber State Coll., 1974; M.S., (Champlin Petroleum scholar), U. Wyo., 1979; m. Susan Crockett, Feb. 27, 1971; children—Megan Bree, Alana Jo. Geologist, field engr. Kemmerer Coal Co., Frontier, Wyo., 1974-76; research asst. Remote Sensing Lab., U. Wyo., Laramie, 1977-78; geologist Conoco, Inc., Denver, 1979-81; sr. geologist Milestone Petroleum Inc., Billings, Mont., 1981—; speaker profl. conf. Mem. Soc. Econ. Paleontologists and Mineralogists, Am. Assn. Petroleum Geologists, Rocky Mountain Assn. Geologists, Sigma Xi, Phi Kappa Phi. Lutheran. Office: First Northwestern Bank Center PO Box 1855 Billings MT 59103

CARLQUIST, J. WILLIAM, video and film executive, consultant, educator; b. Los Angeles, Sept. 18, 1948; s. Robert William and Delight (Shaffer) C.; m. Stephanie Jean Hurley, June 19, 1976; children—Nicholaus William, Hillary Jean. B.S.E.E., Calif. Poly. U., 1972. Owner Audio/Video Products, Inc., Burbank, Calif., 1971—; owner, Horizontal Editing Studios, Burbank, 1977—; instr. UCLA extension, 1979—. Mem. IEEE, AIA, Soc. Motion Picture and TV Engrs. Office: 2625 W Olive Ave Burbank CA 91505

CARLSEN, BEN ALFRED, JR., county ofcl.; b. Seattle, Dec. 7, 1941; s. Ben Alfred and Dorothy May (Wright) C.; B.S., U. Wash., 1963; postgrad. Calif. State U., Long Beach, 1973, Calif. State U., Los Angeles, 1976; M.B.A., Pepperdine U., 1978. Dept. supr. Barker Bros. Corp., Los

Angeles, 1964; corr. Union Carbide Corp., Los Angeles, 1964-66; caseworker County of Los Angeles, 1967-68, social services supr., 1968-69, data systems analyst, 1969-70, sr. fiscal analyst, 1970-71, prin. fiscal analyst, 1972-79, chief mgmt. systems Dept. Health, 1979—; cons. nationwide demonstration project on computer based info. systems; cons. adminstrv. cost control State of Calif., 1976; instr. Community Coll., 1979—, Calif. State U.-Dominguez Hills; Los Angeles rep. Calif. Welfare Dirs. Fiscal Com., 1977-79; community rep. UCLA Health Adminstrn. Task Force, 1980-81. Cert. in data processing, supervisory mgmt., public sector labor-mgmt.; notary public; real estate licensee, Calif. Mem. Am. Mgmt. Assn., Los Angeles County Mgmt. Council, WHO, Am. Public Health Assn., Health Mgmt. Systems Soc., Advocates for Public Health, Los Angeles County Mgmt. Forum, Assn. Systems Mgmt. (pres. So. Calif. chpt., program com. internat. Conf. 1982, 83; Merit award), Nat. Notary Assn., U. Wash., Pepperdine U. alumni assns., Productivity Council of South-West (dir. white collar productivity), World Future Soc. Republican. Clubs: Toastmasters, Internat. Entrepreneurs (Los Angeles); Century (Malibu). Author: Evaluation of Feasibility of Staggering Welfare Payments, 1978; Dissecting the Productivity Animal, 1983; contbr. articles to profl. jours. Home: 1553 Randall Ct Los Angeles CA 90065 Office: 313 N Figueroa St Los Angeles CA 90012

CARLSON, BARBARA COIN, psychologist; b. Davenport, Iowa, July 27, 1927; d. William F. and Jule I. (Mulcahy) Coin; m. Douglas D. Carlson, May 8, 1948; children—Eric, Matt, Kurt. A.A. in Nursing, Los Angeles Valley Coll., 1964; B.S. in Nursing, Calif. State U.-Los Angeles, 1969, M.A., in Psychology, 1975; Ph.D. in Profl. Psychology, U.S. Internat. U., San Diego, 1976. Clin. psychologist, Rowland Heights, Calif., 1977—; staff psychologist Spectrum Counseling Services, Arcadia, Calif., 1975—; prof. nursing Cerritos Coll., Norwalk, Calif., 1972—; cons. to hosps. and industry. Mem. Am. Psychol. Assn., Calif. Psychol. Assn., Calif. Tchrs. Assn., NEA, Am. Nurses Assn., Calif. Nurses Assn., Assn. Holistic Health, Profl. Assn. Continuing Edn. (pres. 1979—). Address: 2304 Cordoza Ave Rowland Heights CA 91748

CARLSON, BRUCE ALLAN, aquarium curator; b. Akron, Ohio, Jan. 8, 1949; s. Richard Bruce and Maxine Lucille (Pringle) C.; B.S., U. Mich., 1971; postgrad. U. Hawaii, 1975—. Research asst. U. Mich. Mus. Zoology, Ann Arbor, 1968-71; lectr. ichthyology U. South Pacific, Fiji, 1975; teaching asst. ichthyology U. Hawaii, Honolulu, 1976-77, curator Waikiki Aquarium, 1977—; NSF student Scripps Inst., 1967, Am. Mus., 1969-70; Peace Corps vol. Smithsonian program Fiji, 1972-75. Fellow Am. Assn. Zool. Parks and Aquariums; mem. Western Soc. Naturalists, Am. Soc. Ichthyologists and Herpetologists, Am. Zool. Soc., Sigma Xi. Contbr. articles to profl. jours. Address: 2777 Kalakaua Ave Honolulu HI 96815

CARLSON, CHARLES RICHARD, college dean; b. Santa Monica, Calif., Oct. 14, 1935; s. Oscar and Esther Frieda (Carlson) C.; A.A., Santa Monica Coll., 1955; A.B., UCLA, 1955-57; M.A., San Fernando Valley State U., 1966; Ph.D., U. So. Calif., 1972; m. Marsha Ann Dolby, 1976. Tchr., Los Angeles City Schs., 1962-66; prof., adminstr., Barstow Coll., 1966-71; dean Bakersfield (Calif.) Coll., 1971—; adj. prof. Chapman Coll., George AFB, Calif., 1968-71, U. Calif. Extension, 1977-80, Calif. State Coll.-Bakersfield, 1981—; cons. ednl. programs for sr. citizens, various colls., univs.; partner Gerontol. Cons. Assos., 1977—. Bd. dirs. Bakersfield Rescue Mission, 1979—, v.p., 1981—; bd. dirs. Bakersfield Devel. Corp., 1979—. Served with AUS, 1957-60. Mem. Calif. Tchrs. Assn., Assn. Calif. Community Coll. Adminstrs., NEA, Western Gerontol. Soc., Downtown Bus. Assn. (dir. 1974-80). Presbyterian (ruling elder 1973—). Club: Kiwanis (dir. 1974-78, 81—). Home: 5205 Eastridge Ct Bakersfield CA 93306 Office: 1801 Panorama Dr Bakersfield CA 93305

CARLSON, ERNEST BERNHARD, III, accountant; b. Carlsbad, N.Mex., May 22, 1950; s. Ernest Bernhard, Jr., and Mary (Windham) C.; m. Cheryl Jan Milner, June 24, 1978; 1 dau., Kirstin Jeanne. B.B.A., N.Mex. State U., 1977. C.P.A., N.Mex., Tex. Sr. acct. Trott & Co., C.P.A.s, Midland, Tex., 1977-79, Elms, Faris & Co., Midland, 1979-81; ptnr. in charge of office, Carlsbad, N.Mex., 1981—. Served with N.G., 1969-76. Mem. Am. Inst. C.P.A.s, N.Mex. Soc. C.P.A.s, Tex. Soc. C.P.A.s, Carlsbad C. of C. Methodist. Clubs: Elks, Masons. Home: 1902 Gwenda Carlsbad NM 88220 Office: 1008 W Pierce Carlsbad NM 88220

CARLSON, HENRIETTA MAE, nurse; b. Beach, N.D., Nov. 4, 1927; d. Andrew and Almeda Mae (Rouse) C.; diploma Gt. Falls div. Mont. State U., 1948; postgrad. in sociology Westmar Coll., 1951-52; B.S. in Nursing, Mont. State U., Bozeman, 1953; M.S. in Nursing Adminstrn., U. Minn., Mpls., 1959. Staff nurse Mont. Deaconess Hosp., 1948-49, Johnston Meml. Hosp., Beach, 1949-51, 52, 53; sch. nurse Westmar Coll., 1951-52; with VA, 1953—, asst. chief nursing service, Miles City, Mont., 1953-58, Sioux Falls, S.D., 1960-63, asst. chief nursing service, Fargo, N.D., 1963-69, Boise, Idaho, 1969-75, chief nursing service VA Med. Center, Ft. Harrison, Mont., 1975—; mem. profl. adv. coms. Vol., Helena Hospice, Helena, Mont.; mem. Fed. Exec. Council, Helena. Recipient spl. advancement for performance VA, 1971. Mem. Am. Nurses Assn., Mont. Nurses Assn. (sec.-treas. chpt. 1953-54), Alpha Tau Delta, Sigma Theta Tau, Epsilon Sigma Alpha (pres. chpt. 1963-64). Lutheran. Clubs: Altrusa (sec. 1979-80, pres. 1981-82) (Helena); Broadwater Athletic. nurse; b. Beach, N.D., Nov. 4, 1927; d. Andrew and Almeda Mae (Rouse) C.; diploma Gt. Falls div. Mont. State U., 1948; postgrad. in sociology Westmar Coll., 1951-52; B.S. in Nursing, Mont. State U., Bozeman, 1953; M.S. in Nursing Adminstrn., U. Minn., Mpls., 1959. Staff nurse Mont. Deaconess Hosp., 1948-49, Johnston Meml. Hosp., Beach, 1949-51, 52, 53; sch. nurse Westmar Coll., 1951-52; with VA, 1953—, asst. chief nursing service, Miles City, Mont., 1953-58, Sioux Falls, S.D., 1960-63, asst. chief nursing service, Fargo, N.D., 1963-69, Boise, Idaho, 1969-75, chief nursing service VA Med. Center, Ft. Harrison, Mont., 1975—; mem. profl. adv. coms. Vol., Helena Hospice, Helena, Mont.; mem. Fed. Exec. Council, Helena. Recipient spl. advancement for performance VA, 1971. Mem. Am. Nurses Assn., Mont. Nurses Assn. (sec.-treas. chpt. 1953-54), Alpha Tau Delta, Sigma Theta Tau, Epsilon Sigma Alpha (pres. chpt. 1963-64). Lutheran. Clubs: Altrusa (sec. 1979-80, pres. 1981-82) (Helena); Broadwater Athletic. Home: 1303 Mountain View Helena MT 59601 Office: Fort Harrison MT 59636

CARLSON, JAMES FREDERICK, architect; b. Seattle, Dec. 3, 1946; s. Julian Frederick and Dorothy C.; A.A., Rio Hondo Coll., 1973; B.S. in Arch., Calif. State Poly. U., Pomona, 1975; m. Astrid Van Ravensberg, Aug. 29, 1970. Archtl. draftsman The Austin Co., Los Angeles, 1975-76, archtl. designer, Irvine, Calif., 1976-78, project planner, Irvine, 1978—; solar cons.; residential archtl. designer; publisher, author; works include: Solar Primer One, 1975, numerous solar residences, indsl. and comml. facilities. Served with USN, 1965-69; Vietnam. Mem. AIA (asso.). Home: Newport Beach CA 92663 Office: 18800 Von Karman Ave Irvine CA 92713

CARLSON, JOHN GREGORY, psychology educator; b. Mpls., Mar. 25, 1941; s. Wentworth Robert and Dorothy Adeline (Neff) C.; m. Melinda Jo Keyser, Aug. 1, 1963 (div.); chldren—Jared Matthew, Sarah Rachel; m. 2d, Betty Knight Clark, July 9, 1981; 1 stepdau., Wendy Carol Franklin. B.A. summa cum laude, U. Minn., 1963, Ph.D., 1967. Trainee Ctr. for Research in Human Learning, U. Minn., Mpls., 1965-67; research psychologist Honeywell, Mpls., 1966; asst. prof. psychology U. Hawaii, Honolulu, 1967-72, assoc. prof., 1972-76, prof., 1976—; vis. prof. U. Colo., 1973, 75, 79, 80, U. Minn., 1974, 76, 82. NSF fellow, 1967; NIMH fellow, 1975. Mem. Biofeedback Behavioral Medicine Soc. Hawaii (pres.), Am. Psychol. Assn., Biofeedback Soc. Am., Phi Beta Kappa. Democratic. Contbr. chpts. to books, articles to profl. jours. Office: 2430 Campus Rd U Hawaii Honolulu HI 96822

CARLSON, LEROY EINAR, real estate investment trust exec.; b. Los Angeles, Oct. 29, 1945; s. Einar Carl and Myrtle Christine (Gaston) C.; divorced; children—Daniel, Kari. B.S., U. So. Calif., 1971; C.P.A., Calif. Acct., Main Hurdman C.P.A.s, Los Angeles, 1971-74; controller-treas. Egsmetro Devel. Constr. Co., Los Angeles, 1974-75; dir., chief fin. officer Real Estate Investment Trust Calif., Santa Monica, 1980—. Mem. Calif. Soc. C.P.A.s, Am. Inst. C.P.A.s. Office: 2444 Wilshire Blvd Santa Monica CA 90403

CARLSON, MARILYN WALTER, investment adviser; b. N.Y.C., Apr. 19, 1935; d. Julius George and Ethel Margaret (Schwinn) Walter; m. Carl H. Carlson, Nov. 4, 1972. A.B., Syracuse U., 1956. Research asst. Smith, Barney & Co., 1956-58, security analyst, 1958-62; sr. security analyst Pickard & Co., 1962-66; v.p. instnl. research W.E. Hutton, 1966-72; dir. research, v.p. Shareholders Mgmt. Co., Los Angeles, 1972-75; v.p., portfolio mgr. Trust Co. of the West, Los Angeles, 1977-80; owner, dir., investment adviser Stonebridge Capital Mgmt. Co., Los Angeles, 1980—; dir. Sunset Industries, Cybix Intelligent Systems. Treas. Commuter Computer, Los Angeles. Conservative Republican. Clubs: Bel-Air Country, The Springs Country, Calif. Yacht. Office: 1880 Century Park E Suite 717 Los Angeles CA 90067

CARLSON, NATALIE LOUISE, tax accountant; b. Butte, Mont., Feb. 12, 1938; d. Frank Vincent and Marie Lynn (DeJohn) Boroni; student Mont. State U., at Bozeman, San Diego Jr. Coll.; B.A. U. Mont.-Missoula, 1984; children—Kym, Kert, Kynny. Various clk. and secretarial positions, 1953-65; tax acct. Calif. Tchrs. Tax Service, San Diego, 1969-70; individual practice tax acctg., San Diego, 1970-73, Missoula, 1973—; cons. various areas of tax law. Mem. acctg. adv. com. Missoula County High Sch., 1977-80, now mem. Citizens' Task Force for Reorgn.; active PTA, Vol. Income Tax Assistance; mem. Title I Parent Adv. Council, Dist. 11 Human Resource Council; team mgr. Bobby Sox Softball for Girls, San Diego, 1969-73; founder Christians in Transition, 1980; athletic dir. Big Sky High Sch. Booster Club, 1981. Recipient Bus. and Profl. Women's Scholarship award, 1979; others. Mem. Am. Soc. Women Accountants, Nat. Assn. Accountants, Assn. Legal Students, Bus. and Profl. Women. C. of C. (small bus. council com.), Mortar Bd. (Pentrailia chpt.), Beta Sigma Phi. Roman Catholic. Club: Soroptimist. Home and office: 2535 W Central St Missoula MT 59801

CARLSON, NELS JAMES, optometrist; b. Seattle, Jan. 1, 1950; s. John Carlyle and Mary Navonne (Surtees) C.; m. Cheryl Lynn Dyer, July 6, 1974; children—Kristina Suzanne, Ana-Lisa. B.A., U. Wash., 1972; O.D., So. Calif. Coll. Optometry, 1977. Pvt. practice optometry, Kirkland, Wash., 1977—; dir. Totem Lake Vision Ctr., Kirkland. Recipient Al Dennis award So. Calif. Coll. Optometry, 1977. Mem. Am. Optometric Assn. (chmn. membership devel. com. 1981, 82, sec. sports vision sect., 1981, 82, vice chmn., 1983, liaison to U.S. Olympic com. sports medicine dept. for Nat. Sports Festival V 1983), Wash. Optometric Assn. Mem. Evergrace Bible Ch. Office: Totem Lake Vision Ctr 11830 NE 128th St Kirkland WA 98033

CARLSON, RALPH WILLIAM, JR., energy resources company executive; b. Oak Park, Ill., Dec. 28, 1936; s. Ralph W. and Evelyn Marie (Benson) C.; m. Donna Drevs, Feb. 9, 1963; children—Daniel, Karen, Susan, Robert, Kathleen. B.A., Mich. State U., 1958; M.B.A., U. Chgo., 1965; J.D., De Paul U., 1976. Bar: Ill. Group product mgr. The Kendall Co., Chgo., 1966-70; dir. mktg. Ovaltine Products Co. div. Sandoz, Inc., Chgo., 1970-76; mgr. new products Arco Polymers, Inc. subs. Atlantic Richfield Co., Chgo., 1976-78, mgr. internat. fleet ops. Arco Transp. Co., Long Beach, Calif., 1978-81; mgr. mktg. planning Arco Solar Industries, Woodland Hills, Calif., 1981—. Mem. Oak Park Sch. Bd., 1976-78. Served to lt. USNR, 1958-63. Mem. ABA, Am. Mktg. Assn., U.S. Naval Inst., Delta Chi. Republican. Roman Catholic. Club: Economic (Chgo.). Home: 9117 Wagner River Circle Fountain Valley CA 92708 Office: 21011 Warner Center Ln Woodland Hills CA 91367

CARLSON, RICHARD WARNER, banker, journalist; b. Boston, Feb. 10, 1941; s. W.E. and Ruth Miriam C.; student U. Miss., 1961-62; m. Patricia Caroline Swanson, Feb. 18, 1979; children—Tucker McNear, Buckley Peck. Editorial asst. Los Angeles Times, 1963-64; gen. assignment reporter, night bur. mgr. UPI, San Francisco and Sacramento, 1964-65; investigative reporter, anchorman ABC-TV, San Francisco, 1965-70, polit. editor, investigative reporter, Los Angeles, 1970-74; producer, writer, dir. documentary films NBC-TV, Burbank, Calif., 1974; anchorman, host Carlson & Co., CBS-TV, San Diego, 1975-76; sr. v.p. San Diego Fed. Savs. & Loan Assn., 1976—; dir. Calif. Gen. Mortgage Assurance Corp., 1976—; lectr., cons. in field. Co-chmn., San Diego Coalition, 1980-81, Citizens for Open Space, 1978; pres. Republican Bus. and Profl. Club, 1980, Actors and Others, Inc., 1971-75; bd. dirs. San Diego chpt. San Diego Muscular Dystrophy Assn., 1977-80, Western Water Found., 1980-81, Nat. Safety Council, 1980-81. Recipient award investigative reporting AP, 1968, 76, 77, award news analysis, 1968, 69, 75; Nat. Headliners award, 1968, Emmy award, 1972, 76, 77; Golden Mike award best documentary, 1972, investigative reporting, 1975, 76, best commentary, 1975; George Foster Peabody award, 1976; Los Angeles Press Club Grand award, 1976; San Diego Press Club award, 1976, 77; award merit San Diego Hist. Soc., 1979; Mexican-Am. Found. Amigo de Distinction, 1979. Mem. Savs. and Loan Clearing House, Calif. C. of C., San Diego C. of C. (v.p., dir. 1977-80), Sigma Delta Chi. Republican. Episcopalian. Clubs: Press, Univ. (San Diego); Thunderbird Country (Palm Springs, Calif.); La Jolla Beach and Tennis; Mid-Ocean (Tuckerstown, Bermuda). Author: History of Women in San Diego, 1978; also articles. Home: 7956 Avenida Alamar La Jolla CA 92037 Office: 600 B St San Diego CA 92183

CARLSON, ROBERT FREDRICK, lawyer; b. Sacramento, Jan. 28, 1928; s. Fred Neil and Kathleen Bridget (Evans) C.; B.A., St. Mary's Coll., 1949; LL.B., U. Calif., 1952, J.D., 1952; m. Barbara J. Werner, Aug. 20, 1975; children by previous marriage—Richard Anthony, Kenneth Michael, Diane Elizabeth. Atty., chief counsel Calif. Dept. Transp., Sacramento, 1952—; pres., mem. bd. adminstrn. Pub. Employees Ret. System, Sacramento, 1971—; mem. adminstrv. bd. Blue Shield of Calif., 1979—; adj. prof. law McGeorge Sch. Law, U. Pacific, Sacramento, 1975—; dir. A.G.E. Mut. Fund; mem. transp. research bd. Nat. Acad. Scis., Washington, 1965—, chmn. legal resources group. Chmn. bd. trustees Sutter Community Hosps., 1979—. Mem. Am., Calif., Sacramento County bar assns., Calif. State Employees Assn. (past pres.), Assembly of Govtl. Employees (past pres.). Democrat. Roman Catholic. Club: K. C. Author: (with others) Selected Studies in Highway Law, 1976. Home: 2120 Lambeth Way Carmichael CA 95608 Office: 1120 N St Sacramento CA 95814

CARLSON, VERNE, writer, cameraman; b. Bridgeport, Conn., Apr. 8, 1926; s. Ralph Ivar and Edna Mae (Marsh) C.; m. Sylvia Eleanor Fleishman, June 1, 1951 (div.). Pres. Sylverne Prodns., San Francisco, 1956-70; exec. v.p. Audio Motion Pictures, San Francisco, 1970-71; pres. Cinesync Inc., Los Angeles, 1971-79; freelance writer, cameraman, 1979—; bus. mgr. Internat. Photographer mag., Hollywood, Calif., 1982—; instr. advanced film Moorpark (Calif.) Coll., 1980-81. Served with USN, 1942-46, USMC, 1948-50. Mem. Internat. Photographers, Am. Soc. Lighting Dirs. Author: (with Sylvia E. Carlson) Professional Cameraman's Handbook, 1970, rev. edit., 1974, 81; Cowboy Cookbook, 1981; translated film/video terms into various langs. Office: Internat Photographer 7155 Sunset Blvd Suite 150 Hollywood CA 90046

CARLSSON, JEANNE DELORME, interior designer; b. Mt. Vernon, Wash., Nov. 5, 1939; d. Lawrence Anthony and Eleanor Louise (Hoier) Reisinger; m. Eigil Carlsson, Jan. 1, 1979; children—Michael, Roland, Lisa, Richmond, Kristen, Shara, Marci. Student U. Puget Sound, Tacoma, 1957-59; diploma in interior design Chgo. Sch. Interior Design, 1970. Freelance designer, 1970-72; drapery cons. Levin's Furniture Co., Bellingham, Wash., 1972-74; interior designer Continental Furniture Co., Bellingham, 1974-76; pres., interior designer DeLorme's, Bellingham, 1976—; cons., tchr. in field. Active local PTA, Boy Scouts, Am. Cancer Soc. Mem. N. Puget Sound Interior Design Assn. (pres. 1978), Whatcom Women in Bus. (pres. 1983). Clubs: Bellingham Yacht, Bellingham Golf and Country. Home and Office: 680 Cherry Ln Bellingham WA 98226

CARLSTROM, STEPHEN PAUL, boat excursion co. exec.; b. San Diego, July 23, 1944; s. Charles William and Irene Elizabeth (Houser) C.; student Grossmont Coll., 1962-64, Ariz. State U., 1964; m. Clara Louise Cochran, May 3, 1968; children—Stephen Paul, Joseph Hall. Buyer, prodn. control supr., new constrn. cost accountant San Diego Marine Constrn. Co., 1967-72; mgr. Star & Crescent Boat Co., San Diego, 1972-76, pres., 1976—. Bd. dirs. San Diego Conv. and Visitors Bur.; past pres. SKAL. Served with USCG, 1965, Res., 1965-71. Mem. Hotel Sales Mgmt. Assn. Home: PO Box 751 San Diego CA 92112 Office: 570 N Harbor Dr PO Box 751 San Diego CA 92112

CARMALT, E. DUANE, physician; b. Pitts., May 11, 1943; s. Emmett Duane and Marie (Bordy) C.; A.B., Johns Hopkins, 1965; M.D., Duke, 1969. Intern U. Okla. Hospitals, Oklahoma City, 1969-70; resident in medicine Wadsworth VA Hosp., Los Angeles, 1972-72; fellow in infectious disease, 1972-74; physician emergency medicine Queen of Angels Hosp., Los Angeles, 1975-76; dir. emergency medicine Encino (Calif.) Hosp., 1976, staff physician emergency dept., 1977—; cons. in infectious disease, emergency medicine Huntington Meml. Hosp., Pasadena, Calif., 1977-79; med. dir. Tarzana (Calif.) Psychiat. Hosp., 1979—; med. staff physician Med. Ctr. Tarzana (Calif.), West Hills Med. Ctr., Canoga Park, Calif., Northridge (Calif.) Hosp., West Park Hosp., Canoga Park, Parkwood Community Hosp., Canoga Park. Served to maj. USMC, 1973. Mem. Am. Coll. Physicians, Am. Coll. Emergency Physicians. Editor: Rounds, Wadsworth VA Hospital, 1972-74; contbr. articles to med. jours. Home: 21844 Corvo Way Topanga CA 90290

CARMAN, E(RNEST) DAY, lawyer, writer; b. Mpls., Nov. 25, 1922; s. Ernest Clarke and Juanita Howland (Day) C.; children—Eric Christian, Brooke Howland, Christiane Marie, Dayna, Heidi. B.A., U. So. Calif., 1944; M.A., Stanford U., 1947; J.D., U. San Francisco, 1957; Dr. es Science Politique, U. Geneva (Switzerland), 1950. Bar: Calif. 1957, U.S. Supreme Ct. 1970. With various law firms, 1958-70; mem. Carman & Mansfield, Corona del Mar and San Jose, Calif., 1970—. Chmn. Santa Clara County Dem. Com., 1966-70; active Children's Home Soc., Cerebral Palsy Assn., others. Served with USMC, 1943-46. Mem. ABA, Assn. Trial Lawyers Am., Calif. Trial Lawyers Assn. Democrat. San Francisco Press, Rotary, Saratoga Swim, Saratoga Tennis. Contbg. author legal jours. Home: 776 Cliff Ave Laguna Beach CA 92651 Office: Carman & Mansfield 2721 Coast Highway Corona del Mar CA 92625

CARMAN, HOY FRED, educator; b. Wallowa, Oreg., July 3, 1938; s. Hoy Ransom and Ruth Nina (Weinhard) C.; B.S., Oreg. State U., 1960, M.S., 1962; Ph.D., Mich. State U., 1964; m. Patricia Marie Gosse, June 4, 1960; children—Susan Marie, Laura Ann. Economist Econ. Research Service, U.S. Dept. Agr., East Lansing, Mich., 1964-65; prof. dept. agrl. econs. U. Calif., Davis, 1967—. Served to capt., U.S. Army, 1965-67. Found. Econ. Edn. fellow, 1968, Fulbright Research fellow New Zealand, 1973. Mem. Am. Agrl. Econs. Assn. (internat. travel grantee 1970), Internat. Assn. Agrl. Economists, Western Agrl. Econs. Assn., Alpha Gamma Rho, Alpha Zeta, Phi Kappa Phi. Republican. Contbr. articles to profl. jours. Home: 1108 Colby Dr Davis CA 95616 Office: Dept Agrl Econs U Calif Davis CA 95616

CARMANY, THOMAS BEAR, pathologist; b. Lebanon, Pa., Dec. 13, 1936; s. Earl F. and Marian (Bowman) C.; B.S., Lebanon Valley Coll., 1958; M.D., Jefferson Med. Coll., 1962; children—Rafael, Peter. Intern, Harrisburg (Pa.) Polyclinic Hosp., 1962-63; resident in pathology Jefferson Med. Coll., Phila., 1963-67; chief pathology Gallup Indian Med. Center (N.Mex.), 1967-69; dir. labs. McKinley Gen. and Rehoboth Christian hosps., Gallup, 1969—; clin. asso. U. N.Mex., 1970—; individual practice medicine specializing in pathology, Gallup, 1967—; pres. Rehoboth-McKinley Christian Health Service, Inc.; dir. N.Mex. Physicians Mut. Liability Co., N.Mex. Med. Labs., Inc.; chief of staff McKinley Gen. Hosp., 1979-80, Rehoboth Christian Hosp., 1981; mem. N.Mex. Cancer Control Program; cons. in field. Chmn. bloodmobile com. McKinley County, N.Mex., 1967-69; chmn. Area Health Coop. Com., 1980-81, Comprehensive Alcoholism Planning Council, 1981. Diplomate Am. Bd. Pathology. Fellow Am. Soc. Clin. Pathologists, Coll. Am. Pathologists; mem. Am. Soc. Cytology, Alpha Omega Alpha. Home: PO Box 1930 Gallup NM 87301 Office: McKinley Gen Hosp Gallup NM 87301

CARMODY, DOUGLAS JAMES, civil and traffic engr.; b. Newark, N.J., Apr. 11, 1924; s. William Alexander and Loretta Frances C.; m. Rosalie Elaine Hicks, July 14, 1945; children—Linda, Brian. B.S., U. Calif.-Berkeley, 1948, M.S., 1954. Registered civil engr., Calif.; registered traffic engr., Calif. Supervising sr. civil engr. Alameda County (Calif.), 1947-54; civil and traffic engr., 1954—; dir. parking and traffic dept. City of Modesto (Calif.), 1954—; cons. numerous Calif. cities on parking and transp. Mem., Downtown Modesto Assn., 1954—. Mem. Inst. Traffic Engrs., ASCE, Transp. Research Bd. Rep. Episcopalian. Home: 1239 Purdue Ave Modesto CA 95350 Office: 801 11th St Modesto CA 95354

CARMODY, SANDRA ELLEN, educator; curriculum specialist; b. Rochester, N.Y., June 14, 1944; d. Leslie Hugh Manley and Jeanette Ellen (Bradstreet) Murphy; m. Brendan William Carmody, Aug. 28, 1965 (div.); children—Theresa Ellen, Patrick William. B.A., Nazareth Coll. Rochester, 1971; M.Ed., U. Nev., 1980. Cert. elem. tchr., elem. and secondary counselor, adminstrn., Nev. Elem. tchr. Sch. Good Shepherd, Henrietta, N.Y., 1966-67, St. Christopher's Sch., Las Vegas, 1972-73, St. Anne's Sch., Las Vegas, 1973-74; elem. tchr. Clark County Sch. Dist., Las Vegas, 1974-79, curriculum cons. elem. phys. edn., dance, movement, 1978—; phys. edn. tchr. hearing impaired, 1981-83; elem. curriculum cons., 1983—. Chmn. dance div. Las Vegas Allied Arts Council, 1978. Mem. Am. Alliance Health, Phys. Edn., Recreation and Dance (Southwest dist. dance div. chmn. 1983), Nev. State Edn. Assn., NEA, Assn. Supervision and Curriculum Devel., Internat. Reading Assn., U. Nev. Alumni Assn. Republican. Roman Catholic. Author dance syllabi and curricula. Home: 5945 W Vegas Dr Las Vegas NV 89108 Office: 600 N 9th St Las Vegas NV 89101

CARMONA, RALPH CHRIS, banker, political scientist; b. East Los Angeles, Calif., Jan. 5, 1951; s. Dario Palacio and Maria Luz (Montanez) C.; m. Graciela Albiar, July 5, 1975; children—Rafael Dario, Alejandro Gabriel. B.A., U. So. Calif., 1973; M.A., U. Calif.-Santa Barbara, 1974, Ph.D., 1983. Cert. community coll. tchr., Calif. Intern, Ho. of Reps.,

Washington, 1972; research asst. dept. polit. sci. U. So. Calif., Los Angeles, 1970-73, lectr., 1977-78; tchr. asst. U. Calif.-Santa Barbara, 1974-75; job devel. specialist City of Los Angeles, 1973; asst. to speaker Calif. State Assembly, Los Angeles, 1976-78; lectr. Los Angeles Trade Tech. Coll., 1979-80; govt. relations officer Bank of Am., Los Angeles, 1980—. Chmn. Am. Soc. Pub. Adminstrn. Panel on Immigration, 1978; discussant Human Relations Commn. Conf. on Integration, 1978; sponsor Community Coll. Forum on Police-Community Relations in Los Angeles, 1980; chmn. Pasadena Scholarship Com. for Ams. of Mexican Descent awards luncheon, 1982; mem. research com. for Congressional mems. Esteban Torres and Matthew Martinez, 1982; del. Nat. Democratic Conv., 1972; mem. All Saints Ch. Parish Council, 1982. Nisei VFW Meml. scholar, 1969; U. So. Calif. scholar, 1969-73; Ford Found. fellow, 1973-76, doctoral fellow, 1978-79; recipient Stanford Bank Simulator Cert., 1981, Outstanding Community Service award Pasadena Scholarship Com. for Ams. of Mexican Descent, 1982. Mem. Am. Polit. Sci. Assn., Calif. Assn. for Bilingual Edn., Politics of Edn. Assn., Hispanic Bankers Assn., Los Angeles County Pub. Affairs Officers Assn. Democrat. Catholic/Episcopalian. Home: 725 E Sacramento St Altadena CA 91001 Office: Bank of America 555 S Flower St Los Angeles CA 90071

CARNAHAN, ORVILLE DARRELL, college administrator; b. Elba, Idaho, Dec. 25, 1929; s. Marion Carlon and Leola Pearl (Putnam) C.; m. Colleen Arrott, Dec. 14, 1981; children—Karen, Jeanie, Darrell, Carla. B.S., Utah State U., 1958; M.Ed., U. Idaho, 1962, Ed.D., 1964. Vocat. tchr., Jordan Sch. Dist., Sandy, Utah, 1958-59; tchr., prin. Valley Sch. Dist., Eden, Idaho; instr., dir. of tng. sch., supr. student tchrs. U. Idaho, Moscow, 1961-64; v.p. Yakima (Wash.) Valley Coll. 1964-66, dir. vocat. edn., 1966-69; chancellor Eastern Iowa Community Coll. Dist., Davenport, 1969-71; pres. Highline Coll., Midway, Wash., 1971-76; pres. So. Utah State Coll.-Cedar City, 1978-81; pres. Utah Tech. Coll., Salt Lake City, 1981—; assoc. commnr. for higher edn., 1976-78. Served with U.S. Army, 1952-54. Mem. Assn. of Community and Jr. Colls., Am. Tech. Edn. Assn., Am. Vocat. Assn., NEA, Salt Lake Area C. of C., Alpha Tau Alpha. Mormon. Club: Rotary. Home: 1088 W Fairhaven Circle Salt Lake City UT 84107 Office: Utah Tech College PO Box 31808 Salt Lake City UT 84131

CARNAHAN, WILLIAM CHARLES, systems analyst; b. New Kensington, Pa., Jan. 31, 1942; s. William Jennings and May Florence (Fricke) C.; student Phoenix Coll. and Ariz. State U., 1959-61; m. Marilyn Bullard, May 8, 1971; children—Marnie, Brian, Kevin. Asst. mgr. data processing Good Samaritan Hosp., Phoenix, 1962-65; mgr. data processing Ramada Inns, Phoenix, 1966-67; dir. systems analysis, edn. and planning Samaritan Health Service, Phoenix, 1968-74, dir. operations analysis and planning research, 1975-77, project mgr. fin. systems implementation, 1978-82; corp. dir. systems Planning Dyna Cor, Phoenix, 1982—; cons. hosps., physicians' offices; seminar tchr.; mem. data mgmt. com. Central Ariz. Health Systems Agy., 1978—, public service award. Mem. prins. adv. com. Senita Elem. Sch., 1980. Mem. Am. Hosp. Assn., Hosp. Mgmt. Systems Soc., Supporters of Senita Assn. Office: 1427 N 3d St Phoenix AZ 85004

CARNAHAN, WILLIAM HARMON, lawyer; b. Chgo., Jan. 9, 1925; s. Charles Everett and Esther Marie (O'Malley) C.; J.D., U. Notre Dame, 1949; m. Patricia Lynn, May 24, 1945; children—Michael, William A., Julie, Shawn, Carrine, Colin, Christopher. Admitted to S.D. bar, 1953, Wis. bar, 1964, Colo. bar, 1976, U.S. Supreme Ct., 1955; individual practice law, Deadwood, S.D., 1957-61; commd. 1st lt. USAF, 1953, advanced through grades to col., 1973; assoc. prof. USAF Acad., 1967-71; command staff judge adv. Third Air Force, Eng.; ret., 1976; individual practice law, Colorado Springs, Colo., 1976—; state's atty., Lawrence County, S.D., 1957-61. Decorated Legion of Merit. Mem. Wis. Bar Assn., Colo. Bar Assn., Colo. Trial Lawyers Assn., Notre Dame Law Assn., Ret. Officers Assn. Republican. Roman Catholic. Clubs: Lions (past pres.), Serra (v.p.), KC (4 deg.). Author: Protection of Computer Programs—A Dilemma, 1973. Office: 6180 Lehman Dr Suite 101 Colorado Springs CO 80907

CARNEVALI, TONY, optometrist; b. Parenti, Cosenza, Italy, Jan. 27, 1944; came to U.S., 1957; s. Fulvio and Amanda Maria (Venneri) C.; m. Franca Sabato, Dec. 6, 1975; children—Amanda Laura, Fulvio Giancarlo. B.A. in Physiol. Psychology, U. Calif.-Berkeley, 1967; O.D. magna cum laude, So. Calif. Coll. Optometry, 1975. Ptnr. Drs. Newman, Goldstone & Carnevali, Burbank, Calif., 1975-76; practice optometry, Glendale, Calif., 1976—; teaching asst. ocular optometry, 1974-75; lectr. vision perception tchrs., parents, students. Served as capt. USAF, 1967-71. Recipient Heard Optical Orthoptics award Heard Optical Lab., 1975. Mem. San Fernando Valley Optometric Soc. (dir. edn. and research 1980-81, pres. 1981-82), Calif. Optometric Assn. (Aux. Scholastic Achievement award 1975, optometric sch. liaison 1979-80, nominating com. 1980-82, Young Optometrist of Yr. 1981, resolutions com. 1983, chmn. communications div. 1983-84), Am. Optometric Assn., So. Calif. Pub. Health Assn., Optometric Care Council So. Calif. (treas. 1981-82), Calif. Scholastic Fedn. (life). Democrat. Roman Catholic. Office: 839 Glendale Ave Glendale CA 91206

CARNICOM, GENE E., social services administrator; b. Miami, Fla., Nov. 13, 1944; s. Francis Eugene and Kathleen (Kitchens) C.; m. Sharon Boisseau Brown, 1966; children—Patrick Dylan, Danielle Brooke; m. 2d, Lillian Helen Baehr, Mar. 22, 1970. B.A. in Social Welfare, San Diego State U., 1971, M.S.S.W., 1972; Ph.D., Southeastern U., 1981. Cert., Acad. Cert. Social Workers. Coordinator, Beach Area Free Clinic, San Diego, 1970-72; program cons. Balt. City Dept. Social Services, 1973; chief of social work Balt. City Jail, 1974-76; hosp. social work dir. Pine Ridge (S.D.) Indian Health Service Hosp., 1980-81; dir. mental health and social service USPHS Indian Health Service Hosp., Mescalero, N.Mex., 1981—; mem. faculty U. Md., 1972-76, Community Coll. Balt., 1973-76, Morgan State U., 1974-76, Webster Coll., 1977-80, Oglala Sioux Community Coll., 1980-81, Park Coll., 1982—, Golden Gate U., 1982—. Steering com. Community Congress San Diego, 1980-82; dir. Innercity N.W. Neighborhood Corp., 1970-72; exec. dir. RETIRED, Inc., 1971-72; site selection task force Community Corrections Program of Md. Dept. Corrections, 1973-74; grad. council Webster Coll., San Antonio, 1978-80; coordinator child protection team Pine Ridge Indian Reservation, 1980-81, sec., Mescalero Apache Indian Reservation Child Protection Team, 1981—; comdr. Sierra Blanca CAP Cadet Squadron, 1982—. Served with USNR, 1962-68, to capt. U.S. Army, 1976-80. Decorated Army Commendation medal; recipient Isolated Hardship Duty award USPHS, 1981, Hazardous Duty award, 1981. Mem. Nat. Assn. Social Workers, Am. Anthrop. Assn., Soc. Med. Anthropology, Assn. Mil. Surgeons U.S., Found. Exceptional Children, Soc. Hosp. Social Work Dirs., Profl. Assn. Commd. Corps of USPHS, Indian Health Service Computer Users Group, Mensa. Democrat. Contbr. articles profl. jours.

CARNOW, LAWRENCE EDWARD, podiatrist; b. Chgo., Feb. 24, 1951; s. Jacob and Marilyn (Shparago) C.; B.S. in Biology, Stanford U., 1973, A.B. in Communications cum laude, 1973; D.P.M., Calif. Coll. Podiatric Medicine, 1977. Practice podiatric medicine, Pico Rivera, Calif.; chmn. podiatry sect. Rio Hondo Hosp., Downey, Calif. Mem. Am. Podiatry Assn., Calif. Podiatry Assn., Los Angeles County Podiatry Assn. (exec. chmn. Central East Los Angeles County 1980, 81), Pi Delta. Club: Kiwanis. Address: 8348 Rosemead Blvd Pico Rivera CA 90660

CAROSELLI, PATRICIA ANN, film production executive; b. Rochester, N.Y., Feb. 21, 1954; d. Patrick R. and Elvira J. (Ciaccia) Caroselli. B.A., SUNY-Buffalo, 1975; M.B.A., U. Conn., 1977; postgrad. European Arts Workshop, summer 1971. Asst. project dir. mktg. research dept. Grey Advt., Los Angeles, 1977-79; prodn. assoc. Blake Edwards and Julie Andrews' film prodn. co. on films —10—, S.O.B., Victor/Victoria, Trail of the Pink Panther, Curse of the Pink Panther, The Man Who Loved Women, 1979—; v.p. prodn. Blake Edwards Entertainment, Los Angeles, 1982—. Vol., Operation Calif.'s world disaster relief program, 1979; mem. Conn. Commn. on the Arts, 1976. U. Conn. scholar, 1976-77. Mem. NOW, ACLU, Am. Assn. Female Execs., Assn. M.B.A. Execs., Women in Film, Am. Film Inst. Club: Advt. Contbr. articles to profl. jours. Office: 1888 Century Park E Suite 1616 Los Angeles CA 90067

CARPENELLO, DONALD RALPH, human resource executive; b. Pittsburg, Calif., June 19, 1931; s. Paul and Anita Marie (Gemingnani) C.; m. Mary Jane Mattevi, Aug. 26, 1956; children—Donald, Teri. B.S., San Jose State U., 1961. Personnel adminstr., mgr. Schlage Lock Co., San Francisco, 1961-69; indsl. relations mgr. Pek, Inc., Sunnyvale, Calif., 1969-71; personnel mgr. Shaklee Corp., San Francisco, 1971-72, dir. indsl. relations, 1972-75, dir. personnel, 1975-78, v.p. personnel, 1979-82, v.p. human resources, 1982—. First vice chmn. bd. dirs. Bay Area Urban League, Inc. Served with USN, 1951-55. Mem. Federated Employers Bay Area (bd. govs.), Am. Soc. Personnel Adminstrn., No. Calif. Human Resources Council. Republican. Roman Catholic. Club: San Francisco Comml. Office: Shaklee Corp 444 Market St San Francisco CA 94111

CARPENTER, BETTY LOU, bank executive; b. Winfield, Kans., Aug. 28, 1934; d. George Owen and Louis (Bailey) Watson; m. E. Reid Graves, June 10, 1955; children—G. Michael, Laurie L. Graves Livesay, Elizabeth M., David L. m. 2d Lester G. Carpenter, Jr., Sept. 17, 1970. Student U. Kans., 1952-54; B.S. in Bus. Adminstrn., Regis Coll., 1983. Vice pres. Midland Fed. Savs., Denver 1967-70; account mgr. Broyles, Allebaugh & Davis, Inc., Denver, 1970-72; v.p. mktg. Central Bank of Denver, 1973—; tchr. Savs. & Loan Inst. Vice chmn., commr. Denver Housing Authority, 1977—; exec. v.p. Advt. Industry of Denver Emergency Sponsors. Recipient 1st place Colo. Savs. & Loan Speech Contest, 1968. Mem. Nat. Assn. Housing and Redevel. Ofcls. (nat. com.), Denver Advt. Fedn. (dir.), Bank Mktg. Assn. (dir. Rocky Mt. chpt.), Automated Clearing House Assn. (chmn. mktg. com. Rocky Mt. chpt.), Savs. and Loan League (mem. nat. com. advt. and pub. relations), Denver C. of C. Democrat. Methodist. Club: Cherry Creek Sporting (Denver). Home: 801 S Ellipse Way Denver CO 80209 Office: Central Bank of Denver 1515 Arapahoe St Denver CO 80292

CARPENTER, C. NEAL, architect, corporate executive; b. Amarillo, Tex., May 10, 1932; s. Clarence Arthur and Ethel Ida (Hill) C.; m. Patricia Ann Powers, May 28, 1932; 2d m. Mary Ann Hahn, Dec. 22, 1945; children—Carol, Lewis, Brian. B.A. in Architecture, Okla. State U., 1956. Registered architect in 5 states. Draftsman, Gordon & Elizabeth Wright Ingraham, Colorado Springs, 1957-58; draftsman Walter H. Weber, Architect, Colorado Springs, 1958-61; prin. architect Nelson, Haley, Patterson and Quirk, 1961-75, Greeley, Colo.; pres. NHPQ Inc., 1975-79; pres. ARIX, P.C., Greeley, 1979—; dir. Greeley Nat. Bank. Bd. dirs. Boys Club, 7 yrs.); pres., dir. Symphony Assn. Served to 1st lt. U.S. Army, 1956-61. Named Disting. Mil. Student, Okla. State U., 1954; recipient Disting. Service award Western Mountain Region AIA, 1973, Disting. Achievement in Design, 1974; service awards Boys Club, City of Greeley, Bldg. Appeals Board, Symphony Assn., Ctr. for Creative Arts. Mem. AIA, Nat. Council Archtl. Registration Bds., Greeley C. of C. (chmn. econ. devel. bd. 1983), Democrat. Unitarian Clubs: Rotary (Service award, Paul Harris fellow), Greeley Country, Elks, Sigma Alpha Epsilon Alumni. Contbr. articles to profl jours. Office: PO Box 2021 Greeley CO 80632

CARPENTER, CARL HATTEN, civil engineer; b. Manti, Utah, Feb. 4, 1932; s. Joseph and Mary (Koch) C.; m. Marcia Tuttle, Sept. 16, 1955; children—Randall, Douglas, Charlotte, Helen, Gerald. B.S.C.E., Utah State U., 1956. Registered profl. engr., Utah. Design engr. Utah Power and Light Co., Salt Lake City, 1956-57; hydraulic engr., U.S. Geol. Survey, Richfield, Utah, 1957-64, Salt Lake City, 1964-65; dist. engr. Central Utah Water Conservancy Dist., Orem, 1965-73, 81—; cons. engr. Neilsen, Maxwell and Wangsgaard, Salt Lake City, 1973-81. Active Springville (Utah) Planning Commn., 1979-80. Served to staff sgt. U.S. Army, 1952-54. Decorated Korean Service Medal. Fellow ASCE; mem. Am. Water Works Assn. Mormon. Contbr. articles to profl. jours. Home: 1246 E 100th St S Springville UT 84663 Office: Central Utah Water Conservancy Dist Orem UT 84057

CARPENTER, DANTE KEALA, state senator, mech. engr.; b. Honolulu, Dec. 3, 1934; s. Vernon Forest and Louise Pomaikai (Kakelaka) C.; student U. Hawaii, 1952-53; B.S. in Marine-Mech. Engring., U.S. Mcht. Marine Acad., 1957; m. E.M. Olan Peltier, Mar. 13, 1958; children—Dante K., Carla K., Darren H., Dee-Ann L. Engr. trainee C. Brewer & Co., Ltd., 1960-61; process engr. Hilo Sugar Co., 1961-63; process engr., then project engr. Hutchinson Sugar Co., 1963-73; staff engr. Hawaiian Sugar Co., 1973-76; sr. mech. engr. Hawaii Agronomics Internat., 1977—. Mem. energy action com. Hawaii Assn. Counties, 1974-75; mem. Gov. Hawaii Temp. Commn. Environ. Planning, 1973; v.p. Naalehu Sch. P.T.A., 1967-68. Councilman, County of Hawaii, 1968-76, chmn. recreation and transp. com., 1974-76, vice chmn. council, 1968-72; mem. Hawaii Senate, 1978—, chmn. com. on health, vice chmn. com. on econ. devel., chmn. judiciary com., vice chmn. health com. Served to lt. comdr. USNR, 1957—. Registered profl. engr., Hawaii. Mem. Hawaiian Sugar Technologists, Hawaii Assn. Profl. Engrs., Kau Hist. Soc. (pres. 1975-77), Hawaiian Civic Club of Kau (pres. 1969-70), Naalehu Community Club (pres. 1966). Democrat. Congregationalist. Clubs: Lions, Kiwanis. Home: 176 Likeke St Hilo HI 96720 Office: PO Box 1801 Hilo HI 96720

CARPENTER, DIXIE ANN, educator; b. Las Vegas, Nev., Sept. 16, 1937; d. Edgar William and Lola Lorrine (Warwick) Davis; B.S., Wash. State U., Pullman, 1959; postgrad. UCLA, 1959-62, M.A. in Secondary Edn., Ariz. State U., 1981; m. Marvin Ross Carpenter, Nov. 9, 1958; children—Clayton, Kent, Megan. Tchr. home econs. Pacioma Jr. High Sch., Los Angeles, 1959-62; tchr. First Meth. Ch. Sch., Tempe, Ariz., 1968-69; dir. pre-sch., home econs. dept. Ariz. State U., Tempe, 1969-70; career edn. curriculum developer Mesa City (Ariz.) Schs., 1972-73; tchr. Hidden Valley Middle Sch., Escondido, Calif., 1975-76; analysis and ins. salesman Am. Pacific Securities, San Diego, 1976-77; home econs. tchr. H.W. Smith Sch., Glendale, Ariz., 1979-82, Horizen Elem. Sch., Glendale, 1982—, dist. chmn. home econs. Glendale Elem. Schs.; home econs. cons. Sta. KTAR, Phoenix, 1979-81. Mem. Nat. Home Econs. Assn., AAUW, Ariz. Home Econs. Assn., Assn. Supervision and Curriculum Devel. (dir.-at-large 1982—), Alpha Delta Pi Alumnae Assn., Delta Kappa Gamma. Lutheran. Home: 18220 N 74th Dr Peoria AZ 85345 Office: 8520 N 47th Ave Glendale AZ 85302

CARPENTER, DONALD ALFRED, judge; b. Greeley, Colo., Jan. 2, 1907; s. Delph E. and Michaela (Hogarty) C.; student Colo. State Coll., 1926-27, Am. U., 1927-28; J.D., George Washington U., 1931; m. Evelyn Ward, Dec. 31, 1941 (dec. 1963); children—William Ward, Ward; m. 2d, Doris Piedalue Baney, June 16, 1965. Admitted to Tex. bar, 1931, Colo. bar, 1949; pvt. practice, El Paso, 1931-34; dir. Colo. Use Tax Div., 1938-40; adminstrv. asst. to Hon. William S. Hill, 1940-43; judge County Ct. Weld County, Colo., 1946-52, Dist. Ct. of 8th Jud. Dist. Colo., 1952-64; chief judge of 19th Jud. Dist., 1964-78; water judge South Platte River System, 1969-78; chief judge Colo. Jud. Dept., 1978—; apptd. to Gov.'s Jud. Conf. Colo., 1957, 58, Colo. Jud. Council, 1958; chmn. Com. on Appellate Practice, 1958; master for Colo. Supreme Ct., 1960-61; adminstrv. judge No. Colo. Water Conservancy Dist., 1965-78; mem. jud. council of chief justice Colo. Supreme Ct., 1973-78; adminstrv. judge Central Colo. Water Conservancy Dist., 1965-78. Pres. Young Rep. League Colo., 1941-42. Served with AUS: ETO, NATOUSA, MTO. Recipient Profl. Achievement award George Washington U., 1982. Mem. Nat. Coll. Probate Judges, Colo. Dist. Judges Assn., World Assn. Judges, Am., Colo., Tex., Weld County bar assns., Union Colony Pioneer Soc. (pres.), Am. Judicature Soc., Nat. Conf. State Trial Judges, Am. Acad. Polit. and Social Sci., Am. Legion, Newcomen Soc. N. Am., V.F.W. Republican. Episcopalian. Mason, Elk. Home: 14953 Weld County Rd 70 Greeley CO 80631 Office: Court House Greeley CO 80631

CARPENTER, DONALD BLODGETT, real estate appraiser; b. New Haven, Aug. 20, 1916; s. Fred Donald and Gwendolen (Blodgett) C.; Ph.B., U. Vt., 1938; m. Barbara Marvin Adams, June 28, 1941 (dec. Aug. 1978); m. 2d, Lee Burker McGough, Dec. 28, 1980. Reporter Burlington (Vt.) Daily News, 1938-39; guide chair operator Am. Express Co., N.Y. World's Fair, 1939; underwriter G.E.I. Corp., Newark, 1939-40; Sales corr. J. Dixon Crucible Co., Jersey City, 1940-41, asst. office mgr., priorities specialist, 1941-42, sales rep., San Francisco, 1946-52; field supr. Travelers Ins. Co., San Francisco, 1952-58; gen. agt. Gen. Am. Life Ins. Co., San Francisco, 1958-59; Western Supr. Provident Life & Accident Ins. Co., San Francisco, 1959-60; brokerage supr. Aetna Life Ins. Co., San Francisco, 1960-61, maintenance cons. J.I. Holcomb Mfg. Co., Mill Valley, Calif., 1961-68; ednl. service rep. Marquis Who's Who, Inc., Mill Valley, 1963-68; sales rep. Onox, Inc., Mendocino, Calif., 1965-68; tchr., coach Mendocino Jr.-Sr. High Sch., 1968; real property appraiser, Mendocino County, Calif., 1968-81. Active numerous civic orgns.; chmn. Community Calendar, 1972—; co-chmn. Citizens for Sewers, 1971-72; mem. Mendocino County Safety Council, 1981. Served with USNR, 1942-46; lt. comdr., comdg. officer res. unit, 1967-68, now ret. Recipient Community Sportsman-of-Year award, 1971; Sec. of Navy Commendation with ribbon, 1946, other awards, certificates; decorated companion Mil. Order World Wars. Mem. Manufactured Housing Appraisal Inst., Internat. Inst. Valuers, Nat. Assn. Rev. Appraisers, Reserve Officers Assn. U.S. (life; chpt. pres. 1954, 56, state v.p. 1958-61), Ret. Officers Assn. (life; chpt. survivors assistance area counselor 1979—), Mendocino Art Center, Save-The-Redwoods League, Marines Meml. Assn., Mendocino County Employees Assn. (dir. 1981), Mendocino County Hist. Soc., Mendocino Hist. Research Inc., Nat. Assn. Uniformed Services (life), Nat. Ret. Tchrs. Assn., Calif. Ret. Tchrs. Assn. (life, dir. 1983—), Naval Order of U.S., Naval Res. Assn. (life), Navy League of U.S., Oceanic Soc. (charter), San Francisco Maritime Mus. Assn., U.S. Naval Inst., Am. Diabetes Assn., Alumni Assn. U. Vt. (founding pres. No. Calif. club 1964), Wilbur Soc., Mendocino Coast Stamp Club, Kappa Sigma (scholarship leadership award 1937-38). Republican. Congregationalist. Clubs: Rotary Internat. (pres. 1975-76, dist. gov. area rep. 1977-78, Dist. Gov. awards 1974, 76, dist. ednl. awards com. 1978-81; dist. group study exchange com. 1981—; Paul Harris fellow 1979—), Nat. Travel, Am. Legion (post comdr. 1972-73, state citation for outstanding community service 1972), Am. Legion Past Comdrs. Calif., Mendocino Cardinal Booster (charter, life mem.; club pres. 1971), U. Vt. Catamount (charter), Old Mill, Redwood Health. Home: Box 87 Mendocino CA 95460 Office: 10801 Gurley Ln Mendocino CA 95460

CARPENTER, DORIS MARIE, accountant; b. Parks, Nebr., Aug. 3, 1924; d. Hector Joseph and Hulda Piedalue; B.A., U. No. Colo., 1971; m. Donald L. Baney, June, 1953 (dec. 1961); m. 2d, Donald A. Carpenter, June 16, 1965; 1 dau., Denise Ann (dec.). Controller, W-E-W, Inc., McCook, Nebr., 1943-53; tchr. public schs., Chase County, Nebr., 1953-59, 61-63; chief acctg. dept. Imperial Coop Equity, Inc., Imperial, Nebr., 1963-65; mem. staff Thompson and Hoover C.P.A.'s, Greeley, Colo., 1973-74; pres. Doris M. Carpenter, C.P.A., Greeley, 1975—. Bd. dirs. Salvation Army, Greeley, 1976—; charter mem. Assistance League of Greeley; sec. Union Colony Pioneer Soc., 1978-80. Mem. Colo. Soc. C.P.A.'s, Am. Inst. C.P.A.'s, No. Colo. Estate Planning Council, Am. Soc. Women C.P.A.'s, Greeley C. of C. Republican. Clubs: Altrusa, Order Eastern Star. Home: 14953 WCR 70 Greeley CO 80631 Office: 912 9th Ave Greeley CO 80631

CARPENTER, FRANK CHARLES, JR., electronics engr.; b. Los Angeles, June 1, 1917; s. Frank Charles and Isobel (Crump) C.; A.A., Pasadena City Coll., 1961; B.S. in Elec. Engring. cum laude, Calif. State U.-Long Beach, 1975, M.S. in Elec. Engring., 1981; m. Beatrice Josephine Jolly, Nov. 3, 1951; children—Robert Douglas, Gail Susan, Carol Ann. Self-employed design and mfgr. aircraft test equipment, Los Angeles, 1946-51; engr. Hoffman Electronics Corp., Los Angeles, 1951-56, sr. engr., 1956-59, project mgr., 1959-63; engr.-scientist McDonnell-Douglas Astronautics Corp., Huntington Beach, Calif., 1963-69, spacecraft telemetry, 1963-67, biomed. electronics, 1967-69, flight test instrumentation, 1969-76; lab. test engr. Northrop Corp., Hawthorne, Calif., 1976-82, spl. engr., 1982—. Served with USNR, 1941-47. Mem. I.E.E.E. (sr.), Amateur Radio Relay League. Contbr. articles to profl. jours. Patentee transistor squelch circuit; helicaland whip antenna. Home: 2037 Balearic Dr Costa Mesa CA 92626 Office: One Northrop Ave Hawthorne CA 90250

CARPENTER, JAMES FLOYD, JR., aerospace co. exec.; b. Baker, Oreg., Nov. 15, 1925; s. James Floyd and Eva Leona (Safford) C.; student Eastern Oreg. Coll. LaGrande, 1946-48; B.A. in Math. and Physics, Willamette U., Salem, Oreg., 1951; M.S. in Physics, Oreg. State U., 1953, Ph.D. in Applied Math., 1956; m. Margery Jean Jacobs, Aug. 12, 1951; children—Mary Ann Carpenter Mosher, Michael James, Melissa Kay. Electron microscopist, fellow Oreg. State Coll., Corvallis, 1951-55; research engr. Boeing Airplane Co., Seattle, 1955-58; sect. head Dalmo Victor Co., Belmont, Calif., 1958-61; prin. dir. communications and radar subdiv. Electronics & Optics div. The Aerospace Corp., El Segundo, Calif., 1961—. Served with USN, 1944-46. Mem. Armed Forces Communications and Electronics Assn., Inst. Navigation, Sigma Xi, Sigma Pi Sigma, Pi Mu Epsilon. Home: 10 Pear Tree Ln Rolling Hills Estates CA 90274 Office: 2350 E El Segundo Blvd El Segundo CA 90245

CARPENTER, JOHN EVERETT, former educator; b. Tarrytown, N.Y., Nov. 27, 1923; s. Everett Birch and Mary (Avery) C.; student Union Coll., 1943; B.A., Iona Coll., 1946; M.A., Columbia, 1949, profl. diploma, 1961; m. Marie F. McCarthy, Nov. 14, 1944; 1 son, Dennis Everett. Tchr., Blessed Sacrament High Sch., New Rochelle, N.Y., 1946-50; tchr., adminstr. Armonk (N.Y.) pub. schs., 1950-62; dir. guidance Ridge Street Sch., Port Chester, N.Y., 1962-64; counselor Rye (N.Y.) High Sch., 1964-66, prin., 1966-78, ret.; guest lectr. Served to lt. USNR; now lt. comdr. ret. Res. Decorated Bronze Star medal. Mem. Middle States Assn. Colls. and Schs. (commn. on secondary schs.), Am. (life), Westchester-Putnam-Rockland (past pres.) personnel and guidance assns., NEA, Am. Legion (past comdr.), Phi Delta Kappa, Kappa Delta Pi. Rotarian (past pres., Paul Harris fellow). Clubs: Tarrytown Boat (past commodore), Green Valley Elks. Home: 321 Paseo de los Conquistadores Green Valley AZ 85614

CARPENTER, MARVIN ROSS, electrical engineer; b. Spokane, Wash., June 20, 1929; s. Ross Thomas and Hazel Ida (Simpson) C.; B.S. in Elec. Engring., Wash. State U., 1959; m. Dixie Ann Davis, Nov. 9,

1958; children—Clayton, Kent, Megan. Elec. engr. Librascope Co., Glendale, Calif., 1959-66, Motorola Semi-Condr. Products div., Mesa, Ariz., 1966-74, Micro-Components orgn. Burroughs Corp., Rancho Bernardo, Calif., 1974-77, Digital Equipment Corp., Peoria, Ariz., 1977-80, Sperry Flight Systems, Phoenix, 1980-83, Motorola, 1983—. Founder, active J.J. Currey Sch. PTO, Tempe, Ariz., 1969-74; Cub Scout pack leader, 1970-74. Served with USMC, 1946-49, 53-55. Mem. IEEE, Wash. State U. Alumni Assn., Delta Chi Alumni. Republican. Lutheran. Club: Optimists (v.p. Tempe 1976).

CARPENTER, MAUDINE HALL, sch. ofcl.; b. Miss., Jan. 5, 1934; d. Coster Delyn and Ada Virginia (Nagle) Hall; student public schs.; m. Billy Franklin Carpenter, Jan. 13, 1951; 1 son, James Bradford. Bookkeeper, loan receptionist Nat. Bank Alaska, Anchorage, 1953-58; loan clk., teller Security Pacific Nat. Bank, Riverside, Calif., 1959-64; purchasing clk., purchasing asst. Riverside Unified Sch. Dist., 1964-67, purchasing agt., 1967—. Mem. Calif. Assn. Public Purchasing Officers, Calif. Assn. Sch. Bus. Ofcls., Riverside Assn. Sch. Mgrs. (treas.), San Gabriel Valley Assn. Purchasing Agts. Democrat. Methodist. Home: 20410 Harvard Way Riverside CA 92507 Office: 3380 14th St Riverside CA 92501

CARPER, DONN ARMISTEAD, sales manager; b. Glendale, Calif., Sept. 30, 1945; s. Armistead Fitzgerrel and Frances Marion (Robertson) C.; m. Meg Johnson, July 18, 1970; children—Todd Armistead, Kellee Francis, Scott Campbell. B.S. in Bus. Adminstrn., U. So. Calif., 1967, Advanced Advt. degree, 1969. Account exec. Hall, Butler, Blatherwick Advt., Los Angeles, 1970-73; account exec. KHJ-TV, Los Angeles, 1973-74; account exec. ABC-TV, Los Angeles, Chgo., N.Y.C., 1974-79, West Coast spot sales mgr., Los Angeles, 1981—; retail sales mgr. KABC-TV, Los Angeles, 1979-81; sponsor Advt. Industry Emergency Fund. Mem. Republican Nat. Com. Mem. Hollywood Radio and TV Soc., Los Angeles Advt. Club. Roman Catholic. Club: Century City Tennis (Los Angeles). Home: 5425 Oakdale Ave Woodland Hills CA 91364 Office: 2020 Ave Stars Suite 250 Century City CA 90067

CARPER, RAYMOND CLIFFORD, JR., financial executive; b. Colorado Springs, Colo., July 15, 1949; s. Raymond Clifford Mary Alyce (McCluer) C.; m. Linda Ann Bryant, Nov. 8, 1975. B.S. in Bus. Adminstrn., U. N.Mex., 1971. Consumer loan officer Security Pacific Nat. Bank, Los Angeles, 1972-75; v.p. Bateman Eichler, Hill Richards, Los Angeles, 1975—; host —Charting the Market—, KWHY-TV. Mem. Pi Kappa Alpha. Republican. Presbyterian. Club: Century. Office: 700 S Flower 27th Floor Los Angeles CA 90017

CARR, ALLAN, film producer, celebrity rep.; b. Chgo., May 27, 1941; s. Albert and Ann (Neimitz) Solomon; B.A., Lake Forest Coll., 1962. Reopened Civic Theater, Chgo., 1962; formed Allan Carr Enterprises; became career mgr. Ann-Margret, Rosalind Russell, Peter Sellers, Marvin Hamlisch, Paul Anka, Melina Mercouri, others; producer nightclub extravaganzas, TV spls., motion pictures; motion picture producer The First Time, 1969, C.C. & Company, 1970, Survive, 1976; co-author and producer Grease, 1978; creative cons. 50th Acad. Awards Show and The Deerhunter, 1979; co-author, producer Can't Stop the Music, 1980; made theatre producing debt in Sunday in New York, Los Angeles; producer Broadway musical The Queen of Basin Street, La Cage aux Folles, 1983. Bd. dirs. Cedars-Sinai Med. Center; founder Dorothy Chandler Music Center; co-sponsor FOCUS Student Film awards. Named Producer of Yr., Nat. Theatre Owners, 1978; recipient People's Choice award for movie of yr., 1978. Office: 1220 Benedict Canyon Dr Beverly Hills CA 90210*

CARR, KENNETH GERALD, manufacturing company executive; b. Iowa Falls, Iowa, May 30, 1937; s. Gerald and De Loris Arlene (Stone) C.; student Carlsbad Jr. Coll., 1957-58, Santa Ana Coll., 1962-63, Golden West Coll., 1968; cert. bus. mgmt. Orange Coast Coll., 1968; cert. indsl. relations UCLA, 1971, in bus. mgmt. Grad. Sch., 1972, in econs. 1977; cert. in mgmt. U. Calif., Irvine, 1976; B.S. in Bus. Mgmt., Pacific Western U., 1979; m. Joan Victoria Vallely, Nov. 8, 1978; children from previous marriage—Kurt Kenneth, Canda Joy, Kevin Dean, Christa Jean. With Ford Aerospace Communications Corp., Newport Beach, Calif., 1962—, sect. supr., 1972-76, mgr. program mfg., 1976-77, mgr. prodn. control dept., 1977—. Chmn. Gloria Dei Lutheran Ch.; bd. dirs. Orange County Indsl. Center, 1980. Served with USMC, 1956-58. Recipient Community Service citation Ford Motor Co., 1974, 78, South Coast YMCA, Jr. C. of C. San Juan Capistrano. Mem. Am. Inventory and Prodn. Control Soc., Am. Mgmt. Assn. (dir. 1980-81). Republican. Club: Irvine Coast Country (Newport Beach). Home: 1038 Sea Ln Corona del Mar CA 92625 Office: Ford Aerospace Communications Corp Ford Rd Bldg 6 Newport Beach CA 92663

CARR, MICHAEL ALAN, technical instrumentation specialist; b. Wichita, Kans., Feb. 28, 1947; s. Joseph Ellsworth and Juanita Opal (Doris) C.; student Pasadena (Calif.) City Coll., 1971-72; m. Robin Ruth Margosian, May 26, 1979; 1 son, Ethan Michael. Lens grinder Teledyne Optics, Monrovia, Calif., 1964-65; apprentice forging shop Calif. Drop Forge Co., Los Angeles, 1965-67; machinist central engring. services Calif. Inst. Tech., 1972-73, tech. instrument specialist geology div., 1973—; propr. Carr Instrumentation, cons. engring. of mass spectrometry; participant lunar neutron probe expt. of Apollo 17, 1972, space telescope wide field/planetary camera project, 1978-83; chief technician 4-Shooter Camera Project, Palomar Obs., 1983—. Served with U.S. Army, 1967-69. Recipient award for black and white exptl. photograph U.S. Army, 1969. Inventor V filament jig, borehole camera, carbon dioxide reaction heads; co-inventor bubble tilt meters. Home: 5605 Canyonside Rd La Crescenta CA 91214 Office: 1201 E California Blvd Pasadena CA 91109

CARR, ROBERT ALLEN, educator; b. Los Angeles, Sept. 28, 1917; s. Harry Newton and Elvaretta (Wilson) C.; m. Ruth Eleanor Holland, Dec. 7, 1946; children—Nancy Ellen, David Allen. A.B., San Francisco State Coll., 1951, M.A., 1953; Ph.D., U. So. Calif., 1959. Orgn. and methods examiner VA, San Francisco, 1946-48; instr. Golden Gate Coll., 1952, coordinator econ. edn. project, 1952-56; lectr. U. So. Calif., 1956-57; asst. prof. Calif. State U., Fresno, 1957-61, asso. prof., 1961-66, prof., 1966-83, emeritus prof., 1983—, asst. head div. bus., 1964-65, chmn. dept. finance and industry, 1965-76. Cons. economist Fresno (Calif.) Planning Dept., 1962-63; cons. Somali Inst. Devel., Adminstrn. and Mgmt., 1982-83. Served to staff sgt., USAAF, 1941-45. Ford Faculty fellow, 1962; E.L. Phillips intern, 1963-64. Mem. Am., Western econ. assns., Am., Western (exec. com., v.p. 1966-67, pres. 1967-68) finance assns., Financial Mgmt. Assn. (dir. 1970-72, v.p. 1973-74), Soc. for Internat. Devel., Am. Statis. Assn. (pres. San Joaquin Valley chpt. 1975-77), Regional Sci. Assn., AAUP. Co-author: The Development of SIDAM: A Program of Action, 1982—; contbr. articles to profl. jours. Home: 5734 N Bond St Fresno CA 93710

CARRAHER, DANIEL PETER, public accountant; b. Hawthorne, Nev., Dec. 27, 1953; s. Martin William and Pernina (Cadwell) C.; student U. Nev., 1971-72; B.S. in Bus. Adminstrn., U. San Francisco, 1975; postgrad. Golden Gate U., 1978—; m. Pamela Marie Peterson, Mar. 22, 1975; 1 dau., Tiffin. Adminstrv. asst. U. San Francisco, 1974-75; staff acct. Alexander Grant & Co., San Francisco, 1975-78; ptnr. Carraher & Carraher, Ltd., C.P.A.s, Reno, 1978-81; prin. Daniel P. Carraher, C.P.A., 1981-82; chief fin. officer Oiltech, Reno, 1982—; sec., treas., chief fin. officer Lassenite Industries, Inc., Reno, 1982—; Western Hills Assocs., Miss Tif Assos.; instr. Western Nev. Community Coll., Reno, part-time 1978. C.P.A., Calif. Mem. Am. Inst. C.P.A.s, Nat. Assn. Accts., Republican. Home: 6355 Plum Hollow Circle Reno NV 89502 Office: 1475 Terminal Way Suite C1 Reno NV 89502

CARRAWAY, MELISSA FAY, educational administrator; b. Ft. Knox, Ky., Mar. 6, 1953; d. Joseph Green and Catherine Joyce (Gundy) C. B.S., Mont. State U., 1975; M.Ed., U. Wash., 1982. Tchr. Bozeman (Mont.) Pub. Schs., 1975-80; asst. prin. Lower Kuskokwim Schs., Bethel, Alaska, 1982-83; prin. Stedman Sch., Petersburg, Alaska, 1983—. Bd. dirs. Project for the Prevention of Child Sexual Abuse. Mem. Nat. Assn. Elem. Prins., Assn. Supervision and Curriculum Devel., Alaska Women in Ednl. Adminstrn., Delta Assn. Edn. Young Children. Home: PO Box 389 Petersburg AK 99833 Office: PO Box 289 Stedman Sch Petersburg AK 99833

CARREL, LARRY JOE, bus. exec.; b. St. Joseph, Mo., July 6, 1935; s. John Morton and Opal Marie (Ramseier) C.; A.A. cum laude, Grossmont Coll., 1970; B.A., Calif. Pacific U., 1977, M.B.A., 1977; m. Imogene Johnson, July 8, 1962; children—John Joseph, Shelly Jean. With Hewlett-Packard Co., San Diego, 1969—, now purchasing mgr., Mem. San Diego Regional Minority Purchasing Council (chmn. 1977-78), Am. Production and Inventory Control Soc., Nat. Assn. Purchasing Mgrs., Mensa. Republican. Home: 16979 Cresta Dr San Diego CA 92128 Office: 16399 W Bernardo Dr San Diego CA 92127

CARRIER, LOUIS MERRICK, JR., aeronautical engineer; b. Clarksville, Tex., Apr. 30, 1941; s. Louis Merrick and Alleen (Goodwin) C.; m. Martha Merino, July 30, 1942; children—Mark, Michael. A.A., Santa Monica (Calif.) City Coll., 1962; B.S. in Engring., Calif. State U.-Los Angeles, 1964. With Rockwell Internat., Lakewood, Calif., 1962—, dir. Avionic Systems Aircraft Ops., 1981—. Recipient Apollo Achievement award NASA, 1965; Inst. of Navigation award, 1979; Space Shuttle STS-1 Flag award, 1981. Mem. Nat. Mgmt. Assn., AIAA, Assn. Old Crows. Republican. Contbr. articles to profl. jours. Home: 18952 Crimson Circle Huntington Beach CA 92646

CARRISON, MURIEL PASKIN, educator; b. N.Y.C., Apr. 27, 1928; d. Jacob and Hattie (Ganeles) Paskin; B.A., Hunter Coll., 1948; M.A., Calif. State U.-Long Beach, 1964; Ed.D. (NDEA scholar, Educare fellow), U. So. Calif., 1969; m. Donald A. Carrison, Aug. 7, 1969; children—Michael, Amy, Peter, David. Tchr. elem. and secondary schs., N.Y.C. and Calif., 1948-64; specialist Tchr. Corps for Disadvantaged Youth, team coordinator Specialist Program for Secondary Tchrs., Los Angeles Unified Sch. Dist., research dir. French Lang. Lab., U. So. Calif., 1964-67; vis. asst. prof. edn. U. So. Calif., Los Angeles, Calif. State U.-Long Beach, Calif. State U.-Fullerton, 1967-68; instr. psychology and sociology Long Beach City Coll., Rio Hondo Jr. Coll., 1968-69; prof. edn. Calif. State U.-Dominguez Hills, 1969—, interim dir. Tchr. Corps. summer 1973; co-dir. Somoan and Bilingual Tchr. Aide Program, Compton (Calif.) Unified Sch. Dist., 1970-71; cons. Inglewood Unified Sch. Dist., 1973; monitor, rev. cons. elem. edn. Calif. Dept. Edn., 1975—; integration evaluator Los Angeles Unified Sch. Dist., 1978, fgn. student advisor, 1979—, dir. internat. student programs, 1980, grad. advisor, 1981—. Leader, Campfire Girls, 1959-66, YMCA Indian Guides, 1956-59; v.p. Lee Sch. PTA, 1961-63; bd. dirs. Fair Housing Found. of Long Beach, 1981. Mem. Am., Pacific sociol. assns., Am. Psychol. Assn., NEA, Internat. Conf. on Edn. of Tchrs., Nat. Council Social Studies, Phi Delta Kappa. Contbr. articles to profl. jours. Office: Calif State U Dominguez Hills Carson CA 90747

CARROLL, CHARLES BONNAFFON, JR., consultant; b. Pitts., May 15, 1933; s. Charles Bonnaffon and Elizabeth (Stickney) C.; B.A., U. Miami, 1957; M.A., U. No. Colo., 1975; m. Marilyn O. Estey, May 28, 1960; children—Craig Bonnaffon, Ann Chase. Commd. 2d lt. U.S. Air Force, 1957, advanced through grades to capt., 1968; utilities dir. City of Englewood, Colo., 1968-77, City of Aurora, Colo., from 1977, now cons., pres. Nev. Ditch Holding Co., Littleton, Colo., 1970-77; mem. Colo. Water and Wastewater Plant Operator Certification Bd., 1975—; chmn. water quality adv. com. Denver Regional Council Govts., 1979. Pres. Arapaho Hills Water Dist., Littleton, 1973-77; chmn. water resources advisory com. Denver Regional Council Govts., 1974. Recipient Distinguished Service award Denver Regional Council Govts., 1977, 82. Mem. Am. Water Works Assn. (past chmn. Rocky Mountain sect.), Water Pollution Control Fedn., S.A.R. Episcopalian. Home: 5460 Manitou Rd Littleton CO 80123 Office: 1470 S Havana Aurora CO 80012

CARROLL, DON EUGENE, TV broadcasting exec.; b. Los Angeles, Feb. 6, 1942; s. Wilson E. and Maxine (Wingo) C.; B.A., San Jose State Coll., 1964; M.B.A., Harvard, 1966; m. Diana Vivian Butta, June 19, 1977; children—Wendy, Jeff, Bari, Adrian. Fin. analyst Oceanic Properties, Inc., Honolulu, 1966-69; v.p., treas. Oceanic Cablevision, Inc., Honolulu, 1969-76; pres., 1976—; pres. Home Communications Services Corp.; cons. Mililani Town, Inc., 1966-69. Counselor, Jr. Achievement, 1967-68; pres. Miliani Town Assn., 1969. Mem. Financial Mgmt. Assn., Hawaii Soc. Corporate Planners, Hawaii Cable TV Assn. (sec.), Cable TV Adminstrv. and Mktg. Soc., Young Presidents Orgn., Waikiki Jr. C. of C. Clubs: Miliani Golf (pres. 1967-68) (Honolulu); Oahu Country. Home: 3964 Old Pali Rd Honolulu HI 96817 Office: 2669 Kilihau St Honolulu HI 96819

CARROLL, JOEL, scientist; b. Hallettsville, Tex., Apr. 8, 1924; s. Norman and Otealia (Hargrove) C.; B.A., Roosevelt U., 1950; M.S., DePaul U., 1952; m. Anne M. Merriweather, Aug. 20, 1960; children—Joel Anson, Bernard Eugene, Harlan Patrick. Analytical statistician U.S. R.R. Retirement Bd., Chgo., 1952-54; asst. mathematician Argonne Nat. Lab., Lemont, Ill., 1954-55; computing engr. N.Am. Aviation, Inc., Los Angeles, 1955-58; mathematician Land-Air, Inc., Point Mugu, Calif., 1958-61, Gen. Precision, Inc., Glendale, Calif., 1961-63; sr. engr. Northrop Corp., Hawthorne, Calif., 1963-65; computer specialist Douglas Aircraft Co., Santa Monica, Calif., 1965-66; mathematician Naval Ocean System Center, San Diego, 1966-80, scientist, 1980—. Served with USNR, 1943-45. Recipient Superior Accomplishment award U.S. Dept. Navy, 1968, Spl. Achievement award Naval Ocean System Center, 1974. Moderator San Diego Assn. United Ch. of Christ, 1980-81. Mem. Am. Math. Soc., Soc. for Indsl. and Applied Math., AAAS, ACLU, Zool. Soc. San Diego, Smithsonian Assos., Town Hall of Calif., Council Basic Edn., Harry S. Truman Library Inst. (hon. fellow), Roosevelt U. Alumni Assn., Pi Mu Epsilon. Congregationalist (past moderator, past treas.). Club: Kiwanis (past sec.). Contbr. articles to profl. jours. Home: 13307 Olive Grove Dr Poway CA 92064 Office: Naval Ocean System Center Bldg 175 San Diego CA 92152

CARROLL, MARTIN HOWARD, optometrist; b. Rock Springs, Wy., Aug. 20, 1955; s. Dean and Joan Marie (Petre) C.; m. Claudia Gail Smith, Oct. 10, 1981. A.A. with honors, Laramie County Community Coll., 1975; B.S. with honors, U. Wyo., 1977; O.D. magna cum laude, So. Calif. Coll. Optometry, 1981. Optometric cons. for Dow Corning Ophthlamics, Denver, summer 1981; mem. clin. staff Cheyenne (Wyo.) Vision Clinic, 1981—; lectr. Recipient Precision Optical award, 1981. Mem. Wyo. Optometric Assn., Am. Optometric Assn., Phi Kappa Phi. Beta Sigma Kappa. Democrat. Roman Catholic. Clubs: Cheyenne Jaycees, Frontier Lions. Office: 1200 E Pershing Cheyenne WY 82001

CARROLL, PATRICIA ANNE, advertising and public relations executive; b. Santa Monica, Calif., June 21, 1939; d. Matthew J. and Frances E. (Michaelsen) C. B.A. in Italian, UCLA, 1961; M.B.A. in Mktg., Pepperdine U., 1980. Coordinator advt. and sales promotion Deluxe Gen. Film Lab., Hollywood, Calif., 1964-73; gen. mgr., prodn. mgr. Adgraphix Advt. Agy., Van Nuys, Calif., 1974-75; mgr. mktg. services Nat. Auto Glass Co., Los Angeles, 1975-78; mgr. advt. and pub. relations Kubota Tractor Co., Compton, Calif., 1978—. Mem. Los Angeles Advt. Women (pres. 1983-84), Ad Club Los Angeles, Nat. AgriMktg. Assn. Office: Kubota Tractor Corp 550 W Artesia Blvd Compton CA 90220

CARROLL, TOM WALTON, photo-illustrator; b. Ft. Smith, Ark., Apr. 3, 1930; s. John M. and Justine (Hayes) C.; attended U. Ark., 1948-49, U. Tex., 1949-50, U. Ariz., 1951-53; m. Karen Lee Casey, June 5, 1971; children—Mary Noelle, Sarah Elizabeth, Ellen Casey. Founding partner Ray Manley Comml. Photography, Tucson, 1953-59; photog. systems cons. Amerind Founds, Inc., 1959-60; dir. photography Joint Casa Grandes Expdn., Chihuahua, Mexico, 1959-60; founder Photog. Internat. Corp., Los Angeles, 1961, pres., 1968-71; owner Tom Carroll Photography, Malibu, Calif., 1971-78, Irvine, Calif., 1978—; instr. mktg. techniques UCLA; instr. creative photography U. So. Calif., Pepperdine U.; lectr. U. Syracuse, Johns Hopkins, USN, USAF,; exhibited at Mus. Modern Art, N.Y.C., 1968. Mem. Soc. Photog. Instrumentation Engrs., Am. Soc. Mag. Photographers, Profl. Photographers Am., Am. Mgmt. Assn., Advt. Photographers Am., Alpha Delta Sigma. Mem. Christian Ch. (deacon, dir.). Contbr. illustrations to Nikon Manual; Golden Issue cover Eastman Kodak's Applied Photography; advance work in time/sound relatively; holographic laser research and solar environ. energy, laser image retrival systems, various computer systems. Address: 26801 Del Gado Capistrano Beach CA 92624

CARROLL, VIRGINIA I., counselor; b. Greenville, Tex., Jan. 1, 1925; d. Thomas F. and Ruth (Dial) Vines; B.S., U. Okla., 1947; M.A., Eastern N.M. U., 1964, postgrad., 1962—; m. Maurice W. Carroll, Jr., June 29, 1947; children—Maurice III, Richard Thomas, Randolph Lynn. Tchr. elementary sch. Hobbs (N.M.) Municipal Schs., 1955-56, secondary sch., 1960-62, counselor secondary sch., 1962-65, counselor coordinator elementary schs., 1965-77, testing and evaluation coordinator, 1977-80, elem. sch. prin., 1980—. Mem. NEA, N.Mex. Edn. Assn., Hobbs Tchrs. Assn., Am. Sch. Counselors Assn., Am., N.Mex. Elementary Sch. Counselors Assn. (pres. 1970-72), N.Mex. (pres. 1973-74), Southeastern N.Mex. (sec. 1962-63) personnel and guidance assns., Lea County Reading Assn. (v.p. 1968-69, pres. 1969-70). Democrat. Presbyterian. Club: Altrusa (sec. Hobbs 1968-70; pres. 1971-72). Home: 226 W Silver St Hobbs NM 88240 Office: PO Box 1040 Hobbs NM 88240

CARROLL, WILLIAM JEROME, civil engineer, consultant; b. Los Angeles, Nov. 23, 1923; s. William Jerome and Adeline Marie (Verden) C.; m. Louise Mae Judson, June 6, 1944; children—Charisse, Jean, Charles Gary, Christine Louise, Pamela Ann. B.S., Calif. Inst. Tech., 1948, M.S., 1949. Registered profl. engr., Calif., 1951. Engr., Los Angeles County, 1949-51; engr. James M. Montgomery, Cons. Engrs., Inc., Pasadena, Calif., 1951-56, v.p., 1956-59, pres., chief exec. officer, 1969-82, chmn. bd., 1982—; pres. Montgomery Engrs. of Nev.; v.p. Montgomery, Engring. Ctr., Engrs. Ltd., Montgomery Research, Inc. Served as lt. USAAF, 1943-46. Recipient Engring. Merit award, 1975; Inst. Advancement Engring. So. Calif. Engr. of Yr., 1983. Mem. Am. Acad. Environ. Engrs., ASCE, Am. Water Works Assn., Water Pollution Control Fedn., Internat. Water Resources Assn., Am. Geophys. Union, World Fed. Engring. Orgns. Republican. Roman Catholic. Clubs: University (Pasadena); Jonathan (Los Angeles). Home: 342 W Starlight Crest Dr La Canada CA 91011 Office: 250 N Madison Ave Pasadena CA 91101

CARR-RUFFINO, NORMA JEAN, business educator, management consultant; b Fort Worth, Dec. 15, 1932; d. Robert (Jack) Leroy and Lorene (Dickeson) Carr; m. Randell Hilton Smith, July 28, 1951; (div.); children—Randy, Brian, Carrie Smith Adams; m. 2d Alfredo Ruffino, Jan. 6, 1979. B.B.A. summa cum laude, Tex. Wesleyan Coll., 1968; M.B.E., North Tex. State U., 1969, Ph.D., 1973. Vice-pres. Randy's Inc., Ft. Worth, 1965-72; vocat. office Edn. coordinator Fort Worth pub. schs., 1969-72; prof. bus. San Francisco State U., 1972—; editor Calif. Bus. Edn. Yearbook, 1975-76. Mem. Acad. of Mgmt., Am. Bus. Communication Assn., Internat. Soc. Bus. Educators, Administr. Mgmt. Soc., Internat. Communication Assn., Nat. Bus. Edn. Assn., Western Bus. Edn. Assn., Calif. Bus. Edn. Assn., Delta Pi Epsilon. Author: Theory Reinforcement and Skill Building, 1975 2d edit., 1981; Writing Short Business Reports, 1980; The Promotable Woman, 1982. Office: Sch of Bus San Francisco State Univ 1600 Holloway San Francisco CA 94132

CARSON, GAIL HALVERSON, psychologist; b. Glendale, Calif., Mar. 28, 1934; d. Homer Allen and Millicent Serena (Scoltock) Halverson; m. Vance Lee Carson, Aug. 17, 1958; children—Devin Lee, Paul Jonathan, Trevor Rory. B.A., Occidental Coll., 1955; M.S., U. Okla., 1958; lic. psychologist, Calif. Vocational psychologist Los Angeles Unified Sch. Dist., 1958-60, psychometrist, part-time, 1964-69, examiner, 1965-73; personnel research analyst, 1973—; statis./programming cons. dept. psychology Occidental Coll., 1978—. Mem. Personnel Testing Council of So. Calif., (pres. 1981, dir.), Los Angeles City Tchrs. Math Assn., Phi Beta Kappa. Democrat. Presbyterian. Club: Toastmasters. Office: 450 N Grand Ave P301 Los Angeles CA 90012

CARSON, MARJORIE E., educator; b. Portland, Oreg., Jan. 25, 1939; d. Ralph R. and Faith M. (Hiatt) Reynolds; B.S. in Bus. Adminstrn., Oreg. State U., 1961; M.S. in Bus. Edn., 1967; postgrad. Portland State U., 1962-63, U. Ariz., 1961; Ed.D. in Curriculum Devel., Utah State U., 1979; m. John T. Carson, June 11, 1960; 1 dau., Kaia Kathleen. Tchr., Centennial High Sch., Gresham, Oreg., 1963-66, Sunset High Sch., Beaverton, Oreg., 1966-68; instr. bus. Portland Community Coll., 1968—; teaching asst. Utah State U., 1976-77. Mem. Internat. Assn. Records Mgrs., Oreg. Assn. Records Mgrs. and Adminstrs., Am. Mgmt. Assn., Nat. Bus. Edn. Assn., Western Bus. Edn. Assn., Oreg. Bus. Edn. Assn., Delta Pi Epsilon, Phi Kappa Phi, Phi Delta Kappa, Alpha Omicron Pi. Contbr. articles in records mgmt. and curriculum devel. to profl. jours. Office: Portland Community College 12000 SW 49th St Portland OR 97219

CARSON, VIRGINIA ROSALIE GOTTSCHALL, biology educator and researcher; b. Pitts., Jan. 22, 1936; d. Walter Carl Gottschall and Rosalie Madelaide (Paulin) G.; m. John Richard Carson, June 12, 1960; children—Margaret Rosalie, Kenneth Robert. Student Swarthmore Coll., 1953-57; B.A., Calif. State U.-Los Angeles, 1960, M.A., 1965; Ph.D., UCLA, 1970. Research aide Calif. Inst. Tech., Pasadena, Calif., 1958-60; asst. clin. research chemist Magaw Labs., Glendale, Calif., 1960-64; mental health trainee Brain Research Inst., UCLA, Los Angeles, 1965-69, postdoctoral trainee dept. pharmacology, 1970-71; asst. prof. biology Chapman Coll., Orange, Calif., 1971-77, assoc. prof. biology, 1977—, premed. advisor, 1974—; asst. research pharmacologist U. Calif.-Irvine, 1972-81, assoc. research pharmacologist, 1981—; assoc. prof. so. Calif. Coll. Optometry, Fullerton, Calif., 1979—. Recipient Outstanding Faculty Mem. award Chapman Coll., 1979-80; postdoctoral fellow UCLA, 1972-74. Mem. AAAS, Am. Pharmacol. Assn., Am. Soc. Pharmacology and Exptl. Therapeutics, IEEE, Soc. Neurosci., Iota Sigma Pi. Republican. Presbyterian. Contbr. numerous articles to profl. jours.

CARSON, WALLACE P., JR., state supreme court justice; b. Salem, Oreg., June 10, 1934; s. Wallace P. and Edith (Bragg) C.; m. Gloria Stolk,

1956; children—Wallace Scott, Carol Elizabeth, Steven Bruce. B.A., Stanford U., 1956; J.D., Willamette U., 1962. Ptnr., Carson & Carson, Salem, from 1962; mem. Oreg. Ho. of Reps., 1967-71, maj. leader, 1969-71; mem. Oreg. State Senate, 1971-78, minority floor leader, 1971-78; now chief justice Oreg. Supreme Ct. Served to 1st lt., USAF, 1956-59. Recipient Comdr. trophy Air Force Flight Sch., 1956, Disting. Service award Salem Jaycees, 1968; named one of 5 Outstanding Young Men of Yr., 1968. Mem. Marion County Bar Assn., Oreg. Bar Assn., ABA, Phi Delta Theta, Delta Theta Phi. Author: Writ of Mandamus, 1964. Republican. Office: Oregon Supreme Court Supreme Court Bldg Salem OR 97310*

CARSTEN, ARLENE DESMET, financial executive, city official; b. Paterson, N.J., Dec. 5, 1937; d. Albert F. and Ann (Greutert) Desmet; student Alfred U., 1955-56; m. Alfred John Carsten, Feb. 11, 1956; children—Christopher Dale, Jonathan Glenn. Exec. dir. Inst. for Burn Medicine, San Diego, 1972-81; founding trustee, dir. Nat. Burn Fedn., 1975-81; chief fin. officer A.J. Carsten Co., Inc., 1981—; Councilwoman City of Del Mar (Calif.), 1982—. Organizer, mem. numerous community groups; chmn. San Diego County Mental Health Adv. Bd., 1972-74, mem., 1971-75; chmn. community relations subcom., mem. exec. com. Emergency Med. Care Com., San Diego, Riverside and Imperial Counties, 1973-74; pub. mem. psychology exam. com. Calif. State Bd. Med. Quality Assurance, 1976-80, chmn., 1977; bd. dirs. Mental Health Assn., San Diego, 1978-79; mem. governing body HSA 14 representing San Diego County Govt., 1980; mem. faculty, lectr. numerous HEW Emergency Med. Service symposia, 1977-79. Mem. Calif. Democratic Central Com., 1968-74, exec. com., 1971-72, 73-74; treas. San Diego Dem. County Central Com., 1972-74; chmn. edn. for legislation com., women's div. So. Calif. Dem. Com., 1972; dir. Muskie for Pres. Campaign, San Diego, 1972; organizer, dir. numerous local campaigns. Bd. dirs. San Dieguito Family Service Assn., 1969-71, San Dieguito Dem. Club, 1965-71. Recipient Key Woman award Dem. Party, 1968, 72; 1st Ann. Community award Belles for Mental Health, Mental Health Assn. San Diego, 1974; citation Alfred U. Alumni Assn., 1979. Mem. Republican Assocs. Contbr. articles to profl. jours. Home: 1415 Via Alta Del Mar CA 92014 Office: AJ Carsten Co Inc 6711 Nancy Ridge Dr San Diego CA 92121

CARSTEN, JACK CRAIG, semiconductor company executive; b. Cin., Aug. 24, 1941; s. John A. and Edith L. C.; m. Mary Ellis Jones, June 22, 1963; children—Scott, Elizabeth, Amy. B.S. in Physics, Duke U., 1963. Formerly mktg. mgr. Tex. Instruments, Dallas and Houston, gen. mgr., 1971-75; v.p. sales and mktg. Intel Corp., Santa Clara, Calif., 1975-79, v.p., gen. mgr. microcomputers, 1979-82, sr. v.p., gen. mgr. components, 1982—; dir. Cimatel, Inc., Paris. Mem. Semicondr. Industry Assn., Am. Mgmt. Assn. Contbr. articles on electronics to profl. jours. Office: 3065 Bowers Ave Santa Clara CA 95051

CART, ROBERT LEE, JR., shopping center executive; b. Rayne, La., Mar. 22, 1945; s. Robert Lee and Lillian Effie (Johantgen) L.; m. Deanna Lee Heckley, Feb. 12, 1972; children—Cristin Dyan, Kimberly Ann. B.S. in Bus. Adminstrn., U. Southwestern La., 1967. Cert. shopping ctr. mgr. Promotion dir. James J. Cordano Co., Sacramento, Calif., 1974-76; mktg. dir., ops. mgr., gen. mgr. Long Beach (Calif.) Plaza, Ernest W. Hahn Inc., 1976—; gen. mgr. Univ. Village, Los Angeles, 1979, Laguna Hills (Calif.) Mall, 1979-81. Bd. dirs. Downtown Long Beach Assocs. Served to capt. USAF, 1968-73. Decorated D.F.C., Air medal with 8 oak leaf clusters. Mem. Internat. Council Shopping Ctrs., Kappa Sigma. Office: 451 Long Beach Blvd Long Beach CA 90802

CARTER, BRIAN ROBERT, judge; b. Paris, France, Nov. 10, 1925; s. David and Jeanne (Richmond) C.; parents Am. citizens; B.S. in Elec. Engring., U. Iowa, 1950; postgrad. U. Kansas City, 1958; J.D., Pepperdine U., 1969; m. Margaret Helen Schwarz, Feb. 14, 1958; children—Brian Robert, Scott David. Staff adviser Westinghouse Electric Corp., Pitts., 1952-54, promotion mgr. Kansas City, Mo., 1954-58, program mgr., Balt., 1958-62; dir. licensing electronics N.Am. Rockwell Corp., 1964-74; admitted to Calif. bar, 1970, practice law, Newport Beach, Santa Ana and San Diego, Calif., 1970-82; judge Mcpl. Ct., Newport Beach, 1982—; judge pro tem Orange County (Calif.) Ct. System, 1976-78. Served with USNR, USMCR, 1943-45. Decorated Purple Heart medal. Mem. State Bar Calif., Orange County Bar, Iowa Alumni Assn. (named to Order Golden Hawk 1956), Beta Kappa Lambda. Episcopalian. Mason. Clubs: Bahia Corinthian Yacht (commodore 1972-73). Contbr. articles on yachting to various mags. Home: 4732 Cortland Dr Corona del Mar CA 92625 Office: Carter and Hobart 601 N Parkcenter Dr Santa Clara CA 92705

CARTER, CALVIN ROSS, energy company executive, financial consultant; b. Ogden, Utah, Oct. 6, 1933; s. Thomas Ross and Florence Regina (Spendlove) C.; m. Bonita Rae Kerr, Apr. 1, 1955; children—Camron Shea, Calene Celeste, Mitchel Ross. B.S. in Acctg. and Econs., Utah State U., 1960, M.B.A., 1961. C.P.A. Calif., N.Y. Audit mgr. Arthur Andersen & Co., Los Angeles and Rochester, N.Y., 1961-70; chief fin. officer Continental Ill. Realty, Los Angeles, 1970-80, Oak Creek Energy Systems Group, Tehachapi, Calif., 1982—; v.p. fin. and adminstrn. Wolf & Vine, Inc., Los Angeles, 1980-82; fin. cons. to JDH Realty Co.; co-owner BCEG Enterprises, Inc., C & G Mktg. Assocs. Served with U.S. Army, 1955-57. Utah State U. research grantee, 1960. Mem. Nat. Rifle Assn., Calif. Rifle and Pistol Assn., U.S. Jr. C. of C. (former v.p., treas. dir.), Am. Inst. C.P.A.s, Calif. Soc. C.P.A.s. Republican. Mormon. Club: Safari. Home: 2496 Via Mariposa St San Dimas CA 91773 Office: Oak Creek Energy Systems Group 441 N Green St Tehachapi CA 93561

CARTER, DANNY MICHAEL, educator; b. Yuma, Colo., Sept. 5, 1948; s. Floyd and Estalene (Haley) C.; m. Patricia Marie Wahrman, Sept. 3, 1940; 1 son, Christopher Adam. B.A., Western State Coll., 1970; M.A., Colo. State U., 1973. Tchr. Wray (Colo.) High Sch., 1970-72; teaching asst. indsl. scis. Colo. State U., Ft. Collins, 1972-73, instr., 1973-74; tchr. Natrona County Sch. Dist., Casper, Wyo., 1974—, East Jr. High Sch., 1974—. Named Indsl. Arts Tchr. of Yr., Am. Indsl. Arts Assn. and Wyo. Indsl. Edn. Assn., 1982. Mem. Wyo. Indsl. Edn. Assn., NEA, Wyo. Edn. Assn., Natrona County Classroom Tchrs. Assn., Am. Vocat. Assn., Wyo. Vocat. Assn., Central Wyo. Indsl. Edn. Tchrs. Assn. Republican. Club: Elks. Office: East Jr High 900 S Beverly St Casper WY 82609

CARTER, DONNA MARION, educator; b. Chgo., Mar. 27, 1931; d. Earl Jesse and Marion Elizabeth (McCormick) Hyett; m. Milburn Carlton Carter, Dec. 29, 1950; children—Lynn Roble, Deborah Yager, Donna T., Sally, John, Nancy, Peter. B.A., San Diego U., 1968, M.A., 1983. Cert. tchr., Calif. Tchr. asst. San Diego City Schs., 1965-66, reader, 1970-71, substitute tchr., 1973-75, jr. high sch. tchr., 1975-83, high sch. tchr., 1983—, computer resource coordinator. Mem. PTA bd., 1964-65; catechism tchr., 1962-65; mgr., scorekeeper Bobby Sox, 1968-70. Mem. Nat. Council Tchrs. Math., Greater San Diego Math. Council, Assn. San Diego Educators for Gifted and Talented, Computer Using Educators. Republican. Roman Catholic. Home: 3898 Ashford St San Diego CA 92111 Office: 4302 Valeta St San Diego CA 92107

CARTER, EDWARD WILLIAM, merchant; A.B. in Econs., U. Calif. at Los Angeles, 1932; M.B.A. cum laude, Harvard, 1937; LL.D., Occidental Coll., 1962; m. 2d, Hannah Locke Caldwell, 1963; children—William Dailey Carter, Mrs. Ann Carter Huneke. Chmn., dir. Carter Hawley Hale Stores, Inc., Los Angeles; dir. Novacor Med. Corp., Lockheed Corp., Pacific Mut. Life Ins. Co., So. Calif. Edison Co., First Interstate Bancorp. Regent U. Calif.; trustee Occidental Coll.; bd. dirs. Stanford Research Inst.; trustee Brookings Instn., Nat. Humanities Center, Com. for Econ. Devel.; mem. council Woodrow Wilson Internat. Center, Rockefeller U.; mem. Sloan Commn. on Higher Edn.; mem. Harvard bd. overseers coms. on art museums and dept. econs., also univ. resources; mem. vis. com. Grad. Sch. Mgmt., UCLA; bd. dirs. Los Angeles Philharmonic Assn.; trustee Los Angeles County Mus. Art, San Francisco Opera Assn.; mem. Bus. Council, Conf. Bd., Council on Fgn. Relations; bd. dirs. James Irvine Found., Santa Anita Found., Los Angeles World Affairs Council. Clubs: Los Angeles Country, California, Pacific Union, Bohemian, Burlingame Country, Cypress Point. Office: 550 S Flower St Los Angeles CA 90071

CARTER, EVERITT A., electronics company executive; b. Phila., May 9, 1919; s. Robert A. and Florence Emma (Everett) C.; B.S. in Mech. Engring., Duke, 1940; m. Mary M. Cragoe, Oct. 9, 1943; children—Nickola Mary, Robert Edward, Timothy John, Susan Catherine. Engring. and sales positions Wright Aeros. div. Curtiss-Wright Corp., 1940-45, dir. sales west coast, 1952-55; dir. sales and service Hughes Aircraft Co., 1945-47; v.p. Faber Labs., N.Y.C., 1947-52; gen. mgr. Curtiss-Wright Can., Ltd., 1955-56; v.p., gen. mgr. Canadian Curtiss-Wright, Ltd., 1957-59; pres. Oak Industries, Inc., 1959-70, chief exec. officer, 1959—, chmn. bd., 1963—, also dir.; dir. Fed. Signal Corp., Johnson Controls, Inc., Home State Bank Crystal Lake. Mem. No. Ill. U. Pres.'s Council; chmn. pattern gifts bldg. fund campaign Lake Region YMCA, Crystal Lake; mem. Chgo. Crime Commn.; bd. dirs. Crystal Lake Hosp. Assn.; trustee Rockford Coll. Mem. Soc. Automotive Engrs., Canadian Aero. Inst., World Trade Council, U.S. C. of C. (membership com.), Chgo. Assn. Commerce and Industry (dir.), U.S.-Korea Econ. Council (dir.), Korean-Am. Midwest Assn. (hon. dir.), Chgo. Council Fgn. Relations (Chgo. com.), Midwest-Japan Assn., Phi Kappa Psi, Delta Epsilon Sigma. Republican. Clubs: Inverness Golf; Turnberry Country; Econ., Chgo., Mid-Am., Univ., Met. (Chgo.); Canadian; Barrington (Ill.) Tennis; Racket (Crystal Lake); West Side Tennis (Forest Hills, N.Y.); Balboa Bay (Newport Beach, Calif.); Escondido (Calif.) Tennis. Office: Oak Industries Inc 16935 W Bernardo Dr Rancho Bernardo CA 92127*

CARTER, GEORGE SZEKERES, lawyer; b. Gyor, Hungary, Jan. 29, 1917; s. Max and Irene (Csillag) Szekeres; A.B., Realgymnasium, Gyor, 1935; LL.B., U. Budapest (Hungary), 1938; LL.B., U. Paris (France), 1941, LL.M., 1942; J.U.D., U. Erlangen (Germany), 1947; J.D., U. Denver, 1954; m. Rose Piroska Voros, Aug. 13, 1949; children—Susan Irene, Agnes Eve, Esther Rose. Came to U.S., 1951, naturalized, 1957. Practiced in Paris, 1941-43, Bamberg, Germany, 1946-49, Munich, Germany, 1949-51; instr. mil. govt. law U. Erlangen Law Sch., 1948-50; admitted to Colo. bar, 1957; adminstrv. asst. to pres. Rocky Mountain Export Co., Inc., Denver, 1955-57; practiced in Denver, 1957—; partner Goldsmith & Carter, 1966-71; legal adviser German Consulate Gen. in San Francisco; lectr. U. Denver Coll. of Law, 1964-65. Mem. Colo. (chmn. internat. and comparative law subcom. 1963-65, chmn. world peace thru law com. 1966-67, chmn. internat. and comparative law com. 1967-68, chmn. community and internat. relations com. 1971-73), Denver bar assns., Assn. Immigration and Nationality Lawyers (chmn. Colo. chpt. 1978-79), Phi Delta Phi. Democrat. Unitarian. Author: Legal Status of Displaced Persons in Germany, 1947; Am. Military Government Law, 1948. Home: 2855 S Winona Ct Denver CO 80236 Office: Am Nat Bank Bldg Denver CO 80202

CARTER, HAROLD RAYMOND TRAFFORD, lawyer; b. Liverpool, Eng., Aug. 25, 1925; came to U.S., 1948, naturalized, 1954; s. Harold and Edith Gertrude Carter. LL.B., U. San Diego, 1961. Bar: Calif., U.S. Supreme Ct. 1971. Practice law, La Jolla, Calif., 1978; pres. Carter Internat., Inc., San Diego and Honolulu, 1978; v.p., gen. counsel, dir. Coleman & Assocs.; pres. The Village Travel Shoppe, Inc.; v.p. China Arts of La Jolla, Inc.; asst. atty. gen. to Govt. of Marshall Islands, Majuro. Served with Brit. and Indian Army, 1944-48. Mem. State Bar Calif., San Diego County Bar Assn. Republican. Episcopalian. Clubs: San Diego Yacht; Royal Overseas (London). Home: 7811 Eads Ave La Jolla CA 92037 Office: 1111 Prospect St La Jolla CA 92037 also PO Box 2548 La Jolla CA 92038 also PO Box 679 Majuro Marshall Islands 96960

CARTER, J. GEOFFREY, editor; b. Noblesville, Ind., June 13, 1946; s. E. Barton and Julia W. (Riley) C.; student Marion Coll., 1964-66; m. Mary Alice Wooten, Feb. 14, 1970; 1 dau., Natalie Rose. Advt. graphic designer, 1970-72; with Advance Sign Co., Ft. Wayne, Ind., 1972-76, Shurtz Unltd., Ft. Wayne, 1976-79; editor St. Rodder mag., McMullen Pub., Anaheim, Calif., 1979—; editorial, graphic and prodn. mgr. Ind. St. Rod Assn., 1978-79. Served with U.S. Army, 1967-69. Mem. Nat. St. Rod Assn., Ind. St. Rod Assn., Minn. St. Rod Assn. Club: Rd. Masters (Muncie, Ind.). Office: 2145 W La Palma St Anaheim CA 92801

CARTER, LOUIS PHILIP, surgeon; b. St. Louis, Feb. 26, 1939; s. Russell G. and Dorothy Ruth (Zerweck) C.; student U. Iowa, 1957-60; M.D., Washington U., 1964; m. Marcia L. Carlson, Aug. 26, 1960; children—Kristin, Melinda Nell, Chad Philip. Intern, King County Hosp., Seattle, 1964-65; resident in surgery St. Luke's Hosp., N.Y.C., 1967-68; resident in neurosurgery Barrow Neurol. Inst., Phoenix, 1968-72, U. Western Ont., 1973; practice medicine specializing in neurosurgery, Phoenix, 1973—; mem. staff St. Joseph's Hosp., John C. Lincoln Hosp., Humane Hosp. Phoenix Baptist Hosp.; neurosurg. cons. Ariz. Emergency Med. Systems, 1977—, VA Hosp., Phoenix, 1973—; attending neurosurgeon Barrow Neurol. Inst., 1973—, dir. Microsurg. Lab., 1976—. Served to capt. M.C., USAF, 1965-67. Internat. Coll. Surgeons Traveling fellow, 1973; diplomate Am. Bd. Neurol. Surgery. Mem. A.C.S., Congress Neurol. Surgeons, Am. Assn. Neurol. Surgeons, Rocky Mountain Neurosurg. Soc., Ariz. Neurosurg. Soc., Ariz. Med. Assn., AMA, Maricopa County Med. Soc., Mamakai Med. Soc. (sec. treas. 1978). Contbr. articles in field to med. jours. Office: 222 W Thomas Ave Phoenix AZ 85013

CARTER, MILDRED BROWN, broadcast exec.; b. Leo, S.C., Feb. 22, 1927; d. Eddie Washington and Hester Lessie Lee (Poston) Brown; student Pace Seminar, 1977, Dale Carnegie, 1977, Am. Mgmt. Assn., 1977; m. Richard Bert Carter, Sept. 6, 1952; children—Paul, Mark, Janis, David. Various secretarial positions, FBI, Washington, 1943-48, adminstrv. asst., 1948-51; adminstrv. asst., office asso. dir., 1952; with Bellevue (Wash.) Sch. Dist., 1965-75; sec., registrar Hyak Jr. High Sch., 1971-75; asst. to exec. v.p. Bonneville Internat. Corp., Salt Lake City, 1975—. Mem. PTA Bd., Yakima, Wash., 1963; treas. PTA, Bellevue, 1973. Mem. Soc. Former FBI Women, Beta Sigma Phi. Mormon. Clubs: Women's Century, Soroptimist. Home: 2180 Elaine Dr Bountiful UT 84010 Office: 36 S State St Suite 2100 Salt Lake City UT 84111

CARTER, NANCY JEAN, mathematics educator; b. Los Angeles, Apr. 12, 1952; d. Lyle Wilbur and Jean Everal (Buchanan) Carter. B.A., Calif. State U.-Chico, 1974; M.S., U. Nebr., 1976; Ph.D., Oreg. State U., 1981. Statis. Researcher USDA, Washington, 1981-82; asst. prof. math. Calif. State U.-Chico, 1982—; statis. cons. Recipient Bank Am. Achievement award in math., 1970. Mem. Am. Statis. Assn., Biometric Soc., AAAS, Phi Kappa Phi, Sigma Xi. Republican. Co-author: The Development of a Fish Passage Model for McNary Dam, 1979. Home: 181 San Gabriel Dr Chico CA 95926 Office: Math Dept Calif State U Chico CA 95929

CARTER, NORMAN DANA, educational administrator; b. San Mateo, Calif., Apr. 7, 1931; s. John Lloyd and Carrie Jean (Barnes) C.; m. Lois Marie Olsen, Aug. 23, 1953; children—Eric Dana, Cristina Marie, John Louis. B.A., San Jose State U., 1953, M.A., 1963; gen. adminstrn. credential Stanford U., 1966. Elem. tchr. Santa Clara (Calif.) Unified Sch. Dist., 1956-58, tchr. academically talented, 1958-62, elem. sch. prin., 1962-65, 1966-69; dir. spl. services, 1965-66, asst. dir. elem. curriculum and edn., 1970—; sr. research sci., cons. Am. Inst. Research in Behavioral Scis., Palo Alto, Calif., 1969-70; dir. Redwood Glen Sch., 1963-80; asst. prof. San Jose State U., 1970-74. Chmn. Santa Clara chpt. ARC (Outstanding Achievement award). Served with U.S. Army, 1954-56. Mem. PTA (hon. life), Assn. Sch. Curricula Developers, Assn. Calif. Sch. Adminstrs. (charter). Republican. Clubs: Commonwealth of Calif., Half Moon Bay Yacht. Office: 1889 Lawrence Rd Santa Clara CA 95051

CARTER, PETER LENN, industrial engineer; b. Albany, Calif., Sept. 28, 1938; s. Lennard James and Emogene (West) C.; A.A., Contra Costa Coll., 1962; student U. Calif., 1963; m. Lucille Ann Incaviglia, Dec. 31, 1972; children by former marriage—Kimberly, Kiersten, Katherine, James. With Bechtel Corp., 1966—, engring. positions, San Francisco, 1966-72, project engr., Beirut, Lebanon, 1972-75, chief control systems engr., San Francisco, 1975-79. Instr. underwater diving activities Alameda County Sheriff's Dept., 1967-70, YMCA, 1965-68; charter mem. Walnut Creek Civic Arts Assn. Served with USN, 1958-59. Registered profl. engr., Calif.; lic. pilot, amateur radio operator. Sr. mem. IEEE, Instrument Soc. Am.; mem. Calif. Soc. Profl. Engrs., Nat. Soc. Profl. Engrs., U.S. Com. on Large Dams, Nat. Rifle Assn., Aircraft Owners and Pilots Assn. Republican. Clubs: Masons (32 deg.), Scottish Rite, Shriners; Athenian Nile. Office: 610 16th St Oakland CA 94612

CARTER, RICHARD BERT, ch. ofcl., ret. govt. ofcl.; b. Spokane, Wash., Dec. 2, 1916; s. Richard B. and Lula Selena (Jones) C.; B.A. in Polit. Sci., Wash. State U., 1939; postgrad. Georgetown U. Law Sch., 1941, Brown U., 1944, Brigham Young U. Extension, 1975-76; m. Mildred Brown, Sept. 6, 1952; children—Paul, Mark, Janis, David. Advt. credit mgr. Elec. Products Consol., Omaha, 1939-40; pub. communications ofcl., investigator FBI, Washington, 1940-41, Huntington, W.Va., 1941, Houston, 1942, Boston, 1943, S. Am., 1943, Providence, 1944-45, N.Y.C., 1945, Salt Lake City, 1945, P.R., 1946-48, Phoenix, 1948-50, Washington, 1950-51, Cleve., 1952-55, Seattle, 1955-75, ret., 1975; assoc. dir. stake and mission pub. communications dept. Ch. Hdqrs., Ch. of Jesus Christ of Latter-day Saints, Salt Lake City, 1975-77. Dist. chmn. Chief Seattle council Boy Scouts Am., 1967-68, Council v.p., 1971-72, council commr., 1973-74, nat. council rep., 1962-64, 72-74. Bd. dirs. Salvation Army, 1963, United Good Neighbors, 1962-63, mem. allocations com., 1962. Served to lst lt., Intelligence Corps, U.S. Army, 1954. Recipient Silver Beaver award Boy Scouts Am., 1964, Vigil Honor, 1971; named Nat. Media Man-of-Month, Morality in Media, Inc., N.Y.C., 1976. Mem. Profl. Photographers Am., Internat. Assn. Bus. Communicators, Am. Security Council (nat. adv. bd.), Internat. Platform Assn., Sons Utah Pioneers (pres. 1982), William Carter Family Orgn. (nat. pres.), Scabbard and Blade, Alpha Phi Omega, Pi Sigma Alpha, Sigma Delta Chi, Phi Delta Theta. Mem. Ch. of Jesus Christ of Latter-day Saints (coordinator pub. communications council Seattle area 1973-75, br. pres. 1944-45, dist. pres. 1954-55, high priest 1958—, pres. stake 1959-64, stake Sunday Sch. pres. 1980-81). Clubs: Bonneville Knife and Fork (bd. dirs. 1982—), Rotary (dir., editor The Rotary Bee, 1982-83, Paul Harris fellow 1982, award for best newsletter in dist. 1983). Assoc. editor FBI Investigator, 1965-75; contbg. author, editor: Biographies of Sons of Utah Pioneers, 1982. Home: 2180 S Elaine Dr Bountiful UT 84010

CARTER, RONALD MARTIN, SR., pharm. co. exec.; b. Chgo., Nov. 18, 1925; s. Jack Edward and Anna P. C.; student U. Ill., 1942-43, 45-46; m. Joy Wolf, Nov. 14, 1946; children—Ronald Martin, Craig Alan. Sales mgr. Preston Labs., Chgo., 1947-52; exec. v.p. Myers-Carter Labs., Inc., Phoenix, 1952-69; pres., chief exec. officer Carter-Glogau Labs., Inc., Glendale, Ariz., 1969—, also dir. Served with U.S. Army, 1943-45. Decorated Bronze Star, Purple Heart. Mem. Assn. Corp. Growth, Nat. Pharm. Alliance (pres.), Nat. Assn. Pharm. Mfrs., Drug, Chem. and Allied Trades Industry, Parenteral Drug Assn. Club: Arizona. Home: 5707 N 40th St Phoenix AZ 85018 Office: 5160 W Bethany Home Rd Glendale AZ 85301

CARTER, ROY GUY, lumber co. purchasing ofcl.; b. Mt. Shasta City, Calif., Jan. 28, 1921; s. Royal Guy and Blanche Edna (Clark) C.; student Woodbury Coll., Los Angeles, 1939-40, U. Idaho, 1966-68; m. Donna Lee Happy, Mar. 15, 1969; children—Susan, Gayle, Camieon, Roy. Asst. purchasing agt. Wells & Wade, Inc., Wenatchee, Wash., 1942-54; purchasing agt. Oreg. Fibre Products, Pilot Rock, 1954-56; mgr. J.E. Haseltine & Co., Spokane, Wash., 1956-62; purchasing agt. Wood Products Group, Potlatch Forests, Inc., Lewiston, Idaho, 1962-70; dir. purchasing Roseburg Lumber Co. (Oreg.), 1970—. Mem. Nat. Assn. Purchasing Mgmt. (cert., nat. chmn. wood products commodity com.), Pacific Logging Congress, Oreg. Logging Congress, Purchasing Mgmt. Assn. Oreg. (pres. Willamette Valley div. 1973-74). Home: 110 Isabell St Roseburg OR 97470 Office: PO Box 1088 Roseburg OR 97470

CARTER, SUSAN MONTGOMERY, actress, business woman; b. Great Falls, Mont.; d. A. Raymond and Jean (Anderson) Montgomery; m. George Robert Carter, III, July 15, 1961 (div.), children—George Robert, Anne Strong. B.A., UCLA, 1961; postgrad. Stanford U. Bus. Sch. Profl. model Vogue mag., 1969-75, Harper's Bazaar mag., 1976-79; actress stage and screen, 1969—, commls., 1970—; mktg. and adminstrv. dir. Landor Assocs., Los Angeles and Hawaii, 1979-82; personal fin. mgr., 1982—. Trustee Strong Carter Dental Clinic, Honolulu, 1963-69; bd. dirs. Hawaii Child and Family Service, 1963-69, Big Bros. Chgo., 1973-75, Northwestern U. Med. Ctr., 1973-75; dir. Hawaii Air/Water Pollution Campaign, 1967; bd. govs. Burlington House, N.Y.C., 1969-75; active Los Angeles Olympic Com., UCLA Chancellors Assocs., Royce 270, Los Angeles Jr. League; patron Vatican Art, Nat. Charity League. Mem. Prytanean Soc. Clubs: San Francisco Met.; Hawaii Outrigger Canoe; Beach (Santa Monica).

CARTER, THOMAS L(EE), ins. co. mgr.; b. La Jolla, Calif., Feb. 10, 1941; s. O. L. and Leila I. (McCall) C.; B.S. in Math., Central Mo. U., 1963; grad. Advanced Mgmt. Conf. U. Mass., 1977; m. Shirley, June 17, 1962; children—Jeffrey, Cindy. With Aetna Life & Casualty Co., 1960—, supt., Los Angeles, 1971-76, claim mgr. Los Angeles met. operation, Panorama City, Calif., 1976—. Leader, Boy Scouts, 1973-75; coach Little League, 1976. Mem. Claim Mgrs. Council, Los Angeles Ins. Arbitration Com. (chmn. 1975), Calif. Ins. Guarantee Assn. (bd. govs., chmn. claim com.), Soc. C.P.C.U.s. Office: 8155 Van Nuys Blvd Panorama City CA 91402

CARTER, VICTOR M., pvt. investor; b. Rostov, Russia, Aug. 21, 1910; s. Mark and Fanya (Rudnick) C.; m. Adrea Zucker, July 15, 1928; 1 dau., Fanya. Dir., 1st Interstate Bank, Hamburger Hamlets, Inc.; mem. exec. com. IDB Bankholding Co.; v.p., dir. So. Calif. Theatre Assn. Past pres. United Way, City of Hope, Japan Am. Soc., Japanese Philharmonic Soc. Bd. dirs. Fedn. Jewish Welfare Orgns., World Affairs Council, Century City Cultural Commn.; hon. chmn. bd. Israel Devel. Corp., Clal (Israel) Ltd., bd. govs. Jewish Agy., Inc. Democrat. Mason; mem. B'nai B'rith. Club: Hillcrest Country. Home: 10375 Wilshire Blvd Los Angeles CA 90024 Office: 10375 Wilshire Blvd Suite 2A Los Angeles CA 90024

CARTER, WENDELL EUGENE, ch. ofcl., former air force officer; b. Lincoln, Nebr., Nov. 19, 1915; s. Joseph Albert and Amanda (Higginbotham) C.; B.B.A., Wichita State U., 1938; M.B.A., Harvard U., 1947; grad. Air War Coll., 1956; m. Helen Rebecca Inness, Aug. 14, 1940; children—Sandra Leigh, David Inness, Karen Lou. Commd. 2d lt. U.S. Army, 1940; advanced through grades to maj. gen. U.S. Air Force, 1966; assigned to Wright Field, 1940-46; with budget directorate USAF Hdqrs., 1947-49; asst. to comptroller USAF, 1949-51; chief adminstrv. mgmt. Air Material Command, 1951-52; chief acctg. div., 1952-55; comptroller Alaskan Air Command, 1956-59; dep. comptroller MATS, 1959-60, comptroller, 1960-63; dep. dir. USAF Budget Directorate, 1963-64; comptroller Air Force Systems Command, 1964-67; dep. asst. sec. of def., 1967-69; ret., 1969; pres. Synod of the S.W. Corp., United Presbyn. Ch., 1979-81, elder, 1971-81, chmn. Synod of S.W. Mission Council, 1979-81; mem. Council Theol. Seminaries Presbyn. Ch., chmn. budget com., 1980-81. Pres., La Vida Llena Corp. Retirement Center. Decorated Disting. Service medal, Legion of Merit (4), AF Commendation medal, Army Commendation medal; named Man of Distinction, Am. Mgmt. Assn., 1966. Mem. Air Force Assn., Ret. Officers Assn., Nat. Def. Preparedness Assn., Am. Security Council, Armed Forces Mgmt. Assn. (dir.), Am. Soc. Mil. Comptrollers (nat. pres.). Republican. Clubs: Harvard-Yale-Princeton (Albuquerque), Kirtland Officers, Masons, Shriners. Contbr. articles to Def. Industry Bull., Navy Mgmt. Rev. Home: 3200 Candlelight Dr NE Albuquerque NM 87111

CARTER, WILLIAM BROCK, safety cons.; b. Bolling, Va., Apr. 15, 1951; s. William P. and Eleanor (Brock) C.; B.Univ. Studies, U. N.Mex., 1974. Account exec. Clayton Brokerage Co., Albuquerque, 1974-75; v.p. Safety Counselling, Inc., Albuquerque, 1975-80, pres., 1980—; mem. adv. com. on constrn. safety and health OSHA, Dept. Labor, Washington. Active Downtown Exchange Club. Mem. Am. Soc. Safety Engrs., N.Mex. Safety Assn. (dir. 1975—), Am. Subcontrators Assn. Office: 3207 Matthew Ave NE Suite B Albuquerque NM 87107

CARTERETTE, EDWARD CALVIN HAYES, psychologist; b. Mt. Tabor, N.C., July 10, 1921; s. John Calvin and Alma Olivia (Fowler) C.; diploma U.S. Army Command and Gen. Staff Coll., 1943; A.B., U. Chgo., 1949; A.B. cum laude, Harvard U., 1952; M.A., Ind. U., 1954, Ph.D. (NSF predoctoral fellow), 1957; m. Patricia Spidel Blum, Jan. 18, 1955 (dec. Jan. 7, 1977); 1 son, Christopher Edward; m. 2d, Noel McSherry, Sept. 27, 1980. Served as enlisted man U.S. Army, 1937-42, commd. 2d lt., 1942, advanced through grades to lt. col., 1946; served in Hawaii, 1937-41; dep. dir. personnel Hampton Roads Port of Embarcation, Newport News, Va., 1942-45; adj. gen. 32d Inf. Div., Philippines and Japan, 1945-46; ret., 1946; mem. research staff acoustics lab. M.I.T., 1952; instr. UCLA, 1956-58, asst. prof. psychology, 1958-63, asso. prof., 1963-68, prof., 1968—; vis. asso. prof. U. Calif., Berkeley, 1966; NSF postdoctoral fellow in physics Royal Inst. Tech., Stockholm and Cambridge (Eng.) U., 1960-61; NSF sr. postdoctoral fellow Inst. Math. Studies in Social Scis., Stanford U., 1965-66; cons. in field; cons. neuropsychology VA Wadsworth Hosp. Center, 1978—; chmn. selection com. Woodrow Wilson Nat. Fellowship Found., 1963-72, chmn., 1966-72; mem. editorial com. U. Calif. Press, 1970-77, co-chmn., 1973-77, mem. bd. control, 1973-77; Disting. visitor Am. Psychol. Assn., 1979—. Fellow Acoustical Soc. Am., AAAS (nominating com. 1981-84), Am. Psychol. Assn., Soc. Exptl. Psychologists (chmn. 1977-78, sec.-treas. 1982); mem. IEEE, Psychonomic Soc., Internat. Neuropsychol. Soc., Soc. Math. Psychology, Sigma Xi. Club: Harvard of So. Calif. (dir. 1982—). Author: Brain Function: Speech, Language and Communication, 1966; (with Margaret Hubbard Jones) Informal Speech, 1974; editor: (with M. P. Friedman) Handbook of Perception, 11 vols., 1973-78, Academic Press Series in Cognition and Perception, 1973—; asso. editor Perception and Psychophysics, 1972—, Music Perception, 1981—. Home: 456 Greencraig Rd Los Angeles CA 90049 Office: Dept Psychology U Calif Los Angeles CA 90024

CARTIER, PAUL KELSO, III, microbiologist; b. Hamilton, Ohio, Oct. 26, 1941; s. Paul Kelso and Ruby Bernice (Pridemore) C.; A.B., U. Calif. at Los Angeles, 1968; m. Sharlene Ellen Tennant, Jan. 25, 1963, one son, Paul Kelso IV. Research asst. microbiology Calif. Inst. Tech., Pasadena, 1968-69, research biologist, 1973—, scientist Jet Propulsion Lab., Pasadena, 1969-73. Mem. Youth Sci. Congress Evaluation Com. NASA-Nat. Sci. Tchrs. Assn., 1970-71. Asso. in devel., evaluation pyrolytic release life detection experiment for Viking mission to Mars. 1969-78. Home: 58 W Grand View Ave Arcadia CA 91006 Office: Calif Inst Tech Pasadena CA 91125

CARTWRIGHT, MARY LOU, clinical laboratory scientist; b. Payette, Idaho, Apr. 5, 1923; d. Ray J. and Nellie Mae (Sherer) Decker; B.S., U. Houston, 1958; M.A., Central Mich. U., 1976; m. Chadwick Louis Cartwright, Sept. 13, 1947. Med. technologist Methodist Hosp., Houston, 1957-59, VA Hosp., Livermore, Calif., 1960-67, Kaiser Permanente Med. Center, Hayward, Calif., 1967-71, United Med. Lab., San Mateo, Calif., 1972-73; sr. med. technologist Oakland (Calif.) Hosp., 1974—; cons. med. lab. tech. Oakland Public Schs. Chmn., Congressional Dist. 11 steering com. Common Cause, 1974-77; consumer mem. Alameda County (Calif.) Health Systems Agy., 1977-78. Served with USNR, 1945-53. Mem. Calif. Soc. Med. Tech., Calif. Assn. Med. Lab. Tech. (Technologist of Yr. award 1968, 78, Pres.'s award 1977, Service award chpt. 1978, 79), Am. Soc. Med. Tech. (chmn. by-laws com. 1981-83), Am. Bus. Women's Assn., Nat. Assn. Female Execs. Democrat. Home: 1539 Delemos Ave Hayward CA 94544 Office: 2648 E 14th St Oakland CA 94601

CARUCCI, RODERIC ALAN, medical company executive, consultant; b. N.Y.C., July 24, 1948; s. Julius John and Vesta Merle (Schroeder) C.; m. Linda Sharon Wallace, Dec. 31, 1977. B.S. in Chemistry, Adelphi U., 1970, M.B.A. cum laude, 1972; postgrad. fellow Fla. State U., 1975-76. Market mgr., Abbott Laboratories, South Pasadena, Calif., 1977-78; dir. mktg. Am. Edwards Laboratories, Santa Ana, Calif., 1978-81; dir. sales, mktg. Mansfield Sci. Inc., Mansfield, Mass., 1981-82; pres. Claremont Med. Software Inc. (Calif.), 1983—; pres. Stanco Med. Co., Fountain Valley, Calif., 1982—; start-up cons. to med. firms. Mem. gen. plan com., City of Claremont, 1980-81. Mem. Am. Mktg. Assn. Home: 123 E Limestone Rd Claremont CA 91711 Office: PO Box 1002 Claremont CA 91711

CARVELL, FRED JOHN, educational and business consulting firm executive; b. N.Y.C., June 22, 1934; s. Douglas and Ada (Cook) C.; m. Joan Barnes, July 3, 1954; children—Lyndall Anne, John Randall. B.A. in Bus. Edn., Calif. State U.-Fresno, 1962, M.A. in Bus., 1963. Instr. bus. Fresno City Coll., 1963-67; cons. Mgmt. and Econs. Research, Palo Alto, Calif., 1967-68, Burlingame, Calif., 1968-69, v.p. Tadlock Assocs., Inc., Los Altos, Calif., 1969-76; pres., sr. cons. Carvell Edn. Mgmt. Planning, Inc., Los Altos, 1976—. Served with USNR. Mem. Calif. Vocat. Edn. Adminstrs., Am. Assn. Community and Jr. Colls., World Future Soc., Am. Vocat. Assn. (life). Author: Human Relations in Business, 1970, 1976, 1980 (transl. in Portuguese 1982); It's Not Too Late, 1971; Breakthrough, 1979-82 (award Excellence Nat. Assn. Vocat.-Tech. Edn. Communicators); and other publs. Office: Carvell Edn Mgmt Planning Inc PO Box 531 Los Altos CA 94022

CARVELL, JOAN BARNES, educational and management consultant firm executive; b. Monterey, Calif., Jan. 10, 1934; d. Henry C. and Violet (Wallace) Barnes; m. Fred Carvell, July 3, 1954; children—Lyndall Anne, John Randall. B.A. with great distinction in Econs., San Jose State U., 1970, M. Urban Planning, 1974. Tchr. pub. schs, Sacred Heart Sch., Fresno, Calif., 1965-67; market researcher URS Research Co., Palo Alto, Calif., 1968-69; planner, cons. Tadlock Assocs., Inc., Los Altos, Calif., 1969-76; v.p., sr. cons. Carvell Edn. Mgmt. Planning, Inc., Los Altos, 1976—. Mem. Am. Vocat. Assn., Am. Vocat. Edn. Research Assn., World Future Soc. Club: Island Yacht. Contbr. chpts. to books, articles to profl. jours. Office: Carvell Edn Mgmt Planning Inc PO Box 531 Los Altos CA 94022

CARVER, BEVERLY ANN, educational software company executive, consultant; b. Douglas, Wyo., Sept. 17, 1934; d. John Emmett and Lillian Beryl (Russell) Carver; m. Raymond Pergeau, July 12, 1958; (div.); children—Natalie Alayne, Raymond James. B.A. (scholar), MacMurray Coll., 1956; Ed.M., Harvard U., 1957; Ph.D. (Charles F. Mott fellow), Ariz. State U., 1980. Cert. tchr., supt., reading specialist, Ariz. Tchr., Anchorage, Alaska, 1957-60, Roseville, Minn., 1960-63; instr. elem. edn. Hamline U., St. Paul, 1963-66; tchr., Scottsdale, Ariz., 1966-70; sch. adminstr. Scottsdale Unified Sch. Dist. 48, 1970-81; v.p. mktg. and product devel. Computing Adventures, Ltd., Glendale, Ariz., 1981—; cons. editorial, small bus. Parent adv. with mentally retarded; precinct committeewoman dist. 28, Scottsdale, 1975-76, sec., 1976. Mem. Am. Assn. Sch. Adminstrs., Computer Users in Edn., Phi Delta Kappa, Pi Lambda Theta. Unitarian. Author poems; developer ednl. software. Office: Computing Adventures Ltd Suite D 49411 N 53d Ave Glendale AZ 85302

CARVER, CAROL LOUISE, community educator; b. Trenton, N.J., Nov. 6, 1948; d. Robert Bruce and Marion Teresa (Maloney) C.; m. George William Exon, July 7, 1978. B.S.N., U. Va., 1970; M.S., U. Calif.-San Francisco, 1976. Nurse Meml. Sloan Kettering, N.Y.C., Martha Jefferson Hosp., Charlottsville, Va., Langley Porter Neuropsychiat. Inst., San Francisco, 1970-74; research asst. U. Calif.-San Francisco, 1974-76; program planner, co-dir. Marin Sr. Day Services, Mill Valley, Calif., 1977-78; county agt., chmn. Coop. Extension Wahkiakum County Wash. State U., 1979—; adult educator San Rafael (Calif.) Sch. Dist., 1975-78. Mem. Health Systems Agency; sec. S. Willapa Hills Solar Energy Assn.; mem. Wahkiakum County Food Buying Club. Mem. Western Gerontol. Soc., Nat. 4-H Agts. Assn., Nat. Assn. Extension Home Economists, Amnesty Internat., Women's Internat. League for Peace and Freedom, Sigma Theta Tau. Office: PO Box 278 Courthouse Cathlamet WA 98612

CARVER, DONALD STANLEY, university administrator, consultant; b. Colfax, Wash., Feb. 22, 1928; s. John Stuart and Martha Jane (Buck) C.; m. Barbara Bristol, Apr. 2, 1949; children—David, John, Steven, Joan, Jane, Beth, Scott. B.S., Wash. State U., 1950; Ph.D., Iowa State U., 1953. With Swift & Co., 1953-54, Gen. Mills, Inc., 1956-63; pres. Ovaltine Food Products Co., Villa Park, Ill., 1963-70; v.p. planning Standard Brands, Inc., N.Y.C., 1971-72; pres. Cracker Jack Co., Chgo., 1972-74; dean Sch. Mgmt. and Bus. Nat. U., San Diego, 1974—. Served to 1st lt. USAF, 1954-56. Recipient Packaging award of Yr., Packaging Inst., 1967, 69. Mem. Grocery Mfrs. Am., Pet Food Inst., Animal Nutrition Research Council, Sales and Mktg. Execs. San Diego, Small Bus. Assn. (dir.), Am. Assembly Schs. Bus., Phi Kappa Phi, Sigma Xi, Phi Delta Theta. Republican. Presbyterian. Club: Executives (Chgo.). Contbr. articles to popular mags., profl. jours. Home: 12102 Rancho Bernardo Rd San Diego CA 92128 Office: Sch Mgmt and Bus Nat U 4141 Camino del Rio St San Diego CA 92108

CARVER, DOROTHY LEE ESKEW (MRS. JOHN JAMES CARVER), coll. dean; b. Brady, Tex., July 10, 1926; d. Clyde Albert and A. Maurine (Meadows) Eskew; student So. Ore. Coll., 1942-43, Coll. Eastern Utah, 1965-67; B.A., U. Utah, 1968; M.A., Cal. State Coll. at Hayward, 1970; postgrad. Mills Coll., 1971; m. John James Carver, Feb. 26, 1944; children John James, Sheila (Mrs. Joseph English), Chuck, David. Instr., Rutherford Bus. Coll., Dallas, 1944-45; sec. Adolph Coors Co., Golden, Colo., 1945-47; instr. English, Coll. Eastern Utah, Price, 1968-69; instr. speech Modesto (Calif.) Jr. Coll., 1970-71; instr. personal devel. men and women Heald Bus. Colls., Oakland, Calif., 1972-74, dean curricula, Walnut Creek, Calif., 1974—. Communications cons. Oakland Army Base, Crocker Bank, U.S. Steel, I. Magnin, Artec Internat. Mem. Gov's. Conf. on Higher Edn. in Utah, 1968; mem. finance com. Coll. Eastern Utah, 1967-69; active various community drives. Judge election Republican party, 1960, 64. Bd. dirs. Opportunity Center, Symphony of the Mountain. Mem. AAUW, Bus. and Profl. Womens Club, Nat. Assn. Deans and Women Adminstrs., Delta Kappa Gamma. Episcopalian (supt. Sunday Sch. 1967-69). Clubs: Soroptimist Internat. (pres. Walnut Creek 1979-80); Order Eastern Star. Home: 20 Coronado Ct Walnut Creek CA 94596 Office: 2085 N Broadway Walnut Creek CA 94596

CARVER, EUGENE PENDLETON, real estate co. exec.; b. Bellingham, Wash., Oct. 15, 1928; s. Nathan Pendleton and Mary Louise (Rautenberg) C.; A.B., Dartmouth Coll., 1950; m. Patricia Louise Sutherland, June 6, 1954; children—Mary K., Sara E., Joan E. Gen. Mgr. Whonnock Lumber Co., Ltd. (B.C., Can.), 1953-56; sr. v.p. Western Mortgage Corp., San Francisco, 1956-69; pres., dir. Hoffman Properties, Inc., Los Angeles, 1969—; chmn. bd. trustees Bankamerica Realty Investors, San Francisco. Mem. Los Angeles World Affairs Council. Served as 1st lt. U.S. Army, 1951-53. Decorated Bronze Star. Mem. Am. Soc. Real Estate Counselors, Bay Area Mortgage Assn. (past pres.), No. Calif. Mortgage Bankers Assn. (past dir., treas., sec.). Republican. Episcopalian. Clubs: Jonathan, King Harbor Yacht. Home: 30032 Avenida Esplendida Rancho Palos Verdes CA 90274 Office: 626 Wilshire Blvd Los Angeles CA 90017

CARVER, JOHN JAMES, mining engr.; b. Dover, Okla., Mar. 30, 1919; s. John Earl and Sarah Eva C.; degree in Metallurgy, Colo. Sch. Mines, 1948; m. Dorothy Lee Eskew, Feb. 26, 1944; children—John, Sheila, Charles, David. With U.S. Steel; former prin. engr. Kaiser Engrs., Inc., Oakland, Calif.; now pvt. cons.; cons. to Dept. Energy on comml. coal mine devel., planning, feasibility. Served with U.S. Army, 1941-45. Decorated Bronze Star. Mem. Am. Inst. Mining and Metall. Engrs. Republican. Episcopalian. Club: Masons. Home and office: 20 Coronado Ct Walnut Creek CA 94596

CARVER, JUANITA, plastic co. exec.; b. Indpls., Apr. 8, 1929; d. Willard H. and Golda M. Ashe; student Ariz. State U.; children—Daniel Charles, Robin Lewis, Scott Alan. Asst. librarian, sec., dir. CAMSCO, 1962—, pres. Carver Corp., Phoenix, 1977—. Bd. dirs. Scottsdale Meml. Hosp. Aux., 1964-65, now asso.; active P.T.A.; den mother Cub Scouts; fund raiser Heart and Cancer campaigns. Republican. Methodist. Patentee latch hook rug yarn organizer. Home: 6255 E Avalon St Scottsdale AZ 85251

CARVER, JULIA, physical education educator; b. Salt Lake City, Sept. 1, 1923; d. William George and Julia Augusta (Sabin) C. Student U. Utah, 1941-45; B.S., Brigham Young U., 1952; M.A., NYU, 1954; Ph.D., U. Oreg., 1964. Instr. phys. edn. Brigham Young U., 1952-53; instr. phys. edn., dance Allegheny Coll., 1954-56; asst. prof. phys. edn. and dance Montclair State Coll., 1956-60; grad. asst. phys. edn. U. Oreg., 1960-62; assoc. prof. phys. edn. and dance, chmn. dept. health and phys. edn. Church Coll. Hawaii, 1962-67; assoc. prof. phys. edn., grad. student adv. Brigham Young U., 1967-68; assoc. prof. phys. edn. and dance, coordinator women's phys. edn. N.Mex. State U., 1968-72; lectr. phys. edn. Calif. State U.-Humboldt, 1972-73; prof. phys. edn. Brigham Young U.-Hawaii, 1973—, head health and phys. edn., 1976-81. Sec.-treas., dir. Carver Sheet Metal Works, Inc., Salt Lake City, 1955—. Mem. NEA (life), AAHPER, others. Mormon. Home: 53-126 Halai St Hauula HI 96717 Office: Brigham Young U Hawaii Campus Laie HI 96762

CARVER, RALPH DANIEL, JR., auto parts co. exec.; b. Denver, Oct. 7, 1932; s. Ralph Daniel and Beulah M. (Hill) C.; ed. high sch.; m. Myrlis Jean Harrelson, Mar. 4, 1978; children by previous marriage—Delphine, Robert, James, Steven. Farmer, Dove Creek, Colo., 1950-56; diesel mechanic, asst. foreman I. Sanders Trucking Co., Naturita, Colo., 1957-60; owner, operator, pres., chmn. C & C Auto Parts Co., Naturita, 1960—, Montrose, Colo., 1963—, Delta, Colo., 1977—; chmn. bd. Ralph Carver Jr. Inc., Montrose, 1966—; land developer, Montrose, 1972—, dir. 1st Nat. Bank, Montrose. Chmn. bd. dirs. Colo. Western Coll., Montrose, 1969-72. Mem. Rocky Mountain Automotive Wholesalers Assn. (dir. Denver 1976—), Airplane Owners and Pilots Assn. Methodist. Clubs: Masons, Shriners, Elks. Home: PO Box 549 Montrose CO 81401 Office: 530 N Townsend St Montrose CO 81401

CARVER, ROYAL THAIR, veterinarian; b. Plain City, Utah, Apr. 19, 1928; s. Royal Gilbert and Ivy Tracy (Skeen) C.; B.S., Utah State U., 1953, M.S., 1969; D.V.M., Wash. State U., 1959; m. Norma Louise Hull, Feb. 8, 1951; children—Alan Thair, Ann Carver Jones, Jill, Jon Hull, Aaron Scott. Veterinarian, Calif. Dept. Agr., Merced, 1959-60; practice vet. medicine Adobe Vet. Hosp., Sacramento, 1960-62; vet. med. officer U.S. Dept. Agr. Animal and Plant Health Inspection Service, Vet. Services, Salt Lake City, also Logan, Utah, 1962—, brucellosis and Tb epidemiologist, hog cholera diagnostician, 1964—, fgn. animal disease diagnostician, 1982. Pres., Wilson Sch. PTA, Logan, 1970-71; mem. Cache Valley troop council Boy Scouts Am., 1964-69. Served with AUS, 1953-54; col. Res. Union Pacific R.R., Carl Raymond Gray scholar, 1946. Mem. AVMA, Utah Vet. Med. Assn. (officer exec. bd., treas. 1975-83), Nat. Assn. Professions, Nat. Assn. Fed. Vets., Res. Officers Assn. Mem. Ch. Jesus Christ of Latter-day Saints (sr. pres. 32d Quorum of 70 1966-74, mem. high council Mt. Logan Stake 1981). Home: 920 E 320 N Logan UT 84321 Office: US Dept Agr Animal Plant Health Inspection Service Vet Services Room 302 Agriculture Bldg 350 N Redwood Rd Salt Lake City UT 84116

CARVILLE, PHILIP PARKER, resort and recreation developer; b. San Francisco, July 15, 1939; s. Leonard Frank and Virginia Anne (Parker) C.; B.S., U. Calif., Berkeley, 1962, M.B.A., 1966; m. Julie Ann Stauffer, Feb. 10, 1962, children—Michael, Jennifer. Data processing sales rep. IBM, San Francisco, 1966-69; exec. v.p., co-founder Computer Synergy, Oakland, Calif., 1969-74; pres. Trimont Land, Subsidiary Fibreboard, Northstar, Calif., 1974-76; gen. mgr. Forest Products Div., Fibreboard, San Francisco, 1977-79; pres. Carville Sierra Corp., Olympic Valley, Calif., 1979—. Served to 1st lt., USMC, 1962-65. Mem. Urban Land Inst., Am. Land Devel. Assn. Home: 100 Wayne Rd Olympic Valley CA 95730 Office: PO Box 2395 1900 Squaw Valley Rd Olympic Valley CA 95730

CARY, ANDREW JAMES LLWELLYN, biostatistician; b. Oakland, Calif., Nov. 9, 1951; s. John Louis and Kathryn Roberta (Halemeier) C.; m. Elizabeth Leigh Futscher, June 14, 1975; children—Alexandra Lisanne, Jennifer Anne. B.S., Calif. State U.-Hayward, 1975, M.S. in Stats., 1976. Asst. lectr. Calif. State U., 1975-76; bioanalyst Syntex Research, Palo Alto, Calif., 1976—. Mem. Am. Statis. Assn. Contbr. articles to profl. jours.

CARY, WILLIAM JEWELL, JR., association executive, clergyman; b. Independence, Mo., Oct. 19, 1924; s. William Jewell and Mildred Elizabeth (Crews) C.; m. Genevieve Campbell, Sept. 7, 1947; children—William Jewell, Christopher C. B.Journalism, U. Mo., 1948; M.S. in Journalism, Northwestern U., 1949. Ordained priest Episcopal Ch. Owner, pub. Fallon (Nev.) Eagle, Fernley (Nev.) Tri-Town Times, 1956-59; bus. editor Portland (Oreg.) Jour., 1959-67; dir. pub. affairs Western Wood Products Assn., 1967-72; asst. dir. pub. info. Ga.-Pacific Corp., 1972-78; exec. v.p. Pacific Logging Congress, Portland, 1978—; chmn. dept. communications Episcopal Diocese of Oreg. Chmn. bd. trustees West Hills Christian Sch., 1972-73; bd. overseers Lewis and Clark Coll., 1969—. Served with U.S. Army, 1943-46, to 1st lt., 1951-53. Mem. Pub. Relations Soc. Am. (v.p. Columbia River Chpt.), Pub. Relations Round Table Portland (pres. 1972), Nat. Assn. Self-Supporting Active Ministry, Sigma Delta Chi. Republican. Lodge: Masons. Office: 217 American Bank Bldg Portland OR 97205

CASADOS, JACK, real estate broker; b. Gallup, N.Mex., Feb. 25, 1914; s. Jacob and Virginia (Padilla) C.; B.A., Woodbury Coll., 1946; m. Letha D. Finley, Nov. 25, 1955; 1 son, Jerry. Auditor, Los Angeles, owner Casados Grocery, Gallup; owner, real estate broker Casados Realty, Gallup, 1970—. Served with AUS, 1943-45. Decorated Combat Inf. Badge, Purple Heart. Mem. Gallup Bd. Realtors (pres. 1974—). Home: PO Box 632 Gallup NM 87301 Office: 308 E 66th Ave Gallup NM 87301

CASALE, ROBERT JOHN, real estate broker; b. N.Y.C., Oct. 13, 1929; s. John Douglas and Elsie Elizabeth (Mazey) C.; student Rutgers U., 1947-48; B.S., Seton Hall U., 1953; children—James, Pamela, Robert John II, Christine Elizabeth, John Douglas II. Real estate asso. Art Leitch Realtors, San Diego, 1956-66; partner, real estate broker C&R Realty, San Diego, 1966—. Dir. Centennial Resources, Inc., 1971—. Served to lt. (j.g.) USNR, 1954-56. Contbr. articles to profl. jours. Home: 3970 Arroyo Sorrento Del Mar CA 92014 Office: 2700 Adams Ave San Diego CA 92116

CASANI, EDWARD KANE, aerospace research and development manager; b. Phila., June 17, 1933; s. John C. and Julia J. (Bateman) C.; children—Anita, Aundrea. C.E., U. Pa., 1959; postgrad. U. So. Calif., UCLA. With Jet Propulsion Lab., Pasadena, Calif., 1958—, mgr. spacecraft system design and integration sect., 1973-76, project mgr. infrared astron. satellite, 1976-80, dep. mgr. Observational Systems div., 1980-81, div. mgr., 1981—; tchr. various univs., guest lectr., cons.; cons. movie Andromeda Strain; v.p. JETS, Ltd.; active design and devel. of Mariner, Viking and Ranger spacecraft. Mem. YMCA. Recipient Exceptional Service medal NASA. Mem. AIAA, Sigma Xi. Contbr. articles profl. jours.

CASCIO, WAYNE FRANCIS, industrial psychologist, educator; b. Jamaica, N.Y., Mar. 2, 1946; s. Francis Bernard and Rose Joan (Ingrao) C.; m. Dorothy Meyers, Aug. 23, 1975; 1 son, Joseph Francis. B.A., Holy Cross Coll., 1968; M.A., Emory U., 1969; Ph.D. in Indsl. and Organizational Psychology, U. Rochester, 1973. Diplomate in indsl. and organization psychology Am. Bd. Examiners Profl. Psychology. Assoc. prof. Sch. Bus. Fla. Internat. U., 1973-80; vis. assoc. prof. psychology and bus. U. Calif., Berkeley, 1980-81; prof. mgmt. and orgn. Grad. Sch. Bus. U. Colo., Denver, 1981—. Served to 1st lt. U.S. Army Res. N.G., 1969-75. Fellow Am. Psychol. Assn.; mem. Acad. Mgmt., Am. Soc. Personnel Adminstrn., Colo. Soc. Personnel Adminstrn. Republican. Roman Catholic. Author: Applied Psychology in Personnel Management, 2d edit., 1982; Costing Human Resources: The Financial Impact of Behavior in Organizations, 1982; (with E. Awad) An Information Systems Approach, 1981. Office: 1100 14th St Denver CO 80204

CASE, BARBARA JONTE, educational administrator; b. Sacramento, Apr. 20, 1947; d. Henry Kenneth and Evelyn Frances (Renshaw) Jonte; m. William A. Case, Jr., Aug. 4, 1967 (div.); 1 dau., Kerry Frances. Student Vassar Coll., 1965-67; B.S. in Edn., U. Tulsa, 1969, M.T.A., 1973. Tchr. social studies Edison High Sch., Tulsa, 1969-72; coordinator The New Social Studies, NSF, 1971; program coordinator alternative high sch. project Tulsa Pub. Schs., 1972-81; asst. prin. Nimitz Jr. High Sch., Tulsa, 1981-82; prin. Centennial Jr. High Sch., Boulder Valley Sch. Dist., Boulder, Colo., 1982—; cons. Ctr. for Ednl. Devel., various sch. dists. Mem. Nat. Assn. Secondary Sch. Prins., Collegial Assn. for Devel. and Renewal of Educators, Colo. Assn. Sch. Execs., Assn. for Supervision and Curriculum Devel. Democrat. Contbr. articles to periodicals. Office: 2205 Norwood Ave Boulder CO 80301

CASE, LORRAINE SUE, adult education adminstrator; b. Bell, Calif., Aug. 11, 1946; d. Gifford R. and Susanna M. (Waggoner) C.; m. Gerald M. Keck, Dec. 19, 1965 (div.); children—Julie L., Matthew A. B.S., Phillips U., 1968. Phys. edn. tchr. Madison Jr. High Sch., Bartleville, Okla., 1969-70; dir. Ctr. Continuing Edn., Rocky Mountain Coll., Billings, Mont., 1975—. Loaned exec. United Way, 1976; v.p. Mont. Assn. Chs., 1976-77; sec. bd. dirs. Pastoral Counseling Ctr., 1978-82. Mem. Nat. Assn. Female Execs., Am. Soc. Tng. and Devel (local bd. dirs.). Democrat. Mem. Disciples of Christ. Home: 935 N 30th Billings MT 59101 Office: 1511 Poly Dr Billings MT 59102

CASE, MARIE, marketing and advertising consultant; b. Akron, Ohio, July 25, 1947; d. Frank and Concetta (Fiore) Case. Student, UCLA, 1969. Paste-up, layout artist, Aspen, Colo., 1970-72; account supr. Ashley/Moore, Aspen, 1972-73; various positions to mktg. dir. Vilcor, Inc., Aspen, 1973-77, Jackson Hole, Wyo., 1977-79; mktg. mgr. Jackson Hole Ski Corp., 1979; owner, operator Marie Case Communications, Jackson, Wyo., 1979—, Precinct woman Democratic Party; pres. Jackson Hole Art Assn.; mem. Jackson Hole Film Commn.; mem. bus. adv. com. Jackson Hole Arts Center. Mem. Jackson Hole Area C. of C.

CASE, MARY KATHERINE, data processing manager, consultant; b. Spokane, Wash., Aug. 6, 1951; d. Warren Stanley and Ann Carol (Clarke) Nechodom; m. M. James Case, Jan. 17, 1973. Student Eastern Wash. State Coll., 1970. With Nat. Student Film Corp., 1975-77; sec. Internat. div. TRW Datacom, Los Angeles, 1978, sr. sec., 1979, internat. accounts coordinator, 1979-80, internat. accounts adminstr., 1980, program analyst, 1981-82, mgr. program ops., 1982—. Served with CAP, 1964-68. Mem. Data Processing Mgmt. Assn. (v.p., dir. Los Angeles chpt.), Nat. Assn. Female Execs., Mensa. Poet. Office: 10880 Wilshire Blvd 1812 Los Angeles CA 90024

CASE, ROBERT EUGENE, educational administrator; b. Oxnard, Calif., Nov. 15, 1929; s. Frank Leslie and Flora (Gregory) C.; m. Patricia Ann Glass, May 8, 1934; children—Geoffrey Alan, Sherolynn Ann, Edward Wayne, Stephen Todd. A.A., Ventura Coll., 1954; A.B., Fresno State Coll., 1956, M.A., 1966. Coordinator social studies, vice-prin. Wawona Jr. High Sch., Fresno, Calif., 1962-73; prin. Tehipite Jr. High Sch., Fresno, 1973-76; asst. adminstr., curriculum staff devel. Fresno Unified Schs., 1976—. Commr., Boy Scouts Am., 1972-74. Served with USNR, 1948-52. Mem. Assn. Calif. Adminstrs., Assn. Supervision and Curriculum Devel., Phi Delta Kappa. Republican. Presbyterian. Office: Education Center Tulare & M Sts Fresno CA 93721

CASE, ROBERT JOSEPH, wood products co. exec.; b. Crawford, Nebr., Jan. 4, 1920; s. Roy Lawrence and Emma Viola (Beckler) C.; B.A., Doane Coll., 1941; postgrad. U. Nebr., 1942-44; m. Gloria Mary Rosenberger, Apr. 9, 1944; children—Robert Joseph, David R., Terry L., Kathy Ann. Fellow, U. Nebr., 1940-41; tchr., coach high sch., Utica, Nebr., 1941-42; plant mgr., sales mgr., v.p. Western Aspen Excelsior Co., Los Angeles, and Arlington, Tex., 1945-56; div. mgr. Am. Excelsior Corp., Arlington, Tex., 1956-58, 60-66, nat. sales mgr., 1966-68; pres. Tex. Excelsior Corp., Dallas, 1958-60; pres., chmn. bd. Southwest Industries, Inc., Gallup, N.Mex., 1969-73; sec., dir. Rob-Roy Enterprises, Gallup, N.Mex., 1972—; pres., chmn. bd. Western Timber & Devel. Corp., Mancos, Colo., 1974—. Active Little League and Sr. League Baseball, Arlington, Tex., 1956-66; mem. Mancos City Council, 1978-82. Served with USAAF, 1941-42. Republican. Methodist. Clubs: Lions, Elks, Masons (32 deg.). Address: PO Box 532 Mancos CO 81328

CASE, ROBERT ORMOND, electronics co. exec.; b. Portland, Oreg., Feb. 3, 1926; s. Robert Ormond and Evelyn (Smith) C.; B.Engring., Yale, 1949, M.Engring., 1950; m. Cynthia Tribou, June 28, 1947; children—Jennifer, Patricia Leigh, Victoria Jane, Robert Ormond. Devel. engr. Oak Ridge Nat. Lab., 1950-51; research engr. N.Am. Aviation, Inc., Downey, Calif., 1951-54, engring. supr., 1954-57, chief preliminary engring. sect., Anaheim, Calif., 1957-61; dir. research Tamar Electronics, Inc., Anaheim, 1962-63, v.p. engring. and marketing 1963-65, also dir.; with Ford Aerospace and Communications Corp., 1965—, dir. radar and intelligence operation, aeronutronic div., 1966-67, dir. air def. systems operation, 1967-72, dir. missile systems operation, 1972-80, asst. gen. mgr. Western devel. labs. div., Palo Alto, Calif., 1980—. Served with USNR, 1943-46. Mem. AAAS, Yale Sci. Assn., Assn. U.S. Army, Am. Def. Preparedness Assn., Air Force Assn., Sigma Xi, Tau Beta Pi. Republican. Methodist. Patentee in electronics field. Home: Saratoga CA Office: 3939 Fabian Way Palo Alto CA 94303

CASE, STEPHEN SHEVLIN, lawyer; b. Mpls., Nov. 16, 1943; s. George Price and Helen (Beckwith) C.; m. Judy Elizabeth Everett, Apr. 5, 1969 (div. Feb. 1979); children—Mackenzie Beckwith, Julia Lee; m. 2d, Pamela Ellen Hansen, Aug. 26, 1949. B.A., Washington and Lee U., 1966, LL.B. with honors, 1969. Bar: Ariz. 1969. Assoc., Fennemore, Craig, von Ammon & Udall, Phoenix, 1969-73; majority atty. (Republican) Ariz. State Senate, 1973; trust counsel First Interstate Bank of Ariz., Phoenix, 1973-76; ptnr. Norris & Case, P.C., Sun City, Ariz., 1976—; sec., dir. The Camel Bank, Inc.; instr. Golden Gate U., Phoenix Campus. Bd. dirs. Central Ariz. Estate Planning Council, 1978-81. Mem. ABA, State Bar Ariz. (chmn. sect. real property, probate and trust law 1981-82, chmn. sect. taxation 1983—), Delta Theta Phi. Clubs: Paradise Valley Country; Rotary (dir. 1977-81) (Sun City, Ariz.). Contbr. articles in field to profl. jours. Office: 10331 Coggins Dr Sun City AZ 85351 also 3020 E Camelback Rd Phoenix AZ 85016

CASEBEER, ROBERT SCOTT, automotive exec.; b. Portland, Oreg., Feb. 20, 1955; s. Richard Roy and Marcia Jane (Wyland) C.; m. Leslie Diane Green, Aug. 7, 1977; children—Matthew, Alexander. Student U. Oreg., 1974-77. Mgr., partner Capitol Chevrolet Cadillac Inc., Salem, Oreg., 1977—; bd. dirs. Cascade Life Ins. Mem. Salem Econ. Devel. Commn.; exec. com. Leadership Salem; active United Way, YMCA, Salem Symphony Assn.; bd. dirs. Salem Art Assn. Mem. Salem New Car Dealer Assn., Chevrolet Post Card Club, Soc. Sales Execs. (Chevrolet div.). Republican. Episcopalian. Clubs: Illahe Hills Country, Rotary, Willamette U. Roundtable. Office: PO Box 12456 Salem OR 97309

CASEBOLT, EDWARD CARMI, JR., ednl. adminstr.; b. Newport, Ky., Apr. 17, 1927; s. Edward C. and Catherine M. (McGill) C.; A.B., Eastern Ky. U., 1949; M.A., San Diego State U., 1960; m. Katherine Sizemore, Mar. 19, 1948. Tchr., Butler High Sch., Vandalia, Ohio, 1949-53; counselor Montgomery Jr. High Sch., San Diego, 1953-61; vice-prin. Pacific Beach Jr. High Sch., 1961-65; vice prin. Dana Jr. High Sch., 1965-67; prin. Horace Mann Jr. High Sch., 1967—. Served with U.S. Army, 1945-46. Recipient hon. service award Sunset Council PTA, 1971; continuing service award Horace Mann Jr. High Sch. PTA, 1980. Mem. Assn. Calif. Sch. Adminstrs., Nat. Assn. Secondary Sch. Prins., Kappa Delta Pi. Home: 4330 Altamirano Way San Diego CA 92103 Office: 4345 54th St San Diego CA 92115

CASELLI, JACLYN RUTH, library coordinator; b. Boston, Mar. 28, 1921; d. Jacob Bates and Eleanor Ruth (Jackson) Abbott; student Pa. State U., 1938-40; A.A., San Jose City Coll., 1970; B.A. with distinction, San Jose State U., 1976, M.L.S., 1979; m. Reginald Louis Caselli, Aug. 18, 1945; children—Pamela Anne, Patrick Bates, Kevin Wade, Reginald Louis, Michele Susan, Suzette Marie. With Yankee Mag., Dublin, N.H., 1940-42; with Eric Clearinghouse on Info. Resources, Sch. Edn., Stanford (Calif.) U.; 1969—, dir. acquisitions, 1970-77, library coordinator Research Libraries Info. Network, 1976—, library user services coordinator Research Libraries Group, 1977—. Served with WAVES, 1942-45. Recipient 2 Gold medals, 1 Silver medal Internat. Sr. Olympics, 1979. Mem. Am., Calif., Spl. library assns., Nat. Wildlife Soc., Audubon Soc., Amateur Athletic Union, Athletic Conf., Sierra Club, Phi Kappa Phi. Home: 1528 Carmel Dr San Jose CA 95125 Office: RLIN Stanford CA 94305

CASEY, CAROL ANNE, management consultant; b. San Mateo, Calif., Dec. 14, 1953; d. Thomas Francis and Barbara Anne (Dyer) C. B.A. in Psychology and Sociology, U. Colo., 1976; M.S. in Counseling, San Francisco State U., 1979. Career cons., Walnut Creek, Calif., 1979-82; career counselor, guidance instr. City Coll. San Francisco, 1979-81; dir. career devel. ctr. John F. Kennedy U., Orinda, Calif., 1980-82, grad. lectr. career devel. program, 1980-82; v.p. Drake Beam Morin, Inc., San Francisco, 1982—. Bd. dirs. H.B. McDaniel Found., 1981-83, sec. bd. dirs., 1981-83; mem. adv. bd. career devel. program John F. Kennedy U. Mem. Am. Soc. Tng. and Devel. (chpt. v.p. 1982), Am. Personnel and Guidance Assn., Nat. Vocat. Guidance Assn., Calif. Personnel and Guidance Assn., Career Planning and Adult Devel. Network. Democrat. Roman Catholic. Club: Oak Creek (Palo Alto). Co-author: Skills Pack: A Technique for Identifying Transferable Skills, 1980; Alternate Careers for Counselors, 1980. Home: 1736 Oak Creek Dr #201 Palo Alto CA 94304 Office: Drake Beam Morin Inc One Embarcadero Ctr 41st floor San Francisco CA 94111

CASEY, DANIEL ABNER, state commissioner; b. Pasadena, Calif., Aug. 17, 1946; s. Buford Abner and Vera Elizabeth (Miller) C.; B.A., U. Calif.-Berkeley, 1972; M.B.A. with high distinction (Baker scholar), Harvard U., 1974. Smokejumper U.S. Forest Service and Bur. Land Mgmt., N.W. U.S., 1966-69; constrn. supt. J. Ray McDermott subs., Cook Inlet, Alaska, 1969-72; constrn. mgr. ARCO, Prudhoe Bay, Alaska, 1976-81, North Slope project mgr., Anchorage, 1981-83; commr. Dept. Transp. and Pub. Utilities, State of Alaska, 1983—. Adminstrv. asst., cons. Alaska Legislature; mem. Gov.'s Council Econ. Advs., 1982; bd. dirs. Alaska Power Authority; mem. Alaska Coastal Zone Policy Council, Alaska Land Use Council. Alaska Businessmen's Assn. scholar, 1970. Mem. Anchorage C. of C., Am. Mgmt. Assn., Soc. Petroleum Mgrs. Club: Tower. Climbed Mt. McKinley. Home: 300 Hermit St #10 Westridge Juneau AK Office: Pouch Z Juneau AK 99811

CASEY, EVA LYN M., lawyer; b. Modesto, Calif., Oct. 31, 1929; d. J. Hugh and Martha (Kuhlman) C.; B.S. in Law, Glendale (Calif.) U., 1974, J.D., 1975. County law librarian, San Luis Obispo, Calif., 1960-69, Santa Barbara, Calif., 1969-77; jury commr., San Luis Obispo, 1961-69; admitted to Calif. bar, 1976; pvt. practice, 1976—; head law librarian Glendale U. Coll. Law, 1977-80, asst. prof., 1977-80; program dir. Glendale Coll. Legal Arts, 1978-81; sec. Calif. Jury Commrs. Assn., 1967-68. Mem. Am. Bar Assn., Am. Assn. Law Librarians, State Bar Calif. (family law sect.), Calif. Conf. County Law Librarians (sec. 1976-77), So. Calif. Assn. Law Librarians (dir. 1979), Los Angeles County Bar Assn., Los Angeles Paralegal Assn., Alumni Assn. Glendale Coll. Law (rec. sec. 1977-80). Author articles in field. Office: PO Box 60731 Los Angeles CA 90060 also 222 S Figueroa St Suite 1218 Los Angeles CA 90012

CASEY, J. JOSEPH, heavy construction and manufacturing company executive; b. 1921; married. Grad. Georgetown U.; postgrad NYU Law Sch. With Dillingham Corp., 1967—, v.p., controller, 1967-70, exec. v.p. Dillingham Corp. of Australia Ltd., 1970-72, pres., chief exec. officer Gordon H. Ball Inc. subs., beginning 1972, then asst. to group v.p.-constrn. and pres. Dillingham Corp., group v.p.-constrn., 1981-82, corp. pres. Honolulu, 1982—, also dir. Office: Dillingham Corp 1441 Kapiolani Blvd PO Box 3468 Honolulu HI 96801*

CASEY, JAMES VINCENT, archbishop; b. Osage, Iowa, Sept. 22, 1914; s. James G. and Nina (Nims) C.; A.B., Loras Coll., 1936, LL.D., 1959; student Gregorian U., Rome, Italy, 1936-40; J.C.D., Cath. U. Am., 1949. Ordained priest Roman Cath. Ch., 1939; asst. pastor St. John's Parish, Independence, Iowa, 1940-44; sec. Archbishop Leo Binz, Dubuque, 1946-49; consecrated Bishop of Lincoln, Nebr., 1957; archbishop of Denver, 1967—. Served to lt. (s.g.), Chaplains Corps, USNR, 1944-46. Office: 200 Josephine St Denver CO 80206*

CASEY, JOHN THOMAS, health care administrator; b. Pensacola, Fla., Oct. 6, 1945; s. J.T. and Sylvia Marie (Bond) C.; B.S. in Econs., Auburn U., 1967; M.S. in Hosp. Adminstrn., U. Ala., Birmingham, 1972; m. Kathryn Camp, Mar. 23, 1968; children—Christopher Lee, Kathryn Welch; m. 2d, Gail Bartosch, Apr. 30, 1982. Asst. dir. Shands Teaching Hosp., U. Fla., Gainesville, 1972-73; adminstr. Cathedral Rehab. Center, Jacksonville, Fla., 1973-76, St. Luke's Hosp., Denver, 1976-79; pres. Presbyn./St. Luke's Med. Center, Denver, 1979—; dir. Colo. Blue Cross-Blue Shield; chmn. bd. Hosp. Shared Services of Colo. Served to lt. (j.g.) USNR, 1968-69. Named Young Hosp. Adminstr. of Yr., Am. Coll. Hosp. Adminstrs., 1981. Mem. Colo-Hosp. Assn. (dir.), Nat. Council Community Hosps., Met. Denver Hosp. Council (pres.). Republican. Episcopalian. Clubs: Denver Athletic, Denver Rotary. Office: 1601 E 19th Ave Denver CO 80218

CASEY, JOHN WESLEY, educational administrator; b. Correctionville, Iowa, Sept. 16, 1926; s. Charles Clark and Amie F. (Tuschoff) C.; B.A. cum laude, Morningside Coll., 1957; M.S., Iowa State U., 1957, Ph.D., 1963; postgrad. (scholar) UCLA, 1964-66; m. Helen Lucille Chamberlain, Dec. 18, 1947; children—John Warren, Terrence Michael, Allen Chamberlain, Andrew Stevenson. Asst. mgr. State Fin. Co., Sioux City, Iowa, 1949-54; br. mgr. Universal C.I.T. Credit Corp., Sioux City, 1954-55; tchr. jr. high sch. and high sch. Oto (Iowa) pub. schs., 1955-57; grad. asst., instr., asst. prof. Iowa State U., Ames, 1957-64; acad. dean Pacific Christian Coll., Long Beach, Calif., 1964-65; dir. higher edn. Okla. State U., Stillwater, 1966-67; asst. to pres. Fullerton (Calif.) Coll., 1965-66, v.p., 1967-69, pres., 1969-77; chancellor Seattle Community Coll. Dist. VI, 1977-83; supt.-pres. Pasadena Area Community Coll. Dist., 1983—; spl. cons. Tchrs. Hall of Fame, 1971—. Bd. govs. Marine Sci. Inst., 1969-77; bd. dirs. N. Orange County YMCA, 1969-72, Coll. Legal Clinic, 1972—; bd. advisors Milligan Coll., 1972—, Emmanuel Sch. Religion, Johnson City, Tenn., 1975—; adv. com., bd. govs. Calif. Community Colls., 1972—; chmn. ednl. div. United Way, 1974-75, chmn. edn. com., 1978-79; mem. Pub. Policy Adv. Bd., Newport Beach, Calif., 1975-77; bd. dirs., v.p. Museum Assn. N. Orange County, 1974—; mem. Gov.'s Task Force on High Tech. Tng. and Advancement. Mem. Am. Assn. Community and Jr. Colls. (dir.), Wash. Assn. Community Colls. (chmn. legis. com. 1978—), Assn. Wash. Community Coll. Adminstrs. (pres.), Puget Sound Community Coll. Consortium for High Tech. Tng., Assn. Coll. Trustees (chmn. adv. com. 1979—), Nat. Alliance Bus. (dir.), Pvt. Industry Council (dir.), Seattle C. of C., Phi Delta Kappa, Gamma Sigma Delta, Alpha Kappa Delta. Office: Seattle Community Coll 300 Elliott Ave W Seattle WA 98119

CASEY, LADEANE OSLER, psychologist; b. Griswold, Iowa, May 27, 1926; d. Albert Lon and Delia Emma (Sasse) Osler; B.A. cum laude, Grinnell Coll., 1947; M.A., Drake U., 1974; Ph.D., Ariz. State U., 1977; m. Donald John Casey, June 21, 1947; children—Kent, Robert, Janice, Diane, Donna, Mark. Physics lab. instr. Grinnell (Iowa) Coll., 1947-48; tutor in chemistry, algebra and trigonometry Iowa State U., Ames, 1954-59; instr. stats., psychology dept. Mesa (Ariz.) Community Coll., 1976-78; instr. ednl. psychology dept. Ariz. State U., Tempe, 1974-75; pvt. practice psychology, Tempe and Scottsdale (Ariz.), 1974—; researcher Devereux Day Sch. and Clinic, Scottsdale, 1976. Leader, Girl Scouts U.S.A., Carroll, Iowa, 1960-74, canoe camp dir., 1969-73, exec. v.p. Lakota council, 1968-71, dir. Mex. trips, 1970, 73. Recipient St. Anne Award for outstanding youth leadership Nat. Cath. Welfare Conf. Am., 1970. Mem. Am. Psychol. Assn., Soc. for Research in Child Devel., Nat. Soc. for Autistic Children (profl. adv. bd. Greater Phoenix chpt.), AVMA Aux., Ariz. Psychol. Assn., Southwestern Psychol. Assn., Am. Assn. Sex Educators, Counselors and Therapists, Phi Beta Kappa, Iota Sigma Pi. Contbr. articles in field to profl. jours. Home: 5939 E Hummingbird Ln Paradise Valley AZ 85253 Office: Mercado del Lago 8300 N Hayden Rd Scottsdale AZ 85258

CASEY, STEPHEN JAMES, adminstrv. elec. engr.; b. Hanford, Calif., Aug. 20, 1948; s. James Alfred and Juanita Alice (Spanke) C.; A.A., Southwestern Coll., Chula Vista, Calif., 1968; B.S. in Elec. Engring., San Diego State U., 1972. With Lockheed Calif. Co., Burbank, 1973—, mgmt. trainee, mfg. br., 1974-75, engr., functional test, 1975, supr. mgr., 1975—, recipient Achievement awards, 1975, 76, 81. Mem. Nat. Mgmt. Assn. Republican. Home: 1304 N Sparks St Burbank CA 91506

CASEY, THOMAS CLARK, trust co. exec.; b. Akron, Ohio, Dec. 17, 1929; s. Thomas Wanton and Portia (Clark) C.; B.A., Bowdoin Coll., 1951; M.B.A., Stanford U., 1957; m. Tanya Seely, July 2, 1958; children—Tate S., Douglas R., John S., Gary L., Bradley W., Nina, Mimi, Thomas W. Sales rep. Reeves Rubber Co., San Clemente, Calif., 1958-60; mgr. Polymer Corp., Santa Ana, Calif., 1960-61; sr. v.p. First Am. Trust Co., Santa Ana, 1965—, Newport Beach, Calif., 1976—; instr. fin. counseling Am. Coll., Grad. Div., Santa Ana, 1975-76. Mem. bd. edn. Newport-Mesa Unified Sch. Dist., 1969-77, pres., 1975-76; pres. Friends of U. Calif., Irvine, 1978-80, Newport Center Assn., 1979, U. Calif.-Irvine Found., 1981-83, Orange County Mental Health Assn., 1981-83; pres. bus. council Newport Harbor Art Mus., 1982—; bd. dirs. So. Calif. Bldg. Fund, 1982—; treas. 552 Club of Hoag Hosp., 1979. Served to 1st lt. U.S. Army, 1951-53. Mem. Calif. Bankers Assn. (com. chmn.), Orange County Estate Plan Council (pres. 1978), Newport Irvine Estate Planning Council. Republican. Clubs: Irvine Coast Country, Big Canyon Country (Corona del Mar, Calif.); Balboa Bay (Newport Beach). Office: 2101 San Joaquin Hills Rd Newport Beach CA 92660

CASEY, WILLIAM JOSEPH, ophthalmologist; b. Balt., Feb. 9, 1936; s. Harry J. and Florence H. (McDivit) C. A.B., Johns Hopkins U., 1958, M.D., 1962. Intern Kaiser Found. Hosp., San Francisco, 1962-63; resident ophthalmology U. Calif. Med. Center-San Francisco, 1963-64, 65-67; postdoctoral fellow NIH, Uppsala, Sweden, 1964-65; lectr. anatomy Makerere U. Coll., Kampala, Uganda, 1965; Heed Ophthalmic fellow Yale, New Haven, 1967; dir. eye bank St. John Ophthalmic Hosp., Jerusalem, Jordan, 1967-69, dir. Eye Bank Fellowship Program, 1969—; prin. investigator for research grant NIH for Glaucoma Research, San Francisco, 1969-77; practice medicine specializing in ophthalmology, San Francisco, 1969—; cons. ophthalmology San Francisco Gen. Hosp., 1969—; assoc. prof. ophthalmology U. Calif.-San Francisco, 1969—; mem. adv. bd. Visual Scis. Info. Center, U. Calif.-Berkeley, 1970-76; expert civilian cons. in ophthalmology, U.S. Army, Letterman Gen. Hosp., Presidio San Francisco, 1972; owner St. Clement Winery, St. Helena, Calif., 1976—. Vice-chmn. Bay Area Graphic Arts Council, Calif. Palace Legion of Honor, San Francisco, 1971-72. Knighted Order Hosp. St. John Jerusalem (Eng.). Diplomate Am. Bd. Ophthalmology. Mem. AMA, Assn. Research Vision and Ophthalmology, Am. Acad. Ophthalmology and Otolaryngology, Pacific Coast Oto-Ophthalmol. Soc., Calif. Med. Assn. Home: 3584 Pierce St San Francisco CA 94123 Office: 490 Post St Suite 934 San Francisco CA 94102

CASHELL, ROBERT (BOB) A., state official; b. Longview, Tex., Apr. 22, 1938; m. Nancy Parker; children—Rob, Patrick, Catherine, Jane. B.S.B.A., Stephen F. Austin State U., 1961. Mgmt. trainee, Houston, then sales rep., Oakland, Calif. Exxon Corp.; now chmn. bd. Boomtown, Inc., nr. Reno, Nev., and chmn. bd. Wild West Enterprises, Winnemucca, Nev., operating Winners Hotel/Casino, Model Truck Stop and Star Casino; lt. gov. State of Nev., Las Vegas, 1982—. Chmn. bd. regents U. Nev. System, 1978-82; mem. adv. bd. Nev. Youth Ctr., chmn. Nev. Comprehensive Health Planning Bd., Nev. Higher Edn. Commn., Nev. Tourism Adv. Council, White House Fellowship Selection Com.; bd. dirs. Sierra Arts Found.; chmn. Sierra Nev. Mus. Art; former bd. dirs. U. Nev.-Reno Wolf Pack Boosters; founder YMCA Youth Soccer; former youth football coach. Mem. No. Nev. Petroleum Retailers, Nat. Assn. Truck Stop Operators (dir.), Reno C. of C. (former dir.). Office: Office of Lt Gov 1100 S Tenth Las Vegas NV 89104*

CASHEN, JOSEPH LAWRENCE, real estate broker; b. Kansas City, Mo., May 10, 1931; s. John Lawrence and Anna May (Sutcliffe) C.; student real estate U. Calif. at Los Angeles, 1965-66; m. Michele Ann Hayes, June 15, 1960; children—Michael, Patricia, Kelly. Sales cons. chems. Economics Lab., Los Angeles, 1954-64; broker Forest E. Olsen Realtors, Canoga Park, Calif., 1964-67; pres. Property World, Inc., Woodland Hills, Calif., 1967-71; pres. Century 21 Real Estate #1, Inc., Woodland Hills, 1971—. Mem. Police Activity League, Woodland Hills, 1973-76; pres., mem. adv. council Pierce Coll. Rotoract, 1974-75. Served with USMC, 1950-54. Mem. San Fernando Valley Bd. Realtors, Calif. Assn. Realtors, Nat. Assn. Realtors, Nat. Inst. Farm and Land Brokers, Nat. Assn. Home Builders, Aircraft Owners and Pilots Assn., Woodland Hills C. of C. (pres. 1976). K.C., Rotarian (pres. 1974-75). Inventor in field. Office: 5959 Topanga Canyon Woodland Hills CA 91367

CASKIE, WILLIAM WIRT, accountant; b. N.Y.C., May 9, 1945; s. John Minor and Rosa Maria (Marchese) C.; B.S. in Physics, Georgetown U., 1967; M.B.A. in Ops. Research, N.Y.U., 1970; B.S. magna cum laude in Acctg., Golden Gate U., 1976. Tchr. math. N.Y.C. pub. schs., 1968-71; statistician Fed. Res. Bank of San Francisco, 1972-74; pvt. practice acctg., Marina Del Rey, Calif., 1977—. Mem. Assn. Bus. and Tax Cons., Nat. Assn. Enrolled Agts., Calif. Soc. Enrolled Agts., Mensa. Home and Office: 557 1/2 Washington St Marina Del Rey CA 90292

CASMIR, FRED LUTZ, communications educator, consultant; b. Berlin, Germany, Dec. 30, 1928; came to U.S., 1954; s. Arthur and Gertrude (Wolter) C.; m. Marjorie M. Rogers, June 2, 1952; children—Karen Anne Casmir Safian, Fred Otis. B.A. in Speech, David Lipscomb Coll., 1950; M.A., Ohio State U., 1955, Ph.D., 1961. Instr. speech Pepperdine Coll., Malibu, Calif., 1956-57, asst. prof. dept. of communications, 1957-62, assoc. prof., 1962-70, marshall of coll., 1958-72, prof. Seaver Coll., Div. of Communication, Pepperdine U., 1970—, marshall of the univ., 1972—; part-time faculty San Fernando Valley (Calif.) State Coll., 1961-73, East Los Angeles Coll., 1973-74; asst. prof. speech Calif. State U.-Northridge, 1965-69, assoc. prof., 1971-73; cons. for oral communications Mgmt. Tng. Corp., 1968-70; radio spokesman Sta. KTYM, Los Angeles, 1969-70; pres. Nat. Edn. Inst., 1972, cons., 1972-74; mgmt. cons., 1975—; presenter numerous seminars, workshops and symposiums, 1962—; lectr. on communications for numerous internat. insts. and groups. Chmn. citizens by choice com. Los Angeles Republican Central Com., 1961-64, state nationalities dir., 1964-65, chmn. 31st congl. dist. com., mem. central com., 1970-72, treas. central com., 1971-72; mem. Calif. State Scholarship and Loan Commn., 1986-76; co-chmn. Citizens Com. for Welfare Reform Los Angeles County, 1971; mem. bicentennial com. Los Angeles City Schools, 1975-76, citizens mgmt. rev. com., 1976-77; sr. advisor to U.S. del. UNESCO, 2d World Confs. on Cultural Policies, Mexico City, 1982; elder Ch. of Christ, Arcadia, Calif., 1979-81; forum developer Pepperdine Ann. Bible Lectureships. Served with German Air Force, World War II. Recipient numerous civic and polit. awards; named Outstanding Tchr. Pepperdine U., 1973. Mem. Speech Communication Assn. (founding editor Internat. and Intercultural Communication ann. 1973-76, chmn. publs. com. mass communications div. 1980-81), AAUP, Internat. Soc. Phonetics, Western Speech Assn., Communications Assn. of the Pacific (hon. dir., sponsor, advisor), Internat. Communication Assn., Soc. for Intercultural Edn., Tgn., Research (coordinating v.p. for N.Am., 1982-83). Author: Interaction: An Introduction to Speech Communication, 1974; Intercultural and International Communication, 1978; Contbr. numerous articles to profl. jours. and books. Home: 1967 Hilldale Dr La Canada CA 91011 Office: Div of Communications Pepperdine U Malibu CA 90265

CASON, MARSDEN STARBUCK, financial services company executive; b. Nashville, Sept. 27, 1942; s. James and Rebecca M. C.; B.A. in Finance, San Francisco State U., 1965; children—Sean, Regan, Jason. Dir., Equitec Fin. Group Inc., Oakland, Calif., 1973—, chmn. and chief exec. officer, 1975—; dir. Equitec Properties Co. Mem. bus. adv. com. San Francisco State U. Mem. Internat. Assn. Fin. Planners (charter), Oakland C. of C. (chmn.), Nat. Assn. Securities Dealers (registered rep.). Clubs: Lafayette (Calif.) Country; World Trade (San Francisco); Lincoln of No. Calif. Home: 1066 Longridge Ave Oakland CA 94610 Office: 7677 Oakport St Oakland CA 94614

CASPERS, CARL FREDERICK, civil engineer; b. Hopkinston, Iowa, Dec. 2, 1927; s. Peter Martin and Johanna Elizabeth (Poppi) C.; m. Delores J. Adams, Sept. 12. 1953. B.S. in Civil Engring., Iowa State U., 1955. Registered profl. engr., Iowa, Ill., N.Mex. With Brown Engring. Co., Des Moines, 1955-66; city engr., dir. pub. works, bldg. officer, zoning enforcement officer, mem. planning commn. City of Urbandale (Iowa), 1966-73; village engr. Village of Carpentersville (Ill.), 1973-82; dir. Pub. works, city engr., Clovis, N.Mex., 1982—. Chmn. transp. com. Central Iowa Regional Planning Commn., 1970-73; mem. Iowa Hwy. Resesrh Bd., Iowa Hwy. Commn., 1971-73. Served with USN, 1945-48, 51-52; Korea. Mem. ASCE (past dir. sect.), N.Mex. Soc. Profl. Engrs., Am. Pub. Works Assn. (past dir. br., sec. 1981-82), Am. Legion (past post comdr.). Methodist. Office: PO Box 760 Clovis NM 88101

CASPERSON, LEE WENDEL, elec. engr., educator; b. Portland, Oreg., Oct. 18, 1944; s. Rudolph Oliver and Effie Marie (Dahlman) C.; B.S. in Physics, M.I.T., 1966; M.S. in Elect. Engring., Calif. Inst. Tech., 1967, Ph.D. in Elec. Engring. and Physics, 1971; m. Susan Diane Lunnam, Oct. 18, 1974; children—Julie Diane, Janet Marie. Asst. prof. Sch. Engring. and Applied Sci., UCLA, 1971-76, asso. prof., 1976-80, prof., 1980—; cons. Northrop Research and Tech. Center, TRW. NASA trainee, 1967-68; Tektronix Found. fellow, 1968-69; Regents Faculty fellow, 1974; NSF grantee, 1972-74, 76—. Mem. Optical Soc. Am., IEEE, Sigma Xi. Republican. Lutheran. Contbr. numerous articles in field of laser physics to profl. jours. Home: 2571 Westwood Blvd Los Angeles CA 90064 Office: 7731D Boelter Hall UCLA 405 Hilgard Ave Los Angeles CA 90024

CASPERSON, RICHARD LEE, engring. and tech. co. exec.; b. McKeesport, Pa., Apr. 9, 1940; s. Robert E. and Beulah B. (Overturf) C.; B.S., Colo. State U., 1963; M.S., U. Colo., 1966, postgrad., 1971—; m. Laura L. James, June 10, 1967; children—Mylee, Lea. Aerospace engr. Boeing Co., Seattle, 1963, Hughes Aircraft Co., El Segundo, Calif., 1964; sr. engr. Martin-Marietta Corp., Denver, 1965-67, 71-72; engring. cons., scientist Idaho Nat. Engring. Lab., Idaho Falls, 1967-68, 72-76; pres., prin. Energy Engring. Group, Inc., Golden, Colo., 1977—; mem. faculty U. Idaho, U. Colo. Mem. Variance Bd. City of Idaho Springs (Colo.), 1976—; mem. planning and study coms. Clear Creek Sch. Dist. RE-1, Idaho Springs, 1978—. Stanley Aviation scholar, 1976-77; Colo. Energy Research Inst.-U. Colo. research fellow, 1977-78; recipient Outstanding Faculty award U. Colo., 1980; registered profl. engr., Colo. Mem. AAAS, ASCE, ASHRAE, Internat. Solar Energy Soc., Natural Resources Def. Council, Idaho Environ. Council, Sierra Club, Wilderness Soc., Audubon Soc. Democrat. Researcher solar energy. Home: 2051 Miner St PO Box 10 Idaho Springs CO 80452 Office: 1115 Washington Ave Golden CO 80401

CASSEDAY, BONNIE LOU, comptroller; b. Terra Alta, W.Va., Oct. 25, 1949; d. James D. and Lola S. (Stouffer) Shaffer; m. Jeffery Hugh Casseday, June 28, 1975. A.B. in Bus. and English, Fairmont State Coll., 1972; student West Va. U., 1975-77. Tchr. bus. edn. Meadowbrook High Sch., Byesville, Ohio, 1972-73, So. High Sch, Oakland, Md., 1974-76, Morgantown High Sch., 1976-78; curriculum writer bus. office dept. Preston County Ednl. Ctr., Kingwood, W.Va., 1973-74; dist. mgr. Franklin Life Ins. Co., Springfield, Ill., 1979-81; fin. comptroller Children's Dental Assocs., P.C., Phoenix, 1981—. Recipient sales awards Franklin Life, 1979. Mem. Beta Sigma Phi. Methodist. Club: Count One Tennis (treas.). Office: Children's Dental Assocs 1728 W Glendale Ave Suite 307 Phoenix AZ 85021

CASSEDY, KEVIN HALSEY, mktg. cons.; b. Cambridge, Mass., Mar. 21, 1932; s. Anthony Burns and Caroline (Finn) C.; B.A., Stanford U., 1955; m. Judith Aileen Roberts, Aug. 22, 1955; children—Anne, Matthew, Brian, Paul, Molly, Betsy. Researcher, Gallup Poll, 1959; area rep. automobile and def. div. Budd Co., 1959-61; area rep. Lear Siegler, Inc., 1961-65; mktg. mgr. Aerojet-Gen. Co., Fullerton, Calif., 1965-69; pres., founder Cassedy & Asso., Laguna Beach, Calif., 1969—. Served with USMC, 1955-58. Republican. Roman Catholic. Home: 150 Cleo Laguna Beach CA 92651

CASSEL, LOUIS A., aerospace engineer; b. Lebanon, Pa., Dec. 9, 1938; s. Russel N. and Edythe M. (Rotunda) C.; m. Pamela J. Bleecker, Aug. 26, 1961; children—Teresa A., Mitchal L. B.A.E., Auburn U., 1960, M.S., 1965; postgrad. UCLA, 1966-68, U. So. Calif., 1967-69. Sect. chief aerodynamics McDonnell Douglas Astronautics Co., Huntington Beach, Calif., 1965-75; div. mgr. flight tech. Sci. Applications, Inc., Irvine, Calif., 1975-79; sect. head maneuvering reentry vehicles TRW Ballistic Missiles Div., San Bernardino, Calif., 1979—. Served to lt. USMC, 1960-63. Mem. AIAA. Contbr. articles to profl. jours. Home: 19973 Grant St Corona CA 91720 Office: TRW PO Box 1310 San Bernardino CA 92402

CASSEL, MYRNA HARRIET, educational administrator; b. North Platte, Nebr., June 11, 1938; d. Howard H. and Ima M. (Callahan) Hewson; div.; children—Barry Steinbrecher, Kevin Cassel. B.S., Chadron State Coll., 1967, M.S., 1969; M.S., Kearney State Coll., 1977; Ph.D., U. Nebr., 1979. Tchr. pub. schs., Western Nebr., 1956-68; grad. asst. Chadron (Nebr.) State Coll., 1968-69, U. Nebr., 1978-79; instr. social scis. Central Tech. Community Coll., 1969-74, assoc. dean students, 1974-79; teaching learning specialist Nebr. Ednl. TV Consortium Higher Edn., 1979-80; dean Sch. Extended and Grade Studies U. Alaska-Juneau, 1980—; cons. in field. Bd. dirs. Alaska Native Tng. Inst., 1981-82; trustee Juneau Arts and Humanities Council, 1982-83. Recipient Master Tchr. award Central Tech. Community Coll., 1971, Educator of Year award, 1975. Mem. Adult Edn. Assn., Nat. Council on Community Services and Continuing Edn., Nat. Univ. Continuing Edn. Assn., Am. Assn. Univ. Adminstrs., Council for Occupational Edn., Nat. Assn. Women Deans, Adminstrs. and Counselors. Contbr. articles to profl. jours. Office: 11120 Glacier Hwy Juneau AK 99801

CASSEL, RICHARD DEE, marketing executive; b. Denver, Feb. 8, 1943; s. Harold Joseph and Florence Mildred (Rankin) C.; m. Judith Renee Reiswig, Aug. 20, 1964; children—Julie, Debra. B.A. in Econs., Calif. State U.-Fullerton, 1967, M.B.A., 1970. Sales rep. MAB Services, Inc., Los Angeles, 1967-70, sales mgr., 1971-74, v.p. mktg. and sales, 1975—; instr. Sch. Bus., Fullerton Community Coll., 1977—. Chmn., Seventh Day Adventist Sch. Bd., 1976-79, 82—. Mem. Nat. Automatic Merchandising Assn., Food Service Execs. Assn. Home: 1749 Baronet Pl Fullerton CA 92633 Office: 2121 W Temple St Los Angeles CA 90026

CASSENS, NICHOLAS, JR., ceramics engr.; b. Sigourney, Iowa, Sept. 8, 1948; s. Nicholas and Wanda Fern (Lancaster) C.; B.S., Iowa State U., 1971, B.S. in Chem. Engring., 1971; M.S. in Material Sci. and Engring., U. Calif., Berkeley, 1979; m. Linda Joyce Morrow, Aug. 30, 1969; 1 son, Randall Scott, Jr. research engr. Kaiser Aluminum & Chem. Corp., Pleasanton, Calif., 1971-72, research engr., 1972-74, sr. research engr., 1974-77, staff research engr., 1977—. Mem. Am. Ceramic Soc. Democrat. Patentee in field, U.S., Australia, S.Am., Europe. Home: 4082 Suffolk Way Pleasanton CA 94566 Office: PO Box 877 Pleasanton CA 94566

CASSIDAY, PAUL RICHARD, corporate estate executive; b. Honolulu, Oct. 9, 1928; s. Benjamin Buckles and Charlotte Harriet (Lucas) C.; m. Fredrica Rose, July 29, 1969; children—Paul Richard, Cochrane Bryan, Lindsey Leinaala, Brooke Hapoiikekuokalani. Inst. exec. Amfac, Inc., Honolulu, 1950-61, mgr. mortgage loan dept., 1961-63, v.p., Los Angeles, 1967-73, sr. v.p., 1973-75, exec. v.p., 1975-78; pres. Amfac Fin. Corp., Honolulu, 1964-71; chmn. Amfac Mortgage Co., 1974-77; trustee Estate of James Campbell, Honolulu, 1979; pres. P.R. Cassiday, Inc., estate trustee, Honolulu, 1979—. Bd. dirs. Island Holidays, 1967-69, Friends of Lolani Palace, 1964-71, Straub Clinic and Hosp. Adv. Bd.; trustee Hawaii Pacific Coll., 1968-73; bd. dirs. Hawaii Visitors Bur., 1979—, chmn., 1979-80; bd. dirs. U. Hawaii Travel Industry Mgmt. Sch., 1981—. Republican. Clubs: Outrigger Canoe, Pacific, Honolulu. Home: 3263 Diamond Head Rd Honolulu HI 96815 Office: P R Cassiday Inc 900 Fort St Suite 1450 Honolulu HI 96813

CASSIDY, DIANNE MARIE, nurse educator; b. Las Vegas, Nov. 16, 1944; d. J. Emmet and Marguerite Louise (Paquet) Cassidy; diploma Jersey City Hosp. Sch. Nursing, 1966; B.A., Jersey City State Coll., 1969; M.A., N.Y. U., 1971; m. Eugene J. Koprowicz, May 20, 1967 (div. 1973). Asst. prof. nursing Calif. State U., San Diego, 1971-73; clin. instr. Cedars Sinai Med. Center, Los Angeles, 1973-75; asst. dir. nursing, 1976; dir. of edn. adminstrn. St. Mary Med. Center, Long Beach, Calif., 1976-80; dir. nursing Huntington Intercommunity Hosp., 1980—; mem. faculty extension div. UCLA, 1976—. NIH grantee, 1969-71. Mem. Nat. League for Nursing Am. Soc. Health Manpower Edn. ad Tng., Mensa, Sigam Theta Tau. Club: Soroptimists. Contbr. articles on nursing and med. therapy to profl. jours. Office: 17772 Beach Blvd Huntington Beach CA 92647

CASSIDY, MICHAEL JOSEPH, urban planner; b. Gulfport, Miss., Jan. 29, 1943; s. John Vincent and Margaret Veronica (Daugherty) C.; student John Carroll U., 1960-61, U. Stranieri, Perugia, Italy, 1961, U. St. Thomas, Rome, 1961-62; Ph.B., St. Albert's Coll., 1965, postgrad., 1965-66; M.City Planning, U. Calif.-Berkeley, 1971; m. Beverly Ann Marie Terlep, Aug. 17, 1968; children—Erin Kathleen, Sean Albert, Christopher Michael. VISTA vol. Protestant Community Services, Detroit, 1967-69; instr., field tng. officer U. Oreg., Eugene, 1969; asst. planner Assn. Bay Area Govts., Berkeley, 1970; dir. planning and evaluation Oakland (Calif.) Community Action Agy., 1971-77, mem. needs assessment tech. adv. com., 1977-78; dir. planning and research Pacific Econ. Resources League, Oakland, 1978—. Bd. dirs. Displaced Homemakers Ctr., 1979-82; chmn. evaluation com. Oakland Youth Work Experience Program, 1975-76. Recipient Baush and Lomb Sci. award, 1960; Armed Forces Relief and Benefit Assn. scholar, 1960-61; Louda D. Lasker fellow, 1969-70; Am. Inst. Planners fellow, 1969-70; R.K. Mellon fellow, 1970-71. Mem. Am. Planning Assn., Nat. Assn. Bus. Economists, U.S. Coast Guard Aux., Am. Radio Relay League. Roman Catholic. Club: Morse Telegraph. Home: 1064 Warfield Ave Oakland CA 94610 Office: Pacific Econ Resource League Suite 930 1330 Broadway Oakland CA 94612

CASSTEVENS, MARILYN TERESE, psychologist, educational administrator; b. San Diego, Dec. 4, 1927; d. Francis and Florence Ruth (Carl) Casstevens; A.A., Sacramento City Coll., 1946; B.A. with honors, Calif. State U. at San Jose, 1948; M.A., Calif. State U. at Sacramento, 1962; Ph.D., Ariz. State U., 1969. Dept. chmn. girls' phys. edn. Turlock (Calif.) High Sch., 1948-57; high sch. counseling dept. chmn. San Juan Unified Sch. Dist., Carmichael, Calif., 1957-63, dist. counseling program specialist, 1963-68, dir. pupil personnel services, 1968-71, psychologist, 1971-77, staff devel. specialist, dir. staff devel., 1977-81; pvt. practice as psychologist, marriage, family and child counseling, Sacramento, 1972—; lectr., cons. on human relationships and communication, 1970—; lectr., counselor edn. dept. Calif. State U., Sacramento, 1969—; co-owner Sprengstoff Giant Schnauzer Kennel, 1980—. Bd. dirs. Sacramento Tchrs. Credit Union, 1965-66; bd. dirs. Calif. Network, Tchrs. Corps Program, 1978-80, mem. exec. bd., 1979-80. Mem. Am., Calif., Sacramento Valley psychol. assns., Calif. Tchrs. Assn., NEA, Sacramento Area Personnel and Guidance Assn. (pres. 1967-68). Home: 5504 Oak River Ct Sacramento CA 95841

CASTAGNA-SCHENCK, JOAN FRANCES, mktg. ofcl.; b. New Rochelle, N.Y., Nov. 20, 1949; d. John Anthony and Lucy Rose (Tozzo) C.; A.A., Monterey Peninsula Coll., 1974; B.S. in Bus. Adminstrn., San Jose State U., 1978; M.A. in Mgmt., U. Redlands, 1981; m. Charles R. Schenck. Office mgr. Career Devel. Center, Monterey, Calif., 1977; mgr. San Jose (Calif.) Residence Club, 1977-78; personnel recruiter Timesavers Temporary Personnel, Inc., Sunnyvale, Calif., 1978-79; sales rep. West-Ward, Inc., generic drugs, Sunnyvale, 1979-81; mktg. adminstr. Central Region, Four Phase Systems, Inc., Cupertino, Calif., 1979-81; office mgr. Glenayie Electronics, Santa Clara, Calif., 1982—; skin care cons. Mary Kaye Cosmetics, 1982—. Santa Clara Valley Personnel scholar, 1978. Mem. San Jose State U. Bus. Alumni Assn. (pres. 1981—), Soc. Advancement of Mgmt., Sierra Club, Alpha Gamma Sigma. Home: 710 Nido Ave Apt 82 Campbell CA 95008

CASTANEDA, ROBERT E., investment banker, fin. planning co. exec.; b. Los Angeles; s. Robert S. and Antonia Dora C.; student Fordham U., 1950-51, Iona Coll., 1951-52; B.S. in Fin., U. Santa Clara, 1957; m. Pierangela Figini, Jan. 30, 1960; 1 dau., Gabrielle Ann. Account exec. Shearson Hamill & Co., Inc., Beverly Hills, Calif., 1967-73; asst. v.p. Sutro & Co., Inc., Beverly Hills, 1973-76; with Shearson Am. Express (formerly Loeb Rhoades Hornblower), Los Angeles, 1976-82, 2d v.p., 1980-82; exec. v.p. Calif. R & J, Inc., 1980-82; 2d v.p. Smith, Barney, Harris, Upham & Co., Inc., Los Angeles, 1982—; dir. Romeo & Juliet Restaurant, Beverly Hills. Named Outstanding Toastmaster of Yr., 1968. Mem. U. Santa Clara Alumni Assn., Los Angeles Stockbrokers Soc., Am. Stock Exchange, Chgo. Bd. Trade, Chgo. Merc. Exchange, Chgo. Bd. Options Trading, N.Y. Stock Exchange. Republican. Roman Catholic. Office: Smith Barney Harris Upham & Co Inc 800 W 6th St Suite 1100 Los Angeles CA 90071

CASTELLANO, JOSEPH ANTHONY, chemist, indsl. engr.; b. N.Y.C., Oct. 28, 1937; s. Joseph John and Marie Antoinette (Gallo) C.; B.Sc., CCNY, 1959; M.Sc., Poly. Inst. N.Y., 1964, Ph.D., 1969; m. Rosalie Ann Fantaci, Aug. 28, 1960; children—Joseph, Thomas, Laura. Research chemist Witco Chem. Co., Paterson, N.J., 1959-62; sr. research chemist Thiokol Chem. Corp., Denville, N.J., 1962-65; mem. tech. staff, project mgr. RCA Labs., Princeton, N.J., 1965-73; chmn., chief exec. officer Princeton Materials Sci. Co., 1973-75; ops. mgr. Fairchild Camera & Instrument Corp., Palo Alto, Calif., 1975-77; mgr. ops. Kylex, Mountain View, Calif., 1977-78; pres. Stanford Resources, San Jose, Calif., 1978—; cons. Princeton U., 1970-72. Recipient Doctoral Study award RCA, 1966, Outstanding Achievement award RCA Labs., 1967; IR-100 award Indsl. Research Mag., 1968; award in sci. David Sarnoff Team, 1969; accredited profl. chemist, Calif. Fellow Am. Inst. Chemists; mem. Am. Chem. Soc., Royal Chem. Soc., Soc. Info. Display, Am. Solar Energy Soc., Profl. and Tech. Cons. Assn. (pres.), Sigma Xi. Roman Catholic. Editor-in-chief Electronic Display World; editor Active and Passive Electronic Components, An Internat. Jour.; contbr. articles, chpts. to profl. publs. on liquid crystal materials and displays. U.S., fgn. patentee in field. Home: 7017 Elmsdale Dr San Jose CA 95120 Office: 1095 Branham Ln Suite 201 San Jose CA 95136

CASTETTER, SANDRA LEA, nursing administrator; b. Seymour, Ind., Jan. 24, 1950; d. Bruno Frank and Vida Mae (Gray) Browalski; 1 son, Alan Lowell. B.S., Ball State U., 1971; M.S., U. Colo., 1979. R.N., Ind., Colo., Calif. Staff nurse Ball Meml. Hosp., Muncie, Ind., 1971, Mesa Meml. Hosp., Grand Junction, Colo., 1971-72; charge nurse Rose Med. Center, Denver, 1972-73; staff nurse to dept. head St. Luke's Hosp., Denver, 1974-79; clin. instr. U. Colo., Denver, 1978-79; asst. dir. nursing St. Joseph Hosp., Denver, 1979-81; asst. adminstr. patient care services, St. Francis Meml. Hosp., San Francisco, 1981—. Mem. Calif. Soc. Nursing Service Adminstrs., Am. Soc. Nursing Service Adminstrs., Nat. League for Nursing, San Francisco Dirs. of Nursing, Assn. Western Hosps., Nursing Adminstrs. Affiliated Hosps. of San Francisco, Nat. Forum for Adminstrs. of Nursing Services. Lutheran. Office: 900 Hyde St San Francisco CA 94109

CASTILE, EUGENE ARTHUR, surgeon; b. Anapolis, Mo., Mar. 23, 1917; s. Arthur Wilson and Cora Ethel (Buxton) C.; student U. Ind., 1937-39; M.D., U. Louisville, Ky., 1943; postgrad. in Medicine, U. Calif., Los Angeles, 1973, U. So. Calif., 1972-76, Coll. of Med. Evangelists, 1952-53, m. Norma Eileen Shidler, July 3, 1956; children—Jeanette Isabell, Barbara Lynn, Donald Lee, Mark Allen, Kathleen Norma. Intern, Queen of Angels Hosp., Los Angeles, 1944; resident in surgery St. Anthony Hosp., Oklahoma City, 1947-48, Hosp. of the Good Samaritan, Los Angeles, 1951-54; practice medicine specializing in surgery, Los Angeles, 1954—; mem. surg. staff Whittier (Calif.) Hosp., Queen Valley Hosp., West Covina, Brea (Calif.) Hosp. Served as capt. U.S. Army, 1944-46. Lic. real estate broker, Calif. Mem. Am., Calif., Los Angeles County med. assns., Soc. Abdominal Surgeons, Am. Bd. Gen. Surgery (certified), Am. Bd. Abdominal Surgery (certified), La Punta C. of C. Republican. Clubs: Southwest Los Angeles Optimists, Elks. Home: 16467 Canelones Dr Hacienda Heights CA 91745 Office: 324 Azusa Ave City of Industry CA

CASTLE, JAMES CAMARON, corporate executive; b. Peoria, Ill., Nov. 4, 1936; m. Dorothy P. Camaron, June 7, 1957; children—James Charles, Patricia Elizabeth. B.S., U.S. Mil. Acad., 1958; M.S.E.E., U. Pa., 1963, Ph.D., 1965. With Gen. Electric Co., 1961-75, 78-80, gen. mgr., then gen. mgr. dept. simulation and control systems, 1978-80; chmn. bd., chief exec. officer HB Network Info. Systems, 1975-78; v.p. ops. small systems and terminal div. Honeywell, 1980-82; exec. v.p. Memorex Corp., Santa Clara, Calif., 1982—. Served with U.S. Army, 1958-61; Germany. Mem. Young Pres.'s Orgn. Office: Memorex Corp San Tomas and Central Expressway Santa Clara CA 95052

CASTNER, MYRA HAHN, educational administrator; b. Cleve., Nov. 5, 1929; d. Edgar A. and Margaret Ellen (Ward) Hahn; m. Thomas J. Castner, Aug. 30, 1952; children—Sarah Lynn, Margaret Jo. B.A. in Edn., U. Mich., 1951; M.S. in Edn. Psychology and Linguistics. Elem. teaching credential, Calif., Mich., Pa.; reading specialist, supervision, jr. coll. teaching credentials, Calif. Mem. research staff Exemplary Ctr. Reading Instrn., Salt Lake City, 1965-67; dist. master tchr., coordinator Early Childhood Edn./Title I/Bilingual Edn., Campbell (Calif.) Union Sch. Dist., 1972-75, prin., 1976—; lectr. lang. arts; participant curriculum devel. Founder, chmn. Bountiful Young People's Theater (Utah), 1964-67; active LWV, 1955-67. Recipient Gold medallion Calif. Reading Assn., 1976. Mem. Calif. Reading Assn., Internat. Reading Assn., Nat. Council Tchrs. English, Assn. Supervision and Curriculum Devel., Assn. Calif. Sch. Adminstrs, Nat. Assn. Elem. Sch. Prins. Republican. Home: 6390 Janary Way San Jose CA 95129 Office: 155 N 3d St Campbell CA 95008

CASTO, CLARENCE EDWIN, accountant; b. Ontario, Oreg., June 13, 1926; s. Edwin and Maude Esther (Kime) C.; m. Susie Anne Howard Brown, Sept. 23, 1951; children—Ginger, Leslie. B.B.A., U. Oreg., 1950. C.P.A., Oreg. Acct., Percy W. Brown & Co., C.P.A., Eugene, Oreg., 1951-52, Mervin L. Hanscam, C.P.A., Sweet Home, Oreg., 1952-53; ptnr. Hanscam & Casto, Sweet Home, 1953, Lakeview, Oreg., 1953—. Served with USN, 1944-46. Named Lake County Jr. Citizen, Lake County C. of C., 1962, Sr. Citizen, 1974. Mem. Oreg. Soc. C.P.A.s, Am. Soc. C.P.A.s, Lake County C. of C. Republican. Episcopalian. Clubs: Rotary, Elks (Lakeview). Office: Hanscam & Casto 19 S G St Lakeview OR 97630

CASTRO, EDNA CARLENE, retail exec.; b. Twin Falls, Idaho, Mar. 25, 1942; d. Leo Walter and Joy Pauline (Rugh) Wright; A.A., Coll. So. Idaho, 1980; m. Robert G. Castro, Jr., June 30, 1971; children—R. Jeffrey, Leslie Joy. Personnel clk. Glendale div. Kellwood Corp., Twin Falls, 1969-71; office mgr. Snake River Area council Boy Scouts Am., Twin Falls, 1972-74; mgr. Nat. Car Rental Co., Twin Falls, 1974-78; personnel mgr. F. W. Woolworth Co., Twin Falls, 1978—; calligrapher, comml. artist. Mem. adv. bd. Distributive Edn. Club Am., 1980-81. Mem. Am. Soc. Personnel Adminstrn., Nat. Assn. Female Execs., Alma Soc., Life Study Fellowship, Am. Soc. Profl. and Exec. Women, Internat. Entrepreneurs Assn. Republican. Mem. Ch. of Christ. Home: 207 Caswell Ave Twin Falls ID 83301 Office: 705 Blue Lakes Blvd N Twin Falls ID 83301

CASTRO, JOHN GONZALES, clergyman, educator; b. San Antonio, Nov. 18, 1935; s. John Riojas and Elvira (Medrano) Gonzales C. B.A. in Philosophy, Oblate Coll. S.W., 1959, M.Div. (equivalent), 1963; Ph.D. in Counseling Psychology, Mich. State U., 1975. Ordained priest Roman Catholic Ch., 1962. Joined Missionary Oblates of Mary Immaculate, 1956; tchr. Spanish, St. Anthony High Sch. Sem., San Antonio, 1972; grad. asst. Mich. State U., East Lansing, 1973-75, coordinator Chicano program com. Coll. Edn., 1972-73; assoc. pastor Our Lady of Guadalupe, Austin, Tex., 1975-78; prof. Mexican Am. psychodynamics, counseling psychology and homiletics, dir. dept. cultural awareness and devel. Oblate Coll. S.W., San Antonio, 1978-81; prof. Hispanic psychodynamics, social, emotional, interpersonal devel., pastoral psychology, homiletics, Spanish, dir. dept. Hispanic ministries Mt. Angel Sem., St. Benedict, Oreg., 1981—; mem. diaconate program teaching staff Archdiocese of San Antonio, 1978-81; trustee El Visitante Dominical, nat. weekly newspaper, 1978—; co-dir. undergrad. coll. program Missionary Oblates of Mary Immaculate, Austin, 1975-76; coordinator master's program Antioch Juarez Lincoln U., Austin, 1976-77; program dir. Mexican Am. Ctr. for Econ. Devel., Austin, 1978-79; psychologist Diocese of Austin, 1975-78; mem. San Salvador Vicariate for Hispanic Affairs, Archdiocese of Portland (Oreg.), 1981—. Charter mem. Juvenile Rev. Bd. Brownsville (Tex.), 1971-72; mem. central council Mental Health and Mental Retardation Adv. Bd., Austin, 1976-77; chmn. adv. bd. Drug Abuse Mental Health and Mental Retardation, Austin, 1976-78; chmn. adv. bd. VISTA, Austin, 1976-77. Mem. Am. Personnel and Guidance Assn.,. Nat. Council Cath. Bishops (trustee N.W. region for Hispanic a-fairs Region XII, 1981—), Priests Organized for Religious, Econ. and Social Rights, Mich. State U. Alumni Assn. Democrat. Club: K.C. Home: 4143 47th Ave NE Salem OR 97301 Office: Mt Angel Seminary Saint Benedict OR 97373

CASTRO, RODOLFO HADER, county ofcl., community services adminstr.; b. Riverside, Calif., May 31, 1942; A.A. with honors, Riverside City Coll., 1967; B.S. with honors in Bus. Adminstrn., Calif. Poly. Coll., 1970; M.B.A., Harvard U., 1973. Dep. dir. Econ. Opportunity Bd., Riverside, 1970; dir. program ops. LULAC Nat. Edn. Center, Washington, 1973-74, asst. dir., 1975, exec. dir., 1975; exec. dir. community services dept. San Bernardino County (Calif.), 1976—; pres. Rodolfo H. Castro & Assos., 1977—. Mem. Calif. Republican Hispanic Assembly, sustaining mem. Calif. Rep. Com.; primary candidate for U.S. Ho. of Reps. from 37th dist. Calif. Mem. Harvard U. Bus. Sch. Alumni Assn., Am. Soc. for Pub. Adminstrn. Club: Palm Springs Harvard (treas. 1982-83). Home: 250 N Phillips Ave Banning CA 92220 Office: 602 S Tippecanoe Ave San Bernardino CA 92314

CASWELL, HELEN RAYBURN, artist, writer; b. Long Beach, Calif., Mar. 16, 1923; d. Odis Claude and Helen Marian (Kepner) Rayburn; m. Dwight Allan Caswell, Dec. 27, 1942; children—Dwight Allan, Philip, Mary (Mrs. Matthew Walsh), Christopher, John. Grad. in fine arts U. Oreg., 1942. One-woman shows: Gallery Americana, Carmel, Calif., Hardie's Heritage Gallery, Saratoga, Calif.; group shows: Soc. Western Artists; mural commns.: Saratoga Federated Ch., Emmanuel Lutheran Ch., Saratoga, San Jose Hosp.; numerous portraits and studies of children in natural and informal settings. Recipient Phelan award for narrative poetry, 1958; award for dramatic monologue San Francisco Browning Soc., 1964. Republican. Episcopalian. Author: Jesus, My Son, 1962; A Wind on the Road, 1964; A New Song for Christmas, 1966; Shadows from the Singing House, 1968; You Are More Wonderful, 1970; Thank You For Being You, 1972; Never Wed An Old Man, 1975. Address: 13207 Dupont Rd Sebastopae CA 95472

CATALANO, FRANK, executive, educator, actor; b. N.Y.C., Sept. 17, 1951. A.A. in Theatre Arts, Nassau Community Coll., 1973; B.A. in Theatre, SUNY-Stony Brook, 1973; M.A. in Drama, U. Hawaii, 1975; M.F.A. in Profl. Writing, U. So. Calif., 1983. Exec. dir., founder So. Calif. Ctr. Arts, Los Angeles, 1976—; producer plays, including Hold Me!, 1982; writer, producer plays including: American Rose Garden, 1976; Evolution, 1973; Saturday Nights, Part I, 1982. Appeared in TV shows including: The Waltons, Days of Our Lives, Hawaii Five-O; career cons. Bd. dirs. Los Angeles Theatre Alliance; com. chmn. Arts Advocacy Calif. Confedn. of Arts. Recipient numerous awards for acting, direction and overall prodn. design, 1979-83. Mem. Screen Actors Guild, AFTRA, Actors Equity Assn., Dramatical Guild Am. Office: 7551 Melrose Ave Suites 5-8 Los Angeles CA 90046

CATALDO, DONALD MARIO, learning disabilities educator, educational administrator; b. Rochester, N.Y., Nov. 1, 1947; s. Mario B. and Marie (Batall) C.; m. Judith Thea Abel, Mar. 19, 1972; children—David, Matthew, Andrea. B.A. in Psychology (Regents scholar), UCLA, 1970, postgrad., 1982—; postgrad. UCLA Sch. Medicine, 1971-73; M.A. in Edn. and Spl. Edn., Calif. State U.-Los Angeles, 1981, postgrad., 1982—. Cert. standard secondary, learning handicaps specialist, adminstrv. services, resource specialist, Calif. Tchr. math. Bishop Amat High Sch., La Puente, Calif., 1974-75; tchr. math. and sci., counselor La Salle High Sch., Pasadena, Calif., 1975-77; specialist in learning disabilities Chaffey High Sch. Dist., Ontario, Calif., 1977—; exec. dir. So. Calif. Learning Ctr., Upland, Calif., 1979—. Served to lt. (j.g.) USN, 1971-74. Anna Bing Meml. and Health Scis. scholar UCLA, 1971. Mem. Assn. Calif. Sch. Adminstrs., Assn. Supervision and Curriculum Devel., Council for Exceptional Children. Roman Catholic. Author: (pamphlet) Reading Problems—A Parent's Guide to Special Education Problems, 1980.

CATALFOMO, PHILIP, univ. dean; b. Providence, Dec. 27, 1931; s. Antonio and Frances (Di Giuseppe) C.; B.S., Providence Coll., 1953, U. Conn., 1958; M.S., U. Wash., Seattle, 1960, Ph.D., 1962; m. Magdalena Wettstein, Jan. 8, 1962; children—Kristina, Anthony Werner. Mem. faculty Oreg. State U., 1963-75, prof. pharmacognosy, 1966-75, head dept., 1966-75; prof. pharmacognosy, dean Sch. Pharmacy and Allied Health Scis., U. Mont., Missoula, 1975—. Served with AUS, 1953-55. Gustavus A. Pfeiffer Meml. research fellow, 1969-70. Mem. Am. Pharm. Assn., Acad. Pharm. Scis., AAAS, Am. Soc. Pharmacognosy, Am. Assn. Colls. Pharmacy, Sigma Xi, Rho Chi. Author research articles on fungal physiology, phytochemistry and metabolism of marine fungi. Home: 33 Willowbrook Ln Missoula MT 59802 Office: Sch Pharmacy U Mont Missoula MT 59812

CATER, JACK ERNEST, underwater acoustician; b. N.Y.C., Apr. 28, 1950; s. Ernest Everett, Jr., and June Mary (Sohigian) C.; S.B.E.E., M.I.T., 1972, S.M. in Ocean Engring., 1974; m. Judy Jerstad, Nov. 24, 1973; 1 dau., Joanne Jerstad. Cons., Lincoln Lab., Lexington, Mass., 1972-73, also research employee M.I.T., 1972-74; sr. engr. Bolt Beranek & Newman Inc., San Diego, 1977—. Asst. scoutmaster Boy Scouts Am., 1976—. Served to lt. USNR, 1974-77. Mem. Acoustical Soc. Am., AAAS, IEEE, N.Y. Acad. Scis., Sigma Xi. Eagle scout. Home: 2386 Botella Pl Carlsbad CA 92008 Office: 3065 Rosecrans Pl Suite 210 San Diego CA 92110

CATES, GILBERT, director, producer; b. N.Y.C., June 6, 1934; s. Nathan and Nina (Peltzman) Katz m. Jane Betty Dubin, Feb. 9, 1957; children—Melissa Beth, Jonathan Michael, David Sawyer, Gilbert Lewis. B.S., Syracuse U., 1955, M.A., 1965. TV producer, dir. Haggis Baggis, NBC-TV, 1959, Camouflage, ABC-TV, 1961-62, Internat. Showtime, 1962-64; producer-dir. Hootenanny ABC-TV, 1962, To All My Friends on Shore, CBS-TV, 1972, The Affair, ABC-TV, 1974, After the Fall, NBC-TV, 1974, Johnny, We Hardly Knew Ye, NBC-TV, 1976, The Kid From Nowhere, NBC-TV, 1981, Country Gold, CBS-TV, 1982, Rapunzel, Goldilocks and The Three Bears Cable TV, 1983, Hobson's Choice, CBS-TV, 1983; film producer, dir. The Painting, 1962, Rings Around the World, 1967, I Never Sang for My Father, 1970, Summer Wishes, Winter Dreams, 1973, One Summer Love, 1976, The Promise, 1978, The Last Married Couple in America, 1979; Oh, God Book II, 1980; theatrical producer You Know I Can't Hear You When the Water's Running, 1967, I Never Sang for my Father, 1968, The Chinese and Doctor Fish, 1970, Solitaire-Double Solitaire, 1971; dir. Voices, 1972, Tricks of the Trade, 1980. Mem. com. 1, Syracuse U. Drama Dept., 1969-73, New Dramatists, N.Y.C. Vice pres. Westchester Reform Temple. Recipient Best Short Film award Internat. Film Importers and Distbrs., 1962, Chancellor's medal Syracuse U., 1974. Mem. Dirs. Guild Am. (pres.), League N.Y. Theaters. Club: Friars. Home: 936 Hilts Ave Los Angeles CA 90024 Office: 195 S Beverly Dr Beverly Hills CA 90212

CATTANEO, JACQUELYN ANNETTE KAMMERER, artist; b. Gallup, N.Mex., June 1, 1944; d. Ralph John and Gladys Agnes (O'Sullivan) Kammer; m. John Leo Cattaneo, Apr. 25, 1964; children—John Auro, Paul Anthony. Student Tex. Woman's U., 1962-64. Portrait artist, Gallup, N. Mex., 1972; one man shows: Gallup Pub. Library, 1963, 66, 77, 78, 81, Gallup Lovelace Med. Clinic, Santa Fe Station Open House, 1981; group shows include: Navajo Nation Library Invitational, 1978, Santa Fe Festival of the Arts Invitational, 1979, N.Mex. State Fair, 1978, 79, 80, Nat. Apaloosa Horse Club, 1980, Catharine Lorillard Wolfe, N.Y.C., 1980, 81; represented in permanent collections: Zuni Arts and Crafts Ednl. Bldg., U. N.Mex., C.J. Wiemar Collection. represented by Rosequist Galleries, Tucson. Mem. Internat. Fine Arts Guild, Am. Portrait Soc. Address: 210 E Green St Gallup NM 87301

CATTANI, MARYELLEN BILLETTE, lawyer; b. Bakersfield, Calif., Dec. 1, 1943; d. Arnold Theodore and Corinne Marilyn (Kovacevich) Cattani; A.B., Vassar Coll., 1965; J.D., U. Calif. at Berkeley, 1968; m. Bernard J. Mikell, Jr., April 1, 1978. Admitted to N.Y. bar, 1969, Calif. bar, 1969; asso. firm Davis Polk & Wardwell, N.Y.C., 1968-69; asso. firm Orrick, Herrington & Sutcliffe, P.C., San Francisco, 1970-74, partner, 1975-81; v.p., gen. counsel Transam. Corp., 1981—; adj. prof. Calif. Pub. Interest Law Center, Lone Mountain Coll., San Francisco, 1973-74. Mem. Am. Bar Assn. (corp., banking, bus. law sect.), State Bar Calif. (investigation panel dist. 4, 1977-78, exec. com. bus. law sect. 1978-82, vice chmn. 1979-80, chmn. 1980-81), Bar Assn. San Francisco (chmn. com. on employment of women in law 1976, fee arbitration panel), Calif. Women Lawyers (jud. qualifications com. dist. 4 1977-78, No. Calif. steering com. 1974), Legal Aid Soc. San Francisco (dir. 1981—), Boalt Hall Alumni Assn. (dir. 1975-78), Am. Corporate Counsel Assn. (dir. 1982—). Home: 2829 Buena Vista Way Berkeley CA 94708 Office: 600 Montgomery St San Francisco CA 94111

CATZ, BORIS, physician; b. Troyanov, Russia, Feb. 15, 1923; s. Jacobo and Esther (Galbmilion) C.; came to U.S., 1950, naturalized, 1955; B.S., Nat. U. Mexico, 1941, M.D., 1947; M.S. in Medicine, U. So. Calif., 1951; m. Rebecca Schechter; children—Judith, Dinah, Sarah Lea, Robert. Intern, Gen. Hosp., Mexico City, 1945-46; prof. adj., sch. medicine U. Mexico, 1947-48; research fellow medicine U. So. Calif., 1949-51, instr. medicine, 1952-54, asst. clin. prof., 1954-59, assoc. clin. prof., 1959-83, clin. prof., 1983—; pvt. practice, Los Angeles, 1951-55, Beverly Hills, Calif., 1957—; chief Thyroid Clinic Los Angeles County Gen. Hosp., 1955-70; sr. cons. thyroid clin. U. So. Calif.-Los Angeles Med. Center, 1970—; clin. chief endocrinology Cedars-Sinai Med. Ctr., 1983—. Served to capt. U.S. Army, 1955-57. Fellow ACP, Am. Coll. Nuclear Medicine (pres. elect 1982); mem. A.M.A., Los Angeles County Med. Soc., Calif. Med. Assn., Endocrine Soc., Am. Thyroid Assn., Soc. Exptl. Biology and Medicine, Western Soc. Clin. Research, Am. Fedn. Clin. Research, Soc. Nuclear Medicine, So. Calif. Soc. Nuclear Medicine, AAAS, N.Y. Acad. Scis., Los Angeles Soc. Internal Medicine, Collegium Salerni, Beverly Hills C. of C., Phi Lambda Kappa. Jewish. Mem. B'nai B'rith. Club: The Profl. Man's (past pres.). Author: Thyroid Case Studies, 1975, 2d edit., 1981. Contbr. numerous articles on thyroidology to med. jours. Home: 300 El Camino Dr Beverly Hills CA 90212 Office: 435 N Roxbury Dr Beverly Hills CA 90210

CAUDILL, JAMES MASON, public relations counselor, corporation executive; b. Detroit, Sept. 16, 1950; s. Estill and Naomi C.; m. Elaine Marie O'Donnell, Oct. 30, 1971; children—Heather, Stacy, Megan. B.A., Wayne State U., 1974; M.A. with honors, Western Mich. U., 1979; postgrad. Bus. Adminstrn., San Francisco State U. Accredited Pub. Relations Soc. Am. Reporter/editor Leader Publs., Dearborn Heights, Mich., 1970-72; pub. relations specialist Dearborn, Benton Harbor and Macomb (Mich.) sch. dists., 1972-79; v.p., pub. relations counselor Carl Byoir & Assocs., Inc., Detroit, 1979-80, San Francisco, 1980—; cons. in field; writer for sch. assns. Bd. dirs. Big Bros./Big Sisters of the Peninsula. Named one of top 10 writers, ann. John Stahr writing contest, Carl Byoir & Assocs., 1979-83. Mem. Pub. Relations Soc. Am. (co-recipient Silver Anvil award 1980), Counselor's Acad., Pub. Relations Round Table, Found. Pub. Relations Edn. and Research. Democrat. Methodist. Regular contbr. publs. including Am. School Board Jour., Executive Educator, Thrust, various ednl. jours. Home: 901 Lurline Dr Foster City CA 94404 Office: 181 Fremont St Mezzanine Suite San Francisco CA 94105

CAUDLE, ALLEN SCOTT, food service director; b. Havelock, N.C., July 23, 1953; s. Forrest E. and Alyce L. (Niskawara) C.; m. Susan Bernstein, Nov. 25, 1978. B.A., Calif. State U., 1975-. Food service mgr. Good Samaritan Hosp. of Santa Clara Valley, San Jose, Calif., 1975-77; assoc. food service dir. Providence Med. Center, Portland, Oreg., 1977-80, food service dir., 1980—. Mem. Am. Soc. Hosp. Food Service Adminstrs. (past pres., chpt.). Office: 4805 NE Glisan St Portland OR 97213

CAUDRON, JOHN ARMAND, administrator, engineering analyst; b. Compton, Calif., Sept. 26, 1944; s. Armand Robert and Evelyn Emma (Hoyt) C.; m. Marilyn Edith Fairfield, Mar. 16, 1968; children—Melita E. M., Rochelle M. Student Calif. State U.-Fullerton, 1964-67, U. Nev., 1975-78, Safety Tng. Inst., 1979; M.S. in Safety, U. So. Calif., 1980. Rep., dealer, auditor Gen. Motors Acceptance Corp., Downey and Redding, Calif., and Reno, 1969-75; mgr. Snyder Research Lab., Inc., Reno, 1976-78, safety engr., Pico Rivera, Calif., 1978-79, v.p., 1979. Served with U.S. Army, 1967-69. Mem. ASCE, Am. Soc. Safety Engrs., Am. Soc. Profl. Cons., Geol. Soc. Am., Firearms Research and Identification Assn. Club: Internat. Mil. Rifle Team. Office: 2535 N Rosemead Blvd South El Monte CA 91733

CAUFIELD, JAMES DAVID, consulting engineer; b. Helena, Mont., Sept. 13, 1924; s. Lee James and Mary Elizabeth (Lenzen) C.; m. Pamela Hillyard Jones, Feb. 14, 1949 (div.). B.E., Yale U., 1944; M.S.E., U. Mich., 1947. Registered profl. engr., Oreg., Wash., Idaho, Nev., N.Y., R.I., Vt., Utah, Alaska, S.D., Ind., Ill. Jr. engr. Moffatt, Nichol & Taylor, Portland, Oreg., 1948-49; design engr. John W. Cunningham & Assocs., Portland, 1949-51; Carl E. Green & Assocs., Portland, 1954-56; ptnr. Caufield & Caufield, Portland, 1956-65; dist. engr. Am. Wood Preservers Inst., Portland, 1965-70; dir. bio-engring. div. UMA Engrs., Inc., Portland, 1970-80; pres. J.D. Caufield & Assocs., Inc., Portland, 1980—. Served to lt. comdr. C.E., USNR, 1944-46, 1952-53. Mem. Am. Fisheries Soc., ASCE, Am. Concrete Inst., Am. Water Works Assn., Nat. Soc. Profl. Engrs., Cons. Engrs. Council Oreg., Profl. Engrs. Oreg. (past pres.), Structural Engrs. Assn. Oreg. (past pres.). Club: City (Portland). Democrat. Congregationalist. Contbr. papers in field.

CAULFIELD, HENRY PATRICK, JR., political science educator; b. N.Y.C., Nov. 25, 1915; s. Henry Patrick and Grace Lenore (Nelson) C.; S.B. cum laude, Harvard U., 1940, M.P.A., 1949; m. Violet M. Green, Apr. 30, 1956; children—Deborah, Laura, Mary, Patrick. Research assoc. Resources for the Future, Washington, 1955-60; asst. dir. resources program staff Office of Sec., Dept. Interior, Washington, 1961-62, dir., 1963-66; exec. dir. U.S. Water Resources Council, Washington, 1966-69; prof. polit. sci. Colo. State U., Fort Collins, 1969—. Mem. Colo. Gov.'s Sci. and Tech. Council, 1975-79; mem. environ. studies bd. NRC, 1976-79; mem. exec. bd. Univs. Council on Water Resources, 1978-81, pres., 1979-80; mem. arid and semi-arid lands subcom. U.S. Com. on Man and Biosphere, Dept. State, 1978—. Served with USN, 1942-45. Mem. Am. Soc. Pub. Adminstrn., Western Polit. Sci. Assn., Policy Studies Orgn., Am. Water Resources Assn., Internat. Water Resources Assn. Democrat. Roman Catholic. Club: Harvard of Rocky Mountains. Contbr. articles to profl. jours. Home: 808 Gregory Rd Fort Collins CO 80524 Office: Dept Polit Sci Colo State Univ Fort Collins CO 80523

CAVALLI-SFORZA, LUIGI LUCA, educator; b. Genoa, Italy, Jan. 25, 1922; s. Pio and Attilia (Manacorda) C.; M.D., U. Pavia (Italy), 1944; M.A., Cambridge U. (Eng.), 1950; D.Sc. (hon.), Columbia U., 1980; m. Albamaria Ramazzotti, Jan. 12, 1946; children—Matteo, Francesco, Tommaso, Violetta. Came to U.S., 1970. Asst. research Istituto Sieroterapico Milanese, Milan, Italy, 1945-48, dir. research, 1950-57; prof. genetics U. Parma, 1958-62; prof. genetics, dir. Istituto di Genetica, U. Pavia, 1962-70; prof. genetics Stanford, 1970—. Vice-pres. Internat. Congress Genetics, Tokyo, Japan, 1968. Served as med. officer, Italian Army, 1947-48. Recipient T.H. Huxley award in anthropology, 1972, Weldon award in biometry, 1975. Fellow AAAS; mem. Am. Assn. Phys. Anthropology, Am. Soc. Human Genetics, Associazione Genetica Italiana, Behavioral Genetic Assn., Biometric Soc. (pres. 1967-68), Genetical Soc. Gt. Britain, Institut Internat. de Statistique, Soc. for Study Evolution, Union Internat. pour L'Etude Scientifique de la Population, Royal Statis. Soc., Am. Acad. Arts and Scis. (fgn. hon.), Japanese Soc. Human Genetics (fgn. hon.), U.S. Nat. Acad. Sci. (fgn. hon.). Author: (with W. Bodmer) The Genetics of Human Populations, 1971; Genetics, Evolution and Man, 1976; (with M. Feldman) Cultural Transmission and Evolution, 1981. Office: Dept Genetics Stanford U Med Sch Stanford CA 94305

CAVANAGH, JOHN CHARLES, advertising agency executive; b. San Francisco, Dec. 19, 1932; s. John Timothy and Alicia Louise (McDowell) C.; m. Mary Ann Andling, Apr. 10, 1959; children—Karen, Brad. Student U. Hawaii, 1950; B.S., U. San Francisco, 1954. Pub. relations rep. Kaiser Industries Corp., Oakland, Calif., 1956-58; pub. relations mgr. Kaiser Cement & Gypsum Corp., Oakland, 1958-63; pub. relations dir. Fawcett-McDermott Assocs., Inc., Honolulu, 1964-66, ops. v.p., 1966-69, exec. v.p., 1969-73, pres., 1973-75, also dir.; pres. Fawcett McDermott Cavanagh Inc., Honolulu, 1975—, also dir.; pres. Fawcett McDermott Cavanagh Calif., Inc., San Francisco, 1975—, also dir. Served to 1st lt. 740th Guided Missile Bn., U.S. Army, 1954-56. Mem. Pub. Relations Soc. Am. (accredited; v.p. 1970, pres. Hawaii chpt. 1971), Advt. Agy. Assn. Hawaii (pres. 1973), Affiliated Advt. Agys. Internat. (chmn. elect), Am. Assn. Advt. Agys. (past chmn. Hawaii council). Clubs: Rotary, Honolulu Press, Honolulu Advt., Outrigger Canoe, Oahu Country, Pacific. Home: 3068 La Pietra Circle Honolulu HI 96815 Office: 1441 Kapiolani Blvd Suite 1500 Honolulu HI 96814

CAVAT, IRMA, art educator, painter; b. Bklyn.; d. Philip and Sylvia Ciavati. Student Bklyn. Mus. Sch., Archipenko Art Sch., New Sch. Social Research. Prof. studio art U. Calif., Santa Barbara, 1964—; one person shows include: Main St. Galleries, Chgo., Santa Barbara Mus., Phoenix Art Mus., Kennedy Galleries, N.Y.C.; group shows include: Mus. Modern Art, N.Y.C., Detroit Inst. Art, Art Inst. Chgo.; permanent collections: Chase Manhattan Bank, Cornell U., Flint (Mich.) Mus., Delgado Mus., New Orleans, also numerous pvt. collections. Mem. Santa Barbara Com. on Art in Public Places, 1982—. Fulbright grantee, 1956-58, creative studies grantee U. Calif., Santa Barbara, 1972-73. Mem. Coll. Art Assn., Santa Barbara Contemporary Arts Forum (dir.). Office: U Calif Santa Barbara Art Dept Santa Barbara CA 93106

CAVE, KRESS K., accountant; b. Elko, Nev., Sept. 8, 1951; s. W.W. and Roberta C. B.S. in Bus. Adminstrn., U. Nev.-Reno, 1974. C.P.A., Oreg., 1981, Nev., 1982. Practice acctg., Carson City, Nev., 1982—; dir. Roberta E. Cave Inc. Office: 508 N Curry St Carson City NV 89701

CAVELTI, PHILIP ALFONS, physician; b. Gossau-St. G., Switzerland, Aug. 21, 1914; came to U.S., 1941, naturalized, 1958; s. Alphons Georg and Margrit (Staerkle) C.; B.A., Bern Gymnasium, 1933; M.D., U. Bern, 1939; m. Else Hedwig Staehelin, Feb. 15, 1941 (dec. 1961); children—Christine Sylvia, Thomas Philip, Nicholas Ernest; m. 2d, Kungolt Alix Barbara Bodmer, Aug. 23, 1962 (div.); m. 3d, Margarete Helene Woehlert, May 22, 1965 (div.); m. 4th, Ursula Loesch Swart, Feb. 23, 1974. Asst. resident in Medicine U. Bern Hosp., 1939-41; Commonwealth Fund fellow George Williams Hooper Found. Mem. Research, also instr. medicine U. Calif. Med. Center, San Francisco, 1942-47; intern Mt. Zion Hosp., San Francisco, 1947-48; asso. Georges Piness Allergy Group, Los Angeles, 1948-50; practice medicine specializing in allergy, Palo Alto, Calif., 1951—; mem. staff Palo-Alto-Stanford Hosp. Center. Diplomate Swiss Bd. Internal Medicine, Am. Bd. Allergy and Immunology. Fellow Am. Acad. Allergy, Am. Coll. Allergy; mem. AMA, N.Y. Acad. Scis., Swiss Allergy Soc., Calif. Allergy Soc., Am. Assn. Immunologists, West Coast Allergy Soc., No. Calif. Allergy Assn. Home: Sonnenbergstrasse 10 8968 Mutschellen Switzerland Office: 1981 Gartenstrasse 33 8002 Zuerich Switzerland

CAVIGGA, MARGARET MADDOX, quilt collector, art consultant, quilt historian; b. Poplar Bluff, Mo., Oct. 31, 1924; d. Thomas Clarence and Octabelle (Peterson) Maddox; m. Albert Anthony Cavigga, Jan. 19, 1952; Student So. Meth. U., 1943, U. Mo., Columbia, 1945; B.A. in Art, Psychology and Sociology, La. State U., 1946; postgrad. in art and edn. UCLA, 1949-53, Calif. State U.-Northridge, 1953-60. Tchr. pub. schs., Los Angeles, 1953-72, master tchr., tchr. tng. program, 1954-72; tour condr. Club Universe Unitours, Los Angeles, 1960-73; owner, operator Margaret Cavigga Quilt Collection, Los Angeles, 1973—; appraiser Am. quilts and collectibles; lectr. on collecting textiles and Americana; curator numerous hist. quilt exhbns. U.S., abroad; TV and radio appearances; bd. dirs. Women In Design, Los Angeles; mem. Decorative Arts Council, Los Angeles County Mus.; mem. Costume and Textile Council, Los Angeles County Mus. Recipient Civic award Los Angeles County Supr., 1981, Mayor of Los Angeles, 1981, Mayor of Santa Monica, 1982, Gov. of Calif., 1982; Senate Resolution, Calif. Senate, 1982. Mem. Am. Soc. Interior Designers (design affiliate), Internat. Soc. Interior Designers (trade mem.), Craft and Folk Art Mus., N.Y. Folk Art Mus., Hancock Park Hist. Soc., Smithsonian Inst., Nat. Trust Hist. Preservation, Los Angeles State U. Alumnae. Methodist. Clubs: Republican of Los Angeles, Republican of Calif. Author: American Antique Quilts, Japanese and English edits., 1981; Quilt Connoisseurship, 1982. Office: 8648 Melrose Ave Los Angeles CA 90069

CAVINESS, GEORGE LEWIS, educator; b. Silver Springs, Md., Apr. 14, 1915; s. Leon Leslie and Agnes L. (Lewis) C.; B.A., Pacific Union Coll., 1937; M.A., U. Calif., Berkeley, 1939; Ph.D. (Univ. Scholar), Ohio State U., 1945; m. Goldie Mae Raley, Aug. 15, 1939; children—William Malcolm, Arthur Roland, Dorothy Jeanne. Mem. faculty, registrar Atlantic Union Coll., South Lancaster, Mass., 1939-47; mem. faculty

Pacific Union Coll., Angwin, Calif., 1947-54, 57-58; affiliation officer Avondale Coll., Cooranbong, N.S.W., Australia, 1954-57; acad. dean Union Coll., Lincoln, Nebr., 1958-66; pres. Newbold Coll., Bracknell, Eng., 1966-71; prof. modern langs. Walla Walla Coll., College Place, Wash., 1971-80, ret., 1980, prof. emeritus, 1980—. Mem. MLA, Am. Assn. Tchrs. of French. Seventh-Day Adventist. Home: 114 NE Cedar Ave College Place WA 99324

CAVNAR, MARGARET MARY (PEGGY), former state legislator, business executive, nurse; b. Buffalo, July 29, 1945; d. James John and Margaret Mary Murtha Nightengale; B.S. in Nursing, D'Youville Coll., 1967; m. Samuel M. Cavnar, 1977; children—Heather Anne, Heide Lynn, Dona Cavnar Hambly, Judy Cavnar Bentrim. Utilization rev. coordinator S. Nev. Meml. Hosp., Las Vegas, 1975-77; v.p. Ranvac Publs., Las Vegas, 1976—; partner Cavnar & Assos., Reseda, Calif., 1976—, C & A Mgmt., Las Vegas, 1977—; pres. PS Computer Service, Las Vegas, 1978—. Mem. Clark County Republican Central Com., 1977—, Nev. Rep. Central Com., 1978—; mem. Nev. Assembly, 1979-81; dir., treas., sec. Nev. Med. Fed. Credit Union, 1976, 81; v.p. Community Youth Activities Found., Inc., Civic Assn. Am.; mem. utilization rev. bd. Easter Seals, 1976—; bd. dirs. Las Vegas Jr. Conservatory, So. Nev. Summer Music Sch., 1981. Mem. Nev. Order Women Legislators (parliamentarian 1981—). Club: Cosmopolitanly Hers Info. (pres.). Office: PO Box 26073 Las Vegas NV 89102

CAVNAR, SAMUEL MELMON, author, publisher, activist; b. Denver, Nov. 10, 1925; s. Samuel Edward and Helen Anita (Johnstone) C.; student public schs., Denver; m. Peggy Nightengale, Aug. 14, 1977; children by previous marriage—Dona Cavnar Hambly, Judy Cavnar Wallen; children—Heather Anne, Heide Lynn. Dist. mgr. U.S. C. of C., various locations, 1953-58; owner Cavnar & Assos., mgmt. cons., Washington, Las Vegas, Nev., Denver and Reseda Calif., 1958—; v.p. Lenz Asso. Advt., Inc., Van Nuys, Calif., 1960—; dist. mgr. Western States Nu-Orm Plans, Inc., Los Angeles, 1947-52; cons. to architect and contractor 1st U.S. Missile Site, Wyo., 1957-58; prin. organizer Westway Corp. and subsidiaries, So. Calif. Devel. Co., 1958—; chmn. bd. Boy Sponsors, Inc., Denver, 1957-59; pres. Continental Am. Video Network Assn. Registry, Inc., Hollywood, Calif., 1967—; pres. United Sales Am., Las Vegas and Denver, 1969—; sr. mgmt. cons. Broadcast Mgmt. Cons. Service, Hollywood, Las Vegas, Denver, Washington, 1970—; pres., dir., exec. com. Am. Center for Edn., 1968—; pub. Nat. Ind., Washington, 1970—, Nat. Rep. Statesman, Washington, 1969—, Nat. Labor Reform Leader, 1970—, Nat. Conservative Statesman, 1975—; owner Ran Vac Pub., Las Vegas and Los Angeles, 1976—; partner P.S. Computer Services, Las Vegas, 1978—, C & A Mgmt., Las Vegas, 1978—, Westway Internat., 1983—; lectr. in field; spl. cons. various U.S. senators, congressmen, 1952—. Nat. gen. chmn. Operation Houseclean, 1966-81; nat. candidate chmn. Citizens Com. To Elect Rep. Legislators, 1966, 68, 70, 72-74; mem. Calif. and Los Angeles County Rep. Central Coms., 1964-70; nat. gen. chmn. Project Prayer, 1962—; exec. dir. Project Alert, 1961—; nat. chmn. Nat. Labor Reform Com., 1969—; sustaining mem. Rep. Nat. Com., 1964—; Western states chmn. and nat. co-chmn. Am. Taxpayers Army, 1959—; area II chmn. Calif. Gov.'s Welfare Reform Com., 1970; chmn. Com. Law and Order in Am., 1975; mem. Nev. State Rep. Com., 1972—; mem. Clark County Rep. Com., 1972—; bd. dirs. Conservative Caucus, Las Vegas, 1980—; Rep. candidate for U.S. Senate from Nev., 1976, 82; nat. chmn. Return Pueblo Crew, 1968; pres., trustee Community Youth Activities Found., 1977—; nat. chmn. Operation Bus Stop, 1970—, P.R.I.D.E. Com., 1981—, Positivics Program, 1982—; co-chmn. Question 8 Com., 1980-82, S.H.A.F.T.E.D. Tax Repeal Com., 1982 C.H.I.C. Polit. Edn. Com., 1977—, People Against Tax Hikes Com., 1983—. Served with USN, 1942-45, USAF, 1950-53; Korea; comdr. USCG Aux., 1959-60. Mem. Am. Legion (comdr. 1947-48, mem. nat. conv. disting. guest com. 1947-52), DAV, VFW, Am. Security Council (nat. adviser 1966—). Author: Run, Big Sam, Run, 1976; The Girls on Top, 1978; Big Brother Bureaucracy, The Cause and the Cure, 1979; Kiddieland West, 1980; Games Politicians Play: How to Clean Up Their Act, 1981; A Very C.H.I.C. President, 1981; How to Clean Up Our Act, 1982. Home: 301A Misty Isle Ln Las Vegas NV 89107 Office: PO Box 26073 Las Vegas NV 89102

CAWOOD, ELIZABETH JEAN, public relations counselor; b. Santa Maria, Calif., Jan. 6, 1947; d. John Stephen and Gertrude Margaret (Shelton) Dille; m. Neil F. Cawood, Jan. 4, 1975; 1 son, Nathan Patrick. B.A., Whitworth Coll., 1968. Dir. pub. info. Inland Empire Goodwill Industries, Spokane, 1967-72; adminstrv. asst. Northwest Assn. Rehab. Industries, Seattle, 1973-74; owner Cawood Communications, Eugene, Oreg., 1974—; pub. relations counselor in field. Bd. dirs. Eugene Action Forum, 1981—, Birth-to-Three, Eugene, 1982—, ARC, Lane County, Oreg., 1983—; treas. LWV Cen. Lane County, Eugene, 1979. Recipient Disting. Leadership award Northwest Assn. Rehab. Industries, Pub. Relations Achievement award Goodwill Industries Am., 1971. Mem. Eugene Pvt. Industries Council (chmn. 1979-81, dir. 1981-83), Nat. Rehab. Assn. (life; state pres. 1980-81), Women in Communications, Inc. (Eugene Profl. Chpt. pres. 1981-83), Bus. Owner's Network Eugene (chmn. 1980-81), Profl. Women's Network Oreg. (dir. 1982), Counselor's Acad. Pub. Relations Soc. Am. (accredited), Eugene Area C. of C. (co-chmn. Econ. Devel. Com. 1982-83). Presbyterian. Editors Work-Oriented Rehabilitation Dictionary and Synonyms (WORDS), 2d edit., 1979; editor Directory of Rehabilitation Acronyms (DORA), 1977; INTERCOM; Family Communicator, 1979-80; Oregon Focus, 1980-81. Office: 144 East 14th Eugene OR 97401

CAYETANO, BENJAMIN JEROME, state senator; b. Honolulu, Nov. 14, 1939; s. Bonifacio Marcos and Eleanor (Infante) C.; B.A., UCLA, 1968; J.D., Loyola U., 1971; m. Lorraine Gyeco, Sept. 20, 1958; children—Brandon, Janeen, Samantha. Admitted to Hawaii bar, 1971; practiced in, Honolulu, 1971—; mem. Hawaii Senate, 1978—; bar examiner Supreme Ct. State Hawaii, 1976-80; adv. U. Hawaii Law Rev., 1981—; mem. Hawaii Ho. of Reps., 1974-78. Mem. bd. regents Chaminade U., 1981—. Democrat. Office: 33 S King St Suite 401 Honolulu HI 96813*

CAZIER, JAMES HENRY, mining engineer; b. Wells, Nev., Nov. 23, 1912; s. Henry Hallowell and Neva (Dewar) C.; B.S. in Mining Engring., U. Nev., 1935; m. Dorothy Lynton, Oct. 5, 1940; children—Barry J., Stanley W. Engr. at various locations Internat. Smelting & Refining Co., Salt Lake City, 1935-41; asst. gen. supt., then gen. supt. Lexington Mining Co., Neihart, Mont.; gen. supt. Callahan Consol. Mines, Inc., Wallace, Ida., 1941-43; supervising engr. mine loan sect. RFC, Phoenix, also Salt Lake City, 1943-48; gen. supt. Goodwin Mining Co., Bagdad, Ariz., 1948-49, Bagdad Copper Corp., 1949-52; ind. mine operator Bagdad, 1952-56; mining mgr. Anschutz Drilling Co., Inc., Denver, 1956-60; pres., dir. Webb Resources, Inc., 1961-68, mgr. mining div., Denver, 1975-79; mining cons., Denver, 1961—; v.p. Black Pearl Mining Co. Registered engr., Nev., Ariz., Colo., Idaho. Served to lt. USNR, 1944-46. Mem. AIME, Colo. Mining Assn., Am. Inst. Profl. Geologists, Rocky Mountain Association of Geologists. Democrat. Club: Petroleum. Home: 2817 S Lansing Way Aurora CO 80014 Office: 1645 Court Pl Denver CO 80202

CAZIER, STANFORD, university president; b. Nephi, Utah, June 11, 1930; B.S. in Philosophy, U. Utah, 1952, M.A. in History, 1956; Ph.D. in History, U. Wis., 1964; m. Shirley Anderson, 1952; children—David, John, Paul. Reader, U. Utah, 1954-56; teaching asst. U. Wis., 1957-58, research asst., 1959; instr. Bronx Community Coll., 1959-60; instr. Utah State U., 1960-62, asst. prof. history, 1962-67, assoc. prof., 1968-69, prof., 1969-71, asst. to pres., 1968-69, chmn. dept. history, 1969, vice provost, 1969-71; Am. Council on Edn. fellow in acad. adminstrn. N.Y. U., 1967-68; pres. Calif. State U.-Chico, 1971-79, Utah State U.-Logan, 1979—; chmn. council of pres.'s Calif. State Univs. and Colls., 1978-79, mem. exec. com. council pres., 1976-79. Served as ensign USN, 1952-53. Named Tchr. of Yr., Robin's award, 1966; Danforth Found. assoc., 1966—. Mem. Am. Assn. Higher Edn., Am. Assn. State Colls. and Univs., Am. Council Edn., Nat. Assn. State Univs. and Land Grant Colls., Western Coll. Assn. (exec. com.), Phi Kappa Phi, Phi Alpha Theta. Contbr. articles to profl. publs.; author: Student Discipline in Higher Education, 1973; bibliography editor history div. Am. Quar., 1968-71. Office: Office of Pres Utah State U Logan UT 84321

CECCARELLI, FRANK EDWARD, JR., physician; b. Bronx, N.Y., Aug. 29, 1927; s. Frank Edward and Agnes (Haddock) C.; B.A., Bowdoin Coll., 1951; M.D., N.Y. U., 1951; m. Mary C. Colletta, Dec. 27, 1957; children—Nance, Joan, Wellington. Intern, New Haven Hosp., 1951-52, resident in surgery and urology, 1952-53; resident Tripler Army Hosp., 1955-57, Brooke Hosp., 1958-61; commd. 1st lt. U.S. Army, 1953, advanced through grades to col., 1968; staff, Korea, 1953-55, Tripler Army Hosp., 1955-57, 67-71, Brooke Hosp., 1958-63, 71-73, Gorgas Hosp., C.Z., 1963-66, ret., 1973; pvt. practice urology, Kailua, Hawaii, 1973—; chief staff Castle Meml. Hosp.; mem. staff Children's Hosp., Queens Hosp. Decorated Bronze Star, D.S.M.; Orden de Vasco Nunez de Balboa (Panama); diplomate Am. Bd. Urology. Mem. Am. Urol. Assn., Societe International d'Urologie, Am. Acad. Pediatrics, Socied d'Urologia de Chile. Contbr. articles to profl. jours. Home: 46-002 Nana Pl Kaneohe HI 96744 Office: 30 Aulike St Suite 602 Kailua HI 96734

CECILIO, CATALINO BAUTISTA, civil engineer; b. Legaspi City, Philippines, Nov. 7, 1937; s. Ramon Santo Tomas and Inocencia (Bautista) C.; came to U.S., 1968, naturalized, 1973; student U. Philippines, 1954-57; B.S. in Civil Engring., Mapua Inst. Tech., 1962; continuing edn. U. Calif., Berkeley, 1970-71, Calif. State U., Sacramento, 1976, U. Calif., Davis, 1977, Colo. State U., 1978; m. Consolacion Ocampo Acuna, Apr. 27, 1963; children—Cielito, Carmelo, Carlino. Resident engr. Western Steel, Inc., Manila, 1963; jr. civil engr. Nat. Power Corp., Manila, 1964-68; computer draftsman Pacific Gas & Electric Co., San Francisco, 1968, engring. designer, 1969-71, sr. engring. designer, 1972, civil engr., 1972-78, sr. civil engr., 1978—, head hydrologic engring. unit, 1976—; proposals reviewer NSF, 1979, 80; participant profl. confs.; hydrology cons. Registered profl. engr., Calif.; registered civil engr., Philippines. Mem. ASCE, U.S. Com. on Large Dams, Pacific Coast Electric Assn., Filipino-Am. Soc. Architects and Engrs. (bd. dirs.). Republican. Roman Catholic. Club: KC. Contbr. articles on hydraulics and hydrology to profl. publs. and NRC manual on dams. Co-developer Am. Nat. Standard, standards for determining design basis flooding at power reactor sites, 1976, 81. Home: 931 Park Pacifica Ave Pacifica CA 94044 Office: Pacific Gas & Electric Co 77 Beale St San Francisco CA 94106

CEDER, ELAYNE BARBARA, film production designer; b. Brookline, Mass., July 23, 1946; d. Arthur and Mollie G. (Fienman) C.; B.A. in Architecture, Case Western Res. U., 1967; M.A. in Environ. Design, UCLA, 1969. Prodn. designer, art dir. motion pictures for TV and theatrical releases, Los Angeles, 1971—, films include Firefox, The Conversation, Every Which Way But Loose, When A Stranger Calls, The Jayne Mansfield Story; assoc. studios including MGM, Paramount, Warner Bros., Columbia; assoc. producer Marvin and Tige, 1983; spl. studies cons. in city planning, Los Angeles and Inglewood, Calif., 1970-72. Accredited art dir., Hollywood Motion Picture Assn. Mem. Soc. Motion Picture Art Dirs., Local 876, Acad. TV Arts and Scis., Acad. Motion Picture Arts and Scis., Synagogue for Performing Arts. Jewish. Home: Los Angeles CA

CEDZO, KAREN LUCILLE, public relations executive; b. Milw., Dec. 10, 1950; d. Joseph Martin and Florence Lucille (Lonski) C.; m. J. Harvey Wieler, June 5, 1979. B.A., U. Wis.-Milw., 1973, M.A., 1975. Ins. agt. Equitable Life Assurance Soc., Milw., 1973-74; reporter, anchor, news dir. No. TV Inc., Fairbanks, Alaska, 1976-78; co-owner, prin. No. Info. Services, Fairbanks, 1978-81; dir. pub. affairs U. Alaska, Fairbanks, 1979—; cons. in field. Co-chmn. pub. relations com. Arctic Winter Games, 1981-82; bd. dirs. Citizens for Mgmt. of Alaska's Lands, 1978-79; mem. Alaska Statehood Day Com., Fairbanks Festival '84. Mem. Pub. Relations Soc. Am., Greater Fairbanks C. of C. Club: Tahana Valley Sportsmen's Assn. Creator radio series: I Didn't Know That, carried statewide in Alaska. Home: PO Box 60316 Fairbanks AK 99706 Office: U Alaska 704 B Gruening Bldg Fairbanks AK 99701

CELANO, JAMES FRED, assn. exec.; b. Newark, Aug. 27, 1930; s. James Vincent and Thelma Mary (Pilone) C.; A.A., Los Angeles City Coll., 1963; student Calif. State U., 1965-74; B.A. in Mgmt., U. Redlands, 1983; m. Bernadette Clara Skolny, Nov. 15, 1958; children—Peter, Michael, Christopher. Ry. express, parcel post clk. May Co., Los Angeles, 1949-50; delivery man Calif. Trimmings Co., Los Angeles, 1950-51; service rep. Automobile Club of So. Calif., Highland Park, Calif., 1959-62, travel tng. instr., 1962-64, supr., asst. mgr., 1964-69, asst. dist. mgr., Long Beach, Calif., 1969-70, dist. mgr., Redlands (Calif.) Dist. Office, 1970-79, San Bernardino Dist Office, 1979—. Mem., Redlands City Traffic Commn., 1973-83; Eucharistic minister Sacred Heart Roman Cath. Ch., Redlands, 1978-81; pres. United Way of Redlands, 1976; mem. San Bernardino Mayor's Traffic Safety Adv. Com., 1979—, chmn., 1980-81; bd. dirs. Boys Club of Redlands, 1976-79, Boys Club of San Bernardino, 1981—, Redlands YMCA, 1973-76, Redlands Community Scholarship Found.; corp. body Redlands Community Hosp., 1976-81; hon. police officer Redlands Police Dept. Served with USAF, 1951-59. Named Redlands Man of Yr., 1979. Mem. Redlands C. of C. (1st v.p. 1979), San Bernardino C. of C. (dir. 1981—, v.p. 1982-83). Republican. Roman Catholic. Clubs: Toastmasters (pres. 1970, Able Toastmaster 1975), Elks, K.C. (rec. sec. Redlands council 1971-76), Kiwanis (pres. Redlands Noon club 1978-79, bd. dirs. San Bernardino club 1983—). Home: 1417 Pleasant View Dr Redlands CA 92373 Office: 808 W 2d St San Bernardino CA 92410

CELEKETIC, RICHARD RADOMIR, upholstery manufacturing executive; b. Belgrade, Yugoslavia, June 15, 1945; s. Zivko and Tomislava (Slepcevic) C.; m. Jean Richie, Jan. 23, 1966; 1 dau., Julie L. B.A. in Bus. Mgmt., Kingsway Coll. (Ont., Can.). Mgr. purchasing, personnel and prodn. control Calif. Prints, Inc. div. Udico Corp., 1966-69; asst. mgr. purchasing Barth and Dreyfuss, Los Angeles, 1969; ops. mgr. Perfect Fit Industries, Zimmer Assocs., Commerce, Calif., 1969-70; v.p. mfg., Ampro Corp., Anaheim, Calif., 1971-80; gen. mgr. Concel Urethane Foam, Anaheim, 1976-80; corp. v.p. mfg. Reliance Upholstery Supply Co., Gardena, Calif., 1980—; dir. On Industries, Inc.; cons. on plastics and vinyls, import activities. Republican. Adventist.

CELENTANO, FRANCIS MICHAEL, artist; b. N.Y.C., May 25, 1928; s. Michael Anthony and Rafaela (Valentino) C.; B.A., NYU, 1951, M.A. in Art History, 1957. Lectr., C.W. Post Coll., L.I., N.Y., 1961-63, N.Y. Inst. Tech., Old Westbury, N.Y., 1965-66; from asso. prof. to prof. Sch. Art, U. Wash., Seattle, 1966—; one-man exhbns. include Foster/White Gallery, Seattle, 1971, 73, 75, 78, Howard Wise Gallery, N.Y.C., 1963, Diane Gilson Gallery, Seattle, 1981, 82, Fountain Gallery, Portland, Oreg., 1983; represented in permanent collections at Mus. of Modern Art, N.Y.C., Albright-Knox Mus., Buffalo, Seattle Art Mus. Fulbright scholar, Rome, 1958. Office: Sch of Art Univ of Wash Seattle WA 98195

CELLER, BEATRICE JOHANNA, state administrator; b. Los Angeles, Sept. 14, 1939; d. Joseph and Dorothy H. (Vorhaus) Hanfling; m. John Cornell Celler, Feb. 22, 1966; children—Leslie, Brian. B.S. cum laude in Polit. Sci./Langs., U. Calif.-Berkeley, 1961; M.S. in Pub. Adminstrn., U. Denver, 1982. Cert. tchr., Calif. TV prodn. asst. Wolper Prodns., Los Angeles, Candid Camera, N.Y., 1963-68; bilingual edn. tchr. Los Angeles Sch. Dist., 1969-73; ombudsman labor, employment Office of Gov. of Colo., 1975-77; employer relations dir,. Colo. Dept. Labor and Employment, 1977-81; dir. bus. info. ctr. Colo. Dept. Regulatory Agys., 1981—; tchr., moderator Smokenders, 1977—. Adv. bd. Colo. Displaced Homemakers. Mem. Am. Soc. Pub. Adminstrn. Democrat. Jewish.

CENARRUSA, PETE THOMAS, state ofcl.; b. Carey, Idaho, Dec. 16, 1917, s. Joseph M. and Ramona G. (Gardoqui) C.; B.S., U. Idaho; m. Ereda Coates, Oct. 27, 1947; 1 son, Joe E. Tchr. high sch., 1940-41, 49-51; mem. Idaho Ho. of Reps., 1950-67, speaker, 1963-67; sec. state Idaho, 1967—; rancher, 1950—; pres. Biskey Land and Livestock Co. Served with USMC, 1942-46, USMCR, 1947-59. Republican. Roman Catholic. Clubs: Kiwanis, Elks. Office: State Capitol Boise ID 83720*

CERF, MILTON, insurance executive; b. San Francisco, Sept. 27, 1928; s. Alvin Edgar and Ida Pauline (Lockwood) C.; m. Adriene Carbone, Aug. 11, 1954; children—James Milton, Dee Dee Reynolds. B.A. in Phys. and Health Edn., San Francisco State U., 1953. Cert. tchr., adminstr., Calif.; C.L.U. Asst. prof., asst. camp dir. San Francisco State U., 1950-53; athletic dir., coach Healdsburg (Calif.) Jr. High Sch., 1954-56; supt. Healdsburg Recreation Dept., 1955-56; head counselor social scis. and phys. edn. depts. Calistoga (Calif.) High Sch., 1956-58; math. tchr., coach Carlmont (Calif.) High Sch., 1958-60; pres. chmn. bd. Calif. Pacific Ins. Services Inc., San Rafael, Calif., 1966—; coach, instr. phys. edn. classes Sonoma State U., 1979-81. Recipient Bankers Life Iowa Achievement award, 1960; Sonoma State U. Mentor award, 1980. Mem. Marin Assn. Life Underwriters, Nat. Assn. Life Underwriters (Builder Contbr. award 1979), Gen. Agts. and Mgrs. Assn., Am. Football Assn. Contbr. articles to profl. publs. Home: 4737 Paradise Dr Tiburon CA 94920 Office: 555 Northgate Dr San Rafael CA 94903

CESERANI, JOHN EDWARD, metallurgical engineer; b. Butte, Mont., Dec. 4, 1938; s. Victor George and Ercel Josephine (Risto) C.; m. Geralynn Rae Alega; children—Kimberly, Rebecca, Victor, Paul, Brad, Ranee. B.S. in Metall. Engring., Mont. Coll. Mineral Sci. and Tech., 1963; M.B.A., Gonzaga U., Spokane, Wash., 1971. Metall. engr. Am Smelting and Refining Co., Selby, Calif., East Helena, Mont., 1963-68; with Kaiser Aluminum and Chem. Corp., 1968-73; foreman, Precision Castparts Corp., Portland, Oreg., 1973—, supr., 1973-75, prodn. mgr., 1976-78, v.p. in charge prodn., corp. officer exec. com., 1983—. Pres., East Helena Jaycees, 1966, govt. affairs chmn., 1967; active Spokane (Wash.) Jaycees, 1968. Served with USMCR, 1958-64. Recipient Spark of Quarter for State Key Man, Jaycees of Mont. and Spokane. Mem. Am. Soc. of Metals, Soc. of Mfg. Engrs., AIME, Am. Mgmt. Assn. Republican. Roman Catholic. Clubs: Pleasant Valley Golf, Portland. Home: 4564 SW Trail Rd Tualatin OR 97062 Office: 4600 SE Harney Dr Portland OR 97206

CETRONE, LINDA LUCILLE, photographer; b. Billings, Mont., March 11, 1942; dau. Wilson Royal Topp and Margaret Elizabeth McKinnon; m. Victor Eugene Cetrone, Aug. 1961; children—Michael Lee, Mark Jeffrey. Grad. Dale Carnegie course in human relations, 1976; student Winona Profl. Photography Sch., 1977, Dale Carnegie Mgt. Semminar, 1980. Co-owner, mgr., photographer, Cetrone Studio, 1975-83, McThrifty Studio, 1983—. Recipient 2d pl. award Mont., 1981. Mem. Profl. Photographers Am., Mont Profl. Photographers Assn. Democrat. Home: 945 Alderson Ave Billings MT 59102 Office: 2419 Broadwater Billings MT 59102

CETTI, WILLIAM CHARLES, utility manager; b. Phoenix, June 5, 1945; s. Fred Robert and Mary Elizabeth (Baker) C.; B.S. in Advt., Ariz. State U., 1972, M.B.A., 1978; m. Mary Jane Stone, Oct. 11, 1963; children—Sherri Kay, William Robert. Mgt. trainee Gen. Electric Co., Phoenix, 1967-72; customer service rep. Ariz. Public Service Co., Globe, 1972-74, sr. public safety rep., Phoenix, 1974-79, Sedona Area mgr., 1979-82, Prescott customer Service supr., 1982-83, Payson dist. mgr., 1983—. Chmn. Citizens Against a Nat. Monument in Sedona; adv. bd. No. Ariz. U. Safety Programs; bd. dirs. Keep Sedona Beautiful ; Yauapai Coll. dist. adv. bd.; charter mem. Payson Indsl. Authority. Cert. safety profl. and hazard control mgr.; named outstanding loss control profl. S.W. Safgty Congress, 1979. Mem. Am. Soc. Safety Engrs. (profl.; pres. Ariz. chpt. 1978-79), Cert. Safety Profls. of the Americas (dir.). Republican. Club: Rotary (dir. Sedona club), Sedona-Oak Creek. Home: 1108 N Camelot Ln Payson AZ 85541 Office: 613 S Beeline Hwy Payson AZ 85541

CHABAFY, ARPAD ANTON, architect; b. Gyor, Hungary; s. Jeno and Theresia (Strouhall) Csabafy; student Tech. U. Budapest; M.Arch., Tech. U. Zurich; degree in urban planning U. Montreal. Design architect, Montreal, 1962; architect Rossmoor Corp., 1963-66; design architect Alexander Ewing & Assos., Princeton, N.J.; pres., prin. Arpad Chabafy Architect, Inc., Newport Beach, Calif.; pres. The Chabafy Co. Inc. Mem. Nat. Republican Congressional Com. Mem. AIA, Soc. Am. Registered Architects, Engrs. and Architects Inst. Office: 2418 MacArthur Blvd Newport Beach CA 92660

CHACON, ANGEL ESPINOZA, safety consultant; b. Morenci, Ariz., Dec. 16, 1950; s. Angel NaFaarte and Lily (Espinoza) C.; m. Rose Mary Huggins, June 8, 1969; children—Monica Lynn, Mathew Jeremy. A.A in Bus., Eastern Ariz. Coll., 1977, A.A.S. in Sci., 1977; B.A. in Edn., U. Ariz., 1979; M.A. in Mgmt., U. Phoenix, 1983. Electrician, Phelps Dodge Mining Corp., Morenci, 1970-78; tchr. secondary edn. Sunnyside High Sch., Tucson, 1979-80; police officer planning and research bur. Phoenix Police Dept., 1980-81; safety cons. Ariz. Compensation Fund, 1981—. Past bd. dirs. League for United Latin Am. Citizens; bd. dirs. Desert Search and Rescue; mem. Chicanos Por La Causa. Served with Ariz. N.G., 1970-76. Recipient letter of commendation Phoenix Police Dept. Mem. Am. Soc. Safety Engrs. Democrat. Presbyterian. Home: 2058 W Hazelwood Pkwy Phoenix AZ 85015 Office: 7141 N 51st Ave Glendale AZ 85301

CHADEY, HENRY FRANK, museum director, educator; b. Superior, Wyo., Feb. 20, 1924; s. Frank and Anna (Glogovsek) C.; m. Helen Puts, Aug. 3, 1957; children—Michael, Katherine, Mary Jo, Jeanne. B.A., U. Wyo., 1949; M.A., 1955. Tchr., Reliance (Wyo.) dist. No. 7, 1949-56; sch. supt. Sweetwater (Wyo.) dist. No. 7, 1956-59; asst. supt. public instrn. Wyo. Dept. Edn., Cheyenne, 1959-61; prin. schs., Glenrock, Wyo., 1961-62, Rock Springs (Wyo.) High Sch., 1962-67; mus. dir. Sweetwater County Hist. Mus., Green River, Wyo., 1967—; instr. Western Wyo. Coll., 1967-75. Adviser, Sweetwater County Recreation Bd., 1967—, Sweetwater County Bd. Edn., 1967—. Served with AUS, 1943-46, ETO, 1950-51, Korea. Mem. Wyo. Secondary Sch. Prins. Assn. (pres. 1956), Wyo. Sch. Bd. Assn., (dir. 1977—, pres. 1980-81), Am. Assn. Mus. Am. Assn. State and Local History, Mt. Plains Mus. Assn., Colo.-Wyo. Assn., Sweetwater County Hist. Soc. (pres. 1958), Wyo. State Hist. Soc. (pres. 1972-73), Slovene Nat. Benefit Soc. Democrat. Roman Catholic. Club: Lions (pres., 1969, 80-82).

CHADWICK, CHARLES ROBB, bank executive; b. Seattle, May 17, 1923; s. Charles Robb and Ernestine (Wright) C.; m. Marion Kerr, Apr. 14, 1945; children—Robin Ann Sieber, Marcy Jean Woodruff. B.A., U. Wash., 1943. Br. mgr. Rainier Bank, Seattle, 1968-69; credit adminstr., 1969-74, sr. credit officer, 1975-81, mgr. comml. banking div., 1981—; pres. Puget Sound chpt. Robert Morris Assocs.; trustee Wash. Student Loan Guaranty Assn. Served to lt. USMC, 1943-46. Club: Wash. Athletic.

CHADWICK, JERRY CLAIR, management consultant; b. Charles City, Iowa, Apr. 8, 1946; s. Gilbert Clarence and Joyce Mae (Ballhagen) C.; m. Kirby Ann, June 7, 1969. B.A., St. Ambrose Coll., 1970; postgrad. LaSalle U., 1972, U. Iowa, 1970. Advt., display asst. Sears & Roebuck Co., Iowa City, 1970-72; zone exec. Circle K. Corp., Phoenix, 1972-75; v.p. PCA Mgmt. Corp., Phoenix, 1975-79; pres., dir. Chadwick & Einig Ltd., Chandler, Ariz., (formerly Town & Country Mgmt. Corp., Higley, Ariz.), 1979—; owner Tanimara Arabians Ranch; cons. in field; dir. numerous corps.; fin. advisor Cherokee Tool Co., 1976. Named Outstanding Zone Exec., Circle K. Corp., 1974; cert. mgmt. cons. Mem. C. of C., Am. Inst. Profl. Cons., St. Ambrose Alumni Assn., Arabian Horse Registry, Internat. Arabian Horse Assn., Ariz. Arabian Horse Assn. Republican. Roman Catholic. Clubs: San Marcos Country, Optimist, K.C. Editor: Farm & Ranch Fin. Planning, 1977-79. Address: 18703 E Via Del Oro Higley AZ 85236

CHAFFEE, PAUL STANLEY, veterinarian; b. Port Huron, Mich., Jan. 23, 1928; s. Walter Henry and Leland Elizabeth (Green) C.; A.S., Port Huron Jr. Coll., 1949; B.S., Mich. State U., D.V.M., 1953; m. Rae Ann Kish, Oct. 16, 1975; children—David P., Daniel P., Richard P., Rob P., Brad W., Cynthia A., Denise J., Mark S. Intern, Peigh Animal Hosp., 1953-54; pvt. practice veterinary medicine McKinley Pet Hosp., 1955-65; veterinarian Roeding Park Zoo, Fresno, Calif., 1960—, dir., 1965—. Served with M.C., U.S. Army, 1947-49. Mem. Am. Assn. Zool. Parks and Aquariums (pres.), Am. Assn. Zoo Veterinarians (pres., sec.). Club: Rotary (Fresno). Office: 894 W Belmont Ave Fresno CA 93728

CHAFFEE, WILLIAM GALBRAITH, JR., physician; b. Wilkes-Barre, Pa., June 24, 1933; s. William Galbraith and Sarah (Ahlborn) C.; B.A., Princeton U., 1955; M.D., Cornell U. Med. Coll., 1962; m. Grace E. Elmendorf, Mar. 3, 1962; children—Tonya, Christopher G. Intern, San Francisco Gen. Hosp., 1962-63, resident, 1964-65; resident U. Calif. Hosps., San Francisco, 1963-64, 1965-66; practice medicine specializing in internal medicine, Berkeley, Calif., 1966-72, Phoenix, 1972—; mem. active staff St. Joseph's Hosp., Good Samaritan Hosp., Phoenix, asst. prof. medicine U. Calif., San Francisco, 1969-72. Bd. dirs. Maricopa County div. Am. Heart Assn., 1973-80, pres., 1978-79. Served with U.S. Army, 1955-57. Diplomate Am. Bd. Internal Medicine. Fellow ACP, Am. Coll. Clin. Pharmacology; mem. AMA, Ariz. Med. Assn., Am. Soc. Internal Medicine, Ariz. Soc. Internal Medicine (pres. 1981-82), Assn. Acad. Clin. Toxicology, AAAS, Calif. Acad. Medicine. Republican. Office: 2200 N 3rd St Phoenix AZ 85004

CHAFFIN, DANIEL SUMNER, physician; b. Boston, Apr. 12, 1929; s. Ira and Miriam Rebecca (Cohan) C.; A.B. magna cum laude, Harvard U., 1950; M.D., Boston U., 1955; m. Sarah Ann Frank, June 9, 1954; children—Thomas Frank, Nancy Marie, David Bernard. Intern in medicine Mass. Meml. Hosps., Boston, 1955-56, resident in preventive medicine, 1956-57; resident in psychiatry, Langley Porter Neuropsychiat. Inst., San Francisco, 1959-62; asst. clin. prof. psychiatry, U. Calif. Med. Center, San Francisco, 1962-66; practice medicine specializing in psychiatry and forensic medicine, San Francisco, 1962—; ind. med. examiner, div. indsl. accidents, State of Calif., 1966-79. Served with M.C., USAF, 1957-59. Recipient various research grants. Diplomate Am. Bd. Psychiatry and Neurology. Fellow Am. Psychiat. Assn.; mem. AMA, San Francisco Med. Soc., No. Calif. Psychiat. Soc. Condr. research on toxic effects of psychotropic drugs, psychiat. wards in gen. med. hosps., hypnosis with hypertensive patients; lectr., contbr. articles in field to med. jours. Office: 2000 Van Ness Ave Suite 301 San Francisco CA 94109

CHAIT, ROBERT JAY, corporate tax attorney; b. Newark, Mar. 22, 1940; s. Nathan and Sophie (Gitlin) C.; m. Arlene Louise Sacks, June 12, 1970. B.S. in Econs., Wharton Sch. Fin. and Commerce, U. Pa., 1962; J.D., N.Y.U., 1965. Bar: Calif., N.C., N.Y. Pension counsel Litton Industries, Beverly Hills, Calif., 1972-74, assoc. tax counsel, pension counsel, 1974-76, assoc. tax, employee benefit counsel, 1976-79, corp. tax, employee benefit counsel, 1978-81, corp. tax counsel, gen. counsel investment com., 1981—. Mem. ABA, Calif. Bar Assn., Los Angeles Bar Assn. Office: 360 N Crescent Dr Beverly Hills CA 90210

CHALFANT, KENNETH PAUL, electronics co. exec.; b. Colorado Springs, Colo., July 31, 1953; s. Harry Ellis and Maxine Eleanor (Blunt) C.; student pub. schs., Colorado Springs; m. Rosemary B. Chandler, May 26, 1979. Technician, Maytronics Co., Colorado Springs, 1971, Western Sci. Co., Colorado Springs 1972, cons. engr. Electric Co., Colorado Springs, 1971—; founder, owner, mgr. Chalfant Research & Devel. Co., Colorado Springs, 1974—; cons. in field. Hewlett Packard grantee, 1967-69; Tektronix Co. grantee, 1972; Bell Telephone Co. grantee, 1970; U. Colo. grantee, 1968. Mem. Florence Pioneer Mus. Hist. Soc. Office: 2842 N Institute St Colorado Springs CO 80907

CHALL, LEO PAUL, sociologist, publisher; b. Daugavpils, Latvia, July 28, 1921; s. Paul and Rose Chall; came to U.S., 1937, naturalized, 1943; B.A., Ohio State U., 1948, M.A., 1952; married. Research asst. sociology Bur. Applied Social Research, Columbia U., N.Y.C., 1950-53; founding editor Sociol. Abstracts, N.Y.C., 1953—, pres., 1962—; pres. Essay Press, Inc., N.Y.C., 1957—; lectr. Bklyn. Coll., 1953-61, instr., 1961; publisher Lang. and Lang. Behavior Abstracts, Reading Abstracts; asso. editor Jour. Sex Research, 1961-70. Mem. New York County Democratic Com., 1962. Served with AUS, 1942-46. Fellow Am. Sociol. Assn.; mem. Soc. Study Social Problems. Contbr. articles to profl. jours. Home: 6002 Beaumont Ave LaJolla CA 92037 Office: PO Box 22206 San Diego CA 92122

CHALMERS, DONALD LEDLEY, automobile dealer; b. Tulsa, May 4, 1948; s. James S. and Marjorie A. (Cohenhour). B.S. in Bus., Okla. State U., 1970. Zone mgr. Ford Motor Co., Houston, 1970-75; sales mgr. Gillespie Ford, San Antonio, 1975-77; gen. mgr., v.p., Sound Ford, Renton, Wash., 1977—; ptnr. Loberg Olds, GMC, Toyota, Renton, Wash., Spokane Lincoln/Mercury, Mazda (Wash.), Sound Mazda, Renton, Wash.; pres. Pacific Automotive Products, Renton, 1977—; v.p., dir. Lariat Life Ins. Co., Renton, 1977—. Recipient Ford Motor Co. disting. dealer's award, 1977. Mem. Wash. State Auto Dealers Assn., Nat. Auto Assn. Renton C. of C. Office: 750 Rainier Ave S Renton WA 98055

CHALMERS, RICHARD HAMILTON, JR., mech. engr.; b. Riverside, Calif., June 3, 1931; s. Richard Hamilton and Margaret Viola (Bradshaw) C.; B.S., Calif. State Poly. U., 1959; postgrad. San Diego State U., 1970-74; m. Lois May Jensen, Apr. 14, 1965; children—Sheryl Ann, Lora Lynn, Richard Hamilton III. Engr., U.S. Naval Ocean Systems Center, San Diego, 1959—, supr. III 1972—. Served with USN, 1950-54. Mem. Soc. Automotive Engrs., ASME, Inst. Environ. Sci. (v.p. region IV 1980-82). Home: 1430 Savoy Circle San Diego CA 92107 Office: US Naval Ocean Systems Center Code 9331 San Diego CA 92152

CHAMBERLAIN, JOYCE ANN, management consultant; b. Denver, Sept. 3, 1942; d. Kenneth Lee and Delores Ann (Rik) C. Student U. Calif.-Berkeley, 1960-62; B.A., UCLA, 1966. Mgr. data processing, dept. real estate UCLA, 1966-68; cons. Peat, Marwick, Mitchell, Los Angeles, 1968-70; supr. systems and programming Larwin Co., Los Angeles, 1970-75; asst. dir. bus. data processing U. So. Calif., Los Angeles, 1975; mgr. systems mainenance and control Mission Equities Corp., Los Angeles, 1975-76; mgr. systems analysis Telecredit, Inc., Los Angeles, 1976-78; sr. cons. Gottfried Cons., Los Angeles, 1978-79; owner, operator Chamberlain & Assos., data processing and mgmt. cons., Los Angeles, 1979—. Mem. UCLA Alumni Assn., World Future Soc., Friends of KCET, Assn. Systems Mgmt., Assn. Humanisitic Psychology, Mensa.

CHAMBERLAIN, OWEN, nuclear physicist; b. San Francisco, July 10, 1920; A.B. (Cramer fellow), Dartmouth Coll., 1941; Ph.D., U. Chgo., 1949; m. 1943 (div. 1978); 4 children; m. June Steingart, 1980. Instr. physics U. Calif., Berkeley, 1948-50, asst. prof., 1950-54, asso. prof., 1954-58, prof., 1958—; civilian physicist Manhattan Dist., Berkeley, Los Alamos, 1942-46; Guggenheim fellow, 1957-58; Loeb lectr. at Harvard U., 1959. Recipient Nobel prize (with Emilio Segré) for physics, for discovery anti-proton, 1959. Fellow Am. Phys. Soc., Am. Acad. Arts and Scis.; mem. Nat. Acad. Scis. Address: Physics Dept U Calif Berkeley CA 94720*

CHAMBERLAIN, RICHARD DENNIS, retail company executive; b. Oroville, Calif., July 8, 1940; s. Ellis Arthur and Addie Vesta (Stiles) C.; m. Ann Burden Thomas, Jan. 25, 1969; children—John, Susan. B.S., Calif. State U., 1963. Retail trainee Emporium-Capwell Co., Oakland, Calif., 1963-66, mgr., N.Y.C., 1967-68, buyer, Oakland, 1968-70; mgr. Morris Dept. Store, Delano, Calif., 1970-75; owner, mgr. City of Paris Dept. Store, Oroville, 1976—. Mem. bus. adv. com. Calif. State U., Chico, 1982—; trustee Med. Ctr. Hosp., 1983—. Mem. Jr. Dept. Stores of Calif., Oroville C. of C. Republican. Congregationalist. Clubs: Mason, Rotary, Commonwealth (San Francisco). Office: City of Paris Dept Store PO Box 1511 Oroville CA 95965

CHAMBERLIN, EUGENE KEITH, historian, educator; b. Gustine, Calif., Feb. 15, 1916; s. Charles Eugene and Anina Marguerite (Williams) C.; B.A. in History, U. Calif. at Berkeley, 1939, M.A., 1940, Ph.D., 1949; m. Margaret Rae Jackson, Sept. 1, 1940; children—Linda, Thomas, Rebecca, Adrienne (dec.), Eric. Tchr. Spanish, Latin, Lassen Union High Sch. and Jr. Coll., Susanville, Calif., 1941-43; tchr. history Elk Grove (Calif.) Joint Union High Sch., 1943-45; teaching asst. history U. Calif., Berkeley, 1946-48; instr. history Mont. State U., Missoula, 1948-51, asst. prof., 1951-54; asst. prof. to prof. San Diego City Coll., 1954-78; vis. prof. history Mont. State Coll., Bozeman, summer 1951, U. Calif. Extension, 1965-68, San Diego State Coll., 1965-68, others; instr., coordinator history lectures San Diego Community Colls.-TV, 1969—; prof. San Diego Miramar Coll., 1978-83, part-time, 1983—; prof. history San Diego Mesa Coll., 1983—. Huntington Library-Rockefeller Found. grantee, 1952; Fulbright-Hays grantee, Peru, 1982; recipient merit award Congress of History San Diego County, 1978; Outstanding Educator award, San Diego City Coll., 1970. Mem. AAUP (various coms., nat. council 1967-70, pres. Calif. conf. 1968-70), San Diego County Congress of History (pres. 1976-77, newsletter editor 1977-78), Am. Hist. Assn. (Beveridge-Dunning com. 1982—), Pacific Coast Council on Latin-Am. Studies, Cultural Assn. of the Californias, The Westerners (Calafia chpt.), E. Clampus Vitus (chpt. pres. 1972-73, dir. 1983—, dir. AUX, 1979—, pres. aux. 1983-84), Phi Alpha Theta (sec. U. Calif. Berkeley chpt. 1947-48, organizer and faculty adv., Mont. State U. chpt. 1948-54). Democrat. Mem. Ch. of the Brethren. Author numerous booklets on SW Am. history and numerous articles on Mexican NW to profl. jours. Home: 3033 Dale St San Diego CA 92104

CHAMBERLIN, MARGARET JEAN, association executive; b. Fairport Harbor, Ohio, Apr. 15, 1937; d. Oscar Wilho and Lillian Irene (Ahlberg) Pasanen; m. John D. Chamberlin, Aug. 19, 1961; 1 son, Robert John. B.A. in Econs., Hiram Coll., 1959; postgrad. Baldwin-Wallace Coll., 1961, Grand Canyon Coll., 1964, Ariz. State U., 1964, 76. Instr. tng. div. Cleve. Trust Co. subs. Ameritrust Co., 1959-62; elem. sch. tchr., Parma, Ohio, 1962-63, Phoenix, 1964-66; asst. buyer Webb's Dept. Store, Glendale, Calif., 1963-64; bookkeeper for atty., Phoenix, 1974-76; with Am. Inst. Banking, Phoenix, 1977—, program developer, 1979-80, exec. dir. Central Ariz. chpt., 1980—. Mem. early childhood edn. com., Pasadena, Calif., 1973-74; mem. adv. bd. Rio Salado Community Coll. Mem. Nat. Assn. Bank Women, Am. Assn. Tng. Devel. Democrat. Episcopalian. Club: Soroptomists (Phoenix). Office: Central Ariz Chpt Am Inst Banking 111 W Monroe Suite 808 Phoenix AZ 85003

CHAMBERLIN, ROBERT THOMAS, employment counselor; b. Oakland, Calif., Sept. 5, 1927; s. Arthur Richard and Sadie (Nieusma) C.; grad. Piedmont High Sch., 1945. Safety engr. trainee Pacific Indemnity, San Francisco, 1954-56; safety engr. Liberty Mut. Ins. Co., Los Angeles, 1957-64; safety engr. Indsl. Indemnity Co., Los Angeles, 1964-67, supervising engr., Fresno, Calif., 1967-68, asst. engring. mgr., Los Angeles, 1968-69, safety services home office mgr., San Francisco, 1969-73, safety engring. mgr., Orange, Calif., 1973-74; dir. loss control Great Am. Ins. Co., Cin., 1974-77; mgr. Allianz, Los Angeles, 1977-78; pres. R.T. Chamberlin Agy., Los Angeles, 1980—. Chmn. health and safety com. Tamarack Dist., Sequoia council Boy Scouts Am., Fresno, 1967-68, chmn. advancement com. Hollywood-Wilshire Dist., Los Angeles, 1968-69. Served with USMC, 1945. Registered profl. engr., Calif. Mem. Am. Soc. Safety Engrs., So. Calif. Indsl. Safety Soc. Republican. Editor: Safety Engring. Standards, 1969-72. Home and Office: 3640 Monon St Unit 203 Los Angeles CA 90027

CHAMBERS, CAROLYN SILVA, communications co. exec.; b. Portland, Oreg., Sept. 15, 1931; d. Julio and Elizabeth Silva; B.A., U. Oreg., 1953; m. Richard Alan Chambers, Dec. 14, 1963; children—William Daniel, Scott Davis, Elizabeth, Clark, Silva. Sec.-treas., bd. mem. McKenzie River Motors, Eugene, Oreg., 1952—; v.p. R.A. Chambers & Assos., Eugene, 1977—; treas., mem. bd. dirs. Liberty Communications, Inc., Eugene, 1960-74, v.p., treas., 1974-79, exec. v.p., treas., 1979-83; pres. Chambers Cable Co., Inc., 1983—; dir. Fed. Res. Bd. Mem. Alton Baker Park Commn.; mem. adv. com. Eugene Hearing and Speech Center; pres., mem. bd. treas. Very Little Theatre; treas., mem. bd., mgr. thrift shop Jr. League Eugene; mem. bd., treas. Eugene Symphony; chmn. Pleasant Hill Sch. Bd.; mem. bd. Sacred Heart Med. Found.; trustee U. Oreg. Found. Mem. Nat. Cable TV Assn. (mem. finance com., chmn. elections and by-laws), Calif. Community TV Assn. (bd. mem., conv. panelist), Oreg. Cable Communications Assn. (pres., mem. edn. com.), Pacific Northwest Cable Communications Assn. (bd. dirs., conv. chmn. 1983). Home: 86220 Dery Rd Pleasant Hill OR 97455 Office: PO Box 7009 Eugene OR 97401

CHAMBERS, DOROTHY ROSE, educator; b. Yakima, Wash., May 8, 1941; d. George Milford and Blance Mary (McCarthy) Hollenbeck; B.S. in Speech and Lang. Therapy, Marquette U., 1964; M.A. in Spl. Edn. (HEW Dept. Rehab. fellow), San Francisco State U., 1969; m. Thomas M. Chambers, Aug. 14, 1971; adopted children—David, Monique, Christopher, George, Elizabeth. Speech pathologist Mpls. Pub. Schs., 1964-65, Milbrae (Calif.) Sch. Dist., 1965-68; reading specialist Dept. Def., Landstuhl, Germany, 1970-71; tchr. children with extreme learning problems Portland (Oreg.) Public Schs., 1971-80, dept. chmn. spl. edn., 1980—; instr. developmental therapy U. Ga., 1982. Mem. Am. Speech and Hearing Assn. (cert. clin. competence), Common Cause. Democrat. Roman Catholic. Author: PEACHES (Pre-Sch. Ednl. Adaptation for Children Who Are Handicapped), 1978. Home: 12414 SE Oatfield Rd Milwaukie OR 97222 Office: 501 N Dixon St Portland OR 97227

CHAMBERS, JACK A., psychologist; b. Hamilton, Ohio, Feb. 26, 1932; s. Glen S. and H. Edna (McCormick) C.; A.B., U. Miami (Fla.), 1954; M.A., U. Cin., 1955; Ph.D., Mich. State U., 1964; m. A. Ruth Coe, Aug. 24, 1957; children—Melissa Ann, Wendy Colleen. Dir. personnel U. S.Fla., Tampa, 1960-66, dir. computer research center, asst. dean adminstrn., 1966-72; prof. psychology, dir. computer ednl. center Mansfield (Pa.) State Coll., 1972-74; prof. psychology, dir. Center Info. Processing, Calif. State U., Fresno, 1974—; dir. Compute Assisted Instruction Coordination Center, Calif. State U. System, 1981—; sr. partner Chambers, Sprecher & Assos., 1978—; cons. NSF. Grantee James McKeen Cattell Found., 1960, U.S. Office Edn., 1969, Calif. State Dept. Edn., 1977; lic. psychologist, Calif., Pa. Mem. Am. Psychol. Assn., AAAS, Assn. Computing Machinery (co-chmn. CAI task force elem. and secondary schs. subcom), Calif. Ednl. Computing Consortium (co-chmn. CAI com.). Author: CAI: Its Use in the Classroom, 1982; contbr. articles to profl. jours. Home: 1637 W Morris Ave Fresno CA 93711 Office: Center Info Processing Calif State Univ Fresno CA 93740

CHAMBERS, KENTON LEE, botany educator; b. Los Angeles, Sept. 27, 1929; s. Maynard Macy and Edna Georgia (Miller) C.; m. Henrietta Laing, June 21, 1958; children—Elaine Patricia, David Macy. A.B. with highest honors, Whittier Coll., 1950; Ph.D. (NSF fellow), Stanford U., 1955. Instr. biol. scis. Stanford U., 1954-55; instr. botany, Yale U. 1956-58, asst. prof., 1958-60; assoc. prof. botany Oreg. State U., Corvallis, 1960-65, prof., 1965—, curator Herbarium, 1960—; program dir. systematic biology NSF, Washington, 1967-68. NSF fellow, 1955-56. Mem. Bot. Soc. Am., Am. Soc. Plant Taxonomists, Soc. Study Evolution, AAAS, Am. Inst. Biol. Scis., Calif. Bot. Soc., Soc. Systematic Zoology, Western Soc. Naturalists, Assn. Tropical Biology. Democrat. Presbyterian. Clubs: Triad, Oreg. State U. Contbr. articles in field to profl. jours. Home: 3220 NW Lynwood Circle Corvallis OR 97330 Office: Herbarium Botany Dept Oreg State U Corvallis OR 97331

CHAMBERS, LOIS I., ins. agent and exec.; b. Omaha, Nov. 24, 1935; d. Edward J. and Evelyn B. (Davidson) Morrison; m. Frederick G. Chambers, Apr. 17, 1981; 1 son, Peter Edward. Ins. clk. Gross-Wilson Ins. Agy., 1955-57; ins. sec., bookkeeper Reed-Paulsen Ins. Agy., 1957-58; office mgr., asst. sec., agent Don Biggs & Assocs., Vancouver, Wash., 1958—. Mem. Citizens Com. Task Force, City of Vancouver, 1976, Block Grant Rev. Task Force, 1978—; chmn. adv. com. Clark Community Coll.; mem. agts. adv. council Safecom Mgmt. Systems, Inc. Mem. Ins. Women of S.W. Wash., Nat. Assn. Ins. Women. Roman Catholic. Club: Soroptimist (Vancouver). Office: 916 Main St PO Box 189 Vancouver WA 98666

CHAMBERS, MILTON WARREN, architect; b. Los Angeles, Aug. 5, 1928; s. Joe Sherwood and Barbara Newell (Harris) C.; student Coll. Sequoias, Visalia, Calif., 1949; m. Elizabeth M. Smith, Nov. 27, 1949; children—Mark, Michael, Daniel, Matthew. Architect, Kaestner & Kaestner, Architects, Visalia, Calif., 1950-57, Wurster, Bernardi & Emmons, Architects, San Francisco, 1958-63; partner with Garo Dorian, Architect, San Francisco, 1964; project architect Claude Oakland, Architect, San Francisco, 1965; architect Bank of Am., San Francisco, 1965-68; pvt. practice architecture, San Rafael, 1968—. Foreman Marin County Grand Jury, 1975-76. Served with U.S. Amry, 1946-48, 50-51. Mem. San Rafael C. of C. (dir. 1973-76), AIA, Nat. Trust for Historic Preservation, Marvelous Marin Breakfast Club. Rotarian (pres. Terra Linda 1974-75). Restorer 1879 Boyd House, 1974. Home: 110 Mt Whitney Ct San Rafael CA 94903 Office: 1505 5th St San Rafael CA 94901

CHAMBERS, PETER R., psychologist; b. Los Angeles, Aug. 23, 1953; s. Ralph James and Eileen Lucy (Allsworth) C. Student U. Calif., Riverside, 1975-77; B.A., Chapman Coll., 1978; M.A., U.S. Internat. U., 1980, Ph.D. Researcher, Rancho Los Amigos Hosp., Downey, Calif., 1972-76; counselor educator Free Clinic of Orange County, Anaheim, Calif., 1976-78; psychotherapist Care Manor Hosp., Orange, Calif., 1978-80; asst. adminstr. Cabrillo Med. Center, San Diego, 1980-81, psychologist Cabrillo Mental Health Group, 1982, ct. evaluation and guidance unit Orange County Mental Health, Orange, 1982—; instr. Calif. Community Coll.; cons. Starlight Hosp. Mem. Am. Psychol. Assn., Assn. Advancement of Behavior Therapy, Soc. Behavioral Medicine, Health Care Execs. Assn. Republican.

CHAMBERS, RICHARD H., retired U.S. circuit judge; b. Danville, Ill., Nov. 7, 1906; s. William R. and Lida J. (Spencer) C.; A.B., U. Ariz., 1929, LL.D., 1976; LL.B., Stanford, 1932; LL.D., U. Pacific, 1972; m. 2d, Mary Martin, Nov. 24, 1945; children by previous marriage—Martha Chambers Froese, Janet Chambers Crews. Admitted to Ariz. bar, 1932; practice law in Tucson, 1932-41, 45-54; judge Ct. of Appeals, 9th Circuit, Tucson, 1954-77, sr. judge, 1977-82. Served from capt. to maj. USAAF, 1942-45. Recipient Law medal Gonzaga U., 1974. Mem. Am. Law Inst., Am. Bar Assn., Phi Gamma Delta. Republican. Club: Old Pueblo (Tucson). Home: 6300 N Campbell Tucson AZ 85718 Office: 55 E Broadway Tucson AZ 85701

CHAMBERS, ROBERT ROOD, scientific company executive; b. Lincoln, Nebr., May 23, 1923; s. Guy Cleveland and Grace (Rood) C.; m. Martha Wayne, 1948; children—Anne E., Guy W., Carl R.; m. 2d, Clytia Capraro, May 28, 1965. A.B., U. Nebr., 1944; Ph.D., U. Ill., 1947; J.D., DePaul U., 1951. Bar: Ill. 1952. From chemist to v.p. research Sinclair Oil Co., 1947-69; v.p. chemicals, nuclear, splty. bus., new bus. ventures, Atlantic Richfield Co., 1969-81; pres. Sandhill Sci. Inc., Pasadena, Calif., 1982—; chmn. Montedoro-Whitney Co. Mem. Am. Chem. Soc. Club: California. Office: Sandhill Sci Inc 2040 E Foothill Blvd Pasadena CA 91107

CHAMBERS, THOMAS WILLIAM, Canadian provincial government official; b. Port Arthur, Ont., Can., July 7, 1928; s. William Edward and Mary Jane C.; m. Margaret Lenore Green, Dec. 22, 1952; children—Steven William, Robert Norris, Joan Maureen, Susan Lenore. B.A.Sc., U. Toronto (Ont.). Petroleum engr.-cons.; mem. Legis. Assembly Alta. (Can.), Edmonton, 1971—, minister of housing and pub. works, 1979-82, minister of pub. works, supply and services, 1982—. Mem. Alta. Assn. Profl. Engrs., Can. Inst. Mining and Metallurgy, Edmonton C. of C., RCAF Assn. Progressive Conservative. Office: 207 Legis Bldg Edmonton AB T5K 2B7 Canada*

CHAMBLISS, DEAN BLAKE, architect; b. Jefferson City, Mo., Nov. 11, 1934; s. Hiram Darden and Florence (Blakemore) C.; B.S. in Archtl. Engring., U. N.Mex., 1956; M.Arch., Harvard U., 1960; m. Dorothy Ann Holland, May 26, 1956 (dec.); children—Karen, Susan, Blake, Peggy, Robert, Diana, Becket. Designer, Shepley Bulfinch Richardson & Abbott, Boston, 1957-58, Eugene D. Sternberg, Denver, 1960; archtl. designer Van Deusen & Bliska, Grand Junction, Colo., 1961-62; prin. Chambliss Assos., Grand Junction, 1963-71; partner Chambliss/Dillon & Assos., Grand Junction, 1972-77; mng. partner Chambliss/Dillon/Jenkins, Architects & Planners, Grand Junction, 1978-80; pres. Chambliss Assos., P.C., Architects and Planners, Grand Junction, 1980—; asst. prof. architecture and city planning Tex. Tech. U., 1962-63. Mem. Colo. Population Adv. Council, 1972; mem. Colo. Housing, Inc., 1971-78, treas., 1972, chmn., 1977, vice-chmn., 1978; chmn. Mesa

County Regional Planning Commn., 1970-72, Grand Junction City Planning Commn., 1967-77; mem. Glenwood Canyon Citizens Adv. Com., 1976—; co-chmn. Colo. Gov.'s Housing Task Force, 1976-77; mem. Gov.'s Public/Pvt. Partnerships Task Force, 1982-83. Recipient award Colo. Easter Seal Soc., 1965; Japan award Jr. Chamber Internat., 1965; Lee F. Johnson award, 1980. Mem. AIA (housing com. 1976—, chmn.-elect 1983; Colo. energy conservation adv. com. 1978-81), Am. Soc. Planning Ofcls., Urban Land Inst., Nat. Trust Historic Preservation, Nat. Assn. Housing and Redevel. Ofcls., U.S. (nat. dir. 1966), Colo. (v.p. 1965, internat. dir. 1967), Grand Junction (pres. 1964) Jaycees. Democrat. Mem. Christian Ch. (Disciples of Christ). Home: 1315 Mesa Ave Grand Junction CO 81501 Office: 930 Main St Grand Junction CO 81502

CHAMP, FREDERICK WINTON, banking and mortgage banking exec.; b. Logan, Utah, July 29, 1930; s. Frederick Percival and Frances (Winton) C.; A.B. in Econs., Stanford U., 1952; M.B.A., Harvard U., 1956; m. June King, Mar. 26, 1960 (dec.). Exec. v.p. Utah Mortgage Loan Corp., Boise, Idaho, 1960-68, also dir.; pres., chief exec. officer First Security State Bank, Salt Lake City, 1968—, also dir.; pres., chief exec. officer First Security Mortgage Co., Salt Lake City, 1977—, also dir.; chmn. exec. com., chief exec. officer First Security Bank of Rock Springs (Wyo.), 1977—, also dir.; dir. First Security Bank of Utah, N.A., Utah Mortgage Loan Corp., Logan. Bd. dirs., treas. Greater Salt Lake YMCA, 1972-75; bd. dirs. Salt Lake City Planning and Zoning Commn., 1972-76. Served as 1st lt. Fin. Corps, Korean War. Mem. Mortgage Bankers Assn. Am., Salt Lake Clearing House Assn. (pres. 1970, dir. 1968-79), Utah Mortgage Bankers Assn. (dir.). Republican. Episcopalian. Clubs: Alta, Univ., Salt Lake Country, Bonneville Knife and Fork, Elks, Masons, Shriners. Office: 381 E Broadway Salt Lake City UT 84110

CHAMP, STANLEY GORDON, sci. co. exec.; b. Hoquiam, Wash., Feb. 15, 1919; s. Clifford Harvey and Edna Winnifred (Johnson) C.; B.S., U. Puget Sound, 1941; postgrad. M.I.T., 1955, 57, UCLA, 1959; m. Anita Knapp Wegener, Sept. 6, 1941; children—Susanne Winnifred Champ Whalen, Colleen Louise Champ Szurszewski. Tchr. Lake Washington Sch. Dist., 1942-48; prof. math. U. Puget Sound, 1948-51; supervisory mathematician U.S. Navy, Bremerton, Wash., 1951-55; research specialist Boeing Co., Seattle, 1955-68; v.p. R.M. Towne & Assos., Seattle, 1968-75; founder, pres. Dynac Scis., Tacoma, Wash., 1975—; active adult edn. U. Puget Sound. Mem. Acoustical Soc. Am., Soc. Naval Architects and Marine Engrs., Phi Delta Kappa. Presbyterian. Author: Noise Radiation from Vibrating Structure, 1970; Mechanical Impedance in Vibration, 1963; How Useful is Your Harmonic Analysis, 1959; Electronic Computing at PSNS, 1953; patentee method and apparatus for determining dynamic parameters of soil insitu. Home and Office: 1540 Fairview Dr Tacoma WA 98465

CHAMPIE, ELLMORE ALFRED, historian, writer; b. Eden, Tex., Sept. 11, 1916; s. Sam Houston and Nora Louise (Sorrell) C.; student Tex. Coll. Mines and Metallurgy, 1941-42; B.A. with highest honors, U. Tex, Austin, 1947, M.A. (Univ. Scholar), 1948; Ph.D. in History (Bayard Cutting Scholar), Harvard U., 1967; m. Rosemary Erter, Sept. 7, 1947 (dec. Nov. 1962); children—Ellmore Alfred, Nora Beatrice; m. 2d, Miriam Helene Boysen Mann, Aug. 28, 1971 (div. Oct. 1974). Archivist, Nat. Archives, 1952-55; historian U.S. Marine Corps Hdqrs., 1955-56, Joint Chiefs of Staff, U.S. Dept. Def., 1956-61; asso. agy. historian Fed. Aviation Agy., 1961-67; agy. historian FAA, Dept. of Transp., 1967-72; hist. researcher and writer, 1972—; mem. tech. com. on history U.S. Inst. of Aeros. and Astronautics, 1970-72; editorial cons. history of FAA and predecessor agys., 4 vols. Served with U.S. Navy, 1936-40; served to 1st lt. USAAF, 1942-45. Mem. Am. Hist. Assn., Am. Acad. Polit. and Social Sci., Am. Soc. for Eighteenth-Century Studies, Am. Soc. for Pub. Adminstrn., Phi Beta Kappa. Democrat. Clubs: Masons, Harvard (So. Ariz.). Author: The Federal Turnaround on Aid to Airports, 1926-38, 1973. Home: 7480 E Rio Verde Dr Tucson AZ 85715

CHAMPINE, DENNIS, mayor, real estate broker; b. Detroit, Mar. 29, 1942; s. Earl and Margaret (Keigher) C.; m. Joanna D'Angelo, Jan. 6, 1961; children—Jeff, Brett, Dana, Earl. Bus. mgr. Am. Motor Sales Corp., Seattle and San Francisco, 1963-69; dist. mgr. Toyota Motor Distbrs., Denver, 1969-73; now regional mgr. Marcus & Millichap, Inc., Denver; mayor City of Aurora (Colo.), 1979—, councilman, 1974-79. Served with USMC, 1960-63. Mem. U.S. Conf. Mayors, Nat. Assn. Republican Mayors. Republican. Office: Office of Mayor City Hall 1470 S Havana St Aurora CO 80012*

CHAMPLIN, PHILIP ALDEN, judge; b. Annapolis, Md., Sept. 1, 1939; s. Jackson Selover and Betty (Trotter) C.; B.A., Yale U., 1961; J.D., U. Calif.-Berkeley, 1964; m. Lynne McWilliams, Nov. 3, 1966; children—Christopher Alden, Catherine Ann. Bar: Calif. 1965. Assoc., Coombs, Dunlap & Dunlap, 1965-66; ptnr. Coombs, Dunlap, Dunlap & Champlin, Napa, Calif., 1967-77; city atty. Yountville, Calif., 1968-77; dep. city atty. Napa, 1966-77; judge Mcpl. Ct. County of Napa, 1978-79; judge Superior Ct., State of Calif., County of Napa, 1979—. Bd. dirs. Napa ARC; bd. dirs. Silverado council Boy Scouts Am., pres., 1983; trustee Napa Community Coll., 1968-77, pres. bd., 1969-71. Mem. Calif. Judges Assn., Phi Delta Phi. Club: Rotary (pres. 1983-84) (Napa). Home: 595 Montecito Blvd Napa CA 94558 Office: Courthouse Napa CA 94558

CHAN, CHANG D(ONG), optometrist; b. San Francisco, May 7, 1946; s. Chack Wing and Victoria Chan; m. May Chau, Aug. 25, 1974; children—Connie, Elaine. B.A. in Biology, San Francisco State U., 1969; B.S. in Physiol. Optics, U. Calif.-Berkeley, 1972, O.D., 1974. Draftsman, Bechtel Corp., San Francisco, summers 1969-74; practice optometry, West Sacramento, Calif., 1974—. Bd. dirs. Mental Health Assn. Yolo County (Calif.). Mem. Am. Optometric Assn., Calif. Optometric Assn., Sacramento Valley Optometric Assn., West Sacramento C. of C. Club: Lions (chmn. sight conservation 1981-83, bull. editor 1981-82, v.p. 1977-79, sec. 1979-80, Sight Conservation and Work for Blind award 1979). Office: 1029 Jefferson Blvd Suite B West Sacramento CA 95691

CHAN, ERIC HONG-CHING, structural and civil engr.; b. Canton, China, Apr. 14, 1930; came to U.S., 1969, naturalized, 1974; s. Sin-Ming and Shun-Ying (Ho) C.; B.S. in Engring., Hong Kong U., 1953; m. Jean Sau-May Wu, June 10, 1955; children—Gaye M.G., Sonia M.S., Anthony S.C. Engr. W. Szeto & Partners, Hong Kong, 1954-58, chief engr., 1958-63, partner, chief engr., 1963-69; structural engr. T.Y. Lin Hawaii Inc., Honolulu, 1969-71, asso., 1971-72, partner, v.p., 1972-79; partner, v.p. KFC & Assos., Inc., Architects and Engrs., Honolulu, 1979—; partner, pres. Fan, Kasamoto & Chan, Inc., Structural Engrs., Honolulu, 1980—. Fellow Instn. Structural Engrs., Eng. (A.E.Wynn prize, 1958); mem. Instn. Civil Engrs., Eng., Nat. Soc. Profl. Engrs., ASCE, Structural Engrs. Assn. Hawaii. Democrat. Office: 615 Piikoi St Suite 1001 Honolulu HI 96814

CHAN, FREDERICK MAN-HIN, architect, developer; b. Hong Kong, June 17, 1947; s. William Chak-Yan and Nancy Sui-Yin (Tse) C.; B.Arch., U. Calif., Berkeley, 1969; M.Arch., Harvard U., 1974. Architect, N.Y. State Urban Devel. Corp., N.Y.C., 1973-74; devel. mgr. community land devel. Ministry of Housing, Toronto, Ont., Can., 1974-78; pres. Nu West R.E.I. Corp., Los Angeles, 1978—, Kingsley Properties, Inc., Los Angeles, 1978—; treas. Pearl City Investments Corp., Los Angeles, 1978—; pres. Nu West Project Mgmt. Inc., Los Angeles, 1981—; project dir. North Broadway Mall Devel. Corp., Los Angeles, 1981—. Mem. Am. Planning Assn., Ont. Assn. Architects, Urban Devel. Inst., Chinese C. of C. Los Angeles (dir.), Internat. Council Shopping Centers, Am. Mgmt. Assn., Los Angeles Jaycees, Urban Land Inst. Clubs: Marina City, Los Angeles Racquet, Internat. Office: 350 S Figueroa St Suite 555 Los Angeles CA 90071

CHAN, LINDA SIM YING, research analyst, biostatistical and research consultant; b. Hong Kong, Aug. 17, 1942; d. Chung Hon Cheung and Kwan (Chan) C.; m. Kenneth Hung-Yip Chan, Sept. 17, 1967; children—Andrew, Kevin, Michael, Stephanie. B.S., U. Calif.-Berkeley, 1966, M.S., Los Angeles, 1967, Ph.D., 1970. Research analyst Los Angeles County/U. So. Calif. Med. Ctr., 1970-79, Instr. dept. community and family medicine, 1970-74, asst. clin. prof., 1974-82, dir. research, planning and evaluation unit 1979—; cons. health related areas. Mem. Am. Statis. Assn., Biometric Soc., Am. Pub. Health Assn., Evaluation Research Soc., UCLA Alumni Assn. Contbr. numerous articles to profl. jours. Office: LAC-USC-MC Room 12-900 1200 N State St Los Angeles CA 90033

CHAN, PETER WING KWONG, pharmacist; b. Los Angeles, Feb. 3, 1949; s. Sherwin T.S. and Shirley W. (Lee) C.; B.S., U. So. Calif., 1970, D.Pharmacy, 1974; m. Patricia Jean Uyeno, June 8, 1974; children—Kristina Dionne, Kelly Alison, David Shoichi. Clin. instr. U. So. Calif., 1974-76; staff clin. pharmacist Cedars-Sinai Med. Center, Los Angeles, 1974-76; 1st clin. pharmacist in ophthalmology Alcon Labs., Inc., Ft. Worth, 1977—, formerly in Phila. monitoring patient drug therapy, teaching residents, nurses, pharmacy students, then assigned to Tumu Tumu Hosp., Karatina, Kenya, also lectr. clin. ocular pharmacology tng. course, Nairobi, Cairo, Athens, formerly dist. sales mgr. Alcon/BP, ophthal. products div. Alcon Labs., Inc., Denver; v.p., gen. mgr. Optikem Internat., Sereine Products Div., Optacryl, Inc., Denver; formerly product mgr. hosp. pharmacy products Am. McGaw div. Am. Hosp. Supply Corp.; now internat. market mgr. IOLAB subs. Johnson & Johnson; dir. SUDCO Internat., Los Angeles; del. Am. Pharm. Assn. House of Dels., 1976-78. Recipient Hollywood-Wilshire Pharm. Assn. spl. award for outstanding service, 1974; licensed pharmacist, Calif. Mem. Am., Calif., Hollywood-Wilshire (bd. dirs. 1972-76) pharm. assns., Am. Soc. Hosp. Pharmacists, Am. Pharm. Assn. Acad. of Pharmacy Practice, U. So. Calif. Gen. Alumni Assn., OSAD Centurions. Democrat. Home: 27341 Viana Mission Viejo CA 92692 Office: IOLAB 861 S Village Oaks Dr Covina CA 91724

CHAN, ROSALIE YUK-KUEN, med. technologist, chemist; b. Canton, China, Apr. 26, 1938; came to U.S., 1961, naturalized, 1966; d. Shong-Ching and Ying-Wah (Leung) Lau; B.S. with high honors, Taiwan U., 1960; postgrad. Calif. State U., 1970; m. Tom Chan, Dec. 30, 1962; 1 dau., Jane W. Tchr. Chinese Community Center, Oakland, Calif., 1961-63; research asst. U. Calif., Berkeley, 1967-68; real estate broker Century 21, San Leandro, Calif., 1978-79; med. technologist Kaiser Hosp., Oakland, 1972-78, sr. med. technologist Kaiser Permanente Med. Group, Berkeley, 1978—. Mem. U.S. Congl. Adv. Bd., Am. Security Council, 1982; active YWCA, Oakland. Mem. Apt. Owners Assn. of So. Alameda County, Am. Soc. Clin. Pathologists (affiliate mem., cert. med. technologist), Calif. Assn. for Med. Lab. Tech. Democrat. Home: 13437 Doolittle Dr San Leandro CA 94577 Office: 1725 Eastshore Hwy Berkeley CA 94710

CHAN, SHU-WING, physician; b. Hong Kong, Sept. 6, 1944; came to U.S., 1970; s. Kwong-Ying and Yee-Lan (Yip) C.; M.B., B.S., U. Hong Kong, 1968; m. Flora Yu-Big Yau, May 19, 1973; children—Mai-Sie, Mai-San, Ming Jeung. Intern, Northwestern Hosp. of Mpls., 1970-71, in internal medicine, 1972-75; fellow in cardiology U. Minn. Hosps., Mpls., 1975-76; practice medicine specializing in internal medicine and cardiology, San Francisco, 1976—; attending physician St. Frances Meml. Hosp., Chinese Hosp., co-dir. ICU, 1980—, asst. chief of medicine, 1979—; pres. Shu-Wing Chan M.D., Inc., San Francisco, 1979—; clin. instr. medicine U. Calif., San Francisco, 1976; med. adv. to YMCA, San Francisco, 1978. Bd. dirs. Chinese Newcomers Service Center, San Francisco, 1980. Diplomate Am. Bd. Internal Medicine. Mem. Am. Heart Assn., San Francisco Med. Soc., AMA, Calif. Med. Assn. Office: 929 Clay St Suite 303 San Francisco CA 94108

CHAN, TONY LEE, pharmacist; b. Rangoon, Burma, July 17, 1951; s. Chin Yaw and Sofia Lee C.; student UCLA, 1971-74, Calif. State U., Long Beach, 1974; Pharm.D., U. Pacific, 1977; m. Virginia Chang, Oct. 7, 1978. Intern, Meth. Hosp. So. Calif., Arcadia, 1972-73, mem. staff, 1977-78; tng. in clin. pharmacy San Diego VA Hosp., 1976-77; pharmacist, pres. Maxson Pharmacy Inc., West Covina, Calif.; clin. pharmacy cons. San Gabriel Valley Regional Center; pvt. practice clin. pharmacy, 1978—; pharmacy student tchr. U. So. Calif., 1980. Mem. Am. Pharm. Assn., Calif. Pharm. Assn., San Gabriel Valley Pharm. Assn., AAAS, Am. Soc. Hosp. Pharmacists, Pharmacy Assos. U. Pacific, Medicinal Chemistry Soc., Am. Inst. Research (exec.), San Gabriel Valley Chinese Assn., Burma Med. Profl. Assn. Home: 1801 Cielito Ave Monterey Park CA 91754 Office: 338 S Sunset Ave West Covina CA 91790

CHAN, VINCENT POWER, newspaper editor; b. San Jose, Calif., Sept. 27, 1921; s. Wah Yoke and Shee (Wong) Chin. A.A., Hartnell Coll., 1948; A.B. in Journalism, San Jose State U., 1955. Corr., Union Gazette, San Jose, 1955; substitute reporter Mountain View (Calif.) Register-Leader, 1957; reporter, sports editor Gilroy (Calif.) Evening Dispatch, 1958-59, mng. editor (Pulitzer Prize nominee 1965), 1959-66; wire editor Salinas Californian (Calif. Newspaper Pubs. Assn. award for Gen. Excellence 1971), 1966-72; editor Hollister (Calif.) Evening Free Lance, 1976—. Served with USAF, 1942-45; ETO. Decorated Air medal with 4 oak leaf clusters. Mem. Gilroy C. of C. (dir. 1962), Internat. Platform Assn., Am. Legion, Sigma Delta Chi. Clubs: Kiwanis (dir. Gilroy chpt. 1979); Commonwealth. Home: 153A Riverside Dr Watsonville CA 95076 Office: Hollister Evening Free Lance 360 6th St Hollister CA 95023

CHAN, WAN HOR, physician; b. Batu Gajah, Malaysia, Dec. 13, 1939; came to U.S., 1971, naturalized, 1979; s. Tong Thye and Seow Ying (Ng) C.; M.B.B.S., U. Singapore, 1964; m. Amy Chan, June 29, 1967; children—Evelyn, Jennifer, Donald. Intern, Loma Linda U., 1971; resident Royal Maternity Hosp., Belfast, No. Ireland, 1967-70; asst. lectr. ob-gyn U. Singapore, 1966; tutor, fellow ob-gyn Queen's U. Belfast, 1967-71; asst. prof. ob-gyn U. So. Calif., 1972-74, Charles Drew Postgrad. Med. Sch., 1972-74; practice medicine specializing in ob-gyn, Los Banos, Calif., 1974—; asst. clin. prof. family practice U. Calif., Davis, 1976-80. William Blair Bell Meml. Research fellow, 1970. Fellow Royal Coll. Surgeons Can., Am. Coll. Obstetricians and Gynecologists, Internat. Coll. Surgeons, Am. Soc. Abdominal Surgeons; mem. Am. Fertility Soc., AMA, N.Y. Acad. Scis., Royal Coll. Obstetricians and Gynecologists (Eng.). Methodist. Club: Rotary. Author: Outline of Obstetrics and Gynecology, 1971. Office: 600 W I St Los Banos CA 93635

CHAN, WAYNE LYMAN, physician; b. San Francisco, Aug. 14, 1938; s. Shau Wing and Anna Mae C.; A.B., Stanford U., 1960; M.D., George Washington U., 1967; m. Elizabeth Lee, May 27, 1967; children—Lisa Anne, Christopher Wayne. Intern, Santa Clara Valley Med. Center, San Jose, Calif., 1967-68; resident in dermatology Stanford (Calif.) Med. Center, 1970-73; practice medicine specializing in dermatology, San Jose, Calif., 1973—; mem. staff Alexian Bros. Hosp., San Jose, Valley West Hosp., Los Gatos, Calif., San Jose Hosp., Presbyn. Hosp., San Francisco, Valley Med. Center, San Jose; clin. instr. Stanford U., 1974-77, clin. asst. prof., 1977—. Diplomate Am. Bd. Dermatology. Fellow Am. Acad. Dermatology, Pacific Dermatol. Assn.; mem. San Francisco Dermatol. Soc., AMA, Calif. Med. Assn., Santa Clara County Med. Soc. Office: 2323 Montpelier Dr #C San Jose CA 95116

CHANCE, GAILYA MONROE, educational administrator, educator, consultant; b. Pearl River County, Miss., May 2, 1937; d. John Thomas and Frankie Dee (Clark) Monroe; m. Dr. Jay Paul Chance, Sept. 30, 1934; children—Jay, Jeffrey. B.S., Miss. U. Women (formerly Miss. State Coll. Women), 1959; M.R.E., Southwestern Baptist Theol. Sem., 1972; Ed.D., in Ednl. Adminstrn., Miss. State U., 1979. Adminstrv. services credential; community coll. teaching credential; children's center supervision teaching permit. Children's center teaching permit, Calif. Dir., Child Enrichment Center, Memphis, 1964-75; dir. Creative Learning Center, Starkville, Miss., 1975-78; instr. bus. mgmt. Miss. State U., Starkville, 1978-80; chmn. dept. early childhood studies, coordinator tchr. tng. lab. Riverside (Calif.) City Coll., 1981—; regional cons. church adminstrn. dept., Southern Baptist Sunday Sch. Bd. Active Friends Mission Inn; trustee Magnolia Ave. Baptist Ch.; mem. fin. devel. com. Calvary-Arrowhead Assn. Calif. So. Baptist Conv.; mem. citizens adv. com. Calif. Baptist Coll. Mem. Acad. Mgmt., Calif. Community Coll. Early Childhood Educators, Calif. Tchrs. Assn., Nat. Tchrs. Assn., Nat. Assn. Edn. Young Children, Phi Delta Kappa. Republican. Author: Church Weekly Early Education Teacher's Guide, Birth-Three, 1977; (with Jean Kirk Reynolds) How to Choose and Use Day Care, 1980; contbr. articles in field to ednl. and religious publs. Home: 5940 Intervale Dr Riverside CA 92506 Office: Riverside City Coll 4800 Magnolia Ave Riverside CA 92506

CHAND, IAN PHILLIP, sociologist, marriage, family and child counselor; b. Roorkee, India, Aug. 15, 1944; came to U.S., 1968; s. Inayat Masih and Phoebe (Mall) C.; m. Pansy Moses, Dec. 26, 1965; children—Ivonne, Iva. B.Th. (Lowry Meml. scholar), Spicer Meml. Coll., India, 1965; M.A., Andrews U., 1969; M.S. (grad. asst.), Pa. State U., 1973, Ph.D., 1980; post doctoral U. So. Calif., 1983. Asst. prof. sociology Lincoln U., Pa., 1975-79; asst. prof. sociology Loma Linda U., Riverside, Calif., 1979-81, assoc. prof., 1982—, coordinator Adminstrn. of Justice Program. Mem. Am. Sociol. Assn., Pacific Sociol. Assn., Rural Sociol. Soc., Nat. Council Family Relations, Am. Assn. Marriage and Family Therapists, Calif. Assn. Marriage and Family Therapists, Alpha Kappa Delta. Author tech. publs., sociology workbook and study guide. Home: 11152 Schuyler Ave Riverside CA 92505 Office: Loma Linda U Loma Linda CA 92350 also Loma Linda U Riverside CA 92515

CHANDLER, CALEB JOHN, state senator, city ofcl.; b. Clovis, N.Mex., Jan. 4, 1943; s. John Caleb and Myrtle Marie (Bishop) C.; student Eastern N.Mex. U., 1962-63; grad. N.Mex. Law Enforcement Acad., 1967, FBI Nat. Acad., 1974; m. Donna Marie Murray, Jan. 8, 1971; children—Sandra Michelle, Tammy Annette, John Caleb, Matthew Edward. Switchman, Santa Fe R.R., 1961-63; foreman Trans-Pecos Dairy, Pecos, Tex., 1963-67; with Dept. Police, City of Clovis, 1967—, dep. police chief, 1977—; mem. N.Mex. Senate, 1976—, chmn. interim criminal justice study com., 1981—. Bd. dirs. YMCA, Clovis, N.Mex. Outdoor Drama Assn. Democrat. Baptist. Club: Sertoma. Office: PO Box 862 Clovis NM 88101

CHANDLER, JOHN HERRICK, college administrator; b. San Francisco, Aug. 7, 1928; s. Ralph William and Gwen Thornton (Herrick) C.; A.B., UCLA, 1952; B.D. (Danforth fellow), U. Chgo., 1958, Ph.D. (fellow), 1963; m. Nancy Gordon Phillips, Dec. 10, 1955; children—John, Seth, Will. Instr. English, Dartmouth Coll., 1961-63; asst. prof. UCLA, 1963-64; assoc. prof., dean spl. programs Ohio U., 1964-67; v.p. Danforth Found., St. Louis, 1967-71; pres. Salem Coll. and Acad., Winston-Salem, N.C., 1971-76, Scripps Coll., Claremont, Calif., 1976—; ordained to ministry Episcopal Ch., 1960. Trustee Newton Coll. Sacred Heart, 1970-75, Thacher Sch., 1977—; dir. Clayton (Mo.) Bd. Edn., 1970-71. Clubs: Univ. (Los Angeles); Twilight. Office: Scripps College Balch Hall Claremont CA 91711

CHANDLER, KRISTIAN, computer consultant; b. Cleveland Heights, Ohio, June 26, 1948; d. Gerhard A. and Hanna R. (Rittmeyer) Hoffmann; m. William D. Chandler, July 1, 1982; children—Karen, Heidi. Student U. So. Colo., 1981—. Owner, mgr. V&W Fgn. Car Service, Canon City, Colo., 1970-80; prin. The Chandlers, Computer Cons., Pueblo, Colo., 1982—; mgr. U. So. Colo. Sch. Bus. microcomputer lab. Bd. dirs. Canon City Community Service Ctr., 1978-80, Canon City Red Cross, 1978-81. Mem. Student Programmers Operators of Computers, Data Processing Mgmt. Assn., USC Honors Soc., (Pueblo). Home and Office: 42 McNaughton Rd Pueblo CO 81001

CHANDLER, LINDA CLINE, investment broker; b. Sioux Falls, S.D.; d. Lawrence Alphonse and Wilba Nell (Leatherwood) Dhaemers; B.S., Iowa State U., 1968, M.A., 1972; m. Terence E. Chandler, Oct. 16, 1976. With Sutro & Co., San Jose, Calif., 1974—, asso. v.p., 1977-78, v.p. investments, 1978—; pres. Chandler Roberts, Inc., Santa Clara, Calif., 1983—; contbg. personal fin. editor Sta. KCSM-TV; fin. commentator Sta. KPEN. Named Fin. Planner of Yr., Am. Home Properties, 1981, 83; named one of nations leading brokers Wall Street Transcript, 1982. UN fellow. Mem. Santa Clara County Profl. Brokers Assn., Santa Clara County Profl. Young Women, AAUW, Phi Kappa Phi, Phi Delta Theta, Alpha Delta Pi. Mehtodist. Clubs: Sutro Century (pres.'s council 1978-81), Sutro Second Century, Sutro Pres. Office: 2900 Gordon Ave Suite 101 Santa Clara CA 95051

CHANDLER, OTIS, publisher; b. Los Angeles, Nov. 23, 1927; s. Norman and Dorothy (Buffum) C.; grad. Andover Acad., 1946; B.A., Stanford, 1950; m. Marilyn Brant, June 18, 1951 (div.); children—Norman, Harry, Cathleen, Michael, Carolyn; m. 2d, Bettina Whitaker, Aug. 15, 1981. Joined Times Mirror Co., 1953, now chmn., editor-in-chief, dir.; pub. Los Angeles Times, 1960-80; chmn. bd., editor-in-chief Times Mirror, Los Angeles, 1980—. Served to 1st lt. USAF, 1951-53. Mem. Am. Soc. Newspaper Editors, Am. Newspaper Pubs. Assn. Clubs: California, Regency. Office: Times Mirror Co Times Mirror Sq Los Angeles CA 90053

CHANDLER, ROBERT WILBUR, newspaper editor; b. Marysville, Calif., May 12, 1921; s. Wilbur Ray and Grace Helena (Johnson) C.; B.A. in Journalism, Stanford U., 1942; m. Nancy Jane Renne, Sept. 7, 1946; children—Janet Chandler Stevens, Margaret Chandler Cushman, Mary Jean Chandler Jordan, Patricia Ann Chandler Moss, Elizabeth Jane Chandler McCool, Robert Wilbur. Reporter San Francisco Chronicle, 1941; reporter, bur. mgr. UP, Portland, Oreg., Helena, Mont., Phoenix and Boise, Idaho, 1941-43; reporter, copy-reader, bus. office Denver Post, 1946-50, William Kostka & Assos., Denver, 1950-52; editor Stanford U. Rev., 1952-53, The Bulletin, Bend, Oreg., 1953-60, 62—; gen. mgr. Los Angeles Mirror, 1960-61; chmn. Western Communications, Inc., Bend, 1966—; dir. Hawaii Newspaper Agy., Inc., Honolulu, 1974—. Mem. Oreg. Constl. Revision Commn., 1961-63, Oreg. Jud. Council, 1966-69, Oreg. State Bd. Edn., 1966-69, Oreg. Jud. Fitness Commn., 1967-82, Oreg. Criminal Law Revision Commn., 1967-73, Oreg. Law Enforcement Council, 1974-75, Oreg. Ednl. Coordinating Commn., 1982—; bd. dirs. Central Oreg. Community Coll., Bend, 1962-66, Am. Press Inst., Reston, Va., 1972—. Served with U.S. Army, 1943-46. Mem. Am. Soc. Newspaper Editors (dir. 1972-79), Sigma Delta Chi (nat. pres. 1970-71). Clubs: Bohemian (San Francisco);

Arlington (Portland). Home: 15 NW Glen Rd Bend OR 97701 Office: The Bulletin Bend OR 97701

CHANDLER, ROD, congressman; b. LaGrande, Oreg., July 13, 1942; m. Joyce Elaine Laremore; children—John, Amanda. B.S. in U.S. History, Oreg. State U. Former news commentator KOMO-TV, Seattle; former asst. v.p. Wash. Mut. Savs. Bank; former ptnr. pub. relations firm Chandler/Corcoran, Inc.; mem. 98th Congress from Wash. Mem. Wash. Ho. of Reps., from 1974; chmn. house edn. com., 1979-81; chmn. ho. ways and means com., 1981-83; mem. King County Met. Council, 1974-75. Mem. Variety Club, Tent 46, AFTRA. Republican. Office: 216 Cannon House Office Bldg Washington DC 20515*

CHANDLER, SANDRA MARILL, interior designer; b. San Francisco, Oct. 16, 1944; d. Robert S. and Cornelia B. (Brutnell) Marill; children—Christopher, Robert. B.A. in Interior Design, San Jose State U., 1966. Designer, Design & Office Concepts, Santa Clara, Calif., 1976; prin. Sandra Marill Chandler Design, Saratoga, Calif., 1977-80; ptnr. Bond and Chandler Design, Mountain View, Calif., 1980—; prin. Sandra Chandler Design Assos., San Francisco; speaker, cons. in field. Mem. AIA (assoc.), Am. Soc. Interior Designers (dir.), Inst. Bus. Designers, San Francisco C. of C. Republican. Episcopalian. Office: 555 DeHaro St #330 San Francisco CA 94107

CHANDRA, APURVA, digital equipment corporation sales executive; b. India, May 7, 1948; came to U.S., 1969, naturalized, 1982; Govind Saran and Shanta Srivastava; m. Vunita Mohini Chandra, Feb. 11, 1977; 1 son, Hamish. B.S.E.E., Indian Inst. Tech., Delhi, 1969; M.S. in Computer Scis., UCLA, 1970. Sales rep. Hewlett Packard Corp., Hollywood, Calif., 1972-74; sales rep. Digital Equipment Corp., El Segundo, Calif., 1974-77, sales unit mgr., 1977-79, sales group mgr., Oakland, Calif., 1979-81, Santa Clara, Calif., 1979-81, dist. sales mgr., San Francisco, 1982—. Home: 208 Echo Ln Portola Valley CA 94025 Office: 100 Bush St 7th Floor San Francisco CA 94104

CHANDRA, DHANESH, research metallurgist; b. Hyderabad, India; s. Narhari and Chetan (Kumari) P.; came to U.S., 1970; B.Engring., Osmania U., 1967; M.S., U. Ill., 1972; Ph.D., U. Denver, 1976. Planning and devel. engr. Hyderabad Asbestos Cement Products, India, 1968-70; grad. research student U. Ill., Chgo., 1971-72; grad. research asst. Denver Research Inst., U. Denver, 1972-76, sr. research metallurgist, mgr. Strategic Materials Center, 1976-82; chmn. of a session, 25th annual Denver X-Ray Conf., 1976; cons. in field. U.S. Bur. Mines grantee, 1976-79. Mem. Am. Soc. Metals, Am. Inst. M.E., Colo. Mining Assn., AAAS, Sigma Xi, Alpha Sigma Mu. Contbr. articles in field to profl. jours. Home: 4904 S S Flower St Denver CO 80123 Office: Strategic Material Center Metallurgy Dept Univ of Denver Research Inst Denver CO 80208

CHANDRAMOULI, RAMAMURTI, elec. engr.; b. Sholinghur, Madras, India, Oct. 2, 1947; s. Ramamurti and Rajalakshmi (Ramamurti) Krishnamurti; B.Sc., Mysore U., 1965, B.E., 1970; M.E.E., Pratt Inst., 1972; Ph.D., Oreg. State U., 1978; m. Ranjani, Dec. 4, 1980. Instr., Oreg. State U., Corvallis, 1978; sr. engr. research and devel. group, mem. tech. staff spacecraft datasystems sect. Jet Propulsion Lab., Pasadena, Calif., 1978-81; staff engr., design automation group Am. Microsystems Inc., Santa Clara, Calif., 1982—; adj. lectr. Calif. State U.-Fullerton, 1981. Sec., South India Cultural Assn., Los Angeles, 1980-81; bd. dirs. Am. Assn. East Indians. Mem. IEEE, IEEE Computer Soc., Sigma Xi, Eta Kappa Nu. Home: 450 N Mathilda #G102 Sunnyvale CA 94086 Office: 3800 Homestead Rd Santa Clara CA 95051

CHANE, KENNETH ROY, marketing executive; b. Phila., Dec. 14, 1933; s. Abraham J. and Frances (Newman) C.; m. Sandra L. Feiner, June 26, 1963; children—Andrew, Peter, Lawrence, Abby. B.S., Temple U., 1955. Lic. pharmacist N.Y., N.J., Pa., Del. Exec. v.p. Mack Drug Stores, Moonachie, N.J., 1973-77; pres. Sun Drug Stores, Butler, Pa., 1977-80; v.p. Gen. Nutrition Corp., Pitts., 1980-81; v.p., gen. mgr. Health and Nutrition div. Carnation Co., Los Angeles, 1981—. Bd. dirs., chmn. loss prevention com. Pitts. C. of C., 1978-81; bd. dirs. N.J. Retail Merchants Assn., 1976-77. Contbr. articles to trade publs. Office: 5045 Wilshire Blvd Los Angeles CA 90036

CHANG, DONALD AWO, physician's assistant, medical society executive; b. Hilo, Hawaii, May 11, 1948; s. Anthony Ah Wo and Margaret C.; B.S. in Med. Sci., Emory U., 1975; A.A., Community Coll. Denver, 1973; m. Karen Toshiko Isemoto, July 28, 1973; 1 dau., Jennifer Lianne. Cert. fitness instr. Am. Coll. Sports Medicine. Asst. clin. instr. respiratory therapy Mercy Hosp., Denver, 1973; physician's asst. Hilo (Hawaii) Med. Group, 1976-83; exec. dir. Hawaii Unit Am. Cancer Soc., 1983—; basic cardiac life support instr. Am. Heart Assn. Mem. Am. Acad. Physician's Assts., Hawaii Acad. Physician's Assts. Club: Lehua Jaycees (sec. 1977-78, individual devel. v.p. 1978-79, dist. dir. 1979-80, dir. awards and competition, 1980-81, exec. v.p. 1981-82, regional dir. 1982-83). Office: 163 Kalakaua Ave Hilo HI 96720

CHANG, SHIH-GER, chemist; b. Taipei, Taiwan, Oct. 24, 1941; came to U.S., 1966, naturalized, 1980; s. T.-Y. and Y.-C. (Tsay) C.; B.S.E., Taiwan Cheng-Kung U., 1964; M.S., U. Detroit, 1968; Ph.D., U. Calif.-Berkeley, 1971; m. Judy Cheu-Yeuh Tsay. Research asso. div. inorganic and material research Lawrence Berkeley Lab., U. Calif., Berkeley, 1972-73, prin. investigator div. applied sci., 1973—. Dept. Energy grantee, 1979—. Mem. Am. Chem. Soc. Contbr. articles, chpts. to profl. publs.; research in atmospheric and scrubber chemistry. Home: 948 King Dr El Cerrito CA 94530 Office: 1 Cyclotron Dr Berkeley CA 94720

CHANG, SIDNEY HSU-HSIN, educator; b. Wuchang, China, Jan. 1, 1934; s. Chung Ning and Wen Jane (Hwang) C.; B.A., Nat. Taiwan U., 1956; M.A., U. Mo., 1959; M.S., Fla. State U., 1961; Ph.D., U. Wis., 1966; postdoctoral research Harvard, 1969-70; m. Elaine Pardue, Sept. 15, 1962; children—Walter Gerald Chi-chung, Gregory Eugene Chi-tung. Asst. prof. history Calif. State U. at Fresno, 1966-69, asso. prof., 1969-73, prof., 1973—; chmn. Asian studies, 1967-69; chmn. bd. dirs. Chinese Culture & Arts Co., Inc., San Francisco, 1975-77; chmn. bd. trustees C.C.Y. Corp., 1972-77; pres. Am. Chinese Hua Hui Co., 1976—; chmn. bd. dirs. Am. Chinese Culture and Arts Co., 1977—; vis. prof. Nat. Chengchi U., 1975-76. Mem. Republican Presdl. Task Force, 1983—. Am. Philos. Soc. research grantee, summers 1967, 69; Wis. Ford Area fellow, 1963-65. Mem. Am. Hist. Assn., Assn. for Asian Studies, Oral History Assn., Asian Studies on Pacific Coast, Asia Sci. Research Assos. Author: Method and Form for Paperwriting: A Manual, 1977. Mem. editorial bd. Am. Asian Rev., 1983—. Contbr. articles to various scholarly jours. Home: 4526 E Santa Ana Fresno CA 93726 Office: Dept History Calif Stae U Fresno CA 93740 also 241 Columbus Ave San Francisco CA 94133

CHANG, THOMAS JOKON, architect, educator; b. New Westminster, B.C., Can., Jan. 31, 1908; came to U.S., 1924, naturalized, 1926; s. Charles and Elizabeth (Wun) C., m. Weifan Chiu, Nov. 21, 1961. B.S., Fu Tan U., Shanghai, China, 1927; postgrad., U. Cin., 1929; B.F.A., B.Arch., U. Pa., 1935; M.Arch., Ecole des Beaux-Arts, Fontainebleau, France, 1936; M.Arch., MIT, 1937. Pvt. practice architecture, Vancouver, 1938-41; mem. architecture design faculty U. Wash., Seattle, 1941-42; plant engr. Boeing Aircraft Co., 1943-45; plant engr. rep. U.S. Army Air Force, 1943-45; project architect The Austin Co., Seattle, 1946, Los Angeles, 1961; project architect Welton Becket Assocs., Los Angeles, 1954, Pereira-Luckman Assoc., 1955-56, D. McLellan Architecture, 1957, Austin, Field & Fry Assoc., Los Angeles, 1958, Ralph M. Parsons Co., Los Angeles, 1959, Holmes and Narver, Inc., Los Angeles, 1960, R. Sealey Architect, Los Angeles, 1962, Eric Cumine, Architect, Hong Kong, 1962-63, William Allen Cons. Co., 1963-64; sr. set designer, asst. art dir. Walt Disney Prodns., 20th Century-Fox, Warner Bros., Seven Arts, Universal Studios, Hollywood, Calif., 1964-68; project architect McNeil Constrn. Co., Honolulu, 1969-71; ptnr. Jew & Chang Assocs., Venice, Calif., 1977—. Mem. AIA, Boston Soc. Architects, Hong Kong Soc. Architects. Clubs: Am. Commons Cin.; Am. (life) (Hong Kong); Grindelwald Ski (life) (Los Angeles). Archtl. works include: Disneyland Hotel, Union Oil Center, environ. missile lauching facilities, ABC TV Studio, Hollywood, Long Beach (Calif.) Marina, Hong Kong Baptist Coll. Campus, North Las Vegas Civic Ctr. Office: 1 N Venice Blvd Suite 208 Venica CA 90291

CHANG, TIEN-LIN, electronics engr.; b. Chekiang, China, Nov. 22, 1943; s. Hsu-Ting and Vie-Wen (Chou) C.; B.S.E.E., Nat. Taiwan U., 1965; M.S. in E.E., Rice U., 1969, Ph.D., 1971; m. Tu-Ming Cheng, Aug. 2, 1971; children—Wayne, Eric. Postdoctoral fellow Rice U., Houston, 1971; mem. tech. staff Rockwell Internat., Anaheim, Calif., 1971—. Mem. IEEE, Sigma Xi, Chinese Culture Assn. So. Calif. Contbr. articles to profl. jours.; patentee in field. Home: 4419 E Emberwood St Anaheim CA 92807 Office: 3370 Miraloma St Anaheim CA 92803

CHANG, WILLIAM WAI, electrical engineer, manufacturing company executive; b. Kwangtung, China, Aug. 15, 1935; came to U.S., 1956, naturalized, 1961; s. Po Wing and Wai Ming C.; grad. Grantham Coll. Edn., Hong Kong, 1955; B.S.E. in Elec. Engring., U. Mich., 1961; M.S.E.E., MIT, 1963; M.B.A., U. So. Calif., 1974, M.S.B.A. in Fin., 1977; m. Anita Chiu-Woon Wong, Apr. 25, 1965; children—Christina Yuen-Men, Tracey Nga-Men. Tchr., Wun Yiu Public Sch., Hong Kong, 1955-56; research asst. High Voltage Research Lab., MIT, Cambridge, 1961-63; research engr. Northrop Corp., Ventura Div., 1963-65, sr. engr., nuclear effects group Northrop Corp. Labs., Hawthorne, Calif., 1965-71, resident rep. for Northrop Electronics Div., M.I.T. Charles Draper Labs., Cambridge, 1971-72, engring. specialist Northrop Corp. Labs., 1972-74, devel. planning specialist div. master planning Aircraft div. Northrop Corp., Hawthorne, 1974-77, ops. research specialist, integrated logistics support, 1977-80, dir. planning systems and methods, programs and ops. planning, 1980-81; mgr. automated planning and info. mgmt. systems, 1982—. Judge, Los Angeles County Sci. Fair, 1978, 80; mem. South Bay-Harbor Industry Edn. Council, adv. com. Palos Verdes Unified Sch. Dist.; vice prin. South Bay Chinese Sch., 1979-80, prin., 1980-81; bd. dirs., 1981—; bd. dirs., sec., treas. So. Calif. Council Chinese Schs., 1980-81; bd. dirs. South Bay Action for Older Citizens/Ret. Sr. Vol. Program, 1981—; mem. steering com. Palos Verdes Sr. Advocacy Center, 1981-82; bd. dirs. Peninsular Srs., 1982—; developer JOY (Joining Old and Young) Concept, 1975, founder JOY Program, 1982, recipient recognitions from various cities. Mem. IEEE, World Future Soc., Sigma Xi, Tau Beta Pi, Eta Kappa Nu, Phi Kappa Phi, Phi Eta Sigma. Clubs: Northrop Mgmt., Toastmasters (pres. Club 212, adminstrv. asst. lt. gov. Div. B, Dist. 1, 1980-81, commr. 1981-82, Most Outstanding Toastmaster award 1980, others). Contbr. articles to profl. publs. Home: 5732 Scotwood Dr Rancho Palos Verdes CA 90274 Office: Northrop Corp Aircraft Div Dept 3327/82 One Northrop Ave Hawthorne CA 90250

CHAO, CHIA-CHUN GEROGE, aerospace engineer; b. Kwei-Yang, Kwei-Chow, China, Nov. 17, 1939; s. Hsueh-Yen and Wen-Ru (Lu) C.; m. Jean Mei-Jen Kong; children—Frank S., Sophia S. B.S., Cheng-Kung U., Taiwan, 1962; M.S. in Aeros., Calif. Inst. Tech., 1964, Aero. Engr., 1966; Ph.D. in Aerospace Engring., UCLA, 1975. Project engr. Aerospace Research Assocs. Inc., West Covina, Calif., 1966-68; sr. engr. Jet Propulsion Lab., Pasadena, Calif., 1968-78; mem. tech. staff Aerospace Corp., El Segundo, Calif., 1968-80, engring. specialist, 1980—. Served to 2d lt. Taiwan Army, 1962-63. Recipient Cheng-Kung U. model youth award, 1961. Mem. AIAA (astrodynamics tech. com.), Chinese Engrs. and Scientists Assn. So. Calif. Republican. Buddhist. Club: Toastmaster. Contbr. articles to tech. jours. Home: 5640 Seaside Heights Dr Rancho Palos Verdes CA 90274 Office: 2350 E El Segundo Blvd El Segundo CA 90245

CHAO, CHIH HSU, research mechanical engineer; b. Shantung, China, Aug. 2, 1939; s. Ching Fung and Ching Chih (Lin) C.; B.S., Nat. Taiwan U., 1962; M.S., U. Calif.-Berkeley, 1965, Ph.D., 1972; m. Grace Yng Chu, Apr. 15, 1967; children—Henry Shaw, Lily Yuin. Research asst., applied mechanics U. Calif.-Berkeley, 1965-72; research engr. Boeing Co., Seattle, 1966-67; research scientist, mgr. engring. analysis, chief engr. Physics Internat. Co., San Leandro, Calif., 1969—; cons. engr. Registered profl. engr., Calif. Mem. ASME (sect. chmn.), Nat. Soc. Profl. Engrs., Calif. Soc. Profl. Engrs., Nat. Apt. and Property Owners Assn. Democrat. Roman Catholic. Contbr. research papers in field to profl. jours. Home: 1018 Contra Costa Dr El Cerrito CA 94530

CHAO, FU-CHUAN, biochemist; b. Hong Kong, Feb. 8, 1919; s. Timothy Yan-Tze and Kwei-Ching (Wan) C.; B.S., Lingnan U., 1941; Ph.D., U. Calif. at Berkeley, 1951; m. Lydia Lai-Yuk Chui, July 1, 1947; children—Francis, Shirley, Thomas. Came to U.S., 1948, naturalized, 1962. Research fellow U. Calif. at Berkeley, 1951-52, jr. research biochemist, 1952-53; research instr. U. Utah, 1953-55; research asso. Stanford, 1955-61; biophys. chemist Stanford Research Inst., Menlo Park, Calif., 1961-74; research chemist VA Hosp., Palo Alto, Calif., 1974-78; biochemist SmithKline Beckman, Inc., 1978—. Am. Heart Assn. research fellow, 1955-57. Fellow Am. Inst. Chemists; mem. A.A.A.S., Am. Inst. Biol. Scis., Am. Soc. Microbiology, Am. Chem. Soc., N.Y. Acad. Sci., Sigma Xi. Methodist. Research in biochemistry. Home: 1524 Channing Ave Palo Alto CA 94303 Office: 485 Potrero Ave Sunnyvale CA 94086

CHAO, JAMES MIN-TZU, architect; b. Dairen, China, Feb. 27, 1940; s. T. C. and Lin Fan (Wong) C.; came to U.S., 1949, naturalized, 1962; B.Arch., U. Calif., Berkeley, 1965; m. Kirsti Helena Lehtonen, May 15, 1968. Intermediate draftsman Spencer, Lee & Busse, Architects, San Francisco, 1966-67; asst. to pres. Import Plus Inc., Santa Clara, Calif., 1967-69; job capt. Hammaberg and Herman, Architects, Oakland, Calif., 1969-71; project mgr. B A Premises Corp., San Francisco, 1971-79; constrn. mgr. The Straw Hat Restaurant Corp., 1979-81, mem. sr. mgmt., dir. real estate and constrn., 1981—; coordinator minority vending program, solar application program Bank of Am. Recipient honorable mention Future Scientists Am., 1955. Certified architect, Calif. Mem. AIA. Republican. Clubs: Encinal Yacht (dir. 1977, 78). Patentee tidal electric generating system. Author first comprehensive consumer orientated performance specification for remote banking transaction.

CHAO, LI-PEN, neurochemist, neurologist; b. Hunan, China, Apr. 14, 1933; came to U.S., 1960, naturalized, 1975; s. Tun-Shu and Chi-Jung (Lei) C.; B.S., Taiwan Chung-Hsing U., 1957; M.S., U. Minn., 1964, Ph.D., 1967; m. Theresa H. Hsu, June 24, 1967; children—Emil Yu-Ming, Jennifer Ray-Ming. Asst. research biochemist dept. neurology U. Calif., San Francisco, 1967-70; asst. research neurologist dept. neurology UCLA, 1970-74, asso. research neurologist, 1974-79, research neurologist, 1979—. Served with Chinese Army, 1957-59. Mem. AAAS, Am. Chem. Soc., Am. Soc. Neurochemistry, Internat. Soc. for Neurochemistry, Soc. for Neurosci., Sigma Xi. Contbr. articles to profl. jours. Home: 2346 Pearl St Santa Monica CA 90405 Office: Dept Neurology Reed Center UCLA Los Angeles CA 90024

CHAO, WEN YING, plastic surgeon; b. Kirin, China, Aug. 18, 1917; s. Sheng and Shih C.; m. Ching Ju, June 6, 1945; children—Schumarry, Schucherry, Arlene, Joanne, Joyce. M.B.C.H.B., Mukden Med. Coll., 1936, M.D., 1941. Lic. physician, Md., Calif. Intern, Mukden Med. Coll. Hosp., 1942, resident in surgery, 1943-45; resident in plastic surgery SUNY-Syracuse, 1952-55; fellow thoracic surgery Washington U. Barnes Hosp., St. Louis, 1948; practice medicine specializing in plastic and reconstructive surgery, Redondo Beach, Calif., 1958-77, Gardena, Calif., 1977—; mem. staff Martin Luther King Hosp.; assoc. prof. surgery U. So. Calif.; asst. clin. prof. surgery Loma Linda U. Mem. Calif. Soc. Plastic Surgeons, Am. Soc. Plastic and Reconstructive Surgeons, Am. Assn. Cosmetic Surgeons. Office: 1141 W Redondo Beach Blvd 211 Gardena CA 90247

CHAPIN, CHARLES, computer software products company executive; b. San Diego, Oct. 21, 1953; s. Charles A. and Helen (Gillette) C.; m. Evelyn Marie Fike, Sept. 22, 1979; 1 dau., Katherine Elizabeth. Student UCLA, Biol. Coll., La Mirada, Calif.; B.A., U. Calif.-San Diego, 1978. Systems programmer Gen. Automation, San Diego, 1977-78; systems programmer U. Calif.-San Diego, 1977; chief cons. Univ. Pascal Cons. Service, San Diego, 1979; mktg. mgr. SofTech Microsystems, Inc., San Diego, 1979-80; owner, pres. Chapin Assocs., San Diego and Ashburn, Calif., 1980—; dir. engring. Am. div. Advanced Data Inst., 1982—. Mem. Assn. Computing Machinery, IEEE, U. Calif.-San Diego System Users Soc. (sec. 1980—). Club: San Diego Yacht. Office: Advanced Data Inst 1215 Howe Ave Sacramento CA 95825 also Chapin Assocs PO Box 749 Ashburn CA 95603

CHAPIN, JUNE ROEDIGER, educator, author; b. Chgo., May 19, 1931; d. Henry and Stephania (Palke) Roediger; m. Ned Chapin, June 12, 1954; children—Suzanne, Elaine. B.A., U. Chgo., 1952, M.A., 1954; Ed.D., Stanford U., 1962. Tchr., Chgo. Pub. Schs. and Redwood City, Calif., 1954-60; mem. faculty U. Santa Clara (Calif.), 1965-67; prof. edn. Coll. Notre Dame, Belmont, Calif., 1967—; cons. Recipient Hilda Taba award Calif. Council Social Studies, 1976. Mem. Nat. Council Social Studies, Am. Sociol. Assn., Am. Ednl. Research Assn., AAUP. Author: Chronicles of Time, 1983; (with Oswald and LaRaus) Windows on Our World Planet Earth, 1976, Our Home, the Earth, 1980; (with Gross) Teaching Social Studies Skills, 1973, Social Studies for Our Times, 1978; others. Home: 1190 Bellair Way Menlo Park CA 94025 Office: Coll Notre Dame Belmont CA 94002

CHAPIN, NED, data processing consultant; b. Port Gamble, Wash., Aug. 8, 1927; s. M. C. and Rose A. (Smallwood) C.; m. June Roediger, June 12, 1954; children—Suzanne, Elaine. M.B.A., U. Chgo., 1949; Ph.D., Ill. Inst. Tech., 1959. Registered profl. engr., Calif. Lectr. to asst. prof. various schs., 1953-56; systems analyst SRI Internat., 1956-61; assoc. prof. San Francisco State U., 1961-64; data processing cons. InfoSci., Inc., Menlo Park, Calif., 1965—; series editor Van Nostrand Reinhold Pub. Co., Inc.; session chmn. Nat. Computer Cons.; dir. InfoSci, Inc., CTS Time Sharing Corp. Served with U.S. Army, 1951-53. Mem. Assn. Computer Programmers and Analysts, Assn. Computing Machinery, Data Processing Mgmt. Assn., Assn. Computers and Humanities, Soc. Mgmt. Info. Systems, Inst. Indsl. Engrs., Soc. Gen. Systems Research, Ops. Research Soc. Am., Inst. Mgmt. Sci., EDP Auditors Assn., Assn. Ednl. Data Systems, Soc. Cert. Data Processors, Am. Econs. Assn., N.Y. Acad. Sci., Sigma Xi, Delta Sigma Rho. Author: Computer: A System Approach, 1971, others; contbr. articles to profl. jours.; patentee in field. Home: 1190 Bellair Way Menlo Park CA 94025 Office: PO Box 7117 Menlo Park CA 94025

CHAPLIN, GEORGE, newspaper editor; b. Columbia, S.C., Apr. 28, 1914; s. Morris and Netty (Brown) C.; m. Esta L. Solomon, Jan. 26, 1937; children—Stephen, Jerri. B.S., Clemson Coll., 1935. Reporter, city editor Greenville (S.C.) Piedmont, 1935-42; mng. editor Camden (N.J.) Courier-Post, 1946-47, San Diego Jour., 1948-49; mng. editor, then editor New Orleans Item, 1949-58; assoc. editor, then editor, then v.p., editor-in-chief Honolulu Advertiser, 1958—. Chmn. Gov.'s Conf. on Yr. 2000, 1970, Hawaii Commn. on Yr. 2000, 1971-74; co-chmn. Conf. on Alternative Econ. Futures for Hawaii, 1973-75; charter mem. Goals for Hawaii; bd. dirs. U. Hawaii Research Corp., 1970-72, Inst. Religion and Social Change, Hawaii Jewish Welfare Fund; vice-chmn., bd. govs. East-West Ctr., Honolulu; mem. Honolulu Symphony Soc., Pacific and Asian Affairs Council; alt. U.S. del. S. Pacific Commn., 1978-81. Served to capt. AUS, 1942-46; editor, officer in charge Stars and Stripes, Mid-Pacific. Decorated: Star of Solidarity (Italy), 1957; Harvard U. Nieman fellow, 1940-41; recipient Overseas Press Club citations, 1961, 72, E.W. Scripps award, 1976, Headliners award, 1962, John Hancock awards 1972, 74; Dartmouth Coll. Champion Media Award for Econ. Understanding, 1981, Clemson U. Disting. Alumni award, 1974. Mem. Am. Soc. Newspaper Editors (pres. 1976-77), Soc. Nieman Fellows, Internat. Press Inst., Nat. Conf. Editorial Writers, World Future Soc., U.S.-Japan Conf. Cultural and Ednl. Interchange, Sigma Delta Chi. Jewish. Clubs: Pacific, Waialae Country. Co-editor Hawaii 2000, Continuing Experiment in Anticipatory Democracy, 1973; contbr. other books. Office: PO Box 3110 Honolulu HI 96802

CHAPLINE, CLAUDIA BEECHUM, educator, artist, choreographer, artist; b. Oak Park, Ill., May 23, 1930; d. Jacob Burwell and Lillian Estella (Schell) Chapline; B.A. cum laude, George Washington U., 1953; M.A., Washington U., 1956; postgrad. Conn. Coll. Sch. Dance, summers, 1954, 56, U. Mo., 1956-57; m. James Nicol Hood, Dec. 22, 1955 (div. June 1974); children—Craig, Randall. Instr. Washington U., St. Louis, 1953-56; dance therapist St. Louis State Hosp., 1953-56; instr. Univ. Mo., Columbia, 1956-57; asst. prof. Calif. State Univ., Northridge, 1961-64; asst. prof. UCLA, 1960-67; performer Doris Humphrey Repertory Group, New London, Conn., 1954; actress Instant Theatre, Los Angeles, 1959-64; dir. Premiere of The Summons, 1964; dir. West Coast Premiere of The Mother of Us All, 1965; performer with Gloria Newman Dance Theater Co., Los Angeles, 1957-59; one person shows include E.B. Crocker Gallery, Sacramento, Calif., 1967, Mus. Art, Downey, Calif., 1970, Humboldt Galleries, 1969-74, Brand Library, Glendale, Calif., 1974, Mus. Art, Palos Verdes, 1975, others; group shows include Corcoran Gallery Art, Washington, 1952, St. Louis Art Mus., 1955, Mus. Art, Laguna Beach, Calif., 1973, Los Angeles County Mus. Art, 1973, Los Angeles Inst. Contemporary Art, 1973; represented in permanent collections E.B. Crocker, Humboldt Galleries, Downey Mus. Art; represented in pvt. collections: founder Claudia Chapline Dance Theatre Co., Los Angeles, 1973; founder, pres., dir. Inst. Dance & Exptl. Art, 1974-82; tutorial staff Internat. Coll./Univ. Without Walls, 1980-81; editorial staff Dance West Mag., 1979-80, The Artists' News, 1980-81; soloist for various groups, 1960-80; tchr. dance UCLA Extension, 1981-82; mem. staff Calif. Arts Council, 1982—, coordinator Artists in Social Instns., 1982—. Mem. adv. bd. Beyond Baroque Found., 1976-81; founder Santa Monica Bay Area Arts Council, 1978-80; mem. art adv. bd. Santa Monica Pub. Library, 1976-78; curriculum cons. in dance Los Angeles City Schs., 1957-58. City Santa Monica grantee, 1977-78, 80-81; Calif. Arts Council grantee, 1978, 80. Mem. Los Angeles Area Dance Alliance, Los Angeles Inst. Contemporary Art, Calif. Assn. Dance Cos., Dance Critics Assn.

CHAPMAN, CAROLYN, media staff dir.; b. Portsmouth, Ohio, Feb. 4, 1933; d. Roger Donald and Flowery Alice (Callaway) Carr; diploma Portsmouth Interstate Bus. Coll., 1954, S. Ohio Manpower Tng. Ctr.,

1965; m. Edward J. Chapman, May 13, 1966; children—Cheryl, Roger, Lisa, Mark, Edmond, Sean. Dep. probation officer Scioto County Juvenile Ct., Portsmouth, 1960-63: coder II, Aid for Aged, Ohio Dept. Pub. Welfare, Columbus, 1964; clk. typist II, Bur. Vital Stats., Dept. Health, Columbus, 1964, clk.-stenographer II, CD Div., 1966; clk.-stenographer ABC, Los Angeles, 1967, ops. coordinator, 1968-72, assoc. dir., on-air dir., 1972—; cons. in video tape and TV prodn.; mem. negotiating com. Teamsters Union, Los Angeles, 1970. Ch. sec. Findlay St. Meth. Ch., Portsmouth, 1959-63, chmn. women's day program, 1962, chmn. commn. on missions, 1959-62, del. ann. conf., Cleve., 1963, sec. ofcl. bd., 1959-62; pres. local chpt. Ohio Republican Council, 1959-62, mem. state bd., 1962, del. from Scioto County to State Rep. Conv., Ohio, 1962; mem. film editing com. Social Health and Hygiene Assn., 1961-62; tribute com. for Tribute to Dorothy Arzner, 1975; Los Angeles Jr. C. of C., 1977. Mem. ABC Employees Assn. (pres. Hollywood branch, 1971-73), Dirs. Guild Am. (council 1981-83). Address: PO Box 43025 Los Angeles CA 90043

CHAPMAN, CARRIE ETHELYN, physician; b. Manchester, N.H., Dec. 17, 1906; d. John Wilbert and Carrie Ethelyn (Crawford) C.; B.S., Fla. State U., 1928; M.D., Tufts U., 1934. Intern, Mass. State Infirmary, Tewksbury, 1934-35, staff physician, 1937; resident anesthesiology Mass. Gen. Hosp., 1937-38, Faulkner Hosp., 1938-41; chief anesthesiology Elliot Hosp., Manchester, N.H., 1941-46; fellow in anesthesiology Mayo Clinic and Found., 1946, fellow phys. medicine and rehab., 1946-49; practice medicine specializing in phys. medicine, rehab. and anesthesiology, Oakland, Calif., 1951-63, Los Angeles, 1963—; asst. to surgeon USPHS, 1944-51, lt. comdr., then comdr., 1950—, chief phys. medicine, rehab. service Oakland Naval Hosp., 1951-53, cons., 1955-63; clin. instr. anesthesiology Postgrad. Med. Sch. Harvard U., 1938-41; cons. dept. occupational therapy San Jose (Calif.) State Coll., 1960-63; asst. clin. prof. phys. medicine and rehab. U. So. Calif. Med. Sch., 1964-70, asso. prof., 1970-76, prof., 1976—; chief phys. medicine, rehab. VA Hosp., Oakland, 1954-63; cons. San Joaquin Gen. and County Hosp., Stockton, Calif., 1962-63; asso. dir. adj. staff Ben R. Meyer Rehab. Center Cedars of Lebanon Hosp., Cedar Sinai Med. Center, 1963, asso. attending, 1964—; cons. VA Hosp., Long Beach, Calif., 1964-65; attending staff Los Angeles County Gen. Hosp., 1965—; liaison officer Am. Acad. Phys. Medicine and Rehab. to AMA Nat. Congress Vol. Health Agys. Chmn., Alameda County chpt. Muscular Dystrophy Assn., 1954-56; mem. Pres.'s Com. Employment Handicapped, 1963—; vice chmn. So. Calif. chpt. Multiple Sclerosis Soc., 1966—, chmn. med. adv. bd., 1968—; mem. adv. bd. East Bay Rehab. Center; mem. med. adv. bd. Diablo Therapy Center, Pleasant Hill, Calif.; chmn. Beverly Hills (Calif.) Com. to Employ Handicapped, 1972-74; founder, pres. Am. Found. Treatment of Burn Injuries, 1970. Recipient award of merit Dept. Calif. Mil. Order Purple Heart, 1958; DAV Nat. citation for Distinguished Service, 1961; certificate of merit A.C.S., 1963; Dr. A.B.C. Nat. Rehab. award, 1974; Distinguished Alumnus award Fla. State U., 1975; Pioneer award Am. Inst. Ultrasound in Medicine, 1980; named Calif. Physician of Year, 1969. Diplomate Am. Bd. Phys. Medicine and Rehab. Fellow Am. Acad. Phys. Medicine and Rehab., Am. Geriatrics Soc., Am. Med. Women's Assn. (life); mem. AMA (certificate of merit 1964), Calif. (asst. sec. sect. phys. medicine 1958-71; chmn. 1960-73), Alameda-Contra-Costa (past rehab. com. chmn.), Pan Am. med. assns., Am. Congress Phys. Medicine and Rehab. (Bronze medal 1962, sec. Western sect.), Calif., Peruvian (hon.) socs. phys. medicine and rehab., Am. Inst. Ultrasonics in Medicine (pres. 1963-64, plaque for outstanding contbns. as pres. 9th ann. meeting 1964), Calif. (chmn. 1970), So. Calif. (pres. 1970-71; exec. bd. 1969—) socs. phys. medicine, Am. Assn. Electromyography and Electrodiagnosis, Assn. Rehab. Centers, Assn. Mil. Surgeons U.S., Assn. Med. Rehab. Dirs. and Coordinators (chmn. med. certification bd.), Tufts Med., Mayo Grad. Sch. Medicine (life), Mass. Gen. Hosp. alumni assns., Nat. Rehab. Assn. (pres. So. Calif. chpt. 1970), Nat. Assn. Sheltered Workshops and Homebound Programs, Pan Am. Med. Women's Alliance, Soc. History of Medicine, Internat. Soc. Burn Injuries (Edinburgh, Scotland), N.Am. Acad. Manipulative Medicine (v.p. 1969-71, pres. 1972), Calif. Phys. Med. Soc. (v.p. So. Calif. 1969, pres. 1970). Contbr. articles to profl. jours. Home and Office: 3522A Bahia Blanca W Laguna Hills CA 92653

CHAPMAN, DEWEY OTIS, JR., investment and real estate devel. exec.; b. Oakland, Calif., June 19, 1920; s. Dewey Otis and Catherine Mae (Graves) C.; student public schs.; m. Betty Jane Ridge, Sept. 11, 1944; children—Denise Lee, Michele Leslie. Joined U.S. Navy, 1942, advanced through ranks to chief petty officer, 1944; service in PTO, World War II; ret., 1962; With Hamilton Mgmt. Corp., 1956-63, regional mgr. No. Calif., 1959-63; regional mgr. Trust Securities Corp., Los Gatos, Calif., 1963-70, Cornerstone Securities Corp., San Jose, Calif., 1970-71; chmn. bd., chief exec. officer Calif.-Hawaii Devel. Inc., Alamo, Calif., 1971—; dir. Profl. Resort Mgmt., Inc. Mem. Nat. Assn. Securities Dealers, Assn. Fin. Planners. Republican. Club: Plaza (Honolulu). Office: 1399 Ygnacio Valley Rd Suite 20 Walnut Creek CA 94598

CHAPMAN, DONALD MASON, III, investment banker, consultant; b. Sherman, Tex., Mar. 17, 1949; s. Donald Mason and Patsy Jean (Jarrell) C.; m. Judith Lee Eckes, June 14, 1969 (div.). B.A. in Econs., San Diego State U., 1971; M.A. in Econs., U. Wash., 1972. Economists, Rapid City, S.D., 1972, asst. dir. 6th planning dist., 1973; project mgr. Comprehensive Planning Orgn., San Diego, 1974-78; dir. mktg. 1st Affiliated Securities, La Jolla, Calif., 1978-79; pres., dir. AFR Securities Corp., Del Mar, Calif., 1979-80, Am. Cinema Group, Del Mar, 1980-81, Angeles Entertainment Group and Angeles Entertainment Funding, LaJolla, 1981—; dir. Pacific Marine Energy, Seattle, 1982-83, Strata Energy, Denver, 1982-83; advisor Leaseby, Inc., Newport Beach, Calif., 1981-83; prof. econs. Nat. U., San Diego, 1974-78; instr. econs. S.D. State U., 1972-73. Active LaJolla Mus. Contemporary Art, 1980—. Econs. fellow U. Wash., 1971-72; recipient Econ. Found. award San Diego 1970. Mem. Internat. Assn. Fin. Planners, Nat. Assn. Security Dealers. Author: Overall Economic Development Plan Western South Dakota, 1973; Growth Management in San Diego, 1975; contbr. articles to fin. jours. Office: 3401 Girard Ave 300 La Jolla CA 92037

CHAPMAN, J. MAYNARD, public affairs officer; b. Ft. Worth, July 18, 1940; s. John B. and Mildred E. (Morrison) C.; m. Patricia Vann, Apr. 4, 1969; children—Carric, Teresa, Tom. B. in Journalism, U. Tex., 1962; M.Th., So. Meth. U., 1970. Pub. info. officer, N.Mex. Environ. Improvement Agy., Santa Fe, 1973-75, N.Mex. Health and Social Services Dept., 1975-76, N.Mex. Health and Environment Dept., 1980-82; spl. projects officer Colo. Dept. Social Services, Denver, 1983—. Served with USAF, 1962-65. Mem. Pub. Relations Soc. Am., Sigma Delta Chi.

CHAPMAN, JAMES ARLEN, paper company executive; b. Portland, Oreg., May 14, 1935; s. Lyle Vernon and Agnes E. (Widell) C.; m. Yvonne Maxine LeGail, Sept. 10, 1955; children—Susan, Lisa, David, Wendy. B.S. in Chem. Engring., Oreg. State U., 1958. Sr. research engr. U.S. Borax Corp., Boron, Calif., 1957-62; engring. mgr. Chem. Products div. Crown Zellerbach, Camas, Wash., 1963-68, gen. mgr., Vancouver, Wash., 1969-81, resident mgr. Flexible Packaging div. Crown Zellerbach, Portland, Oreg., 1981—. Mem. Clark County Health and Welfare Planning Council, 1974-80; allocations chmn. Clark County CETA Bd., 1978-80; fin. chmn. State Senator Zimmerman, 1980; trustee S. West Wash. Hosps., 1980—; trustee Clark Coll. Found., v.p., 1983. Mem. Am. Inst. Chem. Engrs., Tau Beta Phi. Club: Columbia Edgewater Country (Portland).

CHAPMAN, JEAN RUSS, publishing exec.; b. Pitts., Aug. 11, 1928; d. John Monroe and Constance (Clarke) Russ; B.A., U. Mich., 1950; postgrad. L.I. U., 1969-71; m. Robert David Rust, Mar. 4, 1957 (div.); 1 dau., Constance Clare; m. 2d, Francis Allan Chapman, Mar. 11, 1972; stepchildren—Allan, Kenneth, Jeanne. Asst. to editor Ladies Home Jour., N.Y.C., 1950-51; asst. editor Child Life Mag., Boston, 1951-55; tchr., Stirling, Scotland, 1955-57; sr. editor, project mgr., then cons. Harcourt Brace Jovanovich, N.Y.C. and San Francisco, 1971-75; adminstr. dept. anesthesiology U. Wash. Med. Center, Seattle, 1976-82; chief book editor Alaska N.W. Pub. Co., Edmonds, Wash., 1982—; instr. Nassau Community Coll., part-time 1970-71. Clk., Congl. Ch., Huntington, N.Y., 1968. Mem. Network Exec. Women, Alpha Phi (chpt. pres. 1967-69). Democrat. Presbyterian. Club: Mercerwood Shore. Sr. editor, project mgr. Bookmark Reading Series, 1973-75. Home: 4307 E Mercer Way Mercer Island WA 98040 Office: 130 2d Ave S Edmonds WA 98020

CHAPMAN, LORING, psychologist, neuroscientist; b. Los Angeles, Oct. 4, 1929; s. Lee E. and Elinore E. (Gundry) Scott; B.S., U. Nev., 1950; Ph.D., U. Chgo., 1955; m. Toy Farrar, June 14, 1954; children—Robert, Antony, Pandora. Research fellow U. Chgo., 1952-54; research asso., asst. prof. Cornell U. Med. Coll., N.Y.C., 1955-61; asso. prof. in residence UCLA, 1961-65; research prof. U. Oreg., Portland, 1965; br. chief NIH, Bethesda, Md., 1966-67; chmn. dept. behavioral biology Sch. Medicine, U. Calif., Davis, 1967-79, prof., 1967-79, prof. psychiatry, neurology and human physiology, 1979-82, vice chmn. div. sci. basic to medicine, 1976-79, prof. psychiatry, chief div. clin. psychology, dir. chronic pain unit, 1979—; vis. prof. U. Sao Paulo, 1959, 77, Univ. Coll., London, 1970, U. Florence (Italy), 1980; clin. prof. Georgetown U., 1966-67; mem. Calif. Center Primate Biology, 1967—; dir. research Fairview Hosp., 1965-66; cons. Nat. Inst. Neurol. Disease and Stroke, 1961—; cons. Nat. Inst. Child Health Devel., 1967—, mem. research and tng. com., 1968-72; cons. NASA, USN, USAF, Calif. State Dept. Corrections, Nat. Cancer Inst., 1967—. Recipient Thornton Wilson prize, 1958; Career award USPHS, 1964; Commonwealth Fund award, 1970; grantee NIH, 1956—, NASA, 1969—, Nat. Inst. Drug Abuse, 1971—; Fogarty sr. internat. fellow, 1980; lic. psychologist, N.Y., Oreg., Calif. Mem. Am. Acad. Neurology, Am. Physiol. Soc., Am. Psychol. Assn., Royal Soc. Medicine (London), Am. Neurol. Assn., Am. Assn. Mental Deficiency, Soc. Neuroscis., Aerospace Med. Assn. Author: Pain and Suffering, 3 vols., 1967; Head and Brain, 2 vols., 1971; (with E. Dunlap) The Eye, 1981; contbr. sci. articles to publs.; research in mental illness, brain function, pain and psychopharmacology. Home: 756 Sycamore St Davis CA 95616 Office: School Medicine Univ Calif Davis CA 95616

CHAPMAN, MARY JO, small business owner, bookkeeper; b. Portland, Oreg., Mar. 15, 1929; d. John Herman and Frances Jo (Smith) Bohlen; student Ins. Agts. Sch., Portland, 1951, IBM Sch., 1956; m. Ruel Earl Chapman, Jan. 6, 1965; 1 son, Charles John. Automobile underwriter Metzger Parker Agy., Portland, 1948-50; ins. underwriter, gen. office worker Doug Henson Ins. Agy., Portland, 1950-52; clk.-typist Alaska Dist. Engrs., Anchorage, 1952-53; asst. statistician North Consol. Airlines, Anchorage, 1953-56; IBM operator Standard Oil Calif., Portland, 1956-59; co-owner, bookkeeper, buyer, mgr. Sand Dunes Frontier, Inc., Florence, 1960—; corp. officer and bookkeeper Timber Dunes, Inc., Florence, 1971—; owner Galeria of Florence, 1983—. Mem. Florence Co-ordinating Council, 1973-74; bd. dirs. Florence Sr. Center, 1973-75. Mem. Oreg. Coast Assn., Oreg. Hosp. and Visitors Assn. Club: Soroptimist (past pres.) (Florence). Club: Ladies of Elks. Home: 777 1st St Florence OR 97439 Office: 83960 Hwy 101 S Florence OR 97439

CHAPMAN, ROBERT GALBRAITH, physician; b. Colorado Springs, Colo., Sept. 29, 1926; s. Edward Northrop and Janet (Johnson) C.; student Westminster Coll., 1944-45; B.A., Yale, 1947; M.D., Harvard, 1951; M.S., U. Colo., 1958; m. Virginia Irene Potts, July 6, 1956; children—Lucia Tully, Sarah Northrop, Robert Bostwick. Intern, Hartford (Conn.) Hosp., 1951-52, jr. med. resident, 1952; med. resident U. Colo. Med. Center, Denver, 1955-58, chief resident, 1957-58; postdoctoral research fellow U. Wash., Seattle, 1958-60; faculty U. Colo., Denver, 1960—, asso. prof. medicine, 1968—; chief staff Denver VA Hosp., 1968-70; asso. dir. Belle Bonfils Meml. Blood Center, Denver, 1973-77, dir., 1977—; attending physician Colo. Gen. Hosp. and Denver VA Hosp., 1960—. Mem. gov.'s adv. com. Sickle Cell Anemia program, 1974—. Served with USN, 1944-45, to capt. USAF, 1953-54. Diplomate Am. Bd. Internal Medicine, Am. Bd. Pathology. Fellow A.C.P.; mem. Am. Soc. Hematology, Am. Assn. Blood Banks, Council Community Blood Centers (v.p. 1979, 80), Western Soc. Clin. Research, Colo., Denver med. socs., AAAS, Alpha Omega Alpha. Mem. United Ch. of Christ. Club: Denver Country. Contbr. articles in field to med. jours. Home: 250 S Eudora St Denver CO 80222 Office: 4200 E 9th Ave Denver CO 80262

CHAPMAN, ROBERT GORDAN, high school academic/vocational counselor; b. Los Angeles, March 26, 1941; s. Robert John and Elizabeth (Wickersham) C.; m. Barbara Ann Myers, Aug. 10, 1963; children—Edward, Lisa, Laurie, Scott. B.A. in Art, San Jose State U., 1964, M.A. in Design and Counseling, 1969. Cert. gen. secondary, spl. secondary, pupil personnel services, jr. coll. adminstrn. Instr., art Piedmont Hills (Calif.) High Sch., 1964-74, West Valley Coll., Saratoga, Calif., 1946-80; vocat./acad. counselor Santa Teresa High Sch., San Jose, Calif., 1975—; mem. master plan for excellence in edn. com., San Jose. Recipient Calif. Expn., hon. mention art award, 1965, 1966, Western U.S. traveling exhbn., 1972, 2d award San Jose Art League, Mem. NEA, San Jose Art League, Smithsonian Inst. Democrat. Roman Catholic. Club: K. C. (San Jose). Contbr. articles to profl. jours.; designer pendant honoring 1st lunar landing. Office: 6150 Snell Rd San Jose CA 95123

CHAPPELIE, NORMAN ANDREW, chemist; b. East Chicago, Ind., May 1, 1940; s. Frank Joseph and Helene Susan (Kasony) C.; B.S., Purdue U., 1962, M.S. (Am. Petroleum Inst. fellow), 1965. Research asso. Standard Oil, Whiting, Ind., 1962; chemist Oreg. State Police, Portland, 1966-68; chemist Chembond Corp., Springfield, Oreg., 1968—, supr. chem. labs., 1976—. Mem. Am. Chem. Soc., AAAS. Clubs: Emerald Empire Gun, Elks (Springfield). Patentee in field. Office: 475 N 28th St Springfield OR 97477

CHAPPELL, DOROTHY TWICHELL, psychologist, educator; b. South Dayton, N.Y., May 10, 1916; d. Evans Truman and Marjorie Emily (Howard) Twichell; m. Raid B. Chappell, Dec. 30, 1950; children—Susan Mensinger, Ann Barbeiro, Lani, Robert, Steven. B.A., U. Buffalo, 1946, M.A., 1947; Ph.D., U. Mich., 1952. Lic. clin. psychologist, Calif. Psychologist, Modesto (Calif.) State Hosp., 1964-67; psychologist Family Service Agy., Modesto, 1967—; instr. Modesto Jr. Coll., 1977—. Home: 3701 E Orangeburg Modesto CA 95355

CHAPPELL, RONALD LEE, accountant; b. Gilroy, Calif., Feb. 1, 1945; s. Maitland Alfred and Nettie Almira (Yearian) C.; m. Colleen Ann Ludwig, Dec. 30, 1967; 1 son, Peter James. B.A. in Acctg., Boise State U., 1970. C.P.A., Idaho, Calif. Cost acct. Idaho Dept. Employment, Boise, 1970-72, sr. acct. fed. reporting, 1977-81; cost acct. supr. Wash. Dept. Employment Security, Olympia, 1972-75; controller, New Life Fin. Mgmt. Inc., Olympia, 1976; pvt. practice C.P.A., Clovis, Calif., 1981—. Served with USN, 1962-66. Mem. Idaho Soc. C.P.A.s, Am. Inst. C.P.A.s, Fresno Enrolled Agts., Full Gospel Bus. Men's Fellowship Internat., Alpha Kappa Psi. Republican. Office: Suite 21A 3097 Willow Ave Clovis CA 93612

CHAPPELL, RUTH, mgmt. devel. cons.; b. Calif., Apr. 20, 1932; d. George and Helen (Finley) Rax; B.A. in Communication, Calif. State U., Sacramento, 1977, B.A. in Psychology, 1977; m. Joseph Chappell, May 10, 1952; children—Valinda, Patricia, Jerome, Kevin. With San Francisco Public Health Dept., 1954-63; lab. technician, technologist Calif. Dept. Food and Agr., 1963-75, affirmative action officer, women's program officer, 1975-76, tng. officer, 1976-77; prof. devel. cons., 1977-79; mgr. adminstrv. services personnel devel. div. Calif. Personnel Bd., 1979—. Vice chmn. legis. com. Calif. State Employees Assn., 1977; legis. chmn. Sacramento Community Commn. on Status of Women, 1976; No. vice chmn. Women's Coalition Calif., 1979; Calif. chmn. Womens' Equity Action League, 1977. Recipient cert. merit (3) Calif. State Govt. Mem. Am. Soc. Tng. and Devel., Labor Relations Assn., Nat. Womens Polit. Caucus, Black Women Organized for Polit. Action, Black Women's Polit. Caucus. Methodist (human rights chmn.). Club: Toastmistresses (regional public relations chmn.). Address: 2551 5th Ave Sacramento CA 95818

CHAPPELL, WILLARD RAY, physics educator, environmental scientist; b. Boulder, Colo., Feb. 27, 1938; s. Willard Bruce and Mildred Mary (Weaver) C.; m. Juanita June Benetin, Mar. 5, 1981. B.A. in Math., U. Colo., 1962, Ph.D. in Physics, 1965; A.M. in Physics, Harvard U., 1963. Postdoctoral research assoc. Smithsonian Astrophys. Obs., Cambridge, Mass., 1965-66, Lawrence Livermore (Calif.) Lab., 1966-67; asst. prof. physics U. Colo., Boulder, 1967-70, assoc. prof., 1970-73, prof., 1973-76; prof. physics, dir. Ctr. for Environ. Scis., U. Colo., Denver, 1976—; chmn. Dept. Energy Oil Shale Task Force, 1978-83; mem. adv. com. to dir. on health scis. Los Alamos Nat. Lab.; mem. Colo. Gov.'s Sci. Adv. Com., 1974-76, chmn., 1975-76. Served with U.S. Army, 1956-58. NSF fellow, 1962-65; Fleishman Found. grantee, 1969-71; NSF grantee, 1971-76; EPA grantee, 1975-79; Dept. Energy grantee, 1976-83; U.S. Bur. Mines grantee, 1979-81. Mem. Am. Phys. Soc., AAAS, Soc. Environ. Geochemistry and Health (exec. com. 1981-83), Phi Beta Kappa. Democrat. Author: Transport and Biological Effects of Molybdenum in the Environment, 1975. Office: 1100 14th St Box 36 Denver CO 80202

CHAPPIE, EUGENE A., congressman; b. Sacramento, 1920. Mem. Calif. State Assembly, 1960-80, chmn. com. on rules, 1968-70, chmn. com. on social welfare, 1966-68; mem. 97th Congress from Calif. 1st dist. Served with U.S. Army, World War II, Korean conflict. Decorated Bronze Star. Republican. Office: 1730 Longworth House Office Bldg Washington DC 20515*

CHAPPLE, GORDON DOUGLAS, food company official; b. Palo Alto, Calif., May 4, 1948; s. John Thayer and Betsy Ann (Gordon) C.; m. Katharine R. Vaughan, May 11; children—Katharine Denise, Christopher Douglas. B.S., U. Calif.-Santa Barbara, 1970, B.A., U. Calif.-Berkeley, 1973. Brand asst. Clorox Co., Oakland, Calif., 1973-75, asst. brand mgr. new products, 1975-76, brand mgr., 1976-78, new products brand mgr., 1979-80; brand mgr. RJR Foods/Del Monte Co., San Francisco, 1980-82, group product mgr., 1982—; lectr. Saint Mary's Coll. Active Walnut Heights (Calif.) Nature Area Adv. Com.; mem. Cling Peach Adv. Bd., Pear Adv. Bd. Office: Del Monte Corp One Market Plaza Box 3575 San Francisco CA 94119

CHAPPLER, RONALD REED, dermatologist; b. Kansas City, Mo., Aug. 13, 1947; s. Milton George and Mary Ann (Ferris) C.; M.D., Kans. U., 1971; m. Karen Ann Kelley, Sept. 3, 1968. Intern, Baylor U. Sch. Medicine, 1971; resident in dermatology U. Calif. Hosps., San Francisco, 1974-76; practice medicine specializing in dermatology, San Francisco, 1977—; asst. clin. prof. U. Calif., San Francisco, 1977—. Served with USN, 1972-73. Diplomate Am. Bd. Dermatology. Fellow Am. Acad. Dermatology; mem. Western Soc. R.R. and Indsl. Surgeons (past pres.), Exptl. Aircraft Assn., Alpha Omega Alpha. Office: 909 Hyde St San Francisco CA 94109

CHAR, WAI SINN, dentist; b. Honolulu, June 14, 1902; s. Man Hoon and Yen Kun (Wong) C.; D.D.S., Creighton U., 1926; m. Bertha Kam Yuk Lum, Aug. 13, 1931; children—David Kingman, John Kingson, Cynthia Moonyeen Char Schwab, Claudia (Moontoy Char Loo, Douglas King Chee. Head dental dept. Hunan-Yale Hosp., Changsha, China, 1926-27; dentist-in-charge Shanghai (China) Red Cross Hosp., 1928-30; gen. practice dentistry, Honolulu, 1934—; mem. staff Kuakini Hosp. Bd. dirs. Woodrose Condominium, 1971-72, active various coms. United Ch. of Christ. Recipient Community Service citation Hawaii C. of C., 1974. Mem. Am., Hawaii State, Hawaii County dental assns., Hawaii Chinese Jr. C. of C. (founder), Chinese Amateur Athletic Assn. (past pres.), C. of C. of Hawaii (life mem.), Assn. Honolulu Artists, YMCA, Ket Fui Ken Assn. Republican. Clubs: Chinese Univ. (treas. 1963, v.p. 1965), Am. Chinese, United Chinese Soc., Nat. Trust Historic Preservation, Internat. Platform Assn., Downtown Improvement Assn., Hawaii Creighton Alumni (founder, pres. 1941-45), numerous others. Columnist Hawaii Chinese Jour., 1951-62. Home: 780 Amana St Apt 601 Honolulu HI 96814 Office: 169 S Kukui St Honolulu HI 96813

CHAREAU, KENET EDWARD, lawyer; b. East Cleveland, Ohio, Feb. 13, 1945; s. Walter J. and Dorothy C.; m. Margo Chareau, Dec. 19, 1970; 1 son, Sean Louis. A.B., John Carroll U., 1967; J.D., Cleve. State U., 1970. Bar: Ohio 1970, Ariz. 1973, U.S. Ct. Mil. Appeals 1970. Mem. firm Kenet & Chareau & Assocs., P.C., Tucson; guest lectr. real estate, various bds. off realtors, insts.; registered rep. Univs. Securities Group, 1980-82, Design Capital Securities, 1982—. Served to capt. JAGC, U.S. Army, 1970-75. Mem. Ariz. Bar Assn., ABA, Ohio Bar Assn., Cochise County Bar Assn., Pima County Bar Assn., Internat. Assn. Fin. Planners, Nat. Assn. Securities Dealers, Real Estate Securities and Syndication Inst. Home: 5961 E San Mateo Dr Tucson AZ 85715 Office: 1141 N El Dorado Pl Suite 201 Tucson AZ 85715

CHARLES, ALLAN HOWARD, periodontist; b. Waukegan, Ill., Apr. 3, 1946; s. Henry David and Jean (Geco) C.; student U. Ill., 1966, D.D.S., 1970; cert. periodontics U. So. Calif., 1972; m. Gay Ballard, Oct. 23, 1979; 1 dau., Katherine. Practice dentistry specializing in periodontics, Pasadena, Calif., 1974—; assoc. clin. prof. U. So. Calif., Los Angeles, 1972-77, lectr. continuing edn., 1975—; lectr. continuing edn. U. Oreg., 1980—. Mem. ADA, Calif. Dental Assn., Am. Acad. Periodontology, Western Soc. Periodontology. Office: 837 S Fair Oaks PAsadena CA 91105

CHARLES, CONRAD JOSEPH, book pub. co. exec.; b. Chicago Heights, Ill., Aug. 7, 1930; s. Conrad and Isabel (Gayton) C.; student parochial schs.; children—Richard, Michael, Rhonda, Cheryl. Prodn. mgr. Childrens Press Pub., Chgo., 1969-71; v.p. adminstr. Henry Regenery Pub. Co., Chgo., 1971-75, Sheed & Ward Pub. Co., Mission, Kans., 1975-77; dir. prodn. and spl. sales Raintree Pubs., Inc., Milw., 1977—. Active local Big Bros./Big Sisters. Served with AUS, 1951-53. Mem. Printing Industry Wis., Chgo. Book Club. Roman Catholic. Club: Chgo. Press. Home: 230 S Monaco Pkwy Apt 308 Denver CO 80224

CHARLES, E. OTIS, bishop; b. Norristown, Pa., Apr. 24, 1926; s. Jacob Otis and Elizabeth Francis (Abraham) C.; B.A., Trinity Coll., Hartford, Conn., 1948; S.T.B., Gen. Theol. Sem., N.Y.C., 1959, D.D., 1983; m. Elvira Latta, May 26, 1951; children—Chirstopher, Nicholas, Emilie, Timothy, Elvira. Ordained deacon Episcopal Ch., 1951, priest,

1951, bishop, 1971; curate St. Johns Ch., Elizabeth, N.J., 1951-53; priest-in-charge St. Andrews Ch., Beacon, N.Y., 1953-59; rector St. Johns Ch., Washington, Conn., 1959-68; asso. dir. Montford House Ecumenical Center, 1968-69; exec. sec. Asso. Parishes, Inc., 1968-71; bishop Episcopal Diocese Utah, Salt Lake City, 1971—; bishop in charge Navajo Episc. Ch., 1976-79; mem. Episcopal Standing Liturgical Commn., 1970-79; dir. Epis. Ch. Pub. Co. Trustee Episcopal Radio TV Found., 1972-78; pres. bd. trustees St. Marks Hosp., Rowland Hall St. Marks Sch.; pres. Hospice of Salt Lake, 1978-81; adviser U. Utah Coll. Nursing, 1980, Utah Camp Fire Council; bd. dirs. Episcopal Urban Caucus, 1981, Planned Parenthood of Utah, 1980; mem. Utah Health Systems Agy., 1980—, Utah State Health Coordinating Council, 1982—; exec. com. Utahns United Against the Arms Race, 1982—. Served with USNR, 1943-46; PTO. Recipient Washington Community Fund grants, 1962, 68. Clubs: Alta (Salt Lake City). Mem. Utah Arts Festival Council, Utah Assn. Autism (adviser).

CHARLES, JOHN PETERSON, applied scientist, consultant; b. Parkers Prairie, Minn., Apr. 20, 1926; s. J. Harold Peterson and Geneva I. (Lindall) C.; m. Marian E. Weidetz, Sept. 13, 1952; children—John Peter, Jan P. B.A. U. Minn., 1950; student U. Edinburg, 1950-51; M.S. Northwestern U., 1958, Ph.D., 1963. Commd. ensign U.S. Navy, 1949, advanced through grades to comdr., 1967; served as human engring. officer Bur. Naval Weapons, head human factors br. Naval Missile Center, and human factors research and devel. officer Office Chief of Naval Ops.; with human factors dept. Logicon Inc., San Diego., 1968-74; sr. scientist, v.p. Appli-mation Inc., San Diego, 1974-77; sr. scientist, pres. Icon Inc., San Diego, 1977—; cons., tchr. Mem. Human Factors Soc., Sigma Chi. Republican. Author numerous tech. reports in field. Home and Office: 3401 Bangor Pl San Diego CA 92106

CHARLTON, IRENE K. ZIMMERS, watercolorist; b. Charleston, Ill., Aug. 7, 1902; d. Edward Lee King and Nettie Mae (Money) K.; m. Charles Philip Zimmers, June 1932 (dec.); children—Philip Hays, Hugh Morley. Student Eastern Ill. State Tchrs. Coll., 1922. Exhibited watercolorist juried shows; artists of the S.W. Los Angeles County Mus., 1954; represented Calif. Group Art Tour, 1982, 83; judge Watercolor shows; demonstrator pure transparent watercolor. Past pres. Morongo Valley Republican Club. Recipient honorable mention Palm Springs Civic Art Assn. award, 1977; Date Festival Indio Calif. award, 1964; N. Mex. Watercolor Soc. Purchase Prize award, 1981. Mem. Watercolor W., N. Mex. Watercolor Soc., Old Bergen Art Guild. Episcopalian.

CHARLTON, JOHN KIPP, pediatrician; b. Omaha, Jan. 26, 1937; s. George Paul and Mildred (Kipp) C.; A.B., Amherst Coll., 1958; M.D., Cornell U., 1962; m. Susan S. Young, Aug. 15, 1959; children—Paul, Cynthia, Daphne. Intern, Ohio State U. Hosp., Columbus, 1962-63; resident in pediatrics Children's Hosp., Dallas, 1966-68, chief pediatric resident, 1968-69; nephrology fellow U. Tex. Southwestern Med. Sch., Dallas, 1969-70; practice medicine specializing in pediatrics, Phoenix, 1970; chmn. dept. pediatrics Maricopa County Gen. Hosp., Phoenix, 1971-78, assoc. chmn. dept. pediatrics, 1979—; med. dir., bd. dirs. Crisis Nursery, Inc., 1977—. Pres. Maricopa County Child Abuse Council, 1977-81; bd. dirs. Florence Critenton Services, 1980—. Served as officer M.C., USAF, 1963-65. Recipient Hon Kachina award for volunteerism, 1980, Jefferson award for volunteerism, 1980. Mem. Am. Acad. Pediatrics, Ariz. Pediatric Soc., Maricopa County Pediatric Soc. (past pres.). Author articles, book rev. in field. Home: 6230 E Exeter St Scottsdale AZ 85251 Office: 2601 E Roosevelt St Phoenix AZ 85008

CHARM, HARRY JOEL, optometrist; b. Phila., Aug. 21, 1946; s. George and Libby C.; m. Judith R. Silberman, July 27, 1969; children—Kenneth Alan, Corine Michele. Student Calif. State U.-Los Angeles, 1969; B.S., Los Angeles Coll. Optometry, 1971; O.D., So. Calif. Coll. Optometry, 1973. Pvt. practice optometry, Anaheim, Calif., 1977—; mem. optometric adv. bd. Calif. Dept. Motor Vehicles, 1980; v.p. Vision Conservation Inst., 1982; chmn. Lions Sight Conservation Commn., 1982; lectr. in field. Named Calif. Young O.D. of the Yr., 1979; recipient Optometric Recognition award for continuing edn., 1979-82. Mem. Am. Optometric Assn., Calif. Optometric Assn. (chmn. communications div. 1981, trustee 1983), Orange County Optometric Assn. (sec. 1978, editor Perceptions 1979, coordinator polit. activities 1980, pres. 1982), Coll. Optometrists in Vision Devel., Optometric Extension Program Found., Omega Delta. Jewish. Club: Masons. Editor Calif. Optometry, 1981. Office: 466 S Anaheim Hills Rd Anaheim CA 92807

CHARNEY, NORMAN MURRY, physician, lawyer; b. Bklyn., July 19, 1931; s. Irving and Hannah (Richman) C.; A.B., Bklyn. Coll., 1953; D.O., Phila. Coll. Osteopathy, 1957; M.D., Calif. Coll. Medicine, 1962; J.D., Western State U. Coll. Law, 1971; children—Mark Alan, Darlene Karen, Ellyn Beth. Intern, Maywood (Calif.) Hosp.; practice medicine specializing in family practice, La Mirada, Calif., 1958—; mem. staff La Mirada Community Hosp., chief of staff, 1972-73; asst. clin. prof. Calif. Coll. Medicine, U. Calif. at Irvine; staff Brea Community Hosp., chief of staff, 1980-83; to Calif. bar, 1971, since practiced law, Fullerton, Calif.; partner firm Charney & Cifarelli; prof. law and medicine Western State U. Coll. Law. Mem. Friends of Library, U. Calif. at Irvine, 1967—, Friends of Coll., Calif. State, Fullerton, 1966—, Los Angeles County Heart Assn., 1960—; health and safety chmn. Los Ranchos dist. N. Orange County Boy Scouts Am., 1967—. Bd. dirs. Jewish Community Council Orange County Diplomate Am. Bd. Family Practice. Fellow Am. Geriatrics Soc., Royal Soc. Health, Am. Acad. Family Practice, Am. Coll. Legal Medicine; mem. Am., Calif., Los Angeles County med. assns., Am. Acad. Family Practice, Am. Bar Assn., Calif. Trial Lawyers Assn., La Mirada C. of C. Jewish (pres. temple 1964-66). Club: B'nai B'rith (dir. lodge). Office: 14930 E Imperial Ave La Mirada CA 90638 also 713 E Chapman Ave Fullerton CA 92632

CHASE, CHARLES ANTHONY, executive engineer; b. Detroit, June 27, 1939; s. Joseph Leon and Marion Katherine (Lukowiak) C.; m. Carole Ann Chaikin, June 10, 1961; children—Carlton, William. B.S.A.E., U. Mich., 1961, M.S.A.E., 1962; D.Engring. A.E., Stanford U., 1968. Design engr. Chem. Systems div. United Technologies Corp., Coyote, Calif., 1962-68, project engr., 1968-71, chief solid propulsion advanced design, 1971-74, chief engr. space motor programs, 1974—. Mem. Monte Sereno Sch. Bd., 1972-77. Recipient Outstanding Service award United Techs. Corp., 1981. Assoc. fellow AIAA (solid rocket com.); mem. AAAS, ASME. Republican. Roman Catholic. Club: Courtside Racquet (Los Gatos, Calif.). Contbr. numerous articles to profl. jours. Patentee in field.

CHASE, C(HARLES) WARD, ind. petroleum landman; b. Hartford, Conn., Feb. 28, 1908; s. Warren D. and Elizabeth S. (Ward) C.; B.A., Princeton U., 1928; m. Olga Memi, Feb. 12, 1966. Drama critic, asst. dramatic editor Billboard mag., 1930-31; ins. editor Real Estate Record and Guide, N.Y., 1940-43; v.p. Butler and Baldwin, Inc., 1931-41; account exec. Johnson & Higgins, 1942, dept. mgr., 1950, v.p., 1953-69, dir., 1956-69; pres., dir. Johnson & Higgins (Can.), Ltd., 1955-63; chmn. bd. Johnson & Higgins Calif., 1964-65; pres. Chase Resources Co., 1970—. Served with USNR, 1943-46. Mem. Soc. Mayflower Descs. Clubs: Eldorado, Indian Wells (Calif.). Home: 45-830 Pima Rd Indian Wells CA 92260 Office: PO Box 1704 Palm Desert CA 92261

CHASE, JULIA P., public relations and advertising company executive, editor; b. Riverside, Calif., May 21, 1942; d. Harold W. and Jean M. (Smith) Peebles. B.A., San Francisco State U., 1965; postgrad. Calif. State U.-Long Beach, U. Calif.-Berkeley, U. Calif.-Irvine, U. So. Calif. Tchr. English, Calif. high schs., 1966-70; assoc. editor Videorecord World mag., Newport Beach, Calif., 1970-71; advt. promotion dir. Technicolor, Inc., 1971; pub. relations cons., Newport Beach, 1971-72; pub. relations account exec. Cochrane Chase & Co., Inc., Orange County, Calif., 1973; community relations dir. McGaw Labs., Irvine, 1976-77; pres. J.P. Chase & Co., Inc. Advt. & Pub. Relations, Newport Beach, 1977—. Rep. council agys., allocations and communications United Way, 1976-83; bd. dirs. United Way North/South, 1980-81. Recipient award Am. Advt. Fedn., 1978; award of merit Western Art Dirs.; award of excellence Arts mag., N.Y. Art Dirs.; award of merit/communication excellence So. Calif. Bus. Communicators; Mem. Pub. Relations Soc. Am., Orange County Sportswriters, Newport Harbor Art Mus., Laguna Beach Mus. Art. Democrat. Presbyterian. Clubs: Orange County Press (dir. 1979), John Wayne Tennis. Editor, pub.: Newport Set mag.; art editor Orange County Illustrated; editor: Add One, 1983, 84. Office: PO Box 8343 Newport Beach CA 92660

CHASE, KRISTINE LOUISE, economist, educator; b. Oakland, Calif., Jan. 16, 1949; d. Keith E. Terrill and Dorothea L. (Lodi) T.; m. Daniel P. Chase, June 9, 1973; children—Karen Louise, Michael Steven. B.A., U. Calif.-Davis, 1970, M.A., 1972; Ph.D. in Econs., U. Md., 1981. Acting asst. prof. Calif. Poly. State U.-San Luis Obispo, 1972-73; instr. and adminstrv. officer U. Md., College Park, 1973-79, asst. prof., Balt. County br., 1981-82; acting asst. prof. U.S. Naval Acad., Annapolis, Md., 1979-81; asst. prof. Mills Coll., Oakland, Calif., 1982—. Mem. Am. Econs. Assn., Am. Enterprise Inst. Contbr. articles to profl. jours. Office: Social Scis Dept Mills Coll Oakland CA 94613

CHASE, LORIENE ECK, psychologist; b. Sacramento; d. Walter and Genevieve (Bennetts) Eck; A.B., U. So. Calif., 1948, M.A., 1949, Ph.D., 1953; m. Leo Goodman-Malamuth, 1946 (div. 1951); 1 son, Leo; m. 2d, Allen Chase, Mar. 4, 1960 (div.); m. 3d, Clifton W. King, 1974. Psychologist, Spastic Children's Found., Los Angeles, 1952-55, Inst. Group Psychotherapy, Beverly Hills, Calif., 1957-59; pvt. practice, 1953—; v.p. VSP Exec. Relocation Consultants. Condr., Dr. Loriene Chase Show, ABC-TV, Hollywood, Calif. 1966—. Cons., Camarillo State Hosp.; bd. dirs., pres.'s circle U. So. Calif.; founding mem. Achievement Rewards for Coll. Scientists; bd. dirs. Chase-King Personal Devel. Center, Los Angeles; exec. bd. Cancer Research Center, Los Angeles. Writer syndicated newspaper column Casebook of Dr. Chase. Served with Waves World War II. Recipient Woman of Year in Psychology award Am. Mothers Com. Mem. Diadames, Assn. Media Psychologists, Les Dames de Champagne, Dame de Rotisseur, Nat. Art Assn. Clubs: Regency, Lakeside Country. Author: The Human Miracle; columnist Westways mag. psychologist; b. Sacramento; d. Walter and Genevieve (Bennetts) Eck; A.B., U. So. Calif., 1948, M.A., 1949, Ph.D., 1953; m. Leo Goodman-Malamuth, 1946 (div. 1951); 1 son, Leo; m. 2d, Allen Chase, Mar. 4, 1960 (div.); m. 3d, Clifton W. King, 1974. Psychologist, Spastic Children's Found., Los Angeles, 1952-55, Inst. Group Psychotherapy, Beverly Hills, Calif., 1957-59; pvt. practice, 1953—; v.p. VSP Exec. Relocation Consultants. Condr., Dr. Loriene Chase Show, ABC-TV, Hollywood, Calif. 1966—. Cons., Camarillo State Hosp.; bd. dirs., pres.'s circle U. So. Calif.; founding mem. Achievement Rewards for Coll. Scientists; bd. dirs. Chase-King Personal Devel. Center, Los Angeles; exec. bd. Cancer Research Center, Los Angeles. Writer syndicated newspaper column Casebook of Dr. Chase. Served with Waves World War II. Recipient Woman of Year in Psychology award Am. Mothers Com. Mem. Diadames, Assn. Media Psychologists, Les Dames de Champagne, Dame de Rotisseur, Nat. Art Assn. Clubs: Regency, Lakeside Country. Author: The Human Miracle; columnist Westways mag. Address: 4925 Tarzana Woods Dr Tarzana CA 91356 also 375 Palomar Shell Beach CA

CHASE, LOUIS RICHARD, publisher; b. Grand Rapids, Mich., Dec. 6, 1917; s. Jacob and Fannie (Kaufman) C.; m. Salley E. Barth, 1938; children—Richard B., Lawrence J.; m. 2d Shirley E. Friedman, 1982. B.S., UCLA, 1957. Mem. tech. staff Hughes Aircraft Co., Culver City, Calif., 1952-57; pres. Richards Lawrence & Co., Santa Monica, Calif., 1958—. Served to lt. (j.g.) USNR, 1942-45; CBI. Mem. IEEE, Greater Los Angeles Press Club, Fgn. Trade Assn. Clubs: Sherman Oaks (Calif.) Tennis (pres. 1967-69), Rogallo Gliding (pres. 1975), Sherlock Holmes Soc. Los Angeles. Author numerous articles on automatic control and inertial guidance systems. Patentee in aircraft nav. equipment. Home: 124 Idaho Ave Santa Monica CA 90403 Office: 309 Santa Monica Blvd Suite 324 Santa Monica CA 90401

CHASE, RICHARD ALLAN, advertising executive; b. Los Angeles, Jan. 7, 1949; s. Ellis Wishnow and Honey (Burnett) C.; m. Marilyn S. Lofland, Sept. 17, 1977; 1 dau., Allison Leigh. B.A. in Bus. Adminstrn., UCLA, 1972. Pres., Elan Assocs., Los Angeles, 1971-78; producer Araiz Condoy, Mexico City, 1978-79; v.p., gen. mgr. Bermudez & Assocs., Beverly Hills, Calif., 1979—. Mem. Los Angeles Advt. Club. Office: 8200 Wilshire Blvd Beverly Hills CA 90211

CHASE, SHERRET SPAULDING, plant research geneticist; b. Toledo, Ohio, June 30, 1918; s. Clement Edwards and Helen (Kelsey) C.; m. Catherine Ross Compton, Nov. 27, 1943. B.S. in Botany, Yale U., 1939; Ph.D. in Plant Cytology, Cornell U., 1947. Asst. and assoc. prof. dept. botany and plant pathology Iowa Expt. Sta., Iowa State U., 1947-53; research geneticist DeKalb AgResearch, Inc. (Ill.), 1954-66, dir. internat. seed ops., 1964-66; Bullard fellow and Cabot fellow in forest genetics Harvard U., Boston, 1966-68, hon. research assoc. and fellow in econ. botany Bot. Mus., 1968-74; prof. genetics dept. biology SUNY-Oswego, 1968-80; dir. plant breeding dept., acting dir. cell biology dept., dir. farm and greenhouse ops. Internat. Plant research Inst., San Carlos, Calif., 1981-82. Founding pres., bd. dirs. Catskil Ctr. for Conservation and Devel., Inc., Arkville, N.Y., 1969-81; bd. dirs. Mid-Hudson Pattern for Progress, Inc., Poughkeepsie, N.Y., 1972-81, Assn. for Protection for Adirondacks, Inc., 1972-81, Hanford Mills Mus., East Meredith, N.Y., 1973-80, Erpf-Catskill Cultural Ctr., Arkville, 1974-80. Served to 1st lt. USAAF, 1942-45. Decorated D.F.C. Mem. AAAS, Am. Inst. Bot. Sci., Am. Soc. Agronomy, Am. Genetics Assn., Genetics Soc. Am., Bot. Soc. Am., Can. Soc. Genetics and Cytology, N.Y. Acad. Sci., New Eng. Bot. Club, Sigma Xi, Phi Kappa Phi, Gamma Sigma Delta. Contbr. numerous articles to profl. jours., abstracts to profl. meetings. Home: 7 Lilly Ln San Carlos CA 94070 Office: Internat Plant Research Inst 853 Industrial Rd San Carlos CA 94070

CHASE, STEPHEN EARL, optometrist; b. Inglewood, Calif., Feb. 27, 1953; s. John Earl and Mildred Lucille (McFerran) C.; m. Rozell Johnson, June 27, 1975; children—Veronica, Vaughn, Ammon, Jared. B.A. in Spanish, Calif. State U.-Dominguez Hills, 1977; B.S., So. Calif. Coll. Optometry, 1978, O.D., 1981. Practice optometry, Torrance, Calif. Bd. dirs. Am. Handicapped Assn. Mem. Am. Optometric Assn., Calif. Optometric Assn., Optometric Extension Program (Knight-Henry Meml. award 1981). Republican. Mormon. Office: 22850 Crenshaw Blvd Suite 104 Torrance CA 90505

CHASES, MARK STEFAN, manufacturing company executive; b. Allentown, Pa., Mar. 20, 1938; s. Morris and Jeanetta (Binder) C.: B.S., Pa. State U., 1960, postgrad. 1962; children—Andrea, Elizabeth. Sr. analyst Gen. Motors Corp., Detroit, 1960-69; corp. controller Cole Nat. Corp., Cleve., 1969-71; treas. Swedlow Plastics (Can.), 1971; fin. v.p. Swedlow, Inc., Los Angeles, 1971-81, pres., chief operating officer, treas., dir., 1979-81; chmn. The Swedlow Group, 1978; exec. v.p., chief operating officer, dir. Custom Weave Carpets, Inc., Fountain Valley, Calif., 1982—; v.p., dir. Customweave Carpets Holding Co., Inc., 1983—; sec., treas. Design Tek, Inc.; guest lectr. Calif. Poly. Inst., Pomona. Bd. dirs. Resources Council So. Calif., 1978—, United Way Orange County, Pacific Symphony Orch. trustee Orange County Repertory Theatre; dir. adv. com. Calif. State Univ., Cominquiz Hills, 1979: exec. council Hoag Meml. Hosp., 1979; mem. bus. council Newport Harbor Mus. Art; mem. Orange County Exec. Council. Served with U.S. Army, 1956-62. Mem. Garden Grove C. of C., Alpha Kappa Psi. Home: 59 Jasmine Creek Dr Corona del Mar CA 92625 Office: 18480 Pacific Ave Fountain Valley CA 92708

CHASTAIN, GARVIN, psychology educator, research director; b. Fort Worth, Feb. 23, 1945; s. Garvin Dunn and Bertha Pearl (Parrish) C.; m. Patricia Jean Ritter, Dec. 16, 1967; m. 2d, Gloria Jean Pollard, Nov. 21, 1975; 1 son, Ross Calvert. Ph.D. in Human Exptl. Psychology, U. Tex., Austin, 1976. Head, computer instn. Durhams Coll., Austin, Tex., 1976-77; research scientist Human Resources Research Orgn., Fort Hood, Tex., 1977-78; asst. prof. psychology Boise State U. (Idaho), 1978-82, asso. prof. and dir. Perceptual Research Labs., 1982—. Mem. Idaho com. of correspondance on creation/evolution, 1982—. Recipient Boise State U. Alumni Assn. award, 1979. Mem. Psychonomic Soc., Am. Psychol. Assn. (exptl. and philos. divs.), AAAS, Freedom from Religion Found. (Rocky Mountain region v.p.), Am Humanist Assn., Psi Chi, Phi Kappa Phi. Libertarian. Contbr. articles to profl. jours. Home: 1819 Tendoy Dr Boise ID 83705 Office: Dept Psychology Boise State U Boise ID 83725

CHASTAIN, HAROLD HERMAN, savs. and loan assn. cons.; b. Grosvenor, Tex., Oct. 25, 1919; s. Homer Hardin and Dora Frances (Baugh) C.; spl. cert. Howard Payne U., 1939; student LaSalle Extension U., 1939-50; m. Mary Francis Sprinkle, Dec. 23, 1939; Bookkeeper-cashier Weatherby Motor Co., Brownwood, Tex., 1939-40; bookkeeper, teller Citizens Nat. Bank, Brownwood, 1940-42; controller Mut. Savs. & Loan Assn., Ft. Worth, 1945-47; Savs. & Loan Assn. examiner for Tex., 1947-50, for Fed. Home Loan Bank Bd., 1950-58; dist. 9 dir. Fed. Home Loan Bank Bd., Little Rock, 1958-77; savs. and loan assn. cons., Albuquerque, 1977—; dir. Security Fed. Savs. & Loan Assn., Albuquerque, 1977—, vice chmn. bd., 1981-82, chmn. audit com. of dirs., 1978-82. Served with AC, USNR, 1942-45. Recipient Outstanding Performance Service certs. Fed. Home Loan Bank Bd., 1972-73, Spl. Recognition certs. Treasury Dept., 1959-75. Mem. Am. Assn. for Ret. People, Nat. Assn. Ret. Fed. Employees, U.S. League Insured Savs. and Loan Assn., N.Mex. League Insured Savs. and Loan Assns. Republican. Club: Four Hills Country. Home: 5604 Cactus Flower Dr NW Albuquerque NM 87120

CHATTERJEE, JOYA BANERJEE, educator, consultant; b. Varanashi, India, Feb. 5, 1946; d. Brahmanya Bhushan Banerjee; came to U.S., 1969, naturalized, 1974; m. Bijoy Gopal Chatterjee, May 22, 1965; children—Arjun Bijoy, Indra Neel. B.A., Calcutta (India) U., 1965; M.A., Glassboro (N.J.) State Coll., 1972; Ed.D., U. San Francisco, 1983. Kindergarten tchr. pub. schs., Avon, Conn., 1973-75; tchr. elem. schs. Berryessa Sch. Dist., San Jose, Calif., 1975-78, tchr. learning handicapped, 1978-81; program specialist Oak Grove Sch. Dist., San Jose, 1981—; cons. World Affairs Council, San Francisco; mem. Stanford Program on Internat. Cross Cultural Edn.; field reader, grant reviewer Office Edn., Washington; mem. com. Outreach Project/Assn. for Asian Studies. Vice pres. Ming Quong Childrens Ctr., Los Gatos, Calif. Fulbright grantee, Peoples Republic China, summer 1983. Mem. Assn. Asian Studies, Assn. Children Learning Disabilities, Asian Am. Educators Assn., Pi Lambda Theta. Hindu. Produced film on China; developed Curriculum materials. Home: 127 Mary Way Los Gatos CA 95030 Office: 6578 Santa Teresa Blvd San Jose CA 95119

CHATTERTON, NORMAN JERRY, physiologist; b. Mapleton, Idaho, Feb. 11, 1939; s. Norman J. and Thelma (Nessen) C.; m. Janeal Spencer, Sept. 6, 1963; children—Julie, Jill, Jeffrey, Jamie. B.S., Utah State U., 1966; M.S., U. Calif.-Riverside, 1968, Ph.D., 1970. Physiologist, Agr. Research Service, U.S. Dept. Agr., Beltsville, Md., 1970-78, supr., lab. chief, 1978-80, assoc. dir. arid southwest, Logan, Utah, 1980—. Mem. Am. Soc. Agronomy, Crop Sci. Soc. Am., Am. Forage and Grassland Council. Mormon. Contr. numerous articles to profl. jours. Home: 2085 N 1600 E Logan UT 84321 Office: USDA-ARS Agr Sci Bldg Utah State U UMC 48 Logan UT 84322

CHATZKY, MICHAEL GARY, lawyer; b. Denver, June 14, 1943; s. Louis and Sylvia Zena (Byer) C. B.S., U. Md., 1966, J.D., 1969. Bar: Calif. 1970, U.S. Dist. Ct. (no. dist.) Calif. 1970, U.S. Tax Ct. 1970, U.S. Ct. Appeals (9th cir.) 1970, U.S. Supreme Ct. 1975. Mem. firm Margolis, Chatzky, Dunnett & Muehlenbeck, P.C., Los Gatos, Calif., 1970-80, Michael Gary Chatzky, A Law Corp., San Jose, Calif., 1980—; lectr. in field; mng. editor Internat. Comparative Tax Law Rev. Sect. of the Common Law Lawyer, Palo Alto, Calif. Chmn. bd. dirs. Santa Clara Valley Chpt. ACLU, 1971-76, coordinator legal screening com., 1977, 80—; co-founder Santa Clara Valley chpt. Campaign for Econ. Democracy, 1977. Mem. ABA (adj. mem. fgn. activities of U.S. taxpayers and U.S. activities of foreigners and tax treaties coms.), Santa Clara County Bar Assn. (exec. com. tax sect.). Contbr. articles to publs. Office: 762 El Paseo De Saratoga San Jose CA 95130

CHAUNCEY, TOM, radio-TV exec.; b. Houston, Jan. 20, 1913; s. Brinkley and Lucille Dunn (Weber) C.; student pub. schs.; m. Dorothy Atwater Wrigley, Feb. 27, 1959; 6 children. Owner, Tom Chauncey Jeweler, 1940-61; v.p., gen. mgr. Sta KPHO, 1941-48; pres. Sta. KOPO, Tucson, 1947-76; v.p., mng. dir. KOOL Radio-TV, Inc., 1948-55, exec. v.p., gen. mgr., 1955-57, pres., gen. mgr., 1957-61, pres., 1961-81, chmn. bd., pres., chief exec. officer, 1981-82, owner, chief exec. officer Sta. KOOL-AM-FM, 1982—; owner H Lazy A Ranches, Tom Chauncey Arabians, Tom Chauncey Properties; pres., mng. dir. Old Pueblo Broadcasting Co., (KOLD-TV), Tucson, 1957-69; daily columnist TV Views, Ariz. Republic, Phoenix Gazette, (weekly) Broadcasting mag., 1960-61; former chmn. bd. CBS TV Network Affiliates 1961-62; dir. Valley Nat. Bank; mem. nat. com. Support Free Broadcasting; rep. of pres. U.S., ambassador, Nigeria, 1960. Grand marshal J.C. World Championship Rodeo and Parade, 1963; former nat. trustee City of Hope; former mem. Ariz. Nat. Livestock Show; past Ariz. chmn. Radio Free Europe; former mem. bd. Phoenix Symphony Assn., Phoenix Art Mus., Muscular Dystrophy Assn. Am.; gen. campaign. chmn. Greater Phoenix-Scottsdale United Fund Campaign; former mem. bd., v.p., pres. Phoenix Better Bus. Bur.; mem. Citizen's Action Com.; voting mem. Ariz. State U. Found.; former mem. Phoenix Baseball Stadium Com., U. Ariz. Found., chmn. Ariz. com. A.R.C.; past dir. at large for Ariz. Am. Cancer Soc.; past dir. and pres. Community Council; exec. v.p., mem. bd., Incorporator, co-founder Barrow Neurol. Inst.; mem. Com. for Phoenix Civic Plaza Dedication Ceremonies, 1972, Ariz. Commn. on Nat. and Internat. Commerce; past nat. chmn. Broadcaster's adv. com. U.S. Savs. Bonds; past dir. United Cerebral Palsey Assn. Central Ariz.; past mem. Phoenix All-Am. City Com.; chmn. Ariz. Motion Picture Adv. Bd.; past chmn. adv. bd. on radio and TV, Ariz. State U.; bd. dirs. Central Ariz. Water Conservation Dist.; Nat. Cowboy Hall of Fame bd. dir. 1979—; pres., bd. dirs. Ariz. Children's Found. Named Man of Yr., City of Hope, 1962, NCCJ, 1967, B'nai B'rith Anti-Defamation League, 1975; Citizen of Yr., Phoenix Real Estate Bd., 1965; recipient Nat. Sch. Bell award, 1961; award U.S. Treasury Dept., 1961; Tom Chauncey award United Fund, 1962; Jesse Owens award; George Foster Peabody award. Mem. Ariz. (past pres., past dir., past mem. legis. com.), Met. Phoenix (past pres., dir.) broadcasters assns., Nat. Assn. Broadcasters,

Nat. Acad. TV Arts and Scis. (Bd. Govs. award Phoenix chpt. 1962, past Ariz. bd. gov.), Mus. Broadcasting (hon.), Nat. Retail Jewelers Assn. (past dir.), Phoenix C. of C., Ariz. Quarterhorse Breeders Assn., Ariz. State Horseman's Assn., Ariz. Heart Inst. 1974—, Arabian Horse Assn. Ariz. (dir. 1972), Ariz. Hereford Assn., Ariz. Retail Jewelers Assn., Am. Gem Soc., TV Pioneers, Phoenix Press Box Assn. (life), Phoenix Thunderbirds, Navy League, Newcomen Soc. N. Am., Sigma Delta Chi. Elk. Clubs: Phoenix Country, Phoenix Execs.; Paradise Valley Country; Rancheros Vistacores; Cowman's. Author: Educational Contributions of Commercial Television, 1960. Tom and Dorothy Chauncey Student Loan Fund established at Ariz. State U. Office: 511 W Adams St Phoenix AZ 85003

CHAUVIN, RICHARD LUCIEN, software co. exec.; b. Manchester N.H., Apr. 6, 1949; s. Lucien F. and Violette G. (LeMay) C.; m. Theresa Ann Pachtner, June 20, 1977; children—Christopher Scott, Michael Andrew. Computer supr. Nat. CSS, San Francsico 1974-76, tech. rep., 1976-77, computer systems programmer, 1977-78, sr. systems programmer, 1978-79; with Fireman's Fund Ins. Co., San Rafael, Calif., 1979-80; with Magnuson Computer Systems, San Jose, Calif., 1979-80, systems software specialist, 1980, mgr. systems software, 1980-82; owner Chauvin Cons., 1982—; chmn. bd., chief fin. officer, sr. exec. v.p. Dovetail Systems, Inc., Sunnyvale, Calif., 1982—. Served with U.S. Air Force, 1968-74. Mem. Assn. Computing Machinery, Aircraft Owners and Pilots Assn. Home: 418 Ridge Rd San Carlos CA 94070 Office: 1030 W Maude Ave Sunnyvale CA 94086

CHAVEZ, ANDRES STEVEN, film director; b. Los Angeles, July 16, 1947; s. Armando and Elena (Quintana) C. B.A., UCLA, 1970; postgrad. U. So. Calif., 1973, Loyola U., 1973. Cons., U.S. Office Edn., 1968-71; student counselor UCLA, 1970, extension program coordinator, 1971; reporter/producer Pacific Found., Sta. KPFK-FM, 1971-73; assoc. producer Reflexciones KABC-TV, ABC, 1973-74; producer/host Impact, KLOS-FM, ABC, 1974-75; free-lance writer and producer, 1975; sta. mgr. Channel 3-B, Napa Coll., 1975; field producer Eyewitness Los Angeles, Sta. KABC-TV, Hollywood, Calif., 1976-79, dir. local film, 1979—. Vice-pres. bd. dirs. East Los Angeles Rape Hotline, 1979-81; pres. bd. dirs. Service for Asian Am. Youth, 1977-81; bd. dirs. E.U.C.L.I.D. Found., 1973; exec. dir. Centro Universitario, 1971. Recipient Emmy certs., 1974, 77. Mem. Am. Film Inst., Calif. Assn. Latinos in Broadcasting, Calif. Chicano News Media Assn., Nat. Space Inst., Planetary Soc. Democrat. Presbyterian. Founder, editor Aztlan, 1971-74; contbg. editor Ednl. Film Strips, 1974—. Office: 4151 Prospect Ave Bldg 18 Hollywood CA 90027

CHÁVEZ, CARLOS CARRASCO, lithography firm exec., portrait painter; b. Guadalajara, Mex., Aug. 27, 1918; came to U.S., 1951; s. Gabriel Vázquez Chávez and Beatriz Gómez (Carrasco) C.; M.A., U. Autónoma de Mex., 1940; m. Altagracia García, Feb. 16, 1944; children—Carlos, Rafael, Gabriel. With Galas of Mex., 1940-48, Pacific Press, 1952-58, Western Lithograph Co., 1958-64; gen. mgr. Modern Graphics, Canoga Park, Calif., 1964-69; owner, pres. Repro-Chrome, 1969-78; exec. v.p. Colorex Lithographers Inc., Alhambra, Calif., 1978—; portrait painter, 1938—; group exhbns. in Mexico City, Los Angeles. Pres., mem. Welfare com. Beneficencia Mexicana, 1971-72; mem. Mex. Civic-Patriotic Com. Served with Mexican Army, 1942-44. Roman Catholic. Clubs: Los Hambriados, Par (founder, pres. 1974-75), Interamerican.

CHAVEZ, CESAR, union ofcl.; b. nr. Yuma, Ariz., Mar. 31, 1927; married; 8 children. Mem. staff Community Service Orgn., Calif., 1952-58, gen. dir., 1958-62; Organized Nat. Farm Workers Assn., 1962, merged with Agrl. Workers Organizing Com. of AFL-CIO, 1966, to form United Farm Workers Organizing Com., Delano, Calif., pres., 1966-72; now pres. United Farm Workers Am., AFL-CIO, Keene, Calif. Served with USNR, 1944-45. Roman Catholic. Address: United Farm Workers Am Box 62 Keene CA 93531

CHAVEZ, FEDERICO, Mexican trade ofcl.; b. Mexico City, June 3, 1945; came to U.S., 1978; s. Jorge and Celia (Barajas) C.; Indsl. Engr. Degree, Engring. Faculty U. Mexico, Mexico City, 1969; Diplome d'Economie (Govt. France scholar), Ecole Coopératif Université de Paris, 1971; m. Jana Hornakova, July 3, 1971; children—Andrei, Jana. Sales and design engr. Procter & Gamble, Mexico City, 1968-69, Foxboro Co., Mexico City, 1969-70; asst. trade commr. of Mexico to Spain, 1973-75; sr. trade commr. to Can., Toronto, Ont., 1975-78, to Western U.S., Los Angeles, 1978—; plant adminstrn. prof. Faculty Engring. U. Mexico, 1968-69. Recipient commendation for public service Lt. Gov. Calif., 1979; Tunisian Govt. research grantee, 1970; Israeli Govt. research grantee, 1971. Mem. U.S.-Mex. C. of C. (founder, chmn. adv. bd. Pacific chpt. 1981—), Los Angeles-Mex. Assn. for Tourism (dir.), Mexican Agys. and Enterprises Reps. Group (pres.). Mexico-Can. Cultural Assn. (founder, dir.). Author: Industrial Development in Third World Countries, 1970; Industrial Cooperatives in Developing Countries, 1972. Office: 8484 Wilshire Blvd Suite 808 Los Angeles CA 90010

CHAVEZ, JOSEPH ARNOLD, art educator, sculptor; b. Belen, N. Mex., Dec. 25, 1939; s. Arnold F. and Rose (Rael) C.; children—Luella, Audrey. B.S. in Edn., U. Albuquerque, 1963; M.A. Art Edn., U. N.Mex., 1967, M.F.A., 1971. Instr., Albuquerque Pub. Schs., 1964—. Served with Air N.G. Mem. Albuquerque Fedn. Teachers. Producer The Art of Carving Stone (video tape), Albuquerque Pub. Sch. system; spokesman on the Creative Process for Channel 5, KNME-TV, Albuquerque. Address: 4618 Sorrel Ln SW Albuquerque NM 87105

CHAVEZ, TERESA L., bank operations officer; b. Los Angeles, Jan. 10, 1935; d. Flavio F. and Marie S. Chavez. A.A., East Los Angeles Coll., 1975; B.A. in Liberal Studies, Calif. State U.-Los Angeles, 1982. Various banking positions Union Bank, Los Angeles, 1960-80, trainer courses, 1960-83, ops. officer, 1983—; lectr. Am. Inst. Banking, 1961—. Mem. Palm Springs Property Owners Assn., Mt. Washington Homeowners Assn., Sacred Heart Alumnae Assn., Mexican Am. Polit. Assn. Clubs: Union Bank Toastmistresses (sec.), Union Bank Bowling League (sec.-treas.). Office: 1000 S Hope St Los Angeles CA 90015

CHAVEZ, TITO DAVID, state senator, lawyer; b. Albuquerque, July 31, 1947; s. Florencio and Maria Agatha (Quintana) C.; m. Beatrice Louise Moya, 1976. B.A. in Econs., U. N.Mex., 1968, J.D., 1975; M.A., U. Ariz., 1972. Personnel adminstr. Edgerton, Germeshausen & Trier, Inc., 1979-71; law clk. Branch, Dickson, DuBois & Wilson, Albuquerque, 1974-76; gen. mgr. Tele Data, Inc., Albuquerque, 1976; real estate mgr., Albuquerque, 1976—; mgr. Plaza Indian Trading Post, Albuquerque, 1977—; mem. N.Mex. State Senate from Dist. 313, 1976—. Mem. GI Forum, Delta Sigma Pi, Beta Pi Alpha, Delta Theta Phi. Roman Catholic. Democrat. Clubs: Econ., Columbus Intramural Athletic, Eagles. Home: 1503 Mountain Rd NW Albuquerque NM 87104 Office: New Mexico State Senate Santa Fe NM 87503*

CHAVEZ, VICTOR BELTRAN, financial officer; b. Los Angeles, Mar. 26, 1945; s. Victor L. and Carmen (Beltran) C.; m. Charlotte M. Tarrin, Aug. 16, 1969; children—Michael, Lisa Marie. B.B.A., Loyola U.-Los Angeles, 1967. C.P.A. Mgr., Arthur Andersen and Co., Los Angeles, 1967-75; v.p., acctg. S.E. Rykoff and Co., Los Angeles, 1975—; pres. Los Molinos PTA, 1982. Mem. Am. Inst. C.P.A.s, Calif. Soc. C.P.A.s, Don Bosco Alumni Assn. (pres. 1982). Republican. Roman Catholic. Office: 761 Terminal St Los Angeles CA 90021

CHECKETTS, MICHAEL BEN, mfg. engr.; b. Brigham City, Utah, Apr. 28, 1953; s. James Kay and LaRue (Olsen) C.; B.S. in Mfg. Engring., Weber State Coll., Ogden, 1975; m. Debra Lynn Thompson, June 22, 1973; children—Mike Anthony, Staci Lynn, Nikki Lee. Mfg. and quality engr. Nat. Semicondr. Co., W. Jordan, Utah, 1975-76; mfg. engr. mining machinery div. EIMCO, Salt Lake City, 1976-77; mfg. project engr., mfg. engring. mgr. Sorenson Research Co., Salt Lake City, 1977—; cons. machine design; owner Photo-Micro-Graphics, photography and custom printing lab. Mem. Soc. Mfg. Engrs. (chpt. membership chmn. 1978-79). A developer intravenous flow control device. Home: 1101 N Sunflower Circle Layton UT 84041 Office: 4455 Atherton Dr Salt Lake City UT 84107

CHEE, PERCIVAL HON YIN, ophthalmologist; b. Honolulu, Aug. 29, 1936; s. Young Sing and Den Kyau (Ching) C.; B.A., U. Hawaii, 1958; M.D., U. Rochester, 1962; m. Carolyn Siu Lin Tong, Jan. 27, 1966; children—Lara Wai Lung, Shera Wai Sum. Intern, Travis AFB Hosp., Fairfield, Calif., 1962-63; resident Bascom Palmer Eye Inst., Miami, Fla., 1965-68, Jackson Meml. Hosp., Miami, 1965-68; partner Straub Clinic, Inc., Honolulu, 1968-71; practice medicine specializing in ophthalmology, Honolulu, 1972—; mem. staffs Queen's Med. Center, St. Francis Hosp., Kapiolani Children's Med. Center, Honolulu; clin. assoc. prof. surgery U. Hawaii Sch. Medicine, 1971—; cons. Tripler Army Med. Center. Mem. adv. bd. Services to Blind; bd. dirs. Lions Eye Bank and Makana Found. (organ bank), Multiple Sclerosis Soc. Served to capt. USAF, 1962-65. Fellow Am. Acad. Ophthalmology, ACS; mem. AMA, Pan Am. Med. Assn., Pan Pacific Surg. Assn., Am. Assn. Ophthalmology, Soc. Eye Surgeons, Hawaii Ophthal. Soc. Pacific Coast Ophthal. Soc., Am. Assn. for Study Headache, Pan Am. Ophthal. Found. Contbr. articles to profl. pubs. Home: 3755 Poka Pl Honolulu HI 96816 Office: Kukui Plaza 50 S Beretania St Honolulu HI 96513

CHEEK, JERRY DALE, civil engineer; b. Yellville, Ark., Apr. 17, 1939; s. Irvin MacDonald and Eva Ivon (Kyles) C.; student Yakima Valley Coll., 1972-74; m. Janice Arlene Wales, Sept. 11, 1959; children—Dawn Antoinette, Janice Karen, Denise Dale. Insp., Dept. Hwys., Walla Walla, Wash., 1957-60, surveyor, 1960-63, project designer, 1963-65, spl. studies engr., Yakima, Wash., 1965-69, needs study engr., 1969-76; asst. project engr. Dept. Transp., Union Gap, Wash., 1976-80; environ. rev. coordinator Dept. Transp., Olympia, Wash., 1981—; pres. Cheek Enterprises, 1981—; mem. engring. tech. adv. com. Yakima Valley Coll., 1976-81; mem. engring. aide/surveying/drafting adv. com. Yakima Valley Vocat. Skills Center, 1977. Registered profl. engr., Wash.; cert. engring. technician Inst. for Certification of Engring. Technicians. Mem. ASCE, Internat. Fedn. Profl. and Tech. Engrs. (trustee 1975-79), Farmers Grange, Ind. Order of Foresters. Club: Eagles. Home: 5418 Box Elder Ct SW Olympia WA 98502 Office: Transp Adminstrn Bldg Olympia WA 98504

CHEHARDY, PEGGY LYNN, educator; b. New Orleans, July 16, 1953; d. Robert Elias and Peggy Joyce (Lamb) C. B.S. in Home Econs., La. State U., 1975; cert. Vocat. Home Econs., U. N.Mex., Albuquerque, 1977, M.S. in Health Edn., 1979. Head tchr. health edn. Eldorado High Sch., Albuquerque, 1977—. Chmn. pub. edn. com. Bernalillo unit Am. Cancer Soc. Recipient cert. Appreciation FDA, 1982, N.Mex. Sch. Health Assn., 1982, U.S. Consumer Product Safety Commn., 1981. Mem. Am. Sch. Health Assn., N.Mex. Sch. Health Assn. (treas. 1980-82), Albuquerque Home Econs. Assn., N.Mex. Vocat. Assn., Phi Delta Phi, Eta Sigma Gamma (v.p. 1979-80). Methodist. Author of health edn. curriculum guide for Albuquerque pub. schs. Home: 6204 Lola St NE Albuquerque NM 87109 Office: Eldorado High Sch 11300 Montgomery St NE Albuquerque NM 87111

CHEKERYLLA, JAMES RAY, computer corp. exec., b. Detroit, Mar. 12, 1949; s. Andrew and Mary (Betanzos) C.; B.S. in Aerospace Engring., U. Mich., 1971, M.A. in Math., 1974; m. Blanca Luz Castillo, June 5, 1976. Design engr. Ford Motor Co., Dearborn, Mich., 1971-73; sr. engr. Boeing Aerospace Co., Seattle, 1974-78; v.p. Advanced System Products, Inc., Seattle, 1979—, also sec.; cons. in computer field. Recipient various coll. scholarships. Mem. IEEE. Office: 26225 SE 158 Issaquah WA 98027

CHELAPATI, CHUNDURI VENKATA, civil engineer, educator; b. Eluru, India, Mar. 11, 1933; s. Lakshminarayana and Anjamma (Kanumuri) Chunduri; came to U.S., 1957, naturalized, 1971; B.E. with honors, Andhra U., India, 1954; M.S., U. Ill., 1959, Ph.D., 1962. Jr. engr. office of Chief Engr., State of Andhra, India, 1954-55; asst. prof. structural engring. Birla Coll. of Engring., Pilani, India, 1956-57; research asst. dept. civil engring. U. Ill., 1957-62; asst. prof. engring. Calif. State U., Los Angeles, 1962-65, assoc. prof. Calif. State U., Long Beach, 1965-70, prof. civil engring., 1970—, vice-chmn. dept., 1971-73, chmn. dept., 1973-79, coordinator profl. rev. and devel. programs for engrs., 1973-81, dir. continuing engring. edn., 1982—; pres. C.V. Chelapati & Assocs., Inc., Cons. Engrs., Huntington Beach, Calif., 1979—; cons. U.S. Navy Civil Engring. Lab., 1962-68, 75—, Holmes & Narver, Inc., Anaheim, 1968-73. Registered profl. cons. civil engr., Calif. Mem. ASCE, Am. Soc. Engring. Edn., Structural Engrs. Assn. So. Calif., Earthquake Engring. Research Inst., Am. Concrete Inst., Am. Inst. Steel Constrn., Seismological Soc. Am., Sigma Xi, Chi Epsilon, Tau Beta Pi, Phi Kappa Phi. Home: 16292 Mandalay Circle Huntington Beach CA 92649 Office: Dept Civil Engring Calif State U Long Beach CA 90840

CHELINI, SUSAN FITZHARRIS, home economics educator; b. Los Angeles, Aug. 31, 1940; d. Cletus James and Genevieve (Staley) Fitzharris; m. John Edward Chelini, July 8, 1967; children—Colleen Marie, Letitia Anne. B.S., U. Calif.-Davis, 1962; M.A., San Francisco State U., 1983. Cert. secondary tchr., adminstr., Calif. Tchr. home econs. Santa Cruz (Calif.) City Schs., 1962-64; tchr. home econs. Tamalpais Union High Sch. Dist., Larkspur, Calif., 1964—; chmn. home econs. dept. Redwood High Sch., Larkspur, 1964—. Mem. Am. Home Econs. Assn., Calif. Home Econs. Assn. (grad. fellow, Home Economist of Yr., Home Econs. Tchr. of Yr. 1980; pres. 1983—), Bay Dist. Home Econs. Assn., Am. Vocat. Assn., Calif. Assn. Vocat. Edn., Home Econs. Tchrs. Assn. Calif., NEA, Calif. Tchrs. Assn., Tamalpais Dist. Tchrs. Assn.

CHEMTOB, CLAUDE MOUSSA, psychologist; b. Alexandria, Egypt, Aug. 4, 1950; s. Elie Moussa and Tony (Fortunee) C. B.A. in Psychology (with honors), U. Calif.-Santa Cruz, 1972; M.A. in Psychology, U. Mich., 1977, Ph.D. in Clin. Psychology, 1980. Sr. research assoc. U. Mich. Med. Sch., 1977-80; clin. psychologist VA, Honolulu, 1980—, dir. research, 1981—; clin. asst. prof. psychiatry U. Hawaii Med. Sch., 1982—; pvt. practice, Honolulu. Mem. Hawaii Psychol. Assn. (co-chmn. programs), Nat. Orgn. VA Psychologists (sterring com.), Am. Psychol. Assn. Democrat. Jewish Contbr. articles to profl. jours. Home: 2957 Kalakaua Ave Apt 306 Honolulu HI 96815 Office: 677 Ala Moana Blvd Suite 413 Honolulu HI 96815

CHEN, CHI-CHU WU, biochemist; b. Changhai, Taiwan, Feb. 16, 1943; d. Tang Chao and Cheong Chi Wu; came to U.S., 1966, naturalized, 1977; B.S., Tunghai U., 1965; Ph.D., U. Ill., 1974; m. Cheng-I Chen, Sept. 14, 1969; children—Eugene, Philana. Research specialist dept. medicine U. Calif., Irvine, 1974-78; sr. profl. chemist Allergan Pharm. Co., Irvine, 1978—; cons. U.S. Indsl. Product Corp., Norwalk, Calif., 1980—. Mem. Soc. for Investigative Dermatology, AAAS, Sigma Xi. Contbr. articles on biology to sci. publs. Home: 28812 Woodcock Dr Laguna Niguel CA 92677 Office: 2525 Du Pont Dr Irvine CA 92713

CHEN, EVAN EVA, statistician, consultant; b. Taiwan, Republic of China, Oct. 31, 1949; d. Yu-kai and Hsi-Ing Grace (Huang) C.; came to U.S., 1972; m. Tang Wu, June 14, 1975; children—Eric J., Albert J. Ph.D., U. Wis.-Madison. Div. statistician Signetics Corp., Sunnyvale, Calif., 1980-82; statistician, statis. cons. ROLM Corp., Santa Clara, Calif., 1982—; liaison rep. stats. and electronics divs. Am. Soc. Quality Control. Mem. Am. Statis. Assn., Am. Soc. Quality Control. Home: 10834 Willowbrook Way Cupertino CA 95014 Office: ROLM Corp 4900 Old Ironsides Dr Santa Clara CA 95050

CHEN, JANEY C., linguist; b. China, Feb. 5, 1922; d. Ching Choi and Sik Yu (Li) Chou; B.Sc., Nat. South-West Associated Univs., Yunnan, China, 1944; M.R.E., Heavenly People Theol. Sem., 1968, Golden Gate Bapt. Theol. Sem., 1980; m. Ti Kang Chen, July 25, 1943; children—David, Julia, Helen. Instr. English, 1st Middle Sch., Kuangchouwan, 1945-46; sr. instr. Taipei Lang. Inst., Taiwan, 1957-64; sr. instr. Chinese U., Hong Kong, 1964-71; founder, prin. Hong Kong Lang. Inst., 1971-75; tchr. German Swiss Internat. Sch., 1975-78; instr. Chinese Tiburon (Calif.) Baptist Ch., 1979—; dir. English/Chinese lang. and Bible classes Lang. Mission, So. Bapt. Conv., 1979—; dir. H.K. World Home Bible League, 1972-77; owner J.C. Publs., 1968-78. Author: A Language Bridge for John, 1967; Cantonese for Foreign Children, 1968; Conversation Drills in Everyday Cantonese, 1969; A Practical English-Chinese Pronouncing Dictionary, 1970; 300 Common Chinese Characters, Mandarin and Cantonese, 2 vols. Home: 19 Miwok Way Shelter Hill Apt Mill Valley CA 94941

CHEN, JOSEPH LIANG-PING, chem. engr.; b. Taipei, Taiwan, Nov. 16, 1942; s. Twang Wang and Shiang (Lin) C.; B.S. in Chem. Engring., Nat. Taiwan U., 1965; M.S., (Univ. fellow, Harrison scholar), U. Pa., 1968, Ph.D. in Chem. Engring., 1970; m. Elizabeth S. Lee, Oct. 3, 1970; children—Thomas J., Theresa B.; came to U.S., 1966, naturalized, 1977. Sr. engr. Westinghouse Elec. Corp., Pitts., 1971-75; sr. research engr. Hooker Chem. & Plastics Corp., Buffalo, 1975-77, Occidental Petroleum Corp., Irvine, Calif., 1977—. Mem. Am. Inst. Chem. Engring. Presbyterian. Patentee in field. Home: 21652 Cabrosa Rd Mission Viejo CA 92691

CHEN, LI-KING, mining engineer, coal company executive; b. Szuchuan Province, China, Dec. 7, 1938; came to U.S., 1968, naturalized, 1977; s. Y.J. and S.W. (Chang) C.; B.S. in Mining Engring., Taiwan Cheng Kung U., 1966; M.S. in Mining Engring., U. Mo., Rolla, 1970; m. Dec. 6, 1967; children—Bob, Alex, Lisa. Sec. gen. and mining engring. Keng Da Coal Mining Co., Taiwan, 1966-73; mine engr. Concinco Am. Inc., Bixby, Mo., 1970-73; project engr. FMC Corp., Green River, Wyo., 1974-75; mine devel. engr. El Paso Energy Co., 1975-76; supt. Energy Fuels Corp., Steamboat Springs, Colo., 1976-79; prin. mining engr. NUS Corp., 1978-79; v.p. ops. GEC Minerals Inc., Florence, Colo., 1979—. Mem. AIME. Club: Lions. Home: 964 Ridgeview Pl Canon City CO 81212 Office: PO Box 225 Florence CO 81226

CHEN, MARJORIE WONG, airline exec.; b. Los Angeles, Oct. 28, 1940; d. Thomas A. and Mayme M. (Moe) Wong; B.A., Goucher Coll., 1962; M.A., U. Calif. at Berkeley, 1965; m. Joseph Tao Chen, July 10, 1965; children—Barbara Joanne, Cynthia Anne. Research economist Fed. Reserve Bank San Francisco, 1964-65; bus. cons., travel industry, 1968-74; marketing analyst The Flying Tiger Line Inc., Los Angeles, 1974-76, systems analyst, 1976-77, mgr. mgmt. reporting and performance analysis, 1977-78; mgr. passenger pricing and fare devel. Continental Airlines, 1978-80, dir. internat. pricing, 1980-83; aviation and mktg. cons. Chen and Assocs., 1983—; dir. Continental Fed. Credit Union. Mem. Calif. Republican Assembly, 1976. Danforth Found. asso., 1968-79. Mem. Nat. Mgmt. Assn. (membership chmn.), World Affairs Council Los Angeles, Town Hall Calif., U. Calif., Marlborough alumni assns. Republican. Conglist. Club: Goucher. Home: 640 N June St Los Angeles CA 90004 Office: 7300 World Way W Los Angeles CA 90009

CHEN, ROBERT I-CHIH, mfg. co. exec.; b. China, Dec. 17, 1947; s. Kon-Yu and H.H. Chen; came to U.S., 1971; B.S., Nat. Taiwan Cheng Kung U., 1970; M.S., S.D. Tech. U., 1973; Dr. Engring., Syracuse U., 1977; m. Lien, Sept. 6, 1975; children—She Rae, She-Reen. Mfg. devel. engr. Delco Electronics, Gen. Motors, Kokomo, Ind., 1973-74; product engr. semiconductor dept. Gen. Electric Co., Syracuse, N.Y., 1974-77; engring. mgr., component engring. dept. Tektronix, Beaverton, Oreg., 1977-78; product mgr. Optoelectronic div. Fairchild Semiconductor, Mountain View, Calif., 1978-79; pres., founder Applied Optoelectronic Tech. Corp., Palo Alto, Calif., 1979—. Mem. IEEE, Soc. Info. Displays, Internat. Soc. Hybrid Microelectronics, Eta Kappa Nu. Patentee in field. Office: 1294 Lawrence Station Rd Sunnyvale CA 94086

CHEN, THOMAS CHUNGMIN, scientist; b. Taichung, Taiwan, June 21, 1926; s. Wunli and Su-o (Chi) C.; came to U.S., 1960, naturalized, 1971; B.S. in Elec. Engring., Cheng Kung U., Taiwan, 1950; M.S. in Elec. Engring., Purdue U., 1961; Ph.D. in Elec. Engring., Ill. Inst. Tech., 1971; m. Peggy Peyu, Mar. 10, 1951; children—William T., Patty Z., Robert T. Dir., Taipei N. Telephone Exchange Office, Taiwan, 1950-63; sr. engr. GTE Automatic Electric Labs., Chgo., 1964-72; tech. specialist ITT Defense Communications Div., Nutley, N.J., 1973-74; sr. mem. tech. staff Litton Data Systems, Van Nuys, Calif., 1975-78; sr. project engr. Hughes Aircraft Co., El Segundo, Calif., 1979-80; sr. staff engr. TRW Inc., Redondo Beach, Calif., 1980—. Mem. IEEE, Sigma Xi. Contbr. articles on communications systems engring. to tech. publs.; patentee (U.S. and internat.) switching systems. Address: 12615 Byron Ave Granada Hills CA 91344 Office: One Space Park Dr Redondo Beach CA 90278

CHEN, TUNG-SHAN, educator; b. Chungking, China, Apr. 17, 1939; s. Sze-Chen Lin and Mary M. Chen; came to U.S. 1962, naturalized, 1976; m. Yolanda Chu, Dec. 26, 1964; children—Andy, Lynn. B.S., Nat. Taiwan U., 1960; M.S., U. Calif.-Berkeley, 1964, Ph.D., 1969. Research chemist Food Tech. Ctr., Taipei, Taiwan, 1961-62; research and teaching asst. U. Calif.-Berkeley, 1962-69; asst. prof. food sci. Calif. State U.-Northridge, 1969-73, assoc. prof., 1973-78, prof., 1978—; vis. assoc. prof. UCLA, 1974; cons. to food industry and govt. agys. Pres. San Fernando Valley Chinese Cultural Assn., 1974-75, bd. dirs., 1975-78. Earl Antony fellow, 1965-69; Nat. Acad. Sci. NRC research fellow, 1969; NSF/Calif. State U.-Northridge research grantee, 1971, 74-76, 81. Fellow Am. Inst. Chemists; mem. AAAS, Am. Chem. Soc., Am. Dietetic Assn., Am. Home Econs. Assn., Inst. Food Technologists, Greater Los Angeles Nutrition Council (bd. dirs. 1978-81), Sigma Xi, Phi Tau Sigma. Contbr. numerous articles to profl. jours. Office: Calif State U Northridge CA 91330

CHENEY, MARSHALL CHIPMAN, lawyer; b. San Francisco, Feb. 15, 1924; s. Marshall Chipman and Penelope (McEntyre) C.; m. Nancy Dunn, June 8, 1944; children—Linda Maureen, Timothy Dunn. B.A., U. Calif.-Berkeley, 1947. LL.B., 1950. Bar: Wyo. 1951, Oreg. 1952. Asst. atty. gen. Oreg., 1953-55; assoc. Koerner, Young, McColloch & Dezendorf, Portland, Oreg., 1955-65; mem. Mize, Kriesien, Fewless, Cheney & Kelley, Portland, 1965-78; mem., sec.-treas Cheney & Kelley, P.C., Portland, 1978—. Bd. regents Oreg. Poly. Inst.; mem. standing and adv. com. Northwestern Sch. of Law, Lewis and Clark Coll.; mem. Multnomah County Republican Central Com., 1960-62. Served to lt. col. USAFR, 1943-72. Mem. ABA, Oreg. State Bar (chmn. com. on lawyer placement 1957-60, 63-67), Multnomah County Bar Assn. Home: 10360 SE Waverley Ct #308 Milwaukie OR 97222 Office: 610 SW Alder St Suite 303 Portland OR 97205

CHENG, ALBERT (ZHENG GUOHE), educational administrator; b. Manila, Sept. 29, 1948; s. Robert Fai A. and Isabel (Wong) C.; B.A. in Biol. Scis., U. Calif., Berkeley, 1969; M.A. in Ednl. Adminstrn., U. San Francisco, 1981; m. Anne Shui-Chun Chen, Aug. 28, 1971; children—Ryan Justin, Lorens Derek. Exec. dir. Chinatown North Beach Youth Council, San Francisco, 1969-71; ombudsman/citizen complaint officer San Francisco Unified Sch. Dist., 1971-75, affirmative action officer, 1975-81, coordinator bilingual-crosscultural/English as 2d lang. edn., 1981-83, coordinator personnel services, 1983—. Bd. dirs. Wah Nei Bilingual Pre-Sch. Program, Mayor's Employment and Tng. Council, Mission YMCA, Chinatown Youth Services Ctr. Mem. Chinese for Affirmative Action, Nat. Assn. Bilingual Educators, San Francisco Assn. Bilingual Edn. (pres.), Nat. Assn. Asian and Pacific Am. Edn., Asian Pacific Am. Advocates Calif., Calif. Assn. Bilingual Edn., Assn. Chinese Tchrs., Jaycees. Office: 135 Van Ness Ave San Francisco CA 94102

CHENG, DAVID GEE, Realtor, real estate developer; b. Shanghai, China, Sept. 1, 1915; s. Tsi Fei and Wai Wen (Liang) C.; came to U.S., 1966, naturalized, 1972; B.S. in Civil Engring., St. John's U., Shanghai, 1939; postgrad. Grad. Sch. of Design, Harvard U., 1966-67; children—David, Vida, Anthony. Pres., Nat. Housing Devel. Corp., Jakarta, Indonesia, 1956-66; minister of city planning and constrn. Republic of Indonesia, 1964-66; devel. dir. Hawaii Council of Housing Action, Honolulu, 1968-70; pres. DGC Devel. Corp., Honolulu, 1971—; asso. DRG Fin. Corp., Washington. Mem. transp. com. Oahu Devel. Conf., 1975-81. Recipient Devel. Achievement medal Republic of Indonesia, 1964. Mem. Nat. Assn. Realtors, Honolulu Bd. Realtors. Roman Catholic. Club: Plaza (charter mem.). Office: Amfac Tower Suite 1928 Honolulu HI 96813

CHENG, LUCIE, sociologist, university administrator; b. Hong Kong, Feb. 11, 1939; came to U.S., 1960, naturalized, 1965; d. She-Wo and Tsung-jang (Shaw) Cheng. M.A., U. Chgo., 1964; Ph.D., U. Hawaii, 1971. Lectr., U. Hawaii, Honolulu, 1966-70; asst. prof. UCLA, 1970-76, acting dir. Asian Am. Studies Center, 1972-76, assoc. prof., 1976-82, dir. China Exchange Program, 1979—, spl. asst. to vice chancellor, 1980—, prof., 1982—, dir. Asian Am. Studies Center, 1976—; cons. in field. Mem. Census Adv. Com. on Asian and Pacific Am. population for the 1980 census, 1976-80; bd. dirs. Chinese Hist. Soc. of So. Calif., 1978-80; mem. Calif. Council for the Humanities, 1981-85. Social Sci. Research Council grantee, 1972; Assn. for Asian Studies grantee, 1974-75; NIMH grantee, 1979-81; NEH grantee, 1982; East-West Center grantee, 1982. Mem. Am. Sociol. Assn. Author: Chinese Immigrant Women in 19th Century California, 1979; Mental Illness Among the Chinese, 1973; Toward a Political Economy of Chinese America, 1975.

CHENG, LUKE, earthquake engineer; b. Taipei, China, Oct. 11, 1952; came to U.S., 1968, naturalized, 1973; s. Philip C. and Louise (Pan) C.; m. Belle W. Y. Wei, Dec. 29, 1978; 1 dau., Martha. B.S. with high honors (James scholar), U. Ill., 1974; M.S., U. Calif.-Berkeley, 1975; postgrad. M.I.T., 1979. Asst. engr. H.K. Ferguson Co., San Francisco, 1976; assoc. engr. URS/John A. Blume & Assocs., San Francisco, 1977-78, sr. engr., 1980—; engr. Weidlinger Assocs., Cambridge, Mass., 1979; lectr. Cogswell Coll., San Francisco, 1981—. Harry H. Hilp fellow, 1974-75; registered profl. engr., Calif., Mass. Mem. ASCE, Earthquake Engring. Research Inst., Am. Concrete Inst. (tech. com. 1980—), Structural Engrs. Assn. No. Calif., Phi Kappa Phi, Chi Epsilon. Office: URS/John A Blume 130 Jessie St San Francisco CA 94105

CHENG, TSEN-CHUNG, elec. engr., educator; b. Shanghai, China, Dec. 24, 1944; came to U.S., 1964; B.S. in Elec. Engring., M.I.T., 1969, M.S., 1970, E.E., 1971, Sc.D., 1974; m. Doris Tin-Gen Lee, Aug. 25, 1974; 1 son, Jason Simon. Mem. research staff M.I.T., Cambridge, summer 1974; asst. prof. elec. engring. U. So. Calif., Los Angeles, 1974-80, asso. prof., 1980—, dir. electric power program, 1974—; dir. Sci. and Engring. Corp., Los Angeles, 1977—; cons. to electric power industry. Named Outstanding Elec. Engring. Faculty Mem., U. So. Calif., 1976; Exceptional Service award Sch. Engring., U. So. Calif., 1981. Electric Power Research Inst. grantee, 1976-80, So. Calif. Edison Co. grantee, 1975-80. Sr. mem. IEEE; mem. Sigma Xi, Tau Beta Pi, Eta Kappa Nu. Contbr. articles on electric power generation and transmission systems and insulation materials to profl. jours. Home: 2937 Sheffield Rd San Marino CA 91108 Office: PHE 634 Univ So Calif Los Angeles CA 90007

CHERAMY, EDWARD ROY, JR., accountant; b. Lawrence, Kans., Aug. 10, 1943; s. Edward Roy and Avis Leona (Crittenden) C.; m. Charlotte Valentic, Oct. 3, 1964; children—Mark, Matthew, Holly. B.S. in Acctg., Calif. State U.-Long Beach, 1970. C.P.A., Calif. With Price Waterhouse, 1970—, ptnr. in charge comprehensive profl. services dept., 1978—; SEC profl. acctg. fellow, Washington, 1976-78. Past pres. adv. council dept. accountancy Calif. State U., past pres. Acctg. Colleagues, mem. adv. bd. Sch. Bus. Served to 2d class petty officer USN, 1964-68. Named Outstanding Grad. Sch. Bus., Calif. State U., 1982. Mem. Am. Inst. C.P.A.s, Calif. Soc. C.P.A.s, Inst. Internal Auditors (internat. profl. practices com., Los Angeles chpt. bd. govs., pres.), Small Bus. High Tech. Inst. (chmn. So. Calif.). Republican. Office: Price Waterhouse 606 S Olive St Los Angeles CA 90014

CHERBERG, JOHN ANDREW, lt. gov. Wash.; b. Pensacola, Fla., Oct. 17, 1910; s. Fortunato and Annie (Rand) C.; B.A., U. Wash., 1933; m. Elizabeth Anne Walker, Aug. 17, 1935; children—Kay Elizabeth Cherberg Cohrs, Barbara Jean Cherberg Tonkin, James Walker. High sch. tchr., athletic coach, 1934-46; football coach U. Wash., 1946-56; lt. gov., Wash., 1957—, pres. Wash. Senate, 1957—. Mem. Nat. Conf. Lt. Govs. (chmn. 1968-69), Wash. Assn. Broadcasters (hon. life), Seattle Tchrs. Union (hon. life), Firefighters Union (hon. life), Sigma Nu. Office: 304 Legislative Bldg Olympia WA 98504

CHERBOSQUE, JORGE, counseling psychologist, cross-cultural communication consultant; b. Mexico City, Mar. 5, 1955; s. Gregorio and Sonia (Zundelevich) Cherbowski. B.S. (hon.), Hebrew U. Jerusalem, 1977; M.A. (hon.), U. So. Calif., 1979, postgrad. in counseling psychology, 1983—; postgrad. in psychoanalytic psychotherapy Wright Inst. Los Angeles, 1982-84. Lic. marriage, family and child therapist. Marriage, family and child counselor Maple Ctr., Beverly Hills, Calif., 1978-81; internat. student adv. Peer Counseling Program, U. So. Calif., Los Angeles, 1978-80, counseling psychologist Counseling Ctr., 1980-82, clin. assoc. counseling dept., 1980-83, cons. Office Internat. Students and Scholars, 1978-80; pvt. practice psychotherapy, Los Angeles, 1980—; instr. adult edn. classes Adat Ariel Adult Studies Inst. Student rep. Internat. Students Task Force, Nat. Assn. Fgn. Student Affairs, U. So. Calif.; cons., trainer peer-counseling programs; active groups ecol. contamination and nuclear arms disarmament. Phi Beta Kappa scholar, 1981; recipient Outstanding Student award Internat. Students Assembly, U. So. Calif., 1981. Mem. Am. Psychol. Assn., Nat. Assn. Social Workers, Am. Personnel and Guidance Assn., Am. Orthopsychiat. Assn., Phi Kappa Phi. Jewish. Club: Centro Deportivo Israelita (Mexico City). Author: The Magic Box, experiential exercise, 1983. Office: 8633 W 3d St Suite 770 Los Angeles CA 90048

CHERIS, SAMUEL DAVID, lawyer; b. Bklyn., Nov. 14, 1945; s. Hyman and Gertrude (Perlman) C.; B.S. cum laude with honors in Econs., Bklyn. Coll., 1967; J.D., Stanford U., 1971, M.B.A., 1971; m. Elaine Gayle Ingram, June 8, 1980; 1 son by previous marriage, Aaron Joseph. Bar: Calif. 1972, U.S. Ct. Claims 1972, Colo. 1973, U.S. Tax Ct. 1974. Law clk. U.S. Ct. of Claims, Washington, 1971-72; asso. atty. Yegge, Hall & Evans, Devner, 1972-75; partner Hall & Evans, Denver, 1976—, mem. exec. com., 1982—; sr. v.p., dir. Am. Stratigraphic Co., Denver, 1976—; dir. Carson's, Inc., Petrofiche, Inc.; adj. prof. U. Denver Sch. Law, 1973—. Vice pres. Stanford Law Sch. Fund, 1970-75; bd. dirs. Jewish Community Center of Denver, 1980—, Internat. Hearing Dog, Denver, 1979—, Congregation Rodef Shalom; 1982-83. Registered investment adv.; recipient Stanford U. Service award, 1976. Mem. ABA (real property probate and trust sect., vice chmn. com. spl. problems of execs. and profls., mem. pub. contracts sect.), Calif. Bar Assn., Colo. Bar Assn., Denver Bar Assn., U.S. Fencing Assn. (v.p. 1982—, ofcls. commn. 1979— asst. fgn. sec. 1981—), Cheyenne Fencing Soc., Colo. Assn. Commerce and Industry (small bus. tax council), Internat. Assn. Fin. Planners, Denver Estate Planning Council, Assn. Jewish Lawyers, U.S. Com. Sports for Israel (state chmn. Colo.), Order of Coif. Editor Stanford Law Rev.; exec. editor Stanford Jour. Internat. Studies; contbr. articles to profl. jours. Home: 5730 Montview Blvd Denver CO 80207 Office: Hall & Evans 2900 Petro Lewis Tower Denver CO 80202

CHERN, WEN SHYONG, economist; b. Taiwan, Mar. 19, 1941; came to U.S. 1967, naturalized 1978; s. Tsai Ching and Yao Cho C.; m. Ann Li-Faung, June 24, 1972; children—Annie Lee, Wenson Roy. B.S., Nat. Chung-Hsing U., 1964; M.S., U. Fla., 1969; M.A., U. Calif.-Berkeley, 1971, Ph.D., 1975. Asst. prof. U. Fla. 1973-74; economist, group leader energy div. Oak Ridge Nat. Lab. 1974-81; vis. assoc. prof. Nat. Chung-Hsing U. 1978; sr. economist, planner Lawrence Livermore (Calif.) Nat. Lab., 1981—; adviser Chinese Petroleum Corp. Served to 2d lt. Chinese Air Force 1964-65. Nuclear Regulatory Commn. grantee 1976-81; Dept. Energy grantee 1977-82; U.S. Dept. Agr. grantee 1980-81. Mem. Am. Econs. Assn., Am. Statis. Assn., Am. Agrl. Econs. Assn., Econometric Soc., Internat. Assn. Energy Economists. Democrat. Author: (with G.S. Madalla) Econometric Studies in Energy Demand and Supply 1978; contbr. articles in field to profl. jours. Home: 5462 Trumpet Ct Castro Valley CA 94546 Office: PO Box 808 L-202 Livermore CA 94550

CHERNICK, MICHAEL ROSS, mathematicial statistician; b. Havre de Grace, Md., Mar. 11, 1947; s. Jack and Norma Leonia (Weiner) C. B.S., SUNY-Stony Brook, 1969; M.A., U. Md., 1973; M.S., Stanford U., 1976, Ph.D., 1978. Mathematician, Army Materiel System Analysis Activity, Aberdeen Proving Ground, Md., 1969-74; math. statistician Oak Ridge Nat. Lab., 1978-80; mem. tech. staff Aerospace Corp., Los Angeles, 1980—. Stanford U. Sch. Engring. fellow, 1974. Mem. Am. Statis. Assn., Inst. Math. Stats., Barnoulli Soc., Soc. Indsl. and Applied Math. Democrat. Jewish. Contbr. articles to math. and statis. jour.

CHERNISS, NORMAN ARNOLD, newspaper editor; b. Council Bluffs, Iowa, July 16, 1926; s. David P. and Esther (Arenson) C.; B.A., State U. Iowa, 1950; postgrad. (Nieman fellow) Harvard, 1958-59, (Haynes fellow) U. Calif. at Los Angeles, 1960-61. Reporter, Council Bluffs Nonpareil, 1942-44; newswriter Sta. KOIL, Omaha, 1946; corr. Internat. News Service, Iowa City, 1948-49; editorial writer Des Moines Register and Tribune, 1949; Evansville (Ind.) Courier, 1951-53; editor editorial pages Riverside (Calif.) Press and Enterprise, 1953-67, asso. editor, 1967-71, exec. editor, 1971—. Vis. lectr. U. Calif. at Los Angeles, 1965-66, U. So. Calif., 1968-69, 71, 79; vis. prof., editor in residence Columbia Grad. Sch. Journalism, 1969-70. Served with USNR, 1944-46. Mem. Am. Soc. Newspaper Editors, Nat. Conf. Editorial Writers, Soc. Nieman Fellows, Kappa Tau Alpha. Home: 2218 El Capitan Dr Riverside CA 92506 Office: Press-Enterprise Co PO Box 792 Riverside CA 92502

CHERNOVE, SHELDON BROOKS, lawyer; b. Los Angeles, July 31, 1949; s. Louis Aaron and Helen Eleanor C.; B.A. cum laude (Outstanding Grad. Sr. Dept. Phys. Edn.), Calif. State U., Northridge, 1971; postgrad. U. Calif., Berkeley, 1971-72; J.D. cum laude (dean's scholar, teaching fellow), Loyola U., 1975; m. Cassandra H. Davis, Nov. 14, 1976; children—Arianna Beth, Ashley Helene. Admitted to Calif. bar, 1975; asso. firm Thorpe, Sullivan, Workman, Thorpe & O'Sullivan, Los Angeles, 1975-78; partner Malley, Yelsky, Chernove & Scott, Beverly Hills, Calif., Washington and Chgo., 1978—; adj. prof. law Valley U. Sch. Law.; settlement officer Los Angeles County Small Claims Ct.; dir. Centre Court Restaurants, Inc., Pacific Tastee Freez, Inc., Equity 1 Credit Corp., Diamond Bar Escrow, Inc. Mem. Myasthenia Gravis Found. Mem. ABA (mem. small bus. subcom. of sect. corp., banking and bus. law), Calif. Bar Assn., Los Angeles County Bar Assn. (mem. econs. of law practice subcom.), Beverly Hills Bar Assn., St. Thomas More Law Honor Soc., Beverly Hills C. of C. (local govt. com.), Calif. Assn. Health, Phys. Edn. and Recreation (div. pres.). Contbr. article to legal review. Office: 9595 Wilshire Blvd #610 Beverly Hills CA 90212

CHERRY, M. RUTH, psychologist; b. Pine Bluff, Ark., Mar. 28, 1950; d. Earl J. and Mary R. C. Ph.D., Calif. Sch. Profl. Psychology, 1976. Psychol. intern Family Services Assn., San Diego, 1973-74, Linda Vista Health Care Center, San Diego, 1974; program evaluator Social Advocates for Youth, San Diego, 1977; psychol. intern Tech. Research Inst., Inc., San Diego, 1974-75, Fed. Defenders, San Diego, 1975, Cath. Community Services, El Centro, Calif., 1978; psychol. asst., San Diego, 1976-78; pvt. practice psychology, San Diego, 1976-82, Oceanside, Calif., 1979—. Mem. Am. Psychol. Assn., Calif. State Psychol. Assn., Acad. San Diego Psychologists. Democrat.

CHERU, FANTU, political scientist, educator; b. Gondar, Ethiopia, Apr. 21, 1949; s. Cheru Tegegne and Woubalech Getahun. B.A. in Polit. Sci., Colo. Coll., 1975; M.S. in Polit. Sci., Portland State U., 1978, Ph.D. in Urban and Pub. Affairs, 1983. Vis. research assoc. Inst. Devel. Studies, U. Nairobi, 1981-82; asst. prof. dept. African/Afro Am. studies Portland (Oreg.) State U., 1982—. Maurie Clark Dissertation fellow, 1981-82. Mem. Am. Polit. Sci. Assn., Pi Gamma Mu. Home: 1845 NW 23d Pl Portland OR 97210

CHESAREK, FERDINAND JOSEPH, business executive, former army officer; b. Calumet, Mich., Feb. 18, 1914; s. Joseph and Mary (Pontello) C.; B.S., U.S. Mil. Acad., 1938; M.B.A., Stanford, 1950; grad. Nat. War Coll., 1956, Advanced Mgmt. Program, Harvard U., 1958; m. Martha Jayne Rullman, Sept. 1, 1938 (dec. 1978); 1 son, John Laymon; m. 2d, Joan Tepe, 1979. Commd. 2d lt. U.S. Army, 1938, advanced through grades to gen., 1968; comdg. officer 28th F.A. Bn., 8th Inf. Div., ETO, World War II, 5th Arty. Group, Korean War; comdg. gen. 4th Logistical Command, Europe, 1959-62; asst. dep. chief staff logistics Dept. Army, 1962-66; comptroller of army, 1966; asst. vice chief staff Army, 1967-68, comdg. gen. U.S. Army Materiel Command, 1968-70; ret., 1970; now owner Chesarek Industries, Inc.; pres. Consol. Investment & Devel. Corp., Luxembourg. Decorated Silver Star, Legion of Merit, Bronze Star, Commendation medal, Air medal, Purple Heart, D.S.M.; Legion of Honor, Croix de Guerre (France); Croix de Guerre (Luxembourg); Order Ulchi (Korea); Order of Republic (Italy). Home: 25706 Elena Rd Los Altos Hills CA 94022

CHESHIRE, DAVID JOSEPH EDWARD, physician; b. Nottingham, Eng., Oct. 3, 1922; s. Daniel and Clara Millicent (Pennington) C.; came to U.S., 1972; M.B., B.S., St. Bartholomew's Hosp., U. London, 1947; m. Elizabeth Anne Gillings, June 24, 1973; children—Barbara Mary Cheshire Porter, Katherine Elizabeth Cheshire DeGroot, Philip Anthony. House physician St. Bartholomew's Hosp., 1947; house surgeon, registrar in orthopaedic surgery Highlands Hosp., London, 1947-50; fellow in spinal cord injuries Stoke Mandeville Hosp., Aylesbury, Eng., 1958-59; med. officer Nat. Coal Bd., 1955-58; dir. Spinal Injuries Centre Victoria, Austin Hosp., Heidelberg, Victoria, Australia, 1959-72; cons. Govt. Tasmania, 1967-72; clin. dir., dir. edn. S.W. Regional System Treatment Spinal Injury, Good Samaritan Hosp., Phoenix, 1972-75, dir., 1975-78, mem. hosp. staff, 1972—; practice medicine specializing in spinal cord injuries and orthopaedics, Phoenix, 1972—; mem. staff St. Joseph's, John C. Lincoln hosps., Phoenix Baptist Med. Center, Good Samaritan Med. Ctr.; med. dir. Phys. and Behavioral Medicine Assocs.; pres. Council Paraplegic and Quadriplegic Assns. Victoria, 1966-67; founding pres. Australian Paraplegic and Quadriplegic Council, 1961-72; mem. council mgmt. Victorian Soc. Crippled Children and Adults, 1962-64; mem. bd. mgmt. Occupational Therapy Sch. Victoria, 1961-72; lectr. in field. Served as officer, M.C., RAF, 1950-55. Diplomate bds. rehab. medicine Eng., Australia, also Bd. Neurol. and Orthopedic Medicine. Fellow Am. Acad. Neurol. and Orthopaedic Surgery; mem. Royal Coll. Surgeons Eng., Am. Spinal Injury Assn. (sec.-treas. 1977-79, dir. 1972-78), Internat. Med. Soc. Paraplegia (v.p. 1969-77, council 1969—), Am. Congress Rehab. Medicine, Internat. Rehab. Medicine Assn., Internat. Soc. Prosthetics and Orthotics, Am. Assn. Automotive Medicine, Australian Orthopaedic Assn., AMA, Ariz. Med. Assn., Maricopa County Med. Assn. Contbr. articles to med. publs. Office: 1010 E McDowell St Suite 405 Phoenix AZ 85006

CHESLEY, MICHAEL VERL, educational adminstrator; b. Burley, Idaho, July 16, 1947; s. Verl Russell and Susie Baugh C.; m. Christine Tilby, June 24, 1966; children—Michelle, Mark, Aaron, Jason, Chris, Mary. B.S., Weber State Coll., 1969; M.A., Birgham Young U., 1974, Ed.D., 1984. Tchr. pub. schs., American Fork, Utah, 1976, Burley, Idaho, 1977-81; prin. pub. schs., Heyburn, Idaho, 1981—. Weber State Coll. scholar, 1965-69; named Outstanding Young Educator, Am. Fork, 1976. Mem. Assn. Supervision and Curriculum Devel., Nat. Assn. Elem. Sch. Prins., Phi Delta Kappa, Kappa Lambda Delta. Republican. Mem. Ch. of Jesus Christ of Latter-day Saints.

CHESNEY, ROBERT, television production company executive; b. Chgo., Dec. 6, 1939; s. Anthony and Irene (Maslowski) C. B.A., U. Miami (Fla.), 1961; m. Joni Morgan, Jan. 1979. Freelance sports broadcaster, Atlanta, 1964-75; owner, pres. The Big Beefster restaurant chain, Atlanta, 1971-75; prin. Chesney & Assocs. comml. sales promotion and tng. films, Hollywood, Calif., 1975—; owner, pres. Chesney Communications; pres. Corp. Previews; exec. producer Window on Wall St. Exec. v.p., pres. Magna Carta Fundamentum; bd. dirs. Easter Seals. Mem. Am. Soc. Tng. Dirs. Clubs: Freemason, Jonathan. Mem. Ch. of Religious Scis. Office: 3225 Verdugo Rd Glendale CA 91208

CHESNUT, CAROL FITTING, economist; b. Pecos, Tex., June 17, 1937; d. Ralph Ulf and Carol (Lowe) Fitting; B.A. magna cum laude, U. Colo., 1971; m. Dwayne A. Chesnut, Dec. 27, 1955; children—Carol Marie, Michelle, Mark Steven. Research asst. U. Colo., 1972; head quality controller Mathematica, Inc., Denver, 1973-74; cons. Mincome Man. (Can.), Winnipeg, 1974; cons. economist Energy Cons. Assocs. Inc., Denver, 1974-79, also dir.; exec. v.p. tng. ECA Intercomp, 1980-81; gen. ptnr. Chestnut Consortium, 1981—; sec., dir. Critical Resources, Inc., 1981-83; staff aide Senator Gary Hart, 1978. Rep., Lakehurst Civic Assn., 1968; precinct capt. Democratic Party, 1982—. Mem. Am. Mgmt. Assn., Soc. Petroleum Engrs., Assn. Women Geoscientists (treas. Denver 1983—), ACLU, NOW, Colo. Assn. Commerce and Industry, Phi Beta Kappa, Phi Chi Theta. Unitarian. Clubs: City (Denver), Century. Office: 419-A St Paul Denver CO 80206

CHESPAK, WALTER, JR., marketing and advertising executive, landscape designer; b. Newark, July 18, 1933; s. Walter and Elsie A. (Repke) C.; m. Mary V. Helstowski, Aug. 6, 1955; children—Lawrence, Ronald, Leslie. B.S., Rutgers U., 1955, M.S., 1956. Nat. sales mgr. RN mag. Litton Publs., Oradell, N.J., 1966-69; dir. mag. ops. Am. Jour. Nursing Co., N.Y.C., 1970-71; dir. mktg. Med. Book Club, Edison, N.J., 1972-78; dir. communications Am. Assn. Critical-Care Nurses, Irvine, Calif., 1979-81; v.p. The Sanborn Co., Newport Beach, Calif., 1981-82; pres. Designage Advt. & Pub. Relations, Newport Beach, 1982—; lectr. continuing edn. courses. Pres. J.F. Kennedy Football Booster Club, Iselin, N.J., 1975-77; cubmaster Boy Scouts Am., Iselin, N.J., 1967-70. Mem. Sales Execs. Club N.Y., Pharm. Advt. Council N.Y., So. Calif. Turfgrass Council, Hortelite Club, Theta Chi, Alpha Zeta. Club: Lake Forest II Assn. Contbr. articles to health care and landscaping trade jours. Home: 22141 Pheasant St El Toro CA 92630 Office: Designage Advt & Pub Relations 4500 Campus Dr Suite 210 Newport Beach CA 92660

CHESS, STEPHEN JOHN, surgeon; b. W.Va., June 29, 1914; s. John and Theresa (Cernalavic) C.; B.S., Marquette U., 1937; M.S., 1939, M.D., 1942; Ph.D. in Surgery, U. Ill., 1949; m. Dorothy Anne Haasch, Nov. 21, 1940; children—Dorothy Anne, Stephanie Jean, Stephen John Gerard, Robert Phillip Michael, Thomas Christopher Paul. Intern, U. Ill. Sch. Medicine Research and Ednl. Hosps., 1942-43, fellow in surgery, 1943-44; resident in surgery Hines (Ill.) VA Hosp., 1946-49; asst. chief surgeon Wesley Meml. Hosp., and mem. teaching staff in surgery Northwestern U., 1949; practice medicine specializing in surgery, Buenaventura Med. Clinic, Inc., Ventura, Calif., 1950—; mem. staff Ojai (Calif.) Community Hosp., St. John's Hosp., Oxnard, Calif.; mem. staff Ventura County Gen. Hosp., 1957—, chief of staff, 1971-72; mem. staff Ventura Community Meml. Hosp., 1950—, chief of staff, 1973, chief of surgery, 1978; cons. in field. Bd. dirs. Am. Cancer Soc., 1974-76. Served to maj. M.C., U.S. Army, 1944-46; PTO. Decorated Bronze Star medal. Diplomate Am. Bd. Surgery, Am. Bd. Abdominal Surgery. Fellow A.C.S.; mem. Ventura County Med. Soc. (pres. 1975), Profl. Standards Rev. Orgn. (pres. Ventura Area chpt.), Calif. Hosp. Assn. (Ventura area rep. state council apptd. by sec. HEW), So. Calif. Hosp. Assn. (med. adv. com. 1975-80). Democrat. Roman Catholic. Contbr. articles to med. jours. Home: 155 Lakewood Ave Ventura CA 93003 Office: 2705 Loma Vista Rd Ventura CA 93003

CHESTER, CHARLOTTE WANETTA, painter, printmaker; b. Columbus, Ohio, Oct. 27, 1921; d. Charles William and Edna Mae Cole (Casteel) Harper; student Oklahoma City U., 1958-59, Pa. Acad. Fine Arts, 1968-69, Phila. Coll. Arts, 1971; B.F.A., Ft. Wright Coll., 1977; m. David Murel Chester, Sept. 27, 1939; children—Carol Chester Landt, Janet Chester Cocklereece, David. Adminstrv. asst. FAA, 1955-68; advanced painting tchr. Community Coll., Mays Landing, N.J., 1968-69; tchr., co-owner gallery Art Is The Key, W.Orange, N.J., 1972-73; owner, operator studio, Reardon, Wash., 1977—; represented in permanent collection: Nat. Air and Space Mus., Smithsonian Inst., Washington; chmn. Atlantic City Art Center. Mem. Ft. Wright Alumni, Wash. Art Assn., League of S. Jersey Artists, Fed. Art Assn., Allied Artists, Artists Equity, Old World Water Color Soc. (London), Am. Pen Women, ACLU, Common Cause, NOW. Unitarian. Home and office: Route 1 Box 53 Reardon WA 99029

CHESTERFIELD, RHYDONIA RUTH EPPERSON, financial company executive; b. Dallas, Tex., Apr. 23, 1919; d. Leonard Lee and Sally F. (Stevenson) Griswold; B.S. Southwestern U., 1952; B.S., N. Tex. U., 1954, M.E., 1956; Ph.D., Bernardean U., 1974, Calif. Christian U., 1974, LL.D. (hon.), 1974; m. Chad Chesterfield, Apr. 21, 1979. Evangelist with Griswold Trio, 1940-58; tchr., counselor Dallas public schs., 1952-58, Los Angeles public schs., 1958-74; pres. Griswold-Epperson Fin. Enterprise, Los Angeles, 1974—; pres. GEC Enterprises, 1979—; guest speaker various schs., chs. and civic orgns. in U.S. and Can. Fellow Internat. Naturopathic Assn.; mem. Los Angeles Inst. Fine Arts, Assn.

of Women in Edn. (hon.), Internat. Bus. and Profl. Women, Pi Lambda Theta (hon.), Kappa Delta Pi (hon.). Author: Little Citizens series, Cathedral Films; contbr. articles on bus. to profl. publs. Office: 10790 Wilshire Blvd 202 Los Angeles CA 90024

CHEVALIER, BARBARA LANSBURGH, interior designer; b. San Francisco; d. S. Laz and Ethel (Newman) Lansburgh; children—Suzanne Chevalier Skolnikoff, Haakon L. Student Mills Coll., 1926; A.B., Stanford U., 1927; postgrad. U. Calif.-Berkeley, 1931. Social worker Fed. Govt., 1936-37; apprentice interior designer, San Francisco, 1938-43; personal sec. to Elizabeth Arden, 1944; owner, mgr. Barbara Chevalier Interiors, San Francisco, 1947—; pres. Chevalier-Rogers, Inc., San Francisco, 1962-70. Home: Stinson Beach CA 94970 Office: Barbara Chevalier Interiors 2033 Baker St San Francisco CA 94115

CHEW, DENNIS W., assn. exec.; b. Hong Kong, Jan. 1, 1941; s. Stephen and Wai (Mui) C.; B.S., U. Redlands, 1963; postgrad. U. Calif., Riverside, 1965; m. Linda Lee Olson, July 23, 1965; children—Stephanie L.S., Erica L.S. Tchr., Riverside (Calif.) Unified Sch. Dist., 1965-71; asst. exec. dir. Sacramento City Tchrs. Assn., 1971-73; negotiations cons. Calif. Tchrs. Assn., Burlingame, 1973-77, asst. exec. dir., 1977-78, assoc. exec. dir., 1979-82, cons., 1982—; instr. U. Calif. extension. Bd. dirs. Redlands Winter Concerts, 1969-71. Mem. AAAS, Am. Arbitration Assn. Office: 6 Garden Estates Ct Alamo CA 94507

CHEW, HERMAN FRANCIS, psychologist; b. Pleasantville, N.J., Oct. 18, 1924; s. Melvin Everett and Clara Regina (Gandy) C.: B.A., San Diego State Coll., 1954, M.A., 1956; m. Eulalia Nadine Jordan, Mar. 11, 1946; children—William Neil, Andrea Claire. Social scientist Rand Corp., Santa Monica, Calif., 1955-57; human factors scientist, sr. scientist System Devel. Corp., Santa Monica, 1957-70; cons. psychologist, Los Angeles, 1970-72; dir. FlexEd program U. So. Calif., 1972—, asso. dir. Center for Study of Pvt. Enterprise. Served with U.S. Navy, 1942-48, 51-53. Mem. Am. Psychol. Assn., Western Psychol. Assn., Assn. Pvt. Enterprise Edn. (pres. 1981-82). Home: 22124 Baltar St Canoga Park CA 91304 Office: Sch Bus U So Calif Los Angeles CA 90007

CHEW, LINDA LEE, public relations specialist; b. Riverside, Calif., Mar. 3, 1941; d. LeRoy S. and Grace (Ham) Olson; m. Dennis W. Chew, July 23, 1965; children—Stephanie, Erica. B.Mus., U. Redlands, 1962. Cert. fund raising exec. Dir. pub. events U. Redlands (Calif.), 1962-69, dir. fin. and communications San Gorgonio council Girl Scouts U.S.A., Colton, Calif., 1969-71; exec. dir. United Cerebral Palsy Assn. Sacramento-Yolo Counties, 1972-73; fin. devel. dir. San Francisco Bay council Girl Scouts U.S.A., 1973-76; chief devel. and pub. info. East Bay Regional Park Dist., Oakland, Calif., 1976—. Bd. dirs. Planned Parenthood Contra Costa County, 1980-82. Recipient Abel Hanson Meml. award Nat. Soc. Fund Raising Execs., 1977. Mem. Nat. Soc. Fund Raising Execs. (nat. vice chmn. 1981—), Pub. Relations Soc. Am., Calif. Park and Recreation Soc., AdMark Club, AAUW (pres. Redlands br. 1968-69), Am. Guild Organists (dean Riverside-San Bernardino chpt. 1969-71). Office: 11500 Skyline Blvd Oakland CA 94619

CHEW, MATTHEW KENYON, accountant; b. Youngstown, Ohio, June 9, 1932; s. Matthew Kates and Seville (Wyckoff) C.; m. Lucile Vernon Clark, Oct. 25, 1952; children—Matthew Kevin, Kenyon Wyckoff, Christopher Clark. B.B.A., Ashland Coll., 1955. C.P.A., Ohio, Ariz. Staff acct. to mgr. Haskins & Sells, Cleve., 1955-61, Phoenix, 1961-74; ptnr. Walker & Armstrong, Phoenix, 1974-79, Allen & Chew, Scottsdale, Ariz., 1979—. Recipient Wall St. Jour. Student Achievement award, 1955. Mem. Am. Inst. C.P.A.s, Ariz. Soc. C.P.A.s, Ohio Soc. C.P.A.s. Republican. Episcopalian (mem. nat. exec. council 1976-82, treas. Ariz. Diocese 1969-75, 79-82). Club: Arizona Country. Home: 3308 N 63d Pl Scottsdale AZ 85251 Office: 7045 3d Ave Scottsdale AZ 85251

CHI, JEFF KUO S., aero. engr.; b. Harbin, China, Feb. 12, 1936; came to U.S., 1961, naturalized, 1972; s. Yung Yeng and Hsu Kuei (Tzu) C.; Ph.D. (Univ. gen. fellow, Deutsch Co. fellow), UCLA, 1972; m. Susana Chao, June 10, 1962; children—Joseph H., Diana H. Mem. tech. staff Rockwell Internat. Corp., Los Angeles, 1973-77; staff engr. Hughes Aircraft Co., El Segundo, Calif., 1977-80; mem. tech. staff Aerospace Corp., El Segundo, 1980—; tchr. UCLA, 1975—; adj. prof. Northrop U., 1981—; hon. cons. engr. Aero Industry Devel. Center, 1977—. Registered profl. engr., Calif.; recipient Outstanding Tech. Achievement award Rockwell Internat., 1975. Asso. fellow AIAA; mem. Sigma Xi. Contbr. articles profl. jours. Office: 2350 E El Segundo Blvd El Segundo CA 90245

CHIANG, ALBERT CHIN-LIANG, electrical engineer; b. Putai, Taiwan, Jan. 25, 1937; s. San Chi and Chiu (Hsu) C.; B.S. in E.E., Nat. Taiwan U., 1959; M.S. in E.E., Chiaotung U., Taiwan, 1963; Ph.D., U. So. Calif., 1968; m. Steffie F.L. Huang, Dec. 24, 1967; children—Margaret, Stacy, Kathy, George. Came to U.S., 1963, naturalized, 1973. Research asst. U. So. Calif., Los Angeles, 1963-68; engr. specialist Litton Industries, Woodland Hills, Calif., 1968-70; dir. internat. sales Macrodata Co., Woodland Hills, Calif., 1970-77; pres. Tritek Internat. Co., Northridge, Calif., 1977—. Mem. IEEE, Sigma Xi, Eta Kappa Nu. Home: 24132 Lupin Hill Rd Hidden Hills CA 91302 Office: 8345 Reseda Blvd Northridge CA 91324

CHIANG, CHIN LONG, statistician, educator; b. Chekiang, China, Nov. 12, 1916; s. Tse Shang and (Chen) C.; came to U.S., 1946, naturalized, 1963; B.A. in Econs., Tsing Hwa U., 1940; M.A., U. Calif., Berkeley, 1948, Ph.D. in Stats., 1953; m. Fu Chen Shiao, Jan. 21, 1945; children—William S., Robert S., Harriet W. Teaching asst. U. Calif., Berkeley, 1948, research asst., 1950-51, asso., 1951-53, instr., 1953-55, asst. prof. biostatistics, 1955-60, asso. prof., 1960-65, prof., 1965—, chmn. div. of measurement scis., 1970-75, chmn. faculty Sch. of Public Health, 1975-76, chmn. Program in Biostatistics, 1970—, co-chmn. group in biostatistics, 1971—; vis. prof. U. Mich., 1959, U. Minn., 1960, 61, Yale U., 1965-66, Emory U., 1967, U. Pitts., 1968, U. Wash., 1969, U. N.C., 1969, 70, U. Tex., 1973, Vanderbilt U., 1975, Harvard U., 1977; cons. WHO, HEW, NIH, others. Nat. Heart Inst. fellow, 1959-60; Fulbright sr. lectr., 1964. Fellow Am. Statis. Assn., Inst. Math. Statistics, Am. Public Health Assn., Royal Statis. Soc., London; mem. Internat. Statis. Inst., Biometric Soc. Democrat. Author: Introduction to Stochastic Processes in Biostatistics, 1968; Life Table and Mortality Analysis, 1978; An Introduction to Stochastic Processes and Their Applications, 1979. Asso. editor: Biometrics, 1972-75, Mathematical Biosciences, 1976—. Mem. editorial bd. WHO Statistical Quar., 1979—. Office: School of Public Health University of California Berkeley CA 94720

CHIANG, WEN-LI, hydrodynamicist; b. Miaoli, Taiwan, Republic of China, Apr. 14, 1946; s. Pen-Hsiu and Shizuko (Yanagi) C.; B.S., Nat. Taiwan U., 1969; M.S., Nat. Central U., 1972; M.S., U. Kans., 1977; Ph.D., U. So. Calif., 1980; m. Hsiu-lan Wang, Dec. 26, 1974; children—Dean Tsung, Charles. Sea grant intern U. So. Calif., 1976-79; sr. engr. Tetra Tech, Inc., Pasadena, Calif., 1979—; part-time sr. lectr. dept. civil engring. U. So. Calif., Los Angeles, 1982—. Served with China Army, 1969-70. Registered profl. engr., Calif. Mem. ASCE, N.Y. Acad. Scis., Sigma Xi, Tau Beta Pi. Home: 1139 Calle Malaga Duarte CA 91010 Office: 630 N Rosemead Blvd Pasadena CA 91107

CHIAPPELLI, FRANCESCO, mental retardation researcher; b. Lausanne, Switzerland, June 11, 1953; came to U.S., 1969; s. Fredi Chiappelli and Aimerica Bollati; B.A. in Biology, UCLA, 1975, M.A. in Research Methods in Edn., 1901, postgrad., 1981—; m. Gloriela Maria Davis, May 23, 1975; 1 dau., Gioia Elvira. Staff research assoc. Mental Retardation Research Ctr., UCLA, 1977—, grantee in biomed. research, 1980, lab. research in phenylketonurea. Mem. N.Y. Acad. Sci., Am. Assn. on Mental Retardation, European Tissue Culture Assn., Am. Psychol. Assn. (nominee), Soc. Psychiatry and Culture, Hastings Ctr., Sigma Xi. Roman Catholic. Club: Nautilus Health. Contbr. papers to profl. publs. in field. Home: 10969 Coventry Pl Los Angeles CA 90064 Office: UCLA/NPI 67 384 760 Westwood Plaza Los Angeles CA 90024

CHIASSON, HAROLD WILLIAM, accountant; b. Newark, Nov. 29, 1942; s. James and Rose M. (Macri) C.; B.S. in Acctg., Bentley Coll., 1971; M.Bus. Taxation, U. So. Calif., 1982; m. Stephanie D. Butler, Apr. 1975; children—Scott, Clarke, Wendy. Acct., Harris, Kerr, Forster & Co., C.P.A.'s, Boston, 1962-63; sr. acct. Pride-Patten & Co., C.P.A.'s, Boston, 1963-66, Touche Ross & Co., C.P.A.'s, Boston, 1967-68, supervisory acct., Los Angeles, 1968-70; prin. Harold W. Chiasson, C.P.A., Pasadena, Calif., 1971-80, Arcadia, Calif., 1980—; instr. in bus., taxation Azusa Pacific Coll. Met. chmn. Christian Businessmen's Com., Pasadena. Served with USMC, 1964-70. C.P.A., Mass., Calif. Mem. Am. Inst. C.P.A.s, Calif. Soc. C.P.A.s, Arcadia C. of C. Republican. Contbr. articles to profl. jours. Home: 390 E Laurel Ave Sierra Madre CA 91024 Office: 20 E Foothill Blvd Arcadia CA 91006

CHIBBER, SURENDER MOHAN, mechanical engineer, consultant; b. New Delhi, India, May 1, 1943; s. Onkar Nath and Vidya Wati (Vaid) C.; m. Shalini Bakshi, Oct. 16, 1972; children—Amitabh, Anuj; B.S. in Mech. Engr., Jammu and Kashmir U., India, 1967; M.S., U. Calif.-Berkeley, 1970. Machine tool enumerator; Govt. of India, 1968-69; supervising engring. cons. piping stress safety analysis of nuclear power plants E D S Nuclear, Inc., 1970—. Mem. ASME. Hindu. Home: PO Box 1201 El Cerrito CA 94530 Office: 220 Montgomery St San Francisco CA 94104

CHICK, ROBERT ARON, insurance company executive; b. Chgo., Mar. 4, 1939; s. Morris and Bessie (Stern) C.; m. Laura Newman, Dec. 10, 1978; children—Andrew, Elizabeth, Kathy, Carrie. B.S. in Pub. Adminstrn., U. So. Calif., 1960; B.A., Brasenose Coll., Oxford U., 1965, M.A., 1972. Sec. to Gov. Calif., 1962-65; v.p., corp. sec. Pierce Nat. Life Ins. Co., Los Angeles, 1967-77; chief exec. officer Lawyers Mut. Ins. Co., Los Angeles, 1978—. Mem. Los Angeles City Bd. Pub. Utilities and Transp., 1977; pres. Los Angeles Bd. Transp. Commrs., 1979—; sec.-treas. Brasenose Coll. Charitable Found. Office: 10701 Riverside Dr North Hollywood CA 91602

CHIDSEY, CHARLES WELLINGTON, JR., newspaper exec.; b. Springfield, Mass., June 12, 1923; s. Charles Wellington and Ruby Isabell (Sleith) C.; B.S., Northwestern U., 1947; postgrad in Bus., U. Calif. at Los Angeles, 1971-73, Columbia U., 1973; m. Mary Jacqueline Randell, June 26, 1948; children—Charles Wellington III, Carol Anne Tucker. Account exec. advt. dept. Chgo. Tribune, 1948-64; account exec. Cresmer, Woodward, O'Mara & Ormsbee, Inc., Chgo., 1965-67; Midwestern sales mgr. Los Angeles Times, 1968-70, asst. dir. mktg. research, 1971-73, dir. mktg. research, 1974—; dir. IAM Corp., Venice, Calif., Sky Harbor Press, Los Angeles; guest lectr. mktg. U. Calif. at Los Angeles, 1972-77, Calif. State U., Los Angeles, 1973-77. Republican precinct capt., Winnetka, Ill, 1954-71. Served with AUS, 1943-46; capt. USAR, 1947-55. Mem. Am. Mktg. Assn., Newspaper Research Council, So. Calif. Research Council, Internat. Newspaper Advt. and Mktg. Execs., Travel and Tourism Research Assn. (dir. 1972-76), Los Angeles C. of C., Western Research Conf. Bd., Nat. Assn. Bus. Economists, Am. Assn. for Public Opinion Research, Assn. for Consumer Research, Republican. Episcoplaian (vestryman 1951-60, jr. warden 1960-63, sr. warden, 1963-66, treas. Chgo. diocese, 1960-63, mem. diocesian council 1954-63). Club: Palos Verdes Yacht. Home: 2200 Paseo del Mar Palos Verdes Estates CA 90274 Office: Los Angeles Times Times Mirror Sq Los Angeles CA 90053

CHIEFFALO, MARIO VICTOR, pub. co. sales exec.; b. Italy, Aug. 24, 1934; s. Rosario and Teresa C.; came to U.S. from Uruguay, 1948, naturalized, 1954, B.S., La. State U., 1961; B. Fgn. Trade, Am. Inst. Fgn. Trade, 1962; m. Mary Ruth Rector, June 3, 1958; 1 dau., Belinda. Export sales mgr. Cotton Producers Assn., Atlanta, 1963-66; mem. advt. sales staff This Week mag., N.Y.C., 1966-69, Am. Home mag., N.Y.C., 1969-71; mem. advt. sales staff Reader's Digest, N.Y.C., 1971-74, advt. mgr. Iberian edit., Spain, 1974; West Coast advt. sales mgr. So. Living mag., San Francisco, 1974—. Served to petty officer USN, 1955-58. Mem. San Francisco Mag. Reps. Club. Club: Moraga Country. Office: 625 Market St San Francisco CA 94105

CHIEN, JOHN CHUNG-JEN, aerospace engineer; b. Taipei, Taiwan, July 11, 1942; came to U.S., 1966, naturalized, 1973; s. Chien Shi Chi and Yu Fong; B.S. with honors in Mech. Engring., Nat. Cheng Kung U., 1964; M.S., U. Pa., 1969; Ph.D., Va. Inst. Tech., 1973; m. Kang Fang, Dec., 1969; children—David, Jennifer. Research engr. Sverdrup/ARO, Inc., Arnold Engring. Devel. Center, Tullahoma, Tenn., Arnold Air Force Sta., 1973-79; mem. tech. staff Aerospace Corp., El Segundo, Calif., 1979-80; staff scientist Sci. Applications, Inc., Canoga Park, Calif., 1981-82; mem. tech. staff Rockwell Internat./NAAO, El Segundo, 1982—. Mem. ASME, AIAA (reviewer). Reviewer, Jour. Fluid Engring.; contbr. in field of computational fluid dynamics. Home: 9341 Larkspur Dr Westminster CA 92683 Office: Rockwell Internat/NAAO 201 N Douglas St PO Box 92098 Los Angeles CA 90009

CHIEN, PERCY HSIN-IH, civil engineering educator, consultant; b. Taichi, Taiwan, June 7, 1940; came to U.S., 1965, naturalized, 1976; s. Chang-Ping and Zu (Wang) C.; m. Linda Ling-Ling Chung, Sept. 9, 1967; children—Andy Jau-Ann, Angela Jan-Chyi. B.S., Nat. Taiwan U., 1962; M.S., U. Houston, 1967; Ph.D., Clemson U., 1972. With Deward Martin & Assocs., Williamsburg, Va., 1972-73, Teledyne Brown, Huntsville, Ala., 1973; mem. faculty Drexel U., Phila., 1973-76; assoc. prof. civil engring. Seattle U., 1976—. Served to 2d lt. Chinese Army, 1961-63. Research asst. U. Houston, 1965-67, Clemson U., 1967-72. Mem. Am. Water Works Assn., Am. Water Resources Assn., Water Pollution Control Fedn., Am. Geophys. Union, Sigma Xi, Tau Beta Pi. Office: Civil Engring Dept Seattle U Seattle WA 98122

CHIGOS, DAVID, university president; b. Scranton, Pa., Mar. 29, 1933; s. Andrew D. and Emma (Kossmann) C.; B.S. in Chemistry, W.Va. Wesleyan Coll., 1954, LL.D. (hon.), 1980; M.A. in Counseling and Guidance, U.S. Internat. U., 1968; Ph.D., U.S. Internat. U., 1972; m. Ruth Elizabeth Chamberlain, May 22, 1954; children—Catherine Mary Chigos Bradley, Carla Jane Chigos Sotelo, Lisa Anne, Laura Elizabeth. Commd. ensign USN, 1957, advanced through grades to capt. Res., 1983; indsl. relations Convair Aerospace div. Gen. Dynamics Corp., San Diego, 1967-70; faculty U. Calif. Extension, San Diego, 1967-81, San Diego State U. Extension, 1968-71, San Diego Evening Coll., 1967-71; pres. Nat. U., San Diego, 1971—; cons. in field; dir. COMBO. Bd. dirs. San Diego Symphony, NCCJ. Mem. Nat. Mgmt. Assn. Gold Knight award 1979), Convair Nat. Mgmt. Assn. (hon. life), San Diego Safety Council (hon.), AAAS, Am. Assn. Pres. Ind. Colls. and Univs., Nat. Ind. Colls. and Univs., Personal Mgmt. Assn., Am. Soc. Tng. and Devel., Naval Res. Assn. (life), Navy League U.S. (life, Scroll of Honor 1979, nat. dir. 1980—, pres. San Diego council 1981-82), Res. Officers Assn. (life). Clubs: San Diego Yacht, Kona Kai, Cuyamaca, University (San Diego); Army-Navy (Washington); Rotary Internat. (hon.). Office: 4141 Camino del Rio San Diego CA 92108

CHIHOREK, JOHN PAUL, electronics company executive; b. Wilkes-Barre, Pa., June 22, 1943; s. Stanley Joseph and Caroline Mary Chihorek; B.S.E.E., Pa. State U., 1965: postgrad. Calif. State U., San Diego, 1970-71; M.B.A., Calif. State U., Sacramento, 1972; m. Christina Maria Marroquin, Dec. 28, 1968; children—Jonathan, David, Crista. Program officer Hdqrs. Air Force Logistics Command, Dayton, Ohio, 1972-75; sr. engr. Hdqrs. Air Force Space Div., Los Angeles, 1975-78; mgr. software systems dept. Logicon Inc., San Pedro, Calif., 1978-82; mgr. software product assurance Ford Aerospace & Communication Corp., Newport Beach, Calif., 1982—; owner investment adv. firm. Mem. Congl. Adv. Bd., 1980; active PTA. Served with USN, 1965-70; Vietnam. Decorated Bronze Star. Mem. IEEE, Air Force Assn. Roman Catholic. Clubs: Lions, Odd Fellows. Office: Ford Rd Newport Beach CA 92663

CHILD, ARTHUR JAMES EDWARD, food company executive; b. Guildford, Eng., May 19, 1910; s. William Arthur and Helena (Wilson) C.; B.Commerce, Queen's U., 1931; grad. Harvard Advanced Mgmt. Program, 1956; M.A., U. Toronto, 1960; LL.D., Queen's U., 1983; m. Mary Gordon, Dec. 10, 1955. Chief auditor Can. Packers Ltd., 1938-52, v.p., 1952-60; pres. Jamar, Inc., Intercontinental Packers Ltd., 1960-66, Ajex Investments, Ltd.; pres., chief exec. officer Burns Foods Ltd., Calgary, Alta., Can., 1966—; chmn., dir. Burns Meats Ltd., A.R. Clarke & Co. Ltd., Palm Dairies Ltd., Scott Nat. Co., Ltd., Canbra Foods Ltd., Food Services Ltd., Stafford Foods Ltd.; dir. Nova, Ronalds-Federated Ltd., Can. Life Assurance Co., LaVerendrye Mgmt. Corp. Ltd., Detroit Marine Terminals Inc., Canoe Cove Mfg. Ltd., Grove Valve and Regulator Inc., Vulcan Assets Ltd., Newsco Investments Ltd., Energy Equipment Systems Inc., Hydroblaster Inc., Imperial Trust Co., WAGI Internat. Corp.; asso. prof. U. Sask., 1964-65. Chmn. Can. West Found. Fellow Chartered Inst. Secs.; mem. Meat Packers Council Can. (past pres.), Inst. Internal Auditors (past pres.), Am. Mgmt. Assn., Inst. for Strategic Studies. Author: Economics and Politics in United States Banking, 1965; (with B. Cadmus) Internal Control, 1953. Home: 1320 Baldwin St SW Calgary AB T2V 2B8 Canada Office: PO Box 2520 Calgary AB T2P 2M7 Canada

CHILD, DAVID LEIGHTON, obstetrician, gynecologist, clin. adminstr.; b. Concord, N.H., May 26, 1936; s. Roswell Towle and Dorothy Emma (Knapp) C.; B.A., Dartmouth Coll., 1958; M.D., U. Md., 1962; m. Eleanor Roberta Cass, June 28, 1958; children—Marilyn Lois, Suzanne Eleanor, Paul Leighton, Rebecca Joy. Rotating intern USPHS, Staten Island, N.Y., 1962-63, chief gen. med. officer USPHS Outpatient Clinic, Hawaii, 1963-65, resident in obstetrics gynecology, USPHS Hosp., New Orleans, 1965-68; postgrad. tng. gynecology oncology USPHS Hosp., Seattle, 1968-71; chief obstetrics-gynecology div. Indian health Phoenix (Ariz.) Med. Center, 197; instr. obstetrics gynecology Tulane Med. Sch., 1966-68, U. Wash., 1969-71. Diplomate Am. Bd. Obstetrics and Gynecology. Fellow Am. Coll. Obstetrics and Gynecology. Republican. Baptst. Home: 9238 N Arroya Vista Dr E Phoenix AZ 85028

CHILDRESS, PAUL DALLAS, engineer, gas company executive; b. Gallup, N.Mex., Aug. 29, 1938; s. Harry Paul and Neva Lorena (Dennis) C.; student Ft. Lewis Coll., 1964-66; B.S. in Civil Engring., Colo. State U., 1968; m. Mona Louise Jones, Mar. 30, 1959; children—Carrie Leigh, Paul Mitchell. Project engr. Shell Oil Co., Anacortes, Wash., 1968-73; field constrn. mgr. Snelson's, Sedro Wooley, Wash., 1973-74; sr. project engr. Hallanger Engrs., Bellingham, Wash., 1974-82, successively project mgr., mgr. projects and design, 1975-76, chief engr. Bellingham Office, 1976-82, mgr. N.W. ops., 1980-82; dir. engring. Colo. Interstate Gas, Colorado Springs, 1982—; tchr. math. techniques and instrumentation design Shell Oil Co. Registered profl. engr., Wash., Colo., Alaska. Mem. Pacific Energy Assn. (bd. dirs. Puget Sound br.), ASCE, N.W. Wash. Engrs. Club (pres. 1977-78), Whatcom County C. of C. (pres. 1982, bd. dirs. 1981—), Chi Epsilon (pres. chpt. 1968-69). Clubs: Rotary, Lions. Office: 2 N Nevada St Colorado Springs CO 80944

CHILDRESS, PHYLLIS ANN, municipal construction manager; b. Fort Wayne, Ind., Feb. 20, 1937, d. Paschal J. and Pietrina M. (Ceccanese) Pallone; B.S. in Commerce, Internat. Coll., 1955; postgrad. Pima Community Coll., 1978-80; m. Kelly W. Childress, Aug. 24, 1973; children—Patricia, William, Jeffrey. Sec. to v.p. trust dept. Lincoln Nat. Bank, Ft. Wayne, Ind., 1955-57; sec. to pres. adminstrn. dept. Internat. Coll., Ft. Wayne, 1957-60; dir., sec. Lightning Homes, Inc., Homebuilders and Developers, Ft. Wayne, 1960-63; sec. to v.p., fin. dept., office mgr. fleet maintenance dept. N.Am. Van Lines, Inc., Ft. Wayne, 1963-71; asst. mktg. dir. ITT Electro-Optical Products, Ft. Wayne, 1972-76; asst. v.p. Empire West Builders, Inc., Tucson, 1977-80; staff constrn. mgmt. Akins Co., Tucson, 1981-82; construction mgr. Archtl. Div., City of Tucson, 1982—. Recipient Appreciation Cert. Nat. Assn. Women Constrn., 1978; named Sec. of yr. Tawasi chpt. Nat. Secs. Assn., 1967, recipient plaque for outstanding service, 1977. Mem. Bus. and Profl. Women, Nat. Assn. Women Constrn. (chpt. pres.). Democrat. Baptist. Club: Internat. Toastmistresses. Contbr. articles to various publs. Home: 2833 N Laurel Ave Tucson AZ 85712 Office: City of Tucson Archtl Div PO Box 27210 Tucson AZ 85726

CHILDRESS, WILLIAM JAMES, educational administrator, clergyman; b. Ft. Worth, Sept. 15, 1928; s. Roy E. and Effie J. (Lott) C.; m. Mildred L. Barnes, Aug. 30, 1947; children—Carolyn Roberts, William James, J. Mark. B.A., Hardin Simmons U., 1949; M.A., U. Colo., 1968; postgrad. Southwestern Bapt. Theol. Sem., 1952-61, N.Mex. State U.-Las Cruces, 1963-65. Ordained to ministry So. Baptist Ch., 1951; elem. sch. tchr. Levelland (Tex.) Ind. Schs., 1949-53; pastor Morningside Bapt. Ch., Levelland, 1951-53; elem. tchr. Plainview (Tex.) Ind. Schs., 1954-56; high sch. tchr., coach, elem. prin. Presidio (Tex.) Pub. Schs., 1956-58; pastor First Bapt. Ch., Presidio, 1956-58; pastor Kendall Bapt. Chapel, Waco, Tex., 1958-61; pastor Pleasant View Bapt. Ch., Dallas, 1961-62; elem. tchr. Farmington (N.Mex.) Mcpl. Schs., 1962-68; elem. prin., 1968-73; dir. instrn. Farmington Schs., 1973-78, dir. elem. edn., 1978—; interim pastor Trinity Bapt. Ch., Farmington, 1962-64, Pleasant View (Colo.) Bapt. Ch., 1966-67, First Bapt. Ch., Dove Creek, Colo., 1967-69. Mem. Assn. Supervision and Curriculum Devel., N.Mex. Assn. Supervision and Curriculum Devel., N.Mex. Assn. Sch. Adminstrs. Democrat. Baptist. Home: 616 Venada Circle Farmington NM 87401 Office: Box 660 Farmington NM 87499

CHILDS, JOHN DAVID, computer hardware and services co. exec.; b. Washington, Apr. 26, 1939; s. Edwin Carlton and Catherine Dorothea (Angerman) C.; student Principia Coll., 1957-58, 59-60; B.A., Am. U., 1963; m. Margaret Rae Olsen, Mar. 4, 1966; 1 son, John-David. Jr. adminstr. Page Communications, Washington, 1962-65; account rep. Friden Inc., Washington, 1965-67; Western sales dir. Data Inc., Arlington, Va., 1967-70; v.p. mktg. Rayda, Inc., Los Angeles, 1970-73, pres., 1973-76, chmn. bd., 1976—; sr. asso. World Trade Assos., Inc., 1976—. Pres. Coll. Youth for Nixon-Lodge, 1959-60, dir. state fedn.; mem. OHSHA policy formulation com. Dept. Labor, 1967. Served with USAFR, 1960-66. Mem. Assn. Data Center Owners and Mgrs. (chmn. privacy com. 1975, sec. 1972-74, v.p. 1974). Democrat. Christian Scientist. Office: 16229 Victory Blvd 120 Van Nuys CA 91406

CHILDS, MARJORIE M., lawyer; b. N.Y.C., July 13, 1918; d. Charles William and Eva May (Tarrant) C.; student Hunter Coll., 1942-46; B.A., U. Calif., Berkeley, 1948; postgrad. Hastings Coll. Law, 1948-49; J.D.,

U. San Francisco, 1956; LL.D., Iowa Wesleyan Coll., 1973. Econ. research analyst Fgn. Service, U.S. Dept. State, Paris, 1949-50, Frankfurt, Germany, 1950-51; legal asst. Dept. Navy, San Francisco, 1956-60; admitted to Calif., bar, 1957, U.S. Supreme Ct. bar, 1969; practiced in San Francisco, 1962-64, 79—; asst. county counsel Humboldt County (Calif.), Eureka, 1960-62; mem. firm Berry, Childs & Berry, San Francisco, 1962-64; commr., referee, judge Juvenile Ct. San Francisco, 1964-79. Bd. dirs. United Cerebral Palsy Assn. San Francisco, United Cerebral Palsy Assn. Calif.; bd. govs. U. San Francisco, 1978-81. Recipient James Harlan award Iowa Wesleyan Coll., 1969. Fellow Am. Bar Found.; mem. Calif. State Bar (com. juvenile justice 1969-76, chmn. 1970-72, adviser 1972-76), Internat. (council 1975-76, del. 1978, 82), ABA (del. 1975-77, sec. family law sect. 1980-82), Fed. Bar Assn. (pres. 1976-77), Nat. Assn. Women Lawyers (pres. 1974-75), Queen's Bench (pres. 1967-68), AAUW (pres. br. 1970-72), Bar Assn. San Francisco. Club: Metropolitan. Contbr. articles to profl. jours. Home: 64 Turquoise Way San Francisco CA 94131 also PO Box 31430 San Francisco CA 94131 Office: 301 Junipero Serra Blvd Suite 260 San Francisco CA 94127

CHILLINSKY, SANDRA JEAN, trucking co. exec.; b. Houston, Aug. 6, 1935; d. Laurence Vernon and Winnie Mae (Pace) Butler; student U. Houston, 1953-54, S. Tex. Law Sch., 1955; m. John Chillinsky, Oct. 12, 1974; children by previous marriage—Claud V. Sherrill, Catherine L. Sherrill. With San Jacinto Fin. Corp., Houston, 1953-54, Guns, Inc., Houston, 1955, Magcobar, Southwestern Indsl. Electronics, Houston, 1956-57; acct. Durban G. Ford, C.P.A., Barstow, Calif., 1960, Dept. Def., Barstow, 1960-61; sec. U.S. Marine Corps Exchange Contracts Div., San Diego, 1961-65; computer analyst, stenographer Rohr Corp., Chula Vista, Calif., 1966-68; office mgr. Mesa Motors, DBA Honda, Lemon Grove, Calif., 1968-72; office mgr. Sky Trucking Co., San Diego 1972—, sec.-treas., 1976—. Trustee, Mark IV Equipment Trust, Alpine Trust, 1978-81. Recipient Cert. of Commendation, Rohr Corp., 1968, 69; Cert. of Recognition, Nat. Republican Congressional Com., 1980. Mem. Cal-West Tariff Bur., Hwy. Carriers Assn., Nat. Right to Work Com., VFW Aux. (trustee, publicity chmn. 1982—). Republican. Lutheran. Office: 187 Mace St Chula Vista CA 92011

CHIMENTO, JAMES JOHN, orthopedic surgeon; b. Pueblo, Colo., May 13, 1943; s. James and Virginia (Minuto) C.; B.A., So. Colo. State Coll., 1965; M.D., U. Colo., 1969; m. Carol Ann Wishart, Sept. 27, 1969. Intern, Walter Reed Army Med. Center, Washington, 1969-70, orthopedic resident, 1971-74; resident in gen. surgery Ft. Bragg (N.C.) Army Hosp., 1970-71; orthopedic dept. Ft. Carson Army Hosp., Colorado Springs, Colo., 1974-76; practice medicine specializing in orthopedic surgery, Pueblo, Colo., 1976—; staff St. Mary Corwin Hosp., Pueblo, Parkview Episcopal Hosp.; clin. instr. dept. family medicine U. Colo. Served to maj. U.S. Army, 1969-76. Fellow Am. Acad. Orthopedic Surgery; mem. AMA, Colo. Med. Soc., Pueblo County Med. Soc. (sec. 1978-80), Western Orthopedic Assn., Rocky Mountain Orthopedic Assn. Office: 2002 Lake Ave Pueblo CO 81004

CHIN, JENNIFER YOUNG, city ofcl.; b. Honolulu, June 22, 1946; d. Michael W.T. and Sylvia (Ching) Young; B.A., San Francisco State Coll,, 1969; M.P.H., U. Calif., Berkeley, 1971; m. Benny Chin, Nov. 16, 1975; children—Kenneth Michael, Lauren Marie, Catherine Rose. Edn. asst. Am. Cancer Soc., San Francisco, 1969-70; intern Lutheran Med. Center, Bklyn., 1971; community health educator Md. Dept. Health and Mental Hygiene, Balt., 1971-74; community health educator Northeast Med. Services, San Francisco, 1975; public health educator child health and disability prevention San Francisco Public Health Dept., 1975—. USPHS grantee, 1970-71. Mem. Soc. No. Calif. Public Health Edn. (treas. 1976, 77), Am. Public Health Assn. Home: 1057 Holly St Alameda CA 94501 Office: CHDP 101 Grove St Room 402 San Francisco CA 94102

CHIN, JIN H., aerospace engineer; b. Kwantung, China, Oct. 15, 1928; s. Bing S. and Ru J. (Liau) C.; m. Jane E. Heng, Sept. 11, 1960; children—Goodwin R., Kingsley N. B.S. in Chemistry, Stanford U., 1950; M.S. in Chem. Engring., U. Mich., 1951, Ph.D. (Eastman Kodak fellow 1951; Rockham fellow 1952-53), 1955. Research assoc. U. Mich., Ann Arbor, 1955-57; heat transfer specialist flight propulsion div. Gen. Electric Co., Evandale, Ohio, 1957-60; with Lockheed Missile & Space Co. Inc., Sunnyvale, Calif., 1960—, sr. staff engr., 1980—; lectr. in field. Mem. AIAA, AAAS. Baptist. Contbr. articles to profl. jours. Home: 727 Christine Dr Palo Alto CA 94303 Office: Lockheed Missile & Space Co Inc Dept 81-11 Sunnyvale CA 94086

CHIN, PEARL GEE, actuarial assistant, programmer; b. Portland, Oreg., June 23, 1948; d. Bill and Nancy Jade (Lum) Chin. B.S. in Math., Oreg. State U., 1970; M.S. in Biostats., UCLA, 1974. Research assoc. dept. epidemiology U. Wash., Seattle, 1975-80, dept. genetics U. B.C., Vancouver, 1980-81; actuarial asst. Howard Johnson & Co., Seattle, 1981—. Mem. Am. Statis. Assn., Am. Soc. Pension Actuaries, Phi Kappa Phi. Home: 6568 4th Ave NE Seattle WA 98115 Office: Howard Johnson & Co 1111 3d Ave Bldg Suite 1700 Seattle WA 98101

CHIN, SUE S.(SUCHIN), painter, photographer, conceptual designer, occult diviner; b. San Francisco; d. William W. and Soo-Up (Swebe) C.; grad. Calif. Coll. Arts, Los Angeles, Mpls. Art Inst., Schaeffer Design Center; student Yasuo Ku-niyo-shi, Rico LeBrun, Cheiro. Photojournalist, All Together Now art show KPIX-TV, 1973, East West News, Third World Newscasting, 1975-78, KNBC Sunday Show, Los Angeles, 1975-78; designer, painter of textiles, wallcoverings, hangings; internat. photographer, conceptual artist, portrait painter, occult diviner; one-woman show: Lucien Labaudt Gallery, San Francisco, 1975; group shows include: Los Angeles County Mus. Art, 1975-77, Calif. Mus. Sci. and Industry, Los Angeles, 1975-78, Capricorn-Asunder, San Francisco, 1972, Peace Plaza, Japan Center, Kaiser Center, Newspace Galleries, New Coll., 1983; also exhibited in Hong Kong and Australia, 1979-81; represented in permanent collections: Los Angeles County Fedn. Labor, Calif. Mus. Sci. and Industry, also corp. and pvt. collections. Del. state conv. Nat. Women's Polit. Caucus, 1977-83, affirmative action chmn. San Francisco chpt., 1978-83. Recipient Honorarium, AFL-CIO Labor Studies Center, Washington, 1976; Bicentennial award Los Angeles County Mus. Art, 1975-76, 77, 78; 1st award for conceptual painting and photography of Far East, Asian Women Artists, 1978-79. Mem. Asian Women Artists (founding v.p. 1978-83), Calif. Chinese Artists (sec.-treas. 1978-81), Japanese Am. Art Council (co-chmn. 1978-82, dir.), San Francisco Women Artists, Artists in Print, Pacific Asian Am. Women's Bay Area Coalition, San Francisco Graphics Guild, Chinatown Council Performing and Visual Arts, Chinese Cultural Ctr. Galleries. Home: PO Box 1415 San Francisco CA 94101

CHINAI, KIRIT BABUBHAI, retail import corp. exec.; b. Bombay, India, July 20, 1937; s. Babubhai Maneklal and Savita (Shah) C.; B.A. in Econs., Jai-Hind Coll., Bombay, 19; m. Rupa K., May 31, 1963; children—Gautam, Monika. Owner, pres. Internat. Imports Inc., Santa Rosa, Calif., 1974—, Santa Maria, Calif., 1975—, Merced, Calif., 1975—, Salinas, Calif., 1976—, Chico, Calif., 1978—, Citrus Heights, Calif., 1976—, Stockton, Calif., 1977—, Petaluma, Calif., 1980—, Internat. Gifts Inc., San Rafael, Calif., 1975—; owner, pres. Chinai Corp. Co-chmn. bus. Sister City of San Francisco and Delhi, 1981. Mem. Assn. Ams. of Indian Origin (chmn. com. culture and art 1981). Democrat. Hindu. Address: 281 Blackfield Dr Tiburon CA 97920

CHINCHINIAN, HARRY, pathologist; b. Troy, N.Y., Mar. 7, 1926; s. John and Armen (Der Arakelian) C.; B.A., U. Colo., 1952; M.S., Marquette U., 1956, M.D., 1959; m. Mary Corcoran, Aug. 22, 1952; children—Armen, Marjorie, Matthew. Intern, St. Elizabeth Hosp., Youngstown, Ohio, 1959-60; resident in pathology Deaconess Hosp., Milw., St. Mary's Hosp., Milw., 1960-64; co-dir. Pathologists Regional Lab., Lewiston, Idaho, 1964, Lewiston-Clarkston Blood Bank, 1964; asso. prof. pathology Wash. State U., Pullman, 1972—; chief of staff Tristate Hosp., Clarkston, Wash., 1968—, St. Joseph's Hosp., Lewiston, 1979-80; cons. Pullman (Wash.) Hosp. Pres., Lewiston Roundup Rodeo, 1976, 77. Served with inf. AUS, 1944-46. Diplomate Am. Bd. Pathology. Fellow Am. Soc. Clin. Pathologists, Coll. Am. Pathologists; mem. Idaho Soc. Pathologists (pres. 1976, 77), AMA, Pacific N.W. Soc. Blood Banks (pres.), Wash. Med. Soc. Contbr. articles to med. jours. Home: Star Route L Clarkston WA 99403 Office: Box 956 Lewiston ID 83501

CHING, DANIEL GERALD, structural engr.; b. Honolulu, Dec. 17, 1948; s. Daniel Kui Fah and Ethel (Lo) C.; B.S.C.E., U. Denver, 1973; M.S., Cornell U., 1974; m. Mei-Yung Chen, Mar. 14, 1976. Estimator, Swinerton & Walberg Co., Honolulu, 1974-75; project engr. E. E. Black Ltd., Honolulu, 1976; structural engr. Alfred A. Yee & Assocs., Honolulu, 1976-80; project mgr. Blackfield, Hawaii, Honolulu, 1980-82; pres. D.G. Ching & Assocs., Honolulu, 1982—. Served with AUS, 1968-71. Mem. ASCE, Nat. Soc. Profl. Engrs. Episcopalian. Home: 1350 Ala Moana Blvd Apt 503 Honolulu HI 96814 Office: 1259 S Beretania St Suite 24 Honolulu HI 96814

CHING, FRED YET-FAN, aerospace engineer; b. China, Mar. 27, 1957; s. Lloyd Lap-Chi and Lena Yuen-Wah (Moy) C.; B.S. with honors in Mech. and Aerospace Engring., Ill. Inst. Tech., 1979; M.S. in Aerospace Engring., Ga. Inst. Tech., 1980. Asst. engr. Miner Enterprises, Chgo., 1977-78; analytical engr. Continental Can Co., Chgo., 1979; engr. scientist McDonnell Douglas Corp., Long Beach, Calif., 1981—. Mem. ASME, AIAA, Pi Tau Sigma. Contbr. articles to profl. jours. Home: 11901 E 176th St Apt 263 Artesia CA 90701 Office: 3855 Lakewood Blvd Long Beach CA 90846

CHING, HUNG WO, airline exec.; b. Honolulu, May 8, 1912; m. Elizabeth Lau, Jan. 11, 1936; children—Han H., Han P. B.S., Utah State U., 1935; Ph.D., Cornell U., 1945; postgrad. Harvard U., 1955; LL.D. (hon.), Utah State U. Pres., Aloha Airlines, Inc., Honolulu, 1958-65, chmn. bd., 1965—; dir. Bishop Ins. of Hawaii, Inc., Hawaiian Western Steel Ltd. Trustee Kamehameha Schs., 1968-82; hon. trustee Com. Econ. Devel.; mem. judicial council Sup. Ct. of Hawaii; mem. adv. bd. Utah State U. Mem. Phi Kappa Phi. Democrat. Congregationalist. Club: Waialae Country. Lodge: Masons. Office: Aloha Airlines Inc Honolulu Internat Airport PO Box 30028 Honolulu HI 96820

CHING, LAWRENCE LIN TAI, retail executive; b. Hanalei, Hawaii, July 23, 1920; s. Young and Ah Har (Dang) C.; student St. Louis Coll., 1936-40; m. Jennie Kim Pang, Dec. 27, 1947; children—Steven L., Michael G. Clk., USAAF, Honolulu, 1942-44; dir. Kauai Realty, CKKS Corp.; pres., dir. Can Corp.; 1946—; owner, pres., mgr. Ching Young Store; dir. Na-Pali Realty, Kauai Times; mem. adv. bd. First Inter State Bank Hawaii. Mem. Kauai Charter Commn., 1964-65. Served with AUS, 1944-46. Democrat. Buddhist. Address: PO Box 426 Hanalei HI 96714

CHING, RICHARD WAH, social worker; b. San Francisco, Feb. 19, 1941; s. Chun Wah and Frances (Low) C.; B.A. in Social Work, San Francisco State U., 1968; M.S.W. (NIMH grantee 1970), U. Hawaii, 1972; married; 2 children. Student counselor Hawaii Corrections Div., 1971-72; acting contracts coordinator, concentrated employment program Honolulu Community Action Program, 1972; med. social worker crippled children's br. Hawaii Dept. Health, Honolulu, 1972-76; sch. social worker Hawaii Dept. Edn., 1976—; Served with USNR, 1964-66; Vietnam. Grantee Rehab. Counseling, 1968. Mem. Nat. Assn. Social Workers (sch. social work liaison for Hawaii chpt.), Acad. Cert. Social Workers, Register Clin. Social Workers, Hawaii Govt. Employees Assn., U. Hawaii Sch. Social Work Alumni Assn. Home: 1801 Keeaumoku St Apt 101 Honolulu HI 96822

CHINN, EUGENE LEE, government official; b. San Francisco, Dec. 7, 1941; s. Kay Yoke and Myrtle Chin; student Monterey Peninsula Coll., 1959-60; A.A., Cabrillo Coll., 1967; B.A., San Francisco State U., 1969, M.B.A., 1970; m. Sylvia Fong Jeong, Nov. 2, 1968; children—Craig Eugene, Lisa Kay. Supervisory mgmt. auditor GAO, San Francisco, 1970-75; pres. Dimensions Unique, Inc., Pacifica, Calif., 1976-77; chief reimbursement and recovery br. health care financing adminstrn. HHS, San Francisco, 1975—. Vice pres. Park Pacifica II Homeowners Assn., 1972, pres., 1973. Served with USAF, 1962-66. Recipient High Quality Performance awards HHS, 1976, 78. Democrat. Club: Commonwealth of Calif. Home: 2751 Summit Dr Burlingame CA 94010 Office: U S Dept HHS 100 Van Ness Ave San Francisco CA 94102

CHINN, RONALD ERNEST, retired political science educator; b. Des Moines, June 11, 1911; s. Thomas and Lillie Cornelia (Linderholm) C.; m. Eleanor Jeannette Jaeger, Aug. 24, 1947; children—Marilyn, Scott. A.B., Stanford U., 1933; M.A., Stanford U., 1937; Ph.D., U. Calif.-Berkeley, 1958. Asst. prof. polit. sci., dept. head Whitworth Coll., Spokane, Wash., 1960-66; prof., head dept. polit. sci. U. Alaska, Fairbanks, 1966-76, part-time faculty, 1976—. Mem. Dist. 19 Democratic Com., Common Cause, Friends Com. on Nat. Legislation. Home: SR Box 30624 Fairbanks AK 99701

CHINN, THOMAS WAYNE, typographic co. exec.; b. Marshfield, Oreg., July 28, 1909; s. Wing Chin and Shee Lee; student U. Calif., 19—; m. Daisy Lorraine Wong, June 8, 1930; 1 son, Walter Wayne Chinn. Propr., Chinn Linotype Co., San Francisco, 1937-42; owner Calif. Typesetting Co., 1949-56; typographer, 1956-71; pres. Gollan Typography, Inc., San Francisco, 1971-80. Mem. San Francisco Mayor's Citizens Com., 1958—; mem. San Francisco Twin Bicentennial History Com., 1974-76; mem. Nat. Am. Revolution Bicentennial Advisory Com. on Racial, Ethnic and Native Am. Participation, 1974-76; governing mem. San Francisco YMCA; founder Chinese Hist. Soc. Am., San Francisco, 1963, first pres. 1963-66, pres., 1975. Recipient awards of merit Conf. Calif. Socs., 1976, 81, Am. Assn. State and Local History, 1976. Mem. Calif. Hist. Soc. (award of merit 1970, trustee 1981), E Clampus Vitus, The Westerners. Clubs: Masons (32 deg.) (past master lodge), Shriners. Editor: A History of the Chinese in California-A Syllabus, 1969; editor, co-pub. 1st newspaper in English for Chinese-Ams., 1935-37; contbr. articles to hist. jours.

CHIRIBOGA, DAVID ANTHONY, psychologist, researcher; b. Boston, Mar. 10, 1941; s. Vicente Eliecer and June Lillian (Rowson) C.; m. Kikue Suzuki, Aug. 16, 1980; B.A., Boston U., 1964; Ph.D., U. Chgo., 1972. Research specialist dept. psychiatry U. Calif.-San Francisco, 1972-73, asst. prof. in residence, 1974-79, project dir. Divorce: Psychosocial Study Adaptation, 1976-78, assoc. prof. psychology and prin. investigator Mental Illness and Divorce: A Life Span Study, 1979—. Mem. Am. Psychol. Assn., Gerontol. Soc. Am., Western Psychol. Assn., Western Gerontol. Soc., Nat. Hispanic Council on Aging. Author: (with M. Fiske and M. Thurnher) Four Stages of Life: A Comparative Study of Women and Men Facing Transitions, 1975; contbr. articles to profl. jours. Home: 2025 Hayes St San Francisco CA 94117 Office: Human Devel & Aging Program U Calif San Francisco CA 94143

CHIRURG, JAMES THOMAS, JR., investment co. exec.; b. Wellesley, Mass., May 21, 1944; s. James Thomas and Virginia Burtt (Low) C.; A.B., Cornell U., 1964; M.B.A., Harvard U., 1969; B.Litt. (Knox fellow), Oxford (Eng.) U., 1972; postgrad. U. Calif., Berkeley. Asst. mktg. mgr. Gen. Mills Inc., Tokyo, 1968; mem. corp. fin. dept. First Boston Corp., N.Y.C., 1969-70; gen. mgr. Protasis Trust, Ltd., London, 1971-72, lead partner, Berkeley, 1973—; dir. Protasis Holdings (S.A.R.L.), Luxembourg; investment adv. AID investment mission, Tanzania, 1980 fellow Salzburg (Austria) Seminar, 1980; lectr. U. Calif. Bd. dirs. World Affairs Council No. Calif., 1973-75; vice chmn. coastal zone com. Marine Tech. Soc., 1977—; mem. com. on maritime preservation Nat. Trust Historic Preservation, 1979—. Served to lt. (j.g.) USNR, 1964-67. Decorated Bronze Star with combat V. Fellow Inst. Dirs. (U.K.), Royal Asiatic Soc. (London); mem. Acad. Internat. Bus., Overseas Devel. Council, Internat. Assn. for Advancement Appropriate Tech. for Developing Countries, Brit. Inst. Mgmt., Am. Econ. Assn., Royal Econ. Soc., Soc. Internat. Devel., Asia Soc., Pacific Sci. Assn., Navy League U.S., Am. Mensa Ltd., Naval Order U.S., Internat. Wine and Food Soc., Mensa, Soc. Asian Art, Chinese Culture Found., Alpha Delta Phi. Clubs: Commonwealth (San Francisco); Union League (N.Y.C.); Harvard (Boston); United Oxford and Cambridge, Royal Naval (London); Internat. House of Japan (Tokyo). Home: 2001 Broadway San Francisco CA 94115 Office: Protasis Trust Ltd PO Box 4000 Berkeley CA 94704

CHITTUM, ROGER DEAN, energy company executive, lawyer; b. Millersburg, Ohio, Mar. 21, 1939; s. John William and Alma Pearl (Spencer) m. Susan Kovacss Dec. 10, 1978. A.B., Coll. of Wooster, 1962; LL.B., Stanford U., 1966. Bar: D.C. 1967, Calif. 1973, U.S. Supreme Ct. 1971. Assoc., Cleary, Gottlieb, Steen & Hamilton, Washington, 1966-71; asst. to pres. The Oil Shale Corp., N.Y.C. and Los Angeles, 1972-73; v.p. Tosco Corp., Los Angeles, 1973-80, sr. v.p. environ. affairs, 1981—. Mem. ABA, State Bar Calf., D.C. Bar Assn. Office: 10100 Santa Monica Blvd Los Angeles CA 90067

CHIU, JOHN CHIH, surgeon; b. Fukien, China, Aug. 6, 1937; s. Stanley L. and T.C. Chin; student So. Meth. U., 1959; M.D., Baylor U., 1963. Intern in surgery Bklyn. Hosp., 1963-64; resident in neurosurgery Mayo Clinic, Rochester, Minn., 1964-66; resident in neuroradiology Baylor U. Coll. of Medicine, Houston, 1966; resident in neurosurgery SUNY Downstate Med. Center, Bklyn., 1967-70, L.I. (N.Y.) Coll. Hosp., 1967-68, Kings County (N.Y.) Hosp., 1968-70; practice medicine specializing in neurosurgery Conejo Neurol. Med. Group, Inc., Thousand Oaks, Calif., 1970—; mem. staff Simi Valley Doctors' Hosp., chief surgery dept., 1976-77, chief of staff, 1979-80; ind. med. examiner neurosurgery Workman's Compensation Appeals Bd., Calif., 1979; Bd. dirs. Westlake Community Hosp., 1976-77. Diplomate Am. Bd. Neurol. Surgery. Fellow Internat. Coll. Surgeons, Soc. Computerized Tomography and Neuro-Imaging, Am. Coll. Angiology; mem. Congress Neurol. Surgeons, Am. Assn. Neurol. Surgeons, So. Calif. Neurol. Soc., Am. Geriatrics Soc., Ventura County Med. Soc., AMA (Physicians Recognition award 1976), Calif. Med. Assn., N.Y. Acad. Scis., Baylor Med. Alumni Assn. Office: Conejo Neurol Med Group Inc 2220 Lynn Rd Suite 208 Thousand Oaks CA 91360

CHIU, KUNG-YUEN, civil-structural-traffic engr.; b. Kwong-Tung, China, Mar. 5, 1943; s. Chun-Wah and Yue-Bing (Leo) C.; came to U.S., 1962, naturalized, 1973; B.S. in Civil Engring., U. Calif., Berkeley, 1974; m. Judy Wan Mark, Sept. 4, 1974. Engring. aid Calif. Div. Hwys., San Francisco, 1970, engring. student asst., 1972; civil-structural design engr. Arthur G. McKee Engring. Co., San Mateo, Calif., 1974-76; asst. civil-structural design engr. Kaiser Engrs. Inc., Oakland, Calif., 1976-78; asst. civil engr. City and County San Francisco, Calif. Bur. Utilities Engring., 1979—. Mem. Nat., Calif. soc. profl. engrs., ASCE, Inst. Transp. Engrs., Am. Concrete Inst., Am. Water Works Assn., Earthquake Engring. Research Inst. Mormon. Club: G U Kung Fu of Am. Home and Office: PO Box 677 Daly City CA 94015

CHIU, WEN CHENG LIANG, nutritionist, educator; b. Chingtao, China, Feb. 2, 1934; d. Shih-chiu Liang and Shih-shu Cheng; m. John S.Y. Chiu, Jan. 31, 1959; children—Andrew C.T., Michael C.M. B.S. in Agrl. Chemistry, Nat. Taiwan U., 1955; M.S. in Home Econs., U. Ill., 1960; Ph.D. in Edn., U. Wash., 1982. Sr. lab. technician U. Wash. Med. Sch., Seattle, 1960-61; lectr. home econs. dept. Taiwan Normal U., Taipei, 1968; instr. continuing edn. U. Wash., Seattle, 1971-73; prof. food and nutrition Shoreline Community Coll., Seattle, 1973—. Mem. Nutrition Today Soc., Am. Home Econs. Assn. Contbr. articles to profl. and gen. interest publs. Office: 16101 Greenwood Ave N Seattle WA 98133

CHIWATA, KOSHIRO, photog. mfg. and distbg. co. exec.; b. Saga, Japan, Feb. 24, 1924; came to U.S., 1976; s. Seiroku and Kane Gosho; diploma Kanto Comml. Sch., Tokyo, 1942; postgrad. U. Ill., Champaign; m. Kazuko Matsuda, Oct. 7, 1957; 1 son, Koichiro. Dir. fgn. trade Asahi Optical Co. Ltd., Tokyo, 1973-76; mng. dir. Asahi Optical (Internat.) Ltd., Hong Kong, 1976; pres. Pentax Corp., Englewood, Colo., 1976—. Recipient Joseph Ehrenreich Human Relations award Am. Jewish Com. photog. div. Address: Pentax Corp 35 Inverness Dr Englewood CO 80112

CHMIEL, LEONARD KENNETH, artist; b. Chgo., Jan. 9, 1942; s. Leonard Albert and Melane (Sierzega) C.; student Art Center Coll. Design, Los Angeles, 1959-61; m. Johanna Rita Pellegrin, June 14, 1975; children—Mary Jae, Julie Melane, Aleksandra Nicole, Kataryna Vivien. Asst. art dir. Cannon and Sullivan Publs., Los Angeles, 1961-63; tech. artist Hughes Aircraft Co., Fullerton, Calif., 1963-67; freelance illustrator, Los Angeles, 1967-71; one-man shows include: Phoenix Gallery, Denver, 1973, Bishop's Gallery, Scottsdale, Ariz., 1973, Birger Sandzen Meml. Gallery, Lindsborg, Kans., 1977, Stremmel Galleries, Ltd., Reno, 1978, 79, 81, 83, Bishop's Gallery, Allenspark, Colo., 1978, 79; group shows include: Sandra Wilson Galleries, Denver, 1974-79, Arvada (Colo.) Center Mus., 1977, Equus, Denver, 1977, Artists of Am., Denver, 1983; represented in permanent collections: State of Wyo., United Banks, Mountain Bell, Cherry Creek Nat. Bank, Johns Manville Corp. Heritage Collection. Recipient David Humphries Meml. award

Allied Artist of Am. show, 1982. Mem. Soc. Animal Artists Am. Home: 555 N 111th Ave Lafayette CO 80026

CHO, LEE-JAY, demographer, sociologist; b. Kyoto, Japan, July 5, 1936; s. Sam-Soo and Kyung-Doo (Park) C.; B.A., Kookmin Coll., Seoul, Korea, 1959; M.A. in Pub. Adminstrn., George Washington U., 1962; M.A. in Sociology, U. Chgo., 1964, Ph.D. in Sociology, 1965; m. Eun-Ja Cho, Feb. 1973; children—Yun-Kyong, Sang-Mun. Statistician, Govt. Korea, 1958-59; sr. statistician Korean Census Council, 1959-62; research asso., asst. prof. U. Chgo., 1965-66, asso. dir. Community and Family Student Center, 1969-70; research asso. Seoul Nat. U., 1966-67, U. Mich., 1967-69; prof. sociology U. Hawaii, Honolulu, 1973—, dir. East-West Population Inst., East-West Center, 1974-80, pres. pro tem center, 1980-81; mem. com. on population and demography Nat. Acad. Scis.; mem. adv. com. for 1980 census U.S. Bur. Census. Mem. Internat. Union Sci. Study Population, Internat. Statis. Inst., Am. Statis. Assn., Am. Sociol. Assn., Population Assn. Am. Office: 1777 East-West Rd Honolulu HI 96821

CHOATE, JUDY LEE, nurse; b. Los Angeles, Oct. 3, 1951; d. Frank John and Jacqueline Lee (Pope) Morrison; grad. Los Angeles County Sch. Nursing, 1972. Staff nurse Los Angeles County U. So. Calif. Med. Center, 1972, head nurse burn surgery, 1973, head nurse main surgery, 1974-76; supervisory nurse Eskaton Colusa (Calif.) Hosp., 1976-77; supr. Eskaton Oakland (Calif.) Hosp. Center, 1977; supr. operating room, central service, outpatient dept. Monterey Peninsula Hosp., Monterey, Calif., 1977—. Mem. Assn. Operating Room Nurses. Democrat. Roman Catholic. Home: 528 Belden Monterey CA 93940 Office: 576 Hartnell St Monterey CA 93940

CHOATE, MELVIN KEITH, coll. adminstr.; b. Portland, Oreg., Oct. 26, 1923; s. Helen Myrtle (Decious) Wheeler; student Western Wash. U., 1941, U. Ill., 1947; B.A., U. Wash., 1954, M.A., 1968; m. Marjorie Mae Forstein, June 6, 1946; 1 son, David K. Acct., Fansteel Metall. Corp., 1947, City of Seattle, 1948; tchr. Franklin High Sch., Seattle, 1954-59; chmn. dept. bus. Ingraham High Sch., Seattle, 1959-62; instr. in acctg. Seattle Community Coll., 1962-68, chmn. dept. acctg., 1968-70; chmn. div. bus. and commerce North Seattle Community Coll., 1970—; vis. lectr. U. Wash., 1956-68; cons. bus., taxes. Served with USN, 1942-47, 50-52. Mem. Am. Acctg. Assn., Nat. Bus. Edn. Assn., Phi Delta Kappa. Clubs: Masons, Shriners. Home: 7525 19th St NW Seattle WA 98117 Office: 9600 College Way N Seattle WA 98103

CHODERA, JERRY LLOYD, mech. engr.; b. Medina, Ohio, May 19, 1947; s. Joseph John and Marcella Ellaine (Damon) C.; B.S. in Mech. Engring., Case Inst. Tech., 1969; postgrad. U. Fla., 1969-70; m. Marie Grace Buonocore, June 29, 1972; children—John Damon, Kristin Ann. Apollo launch crew engr. Boeing Atlantic Test Center, Cape Canaveral, Fla., 1969-70; sr. plant engr. B. F. Goodrich Co., Akron, Ohio and Los Angeles, 1970-75; sr. project engr. AMF-Tire Equipment Div., Santa Ana, Calif., 1975-78; chief engr. Wescal Industries, Rancho Dominguez, Calif., 1978—; v.p. Calplant Engring., 1978. Recipient Bausch and Lomb Sci. award, 1965. Mem. ASME (dir. plant engring. and maintenance div.), Am. Electroplaters Soc., Soc. Die Cast Engrs., Case Inst. Tech. Alumni Assn. Presbyterian. Office: 18033 S Santa Fe St Compton CA 90221

CHODOROW, JOAN MARIE, movement psychotherapist, educator; b. N.Y.C., May 29, 1937; d. Eugene Aaronovitch and Lillian (Kleidman) Chodorow; 1 dau., Laurene Kim Smallwood. Dance therapy tng. Trudi Schoop and Mary Whitehouse, 1963-65; M.A. in Dance Therapy, Goddard Coll., Plainfield, Vt., 1972; analyst tng. program C. G. Jung Inst. of Los Angeles, 1977—. Registered dance therapist, Am. Dance Therapy Assn., 1972; lic. marriage, family, child therapist, Calif. Dancer, choreographer, tchr. So. Calif. area, 1953-64; dance therapist County Gen. Hosp., Los Angeles, 1964-66, Santa Barbara Psychiat. Med. Group, 1968-73, Cottage Hosp., Santa Barbara, 1968 ; pvt. practice dance therapy and Jungian analysis, Santa Barbara, 1977—; lectr. continuing edn. programs Santa Barbara Community Coll., U. Calif.-Santa Barbara, 1968—; cons. to insts. Los Angeles, Houston, Madison, Wis., Israel, Can. Mem. Am. Dance Therapy Assn. (pres. 1974-76), Am. Psychol. Assn., Calif. Assn. Marriage and Family Therapists. Jewish. Author chpts. in profl. books; editor: Proc. First Calif. Regional Conf. Am. Dance Therapy Assn., 1972; co-editor: What Is Dance Therapy, Really?, 1973. Home and office: 1821 La Coronilla Dr Santa Barbara CA 93109

CHODOROW, NANCY JULIA, sociologist, educator; b. N.Y.C., Jan. 20, 1944; d. Marvin and Leah Ruth (Turitz) Chodorow; m. Michael Reich, June 19, 1977; children—Rachel Esther, Gabriel Isaac Chodorow-Reich. A.B. summa cum laude in Social Relations, Radcliffe Coll., 1966; Ph.D. in Sociology, Brandeis U., 1972; postgrad. London Sch. Econ. and Polit. Sci., 1966-67, Harvard U., 1967-68. Instr. women's studies Wellesley Coll., 1973-74; lectr. Bd. Studies Sociology, U. Calif.-Santa Cruz, 1974-76, asst. prof., 1976-79, assoc. prof., 1979—; assoc. research sociologist Inst. Personality Assessment and Research, U. Calif.-Berkeley, 1981-83; Fellow Brandeis U., 1969-70, NSF, 1970-72, NIMH, 1966-68, 72-73, Ctr. Advanced Study Behavioral Scis., 1980-81; research grantee U. Calif.-Santa Cruz, 1975-82, Russell Sage Found., 1981-83, NEH, 1982-85. Mem. Am. Sociol. Assn. (Jessie Bernard award 1979), Nat. Women's Studies Assn., Sociologists Women in Soc., Phi Beta Kappa. Cons. editor Feminist Studies; mem. editorial bd. Signs; contbr. articles to profl. jours. Office: Merrill College U Calif Santa Cruz CA 95064

CHOE, WON-GIL, video executive; b. Gang-Nung, Korea, Apr. 24, 1932; s. Chan-Jang and Sook-Ja (Shim) C.; came to U.S., 1957, naturalized, 1970; B.S., Ariz. State U., 1960; M.S., Stanford U., 1962, Ph.D., 1975; m. Grace T. Han, Oct. 17, 1965; children—Iliad, Christopher, Charlotte. Engr. Fairchild Semiconductor, 1962-64; project mgr. Memorex Corp., 1966; mgr. indsl. engring. Internat. Video Corp., 1967-68; v.p. ops. Dole Electro-Systems, Inc., Palo Alto, Calif., 1968-70; v.p. ops. Intellex Corp., Palo Alto, 1970-72; v.p. fin. Vacu-Blast Corp., Belmont, Calif., 1972-74, exec. v.p., 1977-79; pres. Tronic Corp., Belmont, 1973-79; v.p. Applied Implant Tech, Santa Clara, Calif., 1979-81; pres., chief exec. officer Video Logic Corp., Sunnyvale, Calif., 1982—. Mem. Am. Mgmt. Assn., Inst. Indsl. Engring. Assn. Republican. Presbyterian. Author: Quality of Profit in Non-Financial Companies, 1975. Home: 11 Cowell Ln Atherton CA 94025 Office: 597 N Mathilda Ave Sunnyvale CA 94086

CHOI, JEI YORK, metall. engr.; b. Kyung Buk, Korea, June 5, 1923; s. Byong Sang and Ko Bang (Kim) C.; B.Engring., Kyushu Inst. Tech., Japan, 1944; B.Engring., Seoul Nat. U., Korea, 1947; M.Engring., Seoul Nat. U., Korea, 1953; postgrad. Carnegie Inst. Tech., 1960-62; Ph.D., Kyushu U., Japan, 1962; m. Yun Han, Jan. 14, 1947; children—Myong Suk, Soojin Paul. Came to U.S., 1967, naturalized, 1972. Instr. Seoul Nat. U., Korea, 1947-54, asst. prof. metallurgy dept., 1954-57; chief metall. engring. sect. Sci. Research Inst., Korea, 1957-60; research metall. engr. Carnegie Inst. Tech., 1962-63; engring. cons. Korea Automobile Industry Coop. Assn., 1963-67; prof., head metall. engring. dept. Han Yang U., Korea, 1964-67; research metall. engr. Carnegie-Mellon U., 1967-68; research staff mem. Raychem Corp., Menlo Park, Calif., 1968—. Mem. Korean Industry Standard Establishment, Ministry Commerce and Industry, Korean Govt., 1964-67; mem. Edn. Korean Words Establishment for Sci. and Engring., Ministry Edn., Korean Govt., 1966-67; mem. Bd. Natural Sci., Seoul City, Korea, 1967. Recipient Emperor Japan award, 1944; Silver Star Wha Rang Decoration, Republic Korea, 1952, Mu Song Chung Mu Decoration, Korea, 1954, Nat. Invention award Korea, 1968. Mem. Am. Inst. Mining, Metall. and Petroleum Engrs., Am. Soc. for Metals, Korean Inst. Metall. Engrs. (pres. 1965-69), Korean Soc. Heat Treatment Metals (pres. 1965-66), Alumni Assn. Metallurgy Seoul Nat. U. Korea (pres. 1964-67), Sigma Xi. Author: Diffusion in Metals, 1965; Thermodynamics of Metals, 1965; Physical Metallurgy, 1966; Heat Treatment of Metals, 1966; Physical Chemistry of Metals, 1968. Contbr. articles to profl. jours. Patentee in field. Home: 1128 Blackfield Way Mountain View CA 94040

CHONG, JOHN KENNETH, plastic surgeon; b. Ipoh, Malaysia, Apr. 4, 1929; s. Francis and Catherine C.; came to U.S., 1967, naturalized, 1973; B.Sc., McGill U., 1951; B.M., B.Ch., Oxford (Eng.) U., 1958, M.A., 1959; m. Junie Choong, Sept. 4, 1954; children—Lavinia Karen, Kenneth Trevor, Clare Vanessa. Intern, St. Bartholomew's Hosp., London, 1959; resident plastic surgery Queen Victoria Hosp., East Grinstead, Sussex, Eng., 1963-67; jr. lectr. surgery U. London, St. Bartholomew's London, 1961-62 asst. prof. plastic surgery Temple U., Phila., 1967-69, asso. prof., 1970-72; practice medicine specializing in plastic surgery, Newport Beach, Calif., 1972—; mem. staff Hoag Meml. Hosp., Newport Beach, U. Calif. Irvine Med. Center; clin. asso. prof. plastic surgery U. Calif., Irvine, 1972—. Diplomate Am. Bd. Plastic Surgery. Fellow A.C.S., Royal Coll. Surgeons Eng., Royal Soc. Medicine; mem. AMA, Pan Am., Calif., Orange County med. assns., Brit. Assn. Plastic Surgeons, Am. Soc. Plastic and Reconstructive Surgeons, Internat., Am. socs. aesthetic plastic surgeons, Robert H. Ivy Soc., Calif. Soc. Plastic Surgeons, Assn. for Academic Surgery, Am. Cleft Palate Assn., Internat. Confedn. for Plastic and Reconstructive Surgery, So. Calif. Chinese Physicians Soc. (pres. 1974-75). Anglican. Clubs: Oxford Soc., McGill Soc. Contbr. articles in field to profl. jours. Office: Suite 803 1401 Avocado Ave Newport Beach CA 92660

CHONG, MARY DRUZILLEA, nurse; b. Fairview, Okla., Mar. 8, 1930; d. Charles Dewey and Viola Haddie (Ford) Crawford; A.A. (Bells scholarship), El Camino Jr. Coll., 1950; R.N., Los Angeles County Hosp. Sch. Nursing, 1953; B.S. in Nursing, Calif. State U., 1968; M. Nyuk Choy Chong, Aug. 24, 1952 (div. 1968); children—Anthony, Dorlinda. Staff nurse neurosurgery Los Angeles County Gen. Hosp., Los Angeles, 1957-58, staff nurse Harbor Gen. Hosp., Torrance, Calif., 1958-59, emergency room staff nurse, 1959-61, asst. head nurse, 1963-64, supr. neurosurgery intensive care unit, 1964-67, part-time relief nurse, 1967-69, head nurse chest medicine, 1969-72; tchr. YWCA Job Corps, 1972-74; emergency room staff nurse mobile intensive care nurse Victor Valley Hosp., Victorville, Calif., 1974-79; dir. nursing San Vicente Hosp., Los Angeles, 1980-82; dir. nursing Upjohn Healthcare Services, Los Angeles, 1983—. Leader, South Bay council Girl Scouts Am., 1968. Mem. AAUW, Nat. Assn. Female Execs., Calif. State U. Los Angeles Alumni Assn. Home: PO Box 697 Lucerne Valley CA 92356 Office: 6430 Sunset Blvd Suite 506 Los Angeles CA 90028

CHONG, THOMAS, comedian, writer, musician; b. Edmonton, Alta., Can., May 24, 1938; s. Stanley and Lorna Jean (Gilchrist) C.; ed. pub. schs. Co-founder rhythm and blues band The Shades; mem. group Bobby Taylor and the Vancouvers until, 1968; founder improvisational theater troupe City Works; formed comedy duo with Cheech Marin called Cheech and Chong; appeared in nightclubs, Can., Los Angeles; recs. include: Cheech and Chong, Big Bambu, Los Cochinos, The Wedding Album, Sleeping Beauty, co-writer, co-star film Up in Smoke, 1978, co-writer title song Up in Smoke. Recipient with Cheech Grammy award for Best Comedy recording Los Cochinos, 1973. Office: care Monterey Peninsula Artists PO Box 7308 Carmel CA 93921

CHORNEY, FREDERICK RICHARD, mfg. co. exec.; b. Lackawanna, N.Y., Jan. 29, 1930; s. Nicholas and Veronica Helen (Knasak) C.; student UCLA, 1952-54, Los Angeles City Coll., 1957, m. Aicha Abassi, Dec. 7, 1976; children—Dennis Curtis, Roman Guillory, Nicole Chorney. Research chemist Bray Oil Co., Los Angeles, 1954-65, Octagon Process Co., Edgewater, N.J., 1966; owner, mgr. U.S. Lubricants Co., Paramount, Calif., 1967—. Served with U.S. Army, 1948-52; Korea. Republican. Roman Catholic. Club: Los Coyotes Country. Patentee in chem. process. Office: 15544 Minnesota Ave Paramount CA 90723

CHOU, PETER WEI-SHIN, clinical chemist; b. Taiwan, China, Jan. 9, 1931; s. Zue and Sophia Shing-Chy (Hsie) C.; m. Sok-Yin Leung, Oct. 11, 1969; children—Stephen Hsien-Hong, Victor Hsien-Ming. B.S. in Food Sci., Oreg. State U., 1958; M.S. in Food Sci., Wash. State U., 1960; Ph.D. in Biochemistry, U. Mo., Columbia, 1968. Diplomate Am. Bd. Clin. Chemistry; lic. clin. chemist, Calif. Teaching and research asst. U. Mo., Columbia, 1964-68, postdoctoral fellow, 1968-69; research asso. Meth. Hosp., Bklyn., 1969-70; research specialist Mendocino State Hosp., Talmage, Calif., 1970-71; clin. chemist Western Labs., Oakland, Calif., 1971-72; chief clin. chemist Nichols Inst. for Endocrinology, San Pedro, Calif., 1973-76; founder, pres., dir. Radioimmunoassay Centre, Inc., Monterey Park, Calif., 1976—, dir. clin. labs.; cons. ICL Sci., Fountain Valley, Calif. Mem. Am. Assn. for Clin. Chemistry, Clin. Ligand Assay Soc., Am. Soc. Clin. Pathologists, N.Am. Chinese Clin. Chemist Assn. (pres. elect 1984). Democrat. Presbyterian. Home: 748 Rodman Circle Monterey Park CA 91754 Office: 1110 Monterey Pass Rd Monterey Park CA 91754

CHOULES, JOHN MAYNARD, civil engineer, contract administrator; b. Salt Lake City, May 28, 1934; s. George and Esther Rosella (Anderson) C.; m. Doris Anne Johnson, Sept. 1, 1952 (div. May 1976); children—Jack Mark, David Victor, Karen Diane, Dale William, Nancy Carol, Stacy Lynn, Grant Alden, Ryan Trent. B.S.C.E., Utah State U., 1956; postgrad. LaSalle Extension U., 1969, Cleve. Inst. Electronics, 1982-83. Registered profl. engr., Calif., Utah. With Pacific Soils Engring. Co., Los Angeles, 1957-60; civil engr. Fresno County, Calif., 1960; dam safety engr., resident engr. State of Calif., 1960-72; engr. Fulton Constrn. Co., 1972; office engr., contract adminstr. Rancho Seco Nuclear Power Sta., Bechtel Power Co., 1972-78; builder fruit juice processing plant and villa Dadco Co., Saudi Arabia, 1979-80; cons. Utah fed. aid projects, 1980-81; site constrn. mgr. Prowswood/Caldwell, Richard & Sorensen, 1981-83; developer apt. housing projects Choules Devel. Co., Inc., Salt Lake City, 1983—; civil engr. Hawthorne Aviation, Dugway Proving Grounds, Utah, 1983; tchr. engring. Bakersfield (Calif.) Jr. Coll. Active nuclear campaign in Calif., 1976. Recipient award for pub. service Bechtel Corp., 1976. Mormon. Club: Orange County Toastmasters (dist. lt. gov.). Home: 5363A Harris St Dugway UT 84022 Office: PO Box 187 Bldg 5474 Dugway UT 84022

CHOW, BRIAN GEE-YIN, physicist, economist; b. Aug. 10, 1941; naturalized Am. citizen, 1976; s. Kai-Chuen and Chi-Shiu (Miao) C.; B.S., Chinese U. of Hong Kong, 1963; Ph.D. in Physics, Case Western Res. U., 1969; M.B.A. with distinction, U. Mich., 1977, Ph.D. in Fin., 1980; m. Pauline Chou, June 14, 1969; children—Kira, Albert E. Research assoc. dept. physics Case Western Res. U., Cleve., 1969; postdoctoral scholar U. Mich., Ann Arbor, 1972-73; asst. prof. dept. physics Saginaw Valley State Coll., University Center, Mich., 1969-73, assoc. prof., 1973-78, prof., 1978-79, chmn. dept., 1970-74, dir. Obs., 1974-76; sr. research specialist Pan Heuristics, Marina del Rey, Calif., 1978—; cons. Arms Control and Disarmament Agy., Dept. Energy, Council on Environ. Quality, Def. Nuclear Agy., Office of Sec. of Def., Trippensee Planetarium Co., law firms. Am. Enterprise Inst. for Public Policy Research grantee, 1974-75. Contbr. articles on nuclear energy, fin., high energy and nuclear physics to profl. jours. Home: 926 Harvard St Santa Monica CA 90403 Office: R and D Assos 4640 Admiralty Way Marina del Rey CA 90291

CHOW, EDWARD ANSON, physician; b. San Francisco, Jan. 30, 1938; s. William Jack and Anne Chow; B.S., U. San Francisco, 1959; M.D., St. Louis U., 1963; m. Loretta Bing Lee, Apr. 11, 1970; children—Cheryl Lyn, Marc Edward. Intern, So. Pacific Meml. Hosp., San Francisco, 1963-64, resident in internal medicine, 1964-67; gen. practice internal medicine, San Francisco, 1969—; dir. Ambulatory Care Center, Harkness Community Hosp., San Francisco, 1970-74; chief of staff Chinese Hosp., San Francisco, 1977-80; bd. dirs. San Francisco Peer Rev. Orgn., 1978—, sec., 1979-80, v.p., 1981—. Trustee, U. San Francisco, 1982—. Served to lt. comdr. M.C., USNR, 1967-69. Mem. AMA, Calif. Med. Assn. (med. staff survey com. 1976—, alt. del. 1981-82, del. 1983—), San Francisco Med. Soc. (dir. 1980-82, editor 1982—), ACP, Am. Soc. Internal Medicine (del. 1981), Calif. Soc. Internal Medicine (asst. sec.-treas. 1978-82, sec.-treas. 1982—), Calif. Acad. Medicine, San Francisco Heart Assn. (bd. govs. 1979—), U. San Francisco Alumni Assn. (1st v.p. 1977-78, pres. 1978-79), Chinese Am. Citizens Alliance, 3d Marine Div. Assn. Episcopalian. Office: Suite 512 490 Post St San Francisco CA 94102

CHOW, EILEEN SIU-HA, investment company executive; b. Hong Kong, Jan. 18, 1951; d. Hin To and Oi (Kuen) Choi; came to U.S., 1969, naturalized, 1983; m. Chun Ping Chow, Aug. 25, 1973; children—Connie, Sandra. B.A. cum laude, UCLA, 1972, M.S., 1973. Systems analyst Gen. Motors Research Lab., Warren, Mich., 1973-77; v.p. Cougar of Calif., Inc., South San Francisco, 1977—, Choice Investment Co. N.V., Netherlands Antilles, 1978—. Mem. Soc. Women Engrs., ACM. Office: 380 Swift Ave Suite 1 South San Francisco CA 94080

CHOW, KAY MARGARET, designer, educator; b. Pullman, Wash., April 22, 1918; d. Ray Alan Wagner and Edna Mable (Ringer) W.; m. Norman Charles Wallace, Aug. 22, 1943; 1 son, Richard Q; m. 2d, David Zai-Chen Chow, Aug. 25, 1957. B.A. cum laude, Wash. State U., 1936; postgrad. Art Students' League, N.Y.C., 1938-39; M.A., Kans. State U., 1942. Fashion illustrator Women's Wear Daily, N.Y.C., 1937-38; instr. Kansas State U., Manhattan, 1939-43; designer Gump's, San Francisco, 1944-45; dir. Home Planning Center, Harbour-Longmire, Oklahoma City, 1946-47; designer W. O. Wagner & Assocs., Pasadena, Calif., 1950-65; coordinator tech. illustration Jet Propulsion Lab., Calif. Inst. Tech., Pasadena, 1965-67; prof. profl. arts Woodbury U., Los Angeles, 1968-81; designer David Chow & Assocs., Pasadena, 1968—; Mem. Inst. Bus. Designers, (v.p. edn. chpt.), Interior Designers Educators Council (cert.), Am. Soc. Interior Designers (edn. affiliate). Club: Order of Eastern Star.

CHOW, TSAIHWA JAMES, chemist; b. Shanghai, China, Oct. 13, 1924; s. Ma Son and Tze (Hsu) C.; B.S., Nat. Chiao-tung U., Shanghai, 1946; M.S., Wash. State U., Pullman, 1949, Ph.D., U. Wash., 1953; postgrad. Stanford, 1954. Came to U.S., 1947, naturalized, 1960. Research asso. oceanography U. Wash., Seattle, 1953-55; research fellow geochemistry Calif. Inst. Tech., Pasadena, 1955-60; asst. research chemist Scripps Inst. Oceanography, U. Calif., San Diego, 1960-65, asso. research chemist, 1966-71, research chemist, 1971—; vis. researcher Royal Inst. Tech., Stockholm, 1962-63; vis. scientist Acad. Sci. People's Republic of China, 1979, Nat. Bur. Oceanography, People's Republic of China, 1981; mem. trace metal subcom. of safe drinking water com. Assembly of Life Sci., NRC, 1976-77; adv. marine productivity project Instituto del Mar del Peru, Lima, OAS, 1976. Mem. Am. Soc. Limnology and Oceanography, Am. Geophys. Union, Geochem. Soc., AAAS, Japan Oceanographic Soc., Sigma Xi. Contbr. numerous articles to profl. jours. Office: Scripps Inst Oceanography U Calif La Jolla CA 92093

CHOW, WINSTON, chemical engineer; b. San Francisco, Dec. 21, 1946; s. Raymond and Pearl C.; B.S. in Chem. Engring., U. Calif., Berkeley, 1968; M.S. in Chem. Engring., Calif. State U., San Jose, 1972; postgrad. Calif. State U., San Francisco, 1975—; m. Lilly Fah, Aug. 15, 1971; children—Stephen, Kathryn. Chem. engr. Sondell Sci. Instruments, Inc., Mountain View, Calif., 1971; mem. research and devel. staff Raychem Corp., Menlo Park, Calif., 1971-72; with Bechtel Power Corp., San Francisco, 1972-79, engr., 1972-76, sr. engr., 1976-77, engring. mech. mgr., 1977-79; supr. water quality control program Electric Power Research Inst., Palo Alto, Calif., 1979—. Registered profl. chem. and mech. engr., Calif. Gov.'s Exec. Fellow, 1982; instr.'s credential Calif. Community Coll. Mem. Am. Inst. Chem. Engrs. (Profl. Devel. Recognition cert.), Nat. Soc. Profl. Engrs., Calif. Soc. Profl. Engrs. (pres. Golden Gate chpt. 1983-84), Water Pollution Control Fedn., Calif. Water Pollution Control Assn., Water Supply Improvement Assn., ASME, Calif. Alumni Assn., Beta Gamma Sigma. Democrat. Presbyterian. Office: 3412 Hillview Ave Palo Alto CA 94303

CHOWDHURI, PRITINDRA, elec. engr.; b. Calcutta, July 12, 1927; s. Ahindra and Sudhira (Mitra) C.; came to U.S., 1949, naturalized, 1962; B.Sc. in Physics with honors, Calcutta U., 1945, M.Sc., 1948; M.S., Ill. Inst. Tech., 1951; D.Eng., Rensselaer Poly. Inst., 1966; m. Sharon Elsie Hackebeil, Dec. 28, 1962; children—Naomi, Leslie, Robindro, Rajendro. Jr. engr. lightning arresters sect. Westinghouse Elec. Corp., East Pittsburgh, Pa., 1951-52; elec. engr. high voltage lab. Maschinenfabrik Oerlikon, Zurich, 1952-53; research engr. High Voltage Research Commn., Daeniken, Switzerland, 1953-56; devel. engr. high voltage lab. Gen. Electric Co., Pittsfield, Mass., 1956-59; elec. engr. research and devel. ctr. Gen. Electric Co., Schenectady, N.Y., 1959-62, engr. elec. investigations transp. systems div., Erie, Pa., 1962-75; staff mem. Los Alamos Nat. Lab., 1975—; lectr. Pa. State U. Behrend Grad. Center, Erie, 1969-75. Fellow Instn. Elec. Engrs. (Eng.), AAAS, N.Y. Acad. Scis.; sr. mem. IEEE. Democrat. Unitarian. Patentee in field. Home: 510 Bryce Ave White Rock NM 87544 Office: PO Box 1663 Los Alamos Nat Lab Los Alamos NM 87545

CHOY, BONG YOUN, educator; b. Korea, May 25, 1914; s. Ki Ok and Bong Nae (Chang) C.; came to U.S., 1938; B.A., U. Calif., 1943, M.A., 1945; Ph.D. (hon.), World U., 1983; m. Jung Suck Lee (dec. 1970); m. 2d, Young Ja Kim, Jan. 14, 1971; children—Sai Chun, Cora, David, Francis, Sunnie. Instr., U. Calif., Berkeley, 1942-46; prof. Seoul Nat. U., 1946-48; vis. prof. Seattle Pacific U., 1949-52; dep. dir. South Korean Interim Govt., 1947-48; prof. Asian studies Contra Costa Coll., 1977—. Trustee Multi-Services Center for Koreans (San Francisco); polit. edn. specialist Am. Mil. Govt. in South Korea, 1946-48. Author: Korean Reader, 1943; Korea: A History, 1971; Koreans in America, 1979. Home: 101 Tamalpais Rd Berkeley CA 94708 Office: Contra Costa College San Pablo CA 94800

CHOY, HERBERT YOUNG CHO, federal judge; b. Makaweli, Kauai, Hawaii, Jan. 6, 1916; s. Doo Wook and Helen (Nahm) C.; B.A., U. Hawaii, 1938; J.D., Harvard, 1941; m. Dorothy Helen Shular, June 16, 1945. Admitted to Hawaii bar, 1941; pvt. practice, Honolulu, 1946-57, 58-71; atty. gen. Territory of Hawaii, 1957-58; judge 9th circuit U.S. Ct. Appeals, Honolulu, 1971—. Trustee Hawaii Loa Coll., 1963-79. Served with AUS, 1942-46. Decorated Order Civil Merit (Republic Korea), 1973. Fellow Am. Bar Found.; mem. ABA, Hawaii Bar Assn. Home: Honolulu HI Office: US Courthouse PO Box 50127 Honolulu HI 96850

CHOY, KOON HIN, pension and estate planning executive; b. Honolulu, Mar. 12, 1925; s. Yin and Wong S. Choy; student La. State

U., 1973; m. Kazuko Tsuchiya, Feb. 19, 1950; children—Roberta Lee Choy Quenzer, Isaac William. Dist. mgr. Honolulu Star Bull., 1942; asst. circulation mgr. Pacific Stars & Stripes, Far East, 1946-60; life ins. agt. West Coast Life, Honolulu, 1961-63; estate and retirement planning cons. Manulife, Honolulu, 1963-73; pres. K.H. Choy & Associates, Inc., Honolulu, 1973—; state chmn. Life Underwriters Polit. Action Com., 1975-76. Served with U.S. Army, 1946-48. Mem. Nat. Assn. Life Underwriters (Nat. Quality award, Sales Achievement award), Hawaii Assn. Life Underwriters (dir.), Assn. for Advanced Life Underwriting, Nat. Assn. Pension Consultants, Am. Soc. of Chartered Life Underwriters, Nat. Fedn. Ind. Bus., Am. Soc. Pension Actuaries (state chmn. 1976-79). Mem. Congregational Ch. Clubs: Elks, Mid-Pacific Country. Home: 3421-A Woodlawn Dr Honolulu HI 96822 Office: 190 S King St Honolulu HI 96813

CHOY, TERENCE TIN-HO, artist; b. Hong Kong, Nov. 26, 1941; s. Yang Fai and Yin Chen (Ng) C.; B.A., San Francisco State U., 1965; M.A., U. Calif., Berkeley, 1967; m. Carol Eastland, Oct. 10, 1975. Instr. art deYoung Mus. Art Sch., San Francisco, 1969-70; asso. prof. art U. Alaska, Fairbanks, 1970-81, prof., 1981—; one man shows Richmond (Calif.) Art Center, 1968, Coll. Holy Names, Oakland, Calif., 1969, Valley Art Gallery, Walnut Creek, Calif., 1970, Alaska State Mus., Juneau, 1972, Anchorage Hist. and Fine Arts Mus., 1974, 81, U. Alaska, Fairbanks, 1975, U. Minn., 1982, Murray (Ky.) State U., 1982, Alma (Mich.) Coll., 1982; exhibited in group shows Massilon (Ohio) Mus., 1975, Honolulu Acad. Art, 1977, Woodson Art Mus., Wausau, Wis., 1977, Nat. Collection Fine Arts, Washington, 1978, Columbus (Ga.) Mus. Arts and Crafts, 1978; represented in permanent collection Alaska State Council Arts, Alaska State Mus., U. Alaska. Mem. art in public place com. Alaska State Council Arts. Rockefeller/Nat. Endowment Arts fellow, 1977-78; Nat. Endowment Humanities fellow, 1979; Andrew W. Mellon Found. grantee, 1980, 81; Alaska State Council Arts travel grantee, 1979. Mem. AAUP, Coll. Art Assn. Am., Am. Assn. Mus., Visual Arts Center Alaska, Fairbanks Art Assn. Home: 4820 Palo Verde Ave Fairbanks AK 99701 Office: Dept Art U Alaska Fairbanks AK 99701

CHOY, WILBUR WONG YAN, clergyman; b. Stockton, Calif., May 28, 1918; s. Lie Yen (Wong Kai Tong) and Ida (Lee) C.; A.A., Stockton Jr. Coll., 1944; B.A., Coll. Pacific, 1946; M.Div., Pacific Sch. Religion, 1949, D.D., 1969; L.H.D., U. Puget Sound, 1973; m. Grace Ying Hom, Sept. 26, 1940 (dec. Dec. 1977); children—Randolph W., Jonathan W., Phyllis W. Choy Uno, Donnell W.; m. 2d, Nancy S. Yamaski, Dec. 30, 1982. Ordained to ministry United Meth. Ch. as deacon, 1947, elder, 1949, consecrated bishop, 1972; assoc. pastor Chinese Meth. Ch., Stockton, Calif., 1943-49, pastor, 1949-54; pastor St. Mark's Meth. Ch., Stockton, 1954-59; assoc. pastor Woodland (Calif.) Meth. Ch., 1959-60; pastor Oak Park Meth. Ch., Sacramento, 1960-69, Chinese Meth. Ch., Sacramento, 1968-69; dist. supt. Bay View Dist., Calif.-Nev. Conf. United Meth. Ch., 1969-72; resident bishop Seattle area, 1972-80, San Francisco area, 1980—; cons. Pacific and Asian Am. Center for Theology and Strategies, Berkeley, Calif., 1972—. Chaplain, Calif. Senate, 1967; mem. exec. com. Nat. Conf. Chinese Chs., 1971-74; exec. com. World Meth. Council, 1972—; mem. gen. bd. ch. and soc. United Meth. Ch., 1972-80, v.p. and chmn. div. gen. welfare, 1972-76; mem. gen. bd. global ministries, 1980—; mem. Meth. Gen. Bd. Temperance, 1952-56; del. Western Jurisdictional Conf., 1952, 56, 60, 64, 72, alt. rep., 1968; del. Gen. Conf., 1972. Chinese Assn. of Stockton rep. Nat. Conf. Chinese Communities in U.S.A., 1954; mem. exec. com. Oak Park Neighborhood Council, Sacramento, 1964-67; bd. dirs. Goodwill Industries, Stockton, 1958-59, Family Service Agy., Stockton, 1958-59, Woodland, Calif., 1959-60, Center for Asian-Am. Ministries Sch. Theology, Claremont, Calif., 1977—; trustee Pacific Sch. Religion, U. Puget Sound; regent U. Pacific, 1980—. Mem. Asian Am. Ministries (mem. adv. com. 1968-72). Clubs: Rainier, Harbor (Seattle). Office: 330 Ellis St PO Box 467 San Francisco CA 94101

CHOY-BERNARDO, TABBY, public relations counsel; b. Honolulu, Mar. 13, 1939; d. Harry H. P. and Ellen Lilinoe (Davis) Choy; m. Ruben O. Bernardo, Oct. 23, 1976. B.J., U. Mo., 1963. Pub. relations asst. Hawaii Med. Service Assn., Honolulu, 1964-70; dir. pub. relations St. Francis Hosp., Honolulu, 1970—. Chmn. polit. action com., bd. dirs. Hawaii Credit Union League; bd. dirs. St. Francis Hosp. Fed. Credit Union, pres., 1973-78; ofcl. Oahu Aloha chpt. Hawaii Credit Union League. Mem. Pub. Relations Soc. Am., Internat. Assn. Bus. Communicators, Hosp. Pub. Relations Assn. Hawaii (pres.). Democrat. Mem. United Churches of Christ. Home: 45-371 Mokulele Dr Apt 55 Kaneohe HI 96744 Office: 2230 Liliha St Honolulu HI 96817

CHRISMAN, ROBERT CHARLES, personnel administrator, educator; b. Port Arthur, Tex., June 1, 1940; B.S., Mo. Valley Coll., 1961; postgrad. in personnel systems Calif. State univs., 1956-76. Asst. dir. personnel Med. Center, Stanford (Calif.) U., 1966-71; dir. indsl. relations Mary's Help Hosp., Daly City, Calif., 1971—; asst. prof. personnel adminstrn. San Francisco State U., 1976—; cons. in field. Served to lt. USNR, 1961-65; Vietnam. Mem. Calif. Hosp. Personnel Mgmt. Assn. (pres. 1971-72), Am. Soc. Hosp. Personnel Adminstrn. (dir. 1973-74), Am. Hosp. Assn., Am. Soc. Tng. and Devel. Home: 503 Headlands Court Sausalito CA 94965 Office: 1900 Sullivan Ave Daly City CA 94015

CHRISMER, DENNY LEE, computer mfg. co. exec.; b. Denver, May 26, 1946; s. Charles Robert and Maxine (Means) C.; B.S. in Elec. Engring., USAF Acad., 1968; M.Internat. Mgmt. with honors, Am. Grad. Sch. Internat. Mgmt., Glendale, Ariz., 1968; m. Sara Jane Moore, Sept. 13, 1975; children—Sunny Dawn, Mitchell Ryan. With Rolm Corp., computer mfg., 1975-82, regional sales mgr. Southeastern U.S., 1977-79, sales mgr. Far East and Latin Am., Santa Clara, Calif., 1979-82; asst. to pres. Auto-Trol Tech. Corp., Denver, 1982—. Served to capt. USAF, 1964-73. Decorated Air medal. Office: 12500 N Washington St Denver CO 80233

CHRISSINGER, JOHN EDWARD, banker; b. Detroit, Mar. 31, 1939; s. Horace Blaine and Edna Allan (Harbeck) C.; m. Marlene Kay Sonju, Mar. 2, 1974; children—Craig, Lynne, Katherine, Theodore. Student Brown U., 1957-59; B.S. in Physics, Stanford U., 1961; M.S. in Physics, Pa. State U., 1969; M.B.A., U. Nev.-Las Vegas, 1977. Commd. 2d lt., U.S. Army, 1961, advanced through grades to maj., 1972; asst. prof. physics U.S. Mil. Acad., West Point, N.Y., 1970-72; ret., 1972; mem. Res.; account exec. Merrill Lynch, Las Vegas, 1972-74; with Nev. Nat. Bank, Reno, 1974—, sr. v.p., mgr. Trust and Investment div., 1981—; vice chmn. Nev. Blue Shield; cons. Washoe County Bar Assn.; lectr. wills and estates Multiple Sclerosis Soc. Pres. Brookdale Park Homeowners Assn. Decorated Bronze Star, Army Commendation Medal with oak leaf cluster; Cross of Gallantry (Vietnam). Mem. Estate Planning Council Reno, Nev. Bankers Assn. (chmn. trust com.). Democrat. Lutheran. Clubs: Stanford Reno (pres.), Elks. Home: 155 Moore Ln Reno NV 89509 Office: 200 S Virginia St Reno NV 89501

CHRISTENSEN, ARNOLD, heating and elec. contractor, state senator; b. Salt Lake City, July 26, 1936; s. Walter A. and Joyce (Pierce) C.; student U. Utah, 1955-56; m. Necia Ann Larsen, May 10, 1956; children—Valerie Ann Cutrer, Cheryl Ann Berrett, Kathy Ann, Bruce Arnold. Owner, operator Christensen Electric Co., Midvale, Utah, 1957—; mem. Utah Senate, 1978—. Adviser, Boy Scouts Am., 1964-65. Republican. Mormon. Office: 7000 South 400 West Midvale UT 84047

CHRISTENSEN, CAROLINE, educator; b. Lehi, Utah, Oct. 5, 1936; d. Byam Heber and Ruth (Gardner) Curtis; m. Marvin Christensen, June 16, 1961; children—Ronald, Roger, Robert, Corlyn, Richard, Chad. B.S., Brigham Young U., 1958, M.S., 1964. Sec. Brigham Young U., Provo, Utah, 1954-58; instr. bus. Sevier Valley Area Vocat. Ctr., Richfield, Utah, 1970—. Historian, Sevier Sch. Dist. PTA, 1968, 69; chmn. Heart Fund Dist., 1983. Mem. Utah Edn. Assn., Am. Vocat. Assn., Utah Vocat. Assn., Nat. Bus. Edn. Assn. Utah Bus. Edn. Assn., NEA, Western Bus. Edn. Assn., Sevier Valley Tech. Tchrs. Assn., Delta Pi Epsilon, Delta Kappa Gamma.

CHRISTENSEN, CHARLOTTE ELSIE ANDERSON, home economist, educator; b. Los Angeles, Dec. 19, 1935; d. Samuel Buena and Virginia Missie (Hamblen) Anderson; divorced; children—Tom, Steve. A.A., El Camino Coll., 1954; M.A., Calif. State U.-Humboldt, 1973. Tchr. Union High Sch., Santa Paula, Calif., 1956-61; demonstrator Ventura Electric Co., 1964-65; tchr. So. Humboldt (Calif.) Unified Sch. Dist., 1971-72; instr. clothing and textiles Solano Coll., Suisun, Calif., 1973—. Ruling elder Presbyterian Community Ch., Miranda, 1972-73. Mem. Calif. Tchrs. Assn., NEA, Calif. Home Econs. Assn., Am. Home Econs. Assn., Costume Soc. Am., Mus. Vintage Fashion, Kappa Omicron Phi. Republican. Clubs: Sierra (San Francisco Bay area); Job's Daughters. Home: 1096 Rose Dr Napa CA 94558 Office: PO Box 246 Suisun CA 94585

CHRISTENSEN, DALE ORRIN, oil company executive; b. Great Falls, Mont., Jan. 31, 1950; s. Wayne Marinus and Helen Katherine (Hickman) C.; m. Myra Louise Keith, Mar. 30, 1953; children—Collette, Trevor, Justin, Taylor. B.S., Brigham Young U., 1974. Controller Harold Square, Inc., Orem, Utah, 1974-75, True Value Home Mart Stores, Orem, 1975-76; comptroller Dunn Oil Co., Salt Lake City, 1976-82, v.p. fin., 1982—. Mem. Sigma Epsilon. Mormon. Office: Dunn Oil Co 711 W 800 S Salt Lake City UT 84104

CHRISTENSEN, DEAN ELMER, vocational education administrator; b. Murray, Utah, Mar. 4, 1938; s. Martin Elmer and Melba (Morgan) C.; m. Ruth Hubbard, Aug. 29, 1963; children—Paul, Van, Kevin, Don. B.S. in Indsl. Edn., Utah State U., 1966; M.S., Brigham Young U., 1976. Cert. profl. adminstr. secondary edn., indsl. edn., Utah. Tchr. indsl. arts Uintah High Sch., Vernal, Utah, 1966-67; tchr. indsl. arts Viewmont High Sch., Bountiful, Utah, 1967-82, adminstrn. intern, 1979-81; supr. indsl. edn. Davis Sch. Dist., Farmington, Utah, 1982-83; asst. dir. vocat. edn. Davis Sch. Dist., 1983—; dir. State of Utah Vocat. Indsl. Clubs Am., 1979-83. Chmn. sustaining membership enrollment Salt Lake council Boy Scouts Am., 1983—. Served with USNG, 1956-66. Named Trade and Indsl. Edn. Tchr. of Yr. Utah Indsl. Edn. Assn., 1973, 80. Mem. NEA, Utah Edn. Assn., Utah Vocat. Assn., Utah Indsl. Edn. Assn., Am. Vocat. Assn., Davis Edn. Assn., Nat. Assn. Trade and Indsl. Edn. Republican. Mormon. Home: 943 N Main St Centerville UT 84014 Office: 45 E State St Farmington UT 84025

CHRISTENSEN, DON LEE, surgeon; b. Salina, Utah, Apr. 20, 1930; s. Paul DeLloyd and Gladys N. (Christensen) C.; B.S., U. Utah, 1952, M.D., 1955; m. Lora Dee Nelson, May 17, 1952; children—Paula, Michele, Tammy, Karla, Terri Lynn, Connie Lee. Intern, U. Wis. Hosps., 1955-56; asst. resident gen. surgery Stanford Hosp., 1956-59, chief resident, 1959-60; chief of surgery Sunrise Hosp., Las Vegas, Nev., 1968-72, chief of staff, 1972-73; practice medicine, specializing in surgery, Las Vegas, 1965—; asso. prof. surgery U. Nev. Med. Sch. Bishop of 24th Ward, Las Vegas East Stake, Ch. Jesus Christ of Latter-day Saints, 1975-80, stake pres. Paradise stake, 1982—. Served with USAF, 1960-65. Recipient Outstanding Intern award U. Wis. Med. Sch., 1956. Diplomate Am. Bd. Surgery. Fellow ACS, Am. Coll. Chest Physicians; mem. AMA, Phi Beta Kappa, Alpha Omega Alpha. Republican. Home: 2044 Mohigan Way Las Vegas NV 89109 Office: 3196 Maryland Pkwy Las Vegas NV 89109

CHRISTENSEN, DONN WAYNE, ins. and mgmt. exec.; b. Atlantic City, Apr. 9, 1941; s. Donald Frazier and Dorothy (Ewing) C.; B.S., U. Santa Clara, 1964; m. Mei Ling Fill, June 18, 1976; children—Donn Wayne, Lisa Shawn; m. 2d, Linda Chang, Oct. 18, 1980; stepchildren—Jim Chang, Mina Chang. West Coast div. mgr. Ford Motor Co., 1964-65; agt. Conn. Mut. Life Ins. Co., 1965-68, Christensen & Jones, Mgmt. and Ins. Services, Los Angeles, 1968—; v.p. Research Devel. Systems Inc. Pres. Duarte Community Drug Abuse Council, 1972-75; pres. Woodlyn Propertys Owners Assn., 1972-73. Recipient Man of year award Los Angeles Gen. Agts. and Mgrs. Assn., 1969, 72, 73. Mem. Nat. Life Underwriters Assn., Calif. State Life Underwriters Assn., Nat. Assn. Music Mchts. and Mfrs., Soc. Pension Actuaries, Foothill Community Concert Assn. (pres. 1970-73). Home: 4234 Alhama Dr Woodland Hills CA Office: 1015 Wilshire Blvd Los Angeles CA 90017

CHRISTENSEN, DOUGLAS KEITH, educational administrator; b. Salt Lake City, Sept. 23, 1947; s. Keith Willmor and Vera (Cahoon) C.; m. Linda Swan, June 19, 1969; children—Caryn, Coray, Camille, Cameron. B.S. in Acctg., Brigham Young U., 1972, postgrad., 1981—. Adminstr. bus. info. and support Brigham Young U., Provo, Utah, 1972—. Mem. Assn. Phys. Plant Adminstrs., Am. Mgmt. Soc., Am. Soc. Tng. and Devel., Nat. Assn. Coll. Univ. Bus. Officers, Delta Pi Epsilon. Mormon. Club: Kiwanis Internat. (Provo). Home: 272 W 1060 S Orem UT 84057 Office: 207 BRWB Brigham Young U Provo UT 84602

CHRISTENSEN, HOWARD BLAIR, statistics educator, consultant; b. Payson, Utah, Dec. 9, 1939; s. Jensen D. and Dorothy (Anderson) C.; m. Bonnie Gayle Heelis, Mar. 15, 1963; children—Derek, Quinn, Devin, Brandon, Jordan, Doran, Trent, Megan, Erin, Diana, Alex. B.S., Brigham Young U., 1964; M.E.S., N.C. State U., 1966, Ph.D., 1975. Mem. Faculty Brigham Young U., Provo, Utah, 1967—, prof. stats., 1975—; sample surveyor statis. research div. Bur. Census, Suitland, Md., 1974-75; cons. Hill AFB, 1968-70, FDA, 1976-78, Brigham Young U. Ctr. Statis. Research, 1979—. NASA fellow, 1964-67. Mem. Am. Statis. Assn. Republican. Mormon. Author: Statistics Step By Step, 1977. Home: 10454 So 1900 W Payson UT 84651 Office: 246 TMCB Brigham Young Univ Provo UT 84602

CHRISTENSEN, JAMES LEE, sales management executive; consultant; b. Aurora, Nebr., May 24, 1933; s. James LeRoy and Gertrude Edna (Woodford) C.; m. Monna Lee Murphy, June 1, 1968; children—Donna Spiegel, Vickie Douthit, Robin. B.A., U. Calif.-Santa Barbara, 1955. Sales rep. Procter & Gamble, Calif., Ariz., Hawaii, 1955-63, gen. sales rep., Ariz., 1963-65; field mgr., southeastern states, 1965-68, regional mgr., Cin., 1968-78; sr. v.p. sales Miller Cascade Foods Inc., Kent, Wash., 1979—; cons., lectr. U. Wash. Served with U.S. Army, 1956-57. Mem. Restaurant Assn. Wash., Oreg. NW Cannery Assn. Home: 17410 NE 40th Pl Redmond WA 98052 Office: 18430 E Valley Hwy Kent WA 98031

CHRISTENSEN, JEAN, school counselor; b. Waterloo, Iowa, Jan. 20, 1947; d. Lloyd Everett and Thelma Gregory C. B.S., Iowa State U., 1969, M.S., 1971; Ph.D., U. Colo., 1980. Tchr. English, Gove Jr. High Sch., Denver, 1970-80, counselor, 1973-80; program mgr. ESEA Title II Basic Skills, 1980-82; counselor Manual High Sch., Denver, 1982—. Precinct committeewoman Republican party, 1976-80; vol. youth sponsor ARC, 1974-76. Mem. NEA (life), Am. Personnel and Guidance Assn., Nat. Assn. Women Deans, Adminstrs. and Counselors (bd. dirs. 1980-82), Assn. Supervision and Curriculum Devel., Colo. Edn. Assn., Colo. Assn. Sch. Execs., Denver Classroom Tchrs. Assn. (bd. dirs. 1977-79), Nat. Council Tchrs. English, Colo. Lang. Arts Soc., Iowa State U. Alumni Assn. (life), U. Colo. Alumni Assn., Phi Delta Kappa (life), Alpha Xi Delta. Republican. Presbyterian. Office: 1700 E 28th Ave Denver CO 80205

CHRISTENSEN, LEE NORSE, architect; b. Passaic, N.J., Apr. 29, 1940; s. Olaf and Elsie Johanna Petri (Reese) C.; B.Arch., U. Ariz., 1966; m. Mary Ellen Lewis, July 27, 1967 (div. 1972); m. 2d Marie Elizabeth Pusch, Nov. 25, 1974 (div. May 1978); children—Katie, Susan, Emily. Asso., John Mascarella & Assos., Tucson, 1963-65, Louis Coon & Assos., Tucson, 1965-72, Schonberger, Straub, Florence & Assos., Phoenix, 1973-75; v.p. Shuart Corp., Phoenix, 1975-76; prin. Lee N. Christensen & Assos., Sedona, Ariz., 1976—. Chmn., Jerome (Ariz.) Design Rev. Bd., 1979-81; chmn. Planning and Zoning Commn., Jerome; bd. dirs. Keep Sedona Beautiful, 1979-81. Recipient award of Merit, City of Tempe (Ariz.), 1975, Verde Valley Art Assn. Mem. AIA, Nat. Council Archtl. Registration Bds., Nat. Trust Historic Preservation, Smithsonian Assos. Office: PO Box 1815 Sedona AZ 86336

CHRISTENSEN, LEW FARR, choreographer, ballet director; b. Brigham City, Utah, May 6, 1909; s. Chris and Mary Isabelle (Farr) C.; m. Giselle Caccialanza, May 10, 1941; 1 son, Chris. Soloist, ballet master Ballet Caravan, N.Y.C., 1936-41, Am. Ballet, N.Y.C., 1941, Ballet Soc., N.Y.C. Ballet, 1946-52; dir. San Francisco Ballet, 1952—. Mem. Adv. Com. on Arts, Washington, 1963-69, Calif. Arts Commn., 1963-66. Served with AUS, 1942-46. Office: San Francisco Ballet 378 18th Ave San Francisco CA 94121*

CHRISTENSEN, PHILLIP REX, tax cons.; b. San Antonio, Feb. 29, 1944; s. LaVerne Edward and Blanche Kathryn (Bennett) C.; student public schs. Phoenix; m. Lorelei Ellen, Sept. 2, 1972; children—Glen, Rory, Lorelei L., Peter, Chrisann. Commissary foreman Dept. Army, Anchorage, 1967-71; mil. account rep., sales rep. Kraft Foods Co., Anchorage, 1971-72; adminstrv. pay technician Alaska Army Nat. Guard, Kodiak, 1972-76; pres. Christensen Enterprises, Inc., Anchorage, 1976—. Libertarian Candidate lt. gov. Alaska, 1982. Served with USAF, 1962-66. Mem. Nat. Soc. Public Accts., Alaska Soc. Ind. Accts. (chmn. tax research div., past pres.). Club: Moose. Research in tax refund errors Alaska Dept. Revenue. Home: 4300 Arctic Blvd #49 Anchorage AK 99503 Office: 4660 Stuart Way Suite A Anchorage AK 99503

CHRISTENSEN, STEVEN FRED, financial planner; b. Salt Lake City, Jan. 9, 1954; s. F. Mac and Joan (Graham) C.; m. Terri L. Romney, Sept. 16, 1976; children—Joshua, Justin, Jared. Student, U. Utah, 1975-79. Vice pres. Mr. Mac Men's Clothing Co., Salt Lake City, 1975-79; fin. cons. Coordinated Fin. Services, Salt Lake City, 1980—, dir. 1983—. Trustee, Deseret Found., Leonard J. Arrington Found. for Mormon Studies, Sunstone Found.; bishop Mormon Ch.; county del. Republican, party; bd. mem. SSS, 1972. Mem. Mormon History Assn., Soc. Bibl. Lit., Soc. Ch. History, Soc. Early Hist. Archeology. Office Coordinated Financial Services 324 S State St Suite 500 Salt Lake City UT 84111

CHRISTENSEN, TED, painter, printmaker, potter; b. Vancouver, Wash., Mar. 20, 1911; s. Ted. and Francine Catherine C. grad. Otis Art Inst., Los Angeles, 1949; student Portland Mus. Sch., 1944, 48, Art Center Los Angeles, 1944-46. Instr. dept. art Coll. of Marin, Kentfield, Calif., 1952-60; various positions in ceramics industry; 51 one-man-shows of paintings, prints and/or pottery, latest being: Sky-Ligh Gallery, Albuquerque, 1974, 75, 76, Jensen Gallery, San Francisco, 1974, 75, 76, Village Gallery, Fairfax, Calif., 1978-80, Arelene Lind Gallery, San Francisco, 1978, Schoolhouse Gallery, Amador City, Calif., 1979, Tivoli Gallery, Los Altos, Calif., 1978, 79, Red Tree Gallery, Bend, Oreg., 1979; numerous group shows, latest being: Oreg. State Fair, Salem (awards), 1942, 43, Portland (Oreg.) Art Mus. (awards), 1946, 48, Marin Soc. Artists (awards), 1952, 55, 57, 58, Sausalito (Calif.) Art Festival (award), 1954, Jack London Outdoor Festival, Oakland (award), 1955, Oakland Art Mus., 1954, Mill Valley (Calif.) Art Festival (award), 1962; represented in numerous permanent collections Dow Chem. Corp., San Francisco, United Calif. Bank, San Francisco, Harney Sch., Vancouver, Wash., Vancouver Public Library, Met. Life Ins., San Francisco, Henderson Galleries, Monterey, Calif., Sausalito Hist. Mus., Mendocino Hist. Mus. (Calif.), others, also numerous pvt. collections in U.S., Canada, Europe, Japan, Chile and Taiwan. Served with inf. U.S. Army, 1940-41. Recipient numerous awards various art shows and art socs.; named Sonoma Treasure, Cultural and Fine Arts Commn. Sonoma, 1983. Mem. Artists Equity Assn., Am.-Scandinavian Artists of the West (sec. 1946-49), Oakland Mus. Assn., Mus. Soc. San Francisco, Mendocino Art Assn., Otis Art Inst. Alumni Assn. Author: Mendocino Sketchbook, 1972. Address: 573 3rd St E Sonoma CA 95476

CHRISTENSEN, VIKTOR ALBERT, public relations executive; b. Svendborg, Denmark, May 11, 1921; came to U.S., 1957; s. Anton Marius and Maren Johanne (Jorgensen) C.; m. Vera Helene Nielsen, July 12, 1945; children—Bjarne, Berit Osborne. B.A., Loma Linda U., 1959; M.A., Fresno State U., 1961; Ph.D., U. So. Calif., 1969. Elem. tchr., prin. schs., Denmark, 1945-57; secondary tchr. pub. schs., Fresno, Calif., 1959-62; prof. phys. edn. Loma Linda U., Riverside, Calif., 1962-67, prof. edn., 1968-81, assoc. dean sch. edn., 1976-81. dir. pub. relations devel., La Sierra campus, Riverside, 1981—. Mem. Citizens Adv. Com. La Sierra/Arlanza Devel., Riverside, 1977-79; mem. Riverside City Centenniel Celebration Steering Com., 1983—. Recipient Twenty Yr. Service award Loma Linda U.; Ten Yr. award Western Assn. Schs. Colls.; Notable Ams. award Hist. Preservations of Am., 1976-77. Mem. Pub. Relations Soc. Am., Council for Advancement Support of Edn., La Sierra C. of C. (dir.), Phi Delta Kappa. Republican. Seventh-day Adventist. Club: Arlington Rotary (sec.). Contbr. articles to profl. jours. Home: 5130 Leon Ct Riverside CA 92505 Office: Loma Linda U La Sierra Campus Riverside CA 92515

CHRISTENSON, CAROLYN (LYN) ELIZABETH, corporate manager; b. Madison, Wis., May 29, 1949; m. Larry R. Christenson, Sept. 4, 1971. B.A. in Journalism, U. Mo., 1971; M.B.A., Pepperdine U., 1981. Pub. relations rep. Varian Assocs., Palo Alto, Calif., 1972-76; mgr. internal communications and community affairs Fairchild Camera and Instrument Corp., Mountain View, Calif., 1976-80; mgr. communications Syntex Corp., Palo Alto, 1980-83; mgr. corp. and fin. relations Burson-Marsteller, Santa Clara, Calif., 1983—. Mem. pub. relations adv. com. Santa Clara County (Calif.), United Way; mem. community adv. council Resource Ctr. for Women, Palo Alto, Calif. Mem. Nat. Investor Relations Inst., Pub. Relations Soc. Am. Contbg. author to publ. in field. Office: 2041 Mission College Blvd Santa Clara CA 95051

CHRISTEY, ROBERT BRUCE, stockbroker; b. San Salvador, El Salvador, Feb. 5, 1952; s. Leroy Scott and Doris Maude (Droskie) C.; m. Diann Cecelia Rasmussen, Aug. 20, 1977; 1 dau., Lisa Diann. B.A. in Econs., Western Wash. U.-Bellingham, 1974, M.A. in Econs., 1976. Teaching asst. dept. econs. Western Wash. U., 1974-76; supr. installment loan dept. Bank of Wash., Bellingham, 1976-79; real estate loan officer Cascade Savs. & Loan, Bellingham, 1979-80; acct. exec. Merrill Lynch, Bellingham, 1980—; lectr. and speaker in field. Loaned exec. United Way of Whatkom County (Wash.). Lutheran. Clubs: Kiwanis, Toastmasters (named Able Toastmaster 1983, best evaluator Dist. 2, 1983) (Bellingham). Home: 2408 Crestline Dr Bellingham WA 98226 Office: 1213 Cornwall Ave Bellingham WA 98225

CHRISTIAENS, BERNARD FRANCIS (CHRIS), state senator, finance and insurance executive, finance consultant; b. Conrad, Mont., Mar. 7, 1940; s. Marcel J. and Virgie Jeanette (Van Spyk) C. B.A. in Chemistry, Coll. of Gt. Falls (Mont.), 1962; postgrad. in Personnel Mgmt., U. Mont., 1963, Mont. State U., 1966. Supr. and claim dir. Equifax, Great Falls, 1963-78; fin. and ins. mgr. Rice Motors, Great Falls, 1978-82, v.p. Rice Motors Fleet Sales and Leasing, 1983—; mem. Mont. Senate, 1982—; instr. Coll. of Gt. Falls; condr. seminars in field. State committeeman Cascade County Dem. Party, 1976-80, fin. chmn., 1974-78, Mont. del. to nat. rules conv., 1980, alt. del. nat. conv., 1980; mem. Mont. Human Rights Commn., 1980-82. Recipient Outstanding Alumni award Coll. Gt. Falls, 1980. Roman Catholic. Clubs: Optimists, Gt. Falls Ski, Toastmasters (v.p. edn., Able Toastmaster 1978, Outstanding Area Evaluator, 1974).

CHRISTIAN, DAVID LYNN, architect; b. Clovis, N.Mex., Nov. 28, 1946; s. Orphane Eugene and Nola Maxine (Rice) C.; student N.Mex. State U., 1964-65; B.Arch., Tex. Tech. U., 1970. Project designer D. A. Wexler Assocs., Palm Springs, Calif., 1970-72; head project architect Kaptur & Lapham, Palm Springs, 1972-76; founder, since pres. Christian Assocs., Palm Springs, 1976. Mem. Palm Springs Archtl. Adv. Bd., 1979—; mem. Com. for Palm Springs Cultural Center, 1979—, Palm Springs Desert Mus., 1976—, Palm Springs Planning Commn., 1980. Recipient various local and nat. archtl. awards including Instns. mag. award of Merit, 1979. Mem. AIA, Nat. Council Archtl. Registration Bds. (cert.). Office: 1000 S Palm Canyon Dr Palm Springs CA 92262

CHRISTIAN, JAMES HOWARD, sales exec.; b. Kansas City, Mo., June 4, 1938; s. Joseph and Thelma Jean (Watts) C.; B.S., U. Mo., 1967; m. Patricia Hoffman, June 17, 1972. Engr., Gen. Dynamics, Pomona, Calif., 1967-69; salesman Hewlett Packard, Fullerton, Calif., 1969-71; dist. mgr. Data Gen., Palo Alto, Calif., 1971-74; br. mgr. Digital Equipment, Honolulu, 1974-79; dir. mktg. Hamilton/AVNET, Culver City, Calif., 1979-80; v.p. sales and mktg. Data Memory Corp., Canoga Park, Calif., 1980—. Registered profl. engr., Mo. Clubs: Data Gen. Million Dollar, Digital Equipment DEC 100. Home: 2102 E Hillcrest Dr Thousand Oaks CA 91362 Office: 6750 Eton Ave Canoga Park CA 91303

CHRISTIANSEN, EDWARD KRISTIAN, newspaper executive; b. Seattle, Feb. 29, 1928; s. Sigvald and Ingeborg C. (Scheldrup) C.; m. Alene Ruth Hubbard, June 10, 1949, children—Claudia Jo Christiansen Herrick, Karen Louise. Student U. Wash. With Riches & Adams, Seattle, 1950-59; with Fairbanks (Alaska) News, 1959—, pres., gen. mgr., 1969—. Pres. operating bd. and found. Fairbanks Meml. Hosp. Served with U.S. Army. Republican. Lutheran.

CHRISTIANSEN, JOYCE L. SOELBERG, newspaper editor; b. Salt Lake City, May 25, 1924; d. Lloyd LeRoy and Irene (Lindberg) Soelberg; student public schs.; m. Ernald Christiansen, Sept. 7, 1947; children—Melodie Joyce, Lynda Lee, Lloyd Randall, Catherine Jill. Sec., COBUSCO Steel, Salt Lake City, 1941-42, Universal Film, Inc., Salt Lake City, 1942-43, Delivery Service Co., Salt Lake City, 1946-47; legal sec. Clearfield Naval Supply (Utah), 1943-45; editor Sunset News, Bountiful, Utah, 1972-75; photographer, journalist, religion writer Deseret News, Salt Lake City, 1976-82; editor, writer, photographer South Salt Lake Bugle, Salt Lake City, 1982—. Pres., Backman Elem. Sch. PTA, 1958-60; 2 v.p. Northwest Jr. High Sch. PTA, 1961-62; active Girl Scouts U.S.A., 1965—, originator Girl Scout Baby award, Utah, 1980; mem. adv. bd. Northwest Multi-Purpose Center, 1972-82, sec., 1973-82; host radio show Get Me to the Church on Time, 1977, mem. Salt Lake Library Bd., 1980—, mem. ops., bldgs. and grounds coms. Recipient 3rd place award Nat. Fedn. Press Women Communication Contest, 1977; numerous first and second place awards Utah Press Women. Mem. Nat. Fedn. Press Women, Utah Press Women (sec. 1978-82, corr. sec. 1982—, 2d v.p. 1980-82). Mem. Ch. Jesus Christ of Latter-day Saints (mem. Sunday sch. bd. Riverside Stake 1955). Clubs. Women's Democratic, Jane Jefferson, Lady Lions (2d v.p. 1979-80). Contbr. articles to Utah Life mag. Home: 755 N 1400 W Salt Lake City UT 84116 Office: Bugle News 55 E Malvern Ave Salt Lake City UT 84115

CHRISTIANSEN, KENT M., univ. adminstr.; b. Moreland, Idaho, Dec. 31, 1928; s. James Loran and Thelma (Park) C.; B.S., Brigham Young U., 1954, M.S., 1958; Ph.D., Mich. State U., 1965; m. Margaret Blood Bird, June 15, 1956; children—Maureen, Mary Ann, Susan, Stephen, Karen, Jane, John, Carolyn. Dir. guidance East Lansing (Mich.) Jr. High Sch., 1961-64; instr., counselor Lansing (Mich.) Community Coll., 1964-65; asst. prof. counselor edn. U. Wyo., Laramie, 1965-66; dir. student services Ariz. State U., Tempe, 1966—. Bishop, Ch. of Jesus Christ of Latter-day Saints, 1971-76; mem. parents adv. com. Tempe High Sch., 1977-78. Served to 1st lt. USAF, 1952-54. Mem. Am. Personnel and Guidance Assn., Am. Coll. Personnel Assn., Am. Soc. for Tng. and Devel., Acad. Affairs Adminstrs. Assn., Assn. Mormon Counselors and Psychotherapists, Kappa Delta Pi (compatriot in Edn. cert.). Republican. Contbr. articles to profl. jours. Home: 18 W Palmcroft Dr Tempe AZ 85282 Office: B-2 Payne Hall Ariz State U Tempe AZ 85287

CHRISTIANSEN, ROBERT MILTON, engineer, manager; b. Chgo., Nov. 5, 1924; s. Milton John and Lillian Marion (Donat) C.; m. Lois Elinor Todd, July 12, 1952; children—Eric Todd, Dana Scott, Lois Martha. B.S., Northwestern U., 1947, M.S., 1949; Ph.D. in Chem. Engring. (Allied Chem. Fellow), U. Pa., 1955. Lic. profl. engr., Colo. Pilot plant engr. Universal Oil Products, Riverside, Ill., 1947-48, jr. engr. Shell Devel. Co., Emeryville, Calif., 1949-52; dir. physics research lab. Owens Corning Fiberglass, Granville, Ohio, 1955-59; chief process engr. Stearns Roger Corp. Denver, 1959-70, mgr. environ. scis. div., 1970—; instr. U. Pa., 1952-54, Ohio State U., 1955-56. Rep., Colo. Polit. Action Com.; pres. home owners assn., Cherry Hills Village, Colo., 1982-83. Mem. Am. Inst. Chem. Engrs., Am. Chem. Soc., Sigma Xi, Phi Lambda Upsilon. United Ch. of Christ. Club: Denver Athletic. Home: 4081 S Holly St Englewood CO 80111 Office: 4500 Cherry Creek Dr S Box 5888 Denver CO 80217

CHRISTIE, HANS FREDERICK, utility executive; b. Alhambra, Calif., July 10, 1933; s. Andreas B. and Sigrid E. (Falck-Jorgensen) C.; B.S. in Business and Finance, U. So. Calif., 1957, M.B.A. in Mgmt., 1964; m. Susan Earley, June 16, 1957; children—Brenda Lynn, Laura Jean. With So. Calif. Edison Co., 1957—, exec. v.p., 1980—; pres. dir. Asso. So. Investment Co.; dir. Electric Systems Co., Energy Services, Inc., Mono Power Co., VSCE Capital Co., So. Sierra Energy Co., Nuclear Mut. Ltd., Nuclear Electric Ins. Ltd., VARCO, Am. Mut. Fund Co., Bond Fund Am., Cash Mgmt. Fund, Tax Exempt Fund, New Economy Fund, Assoc. Electric & Gas Co. Trustee So. Calif. chpt. Multiple Sclerosis Found.; treas. United Way of Los Angeles; trustee Occidental Coll. Mem. Pacific Coast Elec. Assn. (dir., treas.), Nat., Los Angeles socs. fin. analysts, Fin. Execs. Inst. Home: 19 Empty Saddle Ln Rolling Hills Estate CA 90274 Office: 2244 Walnut Grove Ave Rosemead CA 91770

CHRISTLIEB, RICHARD, educator; b. Aboite, Ind., Feb. 25, 1932; s. Lloyd Franklin and Myrel Lou (Heck) C.; m. Della Lou Swapp, Mar. 1, 1953; children—Brenda Edwards, Nancy Gibson, Kayla Hall, Roger, Grant, Heidi, Julie, Diane, Richelle. B.S., Brigham Young U., 1962, M.S., 1963. Cert. tchr., Utah. Tchr. Granite Sch. Dist., Salt Lake City, 1963-64; tchr. indsl., distributive edn. Provo (Utah) High Sch., 1964—. Del. to Republican State Conv., Utah County Conv., 1966; Rep. dist. voting chmn.; active Boy Scouts Am. Served with U.S. Army, 1950-53. Recipient Silver Beaver award Boy Scouts Am., 1976. Mem. Am. Vocat. Assn., Utah Vocat. Assn., Utah Edn. Assn., NEA, Provo Edn. Assn. (pres. 1973-74), Phi Delta Kappa. Mormon. Club: Provo Lions. Home: 1361 N 1160 W Provo UT 84604 Office: Provo High Sch 1125 N University Ave Provo UT 84601

CHRISTMAN, HELEN DOROTHY NELSON, resort exec.; b. Denver, Nov. 25, 1922; d. Hector C. and Dorothy C. (Hansen) Russell; student Colo. U., 1940-42; m. James Ray Christman, Aug. 7, 1942; children—J. Randol, Linda Rae. TV producer KRMA, Denver, 1960-62; resident mgr. Mana Kai Maui, Maui, Hawaii, 1974-76, exec. coordinator, 1976—; sec.-treas. Resort Apts. Inc., 1973—; v.p. HDC, Inc., 1976—; producer Gourmet Cooking Show, KRMA-TV, 1960-62. Pres., Stephen Knight PTA, Denver, 1957; radio and TV chmn. Colo. PTA, 1958-59; producer ednl. TV programs for PTA, Denver County, 1960-61. Bd. dirs. Kihai Aloha Assn., 1977-78, Maui United Way, 1983—. Mem. Delta Delta Delta. Address: 2960 S Kihei Rd Kihei Maui HI 96753

CHRISTMAS, RICHARD JUDSON, counselor, educator; b. Vicksburg, Miss., May 10, 1945; s. James Yancy and Elva (Downing) C.; m. Nancy Lou Napier, Aug. 20, 1966. B.S., U. So. Miss., 1967; M.A., U. No. Colo., 1972, Ed.S., 1974, Ph.D., 1980. Counselor, VA Info. Ctr., U. No. Colo., Greely, 1971-73; social sci. program specialist U.S. Army, Germany, 1974-75; guidance counselor, Bad Aibling, W.Ger., 1975-78; counselor, guidance and placement specialist Colo. Mountain Coll., Leadville, 1980—. Vice pres. Leadville Raiders, 1982-83. Served to capt. U.S. Army, 1967-70. Mem. Am. Vocat. Assn., Colo. Vocat. Assn., Colo. Guidance and Personnel Assn. Club: Lions (pres. 1983-84), Elks, Leadville Raiders (v.p. 1983). Office: Colo Mountain Coll Leadville CO 80461

CHRISTOFFERSEN, RALPH EARL, univ. adminstr.; b. Elgin, Ill., Dec. 4, 1937; s. Arthur and Mary (Frank) C.; B.S., Cornell Coll., 1959; Ph.D. (NIH predoctoral fellow), Ind. U., 1964; postgrad. (NIH Postdoctoral fellow), U. Nottingham (Eng.), 1964-65, Iowa State U. (NIH Postdoctoral fellow), 1965-66; m. Barbara L. Hibbard, June 10, 1961; children—Kirk Alan, Rachel Anne. Asst. prof. chemistry U. Kans., Lawrence, 1966-69, asso. prof., 1969-72, prof., 1972-81, asst. vice chancellor acad. affairs, 1974-75, asso. vice chancellor acad. affairs, 1976-79, vice chancellor acad. affairs, 1979-81; pres. Colo. State U., Fort Collins, 1981—; cons., 1969—; frequent speaker Kans. High Sch. Honors Banquets, civic clubs. Standard Oil scholar, 1958-59; Alfred P. Sloan fellow, 1971-73; Vis. Fgn. Scientist award Govt. W. Ger., 1970. Mem. Am. Chem. Soc., Am. Phys. Soc., Am. Inst. Chemists, AAUP, Internat. Soc. Quantum Biology (pres. 1977-79), Sigma Xi. Editorial adv. bd. Computers in Chemistry, 1975-81, Jour. Medicinal Chemistry, 1975-79. Contbr. numerous articles to profl. publs. Office: 102 Administration Bldg Colorado State U Ft Collins CO 80523

CHRISTOFFERSON, JOHN D., interior designer, interior design educator; b. Lehi, Utah, July 14, 1951; s. Dean DeWitt and Lucile (Chamberlain) C.; m. Shauna Jean Thompson, Oct. 8, 1975; children—Timothy, Daniel, Melissa. B.S., Brigham Young U., 1977. Cert. Nat. Council Interior Design Qualification. With Bel-Marin Interiors, Pleasant Grove, Utah, 1974-75; interior designer Woodmere Interiors, Bountiful, Utah, 1977; sr. interior designer planning and archtl. div. Brigham Young U., 1977—, also instr. comml. interior design; owner, designer Chris Designs, Ltd., Orem, Utah, 1979—. Served with Army N.G., 1969-77. Recipient Outstanding Sophomore award Brigham Young U., 1975; Jack H. West Design scholar, 1976. Mem. Am. Soc. Interior Designers. Republican. Mormon. Designer 4 bldgs. and 2 bldg. additions Brigham Young U., 1977-82. Home: 1128 W 1420 N Orem UT 84057 Office: 240 Brewster Bldg Brigham Young U Provo UT 84602

CHRISTOFFERSON, LEONARD ISAAC, ironworks company executive, structural engineer; b. Rock Springs, Wyo., Dec. 11, 1930; s. Isaac and Mildred (Mouritsen) C.; m. Mildred Jean Case, June 4, 1954; children—Bonnie Lee, Clair Leonard; m. 2d, Kate Mary Wilding, July 2, 1966. B.S. in Civil Engring., U. Tah, 1956. Registered profl. engr., Utah. Field engr. Chgo. Bridge and Iron Co., 1956-58, design engr., 1958-59, shop engr., 1959-64, shop supt., 1964-67, mfg. mgr., Houston, 1967-69, mfg. mgr., Australia, 1969-72, ops. mgr., 1972-74, mfg. mgr., Salt Lake City, 1974-83, project mgr. Golden Gate Bridge deck replacement, 1983—; dir. Indsl. Relations Council. Active Salt Lake City Jr. Achievement. Served with U.S. Army, 1951-53. Mormon. Club: Fort Douglas.

CHRISTOPHER, RICHARD SCOTT, journalist, editor, marketing executive; b. Chgo., May 21, 1953; s. James J. and Geraldine A. (Kaulback) C. B.J., U. Mo.-Columbia, 1975. Gen. assignment reporter Salem (Mo.) News, 1975; news editor, tech. writer AVMA Schaumburg, Ill., 1975-77; sports reporter Paddock Publs., Arlington Heights, Ill., 1977-78; assoc. editor, mktg. coordinator Farm and Land Inst/Nat. Assn. Realtors, Chgo., 1978-80; mgr. project services Kiwanis Internat., Chgo., 1980-82; acct. exec. Eckis Advt. & Design, Irvine, Calif., 1982-83; mktg. media specialist TRW, Orange, Calif., 1983—; editor, advt. mgr. Nat. Assn. Ind. Ins. Adjusters, Chgo., 1982—. Recipient Bronze award Internat. Film & TV Festival of N.Y., 1981, 82. Mem. Internat. Assn. Bus. Communicators, Pub. Relations Soc. Am. Roman Catholic. Club: Kiwanis.

CHRISTOPHER, STEVEN LEE, clergyman; b. Long Beach, Calif., May 29, 1956; s. Lehland James and Harriet Ann (Werner) C.; B.S. in Edn., Luth. Tchrs. Diploma, Dir. Christian Edn. cert., Concordia Tchrs. Coll., Seward, Nebr., 1979; m. Doris Dianne Deterding, Aug. 19, 1978. Dir. Christian edn. intern Peace Luth. Ch., Texas City, Tex., 1977-78; minister youth and edn. Bethany Luth. Ch., Long Beach, Calif., 1979—; workshop leader S.D. Luth. Dist. Youth Gathering, 1977; facilitator Tex. Dist. Luth. Youth Gathering, 1977; mem. Dir. Christian Edn. curriculum rev. com. Concordia Tchrs. Coll., Seward, 1979; chmn. planning com. So. Calif. Luth. Dist. High Sch. Youth Camp, 1980; mem. So. Calif. Luth. Dist. Youth Com., 1980—, facilities chmn. So. Calif. Luth. Dist. Youth Gathering, 1981, group life chmn., chmn., 1983—; 1982; workshop leader So. Calif. Dist. Sunday Sch. Conv., 1981, 83; mem. back home ministries Com. Luth. Ch.-Mo. Synod Youth Gathering, 1983; planning com. So. Calif. Dist./Calif.-Nev.-Hawaii Dist. Dir. Christian Edn. Conf., 1984. Mem. Luth. Edn. Assn.-Theol. Educators in Asso. Ministries. Contbr. articles to religious jours. Office: 4644 Clark Ave Long Beach CA 90808

CHRISTOPHERSON, DANIEL ALFRED, marketing executive; b. Ames, Iowa, Nov. 21, 1947; s. John L. and Simone H. (Mathis) C.; m. Anne Prochoruk, Dec. 20, 1969; 1 dau., Stephanie Anne. B.S. in Journalism, U. Colo., 1970. Sports writer Colorado Springs (Colo.) Sun, 1970; dir. pub. relations First Nat. Bank of Denver, 1970-78; writer Denver Post, 1972; pub. relations dir. Vail (Colo.) Assocs., 1978-80; dir. mktg. Beaver Creek (Colo.), 1980; v.p., dir. mktg. Empire Savs., Denver, 1980—; cons. in mktg. Mem. organizing com. Jerry Ford Celebrity Ski Cup, 1980; media ops. dir. Gerald Ford Invitational Golf Tournament, 1978-80; active Denver Internat. Film Festival, 1978-82, chmn., pres., 1981-82. Mem. Pub. Relations Soc. Am. (accredited, Golf Pick award for best spl. event 1982), Denver Advt. Fed. (bd. dirs. 1983—, 1 Grant Alfie, 2 Alfie awards 1982, 83), Sales and Mktg. Execs. Internat. (bd. dirs. 1983—), Savs. Inst. Mktg. Soc., Internat. Assn. Bus. Communicators (pres. Colo. chpt. 1976). Lutheran. Writer and asst. dir. spl. Olympics TV documentary, 1983. Office: Empire Savings 1654 Calif St Denver CO 80202

CHRISTOPHERSON, TERRY LEE, fire fighting equipment sales consultant; b. Portland, Oreg., Aug. 18, 1950; s. Lee V. and Ruth E. (Grove) C.; m. Stephanie Lee Patrick, Dec. 15, 1970; children—Aaron Lee, Adam Lee. Student Portland State U., Multnomah Sch. of the Bible, 1972. Fire fighting equipment sales cons. Huser Sales and Service, Portland, 1981—. Recipient various co. sales awards. Mem. Am. Soc. Safety Engrs., Internat. Soc. Fire Service Instrs. Republican. Baptist.

CHRISTY, JAMES WALTER, astrophysicist; b. Milw., Sept. 15, 1938; s. Walter W. and Mary (Nistor) C.; m. Charlene M. Crockett, Nov. 22, 1975; children—David J., Teresa E., James R., Nola M. B.S., U. Ariz., 1967. Astronomer, U.S. Naval Obs., Flagstaff, Ariz., 1962-71, U.S. Naval Obs., Washington, 1971-82; physicist Hughes Aircraft Co., Tucson, 1982—; astronomer U. Ariz., Tucson, 1983—. Mem. Internat. Astron. Union, Am. Astron. Assn., Astron. Soc. of Pacific. Club: Explorers (N.Y.C.). Research and publs. on spectrography and radial velocities of stars, color photography of galaxies, astronomy of nearby stars, double stars, planetary satellites; Discoverer and named Charon, the moon of Planet Pluto, 1978. Office: PO Box 11337 Bldg 802-2 Tucson AZ 85734

CHRISTY, WALTER KEITH, educational administrator; b. Lawrence, Kans., Sept. 20, 1942; s. Raymond Wayne and Edith Elizabeth (Mollhagen) C.; m. Randi Augusta Gerretson, June 10, 1961; children—David Wayne, Dana Lynn. B.A., U. No. Colo., 1963; M.A., U. Colo., 1967, Ed.D., 1977. Cert. adminstr., Colo. Tchr. Colorado Springs (Colo.) Pub. Schs., 1963-69, elem. sch. prin., 1969-77; adminstrv. prin., area supt. 1977-78, asst. supt. instrn., 1978—; adj. prof. U. Colo.-Colorado Springs; cons. Colo. Dept. Edn. Deacon, elder 1st Presbyterian Ch.; mem. Palmer Drug Abuse Community Service Bd. Mem. Am. Assn. Sch. Adminstrs., Colo. Assn. Sch. Execs., Assn. for Sch. and Curriculum Devel. (bd. dirs. Colo. 1980—). Republican. Presbyterian. Home: 2119 Bryant Ave Colorado Springs CO 80909 Office: 1115 N El Paso St Colorado Springs CO 80903

CHU, HILBERT KWOK-HO, acct.; b. Hong Kong, Oct. 17, 1950; s. Man Yui and Shuk Hin (Wong) C., A.B. with distinction, U. Calif., Berkeley, 1972, M.B.A., 1974; J.D., U. San Diego, 1982; m. Peggy Mak, Sept. 6, 1975; children—Agnes, Jennifer. Sr. tax specialist Peat Marwick Mitchell & Co., San Diego and Tucson, 1974-77; pres., chmn. bd. KCOO Devel. Co., Inc., San Diego, 1979—; prin. Hilbert K. Chu, C.P.A., San Diego, 1977—. Treas., 1st Chinese So. Baptist Ch., San Diego, 1977-78, 82—; mem. fin. com. So. Baptist Assn. of San Diego, 1978-81. Mem. Am. Inst. C.P.A.s, Calif. Soc. C.P.A.s. Clubs: Kiwanis, Christian Businessmen's Com. Office: 3434 4th Ave Suite 120 San Diego CA 92103

CHU, JUDY MAY, psychologist, educator; b. Los Angeles, July 7, 1953; d. Judson and May (Lum) Chu; m. Michael Francis Eng, Aug. 8, 1978. B.A. in Math., UCLA, 1974; M.A., Calif. Sch. Profl. Psychology, 1977, Ph.D., 1979. Instr., UCLA Asian Am. Studies, 1980—; asst. prof. psychology Los Angeles City Coll., 1981—. Co-chmn., Orgn. Chinese Am. Women, Los Angeles 1982. U. Calif. Regents scholar, 1970-74; Am. Psychol. Assn. minority fellow, 1978-79. Mem. NOW (co-chmn. minority women's task force), Asian Pacific Women's Network (dir.), Am. Psychol. Assn., Calif. Psychol. Assn., Western Psychol. Assn., Nat. Women's Studies Assn. Contbr. articles to profl. jours. Office: 855 N Vermont Ave Los Angeles CA 90029

CHU, KWANG-WEN, economist, educator, researcher; b. Jiangsu Province, China, May 5, 1935; came to U.S. 1960, naturalized 1974; s. Chih-tang and Shu-shan (Yuan) C.; m. Stella C. Chu, June 15, 1968; 1 son, Eric. B.A., Nat. Taiwan U., 1958; M.A., U. Minn., 1962; Ph.D., UCLA, 1972; cert. real estate proficiency Fullerton Coll., 1977. Research assoc. dept. econs. UCLA, 1966-67, asst. prof. Grad. Sch. Bus., U.S. Internat. U., 1967-70; asst. prof. econs. Calif. State U., 1970-74, assoc. prof., 1974-79, prof., 1979—; del. Calif. State House Conf. on Aging, 1981. Pres., Chinese Cultural Renaissance Assn. So. Calif., 1980—. Sun Yat-sen fellow, 1960-62; recipient United Chinese-Am. League Spl. award, 1978. Mem. Am. Econs. Assn., Western Econs. Assn., Econometric Soc., Chinese Am. Profl. Soc. Pi Gamma Nu, Beta Gamma Mu, Omicron Delta Epsilon. Contbr. to profl. jours. Office: Dept Econs Calif State U Fullerton CA 92634

CHU, LILY, psychologist, educator; b. Tai Wan, Jan. 4, 1942; d. Hui-Ping and Zanna Chu; m. Harold M. Bergsma, July 14, 1974; children—Phyllis, Harley. B.S., Nat. Taiwan U., 1963; M.A., U. N.Mex., 1970, Ph.D., 1973. Cert. sci. tchr., N. Mex. Med. technologist St. Joseph Hosp., Albuquerque, 1968-70; asst. prof. Lake Superior State Coll., Sault Ste. Marie, Mich., 1973-77; dir. project minorities women N. Mex. State U., 1977-79; asst. prof. U. Tex.-El Paso, 1979—. Vice chmn. Las Cruces chpt. Friends Free China. Nat. Inst. Edn. multipurpose model grantee, 1977-79; office Edn. health professions grantee, 1979-80. Mem. Am. Psychol. Assn., Am. Ednl. Research Assn., Am. Soc. Clin. Pathologists, Asian-Am. Mental Health Research Center. Contbr. articles to profl. jours. Office: Dept Educational Psychology U Tex El Paso TX 79968

CHUANG, HAROLD HWA-MING, accountant; b. Hong Kong, Feb. 13, 1941; s. Hung-Chuan and Chih-Chuan (Wu) C.; M.B.A., UCLA, 1969; m. Christina Chu, Apr. 1974; children—Harrison, William. Sr. in charge Touche Ross & Co., Los Angeles, 1970-75; div. controller Standex Internat., Los Angeles, 1975-77; mng. partner Hwang & Chuang Accountancy Corp., Los Angeles, 1977—. Bd. dirs. So. Calif. Chinese Businessmen's Assn., 1979-81; mem. U.S.A.-Republic of China Econ. Council, 1979-81. C.P.A., Calif. Mem. Calif. Soc. C.P.A.'s, Am. Inst. C.P.A.'s, Calif. Tamkang U. Alumni Assn. (pres.), Chinese U. Alumni Assn. Am. (chmn.). Club: Los Angeles Athletic. Office: 707 Wilshire Blvd Suite 1760 Los Angeles CA 90017

CHUBB, HENDON, psychologist; b. N.Y.C., Mar. 1, 1933; s. Percy and Corinne Roosevelt (Alsop) C.; m. Nita Colgate, June 7, 1958; children—Ann Caroline, Oliver; m. 2d, Phyllis Lancaster Nauts, June 12, 1982. B.A., Yale U., 1954, M.A., Adelphi U., 1976, Ph.D., 1978. With Chubb & Son Inc., N.Y.C., 1957-74, dir., chief fin. officer, sr. v.p., 1970-74, also dir. and/or sr. v.p. and/or chief fin. officer Chubb Corp., Fed. Ins. Co., Vigilant Ins. Co., Colonial Life Ins. Co. Am., United Life and Accident Ins. Co., Fed. Bus. Products; sr. psychologist Kings County Hosp., Bklyn., 1977-80; psychologist Kaiser Permanente Med. Center, Martinez, Calif., 1980—; pres. Chubb Found., 1967-74. Mem. Council Fgn. Relations, N.Y.C. Served with U.S. Army, 1954-56. Mem. Am. Psychol. Assn. Democrat. Author: John La Farge and The Ascension, An Early Case of Japanese Influence on An American Intellectual, 1961; Strategic Brief Therapy in A Clinic Setting, 1982. Home: 722 Santa Barbara Rd Berkeley CA 94707 Office: 200 Muir Rd Martinez CA 94552

CHUCK, THOMAS EDWARD, computer sales representative; b. Chgo., Feb. 11, 1947; s. Harris and Muriel Eileen Chuck; A.A., Palomar Coll., 1968; B.A., U. San Diego, 1972; M.B.A., Nat. U., 1981. Store mgr. Hoagy's Corner, Pacific Beach and Oceanside, Calif., 1977-78; retail sales clk. Boise Cascade BMC Co., Oceanside, 1978-79; sales rep. Mktg. Profls., Inc., San Marcos, Calif., 1979-80, San Diego Floor Covering Supply, San Marcos, 1980-82, DBS Computer Systems, 1982-83, Westrim Computer Solutions, 1983—. Sec., Oceanside-Carlsbad Jaycees,

1978, pres., 1980; mem. North San Diego County Vets. Employment Com.; softball umpire Margarita Ofcls. Assn., 1982. Served with USMC, 1969-71, 72-75; mem. Res. Mem. Marine Corps Res. Officers Assn. (v.p. San Luis Rey chpt. 1980, pres. chpt. 1981), Res. Officers Assn. Home: 1507 San Jose Oceanside CA 92054 Office: 2382-K Camino Vida Roble Carlsbad CA 92008

CHUCK, WALTER G(OONSUN), lawyer; b. Wailuku, Maui, T.H., Sept. 10, 1920; s. Hong Yee and Aoe (Ting) C.; Ed.B., U. Hawaii, 1941; J.D., Harvard, 1948; m. Marian Chun, Sept. 11, 1943; children—Jamie Allison, Walter Gregory, Meredith Jayne. Navy auditor, Pearl Harbor, 1941; field agt. Social Security Bd., 1942; labor law insp. Terr. Dept. Labor, 1943; admitted to Hawaii bar, 1949; law clk. Ropes, Gray, Best, Coolidge & Rugg, 1948; asst. pub. prosecutor City and County of Honolulu, 1949; with Fong, Miho & Choy, 1950-53; mem. Fong, Miho, Choy & Chuck, 1953-58; practicing individually, Honolulu, 1958-65; partner firm Chuck & Fujiyama, 1965-74, Chuck, Wong & Tonaki, 1974-76, Chuck & Pai, 1976-78; individual practice law, Honolulu, 1978—; mem. Walter G. Chuck, A Law Corp., 1980—; treas. M. & W, Inc.; gen. partner Tripler Warehousing Co., Kapalama Investment Co.; dir. Pacific Resources, Inc., Hawaiian Ind. Refinery, Inc., Enerco, Inc., Gasco, Inc., Princess Pauahi Coffee Shop Inc. Dist. magistrate Dist. Ct. Honolulu, 1956-63; Hawaii Employment relations Bd., 1955-59; dir. Nat. Assn. State & Labor Relations Bd., 1957-61; chief clk. Ho. of Reps., 1951, 53; govt.- appeal agt. SSS, 1953-72; clk. of senate State of Hawaii, 1959-61;mem. Jud. Council, State of Hawaii. Served as captain inf. Hawaii Territorial Guard. Mem. Bar Assn. Hawaii (pres.). Am. (ho. of dels.), Hawaii bar assns. (mem. exec. com., jud. appointment com.), Asso. Students U. Hawaii, Chinese C. of C., Internat. Soc. Barristers, Law-sci, Inst. Republican. Clubs: Waialae Country (pres., dir.); Pacific Oahu Country. 2691 AAliamanu Pl Honolulu HI 96813 Office: Suite 200 1022 Bethel St Honolulu HI 96813

CHUKS-ORJI, CHARLES EJIMOFOR, mfg. co. exec.; b. Enugu, Nigeria, Nov. 21, 1940; s. Orji and Maria (Nneze) (Nwachukwu); B.A., U. San Francisco, 1964, M.B.A., 1968; Ph.D., Calif. Christian U., Los Angeles, 1978. Came to U.S., 1960, naturalized, 1968. Ins. staff Golden State Mut. Ins. Co., Los Angeles, 1968-69, staff mgr., 1969-71; owner, operator franchise McDonald's, Oakland, Calif., 1971—; founder, owner Milanco Export Corp., Oakland, 1976—; dir. McDonald's Operators of Oakland, Unux Exco Co.; pres. Chuks-Orji Consol. Services, Oakland, 1977—; dir. Chuks-Orji Fin. and Ins. Co., Oakland, 1979—; chmn. exec. com. Macon's Group of Cos. Ltd., 1979—; group dir. Macon's Group (U.K.) Ltd., 1979—; pub. Oakland First mag., 1982; exec. producer Total Entertainment Networks. Mem. Am.-Nigerian C. of C., Nigerian-Calif. C. of C. (founder). Republican. Roman Catholic. Rotarian. Home: 919 45th St PO Box 3001 Oakland CA 94609 Office: McDonald's 4514 Telegraph Ave Oakland CA 94609

CHUN, DAI HO, educational consultant; b. Waipio, Hamakua, Hawaii, Jan. 8, 1905; s. Hin and Shee (Kwock) C.; B.A. with honors, U. Hawaii, 1930, M.A., 1937; Ph.D., Ohio State U., 1947. Tchr. pub. schs. Hawaii, 1930-41; dir. placement and ednl. vocat. guidance, 1941-42; asst. prof. edn., supr. practice teaching U. Hawaii, Honolulu, 1945-51, asso. prof. edn., 1951-56, prof., 1956-70, prof. emeritus, 1970—; dir. Internat. Coop. Center Hawaii, 1956-61; exec. dir. Inst. Tech. Interchange, East-West Center, 1961-69, dir. Tech. and Devel. Inst., 1969-70; internat. ednl., mgmt. and devel. cons., Honolulu, 1970—; adviser Hawaii Tng. Council, 1968-70, Utah State U. East-West Inst., 1972—; cons. to Pacific Investment Fund, 1957-58, Pacific Mgmt., Ltd., 1957-58; dir. Security Assos. Ltd., Honolulu, 1956-60. Mem. Gov.'s Commn. on Pub. Edn., 1956-60; state chmn. 11th Anniversary UN, 1956; mem. bd. mgrs. Mid-Pacific Inst., 1946-47, sec., 1946; mem. Community Chest Steering Com., Honolulu, 1960-61. Served to lt. col. USAAF, 1942-45. Recipient Distinguished Service award U. Hawaii Alumni Assn., 1959; trustees' award U. Hawaii Found., 1982; fellow Ohio State U., 1951; research fellow Joint Council on Econ. Edn., 1952. Fellow Progressive Edn. Assn., Internat. Inst. Arts and Letters.; mem. Mensa, AAUP (v.p. Hawaii chpt.1955-56), Internat. Platform Assn., John Dewey Soc., Soc. Internat. Devel., Air Force Assn., Hawaii Union (pres. 1929-30), Phi Beta Kappa (counselor 1953-55), Phi Kappa Phi, Pi Gamma Mu (sec.-treas. 1947), Delta Sigma Rho, Phi Delta Kappa. Club: Rotary (dir. 1960-62). Author: Mooneys Problem Check List, 1942; Personal Problems of Adolescent Youth (script and film strip), 1952; editor: University High School Curriculum Guide, 1955; Hawaii-U.S.A.: Resources for Technical Assistance, 1958; Hawaii's Training Resources, 1959. Home and Office: 1588 Laukahi St Honolulu HI 96821

CHUNG, ANNA WON KYUNG, optometrist; b. Honolulu; d. Earl C. Chung and Chai Bok Kim Chung. Student U. Hawaii, 1945-47; O.D., Pa. Coll. Optometry, 1950. Lic. optometrist, Hawaii, Pa., N.C. Pvt. practice optometry, Honolulu, 1951—; mem. Nat. Save Your Vision Week TV panel, 1955; bd. examiners optometry State of Hawaii, 1981—, v.p., 1982-83. Bd. regents U. Hawaii, 1975-79; bd. dirs. Goodwill Industries, 1970-83; pres. Friends of East-West Ctr., 1968; mem. Honolulu City and County Status of Women Commn., 1971-75, vice chmn., 1973. Mem. Hawaii Optometric Assn. (officer 1953-55), Am. Optometric Assn. Episcopalian. Office: 1154 Fort St Mall Suite #310 Honolulu HI 96813

CHUNG, HARVEY HSIU-HSIONG, engineer, corporate executive; b. Taiwan, July 6, 1940; s. Chuan and Chien (Yang) C.; m. Sharon Lee, July 16, 1966 (div. Sept. 15, 1983); children—Kevin, Tanya, Alica. Diploma in Chem. Engring., Taipei (Taiwan) Inst. Tech., 1972; B.S. in Chem. Engring., U. Maine, 1966; M.S. in Plastics, Lowell Tech. Inst., 1977. Research chem. engr. Am. Cyanamid Co., Havre de Grace, Md., 1967-70; sr. devel. chemist U.S. Polymeric Inc., Santa Ana, Calif., 1970-72; staff scientist Avco, Lowell, Mass., 1972-74; materials and processing mgr. Aldila Inc., San Diego, 1974-76; sr. research engr. Lockheed Aircraft Corp., Burbank, Calif., 1976-78; pres. KTA Co. Inc., Westminster, Calif., 1978—. Mem. Soc. Aerospace Material and Processing Engrs. Developer resin system for graphite tennis racket use. Home: 9799 Red River Circle Fountain Valley CA 92708 Office: 7382 Bolsa Ave Westminster CA 92683

CHUNG, JIN SOO, ocean mining and offshore mining engr.; b. Seoul, Korea, Jan. 27, 1937; s. Hyun Mo and Soon Mo (Yoo) C.; B.S.E. in Naval Architecture, Seoul Nat. U., 1961; M.S., U. Calif., Berkeley, 1964; Ph.D. in Engring. Mechanics, U. Mich., 1969; m. Yang Ja Park, Aug. 11, 1967; children—Claude H., Christine M. Sr. research engr. Exxon Prodn. Research Co., Houston, 1969-73; staff engr. Lockheed Missiles & Space Co., Sunnyvale, Calif., 1973-80; prof. Colo. Sch. Mines, Golden, 1980—; cons. in hydrodynamics to Inter-Govtl. Maritime Consultative Orgn., UN, 1981; chmn., editor Proceedings of 1st Offshore Mechanics/Arctic Engring./Deepsea Systems Symposium, New Orleans, 1982, chmn., editor 2d Internat. Symposium, Houston, 1983, 3d Internat. Symposium, New Orleans, 1984. Recipient Eugene W. Jacobson award Energy Tech. Conf., Houston, 1978. Mem. ASME (Ralph James award 1980, policy bd. communication 1981—, chmn. offshore mechanics com., 1982—, paper revs. chmn. Petroleum Div. 1980—), Am. Inst. Mining Engrs., Soc. Petroleum Engrs., Soc. Naval Architects Japan, Sigma Xi. Sr. editor Transactions Jour. of Energy Resources Tech., 1980—; pioneer in advanced tech. devel. and position control simulation of deep ocean mining system. Home: 12757 W 57th Dr Arvada CO 80002 Office: Colo Sch Mines Golden CO 80401

CHURCH, JOHN HARTLEY, county ofcl.; b. Monson, Mass., Jan. 24, 1931; s. Leon Henry and Gertrude Audrey (Madden) C.; B.S., Seattle U., 1966; m. Clarine Helen Lund, June 11, 1966; children—Phillip Irvine, Gerald Ernest, Dennis Emmett, Michael John. Office mgr. Seattle-King County Health Dept., Seattle, 1958-66, fiscal mgr., 1968—; accountant United Aircraft Corp., East Hartford, Conn., 1966-68. Mem. Com. to Organize Dept. of Social and Health Services, State of Wash., 1971. Served with U.S. Army, 1948-54. Decorated Bronze Star, Purple Heart. Mem. Wash. State Public Health Assn. (exec. dir. 1970-76), Am. Acad. Health Adminstrn. (pres. 1975), Am. Public Health Assn. Home: 28607 SE 225th St Maple Valley WA 98038 Office: 7th Floor 400 Yesler Bldg 400 Yesler Way Seattle WA 98104

CHURCH, LARRY JAMES, vocational agriculture educator, farmer; b. Ontario, Oreg., July 17, 1946; s. Joseph P. and Leona L. (Huber) C.; m. Gail Marie Nuttman, Aug. 10, 1968; children—Dianna, Jeff, Bob, Jacque. B.S. in Agrl. Edn., U. Idaho, 1968, M.S., 1973. Vocat. agr. instr., Future Farmers Am. adviser Vallivue High Sch., Caldwell, Idaho, 1968—. Religious edn. tchr. St. Aloysious Catholic Ch. Recipient Hon. State Farmer degree Idaho Future Farmers Am. Assn., 1976, Hon. Am. Farmer degree Nat. Future Farmers Am. Assn., 1980. Mem. Idaho Vocat. Agr. Tchrs. Assn., Idaho Vocat. Assn., Nat. Vocat. Agr. Tchrs. Assn., Idaho Duroc Assn., Southwest Idaho Pork Producers Assn., Nat. Pork Producers Assn. Home: Rt 1 PO Box 201-A Fruitland ID 83619

CHURCH, NATHAN, clinical sociologist, educational administrator; b. Helena, Mont., Nov. 27, 1951; s. Jack Levain and Bertie Lou (Lancaster) C.; m. Deborah Gail Chivers, Sept. 2, 1972; children—Nate, Tasha. B.S. in Sociology and Psychology, Portland State U., 1975, M.S. in Sociology, 1977; Ph.D. in Sociology, Rutgers U., 1981. Mem. faculty Columbia Christian Coll., Portland, Oreg., 1975-77; teaching asst. sociology dept. Douglass Coll. Rutgers U., New Brunswick, N.J., 1978-80; adminstrv. dir. health, counseling, career services, adj. prof. sociology Pepperdine U., Malibu, Calif., 1980—; leader workshops on marriage, famiy, sexuality, clin. sociology. Mem. Am. Sociol. Assn., Clin. Sociology Assn., Soc. for Sci. Study Religion, Am. Coll. Health Assn., Am. Personnel and Guidance Assn. Mem. Churches of Christ. Home: 4327 Kimberwick Ln Moorpark CA 93021 Office: Counseling Services Pepperdine U Malibu CA 90265

CHURCH, PEARL DEE, artist; b. N.Y.C., Nov. 16, 1907; d. Harry and Mollie (Miller) Friedman; B.A., Barnard Coll., 1928; postgrad. U. Mich., 1936, Am. U., 1956; M.A., Ohio U., 1938; m. Donald E. Church, June 16, 1929; 1 son, Russell M. Advt. research Churchill-Hall, N.Y.C., 1928-30; vocat. counselor USES, 1936-38; dir. Athens (Ohio) Guidance Bur., 1938-41; occupational research Office Def. Moblzn., 1942-43; profl. artist, 1955—; originator stone collage and mazdalith techniques; one man shows Madison Gallery, N.Y.C., 1961, Collectors Gallery, Washington, 1958, 62, Bridge Gallery, N.Y.C., 1964-66, Massillon (Ohio) Mus. Arts, 1967, Internat. Gem Show, 1969, Town East Gallery, 1970, Goldman Fine Arts Gallery, 1972-75; one-man traveling shows at Arlington and Alexandria (Va.) pub. libraries, 1966, also tour at 10 Southwest museums, 1972-73; works permanently exhibited Nat. Petroleum Council, Smithsonian Inst., Nev. Mus. Art (Reno), Wellfleet Art Gallery, Aden Gallery, Massillon Mus. Art, Am. Mus. Immigration, Randolph Macon, Houston Mus. Sci. Asst. dir. tng. Am. Women's Voluntary Services, 1941-42; vol. work neurospsychiat. wards at White Plains (N.Y.) Mental Hosp., USN Med. Center, St. Elizabeth's Hosp. (Washington); dir. Workshop Center of the Arts; mem. adv. council Sun City-Phoenix Art Mus., 1979-81, sec. pres., trustee, 1981—. Mem. adv. com. Nat. Acad. Scis. Recipient First prize S.E. Regional Art Exhibit, 1956, 60, Am. Pen Women's Art Exhibit, 1958, 61, 75. Mem. Nat. League Am. Pen Women (nat. art chmn.; past pres. Capital br.), Internat. Platform Assn. (bd. govs.; best in show 1967), Ikebana Internat. (pres. 1981-82), Artists Equity. Home and studio: 13401 N 107th Dr Sun City AZ 85351

CHURCHILL, LYNN FRANK, compensation and benefits executive, organization analysis manager; b. Port Huron, Mich., Sept. 13, 1942; s. Frank James and Dorothy Minnie (Treleaven) C.; m. Patricia Nann Cole, July 3, 1965; children—Heather Irene, Holly Ann. Student Gen. Motors Inst., 1960-62; B.S., Mich. State U., 1964; M.A., Central Mich. U. 1974. Coop. engring. student Buick Motor div. Gen. Motors Corp., Flint, Mich., 1960-62, mgmt. trainee personnel, Fisher Body div., Flint, 1966; asst. personnel dir. Central Mich. U., Mt. Pleasant, 1969-74; mgr. wage and salary adminstr. U. Mo.-Columbia, 1974-77; dir. compensation Gold Circle Stores div. Federated Dept. Stores, Columbus, Ohio, 1977-80; dir. compensation Freightliner Corp. div. Daimler-Benz, A.G., Portland, Oreg., 1980—. Served as lt. USNR, 1966-69. Mem. Am. Compensation Assn., Western Pension Conf. Mem. Christian Ch. (Disciples of Christ). Home: 14675 Sunrise Ln Tigard OR 97223 Office: 4747 N Channel Ave Portland OR 97208

CHURCHILL, PETER D., commercial photographer, and marketing consultant; b. N.Y.C., June 23, 1940; s. Clarence H. and Vivian L. (Baker) Drown; children—Mark, Christina, Michelle. B.A., U. Pacific, 1963; M.A., Calif. State U., Los Angeles, 1971; J.D., Am. Coll. Law, Anaheim, Calif., 1978. Mgr. store ops. Shakey Inc., Los Angeles, 1965-67; sales tng. mgr. Hallmark Cards, Inc., Los Angeles, 1967-77; asso. Purcell Real Estate, Inc., Los Angeles, 1977-78; nat. sales tng. coordinator Datsun, Los Angeles, 1978-80; gen. partner P & L Assos., Renton, Wash., 1980-82; regional mgr. Burns Internat. Security Services, Inc., 1980-82; owner Peter Churchill & Assocs., 1982—, Churchill Pictures, 1979—. Recipient Silver award for Datsun-The Front Runner, Internat. Film and TV Festival, 1980; Gold awards for A Matter of Pride, Houston Internat. Film Festival, 1981, U.S. Indsl. Film Festival, 1981. Mem. Am. Soc. Indsl. Security, Am. Mgmt. Assn., Am. Soc. Tng. and Devel., Assoc. Photographers Internat., Aircraft Owners and Pilots Assn., Nat. Assn. Underwater Instrs., Photographic Soc. Am., Am. Film Inst., Phi Kappa Tau, Phi Mu Alpha, Alpha Kappa Phi. Office: PO Box 276 Sunset Beach CA 90742

CHURCHILL, WILLIAM DELEE, educator, psychologist; b. Buffalo, Nov. 4, 1919; s. Glenn Luman and Ethel (Smith) C.; A.B., Colgate U., 1941; M.Ed., Alfred U., 1951; Ed.D., U. Rochester, 1969; m. Beulah Coleman, Apr. 5, 1943; children—Cherylee, Christie. Tchr. secondary sci., Canaseraga, N.Y., 1947-56; dir. guidance Alfred-Almond Sch., Almond, N.Y., 1956-63; grad. asst. U. Rochester, 1963-65; asst. prof. psychology Alfred (N.Y.) U., 1965-66; asso. prof. edn. Ariz. State U., Tempe, 1966—. Served to lt. col. USAAF, 1942-46; PTO. Mem. Am., Western, Ariz. psychol. assns., Am. Ednl. Research Assn. Author: Career Survey of Graduates, 1973. Home: 11454 N 85th St Scottsdale AZ 85260 Office: Univ Counseling Service Ariz State U Tempe AZ 85281

CHURCHMAN, VALERIE JOY, educator, reading consultant; b. Salt Lake City, July 19, 1932; d. A. Clark and Violet (Robinson) Robison; m. Wilson F. Churchman, Nov. 26, 1950; children—Terri Churchman Schmidt, Stacie Churchman Briggs, Leslie Churchman Knowles, Dan, David. B.A., Idaho State U., 1970; M.A. in Reading, Boise State U., 1980. Tchr. Shoshone (Idaho) Sch. Dist., coordinator basic skills, dir. Title 1 program; rep. Basic Skills Instrn. task force, 1980-82. Mem. Nat. Council Tchrs. English, Internat. Reading Assn., Assn. Supervision and Curriculum Devel. Roman Catholic. Co-author: Your Child Grows Through Discovery, 1974; Discover the Road to Success, 1981; Teen Trail to Success, 1982. Home: 210 W C St Shoshone ID 83352 Office: 410 Apple St Shoshone ID 83552

CHURCHWELL, RICHARD NELSON, mech. engr.; b. Oklahoma City, Feb. 20, 1955; s. Durward Joseph and Betty Ruth (Mead) C.; A.A., Glendale Community Coll., 1977; m. Lisa Carole Sutton, Nov. 21, 1976; 1 son, Joseph Wayne. Technician, Neubeck Engring., Phoenix, 1976-77; design draftsman Penn Athletic Products div. Gen. Tire & Rubber, Phoenix, 1977; mgr. research and devel. Ramada Energy Systems, Inc., Tempe, Ariz., 1977-81; engring. mgr. Gila River Products, Chandler, Ariz., 1981—. Home: 4013 S Mitchell Dr Tempe AZ 85282

CHURILLA, KENNETH R(AYMOND), mgmt. cons.; b. Hartford, Conn., Apr. 20, 1941; s. Albert Michael and Helen Anne (Smetana) C.; B.A., U. Conn., 1966; m. Miryam Elena Fortich, July 1, 1976. English master Laurelcrest Prep. Sch., Bristol, Conn., 1966-67; mktg. rep. IBM data processing div., New Haven, Conn., 1968; mktg. rep. IBM Service Bur. Co., N.Y.C., 1968-72; dir. data processing Delafield, Harvey, Tabell, Princeton, N.J., 1972-74; mgr. fin. mktg. Tymshare, Inc., Cupertino, Calif., 1974-80; sr. cons. for info. processing industry Input, Inc., Palo Alto, Calif., 1980—; propr. Almaden Stained Glass Co., San Jose, Calif., 1980—. Mem. Am. Mgmt. Assn., Nat. Computer Graphics Assn. Home: 6214 Meridian Ave San Jose CA 95120 Office: 2471 E Bayshore Rd Suite 600 Palo Alto CA 94303 also 4666 Meridian Ave San Jose CA 95118

CHUTE, PHILLIP BRUCE, business consultant, writer; b. Saugus, Mass., Aug. 19, 1938; s. Ernest Yorke and Dorothy Maude (Bruce) C.; m. Elizabeth Simpson Boyd, Apr. 2, 1960; children—Brian R., Elaine. Student Northeastern U., Boston, 1961-62; A.A., Pasadena City Coll., 1965; B.S., Calif. State U.-Los Angeles, 1977. With Dun & Bradstreet, 1961-62, Crocker Citizens Bank, 1962-64, Consol. Rock Products, 1965-67; numerous acctg. positions until 1974; pres. Phillip B. Chute Corp., 1975—. Served with U.S. Army, 1957-60. Mem. Nat. Assn. Pub. Accts., Nat. Soc. Enrolled Agts., Riverside C. of C., Riverside County Tax Cons. (pres. 1978). Author: Small Business and Computer Handbook, 1983. Home: 5608 Date St Alta Loma CA 91701 Office: Phillip B Chute Corp 6876 Indiana Ave Riverside CA 92506

CHVOSTAL, PAUL JOHN, mechanical engineer; b. McKees Rocks, Pa., May 17, 1930; s. John Martin and Mary Ann (Raynak) C.; m. Joan Paula Potocki, Sept. 6, 1952; children—Paula Jay, Paul John, Jay Ann, John Joseph. Engring. aide U.S. Army C.E., 1953-55; field engr. Civil Constrn., 1956-58; constrn. engr. Atlas and Titan missile sites, 1958-62; engr. technician and lab. mgr. Apollo Spacecraft Program and Unmanned Satellites, 1962-73; engring. mgr. Multi Link Electronics div. Odetics, Anaheim, Calif., 1973-80; mfg. mgr. Ametek Microelectronics, El Segundo, Calif., 1980-81; mech. engr., then mfg. mgr. Kode Inc., Tustin, Calif., 1981—. Served with USAF, 1947-53; Korea; Res. ret. Recipient citation NASA, 1977. Mem. AIAA, AF Assn., Am. Def. Preparedness Assn., U.S. Naval Inst., U.S. Strategic Inst. Democrat. Roman Catholic. Clubs: Jednota, Foresters. Inventor microminiature wire welder. Home: 6843 Mount Waterman Dr Buena Park CA 90620 Office: Tustin CA

CHYKALIUK, PETER BOHDAN, product development representative; b. Newark, Sept. 12, 1955; s. John and Oxana (Federuk) C.; m. Amanda Brigman, Jan. 6, 1979. B.S., Rutgers U., 1977; M.S. Tex. Tech. U., 1979; Ph.D., Okla. State U., 1981. Technician, Texas A&M Exptl. Sta., Lubbock, Tex., 1977; research asst. Tex. Tech. U., Lubbock, 1978-79; technician Monsanto Co., Lubbock, 1979; research asst. Okla. State U., Stillwater, 1979-81; product devel. rep. III Monsanto Co., 1981—. Recipient Wimberly Small Grains Grad. Achievement award Agronomy Dept., Okla. U., 1981. Mem. Council Agrl. Sci. and Tech., Weed Sci. Soc. Am., North Central Weed Control Conf., Western Weed Sci. Soc., Soil Conservation Soc., Wyoming Pest Council. Baptist. Contbr. articles to profl. jours.

CIARANELLO, ROLAND DAVID, physician, biomed. researcher; b. Schenectady, Feb. 27, 1943; s. Roland Victor and Carmella (Vertucci) C.; B.S., Union Coll., 1965; M.D., Stanford U., 1970; m. Nancy Jane Rogers, June 29, 1968; 1 dau., Andrea Lynne. Research asso. NIH, Bethesda, Md., 1971-74, intern, 1974-75; resident in psychiatry, child psychiatry Stanford U., 1974—, biomed. researcher, 1965—, asst. prof., 1977-81, asso. prof., 1981—, dir. Lab. Developmental Neurochemistry, 1976—, fellow in psychiatry, 1970-71. NIH research grantee, 1975—, Career Devel. award, 1978; NSF research grantee, 1978—. Mem. Am. Soc. Pharmacology and Exptl. Therapeutics, Am. Psychiat. Assn., Am. Coll. Neuropsychopharmacology Soc. Neurosci., AAAS, Sigma Xi. Contbr. articles to profl. publs.; researcher biochemistry, biochem. genetics, metabolic regulation, 1965—. Home: 996 Wing Pl Stanford CA 94305 Office: Dept Psychiatry Stanford Med Center Stanford CA 94305

CIARLO, JAMES ANTHONY, research psychologist; b. Steger, Ill., Nov. 12, 1933; s. Anthony Joseph and Bernice (Douglas) C.; B.A., U. Ill., 1955; A.M., Washington U., 1959; Ph.D., Harvard U., 1964; m. Dorothy Ann Day, Aug. 11, 1963; children—Catherine Hope, David Michael. Instr. asst. prof. psychology Wesleyan U., Middletown, Conn., 1963-65; research assoc., lectr. psychology U. Mich., Ann Arbor, 1965-68; dir. mental health research and evaluation Denver Dept. Health and Hosp., 1968-76; adj. asso. prof. psychology U. Denver, 1971-76, vis. asso. prof., 1976-77, vis. prof., 1977-80, research prof., 1980—; chmn. research and evaluation council Nat. Council Community Mental Health Centers, 1976-78; vis. faculty NIMH staff coll., 1976-78. Served with USAF, to 1st. lt., 1955-57. USPHS trainee in clin. psychology, 1959-62, research fellow, 1963; NIMH grantee in research, program evaluation, 1971—. Mem. Am. Pub. Health Assn. (council mental health sect. 1974-76), Colo. (dir. 1974-76), Am. psychol. assns., Phi Beta Kappa, Lambda Chi Alpha. Author books. Co-editor Community Mental Health Jour., 1979-81. Contbr. articles to profl. publs. Research in program evaluation community mental health centers. Home: 2365 Bellaire St Denver CO 80207 Office: 70 W 6th Ave Denver CO 80204

CIAVARELLI, ANTHONY PAUL, psychologist; b. Mincola, N.Y., Sept. 14, 1942; s. Anthony Peter and Anne (Imperato) C.; student U. Calif., Santa Barbara, 1963-66; B.A., Calif. State U., Los Angeles, 1968, M.A. in Exptl. Psychology, 1974; m. Carol Lee Souza, Sept. 5, 1964; 1 dau., Gina Lynn. Staff scientist Dunlap and Assos., Inc., Santa Monica, Calif., 1967-69, mng. scientist Western div., 1975-81; mng. performance measurement systems CUBIC Corp., San Diego, 1981—; sr. scientist Integrated Scis., Inc., Santa Monica, 1969-71; sr. research analyst Boeing Aerospace Co., Seattle, 1971-75. Chmn. ways and means com. Stella Maris Acad., La Jolla, 1979-80. Mem. Human Factors Soc., Soc. Info. Display. Republican. Roman Catholic. Club: Optimist (pres. 1978-79, hon. life mem.)(University City, Calif.). Editor-in-chief Tng. Tech. Jour. Home: 4171 Combe Way San Diego CA 92122 Office: 9333 Balboa Ave San Diego CA 92123

CIESNIEWSKI, ANTHONY RICHARD, business exec.; b. Chgo., Apr. 11, 1945; s. John and Josephine (Ernest) C.; ed. public schs.; children—Lisa Ann, Renee Marie. With ABC-TV, Chgo.; asst. chief engr. WTTW-TV, Chgo.; formerly dir. engring. Golden West Broadcasters, Los Angeles; now dir. engring. MetroTape/Metromedia, Los Angeles. Mem. Soc. Motion Picture and TV Engrs., Soc. Broadcast Engrs., Acad. TV Arts and Scis., Soc. TV Engrs. Office: 5746 Sunset Blvd Los Angeles CA 90028

CIHACEK, LARRY JOSEPH, plant nutritionist; b. North Bend, Nebr., Apr. 21, 1948; s. Albin Louis and Ceclia Georgia (Sousek) C.; B.S., U. Nebr., 1970, M.S., 1972; Ph.D., Iowa State U., 1979; m. Karen

Kay Fossler, Nov. 23, 1973; 1 dau., Laura Jean. Research asst. U. Nebr., Lincoln, 1970-73; research asst. Iowa State U., Ames, 1973-76, research asso., 1976-78; area research and extension plant nutritionist N.Mex. State U., Artesia, 1978—. Served to capt. N.Mex. N.G. Mem. Internat. Soc. Soil Sci., Am. Soc. Agronomy, AAAS, Soil Sci. Soc. Am., Council Agrl. Sci. and Tech., Sigma Xi, Alpha Zeta, Gamma Sigma Delta. Contbr. articles to profl. jours. Office: Route 1 Box 121 Artesia NM 88210

CIMINO, RICHARD ANGELO, broadcasting personality, actor; b. Gilroy, Calif., Dec. 17, 1929; s. Angelo and Laura Maria (Macchione) C.; student Hartnell Coll., 1948-50; m. Enid Lucile Kilburn, Dec. 9, 1962. Program mgr. Sta. KCRA, Sacramento, 1966-68; morning program host Sta. KNEW, Oakland, 1968-72; afternoon program host Sta. KSFO, San Francisco, 1974-77; ptnr. Charles Jewelry; owner Paradox Rehearsal Studios; pres. Rick Cimino, Inc.; owner comml. fishing vessels Zulu and African Queen; instr. voice, acting; freelance advt. voice. Served with U.S. Army, 1951-53. Recipient Best Radio Personality award TV-Radio Mirror mag., 1969; 4 CLIO awards, 1976, 2 awards, 1982; 2 Nat. Acad. TV Arts and Scis. awards, 1981; Gold medal 1982 Internat. Film Festival. Mem. Am. Advt. Fedn. (radio div. chmn. Am. Advt. Best in West awards), AFTRA, Screen Actors Guild, Italian Am. C. of C. Pacific Coast. Club: Il Cenacolo. Home: 7352 Stockton Ave El Cerrito CA 94530

CIOCCA, ARTHUR A., wine industry exec.; b. Tarrytown, N.Y., Dec. 5, 1937; s. Angelo Arthur and Helen Theresa C.; B.S., Coll. Holy Cross, 1959; M.B.A., Roosevelt U., 1963. Group product mgr. Gallo Winery, Modesto, Calif., 1968-73; gen. mgr. grocery products div. Oroweat, San Francisco, 1973-74; v.p. mktg. Franzia Winery, Ripon, Calif., 1974-75, pres., chief exec. officer, 1975-79; pres. The Wine Group Inc., Ripon, 1979-81; pres., owner, 1981—; v.p. Coca-Cola Bottling Co. Served with USNR, 1962. Mem. Calif. Wine Inst. (dir., mem. exec. com.), Young Pres. Orgn. Office: 177 Post St San Francisco CA

CIPRIANO, PATRICIA ANN, educator, consultant; b. San Francisco, Apr. 24, 1946; d. Ernest Peter and Claire Patricia (Croak) C. B.A. in English, Holy Names Coll., Oakland, Calif., 1967; M.A. in Edn. of Gifted, Calif. State U.-Los Angeles, 1980. Cert. tchr., tchr. spl. edn., adminstrv. service, Calif. Tchr. English, math. and bus. Bancroft Jr. High Sch., San Leandro, Calif., 1968-69, coordinator gifted edn., 1971-79; tchr. English, math. San Leandro High Sch., 1979—, coordinator gifted and talented edn., 1981—; cons. Calif. State Dept. Edn., various Calif. sch. dists. Recipient Hon. Service award Tchr. of Yr., Bancroft Jr. High Sch. PTA, 1973. Mem. Calif. Assn. for Gifted (rep. Region 3 tchr. com.), Assn. for Gifted, Nat. Assn. for Gifted, World Council Gifted and Talented, Central Calif. Council of Tchrs. English, Calif. Assn. Tchrs. English, Nat. Council Tchr. English, San Leandro Tchrs. Assn., Calif. Tchrs. Assn., NEA, Delta Kappa Gamma. Roman Catholic. Contbr. articles in field. Office: 1100 Bancroft Ave San Leandro CA 94577

CISCH, DOUGLASS STEPHEN, oil co. exec.; b. Hamilton, Ohio, Nov. 22, 1938; s. Alexander George and Helen Margaret (Stephenson) C.; B.S., Miami U., Ohio, 1960; postgrad. in Bus., U. Calif., Los Angeles, 1963-64; m. Carol Ann Campbell, Mar. 17, 1960; children—Jeffrey, Dawn, Bryan, Shannon. Accounting trainee Marathon Oil Co., Findlay, Ohio, 1960-61; accountant Price Waterhouse & Co., Los Angeles, 1965-71; controller-treas. Kern County Refinery, Inc., Long Beach, Calif., 1971-72, Bakersfield, Calif., 1972-75; v.p. fin. Kern County Refinery, Bakersfield, 1976-80, exec. v.p., Long Beach, 1980-82, also dir. pres. Kern Oil & Refining Co., Long Beach, 1982—. Councilman YMCA Indian Guides, 1976-77. Served with USN, 1961-65; Vietnam. C.P.A., Calif. Clubs: Town Hall of Calif., Petroleum of Bakersfield (dir. 1979-80). Republican. Home: 3541 Starline Dr Rancho Palos Verdes CA 90274 Office: 180 E Ocean Blvd Long Beach CA 90802

CITERLEY, RICHARD LEE, research company executive; b. Sacramento, Calif., Mar. 25, 1932; s. Clark Granville and Laura (Sousa) C.; m. Barbara Frances Kelley, July 9, 1955; children—Sharon L., Cara L. B.S.M.E., U. Calif.-Berkeley, 1955, M.S.M.E., U.S. Naval Postgrad. Sch., 1961. Registered profl. engr., Calif. Stress engr. Firestone Tire & Rubber Co., Los Angeles, 1955-58, United Tech. Ctr., Sunnyvale, Calif., 1962-65; systems engr. Dalmo Victor Co., Monterey, Calif., 1958-60; asst. prof. dept. aeros. U.S. Naval Postgrad. Sch., Monterey, Calif., 1957-61; v.p. Anamet Labs. Inc., San Carlos, Calif., 1965—. Mem. AIAA, ASME, Am. Acad. Mechanics. Republican. Home: 476 Birch Way Santa Clara CA 95051 Office: Anamet Labs Inc 100 Industrial Way San Carlos CA 94070

CLABAUGH, ELMER EUGENE, JR., lawyer; b. Anaheim, Calif., Sept. 18, 1927; s. Elmer Eugene and Eleanor (Heitschusen) C.; B.B.A. cum laude, Woodbury Coll., 1951; B.A. summa cum laude, Claremont Men's Coll., 1958; J.D., Stanford, 1961; m. Elizabeth Ellen Chapman, Dec. 25, 1954 (div. July 1966); children—Christopher Chapman, Matthew Martinson; m. 2d, Donna Marie Organ Donkers, Dec. 19, 1968 (div. Apr. 1982). Fgn. service staff U.S. Dept. State, Jerusalem and Tel Aviv, 1951-53; field staff Public Adminstrn. Service, El Salvador, Ethiopia, U.S., 1953-57; admitted to Calif. bar, 1961; dep. dist. atty. Ventura County, Calif., 1961-62; practice law, Ventura, 1962—; mem. firm Hathaway, Clabaugh Perrett and Webster, 1962-79, Clabaugh & Perloff, 1979—; city atty. Thousand Oaks (Calif.), 1964—, Simi Valley, Calif., 1969—; state inheritance tax referee, Ventura County, 1968-78. Bd. dirs. Ventura Community Meml. Hosp., Sch. Bd. Ojai Unified Sch. Dist., San Antonio Water Conservation Dist. Served in USCGR, 1944-46, USMCR, 1946-48. Mem. Calif. Bar, Town Hall of Calif., Am. Arbitration Assn., Phi Alpha Delta. Mason (32 deg., Shriner), Lion. Home: 241 Highland Dr Channel Islands Harbor CA 93030 Office: 1190 S Victoria Ave Suite 305 Ventura CA 93003

CLACK, DICK SCOTT, import co. exec.; b. Celina, Tex., Nov. 13, 1927; s. Clyde William and Tink (Blakemore) C.; B.S. in Wildlife Conservation, Okla. State U., 1952; postgrad. Hokkaido U., Sapporo, Japan, 1953-54, U. Hawaii, 1979; m. Yoshiko Eguchi, Oct. 1, 1955; children—Michael Bruce, Meiling Jade. Served as enlisted man U.S. Army, 1945-52, commd. 2 lt., 1952, advanced through grades to lt. col., 1967, ret., 1970; asst. v.p. Makaha Surfside Devel. Co., Honolulu, 1970-72; pres. D. Clack Inc., public relations cons., Honolulu, 1972-74; v.p. PCO Inc., Honolulu, 1974-76; exec. trustee Hawaii Army Museum Soc., Honolulu, 1976-78, trustee, 1976-81; v.p., dir. mktg. Traders Pacifica Ltd., Honolulu, 1979-81; propr. C&S Imports, Honolulu, 1981—; chmn. bd. dirs. Makaha Surfside Assocs.; dir. Agri Trade Internat. Unlimited, Honolulu, Agri Trade Internat. Ltd., Rakotonga, Cook Islands, South Seas Airlines. Bd. dirs. Société Tahitienna de Developpement Agri-Industrielle et Touristique, Papeete, 1982—. Decorated Legion of Merit, Army Commendation medal with 3 oak leaf clusters; named hon. mem. City Council Kumagaya (Japan), 1954; recipient cert. of commendation Gumma Prefectural Govt. Japan, 1955, Saitama Prefecture Govt. Japan, 1955; named Okla. Col., 1957, Ark. Traveler, 1962, La. Col., 1963, Hon. Citizen New Orleans, 1964. Mem. Assn. U.S. Army (exec. com. Hawaii chpt. 1967-80), Mil. Order World Wars, War Mus. Can., Japan-Am. Soc. Democrat. Clubs: Rotary (dir. public relations Dist. 500, 1974, 79, dir. world understanding Dist. 500, 1980-81), Honolulu Press, Adventurers, VFW (chief of staff Hawaii 1973). Office: PO Box 22367 Honolulu HI 96822

CLAES, DANIEL JOHN, physician; b. Glendale, Calif., Dec. 3, 1931; s. John Vernon and Claribel (Fleming) C.; A.B. magna cum laude, Harvard U., 1953, M.D. cum laude, 1957; m. Gayla Christine Blasdel, Jan. 19, 1974. Intern, UCLA, 1957-58; Bowyer Found. fellow for research in medicine, Los Angeles, 1958-61; practice medicine specializing in internal medicine, Los Angeles, 1962—; v.p. Am. Eye Bank Found., 1978-83, pres., 1983—, dir. research, 1980—; pres. Heuristic Corp., 1981—. Mem. Los Angeles Mus. Art, 1960—. Mem. AMA, Calif. Med. Assn., Los Angeles County Med. Assn. Clubs: Harvard and Harvard Med. Sch. of So. Calif. Contbr. papers on diabetes mellitus, computers in medicine to profl. lit. Office: 845 Via de la Paz Suite A236 Pacific Palisades CA 90272

CLAEYS, MAURICE FRANCIS, banker; b. Seattle, Nov. 25, 1927; s. Remi Henry and Flore Helene (De Bels) C.; m. Susan Anne Ellertson, July 9, 1960; children—John, Thomas, Scott. B.A., Seattle U., 1947; postgrad. U. Wash. With Nat. Bank of Commerce, Seattle, 1947-73, br. mgr., 1963-67, corporate planner, 1967-73, dir. urban affairs, 1968-73; mgr. asset and liability mgmt. planning and analysis Rainier Nat. Bank, Seattle, 1974-81, sr. v.p. credit adminstrn. deputy, 1981—; dir. BANK-WIRE. Bd. dirs. DePaul, Mt. St. Vincent; mem. Council for Wash.'s Future; Chmn. steering com. Alts. for Washington, 1975. Served with USN, 1951-53. Mem. Robert Morris Assocs. Roman Catholic. Office: 1301 5th Ave Seattle WA 98122

CLAFFEY, WILLIAM JOSEPH, JR., educator; b. Boston, Mar. 1, 1925; s. William Joseph and Grace (Hanson) C.; B.S., Boston U., 1950; M.S., U. So. Calif., 1965; m. Patricia Ruth Hutchings, May 6, 1972; children—Sheila, Leslie, Brent, Scott, Devin. Tchr. Westwood (Mass.) High Sch., 1950-51; asso. prof. Reno Bus. Coll., 1951-52; mgr. Occidental Life Ins. Co., Los Angeles, 1952-56; chmn. bus. dept. Buena Park (Calif.) High Sch., 1957-61; dir. data processing Fullerton (Calif.) Coll., 1961-73; bus. div. chmn. Cypress (Calif.) Coll., 1973-80, assoc. dean admissions and records, 1980—; cons. in bus. edn., State of Calif.; bd. dirs. Patti-Ruth Originals. Served with USN, 1942-46. Summer fellow U. Calif. Los Angeles, 1970. Mem. Internat. Word Processing Assn. (charter), Calif. Tchrs.' Assn., Calif. Bus. Edn. Assn., Pacific Assn. Coll. Registrars and Admissions Officers, Calif. Community Coll. Assn. Republican. Methodist. Clubs: Fullerton Aquatics (pres. 1966-67), Wentworth Riding and Polo, Elks. Author texts: Principles of Data Processing, 1967; Principles of Programming the IBM 1620, 1968; Key Punch Operation, 1970; textbook editor. Home: 13266 La Quinta St La Mirada CA 90638 Office 9200 Valley View St Cypress CA 90630

CLAIBORNE, HARRY E., judge; b. McRae, Ark., July 2, 1917; student Ouachita U., 1934-37; LL.B., Cumberland U., 1941, J.D., 1969. Bar: Ark. 1942, Nev. 1946, U.S. Supreme Ct. 1965; sole practice law, Las Vegas, after 1946; former U.S. dist. judge, now chief justice U.S. Dist. Ct., Las Vegas; mem. Nev. Assembly, 1949, chmn. judiciary com.; asst. dist. atty. Clark County, Nev., 1946-48; city atty. City of North Las Vegas, 1948-55. Fellow Am. Coll. Trial Lawyers; mem. Nat. Assn. Trial Lawyers, Am. Assn. Criminal Def. Lawyers, Am. Bar Assn., Am. Bd. Trial Advs. (adv.). Office: US Dist Ct 300 Las Vegas Blvd S Las Vegas NV 89101*

CLAIR, CASEY MAXWELL, advertising executive; b. Los Angeles Calif., May 23, 1949; d. Eddie and Eve (Whitney) Maxell; divorced; children—Melanie, Tiffany. B.A., UCLA, 1972. Freelance art dir. Los Angeles, 1974-79; art dir. Warner Bros. Studio, Los Angeles, 1979-81; dir. advt. and promotion ABC Motion Pictures, Inc., Century City, Calif., 1981—. Office: ABC Motion Picutes Inc 2020 Ave of the Stars 5th Floor Century City CA 90067

CLAIR, THEODORE NAT, ednl. adminstr.; b. Stockton, Calif., Apr. 19, 1929; s. Peter David and Sara Renee (Silverman) C.; A.A., U. Calif. at Berkeley, 1949, A.B., 1950; M.S., U. So. Calif., 1953, M.Ed., 1963, Ed.D., 1969; m. Laura Gold, June 19, 1961; children—Shari, Judith. Tchr., counselor Los Angeles City Schs., 1957-63; psychologist Alamitos Sch. Dist., Garden Grove, Calif., 1963-64, Arcadia (Calif.) Unified Sch. Dist., 1964-65; head psychologist Wiseburn Sch. Dist., Hawthorne, Calif., 1966-69; asst. prof. spl. edn., coordinator sch. psychology program U. Iowa, Iowa City, 1969-72; dir. pupil personnel services Orcutt (Calif.) Union Sch. Dist., 1972-73; adminstr. Mt. Diablo Unified Sch. Dist., 1973-77; program dir. San Mateo County Office of Edn., Redwood City, 1977—; assoc. prof. John F. Kennedy U. Sch. Mgmt., 1975-77; pvt. practice as ednl. psychologist and marriage and family counselor, Concord, Calif., 1972-77, Menlo Park, Calif., 1977—; dir. Peninsula Vocat. Rehab. Inst., 1978—. Served with USNR, 1952-54. Mem. Calif., San Francisco Bay Area assns. for spl. edn. adminstrs., Calif. Assn. Marriage and Family Counselors, Am. Psychol. Assn., Nat. Rehab. Assn., Phi Delta Kappa. Club: Palo Alto B'nai B'rith (pres.). Author: Phenylketonuria and Some Other Inborn Errors of Amino Acid Metabolism, 1971; mem. editorial adv. bd. Psychology in Schs., 1972—; contbr. articles to profl. jours. Home and office: 56 Willow Rd Menlo Park CA 94025

CLANAHAN, BARKLEY LAX, lawyer; b. Springfield, Ill., Aug. 24, 1914; s. Robert C. and Helen (Lax) C.; m. Virginia Lucile Blomgren, Sept. 11, 1941; children—Diane Clanahan Conn, Denis B. B.S., U. Ill., 1937; LL.B., U. S.D., 1939. Bar: Ill., 1939, S.D. 1939, Colo. 1946. With FBI, 1940-46; ptnr. Clanahan, Tanner, Downing & Knowlton, Denver, 1954—. Mem. ABA, Colo. Bar Assn., Denver Bar Assn. Republican. Episcopalian. Clubs: Denver Country, Mile High, Law, Arlberg, Gyro (Denver). Home: 240 S Birch St Denver CO 80222 Office: 718 17th St Suite 1950 Denver CO 80202

CLANCEY, MICHAEL PATRICK, lawyer, univ. dean; b. Detroit, Nov. 8, 1946; s. Harry L. and Gloria (Forster) C.; A.A., Santa Ana Coll., 1968; B.S. in Law, Western State U., Fullerton, Calif., 1972, J.D., 1973; m. Sandra Kay Griswold, Aug. 1, 1969; children—Erin Heather, Kelly O'Brien. Admitted to Calif. bar, 1974, U.S. Supreme Ct. bar, 1978; pvt. practice law, Orange County, Calif., 1974-76, Sacramento County, 1979—; partner firm Clancey & Colletta, Laguna Hills, Calif., 1976-79; judge pro tem Mcpl. Ct. Orange County, Harbor Jud. Dist., 1975—; founder, dean Sch. Law, Davis U., 1982—. Mem. Calif. Republican Com., Calif. Rep. Assembly, Rep. candidate for Congress, 1976, 82. Served with USMC, 1966-68; Vietnam; capt. J.A.G., U.S. Army Res., 1979—. Decorated Purple Heart. Community coll. teaching credential, Calif. Mem. Am., Sacramento, Orange County bar assns., Calif. Bar. Club: Lions (past pres. Laguna Niguel). Office: 455 Capitol Mall Suite 415 Sacramento CA 95814

CLANTON, GORDON, sociologist, lecturer, consultant; b. Bayonne, N.J., Mar. 25, 1942; s. Robert G. and Vivian (Singletary) C. B.A., La. State U., 1964; M.Divinity, Austin Presbyn. Theol. Sem., 1967; Ph.D., Grad. Theol. Union, U. Calif.-Berkeley, 1973. Lectr. dept. religion Rutgers U., New Brunswick, N.J., 1970-73; now lectr. sociology San Diego State U. Mem. Am. Sociol. Assn., Nat. Council Family Relations, Soc. Sci. Study Religion, Groves Conf. Marriage and Family, Soc. Values in Higher Edn., Pacific Sociol. Assn. Author: Face to Face to Face, 1975; Jealousy, 1977, Social Forces and the Changing Family, 1983. Office: Dept Sociology San Diego State U San Diego CA 92182

CLAPP, NORTON, bldg. materials co. exec.; b. Pasadena, Calif., April 15, 1906; s. Eben Pratt and Mary Bell (Norton) C.; A.B., Occidental Coll., 1928, LL.D., 1958; Ph.B., U. Chgo., 1928, J.D., 1929; D.C.L., U. Puget Sound, 1958; m. Mary Cordelia Davis, July 8, 1929 (dec.); children—James Hayes (dec.), Matthew, Ralph (dec.), Roger (dec.); m. 2d, Evelyn Beatrice Booth, Jan. 15, 1941 (dec.); children—William Hayes, Stephen Gilbert; m. 3d, Jane Bumiller, Apr. 19, 1952 (div.). Admitted to Calif., Wash. bars, 1929, practiced in Tacoma, 1929-42; pres. Pelican (Alaska) Cold Storage Co., 1947-60, chmn., 1960-77; pres. Boise (Idaho) Payette Lumber Co., 1949-55; pres. Laird Norton Co., bldg. materials, Winona, Minn., 1950-60, chmn., 1960—; v.p. Weyerhaeuser Co., 1956-57, chmn. bd., 1957-60, 66-76, pres., 1960-66. Mem. nat. adv. bd., hon. v.p. Boy Scouts Am., nat. pres., 1971-73. Chmn. bd. trustees U. Puget Sound, Tacoma; life trustee U. Chgo.; trustee Menninger Found., Econ. Devel. Council Puget Sound, Episcopal Ch. Found., Nat. Park Found. Served as lt. comdr. USNR, 1942-46. Mem. Seattle C. of C. (pres. 1970-71). Republican. Episcopalian. Clubs: Harbor, Rainier, University, Overlake Golf and Country, Yacht (Seattle); Tacoma Country and Golf, Yacht (Tacoma). Home: PO Box 99 Medina WA 98039 Office: Norton Bldg Seattle WA 98104

CLAPP, RODGER CORDREY, aerospace company official; b. Ft. Lauderdale, Fla., Apr. 14, 1950; s. Roger Houghton and (stepmother) Simone (Chiraki) C.; student public schs., Ft. Lauderdale; m. Debra L. Clapp, Dec. 1, 1979; children—David Allen, Bryan Christopher, Steven Cordrey. Electrician, San Diego, 1978; sr. engr., ops. supr. cruise missile program McDonnell Douglas (TVL), San Diego, 1978—. Served with USN, 1968-78. Mem. Nat. Mgmt. Assn., Convair Mgmt. Assn. Republican. Club: Navy Amateur Radio Sta. (San Diego). Home: 7566 Alonda Way San Diego CA 92126 Office: McDonnell Douglas (TVL) PO Box 80847 San Diego CA 92138

CLAPPER, JOHN FRANKLIN, army officer, pediatrician; b. Whitefish, Mont., Apr. 12, 1947; s. John Jospeh and Jacqueline (Jensen) C.; m. Cynthia Anne Gwinn, Mar. 16, 1974; children—Jonathan, Jennifer, Caroline, Melissa. B.S., U.S. Mil. Acad., 1969; M.D., U. Wash., 1975. Diplomate Am. Bd. Pediatrics. Commd. lt. col. M.C., U.S. Army, advanced through grades to lt. col., 1980; intern, resident in pediatrics Tripler Army Med. Center, Honolulu, 1975-78; fellow in developmental pediatrics Boston Childrens Hosp., 1980; pediatrician Army Hosp., Fort Knox, Ky., 1978-81; pediatrician Madigan Army Med. Center, Tacoma, 1981—; asst. prof. U. Louisville, 1978-81, U. Wash., Seattle, 1981—. Mem. Am. Acad. pediatrics, Officers Christian Fellowship, Christian Med. Soc. Home: 11614 66th Ave Ct SW Tacoma WA 98499 Office: Box 859 Madigan Army Med Center Tacoma WA 98431

CLARE, MICHAEL COLIN, pharmacist; b. London, June 10, 1942; came to U.S., 1953, naturalized, 1958; s. Henry and Henrietta (Levy) C.; A.A., Long Beach (Calif.) City Coll., 1964; Pharm.D., U. Calif.-San Francisco, 1968; div.; children—Lisa Erin, Scott Howard. From pharmacy student to asso. dir. pharmacy services Cedars-Sinai Med. Ctr., Los Angeles, 1969-77; dir. pharmacy Daniel Freeman Meml. Hosp., Inglewood, Calif., 1977—; clin. instr. U. So. Calif. Sch. Pharmacy, 1976—; mem. hosp. pharmacy technician adv. com. Los Angeles Harbor Coll., 1977; cons. Computer Scis. Corp., Monterey Park Hosp., Syncor Internat. Recipient Pharmacy Dept. of Year award Daniel Freeman Meml. Hosp., 1977. Mem. Am. Soc. Hosp. Pharmacists, Am. Pharmacists Assn., Calif. Soc. Hosp. Pharmacists (dir.), Calif. Pharmacists Assn., So. Calif. Soc. Hosp. Pharmacists (pres. 1980-81). Office: 333 N Prairie Ave Inglewood CA 90301

CLARIDGE, LOIS WESSLUND, social worker, nurse; b. Paxton, Ill., Oct. 8, 1921; d. Anton Edgar and Ellen Esther (Pearson) Wesslund; diploma in nursing Evanston Hosp. Sch. Nursing; B.S., Northwestern U., 1945; m. Samuel Ray Claridge, Oct. 8, 1948; children—Clifford, Lynne, Lois R.N. Clin. instr. in med. and surg. nursing Evanston Hosp. Sch. Nursing and Northwestern U., 1945-46; office nurse Safford Clinic (Ariz.), 1946-50; cattle rancher Bonita Creek Ranch, Safford, 1949-72; sch. nurse Safford Schs., 1953-65; caseworker Ariz. Dept. Public Welfare, 1965-72, eligibility and payments supr., 1972—; office coordinator for Graham County, Ariz. Dept. Econ. Security, 1978—. Bd. dirs. Ariz. Easter Seal Soc., 1955—; mem. Gov.'s Adv. Com. on Mental Health, 1963-65; vice chmn. Graham Greenlee Comprehensive Health Planning Council, 1974; mem. Graham area adv. bd. Health Systems Agy. of Southeastern Ariz., 1980—. Mem. Ariz. Nurses Assn., Am. Nurses Assn., Ariz. Cattle Growers Assn., Am. Nat. CowBelles (pres. 1962), Ariz. Cow Belles (pres. 1959). Republican. Methodist. Home: 1507 W Relation St PO Box 388 Safford AZ 85546 Office: 106 8th Ave PO Box 1019 Safford AZ 85546

CLARK, ALICE SANDELL, librarian; b. Oneonta, N.Y., Nov. 24, 1922; d. George Harold and Gertrude (Northrup) Sandell; B.A., State Univ. Coll., Oneonta, 1967, M.L.S., Albany, 1968, M.A. in History, 1978; m. Dewey Clark, Jr., Sept. 13, 1941; children—Malcolm Bruce, Peter D. Lectr. library Sci. SUNY-Albany, 1968; asst. head, personnel, Ohio State U. Libraries, Columbus, 1968-69, reference librarian, 1969-70, head undergrad. libraries, 1970-74; asst. dean readers services U. N.Mex. Library, Albuquerque, 1974—. Recipient grants Greater U. N.Mex. Fund. Mem. ALA (councilor 1977-81), N.Mex. Library Assn., AAUP, Greater Albuquerque Library Assn., Beta Phi Mu, Phi Kappa Phi, Kappa Delta Pi. Author: Managing Curriculum Materials in the Academic Library, 1982. Contbr. articles to profl. jours. Home: 8608 Chambers Pl NE Albuquerque NM 87111 Office: Zimmerman Library Univ New Mexico

CLARK, ARTHUR JOSEPH, JR., mech. and elec. engr.; b. West Orange, N.J., June 10, 1921; s. Arthur Joseph and Marjorie May (Courter) C.; B.S. in Mech. Engring., Cornell U., 1943; M.S., Poly. Inst. Bklyn., 1948; M.S. in Elec. Engring., U. N.Mex., 1955; m. Caroline Katherine Badgley, June 12, 1943; children—Arthur Joseph, III, Durward S., David P. Design engr. Ranger Aircraft Engines Co., Farmingdale, N.Y., 1943-46; sr. structures engr. propeller div. Curtis Wright Co., Caldwell, N.J., 1946-51; mgr. space isotope power dept., also aerospace nuclear safety dept. Sandia Labs., Albuquerque, 1951-71, mgr. environ. systems test lab., 1971-79, mgr. mil. liaison dept., 1979—; mem. faculty U. N.Mex., 1971-75; invited lectr. Am. Mgmt. Assn. Pres. Sandia Base Sch. PTA, 1960-61; chmn. finance com. Albuquerqe chpt. Am. Field Service, 1964-66; chmn. Sandia Labs. div. U.S. Savs. Bond drive, 1972-74, chmn. employee contbn. drive, 1973-75; active local Boy Scouts Am., 1958-66. Recipient Order Arrow, Boy Scouts Am., 1961, Order St. Andrew, 1962, Scouters Key award, 1964; certificate outstanding service Sandia Base, 1964. Sr. mem. IEEE; mem. ASME (nat. v.p. 1975-79), past chmn. N.Mex. sect.), Cornell Engring. Soc., Theta Xi. Clubs: Kirtland Officers, Four Hills Country. Home: 905 Warm Sands Trail Albuquerque NM 87123 Office: Sandia Labs Dept 7210 Albuquerque NM 87185

CLARK, BARBARA, automobile club executive; b. Santa Monica, Calif., Sept. 18, 1940; d. Cyrus Lowell and Anna Gretta (Mack) C. A.A., Santa Monica Coll., 1960; B.A. in psychology with honors, UCLA, 1962; M.A. in Indsl. Psychology, Calif. State U.-Los Angeles, 1982. Compensation asst. System Devel. Corp., Santa Monica, 1960-68; compensation analyst, 1968-70; compensation analyst Automobile Club So. Calif., Los Angeles, 1970-72, research adminstr. compensation and benefits, 1972-74, compensation mgr., 1974—. Mem. Am. Compensation Assn., Calif. Inst. Tech. Mgmt. Discussion Group, Los Angeles County Mus. Art Assn. Republican. Mormon. Contbr. articles to profl. jours. Office: 2601 S Figueroa St Los Angeles CA 90007

CLARK, BILLY RAY, ins. agy. exec.; b. Little Falls, Minn., Mar. 18, 1928; s. William Edward and Cora Esther (Crabtree) C.; B.A. in Bus.

Adminstrn., Bemidji State U., 1953; m. Elsie Helen Torgerson, Oct. 28, 1951; children—Nancy Jo, Kathryn Jean, Julie Rae, Janice Renee. Field supr., supt. Fidelity and Surety Lines, Travelers Ins. Co., Mpls., Denver, 1953-63; account exec. Talbert Corp., Denver, 1963-65, v.p. sales, 1965-73, pres., chmn. bd., 1973—; chmn. bd. Continental Surety & Fidelity Ins. Co.; pres. Surety Mgmt., Inc.; lectr. engring. dept. U. Colo., 1972-79; lectr. constrn. mgmt. Colo. State U., 1972-79. Mem. panel of arbitrators Am. Arbitration Assn.; adv. com. Indsl. Constrn. Mgmt. Program, Colo. State U., also mem. constrn. com. Bus.-Econ. Outlook Forum. Served with USN, 1946-48, 51-53. Named Agt. of Yr., Travelers Ins. Co., 1981. Mem. Nat. Assn. Surety Bond Producers pres. Nat., Colo. assns. ins. agts., Profls. for Colo. Contractors Council (past pres.), Colo. Transp. Assn. Republican. Lutheran. Club: Columbine Country (Littleton, Colo.). ins. agy. exec.; b. Little Falls, Minn., Mar. 18, 1928; s. William Edward and Cora Esther (Crabtree) C.; B.A. in Bus. Adminstrn., Bemidji State U., 1953; m. Elsie Helen Torgerson, Oct. 28, 1951; children—Nancy Jo, Kathryn Jean, Julie Rae, Janice Renee. Field supr., supt. Fidelity and Surety Lines, Travelers Ins. Co., Mpls., Denver, 1953-63; account exec. Talbert Corp., Denver, 1963-65, v.p. sales, 1965-73, pres., chmn. bd., 1973—; chmn. bd. Continental Surety & Fidelity Ins. Co.; pres. Surety Mgmt., Inc.; lectr. engring. dept. U. Colo., 1972-79; lectr. constrn. mgmt. Colo. State U., 1972-79. Mem. panel of arbitrators Am. Arbitration Assn.; adv. com. Indsl. Constrn. Mgmt. Program, Colo. State U., also mem. constrn. com. Bus.-Econ. Outlook Forum. Served with USN, 1946-48, 51-53. Named Agt. of Yr., Travelers Ins. Co., 1981. Mem. Nat. Assn. Surety Bond Producers pres. Nat., Colo. assns. ins. agts., Profls. for Colo. Contractors Council (past pres.), Colo. Transp. Assn. Republican. Lutheran. Club: Columbine Country (Littleton, Colo.). Home: 5186 Tule Lake Dr Littleton CO 80123 Office: 1001 Lincoln St Denver CO 80203

CLARK, BRIAN THOMAS, mathematical statistician; b. Rockford, Ill., Apr. 7, 1951; s. Paul Herbert and Martha Lou (Schlensker) C. B.S. cum laude, No. Ariz. U., 1973; postgrad. Ariz. State U., 1980-82. Math. aide Center for Disease Control, Phoenix, 1973-74, math. statistician, 1979—; math. statistician U.S. Navy Metrology Engring. Center, Pomona, Calif., 1974-79. Mem. Am. Statis. Assn., Biometric Soc. Republican. Lutheran. Office: Center for Disease Control 4402 N 7th St Phoenix AZ 85014

CLARK, CALEB MORGAN, polit. scientist; b. Washington, June 6, 1945; s. Tanner Morgan and Grace Amanda (Kautzmann) C.; B.A., Beloit Coll., 1966; Ph.D., U. Ill., 1973; m. Janet Morrissey Sentz, Sept. 28, 1968; children—Emily Claire, Grace Ellen, Evelyn Adair. Lectr., N.Mex. State U., Las Cruces, 1972-75, asst. prof., 1975-78, assoc. prof. govt., 1978-81; assoc. prof. polit. sci. U. Wyo., Laramie, 1981—. NDEA fellow, 1966-69; Woodrow Wilson dissertation fellow, 1969-70; N.Mex. Humanities Council grantee, 1975; Am. Council Learned Socs. grantee, 1976; Met. Life Ednl. grantee, 1978-80; Nat. Endowment for Humanities grantee, 1978; NSF grantee, 1981. Mem. Am. Polit. Sci. Assn., Am. Assn. Advancement Slavic Studies, Rocky Mountain Assn. Slavic Studies, Western Polit. Sci. Assn., Western Social Sci. Assn., Internat. Studies Assn. (exec. dir. West 1981—), Phi Beta Kappa, Pi Eta Sigma, Phi Kappa Phi. Author: (with Robert L. Farlow) Comparative Patterns of Foreign Policy and Trade, 1976; (with Karl F. Johnson) Development's Influence on Yugoslav Political Values, 1976; (with Donna Bahry) Communist Regimes: What are the Bases of Power?, 1983; cons., asso. editor Soviet Union, 1974-77, World Affairs, 1975—, Social Sci. Jour., 1978-80; contbr. articles to profl. jours. Home: 519 S 12th St Laramie WY 82070 Office: Dept Polit Sci U Wyo Laramie WY 82071

CLARK, CARL ROGER, public administrator; b. Auburn, Calif., Oct. 27, 1948; s. Alexander Alan and Joy Mildred (Griffith) C.; B.A., Calif. Lutheran Coll., 1970; m. Holly Catherwood Strandberg, Mar. 8, 1975; children—Ivy Leanne, Amy Lynn, Kyle Timothy. Recreation supr. Conejo Recreation & Park Dist., Thousand Oaks, Calif., 1970-73; gen. recreation supr. Auburn (Calif.) Area Recreation & Park Dist., 1973-76; dist. adminstr. Mendocino Coast Recreation & Park Dist., Fort Bragg, Calif., 1976-78; dist. adminstr. Hesperia (Calif.) Recreation and Park Dist., 1978—. Recipient Spl. Service trophy Hesperia Wranglers Inc., 1981, Outstanding Achievement award Auburn C. of C., 1976; Pres.'s scholar, 1966-70. Mem. Calif. Recreation and Park Soc. (adminstr. dist. XI, treas. 1980, pres. 1982), Hesperia C. of C. (dir. 1978—, pres. 1981—), Calif. Assn. Recreation and Park Dists. (workers compensation self-ins. program bd. govs. 1978—), Auburn Fair Boosters Assn. (dir.), Redwood Sports Ofcls. Assn. (assignment commr.), Nat. Recreation and Park Assn., Am. Mgmt. Assn., So. Calif. Mcpl. Athletic Assn. Republican. Clubs: Rotary, Inland Sports Ofcls. Assn., Nat. Baseball Congress. Office: PO Box 1055 Hesperia CA 92345

CLARK, CHARLENE ELIZABETH, nursing educator; b. Spokane, Wash., Jan. 8, 1941; d. Carl G. and Anna E. Miller; diploma Sacred Heart Sch. of Nursing, 1962; B.S. in Biology, Whitworth Coll., 1965, Ed.M., 1974; m. Robert Stephen Clark, Apr. 14, 1962; children—Robert Stephen, Jeffrey Craig. Asst. clin. instr. Sacred Heart Sch. Nursing, Spokane, 1963-66; instr. Spokane Community Coll., 1968; lectr. Ctr. for Nursing Edn., Spokane, 1972-73, instr., 1973-74; asst. prof. Intercollegiate Ctr. for Nursing Edn., Spokane, 1974-83, assoc. prof., 1983—, also dir. learning resources unit; cons. in nursing edn., 1975—; vol. Immunization Clinics, 1976; mem. Community Health Edn. Consortia, 1977—. Asst. Cub Scout den mother Inland Empire council, 1972-73; youth group adviser Westminster Congregational Ch., 1962-64, Sunday sch. tchr., 1963-65; judge for first aid competition Inland Empire council Boy Scouts Am., 1977; bd. dirs. Community Concerts Assn., Spokane, 1969-74, exec. sec., 1970-71. Tb League Nursing scholar, 1959. Mem. Nat. League for Nursing, Am. Nurses Assn., Health Edn. Media Assn., Assn. for Ednl. Communications and Tech., Sigma Theta Tau. Club: Order Eastern Star. Home: N 9923 Excell Dr Spokane WA 99218 Office: W 2917 Ft George Wright Dr Spokane WA 99204

CLARK, CHARLES ALBERT, JR., electronics engr.; b. Enterprise, Ala., Feb. 3, 1944; s. Charles A. and Sarah Gene (Williams) C.; B.S.E.E., UCLA, 1965, M.S.E.E., 1968; postgrad. U. So. Calif., 1970-72; m. Anne Jennifer Keslin, July 16, 1966; 1 dau., Courtney Amber. Mem. engring. staff RCA Def. Electronic Products, Van Nuys, Calif., 1966-72, sr. mem. design and devel. staff, ind. research and devel. coordinator Electromagnetic and Aviation Systems, 1973-75, prin. mem. engring. staff Avionics Systems div., 1975-81; prin. mem. engring. staff Sperry Flight Systems, Van Nuys, 1981-82; sr. systems engr. TELOC, Inc., 1982—; cons. magnetics design, high efficiency power supplies. Recipient David Sarnoff award RCA, 1978. Mem. IEEE (sr.). Patentee radar, high voltage, pulse, cathode ray tube circuits. Office: Van Nuys CA

CLARK, CHARLES SUTTER, interior designer; b. Venice, Calif., Dec. 21, 1927; s. William Sutter and Lodema Ersell (Fleeman) C. Student Chouinard Art Inst., Los Angeles, 1950-51. Interior designer LM.H. Co., Gt. Falls, Mont., 1956-62, Andreason's Interiors, Oakland, Calif., 1962-66, Western Contact Furnishers Internat., Oakland, 1966-70, Design Five Assocs., Lafayette, Calif., 1972-73; owner, interior designer Charles Sutter Clark Interiors, Greenbrae, Calif., 1973—. Served with USAF, 1951-55. Recipient prizes Mont. State Fair, 1953-55. Mem. Am. Soc. Interior Designers. Home: 405 Via Castas Apt 7 Greenbrae CA 94904

CLARK, CHASE GORDON, JR., commercial flooring consulting executive; b. Chgo., Apr. 21, 1928; s. Chase Gordon and Eleanor Marie C.; m. Mary Jo Ann Woolsey, Nov. 29, 1952; children—Brenda, Diane. Student Kansas City Jr. Coll., 1945-47, U. Mo., 1947-49. With Fibreboard Paper Products, various locations, 1954-65; dist. sales mgr. Comml. Carpet Corp., Los Angeles, 1965-78; contract mgr. Westwood Carpet, Los Angeles, 1978-80; pres. Chase Clark & Assocs., Inc., Beverly Hills, Calif., 1980—. Served with U.S. Army, 1950-52. Republican. Methodist. Clubs: Mercedes Benz, Masons, Shriners.

CLARK, CLAUDE LOCKHART, artist, educator, business exec.; b. Phila., Mar. 28, 1945; s. Claude and Daima M. Lockhart-Clark; B.A. (scholar), Calif. Coll. Arts and Crafts, 1968; teaching credential, U. Calif., Berkeley, 1969, M.A., 1972. Lectr. Afro-Am. art San Jose (Calif.) State U., 1974—, U. Calif., Berkeley, 1974-79, Calif. Coll. Arts and Crafts, Oakland, 1970—; founder, propr. House of Vai, Oakland, 1977—; photographer, poster artist, sculptor, wood carver; wood carvings include myrtle stool, Council, 1979, live oak stool, Ananse, 1975; felt brush and ink drawings include Cathedral, 1974, Graphics, 1967; sculptures include, cast bronze Fugue, 1963, clay bust Figg, 1960; one-man show First Unitarian Ch., San Francisco, 1966; two-man shows with father, San Francisco and Oakland, 1969, Hayward, Calif., 1967; award shows Oakland and Dearborn, Mich., 1960; catalogue exhibits include San Francisco Mus. Art, 1974, Fisk U., Nashville, 1975-76; mus. exhibits include Oakland Public Mus., 1962, Montgomery (Ala.) Mus. Fine Arts, 1972, San Francisco Mus. Art, 1974; out of state exhibits include Worlds Fair, Spokane, Wash., 1974, Brooks Meml. Art Gallery, Memphis, 1979. Demonstrated African woodcarving principles community workshops, 1962, 74, 75-78. Recipient first place award Oakland Mus. exhibit for public schs., 1960, third place Nat. Ford Indsl. Arts award contest, Dearborn, Mich., 1960. Mem. Center for Visual Arts, Bay Area Black Artist Assn., Assn. Africans and African Americans. Co-author, illustrator A Black Art Perspective, 1970. Office: House of Vai PO Box 8172 Oakland CA 94662

CLARK, COLLEEN ANN, television executive; b. Eugene, Oreg., Apr. 22, 1957; d. Earle Henry and Dorothy Murray (Davies) Clark; m. Michael Kirby Hawkins, June 18, 1977 (div.). B.A. in Broadcast Media Communications, Oreg. State U., 1978. Floor dir. Sta. KATU-TV, Portland, Oreg., 1978; asst. dir., producer Video Prodns., Portland, 1978-79; freelance TV asst. producer/dir., Portland, 1978-80; asst. ops. mgr. Sta. KGW-TV, Portland, 1980-81; promotion mgr. Sta. KECH22-TV, Salem, Oreg., 1981—. Mem. Broadcast Promotion Assn. Democrat. Presbyterian. Home: 5548 Kayak Way NE Salem OR 97303 Office: Sta KECH22 TV 4923 Indian Sch Rd NE Salem OR 97303

CLARK, DONALD CLAYTON, educator; b. Los Angeles, Feb. 28, 1937; s. John Clayton and Grace Eleanor (Link) C.; m. Sally Newbert, Jan. 26, 1957; children—Susan Lynn, Janet Kathleen. A.B., Pasedena Coll., 1959; M.A., Calif. State U.-Los Angeles, 1963; Ed.D., U. So. Calif., 1971. Tchr., Duarte (Calif.) Unified Sch. Dist., 1959-65; dir. curriculum Monrovia (Calif.) Unified Sch. Dist., 1965-71; prof. secondary edn. U. Ariz., Tucson, 1971—; cons. in curriculum; researcher in early adolescent edn. Named Outstanding Young Man, U.S. Jaycees, 1971. Mem. Assn. Supervision and Curriculum Devel., Nat. Assn. Secondary Sch. Prins. Republican. Methodist. Author: A Survey of Middle Level Principals and Programs, 1981; The Effective Middle Level Principal, 1983; contbr. numerous articles to profl. jours. Office: Education Dept Room 617 U Arizona Tucson AZ 85721

CLARK, DONALD EDWARD, county ofcl., educator; b. Silverton, Oreg., Apr. 25, 1933; s. Harold Edward and Vera Mary (Lang) C.; student Vanport Coll., 1951-53; A.B., San Francisco State Coll., 1956; postgrad. Portland State Coll., 1958-60, 65—; m. Shirley Paulus, May 5, 1971; children—Donald Edward, Donna Kim. Correctional officer Calif. Dept. Corrections, San Quentin Prison, 1954-56; investigator U.S. Civil Service Commn., Seattle, 1957; tchr. elementary schs., Portland, Oreg., 1959-61; dep. sheriff Multnomah County (Oreg.), Portland, 1956-57, 59-62, sheriff, 1963-67; asso. dir. law enforcement programs Urban Studies Center, Portland State Coll., 1967-68; cons. commr. Multnomah County, 1969-74, chmn., 1975-79, county exec., 1979-82; police cons., 1967—; cons. Pres.'s Commn. on Law Enforcement and Adminstrn. Justice, 1966; mem. Vice Pres.'s Task Force on Order and Justice, 1968; panelist nat. conv. NAACP, Los Angeles, 1966; moderator Nat. Inst. Program on civil rights, police sci. dept., N.Y. State U., 1966; mem. Oreg. Criminal Law Rev. Commn. Sr. assoc. Cogan and Assocs., Portland. Chmn. City-County Health Com.; founder Project Health, 1973. Mem. adv. bd. Boys' Club Portland, 1963—; bd. dirs. Boys' Clubs Oreg., Boys and Girls Aid Soc.; chmn. govt. div. United Way, 1983; fellow Lewis and Clark Law Sch. Mem. Nat. (life), Oreg. sheriffs assns., Internat. Assn. Chiefs Police, Mil. Police Assn., Am. Correction Assn., Am. Soc. Criminology, Oreg. Edn. Assn., Isaac Walton League, Oreg. Hist. Soc., Portland Classroom Tchrs. Assn., Columbia Region Assn. Govts. (exec. bd.), Urban League, AAUP. Club: City (bd. govs. 1983) (Portland). Author: (with Samuel G. Chapman) A Forward Step: Educational Backgrounds for Police, 1966; also articles. Office: 1120 SW 5th Ave Room 1500 Portland OR 97204

CLARK, EARNEST HUBERT, JR., mfg. co. exec.; b. Birmingham, Ala., Sept. 8, 1926; s. Earnest Hubert and Grace May (Smith) C.; B.S. magna cum laude in Mech. Engring., Calif. Inst. Tech., 1946, M.S. in Mech. Engring., 1947; LL.D. (hon.), Pepperdine U., 1975; m. Patricia Margaret Hamilton, June 22, 1947; children—Stephen D., Kenneth A., Timothy R., Daniel S., Scott H., Rebecca G. With Baker Oil Tools, Inc., Huntington Park, Calif., 1947-76, pres., gen. mgr., 1962-65, pres., chief exec. officer, 1965-69, pres., chmn. bd., 1969-76; pres., chief exec. officer Baker Internat. Corp., Orange, Calif., 1976-80, pres., chmn. bd., 1980—; dir. Beckman Instruments Inc., CBI Industries. Trustee Harvey Mudd Coll.; active YMCA Met. Los Angeles, Downey (Calif.) YMCA, Nat. Council YMCA's. Served with USNR, 1944-46, 51-52; Korea. Recipient Martin Luther King, Jr., Humanitarian award YMCA Met. Los Angeles, 1980. Mem. Petroleum Equipment Suppliers Assn. (dir. 1962—, pres. 1973-74), AIME, Am. Petroleum Inst., Nat. Petroleum Council. Republican. Roman Catholic. Clubs: Calif., Big Canyon. Office: 500 City Pkwy W Orange CA 92668

CLARK, EDGAR SANDERFORD, insurance broker, consultant; b. N.Y.C., Nov. 17, 1933; s. Edgar Edmund, Jr., and Katharine Lee (Jarman) C.; student U. Pa., 1952-54; B.S., Georgetown U., 1956, J.D., 1958; postgrad. INSEAD, Fountainbleau, France, 1969, Golden Gate Coll., 1973, U. Calif., Berkeley, 1974; m. Nancy E. Hill, Sept. 13, 1975; 1 dau., Schuyler; children by previous marriages—Colin, Alexandra, Pamela. Staff asst. U.S. Senate select com. to investigate improper activities in labor and mgmt. field, Washington, 1958-59; underwriter Ocean Marine Dept., Fireman's Fund Ins. Co., San Francisco, 1959-62; mgr. Am. Fgn. Ins. Assn., San Francisco, 1962-66; with Marsh & McLennan, 1966-72, mgr. for Europe, resident dir. Brussels, Belgium, 1966-70, asst. v.p., mgr. captive and internat. div., San Francisco, 1970-72; v.p., dir. Risk Planning Group, Inc., San Francisco, 1972-75; sr. v.p. internat. div. Alexander & Alexander Internat. Inc., San Francisco, 1975—; lectr. profl. orgns.; guest lectr. U. Calif., Berkeley, 1973, Am. Grad. Sch. Internat. Mgmt., 1981, 82. Served with USAF, 1956-58. Mem. Am. Mgmt. Assn., Am. Risk and Ins. Assn., Chartered Ins. Inst., Am. Soc. Internat. Law. Episcopalian. Club: Meadow (Fairfax, Calif.). Editorial adv. bd. Risk Mgmt. Reports, 1973-76. Home: 72 Millay Pl Mill Valley CA 94941 Office: Suite 1700 Three Embarcadero Center San Francisco CA 94111

CLARK, (EDYTHE) AUDREY, home economics educator; b. Jeffersonville, Ind., Dec. 26, 1929; d. (John) Foster and Martha Willey (Long) Eberts; m. Paul Stoner Clark, Sept. 9, 1950; children—Robert Foster, Randall Paul, Barbara Joan, Steven Wesley. B.S., Northwestern U., 1951; M.S., Calif. State U.-Northridge, 1971; Ph.D., U. So. Calif., 1978. With Sibley, Lindsay & Curr Co., Rochester, N.Y., 1951-53; with Calif. State U.-Northridge, 1970—, dir. Presch. Lab., 1971-82, acting chairperson dept. home econs., 1982-83, chairperson, 1983—. USDA grantee, 1979-81; Calif. State U.-Northridge grantee, 1978; Los Angeles Dist. Calif. Home Econs. Assn. grantee, 1976. Mem. Am. Home Econs. Assn. (pres.-elect Los Angeles dist.), Am. Ednl. Research Assn., Calif. Profs. Early Childhood Edn. (mem. editorial bd. quar. rev.), Nat. Assn. Edn. Young Children, So. Calif. Assn. Edn. Young Children, San Fernando Valley Child Care Consortium (dir.), Delta Epsilon. Presbyterian. Contbr. articles to profl. jours. Office: Home Econs Dept 18111 Nordhoff St Northridge CA 91330

CLARK, EDYTHE MIDDLETON, religious exec.; b. Queen, N.Mex., Apr. 18, 1912; d. John Reagan and Rhoda J. (Tulk) M.; student Coll. Indsl. Arts, 1928-30; L.H.D., Inst. Religious Scis., 1967, D.D., 1974; m. Alton Herbert Clark, Feb. 17, 1936; children—Carolynn, Farris. Rancher, N.Mex., 1936-56; farmer, Tex., 1939—; oil operator, Roswell, N.Mex., 1952—; ordained to ministry United Ch. Religious Sci., 1960; pres. bd. dirs. Pala Dura Uranium, Amarillo, Tex., 1955-56; partner Alton H. Clark Royalty Co., Roswell, 1952-74; part-owner Clark & Clark Oil & Uranium, Roswell, 1954-58; asst. minister Founder's Ch. of United Ch. Religious Sci., Los Angeles, 1960-73, first exec. sec., 1973-74, corp. sec., sec. bd. trustees, 1974-76, v.p. in charge adminstrn., 1975, adminstrv. exec. of bd. trustees, 1977—, nat. and internat. dir. dept. member chs., 1977—; faculty Inst. Religious Sci. of United Ch. of Religious Sci. Sch. Ministry, 1960—. Recipient Meritorious Service award United Ch. of Religious Sci., 1976, Ernest Holmes award, 1981. Mem. United Clergy Religious Sci., Internat. New Thought Alliance. Compiler, editor, pub. eight volumes Jr. Ch. material for United Church Religious Sci. Home: 691 S Irolo St Apt 203 Los Angeles CA 90005 Office: 3251 W Sixth St Los Angeles CA 90075

CLARK, HAROLD VICTOR, elec. engr.; b. Winterset, Iowa, May 20, 1927; s. Delbert L. and Jessie M. (Jackson) C.; B.A., Union Coll., 1949; M.S. in Elec. Engring., Stanford U., 1955; m. Dorothy Vernice Simpson, Apr. 16, 1967. Instr., dept. of physics, Union Coll., Lincoln, Nebr., 1950; elec. engr. Ampex Corp., Redwood City, Calif., 1955—, sr. staff engr. Audio-Video Systems Div., 1971—. Served with U.S. Army, 1950-52. Mem. IEEE. Contbr. tech. papers in field, patentee in field. Home: 11556 Hillpark Ln Los Altos CA 94022 Office: Mail stop 3-59 401 Broadway Redwood City CA 94063

CLARK, HENRY BENJAMIN, JR., food company executive; b. Chevy Chase, Md., Oct. 8, 1915; s. Henry Benjamin and Lena (Sefton) C.; B.C.S., Northwestern U., 1937; M.B.A., Harvard, 1940; m. Geraldine D. Putman, July 25, 1942; children—Putman D., Sefton R. Analyst, Castle & Cooke, Inc., Honolulu, 1946-50, asst. sec., 1950-58, asst. treas., 1956-58, treas., 1958-70, v.p., 1962-70, exec. v.p., dir., from 1970, vice chmn. bd., 1980-81, chmn. bd., 1981—; dir. Hawaiian Telephone Co., Honolulu Gas Co., Pacific Resources, Inc., Hawaiian Ind. Refinery, Inc., Hawaiian Airlines, Bunker Hill Income Securities. Mem. Gov.'s Com. Employment of Handicapped; bd. dirs. Honolulu YMCA, Hawaii Loa Coll., Bishop Mus., Honolulu Acad. Arts (pres.), Honolulu Symphony Soc. (chmn.), McInerny Found., Goodwill Industries, Palolo Chinese Home, Pacific and Asian Affairs Council, Rehab. Hosp. Pacific; pres. Hawaii Prep. Acad., Aloha United Way. Served to lt. comdr. USNR, 1940-45. Mem. C. of C., Phi Kappa Psi. Clubs: Pacific, Outrigger, Pacific-Union. Office: Castle & Cooke Inc 130 Merchant St Honolulu HI 96813

CLARK, JACK LELAND, health and fitness center executive; b. San Bernardino, Calif., Oct. 11, 1930; s. Lealand Quency and Faye Loretta (Vaughn) Kindstrom; m. Marcella Newton, 1951 (div.); children—Jack L., Larry, Colleen; m. 2d, Lee D. Clark, Nov. 4, 1973. Student San Bernardino Valley Coll., 1948-50. With Santa Fe R.R., 1948; exec. v.p. Vic Tanny Internat., N.Y.C., 1950-58; founder, pres. Chgo. Health Clubs, 1962—; exec. v.p. Health & Tennis Corp., Los Angeles, 1975—; pres. Health Spa Fin.; v.p., dir. Finco Corp., Detroit; ptnr., investor Richard Simmons Anatomy Asylum. Mem. Phys. Fitness Assn. Am. Republican. Clubs: LaJolla Beach and Tennis, Kona Khi (San Diego). Investor gov.'s working bench Santa Fe R.R., kicking toe for football conversions. Office: 2810 One Century Plaza Los Angeles CA 90067

CLARK, JAMES GILBERT, pharmacist; b. Duluth, Minn., Aug. 27, 1927; s. Gilbert Rolph and Edith (Briggs) C.; student U. Minn., 1946-50; B.S. in Pharmacy, U. So. Calif., 1951; m. Betty Marie Larson, 1949 (div., 1966) children—Lor-Anne, Paula. Pharmacist, Cameron Pharmacy, Huntington Park, Calif., 1951-57; pharmacist, owner Clark Pharmacy, Long Beach, Calif., 1957-69, Abrams and Clark Pharmacy, Long Beach, 1969-77. Licensed pharmacist, Calif., Nev.; preceptor, Calif. Mem. Nat. Assn. Retail Druggists, Calif., Palm Springs-Coachella Valley pharm. assns., Pacific R.R. Soc. Home: 2235 Los Patos Dr Palm Springs CA 92264

CLARK, JAMES GORDON, vocational educator; b. Oakland, Calif., July 19, 1948; s. Donald Lurvey and Kay Jane (Klemgard) C.; m. Shawn Augusta Dyck, Jan. 18, 1975; 1 son, Kevin James. B.S. in Agr. and Agrl. Edn., Wash. State U., 1972, 78. Mgr. trainee Cenex Coop., Baker, Oreg., 1972; salesman agrl. chems. Oxychem., Tulelake, Calif., 1975; vocat. agrl. instr. McLoughlin High Sch., Milton-Freewater, Oreg., 1978—. Adv., Future Farmers Am. Served with Air N.G., 1967-72. Mem. Oreg. Vocat. Agrl. Tchrs. Assn., Nat. Vocat. Agrl. Tchrs. Assn., Am. Vocat. Assn., Oreg. Vocat. Assn., Oreg. Ednl. Assn., McLoughlin Future Farmers Am. Alumni Assn. Club: Elks (Milton-Freewater). Home: 118 SE 7th St Milton-Freewater OR 97862 Office: 120 S Main St Milton-Freewater OR 97862

CLARK, JAMES HOWARD, environmental engineer; b. Vancouver, Wash., Sept. 22, 1953; s. Robert Wallace and Florence Inez (Krein) C.; B.S.C.E. cum laude, Wash. State U., 1975, M.S. in Environ. Engring., 1976, cert. profl. preparation, 1975. Lectr., research asso. Wash. State U., Pullman, 1976-77; research san. engr. Pentech Houdaille, Cedar Falls, Iowa, 1977-78, regional san. engr., Napa, Calif., 1979-80; v.p. Treatment Equipment Co., Lake Oswego, Oreg., 1980—. Registered profl. engr., Wash., Calif., Oreg. Mem. Water Pollution Control Fedn., Pacific N.W. Pollution Control Assn., ASCE (asso.), Tau Beta Pi. Presbyterian. Contbr. articles to profl. publs.

CLARK, JANET EILEEN, political scientist, educator; b. Kansas City, Kans., June 5, 1940; d. Edward Francis and Mildred Lois (Mack) Morrissey; A.A., Kansas City Jr. Coll., 1960; A.B., George Washington U., Washington, 1962, M.A., 1964; Ph.D., U. Ill., 1973; m. Caleb M. Clark, Sept. 28, 1968; children—Emily Claire, Grace Ellen, Evelyn Adair. Staff, U.S. Dept. Labor, Washington, 1962-64; instr. social sci. Kansas City (Kans.) Jr. Coll., 1964-67; instr. polit. sci. Parkland Coll., 1970-71; asst. prof. govt., N.Mex. State U., Las Cruces, 1971-77, assoc. prof., 1977-80; assoc. prof. polit. sci. U. Wyo., 1981—. Wolcott fellow, 1963-64, NDEA Title IV fellow, 1967-69. Mem. NEA (pres. chpt. 1978-79), Western Social Sci. Assn. (exec. council 1978-81, pres.-elect 1983-84), Am. Polit. Sci. Assn., Western Polit. Sci. Assn., Women's Caucus for Polit. Sci. (treas. 1982), LWV (exec. bd. 1980-83), Women's Polit. Caucus, Beta Sigma Phi (v.p. chpt. 1978-79), Phi Beta Kappa, Chi Omega (prize 1962), Phi Kappa Phi. Democrat. Lutheran. Book rev.

editor Social Sci. Jour., 1982—. Contbr. articles to profl. jours. Home: 519 S 12th St Laramie WY 82070

CLARK, JEFFRY RUSSELL, counseling psychologist, consultant, researcher; b. Wareham, Mass., Oct. 12, 1950; s. John Russell and Barbara Jean (Roberts) C.; 1 son, Stephen Russell. B.S., Trinity Coll., 1975; M. Ed., Am. U., 1979; Ph.D., Stanford U., 1983. Social worker Monmouth Family Ctr., Middletown, N.J., 1975-76; counselor Annandale Correctional Ctr., Annandale, N.J., 1977, Temple Hills Counseling (Md.) Ctr., 1977-79; dir. Stanford (Calif.) Counseling Inst., 1979—; counselor Emergency Treatment Ctr., Palo Alto, Calif., 1981—; cons. Peninsula Children's Ctr. Pres. Annandale (N.J.) Jaycees, 1978-79. Served with USMC, 1969-71. Mem. Am. Psychol. Assn. Am. Personnel and Guidance Assn., Assn. Advancement Behavior Therapy, Western Psychol. Assn. Democrat. Research on children of divorce. Home: 115D Escondido Village Stanford CA 94305

CLARK, JERRY DANIEL, electronics company official; b. Denver, May 10, 1951; s. Edwin A. and Helen Clark; B.S. in Math., Whitworth Coll., 1973. Jr. programmer Am. Sign and Indicator, Spokane, Wash., 1973-75, system programmer, 1975-80, mgr. tech. support, 1980-82, mgr. mgmt. info. systems, 1982—. Mem. Assn. Systems Mgmt. Office: Am Sign & Indicator PO Drawer 2727 Spokane WA 99220

CLARK, JOHN FRANCIS, computer engineer; b. Phila., Feb. 27, 1940; s. John Francis and Mary Louise (Burghardt) C.; B.S., in Elec. Engring., Drexel U., Phila., 1963; M.S. in Engring., John Hopkins, 1968; m. Sally Ann Spangler, June 18, 1960; children—John, Eric, Kevin, Kara. Coop. engr. Philco Corp., Phila., 1959-63; sr. staff engr. Applied Physics Lab., Johns Hopkins, 1963-69; with Magnavox Research Lab., Torrance, Calif., 1969—, mgr. computer systems dept., 1973—, asst. dir. engring. and research, 1978-80, asst. dir. tech. ops., 1980-81, dir. computing resources, 1981—; pres. Computing Applications & Software Tech. Corp., 1981—. Active local Little League, Indian Guides. Mem. Inst. Nav., IEEE. Author papers in field. Home: 6165 Jeffrey Mark Cypress CA 90630 Office: 2829 Maricopa St Torrance CA 90503

CLARK, JOHN HAMILTON, chemist; b. San Gabriel, Calif., Nov. 22, 1949; s. Charles Warren and Nellie May (Hamilton) C.; A.B. with highest honors (Nat. Merit scholar 1967-71, Regent's scholar 1967-71, Pres.'s fellow 1970-71), U. Calif., Santa Barbara, 1971; Ph.D. (Chancellor's Sci. fellow, 1971-72, Kofoid eugenics fellow, 1972-73), U. Calif., Berkeley, 1976; m. Piyanud Ruth Hussey, June 12, 1971. J. Robert Oppenheimer research fellow Los Alamos Sci. Lab., 1976-79, asst. group leader for laser photochemistry, 1979; asst. prof. chemistry U. Calif., Berkeley, 1979—, prin. investigator materials and molecular research div. Lawrence Berkeley Lab., 1979—, Henry and Camille Dreyfus Tchr. scholar, 1981—; cons. on applications of lasers to chem., electronics and instrument mfrs. Grantee, Research Corp., 1980-81, Dept. Energy, 1980-83, Am. Heart Assn., 1980-82, Dow Chem. Co., 1981-83, Gen. Atomic Co., 1981; Alfred P. Sloan research fellow, 1982—; Dow Chem. Co. Found., 1981-83, Gas Research Inst., 1982-85, Office Naval Research, 1982-85. Mem. Am. Chem. Soc., Am. Phys. Soc., AAAS, Phi Beta Kappa, Sigma Xi. Co-author books, including: Laser Chemistry, 1977; Chemical and Biochemical Applications of the Laser, 1980; research, numerous publs. in field; patentee in laser chemistry. Office: Dept Chemistry U Calif Berkeley CA 94720

CLARK, JOSEPH FLYNN, high technology company executive; b. San Francisco, Aug. 21, 1949; m. Clara Sue Yamada; children—Joseph F., Jr., Stephanie M.; m. 2d, Marilyn J. Frigard Wendler, Feb. 14, 1981; 1 son, Jerry D. Bathn. B.S. in Bus. Adminstrn., U. San Francisco. With Nat. Cash Register, 1967-71; with Singer Bus. Machines, 1971-75; dir. mktg. northeast region Nat. Data Corp., N.Y.C., 1975-76, v.p. mktg. western region, Los Angeles, 1976-77; dir. mktg. Tymshare Trans. Services, San Francisco, 1977-78; v.p. assoc. Stanley, Barber, Southard, Brown & Assocs., San Francisco, 1978-79; nat. sales mgr. Tellus MSI Data Corp., Costa Mesa, Calif., 1979-80; dir. mktg. Itel-Systemix, Costa Mesa, 1980; v.p. mktg. Pierce Assocs., San Francisco, 1980-82; founder, pres. Joseph Clark & Co., Sunnyvale, Calif., 1982—; v.p. sales Excalibur Technols. Corp., Sunnyvale, 1982—. Vice pres. Santa Clara County council Boy Scouts Am., 1981-82, mem. nat. exec. com., 1981-82. Mem. Peninsula Mktg. Assn. (v.p. membership 1983-84), Peninsula Women in Advt. Republican. Club: Rotary (sec. 1982-83) (Sunnyvale). Home: 802 Revere Dr Sunnyvale CA 94087 Office: 1250 Oakmead Pkwy Suite 210 Sunnyvale CA 94086

CLARK, KENNETH JACKSON, technical and vocational educator; b. Joliet, Ill., Sept. 23, 1945; s. Kenneth Reese and Mae Iris (Jackson) C.; m. Harriett Iona, Mar. 22, 1970; children—Steven Brian, David William, Amy Kathryn. B.S. in Technology and Indsl. Edn., So. Ill. U., 1967, M.S. in Ednl. Adminstrn., 1972, specialist in Counseling, 1975; Ph.D. in Edn., St. Louis U., 1980. Cert. tchr., gen. adminstr., Ill. Tchr. indsl. edn. Pontiac (Ill.) Central Grade Sch., 1967-68, Collinsville (Ill.) High Sch., 1970-72, O'Fallon (Ill.) High Sch., 1972-80; asst. prof. edn., coordinator B.S. in occupation edn. So. Ill. U.-Carbondale, Norton AFB, Calif., 1980—; lectr. workshops Whitehead Ctr., U. Redlands, Calif. Trustee Valley Prep. Sch., 1981-82. Served with U.S. Army, 1968-70. Mem. Am. Vocat. Edn. Assn., Ill. Vocat. Edn. Assn., Planning Execs. Inst., Assn. Devel. of Computer-Based Instructional Systems, Kappa Delta Pi. Mem. Ch. of Christ.

CLARK, LEALAND L., physician; b. Pleasant Grove, Utah, July 13, 1931; s. Lealand A. and Ellna Bell (Cooper) C.; M.D., Columbia U., 1956; postgrad. U. Utah, 1957; m. Patricia Hanlon, Feb. 19, 1956; children—Elizabeth, David, Jennifer. Intern, U. Utah Hosp., Salt Lake City, 1956-57; resident Mayo Clinic, Rochester, Minn., 1957-60; practice gen. medicine, Salt Lake City, 1960—; clin. cons. dermatology U. Utah Hosp., 1960—; courtesy staff Cottonwood, Holy Cross, Latter Day Saints, St. Mark's hosps. Mem. fin. com. Unitarian Ch., Salt Lake City, 1960—, Sunday sch. tchr., 1960—. Served with M.C., U.S. Army, 1961-62. Recipient Mayo Centennial award, 1964; Columbia nat. scholar, 1949-53; Mayo Clinic fellow, 1957-60; diplomate Nat. Bd. Med. Examiners, Am. Bd. Dermatology. Mem. Intermountain Dermatologic Soc. (pres. 1969), AMA, Salt Lake County Med. Soc., Utah Med. Soc., Am. Acad. Dermatology, Pacific Dermatologic Assn., Utah Archaeol. Soc. Republican. Contbr. articles to profl. jours. Office: 1002 E S Temple St Salt Lake City UT 84102

CLARK, LLOYD, state ofcl.; b. Belton, Tex., Aug. 4, 1923; s. Lloyd C. and Hattie May (Taylor) C.; B.S. in Journalism, So. Meth. U., 1948; B. Fgn. Trade, Am. Grad. Sch. Internat. Mgmt., 1949; M. Pub. Adminstrn., Ariz. State U., 1972; m. Jean Reeves, June 17, 1950; children—Roger, Cynthia, Candyce. String corr. A.P., Dallas, 1941-42; editor, pub. Ex-Press, Arlington, Tex., 1945-48; publicity mgr. Advt. Counselors Ariz., Phoenix, 1949; reporter Phoenix Gazette, 1949-65; asst. pub. Ariz. Weekly Gazette, 1965-66; founder Council on Abandoned Mil. Posts-U.S.A., 1966; project cons. City of Prescott, Ariz., 1971-72; dep. dir. adminstrv. services No. Ariz. Council Govts., Flagstaff, 1972-73; regional adminstr. SouthEastern Ariz. Govts. Orgn., Bisbee, 1973-75; local govt. assistance coordinator Ariz. Dept. Transp., Phoenix, 1975-80, program adminstr., 1980—; editor and pub. Clark Biog. Reference, 1956-62. Served to lt. AUS, 1942-46; maj., 1966-70; col. Res. Recipient Ariz. exemplary gen. news coverage award, 1960, outstanding news reporting, 1961. Mem. Am. Grad. Sch. Internat. Mgmt. Alumni Assn. (pres. Phoenix chpt. 1965), Am. Soc. for Pub. Adminstrn., Res. Officers Assn., Ex-Students Assn. U. Tex. at Arlington (life mem., pres. 1946-48), Sigma Delta Chi (pres. Valley of Sun chpt. 1964). Author: Lloyd Clark's Scrapbook, Vol. 1, 1958, Vol. 2, 1960. Address: PO Box 13344 Phoenix AZ 85002

CLARK, MARK WILLIAM, educator, sport sociologist; b. Jacksonville, N.C., July 19, 1945; s. Herbert Philo and Elsa Marion (Hulbert) C.; m. Reiko Watanabe, Jan. 10, 1969; children—Midori, Saori. B.A., U. Calif.-Berkeley, 1973, M.A., 1976; Ph.D., Stanford U., 1980. Instr., Stanford (Calif.) U., 1977; asst. prof. dept. sociology Hofstra U., Hempstead, N.Y., 1977-80; mem. adj. grad. faculty dept. phys. edn. Adelphi U., Garden City, N.Y., 1981; asst. prof. dept. health and phys. edn. Sch. Edn., U. Mont., Missoula, 1981—. Served with USN, 1964-70; with USNR, 1970-74. Mem. AAHPER, Am. Sociol. Assn., Am. Assn. Leisure and Recreation, N.Am. Soc. for Sociology of Sport, Assn. for Anthrop. Study of Play, Internat. Soc. for Comparative Phys. Edn. and Sport, Mont. State Assn. for Health, Phys. Edn., Recreation and Dance, Phi Delta Kappa. Contbr. articles and papers to profl. jours. and assns. Home: 15 September Dr Missoula MT 59802 Office: 211 FH U Mont Dept Health and Phys Edn Missoula MT 59812

CLARK, MYRNA BAKER, art educator; b. Sturgis, S.D., July 25, 1937; d. Glenn Phillip and Holly Isabell (Howie) Baker; 1 son, Brooks. B.F.A. in Comml. Art and Edn., U. S.D., 1959; M.Ed., Mont. State U., 1981. Art supr. West Sioux Community Schs., Hawarden, Iowa, 1959-61; sec. to dir. library services Rocky Mountain Coll., Billings, Mont., 1967-68; proof reader Vermillion (S.D.) Plain Talk, 1965-66; tchr. art Ross High Sch., Hamilton, Ohio, 1968-70; asst. art dir. Sch. Dist. 2, Billings, 1970-80; art cons. State of Mont., also Mont. Migrant Workers Program; now art supr. Anchorage Sch. Dist. Bd. dirs. Midland Empire Council for Arts and Humanities. Delta Kappa Gamma scholar, 1979-80. Mem. Nat. Art Edn. Assn. (awards 1979, 80), Mont. Art Edn. Assn., Billings Art Assn., Mont. Inst. of Arts, Alaska Art Edn. Assn. (state div. dir. supervision and adminstrn.), Alaska Talent Bank, Cook Inlet Admirals Assn., Delta Kappa Gamma. Republican. Episcopalian. Clubs: Kappa Alpha Theta Alumnae (pres. 1976-78), Gourmet, Thread Benders. Home: 1790 Morningtide Ct Anchorage AK 99501 Office: Anchorage Sch Dist 5100 E 4th Ave Anchorage AK 99504

CLARK, NEWTON, III, oil company and trading company executive, business executive; b. Hood River, Oreg., May 9, 1937; s. Newton and Hallie Augusta (Puddy) C.; children—Scott, Charles. B.A. in Econs., Wash. State U., 1959. Chmn. bd. Pacific No. Oil Corp., Seattle, 1973—, v.p., 1980—; chmn. bd. Pacific No. Marine Co., Chempro of Oreg., 1979—, v.p., 1980—; dir. Pacific Futures, pres., 1983—; chmn. bd. Norwester Mgmt. Corp., 1983—, Norwester Securities Corp., 1983—. Trustee Alki Found.; mem. bus. adv. bd. Wash. State U. Coll. Bus. and Econs. Mem. Seattle C. of C. (trustee). Clubs: Seattle Yacht, Queen City Yacht, Wash. Athletic. Lodge: Masons. Office: 1723 8th St N Seattle WA 98109

CLARK, R. BRADBURY, lawyer, business executive; b. Des Moines, May 11, 1924; s. Rufus Bradbury and Gertrude Martha (Burns) C.; B.A., Harvard U., 1948, LL.B., 1951; Dipl.L., Oxford U., 1952; L.H.D. (hon.), Ch. Div. Sch. of Pacific, 1983; m. Polly Ann King, Sept. 6, 1949; children—Cynthia Clark Maxwell, Rufus Bradbury, John Atherton. Admitted to Calif. bar, 1952; assoc. atty. O'Melveny & Myers, Los Angeles, 1952-62, partner, 1962—; chancellor Episcopal Diocese Los Angeles, 1966-69; hon. canon Diocese of Los Angeles; dir. First Charter Fin. Corp., So. Calif. Water Co., Brown Internat. Corp., Automatic Machinery & Electronics, Inc., Econ. Resources Corp. Pres. bd. dirs. John Tracy Clinic, Los Angeles. Served with U.S. Army, 1943-46. Decorated Bronze Star with oak leaf cluster, Purple Heart with oak leaf cluster, Belgian Fourregere. Fulbright fellow, 1951-52. Mem. Am. Bar Assn., Calif. Bar Assn., Los Angeles County Bar Assn. Clubs: Calif., Chancery (Los Angeles); Alamitos Bay Yacht (Long Beach, Calif.). Editor: Ballantine and Sterling, California Corporation Laws, 1976—. Contbr. articles and monographs on bus. law subjects. Home: 615 Alta Vista Circle South Pasadena CA 91030 Office: 400 S Hope St Los Angeles CA 90071 2899

CLARK, RICHARD EDWARD, educational psychology, educator; b. Howell, Mich., Sept. 15, 1940; s. Emmett John and Virgilene Ann (Terhune) C.; m. Ruth Ann Colvin, 1982; children—Vincent, Katheryn, Diane, Jason. B.A., Western Mich. U., 1963; M.A. (Anneburg fellow), U. Pa., 1965; Ph.D. (U.S. Office of Edn. fellow), Ind. U., 1970. Dir. broadcasting Western Mich. U., Kalamazoo, 1968-70; lectr. Ind. U., 1968-70; dir. Communications Research Center, Calif. State U.-Sacramento, 1970-71; dir. Inst. Tech., Stanford U., Menlo Park, Calif., 1971-75; prof. instructional tech. and ednl. psychology Syracuse (N.Y.) U., 1975-78; prof. ednl. psychology and dir. Center for Instructional Research, U. So. Calif., Los Angeles, 1978—. Nat. Inst. Edn. fellow, 1980. Mem. Am. Psychol. Assn., Am. Ednl. Research Assn. Contbr. articles to profl. jours.

CLARK, RICHARD JAMES, advertising and marketing executive; designer, artist; b. Attica, N.Y., Aug. 19, 1945; s. Claude Jones and Rita Elizabeth (McKerna) C.; m. Joy Lynne, Dec. 22, 1966. B.S., SUNY-Buffalo, 1964, B.A., 1969; postgrad. Yale U., summer 1965; M.A., SUNY-Buffalo, 1970. Designer, Calspan Corp., Buffalo, 1966-69; mktg. exec. Erie Bank, Buffalo, 1969-71; designer Design for Industry, Buffalo, 1972-77; v.p. creative dir., 1978—; ptnr. Design Graphics, Buffalo, 1977—; pres., chmn. bd. Nat. Design Concepts, Huntington Beach, Calif., 1979—; cons., tchr. SUNY. Recipient Western N.Y. Communicators award, 1981, 82, 83; Clio award. Mem. Orange County Advt. Fedn., Bus. and Profl. Advt. Assn., Western N.Y. Communicators, Huntington Beach C. of C. Art editor Scene Mag.; exhibited several one man shows. Office: Nat Design Concepts 16152 Beach Blvd Suite 140 East Bldg Huntington Beach CA 92647

CLARK, RICHARD LEFORS, systems research scientist; b. Aberdeen, S.D., Oct. 29, 1936; s. Robert Montgomery and Marion (Shook) C.; B.A., Pacific Western U., 1974, M.S., 1975, Ph.D., 1978; B.S. in Engring. and Applied Sci., Jackson State Coll., 1968, M.A. in Bus. Mgmt., 1972; m. Barbara Louise Battersby, Mar. 28, 1980; 1 son, Robert James. Technician, Honeywell Co., 1957-58; quality assurance Martin Co., 1958-59, Remington Rand, 1959; engr. Gen. Dynamics/Electronics, 1959-68; supr. Graco, Inc., 1971-74; with Internat. Harvester, 1975-81, Caterpiller Tractor Co., 1981—; systems research in fusion power, parapsychology and physics, San Diego, 1975—; lectr. gravity/Maxwell-Faraday physics systems and devices. Served with U.S. Army, 1954-57. Fellow Am. Soc. Psychical Research; mem. Soc. Indsl. and Applied Math., Math. Assn. Am., Am. Chem. Soc., Internat. Platform Assn., Am. Nuclear Soc., Am. Research Soc., Assn. M.B.A. Execs., Am. Hist. Soc., N.Y. Acad. Scis., Am. Math. Soc., AAAS, Spacecraft Research Found., Psychical Research Found. (field reporter). Inventor vortex fusion engine; author tech. papers. Home: 4015 Crown Point Dr P-3 San Diego CA 92109

CLARK, RICHARD LYON, advertising agency exec.; b. New Haven, Dec. 19, 1929; s. Ralph Irving and Margaret Mary (Lyon) C.; student San Diego State Coll., 1947-49; B.Profl. Arts, Art Center Los Angeles, 1953; m. Roberta Jane Thomas, June 6, 1953; children—Robin, Leslie, Katherine, Patricia, Timothy. Art dir. Leo Burnett, Chgo., 1956-58, Campbell Ewald, Detroit, 1958-62, J. Walter Thompson, N.Y.C., 1962-64, Batten, Barton, Durstine & Osborne, N.Y.C., 1964-66, McCann Marschalk, N.Y.C., 1966-67; v.p. Kenyon & Eckhardt, N.Y.C., 1967-69; free lance writer, illustrator, 1969-72, contbr. articles illustrations to Yachting, True, Motor Boating, Rudder, and Sea mags.; owner, operator Richard Lyon Clark Advt. Agency, Newport Beach, Calif., 1972—; tchr. Art Center Coll. Design, Pasadena, Calif.; prin. Carib Dory Corp., Del. Served with U.S. Army, 1953-55. Recipient awards, including N.Y. Art Dirs.' Club, 1965-66, Detroit Art Dirs.' Club, 1963-64. Author, illustrator: What's Your Position?, 1980. Designer U.S. postage: Franklin Roosevelt stamp, John Dewey stamp. Home: 5892 Sierra Siena Irvine CA 92715

CLARK, ROBERT EDWARD, radiologist; b. Duluth, Minn., July 21, 1942; s. Ronald Elvyn and Elizabeth Jean (Linden) C.; M.D., U. Mich., 1966. Intern, Santa Monica (Calif.) Hosp., 1966-67; resident in diagnostic radiology U. Calif. Med. Sch., San Francisco, 1967-70, clin. instr., 1970-71, asst. prof. radiology, 1974-76, clin. asst. prof., 1976—; radiologist St. Francis Hosp., San Francisco, 1976—. Served to maj. U.S. Army, 1971-74. Mem. Radiol. Soc. N.Am., Uroradiol. Soc., San Francisco Med. Soc., San Francisco Radiol. Soc. Contbr. articles to profl. jours. Office: 900 Hyde St San Francisco CA 94109

CLARK, ROBERT EDWARD HOLMES, astrophysicist; b. Washington, July 8, 1947; s. Austin Bryant Jackson and Barbara (McClenon) C.; B.S., Frostburg (Md.) State Coll., 1969; M.S., Pa. State U., 1978, Ph.D., 1980; m. Charlsea Dee Shipp, July 18, 1970; children—Robin Ann, Victoria Gayle. High sch. physics tchr., Prince Georges County, Md., 1969-75; teaching asst. Pa. State U., 1975-76, 79-80, research asst., 1976-79, research asso., 1980; research asst. Sacramento Peak Obs., 1978; postdoctoral Los Alamos Nat. Lab., 1980-82, mem. staff, 1982—. Mem. Am. Phys. Soc., Sigma Xi, Phi Kappa Phi. Republican. Mem. Christian Ch. Contbr. numerous articles to sci. jours. Home: 110 Yosemite Dr Los Alamos NM 87544 Office: Los Alamos Sci Lab Group X-7 MSB257 Los Alamos NM 87545

CLARK, ROGER, mgmt. co. exec.; b. Madison, Wis., Dec. 13, 1934; s. Frank R. and Florence (Sirrine) C.; B.S. in Mech. Engring., Tex. A&M U., 1956; m. Marion Hursey, Apr. 30, 1960; children—Russell S., Randall S., R. Sean, R. Seth. With Babcock & Wilcox Co., 1956-72, sales engr., Houston, Amarillo, Midland (Tex.), Pitts., then sales mgr., Augusta, Ga.; product mgr. Johns Manville Corp., Denver, also product group mgr. and mdse. mgr. Indsl. Products div., 1972-81; owner Clarkson Co., mgmt. and sales tng., 1982—. cons. furnace/kiln constrn., refractory products. Scoutmaster, Boy Scouts Am., 1976-78; mem. vestry (Episcopal) Ch. of Good Shepherd. Served to 1st lt. U.S. Army, 1956-58. Registered profl. engr., Tex. Mem. ASME, Am. Ceramic Soc., Colo. Apt. Assn. (dir.). Republican. Patentee in refractory products; contbr. numerous articles to profl. jours. Home: 3347 E Geddes Dr Littleton CO 80122 Office: Box 2053 Littleton CO 80122

CLARK, ROLLIN F., real estate broker; b. Lexington, Nebr., Aug. 9, 1928; s. William Louis and Sarah Elizabeth (Mowery) C.; B.A. in Bus., Kearney (Nebr.) State Coll., 1962; m. Audrey H. White, June 30, 1949; 1 dau., Marlene Joyce. Self-employed farmer, Lexington, 1950-62; fur distbr., pres. Loveland Chinchilla Ranch, Inc., Loveland, Colo., 1962-65; real estate broker, Loveland, Colo., 1965—, pres. Clark Realty, Inc., Loveland, 1968—. Active Loveland United Fund; mem. Loveland Devel. Fund, 1975-77, Loveland Mus. Bd., 1976-80; precinct committeeman Republican party, 1958-62; treas. Dawson County Young Reps., 1959, organizational dir. Nebr. Young Reps., 1960, treas., 1961; city councilman, Loveland, 1972-74; mem. Loveland Bd. Adjustment, 1980-83, chmn., 1981-82. Named Realtor of Yr., 1982. Mem. United Chinchilla Assos. Inc. (sec.-treas. 1965-69, ed. newsletter 1967), Loveland Bd. Realtors (pres. 1969-70), Green Meadows Water Assn. (pres. 1972-73), Loveland C. of C., Pi Omega Pi. Republican. Mem. Christian Ch. (vice chmn. 1970-71, chmn. 1972-73). Elk, Rotarian. Home: 1701 W 22d St Loveland CO 80537 Office: 216 W 8th St Loveland CO 80537

CLARK, R(UFUS) BRADBURY, lawyer; b. Des Moines, May 11, 1924; s. Rufus Bradbury and Gertrude Martha (Burns) C., m. Polly Ann King, Sept. 6, 1949; children—Cynthia Clark, Rufus Bradbury, John Atherton. B.A., Harvard U., 1948, J.D., 1951; Dipl. Law, Oxford U., 1952. Bar: Calif. 1952. Assoc. O'Melveny & Myers, Los Angeles, 1952-61, ptnr., 1962—; dir. First Charter Fin. Corp., Beverly Hills, Calif., So. Calif. Water Co., Los Angeles, Econ. Resources Corp., Los Angeles, Brown Internat. Corp., Covina, Calif., Automatic Machinery and Electronics Corp., Covina. Chancellor, Episcopal Diocese of Los Angeles, 1967—; pres. bd. dirs. John Tracy Clinic, Los Angeles. Served with U.S. Army, 1943-46. Decorated Purple Heart with oak leaf cluster, Bronze Star with oak leaf cluster. Fulbright grantee, 1951-52. Mem. ABA, State Bar Calif. (chmn. drafting com. on gen. corps. law 1973-81, chmn. drafting com. on non-profit corps. law 1980—, mem. exec. com. bus. law sect. 1977-78), Los Angeles County Bar Assn., Calif. Bar Assn. Clubs: California, Chancery, Alamitos Bay Yacht. Editor: California Corporation Laws, 4th edit., 6 vols., 1976. Home: 615 Alta Vista Circle South Pasadena CA 91030 Office: 400 S Hope St Los Angeles CA 90071

CLARK, STEPHEN C(UTTER), III, ednl. research exec., lecturer; b. Salt Lake City, Mar. 21, 1918; s. Stephen Cutter, Jr. and Helen M. (Moodey) C.; student Calif. Inst. Tech., 1935-37; B.A., U. Wash., 1941, M.A. (Univ. fellow), 1945; Ph.D. (Univ fellow), Yale U., 1949; m. Anne A. Beaudin, Sept. 30, 1945 (dec. Jan. 1962); children—Margaret Andrews, Katherine Clark Hanberry, Elizabeth Clark Leone; m. 2d, Caroline P. North, Oct. 18, 1972. Lectr. in English, 1st Higher Sch., Tokyo, 1940-41; acting instr. in physics U. Wash., 1943-45; asst. to dir. student personnel U. New Haven, 1947-49; chmn. dept. psychology Alfred (N.Y.) U., 1949-51; prof. psychology John Muir Coll., Pasadena, Calif., 1951-55; test officer Calif. State Coll. at Los Angeles, 1955-60; dir. research info. center, research assoc. Calif. Tchrs. Assn., Los Angeles and Burlingame, 1958-62; dir. adminstrv. research San Diego United Sch. Dist., 1962-63; sr. staff ednl. applications IBM Systems Research and Devel. Ctr. Los Angeles and Irvine, Calif., 1963-66; edn. and social sci. research analyst HEW, Washington, 1966-67, 71-80; sr. scientist, prin. investigator Am. U., Washington, 1967-68; sr. ops. analyst, asst. to pres. Pacific Tech. Analysts, Inc., Saigon and Honolulu, 1968-69; sr. scientist computer devel. div. Univac div. Sperry Rand Corp., Washington, 1970; pres. DekaMeter Testing Service, 1972—. Served with USNR. Fellow AAAS; life mem. Am. Personnel and Guidance Assn., NEA, Nat. Vocat. Guidance Assn.; mem. Am. Psychol. Assn., Am. Ednl. Research Assn., Smithsonian Assocs., Common Cause, Internat. Platform Assn., Sierra Club, Phi Delta Kappa. Episcopalian. Clubs: Lions; Commonwealth (San Francisco). Author: Clark Occupational Knowledge Inventory, 1970; contbr. to College and Life (M.E. Bennett), 1941, 52, 60. Inventor DekaMeter Testing Terminal. Home and Office: 2161 Ptarmigan Dr No 4 Walnut Creek CA 94595

CLARK, SUE JANET, literary agent, writer; b. Vancouver, Wash., Oct. 17, 1929; d. Day Walter and Dorothy Janet (White) Hilborn; A.A., Stephens Coll., Columbia, Mo., 1949; student Northwestern U., Evanston, Ill., 1949-51; B.A., U. Wash., Seattle, 1952; children—Leslie Lora, Kyle Scott, Sidne Suzanne, Brian Casey. Continuity dir. KING-TV, Seattle, 1952-54; traffic mgr. KTNT-TV, Tacoma, 1954; free lance pub. relations cons., 1966-70; continuity dir. KTIM, San Rafael, Calif., 1966-68; coordinator vol. services Sunny Hills Residential Treatment Center for Emotionally Disturbed Adolescents, San Anselmo, Calif., 1968-73; dir. univ. relations U. Calif., San Francisco, 1973-77; real estate salesperson Home & Land Co., 1977-80; pres. Lindberg-Clark, Inc., mgr. Hotel Léger, 1978-82; owner S.J. Clark Lit. Agy., 1982—; free-lance writer. Past bd. dirs. Vol. Bur. Marin County. Cert. Am. Assn. Vol. Services Coordinators. Mem. Nat. Soc. Fund Raisers (charter), San

Francisco Easter Seal Soc. (past dir.), Pub. Relations Soc. Am., Calaveras County C. of C. (bd. dirs.), Alpha Delta Pi, Phi Beta. Republican. Presbyterian (elder). Home: Route 1 625 Hildebrandt San Andreas CA 95249 Office: Route 1 625 Hildebrandt San Andreas CA 95249

CLARK, SUSAN MARJORIE, flight instructor, lecturer; b. Reading, Pa., Oct. 21, 1944; d. Ralph Crestman and Elizabeth Marie (Frantz) Bolton; m. David William Clark (div.). Cert. pilot, flight instr., ground instr. Flight instr. Stone Mountain (Ga.) Aviation, 1972-73, Golden State Aviation, San Diego, 1973-75; owner Scarf N Goggles Flying Club, San Diego, 1975-79; chief flight instr., flight ops. mgr. Navajo Aviation, Concord, Calif., 1979—, accident prevention counselor FAA, 1973-79, also flight test examiner, written test examiner; instr. pilot courses USN ROTC, Palomar Jr. Coll., San Diego Mesa Coll., 1975-79; flew traffic watch sta. KSFO, San Diego, 1975-79; coordinator Pacific Air Race, 1977; mem. com. for recommendations for air safety, San Diego, 1978; charter pilot. Active various community programs. Mem. Aircraft Owners and Pilots Assn., Ninety Nines. Developer pinch-hitter course for flying companions. also 531 Mount Dell Dr Clayton CA 94517

CLARK, TERRENCE TOWN, optometrist; b. South Bend, Ind., July 4, 1949; s. Ora Town and Thais Marie (Seidel) C.; m. Rosemarie Price, June 25, 1971; children—Emily, Allison. B.S., U. Wash., 1971, M.A., 1973; O.D. with distinction, Pacific U., 1978. Lic. optometrist, Wash. Pvt. practice optometry, Marysville, Wash., 1981—. Active Marysville Maryfest. Served to capt. U.S. Army, 1978-81. Mem. Am. Optometric Assn., Snohomish County Optometric Soc. (past sec.-treas., pres. 1983-84), Wash. State Optometric Assn., Am. Optometric Found. (J. Harold Bailey award 1978), C. of C. Club: Lions (bd. dirs. 1983). Office: Professional Ctr 1375 State Ave Marysville WA 98270

CLARK, THOMAS JOSEPH, optometrist, former mayor Long Beach (Calif.); b. San Diego, July 13, 1926; s. Thomas Joseph and Marjorie Sarah (Harper) C.; B.S., U. Calif.-Berkeley, 1950, M.S., 1951, D.Optometry, 1951; m. Lois Olney, Feb. 22, 1952; children—Paul, James, Carol. Pvt. practice optometry, Long Beach, 1951—; mem. park commn. City Long Beach, 1963-66, mem. city council, 1966—, mayor, 1975-80, 82—; 82—; pres. Los Angeles County div. League of Cities, 1978-79; pres. League of Calif. Cities, 1981-82. Chmn. Los Altos (Calif.) YMCA, 1959-61. Served with AUS, 1944-46. Mem. Am., Calif. optometric assns., Long Beach Optometric Soc. (pres. 1955-56), Ind. Cities Los Angeles County (pres. 1968-69). Republican. Methodist. Clubs: Masons, Lions, Rotary. Home: 2267 Albury Ave Long Beach CA 90815 Office: 5479 Abbeyfield St Long Beach CA 90815

CLARK, TIM WILLIAM, wildlife researcher, consultant; b. Muskogee, Okla., Oct. 23, 1942; s. Robert D. and Edwina (Ostrander) C. B.S. in Biology, N.E. Okla. State U., 1964; M.S. in Zoology, U. Wyo., 1969; Ph.D., U. Wis. Madison, 1973. Chmn. depts. biology and natural resources Wis. State U., Medford, 1969-71; teaching and research positions U. Wis.-Madison, 1971-75, Wis. Regional Primate Research Center, 1971-73; adj. faculty biology, grad. faculty Idaho State U., 1975—; dir. Yellowstone Inst., 1978-80; pres. Biota Research and Cons., Inc., Jackson, Wyo., 1980—. Bd. dirs. Jackson Hole Alliance for Responsible Planning, 1980—. Nat. Geog. Soc. grantee, 1973, 74, 76, 77, 82; U.S. Nat. Acad. Scis. grantee, 1975, 74. Nat. Audubon Soc. grantee, 1974, 75. Wildlife Preservation Trust Internat. grantee 1981, 82. N.Y. Zool. Soc. Animal Research and Conservation Center grantee, 1982. Mem. The Wildlife Soc., Ecol. Soc. Am., N.W. Sci. Assn., Am. Soc. Mammalogists, Am. Inst. Biol. Scis., others. Editor: (with R.D. Dorn) Rare and Endangered Vascular Plants and Vertebrates of Wyoming; author: Ecology of Jackson Hole, 1980; contbr. numerous articles of black-footed ferrets, prairie dogs, grizzly bears, Japanese monkeys, pine martens and mule deer to profl. jours. Address: Box 2705 Jackson WY 83001

CLARK, TIMOTHY GENEREUX, management consultant; b. Pasadena, Calif., May 24, 1939; s. Benjamin C. and Margaret J. (Genereux) C.; m. Diana Martell, Sept. 27, 1962; 1 dau., Pamela. A.B., U. So. Calif., 1961; M.B.A., Harvard U., 1965. Assoc., Booz, Allen & Hamilton, Los Angeles, 1968-73; v.p., Los Angeles, N.Y.C., 1975-81; v.p. mktg. Arrowhead Pumtas Div., Coca Cola Bottling Co. of Los Angeles, 1973-75; ptnr., mgmt. cons. Coopers & Lybrand, Los Angeles, 1981—. Chmn., Center for Non-Profit Mgmt., 1981-82. Mem. So. Calif. Corp. Planners Assn., Harvard Bus. Sch. Assn. of So. Calif. (pres. 1982-83). Republican. Clubs: Annandale Golf (Pasadena); Jonathon (Los Angeles); Millbrook (Greenwich, Conn.); Harvard (N.Y.C.). Home: 2110 Homet Rd San Marino CA 91108 Office: 1000 W 6th St Los Angeles CA 90017

CLARK, WILLIAM ROY, safety supervisor, b. Scotia, Calif., May 12, 1951; s. William Clyde and Leola Gene (Taylor) C.; m. Karen Ann Hager, May 29, 1976; 1 dau., Tiffany Elizabeth. Student Clark Coll., Vancouver, Wash., 1971; B.S. in Math., U. Oreg., 1973; M.S. in Indsl. Relations, 1982; cert. supervisory mgmt. 1979. Math. instr. Elmira High Sch., 1973-75; with rd. constrn. Internat. Paper Co., Vaughn, Oreg., 1975-76, surveyor, engr., 1977, head powderman, 1977-79, safety supr., 1979-81, regional woodlands safety supr., 1981—. Mem. adv. bd. Fernridge Med. Clinic, 1980-81. Mem. Am. Soc. Safety Engrs. Democrat. Club: Eugene Slowpitch Softball (most valuable player 1981).

CLARKE, BONNIE LEE, sales exec.; b. Stockton, Calif., Oct. 20, 1941; d. Lloyd John and Verle Marianne (Wilson) Houghtaling; B.S. in Bus. Adminstrn., San Jose State U., 1964; children—Timothy John, Sally Esther. Asst. buyer Roos-Atkins, San Francisco, 1964-66; student advisor, instr. fashion merchandising and secretarial careers Patricia Stevens Career Coll., San Francisco, 1966-69; office mgr. PSNM Careers Ltd., Seattle, 1970-72, fashion merchandising coordinator, adminstr. Carolyn Hansen Fashion Coll., Seattle, 1976-80; in sales Nordstrom, Seattle, 1980—. Bd. dirs. Wash. State Commn. for Vocat. Schs.; mem. Vocat. Sex Equity Adv. Council; ch. clk. Community Bapt. Ch., Issaquah, Wash., 1981—. Mem. Wash. Personnel and Guidance Counselors Assn., Wash. Vocat. Assn., Am. Mktg. Assn., Western Mktg. Edn. Assn., Seattle Opera Guild. Home: 3006 241st St SE Issaquah WA 90827 Office: Bellevue Square Bellevue WA 98004

CLARKE, CHARLES LEE, JR., obstetrician and gynecologist; b. Danville, Va., Mar. 4, 1941; s. Charles Lee and Marian (Luther) C.; B.A. in English, U. N.C., 1963, M.D., 1967; m. Karen Lee Spangler, Dec. 22, 1963; children—Robin Elizabeth, Gray Ballengee (twins). Intern, U. Wash., 1967-68; resident in ob-gyn Bernalillo County Med. Center, Albuquerque, 1971-74; practice medicine specializing in ob-gyn, Roswell and Las Vegas, N.Mex.; former chief of staff Las Vegas Hosp. Served to capt. M.C., USAF, 1968-74. Diplomate Am. Bd. Ob-Gyn. Fellow Am. Coll. Obstetricians and Gynecologists; mem. San Miguel County Med. Soc. (sec.-treas. 1982—).

CLARKE, ERNEST PARRISH, architect; b. Valdosta, Ga., May 1, 1938; s. William David and Margaret Emma (Parrish) C.; student U. Fla., 1958; A.A. in Architecture, Fullerton Coll., 1969; student Laguna Beach Sch. Art, 1977. Architect, planner in pvt. practice specializing in ch. architecture, Santa Ana, Calif., 1977—; works include Linda Vista Ch. of Nazarene, San Diego, Rose Drive Bapt. Ch. Sanctuary, Yorba Linda, Calif., Immanuel Bapt. Ch. Sanctuary, San Bernardino, Calif., College Park Bapt. Ch. Sanctuary, Las Vegas. Lic. architect, Calif., Nev., Ariz.; cert. Nat. Council Archtl. Registration Bds. Mem. AIA. Baptist. Club: Tall of Orange County. Office: 2431 N Tustin Ave Suite O Santa Ana CA 92705

CLARKE, FRANK, physician, health systems administrator; b. Blythe, Calif., Nov. 11, 1921; s. Francis Dodsworth; grad. cum laude Los Angeles City Coll., 1942; B.S., UCLA, 1946; M.D., St. Louis U., 1950; postgrad. U.S. Naval Med. Sch., 1951-52; MPH, U. Calif.-Berkeley; m. Pearl Tucker, children—Michael A., Timothy L., Stephen, Teressa, M. Robert, Sha-ni. Diplomate Am. Bd. Family Practice. Intern, USN Hosp., Oakland, Calif., 1950-51; resident Tulare County Gen. Hosp., Tulare, Calif., 1953-54; practice medicine and surgery, Woodlake, Calif., 1974-75; mem. staff Kaweah Delta Dist. Hosp.; chief staff Exeter Meml. Hosp., 1954-56; team physician Coll. of Sequoias, 1968-75; med. dir. USPHS; clin. dir. Albuquerque Indian Hosp., 1975—; lecturer U. Calif. at Santa Cruz, 1971-73; asst. clin. prof. dept. family and community medicine Georgetown U., 1980—. Trustee, Woodlake Union Elementary Sch. Dist., 1956-60, pres. bd. trustees, 1958-60; chmn. Citizens Adv. Com., Title I Funds, 1969-73. Bd. dirs. D-Q. U., 1971. Served with USN, 1942-46, 50-53. Recipient fellowship and grant John Hay Whitney Found., 1950; Indian achievement award Indian Council Fire Chgo., 1961; named Man of Year, City of Woodlake, 1962. Charter fellow Am. Acad. Family Physicians; mem. Assn. Am. Indian Physicians (pres. 1973-74), Nat. Council Clin. Dirs. (chmn. 1977-79), Phi Chi, Tau Alpha Epsilon. Episcopalian (del. 1969-73). Home: 10 Cedar Hills Dr Pocatello ID 83204 Office: USPHS Indian Health Ctr PO Box 317 Fort Hall ID 83203

CLARKE, GEORGE WHITAKER, lawyer, state senator; b. Perry, Iowa, June 22, 1906; s. Fred Greene and Mabel May (Moss) C.; J.D., U. Wash., 1927; m. Helen Vinal, July 5, 1930; children—Louise, George Whitaker, Jr., Keith; m. 2d, Mary Borkenmeyer, May 23, 1976. Admitted to Wash. State bar, 1927, since practiced in Seattle; mem. firm Clarke, Bovingdon & Cole, Seattle, 1971—; gen. mgr. Wash. Surveying and Rating Bur., Seattle, 1957-71; mem. Wash. Ho. of Reps., 1967-71; mem. Wash. Senate, Seattle, 1971—. Mem. Mercer Island Sch. Bd., 1947-67. Served to lt. USNR, 1944-45. Mem. Am. Bar Assn., Seattle C. of C. Office: 1111 Hoge Bldg Seattle WA 98104

CLARKE, JAMES WESTON, political science educator; b. Elizabeth, Pa., Feb. 16, 1937; s. Alonzo Peterson and Beatrice (Weston) C.; children—Julianne, Michael. B.A., Washington and Jefferson Coll., 1962, M.A., 1964, Ph.D., 1968. Asst. prof. Fla. State U., 1967-71; assoc. prof. U. Ariz., Tucson, 1971-76, prof. polit. sci., 1976—, dept. chmn., 1973-78. Served with USMC, 1955-58. Recipient James Gillespie Blaine prize Washington and Jefferson Coll., 1962, Matthew Brown Ringland prize, 1962. Mem. Internat. Soc. Polit. Psychology, Soc. Southwestern Authors, Am. Polit. Sci. Assn., Midwest Polit. Sci. Assn., Sierra Club, Wilderness Soc., Nature Conservancy. Democrat. Author: American Assassins: The Darker Side of Politics, 1982. Office: 315 Social Sci Bldg U Ariz Tucson AZ 85721

CLARKE, JOHN EDWARD, mgmt. recruitment co. exec.; b. Vancouver, B.C., Can., Dec. 13, 1937; s. William James and Laura Mackay C.; B.A., Oberlin Coll., 1960; m. Joanne Saltsman, June 10, 1958; children—Sheryl, Lynn, Bill. Comml. mgr. Ohio Bell Telephone Co., Cleve., 1960-66; mgr. staff recruiting Booz, Allen & Hamilton, Inc., N.Y.C., 1966-69; spl. asst. to postmaster gen. U.S. Post Office Dept., Washington, 1969-70; exec. asst. to dir. OEO, Washington, 1970-71; staff asst. to Pres., White House, Washington, 1971-73; v.p. S.E. Banking Corp., Miami, Fla., 1973-74; mng. dir. nat. spltys., mem. exec. com., sr. officer Korn/Ferry Internat., Los Angeles, 1974-81; pres. Clarke & Assos., mgmt. recruiters, Westlake Village, Calif., 1981—.

CLARKE, JOYCE ANNE, biochemist; b. Sheffield, Eng., Sept. 17, 1947; came to U.S., 1968; d. Fred A. and Annie (Johnson) C.; m. Frank Ogawa, 1982. B.A. with honors, Girton Coll., Cambridge U., Eng., 1968, M.A., 1972; Ph.D. (fellow) in Biochemistry, U. Calif.-Riverside, 1974. Research asst. dept. biochemistry U. Calif.-Riverside, 1968-73; lectr. dept. life scis. Middle East Tech. U., Ankara, Turkey, 1974-76; Dept. Energy research asso. Plant Research Lab., Mich. State U., East Lansing, 1976-78; assoc. biochemist dept. plant scis. U. Calif., Riverside, 1979—, communications coordinator Internat. Club, 1979—. NSF fellow, 1976-78; Phi Beta Kappa scholar, 1972-73. Mem. Am. Soc. Plant Physiologists, Brit. Film Inst., Sigma Xi. Club: University. (Riverside); Anglo-Am. Friendship. Episcopalian. Contbr. articles on plant psysiology and jojoba biochemistry to profl. jours. Home: 955 Via Zapata St Riverside CA 92507 Office: Dept Botany and Plant Sciences Univ of California Riverside CA 92521

CLARKE, JULIE WILLIAMSON (MRS. L.P. MYERS), design company executive; b. Oakland, Calif., May 13, 1939; d. Arthur Douglas and Doris (Dana) Williamson; m. Jerry Eugene Clarke, Apr. 3, 1964; m. 2d, Lawrence Paul Myers, Feb. 7, 1981. B.A. in Interior Design, San Jose State U., San Jose, Calif., 1962. Designer, Maynard-Lyon, 1962-63, Young and Assos., 1963-67, sales Ferguson Hildreth, 1968-76; pres., co-founder Baldwin-Clarke Assos., Inc., San Francisco, 1976—; lectr. schs., univs., profl. groups. Bd. dirs. San Francisco YMCA, 1982—. Named Disting. Alumni San Jose State U., 1982. Mem. Am. Soc. Interior Designers, Inst. Bus. Designers (pres. chpt.). Contbr. articles in field to mags. and bus. jours. Office: 700 Sansome St San Francisco CA 94111

CLARKE, KENNETH VINCENT, computer consulting company executive; b. N.Y.C., Feb. 21, 1943; s. Charles E. and Lillian A. (Borrelli) C.; children—Charles, Kenneth. B.B.A., CUNY, 1971. Mgr. systems and programming L.I. Coll. Hosp., Bklyn., 1970-75; dir. info. systems Ch. Charity Found. of L.I., Garden City, 1975-79; sr. cons. Hosp. Fin. Services, Newport Beach, Calif., 1979-80; pres. West End Computer Assn., Irvine, Calif., 1980—. Mem. Hosp. Fin. Mgmt. Assn., Electronic Computing Health Oriented, Assn. Hosp. Computer Systems (past pres.). Home: 19612 Constellation Ln Huntington Beach CA 92646 Office: 9550 Warner Ave Suite 250 Fountain Valley CA 92708

CLARKE, MICHAEL, city and county ofcl.; b. Chgo., June 24, 1928; s. Edward and Tessie (O'Donnell) C.; student U. So. Calif., No. Ill. U.; B.S., Naval Postgrad. Sch., Monterey, Calif., 1963; M.P.A., U. Colo., 1980; m. Catherine Barbara James, Dec. 30, 1961; children—Katherine Ann, Mary Therese, Patricia Jean. Co. pilot King Resources Co., Denver, 1969-70; tech. writer Jeppesen Sanderson Co., Denver, 1973-74; safety coordinator Parks and Recreation Dept., Denver, 1974-76, Risk Mgmt. Office, City and County of Denver, 1976—; speaker Colo. Safety Congress. Served with USN, 1946-69. Cert. safety profl. Mem. Am. Soc. Safety Engrs. (chpt. v.p.), Public Employees Safety Com. Republican. Roman Catholic. Clubs: KC, Arapahoe Valley Optimist (Littleton, Colo.). Stunt pilot for movie Tora - Tora - Tora, 1968. Home: 6877 S Fillmore Ct Littleton CO 80122 Office: 3840-H York St Denver CO 80205

CLARKE, ROBERT FRANCIS, metallic ore processing research co. exec.; b. Mpls., Mar. 20, 1915: s. Charles Patrick and Maurine Elizabeth (Clark) C.; B.S. with honors, U. Fla., 1948; M.S., U. Ariz., 1971; m. Charlotte Adele Radwill, July 24, 1966; children—Robert, Carol, David. Meteorologist, U.S. Weather Bur., 1940-42, 48-50, 52-55; supervisory electronics engr. U.S. Army Electronics Proving Ground, 1956-58, nuclear physicist, chief scientist nuclear surveillance div., 1958-62; aerospace engr. NASA, Lewis Research Ctr., 1962-66; physicist Hughes Aircraft Co., 1966-68; instr. Math. Pima Community Coll., and San Juan campus N.Mex. State U., 1974-75; instr. math. Am. Internat. Sch., Kabul, Afghanistan, 1976-78; dir. Polaris Internat. Metals Corp., Tucson. Radiol. def. officer Fed. Emergency Mgmt. Agy., CAP. Served with U.S. Army, 1942-46, USAF, 1950-52; res. ret. as col., 1975. Recipient nat. award for best articles in Officer Rev. Sr. mem. IEEE, AIAA; mem. Am. Nuclear Soc., Soc. Photo-Optical Instrumentation Engrs., Am. Meteorol. Soc., Am. Optical Soc., Soc. Unmanned Vehicle Systems, Arctic Inst. N.Am., AAUP, Assn. Former Intelligence Officers, Am. Def. Preparedness Assn., Scientists and Engrs. for Secure Energy, N.Y. Acad. Scis., Ariz.-Nev. Acad. Scis., Navy League, Am. Legion, VFW, AMVETS, Ret. Officers Assn., U.S. Naval Inst., Assn. U.S. Army, Air Force Assn., Mil. Order World Wars. Club: Army and Navy. Lodges: Odd Fellows, Kiwanis. Contbr. articles in aerospace and nat. def. to mags., jours. Home: 5846 E South Wilshire Dr Tucson AZ 85711 Office: 1745 E Factory Ave Tucson AZ 85719

CLARKE, URANA, musician, writer, educator; b. Wickliffe-on-the-Lake, Ohio, Sept. 8, 1902; d. Graham Warren and Grace Urana (Olsaver) C.; artists and tchrs. diploma Mannes Music Sch., N.Y.C., 1925; certificate Dalcroze Sch. Music, N.Y.C., 1950; student Pembroke Coll., Brown U.; B.S., Mont. State U., 1967, M.Applied Sci., 1970. Mem. faculty Mannes Music Sch., 1922-49, Dalcroze Sch. Music, 1949-54; adv. editor in music The Book of Knowledge, 1949-65; v.p., dir. Saugatuck Circle Housing Devel.; guest lectr. Hayden Planetarium, 1945; guest lectr., bd. dirs. Roger Williams Park Planetarium, Providence; radio show New Eng. Skies, Providence, 1961-64, Skies Over the Big Sky Country, Livingston, Mont., 1964-79, Birds of the Big Sky Country, 1972-79, Great Music of Religion, 1974-79; mem. adv. com. Nat. Rivers and Harbors Congress, 1947-58; instr. continuing edn. Mont. State U. Chmn., Park County chpt. ARC, co-chmn. county blood program, first aid instr. trainer, 1969—; instr. ARC cardio-pulmonary resuscitation, 1976—; mem. Mont. Commn. Nursing and Nursing Edn., 1974-76, Park County Local Govt. Study Commn., 1974-76. Mem. Am. Acad. Polit. Sci., Am. Musicol. Soc., Royal Astron. Soc. Can., Inst. Nav., Maria Mitchell Soc. Nantucket, N.Am. Yacht Racing Union, AAAS, Meteoritical Soc., Internat. Soc. Mus. Research, Skyscrapers (sec.-treas. 1960-63), Am. Guild Organists, Park County Wilderness Assn. (treas.), Trout Unlimited, Nature Conservancy, Big Sky Astron. Soc. (dir. 1965—), Sierra Club. Lutheran. Club: Cedar Point Yacht. Author: The Heavens are Telling (astronomy), 1951; Skies Over the Big Sky Country, 1965; also astron. news-letter, View It Yourself, weekly column Big Skies; contbr. to mags, on music, nav. and astronomy. Pub. Five Chorale Preludes for Organ, 1975; also music elementary two-piano pieces. Inventor, builder of Clarke Adjustable Piano Stool. Address: Log-A-Rhythm 9th St Island Livingston MT 59047

CLARKE, WILLIAM EDWARD, educational administrator; b. Alexandria, Ind., Mar. 22, 1927; s. Albert Lafayette and Orpha Blanche (Kilgore) C.; m. Louise Fern Hershberger, Dec. 20, 1948; children—Fred William, Marjorie Louise. A.B., Manchester Coll., 1949; M.S., Ind. U., 1951; Ed.D., Mich. State U., 1960. Tchr., Chester Schs., North Manchester, Ind., 1949-51; counselor Birmingham (Mich.) Schs., 1951-56; head resident advisor Mich. State U., East Lansing, 1956-58; guidance coordinator San Diego County (Calif.), 1958-62, 75-82; dean of students U.S. Internat. U., San Diego, 1962-70; dir. Universidad Internat. de Mex., Mexico City, 1970-73; assoc. prof. U.S. Internat. U., San Diego, 1973-74; dir. Internat. Univ.-Europe, Evian, France, 1975; regional dir. San Diego County, Calif. Office Edn., 1982—. Served with USN, 1945-46. Mem. Assn. Supervision and Curriculum Devel., Am. Ednl. Research Assn., Assn. Calif. Sch. Adminstrs., NEA, Calif. Tchrs. Assn. Methodist. Home: 3548 Mount Carol Dr San Diego CA 92111 Office: 6401 Linda Vista Rd San Diego CA 92111

CLARKE, ZONA MARIE, hospital administrator; b. Baker, Oreg., May 6, 1923; d. Ray Henry and Nell Rhea (Colton) Miller; R.N., Sacred Heart Hosp., Spokane, 1945; B.S., Eastern Oreg. State Coll., 1982; m. Francis Bailey Clarke, Aug. 17, 1947; children—Vicki L., Patti Z. Clarke Howell, Terri J. Clarke Bell, J. Tabor, Nelson C., Michael S. Charge and spl. duty nurse St. Elizabeth Community Hosp., Baker, 1949-66, inservice coordinator, 1973-75, asst. dir. nursing, 1974-75, dir. nursing, 1975-77, v.p. nursing, 1977-82; dir. nursing Cedar Manor Nursing Home, 1968-73, 83—; adv. bd. Council Med. Edn., Eastern Oreg. State Coll.; exec. bd., past sec. Council Med. Edn.; adv. council Oreg. Continuing Edn. for Nurses; adv. bd. Baker County Health Occupations, 1976-80. Served to 1st lt. Nurse Corps, AUS, 1945-47. Mem. Am. Nurses Assn. (nat. accreditation bd., mem. site visitor pool), Oreg. Nurses Assn., Eastern Oreg. Soc. Nursing Adminstrs. (sec.-treas., past pres., mem. council), Am. Soc. Nursing Service Adminstrs., Oreg. Soc. Nursing Adminstrs. (adv. council), Nat. League Nursing, Wingville Grange, AAUW. Republican. Roman Catholic. Clubs: Rotary Ann, Baker Country. Home: 1085 11th St Baker OR 97814 Office: 3325 Pocahontas Rd Box 766 Baker OR 97814

CLARKSON, DAVID MICHAEL, software products co. exec.; b. San Angelo, Tex., Jan. 21, 1948; s. William George and Ruth Garvene (Carlin) C.; B.B.A. (Rotary scholar, U. Tex. Chancellor's scholar), U. Tex., Austin, 1970, postgrad., 1970-77; m. Martha Jane Bradley, Nov. 9, 1968; 1 son, Robert Michael. Computer systems devel. Tracor, Inc., Austin, 1969-71, MRI Systems corp., Austin, 1971-72; exec. v.p. Data Base Mgmt. Systems, Inc., Miami, Fla., 1972-76; v.p., dir. data base mgmt. systems research and devel. Calif. Software Products, Inc., Santa Ana, 1976-80; pres. CORION Internat., Inc., Newport Beach, Calif., 1980—; instr. data base mgmt. U. Calif., Santa Cruz. Mem. Assn. Computing Machinery, Internat. Brotherhood of Magicians. Club: Photography. Reviewer tech. papers, books. Designer, implementer registered data base mgmt. system. Home: 24446 Caswell Ct Laguna Niguel CA 92677 Office: PO Box 8190 Newport Beach CA 92660

CLARO, WANDA IRENE, dentist; b. Orange, Calif., Apr. 2, 1951; d. Albert and Cecile (Horowitz) Lagmay; B.S., U. Calif., San Francisco, 1977, D.D.S., 1977; m. Vaughn Arlen Woodruff, Sept. 2, 1973; children—Meaghan Hall, Tyree LaVonne. Adminstrv. asst. minority relations Placement Center, Calif. State U., Fullerton, 1971-73, tutor, 1973-75, dir. summer orientation, 1974-75; interviewer psychol. study U. Calif., San Francisco, 1976-77; peer dentist, dir. clinic United Health Center, Parlier, Calif., 1977-79; pvt. practice dentistry, Visalia, Calif., 1979—. Calif. Regents scholar, 1973-77; Fleming scholar, 1974. Mem. ADA, Am. Assn. Women Dentists, Calif. Dental Soc., Tulare-Kings County Dental Soc., Bus. and Profl. Women's Orgn. Democrat. Office: 507 W Willow Suite D Visalia CA 93291

CLASQUIN, LORRAINE ALICE, lawyer; b. St. Louis, June 4, 1950; d. Frank Frederick and Signe Elizabeth (Henriksen) Clasquin; m. Eric Ferrand Harslem, May 5, 1979. B.A., Wellesley Coll., 1972; J.D., U. So. Calif., 1977. Bar: Calif., 1977. With Rand Corp., Santa Monica, Calif., 1972-76; assoc. Barrett, Stearns, Collins, Gleason & Kinney, Torrance, Calif., 1977-82, Boren, Elperin, Howard & Sloan, Los Angeles, 1982-83, Burkley, Moore, Greenberg & Lyman, Torrance, Calif., 1983 [illegible]. Home: 869 Muskingum Ave Pacific Palisades CA 90272

CLAUSEN, ORVEL WILLIAM, engineer; b. Decatur, Ill., Oct. 14, 1934; s. Orvel Thomas and Vivian Dorothy (Hoyt) C.; m. Karen Joyce Kusenda, June 18, 1955; children—Laurie Kay, Bradley William. B.S. in Mech. Engring., U. Ill., 1956, M.S., 1961. Asst. mgr. Viking Biology Instrument, TRW Inc., Redondo Beach, Calif., 1974-76, project mgr. applied tech. div., 1976-78, mgr. design dept., 1978-81, mgr. hardware engring. lab., 1981—. Active youth soccer and softball programs,

Huntington Beach, Calif. Mem. ASME, AIAA. Contbr. articles to profl. jours. Home: 16362 Underhill Ln Huntington Beach CA 92647 Office: One Space Park 01/2080 Redondo Beach CA 90278

CLAUSSEN, PAULA ANN, found. exec.; b. Spokane, Sept. 26, 1935; d. William Henry and Marguerite Katherine (Oos) Quine; student Eastern Wash. U.; m. Gerald F. Claussen, Aug. 1, 1953; children—Gerald M., Paul A., Mark R., Dental asst., Spokane, 1952-63; office mgr., dental asst., Spokane, 1963-73; vol. adviser Wash. March of Dimes, Spokane, 1970-74; chmn. Mothers March, Spokane County March of Dimes, 1973-74; coordinator Mothers March, Birth Defects Found., 1974-78; field tng. specialist March of Dimes-Birth Defects Found., 1978-80, coordinator field services, 1980-81, Mpls., 1981-83, spl. asst. dept. devel., hdqrs., 1983—. Mem. Wash. Fedn. Women's Clubs (dir. jrs. 1968-70, advisor jr. membership 1978-80), Am. Soc. Trainers and Developers, Nat. Assn. Female Execs. Home: W 3308 Rockwell Ave Spokane WA 99205

CLAVREUL, GENEVIEVE MARCELLINE, management consultant; b. Paris, May 18, 1940; d. Marcel Henri and Emilie (Cauchois) Clavreul; children—Patricia, Christina, James E., Eric P. B.A. in Psychology, Columbus (Ga.) Coll., 1976, M.Ed., 1977; M.A. in Pub. Adminstrn., Calif. State U.-Bakersfield, 1979. Registered nurse, Ga., Calif., S.D. Head nurse Med. Ctr. Columbus (Ga.), 1974-77; asst. dir. nursing Sioux Valley (S.D.) Hosp., 1977-78; dir. nursing San Joaquin Community Hosp., Bakersfield, 1978-79; coordinator quality assurance Cedar-Sinai Med. Ctr., Los Angeles, 1978; pres. mgmt. cons. firm C.C.M.C., Los Angeles, 1978—; cons., lectr. U. Calif.-Irvine, Stanford U., State N.J., Calif. State U.-Bakersfield, Phoenix U., Columbus Coll. Mem. Hosp. Council So. Calif., Calif. Hosp. Assn., Assn. Western Hosps., Am. Soc. Healthcare Edn. Tng., Hollywood C. of C., West Hollywood C. of C. Contbr. articles to profl. jours. Home: 4119 Los Feliz Blvd Suite 9 Los Angeles CA 90027

CLAWSON, RAYMOND WALDEN, independent oil producer; b. San Jose, Calif., Nov. 15, 1906; s. Benjamin B. and Mae Belle (Names) C.; LL.B., Am. U., 1936; m. Barbara M. Robbins, 1965. Vice pres. C.C. Warren & Co., Oakland, Calif., 1924-27; Ind. operator, exploration and devel. oil properties, 1936—; pub. Los Angeles Mirror, 1945-47; pres. Ariz. Securities, Phoenix, 1947-50, Transcontinental Oil Co., Los Angeles, 1947-49; geophys. cons. in offshore drilling ops. Gulf of Mexico, 1963—, North Sea, 1970—; chmn., chief exec. officer Clawco Petroleum Corp., Newport Beach, Calif., 1979—. Clubs: Balboa Bay, Acapulco Yacht. Office: PO Box 2102 Newport Beach CA 92663

CLAY, CAROLYNE, metallurgist; b. Chgo., Apr. 30, 1952; d. Calvin and Leanet (May) C.; B.S. (Joseph Blazek scholar, Internat. Nickel Co., Inc. scholar), Rensselaer Poly. Inst., 1974; M.S. (Julian Avery scholar), M.I.T., 1976, Metall. Engr., 1978. Research asst. M.I.T., Cambridge, 1975-77; research metallurgist Ford Motor Co. Sci. Research Lab., Dearborn, Mich., 1977-79; sr. metallurgist Kaiser Aluminum & Chem. Corp., Trentwood Works, Spokane, Wash., 1979—; mem. vis. com. M.I.T. Materials Sci. and Engring. Corp., 1978—. Recipient Karl T. Compton award, 1977, Scott MacKay award, 1974. Mem. Am. Soc. Metals, AIME, Nat. Soc. Profl. Engrs., NAACP, Sigma Xi, Delta Sigma Theta. Congregationalist. Office: Trentwood Works PO Box 15108 Spokane WA 99215

CLAYSON, SHELBY JEAN, educator; b. Mpls.; s. Orville Jasper and Violet Mildred (Paul) C.; B.S., U. Minn., 1960; M.S., U. Colo., 1966. Staff phys. therapist St. John's Hosp., St. Paul, 1960-61; phys. therapist U. Minn., 1961-62, sr. phys. therapist, 1962, asst. supr. phys. therapists, 1962-64, instr. phys. therapy, 1966-70; instr. phys. therapy U. Wash., 1970-72, asst. prof., 1972-73; asst. prof. occupational therapy U. Puget Sound, Tacoma, 1973-75, asso. prof. occupational therapy, 1975-76, asso. prof., dir. phys. therapy, 1976-80, asso. prof., 1980-82, prof., 1982—. HEW grantee, 1975-78. Mem. Am. Phys. Therapy Assn. (Dorothy Briggs award for sci. inquiry 1972), Soc. Behavioral Kinesiology, Sigma Delta Epsilon. Methodist. Contbr. articles to profl. jours. Office: 1500 N Warner St Tacoma WA 98416

CLAYTON, E. BERNEICE LOWE, educator, counselor, social worker, b. Clanton, Ala., Jan. 21, 1923; d. Rueben Willis Lowe and Martha Ruth (Smith) L.; M. Norman Dale Clayton, June 30, 1948; children—Alan Foster, Stephen Fremont, Douglas Lowe. B.A. magna cum laude, U. Ala., 1945; M.A., U. Chgo., 1948; postgrad. Calif. State U.-Sacramento, 1956-60, U. Pacific, 1971-72; Ed.D., U. Nova, 1975. Lic. child, family, marriage counselor, Calif. Psychiat. social worker Calif. State Mental Hygiene Clinic, 1948-49; dir. Sutterville Coop. Sch., Sacramento, Calif., 1954-58; presch. and parent educator Sacramento City Unified Sch. Dist., 1960-64, sch. social worker, 1965-68, coordinator parent and presch. edn., 1967-68; instr., dir. Early Childhood Edn., Sacramento City Coll., 1968—, chmn. family and consumer sci. dept., 1971—, chmn. early childhood edn. and family and consumer sci. dept.; cons. pvt. and pub. presch. programs, children and child care ctrs. Bd. dirs. Grace Day Home, 1973—; active Sacramento Child Care Commn., 1973—. Recipient outstanding Calif. home econs. prof. award Calif. Community Colls., 1982-83. Mem. Sacramento Valley Assn. Edn. Young Children (pres. 1976), Calif. Community Colls., Early Childhood Educators (treas. 1975-76). Democrat. Club: Park Terr. Swimming and Tennis (Sacramento). Author: An Administrative Design for Group Infant Care, 1975. Home: 79 Lakeshore Circle Sacramento CA 95831 Office: Sacramento City Coll 3835 Freeport Blvd RS 284 Sacramento CA 95822

CLAYTON, INA SMILEY, educator; b. Montrose, Miss., Mar. 2, 1924; d. Oscar Ruben and Leverett (Jones) Smiley; B.S., Jackson State U., 1946; M.A., Syracuse U., 1955; Ph.D., U.S. Internat. U., 1977; m. O. L. Clayton, July 21, 1959; 1 dau., Felicia Tulikka. Head tchr. Taylorsville, Miss., 1946; Jeanes supr. Covington County (Miss.), Collins, 1947-54, elem. supr. all Black schs. Covington County, 1947-54; tchr., vice prin., prin. elem. schs., Laurel, Miss., 1955-67; tchr., lang. instr. Los Angeles City Schs., 1968—. Vice pres., pres. United Meth. Women's Club, 1979-80, NAACP, 1980. Recipient certs. of appreciation ch. and PTA groups. Mem. NEA, Calif. Teachers Assn., United Tchrs. Los Angeles, Doctoral Soc. of U.S. Internat. U., Council for Basic Edn., Inst. Children's Lit., Sigma Gamma Rho. Democrat. Club: Order Eastern Star. Home: 1717 W 57th St Los Angeles CA 90062 Office: 1916 E 102nd St Los Angeles CA 90062

CLEARY, JAMES W., univ. pres.; b. Milw., Apr. 16, 1927; Ph.B., Marquette U., 1950, M.A., 1951; Ph.D. (univ. fellow 1954-55), U. Wis., 1956; m. 1950. Instr., dir. forensics high sch., Wis., 1949-51; instr. speech, head coach debate Marquette U., 1951-53; from instr. to asst. prof. speech, 1956-61, asso. prof. speech, 1961-63, prof. speech U. Wis., 1963-66, then vice chancellor acad. affairs, 1965-69; pres. Calif. State U., Northridge, 1969—. Bd. dirs. Region I United Way. Served to 2d lt. AUS, 1945-47. Recipient Outstanding Teaching award Central States Speech Assn., 1959; Alumni award for coll. teaching Marquette U., 1960; Wm. H. Kiekhofer Meml. award for excellence in teaching U. Wis., 1960, Alumnus of Year award, 1973. Mem. Western States Speech Assn., Speech Assn. Am., Am. Inst. Parliamentarians (bd. dirs.), Am. Assn. State Colls. and Univs. (chmn. 1982-83). Author articles in field. Editor Bibliog. Rhetoric and Public Address, 1964; Robert's Rules of Order Newly Revised, 1970, 80; John Bulwer's Chirologia-Chironomia, 1644: A Critical Edition, 1974. Address: 18111 Nordhoff St Northridge CA 91330

CLEMANS, BETTIE KING, college administrator; b. Gibbon, Nebr., Sept. 10, 1927; d. Lewallan C. and Opal (Houtz) King; A.A., Central Ariz. Coll., 1972; B.A., Ariz. State U., 1975, M.A., 1977; m. Richard G. Clemans, Sept. 1, 1961; children—Michael James, Richard Alan, Robin Ann and Dana Ellen (twins), James Roy. Office mgr. R.G. Clemans, Atty., Casa Grande, Ariz., 1957-62; adminstrv. asst. Community Action Program, Coolidge, Ariz., 1962-67; pres.'s adminstrv. asst. Pinal County Community Coll. Dist., Coolidge, 1967-78, research asst., 1978-79; coordinator grants devel. Central Ariz. Coll., Coolidge, 1979—. Pres., Pinal County Fine Arts Council, Inc.; mem. Nat. Council on Resource Devel., Am. Assn. Community and Jr. Colls. (intern 1978), Bus. and Profl. Women (past pres. Coolidge Club, asst. dir. Ariz. dist. 3), Nat. Secs. Assn. (cert. profl. sec., founding pres. Desert Rose chpt.), Nat. Bus. Educators Assn., Ariz. Coordinating Council on Resource Devel. (pres. 1979-80), Pi Omega Pi, Kappa Delta Pi. Club: Zonta Internat. Author: Sixty Seasons: A History of Pinal County Community College District, 1976. Office: Central Ariz Coll Woodruff at Overfield Rd Coolidge AZ 85229

CLEMENS, CHARLES JOSEPH, insurance executive; b. Phila., Mar. 1, 1942; s. Charles Wesley and Jane Elizabeth (Nesselhauf) C.; B.A. in Fin., Calif. State U., 1970; M.B.A., U. So. Calif., 1972; m. Keiko Arisugawa, Aug. 12, 1965; 1 son, Charles Shuji. Field supr. Equifax, Inc., Orange County, Calif., 1966-71; agt., then asst. agy. mgr. N.Y. Life Ins. Co., Anaheim, Calif., 1971-75; propr. Charles Clemens Agy., Santa Ana, Calif., 1975-77; brokerage mgr. N.Am. Life & Casualty Co., Santa Ana, 1977-80; mgr. INA Life Ins. Co., Santa Ana, 1980—; instr. Santa Ana Community Coll. Bd. dirs. Orange County Explorers council Boy Scouts Am.; mem. ins. adv. com. Santa Ana Coll.; pres. Parent's Guild, St. Catherine's Mil. Sch., Anaheim, Calif., 1983-84. Served with USAF, 1961-65; mem. Calif. Air N.G., 1974-78. Recipient ins. sales award, nat. quality award. C.L.U. Mem. Nat., Calif. Assn. life underwriters, No. Orange County Life Underwriters Assn. (pres. 1976, 80, dir.), Assn. M.B.A. Execs., Air Force Assn. Republican. Club: Santa Ana North Rotary (treas.). Office: 2200 Orangewood Suite 201 Orange CA 92668

CLEMENT, JOHN PAUL, traffic engineer; b. Bakersfield, Calif., Aug. 15, 1946; s. Phil Francis and Arlene Joan (Gundlach) C.; m. Carol May Kline, Nov. 8, 1980; 1 dau., Pauline Carol. B.S., Calif. Poly. State U., 1969. Registered profl. engr., Calif., Ariz., Oreg., Wash., Colo., Wyo. Civil engr. Cal Trans, Los Angeles, 1969-73; city traffic engr. City of Thousand Oaks (Calif.), 1973—; prin. J.P. Clement, Camarillo, Calif., 1979—. Fellow Inst. Transp. Engrs. Democrat. Roman Catholic. Home: 350 Spindlewood Ave Camarillo CA 93010 Office: 401 W Hillcrest Dr Thousand Oaks CA 91360

CLEMENT, PAUL WAYNE, clinical psychologist, educator; b. Aberdeen, Wash., Mar. 6, 1939; s. Albert Wayne and Helen Marguerite (Norin) C.; m. Katherine Majovski, June 13, 1959; children—Paul, Blake, Erika. Student Pepperdine Coll., 1957-58; B.S., U. Wash., 1960, B.A., 1961; M.A., Pepperdine Coll., 1962; Ph.D. (USPHS fellow), U. Utah, 1965; lic. psychologist, Calif.; diplomate Am. Bd. Profl. Psychology. Instr. to asst. prof. med. psychology in residence UCLA, 1965-67; clin. psychologist II, Harbor Gen. Hosp., Torrance, Calif., also asst. prof. to prof. psychology, 1967—; dir. clin. tng. Grad. Sch. Psychology, Fuller Theol. Sem., Pasadena, Calif., 1967-76, dir. Psychol. Center, 1976—; cons. to hosps., clinics, schs., editorial bds. Named Health Service Provider in Psychology, Council Nat. Register Health Service Providers in Psychology, 1975; recipient Alumni Bd. Dirs. award Pepperdine U., 1975; named Disting. Mem. Western Assn. Christians for Psychol. Studies, 1977; Harbor Gen. Hosp. grantee, 1965-66, USPHS grantee, 1966-67, 68-71, 74-76. Fellow Am. Psychol. Assn.; mem. Western Psychol. Assn., Calif. Psychol. Assn. (pres. 1975, award 1977), Assn. Aviation Psychologists, Flying Psychologists, Pasadena Area Psychol. Assn. (pres. 1970), Council Univ. Dirs. Clin. Psychology. Nat. Council Schs. Profl. Psychology (sec.-treas. 1982—), Sigma Xi, Phi Delta Kappa, Psi Chi. Presbyterian. Co-author: Clinical Procedures for Behavior Therapy, 1981; also articles. Office: Psychol Center Fuller Theol Sem 447 N El Molino Ave Pasadena CA 91101

CLEMENT, WALTER HOUGH, railroad exec.; b. Council Bluffs, Iowa, Dec. 21, 1931; s. Daniel Shell and Helen Grace (Hough) C.; A.A., San Jose (Calif.) City Coll., 1958; m. Shirley Ann Brown, May 1, 1953; children—Steven, Robert, Richard. Designer, J.K. Konerle & Assocs., Salt Lake City, 1959-62; with U.P. R.R. Co., 1962—, class B draftsman, Salt Lake City, 1971-75, sr. right of way engr. real estate dept., 1975-80, asst. dist. real estate mgr., 1980—. Mem. Republican Nat. Com., Rep. Congl. Com. Served with USN, 1950-54; Korea. Lic. realtor, Utah. Mem. Am. Ry. Engring. Assn., Execs. Info. Guild (asso.), Bur. Bus. Practice. Republican. Methodist. Home: 290 West 1200 North Bountiful UT 84010 Office: 406 West 100 South Salt Lake City UT 84101

CLEMENTE, PATROCINIO ABLOLA, ednl. psychologist; b. Manila, Philippines, Apr. 23, 1941; s. Elpidio San Jose and Amparo (Ablola) C.; came to U.S., 1965; B.S.E., U. Philippines, 1960; postgrad. Nat. U., Manila, 1961-64; M.A., Ball State U., 1966, Ed.D., 1969; postgrad. U. Calif., Riverside, 1970, Calif. State Coll., Fullerton, 1971-72. High sch. tchr. gen. sci. and biology, div. city schs., Quezon City, Philippines, 1960-65; doctoral fellow dept. psychology Ball State U., Muncie, Ind., 1966-67, dept. spl. edn., 1967-68, grad. asst. dept. gen. and exptl. psychology, 1968-69; tchr. educable mentally retarded high sch. level Fontana (Calif.) Unified Sch. Dist., 1969-70, intermediate level, 1970-73, dist. sch. psychologist, 1973-79, bilingual edn. counselor, 1979-81; resource specialist Morongo (Calif.) Unified Sch. Dist., 1981 ; adj. instr. Chapman Coll., Orange, Calif., 1981—. Adult leader Girl Scouts of Philippines, 1963-65. State bd. scholar Ball State U., 1965-66. Mem. Council for Exceptional Children, Am. Assn. on Mental Deficiency, Am. Assn. Psychiat. Services for Children, Nat. Assn. of Sch. Psychologists, Internat. Assn. Sch. Psychology, Found. Exceptional Children, Assn. for Children with Learning Disabilities, N.Y. Acad. Scis., AAAS. Roman Catholic. Home: PO Box 637 Twentynine Palms CA 92277

CLEMENTS, LOUIS J., educator, author; b. Rigby, Idaho, Feb. 25, 1939; s. Raymond J. and Louie Scott (Neville) C.; m. Diane Hegsted, Mar. 8, 1963; children—Bradley, Shaun, Kristen, Kimberley, Leslie. A.S., Ricks Coll., 1959; B.S., Brigham Young U., 1963, M.A., 1964. Tchr., Madison High Sch., Rexburg, Idaho, 1964—, chmn. social studies dept., 1965—. Bd. dirs. Upper Snake River Valley Hist. Soc., Rexburg, 1983—, pres., 1977-82; chmn. Rexburg Centennial Com., 1982-84. Named Outstanding Young Educator, Rexburg Jr. C. of C., 1969. Mem. Am. State and Local History Assn., Mormon History Assn., NEA, Idaho State Hist. Soc., Idaho Edn. Assn. Club: Kiwanis. Mem. Ch. of Jesus Christ of Latter-day Saints. Author: History of Teton Valley, 1970; Making of a State, 1971; Pioneering the Snake River Fork Country, 1972; Upper Snake River Area History, 1974; editor: Snake River Echoes, 1971-75. Home: Route 2 Box 307 Rexburg ID 83440 Office: 51 N Center St Rexburg ID 83440

CLEMENTS, MICHAEL REID, engineering executive; b. Los Angeles, Apr. 21, 1943; s. Reid William and Phyllis Marie (Hoopes) C.; m. Genay Shumway, Aug. 30, 1967; children—Tamara, Michelle, Reid, Sean, Scott. A.A., Ricks Coll., Rexburg, Idaho, 1965; B.E.S., Brigham Young U., Provo, Utah, 1968; postgrad. Stanford U., 1968-69. Engr., IBM, Menlo Park, Calif., 1968-69; sr. engr. Multi-Access Systems, Cupertino, Calif., 1969-70; system design mgr. Amdahl Corp., Sunnyvale, Calif., 1970-75, dir. computer devel., 1977-78, corp. v.p. engring., 1978—; mgr. electronic design and data systems EG & G Idaho Falls, Idaho, 1975-77. Mem. IEEE, Am. Mgmt. Assn., Tau Beta Pi. Republican. Mormon. Patentee in field. Home: 95 W Sunset Circle Rexburg ID 83440 Office: 1250 E Arques Ave Sunnyvale CA 94086

CLEMMONS, PENNY, psychologist; b. Chgo., Aug. 16, 1947; d. Trefin D. and Garnet Hope (Murray) Paganis. B.A., U. Ill., 1970; M.A., Roosevelt U., 1976; Ph.D., Calif. Grad. Inst., 1979. Tchr. Archdiocese of Chgo., 1967-69; outpatient treatment coordinator Grant Hosp., Chgo., 1969-74; marriage and child counselor, 1977—; pvt. practice clin. psychology, Los Angeles, 1981—; assoc. prof., dean students Calif. Grad. Inst., Los Angeles, 1979-82; asst. program dir. Fielding Inst., Santa Barbara Calif., 1982—; clin. dir. Inst. for Psychotherapy and Counseling, Los Angeles, 1980—. Pres. bd. dirs. San Fernando Valley Counseling Ctr., 1978-80; v.p. bd. dirs. Ill. Alcoholism and Drug Dependence Assn., 1972-76. Recipient Pub. Service award State of Ill., 1976. Mem. Am. Psychol. Assn., Calif. Psychol. Assn., Nat. Assn. Advancement Psychoanalysis, Am. Orthopsychiat. Assn., Assn. for Interdisciplinary Studies, Am. Personnel and Guidance Assn. Contbr. articles to profl. jours. Office: Fielding Inst 2112 Santa Barbara St Santa Barbara CA 93105

CLEMONS, ELIZABETH CAMERON (MRS. NELSON T. NOWELL), author; b. Berkeley, Calif.; d. Alfred George and Edith (Catton) Cameron; A.B., San Jose State Coll., 1928; M.A., Stanford U., 1937; m. Wood Clemons, Dec. 22, 1946 (div. Dec. 1958); m. 2d, Arthur G. Robinson, May 27, 1961 (dec. Jan. 1967); m. 3d, Nelson T. Nowell, Feb. 15, 1969 (dec. Sept. 1973). With edn. dept. San Jose State Coll., 1928-39; inservice tng. U. Calif. Extension Div., 1939-42; elem. editor The John C. Winston Co., 1942-43, Silver Burdett Co., 1943-44, D.C. Heath, 1944-46; instr. English dept. U. Minn., 1947; writing, editing publs. services Gen. Mills, 1947-50; free-lance writer, 1950—; mem. faculty Monterey Peninsula Coll., Monterey, Calif., 1978—; reading cons. Monterey City Sch., 1959-62; asso. editor Calif. edit. Am. Home Mag., 1965-69. Bd. dirs. Peninsula Community Hosp. Aux., Harrison Meml. Library, 1971-76, Monterey County Symphony Assn., 1974-75; vestryman St. Dunstan's Episcopal Ch., 1974-77; judge Golden Thimble Exhbn. IV V and VII, Aux. of Hosp. of Good Samaritan, Los Angeles, 1977, 79, 80, 82, 83, Montalvo Center for Arts, Saratoga, Calif., 1980, 82, others. Mem. Nat. League Am. Pen Women, Nat. Standards Council Am. Embroiderers, LWV, Nat. Embroidery Tchrs. Assn. (nat. dir. 1977—, seminar faculty 1979—), Authors Guild, Embroiderers Guild Am. (dir., chpt. pres. 1977-78, seminar faculty 1979—, cert. bd. 1974-79), Kappa Alpha Theta, Pi Lambda Theta, Delta Phi Upsilon, Kappa Delta Pi, Delta Kappa Gamma. Republican. Clubs: Women's City, Casa Abrego, Soroptimist, Monterey Peninsula Golf and Country. Author: The Pixie Dictionary, 1953; The Catholic Child's First Dictionary, 1954; The Winston Dictionary for Canadian School Children, 1955; Away I Go, 1956; All About Baby, 1956; I Live on A Farm, 1956; A Wish for Billy, 1956; Wings, Wheels, and Motors, 1957; The Big Book of Real Fire Engines, 1958; The Big Book of Real Trains, 1958; The Big Book of Real Trucks, 1958; Rodeo Days, 1960; Shells Are Where You Find Them, 1960; Rocks and The World Around You, 1960; Big and Little, 1961; Tide Pools and Beaches, 1964; Tides, Waves, and Currents, 1967; Here and There Stories; Now and Then Stories, 1967; Near and Far Stories, 1967); A Source Book for the Teaching of Literature for Children, 1967; The Seven Seas, 1971; The Friendly Frog, 1971; What I Like, 1971; also feature articles in nat. mags. Home: Box 686 Carmel CA 93921

CLEMONS, J. KING, insurance executive; b. Columbus, Ohio, Jan. 21, 1936; s. Frank M. and Ethel K. Clemons; B.S. in Physics, Colorado Coll., 1958; M.S. in Stats., U. Iowa, 1966; m. Ann Douglass, June 2, 1959; children—Mike, Steve, Karl. Research physicist White Sands Missile Range, N.Mex., 1958; actuarial asst. A.S. Hansen, Inc., Lake Bluff, Ill., 1966-67, cons. in tng., Lake Bluff, 1967-69, subject cons., Milw., 1969-70, subject cons., Los Angeles, 1970-72; pres. Western Res. Life Ins. Co., Grand Junction, Colo., 1972 ; propr., broker Top Realty Co., 1972—. Pres., Grand Junction Eagles Baseball, 1976—; active YMCA Fund Drive, Milw., 1969; chmn. Grand Junction/Mesa County Indsl. Devel. Revenue Bond Com., 1981—. Served to capt., Ordnance Corps, U.S. Army, 1958-64. Recipient Disting. Service award YMCA, 1969. Mem. Western Colo. Estate Planning Council, North Ave. Trade Assn. (dir. 1978—), Grand Junction C. of C. (pres. 1980). Republican. Club: Lions. Home: 2561 I Rd Grand Junction CO 81501 Office: 2755 North Ave Grand Junction CO 81501

CLENDENNING, EDWARD WALLACE HAMPTON, marine engineering company official; b. Vancouver, B.C., Can., May 4, 1931; came to U.S., 1958, naturalized, 1965; s. Edward Thomas and Annie Margarite (Hicks) C.; m. Kathleen Van Vorst, Mar. 26, 1953; m. Brenda Lee Baber, Feb. 14, 1965; m. Joyce Anne Haberstich, June 18, 1977; children—Kalee Jane Hunt, Lacey Darlene. Grad. high sch. Gen. ship constrn. and repair apprentice Burrard Dry Dock, North Vancouver, B.C., 1949-54; asst. repair supr. Union Steamships, Vancouver, 1955-58; hull designer Pillsbury & Martingnoni, San Francisco, 1958-62; hull designer W.C. Nickum & Sons (now Nickum & Spaulding Assocs. Inc.), Seattle, 1962-68, project mgr., contract adminstrn., personnel mgr., assoc. and dir., 1968—. Mem. Soc. Naval Architects and Marine Engrs. Clubs: Army Navy and Air Force Vets of Can. (Richmond, B.C.); Elks (Elk of Yr. 1968-69). Home: 3213 151st St SW Lynnwood WA 98036 Office: 2701 1st Ave Suite 350 Seattle WA 98121

CLES, SHIRLEY LAVONNE, registered nurse; b. Denver, Mar. 6, 1926; d. Richard Samuel and Nellie Marie (Pence) Phelps; A.A.S., Casper Coll., 1974; R.N., Natrona County Community Hosp., 1976; m. Alvin B. Cles, Mar. 9, 1970; children by prevous marriages—Richard Holmes, Deanna Holmes Christian, John Walter Williams III, Jim Williams. Owner, operator Cinderella Beauty Salon, Casper, Wyo., 1956-73; staff nurse Natrona County Meml. Hosp., Casper, 1974-76, also developed and directed recreational therapy program; vol. VISTA, 1978—, working with Advocates for Better Care, Nat. Coalition for Nursing Home Reform. Craftswoman, tchr. internal carving and sculpting. Mem. Concerned Citizens of Mountain View (pres.), LWV. Democrat. Episcopalian. Home: 5000 Marmon St Casper WY 82604 Office: 111 S Wolcott Room 305 Casper WY 82601

CLETCHER, JOHN OTIS, JR., orthopedic surgeon; b. Decatur, Ill., Feb. 4, 1928; s. John Otis and Jessie Irene (Wilson) C.; A.B., Harvard, 1950; B.S., U. Ill., 1952, M.D., 1955; m. Polly Catherine Laun, Aug. 20, 1950 (div. 1972); children—John Laun, Scott Wilson, Amy Catherine; m. 2d, Jacqueline Rae Haskett, Nov. 23, 1974. Intern, San Diego County Gen. Hosp., 1955-56; pvt. practice specializing in family practice, Rochelle, Ill., 1958-64; chief of staff Rochelle Community Hosp., 1963-64; resident in orthopedic surgery Denver Gen. Hosp., 1964-67; pvt. practice specializing in orthopedic surgery, Denver, 1967-69, Berkeley, Calif., 1969-71, Longmont, Colo., 1971—. Served with M.C., USNR, 1956-58. Diplomate Am. Bd. Orthopedic Surgery. Mem. Western Orthopedic Assn. (v.p. Rocky Mountain chpt. 1978), Am. Acad. Orthopedic Surgeons, Boulder County Med. Soc. (pres. 1980-81), Ogle County Med. Soc. (pres. 1962-64). Club: Masons. Home: 7421 Nelson Rd Longmont CO 80501 Office: 1331 Linden St Longmont CO 80501

CLEVE, GEORGE, conductor; b. Vienna, Austria, 1936; student Mannes Coll. Music, N.Y.C.; studies with Pierre Monteux, George Szell, Franco Ferrara; D.F.A. (hon.), U. Santa Clara. Music dir., co-founder Midsummer Mozart Festival; music dir. Winnipeg Symphony; music dir., condr. San Jose Symphony, 1972—; guest condr. San Francisco Symphony, Royal Philharm., London, Minn. Orch., Kansas City Philharm., St. Louis Symphony, Boston Symphony, St. Paul Chamber Orch., N.Y. Philharm., Cleve. Symphony, Pitts. Symphony, Denver Symphony, Honolulu Symphony, Balt. Symphony, Mostly Mozart Festival, N.Y.C. Recipient 1st Community Arts program award City of San Jose. Address: San Jose Symphony Orch 170 Park Center Plaza Suite 100 San Jose CA 95113*

CLEVELAND, KENNETH CHARLES, JR., management consultant; b. Pasadena, Calif., Feb. 7, 1933; s. Kenneth Charles and Marjory M. (Mingle) C.; m. Suzi McClure, May 26, 1979; 1 dau., Carolyn Ruth. B.S. in Fin., UCLA, 1956. Controller, asst. sec. Documentation, Inc., Washington, 1960-61; controller Benson Lehner Corp., Los Angeles, 1961; asst. to controller TRW Systems, Los Angeles, 1962-63, mgr. capital planning, 1963-64, mgr. adminstrn. and fin., 1966-68; controller, sec. Nat. Engring. Sci. Co., Pasadena, Calif., 1966-68; v.p., sec.-treas., dir. Houston Fearless Corp., Los Angeles, 1968-69; pres., dir. Dymat Internat. Corp., Santa Monica, Calif., 1969-73; v.p. Terminal Data Corp., Van Nuys, Calif., 1973-74; pres., dir. Tor Corp., Van Nuys, 1974-76; pres., dir. Audiomobile, Inc., Long Beach, Calif., 1976; sr. partner Kenneth Cleveland Assos., Malibu, Calif., 1977—. Pres., Malibu La Costa Owners Assn., Inc., 1979. Served to 1st lt. U.S. Paratrooper, 1956-58. Mem. Western Internat. Trade Group, Nat. Def. Exec. Res., Phi Kappa Psi. Republican. Office: 21344 Rambla Vista Malibu CA 90265

CLEVELAND, ROBERT MARTIN, advertising, catering consultant; b. Opportunity, Wash., Sept. 27, 1930; s. Boyd J. and Amanda L. (Lemke) C.; children—Lisa A., Martin Allan. B.S., Whitworth Coll., Spokane, Wash., 1957. cert Am. Assn. of Advt. Agys. Account exec. Ralph Summers Advt. Agy., 1957-58; mgr. Givens Davis Advt. Agy., 1958-59; ptnr. Soderberg & Cleveland Advt. Agy., 1959-71; pres. Cleveland/McKeehen Advt. Agy., 1971-78, Cleveland & Assocs., 1978-82, Cleveland/Lyman and Assocs., 1982—; owner, operator Stimson Green Mansion; cons. Assoc. Wash. Bus. Served with USN, 1952-56. Mem. Assn. Am. Bus., Assn. Wash. Bus. Republican. Lutheran. Clubs: Wash. Athletic, Bellevue Athletic. Office: 1212 Minor Ave Seattle WA 98101

CLEVENGER, GALEN WILLIAM, research and tech. ofcl.; b. Palo Alto, Calif., July 1, 1916; s. Galen Howell and Alice Emily (Clemens) C.; B.S., Washington and Jefferson Coll., 1939; M.B.A., Internat. Corr. Schs., 1956; m. Cynthia Jones, Aug. 24, 1940; children—Galen Malcolm, Jeffrey Griswold. Metallurgist U.S. Smelting Co., Boston, 1939-40; plant and metall. supt. Am. Zinc Co., St. Louis, 1940-48; sr. staff research engr. M.I.T., Cambridge, 1948-51; research engr. Am. Cyanamid Co., Watertown, 1951-54; mgr. metallurgy dept. Raw Materials Devel. Lab., AEC, Winchester, 1954-59; dir. research White Pine Copper Co. (Mich.), 1959-60; chief metallurgist Shattuck Denn Mining Corp., N.Y., 1960-67, Vitro Mineral & Chem. Co., Salt Lake City, 1967-68; supr. research, extractive metallurgy research lab. Phelps Dodge Corp., Morenci, Ariz., 1968-79, dir. research and tech. services, 1979-81; pres. Metall. Services, Inc., Prescott, Ariz., 1981—. Registered profl. engr., Ariz. Mem. AIME, Mining and Metall. Soc. Am., AAAS, Can. Inst. Mining and Metallurgy, Kappa Sigma. Rotarian. Patentee in field. Contbr. articles to publs. Home: 1825 Hazelwood Ln Prescott AZ 86301 Office: PO Box 431 Prescott AZ 86302

CLEWETT, RAYMOND WINFRED, mech. design engr.; b. Upland, Calif., Nov. 7, 1917; s. Howard Jasper and Pansy Gertrude (Macy) C.; student Chaffey Jr. Coll., 1937; m. Hazel Royer, June 11, 1938; children—Alan Eugene, Patricia Gail, Charles Raymond, Richard Howard, Beverly Lynn. Exptl. mechanic Douglas Aircraft Co., Santa Monica, Calif., 1937-51; shop foreman, exptl. designer Lear, Inc., Los Angeles, 1945-51; design engr., shop mgr. The RAND Corp., Santa Monica, Calif., 1951—; owner, mgr. HY-TECH Engring. and Devel. Lab., Malibu, Calif.; works include mech. design of JOHNNIAC early model electronic computer on permanent display Los Angeles County Mus.; designer various computer input/output devices, 1953-70; developer low vision reading aids for the blind, 1970-75; mech. design cons. Mem. AAAS, Soc. Mfg. Engrs., Am. Soc. Metals. Republican. Patentee in field. Home: 7069 Fernhill Dr Malibu CA 90265

CLIFFORD, DENNIS JOHN, clinical psychologist, mental health consultant; b. N.Y.C., June 24, 1939; s. James and Beatrice (Camardi) C.; m. Jane Mary Hartley, July 13, 1963; children—Paul, John. M.A. in Psychology, Columbia U., 1963; postgrad. in counseling psychology U. N.Mex. Lic. sch. psychologist, N.Y., N.J.; guidance counselor, N.Mex. Sch. psychologist Bur. Child Guidance, N.Y.C., 1970-76; clin. psychologist Child Devel. Ctr., Santa Fe, 1976-81, N.Mex. Dept. Corrections, Santa Fe, 1981—; grad. asst., counselor edn. dept. U. N.Mex. Troop com. chmn. Boy Scouts Am., Santa Fe. Mem. Am. Personnel and Guidance Assn., Assn. Counseling Edn. and Supervision, Am. Sch. Counselor Assn., Am. Mental Health Counselors Assn., N.Mex. Psychol. Assn., Assn. Existential Psychologists and Psychiatrists. Contbr. articles to profl. jours. Home: 2800 Cerrillos Rd #179 Santa Fe NM 87501

CLIFFORD, JOHN CHARLES, ballet dancer, choreographer; b. Los Angeles, June 12, 1947; s. Robert and Betty Louise (Cadwell) C.; student Sch. Am. Ballet, Am. Sch. Dance. Dancer, N.Y.C. Ballet, 1966-73; choreographer works of Stravinsky, Tchaikovsky, Kodaly, Gershwin, Bernstein, Debussy, Gottschalk, Vaugh-Williams for N.Y.C., San Francisco ballet cos., Royal Winnipeg (Can.) Ballet Deutsche Opera Co., West Berlin; leading dancer, ballet master Los Angeles Ballet, 1973-74, artistic dir., 1974—, choreographer works Bach, Chapi, Varèse, Mayuzomi, Brahms; guest artist Paris Opera. Office: Los Angeles Ballet 1035 N McCadden Pl Los Angeles CA 90038*

CLIFT, RUSS, photographer; b. Bellingham, Wash., Mar. 6, 1916; s. Frank Lippincott and Georgia Wilda (Bruce) C.; M. Photography, Profl. Photographers Am., 1963; m. Grace Lorraine Doble, July 4, 1938; children—Michael Edward, Shirlee Ann Clift Dickerson, Laura Kathleen. Photog. apprentice Vinson Studio, Bellingham, 1938; comml. photographer Nelson Studio, Spokane, Wash., 1938-39, Knight Studio, Bellingham, 1939-41; v.p. Jukes, Inc., Bellingham, 1941-49, pres., 1949-52; owner, mgr. Russ Clift Studio, Bellingham, 1952—; tchr. Winona Lake (Ind.) Sch. Profl. Photography, 1966-68, West Coast Sch. Profl. Photography, Santa Barbara, Calif., 1968, 69, Whatcom Community Coll., Bellingham, 1973. Recipient Nat. Service award Profl. Photographers Am., 1963, Photog. Craftsman degree, 1966. Fellow Profl. Photographers B.C. (hon.), Profl. Photographers Wash. (pres. 1951, 63); mem. Camera Craftsmen Am. (sec.), Profl. Photographers Can. (hon.), Alta. Profl. Photographers Assn., Royal Photog. Soc. Gt. Britain (asso.), Mont. Photog. Soc., Inst. Brit. Photographers (asso.), Am. Soc. Photographers (nat. pres. 1970), Profl. Photographers Am. (judge, nat. councilman 1968—). Clubs: Toastmasters, Optimists, Elks. Researched and perfected Low Key techniques. Office: 1905 Cornwall Ave Bellingham WA 98225

CLINCH, HARRY ANSELM, bishop; b. San Anselmo, Calif., Oct. 27, 1908; s. Henry Joseph and Mary (McLaughlin) C.; student St. Joseph Sem., Mountain View, 1928-30, St. Patrick's Sem., Menlo Park, Calif., 1930-36. Ordained p.lpriest Roman Catholic Ch., 1936; founder, dir. Camp Santa Teresita Youth Camp, 1937-41; diocesan dir. Soc. for Propagation of Faith, 1936-48; editor Central Calif. Register, 1939-48; pastor, Taft, Calif., 1948-58, Mission Carmel, Calif., 1958—; consecrated bishop, 1957, aux. bishop Diocese Monterey-Fresno; bishop Diocese of Monterey, 1967—. Past mem. bd. dirs. Fresno and Taft chpts. ARC. Club: Kiwanis. Office: 580 Freemont Blvd Monterey CA 93940*

CLINE, CAROLYN JOAN, plastic and reconstructive surgeon; b. Boston, May 15, 1941; d. Paul S. and Elizabeth (Flom) Cline. B.A., Wellesley Coll., 1962; M.A., U. Cin., 1966; Ph.D., Washington U., 1970, postgrad. 1971-73; M.D., U. Miami (Fla.) 1975. Research asst. Harvard Dental Sch., Boston, 1962-64; research asst. physiology Laser Lab., Children's Hosp. Research Found., Cin., 1964, psychology dept. U. Cin., 1964-65; intern in clin. psychology St. Elizabeth's Hosp., Washington, 1966-67; psychologist Alexandria (Va.) Community Mental Health Ctr., 1967-68; research fellow NIH, Washington, 1968-69; chief psychologist Kingsbury Ctr. for Children, Washington, 1969-73; sole practice clin. psychology, Washington, 1970-73; assoc. Nat. Acad. Scis., 1974; intern internal medicine U. Wis. Hosps., Ctr. for Health Sci., Madison, 1975-76; resident in surgery Stanford U. Med. Ctr., 1976-78; fellow microvascular surgery dept. surgery U. Calif.-San Francisco, 1978-79; resident in plastic surgery St. Francis Hosp., San Francisco, 1979-82; practice medicine, specializing in plastic and reconstructive surgery, San Francisco, 1982—. Contbr. articles to profl. jours. Address: 450 Sutter St Suite 2431 San Francisco CA 94108

CLINE, JACK STANLEY, constrn. co. exec.; b. Walsenburg, Colo., Jan. 24, 1924; s. Clarence Eving and Rose (Brunelli) C.; student Rockhurst Coll., Kansas City, Mo., 1940, Purdue U., 1943-44; m. Mary Lucille Todero, Jan. 26, 1951; children—Jack R., Donna F., Kim K. Constrn. supt. Gottula Trucking Co., Pueblo, Colo., 1948-64; project mgr. State, Inc., indsl. constrn., Pueblo, 1964-74, v.p., 1974-83, chief engr., 1983—, also co. safety mgr., affirmative action officer; chmn. So. Colo. Iron Workers and Employeers Tng. Program. Served with AUS, 1942-46. Mem. Nat. Soc. Profl. Engrs. Roman Catholic. Club: Elks. Home: 4 Milagro Ln Pueblo CO 81005 Office: PO Box 718 Pueblo CO 81002

CLINE, PLATT HERRICK, author; b. Mancos, Colo., Feb. 7, 1911; s. Gilbert T. and Jessie (Baker) C.; grad. N.Mex. Mil. Inst., 1930; postgrad. Colo. U., 1930-31; Litt.D., No. Ariz. U., 1966, B.S. in Gen. Studies, 1982; m. Barbara Decker, Sept. 11, 1934. Advt. solicitor Denver Post, 1931; enrolee Civilian Conservation Corps, 1934-36; Nat. Monument ranger, 1936; publisher Norwood (Colo.) Post, 1937-38; advt. mgr. Coconino Sun, Flagstaff, Ariz., 1938-41; mng. editor Holbrook Tribune-News, 1941-45; editor Coconino Sun, 1945-46; mng. editor Ariz. Daily Sun, 1946-53, publisher, 1953-69, pres., 1969-76, v.p., 1976—; research assoc. Mus. of No. Ariz., 1976—; adj. prof. emeritus history No. Ariz. U., 1983—; founding dir. Bank of No. Ariz., 1978. Mem. Ariz. Commn. Indian Affairs, 1952-55; mem. Norwood (Colo.) Town Council, 1937-38; permanent chmn. Flagstaff Citizen of the Yr. Com., 1976—; bd. dirs., past pres. Raymond Edn. Found.; bd. dirs., past pres. No. Ariz. U. Found.; bd. dirs. Transition Found.; pres. adv. council No. Ariz. U., 1980—; trustee Flagstaff Community Hosp., 1954-58. Recipient Ariz. Master Editor-Pub. award, 1969, El Merito award Ariz. Hist. Soc., 1976; named Flagstaff Citizen of Yr., 1976, Disting. Citizen, No. Ariz. U. Alumni, 1983. Mem. Ariz. Newspapers Assn. (past pres.), No. Ariz. Pioneers Hist. Soc. (trustee 1972-75), Sigma Delta Chi, Phi Alpha Theta. Mason (32 deg.). Author: They Came to the Mountain, 1976; Mountain Campus, 1983. Home: PO Box 578 Flagstaff AZ 86002 Office: 417 W Santa Fe Ave Flagstaff AZ 86001

CLINE, WILSON ETTASON, ret. lawyer; b. Newkirk, Okla., Aug. 26, 1914; s. William Sherman and Etta Blanche (Roach) C.; student U. Ill., 1932-33; A.B., U. Okla., 1935, B.S. in Bus. Adminstrn., 1936; J.D., U. Calif., Berkeley, 1939; LL.M., Harvard U., 1941; m. G. Barbara Verne Pentecost, Nov. 1, 1939 (div. Nov. 1960); children—William, Catherine Cline MacDonald, Thomas; m. 2d, Gina Lana Ludwig, Oct. 5, 1969; children—David Ludwig, Kenneth Ludwig. Admitted to Calif. bar, 1940; atty. Kaiser Richmond Shipyards, 1941-44; pvt. practice, Oakland, 1945-49; atty., hearing officer, asst. chief adminstrv. law judge Calif. Pub. Utilities Commn., San Francisco, 1949-80, ret., 1981, dir. gen. welfare Calif. State Employees Assn., 1966-67, chmn. retirement com., 1965-66, mem. member benefit com., 1980-81, mem. ret. employees div. council dist. C, 1981—. Trustee Cline Ranch Trust, various family trusts. Mem. ABA, State Bar Calif., Conf. Calif. Pub. Utility Counsel (steering com. 1967-71), Am. Judicature Soc., Boalt Hall Alumni Assn., Phi Beta Kappa (pres. No. Calif. assn. 1969-70), Beta Gamma Sigma, Delta Sigma Pi, Phi Kappa Psi, Phi Delta Phi, Pi Sigma Alpha. Republican. Mem. United Ch. Christ. Clubs: Harvard, Commonwealth (San Francisco); Sleepy Hollow Swim and Tennis (Orinda, Calif.); Masons, Sirs (Peralta chpt. 12). Home: 110 St Albans Rd Kensington CA 94708 Office: PO Box 339 El Cerrito CA 94530

CLING, B. J., psychologist; b. N.Y.C., Nov. 22, 1943; d. Isidore Irving and Josephine Jean (Friedman) Rosenbaum; m. James Warren Ingersoll, Sept. 12, 1971 (div.). B.A., CUNY, 1966; M.A., NYU, 1968, Ph.D., 1980; postgrad. Inst. Psychiatry, Law and Behavioral Sci., U. So. Calif., 1982. Lic. clin. psychologist, Calif. Instr. psychology Adelphi U., 1969-70; asst. prof. psychology La Guardia Coll., CUNY, 1970-71; editor Program Practices-Children CBS, Los Angeles, 1978; producer women's series Sta. KPFK, Los Angeles, 1980-81; pvt. practice clin. psychology, Los Angeles, 1980—; instr. UCLA Extension, 1979—; clin. instr. Inst. Psychiatry, Law and Behavioral Scis., U. So. Calif., 1982—. Past bd. dirs. Women's Equal Rights Legal Def. and Edn. Fund. Mem. Screen Actor's Guild (past chmn. women's com.), Am. Psychol. Assn. Office: 11980 San Vicente Suite 607 Los Angeles CA 90049

CLINKUNBROOMER, PAUL JAMES, aviation artist, historian; b. Chgo., Aug. 20, 1937; s. Harry Charles and Louise Veronica (Mukavitz) C.; m. Renée Ann Morrison, Nov. 5, 1971; children—Michael, Dawn, Jill. Student Sch. of Art Inst. Chgo., 1958-60; B.A., U. Ill.-Chgo., 1969; postgrad. No. Ill. U., 1969-70. Artist-illustrator Am. Airlines, Inc., Chgo., 1960-62; asst. dist. advt. mgr. Montgomery Ward & Co., Phoenix, 1962-64; tng. asst., illustrator Flick-Reedy Corp., Bensenville, Ill., 1965-67; owner, operator A.D.S. Art Studio, Chgo., 1970-71; designer Sunset House, Inc., Los Angeles, 1972; instr., illustrator Calif. Mil. Dept., Van Nuys, 1973-77; art dir. Wallace Berrie & Co., Inc., Van Nuys, 1977—; muralist, aviation history artist; works include: exhibits in U.S. Marine Corps Aviation Mus., Quantico, Va., Calif. Air Nat. Guard, Van Nuys; represented in pvt. collections. Retail com. chmn. Franklin Park (Ill.) C. of C., 1963-64. Served with USAF, 1954-58, with USAFR, 1959-70, with Calif. Nat. Guard, 1971—. Decorated Air Force Meritorious Service Medal (U.S.), Gallantry Cross with palm (Vietnam), Calif. Commendation Ribbon with pendant. Mem. U. Ill. Alumni Assn., Am. Aviation Hist. Soc., Coll. Art Assn., Christian Men's Advt. Club Los Angeles, Art Dirs. Club Los Angeles, Alpha Delta Sigma. Author: Vanguard 50, 1974.

CLINTON, JOHN HART, lawyer, publisher; b. Quincy, Mass., Apr. 3, 1905; s. John Francis and Catherine Veronica (Hart) C.; A.B., Boston Coll., 1926; J.D., Harvard U., 1929; m. Helen Alice Amphlett, Feb. 18, 1933 (dec. 1965); children—Mary Jane Clinton Zirkel, Mary Ann Clinton Gardner, John Hart; m. 2d, Mathilda A. Schoorel van Dillen, Feb. 22, 1969. Admitted to Calif. bar, 1930, Mass. bar, 1930, since practiced in San Francisco; asso. firm Morrison, Foerster, Holloway, Clinton & Clark and predecessor, 1929-41, partner, 1941-72; of counsel firm Morrison & Foerster, 1972—. Vice pres., gen. counsel Indsl. Employers and Distbrs. Assn., Emeryville, 1944-72; pres. Leamington Hotel, Oakland, Calif., 1933-47, Amphlett Printing Co., San Mateo, Calif., 1943—; pub. San Mateo Times, 1943—, editor, 1960—. Hon. mem. exec. com. San Mateo County council Boy Scouts Am.; bd. dirs., pres. Calif. Jockey Club Found.; regent emeritus Notre Dame Coll., Belmont, Calif. Decorated Knight Equestrian Order of Holy Sepulchre of Jerusalem. Mem. FCC, Am. Bar Assn., San Francisco Bar Assn., San Mateo County Bar Assn., State Bar Calif. (past chmn. state bar fair trial/free press com., past co-chmn. Calif. bench/bar media com., public affairs com., past mem. editorial bd. California Lawyer), Am. Judicature Soc., Nat. Lawyers Club, Am. Law Inst., San Mateo County Devel. Assn. (pres. 1963-65), San Mateo County Hist. Assn. (pres. 1960-64), Calif. Press Assn. (pres. 1970, chmn. membership com.), Am. Newspaper Pubs. Assn. (mem. govt. affairs com., press/bar relations com., Am. Bar Assn.-Am. Newspapers Pubs. Assn. task force), Calif. Newspaper Pubs. Assn. (pres. 1969), Wine and Food Soc. San Francisco, Am. Soc. Newspaper Editors, Assn. Cath. Newsmen, Nat. Press Photographers Assn., Internat. Platform Assn., Newcomen Soc. Clubs: Commonwealth of Calif. (past pres.), San Francisco Comml., Bohemian (San Francisco), San Mateo Rotary (past pres.), Elks. Home: 131 Sycamore St San Mateo CA 94402 Office: 1080 S Amphlett Blvd San Mateo CA 94402

CLOTHIER, CHRISTINE MARIE, nurse; b. Detroit, Nov. 29, 1951; d. Sigmund Peter and Irene Frances (Vallad) Stone; m. Michael Wayne Clothier, Jan. 14, 1977; 1 stepdau., Dawn Nichole. B.S. in Nursing, U. Mich., 1973; postgrad. in bus. adminstrn. Calif. State Poly. U., 1982—. R.N., Calif. Staff nurse Tustin (Calif.) Community Hosp., 1973-74; enlisted U.S. Air Force, 1974, advanced through grades to capt., 1976; staff nurse, 1974-77, group instr. supr., 1978-81; staff nurse Western Med. Ctr., Santa Ana, Calif., 1981; quality assurance coordinator Glendora (Calif.) Community Hosp., 1981—. Recipient USAF Humanitarian Service award, 1980; commendation medal with oak leaf cluster. Mem. Nat. Assn. Quality Assurance Profls. (membership com., profl. standards com., credentials com. 1983), Calif. Assn. Quality Assurance Profls. (bylaws com. 1983), Quality Assurance Profls. San Gabriel/Pomona Valley (pres.-elect 1983), Calif. Soc. Hosp. Risk Mgrs., Alpha Xi Delta.

CLOUD, BARRETT EDWARD, electronic engr.; b. Santa Barbara, Calif., Apr. 25, 1945; s. Noah Edward and Frances Eloise (Ludlow) C.; B.S.E.E., Calif. State U., Long Beach, 1968; m. Nancy Lee Willoughby, Feb. 11, 1967; children—Joel Edward, Darrell James. Project engr. Seymour Instruments, Orange, Calif., 1968-73; chief engr. Flowcon Systems div. Bower Industries, Orange, 1973-77; dir. electronic devel. HIAC Instruments div. Pacific Scientific, Montclair, Calif., 1977-79; electronic engring. cons. Dymaxion Systems, Orange, 1979—, Barrett Engring., Orange, 1979—. Ruling elder Trinity United Presbyn. Ch., Tustin, Calif., 1973-76. Recipient award Particle Size Analysis System, Indsl. Research and Devel. mag., 1980; profl. engr., Calif. Mem. IEEE Computer Soc., Tau Beta Pi, Eta Kappa Nu. Contbr. articles to profl. publs. Home and Office: 1008 E Chalynn Ave Orange CA 92666

CLOUD, JAMES DOUGLAS, aerospace company executive; b. Dover, Ohio, Mar. 29, 1928; s. Joseph Douglas and Vieleta (Stiffler) C.; m. Virginia Jane Hensley, Aug. 9, 1946; children—Joy Cloud Evans, Jay, Paul, Dayne, Blake. B.S. in Elec. Engring., Purdue U., 1951, M.S. in Elec. Engring., 1952. With Hughes Aircraft Co., Culver City, Calif., 1952—, mgr. systems engring. and analysis lab., 1965-67, asst. program mgr. engring. and mfg. Surveyor, 1967-68, assoc. mgr. system labs., 1968-69, assoc. mgr. advanced system labs., 1969-70, mgr. systems engring. and analysis lab., 1970-73, assoc. mgr. def. systems div., 1973-76, mgr. tech. div., 1976-79, group v.p., mgr. space sensors div., from 1979—; now group v.p. electro-optical and data systems group, El Segundo, Calif. Phi Eta Sigma scholar, 1951. Assoc. fellow AIAA; mem. IEEE (sr.), Eta Kappa Nu, Tau Beta Pi, Sigma Pi Sigma. Office: Hughes Aircraft Company Bldg EL MS C170 PO Box 902 El Segundo CA 90245

CLOUD, JAMES MERLE, univ. admissions adminstr.; b. Winston-Salem, N.C., Feb. 16, 1947; s. Merle Vail and Jane Crawford (Moore) C.; B.A., U. N.C., 1970; Ph.D., Columbia Pacific U., 1979. Co-founder Wholistic Health and Nutrition Inst., Mill Valley, Calif., 1974, dir. edn., 1974-76, dir. health resource consultation, 1976-78; admissions dir. Columbia Pacific U., 1978—, sec.-treas., dir., 1978—; dir. Wholistic Health and Nutrition Inst., 1974—. Mem. Assn. Holistic Health (v.p. 1976). Mem. Airplane Owners and Pilots Assn. Club: U.S. Chess Fedn. Author: The Healthscription, 1979; anthologies of poems: Aeolus, 1971, No One Loves With Solitude, 1970. Home: 629 Eastwood Mill Valley CA 94941 Office: 150 Shoreline Hwy Mill Valley CA 94941

CLOUES, RICHARD WENUELL, civil engineer; b. Shrewsbury, Mass., Jan. 24, 1917; s. William Arthur and Ethel (Walker) C.; B.S. in Civil Engring., Worcester Poly. Inst., 1938; cert. in bus. mgmt. U. Calif. at Berkeley, 1972; m. Doris Verne Dickinson, June 22, 1938; children—Richard W. Jr., Stephen L., Philip W., John A. Engr. Aetna Steel Co., Jacksonville, Fla., 1938-47, chief engr., 1947-54; cons. structural engring., Jacksonville, 1954-55, Pitts., 1955; chief engr. Pitts. Bridge and Iron Works, 1955-57; with machinery div. Dravco Corp., Pitts., 1957-65, asst. chief design engr., 1962-64, coordinator estimates and proposals, 1964-65; with Bechtel Corp., San Francisco, 1965-82, supr. planning and scheduling, 1967-70, mgr. planning and scheduling, 1970-73, project engr. engring., 1973-82, assignments in Jordan, Saudi Arabia, Kuwait, and Venezuela, 1976-80; pres., chief exec. officer Cloues & Sons Enterprises Inc., 1982—. Founder, past pres. Bellevue (Pa.) High Counselors, 1960; mem. troop com. Ohio Valley-Allegheny council Boy Scouts Am., 1957-64; div. rep. Pitts. Community Chest, 1964. Vice pres. Bellevue Boro Sch. Authority, 1961-63. Registered profl. engr., Calif., Fla., Ga., Ill., Mich., N.H., N.Y., Ohio, Pa., W.Va. Fellow ASCE (life; exec. com. 1961); mem. Am. Welding Soc. (life mem.), Nat., Calif. (life mem., pres. chpt. 1971) socs. profl. engrs., Structural Engrs. Assn. No. Calif., Welding Research Council, Project Mgmt. Inst. (dir.), United Christian Missionary Soc. Baptist (deacon, bd. chmn. 1974-76). Club: Masons. Address: 241 Marcella Way Millbrae CA 94030

CLOUGH, ELAINE BUCHHOLZ, librarian; b. Green Bay, Wis., July 2, 1921; d. Helmuth Henry and Lenora Elizabeth (Augustine) Buchholz; B.A., U. Wis., 1943; B.L.S., Simmons Coll., Boston, 1944; m. Robert Francis Clough, June 5, 1943; children—Betty Elaine, Jeanette Marie. Research librarian Turck, Hill & Co., N.Y.C., 1944-48; br. librarian Conejo Library, Thousand Oaks, Calif., 1967-70; bus. research librarian Ventura County Library Services Agy., Ventura, Calif., 1970—; bus. librarian Calif. Lutheran Coll., Thousand Oaks, 1978—. Trustee, Pequannock Twp. Public Library, Pompton Plains, N.J., 1961-65, pres., 1963-65; Pequannock Twp. neighborhood chmn. Morris Area council Girl Scouts U.S.A., 1962-65; SCORE/ACE Counseling Program, SBA, 1974—; v.p. LWV, Pompton Plains, 1959-62. Mem. Spl. Libraries Assn., Calif. Library Assn., ALA, AAUW, Wis. Alumni Assn., Simmons Coll. Library Sch. Alumni Assn., Ventura County Profl. Women's Network. Home: 1324 Buckingham Dr Thousand Oaks CA 91360 Office: PO Box 771 651 E Main St Ventura CA 93001

CLOW, JOHN W., accounting and financial consultant; b. Denver, Oct. 14, 1930; s. John Bailey and Louise (Warner) C.; A.B., Dartmouth, 1952; M.B.A., U. Calif. at Berkeley, 1954; m. Martha H. de Mey, Apr. 10, 1956 (separated Jan. 1981); children—Eric deMey, Gregory Vincent, Amelia Bayley, Guy Rowan, Louise Crankshaw. Dept mgr. J.C. Penney Co., San Francisco, 1954-58; mem. staff Webb & Webb, C.P.A.s, San Francisco, 1958-62, ptnr., 1962-71; pres. Clow Accountancy Corp., San Francisco, 1972-76; ptnr. Main Hurdman and predecessor firm, San Francisco,

1976-79; acctg. and fin. cons., 1979—. Treas. Calif. Young Republicans, 1962, nat. committeeman 1963; trustee Calif. C.P.A. Found. for Edn. and Research, 1979—. Served with USAF, 1952-54. C.P.A., Calif. Mem. Am. Inst. C.P.A.s (council 1977-80), Calif. (dir. 1971-74, treas. 1974-77), San Francisco (pres. 1972-73) socs. C.P.A.s, Dartmouth Alumni Assn. (pres. No. Calif., Nev. 1962-63). Club: U. San Francisco. Home: Laurel Grove Ave Ross CA 94957 Office: PO Box 1448 Ross CA 94957

CLOW, MAURINE, educator; b. Grafton, N.D., Sept. 30, 1908; d. Chester W. and Ellen C. (Terrill) C.; student U. N.D., 1926, 28-30; B.A., Stanford U., 1934, M.A., 1936, Ph.D., 1946; summer study Columbia U., 1942. Counselor, English tchr. Sarah Dix Hamlin Sch., San Francisco, 1935-36; resident asst. to dean of women Stanford U., 1936-38; dean women Whitman Coll., Walla Walla, Wash., 1938-46; assoc. dean students, prof. psychology U. Mont., Missoula, 1946-73, emeritus, 1973—. Mem. Am. Coll. Personnel Assn., Nat. Assn. Women Deans and Counselors (citation 1972), AAUW (pres. Walla Walla br., Wash. ednl. chmn. 1943-44), P.E.O., Mortar Board, Sigma Xi, Pi Lambda Theta, Psi Chi, Delta Gamma (Shield award 1972), Delta Kappa Gamma (Matrix Table award 1971). Republican. Presbyterian (co-chmn. canvass program 1960, elder 1960—). Club: Order Eastern Star. Home: 23 Greenbrier Ln Missoula MT 59802

CLOWER, ROBERT W(AYNE), economist, educator, consultant; b. Pullman, Wash., Feb. 13, 1926; s. Fay Walter and Mary Valentine (Gilchrist) C.; m. Frances Hepburn, Jan. 7, 1946; children—Ailsa, Leslie, Robert, Stephanie, Valerie; m. Georgene Thousendfriend, Jan. 30, 1976; children—Anastasia, Kathryn. B.A., Wash. State U., Pullman, 1948, M.A. in Econs., 1949; M.Litt. in Econs. (Rhodes scholar, Nuffield student), Oxford U., 1952, D.Litt., 1978. Asst. prof. Wash. State U., 1952-57; prof.; chmn. dept. econs. Northwestern U., 1958-71; dean Sch. Social Studies, U. Essex, 1968-69; prof. econs. UCLA, 1971—; John Maynard Keynes research prof. U. Essex, 1965-66. Served as warrant officer AUS, 1943-46. Guggenheim fellow, 1965; hon. fellow Brasenose Coll., Oxford, 1978—. Fellow Econometric Soc.; life mem. Royal Econ. Soc.; mem. Am. Econ. Assn. (exec. com. 1978-80), Western Econ. Assn., Assn. Am. Rhodes Scholars, Phi Beta Kappa. Author: Monetary Theory, 1968; Microeconomics, 1972; Anatomy of Monetary Theory, 1977; mng. editor Am. Econ. Rev., 1980—; mng. editor Econ. Inquiry, 1973-80; Am. cons. editor Penguin Books (U.K.), Ltd., 1967—; contbr. numerous articles to profl. jours., chpts. in books. Office: Dept Econs UCLA Los Angeles CA 90024

CLOYD, MILES WALLACE, med. scientist; b. Livingston, Mont., Nov. 17, 1948; s. Wallace Walker and Beryl Maxine (Tandy) C.; B.A., U. Mont., 1971; M.S., U. N.D., 1973; Ph.D. (NIH fellow), Duke U., 1977; m. Debbra J. Bliler, Aug. 3, 1969; children—Michael Todd, Tristan Dane. Grad. teaching asst. U. N.D., 1971-73, Damon Runyon-Walter Winchell Cancer Fund fellow Nat. Inst. Allergy and Infectious Diseases, NIH, Bethesda, Md., 1977-80; sr. staff fellow Rocky Mountain Lab., Hamilton, Mont., 1980—. Mem. N.D. Acad. Scis., AAAS, N.Y. Acad. Scis., Sigma Xi. Contbr. articles to sci. jours. Home: PO Box 1174 Hamilton MT 59840 Office: Rocky Mountain Lab Hamilton MT 59840

CLOYED-LEONHARDT, GLENNA MAY, systems auditor; b. Ottumwa, Iowa, Nov. 6, 1948; d. Clifford Ernest and Darlene Alice (Lindgren) C.; student (NSF scholar 1967) U. Iowa, 1967-71; B.A.I., U. Wis., 1979. Stock transfer clk. R. G. Dickinson & Co., Des Moines, 1967-68; common trust fund acct. Mchts. Nat. Bank, Cedar Rapids, Iowa, 1968-72; trust auditor Calif. Canadian Bank, San Francisco, 1973-76, asst. v.p., dep. auditor, 1978-79, asst. mgr. ops., 1979-80, EDP auditor, 1980—; dir. EDP Auditors Assos. Inc., San Francisco. Cert. info. system auditor. Mem. Nat. Assn. Bank Women (sec.), Bank Adminstrn. Inst., Bus. and Profl. Women's Club, Inst. Internal Auditors, EDP Auditors Assn., U. Calif. Alumni Assn. Democrat. Office: 344 Pine St San Francisco CA 94104

CLUFF, CHARLES EUGENE, marriage counselor; b. Pomona, Calif., Feb. 4, 1937; s. Harold Eugene and Thelma C.; B.A., Calif. Bapt. Coll., 1958; M.Div., Am. Bapt. Sem. West, 1961; D. Min., San Francisco Theol. Sem., 1975; m. Betty Lou Faulkner, May 24, 1958; children—Mark E., Carrie Lynn. Ordained to ministry American Baptist Ch., 1961; pastor Temple Bapt. Ch., Norwalk, Calif., 1960-65, Lemoore 1st Bapt. Ch., 1965-68, Merced (Calif.) Bapt. Ch., 1968-72; Lemoore Naval Air Sta., counselor, 1966-68; pvt. practice marriage and family counseling, Merced, 1970—; pres. Cluff Family Counseling, Inc., 1972—, Premarital Experience, Inc., 1977 . Bd. dirs. YMCA, United Way; past pres. Mental Health Assn., 1971-73; past pres. bd. incorporators Merced Symphony. Mem. Am. Bapt. Ministers Council, Calif. Assn. Marriage and Family Therapists, Nat. Alliance for Family Life. Republican. Clubs: Rotary, Racquet. Author: Parapsychology and the Christian Faith, 1976; Premarital Experience Manual and Workbook, 1977. Address: 1750 Cypress Way Merced CA 95340

CLUFF, LLOYD STERLING, geologist; b. Provo, Utah, Sept. 29, 1933; s. Colvin Sterling and Melba W. Cluff; B.S., U. Utah, 1960; m. Janet L. Peterson, Dec. 21, 1977; children—Tanya, Sasha. Jr. geologist El Paso Natural Gas Co., Salt Lake City, 1957-59; geologist Lottridge Thomas & Assocs., Salt Lake City, 1960; vis. assoc. prof. geology U. Nev.-Reno, 1968-73; staff geologist to v.p., prin. and dir. Woodward-Clyde Cons., San Francisco, 1960—; dir., v.p. Geoscis., 1968-73. Served with U.S. Army, 1954-56. Recipient Hogentagler award ASTM, 1968. Mem. Nat. Acad. Engring., Seismol. Soc. Am. (pres. 1982), Earthquake Engring. Research Inst., Geol. Soc. Am., Internat. Assn. Engring. Geologists, Structural Engrs. Assn., Utah Geol. Assn. Contbr. articles to profl. jours.

CLURMAN, IRENE, journalist; b. San Francisco, Mar. 2, 1947; d. Charles Isaac and Miriam (Grant) Clurman. B.A., Stanford U., 1969. Reporter, city editor Gallup (N. Mex.) Independent, 1970-72; copy editor Rocky Mountain News, Denver, 1972-73, feature writer, 1973-75, art critic, dance critic, 1975—. Founding mem., treas. Denver Internat. Film Festival, 1978. Mem. Dance Critics Assn., Phi Beta Kappa. Author numerous critical art and dance revs. for profl. jours. Home: Box 6713 Denver CO 80206 Office: Rocky Mountain News Box 719 Denver CO 80201

CLYMER, ALBERT ANDERSON, painter, architectural designer; b. Memphis, Feb. 16, 1942; s. Albert Andrew and Viola Ann (Anderson) C.; m. Susan Irene Clymer, Jan. 12, 1980; 1 dau., Helen Anne. Student in architecture Tex. A&M U., 1960-64; A.A., Napa Coll., 1982. Archtl. designer Keneth Wing, Long Beach, Calif., 1966; with Rossmore Leisure World, Laguna Beach, Calif., 1966-68, Oakland (Calif.) Redevel. Agy., 1966-68; pvt. practice archtl. design, Yountville, Calif., 1968—; group shows include: Oakland Mus. Modern Art (1st prize in oils), 1968, Vintage 1870 Internat. Exhibit (1st prize in oils), 1968, Santa Rosa (Calif.) Statewide Ann. (1st prize in oils), 1969-71, San Francisco Mus. Modern Art (1st prize in oils), 1970, Berkeley Mus. Modern Art (1st prize in oils 1971); represented in permanent collections: Mus. Modern Art, Newport, The Nut Tree-Fine Art Prints, Oakland Mus.; works include U.S. Army recruiting posters, 1977; bd. dirs. Depot Gallery; pres. bd. dirs. Berkeley Arts and Crafts Coop. Served to maj. USAR, 1966—. Decorated Army Achievement medal with 2 oak leaf clusters. Episcopalian. Club: Wine Group (Yountville). Office: PO Box 2278 Yountville CA 94599

CLYMER, CHRISTINE J., savings and loan official; b. Seattle, May 25, 1953; d. Gerald F. and Elaine Ruth (Hilgendorf) C.; 1 son, Geoffrey; m. Patrick J. Silvagnia, June 14, 1981. B.A. in Psychology, San Francisco State U., 1978. Personnel adminstr. Homestead Savs. & Loan, Burlingame, Calif., 1979-80; affirmative action officer Central Bank, Oakland, Calif., 1980-81; employee relations mgr. Bay View Fed. Savs., San Mateo, Calif., 1981-83, product devel. officer, 1983—. Western coordinator youth vol. activities Nat. Easter Seals, 1971-73. Named Outstanding Youth Vol. of Yr., San Mateo County, 1971. Mem. Am. Soc. Personnel Adminstrs., Savs. Instns. Mktg. Soc. Am., Kappa Kappa Gamma, Gamma Zeta. Office: 2121 S El Camino Real San Mateo CA 94403

COATE, LESTER EDWIN, environmental engineer, government agency official; b. Albany, Oreg., Jan. 21, 1936; s. Lester and Mildred Roxanne (Clark) C.; B.S., Oreg. State U., 1959; M.A., Calif. State U. at San Diego, 1969; Ph.D., U.S. Internat. U., 1973; m. Cheryl Mizer, Dec. 22, 1973; children—Steven Allen, David Scott, Carol Maureen. Civil engring. asst. Los Angeles County Flood Control Dist., 1959-61; gen. mgr., partner Robinson & Coate, Valley Center, Calif., 1961-64; gen. mgr., chief engr. Valley Center Municipal Water Dist., 1964-70; White House fellow, spl. asst. to chmn. Council on Environ. Quality, Exec. Office Pres., Washington, 1970-71, staff asst. to Pres. for environ. affairs, 1971; dir. Integrated Regional Environ. Mgmt. Project, San Diego, 1971-73; dep. regional adminstr. U.S. EPA, Seattle, 1973—; affiliate asso. prof. environ. studies U. Wash., Seattle, 1974—. Served to 1st lt. AUS, 1959-60. Recipient John Murdoch State and Nat. Advancement award Am. Water Works Assn., 1966; named Outstanding Young Civil Engr., ASCE, 1966, Bronze medal Environ. Protection Agy., 1975, Silver medal, 1977. Registered profl. engr., Calif., Wash., Oreg., Alaska. Diplomate Am. Acad. Environ. Engrs. Mem. Calif. C. of C. (v.p. 1965-67). Club: Rotary (pres.). Author: A Case Study in Implementation of Environmental Impact Report Requirement, 1973; Regional Environmental Management; Selected Proc. Nat. Conf., 1975. Home: 12913 NE 72d St Kirkland WA 98033 Office: 1200 6th Ave Seattle WA 98101

COATS, HUBERT S., JR., banker; b. Julesberg, Colo., Feb. 26, 1927; s. Hubert S. and Ruth (Lang) C.; pre-standard cert. Am. Inst. Banking, 1951, standard cert., 1955; grad. Pacific Coast Bankers Sch., 1970; m. Edna Mae, July 13, 1946; children—Larry Dale, Matthew Daniel. With First Security Bank, Jerome, Idaho, 1946-55, 57-59, asst. mgr. timeway credit, 1953-55, asst. mgr., 1957-59; asst. mgr. Hailey (Idaho) First Security Bank, 1955-57; v.p., cashier First Security Bank Twin Falls (Idaho), 1959-67; mgr. First Security Bank, Rupert, Idaho, 1967-69; v.p. ops. eastern div. First Security Bank, Pocatello, Idaho, 1967-72, v.p., asst. mgr., 1972-73, mgr., 1977; mgr., v.p. First Security Bank, Coeur d'Alene, Idaho, 1973-77; v.p., area mgr. Idaho Bank & Trust Co., Boise, 1977-78, sr. v.p., 1978—. Pres. PTA, Hailey, Idaho, 1955-56; treas. Pocatello Jr. Achievement, 1970-71, pres., 1969-70; chmn. bd. trustees First Methodist Ch., Coeur d'Alene; treas. Kootenai County (Idaho) YMCA, 1972-75, dir., 1972—; chmn. Idaho Housing Agy.; chmn. St. Luke's Charity Ball, 1983; bd. dirs., chmn. gen. div. United Way, Boise. Served with USN, 1944-46. Named Businessman of Yr., Twin Falls Credit Women's Club, 1954, Man of Yr., Kootenai Family YMCA, 1975; recipient Disting. Service award Coeur d'Alene C. of C., campaign award Kootenai County United Way, 1976. Mem. Idaho Bankers Assn. (chmn. public relations com. 1979-80), Boise C. of C. Clubs: Hillcrest Country, Arid (Boise). Home: 817 Argyll Dr Boise ID 83702 Office: PO Box 2800 Boise ID 83701

COBB, BRIAN ERIC, broadcasting executive; b. Berlin, N.H., Jan. 3, 1945; s. Everett Bryan and Eleanore (Bouchard) C.; children—Jennifer Kay, Heather Christine. B.A., U. Nev., 1967. Nat. sales mgr. Sta. KOA-TV, Denver, 1970-71; mgr. mktg. Sta. WNGE-TV, Nashville, 1972-75, v.p., gen. mgr. Sta. WNGE-TV, WSIX-AM-FM, 1976-77; v.p., gen. mgr. Sta. KOA-TV, KOA-Am, KOAQ, Denver, 1978-81, v.p. bus. communications, 1982—. Bd. dirs. Vanderbilt Children's Hosp., 1975-77; comml. chmn. Mile High United Way, 1980. Mem. Nat. Assn. TV Program Execs., Nat. Assn. Broadcasters. Club: Rotary. Office: 1044 Lincoln St Denver CO 80210

COBB, JEWEL PLUMMER, cell physiologist, university president; b. Chgo., Jan. 17, 1924; A.B., Talladega Coll., 1944; M.S., NYU, 1947, Ph.D. in Biology, 1950; div.; 1 child. Fellow Nat. Cancer Inst., 1950-52; instr. anatomy U. Ill. Coll. Medicine, 1952-54; research surgery Postgrad. Med. Coll., NYU, 1955, asst. prof., 1955-60; Cancer Research Found. prof. biology Sarah Lawrence Coll., 1960-69; prof. zoology, dean Conn. Coll., 1969-76; prof. biology, dean Douglass Coll., Rutgers U., 1976-81; pres. Calif. State U.-Fullerton, 1981—; spl. research on tissue culture studies human neoplasms, changes produced by promising chemotherapeutic agts., mechanisms normal and abnormal pigment cell metabolism. Dir. Travelers Ins. Co. Former mem. commn. on acad. affairs Am. Council on Edn. Bd. dirs. 21st Century Found., Nat. Center Resource Recovery, Nat. Sci. Bd., 1974-80, Nat. Inst. Medicine. Recipient Alumnae Women of Yr. award N.Y. U., 1979. Fellow N.Y. Acad. Scis., Tissue Culture Assn.; mem. AAUW, Sigma Xi. Home: 2963 Persimmon Place Fullerton CA 92635 Office: Calif State U Fullerton CA 92634

COBB, ROY LAMPKIN, JR., manufacturing company executive; b. Oklahoma City, Sept. 23, 1934; s. Roy Lampkin and Alice Maxine (Ellis) C.; B.A., U. Okla., 1972; postgrad. U. Calif., Northridge, 1976-77; m. Shirley Ann Dodson, June 21, 1958; children—Kendra Leigh, Cary William, Paul Alan. Naval aviation cadet U.S. Navy, 1955, advanced through grades to comdr., 1970; ret., 1978; mktg./project staff engr. Gen. Dynamics, Pomona, Calif., 1978-80; prin. engr. Advanced Tech., Inc., Camarillo, Calif., 1980—. Decorated Navy Commendation medal, Air medal. Mem. Ret. Officers Assn. Republican. Methodist. Club: Las Posas Country. Home: 2481 Brookhill Dr Camarillo CA 93010 Office: Advanced Tech Inc 1000 Paseo Camarillo Camarillo CA 93010

COBB, SHIRLEY ANN, public relations specialist, journalist; b. Oklahoma City, Jan. 1, 1936; d. William Ray and Irene (Fewell) Dodson; m. Roy Lampkin Cobb, Jr., June 21, 1958; children—Kendra Leigh, Cary William, Paul Alan. B.A. in Journalism with distinction, U. Okla., 1958, postgrad., 1972; postgrad. Jacksonville U., 1962. Info. specialist Pacific Missle Test Ctr., Pt. Mugu, Calif., 1975-76; corr. Religious News Service, N.Y.C., 1979-81; splty. editor fashion and religion Thousand Oaks (Calif.) News Chronicle, 1977-81; pub. relations cons., Camarillo, Calif., 1977—. Trustee Ocean View Sch. Bd., 1976-79; pres. Pt. Mugu Officers' Wives Club, 1975-76; bd. dirs. Camarillo Hospice, 1983—. Recipient Spot News award San Fernando Valley Press Club, 1979. Mem. Sigma Delta Chi, Pub. Relations Soc. Am., Phi Beta Kappa. Republican. Club: Las Posas Country. Contbr. articles to profl. jours. Home: 2481 Brookhill Dr Camarillo CA 93010 Office: 2481 Brookhill Dr Camarillo CA 93010

COBB, STEPHEN HENRY (STEVE), state senator; b. Honolulu, Dec. 5, 1942; s. William B. and Olivine (Steffens) C.; student U. Hawaii, 1961-64; B.A. in Journalism, Calif. State U.-Los Angeles, 1966. With mktg. and loans dept. Bank of Hawaii, 1970-72; adminstrv. asst. Pacific Resources Inc., 1976; mem. Hawaii Ho. of Reps. from 8th Dist., 1972-78, Hawaii Senate from 7th Dist., 1978—, chmn. consumer protection and commerce com., 1979-84, majority floor leader, 1981-84. Treas., Hawaii Little League Baseball, 1971-75. Bd. dirs. Hawaii Young Dems., 1971-72; active numerous Dem. campaigns, 1960—. Served with AUS, 1966-70; Vietnam. Decorated Silver Star, Bronze Star medal, Army Commendation medal, Air medal. Named Kiwanis Vet. of Yr., Hawaii, 1970. Mem. DAV, Sigma Delta Chi. Roman Catholic. Home: 4246 Kilauea Ave Honolulu HI 96816 Office: Room 215 State Capitol Bldg Honolulu HI 96813

COBB, WILLIAM THOMPSON, research scientist; b. Spokane, Wash., Nov. 10, 1942; s. Elmer Jean and Martha Ella (Napier) C.; B.A. in Biology, Eastern Wash. U., 1964; Ph.D., Oreg. State U., 1973; m. Sandra Lee Hodgson, Aug. 30, 1964; children—Michael, Melanie, Megan, William Thompson. Mgr./agronomist Sun Royal Co., Royal City, Wash., 1970-74; sr. scientist Lilly Research Labs., Kennewick, Wash., 1974-78, research scientist, 1978—; plant pathology instr. Columbia Basin Coll., 1971, 73, 75, 77. Mem. sch. bd., Royal City, Wash., 1973-74; scoutmaster Boy Scouts Am., Royal City, 1972-73. Served with U.S. Army, 1964-66. Decorated Army Commendation medal. Cert. profl. agronomist. Mem. Am. Soc. Agronomy, Am. Phytopath. Soc., Weed Sci. Soc. Am., Council Agrl. Sci. and Tech., Sigma Xi. Address: 815 S Kellogg Kennewick WA 99336

COBBLE, JAMES WIKLE, chemist; b. Kansas City, Mo., Mar. 15, 1926; s. Ray and Crystal Edith (Wikle) C.; B.A., No. Ariz. U., 1946; M.S., U. So. Calif., 1949; Ph.D., U. Tenn. and Oak Ridge Inst. Nuclear Studies, 1952; m. Margaret Ann Zumwalt, July 9, 1949; children—Catherine Ann, Richard James. Chemist, Oak Ridge Nat. Lab., 1949-52; postdoctoral research asso. U. Calif., Berkeley, 1952-55, instr., 1954; asst. prof. to prof. chemistry Purdue U., West Lafayette, Ind., 1955-73; prof. chemistry, dean Grad. Div. and Research, San Diego State U., also v.p. San Diego State U. Found., 1973—; Welch Found. lectr., 1971; chmn. ad hoc com. geothermal energy Nat. Materials Adv. Bd., Nat. Acad. Scis./Nat. Research Council, 1977-78; corrosion adv. com. Elec. Power Research Inst.; mem. Joint Grad. Bd. of U. Calif. and Calif. State Univ. and Colls., 1978—, Calif. Postsecondary Commn. Joint Grad. Bd., 1978—. Served to lt. (j.g.), USNR, 1945-46. Guggenheim fellow, 1966; recipient E.O. Lawrence award A.E.C., 1970; recipient grants A.E.C., NSF, AF Office Sci. Research, Office of Saline Water, E.I. DuPont de Nemours & Co., Gen. Elec. Found., Purdue Research Found., Advanced Research Projects Agy., Elec. Power Research Inst., E.R. Squibb & Sons. Fellow Am. Phys. Soc.; mem. Am. Chem. Soc., Assn. Western Univs. (exec. com., bd. dirs.), Western Assn. Grad. Schs., Sigma Xi, Phi Kappa Phi, Alpha Chi Sigma, Phi Lambda Upsilon. Contbr. articles and revs. to tech. jours. Home: 1380 Park Row La Jolla CA 92037 Office: Graduate Division and Research San Diego State University San Diego CA 92182

COBBS, PRICE MASHAW, psychiatrist; b. Los Angeles, Nov. 2, 1928; s. Peter Price and Rosa (Mashaw) C.; A.B., U. Calif. at Berkeley, 1953; M.D., Meharry Med. Coll., 1958; children—Price P., Marion Renata. Intern, San Francisco Gen. Hosp., 1958-59; resident in psychiatry Mendocino State Hosp., 1959-61, Langley Porter Neuropsychiat. Inst.; practice medicine specializing in psychiatry, San Francisco, 1962—; asst. clin. prof. psychiatry U. Calif. at San Francisco, 1966-67. Mem. Dem. Policy Council, 1969—. Pres., Pacific Mgmt. Systems, San Francisco, 1974—. Served with AUS, 1951-52. Mem. Nat. Med. Assn., A.M.A., Am. Psychiat. Assn., Inst. of Medicine of Nat. Acad. Scis., Authors Guild. Co-author: Black Rage, 1968; The Jesus Bag, 1971. Office: 3528 Sacramento St San Francisco CA 94118

COBURN, MARJORIE FOSTER, psychotherapist, Montessori/special educator; b. Salt Lake City, Feb. 28, 1939; d. Harlan A. and Alma (Ballinger) Polk; m. Robert Byron Coburn, July 2, 1977; children—Robert Scott Coburn, Kelly Anne Coburn, Polly Klea Foster, Matthew Ryan Foster. B.A. in Sociology, UCLA, 1960; Montessori Internat. Diploma honor grad. Washington Montessori Inst., 1968, M.A. in Psychology, U. No. Colo., 1979; Ph.D. in Counseling Psychology, U. Denver, 1983. Probation officer Alameda County (Calif.), Oakland, 1960-62, Contra Costa County (Calif.), El Cerrito, 1966, Fairfax County (Va.), Fairfax, 1967; dir. Friendship Club, Orlando, Fla., 1963-65; tchr. Va. Montessori Sch., Fairfax, 1968-70; spl. edn. tchr. Leary Sch., Falls Church, Va., 1970-72, sch. administr., 1973-76; tchr. Aseltine Sch., San Diego, 1976-77, Coburn Montessori Sch., Colorado Springs, Colo., 1977-79; psychotherapist, supervised pvt. practice, Colorado Springs, 1979-82, San Diego, 1982 ; cons. spl. edn., agoraphobia, women in transition. Mem. Am. Psychol. Assn., Am. Orthopsychiat. Assn., Phobia Soc., Council Exceptional Children, El Paso Psychol. Assn., Calif. Psychol. Assn., AAUW, NOW, Mensa. Contbr. articles to profl. jours.; author: (with R.C. Orem) Montessori: Prescription for Children with Learning Disabilities, 1977.

COCHETTI, MARIE GOODMAN, professional association executive; b. Phila., Jan. 18, 1924; s. Morris and Ethel Margaret (Heebner) Goodman; m. Daniel Philip Cochetti; children—Jay Marc, Kip Tyler, Joy Leslie. Student Temple U., 1945; B.S., Phila. Bible Coll., 1946. Dir. James Industries, Phila., 1945-51; mgr. Angeles Termite Co., Los Angeles, 1951-56; dir. Rehab. Ctr. for Teenage Wards of the Ct., Los Angeles, 1956-74; dir. Associated Photographers Internat., Los Angeles, 1975—. Bd. dirs. Youth Employment Service, 1968-69; dir. Action Life, a Drug Rehab. Group, 1969-74. Recipient Los Angeles County Suprs. award for community service, 1971. Republican. Clubs: Farmer's and Charmers Square Dance, Rockwell Recreation Ctr. Home: 7635 Pomelo Dr Canoga Park CA 91304 Office: 21822 Sherman Way Suite 102 Canoga Park CA 91303

COCHRAN, CHRISTOPHER CRAIG, soil scientist; b. Oak Park, Ill., Dec. 18, 1951; s. Howard William and Olive Anne (Milne) C.; B.S. in Forestry (Ill. State scholar), U. Ill., 1974. Soil scientist Soil Conservation Service, U.S. Dept. Agr., Batavia, Ill., 1974-75, Champaign, Ill., 1975-77, 78-79, Silver City, N.Mex., 1977-78, soil scientist, survey leader, Macomb, Ill., 1979-80, Tucson, 1980—. Mem. Am. Soc. Agronomy, Soil Sci. Soc. Am., Ill. Soil Classifiers Assn., U.S. Jaycees (Presdl. award of honor), Order of Arrow. Contbr. articles to profl. publs. Office: 3241 N Romero Rd Tucson AZ 85705

COCHRAN, FRED L(LOYD), author, editor, nuclear science consultant; b. Hobart, Ind., July 24, 1936; s. Fred G. and Grace Jewel (Stark) C.; m. Joan Boertje, Dec. 19, 1959; children—Elizabeth, Danielle. Lab. chemist U.S. Steel Corp., Gary, Ind., 1954-55; research asst. materials research Collins Radio Co., Burbank, Calif., 1955-56; sr. research analyst Atomics Internat., Canoga Park, Calif., 1956-58, research engr., 1958-60; research chemist Culligan Inc., San Bernardino Calif., 1958-59; chief metallographer Gulf Gen. Atomic Inc., San Diego, 1960-72; editor-in-chief Mountain Messenger, v.p. Roos-Cochran Publs., Downieville, Calif., 1973—; mem. com. on metallography AEC. Served with USAFR 1954-62. Mem. Internat. Metallographic Soc. (co-founder, v.p. 1967-72), Am. Nuclear Soc., ASTM, Am. Soc. Metals, Internat. Microstructural Analysis Soc., Authors League (N.Y.C.), Authors Guild, Sigma Delta Chi. Republican. Jewish. Author: Handbook of Optical Metallography, 1968-70; 5 novels; contbr. articles to sci. publs. Home: PO Box 475 Downieville CA 95936 Office: The Mountain Messenger Downieville CA 95936

COCHRAN, PATRICK EUGENE, food sci. technologist; b. Myrtle Point, Oreg., Dec. 13, 1948. Dir. sanitation and safety Loma Linda Foods, Riverside, Calif., 1973-74, food sci. technologist, dir. quality assurance, 1977-82, sensory evaluation, product devel. research scientist, 1982—; plant sanitarian H.J. Heinze-Starkist, Terminal Island, Long Beach, Calif., 1974-75; food industry tech. rep. Penwalt Corp., Speciality Chem. Div., So. Calif., 1975-77; pvt. practice cons. to food industry on quality control and regulatory compliance, 1975—. Cert. comml.

applicator, State of Calif., Dept. Food and Agr. Mem. Inst. Food Technologists, Internat. Assn. Milk, Food and Environ. Santarians, Calif. Assn. Dairy and Milk Sanitarians, Am. Soc. Quality Control, AAAS. Office: 11503 Pierce St Riverside CA 92515

COCHRAN, SAMUEL VERNE, ins. exec.; b. Santa Ana, Calif., Apr. 20, 1925; s. Henry A. and Mary Ethel (Turner) C.; diploma acctg. Johnson Bus. Coll., Santa Ana, Calif., 1947; diploma agy. mgmt. Stanford U., 1955; cert. ins. cons., Orange Coast Coll., Costa Mesa, Calif., 1965; Ph.D., London U., 1973, Calgary (Alta., Can.) Coll. Tech., 1976; m. Geraldine Kerley, June 3, 1947; children—James Lee, Ronald Wayne, Susan Elaine, Gary Samuel. Engaged in ins. bus., 1947—; propr. Advanced Ins. Mktg., Garden Grove, Calif., 1949—; mem. faculty Orange Coast Coll., 1960—; trustee Griffith Found., Ohio State U., 1972—; lectr. in field, 1965—. Bd. dirs. So. Calif. Coll., Costa Mesa, 1955-77. Founder, pres. laymen div. Light for the Lost, 1953, exec. v.p., 1975—. Mem. Ind. Ins. Agts. Assn. Calif. (past mem. ednl. bd.), Am. Soc. Cert. Ins. Cons. (founder), Nat. Assn. Ind. Ins. Agts. Republican. Mem. Assemblies of God Ch. Author textbooks, manual. Address: PO Box 858 Garden Grove CA 92642

COCHRAN, VERLAN LEYERL, soil scientist; b. Declo, Idaho, Feb. 19, 1938; s. Harley Earl and Anna Helene (Christensen) C.; B.S. in Soil Sci. with honors, Calif. Poly. State U., 1966; M.S. in Soil Sci., Wash. State U., 1971; m. Diana Larraine Dennis, June 21, 1969; children—Dean Scott, Vincent Lee. Research asst. Agrl. Research Service, Dept. Agr., Pullman, Wash., 1966-74, soil scientist Sci. and Edn. Adminstrn., 1974—. Served with AUS, 1959-62. Mem. Am. Soc. Agronomy, Soil Sci. Soc. Am., Western Soc. Soil Sci., Soil Conservation Soc. Am., Sigma Xi. Club: Palouse Lions (sec. 1980). Contbr. articles profl. jours. Home: Rt 1 Box 186A Palouse WA 99161 Office: 215 Johnson Hall Wash State U Pullman WA 99164

COCHRAN, WILLIAM MORGAN, JR., psychologist, consultant; b. Parker's Landing, W.Va., Nov. 11, 1934; s. William Morgan and Frances Imogene (Burn-Field) C. B.A., U. Va., Charlottesville, 1955; M.A., W.Va. U., Morgantown, 1958; A.B.D., U. Pitts., 1963. Vice-pres., research dir. Ketchem, MacLeod & Grove, Pitts., 1973-75; dir. Dentsu Corp. Am., Los Angeles, 1975-79; mng. dir. Research Assocs., Ltd., Los Angeles, 1980-82; v.p., mktg. research dir. Kenyon & Eckhardt, Inc., Los Angeles, 1982—; cons. U.S. Dept. Commerce, 1982—. Mem. Am. Psychol. Assn., Am. Mktg. Assn. Democrat. Episcopalian. Home: 1865 Greenfield Ave Los Angeles CA 90025 Office: 1100 Glendon Ave Suite 725 Los Angeles CA 90024

COCHRANE, PEGGY, architect, writer; b. Alhambra, Calif., July 9, 1926; d. E. Elliott and Gladys (Moran) C.; B.A., Scripps Coll., 1945; postgrad., U. So. Calif., 1951-52, Columbia U., 1954; m. Hugh Bowman, Nov. 24, 1954 (div.). Job capt. Kahn and Jacobs, N.Y.C., 1954-55; project architect Litchfield, Whiting, Panero & Severud, Teheran, Iran, 1956; archtl. designer Daniel, Mann, Johnson and Mendenhall, Los Angeles, 1956-59; individual practice architecture, Sherman Oaks, Calif., 1966—. Recipient Architecture prize Scripps Coll., 1945. Mem. Assn. Women in Architecture (life), Union Internationale des Femmes Architects. Republican. Episcopalian. Club: Dionysians (S. Pasadena). Author (musical) Yucatan, 1979; (play) I Gave at the Office, 1980; The Witch Doctor's Manual; mem. editorial bd. Los Angeles Architect, 1978—; contbr. to Contemporary Architects. Home and office: 3888 Sherview Dr Sherman Oaks CA 91403

COCKRELL, WILLIAM JASPER, III, accountant; b. Jacksonville, Fla., July 7, 1942; s. William Jasper and Bethel Aurora (Hughes) C.; B.S.B.A., Calif. State Coll., Los Angeles, 1968; M.B.T., U. So. Calif., 1974; M.B.A., Pepperdine U., 1978; m. Sharon Lee Gerrie, Sept. 9, 1967. Tax supr. Laventhol & Horwath, Los Angeles, 1973-74; prin. Palmer, Wiggs & Heston, Agana, Guam, 1974-75; tax supr. Laventhol & Horwath, Los Angeles, 1975-76; tax mgr. Arthur Young & Co., Beverly Hills, Calif., 1977-78, Price, Waterhouse & Co., Newport Beach, Calif., 1978-79; pvt. practice acctg., Newport Beach, 1979—; mem. Club 1000, U. So. Calif., 1981—; dir. MBAN V, Inc., Newport Beach, 1978—; instr. Northrop U., 1976-77. Co-trustee T.F. Haller Trust, 1978—; active World Trade Center Assn. Orange County. Served with USN, 1960-61. C.P.A., Calif., Guam. Mem. Am. Inst. C.P.A.'s, Calif. Soc. C.P.A.'s (ethics com., taxation com.), Practicing Law Inst., U. So. Calif. Alumni Assn. Phi Kappa Tau. Newport Beach-Irvine Estate Planning Council, Newport Harbor C. of C. Club: Athletic (Los Angeles). Contbr. articles to profl. jours. Office: PO Box 337 Balboa Island CA 92662

COCKRIEL, STEPHEN EUGENE, lawyer; b. Long Beach, Calif., June 8, 1948; s. John Robert and Patricia Doreen (Carroll) C.; m. Helen Kathleen Mulford, Dec. 19, 1968; children—Jonathan Ryan, Timothy James. B.S. in Fin., U. So. Calif., 1970; J.D., Loyola U., 1973. Bar: Calif. 1973. Ptnr., Bergmann, Cockriel & Forrester, Long Beach, 1978—; legal counsel U.S. Jaycees, 1979-80. Asst. sec. Long Beach Local Devel. Corp., 1980-82. Mem. Calif. Bar Assn., Long Beach Bar Assn., Long Beach Jaycees (past pres.). Republican. Methodist. Office: 2105 E 4th St Long Beach CA 90814

COCKRUM, RICHARD HENRY, elec. engr.; b. Culver City, Calif., Sept. 23, 1950; s. Richard Donald and Irma Lucille (Schilling) C.; diploma in engring. tech. Santa Monica Coll., 1971; B.S.E.E., Calif. State Poly. U., 1973, M.Engring., 1975; postgrad. UCLA, 1976; m. Christie Lynn Howard, Feb. 19, 1978; 1 dau., Tawny Lynn. Engr., Jet Propulsion Lab., Pasadena, Calif., 1973-80, sr. engr., 1980—; lectr. Calif. State Poly. U., Pomona, 1975-80, asso. prof., 1980—; cons. thin film semicondr. materials group Jet Propulsion Lab. Recipient Sloane Meml. award, 1970, NASA awards. Mem. IEEE, Electron Device Soc., Calif. Poly. Alumni Assn. (v.p., dir.), Sigma Xi, Eta Kappa Nu. Contbr. articles to tech. jours. Home: 4531 Denver St Montclair CA 91763 Office: 3801 W Temple Ave Pomona CA 91768

COCKRUM, WILLIAM MONROE, III, investment banker; b. Indpls., July 18, 1937; s. William M. and Katherine J. Moore (Jaqua) C.; A.B. with distinction, DePauw U., 1959; M.B.A. with distinction, Harvard U., 1961; m. Andrea Lee Deering, Mar. 8, 1975; children—Catherine Ann, William M. With A.G. Becker Paribas Inc., Chgo., N.Y.C. and Los Angeles, 1961—, mgr. nat. corp. fin. div., 1968-71, mgr. pvt. investments, 1971—, sr. v.p., 1975-78, vice chmn., 1978—, also dir.; dir. Burrows Inc., Pacific Express Inc., Masti-Kure Inc., Transcon Lines, Knapp Communications Corp., Gen. Hydrocarbons, Inc., Healthgroup Internat. Mem. Delta Kappa Epsilon. Clubs: University (Chgo.); Monterey (Palm Desert, Calif.). Home: 666 Sarbonne Rd Los Angeles CA 90077 Office: 2029 Century Park E Suite 3400 Los Angeles CA 90067 also 55 Water St New York NY 10041

CODDINGTON, DEAN CLINTON, research economist; b. Sioux Falls, S.D., June 11, 1932; s. E.C. and Janice (Rosenberger) C.; m. Judy L., June 26, 1955; children—David, Susan, Michael, Lisa. B.S. in Engring., S.D. State U., 1954; M.B.A., Harvard U., 1959. Research economist Research Inst., U. Denver, 1959-70; mng. ptnr. Browne, Bortz & Coddington, Denver, 1970—. Trustee Swedish Med. Center, Englewood, Colo. Served to 1st lt. USAF, 1954-57. Mem. Internat. Assn. Energy Economists. Democrat. Baptist. Clubs: Internat. Athletic, Rotary (Denver). Contbr. articles to bus. jours. Home: 6571 S Marion St Littleton CO 80121 Office: 155 S Madison St Denver CO 80209

CODY, DENNIS JAMES, testing laboratory executive; b. Los Angeles, Nov. 6, 1947; s. Robert J. and Phyllis L. (Jackman) C.; m. Jo Ann Turnbull, Dec. 31, 1966; children—Johnny Horton, Dayna Jo, Denise Jeanne. Student Adams State Coll., 1965-66. Project materials technician Colo. State Hwy. Dept., 1966, 67, 68; draftsman, project researcher, insp. Morcan Engring., Delta, Colo., 1968-69; lab. technician, inspector, lab. asst. mgr. N.W. Testing Labs., Inc., Portland, Oreg., 1975—, now mgr. Salem br. Mem. Oreg. Fair Share, 1980-81. Mem. Am. Welding Soc. (chmn. Willamette Valley chpt. 1981-83), Oreg. Concrete and Agregate Producers Assn. (mem. tech. com.). Democrat. Clubs: Elks, Nat. Write Your Congressman. Office: 3385 34th St NE Salem OR 97303

COE, HENRY SUTCLIFFE, rancher, mgmt. cons.; b. Oakland, Calif., May 30, 1906; s. Henry Willard and Rhoda Dawson (Sutcliffe) C.; student U. Pacific, 1924-26; A.B., Stanford U., 1929; LL.B., Blackstone Coll. Law, 1941, J.D., 1942; m. Pearle Hersey, Oct. 9, 1928; children—Nancy P., Winnifred Hannah Coe Verbica. Pub. accountant, San Jose, Calif., 1928-29; bookkeeper U.S. Steel, San Francisco, 1929; salesman James A. Clayton Co., real estate, 1929; bookkeeper Calif. Packing Corp., 1930; cattle rancher, San Jose, 1932—; property mgmt. cons., San Jose, 1943—, Bangor, Maine, 1943—. Bd. dirs., trustee Met. YMCA, San Jose. Elected to Wisdom Hall of Fame. Mem. Am. Def. Preparedness Assn., Am. Nat. Livestock Assn., Am. Forestry Assn., Calif. Hist. Soc., Arabian Horse Registry, Arabian Horse Club No. Calif., Calif. Cattlemen's Assn., Maine Forest Products Council, Santa Clara, Calif., San Jose chambers commerce. Republican. Episcopalian. Clubs: Masons (32 deg.; Hiram award), Shriners; Commonwealth of Calif. (San Francisco); San Jose Country. rancher, mgmt. cons.; b. Oakland, Calif., May 30, 1906; s. Henry Willard and Rhoda Dawson (Sutcliffe) C.; student U. Pacific, 1924-26; A.B., Stanford U., 1929; LL.B., Blackstone Coll. Law, 1941, J.D., 1942; m. Pearle Hersey, Oct. 9, 1928; children—Nancy P., Winnifred Hannah Coe Verbica. Pub. accountant, San Jose, Calif., 1928-29; bookkeeper U.S. Steel, San Francisco, 1929; salesman James A. Clayton Co., real estate, 1929; bookkeeper Calif. Packing Corp., 1930; cattle rancher, San Jose, 1932—; property mgmt. cons., San Jose, 1943—, Bangor, Maine, 1943—. Bd. dirs., trustee Met. YMCA, San Jose. Elected to Wisdom Hall of Fame. Mem. Am. Def. Preparedness Assn., Am. Nat. Livestock Assn., Am. Forestry Assn., Calif. Hist. Soc., Arabian Horse Registry, Arabian Horse Club No. Calif., Calif. Cattlemen's Assn., Maine Forest Products Council, Santa Clara, Calif., San Jose chambers commerce. Republican. Episcopalian. Clubs: Masons (32 deg.; Hiram award), Shriners; Commonwealth of Calif. (San Francisco); San Jose Country. Home: San Felipe Valley 8610 San Felipe Rd San Jose CA 95121 Office: PO Box 877 San Jose CA 95106 also PO Box 676 Bangor ME 04401

COE, JOHN CLARK, airline executive; b. Crary, N.D., Mar. 12, 1924; s. James Charles and Margaret Maybelle (Calderwood) C.; m. Joy Eames, Nov. 27, 1954; children—Robert Eames, Nancy Louise. B.S. in Bus., U. Colo., 1946. Flight steward, sta. agt., sta. mgr., maintenance cost acct. Monarch AirLines, Denver, 1947-50; acct. Frontier Airlines, Inc., Denver, 1950-51, dir. econ. research, 1952-66, staff v.p. econ. planning, 1967-68, v.p. econ. planning, 1969-81, v.p. corp. planning, 1982—; forensic econ. analyst air transp. Active Denver Botanic Gardens, Nat. Cathedral Assn., Washington. Mem. N.Am. Soc. Corp. Planning. Congregationalist.

COE, ROBERT CAMPBELL, surgeon; b. Seattle, Nov. 14, 1918; s. Herbert Everett and Lucy Jane (Campbell) C.; B.S., U. Wash., 1940; M.D., Harvard U., 1950; m. Josephine Austin Weiner, Mar. 24, 1942; children—Bruce Everett, Virginia Austin, Matthew Daniel. Intern, asst. resident Mass. Gen. Hosp., Boston, 1950-54, chief resident, 1955, chief surg. clinics, 1956; instr. surgery Harvard U. Med. Sch., Boston, 1956; practice medicine specializing in thoracic and vascular surgery, Seattle, 1957—; mem. hon. staff Children's Hosp.; hon. staff Harborview Hosp.; cons. thoracic surgeon Firland San., Seattle, 1957-68, Children's Hosp. Tumor Clinic, 1968-80; attending surgeon Swedish Hosp.; mng. partner Invex & Inpark med. offices, Seattle, 1970—; clin. prof. U. Wash. Med. Sch., 1973—; mem. Wash. State Med. Disciplinary Bd., 1981—; pres. 1st Mercer (Wash.) Corp., 1973-76, treas., 1977—; owner, operator Hidden Valley Guest Ranch, Cle Elum, Wash., 1969—; developer Kula Estate, Maui, Hawaii. Chmn. bd. Northwest Seaport Inc., hist. mus., Kirkland, Wash., 1974-75; mem. Mayor's Harbor Adv. Commn., 1960-63; mem. vis. com. Sch. Nursing, U. Wash., 1983—. Served with USNR, 1941-46. Diplomate Am. Bd. Thoracic Surgery, Am. Bd. Surgery. Fellow ACS; mem. N. Pacific Surg. Assn. (sr.), Pacific Coast Surg. Assn. (sr.), Seattle Surg. Soc. (pres., 1969), Psi Upsilon. Episcopalian. Clubs: Cruising of Am., Seattle Yacht. Contbr. articles to profl. jours. Editor King County Med. Soc. Bull., 1964-70; editorial bd. N.W. Medicine, 1961-66; trustee Pacific Northwest, sci. mag. Home: 7260 N Mercer Way Mercer Island WA 98040 Office: 1117 Columbia St Seattle WA 98104

COE, SUSAN JOYCE, educator; b. Pinedale, Wyo., May 22, 1954; d. Cecil J. and Geraldine A. Coe. B.S., Chadron State Coll., 1976, M.S., 1977. Cert. tchr., emotionally disturbed tchr., psychol. technician, Wyo. Elem. sch. tchr., Alliance, Nebr., 1976-77; social worker Community Action, Cheyenne, Wyo., 1978-79; tchr. Cole Sch., Cheyenne, 1979-82, tchr. of gifted and talented, 1982—. Mem. Laramie (Wyo.) County Task Force for Gifted and Talented. Active Laramie County Assn. Children with Learning Disabilities, 1980-81, Community Commn., 1979—. Named Working Woman of Day, radio sta., 1982. Mem. NEA, Cheyenne Tchr. Edn. Assn., PEO. Republican. Presbyterian. Office: Cole School 820 O'Neil St Cheyenne WY 82007

COE, WILLIAM CHARLES, psychologist, educator; b. Hanford, Calif., Oct. 22, 1930; s. Bernard and Bertha (Vaughan) C.; children—Karen Ann, William Vaughan. B.S., U. Calif.-Davis, 1958; postgrad. Fresno State Coll., 1960-61; Ph.D., U. Calif.-Berkeley, 1964. Research helper Fresno State Coll., 1960-61; research asst. U. Calif.-Berkeley, 1961-62, NSF research fellow, 1963-64, instr. corr. div., 1967-81; clin. psychology trainee VA Hosp., San Francisco, 1962-63; staff psychologist Langley Porter Neuropsychiat. Inst., San Francisco, 1964-66; asst. clin. prof. med. psychology U. Calif. Sch. Medicine, San Francisco, 1965-66; asst. prof. psychology Fresno State Coll., 1966-68; assoc. prof. psychology Calif. State U.-Fresno, 1968-72, prof., 1972—, chmn. dept. psychology, 1979—; pvt. practice psychology, Fresno, 1965—; instr. Calif. Sch. Profl. Psychology, Fresno, 1973, Northeastern U., Boston, 1974; research asso. U. Calif., Santa Cruz, 1975; vis. prof. U. Calif.-Santa Cruz, 1979, U. Queensland (Australia), 1982; cons. in field. Served with USAF, 1951-55. Decorated D.F.C., Air medal with oak leaf cluster. NSF grantee, 1967, 71. Fellow Am. Psychol. Assn.; mem. Psychol. Assn., Calif., Psychol. Assn., San Francisco, Psychol. Assn. (editor San Francisco Psychologist, 1966), Central Calif. Psychol. Assn. (pres. 1969, dir. 1972-73) psychol. assns., Soc. Clin. and Exptl. Hypnosis, Assn. Advancement Behavior Therapy, Phi Beta Kappa, Sigma Xi, Phi Kappa Phi, Psi Chi. Author: (with T.R. Sarbin) The Student Psychologists Handbook: A Guide to Sources, 1969; (with T.R. Sarbin) Hypnosis: A Social Psychological Analysis of Influence Communication, 1972; Challenges of Personal Adjustment, 1972; (with L. Gagnon and D. Swiercinsky) Instructors Manual for Challenges of Personal Adjustment, 1972; Psychology X118: Psychological Adjustment, 1973. Contbr. articles to profl. jours. Office: Dept Psychology Calif State U Fresno CA 93740

COELHO, TONY, congressman; b. Los Banos, Calif., June 15, 1942; s. Otto and Alice C.; B.A., Loyola U. of Los Angeles, 1964; m. Phyllis, June 10, 1967; children—Nicole, Kristin. Asst. for agr. to Congressman B.F. Sisk, 1965-70, adminstrv. asst., 1970-78; mem. 96th-98th Congresses from 15th Dist. Calif., chmn. Democratic Congl. Campaign Com., 1981—, majority whip-at-large, 1981—, mem. Dem. Steering and Policy Com., 1981—. Office: 403 Cannon House Office Bldg Washington DC 20515

COEN, GEORGE MELBOURNE, management and engineering services company executive; b. Albuquerque, June 28, 1946; s. George Francis and Bettie Millicent (Woods) C.; B.B.A., U. N.Mex., 1971; M.B.A., Calif. State U., 1977; 7; m. Linda Lou Boyd, Sept. 9, 1967; children—Scott M., Dawn M. Contracts supt. Dravo Corp., Pitts., 1976-77; materials mgmt. supr. Public Service Co. N.Mex., Farmington, 1977-80; pres. ISTS-West, Inc., Farmington, 1980-81; pres. G.M. Coen & Assocs., Inc., 1981—. Served with U.S. Navy, 1964-67. Mem. Am. Assn. Cost Engrs., Am. Mgmt. Assn. Republican. Clubs: Negative Thinkers Camera, Elks. Home: 5001 Horvath St Farmington NM 87401 Office: 3005 Northridge Suite E Farmington NM 87401

COFFER, HERBERT LEE, industrial arts educator, photographer; b. Lovington, N.Mex., Nov. 21, 1949; s. Paul and Maxine (Fleming) C.; m. Malta Lou Vowell, Dec. 22, 1972. Student, N.Mex. Jr. Coll., 1967-69; B.S. in Indsl. Edn., Eastern N.Mex. U., 1971, M.Ed., 1976. Indsl. arts tchr. Roswell (N.Mex.) Ind. Sch. Dist., 1971-78, high sch. math. tchr., 1978-79; draftsman Transp. Mfg. Corp., Roswell, 1979, Mann Engring., 1980; indsl. arts, photography tchr. N.Mex. Rehab. Center, Roswell, 1980—; pvt. practice photography, Roswell, 1976—. Mem. Inst. Drafting Tech., N.Mex. Rehab. Assn., N.Mex. Vocat. Assn. Contbr. articles in field to profl. jours. Home: PO Box 1223 Roswell NM 88201 Office: NMex Rehab Center D at E Eyman St Roswell NM 88201

COFFEY, HELEN ELIZABETH, physicist; b. Chelsea, Mass., Nov. 17, 1944; d. Timothy Patrick and Helen Williamina (Stevens) C. B.S., Merrimack Coll., 1966; M.S., U. Colo., 1969. Mem. staff M.I.T., Cambridge, 1969-70; physicist NOAA, Boulder, 1972—, br. chief solar and high atmosphere br., 1977—; sec. Internat. Ursigrams and World Days Service, 1981—. High Altitude Obs. Astrogeophysics fellow, 1966-67. Mem. Internat. Astronom. Union (commn. X working group internat. programs), Am. Geophys. Union, Am. Meteorol. Soc., Am. Astron. Soc., AAAS, Sigma Xi. Democrat. Roman Catholic. Club: Zonta (v.p. 1981—). Editor: Solar-Geophysical Data, 1977—; geomagnetic and solar data table Jour. Geophys. Research, 1981—. Home: 7659 Nikau Dr Longmont CO 80501 Office: World Data Center A Solar Terrestrial Physics NOAA E/GC2 325 Broadway Boulder CO 80303

COFFEY, MARVIN DALE, biology educator; b. Midvale, Idaho, Apr. 25, 1930; s. Raymond Standfield and Agnes (Hutchinson) C.; m. Wanda Kirchgestner, Apr. 29, 1934; children—Susan, Gregory, Lorilee, Mark, Todd. Student Whitman Coll., 1948-49; A.B. in Zoology, Brigham Young U., 1952, M.A., 1953; Ph.D. in Entomology, Wash. State U., 1957. Instr. dept. biology So. Oreg. State Coll., Ashland, 1957-59, asst. prof., 1959-63, assoc. prof., 1963-67, prof. 1967—, chmn. dept. biology, 1965-70; asst. prof. biology Fresno (Calif.) State Coll., 1964-65; vis. prof. U. Ky., Lexington, 1976-77; cons. in field. Mem. AAAS, Am. Inst. Biol. Scis., Entomol. Soc. Am., Wash. State Entomol. Soc., Oreg. Entomol. Soc. Mormon. Contbr. articles to profl. jours. Office: Dept Biology So Oreg State Coll Ashland OR 97520

COFFEY, PHILIP JOHN, civil engr.; b. Holyoke, Mass., Dec. 6, 1910; s. John and Mildred (Knappett) C.; B.S. in Civil Engring. (scholar 1930-32). MIT, 1933; M.A. in Journalism, U. Colo., 1970; m. Lydia Spomer, Aug. 15, 1942; 1 son, Cecil. With USPHS, Chgo., San Francisco, Addis Ababa, Ethiopia. Cin., Denver, 1936-42, 57-68, san. engr. dir., until 1968; san. hydraulic engr. Calif. Depts. Fin. and Water Resources, San Francisco, Sacramento, 1946-48, 51-57; san. engr. Inst. Inter-Am. Affairs, Asuncion, Paraguay, 1949-51; spl. exam. commr. Calif. Bd. Registration for Profl. Engrs., Sacramento, 1952; mem. tech. adv. com. Calif. Senate Com. Radiation Protection, Sacramento, 1956-57; mem. faculty Water and Sewage Plant Operators' Sch., U. Colo., 1966-67. Served to lt. col., C.E., AUS, 1942-46. Registered profl. engr., Calif., Colo. Mem. Ret. Officers Assn., Kappa Tau Alpha. Lodge: Masons. Contbr. articles to tech. publs. Address: 67 S Benton Dr Lakewood CO 80226

COFFEY, SUSAN MARIE, chemist, microbiologist; b. Portland, Oreg., June 8, 1951; d. James R. and Virginia K. (Velega) Coffey; m. Harlan B. Haynie, Sept. 19, 1982; 1 child. Student U. Portland, 1969-70; B.S. in Microbiology, Oreg. State U., 1973. Chemist, MEI-Charlton, Portland, 1974-76; microbiologist, chemist Bull Run Water Shed, Portland Water Dept., 1976-80; pres. Coffey Labs., Portland, 1978—. Mem. Portland Indsl. Chemist Assn. (past pres.). Club: Crotain Fraternal Union. Office: 4914 NE 122d St Portland OR 97230

COFFEY, THOMAS ROLLAND, mech. engr.; b. Alamosa, Colo. Oct. 24, 1918; s. Thomas Herbert and Irene (Warren) C.; student, Mesa Coll., 1939, U. Wis., 1941; m. Marion Grace Egtvedt, Oct. 10, 1942. Mech. engr. Allis Chalmers Mfg. Co., Milw., 1941-69; cons. engr., pvt. practice, Grand Junction, Colo., 1967—. Instr., Mesa Coll., 1967-72; cons. engr. Air Photo Surveys Global Engring., Inc.; cons. engr. James F. Squirrel & Assos., 1972-76; pres. TMC Philogiston Corp., research program dir. Coal Fired Gas Turbine Power Plant, 1977—; adj. asso. prof. Mesa Coll., 1980. Registered profl. engr., Colo. Mem. Nat. Soc. Profl. Engrs., Profl. Engrs. Colo. (asso.), Colo. Soc. Engring., ASME (asso.). Home: 2784 Cheyenne Dr Grand Junction CO 81503

COFFILL, MARJORIE LOUISE (MRS. WILLIAM CHARLES COFFILL), civic leader; b. Sonora, Calif., June 11, 1917; d. Eric J. and Pearl (Needham) Segerstrom; A.B. with distinction in Social Sci., Stanford U., 1938, M.A. in Edn., 1941; m. William Charles Coffill, Jan. 25, 1948; children—William James, Eric John. Asst. mgr. Sonora Abstract & Title Co. (Calif.), 1938-39; mem. dean of women's staff Stanford, 1939-41; social dir. women's campus Pomona Coll., 1941-43, instr. psychology, 1941-43; asst. to field dir. ARC, Lee Moore AFB, Calif., 1944-46; partner Riverbank Water Co., Riverbank and Hughson, Calif., 1950-68. Mem. Tuolumne County Mental Health Adv. Com., 1963-70; mem. central advisory council Supplementary Edn. Center, Stockton, Calif., 1966-70; mem. advisory com. Columbia Jr. Coll., 1972—, pres., 1980—; pres. Columbia Found., 1972-74, bd. dirs., 1974-77; mem. Tuolumne County Bicentennial Com., 1974- ; active PTA, ARC. Pres., Tuolumne County Republican Women, 1952—, asso. mem. Calif. Rep. Central Com., 1950. Trustee Sonora Union High Sch., 1969-73, Salvation Army Tuolumne County, 1973—; bd. dirs. Lung Assn. Valley Lode Counties, 1974—. Recipient Pi Lambda Theta award, 1940; Outstanding Citizen award C. of C., 1974. Mem. AAUW (charter mem. Tuolumne County br., pres. Sonora br. 1965-66). Episcopalian (mem. vestry 1968, 75). Home: 376 E Summit Ave Sonora CA 95370

COFFMAN, ARTHUR RAY, automobile exec.; b. Seattle, Sept. 23, 1924; s. Arthur Ray and Edith Christine (Warwick) C.; m. Donna Zoe Hammer, Apr. 25, 1947; children—Adrienne, Toni, Stacey. B.A., U. Wash., 1949. Salesman, Pennzoil Oil Co., Seattle, 1950-54, Westside Ford Inc., Seattle, 1954-55; sales mgr. Harris Ford Inc., Lynnwood, 1955-59, v.p. gen. mgr., 1960-71, pres., 1972—; pres. AAA Leasing-Harris Isuzu Inc., 1972—; dealer Everett Aviation, 1972-78; pres. Harris DeLorean, 1979-82; pres. Harris Isuzo Inc., 1980—; dir. Wash. Life Ins. Co. Served with USAAC, 1943-46. Recipient numerous Ford Motor Co. awards. Mem. Aircraft Owners and Pilots Assn., Assn. Wash. Gens., Puget Sound Isuzu Dealers Adv. Assn. (dir.). Republican. Roman Catholic. Clubs: Everett Golf & Country (Everett, Wash.). Home: 15316 39th NW Stanwood NW 98292 Office: 20006 64th W Lynnwood WA 98036

COFIELD, MICHAEL, psychologist, cons.; b. Phoenix, June 12, 1949; s. Eva Maye (McGill) C.; m. Mary Ann Picardo, Nov. 25, 1981. Ph.D. in Psychology, Ariz. State U., 1978. Pvt. practice psychology, Phoenix and Sun City, Ariz., 1978—; cons. psychologist Phoenix Community Mental Health Ctr.'s Children and Family Program, 1978-82; founder, prin. S.W. Behavioral Cons., Phoenix, 1979—; pub. speaker, radio appearances on health-related subjects, including stress and illness, alcoholism in industry. Ariz. State Judo Champion, 1965-68; So. States Karate Champion, 1971; Southwestern Grand Champion, 1970; Western States Karate Champion, 1975; Ariz. State Karate Champion, 1976. Mem. Nat. Register Health Service Providers in Psychology, Am. Psychol. Assn., Soc. Behavioral Medicine, Ariz. State Psychol. Assn., Employee Assistance Resources Ariz. Developed hosp. employee assistance program Boswell Meml. Hosp., Phoenix, 1979, established behavioral medicine service, 1982. Office: 4602 N 16th St Suite 202 Phoenix AZ 85016

COGAN, ARNOLD MAURICE, urban regional planner; b. Bath, Maine, Dec. 3, 1932; s. David Solis and Anna (Arick) C.; m. Elaine Rosenberg, Dec. 21, 1952; children—Mark, Sue, Leonard. B.S.C.E., Oreg. State U., Corvallis, 1954; postgrad. Portland State U., 1959-61, U.S. Army Engring. Sch., 1957-58. Registered profl. engr., Oreg. Civil engr., Moffatt, Nichol & Taylor, Portland, Oreg., 1955-56, 58-60; city planner Portland City Planning Commn., 1960-62; planning dir. Port of Portland, 1962-67; state planning coordinator, office of Gov. Tom McCall, Salem, Oreg., 1967-69; dir. planning, econs., assoc. v.p. Daniel, Mann, Johnson & Mendenhall, Los Angeles, 1969-74; dir. Oreg. State Dept. Land Conservation and Devel., Salem, 1974-75; mgr., ptnr. Cogan & Assocs., Portland, 1975—; lectr. community planning Portland State U., 1965-82, Reed Coll., 1978-82, Willamette U., 1978-80, and numerous civic, profl. orgns. Pres. Portland Beautification Assn., 1964-66. Served in U.S. Army, 1956-58. Recipient awards of excellence for developing planning projects Hayden Island in Columbia River, 1980, 10-yr. strategic plan for Portland Met. Family Service, Oreg. chpt. Am. Planning Assn., 1981. Mem. Am. Planning Assn., Urban Land Inst., Am. Inst. Cert. Planners. Democrat. Jewish. Clubs: City of Portland, World Affairs Council (Portland). Co-author: Handbook Public Involvement for Regional and State Planning, 1982; Statewide Policy Instruments, 1977; Techniques of Citizen Involvement, 1977. Office: 71 SW Oak St Portland OR 97204

COGAN, MICHAEL BARR, lawyer; b. N.Y.C.; s. Alan B. and Phyllis S. C.; m., Dec. 17, 1978; 1 son, Benjamin Thomas. B.S., Cornell U., 1967; J.D., UCLA, 1975, M.B.A., 1975. Bar: Calif. Ptnr. firm Kelly, Knapp, Sanders & Cogan, 1976-77, Sklar, Coben, Stashower, Kelly & Knapp, Inc., 1977-78, Kelly, Knapp & Cogan, 1978-79; ptnr. firm Kelly & Cogan, & Kelly & Cogan, P.C., Santa Monica, 1979—, now pres. Founder L. Proyecto del Barrio. Recipient Outstanding Service award Pacoima Optimist Club, commendation award Mayor of Los Angeles, 1978-79; scholar Cornell U.; merit scholar, UCLA. Mem. ABA, State Bar Calif. (bus. sect.), Los Angeles County Bar, Los Angeles Trial Lawyers Assn., Italian-Am. Lawyers Assn. Office: 2632 Lincoln Blvd Santa Monica CA 90405

COGAN, RONALD JAMES, advertising, public relations and editorial services co. exec., photographer; b. Cleve., Dec. 5, 1952; s. John Patrick and Alice Marie (Zollner) C.; student Calif. State Poly. U., 1971-74; m. Sheree K. Gardner, Nov. 20, 1982. Staff writer newsletter Biomed. Safety and Standards, Industry, Calif., 1974; sr. staff writer Select Promotions, Irvine, Calif., 1975; sr. editor Petersen's Vans & Pickups/4 Wheel and Off-Road/Hot Rod Specialty Publs., Los Angeles, 1977-80; editor Custom Rodder mag., Anaheim, Calif., 1980; prin. R. J. Cogan & Assocs., Montclair, Calif., 1980—; co-pub. Foothills mag., Montclair, 1980—; cons. to mags. Editor: Hot Rod's Kit Car Annual #2, 1981; Hot Rod's VW Classics Annual #1, 1981; Petersen's Big Book of Volkswagens, 1981; author curriculum materials for Am. Corr. Schs. Home: 7479 Arroyo Vista Ave Rancho Cucamonga CA 91730

COGBURN, MARTIN ARTHUR, accountant, real estate broker; b. Fancy Hill, Ark.; s. Francis Marion and Mary Isabell (Beezeley) C.; student U. Calif. at Berkeley, 1932-34; B.S., Golden Gate U., 1940; grad. Realtors Inst.; m. Metta Naomi Stockdal, Feb. 18, 1956; children—Martin Arthur, Thomas Stockdal; children from previous marriage—Robert F., Nancy Ann. Instr., Golden Gate U., 1945-49; accountant, San Francisco, 1944—; prin. Cogburn Realty, San Francisco, 1963—, Cogburn Mortgage & Investment Co., San Francisco, 1963—. Councilman, City of Lafayette (Calif.), 1968-70; treas. Springhill Valley Assn., 1967; pres. Lafayette-Morage-Orinda Republican Assembly, 1967-68, 1970-73, congressional dist. state dir., 1971-73. C.P.A., Calif.; cert. comml. investment mem. Realtors Nat. Mktg. Inst. Mem. Calif. Soc. C.P.A.s, Calif., Nat. assns. realtors, San Francisco Bd. Realtors, Contra Costa Bd. Realtors, Sierra Club, Tower and Flame, Beta Alpha Phi. Republican. Clubs: Commonwealth, Masons, Shriners. Home: 3447 Black Hawk Rd Lafayette CA 94549 Office: 1910 Olympic Blvd Suite 100 Walnut Creek CA 94596

COGGIN, CHARLOTTE JOAN, cardiologist, ednl. adminstr., educator; b. Washington, Aug. 6, 1928; d. Charles Benjamin and Nanette (McDonald) Coggin; B.A., Columbia Union Coll., 1948; M.D., Loma Linda U., 1952. Intern, Los Angeles County Gen. Hosp., Los Angeles, 1952-53, resident in medicine, 1953-55; fellow in cardiology Children's Hosp., Los Angeles, 1955-56; research asso. in cardiology, house physician Hammersmith Hosp., London, 1956-57; resident in pediatrics and pediatric cardiology Hosp. for Sick Children, Toronto, Ont., Can., 1965-67; asst. prof. medicine Loma Linda U., 1961-73, asso. prof., 1973—, asst. dean Sch. Medicine Internat. Programs, 1973-75, asso. dean, 1975—, co-dir., cardiologist heart surgery team missions to Saigon, Vietnam, 1974, 75, to Saudi Arabia, 1976—; mem. Pres's. Advisory Panel on Heart Disease, 1972—. Appointed to Med. Quality Rev. Com.-Dist. 12, 1976-80. Recipient award for service to people of Pakistan City of Karachi, 1963, Medallion award Evangelismos Hosp., Athens, Greece, 1967, Gold medal of health South Vietnam Ministry of Health, 1974, Charles Elliott Weinger award for excellence, 1976; named Honored Alumnus Loma Linda U. Sch. Medicine, 1973, Outstanding Women in Gen. Conf. Seventh-day Adventists, 1975; diplomate Am. Bd. Pediatrics. Mem. Am. Coll. Cardiology, AMA (physicians adv. com.) Calif. (com. on med. schs., com. on member services), San Bernardino County (Calif.) (chmn. communications com. 1975-77, editor bull. 1975-76) med. assns., Am. Heart Assn., AAUP, Med. Research Assn. Calif., AAUW, World Affairs Council, Internat. Platform Assn. Calif. Museum Sci. and Industry MUSES (Outstanding Woman of Year in Sci. 1969), Am. Women in Radio, TV, Alpha Omega Alpha. Author: Atrial Septal Defects, motion picture (Golden Eagle Cine award and 1st prize Venice Film Festival 1964); contbr. articles to med. jours. Home: 11495 Benton St Loma Linda CA 92354 Office: Loma Linda U Med Center Loma Linda CA 92354

COGGINS, THOMAS WAYNE, SR., tng. co. exec.; b. Henderson, N.C., Feb. 11, 1941; s. George Grady and Reba Alline (Garrett) C.; student U.S. Navy Enlisted Tech. and Mgmt. Schs., 1960-78; children—Debra Diane, Thomas Wayne, Mari Ellen. Enlisted in U.S. Navy, 1958, advanced through grades to chief petty officer, 1975, ret., 1978; chmn. bd. curriculum Devel. & Cons., Inc., San Diego, 1977—, cons., pres., 1979—; dir. Nav Tech Services Inc., San Diego, S.K. Tourney & Assos., San Diego. Decorated Silver Star, Purple Heart, Air medal. Mem. Nat. Soc. Performance and Instrn. Republican. Baptist. Club: Vikings of Scandia. Contbr. articles to profl. jours. Home: 9171 Ellingham St San Diego CA 92129 Office: 7525 Mission Gorge Rd Suite F San Diego CA 92120

COHAGEN, CHANDLER CARROLL, architect; b. nr. Sioux City, Iowa, Apr. 24, 1889; s. John and Mary Frances (Turner) C.; B.S. in Architecture, U. Mich., Ann Arbor, 1915; m. Flora Brown, Sept. 18, 1917. Pvt. archtl. practice, Billings, Mont., 1915-42, 45—; chief architect U.S. Ordnance Plant, Eau Claire, Wis., 1942-43, war plant, Muscatine, Iowa, 1943-45; past pres. Mont. Bd. Archtl. Examiners; pres. Nat. Council Archtl. Registration Bds., 1962. Alderman, City of Billings, 1936. Fellow AIA (past pres. Mont. chpt.; Scholastic medal 1915), Internat. Inst. Arts and Letters; life mem. Am. Soc. Heating and Ventilating Engrs.; mem. Billings C. of C. (past pres.), Alpha Rho Chi (founder), Delta Phi. Republican. Mem. Christian Ch. (Disciples of Christ). Club: Masons (grand master), DeMolay (treas. internat. supreme council). Address: 19 Burlington Ave Billings MT 59101

COHAN, EDWARD MICHAEL, lawyer; b. Milw., Mar. 26, 1941; s. Edward J. and Norma A. (Hinkel) C.; m. Cynthia K. Tubbs, Oct. 30, 1971; children—Amanda K., Kimberly A. B.S., Marquette U., 1962; M.B.A., U. Ariz., 1967; J.D., U. So. Calif., 1971. Bar: Calif. 1972, U.S. Dist. Ct. (cen. dist.) Calif. 1972, U.S. Dist. Ct. (so. dist.) Calif. 1974, U.S. Ct. Apls. (9th cir.) 1974. Assoc., McCutchen, Black, Verleger & Shea, 1971-72; assoc. Tuttle & Taylor, Los Angeles, 1972-75; assoc. Levin, Saphier & Rien, Los Angeles, 1975-78; ptnr. Seider & Cohan, P.C., Los Angeles, 1978—; instr. Sch. Bus. Adminstrn. U. So. Calif., 1977-78; arbitrator Los Angeles County Superior Ct., 1981—. Vice pres., bd. dirs. Hollywoodland Assn. Served with USAR, 1970-71. Mem. Maritime Law Assn., Bus. Trial Lawyers Assn., Order Coif. Editor: University So. Calif. Law Rev., 1970-71. Office: 10960 Wilshire Blvd Suite 1526 Los Angeles CA 90024

COHAN, JOHN ROBERT, lawyer; b. Arnhem, Netherlands, Feb. 10, 1931; s. Max and Ann (deWinter) C.; came to U.S., 1940, naturalized, 1945; B.S. in Bus. Adminstrn., U. Ariz., 1952; LL.B., Stanford U., 1955; m. Joan B. Golloh, Sept. 6, 1954; children—Deborah Joyce, Steven Mark, Judson Seth; m. 2d, Patricia S. Cohan, Nov. 8, 1970; m. 3d, Roberta Halpern, Nov. 23, 1980. Bar: Calif. 1956. Assoc., Irell & Manella, Los Angeles, 1955-61, ptnr., 1961—. Mem. Los Angeles County Bar Com. on Fed. and Calif. Death and Gift Taxation, 1965—, Calif. State Bar Probate and Trust Com., 1971-74; adj. prof. U. Miami Sch. Law, 1975—; lectr. fed. income taxation U. So. Calif. Sch. Law, 1961-63; lectr., writer Calif. Continuing Edn. Bar Program, 1959—, Practicing Law Inst., 1968—, also various tax and probate insts. Pres., Portals House, Inc., 1966-69; chmn. Jewish Big Bros., Los Angeles, 1963-65, trustee, 1978—; bd. dirs. Hope for Hearing Research Found., 1965-77, pres., 1972; chmn. charitable founds. com. Big Bros./Big Sisters Am., 1965-67, chmn. internat. expansion, 1967—, pres. Western region, 1977-78, also bd. dirs.; bd. dirs., sec. San Fernando Valley Cultural Soc. Found., 1983—; mem. planning com. U. So. Calif. Tax Inst., 1969—, chmn., 1983—; mem. planning com. U. Miami Estate Planning Inst. Bd. dirs. Los Angeles Campus Hebrew Union Coll., 1974-77. Mem. ABA, (vice chmn. sect. taxation, estate and gift tax com.), Los Angeles Bar Assn., Beverly Hills Bar Assn. (past chmn. lawyer placement com. and probate com.), Internat. Acad. Probate and Trust Law (exec. com.), Town Hall of Los Angeles (exec. com., past pres. Western div.), Beta Gamma Sigma, Alpha Kappa Psi, Phi Alpha Delta; fellow Am. Coll. Probate Counsel. Editor: Drafting California Revocable Trusts, 1972; Drafting California Irrevocable Trusts, 1973; Inter Vivos Trusts, Shephard's Citations, 1975; bd. editors Community Property Law Jour., CCH Fin. and Estate Planning Service. Contbr. articles on tax, estate planning, probate law to prof. jours. Home: 4233 Aleman Dr Tarzana CA 91356 Office: 1800 Ave of Stars Century City Los Angeles CA 90067

COHEN, DANIEL MORRIS, museum curator; b. Chgo., July 6, 1930; s. Leonard U. and Myrtle (Gertz) C.; m. Anne Constant, Nov. 4, 1956; children—Carolyn A., Cynthia S. B.A., Stanford U., 1952, M.A., 1953, Ph.D., 1958. Asst. prof. biology and curator fishes Fla. State Mus., U. Fla., 1958-59; ichthyologist Systematics Lab., U.S. Nat. Marine Fisheries Service, Washington, 1959-60, lab. dir., 1960-81; sr. scientist N.W. Alaska Fisheries Ctr., Seattle, 1981-82; chief curator Div. Life Scis., Los Angeles County Mus. of Natural History, 1982—; vis. prof. Suffolk U., 1978; adj. prof. biology U. Miami, 1973-74; mem. faculty Marine Biol. Program, Stanford U., 1965, acting asst. prof. biology, 1962; affiliate prof. Coll. Fisheries, U. Wash., 1982-83; research assoc. Smithsonian Instn., 1967—. Mem. AAAS, Soc. Systematic Zoology, Am. Soc. Ichthyologists and Herpetologists v.p. 1969-70) Soc. Bibliography Natural History, Japanese Soc. Ichthyologists, Soc. Francaise. Ichtyologie, Indian Soc. of Ichthyologists, Challenger Soc., Biol. Soc. of Wash. (pres. 1971-72), Western Soc. Naturalists. Contbr. articles to profl. jours. Office: Los Angeles County Mus Natural History 900 Exposition Blvd Los Angeles CA 90007

COHEN, DAVENE VINES, child development specialist; b. Portland, Oreg., Sept. 30, 1933; d. Alex and Marian (Miller) Vines; B.A., U. Wash., 1954; M.S., Portland State U., 1967; m. Gerald R. Cohen, Aug. 7, 1955; children—Daniel, William, Thomas, Shaari. Tchr. Public Schs. Clackamas County, Portland, Oreg., 1954-65; child devel. specialist Clackamas County Child Devel. Clinic, 1965-66; child services coordinator Owen O. Sabin Occupational Skills Center, 1967-74; ednl. specialist N.W. Regional Ednl. Lab., Portland, 1974-75; program devel. specialist Multnomah County Juvenile Ct., Portland, 1975-83; program devel. specialist Multnomah County Social Services Div./MED, 1983—; chmn. occupational adv. council Clackamas Community Coll., 1980—; mem. profl. standards and tng. com. Oreg. Juvenile Services Commn.; cons. in field. Pres., Clackamas County Child Day Care Assn., 1968; chmn. Oak Lodge Community Council, 1977; chmn. Juvenile Justice subcom. on Youth; mem. youth panel United Way, 1982. Mem. Nat. Assn. Edn. of Young Children, Oreg. Assn. Edn. of Young Children (pres. 1966-68), Assn. Supervision and Curriculum Devel., Council Exceptional Children, Council Children with Behavior Disorders, Joint Council Early Childhood Edn. (chmn. 1965-67), Talented and Gifted Assn., Delta Kappa Gamma. Jewish. Co-author: Parenting: Four Patterns in Child Rearing, 1978. Office: 426 SW Stark Portland OR 97204

COHEN, DAVID EDWARD, newspaper executive; b. Springfield, Mass., Nov. 17, 1950; s. Philip J. and Marjorie P. (Rednor) C.; m. Barbara Elia, Dec. 31, 1979; 1 son, Daniel Elia. B.A. in History cum laude, Windham Coll., 1972; postgrad. Inst. Comparative Studies History, Philosophy and Scis., Eng., 1974-75. Pres., Oriental Imports, Inc., 1976-77; advt. mgr. Valley Advocate Newspaper, New Mass Media, Inc., Springfield, Mass., 1977-79; advt. mgr. Los Angeles Weekly Newspaper, 1979-80, advt. dir., 1980—; co-founder, v.p., treas. Health Incentives Internat., Inc., 1982—, also dir. Mem. Calif. Newspaper Advt. Execs. Club: Advt. (Los Angeles). Patentee vitamin/mineral supplement. Office: Los Angeles Weekly Advt Dept 5325 Sunset Blvd Los Angeles CA 90027

COHEN, EDWIN, fund-raising executive; b. Sunbury, Pa., Feb. 2, 1931; s. Saul and Bessie Mildred (Saxe) C.; m. Shirley Jane Korz, Aug. 21, 1966; children—Lisa Michelle, David Saul. B.A., Calif. State U.-Long Beach, 1956, M.A., 1964; Ph.D., U. So. Calif., 1971. Tchr., Orange (Calif.) High Sch., 1957-59, Downey (Calif.) High Sch., 1961-68; instr. U. So. Calif., Los Angeles, 1968-71, Central Mich. U., Mt. Pleasant, 1971-74, Purdue U.-Calumet, Hammond, Ind., 1974-82; exec. dir. N.W. region Friends of Shaare Zedek Hosp. in Jerusalem, Daly City, Calif., 1982—. Served with AUS, 1952-54. Mem. AAUP, Am. Soc. Tng. and Devel., Speech Communication Assn., MENSA. Lodge: B'Nai Brith. Author: Oral Interpretation: The Communication of Literature, 1977; Speaking the Speech, 2d edit., 1983. Address: 24 Lake Meadow Dr Daly City CA 94015

COHEN, ELEANOR MARCIA COBERLY, councilwoman; b. Los Angeles, July 20, 1940; d. Chester C. and Sylvia S. (Sternberg) Coberly; m. Larry W. Cohen, July 19, 1959; children—Ronald, Jeffrey. B.S. summa cum laude, UCLA, 1961. Chmn. Claremont Environ. Resources Task Force, 1970; mem. Claremont Planning Commn., 1971-74; mem. Claremont City Council, 1974—, mayor, 1980-82; mem. exec. com. So. Calif. Assn. Govts. Asst. dir. Calif. Inst. Pub. Affairs, coordinator Calif. Farmlands Project, 1982-83. Recipient Comml. Devel. award Claremont C. of C., 1981; Woman Achiever award Progress-Bull., 1981. Mem. Calif. Elected Women's Assn. for Edn. and Research. Author: Expanding the Environmental Responsibility of Local Government, 1972. Home: 440 Greensboro Ct Claremont CA 91711 Office: 207 Harvard Ave Claremont CA 91711

COHEN, ELINOR IRISH (MAISIE), computer consultant; b. Pasadena, Calif., Apr. 16, 1930; d. John Marion and Elizabeth (Herrington) Irish; m. William Cohen, June 16, 1956; children—David, Cathy, Andrew, Deborah, Michael, Daniel. B.A., U. Calif.-Berkeley, 1951; M.A. summa cum laude, Stanford U., 1952. Tchr. high sch., China Lake, Calif., 1952-56, Arlington County, Va., 1956-61; info. specialist, programmer analyst Informatics, Inc., Washington, 1967-71; cons., tech. writer Culler Harrison Inc. Systems, Santa Barbara, Calif., 1976-77; tchr. English dept. Santa Barbara City Coll., 1978-79; cons. MicroXchange, Santa Barbara, 1979—. Mem. Data Processing Mgrs. Assn. (chmn. edn. com. chpt. 1982, dir.-at-large 1983), Santa Barbara C. of C., Assn. Computer Users (editorial bd.), Ind. Computer Cons. Assn., Data Entry Mgmt. Assn., Internat. Info./Work Processing Assn., Nat. Assn. Computer Stores, Phi Beta Kappa, Delta Kappa Gamma. Club: Santa Barbara Piano (founder). Office: 222 E Carrillo St #101 Santa Barbara CA 93101

COHEN, E(MANUEL) RICHARD, physicist; b. Phila., Dec. 14, 1922; s. Harry and Rose (Brodsky) C.; A.B., U. Pa., 1943, M.S., Calif. Inst. Tech., 1946, Ph.D., 1949; m. Gilda Raye Rosenblatt, Oct. 18, 1953; 1 dau., Shelly Fern. Research engr. N.Am. Aviation Inc. (merged to form Rockwell Internat. Corp.), El Segundo, Calif., 1949-56, research adviser, 1956-61, asso. dir. research Atomics Internat. div., 1961-62, asso. dir. Sci. Center, Rockwell Internat. Corp., Thousand Oaks, Calif., 1962-69, mem. tech. staff, 1969—, disting. fellow Sci. Center, 1974—, lectr. in field; sr. research assoc. Calif. Inst. Tech., 1965-72. Sec., Internat. Union Pure and Applied Physics Commn. Atomic Masses and Fundamental Constants, 1969-72, chmn., 1972-78; chmn. task group fundamental constants Com. Data for Sci. and Tech., 1969—, exec. com., 1982—. Recipient E.O. Lawrence award, AEC, 1968. Fellow Am. Phys. Soc., Am. Nuclear Soc., AAAS; mem. Assn. Computing Machinery, Sigma Xi, Pi Mu Epsilon. Author: Fundamental Constants of Physics (with K.M. Crowe and J.W.M. DuMond), 1957. Patentee in field. Editorial adv. bd. Nuclear Sci. and Engring., 1959—, Jour. Statis. Physics, 1969-75; editorial bd. Metrologia, 1976-80. Home: 17735 Corinthian Dr Encino CA 91316 Office: 1049 Camino Dos Rios Thousand Oaks CA 91360

COHEN, EVE, administrative law judge; b. Jerusalem, July 22, 1940; d. Morris and Sara (Lubliner) Sternlight; m. Howard Ira Cohen, Sept. 10, 1960; children—Darrel Phillip, Sheri Dana, Halli Frances, Daniel Matthew. B.A., UCLA, 1957; J.D., Loyola U.-Los Angeles, 1964. Assoc., Marvin Cahn, Hollywood, Calif., 1965-66; sole practice, Hollywood, 1966-71, Century City, Calif., 1971-72; adminstrv. law judge Calif. Unemployment Ins. Appeals Bd., Van Nuys, 1972—; instr. in field. Chmn., Speaker's Bur. San Fernando Valley, 1972. Mem. Lawyers Club Los Angeles City (dir. 1975), San Fernando Valley Bus. Profl. Assn., Religion in Media. Republican. Jewish. Author: Diary of a Sabra - Faith in Action, 1980; Your Way to Kingdom Living, 1982. Office: 14435 Sherman Way PO Box 9203 Van Nuys CA 91409

COHEN, HERBERT, clin. psychologist; b. Bklyn., Dec. 13, 1924; s. Abraham and Anna (Kaplowitz) C.; B.A., George Washington U., 1949, M.A., 1950; Ph.D., Calif. Sch. Profl. Psychology, 1972; m. Carmella June, June 27, 1980; children—Robin, Roselle, Martin. Staff psychologist East St. Louis (Ill.) Child Guidance Clinic, 1957-62, St. Louis State Hosp., 1952-62, Atascadero (Calif.) State Hosp., 1962-66, Met. State Hosp., Norwalk, Calif., 1968-74; clin. psychologist St. John's Hosp. & Health Center, Santa Monica, Calif., 1972-78; community mental health psychologist Los Angeles County Dept. Mental Health, 1980—. Served with USAAF, 1943-46. N.Y. War Service scholar, 1947-48. Mem. Am. Psychol. Assn., Calif. Psychol. Assn., Los Angeles County Psychol. Assn., Calif. Neuropsychology Soc. Office: 1720 E 120th St Los Angeles CA 90059

COHEN, HERBERT IRVING, internist; b. San Jose, Calif., Feb. 21, 1931; s. Herbert and Bluma Florence (Levy) C.; A.B., Stanford U., 1952, M.D., 1955; children—Thomas Marc, Susan Marie, Andrew Joel. Intern, King's County Hosp., Bklyn., 1955-56; resident in thoracic medicine Santa Clara County Hosp., 1961-62, resident in internal medicine, 1963-64; resident in internal medicine Presbyn. Med. Ctr., San Francisco, 1962-63; fellow in medicine (cardiopulmonary) Stanford U.-VA Hosp., Palo Alto, Calif., 1964-65; chief pulmonary disease Orange County Med. Ctr., Orange, Calif., 1965-68; dir. pulmonary rehab. Olive View Hosp., Sylmar, Calif., 1968-70; practice medicine specializing in pulmonary medicine (internal medicine), Newport Beach, Calif., 1970-79; asst. clin. prof. medicine U. Hawaii, 1979—; chief TB br. Hawaii Dept. Health, 1979—; former asst. clin. prof. medicine (pulmonary) U. Calif., Irvine. Served with USAF, 1955-61. USPHS Occupational Medicine grantee, 1966-68. Fellow Am. Coll. Chest Physicians; mem. AMA, Am. Thoracic Soc., Calif. Thoracic Soc., Calif. Med. Assn., Am. Soc. Clin. Hypnosis, So. Calif. Soc. Clin. Hypnosis, Orange County Soc., Hawaii Med. Assn., Honolulu County Med. Soc., Trudeau Soc. Los Angeles County, Orange County Med. Assn. Democrat. Office: 1700 Lanakila Ave Honolulu HI 96817

COHEN, HERBERT LEONARD, lawyer, state ofcl.; b. N.Y.C., Feb. 3, 1928; s. Benjamin and Cecile (Pate) C.; A.B., U. Calif. at Santa Barbara, 1949; LL.B., U. Calif. at Berkeley, 1952; m. Shirley Mason, June 24, 1951; children—Bruce, Annette, Carol, Debra. Admitted to Calif. bar, 1952; atty. aircraft procurement contracts USAF, 1956-58; atty. Calif. Dept. Alcoholic Beverage Control, 1958-62; chief counsel Calif. Dept. Food Agr., Sacramento, 1962—; lectr. on law of pesticide controls, also weights and measures. Served with USAF, 1953-56. Mem. Phi Alpha Delta. Author: California Administrative Agency Practice-Agriculture, 1970. Contbr. articles to profl. jours. Home: 6140 Holstein Way Sacramento CA 95831 Office: Calif Dept Food and Agr 1220 N St Sacramento CA 95814

COHEN, JACK, pharmaceutical company executive; b. N.Y.C., Jan. 31, 1937; s. Albert and Diana Orman C.; m. Betty Rosenberg, Sept. 12, 1959; children—Craig, Kimi, Corey. B.S., Columbia U., 1957; M.S., U. Iowa, 1959, Ph.D., 1961. Registered pharmacist, Iowa, Ill. Chemist, Lakeside Labs., Milw., 1961-62; chemist, Pfizer Co., Groton, Conn., 1962-65; dept. head Syntex Research Palo Alto, Calif., 1965-73, asst. dir., 1973-78, dir. quality control Syntex Labs., Inc., 1978-81, v.p. quality assurance, 1981—. Am. Found. Pharm. Edn. fellow, 1960-61. Mem. Am. Pharm. Assn., Am. Chem. Soc., Am. Soc. Quality Control, Rho Pi Phi, Rho Chi. Office: Syntex Labs Inc Stanford Indsl Park Palo Alto CA 94303

COHEN, JEFFREY LEWIS, counselor; b. N.Y.C., Jan. 17, 1950; s. Irving and Betty (Sussman) C.; B.A. cum laude in English, L.I. U., 1972; M.S. in Counseling, Calif. State U.-Los Angeles, 1975. Counselor Career Center, Los Angeles Pierce Coll., Woodland Hills, Calif., 1977—; pvt. practice marriage and family therapy, 1982—. Democrat. Jewish. Researcher books and author articles. Office: Los Angeles Pierce Coll 6201 Winnetka Ave Woodland Hills CA 91371

COHEN, JOANNE E., educator; b. Rochester, N.Y., May 19, 1954; d. Harvey and Doris B. Cohen. B.S. in Edn. and English, SUNY-Cortland, 1976; M.A. in Speech Communication, U. Denver, 1980. Cert. tchr., N.Y. Tchr. English and speech Elmira (N.Y.) Free Acad., 1976-78; tchr. English, Broadway Jr. High Sch., Elmira, 1978-79; tchr. English, speech and drama Southside High Sch., Elmira, 1978-80; instr. pub. speaking Community Coll. Denver, Aurora, Colo., 1982—; tng. coordinator UNIPAC Service Corp., Aurora, 1981—; cons. Bd. dirs., adviser Pupil Assistance in Learning Club, Big Brother/Sister Orgn., Elmira, 1977-80. Mem. Am. Soc. Tng. and Devel., Exec. Profl. Women's Council. Home: 3300 S Tamarac Dr Apt M 105 Denver CO 80231 Office: 3015 S Parker Rd Suite 400 Aurora CO 80014

COHEN, JOYCE E., state senator, business executive; b. McIntosh, S.D., Mar. 27, 1937; d. Joseph and Evelyn (Sampson) Petik; m. Stanley N. Cohen, 1959; children—Julia Jo, Aaron J. Grad. Coll. Med. Tech., Minn., 1955; student UCLA, 1957-78, Santa Ana Coll., 1961-62. Med. research technician dept. surgery U. Minn., 1955-58, dept. tech. U. Calif., 1958-59, dept. bacteriology, 1959-61; med. research scientist Allergan Pharms., Santa Ana, Calif., 1961-70; ptnr. Co-Fo Investments, Lake Oswego, Oreg., 1978—; mem. Oreg. Ho. of Reps., from 1979, now Oreg. state senator. Chmn. Environ. Service Citizen Adv. Com., Columbia Regional Assn. Govts., 1977-78; vice chmn. State Energy Policy Rev. Commn., 1977-78; chmn. legis. rules and ops. com. Oreg. Ho. of Reps., 1979-80, housing and urban devel. com. and judiciary subcom.; mem. Jud. Br. State Energy Policy Rev. Com., 1979. Mem. Assn. Family Conciliation Cts., Citizens Council of Cts., LWV, Oreg. Environ. Council, Oreg. Women's Polit. Caucus. Democrat. Home: 100 Leonard St 3-3 Box 385 Lake Oswego OR 97034 Office: Oregon State Senate Salem OR 97310*

COHEN, JULIUS MILTON, retired association executive; b. Rochester, N.Y., Feb. 14, 1914; s. Abraham V. and Lillian (Pontesof) C.; B.A., Cornell U., 1935; postgrad. Rochester Bus. Inst., 1939, Columbia, 1943, U. N.C., 1948, Stanford, 1954; m. Sophie Katz, Feb. 14, 1956. Mng. editor, columnist Jewish Ledger Publs., Rochester, 1935-43; area dir. U.S.O.-Nat. Jewish Welfare Bd., 1943-63, So. Calif. area, Los Angeles, 1952-63; community devel. dir. Gateways Hosp., Los Angeles, 1963-65; exec. dir. Western region Am. Jewish Congress Los Angeles, 1965-81, ret., 1981. Mem. Los Angeles City Atty.'s Task Force Nursing Home Reform, 1972-74; bd. dirs. Inter-racial Council Bus. Opportunity, 1966-78, Bus. Devel. Center, 1979—, North Seal Beach Sr. Citizens Ctr., 1981—; pres. Leisure World Congregation Sholom, 1981—. Recipient USMC award, Los Angeles, 1960; 6th Army award, 1963; Gateways award, 1965; City of Los Angeles Bicentennial Salute, 1980, 40th Anniversary award USO, 1981, Adv. Council award for disting. service to sr. citizens of Orange County, 1983, others. Mem. Nat. Assn. Jewish Center Workers (past pres. Western states sect.), Acad. Certified Social Workers (charter), Nat. Assn. Social Workers (charter), Nat. Assn. Inter-Group Relations Ofcls. (v.p. So. Calif.), Assn. for Study Community Orgn. (sec.). Mem. B'nai B'rith (past pres. Rochester, Distinguished Service award 1961). Columnist Seal Beach Jour., Huntington Harbour Sun, 1981—. Home: 13200 Del Monte Dr Seal Beach CA 90740

COHEN, MELVIN, aerospace executive; b. Richmond, Va., Mar. 26, 1927; s. Charles and Goldie (Berman) C.; m. Margaret Mary O'Kane, Dec. 3, 1962; children—Mark, Eric, Dean, Jill, Paul, Melisa, Catherine. B.S., Va. Poly. Inst., 1948; J.D., George Washington U., 1957. Chem. engr. Devoe & Raynolds Paint Co., Louisville, 1948-50; project engr. Atlantic Research Corp., Alexandria, Va., 1950-55; chief propulsion br. U.S. Navy, Washington, 1955-58; v.p. chem. systems div. United Technologies Corp., Sunnyvale, Calif., 1959—, v.p. bus. devel., 1977—. Served to lt. (j.g.) USN, 1945-46. Mem. AIAA, Am. Def. Preparedness Assn., Assn. U.S. Army, D.C. Bar Assn., Tau Beta Pi. Democrat. Jewish. Club: Elks (Palo Alto, Calif.). Patentee in field. Home: 1750 Bryant St Palo Alto CA 94301 Office: 1050 Arques St Sunnyvale CA 94086

COHEN, MICHAEL DAVID, accountant; b. Pitts., Aug. 18, 1942; s. Nathan David and Jacqueline Blanche (Radner) C.; B.A. in Bus. Adminstrn., Calif. State U., Fullerton, 1973; m. Renate Herkommer, May 1,1965; children—Kira Danielle, Sabrina Mylene. Staff acct. Marriott and Held, C.P.A.s, Alhambra, Calif., 1970-72; prin. Cohen & Assos., Bookkeeping and Tax Service, Brea, Calif., 1972-74; pres. Cohen & Christianson Accountancy Corp., Brea, 1974—. Commr. Recreation and Parks, City of Brea, 1976-82; pres. Brea Hills Bobby Sox Softball League, 1979-80; chmn., bd. dirs. Help for Brain Injured Children; trustee Cornelia Connelly Sch. of Holy Child, Anaheim, Calif. Served with U.S. Army, 1960-63. Recipient Disting. Alumnus award Calif. State U., Fullerton, 1978. Mem. Am. Inst. C.P.A.s, Calif. Soc. C.P.A.s, Brea C. of C. Democrat. Jewish. Clubs: Rotary (pres. 1980-81); Masons. Home: 560 Bonita Canyon Way Brea CA 92621 Office: 203 N Brea Blvd Brea CA 92621

COHEN, MICHAEL FREDERICK, psychologist, coll. dean; b. N.Y.C., Oct. 29, 1941; s. Joseph Nathaniel and Lee (Nagler) C.; m. Sharna Delaine Eberlein, Apr. 1, 1975; children—Isa, Alexandra, Theodore. B.A. with honors, Fla. State U., Tallahassee, 1962; M.S., U. Wis. Madison, 1965, Ph.D. (USPHS fellow), 1968. Lic. psychologist, Calif. Program adminstr. Community Workers' Program, Santa Clara County Mental Health, San Jose, Calif., 1968-71; chmn. community psychology program Calif. Sch. Profl. Psychology, San Francisco, 1971-75; pres. and dir. evaluation Inst. Study Social and Health Issues, San Francisco, 1971—; campus dean Profl. Sch., San Francisco, 1978—; pvt. practice clin. psychology, Rohnert Park, Calif., 1981—; orgn. and evaluation cons., 1971—. HEW grantee, 1971-77; Inst. for Study Social and Health Issues fellow, 1971. Mem. Am. Psychol. Assn., Soc. Psychol. Study Social Issues. Jewish. Author: A Systems Approach to Health Manpower Utilization: A Technical Procedures Manual, 1971; Procedures for the Development of a Career Opportunity System: A Technical Manual, 1973; also articles. Office: 1714 Lombard St San Francisco CA 94123

COHEN, PAUL BRUCE, physician; b. Bklyn., Oct. 26, 1945; s. Abraham B. and Anne (Rubin) C.; A.B., Brown U., 1967; M.D., Boston U., 1971; M.P.H., U. Calif., Berkeley, 1974, fellow in day care, 1974. Intern, Childrens Hosp. of D.C., Washington; resident Childrens Nat. Med. Ctr. and George Washington Med. Ctr., Washington; clin. instr. pediatrics and gen. medicine George Washington U. Med. Ctr., 1972-73; emergency room physician St. Luke Hosp., San Francisco, 1974-76; staff physician Juvenile Hall, San Leandro, Calif., 1975-76; physician Yuba Feather Health Center, Brownsville, Calif., 1976-80; clin. instr. in family practice U. Calif., Davis, 1979-80; pediatric cons. Calif. Children's Services, 1981—; med. dir. Lindhurst Family Health Ctr., 1981-83. Mem. Gold Empire Health Systems Agy. Task Force in Perinatal Health Care, 1977; mem. Yuba Sutter Symphony Orch., 1982—. Served with USPHS, 1976-80. NSF Summer Research grantee, 1966. Diplomate Am. Bd. Pediatrics. Fellow Am. Acad. Pediatrics; mem. Calif. Med. Assn., Yuba Sutter Med. Soc. Club: California Old Time Fiddlers Assn. Office: 1002 Live Oak Blvd Suite C Yuba City CA 95991 also PO Box 86 Brownsville CA 95919

COHEN, ROBERT ROY, educator, biologist; b. Duluth, Minn., June 3, 1939; s. Peter Harry and Minnie (Goldstein) C. B.A. in Zoology, U. Minn., Duluth, 1961; Ph.D. in Zoology, U. Colo., Boulder, 1965. Asst. prof. biology U. Sask., Saskatoon, 1965-67, N.Mex. Inst. Mining and Tech., Socorro, 1967-69; assoc. prof. biology Met. State Coll., Denver, 1969-76, prof. biology, 1976—. Recipient F. Alexander Bergstrom and Paul A. Stewart awards for ornithol. research, 1979, 80, 81. Mem. Am. Ornithologists Union, Wilson Ornithol. Soc., Cooper Ornithol. Soc., AAAS, Sigma Xi. Contbr. articles to profl. jours. Research on avian breeding biology, population dynamics and demography. Office: Box 53 1006 11th St Denver CO 80204

COHEN, RONALD BRUCE, chemical physicist; b. N.Y.C., Dec. 18, 1939; s. Bertram and Florence (Cohen) C.; m. Beverly Joyce Jamattona, Mar. 15, 1964; children—Victor, Jessica, Jonathan. B.S., Bklyn. Coll., 1960; Ph.D., Pa. State U., 1966. Scientist, Physikalische-Technische Bundesonstalt, Braunschweig, W.Ger., 1966-67; research assoc. Space Research Coordination Ctr., U. Pitts., 1967-69; asst. prof. Ill. Inst. Tech., Chgo., 1969-75; mem. tech. staff Aerospace Corp., El Segundo, Calif., 1975-81, mgr. plasma kinetics and trace detection, 1981—. Mem. AIAA, Am. Phys. Soc. Club: Great Books Reading Group (Torrance, Calif.). Contbr. articles to profl. jours.

COHEN, SALLY ANN SEIFERT, university administrator; b. Zanesville, Ohio, Mar. 20, 1942; d. Walter W. and Helen J. (Bateman) Seifert; B.A. in English, Miami U., Oxford, Ohio, 1964; M. Degree with honors in Counseling and Guidance, Loyola Marymount U., Los Angeles, 1976; m. Donald B. Cohen, Sept. 16, 1967. Mem. staff Calif. Med. Group, Los Angeles, 1971-73; adminstrv. asst. Loyola Marymount U., Los Angeles, 1973-76; mem. adminstrv. staff UCLA, 1976—, also resource mentor; researcher women's status in U.S. labor market. Recipient award for superior mgmt. capabilities USAF, 1979; award for outstanding performance UCLA, 1983. Mem. Calif. Personnel Guidance Assn., Calif. Women Higher Edn., U. Calif. Staff Assn. (chmn. career advancement com. 1978-79), Am. Personnel and Guidance Assn. Libertarian. Home: 804 Hillcrest St El Segundo CA 90245 Office: 251-A Dodd Hall Univ California Los Angeles CA 90024

COHEN, SANFORD, economist, educator, labor arbitrator; b. Cleve., Sept. 19, 1920; s. Louis Jacob and Celie (Schonberg) C.; m. Julia Catherine Beach, June 10, 1955; children—Elizabeth, Melanie. B.A., Ohio State U., 1943, M.A., 1947, Ph.D., 1951. Examiner, NLRB, Cleve., 1948-49; br. chief Wage Stblzn. Bd., Cleve., 1951-53; asst. prof. Western Res. U., Cleve., 1953-57; prof. econs. Butler U., Indpls., 1957-62; vis. prof. U. Ill., Urbana, 1962-63; U. Mich., 1964-66; prof. econs. U. N.Mex., Albuquerque, 1966—; UN and U.S. Govt. assignments in Bolivia, Venezuela, Senegal, Bangkok; arbitrator labor disputes. Served with U.S. Army, 1943-45. Fund for Advancement of Edn. fellow, 1955. Mem. Am. Econ. Assn., Indsl. Relations Research Assn., Nat. Acad. Arbitrators, Phi Beta Kappa. Author: State Labor Legislation, 1948; Labor in the United States, 5th edit. 1979; Labor Law, 1964; (with C. Rehmus) Management Preparation for Collective Bargaining, 1966. Editor: Issues in Labor Policy, 1977. Home: 8209 Guadalupe Trail NW Albuquerque NM 87114 Office: Dept Econs U N Mex Albuquerque NM

COHEN, SEYMOUR I., lawyer, accountant; b. N.Y.C., Apr. 15, 1931; s. Fred and Nettie (Sederer) C.; m. Rhoda Goldner, July 22, 1956; children—Cheryl Lynn, Marcy Ann, Lori Beth. B.B.A., CCNY, 1951; LL.B., Bklyn. Law Sch., 1954, J.D., 1967; M.B.A., N.Y.U., 1961. Bar: N.Y. 1954, Calif. 1973. C.P.A., Ohio, Calif. Practice law, Torrance, Calif.; client trust commr. State Bar Calif. Served with U.S. Army, 1954-56. Mem. Nat. Assn. Accts., Calif. Soc. C.P.A.s, Ohio Soc. C.P.A.s, N.Y. Soc. C.P.A.s, South Bay Bar Assn. (treas.; service award), Los Angeles County Bar Assn., South Bay Estate Planning Council (treas.). Club: Internat. Health, B'nai Brith. Home: 30691 Via La Cresta Rancho Palos Verdes CA 90274 Office: 18411 Crenshaw Blvd Suite 411 Torrance CA 90504

COHEN, WILLIAM ALAN, educator; b. Balt., June 25, 1937; s. Sidney Oliver and Theresa (Bachman) C.; B.S., U.S. Mil. Acad., 1959; M.B.A., U. Chgo., 1967, M.A., Ph.D., Claremont (Calif.) Grad. Sch., 1978; m. Nurit Kovnator, May 28, 1967; children—William Alan, Barak, Nimrod. Commd. 2d lt. U.S. Air Force, 1959, advanced through grades to maj., 1970, resigned, 1970; subsystem mgr. Israel Aircraft Industries, 1970-73; mgr. research and devel. Sierra Engring. Co., Sierra Madre, Calif., 1973-76; pres. Global Assos., Pasadena, Calif., 1973-81; mgr. advanced tech. mktg. McDonnell-Douglas Astronautics Co., Huntington Beach, Calif., 1976-79; prof. mktg., dir. Bur. Bus. and Econ. Research, Calif. State U., Los Angeles, 1979—, bd. dirs. Ctr. for Info. Research Mgmt. Decorated D.F.C. with 3 oak leaf clusters, Air medal with 11 oak leaf clusters. Registered profl. engr., Calif. Mem. Am. Mktg. Assn., Direct Mktg. Assn., West Point Soc. (bd. govs., pres. 1981-82), Direct Mktg. Club So. Calif. (dir.), Assn. Grads. U.S. Mil. Acad., Res. Officers Assn. U.S. Republican. Jewish. Author: Executive's Guide to Finding A Superior Job, 1978, 2d edit., 1983; Principles of Technical Management, 1980; How to Sell to the Government, 1981; Successful Marketing for Small Business, 1981; Building a Mail Order Business, 1982; Entrepreneur Small Business Problem Solver, 1983. Editorial adv. bd. Government Sales Strategist, Mail Order Connection. Contbr. articles to profl. jours.; patentee various tech. items including star motion calculator. Office: Calif State U Sch Bus and Econs 5151 State University Dr Los Angeles CA 90032

COHN, BENEDICT, aero. engr.; b. Bucarest, Romania, Mar. 21, 1913; came to U.S., 1920, naturalized, 1928; s. Lazar and Tzipa C.; B.Aero.Engring. with distinction, U. Minn., 1934; M.S., N.Y. U., 1936; cert. engring. UCLA, 1961; m. Margaret Benezra, Aug. 28, 1938; children—Linda Ann, Arthur Morris, Judith Lee. Chief wind tunnell N.Y. U., 1934-36; with Boeing Co., 1936-78, mgr., dir. engring. So. Calif., 1956-62, sci. adv., 1962-78; pres. Aero Concept Evaluation, Inc., Los Angeles, 1978—; mem. transonic aero. and high speed aero. subcom. NACA, 1946; chmn. So. Calif. Industry Planning Seminar, 1964; mem. Calif. Tech. Arms Control Seminar, 1960; assoc. Ctr. for Internat. and Strategic Affairs, UCLA. Asso. fellow AIAA; mem. AAAS, Am. Astron. Soc., Air Force Assn., Am. Technion Soc., Nat. Security Indsl. Assn., Calif. Seminar Internat. Security and Fgn. Policy, Tau Beta Pi, Sigma Alpha Sigma. Club: Rancho Golf. Home: 344 N Palm Dr Beverly Hills CA 90210

COHN, CECELIA ILENE, accountant; b. Kansas City, Mo., Jan. 25, 1939; d. Phillip and Jeanette (Skoler) Gilberg; student Tex. State Coll. for Women, 1957, Tusculum Coll., 1958; B.A. in Econs., Met. State Coll., Denver, 1975; m. Gershon George Cohn, Aug. 31, 1958; children—Howard Allan, Barbara Richelle. Mgr., Greeneville Pool, 1957, swimming instr., 1961-69; tax cons., mgr. exec. tax service, coordinator real estate sch. Met. Denver area H & R Block, 1969-81; owner, operator Block Bookkeeping, Denver, 1978—. Pres. Northglenn Jaycee-ettes, 1965, 67, Northglenn Toastmistress Club, 1968, br. 65 Nat. Assn. Postal Suprs. Aux., 1970, 75, Colo.-Wyo. Bi-state pres., 1976-78; ednl. v.p., pres. Orators TM Club, 1978, dist. 26 Met. 2 area gov., 1979-80, dist. 26 gov., 1981-82, adminstrv. lt. gov., 1980-81. Recipient Girl of Yr. award Northglenn Jaycee-ettes, 1963, 64; Outstanding Area Gov. award Dist. 26, 1979-80. Mem. Colo. Public Accts. Soc., Nat. Parliamentarians, Toastmasters (Disting. Toastmaster award 1982), Omega Rho Alpha. Democrat. Jewish. Home: 771 S Holly St Denver CO 80222

COHN, DAVID D., investment holding co. exec.; b. Chgo., Dec. 30, 1937; s. Albert H. and Helen F. (Baker) C.; student (research honors) Am. U., 1958; B.A., Pomona Coll., 1959; M.A. in Social Service Adminstrn., U. Chgo., 1977; m. Elizabeth Ann Curtis, Dec. 29, 1960; children—David Curtis, Robert Curtis. Salesman, Universal Battery Co., Chgo., 1959-62, v.p., 1962-66, pres., 1966-69, pres. Universal Battery div. Whittaker Corp., Chgo., 1969-70; pres., dir. Universal Res. Corp., Tucson, 1966—; cons., lectr. employee assistance programs, orgns. and industry. Vice pres. Francis W. Parker Sch. Alumni Assn., 1969-71; bd. dirs. Albert H. Cohn Found., Tucson Symphony, 1979—, Tucson Urban League, 1982—, Ariz.-Sonora Desert Mus. Found., 1982—; trustee Green Fields Country Day Sch., 1979-82, exec. com., 1980-82; mem. adv. bd. Ariz.-Sonora Desert Mus., 1981—. Mem. Nat. Assn. Social Workers, Council Social Work Edn. Unitarian. Clubs: Standard (Chgo.); Tucson Country, Skyline Country Tucson); Pres.'s (U. Ariz. Found.). Research in field; speaker profl. confs. Home: 5455 E Camino Bosque Tucson AZ 85718 Office: 6801-A E Camino Principal Tucson AZ 85715

COHN, GARY DAVID, educator; b. Seattle, June 22, 1955; s. Gerald Clifford and Rosanne (Stern) C. B.A., U. Puget Sound, 1977. Cert. secondary, vocat. edn. tchr., Wash. Mktg. rep. Four-Phase Systems Inc., Kirkland, Wash., 1977-80; instr. Eastern Wash. U., Cheney, 1980; tchr.-coordinator mktg. and distributive edn. Northshore Sch. Dist., Inglemoor High Sch., Bothell, Wash., 1980—; chmn. bus. edn. adv. com. Mercer Island Sch. Dist. Mem. CAP, U. Puget Sound Alumni Com., Northshore YMCA, U.S. Assn. Blind Athletes. Mem. Wash. Assn. Mktg. Educators, Wash. Vocat. Assn., Am. Vocat. Assn., NEA, Wash. Edn. Assn., Northshore Edn. Assn.

COHN, JAY BINSWANGER, psychiatrist, educator, lawyer; b. Pelham, N.Y., Feb. 2, 1922; s. Louis Marbe and Beatrice (Binswanger) C.; m. Sally Elaine Rosenfeld, June 27, 1945; children—Joanne, Laurie. B.A., Amherst (Mass.) Coll., 1942; M.D., Yale U., Ph.D., U. Calif.-Irvine, 1974; J.D., Am. Coll. Law, Anaheim, Calif., 1982. Diplomate Am. Bd. Psychiatry and Neurology. Instr., Case Western Res. U., Cleve., 1951-53; asst. prof. UCLA, 1959-65; assoc. prof. U. So. Calif., 1965-71; prof. psychiatry, social sci. U. Calif.-Irvine, 1971—; clin. prof. UCLA, 1982—; cons., VA; examiner Workman's Compensation Bd. Served to capt. U.S. Army, 1946-48. Mem. Am. Psychol. Assn., AMA, Calif. Med. Assn. Co-author: Emergency Care: Principles and Practice for the EMT-Paramedic, 1978; Emergency Medical Conditions, Psychiatric Sect., Principles and Practice for the EMT-Paramedic, 1982; contbr. articles to profl. jours. Home: 1315 S Roxbury Dr Los Angeles CA 90033 Office: Dept Psychiatry UCLA Los Angeles CA 90024

COHN, LAWRENCE STEVEN, physician, medical educator; b. Chgo., Dec. 21, 1945; s. Jerome M. and Francis C.; B.S., U. Ill., 1967, M.D., 1971; m. Harriett G. Rubin, Sept. 1, 1968; children—Allyson and Jennifer (twins). Intern, Mt. Zion Hosp., San Francisco, 1971-72, resident, 1972-73; resident U. Chgo., 1973-74; practice medicine specializing in internal medicine, Paramount, Calif.; pres. med. staff Charter Suburban Hosp., 1981-83; mem. staff Long Beach Meml. Hosp., Harbor Gen. Hosp; clin. asst. prof. medicine UCLA. Served to maj. USAF, 1974-76. Recipient Disting. Teaching award Harbor-UCLA Med. Center, 1980; diplomate Am. Bd. Internal Medicine. Mem. A.C.P., AMA, Calif. Med. Assn., Los Angeles County Med. Assn., Am. Heart Assn., Soc. Air Force Physicians, Phi Beta Kappa, Phi Kappa Phi, Phi Lambda Upsilon, Phi Eta Sigma, Alpha Omega Alpha. Home: 6608 Via LaPaloma Rancho Palos Verdes CA 90274 Office: 16243 Colorado Ave Paramount CA 90723

COHN, SANFORD JAY, educator; b. Hanover, Pa., Nov. 29, 1945; s. Benjamin Kahanovitz and Rose Hilda (Goldman) C.; B.A., Johns Hopkins U., 1967, M.Ed., 1976, M.A., 1978, Ph.D., 1980. Project asso. intellectually gifted child study group Johns Hopkins U., Balt., 1974-76, project asso. study of mathematically precocious youth, 1976, asst. dir. study, 1977-79, editor Intellectually Talented Youth, Bull., 1977-79; now asst. prof. dept. spl. edn. and dir. project for study of acad. precocity Ariz. State U., Tempe; cons. Nat. Interagency Task Force on Gifted and Talented Youth, 1978; mem. adv. com. on educating the gifted State of Ariz.; speaker profl. confs. including internat. conf. on educating gifted children, Jerusalem, 1979. Mem. Am. Psychol. Assn., Am. Ednl. Research Assn., Council for Exceptional Children/Assn. for Gifted, Ariz. Assn. for Gifted and Talented (treas.), Sigma Xi, Phi Delta Kappa, Phi Beta Kappa, Omicron Delta Kappa, Phi Lambda Upsilon, Delta Phi Alpha. Jewish. Author: Educating the Gifted: Acceleration and Enrichment, 1979; contbr. articles to med. and sci. jours. Home: 2107 E Carson Dr Tempe AZ 85282 Office: Dept Spl Edn Ariz State U Tempe AZ 85287

COHRS, MELANIE CAROL, interior designer; b. Holdrege, Neb., Nov. 30, 1945; d. Malcolm Edward and Margaret Ann (Swanson) Harris; m. Robert Lynn Cohrs, Sept. 20, 1969. Student San Jose State Coll., 1963-64; diploma Internat. Inst. Interior Design, 1966, U. Grenoble (France), 1967. Jr. designer Woodward & Lothrop, Alexandria, Va., 1967-69; mgr. Jordan Marsh, Burlington, Mass., 1971; buyer, interior designer Elliots Fine Furnishings, Burbank, Calif., 1974-77; co-owner Pettits Lighthouse & Interiors, La Jolla, 1977—. Founder, Child Abuse Prevention Found. Aux.; mem. Scripps Hosp. Aux., La Jolla Town Council; mem. home furnishings adv. com. San Diego Unified Sch. Dist. Mem. Am. Soc. Interior Designers. Democrat. Methodist. Club: Sorotimists (2d v.p.). Home: 5166 Chelsea La Jolla CA 92037 Office: 7851 Girard Ave La Jolla CA 92037

COIT, R. KEN, personal fin. planner; b. Los Angeles, Aug. 26, 1943; s. Roger L. and Thelma D. C.; B.S., U. Ariz., 1967; M.B.A., Pepperdine U., 1981; doctoral candidate Golden Gate U.; m. Donna M. Schemanske, Oct. 8, 1977; 1 dau., Kristin M. Co-founder, Orinda Fin. Group (Calif.), 1973; pres. R. Ken Coit, certified fin. planner, Inc., Orinda, 1978—; mem. adj. faculty Coll. Fin. Planning, Denver, 1978-79. Mem.

Internat. Assn. Fin. Planners (chpt. pres. 1978-79), Inst. Cert. Fin. Planners, Fin. Planners Equity Corp., Sales and Mktg. Execs. Assn. Methodist. Clubs: Toastmasters, East Bay Gourmet. Office: 43 G Avenida De Orinda Orinda CA 94563

COKE, FRANK VAN DEREN, photographer, educator; b. Lexington, Ky., July 4, 1921; s. Sterling Dent and Elisabeth (Van Deren) C.; B.A., U. Ky., 1956; M.F.A., Ind. U., 1958; postgrad. Harvard, 1958, 60-61; m. Eleanor Browning Barton, Mar. 1, 1943 (div. 1980); children—Sterling Van Deren, Eleanor. Vice pres. Van Deren Hardware Co., Lexington, 1946-53, pres., 1953-56; asst. prof. U. Fla., Gainesville, 1958-61; asso. prof. Ariz. State U., Tempe, 1961-62; prof., chmn. dept. art U. N.Mex., Albuquerque, 1962-70, prof. art, dir. Art Mus., 1972-79; dir. dept. photography San Francisco Mus. Modern Art, 1979—; dep. dir. Internat. Mus. Photography, Rochester, N.Y., 1970-71, dir., 1971-72; cons. art Lincoln First Bank Rochester, 1971-74, First Nat. Bank in Albuquerque, 1972-75, Arts Council of Gt. Britain, 1975—; vis. lectr. St. Martin's Sch. Art, London, Eng., 1970; vis. prof. U. Calif.-Berkeley, 1973; distinguished vis. prof. U. Calif.- Davis, 1974; chmn. fine arts advisory com. City Albuquerque, 1964-69; Cooke-Daniels Meml. lectr. Denver Art Mus., 1973; one-man shows of photography Witkin Gallery, N.Y.C., 1973, Oakland (Calif.) Mus., 1974, Galerie die Brucke, Vienna, Galerie A. Nagel, Berlin, 1975, Schoelkopf Gallery, N.Y.C., Photo Galerie, Paris, Susan Spiritus Gallery, Newport Beach, Calif., 1976, Art Mus. U. Ky., Chgo. Center Creative Photography, 1982. Bd. dirs. Internat. Folk Art Found., 1966-75, 78-79, v.p., 1970; bd. dirs. Harwood Found., 1972-75, Guadalupe Found., Santa Fe, 1977-79. Served with USNR, 1942-45; PTO. Research grantee U. N.Mex., 1964, 70, 72, 76; Guggenheim fellow, 1975. Mem. Coll. Art Assn. (dir. 1972-76), Soc. Photog. Edn. (dir. 1965-70). Author: Taos and Santa Fe: The Artists Environment, 1963; Impressionism in America, 1965; The Drawings of Andrew Dasburg, 1966; Young Photographers, 1968; Marin in New Mexico, 1968; Nordfeldt the Painter, 1972; The Painter and the Photograph, 1972; Van Deren Coke: Photographs 1956-1973; A Hundred Years of Photographic History, 1975; History of Photography in New Mexico, 1979; Andrew Dasburg, 1979; Avant-Garde Photography in Germany, 1919-1939, 1980; Brett Weston Photographs: 1925-30 and 1980-82, 1982; Val Telberg, 1983. Editor Image, Jour. Internat. Mus. Photography, 1970-72. Home: 4080 20th St San Francisco CA 94114

COKER, FRANK BETHELL, aerospace company executive; b. San Diego, Dec. 26, 1925; s. Robert Noble and Harriet Davis (Petrie) C.; B.E.E. cum laude, U. So. Calif., 1951, M.S. in Elec. Engring., 1953; Ph.D. in Bus. Adminstrn., 1981; m. Wilma Lee Sheets, Dec. 22, 1947; children—Pamela Lee, Tracy Drake. Vice pres., gen. mgr. United ElectroDynamics, Inc., Pasadena, Calif., 1951-63; asst. to pres., mgr. corp. advanced programs office Whittaker Corp., Los Angeles, 1962-65; gen. mgr. Western ops. System Devel. Corp., Santa Monica, Calif., 1965-68; group v.p., gen. mgr. tech. group Sci. Resources Corp., Montgomeryville Pa., 1968-70; v.p., gen. mgr. Telautograph Corp., Los Angeles, 1970-73; founder, pres. Reko Industries, Glendale, Calif., 1973—; pres. Pub. Engrs., Inc., Los Angeles, 1969-70; dir. Digital Seismic Corp., Computer Sharing, Inc., Hybrid Systems, Inc. testifier to Joint Com. on Atomic Energy, Congress of U.S., on tech. aspects of detection and inspection controls of a nuclear weapons test ban, 1960. Bd. dirs. Los Angeles County Industry Edn. Council, 1965-68; prin., bd. dirs. Airport Planning Group, 1965—. Served with USN, 1944-46. Recipient Classic Paper award Geophysics mag., 1960; cert. U.S. patent agt. Mem. Am. Mgmt. Assn., Research Soc. Am. (pres. 1960-63), Archimedes Circle, Soc. Exploration Geophysicists, IEEE, Seismol. Soc. Am., Am. Ordnance Assn., Eta Kappa Nu (past pres.), Tau Beta Pi, Phi Kappa Phi. Contbr. articles to profl. jours.; patentee in field. Home: 333 Chester St Glendale CA 91203

COKER, SYBIL JANE THOMAS, educator, freelance writer; b. Elizabeth, La., Aug. 16; d. Andrew Jackson and Lillie Mae (Miller) Thomas; A.A., Los Angeles City Coll., 1952; B.A., Calif. State U., Los Angeles, 1955; B.A., Pepperdine U., 1957; M.S. in Edn., Mt. St. Mary's Coll., 1980; m. Charles M. Coker, July 1978. With Amos 'n Andy TV series, 1952; elementary tchr. Barton Hill Sch., 1957-58, 96th St. Sch., 1958-63, Hooper Ave. Sch., 1963-65, Vermont Ave. Sch., 1965-68, Hooper Sch., 1968-70, Angeles Mesa Sch., 1970—; entertainment and society editor Los Angeles Gazette, 1972-73; soc. editor Herald-Dispatch, Los Angeles, 1966-67, 75—, women's page editor, movie critic, 1970—; writer Los Angeles Entertainment Digest, 1970-71, Los Angeles Defender, 1974, A.C.C. Ch. and Community News, 1969-70, Celebrity Newspaper, 1970-71, CRS mag., 1978—; fashion show commentator-coordinator, wedding cons. Founder 2d Baptist Drama Guild, 1957-67. Recipient resolution U.S. Congress. Mem. NEA, Calif. Tchrs. Assn., United Tchrs. Los Angeles, Women in Communications, Nat. Fedn. Press Women, Nat. Assn. Media Women (pres. Beverly Hills/Hollywood chpt., Nat. Pres.'s award 1977), NAACP (life), Nat. Council Negro Women (life), Black Women's Forum, Am. Personnel and Guidance Assn., Christian Women on the Move, United Tchrs. Los Angeles, Delta Sigma Theta (Communications award Los Angeles Alumnae chpt. 1977), Greater Los Angeles Press Club, Sigma Delta Chi, Delta Sigma Theta. Democrat. Club: Emanon.

COLAIANNIA, LOUIS MARIO, dentist; b. Denver, Jan. 28, 1955; s. Louis Andrew and Rose Mary (Mangone) C.; m. Cynthia Ann DeLaney, Jan. 28, 1982. Student U. Colo., Denver, 1976, D.D.S., 1980. Dentist, John F. Kennedy Center for Handicapped, Denver, 1980; pvt. practice dentistry, Elizabeth, Colo., 1980—; mem. staff Aurora (Colo.) Community Hosp.; owner Elizabeth Fitness Center; cons. Elizabeth Sch. Dist.; adv. Elizabeth Family Health Center. Chmn. Elbert County (Colo.) First Precinct Democratic Party; mem. U.S. Congl. Adv. Com.; adv. Elizabeth High Sch. Future Bus. Leaders Am. Mem. Am. Assn. Endodontists (hon.). Roman Catholic. Author honor code at U. Colo. Sch. Dentistry, 1979-80; research on effects of Piezo electricity on bone regeneration. Home: 465 Paddock Elizabeth CO 80107 Office: 187 Hwy 86 Elizabeth CO 80107

COLANGELO, JERRY JOHN, profl. sports exec.; b. Chicago Heights, Ill., Nov. 20, 1939; s. Larry and Sue (Drancek) C.; B.A., U. Ill., 1962; m. Joan E. Helmich, Jan. 20, 1961; children—Kathy, Kristen, Bryan, Mandie Brooke. Ptnr. House of Charles, Inc., 1962-63; assoc. D.O. Klein & Assocs., 1964-65; dir. merchandising Chgo. Bulls basketball club, 1966-68; gen. mgr. Phoenix Suns basketball club, 1968—. Recipient Am. Heritage award Anti-Defamation League of B'nai B'rith, 1976; named Ariz. Sports Personality of Yr., Phoenix Press Box Assn.; NBA Exec. of Yr., Sporting News, 1976, 81. Mem. Basketball Congress Am. (exec. v.p., dir.), Phi Kappa Psi. Republican. Baptist. Clubs: Univ., Phoenix Execs. Office: Phoenix Suns 29 10 N Central Phoenix AZ 85012*

COLBERT, GREGORY ALLEN, city official; b. Eldorado, Ill., Feb. 2, 1950; s. Louis Burrel and Verna Mae (Smith) C. B.S. in Psychology, U. Ill., 1970, M.S. in Indsl. Psychology, 1971; Ph.D. in Ednl. Psychology, U. Hawaii, 1979. Human resources researcher State Farm Ins. Co., Bloomington, Ill., 1971-77; employment testing specialist City and County Honolulu, 1977-79, personnel research psychologist, 1979-81, exec. asst. to mng. dir., 1981—. Mem. Mayor's Council on Law and Order. Mem. Am. Psychol. Assn., Hawaii Psychol. Assn., Internat. Personnel Mgmt. Assn. Democrat. Contbr. articles to profl. jours. Office: Office of Mng Dir City and County Honolulu Honolulu HI 96813

COLBY, ARTHUR HAROLD, city official; b. Amesbury, Mass., Aug. 5, 1919; s. Albert Louis and Hazel (Maines) C.; B.S., La. State U., 1942; postgrad. U. Colo., 1948-50; m. Johanna Austin, May 23, 1972; children by previous marriage—Ann Francis and Linda Louise (twins), Sally Ann Simpson. Contract mgr. Dept. Navy, Pensacola, Fla., 1950-53; partner Colby Schuman Co., Hutchinson, Kans., 1953-55; pub. works dir., Hutchinson, 1955-58; city mgr., Nyssa, Oreg., 1958-64; city mgr., Thornton, Colo., 1964-68, Blue Ash, Ohio, 1968-69, Kennewick, Wash., 1969-76; gen. mgr. Port of Kennewick, 1976-81; prin. Mem. Denver Area Transp. Tech. Steering Com., 1965-68, Adams County Air Pollution Variance Bd., 1966-68; dist. chmn. Park Adams dist. Boy Scouts Am., 1965-68; trustee Community Improvement Corp. Served to capt. AUS, 1942-45; ETO. Decorated Purple Heart; recipient Disting. Service award Jr. C. of C., 1954. Mem. Nat. Soc. Profl. Engrs., Tri-City C. of C. Am. Legion (past comdr.), V.F.W., Internat. City Mgmt. Assn., U. Colo. Alumni Club, Phi Delta Theta. Methodist. Clubs: Masons (Shriner), Elks, Lions (past pres.), Tri-City Country (past pres.), Aviation, Toastmasters (past pres.), Kiwanis (past pres.). Contbr. articles to profl. publs. Home and Office: 5005 S Ely Kennewick WA 99336

COLBY, BARBARA DIANE, interior designer; b. Chgo., Dec. 6, 1932; d. Raymond R. and Mertyl Shirley (Jackson) C.; 1 son, Lawrence James. Student Wright Jr. Coll., 1950, Art Inst. Chgo., UCLA. Owner, F.L.S., Los Angeles, 1971-77; ptnr. Ambiance Inc., Los Angeles, 1976-77; owner Barbara Colby, Ltd., Los Angeles, 1977-81; bus. adminstr. Internat. Soc. Interior Designers, Los Angeles, 1982—; instr. Recipient award for Best Children's Room, Chgo. Furniture Show, 1969. Mem. Am. Soc. Interior Designers, Internat. Soc. Interior Designers. Contbr. to profl. jours. Home: 1230 N Sweetzer #214 Los Angeles CA 90069 Office: PO Box 2906 Beverly Hills CA 90213

COLDREN, LINDA L., software engineer; b. Bethesda, Md., Mar. 31, 1952; d. Douglas E. and Violet E. (Shurr) C.; m. Dennis R. Hornberger, Sept. 4, 1971 (div.); children—Brian M. II. B.S., Kutztown State U., 1977; M.S. in Mgmt. Sci., Info. Systems, Colo. State U., 1980. Auditor, Bank & Trust Co. of Pa., 1977-78, fin. analyst, 1978-79; grad. teaching asst. Colo. State U., Ft. Collins, 1979; software quality assurance engr. Ft. Collins div. Hewlett-Packard Co., 1979-80; programmer-analyst Computer Systems div., 1980-82; software engr. ASK Computer Systems, Inc., Los Altos, Calif., 1982—. Mem. Am. Prodn. and Inventory Control Soc., LWV, Mensa. Democrat. Lutheran. Home: 10870 N Stelling Rd #20-B Cupertino CA 95014 Office: ASK Computer Systems Inc 730 Distel Dr Los Altos CA 94022

COLE, BRUCE HERMAN, advertising executive; b. Chgo., July 22, 1928; s. Leo L. and Kate (Mandelkern) C.; m. Jane Renwick Bagby, June 7, 1953; children—Rosemary Nielsen, Dorothy, Robert Bagby, Frances. Student U. So. Calif., 1948-50; A.B., Grinnell Coll., 1953. Advt. mgr. Gen. Electric Co., Schenectady, 1953-59; account exec. Reincke, Myer & Finn, Inc., Chgo., 1959-60; v.p., gen. mgr. Marsteller Inc., Chgo., 1960-74, exec. v.p., 1974-78, also dir.; sr. v.p., gen. mgr. Glenn, Bozell & Jacobs, Phoenix, 1978-80; pres. Cramer-Krasselt/SW, Phoenix, 1980-83; chmn. bd., pres. Bruce H. Cole Co., Inc., Phoenix, 1983—; dir., sec. Piston Powered Products, Inc., Chandler, Ariz.; dir. Inertia Dynamics Corp., Phoenix; lectr. Ariz. State U., 1980-82. Trustee, United Way, Phoenix-Scottsdale, 1979-80, Combined Met. Phoenix Arts, 1979-80; adv. bd. Salvation Army, 1978—; bd. dirs. Health Evaluation and Longevity Planning Found., Inc., 1979—, Ariz. Heart Assn., 1980—, Phoenix Symphony Assn., 1979—, Maricopa council Boy Scouts Am., 1981—, Phoenix Met. Sports Found., 1983—. Served with USN, 1946-48. Mem. Am. Mgmt. Assn., Am. Assn. Advt. Agys., Grinnell Coll. Alumni Assn., Sigma Delta Chi. Clubs: University, Arizona, Plaza, Phoenix Advt. Home: 4701 E Sparkling Ln Paradise Valley AZ 85253 Office: Bruce H Cole Co 3550 N Central Ave Phoenix AZ 85012

COLE, CHARLES WESLEY, mgmt. educator; b. Springfield, Oreg., Jan. 21, 1929; s. Edward Charles and Lucille Ruth (Lambert) C.; m. Colleen Kohler, Mar. 20, 1949; children—Gregory, Sara Moore. B.S., Oreg. State U., 1950; postgrad. U.S. Naval Postgrad. Sch., 1955; M.A., George Washington U., 1964; postgrad. Armed Forces Indsl. Coll., 1969-70. Commd. ensign U.S. Navy, 1950; advanced through grades to capt., 1970; various mgmt. and command positions, 1950-69; asst. chief staff ops. and chief staff Amphibious Group Eastern Pacific, Coronado, Calif., 1970-74; chief mut. def. assistance office Am. Embassy, Tokyo, 1974-77; comdr. Naval Inactive Ship Maintenance Facility, Bremerton, Wash., 1977-79; ret., 1979; exec. dir. bus. regulation study ctr. Coll. Bus. Adminstrn., U. Oreg., Eugene, 1979—, instr. grad. sch. mgmt., 1981—. Chmn. Eugene-Springfield Met. Area Planning Adv. Com. Decorated Silver Star, Legion Merit, Bronze Star (2); named Outstanding Citizen Lane Council Govts., 1982. Mem. Am. Mgmt. Assn. Republican. Lutheran. Clubs: Ret. Officers Assn. (Eugene); Elks. Home: 1245 Inglewood Ave Eugene OR 97401 Office: Coll Bus Adminstrn U Oreg Eugene OR 97403

COLE, DANA ALEXANDRA, communications executive; b. Syracuse, N.Y., Aug. 28, 1935; d. William Alexander and Eldora Venecia (Carroll) Rewak. B.A. summa cum laude, Coll. Our Lady of Mercy, Burlingame, Calif., 1963; M.A. in Counseling Psychology, U. Santa Clara (Calif.), 1973. Tchr., Sisters of Mercy, Burlingame, 1960-69; personnel trainer Standard Oil Co., San Francisco, 1969-70; tng. dir. World Savs. and Loan Assn., Oakland, Calif., 1970-72; personnel coordinator SAI, San Diego, 1973-74; cons. Van Housen, Liberman & Teel, Seattle, 1975-77; personnel dir. Mannesmann Tally Corp., Kent, Wash., 1977-83, dir. corp. communications, 1983—; instr. City Coll. Seattle, 1977-79, Green River Community Coll., Auburn, Wash., 1977-79, Bellevue (Wash.) Community Coll., 1980. Mem. Am. Soc. Personnel Adminstrn., Pacific N.W. Personnel Mgrs. Assn. (dir.), Am. Assn. Handwriting Analysts. Republican. Home: 15255 Sunwood Blvd Tukwila WA 98188 Office: 8301 S 180th St Kent WA 98031

COLE, DAVID MACAULAY, newspaper and magazine editor, computer consultant; b. Richmond, Calif., Feb. 17, 1954; s. Frederick George and Norma Ann (Caudle) C.; Student San Francisco State U., 1972-77. Mng. editor feed/back, The Calif. Journalism Rev., San Francisco, 1974-77, exec. editor, 1977-82, editor, gen. mgr., 1982—; editorial asst. Rolling Stone, San Francisco, 1976-77; asst. news editor San Francisco Examiner, 1977-80, systems editor, 1980—; guest lectr. U. Calif.-Berkeley, Stanford U., San Francisco State U. Bd. dirs. West Contra Costa ARC, 1970. Mem. Media Alliance, Sigma Delta Chi, San Francisco Press Club. Home: 873 Ashbury St San Francisco CA 94117 Office: 1600 Holloway St San Francisco CA 94132 or 110 5th St San Francisco CA 94103

COLE, DAVID RODNEY, mining association executive; b. White Plains, N.Y., July 13, 1931; s. Thomas Harris and Louise Helene (Fischer) C.; m. Marjorie Ann Davis, Nov. 7, 1959; 1 son, John William Owen. E.M., Colo. Sch. Mines, 1952, M.S., 1956. Registered profl. engr., Colo. Mining engr. Colo. Standard Lead-Zinc Mines, Inc., Lake City, 1952, Tech-Ser Mining Co., Silverton, Colo., 1956-57; mining engr., project engr. Idarado Mining Co., Ouray, Colo., 1957-61; sr. metal mine insp. Colo. Bur. Mines, Grand Junction, 1961-67; ops. mgr. Strategic Minerals Exploration Co., Grand Junction, 1967-69; pres. Colo. Mining Assn., Denver, 1969—; dir. Polaris Resources, Inc., Polaris Oil & Gas, Inc., Colo. Hwy. Users Conf.; sec./treas./dir. Colo. Mining Assn. Edn. Found., Inc.; mem. Nat. Def. Exec. Res. Emergency Minerals Adminstrn. U.S. Dept. Interior; mem. bd. western govs. Am. Mining Congress. Sec. Applewood Knolls Homeowners Assn., 1983. Served with AUS, 1952-54. Recipient Disting. Achievement award Colo. Sch. Mines, 1982. Mem. Nat. Soc. Profl. Engrs., Colo. Soc. Profl. Engrs., Soc. Mining Engrs. of AIME, Am. Soc. Assn. Execs., Colo. Soc. Assn. Execs., Colo. Sch. Mines Alumni Assn. (pres.), Mines Sigma Nu (pres. 1980-83). Republican. Clubs: Denver Petroleum, Elks. Patentee ski-stack; editor Mining Yearbook. Office: 1515 Cleveland Pl Suite 410 Denver CO 80202

COLE, DONALD W(ILLARD), clergyman, educator, cons. psychologist.; b. San Diego, Jan. 12, 1920; s. Rolland Ames and Genevieve (Bender) C.; student U. Redlands; A.B., Stanford, 1942; M.Div., Eastern Bapt. Theol. Sem., 1945; Ed.D., Southwestern Bapt. Theol. Sem., 1952; Ph.D., U. of London, 1962; m. Ann Bradford, Sept. 18, 1942; 1 son, Timothy Bradford. Ordained to ministry Bapt. Ch., 1945; pastor Linden Ch., Camden, N.J., 1944-46; asso. pastor First Ch., San Diego, 1946-48; univ. pastor, dir. Bapt. student work So. Calif., 1948-52, dean, dir. Bapt. confs., camps, coll., univ. students, 1948-52; pres. Calif. Bapt. Theol. Seminary and Coll., 1952-59; British Nat. Health Service fellow, 1959-61; dean of students, prof. psychology Fuller Theol. Sem., Calif., 1962-70; pvt. practice family cons. services, San Clemente, Calif., 1970-74; pastor South Shores Bapt. Ch., Laguna Niguel, Calif., 1974—. Fellow Royal Geog. Soc., London; mem. Am., Calif., Western psychol. assns., Alpha Gamma Nu, Alpha Phi Omega. Republican. Author: The Place of the Question in the Teaching Ministry of Jesus, The Role of Religion in the Development of Personality. Contbr. religious publs. Home: 245 Via Ballena San Clemente CA 92672 Office: 32712 Crown Valley Pkwy Laguna Niguel CA 92677

COLE, DOROTHY ANN, developmental educator; b. San Francisco, Sept. 1, 1951; d. Thomas Oliver and Rae Cole. B.S. cum laude, U. Calif., 1974; B.A., Evergreen State Coll., 1977; M.Ed., U. Sheffield (Eng.), 1982. Forestry-biol. technician U.S. Forest Service, McCloud, also Berkeley, Calif., 1973-74; tchr. Shelton (Wash.) High Sch., 1975-76; curriculum design specialist Olympic Coll. Extension Ctr., 1977-82; gem salesperson Alaskan Precious Metals, Anchorage, 1982-83; owner Ednl. Cons. and Organizational Services, 1983—; tutor-trainer Laubach Literacy. Pres. student cabinet YWCA, 1972-73; pres. Shelton Family Planning Assn., 1975-76; mem. Mason County Literacy Council, 1977-80. Rotary Found. grad. fellow, 1980-81; NSF scholar, 1978-79; Standard Oil Co. scholar, 1973. Mem. Assn. Supervision and Curriculum Devel., Shelton Edn. Assn., Olympic Coll. Higher Edn. Assn., NEA, Wash. Edn. Assn.

COLE, JEANETTE TILLMAN, counselor; b. Valdosta, Ga., July 18, 1933; d. Henry Young and Neva Ella (Mathis) Tillman; m. Luther Melanchthon Cole, Jr., Oct. 26, 1951 (dec.). B.S. in Elem. Edn., U. Ala., 1961; M.S. in Psychology, Counseling & Guidance, U. No. Colo., 1971, postgrad., 1971-74. Cert. tchr., Colo.; cert. sch. counselor, Colo. Tchr., Jefferson County (Colo.) Pub. Schs., 1961-67, 68-74, Greensboro (N.C.) Pub. Schs., 1967-68; counselor Evergreen (Colo.) Jr. High Sch., 1974—. Mem. NEA, Colo. Edn. Assn., Jefferson County Edn. Assn., Am. Personnel and Guidance Assn., Colo. Personnel and Guidance Assn., Jefferson County Counselors Assn. Office: 2052 Colorado Hwy 74 Evergreen CO 80439

COLE, JEANNETTE MARIE, marketing exec.; b. Sayre, Pa., Dec. 30, 1943; d. James Edward and Catherine (Burkhart) Smith; R.N., Sacred Heart Coll., Allentown, Pa., 1964, M.B.A., Pepperdine U., 1977. Rehab. nurse Liberty Mut. Ins. Co., Los Angeles, 1970-73; sales rep. Organon Pharm. Co., Los Angeles, 1973-74; sales rep. Edwards Labs., Los Angeles, 1974-75, mgr. market ops., Santa Ana, Calif., 1975-76, mgr. market research, 1976-79; pres. Creative Mktg. Strategies, Dana Point, Calif., 1979-81; v.p. Vorhauer Labs. (now VLI Corp.), Costa Mesa, Calif., 1981—; cons. in field. Vice-pres. bd. dirs. Dana Light Homeowners Assn., 1977. Mem. Am. Mktg. Assn., Am. Mgmt. Assn., Mgmt. Women. Home: 24045 Vista Corona Dana Point CA 92629

COLE, JEFFREY SHERMAN, manufacturing company official; b. Honolulu, Sept. 22, 1941; s. Perry S. and Margaret V. (Jeffrey) C.; m. Sherry V. Vincent June 7, 1966 (div.); children—Kevin, Melissa, Mark. B.S. in Mktg., U. Mo., 1965. Dist. sales mgr. Griffin Pipe Co., Lakewood, Colo., 1967—. Mem. Am. Water Works Assn. Republican. Methodist. Club: Lyons. Home: 445 Union Blvd Lakewood CO 80228

COLE, MALVIN, physician, educator; b. N.Y.C., Mar. 21, 1933; s. Harry and Sylvia (Firman) C.; A.B. cum laude, Amherst Coll., 1953; M.D. cum laude, Georgetown U. Med. Sch., 1957; m. Susan Kugel, June 20, 1954; children—Andrew James, Douglas Gowers. Intern, Seton Hall Coll. Medicine, Jersey City Med. Ctr., 1957-58; resident Boston City Hosps., 1958-60; practice medicine specializing in neurology, Montclair and Glen Ridge, N.J., Montville, N.J., 1963-72, Casper, Wyo., 1972—; teaching fellow Harvard Med. Sch., 1958-60; Research fellow Nat. Hosp. for Nervous Diseases, St. Thomas Hosp., London, Eng., 1960-61; instr. Georgetown U. Med. Sch., 1961-63; clin. asst. prof. neurology N.J. Coll. Medicine, Newark, 1963-72, acting dir. neurology, 1965-72; clin. asso. prof. neurology U. Colo. Med. Sch., 1973—; mem. staff Martland Hosp., Newark, Meml. Hosp., Natrona County, Wyo., U. Hosp., Denver. Served to capt. M.C., AUS, 1961-63. Licensed physician, Mass., N.Y., Calif., N.J., Colo., Wyo.; diplomate Am. Bd. Psychiatry and Neurology, Nat. Bd. Med. Examiners. Fellow Am. Acad. Neurology, Royal Soc. Medicine; mem. Assn. Research Nervous and Mental Disease, Acad. Aphasia, Internat. Soc. Neuropsychology, Harveian Soc. London, N.Y. Acad. Sci., Osler Soc. London, Alpha Omega Alpha. Contbr. articles to profl. jours. Home: Spring Valley Ranch West of Casper WY 82644 Office: 246 S Washington St Casper WY 82601

COLE, PETER WILLIAM, financial executive; b. Berkeley, Calif., Oct. 8, 1939; s. William Robertson and Bernadette Marie (Jordan) C.; B.S. in Engring., U. Calif., Berkeley, 1962; M.B.A., U. So. Calif., 1965; m. Sharleen Martin, June 7, 1969; children—Peter Martin, Megan McKenzie, Christian Granger (dec.), Meredith Elizabeth. Self employed investor, fin. adviser Peter Cole Co., Piedmont, Calif., 1978—; asst. to v.p. Bechtel Corp., San Francisco, 1965-70; investment officer Am. Express Investment Mgmt. Co., San Francisco, 1970-76; investment officer Bank Am. Capital Corp., San Francisco, 1976-78; mng. gen. ptnr. Menlo Park Assocs., dir. Transworld Energy Corp., Applications Services Corp., Switchmaster Corp. Served with U.S. Army, 1962. Mem. Nat. Assn. Petroleum Investment Analysts, U. Calif. Engring. Alumni Soc. Address: 158 Mountain Ave Piedmont CA 94611

COLE, RALPH, lawyer, rancher, state senator; b. Plattsmouth, Nebr., 1915; B.A., LL.B., U. Denver, 1940; m. Jean Cole, June 1, 1948. Practice law, Littleton, Colo.; mem. Colo. Ho. of Reps., 1964-72; mem. Colo. Senate, 1972—, chmn. judiciary com. 52d Gen. Assembly, majority leader 53d Gen. Assembly. Served to capt. JAGC, U.S. Army, 1942-46; col. Res. Mem. Colo. Bar Assn., Denver Bar Assn. Clubs: Masons, Elks. Republican. Office: 1224 Bannock St Denver CO 80204

COLE, WARD KENNETH, musician, educator; b. Helena, Mont., Jan. 17, 1922; s. Ward B. and Helen H. (Reeves) C.; B.A., U. Wash., 1948; postgrad. Juilliard Sch. Music, 1951; M.A. (fellow), Tchrs. Coll., Columbia U., 1952, Ed.D., 1954; m. Carolyn Jean Clark, Nov. 14, 1947. Trumpeter, Seattle Symphony Orch., 1947-49, Ted Weems Orch., 1949-51, Radio City Music Hall, 1952-56, Fred Waring Orch., 1954-56; prof. music, chmn. dept. Frostburg (Md.) State Coll., 1956-64; asso. prof. music U. Toronto (Ont., Can.), 1964-68; prof. music, chmn. dept.

U. Calgary (Alta., Can.), 1968-73, prof. music, 1973-82; condr. Cumberland (Md.) Civic Symphony, 1957-59, Rameses Concert Band, Toronto, 1965-68; guest condr. Tamagawa U., Tokyo, 1980; arranger of stage band series Shawnee Press, Delaware Watergap, Pa., 1962-64; pres. Md. Music Educators, 1963-64; sec.-treas. Alta Music Conf., 1971-73. Served with USAAF, 1943-45. Recipient Deutscher Akademischer Austauschdienst Study award, 1974. Mem. Internat. Trumpet Guild (dir. 1975-77), U. Calgary Faculty Club, Phi Delta Kappa, Kappa Delta Pi, Delta Upsilon, Phi Mu Alpha. Clubs: Calgary Shriners, Montana Club, Masons. Composer: Blues Muse, 1963, Bobcat Rock, 1963, Brazilia, 1964. Jazz editor Canadian Band Dirs. Assn. Jour., 1980—; Home: 2316 Sovereign Crescent SW Calgary AB T3C 2M2 Canada

COLEGROVE, BOONE CLARK, state ofcl.; b. Salt Lake City, Apr. 7, 1936; s. James Vernal and Thelma Jane (Cahoon) C.; B.S., U. Utah, 1958, M.Ed., 1973; postgrad. Brigham Young U., 1964, Pepperdine Coll., 1972; m. Margo Marie Luckau, Apr. 28, 1978; children—Jeffery, Norrie, Joel, Craig, Emilie. Clk., Safeway Stores, Salt Lake City, 1958-68; tchr. Jordan Sch. Dist., Sandy, Utah, 1958-74, supr. social studies, 1970-74; social studies specialist Utah State Office Edn., Salt Lake City, 1974—. Utah del. Democratic Conv., 1976. Recipient Disting. Service award Utah Acad. Scis.; Outstanding Service award Utah Council Social Studies, 1979. Mem. NEA, Utah Edn. Assn., Jordan Edn. Assn., Assn. Supervision and Curriculum Devel., Nat. Council Social Studies, Utah Council Social Studies, Social Studies Suprs. Assn., State Social Studies Specialists Assn., Utah Council Tchrs. Driver Edn., Phi Delta Kappa. Mormon. Club: Rotary. Contbr. articles to profl. jours. Home: 6223 Rainsborough Circle Salt Lake City UT 84121 Office: 250 E 500 S Salt Lake City UT 84111

COLEMAN, ALVIN TRAVIS, elec. engr.; b. Ashburn, Ga., Dec. 23, 1928; s. James Allen and Lilly Missouri (Carter) C.; B.S. in Elec. Engring., U. Tex., Arlington, 1972; m. Lillian Clarissa Gran, Nov. 10, 1952; children—Betty Jo, Cindy Annetta, Donna Lynn, Carol Colleen. Flight test engr. Bendix Corp., Teterboro, N.J., 1956-63; project logistics support engr. Gen. Dynamics Corp., Ft. Worth, 1963-73; group engr. Gates Learjet Corp., Wichita, Kans., 1973-77, chief elec. and avionics liaison, Tucson, 1978—; engring. rep. FAA. Served with USN, 1945-48. Registered profl. engr., Ariz., Tex. Mem. Nat. Soc. Profl. Engrs. Methodist. Club: Moose. Home: 3685 N Tanuri Dr Tucson AZ 85715 Office: 7777 S Nogales Hwy Tucson AZ 85734

COLEMAN, CARLA SWAN, clinical psychologist; b. Denver, Apr. 5, 1908; d. Henry and Carla (Denison) Swan; m. Albert Jones Coleman, Oct. 11, 1952. A.B., Bryn Mawr Coll., 1929; M.A., Yale U., 1936, Ph.D., 1938. Cert. psychologist Am. Bd. Psychologists in Pvt. Practice. Psychol. tester Denver Pub. Schs., 1929-32, tchr. parent edn. and pre-sch. program, 1938-45; research asst. Guidance Nursery, Yale Inst. Human Relations, 1932-38; pvt. practice clin. psychology, Denver, 1945-72, part-time, 1972—; dir., psychol. cons. Innsmont Ctr. for Children, Denver, 1967-72; vol. counselor with pediatricians, psychiatrists, psychologists, 1945—. Bd. dirs. Colo. State Children's Home, 1947-60. Mem. Am. Psychol. Assn., Colo. Psychol. Assn. (Disting. Service award 1970), AAAS, Assn. Gifted and Talented, Colo. Ednl. Assn., Colo. Women Psychologists, Mental Health Assn. Colo., Colo. Assn. Mental Hygiene, Colo. Assn. Children with Learning Difficulties, Colonial Dames Am., Sigma Xi. Republican. Episcopalian. Clubs: University, Fortnightly, Garden of Denver. Address: 475 Humboldt St Denver CO 80218

COLEMAN, DOROTHY IRENE HART, public relations executive; b. Juneau, Alaska, Nov. 9, 1924; d. Julius Harold and Dorothy (Canfield) Hart; m. Don Coryell, May 20, 1952 (div. 1957); m. 2d, Patrick Coleman, Dec. 15, 1957; children—Mary Patricia and Anne Dorothy (twins). B.A., U. Wash., 1947, postgrad., 1947-50; postgrad. UCLA, 1956-60. Asst. to dir. U. Wash. Sch. Journalism, Seattle, 1947-50; reporter Seattle Post-Intelligencer, 1945-57, 50-52; columnist Honolulu Star-Bull., 1952-53; women's editor Vancouver (B.C.) News Herald, 1953-54; pub. relations dir. U. B.C., Vancouver, 1954-55; news editor Wenatchee (Wash.) Daily World, 1955-56; feature writer Los Angeles Mirror, 1956-59, women's editor, 1959-62; asst. family sect. editor Los Angeles Times, 1962; women's editor Los Angeles Herald-Examiner, 1963-68; pub. relations dir. Hollywood Presbyn. Hosp., 1968-72; pres. Dorothy Coleman Pub. Relations, Los Angeles, 1972-73; dir. communications Braille Inst. Am., Inc., 1973-82; dir. community relations Meml. Med. Centers, Inc., 1982—. Served to lt. comdr., USNR, 1950-65. Mem. Los Angeles Press Club, San Francisco Press Club, Honolulu Press Club, Wash. State Press Club, Can. Women's Press Club, Am. Women in Radio and TV, Am. Coll. Pub. Relations Assn., Women in Communications (chpt. pres. 1964), Pub. Relations Soc. Am., Los Angeles Advt. Women, Los Angeles Publicity Club, Gifted Children's Assn., Kappa Alpha Theta. Home: 32 Cedar Tree Ln Irvine CA 92715 Office: 1111 W La Palma Ave Anaheim CA 92803

COLEMAN, JAMES SMOOT, political science educator; b. Provo, Utah, Feb. 4, 1919; s. Jacob and Allie (Smoot) C.; m. Margaret Tate, Feb. 4, 1944; children—James S. Jr., Robert L.; m. 2d, Ursula Maria Finken, June 20, 1965. B.A., Brigham Young U., 1947; M.A., Harvard U., 1948, Ph.D., 1953. Teaching fellow Harvard U., 1949-50, 53; from instr. to prof. polit. sci. UCLA, 1953-65, dir. African Studies Ctr., 1960-65; rep. Rockfeller Found. in East Africa and Zaire, 1967-78; prof. polit. sci., chmn. council internat., comparative studies UCLA, 1978—; cons. Rockefeller Found. Served to lt. col. U.S. Army, 1941-46. Decorated M.B.E. (Brit. Commonwealth); recipient Woodrow Wilson Found. award Am. Polit. Sci. Assn., 1959; Ctr. Advanced Study Behavioral Scis. fellow, 1963-64; grantee Carnegie Corp., Ford Found., Rockefeller Found. Fellow Am. Acad. Arts and Scis.; mem. Am. Polit. Sci. Assn., Council Fgn. Relations N.Y.C., Internat. Studies Assn., Comparative and Internat. Edn. Soc. Democrat. Unitarian. Club: Harvard (N.Y.C.). Author: Nigeria: Background to Nationalism, 1958; co-editor/co-author: The Politics of the Developing Areas, 1960; Political Parties and National Integration in Tropical Africa, 1964; Government and Rural Development in East Africa, 1977; Social Science and Public Policy in the Developing World, 1981; editor and co-author Education and Political Development, 1971. Home: 12315 Darlington Ave Los Angeles CA 90049 Office: UCLA 405 Hilgard Ave Bunche Hall 11343 Los Angeles CA 90024

COLEMAN, JENNIFER WALKER, meeting planner, group travel and internat. trade cons. co. exec.; b. San Francisco, Feb. 9, 1949; d. Leon and Rebecca (Hudson) Walker; B.A. in Social Sci., Calif. State U., San Jose, 1973; m. Curley Coleman, Sept. 4, 1976. Fiscal technician NASA Ames Research, Moffit Field, Calif., 1972-73; account technician Oakland (Calif.) Head Start, 1973-74; free-lance cons., 1974-76; sr. accountant San Francisco Housing Authority, 1976-78, internal auditor, 1977-78; group travel coordinator Atlas Travel Service, San Francisco, 1977—; controller D.D.&A., Cons., San Francisco, 1978-79, also dir.; owner, operator Bus. Interaction Exchange, Oakland, 1979—; affirmative action counselor NASA; bd. dirs. Oakland Small Bus. Export Task Force. Exec. sec. East Bay chpt. Black C. of C.-Oakland, 1980—; mem. conv. activity com. Oakland-Conv. and Tourist Bur., 1980—. Recipient Sales award Norwegian Caribbean Cruise Line, 1978. Mem. Am. Entrepreneurs Assn., Black Am. Polit. Assn. Calif., Black C. of C., Black Women Organized for Polit. Action, Inst. Reading Devel., NAACP, Oakland C. of C. (internat. trade com. 1980—), Oakland Together, Meeting Planners Internat. Democrat. Baptist. Choreographer for plays Calif. State U., San Jose, 1971-72. Home: 4136 Carrington St Oakland CA 94601 Office: 1247 5th Ave Suite 4 Oakland CA 94606

COLEMAN, MELVIN ASHER, endodontist; b. N.Y.C., Sept. 20, 1932; s. William and Ray C.; B.A., Western Res. U., 1954, D.D.S., 1958; children—Michael, Mitchell. Private dentistry specializing in endodontics, Orange, Calif., 1962—; cons. in endodontics VA Hosp., Long Beach, Calif. Served with USAF, 1959-62. Mem. ADA, Calif. Dental Assn., Orange County Dental Soc., So. Calif. Acad. Endodontics (pres. 1975-76), Western Soc. Periodontology. Office: 1000 W La Veta Ave Suite 402 Orange CA 92668

COLEMAN, MICHAEL B., painter; b. Provo, Utah, June 25, 1946; s. Blaine L. and Kathryn (Anderson) C.; m. Jacqueline Morgan, June 1, 1978; children—Michael, Jennifer, Nicholas. Student Brigham Young U., 1968. Group shows include: Springville Mus., Nat. Cowboy Hall of Fame, Oklahoma City, Wunderlich & Co., N.Y.C.; represented in permanent collections: Buffalo Bill Hist. Mus., Cody, Wyo., Kennedy Gallery, N.Y.C.; dealer: Kennedy Gallery.

COLEMAN, MIKI LYNNE, applied biostatistician; b. Butler, Pa., June 20, 1949; d. Otis William and Clara Louise Bosworth. B.S. in Math., Utah State U., 1971, M.S. in Applied Stats, 1972. Math. programmer Kaiser Engineers, Oakland, Calif., 1972; asst. data processing mgr. Huish Distbg. Co., Salt Lake City, 1973; biostatistician, programmer div. of biostats. U. Utah Coll. of Medicine, Salt Lake City, 1972-75, assoc. instr., 1975-78, applied biostatistician, 1978—. Mem. Am. Statis. Assn., Biometric Soc.

COLEMAN, NORMAN ARTHUR, insurance company executive; b. New Philadelphia, Ohio, Mar. 4, 1923; s. Harrison Arthur and Margaret Ersman (Campbell) C.; B.S., Northwestern U., 1947; postgrad. U. Ky., 1947-48; m. Yvonne Lou Cotterman, Apr. 7, 1956; 1 son, Matt Arthur. Salesman, Youngen Ins. Agy., New Philadelphia, 1949-59; pres. CBS Ins., Colorado Springs, Colo., 1959—; dir. Air Acad. Nat. Bank. Trustee U.S. Naval Acad. Found. Served to rear adm. USNR. Mem. Soc. C.P.C.U.s, Navy League U.S., Naval Reserve Assn. Clubs: Army and Navy, Broadmoor Golf. Home: 2223 Glen Summer Rd Colorado Springs CO 80909 Office: PO Box 1900 Colorado Springs CO 80901

COLEMAN, REXFORD LEE, lawyer; b. Hollywood, Calif., June 2, 1930; s. Henry Eugene and Antoinette Christine (Dobry) C.; student Claremont McKenna Coll., 1947-49; A.B., Stanford U., 1951, J.D., 1955; M.Jurisprudence, Tokyo U., 1960; m. Aiko Takahashi, Aug. 28, 1953 (div.); children—Christine Eugenie, Douglass Craig; m. 2d, Sucha Park, June 15, 1978. Bar: Calif. 1955, Mass. 1969. Mem. faculty Harvard U., 1959-69; mem. firm Baker & McKenzie, San Francisco, 1969-83, income ptnr., 1971-73, capital ptnr., 1973-83, head Tokyo office, 1971-78; sr. ptnr. Coleman & Gresser (The Pacific Law Group), Los Angeles, 1983—; cons. U.S. Treasury Dept., 1961-70; counselor Japanese-Am. Soc. Legal Studies, 1964—; guest lectr. Ford Seminar Comparative History, MIT, 1968; lectr. Legal Tng. and Research Inst., Supreme Ct. Japan, 1970-73; chmn. fgn. bus. customs consultative com. Bur. Customs, Ministry of Fin., Japan, 1971-72, chmn. fgn. bus. consulatative commn. Japanese Ministry of Internat. Trade and Industry, 1973-76. Served to 1st lt., inf., AUS, 1951-53; now lt. col. Res. Mem. Japanese-Am. Soc. Legal Studies, Internat. Law Assn. Japan, Nihon Shiho Gakkai, Nihon Kokusai Ho Gakkai, Nihon Kokusai Shiho Gakkai, Sozei Ho Gakkai, Nihon Sozei Kenkyu Kyokai, Assn. Asian Studies, Am. Polit. Sci. Assn., Internat. Studies Assn., Internat. Fiscal Assn. (Japan and U.S.), Acad. Polit. Sci., Am. Acad. Polit. and Social Sci., Am. Soc. Internat. Law, Am. Fgn. Law Assn., Am. Bar Assn., Am. C. of C. in Japan, Mil. Govt. Assn., Res. Officers Assn. (v.p. army dept. Far East 1974-75), Pacific Basin Econ. Council, State Bar Calif., Mass. Bar Assn., Japan-Calif. Assn., U.S. Army JAG Sch. Alumni Assn., Internat. House Japan, Stanford U. Alumni Assn., Phi Alpha Delta, Gakushi Kai. Episcopalian. Clubs: Tokyo Am.; Harvard (N.Y.C.); Los Angeles Marina City; North Ranch Country. Author: American Index to Japanese Law, 1961; Standard Citation of Japanese Legal Materials, 1963; The Legal Aspects Under Japanese Law of an Accident Involving a Nuclear Installation in Japan, 1963; An Index to Japanese Law, 1975; editor: Taxation in Japan, World Tax Series, 1959—; Japanese Ann. Internat. Law, 1970—; chmn. bd. editors Law in Japan: An Ann., 1964-67. Office: 1900 Ave of Stars 4th Floor Los Angeles CA 90067

COLEMAN, ROBERT TRENT, vocational rehabilitation counselor, consultant human relations; b. Gary, Ind., Feb. 4, 1936; s. Robert Clinton and Lucille Verna C.; m. Dorothy Agnes, Aug. 1957; children—Sean, Bryce, Daniel; m. 2d, Patricia Lou, June 13, 1976. B.A. in Speech Therapy, U. Wash., Seattle, 1962; postgrad. in speech U. Redlands, 1963-64; M.S. in Rehab. Counseling, U. Oreg., 1971. Cert. rehab. counselor; nat. cert. counselor. Social worker, San Bernardino City Welfare Dept., 1963-64; correctional counselor Calif. Rehab. Center, Norco, 1964-67; sr. counselor Job Corps, Clearfield, Utah, 1967; assoc. dir. Ednl. Systems Corp., Washington, 1968-69; ptnr. Black Fir Jade Mines, Big Sur, Calif., 1971-76; vocat. specialist Internat. Rehab. Assn., San Diego, 1976-77; vocat. rehab. counselor Sharp Hosp., San Diego, 1977-80; clin. coordinator San Diego Pain Inst., 1981; cons. in rehab. counseling, career guidance, human relations, Carlsbad, Calif., 1981-83; Commr., cons. human resource mgmt., Escondido and San Diego, 1983—. Commr., Handicapped Appeals Commn., San Marcos, Calif., 1981—. Served with U.S. Army, 1955-58. Mem. Am. Personnel Guidance Assn. (pres.), San Diego Career Guidance Assn. (pres. 1984), Assn. Indsl. Rehab. Reps. (pres. 1983), Am. Rehab. Counseling Assn. Republican. Home: 538 Glenheather Dr San Marcos CA 92069 Office: 2165 San Diego Ave Suite 106 San Diego CA 92110

COLEMAN, ROGER DIXON, bacteriologist; b. Rockwell, Iowa, Jan. 18, 1915; s. Major C. and Hazel Ruth Coleman; A.B., UCLA, 1937; postgrad. Balliol Coll., Oxford (Eng.) U., 1944; M.S., U. So. Calif., 1952, Ph.D., 1957; m. Lee Aden Skov, Jan. 1, 1978. Sr. laboratorian Napa (Calif.) State Hosp., 1937-42; dir. Long Beach (Calif.) Clin. Lab., 1946—, pres., 1980—; mem. Calif. State Clin. Lab. Commn., 1953-57. Served as officer AUS, 1942-46. Diplomate Am. Bd. Bioanalysts. Mem. Am. Assn. Bioanalysts, Am. Assn. Clin. Chemists, Am. Soc. Microbiologists, Am. Chem. Soc., Am. Venereal Disease Assn., AAAS (life), Calif. Assn. Bioanalysts (past officer), Med. Research Assn. Calif., Bacteriology Club So. Calif., Sigma Xi, Phi Sigma (past chpt. pres.). Author papers in field. Home: 978 Palo Verde Ave Long Beach CA 90815 Office: 320 Pine Ave Suite 415 Long Beach CA 90802

COLEMAN, WILLIAM EDWARD, psychologist; b. Utica, N.Y., May 30, 1921; s. Michael and Mildred (Hoffman) C.; B.A., Ohio State U., 1942, M.A., 1946, Ph.D., 1949; m. June Charna Juster, Oct. 3, 1943; children—Nancy, Lawrence, Karen. Asst. prof., then dir. testing and guidance U. Tenn., 1947-56; human factors scientist RAND Corp., 1956-60; dir. psychol. services Ward J. Jensen Co., 1960-61; pres. Coleman & Assocs., mgmt. psychologists, Santa Monica, Calif., 1961—; instr. UCLA; lectr. Calif. Inst. Tech. Bd. dirs. Santa Monica Area NCCJ, 1970-73. Served with U.S. Army, 1942-46. Decorated Bronze Star, Purple Heart. Fellow Am. Psychol. Assn.; life mem. Am. Personnel and Guidance Assn. Democrat. Author: Pictorial Intelligence Test, 1960, Life Goals Inventory, 1966. Home: 349 Euclid St Santa Monica CA 90402 Office: 1640 5th St Santa Monica CA 90401

COLENZO, SALVATORE JOHN, psychiat. social worker; b. Utica, N.Y., Dec. 14, 1942; s. Lugo Peter and Concetta Margaret (Armao) C.; B.A., U. Toronto, 1964; M.S.W., U. Ottawa, 1966; m. Patricia Jean Posney, Nov. 26, 1970; children—Karin Jean, Kenneth John, Kristi Joy. Caseworker, Family Service Agy. of Greater Utica, 1966-67; clin. instr. social work U. Calif., Davis, 1974-78, asst. clin. prof., 1978-80; clin. social worker, coordinator partial hospitalization program U. Med. Center, Sacramento, 1970-79; caseworker Yolo County (Calif.) Family Service Agy., Davis, 1978-81; clin. social worker Kaiser Permanente Med. Center, Sacramento, 1979—; instr. Solano Community Coll., 1970-78; instr. Calif. State U., Sacramento, 1975-76, adj. prof., 1979-80; oral commr. Calif. Lic. Clin. Social Work Exams., 1977—, Calif. Marriage, Family and Child Counselor Exams, 1982—. Bd. dirs. Sacramento Drug Abuse Coordinating Council, 1971-72, mem. adv. bd., 1972-73; mem. Sacramento County Tech. Adv. Bd. Drug Abuse, 1973-74; cons. Yolo County Pregnancy Hotline, 1979—. Served to capt., USAF, 1967-70; Vietnam. Decorated Bronze Star; lic. clin. social worker, marriage, family and child counselor, Calif.; cert. social worker, N.Y.; cert. jr. coll. tchr., Calif. Mem. Nat. Assn. Social Workers, Acad. Cert. Social Workers. Democrat. Roman Catholic. Home: 812 Burr St Davis CA 95616 Office: 2008 Morse Ave Sacramento CA 95825

COLER, JOEL H., motion picture company executive; b. Bronx, N.Y., July 27, 1931; s. Irving A. and Pauline (Leader) C.; B.A. in Journalism and Sociology, Syracuse U., 1953; m. Sandra Cohen, Oct. 10, 1959; children—Karen, Linda. With NBC, N.Y.C., 1955-59, advt. asst., 1955-59; asst. account exec. Grey Advt. Inc., N.Y.C., 1959-64; dir. internat. advt. and publicity 20th Century Fox Film Corp., Los Angeles, 1964-81, v.p. advt. and publicity 20th Century Fox Internat., 1981—; film industry rep. Scandinavia Today Com. Mem. adv. bd. local pvt. schs.; mem. Los Angeles Olympic Adv. Com., 1982—. Served to capt. USAF, 1953-55. Mem. Motion Picture Acad., N.Y. Fgn. Press Assn. Home: 18744 Kenya St Northridge CA 91326 Office: 10201 W Pico Blvd Los Angeles CA 90213

COLES, FRANCES SCOTT, criminal law educator; b. Dumfries, Scotland, Nov. 23, 1947; came to U.S., 1969; s. Francis Eagland and Isabella Miller (Scott) C.; LL.B. with honors, Edinburgh U. (Scotland), 1969; M. Criminology U. Calif.-Berkeley, 1970, D.Criminology, 1975. Assoc. dir. Women's Ctr., U. Calif.-Berkeley, 1972-73; coordinator criminal justice Claremont (Calif.) Grad. Sch., 1975-77; dean admissions and fin. aid Boalt Hall Law Sch., U. Calif.-Berkeley, 1973-75; lectr. U. Calif.-Irvine, 1977-78; assoc. Prof., chair. criminal justice dept., coordinator paralegal programs Calif. State Coll., San Bernardino, 1978—; sentencing cons. Bd. dirs. San Bernardino County Sexual Assault Services. Edn. Abroad scholar, 1969; Richard Brown scholar, 1969. Mem. Am. Soc. Criminology, Am. Sociol. Assn., Western Soc. Criminology, Pacific Sociol. Assn., Assn. Criminal Justice Research (dir.). Contbr. articles to profl. jours. Office: 5500 State Coll Parkway San Bernardino CA 92407

COLES, JOAN DARLENE, retail exec.; b. Webb City, Mo., Jan. 17, 1941; d. Francis Wesley and Lottie Elizabeth (Benson) Lorton; A.A., Pasadena City Coll., East Los Angeles Coll., 1970; degree in Psychology, Calif. State U., Los Angeles, 1975; m. Clarence W. Coles, Jan. 18, 1981; children—Lottie Elizabeth, Mark Andrew Van Volkenburg; foster son, Michael Raymond Morris. Sec., Los Angeles Public Defender, 1958; sec. Methodist and Presbyterian ministers, 1966-70; receptionist Pennington Wholesale Grocery Co., Los Angeles, 1972, order desk, 1973-74, sales supr., 1975-78, sales mgr., 1978-81; owner The Wabbitt Hutch restaurant, Arcadia, Calif., 1981—; pres. JC and CJ, Inc., Arcadia, 1981—; v.p., ptnr. Seloc Publs. Active PTA, Liaison League, Found. Jr. Blind, Calif. Taxpayers Assn. Mem. Retail Mchts. Assn., Arcadia C. of C., Bay Area Restaurant Assn., LWV, NOW. Office: 10693 Civic Center Dr Rancho Cucamonga CA 91730

COLESBERRY, HARRY THOMAS, food company executive; b. Washington, Pa., Dec. 2, 1947; s. Harry Collingswood and Henrietta Ann (Gobleck) C.; m. Darlene Jean Beward, Mar. 5, 1968; m. 2d, Rosanna Marie Martin, June 9, 1979; children—Julian Thomas, Danielle Lorraine. B.S., Pa. State U., 1969; M.B.A., Pepperdine U., 1977. C.P.A., Calif. Acct., Coopers & Lybrand, Pitts., 1969-71, Golub, Frankel & Lodgen, Encino, Calif., 1971-75; controller L.A. Beefland, Inc., Los Angeles, 1975-79; fin. analyst Calif. Growers Winery, Cutler, 1979-80; v.p. fin., sec., controller Ruiz Food Products, Inc., Tulare, Calif., 1980—; cons. in field. Bd. dirs., vol. fitness dir. Visalia (Calif.) YMCA. Served with USMC, 1969-71. Democrat. Roman Catholic. Club: Rotary. Home: 2133 E Westcott Ave Visalia CA 93277 Office: Ruiz Food Products Inc 1025 E Bardsley Ave Tulare CA 93275

COLGIN, RUSSELL WEYMOUNT, clinical psychologist, consultant screenwriter, producer; b. Ontonagon, Mich., May 10, 1925; s. Russell W. and Signe E. (Peterson) C.; divorced; children—Dennis, Russell, Marc, Kevin, Sean, Siobhan. B.S., Lake Forest Coll., 1949, M.A., 1950; Ph.D., Northwestern U., 1953. Cert. clin. psychologist, Calif. Psychologist VA Hosp., Downey, Ill., 1949; asst. prof. Lake Forest Coll. (Ill.), 1950-53; asst. prof. North Park Coll., Chgo., 1951-53; pvt. practice clin. psychology, 1953—; cons. to Big Bros. of Los Angeles 1965-78, Midtown Sch., Los Angeles, 1968-78; instr. Los Angeles State U., Northridge, 1965-66; producer, chmn. bd. Star Cinema Prodns., Hollywood, Calif., 1980—. Served with USN, 1942-45. Mem. Am. Psychol. Assn., Los Angeles County Psychol. Assn., AAUP, Los Angeles World Affairs Council, Sigma Xi. Club: Rotary of Los Angeles. Contbr. articles to profl. jours.; screenwriter Young Warriors, 1982. Office: 648 N Doheny Dr Los Angeles CA 90069

COLLAS, JUAN G., lawyer; b. Manila, Philippines, Apr. 25, 1932; s. Juan D. and Soledad M. (Garduno) C.; m. Maria L. Moreira, Aug. 1, 1959; children—Juan Jose, Elias Lopes, Cristina Maria, Daniel Benjamin. LL.B., U. Philippines, 1955; LL.M., Yale U., 1958, J.S.D., 1959. Assoc. Sycip, Quisumbing, Salazar & Assocs., Manila, Philippines, 1956-57; atty. N.Y., New Haven & Hartford R.R. Co., New Haven, 1959; assoc. Baker & McKenzie, Chgo., 1960-63, ptnr., Manila, 1963-70, San Francisco, 1970—. Mem. San Francisco Manila Sister Cities Com. Named Outstanding Filipino Overseas in Law, 1979. Mem. Filipino-Am. C. of C. (v.p.), Filipino Profls. and Businessmen's Assn., Calif. State Bar Assn., Ill. State Bar Assn., Integrated Bar Philippines, ABA, San Francisco Lawyers Club. Republican. Roman Catholic. Clubs: San Francisco Comml., Villa Taverna (San Francisco); Greenhills Country (Millbrae). Contbr. articles to profl. jours.

COLLER, RICHARD WALTER, sociology educator; b. St. Paul, Aug. 29, 1925; s. Walter A. and Helen E. (Kretz) C.; m. Alicia Mabuhay Peruda, Aug. 12, 1950; children—Louis, Margarite, Ann, James, Katherine, Susan, William, Mark, Clair, Ruth, Patrick. B.A., U. Minn., 1948, Ph.D., 1959; M.A., U. Hawaii, 1951. Lectr., U. of East, Manila, 1951; instr., then prof. sociology U. Philippines, Quezon City, 1952-62; tng. instr. Peace Corps, Hilo, Hawaii, 1962-66; prof. sociology Kauai Community Coll., Lihue Kauai, Hawaii, 1966—. Served with U.S. Army, 1943-46. Mem. Community Coll. Social Sci. Assn., Soc. Applied Anthropology, Am. Sociol. Assn., Philippine Studies Assn. Roman Catholic. Club: Filipino Cath. of St. Catherine's Parish. Author: Barrio Gacao, 1962; co-author: Sociology in the Philippine Setting, 1954. Home: 4911 Lani Rd Kapaa HI 96746 Office: 3-1901 Kaumualii Hwy Lihue HI 96766

COLLETTE, CRAIG DELORNE, banker; b. Boise, Idaho, Aug. 9, 1942; s. Dale DeLorne and Grace (Leatham) C.; m. Penny, Jan. 29, 1965; children—Jason, Shannon, Todd. B.A., Brigham Young U., 1966;

M.B.A., U. So. Calif., 1968. Investment banker Birr-Wilson, San Francisco, 1968-70; regional v.p. Bank Calif., San Francisco, 1970-78; pres., chief exec. officer, dir. Landmark Bank, La Habra, Calif., 1979—; dir. local devel. corp.; prof. bus. Calif. State U.-Los Angeles. Active Orange County C. of C.; v.p., dir. Neighborhood Housing Services; bd. dirs. Boys' and Girls' Club La Habra. Recipient Businessman of Yr. award City of Oakland, 1975, YMCA, 1975; Claremont fellow, 1970. Mem. Calif. Bankers Assn., Western Ind. Bankers Assn. Republican. Mem. Ch. Jesus Christ of Latter-day Saints Club: Rotary.

COLLEY, NATHANIEL SEXTUS, lawyer; b. Carlowsville, Ala., Nov. 21, 1918; s. L.D. and Fannie C. (Jones) C.; B.S. with highest honors, Tuskegee Inst., 1941; LL.B., Yale U., 1948; m. Jerlean Jackson, May 16, 1942; children—Jerlean Evelyn (Mrs. Jack L. Daniel), Ola Marie (Mrs. O. Alfred Brown), Natalie Suzanne (Mrs. Gary P. Lindsey), Sondra Aileen, Nathaniel Sextus. Bar: Calif. 1949. Mem. firm Colley & Sakuma, 1952-56; sr. ptnr. Colley & McGhee, Attys. at Law, Sacramento, 1963-71; Nathaniel S. Colley, Inc., 1973—; lectr. U. Calif. Continuing Edn. of Bar Program, 1965-71, Calif. Trial Lawyers Seminars, 1968-74; part-time prof. law U. of Pacific, 1971—. Pres. Calif. Fedn. Civic Unity, 1963-64; mem. Calif. State Bd. Edn., 1960-63; commr. Calif. Horse Racing Bd., chmn., 1977—; bd. dirs. Nat. Com. Against Discrimination in Housing, 1967-70, Charles F. Kettering Found., 1973—; trustee Tuskegee Inst. Served to capt. AUS, 1942-44. Mem. ABA, Calif., Sacramento County (dir. 1967-70) bar assns., Am., Calif. trial lawyers assns., NAACP (nat. dir. 1958—, Western regional counsel 1958—, chmn. nat. legal com. 1982—), Yale Law Sch. Assn. (exec. com.). Home: 5441 Pleasant Dr Sacramento CA 95822 Office: 1810 S St Sacramento CA 95814

COLLIER, BARBARA ANN, management training firm executive, consultant; b. Dallas, Tex., Jan. 1942; d. Eugene Ross and Thelma Cleo (Morris) C.; m. Richard William Deilke, Mar. 20, 1965 (div.); 1 son, Ross Addison Deilke. B.A. in English and Latin, Tex. Tech. U., 1964; postgrad. Pepperdine U., 1974-75; M.A. in Human Resource Devel., Univ. Assocs., San Diego, 1981. Secondary teaching cert. Caif., Tex., S.C., N.J. Tchr. high shcs. Tex, N.J., S.C., 1964-68; supr. social services San Diego County, San Diego, 1968-74; tng. specialist employee devel. and tng., 1974-79; prin. Collier Enterprises, San Diego, 1979—; regional rep. Monroe Inst. Applied Scis. (Va.); lectr. Recipient Helen Reddy award San Diego Women's Opportunity Week, 1981. Mem. Am. Soc. Tng. and Devel. (v.p. fin.; 1984 conf. chmn.), San Diego Career Guidance Assn. (dir.). Author: Career Transitions Guide, 1981. Home: 8552 Golden Ridge Rd Lakeside CA 92040 Office: 929 Turquoise St San Diego CA 92109

COLLIER, DOUGLAS WAYNE, JR., food service design and construction company executive, consultant, b. Indpls., Sept. 23, 1940, s. Douglas Wayne and Ethel Jeanne (Workman) C.; m. Judith Sue Pruyn, Nov. 27, 1963 (div.); m. 2d, Catherine Leach, Sept. 13, 1980; 1 son, Douglas Wayne III. Student Purdue U., 1962, Los Angeles Valley Coll., 1963-66, UCLA, 1970-71. Cert in real estate and site selection Nat. Restaurant Assn. Designer, Parvin Dohrmann Corp., Los Angeles, 1963-68; dir. equipment and fixtures Internat. Industries, Inc., Beverly Hills, Calif., 1968-76; v.p. Design Concept, Inc., Phoenix, 1976-80; pres. Dougals Collier & Assocs., Inc., Phoenix, 1980—; cons. food service; lectr. Purdue U., Scottsdale Community Coll., Ariz. State U.; mem. Nat. Housing Adv. Panel, 1979. Chmn., Republican Legis. Dist., Phoenix, 1980-82; pres. Scottsdale (Ariz.) Rep. Forum, 1982; program chmn. Phoenix Rep. Forum, 1981-83, mem. Ariz. Rep. State Com., 1980-84, bd. dirs. Central Ariz. Mus. History, Phoenix. Served with USMC, 1958-66. Recipient award of commendation, Ariz. State U. Coll. Architecture, 1981; Food Facilities Design award Sheraton Tucson El Conquistador Golf and Tennis Resort, 1983. Mem. Internat. Foodservice Execs. Assn., Ariz. Restaurant Assn., Ariz. Hotel/Motel Assn., Am. Polit. Items Collectors, Ariz. Archeol. Soc., Ariz. Assn. Fine Woodworkers. Club: Masons (Scottsdale). Designer numerous projects including: MGM Grand Hotel fire remodel and new tower, Las Vegas, Nev., El Conquistador Resort and Conf. Center, Tucson, Villa Monterey Country Club, Scottsdale, Wrangler's, Scottsdale, Missouri & Phoenix, Metro Plaza Hotel Phoenix, and Beside the Pointe, Phoenix. Office: 1627 N 40th St Phoenix AZ 85008

COLLIER, RICHARD BANGS, found. exec.; b. Hastings, Nebr., Aug. 12, 1918; s. Nelson Martin and Stella (Butler) C.; B.A., U. Wash., 1951. Fgn. aid officer GS14, civil aviation Am. embassy, Bangkok, Thailand, 1958-63; founder, dir. Pleneurethic Internat., Spokane, Wash., 1963—. Carnegie fellow Inst. Public Affairs, Grad. Sch., U. Wash., 1950-51. Nat. adv. bd. Am. Security Council. Served to capt. USAF, 1965-66. Mem. Assn. Supervision and Curriculum Devel., Acad. of Polit. Sci., AAAS, Royal Inst. Philosophy (Eng.), Senatorial Club. Republican. Author Pleneurethic, 13 vols., 1964-81. Home: PO Box 6326 Kennewick WA 99336

COLLIER, ROBERT MICHAEL, specialty packaging company executive; b. San Francisco, July 24, 1929; s. William Alfred and Ruby Edith (Pronzzeni) C.; m. Lou Ann Phillips, Aug. 21, 1956; 1 son, William Todd. A.A., Coll. San Mateo, 1956; B.A., San Francisco State Coll., 1957; M.B.A., Stanford U., 1960. Gen. mgr. sales Mobil Chem. and Mobil Plastics, 1960-70; v.p., mng. dir. European ops. Mobil Chem., 1970-72, v.p., gen. mgr. Mobil Plastics, 1973-77; v.p., gen. mgr. flexible packaging Crown Zellerbach, 1978-82; sr. v.p., gen. mgr. Splty. Packaging & Chem. Co., San Francisco, 1982—. Vice pres., bd. dirs. Woodland (Calif.) United Fund, 1968-71; mem. adv. bd. taxation Woodland City Council, 1970-71; bd. dirs. Rochester (N.Y.) United Fund, 1974-76. Served to 1st lt. U.S. Army, 1949-54. Mem. Nat. Flexible Packaging Assn. (West Coast chmn. 1969-70), Packaging Edn. Found. (v.p., dir.), Flexible Packaging Assn. (dir.). Republican. Roman Catholic. Club: San Francisco Stock Exchange. Home: 3484 LaMesa St San Carlos CA 94070 Office: 1 Bush St Suite 1863 San Francisco CA 94104

COLLIER, WILLYE PEARL JORDAN, nutritionist, educator; b. Hattiesburg, Miss., Sept. 26, 1922; d. Eugene M. and Effie A. (Campbell) Jordan; m. Petros B. Mdodana, Aug. 29, 1949 (dec.); m. 2d Cisero V. Collier, Dec. 20, 1973; B.S. Tuskegee Inst., 1943; M.S. U. Wis., 1946. Head, Home Econs. Dept. Benedict Coll., Columbia S.C., 1946-49; home economist, mgr. sch. lunch program, S.C. Pub. Schs., Columbia, 1949-56; dir. Dietetic Program So. U., Baton Rouge, 1956-58; dietetic cons. Los Angeles and San Luis Obispo Counties, Calif., 1958-64; chmn. home econs. dept., San Luis Obispo City Schs., 1960-64; prof. food, nutrition, dir. dietetic program, Bakersfield (Calif.) Coll., 1964—. Mem. Am. Heart Assn., Mental Health Assn. Kern County (Calif.), Nat. Council Negro Women; LWV, NAACP, YWCA. Recipient Who award, Calif. Higher Edn. Assn. Mem. Am. Home Econs. Assn., Calif. Home Econs. Assn. (Outstanding Home Economist), Internat. Home Econs. Assn.; Calif. Tchrs. Assn.; NEA; Am. Dietetic Assn., Calif. Dietetic Assn. Democrat. Baptist. Club: Links, Inc. (Bakersfield). Home: 422 9th St Bakersfield CA 93304 Office: 1801 Panorama Dr Bakersfield CA 93305

COLLIER-EVANS, DEMETRA FRANCES, vocational educator, social worker; b. Nashville, Dec. 18, 1937; d. Oscar and M. Earllee (Williams) Collier Sheffield; m. Richard A. Gotha, Feb. 2, 1961; m. 2d George P. Evans, Dec. 21, 1966; 1 son, Richard E. A.A., Soland Community Coll., 1974; B.A. in Sociology and Econs., Chapman Coll., 1981. Cert. tchr., Calif. Wives ombudman Naval Schs. Command, Vallejo, Calif., 1972-74; case responsible person State of Calif., 1975-82; vocat. tchr. pub. adminstrn. service San Diego Community Coll. Dist., 1982—; cons. women's seminars. Rec. sec. San Diego chpt. NAACP, 1981-82; mem. San Diego Mus. Art, Ctr. Women's Studies Service, San Diego, Nat. Assn. YWCA, Friends of San Diego Pub. Library. Served in USAF, 1956-59. Recipient Cert. of Excellence, San Diego Employer Adv. Bd., 1981, Cert. of Leadership, Nat. U. San Diego, 1981. Mem. Nat. Assn. Female Execs., Black Advs. in State Service (San Diego chpt.), DAV, Chapman Coll. Alumni Assn., AAUW, Alpha Gamma Sigma. Clubs: Commanders, Base (San Diego). Created women's seminar for women's opportunity week, San Diego, 1982. Office: Educational Cultural Complex 4343 Oceanview Blvd San Diego 92113

COLLIGNON, FREDERICK CONRAD, JR., economist, city planner; b. Balt., Dec. 17, 1943; s. Frederick Conrad and Margaret Ann (Roeder) C.; B.A. summa cum laude (Carnegie Found. European Research fellow), Columbia U., 1965; M.A. in Polit. Economy and Govt., Harvard U., 1968, Ph.D. (V.O. Key fellow), 1973; m. Joan Frenier Hauserman, Apr. 11, 1970; children—Katherine DuBois, Genevieve Anne, Robert Frederick Hauserman. Legis. asst. to U.S. Rep. Clarence D. Long, Md., Washington, 1963, 65; program analyst and budget examiner Bur. of Budget, Exec. Office of Pres., Washington, 1966-67; sr. economist Abt Assos., Inc., Cambridge, Mass., 1968-70; chmn., asso. prof. dept. city and regional planning U. Calif., Berkeley, 1970—, chmn. dept., 1981—; pres. Berkeley Planning Assos., Berkeley, 1973—; econ. cons. Pres.'s Conf. on Inflation, 1975; mem. Nat. Task Force for Program Evaluation for Employment Programs for Disabled, 1972; cons. to govtl. agys. Mem. adv. bd. Center for Independent Living, Berkeley, 1973—; mem. adv. bd. City of Berkeley Planning Commn., 1977-82, pres., 1979-82; mem. adv. bd. City of Berkeley Univ.-Community Affairs Commn., 1974-75, City of Berkeley Housing Task Force, 1973-74, 80-81; pres. Tom Paine Democratic Club, Berkeley, 1973-75; co-chmn. Berkeley Dem. Alliance, 1978-79. Recipient numerous research grants. Mem. Am. Inst. of Planners, Am. Econ. Assn., Am. Polit. Sci. Assn., Regional Sci. Assn. Author: Evaluation of Federal Interagency Demonstrations for Neighborhood Service Center Programs, 1968; The Causes of Rural to Urban Migration Among the Poor, 1970; Benefit-Cost Analysis and Evaluation of Federal Vocational Rehabilitation Programs, 1973; Evaluation of National Demonstrations for Child Abuse and Neglect, 1977. Home: 2615 Woolsey St Berkeley CA 94705 Office: Berkeley Planning Associates 3200 Adeline St Berkeley CA 94703

COLLINGS, MICHAEL ROBERT, educator; b. Rupert, Idaho, Oct. 29, 1947; s. Ralph Willard and Thella Marie (Hurd) C.; A.A., Bakersfield Coll., 1967; B.A., Whittier Coll., 1969; M.A. (NDEA fellow 1971-73), U. Calif., Riverside, 1973, Ph.D., 1977; m. Judith Lynn Reeve, Dec. 21, 1973; children—Michael Brent, Erika Marie, Ethan Hunt, Kendra Elayne. Teaching asst., assoc. in English, U. Calif., Riverside, 1973-78; instr. English lit. and creative writing San Bernardino (Calif.) Community Coll., Crafton Hills Coll., 1976-78; lectr. English, UCLA, 1978-79; assoc. prof. Pepperdine U., Malibu, Calif., 1979—. Mem. Poets and Writers, Inc., So. Calif. C.S. Lewis Soc. (editor Lamp-Post), Sci. Fiction Poetry Assn., Sci. Fiction Research Assn., Small Press Writers and Artists Assn. Author: A Season of Calm Weather (poetry), 1974. Contbr. poetry, fiction and critical articles in field to profl. jours. Office: Pepperdine Univ Communications Div Malibu CA 90265

COLLINS, BRUCE ALAN, consulting geologist; b. Greensboro, N.C., Dec. 27, 1944; s. Alan Charles and Beatrice Irene (Bramble) C.; B.A., Coll. Wooster, 1966; M.Sc., Colo. Sch. Mines, 1971, Ph.D., 1975; m. Betty Jeanne Estes, Aug. 19, 1966; children—Brian Scott, Bethany Alana. Geologist, Eastern Associated Coal Corp., Pitts., 1971-74, Mid-Continent Coal & Coke Co., Carbondale, Colo., 1974-78; dir. property devel. Western Associated Coal Corp., Denver, 1978-83; cons. geologist, 1983—; supt. Blue Ribbon Coal Co., 1981. Gulf Oil Corp. fellow, 1969-71. Mem. AAAS, Am. Chem. Soc., Am. Assn. Petroleum Geologists, Nat. Ry. Hist. Soc., Soc. Mining Engrs., Rocky Mountain Coal Mining Inst., Rocky Mountain Assn. Geologists, Geol. Soc. Am., Soc. Econ. Paleontologists and Mineralogists, Ry. and Locomotive Hist. Soc., Sigma Xi. Contbr. articles in field to profl. jours. Home: 1398 4060 Rd Paonia CO 81428 Office: 1398 4060 Rd Paonia CO 81428

COLLINS, DANIEL ANDREW, dentist; b. Darlington, S.C., Jan. 11, 1916; s. Andrew Sumner and Lucy (Miller) C.; A.B., Paine Coll., 1936; D.D.S., Meharry Med. Coll., 1941; certificate, Guggenheim Dental Clinic for Children, 1942; M.S.D., U. Calif., 1944; m. DeReath Curtis James, Aug. 28, 1941; children—Daniel A., Edward J., Charles M., Craig S. Mem. faculty U. Calif., 1942-60, asst. prof. Coll. Dentistry, 1949-60; pvt. dental practice, San Francisco, 1945-76; founder, sec. Beneficial Savs. and Loan Assn., Oakland, Calif.; exec. dir., pres. urban edn. div. Harcourt Brace Jovanovich, Inc., San Francisco, also dir., N.Y.C.; sr. v.p. H.B.J. Properties Inc.; dir. Natomas Co., San Francisco. Mem. Pres.'s Nat. Adv. Com. SSS; mem. Gov.'s Com. on Med. Aid and Health Mayor's Com. on Youth; mem. Calif. Bd. Pub. Health, 1961-63, Calif. Bd. Edn., 1963-69, Pres.'s Health Resource Adv. Com. bd. dirs. San Francisco br. NAACP, Radio Free Europe, Radio Liberty, San Francisco Found. for Aged Colored People, Plan of Action for Changing Times (PACT), Youth Service United Bay Area Crusade, Booker T. Washington Community Center chmn. bd. trustees Paine Coll.; trustee Meharry Med. Coll., Golden Gate U. Served to lt. col., Dental Corps, AUS. Recipient Distinguished Alumnus award United Negro Coll. Fund, 1953. Diplomate Am. Bd. Oral Pathology. Fellow Internat. Coll. Dentistry, AAAS, Royal Soc. Health, Sigma Xi; mem. Am., Nat., Calif. (del.) dental assns., Am. Acad. Oral Pathology, Fedn. Dentaire Internat., San Francisco Dental Soc. (dir.), Internat. Assn. Pathology, U. Calif. Dental Coll. Alumni Assn., Nat. Urban League (trustee, v.p.), Omicron Kappa Upsilon, Alpha Phi Alpha, Sigma Pi Phi. Democrat. Author: Your Teeth: A Handbook of Dental Care for the Whole Family, 1967; also articles in profl. jours. Contbr. to Growth and Development of the Negro in Dentistry in U.S., 1952, Oral Pathology. Address: 2449 Sutter St San Francisco CA 94115

COLLINS, DONNA JEAN, business management consultant; b. San Diego, Aug. 4, 1949; d. Jean Curtis and Irene Winifred (Tabbert) Waddell; B.S. in Bus. Adminstrn. (Dean's scholar), San Jose (Calif.) State U., 1978; m. James P. Collins, Apr. 15, 1973; children—Sean Jean Caywood, Tyler Douglas Collins. Clk., City of Newark (Calif.), 1974-77; personnel officer Asso. Students, San Jose State U., 1977-78; gen. mgr. Asso. Students, Humboldt State U., Arcata, Calif., 1978; bus. mgr. Fred C. Hart Assos., Denver, 1979-81; mgr. compensation and benefits Susquehanna Corp., 1981—. Mem. Am. Mgmt. Assn., San Jose State U. Sch. Bus. Alumni Assn. Home: 1105 W Center Ave Lakewood CO 80226 Office: 7400 S Alton Ct Englewood CO 80112

COLLINS, DOROTHY (MRS. AKIBA EMANUEL), advt. and public relations agy. exec.; b. Salt Lake City; d. Jospeh L. and Dorothy (Frey) C.; A.B., U. Denver; m. Akiba Emanuel; 1 dau., Lynn Collins. Woman's page editor Rocky Mountain News, Denver; fashion editor NBC, N.Y.C.; pub. relations dir. Shwayder Bros., Denver; account exec. Ellington & Co., N.Y.C.; v.p. Infoplan, N.Y.C.; v.p., mgr. consumer group Burson-Marsteller, N.Y.C.; sr. v.p., chief exec. officer Public Relations div. Sam Lusky Assos., Inc., Denver, 1981-83; v.p., dir. consumer mktg. Burson Marsteller, Denver, 1983—. Former nat. dir. women's activities Nat. Jewish Hosp., Denver; active Girl Scouts U.S.A.; trustee Marymount Coll., 1979-80. Mem. Nat. Home Fashions League (pres. N.Y. chpt. 1977-79), Women's Forum, Am. Women in Radio and TV, Exec. Women in Pub. Relations. Club: Denver Women's Press. Home: 2950 Albion St Denver CO 80207 Office: 5500 S Syracuse Circle Denver CO 80111

COLLINS, GARELD JEFFERSON, automotive supply company executive; b. Sask., Can., July 4, 1913; s. Andrew Jackson and Amelia (Hartsook) C.; came to U.S., 1922, naturalized, 1968; student pub. schs.; m. June Blevins, July 1, 1940; children—Michael Lee, Lael Gareld. With Civilian Conservation Corps, Pistol River, Oreg., 1933-34; mechanic Del Rogue Garage, Grants Pass, Oreg., 1935-36; shipping clk. Western Auto, Grants Pass, 1937-39; sales rep. George Lawrence Co., Portland, Oreg., 1939-40; shipping clk. Littrell Parts, Yreka, Calif., 1940-41, sales rep., 1942-45, sales mgr., 1945-64, v.p., 1952-64, pres., 1965—; pres. Collins Enterprises, Inc., Yreka, 1970—, Littrell Welding Supply, Inc., Medford, Oreg., 1970—, Littrell Welding Supply, Redding, Calif., 1971—; dir. Timberline Community Bank; dir. Auto Parts Assn. Fed. Credit Union, 1979—, v.p., 1982, pres., 1983. Sec., Siskiyou County (Calif.) Sheriff's Posse, 1967-74. Bd. dirs. Am. Buckskin Registry Assn., 1966-74, pres., 1972. Mem. Calif. Automotive Wholesalers Assn. (dir. 1974—). Clubs: Masons, Shriners, Rotary (dir. 1980-81). Home: Route 1 Box 504 Yreka CA 96097 Office: 404 S Main St Yreka CA 96097

COLLINS, GAYLE MINETTE, educator; b. Kalispell, Mont., Oct. 24, 1953; d. Earl William and Janet Kerr (DeLandelles) Mohn. Student Flathead Community Coll., 1971-74; B.A., U. Mont., 1976; postgrad. Mont. State U., 1979, No.Mont. Coll., 1980, U. Mont., 1983. Tchr. bus. edn. Willow Creek (Mont.) Pub. Schs., 1976-77, St. Regis (Mont.) Pub. Schs., 1978—; sponsor sr. class, jr. class, honor soc., yearbook. Mem. Am. Vocat. Assn., Nat. Bus. Edn. Assn., Mont. Edn. Assn. Presbyterian. Author of bus. edn. programs for Mont. high schs. Office: St Regis Pub Schs Drawer K St Regis MT 59866

COLLINS, JAMES PHILIPP, lawyer, mayor; b. Detroit, Mar. 14, 1945; s. Raymond E. and Gladys A. (Philipp) C.; m. Mary Jo Cook, Nov. 19, 1966; children—Kimberly Anne, Heather Leigh, Elizabeth Anne, Christopher Philipp. B.B.A., Western Mich. U., Kalamazoo, 1967, M.B.A., 1970; J.D., U. Denver, 1975. Bar: Colo. 1977. Asst. personnel dir. City of Kalamazoo, 1967-69; personnel dir., asst. city mgr., acting city mgr., community devel. dir. Urban Renewal Authority, Littleton, Colo.; exec. dir., fed. programs coordinator City of Littleton, 1969-73; pres., mgr. Local Govt. Mgmt. Cons., Inc., Denver, 1973-78; ptnr. Collins & Cockrel, P.C., Denver, 1978—; mayor pro tem City of Littleton, 1977-79, mayor, 1979-83. Mem. Denver Met. Council Organizing Commn., 1981; mem. Gov.'s Met. Water Roundtable, 1981. Mem. Spl. Dist. Assn. Colo. (exec. v.p., sec.-treas. 1975—), Colo. Bar Assn., Denver Bar Assn., Arapahoe Bar Assn., Internat. City Mgmt. Assn. Republican. Lutheran.

COLLINS, KEITH ROGER, medical imaging company executive; b. St. Louis, Aug. 29, 1946; s. Malcolm Keith and Joan Mary (Brown) C. B.S., U. Portland, 1968. Sales engr. Gen. Electric Med. Systems, Glendale, Calif., 1972-75, Rohe Sci. Corp., Santa Ana, Calif., 1975-76; systems cons. ADAC Labs., Sunnyvale, Calif., 1977-81; field sales mgr. Schiff Photo-Mechanics, Santa Ana, 1981—. Mem. Soc. Nuclear Medicine, Am. Inst. Ultrasound in Medicine, Am. Diabetes Assn. Republican. Home: 7890 E Spring St Number 18F Long Beach CA 90815 Office: Schiff Photo-Mechanics 647 E Young St Santa Ana CA 92705

COLLINS, NANCY WHISNANT, foundation administrator, b. Charlotte, N.C., Dec. 20, 1933, d. William Ward and Marjorie Adele (Blackburn) Whisnant; student Queens Coll., 1951-53; B.A. in Journalism, U. N.C., 1955, M.S. in Personnel Adminstrn., 1965-67; postgrad. (fellow) Cornell U., 1955-56; m. Richard F. Chapman, May 29, 1982; children from previous marriage—James Q. III, Charles L., William R. Dir. jr. exec. placement Scofield Cons., San Francisco, 1956-57; free lance journalist, London, Paris, Frankfort, W. Ger., 1957-59, program dir. Area Leaders Girl Scouts U.S.A. Hampton, Va., 1959-61; dir. Oriental Tour Tokyo, Hong Kong, Bangkok, Singapore, 1965; asst. dir. Sloan Program, Grad. Sch. Bus. Stanford (Calif.) U., 1968-78, corp. devel. officer Grad. Sch. Bus., 1978-79; asst. dir. Hoover Instn., Stanford, 1979-81; asst. to pres. Palo Alto Med. Found., 1981—. Vice pres. YWCA; mem. Charter Rev. Com., San Mateo County, Calif.; bd. dirs. Coro Found., 1978—; mem. council Trinity Parish, 1978—; bd. dirs. personnel council City of Menlo Park (Calif.), 1979—; mem. exec. bd. Stanford council Boy Scouts Am.; mgr. Nat. Network Conf. Profl. Women. Richardson Found. research grantee. Mem. Am. Mgmt. Assn., AAUP, Internat. Platform Assn., Peninsula Profl. Womens Network (adv. council), Kappa Delta. Episcopalian. Clubs: Overseas Press. Author: Professional Women and Their Mentors, 1983. Home: 1850 Oak Ave Menlo Park CA 94025 Office: Palo Alto Med Found 400 Channing Ave Palo Alto CA 94301

COLLINS, RICHARD LEO, orthopaedic surgeon; b. Boston, July 20, 1937; s. Francis Joseph and Sarah Ruth (Lapsley) C.; student Mass. Inst. Tech., 1956-57; B.S., U. Notre Dame, 1959; M.D., N.J. Coll. Medicine, 1963; m. Mary Lee Bonnell, Sept. 26, 1964; children—Kelly, Sandra, Nancy. Intern, USPHS Hosp., San Francisco, 1963-64, resident in orthopaedic surgery, 1964-65, 67-68; resident in orthopaedic surgery Charity Hosp., Tulane U. Sch. Medicine, New Orleans, 1965-67; chief of orthopedics Phoenix Indian Med. Center, 1968-69; practice medicine specializing in orthopaedic surgery, Phoenix, 1969-71, Scottsdale, Ariz., 1971—; mem. staff Scottsdale Meml. Hosp., Maricopa County Gen. Hosp., Phoenix, Ariz. Children's Hosp., Tempe; incorporator Bank of Paradise Valley. Served with USPHS, 1963-69. Diplomate Nat. Bd. Med. Examiners, Am. Bd. Orthopedic Surgery. Fellow Am. Acad. Orthopedic Surgeons, A.C.S.; mem. AMA, Ariz. Med. Assn. (dir. 1978—), Central Ariz. Orthopaedic Soc. (v.p. 1976), Maricopa County Med. Soc. (pres. 1980), C. of C. Scottsdale, Cath. Physicians Guild (pres. 1972). Republican. Roman Catholic. Clubs: Scottsdale (Ariz.) Racquet; Notre Dame (v.p. 1972-75) (Phoenix). Home: 7422 E Berridge Ln Scottsdale AZ 85253 Office: 7331 E Osborn Dr Scottsdale AZ 85251

COLLINS, ROBERT FLOYD, optometrist; b. Cleve., Aug. 11, 1935; s. Aaron J. and Ethel M. (Zalkind) C.; m. Shari A. Ballonoff, Dec. 2, 1956; m. 2d Sheila Joan Berkley, Nov. 28, 1981; children—Robyn, Wendy, Teri, Jay, Mark, Wayne. B.S., U. So. Calif., 1961; O.D., So. Calif. Coll. Optometry, 1964. Lic. optometrist, Calif. Pvt. practice optometry, North Hollywood, Calif., 1966—; dir. Vision Safeguard Health Plan, Whittier, Calif., 1982—. Office: 6765 Lankershim Blvd North Hollywood CA 91606

COLLINS, ROBERT HILLIARD, III, natural resource co. exec.; b. Beverly Hills, Calif., May 5, 1935; s. Robert Hilliard and Nancy (Morgan) C.; B.S., Stanford, 1957, M.A., 1959; m. Emily Ann Banks, Apr. 24, 1970. Engr., Pacific Gas & Electric Co., San Francisco, 1957; project engr. Best Industries div. Occidental Petroleum Corp., Lathrop, Calif., 1959-60, chief engr., 1960-61, asst. to v.p. Best Fertilizer Co. div., 1961-62; div. gen. mgr. Cyprus Oil Co., Houston, 1961-64; subsidiary v.p. Anvil Mining Corp. Ltd., Vancouver, B.C., Can., 1964-67; asst. to sr. v.p. Cyprus Mines Corp., Los Angeles, 1964-67; cons., bd. advisers Atlas Explorations Ltd., Vancouver, 1967; pres. Collins Investments, Los Angeles, 1967—, Inter-Tech Resources Inc., Los Angeles, 1969-74, Getty Synthetic Fuels, Inc., Signal Hill, Calif., 1974—. Served with USNR, 1957-59. Mem. Am. Inst. M.E., Am. Soc. Mining Engrs., Assn. Petroleum Engrs., Am. Inst. Chem. Engrs., Stanford Alumni Assn. Clubs: Buck of Month and Block S Orgn., Engrs. of So. Calif., Petroleum, Jonathan, Balboa Bay, Bel Air Country. Home: 2387

Kimridge Rd Beverly Hills CA 90210 Office: 2750 Signal Pkwy Signal Hill CA 90806

COLLINS, TERRENCE LEE, human resources executive, retired army officer; b. Los Angeles, Aug. 31, 1942; s. Albert Newton and Martha Zeta (Merrill) C.; m. Cheryl Jean Brokaw, Jan. 25, 1978; children—Sean Alexander, Patrick Dean, Michael Paul. B.S. in Bus. Adminstrn., Columbia Coll., 1977; M.B.A., Pepperdine U., 1979. Cert. instr. effectiveness mgmt., U.S. Army Organizational Tng. Inst. Enlisted U.S. Army, 1959, commd. capt., 1973, advanced through grades to maj., 1977; multiple assignments primarily in human resources mgmt.; ret., 1979; profl. relations mgr. Nat. Med. Enterprises Inc., Los Angeles, 1979-81; personnel mgr. HR Textron Inc., Valencia, Calif., 1981—. Mem. legis. liaison com. Santa Clarita Valley C. of C. Decorated Legion of Merit, 2 Bronze Stars, 4 Meritorious Service medals, Air medal, Army Commendation medal, Nat. Def. Service medal; Vietnam Cross Gallantry, Vietnam Service medal. Mem. Am. Soc. Tng. and Devel., Employment Mgmt. Assn., Am. Soc. Personnel Adminstrs., Army Assn. U.S., Nat. Mgmt. Assn. Republican. Methodist. Author textbook for sr. Army ednl. tng. course. Home: 1068 Bollin Ave Camarillo CA 93010 Office: 25200 W Rye Canyon Rd Valencia CA 91355

COLLMER, RUSSELL CRAVENER, data processing exec.; b. Guatemala, Jan. 2, 1924; s. G. Russell and Constance (Cravener) C.; B.S., U. N.M., 1951; postgrad. Calif. Inst. Tech., 1943-44; M.S., State U. Iowa, 1955; m. Ruth Hannah Adams, Mar. 4, 1950; 1 son, Reed Alan. Staff mem. Mass. Inst. Tech., Lincoln Lab., Lexington, 1955-57; mgr. systems modeling, computer dept. Gen. Electric, Phoenix, 1957-59; mgr. ARCAS Thompson Ramo Wooldridge, Inc., Canoga Park, Cal., 1959-62; asso. mgr. tech. dir. CCIS-70 Bunker-Ramo Corp., 1962-64; sr. asso. Planning Research Corp., Los Angeles, 1964-65; pres. R. Collmer Assos., Benson, Ariz., 1965—; pres. Benson Econ. Enterprises Corp., 1968-69. Lectr. computer scis. Pima Community Coll., Tucson, 1970—. Served with USAAC, 1942-46, to capt. USAF, 1951-53. Mem. IEEE, Am. Meteorol. Soc., Assn. for Computing Machinery, Phi Delta Theta, Kappa Mu Epsilon. Republican. Baptist. Home: 191 E 8th St Benson AZ 85602 Office: PO Box 864 Benson AZ 85602

COLLOPY, GEORGE FRANCIS, printing co. exec.; b. San Francisco, Sept. 12, 1921; s. James Edward and Gertrude Frances (Wilhelm) C.; B.A., St. Mary's Coll., 1943; student Jean Turner Art Cntr., 1938-43, Calif. Sch. Fine Arts, 1946-48, Golden Gate Coll., 1946-47; m. Dorothy Rose O'Leary, Aug. 25, 1946; children—Christopher, Kevin, Michael, Jon, Liam, Siobhan. Art dir. Pan Am. World Airways, San Francisco, 1946-59; v.p. Michelson Advt., Palo Alto, Calif., 1959-64; mgr. communications Raychem Corp., Menlo Park, Calif., 1964-74; art dir. George Group Printing Cos., San Francisco, 1975—; developer art standards for State of Calif. Apprenticeship Program. Bd. dirs. Burlingame Art Assn., 1968-69; mem. Archdiocese Commn. of Worship, Art and Music, Roman Catholic Ch., 1978-81. Served with USAAF, 1943-46. Recipient awards Nat. Cath. Press Assn., 1974-81, 1st award Peninsula Art Assn., 1960. Mem. Am. Inst. Graphic Arts, Soc. Western Art Dirs., San Francisco Art Dirs. Club, San Francisco Soc. Communicating Arts. Contbg. author: Modern Liturgy Handbook (John F. Mossi), 1976; illustrator: Celebrating, 1979, A Festival Day Book (Thomas Kane), 1979. Home: 1345 Cabrillo Ave Burlingame CA 94010 Office: 650 2d St San Francisco CA 94107

COLOMBO, ARTHUR FRANK, metallurgist, research executive; b. Gilbert, Minn., Nov. 23, 1931; s. Arthur and Agnes Colombo; Assoc. Sci., Eveleth Jr. Coll., 1951; B.Mining Engring., U. Minn., 1954, M.S., 1958, Ph.D., 1974; m. Susan M. Woods, Apr. 4, 1959; children—Arthur F., John G., Mary T., Kathryn A., Michael P., Daniel T. Metallurgist, Twin Cities Research Ctr., U.S. Bur. Mines, U.S. Dept. Interior, Mpls., 1956-61, research metallurgist, 1961-63, research extractive metallurgist, 1963-68, metallurgist, project leader, 1968-77, research supr., 1976-80, research dir. Reno (Nev.) Research Ctr., 1980—. Bd. dirs. Reno Fed. Exec. Council, 1980—, pres., 1983; chmn. combined fed. campaign United Way No. Nev., 1983; mem. natural resources and environ. com. Twin Cities Fed. Exec. Bd., 1976. Served with U.S. Army, 1954-56. U.S. Bur. Mines fellow, 1956-58; recipient Spl. Achievement awards U.S. Bur. Mines, 1973, 79. Mem. AIME, Minn. Soc. Profl. Engrs. Roman Catholic. Club: Squaw Valley Jr. Hockey. Office: 1605 Evans Ave Reno NV 89512

COLONIAS, JOHN STAVROS, physicist; b. Athens, Greece, June 8, 1928; came to U.S., 1954, naturalized, 1964; s. Stavros J. and Eve M. (Marcoe) C.; m. Irene Jansson, Sept. 26, 1981; children—Elisabeth, John. B.S.E.E., Oreg. State U., 1959; postgrad in computer sci. U. Calif.-Berkeley, 1965; Ph.D. in Physics, U. Uppsala (Sweden), 1980. Research engr. Pacific Power & Light Co., Portland, Oreg., 1959-64; staff scientist Lawrence Berkeley Lab., U. Calif.-Berkeley, 1964-73, applications group leader dept. computation, 1973—; cons. to numerous U.S. fgn. firms; instr. U. Calif.; pres. cons. firm; Fulbright vis. fellow, CERN, Geneva, Switzerland, 1970. Served to lt. Greek Army, 1951; Korea. Decorated Bronze Star, D.S.C. (Greece); Tsougmou with gold star (Korea). Mem. Sigma Xi. Republican. Sigma Xi. Author: Particle Accelerator Design, 1974; contbr. numerous articles to profl. jours. Home: 371 Ridgeview Dr Pleasant Hill CA 94523 Office: U Calif Lawrence Berkeley Lab Berkeley CA 94720

COLON-VELEZ, SERGIO ANTONIO, human development counselor; b. Hatillo, P.R., Mar. 3, 1942; s. Pedro and Rosalie (Velez) C.; m. Elsa Socorro Landrau, July 2, 1966; 1 dau., Auria Lydia. B.A. in Philosophy, Coll. of William and Mary, 1975; A.A.S., Community Coll. of Air Force, 1977; M.A. in Counseling, Pepperdine U., 1978; Ed.S., Vanderbilt U., 1982. Enlisted U.S. Air Force, 1966, advanced through grades to tech. sgt., 1979; various assignments including Charleston AFB, 1967, Nha Trang AFB, Vietnam, 1968-69, McCoy AFB, 1969, Hickam AFB, Hawaii, 1970-74; counselor Langley AFB, Va., 1975-78; counselor, supr. Royal AFB, Lakenheath, Eng., 1978-81, Edwards AFB, Calif., 1981—, officer-in-charge of drug/alcohol sect. of social actions; cons. for command personnel. Commdg. officer CAP, 1970—. Decorated Vietnamese Cross for Gallantry. Recipient various achievement awards. Mem. Am. Personnel and Guidance Assn., Am. Rehab. Counseling Assn., P.R. Psychol. Assn. Democrat. Roman Catholic. Club: Edwards Air Force Aero.

COLOSSY, DAN A., airline company executive; Grad. U.S. Coast Guard Acad., 1953; M.B.A., Harvard U., 1965. Advt. exec. Wells, Rich and Green; v.p. mktg. Pan Am. Airlines Co., 1970, pres., 1978-80; pres., chief operating officer Can. Pacific Air Lines Co., Vancouver, B.C., 1982—. Office: Can Pacific Air Lines One Grant McConachie Way Vancouver Internat Airport Vancouver BC V7B 1V1 Canada*

COLT, JOHN ERNEST, engineer, medical center administrator; b. Yonkers, N.Y., May 8, 1943; s. John E. and Alma (Negrini) C.; m. Beth Turner, June 13, 1976 (div.); 1 dau., Rebecca. B.S. Otterbein Coll., 1963; M.S. in Engring., Delaware Valley Agronomy Engr. Coll., 1966. Fgn. service officer U.S. Dept. State Frankfurt, W.Ger., 1967-68; engr. U.S. Postal Service, Washington and Pitts., 1973-75; dir. plant service Presbyn. U. Hosp., Pitts., 1975-81; founder, pres. Unique Cuisine Inc., Pitts., 1976-81; dir. plant ops. Cedars Sinai Med. Ctr., Los Angeles, 1981; assoc. prof. evening div. U. Pitts. Served to capt. U.S. Army, 1968-73. Decorated Air Medal, Purple Heart, Bronze Star. Mem. Am. Inst. Plant Engrs., Assn. Energy Engrs., Am. Hosp. Assn., Nat. Fire Protection Assn., Calif. Soc. Hosp. Engrs. Home: 18875 Kirkcohm Ln Northridge CA 91326 Office: Cedars Sinai Med Ctr 8700 Beverley Blvd Los Angeles CA 90048

COLTER, MEL A., business educator; b. Conway, Iowa, June 11, 1947; s. Archie B. and Jessie E. (Brown) C.; B.S. in Physics, Iowa State U., 1969; Ph.D. in Mgmt. Sci., U. Iowa, 1975. Lab. asst. Ames Lab., Iowa State U., Ames, 1966-69; teaching asst. Coll. Bus., U. Iowa, Iowa City, 1970-75, vis. asst. prof., 1976-79; project dir. Computer Cons. Service, Dubuque, Iowa, 1975-76; assoc. prof. bus. U. Colo., Colorado Springs, 1979—, mem. univ. computing policy com.; cons. and lectr. in field. Mem. ACM. Co-author: (with J.D. Couger & R. Knapp) Advanced System Development/Feasibility Techniques, 1982; (with J. Daniel Couger) Motivation of the Maintenance Programmer, 1983; contbr. research reports and articles to profl. jours. Home: 2860 Purgatory Dr Colorado Springs CO 80918 Office: Coll Bus and Adminstrn U Colorado Austin Bluffs Pkwy Colorado Springs CO 80907

COLTON, ROY CHARLES, management consultant; b. Phila., Feb. 26, 1941; s. Nathan Hale and Ruth Janis Baylinson) C.; B.A., Knox Coll., 1962; M.Ed., Temple U., 1963. With Sch. Dist. of Phila., 1963-64; systems analyst Wilmington Trust Co., 1967-69; exec. recruiter Atwood Consultants Inc., Phila., 1969-71; pres. Colton Bernard Inc., San Francisco, 1971—; occasional lectr. Fashion Inst. Tech., Phila. Coll. Textiles and Scis. Served with AUS, 1964-66. Mem. San Francisco Fashion Industries, San Francisco C. of C., Calif. Exec. Recruiter Assn., Am. Apparel Mfrs. Assn. Office: Colton Bernard Inc 417 Spruce St San Francisco CA 94118

COLVARD, RICHARD MALTBY, sociologist, educator; b. Weiser, Idaho, Oct. 22, 1928; s. Freeland A. and Ruth (Maltby) C.; m. Patricia McGregor; m. 2d, Christine De Nering. Instr. U. Oreg., 1957; instr., asst. prof. U. Tex., 1957-62; assoc. prof. SUNY, Buffalo, 1963-70; prof. So. Oreg. State Coll., Ashland, 1971—. Mem. Soc. Study of Social Problems, Sociologists for Women in Soc., Am. Sociol. Assn., Pacific Sociol. Assn. Co-editor: Women and Work: Problems and Perspectives, 1982; editor: Social Problems, 1978-81; contbr. articles to profl. jours. Home: PO Box 514 Ashland OR 97520 Office: Southern Oreg State College Dept Sociology Ashland OR 97520

COLVER, CHARLES GORDON, forester; b. Pomona, Calif., Dec. 2, 1920; s. William Charles and Myrtle Florance (Maxfield) C.; m. Mary Curtiss, Sept. 29, 45; children—John (dec.), Edward, Marylou. A.A., Chaffey Coll., Ontario, Calif., 1941; postgrad. Citrus Coll., Azusa, Calif., Calif. State Poly. U., Pomona, 1974. With Douglas Aircraft Corp., Long Beach, Calif., 1941-44; with U.S. Forest Service, 1946—, mgr. San Dimas Exptl. Forest Sta., Glendora, Calif., 1962—; Calif. South Zone fire dispatcher, 1972-77; mem. U.S. Assay Commn., 1974; v.p. Covina Irrigating Co., 1974—. Councilman, City of Covina (Calif.), 74—, mayor pro tem, 1976-78, mayor, 1980-82, mayor pro-tem, 1982—; mem. president's adv. commn. Mt. San Antonio Coll., Walnut, Calif.; mem. Covina Bd. Library Trustees, 1970-74. Served with U.S. Army, 1944-46; ETO. Decorated Bronze Star, Purple Heart, Combat Inf. badge; recipient Numismatic Ambassador award Krause Publs., 1974. Mem. Am. Forestry Assn., Am. Numismatic Assn., Calif. State Numismatic Assn. (sec. 1964-81, v.p. 1981-83, pres. 1983—, medal of merit 1970, Silver lit. medal 1965, 70), 45th Inf. Div. Assn., Nat. Rifle Assn., Covina Valley Hist. Soc (founding pres., dir., mem. com. for preservation and restoration Old San Francisco Mint), Soc. Paper Money Collectors (dir.), Covina Coin Club (past pres.). Republican. Presbyterian. Club: Toastmaster, (communication achievement award 1982). Home: 611 N Banna Ave Covina CA 91724 Office: 110 N Wabash Ave Glendora CA 91740

COLWELL, ARTHUR RALPH, JR., physician; b. Chgo., Mar. 27, 1924; s. Arthur Ralph and Jeane (Haskins) C.; B.S., Northwestern U., 1945, B.M., 1947, M.D., 1948; M.A., U. Toronto (Ont., Can.), 1950; m. Bettie Jane Norton, Sept. 4, 1948; children—Christina Jeane, Arthur Ralph, E. David, Julia Beth. Rotating intern Abington (Pa.) Meml. Hosp., 1947-48; resident in internal medicine Evanston (Ill.) Hosp., 1950-51, 53, chief div. rheumatology, 1972-78, attending physician, 1955-79; attending physician VA Research Hosp., Chgo., 1954-55; attending physician Boswell Meml. Hosp., Sun City, Ariz., 1979—; fellow Northwestern U. Med. Sch., 1954-65, asst. prof. medicine, 1965-71, asso. prof., 1971-80; cons. Ill. Div. Services Crippled Children, 1955-79; speaker, hon. lectr. 33d Ann. Phi Delta Epsilon meeting at U. Louisville, 1974. Served as capt. U.S. Army, 1951-53; Japan. NIH grantee, 1966-69. Diplomate Am. Bd. Internal Medicine. Fellow A.C.P.; mem. Am. Diabetes Assn., Am. Rheumatism Assn., Am. Fedn. Clin. Research, Sigma Xi. Republican. Episcopalian. Club: Palmbrook Country (Sun City). Author: Understanding Your Diabetes, 1978. Home: 10325 Bayside Rd Sun City AZ 85351 Office: 10503 W Thunderbird Blvd Sun City AZ 85351

COLWELL, BUNDY, mortgage banker; b. Ely, Nev., Aug. 24, 1912; s. Alfred Bundy and Pearl (O'Brien) C.; B.S. in Bus. Adminstrn., U. So. Calif., 1934, J.D., 1936; m. Anne Foster Jackson, Aug. 28, 1940; children—Stephen B., Penelope Anne. Admitted to Calif. bar, 1936; individual practice law, Los Angeles, 1936—; formerly v.p., dir. Calif. Fed. Savs. and Loan Assn., Los Angeles; chmn. The Colwell Co., mortgage bankers, Los Angeles. Served with USAAF, 1943-44. Mem. Am., Los Angeles bar assns., Nat. Assn. Real Estate Bds., Nat. Home Builders Inst., Nat. Inst. Real Estate Brokers, Mortgage Bankers Assn. Am. (gov., regional v.p.), Calif., So. Calif. mortgage bankers assns., U.S., Calif., Los Angeles chambers commerce, Alpha Kappa Psi, Phi Kappa Tau, Lambda Alpha, Phi Alpha Delta. Conglist. (past moderator, trustee). Mason (Shriner). Clubs: Jonathan (Los Angeles); Trojan. Office: 3223 W 6th St Los Angeles CA 90020

COLWILL, RICHARD HENRY, research and devel. co. exec.; b. Dublin, Ireland, Apr. 14, 1909; came to U.S., 1927, naturalized, 1938; s. William Henry and Daisy Florence (Mann) C.; m. Ethel Conet Smith, Dec. 12, 1935; children—Phyllis Dianne, Thomas Richard, William Henry. Student Chgo. Y.M.C.A. Coll. Machinist, exptl. engr. UARCO, Chgo., 1929-42; tool maker, foreman Dodge Motor Co. Plant, Chgo., 1942-46; engr. Machinery Devel., Chgo., 1946-49; sales engr. Center Tool, Chgo., 1949-50; sr. engr. A. O. Smith, Milw., 1950-51; chief engr. J. Curry Mendes, Chgo., 1951-56; project engr., sr. engr. Burroughs Corp., Rochester, N.Y., 1956-71; owner, mgr. Colwill Co. (and predecessor co.), Monterey, Calif., 1971—; free-lance design for Xerox; Webster. Committeeman Boy Scouts Am., 1950; mem. Hobson Road Sch. Bd., Naperville, Ill., 1954. Mem. Tech. Engrs. Assn. Patentee collating and printing tech.; tools; household improvements; verti-slide medicine cabinet, recirculating feeder for copier. Address: 1007 Hellam St Monterey CA 93940

COMANOR, WILLIAM S., economist, educator; b. Phila., May 11, 1937; s. Leroy and Sylvia (Bershad) C.; m. Lorraine G. Hanlon, Dec. 17, 1967; children—Christine, Katherine. A.B., Haverford Coll., 1959; Ph.D., Harvard U., 1964. Asst. prof. econs. Harvard U., 1966-68; spl. econs. asst. to asst. atty. gen. antitrust div. U.S. Dept. Justice 1965-66; assoc. prof. econs. Stanford U., 1968-73; prof. econs. U. Calif.-Santa Barbara, 1975—; dir. Bur. Econs., FTC, 1978-80; cons. in field. Mem. Am. Econ. Assn. Author: Advertising and Market Power, 1974; National Health Insurance In Ontario, 1980; contbr. articles to profl. jours. Office: Dept Econs U Calif Santa Barbara CA 93106

COMARR, AVROM ESTIN, urologist, educator, author; b. Chgo., July 15, 1915; s. Louis and Esther (Massel) C.; A.B., U. So. Calif., 1937; M.B., Chgo. Med. Sch., 1940, M.D., 1941; m. Ruth Harriette Litchman, Sept. 4, 1938; 1 dau., Cynthia Ester. Intern, Evang. Deaconess Hosp., Cleve., 1940-41; resident Polyclinic Hosp., Cleve., 1941-42, Birmingham Gen. Hosp., Van Nuys, Calif., 1946-50, VA Hosp., Long Beach, Calif., 1950-52; practice medicine specializing in neurol.-urology, Van Nuys, Calif., 1946-50, Long Beach, Calif., 1950-73, Lakewood, Calif., 1973-76; asst. chief spinal cord injury service VA Hosp., Long Beach, Calif., 1946-70, chief of spinal cord injury service, 1970-73, med. adviser of veterans assistance, 1970—; chief urology service Rancho Los Amigos Hosp., Downey, Calif., 1954-73, cons. spinal cord injury service, 1954-73, med. dir. outpatient clinic services, 1980—; jr. attending physician urology service Los Angeles County, U. So. Calif. Med. Center, 1955-70, sr. attending physician, 1970-82, emeritus, 1982—; cons. spinal cord injury service VA Hosp., Long Beach, Calif.; dir. spinal cord injury clinic Loma Linda (Calif.) U. Med. Center, 1973-80; hon. staff mem. Casa Colina Hosp. for Rehab. Medicine, 1979—; clin. instr. in urology U. Calif. Sch. Medicine, Los Angeles, 1953-55; asst. clin. prof. urology Loma Linda U., 1955-58, asst. prof. urology, 1958-59, asso. clin. prof. urology, 1959-66, clin. prof. urology, 1966-82, prof. emeritus, 1982—; clin. prof. surgery U. So. Calif., Los Angeles, 1966-82, prof. emeritus, 1982—; vis. prof. Temple U., Phila., 1970, U. Ala., Birmingham, 1973, Ohio State U., Columbus, 1971, U. Calif., Los Angeles, 1971, Southwestern Med. Sch., U. Tex., Dallas, 1973, U. Tel-Aviv, Israel, 1974; cons. to Children's Hosp., Los Angeles, 1969-82, emeritus staff, 1982—. Orthopedic Hosp., Los Angeles, 1969—. Served to maj., M.C., U.S. Army, 1942-46. Decorated Bronze Star; recipient Sr. Physician award VA, 1972, 30 Year Service award VA Hosp., 1972, Disting. Career award VA, 1973, William H. and Carrie Gottsche Found. Tutelary Saint award, 1966; silver bowl Casa Colina Hosp. for Rehab. Medicine Med. Staff, 1979; diplomate Am. Bd. Urology. Fellow A.C.S., Internat. Coll. Surgeons; mem. Am. Urol. Assn., VA Urol. Assn., Am. Paraplegia Soc. (founder 1954, pres. 1954, 67), Los Angeles Urol. Soc. (pres. 1977, dir. 1978-79), Calif., Los Angeles County med. assns., AMA (Recognition award 1969—), Soc. of Govt. Service Urologists, Internat. Med. Soc. of Paraplegia, World Med. Assn., Am. Bd. Spinal Cord Injury (founding dir. 1978, founding chmn. 1978—), Alumni Assn. of Chgo. Med. Sch. (1st ann. Sci. Meritorious award 1963), Kappa Zeta, Phi Delta Epsilon, Phi Lambda Kappa, Tau Epsilon Phi. Author: (with E. Bors) Neurological-Urology, 1971; contbr. numerous articles in neurol.-urology to med. jours.; pioneer in spinal cord injury field of medicine. Home: 4235 Clubhouse Dr Lakewood CA 90712

COMBS, ALAN EDWARD, retail company executive; b. Long Beach, Calif., Nov. 2, 1952; s. Paul Edward and Shirley Rose C.; m. Debra K. Leavitt, Dec. 31, 1974; children—Ryan L., Nathan E., Heather D. B.S., Brigham Young U., 1976; M.B.A., Pepperdine U., 1980. C.P.A., Utah. Auditor, Delloitte, Haskins & Sells, Santa Ana, Calif., 1976-77; controller Self Enterprises, Inc., 1977-79, Air Industries Corp., Garden Grove, Calif., 1980; fin. v.p. Stokes Brothers, Inc., Midvale, Utah, 1981—. Mem. Am. Inst. C.P.A.s, Utah, Retail Fin. Execs. Assn. Republican. Mormon. Home: 9161 Morning Mist Ct Sandy UT 84092 Office: Stokes Brothers Inc 6885 S State St Midvale UT 84047

COMEAU, CAROL SMITH, elementary educator; b. Berkeley, Calif., Sept. 4, 1941; d. Floyd Franklin and Bessie Caroline (Campbell) Smith; m. Dennis Rene Comeau, Dec. 27, 1962; children—Christopher, Michael, Karen. B.S. in Edn., U. Oreg., 1963; postgrad. in Pub. Sch. Adminstrn., U. Alaska, 1982—. Third grade tchr., Springfield, Oreg., 1963-64; elem. sch. tchr. Ocean View Elem. Sch., Anchorage, 1975—, 6th grade tchr., 1977—; community activist ednl. issues. Named Tchr. of Yr., Anchorage Sch. Dist. PTA Council, 1976. Mem. Anchorage Edn. Assn., NEA, Nat. Council Tchrs. English, Alaska Tchrs. English, Am. Soc. Curriculum and Devel., Nat. Council Tchrs. Math., Nat. Council Social Studies, Phi Delta Kappa. Democrat. Home: 13632 Jarvi Dr SRA Box 801-B Anchorage AK 99502 Office: Ocean View Elementary School SRA Box 3117-A Anchorage AK 99502

COMEAU, JEROME FRANKLIN, business management and consulting company executive; b. Norfolk, Nebr., Feb. 25, 1933; s. William. J. and Mabel Olivia (Kindschy) C.; diploma Boise Jr. Coll., 1955; postgrad. Portland State Coll., 1957-58; m. Beverly Irene Fox, Aug. 21, 1953; children—Pamela Irene, Barbara Jean, William Jerome. Asst. credit mgr. Van Waters & Rogers, Inc., Portland, 1955-60; asst. credit mgr. Lou Johnson Co., Portland, 1960-62; exec. dir. Profl. Bus. Services, Portland, 1962-68; founder, chmn., pres. Profl. Bus. Services, Inc., Portland, 1968—; founding partner Our Enterprises, Portland, 1980—. Pres., Mt. Olivet Lutheran Ch., Portland, 1961-63. Mem. Soc. Profl. Bus. Cons. (dir. 1970-73, chmn. nat. membership 1970-73, chmn. nat. com. ethics 1980-83, pres.-elect 1983-84), Med. Group Mgmt. Assn. Republican. Club: Masons. Office: 12788 SE Stark St Portland OR 97233

COMEAU, PAUL THEODORE, educator; b. New Bedford, Mass., Sept. 21, 1926; s. Laurent H. and Leda (Henley) C.; m. Ruby J. Klindt, Sept. 1, 1929; children—Stephen P., Michael F., Lisa Comeau MacMillan. B.A. in Pre-Med. and Philosophy, Assumption Coll., Worcester, Mass., 1949; M.A. in French, Princeton, 1964, Ph.D. in Romance Langs., 1968. Enlisted U.S. Army, 1945; enlisted U.S. Air Force, 1950, commd. 2d lt., 1952, advanced through grades to lt. col., 1969, ret., 1975; intelligence officer USAF, Colo., Mass., Washington, Japan and Tex., 1950-62; mem. faculty USAF Acad., Colo. and France, 1964-70; instr. USAF ROTC, Ala., N. Mex. and Cambodia, 1970-75; assoc. prof. French and Latin, head dept. fgn. langs. N. Mex. State U., Las Cruces, 1975—. Chmn. div. United Way, 1976-79. Decorated Meritorious Service medal with cluster, USAF Commendation medal. Nat. Endowment Humanities fellow U. Pitts., summer 1977; N. Mex. State U. Found. research grantee, 1978. Mem. MLA, Am. Council on Teaching Fgn. Langs., Am. Assn. Tchrs. of French (v.p., pres. N.Mex. chpt. 1981-83), Rocky Mountain MLA, Am. Translators Assn., Am. Lit. Translators Assn., Classical Assn. S.W. U.S. Democrat. Roman Catholic. Club: Rotary (pres. 1979-80) (Las Cruces). Author workbook: Latin: An Introductory Course (Wheelock), 1980, rev. edit., 1982; contbr. articles to profl. jours. Home: 1023 Avondale Dr Las Cruces NM 88005 Office: Box 3L Dept Fgn Langs New Mexico State Univ Las Cruces NM 88003

COMES, ROBERT GEORGE, sr. research scientist; b. Bangor, Pa., July 7, 1931; s. Victor Francis and Mabel Elizabeth (Mack) C.; student U. Detroit, 1957-58, Oreg. State Coll., 1959-60, U. Nev., 1960, Regis Coll., 1961-62; m. Carol Lee Turinetti, Nov. 28, 1952; children—Pamela Jo, Robert G. II, Shawni Lee, Sheryl Lynn, Michelle Ann. Tech. liaison engr. Burroughs Corp., Detroit, 1955-60, mgr. reliability and maintainability engring., Paoli, Pa., 1962-63, Colorado Springs, 1963-67; sr. engr. Martin Marietta Corp., Denver, 1960-62; program mgr., research scientist Kaman Scis. Corp., Colorado Springs, 1967-75; dir. engring. Sci. Applications, Inc., Colorado Springs, 1975-80; mgr. space def. programs Burroughs Corp., Colorado Springs, 1980-82; tech. staff Mitre Corp., Colorado Springs, 1982—; chmn. Reliability and Maintainability Data Bank Improvement Program, Govt.-Industry Data Exchange

Program, 1978—; cons. in field. Youth dir. Indian Guides program YMCA, 1963-64; scoutmaster Boy Scouts Am., 1972-73; chmn. bd. dirs. Pikes Peak Regional Sci. Fair, 1972—. Served with USAF, 1951-55. Mem. AAAS, IEEE, Inst. Environ. Scis., Soc. Logistics Engrs., Am. Soc. Quality Control. Lutheran. Club: Colorado Springs Racquet. Author: Maintainability Engrineering Principles and Standards, 1962. Inventor Phase Shifting aircraft power supply, 1957. Home: 4309 Tipton Ct Colorado Springs CO 80915 Office: 1275 Lake Ave Colorado Springs CO 80906

COMI, GLADYS ROSE, city planner; b. Pueblo, Colo., Mar. 6, 1926; d. Sylvester Thomas and Vida Estelle (Potter) C.; A.A., Pueblo Jr. Coll., 1947; B.S., U. So. Colo., 1971; M.A., U. No. Colo., 1975; div.; children—Stephanie Louise, Thomas J. Sec. to dir. Pueblo Regional Planning Commn., 1960-61, office mgr., statistician, 1962-66, planning technician, planner, 1967-73, asst. to dir., 74-79, asst. dir., 1979-80; dir. Pueblo City Community Devel. Dept., 1980—. Pres., El Pueblo Boys' Ranch, 1977; v.p. Pueblo Symphony Assn., 1973; mem. exec. bd. Sangre de Cristo Arts & Conf. Center, 1975-77; sec. Pueblo Arts Council, 1968, pres., 1971; pres. Impossible Players, 1969; mem. exec. com. Pueblo Beautiful Assn., 1969—, pres., 1970-71; mem. Pueblo Environ. Policy Adv. Com., 1981—; pres. Colo. Mcpl. League Dist. 7; bd. dirs. Pueblo County Easter Seal Soc., 1979—. Recipient Century 2 award C. of C., 1971; Good Citizen award Pueblo Beautiful Assn., 1980; Disting. Service citation Pueblo Regional Planning Assn., 1980. HUD grantee, 1973-74. Democrat. Episcopalian. Club: Order Eastern Star. Home: 1905 West St Pueblo CO 81003 Office: 1 City Hall Pl Pueblo CO 81003

COMMON, KENNETH DOUGLAS, optometrist; b. Jersey City, Oct. 8, 1949; s. William Kenneth and Ida May (See) C.; m. Roxie M. Shannon, Mar. 11, 1978; children—Ronni, Paula, Jennifer, Daniel. B.A., Rutgers U., 1971; O.D., Mass. Coll. Optometry, 1976. Owner, optometrist Sea-Tac Vision Clinic, Seattle, 1981—; staff optometrist Seattle Pub. Health Hosp., part time, 1982—; instr. So. Calif. Coll. Optometry, 1982. Served to lt. USN, 1976-81. Mem. Am. Optometric Assn., Wash. Optometric Assn., King County Optometric Soc., B & L Council Sports Vision. Baptist. Home: 126 Bremerton Ave SE Renton WA 98056 Office: 16238 42d Ave S Seattle WA 98188

COMMONS, DORMAN L., shipping co. exec.; b. Denair, Calif., 1918; student Stanford U., 1943-47. Staff acct. John F. Forbes & Co., 1943-47; sr. v.p., dir. Douglas Oil Co., 1947-64; sr. v.p. fin., dir. Occidental Petroleum Co., 1964-72; pvt. practice fin. cons., 1972-73; pres., chief exec. officer Natomas Co., 1974—, also dir.; with Am. Pres. Lines subs. Natomas Co., San Francisco, 1974—, chmn. bd., chief exec. officer, pres., 1977—, also dir. Office: Natomas Co 601 California St San Francisco CA 94108*

COMPAGNONI, LAWRENCE, family, marriage and child counselor; b. Santa Cruz, Calif., May 10, 1947; s. Albert Lincoln Compagnoni and Lola Leota (Massey) Compagnoni Ludlow; A.A. in Social Scis., Cabrillo Community Coll., 1968; B.A. in Sociology, St. Patrick's Coll., 1971; M.A. in Theology, St. Patrick's Sem., 1973; M.A. in Marriage, Family and Child Counseling, U. Santa Clara, 1978; m. Marsha Darleen Stowell, Dec. 4, 1976. Tchr., chmn. Transcendental Mediation Program Santa Clara Valley World Plan Center, San Jose, Calif., 75-77, part-time, 1977—; sr. coordinator Personal Dynamics Inst., 1977; marriage, family counseling intern Bill Wilson Center, Santa Clara, 1978; counseling intern subacute psychiat. residential treatment program Rehab. Mental Health Services, San Jose, Calif., 1978; child counselor spl. edn. dept. Mountain View (Calif.) Sch. Dist., 1978-79; prin. alcohol-impaired drivers' sch., group facilitator youth and adult programs Nat. Traffic Safety Inst., San Jose, 1978—; dir. clin. services and staff family therapist Community Health Abuse Council, Mountain View, 1979-82; counselor El Camino Hosp., Mountain View, 1983—, alcohol group counselor and workshop leader Met. Adult Edn. Programs, San Jose, 1979-80; pvt. practice marriage, family and child counseling, 1980—; alcohol and drug abuse cons. to pvt. industry, 1980—. Mem. Monterey Diocese Vocation Commn., Roman Catholic Ch., 1970-71, 72-73, mem. Monterey Diocese Youth Search Bd., 1970-71, mem. No. Santa Clara County Alcohol Service Bur. Adv. Bd., 1979-80; mem. North County Child Abuse Adv. Council, 1980—; pres. Santa Clara Valley chpt. Spiritual Regeneration Movement, 1975. Lic. marriage, family and child counselor, cert. hypnotherapist Calif. Bd. Behavioral Sci. Examiners; cert. instr. and adminstr. for Transcendental Mediation Program, World Plan Exec. Council of U.S. Mem. Am. Personnel and Guidance Assn., Calif. Assn. Marriage and Family Counselors, Internat. Transactional Analysis Assn. Home: 164 Villa Ave Los Gatos CA 95030 Office: 650 Castro St Mountain View CA 94041

COMPEAN, RICHARD EDWARD, educational administrator; b. Globe, Ariz., Sept. 21, 1945; s. Albert and Carmen (Quijada) C.; A.B. with honors, U. San Francisco, 1967; M.A., U. Calif.-Davis, 1969, Ph.D., 1973. Tchr., cons. U. Calif.-Davis, 1969-73, 78-80; tng. analyst Calif. Dept. Social Services, 1973-74; tng. dir. Calif. Pub. Utilities Commn., San Francisco, 1974-76; sr. tng. analyst Western States Bankcard Assn., Crocker Nat. Bank, 1976-77; regional coordinator continuing profl. edn. Kaiser Permanente Med. Care Program, Oakland, Calif., 1977—; tchr., cons. U. San Francisco, San Francisco Community Coll. Dist., Civil Service Coll., San Francisco Community Tng. and Devel. Project; teaching assoc. U. Calif., Davis, 1969-73. Mem. Am. Soc. Tng. and Devel., Orgn. Devel. Network, Am. Soc. Health Care Edn. and Tng. Democrat. Roman Catholic. Editor Am. Soc. Tng. and Devel. Newsletter, 1976-77, 80-82. Home: 2448 Golden Gate Ave San Francisco CA 94118 Office: 3505 Broadway Oakland CA 94611

COMPTON, DALE LEONARD, government executive; b. Pasadena, Calif., June 18, 1935; s. John Leonard and Gladys Imnachuck (Foster) C.; m. Marilyn Doris Garland, June 21, 1959; children—David, Debora. B.S., Stanford U., 1957, M.S., 1958, Ph.D., 1969; M.M.S., MIT, 1975. Research scientist NASA-Ames Research Ctr., Moffett Field, Calif., 1957-72, tech. asst. to dir., 1972-73, dep. dir. astronautics, 1973-74, chief Space Sci. div., 1974-80, mgr. IRAS Telescope Project, 1980-81, dep. dir. astronautics for projects, 1981-82, dir. engring. and computer systems, 1982—. Mem. AIAA, AAAS, Sigma Xi, Tau Beta Pi. Contbr. articles to profl. jours. Office: Ames Research Center Moffett Field CA 94035

COMPTON, ESTHER ELIZABETH, educational administrator, educator; b. West Point, Nebr., Oct. 21, 1938; d. William J. and Elizabeth C. (Ortmeier) Maly; m. Thomas N. Compton; children—Shawn, Kevin, Shannon, Corey, Tommy (dec.). B.A. summa cum laude, Adams State Coll., 1975; M.A., Colo. State U., 1979; postgrad. Adams State Coll., Colo. State U., U. No. Colo. Tchr. coordinator Alamosa (Colo.) High Sch., 1975-79; community edn. coordinator Sch. Dist. RE11J, Alamosa, 1979-80, tchr., job coordinator Co-op G, Alamosa High Sch. Disadvantaged, 1980—; mem. State Adv. Council for Vocat. Edn.; tchr. adult stress mgmt., bus. County coordinator Senator Cary Hart, 1980, Congressman Ray Kogovsek, 1982; sec. Alamosa County Democratic. Party, 1981—; mem. Dem. State Central Com., 1983. Mem. Colo. Vocat. Assn., Am. Vocat. Assn., Colo. Edn. Assn., NEA, Crime Stoppers (bd. dirs.), AAUW, Phi Delta Kappa. Democrat. Roman Catholic.

COMPTON, JOHN MICHAEL, neuropsychologist, educator; b. Tulsa, April 8, 1940; s. John T. and Johnnie M. (Yount) C.; divorced; children—Bonnie T., Michele M. B.A., Princeton U., 1962; M.A., U. Hawaii, Mano., 1964; Ph.D., Bowling Green State U., 1973. Field assessment officer U. Hawaii Peace Corps Tng. Programs, 1965-66, 68, 70; psychologist Ohio Mental Hygiene Dept., 1968-71; mem. faculty dept. psychology Ohio State U., 1971-74; asst. prof. psychiatry U. Hawaii Med. Sch., Honolulu, 1974-75; psychologist Hilo Counseling Ctr., 1975-82; neuropsychologist Hawaii State Neuropsychology Service, Hawaii State Hosp., Kaneohe, 1982—; cons.; Named Outstanding Tchr., Ohio State U., 1971. Mem. Am. Psychol. Assn., Hawaii Psychol. Assn., Internat. Soc. Research on Aggression; Psi Xi. Contbr. articles to profl. jours. Home: PO Box 1043 Hilo HI 96720 Office: Neuropsychology Service Hawaii State Hosp Kaneohe HI 96744

COMRIE, DAVID STANLEY, accountant; b. Nottingham, Eng., Nov. 14, 1939; s. Alfred Stanley and Emily Ellen (Topham) C.; came to U.S., 1975; cert. elec. engring., Peoples Tech. Inst., Rugby, Eng., 1963; m. Donna Lee Snyder, Oct. 18, 1975. Elec. and hydraulic engr. B.I.C.C. Ltd., Belvedere, Kent, Eng., 1960-76; sec., office mgr. M & M Trailer Sales, Inc., Grand Coulee, Wash., 1976-82; owner, prin. Comrie Acctg. Services, 1983—, also dir. assoc. mem. Inst. Gen. Technician Engrs. (Eng.). Conservative. Mem. Ch. of Eng. Clubs: Moose, Eagles, Masons. Home: 327 Fortuyn Rd Grand Coulee WA 99133 Office: 102 Main St Grand Coulee WA 99133

COMSTOCK, NANCY MURRAY, educator, consultant; b. Phoenix, Sept. 16, 1933; d. George Harold and Mary Lois (Lambert) Crose; m. William Clarence Comstock, Feb. 26, 1932; children—William G., Jeanne Marie Comstock Weber, Cynthia Ann Comstock Jenkins. B.A., Fresno State U., 1966; M.A., Bakersfield State Coll., 1976. Cert. elem., secondary, adminstrv., reading specialist, Calif. Jr. high sch., reading tchr., Bakersfield, Calif., 1966-72; resource tchr. Lerdo Sch. Dist., Bakersfield, 1972-76; primary cons. Kern County Supt. Schs. Office, Bakersfield, 1976-79, reading cons., 1979-82, staff devel. cons., 1979-82, tchr. edn., computer ctr. dir., 1982—. Mem. Calif. Tchrs. Assn., Assn. Calif. Sch. Adminstrs., Assn. Supervision and Curriculum Devel., Internat. Reading Assn., Calif. Reading Assn., Delta Kappa Gamma, Phi Delta Kappa. Democrat. Roman Catholic. Author publs. in field. Home: 6404 Landfair Dr Bakersfield CA 93309 Office: Kern County Supt Schools Office 5801 Sundale Bakersfield CA 93309

CONANT, CHESTER MAVIS, JR., bank exec.; b. San Antonio, July 18, 1943; s. Chester Mavis and Mary Ruth (Lemon) C.; B.B.A., Tex. A. and M. U., 1963; m. Jane, July 29, 1978; 1 son, Randall Dean. Unit mgr. S.W. Bell Telephone Co., 1963-68; group mgr. credit services Foley's Dept. Stores, Houston, 1968-79; v.p., bus. mgr. Citicorp, San Mateo, Calif., 1979—. Chmn. Hardin County United Fund campaign; mem. Kountze (Tex.) Sch. Bd. Served to lt. USMC, 1960-62. Named Man of Yr., Graphic Communication Council Houston, 1977. Mem. Nat. Microfilm Assn. (pres. SW chpt., Man of Yr., SW chpt. 1978), Houston Retail Credit Assn. (bd. dirs.). Democrat. Methodist. Clubs: Rotary (v.p.), Kiwanis (pres.) DeMolay (life). Home: 668 Fathom Dr San Mateo CA 94404 Office: Citicorp PO Box 5937 San Mateo CA 94404

CONATY, CHARLES FRANCIS, film co. exec.; b. Los Angeles, Sept. 15, 1948; s. Charles Clement and Katherine Buckley (Roddy) C.; children—Garrett Michael, Gavin Charles. B.S. in Elec. Engring., U. So. Calif., 1971. Sales engr. Spectra Sonics, Los Angeles, 1971-72; engr. Hannon Engring., Los Angeles, 1972-73; v.p. United Sound, Inc., Burbank, Calif., 1973-77; v.p. sound systems, exec. dir. tech. div. Paramount Pictures Corp., Los Angeles, 1977—. Mem. tech. adv. com. Calif. Republican Com., 1981—. Mem. Soc. Motion Picture and TV Engrs., Audio Engring. Soc., Assn. for Computing Machinery. Club: Toastmasters. Office: 5555 Melrose Ave Los Angeles CA 90038

CONBOY, CHARLES EDWARD, real estate broker; b. Swampscott, Mass., Dec. 29, 1909; B.A., U. Hawaii, 1963; m. Muriel Veronica Abbey, Mar. 1, 1937; children—Alan Joseph, Charles Edward. Enlisted USN, 1928, advanced through grades to comdr., 1952, ret., 1958; salesman Windward Oahu Realty, Kailua, Hawaii, 1964-66; salesman, real estate broker Tropic Shores Realty, Honolulu, 1967-68; staff appraiser Hambleton & Asso., Inc., Honolulu, 1968-69, prin. broker, 1968-70; ind. fee appraiser, Honolulu, 1969—; ind. real estate broker, Honolulu, 1970—. Bd. dirs. Community Council Kailua, 1971-76; pres. Community Assn., Hawaii; treas. 25th dist. Republican party Hawaii, 1967-79. Mem. Am. Right of Way Assn., Honolulu Bd. Realtors, Nat. Assn. Realtors, Hawaii Assn. Real Estate Bds., Am. Soc. Appraisers (sr.), Navy League U.S. Roman Catholic. Home: 1423 Mokolea Dr Kailua HI 96734 Office: 733 Bishop St Suite 1616 Honolulu HI 96813

CONDÉ, RICHARD LOUIS, psychiatrist; b. Waterloo, Iowa, Sept. 16, 1922; s. Leon and Mildred Lucille (Kunce) C.; B.S. in Medicine, U. Minn., 1946, M.D., 1949; m. Mary Lou McLear, Apr. 10, 1948; children—Thomas John, Ann Louise, Mary Elizabeth. Intern, Ancker Hosp., St. Paul, 1948-49; resident Walter Reed Army Hosp., Washington, 1952-54; clin. dir. Anoka (Minn.) State Hosp., 1956-57; practice medicine specializing in psychiatry Colorado Springs, Colo., 1957—. Served to maj. U.S. Army, 1950-56. Decorated Bronze Star. Mem. AMA, Colorado Springs Psychiat. Soc. (pres. 1975-76) Colo. Med. Soc. (chmn. council pub. health 1968-75, chmn. com. alcoholism and drug abuse 1966-75), Am. Psychiat. Assn. Clubs: Cheyenne Mountain Country, Garden of the Gods, Broadmoor Golf. Home: 11 El Encanto Colorado Springs CO 80906 Office: 2131 N Tejon St Colorado Springs CO 80907

CONDIE, HELEN CROWTHER, home economics educator; b. Salt Lake City; d. Norman W. and Gwenfred (Jones) C.; m. Wilmar W. Condie, July 22, 1950; children—Gwendalyn Condie Lloyd, Steven Norman. B.S. in Home Econs. Edn., Utah State U.-Logan, 1948, M.S., 1954; Ed.D., Brigham Young U., 1983. Cert. tchr., Idaho. Tchr. home econs. Provo (Utah) High Sch., 1948-50, Preston (Idaho) High Sch., 1950-55; with dept. home econs. Idaho State U., Pocatello, 1956—, prof. consumer econs., 1970—; condr. workshops Idaho State Bd. Vocat. Edn. Recipient Idaho Vocat. Edn. Disting. Service award, 1976; Idaho Future Homemakers of Am. Award of Merit, 1982. Mem. Am. Home Econs. Assn., Idaho Home Econs. Assn. (cert. award 1981), Am. Vocat. Assn., Idaho Vocat. Assn., Home Econs. Edn. Assn., Nat. Assn. Home Econs. Tchr. Educators. Republican. Mormon. Authored curriculum guides; contbr. article to profl. jour. Office: Idaho State U Pocatello ID 83209

CONDIFF, DAVID WESLEY, psychologist, counseling center exec.; b. St. Paul, Sept. 22, 1943; s. Howard Lee and Hazel (Rice) C.; student U. Minn., 1961-62; B.A. summa cum laude, Bethel Coll., 1965; Ph.D., Fuller Grad. Sch., 1972; m. Lorraine Shelden, Aug. 28, 1965; children—Deborah Lorraine, David Wesley. Lab. technician Archer Daniels Midland Co., Mpls., 1962-65; minister of youth Glendale (Calif.) Alliance Ch., 1965-68; psychology clk. mental health unit Glendale Adventist Hosp., 1968-69, social worker asst., 1969-70; psychology intern San Fernando Valley Child Guidance Clinic, Van Nuys, Calif., 1969-70, Ingleside Mental Health Center, Rosemead, Calif., 1970-71; psychol. asst. Foothill Psychiat. Med. Group, Glendora, Calif., 1971-73, clin. psychologist, 1973-75; founding dir. Live Oak Counseling Center, Glendora, 1973—; clin. psychologist, marriage, family, child counselor, Glendora, 1973—; asso. staff mem. Sierra Royale Psychiat. Hosp., Azusa, Calif., 1978—; cons. to bus., chs., 1975—. Mem. Am. Psychol. Assn., Pi Epsilon Mu. Democrat. Office: Live Oak Counseling Center 1114 E Alosta Ave Glendora CA 91740

CONDON, CHARLES ROBERT, management consultant; b. Tacoma, Wash., Mar. 10, 1945; s. Lester Milo and Ruby Elizabeth (Elson) C.; m. Judy Baihly, Oct. 15, 1969; 1 dau., Mikal Jenna. B.S., U. Wash., 1968, M.B.A., 1973. With Olympic Assocs. Co., Seattle, 1973—, v.p., 1980—; also dir. Served with NOAA, 1968-71. Standard Oil scholar, 1972. Mem. Am. Assn. Cost Engrs. Presbyterian. Office: 1319 Dexter Ave N PO Box 9445 Seattle WA 98109

CONE, ANNE DIMARIA, lawyer; b. Palo Alto, Calif., Feb. 16, 1949; d. Philip A. and E. Carolyn (Chase) DiMaria; m. Samuel A. Ferguson, Mar. 19, 1968; children—Elizabeth Anne, Philip; m. 2d, Steven J. Cone, June 19, 1982. LL.B., Lincoln U., San Jose, Calif., 1978. Bar: Calif. 1979. Ptnr. DiMaria & Cone, 1979—. Mem. Santa Clara County Bar Assn., Palo Alto Bar Assn., Calif. Trial Lawyers Assn., Assn. Trial Lawyers Am., Peninsula Execs. Assn. Republican. Office: DiMaria & Cone 425 Sherman Ave Suite 320 Palo Alto CA 94306

CONE, LAWRENCE ARTHUR, physician, researcher, clin. adminstr.; b. N.Y.C., Mar. 23, 1928; s. Max and Ruth (Weber) C.; A.B., N.Y. U., 1948; M.D., U. Berne, Switzerland, 1954; m. Mary Elisabeth Osborne, Aug. 20, 1960; 1 son, Lionel Alfred. Interne, Meth. Hosp., Dallas, 1954-55, resident in medicine, 1955; resident in medicine Flower 5th Ave. Hosp., Met. Hosp., N.Y.C., 1957-60; asst. prof. medicine N.Y. Med. Coll., N.Y.C., 1962-68, asst. prof. microbiology, 1962-72, asso. prof. medicine, 1968-72; chief, immunology and infectious disease, 1962-72; practice internal medicine, N.Y.C., 1968-72, Rancho Mirage, Calif., 1972—; active staff Eisenhower Med. Center, Rancho Mirage, 1972—, chief sect. oncology, immunology and infectious disease, 1972—, chmn. dept. medicine, 1975—; Career Scientist Health Research Council N.Y., 1962-68; cons. infectious disease Good Samaritan Hosp., N.Y.C., 1966-72, Physicians Hosp., N.Y.C., 1965-72, Desert Hosp., 1977—. USPHS research fellow, immunology infectious disease, N.Y. U. Sch. Medicine, 1960-62. Diplomate Am. Bd. Internal Medicine, Am. Bd. Allergy and Immunology, Am. Bd. Infectious Disease, Am. Bd. Oncology. Served to capt. M.C. U.S. Army, 1955-57. Fellow Am. Coll. Physicians, Royal Soc. Medicine; mem. Am. Acad. Allergy, Am. Soc. Microbiology, Harvey Soc., Reticuloendothelical Soc., AMA, Calif. Med. Assn., Riverside County Med. Soc., Am. Fedn. Clin. Research, N.Y. Acad. Scis. Republican. Clubs: Tamarisk Country, Wild Wings (Palm Springs). Contbr. articles to med. jours. and books. Home: 765 Via Vadera St Palm Springs CA 92262

CONERLY, WILLIAM BOOTH, economist; b. San Diego, Jan. 12, 1952; s. Tom B. and Lila (Faught) C. B.A., New Coll., 1974; M.A., Duke U., 1976, Ph.D., 1980. Instr. econs. St. Andrews Presbyterian Coll., Laurinburg, N.C., 1977-80; econ. analyst Pacific Gas and Electric Co., San Francisco, 1980-81, sr. economist, 1981—; cons. Alpha Gen. Corp. Chmn. Libertarian Party of N.C., 1978-80; dir. N.C. Fund for Individual Rights, 1980. Donner Found. fellow, 1976-77. Mem. Am. Econ. Assn., Nat. Assn. Bus. Economists. Clubs: Commonwealth, Marina Sailing Soc. Office: 77 Beale St San Francisco CA 94501

CONFER, HARRY EDWARD, podiatric physician, surgeon; b. New Castle, Pa., Apr. 19, 1947; s. Clarence and Ruth E. (Byler) C.; B.A., Youngstown State U., 1970; Dr. Podiatric Medicine, Ohio Coll. Podiatric Medicine, 1977. Resident, Foot Clinic of Youngstown (Ohio), Community Hosp. Warren (Ohio), 1978; owner Foothills Podiatry Group, Tustin, Calif., 1979—; partner Pico Rivera (Calif.) Podiatrists Group, 1979—, West Covina (Calif.) Podiatrists Group, 1981—; mem. staffs Buena Park (Calif.) Community Hosp., Rio Honda Gen. Hosp., Pico Rivera, Calif., Tustin (Calif.) Community Hosp., Pico Rivera Community Hosp., Downey (Calif.) Community Hosp., Beverly Hosp., Montebello, Calif., Whittier (Calif.) Gen. Hosp., Good Samaritan Hosp., Anaheim, Calif., Queen of Valley Hosp., West Covina, Calif., West Covina Community Hosp. Diplomate Nat. Bd. Podiatric Examiners. Mem. Execs. Assn. Orange County Calif., Am. Podiatry Assn., Calif. Podiatry Assn., Orange County Podiatry Assn., Am. Assn. Hosp. Podiatrists, Tustin C. of C., Ohio Coll. Podiatric Medicine Alumni Assn., Youngstown State U. Alumni Assn., Am. Joggers Assn., Alpha Gamma Kappa. Club: Masons. Home: 747 Promontory Dr W Newport Beach CA 92660 Office: 8715 Washington Blvd Pico Rivera CA 90660 also 1212 S Glendora Ave West Covina CA 91790 also 105 S Prospect Ave Tustin CA 92680

CONFORTI, EMILE RALPH, plastics mfg. co. exec.; b. Torrington, Conn., Oct. 22, 1928; s. Emile Domenic and Catherine C.; B.A., Providence Coll., 1950; m. Kathleen Ann Zullo, Dec. 27, 1953; children—Diane, Donna, David. Mktg. mgr. Monsanto Co., St. Louis, 1956-68; pres., chief exec. officer Hollywood Plastics subs. Shell Chem., Los Angeles, 1968-73; exec. v.p., chief exec. officer, dir. Ampro Corp., Anaheim Calif., 1974, now pres., chief exec. officer; vice chmn. bd. Western Empire Savs. and Loan. Mem. Planning Commn. City of Placentia. Served with U.S. Army, 1951-53. Mem. Soc. Plastic Engrs., ASTM, Anaheim C. of C., Ostomy Assn. Orange County (pres.). Club: Yorba Linda Country. Office: 1340 N Jefferson St Anaheim CA 92807

CONGER, HARRY M., mining company executive; b. Seattle, July 22, 1930; s. Harry M. and Caroline (Gunnell) C.; m. Phyllis Nadine Shpeard, Aug. 14, 1949; children—Harry Milton, Preston George. Engr. Mines, Colo. Sch. Mines, 1955. Registered profl. engr., Ariz., Colo. Shift foreman Asarco, Inc., Silver Bell, Ariz., 1944-64; mgr. Kaiser Steel Corp., Eagle Mountain Mine, 1964-70; v.p., gen. mgr. Kaiser Resources, Ltd., Fernie, B.C., Can., 1970-73; v.p., gen. mgr. Midwestern div., Consolidation Coal Co., Carbondale, Ill., 1973-75; v.p. Homestake Mining Co., San Francisco, 1975-77, pres., 1977-78, pres., chief exec. officer, 1978-81, chmn., pres., chief exec. officer, 1981—; dir. Calif. Portland Cement Co., Pacific Gas & Elec. Co. Served with C.E., U.S. Army, 1956. Recipient Disting. Achievement medal Colo. Sch. Mines, 1978. Mem. AIME, Mining and Metallurgy Soc. Am., Am. Mining Congress (vice chmn.), Conf. Bd. Republican. Episcopalian. Clubs: Mining, Commonwealth, Pacific Union, Bankers, World Trade, Diable Country. Home: 1879 Piedras Circle Danville CA 94526 Office: 650 California St San Francisco CA 94108

CONKEY, HARLAN DON, educator, apt. rental co. exec.; b. Edmond, Kans., May 1, 1934; s. Howard B. and Lola G. (Pillmone) C.; m. Judy White, Aug. 17, 1958; children—Janet, Jeff, Jill. B.S., U. Kans., 1959, M.S. 1961; Ed.D. (Mabee fellow), U. Tulsa, 1964. Asst. prof. audiology Oreg. State U., 1969-71, assoc. prof., 1971-74, prof., 1974—; pres. Conkey Apts., Monmouth, Oreg., 1969—; pres. Beaver State Savs. & Loan, Monmouth, Oreg., 1975-79; dir. Baldwin Tool, HCI Industry. Served with U.S. Army, 1953-55. Club: Elks. Home: PO Box 125 Monmouth OR 97368 Office: Oreg State U Corvallis OR 97331

CONKEY, MAURICE CAMERON, civil engr.; b. Carthage, Mo., Nov. 4, 1901; s. Maurice Cameron and Irma (Strock) C.; student U. Calif. at Santa Barbara, 1920-22, Mass. Inst. Tech., 1922-25; m. Edith Grace Bond, May 12, 1961. Draftsman, Am. Bridge Co., Pa., 1925-27; bridge draftsman, designing engr. B&O R.R., 1927-37; asst. engr. J.E. Greiner

Co., Balt., 1937-44; chief structural engr. Del Monte Corp., San Francisco, 1947-54; project engr. H.K. Ferguson Co., San Francisco, 1955-65; cons. civil engr., Santa Barbara, 1965—. Registered profl. engr., Calif. Mem. Soc. Colonial Wars (treas. 1971-73, gentleman of the council 1978-80), Santa Barbara Hist. Soc. (life), Soc. War 1812. Republican. Episcopalian. Clubs: Coral Casino Cabana and Beach. Contbr. articles to profl. jours. Home: 1819 Olive Ave Santa Barbara CA 93101

CONKLE, GALEN EUGENE, accountant, corp. dir.; b. Clark, Ohio, Feb. 26, 1933; s. Maynard S. and Mary (Parks) C.; B.S. in Accounting, Sacramento State Coll., 1959; m. Lureen A. Edgar, Apr. 27, 1962; children—Galen John, Ramona Jean, Rebecca Lureen; stepchildren—Stephen, David, Ruth Strawn. Prin., Galen E. Conkle, C.P.A., Oceanside, Calif., 1963-66; partner Conkle, Sigrist & Co., C.P.A.'s, Oceanside, Calif., from 1966; later Partner Reschly & Conkle, C.P.A.s, Escondido; prin. Galen E. Conkle, C.P.A. Escondido, Calif.; now corp. dir.; instr. accounting and fed. income taxes Palomar Coll., San Marcos, Cal., 1964-68, 75-79. Served with USNR, 1951-55. Mem. Calif. Soc. C.P.A.'s. Republican. Home: Route 1 Box 532 Ramona CA 92065 Office: Conkle CPAs 420 W 5th Ave Escondido CA 92025

CONKLIN, ERNEST EMERY, accountant; b. Newton Falls, Ohio, Jan. 22, 1938; s. Wayne Hall and Virginia Almeta (Bailey) C.; m. Tima Ernest El-Sheikh, Dec. 18, 1971; 1 dau., Sara. B.S., Kent State U., 1961; M.S., Am. U. Beirut, Lebanon, 1975; postgrad. Drew U., Rider Coll., U. Nebr. C.P.A., Ohio, Calif. Staff auditor Coopers & Lybrands, C.P.A.s, Cleve., 1961-64; comptroller Hiram (Ohio) Coll., 1964-69; comptroller Am. U., Beirut, Lebanon, 1969-76; fin. dir. Modern Arab Contractor, Al-Khobar, Saudi Arabia, 1976-80; pres. Conklin Profl. Services, San Diego, 1980—; cons. Ford Found., United Negro Coll. Fund, Am. Univ. Assocs.; acctg. instr. Hiram Coll., Am. U. Beirut. Recipient Ernest Conklin Day award Hiram Village, 1969. Mem. Am. Inst. C.P.A.s, Calif. Soc. C.P.A.s, Ohio Soc. C.P.A.s, Peninsula C. of C. Republican. Club: Optimists Internat. Home: 2310 Caminito Estero San Diego CA 92107 Office: 1537 Rosecrans Suite G San Diego CA 92106

CONKLIN, MARILYN ALICE, nurse, educator; b. Spokane, Wash., Nov. 19, 1937; d. Charles Hobart and Agnes Alzina (Warriner) Solomon; m. John Louis Conklin, Sept. 25, 1973. Diploma in nursing Sacred Heart Sch. Nursing, 1964; B.S. in Health Sci. in Edn., Whitworth Coll., 1979; postgrad. Eastern Wash. U., 1983—. R.N., Wash. Staff nurse pediatrics Sacred Heart Hosp., Spokane, 1965-66, charge nurse orthopedics, 1969-71; nurse therapist Child Psychiat. Day Care Unit, U. Wash., Seattle, 1966-68; office nurse, Everett, Wash., 1968-69; nurse maternity dept. Everett Gen. Hosp., 1971-72; staff nurse Holy Family Hosp., Spokane, 1972-75, instr. ednl. services, 1975-76, co-dir. ednl. services, 1976-78, dir., 1978—; health care seminar leader. Mem. Am. Soc. Tng. and Devel., Am. Soc. Health Edn. and Tng. of Am. Hosp. Assn. (past pres. eastern Wash./Idaho chpt.). Developed program Human Aspects of Health Care. Home: W 3231 Boone Ave San Souci West #127 Spokane WA 99201 Office: N 5633 Lidgerwood Ave Spokane WA 99207

CONKLIN, RICHARD GRIDLEY, architect; b. Santa Barbara, Calif., July 22, 1931; s. George Ellis and Ella Mae (Freeman) C.; student NW Nazarene Coll., Nampa, Idaho, 1949-50, Portland State U., 1955-57; B.Arch. summa cum laude, U. Oreg., 1960; m. Solveig Birgitte Jorgensen, June 13, 1953; children—Richard, David, Julie, Nancy. Architect with Stanley M. Morse, Denver, 1960-61, Fisher and Davis, Denver, 1961-63, Earl Morris Assos., Denver, 1963-64, Arbogast-Jones-Reed Assos., Los Angeles, 1964-65, Daniel, Mann, Johnson & Mendenhall, Los Angeles, 1965, v.p., 1978—; bds. dirs. SOLARCOA, Parker Corp.; lectr. Calif. State Poly. U., Pomona, tech. and media confs. U. So. Calif.; annual speaker Women in Industry, Los Angeles Chpt. Served with Intelligence, USAF, 1951-55. Recipient nat. archtl. design awards: Peoria Detention Facility, Fla. Jr. Coll., Jacksonville, Santa Monica City Coll. Library, Universidad Santa Maria La Antigua, Panama, Butte Coll., Calif. local and nat. design awards for various facilities Ch. of the Nazarene; registered architect, Colo., Calif., Kans., Oreg., Idaho, Mo., Wash., Nev. Mem. AIA (chmn. nat. com. architecture for justice 1981; v.p. design and public awareness Calif. council, dir. 1979-81, fin. com. 1981, justice systems com. 1974-79; dir. Los Angeles chpt. 1979-81, continuing edn. com. 1980, public bldgs. com. 1977), Am. Correctional Assn., Nat. Council Crime and Delinquency, Assn. Community Coll. Trustees (workshop chmn. nat. conv.), Council Ednl. Facility Planners, Los Angeles C. of C. (So. Calif. Dist. planning com.). Mem. Church of Nazarene (dir.). Clubs: Los Angeles Athletic, Rotary. Author AIA slide presentation: The Greening of Grey Granite, 1978; photographer, author lectures on architecture of Portugal, Saudi Arabia, Japan, Philippines, Mex., Eng., Bangkok, Indonesia, Australia, Panama; seminar speaker, TV panelist. Home: 3462 Yellowtail Dr Los Alamitos CA 90720 Office: 3250 Wilshire Blvd Los Angeles CA 90010

CONKLING, RALPH FRANK, criminology educator; b. Buffalo, Dec. 6, 1925; s. Ralph E. and Jennie (Russo) C.; m. Jean Louise Philipps, Aug. 14, 1948; children—Betty Martin, Joann Lepsch. Ph.D. in Criminology, U. Beverly Hills, 1981. Undercover agt., security supr. Sears, Roebuck & Co., Los Angeles, 1946-55; chief spl. agt. Thrifty Drug Co., Los Angeles, 1955-78; corp. dir. security and safety Glaser Bros., Los Angeles, 1978—; prof. criminology U. Beverly Hills, 1983—. Bd. dirs. Tierra Del Sol, Sch. for Retarded, 1982—. Served with USMC, 1943-46. Roman Catholic. Office: 3130 Leonis Blvd Vernon CA 90058

CONKLING, ROGER LINTON, consultant, retired utility company executive; b. Bloomington, Ill., July 12, 1917; s. Robert Edwin and Helen (Ricketts) C.; B.B.A., Northwestern U., 1941; M.A., U. Oreg., 1948; LL.D., U. Portland, 1972; m. Meta Baskerville, Apr. 4, 1941; children—Mary Beth, Jane Linton, Roger Marc. With Pub. Service Co. of No. Ill., Chgo., Joliet, Ill., 1936-42; economist Bonneville Power Adminstrn., Portland, Oreg., 1945-47, asst. to power mgr., 1948-51, chief system devel., 1952-53, chief customer service, 1954, dir. budget and mgmt., 1955-56, asst. to adminstr., 1957, past mem. adv. council; v.p., asso. H. Zinder & Asso., Inc., Washington, 1958-61; pres. Conkling, Inc., cons., Portland, 1962-67; v.p. N.W. Natural Gas Co., Portland, 1967-76, sr. v.p., 1976-82; nat. energy econs. cons.; trustee Assn. Wash. Gas Utilities, 1970-82; former pres., dir. Pacific Western Pipeline Corp., Portland. Mem. faculty Northwestern U., grad. faculty Oreg. System Higher Edn., Portland, 1946-56. Past pres., chmn. Oreg. United Appeal; pres. Delauney Inst. Mental Health, 1964; mem. Gov.'s Com. Child Care, 1964; bd. dirs. Cath. Charities, Inc., Portland, 1957-58, 61-64, Parry Center; pres. Oreg. State Soc., Washington, 1960; chmn. exec. com. Nat. Found., Washington, 1958-60; chmn. March Dimes Campaign, Portland, 1957; bd. dirs. Mental Health Assn., 1957-58, Cath. Services for Children, 1954-57, Nat. Found. for Infantile Paralysis, Portland, 1956-58, Found. Oreg. Research and Edn., 1967—, Oreg. Ind. Coll. Found.; chmn. bd. regents U. Portland; trustee Providence Children's Center; bd. dirs. NCCJ; bd. dirs. Oreg. Symphony Assn., chmn. ann. fund campaign, 1981. Served with USNR, 1942-45. Recipient Distinguished Service award Dept. Interior; Arthur S. Fleming award Jr. C. of C. Mem. Am. Econ. Assn., Western Econ. Assn., Fed. Govt. Accountants Assn., Am. Gas Assn., Pacific Coast Gas Assn., Beta Gamma Sigma, Delta Mu Delta. Clubs: Multnomah Athletic (Portland, Oreg.). Home and Office: 2539 SW Hill Crest Dr Portland OR 97201

CONLAN, JOHN GREGG, dentist; b. Susanville, Calif., Mar. 28, 1931; s. John Patrick and Anita (Barclay) C.; B.S., St. Mary's Coll., 1952; D.D.S., Coll. Physicians and Surgeons, 1956; m. Joan Anderson, June 19, 1956; children—Susan, Amy, Kathleen. Pvt. practice dentistry for children, Eureka, Calif., 1958—; clin. instr. pedodontics U. Pacific Sch. Dentistry, San Francisco, 1970-73; mem. staff St. Joseph's Hosp., Gen. Hosp., both Eureka. Served to capt. USAF, 1956-58. Mem. Acad. Dentistry for Handicapped, Calif. Soc. Pediatric Dentists, Calif. Soc. Dentistry for Children, Am. Acad. Pedodontics, Calif. Dental Assn. (pres. 10th dist. 1965), Flying Dentists Assn., Delta Sigma Delta. Home: 3186 Lucia Ave Eureka CA 95501 Office: 2460 Buhne St Eureka CA 95501

CONLEY, BRYAN CHARLES, economist; b. Vancouver, B.C., Can., Sept. 28, 1942; s. Charles Nelson and Margaret (Robinson) C.; m. Mary Libbey, Apr. 8, 1972; children—Sarah, Laura. B.A., U. Wash., 1964; Ph.D., U. Calif.-Santa Barbara, 1972. Research asst. UCLA, 1967-70; lectr., asst. prof. bus. econs. U. So. Calif., Los Angeles, 1974-79; prin. Bryan Conley, litigation support cons., Pacific Palisades, Calif., 1979—. NDEA fellow, 1964; Resources for the Future fellow, 1966. Mem. Am. Econ. Assn., Western Econ. Assn. Episcopalian. Author: (with others) Program Budgeting for Health and Welfare, 1974; mem. editorial com. Anns. of Regional Sci., 1969-75; contbr. articles to profl. jours. Home and Office: 1146 Fiske St Pacific Palisades CA 90272

CONLEY, ZEB BRISTOL, JR., art gallery dir.; b. Andrews, N.C., Feb. 12, 1936; s. Zeb Bristol and A. Elizabeth (Faircloth) C.; student N.C. State Coll., 1954-55, Mars Hill Coll., 1955-57, Coll. William and Mary, 1957-61; m. Betty Ann Wiswall, May 25, 1974; stepchildren—Peter Wiswall Betts, Stephen Wood Betts, Frederick Beale Betts, III. Designer, Seymour Robins, Inc., N.Y.C., 1961; with First Nat. Bank, Las Vegas (N.Mex.), 1964-65; gen. mgr. Swanson's Inc., Las Vegas, 1965-73, v.p., 1969—; dir. Jamison Galleries, Sante Fe, 1973—, sec. Marbasconi, Inc., d.b.a. Jamison Galleries, 1974-80, pres., 1980—. Bd. dirs. Las Vegas Mental Health Assn., 1963-65; office mgr. Las Vegas Opera Guild, 1971-73. Republican. Home: PO Box 2534 Santa Fe NM 87501 Office: The Jamison Galleries 111 E San Francisco St Santa Fe NM 87501

CONLY, JOHN FRANKLIN, engineering educator; b. Ridley Park, Pa., Sept. 11, 1933; s. Harlan and Mary Jane (Roberts) C.; m. Jeanine Teresa McDonough, Apr. 15, 1967; children—Mary Ann, John Paul. B.S. in Mech. Engring., U. Pa., 1956, M.S. in Mech. Engring., 1958; Ph.D., Columbia U., 1962. Asst. instr. U. Pa., Phila., 1956-58; research asst. Columbia U., N.Y.C., 1960-62; asst. prof. San Diego State U., 1962-65, assoc. prof., 1965-70, prof., 1970—, chmn. dept. aerospace engring. and engring. mechanics, 1970-74, 78—, wind tunnel dir., 1978—. Daniel and Florence Guggenheim fellow, 1958; Am. Soc. Engring. Edn.-NASA fellow, 1968. Assoc. fellow AIAA (chmn. San Diego sect. 1970); mem. Am. Soc. Engring. Edn., AAUP, Calif. State Edn. Assn. Club: San Diego State U. Faculty-Staff. Office: Dept Aerospace Engineering San Diego State University San Diego CA 92182

CONN, RICHARD GEORGE, museum curator; b. Bellingham, Wash., Oct. 28, 1928; s. Bert Grover and Mary Ann (Slack) C. B.A., U. Wash., 1950, M.A., 1955. Curator Indian art Denver Art Mus., 1955-59, curator native arts, 1973—; dir. Eastern Wash. Hist. Soc., Spokane, 1959-66; chief human history Man. (Can.) Mus., Winnipeg, 1966-72; dir. Mus. of Albuquerque, 1973; adj. prof. anthropology U. Colo., Denver. Works include: Robes of White Shell and Sunrise, Denver Art Mus., 1974, Native American Art, 1979; Circles of the World, 1982. Served to cpl. U.S. Army, 1951-53. McCloy fellow in art, 1979. Mem. Am. Assn. Mus. Methodist.

CONNELLEE, BARBARA GALBRAITH, laboratory administrator; b. Hereford, Tex., Dec. 4, 1929; d. Herman and Audrey Stella (Carroll) Galbraith; m. Rodger Sadosa Connellee, Oct. 1, 1950; children—Alison Elaine, Rebecca Diane Connellee Crabtree. B.S., U. N.Mex., 1976, M.B.A., 1981. Mem. adminstrv. staff U. Calif. Los Alamos Nat. Lab., 1976—. Pres., Wesleyan Service Guild, 1958. Recipient Women at Work award region 8 Dept. Labor Council on Working Women, 1983. Mem. Nat. Assn. Female Execs., Laser Inst. Am., Optical Soc., Women in Sci. United Methodist (past dir. edn.). Office: PO Box 1663 MS E 505 Los Alamos NM 87544

CONNELLY, DONALD PATRICK, health services administrator; b. St. Louis, Apr. 14, 1924; s. Patrick Joseph and Angela Mary (Dryer) C.; m. Mary Eileen, Oct. 28, 1950; children—Mary Colleen Connelly Braswell, Donald Patrick, Jr., Megan Ann, Maureen Lynn Connelly McNally. B.A., Wayne State U., 1951; lic. nursing care adminstr. #101, Ariz. 1976. Staff mem. Gen. Motors Inst., Flint, Mich., 1958; asst. dir. Sinai Hosp., Detroit, Mich., 1958-64; pres. Devon Gables Health Care Center, Tucson, Royale Convalescent Hosp., Santa Ana, Calif., San Gabriel Valley Convalescent Hosp., El Monte, Calif., Desert Manor Nursing Home, Yuma, Ariz., 1964—. Served with AUS, 1943-46. Mem. Assn. Healthcare Facilities, Am. Coll. Nursing Home Adminstrs., Western Gerontological Soc., Am. Hosp Assn., Ariz. Bur. Health Econs.

CONNELLY, THEODORE SAMPLE, communications executive; b. Middletown, Conn., Oct. 15, 1925; s. Herbert Lee and Mabel Gertrude (Wells) C.; B.A., Wesleyan U., 1948, postgrad., 1951; postgrad. U. Paris, 1950. Sec., Nat. Com. on Edn., Am. Trucking Assn., Inc., Washington, 1952-54; dir. public affairs Nat. Automobile Club, San Francisco, 1955-62; pres., chmn. Connelly Corp., San Francisco, 1963—; treas. Ednl. Access Cable TV Corp.; dir. Mission Neighborhood Centers, Inc., Neighborhood Devel. Corp.; mem. adv. com. on Calif. motor vehicle legis., 1955-62, Calif. State C. of C. com. on hwys., 1958-62. Trustee, sec., v.p. Lincoln U.; sec. Lincoln U. Found., 1968-80; bd. dirs. San Francisco Program for Aging; founder Communications Library, 1963, Communications Inst., 1978; founding mem. Calif. Council for UN Univ., 1976; organizer Internat. Child Art Collection; co-founder African Research Commn., 1970; established Connelly Fund, 1981. Served with USNR, 1943-54. Recipient cert. of merit San Francisco Jaycees, 1959; award of merit USPHS, 1980, citation, 1981. Mem. AAAS, AAUP, Public Relations Round Table San Francisco, Atlanta Hist. Soc., Asian Mass Communication and Info. Centre (Singapore), NAACP, SAR, Press Club San Francisco, UN Assn. U.S.A., Nat. Sci. Tchrs. Assn. (bus.-industry sect.). Club: Dolphin Swimming and Boating (San Francisco). Author/compiler: BCTV Bibliography on Cabletelevision, 1975—; Electromagnetic Radiation, 1976; CINCOM: Courses in Communications, 1978; editor: An Analysis of Joint Ventures in China, 1982; contbr. articles to profl. jours.; producer, writer, dir. numerous TV programs. Office: Communications Inst 1550 Bryant St San Francisco CA 94103

CONNER, FINIS FREDRICK, manufacturing company executive; b. Gadsden, Ala., July 28, 1943; s. William Otis and Vera Belle (Beasley) C.; m. Julie Manchura, July 15, 1972. B.S. in Indsl. Mgmt., San Jose State U., 1969; grad. U. Santa Clara, 1971. Pres., Mastec Corp., Cupertino, Calif., 1969-71; original equipment mfr. market mgr. Memorex, Santa Clara, Calif., 1971-79; founder, western regional mgr. Shugart Assocs., Sunnyvale, Calif., 1973-79; founder, exec. v.p. Seagate Tech., Scotts Valley, Calif., 1979—, also dir. Served with USN Air Res. Democrat. Clubs: The Vintage, Indian Wells Country (Palm Springs, Calif.); Castle Pines Country (Denver). Office: Seagate Technology 920 Disc Dr Scotts Valley CA 95066

CONNER, LARRY MICHAEL, optometrist, consultant; b. Phoenix, Feb. 25, 1947; s. Louis M. and Ida Louise (Kurtz) C.; m. Joan Marie Yachon; children—Linda, Karen, Brian. O.D., La Verne U., 1969; O.D., So. Calif. Cool. Optometry, 1972. Lic. optometrist. Practice optometry, Glendale, Ariz., 1972—; researcher soft contact lenses; cons. vision specialist Sperry Flight Systems. Pres. Bicentennial commn., Glendale, Airz.; v.p. charter com. Boys Club: active Boy Scouts Am.; mem. adv. bd. Samaritan Health Services. Mem. Am. Optometric Assn. (Consumer Edn. award 1980), Better Vision Inst., Ariz. Mineral. Soc. (bd. dirs.). Republican. Mormon. Clubs: Optimist (pres.), Lions (Vision Service award 1978) (Glendale). Home: 8420 N 49th Ave Glendale AZ 85302 Office: 8503 N 51st Ave Glendale AZ 85302

CONNER, RICHARD LOUIS, computer services executive, consultant, lawyer; b. North Charleroi, Pa., Mar. 17, 1934; s. Rupert Dean and Catherinne Modistine (Dulak) C. A.B., Shimer Coll., 1954; J.D., U. Chgo., 1975. Bar: Ill. 1975, Calif. 1977, U.S. Supreme Ct. 1979. Program mgr. advanced systems tech. IBM Corp., 1959-69; mng. dir. Cia, Real de Processamento de Dados, Sao Paulo, Brazil, 1969-71; mgr. systems devel. U. Calif.-Berkeley, 1971-72; asst. atty. gen. Ill., 1976-77; prin. Custom Computer Services, San Francisco, 1977—. Served to capt. USAF, 1955-59. Mem. ABA, Assn. Systems Mgmt., San Francisco Bar Assn., Lawyers Club San Francisco. Roman Catholic. Clubs: Jockey (Sao Paulo, Brazil); San Francisco Yacht (Tiburon, Calif.); Commonwealth. Home and Office: 1243 Pine St San Francisco CA 94109

CONNETT, ROGER LEE, coal co. exec.; b. St. Francis, Kans., May 28, 1948; s. Wilbur G. and C. Lorraine (Elley) C.; student Casper Coll., 1966-67, Central Wyo. Coll., 1978-79; m. Sally Conrad, Feb. 12, 1967; children—Janeen, Tori. Foreman, Gilpatrick Constrn. Co., Riverton, Wyo., 1969-77; planning supr. American Partners Co., Gas Hills, Wyo., 1977-79; sr. supt. mech. maintenance Thunder Basin Coal Co., Gillette, Wyo., 1979—. Mem. adv. bd. Sheridan Coll., 1980. Mem. Wyo. Area Master Mechanics. Republican. Methodist. Clubs: Elks, Masons, Shriners. Office: PO Box 406 Wright WY 82732

CONNICK, C(HARLES) MILO, clergyman, educator; b. Conneaut Lake Park, Pa., Mar. 23, 1917; s. Walter and Iola Belle (Wintermute) C.; A.B., Allegheny Coll., 1939, D.D. (hon.), 1960; S.T.B. magna cum laude, Boston U., 1942, Ph.D., 1944; postgrad. Harvard U. Episcopal Div. Sch., 1942-44; m. Genevieve Shaul, June 7, 1941; children—Joy Connick Parker, Christopher Milo, Nancy Connick Jankowski. Ordained to ministry United Meth. Ch., 1941; asso. minister St. Paul's Meth. Ch., Lowell, Mass., 1940-41, Copley Meth. Ch., Boston, 1941-42; dir. Wesley Found., Harvard U., summers 1943, 44; sr. instr. Curry Coll., Boston, 1942-44; head Bible dept. Northfield (Mass.) Sch., 1944-46; prof. religion Whittier (Calif.) Coll., 1946-82, prof. emeritus, 1982—, trustee coll., 1982—, chmn. dept., 1946-82; editorial cons.; pres. I-TAC, 1976—. Pres., ACLU, Whittier, 1953-56. Recipient Disting. Alumnus award Boston U., 1971. Danforth Found. fellow; Haynes Found. fellow; Roswell R. Robinson fellow, 1942-43; Danforth Found. asso., 1959. Mem. Am. Acad. Religion (pres. Western region 1953-54), Soc. Bibl. Lit., AAUP (pres. Whittier 1970-72), Am. Christian Assn. for Israel (nat. adv. com. 1964-69), Kappa Phi Kappa, Omicron Delta Kappa, Phi Sigma Tau, Chi Delta Sigma. Democrat. Author: Build on the Rock, You and the Sermon on the Mount, 1960; Jesus—The Man, The Mission, and the Message, 1963, 74; The Message and Meaning of the Bible, 1965; The New Testament, An Introduction to Its History, Literature and Thought, 1972, 78; contbr. articles to nat. mags. and profl. jours. Home: 6249 Roundhill Dr Whittier CA 90601 Office: Dept Religion Whittier Coll Whittier CA 90608

CONNOLLY, HUGH FRANCIS, lawyer; b. N.Y.C., Sept. 16, 1928; s. John Patrick and Helen Marie (Reid) C.; m. Paulette Marie Tobin, Feb. 9, 1952; children—Colleen, Maureen Connolly Holmes, Brian, Thomas, Christopher. A.B. in Greek, Fordham U., 1951, J.D., 1958. Admitted to Calif. bar, 1958; ptnr. firm Anderson, McMillan & Connolly, Burlingame, Calif., 1958-82; individual practice law, Burlingame, 1982—; instr. real estate law Coll. of San Mateo, 1968-74; pres. Seton Med. Office Ctr., Inc.; gen. counsel Seton Med. Ctr., St. Catherine Hosp., San Mateo-Burlingame Bd. Realtors, Redwood City-San Carlos-Belmont Bd. Realtors, North San Mateo County Bd. Realtors, South Lake Tahoe Bd. Realtors. Pres., Cath. Social Service San Mateo County, Cath. Social Service San Francisco Archdiocese, Serra High Sch. Bd. Edn., San Mateo County Easter Seal Soc., chmn. legal affairs com. Cath. Health Assn. U.S. Served to 1st lt., AUS, 1951-53. Recipient Vol. of Yr. award San Mateo County Easter Seal Soc., 1977. Mem. ABA, Am. Soc. Hosp. Attys., Burlingame C. of C. (pres.), Calif. Assn. Cath. Hosps. (pres.). Republican. Roman Catholic. Club: Burlingame Kiwanis (pres.). Office: 1450 Chapin Ave Burlingame CA 94010

CONNOLLY, JOHN EARLE, surgeon, educator; b. Omaha, May 21, 1923; s. Earl A. and Gertrude (Eckerman) C.; A.B., Harvard U., 1945, M.D., 1948; m. Virginia Hartman, Aug. 12, 1967; children—Peter Hart, John Earle, Sarah. Intern in surgery, Stanford U. Hosps., San Francisco, 1948-49, asst. resident surgeon, 1950-52, chief resident surgeon, 1953-54, surg. research fellow, 1949-50, surg. pathology fellow, 1954, instr. surgery, 1957-60, from asst. prof. to asso. prof., 1960-65, John and Mary Markle scholar in med. scis., 1957-62; prof., chmn. Dept. Surgery, U. Calif.-Irvine, 1965-78, chmn. thoracic and vascular surgery, 1978—; surg. registrar profl. unit St. Bartholomew's Hosp., London, 1952-53; resident in thoracic surgery Bellevue Hosp., N.Y.C., 1955; resident in thoracic and cardiovascular surgery, Columbia-Presbyn. Med. Center, N.Y.C., 1956; attending surgeon Stanford Med. Center, Palo Alto, Calif., 1959-65; cons. Long Beach (Calif.) VA Hosp., Long Beach Naval Hosp., 1965—; chmn. cardiovascular and thoracic surgery U. Calif., Irvine Med. Center, 1968—; staff St. Joseph's-Children's Hosp., Anaheim Meml. Hosp., 1968—; adv. council Heart, Lung & Blood Inst., NIH, Bethesda, Md., 1981—. Served with U.S. Army, 1943-44. Diplomate Am. Bd. Surgery (dir. 1976-82), Am. Bd. Thoracic Surgery. Fellow ACS (gov. 1964-70, regent 1973-82), Royal Coll. Surgeons (Eng.) (hon.), Royal Coll. Surgeons (Ireland) (hon.); mem. Am. Surg. Assn., Soc. Univ. Surgeons, Am. Assn. Thoracic Surgery, Pacific Coast Surg. Assn. (recorder 1973-79), San Francisco Surg. Soc., Los Angeles Surg. Soc., Soc. Vascular Surgery, Western Surg. Assn., Internat. Cardiovascular Soc. (pres. 1977), Soc. Internat. Chirgirie, Soc. Thoracic Surgeons, Samson Thoracic Surg. Soc. (pres. 1978), Audio-Digest Found. (dir. 1975—), Franklin Martin Found. (bd. dirs. 1974-80). Clubs: Calif. (Los Angeles), San Francisco Golf, Pacific-Union, Bohemian (San Francisco); Cypress Point (Pebble Beach, Calif.); Harvard (N.Y.C.). Contbr. articles to profl. jours.; editorial bd. Jour. Cardiovascular Surgery, 1974—, Western Jour. of Medicine, 1975—, Jour. Stroke, 1979—, Jour. Vascular Surgery, 1983—. Home: 5135 Altoona Ln Irvine CA 92715 Office: Dept Surgery Univ Calif Irvine CA 92717

CONNOLLY, THOMAS JOSEPH, bishop; b. Tonopah, Nev., July 18, 1922; s. John and Katherine (Hammel) C.; student St. Joseph Coll., Menlo Park, Calif., 1936-42, St. Patrick Sem., 1942-47; J.C.L., Cath. U., Washington, 1951; J.C.D., Pontifical U., Rome, 1952; D.H.L. (hon.), U. Portland (Oreg.), 1972. Ordained priest Roman Cath. Ch., 1947; asst. priest St. Thomas Aquinas Catherdral, Reno, 1947; rector, 1953-55; asst. priest Little Flower Ch., Reno, 1947-48; sec. to bishop, Diocese of Reno, 1948-49; tchr. Manogue High Sch., Reno, 1948-49; asst. priest St. Albert Great Ch., Reno, 1952-53; pastor, 1960-68; pastor St. Joseph Ch., Elko, Nev., 1955-60; pastor St. Teresa Ch., Carson City, Nev., 1968-71; consecrated bishop, 1971; bishop, Diocese of Baker (Oreg.), 1971—; mem. adminstrv. com. Nat. Conf. Cath. Bishops, 1973-76; mem. adv. council, 1974-76; mem. adminstrv. bd. U.S. Cath. Conf., 1973-76; bd. dirs. Cath. Communications N.W., 1978-81; mem. Bishops' Com. for N.Am. Coll., 1978—; chmn. of Bishops of Region XII, 1980—. Office: Box 826 2215 1st St Baker OR 97814

CONNOR, GARY EDWARD, manufacturing company executive; b. S.I., N.Y., Nov. 13, 1948; s. Everett M. and Josephine (Amato) C.; B.S. in Elec. Engring., U. Md., 1973; M.B.A., U. Santa Clara (Calif.), 1979. Quality assurance engr. Frankford Arsenal, 1973; quality assurance engr., field service engr. Lockheed Electronics Co., 1973-74; group leader memory test engring. sect. head bipolar product engring. Nat. Semicondr. Corp., 1975-79; internat. mktg. mgr. Am. Microsystems Inc., 1979-80; mktg. mgr. GenRad-STI, Santa Clara, 1980-82 prodn. mktg. exec., mgr. interface product mktg. AMD, Sunnyvale, Calif., 1982—. Mem. IEEE, Electronics Internat. Adv. Panel, Am. Security Council (nat. adv. bd.), Franklin Mint Collectors Soc. Republican. Home: 800 Saratoga Ave #206A San Jose CA 95129 Office: 901 Thompson Pl PO Box 453 Sunnyvale CA 94086

CONNORS, STEPHEN WILFRED, lawyer; b. Monroe, Wis., Mar. 11, 1918; s. Patrick J. and Alice (Norder) C.; student U. Wis., 1937-41, U. Minn., 1951; B. Sci. Law, St. Paul Coll. Law, 1950, LL.B. cum laude, 1952; J.D., William Mitchell Coll. Law, 1969; m. Louise Pharr, Feb. 4, 1946; children—Maureen, Patricia, Constance, Mary, Michele, Kelly. Admitted to Ariz. bar, 1953, Minn. bar, 1952; practiced in Phoenix, 1953—; pres. Olympia Realty, Inc.; dir. Truten Investment Corp. Mem. Ariz. State Athletic Commn., 1961; mem. adv. council Am. Security Council; precinct committeeman Democratic Party, 1954-59, 61-72, mem. Dem. State Central Com., 1954-59, 61-72. Served as sr. pilot USAF, 1943-53, disch. capt. Mem. Am., Ariz., Maricopa County, Minn., Ramsey County bar assns., VFW (life), Am. Legion, Amvets, Hump Pilots Assn. (life), Mil. Flight Service (life dir., legal officer), Fraternal Order of Police, Friendly Sons of St. Patrick, Am. Trial Lawyers Assn., Internat. Assn. Jewish Lawyers and Jurists, Internat. Acad. Law and Sci., Am. Judicature Soc., Academia Internationali Lex et Scientia. Roman Catholic. Moose. Clubs: Phoenix Execs., Prescott Mountain, Phoenix Press, Terrace, Arizona. Home: 8650 E Sandalwood Dr Scottsdale AZ 85253 Office: 810 Clubhouse Dr Prescott AZ

CONOVER, ROBERT WARREN, librarian; b. Manhattan, Kans., Oct. 6, 1937; s. Robert Warren and Grace Darline (Grinstead) C.; B.A., Kans. State U., 1959; M.A., U. Denver, 1961. Librarian, supervising librarian County of Fresno, Calif., 1961-66; county librarian County of Yolo, Woodland, Calif., 1967-68; dir. City of Fullerton (Calif.) Public Library, 1968-73, City of Pasadena (Calif.) Public Library, 1973-80, Palos Verdes Library Dist., Palos Verdes Peninsula, Calif., 1980—. Bd. dirs. Rancho de los Palos Verdes Hist. Soc., 1981. Recipient Pres.'s award Fresno Jaycees, 1963. Mem. ALA, Orange County Library Assn. (pres. 1971), Spl. Libraries Assn., Calif. Library Assn. (pres. Yosemite chpt. 1965), mem. council 1981), Libraria Sodalitas (dir. 1981), Santiago Library System Council (pres. 1972), Palos Verdes C. of C., Pi Kappa Alpha. Republican. Episcopalian. Clubs: Rotary, Univ. (Pasadena). Office: 650 Deep Valley Dr Palos Verdes Peninsula CA 90274

CONOVER, THEODORE ELBERT, journalism educator; b. Phila., Pa., Aug. 10, 1921; s. Elbert M. and Ethel (Holdcraft) C. m. Edna Florence Harsha, May 13, 1944; children—David Paul, Nancy Ann, Linda S. Conover Wampler. Student MIT, 1943, U. R.I., 1944, Wittenburg U., 1949; B.S. in Journalism, Ohio U., 1959, M.A., 1960; postgrad. U. Nev., 1961, 63. Owner, pub. Twin City News, Balt., 1946-47, Miami Gazette, Waynesville, Ohio, 1947-48, West Liberty (Ohio) Banner, 1950, Centerburg (Ohio) Gazette, 1953-60; mng. editor Daily Standard, Celina, Ohio, 1951-52; founder, pub. Reynoldsburg (Ohio) Record, 1958-60; asst. prof. U. Nev.-Reno, 1960-65, assoc. prof., 1965-69, prof., 1970—, chmn. dept. 1967-77; state mgr. News Election Service, 1978-79; with election coverage, NBC News, 1975-77. Served with U.S. Army, 1944-46. Decorated Purple Heart with oak leaf cluster. Fellow Pub. Relations Soc. Am., Am. Bus. Press; mem. Am. Soc. Journalism Sch. Adminstrs. (pres. 1973-74), Newspaper Assn. Mgrs., Assn. for Edn. in Journalism, Am. Journalism History Assn., Kappa Tau Alpha, Sigma Delta Chi. Methodist. Club: Lions. Contbr. numerous articles to profl. jours. Home: 13305 S Hills Dr Reno NV 89511 Office: Dept Journalism U Nevada Reno NV 89557

CONQUEST, LOVEDAY LOYCE, biostatistics educator, statistical consultant; b. Hilo, Hawaii, Jan. 22, 1948; d. Jay Walter and Daisy Eloise (Yamaguchi) C. B.A. in Math., Pomona Coll., 1970. M.S. in Stats., Stanford U., 1972; Ph.D. in Biostats., U. Wash., 1975. Asst. prof. biostats., dept. pub. health scis. U. Hawaii, Honolulu, 1975-76; vis. asst. prof. Ctr. Quantitative Sci., U. Wash., Seattle, 1976-77, asst. prof., 1978-83, assoc. prof., 1983—; vis. asst. prof. Sch. Bus. Adminstrn., 1977-78; statis. cons. to local bus. and govt. Mem. ch. council Univ. Congregational Ch., 1980—. Mem. Am. Statis. Assn., Biometric Soc., AAAS, Am. Women in Sci., Assn. Women in Math., U. Wash. Pub. Health Alumni Assn. (pres. 1980—), Belvedere Soc. (Pres. 1982—), Phi Beta Kappa (pres. 1983—, trustee), Sigma Xi (pres. 1982-83). Club: City (Seattle). Office: Ctr Quantitative Sci HR-20 U Wash 3737 15th Ave NE Room 304 Seattle WA 98195

CONRAD, HAROLD THEODORE, psychiatrist; b. Milw., Jan. 25, 1934; s. Theodore Herman and Alyce Barbara (Kolb) C.; A.B., U. Chgo., 1954, B.S., 1955, M.D., 1958; m. Elaine Marie Blaine, Sept. 1, 1962; children—Blaine, Carl, David, Erich, Rachel. Intern USPHS Hosp., San Francisco, 1958-59; commd. sr. asst. surgeon USPHS, 1958, advanced through grades to med. dir., 1967; resident in psychiatry USPHS Hosp., Lexington, Ky., 1959-61, Charity Hosp., New Orleans, 1961-62; chief of psychiatry USPHS Hosp., New Orleans, 1962-67, clin. dir., 1967; dep. dir. div. field investigations NIMH, Chevy Chase, Md., 1968; chief NIMH Clin. Research Center, Lexington, 1969-73; cons. psychiatry, region IX, USPHS, HEW, San Francisco, 1973-79; dir. adolescent unit Alaska Psychiat. Inst., Anchorage, 1979-81, supt., 1981—; clin. instr. psychiatry La. State U. Med. Sch., New Orleans, 1962-67; clin. asst. prof. psychiatry U. Ky. Med. Sch., Lexington, 1969-73. Decorated Commendation medal; recipient various community awards for contbns. in field of drug abuse and equal employment opportunity for minorities. Diplomate Am. Bd. Psychiatry. Fellow Royal Soc. Health; mem. Am., So. psychiat. assns., A.M.A., Alpha Omega Alpha, Alpha Delta Phi. Contbr. to publs. in field. Home: SRA Box 2190 Snowline Trail Anchorage AK 99507 Office: 2900 Providence Ave Anchorage AK 99504

CONRAD, PAUL RAWSON, trade association executive; b. Omaha, Oct. 24, 1927; s. Paul E. and Clara Katherine (Beaver) C.; B.S. in Journalism, U. Kans., 1949; LL.B., George Washington U., 1952, LL.M., 1968; m. Shirley Martindale, Sept. 16, 1949 (div. 1970); children—David Rawson, Richard Martin, Paula Dale. Clk. and research asst. Rep. Albert M. Cole, Washington, 1949-52; admitted to Kans. bar, 1953; asst. mgr. Kans. Press Assn., Topeka, 1952-53; editor-mgr. Gt. Bend (Kans.) Herald-Press, 1954; editor Gt. Bend Daily Tribune, 1954-62; gen. counsel Nat. Newspaper Assn., Washington, 1966-70; exec. dir. Allied Daily Newspapers, Olympia, Wash., 1963-66, Seattle, 70-80, Tacoma, 1980—. Served with U.S. Army, 1946-47; Japan. Named Outstanding Young Man of Kans., Kans. Jaycees, 1962. Mem. Newspaper Assn. Mgrs. (pres. 1972-73), Order of Coif, Sigma Delta Chi (pres. Western Wash. chpt. 1974-75), Beta Theta Pi, Phi Delta Phi. Club: Rotary (Tacoma). Author: U.S., Washington State Statutes and Regulations Affecting Advertising, 1975; U.S., Alaska State Statutes and Regulations Affecting Advertising, 1980. Home: 1524 S Oakes St Tacoma WA 98405 Office: PO Box 11128 Tacoma WA 98411

CONRADS, EDWARD CHARLES, banker; b. Kewanee, Ill., Aug. 8, 1928; s. Paul Edward and Beatrice Helen (Holzbach) C. B.A., Lawrence U., 1950; postgrad. Occidental Coll., 1953-54. Teller, escrow clk. Bank of Am., Glendale and Montrose, Calif., 1954-55; personnel asst. Gen. Motors Corps., Van Nuys, Calif., 1955-56; underwriter Hartford Ins. Co., Los Angeles, 1956-64; asst. trust officer Security Pacific Nat. Bank, Los Angeles, Pomona and Pasadena, Calif., 1964-73; trust officer 1st Nat. Bank & Trust Co., Rockford, Ill., 1973-80; fin. cons., 1980-81; asst. v.p. 1st Trust Bank, Ontario, Calif., 1981—. Mem. Am. Inst. Banking (basic and gen. certs., former instr.), Lawrence U. Alumni Assn., Phi Kappa Tau. Republican. Clubs: Masons, Shriners, Mayan Order. Home: 450 S 2d Ave Covina CA 91723 Office: 1st Trust Bank Ontario CA

CONRADS, EDWARD CHARLES, banker; b. Kewanee, Ill., Aug. 8, 1928; s. Paul Edward and Beatrice Helen (Holzbach) C. B.A., Lawrence U., 1950; postgrad. Occidental Coll., 1953-54; cert. Am. Inst. Banking, 1964-70. Teller, escrow clk. Bank of Am., Glendale, Calif., 1954-55; personnel asst. Gen. Motors Co., Van Nuys, Calif., 1955-56; underwriter Hartford Ins. Co., Los Angeles, 1956-64; asst. trust officer Security Pacific Nat. Bank, Pasadena, Calif., 1964-73; trust officer First Nat. Bank & Trust Co., Rockford, Ill., 1973-80; asst. v.p., investment officer First Trust Bank, Ontario, Calif., 1981—; instr. Am. Inst. of Banking. Served with U.S. Army, 1951-53. Mem. Phi Kappa Tau. Republican. Methodist. Clubs: Optimists (Pomona), Masons, Shriner, Mayan Order. Home: 450 S 2d St Apt 9 Covina CA 91723 Office: 437 W Euclid Ave Ontario CA 91762

CONROD, JAMES HENRY, clergyman; b. Chgo., Sept. 14, 1930; s. James Andrew Conrod and Frieda (Steffens) Conrod Johanson; m. Barbara Ann Chesnut, July 25, 1950; children—Rebecca, James, Sharon, Daniel, Paul. Th.B., No. Bapt. Sem., 1953; B.A., Roosevelt U., 1956; B.D., No. Bapt. Sem., 1959; M.Div., 1971; D.Ministry, Am. Bapt. Sem. West, 1974. Ordained to ministry Am. Baptist Chs. in U.S.A., 1953; pastor Logan Sq. Bapt. Ch., Chgo., 1953-59; organizer, pastor Am. Bapt. Ch., Longview, Wash., 1959-73, 74—; founder, bd. dirs. Longview Christian Sch., 1966— Campus Towers Retirement Residence, 1968—; dir. Wayron Corp., 1974—, Brudi Equipment Co., 1968—, New Hope Farms, 1978—. Chmn. fund drive Am. Cancer Soc., 1969-70, pres. Cowlitz Wahkiakum counties unit, 1971-72; bd. dirs. 5 County Task Force on Aging, 1974-77, C.W. Governmental Conf. Housing Task Force, 1979—. Club: Rotary. Address: 2604 Ocean Beach Hwy Longview WA 98632

CONROY, DIANE WORRELL, banker; b. Clovis, N.Mex., Mar. 26, 1941; d. Iva Dannelly and Dorothy E. (Schlee) Worrell; m. Donald Eugene Conroy, Jan. 20, 1973 (separated); children—Danyel Diane, Dason Eugene. Student Stephen Coll., 1961; honors grad. Pacific Coast Banking Sch., 1981. With Citizens Bank, Clovis, 1961-68; staff officer-ops. First Nat. Bank Ariz., Phoenix, 1968-74; v.p. Great Western Bank & Trust, Phoenix, 1974-82; v.p., cashier N.Am. Bank, Phoenix, 1982-83, First Central Bank, Phoenix, 1983—. Mem. Nat. Assn. Bank Women (chmn. state conf. 1983), Ariz. Bankers Assn. (bank card, security, personnel and ops. coms.); Phoenix Met. C. of C. (criminal justice task force). Co-author: Bank Operations, 1982; IRA/Keough Implementations Manual, 1981. Office: 3443 N Central Ave Phoenix AZ 85012

CONROY, THOMAS FRANCIS, insurance company executive; b. Chgo., Sept. 26, 1938; s. Thomas Francis and Eleanor Althea (Heatherly) C.; m. Mary Elizabeth Schaeffer, June 6, 1965; children—Alexander, Blance, Margaret, Eleanor. B.S.C., DePaul U., 1959; M.B.A., U. Chgo., 1969, C.P.A.; cert. data processing. Mgr., Ernst & Whitney Co., Chgo., 1959-74; v.p., controller Security Life of Denver, 1974—. Served to 1st lt. U.S. Army, 1960-62. Fellow Life Mgmt. Inst.; mem. Am. Inst. C.P.A.s, Colo. Soc. C.P.A.s. Home: 3970 S Narcissus Way Denver CO 80237 Office: Security Life of Denver Glenarm Pl Denver CO 80202

CONSALES, PAUL RICHARD, mental health therapist; b. Boston, July 12, 1945; s. Peter A. and Clymena B. (Dwelley) C. B.A., Roanoke Coll., 1967; M.Ed., cert. advanced study, Springfield Coll., 1969. Adminstr. Chetwynde Nursing Homes, Mass., 1970-74; health planner Ariz. Dept. Health Services, Phoenix, 1974-80; pvt. practice counseling, Phoenix, 1980—; mfr.'s. rep., Phoenix, 1982—. Past co-chmn. Alternative Relations Ctr., Phoenix. Mem. Am. Pub. Health Assn., Am. Mental Health Assn., Nat. Rehab. Assn., Assn. Gay Psychologists. Home and Office: 502 E Tam-O-Shanter Dr Phoenix AZ 85022

CONSIDINE, SHARON CULVER, restaurant and clerical services company executive; b. San Diego, June 6, 1942; s. Harold B.W. and Elaine Lois (Smith) Culver; m. Timothy M. Considine, Aug. 18, 1962; children—Kevin Charles, Kenneth Culver, Kelly Elaine. Student San Diego State U., 1960-63. Ptnr., travel agt. TNT Travel Co., San Diego, 1975—; real estate agt. Sun and Sea Co., San Diego, 1976—; ptnr., restaurant mgr. Mex.-Pac Inc., San Diego, 1973—; ptnr., mgr. clerical services Seeseeanoh Inc., San Diego, 1971—; dir. Bank So. Calif. Pres. Aztec Athletic Found., San Diego State U., 1983. Mem. Calif. Restaurant Assn. (bd. dirs., pres. San Diego chpt.), San Diego U. Alumni Assn. (bd. dirs.). Republican. Roman Catholic. Office: Seeseeanoh Inc 734 1st Ave San Diego CA 92101

CONSIDINE, TIMOTHY MALCOLM, accountant; b. Palo Alto, Calif., Nov. 20, 1940; s. Charles Ray and Thalia Houston (Kelly) C.; m. Sharon Elaine Culver, Aug. 18, 1962; children—Kevin Charles, Kenneth Culver, Kelly Elaine. Student, Cornell U., 1958-60; B.S. in Acctg., San Diego State U., 1962. With Considine & Considine, San Diego, 1961—, ptnr., 1965-72, pres., 1972—; tchr. univs. and community colls., San Diego. Co-chmn. San Diego County Econ. Coordination and Planning Commn. Active San Diego County Tax Appeals Bd.; pres. San Diego County Civil Service Commn.; bd. dirs. San Diego State U. Found. Named Outstanding Young Man, San Diego Jaycees, 1973, Outstanding Alumnus, Bus. Sch. San Diego State U., 1981. Mem. Am. Inst. C.P.A.s, Calif. C.P.A. Soc. Republican. Roman Catholic. Office: 734 1st Ave San Diego CA 92101

CONSOLACION, FRANCO HERMINIA, accounting executive; b. Phillipines, Dec. 11, 1938; s. Jose De Los Santos and Coleta Sanchez (Herminia) C.; m. Lourdes Siazon Ancheta, May 14, 1966; children—Franco, Rosavilla, Garry. A.C.S., U. of the E., 1959; B.B.A., 1962; M.B.A., John F. Kennedy U., 1977. C.P.A., Phillipines, Calif.; cert. teacher. Sr. bank examiner Central Bank Phillipines, Manila, 1967-73; sr. acct. U. Calif.-San Francisco, 1973-81; gen. mgr. C&C Profl. Cons. Co., San Francisco, 1981-82; pres., gen. mgr. Consolacion & Partible C.P.A.s, Inc., 1982—; prof. U. of East, Manila, 1966-73; instr. City Coll. San Francisco, 1980; lectr. San Francisco State U., 1980-81, Golden Gate U., 1981-82; auditor Filipino-Ams. of Contra Costa, Inc. Regional dir. Congress of Filipino-Am. Citizens; mem. Cursillos in Christianity; mem. human relations com. Richmond Unified Sch. Dist. Bd. Edn. Recipient Outstanding leadership award San Francisco Bd. Suprs., 1981; Pub. Service award as Most Outstanding Filipino Acct. Phillipine Consul Gen., 1981; named Outstanding Filipino Acct. of Decade, Supr. Carol Ruth Silver, 1981; cited for Outstanding Leadership Calif. State Bd. Acct., 1983, Calif. Legislature, 1983. Mem. Am. Inst. C.P.A.s, Filipino Accts. Assn. (founder, pres. 1974-82, chmn. bd., Outstanding Leadership plaque of Appreciation. 1982). Democrat. Roman Catholic. Home: 1835 Hoke Ct Pinole CA 94564 Office: Consolacion & Partible CPAs Inc 833 Market St Suite 708 San Francisco CA 94103

CONSTANT, CLINTON, chemical engineer; b. Nelson, B.C., Can., Mar. 20, 1912; came to U.S., 1936, naturalized, 1942; s. Vasile and Annie (Hunt) C.; m. Margie Robbel, Dec. 5, 1965. B.Sc. with honors, U. Alta., 1935, postgrad., 1935-36; Ph.D., Western Res. U., 1939. Registered profl. engr. Devel. engr. Harshaw Chem. Co., Cleve., 1936-38, mfg. foreman, 1938-43, sr. engr. semi-works dept., 1948-50; supt. hydrofluoric acid dept. Nyotex Chems., Inc., Houston, 1943-47, chief devel. engr., 1947-48; mgr. engring. Ferro Chem. Co., Bedford, Ohio, 1950-52; tech. asst. mfg. dept. Armour Agrl. Chem. Co. (name formerly Armour Fertilizer Works), Bartow, Fla., 1952-61, mfg. research and devel. div., 1961-63, mgr. spl. projects Research div. (co. name changed to USS Agri-Chems 1968), 1963-65, project mgr., 1965-70; chem. adviser Robert & Co. Assocs., Atlanta, 1970-79; chief engr. Almon & Assocs., Inc., Atlanta, 1979-80; project mgr. Engring. Service Assocs., Atlanta, 1980-81; v.p. engring. ACI Inc., Hesperia, Calif., 1981—. Fellow AAAS, Am. Inst. Chemists, Am. Inst. Chem. Engrs., N.Y. Acad. Scis., AIAA (assoc.); mem. Am. Chem. Soc., Am. Astron. Soc., Astron. Soc. Pacific, Royal Astron. Soc. Can., Am. Water Works Assn., Ga. Water and Pollution Control Assn., Ala. Assn. Water Pollution Control, Soc. Mfg. Engrs. Author tech. reports, sci. fiction; patentee in field. Office: PO Box 204 2042 Hesperia CA 92345

CONSTANTEN, CARL PHILIP, mech. engr.; b. Hackensack, N.J., Sept. 20, 1951; s. Frank Costos and Lillian Barbara (Sture) C.; B.S. in Engring. and Applied Sci., Calif. Inst. Tech., 1972, M.S. in Mech. Engring., 1973; M.B.A., U. So. Calif., 1982; m. Roberta Kay McDermott, Nov. 13, 1975. Cons. engr. Dino A. Morelli, Inc., Pasadena, Calif., 1972-73; lead engr. F-5 hydraulic systems Northrop Corp., Hawthorne, Calif., 1973-82, mgr. F-5/F-20 mech. design, 1982—. Area chmn. Calif. Inst. Tech. Alumni Fund, 1978—. Howard R. Hughes scholar, 1968-69; Gen. Motors scholar, 1970-71. Mem. Soc. Automotive Engrs., Beta Gamma Sigma. Republican. Home: 3213 Onrado St Torrance CA 90503 Office: 1 Northrop Ave Hawthorne CA 90250

CONSTANTINE, THOMAS JAMES, lawyer; b. Denver, May 7, 1940; s. Joseph Paul and Anita Margaret (Cumero) C.; A.B., Regis Coll., Denver, 1962; student Loyola U., Los Angeles, 1960-61; J.D., U. Denver, 1965; m. Sharon Ann O'Loughlin, June 15, 1963; children—Thomas James, Jennifer Lynn, Leslie Catherine, Susan Margaret. Admitted to Colo. bar, 1965; practiced in Denver, 1965—; individual practice, 1965-68; v.p., gen. counsel Petro-Nuclear Ltd., 1969-70; ptnr. firm McKibben, Constantine & Pred, 1970-73; dir. firm Hindry & Meyer, 1973-78; pres., dir. firm Constantine & Prochnow, 1978—. Bd. govs. Regis Coll. Recipient Am. Citizenship award, 1968; named Outstanding Young Man of Am., 1969. Mem. Am. Bar Assn., Colo. Bar Assn., Am. Trial Lawyers Assn., Colo. Trial Lawyers Assn. (dir.), Colo. Mining Assn., Am. Arbitration Assn., Am. Soc. Sci. and Politics, Regis Coll. Alumni Assn. (past pres., dir.), Alpha Delta Gamma, Phi Delta Phi, Alpha Sigma Nu. Democrat. Roman Catholic. Clubs: Pinehurst Country, Denver Athletic, Denver Petroleum. Home: 23 Belleville Ln Littleton CO 80121 Office: 5650 DTC Pkwy Englewood CO 80110

CONTER, MARIALYCE, educational administrator, consultant; b. Princeton, Mo., Aug. 6, 1946; d. King Evans and Nancy Beatrice (Owens) Girdner; m. Robert Victor Conter, June 9, 1968. B.A. in Journalism, Philosophy, U. Ariz., 1968, M.Ed. in Adminstrn., 1978. Coordinator publs. U. Ariz., Tucson, 1969-73, advisor Continuing Edn., 1973-74, coordinator Continuing Edn., 1974-75, dir. Opportunities for Women Program, 1975-83; tng. and devel. mgr. Home Fed. Savs., Tucson, 1983—; cons. mgmt. devel., co owner Sun Country Cons.; workshop leader Sun Country. Recipient Regional Rep.'s award of Excellence U.S. Dept. Edn., 1983; Outstanding Leadership, Service award Exec. Women's Council, 1982; award of Merit YWCA, 1982. Mem. Am. Assn. Higher Edn., Nat. Univ. Continuing Edn. Assn., State Job Tng. Coordinating Council, Tucson Bus. Industry Edn. Council, Higher Edn. Resource Services, Am. Soc. Tng. and Devel., Am. Vocat. Assn., Nat. Assn. Women Deans, Adminstrs. and Counselors, Am. Mgmt. Assn., Assn. Am. Colls., Nat. Assn. Female Execs. Republican. Methodist. Club: Soroptimists. Author ednl. publs.

CONTER, ROBERT VICTOR, educational administrator; b. Des Moines, Oct. 18, 1946; s. Louis Victor and Ethyle (Shaffer) C.; m. Marialyce Girdner, June 9, 1968. B.S., U. Ariz., 1968, M.B.A., 1973, M.S., 1976, Ph.D., 1983. Dept. mgr., customer services mgr. Sears, Roebuck & Co., Tucson, 1969-73; coordinator specialized bus. programs U. Ariz., Tucson, 1973-76, asst. dir. continuing edn., 1976-79, dir. spl. projects, 1979—; sr. assoc. Alternatives, Assocs. in Cons., Tucson. Bd. dirs. Southwestern Ctr. Behavioral Health Studies, 1982—; mem. Senator Deconcini Campaign Liaison Com., 1982. Fellow Am. Mktg. Assn.; mem. Nat. Continuing Edn. Assn., Western Gerontol. Assn. Republican. Methodist. Club: Elks. Contbr. articles to profl. jours.

CONTI, SAMUEL, judge; b. Los Angeles, July 16, 1922; s. Fred and Katie (Lencioni) C.; B.S., U. Santa Clara, 1945; LL.B., Stanford, 1948, LL.D.; m. Dolores Crosby, July 12, 1952; children—Richard, Robert, Cynthia. Admitted to Calif. bar, 1948; pvt. practice, San Francisco and Contra Costa County, 1948-60; city atty., Concord, Calif., 1960-69; judge Superior Ct. Contra Costa County, 1968-70; judge U.S. Dist. Ct., No. Dist. Calif., San Francisco, 1970—. Mem. Bd. Edn., Pittsburg Unified Sch. Dist., 1952-58, mem. Sch. Redistricting Com. for Contra Costa County, 1956-58. Served with AUS, 1940-44. Mem. Central Contra Costa Bar Assn. (pres.), Concord C. of C. (pres.), Alpha Sigma Nu. Office: US Dist Court House PO Box 36060 San Francisco CA 94102

CONTO, ARISTIDES, advertising agency executive; b. N.Y.C., Feb. 10, 1931; s. Gus Dimitrios and Osee (Kenney) C.; B.A., Champlain Coll., 1953; M.S. in Journalism, U. Calif., Los Angeles, 1958, certificate in indsl. relations, 1965; m. Phyllis Helen Wiley, June 22, 1957; 1 son, Jason Wiley. Reporter, City News Service, Los Angeles, 1958; dir. pub. relations Galaxy Advt. Co., Los Angeles, 1959-60; news media chief Los Angeles County Heart Assn., 1960-61; pub. relations asso. Prudential Ins. Co., Los Angeles, 1961-64; advt. mgr. Aerospace Controls Co., Los Angeles, 1964-65; comml. sales promotion coordinator Lockheed-Calif. Co., Burbank, 1965-73; pres. Jason Wiley Advt. Agy., Los Angeles, 1973—; dir. Tower Master, Inc., Los Angeles. Served with U.S. Army, 1955-56. Recipient advt. awards. Mem. Nat. Soc. Published Poets, Los Angeles Press Club, Bus.-Profl. Advt. Assn. Los Angeles, Public Relations Soc. . Author: The Spy Who Loved Me, 1962; The Diamond Twins, 1963; author screenplays: Lannigan, 1973; Haunted Host, 1976; Captain Noah, 1977. Office: 3598 Beverly Blvd Los Angeles CA 90004

CONTRERAS, DARLENE ROWELL, rancher; b. Seneca, Mo., June 16, 1926; d. Myrlen and Ada (Ruggles) Rowell; grad. high sch.; m. John L. Contreras, Feb. 15, 1957 (dec. 1978); children—Patricia, Pamela. Service rep. Pacific Telephone Co., 1955-66; bookkeeper Mobil Oil plant, Fairfield, Calif., 1967-75, distbr., 1978-81; owner, mgr. ranch, Vacaville, Calif. 1978—. Mem. Calif. Farm Bur. Fedn., Internat. Platform Assn. Club: Yolo Fliers Country. Address: 507 Buck Ave Vacaville CA 95688

CONVERTI, VINCENZO, electrical utility executive; b. Roseto, Italy, Nov. 27, 1925; s. Rocco and Antoinette (Russo) C.; m. Marjorie Ruth Pefley, Sept. 12, 1951; children—Mark, David, Paul, Cathy. B.S., U. Ariz., 1952, M.S., 1956. Registered profl. elec. engr., Ariz. Elec. engr. Ariz. Pub. Service Co. Phoenix, 1952-55, researcher Ariz. computer research program, 1956-59, supr. systems engring., 1960-67, mgr. systems engring., 1967-75, mgr. computer services, 1976—; adj. prof. Ariz. State U. Served with USAF, 1944-48, Italy. Fellow, IEEE; mem. Soc. Mgmt. Info. Systems, Pacific Coast Elec. Assn. Republican. Contbr.

articles to tech. jours. Home: 7039 N 14th St Phoenix AZ 85020 Office: PO Box 21666 Phoenix AZ 85036

CONWAY, ARCH WILSON, electronic company executive; b. Hartman, Ark., June 3, 1936; s. Arch David and Thelma Bess (Wilson) C.; m. Barbara McCutchan, Sept. 13, 1959; children—Michael, Cheryl, Laura. B.S. in Elec. Engring., Calif. State Poly. U., 1963; postgrad. U. Calif.-Irvine, 1964. Electronic engr. Gen. Dynamics, Pomona, Calif., 1962-65, Interstate Electronics, Anaheim, Calif., 1965-68; v.p. engring. and ops. Racal-Dana Instruments, Irvine, Calif., 1968-83; v.p. ops. Hilevel Tech., Irvine, 1983—. Mem. IEEE. Club: Toastmasters (Lake Forest, Calif.). Contbr. articles on electronic engring. to profl. jours.; patentee in field.

CONWAY, CASEY ANTHONY, regulatory compliance official; b. Portland, Oreg., Mar. 11, 1953; s. James William and Wanna Donna (Caspers) C.; A.A., Orange Coast Coll., 1974; B.A. in Bus. Adminstrn., Calif. State U.-Fullerton, 1976; M.S. in Safety, U. So. Calif., 1978. Safety and environ. technician Energy Mining div. Union Oil Co. Calif., 1979, Rawlins, Wyo., safety trainer, 1979-80, safety supr., 1980-82, regulatory compliance coordinator oil shale ops., Parachute, Colo., 1983—. Instr. CPR, Wyo. chpt. Am. Heart Assn. Cert. instr./trainer in surface/underground mine safety Mine Safety and Health Adminstrn; cert. mine foreman, surface uranium, Wyo. State Bd. Mine Examiners; cert. emergency med. technician, Wyo.; cert. audiometric technician; lic. amateur radio operator. Mem. Am. Soc. Safety Engrs. (membership chmn. Wyo. chpt. 1981-82, sec. 1982-83), Soc. Mining Engrs., Carbon County Amateur Radio Assn. (pres. 1980), Wyo. Safety Congress (program com. 1982), Am. Mgmt. Assn., Grand Mesa Repeater Soc., Am. Radio Relay League. Roman Catholic. Lodge: Elks. Home: PO Box 40207 Grand Junction CO 81504 Office: PO Box 76 Parachute CO 81635

CONWAY, EDWARD ROBERT, real estate broker; b. Concord, N.H., Aug. 27, 1925; s. Edward James and Frances (O'Brien) C.; B.S., U. N.H., 1950; postgrad. San Diego State U., 1970-72; cert. in real estate U. Calif.-San Diego, 1974; grad. Realtors Inst. Calif.; children—Craig William, Margaret Kathleen. Commd. 2d lt. U.S. Army, 1950, advanced through grades to lt. col., 1967, ret. 1969; real estate investment and exchange broker Conway Investment Realty, Rancho Santa Fe, Calif., 1972—. Served with AUS, 1942-46. Decorated Legion of Merit, Army Commendation medals (4). Mem. San Dieguito Bd. Realtors (treas., dir. 1975—), Calif. Assn. Realtors (dir.), CCIM Real Estate Brokers (v.p. So. Calif. chpt.), Real Estate Cert. Inst., U. N.H. Alumni Assn., Ret. Officers Assn., Kappa Sigma. Republican. Address: Box 1777 Rancho Santa Fe CA 92067

CONWAY, FRANKLIN DANIEL, real estate investor; b. Denver, June 13, 1921; s. Franklin Daniel and Clara Belle (Phelps) C.; student San Francisco State Coll., 1947, San Mateo Jr. Coll., 1948, 52, also Air U.; m. Carol F. Upchurch, Nov. 21, 1972; children by previous marriage—Claire Conway Spence, Ivka, Marian; 1 stepdau., Jane Russell Parris. Diesel engr. Delta Lines, 1947; sr. technician, tng. supr. Pacific Tel. & Tel. Co., 1979; engaged in real estate investing, 1959—. Served as capt. CAP, 1950-59. Served with USNR, 1941-45. Mem. Telephone Pioneers Assn., Aircraft Owners and Pilots Assn., Air Force Assn. Aux., Am. Legion (post vice comdr. 1958, chmn. nat. def. com. 1956-57). Republican. Roman Catholic. Clubs: Elks, Commonwealth Calif. Address: 12160 Mellowood Dr Saratoga CA 95070

CONWAY, STELLA ANNE, designer, silk screener, orthoptist, model, dancer; b. Portsmouth, Hampshire, Eng., Mar. 8, 1933; d. Frederick Leonard Sealey and Dorothy Singleton (Gates) S.; m. Charles Quinlan Conway, June 15, 1957; children—Kerri, John, Christopher, Mark, Shelagh. A.A., U. Alaska, 1976; degree Oxford U. Sch. Orthoptics, 1954. With Addeubrookes Hosp., Cambridge, Eng., 1954-56; orthoptist Orthoptic Clinic, Seattle, 1956-58, Everett (Wash.) Gen. Hosp., 1956-58, Children's Hosp. Tacoma, 1956-58, Eyeclinic, Bremerton, Wash., 1956-58, Eyeclinic, Yakima, Wash., 1956-58, State of Alaska, 1958—, pvt. practice orthoptics, Alaska, 1974-77; orthoptist Sitka (Alaska) pub. schs., 1974-77; pres. Stella Designs, Inc., Anchorage, 1977—. Mem. Alaska Visitors Assn., Beta Sigma Phi. Republican Roman Catholic. Clubs: Networking, British Womens (Anchorage). Designer Jewelry and T-Shirts. Office: 2604 Spenard Rd Anchorage AK 99503

CONZELMAN, BRUCE THOMAS, developer; b. St. Louis, May 9, 1935; s. Fred H. and Lily Margarite (Kern) C.; B.S. in Elec. Engring., U.S. Naval Acad., 1958; postgrad. U. Calif. at La Jolla, 1972. Founder, pres. Beach & Towne Realty, San Diego, 1965-72; exec. v.p., dir. new home mktg. Grubb & Ellis Co., San Diego, 1974-78; pres. Mktg. Advisors, Inc., San Francisco, 1974—. Served to lt. USN, 1958-62. Mem. Am. Mktg. Assn., Building Contractors Assn., San Diego C. of C., U.S. Naval Acad. Alumni Assn. Home: 1022 Powell St Apt 2 San Francisco CA 94108 Office: 150 California St Suite 302 San Francisco CA 94111

CONZELMANN, RICHARD THEODORE, park and recreation administrator; b. San Francisco, Nov. 14, 1933; s. Richard and Eleanor Lorraine (Weber) C.; m. Shirley Ann Knapp, Jan. 30, 1955; children—Diana Rae Bray, Kirk Richard, Sandra Elise, Heidi Anne. B.S., San Jose State U., 1955; postgrad. Calif. State U.-Sacramento, 1964-66. Supr. sports, acquatics and recreation City of Salinas (Calif.), 1958-62; dir. parks and recreation Terra Linda Recreation Park Dist., San Rafael, Calif., 1962-64; dir. parks and recreation Fulton-El Camino Recreation and Park Dist., Sacramento, 1964-69; dir. parks and recreation, asst. city mgr. City of Eureka (Calif.), 1969-77; adminstr., gen. mgr. Greater Vallejo (Calif.) Recreation Dist., 1977—; cons. Vice pres., advisor, bd. dirs. Humboldt County Boys' Club; bd. dirs. Redwood div. ARC, 1969-71. Mem. Eureka C. of C., Vallejo C. of C. (mem. govt. affairs com., visitors and conv. bur., mem. legis. com.), Calif. Park and Recreation Soc. (pres. 1976, dir.), Nat. Recreation and Park Assn. (trustee). Republican. Methodist. Club: Rotary. Home: 232 Lexington Dr Vallejo CA 94591 Office: 395 Amador St Vallejo CA 94590

COOGAN, JOHN LESLIE (JACKIE), actor; b. Los Angeles, Oct. 26, 1914; s. John Henry and Lillian Rita (Dolliver) C.; student Santa Clara U., 1931-32, U. So. Cal., 1933-34; m. Dorothea Odetta Hanson, May 27, 1950; children—John Anthony, Joann Dolliver, Leslie Diane Coogan Franklin, Christopher Fenton. Appeared in numerous motion pictures, 1916—, including Skinner's Baby, 1916, The Kid, 1919, The Actress, 1953, Fine Madness, 1965, Shakiest Gun In The West, 1967, Rogues Gallery, 1967, Little Sister, 1968, Marlo, 1968; appeared on numerous TV shows, 1947—, including Playhouse 90, 1955, Studio One, 1956, Johnny Carson, 1965, Mike Douglas, 1965, Regis Philbin, 1966, Les Crane, 1966, Joey Bishop Show, 1967, U Don't Say, 1967, Truth or Consequences, 1967, Woody Woodbury, 1967, Name of the Game, 1968, 69, 70, Red Skelton, 1970, Jeanie, 1970, Julia, 1970, The Interns, 1970, Partridge Family, 1970, Stump the Stars, 1970, Barefoot in the Park, 1970, Matt Lincoln, 1970, This Is Your Life, 1977, Adams Family, 1977, Hawaii 50 and San Francisco Beat, 1970's; appeared on television series Cowboy G-Men 1951-53, McKeever and Colonel, 1960s, Addams Family, 1963-65; appeared in stage plays Blue Denim, 1967, Make a Million, 1968, Sweet Bird of Youth, 1968, Odd Couple, 1969, Come Blow Your Horn, 1969; toured U.S. and Europe with Donald O'Connor, 1950; toured U.S. with Ted Cassidy, summer stock 1963-65. Served with USAAF, 1941-45; CBI. Decorated D.F.C., Air medal; recipient Papal medal Pope Pius 10th, 1924, Order of King George (Greek Govt.), 1924, Justinian Cross, Greek Orthodox Ch., 1924. Mem. Screen Actors Guild, A.F.T.R.A., Am. Guild Variety Artists, Equity, Acad. Motion Picture and Television Arts and Scis. World War II Glider Pilots Assn., 1st Air Commandos, Star of Burma Assn. Author: Jackie Coogan Child Labor Law, 1937. Home: Palm Springs CA Office: care Kitty Davis Publicist Box 1305 Hollywood CA 90028

COOK, ARLENE ETHEL, author; b. Escondido, Calif., July 1, 1936; d. Oscar Emil and Leona Lucy (Wells) Knappe; B.A. in Elementary Edn., San Diego State Coll., 1958; m. Richard H. Cook, Dec. 23, 1964; children—Alan Jason, Alyse Jennifer, Jon Andrew. Home tchr., substitute tchr. elementary grades, Escondido, 1961-62; jr. high sch. tchr. Poway (Calif.) Unified Sch. Dist., 1962-67; office mgr. Shuster Oil & Chem., Escondido, 1969—; pres. Profiles Plus, Escondido, field mgr. Performex Systems, Inc.; founder, adviser 8 ladies stock investment clubs in Escondido, 1970; stringer Nat. Enquirer, 1978-81; extension instr. U. Calif., San Diego, 1979; instr. adult edn. Poway Unified Schs., 1978-79; condr. seminars for adults, 1982—. Mem. Mayor Escondido 1st Blue Ribbon Com., 1973. Winner grand prize nat. writing competition Writer's Digest, 1982. Mem. Nat. League Am. Pen Women (pres. Escondido 1970-72), Nat. Assn. Investment Clubs (v.p. San Diego 1970-73), Nat. Press Women, Calif. Press Women, Scribblers. Republican. Lutheran. Author: (under pen name Cannon Cole) From the Ashes of Hell, 1973; (with others) The World of Long Ago, 1971; contbr. to nat. mags., 1966—. Home: 371 Cypress Crest Terr Escondido CA 92025 Office: PO Box 184 Escondido CA 92025

COOK, BARRY PAUL, optometrist; b. Price, Utah, Mar. 27, 1951; s. Paul W. and Patricia C.; m. Julee Orme, Dec. 28, 1974; children—Brent, Mark, Diane. A.S., Coll. Eastern Utah, 1973; student Brigham Young U., 1973-74; O.D., Ill. Coll. Optometry, 1978. Practice optometry, Price, Utah, 1978—. Mem. Am. Optometric Assn., Utah Optometric Assn., Carbon County Optometric Soc., Carbon County C. of C. Mem. Ch. of Jesus Christ of Latter Day Saints. Club: Lions (pres. club). Home: 146 E 900 N Price UT 84501 Office: 92 N 400 E Price UT 84501

COOK, BERNARD LEON, traffic engr.; b. Jamaica, Iowa, Dec. 16, 1927; s. James Roy and Olive (Cabelka) C.; B.S. in Civil Engring., U. Wash., 1954; M.E. in Transp., U. Calif., Berkeley, 1958; m. Shirley J. Reeder, Apr. 7, 1956; children—Sharon Kay, Walter Roy. With Engring. Dept., City of Seattle, 1958—, transp. planner, 1959-62, asst. city traffic engr., 1962-74; transp. planner transit studies and elderly handicapped transp. study Urban Mass Transp. Adminstrn., 1974-77, project mgr., 1974—. Com. chmn., den leader Cub Scouts, 1975-76. Served with USMC, 1946-48. Recipient Pub. Service award Puget Sound Engring. Council, 1971, 25 year service award City of Seattle, 1980; lic. profl. engr., Wash. Mem. Inst. Transp. Engrs. (past pres. Wash. sect.). Republican. Editor, pub. proceedings of western sect. Inst. Transp. Engrs., 1959, 67. Home: 12711 9th Ave NW Seattle WA 98177 Office: 806 Municipal Bldg Seattle WA 98104

COOK, CHRISTOPHER DIXON, communications company exec.; b. Santa Monica, Calif., Sept. 14, 1942; s. Albert Leon and Virginia Patricia (Dixon) C.; B.A., N.C. State U., 1964; M.A., U. Va., 1966; m. Elizabeth L. Burkman, June 18, 1966; children—Christopher Dixon, Lisa Christina. Instr. English, U. N.C., Charlotte, 1966-69; account exec. Editorial Assos./K. Drake Assos., Detroit, 1969-72; pub. relations account supr., advt. account exec. Cochrane Chase & Co., Newport Beach, Calif., 1972-76; pres. Cook Communications Services, Inc., Newport Beach, 1976—; freelance mag. writer. Editor, Sierra Broadmoor Community Assn. Newsletter, Irvine, Calif., 1972-73. Mem. Pub. Relations Soc. Am. (Prism award for outstanding mktg. program in So. Calif., Los Angeles chpt. 1975, several awards Orange County chpt. 1976—, mem. counselors sect.), U. Va. Alumni Assn. So. Calif., Publicity Club Los Angeles, Asso. Bus. Writers Am. Episcopalian. Contbr. articles to various publs. Home: 19301 Sierra Inez Irvine CA 92715 Office: Suite 101 4630 Campus Dr Newport Beach CA 92660 also PO Box 4392 Station Irvine CA 92716

COOK, DAN, editor; b. Cin., Apr. 16, 1942; s. George Thomas and Evelyn Margaret (Hill) C. B.A. in Polit. Sci., Stanford U., 1969. Investigator, U.S. Ho. of Reps. Com. Govt. Ops., Washington, 1976-79; v.p. communications Pilots Lobby, Inc., Washington, 1978-80; sr. editor Exec. mag., San Francisco, 1979-81; dir. communications Am. Electronics Assn., Palo Alto Calif., 1981-82; exec. editor The Recorder, San Francisco, 1982—; contbr. numerous articles to newspapers, mags. Alt. mem. San Mateo County (Calif.) Democratic Central Com., 1980-81. Served in U.S. Army, 1964-70. Mem. Peninsula Press Club (founding pres., dir.), POETS Club (Washington), Aviation/Spacewriters Assn., Taurine Bibliophiles Am. Clubs: Peña Sol y Sombra (dir.) (San Francisco); Peña Maisonnave (Spain). Home: 1200 E Hillsdale Blvd Apt 220 Foster City CA 94404 Office: The Recorder 99 Van Ness Ave San Francisco CA 94103

COOK, DAVID LAWRENCE, pharmacist; b. Bremerton, Wash., July 1, 1942; s. Joe Lawrence and Louise (Powell) C.; student U. Hawaii, 1960-62; B.S., U. Wash., 1967; m. Lynn Maureen Jacobson, Dec. 22, 1963; 1 dau., Elizabeth Louise. Pharmacist, Castle & Cooke, Bremerton, 1968-70, pharmacy mgr., Honolulu, 1971-78; pharmacist Long's Drugs, Honolulu, 1970-71, Pay 'n Save Drugs, 1980—. Cons. Hawaii State Senate health com., 1975-78; mem. Hawaii Health Interim Com. on Family Planning, 1976-78; mem. neighborhood bd. City and County of Honolulu, 1977-78. Recipient Lederle Labs. Public Service award, 1973; Blood Bank of Hawaii Public Service award, 1975. Mem. Hawaii (pres. 1975-76), Am., Wash., Calif. pharm. assns. Home: 1202 12th St Bremerton WA 98310 Office: 2860 NW Bucklin Hill Rd Silverdale WA 98383

COOK, DONALD E., pediatrician; b. Pitts., Mar. 24, 1928; s. Merriam E. and Bertha (Gwin) C.; B.S., Colo. Coll., 1951; M.D., U. Colo., 1955; m. Elsie Walden, Sept. 2, 1951; children—Catherine, Christopher, Brian, Jeffrey. Intern, Fresno County Gen. Hosp., Calif., 1955-56; resident in gen. practice Tulare (Calif.) County Gen. Hosp., 1956-57; resident in pediatrics U. Colo., 1957-59; practice medicine specializing in pediatrics, Aurora, Colo., 1959-64, in pediatrics, Greeley, Colo., 1964—; clin. faculty U. Colo., 19—, clin. prof., 1977—; mem. adv. bd. Nat. Center Health Edn., San Francisco, 1978-80. Mem. Weld County Dist. 6 Sch. Bd., 1973-83, pres., 1973-74, 76-77, chmn. dist. 6 accountability com., 1972-73. Served with USN, 1946-48. Recipient Disting. Service award Jr. C. of C., 1962, Disting. Citizenship award Elks, 1975-76, Service to Mankind award Sertoma Club, 1972; Community Service award Phi Delta Kappa, 1981, Spark Plug award U. No. Colo. diplomate Am. Bd. Pediatrics. Mem. Colo. Soc. Sch. Health Com. (chmn. 1967-78), Am. Acad. Pediatrics (chmn. sch. health com. 1975—, chmn. Colo. chpt. 1982), AMA (chmn. sch. and coll. health com. 1980-82), Adams Aurora Med. Soc. (pres. 1964-65), Weld County Med. Soc. (pres. 1968-69), Colo. Med. Soc. (A.H. Robbins Community Service award 1974), Centennial Pediatric Soc. (pres. 1982—). Republican. Methodist. Club: Rotary. Home: 1710 21st Ave Greeley CO 80631 Office: 1650 16th St Greeley CO 80631

COOK, FRANK RICHARDSON, investment company executive; b. Dec. 23, 1910; s. William Felder and Helena May (Richardson) C.; m. Lois Lorton, June 24, 1935; children—William, Grady; m. 2d, Ines Fisher, Dec. 20, 1966. S.B., MIT, 1932; Ph.D., U. Calif.-Irvine, 1980. Commd. 2d lt. U.S. Army Air Force, 1935, advanced through grades to col. U.S. Air Force, 1942, resigned, 1949, chief research br., plans and policy br. Hdqrs. U.S. Air Force, 1947-49; dir. aero. research and engring. Honeywell, Inc., Mpls. 1949-55; founder, pres. Frank R. Cook Co., Denver, 1955—, Sci. Mgmt. Corp., Irvine, Calif., 1958—. Decorated Legion of Merit with oak leaf cluster. Assoc. fellow AIAA; mem. Air Force Assn., Am. Security Council, Population Council Am., Mensa. Republican. Episcopalian. Club: Town Hall. Office: Science Management Corp 13635 Espirit Way Irvine CA 92714

COOK, HAROLD E., company executive, human resources consultant; b. Bristol, Conn., Nov. 15, 1929; s. Harold E. and Amy E. C.; m. Helen Gough, Feb. 14, 1969; children—Harold, Deborah, Peter, Jody. Student Hartford Coll., 1947-50. Prodn. control mgr. Sessions Clock Co., Forestville, Conn., 1947-60; material mgr. Haydon div. Gen. Time, Torrington, Conn., 1960-67; material dir. Litton Industries, Ft. Wayne, Ind., 1967-68; owner, gen. mgr., v.p. Roth Young Personnel, Los Angeles, 1969-82; owner Search Alternatives, Tustin, Calif., 1982—; pres. The Thomaston Group Inc., Mission Viejo, Calif., 1982—. Served with U.S. Army, 1947-53. Mem. Inst. Food Technologists, So. Calif. Grocers Assn. Home: 23622 Amalia Pl Mission Viejo CA 92691 Office: 17291 Irvine Blvd Suite 313 Tustin CA 92680

COOK, HAROLD V., city official; b. Denver, Jan. 6, 1920; s. Louis and Susan (Finer) C.; m. Leanor E. Stark, July 3, 1947; children—Kathleen Rae Waldron, Kelsey D. Cook. B.M.E., U. Colo., 1941; M.S., Calif. Inst. Tech., 1942. Registered profl. engr., Colo., N.Mex. Engr., U.S. Bur. Reclamation, Denver, 1946-47; pres. Louis Cook Plumbing & Heating Co., Denver, 1947-72; dep. mayor, mgr. pub. works City and County of Denver, 1971—, chmn. Denver Planning Bd., 1972-74, pres. Denver City and County Bd. County Commrs., 1972—, chmn. Bd. Equalization of Bd. County Commrs., 1972—. Pres., Multiple Sclerosis Soc. Colo., 1969-71; v.p. Denver Ctr. for Performing Arts, 1975—; chmn. Met. Denver Sewage Disposal Dist. 1, 1973-74; chmn. exec. com. Downtown Denver Mall, 1982—. Served to lt. col. USAAF, 1942-46. Decorated Bronze Star medal. Mem. Am. Soc. Heating and Ventilating Engrs., Am. Pub. Works Assn., Profl. Engrs. Colo. Democrat. Jewish. Clubs: Masons, Shriners, Green Gables Country. Office: City and County Bldg Room 379 Denver CO 80202

COOK, HOLLIS N., park manager; b. Mena, Ark., May 22, 1943; s. Fred and Geneva E. (Rollins) C.; m. Shirley F. Armstrong, Oct. 9, 1965; children—Holly, Sonia. B.A., Grand Canyon Coll., 1967. Ranger, Nat. Park Service, Casa Grande Ruins, 1964; with City of Casa Grande Parks Dept., 1965; park ranger Ariz. State Parks, Lake Hauasu, 1970, Fort Verde, 1971; park mgr. Tubac Presidio, 1971-80; park mgr. Tombstone Courthouse State Park (Ariz.), 1980—. Recipient Anza Bicentennial medal Tubac Hist. Soc., 1975. Mem. Am. Assn. State and Local History. Democrat. Baptist.

COOK, JOSEPH VERNON, physician; b. Brigham City, Utah, Sept. 7, 1935; s. Joseph Vernon and Cleo Berniece (Kimball) C.; B.S., Utah State U., 1959; M.D., U. Utah, 1962; m. Nancy Louise Carlson, July 7, 1958; children—Joseph David, John Carlson, Paul Carlson. Intern, U. Okla., Oklahoma City, 1962-63; gen. practice medicine, San Mateo, Calif., 1967—; clin. asst. prof. U. Calif. at San Francisco, 1974—, advisor family practice pathway, 1974-81; chief gen. practice sect. Mills Meml. Hosp., San Mateo, 1975-79. Stake pres. Ch. of Jesus Christ of Latter Day Saints, Pacifica, Calif., 1975-82, San Francisco, 1982—, bishop, 1969-72. Served with USN, 1963-67. Diplomate Am. Bd. Family Practice. Fellow Am. Acad. Family Practice (chpt. dir. 1971—, chpt. pres. 1973-76); mem. Am., Calif. med. assns., Mid-peninsula PSRO (pres. 1980-81), Blue Key, Phi Kappa Phi, Alpha Epsilon Delta, Pi Kappa Alpha. Republican. Club: Rotary. Home: 406 Costa Rica St San Mateo CA 94402 Office: 1 Baywood St San Mateo CA 94402

COOK, JULIA ARDIS, art center administrator; b. Michigan City, Ind., Jan. 25, 1958; d. Charles Miller Cook and Marcelline Ann (Ardis) Woodson. B.F.A. cum laude, Miami U., Oxford, Ohio, 1980. Asst. dir. Community Gallery of Lancaster (Pa.), 1980-81; dir. Custer County Art Ctr., Miles City, Mont., 1981—. Presbyterian. Home: PO Box 165 Miles City MT 59301 Office: PO Box 1284 Water Plant Rd Miles City MT 59301

COOK, LYLE EDWARDS, fund-raising found. exec.; b. Astoria, Oreg., Aug. 19, 1918; s. Courtney Carson and Fanchon (Edwards) C.; A.B. in History, Stanford U., 1940, postgrad., 1940-41; m. Olive Freeman, Dec. 28, 1940; children—James Michael, Ellen Anita (Mrs. James R. Otto), Mary Lucinda (Mrs. Lee D. Vaage), Jane Victoria. Instr. history Yuba Jr. Coll., Marysville, Calif., 1941-42; methods analyst Lockheed Aircraft Corp., 1942-45; investment broker Quincy Cass Assocs., Los Angeles, 1945-49; mem. staff Stanford U., 1949-66, assoc. dean Sch. Medicine, 1958-65; sr. staff mem. Lester Gorsline Assocs., Belvedere, Calif., 1966-72; v.p., 1967-70, exec. v.p., 1970-72; v.p. univ. relations U. San Francisco, 1973-75; fund-raising and planning cons., 1975; dir. fund devel. Children's Home Soc. Calif., 1976-78; exec. dir. That Man May See, Inc., San Francisco, 1978—; trustee, chmn. bd. The Fund Raising Sch., 1978—; spl. cons. NIH, 1960-62. Mem. Devel. Execs. Round Table, Nat. Soc. Fund Raising Execs., Stanford Assocs., Theta Delta Chi. Episcopalian. Clubs: Belvedere Tennis, Lake of Pines Country. Home: 1750 Lagoon View Dr Tiburon CA 94920 Office: 374 Parnassus Ave Suite 312 San Francisco CA 94143

COOK, MARGUERITE FLORENCE, hotel executive; b. Buffalo, Feb. 24, 1940; d. James and Marguerite Florence (Bessel) McLachlan. A.A., Santa Monica City Coll., 1959; postgrad. in Edn., UCLA, 1960-61. Mktg. rep. Bank of Calif., 1970-72; corp. sales mgr. Biltmore Hotel, Los Angeles, 1972-74, dir. pub. relations and advt., 1974—. Founder Los Angeles Downtowners, 1982—; pres. Civic Angels, 1979-80, Pacesetters, 1973; mem. Los Angeles Conservency, 1980—. Mem. Am. Women in Radio and TV, Hotel Sales Mgmt. Assn. Republican. Presbyterian. Club: Los Angeles Athletic. Office: Biltmore Hotel 515 S Olive St Los Angeles CA 90013

COOK, MARY JANE, reading cons.; b. Mpls., Aug. 27, 1930; d. Corliss Bruce and Helen Bertha (Ruppert) Von Housen; student U. No. Iowa, 1948-50; B.A., Ariz. State U., 1969, M.A., 1971; Ed.D., Nova U., 1982; m. Walter F. Cook, Aug. 20, 1950; children—David Von, Cynthia Sue. Tchr. elem. sch., Iowa, 1950-53; tchr. spl. edn. for mentally handicapped, Phoenix, 1966-67, tchr. emotionally handicapped, Scottsdale, Ariz., 1969-70; reading cons., Phoenix, 1971-74, Westford, Mass., 1974-76; coordinator gifted edn., Phoenix, 1977-78; reading cons. Paradise Valley Sch. Dist., Phoenix, 1978—. Ariz. Dept. Edn. grantee, 1976; recipient Ariz. Sch. Bd. Assn. Golden Bell award, 1983. Mem. Assn. Supervision and Curriculum Devel., Ariz. Reading Council, Internat. Reading Assn., Ariz. Assn. Gifted and Talented. Republican. Mem. United Ch. Christ. Home: 7145 N 7th Ave Phoenix AZ 85021 Office: 15833 N 29th St Phoenix AZ 85032

COOK, PATRICIA COCHRAN, publisher; b. Des Moines, Mar. 13, 1927; d. Charles Elmer and Rachel Marion (Smith) Cochran; m. Harlin Maurice Cook, June 9, 1948 (div.); children—Paul Harlin, Lisa Louise Cook Foreman. A.A., Colo. Womens Coll., 1947; B.F.A., U. Ariz., 1950. Writer, Sta. KOOL-AM, Phoenix, 1947, Sta. KPHO-TV, Phoenix, 1953-57; owner, mgr. Edit. & Publ. Co., Phoenix, 1957-60; ptnr. Cook & Rau Advt. & Publ., Phoenix, 1960-65; co founder, pres. COMCO Pub. Relations, Inc., Phoenix, 1965-75, Phoenician Books, Inc., Phoenix, 1968-77; media coordinator No. Ariz. U., Flagstaff, 1977-82; owner, mgr. Cochran Press, Flagstaff and Phoenix, 1982—; instr. Phoenix Community Coll., 1967-74; instr. public relations No. Ariz. U., 1980-81. Mem. community devel. com. Phoenix Forward, 1968-72; chmn. media auction Goodwill Industries, 1981. Mem. Pub. Relations Soc. Am. (pres. 1970; Percy award 1971), Internat. Assn. Bus. Communicators (pres. 1967), Am. Women in Radio and TV (pres. 1956), Ariz. Press Women (state pres. 1974), Nat. Fedn. Press Women, Women in Communications (pres. 1974-75), Gamma Alpha Chi. Democrat. Home: 77 W Coolidge #121 Phoenix AZ 85013 Office: PO Box 16847 Phoenix AZ 85011

COOK, PAUL M., electrical machinery company executive; b. Ridgewood, N.J.; B.S. in Chem. Engring., M.I.T., 1947. With Stanford Research Inst., Palo Alto, Calif., 1949-53, Sequoia Process Corp., 1953-56; with Raychem Corp., Menlo Park, Calif., 1957—, pres., chief exec. officer, to 1983, chmn., chief exec. officer, 1983—, also dir. Office: Raychem Corp 300 Constitution Dr Menlo Park CA 94025

COOK, ROBERT C., research scientist; b. New Haven, June 5, 1947; s. Russell C. and Tensia (Veazey) C.; (div.); children—Andrew, Daniel. B.S., Lafayette Coll., 1969; M.Ph., Yale U., 1971, Ph.D., 1973. Mem. faculty dept. chemistry Lafayette Coll., Easton, Pa., 1973-81; vis. prof. Dartmouth Coll., Hanover, N.H., 1977, 78, 79; Colo. State U., 1980; research scientist Lawrence Livermore (Calif.) Nat. Lab., 1981—. ACS grantee, 1974-78; Research Corp. grantee, 1979, 80-81; Petroleum Research Fund grantee, 1980-81. Mem. Am. Chem. Soc., Am. Phys. Soc., Sigma Xi. Contbr. numerous articles to sci. jours. Office: Lawrence Livermore Nat Lab L-338 Livermore CA 94550

COOK, ROBERT DONALD, business exec.; b. Chicago Heights, Ill., Nov. 1, 1929; s. Webster Warren and Gladys (Miner) C.; B.S. in Bus., U. Md., 1956; grad. advanced mgmt. program Harvard U., 1973; m. Maxine Jensen, Nov. 11, 1950; children—Carolyn Jean, Robert Donald II. Audit mgr. Arthur Andersen & Co., C.P.A.'s, Washington, 1956-63; comptroller Peoples Drug Stores, Washington, 1963-68; v.p., controller Booz, Allen & Hamilton Inc., Chgo., 1968-72; pres. Cookemper Rentals, Inc., Barrington, Ill., 1971-73; controller Esmark, Inc., Chgo., 1973-77; exec. v.p. fin. and adminstrn. Castle & Cooke, Inc., San Francisco, 1977—. Served with USNR, 1948-52. C.P.A., Md. Mem. . Inst. C.P.A.'s, Financial Execs. Inst., Beta Alpha Psi. Mason (32 deg., Shriner). Home: 75 Rolling Hills Rd Tiburon CA 94920 Office: 50 California St San Francisco CA 94111

COOK, RONALD WILLIAM, public relations executive; b. Denver, Apr. 17, 1932; s. Milward Thomas and Anne Kathryn (Frazier) C.; B.S. in Speech, Northwestern U., 1955; m. Katherine Leontieff, July 1, 1967; children—Jill, Debbie, Richard. Field advt. and publicity rep. Warner Bros. Pictures, Inc., N.Y.C., 1954-56; public relations rep. Bank of Am., Los Angeles, 1956-58; mgr. product publicity and advt. Martin-Marietta Corp., Denver, 1958-61; account exec. Carl Byoir & Assos., Mpls., 1961-63; dir. communications microelectronics group Rockwell Internat. Co., Anaheim, Calif., 1963-76; dir. public relations and advt. Calif. Computer Products, Inc., Anaheim, 1976-80; v.p. corp. communications Nat. Med. Enterprises, Inc., Los Angeles, 1980—; dir. advt. Orange County Met. chpt. Nat. Alliance Businessmen, 1970-72. Bd. dirs., v.p. Orange County Music Center, 1976-82; v.p., trustee Anaheim Meml. Hosp. Found., 1977-79; dist. mgr. Jr. Achievement So. Calif., 1975-76. Mem. Public Relations Soc. Am., Nat. Investor Relations Inst. Republican. Episcopalian. Club: Greater Los Angeles Press. Office: 11620 Wilshire Blvd Los Angeles CA 90025

COOK, RUDOLPH EMANUEL, psychologist; b. Chgo., May 30, 1928; m. Shirley Thrower, Aug. 3, 1973. Ph.B., Northwestern U., 1949; M.A., Loyola U., Chgo., 1956; Ph.D., U. Oreg., 1965. Lic. psychologist, Calif. Boys' counselor Cook County Juvenile Home, Chgo., 1952-56; psychologist Elgin (Ill.) State Hosp., 1956-62; teaching asst. U. Oreg., Eugene, 1962-65; poverty worker Portland (Oreg.) Urban League, 1965-66; psychol. counselor San Jose (Calif.) State U., 1966—; forensic evaluator Santa Clara County (Calif.) Superior Ct.; psychologist Calif. Disability Evaluation Div. Recipient Service award Continental Socs., 1982-83. Fellow Am. Orthopsychiat. Assn., Royal Soc. Health; mem. Nat. Register Health Service Providers in Psychology, Pathway Socs. (Service award 1977), Afro-Am. Community Ctr., Campus Christian Ctr., Kappa Alpha Psi (Service award 1975, 76). Democrat. Home: 1094 Pomeroy Ave Santa Clara CA 95051 Office: Adm 201 San Jose State Univ San Jose CA 95192

COOK, STANLEY JOSEPH, linguist; b. Spicer, Minn., June 9, 1935; s. William Joseph and Lillie Esther (Feeland) C.; B.A., U. Minn., 1957; M.A., U. Utah, 1966, Ph.D. (NDEA fellow), 1969; m. Janet Lucille Terry, Oct. 9, 1964; children—John Hildon, Laurel Erin. Project specialist in English, U. Wis., Madison, 1967; instr. English, U. Utah, Salt Lake City, 1968-69; prof. English and modern langs. Calif. State Poly. U., Pomona, 1969—; cons. communications. Served with USMCR, 1958-64. NSF grantee, 1966; Calif. State U. and Colls. grantee, 1973-74. Mem. Dialect Soc., Western Photog. Soc., Phi Beta Kappa. Democrat. Unitarian. Editor: Language and Human Behavior, 1973; Man Unwept: Visions from the Inner Eye, 1974; The Scope of Grammar: A Study of Modern English, 1980. Home: 1744 N Corona Ave Ontario CA 91764 Office: 3801 W Temple Ave Pomona CA 91768

COOK, SUSAN PAULA, retail executive; b. Rochester, N.H., Feb. 16, 1947; d. Israel J. and Molly (Landes) Cook; A.B. cum laude, N.Y. U., 1968; student U. Madrid, 1966-67. Supr. customer service operation Bloomingdale's, 1968, personnel rep. for home furnishings div., 1969-70, personnel mgr. Stamford (Conn.) store, 1971, corp. tng. mgr., N.Y.C., 1972-73; personnel mgr. Macy's Calif., Palo Alto, 1973-74, divisional staff tng. mgr., San Francisco, 1974-75, adminstr. tng., 1975-77, v.p. personnel devel., 1977-80, v.p. exec. personnel and devel., 1980-82, v.p. personal services, 1982; mgr. employee devel. Apple Computer, Cupertino, Calif., 1982—. Mem. United Way Mgmt. Assistance Program. Mem. Profl. Women's Alliance, Am. Soc. Tng. and Devel. (exec. com. 1979), Internat. Assn. Bus. Communicators, Nat. Soc. Performance Improvement, Am. Soc. Personnel Adminstrs. Democrat. Jewish. Home: 21100 Gary Dr Apt 309 Hayward CA 94546 Office: 20525 Marioni Ave Cupertino CA

COOK, SUZANNE MARY, educator; b. Odessa, Tex., Feb. 26, 1940; d. Raymon Leslie and Jeane Louise (Miller) Halbrook; B.B.A., Tex. Tech. Coll., Lubbock, 1962, M.B.A., 1970, D.B.A., 1973; divorced; children—Kimberley Jeane, Deborah Sue. Teaching asst. Tex. Tech. U., 1970-73; asst. prof. mgmt. Idaho State U., Pocatello, 1973-74; mem. faculty Ariz. State U., Tempe, 1974—, asso. prof. mgmt., 1978—; condr. seminars. Bd. dirs. Mayor Phoenix Com. Employment Handicapped, 1976—. Mem. Acad. Mgmt., Soc. Personnel Adminstrs., Soc. Advancement Mgmt., Phoenix Personnel Mgmt. Assn., Am. Bus. Women's Assn., Sigma Iota Epsilon, Omicron Delta Epsilon, Alpha Kappa Psi, Alpha Phi. Methodist. Contbr. to profl. publs. Home: 407 E Aepli Dr Tempe AZ 85282 Office: Dept Mgmt Coll Bus Ariz State Univ Tempe AZ 85282

COOK, SYBILLA POMEROY AVERY, librarian; b. Buffalo, Aug. 20, 1930; d. Edward C. and Elizabeth A. (Boorum) Avery; m. John D. Cook, June 12, 1951; children—Harold John, Robert Sherman, Raymond Avery. Student Smith Coll., 1948-50; B.S., Northwestern U., 1951; M.A.L.S., Rosary Coll., 1968; M.A., U. Oreg., 1982. Cert. tchr., Ill., Oreg. Librarian Sch. Dist. 103, Deerfield, Ill., 1968-69; media specialist Sch. Dist. 62, Des Plaines, Ill., 1969-76; librarian Sch. Dist. 116, Dillard, Oreg., 1976-78; library media specialist Sch. Dist. 12, Glide, Oreg., 1978—. Active Umpqua Valley Arts Assn., Umpqua Actors Community Theatre, Roseburg (Oreg.) Symphony Assn., Community Concert Assn., Friends of the Douglas County Library, Safari Game Search Found. Mem. ALA, Oreg. Ednl. Media Assn., Oreg. Library Assn., Pacific N.W. Library Assn., Soc. Children's Book Writers. Contbr. numerous articles to profl. jours. Office: Library 1477 Glide Loop Rd Glide OR 97443

COOK, WILLARD EUGENE, SR., automotive executive; b. Mandan, N.D., Aug. 18, 1912; s. Valentine Ralph and Myrtle Eugenia (McVey) C.; m. Anne Elizabeth Sanders, July 27, 1938; children—Willard, Stephen B., Judith Anne Cook Garber, Janet R. Grad. high sch., Great Falls. Bookkeeper, Mont. Power Co., Great Falls, 1929-34; credit desk Gen. Motors Acceptance Corp., Great Falls, 1934-36; sales Gen. Mills., Inc., Mpls., 1937-47; v.p. Scales Motor Co., Sheridan, Wyo., 1947-54; pres. Cook Ford Sales, Inc., Sheridan, 1954—. Trustee, Sch. Dist. #7, 1950-68; mem. Sheridan County Welfare Bd., 1960-65; pres., bd. dirs. Sheridan chpt. Salvation Army; bd. dirs. YMCA, 1966-78, Whitney-Benefits, Inc., 1970-83; mem. Wyo. Gov.'s Commn. on Edn., 1963-64; deacon, trustee, elder Presbyterian Ch., 1955-75. Recipient Golden Bell award Wyo. Sch. Bd. Assn., 1968; 1st pl. Quality Dealer award Time mag., 1975; Disting. Service in Bus. award Coll. Commerce, U. Wyo., 1976. Mem. Nat. Auto Dealers Assn., Sheridan Auto Dealers Assn. (past pres.), Wyoming Auto Dealers Assn. (dir.), Ford Registered Dealers Council, Rocky Mountain Ford Dealers Advt. Assn., Future Farmers Am. (hon. life). Presbyterian. Clubs: Sheridan Country, Lions (past pres.), Executive (dir.) Sportsman, Elks, Masons, Shriners. Home: 566 W Loucks St Sheridan WY 82801 Office: 103 N Gould St PO Box 863 Sheridan WY 82801

COOKE, EDNA MARIE, fire protection co. exec., restaurant owner; b. Hogansburg, N.Y., Dec. 27, 1935; d. Thomas and Agnes E. (Jock) Lazare; student Pasadena Coll., 1965, Citrus Coll., 1966-67; m. Charles Ronald Cooke, July 2, 1955 (div.); children—Leanna Jane, Ramona Gale, Craig Ronel. Various positions, 1953-65; sec.-treas., part owner Vanguard Automatic Sprinkler Co., Santa Fe Springs, Calif., 1967-74; owner LaZar House of Beauty, Glendora, Calif., 1974—, Jacques Restaurant, Glendora, 1974—; pres., owner Eagle Fire Protection, Glendora, 1974—. Ways and means chairperson San Gabriel Valley Symphony Assn., 1966. Mem. Glendora C. of C., Calif. Restaurant Assn. Democrat. Roman Catholic. Club: Glendora Country. Office: 2264 E Alosta Glendora CA 91740

COOKE, PHYLLIS, psychologist; b. Cleve., Sept. 6, 1933; d. Reuben and Margaret Swanson; B.A., Baldwin Wallace Coll., 1969; M.A., Cleve. State U., 1971; Ph.D., Kent State U., 1974; m. Thomas L. Cooke, Apr. 11, 1952 (div. 1974); 1 son, Thomas Lee. Psychologist, cons. Cleve. Bd. Edn., 1970-77; instr. Kent State U., 1971-75; pvt. practice clin. psychology, Beachwood, Ohio, 1970-77; dean grad. program in human resource devel. Univ. Assos. Cons.'s and Pubs., Inc., San Diego, 1979—, dean lab. edn. intern program, 1977—, dir. profl. services, 1977—. Mem. Am. Psychol. Assn., Calif. Psychol. Assn., Acad. Mgmt., Am. Soc. Tng. and Devel. Office: 8517 Production Ave San Diego CA 92121

COOKE, RALPH KENT, advertising executive, real estate developer; b. Toronto, Ont., Can., Apr. 29, 1937; s. Jack Kent and Jean (Carnegie) C.; m. Carolyn Rozelle; m. 2d, Barbara Simon, May 17, 1975; children—Jeannie, Jack II, Ralph II, Philip. Student St. Andrews Coll., Aurora, Ont., Can., 1947-50, Upper Can. Coll., Toronto, Can., 1953-57, U. Western Ontario, 1957-59. Sales mgr. CKEY radio, Toronto, Ont., Can., 1959-61; gen. mgr. KMBY radio, Monterey, Calif., 1961-62; owner RKC, Inc., Cooke Racing, Carnegie/Cooke Properties, Ltd., Cardinal Prodns., Inc., Los Angeles, 1963—. Founder, patron Huntington Hartford theatre, mem. Friends of Music Ctr.; founder Mus. Contemporary Art; mem. Republican Nat. Com. Club: Bel Air Country. Home: 1950 Tollis Ave Santa Barbara CA 93108 Office: 814 S Westgate Ave Los Angeles CA 90049

COOKSON, JOHN (JACK) WILLIAM, Canadian provincial government official; b. Lougheed, Alta., Can., Oct. 29, 1928; s. Herbert and Catherine Cookson; m. Winnifred Ann Doupe, June 23, 1956; children—Bruce, John, Robert, Sally. B.Sc. in Agri. Profl. Cert. Edn., U. Alta., 1956. Farm operator; mem. Legis. Assembly Alta., Edmonton, 1971—, party whip, 1971-75, minister of environment, 1979—; county councillor Lacombe, 1964-71. Progressive Conservative. Office: 222 Legis Bldgs Edmonton AB T5K 2B7 Canada*

COOLEY, ELEANOR NEWCOMB, ret. editor; b. Melba Idaho, Nov. 30 1915; d. Lewis Elmer and Helen Alice (Prisk) Newcomb; student Coll. of Idaho, 1934-35, U. Colo., 1935-37, Ariz. State U., 1960; m. Robert Miller Cooley, July 1, 1937; 1 son, Richard Lewis. Co-pub., soc. editor, office mgr. Mountain Home (Idaho) News, 1946-53, part-time editor, proofreader, copyreader, 1979—; soc. editor Ariz. Daily Sun, Flagstaff, 1966-67; editor Pine alumni mag. No. Ariz. U., Flagstaff, 1971-79. Co-chmn. publicity Coconino unit Am. Cancer Soc., 1971-73. Mem. Sigma Delta Chi, Theta Sigma Phi, Chi Omega, Beta Sigma Phi, Daus. of Nile. Republican. Episcopalian. Home: 5100 Umatilla Ave Boise ID 83709

COOLEY, RICHARD P., banker; b. Dallas, Nov. 25, 1923; s. Victor E. and Helen (Pierce) C.; B.S., Yale U., 1944; children—Leslie Ann, Pierce, Sheila, Sean, Mark. With Wells Fargo Bank, San Francisco, 1949-1982, sr. v.p., 1964-65, exec. v.p., 1965-66, pres., 1966-79, chmn., 1979-1982, chief exec. officer, 1966-1982, also dir.; chmn., chief exec. officer, dir. Wells Fargo & Co., 1968-1982; chmn. chief exec. officer, pres. Seattle-First Nat. Bank, 1983—; dir. Howmet Turbine Components Corp., UAL, Inc., Pechiney Ugine Kuhlmann Corp. Trustee Rand Corp., Calif. Inst. Tech., Pasadena. Served to 1st lt. Armed Services. Decorated Air medal. Mem. Assn. Res. City Bankers, Smithsonian Instn. Nat. Assocs. (dir.), Calif. C. of C. (dir.). Office: 1001 4th Ave Seattle WA 98124

COOLEY, THOMAS FERGUSON, economics educator; b. Rutland, Vt., Jan. 3, 1943; s. Thomas J. and Marjorie (Batchelder) C.; m. Patricia Bower, Nov. 26, 1977; children—Aaron, Joshua, Noah. B.S. (Irving Scholar), Rensselaer Poly. Inst., 1965; M.A. (NSF fellow), U. Pa., 1970, Ph.D., 1971. Asst. prof. econs. Tufts U., Medford, Mass., 1970-76; research assoc. Nat. Bur. Econ. Research, Cambridge, Mass., 1973-77; faculty assoc. Joint Center Urban Studies MIT and Harvard U., Cambridge, 1976-80; prof. U. Calif.-Santa Barbara, 1976—; cons. govt. depts., pvt. industry. Mem. Am. Econ. Assn., Econometric Soc., Am. Statis. Assn. Contbr. articles in field to books, profl. jours. Office: Dept Econs U Calif Santa Barbara CA 93106

COOLIDGE, ROBERT CANODE, computer co. exec.; b. Bloomington, Ill., Feb. 11, 1933; s. Clifford Newell and Margaret Jane (Canode) C.; student DePauw U., 1951-53, San Francisco State U., 1966-67, Advanced Mgmt. Program, Stanford U., 1976; m. Marie Ann Handley, Apr. 6, 1975; children—Kimberly, John Case, Robert Todd, Christopher Lawrence. Western area mgr. Minn. Mining & Mfg. Co., St. Paul, 1959-67; regional mgr. Stromberg Data Graphics, Inc., San Diego, 1967-69; v.p. mktg. Distbn. Scis., Inc., Hinsdale, Ill., 1969-72, also dir.; exec. v.p. Boole & Babbage, Inc., Sunnyvale, Calif., 1972-80, also dir.; chmn. bd., pres. Internat. Data Processing Services, Inc., San Francisco, 1980—; pres. Shasta Gen. Systems, Sunnyvale, Calif., 1981—; dir. Computer Program Products, Ltd., London, European Software Co., The Hague, Netherlands, Inst. Software Engring., Menlo Park, Calif., Calif. Software Co., Los Angeles. Served with U.S. Army, 1953-55. Mem. Users of Automated Data Processing Equipment (past nat. dir.), Western Electronic Mfrs. Assn., Assn. Data Processing Services Orgn., Inc., Mill Valley Jaycees (founder, past pres.). Republican. Home: 354 Pine Hill Rd Mill Valley CA 94941

COOLIDGE, WINTHROP KNOWLTON, investment co. exec.; b. Chgo., Nov. 14, 1901; s. Winthrop and Marie (Knowlton) C.; S.B., Mass. Inst. Tech., 1923; m. Laetitia B. Kelly, July 20, 1935 (div. Jan. 1961); children—Laetitia (Mrs. Robert G. Allen Jr.), Deborah Jean (dec.), Olga Elizabeth, Dexter Knowlton, Carol Marie (Mrs. Alexander Breckinridge); m. 2d, Catharyn June Cook, Dec. 30, 1968. With sales dept. Standard Oil Co. (Ind.), 1923-26; with Chgo. Copper & Chem. Co., 1927—, pres., 1949—. Mem. English Speaking Union, SAR, Delta Kappa Epsilon. Clubs: Saddle and Cycle (Chgo.); White Lake (Mich.) Golf, White Lake Yacht; Tucson Country. Address: 2640 N Camino Valle Verde Tucson AZ 85715 also Michillinda Beach Assn Whitehall MI 49461

COOMBES, ROBERT FREEMAN, scientist; b. Dallas, Mar. 29, 1943; s. Zachariah Ellis and Bertha C.; B.S., U. Tex. at Arlington, 1969; Ph.D., U. Houston, 1972; m. Wanda Beth Dikes, Apr. 5, 1970. Postdoctoral fellow U. Calif. at Riverside, 1972-73; sr. research chemist Curtis Nuclear Corp., Los Angeles, 1973-75; chief scientist Diagnostic Products Corp., Los Angeles, 1975—. NDEA Grad. fellow, 1969-72; U. Calif. Cancer grantee, 1972-73. Mem. Am. Assn. Clin. Chemistry, Am. Chem. Soc., Sigma Xi, Phi Kappa Phi. Republican. Reviewer, Jour. Clin. Chemistry, 1980—. Home: 1716 Goodman Ave Redondo Beach CA 90278 Office: 5700 W 96th St Los Angeles CA 90045

COOMBS, ARTHUR FERRELL, JR., educator, consultant; b. Salt Lake City, May 26, 1930; s. Arthur Ferrell and Olive (Woolley) C.; m. Mignon Peterson, Feb. 17, 1955; children—Cary, Linda, Art, Kay, Mike, Holly. B.A., U. Utah, 1950, M.S., 1955; Ph.D., Stanford U., 1970. Research asst. Stanford U., Palo Alto, Calif., 1965-69; pres. corp. hdqrs. Edn. Coordinates, Palo Alto, 1969-72, chmn. bd., edn. coordinator, Sunnyvale, Calif., 1972-79; dir. Sysorex Inst., Cupertino, Calif., 1979—; cons. in field. Ecclesiastical leader Ch. Jesus Christ of Latter-day Saints, Cupertino and Santa Clara. Mem. Am. Soc. Tng. and Devel., Phi Beta Kappa. Republican. Mormon. Author: The Teachers' Handbook/Flexible Scheduling by Computer, 1971.

COOMBS, ROBERT HOLMAN, educator, researcher, consultant, author; b. Salt Lake City, Sept. 16, 1934; s. Morgan Scott and Vivian (Holman) C.; m. Carol Jean Cook, May 29, 1958; children—Robert Scott, Kathryn, Lorraine, Karen Youn Jung, Holly Ann, Krista Ho Jung, David Jeremy. B.S. in Sociology, U. Utah, 1958, M.S. in Sociology, 1959; Ph.D. in Sociology, Wash. State U., 1964; postdoctoral fellow Bowman Gray Sch. Medicine, Wake Forest U., 1966. Instr. sociology Iowa State U., Ames, 1963-64, asst. prof. sociology, 1964-66; asst. prof. sociology Wake Forest U., Bowman Gray Sch. Medicine, Winston-Salem, N.C., 1966-68, assoc. prof., 1968-70; career research specialist UCLA Neuropsychiat. Inst., 1970-73, assoc. research sociologist, 1973-77, assoc. adj. prof. behavioral Scis., 1977-78, prof., 1978—, asst. dir. research, 1978-81, dir. office edn., 1980—; chief Research Ctr., UCLA/Camarillo, Calif., 1970-81; adj. faculty U. Without Walls., Antioch Coll., 1971-75; dir. UCLA Family Learning Ctr., Oxnard, Calif., 1977—; chief research Camarillo State Hosp., Calif., 1970-81; chmn. Instl. Rev. Bd. Calif. Dept. Health and Human Services, 1970-71, Calif. Council Criminal Justice, 1973; mem. planning com. Los Angeles Regional Criminal Justice Bd., 1975; NSF grant referee, 1982; counselor; cons.; educator. Del. White House Conf. Children and Youth 1970; adv. com. alcohol Ventura County, Calif., 1973-74; adv. com. drugs Ventura County, 1973-74; bd. dirs. Camarillo Family Inc., 1973-76; dirs. adv. com. UCLA Drug Treatment Program, 1976; cons. Father Flanagan's Boys' Home, Boys Town, Nebr., 1977-78; exec. council UCLA Alcohol Research Ctr., 1977-82; Calif. State Adv. Com. on Peace Officer Standards and Tng., 1979-81; Family Health Task Force, 1979-80; participant White House Conf. on Families, 1980. Served with U.S. Army, 1956-64. NSF fellow 1962, 63, NIMH grantee 1968-73, 82-83; Nat. Fund Med. Edn. grantee 1969-71; Nat. Inst. Drug Abuse grantee 1977-80; Father Flanagan's Boys' Home Found. grantee 1977-79, U.S. Dept. Labor grantee 1978; UCLA Research Ctr. grantee 1977-82. Mem. Sigma Xi, Phi Kappa Phi, Alpha Kappa Delta, Kappa Delta Pi. Democrat. Mormon. Author: Junkies and Straights: The Camarillo Experience, 1975; Mastering Medicine: Professional Socialization in Medical School, 1978; (with J. St. John) Making It in Medical School, 1979; editor (with C.E. Vincent) Psychosocial Aspects of Medical Training, 1971; (with L.J. Fry and P. Lewis) Socialization in Drug Abuse, 1976; author numerous jour. articles, tech. reports, book chpts. Home: 1612 Hobart Dr Camarillo CA 93010 Office: UCLA Neuropsychiat Inst 760 Westwood Plaza Los Angeles CA 90024

COOMBS, WILLIAM ELMER, accountant, lawyer; b. Keosauqua, Iowa, Jan. 17, 1911; s. Elmer Clyde and Myra (Moon) C.; A.B., U. Calif. at Los Angeles, 1933; J.D., Loyola U., Los Angeles, 1954; m. Katheryn Rose Logan, Oct. 20, 1934; children—Katheryn M. Kirkendoll, Rose Ann (Mrs. Luciano Siracusa). Acct., Shell Oil Co., Los Angeles, 1933-36, So. Calif. Edison Co., Los Angeles, 1936-37; auditor State of Calif., Los Angeles, 1937-41; sr. acct. Arthur Andersen & Co., 1941-43; controller Case Constrn. Co., San Pedro, Calif., 1943-46; C.P.A., Roberts & Coombs, 1946-49, Deloitte, Plender, Griffths & Co., 1949-52; controller Ford J. Twaits Co., Los Angeles, 1952-55; overseas auditor Morrison-Knudsen Internat., San Francisco, 1955-56; asst. prof. bus. Calif. State U., Chico 1956-58; sec.-treas., dir. Matich Corp., Colton, Calif. 1958-61; admitted to Calif. bar, 1955; practiced in Rialto, 1952-58 mem. Calif. Senate, 1967-73; city atty. Rialto, 1977-81, Big Bear Lake, Calif., 1980-82. Mem. Rialto City Planning Commn., 1960-62; councilman, Rialto, 1962-67; bd. dirs. Regional Econ. Devel. Council, 1964-67, pres., 1965-66. C.P.A., Calif. Mem. State Bar Calif., ABA, Am. Inst. C.P.A.s, Calif. Soc. C.P.A.s, Calif., San Bernardino County (pres. 1966-67) taxpayers assns. Rotarian. Author reference book: Construction Accounting and Financial Management. Home: 5810 Date Ave Rialto CA 92376 Office: 225 S Riverside Ave Rialto CA 92376

COON, ARNOLD WILDING, cons. engr.; b. Salt Lake City, Sept. 24, 1925; s. Chester Nelson and Clara Cornelia (Wilding) C.; S.B., U. Idaho, 1943; B.S. in Civil Engring., U. Utah, 1949; m. Arlene Elenor Pesina, July 8, 1947; children—Steven, Deborah, Gregory, Gary, Lori, Mark, Heidi. Asst. project engr. Utah Constrn. Co., Lark, 1949; structural engr. H.C. Hughes Co., Salt Lake City, 1950-54; self-employed, Salt Lake City, 1955-56; cons. engr., partner Coon & King, engrs., Salt Lake City, 1956-62; cons. engr., chmn. bd. Coon, King & Knowlton Engrs., Salt Lake City, 1962-82; owner Arnold W. Coon, forensic engrs., Salt Lake City, 1982—. Dist. chmn. Republican Party; del. county and state Reps. cons. Recipient Distinguished Civil Engring. Alumnus award U. Utah, 1975. Mem. Utah Council Land Surveyors (pres. 1969-70), Cons. Engrs. Council Utah (pres. 1959; Excellence in Engring. Design award 1975), Am. Cons. Engrs. Council (dir. 1964-65), Am. Concrete Inst. Mormon. Club: Star Valley Country. Home: 3679 Oakview Dr Salt Lake City UT 84117 Office: 5330 S 900 E Salt Lake City UT 84117

COONEY, DANIEL ELLARD, aeronautical engineer; b. DeLand, Fla., Oct. 25, 1949; s. William Phillip and Ruth Eleanor (Weins) C. B.S. in Aerospace Engring., U. Fla., Gainesville, 1972. registered profl. aero. engr., Kans. Aero. engr. Bede Aircraft, Newton, Kans., 1972-76, chief engr., 1977-78; propulsion design supr. Lear Fan Corp., Reno, Nev., 1978-80, mgr. computer aided design dept., 1981—; flight and ground sch. instr. Mem. Soc. Automotive Engrs., AIAA. Contbr. articles to profl. jours.; patentee electromechanical propeller speed gov. system, aircraft engine mount. Office: PO Box 12010 Reno NV 89510

COOPER, ANITA LUCILE, chamber of commerce executive; b. Rocky Ford, Colo., June 23, 1909; d. Frank Alan and Eunice Harriet (Casebeer) Crowe; m. Roy Doig Cooper, May 27, 1936; children—Alice Eunice Deatherage, Virginia Jessie Grimsley. Cert., Colo. State Tchrs. Coll., Greeley, 1929, student summer 1931. Elem. sch. tchr. rural schs. Bent and Otero counties, Colo., 1929-36; vol. community work, 1936-75; sec.-mgr. Las Animas-Bent County C. of C., 1976—. 4-H club leader, Rixey, Colo.; past officer various community orgns. Recipient Santa Fe Trail Day award as Outstanding Citizen of the Community of Las Animas, Las Animas High Sch., 1980; Citizen of the Year award for Outstanding Community Service, Las Animas-Bent County C. of C., 1981. Republican. Presbyterian. Clubs: Eastern Star, Rixey Country Club., PEO. Office: 233 6th St Las Animas CO 81054

COOPER, CHARLES FISHER, ecologist; b. Kenosha, Wis., Sept. 26, 1924; s. Ralph Yocum and Mildred (Todt) C. B.S., U. Minn., 1950; M.S., U. Ariz., 1957; Ph.D., Duke U., 1958. Forester, range conservationist U.S. Bur. Land Mgmt., Colo. and Ariz., 1950-54; asst. prof. Humboldt State Coll., Arcata, Calif., 1958-60; research scientist U.S. Agrl. Research Service, Boise, Idaho, 1960-64; assoc. prof. to prof. Sch. Natural Resources, U. Mich., Ann Arbor, 1964-69; program dir. ecosystem studies NSF, Washington, 1969-71; prof. biology, dir. Ctr. for Regional Environ. Studies, San Diego State U., 1971—; Fulbright research fellow, Australia, 1962-63; fellow Woodrow Wilson Internat. Ctr. for Scholars, Smithsonian Instn., Washington, 1977; mem. mgmt. authority Tijuana River Nat. Estuarine Sanctuary, 1982—. Bd. dirs. San Diego County Water Authority, 1973—; trustee The Inst. Ecology, 1976-81; bd. dirs. Planning and Conservation League of Calif., 1979—. Fellow AAAS; mem. Am. Geophys. Union, Soc. Am. Foresters, Assn. Tropical Biology, Ecol. Soc. Am. (chmn. applied ecology sect. 1979-81), Sigma Xi. Club: Commonwealth of Calif. (San Francisco). Contbr. numerous articles on ecology and climate change to profl. jours., periodicals. Home: 9302 La Jolla Farms Rd La Jolla CA 92037 Office: Dept Biology San Diego State U San Diego CA 92182

COOPER, DOUGLAS ELHOFF, chemist, consultant; b. New Boston, Ohio, May 21, 1912; s. Frank Edward and Norma Irene (Elhoff) C.; m. Anita H. Hansen, Sept. 26, 1959. B.S., Eastern Ky. State U., 1939; M.S., U. Tenn., 1940; Ph.D., Purdue U., 1943. Chief chemist, Bristol Labs., Syracuse, N.Y., 1943-52; research assoc. Ethyl Corp., Detroit, 1952-69, market analyst, Baton Rouge, 1969-77; cons. Occupational Health, Rocklin, Calif., 1977—. Mem. Am. Chem. Soc., AAAS, Health Physics Soc., Am. Indsl. Hygiene Assn. Patentee in field of drugs and catalysts. Home: 3065 Argonaut Rocklin CA 95677 Office: 3065 Argonaut Rocklin CA 95677

COOPER, EDWARD MARK, marketing educator, consultant, researcher; b. Bklyn., Apr. 6, 1950; s. Jack J. and Evelyn (Weinfeld) C.; m. Anita J. Ross, June 6, 1970. B.A. in Psychology and Sociology, U. Colo., 1973, M.A. in Counseling and Personnel, 1976, Ph.D. in Higher Edn. Adminstrn. and Mktg., 1979. Research assoc. Nat. Ctr. for Higher Edn. Mgmt. Systems, Boulder, Colo., 1975-77; dir. instl. research, dir. program evaluation and outcomes research Met. State Coll., Denver, 1977-79, assoc. prof. mktg., 1979—; co-founder, dir., v.p. mktg. Internat. Data Systems, Inc., Denver, 1982; founder Cooper/Marcum Advt., Denver; pres., chmn. Mktg. and Mgmt. Services of the Rockies, Inc. Chmn. Met. State Coll. United Way Campaign, 1981-82; mem. Needs Assessment Com., Mile High United Way, internat. sci. vis. host. El Rancho Colo. Corp. grantee, 1982. Mem. So. Mktg. Assn., Southwestern Mktg. Assn., Internat. Assn. for Instl. Research (chmn. internat. forum), Colo. Assn. Planners and Instl. Researchers (pres. 1980-81). Democrat. Jewish. Contbr. writings to publs. in field. Office: Box 13 Mktg Dept 1006 11th St Denver CO 80204

COOPER, FRANK, financial executive; b. Seattle, Nov. 28, 1928; s. Frank H. and Marguerite (Madison) C.; m. Erlene Johnson, June, 1952; children—Dawn, Frank Jr. B.A., U. Wash., 1951, M.B.A., 1968. Commr. banking Wash. state, 1968-71; pres., dir., chief exec. officer Bank Honolulu, 1971-75; prin. Frank Cooper & Assocs., Honolulu, 1975-80; pres., dir., chief exec. officer Equitable Savs. & Loan, Huntington Beach, Calif., 1980—; mem. Wash. legislature, 1964-68. Del. Republican Nat. Convs., 1964, 68, 80; chmn. Rep. Party Hawaii, 1978-80; mem. Rep. Nat. Com.; trustee U. Wash. Grad. Sch. Banking, Annie Wright Girls Acad.; dir. Nat. Assn. Bank Commrs., Am. Athletic Assn. Pacific Coast Baseball League, Jessie Dslyn Boys Ranch, Mary Bridges Childrens Hosp., Wash. State Community Coll. Assn.; chmn. Tacoma Community Coll. Served with U.S. Army, 1945-47. Mem. Young Mens Bus. Club (pres.), Navy League U.S. Clubs: Univ. Union (Tacoma); Outrigger Canoe, Oahu Country, Pacific, Waikiki Yacht, Plaza (Honolulu); Elk, Mason, Shriner.

COOPER, FREDERICK MICHAEL, physicist; b. N.Y.C., Apr. 1, 1944; s. Ernie E. and Lottie (Silverman) C.; B.S. (Woodrow Wilson fellow), City Coll. N.Y., 1964; Ph.D. in Physics (Harvard fellow, NSF fellow), Harvard, 1968; m. Necia Grant, May 21, 1972; children—Lottie Grant, David Grant. Research asst. Inst. Space Studies, NASA, N.Y.C., 1963-64; lectr. physics CCNY, 1964; instr. physics Cornell U., Ithaca, N.Y., 1968-70; asst. prof. physics Belfer Grad. Sch. Sci., Yeshiva U., 1970-75; mem. Inst. Advanced Study, 1977; dep. group leader T-8, theory div. Los Alamos Sci. Lab., 1975—. Democratic committeeman Bronx County, N.Y.C., 1971-74. Frederick Cottrell grantee, 1971-72, NSF grantee, 1971-74. Mem. Am. Phys. Soc., N.Y. Acad. Sci., Phi Beta Kappa. Contbr. articles to profl. jours. Home: 1117 S Plata Circle Santa Fe NM 87501 Office: Box 1663 Los Alamos NM 87544

COOPER, GENE ALFRED, fin. exec.; b. Bryan, Ohio, Sept. 26, 1936; s. George Wayne and Agnes Anibel (Fisher) C.; B.S., Bowling Green State U., 1958; M.B.A., U. Toledo, 1960; m. Carolyn Marie Bearss, Apr. 14, 1962; children—Steven William, Jeffrey Wayne. Sr. acct. Arthur Young & Co., Toledo, Ohio, 1960-64; asst. to controller Princeton U., 1964-67; controller Kenyon Coll., Gambier, Ohio, 1967-69; sr. internal auditor, staff asst. policies and procedures, mgr. corp. reporting, beverage div. controller Westinghouse Electric Corp., Vernon, Calif., 1969-79, beverage bus. unit controller, 1979-83, v.p., controller, 1983—; instr. Bowling Green U., 1963-64, Rider Coll., 1965-67. Bd. dirs., treas. Wesley Found., Princeton U. C.P.A., Ohio, N.J., Pa. Mem. Am. Inst. C.P.A.s, Nat. Soft Drink Assn., Am. Mgmt. Assn., Nat. Assn. Accts., Am. Acctg. Assn., Ohio Soc. C.P.A.s, Beta Alpha Psi, Sigma Phi Epsilon. Methodist. Home: 1694 Elmsford Pl Westlake Village CA 91361 Office: 3220 E 26th St Vernon CA 90023

COOPER, HAL, TV director, producer; b. N.Y.C., Feb. 23, 1923; s. Benjamin and Adeline (Raichman) C.; B.A., U. Mich., 1946; m. Marta Lucille Salcido, June 26, 1971; 1 son, James Benjamin; children by previous marriage—Bethami, Pamela. Performer, Big Bro.'s Rainbow House, Mut. Network, 1936-41; asst. dir. Dock Street Theatre, Charleston, S.C., 1946-48; writer, producer TV Babysitter, DuMont TV Network, 1948-52, The Magic Cottage, 1950-56; dir., producer various daytime TV shows including Search for Tomorrow, Valiant Lady, Portia Faces Life, Kitty Foyle and others, 1950-57; producer The Troublemakers, stage play, London, England, 1952; dir. TV shows including Death Valley Days, Dick Van Dyke, I Dream of Jeannie, I Spy, That Girl, Mayberry RFD, Courtship of Eddie's Father, Odd Couple, Mary Tyler Moore, All in the Family, 1960—; dir., exec. producer Maude, CBS, Hollywood, Calif., 1972-78, Love, Sidney NBC, 1982-83. Served to lt. (j.g.) USNR, 1943-46. Mem. Writers Guild Am., Screen Actors Guild, AFTRA, Actors Equity, ASCAP, Dirs. Guild Am. (guild sec. 1981-84, mem. dir.'s council 1964-83, trustee pension plan 1964-75). Address: 2651 Hutton Dr Beverly Hills CA 90210

COOPER, IVAN ARTHUR, civil/environ. engr.; b. Bronx, N.Y., Apr. 29, 1949; s. Samuel and Hilda Beatrice (Krause) C.; B.S.C.E. (N.Y. State Regents scholar, Water Pollution Control agy. fellow), Union Coll., 1971; M.S.C.E., Northwestern U., 1975, postgrad., 1975; m. Rosalind Wasserman, Aug. 21, 1971; children—Alana, Micah, Shira. Design engr. Consoer Townsend & Assos., Chgo., 1971-72; project mgr. HMG Group, Libertyville, Ill., 1972-78, v.p., Aurora, Colo., 1978-79; sr. project mgr. Henningson Durham and Richardson, Denver, 1979—; pres., chief exec. officer Certified Inspection Services, Boulder, Colo., 1978—; guest lectr. in san. engring. Northwestern U., 1977; cons. and lectr. small wastewater treatment systems seminars EPA. Democratic precinct capt. Abner Mikva for Ill. Congressman, 1978; bd. dirs. Congregation B'nai Shalom. mem. adv. bd. Aurora (Colo.) Votech Sch. System, 1978-79; bd. dirs. Boulder (Colo.) Parent Tchrs. Orgn., 1980-82, pres., 1982-83. Registered profl. engr., Wis., Ill., Mich., Ind., Colo. Mem. Water Pollution Control Fedn. (chmn. tech. activities com. 1979-80), Am. Water Works Assn. Author: Septage Management, 1980; Vacuum Sewer Technology, 1981; prin. designer Sheridan (Wyo.) Wastewater Facility, Littleton/Englewood (Colo.) Wastewater Facility. Club: Meadows Country (Boulder). Home: 840 Racquet Ln Boulder CO 80303 Office: 1100 Capitol Life Center Denver CO 80209

COOPER, JAMES H., book publishing company executive, lawyer; b. Bklyn., May 20, 1929; s. James H. and Helen M. (Hofeditz) C.; m. Vera D. Duboy, May 28, 1958; children—James K., Jonathan S. A.B., Columbia U., 1951, J.D., 1957. Bar: N.Y. 1957, U.S. Supreme Ct. 1965. Sole practice, Millerton, N.Y., 1957-58; law editor Lawyers Coop. Pub. Co., Rochester, N.Y., 1958-63, mng. editor, editor-in-chief, 1973-78; legal advisor NASA, Washington, 1963-65; asst. mng. editor, editorial dir. Bancroft Whitney Co., San Francisco, 1965-73; pres. Shepard's/McGraw-Hill, Colorado Springs, Colo., 1978—; dir. First Nat. Bank of Colorado Springs. Bd. dirs. Colorado Springs Symphony, Colo. Opera Festival. Served to capt. USMC, 1951-64. Decorated Bronze Star. Mem. ABA, Assn. Trial Lawyers Am., Fed. Bar Assn., Colorado Springs C. of C. (vice chmn. mgrs. group). Club: El Paso (Colorado Springs). Office: Shepard's/McGraw-Hill 420 N Cascade St Colorado Springs CO 80902

COOPER, KATHLEEN MARIE, economist; b. Dallas, Feb. 3, 1945; d. Patrick Joseph and Ferne Elizabeth (McDougle) Bell; m. Ronald James Cooper, Feb. 6, 1965; children—Michael Patrick, Christopher Phillip. B.A. in Math., U. Tex., 1970, M.A. in Econs., 1971; Ph.D. in Econs., U. Colo., 1980. Econ. research analyst United Banks of Colo., Denver, 1971-73, economist, 1973-75, corp. economist, 1975-80, chief economist, 1980-81; v.p., sr. fin. economist Security Pacific Nat. Bank, Los Angeles, 1981—; v.p. Bunker Hill Income Securities, Inc., 1983—; mem. Gov.'s Revenue Estimating Adv. com., Denver, 1976-81. Mem. Nat. Assn. Bus. Economists (exec. council 1975-78), Am. Econ. Assn. Roman Catholic. Office: 333 S Hope St H8-13 Los Angeles CA 90071

COOPER, MARGARET KATHRYN HUNT, secondary sch. tchr.; b. Hugo, Okla., June 23, 1929; d. Jodie and Josephine (Henry) Hunt; B.A., Langston (Okla.) U., 1951; M.L.S., U. Okla., 1957; Ph.D., U. Calif. at Berkeley, 1976; m. Reginald D. Cooper, May 31, 1952; 1 son, Rupert McLloyd. Tchr., librarian schs. in Okla., 1951-56; asst. circulation librarian, asst. sci. librarian U. Nebr., 1957-62; head librarian Fremont Jr. High Sch., Stockton, Calif., 1962-69; reading and math. project dir. Marshall Jr. High Sch., Stockton, 1970-71; tchr. Webster Jr. High Sch., Stockton, 1972—; dir. instructional media services Stockton Unified Sch. Dist., 1974—; cons. in field. Mem. NEA, Calif. Stockton (v.p. 1967-68) tchrs. assns., Black Tchrs. Alliance, AAUW, NAACP, Links, Delta Kappa Gamma (chpt. v.p. 1968-70), Pi Lambda Theta, Alpha Kappa Alpha. Democrata. Roman Catholic. Contbr. articles to profl. jours. Home: 44 E Pine St Stockton CA 95204 Office: 1525 Pacific Ave Stockton CA 95204

COOPER, MARTIN MICHAEL, communications executive, author; b. Phila., Aug. 13, 1941; s. Al and Anne Rae (Katzen) C.; m. Barbara A. Roisman, Aug. 13, 1960. B.A., UCLA, 1963. Advt. and promotion mgr. Disneyland, Anaheim, Calif., 1963-69; mktg. dir. recreation div. Universal City (Calif.) Studios, 1968-70; sr. v.p. pub. relations Harshe-Rotman & Druck, Inc., Los Angeles, 1970-79; sr. v.p. corp. communications and corp. mktg. dir. Playboy Enterprises, Inc., Los Angeles, 1979-82; pres. Cooper Communications, Inc., Los Angeles, 1982—; instr. mag. writing UCLA Extension Div.; speaker pub. relations seminars; author: Academy Awards Oscar Annual, 1979; contbr. chpt. to book, articles to mags. Chmn. pub. relations adv. com. sta. KCET, Los Angeles. Recipient Gold Key award Pub. Relations News, 1980, 81, Pro awards, Publicity Club of Los Angeles, 1974-76, 78, So. Calif. Chpt. of Am. Mktg. Assn. award, 1980, Los Angeles Advt. Women award, 1980. Mem. Acad. Motion Pictures Arts and Scis., Pub. Relations Soc. Am. (Silver Anvil award 1974, Prisms award 1978). Am. Film Inst., Acad. TV Arts and Scis. (co-chmn. Emmy adv. council). Office: 16250 Ventura Blvd Suite 335 Encino CA 91436

COOPER, MARY FOLEY, personnel adminstrator; b. Gloucester, Mass., Apr. 2, 1947; d. Clifford Francis and Margaret Mary (Flatley) Foley; m. Thomas A. Cooper Jr., Aug. 21, 1971; 1 dau., Kimberly Ann. B.A. in English, Manhattanville Coll., 1969; M.A. in Lang. Arts, Webster Coll., 1974. Sec. sociology dept. Simmons Coll., Boston, 1971; tchr. Laurelcrest, Bristol, Conn., 1971; dir. Learning Ctr., Nerinx Hall, St. Louis, 1971-74, asst. personnel mgr., 1974-75; personnel mgr. Macy's Calif., 1976-77, Bell Savs. and Loan, San Mateo, Calif., 1977-78; personnel mgr., adminstrv. services mgr. Addison Wesley Pub., Menlo Park, Calif., 1978—. Class coordinator Manhattanville Coll. Mem. Nat. Personnel Assn. (founding mem. South Bay chpt.), Bay Area Profl. Women's Network (program chmn.). Roman Catholic. Office: 2725 Sand Hill Rd Menlo Park CA 94025

COOPER, PETER DIRR, insurance co. executive, attorney; b. San Francisco, July 19, 1940; s. Tom Richardson and Marion (Dirr) C.; m. Ann Catherine Cady, Sept. 1, 1962; children—Catherine Marion, Joseph Cady. B.A., U. Calif.-Berkeley, 1962, LL.B., 1965. Bar: Calif. Assoc. MacMahon, Nelson & Tilson, Los Angeles, 1965-66; house counsel, Auto Club So. Calif., Los Angeles, 1967-69; assoc. gen. counsel Occidental Life Ins. Co., Los Angeles, 1969-74; gen. counsel Calif. Life Ins. Co., Los Angeles, 1974-76; pres. Pierce Nat. Life Ins. Co., 1977—. Bd. dirs. Ins. Council So. Calif. for City of Hope, 1979—. Mem. Assn. Calif. Life Ins. Co. (dir., mem. exec. com.), Conf. Ins. Counsel. Clubs: Los Angeles, Rancho Las Palmas. Home: 1845 McFarlane St San Marino CA 91108 Office: 3807 Wilshire Blvd Los Angeles CA 90010

COOPER, RICHARD LEE, educator; b. Yakima, Wash., Feb. 11, 1945; s. Elmer Leone and Marion Barbara (Sawyer) C.; m. Linda Jeanne Webb, Feb. 24, 1968; children—Christi Lee, Kimberly Jeanne. A.A., Yakima Community Coll., 1965; B.S. in Agr., Wash. State U., 1967. Cert. vocat. tchr. Tchr. vocat. agr., Elma, Wash., 1968-70, Evergreen High Sch., Vancouver, Wash., 1970-81, tchr. Mountain View High Sch., Vancouver, 1981—, also chmn. dept. Mem. Satsop Grange, 1969. Recipient Hon. Chpt. Farmer degree Evergreen Future Farmers Am., 1976, Hon. State Farmer degree Wash. State Future Farmers Am., 1977. Mem. Nat. Future Farmers Am. Alumni, Wash. Future Farmers Am. Alumni, Evergreen/Mountain View Future Farmers Am. Alumni, Wash. Vocat. Assn., Am. Vocat. Assn., NEA, Nat. Vocat. Agr. Tchrs. Assn., Wash. Vocat. Agr. Tchrs. Assn., Elma Edn. Assn., Am. Fedn. Tchrs., Evergreen Edn. Assn., Elma McCleary Jr. C. of C., Alpha Tau Alpha. Democrat. Presbyterian.

COOPER, RICHARD WALTER, credit union executive; b. Bend, Oreg., Feb. 15, 1955; s. Jake Q. and Darlene M. (Anderson) C. Student U. Alaska, 1973-76. Mem. services supr. Alaska Sch. Employees Fed. Credit Union, Anchorage, 1976-77; mktg. dir. Fedalaska Fed. Credit Union, Anchorage, 1977-80; spl. services mgr. Flying Tigers Employees Fed. Credit Union, Los Angeles, 1980—. Program chmn. Costa Del Sol Ednl. Conf. Mem. Mass Media Council, Calif. Credit Union League (chmn. chpt.). Club Rotary (Alaska). Office: Flying Tigers Employees Federal Credit Union 8636 S Sepulveda Blvd Los Angeles CA 90045

COOPER, STEVEN JON, health care mgmt. cons., educator; b. Oct. 19, 1941; B.A., U. Calif., Los Angeles, 1966; M.Ed., Loyola U., 1973; postgrad. Union Sch., 1977—; m. Sharon M. Lepack; children—Robin E., Erik S. Ednl. coordinator dept. radiology Mt. Sinai Hosp. Med. Center, Chgo., 1969-72; chmn. dept. radiol. scis. U. Health Scis., Chgo. Med. Sch., VA Hosp., North Chicago, 1972-79; v.p. C&S Inc., Denver, 1980-81; pres. Healthcare Mktg. Corp., Englewood, Colo., 1981—; cons. HEW; lectr. in field. Served with USAF, 1960-64, USAFR, 1964-66. Mem. W.K. Kellogg Found. grantee. Mem. Am. (mem. edn., curriculum review coms., task force), Ill. (chmn. annual meeting 1976, program Midwest conf., 1977) socs. radiol. tech., Coll. Radiol. Scis., Am. Hosp. Radiology Adminstrs. (mem. edn. com., treas. Midwest region, nat. v.p.), AMA (com. on allied health edn. and accreditation), Sigma Xi. Author numerous publs. in field. Home: 8522 E Dry Creek Pl Englewood CO 80112 Office: 7346A S Alton Way Englewood CO 80112

COOPER, THEODORE WILBUR, scientist/author; b. Hillman, Mich., Apr. 27, 1923; s. Clayton T. and Vila M. (Spencer) C.; B.S., Mich. Tech. U., 1952, M.S., (R.R. Seeber research scholar 1952-53), 1953; Sc.D., Colo. State Christian Coll., 1973; m. Calla M. Francisco, Aug. 8, 1942 (div. Apr. 1968); children—Jeannie, Gary A.; m. 2d, Gwendolyn Anne Gleeson, May 16, 1970. Project engr. transistor devel. sect. Hughes Semiconductor, 1953-56, head, transistor engr. dept., 1956-60; ops. mgr. Micro Systems, Inc., 1960-61, head microelectronic enging. Electro Optical System, 1961-63; mgr. product devel. dept. Centralab div. Globe Union, Inc., 1963-66; pres. Technicon Assos., Inc., 1966-69; pres., gen. mgr. Gen. Technicon Co., 1969—. Mem. nat. adv. bd. Am. Security Council. Served with AUS, 1942-45. Mem. IEEE, AAAS, Internat. Platform Assn., Acad. Polit. Sci., Fedn. Am. Scientists, Am. Security Council Edn. Found., Smithsonian Assos., Tau Beta Pi. Author: By Popular Choice: Why Not Vocalize the Silent Majority?, 1975; discoverer, author: Functionality: A Revelation for Science, 1978. Patentee anti-pollution system for internal combustion engines; Creator objective br. Plan for fed. govt. Home: 1269 Parkwood Dr Novato CA 94947

COOPER, THOMAS MCNEIL, agrl. engr.; b. Wallace, Idaho, Jan. 14, 1951; s. John W. and Jean E. (McNeil) C.; B.S., Coll. of Idaho, 1973; M.S., Western Wash. U., Bellingham, 1979; postgrad. Oreg. State U. Lab. asst. Coll. of Idaho, 1971-73; with Atlantic Richfield, Hanford, Wash., 1971; chief chemist N. Idaho Phosphate Co., Kellogg, 1973-75; teaching asst. Western Wash. U., 1977-79; research chemist Rockwell Hanford Ops., Richland, Wash., 1977; research asst. Oreg. State U., Corvallis, 1980—; bus. mgr. Western Wash. U. Sailing Facility, Lakewood, 1978-79. Mem. Sigma Xi. Club: Western Wash. U. Sailing. Office: Dept Agrl Engring Oreg State Univ Corvallis OR 97331

COOPER, WILLIAM CLARK, physician; b. Manila, P.I., June 22, 1912 (father Am. citizen); s. Wibb Earl and Pearl (Herron) C.; M.D., U. Va., 1934; M.P.H. magna cum laude, Harvard U., 1958; m. Ethel Katherine Sicha, May 1, 1937; children—Jane Willoughby, William Clark, David Jeremy, Robert Lawrence. Intern, asst. resident U. Hosps., Cleve., 1934-37; commd. asst. surgeon USPHS, 1940, advanced through grades to med. dir., 1952; chief occupational health Field Hqrs., Cin., 1952-57; mem. staff div. occupational health USPHS, Washington, 1957-62, chief div. occupational health, 1962-63; ret., 1963; research physician, prof. occupational health in residence Sch. Pub. Health, U. Calif.-Berkeley, 1963-72; med. cons. AEC, 1964-73, Calif. Dept. Pub. Health, 1964—; sec.-treas. Tabershaw-Cooper Asso., Inc., 1972-73, v.p., sci. dir., 1973-74; v.p. Equitable Environ. Health Inc., 1974-77; cons. occupational medicine, 1977—. Served to 1st lt. M.C., U.S. Army, 1937-40. Diplomate Am. Bd. Internal Medicine, Am. Bd. Preventive Medicine, Am. Bd. Indsl. Hygiene. Fellow AAAS, Am. Pub. Health Assn., Am. Coll. Chest Physicians, Am. Occupational Medicine Assn., Am. Acad. Occupational Medicine, Royal Soc. Medicine (London); mem. Permament Commn. and Internat. Assn. Occupational Health, Western Occupational Med. Assn., Am. Indsl. Hygiene Assn. Club: Cosmos (Washington). Contbr. articles to profl. jours. Home: 8315 Terrace Dr El Cerrito CA 94530 Office: 2150 Shattuck Ave Suite 401 Berkeley CA 94704

COORPENDER, PAUL BRUCE, software engr.; b. Longview, Tex., Dec. 14, 1942; s. June Feltus and Helen Lee (Haines) C.; B.S. in Math., U. Tex., Arlington, 1974, M.S. in Computer Sci., 1977; m. Laura Marie Anderson, Nov. 2, 1974. Sci. programmer Herman Blum Engrs., Dallas, 1968-74; cons. Tex. Christian U., Ft. Worth, 1974; project engr. Herman Blum Engrs., Dallas, 1974-75; program mgr. Trailways, Dallas, 1975-78; hardware/software engring. mgr. Tektronix, Beaverton, Oreg., 1978—; pres. Ancor Analytical, Inc. Mem. Assn. Computing Machinery (exec. council Dallas chpt. 1976-78), Data Processing Mgmt. Assn., IEEE, Computer Soc. Upsilon Pi Epsilon. Home: 10715 SW 41st St Portland OR 97219 Office: PO Box 500 Beaverton OR 97005

COORS, WILLIAM K., brewery executive; b. Golden, Colo., 1916. Chmn. bd., chief exec. officer Adolph Coors Co., Golden. Home: Route 5 Box 763 Golden CO 80401 Office: Adolph Coors Co Golden CO 80401

COPE, CONNIE LOU, accountant, educator; b. San Diego, July 22, 1944; d. Arlise Lanesome and Mary Norbourne (Gordon) Cope, Jr.; m. John W. Prather, Jan. 26, 1965; m. 2d, Gearl Bennett, July 9, 1977; children—Robert Neat Bennett, Terri Ann Bennett Minney Shields, Gearl Don Bennett, Danny Lynn Bennett, Johnny Ray Bennett. A.A. in Secretarial Sci., Western N.Mex. U., 1964, B.A. in Bus. and History Edn., 1972; postgrad. Eastern N.Mex. U., 1979-81. Cert. tchr., Tex., N.Mex.; lic. gen. contractor, N.Mex. Tchr., counselor Allstate Bus. Coll., Dallas, 1973-77; tchr. Hobbs (N.Mex.) Pub. Schs., 1977-78; tchr. N.Mex. Jr. Coll., Hobbs, 1978-80; owner, mgr. Energy Coating Co., Hobbs, 1980-82; acct. Guidance Ctr. Lea County, Hobbs, 1982—. Mem. Am. Soc. Tng. and Devel., N.Mex. Farm and Livestock Bur. Presbyterian. Club: Women of Moose (Hobbs). Office: 920 W Broadway St Hobbs NM 88240

COPE, DAVID HOWELL, university provost, composer, author, educator; b. San Francisco, May 17, 1942; s. Howell Nicholson and Charlotte Evlyn (Schleicher) C.; m. Mary Jane Stluka, Aug. 12, 1967; children—Tim, Stephen, Brian, Gregory. B.M., Ariz. State U., 1963; M.M., U. So. Calif., 1965. Instr., Kans. State Coll., Pittsburg, 1966-68; vis. composer Calif. Luth. Coll., 1968-69; instr. Cleve. Inst. Music, 1970-73; assoc. prof. Miami U., Oxford, Ohio, 1973-77; prof. music U. Calif.-Santa Cruz, 1977—, dir. arts and provost Porter Coll., 1982—; compositions include: Threshold and Visions, 1977; The Way, 1982;

Afterlife, 1983; Corridors of Light, 1983. Vol., Nat. Heart Assn. NEA grantee, 1975, 80. Mem. ASCAP (ann. awards 1971—), Am. Soc. Univ. Composers. Author: New Directions in Music, 4th edit., 1983; New Music Notation, 1976; New Music Composition, 1976. Office: Dir of Arts U Calif Santa Cruz CA 95064

COPE, KENNETH WAYNE, chain store executive; b. Rifle, Colo., May 31, 1924; s. William Grant and Mary (Park) C.; m. Patricia Miller, Feb. 1, 1946; children—Kimberly Ann, Bradley Mark. B.A., La Sierra Coll., Arlington, Calif., 1948; postgrad. U. Wash., 1948-50. Staff acct. to mgr. Price Waterhouse & Co., C.P.A.s, Los Angeles, 1950-58, resident mgr., Phoenix, 1959-63; regional controller Lucky Stores, Inc., San Leandro, Calif., 1963-68, v.p., corp. controller, 1968—. Served with AUS, 1943-46. C.P.A., Calif. Mem. Fin. Execs. Inst., Am. Inst. C.P.A.s, Calif. Soc. C.P.A.s. Republican. Episcopalian. Home: 1683 Graff Ave San Leandro CA 94577 Office: 6300 Clark Ave Dublin CA 94566

COPELAND, EUGENE LEROY, lawyer; b. Fairfield, Iowa, Mar. 5, 1939; B.A., Parsons Coll., 1961; J.D. with distinction, U. Iowa, 1965. Admitted to Colo. bar, 1965, Iowa bar, 1965, U.S. Supreme Ct. bar, 1966; individual practice law, Denver, 1965-66; sr. v.p., gen. counsel, sec. Security Life of Denver, 1966—; lectr., speaker at legal and industry convs., seminars, meetings; participant contemporary issue program Today show NBC, 1980. Bd. dirs. Buffalo Mountain Met. Dist., Summit County, Colo.; bd. dirs., chmn. investment com. Friends Found. of Denver Pub. Library; bd. dirs., 1st v.p. Adult Edn. Council Met. Denver. Served with inf. U.S. Army. Fulbright scholar. Mem. Inter-Am. Bar Assn., ABA, Colo. Bar Assn., Denver Bar Assn., Iowa Bar Assn., Assn. Life Ins. Council, Am. Council Life Ins. (state v.p. 1973-83), Colo. Life Conv. (legis. chmn. 1973—), Colo. Assn. Corp. Counsel, Denver Estate Planning Council, Colo. Assn. Life Underwriters (co-author learning guide 1978), Law Club Denver, Phi Kappa Phi. Unitarian. Author: Preventive Law for Medical Directors and Underwriters, 1973; Underwriting in a New Age of Legal Accountability, 1978; Insurance Law, 1982; bd. editors Iowa Law Rev., 1965. Office: #700 Security Life Bldg 1616 Glenarm Pl Denver CO 80202

COPELAND, PHILLIPS JEROME, educational administrator, former air force officer; b. Oxnard, Calif., Mar. 22, 1921; s. John Charles and Marion Moffatt) C.; student U. So. Calif., 1947-49; B.A., U. Denver, 1956, M.A., 1958; grad. Air Command and Staff Coll., 1959, Indsl. Coll. Armed Forces, 1964; m. Alice Janette Lusby, Apr. 26, 1942; children—Janette Ann Copeland Bosserman, Nancy Jo Copeland Briner. Commd. 2d lt. USAAF, 1943, advanced through grades to col. USAF, 1964, pilot 8th Air Force, Eng., 1944-45; various flying and staff assignments, 1945-51; chief joint tng. sect. Hdqrs. Airsouth (NATO), Italy, 1952-54; asst. dir. plans and programs USAF Acad., 1955-58; assigned to joint intelligence, Washington, 1959-61; plans officer Cincpac Joint Staff, Hawaii, 1961-63; staff officer, ops. directorate, then team chief Nat. Mil. Command Center, Joint Chiefs Staff, Washington, 1964-67; dir. plans and programs USAF Adv. Group, also adviser to Vietnamese Air Force, Vietnam, 1967-68; prof. aerospace studies U. So. Calif., Los Angeles, 1968-72, exec. asst. to pres., 1972-73, asso. dir. office internat. programs, 1973-75, dir. adminstrv. services Coll. Continuing Edn., 1975-82, dir. employee relations, 1982—. Decorated D.F.C., Bronze Star, Air medal with 3 clusters; Medal of Honor (Vietnam). Mem. Am. Econ. Assn., Air Force Assn., Order of Daedalians. Home: 81 Cypress Way Rolling Hills Estates CA 90274 Office: U So Calif Los Angeles CA 90007

COPELAND, THOMAS EARL, financial educator; b. Coatesville, Pa., Aug. 14, 1946; s. George B. and Irene C.; m. Karen L. Copeland, Aug. 24, 1969; 1 dau., Amanda L. B.A. in Econs., Johns Hopkins U., 1968; M.B.A., U. Pa., 1969, Ph.D. in Applied Econs., 1973. Assoc. prof. fin. UCLA, 1979—; dir. Kalama Chem. Co., Seattle. Served with USAR, 1969-75. Mem. Am. Fin. Assn., Am. Econs. Assn., Western Fin. Assn. Author: Financial Theory and Corporate Policy 1979; assoc. editor: Fin. Rev., 1982—; contbr. articles to profl. jours. Office: Grad Sch Mgmt UCLA Los Angeles CA 90024

COPLAN, DANIEL JONATHAN, financial analyst, entertainment entrepreneur; b. N.Y.C., Oct. 4, 1955; s. Robert Saul and Constance Joan (Karl) C. B.A. in Film, NYU, 1977; postgrad. Southwestern U. Sch. Law. Exec. producer NCL Films, N.Y.C., 1975-77; ptnr. Kizer/Coplan Co., N.Y.C., 1978; agt. for feature film Just Before Dawn, D.J. Coplan Entertainment Entrepreneur, 1979; mgr., asst. film buyer Walter Reade Orgn., N.Y.C., 1979-81; entertainment entrepreneur D.J. Coplan, Los Angeles, 1981—. Recipient Silver medal Atlanta Internat. Film Festival, 1974; Golden Image cert. L.I. Internat. Film Festival, 1975. Author, producer, dir.: Of Mirrors, The Mind and Time, producer: 1973; (short subject) The Incredibly Awful Dr. Sporgo, 1973; exec. producer/writer: (film) The Dream Factory, 1977.

COPLEN, HERMAN LEROY, JR., mech. engr.; b. Rochester, Ind., July 16, 1915; s. Herman Leroy and Eunice May (Barkman) C.; B.S. in Mech. Engring., Purdue U., 1937; postgrad. nuclear and mech. engring., UCLA, 1953; m. Betty Jo Buckles Walker, June 27, 1969; children by previous marriage—Janet Virginia, Russell Bruce, Phillip Eugene. Research and field engr. Bailey Meter Co., Cleve., 1937-42; control projects engr. Los Angeles Bur. Light and Power, 1942-43; with engring. div. Aerojet-Gen. Corp., Sacramento, 1943-61, mgr. engring. div., 1961-65, Apollo program mgr., 1965-69; program mgr. LOFT, Aerojet Nuclear Corp., Idaho Falls, Idaho, 1969-75; prin. EnCoTech, engring. cons., Shingle Springs, Calif., 1975—. Recipient Outstanding Performance award for Apollo program mgmt. Aerojet-Gen. Corp., 1969; registered profl. engr., Calif. Mem. ASME, Am. Nuclear Soc. Democrat. Club: Engineers (San Francisco). Address: 3092 Sudbury Rd Shingle Springs CA 95682

COPLEY, HELEN KINNEY, newspaper publisher; b. Cedar Rapids, Iowa, Nov. 28, 1922; d. Fred Everett and Margaret (Casey) Kinney; m. James S. Copley, Aug. 16, 1965 (dec.); 1 son, David Casey. Assoc. Copley Press, Inc., San Diego, 1952—, chmn. bd., chmn. exec. com., dir., 1973—, chief exec. officer, sr. mgmt. bd., 1974—; chmn. bd. Copley News Service, San Diego, pub. The San Diego Union and The Tribune, trustee, chmn. bd. James S. Copley Found., 1973—; chmn. editorial bd. Union-Tribune Pub. So., San Diego, 1976—. Mem. Friends of Internat. Ctr., La Jolla, Calif., La Jolla Mus. Contemporary Art, La Jolla Town Council, Inc.; life patroness Makua Aux.; charter mem. San Diego Women's Council, Navy League U.S.; life mem. San Diego Hall Sci.; mem. San Diego Soc. Natural History, women's com. San Diego Symphony Assn., Scripps Meml. Hosp. Aux., Social Service League La Jolla; life mem. Star India Aux., Zool. Soc. San Diego; mem. YWCA; hon. chmn., bd. dirs. Washington Crossing Found.; trustee, bd. dirs. Freedoms Found. at Valley Forge; trustee, devel. com. Scripps Clinic and Research Found.; trustee U. San Diego. Mem. Internat. Press Assn., Am. Press Assn. (dir.), Calif. Press Assn., Am. Soc. Newspaper Editors, Am. Press Inst., Calif. Newspaper Pubs. Assn., Greater Los Angeles Press Club, National Press Club, San Diego Press Club, San Francisco Press Club, Nat. Newspaper Assn., Western Newspaper Found., Sigma Delta Chi. Clubs: Aurora (Ill.) Country; Cuyamaca, San Diego Yacht, University, U. San Diego, Presidents (San Diego); De Anza Country (Borrego Springs, Calif.); La Jolla Beach and Tennis, La Jolla Country. Republican. Roman Catholic. Home: 7007 Country Club Dr La Jolla CA 92037 Office: PO Box 1530 La Jolla CA 92038

COPPOLA, FRANCIS FORD, motion picture writer, producer, dir.; b. Detroit, Apr. 7, 1939; s. Carmine and Italia C.; B.A. in English, Hofstra U., 1960; M.F.A., UCLA, 1967; m. Eleanor Neil, Feb. 2, 1963; children—Gian-Carlo, Roman Francios, Sofia Carmina. Pres., chmn. bd. Am. Zoetrope Corp., San Francisco, 1969—; dir. motion pictures: Dementia 13, 1963, You're A Big Boy Now, 1967, Finian's Rainbow, 1968, The Rain People, 1969; writer Patton (Acad. award), 1970, This Property is Condemned, 1966, Reflections in a Golden Eye, 1967, The Rain People, 1969, Is Paris Burning?, 1966, The Great Gatsby, 1974; writer-producer, dir. The Conversation, 1974, The Godfather (Acad. award), 1972, The Godfather, Part II (Acad. award), 1974, Apocalypse, Now, 1977; producer American Graffiti, 1974, THX 1138, 1971; exec. producer The Black Stallion, 1978. Mem. Writers Guild Am., West, Acad. Motion Picture Arts and Scis. Office: care Zoetrope Studios 1040 N Las Palmas Los Angeles CA 90038

COPPOLINO, DOMENIC ANTHONY, JR., optometrist; b. South Kingstown, R.I., Nov. 9, 1954; s. Domenic Anthony and Matilda Ida (Sciola) C.; m. Carolyn Anne Rush, Aug. 31, 1957; children—Jamison, Michael. B.S., U. R.I., 1976; B.S., Coll. Optometry Pa., 1977, O.D., 1980. Commd. 1st lt. U.S. Army, 1981, advanced through grades to capt., 1981; chief optometry U.S. Army Health Clinic, Yuma Proving Ground, Ariz., 1981—. Mem. Am. Optometric Assn., Armed Forces Optometric Soc., Assn. U.S. Army. Roman Catholic. Home: PO Box 3015 Yuma Proving Ground AZ 85365 Office: US Army Health Clinic Yuma Proving Ground AZ 85365

CORBELL, CAROLYN ALLEN, state official; b. El Paso, Tex., Aug. 23, 1945; d. Richard Weldon and Opal Downing Allen. B.A. cum laude, Western N.Mex. U., 1968, M.A., 1980. Bus. edn. tchr., Lordsburg, N.Mex., 1968-82; supr. N.Mex. Bus. and Office Edn., Santa Fe, 1983—. Mem. Gov.'s Career Devel. Conf., 1983. Named Lordsburg Tchr. of the Year, K.P., 1980. Mem. Am. Vocat. Assn., Nat. State Suprs. Bus. Edn., N.Mex. Vocat. Assn., N.Mex. Bus. Edn. Assn., Office Edn. Assn. (state supr. 1983—), Beta Sigma Phi. Democrat. Methodist. Office: Dept Edn Edn Bldg Santa Fe NM 87501

CORBETT, JAMES ARTHUR, oil company official; b. Albany, N.Y., Feb. 1, 1948; s. Arthur Daniel and Henrietta Levy (Mosher) C.; children—Kevin Michael, Jonathan Daniel. B.S. in Indsl. Mgmt., Clarkson Coll. Tech., 1970; M.B.A., U. So. Calif., 1975. Credit sales mgr. Goodyear Tire & Rubber Co., Troy, N.Y., 1970; sales mgr. Prudential Ins. Co., Albany, 1973-74; mgr. adminstrn. Union Oil Co., Los Angeles, 1975—. Served with U.S. Army, 1970-73. Mem. Assn. Systems Mgmt. (dir.; facilities dir. So. Calif. chpt.), Am. Mgmt. Assn., Los Angeles C. of C. (co-chmn. Los Angeles Open Project 1977), Alpha Kappa Psi, Alpha Phi Omega. Home: 13000 Valleyheart Dr #12 Studio City CA 91604 Office: Union Oil Co 461 S Boylston Suite M-201 Los Angeles CA 90017

CORBETT, JOHN PHILIP, vocational educator; b. Phoenix, Mar. 26, 1935; s. Harry Ledyard and Miriam Madelyn (Younce) C.; m. Mildred Lew Bowman, Aug. 9, 1958; children—Daniel Owen, Elizabeth Michelle. Student, Ariz. State U., 1958-59, Adams State U., 1960-61, U. N.Mex., 1966; B.A., Eastern N.Mex. U., 1960, M.A., 1967. Indsl. edn. tchr., Pagosa Springs, Colo., 1960-63; parts mgr. Post Chevrolet, Pagosa Springs, 1964; jr. engr. Colo. Dept. Hwys., Durango, 1964; tchr. indsl. edn., Roswell (N.Mex.) Ind. Sch. Dist., 1964-71, Roswell High Sch., 1971—; vocat. instr., curriculum writer Thiokol Chem. Corp. Served with USN, 1953-57. Mem. Am. Vocat. Assn., Indsl. Arts Assn., N.Mex. Vocat. Assn. (pres. trade and indsl. div.). Democrat. Episcopalian. Clubs: Kiwanis, Masons, Elks. Developer curriculum, Indian Tng. Sch., Roswell, 1974-75; contbr. articles to N.Mex. Indsl. Arts Jour. Office: 500 W Hobbs Roswell NM 88201

CORBETT, MAURICE CLARK, dentist; b. Turlock, Calif., Feb. 4, 1935; s. Maurice Virgil and Opal (Clark) C.; student Fresno State Coll., 1954; A.A., Coll. Sequoias, 1955; D.D.S., U. Calif. at San Francisco, 1959; postgrad. U. Calif., 1971-73; children—Sandra Lea, Christin Ann, Maurice Virgil. Individual practice dentistry specializing in children, San Jose, Calif., 1962-73; practice dentistry, specializing in orthodontics, San Jose, 1973—; clin. instr., lectr. U. Calif. Dental Sch., San Francisco, 1963-67; mem. staff O'Connor Hosp., San Jose. Founder, exec. dir., treas. Found. for Advanced Continuing Edn. Served with USN, 1958-62. Mem. Calif. Soc. Dentistry for Children (pres.), Am. Acad. Pedodontics, Santa Clara Valley Pedodontic Acad. (pres. 1965-66), Am. Assn. Orthodontists. Rotarian. Home: 14 Aliso Rd Carmel CA 93924 Office: 100 O'Connor Dr San Jose CA 95128

CORBIN, EUGENE FELTS, office furniture and partitioning co. exec.; b. Delevan, Calif., Aug. 31, 1906; s. William Miller and Georgia (Felts) C.; B.S., U. Calif., Berkeley, 1927; m. Louise Elizabeth Dortch, Sept. 22, 1945. Mgr., Calif. Pelican, U. Calif., 1927; sales and dist. mgr. Paraffine Cos., Inc., Dallas and San Francisco, 1927-42; mem. sales staff Sacramento Daily Union, 1946-49; mem. advt. staff News Publ. Co., Sacramento, 1949-53; pres., gen. mgr. E.F. Corbin Co., Sacramento, 1953—; pres. Calif. Office Products Conf., 1970; mem. adv. com. Sacramento Public Radio; bd. dirs. Sacramento Builders Exchange. Served to maj., inf., AUS. 1942-46. Mem. Sacramento Met. C. of C. (chmn. crime prevention com., chmn. quality of life com.; Pres.'s award 1976), Nat. Office Products Assn., Western Assn. Coll. Comics (pres.). Republican. Christian Scientist. Club: Lions. Home: 1415 43d St Sacramento CA 95819 Office: 1810 13th St Sacramento CA 95811

CORBIN, KRESTINE MARGARET, fashion designer, columnist, educator; b. Reno, Apr. 24, 1937; d. Lawrence Albert and Judie Ellen (Johnston) Dickinson; m. Lee D. Corbin, May 16, 1959 (div.); children—Michelle Marie, Sheri Karin. B.S., U. Calif., 1958. Asst. prof. home econs. Bauder Coll., Sacramento, 1974—; columnist McClatchy newspapers, Sacramento, 1976-81; owner Creative Sewing Co., Sacramento, 1976—; pvt. practice fashion consulting, 1974—; lectr. in field. Mem. Crocker Art Gallery Assn., Sacramento, 1960-78; mem. Republican Party Elections Com., Sacramento, 1964, 68. Mem. Home Economists in Bus., Am. Home Econs. Assn., Internat. Fashion Group, Inc., Women's Fashion Fabrics Assn. New York, Omicron Nu. Author: Suede Fabric Sewing Guide, 1973; Creative Sewing, 1978; (audio-visual) Fashions in the Making, 1974. Office: 532-4 Woodside Oaks Sacramento CA 95825

CORBIN, ROBERT KEITH, lawyer; b. Worthington, Ind., Nov. 17, 1928; m., 3 daus. B.S. in Bus., Ind. U., 1952, J.D., 1956. Bar: Ind. 1956, Ariz. 1958. Sole practice, Phoenix, 1958-76; county atty. Maricopa County (Ariz.), Phoenix, 1965-68; mem. Maricopa County Bd. Suprs., 1973-76, 77-78; atty. gen. State of Ariz., Phoenix, 1979—. Mem. Ariz. Bar Assn. (ethics com.), Ariz. County Attys. and Sheriffs Assn., Ams. for Effective Law Enforcement (pres. 1974), Nat. Rifle Assn. Republican. Lodge: Masons. Office: Office of Atty Gen State Capitol 1700 W Washington Phoenix AZ 85007*

CORBIN, WALTER EUGENE, family therapist; b. Hastings, Nebr., Nov. 4, 1937; s. Orris Kenneth and Clara Ruth (Gordon) C.; B.A. cum laude, Calif. Western U., 1960; M.A., U.S. Internat. U., 1974; Ph.D., Calif. Pacific U., 1979; m. Lynda Ruth Green, June 14, 1958. Social caseworker San Diego Dept. Public Welfare, 1960-62; probation officer, supr. San Diego County Probation Dept., 1962—; pvt. practice family therapy, San Diego, 1975—; cons. govtl. agys. and community orgns. Lic. marriage, family and child counselor, Calif. Mem. Am. Personnel and Guidance Assn., Am. Rehab. Counselor Assn., Am. Assn. Marriage and Family Therapy (clin. mem.), Calif. Assn. Marriage and Family Counselors, Calif. Probation, Parole and Correctional Assn. Democrat. Methodist. Home: 2365 Beryl St San Diego CA 92109 Office: 2901 Meadowlark Dr San Diego CA 92123

CORBRIDGE, JOHN, lawyer; b. Casper, Wyo., July 25, 1925; s. W. J. and Juanita (Oldham) C.; m. Doris M. Fricke, Nov. 25, 1950; children—Anne, Thomas. B.S., U. Colo., 1950; J.D. cum laude, U. Denver, 1956. Bar: Colo. 1956. C.P.A., Colo., 1954. Pub. acct., Denver and Casper, 1950-54; sole practice law, Denver, 1956—. Served in U.S. Army, 1943-46. Decorated Bronze Star, Purple Heart. Mem. ABA, Colo. Bar Assn., Am. Judicature Soc. Colo. Soc. C.P.A.s, Am. Arbitration Assn. (comml. panel), SAR, DAV, 94th Inf. Div. Assn. Republican. Office: 1075 Capitol Life Center Denver CO 80111

CORBY, NANCY HAWKINS, psychologist, researcher; b. Los Angeles, Nov. 2, 1937; d. John N. A. and Retha Alberta (Gompertz) Hawkins; m. Grant White Corby, June 22, 1957 (div.); m. 2d, Fen Rhodes, Nov. 26, 1977; stepchildren—Neil Rhodes, Carolyn Rhodes, Richard Rhodes. A.A., City Coll. San Francisco, 1957; B.A., U. Calif.-Irvine, 1972; Ph.D. (Univ. scholar 1973-75, NIMH tng. fellow 1974-75), U. So. Calif., 1977. Lic. psychologist, Calif. USPHS postdoctoral research fellow dept. psychiatry SUNY-Stony Brook, 1977-78; instr., research technologist U. So. Calif., 1978-79, acad. coordinator geriatrics, research asst. prof. gerontology Andrus Gerontoloty Center, and Sch. Medicine, 1979-83, asst. clin. prof. psychiatry, assoc. dir. Div. Geriatric Psychiatry, Sch. Medicine, 1981-83; dir. psychol. service Alzheimer's Assessment Center, Long Beach (Calif.) Community Hosp., 1983—; research cons. Consumers Union, Mt. Vernon, N.Y., 1977-82; fellow UCLA/U. So. Calif. Long-Term-Care Gerontology Ctr., 1981—. Mem. Am. Psychol. Assn., Gerontol. Soc. Am. (Internat. Travel award 1981), Am. Pub. Health Assn. Contbr. articles to profl. jours., chpts. to reference and text books. Home: 12111 Nieta Dr Garden Grove CA 92640 Office: 1760 Termino Ave Suite 101 Long Beach CA 90804

CORCORAN, CHRISTOPHER MATTHEW, public relations executive; b. Los Angeles, Sept. 19, 1951; s. James George and Anne Giovana (DeLuca) C.; m. Carol Ann O'Halloran, Nov. 9, 1974; 1 son, Christopher Matthew. Student Loyola U., Los Angeles, 1968-73; B.S.L., Irvine U. Sch. Law, 1977. Pres., Ultimate Performance Group, Anaheim, Calif., 1976—; dir. communications United Technologies Corp., Santa Ana, Calif., 1978-80; mktg. dir. Promotion Ltd., Santa Ana, 1980-81; mgmt. supervisor Dailey & Assocs., Los Angeles, 1981—; cons., lectr. in field. Bd. dirs., producer Hollywood Bowl Easter Sunrise Service, 1974-79. Mem. Pub. Relations Soc. Am. Roman Catholic. Office: 3055 Wilshire Blvd Los Angeles CA 90010

CORCORAN, JOHN JAMES, accountant; b. Chgo., Feb. 6, 1941; s. Vincent A. and Mae (DeNardo) C.; m. Barbara Ann Latoza, June 13, 1964; children—Aubrey Joy, Jon Ashley. B.B.A., Loyola U., Chgo., 1976. C.P.A., Ill., Ariz. Acct., Rauch, Tolliver & Corcoran, Ltd., Phoenix, 1975-76; prin. John J. Corcoran, Ltd., Phoenix, 1976-78; v.p. fin., chief fin. officer Provident Energy Co., Inc., Phoenix, 1978—, also dir. Dir. Provident Holding Corp.; v.p. Superpumper, Inc., 1982-83. Bd. dirs. Esperanca Inc., 1980-83; v.p. Mccormick Ranch P.O.A., 1977-83. Mem. Am. Inst. C.P.A.s, Ariz. Soc. C.P.A.s. Democrat. Roman Catholic. Club: Plaza. Office: Provident Energy Co Inc 3003 N Central Ave Suite 2510 Phoenix AZ 85012

CORCORAN, RICHARD ALAN, optometrist; b. Portland, Oreg., Aug. 1, 1954; s. Raymond Ervin and Gwendolyn Jean (Currie) C. B.S. in Biology, U. Oreg., 1977; O.D. with distinction, Pacific U., 1981. Lic. optometrist, Oreg., Calif. Practice optometry, Marina, Calif., 1981—. Mem. Am. Optometric Assn., Marina C. of C. Democrat. Club: Lions (Marina). Home: 1 Surf Way Apt 235 Monterey CA 93940 Office: 3172 Del Monte Blvd Marina CA 93933

CORD, MICHAEL JONAS, diversified co. exec.; b. Owyhee, Nev., Feb. 28, 1949; s. John Joseph and Rosa Elizabeth (Campbell) Gallagher; student Links Bus. Coll., Boise, Idaho, 1967-68; m. Susan Hester Brunelle, Nov. 11, 1977; children—Sean Michael, Justin Bleu and Melissa Rose (twins), Shannon Dawn. Computer operator Paine Webber, Los Angeles, 1969-70; owner Hippodrome Boutiques, Los Angeles, 1970-72; owner Cord Artist Mgmt. & Public Relations, Beverly Hills, Calif., 1971-74, Cordco-Mail Order, Los Angeles, 1972-76; dist. mgr. Luzier Cosmetics, Los Angeles, 1975-76; broker Hollywood Properties, Los Angeles, 1979-80; owner Famous Designers Forum, Beverly Hills, 1976-80, Graffiti Guard Splty. Coatings, Van Nuys, Calif., 1979—, Cord Diversified Industries, Van Nuys; pub. Properties Illustrated, Van Nuys, 1981—. Mem. Beverly Hills C. of C., Hollywood C. of C., Jaycees, Small Businessmen's Assn. Los Angeles, San Fernando Valley Bd. Realtors, Beverly Hills Bd. Realtors. Democrat. Mem. Ch. of Religious Sci. Home: 15946 Vanowen St Van Nuys CA 91406

CORDINGLEY, WILLIAM ANDREW, JR., advertising executive; b. Mpls., July 18, 1948; s. William Andrew and Mary Jeannette (Bowles) C.; m. Pamela Cotter, Apr. 2, 1950. A.B., Harvard Coll., 1971; M.B.A., M.S., Columbia U., 1975. Account mgr. Ogilvy & Mather, N.Y.C., 1975-77, Foote, Cone & Belding/Honig, San Francisco, 1977-80; pres. Bill Cordingley Advt., San Anselmo, Calif., 1980—. Mem. Harvard Fund, San Francisco area Harvard Campaign com., 1982; founder, pres. San Anselmo Resident's Forum; chmn. tax initiative San Anselmo, 1982; co-chmn. Town Council candidate election campaign, 1982. Home and Office: 10 Elkhorn Way San Anselmo CA 94960

CORDONNIER, WILLIAM RICHARD, mgmt. cons.; b. Russia, Ohio, Nov. 8, 1942; s. August J. and Freda C.; B.S., Ohio U., 1966; m. Feb. 17, 1968; children—Nicole, Brett. Prodct mgr., sales mgr. Merrell Nat. Labs., San Francisco, 1966-76; founder, v.p. Mgmt. Recruiters of Sacramento, 1976—. Vol., Handgun Control Lobby. Served with Army NG, 1960-64. Home: 6202 Lou Ct Roseville CA 95678 Office: 1900 Point West Way #281 Sacramento CA 95815

CORDOVA, ALEX AGUIRRE, municipal finance executive; b. Pheonix, Sept. 14, 1920; s. Luis H. and Carmen A. C.; m. Violet Moreno, June 28, 1942; children—Alex M., Debra Louis. B.S. in Acctg., Ariz. State U., Tempe, 1948. Acct., auditor C.P.A. firm, 1948-50; auditor Office Price Stabilization, 1950-52; successively acct., city assessor, real estate dir., fin. dir. City of Phoenix, 1952-83. Served with USCG, 1942-45. Mem. Mpl. Fin. Officers Assn., Ariz. Fin. Officers Assn., Am. Soc. Pub. Adminstrn., Am. Right of Way Assn. Democrat. Roman Catholic. Clubs: Vesta (past pres.), Optimist. Home: 3411 E Garfield St Phoenix AZ 85008 Office: 251 W Washington St Suite 405 Phoenix AZ 85003

CORETTE, ROBERT DRISCOLL, lawyer; b. Butte, Mont., Jan. 15, 1911; s. John Earl and Mary Taafe (Driscoll) C.; A.B., LL.B., Mont. State U., 1934; m. Lora Berta Holt, Sept. 6, 1934; children—Constance Corette Kenney, Robert Driscoll, Susan Corette Matule, Holt. Admitted to Mont. bar, 1934, U.S. Supreme Ct. bar, 1974; pres. firm Corette Smith Pohlman & Allen, 1934—; counsel, dir. Mont. Power Co., 1957-83; past dir. Northwestern Resources Co., Western Energy Co., Intercontinental Energy Corp., Altana Exploration Co. Served with USMC, World War II. Fellow Am. Coll. Trial Lawyers, Am. Coll. Probate Counsel; mem. Am., Silver Bow County bar assns., State Bar Mont. (pres. 1980-81), Am. Judicature Soc., Nat. Cowboy Hall of Fame (charter), U.S. C. of C. (dir. 1966-70), Mont. (pres. 1960), Butte (pres. 1955-56) chambers commerce. Clubs: Nat. Pony of the Ams. (pres. 1963-64), Elks, Butte

Country, Montana. Home: 1201 W Platinum St Butte MT 59701 Office: Prudential Fed Savs Bldg 49 N Main Butte MT 59701

COREY, DIANA LYNNE, property mgr.; b. Seattle, Sept. 15, 1954; d. Eugene A. and Betty (Bertsch) B.; B.A. magna cum laude in Bus. Adminstrn., 50 U. Wash., 1976. Property mgr. PACCAR Inc., Bellevue, Wash., 1976-81; property mgr. Evergreen Mgmt. Co., Bellevue, 1981—. Vice pres. bd. dirs. Midlakes Homeowners Assn. Lic. real estate sales agt., Wash. Mem. Bldg. Owners and Mgrs. Assn. (cert. real property adminstr.), Bellevue Downtown Assn. (dir.), Soc. Real Property Adminstrs., Phi Beta Kappa, Sigma Kappa. Office: 1721 132d Ave NE Bellevue WA 98005

COREY, ROBERT LESTER, mfg. co. exec.; b. San Diego, Nov. 6, 1941; s. Lester Wilson and Frances Jane (Hartman) C.; B.A. in English, Calif. State U., 1965; M.A., U. Nebr., 1970; Ph.D., U. Tulsa, 1973; M.B.A., Pepperdine U., 1980; m. Margaret Ellen Wallis, June 11, 1965; children—Christopher Robert, Katherine Anne. Prodn. mgr. heat tracing Nelson Electric div. Sola Basic Industries, Tulsa, 1973-75; project adminstr. Sohio Pipeline Project, Williams Bros. Engring. Co., Tulsa, 1976-77; dir. program definition Data-Design Labs., Arlington, Va., 1977-80; mgr. product devel. Ordnance div. IRT Corp., San Diego, 1980—. Mem. tech. writing adv. bd. Okla. State U. Tech. Inst., 1976-77; mem. San Bernardino Lung Assn., 1979-80. Served with USAF, 1959-65. U. Tulsa grad. fellow, 1970-73; recipient award for disting. tech. communications Soc. Tech. Communication, 1975. Mem. Soc. Tech. Communications (chpt. chmn. 1977), Am. Assn. Cost Engrs., Naval Inst., Air Force Assn., Assn. U.S. Army, Am. Def. Preparedness Assn. Guest editor fall 1978 issue Jour. Tech. Communications; contbr. articles to profl. jours. Home: 14441 Yazoo St San Diego CA 92129 Office: 7650 Convoy Ct San Diego CA 92138

CORFIELD, TIMOTHY L., history educator, rodeo coach, association executive; b. Nyssa, Oreg., July 1, 1943; s. Chet and Leona C.; m. Marilyn M. Foster, Aug. 22, 1964; children—Sabrina L., Ashley Ann. B.S. in History, Eastern Oreg. State Coll., 1967; M.S., Walla Walla Coll. High sch. tchr., 1967-77; history instr., rodeo coach Walla Walla (Wash.) Community Coll., 1973—; founder Wash. High Sch. Rodeo Assn., 1973; exec. sec. Nat. Intercollegiate Rodeo Assn., 1979—; cons. various jr. rodeo assns., univs., corp. sponsors in rodeo and related areas. Recipient Outstanding Service award Nat. Intercollegiate Rodeo Assn., 1980. Mem. Am. Assn. Higher Edn. Episcopalian. Clubs: Exchange (Walla Walla, founder first coll. rodeo), Elks. Editor-in-chief College Rodeo Mag. Office: 500 Tausick Way Walla Walla WA 99362

CORKER, ROBERT STEPHEN, advt. and public relations exec.; b. Portland, Oreg., July 4, 1941; s. William Brigham and Marian Celeste (Wright) C.; B.A. in Polit. Sci., Stanford U., 1963; m. Stacia Ann Routh, Sept. 13, 1978; children—Dalton Gann, Miranda Jane. Internat. travel exec., 1963-77; dir. Internatl Travel Services, People-to-People Internat., Kansas City, Mo., 1963-67; pres. Security Travel Service, Oakland, Calif., 1967-68; pres. Nat. Academic Services, N.Y.C., 1968-71; v.p. Ednl. Travel Co., Spokane, Wash., 1971-77; co-owner Coons, Corker & Assocs., Inc., Spokane, 1978—; assoc. prof. advt. Gonzaga U., Spokane, 1981—. Chmn., Spokane County Democratic party, 1979-81; chmn. Coop. Health Plan, 1975-81; trustee Ft. Wright Coll., 1976-80; mem. exec. com., trustee People-to-People Internat., 1970-80; del. Nat. Dem. Conv., 1976; mem. Oreg. Gov.'s Com. on Children and Youth, 1958-59. Wash. States Humanities grantee, 1977-78. Mem. Am. Soc. Travel Agts., Am. Acad. Polit. and Social Sci., Acad. Polit. Sci., Am. Acad. Arts and Scis., Wash. State Arts Alliance, UN Assn., Stanford Alumni Assn., ACLU, NOW, NAACP, Planned Parenthood, Sigma Nu, Pi Sigma Alpha. Episcopalian. Clubs: Exchange. Polit. columnist Community Press, Spokane, 1979-81, KREM-TV, Spokane, 1981—. Home: S 1728 Lincoln St Spokane WA 99203 Office: W 1614 Riverside Ave Spokane WA 99201

CORKINS, JACK PHILIPS, chemist; b. Bozeman, Mont., Feb. 13, 1921; s. Clifford Leon and Bessie Barbara (Philips) C.; B.Sc., Mont. State U., 1950; m. Sylvia Lou Stevens, Feb. 13, 1954; children—John Stevens, Timothy Glen, Sylver Lou, Melodie Lou. Mgr. farm sci. dept. Occident Elevators, Billings, Mont., 1946-49; asst. state entomologist Mont. State U., Bozeman, 1949-54; field entomologist Skyway Flying Service, Great Falls, Mont., 1955; area supr. Uniroyal Chem. div. Uniroyal Inc., Porterville, Calif., 1955-65, research scientist, 1966-75, sr. research scientist, Western Research Sta., 1976—; dir. Calif. Weed Conf., 1966. Served with U.S. Army, 1940-45. Recipient Uniroyal Patent award, 1971. Mem. Weed Sci. Soc., Entomol. Soc. Am., Registry Cert. Entomologists, Am. Soc. Plant Physiologists. Republican. Episcopalian. Clubs: Masons, Order Eastern Star. Patentee in field. Home: 1696 S Leggett St Porterville CA 93257

CORLESS, JOE DONALD, pediatrician; b. Walla Walla, Wash., June 4, 1934; s. Donald Edward and Elizabeth (Gilmore) C.; B.S., U. Idaho, 1955; M.D., Baylor U., Houston, 1959; m. Judy Lenore Thralls, Sept. 30, 1978; 1 son, Jeffrey; children by previous marriage—Ruth, Philip. Rotating intern, then resident in pediatrics Orange County Gen. Hosp., Orange, Calif., 1959-63; resident, then chief resident in pediatrics William Beaumont Gen. Hosp., El Paso, Tex., 1963-65; practice medicine specializing in pediatrics, Santa Ana, Calif., 1967—; mem. staff Children's Hosp. Orange County, chief staff, 1983—; mem. staff St. Joseph's Hosp., Orange, Chapman Gen. Hosp., Orange, U. Calif. Irvine Med. Center, Orange; chmn. dept. pediatrics Western Med. Center, 1974-80; clin. asst. prof. U. Calif. Med. Sch., Irvine; mem. Flying Samaritans Orange County. Active local Boy Scouts Am. Served to maj. M.C., U.S. Army, 1960-62, 63-67. Decorated Army Commendation medal; Order Cloud and Banner (China); grantee Nat. Found., 1957-58; diplomate Am. Bd. Pediatrics. Fellow Am. Acad. Pediatrics (regional exec. com.); mem. S.W. Pediatrics Soc., Orange County Med. Assn. (chmn. perinatal mortality com. 1972-77; presdl. citation 1977), Orange County Pediatric Soc. (pres. 1977-78, dir. 1974—), Phi Beta Kappa. Presbyterian. Contbr. articles to med. publs. Office: Suite 105 705 W LaVeta Orange CA 92668

CORLETT, DONNA JEAN, university administrator, educator, writer; b. Seattle, Sept. 28, 1933; d. Joseph Earl and Margaret (Whitehall) Broyles; 1 child by previous marriage, Shannon Hayes. B.A., U. Idaho, 1953; M.Ed., U. Oreg. 1964; Ed.D., U. Portland, 1969. Cert. tchr., Idaho, Wash. Tchr. pub. schs., Idaho and Wash., 1955-60; instr. reading Portland (Oreg.) State U., 1965-67; assoc. prof. U. Portland, 1968—, coordinator elem. edn., 1975—. Mem. LWV, AAUW, Internat. Reading Assn., Am. Assn. Coll. Tchrs. Educators, Assn. Supervision and Curriculum Devel., Phi Delta Kappa (v.p.). Clubs: Willamette Writers, Mazama. Contbg. author: Handbook of Materials to Study, 1979; contbr. articles in field to profl. jours. Office: U Portland 5000 N Willamette St Portland OR 97203

CORLETT, EMMA JEAN, social worker; b. Knox City, Tex., Aug. 4, 1926; d. LeRoy and Luella (Burns) Massey; m. John Paul Corlett, Jan. 1, 1946 (dec.); children—Jeanne Marie, Thomas Lee, Jan Louise. B.A. in Secondary Edn. cum laude, N.W. Nazarene Coll., 1965; M.S.W., U. Utah, 1972. Feature writer Statesman Newspaper, Boise, Idaho, 1960-63; caseworker Idaho Dept. Public Assistance, Boise, 1965-68; mental health counselor Community Inst. Human Resources, Boise, 1969-70; dir. patient and family counseling Mercy Med. Center, Nampa, Idaho, 1972-75; edn. counselor U.S. Army, Seoul, South Korea, 1975-76; med. social worker Kern Med. Center, Bakersfield, Calif., 1976-78, dir. med. social services, 1978-79; dir. med. social services Santa Barbara Cottage Hosp., Calif., 1979—. Mem. Nat. Assn. Social Workers, AAUW, Acad. Cert. Social Workers, Internat. Register Clin. Social Workers, Soc. Hosp. Social Work Dirs., Am. Hosp. Assn., U.S. Postal Clks. Aux. (nat. v.p. 1959-63), Phi Delta Lambda. Office: Santa Barbara Cottage Hosp Pueblo at Bath St Santa Barbara CA 93105

CORLEY, ROBERT MICHAEL, sales exec.; b. Little Rock, Mar. 5, 1944; s. Vernard Flynn and Mary Lelia (Reynolds) C.; m. Chalona Corson, Feb. 8, 1969; children—Brian Kevin, Scott Chalon. B.A., U. Ark., 1966. Plastics devel. engr., Plastics Tech. Ctr., Phillips Chem. Co. sub. Phillips Petroleum Co., Bartlesville, Okla., 1966-67, plastics sales engr., Chgo., 1967-72, Kansas City, 1972-76, Detroit, 1976-79, Far West area sales mgr., Los Angeles, 1979-82, Western area sales mgr., 1982—. Mem. Soc. Plastics Engrs., Soc. Plastics Industry, U. Ark. Alumni Assn., Phi Delta Theta. Home: 24541 Via Tonada El Toro CA 92630 Office: PO Box 792 Pasadena TX 77501

CORMIE, DONALD MERCER, investment co. exec.; b. Edmonton, Alta., Can., July 24, 1922; s. George Mills and Mildred (Mercer) C.; B.A., U. Alta., 1944, LL.B., 1945; LL.M., Harvard, 1946; m. Eivor Elisabeth Ekstrom, June 8, 1946; children—John Mills, Donald Robert, Allison Barbara, James Mercer, Neil Brian, Bruce George, Eivor, Robert. Admitted to bar, 1947; Queens counsel 1964; sessional instr. faculty law U. Alta., 1947-53; sr. partner Cormie, Kennedy, Fitch & Patrick, Edmonton, 1954—; dir. Prin. Equity Fund, Inc., Prin. World Fund, Prin. Cash Mgmt. Fund, Inc., Prin. Mgmt., Inc. instr. real estate law Dept. of Extension, U. Alta., 1958-64; pres., dir. Prin. Group Ltd., Prin. Life Ins. Co. Can., Collective Securities, Ltd., Collective Mut. Fund Ltd., Cormie Ranch, Ltd., Prin. Certificate Series, Inc., Prin. Investors Corp., Prin. Venture Fund Ltd.; chmn., dir. Prin. Savs. & Trust Co.; dir. Prin. Equity Fund, Inc., Prin. Cash Mgmt. Fund, Inc., Prin. Mgmt., Inc. Served with Canadian Mcht. Marine, 1943-44. Recipient Judge Green Silver medal in Law. Mem. Law Soc. Alta., World Bus. Council, Chief Execs. Forum (dir. 1976—), Canadian Bar Assn. (mem. council 1961—, chmn. adminstrv. law com. 1963-66, chmn. taxation 1972-82, v.p. Alta. 1968-69). Home: 12436 Grandview Dr Edmonton AB T6H 4K4 Canada Office: 3000 Principal Plaza Edmonton AB T5J 3NG Canada

CORN, NANCY RAYDENE, charitable organization executive; b. Ajo, Ariz., June 30, 1951; d. Calvin Ray and Clydene Elizabeth (Harrison) Workman; m. Ronald Wayne Corn, May 10, 1983; 1 dau., Erica Day. Grad. grantsmanship tng. program, Boulder, Colo., 1980; grad. grantsmanship fundraising tng. program, Las Vegas, 1982. Purchasing agt. H.A. Briggs, Washington, 1970; adminstrv. asst. U. Ariz., 1976-80; dir. devel. Goodwill Industries of Tucson, Inc., 1980—. Recipient award for service to field of rehab. Valpar Corp., 1980. Mem. Devel. Execs. Roundtable of So. Ariz., Nat. Assn. Exec. Females. Democrat. Office: Goodwill Industries 1770 S Cherrybell St Tucson AZ 85713

CORN, RANDALL LEE, hosp. adminstr.; b. Tucson, Apr. 15, 1952; s. Clarence Adrian and Vivian Lucille (Ogborn) C.; B.S. in Biol. Scis., U. Ariz., 1974; m. Malana Linda Watt, Aug. 2, 1975; 1 dau., Solera Nicole. Operating room instrument technician Tucson Med. Center, 1974-76; supply processing and distbn. instrument technician St. Joseph Hosp., Tucson, 1976-78; supr. pharmacy and supply Univ. Hosp., Ariz. Health Scis. Center, Tucson, 1978—; ethylene oxide control cons. Ariz. Hosp. Engring. Services; speaker on ethylene oxide control at numerous seminars. 3M grantee, 1978-79; Sybron Castle grantee, 1979; Union Carbide grantee, 1982; Crown Zellerbach grantee, 1980-81. Mem. Am. Soc. Hosp. Central Service Personnel (chpt. pres., 1980, dir. 1982-84, chmn. research and devel. com. 1982-84; Disting. Membership Recognition award 1982). Office: 1501 N Campbell Ave Tucson AZ 85724

CORNABY, KAY STERLING, lawyer, state senator; b. Utah, Jan. 14, 1936; s. Sterling A. and Hilda Grace (Stoker) C.; B.A., Brigham Young U., 1960; postgrad. U. Heidelberg (Germany), 1961-63; J.D., Harvard U., 1966; m. Linda Rasmussen, July 23, 1965; children—Alyse, Derek, Tara, Heather, Brandon. Admitted to N.Y. bar, 1967, Utah bar, 1969, U.S. Patent and Trademark Office, 1967; asso. firm Brumbaugh, Graves, Donahue & Raymond, N.Y.C., 1966-69; partner firm Mallinckrodt & Cornaby, Salt Lake City, 1969-72; individual practice law, Salt Lake City, 1972—; mem. Utah Senate, 1977—, majority leader, 1983—. Chmn., North and East Regional Council of Neighborhood Assns., 1976-77; chmn. Utah Health Cost Found., 1979—; chmn. 2d Congl. Dist., Republican Com., 1973-77; mem. council legal advisors Rep. Nat. Com., 1981—; mem. Salt Lake County Commn. on Youth, 1979—; bd. dirs. Friends of KUED-Channel 7, 1982—. Mem. ABA, Utah Bar Assn. (chmn. com. Law Day and Americanization 1975-76, chmn. client security fund com. 1979-80), Harvard U. Alumni Assn. Utah (pres. 1977-79), Harvard U. Law Sch. Assn. Utah (vice chmn. 1979—). Office: 559 E South Temple St Salt Lake City UT 84102

CORNELIUS, IRA EARL, aerospace executive, consultant; b. Pella, Iowa, Feb. 29, 1916; s. Jacob Earl and Kitty Mae (Bickford) C.; m. Lois M. Geronime. B.A., Central U. Iowa, 1947; Ph.D., St. Andrews Episc. U., 1967; postgrad, UCLA, 1977. Registered profl. engr., Calif., 1967. Methods engr. Montgomery Ward & Co., 1947-53; group supr. indirect methods analysis Northrop Corp., 1953-54; various mgmt. positions Hughes Aircraft Co., 1957-60; sr. corp. planner Lockheed Corp., 1960-61; various mgmt. positions Space Transp. and Systems Group, Rockwell Internat., 1961—, sr. exec. advisor Advanced Space Systems, 1970—; lectr. West Coast U., Calif. State U. Served with U.S. Army, 1943-45. Recipient numerous awards NASA. Mem. AIAA, AIIE. Contbr. articles to profl. jours. Office: Rockwell Internat Corp 12214 Lakewood Blvd Downey CA 90241

CORNELIUS, MARION E(DNA), biological sciences educator; b. Aurora, Mo., Mar. 10, 1930; d. Delmar Marion and Bessie (Orine) Standridge; m. Robert A. Cornelius, Sept. 4, 1949; children—David Andrews, Deborah Ruth, E. Diana. B.S.S.E., John Brown U., 1952; M.S., Kans. State Tchrs. Coll., 1965; D.Ed., U. Ariz., 1980. Cert. childbirth educator. Tchr., Brown Mil. Acad., 1949-53, Springdale (Ark.) Jr. High Sch., 1954-55, Stella (Mo.) High Sch., 1955-57, Goodman (Mo.) High Sch., 1957-59, Arrowhead Jr. High Sch., Bethel, Kans., 1959-60, Gorin (Mo.) High Sch., 1960-61; tchr., sci. supr. Southeast High Sch., Kansas City (Mo.) Pub. Schs., 1961-70; prof. biol. scis. Central Ariz. Coll., Coolidge, 1970—; acad. advisor. Chmn., Pinal County March of Dimes, 1982, 83; Town Hall del., 1979. NSF grantee summers 1961, 62, 63; Title III grantee, 1980-81. Mem. Nat. Sci. Tchrs. Assn., Nat. Assn. Biology Tchrs., Ariz. State Tchrs. Assn., Ariz. Biol. Conf., Central Ariz. Coll. Faculty Senate. Republican. Baptist. Author curriculum guides, Kansas City Pub. Schs., 1967; contbr. articles to profl. publs. Home: 842 Palm Parke Circle Casa Grande AZ 85222 Office: Central Ariz Coll Coolidge AZ 85228

CORNELL, DAVID ROGER, hospital administrator; b. Glens Falls, N.Y., Apr. 5, 1944; s. Junius R. and Isabelle R. C.; B.A., U. Vt., 1966; cert. phys. therapy Duke U., 1967; M.B.A., U. S.C., 1973; m. Alma Files Cornell, Dec. 16, 1967; children—Kimberley Anne, Kelly Elizabeth. Dir. phys. therapy Univ. Hosp., Augusta, Ga., 1970-72, adminstrv. resident, 1972; adminstrv. asst. Drs. Hosp., Augusta, 1973-74; asst. adminstr. Cypress Community Hosp., Pompano Beach, Fla., 1974; assoc. adminstr. N. Ridge Gen. Hosp., Ft. Lauderdale, Fla., 1975-77, adminstr., 1977-79; adminstr. Mont. Deaconess Med. Center, Great Falls, 1979—; dir. Blue Cross of Mont., First Bank West Great Falls. Bd. dirs. Mont. unit ARC, Mont. Heart Assn. Served with U.S. Army, 1968-69. Fellow Am. Acad. Med. Adminstrs., Am. Coll. Health Care Adminstrs.; mem. Am. Coll. Hosp. Adminstrs., Am. Hosp. Assn., Mont. Hosp. Assn., Beta Gamma Sigma. Clubs: Rotary, Meadowlark Country. Office: 1101 26th St S Great Falls MT 59405

CORNELL, DAVID WILLIAM, naval aviator; b. Plainfield, N.J., Aug. 12, 1951; s. Rodman Munn and Barbara Evelyn (Burtis) C.; B.S. in Aerospace Engring., U.S. Naval Acad., 1973; M.S. in Aero. Engring., Naval Postgrad. Sch., 1983; m. Barbara Ann Frankhouser, June 9, 1973; children—Jennifer Lynn, David William, Michael Rodman. Commd. ensign U.S. Navy, 1973, advanced through grades to lt. comdr., 1981, designated naval aviator, 1974, designated plane comdr., 1977; detailed to U.S.S. Constellation, to Naval Postgrad. Sch., Monterey, Calif., 1981—. Mem. AIAA, U.S. Naval Inst. Episcopalian. Home: 1026 Spruance Rd Monterey CA 93940 Office: NPS Monterey CA 93940

CORNWALL, BRUCE MILLEN, general contractor; b. Salt Lake City, Sept. 30, 1947; s. Stephen L. and Jaclyn (McAllister) C.; m. Roxanne Kay Amundson, Aug. 5, 1974; children—Lori, Jared, Nikole. B.S. in Bus. Mgmt., U. Utah, 1973. With Cannon Constrn., 1965-68, Sterling Constrn., 1968-69, Stephen L. Cornwall Constrn., 1970-78, v.p., 1980—; v.p. Concrete Coring Co.; owner Bruce M. Cornwall Co., West Valley City, Utah, 1980—. Mem. West Valley City Flood Control Com. Mem. Assoc. Builders and Contractors (dir.). Club: Granger Lions. Office: PO Box 20323 3460 S Redwood Rd Suite 204 West Valley City UT 84120

CORNWALL, JOHN RICHARD, JR., leasing executive; b. Lorain, Ohio, June 11, 1942; s. John R. and Thyra N. (Wallace) C.; m. Judith Ann Leonard, Feb. 16, 1945; 1 son, John Jay B. Lic. comml. and instrument ratings pilot. Dist. br. mgr. U.S. Leasing, Louisville and Cleve., 1970-73; br. mgr. CitiCorp Leasing, Cin., 1973-74; v.p. mktg. Lease Am., Cedar Rapids, Iowa, 1974-77; v.p. mktg. Seafirst Leasing, Seattle, 1977-79, pres., 1979—. Mem. Am. Assn. Equipment Lessors (dir.). Republican. Clubs: Bellevue (Wash.) Athletic; Sahalee Golf and Country (Redmond, Wash.); Coll. (Seattle). Office: PO Box 3977 Seafirst Fifth Ave Plaza Seattle WA 98124

CORNWALL, LINDA MARIE, concrete company executive; b. Pueblo, Colo., May 14, 1940; d. Sidney S. and Kathryn E. (McKinstry) Crain. Student pub. schs., Coachella, Calif., 1954-58. Office mgr. C.C.I. Builders Co., Colorado Springs, Colo., 1974-77; controller Tom Hall Bldg. Corp., Pueblo, 1977—; pres. L.T.C., Inc. (Montano Concrete Corp.); Pueblo, 1977—. Mem. Female Execs. Assn., Nat. Assn. Home Builders, Nat. Assn. Women in Constrn. Club: Gold Star Wives (Colorado Springs). Office: Tom Hall Bldg Corp 3559 Baltimore St Pueblo CO 81008

CORONA, PETER, supt. schs.; b. San Diego, Dec. 22, 1928; s. Joseph and Mary (Piranio) C.; A.B., U. Calif., Berkeley, 1953, postgrad., 1957-62; M.A. San Francisco State, 1957; Ph.D., U.S. Internat. U., San Diego, 1969; m. Yolanda Della Zoppa, June 20, 1954; children—Joel David, Marvee Anne. Asst. varsity baseball coach U. Calif. Berkeley, 1952-53; tchr. Walnut Creek Schs., 1955-59, adminstr., sch. prin., coordinator, 1960; supt. schs., Sunol, Calif., 1960-70, Benicia, Calif., 1970-73, Montebello, Calif., 1974-77, San Jose, Calif., 1977—; mem. Western Assn. Schs. and Colls. Evaluation Team for Accreditation of Secondary Schs., 1966—. Pres., Walnut Creek Parks and Recreation Commn., Amador-Livermore Valley Hist. Soc., 1965-66; mem. admissions and budget com. United Fund Solano and Napa Counties; active Montebello-Iguala and Montebello-Ashiya sister city programs; bd. dirs. Lynnewood Found., cultural center Amador-Livermore Valley, Beverly Hosp., Montebello. Mem. Am., Calif. (instrn. com., resolution com., urban affairs com., equal edn. opportunity com.) assns. sch. adminstrs., Calif. Tchrs. Assn., Calif. Assn. Sch. Bus. Ofcls., Solano County Sch. Adminstrs. Assn. (pres. 1973-74), Alameda County Adminstrs. Assn., Montebello Sch. Adminstrs., Montebello C. of C. (dir.), Montebello Hist. Soc., Phi Delta Kappa. Clubs: Rotary (v.p. Pleasanton 1965-66, pres. 1966-67); Scottsdale Swim (Walnut Creek) (v.p. 1967), Commonwealth of Calif. Author: Role of the Superintendent as Perceived by Community Leaders and School Administrators, 1969. Toured schs. of U.S.S.R., Czechoslovakia, Poland, E. and W. Berlin, Denmark, Finland, Austria (sponsored by NEA and Am. Assn. Sch. Adminstrs.), 1966; lectr. on life and edn. in U.S.S.R. and countries of communist E. Europe. Home: 98 Las Lomas Way Walnut Creek CA 94598 Office: 4727 San Pablo Ave Emeryville CA 94608

COROTTO, LOREN VINCENT, psychology consultant; b. Hollister, Calif., Nov. 20, 1929; s. Antone B. and Anna (Angoustures) C.; m. Barbara Joan Haney, Aug. 10, 1957; children—Anna Jean, Loren Vincent, Jr., Ellen Kathleen, Hilary Rose, Claire Marie. B.A., San Jose State Coll., 1951, M.A., 1952; Ph.D., U. Houston, 1958. Lic. psychologist, Calif. Staff clin. psychologist, Napa State Hosp., Calif. Dept. Mental Health, Imola, 1958-64, sr. psychologist, 1965-70, asst. program dir., 1971, psychology cons. Office of Program Rev., 1972—. Served with U.S. Army, 1953-55. Mem. Am. Psychol. Assn., Western Psychol. Assn. Republican. Roman Catholic. Contbr. articles to profl. jours. Home: 1056 Vassar Dr Napa CA 94558 Office: Box A Napa State Hosp Imola CA 94558

CORPSTEIN, PETER JOSEPH, state senator; b. Phoenix, Feb. 20, 1930; s. William and Edith Mercy (Norton) C.; m. Alice P. Daley, July 29, 1961; children—Joanne, Peter. Student U. Ariz. Chmn. bd. Valley Seed Co., 1981—; officer, dir. Ariz. Sash and Door Co., 1961—; mem. Ariz. Ho. of Reps., 1973-82, Ariz. Senate, 1983—. Chmn. Trunk 'N Tusk Com., 1970; pres. St. Luke's Hosp. Men, 1971-72; bd. dirs. Sun Angel Found. of Ariz. State U.; past bd. dirs. Phoenix Jr. Achievement. Served to 1st lt. U.S. Army, 1952-54. Recipient Exceptional and Outstanding Service award Ariz. Pharmacy Assn., 1982. Mem. Paradise Valley C. of C. Republican. Episcopalian. Clubs: Phoenix Country, Valley Field Riding and Polo. Home: 4342 E Highlands Dr Paradise Valley AZ 85253 Office: 1700 W Washington Suite 312 Phoenix AZ 85007

CORRADINI, DEEDEE MCMULLEN, public relations consultant; b. Providence, Apr. 11, 1944; d. Horace Martin and Marie Louise (Strehlau) McMullen; student Drew U., 1961-63; B.S., U. Utah, 1965, M.S. (HEW grantee), 1967; m. Yan M. Ross; children—Andrew Stafford, Andrea Marie. Adminstrv. asst. for pub. info. Utah State Office of Rehab. Services, Salt Lake City, 1967-69; pub. relations cons. State of Utah, 1971-72; media dir. and press sec. Wayne Owens for Congress campaign, Salt Lake City, 1972-73; press sec. to Congressman Wayne Owens, Washington, 1973-74; spl. asst. to Rep. Richard Ottinger, Washington, 1974-75; asst. to pres. and dir. public relations, Snowbird Corp., Salt Lake City, 1975-77; exec. v.p., partner Bonneville Group, Inc., Salt Lake City, 1977—; pres. Bonneville Assocs., Inc., Salt Lake City, 1980—; mem. faculty Taft Inst. of Politics, U. Utah, 1973-79; lectr. U. Utah, 1973—; dir. Utah Power & Light Co., trustee Intermountain Health Care Inc. Del. to Salt Lake County and Utah State Democratic Convs., 1968, co-chmn. Salt Lake City Blue Ribbon Com. on Revenue and Taxation; bd. advs. U. Utah Sch. Bus.; mem. nat. adv. bd. Snowbird Inst. for Arts and Humanities; trustee Ballet West; bd. advisers U. Utah Grad. Sch. Bus.; bd. dirs. Utah Symphony; chmn. Salt Lake County Bus./Govt. Alliance. Recipient awards HEW Office of Rehab. Services, 1968, Best Editor award Intermountain Assn. of Indsl. Editors, 1968. Mem. Salt Lake Area C. of C. bd. govs. 1979-81, U.S. C. of C. (natural resources com.). Democrat. Mem. United Ch. of Christ. Home: 787 17th

Ave Salt Lake City UT 84103 Office: Bonneville Assos Inc 200 E South Temple Suite 300 Salt Lake City UT 84111

CORRELL, WILLIAM ROY, JR., manufacturing company executive; b. Bristol, Tenn., Oct. 15, 1932; s. William Roy and Francis (Dollinger) C.; m. Jo Ann Duval, May 5, 1957; 1 son, William Roy. B.A., U. Calif.-Hayward, 1972. Commd. officer U.S. Marine Corps, 1952, advanced through grades to maj., 1965, ret., 1967; with AMFAC Fluid Power, Hayward, Calif., 1974—, br. mgr., 1979—. Republican.

CORRIERE, RICHARD JOSEPH, psychologist, author; b. Chgo., June 23, 1947; s. Joseph Angelo and Loretta Marie C.; m. Konni Pederson, Sept. 26, 1974; 1 child, Signe. B.A., U. Calif.-Irvine, 1969, Ph.D., 1974. Lic. clin. psychologist. Dir. Research Ctr. Found., Los Angeles, 1976-78; dir. Clinic for Functional Psychotherapy, Los Angeles, 1978-80; pvt. practice clin. psychology, 1980—. Mem. Am. Psychol. Assn., Soc. Behavioral Medicine. Club: Aspen Polo. Author: The Dream Makers: Discovering Your Breakthrough Dreams, 1977; Psychological Fitness: 21 Days to Feeling Good, 1978; Dreaming and Waking: The Functional Approach to Using Dreams, 1980.

CORRIGAN, CHRISTINE HELEN, hospital administrator; b. Hannover, Germany, Feb. 6, 1954; came to U.S., 1957; d. Henry and Ruth (Bonisch) Zurawek. B.S., U. Conn., 1976. Cert. med. staff coordinator, Calif. Adminstrv. asst. Hartford (Conn.) Surg. Ctr., 1977-78; dir. med. staff services Centinela Hosp. Med. Ctr., Inglewood, Calif., 1978-81; coordinator med. staff services Daniel Freeman Hosp., Inglewood, 1981; coordinator, dir. med. staff services South Bay Hosp., Redondo Beach, Calif., 1981—; aerobic dance and calisthenic instr. Mem. Calif. Assn. Med. Staff Services (pres. Los Angeles chpt. 1984), Am. Lung Assn., Nat. Assn. Female Execs., Affiliated Network Exec. Women (former pres., chmn. bd.). Home: 311 Richmond St Apt C El Segundo CA 90245 Office: South Bay Hosp 514 Prospect St Redondo Beach CA 90277

CORRY, LAWRENCE LEE, sugar company executive; b. Portland, Oreg., Oct. 31, 1939; s. Rowland Parry and Clara Hannah (Orton) C.; m. Rhea Kathleen Reeder, May 29, 1964; children—Kamille, Todd L., Matthew D., Jill, Steffani, Melanee. A.S. in Bus. Mgmt., Weber State Coll., 1959; B.A., Brigham Young U., 1963, M.B.A., 1965. Indsl. engr. Arabian Am. Oil Co., Saudi Arabia, 1958; fin. analyst Standard Oil Co. Calif., San Francisco, Houston, 1965 68; fin. analyst, asst. to pres. Amalgamated Sugar Co., Ogden, Utah, 1968-73, dist. agrl. mgr., Nampa, Idaho, 1973-75, dir. indsl. and pub. relations, Ogden, Utah, 1975-77, v.p., 1977—; mem. Dept. Agr. Mktg. Allotment Task Force, 1968-74; dir. Curtis Grain Co. Mem. North Ogden City Citizens Planning Commn., 1973. Mem. Am. Soc. Sugarbeet Technologists. Clubs: Rotary (Nampa); Kiwanis (Ogden). Mormon. Home: 5547 S 100 East St Ogden UT 84403 Office: Amalgamated Sugar Co 2400 Washington Blvd Ogden UT 84401

CORSON, GALE CHAPMAN, engring. and mgmt. cons.; b. Los Angeles, Apr. 15, 1934; s. Asa LeRoy and Merna Louise (Chapman) C.; B.S. in Bus. Adminstrn. with honors, Aurora Coll., 1955; B.S. in Engring., UCLA, 1960, M.B.A., 1964; m. Anita Jeanne Durr, June 12, 1953; children—Don, Glen, Diana. Engr., Aeroquip Corp., Burbank, Calif., 1955-59; engr. Parker Hannifin Corp., Los Angeles, 1960-61; contracts adminstr. Hughes Aircraft Corp., Culver City, Calif., 1962-65; treas., bus. mgr. Aurora (Ill.) Coll., 1965-74; chief engr. Nissen Corp., Cedar Rapids, Iowa, 1974-76; gen. mgr., pres. Center 4 Engring., Redmond, Oreg., 1977—. Chmn., Central Oreg. Energy Policy Com., 1979-81. Registered profl. engr., Calif., Oreg., Iowa. Mem. Architects Engrs. Soc. Central Oreg. (past pres.), Am. Mgmt. Assn., ASME, IEEE, ASTM, ASHRAE. Methodist. Author: Hydroelectric Power Resources in the Pacific Northwest, 1981; contbr. articles to profl. jours. Home: 594 SE Craven Rd Bend OR 97702 Office: Redmond OR 97756

CORTADA, RAFAEL LEON, college president, historian; b. N.Y.C., Feb. 12, 1934; s. Rafael Cortada-Forgas and Yvonne Bernier-Hernandez; m. Selonie Jolissaint-Head, June 24, 1961; children—Celia, Natalia, Rafael. A.B., Fordham U., 1955; M.A., Columbia U., 1974; cert. Inst. Ednl. Mgmt., Harvard U., 1974. Instr., New Rochelle (N.Y.) High Sch., 1957-64, CUNY, Bronx, 1958-64, asst. prof. U. Dayton (Ohio), 1964-66, cons. Fgn. Service Inst., Dept. State, Washington, 1966, desk officer W.I., 1966-69; assoc. prof. history Fed. City Coll., Washington, 1968-69, assoc. provost, prof. history, 1969-70; prof. history, dean community edn. and urban resources Medgar Evers Coll.-CUNY, Bklyn., 1970-71; prof. history, v.p. acad. affairs Hostos Community Coll., Bronx, 1971-74; pres. Met. Community Coll., Mpls., 1974-77, Community Coll. Balt., 1977-82; pres., supt. El Camino Coll./El Camino Community Coll. Dist., Torrance, Calif., 1982—; vis. assoc. prof. Caribbean history Howard U., Washington, 1967-68; mem. adv. bd. grad. fellowship program Danforth Found., 1976-81; mem. adv. com. Am. Assn. Community and Jr. Colls. Internat. Edn. Consortium, 1975-79; mem. state licensure tean N.J. Dept. Edn., 1972; mem. overseas liaison com. Am. Council Edn., 1971-80; mem. acad. adv. bd. East Harlem Exptl. and Bilingual Inst., 1971-75; mem. accreditation teams Middle States Assn. Colls. and Secondary Schs., 1970—; mem. internat. adv. council Media Systems Corp., 1976-78; mem. adv. com. creative programming Sta. KTCA-TV, Mpls., 1976-77. Mem. Balt. Mayor's Literacy Commn., 1981, Health and Welfare Council Central Md., Balt., 1981-82; pres. N.E. region Council Black Am. Affairs, 1980-82; mem. U. S. Nat. Commn. UNESCO, 1979—, vice chmn., 1980; mem. cabinet Mayor of Balt., 1978-82; mem. community adv. bd. Pub. Broadcasting System Md., 1978-82; trustee Woodbourne Sch., Balt., 1979-82, vice chmn., 1980, chmn., 1981-82; pub. corp. mem.; trustee Blue Cross/Blue Shield, 1976-77; bd. govs. U. Guayana, 1971—. Served to 1st lt. U.S. Army, 1955-57; Korea. Mem. African Studies Assn. (v.p. Washington task force African affairs 1969—), Am. Hist. Assn. (program planning com. conv. 1970), Author: Echoes of World Civilizatin 2 vols., 1963; Black Studies: An Urban and Comparative Curriculum, 1975; collaborator TV series The College and Urban Problems, 1970; contbr. articles to profl. jours. Office: 16007 Crenshaw Blvd Torrance CA 90277

CORTEWAY, ROBERT C., bank exec.; b. Milw., Mar. 28, 1944; B.S., Calif. State U., 1966; M.B.A., UCLA, 1967; children—Nelson T., Robert C. With Security Pacific Nat. Bank, 1967—, chief credit and mktg. officer London br., sr. corp. account officer, N.Y.C, credit adminstr. internat. banking, Los Angeles, chief mgr. subs. The Bank of Canton, Ltd., Hong Kong, sr. v.p. and adminstr. Asia-Australasia hdqrs., Hong Kong, now adminstr. corp. banking group. Office: Security Pacific Nat Bank 333 S Hope St Los Angeles CA 90071

CORTOPASSI, RONALD FRANK, pharmacist, hosp. official; b. San Francisco, Sept. 12, 1949; s. Orlando Frank and Rena Virginia (Pellicci) C.; m. Jenine Marie Tardelli, June 29, 1974; children—Elisa Marie, Anthony Frank. A.A., Coll. of San Mateo, 1969; B.A. in Biol. Sci., U. Calif.-Santa Barbara, 1971; Pharm.D., U. Calif.-San Francisco, 1975. Hosp. pharmacy resident U. Ill. Med. Ctr., Chgo., 1975-76; staff pharmacist, coordinator clin. edn. Mt. Diablo Hosp. and Med. Ctr., Concord, Calif., 1976-78; asst. dir. pharmacy services Fresno (Calif.) Community Hosp. and Med. Ctr. 1979—; adj. prof. Sch. Pharmacy, U. Pacific, Stockton, Calif., 1977—; lectr. numerous profl. assns., univs. Named Preceptor of Yr., U. Pacific Sch. Pharmacy, 1978, acknowledgement for outstanding service Contra Costa unit Am. Cancer Soc., 1979. Mem. Am. Hosp. Hosp. Pharmacists, Calif. Soc. Hosp. Pharmacists (contbg. editor Voice, 1980—, mem. council on clin. pharmacy and therepeutics 1980—), Sierra Soc. Hosp. Pharmacists (v.p. 1981, pres. 1982), No. Calif. Oncology Group (pharmacy com. 1980—), No. Calif. Soc. Hosp. Pharmacists (pres.-elect 1979). Contbr. articles to profl. jours. Office: Dept Pharmacy Fresno Community Hosp Fresno and R Sts Fresno CA 93711

CORWIN, DOUGLAS BRUCE, publishing executive; b. Rome, N.Y., Nov. 20, 1943; s. Bernard David and Bertha Jerrie (Wanderone) C.; m. Linda Susan Mortensen, Apr. 13, 1974. B.A. in Fine Arts, U. N. Mex., 1967. Pub. San Francisco Theatre mag., 1976-79; dir. advt. Greenpeace Chronicles, San Francisco, 1979, pub. The Twelfth Night Repertory Co., Mill Valley, Calif., 1980; advt. dir. Oceans, San Francisco, 1980—. Mem. San Francisco Advt. Club, San Francisco Mag. Reps. Club. Democrat. Lutheran. Office: Oceans Ft Mason Center San Francisco CA 94123

CORY, CHARLES ERNEST, engineering company executive; b. Toronto, Ohio, May 6, 1927; s. George E. and Eugene (Howard) C.; B.S. in Mech. Engring., Stanford U., 1951; m. Diane Dix Druehl, Aug. 22, 1953; children—Carolyn, James, Christopher. Engr. FMC, San Jose, Calif., 1951-53, Oakland, Calif., 1954-63; sr. engr. Rietz Mfg. div. Bepex Corp., Santa Rosa, Calif., 1963-71, mgr. research and devel., 1972-77; pres. Cory Engring. Co., Sebastopol, Calif., 1977—; tchr. math., Miranda, Calif., 1953-54. Bd. dirs. Jr. Achievement, 1967-76. Served with USN, 1945-46. Registered mech. engr., Calif. Republican. United Ch. Christ. Patentee in field. Home: 5215 Vine Hill Sebastopol CA 95472 Office: 150 Todd Rd Santa Rosa CA 95402

CORY, JOHN SLANE, research engineering executive; b. Parsons, Kans., Oct. 6, 1930; s. Thomas Cantwell and Lucile Irene (Slane) C. B.S. in Chem. Engring., Kans. State U., 1948, M.S. in Physics, 1958; M.A. in Engring., Princeton U., 1969, Ph.D. in Engring., 1971. Quality control supr., field engr. Hercules Powder Co., Lawrence, Kans., 1952-54; research engr. Atlas Missile project, Gen. Electric, Schenectady, N.Y., 1956-58; prin. investigator McDonnell Douglas, Los Angeles, 1962-65, sr. scientist, program mgr., Richland, Wash., 1965-69; pres. Cory Labs. Inc., Escondido, Calif., 1971—. Mem. AIAA, Am. Physics Soc., AAAS. Republican. Contbr. articles to profl. publs. Address: 1436 View Point Escondido CA 92027

CORY, VIRGINIA JEAN, nursing educator; b. Bridgeport, Conn., June 7, 1923; d. Oscar William and Helen Louise (Klemas) Kuchner; m. George Joseph Cory, Feb. 25, 1961; 1 son, James Scott. B.S., Simmons Coll., 1957; M.S. in Nursing, Cath. U. Am., 1960; postgrad. NYU at Buffalo, 1976; R.N., Oreg. Coordinator nursing edn. Children's Hosp. Med. Ctr., San Francisco, 1963-65; asst. dir. nursing service Golden State chpt. ARC, Burlingame, Calif., 1965-68; asst. prof. med.-surg. nursing U. Oreg. Sch. Nursing, Portland, 1968-78; coordinator nursing edn. St. Vincent Hosp. and Med. Ctr., Portland, 1978—; mem. Oreg. State Bd. of Nursing, 1977-83. Mem. Oreg. Nurse Assn. (dist. 1 pres. 1978-80), Med. Adv. Council for Prescriptive Writing Privileges, Oreg. Thoracic Assn., Oreg. Heart Assn., Sigma Theta Tau. Office: 9205 SW Barnes Rd Portland OR 97225

CORYELL, DONALD DAVID, football coach; b. Seattle, Oct. 17, 1924; B.A., U. Wash., 1950, M.A., 1951. Asst. coach Punahou Acad., Honolulu, 1951; head coach Farrington High Sch., Honolulu, 1952; asst. coach U. Wash., 1953-54; head coach, athletic dir., Ft. Ord, Calif., 1956; asst. coach U. So. Calif., 1960; coach San Diego State U., 1961-71, St. Louis Cardinals, 1973-77, San Diego Chargers, 1978—. Named NFL Coach of Yr., Sporting News, 1974. Office: San Diego Chargers San Diego Stadium PO Box 20120 San Diego CA 92120*

COST, JAMES PETER, artist; b. Phila., Mar. 3, 1923; s. Peter and Rose (Perry) C.; B.A., U. Calif. at Los Angeles, 1950; M.S., U. So. Calif., 1959; m. Betty Jo Root, Apr. 17, 1957; children—Curtis, Shelley, Janet and Nancy Pamela. Former art tchr. art shows Carmel (Calif.), James Peter Cost Gallery; art instr. Principia Coll., summer 1975; exhibited in group shows at Artists Guild Gallery Am., Carmel, 1961-63, Carmel James Peter Cost Gallery, 1964—, Mus. Fine Arts, Springfield, Mass., 1965, Nat. Arts Club, N.Y.C., 1966, represented in collection R.W. Morton Mus., Shreveport, La., also numerous pvt. permanent collections; one-man retrospective show R.W. Norton Gallery, Shreveport, La., 1971; one-man show and lectr. Northwood Inst., Midland, Mich., 1971; lectr. Northwood Inst., Dallas, 1971; newspaper columnist Carmel Pine Cone, 1970; covers for mags., including Reader's Digest, No. Calif. Golf Assn. Impressario. Pres., Carmel Bus. Assn., 1970; mem. Calif. State Republican Central Com., Monterey County Rep. Central Com., 1981—; Rep. candidate for Calif. State Assembly, 1982. Served with USCG, 1942-45. Recipient Gold medal in nat. marine competition Franklin Mint, 1974. Christian Scientist. Home: Pebble Beach CA 93921 Office: Box 3638 Carmel CA 93921

COSTANTINO, MARSHALL UGO, credit analyst; b. West Palm Beach, Fla., Apr. 19, 1949; s. Ugo A. and Gloria R. C.; m. Sharon London, Sept. 22, 1974; 1 son, David Adam. B.S., U. Fla., 1972; M.S., S.D. State U., 1975. Credit research mgr. Diners Club Internat., Denver, 1976-79; credit policy mgr. Citicorp Person-to-Person Fin. Services, Inc., Aurora, Colo., 1979-83; credit analysis mgr. Citicorp Retail Services, Inc., Englewood, Colo., 1983—. Served to capt. USAF, 1972-76. Mem. Ops. Research Soc. Am. (chpt. treas. 1982-84). Author: A Handbook for Time Series Analysis and Prediction, 1981. Home: 8062 S Niagara Way Englewood CO 80112 Office: Citicorp Retail Services Inc 5889 S Syracuse Circle Englewood CO 80111

COTA-ROBLES, ENRIQUE GERARDO, hosp. fin. adminstr.; b. Tucson, July 15, 1947; s. Alfonso and Otilia (Maldonado) Cota-R; student U. Ariz., 1965-68; m. Linda E. Jones, Dec. 29, 1979; 1 son, Ty; children by previous marriage—Christopher, Jennifer, Matthew. Mgr. Interstate Securities Co., Kansas City, Mo., 1969-71; dir. patient accounts Tucson Med. Center, 1971-82; asst. dir. fin. U. Calif.-San Diego Med Center, 1982—. Bd. dirs. Tucson Family Debt Counselors, 1969—, pres., 1977; founder, credit com. chmn. Tucson Med. Center Employees Fed. Credit Union, 1975—. Served with USAR, 1966-77. Mem. Hosp. Fin. Mgmt. Assn. (bd. dirs. 1978—, chpt. sec. 1980, chpt. v.p. 1981), Credit Execs. of Tucson (pres. 1976), Internat. Consumer Credit Assn.

COTCHETT, JOSEPH WINTERS, lawyer; b. Chgo., Jan. 6, 1939; s. Joseph Winters and Jean (Renaud) C.; B.S. in Engring., Calif. Poly. Coll., 1960; LL.B., U. Calif. Hastings Coll. Law, 1964; m. Catherine C. Schad, June 12, 1959; children—Leslie F., Charles P., Rachael E. Admitted to Calif. bar, 1965; since practiced in San Mateo; mem. Calif. Jud. Council. Chmn. San Mateo County Heart Assn., 1967, 68; pres. San Mateo Boys Club, 1971. Bd. dirs. Roscoe Pound Found., Am. Trial Lawyers Found., Cambridge, Mass. Served with Intelligence Corps U.S. Army, 1960-61; now col. Judge Adv. Gen.'s Corps, Res. Fellow Am. Bar Found., Am. Bd. Trial Advocates, Internat. Acad. Law and Sci.; mem. Calif. Trial Lawyers Assn. (gov. 1969-72, v.p. 1972), Nat. Bd. Trial Advocates (diplomate civil trial advocate), State Bar Calif. (gov. 1972-75, v.p. 1975). Clubs: Commonwealth, Press (San Francisco). Author: (with R. Cartwright) California Products Liability Actions, 1970; (with F. Haight) California Courtroom Evidence, 1972; (with A Elkind) Federal Courtroom Evidence, 1976. articles to profl. jours. Office: 4 W 4th Ave San Mateo CA 94402 also 9454 Wilshire Suite 907 Beverly Hills CA 90212

COTE, JOSEPH TERRANCE, foundation executive; b. Muskegon, Mich., Sept. 27, 1943; s. Raymond A. and Bernice C. (McGarvie) C.; m. Gloria A. McDowell, Dec. 11, 1964; children—Thomas A., Angela C. B.S., Ferris State Coll., 1967; M.A.S., U. Ill., 1971. C.P.A., Mich. Staff acct. Arthur Andersen & Co., Detroit, 1967-70; teaching asst. U. Ill., Champaign, 1970-71; instr. Ferris State Coll., Big Rapids, Mich., 1971-73; controller Lorin Industries, Muskegon, Mich., 1973-74; project mgr., tech. adminstr. Am. Inst. C.P.A.s, N.Y.C., 1974-78; dir. continuing profl. edn. Calif. C.P.A. Found., Palo Alto, 1978—. Recipient Achievement award Ernst & Ernst, 1968. Mem. Am. Inst. C.P.A.s, Mich. Assn. C.P.A.s, Calif. Soc. C.P.A.s, Am. Acctg. Assn., Am. Soc. for Tng. and Devel. Contbr. articles to tech. publs. Office: California CPA Foundation 1000 Welch Rd Palo Alto CA 94304

COTHRAN, DAN ALLEN, political science educator; b. Carlisle, Ark., Feb. 24, 1941; s. Walter Marvin and Retha Louise C.; m. Cheryl Cole, July 15, 1977; children—Leslie, Amanda. B.A., U. Calif.-Berkeley, 1963; Ph.D., Cornell U., 1979. History tchr. Chaffey High Sch., Ontario, Calif., 1967-70; asst. prof. Faculty of Commerce, U. B.C. (Can.), Vancouver, 1977-81; auditor Office of Auditor Gen. State of Calif., Sacramento, 1981; assoc. prof. polit. sci. No. Ariz. U., Flagstaff, 1981—. Mem. Planning and Zoning Commn. Coconino County, 1982—. Grantee in field. Mem. Am. Polit. Sci. Assn., Policy Studies Assn. Contbr. articles to profl. jours. Office: Polit Sci Dept No Ariz U Flagstaff AZ 86011

COTLER, SUSAN MORGAN, college adminstrator; b. Chgo., July 18, 1943; d. William Clarence and Mildred (Stern) Morgan; m. Sherwin B. Cotler, Mar. 2, 1941; children—Stacy Renee, Lisa Michelle; m. John A. Bohannon, Jan. 29, 1936. B.A., Calif. State U.-Long Beach, 1965; M.A., Wash. State U., 1969. Tchr., Long Beach (Calif.) Unified Sch. Dist., 1965-66; lectr. Long Beach City Coll., 1972-76, dir. Coll. Children's Ctr., 1976-79, coordinator employment tng. program, 1979-82; adminstrv. asst. tech. div. Cerritos Coll., Norwalk, Calif., 1982—; cons. Calif. Community Colls. Chancellor, Calif. Dept. Edn., 1981. Credentialing Women in the Trades grantee, 1980. Mem. NOW, Am. Vocat. Assn. (life), Am. Vocat. Edn. Assn. (region V dir.), Calif. Assn. Women Adminstrs. and Counselors (pres. 1982-83), Long Beach Area C. of C. Office: 11110 E Alondra St Norwalk CA 90650

COTTER, MAUREEN HELEN, exec. search co. exec.; b. Lawrence, Mass., Jan. 25, 1943; d. John Joseph and Helen Theresa (Kavanagh) C.; B.A. in Theatre Arts, Pasadena Playhouse, 1963; B.A., Calif. State Coll., 1970. Chaplain's asst. Pacific State Hosp., Pomona, Calif., 1967-68; correctional counselor Calif. State Penintentiary for Women, Frontera, 1969-70; mgr. Forum, Los Angeles, 1971-72; account dir. V.I.P., Los Angeles, 1972-74; owner, pres. Actuarial Search Assocs., Beverly Hills, Calif., 1974—. Mem. NOW, Nat. Assn. Female Execs., Am. Entrepreneurs Assn., Women in Bus. Los Angeles. Home: 902 S Curson Ave Los Angeles CA 90036 Office: 910 S Curson Ave Los Angeles CA 90036

COTTER, SID CURTINS, advertising representative, restaurant sales consultant; b. Peoria, Ill., Sept. 26, 1952; s. Phillip Clyde and Martha Helen (Hatmaker) C.; m. Linda Jane Montgomery, July 31, 1976 (div. 1983). A.A., Central Ariz. Coll., 1973; B.A. in Broadcast Journalism, Ariz. State U., 1976. Dir. Mktg. Hardee's Food Systems, Norman, Okla.; regional mktg. mgr. Pizza Hut Co., Los Angeles, 1981-82; dir. patient services mktg. Ident Co., Glendale, Calif., 1982; regional media rep. Stroh Media Services, Van Nuys, Calif., 1982—. Recipient Nat. Promotion award, Sambo's Restaurants. Mem. Am. Mgmt. Assn., Nat. Acad. TV Arts & Scis. Office: Stroh Media Services 7521 Woodman St Van Nuys CA 91405

COTTON, CHESTER CHRISTIE, management educator; b. Los Angeles, Nov. 17, 1939; s. Chester McKendree and Thelma Pauline (Lake) C.; B.S., San Jose State U., 1962, M.S., 1964; Ph.D., U. Oreg., 1974; m. Eileen Marie Giuffré, Apr. 3, 1971. Procurement specialist Lockheed Missiles & Space Co., Sunnyvale, Calif., 1962-64; instr. bus. adminstrn. Shasta Coll., Redding, Calif., 1965-67; grad. teaching asst. U. Oreg., Eugene, 1967-70; asst. prof. orgn. behavior Calif. State U.-Sacramento, 1970-72; asst. prof. mgmt. Calif. State U.-Chico, 1972-76, asso. prof. mgmt. 1978-82, prof. mgmt., 1982—; mgmt. cons. in orgn. devel. and human resources, 1970—. Fed. faculty fellow Dept. Agr., 1976-78. Mem. Acad. Mgmt., Am. Psychol. Assn., Internat. Assn. Applied Psychology, Beta Gamma Sigma, Sigma Iota Epsilon, Pi Gamma Mu, Omicron Delta Epsilon, Delta Sigma Pi. Contbr. articles on mgmt. and bus. adminstrn. to prof. jours. Office: Dept Mgmt Calif State Univ Chico CA 95929

COTTON, DANIEL FRANCIS LEIGH, hosp. mgmt. co. exec.; b. Mt. Vernon, N.Y., Jan. 16, 1931; s. Harold Heath and Dorothy Submit (Avery) C.; B.A., Pacific Union Coll., Angwin, Calif., 1952; M.A., Andrews U., Berrien Springs, Mich., 1954, B.D., 1956; m. Marilyn Dillow, Feb. 27, 1955; children—Patrice Lynn, Jennifer Leigh, Elizabeth Anne, Lori Jean. Ordained to ministry Seventh-day Adventist Ch., 1959; assoc. prof. religion Columbia Union Coll., Takoma Park, Md., 1959-62; assoc. prof. religious philosophy Loma Linda (Calif.) U., 1962-69; developer, pres. Heritage Health Care Inc. Loma Linda, 1966—; developer, pres. Loma Linda Community Hosp., 1972-82; pres. Colorado Springs Community Hosp., 1974-78; chmn. bd., chief exec. officer United Med. Mgmt. Inc., 1978—. Chmn. bd. Nat. Child Health Council, 1977—; pres. Loma Linda Health Care Found., 1979-82. Fellow Am. Coll. Health Care Adminstrs.; mem. AAUP, Hosp. Fin. Mgmt. Assn., Loma Linda C. of C. (past dir.). Republican. Club: Rotary. Home: 1300 Propsect Dr Redlands CA 92373 Office: 25271 Barton Rd Loma Linda CA 92354

COTTON, EILEEN GIUFFRÉ, educator; b. Oakland, Calif., Apr. 23, 1947; d. Leonard and Helen Marie (Weiss) Giuffré; B.A., Calif. State U., Hayward, 1968; M.A. in Edn., Calif. State U., Sacramento, 1976; Ph.D. in Adminstrn., Supervision and Curriculum, U. Md., 1979; m. Chester C. Cotton, Apr. 3, 1971. Elem. tchr. Hayward (Calif.) Unified Sch. Dist., 1969-70, Rescue (Calif.) Union Sch. Dist., 1970-72, Chico (Calif.) Unified Sch. Dist., 1972-76; curriculum dir. Crownsville (Md.) Hosp. Center, 1976-77; vis. asst. prof. edn., Calif. State U., Chico, 1978-82, vis. assoc. prof., 1982—. Mem. Am. Psychol. Assn., Am. Edn. Research Assn., Calif. Reading Assn., Assn. Supervision and Curriculum Devel., Internat. Reading Assn., Internat. Assn. Sch. Adminstrs., Assn. Calif. Sch. Adminstrs., Phi Delta Kappa, Kappa Delta Pi. Author: A Guide to Community Re-entry, 1977; contbr. to ednl. jours. Office: Dept Edn Calif State U Chico Chico CA 95929

COTTON, JOHN CARL, investment banking firm executive, consultant; b. Washington, Sept. 24, 1938; s. John and Marion (Hoglund) C.; m. Janet Hobbs; children—John, Dawne, Elizabeth, Mark. B.A., U. Chgo., 1959, M.B.A., 1967. Pres. Citizens State Bancorp, Vineland, N.J.; exec. v.p. Patagonia Corp., Tucson; pres. Gt. Western Bank & Trust Co., Phoenix; pres. Maricopa Partnerships Inc., Paradise Valley, Ariz. Pres. Phoenix Conv. and Visitors Bur., 1980. Mem. Phoenix C. of C. (pres. 1982-83), Ariz. State Bankers Assn. (pres. 1982). Republican. Episcopalian. Lodge: Kiwanis (pres. 1982-83) (Phoenix). Office: 7526 N Eucalyptus Dr Paradise Valley AZ 85253

COTTON, KATHLEEN LAURA, investment adviser; b. Camas, Wash., Dec. 20, 1940; d. Charles Hershel and Gladys Louise (Coffey) Miller; m. David Cotton, July 10, 1971 (div.); children—Laura, Stephen, Thomas. B.S. with honors, City U., Bellevue, Wash., 1982. Dept. sec. Gen. Electric Co., Richland, Wash., 1959-64; exec. sec. Gen. Telephone, Everett, Wash., 1969-72; membership mgr. Yakima C. of C. (Wash.), 1978-79; office supr. Gen. Telephone, Kirkland, Wash., 1979-82; registered investment adviser, fin. planner Painter Fin. Group Ltd.,

Bellevue, 1982—. Loaned exec. United Way, 1980-81; Gen. Telephone coordinator United Way, 1982. Mem. Kirkland C. of C. (new bus. devel. chairperson 1983), Internat. Assn. Fin. Planners, Forum East Network. Episcopalian. Home: 12034 Slater Ave NE #A7 Kirkland WA 98033 Office: 2223 112th St NE Bellevue WA 98004

COUCH, MICHAEL DOUGLASS, real estate development company executive; b. San Francisco, May 25, 1941; s. Marcus Douglass and Roberta Ann (Brunn) C.; m. Jean McWilliams, Aug. 2, 1969; children—Matthew, Whitney. B.S., U. Oreg., 1964; M.B.A., U. Santa Clara, 1969; postgrad. exec. program for smaller cos. Stanford U., 1979. With Doug Couch, gen. contractor, 1965-68, Coldwell Banker Comml. Brokerage Co., 1968-72; project engr. Sutter Hill Ltd., Palo Alto, Calif., 1972-75, v.p., 1975-76, sr. v.p., 1976-77, exec. v.p., 1977-78, pres., 1978-81; pres. Bren Investment Properties, Inc., Menlo Park, Calif., 1981—; pres. Vintage Properties Investment Co., Menlo Park, Calif. Bd. dirs. Big Bros./Big Sisters of Peninsula, 1976-81, mem. exec. com., 1978-81, pres., 1980-81; bd. dirs. Key Sch., Palo Alto; bd. dirs. YMCA, Palo Alto, mem. com. Y-Fitness Ctr. Mem. Urban Land Inst., Internat. Council Shopping Ctrs. (Idea exchange panelist 1978-81, mem. faculty 1978-80), Theta Chi. Republican. Club: Foothills Tennis and Swimming. Home: 26790 St Francis Dr Los Altos Hills CA 94020 Office: 3000 Sand Hill Rd Bldg 3 Suite 255 Menlo Park CA 94025

COUGHLIN, MICHAEL B., state agy. adminstr.; b. Utica, N.Y., May 28, 1943; s. Roland D. and Margaret G. C.; student Syracuse (N.Y.) U., 1961-63; B.S. in Edn., Castleton (Vt.) State Coll., 1966; postgrad U. Alaska, 1967-70; M.B.A., U. Miami, 1978; m. Twyla D. Garland, May 30, 1970. Tchr. pub. schs., Stamford, Vt., 1966-67, Juneau, Alaska, 1968-69; math. specialist Skagway (Alaska) Pub. Sch., 1969-77; owner, mgr. Grubstake Charlies Pancake Ho., Skagway, 1974-77; retirement specialist State of Alaska, Juneau, 1979—. Bd. dirs. Skagway Fine Arts Council, 1971-73. Mem. MBA Execs. Assn., Aircraft Owners and Pilots Assn., Nat. Rife Assn. Democrat. Club: Elks. Home: 9151 Parkwood Dr Juneau AK 99801 Office: Div of Retirement and Benefits Pouch CR Juneau AK 99811

COULETTE, JACQUELINE JUNE, high school administrator; b. Los Angeles, Aug. 19, 1929; d. Bernard James and Mildred E. (Dillow) Meredith; m. Henri Coulette, Dec. 27, 1950 (div. Dec. 1979). B.A., Calif. State U.-Los Angeles, 1952. Cert. tchr., adminstr., Calif. Tchr., Iowa City Schs., 1952-58; tchr. English, U. Iowa, 1958; tchr. Alhambra Schs. (Calif.), from 1959; tchr. English, drama, art Century High Sch., Alhambra, 1969-74, work experience coordinator, 1974-83, asst. prin., 1983—, adminstr. CETA program, summer 1983. Treas., bd. dirs. Monterey Park Girls and Boys Club; pres. Industry Edn. Council of San Gabriel Valley (Calif.), South Pasadena Rose Tournament Assn.; mem. Craft and Folk Art Mus., Los Angeles, charter mem. Mus. Contemporary Art, Los Angeles. Recipient Order of the Black Rose award for design of poetry pamphlet, Krakow, Poland, 1972. Mem. Calif. Tchrs. Assn., NEA, Alhambra Mgmt. Assn., Sierra Club. Democrat. Club: Soroptimist Internat. (v.p. 1982-83). Designer 3 award-winning floats for Rose Parade; designer logo for Industry Edn. Council, 1982.

COULSON, JOHN EDMUND, psychologist; b. Atlanta, Mar. 11, 1929; s. Cyril E. and Marion Olive (Bullard) C.; B.S., U. Ariz., 1950, B.A., 1952; M.A., Columbia U., 1953, Ph.D., 1956; m. Anne Hersey, Feb. 26, 1956. Tng. specialist Rand Corp., Santa Monica, Calif., 1955-57; sr. research leader System Devel. Corp., Santa Monica, 1958-62, dep. dept. mgr., 1963-79, mgr., studies and eval. dept., 1979—; cons. UCLA, Los Angeles Unified Sch. Dist. Served to 1st lt. USAR, 1950-62. Fellow Am. Psychol. Assn.; mem. Am. Ednl. Research Assn., Nat. Council Measurement in Edn., Western Psychol. Assn. Republican. Episcopalian. Editor: Programmed Learning and Computer Based Instruction, 1962; contbr. articles to profl. jours. Home: 1743 Bryn Mawr Santa Monica CA 90405 Office: 2500 Colorado Ave Santa Monica CA 90406

COULSON, ROY, fuel company executive; b. Ernest, Pa., Jan. 7, 1922; s. Joseph and Jane (McCaw) C.; m. Bernice Bouch, June 2, 1943 (div. Aug. 1980); children—Roy Ann, Roybn Lu, Timothy Galen; m. 2d, Beverly Coulson, Sept. 26, 1980. B.S. in Mech. Engring., U. Pitts., 1949. Maintenance supr., maintenance engr., maintenance foreman Rochester and Pitts. Coal Co., Indiana, Pa., 1949-55; Wyo. div. supt. Vitro Minerals Corp., Riverton, 1955-64, mgr. Alaskan ops., 1964-65; v.p. Kemmerer Coal Co., Frontier, Wyo., 1965-71, exec. v.p., 1971-72, pres., 1972-82, also dir.; sr. v.p. Pitts. & Midway Coal Mining Co., 1982— , v.p. engring., 1982; exec. v.p. Gunn Quealy Coal Co., 1971-72, pres., 1972-80; pres. Continental Livestock Co., 1972-81, Uinta Improvement Co., 1972-81, Lincoln Service Corp., 1978-80. Mem. Wyo. Bd. Mines, 1957-62, sec., 1958. Vice pres., mem. bd. Wyo. Council for Econ. Devel., 1961-63; mem. exec. council Wyo. State Rural Areas Devel. Com., 1962-63; mem. bd. Sch. Dist. No. 25, 1959-63, pres. bd., 1961-62; mem. Lincoln County Sch. Reorgn. Com., 1969-71; bd. dirs. Wyo. Taxpayers Assn., 1974-82. Served with USNR, 1942-45. Mem. AAAS, Am. Inst. Mining Engrs., Wyo. Mining Assn. (pres. 1961-62, dir.), Am. Mining Congress (bd. govs. 1960), Nat. Coal Assn. (dir. 1973-82), Rocky Mountain Coal Mining Inst. (v.p. for Wyo. 1972-73, pres. 1974-75, dir.). Republican. Episcopalian. Mason (32 deg., Shriner), Elk. Home: Parker CO 80134 Office: Pitts & Midway Coal Mining Co Denver CO 80222

COULTER, MYRON LEE, university administrator; b. Albany, Ind., Mar. 21, 1929; s. Mark Earl and Thelma Violet (Marks) C.; B.S., Ind. State Tchrs. Coll., 1951; M.S., Ind. U., 1956, Ed.D., 1959; H.L.D. (hon.), Coll. Idaho, 1982; m. Barbara Bolinger, July 21, 1951; children—Nan and Benjamin (twins). Tchr. English, Reading (Mich.) Pub. Schs., 1951-52; tchr. elem. grades Bloomington (Ind.) Pub. Schs., 1954-56; instr. edn. Ind. U., Bloomington, 1958-59; asst. prof. Pa. State U., 1959-65, asso. prof., 1965-66; vis. prof. U. Alaska, Fairbanks, 1965; asso. dean edn. Western Mich. U., Kalamazoo, 1966-68, v.p. for adminstrn., prof. edn., 1968-76, interim pres., 1974; pres. Idaho State U., Pocatello, 1976—; cons. in fields. Bd. dirs. Kalamazoo C. of C., 1975-76; lay leader Kalamazoo Meth. Ch., 1971-74; trustee Bronson Hosp., Kalamazoo, 1975-76; bd. dirs. Pocatello Jr. Achievement. Served with U.S. Army, 1952-54. Named Distinguished Alumnus, Ind. State U., 1975; recipient award Western Mich. U. Alumni Assn., 1974, resolution of tribute Mich. State Legislature, 1976, Pres.'s medallion Idaho State U., 1978. Mem. Internat. Reading Assn., Am. Assn. State Colls. and Univs. (dir.), Nat. Council Tchrs. of English, Nat. Soc. for Study Edn., Pocatello C. of C. (dir.), Phi Delta Kappa, Omicron Delta Kappa. Club: Pocatello Country. Author school textbooks. Office: Campus Box 8310 Idaho State U Pocatello ID 83209

COUMIDES, ANDREAS DEMOSTHENOUS, mining company executive; b. Limassol, Cyprus, Feb. 10, 1928; came to U.S., 1947, naturalized, 1952; s. Demosthenis C. and Christalia A. (Philippou) C.; m. Amalia Aragon, Nov. 17, 1957; children—Michael A., Andreas Demosthenous, Francisco X. B.S. with high distinction in Bus. Adminstrn., U. Ariz., 1951. Various acctg. position Asarco Inc., El Paso, Tex., 1951-53, Mex., 1953-59, mgr. mining unit, Mex., 1960-63, co. treas., Mexico City, 1963-65, various managerial acctg. positions, southwestern mining dept. Tucson, 1965-79, asst. to v.p. mining, Tucson, 1979—; v.p., dir. Midetco, Ltd.; dir. United Park City Mines Co.; dir.-examiner Mex. Desarrollo Indsl. Minero and various subs. Mem. research com. Ariz. Acad. Recipient award citation Jr. Achievement, 1969. Mem. AIME, Ariz. Mining Assn., Ariz. Tax Research Assn. (dir.), Inst. of Property Taxation, Alpha Kappa Psi, Beta Gamma Sigma, Phi Kappa Phi. Democrat. Roman Catholic. Club: Mexico City Bankers. Home: 3625 Calle Del Prado Tucson AZ 85716 Office: Asarco Inc 1150 N 7th Ave Tucson AZ 85705

COUNTER, BENJAMIN FRINK, canning co. exec.; b. Denver, May 16, 1912; s. Benjamin Tucker and Marguerite Ruth (Frink) C.; B.S. in Chemistry, Colo. State U., 1934; m. Marjorie Lois Little, June 24, 1934; children—Ann Counter Tate, Benjamin T., James Dana, Karna Counter Wells. With Fort Lupton Canning Co. (Colo.), 1934—, chmn. bd., 1956—, pres. 1972—. Mem. Fort Lupton Sch. Bd., 1940-41, Weld County (Colo.) Exec. Com., 1956—; pres. Weld County Bd. Health, 1952-61; sec. Platte Valley Soil Conservation Dist. Bd., 1957-59; adv. bd. Colo. State U. Served to maj. AUS, 1941-46. Decorated Bronze Star. Mem. Nat. Canners Assn. (dir.), Rocky Mountain Canners Assn. (pres. 1963), Old Guard Soc. (v.p. 1974, pres. 1975), Chemistry Club, Euclidean Club, Scabbard and Blade Am. Legion, VFW, Alpha Tau Omega. Republican. Methodist. Club: Rotary (pres. 1978). Contbr. articles to tech. publs. Home: PO Box 208 Fort Lupton CO 80621 Office: 511 McKinley Ave Fort Lupton CO 80621

COUPER, GRETA ELENA, project mgr., art historian; b. Santa Barbara, Calif., June 4, 1943; d. Clive Richard Hamilton and Louisa Victoria (Prill) Couper. B.A., UCLA, 1964; M.A., Smith Coll., 1965. Project leader Systems Devel. Corp., 1966-69; cons. Microspace, Van Nuys, Calif., 1969-70; mem. tech. staff TRW Systems, Redondo Beach, Calif., 1969-70; sr. systems analyst Inventory Mgmt. Systems, Brentwood, Calif., 1970-71; project mgr. Citicorp., Santa Monica, Calif., 1971—; cons. in areas of home banking design, mktg. research and mgmt. Recipient Zonta Club award in Math., 1962; Bus. and Profl. Women's Club award in Math., 1962. Mem. Am. Mktg. Assn., Women in Bus., Am. Soc. Interior Designers (assoc.), World Affairs Council, Los Angeles County Mus., Decorative Arts Council, Patrons of Italian Culture, Los Angeles Conservancy, John Paul Getty Mus. Author: The Works of Sculptor Thomas Ball, 1978; The Works of Sculptor William Couper, 1979. Office: 3100 Ocean Park Blvd Santa Monica CA 90405

COURCHENE, JOHN EDWARD, water utility executive; b. Seattle, Feb. 13, 1926; s. Percy Edmond and Mary Agnes (White) C.; m. Elaine Patricia Heath, Aug. 24, 1958; children—Mary Ann Courchene Chin, Christopher L., Michael E. B.S. in Biology, Seattle U., 1950, M.S. in Biology, 1953. Cert. water distbn. mgr. IV, Wash. Instr. Seattle U., 1952-53, asst. prof. biology, 1953-60; san. engr. Seattle Water Dept., 1960-65, dir. water quality, 1965—. Active Seattle council Boy Scouts Am., 1969-83. Served with USN, 1944-46. Recipient Activities award Pacific N.W. sect. Am. Water Works Assn., 1978. Mem. Am. Water Works Assn. (chmn. bd. trustees water quality div. 1982-83), Am. Soc. Microbiology, Seattle Mgmt. Assn. (bd. dirs. 1972-73). Roman Catholic. Contbr. numerous tech. articles to profl. jours. Home: 1622 N 51st St Seattle WA 98103 Office: Seattle Water Dept 1509 S Spokane St Seattle WA 98144

COURSEN, JEFFREY TYLER, electronic engineer; b. Bakersfield, Calif., Nov. 14, 1952; s. Marshall Edward and Sylvia C.; student Bakersfield Coll., 1970-72; B.S. in Electronic Engring. with highest honors, Calif. Poly. State U., 1976. Microwave test engr. Microwave Test Facility, Rockwell Internat., Lamont, Calif., 1976-78, test supr., quality assurance engr. Collins Communications Systems div., Santa Ana, Calif., 1978—. Recipient Phys. Sci. award Bakersfield Coll., 1972; FCC amateur radio operator. Mem. Am. Soc. Quality Control (cert. quality engr.), Creation Sci. Assn. Orange County, Calif. Scholarship Fedn. (life), Phi Kappa Phi. Republican. Baptist. Home: PO Box 1881 Huntington Beach CA 92647 Office: 3731 W Warner Ave Santa Ana CA 92704

COURT, ARNOLD, climatologist; b. Seattle, June 20, 1914; s. Nathan Altshiller and Sophie (Ravitch) C.; B.A., U. Okla., 1934; postgrad. U. Wash., 1938, M.S., 1949; Ph.D., U. Calif., Berkeley, 1956; m. Corinne H. Feibelman, May 27, 1941; children—David, Lois, Ellen. Reporter, city editor Duncan (Okla.) Banner, 1935-38; observer, meteorologist U.S. Weather Bur., Albuquerque, Washington, Little Am., Los Angeles, 1938-43, chief meteorologist U.S. Antarctic Service, 1939-41, recipient Spl. Congressional medal, 1944; climatologist Office Q.M. Gen., U.S. Army, Washington, 1946-51; research meteorologist U. Calif., Berkeley, 1951-56; meteorologist U.S. Forest Service, Berkeley, 1956-60; chief applied climatology Cambridge Research Labs., U.S. Air Force, Bedford, Mass., 1960-62; sr. scientist Lockheed-Calif. Co., Burbank, 1962-65; prof. climatology, dept. geography San Fernando Valley State Coll., (became Calif. State U. 1972), Northridge, Calif., 1962—, chmn. dept., 1970-72. Served to 1st lt. USAAF, 1943-46. Fellow Am. Meteorol. Soc., AAAS, Royal Meteorol. Soc.; mem. Am. Geophys. Union, Am. Statis. Assn., Assn. Am. Geographers, Assn. Pacific Coast Geographers (pres. 1978-79), Bernouilli Soc. for Math. Stats. and Probability, Calif. Council for Geog. Edn., Weather Modification Assn. (trustee 1973-76), Western Snow Conf., Phi Beta Kappa, Sigma Xi. Contbr. articles, revs., notes in field to profl. jours. Editor: Eclectic Cimatology, 1968; asso. editor Jour. Applied Meteorology, 1978—; chmn. editorial bd. Jour. Weather Modification, 1978—. Home: 17168 Septo St Northridge CA 91325 Office: Dept Geography Calif State U Northridge CA 91330

COURTIS, WILLIAM STUART, biologist, foundry exec., educator; b. Detroit, May 31, 1937; s. Joseph Weber and Martha Francis (Eurich) C.; B.S., U. Miami, 1960, M.S., 1964; Ph.D., So. Ill. U., 1972; 1 dau., Lorraine Elizabeth. Mus. asst. U. Miami, 1955-58, lab. asst., 1958-61, research asst., 1961-64; grad. research asst. So. Ill. U., 1964-65, HEW trainee, 1965-68, teaching asst., 1968-70, instr. zoology, 1970-71; instr. biology Ind. U.-Purdue U., Indpls., 1971-72, asst. prof., 1972-78; staff biologist Am. Village Inst., Marcus, Wash., 1978-80; owner, researcher Phoenix Foundry, Marcus; instr. biology Colville Community Coll., 1980—. Chief, Marcus (Wash.) Vol. Fire Dept. Mem. AAAS, Sigma Xi. Contbr. articles to profl. jours.; patentee in field. Home: 912 Minter Ave Marcus WA 99151 Office: 1110 Overlook Blvd Marcus WA 99151

COURTRIGHT, MORRIS, JR., engineering company executive, state legislator; b. Saginaw, Mich., May 2, 1930; s. Morris Alexander and Helen Esther (Gould) C.; B.S., U. Colo., 1963; m. Phyllis J. Jones, Mar. 1, 1952; children—Helen Courtright Bates, Patricia Courtright Blackman, Pamela Courtright Heyer, Michael, Deborah Courtright Schreiber, Elaine Courtright Ruffconn, Eileen Courtright Hernandez, David, Gregory, Kathleen, Brenda. Photographer, salesman Wright's Studio, Midland, Mich., 1944-50; commd. officer USAF, 1950, advanced through grades to maj., 1966, ret. 1971; cons. engr., pres. Courtright Engring., Inc., Yuma, Ariz., 1971—. Dist. mgr. broadcast div. Rockwell Internat./Collins Radio, Dallas, 1972-79; cons. engring. dept. No. Ariz. U., Flagstaff, 1971-73. Fire chief Doney Park Fire Dept., Flagstaff, 1971-74; planning and zoning commr. Coconino County, 1972-74; mem. Yuma City Bd. Appeals, 1975-78; mem. Ariz. Ho. of Reps., 1979-82. Registered profl. engr., Ariz., N.Mex., Fla., Calif., Tex. Mem. Nat. Soc. Profl. Engrs. (sec., treas. 1972-74), IEEE, Soc. Broadcast Engrs. (nat. dir. 1977-81), VFW. Club: KC (fin. sec. 1972-73, 76-82, grand knight 1973-74, dist. dep. 1974-76, 77-78, faithful nav. 1975-76, state adv. 1982). Automation editor: Broadcast Engring. Mag., 1968-73; facilities editor Broadcast Communications mag., 1979-83; contbr. articles to profl. engrs. Home and office: 1450 W Arroyo Dr Yuma AZ 85364

COURTWRIGHT, DELIGHT ELIZABETH, editor; b. Winnemucca, Nev., Feb. 19, 1928; d. George Blackburn and Aloise Emma (Hawley) Williams; student San Francisco City Coll., Golden Gate Coll., U. Calif., San Francisco; m. Kenneth Petz (dec.); m. Mr. Courtwright (dec.); children—Denise Elizabeth Willson, Daniel John Petz. Reporter, editor Solano Republican, Fairchild, Calif., 1954-56; writer, broadcaster Armed Forces Network Radio, Morocco, 1956-57; copywriter, account exec. Sta. KMEN, continuity dir. Sta. KCHU-TV, San Bernardino, Calif., 1962-64; with Overseas Weekly, Frankfurt, Ger., 1964-66; account exec. Bozell & Jacobs, Inc., Phoenix, 1966-72; statewide public relations dir. Rossmor Ariz. Devel. Co., Phoenix, 1972-73; editor trade newsletter, promotions mgr. Phoenix mag., 1974—, asst. to pub.; now mng. editor Ariz. Living mag., Phoenix. Mem. Phoenix Mayor's Com. for Bicentennial; mem. media adv. com. ARC, March of Dimes; active Cancer Crusade, 1980-81; founder, pres. women's network Bosom Buddies. Mem. Phoenix Advt. Club, Nat. Acad. TV Arts and Scis., Am. Women in Radio and TV, Public Relations Soc. Am. Republican. Editor Phoenix Advt. Newsletter, 1981-83. editor; b. Winnemucca, Nev., Feb. 19, 1928; d. George Blackburn and Aloise Emma (Hawley) Williams; student San Francisco City Coll., Golden Gate Coll., U. Calif., San Francisco; m. Kenneth Petz (dec.); m. Mr. Courtwright (dec.); children—Denise Elizabeth Willson, Daniel John Petz. Reporter, editor Solano Republican, Fairchild, Calif., 1954-56; writer, broadcaster Armed Forces Network Radio, Morocco, 1956-57; copywriter, account exec. Sta. KMEN, continuity dir. Sta. KCHU-TV, San Bernardino, Calif., 1962-64; with Overseas Weekly, Frankfurt, Ger., 1964-66; account exec. Bozell & Jacobs, Inc., Phoenix, 1966-72; statewide public relations dir. Rossmor Ariz. Devel. Co., Phoenix, 1972-73; editor trade newsletter, promotions mgr. Phoenix mag., 1974—, asst. to pub.; now mng. editor Ariz. Living mag., Phoenix. Mem. Phoenix Mayor's Com. for Bicentennial; mem. media adv. com. ARC, March of Dimes; active Cancer Crusade, 1980-81; founder, pres. women's network Bosom Buddies. Mem. Phoenix Advt. Club, Nat. Acad. TV Arts and Scis., Am. Women in Radio and TV, Public Relations Soc. Am. Republican. Editor Phoenix Advt. Newsletter, 1981-83. Home: 1926 E Colter St Phoenix AZ 85016 Office: 5046 N 7th St Suite C Phoenix AZ 85014

COUSINS, ANN VICTORIA, aerospace company official; b. Glastonbury, Eng., Mar. 11, 1947; d. Richard Michael and Edith Bessie (Dixon) Sellens; m. William Russell Cousins, Nov. 26, 1981. Student Holy Names Coll., Oakland, Calif., 1965-67; B.A. in Humanities, Russell Coll., 1970; M.S. in Adminstrn., Calif. State U.-Dominguez Hills, 1980. Tchr., adminstr. Mercy High Sch., Burlingame, Calif., 1969-72; tchr., athletic dir. St. Bernard High Sch., Playa Del Rey, Calif., 1973-77; with Space and Communications Group, Hughes Aircraft Co., El Segundo, Calif., 1977—, supr. group support services, 1978-79, supr. mail services, 1979-80, head operating services, 1980—; instr. indsl. edn. Govt. Ednl. Center, Los Angeles, 1980-83. Co-chmn. Inglewood 902 Postal Customer Council, 1981-83. Mem. Nat. Assn. Fleet Adminstrs. Club: Toastmasters (gov. dist. 1 Los Angeles area). Office: PO Box 92919 S22/E316 Los Angeles CA 90009

COUZENS, JOHN KEITH, agrl. engr.; b. Boise, Idaho, Apr. 18, 1944; s. Samuel O. and Lois Myrtle (Jones) C.; B.S. in Agrl. Engring., U. Idaho, 1967, M.S., 1969; m. Wanda Beth Bevan, Aug. 19, 1972. With N.Mex. Div. Water Resources, and predecessor, Santa Fe, 1971-81, water resource engr. specialist, chief hydrology sect., 1979-81; sr. hydrologist Phillips Uranium Corp., Albuquerque, 1981; sr. water resources engr. Phillips Petroleum Co., Denver, 1981—. NDEA fellow, 1968-71; registered profl. engr., N.Mex., Colo. Mem. Am. Soc. Agrl. Engrs., Am. Geophys. Assn., Nat. Water Well Assn., Colo. Ground Water Assn., Sigma Xi, Alpha Epsilon, Alpha Zeta. Mem. Ch. of Nazarene. Author papers in field. Home: 16092 E Loyola Pl Aurora CO 80013 Office: 8055 E Tufts Ave Pkwy Denver CO 80237

COVARRUBIAS, MARIA MABI, city clk.; b. Oxnard, Calif., Nov. 16, 1953; d. Jose Manuel and Maria del Socorro (Ponce) C.; grad. Sawyer Coll., 1972. Legal sec. law firm Holt, Taylor & McCord, Ventura, Calif., 1972-74; legal sec. law firm Richard Hanawalt, Oxnard, Calif., 1975-76; clk. stenographer City of Oxnard, 1976-77, dep. city clk., 1977-80, city clk., 1980—. Mem., Oxnard Sister City Com., 1980—, dir., 1981-82, 83-84). Mem. Mexican-Am. C. of C., Oxnard C. of C., (sec. women's div. 1980), Ventura County Legal Secs. Assn., Internat. Inst. Mcpl. Clks., Calif. City Clks.' Assn., Ventura County City Clks. Assn., So. Calif. City Clks. Assn. Roman Catholic (sec. women's council 1982—). Office: 305 W 3d St Oxnard CA 93030

COVELL, JOSEPH SYLVESTER, mgmt. cons.; b. Wilkes-Barre, Pa., June 22, 1911; s. John Joseph and Marie (Bogdan) Koval; A.B., Pa. State U., 1933; postgrad. Sch. Bus., Columbia, 1934-35, Franklin U. Law Sch., 1938-39; m. Carlyn Sessler Goldsmith, Oct. 13, 1934 (div. Aug. 1949); children—Carl John, Gerald Edward; m. 2d, Lillian Erbe Taubel, Sept. 21, 1955 (dec. Nov. 1958). Sec., Bus. Jour., Wilkes-Barre, Pa., 1932; with Gen. Electric Co., Schenectady and N.Y.C., 1933-46; owner Joseph S. Covell and Assos., 1946-49; founder mgmt., engring. design and systems cons. firm J. Sylvester Covell & Assos., 1950-58; with Internat. Latex Co., Dover, Del., 1949-50; with George S. May Co., N.Y.C., 1958-62; pvt. cons., 1963; founder, editor, pub. N.Mex. Legionnaire, Albuquerque, 1967-70, N.M. Food and Beverage News, Albuquerque, 1963-67; mgmt. cons., dir. advt. N.Mex., Transporter publ. of N.Mex. Motor Carriers Assn., 1970—; now exec. supr. George S. May Internat. Co.; pub. relations and advt. dir. N.Mex. Banker mag., 1972-73; lectr. in field. Former nat. cons. Nat. Citizens Com. for the Hoover Report; bd. dirs. New Mexicans for Improvement Jud. System. Mem. Toastmasters Internat. (Distinguished Toastmaster award, mem. Hall of Fame), Albuquerque Press Club. Elk, Moose. Club: Edelweiss Am Rio Grande German American (Albuquerque). Contbr. articles to profl. jours. Home: 2720 Pennsylvania NE Albuquerque NM 87110

COVEN, BERDEEN EDYTHE, human resource specialist; b. Portland, Oreg., July 24, 1941; d. Sylvan Stanley and Helen Lillus (Wolfman) Saperstein; m. Lee Coven, May 5, 1962; children—Cynthia, Andrew. B.A., San Jose State U., 1965; M.A., U. Santa Clara, 1976. Lic. marriage, family and child counselor. With Calif. Youth Authority, Santa Clara, 1975-77; tchr. Gavilan Community Coll., Gilroy, Calif., 1977; career devel. specialist Four-Phase Systems, Inc., Cupertino, Calif., 1978-82; pvt. practice marriage and family counseling, Cupertino, 1975—; cons. Good Life Clinic, Mountain View, Calif., 1982-83; condr. seminars. Mem. Mayor's Task Force on Condos and Townhouses, Cupertino, 1978. Mem. Calif. Assn. Marriage, Family and Child Counselors, Am. Personnel and Guidance Assn., Am. Soc. Tng. and Devel., Employee Resources Group, Assn. Labor Mgmt. Adminstrs., Cons.'s on Alcoholism.

COVEY, ROBERT EUGENE, engr.; b. Pasadena, Calif., Dec. 10, 1927; s. Howell Eugene and Dorothy Margaret (Collins) C.; A.A. in Engring., Pasadena City Coll., 1949; B.S. in Mech. Engring., Calif. Inst. Tech., 1951, M.S. in Aero. Engring., 1952; P.E., Carnegie-Mellon U., 1970; m. Joyce L. Hanson, June 30, 1951; children—Alan Reed, Janis Lorraine, Paul Robert. Test engr. Jet Propulsion Lab., Calif. Inst. Tech., Pasadena, 1952-54, ops. engr., 1954-56, supr. wind tunnel ops., 1956-60, asst. chief wind tunnels and environ. facilities, 1960-61, mgr. aerodynamic facilities sect., 1961-64, mgr. space simulators and facility engring., 1964-65, dep. div. mgr. environ. sci. div., 1965-71, mgr. affirmative action program, 1971-72, dep. mgr. applied mechanics div., 1972-76, mgr. electronic parts engring., 1976—, chmn. mission assurance conf., 1980. Pres., La Canada coordinating council, troop chmn., advisor explorer posts Boy Scouts Am.; chmn. various civic action coms. Served with U.S. Army, 1946-48. Recipient Calif. scholarship fedn. award, 1949, outstanding graduating student engr. award, 1949, Los Angeles County Community Service award, 1979; named So. Calif. Engr. of Month, 1962. Asso. fellow AIAA (chmn. aerotesting conf. 1964, microprocessor conf. 1977); mem. Inst. Environ. Sci. (sr.), Space Parts Working Group, NASA Standard Parts Com., Am. Philatelic Soc., Studebaker Drivers Club, Calif. Hist. Vehicles Assn., First Mars Landing Soc. Author: Wind Tunnel Data Processing, 1964; contbr. articles to profl. publs. Home: 5007 Princess Anne Rd La Canada CA 91011 Office: 4800 Oak Grove Dr Pasadena CA 91109

COVINGTON, DONALD PATRICK, design educator, cons.; b. Dallas, Mar. 29, 1929; s. Loyd John and Dortha Kathleen (Dooley) C.; m. Karon Kay Kinnamon, Oct. 28, 1953; children—Lili Nanine Vidal, Milo Paul, Craig William, Matthew Evan. B.A., So. Meth. U., 1948-52; M.A., UCLA, 1957; student Study Centre Fine & Decorative Arts London, 1976. Assoc., UCLA, 1957-58; assoc. prof. Colo. State U., Ft. Collins, 1958-65; coordinator environ. design, prof. environ. design San Diego State U., 1965—; mem. accreditation com. Found. Interior Design Edn. and Research. Served with U.S. Army, 1953-55. Nat. Soc. Interior Designers Attingham fellow, 1973; Interior Design Educators Council fellow, 1980; San Diego State U. Faculty fellow, 1975. Mem. Interior Design Educators Council (cert.), Am. Soc. Interior Designers (cert.), Found. Interior Design Edn. and Research, Illuminating Engrs. Soc., Inst. Bus. Designers, Soc. Archtl. Historians. Contbr. articles to profl. jours.; mem. editorial bd. Jour. Interior Design Edn. and Research. Office: Dept Art San Diego State U San Diego CA 92182

COVITZ, CARL D., real estate and investment executive; b. Boston, Mar. 31, 1939; s. Edward E. and Barbara (Matthews) C.; m. Aviva Habert, May 15, 1970; children—Philip, Marc. B.S., Wharton Sch., U. Pa., 1960; M.B.A., Columbia U., 1962. Product mgr. Bristol-Myers Co., N.Y.C., 1962-66; dir. mktg. Rheingold Breweries, N.Y.C., 1966-68; nat. mktg. mgr. Can. Dry Corp., N.Y.C., 1968-70; v.p. mktg., dir. corp. devel. ITT/Levitt & Sons, Lake Success, N.Y., 1970-73; owner, pres. Landmark Communities, Inc., Beverly Hills, Calif., 1973—. Exec. com. Presl. Commn. Cost Control and Efficiency; co-chmn. Dept. Def. Task Force; chmn. ops. com. Mus. Contemporary Art Los Angeles; vice chmn. Los Angeles County Delinquency and Crime Commn.; dir. Columbia U. Grad. Bus. Sch. Alumni Assn. Mem. Young Pres. Orgn. Home: 818 Malcolm Ave Los Angeles CA 90024 Office: 9595 Wilshire Blvd Beverly Hills CA 90212

COWAN, GARY GLENN, financial executive; b. Ventura, Calif., Sept. 28, 1936; s. John F. and Phyllis M. (Dunn) C.; B.S., UCLA, 1959, M.B.A., 1960; m. Jo Ella A. Miller, June 16, 1956; children—Gregory Gavin, Joleen Aimee. Instr., UCLA, 1959; asso. Price Waterhouse & Co., C.P.A.'s, Los Angeles, 1960-63; treas. Networks Electronic Corp., Chatsworth, 1963-64; asst. controller, coordinator profit planning Tidewater Oil, Los Angeles, 1964-66; v.p. financial analysis and rev. Dart Industries Inc., Los Angeles, 1966-69, pres. Dart Properties div., 1969-73; exec. v.p. Coastland Corp., Virginia Beach, Va., 1973-77; sr. v.p., chief fin. officer Leisure Technology Corp., Lakewood, N.J., 1977-79; sr. v.p.-fin. and adminstrn. Superscope Inc., Chatsworth, Calif., 1979-81; sr. v.p. U.S. Vacation Resorts, Inc., Los Angeles, 1982—. Mem. Am. Inst. C.P.A.s. Home: 3714 Carbon Canyon Malibu CA 90265

COWAN, JOANN, accountant, computer programmer; b. Vernon, B.C., Can., Jan. 14, 1946; d. George Matthew and Bernadette Rita (Desmarais) C. B.A. in History, Stanford U., 1967. C.P.A., Wash. Student asst. Stanford U. Library, 1963-67; sec. Touche Ross & Co., Seattle, 1967-71; acct. Jacobson, Gattis & Lawrence, Seattle, 1971-74; acct. Gattis & Co., P.S., Seattle, 1974-81; owner, Gattis, Cowan & Co., P.S., Seattle, 1981—. Mem. Am. Inst. C.P.A.s, Wash. Soc. C.P.A.s, Am. Women's Soc. C.P.A.s. Office: 2001 Western Ave Suite 330 Seattle WA 98121

COWAN, LINDA GAIL, banker; b. Akron, Ohio, Feb. 2, 1952; d. James Robert and Ruth Geraldine (Akers) Blankenship; m. Jeffrey Roger Johnston, Sept. 14, 1974; m. Gerald Owen Cowan, June 20, 1981. B.A. in English, Westmont Coll., 1974. Teller, Barclays Bank, Santa Barbara, Calif., 1974-77, note teller, 1977-78, ops. officer, 1978-79; ops. officer Santa Barbara Bank and Trust, 1979-81, asst. v.p., mgr., 1981—. Mem. Nat. Assn. Bank Women, Montecito Area Bus. Council. Republican. Home: 1296 Las Manos Ln Santa Barbara CA 93109 Office: 1483 E Valley Rd Santa Barbara CA 93108

COWAN, ROBERT HARVEY, bldg. maintenance co. exec.; b. Fullerton, Calif., Feb. 26, 1946; s. James Henry and Helen Virginia (Croft) C.; A.A., Sierra Community Coll., 1965; B.A., Calif. State U., Sacramento, 1968, postgrad., 1968-71; diploma MTI Bus. Coll., 1971; m. Mary Ann Rittscher, Dec. 14, 1973; 1 son, Bryan Robert. Tchr. elementary sch., Roseville, Calif., 1968-71; electronic mechanic, guidance counselor, prodn. mgmt. specialist McClellan AFB, Calif., 1971-79; chief adminstrv. officer and pres. Buena Vista Maintenance, Roseville, Calif., 1980—. Active Boy Scouts Am. Decorated knight Imperial Order St. Eugene of Trebizonda Mem. Am. Coll. Heraldry, Ark. Geneal. Soc., Am. Motors Owners Assn., Aid Assn. Lutherans. Republican. Lutheran. Author: The Cowan Family, 1971. Home: PO Box 1127 Roseville CA 95678 Office: PO Box 1127 Roseville CA 95661

COWDEN, CHESTER LYLE, accountant; b. Cedar Rapids, Iowa, Oct. 6, 1917; s. James Fenimore and Beulah Hayes (Gilchrist) C.; m. Kathryn Roseanna Phillips, Mar. 21, 1943; children—James Franklin, Patricia Kathryn Cowden Seifert. B.S., U. Iowa, 1942, M.A., 1948. C.P.A., Iowa, Calif. Acting head cost dept., head br. factory ledger acct. Cherry-Burrell Corp., Cedar Rapids, Iowa, 1942-48; semi-sr. acct. Allen & Co., C.P.A.s, Des Moines, 1948-50; stores auditor, trainee fgn. asst. controllership Firestone Tire & Rubber Co., Des Moines, 1950-52; internal auditor Contra Costa County, Martinez, Calif., 1952-57; staff acct. Heruth-Thyken & Smith, 1954-55, Cowden and Koskinen, C.P.A.s, 1958-64, Cowden, Koskinen & Westenrider, C.P.A.s, 1964-65; pvt. practice acctg., Concord, Calif., 1965—. Mem. Am. Inst. C.P.A.s, Am. Acctg. Assn., Nat. Assn. Accts. (sec., dir. Oakland-East Bay chpt., Most Valuable mem. 1961-62, 63-64), Calif. Soc. C.P.A.s, Estate Planning Council Diablo Valley, Concord C. of C. (dir. 1962-65). Republican. Presbyterian. Clubs: Masons, Elks, Kiwanis (dir., treas., v.p.) (Concord, Calif.). Home: 4649 Benbow Ct Concord CA 94521 Office: 1875 Willow Pass Rd Suite 306 Concord CA 94520

COWEN, DONALD EUGENE, physician; b. Ft. Morgan, Colo., Oct. 8, 1918; adopted s. Franklin and Mary Edith (Dalton) C.; B.A., U. Denver, 1940; M.D., U. Colo., 1943; m. Hulda Marie Helling, Dec. 24, 1942; children—David L., Marilyn Marie Cowen Dean, Theresa Kathleen Cowen Cunningham, Margaret Ann. Intern, U.S. Naval Hosp., Oakland, Calif., 1944; gen. practice medicine, Ft. Morgan, 1947-52; resident internal medicine U. Colo. Med. Center, Denver, 1952-54; practice medicine specializing in allergy, Denver, 1954—; mem. staff Presbyn. Med. Center, Denver, Porter, Swedish hosps., Englewood, Colo.; clin. asst. prof. medicine U. Colo. Med. Center, 1964—; postgrad. faculty U. Tenn. Coll. Medicine, Memphis, 1962—; cons. Queen of Thailand, 1973, 75, 77. Pres. Community Arts Symphony Found., 1980-82. Served to lt. M.C., USN, 1943-47. Fellow ACP, Am. Coll. Chest Physicians (vice chmn. com. on allergy 1968-72, 75—, sec.-treas. Colo. chpt. 1971-77, pres. 1978-80), Am. Coll. Allergists, Am. Assn. Clin. Immunology and Allergy, Soc. Clin. Ecology (charter mem.), Acad. Internat. Medicine, West Coast Allergy Soc., Southwest Allergy Forum, Am. Acad. Otolaryngic Allergy; mem. Am. Soc. Opthalmologic and Otolaryngologic Allergy, Am., Colo. socs. internal medicine, Am. Thoracic Soc., Colo. Allergy Soc. (past pres.), Ill. Soc. Opthalmology and Otolaryngology (hon.), Denver Med. Soc. (chmn. library and bldg. com. 1963-73). Presbyterian (ruling elder 1956—). Club: Lions. Contbr. numerous articles to profl. jours. Home: 1501 E Quincy Ave Cherry Hills Village Englewood CO 80110 Office: 3510 S Marion St Englewood CO 80110

COWLES, JEANNINE BOUCHARD, personal services co. exec.; b. Memphis, Oct. 14, 1928; d. Horace Louis and Melissa Oldham (Boyd) Bouchard; student Phila. Acad. Vocal Arts, 1948-51, Hartt Coll. Music, 1963-65; 1 dau. by previous marriage, Ann. Singer, actress, Broadway, summer stock, opera, 1951-67; mem. Am. Opera Co., Phila., then Hartt Opera Theatre, Hartford; pres., chief exec. officer Weight Watchers of Oreg., Inc., Portland, 1969—. Mem. Portland Met. Performing Arts Theatre Task Force, 1976-77, City of Portland Downtown Housing Adv. Com., 1978-79; bd. dirs. Portland Opera Assn., 1973-79, chmn. personnel com., 1977-78. Mem. Portland C. of C. (chmn. cultural resources com. 1976-77, dir. 1977-80), Women's Advt. Club (dir. 1977-78). Episcopalian. Club: Multnomah Athletic. Home: 2221 SW 1st Ave Portland OR 97201 Office: 9200 Barnes Rd SW Portland OR 97225

COWLES, WILLIAM HUTCHINSON, 3D, newspaper pub.; b. Spokane, Wash., Mar. 4, 1932; s. William Hutchinson and Margaret (Paine) C.; B.A., Yale U., 1953; J.D., Harvard U., 1959; m. Allison Stacey, Mar. 28, 1959; children—William Stacey, Elizabeth Allison. Bar: Wash. 1959. Pres., pub. Cowles Pub. Co. (pubs. The Spokesman-Rev., Spokane Chronicle), N.W. Farmer-Stockman, Inc. (pubs. Wash. Farmer-Stockman, Oreg. Farmer-Stockman, Idaho Farmer-Stockman, Utah Farmer-Stockman), Spokane, 1970—, Mont. Farmer-Stockman, Inc. (pubs. Mont. Farmer-Stockman), Billings 1970—; v.p., dir. Inland Empire Paper Co., Millwood, Wash., 1964—; dir. AP, 1974-83, 1st vice chmn., 1982-83. Bd. dirs. United Crusade of Spokane County, 1963—, pres., 1970; bd. dirs. Inland Empire council Boy Scouts Am., 1960—, Spokane Symphony Soc., 1961-78; bd. overseers Whitman Coll., 1966—. Served to lt. USNR, 1953-56. Mem. Am. Soc. Newspaper Editors, Am. Newspaper Pubs. Assn. (dir. 1980—), Newspaper Advt. Bur. (dir. 1968—, chmn. 1978-80), Allied Daily Newspapers (dir. 1970-71, pres. 1972-74), Beta Theta Pi, Sigma Delta Chi. Club: Spokane. Office: The Spokesman-Review Spokane WA 99210

COWLEY, GERALD DEAN, architect; b. Great Bend, Kans., Oct. 2, 1931; s. Stone Oden and Elizabeth (Lillach) C.; student Fort Hays State Coll., 1955-57; B.Arch., Kans. State U., 1960; m. Lois Esther Traudt, Aug. 10, 1957; children—Tara Elizabeth, Craig Stone. Project architect, assoc. Johnson/Hopson & Assocs., architects, planners, Denver, 1963-74; partner, prin. Johnson/Hopson & Ptnrs., 1974—. Served with USAF, 1951-55. Mem. AIA, Constrn. Specifications Inst. Home: 10855 N Polar Ln NW Douglas County Chatfield Lake Littleton CO 80125 Office: 3400 E Bayaud Ave Denver CO 80209

COWLEY, JOHN MAXWELL, physics educator; b. Peterborough, South Australia, Feb. 18, 1923; s. Alfred Ernest and Doris (Milway) C.; B.Sc., U. Adelaide (Australia), 1942, M.Sc., 1945, D.Sc., 1957; Ph.D., Mass. Inst. Tech., 1949; m. Roberta Joan Beckett, Dec. 15, 1951; children—Deborah Suzanne, Jillian Patricia. Came to U.S., 1970. Research officer Commonwealth Sci. and Indsl. Research Orgn., Melbourne, Australia, 1945-62, chief research officer, head crystallography sect., 1960-62; prof. physics U. Melbourne (Australia), 1962-70; Galvin prof. physics Ariz. State U., Tempe, 1970—. Mem. U.S. Nat. Com. for Crystallography, 1973-78. Fellow Australian Acad. Sci., Inst. Physics (London), Australian Inst. Physics, Royal Soc. (London); mem. Internat. Union Crystallography (mem. exec. com. 1963-69), Am. Inst. Physics, Am. Crystallographic Assn., Electron Microscope Soc. Am. (dir. 1971-75). Author: Diffraction Physics, 1975. Editor: (with others) Acta Crystallographica, 1971-80. Contbr. articles to profl. jours. Office: Dept Physics Ariz State Univ Tempe AZ 85281

COX, BENJAMIN VINCENT, elec. engr.; b. Chgo., Jan. 25, 1934; s. Benjamin and Lorretta Deloris (Jozwiak) C.; B.S. in Elec. Engring., U. Utah, 1963, M.S., 1969, Ph.D., 1979; m. Mary Patricia Mitchell, Apr. 18, 1959; children—Linda Marie, Stephen Martin. With Sperry Univac Co., 1963-73, 74—, staff engr., 1974-78, engring. mgr., advanced research and devel., prin. staff cons., Salt Lake City, 1978—; engring. dir. Naval Civil Engring. Lab., Port Hueneme, Calif., 1973-74; adj. prof. U. Utah. Served with U.S. Army, 1954-57. Mem. AIAA (council Utah chpt. 1980-81), IEEE, Am. Def. Preparedness Assn., Air Force Assn., Assn. Old Crows. Author papers, reports in field. Home: 2760 E Blue Spruce Dr Salt Lake City UT 84117 Office: 640 E 2200 West Salt Lake City UT 84116

COX, CATHLEEN RUTH, zoologist, educator; b. Vallejo, Calif., Oct. 20, 1948; d. Charles W. and Betty A. (Born) Cox; B.A., U. Calif.-San Diego, 1970, Ph.D., Stanford U., 1976; m. Robert A. Pugsley, Mar. 18, 1978. Postdoctoral fellow Am. Mus. Natural History, N.Y.C., 1976-78; research assoc. Barnard Coll., N.Y.C., 1978-79; research zoologist UCLA, 1979-82; asst. prof. Calif. State U.-Northridge, 1980—; dir. research Los Angeles Zoo, 1981—. Recipient W.C. Allee award Animal Behavior Soc., 1976; NSF research grantee, 1978. Mem. Assn. Women in Sci. (exec. bd. Los Angeles chpt.), Am. Assn. Zool. Parks and Aquaria, Am. Ornithol. Union, Animal Behavior Soc., Am. Primatol. Soc. Contbr. articles to profl. jours. Office: 5333 Zoo Dr Los Angeles CA 90027

COX, CLARK BURGESS, dentist; b. St. George, Utah, Feb. 23, 1929; s. Emerald Lane and Elsie (Burgess) C.; Asso. Sci., Dixie Jr. Coll., 1949; D.D.S., U. So. Calif., 1953; m. Donna Anderson, July 15, 1949; children—David C., Craig E., Suzanne, Dianne, Gary L., Cynthia. Practice dentistry, Delta, Utah, 1955—; v.p. Habb Corp., Delta, 1962—, Cox Trucking Inc., Delta, 1976—; farmer, livestock rancher, 1960—; dir. Del-Tex Corp., Oasis Seed Corp.; partner Fransworth-Cox Real Estate; vice chmn. W. Millard Soil Conservation Service, 1970-76. City councilman, Delta, 1968-76, mem. bd. adjustment, 1978—. Served with Dental Corps, AUS, 1953-55. Mem. Acad. Gen. Dentistry, Am., Utah, Provo Dist. dental assns., Brigham Young U. Acad. Dentists (charter), Alpha Tau Epsilon, Psi Omega. Mem. Ch. Jesus Christ of Latter-day Saints (Delta 2d ward bishopric 1962-65, high councilor Delta West stake). Home: 173 N 300th St W Delta UT 84624 Office: Hobb Bldg Main St Delta UT 84624

COX, ENID ELAINE, home economist; b. Eugene, Oreg., Feb. 28, 1935; d. James Artie and Bessie Agnes (Foster) Tanner; student Central Oreg. Coll., 1956; B.S., Oreg. State U., 1958, M.S., 1964; m. Manuel Ernest Cox, Jan. 7, 1950; children—Kathryn A., Carol A. Tchr. vocat. homemaking, chmn. dept. Scappoose (Oreg.) High Sch., 1958-67; instr. home econs. Marylhurst (Oreg.) Coll., 1967-68; coop. ext. agt. Wash. State U., Pullman, 1968; ext. agt. 4-H youth Clark County, Wash., 1968-75, home economist, 1975-82; coop. extension agt., home economist Walla Walla County (Wash.), 1982—. Mem. Nat. Elec. Women's Round Table (bd. dirs., chmn. Oreg. chpt. 1978-79), Nat. Extension Home Economists Assn., Blue Mountain Home Econs. Assn. (pres. 1982-83), Am. Econs. Assn., Wash. Home Econs. Assn. (sec. 1983—). Lutheran. Clubs: Daughters of Pioneers of Wash., Scappoose Woman's (past pres.). Home: 309 W Alder St Walla Walla WA 99362 Office: 314 W Main St Walla Walla WA 99362

COX, EXUM MORRIS, investment company executive; b. Santa Rosa, Calif., Feb. 5, 1903; s. Exum Morris and Mary Eleanor (Anderson) C.; A.B., U. Calif., 1924; M.B.A., Harvard U., 1928; m. Elsie Margaret Storke, Sept. 6, 1934; children—Cynthia Cox Huntting, Susana More Cox Fousekis, Thomas Storke. With firm Dodge & Cox, 1933—, partner, 1933-59, pres., 1959-72, chmn., 1972-77, hon. chmn., 1977—; chmn. bd. Dodge & Cox Balanced Fund, 1933-80, trustee, 1980—; dir. Dodge & Cox Stock Fund. Mem. Calif. Delinquency Prevention Commn., 1963-67; mem. San Francisco Library Commn., 1963-64; vice chmn. Citizens Adv. Com. to Atty. Gen. Calif. on Crime Prevention, 1954-58; bd. dirs., v.p. Community Chest San Francisco, 1946-48; bd. dirs. San Francisco Tb Assn., 1948-52, Bay Area Ednl. TV Assn. (KQED), 1961-70; trustee San Francisco Mus. Contemporary Art, pres., 1955-60; trustee Katherine Branson Sch., 1950-57; trustee U. Calif. Berkeley Found., 1972—, v.p., 1974-77, pres., 1977-79; trustee U. Calif. Hastings Law Center Found., 1974—, pres., 1980—. Mem. Investment Counsel Assn. Am. (gov. 1955-58, 61-67), Calif. Acad. Scis. (trustee 1961-73, chmn. bd. trustees 1967-73, treas. 1963-67), Sigma Chi. Clubs: Bohemian, Pacific-Union, Bankers; Anglers (N.Y.C.). Home: 2361 Broadway San Francisco CA 94115 Office: 3500 Crocker Plaza San Francisco CA 94104

COX, HUGH LENNEOUS, mech., aero. engr.; b. Greensboro, N.C., Jan. 8, 1928; s. Basil Sebastian and Mabel (Moffitt) C.; B.C.E., N.C. State U., 1949; M.S., U. Ill., 1952, Ph.D., 1953; m. Chrissa Middleton, Aug. 31, 1979; children—Craig Albert, Carmen Elisa. Exec. v.p. Structure Specialties Corp., Santa Monica, Calif., 1956-57; cons. Kirk Engring. Co., Los Angeles, 1957-59; cons. engr. H. L. Cox & Assos., Littleton, Colo., 1959-66; chief advanced ground systems Martin Marietta Corp., Denver, 1959-69; chmn. bd., pres. Electroculture Corp., Denver, 1969—; prof. U. Ala., 1955; cons. aero., aerospace and mech. engring. Served with AUS, 1954-56. Mem. Am. Inst. Aeros. and Astronautics, Aircraft Owners and Pilots Assn., Sigma Xi, Tau Beta Pi, Phi Eta Sigma, Phi Kappa Phi. Club: Pinehurst Country (Denver). Contbr. articles to profl. jours. Home: 2880 S Locust 705 N Denver CO 80222 Office: 3025 S Parker Rd Aurora CO 80014

COX, JIM DALE, gen. contracting co. exec.; b. Harris, Mo., Nov. 24, 1931; s. John Clarence and Helen LuVern (Holiday) C.; A.A. in Indsl. Mgmt., Independence (Kans.) Jr. Coll., 1951; B.S. in Real Estate and Constrn., U. Denver, 1956, M.B.A. in Fin., 1970; m. Joan Gregerson Green, Mar. 14, 1980; children—Susan J., John H., Charles Green, Andrea Geeen. Gen. mgr. Hopkins Mfg. Co., 1951-53, Shepard Constrn. Co., 1957-60; pres. Cox Constrn. Co., Colorado Springs, Colo., 1960-70, Village Contractors, Inc., Colorado Springs, 1980—; ptnr. SCS Co., constrn. mgmt., Colorado Springs, 1970—, Village Cos., Colorado Springs, 1972-80; dir. First Bank Colorado Springs, Colo. Western Properties, Denver; lectr. U. Denver, 1965—. Mem. El Paso County Courthouse Com., 1969-72, Colo. Small Bus. Council; vice chmn. Colorado Springs Contractors Bd., 1964-65; chmn. Colorado Springs Fire Bd., 1979—. Mem. Home Builders Assn. Met. Colorado Springs (pres. 1963-64), Colorado Springs C. of C. Republican. Episcopalian. Clubs: El Paso, Garden of Gods, Country of Colo., Jaguar Clubs N. Am., U. Denver Pikes Peak Alumni (pres.). Home: 52 Polo Dr Colorado Springs CO 80906 Office: 518 N Nevada Ave Suite 220 Colorado Springs CO 80903

COX, LARRY GLEN, engineering and construction company executive; b. Pampa, Tex., Jan. 16, 1938; s. Odis and Dorothy Izela (Woods) C.; B.S., U.S. Naval Acad., 1960; children—Terri, David. Commd. ensign, U.S. Navy, 1960, advanced through grades to lt. comdr.; with Polaris Nuclear Submarine Service, 1960-69; engr., mgr. prodn. ops. Exxon Gas System, King Ranch Gas Plant, Gulf Coast, Tex., 1969-76; mem. mgmt. staff Prudhoe Bay Prodn. Facilities Project, Pasadena, Calif., div. supervising engr., 1976-79; v.p. ops. Williams Instrument Co., Inc. and partner U.S.A. Industries, Inc., Valencia, Calif., 1979-81; prin. project mgr. The Ralph M. Parsons Co., Pasadena, Calif., 1981-82; pres., partner Chem. Treatment Products, Inc., Valencia, 1982—. . Active Boy Scouts Am.; elder 1st Presbyterian Ch., Newhall, Calif. Registered profl. engr., Tex. Mem. ASME, Calif. Export Mgrs. Assn., Soc. Petroleum Engrs., Pacific Energy Assn., Pacific Coast Gas Assn. Club: Rotary. Home: 16944 W Shinedale Dr Canyon Country CA 91351 Office: 100 W Walnut St Pasadena CA 91124

COX, LYLE ASHTON, physicist; b. Atchison, Kans., Nov. 16, 1921; s. George King and Jessie Viola (Prather) C.; m. Jane Leecraft, Mar. 1, 1947; 1 son, Lyle A. B.S., U.S. Naval Acad., 1944; M.S. in Physics, MIT, 1953. Commd. ensign U.S. Navy, 1944, advanced through grades to comdr., 1960; served on U.S.S. Enterprise, 1944-45; student aviator, Corpus Christi, Tex., Pensacola, Fla., 1946-47; naval aviator, naval ordnance engr., Norfolk, Va., and other bases, 1947-64; physicist and dep. assoc. dir. Lawrence Livermore Nat. Lab., U. Calif., 1964—. Mem. AIAA, Sigma Xi. Republican. Club: Commonwealth of Calif. Home: 569 Escondido Circle Livermore CA 94550 Office: Lawrence Livermore Nat Lab U Calif Livermore CA 94550

COX, MARCUS BUD, educational administrator; b. Miami, Ariz., Aug. 5, 1944; s. Bud and Mildred (Bell) C.; m. June Arlene Milne, June 26, 1971; children—John David, Arlene Rebecca. B.A. in Elem. and Spl. Edn., U. Ariz., 1969, M.Ed. in Counseling and Guidance, 1977, M.Ed. in Ednl. Adminstrn., 1979. Tchr. Savannah Sch. Dist., Anaheim, Calif., 1969-71, Coolidge (Ariz.) Unified Schs., 1971-78, supr. counselor, dir. Indian edn., 1978-79, asst. prin., 1979-82; elem. sch. prin. Casa Grande (Ariz.) Elem. Dist. 4, 1982—. Scoutmaster Boy Scouts Am., 1974-75; coach Little League, 1982—. Mem. Ariz. Sch. Administrs., Nat. Assn. Elem. Sch. Prins., Am. Ednl. Research Assn. Republican. Roman Catholic. Club: Lions Internat. Co-author physical edn. handbook, special edn. plan. Home: 1143 Mesquite Ln Coolidge AZ 95228 Office: 501 S Florence St Casa Grande AZ 85222

COX, MILLICENT ANN, social scientist, researcher, educator; b. Pasadena, Calif., Sept. 5, 1944; d. Richard Horton and Hester Virginia (Smith) C.; m. Larry J. Kimbell, Aug. 24, 1974; 1 son, Richard Sterling. B.A., NYU, 1966; M.A. Claremont Grad. Sch., 1968; Ph.D., U. So. Calif., 1975. Research asst. U. Wash., Seattle, 1968; economist Bank Am., Los Angeles, 1969; planning asst. Los Angeles County, 1970; research asst. U. So. Calif., Los Angeles, 1971, project dir., 1972-75, instr., 1973-80; social scientist RAND Corp., Santa Monica, 1975—; cons. various Los Angeles govt. agys.; instr. Bellevue (Wash.) Community Coll. Bd. dirs. Ctr. for New Corp. Priorities, 1973-79; chmn. Los Angeles Sch. Monitoring Com., 1979-80; corp. mem. Am. Friends Service Com., 1975—. NDEA Title IV fellow, 1966; recipient Founder's Day award NYU, 1965; Mem. Am. Econ. Assn., Western Econ. Assn., Phi Beta Kappa. Democrat. Quaker. Contbr. articles to profl. jours. Home: 2731 Woodshire Dr Los Angeles CA 90068 Office: 1700 Main St Santa Monica CA 90406

COX, MILO LAWSON, educator; b. Denison, Tex., Aug. 27, 1916; s. Milo Rockwell and Effie Maude (Price) C.; student U. Tex., 1935-37; B.S., Tex. A&M U., 1941; M.S. (Aksarben scholar), U. Nebr., 1955, Ph.D., 1957, Ph.D. (hon.), 1976; postgrad. Johns Hopkins U., 1962; m. Thelma Ann Thomson, Nov. 24, 1942; children—Karen Ann, Kelly Brent. Ecologist, Tex. State Govt., 1940-41, 46-48; aquatic biologist Lake Improvement Co., 1948-49; ecologist Tex. Research Found., 1949-51; asst. prof. U. Nebr., 1954-57; agrl. devel. specialist AID, Asia, Africa, S. Am., 1957-75; prof. Sch. Renewable Natural Resources, U. Ariz., Tucson, 1975—; remote sensing DIA/NASA; cons. AID, Brookings Instn., NSF, Nat. Acad. Sci., Dept. State, Rockefeller Found. Served as pilot U.S. Navy, 1941-46. Recipient sr. faculty award Fgn.

Service Inst., Dept. State., 1973. Mem. Am. Soc. Agronomy, Range Mgmt. Soc. Roman Catholic. Author: A Simplified Approach to Agricultural Systems, 1979; contbr. chpts. to books, articles to profl. jours. Home: 3356 E 5th Tucson AZ 85716 Office: School Renewable Natural Resources U Arizona Tucson AZ 85721

COX, RICHARD HORTON, engineering executive; b. Paia, Hawaii, Oct. 10, 1920; s. Joel Bean and Helen Clifford (Horton) C.; m. Hester Virginia Smith, Dec. 12, 1942; children—Millicent, Janet, Lydia, Evelyn, David, Samuel. B.S., Calif. Inst. Tech., 1942, M.S., 1946. Range supr. Calif. Inst. Tech., Pasadena, 1942-46; civil engr. McBryde Sugar Co., Eleele, Hawaii, 1946-56; with Alexander and Baldwin Inc., Honolulu, 1956—, v.p., 1971—. Active C. of C. Hawaii. Mem. ASCE, Nat. Soc. Profl. Engrs., Am. Geophys. Union, AAAS, Hawaiian Sugar Technologists. Home: 1951 Kakela Dr Honolulu HI 96022 Office: PO Box 3440 Honolulu HI 96801

COX, STEVEN RICHARD, economics educator; b. Madison, Wis., Apr. 8, 1944; s. Richard Phillip and Sue Ruth (Scheldrup) C.; m. Carol Ann Cox, June 20, 1970; children—Reid Alan, Mark Ryan. B.S., U. Wis., 1966; M.A., U. Mich., 1968, Ph.D., 1971. Asst. prof. econs. Ariz. State U., 1970-75, assoc. prof., 1975—; cons. FTC. NSF grantee, 1980—. Mem. Am. Econ. Assn. Democrat. Roman Catholic. Contbr. articles to profl. jours. Home: 3324 S Terrace Rd Tempe AZ 85282 Office: Dept Economics Ariz State U Tempe AZ 85287

COX, THOMAS RICHARD, educator; b. Portland, Oreg., Jan. 16, 1933; s. James Louis and Helen Melissa (Case) C.; student Whitman Coll., 1951-52; B.S., Oreg. State Coll., 1955; postgrad. U. Hawaii, 1963-64; M.S., U. Oreg., 1959, Ph.D., 1969; m. Mary Margaret MacGillivray, Nov. 24, 1954; children—Dianne Lynne Tongco, James Kimberley, Cynthia Ann, Michael William. Tchr. pub. high schs., Sisters, Oreg., 1956-59, Tulelake, Calif., 1959-63; teaching asst. U. Oreg., 1964-67; asst. prof. history San Diego State U., 1967-70, asso. prof., 1970-74, prof., 1975—; Tchr. Interchange fellow East-West Center, 1963-64; Fulbright prof., Japan, 1975-76. Mem. Sisters City Council, 1958-59. Recipient Max Savelle prize Phi Alpha Theta, 1965, Theodore Blegen award Forest History Soc., 1974, 82, forest history fellow, 1979-80; Huntington Library fellow, 1981; Nat. Endowment for Humanities grantee, 1976-77. Mem. Orgn. Am. Historians, Forest History Soc. (dir. 1974-83, pres. 1978-80), Agrl. History Soc., Western History Assn., United Profs. Calif. Author: Mills and Markets, 1974 (Emil and Kathleen Sick Lecture-Book award 1975). Bd. editors Jour. Forest History, 1973—. Contbr. articles to hist. jours. Home: 8615 Hudson Dr San Diego CA 92119 Office: History Dept San Diego State U San Diego CA 92182

COX, VELMA MARIE, sales exec., tax cons.; b. Goodland, Kans., Sept. 13, 1930; d. Forrest Seth and Emma Eliza (Zuspann) Higgs; student public schs., Fowler, Colo., 1947; m. Charles L. Cox, June 24, 1960; children—Mary Jane Cox Mayer, Karon Rae, Gary Lynn, Penny Kae Cox Saunders, Jonell, Chyral Ann. Sec., office mgr. Keck Buick-Pontiac, LaJunta, Colo., 1959-62; bookkeeper, office mgr. Harry Ritchie's Jewelry, Eugene, Oreg., 1962-63; pvt. practice bookkeeping and tax cons., Eugene, Oreg., 1964—; area mgr. Am. Bankers Life Assurance Co., Miami, Fla., 1972-79; exec. sales dir. Money Concepts Internat., Inc. of Pacific N.W., Eugene, 1979—. Recipient award of Excellence, Am. Bankers Life Oreg. region, 1973, Woman of Year award Oreg. region, 1977. Mem. Assn. Tax Cons., Ins. Women Eugene-Lane County, Inc. Democrat. Methodist. Club: Eagle Aux. Home and Office: 1360 Flintridge Ave Eugene OR 97401

COX, WENDELL, fin. co. exec.; b. Los Angeles, Dec. 14, 1944; s. Raymond and Shirley (Miller) C.; student U. So. Calif., 1963-65; B.A. in Polit. Sci., Calif. State U.-Los Angeles, 1968; M.B.A., Pepperdine U., Los Angeles, 1981; m. Valerie Woody, 1965; children—Deanna, Jeffrey, Gregory. Credit mgr. Marshall Imports Co., Los Angeles, 1967-68; asst. credit mgr. Bishop Industries, Union, N.J., 1969; mem. credit dept. United Factors (named changed to Crocker Comml. Services, 1977), Los Angeles, 1969-73, mgmt. cons., 1973-76, asst. mgr. credit services dept., 1977-78, mgr., 1978-79, mgr. client services, 1979-82; mktg. mgr. Crocker Nat. Bank, Los Angeles, 1983—. Chmn., Mayor's San Fernando Valley Adv. Com. on Transp., 1975-76; mem. Calif. Dept. Transp., I-405 Diamond Ln. Adv. Com., 1976, mem. transit performance measures project rev. com., 1981—; mem. Los Angeles County Transp. Commn., 1977—, chmn. service coordination com., 1978—, mem. fin. rev. com., 1978—, chmn. energy task force, 1979, mem. ad hoc rapid transit com. 1981—; chmn. Nat. Conf. on Energy Contingency Planning in Urban Areas, Houston, 1983; mem. Urban Mass Transit Adminstrn. Bus Line Costing Procedures Rev. Panel, U.S. Dept. Transp., 1981—, Subsidy Allocation Rev. Panel, 1982—; bd. govs. Tng. Rev. Panel, 1982—; mem. Pvt. Sector Operation of Pub. Transit Rev. Panel, 1982—; mem. pvt. sector/public sector commuter bus study com. So. Calif. Assn. Govts., 1981—; vice chmn. Crocker People Care Charitable Contbn. Campaign, 1983. Mem. Transp. Research Bd. (chmn. energy contingency planning com. 1982—, mem. com. on pub. cooperation in providing pub. transit service 1982—), Am. Pub. Transit Assn. (mem. performance indicators com. and governing bds. com., chmn. policy and planning com. 1982—). Presbyterian. Contbr. articles to profl. publs. Home: 22218-2 Germain St Chatsworth CA 91311 Office: 333 S Grand Los Angeles CA 90011 also 354 S Spring Los Angeles CA 90013

COX, WESLEY DANIEL, speech pathologist, educator; b. Pasadena, Calif., May 24, 1929; s. Jesse Carl and Margaret May (Wallace) C.; A.A., San Bernardino Valley Coll., 1954; B.A., U. Redlands, 1956, M.A., 1958; postgrad. Fresno, San Francisco state univs. With State of Calif. Dept. Health, 1952—, tchr. mentally retarded children Porterville State Hosp. (Calif.), 1958-78; tchr. speech correction and devel., 1979—; instr. speech and hearing courses Calif. State Coll. at Bakersfield, 1970—. Mem. Am. Assn. Mentally Deficient, Calif. Speech and Hearing Assn. (pres. Porterville state tchrs. group 1963-65, 75-76, 79—), Council Exceptional Children (pres. 1972-74, membership chmn. 1974-76). Home: 890 N Lime St Porterville CA 93257 Office: PO Box 2000 Porterville CA 93257

COY, JACKIE THOMAS, SR., dentist; b. Walsenburg, Colo., Feb. 6, 1931; s. Thomas and Ada Florence (White) C.; B.S., Portland State U., 1955; D.M.D., U. Oreg., 1959, cert. in hypnosis, 1969, cert. in sci. implantology, 1971, cert. in occlusal studies, 1978; m. Mary Lou Anna Stapleton, Mar. 17, 1956; children—Diana Kay, Nancy Fay, Jackie Thomas, Barbara Gay. Gen. practice dentistry, Tillamook, Oreg., 1959—. Scholarship chmn. March of Dimes, 1965-68; former chmn. bd. Tillamook Sch. Bd.; former bd. dirs. YMCA; mem. Medicare bd. Tillamook County Hosp., 1967. Served with AUS, 1951-53. Mem. Tillamook Dental Soc. (past pres.), N.Y. Acad. Scis., Soc. Occlusal Studies, Internat. Congress Oral Implantologists, Tillamook C. of C. Republican. Club: Elks. Office: 905 Pacific St Tillamook OR 97141

COY, LUCIEN HARDING, JR., civil systems cons.; b. Atlanta, Dec. 10, 1921; s. Lucien H. and Lucille (Clay) C.; E.E., N.C. State Coll., 1942; m. Wilma Theresa Kirnbauer, Oct. 15, 1949; children—Carol Ann, Norman John. With Gilfillan Corp., Los Angeles, 1947-49, Northrop Corp., Hawthorne, 1949-53; systems engr. Coleman Engring. Co., Inc., Torrance, 1953-59; mem. tech. staff TRW Systems, Redondo Beach, 1959-70; founder Can. Systems Group (ELST) Ltd., Toronto, Ont., Can., 1970-71; cons. IBM Corp., Fishkill, N.Y., Calif. Dept. Housing and Community Devel., Sacramento, Dept. Pub. Social Services, County of Los Angeles, Security Pacific Nat. Bank; lectr. on humanitarian technology. Served with USMCR, 1943-47. Mem. IEEE, Am. Geophys. Union, Town Hall of Calif., ACLU. Developer computer-based information systems, application of algorithmic and heuristic methods in solution of urban planning, social welfare and environ. problems. Home: 4024 W 234th St Torrance CA 90505 Office: Security Pacific Plaza Suite 4100 Los Angeles CA 90071

COYNE, JACK EUGENE, public health adminstr.; b. Uniontown, Pa., Aug. 30, 1928; s. Joseph and Mavorneen Rose (Dewalt) C.; A.B., San Francisco State U., 1961; M.P.H., U. Calif., Berkeley, 1962; m. Inger Beltoft Nielsen, Sept. 4, 1948; children—Julieann, Jack, Jeffrey, Jonathan, Inger. Sanitarian, Monterey County Health Dept., 1950-54, Oakland (Calif.) Dept. Public Health, 1954-59; environ. health insp. San Francisco Dept. Public Health, 1959-65, sr. insp., 1965-66, prin. insp., 1966-69, dir. Bur. Environ. Health, San Francisco, 1969—. Served with USNR, 1945. Mem. Nat. Assn. Dirs. Environ. Health, Am. Public Health Assn., San Francisco Mcpl. Execs. Assn. Lutheran. Home: 125 Los Palmos Dr San Francisco CA 94127 Office: 101 Grove St San Francisco CA 94102

COYNE, JULIEANN KATHRYN, mgmt. cons.; b. Salinas, Calif., Sept. 1, 1949; d. Jack Eugene and Inger B. (Nielsen) Coyne; B.A., U. Calif., Berkeley, 1971; M.S., Calif. State U., San Francisco, 1976. Opns. officer Bank of Am., San Francisco, 1969-74, tng. officer, 1974-75; tng. officer Crocker Bank, San Francisco, 1975-76, v.p., dir. personnel Imperial Bank, Inglewood, Calif., 1976-80; owner Coyne & Assos., mgmt. cons. firm, Encino, Calif., 1980—. Bd. dirs. United Cerebral Palsy, Cystic Fibrosis. Mem. faculty Calif. State U., Los Angeles, 1978-79. Mem. Am. Soc. Tng. and Devel., Women in Bus., Nat. Assn. Women Bus. Owners, Personnel and Indsl. Relations Assn. Office: 16055 Ventura Blvd Suite 719 Encino CA 91436

COYOLI, EDMUND CHARLES, advertising account executive, consultant; b. Kansas City, Mo.; s. Edmundo S. and Edna Jane (Taylor) C.; m. Kathleen Michelle Haddow, June 10, 1972; 1 son, Christopher Edmund. B.A. in Liberal Studies, Calif. State U.-Northridge, 1977; postgrad. UCLA, 1981—. Gen. mgr. Stanley Holden Dence Center, West Los Angeles, Calif., 1971-74; account exec. classified, Los Angeles Times, 1974-77, advt. account exec. display, 1977-80; sr. advt. account exec. Bernard Hodes Advt., Inc. div. Doyle Dane Bernbach, Encino, Calif., 1980—; free lance advt. cons.; chmn. bd. Los Angeles Area Dance Alliance, also mktg. and advt. dir. Adv. bd. Long Beach Ballet & Westside Ballet; bd. dirs. Valencia South Valley Home-owners Assn., editor newsletter. Mem. Music Center Dance Assn., Los Angeles Area Dance Alliance. Republican. Roman Catholic. Advt. dir. for Dance Flash. Home: 25764 Salceda Rd Valencia CA 91355 Office: 16027 Ventura Bldg #300 Encino CA 91436

COZART, MARJORIE LEE, software executive, consultant; b. Kensington, Kans., Dec. 19, 1930; d. Ervin Wayne and Clementine Elizabeth (Zrubec) Oliva; m. Jack Dean Conway, Dec. 25, 1947; m. 2d, Cornelius Garrett Cozart, July 22, 1975; children—Judith Conway Hawkins, Douglas Jack Conway. Student, Parks Bus. Coll., Denver, 1963-64. Lic. real estate salesman. Property mgr., acct. Van Schaack & Co., Denver, 1958-63; office mgr. Computer Listing Services, Denver, 1961-65, Pennant Petroleum Co., Denver, 1965-66; v.p. Petroleum Data Systems, Denver, 1967-71; pres., owner Oil-Tronix Ltd., Denver, 1972—; computerized oil and gas accting. software and timesharing services, land mgmt. cons., application software designer. Mem. Denver Assn. Petroleum Landmen, Am. Assn. Petroleum Landmen. Democrat. Clubs: Denver Country, Eastern Star. Author: publs. in field. Home: 1299 Gilpin Park Towers #5W Denver CO 80218 Office: Oil-Tronix Ltd 1580 Lincoln Suite 1240 Denver CO 80203

COZEN, LEWIS, orthopedic surgeon; b. Montreal, Que., Can., Aug. 14, 1911; s. Lester and Sarah (Jones) C.; A.B., U. Calif., 1933, M.D., 1934; m. Ruth Stein, Jan. 22, 1948; children—Robert, Jane. Intern. San Francisco Hosp., Mass. Gen. Hosp., resident Boston Children's Hosp., U. Iowa Hosp., 1934-39; practice orthopedic surgery, Los Angeles, 1940—; mem. staff Orthopedic Hosp.; cons. USPHS; asso. clin. prof. UCLA Sch. Medicine, 1955—; sr. attending orthopedic surgeon Cedars Sinai Hosp.; emeritus sr. attending orthopedic surgeon Los Angeles County Hosp. Served to lt. col. M.C., U.S. Army, 1940-46; ETO. Mem. Am. Acad. Orthopedic Surgeons, Western Orthopedic Assn., So. Calif. Rheumatism Soc. (pres.), Alpha Omega Alpha. Author: Operative Orthopedic Clinics, 1950; Office Orthopedics, 4th edit., 1975; Atlas of Orthopedic Operations, 1969; Difficult Orthopedic Diagnoses, 1974; also numerous articles in field. Office: 6221 Wilshire Blvd Los Angeles CA 90048

COZENS, ROGER ALLEN, plant engr.; b. Boulder, Colo., Oct. 1, 1950; s. Roger William and Alice Lorraine (Dralle) C.; B.S.M.E., U. Colo., 1973; M.B.A., U. Denver, 1983; m. Vivian Kattler, Mar. 23, 1973; children—Emily Evalyce, Andrew Eugene. Campus minister Conservative Bapt. Home Mission Soc., San Jose, Calif., 1973-75; corp. project engr. Monfort of Colo., Greeley, 1975-79; plant engr. Gen. Cable Co., Westminster, Colo., 1979—; dir. Techmet Industries, Inc., Broomfield, Colo. Recipient 1st pl., grad. awards program James F. Lincoln Arc Welding Found., 1973; registered profl. engr., Colo. Mem. ASME (asso. 2 pl. award Region VIII Student Conf. 1973), ASHRAE (asso.), Greeley C. of C. (accreditation com.), Delta Upsilon. Research on energy conservation products. Office: 5600 W 88th Ave Westminster CO 80030

CRABBS, ROGER ALAN, college president, business educator; b. Cedar Rapids, Iowa, May 9, 1928; s. Winfred Wesley and Faye (Woodard) C.; B.A. in Sci., State U. Iowa, 1954; M.B.A., George Washington U., 1965, D.B.A., 1973; M. Christian Leadership, Western Conservative Bapt. Sem., 1978; m. Marilyn Lee Westcott, June 30, 1951; children—William Douglas, Janet Lee, Ann Lee. Clk., U.S. P.O., Cedar Rapids, 1944-46; commd. 2d lt. U.S. Air Force, 1950, advanced through grades to lt. col., 1968; statis. staff officer, Colo., 1951; spl. weapons def. officer, Korea, 1952-53; radiol. and ops. officer, Armed Forces Spl. Weapons Project, N.Mex., 1953-56; research and devel. staff officer Air Force Ballistic Missile Div., Calif., 1956; aide to comdr. Air Force Systems Command, Andrews AFB, Md., 1957-59, research and devel. staff officer, 1960-63; manpower and orgn. mgmt. staff officer D.C. and C.Z., 1965-72; ret., 1972; asst. prof. mgmt. U. Portland (Oreg.), 1972-74, assoc. prof., 1974-79; prof. bus. George Fox Coll., Newberg, Oreg., 1979-83; pres. Judson Bapt. Coll., Dallas, Oreg., 1983—; pres. Crabbs, Braden & Pamplin, Inc., 1974-77, Walt Morgan Travel and Tours, Inc., 1976-77, Plain & Fancy Fencing, Inc., 1979-80; chmn. bd. Micro-Tech, Inc.; treas., dir. Blasem B Corp.; dir. Embarcadero, Inc., EDRM, Inc., Climax Mfg., Inc., Yaquina Rental Agy., Inc.; cons. to various orgns., corps. and agys. Pres., bd. dirs. Living Rehab. Center, Inc., 1975-79; v.p., bd. dirs. Young Audiences of Oreg., Inc., 1975-78; bd. dirs. George Fox Coll. Found., Inc.; chmn. bd. dirs. Western's Mt. Tabor Ednl. Services Found.; mem. City of Portland Exec. Selection Panel; trustee Western Conservative Bapt. Sem. deacon, mem. long-range planning com. N. Am. Bapt. Conf.; mem. Small Bus. Adv. Council, Oreg. Dist. SBA, 1983—. Decorated Air Force Commendation medal with oak leaf cluster, Meritorious Service medal Dept. Def.; rated Command Air Force Missileman; recipient regional, dist. and nat. awards SBA; U. Portland grantee, 1976-78. Mem. Acad. of Mgmt., Am. Soc. Personnel Adminstrn., Am. Soc. Tng. and Devel., Am. Soc. Public Adminstrn., Small Bus. Inst. Dirs. Assn., Am. Arbitration Assn., Service Corps Ret. Execs./Active Corps of Execs., Air Force Assn., Alpha Kappa Psi, Delta Epsilon Sigma. Democrat. Baptist. Clubs: Portland Officers. Author: The Storybook Primer on Managing, 1976; The Infallible Foundation for Management - The Bible, 1978; The Secret of Success in Small Business Management—Is in the Short Range, 1983. Home: 14930 NW Northumbria Ln Beaverton OR 97006 Office: Judson Baptist Coll 400 E Scenic Dr The Dalles OR 97058

CRAFT, BERNADINE LOUISE, guidance counselor; b. Rock Springs, Wyo., Jan. 15, 1950; d. Ralph Donald and Agnes Louise (Larsen) Craft; B.A. cum laude, U. Utah, 1972, teaching certificate, 1972, M.A. in Ednl. Psychology, 1974; counseling certificate, 1974; postgrad. U. Wyo., 1976. Guidance counselor East High Sch., Salt Lake City, 1973-74, Skyline High Sch., Salt Lake City, 1974-75; Hatha Yoga instr. Western Wyo. Community Coll., 1976—, also guidance counselor White Mountain Jr. High Sch., Rock Springs, 1975—; facilitator, trainer Wyo. Dept. Humanistic Edn. Programs, 1978; guest instr. U. Wyo.; mem. Wyo. Guidance Adv. Council, 1980—; speaker workshops, in-service programs; cons. Title IV Standardized Test Evaluation Program, Sch. Dist. No. 1. Mem. Sweetwater County Child Protection Council, 1976-78; sec. bd. dirs. Sweetwater County Youth Home, 1981—; pres. Sweetwater County Performing Arts Assn., 1982— mem. Wyo. Human Resource Council; tutor Right-to-Read Adult Literacy Program, 1975—; vol. tchr. Headstart, 1974, Salt Lake County Detention Center, 1974; mem. adv. council Cathedral Home for Children, 1980—; performer Rock Springs Dinner Theatre, 1975; hdqrs. sec. Community Concert Assn., 1972-76; Yoga instr. YWCA, 1977—; ch. and choir organist. Named to Nat. Sorority Hall of Fame, 1972. Mem. Am. (state chmn. human rights commn. 1976—, Western Region br. senator 1980—, nat. div. 1983—), Wyo. (exec. council, area reporter jour. 1976—, editorial bd. 1976—, pres. 1979-80, Disting. Service award 1979, govt. liaison worker 1981—) personnel and guidance assns., Assn. Specialists in Group Work, Am. Sch. Counselors Assn. (Wyo. del. 1978), Wyo Sch. Counselor Assn. (pres. 1978-79), Classroom Tchrs. Assn. (treas. 1979-80), NEA, Wyo. Edn. Assn., Assn. Humanistic Edn. and Devel., Mortar Bd., Rock Springs Community Theatre, Alpha Delta Pi (Dorothy Shaw Leadership award 1972, Greek Woman award 1972, state membership chmn. alumnae assn. 1975—). Episcopalian (vestry 1978-81, newsletter editor 1980—, Wyo. Diocesan Council 1982—). Club: Internat. Order Job's Daus. Advt. editor Wyo. Personnel and Guidance Assn. Jour., 1977-78, 80—; contbr. articles to profl. jours. Home: Box 63 522 B St Rock Springs WY 82901 Office: White Mountain Jr High Sch Foothill Blvd Rock Springs WY 82901

CRAFTS, ALAN LEWIS, lawyer; b. Riverside, Calif., Oct. 5, 1945; s. G. Lewis and M. Katherine (Gould) C.; m. Susan Teig, June 26, 1982. Student, Riverside City Coll., 1963-65; B.S. in Bus., Calif. Poly. U., 1967; J.D., U. Calif.-Hastings Coll. Law, 1970. Bar: Calif. 1971; cert. specialist in family law Calif. Bd. Legal Specialization. Tchr., Riverside (Calif.) Unified Sch. Dist., 1970-72; assoc. atty. firm Badger & Biddle, Riverside, 1972-75; instr. community property Citrus Belt Law Sch., Riverside, 1973-74; ptnr. Falsetti, Crafts, Pritchard & Darling, Riverside, 1975—. Mem. State Bar Calif., Riverside Bar Assn. (chmn. family law sect.), Riverside Jaycees (pres. 1972-82). Club: Magnolia Center Exchange (pres. 1974—). Office: Falsetti Crafts Pritchard & Darling 7121 Magnolia Ave Riverside CA 92504

CRAGIN, ROBERT OWEN, leasing company executive; b. Quincy, Mass., Mar. 23, 1940; s. Edward Thomas and Mary Theresa (McCarthy) C.; B.S. in Commerce, U. Santa Clara (Calif.), 1962; M.B.A., U. Calif., Berkeley, 1971; m. Adele M. Brown, May 8, 1971; children—Michael Robert, Scott Edward. Stock broker Sutro & Co., Inc., San Francisco, 1965-66; credit officer Wells Fargo Bank, San Francisco, 1966-69; v.p., mgr. leasing div. Security Nat. Bank, Walnut Creek, Calif., 1972-77; v.p., gen. mgr. Nev. Exec. Leasing Co., Reno, 1977-81; gen. mgr. Eastland Leasing Co., Los Angeles, 1982-83; regional sales mgr. Citicorp Indsl. Credit, Inc., 1983—. Served as officer AUS, 1962-65. Mem. Western Assn. Equipment Lessors, Western Vehicle Leasing Assn. Republican. Roman Catholic. Home: 10142 Suntan Circle Huntington Beach CA 92646

CRAIG, ELLIS EDWARD, advt. exec.; b. Pima, Ariz., Apr. 18, 1915; s. William Edward and Diantha (Smith) C.; student Gila Jr. Coll., 1932-33, Ariz State U., 1934-35; m. Jan Boyd, Mar. 14, 1961; children—Diana (Mrs. Alex Uhrich), Michael, Jan, Gery, Ellis, Jon, Lynda. Radio announcer KOY Phoenix, 1937-39; program dir. Lockheed Aircraft Corp., 1940-44; account exec. advt. Universal Advt. Agy., Inc., 1946-48; founder Craig & Reid, Inc., Hollywood, Calif., 1949, pres., 1949-54, chmn., 1954—; sec.-treas. Great Western Horizons, Inc., Los Angeles, 1968—; partner Langford & Craig Oil & Gas Exploration & Prodn., 1971—, Park-Craig, Inc., 1971—, Canyon Devel. Co., 1972—; pres., chmn. Primal Power Corp., Salt Lake City. High priest Ch. of Jesus Christ of Latter-day Saints, 1950—, mem. high council Burbank-North Hollywood area, 1970—. Pres. Shadow Hills Civic Assn., Sunland, Calif., 1953-54. Treas. Lyndon B. Johnson for Pres. Clubs, 1959-60. Pres. Theo-Sci., Inc. Found., Hollywood, 1968—. Served with AUS, 1944-46. Home: 1176 Oak Hills Way Salt Lake City UT 84108 Office: 1313 Foothill Dr Salt Lake City UT 84108

CRAIG, GENEVA ELLEN, transportation executive; b. Aberdeen, Wash., July 11, 1918; d. Traverse and Thelma (Howell) Radcliffe; m. William Craig, July 7, 1944. Student Grays Harbor Jr. Coll., Grays Harbor Bus. Coll. Librarian Aberdeen Pub. Library, 1938-42; jr. aircraft mechanic Spokane Army Air Depot (Wash.), 1942-44; recruiter Guy F. Atkinson Constrn. Co., Anchorage, 1945; clk. Alaskan Dept. Engrs., Anchorage; chief procurement Army and Air Force Exchange Service, Anchorage, 1945-54; v.p. passenger service Reeve Aleutian Airways, Inc., Anchorage, 1955—, also dir. Mem. Citizens Council Community Improvement, Anchorage, 1960-67, co-chmn., 1966-67. Mem. Aux. U.S. Army, Am. Soc. Profl. and Exec. Women. Clubs: Pioneers of Alaska, Soroptimist. Home: Box 82 SRA Craig Circle Anchorage AK 99507 Office: 4700 W Internat Airport Rd Anchorage AK 99502

CRAIG, IRVIN MILNE, educational administrator; b. Honolulu, June 26, 1921; s. Irvin Fish and Emily (Milne) C.; m. Patricia Leilani Jacobson, Aug. 17, 1967; children—Michael D., Suzanne M. Craig Hewey, Andrew J. A.B., Calif. State U.-Fresno, 1947; M.A., U. So. Calif., 1949. Lic. psychologist, Calif. Speech therapist Kern County Schs., Bakersfield, Calif., 1949-52; psychologist Kings County Schs., Hanford, Calif., 1952-54, psychologist, dir. spl. edn., 1954-56, asst. supt., 1956—. Served with USAAF, 1943-46; PTO. Pres., Kings Rehab. Workshop, Inc., 1977-78, Kings County Easter Seal Soc., Kings County Mental Health Adv. Bd. Mem. Council for Exceptional Children (state fedn. pres. 1964-65), Calif. Adminstrs. of Spl. Edn. (pres. 1967-68). Home: 1122 Robinson Ct Hanford CA 93230 Office: Govt Center Hanford CA 93230

CRAIG, LARRY EDWIN, congressman, farmer, rancher; b. Council, Idaho, July 20, 1945; s. Elvin and Dorothy C.; B.A. in Polit. Sci. and Agrl. Econs., U. Idaho, 1969; postgrad. George Washington U. Farmer, Idaho, 1974-80; past mem. Idaho Senate; now mem. 98th Congress from 1st Idaho Dist., mem. Interior & Insular Affairs com., Govt. Ops. com., Select Com. on Aging. Adv. to HEW on vocat. edn. in public schs., 1971-73; mem. Republican Nat. Com., 1974-79; chmn. Idaho Republican State Senate races, 1976-78. Methodist. Clubs: Elks, Shoepeg Grange. Office: 1318 Longworth House Office Bldg Washington DC 20515

CRAIG, LEXIE FERRELL, vocational guidance counselor; b. Halls, Tenn., Dec. 12, 1921; d. Monroe Stancil and Hester May (Martin) Ferrell; m. Philip L. Craig, May 19, 1951; children—Douglas H., Laurie K., Barbara J. B.S. magna cum laude, George Peabody Coll., Vanderbilt U., 1944, M.A. with honors, 1965; postgrad. Colo. U., 1972—, Colo. State U., 1964—, U. No. Colo., 1964—. Cert. local vocat. adminstr., vocat. guidance specialist, vocat. bus. specialist, vocat. home econs. specialist, reading specialist, nat. recreation dir. specialist. Danforth grad. fellow Mich. State U., East Lansing, 1944-46; nat. student counselor, field dir. student counseling dept. higher edn. Am. Bapt. Conv., summer service career projects dir. U.S. and Europe, 1946-51; coordinator religious and career activities counselor, Colo. U., 1951-52; tchr. home econs., phys. edn., counseling, dist. 96, Riverside, Ill., 1952-54; substitute tchr., psychometrist, reading specialist part time, Deerfield, Ill., 1956-59; substitute tchr. Littleton (Colo.) Dist. VI, 1961-63, guidance and career counselor Littleton Pub. Schs., 1963-67, 68—, now career vocat. specialist, guidance counselor, Powell Sch., Dist. VI, also mem. vocat. needs and assessment com., career task force; dir., counselor YWCA Extension Program, Job Corps, Denver, 1967-68; tchr. adult edn. home econs. evenings, 1963-66; mem. Colo. Career Task Force, Lay conf. rep. Meth. Ch. Pastor/Parish Commn.; bd. dirs. Powell Careers Post Council Boy Scouts Am., also mem. Colo. Career Awareness Council; bd. dirs. So. Suburban Recreation, Littleton Community Arts Ctr.; bd. dirs., adv. council Powell PTO, Home Econs. in Homemaking; mem. local caucus com. Republican Party; mem. Dist. Environ. Sci. Council. Didcott scholar, 1942; Danforth home econs. and leadership scholar, 1943; Am. Leadership Camp Found. scholar, Shelby, Mich., 1942-45; Hildegarde Sweet Scholar, 1983; recipient Sullivan award and grant, named outstanding grad., 1944; named Littleton Mother of Year, 1977, Colo. Vocat. Counselor of Year, 1978; recipient plaque for recruiting and career guidance Navy and Air Force, 1980. Mem. NEA, AAUW, Colo. Edn. Assn., Littleton Edn. Assn., Am. Vocat. Assn., Colo. Vocat. Assn., Am. Personnel and Guidance Assn., Colo. Personnel and Guidance Assn. (pres., exec. bd.), Nat. Vocat. Guidance Assn. (Colo. rep.), Colo. Sch. Counselors Assn., Am. Field Service (pres. Littleton chpt.), Lit. Book Club Littleton Arts Ctr., Phi Delta Kappa, Delta Kappa Gamma (v.p.), Delta Pi Epsilon (past pres.), Pi Omega Pi (past pres.), Pi Gamma Mu (past pres.), Kappa Delta Pi. Clubs: Order Eastern Star, Country Western Dance, Editor, pub. Join in a Song, 1949; editor The Church Follows Its Youth, 1950, curriculum units in consumer edn., home econs., careers.

CRAIG, MAYADELLE JANE, counselor, organizational development consultant; b. Wildrose, N.D., June 14, 1937; d. Willie O. and Olive May (Holland) Evenson; m. William L. Craig, Nov. 4, 1972 (div.); children—Cynthia, Joni. B.A. U. Nev., Las Vegas, 1978; M.A., Whitworth Coll., 1982. Cert. alcoholism counselor Wash. State Profl. Staff Soc., 1982. Counselor, group therapist Ct. Referral Services, Las Vegas, 1977-79; counselor, employee assistance program facilitator Southwest Community Alcohol Ctr., Seattle, 1979-81; pres. Dell Craig Therapists Inc., Des Moines, Wash., 1981—; developer, cons. employee assistance programs; franchiser catalyst plans on alcoholism recovery, organizational enhancement. Mem. Wash. State Council on Alcoholism, Am. Personnel and Guidance Assn., Psi Chi. Club: Toastmasters (Buren, Wash.). Office: Dell Craig Therapists 22030 7th Ave S Suite 204 Des Moines WA 98188

CRAIG, PAUL LAWRENCE, clinical psychologist; b. Oklahoma City, Nov. 20, 1953; s. John Odra and Edith Margritz C.; m. Carol Ann Hult, Dec. 6, 1953; 1 dau., Marie Hult. B.S. with distinction, Nebr. Wesleyan U., Lincoln, 1975; M.S., U. Wyo., Laramie, 1978, Ph.D., 1980. Lic. psychologist, Alaska. Psychology intern U. Minn. Health Scis. Ctr., Mpls., 1979-80; post-doctoral psychology fellow U. Wash. Sch. Medicine, Seattle, 1980-81; program dir. Community Mental Health Ctr., Homer, Alaska, 1981—; cons. neuropsychology; part-time tchr. NIMH tng. fellow U. Wyo., 1976, Clark scholar, U. Wyo., 1979. Mem. Am. Psychol. Assn., Alaskan Psychol. Assn., Internat. Neuropsychol. Soc., Nat. Acad. Neuropsychologists, Inter-Am. Soc. Psychology, Homer C. of C., Phi Beta Kappa. Contbr. articles to profl. jours.; mem. editorial adv. bd. Clin. Neuropsychology.

CRAIG, ROBERT WALLACE, ednl. center adminstr.; b. Long Beach, Calif., Sept. 16, 1924; s. Harold Fleming and Ellen Amelia (Stagg) C.; B.A. cum laude, U. Wash., 1949, B.S., 1950; M.A., Columbia U., 1951; m. Carol Williams Gallun, Nov. 5, 1957; children—Kathleen Elizabeth, Jennifer Courtney, Michael Brian. Cons. on equipment, mountain and cold weather tng. Dept. of Army, 1951-54; exec. dir., v.p., sec. Aspen (Colo.) Inst. Humanistic Studies, 1954-64; v.p., dir. Unimark Internat. Design, Inc., Chgo. and Aspen, 1965-71; prin. Robert Craig & Assocs., 1965-73; partner, dir. Genesis, Inc., 1971-73; partner Rieben & Craig, Denver, 1973-75; pres. Keystone (Colo.) Center, 1975—. Trustee, Aspen Center for Physics, Snake River Health Ctr. Served to lt. (j.g.) with USN, 1943-46; PTO. Mem. Washington Inst. Fgn. Affairs, Democrat. Episcopalian. Clubs: Denver, Cactus (Denver); Bohemian (San Francisco); Am. Alpine. Author: (with Robert Bates and Charles Houston) K2, The Savage Mountain, 1954; Storm and Sorrow, 1978; leader Am. Everest West Ridge Expdn., 1983. Office: Keystone Center Box 38 Keystone CO 80435

CRAIG, SONJA SORENSEN, newspaper executive; b. Des Moines, Aug. 10, 1945; d. Raymond E. and Willa S. (Crane) Sorensen; m. John S. Craig, Nov. 29, 1963; children—J. Stephen, Ann Sorensen. B.A., U. No. Iowa, 1968. Personnel asst. Des Moines Register & Tribune, 1969-72; personnel mgr. Madison (Wis.) Newspapers Inc., 1972-80; gen. mgr. Billings (Mont.) Gazette, 1980—. Bd. dirs. Eastern Mont. Coll. Found.; bd. dirs., chmn. 1983 campaign United Way Yellowstone County. Mem. Am. Newspaper Pubs. Assn., Mont. Assn. Female Execs. (pres.). Office: 401 N Broadway Billings MT 59101

CRAIG, STEPHEN WRIGHT, lawyer; b. N.Y.C., Aug. 28, 1932; s. Herbert Stanley and Dorothy (Simmons) C.; A.B., Harvard, 1954, J.D., 1959; m. Margaret M. Baker, June 10, 1958; children—Amelia Audrey, Janet Elizabeth, Peter Baker. Reporter, Daily Kennebec Jour., Augusta, Me., 1956; engaged in pub. relations with Am. Savoyards, 1957; atty. IRS, San Francisco, 1959-61; atty.-adviser U.S. Tax Ct., 1961-63; partner firm Snell & Wilmer, 1963-78, Craig, Greenfield & Irwin, Phoenix, 1978-81, Winston & Strawn, Phoenix, 1981—; guest lectr. Amos Tuck Sch. Bus., Dartmouth, 1962; lectr. Ariz. and N.Mex. Tax Insts., 1966-67. Chmn. Jane Wayland Child Guidance Center, 1968-70 mem. Maricopa County Health Planning Council, chmn. mental health task force. Mem. Ariz. Republican Com., 1967-72. Bd. dirs. Combined Met. Phoenix Arts, 1968, adv. bd., 1968-69; adv. bd. Ariz. State U. Tax Insts., 1968-70; bd. dirs. Phoenix Community Council, 1970-73, Ariz. Acad., Scottsdale Center Arts. Served with AUS, 1954-56, Mem. Am. County bar assns., state bars Ariz., Calif., Maine, Hasty Pudding Inst., Sigma Alpha Epsilon. Episcopalian (sr. warden, diocesan council). Home: 4615 N 22d St Unit 101 Phoenix AZ 85016 Office: SW Fin Plaza 3101 N Central Ave Phoenix AZ 85012

CRAIG, WALTER EARLY, fed. judge; b. Oakland, Calif., May 26, 1909; s. Jubal Early and Marie (Craig) C.; A.B., Stanford, 1931, LL.B., 1934; LL.D., Ariz. State U., 1963, U. San Diego, 1964; S.J.D., Suffolk U., 1964; m. Meta Elizabeth Jury, Oct. 25, 1935; children—William Early, Meta Lucille. Admitted to Calif. bar, 1934, Ariz. bar, 1936; legal dept. regional office HOLC, 1934-36; practice law, Phoenix, 1936-64; spl. counsel to Pres.'s Commn. on Assassination of Pres. Kennedy, 1963-64, judge U.S. Dist. Ct., Ariz. Dist., Phoenix, 1964—, chief judge, 1973-79. Mem. Ariz. Code Commn., 1951-56; appeal agt. Maricopa County Selective Ser., 1945-64; mem. Ariz. Jud. Council, 1950-63; chmn. Nat. Conf. Fed. Trial Judges, 1973-74. Bd. dirs. Am. Bar Endowment, pres., 1979-81; bd. dirs. Sun Angel Found., Ariz. State U. Found., Ariz. Community Found., Forensic Scis. Found.; trustee Nat. Inst. Trial Advocacy, Harry S. Truman Scholarship Found., 1975-79. Served with USNR, World War II. Decorated Order So. Cross (Brazil). Fellow Am. Bar Found.; mem. Am. Law Inst., Am. (pres. 1963-64), Ariz. (pres. 1951-52), Maricopa County (pres. 1941), Inter-Am. (mem. council 1963-73), Internat. (mem. council 1964-69), Can. (hon.) bar assns., Am. Judicature Soc., Assn. Bar City N.Y., 9th Circuit Dist. Judges Assn. (pres. 1973-75), El Illustre y Nacional Colegio de Abogados de Mexico (hon.), Barra Mexicana (hon.), El Colegio de Abogados de la Ciudad de Buenos Aires (hon.), Colegio de Abogados del Uruguay (hon.), Western States Bar Council (pres. 1956-57), Am. Legion, Phi Gamma Delta, Phi Delta Phi. Clubs: Elks, Rotary, Ariz., Phoenix Country, Kiva, Stanford (pres. 1948-56), Thunderbirds (pres. 1948-49) (Phoenix). Home: 2020 E Bethany Home Rd Phoenix AZ 85016 Office: US Courthouse Phoenix AZ 85025

CRAIGMILE, THOMAS KAY, neurol. surgeon; b. Muncie, Ind., Dec. 28, 1924; s. William Wallace and Hallie (Metzker) C.; B.S., Northwestern U., 1946, M.B., 1948, M.D., 1949; m. Doris Wolfe, Apr. 15, 1950; children—Suzanne, Christine, Elizabeth, Marianne, Kathleen. Intern, Chgo. Wesley Meml. Hosp., 1949; resident neurol. surgery Northwestern U., 1952-54; asst. resident neurology Presbyn. Hosp., N.Y.C., 1956-57; chief resident neurol. surgery U. Colo. Med. Center, Denver, 1957-58, clin. instr. neurosurgery, 1959-61, asst. clin. prof. neurosurgery, 1961-69, asso. clin. prof. neurol. surgery, 1969—. Served to capt., M.C., USAF, 1954-56. Diplomate Am. Bd. Neurol. Surgery. Fellow A.C.S.; mem. Am. Assn. Neurol. Surgeons, Congress Neurol. Surgeons, Rocky Mountain Neurosurg. Soc. (sec. 1966-69, pres. 1970-71), Western Neurosurg. Soc. (v.p. 1974-75, pres. elect 1982-83), Colo Neurosurg. Soc. (pres.-elect 1977). Home: 4431 E 6th Ave Denver CO 80220 Office: 2045 Franklin St Denver CO 80205

CRAIN, BRIAN J(OHN), optometrist; b. Winnipeg, Man., Can., Dec. 6, 1942; came to U.S., 1948, naturalized, 1956; s. Irvin J. and Phyllis M. (Howick) C.; m. Joyce Carol Knudsen, Sept. 24, 1966; children—Sean Brian, Aaron John. B.A. in Journalism, U. Wash., 1966; postgrad. Pacific Luth. U., 1973; O.D., Pacific U., 1978. Advt. mgr., asst. Assoc. Grocers, Seattle, 1968-73; practice optometry, Auburn, Wash., 1978—; instr. optometric technician program Tacoma Community Coll., 1979-80; instr. continuing edn. for optometric technicians. Bd. dirs. Auburn Parks and Recreation Dept., 1982—; deacon bd. N.Am. Bapt. Ch., 1979—. Mem. Am. Optometric Assn., Wash. Optometric Assn., Optometric Editors Assn., Beta Sigma Kappa. Club: Rotary (dir. Auburn 1980—). Editor Wash. Optometry Today, 1979—. Home: 1235 25th St SE Auburn WA 98002 Office: 815 Harvey Rd Auburn WA 98002

CRAIN, RICHARD HARRY, ski sch. ofcl.; b. Schenectady, Nov. 11, 1939; s. Leslie H. and Mary C.; B.S., SUNY, Cortland, 1962; postgrad. SUNY, Cortland, Adelphi U., C. W. Post Coll., SUNY, Oneonta. Instr. phys. edn., coach Wm. Floyd High Sch., Shirley, N.Y., 1962-64; instr. sci., coach Cooperstown (N.Y.) Central Sch., 1964-66; tchr. sci. Farmingdale (N.Y.) Public Schs., 1966-68; mgr. Ski Mart Aspen (Colo.), 1968-69; supr. Steamboat Ski Sch., Steamboat Springs, Colo., 1969—; ski sch. cons.; owner, mgr. rental car agy. Mem. Rocky Mountain Ski Instrs. Assn. (dir.; examiner), Profl. Ski Instrs. Am., N.W. Colo. Bd. Realtors, Colo. Guide and Outfitters Assn. Methodist. Home: Box 1342 Steamboat Springs CO 80477 Office: Box 1560 Steamboat Springs CO 80477

CRAIN, WILLIAM JAMES, vocational educator; b. Pueblo, Colo., Aug. 16, 1937; s. William James and Edith Esther (Donley) C.; m. Eleanor Ann Liesen, Aug. 24, 1967; children—James, Tomas. A.A.S., Pueblo Coll., 1957; B.A., Adams State Coll., Alamosa, Colo., 1960, M.A., 1962; Ph.D., Colo. State U., 1973. Cert. gen. mechanic Nat. Inst. Automotive Service Excellence. Owner, operator Bill Crain's Auto Repair, Pueblo, Colo., 1957-62; instr., dept. head auto mechanics Trinidad (Colo.) State Jr. Coll., 1962-65; prof. auto mechanics U. So. Colo., Pueblo, 1965-77, program dir., acting dir. mech. area, 1970-76; program dir., prof. auto mechanics Pueblo Community Coll., 1979—; cons. Colo. Dept. Health. Asst. leader 4-H club, 1979—. Served with U.S. Army, 1960-66. Nominated outstanding faculty member Pueblo Community Coll., 1982-83. Mem. Colo. Automotive Tchrs. Assn., Colo. Vocat. Assn., Am. Vocat. Assn., Phi Delta Kappa. Christian Scientist. Clubs: Elks, Masons. Author: The Development and Field Testing of an Occupational Competency Examination for Auto Mechanic Teachers, 1973. Home: Rural Route 3 Box 83 Pueblo CO 81004 Office: 900 W Orman Ave Pueblo CO 81004

CRAKER, GEORGE GLENN, banker; b. Dallas, May 19, 1944; s. Glenn Everett and Rita Mae (Sullivan) C.; student U. Dallas, 1962-63, N. Tex. State U., 1963-66. Vice pres. Apt. Owners Services Co., Dallas, 1968-69; regional mgr. Am. Nat. Enterprises Co., Salt Lake City, 1969-72; exec. v.p. Ambassador Releasing Co., Salt Lake City, 1972-76; fin. cons. motion pictures, Salt Lake City, 1976-77; pres. Trans-Am. Advt. Agy., Salt Lake City, 1977—; loan officer Am. Savs. & Loan, Salt Lake City, 1978-81; v.p. Petroleum Services, Inc., Salt Lake City, 1981-82; mortgage banking officer Banco Mortgage Co., 1982—. Served with U.S. Army, 1966. Mem. Variety Club Internat. Republican. Roman Catholic. Home: 1187 Bellcastle Circle Sandy UT 84070 Office: 965 E 4800 S Salt Lake City UT 84117

CRAMER, BRADLEY ALAN, advt. exec.; b. Los Angeles, June 7, 1953; s. Harold Morton and Arlyne Hope (Alberts) C.; B.Communications, Calif. State U., 1975. Pub. relations dir. Davis Broadcasting Co., Santa Ana, Calif., 1972-75; div. promotion mgr. CBS, Inc., Los Angeles, 1976-79; pres. advt./mktg. Impressive Media, La Mirada, Calif., 1980—; faculty communications Rio Hondo Coll., Whittier, Calif., 1980—; guest lectr. UCLA, 1978—. Mem. Am. Mgmt. Assn., Am. Fedn. TV and Radio Artists. Home: 14745 E Valeda Dr La Mirada CA 90638

CRAMER, CYNTHIA JEANETTE, real estate broker, assn. exec.; b. N.Y.C., May 7, 1943; d. Morgan J. and Miriam Jeanette (Fuchs) C.; student Katherine Gibbs Secretarial Sch., 1961-62. Exec. comml. producer Lennen & Newell, Inc., N.Y.C., 1962-68; asst. to dir. public info. Lehigh U., Bethlehem, Pa., 1969-70; adminstrv. asst. to pres. Morgan J. Cramer Associates, Inc., N.Y.C., 1970-72; public relations dir. Greater Bethlehem Area United Fund, 1972-73; v.p. Cramer Assos., Inc., Allentown, Pa., 1973-77; asst. to convention coordinator Girl Scouts U.S.A., 1977-78; realtor asso. Ernie Palmer Realty, Fountain Hills, Ariz., 1979-80; broker Fountain Hills Real Estate Center, 1980-81; sales asso. Estes Homes, Phoenix, 1981-82; exec. dir. Chandler (Ariz.) United Way, 1982—. Bd. dirs. Sayre Child Center, 1973-76, Lehigh Valley of the Performing Arts, 1973-76. Mem. Dalmatian Club of Greater Phoenix (dir. 1980-82). Republican. Episcopalian. Home: 1124 S Chestnut St Mesa AZ 85204 Office: PO Box 567 Chandler AZ 85224

CRAMER, DOUGLAS SCHOOLFIELD, broadcasting executive; b. Louisville, Aug. 22; s. Douglas Schoolfield and Pauline (Compton) C.; student Northwestern U., 1949-50, Sorbonne, Paris, 1951; B.A., U. Cin., 1953; M.F.A., Columbia U., 1954; m. Joyce Haber, Sept. 25, 1966 (div. 1973); children—Douglas Schoolfield III, Courtney Sanford. Prodn. asst. Radio City Music Hall, 1950-51; with script dept. Metro-Goldwyn-Mayer, 1952; mng. dir. Cin. Playhouse, 1953-54; instr. Carnegie Inst. Tech., 1955-56; TV supr. Procter & Gamble, 1956-59; broadcast supr. Ogilvy, Benson & Mather, 1959-62; v.p. program devel. ABC, 1962-66, Twentieth Century-Fox-TV, Los Angeles, 1966-68; exec. v.p. in charge prodn. Paramount TV, 1968-71; ind. producer, pres. Douglas S. Cramer Co., 1971—; exec. v.p. Aaron Spelling Prodns., 1976—; exec. producer Bridget Loves Bernie, CBS-TV, 1972-73, QB VII, 1973-74, Dawn: Portrait of a Teenage Runaway; co-exec. producer Love Boat, Vegas, Aloha Paradise ABC, 1977-80, Wonder Woman, ABC, 1975-77, CBS, 1977-79, Matt Houston, Dynasty, Hotel. Served with AUS, 1954. Mem. Beta Theta Pi. Club: University (N.Y.C.). Author: (plays) Call of Duty, 1953; Love Is A Smoke, 1957; Whose Baby Are You, 1963. Office: Warner Hollywood 1041 N Formosa Ave Los Angeles CA 90046

CRAMER, ESTHER RIDGWAY, supermarket exec.; b. La Habra, Calif., Jan. 17, 1927; d. Claude Arthur and Ida Alma (Leutwiler) Ridgway; B.A., Pomona Coll., 1948; postgrad. U. So. Calif., 1949, Calif. State Coll., 1960-67; m. Stanley E. Cramer, June 17, 1948; children—Cynthia Ann Cramer Freeman, Melinda Cramer Ching, Janet Cramer Esguerra. Supr. phys. edn. Fullerton (Calif.) Schs., 1948-51; writer, historian, pub. relations adminstr. Alpha Beta Co., La Habra, Calif., 1973-74, dir. consumer affairs, 1974-81, v.p. community relations, 1981—; chmn. consumer affairs council Food Mktg. Inst., 1979-81. Mem. Orange County Hist. Commn., 1973—; mem. Orange County Bicentennial Com., 1969; chmn. La Habra City Anniversary and Am. Bicentennial Com., 1973-77. Vice pres. bd. govs. Patrons of Library, Calif. State U., Fullerton, 1971-77; bd. dirs. La Habra Boys and Girls Club, 1978—. Named Woman of Distinction, La Habra, 1976, Citizen of Year, 1978; Bicentennial Woman of Year, Bus. and Profl. Women, 1976. Mem. Calif., Orange County (pres. 1971-72) hist. socs., Calif. Conf. Hist. Socs., La Habra Old Settlers' Hist. Soc. (dir. 1973, historian 1973—, pres. 1976-77), Los Angeles Businessmen's Assn. (dir. 1981—), Los Angeles Public Affairs Officers Assn., Orange County and La Habra C. of C. (dir. 1978-79, 81—), Mortar Bd., Phi Beta Kappa. Club: Soroptomist (hon). Author: La Habra: The Pass through the Hills (award Am. Assn. for State and Local History 1970, U. Calif. at Irvine outstanding author award 1970), 1969; The Alpha Beta Story, 1973. Office: 777 S Harbor La Habra CA 90631

CRAMER, GARY MICHAEL, fin. adviser; b. Los Angeles, June 18, 1942; s. Alphonse Michael and Lynette (Hamm) C.; student U. Calif. at Berkeley, 1960-61; B.S., U. So. Calif., 1965; children—Deborah Rene, Lori Lynn. Auditor, Price Waterhouse & Co., Los Angeles, 1965-67; personal financial adv. Jack L. Warner, motion picture producer, 1967-79; treas. Crestview Realty Co., Beverly Hills, Calif., 1967-71, dir., 1967-71; pres. Sirice Assos., investment partnership, Los Angeles, 1968-69; dir. Ann B. and Jack L. Warner Found., Inc., Sigma Phi Epsilon House Inc. Ltd. Served with U.S. Army, 1965-71. C.P.A., Calif. Mem. Town Hall of Calif., Ranchview Homeowner's Assn. (pres. 1972-73), Am. Inst. C.P.A.'s, Calif. Soc. C.P.A.'s, Nat. Assn. Accountants, Commerce Assos. U. So. Calif., Alumni Assn. U. So. Calif., Los Angeles World Affairs Council, Sigma Phi Epsilon. Home: 705 S Broadway Redondo Beach CA 90277 Office: 1900 Ave of the Stars Suite 1065 Los Angeles CA 90067

CRAMER, GLENN A., airline company executive; b. 1921. With Calif. Eastern Airways Co., 1946-56, Calif. Eastern Aviation Inc., 1957-59; sales mgr. Lockheed Calif. Co., 1959-62; with Transamerica Airlines Inc., Oakland, Calif., 1962—, pres., 1964, chmn. bd., 1969—, also dir. Office: Transamerica Airlines Inc 7901 Oakport St Oakland CA 94621*

CRAMER, HARRISON EMERY, meteorological consultant; b. Johnstown, Pa., May 27, 1919; s. Frank Wilson and Ella Field (Emery) C.; A.B., Amherst Coll., 1941; S.M., M.I.T., 1943, Sc.D., 1948; m. Virginia Myrtle Viets, Dec. 21, 1942; children—Anne Cramer Tupker, Dorothy Cramer Kitchen, Nancy Cramer Donoghue, William. Instr., M.I.T., Cambridge, 1942-44, research asso., 1946-49, research meteorologist, 1949-65; v.p., dir. environ. scis. lab. GCA Corp., Bedford, Mass., 1965-72; pres. H. E. Cramer Co., Inc., Salt Lake City, 1972—. Served with USNR, 1944-46. Amherst Meml. fellow, 1941-42. Fellow Am. Meteorol. Soc., Royal Meteorol. Soc., AAAS; mem. Am. Geophys. Union, Air Pollution Control Assn., N.Y. Acad. Scis., Phi Beta Kappa, Sigma Xi. Office: 540 Arapeen Dr Salt Lake City UT 84108

CRAMER, JAMES DALE, physicist, sci. co. exec.; b. Canton, Ohio, Aug. 4, 1937; s. Dale and Vera Arlene (Lindower) C.; B.S., Calif. State U. at Fresno, 1960; M.S., U. Oreg., 1962; Ph.D., U. N.Mex., 1969; m. Geraldine M. Bendoski, July 20, 1957; children—Karen Lynn, Eric James. Mem. tech. staff U. Calif., Los Alamos, 1962-70; v.p., Davis-Smith Corp., San Diego, 1970-73; mem. tech. staff Sci. Applications Inc., LaJolla, Calif., 1970-73, group v.p., Albuquerque, 1973—, dir., 1974—; pres. Sci. & Engring. Assocs., Inc., Albuquerque, 1980—; cons. in field. Pres. Albuquerque Mus. Found., 1981—. Mem. Am. Phys. Soc., IEEE. Contbr. articles to profl. pubs. nuclear physics. Home: 4152 Dietz Farm Circle NW Albuquerque NM 87107 Office: 2500 Louisiana Blvd NW Albuquerque NM 87110

CRAMER, LORN WAYNE, organizational effectiveness specialist, army non-commissioned officer; b. Julesburg, Colo., May 3, 1944; s. John Calvin and Sylvia Laverne (Elmquist) C.; m. Norma Elree Dick, May 30, 1965; children—Lora Jolynn, Donna Lorraine. Grad. in basic med. lab. procedures Acad. Health Scis., Ft. Sam Houston, Tex., 1967, grad. in advanced med. lab. procedures, 1971; grad. Non-Commd. Officers Advanced Mgmt. Course, 1972; cert. in organizational effectiveness cons. U.S. Army Organizational Effectiveness Ctr. and Sch., 1982; B.S., U. San Francisco, 1981. Enlisted in U.S. Army, 1966, advanced through grades to master sgt. 1984; organizational effectiveness cons. Hdqrs. Command Group, Sixth Army, San Francisco, 1982—; tchr. group dynamics and strategic planning to groups; resoutrce mgmt. trainer. Decorated Bronze Star, Meritorious Service medal, Army Commendation medal with oak leaf cluster, Army Achievement medal; Cross of Gallantry with palm leaf (Vietnam). Mem. Am. Soc. Tng. and Devel., Non-Commd. Officer Assn., Assn. U.S. Army. Republican. Club: Masons. Home: 129-B Riley Ave Presidio San Francisco CA 94129 Office: Hdqrs 6th Army AFKC-OE San Francisco CA 94129

CRAMER, MARY THIEL, government lobbyist; b. Plymouth, Wis., Feb. 12, 1957; d. Joseph Donald and Ruth Eleanor (Dell) Thiel; m. Steven Edward Cramer, Dec. 18, 1982. B.S., Western Ill. U., 1978. Regional polit. rep. Nat. Assn. Realtors, Chgo., 1978-80; govt. relations dir. Colo. Assn. Realtors, Denver, 1980-83; lobbyist Rocky Mountain region Getty Oil Co., Denver, 1983—. Active Colo. Republican party; fin. chmn. Adams County Rep. Party, 1982-83; rec. sec. Mile High Rep. Women's Forum, 1982-83; bd. dirs. Adams County Mental Health Ctr. Recipient Young Career Woman of Yr., Bus. and Profl. Women's Club, 1981. Mem. Colo. Pub. Affairs Council, Colo. Assn. Commerce Industry, Am. Soc. Assn. Execs., Colo. Soc. Assn. Execs., Rocky Mountain Oil and Gas Assn., Colo. Petroleum Assn., Utah Petroleum Assn., Wyo. Petroleum Assn., N.D. Petroleum Assn., Mont. Petroleum Assn. Republican. Presbyterian. Club: Ranch Country (Denver). Contbr. articles to profl. jours. Home: 11828 Vallejo St Westminster CO 80234 Office: 1670 Broadway Denver CO 80202

CRAMER, RICHARD LOUIS, editor; b. Los Angeles, Apr. 5, 1947; s. Martin Michael and Charlotte Sonia (Kessel) C.; B.S.B.A., Calif. State U., 1969; m. Arlene Renee Jacobs, June 15, 1969; children—Matthew Hunter, Brandon Lloyd. Editor-in-chief Environ. Quality Mag., Los

Angeles, 1970-73; editor East/West Network, Los Angeles, 1973-75; editor-in-chief Denver Mag., 1975-76; sr. editor Los Angeles Mag., 1976-77; West Coast editor Playboy Mag., Los Angeles, 1977; editor-in-chief, assoc. pub. Oui Mag., Los Angeles, 1977-80; pres. FourWay Communications, Los Angeles, 1980—. Served with USAFR, 1966-70. Mem. Am. Soc. Journalists and Authors. Office: 2052 Cotner Ave West Los Angeles CA 90025

CRAMER, WILLIAM WAYNE, accountant, court commissioner; b. Lancaster, Pa., Apr. 20, 1949; s. Wayne W. and Frances Jane (Herr) C. B.S., Drexel U., 1972. C.P.A., Md., Wyo. With Peat, Marwick, Mitchell & Co., Balt., 1970-75, sr. staff acct., 1973-75; pvt. practice acctg., Pinedale, Wyo., 1975—; justice of peace, Sublette County, 1979—; apptd. commr. Dist. Ct., 1979—. Mem. Am. Inst. C.P.A.s, Wyo. Assn. Cts. of Limited Jurisdiction, Wyo. Jud. Council. Republican. Home and Office: Box 975 Bondurant WY 82922

CRANDALL, BLISS HANSEN, data processing executive, biometrician; b. Springville, Utah, Dec. 27, 1913; s. E. Vernon and Sylvia May C.; m. Mildred Johnson, June 23, 1937; children—Vern J., B. Lynn, Ken Lee. B.S., Utah State U., 1937, D.Sc. (hon.), 1977; M.S., Iowa State U., 1942. Agronomist, Dept. of Agr., Lincoln, Nebr., 1943-48; prof. applied stats., asst. dir. agrl. expt. sta. Utah State U., 1949-54; dean admissions and records Brigham Young U., 1955-58; pres., chmn. bd. DHI Computing Service, Inc., Provo, Utah, 1958—. Mem. Provo Sch. Bd., 1963-74, pres., 1969-70. Recipient service award Nat. Dairy Herd Improvement Assn., 1973; guest of honor Dairy Shrine Club, 1980. Mem. Am. Statis. Assn., Am. Dairy Sci. Assn. (Disting. Service award 1979). Mormon (stake pres. 1961-72). Developer computer system for eval. of dairy cattle prodn. Home: 1268 E 700 S Provo UT 84601 Office: 1625 W 820 N Provo UT 84601

CRANDALL, DANIEL TAYLOR, museum administrator; b. Ames, Iowa, Feb. 17, 1951; s. Perry Clarence and Margaret Ruth (Taylor) C.; m. Marilyn Alene Backman, June 27, 1976. A.A., Clark Coll., 1971; B.A., U. Wash., 1973, M.A., 1975. Asst. to curator ethnology Thomas Burke Meml., Wash. State Mus., 1971-75; dir. Cowlitz County Hist. Mus., Kelso, Wash., 1975-80; dir. Pittock Mansion, Portland, Oreg., 1980—. Mem. Hist. Preservation League Oreg. (bd. dirs.), Am. Assn. State and Local History (state membership chmn.), Nat. Trust Hist. Preservation, Oreg. Hist. Soc., Oreg. Mus. Assn. Wash. Trust Hist. Preservation. Methodist. Home: 3637 NE Alameda St Portland OR 97212 Office: 3229 NW Pittock Dr Portland OR 97210

CRANDALL, GARY JOSEPH, real estate devel. co. exec.; b. Pratt, Kans., June 4, 1947; s. Joseph Walter and Arlene Kay C.; B.B.A. (Wall St. Jour. Achievement award), U. N.Mex., 1969, M.B.A. (Sam Angel Meml. scholar), 1973; m. Jane Ellen Russell, Sept. 2, 1966; children—Melanie Anne, Martin Leslie, Maurice Spencer. Prin., corp. treas. Energy Conversion Systems, Inc., Albuquerque, 1969-70; mgr. acctg. Computer Micro Image Systems, Inc., Los Angeles, 1970-71; trainee Bank of N.Mex., Albuquerque, 1971-72, asst. v.p., mgr. credit dept., 1972-73, v.p., comml. loan officer, 1973-77; exec. v.p., prin. Bruce J. Pierce & Assos., Inc., Albuquerque, 1977—; v.p., dir. AMCO Services, Inc., 1981—; instr. Am. Inst. Banking, 1975-76. Loaned exec. United Fund, Albuquerque, 1974; mem. Gov.'s Devel. Credit Corp. Adv. Com., 1976; mem. Urban Devel. Action Task Force, Albuquerque Ctr. Mem. Albuquerque Assn. Credit Mgmt. (past pres., dir.), Internat. Bldg. Owners and Mgrs. Assn., Albuquerque Conservation Assn. (dir., mem. exec. com.), Albuquerque C. of C. (public safety com. 1976), Pi Kappa Alpha Alumni Assn. Republican. Clubs: Petroleum, U. N.Mex. Lobo. Home: 1701 Kit Carson SW Albuquerque NM 87104 Office: Bruce J Pierce & Assos Inc Suite 30 320 Central Ave SW Albuquerque NM 87102

CRANDALL, IRA CARLTON, consulting electrical engineer; b. South Amboy, N.J., Oct. 30, 1931; s. Carlton Francis and Claire Elizabeth (Harned) C.; B.S. in Radio Engring., Ind. Inst. Tech., 1954, B.S. in Elec. Engring., 1958; B.S. in Electronics Engring., U.S. Naval Postgrad. Sch., 1962; Ph.D., (postdoctoral fellow), U. Sussex, 1964; M.A., Piedmont U., 1967, D.S. Sc. (hon), 1968; LL.B., Blackstone Sch. Law, 1970; D.Litt., St. Matthew U., 1970; Ed.D., Mt. Sinai U., 1972; Asso. Bus., LaSalle U., 1975; m. Jane Leigh Ford, Jan. 29, 1954; children—Elizabeth Anne, Amy Leigh, Matthew Garrett. Tchr., Madison Twp. (N.J.) Pub. Schs., 1954-55; commd. ensign USN, 1955, advanced through grades to lt. comdr., 1965, released to inactive duty, 1972; engring. cons., Concord, Calif., 1972—. Pres. 7Cs Enterprises, Concord, 1972—; v.p. Dickinson Enterprises, Concord, 1973-77, Williamson Engring., Inc., Walnut Creek, Calif., 1974-82; pres., chmn. bd. I.C. Crandall and Assos., Inc., Concord and Westminster, Calif., Tigard, Oreg., 1976-82; pres. Internat. Research Assocs., Concord, 1982—; chief elec. engr. Gayner Engring. Inc., San Francisco, 1982—. Vice pres. PTA, Concord, 1969; tribal organizer Mt. Diablo YMCA Indian Guide Program, 1971—; pres. Mt. Diablo Unified Schs. Interested Citizens. Decorated Vietnamese Cross of Valor. Fellow Am. Coll. Engrs.; mem. U.S. Naval Inst. Am. Naval Assn., Assn. Elec. Engrs., IEEE, Am. Inst. Tech. Mgmt. (sr.), Soc. Am. Mil. Engrs., Nat. Model Ry. Assn., Concord Homeowners Assn., Concord Chamber Singers, Concord Blue Devils, S.A.R., Pi Upsilon Eta, Gamma Chi Epsilon, Alpha Gamma Upsilon. Republican. Methodist (adminstrv. bd. ch. 1971—). Clubs: Navy League, Century, Optimist (pres.). Address: 5754 Pepperridge Pl Concord CA 94521

CRANDALL, JERRY ROGER, educator; b. Portland, Oreg., June 9, 1930; s. Ralph Huff Crandall and Geraldine (Cole) Ellis; B.A. with honors, U. Oreg., 1957, Ed.M., 1962; children—Clyde Scott, Guy Thomas, Corbi Lyn, Daphne Sue, Kent Gawain. Grad. asst. instr. U. Oreg., 1957-59; head English dept. Pacific High Sch., Port Orford, Oreg., 1959-60, U.S. Grant High Sch., Portland, 1960-62; asst. prof. English, Coll. of So. Idaho, Twin Falls, 1962-63, Southwestern Oreg. Community Coll., Coos Bay, 1963-64; instr., chmn. dept. English, West Valley Coll., Saratoga, Calif., 1964—. Mem. Shakespeare Assn. Am., MLA, Nat. Council Tchrs. English, Coll. Conf. on Composition and Communication, Faculty Assn. Calif. Community Colls. (bd. govs. 1965-71, 74-77, pres. 1978-79), ACLU, Sierra Club, Friends of Earth, CEW, Inc. (pres.). Home: 1078 Polk Ln San Jose CA 95117 Office: English Dept West Valley Coll 14000 Fruitvale Ave Saratoga CA 95070

CRANDALL, KATHARINE JUNE WENDT, educational consultant; b. Kalispell, Mont., June 25, 1939; d. Otto Richard and Kathleen Maria (Chambers) Wendt; m. Larry Walter Crandall, Aug. 23, 1960; children—Darolyn Marie, Debora Ann, Craig Steven, Danielle Lucille. B.S., No. Mont. Coll., 1960; M.S., Wash. State U., 1975, Ph.D., 1983. Cert. tchr. Mont., Nev., Wash.; cert. state prin., supt. Wash. High sch. tchr., Mont., Wash., 1960-61; instr. Western Nev. Community Coll., Carson City, 1972-74; Nev. state supr. bus. and office occupations, 1975-78; teaching asst. Coll. of Bus., Wash. State U., Pullman, 1979-81; co-dir. Instructional Devel. Ednl. Assocs., Pullman, 1974—. Mem. Nev. State Career Edn. Adv. Com. 1977-78, Nev. Fleishmann Scholaship Comm. 1975-78, Washoe County (Nev.) CETA Clerical Tng. Adv. Council. Recipient Vocat. Edn. Grad. Leadership Devel. award Office Edn. Washington, 1978. Mem. Wash. State Assn. Adminstrv. Women in Edn., Am. Vocat. Assn., Nat. Assn. State Suprs. Bus. Edn., Nat. Fedn. Bus. and Profl. Women, AAUW, Phi Kappa Phi, Phi Delta Kappa. Democrat. Roman Catholic. Author: publs. in field. Home: NE 1255 Cove Way Pullman WA 99163

CRANDALL, MARJORIE ANN, mycologist; b. Bklyn., Mar. 15, 1940; d. George Henry and Beatrice Louise (Hart) Krautter; B.S., Cornell U., 1961; Ph.D., Ind. U., 1968; m. Jack Kenneth Crandall, Feb. 2, 1960; children—Laura Lynn. Lectr., Ind. U., Bloomington, 1971-74; instr. Bklyn. Coll., 1974; asst. prof. U. Ky., Lexington, 1974-80; assoc. research prof. Harbor-UCLA Med. Ctr., Torrance, Calif., 1980—. Mem. Am. Soc. Microbiology, Genetics Soc. Am., Med. Mycological Soc. Am., NOW, Sierra Club. Democrat. Unitarian. Contbr. articles to profl. jours. Home: 23930 Los Codona Apt 115 Torrance CA 90505 Office: Harbor-UCLA Med Center E-5 Torrance CA 90509

CRANE, FENWICK JAMES, insurance company executive; b. Cleve., July 9, 1923; s. Reginald J. and Ellie G. (Combes) C.; m. Vivian I. Crane, Oct. 11, 1947; children—Patricia Tadlock, Susan McLean. B.A., U. Mich., 1947. C.L.U. Home office rep. Aetna Life Ins. Co., Detroit, 1947-51; v.p. N.Y. Life Ins. Co., N.Y.C. and San Francisco, 1951-66; v.p. Ins. and Securities, Inc., San Francisco, 1966-69, also dir.; pres., chmn. bd. Family Life Ins. Co., Seattle, 1969—; dir. Merrill Lynch & Co., Inc., Pay 'n Save Corp., Prudential Bank. Trustee, Virginia Mason Research Ctr.; past pres. Seattle-King County Conv. and Visitors Bur.; past v.p. Seafair, Inc.; bd. dirs. Downtown Seattle Devel. Assn., Jr. Achievement Greater Seattle, Evergreen Safety Council; mem. devel. fund bd. U. Wash., past chmn. athletic adv. bd.; mem. devel. council, corp. relations com. U. Mich.; mem. exec. adv. council Sch. Bus. and Econs., Seattle Pacific U. Served with USMC, 1943-46. Clubs: Seattle Rotary, Broadmoor Golf, Rainier, Wash. Athletic; El Dorado Golf (Indian Wells, Calif.). Office: Park Place Seattle WA 98101

CRANE, JULES MELVIN, biology educator; b. N.Y.C., Sept. 5, 1928; s. Jules Maurice and Minnie A. Crane; m. Patricia Lee Watkins, Dec. 21, 1955; children—Ann, Dan, Susan, Elizabeth. A.B., NYU, 1954; M.A., Calif. State Coll.-Los Angeles, 1963; postgrad. Stanford U., 1961-65. Sci. tchr. Pub. Schs. Los Angeles, 1957-62; prof. dept. biology Cerritos Coll., Norwalk, Calif., 1963—, chmn. dept. biology, 1964-70, 74-78. Served to lt. AUS, 1950-53. Fellow So. Calif. Acad. Scis. (dir. 1968—, past pres.); mem. AAAS, Am. Soc. Ichthyologists and Herpetologists, Sigma Xi. Democrat. Jewish. Author: Introduction to Marine Biology, 1973; contbr. articles to profl. jours. Home: 165 Stanford Ln Seal Beach CA 90740 Office: Cerritos Coll 11110 E Alondra Blvd Norwalk CA 90650

CRANE, TERESE ANN, educator; b. Van Nuys, Calif., Oct. 3, 1947; d. Walter James and Leontine Emma (Karle) Riendeau; A.A. (Associated Student Body grantee 1966-67), Los Angeles Valley Coll., 1967; B.A., Mt. St. Mary's Coll., 1969; M.A., Calif. State U., Los Angeles, 1978; postgrad. (regents intern 1980-81) UCLA, 1978—; m. Bruce Allen Crane, Dec. 21, 1968; children—Matthew Allen, Adam Andrew. Tchr., Our Lady of Peace Sch., Sepulveda, Calif., Archdiocese Los Angeles, 1969-74, St. Didacus Sch., Sylmar, Calif., 1976-77, St. Jane France Sch., North Hollywood, Calif., 1977-78, Our Lady of Lourdes Sch., Tujunga, Calif., 1980-81; substitute tchr. Sulphur Springs Union Sch. Dist., 1979-80; tchr. St. Genevieve Sch., Panorama City, Calif., 1982-83; tchr., asst. prin. Our Lady of Peace Sch., Sepulveda, 1983—; lectr. St. Mary's Coll., summer 1982. Mem. Am. Soc. Curriculum Devel., Am. Ednl. Research Assn., Confluent Edn. Devel. and Research Center, Pi Lambda Theta, Phi Delta Kappa. Roman Catholic. Home: 17906 Wellhaven St Canyon Country CA 91351 Office: 9028 Langdon St Sepulveda CA 91343

CRANSTON, ALAN, U.S. senator; b. Palo Alto, Calif., June 19, 1914; s. William MacGregor and Carol (Dixon) C.; student Pomona (Calif.) Coll., 1932-33, U. Mex., 1935; A.B., Stanford U., 1936; m. Norma Weintraub, 1978; children—Robin MacGregor (dec.), Kim MacGregor. Fgn. corr. Internat. News Service, Eng., Italy, Ethiopia and Germany, 1936-38; Washington rep. Common Council for Am. Unity, Washington, 1940-41; chief fgn. lang. div. O.W.I., 1942-44; exec. sec. Council for Am.-Italian Affairs, Inc., Washington, 1945-46; with bldg. and real estate bus. Ames-Cranston Co., Palo Alto, Calif., 1947-58; controller State of Calif., 1959-67; pres. Homes for a Better Am., Inc., 1967-68; v.p. Carlsberg Fin. Corp., 1968; mem. U.S. Senate, 1969—, Dem. whip, 1977—, mem. banking, housing and urban affairs com., mem. fgn. relations com., ranking minority mem. vets. affairs com.; columnist Los Angeles Times, other newspapers, 1967-68; chmn. and rep. first meeting of UN, Dublin Conf. Com., 1945-46. Exec. com. Calif. Democratic Central Com., 1954-60; pres. Calif. Dem. Council, 1953-57. Served with AUS, 1944-45. Mem. United World Federalists (nat. pres. 1949-52), Overseas Press Club, Los Angeles Press Club. Author: (play) The Big Story (with Lee Falk), 1940; The Killing of the Peace, 1945; lectr. world affairs; contbr. numerous articles to newspapers, mags. Office: Senate Office Bldg Washington DC 20510

CRANZ, GALEN, architectural design educator; b. Seattle, Apr. 7, 1944; s. Richard F. and Phyllis (Whitaker) C.; B.A., Reed Coll., 1966; Ph.D., U. Chgo., 1971. Vis. asst. prof. Ill. Inst. Tech., 1969-71; asst. prof. Princton (N.J.) U., 1971-75; asst. prof. U. Calif.-Berkeley, 1975-81, assoc. prof. dept. architecture, 1981—; cons. in field; juror Progressive Arch. Design awards, 1980. NIMH fellow, 1966-68; USPHS fellow, 1968-69; Graham Found. grantee, 1973-78; Kellogg Nat. fellow, 1981—. Mem. Am. Sociol. Assn., Environ. Design Research Assn., Women's Study Group on Environ. Issues in China, Orgn. Women Architects. Author: Politics of Park Design: A History of Urban Parks in America, 1982; User Based Evaluation of Housing for the Elderly, 1975. Office: Dept Arch U Calif Berkeley CA 94720

CRARY, ELIZABETH ANN, parenting educator, author, consultant; b. New Orleans, May 18, 1942; d. Charles Harold and Lora Anne (Briggs) Deinken; m. Fred Dailey Crary, Aug. 14, 1966; children—Karl, Karen. B.S., La. State U., 1964, M.S., 1966. Research asst. Food Research Inst., U. Wis., 1966-70, food sci. dept., 1971-77; founder, dir. Parenthood Edn. Programs, Madison, Wis., 1974-77; instr. parent edn. North Seattle Community Coll., 1977—; pub. Parent Press, 1978—; co-dir. Parent Edn. Assocs., 1980—; Active Girl Scouts U.S.A. Mem. Nat. Assn. Edn. Young Children. Methodist. Author: Without Spanking or Spoiling, 1979; I Want It, 1981; I Can't Wait, 1981; I Want to Play, 1981; My Name Is Not Dummy, 1982. Office: 7750 31st Ave NE Seattle WA 98115

CRAVEN, HOMER HENRY, JR., pilot; b. Seattle, Jan. 31, 1925; s. Homer Henry and Juanita Normah (Briscoe) C.; student S.W. Tex. State Coll.; m. Mary Kathleen Weaver, May 3, 1945; children—James Michael, Scott Marshall, Anne Elizabeth Craven McDonald. With Boeing Airplane Co., Seattle, 1946-48, Smith Aviation, Renton, Wash., 1948-52; pilot Northwest Orient Airlines, Seattle, 1952—, B-747 capt., 1976—; aviation cons. 19—. Served with USAAF, 1943-45; PTO. Decorated Air medal. Mem. Am. Soc. Aerospace Edn., Nat. Aero. Assn., Exptl. Aircraft Assn., Aircraft Owners and Pilots Assn., 14th Air Force Assn., Northwest Captain's Club, Confederate Air Force. Episcopalian. Author research papers on fuel conservation. Home: 1060 89th St NE Bellevue WA 98004 Office: Northwest Airlines Sea-Tac Airport Seattle WA 98001

CRAVEN, WILLIAM A., state senator, businessman; m. Mimi Craven; children—William A., Tricia (Mrs. Don Worley), John. B.S., Villanova U. Sales mgr., sec. own corp.; Eastern sales rep. Philco Corp.; gen. mgr. concessions firm, Los Angeles; mem. Calif. State Assembly, 80th Assembly Dist., 1973-74, 76th Assembly Dist., 1975-78, former mem. local govt. com.; mem. Calif. State Senate, 38th Senatorial Dist., vice chmn. elections and repportionment com., mem. rules, agr. and water, local govt. coms., bus. and profl., joint legis. ethics coms. Chmn., exec. asst. San Diego County Bd. Suprs.; sr. analyst, county chief adminstrv. officer, county info. officer, city mgr., San Marcos, Calif. Served to maj., USMC, 1942-46, 50-53. Mem. Jaycees (past nat. dir.), Am. Soc. Adminstrs., San Diego County Local Agy. Formation Commn. (past chmn.), San Diego Regional Coastal Commn. (past vice chmn.). Republican. Home: 2318 Hogan Way Oceanside CA 92054 Office: California State Senate Sacramento CA 95814*

CRAWFORD, ARTHUR WALLACE, investment broker; b. Chgo., Mar. 24, 1921; s. Arthur Wallace and Elizabeth (Merrill) C.; A.B. cum laude, Harvard, 1941; m. Genevieve Byers Johnston, July 16, 1941 (div. 1976); children—Priscilla, Marie (Mrs. Charles Saale), Carol, Susan; m. 2d, Norma Silvas Myers, May 21, 1976. Market research analyst L. E. McGivena & Co., N.Y.C., 1941; exec. asst. N.Am. Aviation, Inc., Los Angeles, 1941-44, 1946-57; investment broker J. Barth & Co., Los Angeles, 1957-65, Dominick & Dominick, Inc., Los Angeles, 1965-67, White, Weld & Co., Los Angeles, 1967-73, Shields & Co., Los Angeles, 1973-75; investment broker Smith, Barney Harris Upham & Co., Inc., Los Angeles, 1975—, v.p.-sales. Served as lt. (j.g.) USNR, 1944-46; in U.S.S. Fred T. Berry. Republican. Clubs: Harvard of So. Calif., Athletic. Lectr. on investments. Author: Practical Portfolio Management, 1971. Home: 9160 Florence Ave #303 Downey CA 90240 Office: 800 W 6th St 11th Floor Los Angeles CA 90017

CRAWFORD, CAROL A., public relations executive; b. San Francisco, Jan. 17, 1945; d. Kenneth H. and Marvella (Schloesser) C. B.A., San Jose State U., 1967; postgrad. Golden Gate U., 1980—. Food publicist J. Walter Thompson, San Francisco 1967-70; asst. mktg and sales promotion dir. Eastridge Shopping Ctr., San Jose, Calif., 1970-72; consumer info. specialist Carl Byoir & Assocs., San Francisco, 1972-78; account supr. Ketchum Pub. Relations, San Francisco, 1978-80; v.p., dir. pub. relations Grey Advt., San Francisco, 1981-82; dir. corp. communications S&O Cons., San Francisco, 1982—; lectr. in pub. relations. Bd. mgrs. YMCA, Embarcadero, 1980-82. Mem. Pub. Relations Soc. Am. (chpt. treas., bd. dirs.), Am. Women in Radio and TV (past chpt. membership chmn.), Home Economists in Bus. (past chpt. chmn., past chmn. nat. pub. relations). Home: 808 Juno Ln Foster City CA 94404 Office: S&O Consultants 575 Sutter St San Francisco CA 94404

CRAWFORD, CHERYL ANNE, university administrator; b. Quincy, Mass., Sept. 18, 1955; d. Roy W. and Anne (Carmichael) C. B.A. in Bibl. and Theol. Studies, Gordon Coll., 1977; M.S. in Edn. Counseling and Adminstrn., U. So. Calif., 1980, Ph.D. in Ednl. Psychology, 1983. Head resident U. So. Calif., Los Angeles, 1978-80; dir. career devel. Biola U., La Mirada, Calif., 1980—; asst. dir., CIT dir. Camp Brookwoods and Deer Run, summers 1975-83, dir., 1983—. Mem. Am. Ednl. Research Assn., Am. Psychol. Assn., Nat. Assn. Student Personnel Adminstrs., Am. Coll. Personnel Assn., Phi Delta Kappa. Author: Life/Work Planning Manual, 1982; Adolescent Leadership: Research and Recommendations, 1982. Office: 13800 Biola Ave SH112 La Mirada CA 90639

CRAWFORD, JOHN ARTHUR, educator; b. Fort Dodge, Iowa, July 24, 1946; s. Joseph R. and Regis V. (Andrews) C.; B.S., Creighton U., 1968; M.S., U. Nebr., Omaha, 1971; Ph.D., Tex. Tech. U., 1974; m. Peggy Ann Clelland, Aug. 19, 1967. Teaching asst. U. Nebr., 1969-71; research asst. Tex. Tech. U., Lubbock, 1971-74; asst. prof. Oreg. State U., Corvallis, 1974-79, asso. prof. wildlife ecology, 1979—. Recipient Outstanding Young Men of Am. award Montgomery, Ala., 1980. Mem. Wildlife Soc., Am. Ornithologists' Union, Cooper Ornithol. Soc., Pacific N.W. Bird and Mammal Soc. Club: Triad Faculty. Home: 680 NW Survista Ave Corvallis OR 97330 Office: Dept Fisheries and Wildlife Oreg State U Corvallis OR 97331

CRAWFORD, JOSEPH BENJAMEN, ednl. adminstr.; b. Sarasota, Fla., Oct. 4, 1934; B.A. with honors in English and German, U. of Fla., Gainesville, 1958; postgrad. in Comparative Lit., Friedrich Alexander U., Erlangen (Germany); Ed.D. in Edn. Adminstrn., Harvard U., 1971; married; 3 children. Asst. supt. Westport (Conn.) Bd. Edn., 1969-72, Mt. Diablo Unified Sch. Dist., Concord, Calif., 1975-79; supt. Oldham County (Ky.) Bd. Edn., 1972-75, Pomona (Calif.) Unified Sch. Dist., 1979—. Mem. Am. Assn. Sch. Adminstrs., Assn. Sch. Bus. Ofcls. U.S. and Can., Assn. Calif. Sch. Adminstrs., NEA (life). Home: 2061 Yorba Dr Pomona CA 91768 Office: 800 S Garey Pomona CA 91766

CRAWFORD, JOYCE CATHERINE HOLMES, sch. psychologist; b. Kansas City, Mo., May 30, 1918; d. Morton Henry and Lillian Catharine (Burton) Holmes; student Kansas City Jr. Coll., 1934-36; B.S. in Edn., U. Mo., 1938; M.A. in Guidance and Counseling, No. Ariz. U., 1957; Ph.D. in Ednl. Psychology, Ariz. State U., 1976; m. Merle Eugene Crawford, Dec. 18, 1938; children—Hal Wayne, Kent Holmes. Tchr., Sedona, Ariz., 1948-49, Verde Valley Sch., 1949-51, Cottonwood, Ariz., 1952-69; sch. psychologist, child study cons., Phoenix, 1971-75, Riverside Sch. Dist., 1972-74, Avondale Sch. Dist., 1971-83. Ranger-naturalist Tuzigoot Nat. Monument, U.S. Park Service, summers 1959-66. Mem. Ariz. Gov.'s Adv. Com. on Mental Health, 1964-65, Ariz. Hosp. Survey and Constrn. Adv. Council, 1965-68; head start chmn. Cottonwood Neighborhood Council, 1967-69; sec. Yavapai County Head Start Policy Adv. Com., 1968-71; bd. dirs. Yavapai County Econ. Opportunity Council, 1967-70, sec., 1968-69. Bd. dirs. Ariz. Assn. Mental Health, 1955-67, sec., 1961-64, founder Verde Valley chpt., 1956, pres., 1959-61; incorporating com. Verde Valley Community Guidance Clinic, 1965, bd. dirs., 1965-70; bd. dirs. No. Ariz. Comprehensive Guidance Center, 1967-69; bd. dirs., recreation chmn. Ariz. Congress Parents and Tchrs., 1954-55; bd. dirs. Westside Mental Health Services, 1980—, pres., 1980, v.p., 1980-81. Cert. Ariz. Bd. Psychologist Examiners. Mem. Nat. Assn. Sch. Psychologists, Ariz. Assn. Sch. Psychologist (chmn. profl. standards com. 1980-81, pres. 1982-83), Am. Psychol. Assn., Ariz. Psychol. Assn., Maricopa Psychol. Soc., Ariz. Assn. Children with Learning Disabilities, Ariz. Assn. Retarded Children, Am. Assn. UN, Common Cause, ACLU, Delta Kappa Gamma. Democrat. Club: Soroptimists. Home: Box 300 606 N 161st Ave Goodyear AZ 85338 Office: 235 W Western Ave Avondale AZ 85323

CRAWFORD, MARVIN LEONARD, SR., ednl. adminstr.; b. Los Angeles, Mar. 12, 1926; s. James and Emily Georgia (Gough) C.; student Los Angeles City Coll., 1944; B.A., Humboldt State Tchrs. Coll., 1950; M.A., Long Beach State Coll., 1958; postgrad. UCLA, 1954—, U. So. Calif., 1964—, Nova U., 1975; m. Ethel Mae Goodwin, Aug. 21, 1948; children—Carmen, Marvin Leonard. Tchr. Willowbrook Dist. schs., 1950-51; tchr. Enterprise Dist. schs., 1951-54, prin., 1954-65, asst. supt., personnel dir. 1965-68, dist. supt., 1968-70; adminstrv. analyst Compton Unified Sch. Dist., Los Angeles, 1970-72, adminstr. Area I schs., 1972-74, asst. supt. elementary schs., 1974-76, disability leave of absence, 1976—. Guidance conf. cons., Sch. Edn., 1969, Tuskegee Inst., Ala., 1969; visitor sch. dists. around the world, 1961-62. Mem. purchasing adv. com. County Los Angeles, 1968-70. Bd. dirs. Compton Welfare Planning Com., 1968-71. Served as sgt. maj. USAAC, 1944-46; PTO. Mem. PTA (life), Enterprise Tchr. Assn. (sec. 1954), Assn. Supervision and Curriculum Devel., Dept. Elementary Sch. Prins., Calif. Tchrs. Assn., Am. Assn. Sch. Adminstrs., NEA, Calif. Elementary Sch. Adminstrs. Assn., Los Angeles County Sch. Adminstrs. and Suprs. Assn., Calif. Assn. Sch. Adminstrs., Compton Ednl. Assn., Assn. Compton Unified Sch. Adminstrs., Phi Delta Kappa. Home: 6432 Langdon Ave Midvale Estates Van Nuys CA 91406 Office: 604 S Tamarind Ave Compton CA 90220

CRAWFORD, NATALIE WILSON, applied mathematician; b. Evansville, Ind., June 24, 1939; d. John Moore and Edna Dorothea (Huthsteiner) Wilson; B.A. in Math., U. Calif., Los Angeles, 1961, postgrad., 1964-67; m. Robert Charles Crawford, Mar. 1, 1969. Programmer analyst N.Am. Aviation Corp., El Segundo, Calif., 1961-64; mem. tech. staff Rand Corp., Santa Monica, Calif., 1964—, project leader, engring. tech., theater conflict and force employment programs, 1975—; cons., joint tech. coordinating group munition effectiveness. Named YWCA Woman of Yr., 1983. Mem. Am. Def. Preparedness Assn., USAF Assn., IEEE. Republican. Home: 20940 Big Rock Dr Malibu CA 90265

CRAWFORD, NEIL STANLEY, lawyer, Canadian provincial government official; b. Prince Albert, Sask., Can., May 26, 1931; s. William Francis and Hannah (Hoehn) C.; m. Catherine May Hughes, Sept. 3, 1951; children—Scot, Teresa, Ian, Elaine, Sandra, Robert. B.A., U. Sask., 1952, LL.B., 1954. Created queen's counsel 1972. Practice law, 1955-61, 63-71; exec. asst. to Prime Minister, 1961-63; mem. Legis. Assembly of Alta., 1971—, minister Health and Social Devel., 1971-75, minister Labour, 1975-79, atty. gen., govt. house leader, 1979—. Served to 2d lt. Royal Can. Army, 1951-60. Mem. Can. Bar Assn., Law Soc. Alta. Progressive Conservative. Office: Legislative Bldg Room 227 Edmonton AB T5K 2B6 Canada

CRAWFORD, PAUL CLINTON, city planner, filmmaker, photographer; b. Chgo., Aug. 24, 1947; s. John Clinton and Elizabeth Byrne (Burch) C.; A.A., Coll. Sequoias, 1967; B.S. in City and Regional Planning, Calif. Poly. State U., 1971; m. Diana Gwenythe Hagberg, June 1969; 1 son, Jeremy Eric; m. 2d, Linda Suzan Lull, Nov. 17, 1978; 1 dau., Wendy Sarah. Jr. planner City of Visalia (Calif.), 1971-73; asso. planner Quad Cos., Visalia, 1973-74; co-owner Osiris Prodns., Santa Barbara, Calif., 1973—; asso. planner San Luis Obispo County (Calif.) Planning Dept., 1975-76, sr. planner, 1976-78; prin. planner, project mgr. land use element, 1978-79, dep. planning dir., 1979-80; planning dir., sec. San Luis Obispo County Area Council of Govts., 1980—; lectr. Calif. State Poly. U., 1980—; pres. Visual Storage, 1980—; producer, dir. motion pictures: Underground Wilderness, 1975, The World Within, 1978, Marathon Seven, 1980; photographs pub. in housing and archtl. mags. Mem. Am. Planning Assn. (editor Central Coast Sect. News 1980—), Nat. Speleological Soc., Urban and Regional Info. Systems Assn., Calif. County Planning Dirs. Assn. Office: County Govt Center San Luis Obispo CA 93408

CRAWFORD, TERRY NORMAN, marketing manager; b. Los Angeles, Apr. 24, 1945; s. Norman Oscar and Harriet (Hedelund) C.; m. Margaret Ann Kliks, Feb. 7, 1970; children—Ian Ross, Jennifer Ann. B.A. in Biology, U. Oreg., 1967; M.B.A., Portland State U., 1979. Salesman Mead Johnson Labs., Walnut Creek, Calif., 1972-73, Becton-Dickinson, Calif., 1973-76; sales mgr. Fiber Optics Engring., Calif., 1976-77; instr. dept. mktg. Portland (Oreg.) State U., 1979-80; customer mktg. engr. Intel, Portland, 1980—. Vestryman Episcopal Ch., 1980-83, jr. warden; coordinator March of Dimes Walkathon, 1978. Served to lt. USN, 1967-72. Mem. Am. Mktg. Assn. (nat. chpt. and Oreg. chpt. newsletter editor 1980-81, v.p. chpt. affairs 1981-82, chpt. pres. 1983—), Jaycees (pres. Concord, Calif. 1973-77), Beta Gamma Sigma. Republican. Club: Sertoma.

CRAWFORD, TIMOTHY ROY, cleaning co. exec.; b. Medford, Oreg., Nov. 27, 1940; s. George J. and Doris E. (Macfarland) C.; student Portland State U., 1962; m. Carole L. Bothwell, June 23, 1959; children—Timothy Roy, Carrie, Chriss, Todd, Teauge. Laundry mgr. Troy Laundry Co., Portland, Oreg., 1957-67; gen. mgr. Alaska Cleaners, Inc., Anchorage, 1967—; gen. mgr. Alaska Cleaners, Alaska Textiles, Alaska Uniform and Work Clothes, Far North Equipment and Supply, Harris & Martens Enterprises. Mem. Linen Supply Assn. Am., Internat. Fabricare Inst., Nat. Inst. Drycleaning, Nat. Muzzle Loading Rifle Assn., Nat. Assn. Primitive Rifleman, Mckinley Mountainmen (pres.), Izaak Walton League (trustee). Contbr. articles to Linen Supply News. Home: 10034 Goodnews Circle Anchorage AK 99502 Office: 610 W Fireweed Ln Anchorage AK 99503

CRAWFORD, WILLIAM RICHARDSON, psychologist; b. Plant City, Fla., Feb. 5, 1936; s. W. R. and Thelma Lorene (Brown) C. B.S., Fla. State U., 1958, M.S., 1960, Ed.D., 1966. Lic. psychologist, Calif. Asst. prof. psychology San Franciso State U., 1967-69; asst. prof. Coll. Medicine U. Ill., Chgo., 1969-72; project coordinator UCLA, 1972-76; postdoctoral fellow Wright Inst., Los Angeles, 1976-78, clin. supr., 1978—; pvt. practice psychology, Los Angeles, 1978—; mem. Psychology Examining Com., Calif. Bd. Med. Quality, 1981—. Served to 1st lt. USAR, 1959-63. Recipient Disting. and Dedicated Service award Los Angeles Soc. Clin. Psychologists, 1979. Mem. Am. Psychol. Assn., Calif. State Psychol. Assn. (treas. 1981), Los Angeles County Psychol. Assn., Am. Ednl. Research Assn., So. Calif. Soc. Clin. Hypnosis, Am. Acad. Behavioral Medicine (diplomate). Democrat. Author: The Psychology of Learning and Instruction: Educational Psychology, 2d edit., 1974; contbr. articles to profl. jours. Home: 12310 Hesby St North Hollywood CA 91607

CREAGER, CLIFFORD RAYMOND, editor; b. N.Y.C., Oct. 8, 1937; s. Clifford Henry and Catherine (Raymond) C.; A.B., U. Mich., 1960; m. Dorothy Ann Carlson, Dec. 18, 1965; children—Christopher, Curtis. Reporter, wire editor, photographer Grand Haven (Mich.) Daily Tribune, 1960-61; reporter, photographer, city editor, editor Covina (Calif.) Sentinel, weekly, 1963-72; mng. editor Car Craft mag., Los Angeles, 1972-75, Motor Trend mag., Los Angeles, 1975-81; free-lance writer, editor, 1981—. Served with AUS, 1961-63. Mem. U. Mich. Alumni Assn., Am. Auto Racing Writers and Broadcasters Assn.

CREAGER, FREDERICK LEON, architect; b. Springfield, Mass., Mar. 9, 1926; s. Frederick Leon and Alma (Jones) C.; m. Evelyn Timmons, Dec. 25, 1949; children—Doric, Kurt. B.S. in Architecture, U. Ill., 1954. Registered architect, Wash., Idaho, Mont., Iowa. Architect various archtl. cos., 1947-69; sec.-treas. Brooks, Hensley, Creager, Architects, P.S., Spokane, Wash., 1969—; vis. prof. Sch. Architecture, U. Hawaii, Manoa, 1982. Commr. Housing Authority Jo Daviess County (Ill.), 1955-62; bd. dirs. Spokane Christian Coalition, 1978-81, Riverview Retirement Home, 1979—, Riverview Convalescent Ctr., 1979—; mem. Luth. Council Greater Spokane, 1972-74. Served with USAAF, 1943-47; to capt. USAF, 1947-74. Ricker Club fellow U. Ill., 1981. Mem. AIA (pres. Wash. Council 1975), Panel Constrn. Arbitrators, Am. Arbitration Assn., Constrn. Specifications Inst., Soc. Archtl. Historians, Inst. Urban Design, Soc. Am. Mil. Engrs., U. Ill. Alumni Assn. Republican. Lutheran. Clubs: U. Spokane, Elks, Masons. Home: S 1212 Wall St Spokane WA 99204 Office: S 121 Wall St Spokane WA 99204

CREAMER, WILLIAM PAUL, banker; b. Aldan, Pa., Nov. 22, 1945; s. Paul T. and Rita E. (Heywood) C.; B.S., Widener U., 1968, M.B.A., 1971; m. Geraldine J. Bluebello, Jan. 13, 1968; children—Darren William, Dorria Jane, Drew Thomas. Cost acct. E.I. DuPont, 1968-72; sr. fin. officer Girard Bank, Phila., 1972-76; with Bank of Am., San Francisco., 1976—, v.p., head corp. cash mgmt. dept., 1976-80, v.p. high tech. sect., 1981; v.p., head internat. sales and mktg. Bank Am. Travelers Cheques Corp., 1981—; prof. mktg. Mem. Tau Kappa Epsilon. Republican. Contbr. articles to profl. jours. Inventor computer model to analyze and forecast corp. growth. Office: 555 California St San Francisco CA 94137

CREDIDIO, STEVEN GEORGE, psychologist; b. Bronx, N.Y., Sept. 5, 1949; s. George G. and Josephine (Persiano) C.; B.S., Fordham U., 1971; M.A., U. Detroit, 1974, Ph.D., 1975. Lectr., Marygrove Coll., Detroit, 1975-76; staff psychologist Mental Hygiene Clinic, dir. biofeedback headache clinic F.D.R. VA Med. Center, Montrose, N.Y., 1976-80; staff psychologist, dir. stress mgmt. clinic VA Outpatient Clinic, Los Angeles, 1980—; clin. asso. prof. Fuller Grad. Sch. Psychology, Pasadena, 1980—; adj. prof. Pepperdine U., 1982. Diplomate in clin. psychology Am. Bd Profl. Psychology. Mem. Western Psychol. Assn., Am. Psychol. Assn., Biofeedback Soc. Am., Calif. Psychol. Assn., Assn. Advancement of Psychology. Author articles on psychophysiol. assessment, stress mgmt. and biofeedback. Home: 12772 Pacific Ave #5 Los Angeles CA 90066 Office: 425 S Hill St Los Angeles CA 90013

CREEDON, JEREMIAH VINCENT, hosp. adminstr.; b. San Francisco, Nov. 26, 1919; s. Jeremiah and Catherine Agnes (McCarthy) C.; B.A., Compton Coll., 1939; m. Jean Helen Willett, June 25, 1941; children—Michael, Thomas, Ann, Jeannie. Commd. aviation cadet U.S. Army Air Force, 1942, advanced through grades to lt. col. U.S. Air Force, 1964; served with 20th Bomb Wing, Saipan, pilot combat missions, 1944-45; staff meteorologist Air Force Safety Directorate, 1964-67; dep. insp. gen. Air Weather Service, 1967-68; ret., 1971; alcoholism counselor Raleigh Hills Hosp., Newport Beach, Calif., 1972-74, adminstr., Fair Oaks, Calif., 1975-76, Newport Beach, 1976-79; dir. facilities devel. Advanced Health Systems, Irvine, Calif., 1979—. Decorated D.F.C., Air medal with 5 oak leaf clusters, Purple Heart, others; recipient award of Merit Raleigh Hills Hosp., 1975, named Employee of Year, 1976. Mem. Am. Meteorol. Soc., Ret. Officers Assn., DAV, Counselors on Alcoholism and Addictions Assn., Nat. Assn. Alcoholism Treatment Programs (charter dir.). Republican. Roman Catholic. Home: 2 Wandering Rill St Irvine CA 92715 Office: 1501 E 16th St Newport Beach CA 92663

CREGO, CLYDE ALLAN, JR., psychologist; b. Missoula, Mont., June 6, 1936; s. Clyde A. and June (Soderholm) C.; m. Marilyn Wendland, Oct. 7, 1978; children—by previous marriage: Terri Jo, Allan Mason. B.A., U. Mont., 1958; Ph.D., Mich. State U., 1966. Lic. psychologist, Va., Mo., Wash. Chief of counseling U. Mo., Columbia, 1971-83; psychologist U.S. Intelligence Community, Washington, 1969-71; asst. prof. psychology Wash. State U., 1967-69, U. N.C., Chapel Hill, 1966-67; dir. dept. counseling and human devel. services Calif. State U.-Long Beach, 1983—; cons. in field. Recipient Spl. commendation, City Council, Columbia, Mo., 1977. Mem. Am. Psychol. Assn. Contbr. articles to profl. jours. Address: Dept Counseling and Human Devel Services Calif State Univ Long Beach CA 90840

CREIGHTON, DAVID EDWARD, JR., civil engr.; b. Los Angeles, Aug. 27, 1923; s. David Edward and Ethel (Collier) C.; B.S., U. Ariz., 1948; student Washington U., 1943-44; m. Judith Matlock, June 3, 1947; children—James Matlock, Nancy Jean, Hannah Pauline, Robert David. Civil engr., dams sect. U.S. Bur. Reclamation, Sacramento, 1948-50, materials engr. Cachuma project, Goleta, 1950, constrn. engr. Cachuma Day, 1951, constrn. mgmt. engr. Cachuma Dam, 1952; plans and estimate engr. U.S. Bur. Reclamation, Goleta and Santa Barbara, 1953-57; planning engr. Cosumnes River div. Central Valley Project, Sacramento, 1957-61, planning coordinator Central Ariz. Project and Pacific S.W. Water Plan, Phoenix, 1961-65, chief planning and reports div. Phoenix Devel. Office, 1965-72, chief environ. reports br. Ariz. Projects Office, 1972-73, projects environ. officer, 1973-77, environ. engr. Regional Office of Environment, 1977; environ. coordinator Western Area Power Adminstrn., Dept. Energy, 1977-78; civil engr. Ariz. Water Commn., Ariz. Groundwater Study Commn., 1978-79; civil engr. phase I Nat. Dam Safety Program, Dept. Water Resources, 1979-81; cons. engr., 1981-83; civil engr. Div. Dam Safety, Ariz. Dept. Water Resources, 1983—. Mem. nominating com. Presbytery of Phoenix, United Prebyterian Ch., 1965-67, mem. rev. Presbytery records com. Synod of Ariz., 1968-72, Synod of S.W., 1973-75, Ganado Commn., 1979; leader environ. impact workshop U. Wis., 1974, chmn. com. T-201, 1968-77, instnl. rep., 1978—; adv. chmn. Boy Scouts Am., Explorer Scouts 1964-69, chmn. Scottsdale Dist. bd. rev., 1966-72, instnl. rep., 1977—. Served with U.S. Army, 1943-45. Decorated Purple Heart; recipient certificate of superior performance U.S. Dept. Interior, 1963, certificate of meritorious service, 1966, performance award, 1973; registered profl. engr., Ariz. Calif. Fellow ASCE; mem. Nat. Rifle Assn (life), Theta Tau. Club: Santa Ynez Valley Rifle and Pistol (v.p. 1955) (Solvang, Calif.). Home: 7308 E Fillmore St Scottsdale AZ 85257 Office: 99 E Virginia Phoenix AZ 85004

CREIGHTON, HOWARD CLEVELAND, real estate broker; b. Oakland, Calif., Dec. 17, 1944; s. Joseph Riggs and Margaret Hitchner) C.; B.A., Oberlin Coll., 1966; M.B.A., Harvard U., 1968; m. Heather Spencer-Green, June 15, 1968; children—Holly, Robin. Asst. v.p. James W. Rouse & Co., San Francisco, 1972-75; v.p., Western regional mgr. DRG Fin. Corp., San Francisco, 1975-79; pres. Creighton Realty Services, Inc., San Rafael, Calif., 1979—; cons. Earl Warren Legal Inst., U. Calif.-Berkeley. Bd. dirs. Ross Valley Ecumenical Housing Assn., 1978—. Served to lt. (j.g.) USNR, 1968-71. Mem. Bay Area Mortgage Assn. (pres. 1979-80). Libertarian. Presbyterian. Home: 39 Moody Ct San Rafael CA 94901

CREIGHTON, LUCY BLACK, economist; b. Birmingham, Ala., Sept. 8, 1927; d. Walter Steele and Winifred Lane (Castleman) Black; m. Thomas Edwin Creighton, Sept. 27, 1952; children—Thomas Edwin, Winifred, Ann, Virginia. A.B., Smith Coll., 1949; M.A., Radcliffe Coll., 1952; Ph.D., Harvard U., 1969. Faculty, Colo. Women's Coll., 1964-77; corp. economist First Nat. Bancorp., Denver, 1978—; dir. First Nat. Bank of S.W.; cons. Mem. Colo. Compensation Commn.; bd. dirs. Colo. Christian Home, Loretto Heights Coll., Highland Neighborhood Housing Service; trustee Park Hill Congregational Ch. Mem. Nat. Assn. Bus. Economists, Am. Econ. Assn., Women's Forum Colo., Nat. Assn. Bus. Economists, Phi Beta Kappa. Democrat. Mem. Ch. of Christ. Office: PO Box 5605 Denver CO 80217

CRENSHAW, JOHN PATRICK, aerospace engineer; b. Atlanta, Apr. 24, 1938; s. Alvin Herman and Martha Virginia (Murphy) C.; children—Elizabeth Anne, Karen Marie. B.S. in Aero. Engring., Ga. Inst. Tech., 1961, M.S., 1963, Ph.D., 1966. Tech. staff mem. Aerospace Corp., San Bernardino and El Segundo, Calif., 1966-74; engring. assoc. PDA Engring., Santa Anns, Calif., 1974-77; staff engr. Acurex Corp., Mountain View, Calif., 1977-80, prin. scientist, 1980—. NASA trainee, 1962. Assoc. fellow AIAA (atmospheric flight mech. tech. com.). Research and publs. in aerodynamics, flight mech. of atmospheric re-entry vehicles. Home: 6578 American Ct San Jose CA 95120 Office: 485 Clyde Ave Mountain View CA 94042

CRENSHAW, THERESA LARSEN, physician; b. Stockholm, Sept. 25, 1942; d. Einar and Ulrika Margaretta (Ehrenborg) Larsen; adopted d. Louis Ferrari, Jr.; came to U.S., 1948, naturalized, 1958; B.A., Stanford, 1964; M.D., U. Calif.-Irvine, 1969; m. Roger Timothy Crenshaw, Aug. 26, 1967 (div. Dec. 1978); 1 son, Brant Eric. Served to lt. comdr. M.C., U.S. Navy, 1969-73; staff U.S. Naval Hosp., Naples, Italy; fellow with Masters and Johnson, Reproductive Biology Research Found., 1974-75; practice medicine specializing in treatment and evaluation of marital and sexual dysfunction, San Diego, 1975—; dir. Crenshaw Clinic; asst. clin. prof. reproductive medicine, co-dir. human sexuality U. Calif. Med. Sch., San Diego; lectr., cons. in field. Mem. Am. Assn. Sex Educators, Counselors and Therapists (co-chmn. Western region 1976-78, nat. v.p. 1979-81), Am. Psychiat. Assn. (assoc.), Am. Acad. Family Practice, Am. Assn. Marriage and Family Counselors. Author: Emergency Care: Emergency Management of Sexual Assault, 1978; Expressing Your Own Feelings, 1980; contbg. editor: Rape: Helping the Victim, 1978; Bedside Manners: A Guide to Better Sex, 1983; contbr. articles to profl. jours.

CRESWELL, DONALD CRESTON, mgmt. cons., mktg. specialist; b. Balt., Mar. 28, 1932; s. Carroll Creston and Verna Moore (Taylor) C.; student Johns Hopkins U., 1951-52; M.B.A., U. Dayton, 1966; postgrad. bus. Stanford U., 1975; m. Terri Sue Tidwell, Dec. 28, 1958; 1 son, Creston Lee. Cons. engr. A.D. Ring & Assos., Washington, 1956-58; sales and mktg. mgr. Ampex Corp., Redwood City, Calif., 1959-68; dir. mktg., magnetic products div. RCA Corp., N.Y.C., 1968-71; staff v.p. sales and advt. Pan Am. World Airways, N.Y.C., 1971-74; mktg. v.p. Rocor Internat., Palo Alto, Calif., 1975; v.p., chief operating officer, gen. mgr., Am. AmBuCar Services, Inc., San Francisco, 1976; prin. mgmt. cons., dir. mktg. services Stanford Research Inst., Menlo Park, Calif., 1977—; dir. Rogerson Aircraft Controls, 1981—; lectr. planning and mktg. mgmt. Am. Mgmt. Assn., 1968-69; program chmn. Grad. Bus. Assn., 1965; rep. to Electronics Industries Assn., 1968-71, to Internat. Air Transport Assn., 1971-74. Bd. dirs. Peninsula Youth Soccer Club, 1981-82; regional chief referee San Carlos Am. Youth Soccer Orgn., 1981—; State dir. assessment Calif. Soccer Assn., 1982—; ofcl. N. Am. Soccer League, 1983. Mem. Am. Theatre Organ Assn. (bd. dirs. 1978-79), Nat. Intercollegiate Soccer Ofcls. Assn., U.S. Soccer Fedn. (cert. soccer referee). Republican. Club: Wings. Home: 3328 Brittan Ave San Carlos CA 94070 Office: 333 Ravenswood Ave Menlo Park CA 94025

CRETSER, GARY ALLEN, educator; b. Santa Monica; Calif.; Apr. 10, 1942; s. Glenn Allen and Phyllis (Renfro) C. B.A. cum laude, U. So. Calif., 1965, M.A., 1967, Ph.D., 1972. Assoc. in sociology U. Calif., San Diego, 1967-68; asst. prof. sociology Calif. State Poly. U., Pomona, 1966-70, assoc. prof., 1971-76, lectr. continuing edn., 1978, 80, chmn. behavioral sci. dept., 1975—, prof. sociology, 1976—; cons. in field. Mem. Am. Sociol. Assn., AAUP, Norsk, Sosioloforening, Pacific Sociol. Assn., Alpha Kappa Delta, Psi Chi. Manuscript reviewer McGraw Hill Book Co., Hill Book Co., Wadsworth Pub.; contbr. articles to profl. jours. Home: 650 W 25 St Upland CA 91786 Office: Calif State Poly Univ Pomona CA 91768

CREWS, MARIE LANTZ, educator; b. Casper, Wyo, Aug. 9, 1931; d. Peter Martinison and Rubie Julia (Lantz) Indergard; m. Clifton Carroll Crews, Apr. 25, 1953. Student Phoenix Coll., 1968-69; B.A., Ariz. State U., 1971, M.A. in Edn., 1973, postgrad., 1973-80. Cert. vocat. educator, Ariz. Sec., Loffland Bros. Drilling Co. and Amoco Petroleum Corp., Casper, 1950-57; legal sec. McLane & McLane, Phoenix, 1957-62; sec. Davis Acctg. Co., Scottsdale, Ariz., 1969-70; instr. Key-Tape Computer, Ambassador Leather Co., Tempe, Ariz., 1971; tchr. bus. dept. East High Sch., Tempe, 1971-72; tchr. Coop. Office edn. coordinator bus. dept. Marcos de Niza High Sch., Tempe, 1972—; condr. surveys. Adviser Future Bus. Leaders Am. Recipient Outstanding Service award bus. dept. Marcos de Niza High Sch.; 1983. Mem. Tempe Secs. Edn. Assn., Am. Bus. Edn. Assn., Nat. Bus. Edn. Assn., Computer Users in Edn. Soc., Word Processors in Ariz., Pi Omega Pi, Kappa Delta Pi. Republican. Lutheran. Co-author: Arizona Business Occupations Curriculum Guide, 1976; mem. com. for Ariz. Bus. Occupations Competency-Based Curriculum Guide, 1980. Home: 5505 S Jolly Roger Rd Tempe AZ 85283 Office: 6000 S Lakeshore Dr Tempe AZ 85283

CREWS, PATRICIA EILEEN, editor; b. Pasadena, Calif., Aug. 24, 1944; d. Joseph Albert and Natalie (Contreras) McCloskey; student Pasadena City Coll., 1962-63; children—Kathleen, J.J., Andrea. With R.C. Modeler and Freshwater & Marine Aquarium mag., Sierra Madre, Calif., 1963—, exec. editor, 1967—, sec.-treas., 1967—. Democrat. Roman Catholic. Address: 120 W Sierra Madre Blvd Sierra Madre CA 91024

CREWS, RICHARD LAWRENCE, university president, psychiatrist; b. N.Y.C., July 11, 1937. B.A. magna cum laude, Williams Coll., 1959; M.D., Harvard U., Boston, 1963. Intern, San Francisco Gen. Hosp., 1963-64; resident in psychiatry Letterman Gen. Hosp., Presidio of San Francisco, 1965-68; practice medicine specializing in psychiatry, Mill Valley, Calif., 1971—; clin. practice homeopathy and nutritional counselling, Mill Valley, 1977-80; co-founder, pres. Columbia Pacific U., 1978—; mem. staff Marin Gen. Hosp., Ross Gen. Hosp., Marin County, Calif.; co-founder Brookwood Gen. Hosp., Santa Rosa, Calif., 1971, mem. staff, 1973-79; cons. Calif. Disability Evaluation Bd., 1974—; lectr. U.S. Army Edn. Ctr., Ft. Bragg, N.C., 1969-70, U. N.C. Grad. Sch. Social Work, 1970-71, Coll. Marin, 1971-72; lectr. and cons. in psychology Dominican Coll., 1972-75; exec. and clin. dir. Creative Living Ctrs. of Marin County, 1972-75; pres. Brookwood Hosp. Corp., 1975-80; exec. and clin. dir. Wholistic Health and Nutrition Inst., Mill Valley, 1977-79, bd. dirs., 1977—; co-founder N.Am. Coll. Natural Health Scis., Mill Valley and San Rafael, Calif., 1978, designer, adminstr., educator nutrition curriculum, 1978-80. Served to maj. M.C., U.S. Army, 1964-71. Decorated Legion of Merit. Mem. MENSA. Author: Introductory Workbook in Homeopathy, 1978. Office: Columbia Pacific U 1415 3d St San Rafael CA 94901

CRICHTON, JOHN HAYES, investment banker; b. Minden, La., July 21, 1920; s. Thomas and Bernard Moore (Hayes) C.; B.S., Davidson Coll., 1942; J.D., La. State U., 1949; Exec. Program, Stanford, 1970; m. 2d Dale Cowgill, July 3, 1967; children by previous marriage—Kate, Bunnie, Lili, John Hayes. Admitted to La. bar, 1949; mem. firm Smitherman, Smitherman & Purcell, 1949-51; mng. dir. Better Hotels of La., Shreveport, 1951-61; exec. v.p., asst. to pres. Allied Properties, San Francisco, 1961-62; pres. Guaranteed Reservations Inc., Palm Beach, Fla., 1962—; pres. Computer Controls Corp., 1967-70; chmn. Commonwealth Group Inc., 1975—; dir. Inverness Corp., Guaranteed Reservations Inc., Commonwealth Group Inc. Served to maj., inf. AUS, 1942-46. Decorated Bronze Star with oak leaf cluster. Mem. La., Am. bar assns., Nat. Assn. Mergers and Acquisitions Consultants, Bankers Club San Francisco, Phi Delta Phi. Republican. Anglican. Club: Bath and Tennis (Palm Beach). Home: 2411 Pacific Ave San Francisco CA 94115 Office: 601 California St San Francisco CA 94108

CRICHTON, JOHN MICHAEL, author, film dir.; b. Chgo., Oct. 23, 1942; s. John Henderson and Zula (Miller) C.; A.B. summa cum laude, Harvard U., 1964, M.D., 1969. Author: (novels) The Andromeda Strain, 1969; The Terminal Man, 1971; The Great Trial Robbery, 1975; Eaters of the Dead, 1976; Congo, 1980; (non-fiction) Five Patients, 1970; Jasper Johns, 1977; dir. films including: Westworld, 1973; Coma, 1977; The Great Train Robbery, 1979; Looker, 1981. Recipient Edgar award Mystery Writers Am., 1968, 80. Mem. Author's Guild, PEN, Writer's Guild of Am. West, Dir.'s Guild, Acad. Motion Picture Arts and Scis. Club: Aesculaepian (Boston). Office: care Mike Ovitz Creative Artists Agy 1888 Century Park E Suite 1400 Los Angeles CA 90067

CRIDDLE, WILLIAM DAVID, psychologist; b. Portland, Oreg., Jan. 9, 1945; s. Frederick Powell and Ella Marie (Swanson) C.; B.S., U. Wash., 1967; M.A., U. B.C., 1969, Ph.D., 1970; m. Marilyn MacRae, Agu. 15, 1970. Psychology intern U. B.C. Med. Sch., 1970; postdoctoral intern Down State Med. Center, Bklyn., 1971, fellow Inst. for Advanced Study in Rational Psychotherapy, N.Y.C., 1971; instr N. Seattle Community Coll., 1972; dir. tng. Inst. for Rational Living N.W., Seattle,

1972-79; pvt. practice psychotherapy, Seattle, 1971—; asst. clin. prof. U. Wash., 1972—; lectr. Seattle U., 1977-78. Lic. psychologist, Wash. Mem. Am. Psychol. Assn., Am. Assn. Sex Edn., Counselors and Therapists, Western Psychol. Assn., Wash. Psychol. Assn., Alpha Epsilon Delta, Psi Chi. Contbr. articles to profl. jours. Home: 5395 Crystal Springs Dr Bainbridge Island WA 98110 Office: 157 Yesler Way 402 Seattle WA 98104

CRIDER, HOYT, health care executive; b. Arley, Ala., June 5, 1924; s. Lindsey C. and Bessie P. C.; student Ga. Sch. Tech., 1942-43; B.S. in Naval Sci. and Tactics, U. S.C., 1946; M.A. in Polit. Sci., U. Ala., 1949; D.Pub. Adminstrn., U. So. Calif., 1954; m. Judie Watkins, Nov. 2, 1951; children—Kim, Marc. Vis. asst. prof., dir. research U. So. Calif. team, Iran, 1954-56; adminstrv. analyst Chief Adminstrv. Offices Los Angeles County, 1956-59; v.p. Watkins & Watkins Constrn. Co., Hanford and Morro Bay, Calif., 1959-64; co-owner, adminstr. Kings Convalescent Hosp., Hanford, Calif., 1964-66; adminstr. Villa Capistrano Convalescent Hosp., Capistrano Beach, Calif., 1966-68; partner Hunt and Crider, San Diego Convalescent Hosp., 1968-70; pres., chief exec. officer Health Care Enterprises, Inc., San Clemente, Calif., 1970—; mem. Regional Health Planning Commn. Kings County, 1963-64. Served with USNR, 1941-46. Fellow Am. Coll. Nursing Home Adminstrs. (pres. 1976-77); mem. Calif. Assn. Health Facilities (past v.p. local chpt. 1964), Gerontol. Soc., AAAS. Club: San Clemente Kiwanis (Kiwanian of Yr. 1970, pres. 1970-71). Home: 214 Calle Cortez San Clemente CA 92672 Office: 407 N El Camino Real Suite C San Clemente CA 92672 also 5053 N Peck Rd El Monte CA 91732 also 3780 Massachusetts Ave La Mesa CA 92041 also 8001 Birmingham Dr San Diego CA 92123 also 1209 W Hemlock Way Santa Ana CA 92707

CRILEY, CHARLES ALBERT, internat. mktg. and fin. co. exec.; b. Sapulpa, Okla., Aug. 20, 1936; s. Wayne and Audrey Frances (Morey) C.; student Va. Mil. Inst., 1954-55; LL.D. (hon.), London Inst. Applied Research, 1972; 1 dau., Laura Lynne. With traffic dept. Pacific No. Airlines, 1958-59, Consol. Freightways, 1959-61, Stor-Dor Forwarding Co., 1962-63, Garrett Freightlines, 1962-64, Sea-Land Service Co., 1965-66, Traffic Service Co., 1964; chmn., chief exec. officer C.A. Criley & Assos., Inc., traffic freight cons., Bellevue, Wash., 1964-80, Met. Shippers Clearings Corp., Bellevue, 1967-73, Los Angeles, 1971-73, Oak Brook, Ill., 1972-73, Hackensack, N.J., 1972-73, Trans-Action Data Systems, Inc., Bellevue, 1969-80; partner Taryl Resources Internat., Seattle, 1970—, Conaway Traffic Co., Los Angeles, 1971-73. Author: The Merchants Shipper Credit Corporation Plan, 1967. Established Criley professorship of transp. computer scis., Stanford, 1972. Home: 3816 138th SE Bellevue WA 98006 Office: Suite 219 Globe Bldg 310 1st Ave S Seattle WA 98104

CRIMINS, NITA RAE, vocational educator, consultant; b. Delmont, S.D., May 29, 1937; d. Christian and Emarie (Hoff) Weber; m. Jerry D. Crimins, Aug. 12, 1969. B.S., Oreg. State U, 1960, M.Ed., 1966; postgrad. Portland State U., 1977—, Oreg. State U., 1978-79. Cert. tchr. Oreg. Tchr. bus. edn. Franklin High Sch., Portland, Oreg., 1960-61, Springfield (Oreg.) High Sch., 1961-64, Clackamas High Sch., Milwaukie, Oreg., 1964-77; dist. coordinator coop. work experience, coordinator sch. community exploration project North Clackamas Sch. Dist., Milwaukie, 1977—; presenter local, state, nat. and regional confs.; mem. Oreg. Adv. Council for Career and Vocat. Edn. Recipient Most Outstanding Contbn. in Effort and Excellence Toward Edn. award Clackamas High Sch., Milwaukie, 1977. Mem. Am. Vocat. Assn., Assn. for Supervision and Curriculum Devel., Confedn. of Oreg. Sch. Adminstrs., Nat. Council of Local Adminstrs., Oreg. Council of Career and Vocat. Adminstrs., Work Experience Coordinators of Oreg. (Outstanding Legis. Achievement award 1980, Outstanding Work Experience Coordinator of Yr. award 1982), Oreg. Vocat. Assn. (chmn. legis. council; Outstanding Achievement award 1980, Oreg. Vocat. Educator of Yr. award 1982), Western Assn. Coop. Work Experience Educators, North Clackamas County C. of C., Alpha Xi Delta Alumni Assn. Lutheran. Contbr. articles to publs. in field; columnist OVA Voice, 1980—. Home: 7915 SE King Rd Apt 11 Milwaukie OR 97222 Office: North Clackamas Sch Dist 14211 SE Johnson Rd Milwaukie OR 97222

CRIMMINS, EILEEN MARY, educator; b. Northampton, Mass., July 21, 1946; s. John P. and Mary M. (Sullivan) C. Ph.D., U. Pa., 1974. Asst. prof. U. Ill.-Chgo., 1973-78, Rutgers U., Camden, N.J., 1978-80, Andrus Gerontology Ctr., U. So. Calif., Los Angeles, 1982—. Office: Andrus Gerontology Center U So Calif Los Angeles CA 91105

CRINAN, JAMES RAYMOND, educator; b. Albany, N.Y., Oct. 17, 1935; s. Lester J. and Mary (White) C.; m. Carol B. Van Ornam, Jan. 26, 1958; children—James Clark, Christine Denise. B.A., Siena Coll., 1960; postgrad. Georgetown U., 1967-68; M.A., Western N.Mex. U., M.A., 1982. Commd. 2d lt. U.S. Army, 1960, advanced through grades to lt. col., 1975; ret., 1978; police officer, Duncan, Ariz., 1978-79; dispatcher Greenlee County (Ariz.) Sheriff's Dept., 1979-80; tchr. social studies/English, Clifton (Ariz.) High Sch., 1980—; police magistrate, Duncan, 1981, councilman, 1981—. Served with U.S. Army, 1953-56; Vietnam. Decorated Legion of Merit, Bronze Star, Meritorious Service medal, Army Commendation medal. Mem. NEA, Ariz. Edn. Assn., Nat. Council Social Studies, Ariz. Assn. Social Studies, Nat. Council Tchrs. of English, Am. Mil. Inst., Phi Alpha Theta. Roman Catholic. Home: PO Box 681 Duncan AZ 85534 Office: PO Box 1567 Clifton AZ 85533

CRIPPEN, BRUCE D., state senator; b. June 13, 1932; grad. U. Mont., U. Mont. Sch. Law, NYU Grad. Sch. Law; m. Mary Crippen; 4 children. Mem. Mont. Senate, 1981—. Office: 3015 Gregory Dr Billings MT 59102*

CRIPPENS, DAVID LEE, television sta. exec.; b. Jefferson City, Tenn., Sept. 23, 1942; s. Nathaniel Alexander and Dorothy Leola (Sharp) C.; B.A., Antioch Coll., 1964; M.S.W., San Diego State U., 1968; m. Eloise Millicent Brown, Aug. 3, 1968; 1 son, Gerald Chinua. Asso. dir. ednl. opportunities San Diego State U., 1968-69; producer Sta. KPBS-TV, San Diego, 1969-71; exec. producer Sta. WQED, Pitts., 1971-73; v.p., sta. mgr. Sta. KCET-TV, Los Angeles, 1973-83, v.p. nat. prodns., 1983—. Mem. Nat. Assn. Ednl. Broadcasters. Home: 4701 Maytime Ln Culver City CA 90230 Office: 4401 Sunset Blvd Los Angeles CA 90027

CRISLER, ROBERT OWEN, psychologist; b. Indpls., Jan. 27, 1926; s. Chester R. and Alma N. Crisler; B.S. in Chem. Engring., Purdue U., 1948; Ph.D., Calif. Sch. Profl. Psychology, San Diego, 1977. Group leader Procter & Gamble Co., Cin., 1948-73; pvt. practice psychology, San Diego, 1977—. Served with C.E., AUS, 1945-46. Mem. Am. Psychol. Assn. Contbr. articles to profl. jours. Home: 2909 Cape Sebastian Cardiff CA 92007 Office: 5333 Mission Center Rd #309 San Diego CA 92108

CRISMAN, MARY FRANCES BORDEN (MRS. FREDRIC LEE CRISMAN), librarian; b. Tacoma, Nov. 23, 1919; d. Lindon A. and Mary Cecelia (Donnelly) Borden; B.A. in History, U. Wash., 1943, B.A. in Librarianship, 1944; m. Fredric Lee Crisman, Apr. 12, 1975 (dec. Dec. 1975). Asst. br. librarian in charge work with children Mottet br. Tacoma Pub. Library, 1944-45, br. librarian, 1945-49, br. librarian Moore br., 1950-55, asst. dir. Tacoma Pub. Library, 1955-70, dir., 1970-74, dir. emeritus, 1975—; hostess program Your Library and You, KTPS-TV, 1969-71. Mem. Gov.'s Com. Employment of Handicapped, 1974; mem. Highland Homeowners League, Tacoma, 1981—, sec., registered agt., 1981-82. Mem. ALA (chmn. membership com. Wash. 1957-60, mem. nat. library week com. 1965, com. on policy implementation 1973-74, ins. for libraries com. 1970-74, chmn. nominating com. library adminstrn. div. 1971, vice chmn. personnel adminstrn. sect. 1972-73, chmn. 1973-74, mem. budgeting, accounting and costs com. 1974-76), Am. Library Trustee Assn. (legis. com. 1975-78, action devel. com. 1978-81, co-chmn. 1979, program and evaluation com. 1978-81), Pacific Northwest, Wash. (exec. bd. 1957-59, state exec. dir. nat. Library Week 1965, treas. 1969-73), library assns., Urban Libraries Council (editorial sec. newsletter 1972-73, exec. com. 1974-75), AAUW (2d v.p., membership chmn. Tacoma 1958-59), Ladies Aux. to United Transp. Union (past pres. Tacoma), Allied Arts of Tacoma, Friends Tacoma Library (sec. 1975-78, pres. 1978-80), Tacoma-Pierce County Presidents Council of Women's Orgns. (treas. 1980), Marquis Library Soc., Smithsonian Assos. Roman Catholic. Club: Quota (sec. 1957-58, 1st v.p. 1960-61, pres. 1961-62, 79-80) (Tacoma). Home: 6501 Burning Tree Ln Tacoma WA 98406

CRISP, MICHAEL JOHN, physicist; b. Inglewood, Calif., Oct. 14, 1944; s. Herbert Barnard and Virginia Nadeene (Murdock) C.; B.S. cum laude, U. So. Calif., 1966; M.S., UCLA, 1968, M.Engr., 1980; M.B.A., Calif. State U., 1974; m. Cheryl Ann Clooney, Sept. 3, 1966; children—Thomas Michael, Andrew David. Physicist, Gen. Dynamics Corp., Pomona, Calif., 1968-72; asst. dir. sales adminstrn. Am. Land Systems Co., Los Angeles, 1972; sr. physicist Gen. Dynamics Corp., Pomona, 1972-77, project engr., 1978-82, mgr., 1982—; corp. controller Versatron Research Corp., Anaheim, Calif., 1975-81. Seely B. Mudd scholar, 1962-66; Outstanding Teaching Asst. award UCLA, 1968. Mem. Am. Chem. Soc., Nat. Mgmt. Assn., Am. Vacuum Soc. (nat. publicity dir. 1978-79), Phi Lambda Upsilon, Beta Gamma Sigma, Pi Kappa Alpha. Democrat. Presbyterian. Inventor in field; contbr. articles to profl. jours. Home: 438 Montessori Ave Placentia CA 92670 Office: PO Box 2507 Pomona CA 91766

CRISPIN, JAMES HEWES, engring. constrn. co. cons.; b. Rochester, Minn., July 23, 1915; s. Egerton Lafayette and Angela (Shipman) C.; A.B. in Mech. Engring., Stanford, 1938; M.B.A., Harvard, 1941; grad. Command and Gen. Staff Sch., U.S. Army, 1943; m. Marjorie Holmes, Aug. 5, 1966. With C.F. Braun & Co., Alhambra, Calif., 1946-62; treas. Bechtel Corp., San Francisco, 1962-73, v.p., mem. finance com., 1967-75, mgr. investment dept., 1973-75; cons. personal investments, 1976—. Trustee, Santa Barbara (Calif.) Mus. Art, 1979—, Santa Barbara Mus. Art, 1979—; Calif. Hist. Soc., 1979—. Served to lt. col. Ordnance Corps. AUS, 1941-46. Registered profl. mech. engr., Calif. Mem. Mil. Order World Wars, Calif. Soc. SR, Soc. Colonial Wars State Calif., Baronial Order Magna Carta, Mil. Order Crusades, Am. Def. Preparedness Assn., World Affairs Council No. Calif. (treas. 1971-73, trustee 1971-76), Beta Theta Pi. Republican. Clubs: California, Chaparral (Los Angeles); Pacific-Union, St. Francis Yacht, San Francisco Golf, World Trade (dir. 1971-78, pres. 1977-78) (San Francisco); Harvard (N.Y.C.); Valley (Santa Barbara, Calif.). Home: 1340 E Mountain Dr Santa Barbara CA 93108 Office: La Arcada Bldg Suite 220 1114 State St Santa Barbara CA 93101

CRISPO, RICHARD CHARLES, artist, ethnologist, minister; b. Bklyn., Jan. 13, 1945; s. Frank C. and Irene M. (Lamont) C. M.F.A., Trinity Hall Coll., 1975; Ph.D., Collegii Romanii, Rome, 1976, Th.D., 1977. Instr. art Monterey Peninsula Coll., 1968-69, instr. ethnic studies, 1976; instr. art history Hartwell Coll.; now coordinator Arts in Corrections, Art Project, Soledad Prison; instr. pub. sch. art, Monterey, Calif., 1967-72; counselor Intrim, Inc., Monterey, 1976; founder Mus. on Wheels, 1973-74; founder World Folk Art Collection, Monterey, 1972; 53 murals and 63 one-man shows; executed half-mile-long mural at Soledad Prison; priest N. Am. Old Roman Catholic Ch. Recipient numerous awards including 1st prize Calif. State Fair, 1964; UNESCO award, 1971-73; Calif. Arts Council grantee. Mem. Artist Equity, Found. for the Community of Artists, Carmel Art Assn., Pacific Grove Art Center. Contbr. articles to art jours.

CRISTIANO, ROBERT JAMES, real estate investment executive; b. Chgo., Feb. 20, 1950; s. Frank and Louise Ann (Simone) C.; m. Judith Lynn Risher, Aug. 16, 1949. B.A., Ohio State U., 1972; postgrad. in psychology U. Miami, 1979; Ph.D. in Psychology, Walden U., 1981. Vice-pres., CCI Fin. Group, Cleve., San Diego, 1972-75; pres., chief exec. officer PHI Corp., Cleve., 1975-81; sr. v.p. mktg. AmeriVest Corp., Newport Beach, Calif., 1981—; dir. research and devel. Environ, Inc. Patron, mem. acquisitions council Newport Harbor Art Mus., 552 Club of Hoag Hosp. Invited to assist U.S. Ski Team during 1978 World Cup, France. Republican. Clubs: Surf (Miami); Pacific (Calif.); Ocean Reef (Key Largo, Fla.) Home: 18851 San Rufino Irvine CA 92715 Office: Ameri Vest Corp 4400 MacArthur Blvd Suite 460 Newport Beach CA 92660

CRISWELL, DAVID RUSSELL, physicist, cons., b. Ft. Worth, Tex., July 17, 1941; s. Lemual David and Nell (Russell) C.; m. Paula Chandler, June 25, 1980; children—Beth, Bruce David. B.S. cum laude in Physics, N. Tex. State U., 1963, M.S. in Physics, 1964; Ph.D. in Physics and Astronomics, William Marsh Rice U., Houston, 1968. Researcher in lunar exploration for Apollo program TRW Systems, Houston, 1968-70; researcher, staff scientist Lunar and Planetary Inst., Houston, 1970-80, adminstr. Lunar and Planetary Rev. Panel, 1971-80; scientist Calif. Space Inst., 1980—; pres. Cis-Lunar, Inc. Houston, 1975. Mem. AIAA, AAAS, Am. Phys. Soc., Am. Acoustical Soc. Contbr. to CRC Handbook on Space Industrilization, 1979, confs., seminars, reports, revs., abstracts, articles to profl. jours; patentee in field; assoc. editor Space Solar Power Revs. Home: 8121 Camino del Sol La Jolla CA 92037

CRISWELL, JOHN FRIES, author; b. Reading, Pa., Feb. 8, 1910; s. William Allen and Edna Irene (Fries) C.; A.B., U. Pa., 1931; M.A., So. Meth. U., 1935; Ph.D. in Psychology, Ind. U., 1938; m. Dorothy Shearer, June 21, 1938; children—John Robert, James David. Tchr., Dallas High Sch., 1931-35; producer audio visual films, 1935-41; founder, dir. prodn. Camerart Pictures, Knight's Ferry, Calif., 1945-68. Audio-visual lectr., tchr., cons., 1946—. Bd. dirs. Knight's Ferry Community Services Dist., 1970-77, pres., 1970-74. Served with AUS, 1942-46. Recipient Chris awards Annual Columbus (Ohio) Film Festival, 1956-70, Golden Reel Film award Film Council Am., 1956. Mem. NEA. Methodist. Mason. Club: Commonwealth (Calif.). Author: Knight's Ferry's Golden Past, 1971; Knight's Ferry's People and Places, 1973; River of Life, 1976; Search for Peace, 1979; Knight's Ferry's Century-Old Structures, 1980; Knight's Ferry's Water Heritage, 1983; author motion picture and TV scripts, study guides for elem. grade subjects. Contbr. fiction and articles to ednl. jours. and other publs. Home: 12812 Dean St Knight's Ferry CA 95361 Office: PO Box I Knight's Ferry CA 95361

CRITTENDEN, EDWIN BUTLER, architect, planner; b. New Haven, Nov. 26, 1915; s. Walter Eaton and Harriet Rosetta (Butler) C.; m. Katharine Carson, June 11, 1943; children—John, Katharine, James, Elizabeth Coulon, Davis, Harriet. B.A., Pomona Coll., 1938; M.Arch., Yale U., 1942; postgrad. M.I.T., 1946-47. Registered architect, Alaska, Calif., Wash. Assoc. Roy Wilson, Santa Paula, Calif., 1945-46; tech. dir. Alaska Housing Authority, Anchorage, 1949-50, exec. dir., 1965-68; prin. Edwin Crittenden, Architect, Anchorage then CCWJ Architects, Anchorage, CCWC Architects, Anchorage, CCC/HOK Architects, Anchorage; chmn. bd. CCC Architects and Planners, Anchorage; mem. Alaska Bd. Architects and Engrs.; chmn. Anchorage Planning Commn.; mem. human ecology panel com. on Alaska earthquake Nat. Acad. Scis.; mem. Alaska Hist. Sites Adv. Com.; participant, presenter numerous confs. on community devel. in Arctic; cons. in field. Bd. dirs. Visual Arts Ctr. Alaska, chmn. bd., 1975-83; bd. elders First Presbyterian Ch., Anchorage. Served to lt. USCGR, 1942-45. Fellow AIA (regional dir. N.W. 1978-81, nat. bd. dirs. 1978-71); mem. Arctic Inst. N.Am., Council Ednl. Facility Planning. Republican. Designs include numerous sch. projects, and others. Spl. ind. archtl. studies, Helsinki, Finland, and Scandanavian North, 1963-64, Russia, 1975. Office: CCC Architects & Planners 431 W 7th Ave Suite 100 Anchorage AK 99501

CRITTENDEN, JOHN WILLIAM NEIL, artist; b. Brandon, Man., Can., Feb. 10, 1939; s. William Neil and Avis Anne Crittenden; m. Sharon Anne Blewett, Apr. 1, 1961; children—Bradley, Kent, Carol. Apprentice in color photolithography, Calgary, Alta., Can., 1959; engaged in printing industry, 1964; freelance painter, printmaker, poet, 1968—; works represented in permanent collections: Nat. Gallery Can., Ottawa, Ont., Met. Toronto Central Library, Glenbow Gallery, Calgary, also pvt. and corp. collections in Can., U.S. and Europe. Address: Site 5 Comp 4 Rural Route 2 Chase BC V0E 1M0 Canada

CRITTENDON, ROBERT RUSSELL, advertising executive; b. Brookhaven, Miss., Sept. 30, 1930; s. Atha Floyd and Birdie Louise (Canady) C.; m. Kelly Ruth Welch, Apr. 17, 1959; children—Kelli Jaye, Tracy Lynn. B.S., Okla. Bapt. U., 1953. Cert. bus. communicator. Account exec. Roger T. Case Assocs., Long Beach, Calif., 1957-59; advt. specialist Beckman Elec. Components, Fullerton, Calif., 1960-63, advt. mgr., 1963-67, advt. mgr. sci. instruments, 1967-69; corp. mgr. Mktg. Communications, 1969—; trustee Center for Mktg. Communications, 1975-78; dir. Media Comparability Council, 1982-83, Bus. Pub. Audit, 1982-83. Nat. bd. dirs. Leukemia Soc. Am., 1982-83. Served to capt. USMC, 1952-55. Recipient Crain Found. award, 1978. Mem. Bus./Profl. Advt. Assn. (internat. pres. 1974-75), Assn. Nat. Advertisers, Advt. Research Found. Republican. Club: El Niguel Country. Contbr. to book. Office: 2500 Harbor Blvd Fullerton CA 92634

CROCKER, MYRON DONOVAN, judge; b. Pasadena, Calif., Sept. 4, 1915; s. Myron William and Ethel (Shoemaker) C.; A.B., Fresno State Coll., 1937; LL.B., U. Calif.-Berkeley, 1940; m. Elaine Jensen, Apr. 26, 1941; children—Glenn, Holly. Admitted to Calif. bar, 1940; spl. agt. FBI, 1940-46; practiced law, Chowchilla, Calif., 1946-58; asst. dist. atty. Madera County (Calif.), 1946-51; judge Chowchilla Justice Ct., 1952-58, Superior Ct. Madera County, 1958-59; U.S. judge Eastern Dist. Calif., Sacramento, 1959—. Mem. Madera County Republican Central Com., 1950—. Named Outstanding Citizen Chowchilla, 1960. Mem. Chowchilla C. of C. (sec.). Lutheran. Lion. Office: US Dist Courthouse 1130 O St Fresno CA 93721

CROCKER, RICHARD GARTH, safety administrator, security director; b. Spokane, Wash., Dec. 23, 1927; s. Philip Garth and Olive Mae (DeMotte) C.; m. Barry Lee Foster, Aug. 26, 1949; children—Christine, John, Scott, Leslie. B.A. in Bus., Salinas Jr. Coll., 1948. Registered sanitarian. Detective, Salinas Police Dept., Calif., 1949-65; plant sanitarian/safety mgr./security dir. Basic Vegetable Products, King City, Calif., 1967—; instr. good food mfg. practices in food plants. Served with USAAF, 1945-47. Decorated Occupational Medal Japan. Mem. Nat. Safety Council, Am. Soc. Safety Engrs., Mounty Bay Coast Safety Council, King City, Okumura Biol. Inst., Am. Inst. Baking. Republican.

CROCKER, SYLVIA FLEMING, therapist, writer; b. Live Oak, Fla., Apr. 10, 1933; d. Tom and Lydia Belle (Compton) Fleming; m. Thomas D. Crocker, Dec. 31, 1961; children—Sarah Lydia, Trena Elizabeth. A.A. in Interior Design, Stephens Coll., 1953; B.A. in Philosophy, U. Mo., 1957, Ph.D. in Philosophy, 1969; M.A. in History and Lit. of Religions, Northwestern U., 1958. Diplomate Gestalt Tng. Center of San Diego. Interior decorating trainee Marshall Field & Co., Chgo., 1953-54; head dormitory counselor Wis. State Coll.-River Falls, 1958-59; asst. Episcopal chaplain Syracuse (N.Y.) U., 1959-60; grad. instr. in philosophy U. Mo.-Columbia, 1960-63; lectr. in philosophy U. Wis.-Milw., 1964-65; asst. prof. philosophy Marquette U., Milw., 1966-70; lectr. Calif. State Coll.-San Bernardino, 1972-73, U. Wyo., Laramie, 1975-76; pvt. practice Gestalt therapy, Laramie, 1979—. Woodrow Wilson fellow. Mem. Am. Personnel and Guidance Assn., Phi Beta Kappa. Club: Soc. Companions of Holy Cross. Contbr. articles to profl. jours. Home and Office: 2225 Sky View Ln Laramie WY

CROCKER, THOMAS DUNSTAN, economics educator; b. Bangor, Maine, July 22, 1936; s. Floyd Merton and Gloria Francis (Thomas) C.; m. Sylvia Mae Fleming, Dec. 31, 1961; children—Sarah Lydia, Trena Elizabeth. A.B., Bowdoin Coll., 1959; Ph.D., U. Mo., 1967. Timber cruiser, surveyor St. Regis Paper Co., Bucksport, Maine, 1952-62; instr. econs. U. Wis., 1963-66, asst. prof., 1966-70; assoc. prof. U. Calif.-Riverside, 1970-75; prof. U. Wyo., 1975—; mem. sci. adv. bd. EPA, 1973-76; mem. com. prevention of significant deterioration Nat. Acad. Scis.-NRC, 1979-81. Grantee in field. Mem. Am. Econ. Assn., Assn. Environ. and Resource Economists. Republican. Author: (with A.J. Roger III) Environmental Economics, 1971; contbr. to profl. jours. Office: Dept Economics U Wyo Laramie WY 82071

CROCKETT, JOEL EDWARD, printing exec.; b. Burbank, Calif., Feb. 22, 1941; s. John Harvey and Helen Elise (Schreyer) C.; children—Kristin Amy, Kelley Anne, Joshua John. Student, Santa Monica City Coll., 1959-64. Paper cons. NoLand Paper, Buena Park, Calif., 1965-67; printing paper mgr., San Diego, 1967-69; sales mgr. Frye & Smith, San Diego, 1969-75; owner, mgr. The Word Shop, San Diego, 1976-77; sales mgr. Metzger Printing, Denver, 1977-79; pres. The Nat. Press, Palo Alto, Calif., 1979—; cons. in field. Pres. Foster City Toastmasters. Recipient San Diego Salesman of Yr. award, 1968. Mem. Printing Industries No. Calif. (dir.). Republican. Clubs: Rotary (San Diego, Denver, Palo Alto). Author The Elements of Direct Mail, 1977; columnist Printing Jour. Home: 1237 Moonsail Ln Foster City CA 94404 Office: 850 Hansen Way Palo Alto CA 94304

CROCKETT, MARY THOMAS, real estate broker and developer, writer; b. San Francisco, Sept. 3, 1909; d. Benjamin Franklin and Charlotte Maddux (Evans) Thomas; student U. Calif., Berkeley, 1926-27, Stanford U., 1930-31, Woodbury Coll., 1932-33, U. Calif., San Francisco, 1951, 57, 59, Foothill Coll., 1960-61, San Francisco State U., 1961, U. Calif. Sch. Real Estate, 1949—. Lit. editor San Francisco Argonaut, 1937-46; subdivider, builder, real estate broker, San Francisco and Palm Springs, Calif., 1930—; pres. Resources Unlimited, La Costa, Calif., 1972—; dir. Crockett-King-Bartoli, Los Angeles; lectr. U. Calif., San Francisco, Mills Coll., Foothill Coll.; mem. Pulitzer Prize nominating com., 1938-46. Founder Woodside-Atherton Jr. Aux., 1930, Peninsula (San Francisco) Vols., 1946; coordinator Menlo Park Fire Dept. and Red Cross, 1941-45; resource person LWV, 1957—; mem. Marian Hollins Girls Polo Team, 1933; horsewoman, 1914—. Recipient various honors schs., publishers, Carmel Pinecone, 1932, Westways, 1933. Mem. Anna Head Alumnae Assn., U. Calif., Berkeley, Alumni Assn., Alpha Gamma Sigma, Kappa Alpha Theta. Designer, builder Downdale, Atherton, Oleander Walk, Palm Springs, Hawaiian Village, The Grove, Little Carmel, Tele-Hill Houses, San Francisco and Peninsula, La Costa. Home: 2851 Levante La Costa Country Club Carlsbad CA 92008

CROFFORD, HELEN LOIS, coll. adminstr.; b. Mesa, Ariz., Sept. 1, 1932; d. Elmer Earl and Lillian Irene (Williams) C.; grad. Lamson Bus.

Coll., Phoenix, 1952. Accountant, Bob Fisher Enterprises, Inc., Holbrook, Ariz., 1964-78; office mgr. for physician, Holbrook, 1978-79; office mgr. Trans Western Services, Inc., Holbrook, 1979; accountant Northland Pioneer Coll., Holbrook, 1980—. Squadron comdr. CAP, 1965-67, mission coordinator, 1970-79, group comdr., 1972-77, mem. regional staff, 1977-79; mem. Navajo County Natural Resource Conservation Dist., 1970—, sec.-treas., 1971—, chmn., 1980—; exec. bd. Ariz. Assn. Conservation Dists., 1977-78, sec., 1979-80, v.p., 1981, pres., 1983; mem. edn. and youth com. Nat. Assn. Conservation Dists., 1981, 83. Mem. Nat. Assn. Search and Rescue, DAR. Democrat. Home: Box 36 Woodruff AZ 85942 Office: 1200 E Hermosa Dr Holbrook AZ 86025

CROFT, ALFRED RUSSELL, SR., forest hydrologist; b. Ogden, Utah, July 29, 1896; s. George Albert and Mary Isabelle (Russell) C.; B.S., Utah Agrl. Coll., 1920, M.S., 1925; postgrad. (Charles Lathrop Pack fellow), Cornell U., 1931-32; H.H.D. (hon.), Weber State Coll., 1979; m. Irene Hutchings, Mar. 26, 1921; children—Alfred Russell, Lois, Robert Hutchings, James Albert. Tchr. public high schs., Utah, Idaho, 1920-23; prof., head dept. biology Weber Coll., 1925-33; dir. Davis County (Utah) Exptl. Watershed, Intermountain Forest and Range Expt. Sta., U.S. Forest Service, 1934-50, chief sect. watershed mgmt., 1950-62; prof. watershed mgmt. U. Ariz., 1964-67; cons. forest hydrology, Ogden, Utah, 1968—; chmn. various regional and nat. profl. orgns., 1940-62; chmn. adv. bd. Ronald V. Jensen Living Hist. Farm, Utah State U., 1974-78. Vice chmn. Weber State Coll. Endowment Fund, 1972-78. Served to 2d lt., F.A., U.S. Army, 1918. Recipient Superior Service award Dept. Agr., 1957, Disting. Service award Ariz. Water Resources Com., 1966; U.S. Pollution Control Adminstrn. grantee, 1966-67. Fellow Utah Acad. Scis. Arts and Letters; mem. Soc. Am. Foresters, Am. Geophys. Union, Soil Conservation Soc. Am., Western Snow Conf., Sierra Club, Weber State Coll. Alumni Assn. (pres. 1950-51), Utah State U. Alumni Assn. (pres. 1943-45), Sigma Xi. Research, numerous publs. on rainstorm flood control, watershed hydrology and restoration, evapo-transpiration, snow evaporation, evaporation from streams and riparian vegetation. Home and Office: 3921 S 895 E Ogden UT 84403

CROFT, SARALEE BOSCACCI, educator, riding instructor; b. Palo Alto, Calif., Dec. 1, 1942; d. Kenneth M. and Elizabeth W. (Clark) Boscacci; m. William R. Croft, Dec. 28, 1963; children—Brian K., David A. B.S., Calif. State Poly. Coll., 1963. Tchr. pub. schs., Orosi, Calif., 1964; tchr. home econs. Redwood High Sch., Visalia, Calif., 1966, Cabrillo High Sch., Lompoc, Calif., 1968-69, Freemont Jr. High Sch., Roseburg, Oreg., 1975-77, Sutherlin (Oreg.) High Sch., 1977-83. Mem. Sutherlin High Sch. Booster Assn. Mem. Oreg. Home Econs. Assn., Oreg. Horsemen's Assn., Am. Quarter Horse Assn., Oreg. Quarter Horse Assn., Oreg. Jr. Quarter Horse Assn. (exec. sec.). Home: Route 1 Box 1750 Sutherlin OR 97479 Office: Home Econs Dept Sutherlin High Sch Sutherlin OR 97479

CROMER, FRED EUGENE, statistics educator, university administrator, consultant; b. Hastings, Neb., Aug. 4, 1945; s. Harry Hershey and Genevieve Louise (Andresen) C.; m. Dee Ann Lines, Apr. 4, 1964; children—Anna-Marie Jean, Gregory James. B.S. in Math., U. Nebr., 1966; M.A.T. in Math., Harvard U., 1967; Ph.D. in Math. and Psychology, George Peabody Coll., 1971. Instr. math. Luther Coll., Decorah, Iowa, 1967-68; research asst. George Peabody Coll., Nashville, 1968-71; asst. prof., chmn. math. dept. U. Petroleum and Minerals, Dhahran, Saudi Arabia, 1971-74, assoc. prof., dir. stats. div., 1975-76, postdoctoral fellow U. Iowa, Iowa City, 1976-77; sr. research scientist Systems Devel. Corp., Santa Monica, Calif., 1977-78; asst. prof. math. U. Alaska, Anchorage, 1978-80, assoc. prof. math., assoc. dean Coll. Arts Scis., 1980—; corp. mem. Am. Coll. Testing; cons. various fed. and state govt. agys., pvt. cos. NSF fellow, 1966, 68; NDEA fellow 1968-71. Mem. Am. Statis. Assn., Am. Ednl. Research Assn., Nat. Council Measurement in Edn., Nat. Council Tchrs. of Math. Contbr. articles to profl. jours. Home: SRA Box 55C 10001 Grover Anchorage AK 99507 Office: U Alaska Anchorage AK 99508

CROMPTON, DALE DWAYNE, elec. engr.; b. Tremonton, Utah, May 22, 1931; s. Dwayne E. and Ellen Marie (Beck) C.; A.A., Chaffey Jr. Coll., 1956; B.S., U. Wash., 1958; m. Dixie Lee Prellwitz, June 19, 1953; children—Debra L., Cynthia L., Perry D. Instrumentation engr. Boeing Airplane Co., Seattle, 1957-59; instrumentation engr. McDonnell Douglas, Long Beach, Calif., 1959-69, sr. project engr. advanced flight devel., 1969-75, sect. chief, 1975-79, br. chief, 1980—. Active Boy Scouts Am., Placentia, Calif., 1966—. Served with USAF, 1951-55. Recipient Golden Bear award Boy Scouts Am., 1971, Silver Beaver award, 1978; Profl. Engr. award Douglas Aircraft Co., 1965; named Engr. of Month, Douglas Aircraft, 1973. Mem. Instrument Soc. Am. Contbr. articles in field to profl. jours. Home: 1232 Limerick Dr Placentia CA 92670 Office: 3855 Lakewood St Long Beach CA 90808

CROMWELL, VIRGINIA LUCILLE, sculptor; b. La Jolla, Calif., Oct. 16; d. Frank E. and Trientje (Bruns) Weerts; student San Diego Acad. Fine Arts, San Diego State U. Art Center, N.Y.C. Sculpture Center; Ph.D., La Jolla U.; pupil of Bob Winston, Nina Winkle, Donald Hord; m. Lincoln Cromwell, Nov. 18, 1955; 1 son, Dean. Tchr. sculpture, 1953—; group shows include: Clay Club, N.Y.C., 1948, Delmar (N.Y.) County Fair, 1951, Fine Arts Soc. and Gallery, 1951, 52, Carlsbad Oceanside Art League, 1954, Ivanhoe Galleries, La Jolla, Calif., 1955, La Jolla Mus., 1956, San Diego Fine Art Mus., 1976; numerous commns. Mem. N.Y.C. Sculpture Center, San Diego Art Guild, San Diego Allied Crafts Assn. Lutheran. Home and office: 7683 Mar Ave La Jolla CA 92037

CRONEMILLER, PHILIP DOUGLAS, physician; b. Altoona, Pa., Aug. 19, 1918; s. Carl Frederich and Marion (Smith) C.; B.S., Juniata Coll., 1939; M.D., U. Pa., 1943; m. Virginia Sones, Nov. 9, 1942; children—Pamela Joan, Philip Douglas, Suzanne Virginia, David Erich. Intern U.S. Naval Hosp., Phila., 1943-44, resident in surgery, 1946-48, staff surgeon, 1952-54, Guantanamo Bay, Cuba, 1949-51, Jacksonville, Fla., 1954, San Diego, 1958-61; chief surgery, dir. research U.S. Naval Hosp., San Diego, 1961-63; practice medicine specializing in surgery, Arcadia, 1963—; attending surgeon Los Angeles County Hosp., City Hope Nat. Med. Center, asso. clin. prof. surgery U. So. Calif., 1963-77, clin. prof., 1977—; pres. Batterson Realty Co. Active various community activities; bd. dirs. Spectrum Counseling Services. Served to capt., M.C., USN, 1943-63. Diplomate Am. Bd. Surgery. Fellow A.C.S., Pan Am. Med. Assn.; mem. Los Angeles County Med. Soc., AMA, Calif. Med. Assn., Los Angeles Surg. Soc., Royal Soc. Medicine London (assoc.), San Diego Soc. Gen. Surgeons (hon.). Republican. Methodist. Mason. Contbr. articles profl. jours. Home: PO Box 1522 Arcadia CA 91006 Office: 1108 S Baldwin St Arcadia CA 91006

CRONIN, MARTHA AUGUSTA, army officer, dietitian; b. Somerville, Mass., Oct. 13, 1943; d. William Edward and Laura Patricia (Falvey) C. B.S., Framingham State Coll., 1965; M.S., U. Nebr., 1972; postgrad. Command and Gen. Staff Coll., 1978, Indsl. Coll. Armed Forces, 1981, Army War Coll., 1983—. Enlisted in U.S. Army 1963, advanced through grades to lt. col., 1980; dietetic intern Fitz Army Med. Ctr., Aurora, Colo., 1965-66; chief food service 130th Sta. Hosp., Heidelberg, Ger., 1969-70, 67th Med. Group, Danang, Vietnam, 1970-71, 3d Field Hosp., Saigon, 1970-71, Brooke Army Med. Ctr., San Antonio, 1972-77; dep. dir. Food Service Directorate, Walter Reed Army Med. Ctr., Washington, 1980-82; dir. food service Fitzsimons Army Med. Ctr., Aurora, 1982-83. Decorated Bronze Star, Meritorious Service medal with one oak leaf clusters, Army Commendation medal with one oak leaf cluster, Nat. Def. Service medal, Vietnam Cross Galantry. Mem. Am. Dietetic Assn., Hosp. Food Service Adminstrs., Omicron Nu.

CRONIN, TOM, communications company executive, political science educator and writer; b. Milton, Mass., Mar. 18, 1940; s. Joseph M. and Mary Jane (Marr) C.; m. Tania Z. Zaroodry, Nov. 26, 1966; 1 son, Alexander D. A.B., Holy Cross Coll., 1961; Ph.D., Stanford U., 1969. Fellow, aide White House, Washington, 1966-67; fellow Brookings Instn., 1969-72, Ctr. for Study Dem. Instns., 1972-74, Brandeis U., 1974-77; pres. CRC, Inc., Colorado Springs Colo., 1980—; prof. polit. sci. Colo. Coll., 1978—; lectr. at numerous univs. and colls. Bd. dirs. Common Cause; trustee Am. Leadership Forum; candidate for U.S. Congress, 1982. Mem. Am. Polit. Sci. Assn., Urban League, Am. Fedn. Scientists, Democrat. Roman Catholic. Author: The State of The Presidency, 1980; co-author: Government by the People, 1981; U.S. vs. Crime in The Streets, 1981. Home: 1425 La Mesa Colorado Springs CO 80904 Office: Dept Polit Sci Colorado Coll Colorado Springs CO 80903

CRONK, MILDRED SCHIEFELBEIN (MILI), educational consultant; b. Waverly, Iowa, May 29, 1909; d. Emil August and Nettie Marie (Berger) Schiefelbein; student Wartburg Coll., Waverly, 1927, Tampa (Fla.) U., 1944-45, Los Angeles City Coll., 1957; B.A. in Psychology, Calif. State U., Los Angeles, 1960, M.A.Ed. in Spl. Edn. Supervision, 1971; m. Dale Cronk, July 20, 1930; children—Barbara Cronk Burress, Bruce, Margaret, Michael. Aircraft communicator, weather observer CAA, Fla. and Calif., 1942-49; dir. Parkview Nursery Sch., Los Angeles, 1956-57; tchr. trainable mentally retarded Hacienda-LaPuente United Sch. Dist., LaPuente, Calif., 1961-74; cons. spl. edn., La Mirada, Calif., 1975—; in-service trainer for tchrs. Mem. Spl. Olympics Southeast Los Angeles County Com., 1977; mem. Very Spl. Arts Festival Com., Orange County, 1977—, Internat. Very Spl. Arts Festival Com., 1981; active Common Cause. Mem. Am. Assn. on Mental Deficiency (bd. dirs. Region II, editor Newsette, 1975-77, chmn. publicity com., 1977-79, presenter ann. confs.), Council for Exceptional Children (bd. dirs. Calif., editor Calif. State Fedn./Council for Exceptional Children Jour., 1977-80, past pres. San Gabriel Valley chpt. 538, mem.-at-large South Calif. Div. Mental Retardation, 1976-79, pres. Calif. Div. Mental Retardation, 1980-81, chmn. com. on officers handbook, nat. council, Div. Mental Retardation, 1977-78, spl. recognition awards, 1976, 77, 78, 79), Nat. Assn. for Retarded Citizens (nat., state, local orgns.), Southeast Assn. for Retarded Citizens (rec. sec. 1980-81), Nat. Soc. Autistic Children (nat., state, local orgns.), Nat. Ret. Tchrs. Assn. (nat., state, local orgns.), Psi Chi. Democrat. Clubs: Am. Ceramic Soc. (design div.), Smithsonian Instn., Wilderness Soc. Author: Create with Clay, 1976; Vocational Skills Taught through Creative Arts, 1978; Career Education for Trainable Mentally Retarded Students-It's for Life!, 1982; others. Home and Office: 13116 Clearwood Ave La Mirada CA 90638

CRONKLETON, THOMAS EUGENE, physician; b. Donahue, Iowa, July 22, 1928; s. Harry L. and Ursula Alice (Halligan) C.; B.A. in Biology, St. Ambrose Coll., 1954; M.D., Iowa Coll. Medicine, 1958; m. Wilma Agnes Potter, June 6, 1953; children—Thomas Eugene, Kevin P., Margaret A., Catherine A., Richard A., Robert A., Susan A., Phillip A. Rotating intern St. Benedict's Hosp., Ogden, Utah, 1958-59; Donahue, Iowa, 1959-61, practice family medicine, Davenport, Iowa, 1961-66, Laramie, Wyo., 1966—; asso. The Davenport Clinic, 1961-63, partner, 1963-66; active staff St. Luke's Hosp., Mercy Hosp., Davenport; staff physician U. Wyo. Student Health Service, 1966-69, 70-71, 74-75; staff physician outpatient dept. VA Hosp., Iowa City, 1969-70: staff physician outpatient dept. VA Hosp., Cheyenne, Wyo., 1971-74, chief outpatient dept., 1973-74; dir. Student Health Service Utah State U., Logan, 1975-76; physician (part-time) dept. medicine VA Hosp., Cheyenne, 1976-81; staff physician U. Wyo. Student Health Service, Laramie, 1976—. Active Long's Peak council Boy Scouts Am., 1970—, scout chaplain Diocese of Cheyenne, 1980—, mem. Diocesan Pastoral Council, 1982—. Served with USMC, World War II, Korea. Recipient Dist. Scouter award Boy Scouts Am., 1974, St. George Emblem, Nat. Cath. Scouter award, 1981. Recipient 5 and 10 yr. service pins Boy Scouts Am. Diplomate Am. Bd. Family Practice. Fellow Am. Acad. Family Practice; mem. Wyo. State Med. Soc., Albany County (Wyo.) Med. Soc., Iowa Med. Soc., Johnson County (Iowa) Med. Soc. Democrat. Roman Catholic. Club: K.C. (4 deg.). Home: 2107 Sheridan St Laramie WY 82070 Office: Univ of Wyo Student Health Service Laramie WY 82071

CROOKS, MARY E(LIZABETH), educator; b. Quincy, Ill., Mar. 2, 1945; d. Charles Camden and Mary Virginia (Hasson) C.; m. Warren Henry Brazas, Aug. 21, 1966 (div.); m. Michael Dewitt Hasbrouck, Dec. 31, 1980 (div.). B.S., Eastern Ill. U., 1967; M.A., U. Colo.-Boulder, 1983. Cert. tchr., Ill., Ariz., Colo. Tchr. pub. schs., Quincy, Ill., 1968-69, Yuma, Ariz., 1969-70; bookkeeper Sproul Homes, Denver, 1971-72; tchr. math., computer sci. Dist. 27J, Brighton, Colo., 1972—. Order of Eastern Star scholar, 1963; State Ill. scholar, 1963-67. Mem. Nat. Council Tchrs. Math., Am. Personnel and Guidance Assn., Colo. Personnel and Guidance Assn., Colo. Council Tchrs. Math., Alpha Delta Kappa. Club: Schussbaumer Ski. Contbr. articles to Arithmetic Jour. Office: 879 Jessup St Brighton CO 80601

CROOM, JULIA JORGENSEN, educator; b. San Diego, Sept. 15, 1940; d. James Franklin and Ola Agnes (Goodwine) Jorgensen; B.A. with honors, San Diego State U., 1962, M.A. in Curriculum and Instrn., 1966; cert. in elem. adminstrn., U.S. Internat. U., 1970; m. Jary Basil Croom, June 16, 1962; children—Christopher Alan, Kathryn Elizabeth. With San Diego City Schs., 1962—, dist. resource tchr., 1969-72, kindergarten tchr., 1975—; tchr. U. Calif. Extension, 1968-72, San Diego State U. Extension, 1968-71; mem. steering com. Sch. for Creative and Performing Arts; initiator Program for Infant Care Services and Edn.; mem. Adv. Com. Sch.-Age Parenting and Infant Devel. Co-chmn. Heart 'n Hand Ball, 1976, food chmn., 1975, 77. Recipient Edn. award Greater San Diego Industry-Edn. Council, 1982. Mem. Greater San Diego Math Council, Assn. Childhood Edn. Internat., Assn. Supervision and Curriculum Devel., Calif. Reading Assn., San Diego Reading Assn., NEA, Calif. Tchrs. Assn., San Diego Tchrs. Assn., Delta Kappa Gamma. Republican. Clubs: Women's Guild, Home of Guiding Hands. Author curriculum publs. Home: 7121 Wandermere Dr San Diego CA 92119 Office: 6425 Cibola Rd San Diego CA 92120

CROSBY, DONALD FRANCIS, historian, educator, clergyman; b. Oakland, Calif., Oct. 12, 1933; s. Arch LeRoy and Vanda Rita (Poggi) C.; A.B., U. San Francisco, 1956; M.A., Gonzaga U., 1963; postgrad. Harvard U., 1968-69; Ph.D. (Univ. scholar 1969-70, Irving and Rose Crown fellow 1970-72), Brandeis U., 1973. Joined S.J., 1956; ordained priest Roman Catholic Ch., 1968; instr. in history Bellarmine Coll. Prep., San Jose, Calif., 1962-65; prof. history Guadalupe Coll., Los Gatos, Calif., 1967; prof. history Loyola U., Los Angeles, summer 1969; asso. prof. history Univ. scholar-in-residence U. Santa Clara (Calif.), 1969—; acad. and personal counselor. Mem. Am. Hist. Assn., Am. Cath. Hist. Assn., Orgn. Am. Historians. Democrat. Researcher, writer, contbr. articles to publs.; author: God, Church, and Flag: Senator Joseph R. McCarthy and the Catholic Church, 1978; photographer, minister. Home: Jesuit Community U Santa Clara Santa Clara CA 95053 Office: Dept History U Santa Clara Santa Clara CA 95053

CROSBY, JOHN O'HEA, opera mgr., condr.; b. N.Y.C., July 12, 1926; s. Laurence Alden and Aileen (O'Hea) C.; B.A., Yale U., 1950; postgrad. Columbia, 1951-55; Litt.D. (hon.), U. N.Mex., 1967; Mus.D. (hon.), Cleve. Inst. Music, 1974, Coll. Santa Fe, 1969; L.H.D. (hon.), U. Denver, 1977. Accompanist, mus. coach and condr., N.Y., 1951-56; gen. dir., mem. conducting staff Santa Fe Opera, 1957—; condr. world premier Carlisle Floyd's Wuthering Heights, 1958, U.S. stage premier Richard Strauss' Daphne, 1964; pres. Manhattan Sch. Music, 1976—; guest condr. various opera cos. in U.S. and Can., 1967—. Served with AUS, 1944-46; ETO. Clubs: University, Metropolitan Opera (N.Y.C.); Century Assn. Office: PO Box 2408 Santa Fe NM 87501

CROSBY, JUNE KUHN (MRS. GEORGE ROBERT CROSBY), writer; b. Chgo., Feb. 27, 1919; d. Leroy Philip and Grace Christine (Engles) Kuhn; student Sarah Lawrence Coll., 1937, UCLA, 1952-59; m. Bob (George Robert) Crosby, Sept. 22, 1938; children—Cathleen D., Christopher D., George Robert, Stephen R., J. Malia. Columnist, Honolulu Star-Bull., 1962-64; pres. June Crosby's Rainbow Kitchen, Inc., Honolulu, 1963-64; columnist San Diego Union, 1965-69, Australian Women's Weekly 1966, Elgin Daily Courier News, Elgin, Ill., 1967-69, Ill. State Jour., Springfield, 1967-69, Sacramento Union, 1966-68, Sarah Lawrence Alumnae Mag., 1967, Woman's Day mag., 1968, Western's World, 1970—, Carte Blanche mag., 1970-71; pres. Crosstown Publs., LaJolla, Calif., 1971—. Hon. co-chmn. San Diego Am. Heart Assn., 1966-69, San Diego Mental Health Assn., 1971—; founder, pres. Belles for Mental Health, 1972; co-chmn. Nat. Assn. Mental Health, 1976; dep. chmn. United Way/Chad campaign, 1977; sec. exec. com. Combined Health Assn. Drive, 1973, 74, Bd. dirs. San Diego County Mental Health Assn., 1972-77, Calif. Assn. Mental Health, 1975—. Mem. AFTRA, Am. Philatelic Assn., China Stamp Soc., Australasian Stamp Soc., Nat. League Am. Pen Women, Women in Communications, Authors Guild, Am. Soc. Journalists and Authors, D.A.R. Author: Serve It Cold!, 1969; San Diego Fare, 1972. Home: 939 Coast Blvd La Jolla CA 92037 Office: PO Box 122 La Jolla CA 92038

CROSE, JAMES GREGORY, engr.; b. Bosworth, Mo., Mar. 27, 1938; s. Paul T. and Eithel Z. (Smith) C.; B.S., Washington U., 1960; M.S., U. Ill., 1962, Ph.D., 1967; m. Judith Kaye Phelps, Dec. 20, 1958; children—Steven Scott, Douglas Todd, Gregory Neil. Engr. Reitz and Jens Cons. Engrs., St. Louis, 1960-64; mem. tech. staff Aerospace Corp., El Segundo, Calif., 1967-72; dir. advanced tech. PDA Engring., Santa Ana, Calif., 1972—. Served to capt. U.S. Army, 1964-66. NDEA fellow, 1960-63. Asso. fellow AIAA; mem. ASCE, Am. Acad. Mechanics, Sigma Xi, Phi Kappa Phi, Tau Beta Pi, Phi Eta Sigma. Democrat. Baptist. Contbr. articles to profl. jours. Home: 10 Columbus St Irvine CA 92714 Office: 1560 Brookhollow Dr Santa Ana CA 92705

CROSS, ALEXANDER DENNIS, chemical company executive; b. Leicester, Eng., Mar. 29, 1932; s. Arthur Lewis and Mary Gladys (Narracott) C.; came to U.S., 1970; B.Sc. in Chemistry, U. Nottingham (Eng.), 1952, Ph.D. (Fulbright scholar), 1955, D.Sc., 1966; m. Antonia Inez Szilas, Dec. 15, 1973; children—Guy Tibor Boscoe, James Tristan. Teaching fellow Imperial Coll., London, 1957, asst. lectr. chemistry, 1958-60, lectr., 1960; with Syntex Corp., 1961-79, pres. Syntex Sci. Systems, 1970-76, pres. Internat. Pharms. div., Palo Alto, Calif., 1974-78, sr. v.p. corp. econ. and strategic planning Syntex Corp., 1978-79; exec. v.p. Zoecon Corp., Palo Alto, 1979-83, pres., chief exec. officer, 1983—, also dir.; dir. Finnigan Corp. Bd. dirs. San Francisco Opera Assn. Fellow Royal Inst. Chemistry (Eng.); mem. Am. Chem. Soc., Chem. Soc. (London). Club: Commonwealth (San Francisco). Author: An Introduction to Practical Infrared Spectroscopy, 1960; bd. editors Jour. Organic Chemistry, 1967-71; contbr. sci. articles to profl. jours. Patentee in field. Home: 286 Park Ln Atherton CA 94025 Office: 975 California Ave Palo Alto CA 94304

CROSS, CRAIG TRAVIS, investment securities executive; b. Eugene, Oreg., Apr. 5, 1951; s. William Travis and Beverly Jean (Briggs) C.; A.A., Menlo Coll., 1971; B.A., Stanford U., 1973. Intern, U.S. Senator Bob Packwood, Washington, 1972; aide Calif. Gubernatorial Candidate, 1974; asst. athletic dir. Calif. State U., Long Beach, 1975-79, with Halbert Hargrove & Co., Long Beach, 1979—. Mem. Stanford U. Alumni Assn., Menlo Coll. Alumni Assn., 49er Athletic Found. Republican. Clubs: Long Beach Rotary, Long Beach Bond, Stanford Buck, Stanford of Los Angeles County (pres. 1983-84). Home: 4442 Sea Harbour Dr Huntington Harbour CA 92649 Office: 200 Pine Ave Suite 409 Long Beach CA 90802

CROSS, IRVIE KEIL, religious orgn. exec.; b. Huntington, Ark., Mar. 21, 1917; s. William Earl and Bertha Frances (Harris) C.; Th.M., Missionary Bapt. Sem., 1938, Th.D., 1944; D.D., Orthodox Bapt. Inst., 1946; D.D., Eastern Bapt. Inst., 1959; D.D., Internat. Free Protestant Episcopal U. of London, 1964; m. Johnnie Maxine Sharpe, June 9, 1939; children—Johnnie Keilene Cross Barnes, Maxine Irviene Cross McCombs. Ordained to ministry Am. Bapt. Assn. 1936; pastor Pauline Bapt. Ch., Monticello, Ark., 1939-41, County Ave Bapt. Ch., Texarkana, Ark., 1941-50, Langdon St. Bapt. Ch., Somerset, Ky., 1950-59; founder, pres. Eastern Bapt. Inst., 1953-67; pres. Eastern Bapt. Assn., 1958-62; founder, dir. office of publicity Am. Bapt. Assn., Texarkana, Ark.-Tex., 1952-67, dir. office of promotion and public relations, Texarkana, 1967-74, v.p., 1974-79, pres., 1978-79, mem. history and archives com., 1974—, mem. chaplains commn., 1964—; adminstrv. v.p. Calif. Missionary Bapt. Inst. and Sem., Bellflower, Calif., 1974—. Mem. adv. bd. Salvation Army, 1947-50; pres. Kidco, Inc., 1962-74, Lake Cumberland-Dale Hollow Tourist and Travel, 1965; mem. Ky. Devel. Council, 1962. Mem. Four States Aviation Assn. (pres. 1946-47), Somerset-Pulaski County (Ky.) C. of C. (pres. 1962), Somerset Ministerial Assn. (pres. 1954), Ky. Guild Artists and Craftsmen (pres. 1963-67). Club: Masons. Author: Truth About Conventionism, 1955; The Church Covenant, 1955; Paul's Lectures, 1956; Non-Denominational Denomination, 1956; I Believe God, 1966; Tongues, 1973; Baptism Holy Spirit, 1973; Great Commission, 1974; Divine Healing, 1974; Lectures on Israel in Prophecy, 1974; Baptist Heritage Abandoned, 1981; Universal Church, 1982; editor Sword, 1944-49, Am. Bapt. Digest, 1949-50, Missionary, 1953-67, Bapt. Sentinel, 1974—, Glover's Church Manual, 1983. Home: 9649 Foster Rd Downey CA 90242 Office: PO Box 848 Bellflower CA 90706

CROSS, ROBERT MICHAEL, banker; b. Eau Claire, Wis., Nov. 26, 1938; s. George H. and Dolly O. Cross; diploma Minn. Sch. Bus., 1958-59; B.S., U. Wis., 1963; m. Judith Ann Kruse, Dec. 26, 1963; children—Michael, David. Asst. v.p. 1st. Southdale Nat. Bank, Edina, Minn., mgr. Calif. 1st. Bank, Newport, 1972-77; v.p. Citizens Bank, Costa Mesa, Calif., 1977-78; pres. Bankers Investors Group, Inc., Irvine, Calif., 1978-80; asst. v.p. Wells Fargo Bank, Anaheim, Calif., 1980—; lectr. in field. Served with USNR, 1963-65. Mem. Newport Harbor (Calif.) C. of C. (dir. 1976—), Bayside Mchts. Assn. (treas. 1974—), Am. Inst. Banking (nat. conv. 1970—), Saddleback Valley Aquatics-Mission Viejo (pres. 1976-77, 79), Wis. Liberal Arts Soc. River Falls. Roman Catholic. Clubs: Bahia Corinthian Yacht, Elks. Home: 25276 Arcadian St Mission Viejo CA 92675

CROSS, WILLIAM CARL, educator; b. Edgemont, Ark., Sept. 20, 1912; s. Arthur and Pearle Z. (Smothers) C.; B.S., Kans. State Coll. at Pittsburg, 1941; Ed.D., U. Utah, 1952; m. Annette Roberts, Feb. 4, 1944 (dec.); children-Nedra (Mrs. Carl Schnoor), Carol Ann (Mrs. Robert Frank); m. 2d, Jo L. Gabbert, Aug. 2, 1980. Tchr., prin. Elgin-Cedar

Vale (Kans.) pub. schs., 1932-38; tchr. secondary sch., Anthony, Kans., 1938-42; tng. officer VA, Price, Utah, 1946-48; instr., counselor Coll. Eastern Utah, 1948-52; asst. supt., dir. secondary edn. Carbon County (Utah) schs., 1952-59; asso. prof. edn., psychology, head, dept. guidance N.Mex. State U., 1959-62, prof. ednl. psychology, 1962-67, prof., 1967-78, prof. emeritus, 1978—. Mem. N.Mex. Gov.'s Study Commn. Vocat. Rehab., 1967-68. Exec. com. Cerebral Palsy Utah, 1956-57, United Fund, Las Cruces, N.Mex., 1964-68. Served with USAAF, 1942-46; CBI. Named Distinguished Faculty Mem., N.Mex. State U., 1962. Mem. Am. Personnel and Guidance Assn., Nat. Vocat. Guidance Assn., Am. Psychol. Assn., NEA, N.Mex. Edn. Assn., AAUP, Profs., Phi Alpha Theta, Phi Delta Kappa, Psi Chi, Pi Gamma Mu. Kiwanian. Address: 335 Townsend Terr Las Cruces NM 88001

CROSS, WILLIAM WATSON, JR., artist, educator; b. Long Beach, Calif., Oct. 10, 1918; s. William Watson and Hazel (Morehouse) C.; June E. Graham, Sept. 5, 1944; children—Cathleen, Joan. B.F.A. (hon.), Chouinard Art. Inst. Instr. in drawing, painting Chouinard Art Inst., 1944-72; lectr. Calif. State U.-Los Angeles, 1971; instr. drawing Art Ctr. Coll. of Design, Pasadena, 1976-79; asst. prof. 2 dimensional media Calif. State U.-Northridge, 1975—; drawing instr. Otis Art Sch., Parsons Sch. Design, Los Angeles, 1979—. Mem. United Tchrs. Calif., AFL-CIO, Nat. Watercolor Soc. (pres. 1953). Democrat. Episcopalain. Exhbns. include: Los Angles County Mus. Ann. 1943-44, Pasadena Art Inst. Ann., 1946-47; Riverside (N.Y.) Mus., Exhibit, 1946, San Francisco Mus. Ann. Exhbn., 1947-47, John Herron Art Inst., Indpls., 1947, Nat. Acad. Galleries, N.Y.C., 1947-50.

CROSSLAND, HARRIET KENT, portrait painter; b. Cleve., Sept. 8, 1902; d. Carl and Harriet Emily (Bacon) Dueringer; pupil of Margaret McDonald Phillips; m. Paul Marion Crossland, Sept. 20, 1959. Portrait painter, 1952—; freelance editor med. papers, 1953-70; represented in permanent collection John F. Kennedy Library, Boston. Fund raiser Am. Cancer Soc.; mem. fund raising com. Vol. Action Bur.; mem. Santa Rosa Symphony League; mem. visual arts com. Luther Burbank Center for the Arts, Santa Rosa, 1982—. Recipient award of merit Am. Cancer Soc., 1979. Mem. Nat. League Am. Pen Women, Artists Round Table, Burbank Center Guild, Stanford U. Alumni Assn., Sonoma County Med. Assn. Aux., Am. Med. Women's Assn. (friend), Am. Cancer Soc., DAR. Clubs: Ret. Officers Wives, Sonoma County Press, Sat. Afternoon. Editor, illustrator: X-Rays and Radium in Treatment of Diseases of the Skin, 1967; donor Crossland Lab. for Audio-visual Learning, Stanford U. Med. Sch. Address: 2247 Sunrise Dr Santa Rosa CA 95405

CROSSLEY, FRANK ALPHONSO, metallurgical engineer; b. Chgo., Feb. 19, 1925; s. Joseph Buddie and Rosa Lee (Brefford) C.; m. Elaine Sherman, Nov. 23, 1950; 1 dau., Desne Adrienne; B.S. in Ch.E., Ill. Inst. Tech., 1945; M.S., 1947, Ph.D., 1950. Instr., Ill. Inst. Tech., 1948-49, sr. scientist IIT Research Inst., 1952-66; prof. foundry engring., head dept. foundry engring. Tenn. Agrl. and Indsl. State U., 1950-52; sr. mem. research lab. Lockheed Missiles & Space Co., Palo Alto, Calif., 1966-74, dept. mgr. productibility and standards, 1974-78, mgr. dept. missile body mech. engring., 1978-79, cons. engr. missiles systems div., 1979—. Served with USNR, 1944-46. Fellow Am. Soc. Metals; mem. Metall. Soc., AIME, AIAA, Soc. Advancement Materials and Process Engrs., Sigma Xi. Conglist. Contbr. articles to tech. jours. Patentee transage titanium alloys. Office: 1111 Lockheed Way Orgn 81-04 Bldg 157-5E Sunnyvale CA 94086

CROSSLEY, H. BUFFINTON, public relations executive; b. Fall River, Mass., Jan. 7, 1925; s. William Cyril and Martha Edward (Smith) C.; m. Lucille Hathaway, Nov. 4, 1943; children—Cheryl, Diane, Christine, H. Buffinton. B.A., Harvard U., 1950. Owner, operator Crossley Pub. Relations, Mission Hills, Calif., 1963—; cons. in polit. pub. relations. Served with USN, World War II. Recipient comendatory resolutions State of Calif. Senate, City of Los Angeles. Mem. Pub. Relations Soc. Am. (accredited), San Fernando Valley Pub. Relations Roundtable (past pres.), SAR. Republican. Unitarian. Clubs: Harvard (Boston), Masons. Home: 4641 Monarca Dr Tarzana CA 91356 Office: Suite 206 10550 Sepulveda Blvd Mission Hills CA 91345

CROSSMAN, HARLAN J(AY), lawyer; b. Bklyn., July 27, 1941; s. Sydney R. and Mary C.; m. Gayla Glascock, July 1, 1964; children—Monica Ann, Avery Naomi. B.A., U. N.Mex., 1962, J.D., 1965. Law clk. Hartley, Olson & Harris, Albuquerque, 1965-66, to chief judge N.Mex. Ct. Appeals, Santa Fe, 1966-67; atty. DNA Legal Services on Navajo Reservation, Window Rock, Ariz., 1967-69; atty. Ariz. Compensation Fund, Phoenix, 1969-72; individual practice law, Phoenix, 1972—; mem. Ariz. Gov.'s Ad Hoc Com. of Workmen's Compensation Legis., 1980-81. Vice chmn. Downtown YMCA Br., Phoenix, 1979—. Mem. ABA, Maricopa County Bar Assn., Ariz. Bar Assn. (sec. sect. workmen's compensation). Democrat. Jewish. Home: 4909 E Flower Phoenix AZ 85018 Office: 11 W Jefferson Suite 322 Phoenix AZ 85003

CROSSMAN, JAMES EDWARD, educator; b. Ft. Richardson, Anchorage, Alaska; s. Harold Albert and Edna Pauline (Gilbertsen) C.; m. Rose Mary Laun, June 1, 1974; 1 son, James Harold. B.A. in Edn., Ariz. State U., 1971, M.A. in Art Edn., 1977. Cert. tchr., Alaska. Tchr. aide, Phoenix, 1975-77; house parent Intermountain Youth Center, Tucson, 1977; graphic artist Alyeska Pipeline Service Co., Anchorage, 1977; tchr., generalist, Nuiqsut, Alaska, 1977—; community edn. tchr.; part-time regional coordinator U. Alaska, Fairbanks. Mem. Alaska Vocat. Assn., Nuiqsut Sch. Bus. Edn. Assn., NEA, Western Bus. Edn. Assn., Bus. Edn. Assn. Alaska, Sandlake Jaycees, Nat. Rifle Assn. Democrat. Roman Catholic. Club: Benjamin Franklin Stamp. Office: care Nuiqsut Sch Nuiqsut AK 99723

CROSSON, BERNARD ALBERT, electrical engineer; b. Taunton, Mass., Feb. 4, 1920; s. Alden Bernard and Ethel Violet (Duffy) C.; grad. Providence Tech. Inst., 1948, Internat. Corr. Schs., 1953; A.S., Pierce Coll., 1965; cert. plant engr. UCLA, 1971; grad. Indsl. Coll. Armed Forces, 1970; student bus. San Fernando U., 1971; B.E.E., Calif. Western U., 1974, M.B.A., 1975, doctoral candidate; m. June Martha Miner, June 19, 1943; children—Susan Diane Crosson Hughes, Nancy Roberta Crosson Walters, Steven Bernard, Carole Ann, Bruce Donald. Plant engr. Brown U., Providence, 1953-56; dir. ops. and maintenance Mass. Gen. Hosp., Boston, 1956-58; plant engr. Columbia Tchrs. Coll., N.Y.C., 1958; project engr. Marquardt Corp., Van Nuys, Calif., 1959; chief engr. Litton Industries, Inc., 1959-64; supr. facilities engr. Northrup Corp., Ventura, Calif., 1964-69; mgr. facilities engring. and maintenance Xerox Corp., Pomona, Calif., 1969-74; supt. facilities ops. exec. U.S. Bulk Mail, Los Angeles, 1974-76; mgr. bldg. services Los Angeles br. Fed. Res. Bank of San Francisco, 1976-77; dir. nat. constrn. and maintenance Collins Foods Internat., Ky. Fried Foods div., 1977—; cons. project engr. engring. mgmt. div. Litton Inc., 1979-80; pres. Crosson's Assocs., engring. mgmt.; engring. mgmt. cons., Saudi Arabia and Manila, Philippines; nat. and internat. facilities engring. cons.; appeared on several TV programs. Committeeman, San Fernando Valley council Boy Scouts Am., 1962-67. Served with USAAF, 1940-44. Decorated Purple Heart; recipient award for community service U.S. Postal Service, 1976; registered profl. engr., Calif. Mem. Plant Engring. Soc., Plant Engring. Soc. San Fernando Valley (chmn. membership and employment com.), IEEE (mem. nat. adminstrv. com., engring. mgmt. group 1980-83), Nat. Soc. Profl. Engrs., Soc. Mfg. Engrs. (cert. mfg engr.), Illumination Engring. Soc., AFTRA, Kappa Delta Phi. Home: 8366 Garden Grove Northridge CA 91325

CROSWAITE, SANDRA JEAN, social worker; b. Bremerton, Wash., Nov. 9, 1948; d. Fritz John and Dorothea Marie (Haase) Jappe; m. Michael Richard Croswaite, Aug. 28, 1971 (div.); 1 son, Trevor James. B.A. in Psychology, Central Wash. U., 1971, B.Ed. in Art and Psychology, 1971, M.S. in Counseling, 1982. Cert. tchr. and sch. counselor, Wash. Owner, mgr. Das Berghaus Restaurant & Bakery, Leavenworth, Wash., 1974-81; sec., receptionist psychology dept. Central Wash. U., Ellensburg, 1981-82; worksite supr. Kitsap Youth Homes, Kitsap County, Wash., Bremerton, 1982—; part-time mental health profl. Kitsap Resources Consol., 1982—; vol. counselor ALIVE Shelter for Battered Women. Luncheon scholar Central Wash. U. Women Staff, 1981-82; recipient letter of commendation mayor of Port Orchard, Wash., 1982. Mem. Am. Personnel and Guidance Assn. Home: 1109 Shorewood Dr Bremerton WA 98312 Office: Kitsap Youth Homes 3721 Kitsap Way Suite 8 Bremerton WA 98312

CROUCH, BARBARA LEE, personnel dir.; b. Sebring, Fla., Oct. 8, 1936; d. Elmer and Emily (Dreiss) Nichols; student Long Beach City Coll., 1975; Cerritos Jr. Coll., 1976; UCLA, 1977-78; m. Ralph Dean Crouch, Dec. 26, 1952; children—Ralph Dean, Barbara Lee, Clair Christopher, Kelly Andrew. Asst. personnel mgr. Zacky Foods, Commerce, Calif., 1973-75; cons. asst. M & M Assn., Los Angeles, 1975—, library mgr., 1978-80; personnel adminstr. T.A.D. Avanti, Inc., 1980-82; mgr. personnel service Ole's Home Center, Pasadena, Calif., 1982—. Mem. Personnel Indsl. Relations Assn. (treas. 1981, program chairperson 1982), Spl. Libraries Assn., VFW Womens Aux. (jr. vice and aux. rep. to 4th dist. 1977-78, sr. v.p. 1978-79), Am. Soc. Personnel Adminstrs. Democrat. Baptist. Club: Moose. Contbr. articles to profl. jours. Office: 3395 E Foothill Blvd Pasadena CA 91107

CROW, MARTHA NELL, travel agent; b. San Francisco, Oct. 29, 1933; d. Harold M. Tucker and Audrey K. (Kirkbride) Tucker Pinney; B.A., Stanford U., 1955; m. Alden Rankin Crow, Feb. 9, 1957; children—Alana Sims, Tucker Rankin. Sales cons. travel agencies, San Francisco, 1955-57, 63-69; v.p., owner Unravel Travel, San Francisco, 1969—. Chmn. historic sites project San Francisco Jr. League, 1972-79. Cert. travel counselor. Mem. Am. Soc. Travel Agts., Pacific Area Travel Assn., Travellarians, Pacific Musical Soc. (dir., corr. sec., v.p. 1982-83). Republican. Congregationalist. Club: Francisca (dir.) (San Francisco). Author: San Francisco at a Glance, 1971; also articles. Home: 35 Yerba Buena Ave San Francisco CA 94127 Office: 600 Market St Suite 210 San Francisco CA 94104

CROWE, DANIEL WALSTON, lawyer; b. Visalia, Calif., July 1, 1940; s. J. Thomas and Wanda (Walston) C.; m. Nancy V. Berard, May 10, 1969; children—Daniel W., Karyn Louise, Thomas Dwight. B.A. in English, U. Santa Clara, 1962; J.D., U. Calif.-San Francisco, 1965. Bar: Calif. 1966, U.S. Dist. Ct. (ea. dist.) Calif. 1969, U.S. Dist. Ct. (cen. dist.) Calif. 1973, U.S. Ct. Appeals (9th cir.) 1973, U.S. Supreme Ct. 1973. Assoc., Crowe, Mitchell, Hurlbutt, Clevenger & Long, Visalia, 1968-71; assoc. Crowe, Mitchell & Crowe, Visalia, 1971-74, ptnr., 1974—. Mem. coms. State Bar; chmn. governing bd. Calif. Continuing Edn. Bar, 1979-81; dir. Exeter Devel. Co. Founding mem., bd. dirs., counsel Visalia Balloon Assn., Inc., 1981—; founder, bd. dirs., sec. Visalia Aeronauts, Inc., 1982—. Served to capt., M.I., U.S. Army, 1965-68; Vietnam. Decorated Bronze Star, Air medal, Purple Heart. Mem. State Bar Calif., ABA, Tulare County Bar Assn., DAV, Am. Radio Relay League, NRA, Visalia C. of C. Republican. Roman Catholic. Clubs: Rotary, Elks, Moose (Visalia). Home: 3000 Hyde Way Visalia CA 93291 Office: Crowe Mitchell & Crowe 2222 W Main St Visalia CA 93291

CROWE, DEVON GEORGE, physicist, engineering consultant; b. Portland, Oreg., Mar. 11, 1948; s. Frank Irving and Jeannie Campbell (Scott) C.; m. Bonnie Jean McPherson, June 8, 1974. B.S. in Astronomy and Math., U. Ariz., 1971, M.B.A. in Ops. Mgmt., 1977, M.S. in Optical Scis., 1980. Sr. research asst. Kitt Peak Nat. Obs., 1975-76; chief systems devel. and ops. Bell Tech. Ops. Corp., Tucson, 1978-80; sr. scientist Sci. Applications, Inc., Tucson, 1980—; cons. in field. Served to lt. USAF, 1971-74. Fellow Brit. Interplanetary Soc.; mem. IEEE, AAAS, Optical Soc. Am. (pres. elect Tucson sect.), Photo-Optical Instrumentation Engrs., Am. Astron. Soc. Contbr. articles in field to profl. jours. Home: PO Box 11755 Tucson AZ 85734 Office: 5151 E Broadway St Suite 1100 Tucson AZ 85711

CROWE, J. THOMAS, lawyer; b. Fond du Lac, Wis., Jan. 5, 1902; s. John T. and Mary E. (Wood) C.; B.S., U. Santa Clara, 1922, J.D., 1923; m. Wanda Walston, July 18, 1936; children—John T., Daniel W., Marilyn. Bar: Calif. 1923. Practice in Visalia; asso. with Power & McFadzean, 1922-28; mem. Power, McFadzean & Crowe, 1928-35; mem. McFadzean, Crowe & Mitchell, 1935-52; sr. mem. Crowe, Mitchell, Crowe, 1952-83, Crowe, Crowe, Crowe & Wiliams, 1983—. chmn. bd. Tulare County Nat. Bank, 1949-59; dir. Knudsen Corp., 1967-74. Bd. govs. State Bar Calif. Fellow Am. Coll. Trial Lawyers, Am. Coll. Probate Counsel, Am. Bar Found.; mem. Tulare County Bar Assn. (pres. 1930-31), C. of C. (pres. 1947-48), State Bar Calif. (pres. 1969-70), Calif. Hawaii Elks Assn. (pres. 1933-34). Rotarian (dist. gov. 1938-39). Club: Visalia Country (pres. 1931-64). Home: 300 Fairway Dr Visalia CA 93291 Office: 2222 W Main St Visalia CA 93291

CROWE, JOHN T., lawyer; b. Cabin Cove, Calif., Aug. 14, 1938; s. J. Thomas and Wanda (Walston) C.; m. Marina Protopapa, Dec. 28, 1968; 1 dau., Erin Aleka. B.A., U. Santa Clara, 1960, J.D., 1962. Practiced in Visalia, Calif., 1964—; ptnr. firm Crowe, Mitchell & Crowe, 1971—; referee State Bar Ct., 1976-82. Bd. dirs. Mt. Whitney Area council Boy Scouts Am., 1966—, pres., 1971, 72; bd. dirs. Visalia Associated In-Group Donors (AID), 1973-81, pres., 1978-79. Served to 1st lt. U.S. Army, 1962-64; col. Res. Decorated Meritorious Service medal, Army Commendation medal; named Young Man of Yr., Visalia, 1973; Senator, Jr. Chamber Internat., 1970; recipient Silver Beaver award Boy Scouts Am., 1983. Mem. ABA, Tulare County Bar Assn., Nat. Assn. R.R. Trial Counsel, State Bar Calif., Visalia C. of C. (pres. 1979-80). Republican. Roman Catholic. Clubs: Rotary (pres. 1980-81), Country (Visalia); Downtown (Fresno, Calif.). Home: 3939 W School St Visalia CA 93291 Office: 2222 W Main St Visalia CA 93291

CROWE, KEVIN DERRYL, industrial rehabilitation therapist; b. New Britain, Conn., Apr. 26, 1954; s. Melvin C. and Dora T. (Serefini) C. B.A., Glassboro State U., 1976; M.Ed., U. Nev., 1978, Ed.D., 1983. Cert. rehab. therapist, vocat. evaluation specialist Nev. Edn. therapist Inst. Living, Hartford, Conn., 1972-73; resource cons. Berlin, Conn. public schs., 1976-77; research coordinator, teaching fellow, U. Nev., Las Vegas, 1977-78; indsl. rehab. therapist Clark Rehab. Ctr., Las Vegas, 1978—; dir. research Wink Corp., Seattle, 1982—. Diplomate Nat. Assn. Psychotherapists (com. cert. work adj. specialist); mem. Am. Personnel and Guidance Assn., Am. Psychol. Assn. Inventor mobile traction jacket (patent pending). Office: 1001 Shadow Ln Las Vegas NV 89106

CROWE, THOMAS HUNTER, corporate executive, consultant; b. Rome, N.Y., July 13, 1935; s. Henry Dye and Hazel Mary (Schele) C.; m. Carol Ann Rowan, Aug. 20, 1960; children—Susan, Mary Beth, Stephen, Brian, Thomas, Jr. B.S., Purdue U., 1958; postgrad. Internat. Sch. Marquette, 1963, Am. Mgmt. Assn., 1974. Sales engr. Allen Bradley Co., Milw., 1958-61; v.p., mktg. mgr., product mgr., internat. mgr. Hayssen Mfg. Co., Sheboygan, Wis., 1961-77; v.p. mktg. WPM Systems, Denver, 1977-78; v.p. Hathaway Corp., Denver, 1979—. Active Republican Party, sustaining mem. nat. com. Recipient various co. and industry awards for mktg. performance. Mem. Am. Mgmt. Assn., IEEE. Club: Hiwan Country. Contbr. articles to profl. jours. Office: Hathaway Corp 5250 E Evans Ave Denver CO 80222

CROWELL, ANN HULT, advt. exec.; b. Chgo.; d. Stanley Earl and Betty (Yakel) Hult; m. Alton Ingram Crowell, Jr., May 29, 1971; 1 dau., Catherine Elizabeth. B.S., U. Ariz., 1960. Participant mgmt. tng. program Joseph Magnin, San Francisco, 1960-61; account exec. Erwin Wasey, Inc., Los Angeles, 1964-66; sr. account exec. Carson/Roberts, Inc., Los Angeles, 1966-68; pres. Crowell McKay, Inc. advt. and pub. relations, Irvine, Calif., 1971—; instr. U. Calif.-Irvine. Bd. dirs. U. Calif.-Irvine Found., Friends of U. Calif.-Irvine; mem. council Laguna Beach. Mus. Art; mem. Los Angeles/Berlin Sister City Com., Indsl. League Orange County. Orphanage Guild Jrs. Los Angeles. Recipient numerous awards for excellence in advt. and promotion Los Angeles Ad Club, N.Y. Ad Club, Bus. and Profl. Advt. Assn., Merchandising Execs. Club Los Angeles, Communications Arts Mag., Los Angeles Ad Women, Orange County Advt. Fedn., Contract Mag. Mem. Am. Advt. Fedn., Am. Assn. Advt. Agys. Club: Chancellor's U. Calif. Office: 17752 Mitchell N Irvine CA 92714

CROWLEY, FRANCIS LEO, JR., lawyer; b. Boston, Sept. 15, 1931; s. Francis Leo and Genevieve Marie (McCarthy) C.; m. Jennie Maffei, Jan. 25, 1955; children—Francis L. III, Maureen Anne. B.S., Georgetown U., 1952, LL.B., 1955. Bar: D.C. 1955, Calif. 1969. Assoc. Covington and Burling, Washington, 1952-55; atty.-adviser Office Gen. Counsel, U.S. Sec. Def., 1960-63; staff v.p., assoc. gen. counsel Litton Industries, Inc., Beverly Hills, Calif., 1963—. Served to capt. JAGC, U.S. Army, 1955-60. Decorated Commendation medal. Mem. ABA, Los Angeles County Bar Assn. Democrat. Roman Catholic. Home: 2693 Basil Ln Los Angeles CA 90077 Office: 360 N Crescent Dr Beverly Hills CA 90210

CROWLEY, JOHN CRANE, real estate developer; b. Detroit, June 29, 1919; s. Edward John and Leah Helen (Crane) C.; B.A., Swarthmore Coll., 1941; M.S., U. Denver, 1943; m. Barbara Wenzel Gilfillan, Jan. 12, 1945; children—F. Alexander, Leonard, Philip, Eliot, Louise, Sylvia. Mem. staff Pub. Adminstrn. Service, Chgo., 1942-46; asst. dir. Mcpl. Finance Officers Assn., Chgo., 1946-48; So. Calif. mgr. League Calif. Cities, Los Angeles, 1948-53; city mgr. Monterey Park, Calif., 1953-56; v.p. Community Facilities Corp., Los Angeles, 1956-59, DSI Corp., real estate devel., Beverly Hills, Calif., 1961—; founder, exec. v.p. Nat. Med. Enterprises, Los Angeles, 1968; pres. Ventura Towne House (Calif.), 1963—; mem. faculty U. So. Calif. Sch. Pub. Adminstrn., 1950-53. Mem. Calif. Com. on Continuing Edn., 1965-66, State Adv. Council on Retirement Housing, 1965-68, Los Angeles County Com. on Affairs of Aging, 1966—; bd. dirs. Pacificulture Found. and Asia Mus., 1971-76, pres., 1972-74; bd. dirs. Pasadena Area Liberal Arts Center, 1962-72, pres., 1965-68; trustee Pacific Oaks Friends Sch. and Coll., Pasadena, 1954-57; chmn. Pasadena Cultural Heritage Comm., 1975-78; city dir. Pasadena, 1979—. Sloan Found. fellow, 1941-43. Mem. Am. Soc. Pub. Adminstrn., Internat. City Mgmt. Assn., Nat. Mcpl. League (nat. council 1980—), Phi Delta Theta. Democrat. Unitarian. Author: Institutional Employee Maintenance Policy, 1947. Contbr. articles to profl. jours. Home: 615 Linda Vista Ave Pasadena CA 91105 Office: PO Box 93223 Pasadena CA 91109

CROWLEY, JOSEPH NEIL, univ. pres.; b. Oelwein, Iowa, July 9, 1933; s. James Bernard and Nina Mary (Neil) C.; B.A., U. Iowa, 1959; M.A., Calif. State U., Fresno, 1963; Ph.D. (Univ. fellow), U. Wash., 1967; m. Johanna Lois Reitz, Sept. 9, 1961; children—Theresa, Neil, Margaret, Timothy. Reporter, Fresno Bee, 1961-62; asst. prof. polit. sci. U. Nev., Reno, 1966-71, assoc. prof., 1971-79, prof., 1979—, chmn. dept. polit. sci., 1976-78, pres., 1978—. Policy formulation officer EPA, Washington, 1973-74; dir. instl. studies Nat. Commn. on Water Quality, Washington, 1974-75; cons. in field. Bd. dirs. Thursday Evening Forum, Center for Religion and Life, Reno, 1970-73, Nev. Ednl. Seminar, 1976-82; del. Democratic Nat. Conv., 1972. Served with USAF, 1954-57. Recipient Thornton Peace prize U. Nev., 1971; Nat. Assn. Schs. Public Affairs and Adminstrn. fellow, 1973-74. Mem. Am. Polit. Sci. Assn., Western Polit. Sci. Assn., No. Calif. Polit. Sci. Assn. Roman Catholic. Club: Rotary. Author: Democrats, Delegates and Politics in Nevada: A Grassroots Chronicle of 1972, 1976; editor: (with Robert Roelofs and Donald Hardesty) Environment and Society, 1973. Home: 1265 Muir Dr Reno NV 89503 Office: Pres's Office U Nev Reno NV 89557*

CROWLEY, REIDUN MARIE, utility company manager; b. Bergen, Norway, July 29, 1945, came to U.S., 1957, naturalized, 1962; d. Reidar and Konny (Halvorsen) Fammestad; m. David Neil Crowley, Dec. 6, 1969; children—Britt Lindsey, Michael Brian. B.A. in Home Econs., U. Wash., 1969; post-grad. U. Puget Sound, 1980—. Home economist Puget Power and Light Co., Bellingham, Wash., 1969-70, Bellevue, Wash., 1970-77, supr. energy info., 1978-79, Mgr. edn. and consumer relations, 1979, mgr. edn. services, 1980, corp. planning adminstr., 1981, mgr. conservation services, 1982—; adv. bd. N.W. Area Found. Active King County Mcpl. League. Recipient Alma award Assn. Home Appliance Mfrs., 1976; Seattle Salute award Seattle Conv. and Visitors Bur., Mem. Am. Home Econs. Assn., Home Economists in Bus., Electrical Women's Round Table, Profl. and Managerial Women's Network, C. of C. Home: 13456 64 Terrace NE Kirkland WA 98033 Office: Puget Sound Light and Power Co Puget Power Bldg Bellevue WA 98009

CROWLEY, RICHARD JAMES, clinical hypnotherapist, lecturer; b. Cambridge, Mass., Apr. 16, 1942; s. John Francis and Anne Rita (Mitchell) C.; B.A. in Psychology, St. Bonaventure U., 1964; M.S.W., Boston Coll., 1966; Ph.D. in Clin. Psychology, U.S. Internat. U., San Diego, 1979. Lic. clin. social worker, marriage family and child counselor, Calif.; cert. hypnotist. Pvt. practice clin. hypnotist, psychol. therapist, 1970—; lectr., cons. Served to capt. M.C., U.S. Army, 1966-68. NIMH fellow, 1969-70. Mem. Am. Psychol. Assn., Am. Soc. Clin. Hypnosis, Am. Soc. Exptl. and Clin. Hypnosis, Calif. State Psychol. Assn., Internat. Soc. Hypnosis. Brit. Soc. Exptl. and Clin. Hypnosis. Author: Hypnosis Dealing with Acute Pain Associated with Podiatric Surgery, 1979. Co-Inventor board game. Home: 4291 Elmer Ave Studio City CA 91602 Office: Mental Health Ctr 10850 Riverside Dr Suite 612 Toluca Lake CA 91602

CROWLEY, ROBERT TINKHAM, physician; b. Galion, Ohio, Dec. 10, 1913; s. Forrest Glen and Frances Mae (Tinkham) C.; grad. Mercersburg Acad., 1930; M.D., Syracuse U., 1937; M.S. in Surgery, Wayne State U., 1946; M.Sc.Med., N.Y. Med. Coll., 1947; m. Cecilia Rita Smith, Dec. 23, 1956. Intern N.Y. Med. Coll., N.Y.C., 1937-38, resident in pathology and medicine, 1938-39; resident surgery Detroit Receiving Hosp., 1939-43, 45-46; adj. attending surgeon Lenox Hill Hosp., N.Y.C., 1947-54, chief women's div. Cancer Detection Clinic, 1950-54; chief surgery Meml. Med. Center, Williamson, W.Va., 1956-62; partner Kinsman (Ohio) Clinic, 1962-67; asst. prof. clin. surgery N.Y. U. Postgrad. Med. Sch., 1948-54; assoc. prof. surgery Wayne State U. Coll. Medicine, 1954-56; practice medicine specializing in thoracic surgery, Lancaster and Palm Dale, Calif.; chief surg. service Palm Dale Gen. Hosp., 1968—; chief surg. cons. Los Angeles County Mira Loma Hosp., 1980—; cons. surgeon Lancaster Community Hosp.; med. cons.

U.S. Dept. Justice, 1979—. Served from capt. to maj., M.C., AUS, 1943-45; ETO. Named Disting. Citizen of Golden State, 1974. Diplomate Am. Bd. Surgery, Am. Bd. Thoracic Surgery, Nat. Bd. Med. Examiners. Fellow ACS, Am. Assn. Surgery Trauma, Royal Soc. Health (London), N.Y. Acad. Medicine; mem. Internationale Societe de Chirurgie, N.Y. Surg. Soc., N.Y. County Med. Soc., Western, Central surg. assns., Am. Coll. Geriatrics, Am. Coll. Angiology, Lyman Brewer II Internat. Surgery Soc. (founder), Internat. Platform Assn., Am. Authors League, Authors Guild, Sigma Xi. Episcopalian. Author: (novels) The Coffer of Saturno, 1961; Some with Steel, 1965; Not Soldiers All, 1967; Contract Surgeon, 1969; (poetry) Haste to The Red Brides Wedding, 1971; Lessons from Fright School, 1976; Robert T. Crowley research collection at Mugar Inst. Creative Writing, Boston U.; contbr. articles to med. jours. Office: PO Box 1058 Palmdale CA 93550

CROWTHER, H. DAVID, aerospace company executive; b. Long Beach, Calif., Mar. 7, 1930; s. Harry Hampton and Florabelle (Reader) C.; m. Helen Jeanette Custer, May 22, 1960; children—John Newton, Kimberly Ann. B.A. in Pub. Relations, Calif. State U.-Long Beach, 1955. Accredited Pub. Relations Soc. Am. Founder, Crowther and Assocs., Long Beach, 1956-59; pub. relations rep. Lockheed Corp., Burbank, Calif., 1959-72, various positions including asst. to v.p. pub. relations, mgr. pub. affairs, dir. pub. relations, 1975-81, v.p. corp. communications, 1981—; asst. to sec., dir. pub. affairs U.S. Dept. Transp., 1972-75. Bd. dirs. John Tracy Clinic, Council for Econ. Edn. Served with U.S. Army, 1951-53. Decorated Silver Star, Purple Heart. Mem. Pub. Relations Soc. Am., Pub. Affairs Council, Calif. Mfrs. Assn. (dir.). Club: Lakeside Golf (Toluca Lake, Calif.) Home: 10459 Camarillo St Toluca Lake CA 91602 Office: PO Box 551 Burbank CA 91520

CROY, RICHARD ALLEN, photographer, lecturer; b. Trenton, Mich., Sept. 11, 1944; s. Charles Raymond and Doris Elizabeth (Porter) C.; m. Peggy Lynn Townsend, May 16, 1976; children—Edward, Shelly, Eric. Student Winona Sch. Profl. Photography, 1965. Lab technician, photographer Ray Manley Studio, Tucson, 1962-69; photographer Internat. Photographic Assoc., Inc., 1969—, Studio Seven Photography, 1969—, I.P.A. Color Lab, 1969—; lectr. photography. Air Nat. Guard, 1966-72. Recipient numerous photog. exhibit awards. Mem. Ariz. Profl. Photographers Assn. (pres. 1967). Baptist. Clubs. Exchange (pres. 1972); Rotary. Office: 4500 E Speedway 90 Tucson AZ 85712

CROYLE, BARBARA ANN, oil co. exec.; b. Knoxville, Tenn., Oct. 22, 1949; d. Charles Evans and Myrtle Elizabeth (Kellam) C.; m. Marc Rene Brosseau, Oct. 2, 1982. B.A. cum laude, Coll. William and Mary, 1971; student Inst. Paralegal Tng., 1971; J.D., U. Colo., 1975; M.B.A., U. Denver, 1983. Bar: Colo., 1976; paralegal asst. Holland & Hart, Denver, 1972-73; law clk. Colo. Ct. Appeals, 1976; assoc. Shaw Spangler & Roth, Denver, 1976-77; with Petro Lewis Corp., Denver, 1977—, mgr. acquisitions/lands, 1982—. Bd. dirs., vol. mediator Ctr. for Dispute Resolution; bd. dirs. Women and Bus. Enterprises Inc.; vol. arbitrator Better Bus. Bur.; vol. mediator Legal Info. Ctr. Mem. ABA, Colo. Bar Assn., Denver Bar Assn., Colo. Women's Bar Assn., Exec. and Profl. Women's Council, Denver Assn. Petroleum Landmen, Nat. Assn. Female Execs., Am. Arbitration Assn. (panel arbitrators). Home: 1835 S Linden Way Denver CO 80224 Office: 717 17th St PO Box 2250 Denver CO 80202

CRUFT, EDGAR FRANK, mining co. exec.; b. London, Feb. 8, 1933; s. William Frank and Rosina Jane (Edgar) C.; B.Sc., Durham U., Eng., 1954; Ph.D., McMaster U., Can., 1962; postdoctoral fellow, Pa. State U., 1962-63; m. Yvonne Odile Corne, Aug. 1952; children—Nicole Yvonne, Deborah Jane, Stephen Edgar; m. 2d, Geraldine Anne Monola, July 9, 1968; children—John Stuart, Elizabeth Rose. Mining and exploration geologist, S. and C. Am., 1954-57, Can., 1957-62; asst. prof., assoc. prof. U. N.Mex., 1963-73; pres., chmn. bd. Nord Resources Corp., Ohio, 1968—; chmn. bd. Nord Kaolin Corp., Ga. U.S.A., Sierra Rutile Ltd., Sierra Leone, West Africa; dir. Nord Mining Co. Ltd., Australia, Trans Air S.W. Inc., Mond Aviation Inc., Shanley Oil Corp., Houston. Recipient Walker Mineral. award Can., 1964; NSF grantee, 1964-67; Cominco fellow Can., 1963. Fellow Inst. Mining and Metallurgy London; mem. Soc. Econ. Geologists, Geol. Soc. Am., Geochem. Soc., Soc. Exploration Geochemists, Inst. Dirs. London. Contbr. articles to profl. jours. Home: 2850 Refugio Santa Ynez CA 93460 Office: 880 Ballard Canyon Rd Solvang CA 93463

CRUICKSHANK, STEPHANI ANN, public relations administrator; b. Baytown, Tex., Aug. 6, 1955; d. Herbert Howard and Janice Faye (Stowe) C.; m. George Keyston III, Oct. 8, 1983. A.A. with honors, Merced Coll., Merced, Calif., 1975; B.A. in Journalism with distinction, San Jose State U., 1976. Reporter, Fresno (Calif.) Bee, 1974-75; reporter, photographer Merced (Calif.) Sun-Star, 1974-77; pub. info. officer Fresno City Coll. (Calif.), 1977-80; dir. communications Aerojet Tactical Systems Co., Sacramento, 1980—. Co.-coordinator United Way Campaign, 1981; Aerojet Tactical Systems Co. coordinator West Coast Nat. Derby Rallies, 1981-83. Mem. Internat. Assn. Bus. Communicators (dir. Sacramento chpt. 1983), Citrus Heights C. of C. (v.p. 1983). Republican. Office: PO Box 13400 Sacramento CA 95813

CRULL, TIMM F., food products company executive; b. 1931; B.A., Mich. State U., 1955; married. Chief operating officer, dir. Norton Simon Inc., 1977-79; with Carnation Co., 1955-77, 80—, exec. v.p., 1980—, also dir. Office: Carnation Bldg 5045 Wilshire Blvd Los Angeles CA 90036

CRUMBAKER, MARY KAY, business coll. adminstr.; b. Gt. Falls, Mont., Oct. 15, 1920; d. Calvin and Kathryn Elizabeth (Harbaugh) C.; B.S., U. Oreg., 1946; M.Ed., Oreg. State U., 1966; Ph.D., Nat. Christian U., Dallas, 1974; m. William Goodman Williamson, Dec. 17, 1941 (dec. Oct. 1970); children—James Calvin, Albert Jerome, Kathryn Erilda. Various secretarial positions, 1941-46; lectr. econs. and music, then head comml. studies Internat. Trade Coll., Chgo., 1946-51; tchr. Am. Legion Tb Hosp., Mich. Dept. Rehab., Battle Creek, 1952-53; tchr. Army Info. and Edn., Kokura, Japan, 1954-56, Clark Bus. Coll., Topeka, 1956-58; dir. charm sch. Eugene Bus. Coll., dir. tng. Eugene (Oreg.) Bus. Coll., 1959-70, tchr. typing and English, 1960—, mgr. corp. sec. Eugene Bus. Coll., 1970-74, pres., 1974—; lectr. Am. econ. system and music Austro-Am. Soc., Vienna, 1946-48. Mem. exec. bd. S.W. Oreg. Mus. Sci. and Industry, 1972-75; pres. Central Lane County Republican Women, 1970; den mother Boy Scouts Am., 10 yrs. Mem. Nat. Fedn. Bus. and Profl. Women (Woman of Year in Eugene 1967), Am. Bus. Women, Rubicon Soc., DAR, PEO, WCTU, Beta Gamma Sigma, Mu Phi Epsilon. Clubs: Eugene Bus. and Profl. Women's Club (pres. 1966, 79), Eugene City, Zonta, Dial (pres. 1973), Order Eastern Star (organist), White Shrine Jerusalem Bethlehem (organist). Mem. Unity Ch. Author: Typing With Less Than Two Hands, 1962.

CRUMP, MICHAEL JOHN, computerized tax services company executive; b. Los Angeles, Oct. 11, 1946; s. Eugene L. and Elizabeth M. (Finn) C.; m. Susan Jane Pendergast, Apr. 5, 1975; 1 dau., Catherine. B.A., U. San Francisco, 1968; J.D., U. San Diego, 1972. Research asst. U.S. Dist. Ct., San Diego, 1974-75; tax analyst Marshall Acctg., Long Beach, Calif., 1975; tax analyst Tymshare Unitax, Anaheim, Calif., 1975-78, tax mgr., 1978—; mem. IRS Task Force, 1982—; lectr. in field. Mem. Nat. Soc. Pub. Accts., Nat. Assn. Computerized Tax Processors (treas. 1978-81, v.p. 1981-82, pres., 1982—), Xplor (v.p. 1980-81). Democrat. Roman Catholic. Author manuals in field. Home: 27022 Red Barn Circle Laguna Hills CA 92653 Office: 639 N Euclid St Anaheim CA 92801

CRUMP, WILLUS WALKER, financial, estate planning company executive; b. Russellville, Ark., Jan. 31, 1913; s. James Jackson and Sally May (Linn) C.; m. Jacqueline Porter Magers, June 1, 1940; children—Jacqueline Mary Crump Harris, Cynthia Mae Crump Hopson. Student San Francisco State U., 1952-54, B.A. in Polit. Sci., 1981, M.B.A., 1983; student U. Okla., 1958-59, U. Md., 1960-66. Enlisted U.S. Army, 1935, advanced through grades to CW4, 1960; served as personnel and adminstrv. officer, Korea, Hdqrs. U.S. Army, Pacific, Europe, 1949-62, Hdqrs. U.S. Army Security Agy., 1962-66, ret. 1966; life underwriter John Hancock Mut. Life Ins. Co., 1967—; owner, operator real estate agy., San Francisco, 1969—, ins. agency, San Francisco, 1977—; incorporator, pres., chief exec. officer Apple Pie and Velvet Fin. Corp., San Francisco, 1978—; incorporator, pres., chief exec., officer Calif. Hosp. Supply Co., Inc., San Francisco, 1981—. Decorated Army Commendation medal; recipient cert. of honor City and County of San Francisco. Mem. Am. Soc. C.L.U.s, Nat. Assn. Life Underwriters, Nat. Assn. Realtors, Nat. Assn. Security Dealers (registered rep.), Ret. Officers Assn. (v.p. San Francisco chpt. 1979-82, pres. 1982-83), DAV (chpt. comdr. 1983), Mil. Order World Wars, VFW. Democrat. Club: Presidio Officers. Home: 2722 40th Ave San Francisco CA 94116 Office: Apple Pie and Velvet Financial Corp 780 Bryant St San Francisco CA 94107

CRUMPLER, HUGH ALLAN, advertising executive; b. Rolla, Mo., Mar. 14, 1918; s. Hugh Dinsmore and Addye Adelle (Alexander) C.; m. Dorothy Virginia Carter, May 26, 1945; children—Hugh, Shelley Ann, Joan Carter. B.J., U. Mo., 1941. Reporter, editor N.Y. Herald Tribune, 1941-43; war corr. UPI, China, Burma, India, Philippines, Okinawa, Korea, Japan, 1944-45; lectr. U. Mo., U. Minn., 1946-49; attaché, pub. affairs officer Am. embassies in Karachi, Ankara, Istanbul, Amman, 1950-60; intelligence and research officer USIA, 1957-60; v.p., Washington rep. Dean Internat., Global Internat., 1960-70; v.p. advt. and pub. relations Four Winds Enterprises, Inc., San Diego, 1970—. Dem. candidate for Congress, 8th Dist. Mo., 1960. Decorated Burma Star. Mem. Pub. Relations Soc. Am., Burma Star Assn., Merrill's Marauders Assn., Sigma Nu. Author: (with Theodore Wertheim) Communist Propaganda: A Fact Book, 1960; columnist CBI Roundup; contbr. articles to mags. Office: 4275 Campus Point Ct San Diego CA 92125

CRUMPTON, EVELYN, psychologist; b. Ashland, Ala., Dec. 23, 1924; d. Alpheus Leland and Bernice (Fordham) Crumpton. A.B., Birmingham So. Coll., 1948; B.S., UCLA, 1953, Ph.D. in Psychology, 1955. Lic. psychologist, Calif. Research psychologist VA Hosp., Brentwood, Los Angeles, 1955-77; asst. chief, psychology service, coordinator clin. training VA Adminstrn. Med. Ctr., Brentwood div., West Los Angeles, 1977—; clin. prof. dept. psychology UCLA, assoc. research psychologist dept. psychiatry, UCLA Sch. Med., 1957—. Recipient Profl. Service award, Assn. Chief Psychologists VA, 1979. Fellow Soc. Personality Assessment; mem. Am. Psychol. Assn., Western Psychol. Assn., Sigma Xi. Contbr. numerous articles to profl. jours. Office: Psychology Service 691/B118B VA Med Ctr West Los Angeles Brentwood Div 11301 Wilshire Blvd Los Angeles CA 90291

CRUMPTON, SANDRA ANN, computer software company executive, consultant; b. Greenville, S.C., Oct. 12, 1945; d. James Albert and Elizabeth Mae (Surett) C. B.A., Mich. State U., 1968; postgrad. U. Calif.-Berkeley, 1976-77, Am. U., 1972-74. Cert. tchr., Mich., Calif.; cert. adminstr., Calif. Tchr., Okemos (Mich.) Pub. Schs., 1968-70, Crete (Ill.) Pub. Schs., 1970-72; master tchr. Am. Community Sch., Athens, Greece, 1972-74; bus. dir. Crested Butte (Colo.) Ski Sch., 1974-76; mktg. rep. data processing div. IBM, San Francisco, 1977-80; mgr. customer support Walker Interactive Products, San Francisco, 1980—; cons. Mem. Nat. Assn. Female Execs., Women in Bus., AAUW. Republican. Clubs: Commonwealth, International. Contbr. articles to profl. jours. Office: 100 Mission St Suite 300 San Francisco CA 94105

CRUSE, ALLAN BAIRD, mathematician, educator; b. Birmingham, Ala., Aug. 28, 1941; s. J. Clyde and Irma R. Cruse. A.B., Emory U., 1959-62, Ph.D., 1974; postgrad. (Woodrow Wilson fellow) U. Calif.-Berkeley, 1962-63, M.A., 1966; teaching fellow Dartmouth Coll., 1963-64. Instr., U. San Francisco, 1966-73, asst. prof. math., 1973-76, assoc. prof., 1976-79, prof., 1979—; vis. instr. Stillman Coll., summer 1967; vis. assoc. prof. Emory U., spring 1978; prof. computer sci. Sonoma State U., 1983—; cons. math edn. NSF fellow, 1972-73. Mem. Am. Math. Soc., Math. Assn. Am., AAUP, Assn. Computing Machinery, U. San Francisco Faculty Assn., Sigma Xi (Dissertation award 1974). Author: (with Millianne Granberg) Lectures on Freshman Calculus, 1971; research, publs. in field. Office: Harney Sci Center U San Francisco San Francisco CA 94117

CRUTCHFIELD, MICHAEL CHARLES, optometrist; b. Washington, Mar. 4, 1951; s. Clyde V. and Joan Elaine (Strasser) C.; m. Kathern Johnson, Nov. 30, 1975; div. B.S., Colo. State U., 1974; B.S. So. Calif. Coll. Optometry, 1978, O.D., 1980. Cert. optometrist, Nev., Calif. Pvt. practice optometry, Las Vegas, 1980—. Mem. So. Nev. Optometric Assn. (pres. 1982-83), Nev. Optometric Assn., Calif. Optometric Assn., Am. Optometric Assn. Democrat. Presbyterian. Home: 4479 Deforest St Las Vegas NV 89103 Office: 901 Rancho Ln Suite 117 Las Vegas NV 89106

CRUZ, MANUEL ISABEL, aerospace engr.; b. Laredo, Tex., Jan. 15, 1947; s. Manuel Avila and Maria Luisa (Rodriguez) C.; m. Adelina Alvillar Garcia, Aug. 28, 1970; children—Maria Isabell, Manuel Nicholas, Erminda Christina. B.S., Tex. A&M U., 1968, M.S., 1969; postgrad. UCLA, 1971. Mem. tech. staff Minute Man and MX weapons system engring. TRW Systems Group, Redondo Beach, Calif., 1969-77; mgr. aerocapture systems research and tech. devel. Jet Propulsion Lab., Calif. Inst. Tech., 1977—; mem. tech. com. Nat. Atmospheric Flight Mechanics. Mem. AIAA, Sigma Gamma Tau, Phi Kappa Phi. Contbr. articles to tech. jours. Office: 4800 Oak Grove Dr Pasadena CA 91103

CRYER, RODGER EARL, ednl. adminstr.; b. Detroit, Apr. 2, 1940. A.B. in Fine Arts, San Diego State U., 1965; M.A. in Edn. Adminstrn., Stanford U., 1972, postgrad. in Edn. Adminstrn., 1975—. Spl. asst. to commissioner N.J. State Dept. Edn., Trenton, 1967-68; cons. N.J. Urban Sch. Devel., Trenton, 1969-70; mgmt. cons. Rodger E. Cryer, Co., Pinole, Calif., 1970-73; adminstrv. asst. Franklin McKinley Sch. Dist., San Jose, Calif., 1973—. Mem. Nat. Sch. Public Relations Assn. (sec. 1975—), Calif. Sch. Public Relations Assn. (pres.). Certified as tchr., N.J., Calif.; gen. adminstrn., Calif. Contbr. articles to profl. jours. Home: PO Box 21917 San Jose CA 95151 Office: 2281 Galveston Dr San Jose CA 95122

CRYSTAL, VEARL C., state senator, rancher; m. Brenda Crystal; 2 children. Rancher, rodeo producer; mem. from 20th Dist., Idaho State Senate; chmn. agrl. affairs com. Served in World War II. Dep. assessor Jefferson County, 2 yrs., assessor Jefferson County, 28 yrs. Mem. Eastern Idaho Rodeo Assn. (dir.), VFW. Office: Idaho State Senate Boise ID 83720*

CSENDES, ERNEST, chemist, fin. exec.; b. Satu-Mare, Romania, Mar. 2, 1926; s. Edward O. and Sidonia (Littman) C.; came to U.S., 1951, naturalized, 1955; B.A., Protestant Coll., Hungary, 1944; B.S., U. Heidelberg (Ger.), 1948, M.S., Ph.D., 1951; m. Catharine Vera Tolnai, Feb. 7, 1953; children—Audrey Carol, Robert Alexander Edward. Research assoc. biochemistry Tulane U., New Orleans, 1952; fellow Harvard U., 1953; research chemist organic chems. dept. E. I. Du Pont de Nemours and Co., Wilmington, Del., 1953-56, elastomer chems. dept., 1956-61; dir. research and devel. agrl. chems. div. Armour & Co., Atlanta, 1961-63; v.p. corp. devel. Occidental Petroleum Corp., 1963-64, exec. v.p. research, engring. and devel., 1964-68, also mem. exec. com.; exec. v.p., dir. Occidental Research & Engring. Corp., 1963-68; pres., chief exec. officer Tex. Republic Industries, Inc., 1968—; gen. ptnr. Tex. Republic Investors, Ltd., 1971-72; pres., chief exec. officer TRI Ltd., Bermuda, 1971—; chmn. TRI Internat., Ltd., Bermuda, 1971—; dir. TRI Holdings, S.A., Luxembourg, 1971—; mng. dir. TRI Capital N.V. (Netherlands), 1971—. Recipient Pro Mundi Beneficio medal Brazilian Acad. Humanitites. Fellow AAAS, Am. Inst. Chemists; mem. Am., German chem. socs., N.Y. Acad. Sci., Chem. Soc. London, Acad. Polit. Sci., Am. Acad. Polit. and Social Sci., Research Soc. Am., Am. Mgmt. Assn., AIM, AIAA, Am. Def. Preparedness Assn. Contbr. articles to profl. jours. Patentee in field. Research in area of elastomers, rubber chemicals, dyes and intermediates, organometallics, organic and biochemistry, high polymers, phosphates, plant nutrients, pesticides, process engring. and design of fertilizer plants, ammonia, urea, sulfur, iron, potash and phosphate ore mining and metallurgy; also acquisitions, mergers, internat. fin. related to leasing, banking, trusts and ins.; regional devel. related to agr. and energy resources. Home: 1601 Casale Rd Pacific Palisades CA 90272 Office: Am Internat Bldg Richmond Rd Pembroke Bermuda

CUADRA, CARLOS ALBERT, information science executive; b. San Francisco, Dec. 21, 1925; s. Gregorio and Amanda (Mendoza) C.; m. Gloria Nathalie Adams, May 3, 1947; children—Mary Susan Cuadra Nielsen, Neil Gregory, Dean Arthur. A.B., U. Calif.-Berkeley, 1949, Ph.D., 1953. Staff psychologist VA Hosp., Downey, Ill., 1953-56; with System Devel. Corp., Santa Monica, Calif., 1957-78, mgr. library and documentation systems dept., 1968-70, mgr. edn. and library systems dept., 1971-74, gen. mgr. Search Service, 1974-78; founder and pres. Cuadra Assocs., Inc., Santa Monica, 1978—. Mem. Nat. Commn. on Libraries and Info. Sci., 1971—. Served with USN, 1944-46. Recipient Miles Conrad award Nat. Fedn. Abstracting and Indexing Services, 1980. Mem. Am. Soc. Info. Sci. (Merit award 1968, Best Info. Sci. Book award 1969, Disting. Lectr. of Yr., 1970), Info. Industry Assn. (Hall of Fame 1980), Spl. Libraries Assn. Contbr. articles on info. sci. to profl. jours. Home: 13213 Warren Ave Los Angeles CA 90066 Office: 2001 Wilshire Blvd Suite 305 Santa Monica CA 90403

CUARON, ALICIA VALLADOLID, educator, community activist; b. Oxnard, Calif., Mar. 1, 1939; d. Rosendo Alfaro and Guadalupe Valladolid (Perez) V.; m. Carlos Alberto Cuaron, June 18, 1966; 1 dau., Alexis Maritza. B.A. in Edn., U. Tex.-El Paso, 1961, M.A. in Adminstrn., 1972; Ed.D. in Curriculum and Instrn., U. No. Colo., Greeley, 1975. Cert. tchr., supr., Tex. Tchr., Pub. Schs. El Paso, 1961-72; asst. prof. edn. Met. State Coll., Denver, 1974-80; social sci. program specialist U.S. Dept. Labor Women's Bur., Denver, 1979; exec. dir. Colo. Econ. Devel. Assn., Denver, 1980; nat. adminstr. Nat. Assn. Constrn. Enterprises, Denver, 1981-82; dir. Hispanic Access to Services Project, Community Coll. Denver, Auraria Campus, 1982—; bilingual/bicultural presch. coordinator Denver Headstart, 1972; project dir. Bilingual/Multicultural Edn. project, 1975; cons. Hispanic Dispaced Homemakers project, 1981. Founder, Nat. Adelante Mujer Hispana Conf., 1980, Nat. Network Hispanic Women, 1981, Colo. Network Hispanas, 1981; chair Colo. Ctr. Women and Work, 1980; mem. Colo. State Fair Commn., Colo. Supreme Ct. Nominating Commn. Recipient award Colo. Big Sisters, 1983. Mem. Nat. Assn. Hispanas in Econ. Devel. and Enterpreneurship (founder), Colo. Women's Forum, League United Latin Am. Citizens, Nat. Assn. Female Execs., Mexican Am. Nat. Women's Assn., Phi Delta Kappa. Democrat. Roman Catholic. Author: Hispana Displaced Homemakers Training Model, 1982; producer/host TV and radio programs, 1981-83. Home: 1000 S Monaco St #30 Denver CO 80224 Office: Community College Denver Auraria 1111 W Colfax Ave Denver CO 80204

CUCCHIARI, JOSEPH SALVATORE, airplane supply co. exec., b. Point St. Joe, Fla., Apr. 22, 1947; s. Salvatore Joseph C., B.A. in Bus. Adminstrn., Coll. Idaho, 1968; 1 son, Joseph Alan. Gen. mgr., v.p. Fairbanks Flight Service, Inc. (Alaska), 1972-74, Polar Airlines, Anchorage, 1974-76; pres. ASA, Inc., Seattle, 1976—; rated airline transp. pilot, gen. and flight instr. Mem. Airplane Owners and Pilots Assn., Wash. Aviation Assn. (dir. pub. relations), Pilots Internat. Assn., Seattle C. of C. (aviation com.). Republican. Address: 7201 Perimeter Rd Seattle WA 98108

CUCCHISSI, MICHAEL SALVATORE, lawyer; b. Bklyn., Aug. 29, 1953; s. Michael Anthony and Grace Anne (Del Casino) C.; m. Barbara Virginia Barbella, Apr. 12, 1980; 1 son, Gregory Lawrence. B.S., MIT, 1975; J.D., U. Pa., 1978. Bar: Calif. 1978. Law clk. to chief judge U.S. Dist. Ct. Hawaii, Honolulu, 1978-79; assoc. Gibson, Dunn & Crutcher, Newport Beach, Calif., 1979—. Recipient Gold Athletic award MIT, 1974, Harold J. Pettegrove award, 1974. Mem. ABA, Orange County Bar Assn. Republican. Roman Catholic. Contbr. articles U. Pa. Law Rev., 1977. Home: 21071 Cranbridge Dr El Toro CA 92630 Office: Gibson Dunn & Crutcher 800 Newport Center Dr Suite 500 Newport Beach CA 92660

CUELLAR, ROBERT ALEMAN, advertising executive, management consultant; b. Fresnillo, Zacatecas, Mex., Oct. 28, 1939; naturalized Am. citizen, 1963; s. Manuel R. and Lida (Aleman) C.; B.A., N. Tex. State U., 1967, M.A., 1969; m. Sylvia Cobos, Feb. 3, 1968; children—Martin Edward, Mark Andrew. Tchr. pub. schs. Mesquite (Tex.) Inds. Sch. Dist., 1967-68; asst. registrar N. Tex. State U., Denton, 1968-69; nat. dep. dir. Jobs for Progress, Inc., (chmn. Angeles, 1969-74; pres., chief exec. officer Adcom Assos., Inc., Phoenix, 1974—; dir. Nuestro Publs., Washington. Served with USAF, 1962-66. Mem. Am. Mgmt. Assn., Am. G.I. Forum of U.S., Southwestern Hist. Soc. Democrat. Roman Catholic. Author: A History of Mexican Americans in Texas, 1976; research on nat. mktg. potential of Spanish speaking population. Home: 1517 Montana Ave El Paso TX 79902 Office: Cuellar Advt 516 San Francisco El Paso TX 79901

CUENY, RICHARD THOMAS, food service company executive; b. Detroit, Aug. 26, 1944; s. Raymond John and Alice Joyce (Hasse) C.; m. Patricia Ann Lowhorn, Jan. 16, 1965; children—Kimberly Ann, Tamara Lynn. B.S.B.A., U. Phoenix, 1980, M.B.A. with distinction, 1982. With Greyhound Food Mgmt., Inc., Phoenix, 1968—, dir. corp. acctg., 1976-82, asst. controller, 1982, controller, 1983—; mem. evening faculty bus.-related courses U. Phoenix, Scottsdale Community Coll. Mem. Tax Execs. Inst., Internat. Assn. Assessing Officers, Mich. Assn. Assessing Officers, Tex. Assn. Assessing Officers. Republican. Home: 8019 Via Costa Scottsdale AZ 85258 Office: Greyhound Tower 3262 Phoenix AZ 85077

CUK, SLOBODAN, educator; b. Zagreb, Yugoslavia, July 16, 1947; came to U.S., 1972, naturalized, 1979; s. Milojko and Julijana (Aleksic) C.; B.S.E.E., Belgrade U. (Yugoslavia), 1970; M.S.E.E., U. Santa Clara, 1973; Ph.D., Calif. Inst. Tech., 1977; m. Nevenka Grubor, Dec. 17, 1972; children—Tanja, Vesna. Instr., Calif. Inst. Tech., Pasadena, 1977, research fellow, 1977, asst. prof. elec. engring., 1977—; chmn. bd., cons. TESLAco, Pasadena, 1979—. Recipient Yugoslav Math. Soc. award, IR 100 award for 1980. Mem. IEEE, Sigma Xi. Inventor in field. Home: 18902 Via Messina Irvine CA 92715 Office: 116-81 Calif Inst Tech Pasadena CA 91125

CULBERTSON, ROY CASS, JR., utilities exec.; b. Kansas City, Mo., July 6, 1926; s. Roy Cass and Evelyn (Spitzer) C.; cert. Dun & Bradstreet Corr. Course, 1971; m. Carol Marie Babros, Sept. 16, 1947; children—Cathlyne Marie Wheat, Lori Ann, Shari Lynn Silva. Acctg. analyst Pacific Gas & Electric Co., Emeryville, Calif., 1947, traveling auditor, San Francisco, 1953-60, internal auditor, 1962-70, sr. EDP auditor, 1970-73, supervising auditor, 1973—; internal auditor Pacific Gas Transmission Co., Spokane, Wash., 1960-62; tchr. EDP courses Am. Mgmt. Assn., Inst. Internal Auditors. Served with AUS, 1944-46. Decorated Meritorious Service award; recipient Thurston award for outstanding article Internal Auditor mag., 1977. Mem. Inst. Internal Auditors (chmn. info. systems tech. com. 1978-82, dir. 1980-81, 83-86), Pacific Coast Gas Assn., Pacific Coast Electric Assn. Democrat. Methodist. Home: 20111 W Ridge Ct #6 Castro Valley CA 94546 Office: 4 Embarcadero Ctr San Francisco CA 94106

CULBREATH, MYRNA LOU, author; b. Dodge City, Kans., June 1, 1938; d. Noel Galen and Anna Leota (Lickteig) C. B.A. cum laude, Colo. U., 1960, postgrad., 1961. Founder, mgr. Culbreath Schs., Colorado Springs, 1962, Los Angeles, 1980, chmn. bd., pres., 1983—; books include: Culbreath School Phonics 44 Games and Methods; (with Sondra Marshak) The Price of the Phoenix, 1977; The Fate of the Phoenix, 1979; The Prometheus Design, 1982; Triangle, 1983; (with S. Marshak and W. Shatner) Shatner: Where No Man ..., 1980; editor: The Fire Bringer, 1971-73; Star Trek, The New Voyages I, 1976, II, 1977. Founding mem., co-author 1st platform Libertarian party, 1972. Mem. Nat. Assn. Female Execs. Home: 1101 LaBoice Dr Glendale CA 91205 Office: 9060 Telstar El Monte CA 91731

CULLER, PAULETTE BARRETT, marketing executive, interior designer; b. Sydney, N.S., Can., Jan. 6, 1948; d. George Henry and Ruth Mildred (Steele) Barrett. B.S. magna cum laude, Woodbury U., Los Angeles, 1977. Design coordinator Mktg. Services, Lesny Devel. Co., Los Angeles, 1978-81; mktg. mgr. Valencia Corp., 1981-82; v.p. mktg. Allwest Devel., Pasadena, 1982—. Mem. Shakespeare League, Pasadena. Recipient Gold Nugget Merchandising award, 1981. Mem. Am. Soc. Interior Designers (bd. dirs. Pasadena chpt.), Sales and Mktg. Council. Episcopalian. Home: 3710 Ballina Canyon Rd Encino CA 91436 Office: Allwest Devel 285 N Hill 200 Pasadena CA 91106

CULLIGAN, PAUL THOMAS, oil industry cons.; b. Glendale, Calif., June 22, 1924; s. Michael Terrence and Selma (Martinson) C.; student Pasadena Jr. Coll., U. Louisville, 1944-46; m. Lorraine Eleanor Walker, Sept. 14, 1951; children—Erin, Mary, Michael, Patrick. Research technician Calif. Inst. Tech., 1949-51; research group leader Petroleum Engring. Assos., Pasadena, Calif., 1951-53; research dir. Oilwell Research, Long Beach, Calif., 1953-56; research dir. Pioneer Chem. Co., Hobbs, N.Mex., 1956-64; exec. v.p. Unichem Internat., Hobbs, 1964-82, also dir.; dir. Simon Oil Services UKK., TR Oil Services, TR Oil Services Arabia, Aguatreat S.A., Mexico, TR Oil services Mideast, Unichem Minerals Inc., Unichem Drilling Fluids, Inc. Served with U.S. Navy, 1943-46. Mem. Soc. Petroleum Engrs., Nat. Assn. Corrosion Engrs. Republican. Home and Office: 1105 Bishops Lodge Rd Santa Fe NM 87501

CULLIGAN, THOMAS JAY, pub. co. exec.; b. Ithaca, N.Y., Nov. 17, 1944; s. Donald J. and Jane E. (Kimple) C.; B.A. in History, Mich. State U., 1966, B.A. in Advt., 1967; m. Patricia Ann Wanek, Oct. 21, 1978. Advt. sales mgr. Chgo. Tribune, 1968-73, mktg. mgr., 1974-75; exec. v.p., gen. mgr. Daily News, subs. Tribune Co., Los Angeles, 1975—; dir. Mary Bartelme Homes, Chgo., 1974-75; dir. Escondido (Calif.) Times. Mem. Internat. Newspaper Advt. and Mktg. Execs. Assn. (bd. dirs.), Calif. Newspaper Pubs. Assn., Valley Indsl. and Commerce Assn. (v.p.), Phi Delta Theta. Club: Woodland Hills Country. Office: 14539 Sylvan St Van Nuys CA 91411

CULLINAN, VINCENT, lawyer; b. San Francisco, Jan. 22, 1911; s. Eustace and Katherine F. (Lawler) C.; m. Elizabeth Erlin, Oct. 16, 1937; children—Terrence, Kathleen Cullinan Merchant, Sheila Cullinan Wheeler. A.B. magna cum laude, U. Santa Clara, 1933; J.D., Stanford U., 1936. Bar: Calif. 1936. Ptnr. Cullinan and Lyons, and predecessors, San Francisco. Served to lt. comdr. USNR, 1941-46. Mem. Am. Law Inst., Am. Bar Endowment, ABA, State Bar Calif. (v.p. 1972), San Francisco Bar Assn. (pres. 1968). Republican. Roman Catholic. Club: Bohemian. Office: 100 Bush St San Francisco CA 94104

CULLISON, THOMAS PATTERSON, educational administrator, investment and marketing consultant; b. Buffalo, Oct. 16, 1941; s. Thomas Patterson, Sr. and Helen (Hannan) C.; m. Paula E. Giangreco, Oct. 7, 1967; children—Gregory, Pamela. B.S. in Mgmt., Fordham U., 1963; M.B.A. in Finance, CUNY, 1972; postgrad. Ariz. State U., 1981—. Fin. planner Thomson & McKinnon, N.Y.C., 1967-70; mut. funds sales mgr. White, Weld & Co., N.Y.C., 1970-72; v.p. Reynolds Securities, Inc., Phoenix, 1972-77; pres. Cullison Corp., Phoenix, 1977-81; chmn. dept. bus. Western Internat. U., Phoenix, 1981—; mktg. cons. Mem. Acad. Mgmt. Home: 13058 N Surrey Circle Phoenix AZ 85029 Office: Western International U 10202 N 19th Ave Phoenix AZ 85021

CULP, GORDON LOUIS, water treatment engineer; b. Topeka, Dec. 30, 1939; s. Russell Louis and Dorothy Marion (Wilson) C.; m. Bette Marlene Dewalt, June 6, 1962; m. 2d, Mary Kay Neering, Sept. 11, 1979; children—David, Steven, Ivan. B.S. in Civil Engring., U. Kans., 1961, M.S. in Environ. Health Engring., 1962. Lic. profl. engr. 20 states; diplomate Am. Acad. Environ. Engrs., 1977. With USPHS, Cin., 1962-64; research mgr. Neptune Microfloc, Corvallis, Oreg., 1964-68, Battelle NW, Richland, Wash., 1968-70; regional mgr. CH2M/Hill Engrs., Richland, 1970-73; pres. Culp, Wesner, Culp Cons. Engrs., Cameron Park, Calif., 1973—. Author 6 textbooks, over 50 tech. publs. in field; patentee in field. Mem. Am. Water Works Assn., ASCE, Water Pollution Control Fedn., Am. Acad. Environ. Engrs. Club: Rotary (pres.) (Cameron Park). Home: 2781 Stonecrest Court Placerville CA 95667 Office: 3461 Robin Ln Cameron Park CA 95682

CULP, MARILYN MARGARET WAGNER, sociologist; b. Milw., Jan. 1, 1945; d. Charles Gustave and Evelyn Eve Wagner; B.A. cum laude, Baldwin Wallace Coll., 1967; M.A. with honors, Bowling Green State U., 1969; m. Ronald Edward Culp, Aug. 9, 1969. Asst. prof. sociology Cuyahoga Community Coll., Parma, Ohio, 1969-75; pvt. practice marriage counseling, 1971—; dir. victims assistance programs Multnomah County Dist. Atty.'s Office, Portland, Oreg., 1975—; instr. Bur. Police Standards and Tng.; speaker in field. Mem. Task Force on Domestic Violence, Task Force on Victims; chairperson Tri County Community Council Safety Com.; bd. dirs. Camp Fire Girls. Named Outstanding Female Prof., Cuyahoga Community Coll., 1969-75. Mem. Am. Sociol. Assn., Am., Oreg. (dir.) assns. marriage and family therapists, Am. Assn. Marriage and Family Therapists. Club: Baldwin Wallace Women's. Home: 12245 NW Maple Hill Ln Portland OR 97229 Office: 1021 SW 4th St Portland OR 97204

CULP, MILDRED LOUISE, marketing executive; b. Ft. Monroe, Va., Jan. 13, 1949; d. William W. and Winifred (Stilwell) C. B.A. in English Lit., Knox Coll., 1971; A.M., U. Chgo., 1974, Ph.D. in Victorian Lit. and Culture, 1976. Coll. faculty mem. and adminstr. for 5 yrs.; dir. Exec. Resumes, Seattle, 1981—; bus. and fin. colunist Seattle Daily Jour. Commerce, Seattle Chinese Post; has appeared on TV and radio; frequent speaker profl. assns.; planning com. managerial series: 1982 Women and Bus. Conf. Admissions advisor U. Chgo., 1981—. Mem. Network Exec. Women (bd. dirs. 1981-82), Am. Soc. Personnel Adminstrn., Pacific N.W. Personnel Mgmt. Assn. Club: U. Chgo. Alumni (bd. dirs. 1982—). Contbr. articles and book revs. to profl. jours. Office: Seattle Tower Suite 505 Seattle WA 98101

CULP, ROBERT DUDLEY, aerospace engineering educator; b. McAlester, Okla., Feb. 28, 1938; s. Chesley Key and Irma Lucille (Combs) C.; m. Elizabeth L. Poor, Dec. 2, 1960; children—Robert Dielman, Thomas Dudley. B.S., U. Okla., 1960; M.S., U. Colo., 1963, Ph.D., 1966. Engr. Convair Co., Ft. Worth, 1959-59; research engr. Martin Denver Co., 1960-62; prof. aerospace engring U. Colo., Boulder, 1966—. Pres. Boulder Tennis Assn., 1972; scoutmaster Boy Scouts Am., 1980-83. Am. Astronautical Soc. fellow, 1981; recipient Leitseizer medal, 1960. Mem. AIAA (assoc. fellow), Am. Astronautical Assn., Am. Soc. Engring. Edn., Sigma Xi, Tau Beta Pi, Sigma Gamma Tau. Methodist. Club: Ranch Country (Denver). Author: Hypersonic and Planetary Entry Flight Mechanics, 1980; Guidance and Control, 1979, 82; contbr. articles to profl. jours. Home: 10536 Lipan Northglenn CO 80234 Office: U Colo Campus Box 429 Boulder CO 80309

CULPEPPER, ROBERT SAMMONS, ins. agy. exec.; b. Farmington, N.Mex., Aug. 23, 1927; s. Charles C. and Ethelywn (Hart) C.; m. Mary Eleanor Hancock, Nov. 15, 1953; children—Charles Chaisaignac II, Mary Eleanor Culpepper Carlsen, Robert Lee. B.S., N.Mex. State Co., 1951. Entomologist, Edmunds Chem. Co., Albuquerque, 1951-54; v.p. Farmington Investment Co. (N.Mex.), 1954-73; pres. Culpepper Ins. Agy., Inc., 1973—; dir. 1st Nat. Bank, Farmington. Mem. N.Mex. Arts Commn., 1971—, vice chmn., 1972-73, chmn., 1973-74. Mem. Farmington City Council, 1970-78, mayor pro tem, 1974-78, mayor, 1978-82; Democratic precinct chmn. 1968-72, mem. exec. council, 1968; chmn. San Juan Regional Com.; mem. Regional Planning Com.; pres. N.Mex. Mcpl. League, 1980-81; mem. N.W. Nat. Agts. Adv. Council; mem. Farmington Pub. Utility Commn. Served with USN, 1945-46. Mem. N.Mex. Assn. Ind. Ins. Agts. (dir. 1969-71, sec.-treas. 1972-73, v.p. 1973-74, pres. 1975-76, chmn. polit. action com.), Farmington Insurors (pres. 1960-61), Farmington C. of C. (dir. 1959-62, 82—, 2d v.p. 1983-84), Phi Kappa Tau. Episcopalian (vestryman 1970-73, 82—, sr. warden 1971-72, 83-84). Clubs: Lions (Farmington pres. 1963-64), Elks (exalted ruler 1966-67). Home: 5703 Woodland Ct Farmington NM 87401 Office: 106 W Main St Farmington NM 87401

CULVER, MARGARET HARRIET, nurse, health educator; b. Kingston on Thames, Surrey, Eng., Sept. 2, 1938; d. Herbert and Grace Ann (Lines) Parkin; m. Richard S. Culver, June 23, 1962; children—Joseph, Robert, Thomas, Lisa. R.S.C.N., Westminster Children's Hosp., London, Eng., 1960; S.R.N., Addenbrooke's Hosp., Cambridge, Eng., 1962; B.A. with distinction, Loretto Heights Coll., 1982. Staff nurse Westminster Children's Hosp., 1960; asst. nursing supr. Ahmadu Bello U., Nigeria, 1968-70; community devel. aide, Jefferson County Extension Service, Colo. State U., Golden, 1973-75, asst. agt., 1975-80, family living, youth agt., 1980—; cons. mental health centers; instr. health edn. classes. Bd. dirs. Jefferson County Mental Health Center, 1976-82, pres., 1978-80; pres. bd. dirs. Basic Mgmt. Systems, Inc., 1983—. Recipient Velsico Environ. Edn. award, 1982. Methodist. Author (with L. Rosenblum) The Selection and Hiring of an Executive Director of a Community Mental Health Center, 1978; Directing Stress: 4-H Leaders Guide, 1983. Office: Home Econs Colo State U 15200 W 6th Ave Golden CO 80401

CULVER, PAUL DODD, marketing cons.; b. Princeton, N.J., JUne 28, 1917; s. H. Paul and Edith Dodd C.; Mech. Engr., Mich. State U., 1940; m. Eleonora Marie van Ingen, Dec. 20, 1944. Commd. aviation cadet USN, 1941, advanced through grades to comdr.; comdr. officer Utility Squadron Three, Pacific Fleet, 1946-47; ops. officer Carrier Group 17, aircraft carrier ops. in Mediterranean, 1950-52; air ops. officer Pacific ops. USS Oriskany, 1955-56; ops. officer missile test ops. USS Norton Sound, 1956-58; head air launched missile sect. Office of Asst. Chief of Naval Ops. for Research and Devel., 1958-61; ret., 1961; various staff positions advanced planning and marketing Northrop Ventura, Newbury Park, Calif., 1961-70; mfrs. rep., Thousand Oaks, Calif., 1970-72; asst. to v.p. aerospace systems advanced planning and new product devel. Teledyne Ryan Aero., San Diego, 1972-78; mktg. cons. and mfrs. rep., Thousand Oaks, Calif., 1978—. Bd. dirs. Lake Sherwood Community Assn. Mem. Ret. Officers Assn., Am. Security Council, Am. Def. Preparedness Assn., U.S. Naval Inst., Assn. Unmanned Vehicle Systems, Assn. Naval Aviation, Tailhook Assn., Air Force Assn., Sierra Club, Audubon Soc. Republican. Club: Masons. Home and Office: 314 Upper Lake Rd Thousand Oaks CA 91360

CULVER, WARREN WATSON, marketing executive; b. Salt Lake City, Jan. 31, 1923; s. Warren Williams and Reva Merideth (Silver) C.; cert. aeros. tech. Sacramento Jr. Coll., 1943; m. Dora Mae Beeman, June 24, 1945; children—David W., Christine M., Lynda S. With Chanslor & Lyon Co., Los Angeles, 1946-53; with Dupont Co., 1953-54; with Culver & McNeill, Inc., Oakland, Calif., 1954-81, ptnr., 1957-81; pres. Western Pacific Mktg., Inc., Oakland, 1981—. Pres., Little League, 1957-58; sec. Babe Ruth League, 1961-63. Served with USN, 1943-46. Mem. Auto Boosters Club, Auto Affiliated Reps. Clubs: Masons, Shriners. Home: 1184 Huron Ln Hayward CA 94545 Office: 300 Market St Oakland CA 94607

CULVERWELL, HOWARD GLENDON, rancher; b. Concordia, Kans., May 18, 1911; s. Albert Sutcliff and Mabel Amelia (Middaugh) C.; student public schs.; m. Erma Frances Martin, Dec. 31, 1939; children—Gerald, Norman, Jon, Carolyn, Melvin, Melodie. Engaged in sheep, cattle, wheat and hay ranching, Craig, Colo., 1946—; past pres. Moffat County Farm Bur. Mem. Dist. 13 Sch. bd., also pres., 9 yrs., then mem. County Wide Bd., 16 yrs. also pres., 9 yrs., then mem. County Wide Bd., 16 yrs. bd. dirs. Colo. Assn. Sch. Bds., 1965-71. Mem. Profl. Farmers Am., Farmers Union, Nat. Farmers Orgn. Republican.

CULWELL, CHARLES LOUIS, manufacturing and marketing corporation executive; b. Putman, Tex., Apr. 26, 1927; s. Willie and Ila Alberta (Crosby) C.; m. Virginia Green, June 10, 1949; children—Andrew Scott, Perry Neal, Curtis Austin, Travis Lee. Student U. Tex., 1944-45; B.S. in Elec. Engring, U.S. Naval Acad., 1949, M.S. in Mgmt., 1969. Enlisted as Midshipman USN, 1945, advanced through ranks to capt., 1969; comdg. officer, Naval Supply Center, Oakland, Calif., 1975-76; asst. to pres. Purex Corp., Lakewood, Calif., 1976-77, v.p., 1977-79, group v.p. and gen. mgr. indsl., instl. and comml. products, 1979—. Active United for Calif. Decorated Legion of Merit, Bronze Star with Combat V, Presl. Unit citation; Korean Presl. Unit citation; Vietnamese Navy disting. service medal. Mem. U.S. Naval Acad. Alumni Assn. Republican. Pesbyterian. Office: 5101 Clark Ave Lakewood CA 90712

CUMBERLAND, WILLIAM GLEN, biostatistics educator; b. Lloydminster, Sask., Can., Feb. 7, 1948; s. Donald John and Ruth Elnora (Johnson) C.; m. Holly Eugenia Smith, Mar. 2, 1974; children—Todd, Robert, James. B.Sc. in Math., McGill U., 1968; M.A. in Stats., Johns Hopkins U., 1972, Ph.D., 1975. Lectr. math. Simon Fraser U., Vancouver, B.C., Can., 1973; asst. prof. biostats. UCLA, 1976-82, assoc. prof., 1982—. Mem. AAAS, Am. Stats. Assn., Inst. Math. Stats., Biometric Soc. Contbr. articles to profl. jours. Office: Dept Pub Health UCLA Los Angeles CA 90024

CUMMINGS, ALBERT ALEX, real estate exec.; b. Mesa, Ariz., June 21, 1927; s. Alexander John and Sophia (Carrillo) C.; student U. Ariz., 1952-53, 58-59, 75-76; m. Carroll Cutter, June 10, 1970; children—Jennifer, Alan, David, Laurel. Organizer, Cummings Realty & Trust Co. (name changed to Cummings Realty & Trust Co., Inc. 1970), Tucson, 1960, pres., 1971—; pres. Exchange-a-Home, Inc., 1970—; dir. Multiple Listing Service Tucson, Inc., 1966-72, sec., 1967, treas., 1970, v.p., 1971-72; instr. edn. course com. Tucson Bd. Realtors, 1969-74, bd. dirs., 1969-74, v.p., 1971, pres., 1972; instr. Realtors Inst., U. Ariz., Tucson, 1970-72, Realtors Inst., Cochise Jr. Coll., Douglas, Ariz., 1972, Realtors Inst., Ariz. Assn. Realtors, 1970—, Inst. Real Estate, 1973-82; mem. curriculum adv. com. Pima Coll., Tucson, 1972-75, instr., 1973. Pres., John B. Wright PTA, Tucson, 1969-70. Served with Signal Corps, AUS, 1950-51. Named Realtor of Year, Tucson Bd. Realtors, 1973; recipient Omega Tau Rho award, 1979. Mem. Nat. Assn. Realtors (dir. 1981-83), Ariz. Assn. Realtors (chmn. license law com. 1971-72, edn. com. 1974, chmn. bd. govs. Realtors Inst. 1975-79, dir. 1971-74, 77-83, 1st v.p. 1982, pres. 1983), Ariz. Assn. Real Estate Exchangors (dir. 1966-67), Am. Arbitration Assn. (mem. comml. panel 1973-83), Realtors Nat. Mktg. Inst. (cert. real estate brokerage mgr. and cert. comml. investment mem.), Farm and Land Inst. (pres. Ariz. chpt. 1977, regional v.p. 1979, chmn. urban land com. 1980, named Farm and Land Broker of Yr. 1978, accredited farm and land mem.), Real Estate Securities and Syndication Inst. (pres. Ariz. chpt. 1982-83, specialist in real estate securities Tucson Bd. Realtors (pres. 1972, pres. Tucson Real Estate Exchange Club 1967). Clubs: Sertoma-Internat. (life mem., gov. Ariz. dist. 1968-69, Disting. Gov.'s award) (Ariz.); Midtown Sertoma (chmn. bd. 1969-70), Desert Sertoma (pres. 1961-62, chmn. bd. 1962-63, dir. 1963-66) (Tucson). Home: 2324 N Madelyn Circle Tucson AZ 85712 Office: 1725 N Swan Rd Tucson AZ 85712

CUMMINGS, ERNEST EARL, educator; b. Portland, Oreg., Apr. 8, 1937; s. Earl Hanson and Grace Marie (Stone) C.; m. Velma Mae Burrows, Oct. 3, 1940; children—Jonni Dee Cummings Belden, Bradley, Robert, Ernest Mason. B.S. in Vocat. Edn., Agr. and Biology, U. Wyo., 1978. Cert. Wyo. State Dept. Edn. Technician Cowan Radio, Basin, Wyo., 1963-65; driver LL Smith Trucking, Riverton, Wyo., 1966-69; miner Fed. Am. Ptnrs., Gas Hills, Wyo., 1970-71; driver Osborn Trucking, Riverton, 1972-74; vocat. agr. instr. Arapahoe Sch. (Wyo.), 1978-83, vacat. dir., 1983—. Mem. Polit. Action Com. on Edn. Served with U.S. Army, 1960. Mem. Nat. Vocat. Agr. Tchrs. Assn., Wyo. Vocat. Tchrs. Assn., Wyo. Edn. Assn. Republican. Baptist. Club: East End Rural Wrestling. Author vocat. agr. instrn. curriculum for 7th, 8th grades.

CUMMINGS, FAY THOMAS, tax practitioner, enrolled agent b. Midland, Tex., Apr. 3, 1929; d. William Emmett and Vernon M. (Lee) Thomas; ed. U. Ark., 1945-46, U. Ga., 1951; B.A. in Acctg., U. Okla., 1954; m. Neale Stinner (dec. 1951); children—Jerry Neale, Fay Marie, Charley Ray, Teryl Lee. Controller, Garrett Corp., Oklahoma City, 1952-63, Condor Pacific, Canoga Park, Calif., 1963-69; individual practice acctg. and tax service, Redondo Beach, Calif., 1974—; lectr. Columbus Sch. Bus. Mem. Assn. Bus. and Tax Cons.'s (pres. 1977-79).

CUMMINGS, JOHN ERNEST, research co. exec.; b. Westerly, R.I., Aug. 1, 1937; s. John James and Catherine Elizabeth (Rossie) C.; B.S., U.S. Coast Guard Acad., 1959; M.S., U. Ariz., 1969, Ph.D., 1970, M.B.A., 1971; m. Pauline L. Devuyst, Sept. 24, 1960; children—Elaine, Christopher. Instr. dept. mgmt. U. Ariz., Tucson, 1970-71; tech. analyst U.S. AEC, Washington, 1971-72; dir. energy programs, optical systems div., asst. to sr. corp. v.p. Itek Corp., Lexington, Mass., 1972-75; program mgr. solar energy Electric Power Research Inst., Palo Alto, Calif., 1975-79, dept. dir. renewable resource systems, 1979—. Served to lt. (j.g.) USCG, 1959-63. Mem. Am. Phys. Soc., ASHRAE, Internat. Solar Energy Soc., AAAS, Sigma Pi Sigma. Republican. Roman Catholic. Contbr. articles to profl. jours. Office: ELectric Power Research Inst PO Box 10412 Palo Alto CA 94303

CUMMINGS, JOHN PATRICK, optometrist; b. Sheridan, Wyo., Dec. 17, 1952; s. John Francis and Ivy Lee (Borksdale) C.; m. Pamela Gwen Miller, Aug. 30, 1981. A.S., Sheridan Coll., 1973; B.S., Pacific U., 1975, O.D., 1977. Gen. practice optometry, Sheridan, Wyo., 1977—; cons. optometrist Sheridan VA Med. Ctr. Mem. Nat. Ski Patrol, asst. patrol leader, 1980, jr. adv., 1980-83, regional first aid adv., 1982-83; mem. Story-Banner Vol. Emergency Service. Recipient Sheridan Community Disting. Service award, 1982; Jaycee of Year award, 1979-80. Mem. Assn. VA Optometrists, Am. Optometric Assn. (charter mem. contact lens sect.) Clubs: Sheridan Jaycees, Transpo-Expo Club-Fly-In (chmn.). Contbr. articles to profl. jours. Office: 116 S Main St Sheridan WY 82801

CUMMINGS, JOSEPH DEVALSON, psychologist; b. Mossoula, Mont., Aug. 25, 1932; s. Joseph Devalson and Alice (Bahen) C.; m. Lora Earnest, 1982; 1 son by previous marriage, Joseph Devalson. B.S., U.S. Naval Acad., 1954; M.A., U.S. Internat. U., 1972, Ph.D., 1974. Ensign, U.S. Navy, 1954, advanced through grades to lt. comdr., 1964, ret., 1974; clin. psychologist in pvt. practice, Chula Vista, Calif., 1974-76; dir. E.C.I. div. R. D. Gen. Corp., La Jolla, Calif., 1974-76; pres. R.D. Gen. Corp., La Jolla, 1976-78, Applied Personal Dynamics, San Diego, 1978—; adj. prof. San Diego State U., 1974-75; prof. Southwestern Coll., 1975—. Pres. Chula Vista Sch. Bd., 1976—. Decorated Meritorious Service medal, Vietnamese Gallantry Cross. Mem. Am., Western, Calif., San Diego psychol. assns., Am., So. Calif. assns. marriage and family therapists, Naval Inst. Home: Box 459 Bonita CA 92002

CUMMINGS, MARY THERESA, museum director, art historian; b. Mpls., May 22, 1951. B.A., U. Minn., 1973, M.A. in Asian Art History, 1976; M.A. in Arts Adminstrn. (fellow), Ind. U., 1981. Curatorial asst. Holburne Mus., Bath, Eng., 1970; asst. dir. Tweed Mus., Duluth, Minn., 1978; instr. Asian art history Mpls. Inst. Arts, 1977-78; instr. art history Macalester Coll., St. Paul, 1977-78; dir. Missoula Mus. Arts (Mont.), 1981—. Co-chmn. Missoula Centennial Com., 1982-83. Mem. Am. Assn. Mus., Am. Assn. State and Local History, Asia Soc., Assn. Asian Studies, Asian Folklore Soc., Mont. Art Gallery Dirs. Assn. (pres. 1982—). Author: The Lives of the Buddha in the Literature and Art of Asia, 1982; M.A.G.D.A. (Mont. Art Gallery Dirs. Assn.) Handbook, 1982. Office: 335 N Pattee St Missoula MT 59802

CUMMINGS, NICHOLAS ANDREW, psychologist; b. Salinas, Calif., July 25, 1924; s. Andrew and Urania (Sims) C.; A.B., U. Calif., Berkeley, 1948; M.A., Claremont Grad. Sch., 1954; Ph.D., Adelphi U., 1958; m. Dorothy Mills, Feb. 5, 1948; children—Janet Lynn, Andrew Mark. Chief psychologist Kaiser Permanente No. Calif., San Francisco, 1959-79, sr. psychologist, 1979—; pres. Inst. for Psychosocial Interaction, Palo Alto, 1980—; co-dir. Golden Gate Mental Health Center, San Francisco, 1959-75; pres. Calif. Sch. Profl. Psychology, Los Angeles, San Francisco, San Diego, Fresno campuses, 1969-76; pres. Blue Psi Inc., San Francisco, 1972-80; pres., chmn. bd. Calif. Community Mental Health Centers Inc., Los Angeles, San Diego, San Francisco, 1975-76; clin. dir. Brodyne Inst., San Francisco and Honolulu, 1976—; dir. Mental Research Inst., Palo Alto, Calif., 1979-80; Mental health adv. bd. City and County San Francisco, 1968-77; bd. dirs. San Francisco Assn. Mental Health, 1965-75. Pres., chmn. bd. Psycho-Social Inst., 1972-80. Served with AUS, 1944-46. Fellow Am. Psychol. Assn. (dir. 1975-81, pres. 1979); mem. Calif. Psychol. Assn. (pres. 1968), Nat. Acads. Practice (named Disting. Practitioner; pres. 1981—), Pioneer prepaid mental health plans, profl. schs. psychology. Office: 2150 Judah St San Francisco CA 94122

CUMMINGS, RICHARD LEE, employee benefit plans cons.; b. Ft. Morgan, Colo., Sept. 3, 1929; s. George F. and Helen L. (Wentz) C.; B.S., Coll. of Pacific, 1956; M.Fgn. Trade Am. Grad. Sch. Internat. Mgmt., 1957; m. Dorothy Govednik, Oct. 24, 1958; children—Gary, Brian, Kevin. Dist. sales rep. Ashland Oil & Refinery, San Francisco, 1958-59; dist. group mgr. N.Y. Life Ins. Co., Mont., 1958-60; regional group pension mgr. Pacific Mut. Ins. Co., San Francisco, 1960-65, Prudential Ins. Co., San Francisco, 1965-78; chmn., chief exec. officer Burr-Cummings & Assos., Inc., Walnut Creek, Calif., 1978—; pres. BCA Adminstrs., Inc., Walnut Creek, 1978—, Burwin, Inc., San Francisco, 1979—. Pres., Altaorinda Homeowners Assn., 1970-73; mem. planning com. Orinda Homeowners Assn., 1973-74; mem. liaison com. Contra Costa/Orinda, 1970-76; active Boy Scouts Am., 1968-72. Served with Signal Corps, U.S. Army, 1948-52. Decorated Purple Heart. Mem. Internat. Found. Employee Benefits, Western Pension Conf., Soc. Profl. Adminstrs., Am. Soc. Practicing Actuaries, Calif. Metal Trades Assn., Orinda Assn., No. Calif. Employee Benefits Council, Internat. Maserati Owners Club, Maserati Club Am., Ferrari Club Am. Republican. Methodist. Clubs: Olympic, Internat. Exchange. Home: 57 Via Floreado Orinda CA 94563 Office: 1700 N Broadway Suite 309 Walnut Creek CA 94596

CUMMINGS, ROBERT MICHAEL, photographic products company official; b. Boston, Jan. 6, 1954; s. James Richard and Nora Agnes (Greene) C. B.A., Boston Coll., 1979; postgrad. Babson Coll., 1979-80, Pepperdine U., 1983—. With Polaroid Corp., 1972—, supr. central distbn., 1979-81, western regional ops. mgr., Santa Ana, Calif., 1981—; cons. Active charities and ednl. insts. in Orange County and Los Angeles areas. Recipient numerous letters of commendation and certs. Club: KC. Office: Polaroid Corp 3232 W MacArthur Blvd Santa Ana CA 92704

CUMMINGS, RULON CAINE, safety engineer; b. Salt Lake City, Nov. 4, 1925; s. James R. and Gwendelyn M. (Caine) C.; B.S., Northwestern Coll. Allied Sci., 1980; Assoc. in Bus., LaSalle Extension U., 1960; m. Jeannine Mae Astler, Aug. 14, 1947; children—Craig S., Rulon K., Douglas W., Celia M., Cynthia L., Anna Lisa. Chief adminstrn. sect. Utah Army Depot, Ogden, 1950-53, adminstrv. asst. engr. supply sect., 1953-59; mgmt, analyst Def. Depot Ogden, 1959-66, asst. chief methods and standards br., 1966-70, safety and health dir., 1970-82, dir. installation services, 1982—; instr. Nat. Safety Council, 1970—; safety and health cons., 1970—; chmn. exec. com. Fed. Safety Council, 1979-80; mem. Clearfield City Council, 1982—. Pres., Wasatch Little League Football, 1959-60; coach Little League Football, 1958-62; coach community softball, volleyball and basketball teams, Clearfield, Utah, 1964—. Served with U.S. Army, 1944-46. Recipient Supply Agy. Meritorious Civilian Service award, 1973, Superior Performance award Defense Depot, 1968-80, Cert. Appreciation, Asst. Sec. Labor, 1980. Mem. Am. Soc. Safety Engrs., Armed Forces Mgmt. Assn., Quartermaster Assn., Soc. Am. Mil. Engrs., Methods Time Measurement Assn. for Standards and Research. Republican. Mem. Ch. Jesus Christ of Latter-day Saints (counselor in stake presidency, high councilor, bishop, clk.). Club: Kiwanis. Home: 749 E 300 South Clearfield UT 84015 Office: 500 W 12th St Ogden UT 84407

CUMMINGS, SUSAN N., educator, cons.; b. Oak Park, Ill., Sept. 6, 1920; d. Howard Ellsworth and Marie Katherina (Kapps) Null; A.A., U. Chgo., B.S., 1944; M.A., Ariz. State U., Ph.D., 1967; m. Edward Albert Cummings, Oct. 4, 1947; 1 stepson, John Bruce. Instr. psychology Phoenix Coll., 1963-70; instr. ednl. founds. Ariz. State U., Tempe, 1964-68, assoc. prof. secondary edn., 1969—, dir. Title XI Project for Teaching of Disadvantaged, 1968-69; cons. human resources Pub. Schs., Assn. Critical Care Nurses, Assn. Supervision and Curriculum Devel., Profl. Trainers Inst. Named Tchr. of Year, Ariz. Edn. Assn., 1970. Mem. Am. Psychol. Assn., World Futurists, Assn. Humanistic Psychology, World Council Curriculum and Instrn. (editor, dir.), Assn. Supervision and Curriculum Devel. Democrat. Author: Handbook for Teachers of Disadvantaged Youth, 1968; Communication for Education, 1970. Home: 1743 E Beth Dr Phoenix AZ 85040 Office: Ariz State U Tempe AZ 85287

CUMMINGS, WALTER JOSEPH, III, financial services company executive; b. Chgo., Apr. 3, 1947; s. Walter Joseph and Therese Farrell (Murray) C.; m. Pauline Field, Sept. 13, 1975; 1 dau., Julie Pierce. B.A., Yale U., 1969; postgrad. Stanford U. Grad. Sch. Bus., 1974, Stanford Law Sch., 1974. Bar: Calif. Law clk. U.S. Dist. Ct. for So. Dist. Calif., San Diego, 1974-75; assoc. Luce, Forward, Hamilton & Scripps, San Diego, 1975-78; counsel Itel Corp., San Francisco, 1978-79; founder, v.p., gen. counsel Savance Corp., San Francisco, 1979—. Served with AUS, 1969-75. Decorated Army Commendation medal. Mem. ABA, Calif. State Bar Assn., Am. Assn. Equipment Lessors. Club: Burlingame Country (Hillsborough, Calif.). Office: Savance Corporation 45 Belden St San Francisco CA 94104

CUMMINGS, WILLIAM BARTON, educational administrator; b. Richmond, Va., Apr. 26, 1929; s. Frank Letelle and Dallas (Burrows) C.; m. Beatrice Martin, Feb. 18, 1950 (div. Jan. 1971); children—William Barton, Thomas, Judith, Scott; m. Lois Anderson, Jan. 7, 1972. B.A., Moravian Coll., 1953; M.A., Temple U., 1968; Ed.D., U. San Francisco, 1979. Cert. tchr., adminstr., Calif. Tchr., adminstr. Centennial Joint Schs., Warminster, Pa., 1954-67; supr. gifted program Pa. Dept. Edn., 1967-68, San Francisco Unified Sch. Dist., 1968-77; dir. curriculum, area supr. Fall River Joint Unified Sch. Dist., Cassel, Calif., 1981—; cons. gifted child edn.; instr. U. Ill., U. San Francisco, San Francisco State U., Dominican Coll. Served with USN, 1946-48. Mem. Assn. for Gifted, Calif. Assn. Gifted (past pres.), Council Exceptional Children, Assn. Calif. Sch. Adminstrs., Assn. Supervision and Curriculum Devel. Home: PO Box 66 Cassel CA 96016 Office: PO Box 89 Cassel CA 96016

CUMMINS, CHARLES CAVETT, JR., state official; b. Jackson, Wyo., June 19, 1939; s. Charles Cavett and Thelma Fife (Dixon) C.; B.S., Brigham Young U., Provo, Utah, 1963, M.Ed., 1966, Ph.D., 1977; m. Elaine Lucas, Aug. 12, 1966; children—Holly, Wylin, Charmay, Richard. Instr., Los Angeles public schs., 1962-63; instr., then prin. Nebo (Utah) Sch. Dist., 1963-68; mem. faculty Stevens-Henegers Coll., Salt Lake City, 1969-72, Utah Tech. Coll., Salt Lake City, 1973-83; adj. prof. Brigham Young U., 1979-83; data processing mgr. ednl. support services Utah Office Edn., 1968—; cons. Sage Inst. Republican precinct chmn., 1978. Served with U.S. Army, 1958-59. NSF grantee, 1964. Mem. Nat. Assn. Secondary Sch. Prins., Utah Assn. Sch. Bus. Ofcls., Phi Eta Sigma, Phi Kappa Phi, Phi Delta Kappa. Mormon. Home: 885 North 200 East Spanish Fork UT 84660 Office: 250 East 500 South Salt Lake City UT 84111

CUMMINS, EMERY JOHN, psychologist, educator; b. Detroit, Mar. 8, 1937; s. Emery John and Georgina (Forrest) C.; m. Patti Carolyn Blakslee, Apr. 9, 1960; children—Chad Parker, Brendan Forrest. B.A., Wheaton Coll., 1958; M.S., U. So. Calif., 1960; Ph.D., Mich. State U., 1964. Lic. psychologist, marriage and family counselor, Calif. High sch. English tchr., La Puente, Calif., 1959-61; residence hall adminstr. Mich. State U., East Lansing, 1961-64; assoc. dean students Wheaton (Ill.) Coll., 1964-66; prof. counselor edn. San Diego State U., 1966—, chmn. dept. counselor edn., 1980—. Elder United Presbyn. Ch. Mem. Am. Psychol. Assn., Am. Personnel Guidance Assn., Assn. Counselor Edn. and Supervision, San Diego Soc. Sex Therapy and Edn., Phi Delta Kappa. Contbr. numerous articles to profl. jours. Office: Counselor Education San Diego State U San Diego CA 92182

CUMMINS, JOHN STEPHEN, bishop; b. Oakland, Calif., Mar. 3, 1928; s. Michael and Mary (Connolly) C.; A.B., St. Patrick's Coll., 1949; M.Div., St. Patrick's Sem., 1973. Ordained priest, Roman Catholic Ch., 1953; asst. pastor Mission Dolores Ch., San Francisco, 1953-57; mem. faculty Bishop O'Dowd High Sch., Oakland, 1957-62; chancellor Diocese of Oakland, 1962-71; exec. dir. Calif. Cath. Conf., Sacramento, 1971—; consecrated bishop, 1974; aux. bishop of Sacramento, 1974-77, bishop of Oakland, 1977—; campus minister San Francisco State Coll., 1953-57, Mills Coll., Oakland, Calif., 1957-71. Trustee St. Mary's Coll., 1968—. Named Domestic Prelate, 1967. Office: 2900 Lakeshore Ave Oakland CA 94610*

CUMMINS, MICHAEL J(OSEPH), accountant, educator; b. St. Louis, May 3, 1948; s. Robert L. and Clara T. (Trousdale) C.; m. Georgett Esque, Jan. 24, 1970; children—Michael A., Christopher R. B.S. in Fin., San Jose State U., 1970, B.S. in Acctg., 1978. C.P.A., Calif. Stockbroker Merrill Lynch, San Jose, Calif., 1971-76; owner, operator Maccar Industries, pub., San Jose, 1976-78; mem. staff Petrinovich, Pugh and Jones, San Jose, 1978-82, ptnr., 1982—; instr. in acctg. U. Santa Clara Bus. Sch. Treas. bd. dirs. Campfire, Inc., Santa Clara County (Calif.), 1979-83. Served with U.S. Army, 1970-71. Mem. Am. Inst. C.P.A.s, Calif. Soc. C.P.A.s (research and devel. conf. planning com.). Columnist Fin. Planning, Ind. Adv. Jour., 1982—; guest writer Santa Clara County Bus. Mag., 1982-83. Office: 100 Park Center Plaza Suite 450 San Jose CA 95113

CUMMINS, NEIL JOSEPH, JR., land surveyor; b. Oxnard, Calif., Sept. 14, 1945; s. Neil Joseph and Helen Louise (Porter) C.; student Claremont Men's Coll., 1962-64, Calif. State Poly. Coll., 1965-67; J.D., Mid Valley Coll. Law, 1978; m. Lynn D. Mealer, Sept. 16, 1967. Designer, Ludwig Engring., San Bernardino, Calif., 1967-69; field supr. Sikand Engring., Van Nuys, Calif., 1969-77; land surveyor, Reseda, Calif., 1977—; lectr. civil engring. Calif. Poly. Coll., Pomona, 1979-80; admitted to Calif. bar, 1978. Registered profl. engr., Ariz., Calif., Nev.; registered land surveyor, Calif., Nev. Mem. ASCE, Am. Congress Surveying and Mapping, Am. Water Works Assn., ABA, Los Angeles County Bar Assn., Calif. Land Surveyors Assn. Office: 18700 Sherman Way Suite 208 Reseda CA 91335

CUNDALL, DONALD ROGER, rancher; b. Glendo, Wyo., May 30, 1925; s. Edwin Paul and Ruth Frances (Troupe) C.; m. Doris Beatrice Moran, May 18, 1946; children—Jerry, Ronald, Tyler, Mike. Ed. St. Mary's U., 19- Mont. Sch. Mines. Mem. Wyo. Senate, 1973-83 majority floor leader, 1980, pres., 1981-82; gen. ptnr., chmn. Cundall Herefords, Guernsey, Wyo. Served with AC, USN, 1943-46. Republican.

CUNDITH, THOMAS JOHN, sporting goods company executive; b. Escondido, Calif., July 21, 1943; s. Thomas Edwin and Betty Jane (Whittenberger) C.; m. Jo De Busk, Jan. 30, 1965; children—Jeff, Julie, Jaime. B.A. in Econs. with honors, U. Calif.-Santa Barbara, 1965; M.B.A., Stanford U., 1967. Sales trainee Procter & Gamble Co., San Mateo, Calif., 1966; corp. trainee, sales mgr., gen. mgr. Jewel Cos., Chgo., 1967-69; mktg./advt. mgr. Boye Needlw Co., Chgo., 1970; founder, pres., chmn., dir. Sunset Designs, Inc., San Ramon, Calif., 1971-81; founder, pres., dir. Tovan Mfg., Inc., Benecia, Calif., 1974—; founder, chief exec. officer, chmn., dir. Westar Sporting Goods, Inc., Pleasant Hills, Calif. Active Boy Scouts Am., 1979-81. Mem. Young Pres. Orgn. Republican. Club: Quail Ct. Athletic (Walnut Creek, Calif.). Home: 1400 Reliez Valley Rd Lafayette CA 94549 Office: Westar Sporting Goods Inc 3496 Buskirk Ave Suite 102 Pleasant Hill CA 94523

CUNNEEN, WALLACE VINCENT, JR., mktg. cons.; b. York, Pa., Sept. 18, 1922; s. Wallace Vincent and Gertrude (Wood) C.; ed. U.S. Naval Acad., 1941-44, U. Pa., 1946-47; m. Joan Eleanor Frederick, Jan. 8, 1955; children—Wallace, Mary, James. Sales rep. Diebold, Inc., Canton, Ohio, 1947-49; v.p. The Cunneen Co., Phila., 1949-57, Welton Becket & Asso., Los Angeles, 1957-64, v.p., dir. John Carl Warnecke Asso., San Francisco, 1964-69; v.p. programs devel. Daniel, Mann, Johnson & Mendenhall, Los Angeles, 1969-71; programs devel. Hoover Assos., Palo Alto. 1972-74; owner mktg.-cons. practice, Los Altos, 1974—; mem. adv. com. AIA Research Corp. Chmn. Santa Clara County, United Fund Los Altos, 1958-62; exec. bd. Stanford Area council Boy Scouts Am., 1977-78; pres. Los Altos PTA, 1961. Served with USN, 1940-47. Mem. Navy League U.S. (pres. Santa Clara Valley council 1979-80, nat. dir., exec. com. 1980-81). Republican. Roman Catholic. Clubs: Fremont Hills (Los Altos Hills); Commonwealth (San Francisco); St. Claire (San Jose, Calif.). Home: 26666 Laurel Ln Los Altos Hills CA 94022 Office: 342 State St Los Altos CA 94022

CUNNINGHAM, DENNIS, elec. engr.; b. N.Y.C., Sept. 24, 1929; s. Joseph Patrick and Alice Rose C.; A.A., Harbor Coll., 1957; B.S.E.E., Calif. State U., Long Beach, 1970; m. Dorothy Jane Laughton, Dec. 7, 1963; 1 son, Kevin Laughton. Field engr. TRW Inc., Redondo Beach, Calif., 1957-62, sr. system engr., 1962-70; mem. tech. staff Hughes Aircraft Co., El Segundo, Calif., 1971, sect. head, 1971; staff engr. ESL Inc., Sunnyvale, Calif., 1971-79; research specialist Lockheed Missiles and Space Co., Sunnyvale, Calif., 1979—. Served with USN, 1948-54. Mem. IEEE, Tau Beta Pi, Eta Kappa Nu. Home: 20269 Northwest Square Cupertino CA 95014 Office: 1111 Lockheed Way Sunnyvale CA 94086

CUNNINGHAM, GARY WATSON, publishing executive; b. Denver, Jan. 15, 1943; s. Benjamin W. and Virginia M. (Lewark) C.; m. Behnaz Ghorbani-Nik, Aug. 26, 1980; children—Erin, Cameron, Kelan. B.A., U. Pacific, 1965; M.S., Eastern Wash. U., 1971. Cert. speech pathologist. Peace Corps cons. for Ministry of Ednl. TV., Medellin, Colombia, 1966-68; cons. to Ministry Spl. Edn., San Jose, Costa Rica, 1973; speech pathologist North Clakamas Sch. Dist., Milwaukie, Oreg., 1973-76; pres. C.C. Pubs., Inc., Tualatin, Ore., 1976—; cons. in field. Recipient cert. of appreciation Lyndon B. Johnson, 1968; Ednl. grantee Eastern Mont. U., 1961, Eastern Wash. U., 1969, 70, 71. Mem. Am. Speech and Hearing Assn., Oreg. Speech and Hearing Assn. Republican. Episcopalian. Club: Partners of Ams. Contbr. articles to profl. jours. Home: 2 Cellini Ct Lake Oswego OR 97034 Office: 19576 SW 90th Ct Tualatin OR 97062

CUNNINGHAM, JAMES ROLLA, university administrator; b. Seaside, Oreg., Feb. 7, 1925; s. James Anthony and Margaret Ingrid (Halberg) C.; m. Norma Jean Olsen, Sept. 1, 1948 (div.); children—Laura Jean, James Randall, Cynthia Ann, Bridget Eilene, Claire Denise. B.S., U. Wash., 1951; Ph.D., U. Oreg., 1968. Lic. psychologist, Calif. Test officer Humboldt State Coll., Arcata, Calif., 1958-76, dir. instnl. research, 1976—. Served with USCG, 1942-46, to lt. USN, 1951-56; Korea. Mem. Am. Psychol. Assn., Assn. Instl. Research. Contbr. articles to various jours. Home: 2170 Grace Ave McKinleyville CA 95521 Office: Nelson Hall W Room 237 Humboldt State University Arcata CA 95521

CUNNINGHAM, JEFFREY BREWSTER, electronics executive; b. Poughkeepsie, N.Y., Nov. 30, 1946; s. Frederick Reed and Emily Beatrice (Flanagan) C.; B.A., Stanford U., 1968, M.B.A., 1973; m. Yvonne Lindquist, Dec. 31, 1977; 1 dau., Kari. With loan office United Bank Calif., San Francisco, 1973-74; corp. fin. analyst Hewlett Packard, Inc., Palo Alto, Calif., 1975; asst. to pres. Argo Systems, Inc., Sunnyvale, Calif., 1975-78; v.p. fin., sec., treas. Chromatix, Inc., Sunnyvale, 1978-81; pres., chief exec. officer Chat Communications Inc., Mountain View, Calif., 1981-83; v.p. fin. RPL Industries, Hayward, Calif., 1983—. Served to 1st lt. USMC, 1968-71. Mem. Stanford U. Alumni Assn., Stanford U. Grad. Sch. Bus. Alumni Assn. Republican. Club: Menlo Circus (Atherton, Calif.). Home: 223 Cerrito Ave Redwood City CA 94061 Office: RPC Industries PO Box 3306 Hayward CA 94540

CUNNINGHAM, JOHN JOSEPH, tax adviser; b. Berlin, Oreg., May 23, 1924; s. Frederick Joseph and Verena B. (Hoffmeister) C. Grad. high sch., Albany, Oreg. Cert. IRS, 1980. Acct., rancher, Oreg. and Calif., 1963-74; pres. The Tax Adviser, Inc., San Rafael, Calif., 1975—; pub. quar. rev. The XYZ of Taxes. Served as officer Fin. Corps, U.S. Army, 1940-62; World War II, Korea. Decorated Bronze Star, Purple Heart. Mem. Nat. Soc. Pub. Accts. Republican. Clubs: Masons, KT. Home: 521 Alameda Del Prado Novato CA 94947 Office: 1050 Northgate Dr Suite 351 San Rafael CA 94903

CUNNINGHAM, KENNETH ROBERT, sociologist, educator; b. Portland, Oreg., Mar. 23, 1935; s. A. Robert and R. Lillian (Simmons) C.; B.A., U. Oreg., 1960, postgrad., 1963; m. Virginia Ann Brown, June 11, 1962. Sr. research analyst Nat. Security Agy., 1957-59; instr. U. Oreg., 1963; instr., then asst. prof. Portland State U., 1963-65; mem. faculty U. Alta. (Can.), Edmonton, 1965—, asso. prof. sociology, 1975—. Served with USAF, 1956-59. NDEA fellow, 1960-63. Mem. Canadian Sociology and Anthropology Assn., Canadian Railroad Hist. Assn., Nat. Assn. Timetable Collectors. Home: 11732 University Ave Edmonton AB T6G 1Z5 Canada

CUNNINGHAM, LIZ, communication and human relations consultant, management consultant; b. Glendale, Calif., Dec. 25, 1942; d. Joseph M. and Sophia A. (Zoric) Bauernfeind; m. Donald K. Cunningham, Aug. 12, 1968; children—Keith, Kristie. B.S. in Nursing, Seattle U., 1964; M.A. in Speech Communication, U. Denver, 1980. Employed in field of nursing adminstrn. and edn., 1964-73; founder, pres. Cunningham Communications, cons. and mgmt., Littleton, Colo., 1980—. Mem. adv. council on communication Arapahoe Community Coll. Mem. Internat. Communication Assn., Speech Communication Assn., Western States Communications Assn., Exec. and Profl. Women's Council, Women's Ednl. Service Assn. Office: PO Box 320 Littleton CO 80160

CUNNINGHAM, LYNNE STRESEN-REUTER, hosp. adminstr.; b. Oak Park, Ill., June 1, 1950; d. Fred A. and Kathryn J. (Beardsley) Stresen-Reuter; m. Glen A. Cunningham, Mar. 27, 1970. B.S. in Journalism and Chemistry, No. Ariz. U., 1970; M.P.A., Calif. State U., 1978. Customer info. specialist European Exchange System, No. Ger., 1971-73; pub. info. asst. Calif. Hosp. Assn., Sacramento, 1973-75; pub. and community relations supr. Kaiser/Permanente Med. Care Program, No. Calif., 1975-80; dir. community relations Sutter Community Hosps., Sacramento, 1980—. Active Am. Heart Assn.; pres. Sacramento-Yolo council Camp Fire Inc., 1982—. Fellow Am. Soc. Hosp. Pub. Relations; mem. Hosp Pub. Relations Assn., Acad. Hosp. Pub. Relations (MacEachern award 1982), Am. Coll. Hosp. Adminstrs., Sacramento Healthcare Mgmt. Assn. Presbyterian. Club: Jr. League Sacramento. Contbr. articles to profl. jours. Office: 2020 I St Suite D Sacramento CA 95814

CUNNINGHAM, MARY (LOUISE), public relations cons.; b. Los Angeles, Feb. 9, 1932; d. Paul LaFrance and Ina (Decoto) Johnson; A.A., Sacramento Coll., 1951; children—David, Diane, Denise. Loan supr., teller, bookkeeper various banks, Calif., Wash., 1951-61; singer, actress, publicist, dir. concert, light opera, civic theatre, 1948-71; free-lance writer, 1975-79, owner PR Northwest, Renton, Wash., 1980—; seminar leader community colls., Wash., Small Bus. Adminstrn. Founder, Shasta Civic Theatre, 1959; actress, publicist. Stockton Civic Theatre, 1966-68; dir., publicist Santa Rosa Players, 1970-71; fund-raising chmn. Children's Home Soc., 1964-69. Recipient Totem award, 1982. Mem. Women Entrepreneurs Network (founder), Pub. Relations Soc. Am., Women's Bus. Exchange, Women in Communications, Pacific N.W. Writers, Tukwila-Sea Tac C. of C. (media rep.). Contbr. articles to profl. jours.; author The Nuts and Bolts of Promoting Your Business, 60 min. cassette tape, 1981. Address: 15450 SE Fairwood Blvd Renton WA 98055

CUNNINGHAM, PATRICIA IHINGER, interior designer; b. Topeka, Aug. 21, 1927; d. Chester Eugene and Josephine Ethel (Rooney) Ihinger; m. William Lloyd Cunningham, Mar. 31, 1950; children—Shalee Cunningham Kelly, Kerry Cunningham Cody, Kyle. B.A., U. Pacific, 1949; student Sacramento State U., 1950, Coll. Notre Dame, 1979, Coll. San Mateo, 1979; A.A. in Interior Design, Can. Coll., 1979. Cert. elem. tchr., Calif., 1951. Elem. sch. tchr., Calif., 1949-71; owner, designer Treehut, Burlingame, Calif., 1971-74; assoc. designer Thea Ramsey Co., Burlingame, 1978-79; owner, designer Pat Cunningham Co., 1979—. Active with Tamarack branch Children's Home Soc., 1963-68; bd. dirs. Hayward Arts Festival, 1963-68; Bluebird and Campfire leader, 1960-63; asst. den mother Cub Scouts, 1971-72; Recipient Hayward Area Festival of Arts award, 1968; Burlingame Recreation Dept. jewelry design award, 1976. Mem. Am. Soc. Interior Designers (assoc.). Republican. Home and Office: 353 Wyndgate Rd Sacramento CA 95825

CUNNINGHAM, ROBERT CLAY, national park superintendent; b. N.Y.C., Feb. 20, 1936; s. Dale B. and Alice S. (Simmers) C.; B.Sc., Indiana U. Pa., 1963, M.Sc., 1967; postgrad. Ohio State U., 1967; m. Betty Deane Kerr, June 6, 1964; children—James Colter, Jr. high sci. tchr., Ebensburg, Pa., 1963-67; sub-dist. ranger Yellowstone Nat. Park, 1967-68; park ranger Theodore Roosevelt Nat. Park, Medora, N.D., 1968-70; instr. Dickinson (N.D.) State Coll., 1969; dist. ranger North Cascades Nat. Park, Stehekin, Wash., 1970-75; research biologist, asst. supt. Gateway Nat. Recreation Area, N.Y./N.J., 1975-80; supt. Denali Nat. Park and Preserve, McKinley Park, Alaska, 1980—. Served with U.S. Army, 1955-58. Recipient Incentive award Nat. Park Service, 1973, Spl. Achievement award, 1974. Mem. Assn. Nat. Park Rangers (Alaska regional rep.). Methodist. Clubs: Lions (pres. Healy Valley), Masons. Author: It's a Dog's Life, 1970; Bison Management Techniques, 1970. Home and Office: PO Box 9 McKinley Park AK 99755

CURD, WILLIAM HUGH, JR., computer systems engineer; b. St. Joseph, Mo., June 24, 1947; s. William H. and Dorotha Josephine (Kadera) C.; B.S.E.E. with high honors, U. Mo.-Rolla, 1970; M.S. in Systems Engring., So. Meth. U., 1971, Ph.D. in Elec. Engring., 1974; student Grand Canyon Coll., 1974, Glendale Community Coll., 1974-76, Phoenix Coll., 1975, Southwestern Bible Coll., 1979-80; m. Dale Ann Keehn, June 5, 1976. Mem. staff data processing dept. Hillyard Chem. Co., St. Joseph, 1966-68; asst. chief engr. Sta. KMSM-FM, Rolla, 1968-69; contract research Collins Radio Co., Dallas, 1971-72, Fed. Bur. Prisons, Seagoville, Tex., 1972, Naval Weapons Lab., Dahlgren, Va., 1972-73; analyst/engr. design automation Honeywell Info. Systems, Phoenix, 1973-77; specialist/applications systems engr. Motorola Microsystems, 1977-78; prin. engr. Codex Corp. Phoenix ops., 1978-80; mgr. system support engring. A.B. Dick, Phoenix Computer Devel. Center, Scottsdale, Ariz., 1980—; pres. Synesys Corp., 1982—. Vol. emergency dept. John C. Lincoln Hosp., Phoenix, 1975, Glendale (Ariz.) Samaritan Hosp., 1975, respiratory therapy dept. Maryvale Samaritan Hosp., Glendale, 1975; jr. high youth coach 1st Christian Ch., Phoenix, 1975-76; bd. dirs., deacon, librarian Chaparral Christian Ch., Scottsdale, Ariz., 1977-80. Cert. emergency med. technician. Mem. IEEE, IEEE Computer Soc., ACM, Creation Research Soc., Tau Beta Pi, Eta Kappa

Nu, Kappa Mu Epsilon, Phi Theta Kappa. Home: Box 31790 Phoenix AZ 85046 Office: Box 30290 Phoenix AZ 85046

CURL, JAMES CRAIG, mathematician, educator; b. Jefferson, Iowa, May 27, 1941; s. Dale Frank and Irene René (Edwards) C.; A.A., Modesto Jr. Coll., 1961; B.A., San Francisco State U., 1963; M.S., U. Santa Clara, 1968; Ed.D., U. No. Colo., 1976; m. Evelyn Ruth Ewen, July 4, 1963 (div. 1982); children—Brian Mitchell, Darren Matthew, Heather Michele. Tchr. math. high sch., San Mateo, Calif., 1964-66, Tracy (Calif.) Joint Union High Sch., 1966-68; instr. math. Modesto (Calif.) Jr. Coll., 1968—; teaching asst. in math. U. No. Colo., 1974-75. Mem. Calif. Math. Council Community Colls. (past pres., founding dir.), Calif. Math. Council, Stanislaus Math. Council (speaker), Nat. Council Tchrs. Math., Math. Assn. Am. Author: Developmental Arithmetic-An Individualized Approach, 1973; Developmental Arithmetic-A Computational Review, 1978, 2d edit., 1980; contbr. articles to profl. jours. Home: 1520 Sylvan A Modesto CA 95355 Office: Modesto Jr Coll College Ave Modesto CA 95350

CURLEY, ARTHUR WALTER, lawyer; b. Arlington, Va., Sept. 4, 1948; s. Wilfred J. and Ella K. (Winchester) C. B.S., U. Calif.-Berkeley, 1970; J.D., Hastings Coll., 1974. Bar: Calif. 1974. Ptnr., Bradley & Curley Law Corp., San Francisco. Mem. faculty U. Pacific. Mem. ABA, Calif. Trial Lawyers Assn., Assn. Trial Lawyers Am., San Francisco Bar Assn., Calif. Bar Assn. Democrat. Roman Catholic. Office: Bradley & Curley 100 Bush St Suite 1812 San Francisco CA 94104

CUROTTO, RICKY JOSEPH, lawyer, real estate exec.; b. Lomita Park, Calif., Dec. 22, 1931; s. Enrico and Nora (Giusso) C.; B.S. cum laude, U. San Francisco, 1953, J.D., 1958; m. Anne Drobac, June 12, 1954; children—Dina Lynn, John Francis, Alexis Joseph. Admitted to Calif. bar, 1958, asso. Peart, Baraty & Hassard, San Francisco, 1958-60; sr. counsel Utah Internat., Inc., San Francisco, 1960—, asst. sec. 1966—; dir. Securities-Intermountain, Inc., Simco Indsl. Mortgage Co., Capstone Capital Corp., Garden Hotels, Inc., Dominican Homes, Inc. Garden Hotels Investment Co.; sec., counsel Ross Valley Homes, Inc. Trustee, Pres.'s Ambassadors, athletic control bd. U. San Francisco. Served to 1st lt. AUS, 1954-56. Recipient Bur. Nat. Affairs award, 1958; Disting. Service award U. San Francisco, 1981. Mem. State Bar Cal., San Francisco Bar Assn., Am. Arbitration Assn. (nat. panel arbitrators), U. San Francisco Alumni Assn., Am. Bar Assn., Calif. Assn. for A.C.T., Phi Alpha Delta, Pi Sigma Alpha. Republican. Roman Catholic. Clubs: Century (past pres., dir.), Commonwealth of Calif. (membership com., past chmn. lawmaking procedures sect.). Contbr. articles to profl. jours. Home: 1071-A Foster City Blvd Foster City CA 94404 Office: 550 California St Room 700 San Francisco CA 94104

CURRAN, CAROL ANNE, comml. real estate co. ofcl.; b. San Francisco, Nov. 2, 1943; d. Andrew Joseph and Verna Maude (Woodman) Geiser; A.A. in Bus., City Coll. San Francisco; A.A. in Bus. Adminstrn., Foothill Coll.; B.S. in Bus. Adminstrn., San Jose State U., M.B.A., 1978; teaching credential Calif. Community Coll. System, 1980. Employee recruiter, employment rep., asst. mgr. Pacific Telephone Co., San Francisco, 1962-65; with Stanford U., 1965-68; with mktg. dept. Varian Assocs., Palo Alto, Calif., 1968-71; with Michael C. Fields, Menlo Park, Calif., 1971-72; adminstrv. asst. editor co. newsletter Time/Data Corp., Palo Alto, Calif., 1972-74; ind. cons. Olson Labs., Anaheim, Calif., 1977-78; office bldg. specialist Coldwell Banker, San Jose, Calif., 1978—. Named Outstanding Office/Comml. Broker of Yr., San Jose C. of C., 1982. Mem. Peninsula Profl. Women's Network, Assn. South Bay Brokers (dir. 1981—), World Affairs Council No. Calif. Office: 226 W Brokaw Rd Suite 150 San Jose CA 95110

CURRAN, JOHN WILLIAM, accountant; b. Washington, Dec. 13, 1939; s. Bertrend Joseph and Mary Helen (O'Mahoney) C.; m. Judith Strang, Dec. 11, 1971; children—Jennifer, Jodie, Jill. B.S. in Acctg., Seattle U., 1962. C.P.A., Wash. Mem. audit staff Ernst & Ernst, Seattle, 1962-70, mem. tax staff, 1970-80; ptnr. Ernst & Whinney, Seattle, 1980—; acctg. adv. bd. dirs. Seattle U. Bd. dirs. Family Services King County (Wash.). Served with U.S. Army, 1958. Mem. Am. Inst. C.P.A.s, Wash. Soc. C.P.A.s. Clubs: Seattle Tennis, Wash. Athletic, Rotary (Seattle). Office: 2700 Seattle First Nat Bank Bldg Seattle WA 98154

CURRAN, LARRY LEE, lawyer; b. Decatur, Ill., Jan. 18, 1937; s. Roy Willard and Iva Marie (Henricks) C.; student Eastern Ill. U., 1955-57, McGeorge Sch. Law, U. Pacific, 1959-64; children—David Roy, Daniel Lee, Larry Lee, II; m. Jean Loye Nielson; children—Vincent Eugene Galewick, Wendy Louise Galewick. With Aerojet Gen. Corp., Nimbus, Calif., 1957-65, engrng. change bd. coordinator, 1961-62, material adminstrn. analyst, 1962-65; admitted to Calif. bar, 1965; contract adminstr. Western Gear Corp., Lynwood, Calif., 1965-66, legal adv. div., 1965-66, corp. atty., 1966-69; individual practice law, Santa Ana, Newport Beach and Huntington Beach, Calif., 1969—. Pres., Concerned Citizens Council, Huntington Beach, 1968-74; bd. dirs. Huntington Beach Public Facilities Corp., 1970-77, also formerly pres. (twice); mem. Huntington Beach City Charter Revision Com.; Huntington Beach rep. Route 57 Freeway Com.; bd. dirs. Huntington Beach Boys Club, 1978-79; pres. bd. dirs. Huntington Beach Library Patrons Found., Inc., 1983—. Mem. Am. Trial Lawyers Assn., Calif. Trial Lawyers Assn., Orange County Trial Lawyers Assn. (past dir., treas.), Calif. Bar Assn., Orange County Bar Assn. (mem. legal-med. com.). Republican. Lutheran. Clubs: Lions (pres. local club 1975-76, dir. 1975-79), Masons (Huntington Beach). Home: 8131 Wadebridge Circle Huntington Beach CA 92646 Office: Larry L Curran & Assos 18090 Beach Blvd Suite 2 Huntington Beach CA 92648

CURRAN, WILLIAM GIBBONS, film producer and dir.; b. Balt., Oct. 22, 1946; s. William Gibbons and Marie Catherine (Cicero) C.; A.B., Loyola Coll., Balt., 1968; M.S., Syracuse U., 1969; M.A., U. So. Calif., 1976. Adminstrv. asst. MPO Prodns. of Hollywood (Calif.), 1971-72; freelance motion picture and video tape prodn. mgr., Los Angeles and San Francisco, 1972-76; pres. Associated Filmakers Internat., Hollywood, 1976-78; creative prodn. cons., producer tv comml., promotional and indsl. film and video tape, Santa Monica, Calif., 1978—; with TV series Tales of the Unexpected, 1981; lectr. UCLA, 1979-81; cons. dept. arts UCLA Extension Program, 1980. Served to capt. U.S. Army, 1969-71. Recipient Am. Legion Cert. of Achievement, 1960; Md. State scholar, 1964-68; named Disting. Mil. Grad., Loyola Coll., 1968. Mem. Dirs. Guild Am., Producers Assn. Hollywood, Nat. Assn. Ind. Comml. Producers, Alpha Sigma Nu, Delta Kappa Alpha. Democrat. Address: 236 Bay St Santa Monica CA 90405

CURRAN, WILLIAM PATRICK, III, developmental optometrist; b. St. Albans, N.Y. Apr. 15, 1953; s. William Patrick II and Mary Lois (Connolly) C. B.A. NYU, 1975; O.D., SUNY Coll. Optometry, N.Y.C., 1980. Lic. optometrist, Ariz. Supervising optometrist Indian Health Service, USPHS, Aberdeen, S.D., 1980; pvt. practice optometry, Glendale, Ariz., 1980—; Ariz. dir. Optometric Extension Program Found., Inc.; chmn. Sun Valley Behavioral Vision Seminar; co-chmn. Forum on Learning Abilities. Bd. dirs. Pulmonary Hypertension Edn. and Recognition, Inc.; sec. St. Vincent de Paul Soc., Glendale. Mem. Central Ariz. Optometric Soc. (pres.), Am. Optometric Assn., Ariz. Optometric Assn., Coll. Optometrists in Vision Devel., Assn. for Children and Adults with Learning Disabilities, Am. Interprofl. Assn. Roman Catholic. Clubs: Kiwanis (v.p.) (Glendale); Holy Name Soc., Irish-Am. Social. Home: 4721 W Aster Dr Glendale AZ 85304 Office: 5806 W Camelback Rd Glendale AZ 85301

CURREY, JANIE POWER, nurse; b. Demming, N.Mex., Oct. 17, 1944; d. John and Dolly Isabelle (Bignell) Power; m. William John Currey, Sept. 2, 1967. A.S. in Nursing, East Los Angeles Coll., 1978; B.A. in Sociology, Calif. State U.-Los Angeles, 1978; M.A. in Human Resource Mgmt., U. Redlands, 1981. Cert. in advanced nursing adminstrn. Am. Nurses Assn. Charge nurse Arcadia Meth. Hosp., 1969-71; supr. lab. outpatient care unit Beverly Hosp., Montebello, Calif., 1971-78, nursing quality assurance coordinator, 1978-80; dir. nursing services Mission Valley Med. Ctr., Lake Elsinore, Calif., 1980—; adj. faculty U. Redlands. Co-investigator fed. grant Multiagency Quality Assurance Com. Mem. Dirs. Nursing Council of So. Calif. (dir.), Inland Area Dirs. Nursing Council (v.p.), Calif. Soc. Nursing Service Adminstrs. Office: 21220 Walnut St Lake Elsinore CA 92330

CURRIE, GORDON A., Canadian provincial government official; b. Siemans, Sask, Can., May 20, 1923; s. Robert and Maryanne (Pool) C.; m. Shirley Clarke, Feb. 27, 1952; children—Robert, Douglas, James. B.A., Athol Coll. of Notre Dame, Wilcox, Sask.; B.Ed., Mt. Allison U. With Regina (Sask.) Sch. Bd., 1947-82, with Balfour Tech. Sch., 20 yrs., v.p., 4 yrs., prin. Cochrane High Sch., 4 yrs., prin. Campbell Collegiate, 7 yrs., also coach hockey, baseball, football; minister edn. and continuing edn. Govt. Sask., Regina, 1982—. Decorated Order Can.; recipient Dad of Yr. award Wascanda Kiwanis Club, 1963, Outstanding Sports Personality of Yr. award B'nai B'rith, 1966, Newsmaker of Yr. award Sask. Press Club, 1976, Outstanding Services to Football in Can. award CFL and Can. Football League, 1978; Gordon Currie Field named by City Regina, 1974; named Can. Amateur Coach of Yr., Air Can., 1975; Gordon Currie Found. established 1977; inducted into Sask. Sports Hall of Fame, 1978. Office: 361 Legis Bldg Regina SK S4S 0B3 Canada*

CURRIE, JAMES WILLIAM, economist, engr.; b. Old Town, Maine, Aug. 8, 1942; s. James Wallace and Edith Mabel (Sage) C.; m. Andrea Jean Miskoski, Aug. 29, 1964; children—Dana Lorelle, James Brandon. B.S.M.E., U. Maine, 1964, M.S. in Resource Geography, Oreg. State U., 1971, Ph.D. in Resource Econs., Civil Engring., 1975. Engr., Smithsonian Astrophys. Obs., Maui, Hawaii, 1964-67; engr. Ga. Pacific Corp., Bellingham, Wash., 1968; sr. researcher, mgr. resource and regional econs. Battelle Pacific N.W. Labs., Richland, Wash., 1974—. Mem. Am. Econ. Assn., Am. Agrl. Econ. Assn., Am. Geophys. Union, Western Econ. Assn., Western Agrl. Econ. Assn. Club: Masons. Contbr. in field. Office: PO Box 999 Richland WA 99352

CURRIE, MADELINE ASHBURN, educator; b. Rankin, Tex., Sept. 28; d. Herman and Ivan G. Vinson; B.S., Tex. Woman's U., 1962; M.A., Calif. State U., 1967; Ed.D., UCLA, 1974; m. Gail G. Currie; children—Robb Ashburn, Mark Ashburn, Michael Ashburn. Tchr., Edgewood High Sch., West Covina, Calif., 1962-69, Tri-Community Adult Sch., West Covina, 1966-68; instr. Rio Hondo Coll., Whittier, Calif., 1968-69; prof., dir. grad. programs Sch. Bus. Adminstrn., Calif. State Poly. U., Pomona, 1969—. Recipient award Alpha Lambda Delta. Mem. dean's council Grad. Sch. Edn., UCLA. Mem. Nat. Bus. Edn. Assn., Calif. Bus. Edn. Assn. (Recognition award), Tex. Woman's U. Alumnae Assn., Delta Pi Epsilon, Pi Lambda Theta. Office: Calif State Poly U Sch Bus Adminstrn Pomona CA 91768

CURRIER, RICHARD PAUL, information systems analyst, designer, educator; b. Orange, Calif., Oct. 1, 1952; s. Myrl L. and Dolores A. (Ervin) C.; m. Karen Lorraine Mair, Aug. 11, 1973; 1 son, Brett. B.A. in Mgmt. Info. Systems, Calif. State U.-Fullerton, 1979. Cert. data processing Inst. Cert. Computer Profls. Systems. Programmer/analyst Rio Hondo Coll., Whittier, Calif., 1979-81; sr. programmer Bourns, Inc., Riverside, Calif., 1981-82; systems analyst Carter Hawley Hale Stores, Inc., Anaheim, Calif., 1981-82; instr. computer ops., devel. new curriculum Rio Hondo Coll. Served with USN, 1971-75. Mem. Assn. Systems Mgmt. Home: 11584 Kiwi Ct Sunnymead CA 92388 Office: Carter Hawley Hale Stores Inc 1600 Kramer Anaheim CA 92806

CURRY, CAROL JEAN, accountant; b. Los Angeles, Dec. 13, 1943; d. Robert Vincent and Marzene Shirely (Draper) Gunther; m. Noel Roger Curry, May 29, 1970; children—Frank R., Ernest R. B.S. in Bus. Adminstrn., Chico State Coll., 1970. C.P.A., Calif. Staff acct. Herbert J. McClanahan, C.P.A., Gridley, Calif., 1968-70, Davis W. Hammon, C.P.A., Oroville, Calif., 1971-74; ptnr. Davis Hammon & Co., Oroville, 1974-77, mng. ptnr. Susanville (Calif.) office, 1977—; ptnr. Lassen Racquetball Club, Susanville; dir. Suter Dental Mfg., Inc. Bd. dirs., treas. Episcopal Churchwomen, Diocese of No. Calif.; mem. adv. com. Lassen Hospice Care; bd. dirs., sec. Lassen Econ. Devel. Council, Inc.; bd. dirs., chmn. Susanville Mcpl. Energy Corp., Inc. Mem. Am. Inst. C.P.A.s, Calif. Soc. C.P.A.s, Lassen County Cattlemen's Assn., Lassen County Cow Bells. Republican. Office: Davis Hammon & Co 30 S Roop St Susanville CA 96130

CURRY, LINDA WILSON, corporate marketing co. exec.; b. Long Branch, N.J., Mar. 17, 1945; d. Sidney and Josephine Barbara (Dremel) Meadow; B.S. in Math., Bucknell U., 1966; M.S. in Numerical Sci., Johns Hopkins U., 1970; m. James Prescott Curry, Aug. 22, 1980. Various positions as mathematician, 1966-69; ops. research analyst Dept. Transp., 1970-73; mgr. Planning Research Corp., 1973-75; exec. v.p. Automated Scis. Group, Inc., 1975-77; pres. Excel Corp., 1978; mgr. info. systems Commonwealth Research Corp., 1978; pres., chmn. bd. Wilson Hill Assocs., Inc., 1978-81; pres. South Bay Introductions, Inc., Manhattan Beach, Calif., 1981-82; corp. dir. mktg. Automated Scis. Group, Manhattan Beach, 1982—. Mem. Nat. Assn. Women Bus. Owners, Nat. Assn. Female Execs., Women's Referral Service, Women in Bus., Am. Mgmt. Assn., Am. Entrepreneurs Assn., Manhattan Beach C. of C., Phi Beta Kappa. Club: Manhattan Beach Soroptomist. Home: 2027 Via Nova Lomita CA 90717 Office: 2100 Sepulveda Blvd Suite 43 Manhattan Beach CA 90266

CURRY, MITCHELL LEE, clergyman, psychiatric social worker; b. Augusta, Ga., Feb. 5, 1935; s. Walter L. and Ernestine B. C.; m. Carolyn D. May, 1974; children—Sonja, Reuben, Rachael, Michele. B.A., Morris Brown Coll., 1960; M.Div., Andover Newton Theol. Sch., 1964; postgrad. Vanderbilt U., 1968; M.S.W. in Psychiat. Social Work, U. Louisville, 1972; L.H.D. (hon.), Reed Christian Coll., Los Angeles, 1976; D.D. (hon.), E. Tenn. Sch. of Religion, 1972; Ph.D. Min., Claremont Grad. Sch. Theology, 1979. Exec. dir. Harlem Upper-Manhattan Div. Protestant Council N.Y.C., 1963-67; ordained to ministry, 1952; minister Miles Meml. Ch., Washington, 1967-69, Lampkins Meml. Ch., Louisville, 1969-72; asst. dir. western regional office Nat. Urban League, Los Angeles, psychiat. social worker Kedren Community Mental Health Center, Los Angeles, 1972-75; minister First United Presbyn. Ch., Los Angeles, 1972-75, Florence Ave. United Presbyn. Ch., Los Angeles, 1978—, Imperial Heights Community Ch., Los Angeles, 1980—; psychiat. social worker Los Angeles County Dept. Mental Health, 1976—; cons. NIMH; instr. LaVerne Coll. Ecumenical Center for Black Ch. Studies. Active NAACP, PUSH, So. Christian Leadership Conf. Served with U.S. Army, 1954-56. Am. Missionary Assn. fellow, 1960-64; Lilly Fellowship grantee, 1962-63; NIMH grantee, 1970-72. Fellow Am. Assn. Pastoral Counselors (cert. clin. pastoral counseling); mem. Acad. Cert. Social Workers, Nat. Assn. Social Workers, Nat. Council Clin. Pastoral Tng., Nat. Assn. Black Social Workers, Alpha Phi Alpha. Democrat. Club: Kiwanis Internat. Author: Religious Experience in Psychotherapy, 1980. Home: 1809 Virginia Rd Los Angeles CA 90019

CURTIN, THOMAS LEE, ophthalmologist; b. Columbus, Ohio, Sept. 9, 1932; s. Leo Anthony and Mary Elizabeth (Burns) C.; B.S., Loyola U., Los Angeles, 1954; M.D., U. So. Calif., 1957; children—Michael, Gregory, Thomas, Christopher. Intern, Ohio State U. Hosp., 1957-58; resident in ophthalmology U.S. Naval Hosp., San Diego, 1961-64; practice medicine specializing in ophthalmology, Oceanside, Calif., 1967—; mem. staff Tri City, Palomar Meml., Scripps Meml. Mercy hosps.; sci. adv. bd. So. Calif. Soc. Prevention Blindness, 1973-76; cons. in field. Trustee, Carlsbad (Calif.) Unified Sch. Dist., 1975—, pres., 1979, 82, 83. Served as officer M.C., USN, 1958-67. Diplomate Am. Bd. Ophthalmology. Mem. Am., Calif. med. assns., San Diego County Med. Soc., Am. Acad. Ophthalmology, Am. Assn. Ophthalmology, Soc. Cryobiology, Aerospace Med. Assn., Pacific Coast Ophthalmology and Otolaryngology Assn., San Diego Acad. Ophthalmology (pres. 1979), Calif. Assn. Ophthalmology (dir.), San Diego Surg. Soc. Republican. Roman Catholic. Clubs: Carlsbad Rotary, El Camino Country. Home: 2014 Ave of Trees Carlsbad CA 92008 Office: 3231 Waring Ct Suite S Oceanside CA 92056

CURTIS, CHARLOTTE ELIZABETH, educator; b. Huntsville, Tex., May 28, 1947; d. Charles Edward and Elizabeth Jane Nelson; m. Chester Montgomery Curtis, Jr., Sept. 5, 1970; 1 son, Charles Michael. B.S. in Home Econs. N. Tex.-Austin, 1969; M.A. in Edn. Leadership, St. Mary's Coll., 1982. Tchr. home econs. Oakland (Calif.) Pub. Schs., 1970-74; tchr. Amador Valley Joint Union High Sch. Dist., 1976—; tchr. Rop Child Care, 1979—, work experience coordinator, 1983—. Mem. edn. adv. com. Alameda County Work Experience Coordinators, St. Mary's Coll. Mem. Assn. Calif. Sch. Adminstrs., Calif. Assn. Work Experience Coordinators, Calif. Tchrs. Assn., Pleasanton C. of C., Alpha Delta Pi Alumni, DAR. Republican. Roman Catholic.

CURTIS, DANA LOUISE, educator; b. Spokane, Aug. 6, 1946; d. Jack E. and June Smith; m. Richard W. Curtis, Sept. 28, 1968 (div.); children—Amy, Richard, Anne. B.A., U. Mont., 1968; M.A., U. Idaho, 1970. Cert. tchr., Idaho. Grad. asst. dept. English, U. Idaho, 1968-70; tchr. reading Bonner County Sch. Dist., 1970-71, tchr. English, 1971-73, home econs., 1971—; dir., tchr. Parent Program, chmn. dept. home econs., 1980—, dir. ABE-GED Sandpoint Program, 1975-76, coordinator Satellite campus, 1974—; instr. English North Idaho Coll., 1973-77; cons. Spokane Community Coll. Mem. Am. Home Econs. Assn. (merit award), Idaho Home Econs. Assn. (Tchr. of Yr. 1983), Idaho Council on Family Relations, NEA, Idaho Edn. Assn., Bonner County Edn. Assn., Am. Vocat. Assn., Idaho Vocat. Assn., Idaho Vocat. Home Econs. Tchrs. Assn., Idaho Alliance Concerned with School Age Parents (pres.). Home: 432 St Clair St Sandpoint ID 83864 Office: PO Box 430 Sandpoint ID 83864

CURTIS, ELIZABETH BROWN, home economics educator; b. Astoria, Oreg., Oct. 1, 1939; d. Homer O. and Margaret E. (McClure) McEntire; m. Richard L. Curtis, Oct. 13, 1963; children—Steven, Kenneth. B.S., Oreg. State U., 1961; postgrad. Oreg. Coll. Edn., 1979-81, U. Oreg., 1981, Portland State U., 1982, Eastern Oreg. Coll., 1980-82. Cert. tchr. home econs., Oreg. Home extension agt. Oreg. State U. Extension Service, 1961-63; substitute tchr. Harney, Grant, and Morrow Counties (Oreg.), 1963-76; sec. Morrow County Fair, 1972-77; tchr. home econs. Heppner (Oreg.) Jr. High Sch., 1977—. Mem. Oreg. Home Econs. Cadre; chmn. Umatilla-Morrow Home Econs. Consortium; leader Seaside Health Team, 1982-83. Chmn., originator Tri-County Home Health Service, 1976-82; leader 4-H Club, 1975-81; coordinator 4-H Labo Japanese Exchange, 1981-83; mem. Hope Lutheran Refugee com., 1982. Mem. Oreg. Nutrition Council, Am. Home Econs. Assn., Oreg. Home Econs. Assn., AAUW, Am. Vocat. Edn. Assn., Tchrs. Home Econs. Oreg., NEA, Oreg. Edn. Assn., Morrow County Edn. Assn. Lutheran. Club: Prairie City Women's.

CURTIS, GEORGE DARWIN, physics cons.; b. Galveston, Tex., Apr. 30, 1928; s. Darwin Agustus and Frances Loyd (Gymer) C.; B.S. in Physics, North Tex. U., 1952, postgrad., 1970-71; m. Alice Kidd, May 10, 1951; children—Carol, Paul, Ann, George. With Mobil Oil Research Lab., Dallas, 1951-52; sr. scientist, prin. investigator Ling-Temco-Vought, Honolulu, 1952-68; dir. systems Pacific div. Control Data Corp., Honolulu, 1968-70; staff U. Hawaii, Honolulu, 1971, lectr. in electronics, 1963-64; ind. cons. in electro-acoustics, Honolulu, 1971—; lectr. electronics U.S. Naval Postgrad. Sch., 1961; pres. Trans-Nova, Inc., Honolulu, 1973—. Bd. dirs. Hawaii chpt. ARC, 1974-76. Served with USMC, 1950-52. Mem. IEEE (chmn. Hawaii chpt. 1978-79), Marine Tech. Soc. (sect. pres. 1982-83), AAAS, Acoustical Soc. Am., CAP (squadron comdr., pilot). Republican. Episcopalian. Home: 47-363C Hui Iwa St Kaneohe HI 96744

CURTIS, HUGH AUSTIN, provincial government official; b. Victoria, B.C., Can., Oct. 3, 1932; s. Austin Ivor and Helen (Shepherd) C.; m. Sheila Diane Halford, Mar. 16, 1957; children—Gary Hugh, David Charles, Susan Diane Helen. Grad. high sch. Sales mgr. broadcasting co.; alderman Dist. Saanich (B.C.), 1962-64, mayor, 1964-73; mem. B.C. Legislature, 1972—, minister of mcpl. affairs and housing, 1975-78, provincial sec., minister govt. services, 1978-79, minister of fin., chmn. treasury bd., 1979—; chmn. Capital Regional Dist.; pres. Union B.C. Municipalities; chmn. Mcpl. Fin. Authority. Co-recipient John Gillin Jr. Meml. award, 1954. Mem. Social Credit Party B.C. Anglican. Club: Union of B.C. Office: Parliament Bldgs Room 103 Victoria BC V8V 1X4 Canada

CURTIS, JESSE WILLIAM, judge, lawyer; b. San Bernardino, Calif., Dec. 26, 1905; s. Jesse William and Ida L. (Seymour) C.; A.B., U. Redlands, 1928, LL.D., 1973; J.D., Harvard, 1931; m. Mildred F. Mort, Aug. 24, 1930; children—Suzanne, Jesse W., Clyde Hamilton, Christopher Cowles. Admitted to Calif. bar, 1931; pvt. practice, 1931-35; mem. Guthrie and Curtis, 1935-40, Curtis and Curtis, 1946-50, Curtis, Knauf, Henry and Farrell, 1950-53; judge Superior Ct. Calif., 1953-62; judge U.S. Dist. Ct. Central Calif., 1963—. Bd. dirs., past pres. YMCA; bd. dirs. Good Will Industries, Crippled Children's Soc., Arrowhead United Fund; chmn. San Bernardino County Heart Fund; adv. bd. Community Hosp. Mem. Am., Los Angeles County bar assns., State Bar Calif., Am. Judicature Soc., Am. Law Inst., Classic Yacht Assn., Town Hall, Los Angeles World Affairs Council, Phi Delta Phi. Democrat. Congregationalist. Club: Newport Harbor Yacht. Home: 305 Evening Star Ln Newport Beach CA 92660 Office: US Courthouse 312 N Spring St Los Angeles CA 90012

CURTIS, JOSEPH ROGER, banking exec.; b. Oakland, Calif., Apr. 29, 1926; s. Harry Lester and Elizabeth C. (Baker) C.; m. Lois Corinne Pippin, Feb. 5, 1944; children—Michael A., Ann E., Mary T. Student U. Redlands, 1947-49; M.B.A., U. So. Calif., 1967. Regional v.p. Citizens Bank of Riverside (Calif.), 1946-57; br. div. adminstr. Security Pacific Nat. Bank, Los Angeles, 1957-69; group mgr., exec. v.p. Seattle First Nat. Bank, 1969-73, vice chmn., 1973—; vice chmn. Seafirst Corp., 1974—, lectr. Pacific Coast Banking Sch.; dir. Westin Hotels. Bd. dirs. Virginia Mason Hosp., Corp. Council for Arts, First Ridge Acad.; chmn. bd. regents Seattle U. Served with USN, 1944-46. Mem. Am. Bankers Assn., Assn. Res. City Bankers. Republican. Roman Catholic. Clubs: Wash. Athletic, Rainier, Seattle Yacht. Home: 25924 Big Valley Rd NE Poulsbo WA 98370 Office: PO Box 3586 HOB-18 Seattle WA 98124

CURTIS, KITT LESTER, coffee company executive; b. County Galway, Ireland; came to U.S., 1950; d. Daniel and Gladys Y. (Taylor) Moloney; m. Wilbur Curtis, Dec. 23, 1967; children—Geraldine,

Siobhan, Veronicia Eileen. B.A., Am. Nat. Inst. for Phys. Research and Devel., 1983. Model, Vogue Mag., N.Y.C., 1950; mgr. in charge of concessions Plaza Hotel, N.Y.C., 1964; office mgr. Dr. R.J. Paden, D.D.S., Encino, Calif., 1966-67, Dr. E.T. Jones, D.D.S., Tarzana, Calif., 1972-77; owner, mgr. Curtis & Curtis Coffee Co. & V.I.P. Coffee Service, North Hollywood, Calif., 1967-71, Konex Corp., Honolulu, 1972-77, Kona Coffee Hawaii, Calabasas, Calif., 1977—, Curtis Roasting Plant, El Monte, Calif., 1982—. Del. Sacramento Small Bus. Conf.; mem. Womens Referral Service, 1980—, bd. dirs., 1988—; Mem. NOW. Home: 5648 Ruthwood Dr Calabasas CA 91302 Office: Curtis Roasting Plant 1706 Potrero St South El Monte CA 91733

CURTIS, MARK RANDOLPH, advertising executive; b. Phoenix, July 26, 1947; s. Mark and Dorothy (Doyle) C.; m. Becky Lynn LeBeau, Mar. 31, 1956; 1 dau., Brittany Leigh. B.J., U. Mo., 1969. Freelance writer/producer Studios Kaminski, 1975-77; founder/creative dir. Pen-Reel Studios (name later changed to Gustin/Curtis Advt.), Reno, 1977-82; sr. v.p., ptnr. creative dir. Dunn/Draper/Gustin/Curtis Advt., Reno, 1982—. Profl. advisor KNPB Channel 5 Pub. TV, Sierra Arts Found. Recipient award of excellence Savs. Insts. Mktg. Soc. Am., 1979; silver award (2) Inst. Residential Mktg., 1982. Mem. Reno Ad Club (Best of Show awards 1979, 81), Reno Creative Club (founder, pres.). Office: 333 W Moana Ln Reno NV 89509

CURTIS, MERIL GENE, agrl. mfg. co. exec.; b. Kooskia, Idaho, Aug. 12, 1937; s. Chester William and Thelma Val Jean (Grove) C.; student North Idaho Jr. Coll., 1955-57, U. Idaho, 1959-61, Kans. State U., 1978; m. Bobbie Jean Fisher, Oct. 17, 1965; children—Matthew Meril, Daniel Mark, David Michael, Nathan Paul. Mgr. Schiff Shoe Store for Shoe Corp. Am., Missoula, Butte and Gt. Falls, Mont., 1963-66; sanitarian ConAgra Inc., flour milling, Gt. Falls, 1966—, safety dir., 1977—; cons., lectr. in field. Foster parent. Served with U.S. Army, 1957-58. Mem. Arrowhead Gem and Mineral Club (pres. 1972—), treas. 1982-83. Home: 9 Morony Star Route Great Falls MT 59401 Office: ConAgra Inc 900 16th St N Great Falls MT 59401

CURTIS, ORLIE LINDSEY, lawyer, physicist; b. Hutchinson, Kans., Feb. 27, 1934; s. Orlie Lindsey and Lillian Esther (Barnes) C.; B.A. with high distinction, Union Coll., Lincoln, Nebr., 1954; M.S., Purdue U., 1956; Ph.D., U. Tenn., 1961, J.D., U. So. Calif., 1977, m. Idella Mae Krueger, June 5, 1955; children—Elizabeth, Victoria. Group chief Oak Ridge Nat. Lab., 1956-63; lab. dir., sci. fellow Northrop Corp., Hawthorne, Calif., 1963-77; partner firm Kroloff, Belcher, Smart, et al, Stockton, Calif., 1977—; vis. lectr. U. Calif. at Berkeley, 1970-71; adv. bd. physics dept. U. Ky., 1970-73. Bd. dirs. So. Calif. Conf. Seventh-Day Adventists, Newbury Park Acad., 1970-74, No. Calif. Assn. Seventh-day Adventists, 1980—; chmn. bd. Stockton Central Seventh-day Adventists Ch., 1980-81, 83—; mem. sch. bd. Lodi Acad., 1978—. Fellow Am. Phys. Soc., IEEE (chmn. radiation effects com. 1970-73), ABA, Calif. Bar, Calif. Adventist Attys. Assn. (pres. 1983-84), Assn. Def. Counsel, Order of Coif. Author: Point Defects in Solids (editor J.H. Crawford, Jr.), 1975. Contbr. articles to profl. jours. Patentee electron beam modulated signal processor, infra-red sensor array. Home: 9794 N Fernwood Rd Stockton CA 95212 Office: 1044 N El Dorado St Stockton CA 95201

CURTIS, ROGER WARD, physician; b. Alamosa, Colo., Sept. 22, 1924; s. Edward B. and Edna P. (Tucker) C.; D.V.M., Colo. State U., 1946, M.D., U. Colo., 1958; M.Ed., Wis. State U., 1954; m. Linda J. Clift, Apr. 7, 1969; children—Beverly, Martha, Polly, Stacey, Benjamin, Brian. Gen. practice vet. medicine, Greeley, Colo., 1946-52; intern USPHS, Seattle, 1958-59; resident U. Colo. Sch. Medicine, Denver, 1975-76; gen. practice medicine, Albany, Oreg., 1959-74; practice medicine specializing in spinal cords, Englewood, Colo., 1977—; mem. staff Craig Hosp; asst. prof. U. Colo., Denver, 1977—. Served with AUS, 1942-43, 52-54. Diplomate Am. Bd. Phys. Medicine and Rehab., Am. Bd. Family Practice, Am. Acad. Electromyography and Electrodiagnosis, Internat. Coll. Surgeons. Mem. AMA, Colo. Med. Soc., Denver Med. Soc.

CURTIS, WESLEY EDWARD, health systems analyst; b. Westfield, N.Y., Aug. 25, 1918; s. Edward James and Annie Mabell (Walker) C.; student Dunkirk (N.Y.) Coll. Center, 1936-37, U. Buffalo, 1937; B.S., Alfred U., 1940; m. Virginia Janet Austin, May 29, 1949; children—Mark Austin, Kipp Allen. Chemist, Atlas Feldspar Corp., 1940-42; research fellow Alfred U., 1942-44; research asso. Woods Hole Oceanographic Instn., 1944-47; physicist U.S. Army Ballistics Research Lab., Aberdeen, Md., 1947-56; system analyst Tech. Ops., Inc., Ft. Belvoir, Va., 1956-67; sr. operations analyst Dikewood Corp., Albuquerque, 1967-80; dir. spl. projects Hancock/Dikewood Services, Inc., Albuquerque, 1980-83; pvt. cons., 1983—. Recipient U.S. Naval Ordnance Devel. award, 1947. Mem. Ops. Research Soc. Am., AAAS, Sigma Xi. Kiwanian. Home: 3329 Santa Clara St SE Albuquerque NM 87106 Office: 1009 Bradbury Dr SE Albuquerque NM 87106

CURTISS, ELDEN F., bishop. Ordained priest Roman Catholic Ch., 1958; consecrated bishop, 1976; bishop of Helena (Mont.), 1976—. Office: 612 Harrison Ave PO Box 1729 Helena MT 59601

CURZON, EUGENE CHARLES, JR., surgeon; b. Los Angeles, Oct. 6, 1930; s. Eugene Charles and Allene Marguerite (Noel) C.; student Stanford U., 1948-50; B.A., U. So. Calif., 1952, M.D., 1957; children—Cammie Jo, Eugene Charles, Teresa Marie, Allyson Margot, Babette Margot, Dirk Barrett Waldron. Intern, Los Angeles County Hosp., 1957-58; resident, Kern Gen. Hosp., Bakersfield, 1958-60, Madigan Army Hosp., 1963-66; practice medicine specializing in obstetrics and gynecology, surgery, San Clemente, Calif., 1969—; chmn. Obstetrics and Gynecology Dept., San Clemente Gen. Hosp., 1973-75, vice chief staff, 1977, chief staff, 1979-81. Bd. chmn. Boys Club of So. Coastal area, 1973. Served with U.S. Army, 1960-69. Decorated Bronze Star Medal. Fellow A.C.S., Am. Coll. Obstetricians and Gynecologists; mem. Am., Calif., Orange County med. assns., Orange County Obstet.-Gynecol. Soc. Republican. Methodist. Clubs: Masons (Shriners), Order of De Molay, 4th of July Yacht. Home: 3913 Via Manzana St San Clemente CA 92672 Office: 653 Camino de los Mares San Clemente CA 92672

CUSHING, STEARNS, econ. cons.; b. Fowler, Colo., Oct. 3, 1908; s. Stearns and Bessie (Parberry) C.; B.A., Willamette U., 1932; M.A., Northwestern U., 1935; cert. in econs. Mich. State U., 1968; m. Elise Kay Brown, Dec. 8, 1962; children—Charlene Anne, Sharon Lou. Supt. plywood dept. Keith Brown Bldg. Co., Salem, Oreg., 1941-48; owner, operator Cushing's Union Service, Salem, 1948-54; real estate agt. Lukinbeam Real Estate, Salem, 1954-60; econ. cons. Oreg. State Employment Div., 1960-73; pvt. practice econ. consulting, 1973-82; econ. cons. Greater Medford (Oreg.) C. of C., 1975-82, bd. dirs., 1970-71; dir. Access Corp., Medford, 1976—; pres. Area Agy. on Aging, 1976-80; mem. Jackson County Econ. Devel. Com., 1966-76; chmn. Title VI programs Jackson-Josephine Job Council, 1972-76; mem. Marion County Exec. Com. Republican Party, 1956-60; mem. Oreg. Gov.'s Commn. Sr. Services, 1981— Named Lion of Year, 1967. Mem. Internat. Assn. Personnel Employment Security, Oreg. State Employees Assn., Salem Bd. Realtors, C. of C., Sigma Chi. Democrat. Methodist. Home and Office: 3306 S Pacific Hwy #58 Medford OR 97501

CUSHMAN, HAROLD ROBERT, agricultural educator; b. Ferrisburg, Vt., Dec. 21, 1920; s. Lynn Stanley and Ruth (Field) C.; m. Natalia Delfinado, Aug. 26, 1970; children—Richard, Robert, Janette, William, Nanette. B.S., U. Vt., 1941, M.A., 1948; Ph.D., Cornell U., 1951. Cert. agr. tchr., Vt. Tchr. agr., Woodstock, Vt., 1946-48; asst. state supv. agr. edn. Vt., 1948-49; head agrl. edn. dept. U. Vt., Burlington, 1951-55; prof. agr. Cornell U., Ithaca, N.Y., 1955—; overseas assignments: Philippines, 1958-60, 68-70, Western Samoa, 1972, Papua, New Guinea, 1980-81; Western Samoa, 1982—. Served as 1st lt., 1942-45. Decorated Bronze Star with three oak leaf clusters, Purple Heart. Mem. Am. Vocat. Assn., Am. Assn. Tchr. Educators in Agr. (Outstanding Service award 1978). Republican. Roman Catholic. Club: Masons. Office: U S Pacific PO Box 890 Apia Western Samoa

CUSHMAN, JUDITH, pub. relations exec.; b. N.Y.C., Nov. 22, 1942; d. David and Hannah C.; B.A., Barnard Coll., 1964; postgrad. Sch. Pub. Communications, Boston U., 1964-66; m. Robert L. Quick, Aug. 1, 1971; children—Jennifer R.L., Geoffrey K.D. Mem. pub. relations staff Lufthansa German Airlines, N.Y.C., 1968-69; service exec. Pub. Relations Bd., Chgo., 1969-70; with employee relations dept. Mobil Oil Corp., N.Y.C., 1966-67; v.p., pub. relations dir. Marshall Cons., Inc., N.Y.C., 1971-80, exec. v.p., Seattle, 1980—. Mem. Women in Communications, Pub. Relations Soc. Am., Internat. TV Assn., Internat. Assn. Bus. Communicators, Women's Network. Office: PO Box 1749 Seattle WA 98111

CUSICK, JOSEPH DAVID, government official; b. Chgo., Oct. 18, 1929; s. Joseph Martin and Rose Mathilda (Gerrity) C.; A.B., Stanford U., 1951, postgrad. (Sloan exec. fellow) Grad. Sch. Bus., 1973; postgrad. U. San Francisco Law Sch., 1956-57; M.B.A., U. Santa Clara, 1963; M.S., San Jose State U., 1976; m. Kathryn V. Moore, Feb. 2, 1952; children—Stephen, Anne, Eileen, Michael, Joseph R., Mary, James, John. Staff, Magna Power Tool Corp., 1956; asst. to plant engr. Lockheed Missiles & Space Co., Sunnyvale, Calif., 1958-61; scheduling supr. Satellite Test Center, U.S. Air Force, Sunnyvale, 1962-66, supr. policies and procedures, 1966-74, mgr. ops. support div., 1974-75, dir. adminstrn., 1975-77, network resource planner, 1977-79, systems acquisition mgr., 1979-81, dep. dir. Consol. Space Ops. Ctr. activation, 1982—. Bd. govs. Stanford Assos. Served to lt. USNR, 1951-56, 61-62. Mem. Stanford Alumni Assn., Santa Clara Alumni Assn., Stanford Block S Soc., Library Assos. (bd. dirs.), Music Guild, Delta Upsilon. Democrat. Roman Catholic. Clubs: Commonwealth (San Francisco); Stanford Faculty, Stanford Buck. Home: 163 Eastridge Dr Los Gatos CA 95030 Office: Satellite Test Center US Air Force Sunnyvale Air Force Sta Sunnyvale CA 94086

CUSTER, JOHN CHARLES, health care executive; b. Chgo., Aug. 30, 1934; s. John Howard and Irene Lillian (McGovern) C.; A.B., Ind. U., 1956; M.H.A., U. Minn., 1966; grad. Advanced Mgmt. Program, Harvard U., 1975; m. Barbara Ann Welcher, Sept. 5, 1959; 1 son, John Thomas. Asst. adminstr. Johns Hopkins Hosp., 1966-67; with Kaiser-Permanente Med. Care Program, 1967—, health plan mgr., 1970-74, v.p. health plan mgr., Oakland, Calif., 1974-79; v.p., mgr. Kaiser-Permanente Adv. Services, 1979 ; lectr. Harvard U. Grad. Sch. Public Health, 1977-79, U. Minn. Ind. Study Program, 1983, U. Calif.-Berkeley Grad. Sch. Pub. Health, 1983; med. services adv. com. Chabot Coll., 1968-69; tech. adv. com. Office Health Maintenance Orgns., Dept. Health and Human Services, 1980—. Bd. dirs., exec. com., v.p. Alameda County Easter Seal Soc.; pres. Aquabears AAU Swim Club. Served to 1st lt. USAR, 1956-58; col. Res. Mem. Am. Coll. Hosp. Adminstrs., Am. Public Health Assn., Am. Hosp. Assn., Calif. Hosp. Assn., Med. Group Mgmt. Assn., Group Health Assn. Am., Internat. Found. Employee Benefit Plans. Episcopalian. Clubs: World Trade, Oakland Athletic, Athenian-Nile. Home: 108 Sullivan Dr Moraga CA 94556 Office: 1 Kaiser Plaza Oakland CA 94612

CUSUMANO, JAMES ANTHONY, chem. co. exec.; b. Elizabeth, N.J., Apr. 14, 1942; s. Charles Anthony and Carmella Madeline (Catalano) C.; B.A., Rutgers U., 1964, Ph.D., 1968; m. Sonja Ingrid Larson, Sept. 13, 1964; 1 dau., Doreen Ann. Chemist, Exxon Research and Engring. Co., Linden, N.J., 1967-74; pres. Catalytica Assos., Inc., Santa Clara, Calif., 1974—, also dir. Henry Rutgers scholar, 1963-64. Mem. Am. Chem. Soc., Catalysts Soc., Am. Phys. Soc. Patentee in catalysis; author: Catalysis in Coal Conversion, 1979. Home: 3376 Villa Robleda Dr Mountain View CA 94040 Office: 3255 Scott Blvd Suite 7E Santa Clara CA 95051

CUSUMANO, WANDA CELESTA, educational administrator; b. Twin Falls, Idaho, Jan. 25, 1944; d. Samuel Benjamin and Inez Mae (Chamberlain) Martin; m. Douglas John Cusumano, Aug. 16, 1969; 1 dau., Christine Ann. B.S. in Edn., U. Idaho, 1966; M.A. in Edn., Stanford U., 1969; postgrad. U. Pacific. Tchr. Salinas City Sch. Dist. (Calif.), 1966-68; tchr. San Juan Unified Sch. Dist., Sacramento, Calif., 1969; resource tchr., tchr. Clovis Unified Sch. Dist. (Calif.), 1970-79, coordinator spl. projects, 1980—; cons. Fresno County Dept. Edn., 1979-80. Active YWCA Edn. for Youth Program, 1974-75, YWCA Fitness Program, 1980-83. Recipient outstanding contbn. award Tchr. Edn. Council, 1981; Stanford U. tchr. fellow, 1968-69; Mem. Calif. Reading Assn., Fresno Reading Assn., Assn. Calif. Sch. Administrs., Assn. for Supervision and Curriculum Devel., Stanford Alumni Club of Fresno, Alumni Assn. U. Idaho. Delta Kappa Gamma (scholar 1983). Contbr. to profl. jours. Office: 5545 E Herndon Ave Clovis CA 93612

CUTHBERTSON, ROBERT FRED, physician; b. Phoenix, Dec. 15, 1929; s. Fred A. and Mary Catherine (Crowell) C.; student Phoenix Jr. Coll., 1947-49, U. Calif.-Berkeley, 1949-50; M.D., U. So. Calif., 1954; m. Shirley June Hermann, June 27, 1953; children—Robert Fred, Karen Suzanne, Susan Lynn. Intern, Los Angeles County Gen. Hosp., 1954-55; resident U.S. Naval Sch. of Aviation Medicine, Pensacola, Fla., 1955-56; practice family medicine, Phoenix, 1958—; pres. Saguaro Med. Center, Phoenix, 1969—; preceptor U. Utah Sch. Medicine, 1974—; chmn. com. designing health edn. State of Ariz., 1973—; bd. dirs. Physicians Health Plan. Bus. project mgr. Jr. Achievement, 1981. Served as lt. comdr., M.C., USNR, 1955-60. Diplomate Am. Bd. Family Practice. Fellow Am. Acad. Family Physicians; mem. AMA, Soaring Soc. Am. Mem. Ch. Jesus Christ of Latter-day Saints. Club: Rotary (past pres.). Office: Saguaro Med Center Ltd 4426 E Indian Sch Rd Phoenix AZ 85018

CUTLER, MARTHA MARIE EMERY, publishing executive; b. Lodi, Calif., Sept. 15, 1939; d. Wallace Haile and Elizabeth Dorothy Emery; m. David H. Cutler, Dec. 6, 1959; children—Geoffrey Horton, Gregory Abbott. B.A. in Elem. Edn., Calif. State U.-Los Angeles, 1965. Corp. v.p. Merchant Mag., Inc., Newport Beach, Calif., 1965—, also dir.; corp. v.p. Cutler Pub., Inc., Newport Beach, 1981—, also dir. Mem. Jr. League Newport Harbor. Recipient award for vol. hours given to Huntington Meml. Hosp., Huntington Meml. Clinic Aux., Pasadena, Calif., 1972. Republican. Episcopalian. Clubs: Newport Beach Tennis, Seaview Swim and Tennis. Home: 2011 Yacht Vindex Newport Beach CA 92660 Office: 4500 Campus Dr Suite 480 Newport Beach CA 92660

CUTLER, NEAL EVAN, gerontologist, educator; b. Chgo., Aug. 31, 1943; s. Philip Arthur and Mary (Becker) C. divorced; children—Kari Philip, Jori Lance. Ph.D. in Polit. Sci., Northwestern U., 1968. Research scientist Oak Ridge Nat. Lab., 1968-69; asst. prof. U. Pa., 1969-73; sr. research assoc. in gerontology prof. polit. sci. U. So. Calif., Los Angeles, 1973—; Fulbright research fellow Helsinki U., 1972-73; profl. staff mem. U.S. Senate Com. Aging, 1979-81; adj. research assoc. Bur. Social Sci. Research, Nat. Council Aging. Author: Aging, Public Policy and Politics, 1983; editorial bd. Aging and Society, The Gerontologist, Exptl. Aging, Aging and Work; contbr. articles to profl. jours. Zoning commr. Hermosa Beach, Calif. Fellow Gerontol. Soc. Am.; mem. Am. Polit. Sci. Assn., Am. Sociol. Assn., Western Gerontol. Soc. Office: Gerontology Center U So Calif Los Angeles CA 90082

CUTLER, RUTH ELLEN LEMON, aircraft company official, publisher; b. York, Nebr., Feb. 26, 1928; d. Harry Oliver and Ruby Elizabeth (Hartgrave) Lemon; student Latter-day Saints Bus. Coll., 1946; m. Harold Max Cutler, Nov. 17, 1944 (div. 1971); children—Sheryl, Harold Max, Pamela. Sec., photostat operator IRS, Salt Lake City, 1951-54; sec. Purdue U. Sch. Civil Engring., West Lafayette, Ind. and engring. firms, 1954-60; exec. sec. Rico Argentine Mining Co., Salt Lake City and Rico, Colo., 1960-63; exec., legal sec. Manpower, Inc., Salt Lake City, 1959-71; owner, operator Mountain View Motel and Country Club Motel, Salt Lake City, 1963-64; exec. sec., adminstrv. asst. to clin. psychologist in pvt. practice, Salt Lake City, 1964-70; legal sec., head office staff Watkins & Faber, attys., Salt Lake City, 1971-73; adminstrv. sec. F-15 Radar div. Hughes Aircraft Co., Culver City, Calif., 1973—; founder, pres., pub., pres. Gallant House, Inc., Heber City, Utah, 1983—; dir., v.p., sec. Cutler Enterprises, Inc., Salt Lake City, 1963-71. State del. Utah Republican party, 1967-69; active various community drives. Mem. League Utah Writers. Address: 2027 S Spaulding Ave Los Angeles CA 90016

CUTTER, DAVID LEE, pharmaceutical company executive; b. Oakland, Calif., Jan. 3, 1929; s. Robert Kennedy and Virginia (White) C.; student U. Calif. at Berkeley, 1947; A.B., Stanford, 1950, M.B.A., 1952; m. Nancy Lee Baugh, Sept. 14, 1950; children—David Lee, Thomas White, William Baugh, Steven Kennedy, Michael Lee. Staff acct. Webb & Webb, C.P.A.'s, San Francisco, 1952-54; with Cutter Labs., Inc., 1954—, pres., 1967-74, chmn., 1974-80, vice-chmn., 1980—, also dir.; dir. Bills Drugs, Inc., Lafayette, Calif., CHAD Therapeutics, Inc., Woodland, Calif. Active various community drives; mem. Citizens Com. to Study Discrimination in Housing, Berkeley, 1961-62; troop committeeman Boy Scouts Am., Berkeley, 1964-74, v.p. Mt. Diablo council, 1975-77, pres., 1978-80; pres. Golden Gate Scounting, Berkeley, Calif., 1981—; mem. Accrediting Commn. on Edn. in Health Services Adminstrn., 1982—. Bd. dirs. Park Hills Homes Assn., 1961-63, Alameda County (Calif.) Taxpayers Assn., 1967-69, Insts. Med. Scis., San Francisco, 1974-76. Hosp. Council No. Calif., 1983—; pres. Cutter Found., Emeryville, Calif., 1973—; mem. adv. bd. Herrick Hosp., 1968-76, trustee, 1976—, pres. bd. trustees, 1978—; trustee San Francisco Bay Area Council, 1968—, United Way of Bay Area, 1981—; mem. adv. council Sch. Bus., San Francisco State Coll., 1966-70. C.P.A., Calif. Mem. Am. Inst. C.P.A.'s, Calif. Soc. C.P.A.'s, Med.-Surg. Mgrs. Assn. (dir. 1971-73), Pharm. Mfrs. Assn. (dir. 1972-78), Stanford Alumni Assn., Berkeley C. of C. (dir. 1977-83), Delta Upsilon. Club: Rotary. Home: 3749 St Francis Dr Lafayette CA 94549 Office: 2200 Powell St Emeryville CA 94608

DAAR, DAVID, lawyer; b. Chgo., May 23, 1931; s. Julius and May (Scheps) D.; A.B., Sacramento State Coll., 1955; J.D., Loyola U., Los Angeles, 1956; m. Thelma Greta Schwartz, Dec. 20, 1953; children—Jeffery Jay, Eric Steven, Karen Lynn. Admitted to Calif. bar, 1956, U.S. Supreme Ct. bar, 1969; prin. firm David Daar & Assos., Los Angeles, 1956-75; prin. firm Daar & Newman, P.C., Los Angeles, 1975-78; prin. firm. Miller & Daar, P.C., Beverly Hills, Calif., San Francisco, Reno, Seattle, and Milw., 1978—; mem. faculty Nat. Coll. Advocacy, Hastings. Sch. Law. Mem. State Bar Calif. (chmn. com. on fed. cts. 1972). Club: Friars (Los Angeles). Office: 9100 Wilshire Blvd Beverly Hills CA 90212

DABELL, RICHARD W., psychologist; b. Idaho Falls, Idaho, Nov. 11, 1951; s. Burdette and Dorothy (Williams) D.; m. Hoda Mahmoudi, June 21, 1975; 1 son, Bijan. B.S., U. Utah, 1974, M.S., 1978, Ph.D., 1979. Lic. psychologist, Utah. Psychologist, Utah Div. Mental Health, Salt Lake County, 1979-82, psychologist div. rehab., 1981—. Recipient Carnegie Hero Fund ednl. award, 1972. Mem. Am. Psychol. Assn., Utah Psychol. Assn., AAAS. Baha'i. Contbr. articles to profl. jours. Home: 3501 Millstream Ln Salt Lake City UT 84109 Office: 1151 S Redwood Rd Salt Lake City UT 84104

DABNEY, WILLIAM KROEHLE, corporation executive; b. Cleve., June 22, 1933; s. John Carpenter and Mary Ellen (Kroehle) D.; m. Valerie Daniels, Aug. 10, 1962; children—Monica Kroehle, Joseph Daniels, Fiona MacFarlane. A.B., Harvard U., 1955; M.B.A., Columbia U., 1960. Treas., Dictaphone Corp., 1969-75; asst. treas. Internat. Paper Co., 1975-78; sr. v.p. fin. Diamond Sunsweet Inc., 1978-79; pres. Diamond Walnut Growers and Sunsweet Growers, Stockton, Calif., 1979-80; exec. v.p. Sun-Diamond Growers of Calif., Stockton, 1980—. Served to capt. USAF, 1956-58. Mem. Fin. Execs. Inst., Dried Fruit Assn., Nat. Council of Farmer Coops., Walnut Mktg. Bd., Prune Mktg. Commn., Calif. Prune Bd. Club: English Speaking Union. Contbr. articles to publs. Office: 1050 S Diamond St Stockton CA 95201

DACKAWICH, S. JOHN, sociologist, educator; b. Loch Galley, W. Va., Jan. 31, 1926; s. Samuel and Estelle (Jablonski) D.; m. Shirley J. Mc Vay, May 20, 1950; children—Robert, Nancy. B.A., U. Md., 1955; Ph.D., U. Colo., 1957. Asst. prof. Colo. State U., 1957-59; asst. prof. to prof. Calif. State U., Long Beach, 1959-70, dept. chmn., 1968-70; prof. Calif. State U., Fresno, 1970—, dept. chmn., 1970-75. Contbr. articles to profl. publs. Fresno County Econ. Opportunity commr., 1971-75. Served with USMC, 1943-46, AUS, 1950-52. U. Colo. grad. fellow, 1955-57. Mem. Am. Sociol. Assn. Quaker. Club: Riverside Mens Golf (Fresno). Office: Calif State U Fresno CA 93720

DADE, PHILIP EUGENE, agronomist; b. Hutchinson, Kans., Feb. 2, 1929; s. Philip Oliver and Gladys Mae (Dean) D.; B.S., Kans. State Coll., 1951, M.S., 1952; Ph.D., Wash. State U., 1959; m. Caroline Anne Esser, Mar. 31, 1956; children—Susanne Jeanne, Norman Eugene, Karen Lee. Research agronomist U.S. Dept. Agr., Prosser, Wash., 1957-67; research agronomist O. M. Scott & Sons Co., Gervais, Oreg., 1967-74, mgr. seed research and prodn., 1974—; mem. tech. subcom. field burning Oreg. Dept. Environ. Quality, 1982—. Served with U.S. Army, 1953-55. Cert. profl. agronomist. Mem. Oreg. Seed Trade Assn. (dir. 1980—, sec.-treas. 1981-82, pres. 1982-83), Am. Seed Trade Assn., Am. Soc. Agronomy, Crop Sci. Soc. Am., Sigma Xi, Alpha Zeta. Office: 7644 Keene Rd NE Gervais OR 97026

DADISMAN, LYNN ELLEN, tax shelter sales executive, writer; b. Los Angeles, Mar. 1, 1946; d. Orlan Sidney and Erna Lou (Harris) Friedman; m. Kent Dadisman, May 1973 (div. 1974). Student UCLA, 1963-65, 71-72, Willis Bus. Coll., 1965-66, Fin. Schs. Am., 1982, Viewpoints Inst., 1970-71. Office mgr. Harleigh Sandler Co., Los Angeles, 1965-67; customer service Investors Diversified Services, West Los Angeles, Calif., 1968-76; exec. sec. McCulloch Oil Corp., West Los Angeles, 1976; mgr. publs. Security 1st Group, Century City, Calif., 1976-80; office mgr. Morehead & Co., Century City, 1980-81; dir. mktg., mgr. customer service Ins. Mktg. Services, Santa Monica, Calif., 1981-82; v.p. Decatur Petroleum Corp., Santa Monica, 1982-83; assoc. dir. Am. Devel. Corp., Los Angeles, 1983—. Mem. Nat. Assn. Securities Dealers, Internat. Assn. Fin. Planning. Club: Migi Car Am. (sec., newsletter editor) (Placentia, Calif.). Fin. and ins. writer; contbr. poetry to UCLA Literary Mag., 1964. Home: 3442 Centinela Ave Apt 15 Los Angeles CA 90066

DAEFIELD, CHARLEEN KAY, tax preparer and consultant; b. Oakland, Calif., Nov. 5, 1950; d. Donald Norbert and Carleen Charlotte (Sappenfield) D. B.S. in Bus. Adminstn. (Acctg.), Calif. State U.-Hayward, 1974, M.B.A. in Taxation, 1979. Enrolled agt., U.S. Dept.

Treasury. Acct., trainer Oakland (Calif.) Park and Recreation Dept., 1977-78; instr. acctg. and taxation Chabot Coll., Hayward, 1979; asst. prof. mgmt. Sonoma State U., Rohnert Park, Calif., 1979-83; pvt. practice tax preparer and cons., Castro Valley, 1977—; dir. Inst. for Small Bus. Devel., Sonoma State U., 1980-82. Mem. Met. Mus. Art, N.Y.C., Williamsburg Found.; mem. Alameda County Hist. Soc., Oakland, Hayward Hist. Soc., Calif. Careers Alive, Inc., San Leandro, Mem. Nat. Assn. Enrolled Agts., Calif. Soc. Enrolled Agts., Nat. Soc. Pub. Accts., Nat. Assn. Accts., Am. Acctg. Assn., East Bay-San Francisco Assn. Enrolled Agts. (bd. dirs. 1982—), Castro Valley C. of C. Republican. Office: Charleen Daefield 20880 Baker Rd Suite 10 Castro Valley CA 94546

DAGESS, GERALD LAWRENCE, data co. exec.; b. New Bedford, Mass., July 28, 1922; s. Arcade Lawrence and Emma Ann (McAuley) D.; B.S., Boston U., 1944; M.S., Columbia U., 1954; m. Stella Duckett, Feb. 22, 1944. Dir. trade relations Atlantic-Richfield Corp., Phila., 1955-62; v.p. trade relations Continental Copper & Steel Corp., NYC, 1962-72; v.p., treas. Diagnostic Data Inc., Mt. View, Calif., 1972—, also dir.; v.p., treas. VOCON Inc., 1970—; pres., chief exec. officer BDN Corp., Sacramento, 1982—; dir. Photo Voltaic div. Columbia Chase Corp., Braintree, Mass. Winn West Inc., 1977—; cons. Terra Fin. Corp. Mem. Met. C. of C., Builders Internat. Assn. Republican. Roman Catholic. Clubs: Met. (N.Y.C.); Sharon Hts., Country, Country Club of New Bedford, Elks, Peninsula Businessmen's, Rancho Murieta Country. Home: 5 Whitney Ct Menlo Park CA 94025 Office: Diagnostic Data Inc 518 Logue Ave Mountain View CA 94043

DAHL, PETER REYNOLD, psychologist; b. St. Paul, Nov. 4, 1946; s. Ervin Reynold and Norah Blythe (Peters) D.; B.A., Macalester Coll., 1968; Ph.D., U. Minn. (NDEA fellow), 1973. Faculty, U. Redlands (Calif.), 1972-74; sr. research scientist Am. Insts. for Research, Palo Alto, Calif., 1974-83; ednl./rehab. program evaluator. NIH grantee, 1979-81; nat. policy fellow Council Chief State Sch. Officers, Washington, 1981-82. Mem. Nat. Center for a Barrier-Free Environment, Rehab. Engring. Soc. N. Am., Council for Exceptional Children, Am. Vocat. Assn. Author: Mainstreaming Guidebook for Vocational Educators, 1978; Vocational Opportunities, 1978; Training the Handicapped for Productive Employment, 1980; editor: Career Information Delivery for Handicapped Individuals, 1981; contbr. articles to profl. jours. Home: 1170 Ribier Ct Sunnyvale CA 94609 Office: PO Box 1113 Palo Alto CA 94302

DAHLBACKA, GLEN HAMILTON, physicist; b. Wakefield, Mich., Jan. 29, 1946; s. Toivo M. and Mildred L. (Korpela) D.; B.S. in Physics with distinction, U. Ill., 1968; Ph.D. in Physics, U. Minn., 1972; m. Rena Rickles; children—Matthew Hamilton, Nara Reitta. With Lawrence Livermore (Calif.) Lab., 1972-76; staff physicist, group leader Physics Internat., San Leandro, Calif., 1976-80, mgr. radiation and plasma physics dept., 1980—. Mem. Livermore Planning Commn., 1974-76; mem. Livermore City Council, 1974-80; mem. Calif. Democratic Central Com., 1976-80; mem. environ. and energy com. League Calif. Cities, 1975-80; past bd. dirs. State Solid Waste Mgmt. Bd. Mem. Am. Phys. Soc., Soc. Profl. Scientists and Engrs. (past bd. dirs.), Livermore Heritage Guild. Unitarian. Contbr. articles to profl. jours. Patentee in laser fusion. Home: 5675 Chappell Pl Oakland CA 94619 Office: 2700 Merced St San Leandro CA 94577

DAHLEN, ALICE LOUISE, nursing administrator; b. Kenmare, N.D., Nov. 22, 1934; d. Gudmund Bernhard and Alice Marie (Gissel) Rundstrom; student Augsburg Coll., 1952-53; diploma in nursing Emanuel Hosp. Sch. Nursing, 1956; B.S. in Nursing, U. Oreg. Health Scis. Center, 1969, M.S. in Nursing Edn., 1971; Ph.D. in Health Services Adminstrn., Columbia Pacific U.; m. Charles Raymond Dahlen, Mar. 16, 1957; children—Kirsten Ann, Lisa Elaine. Sch. nurse Hillcrest Sch. for Girls, 1957-58; nursing home adminstr. Salem (Oreg.) Methodist Home, 1963-64, Willamette Lutheran Home, Salem, 1966-67; asst. dir. nursing service Emanuel Hosp., Portland, 1970-73; dir. nursing service Meridian Park Hosp., Tualatin, Oreg., 1973—; mem. clin. faculty U. Oreg. Health Scis. Center, 1974—. Mem. Oreg. League Nursing (pres. 1980-82), Nat. League Nursing (bd. dirs., exec. com. 1983-85), Am., Oreg. (past pres. dist. 1) nurses assns., Am. Soc. for Hosp. Nursing Service Adminstrs., Portland Council Dirs. Nursing Service and Edn. (chmn. 1976), Oreg. Soc. Nursing Adminstrs. (chmn. 1977, pres. 1978), Sigma Theta Tau. Republican. Lutheran. Home: 7455 Bunker Post Ct Charbonneau Wilsonville OR 97070 Office: 19300 SW 65th Ave Tualatin OR 97062

DAHLEN, GARY WAYNE, air force officer; b. Fargo, N.D., Apr. 27, 1948; s. Lawrence Harold and Helen Elizabeth (Johnson) D.; B.S., U.S. Air Force Acad., 1970; M.B.A., U. Denver, 1978. Commd. 2d lt. U.S. Air Force, 1970, advanced through grades to maj. 1982; pilot tng., Craig AFB, Ala., 1970-72; space def. systems analyst 1st Aerospace Control Squadron, Colorado Springs, 1972-73; sensor space surveillance officer Shemya AFB, Alaska, 1973-74; space systems staff officer 14th Aerospace Force, Ent AFB, Colo., 1974-75; space def. systems staff officer Hdqrs. N. Am. Air Def. Command-Aerospace Def. Command, Colorado Springs, 1975-78; student Air Command and Staff Coll., Colorado Springs, 1978-79; system program mgr. Maui (Hawaii) Optical Sta., Def. Advanced Research Project Agy., 1979-82; space systems staff officer Hdqrs. Space Command, Peterson AFB, Colorado Springs, Colo., 1982—. Decorated Air Force Commendation medal (2), Def. Meritorious Service medal. Mem. Assn. M.B.A. Execs., Assn. Grads. USAF Acad. Republican. Lutheran. Home: 4 Escondido Valle Manitou Springs CO 80829 Office: Hdqrs Space Command DOZ Peterson AFB CO 80914

DAHLGREN, RONALD EARL, hospital administrator; b. Los Angeles, Oct. 16, 1939; s. Harold Oscar and Doris Goldie (Jones) D.; m. Elizabeth Dahlgren; children—Jeff, Nels, Jonas. A.A., Fullerton Jr. Coll., 1960; B.A., Whittier Coll., 1962; M.P.H., UCLA, 1971. Tchr., South Whittier (Calif.) Sch. Dist. and Lowell Joint Sch. Dist., 1962-65; dist. mgr. Los Angeles chpt. ARC, South Gate, Calif., 1966-69; dir. edn. and tng. St. Francis Hosp., Lynwood, Calif., 1969; hosp. adminstr. Grossmont Dist. Hosp., La Mesa, Calif., 1971—; adj. prof. San Diego State U., 1981—. Mem. community health com. Health Systems Agy. of San Diego and Imperial Counties; mem. coalition action program rev. com. San Diego Med. Care Found; bd. dirs. Grossmont Coll. Found. Mem. Calif. Sch. Bd. Assn., Am. Coll. Hosp. Adminstrs., Health Care Execs. Assn. San Diego County, Health Care Fin. Mgmt. Assn., Hosp. Council of San Diego and Imperial Counties. Quaker. Lodge: Kiwanis. Office: Grossmont Dist Hosp 5555 Grossmont Ctr Dr La Mesa CA 92041

DAHLGREN, THEODORE EUGENE, hosp. adminstr.; b. Hallock, Minn., Apr. 4, 1929; s. John Elmer and Lily Minetta (Nelson) D.; A.A., Luther Coll., 1949; B.Sc., Omaha U., 1956; M.H.A., Washington U., St. Louis, 1958; m. Carol Jean Nelson, June 10, 1949. Salesman, Firestone Tire & Rubber Co., Council Bluffs, Iowa, 1949-51; accountant Nebr. Bridge Supply & Lumber Co., Omaha, 1951-52, 54-55, Bishop Clarkson Meml. Hosp., Omaha, 1955-56; adminstrv. resident Bethany Hosp., Kansas City, Kans., 1957-58; adminstrv. asst. Luth. Hosp. Soc. So. Calif., Los Angeles, 1958-59, asst. controller, 1959-60, controller, 1960-63, regional v.p., 1972-75; asst. adminstr. Calif. Hosp., Los Angeles, 1963-65; exec. dir. Martin Luther Hosp., Anaheim, Calif., 1965-73; dir. Hosp.-Pathologist Central Lab. Orange County, treas., 1970-71, sec., 1971-72, pres., 1972-73; v.p. Hosp. Asso. Supply Services Corp., 1974-75; sr. v.p. Pacific Health Resources, Inc. subs. Luth. Hosp. Soc. So. Calif., 1975—; mem. adv. com. Blue Cross, 1973-75; dir. Orange County Health Planning Council, 1974-79; bd. dirs. Calif. Luth. Homes, 1974—, pres., 1981—. Served with AUS, 1952-54; ETO. Mem. Am. Coll. Hosp. Adminstrs., Calif. Health Care Providers Assn. (treas. 1971-74, pres. 1974-75), Hosp. Council So. Calif. (dir. chmn. ins. com. 1962-72), Washington U. Hosp. Adminstrn. Alumni Assn. (pres. 1962-63), Anaheim C. of C. (dir. 1972-75), Delta Sigma Pi. Republican. Lutheran. Home: 1327 Dana Pl Fullerton CA 92631 Office: 1423 S Grand Ave Los Angeles CA 90015

DAHLQUIST, RALPH LEON, atomic spectroscopist; b. Springfield, Minn., Jan. 21, 1941; s. Clair W. and Elizabeth M. (Foy) D.; children—Russell, Hannah, Robert. Quality assurance tech. rep. Jefferson Electronics, Santa Barbara, Calif., 1959-64; research scientist Hasler Research Center, Santa Barbara, 1964-77; research spectroscopist Applied Research Labs, Sunland, Calif., 1978-80, div. staff, analytical cons., 1980—. Recipient IR-100 award, 1975; Pres.'s award for outstanding tech. achievement, 1981. Mem. AAAS, Soc. for Applied Spectroscopy. Contbr. numerous publs. and holder patents in field of spectrochemistry. Office: Applied Research Labs 9545 Wentworth Blvd Sunland CA 91040

DAHN, WILLIAM JOHN, accountant; b. Billings, Mont., June 21, 1946; s. John Charles and Mirriam C. (Delong) D. A.A. with honors, Oreg. Tech. Inst., 1967; B.S., So. Oreg. Coll., 1969. C.P.A., Oreg. Sr. acct. Barret, Chamberlain & Co., Gardena, Calif., 1970-74; acct., Los Angeles, 1974-77; fin. v.p. Marco Dental Products Co., North Plains, Oreg., 1977-79; internal auditing dept. head Am. Guaranty Fin. Corp., Portland, Oreg., 1979-80; C.P.A. practice, Beaverton, Oreg., 1980—. Treas., Metzger Meth. Ch. Mem. Oreg. Soc. C.P.A.s, Phi Theta Kappa. Democrat. Office: 8196 SW Hall St Suite 206 Beaverton OR 97005

DAHY, EDWARD JOHN, education specialist; b. Los Angeles, June 21, 1930; s. Edward John Jr. and June Claudia (Thompson) D.; m. Nancy Ann Paul, Sept. 24, 1952; children—Edward John, James Patrick, Mary Elizabeth, Paul Christopher. A.B., Gonzaga U., 1952; M.A., Mont. State U., 1957, Ed.D., 1977. Tchr., Absarokee, Belt, Mont., 1955-57; Served with USMC, 1957-71; moved up through ranks to lt. col., 1970; supr. student tchrs. Coll. Gt. Falls, Mont., 1971-72; prin., Centerville, Mont., 1973-77; Navy Edn. specialist State Mont., Butte, 1977—. Decorated Bronze Star with V, others; recipient Edn. Specialist of Yr. award, 1982. Mem. NEA, Am. Personnel and Guidance Assn., Am. Vocat. Assn., Mil. Educators and Counselors Assn., Marine Corps Assn., Phi Delta Kappa. Roman Catholic. Home: 104 Star Ln Butte MT 59701 Office: NRAS Butte Finlen Complex 100 E Broadway Butte MT 59701

DAILEY, CHARLES ANDREW, mus. dir.; b. Denver, May 25, 1935; s. Avery and Lollie (Johnson) D.; B.A., U. Colo., 1962; m. Carol Jo Kane, Jan. 31, 1959; children—Travis Ashkee, Buffy Jo. Mus. preparator, dioramist U. Colo., Boulder, 1958-60; exhibit specialist Mus. No. Ariz., Flagstaff, 1961-62; curator in charge exhbns. Mus. N.Mex., Santa Fe, 1964-72; dir. Inst. Am. Indian Art, Santa Fe, 1972—; one-man shows include: U. Colo., 1961, Gallery Five, Santa Fe, 1965; group shows include: J. F. Kennedy Performing Arts, Washington, 1972; Fiesta Biennial, 1964, 65, 68, SW Biennial, 1968, Mus. of N. Mex., N.Mex. State Fairs 1968, Coll. of Santa Fe, 1981; represented in Vt. collections. Mem. Nat. Profl. Ski Patrol, 1962-74; coach Jr. League Soccer Program, Santa Fe grade schs., 1975—. Served with USMC, 1954-56. Recipient Student award Inst. Am. Indian Art, 1977, 82. Mem. Am. Assn. Museums, N.Mex. Assn. Museums, Mountain Plains Mus. Assn., Canadian Mus. Assn., N.Mex. Soccer League. Author: Creating A Crowd, 1970; Museums Problems Handbook, 1974; Museum Theory Handbook, 1974; Setting Up A Small Museum, 1979. Home: 1369 Cerrillos Rd Santa Fe NM 87501 Office: 1300 Cerrillos Rd Santa Fe NM 87501

DAILEY, FRED WILLIAM, hotel exec.; b. Aurora, Ill., Feb. 3, 1908; s. Louis A. and Frances (McCoy) D.; m. Elizabeth Murphy, Apr. 22, 1946; 1 son, Michael K. Builder, operator tourist resorts, 1933-42; builder, So. Calif., 1946-52; pres. Mokuleia Assos., Mokuleia Polo Farms, Inc., Waikiki Corp., A.D. Corp. Adv. bd. Hawaii, Army; past mem. Honolulu Bd. Water Supply. Served as maj. AUS, World War II. Decorated Purple Heart. Mem. U.S. Air Force Assn., C. of C., Hawaii Hotel Assn. (past pres.), Hawaii Horse Show Assn. (past pres.), Hawaii Polo and Racing Assn. (pres.), U.S. Polo Assn. (past gov.). Clubs: Los Angeles Athletic; Army and Navy (Chgo. and N.Y.C.); Waikiki Polo (Honolulu); Santa Barbara Polo; Big Bend Ranch (pres.) (Korbel); Mad River Polo. Author: Blood, Sweat and Jeers; One Man's Meat. Address: Waikikian Hotel Honolulu HI 96815 also Mokuleia Polo Farm Inc Oahu HI 96815

DAILEY, MICHAEL DENNIS, painter; b. Des Moines, Aug. 2, 1938. B.A., M.F.A., U. Iowa. Exhibited in one-man shows: Tacoma Art Museum, 1966, 75, U. Wis., Madison, 1967, Francine Seders Gallery, Seattle, 1971, 73, 76, 78, Fountain Gallery, Portland, Oreg., 1971, 73, 77, William Sawyer Gallery, San Francisco, 1972, 74, 76, U. Idaho, Moscow, 1974; group shows: Mercyhurst Col. (Purchase award), Erie, Pa., 1965, Ohio U., Athens, 1965, St. Paul Art Ctr., 1966, 68, Wash. State U., (First Pl. award in painting), 1967, Seattle Art Mus. (N.W. Watercolor Soc. award), 1970, Denver Art Mus., 1971, San Francisco Mus. Art, 1975, Smithsonian Inst., Washington, 1974; represented in permanent collections: Smithsonian Inst., Munic Gallery Modern Art, Dublin, Ireland, Seattle Art Mus., Mercyhurst Coll., Mus. Modern Art, N.Y.C.

DAINA, BERNARD LEONARD, clinical psychologist, air force officer; b. Bklyn., Apr. 18, 1950; s. Mordecai Max and Gertrude Rose (Klahr) D.; m. Susan Keller, Mar. 10, 1974; 1 dau., Amber Deborah. B.A. in English, Rutgers Coll., 1972; M.S. in Psychology, Howard U., 1976, Ph.D. in Clin and Community Psychology, 1980. Lic. clin. psychologist, Colo. Commd. 2d lt. U.S. Army Res., 1972; advanced through grades to capt. U.S. Air Force, 1980; fed. intern, social sci. analyst U.S. Census Bur., Washington, 1975-76; extern clin. psychology NIMH St. Elizabeths Hosp., Washington, 1977-78; intern clin. psychology McLean Hosp., Belmont, Mass., clin. fellow psychology Harvard Med. Sch., Boston, 1979-80; clin psychologist U.S. Air Force 3320th Correction and Rehab. Squadron, Lowry AFB, Colo., 1980—; part-time pvt. practice psychology, 1983—. Mem. Am. Psychol. Assn., Colo. Psychol. Assn., Air Force Soc. Clin Psychologists. Jewish. Contbr. articles to profl. jours. Home: 11679 E Dakota Ave Aurora CO 80012 Office: 3320th Correction and Rehab Squadron Lowry AFB CO 80230

DAINES, DELVA, education educator, author; b. Smithfield, Utah, Jan. 12; d. Hazen Benjamin and Sarah E. (Buck) Daines; 1 dau., Sally Ann. B.S., Utah State U., M.S.; Ed.D., Wash. State U.; postgrad. Tchrs. Coll., Columbia U. Nursery sch., elem. tchr., Utah; teaching asst. U. Minn.; supr. Bonneville County Elem. Schs., Idaho Falls, Idaho; dir. student teaching Ricks Coll., Rexburg, Idaho; supr. elem. edn. Idaho State, Boise; now prof. edn. Brigham Young U., Provo, Utah; adv. com. chmn. numerous doctoral candidates, presenter numerous profl. confs., workshop leader. Del. Women's State Legis. Council; bd. dirs. Brigham Young U. credit union; mem. Women's County Legis. Council; fundraiser March of Dimes, Easter Seals for Crippled Children; mem. Gov.'s Subcom. on Women. Research grantee McKay Inst., Coll. Edn., 1979-80, 82-83, 83-84, Brigham Young U., 1968; recipient Utah Internat. Reading Assn. award, 1981, Utah Woman Educator Achievement award, 1975, Karl G. Maeser disting. teaching award Brigham Young U., 1983. Mem. Internat. Reading Assn., Assn. Tchr. Educators, Nat. Council Tchrs. English, Assn. Supervision and Curriculum Devel., Nat. Conf. Research in English, Am. Ednl. Research Assn., Delta Kappa Gamma, Phi Kappa Phi. Republican. Mormon. Author: Reading in the Contents Areas: Strategies for Teachers, 1982. Numerous other publs. in field. Office: McKay Bldg Brigham Young U Provo UT 84602

DAJANI, JARIR SUBHI, civil engineer; b. Jerusalem, Apr. 5, 1940; s. Subhi T. and Lisa (Stori) D.; came to U.S., 1965, naturalized, 1974; B. Engring., Am. U. of Beirut, 1961; M.S., Stanford U., 1966; Ph.D. in Urban Systems Engring., Northwestern U., 1971; m. Rihab Dajani, Aug. 23, 1965; children—Jumana, Subhi, Dina. Asst. resident engr. Riyadh and Al-Khobar, Asso. Cons. Engrs., Saudi Arabia, 1961-62, resident engr., 1962-63, mgr. br. office, Amman, Jordan, 1963-65; estimator Bechtel Corp., San Francisco, 1966; project engr. Asso. Cons. Engring., Beirut, Lebanon, 1966-67; instr. constrn. mgmt. and bldg. constrn. Vocat. Tng. Center, Jerusalem, 1967-68; research asst. Northwestern U., Evanston, Ill., 1968-71; part-time asso. transp. and community planning, DeLeuw, Cather & Co., Chgo., 1968-71; asst. prof. civil engring. Duke U., Durham, N.C., 1971-75, asst. prof. civil engring. and policy scis., 1974-75, asso. prof. civil engring. and policy scis., 1975-76; asso. prof. civil engring., chmn. urban studies com. Stanford (Calif.) U., 1976-82; sr. tech. adv. Abu Dhabi Fund for Econ. Devel., 1982—; cons. to AID, 1978—, EPA, 1978—, FAA, 1976-77, IBRD (World Bank), 1979—; v.p. Public Systems Assos., Inc., Durham, 1974-78; mem. Transp. System Planning Group, Transp. Research Bd., NRC, 1971-76. Mem. ASCE, Am. Soc. Pub. Adminstrn., Ops. Research Soc. Am., Regional Sci. Assn., Am. Planning Assn., Sigma Xi. Author: (with Dennis Warner) Water and Sewer Development in Rural America, 1975; contbr. articles on urban systems engring. and planning to profl. jours.; asso. editor Jour. of High Speed Ground Transportation, 1977—; editorial bd. Policy Analysis and Information Systems, 1977—. Home: 1565 Klamath Dr Sunnyvale CA 94087 Office: PO Box 814 Abu Dhabi United Arab Emirates

DAKE, GLORIA HOPE REITZ, clinical psychologist; b. Hancock, Minn., Mar. 13, 1922; d. Herman Richard and Alvina Maria (Erdman) Reitz; m. D.C. Dake, Aug. 8, 1953; children—Shawn, Sanna Lee, Bruce. B.S., St. Cloud U., 1951; postgrad. U. Minn.; M.A., Long Beach State U., 1964; Ph.D., U.S. Internat. U., San Diego, 1974; lic. psychologist, Calif. Tchr. schs., Minn., Calif., Japan, 1942-53; psychometrist Long Beach (Calif.) Unified Sch. Dist., 1961-64; tchr. ednl. handicapped public schs., Bellflower, Calif., 1968-71; pvt. practice clin. psychology, Long Beach, 1969—, Lakewood, Calif., 1974—. Mem. Am. Psychol. Assn., Calif. Psychol. Assn. Democrat. Office: 5140 Palo Verde Ave Lakewood CA 90713

DALAL, ABDULHUSEIN SULEMAN, mental health consultant; b. Daressalaam, Tanzania, Feb. 17, 1926; came to U.S., 1964, naturalized, 1977; s. Suleman and Kulsum (Nanji) D.; B.A. with honors, Wadia Coll., Poona, India, 1950; M.A., U. Poona, 1961; postgrad. Boston U., 1964-66; Ph.D., Western Colo. U., 1973. Fellow, Postgrad. Center for Mental Health, N.Y.C., 1966-70; sr. clin. psychologist County Mental Health Center, Perth Amboy, N.J., 1967-69; dir. Klamath Mental Health Center, Klamath Falls, Oreg., 1971-81; co-dir. Inst. Integral Psychology, Ojai, Calif., 1982—. Recipient Sir Cusrow Wadia gold medal, 1950. Mem. World Union Internat. (Pondicherry, India) (life), Am. Psychol. Assn., Internat. Council Psychologists, Aurodarshan Internat. (dir.). Home and Office: 614 Grand Ave Box G Ojai CA 93023

DALBEY, DIANE, writer, magazine editor; b. Pasadena, Calif., Feb. 23, 1947; d. Marion Don and Lois Elizabeth Dalbey; student U. Ariz., Guadalajara, Mex., 1967; B.A. in English Composition, DePauw U., Greencastle, Ind., 1969; Asso. editor, then mng. editor Beverly Hills (Calif.) Courier, 1969-71; freelance writer, creative coordinator Joseph Byrd Prodns., 1971-72; asso. editor Tiger Beat, also Fave mags., 1972; editor Rona Barret spl. mags., 1972-73, Rona Barrett's monthly, 1973-77; sr. editor adult mag. div. Laufer Co. (name now D.S. Mags. Inc.), 1978-81, editor in chief Daytimers/Real Life mag., 1982-83; comedy writer Rick Dees RKO radio show, 1980; author teleplay Please StandBy, TV sitcom., 1979; contbg. editor Sat. Eve. Post, De Pauw U. Alumnus, Big Valley mag., TV Guide-Can.; promotions editor CBS-TV, Paramount-TV. Mem. Writers Guild Am., DePauw U. Alumni Assn., Kappa Kappa Gamma. Club: Hollywood Women's Press (bd. dirs. 1981—, rec. sec. 1981-83).

DALE, GARY CLIFFORD, advt. and mktg. exec.; b. Ellensburg, Wash., Apr. 6, 1944; s. Clifford T. and Evelyn R. D.; B.A. in Edn., Central Wash. State Coll., 1966; m. Sharon Horne, Nov. 22, 1980; children by previous marriage—Josh, Sara, Tracy. Tchr., Portland (Oreg.) Pub. Schs., 1966-67; sales, sales mgr. Cone Heiden Co., Seattle, 1967-75; sales Stein Co., Atlanta, 1975-76; pres. Dale Co., Seattle, 1976—. Mem. C. of C., Mcpl. League Seattle. Republican. Presbyterian. Clubs: Toastmasters, Fly Fishing of Wash. Office: 404 Larson Bldg Yakima WA 98901

DALE, JOHN MCCLELLAN, educational administrator; b. Fayetteville, Ark., June 24, 1934; s. Gilbert R. and Arna (Pursell) D.; m. Frances A. Bruner, Aug. 18, 1958; children—Elizabeth, John E., Sara. B.A., U. Colo., 1956; M.A., Colo. Coll., 1962; student Denver U. Profl. Ctr., 1968-70. Tchr., Pueblo, Colo., 1956-62, Barcelona Sch., Albuquerque, 1962-63; tchr., Aurora, Colo., 1963-66, prin., 1971—; instr. Met. State Coll., Denver. Bd. dirs. Denver Catholic Community Services; chmn. credit com. Aurora Pub. Sch. Fed. Credit Union; mem. Hoffman Heights Neighborhood Assn. Mem. Nat. Assn. Elem. Sch. Prins., Assn. Supervision and Curriculum Devel., Colo. Assn. Sch. Execs., Aurora Assn. Adminstrs. and Edn. Specialists (pres.), Dalton PTA, Sch. Execs. Aurora, Phi Delta Kappa, Phi Alpha Theta. Democrat. Contbr. articles to profl. jours. Home: 1179 Salem St Aurora CO 80011 Office: 17401 E Dartmouth Ave Aurora CO 80013

DALE, LEON ANDREW, educator; b. Paris, May 9, 1921; B.A., Tulane U., 1946; M.A., U. Wis., 1947, Ph.D., 1949; m. Arlene R. Dale; children—Glenn Roy, Melinda Jennifer. Asst. prof. economics U. Fla., 1949-50; internat. economist AFL, Paris, 1950-53, U.S. Dept. Labor, Washington, 1956-59; prof., chmn. dept. mgmt. and indsl. relations U. Bridgeport (Conn.), 1960-69; prof. mgmt. scis. and prodn. Calif. State Poly. U., Pomona, 1969—, acting chmn. bus. mgmt. dept., summer 1973; vis. prof. Columbia, 1966, 67; ind. cons., arbitrator, fact-finder; lectr. U. Wis., Milw., 1960. Served with AUS, 1942-45. Mem. Internat. Symposium on Small Bus. (U.S. steering com.), Am. Arbitration Assn. (nat. panel arbitrators, nat. pub. employment disputes settlement panel), Am. Econ. Assn., Acad. Polit. Sci., Am. Acad. Polit. and Social Sci., Indsl. Relations Research Assn., Soc. Profls. Dispute Resolution (charter). Author: Marxism and French Labor, 1956; A Bibliography of French Labor, 1969. Contbr. articles to profl. jours. Home: 30 S La Senda South Laguna CA 92677 Office: Calif State Poly U Pomona CA 91768

DALE, THERESA MARIE, writer/advertising specialist; b. Loma Linda, Calif., July 2, 1957; d. Colburn and Ruth E. Dale. B.A. in Communications/English cum laude, U. Redlands, 1979. Staff asst. Mobil Oil Corp., Los Angeles, 1979-80; promotional copywriter Beckman Instruments, Fullerton, Calif., 1980-82, advt. specialist, Carlsbad, Calif., 1982—; speaker, cons. in field. Mem. Am. Film Inst., Nature Conservancy. Mem. Bus./Prof. Advertisers Assn., Internat. Assn. Bus.

Communicators. Republican. Roman Catholic. Office: Beckman Instruments 6200 El Camino Real Carlsbad CA 92008

DALESSIO, DONALD JOHN, physician; b. Jersey City, Mar. 2, 1931; s. John Andre and Susan Dorothy D.; B.A., Wesleyan U., 1952; M.D., Yale U., 1956; m. Jane Catherine Schneider, Sept. 4, 1954; children—Catherine, James, Susan. Intern, N.Y. Hosp.-Cornell Med. Center, 1956-57, resident, 1959-61; resident Grace New Haven-Yale Med. Center, 1961-62; practice medicine specializing in neurology, La Jolla, Calif.; mem. staffs Green Hosp. of Scripps, Clinic, Univ. Hosp.; head, div. neurology Scripps Clinic & Research Found., La Jolla, Calif., 1964-71, chmn. dept. medicine, head, div. neurology, 1973-80, chief of staff Green Hosp. of Scripps Clinic, 1974-78, mem. Scripps Med. Group, 1980—; asso. dean for clin. affairs, prof. U. Ky., Lexington, 1971-72; clin. prof. neurology U. Calif., San Diego, 1974—. Pres., Nat. Migraine Found., 1977-80. Served to capt. M.C., U.S. Army, 1957-59. Fellow A.C.P., mem. Fedn. Western Socs. Neurol. Sci. (chmn. 1977), Am. Assn. Study Headache, Am. Acad. Neurology. Republican. Roman Catholic. Club: Torrey. Editor: Jour. Headache, 1964-74, 79—; editorial bd. Jour. AMA, 1977—. Home: 8891 Nottingham La Jolla CA 92037

DALEY, JOSEPH ANDREW, public relations consultant, labor arbitrator; b. Rome, N.Y., Sept. 18, 1927; s. Joseph A. and Catherine A. (Murphy) D.; m. Loraine Mathilda Hagemann, Oct. 5, 1955; 1 dau., Debora. A.B., Villanova U., 1951. Sr. v.p. Edward Gottlieb & Assocs., N.Y.C., 1955-68; v.p. pub. relations Continental Airlines, Los Angeles, 1968-80, Pan Am. World Airways, N.Y.C., 1980-82; cons. pub. relations, Tarzana, Calif., 1982—; lectr. in field. Recipient Pub. Relations award Am. Aviation and Space Writers Assn., 1978. Mem. Am. Arbitration Assn. Author: Exit With Drums, 1970; Spicy Lady, 1974. Home and Office: 18900 Ringling St Tarzana CA 91356

DALEY, VIRGINIA BROWN, retired educator, reading consultant; b. Chico, Calif., Nov. 7, 1918; d. Walter W. and Alice A. (Kinner) B.; B.A., San Francisco State Coll., 1953; M.A., U. LaVerne (Calif.), 1971; m. John W. Daley, Nov. 10, 1939; children—Virginia, Pamela. Elem. sch. tchr., then reading specialist schs. in Calif., 1949-70; reading specialist Lehigh Elem. Sch., Montclair, Calif., 1971-81; reading cons. West End Child Devel. Ctrs. Inc., 1981—; extension instr. U. Calif., Riverside, 1973, summer sch. lead tchr., 1974; cons., speaker in field. Mem. Internat. Reading Assn., NEA, Calif. Reading Assn., Reading Specialists Calif., Native Daus. Golden West (past chpt. pres.), Delta Kappa Gamma (past chpt. pres.). Republican. Episcopalian. Clubs: Order Eastern Star, Pomona Valley Lady Anglers.

DALISA, ANDREW LAWRENCE, business executive; b. Bklyn., July 30, 1940; s. Andrew Albert and Marie (Campbell) D.; B.S. in Physics, Poly. Inst. Bklyn., 1962; Ph.D., Adelphi U., 1966; m. Geraldine Theresa Spera, June 16, 1962; children—Christine, Andrew, Douglas. Prof., Monmouth Coll., West Bank, N.J., 1967-68; staff physicist CBS Labs., Stamford, Conn., 1968-69; program mgr. Philips Labs., Briarcliff Manor, N.Y., 1969-78; prof. Briarcliff Coll., 1970-73; gen. mgr. EPID div. Exxon Enterprises, Sunnyvale, Calif., 1978-82; founder, chief exec. officer, chmn. bd. Protolite Corp., San Jose, Calif., 1982—. Served to capt. C.E., AUS, 1966-68. NASA fellow, 1964-66; recipient Patent/Innovation award N.Am. Philips, 1971. Mem. Am. Phys. Soc., IEEE. contbr. to Display Devices, Vol. 40, 1978; contbr. articles to profl. jours. Patentee in field. Office: 985 Timothy Dr San Jose CA 95133

DALIVA, IRENEO DANCEL, pharm. mfg. corp. exec.; b. Makati, Philippines, Aug. 31, 1950; s. Ireneo C. and Iluminada C. (Dancel) D.; came to U.S. 1969, naturalized, 1976; B.Sc., Adamson U., Manila, 1969. Chemist, Peroxide & Spltys., San Francisco, 1969; head quality control Whiteworth, Inc., Gardena, Calif., 1970-73; partner Noren Co., Compton, Calif., 1973-75; pres., chmn. bd. Irenda Corp., Gardena, Calif., 1973—, cons. Pharmac Labs., Anpak Drugs, Wallich Labs., 1973-74. Mem. Am., Calif. pharm. assns., Los Angeles Jr. C. of C. Home: 12942 Crowley St Arleta CA 91331 Office: Irenda Corp 1852 W 169th St Gardena CA 90247

DALLAS, MERRY JO, textiles and clothing educator; b. Greeley, Colo., Jan. 3, 1941; d. Harold W. and Margaret (Tomlinson) Stewart; m. Don J. Dallas, Jr., Sept. 15, 1963; children—Angie, Susie. B.S., Colo. State U., 1962, M.S., 1965. Extension home agt. Arapahoe County, Colo., 1962-63; tchr. adult edn. Poudre R-1 Schs., (Colo.), 1963-65; temporary instr. Colo. State U., Ft. Collins, 1965-70, instr. textiles and clothing, 1971-77, asst. prof., 1977—. Biomed. Scis. Research grantee, 1975-76, Am. Home Econs. Assn. Found. research grantee, 1977, 83, Am. Home Econs. Assn. Vocat. Rehab. Assn. tng. grantee, 1963. Mem. Colo. Home Econs. Assn., Am. Home Econs. Assn., Assn. Coll. Profs. and Textiles and Clothing (sec. Western regional bd., chmn. publs., nat. editor), Omicron Nu. Contbr. articles to profl. jours. Home: 1408 Longs Peak Dr Fort Collins CO 80524 Office: Dept Textiles and Clothing Colo State U Fort Collins CO 80523

DAL PRA, CHRISTOPHER JOSEPH, mental health therapist; b. Rockford, Ill., Nov. 26, 1953; s. Virginio Peter and Mary Jane (Conus) Dal P.; m. Rhea White, May 31, 1975; 1 son, Christopher Joseph. B.S., Rockford Coll., 1975; M. Counseling, Ariz. State U., 1980. Asst. mgr. Mid-West Punch & Die Co., Rockford, Ill., 1975; psychiat. asst. Camelback Hosp., Phoenix, 1976; youth counselor St. Lukes Med. Ctr., Phoenix, 1977-80; mental health counselor Maricopa County Atty.'s Office, Phoenix, 1980; dir. Youth Service Bur., Chandler, Ariz., 1980—; cons. and youth counselor. Mem. Am. Personnel and Guidance Assn., Am. Mental Health Counselors Assn. Office: 250 E Commonwealth St Chandler Ariz 85224

DALRYMPLE, ROBERT MERRITT, physician; b. Morristown, N.J., Dec. 28, 1917; s. John Henry and Mabel (Winans) D.; A.B., Columbia U., 1939; M.D., Cornell U., 1943; m. Nancy Marion Crosland, May 6, 1944; children—Anne Winans (Mrs. Paul J. Meeks, Jr.), Paul Fisher, Deborah Jane (Mrs. Robert Penn), Nancy Lynn (Mrs. Brad Strong). Intern, resident Orange (N.J.) Meml. Hosp., 1943-44; resident internal medicine U. Utah, 1947-49; practice medicine specializing in internal medicine, Salt Lake City; asst. clin. prof. U. Utah 1967—; chief of staff St. Marks Hosp., Salt Lake City, 1962. Served with M.C., AUS, 1944-47. Diplomate Am. Bd. Internal Medicine. Mem. AMA, Utah Med. Soc. (treas. 1957-59), Salt Lake County Med. Soc. (pres. 1965), Am. Soc. Internal Medicine, Sigma Chi, Alpha Omega Alpha. Episcopalian. Home: 3689 Honeycut Rd Salt Lake City UT 84106 Office: St Mark's Office Bldg 1220 E 3900 S #4G Salt Lake City UT 84117

DALTON, DOUGLAS, lawyer; b. Astoria, Oreg., Sept. 1, 1929; s. Mervyn E. and Julia M. Dalton; B.A., UCLA, 1951; LL.B., U. So. Calif., 1956; m. Shirley Kirkpatrick. Aug. 29, 1953; children—Julie, Douglas, John, Matthew, Bartholomew. Admitted to Calif. bar, 1956, U.S. Supreme Ct., 1973; city prosecutor City of Long Beach (Calif.), 1956-60; partner firm Ball, Hunt, Hart, Brown and Baerwitz, Long Beach and Los Angeles, 1960-77; pres. Douglas Dalton, a Law Corp., Los Angeles, 1977—; adj. prof. law Pepperdine U., 1978-80; lectr. continuing edn. State Bar Calif., 1978, 80; counsel Pres.'s Commn. on Campus Unrest, 1970. Served with USN, 1951-53. Fellow Am. Coll. Trial Lawyers; mem. Am. Bar Assn., State Bar Calif., Los Angeles County Bar Assn. Republican. Home: 128 Fremont Pl Los Angeles CA 90005 Office: 3660 Wilshire Blvd Los Angeles CA 90010

DALY, DONALD FREMONT, writer; b. Hamilton, Mont., Aug. 8, 1904; s. Charles Fremont and Annie Laurie (Johnson) D.; ed. public schs., apprenticeship tng., tech. sch.; m. Clara Elizabeth Rawlins, Feb. 7, 1936. Writer, Bakersfield, Calif.; books include: The Refrigeration Contractors Estimating Guide, 1948; Know Your Union, 1964; Aim for a Job in Air Conditioning and Refrigeration, 1968; Aim for a Job in the Pipe Trades, 1969; Aim for a Job in the Building Trades, 1970; Indirections for Vocational/Technical Education, 1974; Your Career in Air Conditioning and Refrigeration and Related Technical Occupations, 1979; Your Career in the Plumbing and Pipefitting Industry, 1980; Tricks of the Trade for the Pipe Trades, 1980. Served with U.S. Navy, 1920-22, U.S. Mcht. Marines, 1923-25, USCG, 1931-33. Mem. United Assn. Journeymen and Apprentices of Plumbing and Pipefitting Industry U.S. and Can., Am. Vocat. Assn. Democrat. Home: 3883 Union Apt 27 Bakersfield CA 93305

DALY, EDWARD JOSEPH, airline executive; b. Chgo., Nov. 20, 1922; s. Edward Michael and Charlotte Grace Daly; student U. Ill., U. Santa Clara, 1967; grad. in applied human relations Dale Carnegie Inst., 1975; m. Violet June Chandler; 1 dau., Charlotte. Vice pres. S. O'Carrol Midway Aviation, Chgo., 1947-48; pres. World Airways, Inc., Oakland, Calif., 1950-83, chmn. bd., 1950—; pres. Skycoach Aircraft Corp.; v.p., gen. mgr. Monarch Air Service; pres. Nationwide Freight Forwarders, Inc.; owner, dir. First Western Bank, 1968-73. Regent, U. Santa Clara. Served to sgt. U.S. Army, 1942-45. Decorated Purple Heart; recipient numerous awards, including: NAACP award, 1969; cert. of honor State Calif., 1975; U.S. award of Merit USO, 1975; U.S. award of honor, U.S. Army, 1975; Easter Seal award Greater San Francisco/Oakland Crusade, 1976-81; Internat. Fellowship medal King Jordan, 1977; United Way award, 1978; Research Philanthropic award Nat. Jewish Hosp., 1978; Achievement award State Md., 1981; Dept. Def. award, 1966; Achievement medal Republic Mali, 1977; named Man of Yr., USO, 1974; Disting. Citizen, State Nev., 1977. Mem. USAF Assn., Internat. Air Carrier Assn., Nat. Air Carrier Assn. (dir.), Flying Samaritans, Nat. Council YMCA's, Nat. Alliance Businessmen, SAR. Roman Catholic. Clubs: Wings, U.S. Aero, Commonwealth Calif., Orinda Country, St. Francis Yacht, Silverado Country, Royal Aero. Office: World Airways Inc PO Box 2330 Oakland Internat Airport Oakland CA 94614

DALY, FREDERICA YOUNG, psychologist, educator; b. Washington, Feb. 14, 1925; d. Samuel Porter and Geneva (Sharper) Young; m. Paul Martineau, June 7, 1965 (dec.); m. 2d, Michael Edward Daly, Mar. 15, 1972. B.S., Howard U., 1946, M.S., 1947; Ph.D., Cornell U., 1956; cert. psychologist, N.Y. Dir. social services George Junior Republic, Freeville, N.Y., 1955-72; assoc. prof. SUNY, 1972-80; coordinator alcohol treatment VA Med. Ctr., Albuquerque, 1981—. Bd. dirs. YWCA, Albuquerque, 1979-81, Nat. Child Labor, 1977-81, St Ministry. Mem. Am. Orthopsychiat. Assn., Internat. Council Psychologists, Am. Psychol. Assn., N.Mex. Alcohol Counselors. Democrat. Unitarian. Home: 526 Hermosa NE Albuquerque NM 87108 Office: VA MC 1163 2100 Ridgecrest SE Albuquerque NM 87108

DALY, KEVIN J. P., architect; b. Bklyn., Feb. 15, 1944; s. Mary Theresa (Gilbane) D.; B.Arch., Kent State U., 1970; m. Joan Ann Cooley, June 7, 1969; children—Tanya Marie, Anastasia Lisa, Kevin Peter, Noah Matthew. Planner/archtl. draftsman Gerald Dake Assos., Jacksonville, Fla., 1970-73; job capt. Robert Broward Architect, Jacksonville, 1973-74; treas., project mgr. Clements/Rumpel/Assos., Jacksonville, 1974-79; architect Am. Indian Engring., Phoenix, 1979-81; prin. Kevin Daly Architect, 1981—; solar cons. Recipient Spl. award of Merit for Innovations in Housing Design Competition, 1978. Mem. AIA, Constrn. Specifications Inst., Internat. Solar Engery Soc. Roman Catholic. Clubs: K.C., Lions. Designer Daly solar residence, 1978. Home: 3146 E Cortez St Phoenix AZ 85028 Office: 6040 N 7th St #101A Phoenix AZ 85014

DALY, PEGGY JEAN, nursing administrator; b. Sacramento, July 22, 1955; d. Albert Eugene and Marilyn (Comb) Daly. B.S. in Nursing, Loma Linda U., 1978, pediatric nurse practitioner, 1978. Cert. pediatric nurse practitioner, R.N., Colo., Calif. Staff nurse, emergency dept. Loma Linda (Calif.) U., 1977-78, day charge nurse, 1978-80; adminstrv. dir. emergency dept. Porter Hosp., Denver, 1981—, instr. in field. Fellow Am. Acad. Pediatrics; mem. Emergency Dept. Nursing Assn. (sec. Denver chpt.), Sigma Theta Tau.

DALY, RICHARD JAMES, computer manufacturing company executive; b. N.Y.C., Nov. 13, 1930; s. James Patrick and Muriel Margaret (Mc Cusker) Daly; B.S. in Mech. Engring., U. Md., 1952; m. Agnes J. Shutty, June 18, 1951; children—Sharon Ann, Brian P. Systems analyst Ford Motor Co., Chgo., 1953-57; program dir. ITT, Chgo., 1957-63, Frankfurt, W. Ger., 1963-67, N.Y.C., 1967-70; pres. Computer Credit Corp., Los Angeles, 1970-74; v.p. ops. DATASAAB, Los Angeles, 1974-82; pres. Roan Engring. Corp., Los Angeles, 1982—. Mem. Mensa. Republican. Roman Catholic. Home: 4514 Ellenita Ave Tarzana CA 91356 Office: 660 Hampshire Rd Westlake Village CA 91361

DALY, WILLIAM RAYMOND, transportation consultant; b. Providence, Mar. 1, 1917; s. William R. and Alice R. (McKenna) D.; m. Margaret M. Cauley, Apr. 6, 1940; children—Maureen Daly McAllister, Patricia, Alicia Daly Lampert, William R., Karen. Cert. mktg. and phys. distbn. tchr., community colls. Calif., 1972. Sec. Maritime Com., Los Angeles C. of C., 1952-57; traffic mgr. Port of San Diego, 1957-69; dir. internat. trade Western Gillette, Inc., Los Angeles, 1969-71, mktg. research dir., 1971-72; owner, mgr. William R. Daly & Assocs., La Mesa, Calif., 1972—; ptnr., cons. San Diego Traffic Services, Inc., 1979—; Calif. Com. Colls., San Diego, 1973—; mem. adv. bd. Pacific Shippers. Mem. transp. and phys. distbn. mgmt. adv. com. San Diego Community Colls., 1972—. Mem. Nat. Def. Transp. Assn. (pres. 1960, 73), Pacific Coast Assn. Port Authorities (chmn. traffic com. 1960-62), Calif. Assn. Port Authorities (chmn. com. on tariffs and practices 1959, 64), Calif. Trucking Assn. (assoc.), San Diego Transp. Club (bd. dirs. 1965), Assn. ICC Practitioners, Assn. Freight Transp. Cons., Propeller Club U.S., Delta Nu Alpha (San Diego chpt. 130 Transp. Man of Yr. 1980-81, Pacific S.W. Region Transp. Man of Yr. 1981-82). Home: 8135 Binney Pl La Mesa CA 92041 Office: 4340 Vandever Ave San Diego CA 92120

DAM, DOROTHY ANN, hosp. services exec.; b. Waukesha, Wis., July 26, 1938; d. Edward Foster and Ruth Elizabeth (Sugden) Perkins; student Carroll Coll., 1956-58; B.A. in Journalism, Marquette U., 1960; m. Nickolaus W. Dam, Dec. 27, 1958; children—Heidi, Jeffrey, Warren. Weekly columnist Country Almanac, Woodside, Calif., 1971-72; clinic asst., Redwood City, Calif., 1971-74; quality care assurance coordinator Kaiser Found. Hosp., Redwood City, 1974-75, patient relations dir., 1975-81, health plan rep., 1981-82, sr. mktg. rep., 1982—; instr. San Mateo Community Coll. Dist. Mem. Calif. Soc. Patient Reps. (charter, bd. dirs., 1977-78, sec., 1978-79), Am. Hosp. Assn., Sigma Delta Chi. Home: 60 Stadler Dr Woodside CA 94062 Office: 1150 Veterans Blvd Redwood City CA 94063

D'AMBROSIO, BLANCHE FADA GRAWE, hotel executive; b. Baton Rouge, Mar. 18, 1926; d. Walter Theodore and Blanche Laura (Cause) Bozant; m. Arthur Nolan Grawe, June 5, 1949; children—Cary Nolan, Geoffrey Allan; m. 2d, Anthony Francis D'Ambrosio, Feb. 18, 1978. Student La. State U., 1943-45, U. So. Calif., 1945-47. Society editor Herald Am. newspaper, Compton, Calif., 1957-61; asst. editor Host mag., Oreg. Restaurant and Beverage Assn., Portland, 1962-66; agt. Oreg. Liquor Control Commn., Portland, 1966-69; dir. sales and catering Cosmopolitan El Mirador, Sacramento, Calif., 1969-71; mgr. Umpqua Hotel, Roseburg, Oreg., 1971-74; gen. mgr. Inn at Spanish Head, Lincoln City, Oreg., 1974—. Mem. Lincoln City Advt. Com.; mem. job service employers com. Dept. Human Resources of Lincoln County. Mem. Nat. Restaurant Assn., Oreg. Hotel and Motel Assn. (past pres., chmn. bd.), Am. Hotel and Motel Assn., Oreg. Motor Hotel Assn. (dir.), Restaurants of Oreg. Assn., Lincoln City Motel Assn. (dir.), Women's Assn. of Allied Beverage Industry (past pres. Portland chpt). Club: Norwalk (Calif.) Jr. Women's (life mem., past pres.). Office: Inn at Spanish Head 4009 S Hwy 101 Lincoln City OR 97367

D'AMBROSIO, CHARLES ANTHONY, economist, educator; b. Chgo., Aug. 31, 1932; s. Anthony and Della (Malpede) D'A.; m. Marilyn Ann Hilgert, June 8, 1957; children—Charles, Margaret, Catherine, Christine, Patricia, Michael, John. B.S.C., Loyola U., Chgo., 1955; M.S., U. Ill., 1958, Ph.D., 1962; cert. Inst. Chartered Fin. Analysts, 1968. Asst. prof. fin. U. Wash., Seattle, 1960-63, assoc. prof., 1963-70, prof., 1970—; fin. cons. Bd. dirs. Inst. for Quantitative Research in Fin. Mem. Am. Fin. Assn., Western Fin. Assn. (pres. 1980-81), Am. Econ. Assn., Seattle Soc. of Security Analysts. Roman Catholic. Author: Principles of Modern Investments, 1976. Editor-in-chief Fin. Analysts Jour., 1982—. Home: 3604 42 Ave NE Seattle WA 98105 Office: Coll Bus Adminstrn U of Washington Seattle WA 98195

DAMERON-LICHTENBERG, CLARICE ELAINE, speech/language pathologist; b. Granite City, Ill., Sept. 9, 1934; d. Leo Alonzo and Cora Frances (Carriger) Dameron; m. Larry Ray Lichtenberg, Dec. 23, 1961; 1 dau., Julia-Isabel. B.S. in Speech Communications, N.E. Mo. State U., 1961; postgrad. Ill. Normal U., 1963, Ariz. State U., 1968-76. Third grade tchr. Harris Sch., Madison, Ill., 1957-59; asst. mgr. Dameron Sheltered Care Home, Roadhouse, Ill., 1959-60; speech-lang. pathologist Washington Elem. Schs., Phoenix, 1969—; dir. learning disabilities program Sweetwater Ch., Glendale, Ariz., 1978-79; supr. Adult Homebound Ministry, The Valley Cathedral, Phoenix, 1979-80; spl. edn. cons. Christian schs., Maricopa County, Ariz.; coordinator nat. patriotism week Washington Elem. Sch. Dist., 1981; pub. relations co-chmn. Ariz. Speech/Hearing Assn. Mktg. analyst Intel, Phoenix, 1983. Pub. relations dir. Federated Women's Club, Bloomington, Ill.; pres. Nat. Asthmatic Club, Bloomington; bicentennial dir. Evangelical Ch. Pageant, Maricopa County. Recipient Am. Educator medal Valley Forge Freedoms Found., 1981. Mem. Am. Soc. Tng. and Devel., NEA, Ariz. Edn. Assn., Nat. Christian Edn. Assn., DAR. Author: Arizona's Heritage Blessed by God Pageant Souvenir Coloring Book, 1975; numerous brochures and newsletters.

DAMES, TRENT R., engr.; b. Bklyn., Oct. 1911; M.S. in Civil Engring., Calif. Inst. Tech., 1934; m. Phoebe Laura Rubins, 1934 (dec.); children—Melissa, Joyce, Roger; m. 2d, Carolyn Nancy Means. Cofounder Dames & Moore, Cons. Engrs., Los Angeles, 1938—, now founding Partner, mem. exec. com.; fin. chmn. engring. industry Com. for Econ. Devel., 1975. Mem. So. Calif. regional adv. council Calif. Inst. Tech., 1975; mem. internat. com. U.S. C. of C., 1968-71. Trustee Mills Coll. Named Constrn. Man of Yr., Los Angeles C. of C., 1975. Fellow Am. Cons. Engrs. Council; mem. ASCE (hon., nat. v.p. 1971-72), Cons. Engrs. Council, Cons. Engrs. Assn. So. Calif., Structural Engrs. Assn. So. Calif., Assos. Calif. Inst. Tech., Cyrus and Susan Mills Soc., Sigma Xi, Tau Beta Pi. Club: Calif. Office: 445 S Figueroa St Los Angeles CA 90071

D'AMICO, MICHAEL, architect, urban planner; b. Bklyn., Sept. 11, 1936; s. Michael and Rosalie (Vinciguerra) D.; B.Arch., U. Okla., 1961; postgrad. So. Meth. U. Sch. Law, 1962-63; m. Joan Hand, Nov. 26, 1955; children—Michael III, Dion Charles. Supr. advanced planning sect. Dallas Dept. City Planning, 1961-63; designer, planner in charge Leo A. Daly Co., San Francisco, 1963-66; project planner Whisler, Patri Assos., San Francisco, 1966-67; architect, urban planner D'Amico & Assocs., San Francisco, N.Y., Guam, 1967-73, pres. D'Amico & Assocs., Inc., Mill Valley, Calif., and Guam, 1973—, Jericho Alpha Inc., 1979-82; cons. architect, planner City of Seaside (Calif.), 1967-72, 79-81; cons. urban redevel. Eureka (Calif.), 1967-82; cons. planner, Lakewood, Calif.; redevel. cons. to Daly City (Calif.), 1975-77; redevel. adviser to Tamalpais Valley Bus. Assn., 1975-77; archtl. and hist. analyst to Calif. Dept. Transp., 1975-77; agt. for Eureka, Calif. Coastal Commn., 1977-79. Mem. steering com. San Francisco Joint Com. Urban Design, 1967-72. Recipient Community Design award AIA, 1970; First prize award Port Aransas (Tex.) Master Plan Competition, 1964. Mem. AIA, Am. Planning Assn., Calif. Assn. Planning Cons. (sec., treas. 1970-72), Am. Soc. Cons. Planners, World Future Soc., Solar Energy Soc. Am. Office: 525 Midvale Way Mill Valley CA 94941 also Agana Guam

D'AMICO, SHEILA, lawyer; b. Newark, Mar. 24, 1941; d. Anthony and Doris Elizabeth (Blaney-Norton) D'Amico; children—Richard Gaughan, Judith Gaughan, David Gaughan, Daniel Gaughan. B.A. cum laude in Polit. Sci., U. Ill.-Chgo., 1972; J.D., Golden Gate U., 1979. Bar: Calif. 1979, U.S. Dist. Ct. (no. dist.) Calif. 1979. Asst. Mitsubishi Internat. Corp., Chgo., 1974; exec. dir. State Ill. Bd. Ethics, Springfield, 1974-76; law clk., researcher Nat. Ctr. State Cts., State Calif. Office Adminstrv. Hearings, San Francisco, 1977-79; sole practice, San Francisco, 1979-81; asst. counsel and compliance specialist Wells Fargo Bank, San Francisco, 1981—; instr. Hastings Coll. Law, 1981-82. Chmn. Hawthorne Community Council, 1972-73; vol. worker John Anderson Presdl. Campaign, 1980, coordinator San Francisco County, 1980; mem. Nat. Women's Polit. Caucus, 1982-83; founding mem. Interstate Adv. Council Ethics, Elections and Disclosure, 1974-77. Recipient Queen's Bench Scholarship award San Francisco Queen's Bench, 1978. Mem. ABA, Lawyers Alliance Nuclear Arms Control (steering com.), Calif. State Bar, Calif. Hist. Soc., Soc. Hist. Preservation, Alliance Francaise (San Francisco). Contbr. articles to profl. jours. Office: Wells Fargo Bank 475 Sansome St San Francisco CA 94111

DAMMAN, RONALD EUGENE, mgmt. services; b. Howell, Mich., Sept. 12, 1941; s. Clayton B. and Carmon Janet (Loree) D.; B.S. summa cum laude, Mich. State U., 1963; M.B.A. summa cum laude (Chrysler Found. fellow), Stanford U., 1969; m. Betty Jean Luckett, Sept. 24, 1970; 1 son, Kirk Ashley. Fin. analyst Ford Motor Co., Ypsilanti, Mich., 1963, 65-67; corp. planning analyst Equitable Life Assurance Soc., N.Y.C., 1969-71, pres., chief operating officer Equico Personal Credit, Inc., subs., N.Y.C., 1971-75, Colorado Springs, Colo., 1975-76, exec. v.p., chief fin. officer, 1976-80, also dir.; pres., dir. Colo. Law Centers of Am. Mgmt. Corp., Colorado Springs, 1980—. Served to lt. U.S. Army, 1963-65. Mem. Phi Kappa Phi, Phi Eta Sigma, Tau Sigma. Club: Masons; Men's Winter Night. First place winner Mich. 4-H musical competition, 1957, 59. Home: 6627 Mesedge Dr Colorado Springs CO 80919 Office: 6627 Mesedge Dr Colorado Springs CO 80919

DAMRON, CARINA KAY CASTAGNETO, educator; b. Longview, Wash., Dec. 26, 1942; d. William James and Beverly Jean (Marshall) Castagneto; B.S.Ed. in Child Devel., Brigham Young U., 1965; postgrad. U. Utah, 1965-76; m. William E. Damron, June 11, 1973. Tchr., Salt Lake City Bd. Edn., 1965-76, Centennial Sch. Dist., Portland, Oreg., 1976—. Active March of Dimes, United Fund, Am. Cancer Soc.; vol. Primary Children's Med. Center, Salt Lake City, 1966-68; active Big Sisters Program, 1967-68; mem. Com. for Defeat of Oreg. Initiative to Limit Property Taxes, 1980. Named Tchr. of Yr., Golden Gleanner Outstanding Woman award Ch. Jesus Christ of Latter-day Saints, 1972. Mem. Salt Lake Tchrs. Assn., Utah Tchrs. Assn., Centennial Edn. Assn., NEA, Oreg. Edn. Assn., Assn. of Early Childhood Educators, Assn.

Early Childhood Edn. Republican. Mem. Ch. Jesus Christ of Latter-day Saints. Club: Women's Century. Home: 15640 SE Millmain Dr Portland OR 97233 Office: 1546 SE 169th Pl Portland OR 97233

DAMSBO, ANN MARIE, psychologist, clinic adminstr.; b. Cortland, N.Y., July 7, 1931; d. Jorgen Einer and Agatha Irene (Schenck) D.; B.S., San Diego State Coll., 1952; M.A., U.S. Internat. U., 1974, Ph.D., 1975; 6 foster children. Commd. 2d lt. U.S. Army, 1952, advanced through grades to capt., 1957; staff therapist Letterman Army Hosp., San Francisco, 1953-54, 56-58, 61-62, Ft. Devers, Mass., 1955-56, Walter Reed Army Hosp., Washington, 1958-59, Tripler Army Hosp., Hosp., Hawaii, 1959-61, Ft. Benning, Ga., 1962-64; chief therapist U.S. Army Hosp., Ft. McPherson, Ga., 1964-67, ret., 1967; med. missionary So. Presbyterian Ch., Taiwan, 1968-70; psychology intern, burn center Univ. Hosp., San Diego, 1975; pre-doctoral intern Naval Regional Med. Center, San Diego, 1975-76, postdoctoral intern, 1975-76, chief, founder pain clinic, 1976—; cons. on forensic hypnosis, law enforcement agys.; guest lectr. U. Calif.-San Diego Med. Sch. Ext.; lectr. in field, U.S., Can., Eng., France, Australia. Fellow Am. Soc. Clin. Hypnosis; mem. San Diego Soc. Clin. Hypnosis (pres. 1980), Am. Psychol. Assn., Am. Phys. Therapy Assn., Calif. Soc. Clin. Hypnosis (bd. govs.), Internat. Soc. Clin. and Exptl. Hypnosis, Internat. Platform Assn. Republican. Methodist. Club: Job's Daus. Contbr. articles to profl. publs.; also chpt. in book. Home: 1062 W 5th Ave Escondido CA 92025 Office: Chief Pain Clinic Naval Regional Med Center San Diego CA 92134

DANCE, MAURICE EUGENE, college administrator; b. Bismarck, N.D., Jan. 14, 1923; s. Alvin Cecil and Jennie (Brown) D.; B.A., U. Wash., 1947; M.S., U. Wis., 1949, Ph.D., 1953; children—Muriel, Maurice C., Marcia, Mark, Michelle, Michael, Myles, Jennifer, Kristina; m. 2d, Anita Ruth Bell, Apr. 10, 1965. Asst. prof. econs. Los Angeles State Coll., 1950-56; prof. econs. San Fernando Valley State Coll., Northridge, Calif., 1956-69, chmn. dept., 1956-64, asst. to v.p. for acad. affairs, 1964-65, dean Sch. Letters and Scis., 1965-69, v.p. acad. affairs, 1964—; econs. cons. Mem. Am. Econs. Assn., Indsl. Relations Research Assn., AAUP. Office: Calif State Coll Hayward CA 94542

DANDOY, JEREMIAH RICHARD, state ofcl.; b. Milw., Sept. 25, 1934; s. Bert Julius and Mildred Eugenia (Masek) D.; B.S. in Finance, UCLA, 1959; M.B.A. in Mktg., U. So. Calif., 1960; m. Suzanne Eggleston, June 14, 1958; children—Kevin, Bret, Jolyn. Asst. to personnel mgr. Los Angeles Times, 1960-66; asst. controller, corp. officer Copley Newspapers, 1966-68; asso. dir. U.S. Peace Corps, 1968-70; state adminstr. developmental disabilities program, dist. I, Ariz. Dept. Econ. Security, Phoenix, 1972-81, asst. dir., 1981—; pres. Loma Resources Ltd., 1980—; instr. Central Ariz. Coll., Ariz. State U.; cons. on found. grants and mgmt. of human service delivery systems to pvt. non-profit orgns. Mem. County Title XX Planning Com., 1976—, State and County Specialized Transp. Com., 1977—; mem. child health services com. Central Ariz. Health Systems Agy., 1977; mem. profl. adv. com. Ariz. Coalition for Persons with Developmental Disabilities, 1977—; mem. Ariz. Task Force on Housing for Spl. Populations, 1980, State Developmental Disabilities Adv. Council, 1981—, Ariz. Council for Deaf, 1981—, Gov.'s Council on Developmental Disabilities, 1981—. Served with U.S. Army, 1954-56. Named Assn. Retarded Citizens Adminstr. of Yr., 1980. Mem. Am. Assn. Mental Deficiency (Ariz. chmn. 1977-78), Nat. Assn. Supts. of Public Residential Facilities for Mentally Retarded, Nat. Assn. Retarded Citizens, Am. Soc. Tng. and Devel., Nat. Assn. State Dirs. Mental Retardation/Developmental Disabilities, UCLA Alumni Assn. (pres. Ariz. chpt. 1978-80), Beta Gamma Sigma, Theta Xi. Mormon. Home: 338 E Loma Vista St Tempe AZ 85282 Office: 1824 E McKinley St Phoenix AZ 85006

DANDOY, MAXIMA ANTONIO, educator; b. Santa Maria, Ilocos Sur, Philippines; d. Manuel and Isidra (Mendoza) Antonio; came to U.S., 1949, naturalized, 1951; teaching cert. Philippine Normal Coll., 1940; A.B., Nat. Tchrs. Coll., Manila, 1947; M.A., Arellano U., Manila, 1949; Ed.D. (John M. Switzer scholar, Newhouse Found. scholar), Stanford U., 1951, postgrad. (Calif. Fedn. Bus. and Profl. Women's Clubs scholar), 1952; m. Apolinario M. Dandoy, Mar. 14, 1947. Tchr. elem. sch., Philippines, 1927-37; lab. sch. tchr. Philippine Normal Coll., Manila, 1938-49; instr. Arellano U., Manila, 1947-49; lab. sch. prin. U. of East, Manila, 1953-54, asso. prof., 1952-55; prof. edn. Calif. State U.-Fresno, 1956-82; curriculum writer, gen. office supr. Manila Dept. Edn., 1944-45; Mem. com. for the selection social studies textbooks for state adoption Calif., 1970-71; vis. prof. UCLA, 1956; Crisologo Meml. lectr. U. No. Philippines, 1977; mem. Calif. Gov.'s Conf. on Traffic Safety, 1962; mem. Calif. Gov's Conf. Delinquency Prevention, 1963. Named Disting. Woman of Year, Fresno Bus. and Profl. Women's Club, 1957, Woman of Achievement award, 1973. Mem. Nat. Council sect. Social Studies (chmn. sec. internat. understanding, nat. conv. 1966), Calif. Fedn. Bus. and Profl. Women's Clubs (state chmn. scholarships 1961-63, treas. Fresno), Calif. Tchrs. Assn., AAUW (liaison Calif. State U. at Fresno 1970-71), Orgn. Filipino-Am. Educators Fresno (pres. 1977-84), Soc. Profs. Edn., Filipino-Am. Women's Club (adv. 1969-74), Internat. Platform Assn., Phi Delta Kappa, Pi Lambda Theta, Kappa Delta Pi (counselor 1972-79, nat. com. attendance and credentials 1975, nat. com. regional confs. 1976). Home: 1419 W Bullard Ave Fresno CA 93711 Office: Calif State U Fresno CA 93740

DANE, BILL, photographer, educator; b. Pasadena, Calif., Nov. 12, 1938; 1 dau., Monet Zulpo-Dane. B.A., U. Calif.-Berkeley, 1964, M.A., 1968. Former tchr., pub. schs., Berkeley, Calif.; exhibited in one-man shows: Gallery Reese Pally, San Francisco, 1970, Museum Modern Art, N.Y.C., 1974, Oakland (Calif.) Mus., 1974, Carpenter Ctr. for Visual Arts, Harvard U., 1975, Wash. State U., Pullman, 1976, Ctr. Creative Photography, U. Ariz., 1976, De Young Mus., San Francisco, 1977, Fraenkel Gallery, San Francisco, 1971, De Saisset Mus., Santa Clara, Calif., 1983, Robert Freidus Gallery, N.Y.C., 1983, Madison (Wis.) Art Ctr., 1983; group shows: Richmond (Calif.) Art Ctr., Hofstra U., L.I., N.Y., 1973, Calif. State U.-Sacramento, 1974, Edinburgh (Scotland) Art Ctr., 1975, Photographers Gallery, London, 1977, Mus. Modern Art, 1978, Fraenkel Gallery, San Francisco, 1981, Mus. Modern Art, 1981; represented in permanent collections: Mus. Modern Art, N.Y.C., Mus. Modern Art, San Francisco, Spencer Mus. Art, U. Kans., Nat. Gallery Can., Ottawa, Ont., Bibliotheque Nationale, Paris, Met. Mus. Art, N.Y.C., Mus. Fine Arts, Boston, Amon Carter Mus., Ft. Worth, Madison Art Ctr., Art Inst. Chgo., Mus. Fine Arts, Houston. John Simon Guggenheim fellow, 1973, 82; Nat. Endowment for Arts fellow, 1976, 77. Office: 1442A Walnut Suite 222 Berkeley CA 94709

DANGERFIELD, GEORGE, author; b. Newbury, Berkshire, Eng., Oct. 28, 1904; came to U.S., 1930, naturalized, 1943; s. George and Ethel Margaret (Tyrer) D.; B.A., Oxford U., 1927, M.A., 1968; m. Helen Mary Deey Spedding, June 28, 1928; m. 2d, Mary Lou Schott, June 29, 1941; children—Mary Jo, Hilary, Anthony. Asst. editor Brewer, Warren & Putnam, N.Y.C., 1930-32; lit. editor Vanity Fair mag., 1933-35; writer, lectr., 1935—; lectr. history U. Calif., Santa Barbara, 1968-72. Served 102d inf. div., AUS, 1942-45. Recipient Bancroft prize in Am. history Columbia U., 1953, Pulitzer prize in Am. history, 1953; Benjamin D. Shreve fellow Princeton U., 1957-58; Guggenheim fellow, 1970. Fellow Soc. Am. Historians; mem. Ams. for Dem. Action, ACLU, Friends of Montecito Public Library, Am. Antiquarian Soc. Author: Bengal Mutiny, 1933; The Strange Death of Liberal England, 1935; Victoria's Heir, 1941; The Era of Good Feelings, 1952; Chancellor Robert R. Livingston of New York, 1960; The Awakening of American Nationalism, 1815-1828, 1965; Defiance to the Old World, 1970; The Damnable Question, 1976; (with Otey M. Scruggs) Henry Adams' History of the United States, 1963; contbr. to Times of Trial (Allan Nevins), 1958, Quarrels That Have Shaped the Constitution (John A. Garraty), 1962, Interpreting American History, Conversations with Historians (Garraty), 1970. Home: 883 Toro Canyon Rd Santa Barbara CA 93108

DANIEL, DELORES (LORI) JANE, city ofcl., recreation adminstr.; b. Mt. Pleasant, Iowa, Jan. 24, 1948; d. Robert Earl and Betty E. (Mark) Carlson; student Iowa Wesleyan Coll., 1968, U. Iowa, 1968-70; B.S., U. No. Colo., 1972; cert. U. Denver, 1978, City of Aurora Police Acad., 1978, Western Revenue Sources Mgmt. Sch., 1978; m. John Wesley Daniel, July 12, 1975; children—Chad Wesley, Valerie Lynn, Chet Alan. Vol. recreation leader Iowa Handicapped Children's Sch., 1968-69; cabin counselor and pioneering dir. Point O'Pines Girls Camp, Brant Lake, N.Y., 1969-70; dir. Cotton Tails Ranch's Saddles 'n Sails Resident/Day Camp, Malibu, Calif., 1970-72; recreation intern Hyland Hills Met. Parks and Recreation Dist., Colo., 1972; recreation program supr. City of Aurora, 1972-75, supt. recreation, 1975—; guest lectr. U. No. Colo., Greeley, 1973—. Recipient Merit award Aurora Rotary Club, 1974. Mem. Nat. Recreation and Park Assn., Colo. Parks and Recreation Soc. (newsletter editor 1973-74, mem. exec. bd. 1973—, award 1973, 76, 78, 79), Nat. Am. Camping Assn. (regional bd. Rocky Mountain sect. 1979—). Republican. Lutheran. Office: 1470 S Havana Aurora CO 80012

DANIEL, ERNEST GARY, food co. exec.; b. Jackson, Tenn., June 24, 1942; s. Ernest Everett and Nellie Brown (Taylor) D.; B.S. in Mech. Engring., U. Tenn., 1965; M.B.A., Memphis State U., 1971; m. Virginia Carol, June 7, 1964; children—Christopher Gary, Marc Andrew. Asso. aircraft engr. Lockheed-Ga., Marietta, 1966-67; process engr. Hunt-Wesson Foods, Inc., Memphis and Fullerton, Calif., 1967-68, asst. refinery supt., 1968-69, plant indsl. engr., 1969-72, sr. facilities planning engr., 1972-74, prodn. mgr., 1974-75; plant mgr. J. Hungerford Smith Co., Inc., Humboldt, Tenn. and Modesto, Calif., 1975-76, v.p. ops., 1976-79; exec. v.p. Silver Mill Frozen Foods, Hart, Mich., 1979-80; dir. mfg. Berrenda Mesa Farms, Fullerton, Calif., 1980-82; pres. Danco Foods, Inc., Modesto, 1982—. Mem. Am. Mgmt. Assn., ASME, Pi Tau Sigma. Republican. Baptist. Clubs: Del Rio Golf and Country, Lions. Home: 2713 Hyannis Circle Modesto CA 95355

DANIEL, MEREDITH GAYLE, insurance broker; b. Calif., Dec. 20, 1946; d. Daniel and Mary Helen (Grass) Winters; student Fresno City Coll., 1965-67; m. D.L. Daniel, Feb. 27, 1963 (div. 1974); children—Vincent L., David W. With Allstate Ins. Co., Menlo Park, Calif., 1969-72; ins. underwriter Cravens Dargan & Co., San Jose, Calif., 1972-75; underwriter, account exec. Alexander & Alexander, San Francisco, 1975-76; account exec. Rollins Burdick Hunter, Palo Alto, Calif., 1976-77; with Reed Stenhouse, Inc., Palo Alto, 1977-82, prodn. mgr., 1978-80, asst. br. mgr., 1980-82, v.p., 1978-82; asst. v.p., br. mgr. Western Internat. Ins. Brokers, Inc., Palo Alto, 1982—. Mem. Ins. Forum Santa Clara Valley, Am. Mgmt. Assn., NOW, Women in Bus. Club: World Trade. Office: Two Palo Alto Sq Palo Alto CA 94306

DANIEL, MONTGOMERY DORAN, advertising management executive; b. Ames, Iowa, Sept. 9, 1956; s. William Kinson and Joan P. (Montgomery) D.; m. Lori Burke, July 27, 1974; children—Brooke Allison, Erin Elizabeth. Student U. Ariz., 1974; B.S., Iowa State U., 1978. Mng. editor New for the Farm mag., Kansas City, Mo., 1978-79; assoc. editor Drovers Jour., Kansas City, 1978-79; advt. promotion mgr. Western Marine Electronics, Seattle, 1979-82; advt. mgr. West Coast ops. Nat. Fisherman mag., Seattle, 1982—. Recipient Focus award Iowa State U., 1978. Contbr. numerous articles to profl. jours. Home: 3853 Pleasant Beach Dr Bainbridge Island WA 98110 Office: 4215 21st Ave West Seattle WA 98199

DANIEL, W. GAYLE, architect; b. Tatum, N.Mex., Aug. 2, 1931; d. Earl W. and Olive M.; B.S., Ariz. State U., 1961; m. Adriana H. Mostert, Mar. 24, 1956; children—Vicki, Chris, Michelle, Gary. Architect, designer Koebig & Koebig, Los Angeles, 1961; chief designer John B. Ferguson & Assos., 1962-65; prin. W. Gayle Daniel Architect, N.Hollywood, Calif., 1966—. Served with USAF, 1951-54. Recipient Los Angeles City Beautiful award, 1973, design awards Soc. Am. Registered Architects, 1970, 73, 74, 76, 78. Fellow Soc. Am. Registered Architects; mem. Prestressed Concrete Inst., Solar Energy Soc. Am. Republican. Baptist. Office: 12160 Victory Blvd North Hollywood CA 91606

DANIELL, LINDA CAROLE, advertising executive; b. Pitts., July 19, 1952; d. James Lachlan and Marcia Wilson (Simblest) D. B.A. in English, Denison U., 1970-74. Reporter, Columbus (Ohio) Citizen-Jour., 1974; editorial coordinator Saturday Evening Post, Curtis Pub. Co., Indpls., also mng. editor The Country Gentleman, 1976-78; founding editor, writer Young Life Outlook, Colorado Springs, Colo.; acting dir. communications RMI Co., Youngstown, Ohio, 1978; account exec. Schenkein Assocs., Denver, 1979-81; pres. Daniell Communications Cons., Denver, 1981—. Campaign dir. Big Brothers-Big Sisters (1983 Challenge Bowl), Denver-Boulder; chmn. Denver Urban Com. Young Life; pres. Denver-Boulder chpt. Denison U. Alumni Soc. Mem. Pub. Relations Soc. Am. Club: Cherry Creek Sporting (Denver). Contbr. numerous articles to profl jours. Office: 1869 S Pearl St #201 Denver CO 80210

DANIELS, DIANE, computer software engineering and development executive; b. Valdosta, Ga., Dec. 4, 1945; d. Harry A. and Mary M. (Curry) Davidson. B.A. with honors, Mich. State U., 1966. With IBM Corp., 1966-73, computer programmer on Apollo II, also Pentagon Intelligence, Washington, Saigon, Vietnam, 1968-70; mgmt. info. systems cons. to Govt. of Iran, Louis Berger Internat., 1973-75, staff, 1978; system engr. automated medicaid and welfare systems, EDS Corp., San Francisco, 1976-77; founder, pres. Info. Orgn. Corp., San Francisco, 1979—. Pres. bd. dirs. Pacific Heights Place Owners Assn., 1980-82, Fairspace Dancing Theatre, 1976-78; chmn. Com. for Ann. Fundraiser for San Francisco Moving Co., Modern Dance, Inc., 1982; Mem. Assn. Records Mgrs. and Adminstrs. (dir. 1980-81, cert. of recognition 1981), Assn. Systems Mgrs. (cert. of recognition 1982), Women Entrepreneurs, Profl. and Tech. Cons. Assn., Profl. Women's Bus. Exchange. Inventor, copyright holder in field. Address: 2295 Vallejo St San Francisco CA 94123

DANIELS, ETHEL MARY, reading specialist; b. Phoenix, Feb. 26, 1942; d. Eddie Ernest and Alberta (Evans) D.; B.A., in Edn., Ariz. State U., 1964; M.A. in Reading, U.S. Internat. U., 1976. Elem. tchr., Phoenix, 1964-67, San Diego, Calif., 1967—; demonstration tchr. reading and math., 1974-75; reading specialist San Diego City Schs., Robert E. Lee Elem. Sch., 1979—. Recipient Service award PTA, 1981. Mem. San Diego Tchrs. Assn., Calif. Tchrs. Assn., NEA, Assn. Supervision and Curriculum Devel. Democrat. Baptist. Clubs: Mountain View Tennis (Service award 1976, 82), Balboa Tennis, Bonita Valley Tennis, Helix South Tennis, Morley Field Tennis. Home: 3041 Picasso Dr Bonita CA 92002 Office: 6190 Childs Ave San Diego CA 92139

DANIELS, LESLIE BETH, city ofcl.; b. Kansas City, Mo., July 14, 1951; d. Charles Lee and Helen Atanasoff D.; B.A., U. Ariz., 1972; M.A., U. Phoenix, 1981; grad. Econ. Devel. Inst., U. Okla., 1983. Copywriter public relations, Tucson, 1972-74, graphic artist/electronic typsetter, 1974-75, polit. campaign mgr., 1972-77; adminstrv. asst. City Mgrs. Office, Annexation/Econ. Devel., City of Tucson, 1978—. Editor, State Republican Com. newspaper, 1975-76; chmn. Pima County Young Rep. League, 1973-74; dist. 9 chmn. Pima County Rep. Central Com., 1974. Mem. Ariz. Assn. Indsl. Developers, Kappa Tau Alpha, Delta Sigma Pi. Republican. Methodist. Club: Pima County Trunk 'n Tusk (publicity chmn. 1974-77). Home: 7369 E 20th St Tucson AZ 85710 Office: PO Box 27210 Tucson AZ 85726

DANIELS, LYDIA M., med. records services adminstr.; b. Louisville, Dec. 21, 1932; d. Effort and Gladys T. (Turner) Williams; student Calif. State U., Hayward, 1967, 69, 70, 71, 72, Golden Gate U., 1979; cert. Samuel Merritt Hosp. Sch. Med. Record Adminstrs., 1959; student Central State Coll., Ohio, 1950-52; children by previous marriage—Danny Winston, Jeffrey Bruce, Anthony Wayne. Sec. chemistry dept. Central State Coll., Wilberforce, Ohio, 1950-52; co-dir. Indian Work-camp, Pala Indian Reservation, Pala, Calif., 1956-58; clk.-typist Camarillo (Calif.) State Hosp., 1956-58; student med. record adminstr. Samuel Merritt Hosp., Oakland, Calif., 1958-59, asst. med. record adminstr., 1962-63, asst. chief med. record adminstr., 1965, chief med. record adminstr., 1965-72; med. record adminstr. Albany (Calif.) Hosp., 1964-65; asst. med. record adminstr. Children's Hosp., San Francisco, 1960; co-dir. interns in community service Am. Friends Service Com., San Francisco, 1960-61; med. record adminstr. Pacific Hosp., Oakland, Calif., 1963-64; med. record cons. Tahoe Forest Hosp., Truckee, Calif., 1969-73; chief med. record adminstr. Highland Gen. Hosp., Oakland, 1972-74; dir. med record services U. Calif. San Francisco Hosps. and Clinics, 1975-82; mgr. patient appointments, reception and registration Kaiser-Permanente Med. Ctr., 1982—; tchr. med. records adminstrn. Golden Gate U., 1978—. Girl scout leader Oakland area council, 1960-62; Sunday sch. tchr. Soc. of Friends, Berkeley, Calif., 1961-63, mem. edn. com., 1965-68; mem. policy and adv. bd. Far West Lab. Demonstration Sch., Oakland, 1973—. Recipient Mgmt. Fellowship award U. Calif., San Francisco, 1979-80. Mem. Am. Med. Record Assn., Calif. Med. Record Assn. (editorial bd. 1976-77, pres. 1974-75), East Bay Med. Record Assn. (chmn. edn. com. 1971-72, pres. 1969-70), Assn. Systems Mgmt., Am. Mgmt. Assn., San Francisco Med. Records Assn. (pres.-elect 1982-83, pres. 1983-84). Author: Health Record Documentation: A Look at Cost, 1981; Inservice Training as a Tool in Managing the Changing Environment in the Medical Record Department, 1983; the Budget as a Management Tool, 1983. Issues editor Topics in Health Record Management, Parts I and II, 1983. Home: 5836 Buena Vista Ave Oakland CA 94618 Office: Kaiser-Permanente Med Ctr 280 W MacArthur Blvd Oakland CA 94611

DANIELS, RICHARD MARTIN, marketing communications company executive; b. Delano, Calif., Feb. 24, 1942; s. Edward Martin and Philida Rose (Peterson) D.; m. Leslea Nan Lorenz, June 19, 1970; m. 2d, Kathryn Ellen Knight, Feb. 28, 1976; children—Robert Martin, Michael Edward. A.A., Foothill Coll., 1965; B.A., San Jose State U., 1967; M.A., U. Mo., 1971. News reporter Imperial Valley Press, El Centro, Calif., summers 1963-66, San Diego (Calif.) Evening Tribune, 1967-68, Columbia Daily Tribune (Mo.), 1969-70; nat. news copy editor Los Angeles Times, 1966-67; fin. writer San Diego Union, 1971-74, real estate editor, 1974-77; v.p. pub. relations Hubbert Advt. & Pub. Relations, Costa Mesa, Calif., 1977-78; ptnr. Berkman & Daniels Mktg. Communications, San Diego, 1979—; lectr. various bus. groups and colls. Dir., chmn. 1983 telethon March of Dimes San Diego County; exec. bd., chmn. pub. relations com. San Diego County council Boy Scouts Am.; bd. dirs. San Diego-Imperial Counties Devel. Services, Inc., Com. of 100, San Diego Downtown YMCA, 1981-82; mem. small bus. adv. com. to U.S. Congressman Duncan Hunter. Served with USN, 1959-62. Recipient Excellence award Communicating Arts Group San Diego, 1981. Mem. Pub. Relations Soc. Am., Building Industry Assn. San Diego County, Nat. Assn. Real Estate Editors (best home sect. in U.S. award 1976, best real estate analysis, consumer oriented story, real estate features awards 1977), Sigma Delta Chi. Republican. Lutheran. Club: San Diego Press (sec. 1975-77). Home: 9080 Oviedo St San Diego CA 92129 Office: Berkman & Daniels Mktg Communications 1717 Kettner Blvd Suite 100 San Diego CA 92101

DANIELSON, WALTER RUSSELL, JR., engring. co. exec.; b. Wharton, N.J., Dec. 30, 1927; s. Walter Russell and Annie May (Lawrence) D.; M.E. with honors, Stevens Inst. Tech., 1951; M.S.A.E., Air Force Inst. Tech., 1954; M.B.A. with honors, U. Chgo., 1962; Air War Coll., 1974; m. Paulette Sazerat, Oct. 30, 1957; children—David Walter, Veronique France, Marc Patrick. System mgmt. and acquisition specialist USAF, advanced through grades to lt. col.; served in Ethiopia, France, Ger., Belgium, Portugal and Guam; ret., 1979; project head DSM System Engring. group System Devel. Corp., Sunnyvale, Calif., 1979-83; support engr. specialist Lockheed Missiles & Space Co., Sunnyvale, 1983—; faculty mgmt. sci. Boston Coll. MSBA program, Brussels, 1978-79. Trustee, St. Andrews Meth. Ch., Cherry Hill, N.J., 1964-65; bd. dirs., treas. Am. Community Sch., Addis Ababa, Ethiopia, 1967-68. Served with USMC, 1946-48. Decorated Meritorious Service Medal with two oak leaf cluusters, Air Force Commendation medal, Joint Services Commendation medal, USAF Outstanding Unit award with 2 oak leaf clusters. Mem. AAAS, Air Force Assn., Mil. Order World Wars, Ret. Officers Assn., Am. Security Council, Armed Forces Communications Electronics Assn. (chpt. dir. 1982-83), Ingenieurs et Scientifics de France, Alliance Francaise, Tau Beta Pi, Beta Theta Pi, Beta Gamma Sigma. Republican. Methodist. Clubs: L'Ile de France, France Am. Scottish Rite Bodies (Masons). Home: 2578 Ohlone Dr San Jose CA 95132 Office: PO Box 504 Sunnyvale CA 94086

DANIHER, JOHN M., engr.; b. LaJunta, Colo., Aug. 2, 1926; s. Gerald and Mary Isabelle (Manly) D.; A.B., Western State Coll., Gunnison, Colo., 1948; postgrad. Idaho State U., 1957-74, U. Idaho, 1974-76; m. Edna Erle Hoshall, Sept. 4, 1948; children—Lyn Mari, Suzanne Laurie, Patricia Gail, Jerome Matthew, Michael Kevin. High sch. tchr., Grand Junction, Colo., 1948-52; salesman Century Metalcraft, Denver, 1952-53; chem. plant supr. U.S. Chem. Corps., Denver, 1953-56; sr. engr. instrument and controls Phillips Petroleum Co., Idaho Falls, 1956-76; project engr. E G & G Idaho, Idaho Falls, 1976—; adv. Eastern Idaho Vocat. Tech. Sch., 1975-80. Cubmaster, Boy Scouts Am., 1970-75, asst. scoutmaster, 1975-80. Recipient Cub Man of Yr., Boy Scouts Am., 1973. Mem. Am. Nuclear Soc. Roman Catholic. Club: K.C. (state dep. 1979-81, Supreme council 1981-83) Home: 250 12th St Idaho Falls ID 83401

DANILOVA, ALEXANDRA, ballet dancer, choreographer; b. Peterhof, Russia; came to U.S., 1934; d. Dionis and Claudia (Gotovtzeva) Danilova; ed. Theatrical Sch. Petograd. Mem. Russian State Ballet, Maryinsky Theater, 1922-24; soloist Diaghileff Ballet, 1925, ballerina, 1929; ballerina Montecarlo Opera House, 1930-31; star Oswald Stoll's prodn. Waltzes from Vienna, Alhambra Theatre, London, 1932; ballerina Col. de Basil's Ballet Russe, 1933-38; prima ballerina Ballet Russe de Monte Carlo, 1938-51; currently head own co. touring various countries, lecture tours, U.S., Europe; guest star, various ballets including: Royal Ballet Covent Garden, 1946; star Song of Norway, 1944, Broadway musical Oh Captain, 1958; choreographer Met. Opera Co., staged Coppelia with George Balanchine for N.Y.C. Ballet, 1974, and Los Angeles Ballet, 1980; staged works for Nijinsky Festival Germany, 1975, for Md. Ballet, 1975; now mem. faculty Sch. Am. Ballet; adjudicator Southeastern Ballet Conf., 1960. Recipient Capezio Dance award, 1958. Greek Orthodox. Address: 100 W 57th St New York NY 10019*

DANNEMEYER, WILLIAM EDWIN, congressman; b. South Gate, Calif., Sept. 22, 1929; s. Henry William and Charlotte Ernestine (Knapp)

D.; B.A., Valparaiso U., 1950; J.D., U. Calif., Hastings Law Sch., 1952; m. Evelyn Hoemann, Aug. 27, 1955; children—Bruce, Kim, Susan. Admitted to Calif. bar, 1952; judge pro tempore Mcpl. Ct., Fullerton, Calif., 1966-76, Superior Ct., 1966-76; asst. city atty., Fullerton, 1959-62; individual practice law, Fullerton, 1957-79; mem. Calif. Assembly, 1963-66, 77-78; mem. 96th-97th Congresses from 39th Dist. Calif., mem. Coms. on Energy and Commerce, Post Office and Civil Service. Bd. dirs. Lutheran Ch., Mo. Synod, So. Calif. Dist.; bd. dirs., pres. bd. Orange County Luth. High Sch.; chmn. spl. gifts Capital Fund Drive, Boy Scouts Am., 1966-67; No. Orange County finance chmn. Billy Graham Crusade, 1969. Served with CIC, U.S. Army, Korean War. Named Outstanding Young Man of Yr., Fullerton Jr. C. of C., 1965. Mem. Orange County Bar Assn. (past dir.). Republican. Office: Longworth House Office Bldg Washington DC 20515

DANNENBERGER, EUGENE PAUL, JR., avionics technician; b. Linton, Ind., Jan. 27, 1954; s. Eugene Paul and Shirley Grace (Knight) D.; A.S. with highest honors in Drafting, Mira Costa Coll., 1974; m. Marye Barbara Walwick, Aug. 29, 1976; children—Christina Anne, Matthew Paul. Engr., Oceanside (Calif.) Police Dept., 1973-75; avionics technician Hughes Aviation Services, Las Vegas, Nev., 1980—. Served with USAF, 1976-80. Honor grad. USAF Air Tng. Command, 1977. Mem. USAF Assn. Democrat. Episcopalian. Home: 2820 Kim Ln #E North Las Vegas NV 89030 Office: 6005 S Las Vegas Blvd Las Vegas NV 89119

DANOFF, DUDLEY SETH, physician, surgeon; b. N.Y.C., June 10, 1937; s. Alfred and Ruth (Kauffman) B.; A.B. summa cum laude, Princeton U., 1959; M.D., Yale U., 1963; m. Hedva Amrani, Oct. 27, 1971. Trainee, intern Inst. Cancer Research, Columbia-Presbyn. Med. Center, N.Y.C., 1969-70; resident in urology Coll. Physicians and Surgeons, Columbia U., N.Y.C., 1969-70; cons. urology, vis. surgeon Sch. Med. Tulane U., New Orleans, 1970-71; practice medicine specializing in urology, Los Angeles, 1971—; clin. chief urology Cedars-Sinai Med. Center, Los Angeles, 1974—; faculty, cons. U. Calif., Los Angeles; mem. staff Cedars-Sinai, Midway, Century City hosps., Beverly Hills Med. Ctr. (all Los Angeles). Bd. dirs. Am. Friends Hebrew U., Los Angeles, also chmn. exec. com. western states; active Am. Technicon Soc., Am.-Israel Pub. Affairs Com., Am. Physicians Fellowship; adv. com. Los Angeles Jewish Fedn. Council; mem. nat. leadership cabinet United Jewish Appeals, Los Angeles; bd. dir. Guardians of Courage, Israel. Served with M.C., USAF, 1969-71. Fellow A.C.S.; mem. Am. Fertility Soc., Soc. Air Force Clin. Surgeons, Soc. Internat. Urology, Am. Urologic Assn., Los Angeles Urologic Soc., Transplant Soc. So. Calif., AMA, Los Angeles County Med. Assn. (bd. govs., past pres.), Los Angeles Profl. Men's Club (exec. com., pres. 1981—), Phi Beta Kappa, Sigma Xi, Alpha Omega Alpha, Phi Delta Epsilon (v.p. com.). Clubs: Hillcrest Country; Mission Hills Golf and Country, Yale, Princeton of So. Calif. Contbr. numerous articles sci. jours. Office: Cedars-Sinai Med Office Tower 8631 W 3d St Los Angeles CA 90048

DANSON, EDWARD BRIDGE, emeritus museum director; b. Glendale, Ohio, Mar. 22, 1916; s. Edward Bridge and Ann (Allen) D.; B.A., U. Ariz., 1940; M.A., Harvard U., 1948, Ph.D. in Anthropology, 1953; m. Jessica Harriet MacMaster, Nov. 2, 1942; children—Jessica Danson Haury, Edward Bridge, III. Asst. prof. anthropology U. Colo., 1948-50; asst. prof. U. Ariz., 1950-56, asst. dir. U. Ariz. Field Sch., 1952 53, acting dir., 1954; asst. dir. Mus. No. Ariz., Flagstaff, 1956-58, dir., 1958-75, dir. emeritus, 1979—, pres. bd. trustees, 1975-79; bd. dirs. S.W. Parks and Monuments Assn., 1958—; mem. Ariz. Hist. Sites Rev. Com., 1967-83; trustee Am. Folklife Center of Library of Congress, 1976—, now chmn. bd. trustees. Mem. adv. bd. Nat. Park Service, 1958-64, mem. adv. council, 1964—. Served with USN, 1942-45. fellow Am. Anthrop. Assn., AAAS, Ariz. Acad. Sci. (pres. 1958-59); mem. Ariz. Hist. Soc. (trustee 1974—), Ariz. Archaeol. and Hist. Soc. (pres. 1955-56), Am. Assn. Museums, Soc. Am. Archaeology, Soc. Hist. Archaeology, Sigma Xi. Episcopalian. Clubs: Sedona Racquet, Phoenix Univ.; Cosmos (Washington). Home and Office: PO Box 379 Sedona AZ 86336

DANSON, RICHARD LEWIS, management consultant; b. N.Y.C., May 18, 1929; s. Richard J. and Julie (Lane) Collins; m. Elaine I. Galuppo, Sept. 27, 1952; children—Richard, Kevin, Brett, Dana, Juliana, Gia, Joshua. A.B., UCLA, 1952, teaching cert. bus. adminstrn., 1957; postgrad. Loyola U. Law Sch., 1962. Mgmt. cons. Miller Assos., cons., Anaheim, Calif., 1962-65; head computer systems services Hughes Aircraft Co., Fullerton, 1965-71; bus. mgr., v.p., dir. The New Standard Co., Inc., med. equipment mfr., Dana Point, Calif., 1971-73; dir. program mgmt. Teleswitcher subs. Astrodata Corp., Dallas, 1973-74; dir. cons. services, planning, control and computer scis. Gottfried Cons. Inc., Los Angeles, 1974—; pres. Danson Cons., Irvine, Calif. Mem. Gov.'s Radiol. Def. Adv. Com., Calif., 1963—. Mayor, City of La Mirada, Calif., 1960-64. Trustee Los Angeles County Sanitation Dist., 1963-64; bd. dirs. Southeast Mosquito Abatement Dist., 1963-64. Served as capt. USAF, 1952-54. Mem. Planning Execs. Inst., Inst. Bus. Appraisers, Phi Delta Phi. Home: 26961 Via la Mirada San Juan Capistrano CA 92675 Office: Danson Cons Inc 2102 Business Center Dr Irvine CA 92715

DANT, ROBERT MICHAEL, real estate investment company executive; b. Portland, Oreg., Oct. 3, 1948; s. Charles Mitchell and Florence Mildred (Stryker) D.; B.S. in Bus. Adminstrn., Oreg. State U., 1970; postgrad. in bus. adminstrn. Portland State U., 1971-76. Vice pres., gen. mgr. Beaverton Transfer Co. (Oreg.), 1971-73; real estate/mortgage loan analyst Standard Ins. Co., Portland, 1973-77; pres., dir. Dant Devel. Corp., Portland, 1977—; dir. Pacat Properties, Inc., San Francisco. Mem., advisor Wilsonville (Oreg.) Planning Commn., 1974-80; mem. Wilsonville Design Rev. Bd., 1978-80, Portland Hist. Landmarks Commn., 1980—; trustee Meridian Park Hosp. Found., Tualatin, Oreg., 1980—. Served with Oreg. Army N.G., 1970-76. Mem. Soc. Real Estate Appraisers (assoc.), Internat. Council Shopping Cntrs. (assoc.), Urban Land Inst. (assoc.). Clubs: Multnomah Athletic, Elks. Office: 808 SW Alder St Suite 200 Portland OR 97205

DANZBERGER, ALEXANDER HARRIS, chemical engineer, consultant; b. N.Y.C., Mar. 23, 1932; s. George Harris and Ruth P. (Alexander) D.; m. Jacqueline P. Pilcher, Mar. 12, 1954; children—Alison, Alexander, Diana, Robert; m. 2d, Anne Griggs Pierson, Apr. 23, 1977; stepchildren—Jennifer Pierson, Priscilla Pierson, Stephanie Pierson. B.S. in Chem. Engring., MIT, 1953. Registered profl. engr., Mass., Colo. Mem. staff Arthur D. Little Inc., Cambridge, Mass., 1953-60; engring. mgr. Linde div. Union Carbide Corp., Tonawanda, N.Y., N.Y.C., 1961-70; chief engr. Booz, Allen & Hamilton, Florham Park, N.J., 1971-72, Marcom Cons., N.Y.C., 1973-75; v.p. Hydrotechnic Corp., N.Y.C., 1976-81; mgr. pollution control group Dames & Moore, Golden, Colo., 1982—. Served to 1st lt. U.S. Army, 1956-68. Recipient Kenneth B. Allen award N.Y. Water Pollution Control Assn., 1983. Fellow Am. Inst. Chem. Engrs. (2d v.p. environ. div.), mem. Am. Acad. Environ. Engrs. (diplomate), Water Pollution Control Fedn., Am. Water Works Assn., ASME, AIME, AAAS. Republican. Presbyterian. Clubs: N.Y. Yacht, Corinthians, Masons. Home: 13245 Willow Ln Golden CO 80401 Office: Dames & Moore 1626 Cole Blvd Golden CO 80401

DANZIG, DANIEL DEVERE, public relations professional; b. Oakland, Calif., Aug. 1, 1953; s. Paul and Mary Devere (Jetmore) D.; m. Dianne Maureen McGregor, July 13, 1980. B.A. in Communications, U. No. Colo., 1975. Field program and news dir. Far East Broadcasting Co., Okinawa, No. Marianas, 1976-80; sr. pub. affairs rep. Kaiser-Permanente Med. Care Program, Kaiser Found. Health Plan, Inc., San Francisco, 1980—. Active Commonwealth Club. Mem. Pub. Relations Soc. Am., Internat. Assn. Bus. Communicators, Hosp. Pub. Relations Assn. Republican. Mem. Covenant Ch. Am. Home: 286 Beachview Ave Apt 32 Pacifica CA 94044 Office: Kaiser Found Health Plan Inc 2266 Geary Blvd San Francisco CA 94115

DANZIGER, JERRY, broadcasting exec.; b. N.Y.C., Jan. 23, 1924; s. Harry and Lillie (Lacher) D.; grad. high sch.; m. Zelda Bloom, Dec. 26, 1948; children—Sydney, Alan, Lee. With WTTV, Bloomington, Ind., 1950-53; program mgr. WTSK-TV, Knoxville, Tenn., 1953; ops. mgr. WTTV, Indpls., 1953-57; v.p., gen. mgr. KOB-TV, Albuquerque, 1957—; mem. Gov. N.Mex. Commn. for Film Entertainment, 1970-71. Bd. dirs. Albuquerque Little Theatre, Albuquerque Public Braodcast, Albuquerque Jewish Welfare Fund, Goodwill Industry N.Mex., Better Bus. Bur. Served with USAAF, 1942-45; hon. comdr. 1550 Tech. Tng. Squadron. Recipient Compadre award Am. Women in Radio and TV, 1978. Mem. AP Broadcasters (dir. 1981-84), N.Mex. Broadcasters Assn. (pres. 1972-73, Broadcaster of Year award 1976, 78), Press Club, Advt. Club. Club: Albuqerque Country. Office: Box 1351 Albuquerque NM 87103

DARAKANANDA, CHONGRAKSA, bus. exec.; b. Nakhon Srithammaraj, Thailand, Dec. 21, 1933; came to U.S., 1977, permanent resident, 1979; d. Hen Jen Lim and Francim Wen; 10th grade cert. Sukit Coll. Sch., 1954; 12th grade cert. Triam-Udom Prep. Sch., 1956; m. Damri Darakananda, Aug. 10, 1957; children—Chutindhon, Aksornprasit, Pinipjporn, Bovornrat, Vacharaphong. Bus. woman, mgr., exec. various trading and mfg. cos., Thailand, 1956-77; dir., treas. Saha-Union Internat. (U.S.A.) Inc., San Francisco, 1977-78, pres., Daly City, Calif., 1978—, exec. dir. fin. and personnel Saha-Union Corp. Ltd., Bangkok, Thailand, 1972-81, v.p., 1981—; guest lectr. middle mgmt., supr. tng. of group, chmn. com. for grievances of group. Mem. Personnel Mgmt. Assn. Thailand (life), Thai Mgmt. Assn. (corp.), Am. Mgmt. Assn. Thailand Chpt. (corp). Buddhist. Club: Royal Bangkok Sports. Home: 455 37th Ave San Francisco CA 94121 Office: 419 Allan St Daly City CA 94014

DARBY, JUNE SCOTT, public relations counsel; b. Topeka, 1917; d. Harry F. and Alberta F. (Sellers) D.; B.J., Kans. State U., 1940; grad. Holmes Coll. Ministry, 1983; m. Jay Ellison, Dec. 30, 1944 (div.); children—Jeremy Jodi, David Scott, John Michael. Broadcaster-writer WMBH Radio, Joplin, Mo., 1940-43; writer KSD Radio, St. Louis, 1943-47; broadcaster, writer KXLW Radio, St. Louis, 1947-50; writer KWK Radio, St. Louis, 1954-57; public relations officer Merc. Trust Co., St. Louis, 1957-75; public relations officer Merc. Bancorp., Inc., St. Louis, 1975-78; owner Ellison Communications, St. Louis and San Francisco, 1978—. Mem. consumer adv. council Better Bus. Bur. Greater St. Louis, 1967-72; adv. council Downtown Activities Unltd. for Downtown St. Louis Inc., 1965-70. Lic. minister Ch. of Religious Sci. Named Advt. Woman of Year St. Louis, 1974-75, Advt. Woman of Year Midwest, 1975-76 (both Am. Advt. Fedn). Mem. Nat. Assn. Bank Women (regional v.p. 1974-75), Mo. Bankers Assn. (chmn. bank mktg. and public relations com. 1975-76), Advt. Women St. Louis Inc., Public Relations Soc. Am., Bank Mktg. Assn., Mo. Press Women, St. Louis Press Club, Women in Communications, Inc., Women's Polit. Caucus. Home and Office: 272 N Carnegie #143 Claremont CA 91711

DARBY, ROBERT LOUIS, interior designer; b. Detroit, Oct. 30, 1921; s. Leo William and Mary Elizabeth (Gilligan) D.; 1 dau., Mariel Elizabeth. Cert. profl. interior designer, Calif. Prin. Robert L. Darby Assocs., Palo Alto, Calif.; guest lectr., tchr. in field. Recipient 1st prize Ohline Corp.'s Design Competition, 1980. Mem. Internat. Soc. Interior Designers (pres. No. Calif. chpt.). Contbr. articles to profl. mags., newspapers. Office: Suite 154 770 Welch Rd Palo Alto CA 94304

DARBY, WESLEY ANDREW, clergyman, educator; b. Glendale, Ariz., Sept. 19, 1928; s. Albert Leslie and Beulah E. (Lamb) D.; student Bible Inst. Los Angeles, 1946, No. Ariz. U., 1946-47, Rockmont Coll., Denver, 1948-50, Ariz. State U., 1965, St. Anne's Coll., Oxford (Eng.) U., 1978; m. Donna Maye Bice, May 29, 1947; children—Carolyn Darby Eymann, Lorna Dale, Elizabeth Darby Bass, Andrea Darby Perdue. Ordained minister Baptist Ch., 1950; pastor Sunnyside Bapt. Ch., Flagstaff, Ariz., 1947-48, First Bapt. Ch. of Clifton, Ariz., 1950-55, West High Bapt. Ch., Phoenix, 1955—; dep. assessor Greenlee County, 1951-55; instr. English lit. and pastoral subjects Southwestern Conservative Bapt. Bible Coll., Phoenix, 1961—. Chmn. bd. Conservative Bapt. Found. Ariz., 1974-83, Gospel Wings, 1960—; v.p. Ariz. Bapt. Conf., 1976-83; pres. Ariz. Alcohol-Narcotic Edn. Assn., 1968—. Recipient God, Family and Country award Freeman Inst., 1981. Mem. Evang. Philos. Soc., Greater Phoenix Assn. Evangelicals (pres. 1960-63). Republican. Club: Ariz. Breakfast (chaplain 1969—). Contbr. articles to profl. jours. Home: 5628 N 11th Dr Phoenix AZ 85013 Office: 3301 N 19th Ave Phoenix AZ 85015

D'ARCY, HENRY WISE, electronics co. exec.; b. St. Louis, Oct. 25, 1940; s. Harry M. and Helen (Wise) D'A.; B.B.A., U. Mo., 1964; M.B.A., San Francisco State Coll., 1968; m. Donna Mirenda, Sept. 9, 1978, 1 dau., Katie; children from previous marriage—Tracey, Jody. Pres., SDR 2 Products & Sales Co., Bellevue, 1971—; partner SDR 2 Mgmt. Services, 1975—; owner D'Arcy Nutcrackers, 1979, D'Arcy Arabian Show Horses; dir. Creative Images Advt. Bellevue. Served with USMC, 1958-63. Mem. Electronic Reps. Assn., Soc. Advancement Mgmt., Seattle Advt. Assn., Pacific N.W. Ski Inst. Assn., Nat. Horse Breeders Assn. Club: Elks. Office: care SDR 2 Products & Sales 14230 NE 8th St Bellevue WA 98007

D'ARCY-CLARKE, EDMUND THOMAS, personnel manager, educator; b. Englewood, N.J., Dec. 21, 1921; s. John Peter and Mary Agnes (Costello) D'Arcy-C.; m. Vera Annaliese Addix, Jan. 12, 1952; children—Peggy Ann, Evelyn Jeanne, Edmund, Charles John. A.A., Riverside City Coll., 1966; B.S. in Bus., Calif. State U.-Fresno, 1973, M.S. in Bus., 1977. Cert. community coll. instr., personnel mgr. Entered U.S. Army, 1942, advanced through grades to master sgt., 1953; ret., 1964; adminstrv. asst. Angeles Nat. Forest, Pasadena, Calif., 1964-65; resource adminstrv. asst. San Bernardino (Calif.) Nat. Forest, 1965-66; personnel mgmt. specialist Sierra Nat. Forest, Fresno, Calif., 1966-69, personnel officer, 1969-76; pre-retirement planning instr. Centers div. San Francisco Community Coll. Dist., 1978—. Mem. curriculum adv. com. Reedley Coll., 1969-74; former mem. Fresno Commn. on Aging. Decorated Bronze Star, Army Commendation medal. Mem. Am. Soc. Personnel Adminstrn., Am. Soc. Tng. and Devel., Am. Assn. Ret. Persons, Nat. Assn. Ret. Fed. Employees. Roman Catholic. Home: 1243 E Escalon Ave Fresno CA 93710

DARDEN, EDWIN SPEIGHT, architect; b. Stantonsburg, N.C., Oct. 14, 1920; s. Edwin Speight and Sallie (Jordan) D.; m. Paula K. Bartlett, Feb. 26, 1944; children—Edwin Speight III, Judith Ann Hulstrom, Diane R. Morgan. B.S. in Arch. Engring., Kans. State U., 1947; lic. architect, Calif. Architect, Fred L. Swartz-William G. Hyberg, Fresno, Calif., 1949-59; architect Nargis and Darden, Fresno, 1959-69; architect Edwin S. Darden Assocs., Fresno, 1969-79, pres., 1979—; mem. state adv. bd. Office of Architecture and Constrn., 1970-78; cons. in field. Mem. Fresno County Bd. Rev., 1975-77. Served to lt. C.E., AUS, 1942-46. Recipient design awards San Joaquin chpt. AIA, 1962 (2), 75, 79, 81; recipient design in steel award Am. Iron and Steel Inst., 1963. Fellow AIA; mem. Alpha Kappa Psi, Sigma Phi Epsilon. Presbyterian. Club: Rotary. Home: 7549 N Toletachi Fresno CA 93711 Office: 5082 N Palm Suite G Fresno CA 93704

DARDEN, LUCILLE ANN, educator; b. Las Cruces, N.Mex., Aug. 6, 1954; d. William Byron and Lucille (Garduño) D. B.S. in Edn., N.Mex. State U., 1976, M.S. in Ednl. Adminstrn., 1982. Elem. teaching cert., ednl. adminstrv cert., N.Mex. Tch. Pub. Schs. Las Cruces, 1976—. Mem. Assn. Supervision and Curriculum Devel., Phi Beta Kappa, Phi Kappa Phi, Pi Beta Phi Alumna. Republican. Office: Alameda Elementary School 301 W Amador St Las Cruces NM 88005

DARKE, CHARLES B(RUCE), dentist, hospital administrator; b. Chgo., Sept. 22, 1937; s. Paul O. and Annie W. (Tennin) D.; m. Annetta Mc Rae, Aug. 15, 1965; 1 son, Charles B. II. A.A., Wilston Jr. Coll., 1960; D.D.S., Meharry Med. Coll., 1964; M.P.H., U. Calif.-Berkeley, 1972. Dir. dental services San Francisco Gen. Hosp., 1973—, asst. adminstr. outpatient dept., 1980—; asst. clin. prof. Sch. Medicine and lectr. Sch. Dentistry U. Calif.-San Francisco; regional cons. Job Corps Tng. Centers, Dept. Labor. Bd. dirs. Calif. Children's Lobby. Served to capt. USAF, 1965-67. Recipient award Royal Soc. Health. Mem. ADA, Nat. Dental Assn. Home and office: 2175 Hayes St San Francisco CA 94117

DARKO, DENIS F., physician; b. Indpls., July 13, 1947; s. Charles O. and Agnes Mary (Lauck) D.; B.S. in Physics, U. Notre Dame, 1969; M.D., Ind. U., 1975. Research technician biols. div. Eli Lilly Co., Indpls., 1970, U. Colo. Sch. Medicine, 1971; resident physician family practice Scotsdale (Ariz.) Meml. Hosp., 1975-76; resident physician psychiatry Good Samaritan Hosp., Phoenix, 1977-80; pvt. practice psychiatry, Scottsdale, Ariz., 1980-83; cons. psychiatrist Phoenix Indian Med. Center, 1980-81; supr. psychiatry residency program Maricopa Med. Center, 1980-83; instr. pre-med. program Ariz. State U., 1980-83; mem. staff Scottsdale Meml. Hosp., instr. family practice residency program, 1980-83; mem. staff Scottsdale Camelback Hosp.; fellow in consultation/liaison psychiatry U. Calif.-San Diego Med. Ctr., 1983—. USPHS fellow, 1972. Mem. Am. Phys. Soc., Am. Chem. Soc., Am. Math. Soc., AAAS, N.Y. Acad. Scis., AMA, ACP, Am. Psychiat. Assn., Central Neuropsychiat. Assn., Am. Psychosomatic Assn., Calif. Med. Assn., Calif. Psychiat. Assn., San Diego County Med. Soc., San Diego Psychiat. Soc., Am. Acad. Family Practice, Am. Assn. Group Psychotherapy, Ariz. Med. Assn., Ariz. Psychiat. Soc., Maricopa County Med. Soc., Phoenix Psychiat. Council. Office: U Calif San Diego Med Ctr San Diego CA

DARLING, BERNARD BENJAMIN, govt. ofcl.; b. Hooper, Nebr., Mar. 6, 1922; s. Benjamin Glenn and Charlotte Margaret Martha (Monnich) D.; B.J., U. Mo., 1948; m. Marian Walsh, May 20, 1950; children—Bruce Bernard, Scott Christopher. Br. mgr. Postal Telegraph Cable Co., Fremont, Nebr., 1941; surveyor Western Natural Gas, Tyler, Tex., 1945; asst. editor Lindsay (Calif.) Gazette, 1948; sports editor, columnist, courthouse reporter Hanford (Calif.) Sentinel, 1948-50; reporter Fresno (Calif.) Bee, 1950-61; asst. press attache, diplomat Am. embassy, Montevideo, Uruguay, 1961-64; press attache Am. embassy, Santo Domingo, Dominican Republic, 1964-67, Quito, Ecuador, 1968-70; congressional staffer, Washington, 1970-72; public info. specialist Animal and Plant Health Inspection Service, U.S. Dept. Agr., Washington, 1973-75; regional info. dir. U.S. Dept. Agr., San Franciso, 1975—. Served with USN, 1941-45. Recipient Superior Service award Dominican Republic Revolution, 1965. Home: 140 Homestead Blvd Mill Valley CA 94941 Office: 630 Sansome St Room 702 San Francisco CA 94111

DARLING, EDWIN EARL, engineer; b. Cheyenne, Wyo., Mar. 17, 1946; s. Earl J. and Lorna M. Darling; m. Lisa Windbigler, July 5, 1968; 1 dau., Laura. B.S. in Engring. Physics, Colo. Sch. Mines, 1968. Lab. mgr. Procter & Gamble Mfg. Co., Kansas City, Kans., 1972-74, mgr. Zest making dept., 1974-76, group leader research and devel., Cin., 1976-78; regional engr. ARATEX Services Inc., Cin., 1978-80, dir. engring., Encino, Calif., 1980-83, v.p. tech. services, 1983—. Served to capt. C.E., U.S. Army, 1969-72. Mem. Am. Soc. Safety Engrs., ASTM Inst. Indsl. Launderers (chmn. energy conservation sub-com.), Blue Key, Scabbard and Blade, Tau Beta Pi, Sigma Gamma Epsilon, Kappa Kappa Psi. Republican. Methodist. Office: PO Box 3000 Encino CA 91316

DARLING, JAMES PAUL, architect; b. Yokohama, Japan, June 19, 1948; came to U.S., 1951; s. Byron Paul and Frances Jacqueline (Barth) D. Registered architect, Calif. Vice pres. Integrated, Inc., Newport Beach, Calif., 1969-79; pres. J.P. Darling & Assocs., Architects, Newport Beach, 1979—. Republican. Presbyterian. Club: Jonathan (Los Angeles). Office: JP Darling & Assocs Architects 3300 Irvine Ave Suite 385 Newport Beach CA 92660

DARLING-ROSENFELD, SANDRA KAYE, educator; b. Portland, Oreg., Aug. 6, 1953; d. Howard Wayne and Ruth Eileen (Russell) Darling; m. Stephen Barry Rosenfeld, June 25, 1983. B.S. in Edn., Portland State U., 1975, M.S. in Edn., 1983. Ticket agt. Meml. Coliseum, Portland, 1971—, Civic Stadium, Portland, 1975—; early childhood educator Portland pub. schs., 1975—. Mem. Portland Assn. Tchrs. (mem. contract maintenance com.), Theatrical Employees Union Local (pres.). Home: 6837 SW 11th Dr Portland OR 97219 Office: 4906 NE 6th Ave Portland OR 97211

DARNALL, ROBERTA MORROW, univ. ofcl.; b. Kemmerer, Wyo., May 18, 1949; d. C. Dale and Eugenia Stayner (Christmas) Morrow; B.S., U. Wyo., Laramie, 1972; m. Leslie A. Darnall, Sept. 3, 1977; 1 dau., Kimberly Gene. Tariff sec., ins. adminstr. Wyo. Trucking Assn., Casper, 1973-75; asst. clerical supr. Wyo. Legislature, Cheyenne, 1972-77; congl. campaign press aide, 1974; pub. relations dir. in Casper, Wyo. Republican Central Com., 1976-77; asst. dir. alumni relations U. Wyo., 1977-81, dir. of alumni, 1981—; exec. com. Higher Edn. Assn. Rockies. Mem. Council Advancement and Support Edn., Higher Edn. Assn. Rockies, Am. Soc. Assn. Execs., Laramie C. of C., PEO, Sigma Delta Chi. Republican. Episcopalian. Clubs: Alumni Scholarship, Cowboy Joe. Home: 1172 Frontera Dr Laramie WY 82070 Office: Box 3137 Univ Station Laramie WY 82071

DARNELL, CHARLOTTE DEANE, psychologist; b. Lamar, Mo., Jan. 15, 1934; d. P.L. and Mary Ambrosia (Burt) Potter; B.A., William Jewell Coll., 1955; M.A., U. Mo., 1958; Ph.D., U. Colo., 1968; m. Donald K. Darnell, Nov. 23, 1951; children—Kelleen, Diana, Kimberly, Daniel. Tchr. elem. sch., Lansing, Mich., 1955-59; social worker, East Lansing, Mich., 1960-62; psychologist, Manhattan, Kans., 1962-65; dir. spl. edn., Manhattan, 1962-65; vis. prof. U. Iowa, 1969-70; coordinator early childhood edn., Boulder (Colo.) Valley Schs., 1971-75; researcher and program evaluator Jefferson County Schs., Lakewood, Colo., 1975—; cons. Colo. Dept. Edn., Colo. Legislature; vis. scholar Harvard U., 1974. Mem. Am. Ednl. Research Assn., Am. Psychology Assn., Nat. Assn. Young Children, Colo. Assn. Edn. Young Children, Assn. Colo. Ednl. Evaluators, Evaluation Network, Phi Delta Kappa. Democrat. Baptist. Contbr. articles to profl. jours. Home: 4497 Grinnell Ave Boulder CO 80303 Office: 1211 Quail St Lakewood CO 80215

DARNELL, MARSHALL CLOYD, school district administrator, consultant; b. Harrodsburg, Ky., Nov. 15, 1937; s. James Milton and Sarah Elizabeth (Robinson) D.; m. Patsy Lucille Pace, Aug. 1, 1964; children—Theresa Michele, James Marshall. B.A., Eastern Ky. State Coll., 1960, M.A., 1964; Ed.D., U. Nev.-Las Vegas, 1977. Cert. adminstr., guidance tchr. Prin., K.O. Knudsen Jr. High Sch., 1969-70,

Valley High Sch., 1970-74, dir. secondary edn. Clark County Sch. Dist., Las Vegas, Nev., 1974-78, dir. vocat. edn., 1978-80, dir. secondary curriculum, vocat. edn., 1980—; cons. in field; Active United Way, Am. Cancer Soc. Recipient Hon. Life Membership K.O. Knudsen PTA, 1969. Mem. Am. Vocat. Assn., Nat. Assn. Secondary Schs. Prins., Phi Delta Kappa. Democrat. Baptist. Clubs: Rotary (Southwest), Masons. Contbr. articles to profl. jours.

DARNELL, PATSY PACE, guidance counselor; b. Clark County, Ky., Oct. 15, 1937; d. Floyd Lockhart and Pattie Lucile (Tudor) Pace; m. Marshall C. Darnell, Aug. 1, 1964; children—Theresa Michele, James Marshall. B.S., Eastern Ky. U., 1960; M.Ed., Ohio U., 1962; postgrad. No. Ariz. U., U. Nev.-Las Vegas. Cert. tchr., counselor, vocat. counselor, Nev. Dir. women's residence halls Eastern Ky. U., 1962-64; jr. high sch. bus. tchr., Las Vegas, 1964-67, high sch. counselor, 1967-69, jr. high sch. counselor, 1974-76; counselor coordinator Bonanza High Sch., 1976-82; counselor Western High Sch., Las Vegas, 1982—. Mem. Clark County Cancer Soc., Matt Kelly PTA. Mem. Am. Personnel and Guidance Assn., Nev. Personnel and Guidance Assn., Clark County Sch. Counselors Assn., Alpha Delta Kappa. Baptist.

DA ROSA, JOSE (JOE) GARCIA, travel agy. exec.; b. San Diego, Oct. 20, 1937; s. Jose Garcia da Rosa and Maria Ascencao (Soares) R.; A.A., Menlo Coll., 1957; B.A., U. Calif., Santa Barbara, 1959; postgrad. (scholar) U. Coimbra (Portugal), 1959; m. Marly Tiburtius Magno de Sa, Mar. 15, 1969; children—Andrea, Ricardo. Asso. editor Gazette-Citizen, Goleta, Calif., 1960-61; vol. Peace Corps, Dominican Republic, 1962-64, U.S. State Dept. fgn. res. officer and Peace Corps state dir. for Alagoas, Brazil, 1965-68, ops. officer for Venezuela, Washington, 1968-69; dep. dir. Latin Am. Devel. and Tng. Center, Escondido, Calif., 1969-71; pres. Balboa Travel Inc., San Diego, 1971—. Mem. Am. Soc. Travel Agts. (past v.p. San Diego chpt., mem. nat. automation com.), Pan Am. Travel Agts. Adv. Council, Pacific Area Travel Assn., San Diego C. of C. Office: 407 Laurel St San Diego CA 92101

D'ARRIGO, STEPHEN, JR., agrl. co. exec.; b. Stockton, Calif., Mar. 8, 1922; s. Stephen and Constance (Picciotto) D'A.; B.S., U. Santa Clara, 1947; m. Rosemary Anne Murphy, Aug. 20, 1949; children—Stephen III, Kathleen Anne, Joanne Marie, Michael Andrew, Dennis Patrick, Patrick Shane. Sec.-treas., D'Arrigo Bros. Co. of Calif., San Jose, 1946—, Salinas, 1962—; sec.-treas. Santa Cruz Farms, Eloy, Ariz., 1947-52; pres., gen. mgr. 1952-70, dir., 1947—. Mem. Nat. Def. Exec. Res., 1973—. Served to 2d lt. AUS, 1943-46. Decorated Bronze Star, Belgian Fouragere, Combat Infantry Badge; recipient Disting. Service award Santa Clara Heart Assn. Mem. Nat. Rifle Assn. (life), NAM, Am. Security Council, Am. Soc. Arms Collectors, Tex. Gun Collectors Assn., Co. Mil. Historians, Nat. Hist. Soc., Assn. U.S. Army, Springfield Armory Mus. (life), Smithsonian Assos. (charter), Mil. Order World Wars. Elk. Club: Commonwealth of Calif. Home: 2241 Dry Creek Rd San Jose CA 95124 Office: PO Box 850 Salinas CA 93901

DARROW, GEORGE FRANCIS, geologist, resource cons.; b. Osage, Wyo., August 13, 1924; s. George Washington and Marjorie (Ord) Darrow; A.B. in Econs., U. Mich., 1945, B.S. in Geology, 1949; m. Elna Tannehill, Oct. 23, 1976; children by previous marriage—Roy Stuart, Karen Josanne, Reed Crandall, John Robin. Pres., Crossbow Corp., 1962—; resource cons., 1959—; pres. Kootenai Galleries, Inc., 1976—; mem. Mont. Ho. of Reps., 1967-69, 71-73, Mont. Senate, 1973-75; chmn. Mont. Environ. Quality Council, 1971-73. Served with USNR, 1943-46. Recipient Hilliard award for outstanding environ. achievement Rocky Mountain Center Environment, 1971. Fellow AAAS; mem. Am. Assn. Petroleum Geologists (past pres. Rocky Mountain sect.), Am. Inst. Profl. Geologists (charter), Mont. Geol. Soc. (charter mem., founder), Billings Petroleum Club. Contbr. articles on resource mgmt. and environmental conservation to profl. jours. Home: 2014 Beverly Hills Blvd Billings MT 59102 also Paladin Farms 1540 Chapman Hill Dr Bigfork MT 59911

DARROW, KERMIT LAWSON, architect; b. Klamath Falls, Oreg., 1928; s. Horace Frederick and Velma Elezibeth (Wescoatt) D.; A.A., Hartnell Coll., 1948; A.B., U. Calif.-Berkeley, 1951; m. Eleanor Sykes Noble, Dec. 10, 1960; children—Matthew, Lizabeth, Joan. Archtl. draftsman Francis A. Lockwood, AIA, Santa Cruz, Calif., 1950-55; pvt. practice architecture, Santa Cruz, 1955—. Mem. City of Santa Cruz Off-St. Parking Commn., 1959-63. Mem. AIA. Republican. Clubs: Rotary, Masons (32 deg.). Works include: Pacific Garden Mall, Santa Cruz, 1971. Home: 2 Thayer Rd Santa Cruz CA 95060 Office: 911 Center St Santa Cruz CA 95060

DASKIVICH, RICHARD ANTHONY, electrical engineer; b. Indiana, Pa., Mar. 26, 1941; s. John and Kathryn Daskivich; m. Patricia Ann Medvetz, June 26, 1965. B.S. in Elec. Engring., Pa. State U., 1963; M.S., Wayne State U., 1967. With Gen. Motors Corp., Detroit, 1963-82, sr. engr. systems, metrology, electronics, friction, lubrication and wear Research Labs., 1963-80, staff engr. advanced engine devel. and reliability Detroit Diesel Allison div., 1980-82; engring. supr. Hughes Aircraft Co., El Segundo, Calif., 1983—, also project mgr. space cryogenics. Mem. Soc. Mfg. Engrs. (sr.). Author research reports. Office: PO Box 902 El Segundo CA 90245

DASWANI, MOTI SADHUMAL, physician; b. Karachi, Pakistan, Oct. 31, 1945; came to U.S., 1971, naturalized, 1981; s. Sadhumal Dhalomal and Ishwari Shewakram (Baharani) D.; m. Ramola Baharani, May 22, 1974; 1 child, Adarsh. M.B., B.S., Grant Med. Coll., Bombay, India, 1969. Diplomate Am. Bd. Internal Medicine, Am. Bd. Nephrology. Intern, Queens Gen. Hosp., N.Y.C., 1971-72; resident in internal medicine Queens Gen. Hosp. affiliation L.I. Jewish Med. Ctr., 1972-75, fellow in nephrology, 1975-77; internist Family Health Program, Long Beach, Calif., 1977-78; practice medicine specializing in nephrology, Long Beach, 1978—; mem. staff Doctors Hosp. of Lakewood (Calif.), Los Altos Hosp., Long Beach, Calif. Mem. AMA, Los Angeles County Med. Assn., Long Beach Soc. Internal Medicine. Office: 3320 Los Coyotes Diagonal Long Beach CA 90808

DATTA, PURNA CHANDRA, psychologist; b. Barisal, Bangladesh, Jan. 1, 1943; s. Jogendra Kumar and Kanak Lata (Ghosh) Datta; m. Anita Rani Datta, Feb. 7, 1969; children—Partha, Aparna. B.A. with honors, Dacca U., 1963, M.A., 1964, M.A. in Psychology, 1967; Ph.D., Newcastle U. (Australia), 1979, M.Psychol., 1982. Lectr. psychology Dacca U., Bangladesh, 1969-73, part-time student counsellor, 1972-73; part-time tutor psychology Newcastle U., New South Wales, 1974; part-time psychologist Morisset Hosp., New South Wales, 1974-76, full time psychologist, 1976-80; program psychologist Fairview State Hosp., Costa Mesa, Calif., 1980—; clin. instr. dept. psychiatry U. Calif.-Irvine, part-time 1981—; cons., lectr. in field. Mem. Australian Psychol. Soc., Australian Behavior Modification Soc., Fairview Psychol. Assn., Am. Psychol. Assn., Morisset Intellectually Handicapped Assn., Assn. for Severly Handicapped, Bangladesh Psychol. Assn. (exec. asst. gen. sec.), Nat. Soc. for Autistic Children, Psychologists in Pub. Service, Am. Assn. Advancement Sci., N.Y. Acad. Sci. Contbr. articles to profl. jours. Home: 2109 A Edinger Ave Santa Ana CA 92704 Office: 2501 Harbor Blvd Costa Mesa CA 92626

DAU, GARY JOHN, nuclear engr.; b. Lewiston, Idaho, Sept. 3, 1938; s. George J. and Marjorie (Konen) D.; B.S., U. Idaho, 1961; Ph.D., U. Ariz., 1965; m. Brenda Graham Brown, June 24, 1961; children—Brent George, Fredric Gary. Research scientist Battelle Northwest, Richland, Wash., 1964-66, sect. mgr. electronic measurements research, 1966-68, dept. mgr. nondestructive testing, applied physics, 1968-74, asso. dept. mgr. nuclear waste tech., 1974-75, staff scientist, 1976-77; nondestructive exam. program mgr. Electric Power Research Inst., Palo Alto, Calif., 1975-76, 77-81, sr. program mgr. system integrity, 1981—; tchr. nuclear engring. Joint Center for Grad. Study, 1967-68; tchr. engring. prins. Columbia Basin Coll., 1968. Co-campaign chmn. County Commr. candidate, 1972; pres. Richland Friends of Library, 1972-74. NDEA fellow, 1961-64; Wash. Water Power Co. scholar, 1957; Standard Oil scholar, 1956; recipient certifcate of appreciation Calif. Soc. Profl. Engrs., 1976; named Outstanding Graduating Mech. Engr., U. Idaho, 1961; registered profl. engr., Calif. Mem. Am. Nuclear Soc., ASME, Am. Soc. for Nondestructive Testing, N.Y. Acad. Scis., Sigma Tau. Home: 3958 Duncan Pl Palo Alto CA 94306 Office: Electric Power Research Inst Box 10412 Palo Alto CA 94303

DAUBERT, RICHARD ALAN, restaurant exec.; b. Seattle, Apr. 9, 1935; s. Albert G. and Virginia Bell (Phipps) D.; B.S. in Elec. Engring., U. Wash., Seattle, 1958, B.S. in Indsl. Engring., 1958; m. Margaret Adelaide Breuer, Dec. 16, 1955; children—Karen Elizabeth, Diane Marie, Sara Jane, James Bruce. Elec. engr. Pacific NW Bell Telephone Co., Seattle, 1956-58, Boeing Co., Seattle, 1958-64; data processing salesman IBM, Portland, Oreg., 1964-66; sr. specialist engr. Boeing Co., 1966-75; pres. Pizza & Pipes, Inc., Tacoma, Wash., 1975—. Pres. Shorewood Community Club, Seattle, 1967-68; div. leader sustaining membership drive Tacoma YMCA, 1976-80; troop committee chmn. Boy Scouts Am., 1981-82; elder Univ. Pl. United Presbyn. Ch., 1979-81. Mem. Tacoma Area C. of C. Republican. Clubs: Beta Theta Pi. Home: 4620 N Lexington St Tacoma WA 98407 Office: 2014 Mildred St W Tacoma WA 98466

DAUM, GORDON ALLAN, real estate company executive, real estate consultant; b. Winnipeg, Man., Can., Aug. 20, 1943; s. Gordon Wilfred and Elizabeth Christine (Kyle) D.; m. Sharon Gay Maloney, June 6, 1970; 1 son, Gregory Allan. B.A., Calif. State U., 1971, M.S., 1974. Lic. real estate broker. Adminstr. City of Anaheim (Calif.), 1971-75; real estate broker Coldwell Banker Co., Santa Ana, Calif., 1976-78; real estate mktg. and devel. mgr. The Irvine Co., Newport Beach, Calif., 1978-80; real estate cons. Frost Spence Trinen, Costa Mesa, Calif., 1980-81; v.p., gen. mgr. The City, Tishman West Mgmt. Corp., Orange, Calif., 1981—. Mem. Econ. Devel. Corp. Orange County; membership com. local Republican party. Served with USNR, 1965-68; Vietnam. Decorated Bronze Star. Mem. Nat. Assn. Corp. Real Estate Execs., Soc. Real Property Adminstrs. (cert. candidate), Internat. Council Shopping Ctr., Orange County C. of C. (chmn. publs. bd.). Office: Tishman West Mgmt Corp Bank of Am Tower The City Orange CA 92668

DAUT, KENNETH RICHARD, facilities engineer; b. Santa Monica, Calif., Aug. 3, 1952; s. Kenneth C. and Betty (Coggins) D.; m. Pamela Jaye Braxton, Feb. 12, 1983; 1 son, Matthew Christopher. B.A., UCLA, 1975. Account exec. Metropolitan Life Ins. Co., Torrance, Calif., 1976-77; bus. devel. officer Community Bank, Huntington Park, Calif., 1977-78; mfg. fin. analyst Northrop Corp., Hawthorne, Calif., 1978-80, indsl. engr. comml. aircraft div., 1980-82, mil. fabrication center, 1982-83, facilities engr., 1983—. Mem. Youth Motivation Task Force, Los Angeles County, 1979-80. Recipient Metropolitan Life Career Booster award, 1976; Northrop Performance award, 1979, Boeing 747 efficiency awards (3), 1982. Mem. Am. Inst. Indsl. Engrs., Nat. Assn. Accts., Hawthorne Jr. C. of C. (sec. 1983), Torrance Jr. C. of C. Democrat. Roman Catholic. Home: 603 Pine Dr Torrance CA 90501 Office: One Northrop Ave Hawthorne CA 90250

DAVI, RICHARD DAVID, med. services adminstr.; b. Pittsburg, Calif., Jan. 1, 1926; s. David T. and Anne Hight (Mancini) D.; B.A., U. Portland, 1952; m. Jeannine Marie Asbill, May 5, 1962; children—Dana Walter, Debra Anne, Malia Diane. Dir. indsl. and public relations Queen's Med. Center, Honolulu, 1957-61; asst. adminstr. Kapiolani Hosp., Honolulu, 1962-63, adminstr., 1964-73, exec. dir., 1973-78; exec. dir. Kauikeolani Children's Hosp., Honolulu, 1976-78; pres. Kapiolani-Children's Med. Center, Honolulu, 1978—; clin. asso. prof. dept. ob-gyn. U. Hawaii Med. Sch., Honolulu, 1969—, lectr., 1972—; chmn. exec. com. Regional Med. Program of Hawaii, 1969-70; cons. hosp. adminstrn. Formosa, Taiwan and Seoul, Korea, 1968. Bd. dirs. Hawaii Health Services Research Center, 1973-74; chmn. Reorgn. Commn. City and County of Honolulu, 1973-75. Served with USN, 1945-48. Recipient Commendation award Reorgn. Commn. of Honolulu, 1975; Disting. Alumnus award U. Portland, 1982. Mem. Assn. Western Hosps. (pres. 1971-72), Hosp. Assn. Hawaii (pres. 1966-67; Outstanding Achievement award 1980), Am. Coll. Hosp. Adminstrs., Indsl. Relations Assn. Hawaii, Hawaii League Nursing (dir. 1969-70), Pacific Health Research Inst., Hawaii C. of C. (chmn. crime com. 1979—, bd. dirs. 1981—), Am. Hosp. Assn. (trustee 1979—, citation for meritorious service 1981), Hawaii Employers Council (bd. govs. 1976-79). Roman Catholic. Clubs: Oahu Country, Outrigger Canoe. Home: 553 Kumukahi Pl Honolulu HI 96825 Office: 1319 Punahou St Honolulu HI 96826

DAVID, KERRY STEVEN, accountant; b. Madera, Calif., Aug. 22, 1948; s. Jack A. and Auburn L. (Meiring) D.; m. Wendy L. Jones, Mar. 25, 1967; children—Kirk, Brian, Jeff, Allison. Student U. Colo., 1966-67, Calif. Lutheran Coll., 1967 Foothill Coll., 1967; A.A., De Anza Jr. Coll., 1970; B.S.C., U. Santa Clara, 1972. C.P.A., Calif., Nev. Ptnr. Limb, Patterson, David & Co., Stateline, Nev., 1976-79; prin. Kerry S. David & Co., Zephyr Cove, Nev., 1979-81, pres. Kerry S. David, Ltd., Zephyr Cove, 1981—; ptnr. Pannell Kerr Forster, Zephyr Cove, 1982—, mng. ptnr. Zephyr Cove office, 1982—; pvt. practice marriage counseling. Mgr. Little League, South Lake Tahoe, Calif., 1973—, Am. Youth Soccer Orgn., South Lake Tahoe, 1980—; trustee South Lake Tahoe (Calif.) Unified Sch. Dist., 1977-81, pres. bd., 1980-81. Served with USN, 1966-67. Mem. Am. Inst. C.P.A.s, Calif. Soc. C.P.A.s, Nev. Soc. C.P.A.s, Club: Optimists (South Lake Tahoe, Calif.). Home: PO Box 13070 South Lake Tahoe CA 95702 Office: PO Box 1968 Zephyr Cove NV 89448

DAVID, LEON THOMAS, judge, educator, former army officer; b. San Francisco, Aug. 25, 1901; s. Leon Kline and Ella Nancy (Thomas) D.; A.B., Stanford, 1924, J.D., 1926; M.S. in Pub. Adminstrn., U. So. Calif., 1935, Dr. Pub. Adminstrn., 1957; m. Henrietta Louise Mellin, May 22, 1927; children—Carolyn L. Eskra, Leon Colby. City editor Vallejo (Calif.) Times, 1920-21; free-lance journalist, 1921-26; admitted to Calif. bar, 1926, U.S. Supreme Ct., 1932; pvt. practice law; mem. Malcolm & David, Palo Alto, Calif., 1926-31; dep. and acting city atty. Palo Alto, 1926-31; mem. faculty Sch. Law, U. So. Calif., 1931-34, Sch. Pub. Adminstrn., 1934-41, 1947-67; sr. asst. city atty. Los Angeles, 1934-41, 46-50; spl. counsel Los Angeles Harbor Commn., 1939-41; judge Municipal Ct., Los Angeles Jud. Dist., 1950-53; judge Superior Court, 1953-67, appellate dept., 1958-60, ret., 1967; asso. justice pro tem Calif. Ct. Appeal, 1969-73. Mem. Calif. Gov.'s Adv. Com. Law Enforcement, 1959-67. Chmn. legal aid com. State Bar Calif. intermittently to 1950, chmn. state bar com. history of law, 1973-78, bd. dirs., past pres. Los Angeles Legal Aid Found. Served from 2d lt. to maj. F.A.-O.R.C., 1924-42; from lt. col. to col. arty. AUS, 1942-46; comdt. U.S. Army Sch. for Spl. Services, 1942-43, chief Spl. Services, N. Africa and Mediterranean theaters of operation, 1943-45; col., USAR (ret.). Decorated Legion of Merit (U.S.), Hon. Officer Order Brit. Empire, Medaille d'Honneur d'Or (France), Medalha do Guerra (Brazil), Comdr. Crown of Italy; recipient Reginald Heber Smith medal for distinguished legal aid service to indigent, 1962. Mem. Los Angeles Bar Assn., Contra Costa County Bar Assn., S.R., Am. Legion (past comdr.), Calif. Judges Assn. (life), Stanford, U. So. Calif. Alumni assns., Calif. Hist. Soc., Mt. Diablo Amateur Radio Club, Phi Alpha Delta, Phi Kappa Phi, Pi Sigma Alpha, Blue Key, Order of Coif. Mason (K.T., 32d degree, Shriner), DeMolay Legion of Honor (life). Presbyn. (elder, mem. laws and regulations com., social edn. and action com. Los Angeles Presbytery, 1965-69). Clubs: Commonwealth, Kiwanis (pres. Palo Alto 1931, Los Angeles 1962, lt. gov. Div. 1 Calif.-Nev.-Hawaii dist. 1967). Author: Municipal Liability for Tortious Acts and Omissions, 1936; Administration of Public Tort Liability in Los Angeles, 1939; Tort Liability of Public Officers, 1940; Law and Lawyers, 1950; Role of the Lawyer in Public Administration, 1957; Law of Local Government, 1966; Old 89, My Horse, and Other Tales, Essays and Verse, 1974; History of State Bar of California, 1979; also articles in field of municipal law, ct. procedure and practice, legal history, legal aid, pub. adminstrn. Home: 240 Kuss Rd PO Box 656 Danville CA 94526

DAVIDSON, GERALD BRUCE, water treatment specialist, educator, consultant; b. Canton, Ohio, Dec. 7, 1943; s. Baine McClelland and June Editha (Johns) D.; m. Pamala Jean Argeri, Dec. 28, 1946; children—Shawn, Heidi Ann. B.S., Coll. Redwoods, 1977. Gen. mgr. water dist. Clearlake Oaks County (Calif.), 1977—; instr. water and wastewater Yuba Coll., Marysville, Calif., 1977—. Cons. Calif. State U.-Sacramento. Served with USN, 1960-63. Mem. Am. Water Works Assn., Water Pollution Control Fedn., Calif. Water Pollution Control Fedn., Lake County Water and Wastewater Assn. Democrat. Roman Catholic. Author chpt.: Water Treatment Plant Ops., Vol. II, Calif. State U.-Sacramento, 1982. Home: 12518 Oak St PO Box 816 Clearlake Oaks CA 95423 Office: Water Dist 12545 Stubbs Island Dr PO Box 736 Clearlake Oaks CA 95423

DAVIDSON, GORDON, theatrical producer, director; b. Bklyn., May 7, 1933; s. Joseph H. and Alice (Gordon) D.; B.A., Cornell U.; M.A., Case Western Res. U.; H.H.D., Bklyn. Coll.; D.Performing Arts (hon.), Calif. Inst. Arts; D.F.A. (hon.), Claremont Univ. Ctr.; m. Judith Swiller, Sept. 21, 1958; children—Adam, Rachel. Stage mgr. Phoenix Theatre Co., Am. Shakespeare Festival Theatre, 1958-60, Dallas Civic Opera, 1960-61, Martha Graham Dance Co., 1962; mng. dir. Theatre Group at UCLA (name changed to Center Theatre Group Mark Taper Forum at the Music Center), 1965-67, artistic dir., 1967—; founder New Theatre For Now, Mark Taper Forum, 1967; produced more than 80 theatrical prodns.; produced and directed numerous plays including: The Deputy, 1965, Candide, 1966, The Devils, 1967, Who's Happy Now?, 1967, In The Matter of J. Robert Oppenheimer, 1968, Murderous Angels, 1970, Rosebloom, 1970, The Trial of the Catonsville Nine, 1971 (also dir. film), Henry IV part one, 1972, Leonard Bernstein's Mass, 1972, 73, Hamlet, 1974, Savages, 1974, Too Much Johnson, The Shadow Box, 1975, 77, Getting Out, Black Angel, 1978, Terra Nova, 1979, Children of a Lesser God, 1979, 80, The Lady and the Clarinet, 1980; including Beatrice and Benedick, Carmen, La Bohème, Cosi Fan Tutte, Il Trovatore, Otello; TV dir. Who's Happy Now? for NET Theatre in Am., It's the Willingness for Visions, PBS, 1979, The Trial of the Catonsville Nine, 1971. Recipient N.Y. Drama Desk award for direction, 1969; Los Angeles Drama Critics Circle award for direction, 1971, 74, 75; Margo Jones award New Theatre for Now, 1970, 76; Obie award, 1971, 77; Outer Critics Circle award, 1977; Tony award for direction, 1977; also awards Nat. Acad. TV Arts and Scis., Nosotros Golden Eagle, N.Y. League Hard of Hearing, N.J. Speech and Hearing Assn., Am. Theatre Assn., Los Angeles Human Relations Commn. Office: Center Theatre Group 135 N Grand Ave Los Angeles CA 90012

DAVIDSON, HERMAN LAMONT, mfg. co. exec.; b. Denver, May 26, 1930; s. William Franklin and Hazel Arnetta (Lenhard) D.; Asso. Sci., Allan Hancock Coll., 1976; m. Virginia Jane Taylor, Oct. 1, 1949; children—Pamela, William, Virginia, David. Mechanic, Leeman Auto Co., Denver, 1948-51; insp. Martin Marietta Co., Denver, 1957-58, engr./supr., 1958-59, quality project chief, 1959-61, chief inspection missile site, Vandenberg, Calif., 1961-68, chief quality assurance, 1968-76, mgr. quality, 1977—, central quality mgr. programs, 1978-82, mgr. quality and safety Vandenberg ops., 1982—. Served with USN, 1951-57; Korea. Registered profl. engr., Calif. Mem. Am. Soc. for Quality Control (sr.), Nat. Mgmt. Assn. (Gold Knight of Mgmt. 1983), Calif. Soc. Profl. Engrs. Air Force Assn., Am. Inst. Aeros. and Astronautics. Home: 937 Empress Circle Santa Maria CA 93454 Office: POB 1681 Vandenberg Air Force Base CA 93437

DAVIDSON, IRA R., aluminum chemical company executive; b. 1925; B.S. in Indsl. Engring., U. Pa.; married. With Kaiser Aluminum and Chem. Corp., mgr. reduction and fabricating facilities U.S. and abroad, 1972, gen. mgr. fabricated products group, 1972, corp. v.p., 1975-80, exec. v.p., 1980—. Office: Kaiser Aluminum & Chem Corp 300 Lakeside Dr Oakland CA 94643*

DAVIDSON, JOAN GRACE, career counselor; b. Grand Island, Neb., Oct. 25, 1941; d. Edwin and Alice Marie (Skolil) Jelinek; m. Loren Ronald Davidson, Dec. 23, 1961 (div.); children—Jackie Charlene, Deborah Diane. B.S. in Edn., U. Neb., 1963; M.A., SUNY-Brockport, 1972; postgrad. Rochester Inst. Tech., 1975. Cert. tchr., guidance counselor N.Y. Sci., music tchr. Panama (Nebr.) Central Sch., 1964-65; counselor Ohio State U., Columbus, 1967-68; sci. tchr. Pittsford (N.Y.) Central Sch., 1969-70; employment counselor Youth Opportunity Ctr., Rochester, N.Y., 1971; guidance counselor Palmyra-Macedon (N.Y.) High Sch., 1971-76; curriculum specialist Singer Career Systems, Rochester, 1977-78; career guidance coordinator Computer Curriculum Corp., Palo Alto, Calif., 1979-80; sr. course developer Rolm Corp., Santa Clara, 1980—. Sec. bd. dirs. Manhattan Playhouse, Palo Alto. Recipient Nat. Forensic League Degree Distinction, 1959. Mem. Am. Soc. Tng. and Devel., Am. Personnel and Guidance Assn., Calif. Personnel and Guidance Assn., Career Planning and Adult Devel. Network, Nat. Assn. Female Execs. Democrat. Methodist. Clubs: Apres Ski (Sunnyvale). Author numerous career guidance guides. Home: 121 Buckingham Dr Apt 56 Santa Clara CA 95051 Office: 4900 Old Ironsides Dr Mailstop 450 Santa Clara CA 95050

DAVIDSON, KEITH THOMAS, electronics company executive; b. Flint, Mich., Oct. 1, 1936; s. Barney Stribling and Dorothy May (Mannor) D.; m. Joan Black, Aug. 19, 1961; children—Dianne, Cynthia, Suzanne. B.S. in Bus. Adminstrn., U. Dayton, 1957; M.B.A. U. Denver, 1962; M.A., Ph.D., Claremont Grad. Sch., 1983. Product devel. mgr. Dow Chem. Co., Midland, Mich., 1962-68; mgr. bus. devel. Boise Cascade Corp., Portland, Oreg., 1968-69; dir. mktg. Mattel, Inc., Hawthorne, Calif., 1969-74; mgr. advt. and customer relations Xerox Corp., El Segundo, Calif., 1974—. Coach, ofcl. Am. Youth Soccer Orgn., 1975-80. Served with USAFR, 1958-64. Mem. Am. Athletic Union. Clubs: Jack Kramer Tennis (Rolling Hills, Calif.); Rancho Las Palmas Country (Rancho Mirage, Calif.). Home: 2903 Via Pacheco Palos Verdes Estates CA 90274 Office: Xerox Corp 880 Apollo St El Segundo CA 90245

DAVIDSON, POLLY ANN, interior designer; b. Exeter, Calif., Nov. 23, 1937; d. Oda Orfus Mann and Ruby Evelyn (Duffy) M.; m. Franklyn Dillard Davidson, Aug. 12, 1956; children—Paul, Peter, Amy. A.A., Fresno City Coll., 1957; B.S. U. Ariz., 1972. Interior designer Avayds Galley of Fine Interiors, Tucson, 1972-73; ptnr., designer, Casual Interiors, Tucson, 1973-74, co-owner, interior designer, Interior Factory, 1974—. Mem. Am. Soc. Interior Designers (cert. 1972). Mem. Parkview

Wesleyan Ch. Clubs: Soroptimist, Women in Tucson. Office: 2937 N Stone Tucson AZ 85705

DAVIDSON, SANDRA LEE ANNE, health equipment co. exec.; b. Long Beach, Calif., Feb. 16, 1947; d. George Anton and Sophia Genevive (Buczynski) Jecmen; A.A., Coll. of the Desert, 1966; B.S. in Bus. Mgmt., Pepperdine U., 1981; m. Craig Stephen Dresman, June 22, 1978. Supr., Kelly Services, Santa Ana, Calif., 1969-71; sales rep. Pacific Personnel Services, Long Beach, 1971-72; account exec. Volt Tech., Alhambra, Calif., 1972-73; territory mgr. Hollister Inc., Chgo., 1974-76; western regional sales mgr. Precision Dynamics Corp., Burbank, Calif., 1976-78; dir. profl. relations, Humana Corp. Westminster (Calif.) Community Hosp., 1978-81; sales rep. capital med. equipment, anethesia and life support equipment Foregger Med. div. Puritan Bennett Corp., 1982—; propr. Sandra L. Davidson Cons., Anaheim; work with Orange County Med. Assn. Active sr. citizens groups in area. Mem. Nat. Assn. Exec. Women, Women in Mgmt. Assn., The Complete Woman, C. of C. Westminster. Republican. Roman Catholic. Author sales tng. manuals and tech. lit. for Culture Tube System; compiler rev. and catalogue for Westminster Community Hosp. Home: 6279 E Woodsboro Ave Anaheim CA 92807 Office: 10th St and Harrison Berkeley CA 94710

DAVIE, EUGENE NEWTON, international language center executive; b. Oakland, Calif., Apr. 3, 1942; s. Eugene Newton and Marjorie Inez (Sifford) D.; m. Mary Jane Whitelam, May 19, 1967 (div. Feb. 1968). B.A., San Francisco State U., 1965; postgrad. Syracuse U., 1968-69, U. Calif. and U. Hawaii, 1961-63. With Burman-Johnson & Assocs., 1965-66; tchr. spl. children San Raphael Mil. Acad., 1966-67; head English dept. St. Hilda's and Hughes Sch., 1969-69; with LanFranco Corp., San Francisco, 1972—, pres., 1976—, chmn. bd., 1979—; guest lectr. Soviet Consulate. Mem. San Francisco Tb and Lung Assn.; bd. dirs. San Francisco Spring Opera, also mem. exec. and planning coms.; mem. San Francisco Opera Fair., English Speaking Union of San Francisco. Tenn. squire, 1973. Mem. Theta Alpha Phi. Episcopalian. Office: One Hallidie Plaza Suite 800 San Francisco CA 94102

DAVIES, DOROTHY FLOYD, pharmacist; b. Mobile, Ala., Jan. 11, 1932; d. Nathan Daniel and Ora Anna (Ellis) Floyd; student Ala. State Coll., 1948-50; B.S. in Pharmacy, Xavier U., 1955; postgrad. Los Angeles City Coll., 1967, UCLA, 1976; children—Erroll, Michael. Staff pharmacist St. Paul's Hosp., Dallas, 1955-59, VA Hosp., Long Beach, Calif., 1959-60, Vitamin Quota Pharmacy, Los Angeles, 1960-63; mgr., pharmacist MDX Pharmacy, Los Angeles, 1963-67, Crenshaw Med. Pharmacy, Los Angeles, 1967-69; owner, pharmacist Vermont & 110th St. Pharmacy Inc., Los Angeles, 1969—, now pres.; pres. Clotilda Internat.; pharm. cons. Drew Ambulatory Care Rev. Team of HEW. Registered pharmacist, La., Tex., Calif. Mem. Am., Central Los Angeles pharm. assns., Am. Bridge Assn., Am. Contract Bridge League, Gamma Phi Delta, Zeta Phi Beta. Democrat. Mem. Science of Mind Ch. Clubs: Harmonett's Bridge, Order of Eastern Star. Office: 10966 S Vermont Ave Los Angeles CA 90044

DAVIES, INGEBURG CHRISTEL, educator; b. Halle, Germany, Nov. 26, 1937; d. Hans Werner and Ursula Anna Helene (Mücke) Kreimann; m. Charles Raymond Davies, Apr. 2, 1963; children—Evelyn Christel, Roxanne Natascha, Charles Ryan. Diplôme de Langue, Alliance Française, Paris, 1956; B.A., U. Utah, 1976, M.A., 1980. Cert. secondary tchr. Utah. Sec., translator West German State Dept., Bonn, 1958-59, Dept. Army, Frankfurt, 1967-71; tchr. Jordan Sch. Dist., Salt Lake City, 1980—; fgn. lang. specialist. Vice chmn. Democratic Voting Dist. 2109; former sec.-treas. Res. Officers' Assn. Ladies. Mem. NEA, Jordan Educators Assn., Utah Educators Assn., Phi Beta Kappa. Lutheran. Author fgn. lang. instrn. text, elem. level. Home: 688 Terrace Hills Dr Salt Lake City UT 84103 Office: 138 Pioneer Rd Midvale UT 84047

DAVIES, JOHN LAWRENCE, advertising executive; b. Utica, N.Y., Dec. 25, 1951; s. Glenn Edwin and Florence B. D.; B.A., SUNY, Fredonia, 1975. Publisher, Artifacts, 1974-75; bur. mgr. Chauquatan Daily, 1975; asst. dean Calif. Law Inst., 1976-78; mktg. dir. Harcourt Brace Jovanovish Legal Publs., Los Angeles, 1977-81, mktg. cons., Santa Barbara, Calif., 1978-81; pres. John Davies Advt., Santa Barbara, 1981—. Bd. dirs. Lawyer Referral Service, 1978-81; bd. dirs., sec. Santa Barbara Middle Sch., 1979-81; bd. dirs. Santa Barbara Med. Found., 1979-81; bd. dirs., treas. Community Resources Info. Service, 1980-83. Mem. U.S. C. of C., Santa Barbara C. of C. Democrat. Roman Catholic. Office: 209 E De La Guerra St Santa Barbara CA 93101

DAVIES, KENT RICHARD, business educator; b. Burns, Oreg., May 12, 1947; s. Richard Griffith and Dorothy Agnes (Buor) D.; B.A. in Bus., Seattle U., 1969; M.B.A., Pacific Lutheran U., 1980; m. D. Sharon Hill, Nov. 30, 1974. Econ. devel. specialist, small bus. cons. VISTA, N.Y.C., 1970-71; econ. devel. specialist Cayuga County Action Program, Auburn, N.Y., 1972-73; dir. citizen participation King County Dept. Youth Services, Seattle, 1974-79; practicum instr. U. Wash. Sch. Social Work, Seattle, 1976-79; trainer Wash. Criminal Justice Tng. Commn., 1975-77; mem. adv. com. Wash. Office Vol. Action, 1976, 77; mem. planning com. Looking Ahead-II Conf., 1978; now adj. prof. Grad. Sch. Bus., U. Puget Sound. Community liaison dir. Halfway House for disabled vets., 1972-74; chmn. adv. com. human and social services div. Edmonds Community Coll., 1976-79; extension chmn. Logan Jaycees, Auburn, 1972-73. Recipient award Logan Jaycees, 1973, Edmonds Community Coll., 1979. Mem. Human Resource Planning Soc., Am. Soc. Tng. and Devel., Greenpeace, Sierra Club, Wash. Wilderness Coalition.

DAVIES, MERTON EDWARD, photog. engr.; b. St. Paul, Sept. 13, 1917; s. Albert Daniel and Lucile (McCabe) D.; A.B., Stanford, 1938, postgrad., 1938-39; m. Margaret Louise Darling, Feb. 10, 1946; children—Deidra Louise (Mrs. Chris Stauff), Albert Karl, Merton Randel. Instr. math. U. Nev., 1939-40; group leader Math. Lofting, Douglas Aircraft Co., El Segundo, Calif., 1940-48; sr. staff Rand Corp., Santa Monica, Calif., 1948-59, 62—, liaison USAF, Washington, 1959-62. U.S. observer inspected stas. under terms Antarctic Treaty, 1967; TV co-investigator Mariner Mars, 1969, 71; Mariner Venus/Mercury 1973 Mission; Voyager Mission; Galileo Mission. Asso. fellow Am. Inst. Aeros. and Astronautics; mem. Am. Soc. Photogrammetry, AAAS. Author: (with Bruce Murray) The View from Space, 1971; (with others) Atlas of Mercury, 1978. Patentee in field. Home: 1414 San Remo Dr Pacific Palisades CA 90272 Office: 1700 Main St Santa Monica CA 90406

DAVIES, PAUL LEWIS, JR., lawyer; b. San Jose, Calif., July 21, 1930; s. Paul Lewis and Faith (Crummey) D.; A.B., Stanford, 1952; J.D., Harvard, 1957; m. Barbara Bechtel, Dec. 22, 1955; children—Laura Davies Mateo, Paul Lewis III. Bar: Calif. 1957. Assoc. Pillsbury, Madison & Sutro, San Francisco, 1957-63, partner, 1963—; dir. FMC Corp., Indsl. Indemnity Co., So. Pacific Co. Trustee Calif. Acad. Scis., chmn., 1973-80; bd. overseers Hoover Instn., chmn., 1976-82; trustee Herbert Hoover Found., Inc.; bd. regents U. Pacific; bd. dirs. Samuel Merritt Hosp., Merritt Peralta Med. Ctr. Served from 2d to 1st lt., U.S. Army, 1952-54. Mem. State Bar Calif. (chmn. com. on corps. 1968-69), Am. Bar Assn., San Francisco Bar Assn., Phi Beta Kappa, Pi Sigma Alpha. Republican. Clubs: World Trade, Pacific-Union, Bohemian, Stock Exchange, Villa Taverna, Bankers (San Francisco); Sainte Claire (San Jose); Claremont Country (Oakland, Calif.); Collectors, Explorers, Links (N.Y.C.); Metropolitan (Washington); Cypress Point (Pebble Beach, Calif.); Chicago, Mid-America (Chgo.); Farmington Country (Charlottesville, Va.). Office: 225 Bush St San Francisco CA 94104

DAVIES, PEARCE GARDINER, public relations counselor; b. Seattle, Dec. 11, 1898; s. D(avid) Thomas and Katharine Easton (Pearce) D.; student U. Wash. Sch. Journalism, Seattle, 1916-17, 20-21; m. Lenore Miller, Oct. 16, 1919; children—Pearce Gardiner, Lenore Katharine Davies Carr. Reporter, dept. editor Everett (Wash.) Herald, 1917, 18-19, Raleigh (N.C.) News & Observer, 1917-18, Yakima (Wash.) Morning Herald, 1920; mem. news staff AP, 1921-37, Calif. state editor, San Francisco, 1933-37; mng. editor San Jose (Calif.) Mercury Herald, 1937-41; asst. 5-state regional dir. Community War Services, San Francisco, 1941-45; public info. dir. surplus property disposal War Assets Adminstrn., 1945-48; editor San Rafael (Calif.) Ind., 1948-49; various public relations positions, 1949-51; mem. faculty San Jose State Coll, 1951-68; owner, operator Praxis, public relations agy., Los Gatos, Calif., 1968—. Served with U.S. Army, 1917. Mem. Public Relations Soc. Am., Public Relations Student Soc. Am. (chpt. life mem.), San Francisco, San Jose, Peninsula pub. relations round tables, Sigma Delta Chi (life), Pi Alpha Nu (founder). Democrat. Clubs: Quest (San Jose); Masons. Address: 1105 Rossmoor Tower I Laguna Hills CA 92653

DAVIES, THOMAS MOCKETT, JR., history educator; b. Lincoln, Nebr., May 25, 1940; s. Thomas Mockett and Faith Elizabeth (Arnold) D.; B.A., U. Nebr., 1962, M.A., 1964; student Universidad Nacional Autónoma de México, 1961; Ph.D., U. N.Mex., 1970; postdoctoral fellow U. Tex., Austin, 1969-70; m. Eloisa Carmela Monzón Abate, June 10, 1968; 1 dau., Jennifer Elena. Lectr., U. N.Mex. Peace Corps Tng. Center, 1964-66; asst. prof. Latin Am. history San Diego State U., 1968-72, assoc. prof., 1972-75, prof., 1975—, dir. Center Latin Am. Studies. Recipient Outstanding Faculty award San Diego State U., 1981; Henry L. and Grace Doherty Charitable Found. fellow, 1966-68; summer research grants San Diego State U. Found., 1971-73, 75, 76, 80, 81; Nat. Resource Ctr. for Latin Am., Dept. Edn. grantee, 1979-84. Mem. Latin Am. Studies Assn., Orgn. Am. Historians, Conf. Latin Am. History (exec. sec. 1979—), Pacific Coast Council Latin Am. Author: Indian Integration in Peru: a Half Century of Experience, 1900-1948, 1974 (co-winner Hubert Herring Meml. award Pacific Coast Council on Latin Am. Studies 1973); (with Victor Villanueva) 300 Documentos Para la Historia del APRA: Conspiraciones Apristas de 1935 a 1939, 1979, Secretos Electorales del APRA: Correspondencia y Documentos de 1939, 1982; (with Brian Loveman) The Politics of Anti-Politics: the Military in Latin America, 1978. Contbr. articles to profl. jours. Home: 4617 Edenvale Ave LaMesa CA 92041 Office: Dept of History San Diego State University San Diego CA 92182

DAVIS, ALEXANDER SCHENCK, architect; b. San Francisco, Jan. 3, 1930; s. William Schenck and Amelia (Francisco) D.; B.A. with honors in Architecture, U. Calif.-Berkeley, 1953, M.A. in Architecture (D. Zelinsky & Sons Found. Grad. scholar), 1957; m. Nancy Leah Barry, Oct. 21, 1953; children—Arthur Barry, Laurel Davis Bowden, Pamela Alexander. With Hammarberg & Herman, Architects, El Cerrito, Calif., 1956-62; project architect Bonelli, Young & Wong, Architects and Engrs., San Francisco, 1962-67; chief architect Earl & Wright, Cons. Engrs., San Francisco, 1967-73; constrn. mgr. Fisher Devel., Inc., San Francisco, 1973-74; project architect Keller & Gannon, Cons. Engrs., San Francisco, 1974-77; individual practice architecture, Albany, Calif., 1977-81. Served with USCGR, 1953-55. Registered architect, Calif., Alaska, U.K.; cert. Nat. Council Archtl. Registration Bds. Fellow Soc. Am. Registered Architects, mem. AIA, Royal Inst. Brit. Architects, Soc. Am. Mil. Engrs., Constrn. Specifications Inst. Home: 928 Contra Costa Dr El Cerrito CA 94530

DAVIS, BARBARA HELEN, nurse, educator; b. Hicksville, N.Y., Aug. 13, 1921; d. James Edward and Florence Julia (Taylor) Allen; m. Lowell Livingston Davis, Sept. 4, 1964. R.N. diploma, Kings County Hosp. Sch. Nursing, Bklyn., 1943; student St. John's U., Jamaica, N.Y., 1943-49, B.S., 1961; M.S., Adelphi U., 1968; Ed.D., Columbia U., 1974. Staff nurse Kings County Hosp., Bklyn., 1943-44, instr., 1944-45, health service dir., 1945-46, asst. adminstr. Arlington Manor Nursing Home, Oceanside, N.Y., 1952-53, nursing dir., 1953-60; instr. Nassau County Med. Ctr., East Meadow, N.Y., 1947-48, head nurse, 1949-51, supr., 1961-64; program coordinator Am. Nurses' Assn., N.Y.C., 1967-71, Kansas City, Mo., 1974-75; nurse coordinator, geropsychiatry UCLA, 1977-79, asst. prof. gerontology nursing, dir. gerontology nursing programs, 1979—; cons. VA, 1981; fellow UCLA/U. So. Calif. Long-Term Care Gerontology Ctr., 1981—; spl. adviser White House Conf. on Aging, 1980-81. Fellow Am. Acad. Nursing, Gerontol. Soc. Am.; mem. Am. Nurses' Assn. (mem. Task Force White House Conf. on Aging 1971, vice chairperson exec. com. Div. Geriatric Nursing Practice 1972-74, vice chairperson exec com. Council Nursing Home Nurses 1982-84), Calif. Nurses' Assn., Western Gerontol. Soc., Am. Pub. Health Assn., Assn. Acad. Women, Am. Geriatrics Soc., Sigma Theta Tau. Democrat. Roman Catholic. Clubs: Marina City (Marina del Rey, Calif.); UCLA Faculty. Contbr. articles to profl. publs.; mem. editorial bd. Jour. Nursing Adminstrn., 1970-78, Jour. Am. Geriatrics Soc., 1974-81, Jour. Gerontol. Nursing, 1974—. Office: Sch Nursing Factor 3-242 UCLA Los Angeles CA 90024

DAVIS, BERTA, psychologist; b. N.Y.C., June 1, 1942; d. Harry and Helen Snyder (Schwartz) D.; M.S., CUNY, 1965; Ph.D., NYU, 1976; m. Benjamin W. Nitzberg, July 23, 1976; 1 son, Hersh Davis-Nitzberg. Tchr., Queens Coll., 1967-70, Lehman Coll., CUNY, 1970-75; dir. study abroad program in open edn., Eng., 1971-72; founder, dir. Inst. Internat. Living, Tokyo and Los Angeles, 1981—. Pacific Air Force grantee, 1978. Mem. Internat. Council Psychologists, Am. Psychol. Assn. Jewish. Weekly columnist On Your Mind, Japan Times, 1981—. Home and Office: 7330 Pyramid Dr Los Angeles CA 90046

DAVIS, BETTY BOURBONIA, real estate co. exec.; b. Ft. Bayard, N.Mex., Mar. 12, 1931; d. John Alexander and Ora M. (Caudill) Bourbonia; B.S. in Elem. Edn., U. N.Mex., 1954; children from previous marriage—Janice Ann Cox Plagge, Elizabeth Ora Cox. Gen. partner BJD Realty Co., Albuquerque, 1977—. Bd. dirs. Albuquerque Opera Guild, 1977-83; membership co-chmn., 1977-79; mem. Friends of Art, 1978—, Friends of Little Theatre, 1973—. Recipient Matrix award for journalism Jr. League. Mem. Maxwell Mus. Assn., Albuquerque Mus. Assn., N.M. Hist. Soc., Albuquerque Symphony Women Assn., Jr. League Albuquerque, Alumni Assn. U. N.Mex. (dir. 1973-76), Alpha Chi Omega. Republican. Methodist. Clubs: Alpha Chi Omega Mother's, Tanoan Country, Internat. Order Eastern Star, Order Rainbow for Girls (past grand worthy advisor N.Mex.). Home: 7816 Vista Del Arroyo NE Albuquerque NM 87109

DAVIS, CHARLES HOMER, consulting agronomist; b. Glendale, Ariz., Feb. 13, 1912; s. Homer and Ollie (Barkley) D.; m. Wilma Butler, Mar. 17, 1937; children—Patricia, Elizabeth; m. 2d, Thelma Packer, Apr. 4, 1964; children—Marilyn, Dennis, Robert. B.S., U. Ariz., 1935; M.S., Iowa State U., 1936, Ph.D., 1939. Asst. prof. U. Ariz., Tucson, 1937-42; asst. agronomist U.S. Emergency Rubber Project, Salinas, Calif., 1942-45; agronomist U.S. Bur. Reclamation, Boulder City, Nev., 1945-52, Ariz. Agri-Chem. Corp., Phoenix, 1952-68; Am. Bioculture, Phoenix, 1968-72; cons. agronomist, 1972—. Dist. chmn. Republican party. Mem. Am. Soc. Agronomy. Methodist. Club: Lions (pres.). Contbr. articles. to profl. jours. and mags.; patentee fertilizer formula. Home and Office: 4415 N 31 Dr Phoenix AZ 85017

DAVIS, CHARLES TRUMAN, ophthalmologist, clergyman; b. El Dorado, Ark., Aug. 16, 1920; s. Jesse Gilbert and Dixie Ethel (Britt) D.; student So. State Coll., Magnolia, Ark., 1939-40, U. Mich., 1945-46, U. Tenn., Knoxville, 1946, M.D., Memphis, 1950; M.S. in Ophthalmology, U. Minn., Rochester, 1955; D.Sc. (hon.), Grove City Coll., 1970; m. Jean Elizabeth Lowe, Aug. 23, 1943; children—Elizabeth Jean (Mrs. Poynter), Nancy Lynn (Mrs. Burritt), Charles Truman. Intern, Gorgas Hosp., Panama Canal Zone, 1950-51; resident Kennedy Hosp., Memphis, 1951-52; fellow in ophthalmology Mayo Clinic, Rochester, 1952-55; staff ophthalmologist Scott & White Clinic, Temple, Tex., 1955-58; pvt. practice medicine specializing in ophthalmology, Mesa, Ariz., 1958—; asst. prof. ophthalmology U. Tex., 1955-58; ordained priest Old Catholic Ch., 1974; pastor Trinity Ch., Anglican, Ind., Mesa, 1973—; mem. staffs Mesa Luth., Doctors, Desert Samaritan hosps. Trustee Grove City Coll., 1969—; pres. Trinity Found., Mesa, 1970—; dir. Trinity Christian Sch., Mesa, 1970—. Served to 1st lt. U.S. Army, 1940-45. Diplomate Am. Bd. Ophthalmology. Fellow Am. Acad. Ophthalmology; mem. Maricopa County (Ariz.) Med. Soc., Ariz., Am. med. assns., Am. Assn. Ophthalmologists (1st v.p. 1973-74), Ariz. Ophthalmol. Soc. (pres. 1964-65), Contact Lens Soc. Ophthalmologists, Alpha Omega Alpha. Republican. Patentee in field. Office: 1150 N Country Club Dr Mesa AZ 85201

DAVIS, CRAIG CARLTON, aerospace co. exec.; b. Gulfport, Miss., Dec. 14, 1919; s. Craig Carlton and Helen Lizette (Houppert) D.; B.S., Ga. Inst. Tech., 1941; J.D., Harvard U., 1949; children—Kimberly Patricia, Craig Carlton. Instr. aeros. Escola Tecnica de Aviacao, Sao Paulo, Brazil, 1946; contract adminstr. Convair, Fort Worth, 1949-51; mgr. contracts and pricing, atomics internat. and autonetics divs. N.Am. Aviation, Anaheim, Calif., 1954-62, asst. corp. dir. contracts and proposals, El Segundo, Calif., 1963-70; dir. contracts Aerojet Electro Systems Co., Azusa, Calif., 1971-81, v.p., 1982—. Served with AUS, 1941-45; USAF, 1951-53, to col. res., 1953-66. Mem. ABA, Fed. Bar Assn., D.C. Bar Assn., Res. Officers Assn., Harvard U. Alumni Assn., Ga. Tech. Alumni Assn. Republican. Episcopalian. Club: Harvard. Home: 10501 Wilshire Blvd Apt 1208 Los Angeles CA 90024 Office: 1100 W Hollyvale St Azusa CA 91702

DAVIS, DAVID E., JR., advertising account executive; b. Denver, Nov. 20, 1946; s. David E. and Jeanne (Gowdy) D. B.A. in Polit. Sci., Coll. William and Mary, 1968. With U.S. Peace Corps, Ethiopa, 1968-70; real estate salesman, Van Schaak & Co., Colorado Springs, Colo., 1973; regional mgr. Transportation Displays Inc., Dallas, 1974-75; asst. brand mgr. Joseph Schlitz Brewing Co., Milw., 1975-81; account exec. Chiat/Day Advt., Inc., Los Angeles, 1981—. Served U.S. Army, 1970-72; Ger. Republican. Presbyterian. Club: Elks. Home: 1119 Sunset Vale Ave Los Angeles CA 90069 Office: Chiat/Day Advt Inc 517 S Olive Los Angeles CA 90013

DAVIS, DAVID PAUL, clinical psychologist; b. Elkhorn, Wis., June 10, 1938; s. Paul A. and Bernice (Schulz) D.; m. Angilie K., Mar. 26, 1970; children—Taree, Cynthia, Daniel. B.A., San Jose State U., Calif., 1961; M.S. in Psychology, San Diego State U., 1968; Ph.D. in Profl. Psychology, U.S. Internat. U., San Diego, 1978. Cert. clin. psychologist, Hawaii; lic. clin. psychologist, lic. marriage, family, child counselor, lic. community coll. tchr., counselor, Calif. Research asst. Western Behavioral Scis. Inst., La Jolla, Calif., 1966-68; tng. devel. officer Peace Corps Tng. Ctr., U. Hawaii, Hilo, 1968-70; instr. Stetson U., DeLand, Fla., 1970-71; dir. continuing edn. and tng. Meml. Hosp. Med. Ctr., Long Beach, Calif., 1971-75, instr. psychology and child devel. Long Beach City Coll., 1971-77, chief mental health clinic Hickam Air Force Base, Hawaii, 1982; pvt. practice; tchr., cons. Mem. Am. Psychol. Assn., Hawaii Psychol. Assn., Soc. Air Force Clin. Psychologists, Soc. Biofeedback and Behavioral Medicine (Hawaii). Contbr. articles to profl. jours. Office: 98-211 Pali Momi St Suite 820 Aiea HI 96701

DAVIS, DONALD ADAMS, architect; b. Los Angeles, Mar. 27, 1919; s. Donald Adams and Grace (Stodart) D.; A.A. in Bldg. Constrn., Fullerton Jr. Coll., 1939; B.S. in Constrn. Engrng., Los Angeles U., 1949; B.Arch., U. So. Calif., 1952; m. Genevieve Rose Krukenberg, May 13, 1945; 1 dau., Diane Annette. Practice architecture, Long Beach, Calif., 1955— , Hawaii, 1959— , Ariz., 1966— , Colo., 1971—. Accident prevention counselor, pilot examiner FAA; mem. airport adv. commn. City of Long Beach. Served to comdr. USNR, 1940-47, ret., 1970. Decorated D.F.C., three Air medals, Presdl. Unit Citation, Lennie pin, U.S. and Internat. Diamond badges pilot soaring. Mem. Exec. Assn. Long Beach (past pres.), AIA, Naval Res. Assn., Soaring Soc. Am. (instr.), Long Beach Soaring Soc. (pres.); hon. mem. Long Beach Police Officers Assn., Q.B., Assn. Naval Aviation, China Painters Calif. Patentee car stacking device; glider and balloon flight instr. Address: 39 Nieto Ave Long Beach CA 90803

DAVIS, DWIGHT M., superintendent of schools; b. Lynnville, Iowa, Mar. 12, 1920; s. Orland G. and Gertrude (McClung) D.; B.A., Iowa State Tchrs. Coll., 1941; M.A., State U. Iowa, 1947, Ph.D., 1953; m. Alice Fredrickson, Aug. 20, 1941; children—Gilbert Kenneth, Trevor Dwight; m. 2d, Arleen M. Schultz, Nov. 2, 1980. Tchr. math. Williamsburg, Iowa, 1941-42, Iowa Falls, Iowa, 1942-43; prin. high sch., dean jr. coll., Bloomfield, Iowa, 1947-48; prin. high sch., Hampton, Iowa, 1948-50, U. High Sch. of State U. Iowa, Iowa City, 1950-53; dean Moline (Ill.) Community Coll., 1953-55; supt. schs. Moline, 1955-65, Des Moines, 1965-80, Colorado Springs, Colo., 1980—. Pres. Girls-Home Sch.; active Community Chest, Boy Scouts Am.; mem. Gov.'s Task Force on Edn.; life mem. P.T.A. Trustee, Joint Council Econ. Edn.; bd. dirs. Mid-Am. Arts Alliance. Served with C.E., AUS, 1943-46. Mem. NEA, Am. Assn. Sch. Adminstrs. (exec. com.), Phi Delta Kappa, Phi Mu Epsilon. Lodges: Rotary, Kiwanis.

DAVIS, EDNA W. secretarial service company executive; b. Los Angeles, Aug. 7, 1950; d. Jerome Wallace and Marian A. (Johnson) Gordon; m. Philip William Davis, May 10, 1975; 1 dau., Gloria. B.A., U. Calif.-San Francisco, 1972; postgrad. U. Calif.-San Diego, 1972-73. Legal sec. various law firms, San Diego, 1972-73, Los Angeles, 1973-75; mgr. bus. office Smith Mfg. Co., Los Angeles, 1978-80; owner, pres. Davis Werik Secretarial Service, Long Beach, Calif., 1980—. Fund raiser Long Beach unit Am. Cancer Soc. Mem. Assn. Cert. Secs., Bus. and Profl. Women's Club, Am. Assn. Women Execs., Phi Mu Alpha. Republican. Roman Catholic. Office: Werik Secretarial Service 3614 Atlantic Ave Long Beach CA 90870

DAVIS, EDWARD MICHAEL, state senator, educator; b. Los Angeles, Nov. 15, 1916; s. Michael and Christine (Hart) D. B.S. cum laude, U.S.C., 1961; LL.D. (hon.), Calif. Grad. Sch. Theology, 1972. Chief Los Angeles Police Dept., 1969-78; mem. Calif. State Senate, 1980—; adj. prof. U. S.C., Calif. State U.-Los Angeles. Served with USNR, 1942-45. Named Man of Yr., Encino Lodge B'nai B'rith, 1974, Headliner of Yr., Greater Los Angeles Press Club, 1975, Outstanding Am., Los Angeles Philanthropic Found., 1977; hon. mayor Chatsworth C. of C. Mem. Am. Legion (comdr. 1957), Internat. Assn. Chiefs of Police (pres. 1976-77). Author: Staff One, 1978. Episcopalian. Home: 10442 Oso Ave Chatsworth CA 91311 Office: California State Senate Sacramento CA 95814*

DAVIS, ELLEN MARY DONNELLY, psychologist; b. Los Angeles, Feb. 21, 1923; d. James Joseph and Lilliam Marie (Daly) Donnelly; B.S. in Nursing, U. Calif., 1944; M.S., Columbia Tchrs. Coll., 1948, M.A., 1953, Ed.D., 1957; postgrad. (Fulbright scholar) U. London, 1953-55; m. Carroll Clifford Davis, Aug. 4, 1962; 1 son, Charles. Dir. for schizophrenia children London U. Sch. Edn. Inst. Psychiatry Psychiat. Clinic, 1953-55; asst. prof. mental health Pitts. U. Sch. Pub. Health, 1956-60; dir., co-investigator research Hartford (Conn.) Vis. Nurse Assn., 1959-64; lectr. Yale Sch. Medicine, 1960-67; dir. research manpower Orange County (Calif.) Dept. Mental Health, 1974-79; asst. clin. prof. med. psychology Sch. Medicine U. Calif., Irvine, 1975—; now coordinator quality assurance Orange County Health Care Agy. cons. in field; mem. Child Abuse Council Orange County. Served to 1st lt. Nurse Corps, U.S. Army, 1945-46. Fulbright scholar, 1953-55; World Health fellow, 1959. Lic. marriage, family and child therapist. Fellow Am. Pub. Health Assn.; mem. Am., Western psychol. assns., Soc. Clin. and Exptl. Hypnosis (asso.), So. Calif. Pub. Health Assn. (bd. govs., v.p.), Am. Psychol. Assn., Mental Health-Psychiat. Nurse Specialists (cert.). Home: 14891 Featherhill Rd Tustin CA 92680 Office: 1440 E 1st St Santa Ana CA 92701

DAVIS, FRANCE ALBERT, clergyman, educator; b. Gough, Ga., Dec. 5, 1946; s. John Hildery and Julia Alberta (Cooper) D.; A.A., Merritt Coll., 1972, Laney Coll., 1972; B.A., U. Calif., Berkeley, 1972; B.S., Westminster Coll., 1977; M.A., 1978; m. Willene Witt, Sept. 1, 1973; children—Carolyn Marie, Grace Elaine, France Albert II. Teaching fellow, communications, U. Utah, Salt Lake City, 1972-73, instr., 1973—; ordained to ministry Baptist Ch., 1971; pastor Calvary Bapt. Ch., Salt Lake City, 1974—; mem. Utah Bd. Corrections, 1975—; mem. Utah Gov's. Black Policy Council, 1974—; cons. theology Westminster Coll., Salt Lake City, 1976-77; moderator Utah-Idaho Gen. Assn. Nat. Bapt. Chs., 1976—; chmn. Utah Opportunities Industrialization Center Bd. Dirs., 1975—; instr. sem. extension, 1978—. Recipient Pres.'s. award NAACP, 1975; Spl. Teaching citation, 1974; Mil. Citizen of Yr. award, 1980. Participant TV and radio programs. Home: 1912 Meadow Dr Salt Lake City UT 84121 Office: Calvary Baptist Church 532 E 7th St St Salt Lake City UT 84102

DAVIS, FRANK STRATFORD, investment management executive; b. Sacramento, Dec. 12, 1924; s. James Rudd and Irene May (Harrington) D.; m. Maxine Mary Sipes; children—Laura Anne, Mark Winston. A.B., U. Calif.-Berkeley, 1945, M.B.A., 1949. Chartered Fin. Analyst. Sr. fin. analyst Commonwealth Group of Mut. Funds, San Francisco, 1950-59; dir. investment research Sutro Co., San Francisco, 1959-67; dir. instl. research Schwabacher & Co., San Francisco, 1967-68; corp. dir., v.p., energy investments head William Hutchinson & Co., Inc., San Francisco, 1968-73; fin. cons., 1974-75; v.p. investment research group, energy investments head Crocker Investment Mgmt. Corp., San Francisco, 1976—; lectr. security analysis and investment principles and practices, U. Calif. Extension, Div., 1955-62. Served with U.S. Army, 1945-46. Mem. World Affairs Council, Middle East Inst., Fin. Analysts Fedn. (former dir.), Inst. Chartered Fin. Analysts, Security Analysts of San Francisco (past pres.), Nat. Assn. Petroleum Investment Analysts, Pi Mu Epsilon. Episcopalian. Clubs: Silverado Country, Calif./Tennis, Commonwealth of Calif. Contbr. reports in field. Home: 111 Santa Paula Ave San Francisco CA 94127 Office: 44 Montgomery St Suite 2100 San Francisco CA 94104

DAVIS, GARY THAYNE, county administrator; b. Topeka, July 22, 1938; s. Kenneth Doud and Ruth Nylene (Grabow) D.; B.S., George Washington U., 1972; M.Sc., Naval Postgrad. Sch., 1974; m. Elizabeth Rae Fritz, Dec. 2, 1966; children—Gary Thayne, Alisa Diane. Enlisted in U.S. Navy, 1955, commd. ensign M.S.C., 1967, advanced through grades to lt. comdr., 1977, ret., 1981; comptroller Naval Regional Med. Clinics, Pearl Harbor, Hawaii, 1981-82; adminstrv. officer Jefferson County Health Dept., Lakewood, Colo., 1982—; acctg. instr. U. Guam, 1976. Mem. Gov.'s Com. for Armed Forces Day, 1976. Decorated Navy Commendation medal (U.S.), Cross of Gallantry (Vietnam). Mem. Assn. Govt. Accts. (cert. of merit, pres. Guam 1976-77), Assn. Mil. Comptrollers, Advanced Hosp. Fin. Mgmt. Assn., Am. Hosp. Assn., Colo. Pub. Health Assn. Republican. Clubs: Nat. Sojourners (pres. Hawaii 1980-81), Hero of '76, Royal Order Jesters, Masons, Shriners. Home: 10147 W Fremont Pl Littleton CO 80127

DAVIS, GEORGE JACK, computer specialist; b. Limoges, France, Nov. 26, 1918 (father Am. citizen); s. Floyd Sylvester and Lucienne A. (Blondeau) D.; student U. Colo., Denver, 1969, 75; student numerous computer sci. and mgmt. courses, 1959—; m. Ruth Allene Southern, Apr. 13, 1952; children—Susan Ann, Diane Rebecca, Cynthia Alice. Mem. data processing staff VA, Denver, 1948-55; supr. data processing Gates Rubber Co., Denver, 1955-59; supr. computer programming Martin-Marietta Co., Denver, 1959-64; mem. computer programming staff Litton Industries, Canoga Park, Calif., 1964-66, Air Force Fin. Center, Denver, 1966-67; supr. br. computer scis. and engring. U.S. Bur. Mines, Denver, 1969—. Mem. Colo. Gov.'s Com. on Vets. Affairs, 1947-48. Served with USAAF, 1942-46; CBI. Recipient Superior Service award U.S. Bur. Mines, 1969; Meritorious Service award Nat. Cath. Community Service, 1949. Mem. Am. Fedn. Musicians, Mensa. Democrat. Roman Catholic. Home: 2551 W Arkansas Ave Denver CO 80219 Office: US Bureau of Mines Denver Fed Center Denver CO 80225

DAVIS, GORDON EDWARD, planning and engineering company executive; b. Chgo., Apr. 15, 1943; s. James Russell and Lois Kathryn (Guither) D.; student LaVerne (Calif.) Coll., 1961-64, Los Angeles City Coll., 1964-65, Mt. San Antonio Jr. Coll., 1964-65; B.Arch., Ariz. State U., 1969; M.Urban Planning, U. Wash., 1971; m. Nancy Lynn Sawyer, Sept. 4, 1964 (div.); 1 son, Keith Alexander. Planner, Walter M. Isaac & Co., Seattle, 1970-71; planner Wilsey & Ham, South Pasadena, Calif., 1971, planner, project profl., Tucson, 1971-74, Portland, 1974-76, asso., 1976-78, v.p., 1978-81, pres., 1981—; guest lectr. Urban Planning program U. Ariz., Geography and Urban Studies programs Portland State U., also Sch. Oceanography, Oreg. State U. Bd. dirs., v.p. strategic planning Columbia-Willamette YMCA, Portland. Served to capt. Army N.G., 1960-71. Recipient Silver medal AIA, 1969; Richard King Mellon fellow, 1970. Mem. Am. Planning Assn., Am. Inst. Cert. Planners. Office: 521 SW 11th Ave Portland OR 97205

DAVIS, HAZEL RUTH GANN, banker; b. Ward, Ark., Jan. 12, 1938; d. Virgel Rupert and Dorothy Camilia Gann; grad. Ariz. State U., 1981; m. William E. Davis, Nov. 3, 1956; children—Karen Kaye, Lisa Gaye. Loan officer, head teller Western Savs., Mesa, Ariz., 1972-75; br. mgr. I, asst. sec., 1975, br. mgr. II, asst. v.p., 1976-80; area mgr., asst. v.p. Home Fed. Savs., Mesa, 1980—. Div. chmn. United Way, Mesa, 1980; mem. steering com. Mesa Leadership, Tng. and Devel., 1981—; bd. dirs. Sister City Assn. Mesa, 1981—. Mem. Mesa C. of C. (dir. 1980—, chmn. membership 1979), Am. Bus. Women's Assn. (chmn. program and edn. 1979-81), Inst. Fin. Edn., Savs. and Loan League, Chandler/Mesa/Tempe Bd. Realtors. Republican. Clubs: Mesa Country, Pilot of East Valley (pres. 1980—). Home: 2244 E Dartmouth Circle Mesa AZ 85203 Office: 1250 S Alma School Rd Mesa AZ 85202

DAVIS, HENRY ALBERT, systems co. exec.; b. Portland, Maine, Feb. 19, 1954; s. Garland J. and Priscilla A. (Dow) D.; student Furman U., 1972-74, N.Mex. Inst. Mining and Tech., 1974-76; m. Irene G. Arthur, May 30, 1974; 1 son, Christopher E. Dir. research Furman U., Greenville, S.C., 1976; microprocessor specialist Activity Systems, Reston, Va., 1977-78; mgr. systems engring. Am. Microsystems, Santa Clara, Calif., 1978—; founder, v.p. tech. Solo Systems, Inc., 1981—; justice of peace, 1972-79. Recipient Electronics Technologist of Yr. award, 1980. Mem. Assn. Computing Machinery, IEEE. Lutheran. Contbr. articles to various publs. Home: 5261 Kentfield Dr San Jose CA 95124 Office: 482 Oakmead Pkwy Sunnyvale CA 94086

DAVIS, HOWARD KENNETH, coll. exec.; b. Pampa, Tex., Nov. 7, 1920; s. Raymond Harry and Virginia Laura (Wallace) D.; student Oklahoma City U., 1948-50; A.B., M.W. Christian Coll. 1950, D.D., 1975; postgrad. Nanzan U., Nagoya, Japan, 1958-59; M.Ed., Central State U., Edmond, Okla., 1970; D.Litt., Berean Christian Sem., 1972; m. Anna Kathryn Giles, Sept. 8, 1939; children—Judith Kathryn Davis Bowers, Janet Ann Davis Layman, Deloras Irene Davis Webb, Edna Rae, Kenneth Howard. Missionary for Christian Ch., Central Japan Mission, Nagoya, Honshu, 1950-64; prof. M.W. Christian Coll., 1965-68, pres., 1968-75; pres. Artesia Christian Coll., 1975—; mem. 120 Man Com., North Am. Christian Conv.; mem. exec. com., v.p., nat. prayer chmn. Nat. Missionary Conv., 1978; mem. archeol. expdn. to Mt. Ararat, 1980. Served with U.S. Army, 1944-46; PTO. Recipient Disting. Ser. award Busan Christian Vocat. Coll., Korea, 1975, award of Honor, Okla. Bicentennial Commn., 1975 Attendance Promoter award Okla. 1971 North Am. Christian Conv.; named Juez-Comisionado on N.Mex. Exec. Staff, Lt. Gov. Robert Ferguson, 1976, col., aide-de-Camp, Gov. Jerry Apodaca of N.Mex., 1976. Mem. N.Mex. Coordinating Council Secondary Schs. and Colls., Berean Christian Fellowship, Internat. Platform Assn., Artesia C. of C. Club: Lions (Artesia). Editor, pub.: Missionary Illustrations, 1964. Home: 2412 Loma Dr Artesia NM 88210 Office: PO Box 9 Artesia NM 88210

DAVIS, JACK J., food company executive; b. Jackson, Calif., Jan. 22, 1938; s. Jack and Gertrude (Malone) D.; m. Catherine Ann Wells, May 3, 1964; children—Beth, Jennifer. B.S. in Chem. Engring., Va. Tech. Inst., 1959; B.S. in Mktg., Delta State U., 1961. Plant mgr. Wilsey Foods, Los Angeles, 1965-67, v.p. mfg., 1967-70, v.p. sales and mktg., 1970-76, exec. v.p., 1976-81, vice chmn., 1981—, pres., 1983—. Mem. Nat. Margarine Mfg. Assn. (dir.), Inst. Edible Oils. Republican. Baptist. Office: 14840 Don Julian Rd City of Industry CA 91746

DAVIS, JAMES FRANK, data processing exec.; b. Weatherford, Tex., Feb. 4, 1937; s. Jennings Price and Bessie Louise (Smith) D.; student U. Hawaii, 1961-64, West Valley Coll., 1965-67; B.S. in Bus. Adminstrn., U. Notre Dame, 1969, postgrad., 1980—; m. Joyceline Wilma Aweau, Mar. 20, 1958; children—James Frank, Jeffrey, Jamie, Jonathan. Systems analyst U.S. Fed. Service, Hawaii, 1962-64; programmer-analyst Lockheed, Sunnyvale, Calif., 1964-68; systems analyst Stanford (Calif.) Med. Center, 1968-70; computer services mgr. AMI Corp., Santa Clara, Calif., 1970-76; dir. computer and adminstrv. services U.S. Fleet Leasing, San Mateo, Calif., 1976-80; analyst SRI Internat., Menlo Park, Calif., 1980—. Bd. dirs., sec., pres. Glenshire Assn., 1975-78; pres. King's Run Assn., 1977; bd. dirs. Branham Homeowner's Assn., 1977. Served with USAF, 1954-60. Republican. Home: 2747 St James Rd Belmont CA 94002 Office: 333 Ravenswood Ave Menlo Park CA 94025

DAVIS, JANET HAYNES MCKIBBEN, ret. child psychologist; b. Council Bluffs, Iowa, Mar. 26, 1910; d. William Alexander and Dora (Pines) McKibben; B.A., Union Coll., Lincoln, Nebr., 1934; M.A., Claremont Coll., 1964; m. Donald Edward Jacobs, Sept. 12, 1935 (div. Oct. 1958); children—William Wallace (dec.), Jenny Ann Jacobs Vierling; m. 2d, Morten Jensen Davis, Apr. 17, 1979. Tchr. elem. schs., Nevada, Iowa, 1929-31; dean of girls Lodi Acad., 1934-35, tchr. English and Spanish, 1936-38; tchr. English and home econs. Battle Creek (Mich.) Acad., 1952-53; tchr. elem. schs., La Grange, Ill., 1953-55, Riverside, Calif., 1955-59; psychometrist, instr. edn. La Sierra Coll., 1959-65; asst. prof. psychology Loma Linda (Calif.) U., 1966-75, clin. instr. psychology dept. psychiatry Sch. Medicine, 1967-78, asso. prof. edn., 1975-78, ret., 1979. Vice chmn. Loma Linda Acad. Sch. Bd., 71-73, chmn., 1973-74. Lic. marriage-family-child counselor, ednl. psychologist, Calif. Mem. Am., Western, Calif., Inland (sec.-treas. 1970, treas. 1977) psychol. assns., Calif. Assn. Sch. Psychologists, Southeastern Counties Sch. Psychologists Assn. (sec. 1970-72). Club: Faculty Women's (pres. 1971-72) (Loma Linda). Contbr. articles to profl. jours. Home: 4648 SE 33d Pl Portland OR 97202

DAVIS, JOHN ELLSWORTH (JAY), broadcaster, educator; b. Cameron, Mo., Aug. 27, 1927; s. John Ellsworth Grant and Ernestine Katherine (Schmitz) D.; B.A., Martin Sch. Communications, 1954; m. Frances Leona Tolete, Nov. 26, 1955; children—Geoffrey, Gregory, Gigi. Chief announcer KORK-TV, Las Vegas, Nev., 1955-56; disc jockey KAFY Radio, Bakersfield, Calif., 1956-57; engr. NBC, Burbank, Calif., 1957; ops. mgr. KRBO, Las Vegas, 1957-58; program dir. KBUC, Corona, Calif., 1958-61; disc. jockey, newsman KEZY, Anaheim, Calif., 1961-71; newsman KNX, Los Angeles, 1965-67; dir. news and public affairs KGER, Long Beach, Calif., 1971-79, dir. ops., 1979—; prof. theatre Calif. State U., Fullerton, 1973-77; faculty Long Beach Community Coll., 1978—. Mem. com. for drafting new charter City of Anaheim, 1963-64. Served with USAF, 1945-52. Recipient Americanism award, Long Beach Elks, 1973. Mem. AFTRA, Anaheim Jaycees (pres. 1962-63). Clubs: Longbeach Rotary, Phoenix (Anaheim). Columnist, On the Go (newspaper), 1964-66. Home: 1630 W Cris Ave Anaheim CA 92802 Office: 3759 Atlantic Ave Long Beach CA 90807

DAVIS, JOHN FRANK, clinical psychologist; b. N.Y.C., Nov. 13, 1942; s. Jack Pierre Bailhe and Pat Cois (Schwartz) B.; m. Virginia Lee Douglas, (div.) Ph.D., Temple U., 1973. Cert. psychologist, Nev. Pvt. practice psychology, Las Vegas, Nev. Mem. Am. Psychol. Assn. Office: 4230 Burnham Suite 202 Las Vegas NV 89109

DAVIS, JOSEPH HOWE, electronics engineer; b. Orlando, Fla., Feb. 6, 1926; s. Joseph Howe and Mary Eugenia (Yates) D.; B.E.E., George Washington U., 1952, postgrad., 1965-67; postgrad. U. Hawaii, 1970; children—Sabine Genevieve Anne, Vincent Joseph Pierre. With Nat. Security Agy., 1949-59; engr., U.S. Army Electronic Labs., Ft. Monmouth, N.J., 1959-65; mem. staff Dept. Army, 1965-67; dep. U.S. Army CEEIA Pacific, Schofield Barracks, Hawaii, 1967-71, chief engr., tech. dir., 1971-73, chief engring. div., 1973-79, chief transmission div. USA Comm, 1979-80, chief field office, 1980-81, asst. to ops. div. USACE WESTCOM, 1981—. Served with USNR, 1944-46. Recipient numerous U.S. govt. awards and commendations. Mem. Assn. U.S. Army (life), Armed Forces Communications-Electronics Assn. (life), Mensa. Mason (32 deg.). Home: 523 Kaimake Loop Kailua HI 96734 Office: USACC WESTCOM Fort Shafter HI 96858

DAVIS, JUDY ANN, manufacturing executive; b. Winchester, Mass., Apr. 4, 1942; d. Merrick Anson and Ethel Margarite (Jewell) Dodge; m. Robin Nigel French Davis, July 15, 1976; children—Robert, Steven, Denise. Grad. Artesia (Calif.) High Sch. Prodn. supr. Narmco div. Celanese, Costa Mesa, Calif., 1973-78; plant supt. Ciba Geigy, Fountain Valley, Calif., head Graphite Composite dept., 1978—. Recipient Orange County chpt. Nat. Safety Council 1st place awards, 1981-83. Mem. Am. Prodn. and Inventory Control Soc., Soc. Advancement Material and Process Engring. Pioneer in devel. carbon graphite composites.

DAVIS, KATHLEEN EDDINS, interior designer; b. Lewistown, Pa., Mar. 15, 1948; d. Arthur Henry and Elizabeth (Weldgen) Eddins; m. John Thomas Malloy, Jr., Apr. 20, 1968; children—John Thomas III, Michele Ann; m. 2d, Charles Joseph Davis, Dec. 27, 1980. B.S., San Jose State U., 1975; A.A., San Jose City Coll., 1971. Asst. interior designer B. Terry Interiors, Campbell, Calif., 1973; asst. interior designer Charles Falls & Assocs., Los Altos, Calif., 1973-75; interior designer W & J Sloane Inc., San Jose, Calif., 1975-79; interior designer, owner Kathleen Malloy, Palo Alto, Calif., 1979—. Chmn., Gamble House Project, City Palo Alto, 1982; v.p. La Entrada PTA, 1982-83. Mem. AAUW, Am. Soc. Interior Designers (pres. Peninsula chpt. 1981-82, recipient presdl. citation 1977, 79, 80). Democrat. Office: 1259 El Camino Real Suite 253 Menlo Park CA 94025

DAVIS, KATHLEEN PERNELL, electronics industry co. exec.; b. Pitts., Aug. 3, 1946; d. Ulysses W. and Kathleen (Waller) D.; B.S., Drexel U., 1969; M.B.A., U. Pa., 1974. Specialist, civil info. Gen. Electric Co., Phila., 1969-74; sr. project mgr., mktg. research Crown Zellerbach Corp., San Francisco, 1974-76, market mgr., bus. and converting papers div., 1976-80; mgr. printer supplies mktg. Diablo Systems, Inc., 1980—. Bd. dirs. La Casa de las Madres, 1980-81, YWCA of San Francisco, 1981—. Mem. Am. Mktg. Assn., Union Sq. Bus. and Profl. Women's Club (pres.), Bay Area Profl. Women's Network. Home: 2903 Carmel St Oakland CA 94602 Office: Diablo Systems Inc 24500 Industrial Blvd Hayward CA 94545

DAVIS, KEVIN WYNSTON, educator; b. Boston, Nov. 11, 1955; s. Robert Lewis and Helen Adeline (Kemp) D.; B.A., Pacific Union Coll., 1977; M.A., Loma Linda (Calif.) U., 1982. Cert. tchr., Calif. Head resident asst. Pacific Union Coll., Angwin, Calif., 1977; ordained to ministry Seventh-day Adventist Ch.; asso. minister Seventh-day Adventist Ch., Los Angeles, 1977-80, elem. tchr., 1980—. Hon. mem. Spl. Olympics Com. Seventh-day Adventist Ch. grantee, 1980. Mem. Calif. Reading Assn., Assn. Supervision and Curriculum Devel. Democrat. Club: Brookinairs. Home: 10000 Imperial Hwy B 105 Downey CA 90242 Office: 15548 Santa Ana Ave Bellflower CA 90706

DAVIS, LARRY ALAN, farm mgr.; b. Delano, Calif., June 1, 1940; s. Thomas Albert and Ina (Bowman) D.; B.A. cum laude in Chemistry (Nat. Merit scholar), LaVerne Coll., 1962; M.S. in Agronomy, U. Calif.-Davis, 1964, Ph.D. in Plant Physiology (NDEA fellow), 1968; m. Nina Irene Boone, June 11, 1960; children—Debra June, Wendy Jean, Pamela Joanne. Asst. mgr. Alina Farms Corp., McFarland, Calif., 1964-65, pres., gen. mgr., 1970-79, dir., tree crops cons., 1979—; mgr. Calcot Pty. Ltd., Wee Waa, New South Wales, Australia, 1968-70, sec., dir., 1968—; sec., dir. Davis Pty. Ltd., Canberra, Australia, 1968—; mng. partner Friendship Farms, 1980—; adj. lectr. biology Calif. State Coll., Bakersfield, 1972-73; dir., research liaison officer Calif. Planting Cotton Seed Dist., 1971-74; dir. San Joaquin Cotton Planting Seed Dist., 1970-80. Sec. Wee Waa Water Users Assn., 1968-70; mem. coordinating com. Namoi Valley Water Users Assn., Australia, 1968-70; chmn. Kern County Cotton Industry Com., 1971-78; dir., vice chmn. McFarland Recreation and Park Dist., 1976—; mem. community adv. com. McFarland Union Elementary Schs., 1972-73; chmn. McFarland Recreation Adv. Com., 1973-74; trustee Ch. of Sequoias, 1973-81, LaVerne Coll. (Calif.), 1972-75; gov. Eccumenical Inst. Chgo.; lic. minister Ch. of Brethren; minister of teaching McFarland Ch. of Brethren, 1976—; pres., dir. ministries Fellowship Christian Farmers, 1980—. Mem. Central Valley Almond Assn. (sec., dir.), Agrl. Leaderships Assos., Council Calif. Growers, Am. Soc. Agronomy, Bot. Soc. Am., Am. Soc. Plant Physiologists, Am. Inst. Biol. Scis., Crop Sci. Soc. Am., Kern County Farm Bur. (dir. 1980—), Sigma Xi, Phi Kappa Phi, Alpha Psi Omega. Home: 12496 Stradley Ave McFarland CA 93250 Office: Route 1 Box 292 McFarland CA 93250

DAVIS, L(LOYD) WAYNE, research co. exec.; b. Medicine Lodge, Kans., July 16, 1929; s. Lloyd and Edith Elda (Furnas) D.; B.S. in Engring. Physics (Summerfield scholar), U. Kans., 1952; M.S. in Elec. Engring. (fellow), U. N.Mex., 1959; m. Betty Louise Pyke, Sept. 7, 1963; 1 son, William W.; children by previous marriage—Robert L., Cheryl S. Staff mem. systems analysis dept. Sandia Corp., Albuquerque, 1952-56, cons., 1956-57; research physicist Dikewood Corp., Albuquerque, 1957-60, sr. research physicist, 1960-64, head weapons effects div., 1964-67, dep. tech. dir., 1967-69, asst. v.p., 1969-72, sec., 1970-80, dir., 1971-82, v.p., 1972-77, sr. v.p., 1977-80, pres., chmn. bd., 1980-82; v.p. Kaman Scis. Corp., gen. mgr. Dikewood div., Albuquerque, 1982—. Mem. IEEE (sr.), Am. Phys. Soc. (S.E. sect.), Air Force Assn., Am. Def. Preparedness Assn., Sigma Xi, Phi Kappa Phi, Tau Beta Pi, Sigma Tau, Sigma Pi Sigma, Kappa Mu Epsilon, Beta Gamma Sigma, Delta Sigma Pi, Sigma Chi. Republican. Mem. Christian Ch. (trustee 1970-73). Research on nuclear weapons effects and phenomenology effects on personnel and complex mil. systems; developed urban nuclear-casualty prediction model for high-yield nuclear bursts from Japanese data base, 1962-70. Home: 4411 Altura Ave NE Albuquerque NM 87110 Office: 1613 University Blvd NE Albuquerque NM 87102

DAVIS, LOWELL LIVINGSTON, thoracic and cardiovascular surgeon; b. Urbanna, Va., Dec. 14, 1922; s. Jordan and Mary Emma (Wright) D.; B.S., Morehouse Coll., 1949; M.S., Atlanta U., 1950; M.D., Howard U., 1955; postgrad. U. Pa. Grad. Sch. Medicine, 1959-60; m. Barbara Helen Allen, Sept. 4, 1964. Rotating intern Jersey City Med. Center, 1955-56; resident in obstetrics Margaret Hague Maternity Hosp., Jersey City, 1956-57; asst. resident in obstetrics and gynecology Elmhurst (N.Y.) Gen. Hosp., 1957-58, chief resident, 1958-59; resident in gen. surgery VA Hosp., Tuskegee, Ala., 1960-61; resident in gen. surgery Meadowbrook Gen. Hosp., Hempstead, N.Y., 1961-63, chief resident, 1963-64; resident and chief resident in cardiothoracic surgery Cook County Hosp., Chgo., 1967-69; fellow in cardiopulmonary surgery U. Oreg. Med. Sch., Portland, 1972; fellow in cardiovascular surgery St. Vincent Hosp., Portland, 1972; fellow in coronary revascularization surgery Med. Coll. Wis., Milw., 1973; fellow in cardiovascular surgery Insts. Med. Scis., Pacific Med. Center, San Francisco, 1974; instr. Meharry Med. Coll., Nashville, 1950-51; instr. surgery U. Ill., 1969; vis. surgeon Hosp. for Sick Children, London, 1977; clin. instr. div. thoracic surgery U. So. Calif., 1981—. Served with USNR, 1943-46; to capt., M.C., USNR, 1971. Diplomate Am. Bd. Surgery, Am. Bd. Thoracic Surgery. Fellow A.C.S., Internat. Coll. Surgeons, Am. Coll. Angiology, Internat. Coll. Angiology, Am. Coll. Chest Physicians, Am. Coll. Cardiology, N.Y. Acad. Medicine; mem. Soc. Thoracic Surgeons, Am. Assn. Thoracic Surgeons, Albert Starr Cardiac Surgery Soc. (founding), Assn. Mil. Surgeons U.S., Lyman Brewer III Internat. Surg. Soc., Royal Soc. Medicine (affiliate), Chi Delta Mu. Home: 4267 Marina City Dr WTS 310 Marina Del Rey CA 90291

DAVIS, MARGARET ROSE TYTLER, sociologist; b. Calcutta, India (parents Brit. citizens); d. Philip and Mary Martha Lillian (Gregory) Tytler; m. Raymond Arthur Davis, Feb. 25, 1956; children—Janet Katharine, Robert Douglas, A.B., Stanford U., 1974, M.A., 1975, Ph.D., 1979. Research and teaching asst. Stanford (Calif.) U., 1973-77; instr. Coll. San Mateo (Calif.), 1977-78; research sociologist SRI Internat., Menlo Park, Calif., 1979-82; sr. orgn. specialist Pacific Gas & Electric Co., San Francisco, 1983—. Active LWV, San Mateo, NIMH fellow, 1976-78. Mem. Am. Sociol. Assn., Pacific Sociol. Assn., Bay Area Organizational Devel. Network. Author: Families in a Working World, 1982. Office: Pacific Gas & Electric Co 215 Market St Room 1600 San Francisco CA

DAVIS, MARSHALL KENT, chemist; b. Gt. Bend, Kans., Dec. 4, 1946; s. Arnold Fay and Mary Marjorie (Harper) D.; m. Sherry Fern Wake, July 19, 1969, children—Jennifer Marie, Aaron Marshall; m. 2d, Constance Elaine Patterson, July 31, 1982. B.A. in Chemistry, U. La Verne, 1969. Water quality analyst III, Am. Water Works Assn. Chemist Sun Kist Orange Products, Ontario, Calif., 1969; with Met. Water Dist. So. Calif., La Verne, Calif., 1969—, supervising chemist 1982—; mem. joint task group standard methods com.; mem. tech. adv. com. Orange and Los Angeles counties water reuse study. Mem. Am. Water Works Assn., Am. Chem. Soc. Home: 637 Sedalia Ave La Verne CA 91750 Office: Met Water Dist So Calif 700 N Moreno Ave La Verne CA 91750

DAVIS, MARY MCGLOTHIN, college administrator, registered nurse; b. Marshall, Tex., Dec. 10, 1942; d. Henry Clay and Annie Bell (Williams) McGlothin; m. Don Albert Davis, Apr. 12, 1963; children—Dianna Alarice, Caryn Janine. B.S., Prairie View A&M Coll., 1963; M.S., U. Colo.-Boulder, 1975, Ph.D., 1983. Registered nurse. Nurse VA Hosp., Waco, Tex., 1963-70; nursing instr. McLennan Community Coll., Waco, 1970-73, Arapahoe Community Coll., Littleton, Colo., 1974-76; dir. health occupations Community Coll. of Denver, 1976-80. HHS, 1980-82; dir. acad. affairs Community Coll. Denver, Aurora (Colo.) Ctr., 1982—; cons. U. Denver nursing curriculum project, Western Interstate Coll. higher edn. nursing project, 1976-78. Bd. dirs. young people's div. Shorter Am. Meth. Epis. Ch. Mem. Am. Vocat. Assn., Am. Assn. Women in Jr. & Community Colls., Am. Soc. Curriculum Devel. Democrat. Contbr. to profl. jours. in field of nursing. Author: Health Teaching in the Mass Media, 1980. Home: 12241 E 48th Ave Denver CO 80239 Office: 791 Chambers Rd #204 Aurora CO 80011

DAVIS, NICHOLAS HOMANS CLARK, securities company executive; b. N.Y.C., Dec. 1, 1938; s. Feltz Cleveland and Loraine Vanderpool (Homans) D.; children—Loraine, Helen, Alexandra, Christopher, Eleanor, Katherine, John. grad. Pingry Prep. Sch., 1956; A.B. in Paleontology with honors, Princeton U., 1961; M.B.A., Stanford U., 1963. Instl. security analyst Fahnestock & Co., N.Y.C., 1963-67; mgr. research dept. Andersen & Co., N.Y.C., 1967-70; instl. sec. research Robert Garrett & Sons, N.Y.C., 1970-71; research partner Boettcher & Co., Denver, 1971-75, also dir.; v.p. White, Weld & Co., Denver, 1976-78; v.p. Paine Webber Jackson & Curtis, Inc., Denver, 1978—; pres., chmn. Colo. Growth Capital, Inc., Denver, 1978—; founder, dir. Colo. Life Ins. Co., Grand Junction, 1977-78. Treas., bd. dirs. Greenwich Village Montessori Sch., N.Y.C., 1965-71. trustee Bonnie Brae Farm Boys, Millington, N.J., 1969-76, Charles Emil Thenen Found., Montclair, N.J., 1965—. Chartered fin. analyst. Mem. N.Y., Denver (dir. 1973—) socs. security analysts, Chartered Fin. Analysts Soc. Clubs: N.Y. Yacht, Racquet and Tennis (N.Y.C.); Denver Petroleum, Denver Country, Mile High (Denver); Quantuck Beach (Westhampton, N.Y.). Author article. Home: 9823 W 83d Ave Arvada CO 80005 Office: 1600 Broadway Denver CO 80202

DAVIS, NISSEN AVROY, public relations executive; b. Windhoek, S.W. Africa, Nov. 21, 1933; s. Sam and Sera (Levin) D.; came to U.S., 1961, naturalized, 1967; student pub. schs., Windhoek; m. Susan Bomar Taylor, Jan. 15, 1977; 1 son, Scott Taylor; children by previous marriage—Janine, Glenn. Public relations mgr. Wynn Oil Co., Azusa, Calif., 1961-67; public relations dir. J. Walter Thompson, Los Angeles, 1967-72; public affairs dir. Action, Peace Corps, Vista, Washington, 1972-74; v.p. public relations and advt. Flying Tiger Line, Los Angeles, 1974-83; v.p. pub. relations Welton Becket Assocs., Santa Monica, Calif., 1983—. Club: Aero of So. Calif. (past pres.). Address: 2900 31st St Santa Monica CA 90405

DAVIS, OAKLEY, JR., mech. engr., mktg. exec.; b. Heilwood, Pa., Sept. 20, 1930; s. Oakley Melvorn and Emabel (Decker) D.; student Ind. U., 1956-57, Carnegie-Mellon U., 1957-58; B.S.M.E., Pa. State U., 1960; m. Gloria Theadora Foresi, Aug. 7, 1957 (dec. 1981); children—Jan Marie, Jeffrey Evan. Asst. designer Pa. Dept. Hwys., Indiana, Pa., 1951-56; design engr. Green Engring. Co., Sewickley, Pa., 1956-58; test and devel. engr. Aerojet-Gen. Corp., Azusa, Calif., 1961-64; v.p., gen. mgr. W.A. Whitney Co., Los Angeles, 1965-68; v.p. mktg. POW-R-TRON, Inc., Home, Pa., 1968-69; v.p., gen. mgr. Fabri-Quipt Systems Co., Arcadia, Calif., 1969—; cons. indsl. econs. Mem. county com. Republican Party, 1956-58, co-ordinating com., 1964; bd. dirs. Am. Baptist Credit Union, 1977—. Served with AUS, 1952-54. Mem. Am. Mgmt. Assn., Soc. Mfg. Engrs. Republican. Baptist. Editor, cons., contbr. articles to indsl. trade publs. Home: 281 W Foothill Blvd Arcadia CA 91006 Office: Fabri-Quipt Systems Co 420 Rolyn Pl Arcadia CA 91006

DAVIS, OLIVE MCFATE, trade show executive; b. Oakland, Calif., Nov. 16, 1922; d. Thomas Albert and Leana Jewel (Combs) McFate; m. Warren Leslie Davis, Jan. 18, 1942 (dec.); children—Jean Davis Cain, Patricia Davis Gualco, Larry, Allan. Student Bonnie Davis Inst. Orgn. Mgmt., 1980-82. Farming ptnr., Linden, Sonora and Mercer, Calif., 1943-69, newspaper correspondent Stockton (Calif.) Record, 1960-73; urban 4-H coordinator U. Calif. Extention Service, San Joaquin County, 1973; hist. researcher S.T. & E. R.R., Stockton, 1974-76; coordinator Central Valley Agrl. Expo, Stockton, 1976-77; staff Greater Stockton C. of C., 1977—, asst. mgr. Stockton Ag Expo, 1977—; mgr. Norcal Expo, Stockton, 1980-83. Chmn. Stockton Cultural Heritage Bd., 1981-82; regional dir. Am. Field Service, 1970-73, pres. Linden chpt., 1967-70; pres. Linden Garden Club, 1976-77; mem. Linden Devel. Commn., 1975. Recipient award Tuolumne County 4-H Council, 1980; Stockton City Planning Commn. award, 1982; Named Citizen of Yr., Linden Lions Club, 1973. Mem. Nat. Agrl. Mktg. Assn., Nat. Assn. Female Execs., Nat. Assn. Am. Pen Women, Calif. Hist. Soc., Jediah Smith Hist. Soc., San Joaquin County Hist. Soc. (pres. 1981-83). Author: Slow Tired & Easy R.R., 1976; contbr. articles to profl. jours., newspapers. Office: 1105 N El Dorado St Stockton CA 95202

DAVIS, PAUL KENSIL, physicist; b. Youngstown, Ohio, Dec. 20, 1943; s. Paul K. and Ruth Adelle (Gledhill) D.; B.S., U. Mich., Ann Arbor, 1965; Ph.D., Mass. Inst. Tech., 1970; m. Joyce Elaine Lindstrom, May 11, 1943; 1 dau., Elise Lorraine. Research assoc. James Franck Inst., Chgo., 1970-71; sr. scientist Inst. Def. Analyses, Arlington, Va., 1971-75; sci. officer ACDA, Washington, 1975-77; sr. analyst Dept. Def., Washington, 1977-79, sr. exec., dir. spl. region studies div., 1979-81, acting dep. asst. sec. for regional programs, 1981; dir. Strategic Assessment Ctr., Rand Corp., Santa Monica, Calif., 1981—. Mem. faculty and adv. bd. Rand Grad. Inst., 1981. Recipient Disting. Civilian Service medal Dept. Def., 1981. Mem. Am. Phys. Soc., AIAA, Sigma Xi. Office: 1700 Main St Santa Monica CA 90290

DAVIS, PETER JOHN, lease fin. co. exec.; b. London, July 13, 1925; s. Jack Henry and Stella (Cohen) D.; came to U.S., 1959, naturalized, 1966; Mgmt. Scis. diploma London Coll. of Commerce, 1949; m. Regina A. Bennett, Oct. 2, 1954; children—Diane Julie, Sorrel Jane, Stuart Victor. Systems analyst IBM Corp., San Jose, Calif., 1959-60; gen. mgr. Laurentide Leasing Co., San Francisco, 1961-68; pres. D.P.I. Systems Inc., Sunnyvale, Calif., 1968-72, Data Pathing Inc., Sunnyvale, 1972, Lease Mgmt. Services Inc., Los Altos Hills, Calif., 1972—; dir. computer Election Systems Inc., Berkeley, Calif., 1971—. Served with RAF, 1943-47.

DAVIS, RETHA MAY, home economist, editor; b. St. Johns, Mich., May 6, 1950; d. Rolland George and Ruth Marie (Dunham) Hankey; m. James Richard Davis, Nov. 29, 1980. B.S. in Community Services, Mich. State U., 1973, M.A. in Adult Edn. and Communications, 1978. Extension 4-H youth agt. Mich. State U., Lansing, 1973-74, extension assoc., 1974-76; dir. home econs. Mich. Beef Industry Commn., Lansing, 1976-78, exec. v.p., 1978-80; cookery editor HP Books, Tucson, 1980—. Recipient Mich. State U. Extension TEAM award, 1974. Mem. Home Economists in Bus., Am. Home Econ. Assn. Congregationalist. Office: 1019 Prince Tucson AZ 85703

DAVIS, RICHARD ALLEN, architect; s. Douglas Arnold and Dorothy Christine (Sievert) D.; B.Arch., U. Nebr., 1968; m. Glenda Rae Busboon, June 29, 1965; 1 dau., Katrina Christine. Designer, Oberg/Hunt/Gilliland Architects, Phoenix, 1968-70, William T. Baker, Architect, Mesa, Ariz., 1970-72; prin. Davis Assos. Architecture/Land Planning, Scottsdale, Ariz., 1972—. Served with USNR, 1959-61. Registered architect, Ariz., Calif., Nev. Mem. AIA, Nat. Council Archtl. Registration Bds., Scottsdale C. of C. Presbyterian. Designer: Plaza De Alamos, Pinnacle Peak, Ariz.; Las Palomas, Scottsdale, Ariz.; Raul Quintana Residence, Paradise Valley, Ariz. Home: 23645 N 83d Pl Scottsdale AZ 85255 Office: 7320 Scottsdale Mall Suite H Scottsdale AZ 85251

DAVIS, RICHARD CARTER, historian; b. El Centro, Calif., Sept. 22, 1939; s. Donald Carter and Ocal Leslie (Pemberton) D.; B.A., U. Calif., Riverside, 1963, M.A., 1965, Ph.D., 1973; cert. in Archives, U. Denver, 1972; M.L.S., U. Ky., 1979. Tchr., Banning (Calif.) Unified Sch. Dist., 1967-68; archives technician Nat. Archives, Washington, 1972-73; research archivist Forest History Soc., Santa Cruz, Calif., 1973-76, research asso., 1979-82; manuscript catalog editor Duke U., Durham, N.C., 1977-78. Mem. Soc. Am. Archivists (recipient Waldo Gifford Leland prize 1977), Am. Hist. Assn. Author: North American Forest History: A Guide to Archives and Manuscripts in the United States and Canada, 1977; Guide to the Cataloged Collections in the Manuscript Department of the William R. Perkins Library, 1980; Ency. of American Forest and Conservation History, 1983. Home: Villa Nueva 51 180 Dakota Ave Santa Cruz CA 95060

DAVIS, RICHARD MALONE, economics educator; b. Hamilton, N.Y., June 2, 1918; s. Malone Crowell and Grace Edith (McQuade) D.; A.B., Colgate U., 1939; Ph.D., Cornell U., 1949. From instr. to assoc. prof. econs. Lehigh U., Bethlehem, Pa., 1941-54; assoc. prof. econs. U. Oreg., Eugene, 1954-62, prof., 1962—. Served with U.S. Army, 1942-45. Mem. Am. Econs. Assn., Western Econs. Assn., Phi Beta Kappa. Republican. Contbr. articles to profl. jours. Home: 1040 Ferry St Apt 503 Eugene OR 97401 Office: Dept Econs Univ Oregon Eugene OR 97403

DAVIS, RICHARD RAYMOND, electro-optics engineer; b. Twin Falls, Idaho, Apr. 20, 1940; s. Richard Reed and Edith Alzina (Bush) D.; m. Pamela Manning, Dec. 27, 1965; children—Richard, Alan, Kimberly, Janell. B.S., Idaho State U., 1968, M.Ed., 1970; Ph.D., Columbia Pacific U., 1983. Instr. electronics Idaho State U.-Pocatello, 1965-73, instr., lab. coordinator electronics, laser/electro-optics, 1973-79, chmn. electro-tech. dept., 1979-81; sr. engr. electro-optics Kentron Internat., Kwajalein, Marshall Islands, 1981—. Served with U.S. Army, 1959-62, Idaho State U. grantee, 1971, 78; U.S. Office Edn. grantee, 1973. Mem. Am. Vocat. Assn. Mormon. Club: Kwajalein Scuba. Contbr. articles to profl. jours. Home: PO Box 1127 APO San Francisco CA 96555 Office: Kentron Internat PO Box 1207 APO San Francisco CA 96555

DAVIS, ROBERT H., fin. exec.; b. Phila., Mar. 26, 1943; s. Robert E. and Dorothy P. (Messmann) D.; student Los Angeles Valley Coll., 1965-67, Alexander Hamilton Inst., 1965-68, Grad. Sch. of Credit and Fin. Mgmt., Stanford U., 1977-80, Pepperdine U. Sch. Law, 1981. 1 dau., Michelle R. Fin. cons., Montepelier, Idaho, 1976-78; credit mgr. Wyo. Machinery Co., Casper, 1978-79; controller/sec.-treas. John E. Burns Drilling Co., Casper, 1979-83; v.p., chief fin. officer Phillips Crosley Assocs., Inc., Winter Park, Fla., 1983—; fin. cons. Western Energy Co., Huey's Smoked Meats, Nashville, Trans-Equip., Casper, Three Percent, Inc., Riverton, Wyo., 1979-80. Adv. bd. dirs. Highland Park Community Ch., 1980—. Served with USNR, 1961-63. Mem. Nat. Assn. Credit Mgmt. (state rep. 1979, 80, founder Casper credit group), Credit Mgrs. Assn. So. Calif. (dir. bus. re-orgn. and bankruptcy 1973-74), Credit Research Found., Am. Mgmt. Assn., Stanford U. Alumni Assn. Club: Order of Demolay (sr. award 1960). Office: PO Box 9082 Casper WY 82609

DAVIS, ROBERT MARK, oil and gas investment broker; b. Bellefont, Pa., May 15, 1955; s. Robert Bennett and Joan Whitmore D.; B.A., U. Wash., 1977. With Touche, Ross & Co., Seattle, 1977-79, sr., 1979; with Ernst & Whinney, Seattle, 1980-81; oil and gas investment broker ENI Corp., Bellevue, Wash., 1981—; instr. Becker C.P.A. Rev. Course, Seattle, 1980—. Mem. Fin. Mgrs. Assn., Am. Inst. C.P.A.s, Wash. Soc. C.P.A.s, Seattle C. of C. Republican. Episcopalian. Clubs: Washington Athletic, SuperSonics Racquet. Office: 1417 116th Ave NE Bellevue WA 98009

DAVIS, ROBERT WILLIAM, clin. psychologist, educator; b. Portland, Oreg., Nov. 1, 1934; s. William Price and Margaret Edith (Schaubel) D.; diploma Vancouver (B.C., Can.) Coll., 1948; B.A., Seattle U., 1956; M.A., U. Portland, 1961, Ph.D., 1964; postgrad. (fellow) N.Y.U., 1969; m. Mary Ann Augustin, Feb. 12, 1971; children—Suzanne, Mary Christine, Molly, Robert Price, Joel Thomas. Counselor, Marion County (Oreg.) Juvenile Dept., 1957-59; exec. sec. Catholic Community Services of Marion-Polk (Oreg.) Counties, 1960-62; instr. Oreg. State U., 1962; clin. fellow Delaunay Inst. Mental Health, Portland, 1962-63; intern Morningside Hosp., Portland, 1963-64; psychologist Interfaith Counseling Center, Portland, 1964-66; psychologist, then chief psychologist Clackamas County Mental Health Clinic, Oregon City, Oreg., 1966-67, 70-71; asst. prof., clin. psychologist Bklyn. Coll. of City U. N.Y., 1967-70; staff and tng. psychologist Lincoln Inst. Psychotherapy, N.Y.C., 1967-70; dir. Clackamas County Mental Health Program and McLoughlin Center for Mental Health, Oregon City, 1971-76; founding pres., dir. Columbia-Pacific Inst. Profl. Devel., Portland, 1971-75; vis. assoc. prof., lectr. psychology Portland State U., 1977-77; pvt. practice, 1976—; chief psychologist, cons. Oreg. Correctional Treatment Services, 1976—; adj. assoc. prof. U. Portland, 1978—; mem. Oreg. Bd. Psychologist Examiners, 1976-80; pres. Oreg. Grad. Sch. Profl. Psychology, 1976—. Served to capt. Med. Service Corps, AUS, 1956-67. Diplomate Am. Bd. Profl. Psychology, Portland Acad. Hypnosis. Fellow Soc. for Personality Assessment, Internat. Soc. Forensic Psychology; mem. Am., Oreg. psychol. assns., Oreg. Acad. Profl. Psychologists. Editor: Toward a Discovery of the Person, 1974. Contbg. author, contbr. articles, book revs., to profl. publs. Asso., cons. editor Jour. Personality 1966-82. Home: 8520 SW Bridletrail Ave Beaverton OR 97005 Office: 2165 SW Main St Portland OR 97205

DAVIS, ROGER TODD, psychologist, educator; b. Balt., Feb. 2, 1926; s. Robert William and Marjory E. (Hendricks) D.; m. Beulah Mae Hill, Jan. 1, 1948; m. 2d Margaret Lucille Davis, Nov. 17, 1975; children—David R., Marjory E., Michael T., Sara L.; stepchildren—Patricia A., Arthur L., Allan R., Walter D., Carol J. Fluharty. B.A., U. Wis., 1947, M.A., 1949, Ph.D., 1953. Teaching and research asst. U. Wis., Madison, 1947-50; instr. to prof. U. S.D., Vermillion, 1950-70; prof. psychology Wash. State U., Pullman, 1970—; vis. prof. U. Tex., Austin, and research scientist Balcones Lab., USAF, 1955-56; vis. prof. U. Oreg., Eugene, 1962-64; visitor Oxford U., 1976. Served with USAAF, 1944-46. Recipient Research Devel. award USPHS, 1965-70; USPHS grantee, 1952-77. Mem. Am. Psychol. Assn., Psychonomic Soc., Phi Beta Kappa, Sigma Xi. Repbulican. Author: Monkeys as Perceivers, 1974; contbr. many articles to profl. jours., chpts. to profl. books; editor: Processes in Animal Memory, 1976. Home: SW 1060 Viento St Pullman WA 99163 Office: Dept Psychology 4830 Wash State U Pullman WA 99164

DAVIS, RUSSELL LEONARD, librarian; b. Blackfoot, Idaho, Oct. 25, 1924; s. John Leonard and Mary Verna (Robertson) D.; student Weber Jr. Coll., 1948-50; B.S., Utah State U., 1952; A.M. in L.S., U. Mich., 1952-53; m. Emma Lou Barnes, June 10, 1949; children—Dan, Kathleen, Kirk, Susan, Eileen, Alan, Julie, Grant. Teaching asst. U. Mich. Library Sch., 1952-53; engring. librarian Utah State U., 1953-54, circulation librarian, 1954-57, instr. library sci., 1953-57, extension librarian, 1955-57; dir. Utah State Library Commn., 1957—. Mem. ALA, Utah Library Assn. (pres. 1960-61), Mountain Plains Library Assn. (pres. 1964-65). Mormon (bishop). Home: 575 E 1350 North Bountiful UT 84010 Office: 2150 S 3d W Salt Lake City UT 84115

DAVIS, STEPHEN EDWARD, water utility exec.; b. Dayton, Ohio, Oct. 28, 1946; s. Melvin Wellington and Frieda (Plummer) D.; B.S., U. Ariz., 1968, M.S., 1971; m. Marvel Elizabeth Fegursky, Aug. 14, 1971. Civil engr./planner Marum & Marum, Tucson, 1971-72; water planning adminstr. Tucson Water, City of Tucson, 1974—; mem. Gov.'s Commn. on Ariz. Environ. Served to capt. USAF, 1972-74. NSF fellow, 1968-71; registered profl. engr., Ariz. Mem. ASCE, Am. Water Resources Assn., Am. Water Works Assn., Ariz. Water and Pollution Control Assn., Internat. Platform Assn., U. Ariz. Alumni Band, Tau Beta Pi, Phi Eta Sigma, Phi Mu Alpha Symphonia. Democrat. Presbyterian (elder, deacon). Club: Tucson Sailing. Contbr. articles to profl. jours. Home: 6602 N Catalina Ave Tucson AZ 85718 Office: 111 E Pennington St Tucson AZ 85701

DAVIS, STEVEN JAMES, optometrist; b. Caldwell, Idaho, Sept. 5, 1952; s. Richard D. and Donna Joyce (McGinnis) D.; m. Eileen Marie (Snavely) Dec. 28, 1974; children—Nicole, Cami. B.S. in Zoology, Coll Idaho, 1974; O.D., Pacific U., 1978. Lic. optometrist, Wash. Practice optometry, Walla Walla, Wash., 1978—; cons. Wash. State Penitentiary. Mem. campaign com. county sheriff, 1982; chmn. profl. div. United Way Walla Walla, 1982. Mem. Wash. Optometric Assn. Am. Optometric Assn., Beta Sigma Kappa. Republican. Club: Exchange (dir.) (Walla Walla). Office: 120 E Birch Suite 1 Walla Walla WA 99362

DAVIS, STEWART L(EE), civil engineer; b. Twin Falls, Idaho, Oct. 21, 1941; s. Clifford L. and Sarah Rachael (Flora) D.; m. S. Joyce Davis, May 23, 1961; children—Michael, Stephen. B.S.C.E., Oreg. State U., 1967, M.S.C.E. in San. Engring., 1968. Registered profl. engr., Oreg., Wash. Application engr. Neptune Microfloc, Corvallis, Oreg., 1968-70, sr. application engr., 1970-73; project engr. CH2M Hill, Portland, Oreg., 1973-74, project mgr., 1975-80, mgr. treatment systems dept., 1980—. Mem. Am. Water Works Assn., Water Pollution Control Fedn. Office: 2020 SW 4th Ave Portland OR 97201

DAVIS, TELFORD ALYNE, physician; b. Las Cruces, N.M., June 18, 1932; s. Rockwell Albert and Mary Alice (Will) D.; B.S. cum laude, N.M. State U., 1956; M.P.H. (N.M. Tb Assn. scholar), U. Mich., 1957; M.D., U. Colo., 1966; children—Mary Patricia, Charles Telford, Thomas Alexander, Stuart Alyne. Health educator N.Mex. Tb Assn., 1957-59; exec. dir. Bernalillo County Cancer Soc., Albuquerque, 1959-60; indsl. hygienist Albuquerque Health Dept., 1960-61; intern Denver Gen. Hosp., 1966-67, practice medicine specializing in family practice, Dolores, Colo., 1967-73, Durango, Colo., 1973—; staff La Plata Community Hosp., 1973—, pres. med. staff, 1982-83; contract physician Ute Mountain Ute Tribe, 1972-73, So. Ute Tribe, 1976—; peer rev. physician Colo. Found. for Med. Care, 1972—; dir. Montezuma County Health Dept., 1968-74; sch. physician Montezuma-Cortez Sch. System, 1968-73; health dir. Little League, 1970-73; health adviser Boy Scouts Am., 1970-73; mem. staff Mercy Hosp., Durango, 1973—; med. adv. San Juan Basin Health Unit; med. dir. Eventide Nursing Home; clin. instr. U. Colo., 1972—, U. Utah, 1972—. Sec.-treas., Camp Ilium, Cortez, Colo., 1970-73; adviser Bluff (Utah) Episcopal Mission Med. Bd.; mem. adv. bd. San Juan Basin Health Unit. Bd. dirs. Club, S.W. Colo. Community Center, 1974-78; pres. 4-Corners Sheltered Workshop, 1979-82. Served with C.E., AUS, 1950-52. Diplomate Am. Bd. Family Practice. Fellow Royal Soc. Health, Am. Acad. Family Physicians (charter); mem. Colo. Med. Soc. (del. 1970-72, 81—, trustee 1974-80, chmn. Public Health Council 1982-83), Montelores Med. Soc. (pres. 1968-70), Tau Kappa Epsilon, Phi Mu Tau. Republican. Episcopalian (sr. warden 1972—, supt. Sunday sch.). Elk, Lion. Home and Office: 3801 N Main St Durango CO 81301

DAVIS, TERRY SERFASS, psychologist; b. Los Angeles, Nov. 6, 1942; d. George Donald and Miriam Allen (Baisden) Serfass; B.A. with distinction, U. Redlands, 1966; Ph.D. (USPHS fellow) U. So. Calif., 1973; children—Sheryl Barak, Janet Barak. Clin. psychology intern, VA, Calif., 1968-69, 72; field placement coordinator, dept. psychology UCLA, 1973-76; lectr. health and safety Calif. State U., Los Angeles, 1975-78; curriculum specialist family rehab. coordinator project, extension health scis. div. UCLA, 1975-76; pres. Rehab. Developers, Los Angeles, 1976-80; dir. family rehab. coordination project UCLA extension, 1976-81, coordinator Alcohol Studies, Alcohol/Drug Summer Inst., 1980—; cons. San Pedro Peninsula Hosp., 1979-80; faculty Antioch U. West, Los Angeles, 1979-82; pvt. practice individual, group and family therapy, Torrance, Calif., 1981—; clin. dir. Charter Pacific Hosp., Torrance, 1981-83. Chmn., Western Los Angeles Alcoholism Coalition, 1976-80; pres., bd. dirs. Felicity House womens recovery home; pres. bd. dirs. CLARE Found.; chmn. bd. dirs. Calif. Assn. Alcoholic Recovery Homes of Los Angeles County; bd. dirs. 361 Found. Mem. Am. Psychol. Assn., Western Psychol. Assn., Calif. Psychol. Assn., Assn. for Women in Psychology. Office: 21150 Hawthorne Blvd Suite 103 Torrance CA 90503

DAVIS, THOMAS AUSTIN, univ. dean; b. Belgian Congo, May 31, 1934 (parents Am. citizens); s. William Ellsworth and Newell (Trimble) D.; B.A. in Math., Denison U., Granville, Ohio, 1956; M.S., U. Mich., 1957; Ph.D., Cambridge (Eng.) U., 1963; m. Patricia Denham, Mar. 31, 1959; children—Nancy, Timothy. Mem. faculty DePauw U., Greencastle, Ind., 1963-73, asso. prof. math., 1967-73, dir. NSF COSIP program, 1971-72; asst. to provost for resource planning Princeton U.-Am. Council Edn. acad. adminstrn. intern, 1971-72; acting pres. U. Puget Sound, Tacoma, 1979, prof. math., dean univ., 1973—. Mem. adminstrv. bd. United Methodist Ch., Greencastle, 1970; mem. steering com. Tacoma Area Council Giftedness, 1980-83; trustee Charles Wright Acad., Tacoma, 1980—. Danforth fellow, 1956; Denison U. Research Found. fellow, 1956. Mem. Am. Assn. Higher Edn., Math. Assn. Am., Soc. Values in Higher Edn., Assn. Acad. Deans, Phi Beta Kappa (past chpt. sec.), Phi Kappa Phi. Presbyterian. Author books, articles, texts on math. Home: 4610 Wayneworth Tacoma WA 98466 Office: Univ Puget Sound Tacoma WA 98416

DAVIS, WILLIAM ALBERT, clergyman, educator; b. Portland, Oreg., Feb. 26, 1934; s. Earl A. and Mary Ruth (Pratt) D.; B.A. in History, Wash. State U., 1961, B.A. in Philosophy, 1962, M.A. in History, 1962; Th.M., So. Meth. U., 1967; postgrad. U. Denver, 1967-73, 79-80; m. Vineta Alice Rensink, July 2, 1960; children—David Albert, Daniel Alyn, Derek Andrew. Tchr. social sci. Wenat High Sch., Wenatchee, Wash., 1962-63; chmn. social scis., asst. to pres. Wenatchee Valley Coll., 1963-64; ordained to ministry United Meth. Ch., 1965, elder, 1967; pastor United Meth. Ch., Celeste, Tex., 1964-67; asso. pastor Burns Meml. United Meth. Ch., Aurora, Colo., 1967-70; polit. scientist, philosophy faculty Community Coll. Denver (now Front Range Community Coll.), 1969—, dir. div. arts and humanities, 1981—. Cons. Denver Urban Observatory, 1970-71; faculty rep. Colo. Bd. Community Colls. and Occupational Edn., 1972-74; treas. Bd. Edn. Adams-Arapahoe Dist. 28J, 1973-75, sec., 1975-77, pres., 1977-79, sec., 1979-81, v.p., 1981-83, dir., 1983—; precinct committeeman Arapahoe County Democratic Party, 1969-71, 1980-82, dist. capt., 1972-73; bd. dirs. Aurora Community Mental Health Center, 1976—, pres., 1981—; trustee Aurora Community Mental Health Found., 1976-78, Aurora Community Living Resources, Inc., 1981—, Aurora Mental Health

Research Inst., Inc., 1981—; trustee Aurora Community Hosp., 1977-80, moderator, 1978-80; mem. Aurora Citizens Utilities Adv. Budget Com., 1983—. Served with AUS, 1954-57, USAR, 1957-62, USNR, 1968-75. Mem. United Ministries in Higher Edn. (chmn. Colo. commn. 1974-75, sec.-treas. 1982—), Colo. Assn. Community Jr. Colls. (pres. faculty unit 1972-74, parliamentarian 1974-75), Am. Legion. Clubs: K.T., Masons (32 deg.), Shriners, Lions (pres. 1965), Optimists (pres. 1980-81). Home: 13257 E Nevada Ave Aurora CO 80012 Office: Front Range Community College Arts and Humanities 3645 W 112th Ave Westminster CO 80030

DAVIS, WILLIAM CLAUDE, linguistics researcher; b. Berkeley, Calif., Mar. 5, 1929; s. Claude Elza and Serena Nichols (Hancock) D.; student U. Nev., 1963-66; B.S. in Edn., Ohio Christian Coll., 1968, M.A., 1971, Ph.D. in Philosophy, 1973; m. Dorothy Jolene Satter White, July 12, 1952; children—Claude Wesley, Dorothy Jane. With Kennametal, Inc., Fallon, Nev., 1960—, also internat. courier; vocat. edn. tchr. U.S. Peace Corps, Black River, Jamaica, 1974; mem. faculty Western Nev. Community Coll.; lectr. police sci. Fla. State Christian Coll., 1970; counsellor boys Ohio Christian Coll., Columbus, 1970-73. Identification officer Mohave County, Ariz., 1967; active New Life Boys Ranch, Columbus, 1971-73, Boy Scouts Am. Served with USAF, 1946-49. Cert. diamond grader. Fellow Internat. Biog. Assn.; mem. Am. Philos. Assn., Linguistic Soc. Am. Club: Explorers Internat. (founder, dir.) (Fallon, Nev.). Author: Infinity and Time Zero, 1971; Concept of Soul, 1972; Lexikos, 1978. Office: 518 Humboldt St Fallon NV 89406

DAVIS, WILLIAM EUGENE, state university system chancellor; b. Wamego, Kans., Feb. 15, 1929; s. Eugene Kenneth and Willa (Dickinson) D.; B.S., U. Colo., 1951; M.A., U. No. Colo., 1958; Ed.D., U. Colo., 1963; m. Pollyanne Peterson, Mar. 17, 1951; children—Deborah, Rebecca, Douglas, Bonnie and Brooke (twins). Asst. to dean men U. Colo., 1951; tchr. English, coach Loveland (Colo.) High Sch., 1954-55, Rapid City (S.D.) High Sch., 1955-59, Greeley (Colo.) High Sch., 1959-60; successively alumni dir., head football coach, dean men U. Colo., 1960-63; exec. asst. to pres. U. Wyo., 1963-65; pres. Idaho State U., Pocatello, 1965-75, U. N.Mex., 1975-82; chancellor Oreg. State System Higher Edn., 1982—. Idaho commr. Western Interstate Commn. for Higher Edn., 1965-75, vice chmn., 1973-74, chmn., 1974-75; bd. dirs. Asso. Western Univs., 1975-82; mem. Selection Com. for Rhodes scholars, N.Mex., 1976-82; mem. pres.'s council Western Athletic Conf., 1975, chmn., 1978-79; mem. N.Mex. Disting. Public Service Awards Council; mem. NCAA Com. on Governance, Orgn. and Services; chmn. Idaho Rhodes Scholarship Selection Com., 1971-75; mem. Theodore Roosevelt award jury Nat. Collegiate Ahtletic Assn., 1974-79; mem. N.Mex. Gov.'s Com. on Tech. Excellence, 1975—; N.Mex. commr. Western Interstate Commn. Higher Edn., 1978-82; bd. dirs. Asso. Western Univs., 1978; mem. N.Mex. Hist. Rev. Bd. Served to capt. USMCR, 1951-54. Mem. Western Coll. Assn. (exec. com. 1981-82), Alpha Tau Omega, Phi Delta Kappa, Omicron Delta Kappa. Methodist. Elk, Rotarian. Author: Glory Colorado—A History of the University of Colorado, 1965; Nobody Calls Me Doctor, 1972. Contbr. articles to profl. jours. Office: Oregon State system of Higher Education Eugene OR 97403

DAVIS-BANKS, PHYLLIS EILEEN, retired city official, artist; b. Shelby County, Ind., May 6, 1918; d. Acy Earl and Grace V. (Crane) Lancaster; student Long Beach (Calif.) City Coll., 1959-61, Art Instituto San Miguel de Allende (Mex.), 1970; m. 2d, Harold Norman Banks, Dec. 24, 1971; children from previous marriage—Linda Ann Davis Hayes, Randal Lee Davis. Legal sec., firm Bingham & Bingham, 1935-36, Herff-Jones, 1936-37; with Curtis Wright, Acct., 1941-42; cashier, fed. govt., San Diego, 1943; legal sec. Western Girl, Kelly Girls, Long Beach, 1960-63, Alaska, 1963-64; sec. Alaska Heart Assn., Anchorage, 1965-68; adminstrv. asst. Community Action Agy., Anchorage, 1968-71; dep. clk. Borough and Municipality of Anchorage, 1973-78, mcpl. clk., 1979-80; one woman shows at The Gallery, Anchorage, 1975, Am. Soc. Arts, Chgo., 1976, Arctic, Anchorage, 1977; exhibited in group show at Anchorage Fine Arts Mus., 1977. Recipient Purchase award Alaska Watercolor Soc., 1977. Mem. Roswell Fine Arts League, N.Mex. Watercolor Soc., Internat. Fine Arts Guild, Nat. Watercolor Soc. Presbyterian. Recipient 1st and 2d prizes portraits Alaska State Fair, 1972, 73. Author: Cocahnia, 1969; Anchorage Fun Book, 1967. Editor: The Alaska Presbyterian, 1965-80; Sierra Blanca Viewpoint, 1982—. Contbr. articles to profl. jours. Home: 1016 Crescent Dr Roswell NM 88201

DAVISON, DONNA JEAN, business executive; b. Glidden, Wis., June 6, 1932; d. William Frederick and Mabel Hesse (Holmes) Bay; m. Taylor Scotford, Apr. 15, 1950; 1 son, Howard; m. John C. Davison, Nov. 24, 1967; children—William, Walter. Student U. Wis., 1959; night school student various colls., 1954-70. Clk., U.S. Post Office, Clam Lake, Wis., 1950-54, also part time at ins. agy.; asst. office mgr. Mass. Mut. Life Ins. Agy., Madison, Wis., 1955-56; office mgr. Somers Lumber Co., Springbrook, Wis., 1957-58; sec. K.E.C. Co., Corona, Calif., 1959-66, sec.-treas., controller, 1966—. Home: 2322 Pacific Dr Corona del Mar CA 92625 Office: KEC Co 200 N Sherman Corona CA 91720

DAVISON, JAQUIE MAY, author; b. Lexington, Ky., May 5, 1938; d. James Abraham and Etta May (Hall) Kirk; student public schs., Lexington; m. Ronald Ray Davison, Jan. 19, 1963; children—John, Mary, Thomas, Regina, Ralph. Founder, pres. Happiness of Womanhood, Kingman, Ariz., 1970—; lectr. on cancer cure to various orgns. Mem. Nat. Press Women's Club. Republican. Mormon. Author: I Am A Housewife, 1972; Cancer Winner, 1977. Office: 1335 Hancock Rd Riviera AZ 86442

DAVISON, LYMAN PARKER, criminal investigator, rancher; b. Peoria, Ill., Mar. 14, 1909; s. William James and Katherin Mary (Lyman) D.; m. Gladys Mary Patton, Aug. 2, 1930; children—Phyllis Anne, Curwood L., Duane R. LL.B.; George Washington U., 1947. Bar: D.C. 1948. Asst. judge adv. claims 5th U.S. Army; personnel dir. 16th Dist. WPA, 1940; insp. hydraulic dredging C.E., 1929-30; complaint supr. Ill. Light Co., 1932-35; warehouse control acct., 1937-41; asst. supt. govt. hosp., Colorado Springs, Colo., 1946; dep. sheriff Chaves County, N.Mex., 1976—; dir. research and testing of tech. equipment Am. Fedn. Police, 1936—; freelance writer. Fellow, contbr. to Cowboy Meml. and Mus. Served to lt. col., AUS, 1941-61. Decorated Air Force Commendation Medal; recipient Outstanding Am. Handgunner award, 1973; award of honor Bicentennial Am. Police Conf., 1976; John Edgar Hoover Disting. Pub. Service award, 1980, fellow Nat. Police Hall of Fame. Fellow Am. Assn. Criminology (registered criminologist); mem. Am. Law Enforcement Officers Assn. (v.p.), N.Mex. Law Enforcement Acad. (cert.), Ret. Officers Assn. (life), Am. Fedn. Police (pres.), Nat. Rifle Assn. (life). Author: (with others) Basic Marksmanship with the Modern Handgun—A Scream in the Night. Oldest ballistics and firearms cons. Home and Office: 3201 N Kentucky St 27 Roswell NM 88201

DAVISON, WALTER FRANCIS, educator; b. Chgo., Apr. 28, 1926; s. Norman Hubert and Lucille Marie (Kuich) D.; B.S., Calif. Inst. Tech., 1951; postgrad. U. Chgo. (NSF fellow), 1951-53; Ph.D. (duPont sr. research fellow), U. Va., 1956; m. Helen Irene Hawk, June 20, 1953 (div.); 1 dau., Linda Ellen. Instr. math U. Mich., Ann Arbor, 1956-60; sr. staff scientist Collins Radio Co., 1960-61; mem. tech. staff Space Gen. Corp., 1961-62; br. head Texas Instruments, Dallas, 1962; pvt. practice electro-optics, Dallas, 1962-63; sr. scientist ITT Fed. Labs., San Fernando, 1963-66; asso. prof. math Calif. State U., Northridge, 1966—. Served with USN, 1944-46. Rackham fellow, U. Mich., 1958; NSF fellow, 1968. Mem. Am. Math. Soc., N.Y. Acad. Scis., U.S. Chess Fedn., Smithsonian Assn., Sierra Club. Patentee in field. Home: 18012 Hiawatha St Northridge CA 91326 Office: Dept Math Calif State Univ Northridge CA 91330

DAWES, DAVID FORD, real estate developer; b. Muskogee, Okla., July 29, 1909; s. Maurice and Ethel (Ford) D.; student Okla. U., 1928; m. Dorothy Louise Snyder, Jan. 5, 1933; children—David Alan, Stuart Edward, Mary Louise (dec.). With Bellante Dawes Realty Co., Inglewood, Calif., 1946-48; owner David Realty, Inglewood and Torrance, Calif., 1948-69; pres. Western Land & Devel. Corp., Carlsbad, Calif., 1969—. Sec., Boys Club Carlsbad, 1973, 74, 76-77, v.p., 1975. Mem. San. and Flood Control Commn. Dist. 1 San Diego County, 1974—. Mem. Calif. Assn. Realtors (state dir. 1959, 60, 74, 75), Carlsbad Bd. Realtors (pres. 1974), Carlsbad C. of C., Gardena Bd. Realtors (past pres.). Clubs: Elks, Rotary, Masons (32 deg.; worshipful master 1984), KT, Shriners. Home: 3428 Don Juan Dr Carlsbad CA 92008 Office: 5200 El Camino Real Carlsbad CA 92008

DAWES, DEXTER BAILEY, investment banker; b. N.Y.C., July 10, 1936; s. Wetmore and Caroline (Foss) D.; B.A., Harvard U., 1958, M.B.A., 1963; m. Jean Rau, Dec. 22, 1961; children—John, James, Adam. Pres., Bangert & Co., San Francisco, 1971-73; chmn. Bangert, Dawes, Reade, Davis & Thom Inc., San Francisco, 1973—; dir. Fold Pak Corp., Newark, N.Y., Internat. Plastics Corp., Colwich, Kans. Served to lt. USN, 1958-63. Mem. Assn. Profl. Bridge Players (dir.). Club: Univ. (San Francisco). Office: Bangert Dawes Reade Davis & Thom Inc 1138 Taylor St San Francisco CA 94108

DAWES, ROBYN MASON, psychology educator; b. Pitts., July 23, 1936; children by previous marriage—Jennifer, Molly. B.A. in Philosophy, Harvard U., 1958; M.A. in Clin. Psychology, U. Mich., 1960, Ph.D. in Math. Psychology, 1963. Researcher Ann Arbor (Mich.) VA Hosp., 1962-67; asst. prof., lectr. U. Mich., Ann Arbor, 1963-67; assoc. prof. psychology U. Oreg., Eugene, 1967-71, prof., 1971—, co-head dept. psychology, 1972-73, acting head, 1979-80, head, 1981—; research scientist Oreg. Research Inst., Eugene, 1967-76, v.p., 1973-74; NATO lectr., The Hague, Netherlands, 1968; vis. prof. U. Calif.-Santa Barbara, 1975-76; cons. numerous insts. and orgns. Rackham Summer fellow, 1961; James McKean Cattell Sabbatical fellow, 1978-79; del. Nat. Acad. Scis. USA-USSR Acad. Scis. Seminar Decision Making, Moscow/Tblisi, USSR, 1979; Ctr. Advanced Study in Behavioral Scis. fellow, 1980-81. Fellow Am. Psychol. Assn.; mem. AAAS, Am. Statis. Assn., Pub. Choice Soc., Psychometric Soc., West Coast Small Group Research Soc. (pres. 1977-78), Sigma Xi. Author: Fundamentals of Attitude measurement, 1972; co-author: (with C.H. Coombs and A. Tversky) Mathematical psychology: An elementary introduction, 1970; contbr. articles to profl. jours; mem. editorial bd., cons. numerous profl. jours. and publs. Address: Dept of Psychology Univ of Oreg Eugene OR 97403

DAWSON, ALSON WILLIAM, free lance writer; b. Reno, Nev., Apr. 10, 1907; s. Dwight A. and Sadie (Phillips) D.; student Calif. Poly. Coll., 1925-27; m. Lillian Wallis Chapman, Aug. 7, 1942; children—Lawrence Dwight, Alison Dian (Mrs. William Blessing). Various positions Scripps Canfield newspapers, San Luis Obispo, Calif., 1928-39, gen. mgr., 1939-40; advt. mgr. City News, Los Angeles, 1940-41; mng. editor Herald-Bulletin, Burley, Idaho, 1946-50, gen. mgr., 1960-67; dist. mgr. Mist Publ. Co., Ontario and St. Helen's, Oreg., Twin Falls, Burley, Idaho, 1951-57; publ.-owner Farm News, Idaho, 1958-60; advt. mgr. S. Idaho Press at Burley, Ida., 1967-70; free lance writer, Burley, Idaho, 1970—; columnist Aroundtown and Western Saga; daily radio program Here We Have Idaho. Area chmn. Idaho Bicentennial Commn., oral history coordinator, 1974-75; area chmn. Idaho Commn. on Arts. Pres. Young Dems., San Luis Obispo, Calif., 1929-30. Served with USAAF, 1942-46. Mem. Cassia County Hist. Soc. (first pres., 1970), Idaho State Hist. Soc. (adv. council), Assn. for Humanities (area chmn.), Nat. Geo. Soc. Pioneer 100 Years of Progress. Author: Western Saga Guide Book, 1974; films: Heritage 76, Here We Have Idaho, 1976, Idaho's Cultural Heritage: Land of the Last Explorer, 1978, Idaho's Cultural Heritage: After Statehood, 1979, The Silver City Masquerade, 1980. Home and Office: 1111 N 6th St Boise ID 83702

DAWSON, DAVID LLOYD, management and computer services exec.; b. Seattle, May 25, 1943; s. Opie Lloyd and Margaret Charlotte (Lash) D.; B.C.S. in Accounting, Seattle U., 1967; M.S. in Mgmt. Sci., Stevens Inst. Tech., 1971; postgrad. N.Y. U., 1978; m. Nedra Marie Boyle, Feb. 16, 1963; children—Deanna, Annette, Janine, Patricia. Systems analyst Sea-Land Service, Inc., Elizabeth, N.J., 1967-71, dir. systems devel., 1971-75; dir. mgmt. info. div. Berkey Photo Inc., N.Y.C., 1975-76; dir. info. services United States Lines, Inc., N.Y.C., 1976-79, mgmt. services exec., 1978-79; v.p. system and computer services and research and devel. Matson Navigation Co., San Francisco, 1979—; tchr. data processing related courses, 1971-75. Mem. internat. data communications systems Maritime Adminstrn., Dept. Commerce. Mem. Data Processing Mgmt. Assn., Soc. for Mgmt. Info. Systems, Am. Mgmt. Assn., World Affairs Council, Nat. Assn. Watch and Clock Collectors, Smithsonian Assos. Republican. Roman Catholic. Clubs: Commonwealth, Bay Point Rod and Gun, Am. Sportsmen, Stevens Inst. Alumni Assn. Home: 232 Clyde Dr Walnut Creek CA 94598 Office: 333 Market St San Francisco CA 94119

DAWSON, DONALD ROY, computer systems company executive; b. Hamilton, Ont., Can., Aug. 7, 1921; s. Roy Elgin and Margaret Hannah (O'Connor) D.; B.A., McMaster U., 1949; M.B.A., U. Toronto, 1951; m. Beatrice K. Kanalele, June 2, 1956; children—Victoria Lani, Kathryn Malia, Donne Leinani, Christopher Burwood. Pres., Dawson Assocs., Honolulu, 1960-63, Dawson Corp., Honolulu, 1963-70; dir. export programs U.S. Dept. Commerce, Honolulu, 1970-80; pres. Dawson Internat. Inc. and Hawaii Prepaid Legal Plan, Honolulu, 1980—. Mem. Pacific Basin Econ. Council; mem. Export Expansion Council. Served with Can. Army, 1939-45. Named Small Businessman of Year, SBA, 1967. Mem. Hawaii World Trade Assn. Republican. Episcopalian. Clubs: Pacific, Plaza, Rotary. Home: 3966 Nuuanu Pali Dr Honolulu HI 96817 Office: Dawson Internat and Hawaii Prepaid Legal Plan Suite 1850 Pioneer Plaza Honolulu HI 96813

DAWSON, EUGENE ELLSWORTH, JR., gerontology educator, clergyman, social worker, consultant; b. Altamont, Kans., June 1, 1937; s. Eugene Ellsworth and Arlene W. Dawson; m. Mary Martha Ide, June 17, 1961; children—Christopher, Gregory, Marta. B.A., U. Redlands, 1959; B.D., Andover Newton Theol. Sch., 1961; M.S.W., Boston U., 1965; Ph.D., Syracuse U., 1977. Cert. social worker; ordained to ministry Am. Baptist Conv., 1961. Asst. minister First Baptist Ch. of Boston, 1962-65; Am. Bapt. chaplain, Boston U., 1962-67; dir. sr. services Onward Neighborhood House, Chgo., 1967-68; asst. prof. social work George Williams Coll., Downers Grove, Ill., 1968-70, Syracuse (N.Y.) U., 1970-77; dir., assoc. prof. gerontology program U. No. Colo., Greeley, 1977—; social work cons. Bonell Good Samaritan Soc.; ednl. dir. Hospice of Weld County, Greeley; mem. Gov. Colo.'s Adv. Com. on Aging, 1980. NIMH grantee, 1966. Mem. Gerontology Assn. in Higher Edn., Western Gerontol. Soc. (chmn. liaison com. 1982—), Colo. Gerontol. Soc. (pres. 1980-82). Democrat. Mem. United Ch. of Christ. Club: Rotary. Author: Intervention with the Elderly, 1975; co-author: Nursing Home Volunteer's Handbook, 1979; contbr. in field. Office: Gerontology Program Univ No Colo Greeley CO 80639

DAWSON, HANES MOORE, oil co. exec.; b. Ardmore, Okla., Aug. 31, 1918; s. David Hepburn and Pearle Juanita (Moore) D.; B.S., U. Okla., 1940; m. Jovan McCullough, July 5, 1941; 1 son, Hanes Moore. With Continental Oil Co., 1947-67, regional landman, Los Angeles, 1958-62, mgr. property acquisitions, Denver, 1962-67; owner Dawson Oil Properties, Denver, 1967—; dir. Pegas Resources, Inc. Served with AUS, 1941-46. Mem. Am., Denver assns. petroleum landmen, Ind. Producers Assn. Am., Rocky Mountain Oil and Gas Assn., Nat., Colo., Denver bds. realtors, SAR, Okla. U. Alumni Assn., Sigma Chi. Republican. Presbyn. (deacon, elder). Clubs: Masons, Shriners, Jesters; Red Cross Constantine; Twenty Six (dir., past pres.), Pinehurst Country; Denver Petroleum (dir., past pres.); Garden of Gods (Colorado Springs, Colo.). Office: 800 First Nat Bank Bldg Denver CO 80293

DAWSON, JAMES PAUL, JR., marketing executive; b. Logansport, Ind., Nov. 11, 1926; s. James Paul and Gwendolyn Virginia D.; B.S., Ind. U., 1954; M.B.A., U. Denver, 1974; m. Janet Marie Waters, Jan. 3, 1950; children—James Paul III, Stephen R., Diane Sharon. Vice-pres. sales J. B. Systems, Inc., Longmont, Colo., 1970-75; v.p., gen. mgr. Arapahoe Aviation, Inc., Englewood, Colo.; pres. J. D. Assos., Broomfield, Colo., 1975-78; dir. mktg. R. V. Lord & Assos., Inc., Boulder, Colo., 1979-82; pres. Adams County Mobility Services, Inc., Thornton, Colo. Planning commr. City of Northglenn (Colo.), 1971-81; city councilman, 1975—, mayor pro tem, 1979-81; mem. Adams County Airport Adv. Commn.; mem. policy com. for fuels, energy and natural resources Nat. League Cities; mem. transp. com. Colo. Mcpl. League. Served with USAAF, 1945-47, USAF, 1951-53; PTO. Mem. Nat. Rifle Assn., Aircraft Owners and Pilots Assn. Republican. Methodist. Club: Masons. Contbr. articles in field to trade jours. Home: 10978 Patterson Ct Northglenn CO 80234

DAWSON, JOHN ALLAN, painter; b. Joliet, Ill., Sept. 12, 1946; s. Thomas Allan and Margaret C. (McRoberts) D.; m. Linda Kay Williams, Mar. 1968. B.F.A. in Painting, No. Ill. U., 1969; M.F.A. in Painting, Ariz. State U., 1974. Grad. teaching asst. in painting and drawing Ariz. State U., 1971-72, 72-73; artist-in-residence, Nat. Endowment for Arts, Mesa (Ariz.) Public Schs., 1973-74; participated in Yaddo artist retreat, summer 1977; one-man shows: Benjamin Mangel Gallery, Phila., 1975, 77, 82, Elaine Horwitch Gallery, Santa Fe, 1976, Scottsdale, Ariz., 1978, 80, 81, 82, Springfield (Mo.) Art Mus., 1980, Gekas-Nicholas Gallery, Tucson, 1981, David Segal Gallery, N.Y.C., 1983; group shows: Art Inst. Chgo., 1971, El Paso Mus. Fine Art, 1972, 74, Meadows Mus. Art, Shreveport, La., 1976, Phoenix Mus., 1975, Huntsville Ala. Mus. Art, 1981; represented in numerous permanent collections. Recipient numerous purchase awards. Reviewed in various profl. art jours. Address: 10246 E Brown Rd Mesa AZ 85207

DAWSON, JOHN HALLAM, banker; b. N.Y.C., Oct. 31, 1936; s. James Robertson and Margaret (Geny) D.; m. Mary D. McVey, Apr. 19, 1975; 1 dau., Elizabeth McVey. B.A., Vanderbilt U., 1958; M.B.A., Harvard U., 1960. Various positions to sr. v.p., dep. head internat. div. 1st Nat. Bank of Chgo., 1961-75; sr. v.p., gen. mgr. internat. div. Crocker Nat. Bank, San Francisco, 1975, exec. v.p., gen. mgr. internat. div., 1975-81, pres., 1981—; pres. Crocker Nat. Corp., Crocker Nat. Bank, also dir. Served with U.S. Army, 1960. Mem. Bankers Assn. Fgn. Trade (past pres.), Calif. Bankers Assn. (pres.). Clubs: Bankers, University (San Francisco); California (Los Angeles); Saddle and Cycle (Chgo.). Office: 333 S Grand Ave Los Angeles CA 90071

DAWSON, KIRK MONTELL, electrical engineer; b. Glendale, Calif., Nov. 15, 1938; s. Harry Kirk and Ruth Ida (Moltz) D.; m. Marjory Elizabeth Burk, June 17, 1961; children—James Kirk, Sheryl Elizabeth. B.A., Physics, Occidental Coll., 1959; B.S., Calif. Inst. Tech., 1961, M.S., 1962. Research engr. Calif. Inst. Tech., Jet Propulsion Lab., Pasadena, 1962-65, group supr., 1965-70, mgr. guidance and control systems and research, 1970-76, mgr. control and energy conversion div., 1976-82, dep. asst. lab. dir. for tech. divs., 1982—. Bd. dirs. Calif. Engring. Found., 1983—. C.F. Braun scholar, 1966-69. Mem. IEEE (chmn. aerospace energy conversion com. 1968-73, treas. aerospace power conditioning specialists conf. 1970), Sigma Pi Sigma, Kappa Mu Epsilon. Clubs: Club 434, Toastmasters Internat. (Verdugo Hills Calif.). Contbr. articles to profl. jours. Home: 4664 El Camino Corto La Canada CA 91011 Office: 4800 Oak Grove Dr Pasadena CA 91103

DAWSON, NORMA ANN, lawyer; b. Detroit, Sept. 11, 1950; d. Emmett Chamberlain and B. Louise (Boddie) D. B.A., Pa. State U., 1971, J.D., U. Mich., 1974. Bar: Calif. 1979, U.S. Ct. Appeals (9th cir.) 1979, U.S. Dist. Ct. (cen. dist.) Calif. 1979. Legal asst. Miller & Daar, Beverly Hills, Calif., 1977-80; assoc. Marvin H. Kleinberg, Inc., Beverly Hills, 1979-81; atty. PennCorp Fin., Inc., Santa Monica, Calif., 1980—; com. chmn. Life and Health Compliance Assn. Mem. ABA, Nat. Bar Assn., Black Women Lawyers Assn., Calif. Bar Assn. (mem. com. group ins. programs). Clubs: Black Porsche Inc., Mensa (Los Angeles). Office: PennCorp Fin Inc 3130 Wilshire Blvd Santa Monica CA 90406

DAWSON, WILLIAM JAMES, JR., orthodontist; b. San Francisco, May 16, 1930; s. William James and Augusta (Rude) D.; A.B., U. Calif. at Berkeley, 1948-52; D.D.S., U. Calif. Med. Center, San Francisco, 1958; m. Judith Elizabeth Riede, Aug. 11, 1962; children—William James, Wendy, Nancy Garms, Sarah Rankin, Evelyn Elizabeth. Pvt. practice orthodontics, San Rafael, Calif., 1958—; clin. instr. oral histology, U. Calif. Med. Center, San Francisco, 1958-61; clin. instr. orofacial anomolies, 1964—, asst. research dentist, 1968—. Mem. bd. adminstrn. Calif. Pub. Employees Retirement System, 1969-76. Mem. adv. com. Marin council Boy Scouts Am., 1965—; chmn. citizen's adv. com. Dominican Coll. San Rafael, 1974-76; mem. city council, Ross, Calif., 1967-69; assn. mem. Calif. Republican Central Com., 1967-68, regular mem., 1971-73; pres. Marin County Property Owners Assn., 1980-82; dirs. Marin County Coalition, 1982-83, Marin County Cancer Soc.; bd. dirs. Terwilliger Found. Served with USAF, 1951-54. Diplomate Am. Bd. Orthodontics (charter mem. Coll. of Diplomates). Fellow Royal Soc. Health; mem. ADA, Am. Assn. Orthodontists, Fedn. Dentaire Internationale, Marin County C. of C. (dir. 1976—), Am. Rifle Assn. (life), Sierra Club (life), Omicron Kappa Upsilon, Chi Phi, Xi Psi Phi. Republican. Episcopalian. Elk, Rotarian (dir. San Rafael 1971-73, pres. 1978-79). Clubs: Lagunitas Country (pres. 1973-75), Bohemian; Lincoln of No. Calif. (vice chmn.). Contbr. articles to profl. jours. Home: PO Box 977 Ross CA 94957 Office: 11 Greenfield Ave San Rafael CA 94901

DAXTON, LAWRENCE EARLE, educator; b. Steamboat Springs, Colo., Sept. 26, 1936; s. William Everett and Olga Nelle (Just) D.; B.A., U. No. Colo., 1961, M.A., 1962; Ph.D., U. Colo., 1971; m. Emily Jane Rosenbach, July 22, 1978; children—Scott, Sandra, Sharon. Tchr., Ft. Collins (Colo.) High Sch., 1962-66; instr. history U. So. Colo., 1966-68, asst. prof., 1968-71, asso. prof., 1971-78, prof., 1978—, chmn. dept., 1972—. Precinct chmn. Pueblo (Colo.) Democratic Com., 1974-76. Served with USAF, 1954-58. Colo. Humanities grantee, 1965, 80. Mem. NEA, Colo. Edn. Assn., Am. Assn. Advancement Slavic Studies, Rocky Mountain Assn. Advancement Slavic Studies, S.W. Labor Assn., Phi Alpha Theta. Contbr. articles to profl. jours. Home: 12 Belaire St Pueblo CO 81001 Office: Dept History U Southern Colorado Pueblo CO 81001

DAY, ANTHONY, newspaper editor; b. Miami, May 12, 1933; s. Price and Alice (Alexander) D.; A.B. cum laude, Harvard, 1955, postgrad. (Nieman fellow), 1966-67; D. Humane Letters (hon.), Pepperdine U., 1974; m. Lynn Ward, June 25, 1960; children—John, Julia. Reporter, Phila. Bull., Phila., 1957-60, Washington, 1960-69, chief Washington bur., 1969; chief editorial writer Los Angeles Times, 1969-71, editor editorial pages, 1971—. Bd. dirs. Calif. Inst. Tech. Served with AUS, 1955-57. Mem. Am. Soc. Newspaper Editors (chmn. freedom of info. com. 1977-79, chmn. com. on internat. communication 1981—, dir. 1979—), Signet Soc. Harvard. Home: 2590 Ridgeway Rd San Marino CA 91108 Office: Los Angeles Times Times Mirror SQ Los Angeles CA 90053

DAY, ARDEN DEXTER, plant sciences educator; b. West Rutland, Vt., Mar. 16, 1922; s. Arden Ward and Callo Lily (Moore) D.; m. Jean Selleck, Jan. 14, 1945 (dec.); children—Vickie L., Peggy A. Smith, Nancy N.; m. 2d, Judith Crabs, Dec. 21, 1982. B.S., Cornell U., 1950; Ph.D., Mich. State U., 1954. Cert. profl. agronomist, crop scientist. Asst. prof. agronomy, asst. agronomist U. Ariz., 1954-56, assoc. prof., assoc. agronomist, 1956-59, prof., agronomist, 1959-75, prof. plant scis., agronomist, 1975—, assoc. head dept. plant scis., 1977—. Fellow Am. Soc. Agronomy; mem. AAUP, Crop Sci. Soc. Am., Western Soc. Crop Sci. Republican. Methodist. Clubs: Vermont Green Mountain, Masons. Contbr. articles to profl. jours. Home: 2909 E Seneca St Tucson AZ 85716 Office: Plant Sci Dept U Ariz Tucson AZ 85721

DAY, COLIEN LONG, educator; b. Roxboro, N.C., Nov. 3, 1927; d. Luther Davis and Cornelia Lou (Allen) Long: student Elon Coll., 1944-45; A.B., Trevecca Nazarene Coll., 1951; M.Ed., U. N.C., Chapel Hill, 1955; postgrad U. Calif., 1965-74, Coll. Idaho, 1967, U. Hawaii, 1970; m. Russell Van Buren Day, July 11, 1964 (dec. 1981). Clk., Burlington Industries, 1945-48; tchr. Caswell County Schs., Yanceyville, N.C., 1951-53, Greensboro (N.C.)/Guilford County Schs., 1953-59; English tch. and librarian Asheboro (N.C.) Schs., 1959-62, Randolph County (N.C.) Schs., 1962-64; English tchr. Marysville (Calif.) Joint Unified Sch. Dist., 1964—, Lindhurst High Sch., 1975—. Mem. Smithsonian Assos., Nat. Assn. Supervision and Curriculum Devel., NEA (life), U. N.C. Alumni Assn., Calif. Tchrs. Assn., Nat. Council Tchrs. English, AAUW, Nat. Trust Hist. Preservation, Marysville Writers Guild. Democrat. Home: 1739 Glen St Marysville CA 95901

DAY, DAVID NATHANIEL, psychologist, educator; b. San Diego, Dec. 12, 1950; s. Wayne Murray and Neva Josephine (Bowman) D.; m. Susan Mary Gallegos, Aug. 26, 1972; 1 dau., Julia Marie. B.A. in Psychology, Westmont Coll., Santa Barbara, Calif., 1974; M.A. in Counseling Psychology, Rosemead Grad. Sch. Psychology, La Mirada, Calif., 1976, Ph.D. in Psychology, 1980. Counselor Child Devel. Ctr., Whittier, Calif., 1975-76; asst. in psychometry South Whittier Sch. Dist., 1976; psychol. asst. Foothill Mental Health Ctr., Glendora, Calif., 1977-78; psychol. intern San Bernardino County (Calif.) Dept. Mental Health, 1978-79; postdoctoral intern Rafa Counseling, Pleasant Hill, Calif., 1979-81; psychology intern Growth Unltd. Psychol. Services, Pleasanton, Calif., 1981—; assoc. prof. Azusa Pacific U., San Jose, 1979—; psychol. asst. Calif. Dept. Consumer Affairs, 1981; cons. in field. Mem. Am. Psychol. Assn., Christian Assn. Psychol. Studies. Democrat. Evangelical Christian. Office: 1811 Santa Rita Rd Suite 200 Pleasanton CA 94566

DAY, GALE EDWARD, land surveyor; b. Lorimer, Iowa, Feb. 25, 1924; s. Ralph and Anna Gertrude (Walters) D.; student Iowa State Coll., 1946-49; m. Maybelle Anna Herbert, Dec. 14, 1959; adopted children—Loretta Mae Archibald, Hazel Louella McNutt, Carolyn Lea Williams. Land surveyor Bush & Gudgell, Inc., Salt Lake City, 1951-68, land surveyor, office mgr., St. George, Utah, 1968—, v.p., 1970—. Served with USMC, 1944-46. Lic. land surveyor, Utah, Nev., Ariz., Mont. Mem. Utah Council Land Surveyors (past pres., sec.-treas.), Utah Home Builders Assn. Methodist. Club: Elks. Home: 356 S 200 East St George UT 84770 Office: 205 E Tabernacle St Saint George UT 84770

DAY, HAROLD EDWARD, hospital administrator; b. Norristown, Pa., June 30, 1948; s. Harold Elsworth and Irene (Whonovitch) D.; m. Melinda S. Dewey, Apr. 3, 1971 (div.); m. Loretta H. Gaines, Aug. 29, 1981. Student U.S. Internat. U., 1970. Pres. RDQ Inc., Dana Point, Calif., 1970—, Capistrano Hosp. Corp., Dana Point, 1970—; chief exec. officer Capistrano by the Sea Hosp., Dana Point, 1968—. Mem. Assn. Mental Health Adminstrs., U.S. C. of C. Office: PO Box 398 Dana Point CA 92629

DAY, JOHN DENTON, wholesale indsl. sales co. exec., horse rancher; b. Salt Lake City, Jan. 20, 1942; s. George W. and Grace (Denton) Jenkins; student U. Utah, 1964-65; B.A. in Econs. and Bus. Adminstrn., Westminster Coll., 1971; m. Susan Hansen, June 20, 1971; 1 dau., Tammy Denton. Riding instr., rangler, Utah and Kans., 1955-58; with Mil. Data Cons., Inc., Los Angeles, 1961-62, Carlseon Credit Corp., Salt Lake City, 1962-65; sales mgr. sporting goods Western Enterprises, Salt Lake City, 1965-69, Western rep. PBR Co., Cleve., 1969-71; dist. sales rep. Crown Zellerbach Corp., Seattle and Los Angeles, 1971-73; pres. Dapco paper, chem., instl. food and janitorial supplies, Salt Lake City, 1973-79; owner, pres. John D. Day, mfrs. reps., 1972—; dist. sales mgr. Surfonics Engrs., Inc., Woods Cross, Utah, 1976-78, Garland Co., Cleve., 1978-81; rancher, Heber, Utah, 1976—; sec. bd. Acquadyne. Group chmn. Tele-Dex fund raising project Westminster Coll. Served with AUS, 1963-64. Recipient grand nat. award for engring. design and craftmanship Internat. Custom Car Show, San Diego, 1962; Key to City, Louisville, 1964; Daily team roping heading and heeling champion, 1982. Mem. Internat. Show Car Assn. (co-chmn. 1978-79), Am. Quarter Horse Assn. (high point champion), Utah Quarter Horse Assn. (champion AMAT reining 1979, 80, AMAT barrel racing 1980), Intermountain Quarter Horse Assn. (champion AMAT reining 1979, 80, 81). Contbr. articles to jours. Home and Office: Rockin D Ranch RFD 1 Box 4 Heber City UT 84032

DAY, L.B., labor union ofcl.; b. Omaha, Feb. 22, 1932; s. L. B. and Neva E. (Grimwod) D.; student U. Nebr., 1949-50; B.A. in Polit. Sci. and Econs., Willamette U., 1958, postgrad. (sr. scholar with honors) Law Sch., 1959, Ph.D. in Civil Law (hon.), 1975; m. Cynthia Rose Lang, Feb. 17, 1961; 1 son, Frank. With Master Service Tire Shop, Salem, Oreg., 1955-59; bus. rep. Cannery Local No. 670, Salem, 1956-70; regional dir. N.W. region U.S. Dept. Interior, Portland, 1970-71; dir. Oreg. Dept. Environ. Quality, 1971-72; public relations dir. Joint Council Teamsters No. 37, 1973; sec.-treas., head adminstrv. officer Teamster Local 670, Salem, 1974—. Mem. Manpower and Vocat. Tng. Devel. Adv. Com., 1962; mem., chmn. Marion County CSC, 1962; legis. council Oreg. Gov.'s Planning Council on Arts and Humanities, 1962; chmn. Portland Fed. Exec. Bd., 1971, Oreg. Land Conservation and Devel. Commn., 1973. Active Family Counseling Service, Marion-Polk County United Good Neighbors, Marion County Health Council, Salem Boys Club, Marion County Juvenile Council, Vol. Services Bur., Marion County Juvenile Bd.; v.p. Oreg. State Fair Savers; mem. adv. com. Salem Vocat. Sch. Mem. Oreg. Ho. of Reps., 1964-70, Oreg. Senate, 1978—. Past mem. bd. dirs. Thomas Kay Hist. Park. Served with USNR, 1951-55; Korea. Named Salem's Jr. 1st Citizen, 1966; One of 4 Outstanding Legislators, Oreg. Press, 1966; One of Top 10 Young Men in Oreg., 1967; Salem's 1st Citizen, 1968; recipient Disting. Alumni award Willamette U., 1972; Citizen of Yr. award Oreg. Assn. Chiropractic Physicians, 1972; Spl. Achievement award River Basins Commn., 1972; tribute of appreciation EPA, 1972; perpetual trophy Oreg. Wildlife Fedn., 1973; Clatsop Environ. Council award as public adminstr. of yr. Public Adminstrs. Oreg., 1973; Oreg. Cup award for conservation achievement, 1973; Leadership in Am. award Time mag., 1974. Mem. Salem Art Assn. (past pres.), Farmers Union, Grange, Salem C. of C. Clubs: Salem City, Masons, Elks. Home: PO Box 3048 Salem OR 97302 Office: 3814 Commercial St SE Salem OR 97302*

DAY, LUCILLE ELIZABETH, educator, author; b. Oakland, Calif., Dec. 5, 1947; d. Richard Allen and Evelyn Marietta (Hazard) Lang; A.B., U. Calif., Berkeley, 1971, M.A., 1973, Ph.D., 1979; m. Frank Lawrence Day, Nov. 6, 1965; 1 dau., Liana Sherrine; m. 2d, Theodore Herman Fleischman, June 23, 1974; 1 dau., Tamarind Channah. Teaching asst. U. Calif., Berkeley, 1971-72, 75-76, research asst., 1975, 77-78; tchr. sci. Magic Mountain Sch., Berkeley, 1977; specialist math. and sci. Novato (Calif.) Unified Sch. Dist., 1979-81; author numerous poems, articles and book reviews; author: (with Joan Skolnick and Carol Langbort) How to Encourage Girls in Math and Science: Strategies for Parents and Educators, 1982. NSF Grad. fellow, 1972-75; recipient Joseph Henry Jackson award in lit. San Francisco Found., 1982. Mem. Am. Inst. Biol. Scis., Nat. Assn. Research in Sci. Teaching, Phi Beta Kappa, Iota Sigma Pi. Democrat. Jewish. Home: 109 Monte Vista Ave Oakland CA 94611

DAY, PATRICIA JOAN, association director, consultant; b. Lansing, Mich., Apr. 9, 1936; d. Louis A. and Johanna (Feringha) Whipple; m. Duane Lee Day, Jan. 7, 1961; children—Kevin Duane, Patricia Kimberely. B.A., Mich. State U., 1958; M.A., Lindenwood (Mo.) Coll., 1979; postgrad. U. So. Calif., 1982-83. Cert. secondary tchr., Calif. Health edn. asst. YWCA, Rochester, N.Y., 1958-59; tchr. jr. high schs., Flint, Mich., 1959-61; tchr. Brookside Acad., Montclair, N.J., 1963-68; adult program dir. YMCA, Long Beach, Calif., 1968-73; community edn. dir. Paramount (Calif.) Unified Sch. Dist., 1973-78; exec. dir. counseling ctr., Arcadia, Calif., 1978-80; sr. citizens program dir. City of Burbank (Calif.), 1981-83; div. dir. Am. Heart Assn., Los Angeles, 1983—; cons. community edn. State Dept. Edn., Fed. Office Community Edn., Los Angeles County Office Edn. Bd. dirs., v.p. Children's Creative Ctr., Long Beach, Calif., 1969-73, Traveler's Aid Soc., 1969-72; vice-chmn. Cerritos YMCA, 1968-73. Mott Found. fellow, 1977-78. Mem. Western Gerontology Assn., Calif. Community Edn. Assn. (sec.-treas., 1974-77), LWV. Democrat. Congregationalist. Club: Soroptimist. Home: 906 E Palm Dr Glendora CA 91740 Office: 929 N Grand Ave Covina CA 91724

DAY, RICHARD ELLEDGE, newspaper editor; b. Denver, June 27, 1939; s. Bartle Henry and Clara Violet (Smith) D.; student Mesa Jr. Coll., 1958-60; B.A., Western State Coll. Colo., 1962. Reporter, Rock Springs (Wyo.) Daily Rocket and Sunday Miner, 1962-64, Casper (Wyo.) Star-Tribune, 1964-66; reporter Montrose (Colo.) Daily Press., 1967-68, mng. editor, 1968—. Mem. accountability adv. com. Montrose County Sch. Dist., 1979—. Republican precinct committeeman, Montrose, 1968—; mem. exec. com. Montrose County Rep. party; bd. dirs. Montrose County United Fund, 1972, Western Slope Tb and Respiratory Disease Assn., 1968-73; trustee Colo. Western Coll., 1971-72. Mem. Nat. Press Photographers Assn., Denver Press Club, AP Mng. Editors Assn., Montrose County C. of C. (dir., chmn. hwy. com. 1973—), Sigma Delta Chi. Mem. Christian Ch. Clubs: Masons, Elks, Kiwanis. Home: PO Box 957 844 N 5th St Montrose CO 81401 Office: PO Box 850 535 S 1st St Montrose CO 81401

DAY, ROBERT WINSOR, research administrator; b. Framingham, Mass., Oct. 22, 1930; s. Raymond Albert and Mildred (Doty) D.; student Harvard U., 1949-51; M.D., U. Chgo., 1956; M.P.H., U. Calif., Berkeley, 1958, Ph.D., 1962; m. Jane Alice Boynton, Sept. 6, 1957 (div. Sept. 1977); m. 2d, Cynthia Taylor, Dec. 16, 1977; children—Cristopher, Nathalia. Intern, USPHS, Balt., 1956-57; resident U. Calif., Berkeley, 1958-60; research specialist Calif. Dept. Mental Hygiene, 1960-64; asst. prof. Sch. Medicine, UCLA, 1962-64; dep. dir. Calif. Dept. Public Health, Sacramento, 1965-67; prof., chmn. dept. health services Sch. Public Health and Community Medicine, U. Wash., 1968-72, dean, 1972-82; dir. Fred Hutchinson Cancer Research Center, Seattle, 1981—; cons. in field. Pres., Seattle Planned Parenthood Center, 1970-72. Served with USPHS, 1956-57. Fellow Am. Public Health Assn., Am. Coll. Preventive Medicine; mem. Soc. Pediatric Research, Assn. Schs. Public Health (pres. 1981-82). Office: Fred Hutchinson Cancer Research Center 1124 Columbia St Seattle WA 98104

DAY, ROBERT WOLCOTT, broadcast advertising executive, radio station owner; b. Springfield, Mass., June 2, 1917; s. Morgan Glover and Ruth Van Buren (Hugo) D.; m. Ann Biehn, May 11, 1958; children—April, Susan, Robert W., Linda, Douglas; B.A., Harvard Coll., 1939. In broadcast advt., Boston, 1937-42; salesman John Hancock Co., 1946-49; advt. and pub. relations exec. Albert Frank-Guenther Law, 1950-77; v.p. radio/TV Foote Cone & Belding, 1977-79; pres. Robert Day Communications, 1979—; chmn. bd. Radio Espanol, owner KOFY, 1976—. Served to lt. comdr. U.S. Navy, 1942-45. Club: Wilshire Country (Los Angeles). Home: 3150 Oakdell Ln Studio City CA 91604 Office: 8826 Dorrington Ave Los Angeles CA 90048 also 8765 Dorrington Ave Los Angeles CA 90048

DAYLEY, ROBERT LEROY, food co. exec.; b. Yreka, Calif., Nov. 14, 1926; s. Dewey L. and Flora M. (Jensen) D.; student Benson Poly., 1941-45; m. Patricia P. Edsall, Nov. 27, 1959; children from previous marriage—Diane (Mrs. Phillip R. Rosebrook), Daniel; stepchildren—Sharon (Mrs. Fite), Connie. With Sears Roebuck, Portland, 1943-49; gen. mgr. Holman Warehouses, Inc., Portland, 1949-55; with Mailliard & Schmiedell, Seattle, 1955—, v.p., gen. mgr., 1969-74, pres., 1974—; v.p., dir. Bromar Inc., 1974—; dir. Mailliard & Schmiedell, 1969-74, pres., 1975—; v.p. Service Assetts Corp., 1976—; dir. Bromar Inc.; mem. brokers adv. council Peter Paul Co., 1978, Gen. Foods, 1979, Libby McNeill & Libby, 1980. Mem. Seattle Food Brokers (pres.). Home: 1015 E Millstream Way Bountiful UT 84010 Office: 436 Bearcat Dr Salt Lake City UT 84115

DAYS, SHEILA TRUNZO, distributing company executive, consultant; b. Charlottesville, Va., Apr. 10, 1946; d. Louis and Beirne Wiley (Moon) Trunzo; m. Timothy Joseph Days, Feb. 25, 1980 (div.). B.S., Radford Coll., 1968; student UCLA-TESOL Inst., 1980, mktg. program, 1981, 82, 83. Cert. secondary sch. tchr., Va. Tchr. French and English, Va. Pub. Schs., 1968-74; writer, researcher Sta. WBRA-TV (PBS affiliate), Roanoke, Va., 1974-75; mgr. Libreria Britanica (English lang. bookstore), Mexico City, 1976-79; promotion mgr. ELS Publs., Los Angeles, 1979-81; rep. Regents Publ. Co., Inc., Los Angeles, 1982; owner, pres. The Lang. Works (publs. distbr.), Los Angeles, 1983—; cons. English as 2d lang. Mem. Nat. Assn. Female Execs., TESOL, Calif. TESOL, Calif. Council Adult Edn., Calif. Assn. Bilingual Educators, Am. Soc. Tng. Dirs. Creator Sta. WBRA-TV (PBS affiliate) show Cast Your Own Shadow, 1975.

DAYTON, GLENN ORVILLE, JR., physician; b. Butte, Mont., June 15, 1922; s. Glenn Orville and Sylvia (Maginn) D.; pre-med. student U. So. Calif., 1940-43; M.D., George Washington U., 1946; M.Sc. in Ophthalmology, U. Pa., 1953; m. Elizabeth Carr Pine, Mar. 4, 1946; children—Elizabeth Bradshaw, Patricia Hunt, Glenn Orville, Diane Pine. Intern, Calif. Hosp., Los Angeles, 1946-48; resident Buffalo Gen. Hosp., 1949-52; pvt. practice as ophthalmic surgeon, Los Angeles, 1952-58; asso. prof. ophthalmic surgery U. Calif. Los Angeles Med. Center, 1966—; mem. staff U. Calif. at Los Angeles Med. Center Hosp., Calif. Hosp., St. Vincent's Hosp. Mem. Los Angeles World Affairs Council. Mem. bd. dirs. Better Vision Inst., also Nursery Sch. for the Blind. Served as maj., M.C., AUS. Diplomate Am. Bd. Opthalmology. Fellow A.C.S.; mem. AMA, Assn. Research Ophthalmology, Am. Ophthal. Soc., Am. Acad. Opthalmology, Otolaryngology, Pan Pacific Surg. Assn., N.Y. Acad. Scis., Pacific Coast Oto-Opthal. Soc., AAAS, Nu Sigma Nu. Pi Kappa Alpha, Alpha Omega Alpha. Republican. Club: Los Angeles Country. Home: 10542 Fontenelle Way Los Angeles CA 90024

DEADY, GENE MARTIN, educator; b. Chardon, Ohio, May 29, 1931; s. Willard Martin and Eva Lucille (Blair) D.; B.A. in Chemistry, Chico State U., 1953, M.A. in Edn., 1961; Ed.D. in Edn., U. Calif., Berkeley, 1969; m. Jo Ann Phelan, Sept. 11, 1954; children—David Martin, Michael Gene. Tchr., Piedmont (Calif.) Unified Sch. Dist., 1955-66; supr. sci. edn. U. Calif., Berkeley, 1966-68; asst. prof. edn. Calif. State U., Chico, 1968-70, coordinator elem. edn., 1970-75, prof. edn., 1975—; mem. exec. panel Far West Lab. Edn. Research and Devel. Mem. Calif. Energy Edn. Forum, Calif. State Univs. and Colls. Energy Edn. Consortium. Mem. Nat. Sci. Tchrs. Assn. (exec. dir. Region XII), Calif. Sci. Tchrs. Assn., Elem. Sch. Sci. Assn. No. Calif., Nat. Assn. Research in Sci. Tchrs., Assn. Edn. Tchrs. Sci., Calif. InterSci. Council, NEA, Calif. Tchrs. Assn., Phi Delta Kappa. Democrat. Methodist. Club: Masons. Home: 4 Lakewood Way Chico CA 95926 Office: 1st St and Normal St Chico CA 95926

DEAL, PATRICIA LOU EISENBISE, educational administrator; b. Reading, Pa., Mar. 25, 1932; d. Jasper Paul and Mae (Rozycki) Eisenbise; m. Robert Lee Deal, May 31, 1955; children—Robert Lee, David Alan, James Edward. B.S., Albright Coll., 1954; postgrad. Temple U., 1965, San Bernadino Valley Coll., 1969, Central Wash. U., 1970, U. Calif.-Berkeley, 1970, U. Puget Sound, 1973; M.A., Pacific Luth. U., 1978. Cert. elem., secondary teaching, provisional secondary prin., occupational info. specialist, vocat. supr., Wash. Tchr. aide instr., coordinator Clover Park Vocat.-Tech. Inst., 1970-79, fed. projects asst., 1979-80, career edn. asst., 1980; asst. dir. elective high sch., Clover Park Sch. Dist., Tacoma, 1981, dir. elective high sch., 1982—. Bd. dirs. Singletree Estates. Recipient United Way award, 1980. Mem. Am. Vocat. Assn., Wash. Vocat. Assn. (bd. dirs. local unit), Wash. Assn. for Career Edn. (bd. dirs. 1982), Nat. Council Local Vocat. Adminstrs., Wash. Assn. Vocat. Adminstrs., Wash. Council Local Adminstrs., Clover Park Local Unit of Wash. Vocat. Assn. (pres. 1983), Lakewood C. of C., Adminstrv. Women in Edn., South Sound Women's Network. Republican. Home: 8401 Woodlawn Ave SW Tacoma WA 98499 Office: 4500 Steilacoom Blvd SW Tacoma WA 98499

DE ALBA, ALFREDO, orthodontist; b. Mexico City, Mar. 25, 1950; came to U.S., 1973, permanent resident, 1978; s. Raul and Leonor (Levy) De A.; D.D.S. cum laude, U. Mex., 1972; M.S., UCLA, 1977; B.S., LaSalle U., 1969; m. Jan Bunch, Nov. 6, 1976. Mem. faculty UCLA Dental Sch., 1975—, asso. prof. orthodontics, dir. clinic orthodontics, 1980—. Named Outstanding Orthodontic Instr., UCLA Dental Sch., 1979-80. Mem. Am. Assn. Orthodontics, Pacific Coast Soc. Orthodontics, Internat. Assn. for Dental Research, Mex. Orthodontic Assn., Mexico City Orthodontic Assn., UCLA Orthodontic Alumni Assn. (pres. 1979-80), Parana Orthodontic Soc. Brazil (hon.), Sigma Xi, Omicron Kappa Upsilon. Author papers in field. Home: 5411 Lemona St Van Nuys CA 91411 Office: Sch Dentistry UCLA Los Angeles CA 90024

DEAMER, MICHAEL L., lawyer, accountant; b. Aurora, Ill., Apr. 8, 1946; s. Jack C. and Jean A. (Purdie) D.; m. Evelyn Warren, Sept. 12, 1969, children—Michelle, Tracy, Deborah, Robin, Michael. B.A. in Acctg., U. Utah, 1970, J.D., 1973. Bar: Utah 1973, U.S. Tax Ct. 1973, U.S. Supreme Ct. 1976; C.P.A., Utah, 1975. Assoc., McKay, Burton, McMurry & Thompson, Salt Lake City, 1973-74; asst. atty. gen. Utah, chief counsel Utah Tax Commn., Salt Lake City, 1974-76, chief dep. atty. gen., 1976-81; corp. counsel Skyline Exploration Co., Salt Lake City, 1981; ptnr. Ungricht, Randle & Deamer, Salt Lake City, 1981—. Life mem. Utah PTA, bd. dirs. Valley Sports Assn.; fund raiser United Way, Am. Cancer Soc.; scoutmaster, Explorer leader Boy Scouts of Am.; bishop Mormon Ch. Served with USAR, 1964-70. Club: Kiwanis (Salt Lake City). Activities described in Norman Mailer's The Executioner's Song. Office: Boston Bldg Suite 514 Salt Lake City UT 84111

DE A'MORELLI, RICHARD, author, psychic researcher; b. Kansas City, Mo., Feb. 1, 1952; adopted son Claude C. and Rowena (Hurlburt) Hale. B.A., Pacifica Coll., 1972, M.Litt., 1974. West Coast corr. Psychic World, 1974-77; psychic reporter Nat. Star, 1977-80; pres. Spectrum Technologies, Inc., 1982—; exec. editor Spectrum Books and Fantasy Publs., 1982—; tech. cons. Burbank Internat. Pictures, Inc. (Calif.) 1976-78; author: Numerology: The Key to Your Inner Self, 1972; Psychic Power: How to Develop Your ESP, 1973; Handbook of Magickal and Occult Rites and Ceremonies, 1977; How to Survive the Future, 1976; Psychic Tests for Everyone, 1976; Whole Being Handbook, 1982; contbr. to numerous anthologies including Irving Wallace's People's Almanac 2; cons., staff The Book of Predictions (Irving Wallace); editor Probe the Unknown, 1976-77, Omen, 1977—; exec. editor The Hefley Report, 1978-79; mng. editor Globe News Service, 1977—; numerous appearances West Coast radio TV programs, 1972—; founder The Majaanian Order; dir. Moonridge Sanctuary and Retreat, 1978—. Mem. World Council Human Understanding, Am. Numerological Fedn. Democrat. Office: Box 7464 Burbank CA 91510

DEAN, JOHN CARL, state ofcl.; b. Elyria, Ohio, May 8, 1924; s. John and Mary (Gallo) D.; B.S., Ohio State, U. So. Calif., 1948; M.B.A., Pepperdine U., 1971; m. Ruth L. Jagels, Nov. 15, 1953; children—Jeffrey J., David R., Marcia R. With Northrop Corp., Van Nuys, Newbury Park, Hawthorne, Calif., 1955-69, acquisitions mgr., 1965-69; chief fiscal and adminstrv. officer, budget and program mgr. IBA & Assocs., Inc., Canoga Park, Calif., 1969—; Martin Co. Denver, Colo. 1959-63; Litton Ind. Woodland, Calif., 1963-67; v.p. fin. and adminstrn., property and personnel mgr. Nartrans Mfg., Div. No. Am. Rockwell, Canoga Park, 1973-74; dep. dir., fiscal mgr., personnel mgr., grants coordinator 7th Step Found., Van Nuys, Calif., 1973-78; with Project Heavy, Calif.; ADEPT, Calif., 1975-76; bus. adminstrn. mgr., controller, dept. dir. and estate executor coordinator LA Luth. High Sch., Burbank, Calif., 1979-81; fin. cons., bud. dir., auditor-examiner State of Calif., Dept. of Corps., Los Angeles, 1981-83; sr. acctg. officer Met. State Hosp., 1983—; cons. in field. Gen. Motors fellow, 1942-48. chrm. Tournament of Roses. Mem. Am. Inst. Indsl. Engrs. (charter mem.), Nat. Assn. of Bus. Budgeting (charter mem.), Budgets Execs. Inst., Am. Inst. of Indsl. Engring.; Nat. Assn. of Accts., Am. Mgmt. Assn., Phi Kappa Tau, Gamma and Pi chpts., Alpha Kappa Psi, Beta Alpha Psi, Bata Gamma Sigma, Phi Kappa Phi. Contbr. articles to profl. jours. Lutheran (chrm., treas. stewardship and evangelism). Home: 5708 Wilhelmina Ave Woodland Hills CA 91367 Office: 11400 Norwalk Blvd Norwalk CA 90650

DEAN, KAY ESTHER, educator; b. Binghamton, N.Y., Apr. 3, 1942; d. Jay Woodruff and Mabel Lucretia (Barney) Axtell; children—Luella Lena and Larella Linda (twins), Lorna Lea. B.S., No. Ariz. U., 1965, M.Ed., 1984. Instr., Maricopa Jr. Coll., Phoenix, 1968-69; tchr. Navajo Indian Reservation, Tuba City, Ariz., 1967-68; tchr. math. St. Francis Sch., Yuma, Ariz., 1968-69; head tchr. Walnut Grove Sch., Kirkland, Ariz., 1971-78; head tchr. Hillside (Ariz.) Sch., 1978-81; head tchr. Skull Valley (Ariz.) Sch., 1981—. Recipient Nat. film award U. Ariz., 1978. Mem. Yavapai Cattle Growers, Yavapai Reading Council (rep.). Mem. Ch. Jesus Christ Latter-day Saints.

DEAN, KENNETH, design executive, educator; b. Chgo., May 10, 1939; s. Wayne Edwin and Genevieve Julia (Kyll) Smith; m. Linda Elizabeth Benitez, Sept. 27, 1980. B.A. in Design, Los Angeles Coll., 1959. Cer. profl. interior designer, Calif. pres. Dean Interior Design, Studio City, Calif., 1971—; dean Los Angeles Sch. Design, 1980—. Debater, lectr. People for the Am. Way. Served to lt. Army N.G., 1955-63. Recipient Award of Merit for Outstanding Design, Los Angeles County Fair, 1979; Best Actor awards, 1962, 1963, 1965. Mem. Am. Soc. Interior Designers, Internat. Soc. Interior Designers. Democrat. Roman Catholic. Contbr. articles to profl. design mags. Office: 13045 Ventura Blvd Studio City CA 91604 also 16507 Soledad Canyon Canyon Country CA 91351

DEAN, LOUISE DANFORTH, educator; b. St. Louis, May 1, 1933; d. Carlton Miles and Christine Alice (Danforth) D.; B.A., Calif. State U., Northridge, 1971, M.A. with honors, 1974; Ed.D., Nova U., 1980; children—Deborah Louise, Lee E., Linda Gail, Laura Dean. Dir., Congl. Presch., Chatsworth, Calif., 1971-74; dir. campus child devel. center Los Angeles Valley Coll., Moorpark, Calif., 1974-75, instr. child devel., 1975—; assoc. prof. to prof. Los Angeles Valley Coll., chmn. dept. family and cons. studies, 1979—; lectr. Calif. State U., Northridge, 1977-78; co-founder, pres. MOM Ednl. Services, 1982—; pres., past pub. policy chmn. Valley chpt. So. Calif. Edn. Young Children; bd. dirs. Child Care Consortium of San Fernando Valley, 1975—; presenter Nat. Adv. Council on Women Hearings, 1979. Mem. Assn. Supervision and Curriculum Devel., Nat. Assn. Edn. of Young Children (nat. presenter 1977), Calif. Assn. Edn. Young Children (pres. 1982), So. Calif. Assn. Edn. of Young Children (editor Newsletter 1981—), Calif. Community Coll. Early Childhood Educators (pres. elect), Child Care Consortium San Fernando Valley, Children's Lobby, Consortium Internat. Edn. (tour prof.), NOW, Phi Kappa Phi, Kappa Kappa Gamma. Presbyterian. Home: 17808 Lemarsh St Northridge CA 91325 Office: 5800 Fulton Ave Van Nuys CA 91401

DEAN, MARY YOUNG, pianist, organist, singer, educator; b. Eldorado, Kans., Nov. 12, 1926; d. Benjamin Warden and Rose Esther (Johnson) Young; Mus.B., Bethany Coll., Lindsborg, Kans., 1946; M.S., Kans. State U., Manhattan, 1949; m. Marvin Glen Dean, Dec. 25, 1950; children—David Allen, Douglas Warner, Deborah Kathryn. Teaching asst. Kans. State U., 1947-49; instr. piano Asbury Coll., 1949-59; asso. prof. piano and voice Taylor U., 1959-65; instr. piano and voice Pasadena City Coll., 1967-68, Pasadena Coll., 1969-73; instr. piano Scottsdale Community Coll., 1973-75; pvt. tchr. piano, voice and organ, Mesa, Ariz., 1973-78, Palm Springs, Calif., 1978—; organist Wayne St. Meth. Ch., Ft. Wayne, Ind., 1963-65, Velda Rose United Meth. Ch., Mesa, 1973-78, Community Ch., Palm Springs, 1978-81; numerous appearances as soprano soloist, profl. accompanist in chs., concerts, TV, Ky., Tenn., Ohio, Ind., Mich., Tex., Calif., Ariz. Mem. Nat. Assn. Tchrs. Singing, Sigma Alpha Iota, Phi Kappa Phi. Republican. Home: 794 El Conquistador Palm Springs CA 92262 Office: 284 S Cahuilla Rd Palm Springs CA 92262

DEAN, RAY BARTLETT, educator; b. Portland, Oreg., Apr. 17, 1901; s. Murray and Hazel (Bartlett) D.; B.S., Whitman Coll., 1925; M.A., U. Wash., 1928; Ed.D., Stanford, 1943; m. Grace V. Burgett, Sept. 2, 1924; children—James, Norma, Robert. Instr., coach high sch., Dayton, Wash., 1925-26; instr., coach, Longview, Wash., 1926-29; playground dir., Longview, 1929; prin. elementary sch., Longview, 1929-30; vice prin. elementary and jr. high sch., Sacramento, 1930-33, prin. elementary sch., 1933-44; instr. Chico State Coll., summers 1936-41, Stanford, summer 1945, U. So. Calif., summer 1948-49; asst. supt. schs., Sacramento, 1945-63; mem. faculty Calif. State U. at Sacramento, 1964-76; dir. men's personnel Bercut-Richards Packing Co., Sacramento. Mem. Calif. State Curriculum Commn., 1944-46. Mem. Sacramento Prins. Assn., Calif. Elementary Prins. Assn., Phi Delta Theta, Phi Delta Kappa. Author numerous tech. articles in profl. jours. Home: 2923 25 St Sacramento CA 95818

DEAN, ROY DANIEL, actor, writer, pub.; b. London, Aug. 2, 1925; s. Henry Charles and Alice Sarah (Hopkins) D.; came to U.S., 1954. Appeared in London plays and film, 1941-54; appeared in films The Music Man, 1962, My Fair Lady, 1964, King Rat, 1965, Sextet, 1978, others; author, photographer: A Time in Eden, 1969, Before the Hand of Man, 1971, The Naked Image, 1972, A World of Nudes, 1974, In Search of Adam, 1976, The Ecstasy of Eden, 1976, Man of Moods, 1977, Roy Dean Nudes, 1978, The Viril Image of America, 1979, Exposures, 1979, The Dean's List, 1982, The Dean's List—Hawaii, 1983; exhibited in Los Angeles, 1979, San Francisco, 1979, N.Y., 1981; pub. Rho-Delta Press, 1971—. Mem. Screen Actors Guild, Actors Equity Assn. Home: 8734 Holloway Dr Los Angeles CA 90069 Office: PO Box 691009 Los Angeles CA 90069

DEAN, VICKI ANN, interior designer, consultant; b. Cherry Point, N.C., Feb. 21, 1951; d. Fredrick M. Fahrion and Shirley A. (Rudolph) F.; m. Raymond Turner Dean, May 15, 1976; 1 dau., Calli Ann. Student Stephens Coll., 1969-70; B.A. in Housing and Design, Colo. State U., 1973. Color coordinator Sherwin-Williams Co., Ft. Collins, Colo., 1975-76; interior designer Furniture Galleries Co., Denver, 1976-78; owner, mgr. Inner Dzyn Co., Ft. Collins, 1979—. Mem. Ft. Collins Symphony Guild. Mem. Allied Bd. of Trade, Am. Soc. Interior Designers (assoc.), Chi Omega. Republican. Presbyterian. Office: PO Box 397 Fort Collins CO 80522

DEANE, GREGORY HOWARD, artist; b. Portland, Oreg., Sept. 27, 1938; s. Alfred Deane and Vida Mae (Piper) Harger; m. Margaret Carter Montgomery, Oct. 23, 1971. B.A., San Jose City Coll., 1963. Interior designer Breuners Home Furnishings, San Carlos, Calif., 1968-71, Fergus Joys Interiors, Los Altos, Calif., 1971-73, Los Altos Design Assos. (Calif.), 1973-74; propr. Gallery Inc., interior design, 1974-76, Gregory Deane/Studio, Palo Alto, Calif., 1976—; one-man exhbns. include Woodlake Spa, San Mateo, Calif., 1972, 101 Most Beautiful Rooms Show, San Francisco, 1973, Los Altos Design Assos./Gallery Inc., 1974, Stanislaus County Free Library, Modesto, Calif., 1975, Gilbert Galleries, San Francisco, 1976, Gallery Hawaii, Honolulu, 1977, 78, Palo Alto, Calif., 1979, Dallas, 1980, 81, 82, 83; group exhbn., N.Y.C., 1981; works represented in newspapers and mags. Recipient 1st and 2d prize Nebr. Coll., 1959, 1st prize Holbrook Palmer Park Art Show, 1977, 1st pl. Atherton (Calif.) Art Show, 1977. Mem. Am. Soc. Interior Designers (past chpt. bd. dirs.). Club: Palo Alto Art.

DEANE, THOMAS ANDERSEN, bank executive; b. Los Angeles, Mar. 20, 1921; s. Thomas Clarke and Dorothy (Milbach) D.; m. Margaret Louise Noble, June 21, 1947; children—James C., William A. B.A., Pomona Coll., 1942; M.B.A., Stanford U., 1948. With Bank Am., Los Angeles, 1948—, exec. v.p., 1974-82, vice chmn., 1982—. Trustee Pomona Coll., Claremont, Calif., St. John's Hosp., Santa Monica, Calif.; bd. dirs. YMCA of Los Angeles; bd. dirs., mem. exec. com. Central City Assn., Los Angeles; mem. exec. com. Soc. Friendly Sons of St. Patrick, Los Angeles. Served to capt. USMC, 1942-46. Mem. Calif. Bankers Assn. (bd. dirs. 1974-80, pres. 1978-79), Assn. Res. City Bankers. Clubs: One Hundred of Los Angeles, Los Angeles Country, Calif. (Los Angeles); Bankers (San Francisco). Office: Bank Am 555 S Flower St Los Angeles CA 90071

DEARBORN, BARRY GEORGE, marketing executive; b. Milford, Conn., Apr. 29, 1941; s. George Martin and Bernice Kelley D.; student U. Conn., 1959-62; B.S. in Bus. Adminstrn., U. Md., 1964; m. Judith Watson, Apr. 5, 1975; children—Dewitt Barry, Kelley Cochran, Kerrey Watson. Communications cons. So. New Eng. Telephone, New Haven, 1965; western regional mgr. Electronic Futures, Inc., North Haven, Conn., 1965-68; v.p. mktg. H C Electronics, Tiburon, Calif., 1968-71; div. sales mgr. Avon Products, N.Y.C., 1971-74; v.p. sales Rusco Electronics, div. Figgie Internat., Inc., Glendale, Calif., 1974-79; group mktg. mgr. Wyle Distbn. Group, Wyle Labs., El Segundo, Calif., 1979-80, group dir. sales, 1980-82; dir. sales Alpha MicroSystems, Irvine, Calif., 1982—. Mem. Nat. Computer Industry Adv. Bd. Served with USAF, 1962-65. Recipient Cert. of Appreciation, Internat. Security Conf., 1978. Mem. Am. Soc. Indsl. Security, Am. Mgmt. Assn., Nat. Mfg. Mktg. Bd., Nat. Assn. Coll. Aux. Services, Sales and Mktg. Execs. Los Angeles. Republican. Clubs: Masons (Thomaston, Conn.); U.S. Senatorial. Office: 17332 Von Karman Irvine CA 92714

DEASY, WILLIAM JOHN, business executive; b. N.Y.C., June 22, 1937; s. Jeremiah and Margaret (Quinn) D.; m. Carol Elyn Lemmons, Feb. 1, 1963; children—Cameron, Kimberly. B.S. in Civil Engring., Cooper Union, 1958; LL.B., U. Wash., 1963. With Morrison-Knudsen Co., Inc., Boise, Idaho, 1970-72, v.p. N.W. region, 1972-75, v.p. mining, 1975-78, group v.p. mining, 1978-83, exec. v.p. mining, shipbldg. and mfg., 1983—; dir. Westmoreland Resources; vice chmn., dir. Nat. Steel and Shipbldg.; pres., dir. Emkay Can. Natural Resources, Ltd.; mem. adv. bd. U. Idaho Coll. Mines. Mem. Soc. Mining Engrs.; Soc. Mil. Engrs. Home: 3770 Coventry Dr Boise ID 83704 Office: PO Box 7808 Boise ID 83729

DEATHERAGE, RICHARD MARION, psychologist; b. Sacramento, Mar. 25, 1943; s. Joseph Marion and Elsie Irene (Richardson) D.; B.S., Pepperdine U., 1966, M.A., 1968; Ph.D., U. So. Calif., 1971; m. Judy Louise Hawley, Oct. 10, 1966; children—Joseph Richard, Mark William, Andrew James, David Hugh. Head consultation dept. John Tracy Clinic, Los Angeles, 1971-72; founder, dir. Family Guidance Center, Fullerton, Calif., 1975-76; dir. North Orange County Child Guidance Center, Fullerton, 1972—, on leave, 1979; aux. staff La Habra Community Hosp., 1976-79; clin. asst. prof. Fuller Theol. Sem., 1976-79; adj. asst. clin. prof. dept. psychiatry Sch. Medicine, U. Calif.-Irvine, 1973-79. Mem. adv. bd. Fairview State Hosp., 1977-79; planning com. United Way Orange County, 1975-76. NIMH grantee, 1973—; Prisoner's Children grantee, State of Calif., 1974—; Compensatory Edn. grantee, State of Calif., 1975—; Henry W. Bull Found. grantee, 1976—; Los Alamitos Found. grantee, 1976—; Fluor Corp. grantee, 1976—; Irvine Found. grantee, 1979; lic. clin. psychologist, Calif., Hawaii; marriage and family counselor, Calif. Mem. Hawaii, Nat. Register Health Service Providers in Psychology, Am., Western, Calif., Orange County psychol. assns., Soc. Pediatric Psychology, Assn. of Psychiatric Outpatient Centers Am., Nat. Assn. Community Mental Health Centers, Assn. for Anthrop. Study of Play. Contbr. papers various state and nat. convs. Address: 2 Scripps Dr Suite 209 Sacramento CA 95825

DEATON, CHARLES, architect, indsl. designer; b. Clayton, N.Mex., Jan. 1, 1921; s. Charles Elmer and Nina (Utter) D.; grad. high sch.; children—Robert, Claudia, Charlee Snow. Aircraft illustrator, engr. Lockheed, also Curtis-Wright, 1941-43; pvt. practice archtl. and indsl. design, Chgo., also N.Y.C., 1943-49, St. Louis, 1951-55, Denver, 1955—; chief designer Bank Bldg. Corp., St. Louis, 1949-52; tchr. design Franklin Sch. Profl. Arts, N.Y.C., 1946-49. Prin. works include: Wyo. Nat. Bank, Casper, 1962; sculptured house, Denver, 1965; Harry S. Truman Sports Complex (in assn. with Kivett & Myers), Kansas City, Mo., 1967; indsl. designs of bank vault equipment, office furniture, comml. lighting equipment. Recipient Horatio Alger award, 1969. Contbr. articles to profl. jours. Patentee in field. Home: Genesee Mountain Golden CO 80401

DEATS, WAYNE LAWTON, JR., oil company executive; b. Houston, Feb. 21, 1941; s. Wayne Lawton and Margaret (Brown) D.; m. Judy Linda Gill, Jan. 4, 1963; 1 son, Wayne Lawton. B.A. in Acctg., U. St. Thomas, Houston, 1974. Data processing and payroll mgr. Ethyl Corp., Houston, 1974-77; cash control mgr. Amerada Hess Oil Co., V.I., 1977-80; corp. sec., controller Berry Holding Co., Taft, Calif., 1980—; dir. Ind. Oil Producers Agy. Vice chmn. Taft Planning Commn.; dir. Taft C. of C.; sr. warden St. Andrew's Episcopal Ch.; active Taft City Personnel Rev. Commn., Taft Community Concerts. Served with USN, 1963-67. Club: Rotary (Taft). Home: 309 Church St Taft CA 93268 Office: Berry Holding Co PO Bin X Taft CA 93268

DEAVER, JAMES S., vocational educator, consultant; b. Laramie, Wyo., Sept. 22, 1938; s. J. Emery and Alice L. (Ackerman) D.; m. Peggy A. Bacus, Sept. 11, 1960; children—Derek, Daren, Dana. B.S. in Bus. Adminstrn., U. Wyo., 1962, M.S. in Vocat. Edn., 1971. Cert. bus. and social studies tchr., Wyo. Fin. officer Associated Discount Corp., Cheyenne, Wyo., 1963-64; tchr. Albany County Sch. Dist., Laramie, 1965-72, dir. Youth Devel. Programs, 1973—; mem. State of Wyo. adv. coms. on edn. Bd. dirs. Albany County Tchrs. Fed. Credit Union, Laramie Youth Baseball, 1980-83, Laramie ARC, 1982-83; mem. Laramie Planning and Zoning Commn., 1974-80, Laramie Fire Master Plan Com., 1980-83. Named Laramie Outstanding Young Educator, 1968; hon. mem. Laramie chpt. Future Farmers Am., 1970; Boss of Yr., Laramie chptr. American Bus. Women's Assn., 1977. Mem. Am. Vocat. Assn., Wyo. Vocat. Assn., NEA, Wyo. Edn. Assn., Albany County Edn. Assn. Club: Elks. Developed tng. program for employment of handicapped, 1978, alternative learning program, 1976. Home: 1964 N 17th St Laramie WY 82070 Office: Albany County Sch Dist 1948 Grand Ave Laramie WY 82070

DEBARTOLO, EDWARD J., JR., owner pro football team; b. Youngstown, Ohio, Nov. 6, 1946; s. Edward J. and Marie Patricia (Montani) DeB.; student U. Notre Dame, 1964-68; m. Cynthia Ruth Papalia, Nov. 27, 1968; children—Lisa Marie, Tiffanie Lynne, Nicole Anne. With Edward J. DeBartolo Corp., Youngstown, Ohio, 1960—, v.p., 1972-75, exec. v.p., 1975-79, pres., 1979—; owner San Francisco 49ers, 1977—, pres., mng. ptnr., 1977-83, chmn. bd., chief exec. officer, 1983—. Bd. trustees Youngstown State U., 1974-77. Served with U.S. Army, 1969. Mem. Internat. Council of Shopping Centers. Roman Catholic. Clubs: Tippecanoe Country, Fonderlac Country. Office: San Francisco 49ers 711 Nevada St Redwood City CA 94061*

DEBARTOLO, JACK, JR., architect; b. Youngstown, Ohio, May 6, 1938; s. Jack and Grace Virginia (Sassinelli) DeB.; B.S., B.Arch., U. Houston, 1962; M.Arch. (William Kinne Fellows traveling fellow 1963-64), Columbia U., 1964; m. Pat McLamore, Aug. 15, 1958; children—Ava, Gina, Jack, III. Sr. v.p., dir. design Caudill Rowlett Scott, 1964-73; sr. v.p. William Wilde & Assos., Tucson, 1973; pres., chief exec. officer, dir. design Anderson DeBartolo Pan Inc. Architecture/Engring., Tucson, 1973—; mem. seminar faculties on hosp. design. Elder, Grace Chapel, Tucson; mem. Tucson Tomorrow/Goals for Tucson. Recipient design awards for CRS Office Bldg., Houston; Joliet (Ill.) Jr. Coll.; Pima Community Coll., Tucson; St. Mary's Convent, Tucson. Fellow, AIA (pres. Ariz. chpt.); mem. Internat. Hosp. Fedn., Am. Hosp. Assn., Assn. Western Hosps., Ariz. Soc. Architects, Tucson Tomorrow. Republican. Club: Tucson Breakfast. Office: 6339 E Speedway Blvd Tucson AZ 85710

DEBELL, ARTHUR GERALD, optical scientist; b. N.Y.C., June 10, 1912; s. David and Jane Eleanor (Caplan) DeB.; student N.Y.U., 1930-31; Chem. Engr., Rensselaer Poly. Inst., 1935; postgrad U. N.Y., 1938-41; m. Beatrice Servetnick, July 11, 1942; children—Gary William, Michael Alan, Margaret Patricia. Instr., Sienna Coll., 1939-41; physicist U.S. Navy Yard, Charleston, S.C., 1942-44; U.S. Naval Weapons Center, 1944-51; physicist, project engr. White Devel. Corp., 1951-55; physics group scientist Rocketdyne and Autonetics, Rockwell Internat., Los Angeles and Anaheim, Calif., 1955-74; research specialist, program mgr. Optical Scis. Center, U. Ariz., Tucson, 1974—. Mem. Optical Soc. Am., Am. Inst. Physics, Soc. Photo Optical Engrs. Patentee in optics. Home: 2155 E Hampton St Tucson AZ 85719 Office: Optical Scis Center U Ariz Tucson AZ 85721

DE BELL, GARRETT, environ. cons.; b. San Francisco, Oct. 30, 1941; s. Wilson Footer and Grace Garrett Hart. A.B. in Biology with distinction, Stanford U., 1966; Ph.C. in Zoology, U. Calif., Berkeley, 1969. Writer, editor, lectr., 1969—; environ. lobbyist, 1970—; mem. full and part-time faculty U. Calif., Berkeley, 1972-74, Sonoma State Coll., 1975-77, Merced Coll., 1975; naturalist on field trips U. Calif., Berkeley, 1973-74; environ. cons. to govt. and industry, 1974—. Served with USAR, 1960-63. Annie M. Alexander Museum scholar, 1966. Mem. Sierra Club, Friends of Earth, Audubon Soc. Author: The Environmental Handbook, 1969; Voter's Guide to Environmental Politics, 1970; The New Environmental Handbook, 1980; also articles. Address: PO Box 757 Yosemite Nat Park CA 95389

DEBENEDETTI,, EDWARD, electronics co. exec.; b. Mountain View, Calif., Mar. 3, 1934; s. John Joseph and Leonora (Boitano) DeB.; student U. Buenos Aires (Argentina), 1951, San Jose State U., 1952; m. Rosemary R. Laurance, Mar. 21, 1964; children—Celia, Diana. Jr. engr. HEC Corp., Redwood City, Calif., 1955-57; engr. Vicon Corp., San Carlos, Calif., 1959-61; engr. AMTEL, San Carlos, 1961-64; project engr. Granger Assos., Palo Alto, Calif., 1964-67; sect. mgr. Ampex Corp., Redwood City, 1967-72; div. pres. Imagex, Inc., Santa Clara, Calif., 1972-75; chmn. bd., pres. Scanco, Inc., Sunnyvale, Calif., 1975—; sr. ptnr. DB Assocs. Internat. Served with arty. U.S. Army, 1957-59. Mem. Soc. Photog. and Instrumentation Engrs., Soc. Info. Display, Aircraft Owners and Pilots Assn. Clubs: Mercedes Benz of No. Calif.; Reid Hillview Flying. Home: 1462 Merry Ln San Jose CA 95128 Office: 1287 Lawrence Station Rd Sunnyvale CA 94089

DEBENHAM, RAY GENE, elec. supply co. exec.; b. Salt Lake City, Oct. 1, 1935; s. Shirley Ray and Lillian Wanda (Grigen) D.; B.S., Alaska Meth. U., 1972; m. Rita Jose Peterson, Aug. 14, 1959; children—Debra, Julie, Michel, Shaun. Field engr. Line Material Industries, Anchorage, 1957-68; pres. Debenham Elec. Supply Co., 1968—, M.A.D. Co., Inc., 1964-79, Debra Rae Chateau Enterprises, 1966-79, Debenham-Alaska Investments, 1979—; pres., gen. partner Debs., Ltd., Steeple Heights, Joel Johnson Constrn. Co. (all Anchorage); chmn. bd. Profl. Bots. Inc., Health of Am. Inc., Health Supplements Inc. (all Ogden, Utah). Trustee Debenham-Alaska Scholarship Fund, 1977—. Served with Air N.G., 1953-62. Mem. Nat. Assn. Elec. Distbrs. (utility com.), Nat. Assn. Contractors, Nat. Assn. Wholesale-Distbrs., Nat. Fedn. Ind. Bus., Resource Devel. Council Alaska, Alaska Rural Elec. Coop., Greater Anchorage C. of C. Mormon. Home: 3435 Fordham Ave Anchorage AK 99503

DEBOER, ROY JOHN, sch. principal; b. Bellingham, Wash., July 23, 1936; s. Harvey Charles and Martha (Hoskin) DeB.; B.A. in Edn., Western Wash. State U., 1962; M.A., U. Puget Sound, 1981; m. Bea C. Meyers, Mar. 18, 1961; children—Nicole, Eric, David. Tchr. high sch. South Kitsap Sch. Dist., Port Orchard, Wash., 1962-73, dir. Indian edn., 1973-82, vice prin., 1978-82; prin. David Wolfle Elem. Sch., North Kitsap Sch. Dist., Kingston, Wash., 1982— vice chmn. Wash. State Adv. Com. to Supt. Public Instruction for Indian Edn. Mem. nat. com. Div. Service and Mission in Am., Am. Luth. Ch., also chmn. devel. assistance com. Served with USAF, 1954-58. Recipient Quill and Scroll award for adult leadership. Mem. Internat. Reading Assn., Assn. Supervision and Curriculum Devel., Phi Delta Kappa. Democrat. Lutheran. Home: 3528 SW Pine Tree Dr Port Orchard WA 98366 Office: D Wolfle Elem Sch Kingston WA

DEBOLT, ALLAN RUSSELL, manufacturing co. executive; b. Cleve., Jan. 21, 1932; s. Russell Allan and Frances Marie (Krasovic) DeB.; children—Michael, Michele, Stephanie, Elizabeth. Student Western Mich. U., 1951. With Purex Corp. Ltd., Cleve., 1957-62, regional mgr., 1959-62; with Armour-Dial Co., Phoenix, 1962—, regional mgr., 1967-79, v.p. spl. markets, 1979—. Bd. dirs. Greentree Recreation Assn., 1977-80. Served as sgt. USAF, 1951-55; Korea. Mem. Am. Logistics Assn. Democrat. Home: 6123 E Redfield Rd Scottsdale AZ 85254 Office: Armour Dial Co Greyhound Tower Phoenix AZ 85077

DEBOLT, HAROLD EUGENE, educator; b. Fredericktown, Ohio, June 9, 1922; s. Paul L. and Edith (Roberts) D.; m. Dolores V. McCreanor, Sept. 21, 1946; children—Mary Ann, Thomas, Rita, Robert, Edith, Patrica. B.S., Carnegie Mellon U., 1947, M.S., 1948, Sc.D., 1949. Sect. mgr. Westinghouse, 1949-50; with Bur. Ships, Washington, 1950-55; mgr. nuclear instrument dept. Fairchild Camera & Instruments, Syosset, N.Y., 1955-60; sr. project scientist Avco Corp., Lowell, Mass., 1960-80; lectr. elec. engring. dept. U. Colo., Boulder, 1980—. Served with Signal Corps, U.S. Army, 1943-45. Roman Catholic. Contbr. articles to profl. jours. Home: 1069 Albion Rd Boulder CO 80303 Office: Univ Colo Boulder CO 80302

DE BONA, MAURICE, JR., author, publisher; b. Chgo., July 25, 1926; s. Maurice and Marguerite (Reuter) De B.; B.A. in Geography, UCLA, 1952. Cartographer, U.S. Geol. Survey, Sacramento, 1952-54; electromech. design cons. aerospace and computer industries, Calif., 1954-75; writer-pub., Culver City, Calif., 1975—; pres. Desserco Pub. Co., 1975—. Served with USN, 1945-46. Mem. Com. Small Mag. Editors and Publishers. Author: God Rejected, 1976. Office: PO Box 2433 Culver City CA 90230

DE BOOM, JAMES L., YMCA exec.; b. Mpls., Oct. 7, 1941; s. Henry and Verna (Carlson) de B.; B.S., George William Coll., Chgo., 1964; postgrad. U. So. Calif.; m. Barbara Adams, Mar. 7, 1970; children—Stacy Lynn, Jodi Anne. Program dir. Westchester YMCA, Los Angeles, 1965-70; program devel. dir. Los Angeles Met. YMCA, 1970-75; gen. dir. Orange Coast YMCA, Newport Beach, Calif., 1975—; instr. sociology Golden West Coll.; adj. prof. George Williams Coll.; mem. Newport Harbor Council Chs. Nat. YMCA fellow, 1970-71. Mem. Assn. Profl. YMCA Dirs., Am. Soc. Tng. and Devel., Calif. Assn. Marriage and Family Counselors, Newport Harbor C. of C. Presbyterian. Club: Newport Balboa Rotary (pres.). Author articles. Office: 2300 University Dr Newport Beach CA 92660

DEBRA, CORINNE CROSBY, journalist; b. Rome, N.Y., Sept. 11, 1956; d. Daniel Brown and Esther (Crosby) DeB. B.A. in Polit. Sci., U. Calif.-Santa Barbara, 1978; M.A. in Pub. Policy, George Washington U., 1981. Research asst. Congressman Bill Royer, Ho. of Reps., Washington, 1979-80; sr. analyst, editor Labat-Anderson Inc., Washington, 1980-82; West Coast asst. editor Telecommunications Mag., Palo Alto, Calif., 1982—. LBJ scholar, 1978. Mem. Am. Polit. Sci. Assn. Presbyterian. Office: 1000 Elwell Ct Suite 234 Palo Alto CA 94303

DEBRETTEVILLE, SHEILA LEVRANT, educator, artist; b. Bklyn., Nov. 4, 1940. Student Barnard Coll.; B.A. in Art History, Columbia U.; M.F.A., Yale U. Group shows include Am. Inst. Graphics Art, 1972, 5e Biennale des Arts Graphiques, Brno Czech, 1972, Whitney Mus., 1974; represented in permanent collections Am. Inst. Graphic Arts, N.Y.,

Mus. Modern Art, N.Y.C., Community Gallery, Los Angeles; commns. include Archtl. League, N.Y., 1965, Yale Art Gallery, 1966, book design Canavese, Olivetti, Milan, Italy, 1968, poster design Calif. Inst. Arts, Valencia, 1970, spl. issue design Art Soc. Wis., 1970; typographer Yale U. Press, 1969-74; co-founder, pres. Woman's Bldg. Community Gallery, 1973—; dir. graphic design dept. Calif. Inst. Arts, 1970-74; co-founder, editor, designer Chrysalis Mag., 1977; design dir. Los Angeles Times, 1978-81; chmn. dept. communication, design and illustration Otis Art Inst., Parsons Sch. Design, Los Angeles, 1981—; judge Nat. Endowment Arts-Civil Service Commn., 1975; lectr. various colls. and univs. Recipient Grand Excellence award Soc. Pub. Designers, 1971, Communication Graphics awards Am. Inst. Graphic Arts, 1972; IBM fellow Interior Design Conf. Aspen, 1974. Mem. Am. Inst. Graphic Arts. Office: Otis Art Institute of Parsons School of Design 2401 Wilshire Blvd Los Angeles CA 90057*

DEBREU, GERARD, educator; b. Calais, France, July 4, 1921; came to U.S., 1950, naturalized, 1975; s. Camille and Fernande (Decharne) D.; m. Francoise Bled, June 14, 1945; children—Chantal, Florence. D.Sc., U. Paris, 1956; Dr.rer.pol. (hon.), U. Bonn, 1977; Docteur en Sciences Economiques (hon.), U. Lausanne, 1980; Dr.Sci. (hon.), Northwestern U., 1981, Université des Sciences Sociales de Toulouse, 1983. Research assoc. Centre National de la Recherche Scientifique, Paris, 1946-48; Rockefeller fellow, 1948-50; research assoc. Cowles Commn. for Research in Econs., U. Chgo., 1950-55; assoc. prof. econs. Cowles Found. for Research in Econs., Yale U., New Haven, 1955-60, vis. prof. econs., 1961, 76; fellow Ctr. for Advanced Study in Behavioral Scis., Stanford (Calif.) U., 1960-61; vis. prof. Ctr. for Ops. Research and Econometrics, U. Louvain (Belgium), 1968-69, 71-72; research assoc. CEPREMAP, Paris, 1980; prof. econs. U. Calif.-Berkeley, 1962—, prof. math., 1975—; vis. prof. U. Canterbury, Christchurch, N.Z., 1973. Served with French Army, 1944-45. Decorated Chevalier de la Legion d'Honneur, 1976; recipient Sr. U.S. Scientist award Alexander von Humboldt Found., U. Bonn., 1977; Guggenheim fellow, 1968-69; Erkskine fellow, U. Canterbury (N.Z.), 1969; overseas fellow Churchill Coll., Cambridge (Eng.) U., 1972. Disting. fellow Am. Econ. Assn.; fellow Am. Acad. Arts and Scis.; mem. Econometric Soc. (pres. 1971), Nat. Acad. Scis. Author: Theory of Value, 1959; Mathematical Economics, 1983; contbr. articles to profl. jours. Office: Dept Econs Univ Calif Berkeley CA 94720

DEBRUGE, PIERRE JOSEPH, aerospace engineer; b. Boma, Zaire, May 5, 1949; s. Rene Henry and Andree Anne (Germanes) B.; B.Sc. in Mech. and Elec. Engring., Ecole Centrale des Arts et Metiers, Brussels, 1973; M.Sc. in Aerospace Engring., Northop U., 1975; postgrad. aero. engring. U. So. Calif., 1975-76; m. Margaret Lucy Metz, Dec. 20, 1976. Engring. trainee Sabena Belgian Airlines, Brussels, 1972-73; design engr. Ahrens Aircraft Corp., Oxnard, Calif., 1976, chief engr., Ramey, P.R., 1976-77, chief engr. Piper Aircraft Corp., Santa Maria, Calif., 1979-81; pvt. engring. cons., Los Angeles, 1974—. Wanson fellow, 1973-74. Mem. Soc. Auto. Engrs., AIAA, Pilots Internat. Assn., Aircraft Owners and Pilots Assn., Tau Beta Pi, Sigma Gamma Tau. Roman Catholic. Office: PO Box 42 Santa Maria CA 93456

DE BRUIN, HENDRIK CORNELIS, college administrator; b. Passaic, N.J., Jan. 3, 1929; s. William and Jane deB.; m. Jo Ann Buck, Nov. 29, 1974. B.A., N.J. State Coll., 1951; M.Ed., U. Ariz., 1953, Ph.D., 1962; student U. Mo., 1955, Carnegie Inst. Tech., 1952, NYU, 1953. Tchr., Tucson (Ariz.) High Sch., 1954-57, prin. Ohio Valley (Ariz.) Pub. Schs., 1957-59; supt. schs., Sanders, Ariz., 1959-61; asst. prof. edn. Mont. State U., 1962-64; dir. grad. studies Butler U., 1964-68; dean coll. edn., prof. edn. Eastern N.Mex. U., 1968-76; chmn. div. edn. Ind. U.-South Bend, 1976-79; head dept. edn., prof. edn. The Citadel, 1979-82; assoc. dir. instrn. U. N.Mex.-Gallup, 1982—. Served with AUS, 1946-48. Westinghouse Sci. fellow, 1952. Mem. Nat. Orgn. Legal Problems of Edn. (past bd. dirs., state chmn.), Ind. Assn. Colls. for Tchr. Edn., Phi Kappa Phi (past pres., v.p.), Phi Delta Kappa (past pres., v.p.). Presbyterian (deacon). Clubs: Masons, Shriners, Elks. Home: 1811 Mariyana St Gallup NM 87301 Office: U NM 200 College Rd Gallup NM 87301

DEBUS, ELEANOR VIOLA, business mgmt. co. exec.; b. Buffalo, May 19, 1920; d. Arthur Adam and Viola Charlotte (Pohl) Debus; student Chown Bus. Sch., 1939. Sec., Buffalo Wire Works, 1939-45; home talent producer Empire Producing Co., Kansas City, Mo., sec. Owens Corning Fiberglass, Buffalo; with public relations and publicity Niagara Falls (Ont., Can.) Theatre, 19—; public relations dir. Woman's Internat. Bowling Congress, Columbus, Ohio, 1957-59; publicist, sec. Ice Capades, Hollywood, Calif., 1961-63; sec. to controller Rexall Drug Co., Los Angeles, 1963-67; bus. mgmt. acct. Samuel Berke & Co., Beverly Hills, Calif., 1967-75; Gadbois Mgmt. Co., Beverly Hills, 1975-76; sec., treas. Sasha Corp., Los Angeles, 1976—; bus. mgr. Dean Martin, Los Angeles, 1976—; pres. Tempo Co., Los Angeles, 1976—. Mem. Nat. Assn. Female Execs., Nat. Notary Assn., Nat. Film Soc., Am. Film Inst., Profl. Dancers Soc. Republican. Club: Order of Eastern Star. Contbr. articles to various mags. Office: Tempo Co 9911 W Pico Blvd Suite 560 Los Angeles CA 90035

DE CAL, MICHAEL THOMAS, newspaper editor; b. Chgo., Nov. 27, 1920; s. Albert Brantley and Cora (Phelps) De C.; student U. Mo., 1936-39; m. Myrtle Margaret Hoyer, Aug. 22, 1965; step-children—Vicki Jo Erickson, Kimberly Linn Erickson. News editor Wichita (Kan.) Beacon, 1939-42; reporter Wichita Eagle, 1938-39; mng. editor Culver City (Calif.) Star News, 1959-66; mng. editor Orange County Evening News, Garden Grove, Calif., 1967-70, Contra Costa Times, Walnut Creek, Calif., 1970-79; editor, gen. mgr. Valley Pioneer, Danville, Calif., 1979—. Served with USMCR, 1942-45. Recipient numerous press awards, 1964-70. Mem. Contra Costa County, East Bay press clubs, A.P. Mng. Editors, CLAN Mng. Editors (chmn. 1964-65). Contbr. short stories to popular mags. Home: 501 Linford Pl San Ramon CA 94583 Office: 322 S Hartz Ave Danville CA 94526

DECAUSEMAKER, RONALD JAMES, computer systems consultant; b. San Francisco, June 23, 1949; s. Richard Edward and Violet Betty DeC.; B.S., E.E.C.S., U. Calif.-Berkeley, 1971; postgrad. Stanford U., 1974; m. Nada Nenadovic; 1 dau., Heidi Hope. Devel. engr. GTE Sylvania, 1972-76; dir. spl. projects Planning Research Corp., Info. Scis. Co., San Jose, 1976-77; mem. tech. staff Intercon Systems, Santa Monica, Calif., 1977-78; owner Yosemite Software, Fresno, Calif., 1978—; dir. ops. Sun Stereo, Fresno, 1980-81; prof. Am. Leadership Coll., Oseola, Iowa, 1980—; computer cons. Ernst & Whinney, 1982. Lic. spiritual cons., Peace Community Ch. Cert. computer programmer, cert. data processor. Libertarian. Address: 5150 N 6th St Suite 105 Fresno CA 93710

DECCIO, ALEX A., state senator; b. Walla Walla, Wash., Oct. 28, 1927; s. Louis and Josephine Deccio; m. Lucille P. Dexter, 1946; children—Barbara Jean Ogle, Janet Marie, Carol Ann, James Paul, Richard A., Patricia E., Teresa M., Catherine Joanne. Student Air Force Officer Sch., 1941. Former mem. Wash. Ho. of Reps.; mem. Wash. State Senate. Precinct committeeman Yakima Republican Party; treas. Young Rep. Club Yakima County, 1948, sec., 1950; del. Yakima County Rep. Conv. from 1955; chmn. platform com., 1960-66; treas. Yakima County Rep. Central Com., 1956-58, sec., 1958-60, chmn., 1971-72; campaign mgr., chmn. fund raising dinners for state and nat. candidates; alt. del. Rep. Nat. Conv., 1960, del., 1972; trustee Yakima Valley Community Coll., 1967—; state committeeman from Yakima County, exec. bd. 4th Congl. Dist., Wash. State Rep. Central Com., from 1973; mem. various coms. Yakima C. of C., 1957-65, dir., 1966-68; drive chmn. United Good Neighbors of Yakima County, 1963; mem. com. to consolidate Yakima Cath. Schs., 1967; dir. Yakima Indian Mus., from 1968; pres. Yakima Valley Visitors and Conv. Bur., 1968-69, dir., 1969—; mem. adv. bd. Pacific Nat. Bank of Wash., Tacoma; mem. Sun Dusters, Yakima, from 1969; dir. Cath. Charities, Yakima Diocese. Served to 1st lt., USAAF, 1940-46; ETO; maj. Res. from 1956. Recipient Presdl. Citation. Mem. Wash. State Ins. Brokers Assn. (legis. chmn.), Yakima County Ins. Brokers Assn., Cath. War Vets. Club: Elks. Home: PO Box 1343 Yakima WA 98907 Office: Washington State Senate Olympia WA 98504*

DECHERT, CURT PETER, geologist; b. Mt. Kisco, N.Y., Oct. 15, 1938; s. Curt Henry and Hedwig Irma (Schropp) D.; A.B., Dartmouth, 1961; M.S., U. Wash., 1963, Ph.D., 1967; m. Yolanda E. Renteria, Nov. 25, 1972; children—Melissa Anne, Monica Lynn. Geologist, Anaconda Co., Yerington, Nev., 1967-68; chief geologist-engr. Fed. Resources Corp., Lordsburg, N.Mex., 1968-72; exploration geologist Phelps Dodge Corp., 1972-78; chief geologist Galli Mineral Assos., 1978-80; chief geologist Transwestern Mining Co., 1980—. Oboeist, Silver City (N.Mex.) Community Orch., 1972-76; founder, dir. Lordsburg Rockhounds, 1970-76. Presiding election judge N.Mex. Primary, U.S. Gen Elections, 1972. Mem. Geol. Soc. Am., AIME, Aircraft Owners and Pilots Assn., U.S. Jr. C. of C. (state v.p. 1970-71), Sigma Xi. Republican. Home: 4015 Mustang Ct Reno NV 89502 Office: PO Box 20728 Reno NV 89515

DECHERT, PETER, photographer, foundation administrator; b. Phila., Dec. 17, 1924; s. Robert and Helen Hope (Wilson) D.; m. Phoebe Jane Booth; children—Sandra, Robin Booth, Caroline. B.A., U. Pa., 1948, M.A., 1950, Ph.D., 1955. Owner, Peter Dechert Assocs., Bryn Mawr, Pa., 1956-68; asst. dir. Sch. of Am. Research, Santa Fe, 1968-71; pres. Indian Arts Fund, Santa Fe, 1971-72; pres. Southwest Found. for Audio-Visual Resources, Santa Fe, 1973-77; self-employed photographer, Santa Fe; tchr., cons. photog. communications, 1964—; pres. St. Vincent Hosp. Found., 1981-83, v.p., 1983—. Served with AUS, 1943-46. Mem. N.Mex. Poetry Soc. (pres. 1969-74), Am. Studies Assn., Am. Soc. Mag. Photographers, SAR, Southwest Assn. Indian Affairs. Club: New Mexico Jazz Workshop. Address: PO Box 636 Santa Fe NM 87504

DECKARD, LAWRENCE ARTHUR, educator; b. Chgo., Nov. 25, 1936; s. Lawrence Alexander and Evelyn (Larson) D.; m. Shirley Adelaide Slight, July 3, 1958; children—Deborah, Daniel, Dawn. B.A., Calif. State U.-Sacramento, 1961, M.A., 1975; Ed.D., U. So. Calif., 1982. Gen. elem. credential; adminstrv. service credential, Calif. tchr. elem. schs. Rio Linda Union Sch. Dist., North Highlands, Calif., 1961—; track coach Grant Unified Sch. Dist., North Highlands, 1979; phys. edn. resource person Oakdale Sch., North Highlands, 1974-77, mem. comprehensive arts com., 1980-81; mem. curriculum support com., 1980—. Hon. life mem. PTA. Mem. Assn. Calif. Sch. Adminstrs., Assn. Supervision and Curriculum Devel., NEA, Rio Linda Edn. Assn., Calif. Tchrs. Assn., Phi Delta Kappa. Democrat. Baptist. Contbr. articles to profl. jours. Home: 7979 Gilardi Rd Newcastle CA 95658

DECKER, RICHARD KELSEY, equipment distribution company executive; b. Monrovia, Calif., Dec. 31, 1929; s. Raymond Grant and Dorothy Irene (Heady) D.; m. Barbara Carolyn Carlson, 1956; children—Richard Brian, Carolyn Ann Decker Johnson. B.S., U. So. Calif., 1952. Cost. acct. S.W. Products Co., Monrovia, 1953-55; controller Scotsman Refrigeration Inc., Monterey Park, Calif., 1955-64; with Scotsman Distbrs. of Los Angeles, Inc., La Verne, Calif., 1964—, pres., chief exec. officer, 1976—. Served with USN, 1945-47. Office: Scotsman Distributors of Los Angeles Inc 1480 Arrow Hwy La Verne CA 91750

DECKER, ROBERT MARSHALL, photographer; b. Lafayette, Ind., Nov. 21, 1910; s. Ralph Howard and Alice (Bezler) D.; student Northwestern U., 1929-30; m. Kathleen Emma Slaughter, Apr. 1, 1934; children—Lewis, William. Asst. prodn. mgr. Crowell, Crane & Williams, advt. agy., Chgo., 1929-30; photographer Austin Studios, Los Angeles, 1931-33, founder, owner Indsl. Photo Service Inc., Los Angeles, 1935—. Chmn., Los Angeles area community orgns. Pres., S.E. dist. bd. dirs. Boy Scouts Am., 1944-45. Mem. So. Calif. Furniture Mgrs. Assn. (dir. supply chpt. 1971-73), Toastmasters Internat. Rotarian (pres. S.E. Los Angeles, 1952-53). Home: 1376 Rainbrook Way Corona CA 91720 Office: 1756 E 64th St Los Angeles CA 90001

DECKER, STANLEY WALLACE, medical group administrator; b. Danville, Ill., Oct. 17, 1936; s. William Howard and Rowena E. (Newlin) D.; B.S., Ill. Wesleyan U., 1958; postgrad. So. Ill. U., 1969. Revenue agt. IRS, 1958-65; v.p. Nat. Bank, Bloomington, Ill., 1965-72; adminstr. Gailey Eye Clinic, Bloomington, 1972-79; adminstr. Casa Blanca Med. Group, Mesa, Ariz., 1979—; dir. Nat. Bank Bloomington, 1978-79. Mem. Med. Group Mgmt. Assn., Am. Coll. Med. Group Adminstrs. Home: 661 W 10th St Mesa AZ 85201 Office: PO Box 1667 Mesa AZ 85201

DECKERT, CURTIS KENNETH, management consultant; b. Whittier, Calif., Jan. 3, 1939; s. Arlen Peter and Ruth Kathrine (Whitaker) D.; m. Janet Kay Newsom, June 18, 1964; children—Denise Joy, Juliet Kay. A.A., Fullerton Coll., 1958; B.S.M.E., U. Ariz., 1960; M.S.M.E., U. So. Calif., 1962, M.B.A., 1968. Cert. mgmt. cons. Sr. engr. Nortronics, Anaheim, Calif., 1960-66; with ITT, Los Angeles, 1966; mem. tech. staff Calif. Computer Products, Anaheim, 1966-70; mgr. research/devel. Universal Graphics, Irvine, Calif., 1971; mgmt. cons., 1971-72; research/devel. engr. Ford Aerospace, Newport Beach, Calif., 1972-75; sr. devel. engr. Abbott Labs., Cerritos, Calif., 1975-76; pres. Curt Deckert Assocs., Inc., Santa Ana, Calif., 1976—; bd. dirs. Alpha Center, Inc., Placentia, Calif., 1972—. Chmn. adminstrv. bd., exec. com. Calvary Ch., Placentia, 1978-83, trustee, 1962-70, treas., 1970-72, elder, 1973-75, 78—. Mem. Instrument Soc. Am., Nat. Assn. Corp. Dirs., Optical Soc. Am., Am. Mktg. Assn., Am. Sci. Affiliation, Soc. Photo-optical Instrumentation Engrs., Assn. Mgmt. Cons., Inst. Mgmt. Cons. Republican. Contbr. articles to profl. jours.; editor bus. sect. Optical Engring., 1978—. Home: 18061 Darmel Pl Santa Ana CA 92705 Office: Koll Center West Tower Suite 3000 4000 MacArthur Blvd Newport Beach CA 92660

DECKERT, HARLAN KENNEDY, JR., manufacturing company official; b. Evanston, Ill., May 22, 1923; s. Harlan Kennedy and Lady Otey (Hutton) D.; B.S., U. Calif., Berkeley, 1949; M.B.A., U. So. Calif., 1962; m. Mary Emma Eldredge, Nov. 27, 1971; children—Mary Adrienne, Christine Ann, Daniel Gregory, Deborah Alice. Systems analyst Northrop Corp., Hawthorne, Calif., 1949-53, supr. engring. adminstrv. services, 1953-57, adminstrv. systems engr., 1957-59; with AiResearch Indsl. div. Garrett Corp., Torrance, Calif., 1959—, systems service adminstr., 1962-72, mgr. adminstrv. services, 1972-75, adminstr. internat. ops., 1975-80, sr. staff advisor Garrett Automotive Products Co., 1980—. Served with USAAF, 1943-46; CBI. Home: 2509 20th St Santa Monica CA 90405 Office: 3201 Lomita Blvd Torrance CA 90505

DECONCILIIS, ANTHONY JOHN, university administrator, psychology educator, counselor, clergyman; b. N.Y.C., July 31, 1941. M.A. in Theology, Holy Cross Coll., Washington, 1967; M.Ed. in Counselor Edn. and Psychology, Lewis and Clark Coll., Oreg., 1979; D.Min. in Pastoral Counseling, Andover Newton Theol., Newton Centre, Mass., 1972. Ordained priest Roman Catholic Ch., 1967. Chairperson, tchr. St. Peter's High Sch., Gloucester, Mass., 1967-70; dir. Drug Program Project NUVA, Mass., 1970-71; dir., counselor univ. ministry Bridgewater (Mass.) State Coll., 1971-75; pastoral counselor, tchr., cons. Northshore Living and Learning Ctr., Vancouver, B.C., Can., 1975-77; asst. prof. psychology U. Portland (Oreg.), 1977—, founder, dir. office counseling and cons., 1980—; cons. Project NUVA, Stonehill Coll., 1970-74, DePaul Ctr. Alcoholism Treatment, Oreg., 1979-81, Project Rebound, 1979. Fellow Am. Assn. Pastoral Counselors; mem. Am. Psychol. Assn., Oreg. Psychol. Assn., Am. Personnel and Guidance Assn., N.W. Coll. Personnel Assn., Assn. Univ. and Coll. Counseling Ctr. Dirs., Am. Mental Health Counselor Assn. Democrat. Developer counseling and ednl. programs in psychology, counseling and gerontology. Home: 5605 N Van Houten St Portland OR 97203 Office: U Portland 5000 N Willamette Blvd Portland OR 97203

DECONCINI, DENNIS, U.S. Senator, lawyer; b. Tucson, May 8, 1937; s. Evo and Ora (Webster) DeC.; B.A., U. Ariz., 1959, LL.B., 1963; m. Susan Margaret Hurley, June 6, 1959; children—Denise, Christina, Patrick Evo. Admitted to Ariz. bar, 1963; practiced in Tucson, 1963-65, 68-73; mem. firm Evo DeConcini, Tucson, 1963-65; partner firm DeConcini & McDonald, Tucson, 1968-73; dep. Pima County atty. Sch. Dist. 1, 1971-72, Pima County atty., 1973-76; mem. U.S. Senate from Ariz., 1977—, mem. Judiciary Com., Appropriations Com., Rules Com., Select Com. on Indian Affairs, Select Com. on Vet. Affairs; ranking Democrat on subcoms: Treasury, Postal Service, Gen Govt.; minority mem. Subcom. on Constitution; mem. subcoms.; Interior and Related Agys., State, Justice, Commerce and Judiciary, Fgn. Ops. past dir. Greater Ariz. Savings & Loan Assn., Johnson-Gallo Machinery Co., Safford, Ariz., Monterey Water Co., Cochise Airlines; past pres., now dir. Shopping Centers, Inc. Chmn. legislative com. Tucson Community Council, 1966-67; mem. major gifts com. St. Joseph's Hosp. Devel. Fund Drive, 1970, Tucson Mus. and Art Center Bldg. Fund, 1971; mem. St. Joseph's Hosp. Devel. Council, 1971-73; adminstr. Ariz. Drug Control Dist., 1975-76; precinct committeeman Pima County, Ariz., Democratic party, 1958—, mem. central com., 1958-67, mem. state exec. com., 1958-68; state vice chmn. State Dem. Com., 1964-66, 70-72; vice-chmn. Pima County Dem. Com., 1970-73; past bd. dirs. Ariz. Land Taxpayers Assn., Inc. Served to 2d lt. JAG, AUS, 1959-60. Mem. Am., Ariz., Pima County bar assns., Nat. Dist. Attys. Assn. (task force on standards and goals 1973-76), Ariz. Acad. Forensic Sci., Am. Judicature Soc., Ariz. Pioneer Hist. Soc., So. Ariz. Estate Planning Council, N.A.A.C.P., U. Ariz. Alumni Assn., Tucson Fraternal Order Police, Phi Delta Theta, Delta Sigma Rho, Phi Alpha Delta. Roman Catholic (pres. parish council 1970-71). Clubs: Nucleus, Old Pueblo, President's of U. Ariz., Latin American Social (Tucson). Office: 328 Hart Senate Office Bldg Washington DC 20510

DE CRISTOFORO, ROMEO JOHN, writer; b. N.Y.C., Apr. 28, 1917; s. Nicholas and Rose (Capello) de C.; grad. high sch.; m. Mary A. Ferrari, June 7, 1942; children—Daniel Taft, David, Ronald John. Freelance writer of how-to books, 1951—, also editorial cons., contbg. editor. Mem. Nat. Assn. Home and Workshop Writers (pres.), Profl. Photographers Assn. Am. Internat. Photographers Assn., Nat. Writers Club. Author books including: The New Carpentry Handbook, 1968; The Practical Handbook of Carpentry, 1969; De Cristoforo's Complete Book of Power Tools, 1972; Concrete Masonry Techniques and Design, 1975; The Practical Handbook of Power Tools, 1975; de Cristoforo's Housebuilding Illustrated, 1977; Handtool Handbook for Woodworking, 1977; Woodworking Techniques Joints and their Applications, 1979; The Magic of Your Radial Arm Saw, 1980; Wood Toys, Gifts and Furniture, 1981. Address: 27861 Natoma Rd Los Altos Hills CA 94022

DECUIR, JOSEPH CHARLES, electronics engineer; b. Pasadena, Calif., Oct. 2, 1950; s. Laurence Edwin and Leota Dorothy (Miller) D.; m. Elizabeth Clare Strauss, Apr. 30, 1982. B.S. in Electronics Engring., U. Calif.-Berkeley, 1972; M.S. in Biomed. Engring. Research asst. Inst. Med. Scis., San Francisco, 1973-75; sr. electronic engr. Atari Inc., Sunnyvale, Calif., 1975-79; dir. engring., dir. Standard Technol. Corp., Berkeley, Calif., 1979—. Bd. dirs. Consumers Coop. Berkeley. Mem. IEEE, AAAS, Assn. Computing Machinery. Democrat. Clubs: Grizzly Cyclists, Strawberry Canyon Aquatic Masters. Patentee in field.

DEDDEH, WADIE PETER, state senator, former educator; b. Bagdad, Iraq, Sept. 6, 1920; s. Peter Joseph and Hannai Mona Deddeh; m. Mary-Lynn Drake, 1951; 1 son, Peter Charles. A.B., U. Bagdad, 1946; M.A., U. Detroit, 1956. Tchr. Arabic lang. Army Lang. Sch., Monterey, Calif., 1949-54; tchr. Sweetwater High Sch., National City, Calif., 1959-62; prof. polit. sci. Southwestern Coll., Chula Vista, Calif., 1962-66; mem. Calif. State Assembly, from 1967, chmn. pub. employees and retirement com., from 1976; now. mem. Calif. State Senate; del. Dem. Nat. Conv., 1980. Mem. Calif. Tchrs. Assn., NEA, Calif. Jr. Coll. Faculty Assn., GI Forum. Roman Catholic. Club: K.C. Home: 368 Surrey Dr Bonita CA 92002 Office: California State Senate State Capitol Sacramento CA 95814*

DEDERICK, DONALD LESLIE, ednl. adminstr.; b. Great Falls, Mont., Jan. 19, 1933; s. Leslie John and Arle Stella (Holliday) D.; B.S., Oreg. State U., 1955; M.Ed., Tex. Tech. U., 1961; Ed.D., U. Wash. at Seattle, 1971; m. Joan Marie Marchek, Sept. 12, 1954; children—Linda, Sherry, Dana, Janelle, Cindy, Mindy. Tchr. sci., math. Federal Way (Wash.) High Sch., 1961-65; dir. adult and vocat. edn. Federal Way Sch. Dist., 1962-68, adminstrv. asst., 1968-69, dir. Title III Project 80, 1969-71; prin. Decatur High Sch., Federal Way, 1970-75, adminstrv. asst. to supt. Area I, 1975-80; asst. supt., Federal Way, 1980-81; supt. Shelton (Wash.) Sch. Dist., 1981—; cons. vocat. tng. Nat. Assn. Pub. Sch. Adult Edn., N.Y.C., 1965, program chmn. nat. conf., 1968; cons. Wash. State Plan Vocat. Edn., 1966; cons. individualized instruction Wash. Assn. Secondary Sch. Prins., 1971, 72; conf. lectr. Wash. Assn. Supervisory and Curriculum Devel., 1972. Mem. Federal Way Community Council, 1966-72, also chmn., 1970; dir. Wayside United Ch. Christ, 1973-74, moderator, 1976-77, bldg. chmn., 1978-79; leader devel. task force United Ministries, 1975-79, chmn., 1978-79; bd. dirs. Federal Way Youth Service Bur., 1973-77, chmn., 1974-76. Served with USAF, 1955-61. Named Outstanding Instr., 1960; recipient Dubach Service award Oreg. State U., 1955, Scholastic Hon. award Phi Kappa Phi, 1961, Disting. Service award Federal Way Community, 1966, Three Outstanding Young Men award Wash. State, 1968, Golden Acorn award Parent Tchr. Student Assn., 1972, Disting. Service award, 1980; Citizen of Month award Federal Way C. of C., 1976. Mem. Federal Way Jaycees (pres. 1963), Wash. Jaycees (state leadership chmn. 1966-68; Outstanding Couple award 1967), Wash. Assn. Pub. Sch. Adult Edn. (state pres. 1967), Nat., Wash. assns. secondary sch. prins., Nat., Wash., Federal Way edn. assns., Wash. Assn. Sch. Adminstrs. (bd. dirs. 1977-80, resolutions com. 1981-83), Phi Delta Kappa. Home: E 1791 Hwy 3 Shelton WA 98584

DEDINAS, DON ANTHONY, electrical engineer, instrumentation consultant; b. Chgo., Nov. 24, 1934; s. Anton and Ann Marie (Balezentis) D.; m. Mary Ann Callen, Nov. 16, 1957; children—Mary, Maureen, Kathleen, Patricia, Don J. B.S. in Elec. Engring., Marquette U., 1960. Design engr. GTE Lenkurt, San Carlos, Calif., 1962-64; sr. design engr. Cushman Electronics, Sunnyvale, Calif., 1964-69; systems engring. mgr. Marin Controls, Belmont, Calif., 1969-71; sr. project engr. Sierra div. Lear Siegler, Menlo Park, Calif., 1971-76; applications, systems engr. Moore Systems, San Jose, Calif., 1976-77; product mktg. mgr. Biomation Corp., Santa Clara, Calif., 1977-78; Western regional sales mgr. Nicolet Instrument Corp., San Jose, 1978—; cons. instrumentation, new bus. Served with U.S. Army, 1954-56. Mem. IEEE.

Republican. Roman Catholic. Office: Nicolet Instrument Corp 691 River Oaks Pkwy San Jose CA 95134

DEDINI, ELDON LAWRENCE, cartoonist; b. King City, Cal., June 29, 1921; s. Grutly Stefano and Oleta Regina (Loeber) D.; A.A., Hartnell Coll., Salinas, Calif., 1942; grad. Chouinard Art Inst., Los Angeles, 1942-44; m. Virginia DeSales Conroy, July 15, 1944; 1 son, Giulio. Staff cartoonist Salinas (Calif.) Index-Jour., Salinas Morning Post, 1940-41; staff story dept. Walt Disney Studios, Burbank, Calif., 1944-46; staff cartoonist Esquire mag., Chgo., 1946-50; New Yorker mag., N.Y.C., 1950—, Playboy mag., Chgo., 1960—. Recipient Best Mag. Cartoonist award Nat. Cartoonists Soc., 1958, 61, 64, ann. award for best color Cartoon Playboy, 1978. Mem. Nat. Cartoonists Soc., Cartoonists Guild Inc. (2d. v.p. N.Y.C. 1970). Author: The Dedini Gallery, cartoon album, 1961; anthologies of New Yorker, Playboy cartoons. Address: Box 1630 Monterey CA 93940

DEE, ANTHONY JAMES, psychiatrist; b. Philippines, Feb. 15, 1940; s. Chuan and Dit (Jao) D.; came to U.S., 1967, naturalized, 1977; B.S. in Physics, U. Philippines, 1961; M.D., U. of East, 1966; M.B.A., U. Hawaii, 1979; children—Jocelyn, Anthony Mark. Intern Kuakini Hosp., Honolulu, 1967; resident U. Hawaii, 1968-70; postdoctoral fellow Yale New Haven Med. Center, 1970-71; practice medicine specializing in psychiatry, 1971—; asst. prof. psychiatry Yale, 1972-75; assoc. prof. psychiatry U. Hawaii, 1975—; chief Diamond Head Mental Health Center, Honolulu, 1975—; attending staff St. Francis Hosp., Honolulu, 1977—, Queen's Med. Center, Honolulu, 1978—. Bd. dirs. Hawaii chpt. Make Today Count, 1976-78, Hawaii chpt. Nat. Sudden Infant Death Syndrome Found., 1977-79, Waikiki Community Center, 1979—, Honolulu YMCA. Served to comdr. M.C., USNR. Fellow Hawaii Inst. Mgmt. and Analysis in Govt.; mem. AAAS, Am. Psychiat. Assn. AMA, Am. Mgmt. Assn. Contbr. articles to med. jours. Home: 4844-2 Kilauea Ave Honolulu HI 96816 Office: 1441 Kapiolani Blvd Suite 621 Honolulu HI 96814

DEERING, FREDERICK ARTHUR, insurance company executive; b. Winfield, Kans., Jan. 12, 1928; s. Frederick Arthur and Lucile (Phillips) D.; m. Isabell Staufenberg, June 14, 1949; children—Anne Deering Buchanan, Kate; m. 2d Elizabeth Kimball, Apr. 12, 1979. B.S. in Bus. Adminstrn., LL.B., U. Colo., 1951. Bar: Colo. 1951. Assoc. Gorsuch, Kirgis, Campbell, Walker & Grover, Denver, 1951-54, ptnr., 1954-62; v.p., gen. counsel Security Life & Accident Co., Denver, 1962-66, pres., 1966-76, pres., chief exec. officer, 1976-82, chmn., chief exec. officer, 1983—, also dir.; chmn., chief exec. officer Midwestern United Life Ins. Co., Ft. Wayne, Ind., 1983—; chmn. bd. Fin. Indsl. Fund, Fin. Daily Income Shares, Fin. Indsl. Income Fund, Fin. Bond Shares, Mental Fabricators, Inc.; dir. Columbia Savs. & Loan Assn., Security Life Denver Ins. Co., First Columbia Fin. Corp. Trustee Huebner Found., 1980—; bd. dirs. Wallace Village for Children, 1970-76; civic adv. com. Porter Hosp.; adv. com. Met. Assn. Retarded Children, 1973-76; adv. panel Denver Research Inst.; former bd. dirs. U. Colo. Found., Inc., Cherry Creek Village Water Dist.; former trustee Cherry Creek Village Civic Assn., Denver Symphony Soc.; chmn. bd. trustees Loretto Heights Coll., 1968—. Named Colo. Businessman of Yr., Alpha Kappa Psi, 1976. Mem. Colo. Life Conv. (past Pres.), Met. Denver Exec. Club (past pres.), ABA, Life Office Mgmt. Assn. (dir. 1977-81), Denver Bar Assn., Colo. Bar Assn., Am. Judicature Soc., Denver Law Club, Assn. Life Ins. Counsel, Am. Life Ins. Assn., Am. Council Life Ins. (dir. 1972-76), Denver C. of C., Sigma Alpha Epsilon, Phi Alpha Delta, Order of Coif. Clubs: Denver (dir. 1972-75), Cherry Hills Country (dir. 1973-76, pres. 1975-76), Univ., Garden of the Gods (Colorado Springs), Old Baldy (Saratoga, Wyo.), Castle Pines Golf, Wigwam. Home: 1551 Larimer St 1701 Denver CO 80202 Office: 1616 Glenarm Pl Denver CO 80202

DEFAZIO, LYNETTE STEVENS, dancer, choreographer, educator, chiropractor; b. Berkeley, Calif., Sept. 29; d. Honore and Mabel J. (Estavan) Stevens; student U. Calif., Berkeley, 1950-55, San Francisco State Coll., 1950-51; D. Chiropractic, Life-West Chiropractic Coll., San Lorenzo, Calif., 1983; children—Joey Panganiban, Joanna Pang. Contract child dancer Monogram Movie Studio, Hollywood, Calif., 1938-40; dance instr. San Francisco Ballet, 1953-64; perfomer San Francisco Opera Ring, 1960-67; performer, choreographer Oakland (Calif.) Civic Light Opera, 1963-70; fgn. exchange dance dir. Academie de Danses-Salle Pleyel, Paris, France, 1966; dir. Ballet Arts Studio, Oakland, 1960—; teaching specialist Oakland Unified Sch. Dist.-Childrens Centers, 1968—; instr. Peralta Community Coll. Dist., Oakland, 197; cons., instr. extension courses UCLA, Dirs. and Suprs. Assn., Pittsburg Unified Sch. Dist., Tulare (Calif.) Sch. Dist., 1971-73; researcher Ednl. Testing Services, HEW, Berkeley, 1974; choreographer San Francisco Childrens Opera, Oakland Civic Theater; ballet mistress Dimensions Dance Theater, Oakland, 1977—; cons. Gianchetta Sch. Dance, San Francisco, Robicheau Boston Ballet, television series Patchwork Family, CBS, N.Y.C.; choreographer Ravel's Valses Nobles et Sentimentales, 1976. Mem. Profl. Dance Tchrs. Assn. Am. Author: Basic Music Outlines for Dance Classes, 1960, rev., 1968; Teaching Techniques and Choreography for Advanced Dancers, 1965; Basic Music Outlines for Dance Classes, 1965; Goals and Objectives in Improving Physical Capabilities, 1970; A Teacher's Guide for Ballet Techniques, 1970; Principle Procedures in Basic Curriculum, 1974; Objectives and Standards of Performance for Physical Development, 1975. Asso. music arranger Le Ballet du Cirque, 1964, Techniques of a Ballet School, 1970, rev., 1974; asso. composer, lyricist The Ballet of Mother Goose, 1968; choreographer: Walses Nobles Et Sentimentales (Ravel); Cannon in D for Strings and Continuo (Pachelbel), 1979. Home and office: 4923 Harbord Dr Oakland CA 94618

DEFFLEY, DAVID GARON, publishing company marketing executive; b. Springfield, Mass., Mar. 26, 1941; s. Thomas Michael and Theresa McCaffrey D.; m. Anne Kathryn Murray, Oct. 30, 1965; children—Mark, Kristen, Kara. B.S., Boston U., 1964; M.S., Springfield Coll., 1965. Tchr., counselor, coach Suffield, Schs. (Conn.), 1965-71; with CTB/McGraw-Hill, Washington, N.Y.C., Monterey, Calif., 1971-79, gen. mgr., 1979-81, gen. mgr., v.p. internat. tng. systems, 1981, dir. mktg., 1981—. Coach recreational programs, Carmel Valley, Calif. Recipient recognition awards McGraw-Hill. Mem. Am. Assn. Sch. Adminstrs., Am. Personnel and Guidance Assn., Am. Mgmt. Assn., Boston U. Alumni Assn., Springfield Coll. Alumni Assn. Roman Catholic. Contbr. articles to newspapers. Home: 36 Miramonte Rd Carmel Valley CA 93924 Office: CTB/McGraw-Hill Del Monte Research Pk Monterey CA 93940

DE FIGH-PRICE, CHERRI, civil engr.; b. Monitor, Wash., Jan. 19, 1953; d. G. Clifford and Doris M. (Gockley) DeFigh; B.S. summa cum laude in Civil Engring., Wash. State U., 1975; m. L. Stephen Price, July 7, 1973. Engr., Battelle Pacific N.W. Labs., Richland, Wash., 1975-76; with Rockwell Hanford Ops., Richland, 1976—, rock mechanic, basalt tech., 1978-80, mgr. engring. mechanics, 1980—. Recipient Young Career Woman award Atlantic Richfield Hanford, 1977. Mem. ASCE (assoc., sec.-treas. Columbia sect. 1981-82), Soc. Women Engrs. (pres. Eastern Wash. 1977-78), Tau Beta Pi. Office: PO Box 800 Rockwell Hanford Richland WA 99352

DE FILIPPO, RITA MARCELLA, budget analyst; b. N.Y.C.; d. Sal and Margaret (Jaeger) DeF.; student Los Angeles City Coll., 1957, City Coll. San Francisco, 1975, U. San Francisco, 1976; cert. acctg. LaSalle U., 1968. Asst. advt. dir. Gump's, Inc., San Francisco, 1959; research statistician Honig-Cooper & Harrington, San Francisco, 1960-61; salesperson Landau Realty, San Francisco, 1962-63; mgmt. analyst Oakland Army Base (Calif.), 1978-80; budget analyst Dept. Army, San Francisco, 1980—. Recipient Outstanding Performance award Fed. Govt., 1979. Mem. Am. Bus. Women's Assn. (treas. 1978-79), Am. Soc. Mil. Comptrollers, Assn. Women in Sci., Assn. U.S. Army, Nat. Fedn. Fed. Employees (trustee 1972), World Affairs Council, Sierra Club. Home: 2820 Scott St San Francisco CA 94123 Office: Presidio of San Francisco CA 94129

DEFLEUR, LOIS B., university dean, sociology educator; b. Aurora, Ill., June 25, 1936; d. Ralph Edward and Isabel Anna (Cornils) Begitske; m. Melvin L. DeFleur (div.). A.B., Blackburn Coll., 1958; M.A., Ind. U., 1961; Ph.D., U. Ill., 1965. Asst. prof. Transylvania Coll., 1963-65, assoc. prof., 1966-67; asst. prof. Wash. State U., 1965-70, assoc. prof., 1970-74, prof. sociology, 1975—, dean Coll. Scis. and Arts, 1981—; Disting. vis. prof. U.S. Air Force Acad., 1976-77; vis. prof. U. Chgo., 1980-81; mem. sociology grad. record com. Ednl. Testing Service, 1980-84. Active Internat. Orgn. Women Pilots; mem. Wash. State Bd. on Correctional Standards and Edn., 1974-77. NIMH doctoral tng. grantee, 1969-79; NSF grantee, 1972-75; Air Force Office Sci. Research grantee, 1978-81. Mem. Am. Sociol. Assn., Pacific Sociol. Assn. (pres. 1980-82), Sociologist for Women in Society Law and Society, Soc. Study Social Problems, Inter-Univ. Seminars on Armed Forces and Soc., Council Colls. of Arts and Scis. (dir. 1982-84), Am. Soc. Criminology, Aircraft Owners and Pilots Assn., Internat. Comanche Soc. Author: Sociology: Human Society, 3d edit. 1981, 4th edit., 1984; The Intergration of Women into All-Male Air Force Units, 1982. Office: 305 Thompson Hall Wash State U Pullman WA 99164

DE FRANCISCO, DAVID ALLAN, English teacher; b. Jamestown, N.Y., Apr. 3, 1945; s. Samuel D. and Alice (Wiborg) DeF.; m. Nancy Ellen Schermerhorn, Jan. 7, 1977. Student St. Bonaventure U., 1963-65, M.S. in Guidance, 1976; A.B. in English, Syracuse U., 1967, M.S. in English Edn., 1968; C.A.S., SUNY, Brockport, 1973; postgrad. U. Rochester, 1977. Tchr. English, Southwestern Central Sch., Jamestown, N.Y., 1968-69, Poughkeepsie (N.Y.) High Sch., 1969-70, Byron-Bergen Central Sch., Bergen, N.Y., 1970-73; tchr. English, guidance counselor Falconer (N.Y.) Central Sch., 1973-76; research asst. U. Rochester (N.Y.), 1976-77; guidance counselor Kingman (Ariz.) High Sch., 1977-80, tchr. English, 1980—. Mem. Nat. Council Tchrs. English, Am. Personnel and Guidance Assn. Club: Elks. Home: 1721 Chicago Ave Kingman AZ 86401 Office: 400 Grandview St Kingman AZ 86401

DEGENHART, PEARL C., artist, educator; b. Phillipsburg, Mont., Feb. 25; d. L.C. and Ellen (O'Neill) Degenhart; A.B., U. Mont., 1923; A.M., Columbia, 1928. Instr. art Arcata (Calif.) Union High Sch., 1928—, chmn. art dept., 1930-65; one-man shows Stafford Inn, Scotia, Calif., 1954, Humboldt State Coll., 1951; exhibited group shows San Francisco Art Assn., 1932, 37, 40; Contemporary Arts Gallery, N.Y.C., 1939; Denver, 1938; Humboldt State Coll., 1935, 45, 54; Spokane Wash., 1948; Oakland Art Gallery, 1948; Humboldt Fed. Gallery, 1966; Eureka Courthouse, 1968, Redwood Art Assn., Eureka, 1976-80, Old Town Art Guild, Eureka, 1977, San Rafael, Calif., 1978-79. Mem. Nat. League Am. Pen Women, Alpha Xi Delta, Delta Phi Delta. Contbr. to art, juvenile mags.; author children's story book. Address: Box 142 Trinidad CA 95570

DEGNAN, JAMES GUILLAUME, lawyer; b. Escanaba, Mich., Sept. 1, 1929; s. James Gerald and Eugenia M. (Thomy) D.; B.A. with distinction, U. Mich., 1951, J.D., 1953; m. Isobel Ann Robinson, Dec. 18, 1954. Admitted to Calif. bar, 1955; asst. gen. counsel May Co., Los Angeles, 1959-67; sr. partner MacFarlane, Schaefer & Haun, Los Angeles, 1967—. Dir. John S. Griffith & Co., Los Angeles. Served to 1st lt. USAF, 1954-56. Mem. Los Angeles County Bar Assn., State Bar Calif., Phi Beta Kappa. Home: 700 S Orange Grove Blvd Pasadena CA 91105 Office: Suite 2204 One Wilshire Bldg Los Angeles CA 90017

DÉ GOLIA, PERSHING, ophthalmologist; b. Oakland, Calif., Aug. 19, 1925; s. Edwin Baldwin and Myra Albertson (Pershing) DeG.; A.B., U. Calif. at Berkeley, 1949; M.D., Stanford U., 1954; m. Frances Vera Schmitt, Aug. 7, 1948; children—Deirdre A. DeGolia Cunningham, Edwin L., Peter C., Victoria A. Intern, San Francisco Hosp., 1953-54; resident family practice Sonoma County Hosp., Santa Rosa, Calif., 1954-56; resident opthalmology San Francisco VA Hosp., 1956-59; practice medicine specializing in ophthalmology, Santa Rosa, Calif., 1959—; mem. staffs Santa Rosa Meml. Hosp., Community Sonoma County, Warrack Hosp. (all Santa Rosa); teaching cons. Community Hosp. of Sonoma County, 1959—; family practice dept. U. Calif. Med. Sch., San Francisco. Bd. dirs. Son-Mend council Boy Scouts Am. Served with AUS, 1943-46. Decorated Purple Heart. Diplomate Am. Bd. Ophthalmology. Fellow Am. Acad. Ophthalmology and Otolaryngology, Royal Soc. Health; mem. Pan-Am. Ophthalmology Assn., Pacific Coast Otolaryngology-Ophthalmology Soc., Los Angeles Research Study Club, Contact Lens Assn. Ophthalmology, Am. Coll. Geriatrics, Soc. Eye Surgeons, Am., Calif., Sonoma med. assns., Santa Rosa C. of C. (dir.). Kiwanian. Home: 3612 Alta Vista St Santa Rosa CA 95405 Office: 1515 Montgomery Dr Santa Rosa CA 95405

DEGRACIE, JAMES SULLIVAN, school district official, educational consultant; b. Marshfield, Wis., Aug. 30, 1939; s. Harold William and Julia Helen DeG.; m. Marlene Louise McDonald, Feb. 5, 1939; children—Debra, Daniel, Donald, Darren. B.S. in Math., Calif. State Poly. Coll., San Luis Obispo, 1962, M.A. in Edn., 1963; M.S. in Stats., Kans. State U.-Manhattan, 1965; Ph.D. in Stats., Iowa State U., 1968. Instr., Iowa State U., 1964-68; sr. statistician Control Data Corp., Dugway, Utah, 1968-70; project mgr. Litton Sci. Support Lab., Ft. Ord, Calif., 1970-71; sr. scientist Human Resources Research Orgn., Monterey, Calif., 1971-72; functioning chief statistician Nat. Ctr. for Edn. Stats., Washington, 1981-82; dir. dept. research adn evaluation Mesa (Ariz.) Pub. Schs., 1972—; vis. prof. No. Ariz. U., Flagstaff, 1979, 80, 81, 83; exec. dir. Info. Analysis Assocs., Mesa, 1973—. Bd. dirs. Community Orgn. for Drug Abuse Systems, 1975-76; mem. adv. bd. Central Ariz. Health Systems, 1976-77. Inst. Ednl. Leadership Edn. Policy fellow, 1981-82. Mem. Am. Ednl. Research Assn. (sec. Div. H, 1982-84, program chmn. 1979, 81), Am. Statis. Assn., Mesa Sch. Adminstrs. Assn. (pres. 1976-77), Sigma Xi, Kappa Mu Epsilon, Phi Kappa Phi. Republican. Roman Catholic. Mem. bd. editorial advisors Education Researcher, 1982; contbr. articles to profl. jours. Home: 2104 E Encanto St Mesa AZ 85203 Office: 549 N Stapley Dr Mesa AZ 85203

DEGRASSE, ROBERT TANE, architect; b. Honolulu, Nov. 19, 1948; s. Robert J. and Kathryn M. Degrasse; B.Arch., Calif. Poly. State U., San Luis Obispo, 1973. Apprentice designer, 1969-73; mgr. design dept. Terranomics, San Luis Obispo, 1973; designer Harold Bakke, AIA, Los Altos, Calif., 1973-75; architect, developer Norman Burdick & Assos., San Jose, Calif., 1975; architect Habitec, Santa Clara, Calif., 1975-77, Ken Wolf & Assocs., Modesto, Calif., 1977—; prin. works include apt. bldgs., office complexes, shopping centers, banks. Mem. AIA, Nat. Council Archtl. Registration Bds., U.S. Nat. Karate Assn. Office: 1031 15th St Suite 4 Modesto CA 95354

DE GRASSI, ALBERTO HURFORD, advertising executive; b. Oakland, Calif., Feb. 3, 1919; s. Alberto Andrea and Ruth (Sharon) de G.; m. Helen Virginia Anderson, Dec. 24, 1941; children—Andy Alberto, Daniel Adrian, Lawrence Lane. A.B., U. Calif.-Berkeley, 1942. City editor Antioch (Calif.) Ledger, 1939-40; account exec. The McCarty Co. Advt. Agy., San Francisco, 1946-48; dir. corp. advt. Kaiser Aluminum & Chem. Corp., Oakland, 1948-72; exec. v.p. Pettler Advt., Oakland, 1972-74; pres. Pettler, de Grassi & Hill Advt. Agy., Oakland, 1974—; lectr. Served with USAF, 1942-46. Mem. Assn. Nat. Advertisers (dir.), Internat. Advt. Assn. (pres. San Francisco chpt.), Assn. Indsl. Advertisers (dir.), East Bay Advt. and Mktg. Assn. (dir.), Oakland Mus. Assn. (dir.), Alpha Delta Sigma. Clubs: Richmond (Calif.) Yacht, Rotary. Home: 9 Brookbank Orinda CA 94563 Office: 5236 Claremont Ave Oakland CA 94618

DEGRASSI, LEONARD RENÈ, educator, art historian; b. East Orange, N.J., Mar. 2, 1928; s. Romulus-William and Anna Sophia (Sannicolo) DeG.; B.A., U. So. Calif., 1950, B.F.A., 1951, M.A., 1956; postgrad. Harvard, 1953, U. Rome, 1959-60, UCLA, 1970-73; m. Dolores Marie Welgoss, June 24, 1961; children—Maria-Christina, Paul. Tchr. art Redlands (Calif.) Jr. High Sch., 1951-53, Toll Jr. High Sch., Glendale, Calif., 1953-61, Wilson Jr. High Sch., Glendale, 1961; faculty Glendale Coll., 1962—, prof. art history, 1974—, chmn. dept., 1972. Decorated knight Order of Merit of Republic of Italy, 1972; knight comdr. Holy Sepulchre (Papal); knight St. John of Jerusalem; knight of Malta. named Outstanding Educator Am., Assn. Outstanding Educators Am., 1971. Mem. Art Educators Assn., Glendale Art Assn., Egypt Exploration Soc. London, Am. Research Center Egypt, Tau Kappa Alpha, Kappa Pi, Delta Sigma Rho. Paintings: Ch. St. Mary, Cook, Minn. high altar, 1968-70, Ch. St. Andrew, El Segundo, Calif., altar screen, 1965-71, altar screen Ch. of the Descent of the Holy Spirit, Glendale. Office: 1500 N Verdugo Rd Glendale CA 91206

DEGRILLA, ROBERT J., real estate executive; b. San Francisco, July 29, 1942; s. Robert M. and Josephine DeG.; m. Barbara G. Gibson, Jan. 27, 1968; children—Angela, Sean, Nicole. Student Pacific U., 1960-62; B.A. in Bus., Real Estate, U. Calif.-San Francisco, 1965. Mgr. Coldwell Banker & Co., San Jose, Calif., 1967-72; v.p. I.D.C. Real Estate, Houston, 1972-75; pres. Wells Fargo Asset Mgmt. Co., Marina del Rey, Calif., 1975—. Served to sgt. U.S. Army, 1965-67. Mem. Nat. Rifle Assn. Home: 10065 Sunn Circle Fountain Valley CA 92708 Office: 330 Washington St Marina del Rey CA 90291

DEGUTES, JOHN MICHAEL, computer co. exec.; b. Milw., May 7, 1937; s. John Warren and Kinga Marie DeG.; B.S. in Math., U. Wis., 1960; m. Mary Malin Carroll, Jan. 18, 1964. Western regional mgr. Incoterm, 1972-75, TRW Bus. Systems Div., 1975-77; v.p. TCW, 1977-79; pres. ICE Internat., San Francisco, Calif., 1979—. Served with USN, 1960-64. Republican. Episcopalian. Club: Olympic (San Francisco). Home: 16 San Felipe Way Novato CA 94947 Office: 1900 Noriega San Francisco CA 94122

DEHAAN, WARREN VERNE, optometrist; b. Des Moines, Sept. 8, 1940; s. Ray John and Jean (Van Gorp) DeH.; student Ottawa U., 1958-59, Long Beach State Coll., 1959-62; O.D. with highest honors, U. Calif.-Berkeley, 1966; m. Caryn Castner, June 8, 1959 (div. Feb. 1969); children—Dyce, Denise; m. 2d, Victoria Parmakian, Jan. 1, 1976. Pvt. practice optometry Table Mesa Med. Center, Boulder, Colo., 1966—; bd. dirs. Colo. Bd. Optometry, 1979—; pres. Colo. Bd. Optometric Examiners, 1982-83. Crusade chmn. Boulder City chpt. Am. Cancer Soc., 1967, Boulder County crusade chmn., 1968-70, Boulder County unit pres., 1969-71, dir. Boulder County unit, 1966-72; cons. pilot vision and factors visual perception aviation. Bd. dirs., sec., treas. Group Assocs., Inc., Boulder, Colo., 1969-72. Cert. flight instr. rated airline transport pilot, helicopter pilot, glider pilot, hot-air balloon pilot. Mem. Am., Colo., Boulder County (pres. 1969-70) optometric assns., Phi Beta Kappa. Author: The Optometrist's and Ophthalmologist's Guide to Pilots Vision. Home: 645 Emporia Rd Boulder CO 80303 Office: Table Mesa Med Center Boulder CO 80303

DEHAVEN, DOUGLAS MARSHALL, mfg. co. mgr.; b. Oxnard, Calif., Aug. 31, 1938; s. Marshall Elwood and Ruby Pearl (Shaffer) De H.; A.A., Orange Coast Coll., 1973; children—David Marshall, Laura Dawn. Methods planner ITT Cannon Electric Co., Santa Ana, Calif., 1961-65; sr. mfg. engr. Pacific Sci. Co., Anaheim, Calif., 1965-74; chief mfg. engr. Sundstrand Corp., Anaheim, 1974-77; mgr. mfg. engring. Dana Corp., Santa Ana, 1977-80; MIS mgr. Gen. Valve Co., Fullerton, Calif., 1980—; cons. in field. Served with USNR, 1958-61. Registered profl. engr., Calif. Mem. Computer and Automated Systems Assn. of Soc. Mfg. Engrs., Numerical Control Soc. Mem. Christian Ch. Home: 824 W Dunton Ave Orange CA 92665

DEHAVEN, KENNETH LE MOYNE, physician; b. The Dalles, Oreg., Mar. 28, 1913; s. Luther John and Dora (Beeks) DeH.; B.S., North Pacific Coll. Oreg., 1935; M.D., U. Mich., 1946; m. Ledith Mary Ewing, Jan. 11, 1937; children—Marya LeMoyne DeHaven Kenth, Lisa Marguerite DeHaven Jordan, Camille Suzanne DeHaven Ludlow. Intern USPHS Hosp., St. Louis, 1947; intern Franklin Hosp., San Francisco, 1947-48, resident, 1949; clinician Dept. Pub. Health, City San Francisco, Dept. V.D., 1949-51; practice gen. medicine, Sunnyvale, Calif., 1955—; mem. staff El Camino Hosp., Mt. View, Calif., San Jose Hosp. (Calif.). Pres. Los Altos Hills Assn. Served to capt., USAF, 1952-55. Fellow Am. Acad. Family Practice; mem. Calif. Med. Assn., Santa Clara County Med. Soc., The Royal Astron. Soc. Can., Brit. Astron. Assn., Astron. Soc. Pacific, Sunnyvale C. of C. (dir. 1955-56), AAAS, Alpha Kappa Kappa. Republican. Mason. Clubs: Press and Union League, Commonwealth, Book (San Francisco). Home: 24915 La Loma Court Los Altos Hills CA 94022 Office: 665 Knickerbocker Dr Sunnyvale CA 94087

DEIGNAN, GERARD MICHAEL, indsl. psychologist; b. Malverne, L.I., N.Y., Mar. 31, 1937; s. Joseph James and Mary Elizabeth (McCarthy) D.; B.A., U. Denver, 1963; M.S., Colo. State U., 1966, Ph.D., 1969; m. Alice Casey Deignan, Feb. 11, 1961; 1 son, Timothy Michael. Adj. faculty U. Colo., 1976—; field assessment officer Peace Corps, Afghan, 1968; sr. behavioral scientist Litton Industries Sci. Lab., Monterey, Calif., 1969-71; adj. prof. Navy Postgrad. Sch., Montry, Calif., 1971; computer-assisted instrn./learning strategies, med. tng. program evaluator A.F. Human Resources Lab., Denver, 1972-78, computer based simulations program evaluator, 1978—; mgmt. cons. to fed. and state govt.; chmn. Denver Fed. Exec. Bd. Intergovtl. Tng. Com., 1978-79; EEO adv. council Lowry AFB, 1980. Coach, Little League Football, 1972-76, Little League Basketball, 1973-76; pack leader Carmel (Calif.) council Cub Scouts Am. Mem. Am. Psychol. Assn., Am. Soc. Tng. and Devel., Rocky Mountain Psychol. Assn., Am. Edn. Research Assn. Contbr. numerous research articles on indsl. psychology to profl. jours. Home: 1261 S Ward Ct Lakewood CO 80228 Office: Air Force Human Resources Lab Lowry AFB Denver CO 80330

DEILE, WILLIAM CHARLES, psychiatrist; b. Adelsheim, Germany, Mar. 12, 1934; s. Charles Andrew and Berenice Constance (Brunetti) D.; A.B., U. Freiburg, 1954; Ph.D., U. Berlin, 1957; M.D. (fellow), U. Vienna, 1959; m. Ernestina Lozano, Apr. 12, 1959; children—Gabriella, Nicholas, Ernestina, Carla, William Charles. Asst., Berlin Psychoanalytic Inst., 1959-60; assoc. psychiatrist Burgholzli Mental Hosp., Zurich, Switzerland, 1960-64, Psychiat. Clinic of Zurich, 1961-65; pvt. practice psychiatry, Basel, Switzerland, 1965-80; vis. prof. psychology Nat. U. Mex., Mexico City, 1980-82, Vienna Psychoanalytic Inst., 1982—. Mem. Internat. Psychoanalytic Assn., World Fedn. for Mental Health. Mem. Swiss Ref. Ch. Club: Rotary. Author: Structure of Psychoanalysis in Social Science, 1965, Empirical Investigation of Free Association, 1967, A Study of Interpersonal Relations in Persons, 1975. Office: Dept Psychology Nat Univ Mex Barcelona 40 Mexico City Mexico

DEINES, HARRY J., agr. and livestock co. exec.; b. Loveland, Colo., Nov. 5, 1909; s. John and Mary (Maseka) D.; B.M.E., U. Colo.; grad. Advanced Mgmt. Program, Harvard; m. Eleanor Vrooman, 1932; children—Gretchen Deines Langston, Mark, Katrina, Stephen. Advt. mgr. Gen. Electric Co., 1930-45; v.p. Fuller & Smith & Ross, 1945-49; gen. advt. mgr. Westinghouse Electric Corp., 1949-53; v.p. J. Walter Thompson, N.Y.C., 1953-56, Fuller & Smith & Ross, N.Y.C., 1956-59; exec. v.p., dir. Campbell, Mithun, Inc., Mpls., 1959-71; mng. partner Deines Agr. & Livestock Co., Ft. Collins, Colo., 1971—; pres. Collectors' Books Ltd. Home and office: 1707 Country Club Rd Fort Collins CO 80524

DEINES, LOIS ANN, b. Los Angeles, Jan. 17, 1923; d. Richard Hart and Ellen Alira (Brownell) Wellington; m. Robert Louis Deines, June 6, 1944; children—Robert Dale, Dean Allen, Dwight Kenneth. B.S., U. So. Calif., 1944, M.L.S., 1967. Catalog and reference librarian San Marino (Calif.) Pub. Library, 1966-69, asst. city librarian, 1970-75, city librarian, 1976—. Mem. ALA, Calif. Library Assn., Women's Archtl. League, San Marino Hist. Soc., Friends of the Old Mill, LWV, Beta Phi Mu, Phi Beta Kappa, Phi Kappa Phi. Home: 2956 Lombardy Rd Pasadena CA 91107 Office: 1890 Huntington Dr San Marino CA 91108

DEIOTTE, CHARLES EDWARD, computer software company executive; b. Gary, Ind., Jan. 31, 1946; s. Raymond Louis and Dorothy Jane (Paulson) D.; A.A., Skagit Valley Jr. Coll., 1966; student Wash. State U., 1970; m. Margaret Williams Tukey, Sept. 11, 1971; children—Raymond, Karl. Programmer, Wash. State U., Pullman, 1969-70; project dir. AGT Mgmt. Systems, Renton, Wash., 1970-72; sr. tech. cons., sect. mgr. McDonnell-Douglas Automation, Bellevue, Wash., 1972-73; sr. engr. Boeing Computer Services, Seattle, 1973-75, computer based instrn. specialist, Tng. div., 1975-79; mgr. microprocessor design support center Boeing Aerospace Co., Kent, Wash., 1979-80; mgr. concept research Federal Express Corp., Colorado Springs, Colo., 1980-81, mgr. microprocessor support group, 1981-82; pres. Deitron Systems, Inc., Auburn, Wash., 1976-81; pres., chmn. bd. Logical Systems Inc., Colorado Springs, 1981—. Neighborhood commr. Chief Seattle council Boy Scouts Am., 1971-72; v.p. REACT alert, Seattle, 1974; advisor Jr. Achievement, Colorado Springs, 1980. Recipient Boeing Aerospace Co. Cert. of Achievement, 1979. Mem. Assn. Computing Machinery, IEEE, Data Processing Mgmt. Assn., Am. Mgmt. Assn., Gamma Sigma Epsilon. Home: 2973 Fascination Circle Colorado Springs CO 80917 Office: 6295 Lehman Dr Suite B-101 Colorado Springs CO 80918

DEISENROTH, CLINTON WILBUR, elec. engr.; b. Louisville, Aug. 9, 1941; s. Clifton Earl and Nell (Pierce) D.; B.E.E., Ga. Inst. Tech., 1965; m. Lisbeth D. Isaacs, May 10, 1974; 1 dau., Susan Michelle. With Raytheon Co., 1966—, div. mgr. Addington Labs., Inc., solid state products div., Santa Clara, Calif., 1975-77, program mgr. electromagnetic systems div., Goleta, Calif., 1977-79, dir. surface navy electronic warfare systems, 1979-81; sr. v.p. systems div. Teledyne-MEC, 1981—. Mem. IEEE, Am. Mgmt. Assn., Am. Def. Preparedness Assn., Navy League, Assn. Old Crows. Home: 1274 Pitman Ave Palo Alto CA 94301 Office: PO Box 10007 Palo Alto CA 94303

DEITRICH, ROBERT FRANKLIN, health care administrator; b. Pitman, Pa., May 24, 1933; s. Thomas Jefferson and Blanche Irene (Wetzel) D.; m. Lillie Esther, Apr. 9, 1955; children—Linda Esther, Lois Elaine. B.A., U. Md., 1966, M.S., U. No. Colo., 1977. Enlisted in USAF, 1951, advanced through grades to capt., 1970; ret., 1977; dir. central services, mgmt. analyst Univ. Hosp., U. Colo. Health Sci. Ctr., Denver, 1980—; faculty mil. sci. U.S. Air Force Sch. Aerospace Medicine, Brooks AFB, Tex., 1960-63. Deocrated Air Force Commendation medal; named Outstanding Registrar, Med. Service Sch., 1967. Mem. Nat. Rifle Assn., Am. Hosp. Assn. Republican. Mem. Evangelical Ch. Club: American Sportsman. Home: 14804 E Iliff Pl Aurora CO 80014 Office: 4200 E 9th Ave Denver CO 80262

DE JANASZ, ANDREW, automotive parts mfg. co. exec.; b. Trembki, Poland, Aug. 20, 1920; s. Gustaw A. and Janina N. (Byszewska) de J.; M.S., Central Agri. Coll., Warsaw, Poland, 1947; m. Bertie Jones, Nov. 25, 1978; children—Christopher G., Antoinette J. Owner, mng. dir. A. de Janasz S.A. (pty) Ltd., Cape Town, S. Africa, 1953-61; founder, pres. Interamerican Motor Corp., Los Angeles, 1962-64; founder, pres. Intercontinental Speed Specialties, Inc., Los Angeles, 1969-71; founder, pres. Janasz Corp., El Segundo, Calif., 1964—. Served with Underground Polish Army, 1941-45. Republican. Office: 137-139 Nevada St El Segundo CA 90245

DEJARNETT, LARRY RAYMOND, mfg. co. exec.; b. Harrisburg, Ill., June 7, 1940; s. Raymond Preston and Fern Berdell (Moye) DeJ.; m. Mary Elizabeth Cotton, June 16, 1962; children—Steven Bradley, Laura Elizabeth. B.S., So. Ill. U., 1962, M.S., 1963. Asst. coordinator systems and procedures So. Ill. U., Carbondale, 1963-64; systems analyst/project leader, systems rev. mgr. Ford Motor Co., Dearborn, Mich., 1964-70, ops. analysis mgr., 1970-72, div. systems mgr., 1973-77, sr. mgmt. services assoc., 1978-79; corp. v.p. info. systems Lear Siegler, Inc., Santa Monica, Calif., 1979—. Mem. Palos Verdes Peninsula Edn. Found., 1980—; mem. adv. com. St. John's Hosp. and Health Ctr., 1982—. Mem. Soc. for Info. Mgmt. (exec. com. So. Calif.), Assn. for Systems Mgmt., Beta Gamma Sigma, Kappa Delta Pi. Republican. Club: Rolling Hills (Calif.) Country. Contbr. articles to profl. jours. Office: Lear Siegler Inc 2850 Ocean Park Blvd PO Box 2158 Santa Monica CA 90406

DE JARNETTE, JAMES EDWARD, psychoanalyst, psychotherapist; b. Atlanta, Mar. 22, 1948; s. Charles Nathan and Sarah Holmes (Phillips) deJ. B.A., Shorter Coll., 1970; M.A., W. Ga. Coll., 1971; Ph.D., Sussex Coll., 1973. Exec. dir. Middle Ga. Counseling Center, Macon, 1972-80; exec. dir. Power Ferry Psychotherapy Clinic, 1976-80, deJarnette and Assos., Beverly Hills, Calif., 1979—; chmn. bd. Leonidas Ltd., Inc.; dir. Alpha-Omega Enterprises, Inc.; chmn. bd. trustees Center for Meditative Living, Inc. Bd. dirs. Ga. Mental Health Assn., 1975, Macon/Bibb County Mental Health Assn., 1975. Fellow Am. Orthopsychiat. Assn., Am. Acad. Behavioral Sci.; mem. Am. Mental Health Couselors Assn., Nat. Psychiat. Assn., Internat. Soc. Adlerian Psychology, Mensa, Tripple Nine Soc. Pi Gamma Mu. Republican. Episcopalian. Contbr. articles to profl. jours. Home: 8535 W Knoll Dr Apt 215 Los Angeles CA 90069

DE JESUS, CESAR BAYQUEN, surgeon; b. Manila, July 6, 1925; s. Zacarias and Juanita (Bayquen) de J.; M.D., U. Philippines, 1950; fellow in urology U. Minn., 1953-55; m. Marilyn Mae Weintz, Feb. 6, 1956; children—Lisa Linda, Tina Marie, Carla Nita, Ricardo, Teresa Mia, Leilani Ann, Tania Renee. Intern, Philippine Gen. Hosp., 1949-50; resident Mpls. Gen. Hosp., 1953-55, Northwestern Hosp., Mpls., 1955-56; chief urology Pacific Med. Assos., Honolulu, 1958-60; staff urologist Queen. Children's, Castle Meml. hosps., Rehab. Hosp. of Pacific, 1961—; pres. Cesar B. de Jesus M.D. Inc. clinic in urology, Honolulu, 1970—; pres. Bayanihan Health Services, 1980—; urol. cons. Bur. Maternal and Child Health, Health Dept. Honolulu, 1961-74; med. examiner ins., 1958—; sr. med. examiner Hawaii, FAA, 1961—; mem. bd., chmn. commn. Comprehensive Health Planning Adv. Council Hawaii, 1968-77; regional adv. group, exec. com. Regional Med. Program Hawaii and Pacific Basin, 1973-76; mem. Imi Hoola admissions com. John A. Burns Med. Sch., U. Hawaii, 1973—, mem. advi. com. health careers opportunity program Sch. Public Health, 1979—; pres. Peoples Investment Co., 1961-62; v.p. Finance Corp. Ltd., 1966-68; co-founder, dir. Bank of Honolulu, N.A., 1971—. Chmn. profl. div. Aloha United Way, 1972-73; chmn. Hawaii State Bd. Health, 1964-74; bd. dirs. Hawaii Med. Service Assn., Friends of East-West Center, 1964-71, Am. Cancer Soc., Health and Community Services Council Hawaii, Honolulu Symphony Soc., 1969-78, ARC Pacific Div.; bd. govs. Goodwill Industries Hawaii, 1973—; bd. regents Chaminade U., 1961-63. Diplomate Am. Bd. Abdominal Surgery. Fellow Am. Bd. Abdominal Surgery; mem. Hawaii Pub. Health Assn. (hon. life), Hawaii Assn. Professions (1st pres., founder 1972-75), Hawaii Med. Assn. (commn. chmn. 1970—), Pan Pacific Surg. Assn. (treas. bd. trustees 1970—), Am. Fertility Soc., Geriatric Soc., Philippine Med. Assn. Hawaii (pres. 1978-80). Kiwanian, Toastmaster. Office: 1441 Kapiolani Blvd Honolulu HI 96814

DE KERCHOVE, GERALD, management consulting company executive; b. Brussels, Apr. 19, 1946; s. Rodolphe and Madeleine (Herry) de K. de Denterghem; B.S., U. Calif.-Berkeley, 1968, M.B.A., 1970; m. Lynn Batchelder, Sept. 6, 1969. Came to U.S., 1965, naturalized, 1976. Ops. research mgr. Sopalin, Paris, 1970-72; sr. analyst Fair, Isaac & Co., San Rafael, Calif., 1972, v.p. fin. and overseas ops., 1972-83, sr. v.p., 1983—, dir., 1972—. Chmn. neighborhood assn., 1978—. Mem. M.B.A. Assocs., Phi Beta Kappa, Beta Gamma Sigma. Republican. Home: 2728 Belrose Ave Berkeley CA 94705 Office: Fair Isaac & Co 55 Mitchell Blvd San Rafael CA 94903

DEKRUIF, ROBERT M., business executive. Pres., H.F. Ahmanson & Co., Los Angeles. Office: HF Ahmanson & Co 3731 Wilshire Blvd Los Angeles CA 90010*

DEKTAR, CLIFFORD, public relations company executive; b. Los Angeles, Dec. 29, 1925; s. Louis and Mollie (Bronson) D.; B.A., U. So. Calif., 1950; m. Joan A. Ahern, Aug. 14, 1955; children—John L., Daniel C., Ellen. Staff writer Los Angeles Mirror, 1950-56; media contact Publicists, ABC-TV, Los Angeles, 1956-65; sr. account exec. McFadden, Strauss & Irwin, Los Angeles, 1965-70, v.p., 1970-75; v.p., account supr. Intercomm Pub. Relations, Los Angeles, 1975—. Pub. relations cons. com. Los Angeles Fire Dept., 1980—; mem. pub. relations adv. com. San Fernando Valley council Girl Scouts Am., 1973-74; bd. dirs. Alisa Ann Rusch Burn Found., 1974-75. Served with AUS, 1944-46. Mem. Pub. Relations Soc. Am. (pres. Los Angeles chpt. 1980), Soc. Profl. Journalists (dir.), U. So. Calif. Journalism Alumni Assn., Los Angeles Press Club, Sigma Delta Chi. Episcopalian (mem. program group communications Los Angeles diocese). Club: Masons. Home: 5047 Bellaire Ave North Hollywood CA 91607 Office: ICPR Public Relations 1900 Ave of the Stars Suite 300 Los Angeles CA 90067

DE LANEY, J. LAWRENCE, transpersonal therapist, educator; b. Sheridan, Wyo., Dec. 9, 1917; s. Edward J. and Mary Rose (Reuter) D.; B.A., Muskingum Coll., 1952; M.A., Calif. State U., Los Angeles, 1967; Ph.D., Brantridge, Sussex, Eng.; m. Gladys Boget, June 1, 1963; children—Bobbie, Irene, Rebecca, Deborah, Susan, Lawrence. Dir. edn. Lake Elsinore (Calif.) Mil. Acad., 1968-72; instr. creative writing Orange Coast Coll., Costa Mesa, Calif., 1964-72, Golden West Coll., Huntington Beach, Calif., 1964-72; dir. Parapsychol. Research Inst. No. Calif., Stockton, 1972—, Calif. Inst. Creative Edn., Stockton; instr. San Joaquin Delta Coll., Stockton, 1972—; tchr. Lodi Unified Sch. Dist.; cons. public relations; polit. speech writer. Served with U.S. Army, 1941-47. Recipient commendations Gen. Milton, United Crusade fund dr., 1972. Fellow Royal Photog. Soc.; mem. Social-Psychology Assn. Eng., Adult Edn. Assn., Psychical Research Inst., Soc. Psychical Research Eng. Composer organ background music Tom Brenneman's Western Home Radio Show, 1947-48, suites and spl. music for Duluth Symphony; author: Cosmogenics; Symbols; Guide to Transpersonal Therapy; Writing is a Business; Teaching Delinquents. Home: PO Box 4703 Stockton CA 95204

DELANEY, MATTHEW SYLVESTER, educator, coll. adminstr.; b. Ireland, Nov. 26, 1927; s. Joseph C. and Elizabeth M. (Berrigan) D.; came to U.S., 1947, naturalized, 1952; student St. John's Coll., 1947-51; B.A., Immaculate Heart Coll., Los Angeles, 1958; M.S., Notre Dame U., 1960; Ph.D., Ohio State U., 1971. Ordained priest, Roman Catholic Ch., 1951; assoc. pastor Los Angeles Cath. Diocese, 1951-55; instr. math., physics Pius X High Sch., Downey, Calif., 1955-58, vice prin., 1960-62; instr. math. Immaculate Heart Coll., Los Angeles, 1962-65, asst. prof., 1965-72, assoc. prof., 1972-76, prof., 1976—; asst. acad. dean, 1973-78; dean acad. devel. Mt. St. Mary's Coll., Los Angeles, 1978-82, acad. dean, 1982—. NSF grantee, 1959-60, 61. Mem. Am. Math. Soc., Math. Assn. Am., Am. Conf. Acad. Deans. Democrat. Contbr. articles to math. publs. Home: 922 S Detroit St Los Angeles CA 90036 Office: Mt St Mary's Coll 12001 Chalon Rd Los Angeles CA 90049

DELANEY, RICHARD JAMES, investment banking co. exec.; b. Pottsville, Pa., Jan. 4, 1946; s. James F. and Ann M. (Giacoia) D.; B.S. in Indsl. Engring., Lehigh U., 1968; M.B.A., Wharton Sch., U. Pa., 1970; m. Mary D. McGuire, Aug. 16, 1969; children—Jennifer, Kelly. With Carrier Air Conditioning Co., N.Y.C., 1968-69; with Dean Witter & Co., San Francisco, 1970; v.p., instl. rep. White, Weld & Co., San Francisco, 1971-78; v.p. Shearson, Hayden-Stone, 1978-79, Donaldson, Lufkin & Jenrette, 1979—; pres., dir. U.S. Global Trading Corp.; dir. Pacific Mellon Corp. Pres. No. Calif. Cystic Fibrosis Found., 1974-75, trustee, 1973-76. Mem. Am. Assn. Indsl. Engrs., Lehigh Alumni of No. Calif. (pres.). Democrat. Roman Catholic. Clubs: San Francisco Bond, Calif. Golf, Wharton Bus. Sch., Lehigh Alumni (pres. 1978—), Elks. Home: 7 Highlands Ct Belmont CA 94002 Office: 555 California St San Francisco CA 94104

DE LA PENA, DONALD JOSEPH, planning, mgmt., transp. cons.; b. Valley Stream, N.Y., Apr. 8, 1936; s. Joseph Alfred and Sophia Marie de la P.; B.C.E., U. Santa Clara, 1959; M. City Planning, U. Calif., Berkeley, 1962; children—Michael Allan, Kimberly Ann, Christine Elaine. Advanced planner Santa Clara County (Calif.) Planning Dept., San Jose, 1962-66; adminstr. City of San Jose, including exec. sec. San Jose Goals Com., head advanced planning City of San Jose Planning Dept., dep. dir. intergovtl. affairs, sr. policy analyst, dir. policy, legislation and grant coordination/implementation, 1967-80; dir. indsl. devel. Ruth and Going, Inc., 1981; planning, mgmt., transp. cons. De la Pena Assos., 1982—; lectr. urban planning, plan implementation, growth mgmt., mgmt. decision-making San Jose State U., 1972-77; lectr. decisionmaking in a cybernetic soc. Stanford (Calif.) U. Assn. Continuing Edn., 1973; adj. prof. community devel. Stanford U., 1980. Mem. Futures Planning Council Episcopal Diocese Calif., 1968-78, chmn., 1973-75; chmn. Guadalupe Coll. Adv. Bd., Los Gatos, Calif., 1967-68; mem. Futures Oriented Com. Santa Clara County, 1966-68; bd. dirs. Opportunities Industrialization E. San Jose, 1967; mem. planning and allocations council United Way of Santa Clara County, 1981—, chmn. community services allocation panel, 1981—. Mem. Am. Planning Assn., Am. Inst. Cert. Planners, Corp. Planners Assn., N.Am. Soc. Corp. Planning, Calif. Planning Roundtable, Calif. Assn. for Econ. Devel. Author articles on corp. involvement in transp., housing, other public issues. Club: Rotary (dir., chmn. community service and fund raising). Office: PO Box 26934 San Jose CA 95159

DE LA PEÑA, RAMON SERRANO, agronomist; b. San Jacinto, Pangasinam, Philippines, Oct. 2, 1936; s. Marcelino Reyes and Maria Serrano de la P.; B.S., U. Philippines, 1958; M.S., U. Hawaii, 1964, Ph.D., 1967; m. Harriet Enriqueta Viloria, Jan. 26, 1963; children—Marjorie Joy Leilani, Ramon, Raynard Don, Ryan Mel. Research asst. U. Philippines, 1958-60; asst. in plant physiology U. Hawaii, 1960-65, jr. soil scientist, 1965-67, asst. agronomist, 1967-76, rice tng. officer, 1968-72, asso. specialist in agronomy Kauai br. sta., Kapaa, 1976-81, supt. sta., 1978-81; asso. agronomist, asso. prof. dept. agronomy and soil sci., 1981-83, agronomist, prof. agronomy, 1983—; dir. econ. devel. County of Kauai, 1973-74; cons. tropical agr. AID, World Bank, Universe Tankships; panel mem. Nat. Acad. Sci. Mem. Kauai County Employment and Tng. Planning Council; mem. Office of Elderly Affairs Policy Bd., County of Kauai. Grantee U.S. Dept. Agr., State of Hawaii, County of Kauai. Mem. Am. Soc. Agronomy, Asian-Pacific Weed Sci. Soc., Hawaiian Acad. Sci., Internat. Soc. Tropical Root Crops, Internat. Soc. Soil Sci., Soil Sci. Soc. Am., Weed Sci. Soc. Am., Weed Sci. Soc. Philippines, Sigma Xi, Gamma Sigma Delta. Democrat. Roman Catholic. Editor Internat. Soc. Tropical Root Crops Newsletter, 1980—; contbr. articles to profl. jours. Home: 6163 Kala Kea Pl Kapaa HI 96746 Office: 7370-A Kuamoo Rd Kapaa HI 96746

DELAPP, KENNETH DEWEY, JR., engring. co. exec.; b. Frederick, S.D., Nov. 8, 1925; s. Kenneth Dewey and Mamie (Parduhn) DeL.; student U. Minn., 1943-44; B.S. in Engring., U. Mich., 1946; M.S. in Engring., 1949; m. Mary Lorraine Kangus, Aug. 29, 1948; children—Kenneth Dewey, Winton Jeffrey, Margot Linda, John Marsden. Structural engr. Giffels & Vallet, Inc., Detroit, 1946-48, 50-52; structural, civil engr. Ayres, Lewis, Norris & May, Ann Arbor, Mich., 1948-50; partner Wood & DeLapp, Cons. Engrs., Santa Fe, 1953-65; owner K.D. DeLapp & Assos., 1965-66; pres. DeLapp & Gordon Engring. Co., 1966-68; pres. DeLapp Engring. Corp., 1968—; dir. Southside Corp., Santa Fe. Neighborhood commr. Kit Carson council Boy Scouts Am., 1964-67, scoutmaster, 1966-68. Served with USNR, 1943-46. Registered profl. engr., N.M., Mich., Colo., Ariz., Tex.; lic. pvt. pilot. Mem. ASCE (pres. N.Mex. sect. 1978-79), Nat., N.Mex. (pres. chpt. 1972-73, state pres. 1977-78) socs. profl. engrs., Am. Concrete Inst., Cons. Engrs. Council N.Mex., Tau Beta Pi. Republican. Methodist. Home: 1828 San Felipe Circle Santa Fe NM 87501 Office: 1300 Luisa St Santa Fe NM 87501

DELAPP, TINA DAVIS, nursing educator; b. Los Angeles, Dec. 18, 1946; d. John George and Margaret (Clark) Davis; m. John Robert D. Lapp, May 31, 1969; children—Julia Ann, Scott Michael. Diploma in nursing Good Samaritan Hosp. Sch. Nursing, Phoenix, 1967; B.S. in Nursing, Ariz. State U., 1969; M.S. in Nursing, U. Colo., 1972. Registered nurse, Alaska, Ariz. Staff nurse Good Samaritan Hosp., Phoenix, 1967-68, Tempe (Ariz.) Community Hosp., 1968-69, Alaska Native Hosp., Bethel, 1969-70; head aide instr. Yukon-Kuskokwim Health Corp., Bethel, 1970-71; instr., then asst. prof. nursing Bacone Coll., Muskogee, Okla., 1972-74; instr. nursing Alaska Meth. U., Anchorage, 1975-76; instr. nursing U. Alaska, Anchorage, 1976-77, asst. prof., 1977-81, assoc. prof., 1981—; bd. dirs. Anchorage Neighborhood Health Ctr., 1980—, vice chmn., 1981-82, chmn., 1982—; instr. basic cardiac life support Alaska Heart Assn., 1977—; mem. health task force Gov.'s Commn. on Status of Women, 1982—. Named Outstanding Instr., Sch. of Nursing, 1979, 83. Mem. Am. Nurses Assn., Am. Assn. Critical Care Nurses, Nat. League for Nursing, Am. Nurses Found., Am. Soc. for Circumpolar Health, Alaska Nurses Assn., Sigma Theta Tau. Roman Catholic. Contbr. articles to profl. jours. Home: SR Box 1561 R Anchorage AK 99507 Office: U Alaska 3221 Providence Dr Anchorage AK 99508

DE LAPPE, ELAINE FRANCES, aerospace co. exec.; b. Detroit, Apr. 19, 1939; d. Oliver and Essellyne Frances (VerHey) Gaathaug; B.S. in Bus. Adminstrn., Bob Jones U., 1962; M.B.A., Seattle U., 1977; m. Robert D. DeLappe, Dec. 1979. Compensation analyst Boeing Co., Seattle, 1970-73; manpower adminstr. salaried payrolls Boeing Aerospace Co., Seattle, 1973-76, manpower adminstr., word processing mgr., 1976-77, personnel mgr., 1977-82, bus. adminstr. Boeing Mgmt. Assn., 1982—. Mem. Word Processing Assn. N.W., Pacific N.W. Personnel Mgmt. Assn., Boeing Mgmt. Assn. (chpt. pres.). Republican. Clubs: Glen Acres Golf and Country, Kelmin Aviation, Boeing Employees Golf Assn. (pres. 1976-78). Home: 4423 193d St SE Issaquah WA 98027 Office: PO Box 3707 M/S 8K-95 Seattle WA 98124

DE LARIOS, DORA, artist; b. Los Angeles, Oct. 13, 1933; d. Elpidio and Concha (Martinez) De L. B.F.A. in Ceramics, U. So. Calif., 1957. Group exhbns. include: Renwick Gallery, Washington, 1977, Everson Mus., Syracuse, N.Y., 1977, Kohler Art Ctr., Sheboygan, Mich., 1977, Mus. Contemporary Crafts, N.Y.C., 1977, Craft and Folk Art Mus., Los Angeles, 1977, Indls. Mus. Art, 1978, Clay and Fiber exhibit, Taos, N.Mex., 1979, Craftsmanship U.S.A., Los Angeles County Mus., Syracuse Nat. Exhbn., 25 Years of Am. Art in Clay, Scripps Coll., Calif. Women in the Crafts, Craft and Folk Art Mus., Los Angeles, West Coast Clay Spectrum, Los Angeles, 1979, Mandell Gallery, Los Angeles, 1980; numerous other one person and group exhbns., numerous commd. works; mem. faculty U. So. Calif., 1959, UCLA, 1979. Address: 8635 W Washington Blvd Culver City CA 90230

DE LASSEN, JAN FOLMER, university administrator; b. Copenhagen, Jan. 25, 1934; came to U.S., 1980, naturalized, 1982; s. Ivar Christian and Edith (Christiansen) De L.; m. Magali Florelia Cumare, Sept. 23, 1972; children—Magalita, Jan Folmer, Jr., Michelle. B.S. in Math. (Gulf Oil Co. scholar), Tex. A&M U., 1959. Computer programmer Mobil Oil Co., Caracas, Venezuela, 1959-60; systems analysis, procedure supr. Gen. Electric of Venezuela, 1961-72; computer ops. mgr. Savoy Group, 1973-75; computer ops. mgr. ACO Group, Caracas, 1976-78; gen. mgr. Boulton Group, Caracas, 1981; asst. dir. computer services Brigham Young U., Provo, Utah, 1980—; cons., computer translations mgr. Computer Translations Inc., Orem, Utah, 1971—; cons. in field. Mem. Assn. System Mgmt. (past pres. Venezuela), Tex. Aggie Former Students Assn. Mormon. Office: 193 TMCB Brigham Young University Provo UT 84602

DE LAVEGA, ENRIQUE MICHAEL, sculptor; b. Los Angeles, June 13, 1935; s. Enrique Alejandro and Eileen Agnes (Shannon) deLaV.; m. Olga Leonor Barcenas, Jan. 19, 1963; m. Susan Mary Lebas, Nov. 9, 1973; children—Leonor, Henry John, Michael, Lisa, Christopher, Nicholas. A.A., Los Angeles City Coll., 1960; M.F.A., Los Angeles County Otis Art Inst., 1964. Apprentice, bronze foundry, 1962-64; art editor Larchmont Chronicle, Los Angeles, 1965-70; freelance sculptor, designer, photographer, Sherman Oaks, Calif., 1964—; archtl. sculpture for chs., parks, pub. bldgs.; executed sculpture, mosaics for St. Francis Assisi Ch., South Windsor, Conn., Nat. Shrine of Milenium, Doylestown, Pa., St. Jude's Chapel, Rochester (N.Y.) Mental Hosp., Little Sisters of the Poor, San Pedro, Calif., St. Hedwig Cemetery, N.J., churches Calif. Served with USAF, 1954-58. Mem. Artists Equity, Internat. Photography Soc. Republican. Roman Catholic. Home: 10965 Strathmore Dr A Los Angeles CA 90024 Office: 4507 Atoll Ave Sherman Oaks CA 91403

DE LAY, BABETTE WALES, public relations consultant, radio broadcaster; b. Buffalo, Sept. 5, 1954; d. Lee R. De Lay and Virginia W. Schive. B.S. in English and Behavioral Scis., Westminster Coll., B.S. in Bus. Communications, 1979. Social worker City Jail, Salt Lake City, 1975-78; exec. editor Rocky Mountain Woman Mag., Salt Lake City, 1976-79; mktg. coordinator Westminster Coll., Salt Lake City, 1979; dir. communications Great Salt Lake area United Way, 1980-82; radio broadcaster Sta. KRCL-FM 91, Salt Lake City, 1981—; pub. relations cons., Salt Lake City, 1979—. Recipient poster of the year award United Way Am., 1982. Mem. Utah Advt. Fedn. (gold, silver awards 1981), Internat. Assn. Bus. Communicators (best poster and merit in photography awards 1981), Pub. Relations Soc. Am. Office: Sta KRCL-FM 208 W 800 South Salt Lake City UT 84101

DELAYO, LEONARD JOSEPH, ednl. adminstr.; b. N.Y.C., Feb. 14, 1921; s. Anthony and Mary (Antonucci) D.; B.S., U. N.Mex., 1949; M.A., Columbia U., 1949; m. Helen Griffith, Apr. 25, 1946; children—Leonard, Donna Marie, Dianne. Tchr., Albuquerque Pub. Schs., 1949-50, prin., 1950-58; research assoc. Tchrs. Coll., Columbia U., N.Y.C., 1958; exec. sec. Tchrs. Assn. Baltimore County, Towson, Md., 1959-63; supt. pub. instrn. State of N.Mex., Santa Fe, 1963—. Chmn. govs. com. to investigate N.Mex. State Hosp. for Mental Defectives, 1956; mem. various gov.'s coms.; mem. Nat. Adv. Com. on Guidance and Counseling, 1969; chmn. Big Six Com. for Edn., 1972-73. Bd. mgrs. N.Mex. PTA, 1952-58; bd. dirs. Council of Chief State Sch. Officers, pres., 1972-73; bd. regents Am. Technol. U.; bd. dirs. St. Vincent's Hosp. Served with USMC, 1943-46. Mem. NEA, Am. Assn. Sch. Adminstrs, N.Mex. Edn. Assn., Phi Delta Kappa, Kappa Delta Pi. Club: Rotary. Home: 114 La Paloma Santa Fe NM 87501 Office: State Capitol Bldg Santa Fe NM 87501

DEL DUCA, CARMELA ROSE, educator, consultant; b. Greensburg, Pa., Mar. 26, 1935; d. Theodore Giovanni and Josephine (Spinella) D. B.A. in Art and Humanities, Holy Names Coll., 1966; M.A. in Spl. Edn. of Gifted, 1974; postgrad. U. La Verne, 1980—. Tchr. elem., secondary religious schs., 1956-69; tchr. spl. edn., coordinator gifted programs Rosemead Elem. Sch., West Covina Unified Sch. Dist., 1969-75; coordinator program for gifted, talented, asst. to dir. of curriculum in staff devel., coordinator Title IX program Paramount (Calif.) Unified Sch. Dist., 1976—; cons. to sch. dists. on gifted edn. Mem. NEA, World Future Soc., Assn. for Curriculum Devel. and Supervision, Calif. Assn. for Gifted, Nat. Assn. for Gifted, Paramount Tchrs. Assn. (Golden Apple award 1981, We Honor Ours award 1982), Delta Kappa Gamma, Kappa Delta Pi. Democrat. Roman Catholic. Co-author art curriculum for Archdiocese of San Francisco, 1968; author curriculum ideas for edn. mag. Home: 506 N Hamlin St Orange CA 92669 Office: 15110 California Ave Paramount CA 90723

DELEEUW, VICTOR JAY, educator; b. Long Beach, Calif., Mar. 3, 1946; s. John and Jeanette (Jongsma) DeL.; student Calvin Coll., 1964-66; B.A., Calif. State U., Long Beach, 1969, cert. athletic trainer, 1974. Asso. athletic trainer Calif. State U., Long Beach, 1967-69; lectr. phys. edn. U. Calif., Riverside, 1969—; cons. on athletic injuries to local high schs.; instr. edn. div. Loma Linda Hosp., 1977; cons. Sports Clinic, Riverside Orthopedic Therapy, 1980—. Mem. Sports Safety and Health Care Soc., S.W. Coll. Sports Medicine, Nat. Athletic Trainers Assn. Democrat. Calvinist. Home: 13311 Dilbeck Dr Sunnymead CA 92388 Office: 50M U Calif Riverside CA 92502 also 6863 Brockton Ave Riverside CA

DELEONE, SAMUEL ANGELO, printer; b. Phila., July 5, 1930; s. Dominick and Rose Carmella DeLeone; B.S., Northeastern U., 1965; m. Consiglia Moeckel, Sept. 11, 1954; children—Gina, Consiglia, Michael, Sam, Paul, Theresa, Dominick, Danielle. Salesman, Globe Ticket Co., Syracuse, N.Y., 1956-59, Boston, 1959-65; salesman Topflight Corp., York, Pa., 1965-68, San Jose, Calif., 1969-72; owner, pres. D & D Assos./The DeLeone Corp., Santa Clara, Calif., also Madras, Oreg., 1972—. Served with U.S. Army, 1951-54. Mem. Printing Industries of Am. Roman Catholic. Club: Elks. Office: PO Box 89 Madras Indsl Park Madras OR 97746 also 3000 Scott Blvd Suite 210 Santa Clara CA 95054

DEL GIUDICE, PAULA JEANNINE, editor; b. Elko Nev., Mar. 26, 1957; d. Paul Joseph and Ollie Mae (Cannon) Del G. B.S. in Bus. Adminstrn., U. Nev., 1983. Nat. advt. mgr. Times-News, Twin Falls, Idaho, 1978-79; sr. editor The Am. Shotgunner, Reno, 1979-82; Nev. state editor Western Outdoors mag., Costa Mesa, Calif., 1982—; free-lance writer, photographer. Mem. Nev. State Republican Central Com., 1981-82, Washoe County Rep. Central Com., 1979-83. Mem. Rocky Mountain Outdoor Writers and Photographers, Outdoor Writers Assn. Am., Future Bus. Leaders Am. Alumni Assn. (No. Nev. pres.). Roman Catholic. Contbr. to Field & Stream, DBI Books, Petersen's Deer Hunting Ann., Am. Shotgunner, Western Outdoors. Home: 4500 Mira Loma Dr Apt 99 Reno NV 89502

DELIGANIS, SAM GEORGE, hosp. adminstr., pharmacist; b. Lewiston, Idaho, Feb. 2, 1943; s. George Sam and Vasiliki (Kostouros) D.; B.Pharmacy, Wash. State U., 1966; M.B.A., U. Puget Sound, 1975; m. Vicki Kovakas, Nov. 5, 1967; children—Anastasia, Chryssa, Zoe, Stephanea. Sr. pharmacist FDA, Arlington, Va., 1966-68; chief pharmacist Meml. Hosp., Pullman, Wash., 1968-70; dir. pharmacy N.W. Hosp., Seattle, 1970-75, dir. pharmacy and materials handling, 1975—; instr. hosp. pharmacy Wash. State U., 1968-70, clin. instr. pharmacy, 1974—; clin. instr. pharmacy U. Wash., 1970—. Chmn. awards com. Wash. State Hosp. Safety Council, 1975. Served with USPHS, 1966-68. Recipient Outstanding Performance award FDA, 1968, Roche Hosp. Pharmacist Grant award Roche Labs., 1975, 79. Mem. Am., Wash. State (pres.) socs. hosp. pharmacists, Am., Wash. State pharm. assns., Kappa Psi (Asklepius Key award 1966). Greek Orthodox. Contbr. articles to pharmacy trade jours., 1973—; editor Pharmacy Reports, Notes, 1972—. Home: 1011 NW 190th St Seattle WA 98177 Office: 1550 N 115th St Seattle WA 98133

DELINE, ROBERT EDWIN, property management corporation executive; b. Denver, June 22, 1930; s. Edwin Francis and Leda Irene (Choquette) D.; B.S. in Mech. Engring., U. Notre Dame, 1952; m. Annabelle Monaghan, Sept. 12, 1953; children—Robert H., Thomas C. Asst. supt. J.H.-N.M. Monaghan Constrn. Co., Denver, 1955-57; estimator Monaghan & Smith Constrn., Co., Denver, 1957-60; gen. mgr. J.H.-N.M. Monaghan Farms Co., Denver, 1960-63; pres. Deline Constrn. Co., Broomfield, Colo., 1963-66, Monaghan Mgmt. Corp., Commerce City, Colo., 1966—; dir. Farmers Mktg. Assn., Denver, 1974-77. Served to lt j.g. USN, 1952-54. Mem. Nat. Assn. Wheat Growers, Nat. Assn. Real Estate Bd., N. Suburban Bd. Realtors, Airplane Owners and Pilots Assn. Republican. Roman Catholic. Club: Centennial Turf (dir. 1980—), (Denver); Coronado (Calif.) Yacht.

DELIS, NICHOLAS PETER, JR., produce dealer, investor; b. San Francisco, Nov. 25, 1949; s. Nick Peter and Pearl S. (Pallios) D.; m. Stephanie A. Morf, Aug. 27, 1972; children—Nicholas III, Katina. B.A. in Mktg., San Francisco State U., 1972. Mktg. and sales dir. Nick Delis Co., Inc., Burlingame, Calif., 1967-75, pres., 1975—, chief exec. officer, 1983—; chief exec. officer Nicholas Peter Delis Investments, 1976—. Mem. Save the Redwood League (life), Nat. Rifle Assn. (life), Save San Francisco Bay Assn. Republican. Greek Orthodox. Club: Pan Cretan Assn. Am. (San Francisco). Office: 851 Burlway Rd Suite 502 Burlingame CA 94010

DELLA, RICHARD P., oceanographic cons.; b. San Francisco, Aug. 28, 1951; s. Raymond P. and Ruth E. Della; B.S., Oreg. State U., 1973; M.S., U. Calif., Berkeley, 1975. Sea Grant research asst. and asso., U. Calif., Berkeley, 1973-74, research engr., 1974; oceanographic engr., project mgr. Tetra Tech, Inc., Pasadena, Calif., 1975-76; pres., chmn. bd. Meridian Ocean Systems, Inc., San Pedro, Calif., 1978—. Mem. Marine Tech. Soc., Internat. Oceanographic Found., Inst. of Navigation. Club: King Harbor Yacht. Developer precision navigation systems for offshore and subsurface navigation, methodologies to evaluate structural condition of underwater structures. Office: 302 W 5th St Suite 201 San Pedro CA 90731

DELLA-DORA, DELMO, educator; b. Detroit, Jan. 20, 1926; s. Vittorio and Rosina (Panicacci) D.-D.; B.S., U. Mich., 1947; M.Ed., Wayne State U., 1952, Ed.D., 1960; married; children—Marilyn, Diane, Joan, Denise. Sci. tchr. St. Clair and River Rouge, Mich., 1947-52; prin., dir. instrn., Erie, Mich., 1952-55: curriculum cons., dep. supt. Wayne County Intermediate Sch. Dist., 1955-63; asso. supt. Dearborn (Mich.) public schs., 1963-65: prof. Eastern Mich. U. on Assignment U.S. AID to Somali Republic, 1965-67; dir. planning Mich.-Ohio Regional Edn. Lab., 1968-69; with Office of Sch. Decentralization, dir. Magnet Sch. Plan, Detroit public schs., 1970-71; prin. Mill Valley (Calif.) Middle Sch., 1971-73; prof. dept. tchr. edn. Calif. State U., Hayward, 1973—, chmn. dept., 1973-78, dir. tchr. corps project, 1979—, assoc. dean Sch. Edn., 1981—; cons. sch. dists Mid-West and Calif.; mem. state task force Calif. Sch. Improvement Comm., 1977-78, steering com. for regional service program Far West Regional Edn. Lab., Calif. State Dept. Edn., 1978-79. Served with USN, 1944-46. Mem. Nat. Assn. for Supervision and Curriculum Devel. (nat. exec. council 1970-72, nat. pres. 1975-76, dir. project on self-directed learning 1977-80, nat. rev. council 1979-83), Nat. Assn. Secondary Sch. Prins., Calif. Curriculum Forum (governing bd. 1976-79, chmn. 1979), United Profs. of Calif. (pres. Hayward local 1980-81), Phi Delta Kappa. Democrat. Pres. Center for Self-Directed Learning, 1977—; contbr. articles to profl. publs. Home: 25115 Oakridge Ct Hayward CA 94541 Office: School Education California State Univ Hayward CA 94542

DELLAMAS, LLOYD RICHARD, city manager; b. Santa Maria, Calif., Aug. 4, 1940; s. Victor Lloyd and Delya Elvanore (Freeman) deL.; m. Caroline Ruth Cox, Nov. 5, 1967; children—Ingrid Dionne, Chelsea Denise; B.S., Calif. State U.-San Diego, 1963; student Calif. State Colls. and Univs., 1975-76. Adminstrv. asst. City of San Diego, 1963-66; sr. asst. to city mgr. City of Torrance (Calif.), 1966-68; city mgr. City of Woodlake (Calif.), 1968-71; city adminstr. City of Lawndale (Calif.), 1971-76; city mgr. City of Monterey Park (Calif.), 1976—. Bd. dirs. Calif. Redevel. Agy., 1981—; asst. chmn. West San Gabriel Valley Manpower Consortium, 1981—; mem. pub. resources adv. bd. Calif. State U.-Los Angeles, 1980—; advisor Nat. Hispanic Field Service Program, 1980—. Mem. League Calif. Cities (mem. safety adv. com. Los Angeles div.), Internat. City Mgmt. Assn., Am. Mgmt. Assn., Urban Land Inst., San Gabriel Valley City Mgrs. Assn. Office: 320 W Newmark Ave Monterey Park CA 91754

DELLAVALLE, NATALE BENEDETTO (NAT), agrl. cons.; b. Madera, Calif., Dec. 9, 1939; s. Alfred and Juanita Grace (Wilson) D.; B.S., Calif. State U.-San Luis Obispo, 1961; m. Ann Margret McMurray, Dec. 29, 1958; children—Mary Janet, Peter Alfred, Angela Grace, Joan Carolyn. Agriculturist, Coit Ranch, Inc., Mendota, Calif., 1961-63; agronomist, lab. technician Brown & Bryant Inc., Shafter, Calif., 1963-68; mgr. Lab. Service Div., T-M-T Chem. Co., Inc., Five Points, Calif., 1968-78; pres., mgr. Dellavalle Lab., Inc., Fresno, Calif., 1978—; mem. Calif. Nematode Diagnosis Adv. Commn. Cert. profl. soil scientist, profl. agronomist. Mem. Soil Sci. Soc. Am., Am. Soc. Agronomy (dir. Calif. chpt.), Council on Soil Testing and Plant Analysis, Soil Conservation Soc. Am., Calif. Assn. Agrl. Labs. (past pres.), Council for Agrl. Sci. and Tech., Am. Mgmt. Assn. Office: 1910 W McKinley St Suite 110 Fresno CA 93728

DELLINGER, (SHIRLEY) KYN, tax and fin. planner; b. Gastonia, N.C., Sept. 15, 1949; d. Kenneth E. and Myrtle R. (Hooper) D.; B.A., Meredith Coll., Raleigh, N.C., 1970; M.A. (Rotary fellow), U. Geneva, 1972. Ptnr., Mar-Kyn Enterprises, San Francisco, 1976—; v.p. Bay Area Tax Cons., Inc., San Francisco, 1978—. Cert. fin. planner; enrolled to practice before IRS. Mem. Women Entrepreneurs, Assn. Enrolled Agts., Internat. Assn. Finl Planners (v.p. San Francisco), Nat. Assn. Security Dealers. Republican. Methodist. Office: 1150 Bayhill Dr Suite 111 San Bruno CA 94066

DELLUMS, RONALD VERNIE, congressman; b. Oakland, Calif., Nov. 24, 1935; A.A., Oakland City Coll., 1958; B.A., San Francisco State Coll., 1960; M.S.W., U. Calif., 1962; m. Leola Roscoe Higgs; 3 children. Psychiat. social worker Calif. Dept. Mental Hygiene, 1962-64; program dir. Bayview Community Center, San Francisco, 1964-65; from assoc. dir. to dir. Hunters Point Youth Opportunity Center, 1965-66; planning cons. Bay Area Social Planning Council, 1966-67; dir. concentrated employment program San Francisco Econ. Opportunity Council, 1967-68; sr. cons. Social Dynamics, Inc., 1968-70; mem. 92d-98th Congresses from 8th Calif. dist. Lectr. San Francisco State Coll., U. Calif., Berkeley. Mem. Berkeley City Council, 1967-71. Served with USMCR, 1954-56. Democrat. Home: Washington DC Office: 2136 Rayburn House Office Bldg Washington DC 20515

DELMAR, EVELYN EMAN, public relations agency executive; b. N.Y.C., Dec. 31, 1949; d. John and Gay (Simon) Eman; m. Larry Edward Delmar, Nov. 26, 1982. Student NYU, 1975-76, Baruch Coll., 1981-82. Asst. mgr. Vanderbilt Athletic Club, N.Y.C., 1967-68; pub. relations mgr. DEC Enterprises, Inc., N.Y.C., 1968-73; exec. interviewer Dun & Bradstreet, Inc., N.Y.C., 1974; pub. relations rep. Parsons & Whittemore, Inc., N.Y.C., 1974-77; corp. mgr. pub. relations NEC Am., Inc., Melville, N.Y., 1977-82; pres. Perception Plus, Colorado Springs, Colo., 1982—. Recipient Merit cert. Publicity Club of N.Y., 1976-77. Mem. Colorado Springs Conv. and Visitors Bur., Internat. Assn. Bus. Communicators, Pub. Relations Soc. Am., Women's Exchange Network Colorado Springs (editor newsletter 1983). Contbg. editor: PR Essay, 1976-77; composer popular songs. Office: Perception Plus 559 E Pikes Peak Ave Suite 307 Colorado Springs CO 80903

DEL MISSIER, RICHARD JEROME, marine furniture mfg. co. exec.; b. Seattle, May 11, 1931; s. Peter F. and Lucy (Roccia) Del M.; B.S. in Civil Engring., U. Wash., Seattle, 1953; m. Constance E. Galvagno, July 11, 1969; children—Deanne, Peter, Sarah, Anthony. From engr. to pres. Acme Iron Works Inc., Seattle, 1955-70; owner, pres. Tri-Way Industries, Inc., Seattle, 1970—. Bd. dirs., past pres. Seattle Hearing and Speech Center. Served with AUS, 1953-55. Recipient Salute to Industry award Seattle-King County Econ. Devel. Council, 1974. Mem. Am. Soc. Naval Engrs., Seattle C. of C. (pres.'s club). Republican. Roman Catholic. Club: Southcenter Rotary (Seattle). Office: 600 Andover Park E Seattle WA 98188

DEL MONICO, PATRICIA, executive, lawyer; b. Schenectady, June 20, 1943; d. Daniel Michael and Margaret (Di Sorbo) Del M. B.A., Pa. State U., 1965; M.S.W., UCLA, 1969, M.B.A., 1983; J.D., Whittier Coll., 1979. Admitted to Calif. bar, 1979. Mental retardation counselor Children's Hosp., Los Angeles, 1969-71; coordinator mental retardation services St. John's Hosp., Santa Monica, Calif., 1971-73; dir. community affairs Harbor Devel. Disabilities Fedn., Torrance, Calif., 1973-78, exec. dir., 1978—. Recipient awards Am. Jurisprudence Assn., 1976, 77; U.S. Child Welfare scholar, 1969. Mem. ABA, State Bar Calif., Los Angeles County Bar Assn., Am. Assn. Mental Deficiency, Calif. Assn. Regional Ctrs. Home: 2815 Greenfield Ave Los Angeles CA 90064 Office: Harbor Devel Disabilities Fedn 21231 Hawthorne Blvd Torrance CA 90503

DELOACH, ROBERT EDGAR, business executive; b. Daytona Beach, Fla., Jan. 6, 1939; s. Ollie Newman and Sally Gertrude (Schrowder) DeL. Student U. Alaska-Anchorage, 1967-69, Alaska Meth. U., 1970, Pacific Luth. U., 1972. Lic. elec. engr. and adminstr., Alaska, 1979; lic. pvt. pilot. Chmn. bd. Alaska Stagecraft, Inc., Anchorage; pres. BG Systems Co., BG Tax & Acctg., Inc., The Electric Doctor, Inc.; former pres. Coastal Electronics, Inc.; former owner-mgr. Bargain Towne, Anchorage. Active Anchorage Community Theatre, Anchorage Theater Guild. Mem. Assn. Ind. Accts., Internat. Assn. Theatrical Stage Employees and Moving Picture Machine Operators U.S. (pres. local 770). Home: 1207 W 47th Ave Anchorage AK 99503 Office: 570 W 53d St Anchorage AK 99502

DELOGU, GAETANO, symphony music dir., condr.; b. Messina, Sicily, 1934; s. Francesco Maria and Maria (Toraldo) D.; grad. U. Catania, 1958; m. Teresa Deluca, Dec. 29, 1960; 1 son, Francesco. Permanent condr. Teatro Massimo di Palermo (Italy), 1975-78; music dir. Denver Symphony Orch., 1978—; guest condr. numerous orchs., including N.Y. Philharmonic, London Philharmonic, others; recs. with London Philharmonic and Czech Philharmonic. Winner Young Condr.'s Competition, Florence, Dimitri Mitropoulos Internat. Competition, N.Y.C., 1968. Roman Catholic. Office: Denver Symphony Orch 1245 Champa St Denver CO 80204

DELONG, PALMER BUNE, civil engr.; b. Ogden, Utah, Mar. 16, 1918; s. Joseph Edmund and Josephine Elizabeth (Bune) DeL.; B.S. in Civl Engring., Utah State U., 1941; m. Rhoda Larson, Oct. 9, 1940; children—Robert Palmer, Alice DeLong Cottle. With U.S. Bur. Reclamation, 1941-75, successively area engr., project constrn. engr., regional planning engr., project mgr. Central Utah project, asst. regional dir., water resource devel. planning and cons. Upper Colo. Basin and Great Basin (Utah, Wyo., Colo., Nev., Ariz., N.Mex., Idaho); profl. cons. Central Utah Water Conservancy Dist., Uintah Water Conservancy Dist., others, 1975—. Recipient Meritorious Service award U.S. Dept. Interior, 1972. Mem. Nat. Soc. Profl. Engrs. Mormon. Home: 721 W Sunny Ln Orem UT 84057

DELONG, WILLIAM JAMES, state senator, business executive; b. Albany, N.Y., Mar. 27, 1930; s. Harry and Pearl Smith (Sickles) DeL.; m. Loretta Strzelecki, 1977; children—Peter, Linda Shackelford, William R., James R., Lee, Robin. Student U. Md., two years. Vice pres. Merodias Constrn. Co., Tucson, 1978, Automated Printing & Mailing, Inc., Tucson, 1979—; gen. mgr. Complete Personnel Service, Tucson, 1978-79, Today's Bus. Mag., Tucson, 1979—; owner Complete Trophy Ctr., Tucson, 1979—; mem. Ariz. Ho. of Reps., from 1981; now Ariz. State Senate. Chief dep. county treas. Pima County, Ariz., 1969-70; city clk. Tucson, 1971-72, manpower dir., 1972-73, asst. city mgr., 1973. Served to maj., JAGC, U.S. Army, 1947-68; Korea, Vietnam. Decorated Legion of Merit, 6 Army Commendation Medals. Mem. Big Bros. (dir.), Council State Govts. Republican. Club: Catalina Midtown Optimist (pres. 1976). Home: 551 S Brighton Ln Tucson AZ 85711 Office: Arizona State Senate Phoenix AZ 85007*

DEL POZO, JOSE LUIS, real estate and resort executive; b. Mexico City, Dec. 6, 1943; s. Jose and Josefina (Austin) Del P.; came to U.S., 1960, naturalized, 1966; B.A., UCLA, 1971; M.B.A., Harvard U., 1973; m. Elizabeth; children—Emilio, Antonio. Resort mgr. Sea Pines Co., Humacao, P.R., 1973-75; regional analyst N.W., ARA Services, Los Angeles, 1975-76, gen. mgr., San Diego, 1976-79, regional mgr. So. Calif., 1979-82; corp. real estate/facilities coordinator Wickes Cos. Inc., San Diego, 1982—; gen. mgr. Bajamar Resort, Ensenada, Mex. Budgeting vice chmn. United Way; trustee Mexican and Am. Found. Served with U.S. Army, 1962-65. Republican. Clubs: Harvard Bus., I.D. (San Diego). Home: 2597 Pinewood St Del Mar CA 92014 Office: 1010 2d Ave San Diego CA 92101

DE LUCA, JOSEPH O., corporate risk manager; b. Long Beach, Calif., Jan. 14, 1940; s. Joseph Daniel and Mary Amelia DeL.; A.B. in Philosophy and Logic, San Diego State U., 1961; postgrad. U. Santa Clara, 1977; M.A. in Mgmt., Sonoma State U., 1980; m. Jacqueline Lee Ross, Aug. 30, 1963; children—Jeanne-Marie, Caren-Elise. Health and safety technician U. Calif., 1964-69; div. safety and security dir. Honeywell, San Diego, 1969-72 corp. safety mgr. Memorex Corp., Santa Clara, Calif., 1972-73; corp. safety mgr. Signetics, Sunnyvale, Calif., 1974; loss control rep. Foremost-McKesson, San Francisco, 1974-77, corp. mgr. safety, 1977-80, corp. mgr. risk control, 1980-81; mgr. corp. ins. Wash. Pub. Power Supply System, Richland, 1981—; mem. Calif. gov.'s select com. on safety and health curriculum rev., 1972-73, State of Calif. Adv. Com. on Occupational Carcinogens, 1975. Served as officer USNR, 1962-64. Cert. workers' compensation self-ins. adminstr., safety profl. Mem. Am. Mgmt. Assn., Nat. Mgmt. Assn., Am. Soc. Safety Engrs., Calif. Mfrs. Assn. Safety and Health Commn. (charter), Calif. Mfrs. Assn. Workers' Compensation Commn., Risk and Ins. Mgmt. Soc., Am. Pub. Power Assn. (ins. com.), Atomic Indsl. Forum (ins. com.). Contbr. articles to publs.; instr. in self-def. and Aikido Dan-Rank; qualified explosives handler; qualified light and heavy duty rescue; instr. first aid and CPR and water safety; qualified shelter mgr. and radiol. def. team leader CD. Office: 6030 W 10th Pl Kennewick WA 99336

DE LUCCIA, EMIL ROBERT, engr.; b. Brighton, Mass., Sept. 20, 1904; s. Emil James and Edna Laura (Hewes) de L.; B.S. in Civil Engring., Mass. Inst. Tech., 1927; m. Margaret McCutcheon, Jan. 16, 1932; children—Margaret Crichton, Jane Hewes. Surveyman and transitman Met. Water Supply Commn., Enfield, Mass., 1927-29; engr. designer Stone and Webster Engring. Corp., 1929-31; engr. insp., designer U.S. Engr. Office, Charleston, W. Va., 1931-33; asso. engr. and chief of design sect., U.S. Engr. Office, Huntington, W. Va., 1933-38, with Fed. Power Commn., 1938-51; v.p., chief engr. Pacific Power & Light Co., 1952-66, sr. v.p., 1966-69; pres. Oreg. Grad. Center, 1969-72; cons. engr., 1969—; v.p. Overseas Adv. Assos., Inc., 1974—; sr. engr. cons. on dams and hydroelectric projects, 1938-40, chief, power supply br. Nat. Def. Power staff, 1940-41; asst. dir. Nat. Def. Power staff and asst. chief Bur. of Elec. Engring. (also cons. on power for O.P.M. and W.P.B), chief Bur. of Power, 1944—. U.S. del. Internat. Conf. on High Dams, Stockholm, 1948, Internat. Conf. on High Tension Elec. Systems, Paris, 1948; chief U.S. delegation Internat. Conf. High Tension Lines, Paris, 1950; U.S. del. World Power Conf., London, Eng., 1950; chmn. Internat. Niagara Falls Engring. Bd.; U.S. ofcl. Negotiation Treaty with Can. for division of water at Niagara Falls; cons. to UN, Japan, 1961, AEC, Nat. Security Resources Bd., Vietnam govt., Saudi Arabia, 1970—; mgmt. and engring. adviser Vietnam Power Co., 1970—; chmn. Internat. Passamaquoddy Bd. Engrs.; chmn. U.S. Com. on Large Dams. Served with R.O.T.C., Mass. Inst. Tech., 2d lt, O.R.C., 1927; from capt. to lt. col, AUS, 1942-45; with SHEAF, 1944; lt. col. Res. (ret.). Mem. Tech. Indsl. Disarmament Com. for German Elec. Power Industry. Decorated Legion of Merit, Am. Victory Medal, World War II; Medal of Merit (South Vietnam); named Oreg. Engr. of Year, 1962. Registered profl. engr., D.C., Oreg. Fellow IEEE, ASCE; mem. Soc. Mil. Engrs. (dir.; Goethals Medal award 1963), A.I.M., V.F.W., Am. Geophys. Union, Am. Legion, Internat. Assn. High Tension Lines, Internat. Hydraulic Research. Mason (Shriner). Clubs: Army-Navy Country (Arlington, Va.); Cosmos (Washington); Arlington, University, Waverly Country (Portland). Home and office: 7225 E Lake Ct Wilsonville OR 97070

DEMARCHI, ERNEST NICHOLAS, aerospace engineering administrator; b. Lafferty, Ohio, May 31, 1939; s. Ernest Costante and Lena Marie (Cireddu) D.; B.M.E., Ohio State U., 1962; M.S. in Engring., UCLA, 1969; m. Carolyn Marie Tracz, Sept. 17, 1960; children—Daniel Ernest, John David, Deborah Marie. With Space div. Rockwell Internat., Downey, Calif., 1962—, engring. mgr., mem. Apollo, Skylab and Apollo-Soyuz missions design team in electronic and elec. systems, mem. mission support team for all Apollo and Skylab manned missions,

1962-74, mem. Space Shuttle design team charge elec. systems equipment, 1974-77, in charge Orbiter Data Processing System, 1977-81, in charge Orbiter Ku Band Communication and Radar System, 1981—. Active, YMCA Indian Guide program, 1969-74, bd. dirs., 1971-74; vol. instr. community program of tech. tng. for high-sch. students, 1973-78; youth athletics coach, 1975-76; pres. Little League, 1976-78; bd. dirs. high sch. athletic boosters club, 1980—. Recipient Apollo Achievement award NASA, 1969, Apollo 13 Sustained Excellent Performance award, 1970, Astronaut Personal Achievement Snoopy award, 1971; Exception-al Service award Rockwell Internat., 1972, Outstanding Contbn. award, 1976; NASA ALT award, 1979; Shuttle Astronaut Snoopy award, 1982; Pub. Service Group Achievement award NASA, 1982; registered profl. engr., Ohio. Mem. ASME (assoc.), Varsity O Alumni Assn. Home: 25311 Maximus St Mission Viejo CA 92691 Office: 25311 Maximus St Mission Viejo CA

DEMARCO, RALPH JOHN, real estate developer; b. N.Y.C., Mar. 22, 1924; s. Frank and Mary (Castriota) DeM.; B.A., Claremont Men's Coll., 1956; m. Arlene Gilbert, July 1, 1945; children—Sheryl DeMarco Grahn, Stephen, Laura DeMarco Wilson. Asso. John B. Kilroy Co., Riverside, Calif., 1960-64, also mgr. operations Riverside, San Bernardino counties, 1960-64; v.p. Marcus W. Meairs Co., 1964-67; pres. Diversified Properties, Inc., Riverside, 1967-72; v.p. Downey Savs. & Loan Assn. (Calif.), 1972-75; exec. v.p. DSL Service Co., 1972-75; pres. Interstate Shopping Centers, Inc., Santa Ana, Calif., 1975—. Mem. City of Riverside Planning Commn., 1955-59, Airport Commn., 1960-70; mem. Urban Land Inst. Served to 1st lt. USAF, 1942-45. Mem. Internat. Council Shopping Centers. Clubs: Monarch Bay, Laguna Niguel Tennis. Home: 23022 Java Sea Dr South Laguna CA 92677 Office: 1505 E 17th St Suite 202 Santa Ana CA 92701

DEMAREE, JULIE ANNE, optometrist; b. Chester, Mont., Sept. 27, 1954; d. Irvin George and Delores Elizabeth (Romain) Hutchison; m. Thomas Lee Demaree, June 10, 1976. B.A., U. Mont., 1975; B.S., Pacific U., 1981, O.D., 1983. Editorial asst. Liberty County Times, Chester, Mont., 1972-75; tchr. sci. Powder River Dist. High Sch., Broadus, Mont., 1975-79; practice optometry, Portland, Oreg., 1983—; low vision externship Lighthouse of N.Y. Assn. for Blind, 1983. AAUW scholar, 1974; Mont. State U. System High Honors scholar, 1972-75. Mem. Am. Optometric Assn., Beta Sigma Kappa, Phi Theta Upsilon. Home: 2334 26th Ave Forest Grove OR 97116

DE MASSA, JESSIE G., librarian; B.S. in Journalism, Temple U., Phila.; M.L.S., San Jose (Calif.) State U., 1967; postgrad. U. Okla., Norman, U. So. Calif., others. Tchr., Palo Alto (Calif.) Unified Sch. Dist., 1966; librarian Antelope Valley Joint Union High Sch. Dist., Lancaster, Calif., 1966-68, ABC Unified Sch. Dist., Artesia, Calif., 1968-72; dist. librarian Tehachapi (Calif.) Unified Sch. Dist., 1972-81, also media specialist; free lance writer, 1981—. Fellow Internat. Biog. Assn.; mem. Calif. Media and Library Educators Assn., Calif. Assn. Sch. Librarians (exec. council), AAUW (bull. editor, asso. editor state bull., chmn. publicity, 1955-68). Contbr. articles to profl. jours. Home: 9951 Garrett Circle Huntington Beach CA 92646

DEMATTIES, NICK F., artist, educator; b. Honolulu, Oct. 19, 1939; s. Ernest and Florence Adele (Sutherland) deM.; children—Seth Demian, Nicholas II. B.A., Calif. State U. 1964; M.S. in Visual Design, Ill. Inst. Tech., 1967. Printmaking instr. Ctr. for Artists and Students, Paris, 1964-65, Oxbow summer sch., Saugutuck, Mich., 1966; teaching asst. Ill. Inst. Tech. Inst. Design, Chgo., 1966-67; printmaking instr. San Diego State U., 1967 69; asst. prof. printmaking Mt. St. Mary's Coll., Los Angeles 1969-70; founder, dir., instr. Pacific N.W. Graphics Workshop, 1970-75; asst. prof. Albion Coll., Mich., 1973-74; asst. prof. Ariz. State U., Tempe, 1974-77, assoc. prof., 1977—; one-man shows: Oreg. Museum Art, Eugene, 1976, Woodward Gallery, Scottsdale, Ariz., 1976, Smithsonian Inst., Washington, 1976, Scottsdale Ctr. for Arts, 1978, Departemento de Bellas Artres, Guadalajara, Mexico, 1978, Phoenix Art Mus., 1980, U. Houston, 1980, Suzanne Brown Gallery, Scottsdale, 1981; group shows: XXII Am. Drawing Biennial, Norfolk, Va., 1967, 9th Nat. Exhbn., Prints, Drawings, Okla. Art Ctr., Oklahoma City, 1967, Boston Printmakers, Boston Mus., 1969, San Diego South Eight Exhibit, Fine Arts Gallery, 1970, Small Image Show, Los Angeles State Coll., 1970, Portland (Oreg.) Mus. Art, 1974, 10th, 11th, 13th, 14th, 15th Southwestern Invitationals, Yuma (Ariz.) Art Ctr. and Phoenix Coll., 1975, 76, 79, 80, 81, 16th Bradley Nat. Print and Drawing Exhbn., Peoria, Ill., 1977, Biennial '77 Phoenix Art Mus., 1977, Cheney Cowles Home Mus. Art, Spokane, Wash., 1977, Parada del Sol invitational Scottsdale (Ariz.) Ctr. for Arts, 1979, State of the Print touring exhibit of Mid Am. Art Alliance, Kansas City, Mo.; Brigham Young U., Provo, Utah, 1980, two-man show at Honey Sharp Gallery, Lenox, Mass., 1980, Gallery 200, No. Ill. U., 1980, Priebe Art Gallery, U. Wis.-Oshkosh; Copper Village Arts and Mus., Anaconda, Mont., 1981, Phoenix Art Mus., 1981, Custer County Art Ctr., Miles City, Mont., 1981; represented in permanent collections: Los Angeles County Mus. Art, Bklyn. Mus. Art, Free Library Phila., Phoenix Art Mus., Cabinet des Estampes, Bibliotheque National de Paris, Library of Congress, San Francisco Mus. Modern Art, Columbia U., U. Chgo., Sheldon Meml. Art Gallery, Omaha, SUNY-Buffalo, Brown U., U. Iowa, Am. Republic Ins. Co., Des Moines, Lowe Art Ctr., Northwestern U., Albion Coll.; juror for printmakers, Oreg. competition, 1973. Recipient continental art award 5th ann. All Calif. Print Exhbn., Los Angeles, 1968; Oreg. Arts Commn. Matching Fellowship grantee, 1972; Western States Arts Found. Printmaking fellow, 1979. Home: 2337 N 10th St Phoenix AZ 85006 Office: Sch Art Ariz State U Tempe AZ 85251

DEMAY, PETER, engineering company executive; b. Bayonne, N.J., Mar. 11, 1926; s. Samuel and Theodosia (Korbelak) D.; m. Olga Kurylo, July 14, 1951; 1 son, Darrin Peter. B.S. in Mech. Engring., U. Mich., 1952; M.S., N.J. Inst. Tech., 1962. Chief project mgr. Exxon Research Engring. Co., 1952-72; v.p. project mgmt. Alyeskia Pipeline Service Co., Anchorage, 1972-77; sr. v.p. ops. Resource Scis. Corp., Tulsa, 1977-78; pres. Williams Bros. Engring. Co., Tulsa, 1978-80; sr. v.p. Fluor Engrs. Inc., Irvine Calif., 1980—. Served with U.S. Army, 1944-46. Office: 3333 Michelson Drive Irvine CA 92730

DEMELLO, STEVEN WAYNE, health planning cons.; b. Oakland, Calif., Nov. 6, 1954; s. Melvin Joseph and Barbara Jean (Correia) DeM.; B.A. in Econs., Claremont Men's Coll., 1977; M.B.A., U. Chgo., 1977. Adminstrv. resident Swedish Covenant Hosp., Chgo., 1976-77; asst. adminstr. profl. services Samuel Merritt Hosp., Oakland, Calif., 1977-80; health planning cons. H.O.M. Group, Inc., San Francisco, 1980—; mem. adj. faculty health services mgmt. program Golden Gate U., San Francisco, 1978—. Service grantee USPHS, 1976-77. Mem. Exec. Assn. Oakland, Alameda-Contra Costa Health Systems Agy., Am. Hosp. Assn. Home: 1001 Warfield Ave Apt 102 Oakland CA 94610 Office: 790 Market St Suite 400 San Francisco CA 94102

DEMETRESCU, MIHAI CONSTANTIN, computer company executive, scientist; b. Bucharest, Romania, May 23, 1929; s. Dan and Alina (Dragosescu) D.; M.E.E., Poly. Inst. of U. Bucharest, 1954; Ph.D., Romanian Acad. Sci., 1957; m. Agnes Halas, May 25, 1969; 1 son, Stefan. Came to U.S., 1966. Prin. investigator Research Inst. Endocrinology Romanian Acad. Sci., Bucharest, 1958-66; research fellow dept. anatomy UCLA, 1966-67; faculty U. Calif.-Irvine, 1967—, asst. prof. dept. physiology, 1971-78, asso. researcher, 1978-79, asso. clin. prof., 1979—; v.p. Resonance Motors, Inc., Monrovia, Calif., 1972—; pres. Neurometrics, Inc., Irvine, Calif., 1978-82; pres. Lasergraphics Inc., Irvine, 1982—. Mem. com. on hon. degrees U. Calif.-Irvine, 1970-72. Postdoctoral fellow UCLA, 1966. Mem. AAAS, Am. Physiol. Soc., IEEE (sr.), Soc. Neurosci. Contbr. articles to profl. jours. Patentee in field. Home: 17761 Palmento Way Irvine CA 92715

DEMETRIADES, ANTHONY, mechanical engineering educator; b. Athens, Greece, June 23, 1930; s. Theodore and Vassiliki (Tsafka) D., m. Donna Lawrence, July 20, 1957; children—Theodore, Lawrence, Donald. A.B., Colgate U., 1951; M.S., U. Minn., 1953; Ph.D., Calif. Inst. Tech., 1958. Sr. research fellow Calif. Inst. Tech., Pasadena, 1958-63; supr. fluid mechanics sect. Ford Aeronutronic, Newport Beach, Calif., 1963-79; prof. mech. engring. Mont. State U., Bozeman, 1979; cons. in field. Pres. Laguna Beach Civic League, 1970-71, bd. dirs., 1968-72. Mem. AIAA, Am. Phys. Soc. Contbr. articles to profl. jours.; patentee in field. Home: 147 Hitching Post Rd Bozeman MT 59715 Office: Dept Mech Engring Montana State U Bozeman MT 59717

DE MEY, MARTHA, actor, artist, author; b. Columbus, Ohio, Nov. 16, 1932; d. Charles Frederic and Amelia Webster (Smith) de Mey; student (Kinsmen Trust scholar) Roedean Sch. for Girls, Brighton, Eng., 1949-50; B.A., Smith Coll., 1954; m. John Warner Clow, Apr. 10, 1956 (div. 1982); children—Eric de Mey, Gregory Vincent, Amelia Bayley, Guy Rowan, Louise Crankshaw. Prodn. asst. advt. Macy's Calif., San Francisco, 1954-56; artist adv. Joseph Magnin Co., San Francisco, 1956-57; free lance artist and writer, 1957—; choreographer Jr. Theater of Marin, 1976, asst. dir., 1977; playground designer. Art cons. and dir. Marin County (Calif.) Dist Atty. election, Presdl. election 1964, Municipal ct. judge election; ofcl. artist Marin Republican Sponsors, 1974-75; vol. Ross Sch. Yearbook adviser, 1975-78, sci. lectr. on Immanuel Velikovsky, 1974—; actor, stage mgr., asst. dir. Ross Valley Players, 1978—; actor, stage mgr. C.A.S.T. Prodns., 1981-82; actor, lighting asst. Coll. of Marin, 1980-82; actor Mill Valley Ctr. Performing Arts, 1980-82; co-chmn. Bicentennial Com.; vice chmn. Marin County Libertarian Party, 1979. Mem. Mill Valley Outdoor Art Club, Marin County Smith Club (pres. 1960-63), Seven Coll. Conf. (pres. 1961-63). Author: Starbreed, 1970. Home: Box 543 Ross CA 94957

DE MICHELE, O. MARK, utility company executive; b. 1934. B.S., Syracuse U., 1955. Vice pres. L. M. Harvey Co. Inc., 1955-61; v.p. pub. reins. Niagara Mohawk Power Corp., 1961-78; v.p. corp. reins. Ariz. Pub. Service Co., Phoenix, 1978, exec. v.p. customer employment and corp. reins., 1981-83, pres., chief operating officer, 1983—. Office: Ariz Pub Service Co Inc 411 N Central Ave PO Box 21666 Phoenix AZ 85036*

DEMING, STEPHEN ARTHUR, civil engr.; b. Kansas City, Mo., Mar. 11, 1906; s. Arthur W. and Anna L. (Groh) D.; B.S., U. Kans., 1932, P.E., 1935; M.S., U. Ariz., 1963, Ph.D., 1971; m. Alma Lorene Burkholder, July 18, 1936. Various positions Mo. State Hwy. Commn., 1926-38; civil engr. various cos., 1938-46, 46-51; chief field engr. Stearns-Roger Mfg. Co., Denver, 1951-53; civil engr. Joseph L. Pohl, Nevada, Mo., 1953-54, W. M. Spann, Kansas City, Mo., 1954, Freese & Nichols, Ft. Worth, Tex., 1954-55, Howard, Needles, Tammen & Bergendoff, 1955; chief field engr. Stearns-Roger Mfg. Co., Denver, 1955-59; civil engr. Tuttle-Ayers-Woodward Engring. Co., Kansas City, Mo., 1959-60; design engr. Ariz. Hwy. Dept., Phoenix, 1964-65; constrn. engr. Stearns-Roger Corp., Denver, Sierrita-Duval Corp., 1967-68; design project engr. Wheeler, Petterson, Coffeen, Inc., engrs., Tucson, 1971-72; cons. engr. Southwest-Ward Engring. Co., Phoenix, 1969-72, Duval Corp., 1975-76; involved in ceramics and solar energy, 1977—. Served from lt. to lt. comdr. USNR, 1941-45. Registered profl. engr. Maine, Mo., Tex., Ariz. Mem. ASCE (life mem.); mem. Assn. Navy Civil Engr. Corps Officers, Alumni Assn. U. Kans. (life), Am. Forestry Assn., Alumni Assn. U. Ariz. (life), Nat. Geol. Soc., Nat. Rifle Assn., Ret. Officers Assn. (life), Theta Tau. Methodist. Mason (32 deg., Shriner). Home: 101 W Vesuvius St Tucson AZ 85704

DEMIRIS, CHRIS, advertising agency executive, development firm executive; b. Salt Lake City, Jan. 21, 1923; s. Peter and Olympia (Mavrides) D.; m. Tina Colichidas, Feb. 3, 1957; children—Marina, Chris. Student U. Utah, 1946-47, Columbia U., 1948-49. Asst. account exec. Grey Advt., N.Y.C., 1948-50; ptnr. Demiris, Rice & Assocs., Salt Lake City, 1954—; co-owner Redwood Bus. Park. Served with AUS, 1943-46. Named to Hall of Fame, Am. Trade Mags., 1970; recipient Coinamatic Service Industry award Utah Artists of Advt. and Editorial Art, 1975; award Utah Artist Fedn. for TV, 1978; Key award Gov.'s Handicapped Com., 1977. Mem. Sales and Mktg. Execs. Utah (past dir.), Utah Advt. Fedn., Utah Assn. Advt. Agys. Greek Orthodox. Clubs: Hidden Valley Country, Masons (Salt Lake City). Home: 2060 Browning Ave Salt Lake City UT 84108 Office: Demiris Rice & Associates 50 S Main St Suite 420 Salt Lake City UT 84144

DEMKO, ADELLE MARY, management consultant; b. Thunderbay, Ontario, Can., Dec. 15, 1946; d. Frank and Anne (Zroback) Demkowich; m. J.A. Baer, III, Aug. 30, 1969; children—Jennifer, Arthur, Matthew. B.A., U. Western Ont., 1968; J.D., Duke U., 1972; M.S. in Pub. and Pvt. Mgmt., Yale U., 1979. Bar: N.Y. 1973. Atty., Amerace Corp., N.Y.C., 1973-77; fin. and strategy cons. Xerox Corp., Stamford, Conn., 1979-81; mgmt. cons. Demko Cons., Los Angeles, 1981—. Pres. N.Y. chpt. Toastmaster's Internat., 1975-76. Mem. ABA, Assn. Bar City N.Y., 1974-81. Episcopalian. Clubs: University (N.Y.C.), Westside Racquet (Los Angeles).

DEMMA, MICHAEL ANTHONY, training and development executive, consultant; b. Natrona Heights, Pa., Mar. 22, 1941; s. Mike Joseph and Sara Marie (Mercurio) D.; m. Joan Marie Sarniak, Oct. 30, 1945; children—Michael, Michelle, Kristine. B.A. in Chemistry, Gannon U., 1963. Product engr. Eastman Kodak Co., Rochester, N.Y., 1966-70, dept. head Colo. div., Windsor, 1970-72, 74-77; project engr., 1972-74, supr. quality, adminstrv. services, 1977-78, supr. tng. and devel., 1978—; mgmt. tng. cons. U.S. Dept. Edn., Bd. dirs. Crossroads; parish council mem. Roman Cath. Ch.; mem. Fort Collins PTO. Served to 1st lt. U.S. Army, 1964-66. Recipient Disting. Service award Colo. State U., 1979. Mem. Am. Soc. Tng. and Devel. (Rocky Mountain chpt.), Colo. Assn. Commerce and Industry (steering com.), Colo. Alliance Bus. (steering com.), Fort Collins C. of C. Club: Elks. Home: 2101 Dover Dr Fort Collins CO 80526 Office: C-11 Kodak Colo Div Windsor CO 80551

DEMMING, VALERIE ANNE, educator; b. Palmer, Alaska, Sept. 24, 1953; d. Richard Edwin and Annie Clara (Hess) D.; m. Thomas Elliott Marsh, Oct. 18, 1980. B.Elem. Ed., U. Alaska, 1975. Tchr. 2d grade Immaculate Conception Sch., Fairbanks, Alaska, 1977-78; tchr. 5th and 2d grades Fairbanks North Star Sch. Dist., 1978-81, tchr. 3d grade, 1982—. Bd. dirs. Fairbanks Crisis Clinic Found., 1980—, pres., 1982-83. Named Vol. of Yr., wife of Gov. Alaska, 1982. Mem. Am. Personnel and Guidance Assn. Episcopalian. Home: 1139 Coppet St Fairbanks AK 99701

DEMMLER, CHARLES FREDERICK, stock broker; b. Hastings-on-Hudson, N.Y., Aug. 28, 1923; s. Charles Robert and Anne Rita (Buckley) D.; student Gen. Motors Inst., 1941-43, Marquette U., 1947-48, George Washington U., 1962-63; B.A., San Diego State U., 1968; m. Clare J. O'Connor, Feb. 16, 1946; children—Robert Charles, Maryanne. Commd. ensign U.S. Navy, 1945; advanced through grades to capt., 1973; comdr. Carrier Air Wing 2, 1964-65, comdg. officer U.S.S. Forrestal, 1969-70, chief of staff 3d Fleet, 1972-73, ret. 1973; asst. v.p. Merrill Lynch Pierce Fenner & Smith, La Jolla, Calif., 1973-83, v.p., 1983—. Decorated Legion of Merit (3). Mem. San Diego Stock and Bond Club (dir. 1975-76), Merrill Lynch Execs., Merrill Lynch Chmns. Club. Clubs: La Jolla Country, Kiwanis, Navy League, K.C. Home: 1561 Calle de Primra La Jolla CA 92037 Office: Merrill Lynch 1225 Prospect St La Jolla CA 92037

DEMONEY, CHARLES LEWIS, II, airline executive; b. Fairplay, Colo., Jan. 18, 1939; s. Charles L. and Margaret A. (Steele) D.; m. Judy Kathryn King, June 11, 1982; children—Jennifer Peterson, James A., Charles Lewis III, Autumn Rea. Grad. Stanford U. Exec. Program, 1975. Passenger service agt., sales rep., dist. sales mgr., regional sales mgr. Frontier Airlines, Inc., Denver, 1958-69, dir. sales, 1969-71, dir. field mktg., 1972-75, v.p., asst. gen. mgr. sales and service, 1975-79, v.p. market planning, 1979-81, sr. v.p. market planning, 1981—. Mem. Am. Soc. Travel Agts. Home: 12390 E LaSalle Pl Aurora CO 80014 Office: 8250 Smith Rd Denver CO 80207

DEMONNIN, JOYCE LORRAINE, public relations counselor, writer; b. Portland, Oreg., Aug. 17, 1952; d. Charles Earnest and Ethelyn Thelma (Shank) DeMonnin. B.A. in Journalism, U. Oreg., 1976. Pub. relations specialist Petrold & Assocs. Advt., 1977-79, Oreg. Pub. Broadcasting, Portland, 1979-81; writer Earthwatch, Portland, 1981-82; owner, pres. DeMonnin Communications, Corvallis, Oreg., 1982—; tchr. advt. Linn Benton Community Coll. Mem. Pub. Relations Soc. Am., Women in Communications, Conv. and Visitors Bur. Corvallis, Corvallis C. of C. (econ. devel. com.). Clubs: Timberhill Athletic, City (Portland). Presbyterian. Contbg. author articles in field. Home: 1480 NE Seavy Corvallis OR 97330 Office: PO Box 207 Corvallis OR 97339

DE MONTE, ROBERT JACK, real estate investment co. exec.; b. Oakland, Calif., July 12, 1942; s. Mervin and Kathleen Irene (Murphy) De M.; B.S., Calif. State U., Hayward, 1964; postgrad. Pepperdine U., 1977-78, Sch. Law, U. San Francisco, 1979-83; m. Suzanne Strachen, Dec. 28, 1963; children—Michele, Margaret. Account supr. Moore Bus. Forms, Inc., Oakland, 1964-68; supr. public acctg. Coopers & Lybrand, San Francisco, 1968-71; dir. housing and community devel., planning and research Gov.'s Office, State of Calif., 1971-74; controller to v.p. fin. and adminstrn. Consol. Capital Cos., Emeryville, Calif., 1974—; exec. v.p. pub. programs treas., trustee Consol. Capital Realty Investors, Consol. Capital Spl. Trust; pres., trustee Consol. Capital Income Trust; dir. Consol. Capital Equities Corp. Trustee, Pitzer Coll., Claremont, Calif. Trustee, mem. exec. com. Peralta Coll. Found. Mem. Am. Inst. C.P.A.s, Calif. Soc. C.P.A.s, Nat. Assn. Real Estate Investment Trusts (bd. govs.). Home: 2045 Oakland Ave Piedmont CA 94611 Office: 1900 Powell St Suite 1000 Emeryville CA 94608

DEMPSEY, PAUL DAVID, plastic and maxillofacial surgeon; b. Winnipeg, Man., Can., Mar. 28, 1947; came to U.S., 1973; s. James Andrew and Edith Gertrude (Bowen) D.: D.M.D., U. Man., 1970, M.D., 1973; m. Donna McVicar, Aug. 21, 1970; children—Justin, Kristin. Intern, resident in gen. surgery U. Tex. Med. Br., Galveston, 1973-75; gen. surgery resident, Winnipeg, 1975-76; plastic surgery resident U. Mich., Ann Arbor, 1976-78; practice medicine specializing in plastic and maxillofacial surgery, Tucson, 1978—; asso. in surgery U. Ariz. Hosp., Tucson, 1979-81; chief plastic surgery El Dorado Hosp., Tucson, 1980-82, Tucson Med. Ctr., 1983-84. Named Surg. Intern of Yr., U. Tex., 1973-74; Fred A. Coller Surg. Soc. scholar, U. Mich., 1977; diplomate Am. Bd. Plastic Surgery. Fellow Royal Coll. Physicians and Surgeons Can., ACS; mem. AMA, Am. Soc. Plastic and Reconstructive Surgeons, Can. Med. Assn., Pima County Med. Soc., Phoenix Acad. Dentistry. Club: Catalina Rotary (Tucson). Home: 8381 E Brookwood Dr Tucson AZ 85715 Office: 5200 E Grant Rd Tucson AZ 85712

DEMPSEY, RICHARD COLEMAN, ins. co. exec.; b. Long Beach, Calif., Aug. 25, 1950; s. Merle H. and Viola M. (Morehouse) D.; B.A. in Polit. Sci., UCLA, 1972. Sales mgr. Sta. KLA, U. Calif., Los Angeles, 1971-72; ins. agt. Merle Dempsey Ins. Co., Long Beach, 1972-74; property and casualty ins. broker Dempsey Ins. Inc., Long Beach, 1974—, v.p., 1974-82, pres., 1982—; guest speaker Cerritos Jr. Coll., Calif., 1977. Bd. govs. Com. of 300 Long Beach Grand Prix, 1976, 77, gov., 1976-80; mem. Long Beach Econ. Devel. Commn., 1981-82. Named Jaycee of Year Long Beach, 1973-74; lic. pvt. pilot. Mem. Ind. Ins. Agts. Am., Ind. Ins. Agts. Assn. Calif., Ind. Ins. Agts. Assn. Long Beach (dir. 1976-79, v.p. 1979-80, pres. 1980-81), Long Beach C. of C., Long Beach Jaycees (dir. 1974-76, v.p. internal affairs 1976-77), UCLA Alumni Assn. Republican. Congregationalist. Home: 2903 Knoxville Ave Long Beach CA 90815 Office: 3639 Atlantic Ave Long Beach CA 90807

DEMPSTER, ANTHONY JOHN, display company executive, designer; b. Los Angeles, Feb. 15, 1942; s. Albert Taylor and Catherine Cajori (Hull) D.; m. Joyce Lynne Kipper, Apr. 20, 1974; children—Adam, Matthew. Student Calif. State U.-Northridge, 1960-62, Art Center Coll. Design, 1962-64, Calif. Inst. Arts, 1965-66. Film designer Tom McGowan Prodns., Los Angeles, 1966; film designer, prodn. illustrator Walt Disney Prodns., 1966-70, Warner Bros. Studios, 1970; art dir., exhibit designer Internat. Displays Inc., Los Angeles, 1970-73; owner, designer Dempster Assocs., Los Angeles, 1973; co-owner, mgr. Carsten Dempster Displays Inc., Los Angeles, 1974—. Mem. Republican Nat. Com., Notre Dame Alumni Club, Art Center Alumni Club, Apartment Assn. San Fernando Valley. Republican. Office: Carsten Dempster Displays Inc 11164 Bradley Ave Pacoima CA 91331

DEMUN, TAYLOR KENT, exhibition mgr.; b. Shreveport, La., Dec. 13, 1929; s. John Russel and Audrey May (Taylor) DeM.; m. LaVolla Mae Light, Mar. 14, 1953; children—Kory Kent, Warren Douglas, Eric Murray, Nancy Gail. B.S., Oreg. State U., 1952; M.B.A., U. Puget Sound, 1980. Commd. ensign U.S. Navy, 1952, advanced through grades to capt., 1972; dep. chief of staff U.S. Atlantic Submarine Force, 1975-78; ret., 1978; ops. mgr. Seattle Trade Ctr., 1978-79, exhbn. dir., 1979-81, exhbn. mgr., 1981—. Bd. dirs. Seattle council Navy League, 1982—; mem. King County Fair Bd., 1982—. Decorated Meritorious Service medal (2), Navy Commendation medal. Mem. Ret. Officers Assn., Sigma Alpha Epsilon. Republican. Club: Washington Athletic. Home: 5720 92nd Ave SE Mercer Island WA 98040 Office: Suite 5101 2601 Elliott Ave Seattle WA 98121

DEMUTH, ALAN CORNELIUS, lawyer; b. Boulder, Colo., Apr. 29, 1935; s. Laurence Wheeler and Eugenia Augusta (Roach) DeM.; B.A. magna cum laude in Econs. and cum laude in Gen. Studies, U. Colo., 1958, LL.B., 1961; m. Ellen Claire Lewis, Mar. 30, 1958; children—Scott Lewis, Evan Dale, Joel Millard. Admitted to Colo. bar, 1961; asso. firm Akolt, Turnquist, Shepherd & Dick, Denver, 1961-68; partner firm Akolt, Dick, Rovira, DeMuth & Eiberger, Denver, 1968-73, Rovira, DeMuth & Eiberger, Denver, 1973-76, DeMuth, Eiberger, Kemp & Backus, Denver, 1976-79, DeMuth, Kemp & Backus, Denver, 1979—; municipal judge Greenwood Village, Colo., 1973-78; conf. atty. Rocky Mountain Conf. United Ch. of Christ, 1970—. Jefferson County central com. and committeeman, 1962-66; del. county, judicial, rep. and del. state convs. and assemblies Republican Party, 1962-72; pres., bd. dirs. Littleton (Colo.) Hockey Assn., 1973-75; chmn. bd. trustees, council of dirs. First United Ch. of Arvada, 1963-71; bd. dirs., exec. com. and chmn. Centers of Mission Commn., Colo. Conf. United Ch. of Christ, 1970-72; bd. dirs. Ecuminical Ministries, Inc., 1968—, Montbello United Parish, 1968—; trustee, sec. Aurorans for an Ice Arena, 1978-79; bd. dirs. Friends of U. Colo. Library, 1978—, treas., 1979; mem. U. Colo. Law Alumni Bd., 1980—. Mem. Am., Colo., Denver, bar assns., Phi

Beta Kappa, Sigma Alpha Epsilon, Phi Delta Phi. Republican. Clubs: The 26, The Village, Denver Law (v.p. 1974). Home: 5121 S Franklin St Littleton CO 80121 Office: Suite 1600 718 17th St Denver CO 80202

DE MUTH, LAURENCE WHEELER, JR., lawyer, utility co. exec.; b. Boulder, Colo., Nov. 22; s. Laurence Wheeler and Eugenia Augusta (Roach) DeM.; A.B., U. Colo., 1951, LL.B., 1953; m. Margaret Evelyn Glasebrook, Jan. 17, 1956; children—Debra Lynn, Laurence Wheeler, III, Brant Hill. Gen. atty. Mountain States Tel. & Tel. Co., Denver, 1968, v.p., gen. counsel, 1968—, sec., 1974—. Mem. Republican Precinct Com., dist. capt., 1957-70; trustee Lakewood (Colo.) Presbyterian Ch., 1965-68; bd. dirs. Colo. Epilepsy Assn., 1973-79, pres. bd., 1978-79; bd. litigation Mountain States Legal Found., 1980—. Served to capt. USAF, 1954-56. Named Disting. Mil. Grad., Air Force ROTC, 1953. Mem. Am., Colo. (chmn. ethics com. 1973-74, bd. govs., fellow found.), Denver bar assns., Am. Judicature Soc., Colo. Assn. Corp. Counsel (pres.), Order of Coif, Phi Beta Kappa, Pi Gamma Mu. Clubs: Univ., 26, Lakewood Country, Paradise Valley Country. Home: 970 Front Range Rd Littleton CO 80120 Office: 931 14th St Room 1300 Denver CO 80202

DENARO, ROBERT PETER, aerospace engineer; b. Glen Rock, N.J., Jan. 28, 1949; s. Angelo and Helene Marie (Warschauer) D.; m. Carolyn Rae McSemek, June 28, 1975; children—Brian Angelo, Tracy Rae. B.S. in Engring. Scis., U.S. Air Force Acad., 1971; M.S. with distinction in Elec. Engring., Air Force Inst. of Tech., Dayton, Ohio, 1973; M.S. in Systems Mgmt., U. So. Calif., 1978. Commd. 2d lt. U.S. Air Force, 1971, advanced through grades to capt., 1975, resigned, 1979; sr. engr. Systems Control Inc., Palo Alto, Calif., 1979-81; founder dir., Theory and Applications Unltd. Corp., Los Gatos, Calif., v.p., mgr. Nav. Systems div. 1981—. Decorated Air Force Commendation medal, Air Force Meritorious Service medal. Mem. IEEE, AIAA, Inst. Nav., Eta Kappa Nu. Republican. Clubs: Kona Kai Swim and Racquet, Los Gatos Athletic. Contbr. numerous articles to tech. jours. Office: 10 Jackson St Suite 101 Los Gatos CA 95030

DENCHFIELD, JERROLD RAY, chemist; b. Garden City, Kans., Nov. 25, 1931; s. Frederick Ray and Mildred Rose (Bowers) D.; B.S. in Chemistry and Math., Ft. Hays (Kans.) State Coll., 1959; m. MarJean Olson, June 10, 1956; children—Vanessa, Pamela, Suzanne. With Sinclair Research Co., Harvey, Ill., 1959-64; sr. research engr. Rocketdyne div. Rockwell Internat. Co., Canoga Park, Calif., 1964-70; research chemist research and tech. dept. Montebello Research Lab., Texaco, Inc., S. El Monte, Calif., 1970—. Served with AUS, 1952-54. Mem. Am. Chem. Soc., Soc. Applied Spectroscopy. Republican. Baptist. Patentee in field. Home: 120 N Palo Cedro Dr Diamond Bar CA 91765 Office: 329 N Durfee St South El Monte CA 91733

DENERIS, KATHLEEN NICHOLES, interior designer; b. Salt Lake City, May 18, 1931; d. Farrell James and Virginia Noble (Gentry) Nicholes; B.S., U. Utah, 1967; m. George Deneris, Sept. 8, 1951; children—Angela, Kimberly, George Angelo. Instr., Utah Tech. Coll., 1972-75; founder, dir. Salt Lake Sch. Interior Design, 1975—. Mem. Interior Design Educators Council, Am. Soc. Interior Designers (edn. affiliate), AAUW (treas. Salt Lake chpt. 1968-70, editor Newsletter, Salt Lake chpt. 1970-72). Democrat. Office: Salt Lake Sch Interior Design 2188 Highland Dr Salt Lake City UT 84106

DENGERINK, HAROLD ARLEN, psychology educator; b. Denver, June 6, 1943; s. Harold W. and Ruth (Hogan) D.; m. Joan Ellen Ham, Oct. 15, 1942; children—Kristin, Erin. B.A. in Psychology, Calvin Coll., 1965; M.S., Kent State U., 1967, Ph.D., 1969. Lic. clin. psychologist, Wash. Asst. prof. psychology Wash. State U., Pullman, 1969-73, assoc. prof., 1973-78, prof., 1978—, dir. clin. tng., 1978—; clin. prof. psychiatry, behavioral scis., U. Wash., Seattle, 1982—; vis. research prof. dept. audiology U. Goteborg (Sweden), 1982. USPHS research fellow, 1967-69; grantee NIMH, Nat. Inst. Alcohol Abuse, 1970-72, USPHS, 1978—. Mem. Am. Psychol. Assn., Midwestern Psychol. Assn., Western Psychol. Assn., Assn. Research Profs. Editor: (with H. Cross) Training Professionals for Rural Mental Health, 1982; (with J. Carr) Behavioral Science in the Practice of Medicine; contbr. chpts. to texts, numerous articles to profl. jours. Office: Dept Psychology Wash State U Pullman WA 99164

DENIRO, DOROTHY ANN, nursing services administrator, vocational educator; b. Green Bay, Wis., Aug. 25, 1940; d. Andrew Vincent and Virginia Bonita (Logerquist) Nejedlo; m. Rocco Thomas DeNiro, Aug. 23, 1962; children—Stephen Lawrence, Susan Marie. Diploma, St. Mary Corwin Sch. Nursing, 1961; B.S. in Behavioral Sci., So. Colo. State Coll., 1967; M.S. in Nursing, U. Tex., 1973. R.N., Colo. Staff nurse St. Mary Corwin Hosp., Pueblo, Colo., 1961, head nurse, 1962-66; psychiat. staff nurse Colo. State Hosp., Pueblo, 1966-79, dir. nursing services, 1979—. Mem. Am. Nurses Assn. Democrat. Roman Catholic. Home: 3101 High St Pueblo CO 81008 Office: 1600 W 24th St Pueblo CO 81003

DENISON, DANA DOYLE, aerospace exec.; b. Hennepin, Okla., Oct. 30, 1927; s. Lumon W. and Francis (Wisdom) D.; A.A., Allen Hancock Coll., 1958; postgrad. Indsl. Coll. Armed Forces, 1959; B.A., UCLA, 1960; B.S. SUNY, 1974; M.B.A., Seattle City Coll., 1978; m. Stephnie Conover, Feb. 4, 1968. Engr. U.S. Army Signal Corps, 1949-53, adminstrn. officer, 1953-60; base mgr. ITT Kellogg, 1960-62, dir. aerospace ops., 1960-64; v.p., dir. range div. ITT Fed. Electric Corp., Vandenberg AFB, Calif., 1964-69, v.p., dir. aerospace ops., Paramus, N.J., 1969-71, v.p., dir. N. Am. ops., 1971-75; v.p. Boeing Services Internat., 1976-78; pres. Talley Services Inc., Mesa, Ariz., 1978—; pres., chief exec. officer DWS Inc., 1980—. Recipient Army Disting. Civilian Service award, 1957; Air Force Systems Command Outstanding Achievement award, 1965, Gold Knight award Nat. Mgmt. Assn., 1969. Mem. IEEE, AIAA, Air Force Assn. Home: 6639 E Sharon Dr Scottsdale AZ 85254 Office: 7170 E McDonald Dr #9 Scottsdale AZ 85253

DENISON, TOM GILES, university dean; b. Pekin, Ill., Oct. 28, 1947; s. John Sylvester and Alta Ella (Rynders) D.; m. Carolyn Gail Goans, Dec. 20, 1970; children—Brook Giles, Ramsey Giles. Ph.D. in Adminstrn. of Vocat.-Tech. Edn., Wash. State U., 1981. Cert. secondary tchr. vocat. welding, Wash. Tchr. vocat. welding Hood River (Oreg.) County Schs., 1971-79; lectr. vocat.-tech. edn. Wash. State U., Pullman, 1980-83, adminstrv. intern, 1982-83; owner, mgr. Tom Denison & Assocs., Pullman, 1981-83; asst. dean Sch. Vocat.-Tech. Edn. Boise (Idaho) State U., 1983—; ednl. cons. career edn.; lectr. in field. Mem. Soc. Mfg. Engrs., Am. Vocat. Assn., Am. Indsl. Arts Assn., Phi Delta Kappa, Epsilon Pi Tau (hon.). Patentee arc and torch cutting simulators. Office: Sch Vocat-Tech Edn Boise State Univ Boise ID

DENISTON, THOMAS GRAHAM, private consultant; b. Richmond, Ky., June 3, 1938; s. Noble Graham and Frankie (DeBoe) D.; student U. Ky., 1956-57, Eastern Ky. U., 1957-60, U. N.Mex., 1976-78; m. May 7, 1967 (div. Dec. 1979); children—Vance Harrison, Blane Edwin, Tod Alan. Sales coordinator Tension Envelope Corp., Memphis, 1970-72; nat. v.p. Paralyzed Vets. Am., Albuquerque, 1973-76, southwestern regional advocacy dir., 1978-80; handicapped affairs coordinator State of N.Mex., Santa Fe, 1980-82; pvt. cons., 1982—; bd. dirs. Energy Consumers N.Mex.; cons. Am. Cert. for Med. Rehab. and Splty. Therapists; chmn. com. on handicapped scouting Gt. S.W. Area council Boy Scouts Am., 1974—; mem. Albuquerque Commn. on Handicapped, 1976-80, chmn., 1978-79; mem. Albuquerque Transit Adv. Bd. Subcom., 1977-82; mem. adv. council N.Mex. Div. Vocat. Rehab., 1979-82; mem. N.Mex. Employment and Tng. Council, 1980-82. Served with USAF, 1960-69. Decorated Air medal with 3 oak leaf clusters, D.F.C.; recipient Outstanding Community Achievement award Pres. Carter, 1979. Mem. Paralyzed Vets. Am., DAV, Wheelchair Pilots Assn., N.Mex. Assn. for Deaf, N.Mex. Registry Interpreters for Deaf, Nat. Spinal Cord Injury Found. Democrat. Baptist. Club: Toastmasters. Home: 3357 Cerrillos Rd Apt 12 Santa Fe NM 87501 Office: Disability Advocates 327 Sandoval St Suite C Santa Fe NM 87501

DENITZ, FREDERICK BERNARD, banker; b. Los Angeles, Nov. 4, 1956; s. Ronald Philip and Betty Joy D.; B.A. cum laude in Psychology and Sociology, UCLA, 1979; grad. Nat. Personnel Sch. Am. Bankers Assn., 1980; m. Jena Novak, Apr. 10, 1983. Cheerleading instr. United Spirit Assn. of Western U.S., 1976-79; spl. programs asst. div. student and campus affairs UCLA, 1978-79; personnel officer, salary adminstrn. research and analysis Lloyds Bank Calif., Los Angeles, 1979-83, corp. banking officer, 1983—. Coordinator, coach acrobatic cheerleading unit Los Angeles Rams, 1980-81. Active Jewish Big Bros. of Los Angeles, 1980-82, award of appreciation for recruitment; water safety instr. ARC, 1975-78; chpt. pres. Nat. Eagle Scout Assn., 1974-77, Silver Wreath award; active Met. YMCA, 1983—, Concern Found. for Cancer Research, 1982—. Recipient cert. of appreciation Mayor Tom Bradley of Los Angeles, 1973. Mem. Am. Soc. Tng. and Devel., Am. Compensation Assn., Democrat. Home: 1831 Barry Ave Los Angeles CA 90025 Office: 612 S Flower St Los Angeles CA 90017

DENKE, CONRAD WILLIAM, motion picture producer and dir.; b. Cottonwood, Ariz., July 23, 1947; s. Lee Ernest and Barbara Ann (Russell) D.; B.A. in Radio-TV Communications and Psychology, U. Wash., 1969; m. Laura Lee Nielson, Aug. 22, 1975; 1 son, Alexander Lee. Dir., Sta. KCTS-TV, Seattle, 1967-69; dir. prodn. Cinema Assos., Seattle, 1973-78; pres. Am. Motion Picture Co., Seattle, Am. Video Lab., Am. Typesetting Co., Am. Tape Duplicating Co., 1978—. Subcom. chmn. cultural arts com. Seattle C. of C., 1979—; bd. dirs. Seattle Children's Ballet, 1980—, Am. Tng. Inst. Served with USAF, 1969-73. Recipient Cine Golden Eagle award Council on Internat. Nontheatrical Events, 1977, 79, Silver Cindy award Info. Film Producers Am., 1977, Gold Camera award U.S. Indsl. Film Festival, 1978. Mem. Internat. TV Assn. (dir. Seattle chpt. 1980—, chpt. pres. 1982-83), Associated Latter Day Media Artists (pres. Seattle chpt.). Republican. Mormon. Club: Elks. Dir. and editor documentary: More Than Bows and Arrows, 1978 (various awards including Western Heritage Arts award for dir. best Western documentary 1978); co-inventor process to transfer slide programs to film. Office: 7017 15th NW Seattle WA 98117 also 7023 15th NW Seattle WA 98117

DENKE, PAUL HERMAN, aircraft engineer; b. San Francisco, Feb. 7, 1916; s. Edmund Herman and Ella Hermine (Riehl) D.; m. Beryl Ann Lincoln, Feb. 10, 1940; children—Karen Denke Mottaz, Claudia Denke Tesche, Marilyn Denke Kunert. B.C.E., U. Calif.-Berkeley, 1937, M.C.E., 1939. Registered profl. engr., Calif. Stress engr. Douglas Aircraft Co., Santa Monica, Calif., 1940-62, mgr. structural mechanics Long Beach, Calif., 1962-65, chief sci. computing, 1965-71, chief structures engr. methods and devel., 1972-78, chief scientist structural mechanics, 1979—; mem. faculty dept. engring. UCLA, 1941-50. Assoc. fellow AIAA; mem. Soc. Automotive Engrs. (Arch T. Colwell merit award 1966), Sigma Xi, Tau Beta, Chi Epsilon. Democrat. Presbyterian. Pioneered and developed finite element method of structural analysis; author numerous technical papers. Home: 753 Via Del Monte Palos Verdes Estates CA 90274

DENMAN, MARY EDEL, educator; b. Pensacola, Fla., Sept. 20, 1922; d. William Wilcox and Louise (Billingsley) Edel; student U. Calif., Los Angeles, 1959-61; B.A. in English, San Diego State U., 1963, M.A. in English, 1969, postgrad., 1971; m. Frank Blaha (dec.); m. 2d, Thomas Denman (div.); children—Frank, Joanna, Mary Lou, William, Thomas, Sarah. Instr. English, San Diego State U., 1966-69, asst. prof. secondary edn., English, 1971, asst. prof. Study Skills Center, 1972, assoc. prof., 1977—; maitre-asst. prof. Am. Studies, U. d' Aix-Marseille, Aix-en Provence, France, 1970; exchange prof. Wuhan U., People's Republic of China, Summer 1982; lectr. in field. Participant in numerous conf's in field. Mem. MLA, Western Reading Assn., Calif. Assn. Tchrs. of English, Nat. Council Tchrs. of English, AAUP, Assn. Humanistic Psychology, Calif. State Psychol. Assn., Phi Delta Kappa. Democrat. Author numerous publs. in field. Office: Study Skills Center San Diego State U San Diego CA 92182

DENMAN, WILLIAM RICHARD, paper company executive; b. N.Y.C., Apr. 26, 1927; s. William Richard and Marion Edith (Fajans) D.; m. Mary Ellen Moody, Oct. 6, 1951; children—William R., Diane, Robert. B.S., U. Wash., 1950; grad. Advanced Mgmt. Program, Harvard U., 1974. Ops. mgr. Simpson Paper Co., Everett, Wash., 1952-62; devel. mgr. Weyerhaeuser Co., Tacoma, 1963-72, v.p. paper, 1973—; dir. cos. Served to lt. USN; World War II, Korea. Mem. Am. Paper Inst. Republican. Episcopalian. Clubs: Seattle Yacht, Rainier (Seattle); Newport Yacht (Bellevue); Northriver Yacht (Ala.). Office: Weyerhaeuser Co Tacoma WA 98477

DENNEHY, RAYMOND LEO, philosopher, educator; b. San Francisco, Aug. 31, 1934; s. Joseph Patrick and Mary Agnes (McGaffigan) D.; A.B., U. San Francisco, 1962; Ph.D., U. Toronto (Ont., Can.), 1973; m. Geraldine Patricia Rine, July 7, 1962; children—Mark, Bridget, Andrea, Rosalind. Asst. prof. philosophy U. Santa Clara (Calif.), 1966-72, prof. philosophy Carmelite Monastery, San Jose, Calif., 1973—; lectr. philosophy, asst. to dir. evening coll. U. San Francisco, 1974—, asso. prof. philosophy, 1979—, mem. founding com., lectr. philosophy St. Ignatius Inst., speaker inst. bio ethics. Co-founder, mem. exec. com. United for Life in San Jose, 1968—. Served with USN, 1954-58; PTO. Mem. Am. Cath. Philos. Assn. (exec. council 1983—), Fellowship Cath. Scholars, Am. Maritain Assn. Author: Reason and Dignity, 1981; Christian Married Love, 1981. Contbr. articles to philos. jour. Lectr. on ethical, social topics to bus., profl. groups, high schs., colls.. and on radio, TV. Home: 64 Westpark Dr Daly City CA 94015 Office: U San Francisco San Francisco CA 94117

DENNEY, AL B., JR., motion picture producer; b. Waco, Tex., Mar. 15, 1935; s. Albert B. and Mary E. (Fason) D.; student San Antonio Jr. Coll., 1953, 57-58, Tex. Chiropractic Coll., 1953, 57-58; 1 son, Rick L. Screen writer, newsreel cameraman; dir., cinematographer Ind. Artists Prodns., Northridge, Calif., 1965—, owner, producer, distbr., 1970—; owner/broker DenReal Co., 1961—; owner/designer Den-Ney Originals, 1972—. Served with USMC, 1953-56. Mem. Internat. Photographers, Internat. Alliance Theatrical Stage Employees, Dirs. Guild Am. (dir. 1978—), Am. Film Inst., Am. TV Arts and Scis., Am. Soc. Lighting Dirs., Underwater Photog. Soc., Internat. Platform Assn., VFW. Republican. Club: Elks. Office: PO Box 5165 Sherman Oaks CA 91403

DENNEY, TALBERT L., cleaning services co. exec.; b. Leedey, Okla., Apr. 23, 1928; s. James Harden and Myrtle Mae (Eaton) D., student pub. schs., Stockton, Calif.; m. Barbara Pilcher, Feb. 17, 1951; children—Melanie Ann, Monica Susan. Owner cleaning co., Portland, Oreg. and Santa Barbara, Calif., 1959-67; pres. Servpro Industries, Inc., Rancho Cordova, Calif., 1967-75, also chmn. bd.; condr. seminars on principles of success. Served with U.S. Army, 1950-52. Mem. Am. Mgmt. Assn., Internat. Franchise Assn, Airplane Owners and Pilots Assn. Office: 11357 Pyrites Way Drawer D Rancho Cordova CA 95670

DENNIE, RICHARD LOE, psychologist; b. Spokane, Wash., July 7, 1921; s. Harold Ramsay and Mabel (Loe) D.; m. Claudia Hahner, Nov. 13, 1948; children—Lynn, Jan, Gail, Bruce, Douglas. Student Wash. State U., 1939-40; B.A. in Psychology, Eastern Wash. U., 1971; M.A., U. Nebr., Lincoln, 1972, Ph.D. in Psychology, 1975. Farmer, Fairfield, Wash., 1941-71; psychology intern VA Hosp., Walla Walla, Wash., 1974-75; dir. counseling services Luth. Social Services, Spokane, 1975-78; pvt. practice clin. psychology, Spokane, 1978—; cons. to Luth. clergymen. Chmn., Fairfield Community Devel. Study, 1960; mem. Fairfield City Council, 1964-70; active Republican Party; pres. Fairfield C. of C., 1961. Mem. Inland Empire Soc. Profl. Psychologists, Am. Psychol. Assn., Western Psychol. Assn., Nat. Register Health Service Providers in Psychology, Internat. Platform Assn. Lutheran. Clubs: Lions, Service, Toastmasters Internat. Home: E 13717 31st Ave Spokane WA 99216 Office: Suite 511 N 4407 Division St Spokane WA 99207

DENNIS, BRANT ALAN, ground water geologist; b. Akron, Ohio, May 10, 1951; s. Francis Alvan and Barbara Ann (Brigeman) D.; B.S. in Geology, Tex. A&M U., 1973; postgrad. Colo. State U., 1974-76; m. Kathleen Julie Brown, Aug. 16, 1975. Staff geologist F.M. Fox & Assos., Wheat Ridge, Colo., 1973-74; field geologist Ameudo & Ivey, Denver, 1974, staff geologist, 1976-77; hydrogeologist Willard Owens Assos., Inc., Wheat Ridge, 1976, Stearns-Rogers, Denver, 1977-79; chief hydrologist Pittsburg & Midway Coal Mining Co., Denver, 1979-80; environmentalist-uranium, Mobil Oil Corp., Denver, 1980-82, cons. ground water geologist, 1982-83; ground water geologist Hydro Dynamics Inc., 1983—; instr. Met. State Coll., Denver, 1978. Active Denver Area council Boy Scouts Am. Served with USN, 1973. Mem. Geol. Soc. Am., Am. Inst. Profl. Geologists, Colo. Ground Water Assn., Sigma Xi. Lutheran. Condr. research in field. Home: 1371 Flintwood Rd Franktown CO 80116

DENNIS, EVERETTE EUGENE, JR., university dean, journalism educator; b. Seattle, Aug. 15, 1942; s. Everette Eugene and Kathryn Marie (Platt) D. B.S., U. Oreg., 1964; M.A., Syracuse U., 1966; Ph.D., U. Minn., 1974; postgrad. Harvard U., 1978-79. Info. officer dept. mental health State of Ill., Chgo., 1966-68; asst. prof. Kans. State U., Manhattan, 1968-72, head mental health mass communication program, 1968-72, acting head dept. journalism, 1971-72; asst. prof., assoc. prof. then prof. U. Minn., Mpls., 1972-81, dir. grad. program sch. journalism and mass communication, 1972-81; prof., dean sch. journalism U. Oreg., Eugene, 1981—; head Project on Future of Journalism and Mass Communication Edn. Mem. Cable Access Adv. Commn., Eugene. Summer fellow, Stanford U., 1969, East-West Communication Inst., Hawaii, 1976; liberal arts fellow in law, Harvard U., 1978-79, vis. Nieman fellow, 1980, John F. Kennedy Sch. Govt. research fellow, 1981. Recipient H. Kreighbaum Under 40 Award for nation's outstanding journalism educator, 1982. Fellow Am. Orthopsychiat. Assn.; mem. Assn. for Edn. in Journalism and Mass Communication (pres. 1983—), Internat. Communication Assn., Soc. Profl. Journalists, Internat. Mass Communication Research Soc. Democrat. Author 10 books including: The Magic Writing Machine, 1971; New Strategies for Public Affairs Reporting, 1976, 2d edit. 1983; The Media Society, 1978; Justice Hugo Black and the First Amendment, 1978; Enduring Issues in Mass Communication, 1978; Reporting Processes and Practices, 1981; Basic Issues in Mass Communication, 1983. Contbr. articles to profl. jours. Home: 2707 Kismet Crest Eugene OR 97405 Office: Sch Journalism U Oreg Eugene OR 97403

DENNIS, JOHN LEE, county ofcl.; b. Anderson, S.C., Mar. 21, 1937; s. Adgie and Bertha (Blount) D.; student Va. Sem. & Coll., 1963-64, Va. Union U., 1964; Asso. in Art, Santa Monica City Coll., 1968; student electronic engring. U. W. Los Angeles, 1968-71, Southwest Coll., Los Angeles, 1970-72; student UCLA extension; 1 son, John II. Various positions, Conn., Va., Los Angeles, 1960-72; eligibility worker County of Los Angeles, 1972-78, supr. employment services Dept. Social Services, 1978-80, supr. foster care med. program So. Calif. area, Alhambra, 1980-81, Mem. Angeles County Dept. Social Services, 1981—. Mem. UCLA Alumni Assn. (life), Calif. Mus. Afro-Am. History and Culture (charter mem.), Nu Beta Epsilon. Democrat. Baptist. Author report: The Naturalist Report, 1976.

DENNISH, GEORGE WILLIAM, III, cardiologist; b. Trenton, N.J., Feb. 14, 1945; s. George William and Mary Ann (Bodnar) D.; A.B. magna cum laude, Seton Hall U., 1967; M.D., Jefferson Med. Coll., 1971; m. Kathleen Macchi, June 28, 1969; children—Andrew Stuart, Brian George, Michael John. Intern, Naval Hosp., Phila., 1971-72, jr. asst. resident, 1972-73, sr. asst. resident, 1973-74; fellow cardiovascular diseases Naval Regional Med. Center, San Diego, 1974-76, dir. coronary care unit, 1977-78; practice medicine specializing in cardiology, San Diego, 1974—, pvt. practice, 1978—; v.p. Splty. Med. Clinic, La Jolla and San Diego, 1982—; staff cardiologist Naval Regional Med. Center, Faculty Medicine, San Diego, 1976—; dir. spl. care units Scripps Meml. Hosp., La Jolla, 1981—; chief medicine Scripps-Encinitas Hosp., 1983—; asst. clin. prof. medicine U. Calif., San Diego, 1976—. Bd. dirs. San Diego County Heart Assn.; founder, pres., Cardiovascular Inst., La Jolla. Served to lt. comdr. USNR, 1971—. Decorated Knight of Holy Sepulchre; recipient Physician's Recognition award AMA, 1974-77; diplomate Am. Bd. Internal Medicine (sub-splty. cert. in cardiovascular diseases), Nat. Bd. Med. Examiners. Fellow ACP, Am. Coll. Cardiology, Am. Heart Assn. (clin. council), Am. Coll. Chest Physicians, Am. Coll. Angrology mem. Am. Soc. Internal Medicine, AAAS, Am. Coll. Clin. Pharmacology, N.Y. Acad. Scis., Am. Fedn. Clin. Research, N.Am. Soc. Pacing and Electrophysiology. Roman Catholic. Club: Old Mission Players, K.C. Contbr. articles to med. jours. Home: 950 Santa Helena Dr Solana Beach CA 92075 Office: 1087 Devonshire Dr Suite 100 Encinitas CA 92024 also 9844 Genesee Ave Suite 400 La Jolla CA 92037

DENNISON, JAMES CLIFFORD, elec. engr.; b. Dexter, Mo., Oct. 7, 1939; s. Clifford Obe and Mary Evelyn (Stuart) D.; B.S., Mich. State U., 1963; M.S., Syracuse U., 1966; Ph.D., U. Colo., 1972; m. Catherine Loretto, Aug. 26, 1961; children—Julie, Timothy, Terese, Betsy. Mem. staff IBM Corp., Poughkeepsie, N.Y., 1963-66, Boulder, Colo., 1966-78, Tucson, Ariz., 1978—, internat. world trade assignee, Europe, 1976, 80; vis research asso. U. Colo., 1973-74, vis. lectr., 1974-75; faculty affiliate Colo. State U., 1977-78. IBM resident study fellow, 1969-72. Mem. IEEE, Pi Mu Epsilon, Eta Kappa Nu. Contbr. articles to sci. jours. Home: 3162 N Longhorn Tucson AZ 85715 Office: IBM Tucson AZ 85744

DENNISON, KEITH ELKINS, museum director; b. Oakland, Calif., Sept. 20, 1939; s. Keith Elsworth and Safa (Smith) D.; m. Theresa Maureen Cushion, June 5, 1971; B.A., San Francisco State U., 1969, postgrad., 1969. Asst. curator edn. Fine Arts Museums San Francisco, 1968-70; visual arts adv. Calif. Arts Commn., State Calif., 1970-72; dir. The Haggin Mus., Stockton, Calif., 1971—; mem. San Joaquin County Arts Commn., 1982—; adj. prof. museology U. Pacific, 1974-76. Served with USAF, 1958-61. Mem. Internat. Council Museums, Am. Assn. Museums, Art Mus. Assn., Calif. Assn. Museums.

DENNISON, MARY ELLEN, nurse; b. Dunn Center, N.D., Feb. 20, 1922; d. Michael Joseph and Alice Bridget (Meehan) McGrath; B.S., U. Calif., San Francisco, 1974, M.S., 1975; m. Lyle Dennison, Sept. 18, 1946 (dec.); children—Mary Elizabeth, Michael Vincent, Kathleen Ann, Georgeanne. Pediatric office nurse-mgr., Oakland, Calif., 1953-65; occupational health nurse Am. Can Co., Oakland, 1965-67; instr. nursing Laney Coll., Oakland, 1967-70; public health nurse Humbolt-

Del Norte County Health Dept., Eureka, Calif., 1976—, dir. pub. health nursing, 1983—; bd. dirs. No. Calif. Health Systems Agy., 1979—. Commr., Humboldt County Commn. on Status of Women, 1981—, co-chair, 1983; bd. dirs. Behavior Devel. Center, Eureka, 1981. Named Woman of Achievement, Humboldt Bay Bus. and Profl. Women, 1982. Mem. Am. Nurses Assn., Nat. Fedn. Bus. and Profl. Women (chpt. pres. 1980-81), U. Calif. San Francisco Alumni Assn., Sigma Theta Tau. Home: 1538 Hayes St Eureka CA 95501 Office: 529 I St Eureka CA 95501

DENNY, JOHN LEIGHTON, JR., mathematics educator, consultant; b. Birmingham, Ala., Oct. 11, 1931; s. John Leighton and Miriam Marie (Stamm) D.; m. Anne Temple Hood. B.A., Stanford U., 1955; Ph.D., U. Calif.-Berkeley, 1962. Asst. prof. math., Ind. U.-Bloomington, 1962-65, U. Calif.-Riverside, 1965-67; assoc. prof. U. Ariz.-Tucson, 1967-70, prof., 1970—; cons. in field. Served with CIC, U.S. Army, 1955-56. NSF grantee, 1965-75. Mem. Am. Math. Soc., Inst. Math. Stats., Am. Statis. Assn., Econometric Soc. Contbr. articles to profl. jours. Office: Dept Math U Ariz Tucson AZ 85721

DENSTEDT, WILLIAM DARRELL, accountant; b. Burns, Oreg.; s. Leslie Darrell and Mable May (Hirsch) D.; student Wash. State U., 1967-70; B.A., Golden Gate U., 1974; m. Rosanne L. Davis, Apr. 8, 1972; 1 dau., Pamela. Asst. mgr. KPUL Radio, Pullman, Wash., 1967-70; adminstrv. technician Dept. Army, Presidio of San Francisco, 1971-74; tax auditor State of Calif., San Francisco, 1974-78; staff acct. Willis Accountancy Corp., Pittsburg, Calif., 1978-80; prin., acct. William D. Denstedt, Vallejo, Calif., 1980-83; ptnr. Denstedt & Miller C.P.A.s, Vallejo, 1983—. Served with AUS, 1961-64. Mem. Calif. Soc. C.P.A.s, Am. Inst. C.P.A.s. Republican. Lodge: Rotary. Home: 2072 Ramona Dr Pleasant Hill CA 94523 Office: 239 Georgia St PO Box 3316 Vallejo CA 94590

DENT, ERNEST DUBOSE, JR., physician; b. Columbia, S.C., May 3, 1927; s. E. Dubose and Grace (Lee) D.; student Presbyn. Coll., 1944-45; M.D., Med. Coll. S.C., 1949; m. Dorothy McCalman, June 16, 1949; children—Christopher, Pamela; m. 2d, Karin Frehse, Sept. 6, 1970. Intern U.S. Naval Hosp., Phila., 1949-50; resident pathology USPHS Hosp., Balt., 1950-54; chief pathology USPHS Hosp., Norfolk, Va., 1954-56; asso. pathology Columbia (S.C.) Hosp., 1956-59; pathologist Columbia Hosp., S.C. Baptist Hosp., also dir. labs., 1958-69; with Straus Clin. Labs., Los Angeles, 1969-72; staff pathologist St. Joseph Hosp., Burbank, Calif., Hollywood (Calif.) Community Hosp., 1969-72; dir. labs. Meml. Hosp. of Glendale, 1972—. Diplomate clin. pathology and pathology anatomy Am. Bd. Pathology. Mem. Am. Cancer Soc., AMA, Los Angeles County Med. Assn. (pres. Glendale dist. 1980-81), Calif. Med. Assn. (councillor 1984—), Am. Soc. Clin. Pathology, Coll. Am. Pathologists (assemblyman S.C. 1965-67; mem. publs. com. bull. 1968-70), Los Angeles Soc. Pathologists, Los Angeles Acad. Medicine, S.C. Soc. Pathologists (pres. 1967-69). Lutheran. Author papers nat. med. jours. Home: 1526 Blue Jay Way Los Angeles CA 90069 Office: 1420 S Central Ave Glendale CA 91204

DENT, HAROLD EDWARD, psychologist, mental health center adminstr., cons.; b. Southampton, N.Y., Aug. 4, 1928; s. Majeskia Cathcart and Mildred Jannette (Hunter) D.; children—Lynne Allison and Leslie Annique (twins). B.A., NYU, 1953; M.A., Denver U., 1955; Ph.D., U. Hawaii, 1966. Asst. coordinator rehab. counseling tng. program, dept. psychology U. Hawaii, 1963-66; mental retardation cons. HEW San Francisco Regional Office, 1966-70; coordinator pupil personnel services Berkeley (Calif.) Unified Sch. Dist., 1970-74; dir. consultation and edn. dept. Wetside Community Mental Health Center, Inc., San Francisco, 1974—; cons. Psychol. and Human Resource Cons., Inc., San Francisco, 1974—; cons. cultural/racial bias in IQ testing and test constrn., cultural aspect of profl. clin. tng., staff devel.; cons. forensic psychology; lectr.; mem. profl. adv. com. Bay View-Hunters Point Growth and Devel. Center, 1972-82. Mem. adv. com. No. Calif. Comprehensive Sickle Cell Ctr., 1978-82. Served with M.C., U.S. Army, 1946-48. Recipient Black Students Psychol. Assn. award, 1972; Euler Dyer award Mothers For Equal Edn., 1976. Mem. Am. Psychol. Assn., Assn. Black Psychologists (Nat. award for Service and Leadership 1980), Bay Area Assn. Black Psychologists (Spl. award 1981), Soc. Indian Psychologists, Western Psychol. Assn., Sigma Xi, Psi Chi. Contbr. articles to profl. jours.

DENTON, PAT, artist; b. Scottsbluff, Nebr., July 20, 1943; d. Dale and Louise (Covington) Redding; student U. Kans., 1961, U. Denver, 1961-62; m. Lawrence E. Denton, Aug. 23, 1964; children—Chip, Lance, Heather. Free-lance comml. artist, Scottsbluff, Nebr., 1964-68; owner Pat Denton Studio & Printage Arts, Lakewood, Colo., 1975—; instr. workshop, Aurora, Nebr., 1980-82; instr. Colo. Inst. Arts, 1983; judge nat. art shows; one-woman shows include: Internat. House, 1972, Foothills Art Center, Golden, Colo., 1974, 80, Art League Nebr., 1975, 76, Warehouse Gallery, Grand Island, Nebr., 1976, 78, others; group exhibitions include: Nebr. Art League, 1974-80, Greeley (Colo.) AAUW, 1976-79, Maxim's, Greeley, 1976-81, Rocky Mountain Watermedia, 1978, 82, Cody Country Art League, 1975-80, Saxon Mountain Gallery, Georgetown, Colo., Maxims of Greeley, Colo.; represented in calendar Artists of Am. Mem. Denver Art Mus. Home: 2948 Pierson Way Lakewood CO 80215

DENTON, SHELA IVA, association executive; b. Bklyn., Aug. 27, 1934; d. Elias and Fannie (Gurowitz) Kalmanowitz; children—Sharon Lee Denton Matloff, David, Marshall Normann. Student Moravian Coll., 1952, Ithaca Coll., 1952-54, Bklyn. Coll., 1957-59. Cert. assn. exec. Vice pres. Acme Jewelry and Color Research, N.Y.C., 1964-73; sec. Fulton Gold Refiners and Esmeraldo Realty, N.Y.C., 1964-73; exec. fir. Nat. Assn. Physical Therapists, West Covina, Calif., 1973—, also elected sec., guest editor Jour. and Newsletter. Active Pres.' Com. on Employment of Handicapped, Calif. Gov.'s Com. on Employment of Handicapped, Mayor's Com. (San Gabriel Valley) Employment of Handicapped, People to People Program, Internat. Yr. of Disabled Persons, Univ. of Judiasm, United Jewish Appeal. Recipient Louis M. London Adminstrv. award div. Nat. Assn. Phys. Therapists, 1980, also Friendship award, 1977, Gold Caduceus award, 1978, 79, 80, Conf. Com. awards, Cert. of Merit, 1977, 78, 79, 80. Mem. Am. Soc. Assn. Execs., So. Calif. Soc. Assn. Execs., Am. Acad. Med. Adminstrs. (cert. of achievement 1978), Nat. Rehab. Assn. Club: Am. Bus. Women (nat. officer, West Covina officer). Office: PO Box 367 West Covina CA 91793

DENTON, WILLIAM RIDLEY, transportation company executive; b. Vancouver, B.C., Can., July 21, 1930; s. Frederick W. and Marjorie R. (Ridley) D.; m. Nanette Massie, Sept. 1, 1954; children—Amanda, Edward. B.A. in Govt., Cornell U., 1952; LL.B., Stanford U., 1956. With law dept. So. Pacific Co., San Francisco, 1956-72, v.p. br., Washington, 1972-77, v.p., San Francisco, 1977-83, v.p., gen. counsel, 1983—; dir. So. Pacific Transp. Co., St. Louis Southwestern Ry. Co. Served with USAF, 1952-54. Mem. ABA, Calif. Bar Assn., D.C. Bar Assn. Clubs: Metropolitan, University, Burning Tree, Congressional Country (Washington), Olympic, World Trade, St. Francis Yacht (San Francisco). Home: 2242 Steiner St San Francisco CA 94115 Office: SP Bldg One Market Plaza San Francisco CA 94105

DENUNZIO, SAMUEL ANTHONY, financial executive; b. Cambridge, Mass., Apr. 8, 1934; s. Samuel and Mary (Bruno) D.; m. Barbara Angela Digiacono, Apr. 8, 1967; children—Joseph, Susan. B.B.A., Suffolk U., 1961. C.P.A., 1966. Various fin. positions Parkland Hosp., Dallas, Meml. Hosp., Worcester Mass., St. Vicents Hosp., Worcestor; dir. fin. Hollywood Presbyn. Med. Center, Los Angeles, 1979—. Served with USAF, 1953-57. Mem. Hosp. Fin. Mgmt. Assn., Am. Inst. C.P.A.s, Calif. Soc. C.P.A.s. Office: 1300 N Vermont Ave Office of Finance Los Angeles CA 90027

DENYES, JOHN STEWART, business executive, musician; b. San Diego, May 22, 1940; s. Gordon Stewart and Isabel Mary (MacLean) D.; m. Eunice Wai Shon Au, Aug. 14, 1965; children—Jill, Caroline, Andrew, Ian. Student, Calif. Inst. Tech., 1958-61; B.S.M.E., U. Calif.-Berkeley, 1963; M.B.A., Harvard U., 1965. Mem. indsl. engring. and planning depts. C. Brewer & Co., Hilo and Honolulu, Hawaii, 1965-68; planning analyst Alexander & Baldwin, Inc., Honolulu, 1968-69, dir. corp. devel., 1981—; head planning to head budget and planning depts. Hawaiian Comml. & Sugar Co., Puunenene, Maui, 1969-81; agribus. cons. Bd. dirs., treas. Big Bros./Big Sisters Maui, 1975-81; bd. dirs. Pacific council Girl Scouts U.S.A., 1981—. Mem. Hawaii Soc. Corp. Planners, Hawaiian Sugar Technologists, Tau Beta Pi, Pi Tau Sigma. Club. Harvard Bus. Sch. Contbr. chpts. to books. Home: 46-379 Nahewai St Kaneohe HI 96744 Office: 822 Bishop St Honolulu HI 96801

DEO, NARSINGH, computer science educator; b. Raniganj, Bihar, India, Apr. 2, 1936; s. Bihari Lal and Durga (Modi) Jee; B.S., Patna U. India, 1956; Dip. I.I.Sc., Indian Inst. Sci. (India), 1959; M.S., Calif. Inst. Tech., 1960; Ph.D., Northwestern U., 1965; m. Karen Ruth Baier, June 29, 1968. Grad. research asst. Calif. Inst. Tech., Pasadena 1959-60; assoc. electronic engr. Burroughs Electro Data Div., Pasedna, Calif., 1960-62; grad. research asst. Northwestern U., Evanston, Ill., 1963-65; sr. engr. Jet Propulsion Lab., Pasadena, 1966-69, mem. tech. staff, 1969-71; v.p. Britt Electronics Corp., Santa Monica, Calif., 1968-69; electronics design cons. Center for Behavior Therapy, Beverly Hills, Calif., 1967-71; faculty engring. extension UCLA, 1965-68; asst. prof. elec. engring. Calif. State Coll., 71; assoc. prof. elec. engring. Indian Inst. Tech., Kanpur, 1971-74, prof., head computer center, 1975-77; vis. assoc. prof. computer sci. U. Ill., Urbana, 1973; vis. prof. computer sci. Wash. State U., Pullman, 1974-75, prof., 1977—, chmn. dept., 1980—; vis. prof. U. Nebr., Lincoln, 1977. Author 4 textbooks, numerous articles. Patentee in field. Home: NW 1620 Kenny Dr Pullman WA 99163

DEPAOLIS, POTITO UMBERTO, food co. exec.; b. Mignano, Italy, Aug. 28, 1925; s. Giuseppe A. and Filomena (Macchiaverna) deP.; Vet. Dr., U. Naples, 1948; Libera Docenza, Ministero Pubblica Istruzione (Rome, Italy), 1955; m. Marie A. Caronna, Apr. 10, 1965. Came to U.S., 1966, naturalized, 1970. Prof. food service Vet. Sch., U. Naples, Italy, 1948-66; retired, 1966; asst. prof. A titre Benevole Ecole Veterinaire Alfort, Paris, France, 1956; vet. inspector U.S. Dept. Agr., Omaha, 1966-67; sr. research chemist Grain Processing Corp., Muscatine, Iowa, 1967-68; v.p., dir. product devel. Reddi Wip, Inc., Los Angeles, 1968-72, v.p. Kubro Foods, Los Angeles, 1972-73, Shade Foods, Inc., 1975—; pres. Vegetable Protein Co., Riverside, Calif., 1973—, Tima Brand Food Co., 1975—. Fulbright scholar Cornell U., Ithaca, N.Y., 1954; British Council scholar, U. Reading, Eng., 1959-60; postdoctoral research fellow NIH, Cornell U., 1963-64. Mem. Inst. Food Technologists, Italian Assn. Advancement Sci., AAAS, Vet. Med. Assn., Biol. Sci. Assn. Italy, Italian Press Assn., Greater Los Angeles Press Club. Contbr. articles in field to prol. jours. Patentee in field. Home: 131 Groverton Pl Bel Air Los Angeles CA 90077 Office: 8570 Wilshire Blvd Beverly Hills CA 90211 also 6878 Beck Ave North Hollywood CA 91605

DE PETRIS, CARLA NICOLE CAPIRONE, fine arts cons.; b. Torino, Italy; came to U.S., 1956, naturalized, 1961; d. Giovanni Giuseppe and Albina Luigia (Ferraris) Capirone di Montanaro; ed. Italian and Calif. schs.; cert. in arts mgmt. U. Calif.; m. Wilmer Anthony DePetris, Dec. 4, 1955; 1 son, Walther Gian Carlo. Internat. cons. fine arts, interior design and hist. preservation, Sonoma, Calif., 1969—; co-owner Fine Arts Research Assos.; tchr. art and art appreciation Sonoma Cath. Elem. Sch.; Arabian horse breeder, Am. Saddlebred breeder. Bd. dirs. Cath. Social Service, 1967-69, treas., 1968; active Pacific Mus. Soc., San Francisco, 1968-69; pres. Sonoma League Hist. Preservation, 1979; sec.-treas. Sonoma Land Trust, 1977-78; founder St. Francis the Ch. Mouse, diocese interior decorator and appraiser; archtl. rev. commr. City of Sonoma; adv. com. Sonoma Parks and Recreation; bd. dirs. Sonoma County Art Council; chmn. spl. events Pres.'s Assos., Sonoma State U. Recipient award Sonoma Parks and Recreation, 1975; Calif. State Office Preservation grantee, 1978. Mem. Associated Photographers Internat. Republican. Research on archtl. style and social devel. from 1840-1940 in So. Sonoma County.

DEPEW, CHRISTINE RAE, hotel sales executive; b. Santa Monica, Calif., Sept. 5, 1951; d. Carlton Roy and Gloria Jean (Richardson) DePew; m. Craig Arthur Thompson, July 6, 1946. A.A., City Coll. San Francisco, 1964. Bellegirl, Quality Inn Hotel, San Francisco, 1973, desk clk., 1973-74, reservations mgr., 1974-76, resident, 1976-78; dir. sales Jack Tar Hotel, San Francisco, 1978-83; dir. sales and mktg. Hotel Union Square, San Francisco, 1983—. Mem. Hotel Sales Mgmt. Assn., Sales Mgrs. Execs. Assn., Hotel Sales Mgmt. Assn. No. Calif. (pres. 1982, chmn. bd. 1983), No. Calif. Soc. of Assn. Execs., Bay Area Passenger Traffic Assn., San Francisco Dist. Merchants Assn., San Francisco Mchts. Assn., Marina Mchts. Assn. (past v.p.). Democrat. Episcopalian. Club: Rotarianne.

DEPICCIOTTO, SOLOMON, computer software exec.; b. Dallas, Nov. 26, 1937; s. Isaac and Leonie (Silvera) DeP.; B.S., Calif. Inst. Tech., 1959, M.S., 1960; m. Phyllis Kay Landy, Nov. 30, 1959 (div. 1975); children—Leonie, Natalie. Staff engr. Hughes Aircraft Co., Los Angeles, 1960-62; project analyst Service Bur. Corp., Los Angeles, 1962-63; computer scis. div. mgr. Application Research Corp., Los Angeles, 1963-69; pres., chmn. bd. Digital Enterprises, Los Angeles, 1969—. Mem. Assn. Computing Machinery, Caltech Alumni Assn. Home: 8725 Clifton Way Beverly Hills CA 90211 Office: 5630 Arbor Vitae Los Angeles CA 90045

DEPNER, ROBERT KURT, architect, planning cons., builder, developer, property mgmt. exec.; b. Calgary, Alta., Can., Sept. 1, 1944; s. Kurt Rudolf and Dagny Kristine (Beim) D.; student U. B.C. (Can.), 1967-69; B.Arch. with distinction, Wash. State U., 1972; m. Linda Kay Butler, June 16, 1979; children—Kendall Ann, Ashley Elizabeth, Cooper Mitchell. Draftsman, designer Calgary (Can.) Regional Planning Commn., 1966-67; designer Expo '74' (Spokane) Architects & Planners, 1972-74; designer Higgins, McClarty and Johnson, 1974-77; v.p. McClarty, Johnson, Depner & Milbrandt, Inc., Bellevue, Wash., 1977-80; pres. Depner Assn., 1980—; owner Depner Properties, 1980—; pres. Depner Architects & Planners, Inc.; v.p. Seamont Homes, 1982—; instr. design Wash. State U., 1975-76, Wash. Realtors Edn. Found. Lic. architect, Wash. cert. Nat. Council Archtl. Registration Bds. Mem. AIA, Nat. Assn. Am. Home Builders, Wash. State Assn. Home Builders (dir.), Wash. State U. Alumni Assn. Office: Hidden Valley Office Park 1750 112th St NE Suite C-225 Bellevue WA 98004

DE PREIST, JAMES ANDERSON, conductor; b. Phila., Nov. 21, 1936; s. James Henry and Ethel (Anderson) DeP.; B.S., U. Pa., 1958, M.A., 1961, L.H.D. (hon.), 1976; student Phila. Conservatory Music, 1959-61; m. Betty Louise Childress, Aug. 10, 1963; children—Tracy Elisabeth, Jennifer Anne; m. 2d, Ginette Grenier, July 19, 1980. Am. specialist music for State Dept., 1962-63; condr.-in-residence, Bangkok, Thailand, 1963-64; Am. debut with N.Y. Philharmonic, 1964; asst. condr. to Leonard Bernstein and N.Y. Philharmonic Orch., 1965-66; prin. guest condr. Symphony of New World, 1968-70; European debut with Rotterdam Philharmonic, 1969; asso. condr. Nat. Symphony Orch., Washington, 1971-75, prin. guest condr., 1975-76; music dir. L'Orchestre Symphonique de Que., 1976—, Oreg. Symphony, 1980—; appeared with Phila. Orch., 1972, Chgo. Symphony, 1973, Boston Symphony, 1973, Cleve. Orch., 1974; condr. Am. premiere Dvorak's First Symphony, N.Y. Philharmonic, 1972. Recipient 1st prize gold medal Dimitri Mitropoulos Internat. Music Competition for Condrs., 1964; Merit citation City of Phila., 1969. Grantee Martha Baird Rockefeller Fund for Music, 1969. Mem. Sigma Pi Phi. Address: L'Orchestre Symphonique de Quebec 350 E St-Cyrille Blvd Quebec City PQ G1R 2B4 Canada also Oregon Symphony Orch 813 SW Alder St Portland OR 97205

DERBALIAN, GEORGE, mech. engr.; b. Beirut, Lebanon, Aug. 30, 1950; came to U.S., 1968, naturalized, 1974; s. Artin and Anahid (Kavouksorian) D.; B.S., Ill. Inst. Tech., 1973; M.S., Stanford U., 1974, Ph.D., 1978; m. Sue Min Lin, July 4, 1980. Cons., Sargent & Lundy Engrs., Chgo., 1972-75; researcher Stanford (Calif.) U., Dept. Mech. Engring., 1974-78; cons. Failure Analysis Assos., Palo Alto, Calif., 1976-78, sr. engr., 1978—; cons. U.S. Naval Weapons Center, China Lake, Calif., 1978—, Electric Power Research Inst., Palo Alto, 1976—, Sandia Nat. Labs., 1982—, Bechtel Power Corp., 1983—, others. Ill. Inst. Tech. scholar, 1969-73; Stanford U. fellow, 1973-74. Recipient Mathematics award, Utica Free Acad., 1969. Mem. ASME, Sigma Xi, Tau Beta Pi, Pi Tau Sigma. Club: Stanford Chardonnay Soc. (founder 1975). Contbr. articles to profl. jours. Home: 65 Park Dr Atherton CA 94025 Office: 2225 E Bayshore Rd Palo Alto CA 94303

DERBES, DANIEL WILLIAM, multi-industry company executive; b. Cin., Mar. 30, 1930; s. Earl Milton and Ruth Irene (Grauten) D.; B.S., U.S. Mil. Acad., 1952; M.B.A., Xavier U., 1963; m. Patricia Ann Maloney, June 4, 1952; children—Donna Ann, Nancy Lynn (dec.), Stephen Paul. Devel. engr. AirResearch Mfg. Co., Phoenix, 1956-58, product line mgr., Los Angeles, 1967-70, asst. gen. mgr., 1970-75, v.p., gen. mgr., 1975—; sales engr. Garrett Corp., Dayton, Ohio, 1958-63, regional sales mgr., Los Angeles, 1963-67, now dir.; pres. Advanced Tech. Group, Signal Cos., Inc., La Jolla, Calif., 1980—, also dir.; dir. Ampex Corp., San Diego Gas & Electric Co. Bd. dirs. Ind. Colls. So. Calif., United Way San Diego, U. S.D., S.D. C. of C., Scripps Meml. Hosp. Found.; mem. exec. bd. Nat. council Boy Scouts Am.; mem. Corp. Fin. Council San Diego, San Diego Mus. Art. Served with U.S. Army, 1952-56. Mem. Atomic Indsl. Forum, Aerospace Industries Assn., West Point Soc. San Diego, San Diego World Affairs Council, Eagle Scout Alumni Assn., Pres.'s Roundtable of San Diego State U. Republican. Roman Catholic. Office: 11255 N Torrey Pines Rd La Jolla CA 92037

DERBY, HOWE ANNA, writer, public relations and marketing consultant; b. Honolulu, Aug. 12, 1932; d. Stephen Arthur and Dora (Cooke) Derby; m. Charles Hoffman Bond, Nov. 26, 1952 (div.); children—Caroline Bond Dvojacki, Susan, Boyd Davis, Sarah Bond Langan, Elizabeth; m. Robert Douglas Howe, Oct. 22, 1974 (dec.). Ed. Vassar Coll., U. Hawaii. Freelance writer and publicist, Honolulu, 1966—; pub. relations dir. YWCA Oahu, 1966-72; exec. dir. Moanalua Gardens Found., Honolulu, 1972-82; spl. agt. Bankers Life Ins. Co., Honolulu, 1982—; mktg. cons., pub. relations, editorial services ANNAgram, 1982—. Active Hawaiian Mission Children's Soc. Mem. Pub. Relations Soc. Am. (accredited). Republican. Episcopalian. Clubs: Honolulu Press, Daughters of Hawaii. Home: 1441 Pi'ikoi St #608 Honolulu HI 96822 Office: 1164 Bishop St #1009 Honolulu HI 96813

DEREGT, JOHN STEWART, real estate devel. exec.; b. San Francisco; s. Christian Anthony and Mary Margaret (Stewart) deR.; B.C.E., U. Santa Clara, 1950; m. Mal Padgett, Mar. 21, 1981; children—Kenneth, Thomas, James, Lauren, Mary, Jordan, Keith. Pres. Carl Holvick Co., Palo Alto, Calif., 1957-75; v.p. Holvick deRegt Koering, Palo Alto, 1960-75, pres., owner 1975—. Indsl. and office park counsel Urban Land Inst., 1978—; bd. dirs. Food Bank, San Jose, Calif., 1980—; bd. regents Bellarmine High Sch., San Jose, 1977—; bd. dirs. San Mateo County Devel. Assn., San Mateo, Calif., 1975—. Served with U.S. Army, 1951-53. Mem. Nat. Assn. Indsl. Office Parks. Club: Sharon Heights Country (Menlo Park, Calif.). Home: 97 Elena Ave Atherton CA 94025 Office: 1230 Oakmead Pkwy 210 Sunnyvale CA 94086

DERELIAN, DORIS VIRGINIA, dietitian, educator, cons.; b. Palo Alto, Calif., Aug. 8, 1945; d. Sarkis and Susan (Karahadian) D.; m. James Joseph Sullivan, Sept. 4, 1976; 1 dau., Stacy Anne. B.S., Calif. State U.-Fresno, 1968; M.S., U. Calif.-Davis, 1973; postgrad. UCLA, 1979—. Supr. food service St. Agnes Hosp., Fresno, 1965-68; nutrition cons. Dairy Council Calif., 1969-72; chief dietitian Unibetic Camps, San Bernardino, Calif., summers, 1968-76; program dir. health scis. Dairy Council Calif., 1973-78; exec. sec. Calif. Dietetic Assn., Playa Del Rey, Calif., 1978-83; edn. and nutrition cons., Los Angeles, 1979—; condr. numerous workshops for profl. assns., univs. Bd. dirs. Los Angeles Metabolic Found., Calif. Council Against Health Fraud. Mem. Am. Council on Sci. and Health, Am. Dietetic Assn., Am. Ednl. Research Assn., Am. Soc. Assn. Execs., Am. Soc. Health Manpower Edn. and Tng., Am. Soc. Profl. and Exec. Women, Calif. Council Against Health Fraud, Calif. Dietetic Assn., Los Angeles Metabolic Found., Nat. Assn. Exec. Women, UCLA Grad. Students Assn. in Edn.

DERGANCE, RALPH HUMBERT, aerospace company manager; b. Medford, Mass., Mar. 22, 1941; s. Raymond Lewis and Olga Marie (Davito) D.; m. Carole Leigh Smith, June 22, 1968; children—Jeannae Marie, Scott Andrew. B.S. in Aero. Engring., B.S. in Mgmt., U. Colo., 1964, postgrad. in mech. engring., 1964-67. Systems analyst, designer Martin Marietta, Denver, 1964-67, propulsion designer, developer Viking Mars Lander, 1967-73, research and devel. program mgr., sect. mgr., 1973-80, mgr. systems/tech. applications, strategic system div., 1980—. Recipient bus. acquistion award Martin Marietta, 1975, author award, 1981. Mem. AIAA, Tech. Mktg. Soc. Am., Denver Sporting House, Friends of Littleton Library, Littleton Soccer Assn. Republican. Presbyterian. Club: Internat. Sportsman (Denver). Contbr. articles to profl. jours. Home: 2454 Park Ln Littleton CO 80120

DERGARABEDIAN, PAUL, space tech. and ground transp. and energy systems co. exec.; b. Racine, Wis., Jan. 19, 1922; s. John and Mary (Hirmizian) D.; B.S., U. Wis., 1948, M.S., 1949; Ph.D. (Shell fellow), Calif. Inst. Tech., 1952; m. Mary A. Jansouzian, Dec. 27, 1947; children—Celeste (Mrs. William Prince), Claudia (Mrs. Larry Shackelford), Clarice (Mrs. John Bowler), Paul. Br. head U.S. Naval Weapons Center, Pasadena, Calif., 1952-55; lab. dir. TRW Systems, Redondo Beach, Calif., 1955-72; dir. Aerospace Corp., El Segundo, Calif., 1972-74, 80—; staff dir. energy systems group TRW, Redondo Beach, Calif., 1974-80; vis. prof. aeros. Calif. Inst. Tech., 1971-72. Served with USAAF, 1943-46. Fellow Am. Astronautical Soc. (pres. 1969-71); mem. Inst. Advancement Engring., Phi Beta Kappa, Sigma Xi. Home: 18 Poppy Trail Rolling Hills CA 90274 Office: 2350 E El Segundo Blvd El Segundo CA

DE RIOS, MARLENE DOBKIN, anthropology educator, adminstrator; b. N.Y.C., Apr. 12, 1939; d. Bernard and Anne (Schwartz) D.; m. Hildebrando Rios, Nov. 7, 1969; children—Evy, Gabriela. B.A. in Psychology, Queens Coll., 1959; M.A. in Anthropology, NYU, 1962; Ph.D. in Anthropology, U. Calif.-Riverside, 1972. Research assoc. San Marcos U., Lima, Peru, 1968-69, U. Calif.-Irvine dept. psychiatry,

1974-75; health sci. adminstr. NIMH, Rockville, Md., 1980-81; prof. anthropology and acting dir. Office of Faculty Research Calif. State U., Fullerton, 1969—. Am. Council Learned Socs. grantee, 1970; Nat. Inst. Drug Abuse grantee, 1973; NIMH fellow, 1975-76; Fulbright grantee, 1979. Mem. Am. Anthrop. Assn., AAAS (travel grantee 1982). Contbr. numerous articles to anthrop. jours.

DER KIUREGHIAN, ARMEN, civil engr., educator; b. Isfahan, Iran, Oct. 4, 1947; s. Sumbat and Arax (Aftandilian) Der K.; came to U.S., 1972; m. Nelly Ouzounian, 1983. M.S. in Civil Engring., Tehran U., 1971; Ph.D. in Civil Engring., U. Ill., 1975. Site engr. Ekbatan-Assad Co., Tehran, 1970-71; teaching and research asst. U. Ill., Champaign-Urbana, 1972-75; asst. prof. civil engring. U. So. Calif., Los Angeles, 1975-78; cons. Agbabian Assos., El Segundo, Calif., 1976-78; asst. prof. civil engring. U. Calif., Berkeley, 1978-81, asso. prof., 1981—; lectr. in field. Participant in Armenian cultural and communal activities. Recipient prizes in intercoll. painting competitions, 1965, 67; Gulbenkian Found. scholar, 1966-70. Mem. ASCE, Structural Engring. Assn. Calif., Seismol. Soc. Am., Earthquake Engring. Research Inst., Sigma Xi, Phi Kappa Phi. Mem. Armenian Apostolic Ch. Contbr. articles to profl. jours. Office: 725 Davis Hall U Calif Berkeley CA 94720

DER MANUELIAN, CHRISTOPHER YEGHIA, portrait photographer, lecturer; b. Beirut, Lebanon, Dec. 6, 1932; s. Yeghia Y. and Zartig K. (Bedrossian) D.; m. Nora S. Ashekian, Oct. 23, 1959; children—Christopher Yeghia, Jennifer. Student engring. Am. U., Beirut, 1953-54, Bradford Durfee Coll., 1956-57, Fresno State Coll., 1957-58. Asst. to photographers, 1958-62; now photographer-owner Christopher, San Mateo, Calif.; exhibited Photokina Exhibits, World Photo Show, Cologne, W.Ger., 1980, 82, Epcot Ctr., Orlando Fla.; featured in Hasselblad camera and Eastman Kodak publs.; represented in permanent collection Carpenter Ctr. Visual Arts, Harvard U.; lectr. on portrait photography and related subjects. Bd. dirs. not-for-profit orgns. Named Propr. of Studio of Yr., Studio Photography Mag., 1982; named to Photography Hall of Fame. Mem. Profl. Photographers Am. (cert. master photographer, awards for photo exhibits), Am. Soc. Photographers, Profl. Photographers Calif. (awards for photo exhibits), Camera Craftsmen of Am. Republican. Mem. United Ch. or Christ. Office: 205 S San Mateo Dr San Mateo CA 94401

DEROECK, (ROBERT) LEE, JR., financial manager, accountant; b. Elmhurst, Ill., Sept. 30, 1952; s. Robert Lee and Glennyce (Wilson) D.; m. Carrie Patrice Spencer, Sept. 25, 1955. B.A. in Acctg., Bus., Western Colo. U., 1975; M.S. in Acctg., Colo State U., 1976. C.P.A. Colo., 1979. Teaching asst. Colo. State U., Ft. Collins, 1975-76; sr. acct. Fox & Co. C.P.A.s, Colorado Springs, 1977-80; mgr. fin., control, mktg. Adolph Coors Co., Golden, Colo., 1983—. cons. tax, aactg. systems. Mem. Am. Inst. C.P.A.s, Colo. Soc. C.P.A.s. Home: 8952 W 31st Ln Arvada CO 80005 Office: Adolph Coors Co Golden CO 80401

DE RONDE, JOHN ALLEN, JR., lawyer; b. Albany, N.Y., July 22, 1947; s. John Allen and Kathleen Francis (Doran) DeR.; m. Marianne Elsie Karlsson, Mar. 19, 1983. B.A. in Polit. Sci., U. Calif.-Davis, 1969; J.D., U. Pacific, 1972. Bar: Calif. 1974, U.S. Supreme Ct. 1981; cert. specialist in family law, Calif. Assoc. DeRonde & Brewer, Fairfield, Calif., 1972-74; sole practice law, Fairfield, 1974-79; ptnr. DeRonde & DeRonde, Fairfield, 1979—; dir. Pietro's Pizza Parlors, Inc., Calif., Hawaii. Winner Jessup Internat. Moot Ct. competition, 1969. Mem. Assn. Trial Lawyers Am., Calif. Trial Lawyers Assn., ABA, Nat. Fedn. Ind. Bus., Bay Area Auto Dismantlers Assn. (hon.) Republican. Roman Catholic. Club: Lions. Contbr. articles to legal jours. Office: DeRonde & DeRonde 627 Delaware St Fairfield CA 94533

DERR, K. T., petroleum executive; pres. Chevron U.S.A. Inc. subs. Standard Oil Co. Calif. Office: Chevron USA Inc 575 Market St San Francisco CA 94105

DERY, GABRIEL, optometrist; b. Rabat, Morocco, July 7, 1938; came to U.S., 1966; s. Albert and Renee Sultana D.; m. Sarah Benudiz, Aug. 21, 1966; children—Mark Alain, Kenneth Jacques. O.D. (valedictorian), Superior Sch. Optometry, 1964; O.D., U. Montreal, 1965; O.D., So. Calif. Coll. Optometry, 1975. Pres., optometrist Gabriel Dery O.D., Inc., Los Angeles, 1975—; mem. med. staff Cedars-Sinai Med. Center; mem. faculty Pa. Coll. Optometry, Ind. Coll. Optometry; cons. spl. visual effects dept. 20th Century Fox; clin. investigator contact lenses, solutions. Bd. dirs. EM Habanim, Tifereth Israel temples. Recipient Bronze medal for services rendered to sci. French Govt., 1978. Fellow Am. Acad. Optometry; mem. Am. Optometric Assn., Calif. Optometric Assn., San Fernando Valley Optometric Assn., Coll. Optometrists Vision Devel., Council of 1000 at So. Calif. Coll. Optometry (cons. sport vision), Grand Prix Humanitaire de France, West Hollywood, Beverly Hills C. of C., Omega Epsilon Phi. Democrat. Contbr. articles to Optometric Mgmt. Jour. Home: 13300 Weddington St Van Nuys CA 91401 Office: Gabriel Dery OD Inc 8235 Santa Monica Blvd Suite 306 Los Angeles CA 90046

DESAI, CHANDRAKANT S., civil and mechanical engineering educator; b. Nadisar, Gujarat, India, Nov. 24, 1936; came to U.S., 1964, naturalized, 1973; s. Sankalchand P. and Kamala M. (Kothari) D.; m. Patricia L. Porter, Apr. 28, 1969; children—Maya C., Sanjay C. B.S., U. Bombay, 1959; M.S. (fellow) Rice U., 1966; Ph.D. (fellow), U. Tex., Austin, 1968. Registered profl. engr., Miss. Engr. various govt. and pvt. agys., India, 1959-64; research civil engr. Waterways, Expt. Sta., U.S. Army C.E., Vicksburg, Miss., 1968-74; prof. dept. civil engring. Va. Poly. Inst. and State U., Blacksburg, 1974-81; prof. dept. civil and mech. engring. U. Ariz., Tucson, 1981—; chmn. Internat. Com. on Numerical Methods in Geomechanics, 1976—; cons. to pvt. and govt. agys. Recipient Meritorious Civilian Service award U.S. Army C.E., 1972; Alexander von Humboldt-U.S. Sr. Scientist award German Govt., 1976; NSF grantee, 1976; Dept Transp. grantee, 1977. Mem. ASCE, Inst. Structural Engrs. (London), Internat. Soc. Rock Mechanics, Internat. Soc. Soil Mechanics and Found. Engrs. Co-author: Introduction to Finite Element Method, 1972; author: Elementary Finite Element Method, 1979; co-editor: Numerical Methods in Geotechnical Engineering, 1977; gen. editor Internat. Jour. for Numerical and Analytical Methods in Geomechanics, 1977—; editor procs. various confs. and symposia; contbr. articles to profl. jours. Home: 6776 N Harran Dr Tucson AZ 85704 Office: Dept Civil and Mech Engring U Ariz Tucson AZ 85721

DE ST. MAURICE, CHARLES EDWARD GOAD, consulting engineer; b. Berkeley, Calif., Apr. 8, 1911; s. Charles Albert and Hattie Belle (Goad) de St. M.; student U. Calif., 1930-32; m. Betty Jane Diller, July 4, 1981; children—Charles, James (dec.). From surveyor to area engr. Sacramento Dist. C.E., 1932-45; engr. H. Earl Parker, Inc., gen. contractors, Marysville, Calif., 1945-50; asso. Charles A. de St. Maurice, cons. engrs., Marysville and Colusa, Calif., 1950-56; pres. succesor M-H-M, Inc., engring., surveying and cons. engrs., Marysville, 1956—, Golden State Mining, Inc., Yuba City, Calif., 1962—, Pacific Mining & Aggregates, Inc., Marysville, 1978—; sec. Yuba-Sutter Counties Com. for Marysville Dam, 1964—. Chmn., Sutter Grand Jury Transp. Com., 1978-79, Sutter County Flood Control Com., 1978-79. Recipient numerous certificates of appreciation, service awards. Mem. ASCE, Calif. Central Valleys Flood Control Assn. (pres.), Am. Arbitration Assn. (nat. panel arbitrators), Am. Congress Surveying and Mapping, Nev. and Calif. Assn. Land Surveyors, Marysville-Yuba County C. of C. (chmn. natural resources com. 1964-67), Colusi County Hist. Soc. Republican. Methodist. Club: Elks. Home: 628 Harris St Marysville CA 95901 Office: 523 J St Marysville CA 95901

DE SALME, WILLA HITCHCOCK, guidance counselor, educator, coach; b. Cisco, Tex., May 30, 1931; d. Thomas Henry and Orphia (Culberson) Hitchcock; children—Charles William, Randy Joe. B.S. in Edn., McMurray Coll., 1953; M.Ed., Tex. Woman's U., 1965. Tchr. Atascosa (Tex.) Pub. Schs., 1953-55, Beeville (Tex.) Pub. Schs., 1955-56, Randolph AFB (Tex.) Pub. Schs., 1957-62, Fallbrook (Calif.) Pub. Schs., 1962-79; coach girls' basketball and track Breckenridge (Tex.) Schs., 1979-80, Ivy High Sch., Fallbrook, 1980—. Mem. Calif. Tchrs. Assn., Tchrs. Assn., NEA, Tex. High Sch. Coaches Assn. Democrat. Baptist. Home: 3237 Carolyn Circle Oceanside CA 92054 Office: Ivy High Sch PO Box 368 Fallbrook CA 92054

DESANTIS, JULIO JUSTIN, insurance agency executive; b. N.Y.C., July 31, 1942; s. Julio and Yolanda Celeste (Firpo) DeS.; student CCNY, 1960-61; B.S., U.S. Mil. Acad., 1965; M.C.E., N.Y. U., 1968; m. Judith Ann Babbitt, Oct. 25, 1969; children—Anne, Rosemarie. Engr., N.Y. dist. U.S. Army C.E., 1965-68; ind. ins. agt., N.Y.C., 1968-72, Mercer Island, Wash., 1972—; pres. Land & Sea Agy., Inc., Mercer Island, 1978—; dir. ViKing One Corp., Seattle. Bd. dirs. St. Brendan Food Coop, Bothell, Wash., 1981—. Served with AUS, 1961-65. Mem. Nat. Assn. Life Underwriters, Assn. Grads. U.S. Mil. Acad., Nat. Wood Carvers Assn. Roman Catholic. Office: 601 Valley St Suite 304 Seattle WA 98109

DE SANTIS, NUNZIO PASQUALE, nuclear pharmacy executive; b. Cansano, Italy, Mar. 24, 1951; s. Luciano and Velia (Di Giacomo) De S.; B.S. in Pharmacy, U. N.Mex., 1974; m. Sherolyn Kay Smith, Aug. 12, 1973; children—Louie, Rhonda. Pres., Radiopharmacy Assocs., Inc., El Paso, 1974-75; dir. Nuclear Pharmacy, Inc., 1975—, mgr. Eastern dist., Phila., 1979, v.p. ops., Albuquerque, 1980, sr. v.p. ops., 1980-81, exec. v.p., 1981—, chief operating officer, 1982—, sec.-treas., 1982—. Mem. Am. Pharm. Assn., Soc. Nuclear Medicine. Democrat. Office: 4272 Balloon Park Albuquerque NM 87109

DE SAPIO, RODOLFO VITTORIO, mathematician, educator; b. N.Y.C., Aug. 16, 1936; s. Martino and Antoinette (Grasso) D.; student City U. N.Y., 1955-57, U. Mich., 1957-59; S.M., U. Chgo., 1961, Ph.D., 1964. Instr. math. Stanford, 1964-66; asst. prof. math. U. Calif. at Los Angeles, 1966-70, asso. prof., 1970—; asso. prof. Belfer Grad. Sch. Sci., Yeshiva U., N.Y.C., 1969-72; vis. mem. Inst. Advanced Study, Princeton, N.J., 1968. Prin. investigator NSF Grants for Research Math. Mem. Am. Math. Soc., AAUP, Math. Assn. Am., N.Y. Acad. Scis. Contbr. articles to profl. jours. Home: 927 Wellesley Ave Los Angeles CA 90049 Office: Dept Math U Calif 405 Hilgard Ave Los Angeles CA 90024

DESCAMP, VICTOR ALFRED, mech. engr.; b. Kirksville, Mo., Sept. 1, 1936; s. Arthur F. and Lucille (Daubresse) DesC.; student Northeast Mo. State Coll., 1954-56; U. Detroit, 1956-57; B.S. in Mech. Engring., U. Mo., 1959; M.S., Chrysler Inst. Engring., 1961; m. Shirley D. Jeffries, Aug. 2, 1959; children—Arthur Stephen, William Curtis, Lori Renee. Devel. engr. Ford Motor Co., Detroit, 1956; design engr. Fairbanks Morse & Co., St. Louis, 1957, Internat. Harvester Co., Chgo., 1958, Chrysler Corp., Detroit, 1959-61; program mgr. Martin-Marietta Corp., Denver, 1961-74; constrn. project engr. Westinghouse Corp., Richland, Wash., 1974—. Registered profl. engr., Colo. Mem. Sigma Tau Gamma, Pi Tau Sigma, Alpha Phi Omega. Republican. Baptist. Patentee in field. Home: 1860 Alder Ave Richland WA 99352 Office: PO Box 1970 Richland WA 99352

DE SILVA, COLIN, developer, fin. broker, author; b. Ceylon, Feb. 11, 1920; s. John William and Rose Mary (Weerasinghe) de S.; came to U.S., 1962, naturalized, 1972; children—Devayani, Cherie-Parakrama Chandrasoma. With Ceylon Civil Service, 1946-56; asst. sec. def., commr. nat. housing Ceylon, 1948-56; mng. dir. Colombo Agys., Ltd., 1957-62; pres. Bus. Investment Ltd., Honolulu, 1964—, Econ. Devel. & Engring. Cons., Inc., 1967—; chmn. Gen. Mgmt. Corp., 1973—; chmn., dir. Condominium Mgmt., Inc. Lectr., cons. Peace Corps, 1964-67; dir. Am. Security Council. Past chmn. bd. Opera Players of Hawaii; bd. dirs. Waikiki Improvement Assn.; past trustee Hawaii Pacific Coll. Mem. Honolulu, Portland (Oreg.) chambers commerce, Screen Actors Guild, McCully Bus. and Profl. Assn. (pres. 1972-73, dir.), Natural History Mus., Smithsonian Instn. Home: 1040 Kealaolu Ave Honolulu HI 96816 Office: Pacific Trade Center Honolulu HI 96813

DE SIMONE, JAMES WILLIAM, construction executive; b. Chgo., Jan. 3, 1932; s. James and Helen Catherine (Lattanzia) DeS.; B.S. in E.E., U. Ill., 1957; J.D., DePaul U., 1961; m. Marilyn Gifford, Apr. 26; children—Deborah, Paula, Michael, John, Stephen. Bar: Ill. 1962. Gen. counsel IIT Research Inst., 1959-65; patent counsel Gen. Dynamics Co., N.Y.C., 1965-69, corp. dir. internat. ops., 1969-73; v.p. IMODCO, Inc., Los Angeles, 1973-75; pres., chief exec. officer Vinnell Corp., Alhambra, Calif., 1975-82 also dir.; chmn., chief exec. officer DMS Internat., Inc., Pasadena, Calif., 1982—, Taser Industries, Inc., El Toro, Calif., 1983—; dir. Security Mut. Casualty Co. Served with U.S. Navy, 1949-53. Mem. ABA, Assn. Gen. Contractors, Am. Def. Preparedness Assn. Roman Catholic. Clubs: Jonathan, Crockfords, Annandale Golf. Home: 1215 Parkview Ave Pasadena CA 91103 Office: Les Bureaux Ctr 720 45 S Hudson Ave Pasadena CA 91101

DESLONDE, JAMES LOUIS, ednl. sociologist; b. Little Rock, Feb. 27, 1939; B.S. in Biology, Xavier U., 1960; M.A. in Urban Edn., Case Western U., 1967, Ph.D. in Ednl. Sociology, 1970; m. Rosalie Deslonde; children—Jimmy, Denise. Tchr., Peace Corps vol., Ethiopia, Cleve. Pub. schs., New Orleans pub. schs., 1962-67; asst. dir. program for Action by Citizens in Edn., Cleve., 1967-69; asst. prof. U. Calif., Riverside, 1970-73, also dir. lab. schs. Western Regional Sch. Desegregation projects; asst. prof. Stanford (Calif.) U. Sch. Edn., 1973-80; co-prin. investigator Violent Juvenile Offender Program, Dept. Justice, San Francisco, 1982—; dir. nat. ethnographic study of Tchr. Corps programs; lectr., cons. on sch. desegregation. Pres. NAACP, Riverside, 1971-72. Mem. Am. Ednl. Research Assn., Nat. Council for the Social Studies, Phi Delta Kappa. Developed survey instruments to assess multicultural social learning climate. Specialist in sch. desegregation, tchr. edn., cultural pluralism in edn., curriculum evaluation, survey research methodology. Office: URSA Inst Pier 1 1/2 San Francisco CA 94111

DESMARAIS, CHARLES JOSEPH, museum director; b. N.Y.C., Apr. 21, 1949; s. Charles Emil and Helen Barbara (Young) D.; m. Sharon McLeod; m. 2d, Patricia Jon Carroll, June 15, 1979. Student Western Conn. State Coll., 1967-71; B.S., SUNY, 1975; M.F.A., SUNY-Buffalo, 1977. Curator, Friends of Photography, Carmel, Calif., 1973-74; asst. editor Afterimage Mag., Rochester, N.Y., 1975-77; dir. Chgo. Center for Contemporary Photography, 1977-79; editor Exposure Mag., Chgo., 1977-81; dir. Calif. Mus. of Photography, U. Calif., Riverside, 1981—. Art critics fellow Nat. Endowment for Arts, 1979. Mem. Am. Assn. Mus., Soc. for Photog. Edn (dir.), Photog. Hist. Soc. N.Y. Author: The Portrait Extended, 1980; Michael Bishop, 1979; Roger Mertin: Records 1976-78, 1978; contbr. articles to publs. including Afterimage, Art in America, Artweek, Modern Photography. Office: Calif Mus Photography Univ Calif Riverside CA 92521

DESMARAIS, ROGER ADRIAN, mgmt. cons.; b. Yakima, Wash., Feb. 7, 1936; s. Adrian Conrad and Elizabeth (Fix) D.; M.A., Gonzaga U., 1963; M.A. Edn., Loyola U., Chgo., 1968; Ph., U. No. Colo., 1972; m. Suzanne Shea, July 1, 1972; children—Michelle Arienne, Jill Allison, Michael Benjamin. Mem. S.J., 1953-71; dir. grad. degree program in adult edn. Seattle U., 1971; dir. tng. Volt Tech. Sch., Kansas City, Mo., 1973-74; dir. tng. and devel. Kaiser Permanente, San Francisco, 1975-77; mgr. orgn. devel. Bechtel Corp., Los Angeles, 1977-78; pres. ODS, Santa Ana, Calif., 1978-80; v.p. Mgmt. Analysis Co., San Diego, 1980-82; pres. Corporate Systemics, Inc., San Diego, 1982—; prof. Seattle U., 1968-72. Mem. Project Mgmt. Inst., Am. Soc. Tng. and Devel., Orgn. Devel. Network, Nat. Tng. Labs., Interact 82. Democrat. Roman Catholic. Author: Adolescent Psychology, 1969; Organization Productivity, 1981. Home: PO Box 2682 Rancho Santa Fe CA 92067 Office: 11085 Sorrento Valley Rd San Diego CA 92121

DESMOND, GARY LEE, architect; b. Detroit, June 24, 1943; s. Bert Lynn and Sandra (D'Onofrio) D.; B.Arch., U. Mich., 1966; m. Rosemary, July 2, 1966; children—Gary Lee, Bryan, Gina Marie. Architect Gunnar Birkerts & Assocs., Birmingham, Mich., 1968-72; asso. Muchow Assocs., Architects, Denver, 1972-78; ptnr. Hoover Berg Desmond, Architects, Denver, 1978—, corp. v.p., sec. Vice pres. coaching Littleton Hockey Assn., also dir.; merit badge counselor Denver Council Boy Scouts Am. First place winner archtl. design competitions, 1976, 77; cert. constrn. specifier. Mem. AIA (chmn. practice mgmt. com. Denver chpt.), Constrn. Specifications Inst., Council of Ednl. Facility Planners. Home: 6074 S Krameria Englewood CO 80111 Office: 1535 19th St Denver CO 80202

DE SOLA, RALPH, author, editor, educator; b. N.Y.C., July 26, 1908; s. Solomon and Grace (von Geist) De S.; student Columbia U., 1927, 29, 31, Swarthmore Coll., 1928; m. Dorothy Clair, Dec. 24, 1944. Collector, N.Y. Zool. Soc., N.Y.C., 1928-29, 30-33, Am. Mus. Natural History, N.Y.C., 1930, Tropical Biology Soc., Miami, Fla., 1933-34; zool. editor Fed. Writers Project, N.Y.C., 1935-39; tech. dir. U.S. Microfilm Corp., N.Y.C., 1939-49; hist. dir. Travel U.S. 90 and Mexican Border Trails Assn., Del Rio, Tex., 1951-54; publs. editor Convair div. Gen. Dynamics Corp., San Diego, 1955-68; instr. tech. English, San Diego Unified Colls., 1962—; author: (with Fredrica De Sola) Strange Animals and Their Ways, 1933; Microstat Technicians Handbook, 1943; Microfilming, 1944; Worldwide What and Where, 1975; compiler: Abbreviations Dictionary, 1958, 7th edit., 1984; Crime Dictionary, 1982; Great Americans Discuss Religion, booklet, 1963; (with Dorothy De Sola) A Dictionary of Cooking, 1969; Great Americans Examine Religion, 1983; editor: International Conversion Tables, 1961; compiler-editor Whitman books, specializing in zool. juveniles, 1937-41; translator: Beethoven-by-Berlioz, 1975; cons. on microfilming to USN, on abbreviations to Dept. Def.; contbr. articles to Copeia, 1928-32, revs. to classical records and concerts to Freeman, Del Rio News-Herald, San Diego Engr., Downtown. Home: 1819 Puterbaugh St San Diego CA 92103

DESOTO, SIMON, mech. engr.; b. N.Y.C., Jan. 8, 1925; s. Albert and Esther (Eskenazi) Soto; B.M.E., CCNY, 1945; M.M.E., Syracuse U., 1950; Ph.D., UCLA, 1965; 1 dau., Linda Jane. Engr., Johns-Manville Corp., N.Y.C., 1946-48; instr. in engring. Syracuse U., 1948-50; research engr. Stratos-Fairchild Corp., Farmingdale, N.Y., 1950-54; research specialist Lockheed Missile Systems div. Lockheed Corp., Van Nuys, Calif., 1954-56; sr. tech. specialist Rocketdyne Rockwell Internat., Canoga Park, Calif., 1956-69; asso. prof. mech. engring. Calif. State U., Long Beach, 1969-72, prof., 1972—; lectr. UCLA, 1954-70; cons. engr.; dir., sec.-treas. Am. Engring. Devel. Co.; mem. tech. planning com. Public Policy Conf: The Energy Crisis, Its Effect on Local Govts., 1973; founding mem. Calif. State U. and Colls. Statewide Energy Consortium and cons. in its tech. assistance program. Served with U.S. Mcht. Marine, 1945-46. Recipient award for faculty providing most stimulation and interest UCLA Engring. Student Body, 1962; Outstanding Faculty award Calif. State U., Long Beach, 1971, 73, 76; lic. profl. engr., Calif., N.Y. State. Mem. AAAS, World Future Soc., Tau Beta Pi, Pi Tau Sigma. Author: Thermostatics and Thermodynamics: An Instructor's Manual, 1963; research, publs. in field. Office: Calif State U Long Beach CA 90840

DESOUZA, PAUL, health foods co. exec.; b. Vidago, Portugal, May 8, 1911; s. Manuel Augusto and Maria Rita (Dias) DeS.; came to U.S., 1920, naturalized, 1933; ed. public schs., univ. extension courses; m. Rosalie Pryor, Nov. 9, 1974; 1 dau. by previous marriage—Silvia. Pub., Portuguese-Am. Mag., 1936-38; sales mgr. Rigid Mfg. Co., East Los Angeles, 1942-44; founder 1st Organic Gardening and Nutrition Club in U.S., 1946; owner, mgr. Health Food Mfg. Co., Glendale, Calif., 1948—; organizer Natural Methods Growers Program, 1955, Escondido (Calif.) Eco-Farming Day, 1956; bus. cons., lectr. World U., Ojai, Calif.; book pub.; tchr. nutrition, health and human relations. Mem. ACLU, Nat. Geog. Soc. Home: 9381 Terra Linda Way Calimesa CA 92320 Office: Desouza's Mini Plaza Banning CA 92220

DESPOL, JOHN ANTON, state deputy labor commissioner; b. San Francisco, July 22, 1913; s. Anton and Bertha (Balzer) D.; m. Jeri Kaye Steep, Dec. 7, 1937; children—Christopher Paul, Anthony John. Student, U. So. Calif., 1931, Los Angeles Jr. Coll., 1929-30. Sec.-treas., council Calif. CIO, Los Angeles, 1950-58, gen. v.p. Calif. Labor Fedn. AFL-CIO, San Francisco, 1958-60; internat. rep. United Steelworkers Am., Los Angeles, 1937-68; with Dempsey-Tegeler & Co., Inc., 1968-70; rep. Bache & Co., 1970-71; commr. Fed. Mediation and Conciliation Services, Los Angeles, 1972-73; indsl. relations cons., 1971-76; dep. labor commr. State of Calif., 1976—; mem. Nat. Steel Panel Nat. War Labor Bd., 1944-45; chmn. bd. trustees Union Mgmt. Ins. Trust Fund, Los Angeles, 1948-68. Mem. Calif. Def. Council, 1939-41, 10th Regional War Manpower Commn., 1942-46; bd. dirs. So. Calif. region NCCJ, 1960-68; bd. dirs. Los Angeles Community Chest; del. Nat. Democratic Conv., 1948, 52, 56, 60; mem. Los Angeles County Dem. Com., 1942-44; mem. exec. com. Calif. Dem. Com., 1952-56; chmn. Calif. Congl. dist., 1954-56; mem. Calif. Legislative Adv. Commn. to State Legislature, 1956-59; del. Nat. Republican Conv., 1968; bd. dirs. Los Angeles World Affairs Council, Braille Inst. Am.; bd. govs. Town Hall, Los Angeles, 1941-44, 67-70, chmn. econ. sect., 1964-65; mem. Los Angeles Com. Fgn. Relations, 1946—; mem. Calif. Job Tng. and Placement Council, 1967-68. Mem. Indsl. Relations Research Assn., Inst. Indsl. Relations. Home: 4717 Willis Ave Apt 7 Sherman Oaks CA 91402 Office: 8155 Van Nuys Blvd Suite 950 Panorama City CA 91402

DESROCHERS, CYNTHIA GAMBLE BILL, educator, consultant; b. Topanga Canyon, Calif., Mar. 16, 1947; d. Joseph Thomas and Louise Warren (Gamble) Bill; B.A., UCLA, 1971, M.Ed., 1972, Ed.D., 1982; m. Michael John Desrochers, Oct. 2, 1971; children—Lawson Raiford, Vanessa Louise. Classroom tchr., supervising and demonstration tchr. Los Angeles Unified Sch. Dist., 1971-74; supervising tchr. Univ. Elem.

Sch., UCLA, 1975-83; prof. Calif. State U.-Northridge, 1983—; state cons. in tchr. edn., 1976—; nat. cons. tchr. edn. and supervision, 1977—; instr. extension classes UCLA. Mem. Am. Ednl. Research Assn., Assn. Supervision and Curriculum Devel., Phi Delta Kappa, Pi Lambda Theta. Democrat. Methodist. Contbr. articles to profl. jours. Office: Calif State U Sch Edn Northridge CA 91330

DESTEFANO, SALLY ANN, stores personnel executive; b. Holyoke, Mass., Jan. 16, 1947; d. Winifield Schley and Dorothy Ann (Williams) Bowers; m. James Vincent DeStefano, Dec. 31, 1971 (div.). B.A., U. Fla., 1969, M.Ed. (equivalent), 1972; student Internat. Found. Employee Benefits, 1980; cert. in employee relations law Inst. Applied Mgmt. and Law, 1982. Instr., counselor Lake-Sumter Community Coll., Leesburg, Fla., 1971-72; tech. editor programming methods div. GTE, N.Y.C., 1972-73; job analyst Fairleigh Dickinson U., Rutherford, N.J., 1973; compensation supr. Stanford U., 1974-75; corp. compensation mgr. Intel Corp., Santa Clara, Calif., 1975-79; dir. human resources The Gap Stores, Inc., San Bruno, Calif., 1979—; tchr. personnel course Resource Ctr. for Women, Palo Alto, Calif. Mem. No. Calif. Human Resources Council, Nat. Assn. Female Execs., Phi Mu. Republican. Presbyterian. Home: 601 Leahy St Apt 302 Redwood City CA 94061 Office: Gap Stores Inc 900 Cherry Ave San Bruno CA 94066

DE TARR, FRANCIS, diplomat; b. Berkeley, Calif., Mar. 15, 1926; s. Adraith and Elizabeth (Henry) De T.; student Yale U., 1944, B.A., 1949, M.A., 1953, Ph.D., 1958; student Sorbonne, 1948, 49-51, U. Geneva, 1947, Nat. War Coll., 1970-71; m. Geraldine Dallas, Aug. 11, 1951; children—Claire, Anne, Charles, Christine. Dock rep. U.S. C.E., Skagway, Alaska, 1943-44; tchr. Lycee Paul Langevin, Suresnes, France, 1949-50; instr., Sorbonne, Paris, 1950-51; curator Lindbergh Collection, Yale U. Library, New Haven, 1954-57; fgn. service officer, U.S. Dept. State, 1957—, vice counsul, Florence, Italy, 1958-60, 2d, sec., Paris, 1961-66, 2d. sec., 1st. sec., Saigon, 1966-68, 1st. sec., Paris, 1968-70, Nat. War Coll., 1970-71, polit. counselor, Rabat, Morocco, 1971-74, diplomat-in-resident, Providence, 1974-75, dir. Office of Ops. Policy, Dept. State, Washington, 1975-77, polit. counselor, Brussels, Belgium, 1977-80; counselor for polit. affairs, American Embassy, Paris, 1980—. Served with USAAF, 1944-45. Recipient Porter prize, Yale U., 1958. Mem. Am. Polit. Sci. Assn., Internat. Polit. Sci. Assn., Soc. for French Hist. Studies. Author: The French Radical Party from Herriot to Mendes-France, 1961. Home: 409 Vermont Ave Berkeley CA 94707 Office: Care Dept of State Washington DC 20520

DETRICK, MARK, orthodontist; b. Hollywood, Calif., Aug. 15, 1939; s. Harold Frederick Detrick and Marka Dorothy (Skidmore) Ritchie; student U. Wis., 1957-59; A.B., U. Calif.-Berkeley, 1961; D.D.S., Coll. Physicians and Surgeons, San Francisco, 1965; postgrad. U. Ill., 1968-70; m. Laurentina Anna Vliegen, May 2, 1982; children— Kimberly Marka, Gregory Caenen. Practice dentistry specializing in orthodontics, El Toro and Newport Beach, Calif., 1970—. Bd. dirs. Met. YMCA, Orange County, 1973-74; bd. mgrs. Saddlebach Valley YMCA, 1972-75, vice chmn., 1974-75. Served with USN, 1965-68, capt. Res. Mem. ADA, Calif., Orange County dental assns., Am. Assn. Orthodontists, Pacific Coast Assn. Orthodontists, Orange County Orthodontic Study Club, Naval Res. Assn., Res. Officers Assn., Mil. Surgeons U.S. Republican. Club. Exchange (sec. 1972-73, pres. 1978-79, dir.). Home: 221 San Joaquin St Laguna Beach CA 92651 Office: 23184 El Toro Frontage Rd El Toro CA 92630

DETTERMAN, ROBERT LINWOOD, energy company executive; b. Norfolk, Va., May 1, 1931; s. George William and Jeanneille (Watson) D.; m. Virginia Armstrong; children—Janine, Patricia, William Arthur. B.S. in Engring., Va. Poly. Inst., 1953; Ph.D. in Nuclear Engring., Oak Ridge Sch. Reactor Tech., 1954; postgrad. Engring. test dir. Foster Wheeler Co., N.Y.C., sr. research engr. Atomics Internat. Co., Canoga Park, Calif., 1959-62; chief project engr. Rockwell Internat. Co., Canoga Park, 1962-68, dir. bus. devel., 1968 ; dir. Bo-Gin, Inc.; dir. Arabian Horse Fed. Credit Union, 1974-82. Trustee, mem. exec. com. Morris Animal Found.; treas., trustee Arabian Horse Trust; chmn. Cal Bred Futurity; Mem. Soc. for the Preservation of Variety Arts, Am. Nuclear Soc., Atomic Indsl. Forum, Acad. Magical Arts, Am. Horse Shows Assn., Am. Horse Council, Tau Beta Phi, Eta Kappa Nu, Phi Kappa Phi. Republican.

DETWEILER, WALTER BOOSER, architect; b. Harrisburg, Pa., Sept 19, 1932; s. Walter B. and Margaret (Wise) D.; B.Arch., Carnegie Mellon U., 1955; postgrad Yale U., 1960-61; m. Virginia Marie Weber, Apr. 27, 1968 (div. 1979); children—Mark Booser (dec.), Devon Elizabeth. Chief designer Adrian Wilson & Assos., Far East Asia, Manila, 1961-66; chief designer Leo S. Wou Assos., Honolulu, 1967; dir. design, partner Meyers, Detweiler & Assos., Architects, Honolulu, 1968-82; pres. Detweiler/Architects/Assocs., Honolulu, 1982—. Served to 1st lt. U.S. Army, 1955-57. Mem. AIA (Merit award Hawaii sect 1978, 83), Am. Acad. Arts and Scis., Nat. Trust Historic Preservation, World Future Soc., Smithsonian Instn. Club: Outrigger Canoe. Home: 2244 Round Top Dr Honolulu HI 96822 Office: 837 Cooke St Suite 200 Honolulu HI 96813

DEUEL, CARL LESLIE, chemist; b. Kansas City, Mo., Sept. 16, 1926; s. Carl Leslie and Enon Rose (Wood) D.; B.S., Tulane U., 1946; m. Rosemary Mullikin, Feb. 23, 1947; children—Teresa, Timothy, Carl, William. Chemist, Clin. Lab., Covina, Calif., 1948-51, Aerojet Gen. Corp., Azusa, Calif., 1951-57, 58-71; self-employed, Alhambra, Calif., 1957-58; co-founder, 1971, since chemist Analytical Research Labs., Inc., Monrovia, Calif., 1971—, dir. gas analysis lab., 1971—. Active local Boy Scouts Am., PTA, Mountain Rescue. Served with USNR, 1944-48. Recipient various service awards, certs. of appreciation. Fellow Am. Inst. Chemists. Republican. Clubs: Order Foresters, Modern Woodmen Am. Author papers in field. Home: PO Box 993 Running Springs CA 92382 Office: PO Box 369 Monrovia CA 91016

DEUEL, JAMIESON KOBY, environmental consulting firm executive; b. Geneva, N.Y., Feb. 23, 1932; s. Melvin Edgerton and Madalene (Koby) D.; B.S., U.S. Naval Acad., 1954; M.B.A., U. N.Mex., 1971; children—Holly, Beth, Martha, Jamieson Koby. Commd. ensign U.S. Navy, 1954, advanced through grades to comdr., 1975; on nuclear submarines Nautilus, Barb, Dace and Lafayette; ret., 1975; sr. engr. Ranchers, Albuquerque, 1975-77; pres. Deuel & Assocs., Inc., Albuquerque, 1977—; gen. mgr., v.p. Ana Cor Labs., Albuquerque, 1982—. Wrestling referee 1972 Olympics, Munich; pres. Ams. for Rational Energy Alternatives, 1977-79; chmn. N.Mex. Youth Soccer Assn., 1978-79; tournament dir. World Schoolboy Wrestling Champs, 1978. Mem. AIME, U.S. Naval Inst., Mensa. Contbr. articles to profl. jours. Office: Deuel & Assocs Inc 7300 Jefferson St NE Albuquerque NM 87109

DEUKMEJIAN, GEORGE, governor Calif.; b. Albany, N.Y., June 6, 1928; s. C. George and Alice (Gairdan) D.; B.A., Siena Coll., 1949; J.D., St. John's U., 1952; m. Gloria M. Saatjian, 1957; children—Leslie Ann, George Krikor, Andrea Diane. Bar: N.Y. 1952, Calif. 1956, U.S. Supreme Ct. 1970. Mem. Calif. State Assembly, 1963-67; mem. Calif. Senate, 1967-79, minority leader; atty. gen. State of Calif., 1979-83; gov. State of Calif., 1983—; past dep. county counsel, Los Angeles. Mem. exec. bd. Long Beach council Boy Scouts Am. Served with U.S. Army, 1953-55. Mem. ABA, Long Beach Bar Assn., Long Beach C. of C. (past dir.), Am. Legion, Navy League. Republican. Episcopalian. Club: Elks. Office: Office of Governor State Capitol 1st Floor Sacramento CA 95814

DEUPREE, ROBERT MARSHALL, physician, ret. govt. ofcl.; b. Elizabeth, Colo., Dec. 26, 1912; s. Elmer Burton and Mary Ayer (Griffin) DeuP.; student Santa Ana Coll., 1930-33, Los Angeles City Coll., 1937-38; D.O., Coll. Osteo. Physicians and Surgeons, 1942; M.D., Met. U., 1948; postgrad. UCLA, 1952-53; A.B., Calif. State U., Fullerton, 1962; M.A., Calif. State U., Long Beach, 1963; postgrad. (Nat. Inst. Dental Health fellow) Purdue U., 1963-64; m. Harriett Ann Janetos, Oct. 11, 1963; children—Carol J., R. Scott. Intern, Wilshire Hosp., Los Angeles, 1942-43, resident in neurology, 1943-44; practice medicine, Los Angeles, 1944-57, El Monte, Calif., 1957-58, Newport Beach, Calif., 1958-59; dir. Rush-Merced Clinic, 1957-58; asso. med. dir. Aerojet Gen. Corp., Azusa, Calif., 1967-69, Am. Airlines, Los Angeles, 1969; ships surgeon U. Calif. Scripps Inst. Oceanography, 1969; area med. officer Div. Fed. Employee Health, USPHS, Los Angeles, 1970—; head dept. internal medicine and radiology Hiss Orthopedic Clinic, Los Angeles, 1953-57; instr. differential diagnosis Coll. Osteo. Physicians and Surgeons, Los Angeles, 1945-49; instr. med. terminology N. Orange Community Coll. Dist., 1966-78; pres., Deustar Internat. Corp.; research fellow VA Hosp., Long Beach State Coll., UCLA Inst. Laryngol. Research, 1962-63. Diplomate in aerospace medicine. Fellow Royal Soc. Health, N.Y. Acad. Scis., Am. Occupational Med. Assn., Am. Aerospace Med. Assn. (assoc.); mem. Royal Soc. Medicine, Aviation Hall of Fame (charter), Asclepiad. Author, editor: DeuPree International Emergency Medical Translations, 1972; co-author: Travis' Handbook of Speech Pathology and Audiology, 1972; editor Jour. Pro-Re-Nata, 1947-50. Home: 2625 W Huckleberry Rd Santa Ana CA 92706

DEUTSCH, BARRY JOSEPH, mgmt. devel. co. exec.; b. Gary, Ind., Aug. 10, 1941; s. Jack Elias and Helen Louise (La Rue) D.; B.S., U. So. Calif., 1969, M.B.A. magna cum laude, 1970; m. Gina Krispinsky, Feb. 20, 1972. Lectr. mgmt. U. So. Calif., Los Angeles, 1967-70; pres., founder Organizational Directions Inc., mgmt. cons. co. tng. upper and middle mgmt., Los Angeles, 1970—, chmn. bd., 1975—. Chmn. bd. govs. Am. Hist. Center, 1980—. Served with M.I., U.S. Army, 1964-66. Mem. Am. Mgmt. Assn., Am. Soc. Bus. and Mgmt. Cons.'s, Am. Soc. Tng. and Devel., Internat. Mgmt. by Objectives Inst. Author: Leadership Techniques, 1969; Recruiting Techniques, 1970; The Art of Selling, 1973; Professional Real Estate Management, 1975; Strategic Planning, 1976; Employer/Employee: Making the Transition, 1978; Managing by Objectives, 1980; Conducting Effective Performance Appraisal, 1982. Home: 2846 Greenbrier Rd Long Beach CA 90815 Office: 3868 Carson St Torrance CA 90503

DEUTSCH, FRANCINE, developmental psychology educator; b. Reading, Pa., Aug. 9, 1948; d. Arthur and Dorace Gertrude (Asher) D. A.B., Albright Coll., 1969; M.S., Pa. State U., 1970, Ph.D., 1972. Instr. child and adolescent devel. Pa. State U., 1969-72, dep. head Pa. Day Care Project, 1972, research assoc. child and family relationships, 1972-73, asst. prof. human devel., 1973-77, asst. prof. child devel., child services, prof.-in-charge child devel. and child services lab., 1977-81; prof. child devel., family relationships San Diego State U., 1981—, dir. Family Life Edn. Project, 1981—. NSF trainee, 1971-72; Danforth fellow, 1979—. Mem. AAAS, Am. Ednl. Research Assn., Am. Psychol. Assn., Am. Home Econs. Assn., Nat. Assn. Early Childhood Tchr. Educators, Nat. Council Family Relations, Orthopsychiat. Assn., Soc. Research in Child Devel. Democrat. Jewish. Author: Life-Span Individual and Family Development, 1977; Adult Development and Aging. A Life-Span Perspective, 1981; Child Services On Behalf of Children, 1982. Contbr. articles to profl. jours.

DEUTSCH, REENA, mathematics educator; b. Englewood, N.J., Aug. 21, 1950; d. Samuel and Helen (Sobel) Deutsch; 1 son, Deven (dec.). B.A. in Math., Boston U., 1971; M.S. in Stats., San Diego State U., 1976, M.B.A., 1978. Mgmt. analyst Nat. Supply Ctr., San Diego, 1972-74; mgmt. analyst, math. statistician Naval Ocean Systems Ctr., San Diego, 1975-79; math., stats. instr. Nat. U., San Diego, 1981—, San Diego State Univ., 1981—, U. San Diego, 1982—; math. tutor. Block capt. Community Alert Program; chmn. alumni recruiting com. Boston U. Mem. Am. Statis. Assn., Am. Inst. Decision Scis. Home: 7886 Hillandale Dr San Diego CA 92120

DEVANEY, EVERETT MAURICE, JR., hosp. adminstr.; b. Peabody, Mass., July 8, 1948; s. Everett M. and Rose E. (Domingos) D.; B.S., Salem State Coll., 1970; M.Public Adminstrn., Golden Gate U., 1973; M.P.H., UCLA, 1975; m. Diane M. Lucey, Oct. 28, 1977; children—Catherine, Meghan. Various positions Los Angeles County Health Services Adminstrn., 1975-76; mgmt. services officer U. Calif., Irvine, 1976-77; asst. adminstr. Doctors Med. Center, Modesto, Calif., 1977-79, asso. adminstr., 1979, adminstr., 1979-82, exec. dir., 1982—. Served with USAF, 1966-69. Mem. Am. Coll. Hosp. Adminstrs., Am. Acad. Med. Adminstrs., UCLA Hosp. Adminstrn. Alumni Assn. Office: Doctors Medical Center PO Box 4138 Modesto CA 95352

DEVAY, JAMES EDSON, plant pathology educator and administrator; b. Mpls., Nov. 23, 1921; s. James Harry and Sarah Mary (Edson) DeV.; m. Mary Alice Bambach, Dec. 27, 1947; children—Susan, Mary, Sally, Joseph, Paula, Michael. B.S., U. Minn., 1949, Ph.D., 1953. Asst. prof., assoc. prof. U. Minn., 1953-57; asst. prof. to prof. plant pathology, U. Calif., Davis, 1957—, dept. chmn., 1980—. Served to lt. (j.g.) USN, 1942-46. Fellow AAAS, Am. Photopathol. Soc.; mem. Mycol. Soc. Am., Scandinavian Soc. Plant Physiology, Sigma Xi, Gamma Sigma Delta. Democrat. Roman Catholic. Contbr. over 200 articles to publs. in field.

DE VENUTA, ANTHONY CHARLES, management consultant; b. Newark, July 11, 1946; s. Anthony Joseph and Mary (Kahanec) DeV.; student Fairleigh Dickinson U., 1964-67; A.A., Monterey Peninsula Coll., 1970; B.A., No. Mich. U., 1971; postgrad. U. So. Calif., 1977-79; m. Francine Mary Ranuio, Oct. 10, 1976; children—Gina Marie, Anthony Joseph, Dominic D. Jr. acct. Fidelity Union Trust Co., Newark, 1965-67; mgmt. intern, indsl. mgmt. analyst Naval Air Rework Facility, Alameda, Calif., 1975-78, supervising indsl. mgmt. analyst, 1979, project mgr., 1979, supervising prodn. controller, project mgr., 1980; pvt. practice indsl. mgmt., systems, office automation cons., Lafayette, Calif.; dir. info. systems devel. Mil. Sealift Command, Oakland, Calif., 1982-83; dir. info. systems, 1983—. Served with U.S. Army, 1967-69. Mem. Assn. Systems Mgrs., Naval Employees Assn. (past dir.), Alameda Def. Mgmt. Assn. (past dir.). Roman Catholic. Home: 3283 Walnut Ln Lafayette CA 94549 Office: 267 4th St Suite 200 Oakland CA 94607

DEVERE, JAMES PATRICK, sporting goods co. exec.; b. N.Y.C., Aug. 7, 1916; s. Leo Bernard and Elizabeth (McCarthy) D.; B.A., UCLA, 1941. Vice pres. Dolly Varden, Inc., Los Angeles, 1945-47; owner The Devere Co., Los Angeles, 1948-63; pres. Devere Co. of So. Calif., Inc., 1963—. Served from 2d lt. to maj. AUS, 1941-45; PTO. Recipient Sporting Goods Dealer Leadership award, 1964. Mem. Sports Council (v.p. 1955-56), Assoc. Western Fishing Tackle Mfrs. Reps. Assn., Nat. Sporting Goods Assn., Tackle Reps. Assn. (pres. 1968—), Hist. Soc. So. Calif., Nat. Wildlife Found., Friends of UCLA Library, Bruin Bench, Sportsmen of the South, Phi Delta Theta. Democrat. Roman Catholic. Clubs: Athletic, Portuguese Bend (Palos Verdes, Calif.). Home: Portuguese Bend Club 114 Spindrift Dr Palos Verdes CA 90274 Office: 273 7th St San Pedro CA 90731

DEVEREAUX, TERENCE MARTIN, corp. adminstrv. specialist; b. Spokane, Wash., Sept. 2, 1941; s. Richard Patrick and Lucille (Downs) D.; A.A., City Coll. San Francisco, 1966; m. Georgia Jean Harlan, Apr. 11, 1964 (div. 1981); children—Coreen, Richard, Keith; m. Katherine Ann McFarland, Jan. 9, 1982. Clk., Wells Fargo Bank, San Francisco, 1958-64; teller First Nat. Bank Daly City (Calif.), 1964-65; sr. adminstrv. account specialist IBM Corp., San Francisco and Eugene, Oreg., 1965—. Chmn. Charitable Solicitation Commn., City of Eugene, 1971-82; pres. Emerald Empire Roundup Assn., 1977-78. Mem. Jaycees (pres. Eugene 1974-75, co-chmn. Eugene Jaycee-City of Eugene All-Am. City Com. 1970, Jaycee Internat. senator 1978, named Eugene Jaycee of year 1976-77, recipient community service award of year 1975-76). Republican. Roman Catholic.

DEVEREUX, DOROTHY VERONICA, vocational evaluator, consultant; b. Stamford, Conn., July 20, 1952; d. Theodore Joseph and Hedwig Mary (Modzelewski) Kaslikowski; m. Christopher John Devereux, May 18, 1974; 1 son, Matthew. M.S., U. Ariz., 1975. Vocat. evaluator Tucson Skill Ctr., 1975-76; program coordinator/counselor U. Ariz., Tucson, 1976-79; chief vocat. evaluator Goodwill Industries, Sacramento, Calif., 1982-83, Vocat. Evaluation Services, Sacramento, 1983—; cons. Mem. Nat. Rehab. Assn. (cert.), Vocat. Evaluation and Work Adjustment Assn., Am. Rehab. Counseling Assn. Democrat. Roman Catholic. Editor Ariz. Assn. Physically Disabled Newsletter, 1978. Home: 6050 Bamford Dr Sacramento CA 95823 Office: Vocat Evaluation Services 1329 Howe Ave Suite 111 Sacramento CA 95825

DEVERMAN, JERONE NELSON, data systems executive; b. Pekin, Ill., July 4, 1938; s. Wilmer Heinrich Gerhardt and Elizabeth Augusta (Reich) D.; m. Wona Annette Dodge, Sept. 4, 1960; children—James Dodge, John Henry. B.S., Purdue U., 1960, M.S., 1962, Ph.D., 1969. Sr. scientist BDM Corp., Albuquerque, 1969-70; mem. tech. staff Sandia Nat. Labs, Albuquerque, 1970-73; sr. research statistician Dikewood Industries, Albuquerque, 1973-77; founder, pres. Med. Data Systems, Albuquerque, 1977—; adj. prof. Anderson Sch. Mgmt., U. N.Mex., clin. assoc. dept. family, community, emergency medicine. Served to capt. U.S. Army, 1966-68. Decorated Disting. Service award. Mem. Am. Statis. Assn., Purdue Alumni Assn. (dir. 1980-83). Lutheran. Club: Purdue of N.Mex. Home: 1206 Cuatro Cerros Trail SE Albuquerque NM 87123 Office: 10701 Lomas Blvd Suite 211 Albuquerque NM 87112

DEVERS, SHEDRICK THOMAS, construction company executive, real estate executive; b. Houston, Mar. 15, 1935; s. James Henry and Daisy (Scott) D.; B.A. in Instrumental Music, Prairie View (Tex.) A. and M. Coll., 1956; m. Carole Gwendolyn Richter, Nov. 28, 1954; children—Reginald T., Carole Yvette, Derrick Howard. Tchr. public schs., Refugio, Tex., 1956-58, Agate, Colo., 1958-61, Denver, 1961-67; real estate salesman Wilhoite Realty, Denver, 1967; dir. housing devel. div. Met. Denver Fair Housing Center, 1967-71, exec. dir., 1971-72; pres. Devers, Inc., Denver, 1968—, Devers Constrn. Corp., Denver, 1974—; owner Devers & Co., real estate brokerage firm, Denver, 1967—; direct distbr. Crown Valley Products; pres. Rainbow Express Corp.; cons. Am. Inst. Housing, 1971-72; chief cons. archdiocesan housing com. Roman Catholic Archdiocese Denver, 1972. Mem. Mayor's Program Policy Adv. Bd., Denver, 1971-72, Democratic precinct committeeman, 1974—; bd. dirs. Margery Reed Day Nursery Sch., Denver, 1970-72, Sr. Service, Inc., Denver, 1971-72, Nonprofit Housing Center, Washington, 1971-73. Named Outstanding Citizen of Year, Omega Psi Phi, 1971. Mem. Nat. Assn. Nonprofit Housing Orgns. (regional v.p. 1970-72), Am. Inst. Housing, Nat. Home Builders Assn. (Denver chpt), Nat., Colo. Denver bds. realtors, Colo. Apt. Assn., No. Colo. Homebuilders Assn., Denver C. of C. (govtl. affairs com. 1973-75). Clubs: Avant Garde, Rotary, Denver. Home: 8106 E Girard Ave Denver CO 80231

DEVINCENZI, STEVEN LEE, business equipment company executive; b. Santa Monica, Calif., Oct. 29, 1943; s. Peter Louis and Jeanne Louise (Simms) DeV.; student El Camino Coll., 1963-65; B.S., Calif. State U.-Long Beach, 1967; m. Cheryl Elaine Higley, Feb. 22, 1974; children—D'Arcy Ann, Anthony David, Dana Ann. Sales mgr. A. B. Dick Co., Los Angeles, 1971-73, br. sales mgr., 1973-74, market planning mgr., Chgo., 1974-75; Western regional mgr. Apeco Corp., Los Angeles, 1975-77; Western region mgr. Royal Bus. Machines, Los Angeles, 1977-79; pres. Pacific Photocopy of Calif., North Hollywood, Calif., 1979—; cons. sales tng. Tratec; PMC Corp.; A.B. Dick Distbrs. Served with USNR, 1961-63. Mem. North Hollywood C. of C., Sun Valley C. of C., Los Angeles C. of C., Nat. Office Machine Dealers Assn., Western Office Machines Dealers Assn., Am. Mktg. Assn. Republican. Home: 2700 Aviation Redondo Beach CA 90277 Office: 15531 Cabrito Rd Van Nuys CA 91406

DEVINE, GRANT, Canadian provincial official; b. Regina, Sask, Can., 1944; Donald William and Bette Jean (Ford) D.; m. Chantal Guillaume, July, 1966; children—Michelle, Monique, David, John William B.S.A. in Agrl. Econs., U. Sask., 1967; M.Sc. in Agrl. Econs., U. Alta. (Can.), 1969, M.B.A. in Mktg., 1970; Ph.D. in Agr. Econs., Ohio State U., 1976. With Agr. Can., Ottawa, Ont., 1967-68, mktg. cons. agrl. commodity legis., 1970-72; grad. asst. Ohio State U., Columbus, 1972-76; assoc. prof. agrl. econs. U. Sask., 1976-79; leader Progressive Conservative Party of Sask., from 1979; mem. Sask. Legis. Assembly for Estevan, 1982—, premier, pres. exec. council, 1982—, also chmn. planning com. Hon. pres. Boy Scouts Sask.; hon. pres. bd. dirs. Sask. Council for Crippled Children and Adults; hon. patron various civic orgns. Recipient Vanier award, 1983. Mem. Agrl. Inst. Can., Sask. Inst. Agrologists, Am. Econ. Assn., Am. Mktg. Assn., Am. Assn. Consumer Research, Can. Agrl. Econs. Soc., Consumer's Assn. Can., Army, Navy and Airforce Vets. (hon. mem. Regina unit 18). Clubs: Wascana Country (hon. v.p.), Assiniboia (hon. mem.). Contbr. numerous articles on agrl. econs. to Can. and U.S. profl. jours. Office: Officer of Premier Legis Bldg 2405 Legislative Dr Regina SK S4S 0B3 Canada

DEVINE, J(AMES) DOUGLASS, manufacturing company executive; b. Boston, Sept. 7, 1940; s. J. James and L. Virginia Devine; A.B., Harvard U., 1962; M.B.A., UCLA, 1971; m. Tee Yarbrough, 5 children. Test pilot Lockheed Aircraft Co., Van Nuys, Calif., 1966-70; mgmt. cons., Los Angeles, 1970-1974; chief exec. officer Flight Adv. Bd., aviation cons., Los Angeles, 1974-1975; dir., chief exec. officer Sunshine Recreation Inc., Westlake Village, Calif., 1975—, Skib Inc., Chatsworth, 1978-80; pres. Sunshine U. Lok Corp., West Lake Village, Calif., 1981—; lectr. in field. Trustee, Community Ch., Encino, 1977-79, mem. ch. choir; coach youth soccer and baseball. Served to capt. AC, USMCR, 1962-66; Vietnam. Decorated D.F.C., Air medal with 26 oak leaf clusters. Mem. Assn. M.B.A.s. Club: Harvard So. Calif. (treas., dir. 1974-76). Office: 31129 Via Colinas Suite 704 Westlake Village CA 91362

DE VINE, WILLIAM EDWARD, JR., real estate broker; b. Clinton, Okla., May 9, 1934; s. William Edward and Lura Estella (Riley) De V.; B.S., Calif. Poly. State U., 1968; children—Wayne, David, William, Dore, Lura, Cory, Eric, Gregory, Annette, Trudy. Electronic technician Naval Air Sta., Alameda, Calif., 1962-64; design engr. IBM Corp., San Jose, Calif., 1968-72; mem. mktg. staff, Honolulu, 1972-75, product planner, Austin, Tex., 1975-77, mktg. mgr., San Francisco, 1977-78; pres. W.E. DeVine & Co., Woodside, Calif., 1972—; exec. dir. DeVine & Wang, 1976—. Served with USAF, 1954-57. Mem. IEEE. Democrat. Club: Lions. Office: 195 Brookwood Rd Woodside CA 94062

DEVINNEY, DOROTHY FLORENCE, chiropractor; b. Greenwood, Miss., Oct. 25, 1942; s. James Murray and Dorothy Florence (OLigher) D.; B.A., Central Wash. U., 1960; M.S., San Jose State U., 1973; student No. Calif. Chiropractic Coll., 1979—; D.C., Palmer Coll. Chiropractic, 1981. Activity center dir. King County (Wash.) Park and Recreation Dept., 1964-67; recreation supr. Kent (Wash.) Parks and Recreation Dept., 1967-69; grad. staff asst. Sunnyvale (Calif.) Parks and Recreation Dept. 1969-71; recreation supr. Santa Rosa (Calif.) Recreation and Parks Dept., 1971-78; bd. dirs. Sonoma County (Calif.) Art Council, 1971-72; chiropractor Pryal Chiropractic Clinic, Alameda, Calif., 1982—. Bd. dirs. chmn. fin. com. Sonoma County Multi-Purpose Sr. Citizen Center, 1976-78, mem. fee and policy com., 1977-78. Mem. Calif. Park and Recreation Soc., Am. Chiropractic Assn., Internat. Chiropractic Assn., Calif. Chiropractic Assn., Gonstead Clin. Studies Soc., Council on Nutrition, Council on Roentgenology, Nat. Assn. Female Execs. Republican. Mem. Unity Ch. Home: 20 Cora Ct Walnut Creek CA 94596

DEVOE, VIOLET ANN, systems analyst; b. Chgo., Sept. 27, 1940; d. Lambert Fred and Jean Mary (O'Hagan) Craemer; B.A. in Math., Mt. St. Mary's Coll., 1962; postgrad. in bus. adminstrn. San Diego State U.; m. Daniel Franklin Devoe, Dec. 29, 1962; children—Debra Jean, Alan Daniel, Lambert Theodore. Research asst. RAND Corp., Santa Monica, Calif., 1962-63; sci. programmer Litton Industries, Canoga Park, Calif., 1964; programmer analyst Lockheed-Calif. Co., Burbank, Calif., 1965-66, 69-72; sr. systems analyst County of San Diego (Calif.), 1972-80; sr. systems analyst Acctg. Corp. Am., San Diego, 1980—. Mem. Data Processing Mgmt. Assn., Coronado Schs. Found., Am. Mensa Ltd. Republican. Roman Catholic. Club: Soroptimists (Coronado, Calif.). Home: 610 First St Coronado CA 92118 Office: 1929 1st St San Diego CA 92101

DE VORE, ZETH BLEVENS, educator; b. Oakland, Calif., 1931; B.A. in Edn., San Francisco State U., 1951, M.A. in Spl. Edn., 1964; married; 3 children. Tchr. trainable mentally retarded Kailua (Hawaii) schs., 1966-69; tchr. educationally handicapped Rich-Mar Sch. Dist., San Marcos, Calif., 1969—, now dist. spl. edn. adminstr. Mem. NEA, Council Exceptional Children (pres. N. County chpt. 1980-81), Am. Assn. Mental Deficiency, Calif., Rich-Mar (pres. 1974-76) tchrs. assns., Calif. Assn. Program Specialists, Assn. Calif. Sch. Adminstrs. Office: 270 San Marcos Blvd San Marcos CA 92069

DEVRIES, CHARLENE LEWIS, office administrator; b. Ord, Nebr., Feb. 10, 1926; d. George Alvin and Alfhild Rigmor (Moller) Munn; m. Ralph Tobias DeVries, Nov. 2, 1978 (dec. July 1982); 1 son from previous marriage, Christian Lewis. B.A., Hastings Coll., 1948. Sec., Robinson-Hannagan, 1955-56; office mgr. Hill & Knowlton, Inc., Los Angeles, 1956-81, office adminstrn. mgr., 1981-83, adminstrv. asst. Western region, 1983—. Vol., Rec. for the Blind, Inc. Hastings Coll. scholar, 1946-48. Mem. Los Angeles Profl. Bus. Women's Club. Methodist.

DEVRIES, DEBORAH DAVISSON, educator; b. Columbus, Ohio, June 14, 1949; d. George Leonard and Eleanor Phyllis (Nappi) Davisson; m. Jan Pieter DeVries, July 15, 1972. B.A. in History, UCLA; M.S. in Edn., U. So. Calif., 1975, Ed.D., 1981. Cert. tchr. Calif.; life cert. in community coll. and adult edn., Ariz., Calif. Dir. Los Angeles City Coll. Overseas Adult High Sch., Japan, 1976-77; dir. individual devel. and edn. advancement program Luke AFB, Ariz., 1978—; instructional designer Computers in Mgmt. TV course, Rio Salado Community Coll., Phoenix, 1982. Active, Republican Women's Coordinating Council, 1982-83; precinct committeeman, 19th dist., 1982-83. Recipient Cert. of Commendation, Tactical Air Command, 1982. Mem. Assn. for Supervision of Curriculum Devel., Am. Soc. Tng. and Devel., Mountain Plains Adult Edn. Assn., Commn. on Adult Basic Edn., Ariz. Adult Edn. Assn. Republican. Roman Catholic. Contbr. presentations to profl. confs. author studies in field. Home: 4840 W Christine Circle Glendale AZ 85308

DE WAART, EDO, condr.; b. Amsterdam, Netherlands, June 1, 1941; grad. with honors for oboe Amsterdam Conservatoire, 1962. Oboist, Concertgebouw Orch., Amsterdam, 1963-64, asst. condr., 1966-67; asst. to Leonard Bernstein, N.Y. Philharmonic, 1965-66; condr. Rotterdam (Netherlands) Philharmonic, 1967-79, prin. condr., music dir.; founding condr. Netherlands Wind Ensemble, 1967-71; condr., music dir. San Francisco Symphony Orch., 1977—; guest condr. orchs. including Amsterdam Concertgebouw, Berlin Philharmonic, Boston Symphony, Chgo. Symphony, Bayreuth Orch., 1979, London Symphony, Cleve. Orch., N.Y. Philharmonic, Phila. Orch.; rec. artist Philips Records; rec. with major European orchs. including: New Philharmonia, English Chamber Orch., Royal Philharmonic Orch., Dresden State Orch., Concertgebouw Orch., Leipzig Gewandhaus Orch. Recipient 1st prize Mitropoulos Competition, N.Y.C., 1964. Office: San Francisco Symphony Orch Davies Symphony Hall San Francisco CA 94102

DEWALD, MAURICE J., accounting firm executive; b. Fort Wayne, Ind., Mar. 20, 1940; s. Maurice J. and Jean (AllGeier) DeW.; m. Carolyn Keefer, Feb. 24, 1962; children—Anne, Colleen, Michelle. B.B.A. in Acctg., Notre Dame U., 1962. C.P.A., Calif., 1968. Acct., Peat Marwick Mitchell and Co., Chgo., 1962-65, San Jose, Calif., 1965-73, ptnr., 1973-76, mng. ptnr., Newport Beach, Calif., 1976—. Pres., Orange County (Calif.) United Way; bd. dirs. Econ. Devel. Corp. Orange County; trustee S. Coast Repertory Theatre, World Affairs Council Orange County. Served to 1st lt. U.S. Army, 1963-65. Mem. Am. Inst. C.P.A.s, Calif. Soc. C.P.A.s, Nat. Assn. Accts. Clubs: Big Canyon Country, Pacific (Newport Beach); Lincoln (Orange County). Office: Peat Marwick Mitchell and Co 4400 MacArthur Blvd Suite 500 Newport Beach CA 92660

DEWALL, ALFRED ATHRON, soil scientist; b. Freeport, Ill., Aug. 9, 1946; s. Joseph Edward and Laura M. DeWall; B.S. in Agrl. Chemistry and Soils, U. Ariz., 1973; m. Janice Beatrice Prentice, Apr. 8, 1967; children—Julianne Lee, Janette Lynn. Soil scientist student trainee Soil Conservation Service, Dept. Agr., summers 1966-67, soil scientist, Phoenix, 1973-75, Safford, Ariz., 1975, soil survey party leader, 1975-78, Holbrook, Ariz., 1978—. Served with USN, 1967-71. Deacon, dir. First So. Baptist Ch., Holbrook; camp treas. Gideons Internat. Mem. Agronomy Soc. Am., Soil Sci. Soc. Am., Soil Conservation Soc. Am., Am. Forestry Assn., Am. Registry Cert. Profls. in Agronomy, Crops and Soils (cert. profl. soil scientist). Author soil survey reports. Office: Dept Agr Soil Conservation Service 152 W Arizona St Holbrook AZ 86025

DEWALL, KAREN MARIE, advertising executive; b. Phoenix, May 31, 1943; d. Merle C. and Agnes M. (Larson) Feller; m. Charles E. DeWall, Sept. 3, 1963; 1 dau., Leslie Karen. A.A., Phoenix Coll., 1969. Media buyer Wade Advt., Sacramento, 1964-66; media dir., Harwood Advt., Phoenix, 1967-71; co-owner, account exec. DeWall & Assocs. Advt. Co., 1971—. Active Jr. League of Phoenix; v.p. Phoenix Arts Coming Together, Inc.; bd. dirs., Florence Crittendon Services of Ariz., Inc. Mem. Am. Women in Radio and TV (v.p. Phoenix chpt.). Republican. Club: Phoenix Country. Home: 32 West Marlette St Phoenix AZ 85013 Office: DeWall and Assocs Advt 737 West McDowell St Phoenix AZ 85007

DEWELL, WENDY ANDERSON WESTOVER, indsl. engr.; b. Denver, Jan. 23, 1950; d. Alden DeLancey and Faye Anderson (Smillie) Westover; B.A. in Math. magna cum laude, UCLA, 1972; M.S. in Ops. Research, Stanford U., 1973; m. David Kent Dewell, Feb. 19, 1978; 1 dau., Elizabeth Anderson; stepchildren—David Todd, Ginger Anne, Thomas Steven. Asso. indsl. engr. IBM, San Jose, Calif., 1973-76, sr. asso. indsl. engr. Gen. Products Div., 1976-77, project engr. indsl. engring., 1977-79, new products program adminstr., 1979-81, project mgr., 1981—. Mem. Soc. Women Engrs. (sec. San Francisco Bay Area sect. 1977-78), Phi Beta Kappa, Alpha Xi Delta (treas. Santa Clara Valley chpt. 1977-79, v.p. 1979-80, pres. 1980-81, regional alumnae dir. 1981—, pres. Alpha Xi chpt. 1971-72. Republican. Presbyterian. Home: 57B Mount Hamilton Rd San Jose CA 95114 Office: 5600 Cottle Rd San Jose CA 95193

DE WETTER, HERMAN PETER, health care corporation executive; b. New Rochelle, N.Y., Jan. 28, 1920; s. Herman and Louise (Hurlbutt) de W.; m. Margaret Belding, Aug. 7, 1943; children—Charles, David, Robert. Grad. Phillips Exeter Acad., Chmn. bd. OK Van & Storage Co., El Paso, Tex., 1952-71; pres., chief exec. officer Bekins Co., Los Angeles, 1971-79; exec. v.p. Nat. Med. Enterprises, Inc., 1979—, also dir.; dir. Beneficial Standard Corp., Conrock Co., Thomas J. Lipton, Inc., Mattel, Inc. Chmn. El Paso Civil Service Commn., 1966-69; mayor City of El Paso, 1969-71; speaker House Com. of 100, 1970-71; pres. El Paso Govt. Council, 1969-71. Served to maj. AUS, 1942-45. Decorated Bronze Star; recipient Humanitarian award NCCJ, 1981; Outstanding Community Service award City of El Paso, 1970; Thanks badge Girl Scouts U.S.A., 1965; Leadership award West Tex. C. of C., 1969. Mem. Los Angeles Area C. of C., Mchts. and Mfrs. Assn., SR, Newcomen Soc. Clubs: Calif., Lincoln, 100, Rotary of Los Angeles, Valley Hunt, Twilight. Office: 11620 Wilshire Blvd Los Angeles CA 90025

DEWEY, RICHARD WILLIAM, automotive company public affairs manager; b. Detroit, June 30, 1930; s. Richard Sydney and Viola Katherine (Rau) D.; m. Dora Belle Byerly, Dec. 27, 1952; children—Steven Richard, Cheryl Katherine Dewey Hartman. B.A., U. Mich., 1955. Reporter, bus. writer Owosso (Mich.) Argus-Press, 1955-56; with pub. relations staff Chrysler Corp., 1956-57, Burroughs Corp., 1957; account exec., pub. relations McCann Erickson, 1958-60, Kenneth Drake Assocs., 1960-61; with Ford Motor Co., 1961—, overseas pub. info. mgr. Ford Tractor Ops., 1965-70, corp. info. mgr. internat. ops., 1970-71, corp. internat. plans mgr., 1971-74, asst. pub. relations mgr. Ford Tractor Ops., 1974-76, asst. mgr. pub. relations Western Region, 1976-83, regional mgr. pub. affairs staff, San Jose, Calif., 1983—. Nat. adv. bd. Northwood Inst., Midland, Mich., bd. dirs. Blue Lake Fine Arts Camp, Twin Lake, Mich., 1972-78; adv. com. Crittendon Hosp., Rochester, Mich. Served to lt. U.S. Army, 1953-55. Mem. Pub. Relations Soc. Am., Detroit Press Club, Los Angeles Press Club.

DEWEY, ROBERT ADDISON, JR., public relations consultant; b. Oakland, Calif., Mar. 1, 1944; s. Robert Addison Dewey and Priscilla (Keefer) Hausbrow. B.A., Oreg. State U., 1966; postgrad. U. Oreg., 1968-69; m. Linda Guynup, Oct. 19, 1974. Editor, Creswell (Oreg.) Chronicle, 1966-67; dir. Stewart Howe Alumni Service of Oreg., 1967-68; copywriter Green Assocs. Advt., Eugene, Oreg., 1968-69; account exec. Pub. Relations div. Cole & Weber, Inc., Portland, Oreg., 1969-72, Daniel J. Edelman, Inc., San Francisco, 1972; dir. info. Ashbrook for Pres. Calif. Com., 1972; v.p. Lowry Russom & Leeper, San Francisco, 1972-79; v.p., prin. Lowry & Ptnrs., Inc., San Francisco, 1979—. Served with USAR, 1966-72. Mem. Pub. Relations Soc. Am., Press Club San Francisco, Sigma Delta Chi. Club: Commonwealth of Calif. (San Francisco). Office: 921 Front St San Francisco CA 94111

DEWHURST, WILLIAM GEORGE, physician, educator; b. Frosterley, Eng., Nov. 21, 1926; s. William and Elspeth Leslie (Begg) D.; B.A., Oxford (Eng.) U., 1947, M.A., 1961, B.M., B.Ch., 1950; postgrad. London Hosp. Med. Coll., 1947-58; Acad. Diploma in Psychol. Medicine with Distinction, London (Eng.) U., 1961; m. Margaret Dransfield, Sept. 17, 1960. Intern, London Hosp., 1950-52, resident, 1954-58; resident Maudsley Hosp., London, 1958-61; practice medicine specializing in psychiatry, London, 1955-69, Edmonton, Alta., Can., 1969—; dir. dept. psychiatry U. Alta. Hosp., Edmonton; prof. psychiatry U. Alta., Edmonton, 1972—, chmn. dept., 1975—; cons. psychiatrist Edmonton Gen. Hosp., Royal Alexandra Hosp., Edmonton, 1976—; sr. lectr. London U., (Can.) (examiner 1973-79), hon. cons. physician Bethlem Royal and Maudsley Hosp., 1965-69; tchr. London U., 1967; lectr., med. registrar Maudsley and London Hosp., 1954-61. Served to capt. M.C., Royal Army, 1952-54. Fellow Royal Soc. Medicine, Royal Coll. Physicians (Can.) (examiner 1973-79), Am. Coll. Psychiatrists, Am. Psychiat. Assn., Royal Coll. Psychiatry; mem. Royal Coll. Physicians London, AAAS, N.Y. Acad. Scis., Can. Psychiat. Assn. (pres. 1983—), Alta. Psychiat. Assn. (pres. 1973-74), Can. Assn. Profs. Psychiatry (chmn. 1976-79), Brit., Canadian med. assns., Can. Coll. Neuropsychopharmacology (pres. 1982—), Collegium Internationale Neuro-Psychopharmacologicum. Club: Faculty (Edmonton). Contbr. articles to profl. jours. Home: 92 Fairway Dr Edmonton AB T6J 2C5 Canada

DEWITT, JOHN BELTON, conservation orgn. exec.; b. Oakland, Calif., Jan. 13, 1937; B.A. in Wildlife Conservation, U. Calif.-Berkeley, 1959; m. Karma L. Sowers, Sept. 17, 1960. With B.R.C. Forest Service, 1956-57; ranger-naturalist Nat. Park Service, U.S. Dept. Interior, 1958-60; land law examiner Bur. Land Mgmt., Sacramento, 1960-64; asst. sec. Save-the-Redwoods League, San Francisco, 1964-71, sec., 1971-74, exec. dir., 1974—. Mem. adv. council Anza-Borrego Desert Com., 1983—; bd. dirs. Friends of the Frederick Law Olmsted Papers, 1981—, Tuolumne River Preservation Trust, 1981—. Recipient Nat. Conservation award DAR, 1982, Golden Bear award Calif. State Park and Recreation Commn., 1982—. Mem. adv. council Trust for Pub. Land, 1975-78. Mem. Nat. Parks Assn., Nature Conservancy (dir. No. Calif. chpt. 1976-77), Sierra Club, Am. Forestry Assn. Office: 114 Sansome St Room 605 San Francisco CA 94104

DEWITT, VALERI JEAN, public relations director; b. San Bernardino, Calif., Jan. 17, 1950; d. Howard William and Beverly Jean (Williamson) DeWitt. B.A. in Journalism, San Diego State U., 1974, student in Bus. Adminstrn. Staff writer San Diego Sentinel Newspapers, 1975-77, Vista Press, San Diego, 1977-78; communications coordinator Home Fed. Savs. & Loan, San Diego, 1978-80; dir. communications Cox Cable, San Diego, 1980-82; dir. corp. communications IVAC Corp., San Diego, 1982—; owner DeWitt & Co. Communications, La Jolla, Calif., 1982—; cons. in field. Named Woman of Achievement Women in Communications, 1981. Mem. Internat. Assn. Bus. Communicators (pres. San Diego chpt.; Communicator of Yr. award 1980), Women in Communications (past pres. San Diego chpt.), Pub. Relations Club San Diego, Pub. Relations Soc. Am., San Diego Writers and Editors Guild. Club: San Diego Press. Writer, San Diego Union Panorama, Tuned In San Diego, The Communicator Mag. Office: 10300 Campus Point Dr San Diego CA 92121 Dewitt & Co Communications 5580 La Jolla Blvd La Jolla CA 92038

DEWOLF, NICHOLAS, electronics co. exec.; b. Chestnut Hill, Pa., July 12, 1928; s. Maurice Mortimer and Marion DeW.; B.S., M.I.T., 1948; m. Margaret Lee Lemle, Oct. 25, 1958; children—Alexander, Nicole, Quentin, Vanessa, Thalia, Ivan. Engr., Gen. Electric Co., Syracuse, N.Y., 1948-52; chief engr. Transitron Electronics Corp., Boston, 1952-60; founder, pres., chmn. bd. Teradyne Electronics Corp., Boston, 1960-77; pres. Nick DeWolf Enterprises, Inc., Aspen, Colo., 1977—. Mem. IEEE, Soc. Motion Picture TV Engrs., Soc. Photog. Scientists and Engrs., Sigma Xi. Republican. Creator, builder Aspen Fountain, 1978-80, Aspen TV Community Bull. Bd., 1981. Contbr. articles in field to profl. jours. Patentee in field. Home and Office: 233 W Bleeker St Aspen CO 81611

DE WOODY, CHARLES OWNBY, lawyer; b. Chgo., Oct. 18, 1914; s. Charles and Oneta (Ownby); student U. Fla., 1931-33, U. Mich., 1933-35, Columbia, 1935-36, Western Res. U., 1936-38; m. Nancy Tremaine, June 15, 1940; children—Charles, Nancy. Office atty. Oglebay, Norton & Co., Cleve., 1939-43; partner Arter, Hadden, Wykoff & Van Duzer, 1943-61; pvt. practice, 1961—; dir. Ferry Cap and Set Screw Co., Nat. Extruded Metal Products Co., Meteor Crater Enterprises, Inc. Bar-T-Ranch. Mem. Am., Ohio, Cleve. bar assns., Cleve. Law Library Assn. Episcopalian. Clubs: Union, Cleve. Country; Cleve. Racquet Club (Pepper Pike, Ohio); Chagrin Valley Hunt (Gates Mills, Ohio); Rancho Santa Fe (Calif.) Tennis. Address: El Mirador Box 1169 Rancho Santa Fe CA 92067

DE WYS, JANE NEGUS, geologist; b. Portland, Oreg., Apr. 24, 1924; d. Howard Curtiss and Cleo (Brockhausen) Negus; B.A. with honors in Geology, Miami U., Oxford, Ohio, 1946; postgrad. U. Wis., 1946-48, U. Wyo., 1947, Ohio State U., 1951-53, U. Calif., Los Angeles, 1964-66, Tex. Tech U. Law Sch., 1969-71; Ph.D., W.Va. U., 1979—; m. Egbert Christiaan deWys, Apr. 7, 1949 (div. 1971); children—Wendela, Tanya, Mark, Matthew. Curator, Geology Mus., U. Wis., Madison, 1946-48; geologist Shell Oil Co., Midland, Tex., 1948-49; instr. geology Case Western Res. U., Cleve., 1949; geologist Mene Grande Corp., Caracas, Venezuela, 1951-53; research asso. Ohio State Research Found. Ohio State U., Columbus, 1953-58; instr. geology adult edn. Van Nuys (Calif.) High Sch., 1958-60; design engr. Sierra Engring., Sierra Madre, Calif., 1960-63; sr. scientist Calif. Inst. Tech. Jet Propulsion Lab., Pasadena, 1963-66; mgr. First Grand Teton Ltd., Jackson, Wyo., 1972-74; gen. mgr. Jackson Hole Cable TV, Jackson, 1974-76, cons. on open univ., 1976—; research geologist, asst. dir. Environ. Studies Lab. U. Utah Research Inst., Salt Lake City, 1976-77; research asso. Devonian Shales Program geology dept. W.Va. U., Morgantown, 1977-81; research specialist Exxon Prodn. Research Lab., Houston, 1981—; lectr. in field; mem. NASA review panel for extraterrestrial resource utilization program U.S. Bur. Mines, 1967-68. Active YWCA, Denver, 1960-70; advisor to sch. bd., Lubbock, Tex., 1970-71. Served with U.S. Cadet Nurse Corps, 1943-44. Recipient NASA citation for Magnet Experiment on Surveyor Spacecraft, 1968; NSF award, 1968. Mem. Geol. Soc. Am., Am. Geophys. Union, Utah Geol. Assn., Nat. Air Pollution Control Assn., Nat. Honor Soc., AAUW, CAP, Sigma Xi, Phi Sigma, Phi Kappa Phi, Sigma Gamma Epsilon, Delta Zeta, Baptist. Contbr. articles to profl. jours. Home: 19 Old Hickory Dr River Plantation Conroe TX 77302 Office: Exxon Prodn Research Co Houston TX

DEXHEIMER, HENRY PHILLIP, II, ins. agy. exec.; b. Dayton, Ohio, Sept. 16, 1925; s. Henry Phillip and Helene Francis (Veach) D.; B.S. in Commerce, U. So. Calif., 1952; children—James Phillip, Jana Helene. Sales account exec. with various cos. and newspapers, 1946-51; broadcasting sales exec. Sta. KBIG, KTLA-TV, Los Angeles, 1952-58; broadcasting sales exec. Sta. KFXM, San Bernardino, Calif., 1956-57, pres., 1956-57; founder, owner, pres. Dexheimer Co., Los Angeles, 1958—. Served with inf. and adj. gen.'s dept. U.S. Army, 1943-46; PTO. Recipient Sammy award Los Angeles Sales Execs. Club, 1955; Silver Sales trophy Radio Advt. Bur. N.Y., 1955; named Agt. of Year, Los Angeles office Travelers Ins. Cos., 1978. C.L.U. Mem. Am. Soc. C.L.U.s (nat. dir. Travelers chpt. 1972-73, 80-81), Am. Coll. Life Underwriters, Advt. Assn. West, Radio and TV Soc. Hollywood, Life Ins. and Trust Council Los Angeles, Los Angeles Life Underwriters Assn. (dir. 1963-65, v.p. 1967-69), Million Dollar Round Table (life), World Affairs Council Los Angeles, Internat. Assn. Fin. Planners, U. So. Calif. Acctg. Circle, Am. Art Council, Decorative Art Council of Los Angeles County Art Mus., Alpha Delta Sigma, Phi Kappa Tau. Republican. Presbyterian. Clubs: Town Hall (Los Angeles); Beverly Hills (Calif.) Men's; Masons, Shriners. Office: Dexheimer Co 3600 Wilshire Blvd Suite 814 Los Angeles CA 90010

DEXTER, RAYMOND ARTHUR, social service exec.; b. Hartford, Conn., Dec. 11, 1923; s. Lyman Arthur and Mona V. (Major) D.; B.S., M.S., MIT, 1947; Ed.D., Stanford U., 1962; m. Kathleen E. Dooley, Aug. 6, 1975; children by previous marriage—Charles Norman, James Sammons, Laurie Francesca. Instr. math. Trinity Coll., Hartford, 1947-49; chief area edn. adviser U.S. Army Southeastern Area Command, Germany, 1949-54; edn. officer Salvation Army Sch. for Officers Tng., San Francisco, 1957-64; territorial edn. dir. Salvation Army, San Francisco, 1966-69, Hawaii state comdr., 1969-73, social welfare dir. Western ty., 1973-74; dir. religious activities Trans-Alaska Pipeline, 1974-77; exec. dir. Salvation Army Comprehensive Alcoholism Services, Anchorage, 1977—; pres. Alaska Human Services Network, 1982—; adv. bd. U. Alaska Center for Alcohol and Addiction Studies, 1980—. Mem. nat. tng. commn. Salvation Army, 1961—; chmn. United Crusade Execs., Spokane, Wash., 1965-66; bd. dirs. Fairbanks Comprehensive Alcoholism Program, 1976-77; pres. Fairbanks Council Chs. Served with USNR, 1942-46. Mem. Res. Officers Assn., San Francisco Psychol. Assn., Mil. Chaplains Assn., Sigma Xi. Clubs: Commonwealth, Rotary. Home: 1634 Stanton Ave Anchorage AK 99508 Office: PO Box 6567 Anchorage AK 99502

DEXTER, WAYNE R., psychologist; b. American Fork, Utah, Dec. 4, 1944; s. James B. and Reta (Robbins) D.; B.S., Brigham Young U., 1967, M.S., 1968; Ph.D., U. Otago (N.Z.), 1973; m. Donna Lee Johnson, Apr. 20, 1964; children—Jon Bryan, Chris Alan, Kimberly, Lindsay. Instr. dept. psychology U. Alaska, Fairbanks, 1969-70, research asso. Inst. Arctic Biology, Arctic Health Research Lab., 1969-71, asst. prof. dept. psychology, 1973-74; lectr., research fellow dept. psychology U. Otago, Dunedin, N.Z., 1971-73; dir. spinal cord injury adjustment project Good Samaritan Hosp., Phoenix, 1974-81, psychologist behavorial scis. dept., 1974-81, dir. dept. psychology Good Samaritan Med. Ctr., 1981—; cons. Nat. Spinal Cord Injury Data Research Ctr., Phoenix, 1975—. Mem. Mayor's Com. on Employment of the Handicapped, Phoenix, 1977-80. Recipient Road Safety Research award N.Z. Ministry of Transport, 1970; Nat. Council Lic. Trade N.Z. grantee. Mem. Am. Psychol. Assn., Western Psychol. Assn., Am. Congress of Rehab. Medicine, Internat. Med. Soc. of Paraplegia, Royal Soc. N.Z., Am. Soc. Clin. Hypnosis, Internat. Soc. Hypnosis, Ariz. Psychol. Assn., Ariz. Assn. Health Psychologists (pres.), Psi Chi. Contbr. articles to jours. in psychology and medicine. Office: 1033 E McDowell Phoenix AZ 85006

DE YARMIN, RAYMOND WESLEY, museum curator, naval historian, author, lectr.; b. Dinuba, Calif., May 25, 1924; s. William Franklin and Helen Augusta (Johnson) de Y.; B.G.S., Chaminade U., 1981; M.P.S., Central Mich. U., 1983; m. Dorothy Jean Mills, Mar. 11, 1949; children—Richard Michael, Karen Sue, Daniel Raymond, Thomas Grady; m. 2d Constance Marie Fedor, July 16, 1966. Curator, Pacific

Submarine Mus., Naval. Submarine Base, Pearl Harbor, Hawaii, 1979—. Served with USN, 1942-77; World War II, Korea, Vietnam. Mem. Am. Mus. Assn., Hawaiian Mus. Assn., Submarine Vets., Naval Submarine League, Fleet Res. Assn., Sierra Club, Sigma Iota Epsilon. Democrat. Episcopalian. Club: Elks (sec.). Author: History of Submarine Base, Pearl Harbor, 1983. Office: Pacific Submarine Mus Naval Submarine Base Pearl Harbor HI 96860

DEYERBERG, ROBERT FRANCIS, aircraft instrument technician; b. Woodhave, N.Y., Mar. 29, 1923; s. Henry Edward and Rose Marie (Zaun) D.; m. Lillian Theresa Clenance, May 6, 1950; children—Carol Jean Trible, Arlene June, Paulene Jane Thompson, Robert P. Demerberg. Student Queens Coll., 1947, Phoenix Coll., 1962-63. Insp. Western Electric Co., N.Y.C., 1947-49; serviceman RCA Service Corp., Flushing, N.Y., 1949-53; customer engr. IBM, Garden City, N.Y., 1953-55; owner Alm Haven Motel & Service Sta., Tunkhannock, Pa., 1956-59; office mgr. Border Products Corp., Phoenix, 1960-63; adjustment dep. Dept. Employment Security, Glendale, Ariz., 1963-66; avionics technician Ariz. Air N.G., Phoenix, 1966—. Served with USN, 1943-46; with U.S. Army, 1950-53. Mem. Am. Fedn. Govt. Employees (pres. 1974-78, sec.-treas. 1978-82), Nat. Campers and Hikers Assn., Am. Legion (dept. fin. officer 1964). Republican. Roman Catholic. Club: Sister City (Glendale). Office: 2001 S 32nd St Phoenix AZ 85034

DE ZONIA, JOHN MICHAEL, air force officer, test pilot; b. Spokane, Wash., Jan. 20, 1948; s. Lawrence Edward and Patricia Anne (O'Sullivan) De Z.; B.S. in Astronautics, Aeros. and Math., U.S. Air Force Acad., 1969; M.S. in Astronautics/Aeros., Purdue U., 1970. Commd. 2d lt. U.S. Air Force, 1969, advanced through grades to maj., 1980; aircraft comdr. 390th Tactical Fighter Squadron, Danang Air Base, South Vietnam, 1971-72, 435th Tactical Fighter Squadron, Ubon Royal Thai AFB, 1972, 43d Tactical Fighter Squadron, Elmendorf AFB, Alaska, 1972-75; F-15 pilot 27th Tactical Fighter Squadron, Langley AFB, Va., 1975-78; F-16 test pilot 422d Test and Eval. Squadron, Nellis AFB, Nev., 1980—. Coach, Little League, Las Vegas; vol. Nev. Spl. Olympics; weekend vol. Desert Developmental Center, Las Vegas. Decorated D.F.C., Air medal with 12 oak leaf clusters, Air Force Commendation medal with oak leaf cluster. Roman Catholic. Home: 4485 Pennwood Ave #305 Las Vegas NV 89102 also 21 Country Club Rd Cocoa Beach FL 32931 Office: 422 TES/DO Nellis AFB NV 89191

DHALIWAL, RANJIT SINGH, educator; b. Bilaspur, India, June 21, 1930; s. Bharpur Singh and Bachan Kaur (Grewal) D.; M.A., Punjab U., 1955; Ph.D., Indian Inst. Tech., Kharagpur, 1960; m. Gurdev Kaur, July 1, 1958; 1 son, Gurminder Singh. Lectr., Indian Inst. Tech., New Delhi, 1961-63, asst. prof., 1963-66; asso. prof. U. Calgary (Alta., Can.), 1966-71, prof. math., 1971—; visitor Imperial Coll. of Sci. and Tech., London, U.K., 1964-65, vis. prof. City U. London, U.K., 1971-72. Mem. Am. Math. Soc., Soc. Indsl. and Applied Math., Canadian Math. Congress, London Math. Soc. Author book; contbr. articles to profl. jours. Home: 6607 Dalrymple Way NW Calgary AB Canada Mailing Address: Clin Assos of Erie 104 E 2d St Erie PA 16507

DHAMOTHARAN, SUNDARAJAN, hydrologist; b. Tamilnad, India, Dec. 31, 1945; came to U.S., 1974, naturalized, 1979; s. A. and S. (Byammal) Sundararajan; B.E. (Govt. India Merit scholar), 1968, M.Sc., 1973; Ph.D. (USDA fellow) U. Minn., 1978; m. Rema Krishnasamy, Nov. 26, 1976; 1 son, Sundar Alvin. Instr., Govt. Poly., Trichy, India, 1968-69; asst. engr. Div. Public Works Tamil Nad, later designs engr., 1969-74; mem. research faculty St. Anthony Falls Hydraulics Lab. U. Minn., 1979-80; mgr. hydrology Morrison Knudsen Co., Inc., Boise, 1980—. Registered profl. engr., Idaho. Mem. Am. Water Resources Assn. (pres. U. Minn. chpt. 1978), ASCE, Soc. Mining Engrs., Sigma Xi, Chi Epsilon. Contbr. articles to profl. jours. Home: 1465 Hancock Dr Boise ID 83706 Office: PO Box 7808 Boise ID 83706

DHARIWAL, ANAND PAUL SINGH, neuroendocrinologist; b. Rahoti, Meerut, India, Dec. 21, 1937; s. Lakhman Singh and Ramkali Davi (Sidhu) D.; B.S., U. Afra, M.D., 1958; Ph.D., U. Ill., 1961; m. Mita Drar, Dec. 19, 1970, children—Meena, Shawn, Pervin. Came to U.S., 1958, naturalized, 1972. Fellow Western Res. U., 1961-64; asso. U. Pa. Sch. Medicine, 1964-66; asst. prof. U. Tex., 1966-70; dir. endocrinology and metabolism Kern Gen. Hosp., 1970-72; dir. research and radioimmunoassays Lucile Reid Cancer Inst. and Gene Reid Nuclear Med. Inst., Bakersfield, Calif., 1972—; clin. prof. U. N.Mex.; mem. Bd. Alcohol Detoxification Kern County; cons. U. So. Calif., Harvard, Stanford, Johns Hopkins; guest lectr. med. centers. Bd. dirs. Kern Detoxification Center, 1979, Kern County Fair, Singh Sabha, Los Angeles; pres. Shri Guausgh Sabha, Los Angeles, 1981, chmn. bd., 1982. Mem. Internat. Soc. Neuroendocrinology (charter), Soc. Study of Reprodn. (charter), N.Y. Acad. Scis., Endocrine Soc., AAAS. Club: Stanford (dir., v.p. 1979-82). Contbr. articles to profl. jours., chpts. to books. Co-discoverer growth hormones inhibiting factor. Home: 4036 Country Club Dr Bakersfield CA 93306 Office: 2131 H St Bakersfield CA 93306

DHARMARAJAN, SANGIAHNADAR, aerospace engineering educator; b. Virudhunager, India, Aug. 10, 1927; s. P.M.S.K. Sangiahnadar and Palammal D.; m. Santha Veilmuthusamy, Sept. 1, 1950; 1 dau., Umarani. B.S.M.E., U. Madras (India), 1950; M.S. in Theoretical and Applied Mechanics, U. Ill.-Urbana, 1958, Ph.D., 1960. Asst. prof. aerospace engring. San Diego State U., from 1960, prof. 1968—, chmn.; dept., 1968-72, cons. Mem. ASTM, AIAA (chmn. sect. 1981-82). Contbr. articles to profl. jours. Home: 5215 College Gardens Ct San Diego CA 92115 Office: San Diego State U Coll Engring San Diego CA 92182

DHAWAN, JAGJIT RAJ KUMAR, mktg. exec.; b. Nowshera, India, Apr. 14, 1944; came to U.S., 1969, naturalized, 1973; s. Badrinath and Savitri Devi (Bhola) D.; B.S. with honors, St. Xavier's Coll., 1967; cert. in exec. program in mgmt., UCLA, 1978; m. Georgene Rose Cain, Aug. 27, 1969. Quality control technician Mobil Chem. Co., Vernon, Calif., 1970-73; math. analyst Jet Propulsion Lab., Pasadena, Calif., 1974; supr. quality control and product control Champion Internat., Monrovia, Calif., 1975-76; tech. dir. Ferro Corp., Culver City, Calif., 1977-80, mktg. dir., 1980—. Bd. dirs., trustee Pan Pacific Centers, Pacific Palisades, Calif., 1974-78. Recipient awards of merit Internat. Vegetarian Congress, 1961, Bombay Humanitarian League, 1962, St. Xavier's Coll., 1967. Mem. Am. Chem. Soc., Am. Mgmt. Assn., Soc. for Applied Material and Process Engring., Internat. Student Assn. Mem. Evangelical Free Ch. Contbr. articles to profl. jours. Office: 8790 National Blvd Culver City CA 90230

DHRUV, HARISH RATILAL, textile chemist/colorist; b. Ahmedabad, India, Mar. 14, 1946; came to U.S., 1970, naturalized, 1978; s. Ratilal Chhaganlal and Shantaben Hariprasad (Dave) D.; B.S. in Chemistry, St. Xavier's Coll., Gujarat U., India, 1966; diploma in textile chemistry M.S. U., Baroda, India, 1967; B.S. in Textile Chemistry, Phila. Coll. Textiles and Sci., 1972; m. Kaumudini Vasudev Vyas, June 21, 1971; 1 child, Nirav H. Trainee supr. Mafatlal Fine Mills, Ahmedabad, 1967-68; supr. Calico Mills, Ahmedabad, 1969-70; quality control, processing mgr. fashion prints U.S. Industries Co., Allentown, Pa., 1972-77; print supt., v.p. mfg. Pacific Fabric Printers, Vernon, Calif., 1977-80; owner textiles importing, converting and printing bus., 1980—. Pres., India Assn. of Lehigh Valley, 1974, 75, 76. Recipient Bicentennial medal, for public service to community City of Allentown, 1977. Mem. Am. Assn. Textile Chemists and Colorists, Am. Chem. Soc., Assn. Western Furniture Suppliers (sec.), West Coast Furniture Fabric Club, Bharatiya Cultural Soc. (pres. 1976). Democrat. Hindu. Home: 269 Saint Albans Ave South Pasadena CA 91030

DIACHUK, BILL W., Canadian provincial government official; b. Vegreville, Alta., Can., Oct. 8, 1929; s. Nick and Helen (Drebit) D.; m. Olga Diachuk, May 31, 1952; children—Glenn, Kenneth, Teresa, Brenda, Lynda. Cert. in social work U. Alta. Social worker Social Services and Community Health, Govt. of Alta. (Can.), 1952-63; pres. Diachuk Mgmt. & Cons. Services Ltd.; mem. Legis. Assembly of Alta. for Edmonton Beverly Constituency, 1971—, minister for workers health, safety and compensation, 1979—. Trustee, Edmonton Cath. Sch. Bd. Mem. Alta. Progressive Conservative Assn., Can. Progressive Conservative Assn., Alta. Cath. Sch. Trustees Assn., Alta. Sch. Trustees Assn. Roman Catholic. Clubs: Lions, Royal Can. Legion, K.C. Office: Legislature Bldg Room 203 Edmonton AB T5K 2B6 Canada

DIAL, OLIVER EUGENE, political science educator, electrical engineer; b. Woodriver, Ill., Nov. 10, 1922; s. Oliver Lee and Julia Lavina (Botkin) D.; LL.B., Blackstone Coll. Law., 1954; B.A., San Diego State Coll., 1959, M.S. in Pub. Adminstrn., 1962; Ph.D. in Polit. Sci. (Grad. Sch. fellow), Claremont Grad. Sch., 1965; m. Bette Jeanne Wynkoop, Dec. 28, 1944; 1 son, Oliver Eugene. Time motion study engr. Owens Ill. Glass Co., Alton, 1940-42; commd. 2d lt. USMC, 1942, advanced through grades to maj., 1953; ret., 1963; lectr. govt. San Diego State Coll., 1963-64; asst. prof. govt. Calif. Poly. Inst., San Luis Obispo, 1964-65; chmn. dept. govt. Idaho State U., 1965-68, dir. Govt. Research Inst., dir. summer sessions, 1966-68; vis. prof. polit. sci. dept., mem. staff Urban Systems Lab., MIT, Cambridge, 1968-69, co-dir. summer studies program Urban Info. Systems, 1968, coordinator asso. activities Urban Systems Lab. Boston Model Neighborhood Project, 1968-69; faculty Joint Center Urban Studies, MIT-Harvard U., 1968-69; mem. staff Boston Health Info. System Project., 1968, summer writing grantee, 1969; mem. subcom. urban regional info. systems div. behavioral scis. Nat. Acad. Scis., Washington, 1968, staff asso. Westin Project computer sci. engring. bd., 1969-70; chmn. dept. polit. sci., supr. grad. program pub. adminstrn. Baruch Coll., City U. N.Y., 1969-70; prof. urban affairs U. Colo. Grad. Sch. Pub. Affairs, Boulder, 1973-81; prof. elec. engring. U. Colo., 1981—; pres. Urban Systems Inst., Inc., 1975—. Research prof., dir. mcpl. info. systems research project U. Center, L.I. U., Greenvale, N.Y., 1969-74; sr. cons. fed. intergovtl. agys. com. urban regional info. systems (USAC), chaired by HUD, Washington, 1968—. Mem. symposium Computer Info. Utilities Social Choice, U. Chgo., 1969; informant subcom. fgn. ops. govt. info. Ho. of Reps., 1973. Mem. Am. Bar Found. (adv. com. land records improvement 1973—) Urban Regional Info. Systems Assn. (pres. Colo. sect. 1976, nat. pres. 1979-80), Am. Polit. Sci. Assn., AAUP, Am. Soc. Pub. Adminstrn., AAAS. Author: Programming and Statistics for Basic Research, 1969; Bibliography on Urban Affairs (B.G. Schumacher), 1970; (with Kraemer, Mitchell, Weiner) Municipal Information Systems: The State of the Art in 1970, 1971, Integrated Municipal Information Systems: The USAC Approach, 1972, Integrated Municipal Information Systems: The Use of the Computer in Local Government, 1973; (with Goldberg) Privacy, Security, Computers and the City: Guidelines for Municipal Information Systems, 1974. Editor policy forum info. systems dedication Bureaucrat, 1972; editor Urban Geocoding, 1975. Contbr. monographs, numerous articles to profl. lit. Home: 7086 Indian Peaks Boulder CO 80301

DIAL, THOMAS FERRON, lawyer; b. Idaho Falls, Idaho, Feb. 9, 1938; s. Edwin and Donna Pearl (Tyner) D.; m. Yvonne Mellies, June 16, 1961 (dec.); children—Cynthia, Paul, Michael, Tamara, Jennifer, Rebecca; m. Cindy Lou Herring, Sept. 18, 1981. B.A., Idaho State U., 1964; J.D., U. Idaho, 1967. Bar: Idaho 1969, U.S. Dist. Ct. Idaho 1969, U.S. Supreme Ct. 1971. Criminal magistrate 6th Dist. Ct., Pocatello, Idaho, 1971-74; assoc. firm Terrill, Green, Service and Gasser, Pocatello, 1975-76; ptnr. firm Dial, Looze & May, Pocatello, 1976—; mem. Idaho Gov.'s Council on Criminal Justice, 1973-75; Idaho del. to Presdl. Commn. on Criminal Justice, Washington, 1973; criminal law faculty advisor Nat. Coll. Trial Judges, U. Nev.-Reno, 1973; mem. criminal rules com. Idaho Supreme Ct., 1976—. Mem. Assn. Trial Lawyers Am., Idaho Trial Lawyers Assn., ABA. Mormon. Home: PO Box 207 Pocatello ID 83201

DIAMOND, ARLYNE MARJORIE, psychotherapist; b. N.Y.C., Jan. 20, 1937; d. George and Bessie (Weshnick) Schwartz; divorced. A.A. with honors, De Anza Coll., Cupertino, Calif., 1967; B.A. with distinction in Psychology, Calif. State U.-San Jose, 1969, M.S., 1972; M.S. in Psychology, Pacific Grad. Sch. Psychology, 1978, postgrad. Lic. marriage, family and child counselor, Calif., 1975. Psychol. asst. Applied Human Systems, Santa Clara, Calif., 1971-73; marriage, family and child counselor Associated Psychologists, Santa Clara, 1973-81; marriage, family and child counselor Diamond Assos., Santa Clara, 1981—. Mem. Am. Psychol. Assn., Calif. State Psychol. Assn., Santa Clara County Psychol. Assn., Am. Psychology Law Soc. (founding pres. Bay area chpt.), Calif. Assn. Marriage, Family Therapists, No. Calif. Consortium of Women Reentry Programs, Parents Without Partners (profl. adv. bd.), Am. Soc. Clin. Hypnosis, Peninsula Profl. Women's Network. Republican. Jewish. Office: 2343 B Homestead Rd Santa Clara CA 95050

DIAMOND, ARTHUR SIDNEY, chem. engring. cons.; b. Bklyn., Sept. 2, 1930; s. Joseph Duke and Rose (Koch) D.; B.Ch.E., Poly. Inst. N.Y., 1951; M.S., U. Rochester, 1958; m. Cecile Tulupman, June 17, 1951; children—Eve Robin, Glenn Michael. Chem. engr. M. W. Kellogg Co., N.Y.C., 1951-53; research chemist Eastman Kodak Co., Rochester, N.Y., 1955-60; lab. supr. Litton Industries, N.Y.C., 1960-61; research mgr. Charles Bruning Co., Mount Prospect, Ill., 1961-67; chief chemist Telautograph Corp., Los Angeles, 1967-68; pres. Diamond Research Corp., Ventura, Calif., 1968—; instr. math. U. Rochester, 1958-59. Served with U.S. Army, 1953-55. Registered profl. engr., N.Y., Ill. Mem. Cons. Chemists Assn. (pres. 1975-79), Am. Chem. Soc., Soc. Photog. Scientists and Engrs., Nat. Micrographics Assn., TAPPI. Contbr. articles to profl. jours.; patentee in field. Home and Office: 9850 Old Creek Rd Ventura CA 93001

DIAMOND, DIANA LOUISE, editor; b. Floral Park, N.Y., Feb. 4, 1937; d. Louis Bartholomew and Helen Stephanie (Strzelecki) Chmielewski; student Middlebury Coll., 1954-56; B.A. in English, U. Mich., 1958; m. Horace Williams Diamond, Jr., June 29, 1958 (div. 1975); children—Bruce Williams, Scott Kenneth, Kent Christopher, Mark Patrick. Editorial asst. dept. higher edn. NEA, Washington, 1958-59; pvt. tchr. art, Sunnyvale, Calif., 1964-68; reporter Pioneer Press, Highland Park, Ill., 1969-70; reporter Lerner Newspapers, Highland Park, 1970-72, mng. editor, 1972-78, suburban coordinator, 1974-78; corr. (part-time) The N.Y. Times, 1975-78; profl. journalism fellow Stanford U., 1978-79; editorial writer, mem. editorial bd. San Jose (Calif.) Mercury News, 1979-80, editor Sunday Opinion sect., spl. projects editor, 1980; editor-in-chief Calif. Lawyer, 1981—; moderator, co-producer League Women Voters TV show Left, Right and Center, 1968. Mem. Sunnyvale Citizens Bond Com., 1966, Sunnyvale Citizens Adv. Com., 1967; exec. sec. Midpeninsula Citizens for Fair Housing, 1966-68; chmn. Art for San Francisco Peninsula, 1967; pres. Deerfield (Ill.) Area Human Relations Com., 1968-70; mem. Deerfield Human Relations Commn., 1969-70; bd. dirs. YWCA, Highland Park, 1977-78, Chgo. Philharmonic Soc., 1977-78, Calif. Republican League, 1962-64; bd. dirs. Midpeninsula Citizens for Fair Housing, pres., 1983—. Recipient Nat. Blue Ribbon Newspaper award, 1976, 77, 78; 3d pl. Ill. Editorial of Year contest, 1974; 1st pl. for Best Feature Story, Ill. Press Assn., 1976, Suburban Newspapers Am., 1977; 2d pl. for Best Column, Nat. Newspaper Assn., 1977. Mem. LWV (dir. Deerfield 1968-70), Sigma Delta Chi. Club: Commonwealth. Home: 4146 Thain Way Palo Alto CA 94306 Office: 535 Franklin St San Francisco CA 94102

DIAMOND, JESS, pediatrician, educator; b. N.Y.C., Sept. 18, 1918; s. Sol and Rose (Lopin) D.; M.D., Royal Coll. Physicians and Surgeons, Glasgow, 1942; m. Ann Kessler, June 20, 1948; children—Jayne Lee, Steven Franklin, Donna Lynn. Intern, Fordham Hosp., 1942-43, resident in pediatrics, 1946-48; resident in contagious diseases Kingston Ave. Communicable Hosp., N.Y.C., 1948; clin. asst. prof. pediatrics Albert Einstein Coll. Medicine, N.Y.C., 1967-71; clin. asso. dept. pediatrics So. Ill. U. Coll. Medicine, Springfield, 1972-75, clin. asst. prof., 1975-79, clin. asso. prof., 1979-80; chmn. dept. pediatrics Kern Med. Center, Bakersfield, Calif., 1980—; adj. asso. prof. dept. pediatrics UCLA Sch. Medicine, 1980—; asso. clin. prof. dept. pediatrics U.C.I. Sch. Medicine, 1981—; also lectr. pediatrics; lectr. pediatrics, emergency med. technician program Lincoln Land Coll.; guest lectr. Sangamon State U.; cons. pediatrician Andrew McFarland Zone Center, Springfield; mem. staff Meml. Med. Center, Springfield, 1969-80; chmn. dept. pediatrics St. Johns Hosp., Springfield, 1970-78, mem. exec. com., 1978-80; cons. pediatrician Abraham Lincoln Med. Group, Lincoln, Ill.; mem. perinatal adv. com. State of Ill.; pres. Found. for Med. Care of Central Ill.; mem. regional perinatal steering com. City of Springfield; mem. adv. bd. Springfield Dept. Health. Served to capt. AUS, 1943-46. Diplomate Am. Bd. Pediatrics. Fellow Am. Acad. Pediatrics, N.Y. Acad. Medicine. Contbr. articles to pediatrics jours. Home: 3512 Panorama Dr Bakersfield CA 93306

DIAMOND, MICHAEL JAY, psychologist; b. Hollywood, Calif., Dec. 4, 1944; Moe and Elaine Julia (Ackerman) D.; m. Linda Ellen Feldscott, July 2, 1981. Ph.D. in Clin. and Exptl. Psychology, 1970. Asst. prof. dept. psychology U. Hawaii, Honolulu, 1970-74; pvt. practice psychology, Los Angeles, 1976—; chief psychologist Airport-Marina Counseling Services, Los Angeles, 1977-79; assoc. clin. prof. dept. psychiatry UCLA, 1978—; Fellow Soc. Clin. and Exptl. Hypnosis; mem. Am. Psychol. Assn. (pres. psychol. hypnosis div. 1982-83), Soc. Calif. Soc. Clin. Hypnosis (pres. 1983-84), Am. Soc. Clin. Hypnosis, Internat. Soc. Hypnosis, Am. Acad. Psychotherapists, Am. Orthopsychiat. Assn., Am. Group Psychotherapy Assn., Running Psychologists, Sigma Xi, Phi Beta Kappa, Phi Eta Sigma. Contbr. numerous articles to profl. jours. Office: 566 S San Vicente Blvd Los Angeles CA 90048

DIAMOND, PHILIP ERNEST, lawyer; b. Los Angeles, Feb. 11, 1925; s. William and Elisabeth (Weizenhaus) D.; B.A., UCLA 1949, M.A., 1950; J.D., U. Calif.-Berkeley, 1953; m. Dorae Seymour Diamond, July 5, 1951 (dec. 1973); children—William, Wendy, Nancy; m. Jenny White Marshall, Sept. 17, 1983. Admitted to Calif. bar, 1954; law clk. Calif. Dist. Ct. of Appeals, San Francisco, 1953-54; assoc. firm Landels, Ripley & Diamond, San Francisco, 1954-60, partner, 1960—; pres. Diamond Wine Mchts. Pres. Contra Costa County Sch. Bds. Assn., 1966-68. Served with USNR, 1943-46. Mem. Am. Arbitration Assn. (arbitrator), Assembly Calif. Sch. Bds. Assn., Am., San Francisco bar assns., Phi Beta Kappa. Democrat. Clubs: Commonwealth, Merchant Exchange. Home: 2 Topside Way Mill Valley CA 94941 Office: 450 Pacific Ave Francisco CA 94133

DIAMOND, STANLEY, physician; b. Portland, Oreg., Dec. 10, 1916; s. Jacob and Jennie (Brown) D.; A.B., U. Calif. at Berkeley, 1940, M.D., 1944; m. Aideen Elizabeth Levy, July 4, 1948; children—Marcia Jean, William Steven. Intern. Mt. Zion Hosp. and Med. Center, San Francisco, 1944-45, now asso. chief ophthalmology; resident in ophthalmology Stanford U. (Calif.), 1947-48; practice medicine specializing in ophthalmology, San Francisco, 1948—; cons. to comml. aviation and allied agys., 1954—; vision com. Armed Forces NRC, 1961—; cons. aerospace ophthalmology, 1954—. Served to lt., M.C., USNR, 1945-46, 52-54. Diplomate Am. Bd. Ophthalmology. Fellow Aerospace Med. Assn.; mem. Calif. Med. Assn., Am. Acad. Ophthalmology and Otolaryngology. Contbr. articles to profl. jours. Research on aerospace and gen. ophthalmology. Home: 1 Stonecrest Dr San Francisco CA 94132 Office: 490 Post St San Francisco CA 94102

DIAS, MILAGRES CONSTANCIO, clinical psychologist; b. Goa, India, Mar. 25, 1937; s. Nicolau P. and Florinda (Coutinho) D.; came to U.S., 1966, naturalized, 1974; B.S., Bombay U, (India), 1958, LL.B., 1961, B.Ed., 1959, M.Ed., 1963; M.Ed., Los Angeles Loyola U., 1967; Ph.D., U. Calif., Los Angeles, 1971; m. Arlette A. Badran, Dec. 4, 1971; children—Colin P., Chantelle R. Tchr., St. Xavier's High Sch., Bombay, India, 1960-63; profl edn. Nirmala Inst. Edn., Goa, 1963-66; clin. psychologist Los Angeles County, 1972—; instr. psychology, cons. East Los Angeles Coll., 1972—; pvt. practice clin. psychologist, Paramount, Bellflower and Hacienda Heights, Calif., 1974—; Licensed psychologist, marriage, family and child counselor, sch. psychologist, Calif. Mem. Nat. Register Health Service Providers in Psychology, Am. Psychol. Assn. Democrat. Roman Catholic. Home: 1626 Oxford Court West Covina CA 91792 Office: 4759 Hollywood Blvd Los Angeles CA 90027

DIAZ, BEDAL, technology educator, administrator, consultant; b. Los Angeles, July 11, 1922; s. Jose Luz and Conception Maria (Alaniz) D.; m. Jennie Mancha, Sept. 28, 1947; children—Nancy Jo Diaz Miller, Norman S., David M., Paul J. B.Vocat. Edn., Calif. State U.-Long Beach, 1967, M.A. in Edn., 1972. Cert. secondary vocat. edn. tchr., supr. With Dept. Water and Power, City of Los Angeles, 1951-63; welding instr. Cerritos (Calif.) Coll., 1963-68, counselor, 1968-80, prof., assoc. dean tech., 1980—; dep. welding insp., welding cons. Served with USAAF, 1943-46, ETO, NATOUSA, with USAF, 1950-51, Korea. Mem. Calif. Tchrs. Assn., AAUP, Faculty Assn. Calif. Community Colls., Calif. Personnel and Guidance Assn., Calif. Schs. Counseling Assn. Democrat. Roman Catholic. Club: K.C.

DIAZ, LUIS F., environmental executive, consultant; b. Lima, Peru, April 20, 1946; s. Julio G. Diaz and Luisa C. (Campodonico) D.; m. Sharon L. Clark, Oct. 19, 1968; children—Daniel, David. B.S. in Mech. Engring, San Jose State U., 1972; M.S., U. Calif.-Berkeley, 1973, Ph.D. in Mech. Engring., 1976. Pres. Cal Recovery Systems, Inc., Richmond, Calif., 1975—; research engr. U. Calif.-Berkeley, 1976-77, instr. 1977; instr. environ. planning San Francisco State U. 1980-81; cons. Served with USAR, 1971-76. Recipient Engring. Award of Distinction, San Jose State U., 1982. Mem. ASME, Am. Soc. Agrl. Engring., Soil Conservation Soc. Am., Sigma Xi. Author: Organic Wastes for Fuel and Fertilizer in Developing Countries, 1980; Resource Recovery from Municipal Solid Wastes, 1982. Contbr. articles to publs.

DIBBLE, GEORGE SMITH, JR., petroleum co. exec.; b. Salt Lake City, July 29, 1933; s. George Smith and Cleone (Atwood) D.; B.S. summa cum laude in Mgmt. and Acctg., U. Utah, 1954, J.D., 1960; M.B.A., Brigham Young U., 1963; m. Ilene Jensen, June 26, 1964; children—Andrea, George Smith III. Admitted to Utah bar, 1960, U.S. Supreme Ct. bar, 1971, Wyo. bar, 1974; individual practice law, Salt

Lake City, 1960-66; asst. to pres., exec. asst. to chmn. bd. Husky Oil Co., Cody, Wyo., 1966-73, v.p., 1973—; co-chmn. petroleum industry task force on land use; vis. prof. various univs. Chmn. Wyo. Gov.'s Adv. Com. on Career Edn.; bd. dirs. North Absaroka Ski Patrol; legis. dir. Nat. Ski Patrol System Inc., recipient Yellow Merit Star award, 1981. Served with USAF, 1954-56, lt. col. Res. ret. Mem. Am. Petroleum Inst. (dir. 1977-80), Rocky Mountain Oil and Gas Assn. (pres. 1977-79, operating com. 1975—), Petroleum Assn. Wyo. (pres. 1975-77). Mormon. Contbr. articles to profl. jours. Office: 6060 S Willow Dr Englewood CO 80111

DICAMILLO, MARK JOSEPH, research company executive; b. Niagara Falls, N.Y., Apr. 2, 1953; s. Joseph John and Olga Marie DiC.; m. Leslie Hughes, Apr. 25, 1982. B.A. cum laude, Harvard U., 1975; M.B.A., Cornell U., 1978. With Field Research Corp., San Francisco, 1978—, now mng. editor Calif. Poll. Mem. Am. Mktg. Assn., Am. Assn. Pub. Opinion Research. Roman Catholic. Clubs: Commonwealth, Harvard, Cornell.

DI CANZIO, ALBERT GEORGE, systems engineer, consultant; b. Washington, Dec. 14, 1942; s. Albert and Cecilia Agnes (Dawes) Di C.; B.S., Georgetown U., 1965; M.S. summa cum laude, West Coast U., 1976, M.B.A., 1978. Mem. tech. staff TRW Systems Group, Redondo Beach, Calif., 1969-70; systems analyst Computer Communications, Inc., Torrance, Calif., 1970-74; project leader software engring. computer spl. systems Digital Equipment Corp., Santa Ana, Calif., 1976-79; computer performance analyst, software quality control engr. Gen. Automation, Inc., Santa Ana, 1979-81, chief designer ILIAD-X Network Operating System, 1980; cons. Di Canzio Enterprises, 1981—; pres. ADASI Systems Corp., 1982—. Mem. Math. Assn. Am. Home: 1602 N Huron Dr Santa Ana CA 92706

DICK, JOHN HALE, lawyer; b. Colorado Springs, Colo., May 25, 1923; s. George A. and Bessie G. (Gross) D.; m. Donna Jean Snyder, June 7, 1947; children—Janna Jean Scudder, John Paul, Eric Robert, Scott Andrew; m. 2d, Maxine Calley, Jan. 5, 1973. B.S. in Bus., U. Idaho, 1950, J.D., 1953. Bar: Ariz. 1954. Sole practice, Chandler, Ariz., 1954—; spl. dep. atty. Maricopo (Ariz.) County, 1957-74; atty. City of Chandler, 1974-79, prosecutor, 1981—. Served in USAF, 1942-45. Decorated Bronze Star (3). Mem. ABA, Ariz. Bar Assn., Maricopa County Bar Assn., Tri-City Bar Assn. Club: Kiwanis (Chandler). Home: 411 N Sunset Ave Chandler AZ 85224 Office: 200 N Chippewa Pl Chandler AZ 85224

DICK, MARTHA SUE, grief counselor, substance abuse counselor; b. Runnells, Iowa, June 20, 1933; d. Ward E. and June Janice (Stevens) Ellison; children—Randall, Cindy; m. James H. Dick, June 15, 1979. Student U. Nev., 1979-81, U. Utah, 1981. Cert. substance abuse counselor, Nev. Pvt. practice substance abuse counseling, Reno, 1978—; juvenile rehab. Oikos Inc., Reno, 1978-80; adult male alcohol counselor Transition House, Reno, 1980-81; dir. Transitior House, Reno, 1981-82; patient rep., grief counselor St. Mary's Hosp., Reno, 1982—; coordinator seminars Nat. Jud. Coll. Democrat. Contbr. articles to profl. jours.

DICK, NANCY, lieutenant governor; m. Stephen Barnett; children—Margot, Timber, Justin. Mem. Colo. Ho. of Reps., 1974-78; now lt. gov. State of Colo. Trustee Denver Symphony Assn.; hon. chairperson Friends of Urban League; chairperson Colo. Rural Council; chairperson regional selection White House Fellows, 1981; mem. adv. panel U.S. Oil Shale Environ. Com., 1974-78; fin. chairperson Fedn. Rocky Mountain States; mem. U.S. Health Care Cost Containment, Fordham Planning Commn., 1981—; mem. exec. bd. Gov.'s Interstate Indian Council, 1981-83; del. Nat. Democratic Conv., 1980; chairperson Colo.-Hunan Indsl. Conf. Planning Com.; Rocky Mountain bd. dirs. Inst. Internat. Edn., 1980-81. Recipient Florence Sabin award Colo. Pub. Health Care Assn., 1980; Outstanding Citizen award Nat. Rural Primary Care Assn., 1981; Outstanding Alumnus award Coll. Bus., Mich. State U., 1981. Office: 144 State Capitol Denver CO 80203

DICKENS, CHARLES GARTH, mech. engr.; b. Tacoma, May 13, 1918; s. Charles Z. and Ruby L. (Nash) D.; B.B.A., U. Puget Sound, 1940; B.S. in Mech. Engring., U. Wash., 1943; postgrad. Westinghouse Grad. Engring. Sch., 1944; m. Betty M. Angel, May 31, 1946; children—Brian J., Lori M., Janet K.; m. 2d Mae H. Kalin, Apr. 15, 1977. Design engr. Westinghouse Electric Corp., Pitts., 1944-50; research engr. Aerojet Gen. Corp., Azusa, Calif., 1951-54; plant engr. Fluid Packed Pump, Los Nietos, Calif., 1954-57; chief engr. Aeroquip Corp., Gen. Logistics Div., Burbank, Calif., 1957-60; proposal mgr. Engineered Systems Div., FMC Corp., Santa Clara, Calif., 1960-80; proposal mgr. ESD Corp., Santa Clara, Calif., 1981—. Pres., Merrivale West Homeowner's Assn.; team capt. Bay Area Indsl. Tennis League; active United Way, Jr. Achievement, Republican Party. Registered profl. engr., Calif. Mem. ASME, Am. Def. Preparedness Assn. Methodist. Clubs: Pacific Coast Magicians Assn., Saratoga Tennis (pres.). Developer computer-controlled automatic order-picking system; designer machines to fill war heads with nerve gas; patentee automatic palletizing machinery. Home: 1359 Cherrywood Sq San Jose CA 95117 Office: ESD Corp 328 Brokaw Rd Santa Clara CA 95052

DICKENSON, RICHARD WAGNER, lawyer; b. Peoria, Ill., Nov. 12, 1910; s. George Love and Erma (Wagner) D.; A.B. with distinction, Stanford, 1932, LL.B., 1935; m. Rosebud Moore, Aug. 31, 1963. Admitted to Calif. bar, 1935; asso. law firm Nutter & Rutherford (later Rutherford, Jacobs, Cavalero and Dietrich), Stockton, Calif., 1936-42; area rent atty. Office Price Adminstrn., Stockton, 1942-43, dist. rent atty., Sacramento, 1943-45, rent atty. regional office, San Francisco, 1945-47; dep. counsel, San Joaquin County, Stockton, 1948-52, asst. counsel, 1952-55, county counsel, 1955-73, spl. asst. to county counsel, 1973—, pub. guardian, 1958-77; instr. U. San Francisco, 1946, instr. Humphreys Coll., 1948-71, dean law sch., 1951-71, 73-78, dean emeritus, 1971-73, counsel to bd. trustees, 1978—; pres., treas., dir. The Georges Co. Adv. bd. Calif. Water Resources Assn.; mem., sec. San Joaquin County Republican Central Com. Mem. Am., Fed., San Joaquin County bar assns., State Bar Calif., Nat. Dist. Attys. Assn., A.A.A.S., C. of C., Phi Beta Kappa, Sigma Delta Pi. Clubs: Commonwealth of Calif., Yosemite, West Lane Racquet. Editor, contbr. Western Water Law Symposium, 1963. Home: 2310 Allston Way Stockton CA 95204 Office: Courthouse Room 711 222 E Weber Ave Stockton CA 95202

DICKER, DORN SUE, corporate relations executive; b. Wichita, Kans., June 27, 1946; d. James Frederick, Jr., and Joan C. (Callais) Barlow; B.A., U. Kans., 1968; M.B.A., U. So. Calif., 1970. Vice pres. for security Pacific Nat. Bank, Los Angeles, 1969-73; dir. adminstrn. Pacific Resources Inc., Honolulu, 1975-76; owner, dir. Island Internat., Honolulu, 1976-79; v.p., dir. corp. relations Parsons Corp., Pasadena, Calif., 1979—; leader seminars and workshops, panelist, speaker. Trustee, v.p. Dispute Resolution Ctr. Pasadena; trustee Pasadena Polit. Action Com.; mem. adv. council Girls Club Pasadena. summer intern U. Kans., 1967; Commerce Assos. fellow, 1968-70; recipient Outstanding Leadership award Am. Cancer Soc., 1982. Mem. Nat. Investor Relations Inst., Pub. Relations Soc. Am., Women in Bus., Pasadena C. of C. (bd. dirs.), Beta Gamma Sigma.

DICKERSON, CAROL ADRIENNE, geologist; b. Greenville, S.C., Apr. 11, 1952; d. Lynn and Brooks (Parker) D. B.S., U. S.C.-Columbia, 1974; M.S., Cornell U., 1977. Geologist, Stauffer Chem. Co., Richmond, Calif., 1977—. AEC fellow, 1974-76. Mem. Am. Assn. Petroleum Geologists, Soc. Econ. Paleontologists and Mineralogists, Am. Inst. Mining Engrs., Assn. Women Geoscientists (com. chmn.), No. Calif. Geol. Soc., Am. Inst. Individual Investors. Office: 1391 S 49th St Richmond CA 94804

DICKERSON, DONALD EDWARD, ophthalmologist; b. Sioux Falls, S.D., May 10, 1932; s. Oren Morris and Jessie Pauline (Martin) D.; A.B., U. Mo., 1953, A.B., B.S., 1955; M.D., Harvard U., 1957; m. Tamra Flower, July 25, 1958; children—Darcie, Shelley. Intern, Bellevue Med. Center, N.Y.C., 1957-58; resident ophthalmology Wadsworth VA Hosp., Los Angeles, 1961-64; practice ophthalmology Santa Monica, Calif., 1964—; asst. clin. prof. surgery UCLA, 1974-80, asso. clin. prof. surgery, 1980—; cons. Los Angeles VA; pres. Santa Monica Eye Med. Group, 1972—; med. exec. bd. Santa Monica Hosp., 1975-80, chief of surgery, 1975-79, chief staff, 1980. Pres., St. Matthew's Parish Sch. Bd., 1974-75. Served to capt., M.C., AUS, 1958-61. Mem. Bay Dist. Los Angeles County (v.p. 1972, pres. 1982), Am., Calif., Los Angeles County med. assns., ACS. Republican. Episcopalian. Clubs: Rotary, Bel-Air Bay. Home: 789 Amalfi Dr Pacific Palisades CA 90272 Office: 1908 Santa Monica Blvd Santa Monica CA 90404

DICKERSON, FRANCIS EDWARD, marketing executive; b. Santa Monica, Calif., Oct. 12, 1952; s. Robert E. and Margaret F. (Budnick) D.; m. Lynne Andrew, Dec. 18, 1976. B.S. in Communication, Stanford U., 1974. Chief copywriter Carter, Callahan & Assocs., San Jose, Calif., 1974-76; asst. v.p., dir. mktg. Pacific Valley Bank, San Jose, 1977-79, v.p., dir. mktg., 1980—. Mem. San Jose Advt. Club (achievement award 1980, 81, v.p., 1982, pres. 1983). Office: 333 W Santa Clara St San Jose CA 95113

DICKERSON, MORGAN WILLIAM FISHER, III, social worker, county/city ofcl.; b. Pueblo, Colo., Apr. 10, 1941; s. Morgan William Fisher and Ellen Morehead (Weddington) B.; B.S., McPherson (Kans.) Coll., 1966; M.S.W., Portland State U., 1972, M.P.A., 1978; m. Patricia A. Pitts, June 16, 1968; children—Laura Noelle, Scott Irving. Asst. rehab. coordinator Goodwill Industries of Oreg., 1968-70; asst. dir. Ret. Sr. Vol. Program, City of Portland/County of Multnomah, Oreg., 1973-74, dir. 1975-76, planner Commn. on Aging, 1974-75, assoc. dir., from 1976, planner Area Agy. on Aging, 1975; now geriatric specialist North/Northeast Community Mental Health Center Inc., 1982-83; adult therapist Ctr. for Community Mental Health, 1983—. Served with U.S. Army, 1966-68. Mem. Nat. Council on Aging, Nat. Assn. Social Workers, Nat. Assn. Black Social Workers. Club: Lions (pres. 1983-84). Office: 6329 NE Union Portland OR 97211

DICKERSON, WILLIAM ROY, lawyer; b. Uniontown, Ky., Feb. 15, 1928; s. Benjamin F. and Honor Mae (Staples) D.; B.A. in Acctg., Calif. State U., Los Angeles, 1952, postgrad., 1952-55; J.D., UCLA, 1958. Admitted to Calif. bar, 1959, U.S. Supreme Ct. bar, 1978; dep. city atty., Glendale, Calif., 1959-62; individual practice law, Los Angeles, 1962-68; mem. firm LaFollette, Johnson, Schroeter and Dehaas, Los Angeles, 1968-73; instr. course N.Mex. Soc. C.P.A.'s, 1977; propr. William R. Dickerson & Associates, Los Angeles, 1973—; instr. Pepperdine U., Los Angeles, 1976; mem. faculty Practicing Law Inst., 1976, 77; speaker in field; arbitrator Los Angeles Superior Ct., 1979—; judge pro tem Los Angeles Mcpl. Ct. Served with U.S. Army, 1946-47. Lic. pub. acct., Calif. Mem. Am. Bar Assn. (mem. com. on profl. and officers and dirs. liability 1975-80, com. on profl. liability litigation sect.), Calif. State Bar, Los Angeles County Bar, Century City Bar, Assn. Trial Lawyers Am., Nat. Soc. Public Accts., Soc. Calif. Accts., San Fernando Valley Criminal Bar, Am. Film Inst., Fed. Bar Assn., Assn. So. Calif. Def. Counsel. Contbr. articles to profl. pubis. Home: 5006 Los Feliz Blvd Los Angeles CA 90027 Office: 3435 Wilshire Blvd Suite 2518 Los Angeles CA 90010

DICKESON, ROBERT CELMER, educator, state official, university president; b. Independence, Mo., June 28, 1940; s. James Houston and Sophie Stephanie (Celmer) D.; A.B., U. Mo., 1962, M.A., 1963, Ph.D., 1968; postgrad. U. No. Colo., 1971, 72; postgrad. inst. ednl. mgmt. Harvard U., 1973; m. Ludmila Ann Weir, June 22, 1963; children—Elizabeth Ann, Cynthia Marie. Adminstrv. asst. U. Mo., Columbia, 1962-64, dir. student activities, 1964-68, asst. dean students, 1968-69; dean student affairs No. Ariz. U., Flagstaff, 1969-70, asso. prof. polit. sci., 1970-76, prof., 1976-81, on leave, 1979-81, v.p. student affairs, 1970-79, v.p. univ. relations, 1973-79; dir. Ariz. Dept. Adminstrn., Phoenix, 1979-81; prof. polit. sci., pres. U. No. Colo., Greeley, 1981—. Nat. vice chmn. Cert. Public Mgrs. Program, 1980-81. Chmn., Gov.'s Commn. on Merit System Reform, 1979-81; active Boy Scouts Am., recipient Dist. award of Merit, 1973, Silver Beaver award, 1975; v.p. Grand Canyon Council, Flagstaff, 1974-76, pres., 1976-78, mem. nat. council, 1976-80; mem. state com. Ariz. Democratic Com., 1970-72. Recipient Distinguished Service award Sigma Alpha Epsilon, 1969. Mem. Am. Polit. Sci. Assn., Am. Soc. for Pub. Adminstrn. (Superior Service award 1981), Am. Acad. Polit. and Social Sci., Nat. Assn. State Budget Officers, Coll. Student Personnel Inst. (mem. acad. council 1969-73), Nat. Assn. Student Personnel Adminstrs. (mem. regional council 1974-79), Phi Kappa Phi. United Methodist (pres. bd. trustees 1974). Club: Kiwanis (pres. 1975-76). Contbr. articles to profl. jours. Office: Office of Pres U No Colo Greeley CO 80639

DICKEY, RICHARD F., publisher; b. Yakima, Wash., July 17, 1936; s. Robert Steven and Metha Lucille (Peterson) D.; m. Carol Lee Spencer, May 3, 1975; children—Richard, Barbara, Kenneth, Samantha. Student Portland (Oreg.) pub. schs. Vice pres., gen. mgr. ABC Distbg. Co., Portland, 1962-68; pres. Clarke Pub. Co., Portland, 1968-72; pres. Community Publs., Inc., Hawaii and Portland, also v.p. Early Calif. Industries, Inc., Los Angeles, 1972-81; pres., chmn. bd. RFD Publs., Inc., Portland and Hawaii, 1981—; newspaper pub. cons.; dir. various corps. Active United Fund, Portland C. of C. Mem. Young Pres.'s Orgn., Nat. Newspaper Assn., Oreg. Newspaper Pub. Assn., Hawaii Newspaper Pubs. Assn. Republican. Presbyterian. Club: Multnomah Athletic (Portland). Office: 6960 SW Sandburg St Tigard OR 97223

DICKEY, RITA M., technical writer, consultant; b. Hartford, Conn., Oct. 16, 1925; d. Joseph and Edwina Curtis (Partridge) Durkee; m. Franklin Miller Dickey, Apr. 19, 1947 (div.); 1 dau., Sarah Coulter Trammell. Student U. Calif.-Berkeley, 1943, 47. Writer, editor, Teaching Machines, Inc., Albuquerque, 1961-64, EVCO, Inc. Behavioral Research & Devel., Albuquerque, 1966-70; editorial dir. Individual Learning Systems, Inc., San Rafael, Calif., 1970-71, mktg. dir., 1972-74; dir. tourism devel. No. Pueblo Enterprises, Santa Fe, 1971-72; v.p. Sipapu Inst., San Francisco, 1976-80, pres., 1980-82; part-time faculty Coll. Bus. Adminstrn., U. San Francisco, 1981; pvt. practice edn./tng. cons., San Francisco, 1976—. Docent Haas-Lilliemthal House; mem. Internat. Visitors Ctr., San Francisco; vol. Com. to Save Cable Cars; mem. Heritage, San Francisco. Mem. Nat. Assn. Female Execs., Soc. Tech. Communication, Media Alliance. Democrat. Club: Commonwealth (San Francisco). Home and Office: 1100 Gough St Apt 12C San Francisco CA 94109

DICKIE, CYNTHIA ANN, counselor for developmentally disabled; b. Detroit, May 14, 1953; d. Richard Clayton and Dorothy Frances (McGeary) Lopus; m. John Edgar Harper, Oct. 22, 1976 (div. 1979); m. 2d., Byron James Dickie, Apr. 19, 1980. B.A., Central Mich. U., 1975, postgrad., 1977-79; postgrad. Mich. State U., 1976. Cert. secondary tchr., Mich. Program coordinator Mid-Mich. Industries, Mt. Pleasant, 1977-80; rehab. coordinator Contra Costa Assn. for Retarded, Walnut Creek, Calif., 1980; counselor Valley Mt. Regional Ctr., Modesto, Calif., 1980—. Mem. exec. bd. service Employee's Internat. Union, 1983. Office: 2105 Lancey Dr #2 Modesto CA 95355

DICKINSON, WADE OAKES, physicist, research and development company executive; b. Sharon, Pa., Oct. 29, 1936; s. Ben Wade Orr and Gladys Grace (Oakes) D.; m. Eleanor Creekmore, June 12, 1952; children—Mark, Katherine, Peter. B.S., U.S. Mil. Acad., 1945; postgrad. Carnegie Inst. Tech., 1949, U. Tenn. 1950, Oak Ridge Sch. Reactor Tech. 1951. Physicist, cons. Rand Corp., 1952-56; tech. adv. Joint Com. Atomic Energy, U.S. Ho. of Reps. and Senate Armed Services Com., 1957-58; prin. engr., cons. Bechtel Corp., 1954-64; pres. W.W. Dickinson Corp., San Francisco, 1960-71; pres. Agrophysics, Inc., San Francisco, 1968—; ptnr. Biophysics, Ltd., San Francisco, 1980—; ptnr. Petrolphysics, Ltd., San Francisco, 1975—; lectr. U. Calif., Berkeley, Davis; cardiology cons. Mt. Zion Hosp. Bd. dirs. Mexican Mus., San Francisco, 1980; chmn. Calif. Med. Clinic Psychotherapy; pres. Young Reps. San Francisco; mem. World Affair Council, 1958-62. Served to capt. USAF, 1945-54. Mem. Soc. Petroleum Engr., Am. Phys. Soc., Masons and Guardsmen, AAAS. Episcopalian. Clubs: Bohemian, Mason. Contbr. numerous articles to profl. jours.; holder 58 patents. Home: 2125 Broderick St San Francisco CA 94115 Office: 187 Steuart St San Francisco CA 94105

DICKINSON, WILLIAM CLARENCE, consultant, retired physicist; b. St. Joseph, Mo., Mar. 15, 1922; s. Thaddeus Stevens and Ethel (Wood) D.; A.B., U. Calif. at Berkeley, 1945; Ph.D., Mass. Inst. Tech., 1950; m. Donna Mae Kuizenga, Feb. 5, 1947; children—William Clarence, Linda Lee. Research physicist Los Alamos (N.Mex.) Scientific Lab., 1950-54; prof. physics and chmn. Dept. Physics, U. Indonesia, Bandung, 1954-57; research physicist, research and devel. group leader Lawrence Livermore (Calif.) Lab., 1957-73, solar projects leader, 1973-82, ret., 1982, cons., 1982—. Mem. Alameda County Charter Review Commn., 1962-63. Served with USN, 1943-46. Mem. Am. Phys. Soc., Internat. Solar Energy Soc., Phi Beta Kappa. Home: 54 Panoramic Way Berkeley CA 94704 Office: Lawrence Livermore Lab Livermore CA 94550

DICKS, EDWARD PICKENS, electronics co. exec.; b. Augusta, Ga., Aug. 14, 1924; s. Edward Pickens and Tommie Emmet (Ponder) D.; B.S. in Indsl. Engring., Ga. Inst. Tech., 1953; B.B.A., Emory U., 1948; postgrad. N.Y.U., 1951-52; m. Barbara Ann Williams, May 5, 1956; children—Phillip. Dee Anne, Edward. Accountant, Price Waterhouse & Co., N.Y.C., 1948-49; accountant Am. Cyanamid Co., N.Y.C., 1949-52; indsl. engr., supr. indsl. engring. GTE Sylvania, Inc., Emporium, Pa., Shawnee, Okla., 1953-62, mgr. facilities, Mountain View, Calif., 1962—. Served with AUS, 1943-46. Registered profl. engr., Calif., Okla. Mem. Am. Inst. Indsl. Engrs., Methods Time Measurement, Assn. for Standards and Research, Mountain View C. of C. (dir.), Calif. Mfrs. Assn., Nat. Mgmt. Assn., Phi Kappa Sigma. Democrat. Baptist. Home: 20940 Pepper Tree Ln Cupertino CA 95014 Office: 100 Ferguson Dr Mountain View CA 94040

DICKS, NORMAN DEVALOIS, congressman; b. Bremerton, Wash., Dec. 16, 1940; B.A. in Polit. Sci., U. Wash., 1963, J.D., 1968; m. Suzanne Callison, 1967; children—David, Ryan. Admitted to Wash. bar, 1968; staff U.S. Senator Warren G. Magnuson, 1968-76, adminstrv. asst., 1973-76; mem. 95th-98th Congresses from 6th Wash. Dist., mem. Appropriations Com. Mem. U. Wash. Alumni Assn., Sigma Nu. Office: 2429 Rayburn House Office Bldg Washington DC 20515

DICKSON, ABIGAIL GILBRIDE, psychol. asst.; b. Portland, Oreg., Feb. 2, 1916; d. Louis and Abigail Sarah (Gardner) Gilbride; B.A. in Psychology, San Diego State U., 1971; M.A., U.S. Internat. U., San Diego, 1973, Ph.D. in Psychology, 1975. Tchr., San Diego schs., 1949-70; intern San Diego State U. Clin. Tng. Center, 1975-76; psychol. asst. to Dr. W.R. Griswold, San Diego, 1956—, partner, 1979—; cons. in field, 1975—. Lic. in standard services personnel services, personnel services, psychometry, pupil counselling, life credentials in psychology, philosophy, human behavior, sociology, Calif. Mem. Am. Psychol. Assn., Calif. Psychol. Assn., San Diego Clin. Psychology Assn., San Diego Psychology-Law Assn. (sec. 1972-76), San Diego Acad. Clin. Psychologists, Psi Chi. Club: University (San Diego). Author research papers. Home: 1027 Adella Ave Coronado CA 92118 Office: 2527 1st Ave San Diego CA 92103

DICKSON, DAVID WILLIAM, metall. testing co. exec.; b. South Gate, Calif., Mar. 7, 1942; s. William and Edna Maurine (Anderson) D.; Metall. Engr., Colo. Sch. Mines, Golden, 1966; m. Judy Sharon Irwin, Dec. 10, 1960; children—Susan Diane, Heather Leigh. Vice pres. Aerocraft Heat Treating Co., Inc., Paramount, Calif., 1966-70; pres. Dickson Testing Co., Inc., South Gate, 1970—. Trustee, Mus. of N. Orange County, Fullerton, Calif. Mem. Am. Soc. Metals. Republican. Club: Virginia County (Long Beach, Calif.). Office: 11126 Palmer Ave South Gate CA 90280

DICKSON, GEORGE HENRY, electrical engineer; b. Tacoma, Wash., Aug. 20, 1928; s. Cecil Leslie and Claire Adelle (Pessemier) D.; B.S. in Econs. and Engring., MIT, 1950; m. Lavonne Irene Schuler, June 7, 1951; children—James Morton, Rodney Glenn, Geoffrey David. Distbn. engr. Puget Sound Power and Light Co., Bellevue, Wash., 1950-58; design engr. Bouillon, Griffith et al, Seattle, 1958-61; ptnr. Miskimen and Dickson, Seattle, 1961-67; dir. engring. Naramore Bain Brady & Johnson, Seattle, 1967-71; asso., exec. engr. R.W. Beck & Assos., Seattle, 1971-78; v.p.-elec. engring. Wood/Harbinger, Inc., Seattle, 1979-80; pres. G.H. Dickson & Assos., Inc., Seattle, 1981-83; gen. mgr. Parkland Light & Water Co., 1983—. Served with U.S. Army, 1951-53. Registered profl. engr., Wash., Alaska, Oreg., Idaho, Calif., Mont., Wyo., Va. Mem. Nat. Soc. Profl. Engrs., Wash. Soc. Profl. Engrs., IES, IEEE (sr. mem.), Sigma Chi. Presbyterian. Club: Kiwanis. Profl. papers presented to regional, nat. pub. power assns., 1974-76. Home: 3911 NE 100th St Seattle WA 98125

DICKSON, LARRY LEE, accountant; b. Seattle, Oct. 19, 1945; s. Floyd Wilson and Lorraine Josephine (Lusk) D.; m. Pamela Lynn Knutson, Aug. 1, 1947; children—Cassandra, Karolyn, Christina. B.S. in Math., Acctg., U. Oreg., 1972. C.P.A., Oreg. Acct., Coopers and Lybrand, Eugene, Oreg., 1972-74; acctg. controller MSI, Inc., 1974-76; systems cons. Internat. Ch. of the Four Square Gospel, 1976-77; ptnr. Young, Koch and Willis, 1977-80; ptnr. Molatore, Gerbert, Rusth & Co., 1980—. Served as lt. U.S. Army, 1967-70. Decorated Bronze Star. Mem. Klamath Falls C. of C. (polit. affairs com.), Full Gospel Businessmen, Christian Businessmen's Com. (chmn.), Am. Inst. C.P.A.s, Oreg. Soc. C.P.A.s. Republican. Mem. Internat. Ch. Four Square Gospel. Club: Toastmasters. Home: 5453 Basin View Dr Klamath Falls OR 97601 Office: 626 S 7th St Klamath Falls OR 97601

DICKSON, MAX CHARLES, career counselor, coordinator; b. Heber City, Utah, Oct. 15, 1924; s. Albert Douglas and Ruth (Hicken) D.; m. Darlene Newbold, May 22, 1944; children—Michael Kent, Dianne Dickson Smith, Ronald N., Kaylene Dickson Murray. B.S., U. Utah, 1950, M.S., 1966, M. Counseling, 1979. Cert. secondary tchr., adminstr., counselor, Utah. Tchr. Utah pub. schs., 1950-59; tchr., media coordinator, student govt. adviser Skyline High Sch., Salt Lake City, 1960-73, career ctr. coordinator/counselor, 1973—. Served with A.C., USN, 1943-45; PTO. Decorated Air medal. Named Tch. of Month, Granite

Sch. Dist. Edn. Assn., Nov. 1961. Mem. Am. Vocat. Assn., Utah Sch. Counselors Assn., NEA, Utah Edn. Assn., Granite Edn. Assn., Sons of Utah Pioneers, Phi Delta Kappa. Democrat. Mormon (past bishop). Developer vocat. guidance program using micro computer.

DICKSON, NAIDA, writer, artist, puzzlesmith, former educator, social worker; b. Thatcher, Ariz., Apr. 18, 1916; d. Charles Edmund and Daisie (Stout) Richardson; B.S., Utah State U., 1940, M.S., 1944; m. Charles Eugene Dickson, Dec. 25, 1942; children—Charles and Clarence (twins). Social worker in Utah, 1941-43; elem., jr. high, spl. edn. tchr., Utah and Calif., 1939-68; part-time adult edn. tchr., 1968-74; children's librarian, Upland, Calif., 1958-59; correctional counselor Calif. Inst. Women, Corona, 1961-62; free-lance writer, 1951—, also puzzlesmith, illustrator; founder Dickson Feature Service, newspaper syndicate distbn. features, 1976, co-dir., Dickson-Bennett Internat. (feature service), 1979—. Vol., Right-to-Life-Line, 1972-80. Fellow social work Latter-day Saints Ch. Relief Soc., 1940-41. Mem. Mensa, Soc. Children's Book Writers, Associated Latter-day Media Artists, Group Against Smoking Pollution (GASP). Mem. Ch. of Jesus Christ of Latter-day Saints (numerous positions). Author, illustrator: The Littlest Helper, 1971; In the Meadow, 1971; I'd Like, 1971; The Toad That Couldn't Hop, 1972; Just the Mat for Father Cat, 1972; The Happy Moon, 1972; Big Sister and Tagalong Teddy, 1973; author: The Best Color, 1971; The Story of Harmony Lane, 1971; About Doctors of Long Ago, 1972; The Biography of a Honeybee, 1974; How to Cope with Smokers, 1979; also poems in anthologies, mags. Puzzles published in puzzle mags., 1963—, sole author 20 spl. puzzle mags. Circle-a-Word and Ring-a-Word, 1973—. Address: 17700 S Western Ave #69 Gardena CA 90248

DICKSON, PATRICK CHARLES, business exec.; b. Phila., Aug. 16, 1941; s. Loris B. and Doris L. (Belknap) D.; B.A., Calif. Luth. Coll., 1967; M.A., Calif. State U.-Northridge, 1969; Ph.D., U. Sarasota, 1973; m. Mina Ann Grimm, June 19, 1965; children—Chad Patrick, Christopher Colin. Pres. Alta Sierra Camps and Sch., Inc.; exec. dir. Alta Sierra Camps, Alta Sierra Prep. Sch.; owner The Travel Sta., Westlake Village, Calif.; pres. Dickson-Slaton & Assocs., profl. mgmt. co.; dist. mgr. Columbus Nat. Leasing Corp. Served with USAF, 1960-64. Mem. Am. Camping Assn. (pres. So. Calif. chpt. 1977-80), Western Assn. Ind. Camps, Calif. Camping Adv. Council. Home: 1902 Stonegate St Westlake Village CA 91361 Office: 973 S Westlake Blvd Suite 101 Westlake Village CA 91361

DICKSTEIN, IRWIN LLOYD, government official; b. Chgo., Apr. 19, 1929; s. Morris and Dorothy (Levin) D.; m. Ina Ruth Pivitz, Sept. 23, 1951; children—Steven, William, Sheila, Margary. B.S., U. Ill., 1951; M.A., Ind. U., 1956, M.B.A., 1957; LL.B., La Salle Law Sch., 1974. Chief chemist Bloomington (Ind.) Dept. Utilities, 1954-64; chief chemistry unit Ohio River Basin Project, Fed. Water Pollution Control Adminstrn., Eumsville, Ind., 1965-67, chief lab. service, 1967-68, chief pollution surveillance, Cin., 1968-69; dir. Office Regulatory Programs, EPA, Cin., 1969-71, dir. enforcement div. R-8, Denver, 1971-78, dir. environ. services div. R-8, 1978—. Served to 1st lt. USAF, 1951-54; lt. col. Res. (ret.). Recipient numerous govt. awards, including Outstanding Service award EPA, 1973, 76, 77, 81, 82, Fed. Womens Program award, 1977. Mem. Am. Chem. Soc., Am. Water works Assn., Water Pollution Control Fedn., Sigma Xi, Sigma Iota Epsilon, Omega Beta Pi. Jewish. Clubs: Optimists, Toastmasters. Home: 6739 S Willow Englewood CO 80112 Office: 1860 Lincoln St Denver CO 80203

DICUS, WILBUR ARTHUR, II, mining co. exec.; b. Cleve., May 26, 1937; s. Wilbur Arthur and Beatrice Leona (Friedeberg) D.; B.S. in Mining Engring., Ohio State U., 1960; m. Delores Lucielle Hyskell, Dec. 24, 1972; children—Melissa Joy, Liana Michelle. Gen. supt. UMAR Oceanics, Key West, Fla., 1960-64; v.p. WADCO Internat., Los Angeles, 1964-68, also dir.; pres., chief exec. officer DMEX Internat., Auburn, Calif., 1968—, also dir.; chief exec. officer Internat. Mineral Services, Sacramento and Miami, Fla., 1976—; cons., investment advisor, Auburn, 1968—. Served with U.S. Army, 1954-56. Cert. master diver; small ship captain; explosive expert; registered investment advisor. Mem. Soc. Mining Engrs., AIME, Marine Tech. Soc., World, Latin Am. dredging assns., Internat. Platform Assn., Internat. Oceanographic Found., Colo. Mining Assn. Republican. Patentee in field of mining and heavy constrn. Office: PO Box 162370 Sacramento CA 95816

DIDOMIZIO, VINCENT JAMES, fin. and strategic planner; b. Waterbury, Conn., Mar. 5, 1939; s. James V. and Carmella M. (Cipriano) DiD.; B.S., Post Coll., 1961; LL.B., LaSalle U., 1965; M.B.A., Calif. Western U., 1974; m. Alexandria Ramanauskas, Oct. 27, 1962; children—Kim, Vincent, Robert. Group controller Timex Corp., 1976-78, dir. planning and control, 1980; dir. planning and control Timex Clock Co., 1978-80; dir. govt. fin. Talley Industries, Mesa, Ariz., 1980-82; pres. VJ Assocs., 1983—; v.p. fin. Dynamic Science, Inc.; dir. Lasting Impressions, Inc. Budget com. United Fund, recipient award. Served with AUS, 1957, 61-62. Recipient Outstanding Fin. Achievement award Timex Corp., 1978. Mem. Nat. Assn. Accts., Nat. Contract Mgmt. Assn., Nat. Indsl. Security Assn. Republican. Roman Catholic. Clubs: KC, Civitan (award). Contbr. articles on acctg., govt. contracting and strategic planning to profl. jours. Home: 7421 Via Camello Del Norte Scotsdale AZ 85258 Office: W Pinnacle Peak Rd Phoenix AZ

DIEDRICK, GERALDINE ROSE, nurse; b. Chgo.; d. Milton Edward and Rose Agnes (Michalski) Goodman; R.N., Mt. San Antonio Coll., Walnut, Calif., 1963; B.S., Calif. State U., Los Angeles, 1966; M.S., UCLA, 1968; divorced; 1 son, Scott Wesley. Nurse, State of Calif., 1960—, dir. nursing Met. State Hosp., Norwalk, 1977—; cons. in mental health, devel. disabilities. Recipient Letter of Commendation, State of Calif., 1974-77. Mem. Am. Nurses Assn., Nat. League Nursing, Am. Assn. Devel. Disabilities, Calif. Nurses Assn. (service awards), Am. Hosp. Assn., World Future Soc., Town Hall Calif. Democrat. Lutheran. Contbr. to profl. jours. Office: 11400 S Norwalk Blvd Norwalk CA 90650

DIEHL, DOLORES, telephone co. public affairs mgr.; b. Salina, Kans., Dec. 28, 1927; d. William Augustus and Martha (Frank) D.; student pub. schs., Kans., 1941-45. Bus. rep. Southwestern Bell Telephone Co., St. Louis, also Kansas City, Mo., 1948-49, Mountain State Telephone Co. Denver, 1949-50; edn. coordinator pub. relations Pacific Telephone, Los Angeles, San Diego, 1950—; cons. Magnet Sch. Los Angeles Unified Sch. Dist., 1977—; pres. Calif. Academic Decathlon, 1979; so. Calif. cons. Industry Edn. Council Calif., 1978-79. Dir. public relations Greater San Diego Sci. Fair, 1960-67; v.p. public relations San Diego Inst. Creativity, 1965-67; mem. exec. com. San Diego's 200th Anniversary Celebration, 1967. Recipient dedication to edn. award Industry Edn. Council, 1964. Mem. Los Angeles area C. of C. (dir. women's council), Calif. Magnet Sch. Consortium of Cities (chairperson), Industry Edn. Council Calif., Los Angeles, San Diego (past pres.) bus. profl. womens' clubs., Delta Kappa Gamma. Republican. Methodist. Home: 691 S Irolo St Los Angeles CA 90005 Office: 1010 Wilshire Blvd Room 516 Pacific Tel Los Angeles CA 90017

DIEHL, RUSSELL REED, investment banker; b. N.Y.C., June 20, 1946; s. Russell Reed and Beverley (Burress) D.; B.A., Lake Forest Coll., 1968; M.S., Am. Grad. Sch. for Internat. Mgmt., 1971; m. Diane Kyle, Aug. 24, 1969; children—Russell Reed, Reed Kyle. With Internat. div. Bank of N.Y., N.Y.C., 1972-75; v.p. Internat. div. Union Bank, Los Angeles, 1975-78; chief exec. officer Peterson, Diehl & Co., Newport Beach, Calif. from 1978; now mng. ptnr. Diehl, Speyer & Brown. Bd. dirs. Rehab. Inst. Orange County. Served with USMC, 1968-71. Mem. Am. Fin. Assn., Nat. Assn. Accountants. Republican. Episcopalian. Home: 40 Westport St Irvine CA 92714 Office: 1201 Dove St Newport Beach CA 92660

DIEHR, PETER EDWARD, computer systems designer and programmer; b. nr. Ann Arbor, Mich., Dec. 29, 1948; s. Harlan John and Olive Jane (Teets) D.; m. Della Marie Arndt, May 26, 1973; 1 dau., Christiana Kelly. Student U.S. Coast Guard Acad., 1967-69; B.S., Eastern Mich. U., 1971, M.B.A., 1974. Programmer, teaching fellow, research asst. Eastern Mich. U., Ypsilanti, 1969-73; data processing mgr. Washtenaw County, Mich., 1973-77; data processing dir. City of Jackson (Mich.), 1977-79; sr. cons. Pacific Mgmt. Systems, Burlingame, Calif., 1979-80; mgr. framework systems devel. Bechtel Power Corp., San Francisco, 1980-82, tech. systems architect, 1982—; systems cons. DNA systems. Served with USCG, 1967-69. Nat. Merit scholar, 1967; Ford Motor Co. scholar, 1967; recipient award for computer systems Lybrand, Ross Bros. & Montgomery, 1972. Mem. Assn. Systems Mgmt. (pres. Ann Arbor chpt. 1978), Assn. Computing Machinery, Am. Arbitration Assn. (panel arbitrators), Mus. Soc., DAV. Republican. Lutheran. Club: Toastmasters (Jackson). Co-developer Eastern Mich. U. Fortran compiler, 1971; author: (with others) Eastern Michigan University Fortran Users Guide and Systems Programmers Manual, 1972. Office: Bechtel Power Corp PO Box 3965 San Francisco CA 94119

DIEL, LEOPOLD, lawyer; b. Fresno, Calif., Nov. 1, 1923; s. Frederick and Mary D.; m. Brunhilda Wallach, Sept. 20, 1947; children—Garrance Stark, Gregory, Mark, Martel. B.A., Princeton U., 1947; J.D., San Francisco Law Sch., 1952. Bar: Calif. 1952. Asst. city atty. City of San Jose (Calif.), 1952-54; ptnr. Bean, Bergna, & Diel, San Jose, 1954-57; sole practice, San Jose, 1957—; arbitrator Superior Ct. of Santa Clara County, 1981—; judge pro-tem San Jose Mcpl. Ct., intermittently 1981—. Served to 1st lt. U.S. Army, 1943-45. Presbyterian. Club: Rotary (Saratoga, Calif.).

DIENER, EVERETT P., public works administrator; b. Portland, Oreg., Jan. 12, 1930; s. Everett Sylvestor and Ruth Marion (Towne) D.; m. Myrle Ewbank, Apr. 15, 1956; children—Lesley K., William S.; B.C.E., U. Wash., 1954; M.C.E., Stanford U., 1962; M.S. in Bus. Mgmt., U. Ark., 1972. Commd. 2d lt. U.S. Army, 1954, advanced through grades to lt. col., 1968, ret., 1973; project mgr. constrn., start-up and maintenance mgr. Operation Trans Alaska Pipeline, 1976-79; dir. pub. works Anchorage, 1979—. Vice-pres., bd. dirs. Alaska Children's Service. Decorated Bronze Star. Episcopalian. Office: Pouch 6-650 Anchorage AK 99502

DIENST, EVELYN RUTH, psychologist; b. Bklyn., Oct. 18, 1943; d. Louis A. and Ann (Hein) D.; m. Robert W. Moulton, Aug. 15, 1973. Student U. Fla., Gainesville, 1961-62; B.A., Bklyn. Coll., 1965; M.A., U. Calif.-Berkeley, 1966, Ph.D., 1971; lic. psychologist, Calif. Research asst. Inst. Human Learning, U. Calif.-Berkeley, 1965-66, teaching asst. Sch. Edn., 1965-66, counseling intern div. counseling psychology, 1966, teaching assoc., 1971, postdoctoral fellow, clin. intern dept. psychology, psychology clinic, 1971-73, research asst., asst. research psychology Ctr. Research and Devel. in Higher Edn., 1966-72; postdoctoral clin. intern VA Hosp., San Francisco, 1972-73; lectr. Calif. State U.-Hayward, 1973-75; vis. scholar Psychologisches Institut, Ruhr Universitat, Bochum, W.Ger., 1973; asst. clin. prof. div. gen. internal medicine dept. medicine U. Calif.-San Francisco, 1975—, dir. program evaluation, 19—; assoc. prof. Calif. Sch. Profl. Psychology, Berkeley, 1982—. N.Y. State Regents scholar, 1962-65. Mem. Am. Psychol. Assn., Assn. Behavioral Scis. and Med. Edn., Psychologists in Family Medicine and Primary Health Care, Soc. Behavioral Medicine, Soc. Research and Edn. in Primary Care Internal Medicine, Evaluation Research Soc., Bay Area Network Women Evaluators, Pi Lambda Theta. Jewish. Contbr. articles to profl. jours. Home: 535 Spruce St Berkeley CA 94707 Office: Univ Calif A-405 San Francisco CA

DIESTELKAMP, DAWN LEA, quality control coordinator; b. Fresno, Calif., Apr. 23, 1954; d. Don and Joy LaVaughn (Davis) Diestelkamp. B.S. in Microbiology, Calif. State U.-Fresno, 1976, M.S. in Pub. Adminstrn., 1983. Cert. clin. lab. Technologist, Calif. Clin. lab. technologist Valley Med. Ctr., Fresno, Calif., 1977-82, quality control coordinator, 1983—; cons., instr. in field. Mem. Nat. Assn. Female Execs., Am. Soc. Pub. Adminstrs. Democrat.

DIETER, ALICE HUNT, journalist; b. Denver, Apr. 16, 1928; d. Thomas Addison and Alice (McCullough) Hunt; B.A. cum laude in English Lang., U. Colo., 1949; m. Leslie Louis Dieter, Sept. 10, 1948; children—Alice Dieter Crowley, Philip Leslie, Paul Wesley. Columnist, reporter, feature writer Intermountain Observer, Boise, Idaho, 1962-72, asst. editor, 1965-72, also TV news reporter Sta. KBOI, and news librarian, 1966-73; stringer Newsweek mag., 1970-73; editorial assoc. corp. communications Boise Cascade Corp., 1973-83; ret., 1983; weekly editorial columnist Idaho Daily Statesman, 1977—. Chair, Idaho Assn. Humanities, 1972-78; bd. dirs. Idaho Farm Workers Services, Inc., 1963-69, pres., 1965-69; mem. Boise Com. Fgn. Relations, 1975—; mem. Idaho Gov.'s Commn. on Excellence in Edn., 1983; pres. Boise LWV, 1957-59; Idaho rep. UNICEF, 1963-65; mem. Boise Valley World Affairs Assn., 1956-65; mem. Boise City Park Commn., 1964-79; co-chair Idaho Johnson for Pres., 1964, Citizens for Andrus for Gov., 1966; del. Women's Conf., Houston, 1978; active YWCA, St. Michael's Episcopal Parish, Boise Philharm., Friends of Boise Library, Idaho Hist. Soc. Recipient Idaho Press awards for feature writing and news photography, 1967. Mem. Idaho Press Club, Phi Beta Kappa. Home: 1147 Santa Maria Dr Boise ID 83712

DIETERICH, JAMES WILLIAM, JR., paper company executive; b. San Rafael, Calif., Aug. 19, 1917; s. James William and Nellie (Wilson) D.; m. Patricia Lee Loomis, Sept. 22, 1945; children—Margaret Ann, William George. B.S. in Commerce, U. Calif.-Berkeley, 1940. Ptnr., Hoefer, Dieterich & Brown, San Francisco, 1945-47; v.p. Clearprint Paper Co., Emeryville, Calif., 1947-68, pres., chief exec. officer, 1968—; chmn. bd., chief exec. officer Dieterich-Post Co., 1982—. Pres., Alameda County Taxpayers Assn., 1978-79, 82—; adv. trustee Alta Bates Hosp., 1979—; trustee U. Calif. Alumni Found., 1967-73, mem. council, 1982—; Bd. govs. NCCJ; mem. exec. Council United Negro Coll. Fund; mem. Pres.'s Airport Access Task Force, 1982-83. Served to col. USAAF, 1940-45, Calif. Air N.G., 1947-50. Mem. Assn. Reprodn. Materials Mfrs., Internat. Reprographic Assn. Republican. Episcopalian (mem. vestry). Club: Rotary. Home: 50 Bolla Ave Alamo CA 94507 Office: 1482 67th St Emeryville CA 94608

DIETERLE, HELLMUTH MICHAEL, transportation company executive; b. Irschenhausen, W. Ger., Oct. 17, 1942; came to U.S., 1960, naturalized, 1965; s. Richard C. and Thusnelda D.; B.A., Golden Gate U., 1970; m. Doris Leone Weber, July 2, 1966; children—Christina, Michael. Traffic mgr. Kaiser Aluminum, Oakland, Calif., also New Orleans, 1963-73; regional mgr. The Harper Group, N.Y.C., 1973-77, now v.p.; lectr. on internat. transp. Republican. Roman Catholic. Office: 545 Sansome St San Francisco CA 94111

DIETLE, CARROLL EUGENE, II, life ins. co. exec., lawyer; b. Toledo, Jan. 4, 1940; s. Carroll Eugene and Martha (Haley) D.; m. Kathleen Anne Keil, Dec. 1, 1978; children—Aimee Marie, Brandon Carroll, Chad Justin. B.A., U. Mich., 1961; J.D., U. Ariz., 1964. Bar: Ariz. 1964. With Anchor Nat. Life Ins. Co., Phoenix, 1968—, gen. counsel, 1968—, asst. sec., 1968-71, sec., 1971, v.p., 1970-78, sr. v.p., 1978-82, exec. v.p., 1982—, dir. 1978—. Mem. ABA, Ariz. Bar Assn., Maricopa Bar Assn. Club: Arizona. Home: 4615 E Arroyo Verde Paradise Valley AZ Office: 2202 E Camelback Rd Phoenix AZ 85016

DIETZ, DOROTHY BRILL, artist-designer; b. San Bernardino, Calif.; d. Henry Edward and Anna Mae (Parfitt) Brill; student San Bernardino Jr. Coll., U. So. Calif., Oreg. State U., Mills Coll., Coll. of Desert, Rudolph Schaefer's Sch. Design, Academie Julian, France, 1959, Art Acad., Honolulu, L'Ecole du Cordon Bleu, France; grad. Japanese Art Center, San Francisco, 1957, Wash. Sch. Art, 1964; grad. Unity Sch. Christianity, 1969; U.S. student Instituto San Miguel de Allende, Mexico, 1960, Sorbonne, France, 1959, Japanese Art Center. One-woman shows: Dietz Galleria, 1959-69, Bank of Am., Palm Desert, Calif., 1962, Ferrall's Playhouse, Palm Springs, 1961, The Villages, San Jose, Calif., Del Mesa Carmel (Calif.), 1980; one-woman and group shows in Calif., Mex., Honolulu; ct. reporter San Bernardino Justice Ct. and San Bernardino Superior Cts. for six years; practice as interior designer, 1947—. Awarded Taka Mizu Dietz, Japanese Govt.; recipient 3 1st place awards and 1 5th place award, nat. art contests. Mem. Assn. of Unity Chs., Carmel Found., Del Mesa Carmel Community Assn., North Shore Animal League, Alpha Chi Omega. Republican. Club: Presidents (Oreg. State U.). Home: 72 Del Mesa Carmel Carmel CA 93921

DIETZ, WILLIAM ANTHONY, product designer; b. New Ulm, Minn., Jan. 14, 1927; s. William Lawrence and Mabel Irene (Simmet) D.; m. Isabel Hamer Smith, Apr. 29, 1978. B.A., St. John's U., 1950. Draftsman Honeywell, Inc., Mpls., Los Angeles, 1951-58; design draftsman Litton Industries, Beverly Hills, Calif., 1958-61; chief design dept. Schurz Corp., Los Angeles, 1966-80; product designer, R G Sloane Mfg. Co., Sun Valley, Calif., 1980—. Served with USAAF, 1945-47. Winner 8th Bachner Award Competition, 1976; San Francisco br. award for unique indsl. plastic product Soc. Plastics Engrs., 1982. Patentee water conditioning control valve, drain valve and fluid coupling. Home: 1564 Talmadge St Los Angeles CA 90027 Office: 7660 N Clybourn Ave Sunvalley CA 91352

DIETZEN, SANFORD RICHARD, vocational rehabilitation counselor; b. Yakima, Wash., Nov. 6, 1948; s. John Fredrick and Elizabeth P. Dietzen; m. Karen Rose Mertens, Aug. 18, 1973; children—Fredrick J., Thadeus R., Rebecca, Elizabeth. B.A. in English, Gonzaga U., 1971, M.Ed. in Guidance and Counseling, 1974. Rehab. counselor State of Wash. Div. Vocat. Rehab., Mt. Vernon, Moses Lake and Pullman, 1974-81; chief case mgmt. for developmentally disabled Valley Mountain Regional Ctr., Inc., Stockton, Calif., 1981—. Chmn. local chpt. Multiple Sclerosis Soc., 1978-79; mem. adv. bd. foster grandparents and foster companion program Stockton State Hosp.; treas. Assn. Regional Ctr. Agys. Mem. Am. Personnel and Guidance Assn., Nat. Rehab. Assn., Nat. Rehab. Adminstrs. Assn. Roman Catholic. Lodge: K.C. Home: 2039 Rosecrans St Stockton CA 95207 Office: 850 N Hunter St Stockton CA 95202

DIEVENDORFF, RICHARD, systems engr.; b. Tsingtao, China, Dec. 30, 1946 (parents Am. citizens); s. Frank and Helen Marion (Haslehurst) D.; B.S. with honors, Calif. State Poly. Coll., San Luis Obispo, 1971; M.S., W. Coast U., Los Angeles, 1976; m. Janet M. Horning; children—Richard, John. Systems programmer Calif. State Poly. Coll. Computer Center, San Luis Obispo, 1969-71; programming supr. Electronic Financial Control Service, Ventura, Calif., 1971-72; sr. systems programmer Automobile Club So. Calif., Los Angeles, 1972-77; sr. systems programmer GTE Data Services, Marina Del Rey, Calif., 1977; sr. systems engr. IBM, Los Angeles, 1977—; cons. in data communications. Served with USN, 1965-69; Vietnam. Mem. Assn. Computing Machinery, Mensa. Home: 433 Forestdale Ave Covina CA 91723 Office: 3424 Wilshire Blvd Los Angeles CA 90010

DIGIOVANNI, MARIO MARTIN, engring. exec.; b. Italy, Dec. 20, 1911; s. Constantine and Antonetta (Raffaelo) DiG.; came to U.S., 1923, naturalized, 1928; B.S. in Mech. Engring., N.Y. U., 1935; postgrad. Princeton, 1943; Ph.D., Calif. Western U., 1976; m. Mary Cordasco, Nov. 6, 1938; children—Ann Marie (Mrs. Leonard Calabro), Martin Robert. Design engr. Glenn L. Martin Co., Balt., 1935-36; supervisory engr. Brewster Aero. Co., L.I., N.Y., 1936-42; project engr. Curtiss Wright Corp., Bloomfield, N.J., 1942-46; dean engring. Stewart Tech. Inst., N.Y.C., 1947-51; with Statham Instruments, Inc., Los Angeles, 1952-71, v.p. engring., 1958-71; v.p. engring., dir. I.C.T. Instruments, Los Angeles, 1973-79, engring. cons. Ametek Controls div., El Segundo, Calif., 1979—; adj. prof. Loyola U., Los Angeles, 1971—. Mem. Los Angeles County Economy and Efficiency Commn., 1975—. Recipient Silver medal Italian Republic, 1968, Order of Merit, 1974; Achievement award N.Y. U. Heights Colls., 1980. Mem. AIAA, ASME, Instrument Soc. Am., Pepperdine U. Assos., Acad. of Scis. (Rome). Clubs: Optimist (past pres.), Unico Nat. (nat. pres. 1967-68). Author textbook on instrumentation; contbr. articles to profl. publs.; patentee in field. Home: 15400 Albright St Pacific Palisades CA 90272 Office: 605 S Douglas Blvd El Segundo CA 90245

DIGNA, JAMES ROBERT, accountant, business executive; b. Oakland, Calif., June 26, 1953; s. Bernard Joseph and Bernice Rose (Isola) D.; m. Susan Marie Grcich, June 25, 1977; children—Katie Marie, Amy Marie. B.S. in Acctg., U. San Francisco, 1975. C.P.A., Calif. Staff acct. Deloite, Haskins & Sells, C.P.A.s, San Francisco, 1975-77; exec. v.p. Pike Rite Inc. (now Rich Pike Rite, Inc.), Escalon, Calif., 1977—; pres. James R. Dignan C.P.A. Inc., Escalon, 1982—. Vice-chmn. Stanislaus County Republican Central Com. Mem. Calif. Soc. C.P.A.s, Am. Inst. C.P.A.s. Club: Elks. Home: 7108 Hillcrest Dr Modesto CA 95356 Office: Pike Rite Inc 19901 S McHenry PO Box 67 Escalon CA 95320

DIGNAM, ROBERT JOSEPH, physician; b. Manchester, N.H., July 8, 1925; s. Walter Joseph and Margaret Veronica (Lowe) D.; B.S., Bates Coll., 1945; M.D., Tufts U., 1949; m. Evelyn Pettitt, Aug. 4, 1951; children—Stephen Mark, Lyn Shore, Margaret Gale. Intern, Boston City Hosp., 1949-50, resident in orthopedic surgery, 1954-57; resident in orthopedic surgery, Lahey Clinic, Boston, 1953-54 practice medicine specializing in orthopedic surgery, Santa Monica, Calif., 1960—; Mem. staff St. Johns Hosp., UCLA Med. Center; clin. prof. orthopedic surgery UCLA. Served to lt. M.C., USN, 1951-54. Fellow A.C.S.; mem. AMA, Mass. Med. Soc., Calif. Med. Assn., Am. Acad. Orthopedic Surgeons. Club: Jonathan. Home: 821 Alma Real Pacific Palisades CA 92072 Office: 2021 Santa Monica Blvd Santa Monica CA 90404

DILBECK, HAROLD ROY, business educator; b. Taft, Calif., May 28, 1932; s. Roy E. and Osalee E. (Swafford) D.; 1 son by previous marriage, Russell. B.S., Fresno State, 1956, M.B.A., UCLA, 1958; Ph.D. in Bus. Adminstrn., 1961. C.P.A., Calif. Grad. research economist UCLA, 1960-61; asst. prof. fin. U. So. Calif., Los Angeles, 1961-65, assoc. prof., 1965-66; vis. assoc. prof. Escuela de Adminstrn. de Negocios Para Graduados (Stanford-U.S. AID Project), Lima, Peru, 1966-69; prof. Calif. State U.-Long Beach, 1969—; pres. Harold Dilbeck Accts., Inc. Served with USMC, 1952-54. Mem. Am. Inst. C.P.A.s, Calif. Soc. C.P.A.s, Am. Fin. Assn., Fin. Mgmt. Assn. Contbr. articles to profl. jours. Home: 18722 Vanderlip Ave Santa Ana CA 92705 Office: 1442 Irvine Blvd Suite 219 Tustin CA 92680

DILGER, PAUL HERMAN, agricultural engineering educator, computer consultant; b. Cin., Jan. 12, 1939; s. Paul George and Dorothy Mae

(Moser) D.; m. Dixie Lee York, Aug. 25, 1966; 1 son, Bryce Edward. A.A. in Chemistry, Los Angeles Valley Coll., 1964; B.S. in Soil Chemistry, U. Calif.-Davis, 1967; M.S. in Agrl. Engring., Calif. Poly. U., 1974. Elec. and telemetry technician Atomics Internat., Chatsworth, Calif., 1961-62; research technician space div. N.Am. Aviation, Canoga Park, Calif., 1962-64, Kearney Found., U. Calif.-Davis, 1964-68; vocat. agr. instr. Cuyama Valley (Calif.) High Sch., 1968-71; assoc. prof. agr. and computers Coll. of Desert, Palm Desert, Calif., 1971—; cons. computers in agr. and bus. Cubmaster and scoutmaster Boy Scouts Am., 1979-83; mem. adv. com. Hemet Future Farmers Am., 1981—. Served with U.S. Army, 1957-59. Mem. Calif. Agr. Tchrs. Assn., Am. Vocat. Assn., Am. Farm Assn., Farm Bur., Fluid Power Soc., Faculty Assn. Calif. Community Colls. Republican. Presbyterian. Clubs: Cuyama Exchange, Anza Valley Lions. Designed particulate control and evaluation for liquid rocket engine fuels; discovered biochemical cause of grass tetany in range land cattle. Home: Indian Hills 34-B Mountain Center CA 92361 Office: 43500 Monterey Ave Palm Desert CA 92260

DILLARD, JOHN MARTIN, lawyer, pilot; b. Long Beach, Calif., Dec. 25, 1945; s. John Warren and Clara Leora (Livermore) D.; student U. Calif., Berkeley, 1963-67; B.A., UCLA, 1968; J.D., Pepperdine U., 1976; m. Patricia Anne Yeager, Aug. 10, 1968; 1 son, Jason Robert. Instr. pilot Norton AFB, Calif., 1973-77; admitted to Calif. bar, 1976; asso. firm Magana, Cathcart & McCarthy, Los Angeles, 1977-80, Lord, Bissell & Brook, Los Angeles, 1980—. Served to capt. USAF, 1968-73; Vietnam. Mem. Am. Trial Lawyers Assn. (aviation litigation com.), Am. Bar Assn. (aviation com.), Fed. Bar Assn., Los Angeles County Bar Assn. (aviation com.), Century City Bar Assn., Internat. Platform Assn., Res. Officers Assn., Sigma Nu. Aircraft comdr. 1st Mil. Airlift Command relief mission for Turkish earthquake, 1976. Home: 19621 Verona Ln Yorba Linda CA 92686 Office: 3250 Wilshire Blvd Suite 1208 Los Angeles CA 90010

DILLER, BARRY, motion picture company executive; b. San Francisco, Feb. 2, 1942; s. Michael and Reva (Addison) D. Vice pres. feature films and movies of week ABC, 1971-73, prime time TV, 1973-74; chmn. bd., chief exec. officer Paramount Pictures Corp., 1974—. Mem. Am. Film Inst., Variety Clubs Internat., Hollywood Radio and TV Soc., Acad. Motion Picture Arts and Scis., ACLU, NCCJ. Office: Paramount Pictures Corp 202 N Cannon Dr Beverly Hills CA 90210*

DILLEY, GREGORY DEAN, electronics co. exec.; b. Boulder, Colo., Feb. 28, 1949; s. William G. and M. Jean (McCarthy) D.; student Weber State Coll., 1968-70, U. Utah, 1971-74; m. Kathryn Geniel Willardsen, Mar. 27, 1975. Electronic technician Spectra Sonics, Ogden, Utah, 1964-75, electronic engr. sales, 1974-75, v.p., 1975—; founder Gregory Devel., 1977; audio cons. Recipient Future Scientist Am. award, 1963. Mem. Audio Engring. Soc., Inc. (vice chmn. Utah sect.), Soc. Motion Picture and TV Engrs., Western State Corvette Council, No. Calif. Corvette Assn. Club: Corvette of Utah. Office: 3750 Airport Rd Ogden UT 84403

DILLEY, JOSEPH WILLIAM, educator; b. Pocatello, Idaho, Nov. 14, 1939; s. Joseph Campbell and Agnes Cynthia (George) D.; m. Barbara Grace Walsh, Apr. 6, 1974; children—Barbara Corlin, Joseph Campbell, George Charles Clyde. B.S., Coll. of Idaho, 1963; cert. in spl. edn. U. Oreg., 1965; postgrad. U. Guam, U. Idaho, U. Mont., U. Alaska, 1965-83. Cert. secondary sch. tchr., Alaska; spl. edn. tchr., Oreg. Constrn. worker Morrison Knudsen, Hells Canyon, Oreg., 1960-61; tchr. sci. Nampa (Idaho) Pub. Schs., 1963-65; tchr. spl. edn Ontario (Oreg.) Pub. Schs., 1965-69; tchr. spl. edn. and sci., adminstrv. asst. dept. edn. Govt. of Guam, Agana, 1969-74; dist.-wide work study coordinator spl. edn., tchr. sci. and ceramics, dir. student activities Soldotna (Alaska) High Sch., Kenai Peninsula Borough Sch. Dist., 1974—. Bd. dirs. Kenai Peninsula Mental Health Clinic, 1979-80. Served with Army N.G., 1957-63. Mem. Am. Fedn. Tchrs. (del. nat. conv. 1980), Kenai Peninsula Fedn. Tchrs., Am. Personnel and Guidance Assn. Republican. Lutheran. Lodge: Elks. Co-author ednl. curriculum for handicapped young adults Kenai Peninsula Borough Sch. Dist., 1975-76; community coll. curriculum for Treasure Valley Community Coll., Ontario, 1966. Home: Box 592 Soldotna AK 99669 Office: Soldotna High Sch Box 3009 Soldotna AK 99669

DILLEY, WILLIAM GREGORY, electronic co, exec.; b. Sterling, Colo., June 6, 1922; s. William Gregory and Ethel (Chandler) D.; B.S., U. Colo., 1951; postgrad. U. So. Calif., 1957; m. Myra Jean McCarthy, May 14, 1944; children—Gregory Dean, Karen Kay. Cons. engr., Denver, 1950-51; commd. officer U.S. Air Force, 1951-68; pres. Spectra Sonics, Ogden, Utah, 1968—; cons. Utah Dept. Vocat. Instrn., 1970-74; cons. electronic mfg. corps. in U.S., 1968—. Served with USAAF, 1943-46; ETO, PTO. Decorated D.F.C., Air medal with nine oak leaf clusters (U.S.); Fourragere (Belgium); recipient U. Colo. Disting. Engring. Alumnus award, 1977; holder U.S., world aircraft speed records. Fellow Audio Engring. Soc.; mem. Soc. Registered Inventors, Soc. Motion Picture and Television Engrs., Internat. Platform Assn., Nat. Assn. Broadcasters, Nat. Aeros. Assn., Caterpillar Club, Aircraft Owners and Pilots Assn., Pi Kappa Alpha. Contbr. articles to profl. jours. Patentee U.S., abroad. Office: 3750 Airport Rd Ogden UT 84403

DILLMAN, DONALD ANDREW, sociology educator; b. Chariton, Iowa, Oct. 24, Joye s. Floyd Andrew and Mildred Arbelle (Gurwell) D.; m. Joye Jolly, Nov. 25, 1964; children—Andrew, Melody. B.S., Iowa State U., 1964, M.S., 1966, Ph.D., 1969. Research assoc. Iowa State U., Ames, 1967-69, asst. prof., 1969-73, dir. social research Ctr. Pub. Opinion Lab., 1970-73; assoc. prof. Wash. State U., Pullman, 1973-78, dept. chmn. rural sociology, 1973-81, prof., 1978—. Nat. Kellogg Found. fellow, 1980-83; recipient Cert. of Merit Rural Sociol. Soc., 1982. Mem. Am. Sociol. Assn., AAAS, Am. Assn. Pub. Opinion Research, World Future Soc., Am. Assn. Housing Educators, Rural Sociol. Soc. (pres. elect N.Am.), Pacific Sociol. Assn. Author: Mail and Telephone Surveys: The Total Design Method; The American Housing Dream: Accommodation to the 1980s; sr. editor Rural Society in the U.S.: Issues for the 1980s; contbr. numerous articles to profl. jours. Office: Dept Rural Sociology Washington State U Pullman WA 99164

DILLON, FRANCIS PATRICK, financial services and human resources consultant; b. Long Beach, Calif., Mar. 15, 1937; s. Wallace Myron and Mary Elizabeth (Land) D.; B.A., U. Va., 1959; M.S., Def. Fgn. Affairs Sch., 1962; M.B.A., Pepperdine U., 1975; m. Vicki Lee Dillon, Oct. 1980; children—Cary Randolph, Francis Patrick, Randee, Rick. Traffic mgr., mgr. personnel services Pacific Telephone Co., Sacramento and Lakeport, Calif., 1966-69; asst. mgr. manpower planning and devel. Pan-Am. World Airways, N.Y.C., 1969-71; mgr. personnel and drgn. devel. Continental Airlines, Los Angeles, 1971-74; dir. personnel Farwest Services, Inc., Irvine, Calif., 1974; dir. human resources Bourns, Inc., Riverside, Calif., 1974-80; dir. employee and community relations MSI Data Corp., 1980-83; pres. Pavi Enterprises, 1983—; mgmt. cons.; pres. Meditrans Inc. Bd. dirs. Health Services Maintenance Orgn., Inc., Youth Services Center, Inc., vol. precinct worker. Served to lt. comdr. USN, 1959-66; asst. naval attaché, Brazil, 1963-65. Recipient Disting. Service award Jaycees, 1969; Jack Cates Meml. Vol. of Year award Youth Service Center, 1977. Mem. Assn. Internal Mgmt. Cons.'s, Am. Soc. Personnel Adminstrn., Personnel Indsl. Relations Assn., Am. Soc. Tng. and Devel. Republican. Episcopalian. Clubs: Mission Viejo Sailing, YMCA Bike, Mission Viejo Ski, Caving, Toastmasters (pres. 1966-67), Have Dirt Will Travel. Home: 27331 Via Armistoso Mission Viejo CA 92692

DILLON, JAMES THOMAS, educator; b. Chgo., Dec. 16, 1940; s. Thomas James and Anna Lorraine (Heineman) D.; m. Virginia K. Greear, 1980; 1 child, Jay LeRoux. Ph.D. in Ednl. Psychology, U. Chgo., 1978. Tchr. high schs., Chgo., 1962-70; asst. prof. edn. Chgo. State U., 1977-79; asst. prof. edn. U. Calif.-Riverside, 1980—. Recipient Harper award U. Chgo., 1973. Mem. Am. Ednl. Research Assn., Am. Psychol. Assn. Author: Personal Teaching, 1971; Resurgence of Religious Instruction, 1977; contbr. articles to ednl. jours. Office: Sch Edn U Calif Riverside CA 92521

DILLON, MARGARET HAFER, educational administrator; b. Chgo., June 25, 1920; d. Lawrence Grover and Beatrice Stella (McGrath) Hafer; m. George Gustave Dillon, Dec. 19, 1942; children—David Lee, Michael George. Telegrapher, Western Union Co., Chgo., 1939-43; disbursing agt. Naval Air Sta., Whidbey Island, Wash. and Seattle, 1943-45; stock control supr. Ship Store Ashore, Atsugi, Japan, 1953-54; dir. purchasing and stores Grossmont Union High Sch. Dist., La Mesa, Calif., 1957—. Bd. dirs. Aztec Athletic Found. San Diego State U., 1982-84. Mem. Calif. Assn. Sch. Bus. Ofcls. (chmn. purchasing com.), Calif. Assn. Pub. Purchasing Officers (pres. San Diego chpt.), San Diego Council Adminstrv. Women, Ednl. Heartland Sch. Adminstrs. Assn. Republican.

DILLON, SVETISLAVA CECILE, marriage, family and child therapist; b. Beograd, Yugoslavia, Jan. 11, 1949; d. Bozidar and Radmila (Djordjevic) Djuknic; m. Dean Herold Smith, Dec. 1, 1977. B.A., Pepperdine U., 1971, M.A., 1974; Ph.D., Calif. Grad. Inst., 1982; lic. marriage, family and child counselor. Psychologist Psychoednl. Cons., Inc., San Marino, Calif., 1972-74; psychoednl. therapist Children's Neurol. Found., Newport Beach, Calif., 1973-74; supervising counselor Trailback Lodge, Long Beach, Calif., 1974-75; asst. team counselor Long Beach Youth Home, 1975-76; marriage, family and child counselor Calif. Ctr. for Counseling and Psychotherapy, Newport Beach, 1975-78; mental health counselor Accacia Cons., Newport Beach, 1979-80; marriage, family and child therapist South Coast Center for Counseling and Psychotherapy, Tustin, Calif., 1977-83; cons. Mardan Sch. Ednl. Therapy, Costa Mesa, Calif., 1981-82, Stepfamily Pacific Counseling, Huntington Beach, Calif., 1982—. Mem. Am. Psychol. Assn., Calif. Psychol. Assn., Calif. Assn. Marriage and Family Therapist, (pres. Orange County chpt. 1979, 80), Stepfamily Assn. Calif. (pres. 1981-82). Office: 16052 Beach Blvd Suite 115 Huntington Beach CA 92647

DILLON, WILLIAM LLOYD, social worker and administrator; b. Spokane, July 29, 1947; s. Robert Carrothers and Helen Kaye (Etheredge) D.; B.A., Eastern Wash. State Coll., 1970; postgrad. Whitworth Coll., 1973-75; M.P.A., Eastern Wash. U., 1980; m. Carole Lynn Schuster, Oct. 6, 1972. Coordinator tutoring program Spokane Community Action Council, 1967-68; founder, dir. North East Youth Center, Inc., Spokane, 1968-70; clin. asso. Spokane Crises Clinic, 1969-70; dir. youth activities Vols. Am., Spokane, 1970-71; coordinator youth services Spokane Parks and Recreation Dept., 1972-79; dir. program assessment/grants-in-aid Youth Help Assn., 1979-80; employment program Coordinator Wash. State Dept. Social and Health Services, Spokane, 1981-82; exec. dir. Northeast Community Center Assn., Spokane, 1982—. Cons., Yakima Center for Youth Devel. and Change, 1973; bd. dirs. Big Bros. of Spokane County, 1973-78; bd. dirs. Youth Alternatives, Spokane, 1975-80, chmn. bd. dirs., 1979-80; mem. tech. advisory com. Spokane Area Youth Com., 1976-78; mem. coordinating council Nat. Assembly Juvenile Justice Program Collaboration, 1976-79. Home: S 2724 Lamonte St Spokane WA 99203

DILLS, JAMES RICHARD, mental health counselor, nurse; b. Weatherford, Tex., Jan. 19, 1948; s. Harold Joseph and Pauline Ada Harkness; B.A. in Edn., Central Wash. U., 1970; postgrad. U. Alta., 1970-71, U. Montreal, 1971, U. Md., 1974-75, U. Chgo., 1977, Bellingham Vocat.-Tech. Inst., 1982-83. Hosp. attendant No. State Hosp., Sedro Woolley, Wash., 1967-70; emergency med. technician United Gen. Hosp., Sedro Woolley, 1976, operating room technician, 1976-77, central service technician, 1977, central service supr., 1978-80; housekeeping mgr. St. Josephs Hosp., Bellingham, Wash., 1980-81; counselor PORTAL program No. State Multiservice Center; Sedro Wooley, 1982—; CPR instrn. coordinator Hosp. Dist. 304, 1980—; dir. Skagit Med. Credit Bur., 1978-80; sec. Wash. Central Service Assn., 1978-80. Served with USAF, 1972-75, Air NG, 1978—. Mem. Assn. Surg. Technologists, Air NG Assn., Wash. Central Service Assn. (sec.). Democrat. Baptist. Club: Skagit-Whatcom Dominion (sec.). Home: 2071 Matson Rd Sedro Woolley WA 98284 Office: 830 Fruitdale Rd Sedro Woolley WA 98284

DILLS, RALPH CLINTON, state senator; b. Rosston, Tex., Feb. 10, 1910; s. Jesse Maro and Viola (Bohannan) D.; A.B., UCLA, 1931; M.A., U. So. Calif., 1933; LL.B., Loyola U., Los Angeles, 1945; LL.D., McGeorge Coll. Law, Sacramento, 1949; J.D., Van Norman U., Los Angeles, 1961; m. Elizabeth Lee, Nov. 18, 1970. Profl. musician; tchr. history, law and govt. Calif. schs. and colls., 1934-51; admitted to Calif. bar, 1945; mem. Calif. Assembly from 69th Dist., 1939-49; gen. practice law, Compton, Calif., 1945-52; justice of peace, Lynwood, Calif., 1949-51, city judge, 1950-51, mcpl. judge, 1952-66; mem. Calif. Senate from 30th Dist., 1966—, chmn. govtl. orgn. com., 1972—. Dist. chmn. Boy Scouts Am., 1961, bd. dirs. Los Angeles, 1961—. Mem. ABA, Calif. Bar Assn., Nat. Soc. State Legislators (pres. 1974). Democrat. Clubs: Masons (33 deg., Shriner), Lions, Elks, Moose. Home: Gardena CA Office: Room 5050 State Capitol Bldg Sacramento CA 95814

DIMARIA, ORLANDO QUINTIN, publishing exec.; b. Greensburg, Pa., Sept. 6, 1918; s. Dominic and Mary Lucy (Vitone) D.; B.A., Pa. State U., 1948; m. Betty Louise Miller, Feb. 6, 1947; children—David J., Betsy Ann (Mrs. Dennis Flynn), With Walworth Co., 1937-40; founder editor, pub. Club Divots, Greensburg, 1940-41; advt. mgr. Madera (Calif.) News-Tribune, 1948-50; asst. advt. mgr. Milton (Pa.) Evening Standard, 1950-51; with Wall Street Jour., 1951-64, asst. retail advt. mgr. Eastern edit., 1951-56, assoc. advt. mgr. nat. edit., 1956-61; spl. projects to design and start Nat. Observer, 1961, advt. mgr. 1961-62, exec. advt. mgr., 1963-64; dir. mktg. Am. Banker, 1965-66; pres. Mardee Enterprises, Inc., pub. Oceanography Newsletter, 1966—, pub. New Med. Tech., 1968—, New Pollution Tech., 1969—; pres. QD Pub., Inc., pub. bank letter, 1966—, Wall Street Newscards, 1975—; founder, pub. Oceanside-Vista (Calif.) Observer, 1974-76; pub. sci. response cards, 1974—; v.p. Soc. West, 1976-77; nat. advt. mgr. Los Angeles Herald-Examiner, 1977—. Trustee, L.I. Library Resources Council. Served from pvt. to 1st sgt. USAAF, 1941-45; ETO. Africa. Mem. Advt. Fedn. Am., Downtown N.Y. Ad Club (organizing chmn.) Navy League U.S., Am. Soc. for Oceanography, Internat. Platform Assn., Internat. Oceanographic Found., Alpha Delta Sigma. Clubs: The Lambs; Lomas Santa Fe Country. Home: 5136 Thorn Tree Irvine CA 92715 Office: Drawer 6249 Huntington Beach CA 92646

DIMASCIO, ROBERT ANTHONY, paper company executive, accountant; b. Phila.; s. Anthony and Lena (Rascona) DiM.; m. Linda Esther Norman, Mar. 25, 1973; children—David Scott, Farrah Hope, Ann Michelle. B.S. in Econs., Villanova U., 1967. C.P.A. Group controller health services group Alco Standard, then asst. to pres., v.p. fin. distbn. group; now exec. v.p. Carpenter Offut Paper Co., Long Beach, Calif. Served with U.S. Army, 1968-69. Mem. Am. Inst. C.P.A.s. Office: PO Box 940 Long Beach CA 90801

DI MILO, ANTHONY JOHN, chemist; b. Phila., May 6, 1924; s. Michael and Adelina DiM.; B.A., Temple U., 1948; postgrad. U. Ind., 1949-50; Ph.D., M.I.T., 1953; m. Mercedes S. Singer, Nov. 1, 1970; children—Michael, Anthony. Research chemist Atlantic Refining Co., Phila., 1953-59; sr. chemist Aerojet Solid Propulsion Co., Sacramento, 1959-78; propulsion devel. engr. TRW Systems, Redondo Beach, Calif., 1978—; adj. prof. chemistry Drexel Inst. Tech., Phila., 1955-59. Served with U.S Army, 1943-46. Decorated Bronze Star. Mem. Am. Chem. Soc., Sigma Xi. Home: 4217 Via Valmonte Palos Verdes Estates CA 90274 Office: 1 Space Park Redondo Beach CA 90278

DIMINO, FRANKLIN JOSEPH, lawyer; b. N.Y.C., Feb. 4, 1933; s. Joseph and Anna (Laserinko) D.; m. Joan Maceli, Dec. 26, 1956; children—Lynn, Mark, Glen, Robyn. B.A., Queens Coll., 1955; J.D., N.Y. U., 1961. Admitted to Calif. bar, 1962; partner firm Parker, Stanbury, McGee, Peckham & Garrett, Los Angeles, Santa Ana, Calif., 1962-68; prin. Garret & Dimino, Inc., law corp., Tustin, Calif., 1968-80, Dimino & Card, 1980—; sec., dir. Motus Chem. Co., Motus Internat., Inc., Bank of San Clemente. Judge pro tem Orange County Superior Ct., 1971-81. Served to capt. USAF, 1955-58. Diplomate Am. Bd. Trial Advs. Mem. ABA, Orange County Bar Assn., State Bar Calif., Am. Trial Lawyers Assn., Lawyer-Pilots Bar; Assn. Trial Lawyers Am., Assn. So. Calif. Def. Roman Catholic. Club: K.C. (4 deg.). Home: 501 Teresa St San Clemente CA 92672 Office: 1633 E 4th St Santa Ana CA 92701 also 300 El Camino Real San Clemente CA 92772

DIMINO, STEPHEN ALEXANDER, management consultant; b. N.Y.C., June 24, 1945; s. Richard Morris and Olga (Tarasuk) Rose; m. Pauline Marie Boucher, Sept. 24, 1977. B.A. with honors in History, St. Francis Coll., 1966; postgrad. Coll. Ins., NYU, 1967-72, M.B.A., 1972. Research and devel. cons. Guardian Life Ins. Co., N.Y.C., N.Y., 1966-69; supr. systems and procedures NYU Med. Ctr., N.Y.C., 1970-73; sr. systems analyst Diamond Internat. Corp., Bangor, Maine, 1973-74, Maine Blue Cross and Blue Shield Co., Portland, 1974-78; supr. systems and programming Blue Cross Mont., Great Falls, 1978-82; mgr. corp. and fin. systems and programming Am. Gen. Corp., Houston, 1982-83; prin. Alpha Mgmt. Assocs., Great Falls, 1983—. Vice chmn. Young Republicans for Lindsay, N.Y.C., 1962-64; sec. Our Lady Tropani Civic Club, 1962-70; town constable Mechanic Falls (Maine), 1974-77, chmn. budget com., 1974-76. Recipient N.Y. State Citizenship award, 1962; N.Y. State Regent scholar, 1962-66. Mem. Assn. Systems Mgmt., Adminstrv. Mgmt. Soc., Duns Scotus, Phi Alpha Theta. Repbulican. Roman Catholic. Contbr. articles to profl. jours. Home: RR 1 S Box 2050 Cascade MT 59421 Office: Alpha Mgmt Assocs Suite 427 600 Central Plaza Great Falls MT 59401

DIMITROFF, ATHANAS ZAHARIEFF, retired mining and electrical engineer; b. Orhanie, Bulgaria, Mar. 3, 1913; s. Zahari Georgieff and Elenka (Hadji) Nicolova; came to U.S., 1932, naturalized, 1945; B.S. in Elec. Engring., Colo. State U., 1936; E.M., Colo. Sch. Mines, 1939; m. Gwen Barker, July 31, 1943 (dec. Sept. 21, 1961); children—Jan Elaine, Mark George; m. 2d, Mildred J. Sherrill, Nov. 18, 1966. With Phelps Dodge Corp., United Verde Mine, Jerome, Ariz., 1939-52; mining, elec. engr., supervising engr. U.S. Bur. Mines, Denver, 1952-69, dist. mgr. Rocky Mountain Dist. metal and nonmetal mine safety, 1969-73; chief Denver Tech. Support Center, Mining Safety and Health Adminstrn., Denver, 1973-83, ret., 1983. Mem. IEEE, Rocky Mountain Coal Mining Inst. (pres. 1960-61), Sigma Tau. Mason, Elk. Home: 1945 Zinnia St Golden CO 80401

DIMMICK, CAROLYN REABER, state supreme ct. justice; b. Seattle, Oct. 24, 1929; d. Maurice Clifford and Margaret (Taylor) Reaber; B.A., U. Wash., 1951, J.D., 1953; m. Cyrus Dimmick, Sept. 10, 1955; children—Taylor, Dana. Admitted to Wash. bar, 1953; asst. atty. gen. Wash. State, 1953-55; dep. pros. atty. King County, 1955-59, 1960-62; practiced in Seattle, 1959-60, 62-65; dist. ct. judge, Bothell, Wash., 1965-75; judge Superior Ct., Seattle, 1976-80; justice State Supreme Ct., Olympia, Wash., 1981—. Named Alumni of Year, John B. Allen Sch., 1978; recipient award World Plan Execs. Council, 1981; Woman of Achievement award Matrix Table, 1981. Mem. Nat. Assn. Women Judges, World Assn. Judges, Am. Judges Assn., Am. Bar Assn., Am. Judicature Soc., Wash. State Bar Assn. Clubs: Wash. Athletic; Wing Point Golf. Home: 10223 Lake City Way NE Seattle WA 98125 Office: Temple of Justice Olympia WA 98504

DIMOND, RICHARD ALLAN, orthopedic surgeon; b. Polk County, Iowa, May 26, 1941; s. Andrew Joseph and Vera Marie (Philp) D.; B.S., U. Iowa, 1962, M.D., 1966; M.A. in Biol. Structure (NIH grantee), U. Wash., Seattle, 1973; m. Brenda Rose Sharer, Aug. 21, 1965; children—Holly Marie, Devrie Rose. Intern, San Bernardino (Calif.) County Hosp., 1966-67; resident in orthopedic surgery U. Wash. Hosps., 1969-74; orthopedic surgeon Group Health Coop., Seattle, 1974—, chmn. dept., 1979—; clin. instr. U. Wash. Med. Center, 1978—. Served as officer M.C., USAF, 1967-69. N. Am. traveling fellow Am. Orthopedic Assn., 1974. Fellow Am. Acad. Orthopedic Surgeons; mem. King County Med. Soc. Club: Lake City Elks (Seattle). Contbr. to med. publs. Address: 200 15th Ave E Seattle WA 98112

DIMUCCIO, MARY-JO, librarian; b. Hanford, Calif., June 16, 1930; d. Vincent and Theresa (Yovino) DiM.; B.A., Immaculate Heart Coll., 1953, M.A., 1960; Ph.D., U.S. Internat. U., 1970. Tchr. parochial schs., San Francisco, 1949-54, Los Angeles, 1954-58; tchr. Govt. of Can., Victoria, B.C., 1959-60; asst. librarian Immaculate Heart Coll. Library, Los Angeles, 1960-62, head librarian, 1962-72; adminstrv. librarian Sunnyvale (Calif.) Pub. Library, 1972—. Bd. dirs. Sunnyvale Community Services, former pres. Mem. ALA, Spl. Libraries Assn., Cath. (past pres. exec. bd.) Calif. library assns., Bus. and Profl. Women (pres. Peninsula Dist.), Calif. Women in Govt. Club: Soroptomists. Office: 1500 Partridge Ave Bldg 7 Sunnyvale CA 94087

DINGMAN, JAMES DANIEL, environmentalist; b. Longmont, Colo., Feb. 1, 1954; s. Leo Willis and Helen Pearl (Fishburn) D.; m. Cheryl Elizabeth Maronde. B.S., Colo. State U., 1976; M.S., U. Denver, 1980. Research technician Colo. State U., Ft. Collins, 1973-76; bioecon. surveyor State of Alaska, Juneau, summer 1977; wildlife technician Colo. Div. Wildlife, Denver, summer 1978; tchr. natural history, ornithology, entomology; research entomologist Denver Mus. Natural History, 1981-82; environmentalist Tri-County Health Dept., 1982—, also cons. Harner-White Ecol. Cons. Grantee, Denver Audubon Soc., 1979-80, U. Denver, 1979-80. Mem. Colo. Environ. Health Assn. (newsletter editor, dir.), Colo. Pub. Health Assn. (dir.), Am. Ornithology Union, Wilson Ornithol. Soc., Colo.-Wyo. Assn. Mus., Oceanic Soc., Sigma Xi. Home: 1516 Mayfield Ln Longmont CO 80501 Office: 4301 E 72d Ave Adams City CO 80022

DINGMAN, MICHAEL DAVID, multi-industry company executive; b. New Haven, Sept. 29, 1931; s. James Everett and Amelia (Williamson) D.; m. Jean Hazlewood, May 16, 1953; children—Michael David, Linda Channing (Mrs. Michael S. Cady), James Clifford. Student, U. Md. Gen. ptnr. Burnham & Co. investment bankers N.Y.C., 1964-70; pres., chief exec. officer, dir. Wheelabrator-Frye Inc., Hampton, N.H., 1970-83, chmn. bd., 1977—; pres., dir. The Signal Cos. Inc., La Jolla, Calif., 1983—; dir. AMCA Internat. Ltd., Time Inc., Ford Motor Co., Pullman Transportation Co. Inc., Mellon Nat. Corp., Pogo Producing Co. Trustee John A. Hartford Found. Mem. IEEE. Clubs: Recess, Links, Board Room, N.Y. Yacht (N.Y.C.); Lyford Cay (Nassau); Union of

Boston; Basin Harbor (Vt.); Cruising Am.; Gulf Stream Golf (Fla.). Office: 11255 Torrey Pines Rd La Jolla CA 92037

DINGMAN, PAUL REVERA, psychologist; b. Palmer, Mass., Sept. 29, 1920; s. Charles Francis and Monna Gertrude (Cox) D.; B.A., Am. Internat. Coll., 1943; Ph.D., Clark U., 1950; m. Ruth I. Taft, Nov. 1, 1942; children—Ann P. Billings, Paul Taft. Clin. psychologist Vets Hosp., Framingham, Mass., 1950; clin. psychologist Brattleboro (Vt.) Retreat, 1950-52; dir. Des Moines Child Guidance Ctr., 1952-69; chief mental health sect. N.Mex. State Dept. Health and Social Services, 1969-70; supt. Grafton (Mass.) State Hosp., 1970-72; dir. Bay-Arenac (Mich.) Community Mental Health Services Bd., 1972-73; dir. univ. counseling and psychol. services, prof. Colgate U., 1973-81; sr. clinician acute admissions unit N.Mex. State Hosp., Las Vegas, 1982—; lectr. Marlboro Coll., 1951-52, Drake U., 1954; cons. State Iowa Div. Child Welfare, 1955-63, Woodward State Hosp. and Sch., 1956-58, Iowa Youth Guidance Service, 1961-65, Iowa Div. Corrections, 1962-65, NIMH, 1963-67, 74—; lectr. Assumption Coll., 1971-72; cons. Joint Commn. on Accreditation Hosps., 1977-79, N.Y. State Office Mental Hygiene, 1979-80, Colgate U., 1981—. Trustee, N.Y. Sch. Psychiatry, 1974, vice-chmn., 1979-80; mem. Iowa Gov's. Adv. Com. on Mental Health, 1965-67; mem. com. on children N.Y. State Dept. Mental Hygiene, 1967; mem. exec. com. N. Central N.Mex. Comprehensive Health Planning Council, 1969-70; mem. N.Mex. Gov's. Adv. Com. on Drug Abuse, 1969-70; bd. dirs. Madison County Mental Health Dept., 1974-81; bd. visitors Hutchings Psychiat. Ctr., 1978-81. Served with U.S. Army, 1942-46. Fellow Am. Psychol. Assn. (council rep. 1961-64), Am. Assn. Mental Deficiency; mem. Am. Assn. Correctional Psychologists, Am. Assn. Psychiat. Services for Children, AAUP, Am. Orthopsychiat. Assn., Am. Pub. Health Assn., Soc. Personality Assessment. Contbr. articles to profl. jours. Home: Vegas Village Apt 18 Las Vegas NM 87701 Office: PO Box 1266 Las Vegas NM 87701

DINNEEN, STEPHEN LAWRENCE, constrn. co. exec.; b. Compton, Calif., Sept. 2, 1946; s. Lawrence Leroy and June (Strueber) D.; B.S. in Fin., Duquesne U., 1973; m. Patricia Ann Wujcik, July 7, 1973. Analyst, Moore, Leonard & Lynch, Pitts., 1973-74; asst. controller Tri-County Truck Co., Oxnard, Calif., 1974-76; sec.-treas. Offshore Crane & Service Co., Port Hueneme, Calif., 1976-78; controller Dean Homes of Beverly Hills (Calif.), 1978-79; v.p. fin. and adminstrn. Wargo Constrn. Co., Ventura, Calif., 1979-82; personal fin. cons. Served with USAF, 1966-70. Lic. life and disability agt., Calif.; lic. real estate salesman, Calif.; notary public, Calif. Mem. Port Hueneme C. of C. (dir. 1978), Delta Sigma Phi. Republican. Roman Catholic. Club: Elks. Home and Office: 2209 Calaveras Dr Camarillo CA 93010

DINNER, NORMAN, business executive; b. Bklyn., Mar. 9, 1927; s. Morris and Pearl (Fine) D.; m. Phyllis J. Hurst, May 30, 1953; children—Wendy, Melanie; m. 2d Norma Grossman, May 1, 1983. B.B.A., Bklyn. Coll., 1952; Cert., Harvard U. Bus. Sch., 1954. Territorial sales mgr. Philip Morris & Co., Bklyn., 1947-52; dist. sale mgr. Curtiss Candy Co., Chgo., 1952-56; Arrco Playing Card Co., Chgo., 1956-50; nat. sales mgr. Polly Gaz Internat., East Rutherford, N.J., 1960-66; eastern sales mgr. Lava Simplex Internat. Co., Chgo., 1966-72; western sales mgr. Heidenberg Textile Co., Closter, N.J., 1972-74, Mission Furniture Co., Los Angeles, 1974-76, Rosen Enterprises, Los Angeles, 1976-77, Products Internat. (Picam Products), Canoga Park, Calif., 1977-78; nat. sales mgr. K. Ogawa & Co., Gardena, Calif., 1978—. Served with USN, 1944-46. Recipient plaque Expo Sure Mag., 1980. Democrat. Jewish. Pub.: Marketech, Inc., Lake Bluff, Ill., 1980. Home: 5132 White Oak Ave Apt 207 Encino CA 91316

DINSMORE, STANLEY HUGH, electronics engineer; b. Huntington Park, Calif., Sept. 25, 1929; s. Daniel George and Margaret (Stone) D.; m. Marcia Dale Shannon, May 15, 1965; children—Daniel Paul, Danika Dale, Kendal Shannon. A.A., Fullerton Jr. Coll., 1949; student U. Calif.-Berkeley, 1950, B.S. in Chemistry, 1955, M.S. in Engring. Sci., 1957. Electronics engr. Bendix Computer, Los Angeles, 1957-63; tech. staff Jet Propulsion Lab., Pasadena, Calif., 1963-69; project engr. Berkeley Computer, 1969-70; sr. engr. Precision Instruments, Palo Alto, Calif., 1970-74, Singer Bus. Machines, San Leandro, Calif., 1974-76, staff engr. Memorex Corp., Santa Clara, Calif., 1975—, mgr. systems engring. magnetic test equipment ops., 1981-82, mgr. systems tech. magnetic test equipment ops., 1982—. Served with USN, 1950-54. Mem. IEEE, Sigma Xi. Republican. Club: Orchid Soc. Calif. Patentee light-activiated keyboard, film duplicator. Home: 1041 Stimel Dr Concord CA 94518 Office: San Tomas at Central Expy Santa Clara CA 95052

DINWIDDIE, DOUGLAS MACARTHUR, mus. adminstr.; b. Salem, Ohio, July 18, 1951; s. Ralph Alonzo and Vernie Mae (Brown) D.; B.A., Western N.Mex. U., 1973, M.A., 1975; postgrad. N. Tex. State U., 1979; m. Rebecca Louise Smith, Aug. 21, 1971; children—Aaron Douglas, Amber Rene. Grad. teaching asst. dept. history and social sci. Western N.Mex. U., Silver City, 1973-74, instr., 1979—, curator Western N.Mex. U. Mus. 1974-77, dir., 1977—. Mem. Am. Assn. Museums, Mountain-Plains Mus. Conf., N.Mex. Assn. Museums, Am. Assn. State and Local History, Hist. Soc. SW N.Mex. Democrat. Presbyterian. Club: Western-ers Internat. Office: Western New Mex U Silver City NM 88061

DINWIDDIE, JANIS ELIZABETH, museum special events director; b. San Gabriel, Calif., Mar. 2, 1948; d. Redfield Towers and Eileen Hilma (Hamilton) Dinwiddie; m. Charles Lindsay Steenrod, Dec. 23, 1976. Student U. Calif.-Irvine, 1965-66; B.A. in Art, Calif. State U.-Fullerton, 1971. Freelance graphic designer, Costa Mesa and Leucadia, Calif., 1972-75; office mgr. Environ. Research Assocs., Del Mar, Calif., 1974-76; bus. mgr. U. Calif.-San Diego, 1976-79, conf. mgr. 1979-82; dir. spl. events Los Angeles County Mus. Art, 1982—. Named Meeting Planner of Yr., San Diego chpt. Meeting Planners Internat., 1982. Mem. Meeting Planners Internat., Los Angeles Olympic Organizing Com. (mem. visitor relations adv. commn. 1980—). Office: 5905 Wilshire Blvd Los Angeles CA 90036

DI PAOLA, SUZANNE MARIE, rehabilitation and vocational evaluation specialist; b. Phoenix, Ariz., Dec. 14, 1952; d. Augustine George and Blanche Bettina (Bosco) Di P.; m. James Sabin Johnson, May 18, 1981; 1 dau., Kristin Leigh. B.S., U. Ariz., 1974; postgrad. Calif. State U.-Sacramento, 1977, McGeorge Sch. Law, 1980—. Spl. services and evaluation intern, U. Ariz.-Tucson, 1973-74; intern dept. rehab., Calif. State U.-Sacramento, 1976; vocat. evaluator San Diego State U. Rehab. Ctr., 1977-78, supr. vocat. evaluation service, 1978-80, adj. faculty dept. counselor edn., 1978-80; owner/dir. Work Assessment Ctr., Sacramento, 1980—; cons. Active Sacramento Women's Network. Mem. Nat. Rehab. Ass., Vocat. Evaluation and Work Adjustment Assn., Am. Personnel and Guidance Assn., Rehab. Profls. Sacramento. Republican. Contbr. Jour Applied Rehab. Office: Work Assessment Ctr 2665 Riverside Blvd Sacramento CA 95818

DIPNER, RANDY WAYNE, systems engineer; b. Columbus, Ohio, July 6, 1949; s. Wayne Elroy and Waneita Mae (Slocum) D.; m. Patricia Kay Peters, Mar. 10, 1973. B.S. in Aero./Astro. Engring., Ohio State U., 1972, B.S. in Computer and Info. Sci., 1972. With Inco, Inc., Colorado Springs, Colo., 1976-81, space object identification tech. advisor, 1978, ADCOM functional event analysis project mgr., 1979, space def. ops. center program mgr., 1981; with Computer Tech. Assocs., Inc., Denver, 1981—; founder Tetrahedron Research Assocs., 1981. Scoutmaster, Boy Scouts Am., Colorado Springs, 1979-80; active participant campaigns Colo. U.S. Senator, and U.S. Rep. Served to 1st lt. USAF, 1972-76. Recipient 1st place award Johns Hopkins U. nat. search for computer applications to aid handicapped, 1981. Mem. Armed Forces Communications and Electronics Assn., IEEE. Republican. Contbr. articles to profl. jours. Home: 3425 Valejo Ct Colorado Springs CO 80918 Office: 6015 Lehman Dr Suite 207 Colorado Springs CO 80907

DIRICCO, LEO, chemist; b. Raymond, Wash., Sept. 16, 1922; s. Ferdinand and Eugenia (delFrate) diR.; B.S., Wash. State U., 1949, M.S., 1950; Ph.D., U. Colo., 1955; m. Cecilia DiFalco, Sept. 22, 1947. Staff engr. IBM, 1960-65; mgr. chem. devel. Singer Bus. Machines, 1965-68; mgr. magnetic media devel. Honeywell Info. Systems, 1968-70; prin. engr. Ampex Corp., 1970-72; cons. Ball Bros. Research, Boulder, 1972-74; mgr. materials and processes devel. Applied Magnetics, Goleta, Calif., 1974-78; mgr. chem. devel. rigid media and components div. Memorex Corp., San Jose, Calif., 1978-83, v.p. research and devel. Kearney Magnetics, San Jose, 1983—. Served with USAF, 1943-47; CBI, ETO. Socony-Vacuum fellow, 1953-54. Mem. Am. Chem. Soc., Sigma Xi, Tau Beta Pi, Phi Lambda Upsilon, Sigma Tau. Republican. Roman Catholic. Patentee in field.

DIRUSCIO, LAWRENCE WILLIAM, advt. agy. exec.; b. Buffalo, Jan. 2, 1941; s. Guido Carmen and Mabel Ella (Bach) DiR.; m. Gloria J. Edney, Aug. 19, 1972; children—Lawrence M., Lorie P., Darryl C., Teresa M., Jack D. With various broadcast stas. and instr., adminstr. Bill Wade Sch. Radio and TV, San Diego, San Francisco, Los Angeles, 1961-69; account exec. Sta. KGB Radio, San Diego, 1969, gen. sales mgr., 1970-72; pres. Free Apple Advt., San Diego, 1972—, Fin. Mgmt. Assocs., Inc., San Diego, 1979—, Self-Pub. Partners, San Diego, 1981—; lectr., writer on problems of small bus. survival. Served with USN, 1958-60. Mem. Nat. Acad. TV Arts and Scis. Democrat. Roman Catholic. Office: 3926 Iowa St San Diego CA 92104

DISANTO, BARTEL JOHN, cons. engr.; b. Matawan, N.J., Oct. 23, 1904; s. Antonio and Maria (Saccone) DiS.; M.E., Cornell U., 1926; M.B.A., N.Y.U., 1949; m. Mary Roman, Sept. 8, 1928; children—Allan, James. Plant engr. Am. Smelting & Refining Co., Perth Amboy, N.J., 1927-37, plant mgr., Perth Amboy, 1938-51, dir. engring., Salt Lake City, 1951-69, sr. cons. Indsl. Minera Mexico SA, Mexico City, 1970—; pres. DiSanto Corp. Pres. Perth Amboy Safety Council, 1950. Life mem. ASME Am. Inst. Chem. Engrs., Nat. Soc. Profl. Engrs., Am. Ordnance Assn.; mem. Canadian Inst. Mining and Metallurgy. Club: Rotary. Author, pub.: Barts Technical File System, 1973; sect. editor: Soc. Mining Engrs. Mineral Processing Handbook, 1978. Patentee in field. Home and Office: 931 Mission Ridge Rd Santa Barbara CA 93103

DISHNO, DUANE ALLAN, educational administrator; b. Missoula, Mont., Oct. 26, 1941; s. Thomas Charles and Nellie Montana (Managhan) D.; m. Pauline Amelia Schwandt, Aug. 17, 1968; children—Joel Thomas, Chris Edward. Student, Wash. State U., 1959-60; B.A., Eastern Wash. U., 1963; M.A., Calif. State U.-Long Beach, 1972; student U. Calif.-Riverside, 1975-76; postgrad. U. La Verne, 1979—. Cert. pre-sch.-adult adminstr., tchr. Classroom tchr., reading specialist, learning analyst Westminster (Calif.) Sch. Dist., 1963-73; lectr. Calif. State U.-Los Angeles, 1973-74; coordinator compensatory edn. Westminster Sch. Dist., 1973-75; prin. Huntington Beach (Calif.) City Sch. Dist., 1975-77, dir. spl. services, 1977-82, asst. supt. ednl. services, 1982—; cons. Calif. State Dept. Edn.; mem. adv. com. bilingual tchr. preparation Calif. State U., 1980-81, mem. adv. com. ethnic heritage studies, 1981-83; adv. com. instructional aide program Goldenwest Community Coll., 1975. Dist. rep. United Crusade, 1975-77; sustaining mem. Calif. Republican Com., 1981—. Mem. Assn. Calif. Sch. Adminstrs., Calif. Soc. Ednl. Program Auditors and Evaluators, Orange County Reading Assn., Calif. Assn. Compensatory Edn., Orange County Adminstrs. Spl. Edn., Educare, Assn. Supervision and Curriculum Devel., West Orange County Tchrs. Center (mem. policy bd., v.p.). Republican. Roman Catholic. Home: 7652 Concordia Pl Westminster CA 92683 Office: 20451 Craimer Ln Huntington Beach CA 92648

DISSELHORST, BYRON FRED, chemical engineer; b. Qunicy, Ill., Oct. 28, 1923; s. Fred William and Lydia Amelia (Wagner) D.; B.S. in Ch.E., Oreg. State U., 1947; m. Eleanor Gertrude Zeller, May 22, 1953; children—Thomas, Suellen, Barry, Lori. Research asst. Calif. Research & Devel. Co., Livermore, 1951-54; engr. Lawrence Livermore Lab., Livermore, 1954-59, Gen. Atomic Co. (now GA Techs. Inc.), San Diego, Calif., 1959—. Served with AUS, 1943-45. Decorated Bronze Star Medal. Registered profl engr., Calif. Mem. Am. Soc. Quality Control (cert.), Am. Chem. Soc., Inst. Nuclear Materials Mgmt., Inst. Nuclear Materials Mgmt., Am. Carbon Soc., Phi Gamma Delta. Republican. Lutheran. Club: Masons, Shriners. Contbr. articles profl. jours. Researcher graphite, uranium, zirconium, uranium measurement control techniques; patentee in field. Home: 181 S Nardo Ave Solana Beach CA 92075 Office: Box 85608 San Diego CA 92138

DISTEFANO, PETER ANDREW, insurance executive; b. N.Y.C., Nov. 26, 1939; s. Peter Julian and Marie Antoinette (Onorato) D.; student City Coll. San Francisco, 1965, Costa Mesa (Calif.)-Orange Coast Coll., 1975; cert. enrolled employee benefits, Wharton Sch., U. Pa., 1980; m. Ann Van Zee; children—Diane, Daniel, Donald, Mark, Nick, Kary. Agt., Mut. N.Y., San Francisco, 1971-73; regional mgr. Hartford Ins. Group, Santa Ana, Calif., 1972-77; v.p. Lachman & Assos., Inc., ins., Lafayette, Calif., 1977-80; pres., owner Distefano Ins. Services, Concord, Calif., 1980—; lectr., cons. risk mgmt., employee benefits. Served with USNR, 1957-62. Recipient various ins. sales awards; registered profl. disability and health ins. underwriter. Mem. Nat. Assn. Health Underwriters, Nat. Assn. Life Underwriters, Soc. Registered Profl. Health Underwriters, Nat. Assn. Security Dealers, Internat. Found. Employee Benefit Plans, Profl. Ins. Agts. Calif./Nev., Oakland/East Bay Assn. Life Underwriters. Greek Orthodox. Club: Elks. Address: 1117 Erickson Rd Suite C PO Box 6628 Concord CA 94524

DISTERDICK, JOHN WILLIAM, financial executive; b. Los Angeles, Mar. 15, 1943; s. Robert Hudson and Alys Marie (Runner) D. B.S. in Engring., Purdue U., 1965; M.B.A., Pepperdine U., 1975; M.S. in Fin. Services, Am. Coll., 1981; J.D., San Fernando Valley Coll., 1978. C.L.U., realtor, cert. fin. planner, Calif. Pres., chief exec. officer Tax and Fin. Programming Inc., Burbank, Calif., 1969—. Co-founder, bd. dirs. U.S. Triathlon Assn; mem. Los Angeles Christian Businessmen's Com., Big Bros. Los Angeles. Mem. Inst. Cert. Fin. Planners, Internat. Assn. Fin. Planning. Author numerous articles for fin. publs.; syndicated fin. TV series Your Money Man, John Disterdick. Home: 4723 Forman Ave Toluca Lake CA 91505 Office: 4303 W Verdugo Ave Toluca Lake CA 91505

DITHRIDGE, BETTY (MRS. ANDREW MORRISON), civic worker; b. Los Angeles, Sept. 11, 1920; d. Thomas Edward and Louise (Miles) Mitchell; student U. Calif. at Los Angeles, 1937-39; m. Andrew Morrison Dithridge, May 11, 1940; 1 son, Andrew Morrison. Boy scout and cub scout leader Los Angeles Orphan's Home Soc., 1952-69, sec. extension com., 1959-61, chmn., 1966-68; vol. worker USO; mem. Los Angeles Jr. Philharmonic Com., 1949—; active Symphonies for Youth Concerts, 1958-59; founder, chmn. San Marino Protection Com., 1971-72; sec. Los Angeles County Grand Jury, 1974-75. Bd. dirs. Pasadena chpt. ARC, 1961-62, Vol. Service Bur. Pasadena; bd. dirs., treas. Wilshire Community Police Council, 1979-81; vol. lab. staffer Orange County Marine Inst.; mem. Los Angeles Olympic Organizing Com., citizens adv. com., hostess com., youth activities com. Recipient awards for work with local youth groups. Mem. Wilshire C. of C. (chmn. women's bur. 1957-59), Los Angeles C. of C., Assos. Los Angeles City Coll., Friends of Huntington Library, DAR, Internat. Platform Assn., Los Angeles Grand Jurors Assn., UCLA Alumni of Orange County, Alpha Phi, Sigma Alpha Iota. Clubs: Los Angeles Tennis, Wilshire Country, Dana Point Yacht. Home: 35411 Beach Rd Capistrano Beach CA 92624

DITMORE, MICHAEL CONRAD, med. co. exec.; b. Mpls., May 14, 1943; s. Conrad William and June Carol (VanNest) D.; student U.S. Air Force Acad., 1961-64; B.A., U. Wash., 1966; M.B.A., Stanford U., 1970; children—Brooke, Nathan. With IBM, Portland, Oreg., 1966-68; dir. European ops. Canberra Industries GmbH, Wiesbaden, Germany, 1970-72; regional sales mgr. Rolm Corp., Santa Barbara, Calif., 1972-73; cons. to NASA-Gen. Research Corp., Santa Barbara, 1973-74; divisional mgr. Gyrex Corp., Santa Barbara, 1974-75; v.p. mktg. and fin. Browne Corp., Santa Barbara, 1975-78; pres. Endotek Corp., Santa Barbara, 1978—. Mem. Montecito Sch. Bd., 1975-79; mem. Santa Barbara alumni bd. Stanford U., 1976-78. Served with USAF, 1961-64. Mem. IEEE, Fgn. Relations Com. Episcopalian. Clubs: Birnam Wood Golf, Channel City. Home: 211 Rametto Rd Santa Barbara CA 93108 Office: 824 E Ortega St Santa Barbara CA 93103

DITTMAN, DEBBIE RUTH, real estate broker; b. Sacramento, Apr. 15, 1932; s. Charles Harwood and Ruth Boice (Potter) Kinsley; m. John Alvin Cardoza, Sept. 1950 (div. 1963); children—Harold, Nancy Cardoza Tolbert, John Allan, Gregory, Janice; m. Edgar Marshall Dittman, Jan. 22, 1967 (dec. Jan. 1982); 5 stepchildren. Student Humprey's Coll., Stockton, Calif., 1966, San Joaquin Delta Coll., 1977; grad. real estate sales Anthony Schs., 1974. Real estate broker, Calif. Sec., Calif. Dept. Water Resources, Patterson and Tracy, 1966-72; hostess Welcome Wagon, Tracy, 1973-74; assoc. realtor Reeve Assocs., Tracy, 1975-80; broker Allied Brokers, Tracy, 1980-83; ptnr. real estate Putt, Fallavena, Willbanks & Dittman, Tracy, 1983—. Mem. Tracy Bd. Realtors (pres. 1981, dir. 1976, 77, 80-83), Calif. Assn. Realtors (dir. 1980-81), Tracy C. of C. Presbyterian. Clubs: Peet Dusters Square Dance, Trot-A-Round Dance. Home: 12134 Midway Dr Tracy CA 95376 Office: 359 W 11th St Suite A Tracy CA 95376

DITZ, JOHN ADAMS, construction executive; b. Stockton, Calif., Mar. 4, 1921; s. George Armand and Janet (Adams) D.; m. Ann Goodwin, June 14, 1947; children—Susan Mary, Elizabeth Ann, Nancy Jane, Janet Sarah. A.B. in Engring., Stanford U., 1942. Vice pres. Ditz Bros., 1948-60; v.p. Ditz-Crane, Santa Clara, 1954-82, pres., 1982—; v.p. Foremost-McKesson Property Co., 1970-75, pres., 1975—; v.p. Foremost-McKesson, Inc., 1975—. Trustee Stanford U., 1982—, Palo Alto Med. Found., 1981—. Republican. Episcopalian. Clubs: Pacific Union, Bohemian (San Francisco). Office: One Post St San Francisco CA 94104

DIVASTO, PETER VINCENT, medical educator, psychologist: b. Bklyn., June 6, 1945; s. Pasquale Robert and Nicoletta (Lotito) DiV. B.S., SUNY-Plattsburgh, 1967; M.A., U. N.Mex., 1973, Ph.D., 1977. Elem. tchr., Ballston Spa, N.Y., 1967-70; tchr. Nazareth Psychiat. Hosp., Albuquerque, 1970-71; psychol. sch. medicine U. N.Mex., Albuquerque, 1973-74, asst. prof. dept. family, community and emergency medicine, dept. psychiatry U. N.Mex., 1977—, dir. undergrad. program, 1982—; cons. in field. Served to capt. Army N.G., 1977—. HEW fellow, 1972. Mem. Am. Psychol. Assn., Soc. Tchrs. Family Medicine, Assn. Rural Mental Health. Contbr. articles to profl. jours. Home: 320 Hermosa St NE Albuquerque NM 87108 Office: Div Family Medicine Univ NMex Albuquerque NM 87131

DIVER, NEIL LONGFELLOW, financial services company executive; b. Ft. Wayne, Ind., Feb. 1, 1938; s. Gordon C. and Josephine L. Diver; B.S., Ind. U., 1960, M.B.A., 1961; m. Christina Bucheit, Jan. 30, 1971; children—Mia Christina, Matthew Longfellow. With Smith, Barney & Co., N.Y.C., 1963-66; v.p. fin. Urban Systems Devel. Corp. subs. Westinghouse Electric Co., Pitts., 1967-72; founder Realam. Homes, Ft. Wayne, 1972-73; exec. v.p. Ticor Mortgage Ins. Co., Los Angeles, 1974-79, pres., 1979, now dir.; sr. v.p., chief fin. officer Ticor, Los Angeles, 1979—. Bd. dirs., mem. audit com., and exec. com. Childrens Hosp., Los Angeles. Served with USAF, 1961-62. Mem. Fin. Execs. Inst., Inst., Calif. Los Angeles C. of C., Newcomen Soc. (treas. So. Calif. chpt.). Republican. Episcopalian. Office: 6300 Wilshire Blvd 21st Floor Los Angeles CA 90048

DIVINE, THEODORE EMRY, electrical engineer; b. Hailey, Idaho, May 27, 1943; s. Theodore Clyde and Muriel Juanita (Kirtley) D.; B.S. in Elec. Engring., U. Wash., Seattle, 1966, M.B.A., 1970; m. Roberta Louise Erickson, Mar. 19, 1966; children—Timothy Shannon, Brianna Kristine, Rachel Melissa. Engr., Gen. Telephone Co. of N.W., 1968-69; mem. tech. staff NW ops. Computer Scis. Corp., 1970-72; mem. staff Battelle Pacific N.W. Labs., Richland, Wash., 1973—, sect. mgr. food and agr., 1978, staff engr. indsl. bus. devel., 1980—. Pres., Mid-Columbia Sci. Fair Assn., 1975-76; ruling elder First Presbyterian Ch., Prosser, Wash., 1982-84. Served as officer USAR, 1966-68; Vietnam. Decorated Bronze Star. Mem. IEEE, Am. Soc. Agrl. Engrs. (com. chmn. 1977-78, 82-83, chmn. nat. conf. on electronics in agr. 1983), Beta Gamma Sigma. Home: 831 Guernsey St Prosser WA 99350 Office: Battelle Blvd Richland WA 99352

DIVOLA, JOHN MANFORD, JR., photographer, educator; b. Santa Monica, Calif., June 6, 1949; s. John M. and Marion (Foster) D.; m. Sheila Divola, Apr. 28, 1979. B.A., Calif. State U.-Northridge, 1971; M.A., UCLA, 1973, M.F.A., 1974. Instr. Calif. Inst. Arts, 1978—, UCLA, 1982. Nat. Endowment for Arts photography fellow, 1973, 76, 79. Mem. Soc. Photog. Edn.

DIX, RONALD LEE, advertising executive; b. Urbana, Ill., Oct. 9, 1951; s. Rex Franklin and Margaret Arleah (Stone) D.; m. Teri Lee Ramey, Sept. 16, 1978; children—Todd, Ryan. B.S. in Fin., U. Ill., 1973, M.B.A., 1978. Fin. analyst Union Pacific Corp., Omaha, 1973-76; advt. exec. Procter & Gamble, Cin., 1978-80, Kahn's & Co., Cin., 1980-82, Gallo Salame, Consol. Foods Co., San Francisco, 1982—. Home: 2846 Bowling Green Dr Walnut Creek CA 94598 Office: 250 Brannan St San Francisco CA 94107

DIXON, HAROLD CONLEY, social work service director, educator; b. Jonesboro, Ark., Aug. 27, 1927; s. Henry and Martilla Conley (Gary) D.; m. Ruth McKinney, Aug. 11, 1951; children—Harold Vincent, Rita Dixon Powell, Gary McKinney, Paula Diane. B.A. in Econs., U. Wash., 1952; B.S. in Social Work, U.B.C., 1959; M. in Social Work, U.Wash., 1962; postgrad., U.S. Internat. U. Reporter Seattle Police Dept., 1951-55; case worker King County Pub. Welfare Dept., Seattle, 1955-59; probation officer King County Juvenile Ct., Seattle, 1960-63; psychiat. social worker VA Med. Ctr., American Lake, Wash., 1963-64; clin. social worker VA Med Ctr., Long Beach, Calif., 1967-69; supr. social work, 1969-72; dir. social work service VA Med Ctr., La Jolla, Calif., 1972—; instr. in field. Bd. dirs. San Diego County Mental Health Assn.; mem. council Health Systems Agy.; adv. com. Calif. Health Tng. Ctr. Served with USN, 1944-45. Mem. Nat. Assn. Social Workers, Soc. for Social Hosp. Dirs., Am. Hosp. Assn., Council for Social Work Edn., Am. Legion, Phi Beta Sigma. Republican. Home: 6655 Ave de las Pescas La Jolla CA 92037 Office: 3350 La Jolla Village Dr La Jolla CA 92037

DIXON, JULIAN CAREY, Congressman; b. Washington, Aug. 8, 1934; B.S., Los Angeles State Coll., 1962; LL.B., Southwestern U., Los Angeles, 1967; 1 son, Cary Gordon. Mem. Calif. State Assembly,

1972-78; mem. 94th-98th Congresses from Calif. 28th Dist. Chmn. Calif. State Democratic Caucus. Served with U.S. Army, 1957-60. Mem. NAACP, Urban League, Calif. Arts Commn. Democrat. Office: Room 423 Cannon House Office Bldg Washington DC 20515*

DIXON, KAREN SUE, psychologist; b. Bloomington, Ill., Mar. 25, 1946; d. Charles Lewis and Faye Lanore (Wantland) Henderson; m. David Thomas Biggs, Dec. 2, 1967; m. 2d, Dean E. Dixon, Jr. Jan. 13, 1973; children—Christopher Andrew, Matthew Patrick. Student Mills Coll., 1963-64; B.A., U. Calif.-Berkeley, 1966; M.S., San Jose State U., 1971; lic. psychol. assoc., Alaska. Dep. probation officer Alameda County Probation Dept., Oakland, Calif., 1967-70; ednl. cons. Cons. Industries, Oakland, summer 1971; cons. psychologist Alviso (Calif.) Econ. Devel. Program, 1972; group counselor II, caseworker Alameda County Probation Dept., 1971-72; instr. psychology Coll. Alameda, 1973-73; parole agt. Narcotic Outpatient Program, State Dept. Corrections, Oakland, 1972-74; faculty adv. coop. edn. U. Alaska Community Coll., Anchorage, 1975-76, instr. psychology, 1974-81; psychiat. social worker Langdon Psychiat. Clinic, Anchorage, 1976-80; cons. Parent Tng. Ctr., Anchorage, 1980-82; psychol. assoc. The Counseling Ctr., Anchorage, 1980—. Mem. Am. Psychol. Assn., Alaska Psychol. Assn. Home: SRA Box 4005D Anchorage AK 99507 Office: 101 E 9th Ave Suite 7 Anchorage AK 99501

DIXON, ROBERT GENE, educator, mechanical company executive; b. Clatskanie, Oreg., Feb. 15, 1934; s. Hobart Jay and Doris Marie D.; m. Janice Lee Taylor, Sept. 19, 1954; children—Linda Dixon Johnson, Jeffrey, David. A.S. in Indsl. Tech., Chemeketa Community Coll., 1978, various special courses, 1978-80. Journeyman machinist, cert. welder, Oreg. Machine apprentice to asst. mgr. A.B. McLauchlan Co., Inc., 1956-69; supt. engrng. and prodn. Stevens Equipment Co., 1969-70; co-owner, operator Pioneer Machinery, 1970-72; supt. constrn. and repair Stayton Canning Co., 1972-73; mgr. Machinery div. Power Transmission, 1973-75; owner, operator Dixon Mech., Salem, Oreg., 1975—; instr. machine shop tech., program coordinator Chemeketa Community Coll., 1975—; cons. Served with U.S. Navy, 1952-56. Named Tchr. of Yr., Chemeketa Deaf Program, 1978, Outstanding Instr. of Yr., Am. Tech. Edn. Assn., 1983. Mem. Am. Vocat. Assn. (Outstanding Tchr. award 1981), Oreg. Vocat. Assn. (Instr. of Yr. 1980; pres. 1984), Oreg. Vocat. Trade Tech. Assn. (Instr. of Yr. 1979; pres. 1981; Pres.'s Plaque 1982), Soc. Mfg. Engrs. (sr.), Am. Welding Soc., Am. Soc. Metals, Chemeketa Edn. Assn. (pres. 1979). Author: Benchwork, 1980; Procedure Manual for Team Approach for Vocational Education Special Needs Students, 1980; designer, patentee fruit and berry stem remover. Home: 4242 Indigo St NE Salem OR 97305 Office: PO Box 14007 Salem OR 97309

DIXON, ROBERT MORTON, soil scientist; b. Leon, Kans., May 30, 1929; s. William Gill and Vivian (Marshall)D.; B.S., Kans. State U., 1959, M.S., 1960; Ph.D., U. Wis., 1966; m. Sharon Ann Youngblood, June 21, 1975; children—James, Curtis, Donna, Gregory. Instr., Kans. State U., Manhattan, 1959-60; irrigation specialist Ford Found., Cairo, 1967; research soil scientist U.S. Dept. Agr., 1960—, Tucson, 1973—. Served with U.S. Army, 1954-56. Mem. Internat. Soc. Soil Sci., Am. Soc. Agronomy, Am. Geophys. Union, Am. Soc. Agrl. Engrs., Soil Sci. Soc. Am., Soil Conservation Soc. Am., Internat. Platform Assn., Soc. Range Mgmt., Ariz.-Nev. Acad. Sci. Democrat. Unitarian. Contbr. articles to profl. jours. Patentee land imprinter. Home: 1231 Big Rock Rd Tucson AZ 85718 Office: US Dept Agriculture-ARS 2000 E Allen Rd Tucson AZ 85719

DIXON, ROSS IVAN, univ. adminstr.; b. New Haven, Conn., Nov. 22, 1920; s. Ross Ivan and Ida May (Bourne) D.; B.A., Yale U., 1942, M.A., 1948. Instr., asst. dean students Yale in China, 1943-47; asst. headmaster Edgewood Sch., Greenwich, Conn., 1948-50, headmaster Kings Point (N.Y.) Sch., 1951-55; dep. dir. Inst. Internat. Edn., N.Y.C., 1956-62; pres. Ross Dixon Assos., N.Y.C., 1962-66; dir. Wiltwyck Sch., Yorktown Heights, N.Y., 1966-68; dean students, exec. v.p. Central New Eng. Coll., Worcester, Mass., 1968-72, pres., 1973-77; asst. dir. Fresh Air Fund, N.Y.C., 1977-78; pres. Inupiat U. of the Arctic, Barrow, Alaska, 1978-80; sr. tech. specialist Inst. Naval Studies, King Abdul Aziz Naval Base, Jubaic, Saudi Arabia, 1981—. Mem. Mass. Postsecondary Edn. Comm., 1977-78; dir. Worcester Consortium for Higher Edn., 1974-77, treas., 1976; mem. Bd. Aldermen, City of New Haven, 1952-54; corporator Worcester Downtown Bus. Dist., 1974-77. Mem. Yale-China Assn., Am. Assn. Univ. Adminstrs. (chmn. nat. assembly III), Internat. Assn. Univ. Pres. Democrat. Episcopalian. Clubs: Petroleum (Anchorage), Worcester; Yale (N.Y.C.), Shanghai Tiffin (N.Y.C.). Home: 4111 Minnesota Dr 1 Anchorage AK 99503

DIXON, STEVEN BEDFORD, lawyer; b. San Bernardino, Calif., Feb. 25, 1945; s. Harold James Dixon and Jane Anna (Bedford) Kennedy; children—Melanie Anne, Zachary David. B.A., U. Hawaii-Hilo, 1975; J.D., Calif. Western Sch. Law, 1978; postgrad. Chaminade U. of Hawaii, Hawaii Tax Inst., 1978-82. Bar: Hawaii. Law clk. firm Linley, McDougal, Meloche & Murphy, El Cajon, Calif., 1976, D. Stephen Boner, San Diego, 1977, Tyson & Churchill, San Diego, 1977; law intern Legal Aid Soc. of Hawaii, 1978; law clk., investigator Stephen Christensen, Hawaii, 1978; gen. ptnr. Altman, Dicker & Dixon, tax attys., Hilo, 1978-79, Altman Dixon & Assocs., tax attys., Hilo, 1979-81; sole practice as tax atty., Hilo, 1981-82; gen. ptnr. Dixon & Okura, Hilo, 1982—; Realtor assoc. with Sanford K. Okura; speaker in field; instr. courses in bus. law U. Hawaii-Hilo, 1979-80. Vice pres. Hawaii Concert Soc.; ann. performer Big Island Press Club Imucelebrity Roast; discharge rev. counsel Vets. Outreach, San Diego, 1976. Served to 1st lt. M.I., U.S. Army, 1967-70. Decorated Bronze Star. Scholarship grantee U. Hawaii-Hilo, 1973. Mem. Hawaii County Bar Assn. Club: Rotary. Regular guest columnist on tax planning Hawaii Tribune Herald, 1981. Home: 1100 Ainalako Rd Hilo HI 96720 Office: 101 Aupuni St Suite 202 Hilo HI 96720

DIXON, THOMAS PATRICK, clin. psychologist; b. St. Paul, Dec. 5, 1947; s. Joseph Thomas and Bernice Louise (Capecchi) D.; B.A. cum laude, U. Minn., 1970; M.S., St. Louis U., 1972, Ph.D. in Psychology, 1975; m. Judy Marie Pates, June 11, 1971; children—Carly Lynn, Julia Marie. Grad. teaching instr. St. Louis U., 1974-75; vis. asst. prof. U. Mo., St. Louis, 1975-76; staff psychologist chronic pain program Casa Colina Hosp., Pomona, Calif., 1976-78, program mgr. spinal cord injury program, 1978—, head dept. psychology, 1982—. Served with USAR, 1967-73. NIMH fellow, 1971-72. Mem. Am. Psychol. Assn., Am. Congress Rehab. Medicine, Assn. Advancement Behavior Therapy. Calif. Assn. Physically Handicapped, Sigma Xi. Home: 3839 Williams Ave LaVerne CA 91750 Office: 255 E Bonita Ave Pomona CA 91767

DIZMANG, OSCAR KIRK, educator, economist, consultant; b. Xenia, Kans., Oct. 2, 1903; s. John Kirk and Carrie Belle (Hammons) D.; m. Marie Georgia Garten, Nov. 14, 1934; 1 dau., Annabelle Ruth. B.S., Kans. State U., Manhattan, 1927; M.A., U. Chgo., 1928, postgrad, 1934. Asst. prof. econs., debate coach Lombard Coll., 1929-30; instr. econs. Beloit Coll. (Wis.), 1930-31; instr. Fenn Coll., Cleve., 1931-32; asst. prof., chmn. dept. econs. and bus. Hanover Coll. (Ind.), 1932-34; prof., chmn. dept. econs. and bus. adminstrn. Whitworth Coll., Spokane, Wash., 1935-45; dist. price economist Inland Empire dist., OPA, Spokane, 1945-46; regional economist, Spokane region, War Assets Adminstrn., 1946-47; asst. prof. econs. and bus. adminstrn., Wittenberg Coll., Springfield, Ohio, 1947-48; gov. reclamation economist, Billings, Mont., 1948; mgr. R & W Supply Co., Spokane, 1949-50; mgr. Spokane Transp. Club, 1950-51; economist, bus. analyst OPS, Spokane dist., 1951-52; adminstrv. asst. Property Mgt. div., AEC, Richland, Wash., 1953-54; assoc. prof. mgmt. Armstrong Coll., Berkeley, Calif., 1954-55; asst. prof. econs. and bus. adminstr. Pacific Luth. U., Tacoma, Wash., 1955-59; acct. Western Boat Co., Tacoma, 1959-60; tchr. St. Georges Sch., Spokane, 1960-61; bursar Lewis and Clark Coll., Lewiston, Idaho; teacher public schs. Wash., 1963-69; in pvt. practice, acctg., taxes, insurance, securities, bus. cons., 1948—. Mem. AAUP. Republican. Lutheran. Clubs: North Star Sr. Citizens Ctr. (treas., bd. dirs.), Huggers (Spokane). Club: Masons. Co-author Principles of Accounting, 1959; Principles of Marketing, 1961; contbr. articles to profl. jours.

DLUGATCH, IRVING, educator; b. Bklyn., Jan. 20, 1910; s. Louis and Lena (Seigle) D.; B.S. in Elec. Engrng., Cooper Union, 1937; B.S. in Elec. Engrng., West Coast U., 1964, M.S. in Systems Engrng., 1965; Ph.D. in Math., Los Angeles U., 1976; m. Helen Rosenberg, Dec. 22, 1935; children—Harvey E., Norman J. Program mgr. TRW, Inc., Redondo Beach, Calif., 1959-61, Hughes Aircraft Co., Culver City, Calif., 1961-66, 69-74; Los Angeles regional dir. Robertson & Assos., Newark, 1974-75; sr. scientist Systems Devel. Corp., Santa Monica, Calif., 1966-68; program dir. Ops. Research, Inc., Silver Springs, Md., 1968-69; dean of students Calif. Western U., 1977-81; dir. Madison Inst., Newark, 1964-51; cons. AID Dept. State, 1966-68; pres. Mgmt. Services Co., Los Angeles, 1970-74. Chmn. Citizens Com. for Better Edn., East Meadow, N.Y., 1952-53; cons. East Meadow Sch. Bd. on Phys. and Recreational Facilities, 1952-53; pres. Westwood (Calif.) Art Assn., 1972-73. Asso. fellow Am. Inst. Aeros. and Astronautics (vice-chmn. conf. 1974); fellow Inst. Advancement of Engrng.; mem. Research Soc. Am., IEEE (sr.; mgr. systems analysis tech. area 1969-72; sec. Los Angeles Council 1973-74). Author: You Can Bet on It, 1973; Dynamic Cost Reduction, 1979; contbr.: Engineering and Indsl. Graphics Handbook, 1982; patentee in field. Home: 5321-A Bahia Blanca Laguna Hills CA 92653

DMYTRYSHYN, BASIL, historian; b. Poland, Jan. 14, 1925; came to U.S., 1947, naturalized, 1951; s. Frank and Euphrosinia (Senchak) Mytrin; B.A., U. Ark., 1950, M.A., 1951; Ph.D., U. Calif., Berkeley, 1955; m. Virginia Roehl, July 16, 1949; children—Sonia, Tania. Asst. prof. history Portland State U., 1956-59, asso. prof., 1959-64, prof., 1964—; vis. prof. U. Ill., 1964-65, Harvard U., 1971, U. Hawaii, 1976, Hokkaido U., Sapporo, Japan, 1978-79; Fulbright-Hays fellow, W. Ger., 1967-68; fellow Kennan Inst. Advanced Russian Studies, Washington, 1978. Mem. state bd. dirs. Oreg. PTA, 1963-64; mem. World Affairs Council Oreg., 1965—. Recipient John Mosser award Oreg. State Bd. Higher Edn., 1966, 67. Mem. Am. Assn. Advancement Slavic Studies (dir. 1972-75), Am. Hist. Assn., Western Slavic Assn., Can. Assn. Slavists, Oreg. Hist. Soc., Nat. Geog. Soc., Conf. Slavic and East European History (nat. sec. 1972-75). Author books, most recent being: Colonial Russian America, 1817-1832, 1976; A History of Russia, 1977; USSR: A Concise History, 3d edit., 1978; The End of Russian America, 1979; contbr. articles to profl. jours. Office: Dept History Portland State U Portland OR 97207

DOAN, ALLEN EDWARD, cardiologist; b. Dayton, Ohio, Sept. 28, 1933; s. Roscius Clinton and Elizabeth Jane (Allen) D.; A.B., Ohio Wesleyan U., 1955; M.D., Case Western Res. U., 1959; m. Marlyn Kay Seaman, Apr. 25, 1959; children—David, Amy, Laura. Intern, Strong Meml. Hosp., Rochester, N.Y., 1959-61; resident U. Wash. Hosp., Seattle, 1961-62, 64-66; chief resident in medicine Seattle VA Hosp., 1965-66; practice medicine, specializing in cardiology Overlake Internal Medicine Assos., Bellevue, Wash., 1966-74; founder Cardiology Clinic, Bellevue, 1974—; founder coronary care unit Overlake Hosp., Bellevue, 1966, founder emergency med. care system, 1971—; med. dir. Bellevue Medic I program, 1971-81. Served with USPH, 1962-64. Diplomate Am. Bd. Internal Medicine. Fellow Am. Coll. Cardiology, ACP; mem. Am. Heart Assn. (pres. Wash. 1977—), AMA, Wash. King County med. assns. Researcher in clin. exercise testing, 1962-64. Office: 1414 116th St NE Bellevue WA 98004

DOAN, CORTLAND CHARLES, educator; b. Glendale, Calif., Aug. 9, 1926; s. Cortland Palmer and Laura (Ott) D.; A.A., Pasadena City Coll., 1951; B.A., U. Calif.-Santa Barbara, 1953; M.A., Calif. State Coll., 1965; m. Virginia Evalyn Malmgreen, Oct. 10, 1947; children—Laurie Evalyn, Charles Cortland, Robyn Lillian. Tchr. indsl. arts San Diego city schs., 1953-56, Citrus Coll., 1959-61, Glendora, Calif., 1959-65; engrng. supr. Consol. Electrodynamics Corp., 1956-59; faculty dept. indsl. studies Calif. State U.-Los Angeles, 1965—, now prof.; engrng. cons. Electro-Mech. Design, 1960—; vocat. edn. adviser to Brit. Honduras, 1970. Planning commr. City Duarte (Calif.), 1961-63. Served with USNR, 1943-46. Recipient Laureate citation Epsilon Pi Tau, 1972; Indsl. Educator of Year Coll. Level, Los Angeles County Indsl. Edn. Assn., 1978. Mem. Calif. Tchrs. Assn., Calif. Coll. and Univ. Faculty Assn., Am. Indsl. Arts Assn., Calif. Indsl. Edn. Assn., Calif. Council of Indsl. Arts Tchr. Educators, Robotics Internat., Soc. Mfg. Engrs. Contbr. articles to profl. jours. Office: 5151 State University Dr Los Angeles CA 90032

DOANE, WINIFRED WALSH, zoology educator, researcher; b. N.Y.C., Jan. 7, 1929; d. Harold Vandervoort and Helen Harper (Loucks) Walsh; m. Charles Chesley Doane, July 5, 1953; 1 son, Timothy Price Doane. A.B. magna cum laude, Hunter Coll., CUNY, 1950; M.S., U. Wis., 1952; Ph.D. (NSF fellow), Yale U., 1960. Teaching asst. U. Wis.-Madison, 1950-51; research asst. Wis. Alumni Research Found., 1951-53; asst. prof. Millsaps Coll., Jackson, Miss., 1954-55; lab asst. Yale U., New Haven, 1956-58, NIH postdoctoral research trainee in genetics, 1960-62, faculty assoc. research, 1962-75, lectr., 1965-75, assoc. prof. biology, 1975-77; prof. zoology Ariz. State U., Tempe, 1977—; NSF grantee, 1969-73; NIH grantee, 1973—; cons., lectr., panelist in field. Recipient Kane prize in biology, 1950; Phi Sigma award, 1950; E. Seringhaus scholar Woods Hole Marine Biology Lab., 1950; named to Hall of Fame, Hunter Coll. Alumni Assn., 1972. Fellow AAAS, mem. Am. Inst. Biol. Scis., Am. Soc. Cell Biology, Am. Soc. Naturalists, Am. Soc. Zoologists, Genetic Soc. Am., Internat. Soc. Biology, Soc. Developmental Biology (sec. 1976-79), Phi Beta Kappa. Author numerous articles, in field; assoc. editor Developmental Genetics, 1979-81.

DOBBIN, MURIEL ISABELLA, newspaper reporter, writer; b. Ayrshire, Scotland; d. George and Isabella Lightbody (Laird) Hunter. Ed. Scottish Acad. Reporter, Ayrshire Post, 1953-57, Rochester (N.Y.) Democrat and Chronicle, 1956-57; reporter Balt. Sun, 1950-62, reporter Washington Bur., 1962, West Coast Bur. chief, San Francisco, 1977—. Clubs: Gridiron, Washington Press (Washington). Author novels: A Taste for Power, 1980; Joe's World, 1983.

DOBBINS, GEORGE C., horticulture educator; b. Courtland, Calif., July 30, 1916; B.A. in Zoology-Botany, U. Calif.-Berkeley, 1946; children—Barbara, Dan (dec.). Dist. nursery insp. Nursery Service, Calif. Dept. Agr., Sacramento, 1953-56; hort. instr. Am. River Coll., Sacramento, 1966—; hort. cons. Rusch Bot. Garden, Citrus Heights, Calif., 1978—. Bd. dirs. Sacramento Tree Found., Inc. Served to 1st lt. U.S. Army, World War II. Mem. Am. Hort. Soc., Calif. Assn. Nurserymen (Bert Kallman award 1967, Edn. award 1971), Calif. Native Plant Soc., Sierra Club. Author: Sacramento: City of Trees, 1980. Home: 7301 Antelope Rd Citrus Heights CA 95610 Office: 4700 College Oak Dr Sacramento CA 95841

DOBBS, BRUCE MARTIN, podiatric surgeon; b. Washington, July 11, 1947; s. Lester and Ann (Kaufman) D.; D.Podiatric Medicine, Pa. Coll. Podiatric Medicine, 1973; M.Surgery, Calif. Coll. Podiatric Medicine, 1974; m. Jane Patricia Cisar, Sept. 28, 1979. Intern, Parkview Hosp., Phila., 1973-74; resident in surgery Calif. Coll. Podiatric Medicine Hosp., 1974-75, mem. faculty, 1975—, asso. prof. surgery, 1979-83, prof., 1983—; pvt. practice podiatry, Daly City, Calif., 1975—. Recipient various certs. merit; diplomate Am. Bd. Podiatric Surgery (bd. dirs.; dir. oral exams.). Fellow Am. Coll. Foot Surgery; mem. Am. Podiatry Assn., Calif. Podiatry Assn. Co-author: Surgical Correction of Hallux Abducto Valgus, 1981; contbr. articles to profl. jours. Office: 1500 Southgate Ave Suite 106 Daly City CA 94015

DOBBS, LINDA LEE, state official; b. San Francisco, Oct. 7, 1948. B.A. in Sociology, Calif. State U.-Los Angeles, 1973; M.S.Ed. (fellow), U. So. Calif., 1980. Cert. community coll. student personnel worker, instr. psychology, counselor, basic pupil personnel services, Calif. Various positions Calif. State U.-Los Angeles, 1972-75; counselor asst. Los Angeles Unified Sch. Dist., 1978; employment and claims asst. State of Calif., Van Nuys, 1976-77, employment devel. officer, El Monte, 1978-80, employment counselor, San Fernando, 1980—; counselor Immaculate Conception Home for Girls, Los Angeles, 1972, McKinley Jr. High Sch., Pasadena, Calif., 1973, Found. for Jr. Blind, Los Angeles, 1978; intern Occidental Coll., Los Angeles and Los Angeles Community Coll. Dist., 1979; family counselor Ctr. for Study of Drug Abuse, Tarzana Psychiat. Hosp., 1979. Mem. LWV; mem. civil service div. Calif. State Employees Assn. Recipient Lit. award St. Vincent High Sch., 1966. Mem. Nat. Soc. Internships and Experiential Edn., Am. Personnel and Guidance Assn., Los Angeles County Personnel and Guidance Assn., Calif. Personnel and Guidance Assn. Office: 1520 San Fernando Rd San Fernando CA 91340

DOBBS, MATTI FOUNTAIN, mgmt. cons.; b. Gordon, Ga., June 5, 1937; d. James F. and Mattie Louise (Fountain) Terry; B.A., Morgan State U., 1959; M.S.W. (John Hay Whitney Found. of N.Y. fellow), Rutgers U., 1964; Ph.D., U. So. Calif. Sch. Public Adminstrn., 1978; m. July 21, 1968. Social worker N.J. Div. Mental Retardation, Hammonton, 1960-64; clin. social worker VA, Newark, 1964-66; sch. social worker Newark Bd. Edn., 1966-67; with Los Angeles County Dept. Mental Health, 1967-78, supervising psychiat. social worker, 1968-73, tng. dir., 1973-78; pres. Dobbs Assos., Mgmt. Cons., Beverly Hills, Calif., 1978—; lectr. in sociology Calif. State U., Los Angeles, 1977-78; vis. lectr. cert. program in exec. mental health adminstrn. Sch. Public Adminstrn., U. So. Calif., 1978—, lectr. Sch. Health Adminstrn., 1978—; lectr. Grad. Sch. Adminstrn., U. Calif., Riverside, 1978-80; lectr. Sch. Mgmt., Calif. State U., Dominguez Hills, 1980—; mem. adv. bd. Center for Improvement Child Caring, 1977-78. Mem. regional planning bd. United Way, Inc., Los Angeles, 1977-78; chairperson bd. dirs. People's Coordinated Services, Los Angeles, 1977-80; bd. dirs. Met. YWCA, Los Angeles, 1980-81; bd. dirs. South Los Angeles Devel. Corp., Women in Bus., Westwood Hosp. Recipient Tribute to Black Women award Women Involved in Student Edn., Los Angeles, 1980. Mem. Am. Soc. Public Adminstrs., Am. Soc. Tng. and Devel., Am. Public Health Assn., Wilshire Bus. and Profl. Women, Women in Bus., Calif. Black Women's Forum (sponsor): Promethean Kappa Tau, Psi Chi. Home: 2539 Westridge Rd Los Angeles CA 90049

DOBBS, WARREN CRAIG, community orgn. exec.; b. Atlanta, Apr. 15, 1928; s. Samuel C. and Marjorie D. (Frampton) D.; student Yale U., 1945-47, various mil. schs., 1950-53, San Francisco State Coll., 1956-57, Coll. Notre Dame, 1966, Wash. State U., 1976; grad. United Community Funds and Councils Inst., 1969; m. Mary Anne Karish, Sept. 27, 1950; children—Marjorie Stanish, Catherine Candler, Warren Craig. Ind. sales contractor, San Francisco, 1957-62; exec. dir. United Cerebral Palsy, Oakland, Calif., 1962-65; area dir. United Crusade, San Francisco, 1965-69, asso. exec. dir., Sacramento, 1969-72; exec. dir. United Way of Benton and Franklin Counties, Kennewick, Wash., 1972-82, United Way Spokane County, 1982—; community orgn. cons. Office Community Devel., State of Wash., 1977-79. Bd. dirs. Benton Franklin Opportunities Industrialization Center, 1978-79; trustee Mid-Columbia Symphony Soc., 1977-79; pres. Mid-Columbia Arts Council, 1975-76. Served with Transp. Corps, U.S. Army, 1950-56; Korea. Republican. Presbyterian. Club: Rotary (pres. Pasco-Kennewick 1981-82). Contbr. articles to profl. jours.; founder of Counterpart, an interracial orgn. community orgn. exec.; b. Atlanta, Apr. 15, 1928; s. Samuel C. and Marjorie D. (Frampton) D.; student Yale U., 1945-47, various mil. schs., 1950-53, San Francisco State Coll., 1956-57, Coll. Notre Dame, 1966, Wash. State U., 1976; grad. United Community Funds and Councils Inst., 1969; m. Mary Anne Karish, Sept. 27, 1950; children—Marjorie Stanish, Catherine Candler, Warren Craig. Ind. sales contractor, San Francisco, 1957-62; exec. dir. United Cerebral Palsy, Oakland, Calif., 1962-65; area dir. United Crusade, San Francisco, 1965-69, asso. exec. dir., Sacramento, 1969-72; exec. dir. United Way of Benton and Franklin Counties, Kennewick, Wash., 1972-82, United Way Spokane County, 1982—; community orgn. cons. Office Community Devel., State of Wash., 1977-79. Bd. dirs. Benton Franklin Opportunities Industrialization Center, 1978-79; trustee Mid-Columbia Symphony Soc., 1977-79; pres. Mid-Columbia Arts Council, 1975-76. Served with Transp. Corps, U.S. Army, 1950-56; Korea. Republican. Presbyterian. Club: Rotary (pres. Pasco-Kennewick 1981-82). Contbr. articles to profl. jours.; founder of Counterpart, an interracial orgn. Home: W 123 13th Ave Spokane WA 99204 Office: PO Box 326 Spokane WA 99210

DOBREI, JOHN, manufacturing company executive; b. Turner, Mich., Nov. 15, 1913; s. John and Fica (Olar) D.; B.S., Wayne State U., Detroit, 1951; M.A. in Edn., Calif. State U., Los Angeles, 1962; m. Gladys Louise Festian, Sept. 19, 1934 (dec.); children—Marilyn Cheroske, Suzanne Taber, Jeanette Weir. Mem. faculty Henry Ford Trade Sch., Dearborn, Mich., 1938-52; tng. dir. Cross Co., Detroit, 1955-58; mgr. tng. Aerojet-Gen. Corp., Azusa, Calif., 1958-65; corp. tng. dir. Norris Industries, Los Angeles, 1966-73, Electronic Memories & Magnetic Co., Hawthorne, Calif., 1973-75; mgr. tng. and devel. Bunker Ramo Corp., Westlake Village, Calif., 1975—; mem. part-time faculty UCLA Sch. Mgmt., Labor and Bus., Mchts. and Mfrs. Assn., Los Angeles. Served to lt. col. CAP, 1944-65. Recipient Gold award United Way Ventura County (Calif.), 1978. Mem. Am. Soc. Personnel Adminstrs. (life; accredited personnel diplomate), Am. Soc. Tng. and Devel. (life; pres. Los Angeles chpt. 1972), Internat. Assn. Bus. Communicators, Nat. Assn. Indsl. Tech. (nat. chmn. industry adv. council 1977-78), Nat. Soc. Programmed Instrn., So. Calif. Industry-Edn. Council, Henry Ford Trade Sch. Alumni Assn. (life), Epsilon Pi Tau. Republican. Baptist. Home: 28648 Conejo View Dr Agoura Hills CA 91301 Office: Bunker Ramo Corp 31717 La Tienda Dr Westlake Village CA 91359

DOBRY, JOYCE ARLENE, educational film producer; b. Nebraska City, Nebr., Mar. 13, 1939; d. Jennings Bryan and Grace (Thurman) Roberts; m. Richard Henry Nalick, Sept. 27, 1959; 1 son, Scott Richard; m. Merlin Austin Dobry, Oct. 27, 1968. Student Pasadena City Coll., 1957-59, Santa Barbara Community Coll., 1978—. Sec., personnel ofcl. Calif. State Coll.-Los Angeles, 1962-65; adminstrv. asst. dept. intercollegiate athletics U. Calif.-Santa Barbara, 1965; office mgr. Film Fair Communications, 1965-67; with personnel dept. Gen. Electric-Tempo, Santa Barbara, 1967-69; mgr. Profl. Career Cons., 1970-83; owner, mgr. Dobry Placement Opportunity Agy., Santa Barbara, 1970-83; pres. Dobry Prodns., 1983—. Adv. com. bus. dept. Santa Barbara City Coll.; dir. United Way Santa Barbara, Santa Barbara C. of C., Good Govt. League, Channel City Women's Forum, Humane Soc. Santa Barbara County; past chmn. Bus. and Profl. Women (Top Hat award); former chmn. vocat. edn. Santa Barbara City Schs. Mem. Calif. Employment

Assn. (pres. Central Coast chpt. 1976-77). Republican. Contbr. articles to local publs. and schs.

DOBSON, JAMES CLAYTON, JR., psychologist, medical researcher, educator; b. Shreveport, La., Apr. 21, 1936; s. James C. and Myrtle G. (Dillingham) D.; B.A., Pasadena Coll., 1958; M.S., U. So. Calif., 1962, Ph.D., 1967; m. Shirley Mae, Aug. 27, 1960; children—Danae, Ryan. Attending staff div. med. genetics Children's Hosp. Los Angeles, 1966-83; assoc. clin. prof. pediatrics U. So. Calif. Sch. Medicine, Los Angeles, 1969-83; dir. radio and TV program Focus on the Family, 460 stas. throughout world, 1977—. Mem. task force White House Conf. on Family, 1980, Nat. Adv. Commn. on Juvenile Justice and Delinquency Prevention, 1982—. Served with U.S. Army, 1958-59. NIH grantee, 1975-77; HEW grantee, 1966-77. Mem. Am. Psychol. Assn., Western Assn. Christians for Psychol. Studies (pres. 1977-78). Republican. Author: Dare to Discipline, 1970; Hide or Seek, 1974; What Wives Wish Their Husbands Knew About Women, 1975; The Strong-willed Child, 1977; Preparing for Adolescence, 1978; Straight Talk to Men and Their Wives, 1980; Dr. Dobson Answers Your Questions, 1982; Love Must Be Tough, 1983; also articles in jours. Home: 348 Harvard Dr Arcadia CA 91006 Office: Focus on the Family 41E Foothill Blvd Arcadia CA 91006

DOBYNS, ZIPPORAH POTTENGER, psychologist; b. Chgo., Aug. 26, 1921; d. William Albert and Martha Cobb (Livingston) Pottenger; B.A. in Anthropology, U. Chgo., 1944; M.A., U. Ariz., 1966, Ph.D. in Clin. Psychology, 1969; m. Henry Farmer Dobyns, Oct. 30, 1948; children—Rique, William, Maritha, Mark. Intern in psychology VA Hosp., Tucson, 1966-67, Tuscon Child Guidance Center, 1967-68; psychol. asst. Los Angeles Psychol. Services Center, 1969-70; minister, research dir. Community Ch. Religious Sci., Los Angeles, 1970—; cons. in field. Mem. Am., Western, psychol. assns., Assn. Humanistic Psychology, Assn. Transpersonal Psychology, Nat. Council Geocosmic Research (dir.), Internat. Soc. Astrological Research (dir.), Fedn. Am. Scientists, AAAS, Am. Soc. Psychical Research, Spiritual Frontiers Fellowship, Psi Chi, Phi Beta Kappa. Author: Evolution Through the Zodiac, 1964; The Zodiac as a Key to History, 1968; The Node Book, 1972; (with Nancy Roof) The Astrologer's Casebook, 1974; Finding the Person in the Horoscope, 1974; Progressions, Directions, and Rectification, 1975; The Asteroid Ephemeris, 1977; Expanding Astrology's Universe, 1982; Astrology, editor Astrologers Annual Reference Book, 1972—. Home: 830 5th Ave Los Angeles CA 90005 Office: Box 45558 Los Angeles CA 90045

DOCKS, EDWARD LEON, chemist; b. Detroit, Jan. 14, 1945; s. Jack and Ann (Getteson) D.; B.S. in Chemistry, Wayne State U., 1967; Ph.D., UCLA, 1972; m. Linda Wolfe, Dec. 28, 1969; children—Andrea Beth, Janene Stephanie. Postdoctoral fellow NIH, Bethesda, Md., 1972-74; sr. research chemist U.S. Borax Research Corp., Anaheim, Calif., 1974—. Petroleum Research fellow, 1970-72, Hoffman LaRoche fellow, 1973-74. Mem. Am. Chem. Soc. Contbr. articles to profl. jours. Home: 1213 E Park Ln Santa Ana CA 92701 Office: 412 Crescent Way Anaheim CA 92801

DOCKSON, ROBERT RAY, savings and loan executive; b. Quincy, Ill., Oct. 6, 1917; s. Marshall Ray and Letah (Edmondson) D.; A.B., Springfield Jr. Coll., 1937; B.S., U. Ill., 1939; M.S. in Fgn. Service, U. So. Calif., 1940, Ph.D., 1946; m. Katheryn Virginia Allison, Mar. 4, 1944; 1 dau., Kathy Kimberlee. Lectr. U. So. Calif., 1940-41, 45-46, prof., head dept. marketing, 1953-59, dean Sch. Bus. Adminstrn. and prof. bus. econs., 1959-69; vice chmn. bd. Calif. Fed. Savs. & Loan Assn., Los Angeles, 1969-70, pres., 1970—, chief exec. officer, 1973—, also dir.; instr. Rutgers U., 1946-47, asst. prof., 1947-48, dir. Bur. Bus. and Econ. Research, 1947-48; economist Western home office Prudential Ins. Co., 1948-52, Bank of Am., San Francisco, 1952-53; dir. McKesson, Inc., IT Corp., Ticor, Pacific Lighting Corp., Olga Co., Transam. Income Shares, Inc. Transam. Capital Fund, Inc., Los Angeles dist. Fed. Res. Bank of San Francisco, Daniel, Mann, Johnson & Mendenhall, Computer Sci. Corp., Internat. Lease Fin. Corp.; also econ. cons. Mem. Town Hall, 1954—, bd. govs., 1963-65, hon. bd. govs., 1965—, pres., 1961-62. Bd. dirs. Music Center Opera Assn.; trustee Orthopaedic Hosp., Rose Hills Meml. Park Assn., Calif. Council Econ. Edn., Com. Econ. Devel., John Randolph Haynes and Dora Haynes Found.; trustee, bd. regents Pepperdine Coll.; bd. dirs. So. Calif. region Nat. Conf. Christians and Jews; mem. Greater Los Angeles chpt. Nat. Safety Council; bd. councilors Grad Sch. Bus. Adminstrn., U. So. Calif. Served from ensign to lt., USNR, 1942-44. Recipient Asa V. Call Achievement award; Whiteney M. Young., Jr. award, 1981; Nat. Housing Conf. Man of Yr. award, 1981; Spirit of Los Angeles award, 1982; decorated Star of Solidarity (Italy). Mem. Calif. (former v.p., pres. 1980, also dir.), Los Angeles (dir. 1970-80, pres. 1975-76), chambers commerce, Am. Econ. Assn., Am. Finance Assn., Am. Arbitration Assn., Newcomen Soc. N.Am., Phi Kappa Phi, Beta Gamma Sigma. Rotarian. Clubs: Bohemian, Los Angeles Country, Lincoln, California, One Hundred, Silver Dollar, Birnam Wood Golf, Thunderbird Country, Los Angeles.

DOCKSTADER, JACK LEE, materiel mgr.; b. Los Angeles, Dec. 14, 1936; s. George Earl and Grace Orine (Travers) D.; student UCLA, 1960-70. Rate analyst Rate Bur., So. Pacific Co., Los Angeles, 1954-57; traffic analyst traffic dept. Hughes Aircraft Co., Fullerton, Calif., 1957-58, Culver City, Calif., 1958-59, traffic mgr. Hughes Research Labs., Malibu, Calif., 1959-70, materiel mgr., 1970-75; materiel mgr. Hughes Aircraft Co., Culver City, 1975-80, prodn. materiel mgr. Electro-Optical and Data Systems Group, El Segundo, Calif., 1980-83, central material mgr., 1983—. Mem. adv. council transp. mgmt. profl. designation program UCLA, 1966-80, mem. Design for Sharing Com., 1977-82; adv. com. transp. program Los Angeles Trade Tech. Coll., 1970-80. Served with USNR, 1954-76. Mem. UCLA Alumni Assn., Nat. Contracts Mgmt. Assn., Naval Enlisted Res. Assn., Hughes Aircraft Co. Mgmt. Club, Delta Nu Alpha (pres. San Fernando Valley chpt. 1965-66, v.p. Pacific S.W. region 1969-71, region man of year 1971). Republican. Presbyn. Home: 2701 Armacost Ave Los Angeles CA 90064 Office: PO Box 902 El Segundo CA 90245

DODART, OLIVER DAVID, skin care products co. exec.; b. Long Beach, Calif., Mar. 18, 1945; s. Oliver Ulysus and Amy Jean (Wood) D.; student Brigham Young U., 1964, Weber State Coll., 1970; m. Jacqueline Marie Ritter, June 18, 1980. Regional v.p. Turner Enterprises, Ohio and Mich., 1970-72, corp. pres., W. Ger., 1972-74; dir. tng. Greentree Realty, Inc., Santa Barbara, Calif., 1974-77; pres., chief exec. officer World Wide Products, Inc., Santa Barbara, 1977—; chmn. bd. Source Investments, Inc.; mem. chmn.'s com. U.S. Senatorial Bus. Adv. Bd. Republican. Mormon. Office: 1224 Coast Village Circle Santa Barbara CA 93108

DODD, JOE DAVID, safety engineer, consultant, business manager; b. Walnut Grove, Mo., Jan. 22, 1920; s. Marshall Hill and Pearl (Combs) D.; m. Nona Bell Junkins, Sept. 17, 1937; 1 dau. Linda Kay Dodd Helmick. Student SW Mo. State U., 1937-39, Wash. U., 1947-55. Cert. profl. safety engr. Calif. Office asst. retail credit co., Kansas City, Mo., 1939-42; bus driver City of Springfield (Mo.), 1945-47; ops., engring., and personnel positions Shell Oil Co., Wood River (Ill.) Refinery, 1947-66; health and safety dept. mgr. Martinez Mfg. Complex, Calif., 1966-83, retired 1983; bus. mgr. Fire Protection Tng. Acad., U. Nev.-Reno; rep. Shell Oil Co., Western Oil and Gas Assn., 1970-81. Mem. Republican Presdl. Task Force. Served with USMC, 1942-45. Decorated Presdl. Citation. Mem. Western Oil and Gas Assn. (Hose Handler award 1972-81, Outstanding mem. award), Am. Soc. Safety Engrs., Veterans Safety, State and County Fire Chiefs Assn., Peace Officers Assn., Nat. Fire Protection Assn. Presbyterian (elder). Established Fire Protection Tng. Acad., U. Nev.-Reno, Stead Campus.

DODD, MARGARET JOANNE, nurse, hospital administrator; b. Billings, Mont., Apr. 13, 1934; d. William and Marie (Heimbichner) Weber; diploma Billings Deaconess Hosp. Sch. Nursing, 1955; B.S.N., Mont. State U., 1967; m. Marvin Lea Dodd, Dec. 21, 1959 (div.); children—Robin Michelle, Randi Marie. Nurse, Billings Deaconess Hosp., 1955, asst. dir. nursing, 1965-70, v.p. for nursing service, 1970-82, v.p. mktg./pub. relations, 1982—; nurse Billings Clinic, 1955-57; registered nurse supr. Monterey County Hosp., Salinas, Calif., 1958-63; nurse Carmel (Calif.) Community Hosp., 1964. Mem. Mont. Nurses Assn. (pres. 1978-80, Dist. #5 Nurse of Yr. 1978, 80), Am. Nurses Assn., Nat. League for Nursing (chmn. planning com.), Forums for Nursing Adminstrs. in West), Mont. League Nursing, Am. Soc. Nursing Service Adminstrs., Mont. Soc. Nursing Service Adminstrs. (pres. 1982—), Mont. Nursing Honor Soc., Sigma Theta Tau. Home: 3020 Stinson Ave Billings MT 59102 Office: PO Box 2547 Billings MT 59103

DODDS, LARRY KEITH, educational executive, consultant; b. Waco, Tex.; Aug. 30, 1944; s. Kenneth Lawrence and Opal June D.; m. Judith Anne Pieper, Aug. 20, 1966; children—Tamara Lynne, Jason Andrew, Sara Elizabeth. B.S. in Edn., Ill. State U., 1966, M.S., 1971; Ed.D., U. Mo.-Columbia, 1980. Cert. tchr., supt., Colo. Math. and phys. edn. tchr. and coach, Middletown, Ill., 1966-67; math tchr., Lincoln, Ill., 1967-71, prin., 1971-74; prin., Clinton, Iowa, 1974-78; math tchr., Columbia, Mo., 1979-80; asst. state dir. Mo. N. Central Assn., U. Mo.-Columbia, 1978-80; assoc. exec. dir. N. Central Assn. Colls. and Schs. Commn. on Schs., Boulder, 1980—. Active YMCA Indian Guides, 1981-83. I.D.E.A. fellow 1974. Mem. Am. Assn. Sch. Adminstrs., Nat. Assn. Secondary Sch. Prins., Assn. Supervision and Curriculum Devel. Lutheran. Contbr. articles to profl. jour. Office: 1540 30th St PO Box 18 Boulder CO 80306

DODGE, CLIFF, broadcaster, state senator; b. Worcester, Mass., Jan. 20, 1939; B.A., Springfield (Mass.) Coll.; m. Gwen Dodge; children—Ken, Nathan. Former jr. and sr. high sch. tchr.; broadcaster; mem. Colo. Ho. of Reps., 1976, vice chmn. HEW Com. 51st Assembly; mem. Colo. Senate from 7th dist. Mem. Correctional Industries Adv. Commn.; mem. adv. bd. Bethesda Mental Health Center. Republican. Office: 1851 S High St Denver CO 80210*

DODGE, DICK, clin. psychologist; b. Oakland, Calif., May 24, 1933; s. Duane and Juanita Francis (Robblee) D.; B.A. cum laude, Chapman Coll., 1972; M.A., 1973; Ph.D., U.S. Internat. U., 1975; m. Carolyn Josephine Renyer, Jan. 31, 1953; children—Sondra Marie, Jeannette Ann, Rhonda Sue, Richard Lornal. Sch. psychologist Beaumont (Calif.) Unified Sch. Dist., 1972-73; psychol. asst. to Mario Levi, Riverside, Calif., 1973-74; clin. psychologist Riverside County (Calif.) Mental Health Day Treatment Center, 1974-75, outpatient clinic, 1975-77; dir. Stress Reduction and Pain Mgmt. Center of Riverside, 1977—; pvt. practice marriage and family counselor, Riverside, 1974—; prof. psychology Chapman Coll.; secondary teaching credential Riverside Unified Sch. Dist.; adj. prof. U.S. Internat. U.; host radio show Something Interresting, Sta. KGGI and KMEN, 1980-83. Chmn., Riverside Mental Health Parents Ad Hoc Com., 1974-75; mem. pub. awareness com. Riverside Child Abuse Council, 1983—; mem. Riverside Inter-Agy. Sexual Abuse Council; chmn. com. recall city councilman, Riverside, 1975; mem. steering com. Calif. Am. Ind. Party, 1975. Served with USAF, 1950-72. Decorated Air medal, Commendation medal; lic. marriage, family and child therapist, Calif.; lic. psychologist, Calif.; cert. sex therapist, clin. biofeedback therapist, bioenergetic analyst, hypnotherapist. Mem. Am., Western, Calif., Inland So. Calif. psychol. assns., Soc. Personality Assessment, Soc. Behavioral Medicine, Internat. Coll. Clin. and Exptl. Hypnosis, Internat. Hypnosis Soc., Internat. Bioenergetic Soc., So. Calif. Bioenergetic Soc., So. Calif. Soc. Clin. Hypnosis, Biofeedback Soc. Calif., Biofeedback Soc., Am. Assn. Sex Educators, Counselors and Therapists, Am. Assn. Biofeedback Clinicians (exec. bd. dirs. 1982), Assn. Holistic Health (exec. bd., chmn. public relations com. 1981), Biofeedback Soc. Calif. (dir. 1983—), Mandala Soc. Mormon (elder). Lodge: Kiwanis. Home: 11754 Terrace View Dr Colton CA 92324 Office: 6900 Brockton Ave Suite 2 Riverside CA 92506

DODGE, EUGENE EDWARD, optometrist; b. Denver, Feb. 21, 1947; s. George Harcourt and Helen Margaret (Moore) D.; m. Lynda Kay Thomsen, June 7, 1969; children—Christian Edward, Casey Lynn, Carrie LeAnne. B.A., U. No. Colo., 1969; O.D., Pacific U., 1974. Lic. optometrist, Colo. Biology tchr. Littleton, Colo., 1969-70; chief optometry sect. 15th Med. Bn., 1st Cav. Div., Ft. Hood, Tex., 1974-77; pvt. practice optometry Aurora, Colo., 1977—. Capt. USAR. Mem. Am. Optometric Assn., Colo. Optometric Assn., Assn. Mil. Surgeons, Res. Officers Assn., Council Sports Vision, Aurora C. of C. Republican. Baptist. Club: Kiwanis (Aurora); Masons. Home: 5376 S Salida Ct Aurora CO 80015 Office: 1390 Chambers Rd Aurora CO 80011

DODGE, ROBERT EDWARDS, emeritus business educator; b. Ashland, Oreg., Sept. 12, 1912; s. Louis I. and Jessie (Edwards) D.; B.A., U. Oreg., 1934, M.A., 1951; Ph.D. in Bus. Adminstrn., N.Y. U., 1959; LL.D., Hokkaido U., 1976; m. Rae Isabell Hull, Aug. 14, 1938; children—Ellen Dodge Rubenstein, William Robert. Buyer, mgr. J.P. Dodge & Sons Furniture Co., Ashland, 1934-50; instr. N.Y. U., N.Y.C., 1951-53; asst. prof. U. Oreg., Eugene, 1953-58, asso. prof., 1958-59; prof. dept. bus. adminstrn. and mktg. Portland (Oreg.) State U., 1959-78, chmn. dept., 1959-67, prof. emeritus, 1978—; dir. sessions Sapporo summer sessions Oreg. State System Higher Edn., Portland State U., 1967, 69, 71, 73; exec. sec. Legis. Com. Trade and Econ. Devel., Salem, Oreg., 1973-74; cons. mktg. and internat. trade Robert E. Dodge Enterprises, 1934—; interim dir. Pacific Basin studies program Pacific U., 1979—. Ford Found. grantee Harvard, 1959. Mem. Oriental Art Study Soc. (chmn. 1971-72, 80-84), Am. Mktg. Assn. (pres. Oreg. chpt. 1962-64), Japanese Garden Soc., Internat. House Japan, Japan-Am. Soc. Oreg., Oreg. Shakespearean Festival Assn. (pres. 1947-49), Eta Mu Pi, Alpha Delta Sigma, Alpha Kappa Psi. Republican. Clubs: Masons, Rotary, Univ. Home: 6345 SW Seymour St Portland OR 97221

DODGEN, JAMES EDWARD, chem. engring. cons.; b. Anniston, Ala., Sept. 15, 1921; s. John Preston and Georgia (Hubbard) D.; B.S. in Chem. Engring., Ga. Inst. Tech., 1943; m. Virginia Mae Korth, Feb. 25, 1972; children—James Edward, Vicki Lynn, Charles Preston, Barbara Mae, Jean Margaret. Sr. chem. engr. Penn Salt Co., Wyandotte, Mich., Phila., 1946-51; gen. dept. mgr. mfg. Lockheed Propulsion Co., Redlands, Calif., 1968-69; mgr. process engring., dir. production Olin Corp., Baraboo, Wis., 1969-72; program mgr. Aerojet Solid Propulsion Co., Sacramento, Calif., 1972-73; mgr. mfg. control Cordova Chem. Co., Sacramento, Calif., 1973-74; pres. Dodgen Engring. Co., Colorado Springs, Colo., 1974—. Served to comdr. USN, 1943-46, 51-68. Registered profl. engr., Colo. Mem. Am. Chem. Soc., Am. Inst. Chem. Engrs., Am. Def. Preparedness Assn., Assn. U.S. Army. Home and office: 2915 Shoreham Circle Colorado Springs CO 80906

DODSON, EDWIN STANTON, education educator; b. Empire, Nev., Mar. 26, 1921; s. George J. and Mary (Larsen) D.; B.A., U. Nev., 1942; M.A., U. Oreg., 1948; M.A., U. Calif., 1966, Ed.D., 1967; m. Rose Arenaz, Aug. 6, 1949 (dec.). Tchr. pub. schs., McGill, Yerington, Reno (all Nev.), 1942-49; elementary sch. prin. Battle Mountain, Nev., 1949, Austin Pub. Sch. (Nev.), 1949-50; supt. schs., Lovelock, Nev., 1950-55; prin. elementary, jr. high, high schs., Reno, Nev., 1955-66; asst. supt. schs., Reno, Nev., 1966-67; asso. prof. sch. adminstrn. U. Nev., Reno, 1967-71, prof., 1971—; cons. Washoe County Sch. Dist., 1967—, Washoe County Tchrs. Assn., 1967-68, Nev. PTA, 1978, Nye County Sch. Dist., 1978, Lander County Sch. Dist., 1978. Nev. Sch. Trustees Assn., 1968, Nev. Dept. Edn., 1968, 78; local coordinator Danforth Sch. Adminstrs. Fellowship Program, 1981-82. Fulbright scholar in comparative edn., Finland, France, 1960. Mem. N.E.A., Nev. Edn. Assn. (dir. 1965-67), Washoe Prins. Assn. (pres. 1963-64), Nev. Assn. Sch. Adminstrs. (exec. sec. 1974-79), Am. Assn. Sch. Adminstrs. (mem. nat. adv. council 1966-69, 75-78), Phi Delta Kappa, Phi Alpha Theta, Phi Kappa Phi. Author: Vocational Education and the Comprehensive High School: A Challenge to Adminstrators, 1968. Home: 425 Vassar St Reno NV 89502

DODSON, JEROME L., financial exec.; b. Oak Park, Ill., May 14, 1943; s. Leo D. and Grace Edith (Shoup) D.; A.B., U. Calif., Berkeley, 1965; M.B.A., Harvard U., 1971; m. Thao Nguyen, Apr. 20, 1975; children—Stephen Jerome, Katrina Kim. Fgn. service officer Am. embassy, Saigon, Vietnam, 1966-68; Am. consul, David, Panama, 1968-69; fin. analyst San Francisco Local Devel. Corp., 1971-73; pvt. practice mgmt. cons., 1974-76; founder, pres., chief exec. officer Continental Savs. & Loan Assn., San Francisco, 1976-82; pres., chief exec. officer Working Assets Money Fund, San Francisco, 1982—. Mem. World Affairs Council No. Calif., ACLU, Found. for San Francisco's Archtl. Heritage, Harvard Bus. Sch. Assn. No. Calif. Clubs: Commonwealth, Harvard (San Francisco). Home: 1427 Shrader St San Francisco CA 94117 Office: Working Assets 230 California St San Francisco CA 94111

DOEH, GIYORA, real estate broker, management consultant; b. Tiberias, Israel, Aug. 12, 1934; s. Benjamin Benzion and Pearl (Kerner) D.; divorced; children—Cole Adam, Tamara Lark Shannan, Thomas David. B.S.M.E., Cooper Union, N.Y.C., 1956; M.S. in Indsl. Mgmt., MIT, 1958. Registered profl. engr., Calif. Adminstrv. asst. Lockheed Aircraft Co., Ontario and Burbank, Calif., 1958-60; mem. tech. staff Hughes Aircraft Co., Los Angeles, 1960-61; sr. systems analyst, Israel Aircraft Industries, 1962-66; sr. indsl. engr. N.Am. Aviation Co., Los Angeles, 1966-67; mgmt. systems advisor TRW Systems Group, Redondo Beach, Calif., 1967-78, sr. staff engr., 1978; cons. Coca Cola Bottling Co., Los Angeles, 1978; pres. Century 21 West LA Realty, Los Angeles, 1979—; cons., mgmt. systems, 1978-81; instr. UCLA, 1970-78, West Coast U., 1972-82. Pres., bd. dirs. South Bay Children's Health Ctr., 1971-74; com. mem. Los Angeles United Way, 1969-75. Mem. ASME, Inst. Mgmt. Sci., Los Angeles Bd. Realtors (arbitration, profl. standards com.). Home: 3432 Colonial Ave Los Angeles CA 90066 Office: 10887 W Pico Blvd Los Angeles CA 90064

DOEPKE, MICHAEL DUBOIS, electronics company executive; b. Cin., Apr. 15, 1953; s. Charles William and Grace Kathryn (DuBois) D.; m. Mary Lorden, Apr. 17, 1982. B.A., Colgate U., 1975; M.B.A., U. Va., 1977. Asst. product mgr. Gen. Foods Corp., White Plains, N.Y., 1977-78, assoc. product mgr., 1978-80, product mgr., 1980-81; product mgr. Mattel Electronics Co., Hawthorne, Calif., 1981-82, dir. mktg., 1982—. Republican. Home: 2806 Green Ln Redondo Beach CA 90278 Office: Mattel Electronics Co 5150 Rosecrans Ave Hawthorne CA 90250

DOERFLING, HANK, aerospace engr.; b. San Pedro, Calif., Nov. 3, 1936; s. Laurence Howard and Julia Margret (Rusbarsky) D.; B.S. in Physics, Oreg. State U., 1958, M.S., 1963; M.Pub. Adminstrn., Pepperdine U., 1975; m. Elaine Carole; children—Howard, Carrie, Cassie, Tony, Evon. Analyst, No. Am. Aviation Co., Downey, Calif., 1963-64; mem. tech. staff TRW Systems Redondo Beach, Calif., 1964-66, adminstrv. and project mgr. Logicon, San Pedro, Calif., 1966-77; project mgr. space and communications group Hughes Aircraft Co., El Segundo, Calif., 1977—. Mem. Hermosa Beach Improvement Commn., 1970-72, chmn., 1971-72; mem. City of Hermosa Beach City Council, 1972-80, mayor, 1973-74, 79-80; pres. South Bay Cities Assn., 1975-76; mem. South Coast (Calif.) Regional Coastal Commn., 1977-80, Calif. Coastal Commn., 1978-80. Served with USN, 1958-61. Home: 1011 2d St Hermosa Beach CA 90254 Office: 1700 Imperial Blvd El Segundo CA 90245

DOERING, HERMAN WILLIAM, management engineer; b. Cleburne, Tex., Aug. 9, 1952; s. Harold Owen and Irma Faye (Berbohm) D.; m. Terresa Jeanne Fickess, Aug. 24, 1975; children—Kirk, Karl. Student So. Missionary Coll., 1971-72; B.A., Andrews U., 1975; postgrad. Colo. State U., 1981—. Hosp. mgmt. intern Porter Meml. Hosp., Denver, 1975-77, methods analyst, 1977-79; mgmt. engr. Adventist Health System, Eastern & Mid-Am. Corp., Denver, 1979-81; dir. mgmt. engring. Porter Meml. Hosp., Denver, 1981—. Mem. Am. Hosp. Assn., Hosp. Mgmt. Systems Soc. Seventh-day Adventist. Contbr. articles to profl. jours.; developer productivity and cost evaluation system for hosps. Office: 2525 S Downing Denver CO 80210

DOERING, RICHARD, sociologist, educator; b. Cleve., May 17, 1939; s. Roy A. and Gertrude (Koubek) D.; m. Clara Mae Weber, Aug. 1, 1969; children—Bart Lee, Karl Curtis, Marlena Rae. B.A., Ohio Wesleyan U., 1960; M.A., Columbia U., 1962; B.S. in Edn., Kent State U., 1967; M.A., U. Calif.-Riverside 1974, Ph.D., 1975. Instr. Central Wyo. Coll., Riverton, 1968-70; research sociologist U. Calif.-Riverside, 1972-74; instr. Orange Coast and Golden West Coll., 1975-76; asst. prof. sociology Calif. State U.-Los Angeles, 1977—; evening instr. Chaffey Coll., 1976—. Recipient Leland Publs. award 1960. Mem. Am. Sociol. Assn., Sociology Edn. Assn., Psi Chi, Kappa Delta Pi, Tau Kappa Epsilon. Contbr. articles to profl. jours. Home: 7286 Nixon Dr Riverside CA 92504 Office: Dept Sociology and Social Work Calif State U Los Angeles CA 90032

DOERMANN, JAMES ALFRED, ednl. cons.; b. Tehachapi, Calif., July 27, 1934; s. Robert and Mary E. (Sanders) D.; B.A., Calif. State U., Fresno, 1959; M.A., 1967; D.D., Litt.D., Internat. Bible Inst. and Sem., 1981; m. Norma E. Courtright, June 26, 1960; children—Teresa Kay, David James. Tchr., adminstr. Calif. schs., 1958—; resource specialist, cons. Fowler Sch., Ceres, Calif., 1977—; author, dir. spl. projects, resource cons., master plan specialist; TV, stage actor including Seven Brides for Seven Bros. Bd. dirs. Pixley Little League; mem. San Joaquin County Central Democratic Com. Served with USMCR, 1951-54; Korea. Mem. An. Assn. Sch. Adminstrs., Assn. Supervision and Curriculum Devel., Nat. Assn. Elem. Sch. Prins., Assn. Calif. Sch. Adminstrs. (chmn. legis. com.), NEA (life), Calif. Tchrs. Assn. (chmn. legis. com. 1966-72). Mormon. Author proposals, curriculum materials, also short stories. Home: 1904 Skylane Way Modesto CA 95350 Office: Fowler Sch PO Box 307 Ceres CA 95307

DOERR, ROBERT DOUGLAS, psychologist, educator; b. Burlington, Vt., Apr. 9, 1944; s. Robert Joseph and Betty Jane Catlin (Whitney) D. B.A., Rollins Coll., 1966; M.A., San Francisco State U., 1969; Ph.D., Humanistic Psychol. Inst., San Francisco, 1978. Cert. biofeedback technician; cert. tchr., Calif. From instr. to prof. Coll. of Alameda (Calif.), 1970—; dir. Alameda Biofeedback Ctr., 1980—; ednl. cons., 1981—. Peace Corps vol., Nepal, 1966-68. Recipient Order of Oseola award Rollins Coll., 1966. Fellow Am. Psychol. Assn.; mem. Biofeedback Soc. Am., Assn. for Humanistic Psychology, Am. Fedn. Tchrs., AAAS. Taoist. Author: 8 books of poetry; contbr. articles to profl. jours.; editor Saybrook Rev., 1979—.

DOGGETT-ELETSKY, VLADIMIR EDOUARDOVICH, THE PRINCE ELETSKY, wholesale trade exec.; b. Los Angeles, Nov. 23,

1920; s. Snell and The Princess Wanda A. Rembiesca Eletska Doggett (adopted son Prince Edouard Eletsky); student U. So. Calif., 1943; m. Lucie Agnes Elfriede Sturtz, Aug. 11, 1958, div. Jan. 1974, remarried, Dec. 24, 1975 (separated 1981); children—Prince Alexander, Princess Kristina; 1 dau. by adoption, Princess Wanda Muriel Shirley-Ann Eletsky Fisher. Pres., Spl. Bus. Products Group, Xerox Corp. (formerly Doggett & Doggett Enterprises), Riverside, Calif.; dir. Fuji-Xerox (merger Xerox and Eletsky Enterprises), Riverside, Walt Disney Enterprises; and direct distbr. Amway Corp., Ada, Mich. Regent, U. Calif.; fellow Hoover Inst. on Dem. Instns. Decorated Order of Merit, Purple Cloud Soc. (Japan); knight grand officer Order White Eagle of Yugoslavia, knight grand cross Order of St. Constantine, knight grand cross Order Holy Cross of Jerusalem; knight grand cross, grand marshall, bailiff Order of St. John of Jerusalem, Knights Hospitallers, knight bachelor, 1962; knight comdr., Order of Temple; knight grand cross with collar Sovereign Mil. Teutonic Order of Levant; knight Order Crown of Thorns; knight comdr. Imperial Mil. Constantinian Order St. George; recipient Toyama prize Black Dragon Soc.; named Environmentalist of Yr., Sierra Club. Mem. Coronet League (pres. 1942—), Radio Officers Union. Imperial Russian Orthodox. Author: Trees and Leaves of California, 1955; Crowns and Coronets, 1957; The Prince Went West, 1939; A Sailor's Guide to the Sea of Japan, 1982; The Prince Goes East, 1983. Office: 6272 Iroquois Rd Westminster CA 92683

DOHEMANN, GORDON HENRY, corp. exec., realtor; b. Fowler, Calif., Apr. 15, 1931; s. Herbert J. and Jean Pool (Bock) D.; student Stanford, 1949-50; B.S., U. Calif., Berkeley, 1957; m. Sharon N. Carwin, 1978; children—Jesse Herbert, Linda Louise, Russell Lawrence, Erik Gordon; stepchildren—Chantele Carwin, Stacy Carwin. Various positions Coldwell, Banker & Co., San Francisco, 1957-59, mgr., 1960-63; v.p. Draper Cos., San Francisco, 1963-64; owner, pres. Dohemann & Co., San Francisco, 1965—, Dohemann Fin. Corp., 1973—; founder, dir. Lincoln Nat. Bank, Santa Rosa, Calif., 1965, chmn. bd., 1968; dir. Redwood Bank, San Francisco. Served to 1st lt. U.S. Army, 1952-55. Office: 350 Rheem Blvd Suite 10 Moraga CA 94556

DOHERTY, GEORGE WILLIAM, psychologist; b. Bronx, N.Y., Oct. 18, 1941; s. William George and Catherine Marguerite (Nierenhausen) D.; B.S., Pa. State U., 1964; M.S., Miss. State U., 1977; postgrad. Baylor U., 1972, North Texas State U., 1979. Cert. Nat. Acad. Cert. Clin. Mental Health Counselors. Program coordinator, dir. Econ. Opportunities Advancement Corp., Waco, Texas, 1968-71; psychol. counselor, parent tng. Counseling or Referral Assistance Services, Phila., 1973-75; psychologist III, Rural Clinics Community Counseling Ctr., Ely, Nev., 1980—. mem. faculty Nev. Community Coll., Ely, 1980—; cons. Served to capt. U.S. Air Force, 1964-68. Mem. Am. Psychol. Assn. (assoc.), Western Psychol. Assn., Tex. Psychol. Assn., Nev. Psychol. Soc. Assn., Psychol. Study of Social Issues, Inter-Am. Soc. Psychology, Internat. Assn. Applied Psychology, Assn. Behavior Analysis, Am. Personnel and Guidance Assn., Biofeedback Soc. Am., Assn. Counselor Edn. and Supervision, Western Assn. Counselor Edn. and Supervision, Assn. Measurement Edn. and Guidance, Am. Mental Health Counselors Assn., Pa. State Alumni Assn. Democrat. Home: Box 187 Ely NE 89301 Office: Community Counseling Ctr Ely NE 89301

DOHERTY, RICHARD MICHAEL, law firm adminstr.; b. San Francisco, Mar. 29, 1943; s. George Daniel and Alice Elizabeth (Kehl) D.; B.S. in Biochemistry, U. Santa Clara, 1965, M.B.A., 1968; m. Karen Lynn Kinney, Aug. 18, 1980; children—Shannon Elizabeth, Matthew John. Mgr. data processing Pacific Telephone Co., San Jose, Calif., 1966-69; mgr. internat. fin. Memorex Corp., Santa Clara, Calif., 1969-73; group controller Rohr Industries, San Diego, 1973-76; v.p. fin. and adminstrn. Photosonics, Inc., Los Angeles, 1976-79; v.p. fin. and adminstrn. Korn/Ferry Internat., Los Angeles, 1979-81; mng. dir., partner firm Cox, Castle, Nicholson, Los Angeles, 1981—; vis. prof. UCLA, U. Calif., Berkeley. Served to lt. U.S. Army, 1965-66. Mem. Nat. Assn. Accts., Am. Inst. Corp. Controllers. Republican. Clubs: Century West, Beverly Hills Gun. Office: 2049 Century Park E Los Angeles CA 90067

DOHERTY, ROBERT JOHN, graphic artist, art center and school director, educator; b. Everett, Mass., Jan. 16, 1924; s. Robert John and Elizabeth Mary (Nugent) D.; m. Esther Fiske, May 7, 1955; children—Jonathan Locke, Anne, Timothy Scott. B.F.A., R.I. Sch. Design, 1951; M.F.A., Yale U., 1954. Dir. graphic design Reynolds Metals Co., 1953-57; dir. devel. R.I. Sch. Design, 1957-59; prof. U. Louisville, 1959-72, dir. Allen R. Hite Art Inst., 1967-72; adj. prof. Rochester (N.Y.) Inst. Tech., 1972-79, U. Rochester, 1972-80, dir. George Eastman House, 1972-80; dir. Salt Lake Art Center & Sch., Salt Lake City, 1981—, dir. Internat. Archives of Photography; adj. prof. U. Utah; cons. museums and publishers. Served with AUS, 1942-45. Recipient awards Am. Inst. Graphic Arts, 50 textbooks of year, AIA, Outstanding Archtl. Lit., Photographic Adminstrs. award for edn.; Fullbright Travel grantee, 1965-66. Mem. Royal Photog. Soc., Deutsches Gesellschaft fur Photographie, Am. Printing Hist. Assn., Am. Assn. Mus., Art Mus. Assn., Am. Fedn. Arts, Friends of Photography. Democrat. Author: Sozial Documentarische Photographie in den USA, 1973; Introduction to Dorothea Lange and the FSA Years, 1935-1940, 1981; The Complete Photographic Work of Jacob A. Riis, 1982; Preservation, 1973; contbr. articles to publs. Office: 20 SW Temple Salt Lake City UT 84101

DOHM, ARNOLD RAY, accounting manager; b. Pearsall, Tex., Sept. 9, 1945; s. Arnold Peter and Lavada Jerlene (Smith) D.; B.S., Loma Linda U., La Sierra Campus, 1969; m. Mary Dawn Perry, July 3, 1966; 1 dau., Linda Dawn. Intern auditor Gen. Conf. 7th.-day Adventists, Loma Linda, Calif., 1969-70; asst. to controller Loma Linda campus Loma Linda (Calif.) U., 1970-71, asst. internal auditor, 1971-73, acct. health prodns., 1973-75, adminstrv. asst., 1975-76, grants fin. mgr., 1976-77, campus controller, 1977-81, pres. credit union, 1979-82; controller Universal Health Care, Inc., San Bernardino, Calif., 1981-82; acctg. mgr. Glendale (Calif.) Adventist Med. Center, 1982—, treas. Fed. Credit Union, 1983—. Bd. dirs. Fairview Jr. Acad., 1979-82; treas. San Bernardino 7th Day Adventist Ch. Mem. Nat. Assn. Accts. Republican. Mem. 7th.-Day Adventist Ch. Home: 25511 Hardt St Loma Linda CA 92354 Office: 1509 Wilson Terr Glendale CA 91206

DOHRMAN, MARGIE MAE, clin. social worker; b. Palisades, Wash., Oct. 23, 1927; d. Charles Joseph and Josie Mae (Gillum) D.; B.A., Seattle Pacific U., 1965; M.S.W., U. Denver, 1968. Engaged in banking, 1946-57; asst. budget analyst Stromberg-Carlson Co., Rochester, N.Y., 1957-59; office mgr. Salvation Army, Rochester, 1959-60; dist. field teller IRS, Anchorage, 1961-64; case worker Denver Dept. Welfare, 1966; social worker VA Neuropsychiat. Hosp., Ft. Lyon, Colo., 1967; sr. clinician, dept. dir. med. social work services, EEO counselor USPHS-Indian Health Service, Alaska Native Med. Center, Anchorage, 1968—; field instr./liason B.S.W. program U. Alaska, 1975—; sec. bd. Anchorage Mental Health Assn., 1970-71; alt. social worker Anchorage Child Abuse Bd., Child Protection Task Force; cons. in field. Recipient Spl. Act award Treasury Dept., 1965. Mem. Acad. Cert. Social Workers, Nat. Assn. Social Workers (treas. chpt. 1974-75, 76-79), Nat. Registry Clin. Social Workers, Soc. Hosp. Social Work Dirs., Am. Public Health Assn., Assn. Retarded Citizens Anchorage, Alaska Mental Health Assn., Seattle Pacific U. Alumni Assn., Chugach Gem and Mineral Soc., Alaskan Prospectors Soc. Author papers, reports in field. Home: PO Box 6377 Anchorage AK 99502 Office: PO Box 7-741 Anchorage AK 99510

DOI, GLENN ISAMI, management engineer; b. Atlanta, Jan. 28, 1955; s. Jimmy and Alice (Okubo) D.; m. Eugenia Gonzales, July 31, 1982. B.S. in Health Systems, Ga. Inst. Tech., 1977. Mgmt. engr. Kaiser Permanente, Los Angeles, 1977-80, Good Samaritan Hosp., Los Angeles, 1980—. Mem. Am. Inst. Indsl. Engrs., Hosp. Mgmt. Systems Soc. Office: 616 S Witmer St Los Angeles CA 90016

DOI, MAKIKO, librarian, educator; b. Okayama, Japan, Feb. 25, 1931; d. Yuichi and Iwa (Kawakami) Nakata; m. Richard T. Doi, Oct. 15, 1954; children—Alice Miwa, Robert Minoru. Student Seiishin Joshi Daigaku, Okayama, 1948-51; B.A., U. of Pacific, 1954; M.L.S., U. Wash., 1970. CatalogerHoover Instn., Stanford U. (Calif.), 1955-57, Columbia U., N.Y.C., 1957-59; reference librarian So. Oreg. Coll., Ashland, 1961-65; asst. librarian Ellensburg (Wash.) Pub. Library, 1970-74; serials librarian Central Wash. U., Ellensburg, 1974—, assoc. prof. librarianship, 1974—. Mem. Japan Library Assn., ALA, Wash. Library Assn. (sec. 1980—), Pacific N.W. Library Assn., Japanese Am. Citizens League (pres. chpt. 1982). Democrat. Author: Small Town Index, 1982; PNLA Quar., 1976. Home: 1202 Vuecrest Rd Ellensburg WA 98926 Office: Central Wash U Library-Serials Dept Ellensburg WA 98926

DOI, MAY YOKO, city clerk; b. Los Angeles, May 30, 1926; d. Paul Mitsugu and Hideko (Nakatani) Horiuchi; m. Carl Kaoru Doi, Aug. 28, 1949; children—Ronald M., Kevin K., Conrad T.; B.S., U. So. Calif., 1971, M.S., 1972; A.A. (Kiwanis scholar), Los Angeles Harbor Coll., 1969; student U. Calif., Santa Cruz, Pepperdine U., Occidental Coll. Sec., Internat. Inst., Detroit, 1946; sec. YMCA, Detroit, 1947-48; sec. Warehousing Service, Los Angeles, 1948-51; sec. Douglas Aircraft, 1952-54; tchr. Los Angeles Unified Sch. Dist., 1971-80; sec. TRW Systems, Redondo Beach, Calif., part-time summers 1974-81; city clk. City of Gardena (Calif.), 1980—. Pres. Gardena Valley Japanese Am. Citizens League, 1983; 2d v.p. Gardena Valley YMCA, 1983—; bd. dirs. ARC; pres. Gardena council PTA, 1966; pres. Amestoy PTA, 1962, hon. life mem.; den mother Los Angeles council Boy Scouts Am., 1960-67. Recipient Resolution of Commendation, City of Gardena, 1980; recognition award Japanese Am. Citizens League, 1981, plaque, 1982. Mem. So. Calif. City Clks. Assn., Calif. City Clks. Assn., Records Mgmt. Assn., Nat. Micrographics Assn., Soc. So. Calif. Archivists, Internat. Inst. Mcpl. Clks., Calif. Hist. Soc., Alpha Gamma Sigma. Baptist (sec. Dorcas Circle 1966). Clubs: Zonta Internat., South Bay (fin. dir., bd. dirs.). Office: 1700 W 162d St Gardena CA 90247

DOI, VINCENT JOSEPH, electric company executive; b. Los Angeles, Aug. 15, 1913; s. Sekizo and Yuki (Kagemasa) D.; grad. Coyne Elec. Sch., Chgo., 1949; m. Agnes Miyeko Inouye, Feb. 2, 1946; children—Marianne Smith, Alan, Philip, Joanne, Arthur. Coil winder Harold E. Saper Co., Chgo., 1945-49; winder Eurton Electric Co., Los Angeles, 1949-65, supr., 1965-69, gen. mgr., 1969—. Pres., Maryknoll Fed. Credit Union, 1962, 65, 79, dir., 1962-67, 70, 76—; troop committeeman Boy Scouts Am., 1952—. Recipient Scouters Key award Boy Scouts Am., 1977, Dist. award of Merit, 1978. Roman Catholic. Home: 2325 Westcott Ave Monterey Park CA 91754 Office: Eurton Electric Co Inc 9920 Painter Ave PO Box 2113 Santa Fe Springs CA 90670

DOKSUM, KJELL A., statistics educator; b. Sandefjord, Norway, July 20, 1940; s. Filip A. and Elise (Olsen) D. A.B. in Math., San Diego State Coll., 1962, M.S. in Math., 1963; Ph.D. in Stats., U. Calif.-Berkeley, 1965. Asst. prof. dept. stats. U. Calif.-Berkeley, 1966-73, assoc. prof., 1973-78, prof., 1978—, asst. dean Coll. Letters and Sci., 1978-80. NSF grantee 1972—. Fellow Inst. Math. Stats. (exec. sec. 1981—); mem. Internat. Statis. Inst. Author: (with Peter J. Bickel) Mathematical Statistics: Basic Ideas and Selected Topics, 1977. Office: Dept Stats U Calif Berkeley CA 94720

DOLAN, BERNARD JOSEPH, optometrist, educator; b. San Francisco, May 23, 1952; s. Lawrence Bernard and Margaret Loretta (Keane) D.; m. Jane Orth Nov. 14, 1981. B.S. magna cum laude, U. San Francisco, 1974, M.S. in Anatomy, 1976; B.S. with honors, U. Calif.-Berkeley, 1978, O.D., 1980. Lic. optometrist, Calif. Resident in hosp-based and rehabilitative optometry VA Med. Ctr., Kansas City, Mo., 1980-81, staff optometrist VA Med. Ctr., San Francisco, 1981—; asst. clin. prof. Sch. Optometry, U. Calif.-Berkeley. Mem. Am. Optometric Assn. (Kansas City VA Victors Program Apollo award 1982), Calif. Optometric Assn., San Francisco Optometric Soc., Nat. Assn. VA Optometrists. Democrat. Roman Catholic. Office: 4150 Clement St Eye Clinic (112A) San Francisco CA 94121

DOLAN, JOSEPH RICHARD, safety and occupational health mgr.; b. Carson City, Nev., Dec. 6, 1935; s. Mark Lorenzo and Murial Elizabeth (Fletcher) D.; m. Marguerite Frances de la Vaux, June 17, 1968; children—Kevin, Charlene, Laura, Cass, Dawn, Roxanne. Student Western Nev. Community Coll., 1978-79. Nat. Guard Bur. Safety and Health Cert., 1981. Warrant officer Nev. Nat. Guard, 1953—, electronic repairman, 1954-64, adminstrv. supply technician, 1964-73, prodn. controller, 1973-77, safety and occupational health mgr., 1977—; CPR instr., 1978—. Chmn. CPR, ARC. Decorated Army Commendation medal, Army Achievement medal. Mem. Am. Soc. Safety Engrs. Republican. Baptist. Home: 2650 Damon Rd Carson City NV 89701 Office: 2525 S Carson St Carson City NV 89701

DOLAND, MICHAEL WARREN, ski industry exec.; b. Kearny, N.J., July 22, 1952; s. Spencer Arnold and Anne Martha (Digirolamo) D.; B.S., Colo. State U., 1974; M.Ed., Ohio U., 1976; m. Linda Kathryn Curtis, June 21, 1975. Market research asst. Copper Mountain (Colo.) Resort, 1976-77, dir. market research and planning, 1977-78; mktg. dir. World Pro Skiing, Aspen, Colo., 1978-79; exec. dir. Profl. Ski Instrs. Am., Boulder, 1979—; rep. to bd. dirs. Am. Ski Fedn., 1979—. Mem. Colo. Ski Country U.S.A. Research Com., 1977—; co-chmn. Western Winter Spl. Olympics, 1978, mem. winter sports adv. com., 1982—; chmn. recreational steering com. Summit County (Colo.) Regional Planning Commn., 1977-78. Mem. Rocky Mountain Ski Writers Assn., Jaycees. Roman Catholic. Home: 1353 Cherryvale Rd Boulder CO 80303 Office: 3333 Iris Boulder CO 80301

DOLD, LARRY ALLAN, data processing educator; b. Indpls., May 19, 1949; s. Leslie Arthur and Anita Ann (Ellis) D.; B.S., Mich. State U., 1971; M.B.A., So. Meth. U., 1979; m. 2d, Donna Jean Vial, May 29, 1981. Assoc. systems analyst Consumers Power Co., Jackson, Mich., 1972-74; systems analyst Lone Star Gas Co., Dallas, 1974-76, Compass Computer Services Co., Dallas, 1976-77; system project mgr. Diamond/Sunsweet Inc., Stockton, Calif., 1977-79, gen. acctg. mgr., 1980; instr. computer sci. San Joaquin Delta Coll. 1980—. Mem. Assn. Systems Mgmt., Tau Beta Pi, Phi Kappa Phi. Republican. Methodist. Home: 6909 N Cox Rd Linden CA 95236 Office: 5151 Pacific Ave Stockton CA 95207

DOLE, CHARLES HERBERT, former banker, sailing coach; b. Honolulu, Oct. 30, 1914; s. James Drummond and Belle (Dickey) D.; A.B., Stanford U., 1936; M.B.A., Harvard, 1938; m. Barbara Jamieson, Apr. 21, 1950; children—Charles Herbert, Elizabeth Dole Hughes, Nancy Dole Mears. Jr. acct. Price, Waterhouse, San Francisco, 1938-39; plantation acct. Castle & Cooke, Ltd., 1939-44; v.p. Cooke Trust Co., 1944-65; v.p., trust officer 1st Hawaiian Bank, Honolulu, 1965-74; sailing coach U. Hawaii, Honolulu, 1980—. Clubs: Waikiki Yacht, Kaneohe Yacht. Home: 2333 Kapiolani St Apt 3501 Honolulu HI 96826 Office: 1337 Lower Campus Rd Honolulu HI 96822

DOLE, JANICE ARNOLD, reading and language arts educator, consultant, researcher; b. Boston, Jan. 31, 1947; d. Walter Francis and Jenny (Sapuppo) Arnold; m. Stephen Eric Dole, Mar. 22, 1975; 1 dau., Melissa. B.A., U. Mass., 1969; M.A., U. Colo., Boulder, 1974, Ph.D., 1977. Tchr. elem. schs., Mass. and Calif., 1969-73; teaching and research asst. U. Colo., 1974-75, 77; asst. prof. reading and lang. arts U. Denver, 1978—; cons. Ctr. Teaching Internat. Relations, 1978-79, Western Regional Resource Ctr., Anchorage, 1980-82, Mid-Continental Regional Ednl. Lab., 1983. Interrelationships Among the Lang. Arts grantee U. Denver, 1981, Predictive Validity of Listening Comprehension, 1983. Mem. Internat. Reading Assn., Am. Edn. Research Assn., Nat. Council Tchrs. English, Phi Delta Kappa. Contbr. articles in field. Office: MRH 119 University of Denver Denver CO 80208

DOLE, MALCOLM, JR., economist; b. Evanston, Ill., Apr. 24, 1935; s. Malcolm and Frances Hibbard (Page) D.; m. Margaret Hoffman Dole, June 30, 1962; children—Malcolm, Heather McAdie. B.A., Northwestern U., 1957; Ph.D., UCLA, 1974. Cert. community coll. instr., Calif. Research asst. UCLA, 1961-64, teaching asst., 1964-67; prof. Calif. State U., 1967-72; sr. economist Calif. State Air Resources Bd., Sacramento, 1973-76, research mgr., 1976—. Recipient award of Appreciation, United Way, 1979. Mem. Am. Econ. Assn., Western Econ. Assn., Western Regional Sci. Assn. Clubs: Commonwealth; Sheridan Shore Yacht (Wilmette, Ill.). Home: 2221-6 Woodside Ln Sacramento CA 95825 Office: PO Box 2815 Sacramento CA 95812

DOLEZAL, FRANK OSCAR, aerospace engineer, consultant; b. San Francisco, Apr. 15, 1923; s. Frank Carl and Teresa (Garcia) D.; m. Barbara Alice Hendrickson, July 15, 1950; 1 dau., Kathryn Alice Cozzens. A.A., San Francisco Jr. Coll., 1948; B.A. in Internat. Relations, U. Calif.-Berkeley, 1950. With prodn. control dept. United Airlines, San Francisco, 1953-54; weights engr. Hiller Aircraft Corp., Palo Alto, Calif., 1954-61, Lockheed Missiles & Space Co., Sunnyvale, Calif., 1961-63; with U.S. Post Office Dept., Mountain View, Calif., 1963-65; weights engr. Electric Boat Co. div. Gen. Dynamics Co., Groton, Conn., 1966, Lockheed Co., Marietta, Ga., 1966-67, Burbank, Calif., 1967-70; stock clk. Tech. Oil and Tool Co., Burbank, 1970-72. Chief stock clk., 1972-76; weight engr. Litton Ship Systems, Culver City, Calif. and Pascagula, Miss., 1972, Rockwell Internat., Inglewood, Calif., 1976-77, Menasco, Burbank, 1978, Convair Gen. Dynamics, San Diego, 1978-79, Hughes Helicopters Co., Culver City, 1979-80, Boeing Aircraft Corp., Everett, Wash., 1980-82; sr. engr. Northrop Aircraft Corp., Hawthorne, Calif., 1982—; cons. in field. Served with USAAF, 1943-46; to 1st lt. USAF, 1950-53. Mem. Soc. Allied Weights Engrs. (sr.), AIAA, Am. Legion. Democrat. Roman Catholic. Office: 5919 Liska Ln Suite 106 San Jose CA 95119

DOLGIN, STEPHEN MARK, social worker, health adminstr.; b. San Francisco, Dec. 22, 1949; s. David Aubrey and Ruth (Ogurak) D.; B.A., U. Minn., 1972, M.S.W., 1976; M.B.A., Golden Gate U., 1982. Social caseworker Contra Costa County Social Services Dept., Richmond, Calif., 1979-81; ins. claims examiner Social Security Adminstrn., Richmond, 1981—. Advisor, Med. Explorers, 1977-79; Jewish lay leader, 1977-79. Served with U.S. Army, 1976-79, to capt. USAR, 1980—. Mem. CAP (squadron sr. mem. of yr. 1980), Nat. Assn. Social Workers, Assn. U.S. Army, Res. Officers Assn. (v.p. med. services Calif. 1983—), Air Force Assn., Am. Philatelic Assn. Club: Toastmasters. Home: 27808 Huntwood Ave Apt 8 Hayward CA 94544

DOLGOW, ALLAN BENTLEY, mgmt. cons.; b. N.Y.C., Dec. 14, 1933; s. Murray and Nettie D.; B.I.E., N.Y. U., 1959, M.B.A., 1972; m. Kun Pok; children—Nicole, Marc, Ginger, Kimbie. Engr., Republic Aviation Corp., Farmingdale, N.Y., 1959-60; mgr. Internat. Paper Co., N.Y.C., 1960-73; project mgr. J.C. Penney Co. Inc., N.Y.C., 1973-75; dir. mfg. and planning Morse Electro Products, N.Y.C., 1975-77, exec. mgr. Morse Electrophonic Hong Kong Ltd., 1976-77; internat. project mgr. Revlon Inc., Edison, N.J., 1977-79: mgmt. cons. SRI Internat., Menlo Park, Calif., 1979—. Served with U.S. Army, 1954-56; Germany. Mem. Nat. Council Phys. Distbn. Mgmt. Home: 2323 Sharon Rd Menlo Park CA 94025 Office: 333 Ravenswood Ave Menlo Park CA 94025

DOLICH, ANDREW BRUCE, baseball executive; b. Bklyn., Feb. 18, 1948; s. Mac and Yetta (Weiselter) D.; m. Ellen A. Fass, June 10, 1972; 1 son, Cory Daniel. B.A. in Govt. and Pub. Adminstrn., Am. U., 1969; M.A. in Edn. and Sports Adminstrn., Ohio U., 1971. Adminstrv. asst. to gen. mgr. Phila. 76ers, NBA, 1971-74; v.p. adminstrn. Md. Arrows, Nat. Lacrosse League, 1974-76; dir. ops. and mktg. Washington Capitals, NHL, 1976-78; exec. v.p., gen. mgr. Washington Diplomats, 1978-80; v.p. bus. ops. Oakland (Calif.) Athletics, 1980—. Bd. dirs. Ohio U., U. Mass. sports studies programs; bd. dirs. Oakland YMCA. Name Ohio U. Outstanding Alumnus, 1982. Office: Oakland Athletics Oakland CA 94621

DOLL, ROBERT WILLIAM, research engr.; b. Glendale, Calif., Feb. 27, 1940; s. Henry Martin and Kathryn Rose (Fox) D.; A.A., Glendale City Coll., 1960; B.S., Calif. State U., Los Angeles, 1964; M.S., U. So. Calif., 1966; Ph.D., U. Calif., Berkeley, 1974; m. Susan Elisabeth Stamps, Feb. 3, 1976; children—Michael, Debra, Kathryn. Project engr., staff engr., test lab. supr. Barry Controls, Burbank, Calif., 1966-69; research asst. U. Calif., Berkeley, 1971-74; mem. tech. staff TRW, Redondo Beach, Calif., 1974—; mem. engring. faculty Calif. State U., Los Angeles, 1967-69. NSF grantee, 1972-74. Mem. U. Calif. Berkeley Alumni Soc., Sigma Xi, Alpha Gamma Sigma, Pi Tau Sigma. Contbr. articles to profl. jours. Office: 1 Space Park Redondo Beach CA 90278

DOLLINGER, ARMAND LEON, pathologist; b. Los Angeles, June 16, 1931; s. G. Glenn and Alethea D. (Morrison) D.; B.A. in Chemistry, La Sierra Coll., 1952; M.D., Loma Linda (Calif.) U., 1956; m. Martha Alice Dobias, June 13, 1975; children by previous marriage—Barbara, John, Robert, Elizabeth, Mary, Rebecca, Andrew, Matthew, Bradley, Kelly. Intern, White Meml. Hosp., Los Angeles, 1956-57; resident in pathology Loma Linda U. Hosp., 1957-63; pathologist, co-dir. Biolabs., Colton, Calif., 1963-73; pathologist, owner, dir. Dollinger Pathology Med. Group, Inc., Hanford, Calif., 1973—; pathologist, lab. dir., past pres. med. staff Hanford Community Hosp.; guest lectr. forensic pathology Loma Linda U. Med. Center, 1972; pathology cons., lab. dir. U.S. Naval Hosp., Livermore, Calif.; adv. bd. Kings County Drug Adv. Bd.; cons. in field, pathologist to coroners' offices. Served with M.C., USNR, 1958-60, now capt. Res. Diplomate Am. Bd. Pathology. Fellow Am. Soc. Clin. Pathologists, Coll. Am. Pathologists; mem. Am. Acad. Forensic Scis., Naval Res. Assn., Nat. Rifle Assn. (life), Kings County Med. Soc. (pres. 1983), Nat. Assn. Med. Examiners, Kings County Peace Officers Assn., Calif. Res. Peace Officers Assn., Calif. Rifle and Pistol Assn. (life), Loma Linda U. Alumni Assn. (life). Republican. Seventh-day Adventist. Author papers in field. Office: 1107 N Douty St PO Box 1308 Hanford CA 93230

DOLLIVER, JAMES MORGAN, justice; b. Ft. Dodge, Iowa, Oct. 13, 1924; s. James Isaac and Margaret Elizabeth (Morgan) D.; B.A., Swarthmore Coll., 1949; LL.B., U. Wash., 1952; m. Barbara Babcock, Dec. 18, 1948; children—Elizabeth, James, Peter, Keith, Jennifer, Nancy. Admitted to Wash. bar, 1952; law clk. Judge Fred Hamley, Wash. Supreme Ct., 1952-53; individual practice law, Port Angeles, 1953-54, Everett, 1961-64; adminstrv. asst. to Congressman Jack Westland, 1955-61, Gov. Daniel J. Evans, 1965-76; justice Supreme Ct. Wash., 1976—. Trustee, Gen. Bd. Ch. and Soc., United Methodist Ch., 1976—; trustee Boy Scouts Am., U. Puget Sound, Swarthmore (Pa.)

Coll., Thurston Youth Soc., State Capitol Hist. Assn., Community Mental Health Center, Wash. 4-H Found., Evergreen Safety Council, Nature Conservancy. Served with USN, 1943-45, USCG, 1945-46. Club: Rotary. Office: Temple of Justice Olympia WA 98504

DOLLY, JOHN PATRICK, univ. dean, ednl. psychologist; b. N.Y.C., May 16, 1942; s. Thomas Joseph and Anna Maria (Baron) D.; m. Carol Ann, Oct. 23, 1966; children—Shelia, Erin. B.S., Manhattan Coll., 1964; M.S., SUNY, 1966; Ed.D., U. Ga., 1973. Area dir. Founds. of Edn., U. S.C., Columbia, 1975-78, asst. dean acad. affairs Coll. Edn., 1978-79, acting dean, 1979-80, asst. dean research and devel., 1980; dean Coll. Edn., U. Wyo., Laramie, 1981—; cons. and lectr. in field. Served to capt. USAF, 1966-70. Vocat. Rehab. Adminstrn. trainee, 1964-66. Mem. Am. Psychol. Assn., Am. Ednl. Research Assn., Phi Delta Kappa, Phi Kappa Phi, Kappa Delta Pi. Co-author: Learning to Teach: A Decision Making System; contbr. articles to profl. jours. Home: 1154 Inca Dr Laramie WY 82070 Office: Coll Edn U Wyo Laramie WY 82071

DOLOWITZ, DAVID AUGUSTUS, otolaryngologist, educator; b. N.Y.C., Nov. 3, 1913; s. Alexander and Florence Reda (Levine) D.; A.B., Johns Hopkins U., 1933; M.D., Yale U., 1937; M.A., U. Utah, 1951, Sc.D. (hon.), 1978; m. Frances Marie Fleisher, May 6, 1937 (dec. 1967); children—David S., Julia Louise, Wilma Florence, Susan Reda, Fridolyn Gimble; m. 2nd Emma Ruth Halvorsen, June 11, 1968. Intern, Morristown (N.J.) Meml. Hosp., 1937-38, Albany (N.Y.) Hosp., 1938-39; resident Johns Hopkins Hosp., Balt., 1939-43; practice medicine, specializing in otolaryngology, Salt Lake City, 1946-78; asst. otolaryngology Johns Hopkins U., Balt., 1938-39, instr., 1942-43; instr. U. Utah, Salt Lake City, 1943-48, asso. clin. prof., 1948-58, asso. prof., chief otolaryngology, 1958-67, clin. prof. otolaryngology, 1967—; staff Holy Cross Hosp., VA Hosp., Salt Lake City, U. Utah Med. Hosp., Primary Children's Hosp., Salt Lake City, all 1946-78; councilman, treas. Town of Toquerville (Utah), 1982—. Chmn. bd. Pioneer Craft House, Salt Lake City, 1965—; mem. gov.'s com. study exceptional children, Utah, 1967. Served with M.C., U.S. Army, 1943-46. NIH fellow, U. Lund, Sweden, 1959-60. Fellow A.C.S.; mem. AMA, Utah Med. Assn., Am. Bd. Otolaryngology, Am. Acad. Otolaryngology, Am. Bd. Clin. Allergy, Am. Otol. Soc., Deafness Research Found., Soc. Univ. Otolaryngologists (adv. com. pulmonary-allergy drugs 1973-78), Am. Laryngology, Rhinology and Otolaryngology Soc., Barany Soc., C. of C. Democrat. Jewish. Author: Basic Otolaryngology, 1964; editor: Allergy in Otolaryngologic Practice: The Otolaryngologic Clinics of North America, 1971; Transactions of Am. Soc. Ophthalmologic and Otolaryngologic Allergy, 1973-78; contbr. articles to profl. jours. Address: PO Box 524 Toquerville UT 84774

DOLSEN, DAVID HORTON, mortician; b. Durango, Colo., Feb. 27, 1940; s. Donald B. and Florence I. (Maxey) D.; B.A., Southwestern Coll., 1962, Mortuary Sci. Degree, Dallas-Jones Coll. Mortuary Sci., 1963; m. Jo Patricia Johnson, Dec. 23, 1962; children—Wendy, Douglas. Apprentice, Davis Mortuary, Pueblo, Colo., 1963-64; bus. mgr. George F. McCarty Funeral Home, Pueblo, 1964-65; owner Dolsen Mortuary, Lamar, Colo., 1965-72; v.p., gen. mgr., dir. Almont, Inc., Lamar, 1972—; sec. Dolsen, Inc., 1967—; treas. Wilson Funeral Dirs. Inc., Itoh-Wilson Funeral Dirs., Inc. Mem. Lamar City Council, 1969-73; mayor City of Lamar, 1971-73. Bd. dirs. Lamar Community Coll., 1967-73, Prowers County Hist. Soc., 1966—, San De Cristo Arts and Conf. Center, 1979—; bd. dirs., sec. Pueblo Met. Mus. Assn., 1975-79; vice chmn. council on fin. and adminstrn. Rocky Mountain Conf. United Meth. Ch., 1976—, del. Gen. Conf., 1979—, mem. Pres.'s Council Nat. Meth. Found., 1978—, trustee, mem. exec. com. Southwestern Coll., Winfield, Kans., 1979—; dist. chmn. Boy Scouts Am., 1981—; treas., mem. exec. com. Girl Scouts U.S.A., 1981—; mem. council on fin. and adminstrn. Western Jurisdiction, United Meth. Ch., 1980—; trustee, gen. council on fin. and adminstrn. United Meth. Ch., 1980—; trustee Meth. Corp., 1980—, United Meth. Ch. Ins. Trust, 1982—; mem. World Service Commn., Meth. Episcopal Ch., 1980—, mem. gen. council on adminstrn., bd. adminstrn. Ch. of United Brethren in Christ, 1980—. Mem. Nat. Funeral Dirs. Assn., Nat. Selected Morticians, Cremation Assn. Am., Monument Builders N.Am., Colo. Funeral Dirs. Assn. Pi Sigma Eta, Pi Kappa Delta, Pi Gamma Mu. Methodist (cert. lay speaker). Clubs: Masons, Shriners, Elks, Rotary (Paul Harris fellow). Home: 3503 Morris Ave Pueblo CO 81008 Office: 401 Broadway Pueblo CO 81004

DOMANSKIS, EDWARD JOHN, plastic surgeon; b. Uffenheim, Ger., Mar. 21, 1945; came to U.S., 1949, naturalized, 1954; s. Van and Alina D. B.S., Loyola U., 1967; M.D., U. Ill., 1971. Intern, Orange County Med. Center, Irvine, Calif., 1971-72; gen. surgery resident U. Calif., Irvine, Santa Barbara Cottage Hosps., 1971-74; resident in plastic surgery U. Calif., San Francisco Hosps., 1974-76; practice medicine, specializing in plastic surgery, Newport Beach, Calif., 1978—; staff Hoag Meml. Hosp., Newport Beach, 1978—, Santa-Ana-Tustin Community Hosp., 1978—. Served to maj. U.S. Army, 1976-78. Diplomate Am. Bd. Plastic Surgery. Fellow A.C.S.; mem. Am. Soc. Plastic and Reconstructive Surgeons, Calif. Soc. Plastic Surgeons, Am. Cleft Palate Assn., Calif. Med. Assn., Orange County Med. Assn. Address: 1441 Avocado Ave Suite 307 Newport Beach CA 92660

DOMENICI, PETE V(ICHI), senator; b. Albuquerque, May 7, 1932; s. Cherubino and Alda (Vichi) D.; student U. Albuquerque, 1950-52; B.S., U. N.Mex., 1954; LL.B., Denver U., 1958; m. Nancy Burk, Jan. 15, 1958; children—Lisa, Peter, Nella, Clare, David, Nanette, Helen, Paula. Tchr. math. Albuquerque Pub. Schs., 1954-55; admitted to N.Mex. bar, 1958; partner firm Domenici & Bonham, Albuquerque, 1958-72; U.S. senator from N.Mex., 1972—, chmn. Budget Com., mem. Com. on Energy and Natural Resources, Com. on Environ. and Public Works, Senate Spl. Com. on Aging. Mem. Gov.'s Policy Bd. for Law Enforcement, 1967-68; chmn. Model Cities Joint Adv. Com., 1967-68; mem. Pres.'s Adv. Bd. on Federalism. Mem. Albuquerque City Commn., 1966-68, chmn. and ex-officio mayor, 1967. Named Outstanding Young Man of Albuquerque, Jaycees, 1967; recipient awards from numerous orgns. including League of United Latin Am. Citizens Nat. Edn. Service Centers, Nat. Fedn. Ind. Bus., Nat. Assn. Bus.; Marconi award Order Sons of Italy in Am. Mem. Nat. League Cities, Middle Rio Grande Council Govts. Office: Suite 4239 Dirksen Office Bldg Washington DC 20510

DOMENICI, ROBERT J., banker; b. Albuquerque, May 15, 1928; s. Antonio and Emma (Giomi) D.; student U. N.Mex., 1944-45; m. Catherine M. Del Frate, May 18, 1952; children—Diane, Karen. With Albuquerque Nat. Bank, 1952-81, v.p., until 1981; sr. v.p. mortgage loan dept. Am. Bank Commerce, Albuquerque, 1981—. Served with AUS, 1950-52. Mem. N.Mex. Mortgage Assn. (pres. 1960, 75), N.Mex. Homebuilders Assn., N.Mex. Bd. Realtors, Albuquerque Bd. Realtors. Republican. Roman Catholic. Clubs: Albuquerque Country, Tanoan Country, Albuquerque Petroleum, Elks. Home: 408 Laguna Blvd SW Albuquerque NM 87103 Office: 200 Lomas NW Albuquerque NM 81703

DOMMARTIN, MAX (MAXIME DUPASQUIER DE DOMPMARTIN), interior designer; b. Luxembourg, Nov. 1, 1925; came to U.S., 1958, naturalized, 1963; s. Marcel and Yvonne (Cuinet) de D.; grad. St.-Cyr Mil. Acad.; M.A., univs. Lille and Paris (France), 1944. Owner, mgr. Max. Dommartin & Co., Interior Design, Los Angeles, 1972—, Art for Ever design imports, 1977—; instr. architecture Woodbury U., Los Angeles, 1976, interior design UCLA, 1975-79. Served as capt. French Marine Corps, 1944-49. Mem. Am. Soc. Interior Designers, French Inst. Interior Architects, Inst. Bus. Designers, Screen Actors Guild, AFTRA. Roman Catholic.

DOMONDON, OSCAR, dentist; b. Cebu City, Philippines, July 4, 1924; s. Antero B. and Ursula (Maglasang) D.; D.M.D., Philippine Dental Coll., 1951; D.D.S., Loma Linda U., 1964; children—Reinelda, Carolyn, Catherine, Oscar. Came to U.S., 1954, naturalized, 1956. Dentist, Manila. (Philippines) Sanitarium and Hosp., 1952, U.S. embassy, Manila, 1952-54; individual practice dentistry, Long Beach, Calif., 1964—. Dentist, Children's Dental Health Center, Long Beach, part-time, 1964-68; past mem. Calif. State Bd. Dental Examiners. Past pres., Filipino Community Action Services, Inc. Served with AUS, 1946-49, 54-60. Fellow Acad. Dentistry Internationale, Acad. Gen. Dentistry, Internat. Inst. Community Service, Acad. Internat. Dental Studies; mem. Am. Soc. Dentistry Children, ADA, Am. Acad. Oral Radiology (award 1964), Internat. Acad. Orthodontists, Am. Soc. Clin. Hypnosis, Am. Endodontic Soc., Western Conf. Dental Examiners and Dental Sch. Deans, Fedn. of Assns. of Health Regulatory Bds., Calif. Assn. Fgn. Dental Grads. (past pres.), Filipino Dental Soc. (past pres.), Philippine Tech. and Profl. Soc. (v.p.), Am. Acad. Dentistry for Handicapped, Am. Assn. Dental Examiners, Nat. Assn. Filipino Practicing Dentists in Am. (v.p.). Republican. Clubs: Lions (past pres.), Elks (chmn. rangers), Masons. Home: 3570 Aster St Seal Beach CA 90740 Office: 3714 Atlantic Ave Long Beach CA 90807

DOMS, MYRA SCOTT, corporation executive; b. San Francisco, May 2, 1947; d. John Raymond and Katherine Jane (June) Scott; m. Donald Willard Hanson, Dec. 27, 1967; 1 son, Conrad John; m. 2d, Richard John Doms, Apr. 17, 1976; 1 dau., Madeline Elaine. Student Coll. of Marin, Calif. State U.-Sonoma, U. Calif.-Berkeley. Instr. Marin Community Coll. Dist., 1974-78; personnel mgr. Gates, Santa Rosa, Calif., 1978-81; v.p. personnel Electroscale Corp. subs. Staveley Industries, Santa Rosa, 1981—. Bd. dirs. Petaluma Boys and Girls Club. Mem. Personnel Assn. Sonoma County (pres.), Am. Compensation Assn., Am. Soc. Personnel Adminstrn., Am. Electronics Assn., Am. Soc. Tng. and Devel. Democrat. Roman Catholic.

DON, MANUEL, research auditory electrophysiology; b. Tucson, May 27, 1942; s. Chun and Shee (Chin) D.; B.A., U. Calif. Berkeley, 1965; M.A., U. Ariz., 1967; Ph.D., Stanford U., 1971; m. Margery Mai Yeung, 1967; children—Kendra Marie, Erica Lynn, Angela Noelle. VA rehab. fellow Stanford (Calif.) U., 1967-69, 1970, NIH fellow, 1971-73; asst. research auditory physiologist, U. Calif. Irvine, 1973-76; Assoc. dir. Auditory Electrophysiology Lab., House Ear Inst., Los Angeles, 1976—, cons., 1976. Mem. Acoustical Soc. Am., Sigma Xi. Democrat. Contbr. articles in field. Home: 5401 Willowick Dr Anaheim CA 92807 Office: 256 S Lake St Los Angeles CA 90057

DONADIO, PATRICK JAMES, clergyman; b. Schenectady, Apr. 17, 1940; s. James Vincent and Florence (Madelone) D.; B.A., Central Bible Coll., 1965; B.S., Valley Forge Christian Coll., 1976; D.D., Fla. Christian Coll., 1978; student Pincrest Bible Inst., 1959-60, Phila. Coll. of Bible, 1960-61; m. Ruth Spuler, Apr. 7, 1962; children—Dale Patrick, Doreen Patricia. Ordained to ministry Gen. Council Assemblies of God Ch., 1965; minister, Athcabascan Indians, Fort Yukon, 1966-67, Arctic Circle, Point Hope, 1968-69, Tok, Alaska, 1970-71, Kenai, Alaska, 1972-77, Eagle River, Alaska, 1978—; counselor Family Christian Service, 1972-75. Capt., CAP, 1974—. Served with AUS, 1973-75. Pres., N. Kenai Playground Assn.; v.p. Anchorage Teen Challenge Internat. Club: Masons. Author: I Should Have Raised Pigs, 1980. Home: PO Box 1172 Preuss Ln Eagle River AK 99577 Office: Corner Eagle River Loop and Baranof St Eagle River AK 99577

DONAHOE, DAVID LEE, mgmt. cons. co. exec.; b. Huntington, W.Va., July 16, 1941; s. Lee F. and Nocha (Maynard) D.; student Palm Beach Coll., 1963-66; m. Georgine Kantzavolos, June 23, 1975; children—David, Cari, Lee J. Systems programmer Pratt & Whitney Aircraft Co., West Palm Beach, Fla., 1963-66; systems programmer Montgomery Ward, Chgo., 1966-67; dir. Midwest ops. Cybernetics Communications, Chgo., 1967; regional mgr. Computer Scis. Corp., Chgo., 1967-71; v.p. Consumer Systems Corp., Chgo., 1971-75; v.p., prin. CARA Corp., Scottsdale Ariz., 1975—, also dir. Served with U.S. Army, 1960-63. Mem. Soc. Mgmt. Info. Systems, Inst. Internal Auditors, Data Processing Mgmt. Assn. Democrat. Methodist. Office: 6900 E Camelback St Suite 303 Scottsdale AZ 85251

DONAHOO, STANLEY ELLSWORTH, orthopaedic surgeon; b. St. Joseph, Mo., Dec. 3, 1933; s. Charles Ellsworth and Opal (Cole) D.; M.D., U. Wash., 1963; m. Sharon Ann Fountain, Sept. 14, 1956; children—Shan Maureen, Brian Patrick, Mary Kathleen, Jane Eileen. Resident, Duke U., Durham, N.C., 1967-68, U.S. Naval Hosp., Oakland, Calif., 1963-67; commd. lt., U.S. Navy, 1963 advanced through grades to lt. comdr. (orthopaedic surgeon), 1971, ret. 1971; practice medicine, specializing in orthopaedic surgery, Roseburg, Oreg., 1971—; chief surgery Mercy Hosp., Roseburg, 1973-74; chief surgery Douglas Community Hosp., Roseburg, 1973, chief of staff, 1974—; cons. Guam Meml. Hosp., co-dir. rehab. unit, 1970-71; cons. orthopaedic surgery VA Hosp., Roseburg, 1971—; chmn. Douglas County (Oreg.) Emergency Med. Services Com., 1973-74. Trustee Douglas Community Hosp., 1975. Served with AUS, 1952-55. Diplomate Am. Bd. Orthopaedic Surgery. Fellow Am. Acad. Orthopaedic Surgeons, N. Pacific Orthopaedic Assn.; mem. Piedmont Orthopaedic Soc., AMA, Oreg. Med. Assn. (mem. sports medicine com., ins. and fee rev. com. 1981), Guam Med. Soc. (pres. 1970), Am. Trauma Soc. (founding mem.), Roseburg C. of C. (bd. govs. 1978—). Home: 1942 NW Oerding Roseburg OR 97470 Office: 1819 W Harvard St Roseburg OR 97470

DONAHUE, CLIFFORD, educator; b. Pitts., May 11, 1950; s. Ralph Vincent and Olga Pauline D.; B.A., Calif. State U., Humboldt, 1973; M.A. (Solano Community Coll. faculty fellow), U. Calif., Davis, 1980; m. Karen Louise Buettner, Sept. 8, 1973; 1 son, Ross Clifford. Tchr., Solano Community Coll., Suisun City, Calif., 1976-82; reading specialist Fairfield (Calif.) High Sch., 1982—; dir. Solano Learning Center, 1978—. Mem. Internat. Reading Assn., Computer Using Educators, Calif. Reading Assn., Council for Basic Edn. Office: Fairfield High Sch Fairfield Ca

DONALD, ERIC PAUL, aeronautical engineer, inventor; b. Sunderland, Eng., Feb. 23, 1930; came to U.S., 1964, naturalized, 1970; s. Norman and Dorothy (Dobson) D.; B.Sc. Int., Sunderland Tech. Coll., 1949; H.N.C., Acton Tech. Coll., 1957; M.Sc., Cranfield Inst. Tech., 1974; m. Christine Juliet Allen, Dec. 26, 1966; children—April Elise America, Paul Allen Hertford. Engr., Fairey Aviation Co., London, 1953-59; research engr. English Electric Co., 1959-64; indsl. engring. cons., N.Y.C., 1965-66; cons. engr. Lockheed Corp., 1966-67, Boeing, 1967-69, Grumman, 1969-70, Hawker Siddeley, 1970-71; chief stress analyst Guided Weapons div. Brit. Aircraft Corp., 1973-79; sr. engr. scientist Douglas Aircraft Co., Long Beach, Calif., 1979—; founder Donald Research, 1978, E.P. Donald Ltd., 1979; mng. dir. Blee-Bolt Indicators, Ltd., 1979—. Served with Brit. Royal Air Force, 1950-52. Recipient Richardson gold medal Inst. Patentees and Inventors, London, 1977. Assoc. fellow AIAA; mem. Royal Aero. Soc., Inst. Patentees and Inventors, Long Beach C. of C. Anglican. Contbr. articles to profl. jours.; patentee in field. Home: 1855 Petaluma Ave Long Beach CA 90815 Office: 3855 Lakewood Blvd Long Beach CA 90846

DONALDSON, CHARLES R., state supreme court justice; b. Helena, Mont.; m. Doris Donaldson. B.A., U. Idaho, J.D., 1948. Practice law, Boise, Idaho; justice of Peace for Ada County, 1960; dist. judge 3d Jud. Dist., 1964; mem. Idaho Supreme Ct., 1969—, chief justice, 1973, 79-81, 83—. Governing com. Idaho chpt. Arthritis and Rheumatism Found.; mem. Idaho Ho. of Reps., 1955-57. Served to capt., U.S. Army, World War II. Mem. Conf. Chief Justices (dep. chmn. 1980-91). Methodist. Lodges: Kiwanis (past pres.), Masons, Shriners. Office: Idaho Supreme Court Supreme Court Bldg Boise ID 83702*

DONALDSON, EDWIN, agronomist; b. Kalispell, Mont., May 20, 1938; s. Walter and Elma (Arnett) D. m. Sue Ann Snell, Mar. 19, 1960; children—Robert, Richard Roger, Becky, Cathy. B.S. in Agronomy, Wash. State U., 1966; PH.D. in Genetics, 1970. Research assoc. Spring Wheat Devel., Wash. State U., Pullman, 1970-72; asst. agronomist Hard Red Winter Wheat Devel., Dry Land Research Unit, Lind., Wash., 1972—. Contbr. numerous articles to tech. publs. Served with Army N.G., 1954-61. Mem. Am. Soc. Agronomy, Western Soc. Crop Sci., AAAS, Sigma Xi. Methodist. Club: Lions. Home: Rodeo Grounds Lind WA 99341 Office: Dry Land Research Unit Lind WA 99341

DONALDSON, GEORGE BURNEY, chemical company executive; b. Oakland, Calif., Mar. 16, 1945; s. George T. and L.M. (Burney) D.; m. Jennifer L. Bishop, Feb. 16, 1974; 1 dau., Dawn Marie. A.S. in Criminology, Porterville Coll., 1972. Police officer City of Lindsay (Calif.), 1966-67; distbn. mgr. Ortho div. Chevron Chem. Co., Lindsay, 1967-73; safety specialist Wilbur-Ellis Co. Fresno, Calif., 1973-77, safety dir., 1977-79, dir. regulatory affairs, 1979—; industry rep. to White House Inter-Govtl. Sci. Engring., and Tech. Adv. Panel, Task Force on Transp. of Non-Nuclear Hazardous Materials, 1980; industry rep. Transp. Research Bd.'s Nat. Strategies Conf. on Transp. of Hazardous Materials and Wastes in the 1980's, Nat. Acad. Scis., 1981, Hazardous Materials Transp. Conf., Nat. Conf. of State Legislatures, 1982. Served with U.S. Army, 1962-65. Mem. Western Agrl. Chems. Assn. (chmn. transp., distbn. and safety com., outstanding mem. of year 1981, govtl. affairs com.), Nat. Agrl. Chems. Assn. (vice chmn. transp. and distbn. com., occupational safety and health com.), Am. Soc. Safety Engrs., Calif. Fertilizer Assn. (transp. and distbn. com.). Republican. Club: Elks. Office: 191 W Shaw Ave Suite 107 Fresno CA 93704

DONART, GARY B., range science educator, consultant, researcher; b. Howard, Kans., Sept. 6, 1940; s. Harry J. and Iris (Bartlett) D.; m. Glenda Avis Stites, Dec. 23, 1961; children—Dana Duane, Michele, Shane. B.S., Ft. Hays (Kans.) State Coll., 1962, M.S., 1963; Ph.D., Utah State U., 1968. Asst. prof. Humboldt State U., 1965-68; asst. prof. Tex. A&M U., 1968-72; prof. range sci. N. Mex. State U., 1972—; cons. to Dept. Interior, mining industry. Active Boy Scouts Am. Mem. Soc. Range Mgmt. (co-Rangeman of Yr. N.Mex. sec. 1974), Am. Soc. Agronomy, Crop Sci. Soc. Am., AAAS. Club: Masons. Author numerous tech. publs. Office: 3-I Dept Animal and Range Scis N Mex State U Las Cruces NM 88003

DONATO, MICHAEL THOMAS, real estate developer; b. Spokane, Wash., Mar. 7, 1942; s. Morris Thomas and Iris Elizabeth (Huggins) D.; m. Betty Lee South, Sept. 21, 1962; children—Michael Ty, Marlo T. Student Ariz. State U., 1961. Lic. real estate broker, builder, developer Ariz. Co-broker Maricopa Realty & Trust Co., Mesa, Ariz., 1963, Ed Post Realty, Scottsdale, Ariz., from 1964; pres. C.A.T. Land & Cattle Co., Scottsdale, Ariz., 1982—, Tom Donato Constrn. Co. Inc., Scottsdale, 1965—; ptnr. Nat. Sports Concepts, Scottsdale, 1982—; quarter horse exhibitor. Bd. dirs. equine sci. dept. Scottsdale Community Coll., Ariz. Nat. Livestock Show; Mem. Ariz. Quarter Horse Breeders Assn., Profl. Rodeo Cowboys Assn. (chmn. Turquoise Circuit Championship Rodeo Finals), Am. Quarter Horse Assn. (judge), Am. Paint Horse Assn. (judge), Ariz. Jr. Rodeo Assn., Ariz. High Sch. Rodeo Assn. Contbr. to movies and TV shows on rodeo; featured in rodeo and horse judging articles in profl. jours.; participant in profl. rodeo activities. Office: 1939 S Sossaman Rd Mesa AZ 85208

DONELAN, LYNN ENGERT, elec. engr.; b. Republican City, Nebr., July 31, 1923; s. Charles Bernard and Matilda Florence (Engert) D., B.S. in Elec. Engring., U. Colo., 1941-48; postgrad. Ill. Inst. Tech., 1949-53, U. Pitts., 1955-57; m. Joanne Leona Birch, Sept. 18, 1971; children—Larry L., Sharon A. Donelan Yurvati, Victoria L. With atomic power div. Allis Chalmers, Milw., 1948-53, engr. in charge design nuclear pump, 1957-63; with Westinghouse Atomic Equipment, 1953-57; mem. tech. staff Atomics Internat., Canoga Park, Calif., 1963—. Served with AUS, 1942-45. Mem. Nat. Rifle Assn., IEEE, Eta Kappa Nu. Patentee in field. Home: 6443 Gross St Canoga Park CA 91304 Office: 8900 Desoto St Canoga Park CA 91304

DONELSON, KENNETH WILBER, lawyer; b. Portland, Oreg.; s. Daniel August and Charlotte (Wilber) D.; m. Irene Witmer, July 25, 1937; children—Carol Ann, Richard Kenneth. B.S., Oreg. State U., 1933; J.D., U. of Pacific, 1940. Bar: Calif. 1940. Supervising auditor, sales tax div. State of Calif., Sacramento, 1935-43, referee, state personnel bd., 1943-45; sole practice, Sacramento, 1945—. Mem. ABA, Calif. Bar Assn., Sacramento County Bar Assn., Nat. Council Juvenile and Family Ct. Judges, Assn. Trial Lawyers Am., Calif. Trial Lawyers Assn., Sacramento Estate Planning Council, Sacramento County Hist. Soc., Sacramento Book Collectors, Sigma Nu. Clubs: Torch (Sacramento); Calif. Writers, Toastmasters (past pres.). Author: (with Irene Donelson) When You Need A Lawyer, 1964, Married Today, Single Tomorrow, 1969, How To Handle Your Legal Problems, 1971. Office: 708 10th St Suite 150 Sacramento CA 95814

DONG, MAE FONG, pharmacist, educator; b. Sacramento, Nov. 21, 1938; d. Johnnie Gwee and Helen (Ho) Fong; Pharm.D., U. Calif. at San Francisco, 1962; m. Richard Gene Dong, May 19, 1968; children—Michael Kenneth, Catherine Elizabeth. Staff pharmacist Mt. Zion Hosp., San Francisco, 1962-68; asst. chief pharmacist Valley Meml. Hosp., Livermore, Calif., 1968-70; tchr. Pre-Sch. P.S. 78, San Ramon Valley Community Center, 1975-79; staff pharmacist G.E.T. Pharmacy, San Francisco, 1980—. Vol., Am. Heart Assn., Am. Cancer Soc.; active alt. edn. program San Ramon Valley Sch. Dist. Licensed pharmacist, Calif., Nev. Mem. Am. Pharm. Assn., U. Calif. Alumni Assn. Home: 38 Hornet Ct Danville CA 94526

DONG, RICHARD GENE, mech. and civil engr.; b. Sacramento, May 16, 1935; s. Chester Q. and May W. (Wong) D.; B.S. in Mech. Engring., U. Calif. at Berkeley, 1957, M.S. in Mech. Engring., 1959, Ph.D. in Civil Engring. (Aerojet-Gen. Corp. scholar), 1964; m. Mae Fong, May 19, 1968; children—Michael K., Catherine E. Dynamic analysis Aerojet-Gen. Corp., Sacramento, 1959-61; research scientist polymeric materials Lawrence Livermore (Calif.) Nat. Lab., 1963-72, group leader, 1966-72, research scientist soils materials, 1972-74, structural analysis and seismic studies, fluid-structure interaction, 1974-78, project mgr. fragilities project of seismic safety margins research program funded by Nuclear Regulatory Commn., 1978-80, dep. mgr. program, 1980-81, mgr. equipment qualification program, 1981-82, sr. staff mem., 1982—; mem. ad hoc cumulative damage subcom. Interagy. Chem. Rocket Propulsion Group, 1968. Active in forming new alternative learning program San Ramon Valley (Calif.) Sch. Dist. Registered profl. engr., Calif. Mem. ASME, Sigma Xi, Tau Beta Pi, Xi Epsilon, Pi Tau Sigma. Contbr. articles to tech. jours. Patentee in field. Home: 38 Hornet Ct Danville CA 94526 Office: Lawrence Livermore Nat Lab PO Box 808 Livermore CA 94550

DONISTHORPE, CHRISTINE ANN, state senator; b. Christina, Mont., May 31, 1932; d. Lambert A. and Ludmilla (Hruska) Benes; m. Oscar Lloyd Donisthorpe, 1951; children—Paul, Karen, Bruce, Brian. Student U. Mont., 1951-53, San Juan Coll., Farmington, N.Mex. and N.Mex. Real Estate Sch., 1958-70. Real estate broker, San Juan County, N.Mex., 1978-81; mem. N.Mex. State Senate, 1979—, mem. edn. com., 1979, fin. com., 1980, edn. study com., 1981. Pres. Bloomfield (N.Mex.) Bd. Edn., 1975-81. Recipient award U.S. Soil and Water Conservation, 1967; hon. state farmer Future Farmers Am., 1975; adv. bd. Salvation Army, 1970-75. Mem. Bloomfield C. of C., N.Mex. Hay Growers Assn. Republican. Methodist. Home: Box 746 Bloomfield NM 87413 Office: New Mexico State Senate Santa Fe NM 87503*

DONLEY, JOHN P., state senator, lawyer; b. Evergreen Park, Ill., Mar. 10, 1939; s. John and Dorothy Donley; m. Sandra Kay Smith, 1961; children—John, Amy, Matt, Grant. A.A., George Washington U., 1957, B.A., 1961; postgrad. Kansas U., 1961-63; J.D., U. Colo., 1966. Counsel, United Agrl. Products, Inc.; co-owner Greeley Recycling Inc.; asst. county atty. Weld County (Colo.); asst. mcpl. judge; asst. city prosecutor; mem. Colo. State Senate, 1982—. Mem. Sigma Xi, Omicron Delta Kappa, Republican. Presbyterian. Clubs: Elks, Lions. Office: State Capitol Denver CO 80203*

DONLEY, RUSSELL LEE, III, cons. engr., state legislator; b. Salt Lake City, Feb. 3, 1939; s. R. Lee and Leona (Sherwood) D.; B.C.E. with honors, U. Wyo., 1961; M.S., U. Fla., 1962; m. Karen Kocherhans, June 4, 1960; children—Tammera Sue, Tonya Kay, Christina Lynn. Cons. engr., prin. Russell L. Donley and Assocs., Inc., Casper, Wyo., 1962—; mem. Wyo. State Ho. of Reps., 1968—, chmn. appropriations com., 1975-78, mem. rules com., 1973-82, majority floor leader, 1979-80, speaker pro-tem, 1981-82, speaker, 1983-84, chmn. rules com., 1983-84, chmn. legis. mgmt. council, 1983-84; chmn. Western Conf., Council State Govt., 1982-83. State chmn. Wyo. Young Republicans, 1967-68; Pres., Casper Family YMCA, 1976-77. Named Wyo. Outstanding Young Engr., 1974, Outstanding Wyo. Engr., 1976, Outstanding Legislator of Yr., Nat. Rep. Legislators Assn., 1981; registered profl. engr., land surveyor, Wyo.; profl. engr., Wyo., Mont., Colo., N.Y., N.J. Mem. Wyo. Engring. Soc., Wyo. Assn. Cons. Engrs. and Surveyors, Am. Waterworks Assn. Home: 1140 Ivy Ln Casper WY 82609 Office: 240 S Wolcott Casper WY 82609

DONNELLY, JOHN DAVID, automotive sales executive; b. Oakland, Calif., Apr. 14, 1934; s. James Howard and Ellen Jane (O'Donnell) D.; B.S. in Fin., U. Notre Dame, 1956; m. Suzanne Shoemaker, Dec. 30, 1961; children—Mary Eileen, John David, Molly Ann. Cons., Monitor program NBC, 1958; asst. editor plant publs. Kaiser Steel Corp., 1959-62, sales rep., Los Angeles, 1962-63; successively sales rep., sales supr., asst. zone mgr., zone sales mgr. AC-Delco div. Gen. Motors Corp., La Mirada, Calif., 1963—. Chmn., Kaiser Steel U.S. Bond drive, 1960-61. Served as lt. (j.g.) USNR, 1956-59. Named Young Exec. of Yr. for San Bernardino County YMCA, 1960. Mem. Am. Mgmt. Assn., U. Notre Dame Alumni So. Calif. (past dir.), United Irish Socs. So. Calif. (dir.), Automotive Service Industry Assn. (Hall of Fame award 1983). Republican. Roman Catholic. Clubs: Notre Dame Alumni (Los Angeles), Orange County Notre Dame Alumni, Elks, Toastmasters (pres. 1961). Editor-in-chief, pub. Checkmate, 1958. Home: 21141 Shaw Ln Huntington Beach CA 92646 Office: 14555 Alondra Blvd La Mirada CA 90638

DONNELLY, MARIAN CARD, ret. educator, art historian; b. Evanston, Ill., Sept. 12, 1923; d. Harold S. and Ethel (Gates) Card; A.B. summa cum laude, Oberlin Coll., 1946, M.A., 1948; Ph.D., Yale U., 1956; m. Russell J. Donnelly, Jan. 21, 1956; 1 son, James Armstrong. Instr. fine arts Upsala Coll., 1948-50; art librarian U. Rochester, 1951-53; research asso. decorative arts Art Inst., Chgo., 1956-57; vis. lectr. U. Chgo., 1965; asst. prof. dept. art history U. Oreg., Eugene, 1966-68, assoc. prof., 1969-73, prof., 1973-81, prof. emeritus, 1981—; participant Attingham (Eng.) Summer Sch., 1972, 75; vis. research scholar in art history U. Copenhagen, 1972; lectr. U. Oreg. Center for Internat. Music, Stuttgart, Germany, 1972. Am. Council Learned Socs. grantee, 1959-60. Fellow Royal Soc. Arts (London); mem. AAUP, Archeol. Inst. Am., Nat. Trust for Historic Preservation, Nat. Trust for Scotland, Soc. for Preservation New Eng. Antiquities, Soc. Archtl. Historians (dir. 1964-67, 78-81), asso. editor newsletter 1966-72, 2d v.p. 1972-74, 1st v.p. 1974-76, pres. 1976-78, gen. chmn. Bicentennial programs 1975-76, Phi Beta Kappa. Author: The New England Meeting Houses of the Seventeenth Century, 1968; A Short History of Observatories, 1973. Contbr. articles to profl. jours. Home: 2175 Olive St Eugene OR 97405

DONNELLY, WILLIAM MICHEAL, JR., obstetrician, gynecologist; b. Holyoke, Mass., Sept. 19, 1930; s. William M. D.; M.D., N.Y. Med. Coll., 1957; children by previous marriage—Michael, Tracey. Intern, Mercy Hosp., Springfield, Mass.; resident Albany (N.Y.) Med. Center Hosp., 1965; chief dept. obstetrics and gynecology U.S. Army Hosp., Berlin, 1965-68; practice medicine specializing in obstetrics and gynecology, Truckee, Calif., 1969—; mem. staff Tahoe Forest Hosp., Truckee, 1969—, chief dept. obstetrics and gynecology, 1969—; pres. Lake Tahoe unit Am. Cancer Soc. Served to maj. M.C. U.S. Army, 1965-68. Fellow Am. Coll. Obstetrics and Gynecology; mem. AMA, Calif. Med. Assn., Nev. Med. Soc. (dir.). Home: 10376 Somerset St Truckee CA 95734 Office: PO Box 507 Truckee CA 95734

DONOVAN, JAMES LAWRENCE, engineering manager; b. Binghampton, N.Y., Mar. 21, 1926; s. Cyril Lawrence and Helen Mildred (Phari) D.; m. Shirley Sliter, Dec. 7, 1947; m. Bee H. Houghton, July 4, 1968; children—Kathleen, John, James, Thomas, William, Nancy. B.S., Syracuse U., 1954; postgrad. Bridgeport Sch. Engring., 1967, NYU, 1970. Registered profl. engr., N.Y., N.J., Conn., Ohio. Process engr. Columbia Nat. Corp., Pace, Fla., 1957-60; project engr. Gulf States Paper Co., Demopolis, Ala., 1960-64; chief process engr. Dorr-Oliver, Stamford, Conn., 1964-68; project mgr. Hoechst-Unde Corp., Englewood Cliffs, N.J., 1968-70, BASF Corp., Ludwigshafen, W.Ger., 1970; dir. projects-teller Environ. Systems, N.Y.C., 1971; chief of design VA Hosp., Bronx, N.Y., 1972; project mgr. Processes Research, Cin., 1973-80; project engring. mgr. Fruco Engrs., Inc., St. Louis, 1980-81, Am. Magnetics, Inc., La Jolla, Calif., 1981—; cons. chem. plant desing. Pres. local PTA, 1958-59. Served with AUS, 1943-46. Mem. Am. Inst. Chem. Engrs., Nat. Soc. Profl. Engrs., VFW. Club: 4522. Home: 2420 Torrey Pines Rd La Jolla CA 92037 Office: 920 Kline St Suite 304 La Jolla CA 90237

DONOVAN, JESSICA ELLEN, geologist; b. Phila., Dec. 17, 1949; d. Neil Benjamin and Dorothy Ellen (Olszewski) D. B.A., Rutgers U., 1975, M.A., Harvard U., 1977. Registered geologist, Calif., 1983. Project geologist, staff geologist Dames & Moore, Honolulu, 1977-79, San Francisco, 1979—; speaker Options in Engring. and Sci., Expanding Your Horizons career confs. Mem. Assn. Women Geoscientist (nat. pres. 1981-82), Geol. Soc. Am., Mineral. Soc. Am., AAAS. Club: Commonwealth (San Francisco). Author conf. abstracts. Office: 500 Sansome St 1st Floor San Francisco CA 94111

DONOVAN, LAWRENCE PERRY, III, chemical engineer; b. San Diego, Feb. 17, 1947; s. Lawrence Perry and JoAnn Louise (Kastrup) D.; B.S. in Chemistry, San Diego State Coll., 1969; J.D., Western State U., 1980. Sr. research chemist Crown City Plating Co., El Monte, Calif., 1972-82; chem. engr. McDonnell Douglas Astronautics Corp., Huntington Beach, Calif., 1982—. Served with U.S. Army, 1969-72. Decorated Army Commendation medal. Mem. Am. Chem. Soc., Am. Electroplaters Soc., Nu Beta Epsilon. Patentee in field. Office: McDonnell Douglas Astronautics Corp 5301 Bolsa Ave Mail Sta 22-Z Huntington Beach CA 92647

DONOVAN, MARGARET ANN, educator; b. Detroit, Aug. 6, 1939; d. Edward Grove and Jean C. Donovan; B.A., U. Detroit, 1961; M.A., Eastern Mich. U., 1969; Ed.D., U. Hawaii, 1977. Elementary sch. tchr., Mich., 1961-69, Hawaii, 1969—; ednl. specialist for spl. edn. Leeward Dist. Office, Waipahu, 1978—; part-time instr. curriculum and instrn. U. Hawaii, 1975—; mem. Title IV Adv. Council, Gifted and Talented Adv. Council. Mem. Internat. Reading Assn., Nat. Council Tchrs. English, Council Exceptional Children, Assn. Supervision and Curriculum Devel., Am. Ednl. Research Assn., Pi Lambda Theta, Delta Kappa Gamma. Club: Zonta. Home: 2185 Aha Niu Pl Honolulu HI 96821 Office: Dept Edn Honolulu Dist Office 4967 Kilauea Ave Honolulu HI 96821

DONOVAN, STEPHEN HENRY, steel company official; b. Oakland, Calif., Feb. 16, 1949; s. Henry Augustine and Francis Dolores (Krieg) D.; B.A., Gonzaga U., 1971; J.D., John F. Kennedy U., 1983; m. Jeanne Yukie Uyehara, June 28, 1975; children—Kristine Mariko, Monica Miyuki. Mgmt. trainee U.S. Steel Corp., Pittsburg (Calif.) Works, 1972-74, foreman continuous and box annealing, 1974-76, labor contract adminstr., 1976-80, supr. personnel and tng., 1980—, staff asst. labor relations, 1980—. Mem. Assn. Iron and Steel Engrs. (past chmn. joint apprenticeship com.), Am. Radio Relay League (life). Roman Catholic. Club: Mount Diablo Amateur Radio. Office: PO Box 471 Pittsburg CA 94565

DONOVAN, THOMAS ANTHONY, nonprofit corporation executive, writer; b. Chgo., Oct. 3, 1938; s. Charles Joseph and Marcelline Mary (Collins) D. B.A. in Liberal Arts, Western Mich. U., 1961; student lang. arts San Francisco State U., 1959-60. Various positions to TV news producer CTS div. CBS, 1961-74; freelance writer, 1974-81; dir. Progressive Epilepsy Network, Phila., 1981-82, now bd. govs.; chmn. bd., pres. Epilepsy Network Service Corp., Van Nuys, Calif., 1982—. Mem. Epilepsy Found. Am., Writers Guild Am. W., AFTRA. Club: Pine Mountain. Home: 2216 Symonds Dr PMC Frazier Park CA 93225 Office: 14164 Sylvan St Van Nuys CA 91401

DONOVAN, WILLIAM CLINTON, JR., state ofcl.; b. Providence, Nov. 12, 1943; s. William Clinton and Elizabeth Helen (Mullen) D.; B.A., Providence Coll., 1967; M.Ed., Boston U., 1972; m. Karen Connelly, Aug. 29, 1970; children— Robert Michael, Kathryn Elizabeth. Child devel. supr. J. Arthur Trudeau Center, Warwick, R.I., 1970-72, asst. exec. dir., 1972-73; adminstr. community services State of R.I., Cranston, 1973-77; exec. dir. Ariz. Gov.'s Council on Devel. Disabilities, Phoenix, 1977—; cons. spl. edn. dept. U. Mass., R.I. Coll., U. Denver, HHS. Co-chmn. Jamestown (R.I.) Cancer Drive, 1976; mem. council, bd. dirs. SW Regional Lab., Los Alamitos, Calif., 1980—. Served with U.S. Army, 1968-69. Decorated D.S.M. Mem. Am. Assn. Mental Deficiency, Nat. Assn. Retarded Citizens, Nat. Assn. Devel. Disabilities Councils (v.p. 1982—). Democrat. Roman Catholic. Contbr. articles to profl. jours. Home: 501 W Hayward Phoenix AZ 85021 Office: 1717 W Jefferson PO Box 6123 Phoenix AZ 85005

DOOLEY, GERALD FRANCIS, univ. adminstr., former marine corps officer; b. Lowell, Mass., Apr. 26, 1935; s. William Edmund and Gertrude Frances (Killeen) D.; m. Eleanor Josephine Bernat, Oct. 31, 1955; children—Deborah Jean, Stephen Patrick, David Gerald. Diploma, U.S. Armed Forces Inst., 1954, U.S. Air Force Sch. Applied Aerospace Scis., 1976; degree in polit. sci. Saddleback Coll., 1979. Enlisted in U.S. Marine Corps, 1953, advanced through grades to lt. col., 1974; presdl. helicopter pilot, 1967-70; ret., 1978; dir. facilities Saddleback Coll. Dist., Mission Viejo, Calif., 1980—; aviation cons. Coach, Metro. Collegiate Baseball League, 1972-79, personnel dir., 1979—; chmn. Workman Med./Rehab. Fund, 1975—; mem. Nat. Republican Congressional Com., 1982. Decorated D.F.C. (2), Air medal (32), Purple Heart; recipient Presdl. Medal of Merit, 1983. Mem. DAV, Mil. Order of Purple Heart, Marine Corps Assn. Roman Catholic. Contbr. articles to profl. jours. Home: 26372 Via Conchita Mission Viejo CA 92691 Office: 28000 Marguerite Pkwy Mission Viejo CA 92692

DOOLEY, RICHARD ROBINSON, pediatrician; b. New Haven, May 4, 1924; s. Vincent Paul and Ultima Anna Marie (Robinson) D.; student Yale U., 1942-43, U. N.H., 1943-44, M.D., L.I. Coll. Medicine, 1947; m. Mary Jane Mackay, Sept. 24, 1976; 1 dau., Sarah Elizabeth; children by previous marriage—Margaret Mary, Karen, Leila, John, Richard. Intern, resident in pediatrics Kings County Hosp., Bklyn., 1947-49; resident in pediatraics Bklyn. Hosp., 1949-50; fellow Children's Med. Center, Boston, 1953-56; practice medicine specializing in pediatrics, Riverside, Calif., 1957-69; chmn. dept. pediatrics San Bernardino County Med. Center, San Bernardino, Calif., 1969—; adj. prof. pediatrics UCLA; prof. biosci. U. Calif., Riverside. Pres. C/F Club Nat. Cystic Fibrosis Found., 1979-80; chmn. adv. bd. Calif. Crippled Children, 1967-77. Fellow Am. Acad. Pediatrics, A.C.P.; mem. Am. Lung Assn., Ambulatory Pediatrics Soc., Western Soc. Pediatric Research, San Bernardino County Med. Soc., Calif. Med. Assn. Democrat. Roman Catholic. Club: Victoria (Riverside). Contbr. articles to profl. jours. Home: 2340 Arroyo Dr Riverside CA 92506 Office: 780 E Gilbert St San Bernardino CA 92404

DOOLIN, JAMES LAWRENCE, artist; b. Hartford, Conn., June 28, 1932; s. Lawrence James and Ruth Jean (Blodgett) D. B.F.A., Phila. Coll. Art, 1954; M.F.A., UCLA, 1971; Community coll. credential, Calif. With Union Carbide Corp., N.Y.C., 1964-65; instr. Praharan Tech. Coll., Melbourne, Australia, 1965-66; instr. dept. art UCLA, 1972-80, instr. extension service, 1971-80; instr. Otis/Parsons Sch. Design, Los Angeles, 1977-80; vis. artist, traveling lectr. Victorian Coll. Arts, Melbourne, 1978; vis. art educator Cerro Coso Community Coll., Ridgecrest, Calif., 1982; one-man shows include Gallery A, Melbourne, 1966, Central Street Gallery, Syndey, Australia, 1967, 70, Boise State U., 1974, Los Angeles Mcpl. Art Gallery, 1977, Victorian Coll. Arts, Melbourne, also 5 other Australian cities, 1978-79, Cerro Coso, Community Coll., 1982; exhibited in group shows including Seth Siegelaub Gallery, N.Y.C., 1964, Am. Gallery, N.Y.C., 1965, Gallery A, Melbourne and Sydney, 1967, Argus Gallery, Melbourne, 1967, Victorian Nat. Gallery, Melbourne, 1968, Art Gallery of New South Wales, Sydney, 1968, Long Beach Mus. Art (Calif.), 1971, Palos Verdes Art Mus. (Calif.), 1972, Cerritos Coll. Art Gallery, Norwalk, Calif., 1976, Artspace Gallery Los Angeles, 1977, DeYoung Mus. Downtown Ctr., San Francisco, 1977, Nev. Art Gallery, Reno, 1978, Rio Hondo Art Gallery, Whittier, Calif., 1982; represented in permanent collections U. Vt., Burlington, Long Beach Mus. Art. Australian Nat. Gallery, Canberra, Nat. Gallery Victoria, Melbourne, Art Gallery New South Wales, Sydney, Australian Nat. U., Canberra. Served with U.S. Army, 1955-57. Guggenheim Found. fellow, 1980-81; Nat. Endowment for Arts grantee, 1981-82. Mem. Los Angeles Contemporry Exhbns. Home and studio: 321 E 3d St Los Angeles CA 90013

DOOLITTLE, JOHN TAYLOR, state senator; b. Glendale, Calif., Oct. 30, 1950; s. Merrill T. and Dorothy Doolittle; B.A. in History with honors, U. Calif., Santa Cruz, 1972; J.D., McGeorge Sch. Law, U. Pacific, 1978; m. Julia Harlow, Feb. 17, 1979; 1 son, John Taylor. Admitted to Calif. bar, 1978; adminstrv. asst. to Sen. H.L. Richardson, exec. dir. Citizens Com. to Stop Crime, 1979-80; mem. Calif. State Senate from 3d Dist., Sacramento, 1980—. Mem. No. Calif. Peace Officers Assn. Republican. Mormon. Office: State Capitol Sacramento CA 95814

DOOLITTLE, PHILLIP LEWIS, financial executive; b. Williams, Calif., Sept. 8, 1953; s. George Lewis, Jr., and Letha M. (Briles) D.; B.A., U. Redlands, 1976; M.Adminstrn., Atkinson Grad. Sch. Adminstrn., Willamette U., 1979. Asst. dir. student activities, student union dir. U. Redlands, Calif., 1976-77, assoc. dean of admissions, 1979-81; planning and budget devel. asst., TRW Corp., San Bernardino, Calif., 1978, bus. mgr., 1981-83, sr. bus. mgr., San Diego, 1983—; research asst. Atkinson Grad. Sch. Adminstrn., Willamette U., Salem, Oreg., 1978-79; cons., counselor SBA, 1978-79; cons. Army C.E., Navigation Div., Waterway Maintenance Br., 1978. Active Friends of Redlands, Abraham Lincoln Meml. Assn., Friends of A.K. Smiley Library, Moore Hist. Found., PARTNERS, Inc.; alumni bd. U. Redlands. Presdl. Mgmt. Intern. Mem. Omicron Delta Kappa, Phi Gamma Nu. Democrat. Congregationalist. Club: Alumni Assn. Chi Sigma Chi (sec.). Condr. research govt. regulations and utility prices, 1978-79. Home: 4057 Brant St San Diego CA 92103 Office: 41040 Sorrento Valley Blvd San Diego CA 92121

DOOLITTLE, WILLIAM HOTCHKISS, internist; b. Cheshire, Conn., June 20, 1929; s. Joseph Delos and Geraldine (Lincoln) D.; B.S., U. Vt., 1956, M.D., 1960; m. Marla M. Rescott; 1 son, William Lawrence. Commd. lt. M.C., U.S. Army, 1959, advanced through grades to lt. col., 1971; intern U.S. Army Hosp., Fort Bragg, N.C., 1959-60; resident in internal medicine Walter Reed Gen. Hosp., Washington, 1961-64, ret., 1973; practice medicine specializing in internal medicine, Fairbanks, Alaska, 1973—; dir. Arctic Med. Research Lab. Alaska, Ft. Wainwright; pres. Fairbanks Internal Medicine and Diagnostic Center; staff Fairbanks Meml. Hosp., chief of staff, 1974-76. Bd. dirs. Fairbanks Meml. Hosp. Found. Served with USAF, 1947-53. Decorated Army Commendation medal, Legion of Merit. Diplomate Am. Bd. Internal Medicine. Fellow A.C.P.; mem. AAAS, AMA, Alaska Med. Assn., Fairbanks Med. Soc., Assn. Mil. Surgeons, Alpha Omega Alpha. Republican. Episcopalian. Club: Rotary. Contbr. articles in field to profl. jours. Home: 666 11th Ave Apt 207 Fairbanks AK Office: 1919 Lathrop St Fairbanks AK 99701

DOPP, CARYLON, real estate broker, educator; b. Wewoka, Okla., July 27, 1945; d. Claude Robert and Lois (Whitaker) Wilson; m. William T. Dopp, Mar. 13, 1963; children—Melannie, Robert, Philip. Grad. Realtors Inst., Nat. Assn. Realtors, 1977; cert. in real estate Contra Costa Coll., 1979. Realtor, assoc. Eyring Realty, El Sobrante, Calif., 1972-74, Locators Real Estate, El Sobrante and Pinole, Calif., 1974-78; sales mgr., Richmond, Calif., 1978-81; sales mgr. Bartels Realtors, Pinole, Calif., 1981—; instr. real estate Contra Costa Community Coll., 1978—. Mem. Nat. Assn. Realtors (cert. residential specialist), Calif. Assn. Realtors (dir. 1979-82), West Contra Costa Bd. Realtors (dir. 1979-80, named Realtor Assoc. of Yr. 1978, Pres. award for spl. services 1979), Pinole C. of C. Office: 3088 Pinole Valley Rd Pinole CA 94564

DOPP, WILLIAM FLOYD, advertising executive; b. Watertown, Wis., Apr. 30, 1942; s. William M. and June K. (White) D.; m. Janet M. Bochnowski, Sept. 8, 1962; children—William J., Douglas F. B.S. in Bus. and Journalism, Ind. U., 1969. With Wall St. Jour., N.Y.C., 1965-68, Chgo. Tribune, 1969-71; v.p., sales mgr. Chicagoland Broadcasters, Inc., 1971-76; pres. TDM Advt., Arlington Heights, Ill., 1976-79; pres., owner Great Western Advt., San Diego, 1979—; seminar leader San Diego State U., Palomar, Calif. Founder, treas. Rancho Bernardo Hist. Soc., San Diego. Mem. Advt. Writers League Calif., Rancho Bernardo C. of C., Escondido (Calif.) C. of C. Sigma Chi. Episcopalian. Clubs: Elks; Ind. U. Alumni (San Diego). Author: Copywriter's Idea Book, 1982. Home: 17212 Carranza Dr San Diego CA 92127 Office: 16766 Bernardo Ctr Dr San Diego CA 92128

DOPULOS, PETER PANTELIS, electric engineering executive; b. Buffalo, Feb. 13, 1925; s. Pantelis Peter and Olga (Maroudas) D.; B.S. in Engring., Wayne U., 1949; m. Ellen Paulos, July 2, 1978; children—Paul, Vincent; stepchildren—Barbara, Kathy, Leslie, Victoria. Chief engr. Lenawee Elec. Co., Adrian, Mich., 1960-64; asst. chief elec. engr. Smith, Hinchman & Gryllis, Detroit, 1964-70; dir. elec. engring. GPRA, Santa Ana, Calif., 1970-74; chief engr. Powerine Oil Co., Santa Fe Springs, Calif., 1974-77; v.p. engring. S&T Western, Inc., Newport Beach, Calif., 1977-82; mgr. elec. engring., power div. DMJM Corp., Los Angeles, 1982—; instr. elec. engring. Calif. State U., Los Angeles, UCLA. Bd. dirs. Long Beach Symphony; pres. Services for the Blind, 1978-80. Served with U.S. Army, 1942-45. Registered profl. engr., Calif., Pa. Fellow Inst. for Advancement of Engring.; mem. IEEE (sr., chmn. Indsl. Application Soc., Los Angeles chpt., 1975), Am. Inst. Plant Engrs. (cert.). Greek Orthodox. Club: St. Luke's Men's (Garden Grove, Calif.). Home: 664 Lausinda Ave Long Beach CA 90803 Office: 3250 Wilshire Blvd Los Angeles CA 90010

DORAN, DOROTHY FITZ, business educator; b. Nekoosa, Wis., Feb. 27, 1934; d. Edwin E. and Ruby E. (Burch) Larson; children—Jean Marie Fitz Harkey, Kenneth Lee, Cynthia Ann Fitz Whitney. B.S. with high distinction in Bus. and English, No. Ariz. U., 1969; M.A. in English, 1971; Ed.D. in Bus., Ariz. State U., 1980. Tchr. English, Cottonwood (Ariz.) Oak Creek Elem. Sch., 1969-70; tchr. bus. and English, Mingus Union High Sch., Cottonwood, 1970-79; mem. faculty dept. office adminstrn. Yavapai Coll., 1979—, chairperson Bus. div., 1981—; cons. Ariz. Dept. Edn. Mem. Ariz. Bus. Edn. Assn. (pres. 1980-81), Nat. Bus. Edn. Assn., Am. Vocat. Assn., Ariz. Edn. Assn., NEA, Internat. Word/Info. Processing Assn., Pi Omega Pi, Delta Pi Epsilon, Phi Kappa Phi, Alpha Delta Kappa, Phi Delta Kappa. Republican. Club: Soroptomists. Editor Ariz. Bus. Edn. Newsletter, 1972-74. Home: 315 E Carleton Prescott AZ 86301 Office: 1100 E Sheldon Prescott AZ 86301

DORAN, MARTHA SUTTON, corporation executive, accountant; b. Escondido, Calif., Mar. 7, 1952; d. Carl Leon and Jean (Godard) Sutton; m. Gary Wayne Doran, Dec. 27, 1975. B.A., Stephens Coll., 1973; postgrad. Ariz. State U., 1979-80. C.P.A., Calif. Acct. Acosta, Cordova & Pittman C.P.A.s, Phoenix, 1978-80, Apodaca, Finocchiaro & Co. C.P.A.s, Pasadena, Calif., 1980-81; controller Bill Palmer Assocs., El Monte, Calif., 1981—. Mem. Stephens Coll. Alumnae Assn. (pres. San Gabriel Valley). Republican. Christian Scientist.

DORAN, TIMOTHY PATRICK, school administrator, educator; b. N.Y.C., July 1, 1949; s. Joseph Anthony and Claire Marie (Griffin) D.; m. Kathleen Matava, Aug. 1, 1981; 1 dau., Claire Marie. B.A. in Econs., Le Moyne Coll., 1971; postgrad. U. Alaska, 1978—. Exec. dir. Project Equality of Northwest, Seattle, 1972-73; exec. dir. Jesuit Vol. Corps, Portland, Oreg., 1973-75; adminstrv. advisor Kaltag (Alaska) City Council, 1975-77; program developer Diocese of Fairbanks (Alaska), 1978-81; adminstr. St. Mary's (Alaska) High Sch., 1981—; mem. nat. com. Campaign for Human Devel., 1980-82; mem. Manpower Planning Council, Tanana Chiefs Conf., Fairbanks, 1976-77. Vol. Jesuit Vol. Corps, 1972-77; pres. Community Council, Sacred Heart Cathedral, Fairbanks, 1978-80. Mem. Assn. Supervision and Curriculum Devel., Coalition S.W. Educators. Office: Saint Marys High Sch PO Box 172 St Marys AK 99658

DORAN, VINCENT JAMES, steel fabricating company executive; b. Ephrata, Wash., June 13, 1917; s. Samuel Vincent and Sarah Anastasia (Fitzpatrick) D.; B. Phil., Gonzaga U., Spokane, 1946; m. Jean Arlene Birrer, Jan. 15, 1949; children—Vincent James, Mollie Jean, Michele Lee, Patrick Michael. Mgr., Flying Service, Coulee Dam, Wash., 1947-58; mgr. constrn. Morrison-Knudsen Co., Wash. and Alaska, 1959-60; co-owner C.R. Foss Inc., constrn., Anchorage, 1961-64; mgr. Steel Fabricators, Anchorage, 1965—. Active Boy Scouts Am.; co-founder, pres. Chugach Rehab. Assn., 1962; mem. Alaska Gov.'s Rehab. Adv. Bd., 1962-63; mem. CAP. Served with USAAF, 1943-45, USAF, 1949-50. Decorated Air medal with 4 clusters. Mem. Anchorage C. of C., Welding Inst. Alaska (co-organizer, dir. 1977-78), Water Pollution Control Fedn. Roman Catholic. Club: Toastmasters. Designer packaged water, sewage treatment plants and water collection systems Arctic communities. Home: 3811 Knik Ave Anchorage AK 99503 Office: Steel Fabricators 2132 Railroad Ave Anchorage AK 99501

DORE, FRED HUDSON, state supreme ct. justice; b. Seattle, July 31, 1925; s. Fred Hudson and Ruby T. (Kelly) D.; B.S.F.S., Georgetown Fgn. Service Sch., 1946; J.D., Georgetown U., 1949; m. Mary S. Shuham, Nov. 26, 1956; children—Margaret, Fred Hudson, Teresa, Tim, Jane. Bar: Wash. 1949. Practiced in Seattle, 1949-77; mem. Wash. Ho. of Reps., 1953-59, Wash. State Senate, 1959-74; mem. Wash. State Ct. Appeals, 1977-80; mem. Wash. State Supreme Ct., Olympia, 1981—. Office: State Supreme Ct Temple Justice Olympia WA 98504

DOREN, BARBARA ANN, home economist, educator; b. San Diego, June 28, 1940; d. Therold Charles and Ann Mary Witte; m. John L. Doren, June 18, 1961; 1 son, John Scott. B.A. with honors, San Diego State U., 1980. Home cons. Thermador Waste King, Calif.; 1970—; tchr. home econs. San Diego Community Coll., 1980—; personal fashion cons. Mem. Home Economists in Bus., Calif. Home Econs. Assn. Republican. Roman Catholic.

DORF, MILTON IRVING, drug store chain exec.; b. Newport News, Va., June 4, 1921; s. Samuel Leonard and Mary Madeline (Moore) D.; A.B. magna cum laude, Washington Coll., Chestertown, Md., 1942; m. Barbara Elaine Levine, Oct. 19, 1949; children—Lauren, Steven. Buyer gen. mdse. Penn Fruit Co., Phila., 1955-60, dir. gen. mdse., 1960-69, also dir. Quaker Drug store chain div., 1967-69; dir. gen. mdse. Bohack Corp., N.Y.C., 1969-71, also v.p. Bohack Super Drugs stores, 1970-71; pres. Drug Pride Corp. div. Food Fair Stores, Inc., Phila., 1971-78; mem. exec. com. J. M. Fields Dept. Store, Phila., 1975—; pres. Argold Press, Inc., 1978—; mem. gen. mdse. com. Supermarket Inst., also Topco Assos.; owner Argold Press (comml. printing co.), 1978—, The Magic Lens. Pres., Laverock Civic Assn., Wyncote, Pa., 1956-69. Served to lt. USCG, 1942-45. Mem. Nat. Assn. Chain Drug Stores. Jewish. Club: Rotary. Home: 1235 Kings Rd #314 Los Angeles CA 90069

DORGAN, JOHN JOSEPH, oil company executive; b. Providence, Sept. 1, 1923; s. John Joseph and Isabelle Regina (Carroll) D.; m. Cynthia Charlton Codrington, June 8, 1946; children—Carroll S., Elizabeth B., Peter M., John C. A.B., Harvard U., 1944, M.B.A., 1948. With Continental Oil Co., 1948-72, treas., dir. supply and transp., London, to 1972; mng. dir. RBP, Belgium, 1972; v.p. Occidental Petroleum Corp., Los Angeles, after 1972, treas., now exec. v.p.-fin.; dir. Can. Occidental Petroleum Ltd., Quimica Hooker S.A., Enoxy Inc. Served to lt. j.g. USNR, 1943-46. Clubs: Harvard, Links (N.Y.C.); Lansdowne (London); Regency (Los Angeles); Am. Petroleum Inst. 25 Yr. Office: 10889 Wilshire Blvd Los Angeles CA 90024

DORIO, EVELYN, author; b. Duryea, Pa.; d. John and Rose Marie (Canonico) D.; B.A., U. So. Calif.; m. Harold J. Nicolais. Freelance writer, 1952—; author essays in Involvement, 1977, children's story in Courage, 1979; contbr. story to Suspense Stories, 1963; author: (juvenile) Pigalee Pink, 1980; also other articles, essays, short stories, poetry. Vol., Interfaith Servicemen's Center, San Clemente, Calif., 1968—. Recipient 1st pl. award contest Spellbinders, Orange County Writers Group, 1974; 2d pl. award (2) contest Press Women Orange County, 1975. Mem. AAUW, Press Women Orange County (awards 1975). Democrat. Presbyterian. Address: 32741 Mediterranean Dr Laguna Niguel CA 92677

DORLAND, FRANK NORTON, art conservator; b. Peru, Nebr., Oct. 11, 1914; s. Frank Norton and Marion Hope (Abbot) D.; student Calif. Christian Coll., 1931-33; San Diego State Coll., 1933-38; m. Mabel Vyvyan Jolliffe, July 29, 1938. Artist preliminary design engring. Convair Co., San Diego, Calif., 1938-49; pvt. practice as art conservator, La Jolla, Calif., 1949-59, San Francisco, 1959-63, Mill Valley, Calif., 1963-73, Santa Barbara, Calif., 1973—; engaged in authentication and classification art objects; cons. art assns. galleries, museums, collectors, churches. Mem. Internat. Inst. for Conservation, Internat. Council Museums, Am. Mus. Assn. Pioneer in use of spl. waxes in painting; inventor oil and water mix wax mediums; engaged in research and devel. waxes and resins and properties and usage of natural quartz crystal, also bio-crystallography, interchange of energies between electronic quartz crystals and the human mind. Address: 1867 Mountain View Dr Los Osos CA 93402

DORMAN, REX LEE, financial executive; b. Boise, Idaho, Jan. 13, 1934; s. Lee R. and Leona D.; m. Marilyn J. Frazier, May 6, 1956; children—Donald, Michael, Diane. A.A., Boise Jr. Coll., 1954; B.S., U. Idaho, 1961; Exec. Program, Stanford U., 1975. C.P.A., cert. internal auditor, Idaho. With Touche, Ross, Bailey & Smart, 1960-66, Low, Viehwig Hill & Grow, 1961-66; internal auditor Boise Cascade Corp., 1966-69, mgr. internal audit, 1969-73, asst. controller, 1973-75, controller, 1975-80, v.p., controller, 1980-82, v.p. fin., 1982—; dir. Boise Cascade Can., Ltd.; mgmt. com. Boise So. Co.; fin. mgmt. com. Am. Paper Inst.; forest products task group Fin. Acctg. Standards Bd.; chmn. bus. adv. bd. U. Idaho. Chmn. Assoc. Taxpayers Idaho, 1981; treas. Boise Civic Opera, 1977-80; Served to lt. (j.g.) USN, 1954-58. Mem. Idaho Soc. C.P.A.s (pres. 1976), Am. Inst. C.P.A.s. Office: PO Box 50 Boise ID 83728

DORN, MARIAN MARGARET, sports management administrator; North Chicago, Ill., Sept. 25, 1931; d. John and Marian (Petkovsek) Jelovsek; m. Eugene G. Dorn, Aug. 2, 1952 (div. 1975); 1 son, Bradford Jay. B.S., U. Ill., 1953; M.S., U. So. Calif., 1961. Tchr., North Chicago Community High Sch., 1954-56; tchr., advisor activities, high sch., Pico-Rivera, Calif., 1956-62; tchr., coach Calif. High Sch., Whittier, 1962-65; instr. phys. edn., chmn. dept., coach, asst. chmn. div. women's athletic dir. Cypress (Calif.) Coll., 1966-82; mgr. Billie Jean King Tennis Ctr., Long Beach, Calif., 1982—; founder, pres. Brymar Enterprises, Inc., Huntington Beach, Calif.; pres. So. Calif. Athletic Conf., 1981. Recipient cert. of merit Cypress Elem. Sch. Dist., 1976. Mem. Calif. (v.p. So. dist.), San Gabriel Valley (pres.) assns. health, phys. edn. and recreation, So. Cal. Community Coll. Athletic Council (sec., dir. pub. relations), NEA, Calif. Tchrs. Assn., AAHPER, Ladies Profl. Golf Assn., AAUW. Republican. Conglist. Author: Bowling Manual, 1974. Office: 7561 W Center St Suite 40 Huntington Beach CA 92647

DORN, ROSE MARIE, advertising executive, interior design consultant; b. Milw., Jan. 23, 1946; d. John Paul and Irene Mary (Korenak) D. B.A., U. Wis.-Milw., 1968. Buyer, McCann-Erickson, Milw., 1968-74; sr. media planner and buyer Eisaman Johns & Laws Advt., Los Angeles, 1974-77; sr. media supr. Chiat/Day Advt., Los Angeles, 1977-79; asst. media dir. Dailey & Assocs., Los Angeles, 1979—; guest lectr. mktg. U. So. Calif. Active McGovern presdl. campaign, 1972, Advt. Industry Emergency Fund, Equal Rights Amendment ratification. Democrat. Roman Catholic. Home: 1522 S Centinela Ave #202 Los Angeles CA 90025 Office: 3055 Wilshire Blvd Suite 1100 Los Angeles CA 90010

DORN, RUSSELL WILLIAM, JR., city manager; b. Jersey City, July 1, 1946; s. Russell William and Catherine Veronica (O'Mara) D.; B.A. in Govt. with honors, U. Ariz., 1968; M.P.A., Fairleigh Dickinson U., 1975. Mgmt. analyst budget div. City of Jersey City, 1972, asst. to bus. adminstr., 1972-73, sr. mgmt. analyst dept. pub. safety, 1973-74; prin. mgmt. analyst budget control office Hudson County, N.J., 1974-76, county adminstr., 1976-78; city mgr. City of Las Vegas, 1978—. Served to 1st lt. U.S. Army, 1970-71. Recipient spl. recognition award Alliance for Volunteerism, Mayor's Awards Program. Mem. Internat. City Mgmt. Assn., VFW. Democrat. Roman Catholic.

D'ORNELLAS, TAMARA LYNN, bank marketing executive; b. Phoenix, Aug. 6, 1957; d. Frederick Thomas and Darlene Ann (Slemons) Meehan; m. Robert William D'Ornellas, Aug. 7, 1982. B.A. in Econs., Bus., U. So. Calif., 1978; Community service rep. Del Taco, Inc., Costa Mesa Calif., 1978-79; mktg. officer, Calif. First Bank, 1979-81, sr. mktg. officer, 1981—. Mem. Orange County C. of C. (econ. devel. council), Orange County Indsl. League, Internat. Econ. Honor Soc.

DORR, AIMEE, educator; b. Los Angeles, Sept. 20, 1942; d. Thomas Osborn and Mary Alice (Perkey) D.; m. Larry John Leifer, Dec. 19, 1962; 1 son, Simeon Kel Leifer; m. 2d, Donald Warren Dorr-Bremme, Aug. 6, 1977; 1 son, John Thomas Dorr-Bremme. B.S., Stanford U., 1964, M.A., 1966, Ph.D. in Psychology, 1970. Acting asst. prof. communication Stanford U., 1967-70, research assoc. in psychiatry and communication, 1970-71, research assoc. in psychiatry, acting asst. prof. communication, childcare policy analyst in Pres.'s Office, 1971-72; asst. prof. edn. Harvard U., 1972-76, assoc. prof., 1976-78; assoc. prof. communications Annenberg Sch. Communication, U. So. Calif., Los Angeles, 1978-81, prof., 1981; prof. edn. UCLA, 1981—; cons. Children's TV Workshop, NBC, Action for Children's TV, others. Fellow Am. Psychol. Assn., Am. Ednl. Research Assn., Soc. Research in Child Devel., Internat. Communication Assn., Amnesty Internat., Friends Com. on Nat. Legis., Action for Children's TV, Friends of South Pasadena Library. Democrat. Contbr. articles to profl. jours. Office: 333 Moore Hall UCLA Los Angeles CA 90024

DORR, MARK ANTHONY, accountant; b. Cheyenne, Wyo., Nov. 9, 1953; s. Billy George Dorr and Dolores Marian (MacGrady) Carver; 1 dau., Ashley. B.S., B.A., U. Denver, 1976. C.P.A., Wyo., Colo. Staff acct. Coopers & Lybrand, Denver, 1976-78; managing ptnr. Dorr & Assocs., Gillette, Wyo., 1978—. Mem. Campbell County Parks and Recreation Bd., past pres. 4th of July Com.; Republican party ward del. Recipient Disting. Service award Jaycees, 1983. Mem. Am. Inst. C.P.A.s (relations with educators com.), Wyo. Soc. C.P.A.s (past chmn. edn. com., mgmt. acctg. practice com.), Colo. C.P.A. Soc., Gillette Soc. C.P.A.s (co-founder, past pres.). Author: Full Disclosure; columnist. Office: Dorr & Assocs Lakeway Profl Ctr Suite 300 Gillette WY 82716

DORRANCE, STURGES DICK, III, broadcasting executive; b. N.Y.C., Jan. 1, 1942; s. Sturges Dick and Marjorie Colt (Wooster) D; m. Pamela Winters, Sept. 21, 1963; children—Elizabeth, Sarah, Meredith, Jennifer. B.A. in English, Dartmouth Coll., 1963. With King Broadcasting, Seattle, 1966—, gen. sales mgr., 1976-82, v.p., gen. mgr. King-TV, 1982—. Past pres. Northwest Chamber Orch. Served to 1st lt. U.S. Army, 1964-66. Mem. Seattle Advt. Fedn. (dir.), TV Bur. Sales Adv. Com. Anglican. Club: Wash. Athletic. Office: King-TV 333 Dexter N Seattle WA 98103

DORSAY, RICHARD HAL, radiologist; b. N.Y.C., Apr. 30, 1939; s. Benjamin Charles and Rose (Tarush) D.; B.S., Tufts U., 1960, M.D. with honors in research, 1964; m. Dorothy Alta Kurzrock, Jan. 19, 1964; children—Adam Akiva, Jennifer Louise. Intern, Montefiore Hosp., Bronx, N.Y., 1964-65, resident in radiology, 1965-69; chmn. dept. radiology Los Gatos (Calif.) Community Hosp., 1970-73; chmn. dept. radiology Kaiser Permanente Hosp., South San Francisco, 1973-78, sec. to med. staff; chmn. chiefs radiology No. Calif. Kaiser Permanente Hosps.; asst. clin. prof. radiology U. Calif. Med. Sch., San Francisco, 1976-77, asso. clin. prof., 1977—; faculty mem. XIV Ann. Congress Radiology, San Salvador, El Salvador, 1975; vol. radiologist Project Hope, Guatemala, 1978. vis lectr. radiology U. Madrid Med. Sch., 1976. Active Am. Cancer Soc. Served with USPHS, 1968-70. Diplomate Am. Bd. Radiology. Mem. AMA, Am. Coll. Radiology, Calif. Radiol. Soc., YMCA. Office: 1200 El Camino Real South San Francisco CA 94080

DORSEY, CHARLES GARFIELD, travel agy. exec.; b. Vinton, Iowa, May 9, 1918; s. Charles Alvey and Elsie (Jensen) D.; A.A., Hancock Coll., 1939; student U. So. Calif., 1939-41; m. Dorothy Mae Barr, June 18, 1943; children—Sandra Jeane, Dianna Lynn. Dist. mgr. Santa Maria Amusement Co. (Calif.), 1945-66; pres., gen. mgr. Santa Maria Travel Center, 1961—, Lompoc Travel Center (Calif.), 1961—, Los Padres Travel, Santa Maria, 1966—; chmn. bd. Los Padres Nat. Bank, 1963-64. Mem. Joint Civilian Orientation Conf., Dept. Def., 1969. Mem. Santa Maria City Planning Commn., 1959-62; city councilman Santa Maria, 1962-65, vice mayor, 1962-65, chmn. council adv. com., 1965-66; mem. County Adv. Com., 1966—. Served with USNR, 1943-45. Named Airways Internat. Licensee of Year, 1968. Mem. Aircraft Owners and Pilots Assn., Valley Developers Orgn., Am. Soc. Travel Agts., Assn. Retail Travel Agts., Santa Maria C. of C. (dir. 1955-65, pres. 1959-60), Three-Valley Pilots Assn. (pres. 1974-75). Republican. Methodist. Rotarian, Elk. Clubs: Executives, Ambassadors. Home: 2106 Glacier La Lake Marie Estates Santa Maria CA 93454 Office: 215 E Main St Santa Maria CA 93454

DORSEY, THOMAS BROOKSHIER, publishing and broadcasting exec.; b. Keokuk, Iowa, Apr. 30, 1928; s. Frank Blinn and Martha Johanna (Brookshier) D.; student DePauw U., 1946-47, State U. Iowa, 1947-50; m. Helen Danner, June 30, 1951; children—Diana, Blinn. Corr., Des Moines Register, 1949-51; pub. affairs dir. Am. Forces Radio and TV Network, Frankfurt, W.Ger., 1954-55; chief European corr. Times Pub. Co., 1954-56; nat. affairs editor Am. Weekend, Washington, 1956-57; editor, gen. mgr. N.Y. Herald Tribune News Service, 1957-59; v.p. Barnet & Reef Assos., Inc., N.Y.C., 1959-63; v.p., dir. internat. div. John Moynahan & Co., N.Y.C., 1963; asso. producer Adlai Stevenson Reports, ABC-TV, 1962-63; dir., editor Newsday Spls. (syndicate) Newsday Inc., 1964-69; v.p., editor Chgo. Tribune-N.Y. News Syndicate, Inc., N.Y.C., 1969-74; sales mgr. Knight News Wire, 1972-74; dir., editor Los Angeles Times Syndicate, 1975-77, dir. Los Angeles Times/Washington Post News Service, 1975-77; chmn., chief exec. officer Dorsey Communications, Inc., 1977—; exec. v.p., chief operating officer Los Angeles Prodn. Group, 1977-79. Served with USAF, 1951-54. Mem. Advt. Club Los Angeles, Aviation/Space Writers Assn., Newspaper Comics Council, Internat. Radio and TV Soc., Internat. Platform Assn., Sigma Delta Chi. Methodist. Clubs: Nat. Press, Deadline (exec. bd., dir.). Home: 9239 Doheny Rd Los Angeles CA 90069 Office: 9239 Doheny Rd Los Angeles CA 90069 also Pink Sands Harbour Island Bahamas

DOSSETT, LAWRENCE SHERMAN, engineering consultant; b. Santa Ana, Calif., May 11, 1936; s. Wheeler Sherman and Eunice Elizabeth (Bright) D.; student U. Ariz., 1957-58, U. Calif., Irvine, 1973-75, Loyola Marymount Coll., 1974; m. Joanne Kallisch; children—Todd Sherman, Garrick Robert (dec.), Dana Shelene, Ryan William. Engring. draftsman Hughes Aircraft Co., Tucson, 1955-57, John J. Foster Mfg. Co., Costa Mesa, Calif., 1958, Standard Elec. Products, Costa Mesa, 1959; engring. mgr. Electronic Engring. Co., Santa Ana, 1959-79; product quality mgr. Farwest Data Systems, Irvine, Calif., 1979-82; cons. Comserv Corp., 1982—, Western Electronic Mfrs. Assn., Am. Prodn. and Inventory Control Soc., 1976-82, Computer Mfrs. Conf., 1980. Cert. in mgmt. Am. Mgmt. Assn., 1968. Mem. Am. Prodn. and Inventory Control Soc. Club: Elks. Co-author patent reel spindle, 1972. Office: Comserv Corp 18411 Crenshaw Blvd Torrance CA 90504

DOST, JEANNE EBBERT, ednl. adminstr.; b. Walla Walla, Wash., Aug. 12, 1929; d. William Clifford and Margie Alice (Patrick) Ebbert; m. Frank Norman Dost, Sept. 3, 1950; children—Karen Elizabeth, Frederick Ebbert. B.A. in Econs., Wash. State U., 1951, M.A., 1953; Ph.D. in Econs., Radcliffe Coll., 1959. Faculty, Kans. State U., 1956-59, Wash. State U., 1959-61; faculty Oreg. State U., Corvallis, 1965—, dir. Women's Studies, 1973—; econ. cons. Founder, Oreg. Women's Polit. Caucus, 1971-74, 1st pres., 1973-74. NSF fellow, 1970. Mem. Am. Econ. Assn., Royal Econ. Soc., Nat. Women's Studies Assn., N.W. Women's Studies Assn., Western Social Sci. Assn., Phi Kappa Phi, Mortar Bd., Phi Chi Theta. Contbr. articles to profl. jours.; author: Beginner's Guide to Women Studies, 1983; Spatial Mobility of Female Worker, 1971; Model of Feminist Development, 1979; Achieving Economic Equity for Homemakers, 1982. Office: Dept Women Studies Oreg State Univ Corvallis OR 97331

DOTO, IRENE LOUISE, statistician; b. Wilmington, Del., May 7, 1922; d. Antonio and Teresa (Tabasso) D. B.A., U. Pa., 1943; M.A., Temple U., 1948, Columbia U., 1954. Engring. asst. RCA-Victor, 1943-44; research asst. U. Pa., 1944; actuarial clk. Penn Mut. Life Ins. Co., 1944-46; instr. math. Temple U., 1946-53; commd. sr. asst. health officer USPHS, 1954, advanced through grades to dir., 1963; statistician Communicable Disease Ctr., Atlanta, 1954-55, Kansas City, Kans., 1955-67; chief statis. and publ. services, ecol. investigations program Ctr. for Disease Control, Kansas City, 1967-73, chief statis. services, div. hepatitis and viral enteritis, Phoenix, 1973—; mem. adj. faculty Phoenix Ctr., Ottawa U., 1982—. Mem. Am. Statis. Assn., Biometrics Soc., Am. Pub. Health Assn., Ariz. Pub. Health Assn. (exec. council), Am. Soc. Quality Control, Ariz. Council Engring. and Sci. Assn. (treas. 1982-83), Bus. and Profl. Women's Club Phoenix, Sigma Xi, Pi Mu Epsilon. Office: Center for Disease Control 4402 N 7th St Phoenix AZ 85014

DOTY, HORACE (JAY), JR., theater administrator, musician; b. St. Petersburg, Fla., May 25, 1924; s. Horace Herndon and Mabel (Bruce) D.; student Sherwood Music Sch., Chgo., 1942-43; B.A. in Music, Pomona Coll., 1950; cert. La Verne Coll., 1969; M.A. in Edn., Claremont Grad. Sch., 1972; m. Wanda L. Flory, Dec. 27, 1947; 1 dau., Janet. Tchr. piano, Claremont, Calif., 1950—; gen. mgr. Hebert's Co., Claremont, 1950-60; propr. Jay Doty's Inc., Claremont, 1960-68; concert mgr. Claremont Colls., 1968-73, supr. Garrison Theater, U. Center Box Office, dir. Auditorium, theater events, coordinator programs, 1973-79, 81—; exec. dir. Flint Ctr. for Performing Arts, Cupertino, Calif., 1979-81. Mem. blue ribbon com. Fox Theater Restoration, Pomona, Calif., 1982. Mem. Claremont Bicentennial Com. for Performing Arts, 1975—, Claremont Coordinating Council, 1966-67, A.R.C., Claremont, 1976 , Claremont Family Service, 1966-67. Served with inf. AUS, 1943-46. Mem. Assn. Coll. and Univ. Concert Mgrs. (dir. 1983—), Western Alliance Arts Adminstrs. (pres. 1975-77), Auditorium Mgrs., Claremont C. of C. (pres. 1965-66). Home: 1115 Oak Hollow Rd Claremont CA 91711 Office: Claremont Colls Center Performing Arts Bridges Auditorium Claremont CA 91711

DOTY, WILLIAM BRYANT, publicity specialist; b. Kansas City, Mo., Feb. 18, 1942; s. Thomas William and Maxine Alva (Daniel) D. B.S. in Journalism, U. Kans., 1965. Field editor Charles Scribners Sons, N.Y.C., 1965-69; dir. prodn. publicity Metromedia Producers Corp., Los Angeles, 1972-83, publicity dir. Merv Griffin Show, 1974-83, dir. prodn. publicity, 1982—. Metromedia liaison Publicity/Press Roundtable U. Calif.-Pomona, 1975; chmn. editorial com. Image mag., 1982; judge Emmy awards, 1979-81. Recipient Gavel award ABA, 1975. Mem. Internat. Alliance Theatrical and Stage Employees (AFL-CIO), S.A.G., Nat. Acad. TV Arts and Scis., Greenpeace, Calif. Scholarship Fedn. (life), Gen. Soc. Mayflower Descs. Office: Metromedia Producers Corp 5746 Sunset Blvd Hollywood CA 90028

DOUGHERTY, CELIA BERNIECE, educator; b. Toronto, Ohio, Aug. 7, 1935; d. Ernest Merle and Dorothy Grace (Erwin) Putnam; student (scholar) Ohio U., 1953-54; B.A., Calif. State U., Fullerton, 1971, M.S., 1974; doctoral candidate U. So. Calif.; m. William Vincent Dougherty, May 14, 1955; children—Marie Collette, Michael Charles. Reading specialist Anaheim (Calif.) Union High Sch. Dist., 1972-78, asst. prin. jr. high, 1978-80; asst. prin. jr. high Orange (Calif.) Unified Sch. Dist., 1980—. Leader, Girl Scouts, 1968-71. Mem. Orange County Reading Assn. (dir. 1978-83, pres. 1982-83), Calif. Reading Assn., Internat. Reading Assn., Assn. Calif. Sch. Adminstrs., Assn. Supervision and Curriculum Devel., Educare. Phi Kappa Phi, AAUW, Phi Alpha Theta, Phi Delta Gamma. Democrat. Home: 860 S Cardiff St Anaheim CA 92806 Office: 370 N Glassell St Orange CA 92666

DOUGHERTY, FREDERICK EARL, county ofcl.; b. Oconomowoc, Wis. June 16, 1929; s. Bert F. and Eleonore L. Dougherty; A.A., Pasadena City Coll., 1949; B.A., Occidental Coll., 1952; M.S., Calif. State U., 1963; postgrad. U. So. Calif., 1963-64; m. Viola M. Takaro, Apr. 21, 1956; children—Frederick Earl, Devon D. Real estate appraiser Los Angeles County, 1957-60, sr. appraiser, 1961-64, prin. appraiser, 1964-69, chief appraiser, 1971-80; ops. mgr. Govt. Ctr., 1968-71, chief spl. services div., 1980-82; chief real estate div. Los Angeles County Assessor, 1982—; tchr. Los Angeles Community Coll. Dist., 1963-68. Active local council Boy Scouts Am.; pres. S. Pasadena Band Parents, 1971-73; mem. exec. com. Pasadena Tournament of Roses, 1976—. Served with U.S. Army, 1953-55. Recipient medal of Merit, Silver Beaver award, Order of Arrow, Boy Scouts Am. Cert. rev. appraiser. Mem. Internat. Assn. Assessors, Nat. Assn. Rev. Appraisers, Soc. Real Estate Appraisers, Assn. Govt. Appraisers, Western Govtl. Research Assn., Sigma Zeta Psi, Pi Sigma Alpha. Methodist. Contbr. articles to profl. jours. Office: 500 W Temple St Los Angeles CA 90012

DOUGHERTY, HOWARD WILLIAM, oil and gas producer; b. Kansas City, Mo., Jan. 5, 1915; s. Frank C. and Elsie (Braecklein) D.; m. Aug. 3, 1940; children—William, Robert, Patrick, Michael, Mary, Peter. B.S. in Earth Sci., Stanford U., 1938. Oil and gas producer, Pasadena, Calif., 1947—; dir. Santa Anita Consol., Inc.; pres. Pioneer Kettleman Co., Book Cliffs Oil & Gas Co. Regent emeritus Loyola Marymount U.; chmn. exec. com. Conservation Com. Calif.; trustee Neuro Scis. Inst. Mem. Ind. Petroleum Assn. Am. (dir.), Beta Theta Pi. Clubs: Los Angeles Country, California, Bohemian, San Francisco Religious Order of Malta, Mil. Order of St. Lazarus (comdr.), Hollywood Turf (past dir.). Office: 77 N Oak Knoll Ave Suite 103 Pasadena CA 91101

DOUGHERTY, PAUL MCCORD, criminalist, lawyer; b. Los Angeles, Apr. 30, 1933; s. Paul Sarsfield and Bernice (McCord) D.; B.S., U. Calif.-Berkeley, 1956; J.D., Lincoln U., 1971; m. JoAnne Logue, Dec. 28, 1955; children—Anne Colleen, Paul Joseph. With San Mateo County (Calif.), 1960—, chief criminalist in charge Lab. Criminalistics, 1967—; admitted to Calif. bar, 1972; lectr. criminalistics and law San Jose State

U., 1973-78; cons. in field. Served with M.I., USNR, 1956-60. Calif. Council Criminal Justice grantee, 1971-73. Fellow Am. Acad. Forensic Scis., Royal Microscopical Soc. Eng.; mem. Calif. Assn. Criminalists, Assn. Firearms Tool Mark Examiners. Home: 1903 Brewster Ave Redwood City CA 94062 Office: 31 Tower Rd San Mateo CA 94402

DOUGHERTY, RALEIGH GORDON, mfr.'s rep.; b. Saginaw, Mich., Aug. 19, 1928; s. Raleigh Gordon and Helen Jean (McCrum) D.; 1 dau., Karen Kealani. Salesman, H.D. Hudson Mfg. Co., Chgo., 1946-48; field sales rep. Jensen Mfg. Co., Chgo., 1948-50; field sales mgr. Regency Idea, Indpls., 1950-54; mgr. Brenna & Browne, Honolulu, 1954-56; owner, pres. Dougherty Enterprises, Honolulu, 1956—. Served with U.S. Army, 1950-52. Mem. Hawaii Hotel Assn., Internat. Home Furnishings Reps. Assn. Republican. Methodist. Club: Elks. (past trustee Hawaii). Home: 1130 Kulauala Way Honolulu HI 96825 Office: PO Box 25400 Honolulu HI 96825

DOUGHERTY, RICHARD L., accountant, educator; b. Redlands, Calif., May 14, 1934; s. Robert L. and Esther L. D.; m. Mary Mann, Sept. 19, 1959; children—Michael, William. B.A. in Econs., U. Redlands, 1956; M.S. in Taxation, Golden Gate U., 1982. C.P.A., Calif. Staff acct. Arthur Andersen & Co., Los Angeles, 1956-60; ptnr. Harris & Corp., C.P.A.s, Los Angeles, 1960-75, Fox & Co., C.P.A.s, Los Angeles, 1975-80; prin. R. L. Dougherty & Co., C.P.A.s, Los Angeles, 1980—; instr. in banking and fin. Golden Gate U.; dir. Calif. Profl. Savs & Loan. Served with U.S. Army, 1957-59. Mem. Am. Inst. C.P.A.s, Calif. Soc. C.P.A.s. Club: Masons. Office: 615 S Flower St Suite 1009 Los Angeles CA 90017

DOUGHERTY, THOMAS ANTHONY, aerospace engr.; b. Wichita, Kans., Dec. 31, 1937; s. Ralph C. and Minnie (Daly) D.; m. Joyce Allegro, June 15, 1963; children—Jennifer, Gregory, Mitchell, Kevin. B.S. in Chemistry, Wichita State U., 1960, M.S. in Chemistry, 1962; Ph.D. in Phys. Chemistry, Iowa State U., 1966. Research engr. Boeing Co., Wichita, 1966-69, sr. research specialist, Seattle, 1969-72; sr. staff scientist Ford Aerospace, Palo Alto, Calif., 1972-78, spacecraft mktg. mgr., 1978-80, spacecraft engring. mgr., 1980-82, dep. program mgr., 1982—. Mem. AIAA, Am. Mgmt. Assn., Phi Lambda Upsilon. Republican. Roman Catholic. Clubs: WDL Golf (Palo Alto), KC. Contbr. articles profl. jours. Patentee in field. Home: 1804 Frobisher Way San Jose CA 95125 Office: 3939 Fabian Way Palo Alto CA 94303

DOUGHTY, DALE, corrosion engineer; b. Sycamore, Ill., Oct. 20, 1944; s. John R. and Dorothy M. (Lambert) D.; m. Shereen T. Stanton, June 11, 1970; children—Theron S., Odette R. B.A. in Edn., U. Wash., 1971, B.S. in Physics, 1976. Registered profl. engr., Wash. physics, chemistry, biology tchr. schs. New South Wales, Australia, 1971-72; engr. Boeing Co., Seattle, 1972-77; project engr. Norton Corrosion Ltd. Inc., 1977—; condr. ann. corrosion control seminar Alaska Profl. Design Council, 1981-83. Democratic Precinct Committeeman, 39th Legis. Dist., 1982. Served with USAF, 1963-67. Mem. Nat. Assn. Corrosion Engrs., Am. Water Works Assn. Ex-Serviceman's Club of Richmond (Australia). Office: Norton Corrosion Ltd Inc 22327 89th Ave SE Woodinville WA 98072

DOUGHTY, LESLIE JOHN TREVALYN (TREVOR DOUGHTY), insurance company executive; b. Wimbledon, Eng., Aug. 20, 1922; s. Reginald John and Ethel Marian (Burch) D.; came to U.S., 1966, naturalized, 1972; student U. London, 1941-42, 47-48, Royal Acad. Dramatic Art, 1942; m. Reine Claire Berger, Feb. 22, 1960 (dec. Oct. 1971); m. 2d, Frances Farwell, Mar. 23, 1974. Tech. mgr. Anglo S. African Devel. Assn., 1948-50; chief purchasing officer PWD-MECH, No. Rhodesian Govt., 1950-56; v.p. First Permanent Bldg. Soc., East Africa Ltd., 1956-66; mgr. Occidental Life Ins. Co., Burbank, Calif., 1967-73, asst. dir. advanced mktg. dept., 1973-78, dir. tech. adminstrn., 1978—; actor and scriptwriter. Served to maj. Brit. Army, 1942-47. C.L.U. Fellow Inc. Soc. Valuers and Auctioneers, Gt. Britain Inst. Estate Agts., Auctioneers and Valuers Rhodesia; mem. Inst. Valuers S. Africa, Glendale-Burbank Life Underwriters Assn. (pres.), Royal Soc. St. George (past pres.). Clubs: Masons, Rotary; Mombasa Yacht; Los Angeles Athletic. Contbr. articles to profl. jours. Home: 740 S Ridgeley Dr Los Angeles CA 90036 Office: Transamerica Center Olive at Hill Sts Los Angeles CA 90015

DOUGLAS, DONALD WILLS, JR., banker; b. Washington, July 3, 1917; s. Donald W. and Charlotte (Ogg) D.; Student Stanford U., 1934-38, Curtiss-Wright Tech. Inst., 1939; m. Molly McIntosh, May 1, 1939 (dec.); children—Victoria, Holly; m. 2d, Jean Cooper, Aug. 17, 1950. With Douglas Aircraft Co., 1939-67, corp. v.p., 1951-57, pres., 1957-67; sr. corp. v.p. adminstrn. McDonnell Douglas Corp., 1971-72; pres., chief exec. officer Douglas Devel. Co., Irvine, Calif., 1972-74; chmn. bd. Capistrano Nat. Bank (Calif.), 1975-82, Capistrano Bancorp., 1981—; 1979—; dir. Partners Real Estate Inc., Des Moines, 1979—; chmn. bd. Biphase Energy Systems, Santa Monica, Calif., 1980-81, sr. cons. market devel., 1981—; dir. Hilton Corp. Chmn. bd. trustees Donald Douglas Mus. and Library, 1975—; mem. Pres. Eisenhower's Com. on Youth Fitness, 1958-59. Decorated chevalier Legion of Honor (France), 1961; named officer Order of Merit Republic Italy. Mem. Nat. Def. Transp. Assn., Aerospace Industries Assn. (chmn. 1964), Clubs: Conquistadores del Cielo; Transpacific Yacht; Los Angeles Country; Confrerie de la Chaine des Rotisseures. Home: 707 Brooktree Rd Pacific Palisades CA 90272 Office: Biphase Energy Systems 2800 Airport Ave Santa Monica CA 90405

DOUGLAS, EDNA, economics educator; b. Asheville, N.C., July 21, 1918; d. Henry and Cora (Skidmore) D.; B.S., U. N.C., 1938, M.A., 1939, Ph.D., 1945. Instr. econs. U. N.C.-Greensboro, 1941-45; asst. and assoc. prof. econs. Iowa State U., Ames, 1945-58; prof. econs. and bus. adminstrn. Wash. State U., Pullman, 1958—; research assoc. Nat. Retail Mchts. Assn., 1945; Fulbright lectr. Norwegian Sch. Econs., Bergen, 1954-55, Swedish Sch. Econs., Stockholm, 1955, Danish Sch. Econs., Copenhagen, 1955, Finnish Sch. Econs., Helsinki, 1955. Mem. Am. Econ. Assn., Western Econ. Assn., Am. Mktg. Assn., Am. Council Consumer Interest. Author: Economics of Marketing, 1975; contbr. articles to profl. jours. Home: NW 430 Dack Ct Pullman WA 99163 Office: Dept Econs Wash State Univ Pullman WA 99164

DOUGLAS, GEORGE MARVIN, telephone co. exec., assn. exec.; b. Durango, Colo., Sept. 10, 1924; s. George and Julia Helen (Steger) D.; student U. Calif., Davis, 1943-44, U. Hawaii, 1944-45, Randall Sch., Denver, 1946-47, Rutgers U., 1961-62, Dartmouth Coll., 1967, U. Pa., 1975; grad. Air War Coll., Air U., 1970, Indsl. Coll. Armed Forces, 1965; m. Ruby Lee Spillman, June 11, 1944; children—Terry Scott, George Bruce. Plant and engring. assignments, long lines dept. AT&T, Denver, Kansas City, 1942-52, plant extensions engr., N.Y.C., 1960-62; planning engr., spl. services engr., def. mgr. Mountain Bell Telephone Co., Denver, 1952-60, dir. mil. communications, Colorado Springs, 1962-67, asst. v.p. ops., Denver, 1967-70, asst. v.p. govt. services, mktg. dept., 1970-78, gen. mktg. mgr., from 1978, now asst. v.p. bus. mktg. Chmn., Gov.'s Mil. Adv. Council for Colo., 1975—; mem. exec. bd. Boy Scouts Am.; bd. dirs. Air Force Falcon Found., Air Force Acad. Found. Served with AUS, 1943-46, U.S. Army Res., 1946-58; to maj. gen. USAF Res., 1958-81. Decorated D.S.M., Legion of Merit, Joint Service Commendation medal, Bronze Star medal, Purple Heart; recipient Outstanding Reservist award Aerospace Def. Command, 1971, Man of Year award Colo. Air Force Assn., 1973. Mem. Assn. U.S. Army (charter mem. 1959—), Res. Officers Assn. (past v.p. for air Colo. dept.), Navy League (past dir. Colorado Springs council), U.S. Naval Inst., Am. Fighter Pilots Assn. (past pres. Denver chpt.), Armed Forces Communications and Electronics Assn. (past dir. Denver chpt.), Def. Orientation Conf. Assn., Air Force Assn. (life mem., Colo. Air Force exec. adv. council 1962—, nat. pres. 1975—, nat. chmn. bd. 1977, trustee Aerospace Edn. Found., meritorious service award, medal of merit 1972, Exceptional Service award 1974, Presdl. citation 1975), Denver C. of C. (chmn. mil. affairs com. 1971-76). Republican. Clubs: Masons, Shriners, Denver Athletic, Brown Palace, Columbine Country, Mt. Vernon Country (Denver); Garden of the Gods (Colorado Springs). Home: 3840 S Hillcrest Dr Denver CO 80237 Office: Room 1150 930 15th St Denver CO 80202

DOUGLAS, JAMES, JR., advertising director; b. Los Angeles, Nov. 8, 1950; s. James and Eleanor (Duarte) D.; m. Cynthia Ann Chadwick, June 2, 1979; children—Leila Carlene, Lauren Ashley. A.A., Pasadena City Coll., 1973; B.A. in Journalism, San Jose State U., 1975; cert. in supervision and mgmt. West Valley Coll., 1976. Asst. advt. dir. Any Mountain, Ltd., Cupertino, Calif., 1976-79; advt. dir. The Outdoorsman, South Lake Tahoe, Calif., 1980—; TV comml. producer; cons. Bd. dirs. Big Bros., South Lake Tahoe, Calif. Served with USAF, 1969-71. Mem. South Lake Tahoe C. of C. (dir.). Produced short Sierra In Season on Good Morning America TV program, Editor Ski Any Mountain mag., 1977-79. Home: PO Box 18346 S Lake Tahoe CA 95706 Office: The Outdoorsman PO Box 8877 S Lake Tahoe CA 95731

DOUGLAS, MARTHA CAROL, communications training consultant; b. San Antonio, Dec. 22, 1937; d. Burrell William and Carolyn (Skillin) Holbrook; m. John R. Douglas; 1 son, Jim. Cert. tchr. Social worker Alameda County (Calif.) Welfare Dept., 1961-63; communications and career tng. coordinator Lesher Communications, Inc., Walnut Creek, Calif., 1976—; cons., 1963—. Author: Go For It, 1969, rev. edit., 1983; contbr. articles newspapers, mags., profl. jours.

DOUGLAS, PAUL JAMES, aerospace engineer; b. Sioux Falls, S.D., Sept. 13, 1930; s. James Paul and Smaragda D. B.S. in Aero. Engring., U. Ill., 1956; m. Marianne P. West, Nov. 14, 1953; children—Pamela, Paula, Patricia, James. With Lockheed Missiles and Space Co., Sunnyvale, Calif., 1956—, advanced systems engring. specialist, 1975—. Served with USAF, 1950-51. Mem. AIAA. Office: PO Box 504 Sunnyvale CA 94088

DOUGLASS, DONALD ROBERT, banker; b. Evanston, Ill., Oct. 7, 1934; s. Robert William and Dorothy (Gibson) D.; B.B.A., U. N.Mex., 1959, M.B.A., 1966; m. Susan Douglas. With Security Pacific Nat. Bank, Los Angeles, 1961—, mgmt. trainee, 1962-63, asst. mgr. Vernon (Calif.) br., 1963-64, asst. mgr. Whittier (Calif.), 1964, asst. v.p., 1965, asst. v.p., credit officer regional adminstrn., Los Angeles, 1966-69, v.p., San Francisco, 1969-74, mgr. corp. accounts credit adminstrn. No. Calif. Corp. Banking, 1974-77; group v.p. Annco Properties, Burlingame, Calif., 1977-79; v.p., sr. loan officer Borel Bank and Trust Co., San Mateo, Calif., 1979-83, sr. v.p., 1983—; instr. Am. Inst. Banking, 1963, Coll. San Mateo (Calif.), 1982—. Served with AUS, 1954-56. Mem. U. N.Mex. Alumni Assn., Sigma Alpha Epsilon, Delta Sigma Phi. Republican. Presbyn. Home: 745 Celestial Lane Dr Foster City CA 94404

DOUGLASS, JOHN MICHAEL, physician; b. Takoma Park, Md., Apr. 13, 1939; s. Jones All and Helen Louise D.; B.A., Columbia Union Coll., Takoma Park, 1959; M.D. (Salerni Collegium scholar), U. So. Calif., 1964; m. Sue Nan Peters, May 15, 1962; children—Dina Lynn, Lisa Michele. Rotating intern Los Angeles County, U. So. Calif. Med. Center, 1964-65, resident internal medicine, 1965-67, home care physician, 1965-68; practice medicine specializing in internal medicine, Cin., 1968-70, Los Angeles, 1970—; physician Pasadena Emergency Center, 1965-68, Deaconess Hosp., 1968-70; postdoctoral fellow automobile safety and trauma research U. Calif., Los Angeles, 1967-68, med. cons. Emergency Med. Services Project, 1970-71; commd. med. officer USPHS, 1968-70; asst. sci. adviser, injury control program ECA, USPHS, Cin., 1968-69, med. specialities cons. Office Product Safety, FDA, USPHS, 1969-70; internal medicine cons. East End Neighborhood Community Health Center, Cin., 1968-70; comdr.-05, USPHS Res. officer, 1970—; internal medicine cons. Hollywood Sunset Free Clinic, 1971-72; sr. med. cons. multidisciplinary hwy. accident investigation unit U. So. Calif., 1971-73; staff internist, coordinator health improvement service Kaiser Found. Hosp., Los Angeles, 1970—; instr. biomedical engring. course U. Calif., Los Angeles, 1968, instr. internal medicine, 1971-74; instr. internal medicine U. Cin. Sch. Medicine, 1968-70; instr. kinesthesiology, traumatic anatomy and head injury U. So. Calif., 1971-74, instr. foodstyle and lifestyle, 1977—; mem. med. adv. bd. Dominican Sisters of Sick Poor, 1969; traffic safety cons. Countywide Conf. on Emergency Med. Services, 1972; mem. nutrition council Las Virgenes Sch. Dist., 1977. Active mgmt. devel. program Boy Scouts Am. Execs., 1966; bd. dirs. Calif. Assn. Pvt. Schs. and Colls., 1967, Coronary Club (adult jogging program), 1967-68; co-organizer Oriental rug exhibit Pacificulture Mus., Pasadena, Calif., 1973; v.p. Los Angeles Med. Milk Commn. Diplomate Nat. Bd. Med. Examiners, Am. Bd. Internal Medicine. Comdr. USPHS Officers Res. Corps. Fellow ACP; mem. AMA, Calif. Med. Assn., Los Angeles County Med. Assn., Am., Calif., Los Angeles socs. internal medicine, Am. Assn. Automotive Medicine (exec. com. Western chpt. 1977-82), Nutrition Today Soc., Internat. Hajji Baba Soc., Decorative Arts Council, Los Angeles Mus. Art, Sierra Club, Phi Delta Epsilon, Alpha Omega Alpha, Phi Kappa Phi. Author: The Lost Language; contbr. articles to profl. jours. Home: 29154 S Lakeshore Dr Agoura CA 91301 Office: 1526 N Edgemont St Los Angeles CA 90027

DOUKE, DANIEL WAYNE, art educator; b. Los Angeles, Sept. 18, 1943; s. Edward Joseph and Geraldine Lucelle (Williams) D.; m. Nadine Margret Foreman, Sept. 8, 1946; 1 dau., Samantha. B.A., Calif. State U.-Los Angeles, 1969, M.A., 1971. Prof. art, dir. fine arts gallery Calif. State U.-Los Angeles, 1975—; group shows include: Drawings by Painters, Long Beach Mus., 1982, Decade, Art Ctr. Coll. Design, Pasadena, Calif., 1982, Nagoya City Mus., Japan, 1982; represented in permanent collections: Israel Mus. Served in USNR, 1968-69. Decorated Navy Cross. Recipient James D. Phelan award San Francisco Found., 1973. Democrat. Methodist. Address: 5151 State University Dr Los Angeles CA 90032

DOUTT, JEFFREY (THOMAS), marketing and management specialist, educational administrator; b. Oakland, Calif., Mar. 30, 1947; s. Richard L. and Lucinda M. (Killian) D.; B.S., U. Calif.-Berkeley, 1968, M.S., 1970, Ph.D., 1976. Assoc. in bus. adminstrn. U. Calif.-Berkeley, 1974; assoc. prof. mgmt. Sonoma (Calif.) State U., 1974-83, prof., 1983—, chmn. dept. mgmt. studies, 1976-80, dean Sch. Social Scis., 1980—; prin. assoc. Mgmt. Devel. Internat.; cons. mktg. and mgmt. Recipient Internat. Exchange award Rotary Found., 1979; Giannini Found. fellow, 1968-70. Mem. Am. Mktg. Assn., Am. Agrl. Econs. Assn., Am. Econ. Assn., Am. Inst. Decision Scis., Acad. Mktg. Sci., Acad. Internat. Bus., Am. Soc. Tng. and Devel., Internat. Communication Assn., Soc. Intercultural Edn. Tng. and Research, Am. Bus. Communication Assn., Western Mktg. Educators Assn., Phi Beta Kappa. Democrat. Club: Rotary. Contbr. articles to profl. jours. Home: 5130 Gilchrist Rd Sebastopol CA 95472 Office: 1801 E Cotati Ave Rohnert Park CA 94928

DOVER, HAROLD, LEON, state senator, building contractor; b. Lewistown, Mont., Oct. 1, 1933; s. John Wesley and Martha Elizabeth (Johnson) D.; B.A., Westmont Coll., Santa Barbara, Calif., 1951-55; m. Marian Leona Prentice, Sept. 1, 1956; children—Stephen Harold, Timothy Prentice, Bryan Hayden. Tchr. elem. sch., Calif. and Mont., 1955-58; gen. bldg. contractor, Lewistown, 1969—; pres. Dover Constrn. Co., Inc.; ordained to ministry Ind. Bible Chs., 1962; pastor, 1958-76; mem. Mont. Senate, 1976—; exec. dir. Nat. Gasahol Commn., 1978-81. Served with USAF, 1956-57. Mem. Lewistown C. of C. (pres. 1975-76). Republican. Club: Rotary (past pres.). Office: 620 Crowley Ave Lewistown MT 59457

DOVER, WILLIAM E., electronic products co. exec.; b. St. Louis, Nov. 26, 1946; s. William M. and Norma E. Dover; B.S. in Bus. Adminstrn., Emporia State U., 1969; m. Mary A. Petrie, Sept. 1, 1968; children—Eric W., David T. Office mgr., salesman Air Products & Chems., Inc., Kansas City, Mo., 1970-74, br. mgr., Broomfield, Colo., 1974-76, S.W. region facility mgr., Houston, 1977; Rocky Mountain div. sales mgr. Sci. Gas Products, Inc., Brighton, Colo., 1978-80; regional sales mgr. ELCHEM, Boulder, Colo., 1980—. Active Cystic Fibrosis Assn., Boulder County. Recipient 1st Pl. Performance award Air Products & Chems., 1975, 76, 77. Mem. Colo. Chem. Club, Am. Welding Soc., Nat. Soc. Cardiopulmonary Tech., Gas Chromatography Discussion Group, Boulder Jaycees (dir. 1976-77). Methodist. Home and Office: 4623 Kirkwood St Boulder CO 80301

DOW, JERRY ALAN, city official, educator; b. Framingham, Mass., Aug. 8, 1946; s. George Stanley and Jeanne (Heron) D.; m. Gloria Jean VanZant, July 3, 1971; children—Veronica Jeanell, Jerry Rodney; B.S.C.E., Wash. State U., 1969; M.S.C.E., U. Wash., 1971; postgrad. profl. program in urban transp. Carnegie-Mellon U., 1977. Registered profl. engr., Wash. Hwy. engr. Wash. State Dept. Hwys., Seattle, 1969-70; research asst. U. Wash., 1971, lectr., 76-79; various positions Municipality of Met. Seattle, 1971-81; mgr. transit devel., 1980—; lectr, Seattle U., 1979-82. Vice chmn. (Social Service and Recreation Bd., Mercer Island, Wash., 1980-81. Wash. State Dept. Transp. fellow Wash. State U., 1969. Mem. ASCE, ASME (keynote speaker nat. conf. transp. 1971); Am. Pub. Transit Assn. (active coms.). Clubs: Wash. State Sports Collectors Assn., Athletic (Seattle). Home: 5819 E Mercer Way Mercer Island WA 98040 Office: 821 2d Ave Seattle WA 98104

DOW, MARY ALEXIS, accountant; b. South Amboy, N.J., Feb. 19, 1949; d. Alexander and Elizabeth Anne (Reilly) Pawlowski; m. Russell Alfred Dow, June 19, 1971. B.S. with honors, U. R.I., 1971. C.P.A., Oreg. Staff acct. Deloitte, Haskins & Sells, Boston, 1971-74; sr. acct. Price Waterhouse, Portland, Oreg., 1974-77, mgr., 1977-81, sr. mgr., 1981—; Mem. fin. com. Oreg. Mus. Sci. and Industry; mem. bd., treas. Legal Advocacy for Women Inc., 1977-80; mem. NOW, treas. Portland chpt., 1976-77. Mem. Am. Inst. C.P.A.s, Oreg. Soc. C.P.A.s, Am. Women's Soc. C.P.A.s, Portland Retail Controllers Group (dir., past pres.). Roman Catholic. Clubs: City (bd. govs.), University (Portland). Contbr. articles to profl. publs. Office: 101 SW Main St Portland OR 97204

DOW, RODNEY LAVERN, mktg., mgmt. and sales cons.; b. Eugene, Oreg., Feb. 26, 1938; s. Marvin LaVern and Mary Margaret (Hilliard) D.; student Lane Community Coll., U. Oreg., various specialized industry courses; diploma Inst. Retail Appliance Mgmt., Western Ky. U., 1978; m. Regina A. Volk, Nov. 29, 1958; children—Kathy A., Debra L., Tammy L., Daren L. With Eugene Planing Mill (Oreg.), 1959-63, 65-81, v.p. mktg., dir., 1975-77, ptnr. R & R Mgmt., Inc., 1977-81, pres., 1981—; grocery owner, mgr., Oakridge, Oreg., 1963-65; with N.Y. Life Ins. Co., 1982. Served with USAF, 1955-58; mem. Res. Mem. Eugene C. of C., Aircraft Owners and Pilots Assn., Mid-Oreg. Advt. (past dir.). Republican. Roman Catholic. Address: 4538 Doyle St Eugene OR 97404

DOWALIBY, PAULINE AGNES, optometrist; b. Portsmouth, N.H., Nov. 23, 1928; d. Abraham Edward and Helen Josephine (Rizk) D. A.A., Los Angeles City Coll., 1948; B. Visual Sci., Los Angeles Coll. Optometry, 1950; O.D., So. Calif. Coll. Optometry, 1951. Pvt. practice optometry, El Segundo, Calif., 1956-60, Beverly Hills, Calif., 1960—; optometrist Los Angeles City Sch. System, part-time, 1957—. Trustee Los Angeles Coll. Optometry, 1961-63. Mem. Am. Optometric Assn., Calif. Optometric Assn., Los Angeles Optometric Soc. (Optometrist of Yr. 1962), Alumni Assn. Los Angeles Coll. Optometry (pres. 1962). Democrat. Author: Healthy Eyes for Your Child, 1981. Office: 9465 Wilshire Blvd Suite 201 Beverly Hills CA 90212

DOWBENKO, URI, advertising and marketing executive; b. Chgo., Dec. 1, 1951; s. Rostyslav and Kateryna (Reshetnyk) D. Student Case Western Res. U., 1969-71, U. Vienna, 1971-72, San Francisco Art Inst., 1973-74. Gen. mgr. sales and prodn. Children of Light, Mars, Pa., 1974-77; copywriter, assoc. editor Summit U. Press, Malibu, Calif., 1978-79; multi-media producer, photographer Kali Prodns., Westlake Village, Calif., 1979-81; pres., creative dir. Uri Dowbenko & Assocs., San Francisco, 1981—; tchr., lectr. on public health issues. Mem. Direct Mktg. Creative Guild, Am. Soc. Mag. Photographers. Author: Homegrown Holography: How to Make Holograms in Your Own Low-Cost Studio, 1978; Encyclopedia of Practical Photography, 1978; contbg. editor Marijuana DoubleTake, 1981. Address: 270 S La Cienega Blvd Suite 301 Beverly Hills CA 90211

DOWD, PETER JEROME, public relations cons.; b. N.Y.C., Oct. 5, 1942; s. Jerome Ambrose and Mary Agnes (Young) D.; A.B., Fordham U., 1964; m. Brenda Badura, Nov. 25, 1972; 1 dau., Kelly Ann. Reporter, UPI, N.Y.C., 1964-66; account exec. Hill & Knowlton, Inc., N.Y.C., 1966-71, v.p., 1971-74, sr. v.p., mgr., Los Angeles, 1974-78, mng. dir. Western region, 1978-80, exec. v.p., 1980; partner Haley, Kiss & Dowd, Inc., 1980-82; pres. Haley, Kiss and Dowd (West), Inc., 1982—; instr. U. So. Calif., Los Angeles, 1977-78. Mem. Dist. Export Council So. Calif., 1976-78; v.p. Town Hall West. Mem. Public Relations Soc. Am. (chpt. dir. 1977-81). Republican. Roman Catholic. Club: Jonathan. Office: 8455 Fountain Ave Los Angeles CA 90069

DOWDEL, CYNTHIA L., safety and health supervisor; b. Sheffield, Ill., Sept. 28, 1939; d. Henry Kellogg Ray and Elizabeth M. (Buckner) Ray; m. Lawrence Joseph Dowdel, Sept. 23, 1961; children—Dennis L., Lawrence Joseph, Marcia L. Grad. Katherine Shaw Bethea Sch. Nursing, Dixon Public Hosp., 1960; B.S., St. Frances Coll., 1975; Registered R.N., Ill. Staff nurse Lincoln Devel. Ctr. (Ill.), 1961-62, 63-64, St. John's Hosp. Premature Ctr., Springfield, Ill., 1962; asst. head nurse Abraham Lincoln Meml. Hosp., Lincoln, 1965-69; plant nurse PPG Industries Inc., Lincoln, 1969-72, supr. safety and health, 1972-79, Valencia, Calif., 1979—; CPR instr., multi media first aid instr. ARC. Recipient Community Service award PPG Industries, 1971, 1973, citation, 1981, outstanding safety performance, 1970, 71, 72, 74, 75, 77, 80, 81. Mem. Am. Soc. Safety Engrs. Nat. Safety Council. Roman Catholic. Home: 21139 Alaminos Dr Saugus CA 91350 Office: 25663 W Ave Stanford Valencia CA 91355

DOWDELL, JOHN LAWRENCE, fin. services co. exec.; b. Sacramento, Sept. 29, 1936; s. Joseph A. and Dorothy F. (Karns) D.; B.A., Stanford U., 1958, M.B.A., 1960; m. Karen Nielsen, June 29, 1958; children—Kirk, Kristen, Bettina. Asst. v.p. comml. loans Crocker Nat. Bank, Sacramento and San Francisco, 1963-70; pres. Delta Investment Co., Inc., and Delta Investment Research Corp., Sacramento, 1970-74; gen. partner Continental Leasing Co., Sacramento, 1970-74; chmn. bd. Medi-Physics, Inc., Emeryville, Calif., 1970-74, Matrix Leasing, San Francisco, 1970-74; pres., chmn. bd., dir. Dowdell Corp., Sacramento, 1974—; vis. lectr. U. Calif., Davis, 1981—. Vice pres., bd. dirs. YMCA, Sacramento, 1975—; pres., bd. dirs. Sacramento Country Day Sch., 1970-80; bd. dirs. Sacramento Civic Theatre, 1978-80, Sacramento History Center, 1981—, Stanford Assn. of Sacramento and Boston, 1960-61, 67-69. Served to capt. USAF, 1960-63. Decorated Air Force Commendation medal; recipient Pres.'s award Crocker Nat. Bank, 1968; YMCA Leadership award, 1981; Nat. Park Service Grand Canyon award, 1978. Mem. Stanford Alumni Assn. (dir. 1969-72), Western Assn. Venture Capitalists, Internat. Assn. Fin. Planners, Western Assn. Equipment Lessors (dir. 1982—), Am. Assn. Equipment Lessors, Calif. Hosp. Assn., United Hosp. Assn., Assn. Western Hosps., Sacramento Bd. Realtors. Republican. Lutheran. Clubs: Rotary (bd. dirs. 1981—), Masons. Author: Hospital Financing—Plan for the 80's, 1981. Home: 1266 Norfolk Way Sacramento CA 95831 Office: 555 Capitol Mall Suite 640 Sacramento CA 95814

DOWDY, WILLIAM LOUIS, tech. corp. ofcl.; b. San Antonio, Dec. 3, 1937; s. Eugene Joseph and Estelle Helen (Schmid) D.; B.S., St. Mary's U. of Tex., 1959; postgrad. U. Ala., 1960-62; M.Engring. (fellow), Tex. A&M U., 1964; children—Mark Allen, John Joseph, Daniel Patrick. Mgr. advanced programs space div. Rockwell Internat., Downey, Calif., 1964-73, managing dir., gen. mgr. air monitoring center, Newbury Park, Calif., 1973-76; cons. W.L. Dowdy Consultants, Thousand Oaks, Calif., 1976-77; mgr. program devel. Electric Power Research Inst., Palo Alto, Calif., 1977-78; dir. new product devel. Envirotech Corp. BSP div., Belmont, Calif., 1978-80; mgr. feasibility studies Lurgi Corp., Belmont, 1980—; cons. tech. devel.; lectr. Tex. A & M U., 1964; invited lectr. various locations. Bd. dirs. Bay Area chpt. March of Dimes, 1980—. Recipient NASA Apollo achievement award, 1969, NASA Tech. Utilization award, 1968; registered profl. engr., Calif., register of chartered engrs., U.K. Asso. fellow AIAA (chmn. nat. tech. com., conf. and session chmn. various times), Royal Aero. Soc.; mem. Am. Mgmt. Assn. Clubs: World Future Soc., K.C., Commonwealth of Calif. Editorial advisory bd. Jour. of Remote Sensing, 1970-71; contbr. articles to tech. and mgmt. publs. Home: 27 Old Spanish Trail Portola Valley CA 94025 Office: 1 Davis Dr Belmont CA 94002

DOWELL, ARMSTRONG MANLY, physicist; b. Torrance, Calif. Aug. 29, 1921; s. Armstrong Manly and Ola Ruth (Thompson) D.; m. Frances Ellen Osborn, Feb. 4, 1950; children—Bruce Albert, Cynthia Ann, Roger Wayne. A.B., UCLA, 1947, M.A., 1949. Clin. lab. technologist Cedars of Lebanon Hosp., Los Angeles, 1950-55; plastics technician Hughes Aircraft Co., Culver City, Calif., 1951-52, mem. tech. staff, 1952-60, mem. tech. staff, head documentation, Fullerton, Calif., 1960—; mem. faculty Cypress Coll., Calif., 1976. Mem. Republican Central Com. Orange County, 1964-66; cubmaster, scoutmaster, commr. Boy Scouts Am., recipient Scouters Key. Served with USN, 1942-46; CBI. Mem. Sigma Xi, Phi Sigma. Home: 2503 E Chestnut Orange CA 92667 Office: PO Box 3310 Fullerton CA 92634

DOWER, EDWARD LOUIS, educator; b. Takoma Park, Md., Jan. 4, 1945, s. Calncy Melvin and Verna May (Thompson) D; m. Donna Fern Piner, Sept. 4, 1966; children—Christine, Carla, Erik. B.A., Pacific Union Coll., 1967; M. Div., Andrews U., 1969, Ed.D., 1980. Ordained to ministry Seventh-day Adventist Ch., 1974; pastor Ill. Conf. Seventh-day Adventists, 1969-73; religion tchr. Spring Valley Acad., Centerville, Ohio, 1973-77, Andrews Acad., Berrien Springs, Mich., 1977-83, Lodi (Calif.) Acad., 1977—; supervising instr. edn. Andrews U., 1977-83. Mem. Religious Edn. Assn., Assn. Supervision and Curriculum Devel., Phi Delta Kappa. Home: 1324 S Central Ave Lodi CA 95240 Office: Lodo Acad 1230 S Central Ave Lodi CA 95240

DOWIS, DALE FRANKLIN, profl. engr.; b. Huntington, W.Va., Nov. 9, 1923; s. Edward F. and Martha (Elkins) D.; B.S., Case Inst. Tech., 1952; postgrad. U. So. Calif., 1954-55; m. May Louise Bernhard, Apr. 11, 1944; children—William F., Robert Dale. Chief applications engr., chief engr. rotating components IMC Magnetics, Maywood, Calif., 1953-58, 60-63; partner Stevens and Grow, Cons. Engrs., Los Angeles, 1958-60; v.p. TEC Magnetics subs. HI-G, Inc., Santa Fe Springs, Calif.; pres. Mandal Enterprises, 1971—; v.p. Trimarco, Inc., Downey, Calif., 1973-79; Western regional mgr. Soladyne, Inc., San Diego, 1979; nat. sales mgr. Astrosyn Am. Inc., Van Nuys, Calif., 1979-82; field sales mgr. Electric Motor Engring., Los Angeles, 1982—. Republican precinct committeeman, Cleve., 1949. Served with USMCR, 1942-45. Registered profl. engr., Calif., Ohio. Mem. AIEE, Nat., Calif. socs. profl. engrs. Mason. Home: 16034 Mariner Dr Huntington Beach CA 92649 Office: 6331 Hollywood Blvd Los Angeles CA 90028

DOWLEY, MARK WILLIAM, physicist, laser manufacturing company executive; b. Dundalk, Ireland, Apr. 28, 1934; came to U.S., 1959, naturalized, 1965; s. Arthur Gerard and Sheila Mary (Williams) D.; m. Mary Donnelly, Mar. 29, 1967; children—A. David, Aoife Mary, Patrick Mark. B.Sc. with 1st class honours, Univ. Coll., Dublin, Ireland, 1956; M.A., U. Toronto, 1957, Ph.D., 1959. Postdoctoral researcher U. Calif.-Berkeley, 1959-61; staff scientist IBM Research Labs., San Jose, Calif., 1961-67; sr. scientist Spectra Physics, Mountain View, Calif., 1967-68; dir. research Coherent, Palo Alto, Calif., 1968-72; founder, chmn., pres., dir. Liconix, Sunnyvale, Calif., 1972—; dir. Sports Software, Inc. Mem. Optical Soc. Am., IEEE, Am. Phys. Soc., Conf. Lasers and Electro Optics. Roman Catholic. Univ. (Palo Alto); Richmond Yacht. Contbr. articles to sci. and engring. jours. Home: 460 Maple St Palo Alto CA 94301 Office: Liconix 1390 Borregas Ave Sunnyvale CA 94086

DOWLIN, KENNETH EVERETT, librarian; b. Wray, Colo., Mar. 11, 1941; s. Ross Everett and Fern Mae (Peterson) D.; B.A., U. Colo., 1963, M.P.A., 1981; M.A., U. Denver, 1966; m. Janice Marie Simmons, Mar. 11, 1961; children—Kevin Everett, Kristopher Everett. Bookmobile librarian, library asst. Adams County Pub. Library, Westminster, Colo., 1961-63; library asst. II Denver Pub. Library, 1963-64; head librarian Arvada (Colo.) Pub. Library, 1964-68; adminstrv. asst. Jefferson County Pub. Library, 1969; dir. Natrona County Pub. Library, Casper, Wyo., 1969-75; dir. Pikes Peak Regional Library Dist., 1975—; instr. Casper Coll., 1971—; vis. instr. U. Denver, 1981, 82; chmn. Colo. Libraries in Cooperation, 1975-76; chmn. Colo. Ad-hoc Com. Networking; cons. video in libraries; mem. Western Interstate Commn. for Higher Edn. Library Network Task Force; del. White House Conf. on Library and Info. Services, 1979, mem. followup com., 1979—; resource person, library and info. service agenda for 80's, U.S. Dept. Edn., 1981. Trustee Wyo. Dept. Library, Archives, and History; bd. dirs. Satellite Library Info. Network; chmn. communications com. First United Methodist Ch., Colorado Springs, 1977-78, also mem. adminstrv. bd.; bd. dirs. Pikes Peak Right to Read Program, 1977-78, Citizen's Goals for Colorado Springs, 1981—. Served with USMCR, 1959-65. Mem. ALA (Hammond Inc. library award jury), Mountain Plains, Colo. (pres. 1968-69, chmn. legis. com. 1976-77) library assns., Denver Council Govts. (chmn. librarians com. 1966), Colo. Mcpl. League (chmn. librarians section, 1967), Bibliog. Center Rocky Mountains (pres. 1972-74), Digital Customer Soc. (chmn. library applications spl. interest group 1978, 79), Pikes Peak Area C. of C. (chmn. cultural affairs com. 1976-77). Mem. bd. Colorado Springs Mag., 1977-78. Office: PO Box 1579 Colorado Springs CO 80901

DOWNES, WARREN WILLIAM, wholesale bldg. materials co. exec.; b. Los Angeles, May 10, 1940; s. Wayne Wallace and Sarah Hayes (Tutt) D.; B.A., San Francisco State U., 1962; m. Christina Reinmiller, Dec. 28, 1968; children—Brant, Shana. With Downes Bldg. Supply Inc., Oakland, Calif., 1962—, pres., chief fin. officer, 1973—. Office: 3401 Wood St Oakland CA 94608

DOWNEY, MARYJO MARIE, local govt. ofcl.; b. Chadron, Nebr., July 22, 1947; d. Ralph Raymond and Mary Elizabeth (McClain) Starkey; B.S., Chadron State Coll., 1969; m. Robert Downey, Dec. 31, 1969; children—Amy Jo, Amber Leigh, Brad Michael. Tchr., Pueblo (Colo.) public schs., 1969-71, Fremont County (Colo.) Schs., 1971-72; program dir. East Central Colo. Opportunity Program, Stratton, 1972-74; exec. dir. East Central Council of Govts., Stratton, 1974—; mem. Gov.'s Tourism Council, 1982—, State Community Service Block Grant Adv. Com., 1982—. Bd. dirs. Kit Carson County Carousel Assn., 1976—, No. Colo. Consortium, 1978-79; mem. No. Area CETA adv. council, 1976—, chmn., 1978, 79; project dir. Kit Carson County Carousel Assn., 1978—; mem. East Central Criminal Justice Planning Council, 1974—; mem. Colo. Balance of State CETA Planning Council, 1977-79. Mem. Colo. Carousel Soc. (dir. 1981—), Colo. Mainstreet Coalition, Econ. Developers Council Colo., Nat. Carousel Assn., Am. Carousel Soc. Roman Catholic. Author: The Other Colorado, 1980. Home: 210 Iowa St Stratton CO 80836 Office: 127 Colorado St Stratton CO 80836

DOWNEY, WILLIAM THOMAS, rehabilitation educator, consultant, trainer; b. San Bernardino, Calif., Nov. 21, 1943; s. Vivan William and Ruth Marie (Helland) D.; m. Patricia Ellen Gorman, Apr. 29, 1972; children—Thomas W., James P. A.A., Barstow Coll., 1963; B.S., Ariz. State Coll., 1965; M.A., No. Ariz. U., 1967; Ph.D., U. Ariz., 1979. Vocat. counselor Ariz. State Employment Service, 1967-71; rehab. counselor Ariz. Div. Vocat. Rehab., 1972-74; instr. dept. rehab. U. Ariz., 1977-78, clin. asst. prof. rehab., 1980—; asst. prof., coordinator undergrad. studies Ctr. Rehab. Studies, North Tex. State U., 1978-80; cons. and trainer Ariz. Rehab. Services Adminstrn. and Rehab. Continuing Edn. Program, Fed. Region IX, Rehab. Services Adminstrn., San Diego, 1976—; mem. Ariz. Adv. Com. on Rehab., 1977-78, 83—. Served in U.S. Army, 1968-70. Decorated Bronze Star, Air medal; Rehab. Services Adminstrn. stipendee, 1974-76, Mem. Nat. Rehab. Assn., Nat. Rehab. Counseling Assn., Am. Personnel and Guidance Assn., Am. Rehab. Counseling Assn. (dir. 1982—), Ariz. Rehab. Assn., Nat. Council Rehab. Edn. (dir. 1982—). Democrat. Home: 4825 E 12th St Tucson AZ 85711 Office: Rehab Dept U Ariz Tucson AZ 85721

DOWNING, DUANE MARCELLES, electrical engineer; b. Scio, Oreg., Dec. 1, 1925; s. Orville C. and Mabel C. (Tietze) D.; B.S. in Elec. Engring., Oreg. State Coll., 1949; m. Elaine Marie Johnson, May 14, 1951; children—Paula E., Donna M. Civilian elec. engr. C.E., U.S. Army, 1949—, chief ops. div. Walla Walla (Wash.) dist., 1965—. Served with USNR, 1944-46. Recipient Meritorious Civilian Service award C.E., 1976; registered profl. engr., Oreg. Mem. Soc. Am. Mil. Engrs. Clubs: Meml. Park Golf, Elks. Devel. and mgmt. of remote and computer controlled multiple purpose hydroelectric projects, 1949—. Home: 766 Wauna Vista Dr Walla Walla WA 99362 Office: Corps Engrs City-County Airport Walla Walla WA 99362

DOWNING, GEORGE (SKIP), interior designer; b. Seattle, Feb. 11, 1937; s. James Bernice and Amy (Neubauer) D.; m. Harriett Hackney, Sept. 13, 1958; m. Dana Madison, June 16, 1974; children—Catherine, Joleen. B.A. in Indsl. Design, U. Wash., 1959. Designer Walter Dorwin Teague, Renton, Wash., 1958-59, Dohrman Hotel Supply, Seattle, 1960-64; lead designer Albert Parvin Co., Los Angeles, 1964-65; chief designer Parvin/Dohrman Co., Seattle, 1966-70; owner, pres. Contract Design Unltd., Seattle, 1970—; cons. speaker, tchr. in field. Served with USNR, 1954-62. Recipient best comml. remodel award Seattle-King County Bd. Realtors, 1979. Mem. Am. Soc. Interior Designers, Food Service Cons. Soc. Internat. Republican. Lutheran. Club: Jaguar Drivers (Mercer Island, Wash.). Contbr. articles to profl. jours. Office: 607 19th Ave E Seattle WA 98112

DOWNING, JOHN FRANCIS, cons. engr.; b. Boston, Sept. 17, 1916; s. Daniel Charles and Elizabeth Mary (Fitzgerald) D.; S.B. in Chem. Engring., M.I.T., 1938; postgrad. Calif. State U., Long Beach, 1963-64; m. Anna Marie Rem, Oct. 20, 1978; children—Frances M., Jacki V., Lawrence S., Michael A., Troy O. Research engr. M.I.T., Cambridge, 1946-47; chem. engr. Cinecolor, Burbank, Calif., 1947-49; chief plant engr. Western Electrochem. Co., Los Angeles, 1949-51; devel. engr. Marquardt Co., Van Nuys, Calif., 1951-53, 63-65; chief applications engr. AMF/Sundstrand-Turbo div., Pacoima, Calif., 1953-60; systems mgmt. cons. Lockheed Aircraft co., Burbank, Calif., 1960-65, Raytheon Co., Sudbury, Mass., 1965-72; pvt. practice cons., Northridge, Calif., 1972—; cons. Boeing Mil. Aircraft Co., Seattle, Wash. and Wichita, Kans., 1977—. Served with USAAF, 1942-45. Mem. Am. Inst. Chem. Engrs., AIAA, AAAS, IEEE. Clubs: Elks, Moose. Home: 15517 SE 48th St Bellevue WA 98006

DOWNING, MICHAEL ROBERT, computer programming company executive; b. San Diego, Aug. 13, 1947; s. Robert Benevan and Hazel Mary (Fisher) D.; B.S. in Physics, San Diego State U., 1970; Electronic engr. Ametek Straza, El Cajon, Calif., 1970-72; mem. tech. staff Bunker-Ramo Corp., Westlake Village, Calif., 1972-78; owner, pres. Internat. Disk, software devel. firm, Woodland Hills, Calif., 1978—; cons. TRW. Mem. IEEE. Home: 20514 Gault St Canoga Park CA 91306 Office: 22458 Ventura Blvd Suite E Woodland Hills CA 91364

DOWNS, FLOYD LEROY, JR., educator; b. Winchester, Mass., Jan. 21, 1931; s. Floyd Leroy and Emma Mildred (Noyes) D.; A.B., Harvard U., 1952; M.A., Tchrs. Coll., Columbia U., 1955; m. Elizabeth M. Lenci, Dec. 29, 1955; children—Karla Christine, John Noyes. Tchr. math. East High Sch. Denver, 1955-60, Kent (Conn.) Sch., 1960-62, Newton (Mass.) High Sch., 1962-63, Hillsdale High Sch., San Mateo, Calif., 1964—. Served with U.S. Army, 1952-54. NSF grantee Harvard U., 1963-64. Mem. Calif. Math Council (pres. 1974-75), Nat. Council Tchrs. Math (dir. 1976-79), Am. Math. Soc., Math Assn. Am., Nat. Council Suprs. Math, NEA, Calif. Tchrs. Assn., Phi Delta Kappa. Author: (with others) Geometry, 1959, 60; (with E.E. Moise) Geometry, 1964, 71, 82; (with others) An In-Service Handbook for Mathematics Education, 1977. Home: 3334 Verdun Ave San Mateo CA 94403 Office: Hillsdale High Sch San Mateo CA 94403

DOWNUM, EVELYN ROSE BENSON (MRS. GARLAND DOWNUM), librarian; b. Chgo., Jan. 21, 1916; d. Arthur E. and Rose (Anderson) Benson; student Oshkosh State Coll. (now Wis. State U.), 1933-35; A.B. (hon.), U. Ill., 1937; M.A., U. Tex., 1938-39; postgrad. Ariz. State Coll. (now No. Ariz. U.), 1955; postgrad. sch. librarianship U. Denver, 1965; m. Garland Downum, June 17, 1939; children—Philip Benson, Carolyn Jean (Mrs. Larry Dale White), Janice Elaine (Mrs. Joe E. Barnett). Instr. history Ariz. State Coll., Flagstaff, 1949, asst. librarian, 1956-59, librarian coll. elem. sch., 1958-66, instr. children's lit., 1965-66, 68—; librarian pub. sch., Flagstaff, 1966-67; librarian elem. sch. of No. Ariz. U., 1967-81, co-dir. 1971 European instructional tour; children's librarian Flagstaff-Coconino County Library, 1982—; library cons. Flagstaff Headstart Program, 1965. Sponsor, Flagstaff Symphony Orch., 1962—; mem. No. Ariz. Univ. Art Gallery, Ariz. Soc. Crippled Children and Adults. Mem. ALA, Ariz. Zool. Soc., No. Ariz. Soc. Sci. and Art, Nat. Council Tchrs. English, Ariz. Library Assn. (exec. bd. sch. library div.), AAUW (various offices, past state treas., v.p.), Internat. Reading Assn., Friends of Smith and Osborne Collection Toronto Pub. Library, M.B.L.S., Vereiningung der Freunde der Internationalen Jugend bibliotek, Internationales Institut fur Jugend literatur und Lesefurschung, children's Lit. Assn., Council Interracial Books, Delta Kappa Gamma, Beta Sigma Phi, Pi Lambda Theta, Phi Kappa Phi, Kappa Delta Pi, Gamma Sigma. Republican. Club: Lake Montezuma Country. Book reviewer, Sch. Library Jour., 1964—, Library Jour., 1964—. Home: 1609 N Aztec St Flagstaff AZ 86001

DOWRICK, PETER WINTON, psychologist, educator; b. Waipukurau, N.Z., Aug. 7, 1944; came to U.S., 1980; s. E. George and Verna May (Sowry) D.; B.Sc., Victoria U. (N.Z.), 1966; M.Sc., U. Auckland (N.Z.), 1971, Ph.D., 1977; postgrad. Trinity Coll., London, 1971. Computer programmer and analyst IBM, Wellington, N.Z., 1966-67; tutor dept. psychology Auckland U., 1968-70, teaching fellow, 1971, asst. lectr., 1972; mgr. computer systems Software Devel. Ltd., Auckland, 1971; research psychologist dept. psychiatry Sch. Medicine, Auckland U., 1974-78; pres. Speld Assn., Auckland Inc., 1976-77, Speld New Zealand Inc., 1977-78; hon. research fellow dept. psychology Birkbeck Coll., U. London, 1979-80; asst. prof. dept. psychology U. Alaska, Anchorage, 1980-82, assoc. prof., 1982—; mem. faculty Alaskan Inst. Family Studies, 1980—; adj. asst. prof. dept. human devel. and family life U. Kans., Lawrence, 1981—; cons. to dept. psychiatry Guys Hosp., London, 1980—, Kiev Co., London, 1980—; cons. Parent Tng. Ctr., Anchorage. Mem. faculty adv. com. Tanaina Child Devel. Center, 1980—. N.Z. Crippled Children Soc. grantee, 1975-77, N.Z. Nat. Children's Health Research Found. grantee, 1977-78, Birkbeck Coll. grantee, 1980. Mem. Assn. for Advancement of Behavior Therapy, Soc. for Behavioral Medicine, N.Z. Psychol. Soc. Contbr. articles profl. jours. Office: 3221 Providence Dr Anchorage AK 99508

DOXEY, ROY WATKINS, educator, ch. adminstr.; b. Ogden, Utah, Feb. 27, 1908; s. Thomas and Bessie (Watkins) D.; A.S., Weber Coll., 1934; A.B., George Washington U., 1938, M.A., 1940; m. Alberta Ophcikens, Aug. 6, 1934; children—Douglas Allen (dec.), Clarke Benson, Kimball Roy, Cheryl Diane (Mrs. Ronald Julian). Economist, FHA, 1935-40, Nat. Housing Agy., 1940-44; pres. Eastern States Mission of Ch. of Jesus Christ of Latter-day Saints, 1944-48; prof. religion Brigham Young U., Provo, Utah, 1948-74, chmn. dept. undergrad. studies in religious instrn., 1963-70, asst. dean Coll. Religious Instrn., 1970-71, dean Coll. Religious Instrn., 1971-74, dean emeritus, 1974—. Vice chmn. bd. Utah Valley Latter-day Saints Hosp., 1965-78; mem. gen. bd. Y.M.M.I.A., 1948-61; pres. Provo Stake, 1963-72, regional rep. of the Twelve, 1972-78; dir. correlation rev. Latter-Day Saints Ch., 1977—. Mem. Phi Kappa Phi, Pi Gamma Mu, Omicron Delta Gamma. Author: The Doctrine and Covenants and the Future, 1957; The Doctrine and Covenants Speaks, vol. 1, 1965, vol. 2, 1970; The Latter-day Prophets and the Doctrine and Covenants, vols. 1-4, 1963-65, rev., 1978; Zion in the Last Days, 1965; Doctrine and Covenants Lessons and Outlines, 1966; Prophecies and Prophetic Promises from the Doctrine and Covenants, 1969; Walk with the Lord, 1973; The Word of Wisdom and You, 1975; Tithing: The Lord's Law, 1976; co-author: Doctrine and Covenants Study Guide, Vols. 1-2, 1971-72. Home: 123 2d Ave N 905 Salt Lake City UT 84103

DOYLE, ALFRED ALAN, advertising agency executive; b. Seattle, June 5, 1946; s. Alfred and Carmen Frances (Impala) D.; student U. Wash., 1968; m. Carol L. Manzanares, Jan. 28, 1965 (dec. Apr. 1982); children—Sandra Renee, Victoria Marie. Sales promotion mgr. KOMO Radio, Seattle, 1968-70; media dir. David Stern, Inc., Seattle, 1970-74; mgr. Pacific N.W. ops. Kelly, Nason, Inc., N.Y.C., 1974-75; pres., owner Doyle Co., Seattle, 1975-80; exec. v.p. David Stern, Inc., Seattle, 1980-82; v.p. Ferguson-Propp & Assos., 1982—; owner Mind Over Matter, creative services, Seattle. Bd. dirs. Bumbershoot Arts Festival, Seattle. Recipient Seattle Art Dirs. silver medals, 1975, 76, 79, gold medal, 1976. Mem. Seattle Advt. Fedn. (dir. 1973-75), Am. Advt. Fedn., Seattle C. of C. Home: 203 W Crockett Seattle WA 98199

DOYLE, EDMOND THOMAS, hospital executive; b. Cin., Jan. 4, 1938; s. Edmund Darr and Regina (Roan) D. B.S. in Psychology, Xavier U., Cin., 1960; M.H.A., St. Louis U., 1972. Resident in hosp. adminstrn. Bethesda Gen. Hosp., St. Louis, 1969, Good Samaritan Hosp., Cin., 1971; HEW trainee dept. hosp. and health care adminstrn. St. Louis U., 1969-70; dir. paramed. services John C. Lincoln Hosp., Phoenix, 1971-73; pres. Alexian Bros. Hosp., San Jose, Calif., 1973-82; pres., chief exec. officer St. Mary-Corwin Hosp. Regional and Med. Ctr., Pueblo, Colo., 1982—, mem. bd. trustees; bd. dirs. St. Mary-Corwin Hosp. Health Care Found., Inc., St. Mary-Corwin Devel. Co.; trustee Sisters of Charity Health Care Systems, Inc. past mem. bd. dirs. Blue Cross No. Calif., Hosp. Council No. Calif., Santa Clara Med. Found.; past pres. Santa Clara County Hosp. Conf. Bd. dirs. Pueblo West Met. Dist. Mem. Am. Coll. Hosp. Adminstrs., Colo. Hosp. Assn., Cancer Info. Service of Colo. (adv. com.), St. Louis U. Alumni Assn. (dir.), Pueblo C. of C. Club: Rotary. Office: 1008 Minnequa Ave Pueblo CO 81004

DOYLE, HENRY LOVELLE, university administrator; b. Tampa, Fla., Sept. 7, 1951; s. Robert Lee and Muriel Antionette Yvonne (Lomas) D. B.A. (KVOR scholar), Colo. Coll., 1973; exchange student Regensburg (Ger.) U., 1971-72; M.Ed., Colo. State U., 1981. Vol., Peace Corps, Ethiopia, 1973-75; teller Nat. City Bank, Denver, 1976-78, Colorado Springs (Colo.) Nat. Bank, 1978-79; grad. asst. residence halls Colo. State U., Fort Collins, 1979-81, coordinator Towers Complex, 1981—, instr. edn., 1980, 81, 82. Mem. Am. Coll. Personnel Assn., Nat. Assn. Student Personnel Adminstrs. Episcopalian. Home and Office: Durward Hall Fort Collins CO 80521

DOYLE, JAMES PATRICK, forest products co. exec.; b. Glen Ridge, N.J., Feb. 23, 1935; s. James J. and Jane F. (Fleming) Doyle; B.S., Seton Hall U., 1959, M.B.A., 1965; m. Mary Ann Ferrera, Nov. 25, 1961; children—James J., John R., Margaret E. Asst. credit mgr. Johnson & Johnson, New Brunswick, N.J., 1961-66; dist. credit mgr. Am. Can Co., N.Y.C., 1966-68; asst. controller-credit Yardley of London, N.Y.C., 1968-71; corp. credit mgr. Indian Head Inc., N.Y.C., 1971-73; asst. treas. Crown Zellerbach Corp., San Francisco, 1973—; bd. dirs. San Francisco Bd. of Trade; cons. minority bus. mgmt. projects. Served with U.S. Army, 1955-57. Recipient outstanding achievement award Greater N.Y. Fund Yardley of London, 1969. Mem. Am. Mgmt. Assn., Nat. Assn. Credit Mgmt., Fin., Credit and Internat. Bus. Assn., Credit Research Found., No. Calif. Credit Mgmt. Assn. Roman Catholic. Clubs: Olympic, Pacific (pres. 1981) (San Francisco); Moraga Country. Home: 710 Crossbrook Dr Moraga CA 94556 Office: 1 Bush St San Francisco CA 94104

DOYLE, JOHN LOUIS, citrus co. exec.; b. Tex., Jan. 21, 1921; s. John Louis and Florence Agnes (Beuhler) D.; B.A., San Diego State U., 1942; M.A., UCLA, 1947; m. Barbara Moore, Apr. 22, 1944; children—John,

Kathleen, Susan. Pres., gen. mgr., dir. Real Gold Co., Redlands, Calif., 1949-64, Calories Ltd., Inc., Redlands, 1964-68; exec. v.p., dir. MCP Foods, Inc., Anaheim, Calif., 1968-72; exec. v.p., gen. mgr. Pure Gold, Inc., Redlands, 1972-73; pres., dir. Valley Foods, Inc., Redlands, 1973—; dir. Webster Internat. Corp.; cons. in field. Pres. bd. trustees Valley Prep. Sch., Redlands, 1957-59; pres., dir. Community Scholarship Found., Redlands, 1974-78; chmn. San Bernardino chpt. ARC, 1967-70, mem. Western area adv. council, 1969-72, v.p., 1971-72, vice chmn. div. adv. council, 1975-77. Served to maj. USMCR, 1942-45. Mem. Calif.-Ariz. Citrus League (chmn. processors council 1970-71), Nat. Juice Products Assn. (dir., pres. 1980-81), Marine Corps Res. Officers Assn., Tau Sigma. Club: Redlands Country. Office: 415 Brookside Ave Redlands CA 92373

DOYLE, PETER THOMAS, architectural co. exec.; b. Chgo., Nov. 22, 1928; s. Peter Vincent and Elizabeth Mary (Maguire) D.; B.A. in Acctg. cum laude, Claremont McKenna Coll., 1955; postgrad. in mgmt. UCLA; m. Mary Leontina Ulrath, Jan. 17, 1953. Staff auditor Price Waterhouse & Co., Los Angeles, 1955-59; asst. treas. Pardee Constrn. Co., Los Angeles, 1959-64, Pacific Western Mortgage Co., Los Angeles, 1959-64; treas. Provident Mortgage Corp., Pasadena, Calif., 1964-67; controller William L. Pereira Assocs., Los Angeles, 1967-72, Hosp. of Good Samaritan, Los Angeles, 1972-73; controller, treas. ArchiSystems Internat., Van Nuys, Calif., 1973-79; v.p., fin., dir. McClellan/Cruz/Gaylord & Assocs., Inc., Pasadena, 1979—; dir. MCG Fin., Bradeis Devel., Inc., Brandeis Constrn., Inc., Bradeis Property and Facilities Mgmt. Co., Inc., The Bannister Group, MCG Properties, Romaine Devel. Corp.; v.p., sec., dir. Doyle Properties, Inc. Bd. dirs. Sunset Mesa Property Owners Assn., 1973-75; mem. Town Hall Calif. Served with AUS, 1946-48. C.P.A., Realtor assoc., Calif. Mem. Am. Inst. C.P.A.s, Calif. Soc. C.P.A.s, Nat. Assn. Accts., Calif. Assn. Realtors, Nat. Assn. Realtors, Simi Valley Bd. Realtors. Republican. Home: 3430 Cloudcroft Dr Malibu CA 90265 Office: 3452 E Foothill Blvd Suite 1100 Pasadena CA 91107

DOYLE, ROBERT HUGH, urban planning cons.; b. Clarkston, Mich., June 9, 1928; s. John Clifford and Virginia D. (Bennett) D.; B.C.E., U. Ky., 1952; B.Arch. with honors, Clemson U., 1955; M. City Planning, Ga. Inst. Tech., 1959; m. Beverly Ann Clark, June 22, 1965; children—Paula, Eileen, Mark, Jon, Daniel. Prin., Peat, Marwick, Mitchell & Co., San Mateo, Calif., 1970—; dir. E. Central Fla. Regional Plan Council, Titusville, Fla., 1962-67; dir. Planning Assistance Program, HUD, Washington, 1967-68; pres. Interplan Corp., Sarasota, Fla., 1969-70. Served with USN, 1946-48. Named Young Man of Yr., Glynn County (Ga.) C. of C., 1962. Mem. Am. Inst. Cert. Planners (nat. bd. examiners 1968-77), Am. Planning Assn. Club: Optimists (lt. gov. Ga. 1961-62). Home: 1280 #30 Sharon Park Dr Menlo Park CA 94025 Office: Peat Marwick Mitchell & Co 400 S El Camino Real San Mateo CA 94402

DOYLE, ROBERT THOMAS, accountant, financial consultant; b. Oakland, Calif., Jan. 18, 1951; s. Henry and Mary (Delpianco) D.; m. Terasita Ashby, Aug. 25,, 1974; children—Shamier, Robert, Philena. B.A. in Acctg., San Francisco State U., 1974; M.B.A. in Taxation, Golden Gate U., 1980. C.P.A., Calif. Supervisory auditor GAO, San Francisco, 1975-80; mgr. Morris, Davis & Co., C.P.A.s, Oakland, 1980-82; ptnr., founder Doyle, Williams & Co., C.P.A.s, Oakland, 1982—. Mem. Oakland Tax Com., Alameda County Com. to Elect George Dukemajian. Recipient Cert. Appreciation, GAO, 1979. Mem. Am. Inst. C.P.A.s, Calif. Soc. C.P.A.s, Nat. Assn. Black Accts., Nat. Assn. Minority C.P.A. Firms, Assn. Govt. Accts., Nat. Assn. Tax Cons., Golden Gate U. Alumni Assn., Men of Tomorrow, Inc., Oakland C. of C., Alpha Psi. Republican. Roman Catholic. Office: 1330 Broadway St Suite 833 Oakland CA 94612

DOYLE, THERESA LIPARI, marketing executive, public relations writer; b. Long Beach, Calif., Aug. 27, 1957; d. Joseph and Joyce Lorraine (Wagle) Lipari; m. Timothy Xavier Doyle, June 26, 1982. B.A., Calif. State U.-Fullerton, 1980. Fund raising asst. Am. Heart Assn., Santa Ana, Calif., 1980; account supr. Kerr & Assocs. Pub. Relations, Huntington Beach, Calif., 1980-83; dir. mktg. Covington Techs., Fullerton, Calif., 1983—; pub. relations cons. Am. Heart Assn., Family Crisis Ctr., Orange County, Calif., 1980—. Recipient Outstanding Pub. Relations award Publicity Club Los Angeles, 1980. Mem. Women in Communications, Inc. (outstanding mag. article award 1980, outstanding pub. relations award 1980), Calif. State U.-Fullerton Alumni Assn. Republican. Roman Catholic. Office: 2451 E Orangethorpe Ave Fullerton CA 92631

DOYLE, WALTER MICHAEL, business executive, physicist; b. Utica, N.Y., Sept. 26, 1937; s. Clarence Michael and Esther Mae (Ruttan) D.; m. Dolores Medeiros, Feb. 11, 1962. B.A. in Physics, Syracuse U., 1959; Ph.D. in Physics, U. Calif.-Berkeley, 1963. Mem. tech. staff Hughes Aircraft Co., Culver City, Calif., 1963-64; sr. scientist Philco Ford Corp., Newport Beach, Calif., 1964-66, prin. scientist, 1966-69; v.p., dir. research, Laser Precision Corp., Utica, 1969-78; pres. Laser Precision Corp., Irvine, Calif., 1978—. Mem. Am. Phys. Soc., AAAS, Am. Mgmt. Assn. Contbr. articles to profl. jours.; patentee optical instruments. Home: 2875 Bernard Ct Laguna Beach CA 92651 Office: 1731 Reynolds Ave Irvine CA 92714

DOYLE, WILLIAM JAMES, artist, ret. pediatrician; b. Utica, N.Y., Mar. 8, 1915; s. William Edward and Elizabeth Mabel (Carroll) D.; B.S., Georgetown U., 1936; M.D., SUNY Downstate Med. Coll.-L.I. Coll. Medicine, 1940; m. Anita V. Figueredo, Aug. 8, 1942; children—William James, Sarita, John, Thomas (dec.). Charles, Anita, Richard, Teresa, Robert (dec.). Intern, L.I. Coll. and Kings County Hosps., Bklyn., 1940-41, resident in pediatrics, 1941-42, 46-47; practice medicine specializing in pediatrics, La Jolla, Calif., 1947-77; painter, 1977—; one-man shows: Athenaeum, La Jolla, 1962, La Jolla Interiors Gallery, 1969, La Jolla Art Assn., Imperial Savs. Gallery, La Jolla, 1982; group shows include: Romanet-Vercel Gallery, N.Y.C., 1963, San Diego Art Inst. (1st award), 1967. Bd. dirs. La Jolla Athenaeum. Lt. of Western Lieutenancy, Equestrian Order of Holy Sepulchre of Jerusalem, 1973-83. Served with M.C., USNR, 1942-46; PTO. Decorated knight Holy Sepulchre, Grand Cross (Vatican); recipient Grumbacher award of Merit, 1963; named to Honor Roll, NCCJ, 1974. Mem. AMA, Calif. Med. Assn., San Diego County Med. Soc., Los Angeles Pediatric Soc., Am. Physicians Art Assn., La Jolla Art Assn., San Diego Art Inst., San Diego Fine Arts Soc., La Jolla Art Assn. (dir.). Roman Catholic. Contbr. articles to med. jours.

DOYLE, WILLIAM THOMAS, biologist, educator; b. Coalinga, Calif., June 1, 1929; s. John Robert and Flora Mary (Hollingsworth) D.; m. Glendawyn A. Cox, Aug. 23, 1955; children—Shelley, Carol, Jean, Mary. B.A., U. Calif.-Berkeley, 1957, Ph.D., 1960. From instr. to asst. prof. Northwestern U., 1960-65; from asst. prof. to prof. biology U. Calif.-Santa Cruz, 1965—, dean div. natural scis., 1980—; dir. Center Coastal Marine Studies, 1976—. Served with USAF, 1948-52. Mem. Bot. Soc. Am., Am. Bryological and Lichonological Soc., AAAS, Am. Inst. Biol. Scis. Club: Santa Cruz Rotary. Office: Dept Biology University of California Santa Cruz CA 95064

DOYON, ERNEST RENE, hosp. adminstr.; b. Waterbury, Conn., July 4, 1937: s. Emile and Bertha Cyr D.; B.A., U. Nebr., Omaha, 1967; m. Beverly Blanner, July 14, 1956; children—Sharleen, Rhonda, Jeffrey, Richard. Enlisted, U.S. Air Force, 1956, advanced through grades to capt., 1971; assoc. adminstr. resource mgmt. div. USAF Hosp., Myrtle Beach, S.C., 1971-73; clinic comdr., adminstr. USAF Clinic, Hancock Field, N.Y., 1973-76; assoc. adminstr. USAF Hosp., Kirtland AFB, N.Mex., 1976-78; ret., 1978; subarea council planner N.Mex. Health Systems Agy., Albuquerque, 1978-79; with Cibola Gen. Hosp., Grants, N.Mex., 1979-82, adminstr., 1982; chief exec. officer N. Am. Surg. Corp., 1982—; dir. Health Mgmt. Services, Inc., Hosp. Home Health Care, Inc. Bd. dirs. Human Resource Ctr., Cibola Gen. Hosp. Found.; bd. advisors Sub area III N.Mex. Health Systems Agy., Sta. KNME-TV, pub. broadcasting. Mem. Am. Coll. Hosp. Adminstrs., N.Mex. Hosp. Assn., Ret. Officers Assn., C. of C. Republican. Roman Catholic. Clubs: Rotary, Kirtland AFB Officers. Home: 1024 Birch St Grants NM 87020 Office: Box 1057 Grants NM 87020

DRAGUN, JAMES, soil chemist; b. Detroit, July 29, 1949; s. Henry George and Stella (Kubilus) D.; m. Noelle Dawn, June 16, 1973. B.S. in Chemistry, Wayne State U., 1971; M.S., Pa. State U., 1975, Ph.D. in Soil Chemistry, 1977; postgrad. in civil engring. U. Calif.-Berkeley, 1982—. Grad. research assoc. Pa. State U., University Park, 1972-77; soil chemist EPA, Washington, 1978-80, sr. soil chemist, 1980-82; project mgr., lab. mgr. Pacific Environ. Lab. div. Kennedy/Jenks Engr., San Francisco, 1982—; cons. Oak Ridge Nat. Lab., EPA. Recipient bronze medal EPA, 1980. Mem. Am. Chem. Soc., Soil Sci. Soc. Am., Soc. Environ. Toxicology and Chemistry, Sigma Xi, Phi Kappa Phi. Contbr. articles to profl. publs. Office: 657 Howard St San Francisco CA 94105

DRAINE, ROBERT WILCOS, real estate executive; b. Los Angeles, Jan. 31, 1925; s. George Neiland and Ruth Ella (Jewett) D.; m. Patricia Lee Hayes, Feb. 1, 1952; children—Janet, Cameron, Steven. Student Occidental Coll., 1943, Ind. U., 1943-44, UCLA, 1944-49. Cert., Soc. Indsl. Realtors. Mgr. Minn. Mining & Mfg., 1952-57; exec. v.p. Coldwell Banker Group, 1957-83; chmn. Robert Draine Group, Pacific Palisades, Calif., 1978—. Chmn. Los Angeles County Econ. Devel. Commn., 1980-81, Calif. Land Use Council, 1977-78, Los Angeles Econ. and Job Devel. Council, 1981-82; trustee UCLA Found.; bd. dirs. Orthopedia Hosp. Served with U.S. Army,, 1943-44. Mem. Soc. Indsl. Realtors (past pres.), Los Angeles C. of C. (past dir., So. Calif. Industrialist of Year, 1971). Presbyterian. Clubs: California Bel Air Bay. Home: 1495 Capri Dr Pacific Palisades CA 90272

DRAKE, CHARLES EDWARD, semi-trailer manufacturing company executive; b. Shreveport, La., Jan. 2, 1947; s. Edward and Charline (Cochran) D. B.S. in Bus. Adminstrn., U. Ark., 1970; M.B.A., U. Denver, 1977. C.P.A., Okla. With Peat, Marwick, Mitchell & Co., Tulsa, 1970-73, CF&I Steel Co., Pueblo, Colo., 1973-76, Leprino Foods Co., Denver, 1977-80; controller, sec. Merritt Equipment Co., Henderson, Colo., 1980—. Mem. Am. Inst. C.P.A.s. Office: Merritt Equipment Co 9339 Hwy 85 Henderson CO 80614

DRAKE, CLAIRE BENTLEY, interior designer; b. Livermore, Calif., July 7, 1927; d. Clyde Edward and Doris (Taylor) Bentley; m. Edward Plumere Drake, Oct. 30, 1949; children—Carolyn Lucille Drake Bowen, Doris Claire, Clyde Bentley. Student U. Calif.-Berkeley, 1945-49, Parson's Sch. Design, 1947, U. Mexico, summer 1946, U. Hawaii, summer 1948, UCLA, 1976. Nat. Council Interior Design qualification, 1979. With Margaret Rugg Design Studio, Berkeley, 1947, Elizabeth Banning Color Cons., 1948; color cons., Hawaii, 1949-52; with Bentley Engrs., Oakland, Calif., 1953, Barkers Westwood Interior Design, Los Angeles, 1960-62; cons. interior design Badgodesberg, Germany, 1962; with Sloane/Mayer, Falls Church, Va., 1964; cons., Paris, 1965; with W & J Sloan, Beverly Hills, Calif., 1969-77, San Francisco, 1977-79, Walnut Creek, Calif., 1980; with Cannell & Chaffin, Design Studio, Los Angeles, 1975-76; interior designer Gumps, San Francisco, 1981-82; interior designer Interior Design Studio, Berman's, Oakland, Calif., 1983—; instr. adult edn. (interior design), Lafayette, Calif. Moderator civic and election meetings LWV, Santa Monica, 1954-60; organizer, 1st pres. Les Marraines Aux. to Children's Home Soc. Los Angeles, 1957. Mem. Am. Soc. Interior Designers (bd. dirs. No. Calif. chpt.; chmn. step program), Pi Beta Phi. Republican. Presbyterian. Office: 650 Grand Ave Oakland CA 94610

DRAKE, HUDSON BILLINGS, aerospace co. exec.; b. Los Angeles, Mar. 3, 1935; s. Hudson C. and Blossom (Billings) D.; A.B., U. Calif., Los Angeles, 1957; M.B.A., Pepperdine U., 1976; m. Joan Johnson, Feb. 9, 1957; children—Howard, Paul. With Autonetics div. Rockwell Internat., Anaheim, Calif., 1957-68, proposal negotiator, 1961-65, dept. mgr. ops., 1965-68; v.p., gen. mgr. Teledyne Ryan Electronics div. Teledyne Industries, San Diego, 1972-80, pres., 1980—; cons. Ash Commn. on Exec. Reorganization, Washington, 1969-70; dir. White House Fellows Commn., 1969-70; dep. undersec. commerce, dep. asst. sec. and dir. Bur. Domestic Commerce, Washington, 1970-72. Bd. dirs. White House Fellows Found., 1972-75; bd. govs. Greater San Diego Youth Sci. Fair, 1976—; bd. dirs. World Affairs Council of San Diego, 1978—; trustee Children's Hosp. and Health Center, 1981—; chmn. bd. Children's Hosp. Research Corp. Served with USNR, 1953-61. White House fellow, 1968-69. Mem. IEEE, Nat. Mgmt. Assn. (Silver Knight of Mgmt. award 1975), Air Force Assn., Inst. Nav., White House Fellows Assn., San Diego C. of C., Phi Delta Phi, Phi Delta Theta. Republican. Episcopalian. Clubs: Stoneridge Country; Internat. (Washington). Home: 18047 Sencillo Dr San Diego CA 92128 Office: 8650 Balboa Ave San Diego CA 92123

DRAKE, HUGH HESS, lawyer; b. Wayne, Nebr., Apr. 30, 1928; s. Hugh Henderson and Bonnie Rose (Hess) D.; B.S. in Elec. Engring., U. Colo., 1950; J.D., DePaul U., 1957; m. Florence Jean Steele, June 13, 1953; children—Richard Paul, Diana Jean, Mary Ellen. Admitted to Ill. bar, 1957, D.C. bar, 1963, Colo. bar, 1967; field engr. Gen. Electric Co., Denver and Washington, 1950-55; law clk., Zenith Radio Corp., Chgo., 1956-57, sr. atty., 1957-67; mem. firm Drake, Crandell & Batchelder, Ft. Collins, Colo., 1967-72; individual practice law, Ft. Collins, 1972—; asst. mcpl. judge, Ft. Collins, 1969-71; co-mgr. Sholine Ranch, Glendevy, Colo., 1968-72; operator Monadnock Ranch, Livermore, Colo., 1973—; dir. various small corps. Pres., PTA, 1960-61; chmn. Sch. Bd. Caucus, 1966; instr. wrestling YMCA, 1962-66; city councilman, Elmhurst, Ill., 1961-65, mem. plan commn., 1962-65, mem. devel. commn., 1961-65; mem. Bd. Local Improvements, 1962-65; mem. Sheriff's Motorized Patrol, 1971-79, capt., 1973-74; trustee St. Lukes Hosp., 1969-71, Episcopal Diocese Colo., 1969-71. Served to lt. (j.g.) USNR, 1946-59. Recipient Golden Tree award YMCA, 1966. Mem. Colo. (chmn. patent sect. 1971), Larimer County, D.C. bar assns., Star and Sextant, Eta Kappa Nu, Sigma Alpha Epsilon, Delta Theta Phi. Club: Elks. Home: Route 1 Livermore CO 80536 Office: 1720 W Mulberry Fort Collins CO 80521

DRAKE, LARRY LEE, instrument engr.; b. Bell, Calif., Feb. 8, 1942; s. Kenneth and Norma Bernice (Bloomquist) D.; B.S., Calif. State U., 1965; m. Susan Marie Skarin, Apr. 11, 1975. Elec. and sr. instrument engr. Atlantic-Richfield, Carson, Calif., 1968-71, 72—; elec. and instrument engr. So. Pacific Pipeline, Los Angeles, 1971-72. Served with USNR, 1965-68. Registered profl. engr. Mem. Tau Beta Pi, Eta Kappa Nu. Mem. Ch. of Christ. Patentee method for storing molten materials. Home: 9211 Tweedy Ln Downey CA 90240 Office: 1801 E Sepulveda Blvd Carson CA 90745

DRAKE, OWEN BURTCH WINTERS, advertising executive; b. N.Y.C., May 22, 1941; s. Owen Burtch Winters and Louise Harrison Gwynn; m. Joan Edwards Draper, Dec. 15, 1961; m. 2d, Deborah Keresey, Jan. 8, 1977; children—Burtch Winters, Frederic Malcolm, Kelley Keresey. Grad. U. Va., 1961. Sr. v.p. Dancer Fitzgerald and Sample, N.Y.C., 1961-78; European area dir. Life Savers Inc., London, 1978-80; sr. v.p. Foote Cone and Belding, N.Y.C., 1981; pres. Dancer, Fitzgerald Sample Inc., San Francisco, 1981—. Served with USMCR, 1959-67. Clubs: Racquet and Tennis (N.Y.C.); University (San Francisco). Office: 1010 Battery St San Francisco CA 94111

DRAKE, SUSAN FREIMER, telecommunications consultant; b. Bklyn., May 23, 1946; d. Leo and Beatrice (Samuels) Freimer; m. Stanley Rosenzweig, July 16, 1967; m. 2d, Richard P. Drake, Nov. 15, 1981. B.A., CUNY, 1967. Communications cons. N.Y. Telephone, N.Y.C., 1970-75; communications analyst Nat. Telephone Planning Corp., Yonkers, N.Y., 1975-78; cons. Peat, Marwick Mitchell & Co., N.Y.C., 1978-79; dir. Los Angeles ops. Contel Info. Systems, Great Neck, N.Y., 1979-82; owner, mgr. Suritel Assocs., Los Angeles, 1982—. Bd. dirs., residential chmn. Am. Cancer Soc., Yonkers, 1977-78. Mem. Internat. Orgn. Women in Telecommunications, Valley Interchange of Exec. Women (founding dir., v.p.), Nat. Assn. Female Execs. Contbr. articles to profl. jours. Home and Office: 18915 Bahama St Northridge CA 91324

DRANEY, NOLAN G., food supplement co. exec.; b. Afton, Wyo., Feb. 22, 1935; s. Elno Foss and Laura (Gardner) D.; B.S., Utah State U., 1957; M.B.A., Harvard U., 1961; m. Joyce Nield, June 30, 1954; children—Jeffrey Nolan, Lisa. Various positions Litton Industries, Van Nuys, Calif., 1961-67; vice-pres. finance Olson Farms, North Hollywood, Calif., 1967-68; exec. vice-pres. Computer Planning Corp., Torrance, Calif., 1968-72; pres. Plus Products, Irvine, Calif., 1972-76; pres., chief exec. officer Wm. T. Thompson Co., Torrance, Calif., 1976—, also dir.; dir. Calif. Nutritional Labs.; Health Mart. Mem. nat. roundtable Utah State U. Served to capt. AUS, 1957-60. Mem. Ch. Jesus Christ of Latter-day Saints. Office: 475 Alaska Ave Torrance CA 90503

DRAPER, LYNN MARIE SPENCER, army officer; b. Tacoma, Wash., July 27, 1955; d. Murvill F. and Barbara (Widmer) Spencer. B.A., U. San Francisco, 1977, postgrad. 1977-79. Service coordinator U. San Francisco Housing Program, 1978-79; commd. 2d lt. U.S. Army, 1979, advanced through grades to capt., 1982; adj. exec. officer Comdt. Hdqrs., Sierra Army Depot, Herlong, Calif., 1982—; evening instr., Lassen Jr. Coll., 1979-81. Republican. Roman Catholic. Home: PO Box 675 Herlong CA 96113 Office: CDR Sierra Army Depot SDSS1-A Herlong CA 96113

DRAPER, SHERRY DIANE, petroleum corporation executive; b. El Dorado, Kans., Oct. 11, 1951; d. Bill D. and June (Richards) D. Student Regis Coll., 1980-83. Billing staff asst. City Clks. Office, Hays, Kans., 1970-73; mem. pub. relations staff Bonfils Blood Ctr., Denver, 1973-78; with Vince Allen & Assoc., Denver, 1978-79; contract adminstrn. clk. Ladd Petroleum Corp., Denver, 1979-80, contract adminstr., 1980-81, sr. contract adminstr., 1981—. Charter mem. Constituent Action Program Ladd Petroleum Corp. Mem. Rocky Mountain Gas Assn. Roman Catholic. Home: 16130 E Gunnison Pl Aurora CO 80017 Office: Ladd Petroleum Corp 830 Denver Club Bldg Denver CO 80202

DRASHNER, DICK DEAN, ins. exec.; b. Kimball, S.D., Feb. 20, 1935; s. Charles Henry and Mary Rose (Pipal) D.; student U. Idaho, 1955-56; B.S., Tome Naval Acad., 1957; m. Mary Ellen Allred, July 10, 1957; children—Valencia, Daniel, Michelle, Christopher. Mgr., Am. Motors Finance Utah, 1959-61; exec. v.p. fin. L & L Furniture Corp., Idaho, 1961-63; pres. Furniture Distbrs. Corp., Denver, 1963-66; exec. Mfrs. Life Ins. Co., Oklahoma City, Okla., 1966-72; v.p. mktg. Teton Nat. Life Ins. Co., Cheyenne, Wyo., 1973; pres. Gem State Securities Corp., Am. Res. Life Ins. Co., Boise, Idaho, 1980—, Western Gen. Ins. Co., Boise, 1981—; partner Drashner-Monk & Co.-Consultants, Boise, 1980—; dir. Idaho Mktg. Corp., Boise. Served with USN, 1953-57. Mem. Sales and Mktg. Execs., Naval Res. Officers Assn., Chartered Life Underwriters Assn., Idaho Life Ins. Co. Council, C. of C. Republican. Roman Catholic. Home: 2953 Leisure Dr Boise ID 83704 Office: PO Box 9327 Boise ID 83707

DRAVIS, BETTY LOUISE, pub.; b. Hamilton, Ohio, Dec. 20, 1928; d. John D. and Felda Mae (Crawford) Barger; student San Diego State U., Foothill Coll. Los Altos, Cabrillo Coll.; children—Debra Rivera, Denyce, Mary Lee, Bob, Mindy Gonzales, Allison. Soc. editor Imperial Beach News, San Diego, 1960-62; editor Gilroy (Calif.) News Herals, 1972, Labor Union Gazette, 1973-78; talk show hostess Gilroy Cable TV, 1972-73; pub., owner Constrn. Labor News, San Jose, Calif., 1978—. Mem. United Way Communications Com. Recipient Santa Clara County Mercury-News Woman of Achievement award; Stanford Heart Disease Prevention award; Gilroy Jaycees award, others. Mem. Internat. Labor Press Assn., San Jose Newspaper Guild, Sigma Delta Chi. Democrat. Author: Zany the Zebra, We're Neat Guitars, 1960. Home: 4644 Calle de Farrar San Jose CA 95118 Office: 2102 Almaden Rd Suite 303 San Jose CA 95125

DRAY, WILLIAM PERRY, lawyer; b. Cheyenne, Wyo., Sept. 20, 1940; s. George N. and Velda M. (Gamble) D.; m. Judy A. Gardner, Aug. 22, 1962; children—Todd, Lisa, Christopher. B.S. in Law, U. Wyo., 1962, J.D., 1964; LL.M. in Taxation, George Washington U., 1968. Bar: Wyo. 1965. Ptnr Hirst, Applegate & Dray, Cheyenne, 1968-75; sole practice, Cheyenne, 1975-76; ptnr. Dray & Madison, Cheyenne, 1976-77, Dray, Madison & Thomson, Cheyenne, 1977—; dir. Am. Bank Corp., Am. Nat. Bank Cheyenne, Univcover Corp., Unicover World Trade Corp., Unicover Internat. Sales Corp. Mem. precinct com. Laramie County Republican Party, 1970-74. Served with JAGC, U.S. Army, 1965-68. Mem Indsl. Devel. Assn., ABA, Wyo. State Bar Assn., Laramie County Bar Assn., Assn. Trial Lawyers Am., Wyo. Trial Lawyers Assn. Methodist. Clubs: Cheyenne Quarterback, Kiwanis. Contbg. articles to profl. jours. Address: 204 E 22d St Cheyenne WY 82001

DRAYTON, HENRY EDWARD, JR., naval officer, naval engr.; b. Port Washington, N.Y., July 1, 1932; s. Henry E. and Phyllis S. (Povah) D.; B.S. in Engring., Yale U., 1954; M.S. in Naval Engring., U.S. Naval Postgrad. Sch., 1963; children—Richard D., Diana H., Stuart H. Commd. ensign U.S. Navy, 1954, advanced through grades to capt., 1975; assigned to U.S.S. Otterstetter, 1954-56, U.S.S. Tiru, 1957-60; navigator in commissioning crew of Polaris submarine U.S.S. U.S. Grant, 1963-65; mem. staff, comdr.-in-chief U.S. Pacific Fleet, 1966-69; engring. duty officer Pearl Harbor Naval Shipyard, 1969-71, asst. repair supt. for submarines, 1970-71; prodn. officer Ship Repair Facility, Guam, 1971-74; submarine sonar div. dir. Naval Sea System Command, 1974-77; chief staff officer Naval Ocean Systems Center, San Diego, 1977-80; comdg. officer Naval Sea Support Center, San Diego, 1980—. Decorated Meritorious Service medal, Meritorious Unit commendation, 1973, Navy Commendation medal, 1977. Mem. Am. Soc. Naval Engrs., Am. Def. Preparedness Assn., Fed. Exec. Assn., Sigma Xi. Republican. Episcopalian. Home: 7281 Golfcrest Dr San Diego CA 92119 Office: Comdg Officer NAVSEACENPAC PO Box 80548 San Diego CA 92138

DREAPER, RICHARD EDWARD, art dealer; b. Mobile, Ala., Aug. 24, 1935; s. Edward Joseph and Emilie Douglas (Poe) D.; A.A., St. Bernard Coll., Cullman, Ala., 1954; postgrad. La. State U., 1955, U. Ariz., 1959-61; B.A., U. Calif.-Irvine, 1969. Asst. to dir. U. Ariz. Art Gallery, Tucson, 1960-61; designer, cons., 1961-69; assoc. Ancient Art, Laguna Beach, Calif., 1969-79; vis. lectr. Chinese art U. Calif.-Irvine. Active Laguna Beach Outreach. Served with USN, 1955-59. Mem. Asia Soc., Alpha Kappa Delta. Democrat.

DREESE, MITCHELL, educator; b. Harrisburg, Pa., Jan. 28, 1901; s. Ira D. and Kathrine M. (Mitchell) D.; B.S., Columbia, 1926, M.A., 1927, Ph.D., 1929; m. Dorothy Coble, June 20, 1925; 1 son, Mitchell Joe. Dir. personnel Grinnell (Iowa) Coll., 1929-31; faculty ednl. psychology George Washington U., Washington, 1931-61, dean Coll. Gen. Studies, 1951-61; prof. edn., Shippensburg (Pa.) State Coll., 1961-66, prof. emeritus, 1966—; freelance writer, lectr. 1966—; cons. extension div. U. Ariz., Tucson, 1973-75. Served to maj. USAAC, 1942-45. Diplomate Am. Bd. Examiners in Profl. Psychology. Fellow Am. Psychol. Assn. (pres. div. counseling psychology 1951-52); mem. Am. Ednl. Research Assn., Am. Personnel and Guidance Assn., Phi Delta Kappa. Author: How to Get the Job, 1941, 70, 77; Military Guidance in Secondary Schools, 1953. Address: 3104 E Broadway Brentwood W Space 124 Mesa AZ 85204

DREIER, DAVID TIMOTHY, congressman; b. Kansas City, Mo., July 5, 1952; s. H. Edward and Joyce D.; B.A., Claremont Men's Coll., 1975, M.A., 1976. Dir. corp. relations Claremont Men's Coll., 1975-79; dir. govt. affairs Indsl. Hydrocarbons, San Dimas, Calif., 1979-80; mem. 97th congress from 35th dist. Calif., 1981—. Mem. Los Angeles County Republican Central Com. Mem. San Dimas C. of C., Nat. Fedn. Ind. Bus. Christian Scientist. Office: 410 Cannon House Office Bldg Washington DC 20515

DREIMAN, HOLLY D., educator; b. Vincennes, Ind., Oct. 31, 1954; s. Dee N. and Barbara L. (Hollingsworth) D. B.S., Purdue U., 1977; M.A. summa cum laude, Ball State U., 1980. Tchr. home econs. Lander County (Nev.) Sch. Dist., 1978-80, Elko County Sch. Dist., Carlin, Nev., 1980—. Mem. Am. Home Econs. Assn., Am. Vocat. Assn. Presbyterian. Home: 190 1/2 W Juniper St Elko NV 89801 Office: Carlin Sch PO Box 797 Carlin NV 89822

DRENNAN, G(EORGE) ELDON, utility company executive; b. Walla Walla, Wash., Mar. 22, 1921; s. George I. and Ella B. (Myrick) D.; student Whitman Coll., 1938-39; B.S., Wash. State U., 1943; grad. Advanced Mgmt. Program, Harvard, 1970; m. Jane Nilsson, June 16, 1943 (dec.); children—Michael E., Barbara A. With Pacific Power & Light Co., Portland, Ore., 1946—, v.p., 1971-74, sr. v.p., 1974-76, exec. v.p., 1976-79, pres., 1979-82, vice chmn. bd., 1982—. Served to lt. USNR, 1943-46. Elk. Clubs: University, Portland Golf, Arlington. Home: 1475 Cherry Crest Dr Lake Oswego OR 97034

DRENNON, JAMES BARRY, life sciences technician; b. Morristown, N.J., Dec. 12, 1944; s. Winfield Kinsley and Rose Marie (Morris) D.; m. Barbara Jo Benavente, Oct. 29, 1962; m. 2d, Marsha Kay Long, Dec. 13, 1969; children—Scott Patrick, Felicia Anne, Jeffrey Todd, Deborah Michele, Laura Nicole. Customer service rep. IBM, Phila., Atlanta, 1966-70; lab. technician Devro Inc., Somerville, N.J., 1970-74; chem. technician Controls for Environ. Pollution, Santa Fe, 1974-76; life scis. technician III U. Calif. Los Alamos Nat. Lab., 1976—. Vestryman, sr. warden, mem. Acolyte Guild, Episcopalian Church. Served with USN, 1963-66. Mem. Am. Soc. Agronomy, Soil Sci. Soc. Am., Calumet Photographic Soc., Western History Assn., N. Mex. Barbed Wire Collectors Assn. Democrat. Contbr. numerous articles to profl. publs. Home: 1607 Salvador Pl Santa Fe NM 87501 Office: PO Box 1663 Los Alamos National Lab Los Alamos NM 87545

DRESSEL, DIANE MARIE, university official; b. Mt. Vernon, N.Y., Dec. 4, 1955; d. Edward George and Mary Alice (Bergines) D. B.S. in Edn., So. Conn. State Coll., 1977; M.S. in Edn., So. Ill. U., 1980. Counselor So. Ill. U., Carbondale, 1978-79, area bus. mgr., 1979-80; resident dir. U. Denver, 1980-81; supr. confs. desks U. San Francisco, 1982, resident dir., 1982—; spl. edn. tchr. Mem. Nat. Assn. Women Deans and Counselors, AAUW, Nat. Assn. Female Execs., NOW. Home: 2305 Golden Gate Ave San Francisco CA 94118 Office: U San Francisco San Francisco CA

DRESSER, JESSE DALE, real estate investor; b. San Diego, May 5, 1906; s. Charlwood Fessenden and Ora (Evans) D.; student pub. schs., San Diego; m. Mary A. Goldsworthy, June 9, 1934; children—Dennis T., Linda A., Brian D. Trainee Union Title Ins. Co., San Diego, 1926; sr. title examiner, chief title officer, v.p. So. Title and Trust Co., 1927-51; v.p., chief title officer Security Title Ins. Co., San Diego, 1951-54; asst. to pres. San Diego Fed. Savs. & Loan Assn., 1954-55, v.p., 1955-56, sec., 1955-62, exec. v.p., 1956-70, dir. 1962-70; v.p., dir. Calif. Gen. Mortgage Service, Inc., 1967-70, S.D. Federated Ins. Agy., Inc., 1967-70, ret., 1969; real estate investor, 1970—. Home: 3833 Acacia St Bonita CA 92002 Office: PO Box 418 Bonita CA 92002

DRESSIN, RONALD MARK, office automation cons.; b. El Paso, Tex., Jan. 20, 1948; s. Sam Aaron and Suzanne Edith (Abrams) D.; B.S. in Engring., U.S. Naval Acad., 1970; M.A. in Human Resources Mgmt., Pepperdine U., 1976; M.S. in Systems Mgmt., U. So. Calif., 1977. Engr. electronics div. Gen. Dynamics Corp., San Diego, 1977-78, software engr. Western Data Support Center, 1978-79; asst. v.p., mgr. orgn. devel. San Diego Fed. Savs. & Loan Assn., 1979-82; office automation mgr. Sci. Applications, Inc., 1982—. Served with USN, 1966-70, USMC, 1970-76. Mem. Am. Inst. Indsl. Engrs., Internat. Info./Word Processing Assn., Fin. Adminstrv. Methods Assn. Home: 7979 Caminito Dia San Diego CA 92122 Office: Sci Applications Inc 1055 Wall St LaJolla CA 92037

DRESSLER, FREDERIC MICHAEL, cable TV executive; b. N.Y.C., Sept. 23, 1941; s. Martin and Anne (Kaufman) D.; m. Betty Brown, Apr. 3, 1966; children—Kevin, Douglas. B.S., Syracuse U., N.Y., 1963; student, U. Denver, 1979; Negotiation Inst., 1981. News reporter, editorial dir. sta. KBTV, Denver 1967-74; exec. news producer Sta. KMGH-TV, Denver, 1974-76; system mgr. Fresno, Calif., 1977; div. mgr. Am. TV and Communications Corp., Englewood, Colo., 1977-80; v.p. Denver, 1980—; pres. Mile Hi Cablevision Inc., Denver, 1982—; also chief exec. officer; lectr. U. Colo., 1971-74. Vice pres., dir. Colo. Easter Seal Soc. 1980. Served USNG, 1963-69. Distinguished Service in Journalism, 1971, Commendation for Investigative Reporting, 1973, Service Recognition Award, Nat. Broadcast Editorial Assn., 1975. Mem. Nat. Cable TV Assn., Nat. Broadcast Editorial Assn. (founding dir., officer, 1972, pres. 1975, Radio-TV Editorial Jour. adv. bd., 1974-76), Alpha Epsilon Rho. Home: 7213 E Hinsdale Pl Englewood CO 80112 Office: Mile Hi Cablevision 1355 S Colorado Blvd Suite 4400 Denver CO 80222

DRESSLER, ROBERT CLAY, cosmetic co. exec.; b. Glen Ridge, N.J., July 22, 1943; s. JohnClay and Maxine Lillian (McLeod) D.; B.S. in Chemistry, Columbia U., 1964. Chemist, Max Factor & Co., Hollywood, Calif., 1966, Revlon Co., N.Y.C., 1967-69; dir. product devel. Elizabeth Arden, 1970-73; v.p. research and devel. Merle Norman Cosmetics, Los Angeles, 1973-79, mem. exec. com., 1976—, sr. v.p., 1979—. Mem. Am. Chem. Soc., Soc. Cosmetic Chemists. Home: 10981 Harrogate Pl Santa Ana CA 92705 Office: 9130 Bellanca Ave Los Angeles CA 90045

DREW, CLIFFORD JAMES, educator; b. Eugene, Oreg., Mar. 9, 1943; s. Albert C. and Violet M. (Caskey) D.; B.S. magna cum laude, Eastern Oreg. Coll., 1965; M.Ed., U. Ill., 1966; Ph.D. with honors, U. Oreg., 1968. Asst. prof. edn. Kent (Ohio) State U., 1968-69; asst. prof., dir. research and spl. edn. U. Tex., Austin, 1969-71; asso. prof. spl. edn. U. Utah, Salt Lake City, 1971-76, prof., 1977—, asst. dean Grad. Sch. Edn., 1974-77, asso. dean, 1977-79, prof. spl. edn. and ednl. psychology, 1979—; cons. HEW, 1969—. Bd. dirs. Far W. Lab. Ednl. Research and Devel., San Francisco. 1974-80; mem. exec. bd. Salt Lake County Assn. Retarded Children, 1971-72; mem. adv. com. Mental Retardation Counseling Service, Tex. Dept. Mental Health Mental Retardation, 1969-70. NDEA fellow, 1965-66, U.S. Office Edn. fellow, 1966-68. Fellow Am. Assn. Mental Deficiency, Council for Exceptional Children; mem. Am. Psychol. Assn., Am. Ednl. Research Assn. Author: (with P. Chinn and D. Logan) Mental Retardation: A Life Cycle Approach, 1975, 2d edit., 1979; Introduction to Designing Research and Evaluation, 1976, 2d edit., 1980; (with M. Hardman and H. Bluhm) Mental Retardation: Social and Educational Perspectives, 1977; (with D. Gelfand and W. Jenson) Understanding Children's Behavior Disorders, 1982; numerous sci. articles. Office: Grad Sch Edn MBH 221 U Utah Salt Lake City UT 84112

DREW, RICHARD CLAYTON, state official; b. Detroit, Feb. 28, 1926; s. William Albert and Bernice Gervave (Topping) D.; student Ariz. State Tchrs. Coll., Flagstaff, 1944; B.S. in Bus. Adminstrn., UCLA, 1949; m. Amelia May Tonoyan, Apr. 24, 1954; children—John, James, Richard, Thomas, William. Safety engr., spl. agt. State Compensation Ins. Fund, Los Angeles, 1950-56; safety engr. Argonaut Ins. Co., Los Angeles, 1956-57; indsl. safety engr. Calif. Div. Indsl. Safety, Los Angeles, 1957-74; dist. mgr. Calif. Div. Occupational Safety and Health, Panorama City, 1974—. Chmn. sweepstakes inspection team Greater Los Angeles chpt. Nat. Safety Council, 1953-54; scoutmaster Bill Hart dist. Boy Scouts Am., 1968-70, 72-79, neighborhood commr., 1971. Served with USNR, 1944; apptd. maj. Calif. Mil. Res., 1979. Recipient award of merit Boy Scouts Am., 1977; cert. safety profl., registered profl. engr., cert. hazard control mgr., Calif. Mem. Am. Soc. Safety Engrs., So. Calif. Indsl. Safety Soc. (gov. 1952), Calif. State Employees Assn., UCLA Alumni Assn. Republican. Am. Orthodox. Office: 3415 Fletcher Ave Suite 204 El Monte CA 91731

DREWS, JEROME DANIEL, chemist; b. Buffalo, Dec. 23, 1942; s. John Alexander and Mary Florence (Poplachowski) D.; B.S., No. Ariz. U., 1973; m. Ann M. Swisher, June 26, 1971; children—Daniel David, Ellen Elizabeth. Lab. technician Ariz. Testing Lab., 1969-71; acting chemist U.S. Geol. Survey, 1972-73; process control chemist Monsanto Co., Seattle, 1973-74; criminalist Wash. State Patrol, Seattle, 1974-75; sr. analytical chemist Pennwalt Corp., Tacoma, 1976-81; design chemist, cons. chemistry, Kent, Wash., 1981—. Served with USAF, 1963-67. Recipient Group Achievement award NASA, 1973. Mem. Am. Chem. Soc., Soc. Applied Spectroscopy. Home and Office: 10582 SE 228th St Kent WA 98031

DREXLER, JOHN ANTHONY, JR., mgmt. psychologist, educator; b. Carnegie, Pa., Oct. 17, 1945; s. John Anthony and Mary Cecelia (Urbanek) D. B.A., Wayne State U., 1968, M.A., 1971; Ph.D., U. Mich., 1975. Asst. project dir. Inst. Social Research, U. Mich., Ann Arbor, 1973-75; research scientist Battelle Meml. Inst., Seattle, 1975-79; lectr. mgmt. and orgn. grad. sch. bus. adminstrn. U. Wash., Seattle, 1979-83; asst. prof. Sch. Bus. Adminstrn., Oreg. State U., Corvallis, 1983—; cons. in field. Mem. Acad. Mgmt., Am. Psychol. Assn., Western Psychol. Assn. Roman Catholic. Contbr. articles to profl. jours. Office: Sch Business Bexell Hall Oreg State U Corvallis OR 97331

DREXLER, KENNETH, lawyer; b. San Francisco, Aug. 2, 1941; s. Fred and Martha Jane (Cunningham) D.; B.A., Stanford U., 1963; J.D., UCLA, 1969. Admitted to Calif. bar, 1970; asso. law offices of David S. Smith, Beverly Hills, Calif., 1970; asso. firm McCutchen, Doyle, Brown & Enersen, San Francisco, 1970-77; asso. firm Chickering & Gregory, San Francisco, 1977-80, ptnr., 1980-82; ptnr. Drexler & Leach, San Rafael, 1982—. Served with U.S. Army, 1964-66. Decorated Army Commendation medal. Mem. Bar Assn. of San Francisco (bd. dirs. 1980-81), Barristers Club (pres. 1976, bd. dirs. 1975-76). Office: 1330 Lincoln Ave Suite 300 San Rafael CA 94901

DREYFUS, EDWARD ALBERT, clinical psychologist; b. N.Y.C., Mar. 27, 1937; s. Herbert and Estelle (Soussi) D.; m. Estelle Dobbs, June 15, 1958; children—David, Ronald, Lydia; m. Judith Kay Jones, Aug. 3, 1980. Ph.D., U. Kans., 1964. Diplomate Am. Bd. Profl. Psychotherapy. Pres. Edward A. Dreyfus, Ph.D. & Assocs., Santa Monica, Calif. 1981—. Home: 1726 Ensley Ave Los Angeles CA 90024 Office: 1421 Santa Monica Blvd Santa Monica CA 90404

DREYFUS, GRACE HAWES (MRS. LOUIS G. DREYFUS, JR.), civic worker; b. Victory, N.Y., Dec. 26, 1892; d. John Bently and Pearl (Van Hoosen) Hawes; student pub. schs., N.Y., Prager Sch., Dresden, Germany; grad. State U. N.Y., 1913; m. Louis G. Dreyfus, Jr., June 14, 1917. Founder, Grace Dreyfus Clinic and Orphanage, Teheran, Iran, 1941; Decorated Elmi 1st class (Iran). Mem. Channel City Women's Forum (charter mem.), Nat. Inst. Arts and Letters (v.p. Santa Barbara), Affiliates U. Calif. (hon. life dir. Santa Barbara br.), Red Lion and Sun (life mem. Iran), Internat. Platform Assn., Nat. Contract Bridge League, English Speaking Union, Channel City Women's Forum. Clubs: Little Town, Valley, Coral Casino, Valley Montecito (Santa Barbara). Home: 370 Hot Springs Rd Santa Barbara CA 93108

DRIGGS, GARY HARMON, financial exec.; b. Phoenix, July 13, 1934; s. Douglas H. and Effie (Killian) D.; student Stanford, 1952-54; B.A., Brigham Young U., 1959; M.B.A., Ind. U., 1960, D.Bus.Adminstrn., 1962; m. Kay Taylor, June 9, 1959; children—Rebecca Taylor, Kimberly, Benjamin. Faculty lectr. Ind. U., 1961-62; exec. v.p., economist Western Savs., Phoenix, 1962-73, pres., 1973—; chmn. bd. Romney Internat. Hotels, 1973; lectr. Ariz. State U., 1962-67; pres. Western Fin. Corp., 1976—. Active Boys Scouts Am.; mem. Ct. Commn. Maricopa County. Chmn. City of Phoenix Sts. Adv. Bd., 1973—; pres. Ariz. Tomorrow; chmn. Gov.'s State Urban Lands Task Force; mem. Ariz. Commn. Nat. and Internat. Commerce. Named Outstanding Young Man of the Year in Ariz., Ariz. Jaycees, 1968, Phoenix Outstanding Young Man, 1969. Mem. Savs. and Loan League Ariz. (pres. 1972-73), Young Pres.'s Orgn. Republican. Mem. Ch. Jesus Christ of Latter-Day Saints. Rotarian. Author: How to Reduce Risk in Apartment Lending, 1966. Home: 7510 Shadow Mountain Rd Paradise Valley AZ 85253 Office: 3443 N Central Ave Phoenix AZ 85011

DRISCOLL, JOHN WAYNE, business official; b. Reidsville, N.C., May 2, 1942; s. John Henry and Inez (Carter) D.; m. Deanne LaRue Yancey, June 14, 1963; children—Suzanne, Debra, Charlotte, David. B. Vocat. Tech. Tchr. Edn. with high honors, Idaho State U., 1982. Reactor operator Argonne Nat. Lab., Idaho Falls, Idaho, 1968-73, tng. specialist, 1974—; tng. specialist Gen. Physics Corp., Columbia, Md., 1973-74; cons. in field. Fin. chmn. Blackfoot dist. Boy Scouts Am., 1981-83; mem. Bingham County Young Republicans, 1969-73. Recipient award of merit Boy Scouts Am., 1982; Argonne Employee scholar, 1981. Mem. Am. Nuclear Soc., Am. Soc. Tng. and Devel. Mormon. Author numerous tng. and procedures publs. Home: 1325 Walker St Blackfoot ID 83221 Office: PO Box 2528 Idaho Falls ID 83401

DRISCOLL, NEIL JOSEPH, III, lawyer; b. Chgo., Nov. 14, 1948; s. Neil Joseph and Regina Frances (Golden) D.; m. Linda Rae Fallon, June 30, 1973; children—Amelia Tara, Ethan Hancock. B.S., Portland State U., 1974; J.D., Lewis & Clark Law Sch., 1977. Bar: Oreg. 1978, U.S. Dist. Ct. Oreg. 1978, U.S. Tax Ct. 1982. Sole practice, Portland, Oreg., 1980—. Served with U.S. Army, 1971-72. Decorated Air medal, Purple Heart, U.S. Army Commendation medal, Armed Forces Honor medal (Vietnam). Mem. Oreg. Bar Assn., Multnomah Bar Assn. Republican. Club: Willamette Athletic (Portland). Home: 6140 SW Burma Rd Lake Oswego OR 97034 Office: 3405 SW Barbur Blvd Portland OR 97201

DROLLINGER, HOWARD BLAINE, II, real estate developer; b. Los Angeles, June 16, 1922; s. Howard Blaine and Ella Margaret (Lewin) D.; student U. Ariz., 1940-42; B.S., U. So. Calif., 1945-47; m. Jewel Eisenhower, Oct. 27, 1950; children—Karen Joy Drollinger Dial, Howard James. Broker, Frank H. Ayres and Son, Los Angeles, 1947-52; mng. partner Ella L. Drollinger Co., Los Angeles, 1952—; pres. H.B. Drollinger Co., Los Angeles, 1952—; founder Fox Hills Savs. and Loan, 1962; founder dir. Gateway Nat. Bank, 1963-70; dir. Wedbush, Noble, Cooke, Inc., 1975-81, also dir. Dir., treas. Westchester YMCA, 1958-62; mem. Los Angeles Bd. Zoning Appeals, 1960-61; mem. Mayor's Com. Capital Improvements, 1963, 65. Served with AUS, 1943-45. Decorated D.F.C., Air medal, Medal, Purple Heart. Mem. Calif. C. of C., Commerce Assos. U. So. Calif., U. So. Calif. Alumni Assn. Mem. Religious Science Ch. Clubs: Westport Beach, Rotary (Westchester). Office: 9100 S Sepulveda Blvd Suite 100 Los Angeles CA 90045

DROSSEL, EUGENE RAYMOND, banker; b. Chgo., Sept. 18, 1921, s. Felix and Julia (Mroczek) D.; B.A., U. Redlands, 1952; postgrad. San Francisco State Coll., 1960-61, U. San Francisco, 1964, Columbia, 1974; m. Ruth MacIver; 1 dau. by previous marriage, Annalee. Supr. heat treat Taylor Pipe & Forge Co., 1939-41; instrument technician Chrysler Corp., Detroit, 1946-49; with Kaiser Steel Co., Oakland, Calif., 1951-80, supr. cinematography, 1956-59, publs. mgr., 1959-64, dir. pub. relations, advt., 1964-74, v.p. pub. affairs, 1977-80; communications dir. Kaiser Industries, 1974-76; mng. dir. Drossel and MacIver, Alameda, Calif., 1976-82; v.p. Fed. Res. Bank, San Francisco, 1982—. Served with USMC, 1942-46. Mem. Public Relations Soc. Am. (accredited), World Affairs Council, Assn. Iron and Steel Engrs., Pub. Relations Round Table. Clubs: Press, Sierra, Commonwealth (San Francisco). Author books and articles. Office: PO Box 7702 San Francisco CA 94120

DROWER, IRIS SHARON, special educator; b. Chgo., June 8, 1954; d. Victor and Harriet (Deutch) Drower. B.S. in Spl., Elem. Edn., No. Ill. U., 1976; postgrad. Ariz. State U., 1979—. Tchr. spl. edn. John Marshall High Sch., Austin High Sch., Chgo., 1976-79; tchr. for handicapped Mesa (Ariz.) Central Vocat. Tech. Ctr., 1979-81; drivers edn. specialist for handicapped, Mesa Sch. Dist., 1981—; tchr. therapeutic horsemanship for handicapped. Camp naturalist Chgo. Youth Ctrs., 1973-78; asst. Spl. Olympics, Ill., 1976-78, Ariz., 1979—. Spl. Edn. scholar Rotary Mesa Club, 1981; recipient award Ariz. Driver and Safety Edn. Assn., Tempe, Ariz., 1983. Mem. Council Exceptional Children, Internat. Found. Bus. and Profl. Women's Club, Driver Safety Assn., Spl. Needs Assn., Found. Exceptional Children, Ariz. Higher and Adult Edn., Assn., Smithsonian Instn., Ariz. Vocat. Assn., Phi Delta Kappa. Home: PO Box 2159 Mesa AZ 85204 Office: 549 N Stapley Dr Mesa AZ 85203

DROWN, EUGENE ARDENT, govt. ofcl.; b. Ellenburg, N.Y., Apr. 25, 1915; s. Frank Arthur and Jessie Kate D.; B.S., Utah State U., 1938; postgrad. Mont. State U., 1939-40; Ph.D. in Public Adminstrn., U. Beverly Hills, 1979; m. Florence Marian Munroe, Mar. 5, 1938; children—Linda Harriett Oneto, Margaret Ruth Lunn. Park ranger Nat. Park Service, Yosemite Nat. Park, 1940-47; forest ranger U.S. Forest Service, Calif. Region, 1948-56; forest mgr. and devel. specialist U.S. Bur. Land Mgmt., Calif., 1956—; forest engring. cons., 1970—; research and devel. coordinator U.S. Army at U. Calif., Davis., 1961-65. Mem. adv. bd. Sierra Coll., Rocklin, Calif., 1962—; active Boy Scouts Am.; instr. ARC, 1954—. Served with AUS, 1941-45. Decorated Bronze Star, Silver Star; registered profl. engr., profl. land surveyor, profl. forester, Calif. Recipient Nat. Service medal ARC, 1964. Mem. Nat. Soc. Profl. Engrs., Soc. Am. Foresters, Am. Inst. Biol. Scientists, Ecol. Soc. Am., Res. Officers Assn. U.S., Nat. Rifle Assn., Internat. Rescue and First Aid Assn., Internat. Platform Assn., Bulldog Sentinels of Superior Calif. Methodist. Clubs: Masons, Shriners. Home: 5624 Bonniemae Way Sacramento CA 95824

DROZ, FRED STEVEN, political/governmental consultant; b. Detroit, Mar. 8, 1945; s. Harry and Florence Droz; m. Heidi Hemmen, Apr. 12, 1969. B.A., Calif. State U.-Fullerton, 1968; J.D., Georgetown U., 1976. Staff assoc. NEA, Washington, 1971-77; pub. involvement liaison, mgmt. analyst Pres.'s Reorgn. Project, Exec. Office of Pres., Washington, 1977; mgmt. analyst Office of Sec., U.S. Dept. Transp., Washington, 1977; pres. Adler & Droz, Santa Ana, Calif., 1978—; lectr. Bd. dirs. Gemco Edn. Found.; mem. alumni bd. dirs. Calif. State U.-Fullerton. Recipient Disting. Alumni award Calif. State U.-Fullerton, 1977; cert. of appreciation Pres. of U.S., 1977; commendation Lt. Gov. Calif., 1978. Mem. Am. Assn. Polit. Cons., Von Strobel Soc. Democrat. Jewish. Office: Adler & Droz 505 N Tustin Ave Suite 282 Santa Ana CA 92705

DROZD, LEON FRANK, JR., lawyer, oil co. exec.; b. Victoria, Tex., Sept. 11, 1948; s. Leon Frank and Dorothy Lucille (Smith) D.; B.B.A., Tex. A and M U., 1971; J.D., U. Denver, 1979. Bar: Colo., U.S. Dist. Ct. Colo. Legis. asst. U.S. Ho. of Reps., also Democratic Caucus, Washington, 1971-74, chief clk. com. on sci. and tech., 1974-75; asst. to dean for devel. Coll. Law, U. Denver, 1975-79; v.p. Braddock Publs., Inc., Washington, 1975-79; land and legal counsel Chevron Shale Oil Co., Chevron Resources Co., 1980—. Colo. elector Anderson/Lucey Nat. Unity Campaign, 1980. Mem. ABA, Colo. Bar Assn., Colo. Trial Lawyers Assn., Denver Bar Assn., Internat. Platform Assn., Denver C. of C. (steering com. 1981-82). Club: Nat. Democratic (Washington). Home: 235 Monaco Pkwy Denver CO 80220 Office: 1625 Broadway Suite 2150 Denver CO 80202

DRUCK, KENNETH MALCOLM, psychologist, social educator; b. Flushing, N.Y., Mar. 11, 1949; s. Charles and Roslyn Sara (Schuster) D.; m. Karen Joan Goldstein, June 5, 1950; children—Jenna, Stephanie. B.A. in Social Sci., Hofstra U., 1971; M.A. in Counseling, Adams State Coll., Alamosa, Colo., 1973; Ph.D. in Clin. Psychol., Fielding Inst., Santa Barbara, Calif., 1982. Registered psychol. asst., Calif. Clin.-community psychologist Spanish Peaks Mental Health Ctr., 1973-79; The Family Life Edn. Series, 1980—; pvt. practice psychotherapy, 1977—; dir.-founder Communication Now Workshop, 1979—; writer, researcher, lectr. on men's changing roles in contemporary life, psychol. wellness and inter-personal health; mem. Colo. Gov.'s Com. on Juvenile Offenders, 1976. Recipient Disting. Service award in community mental health, State of Colo., 1974. Mem. Am. Psychol. Assn. Author: Alice and Male. Home and office: 387 West I St Encinitas CA 92024

DRUE, ROGER HAMILTON, hosp. adminstr.; b. Stockton, Calif., Nov. 7, 1943; s. Roger Hamilton and Fanita Yewing (Yoakum) Druehl; B.S., U. Calif., 1967; M.B.A., U. Chgo., 1969; m. Margaret Randolph, Sept. 10, 1966; children—Christen, Scott, Brian. Vice pres. Meml. Hosp. Med. Center, Long Beach, Calif., 1972-79; pres. Mills Meml. Hosp., San Mateo, Calif., 1979—. Bd. dirs. Bay Pacific Health Plan, San Mateo. Served with U.S. Army, 1969-72. Decorated Bronze Star. Mem. Am. Hosp. Assn., Am. Coll. Hosp. Adminstrs. Club: Rotary. Home: 1405 Avondale Rd Hillsborough CA 94010 Office: 100S San Mateo Dr San Mateo CA 94401

DRUGG, WARREN SOWLE, palynologist; b. Sitka, Alaska, Jan. 29, 1929; s. Nels Martin Edward and Edith Marguerite (Newhall) D.; B.S. in Geology, U. Wash., Seattle, 1952, M.S., 1958; Ph.D. in Botany, Claremont Grad. Sch., 1966; m. Marlene May Boivin, Apr. 12, 1958; children—Martin E., Gordon M., Karen K. Geologist, Calif. Exploration Co., San Francisco, 1958-60; geologist Chevron Oil Field Research Co., La Habra, Calif., 1960-77, sr. research asso., 1977—. Served to 1st lt. USAF, 1952-56. Mem. Am. Assn. Petroleum Geologists, Am. Assn. Stratigraphic Palynologists, Paleontol. Soc., Soc. Econ. Paleontologists and Mineralogists, Paleobot. Soc. Am., Biol. Soc. Wash., Sigma Xi. Republican. Lutheran. Club: Clan Donnachaid. Home: 1820 E Stearns Ave La Habra CA 90631 Office: PO Box 446 La Habra CA 90631

DRUM, WILLIAM ORTON, educator; b. Circleville, Ohio, July 27, 1937; s. Orwin D. and Wilhelmina B. (Strehle) D.; B.A. with distinction, U. Ariz., 1959, M.Ed., 1964; m. Peggy Jo Hoover, Aug. 12, 1962; children—David Michael, Douglas Allen. Tchr., Ohio, 1959-62; chmn. dept. bus. edn. Rincon High Sch., Tucson, 1962—; mem. asso. faculty Pima Community Coll., U. Ariz. Mem. NEA, Computer Users in Edn., Ariz. Edn. Assn., Ariz. Bus. Edn. Assn., Tucson Edn. Assn., Tucson Bus. Educators Assn., Phi Kappa Phi, Pi Omega Pi. Republican. Co-author: Structured Basic Programming, 1982. Home: 801 N Sahuara Ave Tucson AZ 85711 Office: 422 N Arcadia Blvd Tucson AZ 85711

DRUMHELLER, GEORGE JESSE, motel chain exec.; b. Walla Walla, Wash., Jan. 30, 1933; s. Allen and Ila Margaret (Croxdale) D.; student Wash. State U., 1951-52, Whittier Coll., 1955-58; m. Carla Rene Cunha, May 4, 1965 (div. 1983); stepchildren—Matthew F., Douglas J. Mosgrove and Sean M. Drumheller. Asst. mgr. Olympic Hotel, Seattle, 1959; jr. exec. Western Internat. Hotels, Seattle, 1959-63; founder, pres. George Drumheller Properties, Inc., motel holding co., Pendleton, Oreg., 1963—; founder, chmn. bd. Dalles Tapadera, Inc., motel and hotel holding co., The Dalles, Oreg., 1964-77; founder, pres. Lewiston Tapadera, Inc. (Idaho), motel holding co., 1970-77; founder, pres. Yakima Tapadera, Inc. (Wash.), 1971-77; founding partner Drumheller & Titcomb (Tapadera Motor Inn), Ontario, Oreg., 1972—; founder Tapadera Budget Inns, Kennewick and Walla Walla, Wash., 1981—; engaged in farming, eastern Wash., 1958-80. Served with USCG, 1952-55. Mem. Am. Hotel and Motel Assn. (nat. dir. 1980—, pres.'s exec. com. 1982—), Oreg. Hotel Motel Assn. (dir. 1973-78), Wash. State Lodging Assn. (dir., v.p. 1976—). Clubs: La Jolla Beach and Tennis, Walla Walla Country, Spokane. Home: 601 Village Way #23 Walla Walla WA 99362 also 8642-1 Villa La Jolla Dr La Jolla CA 92037 Office: George Drumheller Properties Inc PO Box 1234 Walla Walla WA 99362

DRUMMER, DONALD RAYMOND, banking exec.; b. Binghamton, N.Y., Oct. 10, 1941; s. Donald Joseph and Louise Frances (Campbell) D.; A. Sci., Broome Community Coll., 1962; B.S., U. Colo., 1972; M.B.A., Regis Coll., 1981; m. Rita Kovac, May 22, 1965; children—Shelley Rita, Adam Donn. With, Lincoln First Bank, Binghamton, N.Y., 1962-69; asst. comptroller Adams & Horne, Denver, 1969; with Colo. State Bank, Denver, 1969—, v.p., 1972-81, comptroller, 1972—, sr. v.p., 1981—; adj. faculty Regis Coll. Mem. fin. com. Holy Family Grade Sch. Mem. Nat. Assn. Accts. (dir. 1975-79, v.p. 1977-79), Am. Acctg. Assn., Am. Taxation Assn. Clubs: Denver Sertoma (past pres.), City (v.p., dir.), Denver Athletic. Editor: Chronicle, 1980-81. Office: Colorado State Bank 1600 Broadway Denver CO 80202

DRUMMOND, GERARD KASPER, mining and natural resource development company executive, lawyer; b. N.Y.C., Oct. 9, 1937; s. John Landells and Margaret Louise (Kasper) D.; m. Donna J. Mason, Sept. 14, 1957; children—Alexander, Jane, Edmund; m. Nadine Johanna Skov, Dec. 31, 1976. B.S., Cornell U., 1959, L.L.B., with distinction, 1963. Bar: Oreg., 1963. Assoc. firm Davies, Biggs, Strayer, Stoel & Boley Portland, Oreg., 1963-64, Smith, Rives & Rodgers, Portland, 1964-69; ptnr. firm Rives, Bonyhadi, Drummond & Smith, Portland, 1969-77; pres. NERCO, Inc., Portland, 1977—; mem. corp. policy group Pacific Power & Light Co., Portland, 1979—. Bd. dirs., pres. Tri County Met. Transit Dist., 1974—; mem. Oreg.-Korea Econ. Cooperation Com., 1981—; trustee Reed Coll., 1982—. Served to 1st lt. USAR, 1959-67. Mem. ABA, Oreg. Bar Assn., Order of Coif, Phi Kappa Phi. Club: Arlington (Portland). Home: 1820 N Shore Rd Lake Oswego OR 97034 Office: 111 SW Columbia St Suite 800 Portland OR 97201

DRUMMOND, HAROLD DEAN, educator; b. Bettsville, Ohio, June 8, 1916; s. Ray Waldo and Velma Tyrone (Foor) D.; student Westminster Coll., 1933-35; A.B., Colo. State Coll., 1937, M.A., 1940; Ed.D., Stanford, 1948; m. Erma Catherine Street, Aug. 30, 1939; 1 son, Harold Evan. Prin., tchr. White Deer (Tex.) Ind. Sch. Dist., 1938-42; prof. elementary edn. George Peabody Coll. for Tchrs., Nashville, 1947-60; acting prof. tchr. edn. Stanford, U. Philippines, 1954-55; prof. elementary edn. U. N.Mex., Albuquerque, 1960-79, asso. dean for curriculum and instrn., 1976-79. Mem. adv. bd. Childcraft, 1957-60, 66-80. Served to lt. USNR, 1942-45; PTO. Mem. Assn. for Supervision and Curriculum Devel. (pres. 1964-65). Nat. Assn. Elementary Sch. Prins., Nat. Council Social Studies, Nat. Council Geog. Edn., Nat. Soc. Study Edn., N.E.A., Profs. Curriculum. Author: (with Charles R. Spain and John I. Goodlad) Educational Leadership and the Elementary School Principal, 1956; Our World Today series, A Journey Through Many Lands, Journeys Through the Americas, The Eastern Hemisphere, The Western Hemisphere, 1960-81. Home: 4311 Pershing Ave SE Albuquerque NM 87108

DRUMMOND, HARRIET ANAGNOSTIS, graphic designer, photographer; b. N.Y.C., Feb. 16, 1952; d. Anthony and Emilie (Tzanzek) Anagnostis; m. Gary Lynn Drummond, Apr. 2, 1956. B.S. in Design and Environ. Analysis, N.Y. State Coll. Human Ecology, Cornell U., 1974. Graphic designer Veco Inc., Anchorage, 1979-81, Lane & Knorr & Plunkett, 1977-79; owner Harriet Drummond Graphics & Photography, Anchorage, 1981—. Mem. Am. Inst. Graphic Arts. Greek Orthodox.

DRUMMOND, OLIVER LEE, city official; b. Van Nuys, Calif., Oct. 7, 1947; s. Joseph Lester and Ollie Lee (Rodabaugh) D.; m. Deborah Louise Clark, Oct. 14, 1970; 1 dau., Deborah Lee. B.S. in Criminology, Calif. State U.-Long Beach, 1974; advanced grad. cert. in exec. mgmt. Pacific Christian Coll., 1979; postgrad. in human behavior Newport U., 1979—; L.H.D. (hon.) Newport Internat. U., 1979; LL.D. (hon.) Van Norman U., 1980. Community coll. lifetime tchr. credential, Calif.; basic, intermediate, advanced and mgmt. certs. Calif. Dept. Justice. Police officer Santa Ana (Calif.) Police Dept., 1970-75, sgt., 1975-78, lt., 1978-82; chief of police Hanford (Calif.) Police Dept., 1982—; instr. Advanced Investigators Acad., Saddleback Coll., 1981-83. Mem. sch. site council Kings River-Hardwick Sch., 1982—, mem. sch. attendance rev. bd., 1982—; bd. dirs. Kings County Vol. Bur., 1982—. Served with Army N.G., 1969-75; served to lt., Mil. Police Corps, USAR, 1972-76. Recipient Profl. Service award Santa Ana Police Dept., 1982; named City Employee of Yr., Hanford C. of C., 1982; Chief of Yr., Calif. Law Enforcement Mgmt. Ctr., 1982. Mem. Internat. Assn. Chiefs of Police, Internat. Police Assn., ABA (criminal justice sect.), Calif. Peace Officers Assn. (law and legis. com.), Calif. Chiefs Assn., Calif. Assn. Police Tng. Officers, Calif. Combat Shooters Assn., Calif. Assn. Adminstrn. of Justice Educators, Calif. Robbery Investigators Assn., Kings County Peace Officers Assn., Hanford C. of C. (dir. 1983, 2d v.p., 1983). Lodge: Rotary. Office: 425 N Irwin St Hanford CA 93230

DRURY, DONALD VICTOR, librarian, stained glass artist; b. London, Oct. 22, 1927; came to U.S., 1957; s. Victor John and Mary Gray (Angus) d.; m. Dorothy Perry, Nov. 25, 1959. B.A., U. Cambridge, 1949, M.A., 1953; M.L.S., U. Calif.-Berkeley, 1972. Dir., mgr. Lowndes & Drury Ltd., London, 1950-57, 69-70; designer, craftsman Cummings Studios, San Francisco, 1957-59, Hogan Studios, San Jose, Calif., 1959-62; owner, mgr. Donald V. Drury Stained Glass Studio, San Francisco, 1962-69; dir. libraries Menlo Coll., Atherton, Calif., 1972—; mem. adminstrv. council S Bay Coop. Library System, 1982—. Bd. dirs. Coop. Info. Network, 1978-82. Mem. ALA, Calif. Library Assn. Democrat. Episcopalian. Home: Menlo Coll Apt 3A Atherton CA 94025 Office: Bowman Library Menlo Coll Atherton CA 94025

DRUVA, ROBERT LEE, engineering executive; b. Pueblo, Colo., Dec. 8, 1921; s. Charles Lee and Anna Elizabeth (Strohmer) D.; m. Lee Titman, Oct. 15, 1941; children—Marianne, Mark, Nancy. B.S. in Mech. Engring., Colo. State U., 1948. Registered profl. engr. Colo. Purchasing engr. Stearns-Roger Engring. Corp., Denver, 1948-51, Washington rep., 1951-53, project engr., Tucson, 1953-56, project mgr. various metall. projects, 1956-63, dir. procurement, 1963-70, v.p. purchasing, 1970-73, v.p. corp. affairs, 1973—; dir. Mentor Corp. Mem. Dist. Export Council; dir. Denver chpt. Am. Cancer Soc.; trustee Colo. State U. Found. Served to sgt. USAF. Mem. Am. Arbitration Assn., ASME (past dir.), AIME, Colo. Safety Assn. (dir.), Colo. Mining Assn. (dir.), Nat. Constructors Assn. (former dir.), Rocky Mountain Elec. League (v.p., dir.), Denver C. of C. (past dir.), Nat. Exec. Res. Clubs: Executive, Denver Athletic, Rotary (Denver). Home: 4800 Wagon Trail Littleton CO 80123 Office: 4500 Cherry Creek Dr Glendale CO 80217

DRUXMAN, MICHAEL BARNETT, public relations executive; b. Seattle, Feb. 23, 1941; s. Harry Irving and Florence Evelyn (Barnett) D.; m. Terry M. Lundy, Mar. 18, 1966 (div. 1979); 1 son, David Michael; m. 2d, Laurie Patricia Singer, July 3, 1983; 1 stepdau., Wendy Lynn Russ. B.A. in Sociology, U. Wash., 1963. Real estate salesman Pope & Talbot, Inc., Seattle, 1963; investigator Retail Credit Co., Los Angeles, 1964-65; owner Michael B. Druxman & Assocs., Los Angeles, 1965—; tchr. pub. relations UCLA, 1980. Author: Paul Muni, 1974; Basil Rathbone, 1975; Make It Again, Sam, 1975; Merv, 1976; Charlton Heston, 1976; One Good Film Deserves Another, 1977; The Musical, 1980; monthly columnist Coronet Mag., 1973-74. Office: 8831 Sunset Blvd Los Angeles CA 90069

DRY, JOHN STEPHEN, bus. equipment co. exec.; b. N.Y.C., Nov. 5, 1935; s. John Daniel and Ann (Gleza) D.; A.A., A.S., Merced Coll., 1976; B.S., U. San Francisco, 1979; M.S., U. So. Calif., 1983; m. Judith Elaine Stefko, Sept. 1, 1971; children—Steven J., Stephen A. Belmonte. Enlisted USAF, 1955, advanced through grades to sr. master sgt., 1977; avionics ops. supr., Guam, Thailand, 1967-72; bombing navigation dept. chief, McCoy AFB, Fla., 1972-73; mission systems br. chief, Castle AFB, Calif., 1973-77; ret., 1977; gen. mgr. Calif. Copy, Inc., Stockton, 1977—. Mem. adv. council Woodruff Regional Occupational Center, 1980. Decorated Bronze Star with oak leaf cluster, Air medal; recipient Disting. Edn. award USAF, 1975. Mem. IEEE, Aircraft Owners and Pilots Assn., Air Force Assn., Adminstrv. Mgmt. Soc., AAAS. Republican. Roman Catholic. Home: 3639 N Monitor Circle Stockton CA 95209 Office: 1743 Grand Canal Blvd Suite 10 Stockton CA 95207

DRYDEN, ROBERT EUGENE, lawyer; b. Chanute, Kans., Aug. 20, 1927; s. Calvin William and Mary Alfreda (Foley) D.; A.A., City Coll. San Francisco, 1947; B.S., U. San Francisco, 1951, J.D., 1954; m. Jetta Rae Burger, Dec. 19, 1953; children—Lynn Marie, Thomas Calvin. Admitted to Calif. bar, 1955; asso. Barfield, Barfield, Dryden & Ruane and predecessor firm, specializing in trial advocacy, San Francisco, 1954—, jr. partner, 1960-65, gen. partner, 1965—; lectr. continuing edn. of the bar, 1971-77. Served with USMCR, 1945-46. Diplomate Am. Bd. Trial Advs. Fellow Am. Coll. Trial Lawyers; mem. Am., San Francisco bar assns., State Bar Calif., Am. Judicature Soc., Assn. Def. Counsel (dir. 1968-71), Def. Research Inst., U. San Francisco Law Soc. (mem. exec. com. 1970-72), Internat. Assn. Ins. Counsel, U. San Francisco Alumni Assn. (bd. govs. 1977), Phi Alpha Delta. Home: 1320 Lasuen Dr Millbrae CA 94030 Office: 1 California St San Francisco CA 94111

DRYDEN, TINA VON, insurance executive, real estate salesperson; b. Carlsbad, N.Mex., Aug. 29, 1953; d. James D. and Billie June (Tidwell) D.; m. William A. Quinones, Jan. 10, 1975 (div.). Student Woodbury Coll., Los Angeles, 1973; B.A. in Bus. Adminstrn, N.Mex. State U., 1975. Co-owner Quinones Constrn Co., Las Cruces, N.Mex., 1974-76; owner Whistle Stop Sta., women's retail apparel, Las Cruces, 1976-81; owner Three Crosses Ins. Agy., Las Cruces, 1981—. Promotional chmn. Whole Enchilada Fiesta. Mem. Ind. Ins. Agts. N.Mex., Ind. Ins. Agts. Las Cruces (v.p.), C. of C. Republican. Baptist. Home: Office: Three Crosses Ins Agy 636 S Alameda Las Cruces NM 88005

DRYER, MURRAY, physicist; b. Bridgeport, Conn., Nov. 4, 1925; s. Sol and Sarah (Shapiro) D.; student U. Conn., 1943-44; B.S., Stanford, 1949, M.S., 1950; Ph.D., Tel-Aviv (Israel) U., 1970; m. Geraldine Gray Goodsell, May 12, 1955; children—Steven Michael, Lisa Gray. Research asst. NACA/NASA Ames Research Center, Calif., 1949, aero. research scientist NACA/NASA Lewis Research Center, Cleve., 1950-59; asso. research scientist Martin Marietta Corp., Denver, 1959-65; chief interplanetary physics Space Environment Lab., Nat. Oceanic Atmospheric Adminstrn. Environ. Research Labs., Boulder, Colo., 1965—; lectr. dept. aerospace engring. scis. U. Colo., 1963-76, dept. astro-geophysics, 1978—; vis. asso. prof. dept. mech. engring. Colo. State U., 1966-67; mem. com. solar terrestrial research Nat. Acad. Sci., 1976-80. Mem. Am. Phys. Soc., Am. Geophys. Union, AAAS, Sci. Com. for Solar-Terrestrial Physics, Internat. Astron. Union, Com. for Space Research, Am. Inst. Aeros. and Astronautics (Space Sci. award 1975), Sigma Xi. Co-author: Solar-Terrestrial Physics in the 1980's. Co-editor: Solar Observations and Predictions of Solar Activity, 1972; Exploration of the Outer Solar System, 1976; Solar and Interplanetary Dynamics, 1980; spl. issue editor Space Sci. Revs., 1976; contbr. articles to profl. jours. Office: Space Environment Lab NOAA/ERL Boulder CO 80303

DRYKERMAN, DAN, numismatist; b. Tel Aviv, Feb. 6, 1948; s. George A. and Celina Drykerman; m. Patricia Antman, May 6, 1970; children—David, Andrew. B.A., Wesleyan U., 1969; cert. appraiser, numismatist. Real estate developer N.Y.C., Jacksonville, Fla., 1969-74; founding pres. Am. Coin Portfolios, Inc., San Diego, 1976—; lectr. in field; dir. San Diego Nat. Bank. Mem. nat. community service com. Anti-Defamation League, B'nai B'rith; mem. Wesleyan Schs. Com. Mem. San Diego C. of C., San Diego Visitors Bur., Soc. U.S. Pattern Collectors, Numis. Assn. So. Calif., Am. Numis. Assn., Calif. Profl. Numis. Assn., Calif. State Numis. Assn., Central States Numis. Assn., Fla. United Numismatists, Appraisers Assn. Am. Clubs: Rotary, San Diego Execs. (San Diego). Home: 11781 Fuerte Dr El Cajon CA 92020 Office: 600 B St Suite 1300 San Diego CA 92101

DUAL, PETER ALFRED, school administrator, management consultant; b. Alexandria, Va., Jan. 27, 1946; s. Peter Lloyd and Averlee Lucritia (Coco) D.; m. Toni Irene Nixon, Aug. 24, 1968; children—Nikki Averlee, Peter Aaron, Tony Ahmaad, Alfred Michael. A.A., Lake Mich. Coll., 1966; B.S., Western Mich. U., 1969, M.A., 1971; Ph.D., Mich. State U., 1973; M.P.H., U. Tex.-Houston, 1975. Counselor Neighborhood Youth Corps, Benton Harbor, Mich., 1967-69; tchr., Benton Harbor, 1968-69, Battle Creek, Mich., 1969-70; adminstrv. asst. to dir. sch. community relations Kalamazoo pub. schs., assoc. corm dir. Western Mich. U., Kalamazoo, 1970-71; counselor multi-ethnic counseling ctr., Mich. State U., East Lansing, 1971-72, asst. to ombudsman, 1971-73; asst. chmn. African and Afro-Am. Studies and Research Ctr., U. Texas, Austin, 1973-74, asst. prof. cultural founds. and ethnic studies, 1973-75; assoc. dir. continuing edn., asst. prof. health behavior and health edn. U. Mich., Ann Arbor, 1975-78, dir., asst. to dean Grad. Sch. Pub. Health, 1978-80; acad. dean, prof. health services adminstrn., Eastern Mich. U., Ypsilanti, 1980-83; acad. dean, prof. pub. health and human services San Diego State U., 1983—. Active Greater Detroit Area Hosp. Council, 1982, Nat. Health Council, 1979. Mem. Am. Council Edn., Am. Pub. Health Assn., Am. Assn. Higher Edn., Nat. Assn. Supervision and Curriculum Devel., Am. Soc. Allied Health Professions, NEA, Adult Edn. Assn., Mich. Pub. Health Assn. Club: Rotary. Contbr. articles to profl. jours.

DUAN, NAIHUA, statistician; b. Taipei, Taiwan, Oct. 31, 1949; s. Albert Chi-Chao and Shu-Hui (Chang), Tuan; m. Chih-Ming Fan, Jan. 20, 1979; 1 son, Charles Syntu. Ph.D., Stanford U., 1980. Research affiliate Stanford U., 1978-79; assoc. statistician Rand Corp., Santa Monica, Calif., 1979—; vis. asst. prof. U. N.C., Chapel Hill, 1982; cons. EPA, 1982. Mem. Am. Statis. Assn. Assoc. editor Jour. Am. Statis. Assn.; contbr. articles to profl. jours. Office: Rand Corp 1700 Main St Santa Monica CA 90406

DU BAIN, MYRON, diversified company executive; b. Cleve., June 3, 1923; s. Edward D. and Elaine (Byrne) Du B.; B.A., U. Calif., Berkeley, 1943; grad. exec. program Stanford Grad. Sch. Bus., 1967; m. Alice Elaine Hilliker, Sept. 30, 1944; children—Cynthia Lynn, Donald Aldous. With Fireman Fund Ins. Co., San Francisco, 1946-83, now chmn. bd. pres. chief exec. officer; former vice chmn., dir. Am. Express; pres. Amfac, Inc., Honolulu, 1983—; dir. First Interstate Bank, Pacific Telephone Co., Pacific Gas & Electric Co., Amfac, Inc., Terra Nova Ins. Co. (London); chmn., trustee AFIA Worldwide Ins., N.Y.C.; dir. SRI Internat. Chmn. bd. dirs. Bay Area Council; mem. adv. council Stanford U. Grad. Sch. Bus.; bd. dirs. San Francisco Opera, San Francisco Symphony; pres., trustee United Way of Bay Area; mem. nat. support council U.S. com. UNICEF; mem. industries adv. com. Advt. Council, Inc.; bd. dirs., past chmn. Invest-In-Am., Inc.; dir. adv. council Jr. Achievement; mem. adv. bd. Center for Study Pvt. Enterprise. U. So. Calif. Served as officer USNR, 1943-46, 50-52. Mem. Nat. Assn. Casualty and Surety Execs. (exec. com.). Calif. Roundtable (dir.), Newcomen Soc. (chmn. No. Calif. com.). Republican. Episcopalian. Clubs: Bohemian, Pacific Union, Calif. Tennis (San Francisco); Links (N.Y.C.); Lagunitas Country; Coral Beach and Tennis (Bermuda). Contbg. author: Property and Casualty Handbook, 1960; The Practical Lawyer, 1962. Office: Amfac Inc PO Box 3230 Honolulu HI 96801

DUBBERLY, RONALD ALVAH, library dir.; b. Jacksonville, Fla., Oct. 25, 1942; s. Chester Alvah and Mary Margaret (Jessup) D.; B.A. in History, Jacksonville U., 1964; M.A. in L.S., Fla. State U., 1965; m. Bonnie Rose Bazemore, June 15, 1963; children—Pamela Rose, Kenneth Alvah. Reader's adviser asst. Jacksonville Pub. Library, 1961-64; reference librarian, br. librarian Baltimore County (Md.) Pub. Library, 1965-67, adminstrv. asst. to dir., 1967-69; dir. Sioux City (Iowa) Pub. Library, 1969-75, Seattle Pub. Library, 1975—; exec. bd. Md. Library Assn., 1969; cons. Iowa State Library, 1970-72; exec. bd. Iowa Library Assn., 1971-73, 75, chmn. legis. com., 1973-75; mem. Wash. Adv. Council Libraries, 1975-77. Recipient Spl. Service award Iowa Library Assn., 1975. Mem. ALA (v.p. 1976-78, pres. public library assn. 1978-80, past-pres. 1980-81), Am. Library Trustee Assn. (bd. dirs. 1980-81), Pacific N.W. Library Assn., Wash. Library Assn., Pub. Library Assn. (chmn. prins. task force 1980-82, mem. goals and standards com. 1982-84), Urban Libraries Council (exec. bd. 1981-83). Club: Seattle Rotary. Editorial bd. Jour. Library Adminstrn., 1979-82. Office: 1000 4th Ave Seattle WA 98104

DUBIN, GERALD ROBERT, advertising executive; b. Los Angeles, Sept. 4, 1944; s. Samuel and Florence May (Rossi) D. A.B., UCLA, 1966; M.A., U. So. Calif., 1969. Various mgmt. and creative positions with major advt. agys. in N.Y.C., Dallas and Los Angeles, 1969-80; pres. Dubin Bunde Assocs., Los Angeles, 1980—. Office: Dubin Bunde Assocs Inc 304 S Broadway Los Angeles CA 90013

DUBLIRER, JAMES SAMUEL, investment co. exec.; b. San Jose, Calif., Oct. 9, 1949; s. Arthur Irving and Eleanor Irene (McFarlane) D.; student U. Calif., San Diego, 1967-69; B.A. in Exptl. Psychology, U. Calif., Los Angeles, 1971; postgrad. McGeorge Law Sch., 1971-73. Engr., State of Calif., Sacramento, 1972-75, County of Sacramento (Calif.), 1975—; pres. Paragon Security Systems, Inc., Sacramento, 1974—; cons. in field. Active REACT, 1975—, Calif. Cadet Corps., Sacramento, 1966-67. Recipient commendation for rescue Calif. State Legislature, 1970. Notary pub., Calif. Mem. Nat. Rifle Assn., Roseville Shooting Club, Nat. Notary Assn., Audio Engring. Soc. Democrat. Inventor automatic telephone monitoring and switching device; patentee automatic burglar alarm and security system. Home: PO Box 255344 Sacramento CA 95865 Office: PO Box 255344 Sacramento CA 95865

DUBOFF, LEONARD DAVID, legal educator; b. Bklyn., Oct. 3, 1941; s. Rubin Robert and Millicent Barbara (Pollach) DuB.; m. Mary Ann Crawford, June 4, 1967; children—Colleen Rose, Robert Courtney. J.D. summa cum laude, Bklyn. Law Sch., 1971. Bars: N.Y. 1974, U.S. Dist. Cts. (so. and ea. dists.) N.Y. 1974, U.S. Ct. Appeals (2d cir.) 1974, U.S. Customs Ct. 1975, U.S. Supreme Ct. 1977, Oreg. 1977. Teaching fellow Stanford (Calif.) U. Law Sch., 1971-72; mem. faculty Lewis & Clark Coll. Northwestern Sch. Law, Portland, Oreg., 1972—, prof. law, 1977—; instr. Hastings Coll. Law Coll. Civil Advocacy, San Francisco, summers 1978, 79. Founder, pres. Oreg. Vol. Lawyers for Arts; mem. lawyers' com. ACLU, 1973-78, bd. dirs. Oreg., 1974-76; mem. Mayor's Adv. Com. Security and Privacy, 1974; bd. dirs. Portland Art Mus. Asian Art Council, 1976-77, Internat. Assn. Art Security, N.Y.C., 1976-80; Gov. Oreg. Com. Employment of Handicapped, 1978-81; cons., panelist spl. projects Nat. Endowment for Arts, 1978-79; mem. Mayor's Adv. Com. on Handicapped, 1979-81; mem. Wash. State Atty. Gen's. Com. to Reorganize Maryhill Mus.; Oreg. Commn. for Blind; Oreg. Com. for Humanities. Recipient Bklyn. Law Sch. Stuart Hirschman Property, Jerome Prince Evidence, Donald W. Matheson Meml. awards, 1st scholarship prize; Hofstra U. Lighthouse scholar 1965-71; recipient Hauser award, 1967, Howard Brown Pickard awardee, 1967-69. Mem. Am. Soc. Internat. Law, Assn. Alumni and Attenders of Hague Acad. Internat. Law, Assn. Am. Law Schs. (chmn. sect. law and arts 1974-80, standing com. sect. activities 1975), ABA, N.Y. State Bar Assn., Oreg. Bar Assn., Delta Kappa Phi, Sigma Pi Sigma, Sigma Alpha. Spl. editor Art Xpress; columnist on craft law, The Crafts Report, Make It with Leather; editor, contbr. materials to legal and art textbooks; author articles for legal and art jours. Home: 12440 SW Iron Mountain Blvd Portland OR 97219 Office: 10015 SW Terwilliger Blvd Portland OR 97219

DUBOFSKY, JEAN E., state supreme court justice; b. 1942; A.B., Stanford U.; LL.B., Harvard U. Admitted to bar, 1967; now justice Colo. Supreme Ct. Office: Judicial Bldg 2 E 14th Ave Denver CO 80203

DUBOIS, EDWARD NEELY, business educator; b. Cheyenne, Wyo., Oct. 31, 1925; s. William Robert and Dora Frances (Slack) D.; m. Jean Charlotte Hall, Aug. 21, 1947; children—Christine Bourne, Katherine, William. B.A., U. Wyo., 1946; M.B.A., U. Pa., 1948, postgrad., 1948-53. Instr. bus. U. Pa., Phila., 1947-53; asst. prof. Pa. State U., University Park, 1953-56; asst., then assoc. prof. St. Louis U., 1956-67; vis. prof. U. Colo., Boulder, 1967-68; assoc., then full prof. Ft. Lewis Coll., Durango, Colo., 1968-78; assoc. prof. U. No. Colo., Greeley, 1978—. Pres. Henry Hough (Mo.) PTA, 1965-66; sr. warden Episcopalian Ch., 1962. Mem. AAUP, Am. Statis. Assn., Phi Beta Kappa, Phi Kappa Phi, Pi Gamma Mu, Beta Gamma Sigma, Alpha Kappa Psi. Republican. Author: Essential Methods in Business Statistics, 1964; Essential Statistical Methods for Business, 1979. Home: PO Box 820 Evans CO 80620 Office: U Northern Colorado Greeley CO 80631

DUBOIS, PHILIP LEON, political science educator; b. Oakland, Calif., Oct. 17, 1950; s. Fernand Edmond and Germaine (Goodrich) D.;

m. Lisa Lewis, Aug. 28, 1976. A.B. with highest honors in Polit. Sci., U. Calif.-Davis, 1972; M.A. in Polit. Sci. (Ford Found. fellow), U. Wis.-Madison, 1974, Ph.D. in Polit. Sci. (scholar), 1978. Asst. prof. polit. sci. U. Calif.-Davis, 1976-82, assoc. prof., faculty asst to vice chancellors, 1982—; cons. profl. jours., comml. book pubs. Jud. fellow U.S. Supreme Ct., 1979-80. Mem. Am. Polit. Sci. Assn. (Edward S. Corwin award, 1978), Law and Soc. Assn., Phi Beta Kappa, Pi Sigma Alpha. Democrat. Author: From Ballot to Bench: Judicial Elections and the Quest for Accountability, 1980; editor: The Analysis of Judicial Reform (Philip L. Dubois), 1982; The Politics of Judicial Reform (Philip L. Dubois), 1982; contbr. numerous articles, book revs. to law revs. and jours., other profl. publs. Home: 6301 Holstein Way Sacramento CA 95831 Office: Dept Polit Sci U Calif Davis CA 95616

DUBOSE, FRANCIS MARQUIS, clergyman; b. Elba, Ala., Feb. 27, 1922; s. Hansford Arthur and Mayde Frances (Owen) DuB.; B.A. cum laude, Baylor U., 1947; M.A., U. Houston, 1958; B.D., Southwestern Baptist Sem., 1957, Th.D., 1961; postgrad. Oxford (Eng.) U., 1972; m. Dorothy Anne Sessums, Aug. 28, 1940; children—Elizabeth Anne Parnell, Frances Jeannine Stevens, Jonathan Michael, Celia Danielle. Pastor, Bapt. chs., Tex., Ark., 1939-61; supt. missions. So. Bapt. Conv., Detroit, 1961-66; prof. missions Golden Gate Bapt. Sem., 1966—, dir. World Mission Center, 1979—; lectr., cons. in 115 cities outside U.S., 1969-80; v.p. Conf. City Mission Supts., So. Bapt. Conv., 1964-66; trustee Mich. Bapt. Inst., 1963-66; mem. exec. bd. San Francisco Conf. Religion, Race and Social Concern. Mem. Am. Acad. Religion, Internat. Assn. Mission Study, Am. Soc. Missiology, Assn. Mission Profs. Co-editor: The Mission of the Church in the Racially Changing Community, 1969; author: How Churches Grow in an Urban World, 1978; Classics of Christian Missions, 1979; God Who Sends: A Fresh Quest for Biblical Mission; book rev. editor Missiology: An Internat. Rev.; contbr. to Toward Creative Urban Strategy; Vol. III Ency. of So. Baptists, also articles to profl. jours. Home: 21 Platt Ct Mill Valley CA 94941 Office: Golden Gate Bapt Sem Mill Valley CA 94941

DU BRAU, RICHARD THEODORE, educator; b. Hamburg, Germany, Nov. 11, 1901; s. Richard Frederic and Alvina (Richter) Du B.; B.A., Concordia Coll., Springfield, Ill., 1926; postgrad. U. Aix-Marseille, 1946, 53, 56; M.A., Stanford U., 1948, Ph.D., 1951; D.D., Concordia Theol. Sem., 1978; m. Louise Lydia Markworth, June 18, 1932; children—Irene Lydia Du Brau Hall, Richard Alfred. Ordained to ministry Lutheran Ch., 1926; minister Luth. Ch., Eureka and Ferndale, Calif., 1926-34, Christ Ch., Los Angeles, 1938-41; grad. student, research asst. Stanford U., 1948-51; prof. classics and humanities Calif. Concordia Coll., 1951-67, prof. humanities, visual arts, world lit., 1967-70, prof. emeritus, 1970-76; prof. emeritus Christ Coll., Irvine, Calif., 1977—; chmn. dept. humanities and langs., 1952-67; tutor, translator. Capt., U.S. Civil Conservation Corps., 1934-38. Served to lt. col. AUS, 1941-47. Mem. Am. Philol. Assn., Save-the-Redwoods League, Egypt Exploration Soc., Res. Officers Assn. U.S., Mil. Chaplains Assn. Club: Commonwealth of Calif. Author: Anatole France & Critique of the Mechanistic Soc., 1948; The Strasbourg Oaths and the Vulgar Latin and Romance Vernacular, 1951; The Romance of Lutheranism in California, 1959; Church in Transition, 1975. Contbr. articles to profl. jours. Address: 236 Willow St Pacific Grove CA 93950

DUBRAY, WYNNE, psychologist; b. Wood, S.D., Apr. 22, 1932; d. Peter Joseph and Lillian Bernice (Rice) DuBray; B.A., San Francisco State U., 1973, M.S.W., 1974; Ph.D. in Ednl. Psychology, U. San Francisco; m. Ken Hanson, Dec. 28, 1949 (div.); children David, Yvonne, Les. Dir. social services Intertribal Friendship House, Oakland, Calif., 1973-77; coordinator human service program Los Medanos Coll., Pittsburg, Calif., 1975-76; coordinator Native Am. social work project San Francisco State U., 1977—, also pvt. practice psychotherapy, Antioch, Calif., 1974—; mem. monitoring action com. Calif. Mental Health Dept.; dir. Intertribal Friendship House, Oakland, 1977-79. Danforth fellow nominee, 1980; cert. tchr. community coll., clin. social worker, Calif. Mem. Council Social Work Educators (ho. of dels.), Soc. Clin. Social Work, Assn. Am. Indian Alaska Native Social Workers, Inc. (treas.), United Indian Edn. Assn. Democrat. Methodist. Office: Box 575 Antioch CA 94509

DUBREUIL, ARTHUR JOHN, JR., educator; b. S. Boston, Mass., Sept. 15, 1925; s. Arthur John and Irene Frances (Bufford) D.; A.A., Mira Costa Coll., Oceanside, Calif., 1976; postgrad. San Diego State U., U. San Diego, La Jolla; m. Dorothy Mary Taraska, Sept. 17, 1949; children—Marlene D., Christopher J., Michele D., Mark S., Kimberley A. Enlisted in USMC, 1942, advanced through ranks to master gunnery sgt., 1969; service in S. Pacific, 194-45, China, 1946-48, Korea, 1950; ret., 1969; dir. printing Mira Costa Coll., 1969-74; instr. graphic arts Palomar Coll., San Marcos, Calif., evenings, 1971-80; instr. graphic arts Midway Adult Center, San Diego Community Coll., 1974-82, prof., 1982—. Decorated Purple Heart with gold star; named Tchr. of Yr., Calif. Council Adult Educators, 1982. Mem. Inplant Printing Mgmt. Assn. (charter, dir. edn.), Printing House Craftsmen, Printing Industries Am., Fleet Res. Assn., Calif. Council Adult Edn., 1st Marine Div. Assn., 4th Marine Div. Assn., Am. Vocat. Assn., Employment and Tng. Assn. Calif. Home: 525 Village View Pl Fallbrook CA 92028 Office: 3249 Fordham St San Diego CA 92110

DUCHARME, MARGARET EDNA, museum dir.; b. Washington, Jan. 22, 1917; d. Ray and Hilda Christina (Anderson) Kellogg; grad. high sch., Lakewood, Ohio; m. Clyde E. DuCharme, Aug. 31, 1940 (dec. 1978); children—Jacqueline, Christina, Mark. Owner Historic Home of H.A.W. Tabor, Leadville, Colo., 1972—. Address: 116 E 5th St Leadville CO 80461

DUCKETT, CHLOE ZELLA, foreign service officer; b. Akron, Ohio, June 25, 1925; d. Owen C. and Audrey Z. (Brown) Sandefur; m. Lee L. Duckett, Apr. 30, 1949 (div.); children—Lee L., Theo Duckett Pierce. B.A. in Psychology, U. Ariz., 1949; M.Ed., 1982. Office mgr. Marsh Aviation, Tucson, 1946-48; real estate saleswoman James C. Grant Realty, Tucson, 1950-51; asst. office mgr. aircraft overhaul Grand Central Aircraft, Tucson, 1952-54; asst. to mgr. Tucson Airport Authority, 1957-74; commd. fgn. service officer Dept. State, 1974; staff officer, Mozambique, 1974-75, Swaziland, 1975-76, Martinique, 1976-78, France, 1979-80, Yemen, 1980-81, San Salvador, El Salvador, 1982—. Navigation instr. CAP, Tucson, 1946-51. Mem. Am. Personnel and Guidance Assn., Am. Assn. Airport Execs., Am. Fgn. Service Assn., Mensa. Club: Altrusa (pres. Tucson 1973-74). Co-author concept requiring apprentices to complete basic first aid tng. program before receiving journeyman cert., adopted by AFL/CIO nationwide, 1964. Home: 2124 E 1st St Tucson AZ 85719 Office: Am Embassy/El Salvador APO Miami FL 34023

DUCKWALL, EUGENE HENDERSON, advt. agy. mgmt. cons.; b. Germantown, Ohio, Oct. 15, 1906; s. Ernest I. and Myrta K. (Henderson) D.; B.S., U. So. Cal., 1933; m. Clara Josephine Brown, Aug. 31, 1935; 1 dau., Carol (Mrs. John Richard Sibley). With Foote, Cone & Belding Advt. Agy., Los Angeles, 1934-65, bus. mgr. broadcast dept., Hollywood, Calif., 1939-44, bus. mgr., San Francisco office, 1944-45, bus. mgr., asst. treas., Los Angeles, 1945-57, v.p., media dir., 1957-65; v.p., mgr. Western region Am. Assn. Advt. Agys., Beverly Hills, Calif., 1965-73; advt. agy. mgmt. cons., Arcadia, Calif., 1973—. Faculty, U. So. Calif. Sch. Bus., 1974-75; participant radio program This I Believe, 1954. Mem. adv. bd. U. Calif. Grad. Dept. Journalism, Los Angeles, 1955-59; bd. mgrs., chmn. pub. relations com. YMCA, Los Angeles, 1962-65. Bd. dirs. Pacific Coast region Am. Assn. Advt. Agys., 1950-51, sec.-treas., 1951-52. Mem. Am. Assn. Advt. Agys. (chmn. So. Calif. council 1949-50), Am. Arbitration Assn. (permanent panel mem.), Alpha Delta Sigma (Spl. Service key 1954), Theta Xi. Contbr. articles to profl. jours. Address: 1712 La Ramada Ave Arcadia CA 91006

DUCKWORTH, ALLAN BURL, real estate broker; b. Denver, Aug. 3, 1947; s. Edwin V.B. and Margaret S. D.; B.S. in Forest Sci., Colo. State U., 1969; m. Peggy Ann Griffin, June 10, 1970. Forest technician U.S. Forest Service, Denver, 1968-71; property mgr. Andrews & Co., Denver, 1971-78; sales rep. Todd & Assos., Rifle, Colo., 1978-80; broker/owner The Duckworth Co., Rifle, Colo., 1980—; sec., dir. Andrews & Co. Instr., trainer first aid and CPR, ARC. Recipient Humanity award and cert. of achievement ARC; Eagle Scout award; NDEA fellow, 1969-71. Mem. Sigma Xi, Xi Sigma Pi, Phi Kappa Phi, Beta Beta Beta, Gamma Sigma Delta, Phi Eta Sigma. Methodist. Clubs: Rotary, Elks (trustee). Home: 532 East Ave Rifle CO 81650 Office: 1984 Highway 13 Rifle CO 81650

DUCKWORTH, GUY, musician, educator, author; b. Los Angeles, Dec. 19, 1924; s. Glenn M. and Laura (Lysle) D.; B.A., UCLA, 1951; M.A. (Florence and William C. Bagley scholar), Columbia U., 1953, Ph.D., 1969; m. Ballerina Maria Farra, May 23, 1948. Piano soloist Metro Goldwyn Mayer Studios, 1936-41, Warner Bros. Studios, 1936-41; piano soloist radio stations KFI, Los Angeles, 1938, KNX, Los Angeles, 1939, KHJ, Los Angeles, 1940; piano concert tours in U.S., 1947-49, Can., 1947-49, Mexico, 1947-49; asst. prof. music U. Minn., Mpls., 1955-60, asso. prof., 1960-62; prof. piano Northwestern U., Evanston, Ill., 1962-70, chmn. dept. preparatory piano, 1962-70; prof. music U. Colo., 1970—; condr. various music festivals, U.S., 1956—; dir. Walker Art Children's Concerts, Mpls., 1957-62; nat. piano chmn. Music Educators Nat. Conf., 1965-71; vis. lectr. scholar 75 univs., colls. and conservatories, U.S., Can., 1964—; cons. to Ill. State Dept. of Program Devel. for Gifted Children, 1968-69. Served with U.S. Army, 1943-46. Recipient All-Univ. Teaching award for excellence U. Colo., 1981. Mem. Music Tchrs. Nat. Assn., Colo. State Music Tchrs. Assn., Coll. Music Soc., Music Educators Nat. Conf., Phi Mu Alpha, Pi Kappa Lambda. Author: Keyboard Explorer, 1963, Keyboard Discoverer, 1963, Keyboard Builder, 1964, Keyboard Musician, 1964, Keyboard Performer, 1966, Keyboard Musicianship, 1970, Guy Duckworth Piano Library, 1974; Guy Duckworth Musicianship Series, 1975; contbr. articles in pedagogy of music to various jours.; producer and performer video tapes in piano teaching; originator, coordinator masters and doctoral programs in mus. arts U. Colo. Home: 1020 15th St Denver CO 80202 Office: Univ Colorado Boulder CO 80302

DUDECK, DIANE FRANTZ, graphic artist; b. Troy, Ohio, Mar. 30, 1955; d. Roger Lamar and Mildred Margaret (Davie) Frantz; B.A. in Journalism, Ind. U., 1977, M.S. in Instructional Systems Tech., 1978; m. John P. Dudeck, Aug. 20, 1977. Photographer, Ind. U. Audio-Visual Center, Bloomington, 1977, graphic designer, 1978; art dir. Pier 39 Inc., San Francisco, 1978-81; graphics mgr. Pizza Time Theatre, Inc., Sunnyvale, Calif., 1981-82; dir. advt. The Good Guys Stereo, Inc., San Francisco, 1982-83; pres. Diane Dudeck Design, Inc., 1983—; cons. in field. Recipient Zellerbach award, 1981; Best in West award Am. Advt. Fedn., 1982; Silver Echo award Am. Mktg. Assn. Mem. San Francisco Advt. Club (Cable Car award for billboard design 1980, color newspaper ad design 1981), Artists in Print, Ind. U. Alumni Assn., Phi Beta Kappa, Alpha Chi Omega. Republican. Club: Olympic. Home: 791 Highland Ave Piedmont CA 94611 Office: 21 Sutter St San Francisco CA 94111

DUDENHOEFFER, FRANK EDWARD, pediatrician; b. Cin., May 24, 1926; s. Frank Joseph and Norma (Simper) D.; B.S., U. Cin., 1949, M.D., 1952; m. Nina Genevieve Fincham, May 31, 1952; children—Ann Lynn, John Edward, Mary Jane, Thomas Martin, Susan Leigh, Anne Malver, Greg Malver. Intern Tripler Hosp., Honolulu, 1952-53; resident Childrens Hosp., Los Angeles, 1954-56; pvt. practice medicine specializing in pediatrics, La Canada, Calif., 1956—; mem. staff developmental and behavioral medicine, learning disabilities Childrens Hosp., Los Angeles, chmn. staff, 1978; staff Verdugo Hills Hosp., Glendale, Calif., chmn. dept., 1974; staff Huntington Meml. Hosp., Pasadena, Calif., Glendale Meml. and Glendale Adventist Hosps., St. Joseph's Hosp., Burbank, Calif.; asst. clin. prof. pediatrics Med. Sch., U. So. Calif., 1956-62, asso. clin. prof., 1962-71, clin. prof. pediatrics, 1971—. Chmn. youth com. Am. Acad. Pediatrics local chpt., 1966—; sex edn. program Crescenta Canada YMCA, 1960—; bd. dirs. Glendale Mental Health Clinic, 1957-61, La Canada Scholarship Found., 1972—, Children's Hosp. of Los Angeles, 1977-82; med. dir. Hillside Learning Center, 1978-80. Served with USAAF, 1944-45, U.S. Army, 1952-54; Korea. Recipient Disting. Service award Children's Hosp. of Los Angeles. Fellow Am. Acad. Pediatrics (nat. adolescent com. 1977-80, sect. on adolescent medicine 1980); mem. Southwestern, Los Angeles pediatric socs., AMA, Am. Orthopsychiat. Assn., Am. Soc. Adolescent Medicine, Calif., Los Angeles med. assns., Los Angeles Physicians Art Soc. (art prizes 1974—), Am. Physicians Art Assn., Sigma Chi, U. Cin. alumni assns. Republican. Roman Catholic. Club: Kiwanis. Home: 4859 Oakwood St La Canada Office: 1346 Foothill Blvd La Canada CA 91011

DUDLEY, JOHN HENRY, wholesale florist; b. Detroit, Nov. 17, 1912; s. Henry Augustus and Margaret Helen (Bigelow) D.; A.B., Mich. State Coll., 1937; m. Elizabeth Baird Dean, June 21, 1940; children—John Henry, Thomas Dean. With John Henry Co., 1937—, pres., gen. mgr., 1939-62, now hon. chmn. Mem. exec. com., v.p. Mich. United Fund; mem. fin. staff Senator Robert Griffin of Mich., 1978; past pres., campaign chmn. United Community Chest Greater Lansing Area; past area chmn. serving Project Hope; past chmn. Ingham County Rehab. Center; mem. adv. bd. YMCA; chmn. spl. study and adv. com. YMCA-YWCA; mem. Pres.'s Commn. on White House Fellowships; presdl. appointee bd. dirs. Student Loan Mktg. Assos.; mem. state bd. Mich. Cancer Soc.; mem. Mich. Gov.'s Spl. Commn. on Traffic Safety. Served from lt. (j.g.) to lt. comdr. USNR, 1942-45. Decorated Navy Marine medal, Bronze Star; col. Honorable Order Ky. Cols.; named to Floriculture Hall of Fame, 1966; Fla. State Florists Hall of Fame, 1978. Mem. Soc. Am. Florists (past pres., trustee, sec.-treas. endowment fund, past chmn. nat. edn. com., nat-advt. council), Mich. Florists Assn. (past pres., past dir.), Florists Transworld Delivery Assn. (past dir.), All Florist Industry Congress (founder, co-chmn.), U.S., Mich., Lansing chambers commerce, Mich. Florists Assn. (past pres., dir., chmn. awards com., mem. publs. com., membership com.), Wholesale Florists and Florists Suppliers Am. (dir., treas.). Clubs: City (pres. 1959), Country (past pres.), (Lansing); Detroit; Met., Capitol Hill (Washington); Lansing Automobile; Met. (N.Y.C.); Los Angeles Country, Regency. Home: Comstock Ave Los Angeles CA 90024

DUDZINSKI, DIANE MARIE, biology educator; b. Erie, Pa., July 23, 1946; d. Maxim John and Sophie (Wisniewski) D. B.S., Villa Maria Coll., 1968; M.S., Fordham U., 1970, Ph.D., 1974. Asst. prof. biology Manhattan Coll., Riverdale, N.Y., 1973-78; assoc. prof. biology Coll. of Santa Fe, 1978-81, prof., 1981—, chmn. math. and sci. dept., 1982—; mem. U.S.-USSR oceanographic expdn. to Bering Sea, 1977. Treas., bd. dirs. N.Mex. Network Women in Sci. and Engring., 1981-82. NSF grantee, 1976-78, 79-81; NIH grantee, 1980-82; NASA/Am. Soc. Engring. Edn. research fellow, 1982-83. Mem. AAAS, Am. Inst. Biol. Scis., Ecol. Soc. Am., Sigma Xi. Roman Catholic. Office: St Michael's Dr Santa Fe NM 87501

DUEL, WANDA FAYE, educator, artist; b. Stigler, Okla., Oct. 15, 1928; d. Clarance Auston and Mozelle (Carolan) Peck; m. Thad Delose Duel, July 14, 1952; children—Thais D. Shapiro, Thera Follett, Lane. B.S. in Home Econs., Panhandle State U., 1952; postgrad. Boise State U., 1966-79; Cert. tchr. elem. edn., art, vocat. edn., Idaho. Tchr. McCall-Donnally Pub. Schs. (Idaho), 1951-56, 66-73, 75—; coordinator Fed. Satellite Tech. Demonstration Project, Goodwell Pub. Sch. (Okla.), 1974-75. Mem. NEA, Idaho Edn. Assn., McCall-Donnally Edn. Assn. Democrat. Lutheran. Art exhibited in group shows in western states, represented in permanent collections gallaries in Idaho, Colo., Okla. Home: 131 Mather Rd McCall ID 83638 Office: Home Econs Dept PO Box 164 McCall ID 83638

DUENSING, DAVID L., food processing company executive; b. 1922; married. Attended Wright Jr. Coll., 1940, U. Fla., 1942. With Armour and Co., 1946-77, 80—, in various advt. and mktg. positions, 1946-60, v.p., dir. mktg. Armour Grocery Products Co. subs. (name changed to Armour-Dial Inc., subs. 1968), 1960-64, pres., 1964-68, exec. v.p. Armour and Co. and pres. Armour-Dial, Inc., 1968-77, ret., 1977-80, exec. v.p. Armour & Co., Phoenix, pres. Armour-Dial Inc., also dir., 1980—; dir. DeSoto Inc., Wayne-Gossard Corp. Served to 1st lt. USAAF, 1942-46. Office: Armour and Co Greyhound Tower 111 W Clarendon Phoenix AZ 85077*

DUERMYER, WILLIAM HARRY, JR., counselor; b. Omaha, Sept. 8, 1947; s. William Harry and Betty Louise (Dobbs) D.; m. Kathryn Joan Happel, Sept. 18, 1971. B.S. in Psychology, U. Iowa, 1973; M.A. in Edn., Guidance/Counseling, 1975; Ph.D. in Vocat. Edn. Candidate Colo. State U. Cert. in secondary edn., Mass., N.Mex., Colo.; Nat. Bd. Exam. cert. counselor. Counselor, Am. Sch. Kuwait, 1975-77, Am. Sch. of Isfahan (Iran), 1977-79; counselor, dir. Career Ctr., San Juan Coll., Farmington, N.Mex., 1980—. Served with U.S. Army, 1969-71; Korea. Mem. Am. Personnel and Guidance Assn., Nat. Vocat. Guidance Assn., Am. Vocat. Assn., Am. Coll. Personnel Assn. Office: San Juan College 4601 College Blvd Farmington NM 87401

DUERR-LEVINE, DIANE, mktg. exec.; b. Tulsa, Mar. 8, 1938; d. Arthur and Reta (Reeves) Duerr; B.A. in Math., U. Mich., 1960; M.B.A., Columbia U., 1963; m. Matthew A. Levine, June 9, 1963; 1 dau., Arielle. Systems engr. Xerox Corp., N.Y.C., 1963-64; products mgr. Lever Bros. Corp., N.Y.C., 1964-68; sr. br. mgr. Am. Home Products Corp., N.Y.C., 1968-71; supr. Honig-Cooper Herrington, San Francisco, 1971-72; v.p. advt. and sales promotion Continental Airlines, Los Angeles, 1973-76; dir. mktg. and communications San Francisco Bay Area Transit Dist., 1976-78; pres., founder Inst. Health Mgmt., San Francisco, 1978—; tech. mktg. cons., 1982—; dir. Pacific Select Corp.; prof. San Francisco State U., 1982—; cons. hosp. groups. Bd. dirs. Resource Center for Women, Palo Alto, Calif.; mem. bus. adv. bd. San Francisco State U.; bd. dirs. Am. Friends Service Com. No. Calif.; cons. Solar Energy Research Inst., No. Calif. Coalition for ERA. Recipient numerous mktg., advt. and direct mail awards. Mem. Columbia U. Grad. Sch. Bus. Alumni Assn., Kappa Kappa Gamma. Recipient numerous mktg. and advt. awards. Democrat. Mem. Soc. of Friends. Author: Vital Living after Fifty, 1982. Office: 101 Lansdale Ave San Francisco CA 94127

DUERSCH, FRED, JR, industrial technology educator, consultant; b. Bklyn., June 15, 1938; s. Fred and Anna (Suess) D.; m. Geraldine Grandy, Sept. 6, 1963; children—Darin, Kevin, Sharla Ann, Janalyn. B.S., Utah State U., 1966; M.S., Brigham Young U., 1970; Ph.D., U. Utah, 1974. Head dept. automotive sci. Skyline Sr. High Sch., Salt Lake City, 1966-73; head dept. automotive sci. Logan (Utah) Sr. High Sch., 1973-76; asst. prof. indsl. tech. Utah State U., 1973—; head dept. Bridgerland Area Vocat. Ctr.; tng. engr. Thiokol Corp., Promontory, Utah; tech. cons. DeLorean Mfg. Co., Ford Motor Co., Wilson Motor Co., Hillyard, Low & Anderson, Hansen & Orton. Served with U.S. Army, 1961-62. Emission Control Tng. grantee, 1977. Recipient Order of Arrow, 30-yr. service award Boy Scouts Am. Mem. NEA (life), Am. Vocat. Assn. (life), Utah Vocat. Assn. (life), Utah Indsl. Edn. Assn. (life, pres. automotive sect. 1975-76), Soc. Automotive Engrs. (Ralph R. Teetor award 1978). Republican. Mormon. Contbr. articles to profl. jours. Home: 868 N 400 E Logan UT 84321

DUFF, MARY KATHLEEN, savings and loan executive; b. Watseka, Ill., May 26, 1945; d. John Wesley and Mary Margaret (Blake) Duff; student Coll. of Wooster, 1963-65, U. Miami (Fla.), 1965-67; B.S., U. Ill., 1968; M.P.A., U. Denver, 1976. Research asst. Tex. Research Inst. Mental Scis., Houston, 1968-69; research assoc. Denver Research Inst.-Indsl. Econs., 1970-75; sr. policy analyst City of Denver, Office of Policy Analysis, 1975-77; spl. project dir. Colo. Civil Rights Commn., Denver, 1977-78; govt. loans coordinator Midland Fed. Savs. & Loan Assn., Denver, 1978-80; pvt. practice cons., 1981—. Bd. dirs., zoning chmn. West Univ. Community Assn., 1976—. Mem. Nat. Assn. Housing and Redevel. Ofcls., Am. Soc. Public Adminstrn. Ofcls., LWV, Pi Alpha Alpha, Sigma Iota Epsilon. Author Tech. Reports And Studies In Areas Of Public Adminstrn.

DUFFER, DON RAY, airline pilot; b. Quinlan, Tex., Aug. 3, 1942; s. Emmett L. and Loyce M. (Mack) D.; student U. Tex., Arlington, 1960-62, Saddleback Coll., 1974-76; m. Linda Jo A. Cooley, Mar. 18, 1967; children—Don, Mark. Pilot, Continental Airlines, Los Angeles, 1967—; owner, mgr. Domar Properties, Dana Point, Calif., 1973—; pres. Domar European Imports, Dana Point, 1979—; v.p. M & M Patchworks, Inc. Asst. scoutmaster Boy Scouts Am., 1979—. Served with USMC, 1962-67, to lt. col. USMCR, 1967—. Decorated Air medal. Mem. Marine Corps Res. Officers Assn., Res. Officers Assn., South Orange County Bd. Realtors. Republican. Clubs: Dana Point Yacht, Coto de Caza Hunting. Home: 33452 Cockleshell Laguna Niguel CA 92677 Office: 7300 World Way W Los Angeles CA 90009

DUFFEY, KENNETH EARL, surgeon; b. San Francisco; s. Earl William and Selma Elaine (Hill) D.; A.B., U. Calif., Berkeley, 1942; M.D., Stanford U., 1952; m. Virginia Marie Smith, Aug. 15, 1941; children—Kenta Kay, Gregory Brooks, Bradford Earl. Intern, San Francisco Gen. Hosp., 1951; asst. resident to sr. resident in surgery So. Pacific Gen. Hosp., San Francisco, 1952-55; practice medicine specializing in surgery, San Francisco, 1956—; pres. Kenneth E. Duffey, M.D., Profl. Corp., San Francisco; mem. clin. faculty Sch. Medicine, Stanford, 1956—; cons. Marine Engrs. Diagnostic Center; Commr. Calif. Gov.'s Auto Accident Study Commn., 1968-70; commr. div. licensing Calif. Bd. Med. Quality Assurance, 1977—. Served to capt., USAAF, 1942-46. Recipient commendation Calif. State Senate, 1970. Diplomate Am. Bd. Surgery. Fellow A.C.S., Royal Soc. Medicine (London); mem. AMA, Calif. Med. Assn., San Francisco Med. Soc., Am. Assn. Automotive Medicine, Nu Sigma Nu. Clubs: Olympic, San Francisco. Co-author: From Fiji Through the Phillippines, 1946. Guest editor Calif. Medicine, 1972. Office: 909 Hyde St San Francisco CA 94109

DUFFIELD, JANE MARIE, nurse; b. Holstein, Iowa, Mar. 24, 1943; d. Orville Elmer and Leone Marion (Dierenfield) Petty; m. Richard McGrath Duffield, Nov. 16, 1965 (div.). R.N., Lutheran Hosp. Sch. Nursing, 1964; adult edn. tchr. credential U. Calif.-Berkeley, 1976; student U. San Francisco, 1979. R.N., Mo., Calif. Nurse various instns., 1964-73; dir. nursing St. Francis Convalescent Pavilion, Daly City, Calif., 1973-78; instr. nurse asst. cert. program Jefferson Union Adult Edn., Daly City, 1976-82; sr. flight nurse Air Ambulance, San Bruno, Calif., 1975-82; office mgr. So. San Francisco (Calif.) Med. Ctr., 1979-80;

occupational health nurse United Parcel Service, San Francisco, 1980—; owner, adv. Board-Care Home for Elderly; instr. CPR, first-aid ARC. Served to capt. USNG, 1976—. Mem. Am. Soc. Tng. and Devel. Lutheran. Home: 482 San Pablo Terr Pacifico CA 94044 Office: United Parcel Service 2222 17th St San Francisco CA 94103

DUFFIN, LORNE HUGH, retail exec.; b. Moose Jaw, Sask., Can., June 30, 1948; s. Jim and Marie Mary (Griffeth) D.; studnt public schs. Sask.; Pres., sr. partner Mr. Entertainment Music Stores, Edmonton, Alta., Can., 1976—; pres. Falher Alfalfa, Alta., 1978-79. Mem. Fedn. Ind. Businessmen. Club: Masons. Composer song: Say I Love You, 1973. Office: 172 Kingsway Mall Edmonton AB Canada

DUFFY, JAMES WILLIAM, N.G. officer; b. Mullan, Idaho, Feb. 17, 1930; s. Bernard Bevan and Mary Teresa (Hrella) D.; student Carroll Coll., 1948-50; grad. Command and Gen. Staff Coll., 1975, CD Mgmt. Sch., 1980; m. Barbara Joan Mergenthaler, Aug. 28, 1954; children—Jeanne, Joan, William, Jeffrey, Daniel. Operator farm, Helena Valley, Helena, Mont., 1950-55; commd. 2d lt., Med. Service Corps, Mont. Army N.G., 1956, promoted to maj. gen., 1981; detachment comdr. Separate Detachment 1049th Engr. Co., 1960-63, detachment comdr. Hdqrs. Detachment, 1963, asst. G-1, 1970, reassigned as asst. G-4, 1972, Mil. Support to Civil Authorities Sect., 1973, dir. State Area Command, 1980, adj. gen., State of Mont., Helena, 1981—. Decorated Army Commendation medal, Meritorious Service medal. Mem. N.G. Assn. of U.S., Mont. N.G. Assn., Helena C. of C., Great Falls C. of C. Democrat. Roman Catholic. Club: Helena Lions. Home: PO Box 961 Montana City Route Clancy MT 59634 Office: PO Box 4789 1100 N Main St Helena MT 59604

DUFRESNE, ARMAND FREDERICK, mgmt. and engring. cons.; b. Manila, Aug. 10, 1917; s. Ernest Faustine and Maude (McClellan) DuF.; B.S., Calif. Inst. Tech., 1938; m. Theo Rutledge Schaefer, Aug. 24, 1940; children—Lorna DuFresne Turnier, Peter. Dir. quality control, chief product engr. Consolidated Electrodynamics Corp., Pasadena, Calif., 1945-61; pres., dir. DUPACO, Inc., Arcadia, Calif., 1961-68; v.p., dir. ORMCO Corp., Glendora, Calif., 1966-68; mgmt., engring. cons., Duarte and Cambria, Calif., 1968—; dir., v.p., sec. Tavis Corp., Mariposa, Calif., 1968-79; dir. Denram Corp., Monrovia, Calif., 1968-70, interim pres., 1970; dir., chmn. bd. RCV Corp., El Monte, Calif., 1968-70; owner DUFCO, Cambria, 1971-82; pres. DUFCO Electronics, Inc., 1982—; pres. Freedom Designs, Inc., Ventura, Calif., 1982—. Bd. dirs. Arcadia Bus. Assn., 1965-69; bd. dirs. Cambria Community Services Dist., 1976, pres., 1977-80; mem., chmn. San Luis Obispo County Airport Land Use Commn., 1972-75. Served to capt. Signal Corps, AUS, 1942-45. Decorated Bronze Star medal. Mem. Instrument Soc. Am. (sr.), Arcadia (dir. 1965-69), Cambria (dir. 1974-75) chambers commerce, Tau Beta Pi. Patentee in field. Home: 901 Iva Ct Cambria CA 93428

DUGGAN, DANIEL LAWRENCE, real estate co. exec.; b. Camrose, Alta., Can., Oct. 11, 1913; s. William George and Margaret (Scanlan) D.; A.B., U. Calif. at Los Angeles, 1937; J.D., U. So. Calif., 1940; m. Jean Druffel, Dec. 6, 1941; children—William Dennis, Richard R., Kathleen Joan. With Coldwell, Banker & Co., Los Angeles, 1940-73, partner, 1952-63, vice chmn. bd., dir., 1963-73. Mem. Town Hall Bd. Govs., Los Angeles, 1970; campaign vice chmn. United Crusade, 1970-72; mem. exec. bd. Los Angeles area council Boy Scouts of Am., 1968—. Bd. dirs. YMCA, Los Angeles, 1970-71; trustee U. Calif. at Los Angeles Found., 1970-79. Mem. Los Angeles County Bar Assn., State Bar Calif., Kappa Alpha, Phi Alpha Delta, Blue Key, Skull and Scales. Club: Los Angeles Country; Newport Harbor Yacht; California. Address: 12751 Evanston St Los Angeles CA 90049

DUGGAN, EDMUND BUCHWALTER, JR., ednl. adminstr.; b. Houston, July 2, 1933; s. Edmund Buchwalter and Grace (Nelson) D.; B.Polit. Sci., U. of South, 1956; M.Sch. Adminstrn., San Jose State U., 1963; m. Nancy Cooper, July 6, 1957; children—Alison Raye, Eddy, Randy. Tchr., curriculum dir. Fremont (Calif.) Unified Sch. Dist., 1961-65; vice-prin. Live Oak Unified Sch. Dist., Morgan Hill, Calif., 1965-66; prin. Shasta High Sch., Redding, Calif., 1967-81; asst. supt. Shasta County Schs., 1981-82, dep. supt., 1982—; chmn. accreditation com. Western Assn. Colls. and Univs. Active Cub Scouts Am.; pres. Little League Baseball; pres. No. Athletic League. Pres., bd. dirs. Shasta County United Crusade, 1969-73; bd. dirs. Community Concert Assn., Redding; pres. Grotefend Scholarship Bd. Served to lt. USNR, 1957-61. Mem. Assn. Calif. Adminstrs., Shasta Secondary Adminstrs. Assn. (pres. 1971-72), Shasta County Adminstrs. Assn. (pres. 1976-77), Omicron Delta Kappa, Blue Key, Pi Gamma Mu, Phi Gamma Delta. Presbyterian. (elder). Clubs: Elk, Rotary (bd. dirs. 1971-73). Clubs: Redding Rotary (pres. 1981-82), Home: 1657 Ganim Ln Redding CA 96001 Office: 1644 Magnolia Redding CA 96001

DUHNKE, HORST, political scientist educator; b. Bad Kreuznach, Germany, May 2, 1922; came to U.S., 1947, naturalized, 1952; s. Helmut and Erna (Kneip) D.; children—Diana Duhnke Fajardo, Michael. B.A., U. Calif., 1951, M.A., 1953, Ph.D., 1964. Mem. faculty Calif. State U.-Hayward, 1964—, assoc. prof. polit. sci., 1966—. Mem. Am. Polit. Sci. Assn., Amnesty Internat. Democrat. Author: Stalinismus in Deutschland, 1955; Die KPD von 1933 bis 1945, 1972.

DUKE, RUSSELL WARREN, chemist; b. Dallas, Mar. 14, 1946; s. Henry Greene and Margaret May (Boatner) D.; m. Pamela Fern Moses, Aug. 19, 1966; children—Geoffrey Russell, Gregory Michael. Ph.D. in Biophys. Chemistry, U. Louisville, 1974. Trainee NSF, 1969-73; instr. chemistry Jefferson Community Coll., Louisville, 1972-74; postdoctoral fellow Laboratoire de Physique des Solides, U. Paris-Sud, Orsay, France, 1974-75, Instituttet for Kemiindustri, Danmarks Tekniske Hojskole, Lyngby, Denmark, 1975-76, Inst. Materials Sci., U. Conn., Storrs, 1976; dir. clin. lab. Doctors Health Facilities, Dallas, 1976-80; tech. dir. Nat. Health Labs., Denver, 1980—. Recipient Statens Teknisk Videnskabelige Forskningsrad (Denmark), 1975; George C. Marshall fellow, 19745-75. Mem. Am. Chem. Soc., Am. Phys. Soc., Biophys. Soc., Am. Soc. Clin. Pathologists, Am. Assn. Clin. Chemists, Sigma Xi, Phi Lambda Upsilon, Kappa Alpha. Home: PO Box 1204 Aspen CO 81612 Office: Nat Health Labs 7127 S Alton Way Denver CO 80110

DUKE, WILLIAM EDWARD, petroleum co. exec.; b. Bklyn., July 18, 1932; s. William Robert and Amy Margaret (Devlin) D.; B.S., Fordham U., 1954; m. Leilani Kamp Lattin, May 7, 1977; children by previous marriage, William Edward, Jeffrey W., Michael R. City editor Middletown (N.Y.) Record, 1956-60; asst. state editor Washington Star, 1961-63; exec. asst. to U.S. Senator from N.Y. State, Jacob K. Javits, Washington, 1963-69; dir. pub. affairs Corp. Pub. Broadcasting, Washington, 1969-72; dir. fed. govt. relations Atlantic Richfield Co., Washington, 1973-78, mgr. nat. programs, Los Angeles, 1978—; cons. in field. Community trustee Greater Washington Ednl. Telecommunications Assn., WETA-TV-FM, chmn. radio com., exec. com., 1976-78; assoc. Georgetown U. Center Strategic and Internat. Studies, 1975—. Mem. Pub. Relations Soc. Am. (accredited, bd. dirs. pub. affairs sec., chmn. nat. issues com.), Am. Petroleum Inst. Clubs: Nat. Press, Internat., Capitol Hill, Los Angeles Athletic, Office: Atlantic Richfield Co 515 S Flower St Los Angeles CA 90071

DUKOW, ALBERT N., financial consultant; cons.; b. Phila., May 28, 1917; s. Jacob and Sarah (Devine) D.; B.Sc., Temple U., 1945; m. Henrietta Underberg, Dec. 25, 1940; children—Vicki J., Jeffrey B., Susan W. Mng. dir. Affiliated Mgmt. Co., fin. mgmt.; pres., tax cons. Dukow & Assocs., Burbank, Calif., 1946—; pres., dir. Edward C. James Co.; dir. Andrew Investment Co., Riverside Properties, Nat. Conveyor Corp. Office: 4150 Riverside Dr Burbank CA 91505

DULBECCO, RENATO, biologist: b. Catanzaro, Italy, Feb. 22, 1914; s. Leonardo and Maria (Virdia) D.; M.D., U. of Torino (Italy), 1936; D.Sc. (hon.), Yale U., 1968; LL.D., U. Glasgow (Scotland), 1970; m. Gulseppina Salvo, June 1, 1940 (div. 1963); children—Peter Leonard, Maria Vittoria; m. 2d, Maureen Muir, July 27, 1963; 1 dau., Fiona Linsey. Came to U.S., 1947, naturalized, 1953. Asst. U. Turin, 1942-47; research asso. Ind. U., 1947-49; sr. research fellow Calif. Inst. Tech., 1949-52, asso. prof., then prof. biology, 1952-63; sr. fellow Salk Inst. Biol. Studies, San Diego, 1963-71; asst. dir. research Imperial Cancer Research Fund, London, 1971-74, dep. dir. research, 1974-77; disting. research prof. Salk. Inst., La Jolla, Calif., 1977—; prof. pathology and medicine U. Calif. at San Diego Med. Sch., La Jolla, 1977-81; vis. prof. Royal Soc. Gt. Britain, 1963-64, Leeuwenhoek lectr., 1974; Clowes Meml. lectr., Atlantic City, 1961; Harvey lectr. Harvey Soc., 1967; Dunham lectr. Harvard U., 1972; 11th Marjory Stephenson Meml. lectr., London, 1973; Harden lectr., Wye, Eng., 1973; Am. Soc. for Microbiology lectr., Los Angeles, 1979; Cori lectr. Roswell Park Meml. Inst., Buffalo, 1981; Latta lectr. U. Nebr., Omaha, 1982. Mem. Calif. Cancer Adv. Council, 1963; mem. adv. bd. Roche Inst., N.J., 1968-71, Inst. Immunology, Basel, Switzerland, 1969—; bd. sci. Counselors div. cancer cause and prevention Nat. Cancer Inst., Bethesda, Md. Trustee, La Jolla Country Day Sch. Decorated grand ufficiale Italian Republic; recipient John Scott award City Phila., 1958; Kimball award Conf. Public Health Lab. Dirs., 1959: Albert and Mary Lasker Basic Med. Research award, 1965; Howard Taylor Ricketts award, 1965; Paul Ehrlich-Ludwig Darmstaedter prize, 1967; Horwitz prize Columbia U., 1973; (with David Baltimore and Howard Martin Temin) Nobel prize in medicine, 1975; Targa d'oro Villa San Giovanni, 1978; named Man of Yr., London, 1975; Italian Am. of Yr., San Diego County, Calif., 1978; Mandel medal Czechoslovak Acad. Scis., 1982; hon. founder Hebrew U., 1981; Guggenheim and Fulbright fellow, 1957-58. Mem. Nat. Acad. Scis. (Selman A. Waksman award 1974), Am. Acad. Arts and Scis., Assn. Cancer Research, Accademia Nazionale dei Lincei, Accademia Ligure di Scienze e Lettre (hon.), Royal Soc. (fgn. mem.). Club: Athenaeum. Office: Salk Inst PO Box 85800 San Diego CA 92138

DULDULAO, FLORENCE MARGARET, personnel executive; b. Nogales, Ariz.; d. Joseph Duffy and Casimira Erang (Portacio) Price; student Skyline Community Coll., 1975-77, La Verne Coll., 1977; B.S. magna cum laude in Bus. Adminstrn., U. San Francisco, 1978, postgrad., 1981; m. Antonio C. Duldulao; children—Antonia Maria, Michael David. Riveter, China Aircraft subs. Douglas Aircraft Co.; clk.-sec. Nat. ARC; with Mt. Zion Hosp. and Med. Center, San Francisco, 1964-82, asst. dir. personnel, 1972-74, acting dir. personnel, 1974-75, personnel dir., 1977-82; personnel dir. San Francisco Newspaper Agy., 1983—. Mem. adv. group on careers and occupations in bus. and industry, disabled student service San Francisco State U.; mem. human resources com. Calif. Hosp. Assn., 1980-81; mem. panel of oral examiners Met. Transp. Commn., 1977; mem. personnel com. San Francisco Filipino-Am. Council; bd. dirs. ARC, 1980-81. Mem. Am. Soc. Hosp. Personnel Adminstrn., Am. Soc. Personnel Adminstrs., Calif. Hosp. Personnel Mgmt. Assn. (state dir. 1978-79, pres.-elect 1979-80 pres. state bd. 1980-81, pres. Bay area chpt. 1979-80), Calif. Hosp. Assn. (human resources com. 1980-81), U. San Francisco Alumni Assn. Democrat. Roman Catholic. Club: Toastmasters. Home: 999 Higate Dr Daly City CA 94015 Office: San Francisco Newspaper Agency 925 Mission St San Francisco CA 94103

DULEY, CHARLOTTE DUDLEY, vocational counselor; b. Lincoln, Nebr., Oct. 2, 1920; d. Millard Eugene and Inez Kathryn (Miller) Dudley; student U. Nebr., 1938-41; M.A. in Guidance Counseling, U. Idaho, 1977; B.S., Lewis and Clark State Coll., 1973; m. Phillip D. Duley, Mar. 28, 1942; children—Michael Dudley, Patricia Kaye. Tchr., Nebr. schs., 1951-56; with Dept. of Employment, Lewiston, Idaho, 1958-81, local office counselor handling fed. tng. programs, 1958-81; ind. job cons. Pres. bd. dirs. Civic Arts, Inc., 1972-81; mem. women's service league Wash.-Idaho Symphony Orch., 1972—; bd. dirs. YWCA, 1980—, treas., 1981—; mem. Am. Festival Ballet League. Mem. Am., Idaho personnel guidance assns., Idaho State Employees Assn., Internat. Assn. Employees in Employment Security, Nat. Employment Counselors Assn., Idaho State Employment Counselors Assn. (pres. 1979-80), Stateline Guidance and Counseling Assn. (sec.-treas. 1964, 76-77), Lewiston Community Concert Assn. (bd. dirs., pres. 1980—). Presbyterian. Club: Altrusa (bd. dirs.). Home: 1819 Ridgeway Dr Lewiston ID 83501

DULING, JOHN ANDERSON, univ. adminstr., psychologist; b. Trinidad, Colo., Sept. 7, 1930; s. Edmund G. and Frances Siple (Shadel) D.; m. Virginia C. Steinbach, Apr. 30, 1955; children—Kenneth, Kathleen, Kevin. B.Mus., Colo. State U., 1952; M.A., Western State Coll., Gunnison, Colo., 1958; Ed.D., U. No. Colo., 1966. Tchr. music pub. schs., Colo., 1952-57; instr., adminstr. Lamar Community Coll., 1959-64; dir. student activities U. No. Colo., 1964-65; assoc. prof. psychology U. Wis.-Stout, Menomonie, 1965-67; dir. counseling and student devel. N.Mex. State U., 1967—; bd. dirs. Crisis Ctr., Las Cruces, N.Mex., 1969-73, pres., 1972-73; mem. lay adv. bd. Las Cruces Pub. Schs., 1972—; pres. bd. dirs. S.W. Community Mental Health Ctr., 1983. Mem. Am. Personnel and Guidance Assn., Coll. Student Personnel Assn., Am. Mental Health Counselors Assn., Am. Coll. Personnel Assn. (chmn. membership and div. rep. N.Mex. 1978-82), N.Mex. Coll. Personnel Assn. (pres. 1983-84), Am. Psychol. Assn., NEA, Univ. and Coll. Counseling Ctr. Dirs. Assn., Nat. Assn. Student Personnel Adminstrs., N.Mex. Psychol. Assn., Mesilla Valley Psychol. Assn. (founding). Author: Counselor's Guide to Selected Colleges in New Mexico, 1970; contbr. articles to profl. jours.; research in field; editor Southwestern Rev., Jour. Research and Opinion for Student Personnel Workers in the Southwest, 1974-76. Home: 985 Mormon Dr Las Cruces NM 88001 Office: NMex State U PO Box 3575 Las Cruces NM 88003

DULMAGE, DONALD WRIGHT, audio-visual producer; b. San Francisco, July 31, 1936; s. Claude Samuel and Archylene Bernice (Wright) D.; m. Bonnie Lillian Goodrich, Nov. 24, 1957; children—Debora Dawn Dulmage Moore, Christopher Wright. B.A., Stanford U., 1958. Dir. photography Sta. KNTV, San Jose, Calif., 1962-69; free lance audio-visual producer, 1964-69; founder Panorama Prodns., Santa Clara, Calif., 1969, pres., owner, 1972—; advisor De Anza Coll., Foothill Coll. Ford Found. fellow, 1957-58; recipient IFPA Cindy awards, SJAC Murphy awards, SFAC awards, others. Mem. Profl. Photographers Am., Info. Film Producers Am., San Jose Ad Club, San Francisco Ad Club, Profl. Photographers Greater Bay Area, Profl. Photographers Calif., others. Republican. Methodist. Club: Decathlon. Home: PO Box 38 New Almaden CA 95042 Office: 2353 De La Cruz Blvd Santa Clara CA 95050

DUMAINE, R. PIERRE, bishop; b. Paducah, Ky., Aug. 2, 1931; student St. Joseph Coll., Mountain View, Calif., 1945-51, St. Patrick Sem., Menlo Park, Calif., 1951-57; Ph.D., Cath. U. Am., 1962. Ordained priest Roman Cath. Ch., 1957; asst. pastor Immaculate Heart Ch., Belmont, Calif., 1957-58; mem. faculty dept. edn. Cath. U. Am., 1961-63; tchr. Serra High Sch., San Mateo, Calif., 1963-65; asst. supt. Cath. schs., Archdiocese of San Francisco, 1965-74, supt., 1974-78; ordained bishop, 1978, bishop of San Jose, Calif., 1981—; dir. Archdiocesan Ednl. TV Ctr., Menlo Park, Calif., 1968-81. Mem. Pres.'s Nat. Adv. Council on Edn. of Disadvantaged Children, 1970-72; bd. dirs. Cath. TV Network, 1968-81, pres., 1975-77; bd. dirs. Pub. Service Satellite Consortium, 1975-81. Mem. Nat. Cath. Edn. Assn., Assn. Cath. Broadcasters and Allied Communicators, Internat. Inst. Communications, Assn. Calif. Sch. Adminstrs. Office: St Patrick Cathedral 389 E Santa Clara St San Jose CA 95113

DUMAS, HERBERT MONROE, JR., research engring. mgr.; b. El Dorado, Ark., Dec. 16, 1927; s. Herbert Monroe and Emma Villa (Woodard) D.; A.B. in Physics, U. Ark., 1953, B.S., 1955, M.S., 1956; m. Patricia Ann Johnson, May 9, 1953; 1 son, Scott. Mem. staff Sandia Lab., Albuquerque, 1956—, supr. advanced energy conversion devices, 1961-65, supr. seismic systems div., 1965-69, div. supr. sensors devel., 1969-75, mgr. space systems, 1976—; cons. in field; mem. panel to evaluate treaty evasion Advanced Research Projects Agy., U.S. Dept. Def., 1969-72. Served with USN, 1946-49. Recipient Physics Achievement award U. Ark., 1955. Mem. Optical Soc. Am., Phi Beta Kappa, Sigma Xi, Sigma Pi Sigma (pres. 1954), Kappa Sigma, Pi Mu Epsilon, Phi Eta Sigma. Democrat. Methodist. Club: U. Ark. Alumni (dir. 1971-73, v.p. 1977) (Albuquerque). Specialist in design, devel., mgmt. of satellite instrumentation systems, optical systems. Home: 1304 Florida St NE Albuquerque NM 87110 Office: Sandia Lab Albuquerque NM 87115

DUMBAULD, RICHARD KEITH, meteorologist; b. Somerset, Pa., Mar. 23, 1932; s. Richard Weigle and Susan Louella (Snyder) D.; m. Dorothy Jean Reiman, June 12, 1953; children—Brett Reagan, Kim Renee, Tawn Alin. B.S., U. Pitts., 1954; postgrad. NYU, 1954-55; M.S., U. Mich., 1959. Cert. cons. meteorologist. Research meteorologist U.S. Weather Bur. Research Sta., Nat. Reactor Testing Sta., Idaho, 1959-62; staff scientist GCA Tech. div. GCA Corp., Salt Lake City, 1962-72; v.p., group scientist H.E. Cramer Co. Inc., Salt Lake City, 1972—. Served to capt. USAF, 1955-58. Recipient Pub. Service Group Achievement award, NASA, 1982. Mem. Am. Meteorol. Soc. (pres. Utah chpt. 1966-67), Am. Geophys. Union, Royal Meteorol. Soc., Air Pollution Control Assn. Contbr. articles to profl. jours. Home: 2738 Pebble Glen Circle Salt Lake City UT 84109 Office: PO Box 8049 Salt Lake City UT 84108

DUMESNIL, CARLA DAVIS, interior designer, educator; b. Plainfield, N.J., Oct. 15, 1946; d. Carlton Carlisle and Jenny (Katz) Davis; m. Randolph Alvin Dumesnil, July 7, 1971 (div.); 1 dau., Bretta Amoura. B.S. with distinction and highest honors, U. Conn., 1969, M.A., 1971; postgrad. in social psychology U. Utah, 1978-79. Instr. art Ga. So. Coll., Statesboro, 1969-71; art dir. Rosenthal Shoes, Athens, Ga. and Atlanta, 1971-72; tchr. art Hart County Jr. High Sch., Hartwell, Ga., 1972-73; drafting designer Harbin Homes, Lavonia, Ga., 1974-75; head interior designer Interior Design Cons., Salt Lake City, 1975—; instr. dept. family and consumer studies U. Utah, Salt Lake City, 1977-80, asst. prof., 1980—; interior design cons.; exhibited Am. Home Econs. Assn. Visual Arts Show, 1978. Mem. nominating com. YWCA, Salt Lake City; coop. art tchr. grades K-2 gifted children program, 1980-82. Recipient interior design excellence award Mansfield State Tng. Sch. (Conn.), 1969; State of Conn. scholar, 1968; David P. Gardner fellow U. Utah, 1982. Mem. Am. Soc. Interior Designers (profl.), Nat. Council for Interior Design Qualification, Environ. Design Research Assn., Internat. Assn. for People and their Surroundings, Phi Upsilon Omicron, Phi Kappa Phi. Author: Study Guide for Interior Design, 1978; co-author: An Invitation to Design, 1982. Home: 361 South 1300 East Salt Lake City UT 84102 Office: 214 AEB U Utah Salt Lake City UT 84112

DUMKE, GLENN, univ. and coll. chancellor; b. Green Bay, Wis., May 5, 1917; s. William F. and Marjorie S. (Schroeder) D.; A.B., Occidental Coll., 1938, M.A., 1939, LL.D. (hon.), 1960; Ph.D., U. Calif., 1942; H.L.D., U. Redlands, 1962, Hebrew Union Coll., 1968, Windham Coll., 1969; LL.D., U. Bridgeport, 1963, Transylvania Coll., 1968, Pepperdine Coll., 1969, Our Lady of the Lake U., 1977, Dickinson State Coll., 1978, Calif. State U., 1982; m. Dorothy Deane Robison, Feb. 3, 1945. Instr. history Occidental Coll., 1940-43, asst. prof., 1943-46, asso. prof. 1947-50, prof. history, 1950, Norman Bridge prof. Hispanic Am. history, 1954, dean faculty, 1950-57; pres. San Francisco State Coll., 1957-61; vice chancellor acad. affairs Calif. State Colls., 1961-62; chancellor Calif. State Univ. and Coll. System, 1962-82, chancellor emeritus, 1982—; pres. Inst. Contemporary Studies, 1982—; lectr. in field; dir. Barclays Bank Calif., Olga Co., Farmers Group Ins., Forest Lawn Co. Past trustee Community TV So. Calif. KCET; past mem. com. on state relations Am. Assn. State Colls. and Univs.; mem. bd. visitors USAF Air U.; past mem. bd. visitors USAF Acad.; bd. commrs. Nat. Commn. on Accrediting, 1959-65, 70-74; trustee Calif. Industry-Edn. Council; trustee U. Redlands, 1970-79, trustee emeritus, 1979—; past chmn. Western Interstate Commn. Higher Edn.; chmn. fin. com., mem. exec. com. Council on Postsecondary Accreditation, 1975-82; chmn. Calif. Selection Com. for Rhodes Scholarships, 1966; bd. visitors Southwestern U. Sch. Law, 1981—; bd. dirs. Am. Council on Edn., 1967-68; founding mem. Civilian/Mil. Inst. USAF Acad. Found. Research fellow Huntington Library, 1943-45; Haynes Found. grantee, 1943; decorated Order of Merit (W.Ger.); comdr. Order of North Star (Sweden); Order St. John of Jerusalem (Eng.); medal of Culture, Taiwan, 1980. Mem. Los Angeles World Affairs Council (dir.), Calif. Council Econ. Edn. (1st chmn. 1968), Calif. Hist. Soc., Joint Council Econ. Edn. (trustee 1969—), Western Coll. Assn. (past chmn. membership and standards com.), Am. Mgmt. Assn. (dir. 1970-73, 74-77, 79-82, trustee, exec. com.), Inst. Internat. Edn. (West Coast adv. bd. 1972—), Calif. C. of C. (dir. 1980—), Newcomen Soc. N.Am., Phi Beta Kappa. Methodist. Clubs: Univ., Bohemian (San Francisco); Commonwealth, Town Hall. Author: The Boom of the Eighties in Southern Calif, 1944; Mexican Gold Trail, 1945; (with Osgood Hardy) A History of the Pacific Area in Modern Times, 1949; (under pseudonym Glenn Pierce) The Tyrant of Bagdad, 1955; co-author, editor: From Wilderness to Empire: A History of California, 1959; contbr. articles to profl. and popular publs. Home: 16332 Meadow Ridge Rd Encino CA 91436

DUMMETT, CLIFTON ORRIN, dental adminstr.; b. Georgetown, Guyana, S. Am., May 20, 1919; s. Alexander Adolphus and Eglantine (Johnson) D; came to U.S., 1936, naturalized, 1946; B.S., Roosevelt U.,

1941; D.D.S., Northwestern U., 1941, M.S.D., 1942, D.Sc. (hon.), 1976; M.P.H. (Julius Rosenwald Fund fellow), U. Mich., 1947; Sc.D. (hon.), U. Pa., 1976; m. Lois Maxine Doyle, Mar. 6, 1943; 1 son, Clifton Orrin. Prof., chmn. dept. periodontics, oral diagnosis, chmn. dental adminstrv. com. Meharry Med. Coll., Nashville, 1942-47, dean, dir. dental edn. Sch. Dentistry, 1947-49; chief dental service VA Hosp., Tuskegee, Ala., 1949-65, VA Research Hosp., Chgo., 1965-66; assoc. project dir., health center dir. Watts Health Center, 1966-68; prof., chmn. dept. community dentistry, assoc. dean extramural affairs, Sch. Dentistry, U. So. Calif., Los Angeles, 1968-76, prof. dentistry, 1968—. Served with USAF, 1955-57. Recipient Pierre Fauchard gold medal; diplomate Am. Bd. Periodontology, Am. Bd. Oral Medicine. Fellow AAAS, Am. Pub. Health Assn., Am. Coll. Dentists, Internat. Coll. Dentists; mem. ADA (hon.), Alaska Dental Soc., Los Angeles Dental Soc. (pres. 1977-78), Omicron-Omicron, Omicron Kappa Upsilon (pres. 1948-49), Internat. Assn. Dental Research (pres. 1969-70), Air Force Assn., Nat. Dental Assn. (ann. award 1952, Disting. Service award 1964, 76), Assn. Mil. Surgeons U.S. (Fones award 1976), Am. Acad. Dental Medicine, Acad. Periodontology, Am. Assn. Dental Editors (pres. 1974-75, Disting. Service award), Am. Acad. History of Dentistry (v.p. 1980-81, pres. 1982-83), Sigma Xi, Delta Omega, Sigma Pi Phi, Alpha Phi Alpha. Home: 5344 Highlight Pl Los Angeles CA 90016 Office: 925 W 34th St Los Angeles CA 90007

DUMONT, VIRGINIA PETERSON (MRS. R. PEASLEE DUMONT), educator; b. Salt Lake City, Jan. 19, 1918; d. Frederick L. and Florence Julia (Carpenter) Peterson; B.A. with honors in English, Mills Coll., 1938; postgrad. (grad. scholar), Bryn Mawr Coll., 1938-39, (spl. fellow), 1939-40; m. R. Peaslee DuMont, Aug. 5, 1940; children—Virginia Patricia (Mrs. Peter Kelly), Peaslee Frederick, Jayne Louise (Mrs. John Mack), Julia Blanche Dumont, Peter Bruce, Lorna Elizabeth (Mrs. James Shinkle), Edward Carroll. Home tchr. Piedmont (Calif.) High Sch., 1970-73; pvt. tutor in English and Social Studies, 1970—. Mem. adv. com. on ednl. philosophy Piedmont Unified Sch. Dist., 1967-68; mem. Friends of Oakland Library; mem. Piedmont bd. Am. Field Service, 1965-69. Mem. Mills Coll. Alumnae Assn. (chmn. continuing edn. pilot study 1957-59, nat. gov. 1958-59, dir. Phila. br. 1939, pres. Washington br. 1946-47, pres. Oakland, Calif. br. 1969-70, v.p. program 1983-84), Calif. Writers Club, LWV (v.p. Piedmont 1978 83), Oakland Mus. Assn., San Francisco Mus. Soc., Phi Beta Kappa. Roman Catholic. Contbr. poetry and articles to profl. books; editorial bd. Mills Coll. Alumnae Quar., 1978—. Address: 212 Carmel Ave Piedmont CA 94611

DUMOVICH, MATT, engr., educator; b. Denbo, Pa., Nov. 25, 1920; s. Joseph and Mary (Skrtich) D.; A.A., Henry Ford Coll., 1954; B.S., Wayne State U., 1956, M.Ed., 1961; postgrad. U. Calif., Los Angeles, 1963-67, San Diego State U., 1965-67. Transmitter engr. Sta. WKMH (now WKNR), Dearborn, Mich., 1947-51, Sta. WDET, Detroit, 1951-52; tchr. of deaf, Ecorse (Mich.) Pub. Schs., 1956-57, San Diego Pub. Schs., 1957—. Served with Armed Forces, 1942-45. Mem. San Diego Tchrs. Assn., NEA. Patentee math. teaching apparatuses. Home: 2151 Illion St San Diego CA 92110

DUMPER, ROBERT SARGENT, JR., real estate devel. co. exec.; b. Chgo., Sept. 22, 1940; s. Robert S. and Terry (Turner) D.; B.A. cum laude, Princeton U., 1962; M.B.A., Stanford U., 1964, m. Janet Kaminski, Mar. 6, 1976; 1 son, Adam; children by previous marriage—David, Audrey. Various acctg. positions Kaiser Hawaii Kai Devel. Co., Honolulu, 1964-68, asst. controller, 1968-69, v.p. and gen. mgr. Marina div., 1970-76; v.p. planning Kaiser Aetna, Oakland, Calif., 1976-77; v.p., gen. mgr. indsl./comml. N.W. div. KACOR Devel. Co., Oakland, 1977—. No. Calif. regional dir. Princeton U. Ann. Giving, 1980—; bd. dirs. Greater Oakland YMCA, 1981—. Mem. Internat. Council Shopping Centers. Republican. Episcopalian. Club: Sequoyah Country. Office: 300 Lakeside Dr Oakland CA 94643

DUNBAR, MAURICE VICTOR, educator; b. Banner, Okla., May 24, 1928; s. Moyer Haywood and Louise Edna (Curry) D.; B.A., U. Calif., Berkeley, 1952; M.A., Calif. State U., Sacramento, 1965; m. Virginia Lee McMeekin, Dec. 17, 1971. Tchr. English, Long Tree Sch., Beale AFB, Calif., 1962-64; tchr. Anna McKenney Sch., Marysville, Calif., 1964-66, Yuba City (Calif.) High Sch., 1966-67; prof. English, Foothill Coll., Los Altos, Calif., 1967—. Served with U.S. Army, 1948-50. Recipient prize Ball State U., 1979. Mem.John Steinbeck Soc., Stanford Library Assos. Clubs: Toastmasters (past pres.), Masons. Author: Fundamentals of Book Collecting, 1976; Books and Collectors, 1980; contbr. articles to John Steinbeck Quarterly. Home: 19904 Merritt Dr Cupertino CA 95014 Office: Foothill College Los Altos CA 94022

DUNBAR, NANCY LEE, govt. ofcl.; b. Geneva, Ill., Aug. 29, 1931; d. Douglas D. and Grace K. (Grant) Hammond; student UCLA, 1975; children—Robert Alan Burns, David Wayne Burns. Adminstrv. dir. Swiftbird Tng. Center, Gettysburg, S.D., 1969-71; secretarial positions U.S. Navy, Port Hueneme, Calif., 1970-74, adminstrv. asst., 1974-75, fed. women's program mgr. Naval Ship Weapon Systems Engring. Sta., 1975—, EEO specialist, 1975—, mgr. handicapped or upward mobility program, 1979—, personnel specialist, 1981, dir. career placement, 1982—; adv. to various community groups, 1960—. Vice pres. YWCA, 1978-80; sec. Braille Transcribers, 1966—; pres. Rio Plaza PTA, 1962-64; mem. adv. com. Rio Plaza Sch. Bd., Calif., 1962-64; mem. adv. bd. edn., Ventura and Oxnard. Mem. Federally Employed Women (pres. Ventura County 1977-79, sec. 1974-77, 79-81). Home: 1286 Cachuma Ave Ventura CA 93004 Office: Code 0610 Naval Ship Weapon Systems Engring Station Port Hueneme CA 93043

DUNBAR, PATRICIA LYNN, banker; b. St. Louis, Feb. 11, 1953; d. William R. and Beryl Ione Ferrand (Noland) Dunbar; m. Michael R. Jeffrey, Oct. 2, 1950. B.S., Northwestern U., 1973, M.F.A., 1975. With NBC-TV, Chgo., 1975-79; regional sales/mktg. mgr. Home Box Office, Chgo., 1979-81; sr. product mgr. Bank of Am., San Francisco, 1981-82, v.p., 1982—. Mem. Women in Cable (1st pres. Chgo. chpt. 1981), Jr. League San Francisco. Episcopalian. Patentee on child's chair, 1973.

DUNBAR, RICHARD DONALD, physician, educator; b. Chgo., Dec. 2, 1935; s. Eldine W. and Ivanette (Green) D.; B.A., Columbia Union Coll. Md., 1958; M.D., Loma Linda U., 1962; m. Marcia Hare, June 11, 1961; children—Jennifer, Richard, Allison. Intern, White Meml. Hosp., Los Angeles, 1962-63, resident in radiology, 1963-65; radiologist U.S. Naval Submarine Med. Center, 1966-68; instr. radiology Med. Sch. Loma Linda (Calif.) U., 1968-70, asst. prof., 1970-78, assoc. prof., 1978—, dir. resident edn. in diagnostic radiology, 1979—; univ. practice radiology; mem. staff Loma Linda U. Med. Center, pres. med. staff, 1981-82. Served with USN, 1966-68. Diplomate Am. Bd. Radiology; fellow in pulmonary radiology Cin. Gen. Hosp., 1970; fellow in radiologic pathologic correlation Armed Forces Inst. Pathology, 1966; fellow in chest radiology Royal Victoria Hosp., McGill U., Montreal, 1975. Fellow Am. Coll. Radiology (counselor); mem. ACP, Calif. Radiol. Soc., Inland Radiol. Soc. (past pres.), Am. Assn. Univ. Radiologists, Am. Roentgen Ray Soc., Radiol. Soc. N.Am., AMA, San Bernardino County Med. Soc. Home: 11559 Hillcrest Ct Loma Linda CA 92354 Office: Barton and Anderson Sts Loma Linda CA 92354

DUNBAR, ROBERT GEORGE, historian, educator; b. LaGrange, Wis., Apr. 30, 1907; s. Charles Sales and Johannah (Van de Vrede) D.; B.A., Milton Coll., 1929; M.A., U. Wis., 1933, Ph.D., 1935; m. Mary Snell Albertson, June 19, 1937; children—Ann Marie, George Roger. High sch. tchr., Colby, Wis., 1929-31; asst. prof. history U. S.D., 1935-37; faculty Colo. State U., 1937-47, asso. prof., 1943-47; faculty Mont. State U., Bozeman, 1947—, prof. history, 1950-72, emeritus prof., 1972—, dir. Center for Intercultural Programs, 1966-72. Served with USNR, 1944-45. Mem. Orgn. Am. Historians, Agrl. History Soc. (pres. 1966-67), Western History Assn. (award of honor 1978), Phi Kappa Phi, Phi Alpha Theta. Author: Farmer and the American Way, 1952; Forging New Rights in Western Waters, 1983; editorial bd. Agrl. History, 1943-77. Home: 715 S Grand Ave Bozeman MT 59715

DUNCAN, ANSLEY MC KINLEY, aerospace co. mgr.; b. Homer City, Pa., Jan. 25, 1932; s. William McKinley and Marion Melissa (Davis) D.; student U. Denver, 1955-57, Pa. State U., 1957-59. Engring. adminstr. RCA, Van Nuys, Calif., 1959-61; program evaluation coordinator N.Am. Aviation, Anaheim, Calif., 1961-66; mfg. supr., Rockwell Internat., Anaheim Calif., 1966-70, program adminstr., 1970-76, program controls mgr., 1976-81, plans/schedule advisor, 1981-83. Served with USN, 1951-55. Home: 12600 Willowood Ave Garden Grove CA 92640 Office: 3370 Miraloma Ave Anaheim CA 92803

DUNCAN, ARTHUR WILLIAM, vocational education adminstrator; b. San Pedro, Calif., Sept. 22, 1942; s. Robert William and Irma Jeanette (Hutchins) D.; m. Shirley Marie Adams, Dec. 11, 1965; children—Robert Dean, Tamera Jeanette. A.A., Ventura Jr. Coll., 1962; B.A., Western State Coll., 1965, M.A., 1966. Grad. teaching asst. phys. edn. Western State Coll., Gunnison, Colo., 1966; tchr. indsl. arts Delta (Colo.) High Sch., Dist. 50, 1966-68; tchr. indsl. arts, varsity cross country coach Montrose (Colo.) High Sch., Dist. RE-1J, 1968-76; tchr. vocat. bldg. trades Delta-Montrose Area Vocat.-Tech. Sch., 1976-79, vocat. guidance specialist, 1979-83, asst. dir., 1983—. Mem. Am. Vocat. Assn., Colo. Vocat. Assn. Republican. Episcopalian. Clubs: Order of DeMolay (life) (Ventura, Calif.); Elks (Montrose). Home: 6 Brown Rd Montrose CO 81401 Office: 1765 US Hwy 50 Delta CO 81416

DUNCAN, GREGORY MICHAEL, researcher, economist, statistician, educator; b. Balt., Mar. 9, 1948, s. Terrence Joseph and Rosemary Cecilia (Acheson) D.; m. Kathleen Freida Frey, July 3, 1969; children—Erin Renee, Mara Colleen, Brian Patrick. B.A. in Econs., U. Wash., 1970; M.A. in Stats., U. Calif.-Berkeley, 1974, Ph.D. in Econs., 1975. Systems analyst/programmer, U. Calif.-Berkeley, 1971-75; asst. prof. econs. Northwestern U., Evanston, Ill., 1975-78; asst. prof. econs., Wash. State U., Pullman, 1978-79, assoc. prof. econs. and stats., 1979—; cons. various govt. agys., referee profl. jours. Track coach Seattle Cath. Youth Assn., 1964-70; coach Pullman Youth Soccer, 1978—. Wash. State U. Bus. Devel. Fund grantee, 1978, 81; Office Grant and Research Devel. grantee, 1979; Nat. Commn. Employment Policy grantees, 1980; NSF grantee, 1981. Mem. Am. Econ. Assn., Am. Stats. Assn., Inst. Math. Stats. Democrat. Roman Catholic. Clubs: Whitman County Sportsman's Assn. Contbr. articles to profl. jours.

DUNCAN, IRA L., ret. state ofcl.; b. Bayard, Nebr., June 7, 1910; s. Earl C. and Emma M. (Casper) D.; B.S., Golden Gate Coll., 1957; div. 1940; 2 sons. Real estate and ins. broker, 1940-61, 78—; with Calif. Dept. Pub. Works, San Francisco, 1960-76, collection agent, to 1976. Served with AUS, 1942-45. Mem. Am. Soc. Mil. Insignia Collectors (sec.-treas.), Japanese Sword Soc. U.S. (treas.), Mil. Hist. Soc. London (dir.). Club: Masons (32 deg.). Home: 744 Warfield Ave Oakland CA 94610

DUNCAN, JAMES HENRY, health systems analyst, b. Germantown, Ill., July 10, 1924; s. Joseph Bernard and Veronica Cecelia (Welling) D.; A.A., Vincennes U., 1948; B.S. in Indsl. Engring., St. Louis U., 1951; student Indsl. Coll. of the Armed Forces, 1970, Air War Coll., 1975; m. Mary Nusbaum, Dec. 6, 1952; children—Madeline Lia, Dan, Matthew, Jeff, James. Engr., The Standard Register Co., Oakland, Calif., 1955-58, supr. production control and planning, 1958-63, production supr., 1963-68; evaluation team supr. dept. of med. methods research Kaiser-Permanente Med. Group, Oakland, 1968-73, health systems analyst, 1973-74, sr. health systems analyst, 1974-79; asst. dir. operational research and evaluation dept. Kaiser Found. Health Plan, 1979-80, mgr. med. systems, 1980—; cons. Holy Family Hosp., Spokane, Wash., Mercy Med. Center, Nampa, Idaho, guest lectr. U. Calif. Grad. Sch. Public Health (Berkeley, 1977—, Golden Gate Grad. Sch. Public Adminstrn., 1978 Bd. dirs. Oakland Indsl. Athletic Assn., 1958-65, Alameda Athletic Assn., 1976—; pres. Alameda Council Boy Scouts Am., 1980—. Served with Submarine Service USN, 1943-46; USAF, 1951-55; col. USAFR (ret.). Fellow Soc. for Advanced Med. Systems; mem. Am. Inst. of Indsl. Engrs. (sr. mem.), Hosp. Mgmt. Systems Soc., AAAS, Med. Entities Mgmt. Assn., Air Force Assn., Reserve Officers Assn., Railway and Locomotive Hist. Soc., Nat. Assn. of Railroad Passengers, Smithsonian Inst. Republican. Roman Catholic. Clubs: British-Am. Club of No. Calif., Knights of Columbus, Elks, VFW. Contbr. articles to med. jours., chpts. to book. Home: 1427 Mound St Alameda CA 94501 Office: 3451 Piedmont Ave Oakland CA 94611

DUNCAN, JOHNNY LEE, electrical engineer; b. Adair, Okla., Feb. 2, 1939; s. Lloyd Talbot and Ruby Adelia (Jeans) D.; A.A., Northeastern Okla. A&M U., 1959; B.S. in Elec. Engring., Okla. State U., 1962; M.S. in Elec. Engring., U. N.Mex., 1964; m. Kerin Dale Boston, June 17, 1961; children—Glenn Keith, David Lloyd, (dec.), Melinda Elizabeth. Mem. staff Sandia Labs., Albuquerqe, 1962—, div. supr., 1969—, test mgr. cruise missile warhead, 1978-82, test and evaluation mgr. Trident II fuze, 1982—. Served with U.S. Army, 1957. Mem. IEEE (sr.). Democrat. Baptist. Home: 10820 Nelle St Albuquerque NM 87111 Office: Kirtland AFB Sandia Labs Albuquerque NM 87185

DUNCAN, MARGARET DUNSMORE (MRS. WILLIAM FOWLER DUNCAN), civic worker; b. Summit, N.J., Sept. 9, 1920; d. James and Margaret (Montgomery) Dunsmore; student Fresno State Coll., 1941; m. William Fowler Duncan, June 17, 1940; children—William Fowler, Laird Douglas, Fraser Scott. Gray lady ARC, Oahu, 1959—, chmn. vols. Langley AFB, chmn. blood replacement program; active Heart Fund Dr., Neuromuscular Disease Dr.; mem. Los Niños Guild, Children's Hosp. Orange County; chmn. missionary cdn. women's assn. Presbyn. Ch., mariner, fellowship chmn., 1973-74, deacon, 1974-76, mem. nominating com.; mem. Am. Chapel Adv. Bd. Norway, 1982-83 active Arthritis Found., Leukemia Found. Recipient 25-yr. service pin ARC, 1981; 10-yr. service award San Clemente Gen. Hosp., 1982. Mem. Air Force Assn., Square and Compass, Aux. S.C. Gen. Hosp., Fairfax Hosp. Aux., Clans of Scotland, U.S.A., Scribe, Internat. Platform Assn., Order of Diana, LWV, Beta Sigma Phi (past chpt. pres.). Republican. Clubs: Ikebana, Air Force Officers Wives (Washington); Neighborhood Garden; Wheeler AFB Officers Woman's (1st v.p. 1960) (Oahu, Hawaii); Langley Officers Wives, Langley Yacht, Langley Golf; San Clemente Women's.; NATO Wives, Am. Wives, Am. Officers Wives (Oslo). Home: 502 Calle DeSoto San Clemente CA 92672

DUNCAN, REBECCA SUSAN, data processing administrator; b. Portland, Oreg., Mar. 11, 1946; d. Vincent Eugene and Eleanor Elizabeth (Munden) Davis; m. Richard F. Duncan, July 14, 1973. Student Multnomah Bus. Coll., Portland State U. With Ga.-Pacific, Portland, 1964-80, mgr., 1980; dir. data conversion Am. Data Services, Portland, 1980—. Chairperson adv. com. Clark Coll.; chairperson United Way, 1981. Mem. Computer Data Input Assn. (past pres.). Home: 13240 SW Juanita Pl Beaverton OR 97005 Office: 4550 SW Macadam Portland OR 97201

DUNCAN, RICHARD LEE, JR., ednl. psychologist; b. Lincoln, Nebr., June 1, 1940; s. Richard L. Duncan; B.A. in Edn., Ariz. State U., Tempe, 1963, M.A. in Counseling and Ednl. Psychology, 1965; Ed.D. in Psychology, Western Colo. U., Grand Junction, 1975; m. Charlotte Fish; children—Dana, Dwight, Derick, Denise, Darlene. Psychologist, Mesa (Ariz.) Pub. Schs., 1969-71, guidance cons., 1971-74, dir. Title III, 1973-74, head psychologist, 1974-76, dir. psychol. services, 1976—; pres. Clin. Communications Systems, 1978—; adj. prof. Ariz. State U., 1982—; vis. faculty Mesa Community Coll., 1969—. Bd. dirs. Maricopa County Youth Services Bur., Tri-City Mental Health Ctr., 1983—; active Boy Scouts Am., YMCA, Right to Life. Mem. Nat., Ariz. (pres. 1970-71) assns. sch. psychologists, Am. Psychol. Assn., Am., Ariz. (pres. 1975-76) personnel and guidance assns., Am., Ariz. sch. counselors assns., Kappa Delta Pi, Phi Delta Kappa. Mormon. Editor: Creative Action Counseling Techniques and Useful Strategies, 1976. Certified elementary and secondary tchr., counselor, psychologist, adminstr. Home: 1530 E Alameda Dr Tempe AZ 85282 Office: 549 N Stapley Dr Mesa AZ 85203

DUNCAN, ROBERT WESLEY, tax cons.; b. Mineral Springs, Ark., May 5, 1920; s. Robert S. and Cora E. (Hutchingson) D.; A.A., Santa Monica Jr. Coll., 1938-40; degree in Public Acctg., Willis Bus. Coll., 1948-50. Acct., Gilbert Drummond, Santa Monica, Calif., 1950-54, State of Calif. San Francisco-Oakland Toll Bridge, 1959-62; tax cons., Santa Monica, 1962-75, Riverside, Calif., 1978—; clk. March AFB, Calif., 1975-78. Usher, 1st A.M.E. Ch. of Riverside, 1972—, bd. dirs. Men's Club, 1972—. Served with USMCR, 1943-46. Mem. Nat. Assn. Tax Cons., Nat. Assn. Notaries Public, Internat. Platform Assn., Nat. Assn. Fed. Ret. Employees, Internat. Assn., Chiefs of Police. Democrat. Home: 2346 9th St Riverside CA 92507

DUNCAN, STUART BLACKWELL, writer, photo illustrator, book reviewer; b. Manchester, N.H., Apr. 21, 1933; s. Laurence Ilsley and Doris Madeline (Hackett) D.; m. Marcia Weston Morse, Aug. 20, 1956. A.B., Dartmouth Coll., 1955. Ptnr. D&H Automotive, Concord, N.H., 1955-59; with Crawford Electric, Concord, 1960-64; pres. Northeast Controls, Inc., Concord, 1965-67; gen. mgr. Fifth Ave./Durant Condominiums, Aspen, Colo., 1967-70; freelance writer, Snowmass, Colo., 1971—; author: Guide to the 1981 National Electrical Code, 1982; The Home Insulation Bible, 1982; The Complete Plywood Handwood, 1981; Plumbing with Plastic, 1980; The Build-It Book of Cabinets and Built-Ins, 1979; How to Build Your Own Log Home and Cabin from Scratch, 1978; The Complete Book of Outdoor Masonry, 1978; How to Make your Own Camping and Hiking Gear, 1978; How to Build Your Own Tennis Court, 1979; The Dream House Think Book, 1977; Camping Today, 1972; contbr. numerous articles to jour.; contbr. to books. Mem. Authors Guild. Home and Office: PO Box 148 1246 Gateway Rd Snowmass CO 81654

DUNCAN, TOMMY DALE, aerospace engr.; b. Winslow, Ark., Dec. 24, 1933; s. John Carson and Juanita Coleen (Hilliard) D.; B.S.M.E., San Diego State Coll., 1957; m. Shirley Ann Papike, June 22, 1957; children—Michael, Mark, Mary. Sr. design engr. Convair div. Gen Dynamics, San Diego, 1955-66; group engr. structural design jet engine packages and nacelles Rohr Industries, Inc., Chula Vista, Calif., 1966-82, chief engr. structural design, 1982—. Pres., Lake Murray Little League, 1970. Mem. Nat. Mgmt. Assn. Democrat. Roman Catholic. Home: 7587 Seton Hall La Mesa CA 92041 Office: PO Box 878 MZ 29R Rohr Industries Inc Chula Vista CA 92012

DUNCAN, VERNE A., state ofcl.; b. McMinnville, Oreg., Apr. 6, 1934; B.A., Idaho State U., 1960; M.Ed., U. Idaho, 1964; M.B.A., U. Portland, 1976; Ph.D. in Ednl. Adminstrn., U. Oreg., 1968; m. Donna R. Nichols, 1964; children—Annette, Christine. Tchr., Arco (Idaho) Elementary Sch., 1954-56, prin., 1962-63; prin. Butte Jr. High Sch., Arco, 1958-59; dir. guidance Butte High Sch., 1960-62; supt. Butte County Pub. Sch. Dist., 1963-66; asst. prof. ednl. adminstrn. U. Oreg., 1968-70; supt. Clackamas County (Oreg.) Intermediate Ednl. Dist., 1970-74; supt. pub. instruction State of Oreg., 1975—; cons. various sch. dists. Mem. Idaho Ho. of Reps., 1962-64; trustee Marylhurst Coll. Served in U.S. Army, 1956-58. Mem. Am. Assn. Sch. Administrs., Edn. Commn. of States, Council of Chief State Sch. Officers, Oreg. Hist. Soc. (trustee), Phi Delta Kappa. Address: State Supt's Office 700 Pringle Park Way Salem OR 97310

DUNCAN, VICKY LEE, personnel service co. exec.; b. War, W.Va., Sept. 3, 1936; d. John Henry and Hazel Margaret (Gross) Stumbo; student Lamar U., Beaumont, Tex., 1974-75; m. Bill Duncan, June 2, 1956; children—Christopher Wayne, William Edward, Kimberly Lynn. Bookkeeper, Security Pacific Bank, Hollywood, Calif., 1955-56; teller Bank of Hawaii, Oahu, 1958-59; credit/collection clk. Montgomery Ward & Co., Houston, 1964-68; counselor mgr. Snelling & Snelling, Beaumont, 1972-75; dir. agy. tng., mem. corp. staff Am. Bus. Service Corp., Newport Beach, Calif., 1976—. Mem. Am. Mgmt. Assn., Am. Employment Assn., Adminstrv. Mgmt. Soc., Bus. and Profl. Women, Am. Bus. Women, Calif. Assn. Personnel Cons., Beta Sigma Phi. Republican. Home: 1202 Genoa St Santa Ana CA 92704 Office: 610 Newport Center Dr Suite 250 Newport Beach CA 92660

DUNCAN, WILLIAM FOWLER, ret. air force officer, aerospace co. exec.; b. Springfield, Mo., July 10, 1915; s. Dorsey Berry and Flora (Turner) D.; student Kansas City (Mo.) Jr. Coll., 1933-35, U.S. Coast Guard Acad., 1935-36; B.S., U. Md., 1965; m. Margaret Dickie Dunsmore, June 17, 1940; children—William F., Laird, Fraser. Commd. 2d lt., USAAC, 1940; advanced through grades to col., USAF, 1960; U.S. Air Attache, Uruguay, 1949, Venezuela, Colombia, Ecuador, 1950-52; dir. ops. Wheeler AFB, 1959-63; dep. for intelligence Hdqrs. Tactical Air Command, Langley AFB, Va., 1965-68; ret., 1968; systems engr. Hughes Aircraft Co., Fullerton, Calif., 1968—. Mem. finance com., troop com. chmn. Decorated Legion of Merit, Air medal, Brit. Africa Star, Presdl. citation with cluster, Air Force Commendation medal. Mem. Ret. Officers Assn., Internat. Platform Assn., Air Force Assn. (past pres. Gen. Curtis E. LeMay chpt.), Mil. Order World Wars, Tau Kappa Epsilon. Presbyterian. Clubs: Langley Air Force Base Officers', Langley Yacht, Langley Golf; NATO Officers; Am. Officers (Oslo, Norway). Home: 502 Calle de Soto San Clemente CA 92672 Office: Hughes Aircraft Co Bldg 606 K-135 Fullerton CA 92634

DUNDAS, DENNIS FRANKLIN, plastic surgeon; b. Los Angeles, Oct. 12, 1942; s. John Arthur and Wanda C. (Yoakum) D.; B.A., Johns Hopkins U., 1964; M.D., U. So. Calif., 1968; m. Zoe Lynn Anderson, Feb. 8, 1969; children—Gregory, Denise. Intern, King County Hosp., Seattle, 1968-69; resident in surgery U. Oreg., Portland, 1972-76; resident in plastic surgery, Phoenix, 1976-78; pvt. practice medicine, specializing in plastic and reconstructive surgery, Kirkland, Wash., 1978—; staff Overlake, Evergreen, Children's Orthopedic hosps. Served with USN, 1969-71. Fellow ACS; mem. Am. Soc. Plastic and Reconstructive Surgeons. Clubs: Seattle Yacht, Bellevue Athletic. Home: 3261 Hunts Point Rd Bellevie WA 98004 Office: 13114 120th St NE Kirkland WA 98033

DUNDAS, GIFFORD WENDOW, concrete company executive; b. Lewiston, Idaho, Nov. 29, 1908; s. Harry Wendow and Mamie Clarin (Gifford) D.; student U. Calif.-San Francisco, 1931-33; m. Dee Ramona Houser, Jan. 29, 1942. Pres., Dunclick Concrete Products Mfg. Co., Lewiston, Idaho, 1945-74, Dunclick Research and Devel. Co., Clarkston, Wash., 1974—; dir. Inland Empire Waterways Assn., 1968-70.

Mem. Lewiston Water Commn., 1962-65; chmn. Lewiston Planning Commn., 1964-65; chmn. Lewiston Beautification Commn., 1965-66; mem. Asotin County (Wash.) Parks and Recreation Bd., 1976. Mem. Lewiston C. of C. (dir. 1964-66), Am. Legion. Clubs: Rotary, Masons, Elks, Clarkston Country, Shriners. Patentee swimming pool heating and cooling system. Home: 2040 Sargent Ln Clarkston WA 99403 Office: 2040 Sargent Ln Clarkston WA 99403

DUNG, WILLIAM MAN HIN, physician, clinic adminstr.; b. Honolulu, July 4, 1929; s. Allen and Agnes (Goo) D.; B.S., U. Wash., 1950, M.D., 1954; diploma Harvard Advanced Mgmt. Program, 1974; m. Daisy Yuk Kwai Pang, June 2, 1956; children—Janice, Lili, Mary, Joseph. Intern, Providence Hosp., Seattle, 1954-55; chief resident St. Francis Hosp., Honolulu, 1955-56; practice medicine specializing in family practice, Honolulu, 1959—; mem. Hawaii Permanente Med. Group, Honolulu, 1959—, staff physician, 1959-66, chief emergency, 1966-68, chief peripheral clinics, 1966-70, bd. dirs., 1968—, pres., 1970—; chief staff Kaiser Found. Hosp., Honolulu, 1971—; clin. asst. prof. community health U. Hawaii Sch. Medicine, 1974—. Mem. Hawaii State Bd. Med. Examiners, 1966—, sec. 1969—. Served to lt. USNR, 1957-59. Mem. Am., Hawaii, Honolulu County med. assns., Am. Assn. Med. Clinics, Hawaii Pub. Health Assn., Health and Community Services Councils of Hawaii, Am. Arbitration Assn. Home: 1556 Ulupuni St Kailua HI 96734 Office: 1697 Ala Moana Blvd Honolulu HI 96815

DUNGY, CLAIBOURNE IRA, pediatrician, educator; b. Chgo., Oct. 29, 1938; s. Jesse W. and Euphemia (Mickens) D.; B.S., Eastern Ill. U., 1962; M.D., U. Ill., 1967; M.P.H., Johns Hopkins, 1971; m. Madgetta Thornton, July 25, 1964; children—Kathryn Renee, Camille Thornton. Intern, U. Utah Hosp., Salt Lake City, 1967-68; resident pediatrics Stanford Hosp., 1968-70; pediatrics research fellow, Lagos, Nigeria, 1970; mem. faculty dept. pediatrics U. Colo., Denver, 1971-75, U. Calif. at Irvine, dir. ambulatory and community pediatrics, 1976-80. Regional med. coordinator head start programs region VIII HEW, 1973-75; mem. Calif. State Child Health Bd., 1977-82; UNICEF cons. Nigeria, 1977; bd. advisers Am. Acad. Physicians Assts. Elder Irvine Presbyn. Ch., 1977-80; bd. dirs. Orange County Urban League, 1982—. Served with AUS, 1956-58. Recipient Disting. Alumnus award Eastern Ill. U., 1979. Diplomate Nat. Bd. Med. Examiners (subcom. med. evaluation 1973-76), Am. Bd. Pediatrics. Fellow Am. Acad. Pediatrics; mem. Western Soc. Pediatric Research, Am. Pub. Health Assn., Ambulatory Pediatric Assn., Los Angeles, Orange County pediatric socs., Beta Beta Beta. Address: Dept Pediatrics U Calif Irvine CA 92717

DUNIHUE, ANNE WUNDUKE, city ofcl., steel co. ofcl.; b. Slovan, Pa., Sept. 22, 1924; d. George and Katherine (Yanchiak) Wunduke; Asso. Sci., Chaffey Coll., 1978; B.S., U. Redlands, 1979; m. George Van Sotraidis, Oct. 9, 1942; children—George Thomas, Steven Barry; m. 2d, Donald Wallace Dunihue, Nov. 5, 1952; 1 son, David Brian. With Kaiser Steel Corp., Fontana, Calif., 1951—, acctg. clk., 1968—; city councilwoman Fontana, 1976—, mayor pro-tem, 1977-79; chmn. bd. dirs. Omnitrans, 1979-80; chmn. Fontana Redevel. Agy., 1979-80; bd. dirs. San Bernardino County Transp. Commn., 1977—, East Valley Transit Service Authority, 1976—, Steelworkers Oldtimers Found., 1965—, YWCA, 1977—, United Way, 1979—; mem. Fontana adv. council Chaffey Coll., 1979—, chmn., 1981—. Mem. Calif. Elected Women's Assn. for Edn. and Research, AAUW (v.p. 1983-84), United Steelworkers Am., Fontana C. of C., San Bernardino Asso. Govts. (dir.), So. Calif. Assn. Govts. (energy and environment com. 1977-80), Fontana Bus. and Profl. Women's Club (pres. 1983-84, Woman of Yr. 1965, Woman of Achievement 1978), San Orco Dist. Bus. and Profl. Women's Club (pres. 1978-79). Democrat. Baptist. Club: Zonta (v.p. 1983-84). Home: 9395 Mango Ave Fontana CA 92335 Office: PO Box 217 Fontana CA 92335

DUNIPACE, IAN DOUGLAS, lawyer; b. Tucson, Dec. 18, 1939; s. William Smith and Esther Morvyth (McGeorge) D.; B.A. magna cum laude, U. Ariz., 1961; J.D. cum laude, 1966; m. Janet Mae Dailey, June 9, 1963; children—Kenneth Mark, Leslie Amanda. Reporter, critic Long Branch (N.J.) Daily Record, 1963; admitted to Ariz. bar, 1966, U.S. Supreme Ct. bar, 1972; assoc. firm Jennings, Strouss, Salmon & Trask, Phoenix, 1966-69, Jennings, Strouss & Salmon, 1969-70, ptnr., 1971—. Reporter, Phoenix Forward Edn. Com., 1969-70; chmn. gen. program com. Downtown Phoenix YMCA, 1973-74, bd. mgmt., 1973-80, sec., 1975—, chmn., 1977-78; bd. dirs. Phoenix Met. YMCA, 1976—, sec., 1980, vice chmn., 1981-83, chmn., 1984—; bd. mgmt. Paradise Valley YMCA, 1979-82, chmn., 1980-81; bd. mgmt. Scottsdale/Paradise Valley YMCA, 1983—, mem. legal affairs com. Pacific Region YMCA, 1978-81; bd. dirs. Beaver Valley Improvement Assn., 1977-79, Pi Kappa Alpha Holding Corp., 1968-72; trustee Paradise Valley Unified Sch. Dist. Employee Benefit Trust, 1980—. Served to capt. AUS, 1961-63. Mem. State Bar Ariz. (com. securities regulation 1970—, com. unauthorized practice of law 1972—, chmn. 1975—, mem. corp. law sect. 1981—, vice chmn. 1983-84), Am., Fed. (sec. Ariz. chpt. 1978-79, treas. 1979-80, pres. 1980-81), Maricopa County bar assns., Ariz. Zool. Soc., Heard Mus. Assn., Smithsonian Assos., Phi Beta Kappa, Phi Kappa Phi, Phi Delta Phi, Phi Alpha Theta, Sigma Delta Pi, Phi Eta Sigma, Pi Kappa Alpha (nat. counsel 1968-72). Democrat. Methodist (mem. met. Phoenix commn. 1968-71, lay leader 1975-78, trustee 1979-81, sec. 1979—, v.p. 1980, pres. 1981; mem. Pacific S.W. ann. conf. 1969-79, lawyer commn. 1980—). Clubs: Masons, Kiwanis, Ariz. Comments editor Ariz. Law Rev., 1965-66. Home: 3601 E Mountain View Phoenix AZ 85028 Office: 7501 E McCormick Pkwy Suite 119-S Scottsdale AZ 85258

DUNIWAY, BENJAMIN CUSHING, U.S. judge; b. Stanford, Calif., Nov. 21, 1907; s. Clyde A. and Caroline M. (Cushing) D.; B.A., Carleton Coll., 1928, LL.D., 1981; LL.B., Stanford U., 1931; B.A. (Rhodes scholar), Oxford U., 1933, M.A., 1964; m. Ruth Mason, Oct. 28, 1933; children—Anne (Mrs. Anne Barker), Carolyn (Mrs. Edward P. Hoffman), John M. Admitted to Calif. bar, 1931; practice in San Francisco, 1933-42, 47-59; partner firm Cushing, Cullinan, Duniway & Gorrill, 1947-59; regional atty. OPA, San Francisco, 1942-45, regional adminstr., 1945-47, asst. to adminstr., Washington, 1945; justice Dist. Ct. Appeals, 1st Appellate Dist. Calif., San Francisco, 1959-61; U.S. circuit judge 9th Circuit Ct. Appeals, 1961-76, sr. judge, 1976—; judge Temp. Emergency Ct. Appeals U.S., 1979—; mem. com. trial practice and techniques Jud. Conf. U.S., 1969-74, mem. com. jud. stats., 1970-76; dir. Schlage Lock Co., 1951-59. Chmn., Gov.'s Commn. Met. Area Problems, 1958-59; pres. Community Chest San Francisco, 1956-57, Calif. Conf. Social Work, 1950, Family Service Agy. San Francisco, 1950-51, Urban League San Francisco, 1952. Trustee Carleton Coll., 1958-71, Stanford, 1962-72; trustee James D. Phelan Found., 1957-71, pres., 1969-71; trustee Rosenberg Found., 1960-75, pres., 1964, 68-70; bd. dirs. Legal Aid Soc. San Francisco, 1955-70, Family and Children's Agy. San Francisco, 1948-51; life gov. Mill Hill Sch., Eng., 1933—. Recipient Presdl. Cert. of Merit, 1947. Mem. ABA, Am. Judicature Soc., Am. Law Inst., Conf. Calif. Judges, Bar Assn. San Francisco (treas. 1958, sec. 1959), Soc. Calif. Pioneers, World Affairs Council San Francisco, Order of Coif, Phi Beta Kappa, Delta Smiga Rho. Clubs: Chit Chat, Commercial (San Francisco). Author (with C.J. Vernier) American Family Laws, Vol. II, 1932. Office: PO Box 547 San Francisco CA 94101

DUNKEL, ARTHUR DALE, ret. govt. ofcl., civil engr.; b. Assumption, Ill., Mar. 6, 1914; s. Walter John and Sylvia (Kemmerer) D.; A.A. in Engring., Santa Rosa Jr. Coll., 1950; B.S. in Agrl. Engring., Calif. State Poly. Coll., 1953; A.S. in Real Estate, Fresno City Coll., 1979; m. Helen Roxa Mitchell, June 29, 1937 (dec. Aug. 1972); children—Arthur Dale, Keith Walter, Lynn Darrel, Margaret LaVonne (Mrs. Frederick K. Cheung), John Clifford, Kay Yvonne (Mrs. Michael Gordon Walden); m. 2d, Thelma Lois Teters Chase, June 1, 1975. Joined USN, 1934, gunners mate 3C USS Saratoga, 1934-38; chief gunners' mate U.S.S. Boise, 1938-45; with U.S. Naval Ammunition Depot, Hawthorne, Nev., 1945-46; USN-NAB Samar and Sangley Point, Phillipines, 1946-48; agrl. engr. U.S. Dept. Agr.-Soil Conservation Service, Fresno, Calif., 1953-54, Visalia, Calif., 1954-61, area (civil) engr., Fresno, 1961-80. Decorated Bronze Star (2); recipient Merit cert. U.S. Dept. Agr.-Soil Conservation Service, 1966. Mem. Am. Soc. Agrl. Engrs., Soil Conservation Soc. Am. (sect. Outstanding Achievement award 1967, sec.-treas. San Joaquin sect. 1969), Nat., Calif. socs. profl. engrs. Home: 4932 E Leisure Ave Fresno CA 93727 Office: 1130 O St Fresno CA 93721

DUNKLE, CHERYL ANN, educational administrator; b. Fargo, N.D., Sept. 23, 1947; d. William Arthur and Dolores June (Flick) Fowler; m. Wayne Christian Dunkle, Dec. 28, 1967; children—Jason, Megan. A.B. in Elem. Edn., U. No. Colo., 1968, A.M. (hon.), 1971. Cert. tchr., elem. adminstr., Colo. Tchr. reading Mapleton Pub. Sch., Denver, 1968-74, elem. guidance counselor, 1974-81, adminstrv. asst., 1981-82; elem. prin. Douglas County Schs., Castle Rock, Colo., 1983—. Mem. Colo. Personnel and Guidance Assn., Colo. Sch. Counselors Assn., NEA, Assn. Supervision and Curriculum Devel., Colo. Assn. Sch. Execs., Phi Delta Kappa, Delta Kappa Gamma. Lutheran. Clubs: Echo Hills Country, Perry Park. Home: 4695 W Red Rocks Dr Larkspur CO 80118 Office: 5449 N Huxtable St Sedalia CO 80135

DUNLAP, EDWIN LEE, bookbinder, b. Springfield, Ill., Aug. 8, 1932; s. Edwin Leslie and Essa Dola (Nicholas) D.; m. Roberta Catherine Dunlap, Nov. 26; children—Sandra, Carol, Debra, William. A.A. Phoenix Coll., 1958. With Messenger Graphics Co., Phoenix, 1961-76, Maricops Printers Co., Phoenix, 1976-77; bindery foreman Sims Printing Co., Phoenix, 1977. Served with USMC, 1951-55. Mem. Graphic Arts Internat. Union. Democrat. Lutheran. Home: 4201 N Westview Dr Phoenix AZ 85015 Office: 1726 N 22nd Ave Phoenix AZ 85009

DUNLAP, GEORGE MICHAEL, accountant; b. Amarillo, Tex., Jan. 21, 1946; s. Clinton Ward and Verda Mae (Fagan) D.; m. Janice Kay Halter, Nov. 7, 1967; 1 son, Ryan Michael; m. Delra June Spradley, June 4, 1978; children—Joshua Clinton, Zachary Paul. B.S., Ind. State U., 1971. C.P.A., Calif. Staff acct. Ernst & Whinney, Sacramento and Phoenix, 1971-75; with Daniells, Phillips, Garner & Vaughan, Bakersfield, Calif., 1975-77, John A. Marta & Co., Yuba City, Calif., 1977-79; owner, operator Dunlap Accountancy Corp., Redding, Calif., 1979—. Dir. Yuba-Sutter County YMCA, 1981; mem. adv. bd. Yuba-Sutter County Easter Seal Soc., 1980-81. Served with U.S. Army, 1966-68. Ernst & Whienney acctg. scholar, 1972. Mem. Am. Inst. C.P.A.s, Calif. Soc. C.P.A.s Mem. Ch. of God. Clubs: Yuba City Lions, Elks. Office: 1650 Oregon St Suite 111 Redding CA 96001

DUNLAP, RILEY EUGENE, sociology educator; b. Wynne, Ark., Oct. 25, 1943; s. Riley William and Freddie Eugenia (Jones) D.; m. Lonnie Jean Brown, Aug. 20, 1966; children—Sara Jean, Christopher Eugene. B.A., San Francisco State U., 1966; M.S., U. Oreg., 1969, Ph.D., 1973. Asst. prof. sociology Wash. State U., Pullman, 1972-76, assoc. prof., 1976—. Resources for Future Doctoral Dissertation fellow, 1971-72. Mem. AAAS, Am. Sociol. Assn. (chmn. sect. environ. sociology), Rural Sociol. Soc. (chmn. natural resources group), Soc. for Study Social Problems (chmn. environ. problems div.). Democrat. Contbr. articles to profl. jours. Home: NW 1200 Douglas Dr Pullman WA 99163 Office: Dept Sociology Wash State U Pullman WA 99164

DUNLAP, ROBERT WILLIAM, cardiologist; b. Grosse Pointe, Mich., Oct. 5, 1939; s. Henry Arthur and Josephine Alice (Burkit) D.; B.S., U. Mich., 1960, M.D. cum laude, 1964; m. Gayle Funnell, Dec. 3, 1966. Intern, U. Calif. at San Francisco, 1964-65; resident internal medicine Mayo Clinic, Rochester, Minn., 1965-67, cardiovascular fellow, 1967-69; dir. cardiology Harkness Hosp., San Francisco, 1971-72; asso. dir. cardiology St. Mary's Hosp., San Francisco, 1972-73, dir., 1973-80, chief of medicine, 1981—; co-dir. cardiology St. Joseph's Hosp., San Francisco, 1973-75; asst. clin. prof. medicine U. Calif. Med. Sch., San Francisco, 1976—; practice cardiology, San Francisco, 1971—. Served to maj. M.C., USAF, 1969-71. Decorated Commendation medal. Diplomate Am. Bd. Internal Medicine, Am. Bd. Cardiovascular Disease. Fellow A.C.P., Am. Coll. Cardiology, Am. Heart Assn.; mem. AMA, San Francisco Med. Soc., Mayo Clinic Cardiovascular Soc., Alpha Omega Alpha. Contbr. med. jours. Address: 301 Blackfield Dr Tiburon CA 94920

DUNLEVIE, ERNIE G., Realtor; b. N.Y.C., Aug. 3, 1917; s. George B. and Adelaide (Thompson) D.; children—Jon Taylor, Scott George, Michael Raymond, Geoffrey Kyle Dunlevie; m. 2d, Joy R. Nicholson, Nov. 8, 1982. Ptnr., Desert Bermuda Devel. Co., Bermuda Dunes, Calif., 1957—; pres. Dunray Land Co., Inc., 1957—, Ernie Dunlevie Assos., Palm Springs, Calif., 1946—. Past pres. Bob Hope Desert Classic. Served with USAAF, 1942-45. Decorated Air medal with 3 oak leaf clusters, D.F.C. Mem. Palm Springs C. of C. (dir. 1958), Calif. Real Estate Assn. (v.p. 1959, dir.), Palm Springs Bd. Realtors (past pres.). Clubs: Bermuda Dunes Country, Bermuda Dunes Racquet; Balboa Bay (Newport Beach); Mt. Kenya Safari (Africa); Catalina Island Yacht. Home: 79-050 Ave 42 Bermuda Dunes CA 92201

DUNLOP, NANCY JEANNE, home economics educator; b. Vallejo, Calif., Mar. 28, 1957; d. John Sears and Mary Helen (Raffety) D. B.S. in Home Econs. Edn., Wash. State U., 1979, also postgrad. Teaching and vocat. certs., Wash. Tchr. home econs. East Valley High Sch., Spokane, Wash., also tennis coach, cheerleader advisor. Mem. NEA. Office: Home Econs Dept East Valley High Sch E 15711 Wellesley Spokane WA 99216

DUNLOP, RICHARD GALBRAITH, retail executive; b. Phila., Nov. 24, 1942; s. Robert Galbraith and Emma Laura (Brownback) D.; m. Kathleen Watson Sittig, Aug. 11; children—Robert Galbraith, Allison Suzanne. B.A., Trinity Coll., Hartford, Conn., 1965; M.B.A., Wharton Sch., U. Pa., 1968. With Acme Markets Inc. subs. Am. Stores Co., 1967-80; exec. v.p., corp. sec. Am. Stores Co., Salt Lake City, 1980—. Republican. Presbyterian. Clubs: Ft. Douglas (Salt Lake City); Skytop (Pa.).

DUNMIRE, WILLIAM WERDEN, national park administrator; b. Alameda, Calif., Feb. 24, 1930; s. Samuel P. and Margaret L. (Dickinson) D.; B.A., U. Calif.-Berkeley, 1954, M.A., 1957; m. Marjorie S. Schoder, June 14, 1952; children—Glenn E., Peter P.; m. 2d, Evangeline L. Blinn, Oct. 18, 1972. Naturalist, Nat. Park Service, 1957-63; chief park naturalist Isle Royale Nat. Park, 1963-66; chief park naturalist Yellowstone Nat. Park, 1968-72; chief div. interpretation Nat. Park Service, Washington, 1973-77; supt. Coulee Dam (Wash.) Nat. Recreation Area, 1977-81; supt. Carlsbad Caverns and Guadalupe Mountains Nat. Parks (N.Mex.), 1981—. Mem. Internat. Good Neighbors Council, 1982. Served with U.S. Army, 1954-56. Recipient Meritorious Service award U.S. Dept. Interior, 1973. Mem. Nat. Parks and Conservation Assn., Wilderness Soc., Sierra Club. Club: Rotary. Home: 1412 W Orchard Ln Carlsbad NM 88220 Office: 3225 Nat Park Hwy Carlsbad NM 88220

DUNN, BRAXTON MINOR, research engr.; b. Washington, Feb. 27, 1934; s. William Hugh and Marion Jane (Smith) D.; m. Klara Jolan Haty; children—Andrew, Colleen; B.S. in Aero. Engring., U. Md., 1957; M.M.E., U. Wash., 1964. Registered profl. engr., Wash. Engr., Boeing Aerospace Co., Seattle, 1957-65; research engr. United Aircraft Research Lab., East Hartford, Conn., 1965-67; research engr. advanced airbreathing propulsion Boeing Aerospace Co., Seattle, 1967—; cons. State of Wash., 1972-78. Mem. AIAA, Flight Research Inst. Republican. Presbyterian. Patentee in field. Office: Boeing Aerospace Co Seattle WA 98124

DUNN, CAL, artist, motion picture producer and director; b. Georgetown, Ohio, Aug. 31, 1915; s. Forester Eugene and Mary Achsa (Calvin) D.; m. Eleanor Francis Little, Sept. 4, 1937; 1 son, Michael Hamilton. Student Cin. Art Acad., 1927, Central Acad. Comml. Art, 1932-34. Engaged in layout and illustration studios and advt. agys., Cin., Detroit, Iowa, 1935-43; freelance cartoonist, 1943; founder Cal Dunn Studios, Inc., Chgo., 1947-79; artist, Santa Fe, 1980—; one-man shows include: A.B. Closson Gallery, Cin., 1941, Etc. Gallery, Chgo., 1952, Tavern Club, Chgo., 1962-81; numerous group shows including: Cin. Art Mus., 1941, Davenport (Iowa) Municipal Art Gallery, 1941, Art Inst. Chgo., 1946, 50, Artists Guild Chgo., 1946, 48, 49, 50-55, 58-63, 65, Santa Fe Festival Arts, 1978, 80; represented in permanent collections Albuquerque Mus., N.Mex. Mus. Fine Art. Recipient numerous awards including Artists Guild Chgo., 1946, 48, 49-51, 55; Bronze medal Am. Watercolor Soc., 1956; Emmy award Acad. TV Arts and Scis., 1959; Best Dir. award Chgo. Audiovisual Producers Assn., 1977. Mem. Am. Watercolor Soc., Artist Guild Chgo. (past pres.), Dirs. Guild Am. Address: Route 3 Box 86L Sunlit Hills Santa Fe NM 87501

DUNN, DAVID CAMERON, marketing executive; b. Juneau, Alaska, Dec. 8, 1941; s. Robert C and Kay (Watson) D.; m. Karen Ann Leonard, Jan. 17, 1970; children—David Cameron, Paige. B.A. in Econs., Stanford U., 1963; M.B.A., U. Pa., 1968. Exec. v.p. mktg./sales Calif. Wine Assn., San Francisco, 1977-79; sr. v.p. mktg./sales The Grange Co., Modesto, Calif., 1979-82; gen. mgr. brand mktg. Foster Farms, Livingston, Calif., 1982-83; v.p. WCC Advt., San Francisco, 1983—; cons. small bus. Served to 1st lt. C.E., U.S. Army, 1964-66. Republican. Roman Catholic. Co-founder Wharton Mag., 1967. Home: 3331 Wycliffe Dr Modesto CA 93555 Office: WCC Advt San Francisco CA 94111

DUNN, HARRY LIPPINCOTT, lawyer; b. Santa Barbara, Calif., Feb. 24, 1894; s. E.P. and Margaret Ann (Robinson) D.; m. Louise Reding, Feb. 7, 1925; m. 2d, Katharine Tilt, Feb. 3, 1955; children—Peter R., Priscilla Flynn. Student U. Calif.-Berkeley, 1915, Law Sch., Columbia U., 1915-16, Harvard Law Sch., 1919-21. Bar: Calif. 1925. Assoc. Cravath Henderson Leffingwell de Gersdorf, N.Y.C., 1921-24; assoc. O'Melveny & Myers, Los Angeles, 1924-27, ptnr., 1927-68, of counsel, 1968—; dir. Lockheed Aircraft Corp., Gen. Telephone Co. Calif. Mem. Commn. for Relief in Belgium, 1916-17, Commn. for Relief in Poland, 1919; mem. Claremont Univ. Ctr. Served as 1st lt. AEF, 1917-19. Decorated Croix de Guerre (France). Mem. ABA, Calif. Bar Assn., Los Angeles Bar Assn., Los Angeles World Affairs Council (v.p.). Republican. Episcopalian. Clubs: California (Los Angeles); Annandale Golf, Valley Hunt, Twilight (Pasadena, Calif.). Home: 1360 Hillcrest Ave Pasadena CA 91106 Office: O'Melveny & Myers 400 S Hope St Los Angeles CA 90071

DUNN, IMA CHARLENE GANT, educational administrator; b. Pueblo, Colo., Jan. 29, 1941; d. William Arthur and Fern Evelyn (Traylor) Gant. A.A., U. So. Colo., 1960; B.A., U. No. Colo., 1962, Ed.D., 1973; M.Ed., Central State U., 1966. Cert. pub. sch. tchr., adminstr., Colo. Tchr. elem. sch., remedial reading, Albuquerque, 1962-65; instr. U. So. Colo., Pueblo, 1966-68; secondary reading coordinator Pueblo Dist. No. 70, 1968-71, coordinator secondary educ., 1973-74, dir. spl. services, 1973—; field experience specialist U. No. Colo., Greeley, 1971-73; mem. Colo. Data, Acquisition, Rev. and Utilization Com.; cons. to single life sessions. Mem. Pueblo Council for Exceptional Children, NEA, Colo. Assn. Sch. Execs., Council Adminstrs. Spl. Edn., Kappa Delta Pi, Phi Delta Kappa, Pi Lambda Theta. Republican. Methodist. Clubs: Order of Eastern Star, White Shrine, Order of Amaranth. Contbr. articles to profl. jours. Office: Pueblo Sch Dist No 70 24951 E Hwy 50 Pueblo CO 81006

DUNN, JAMES MICHAEL, physician, pharm. co. exec.; b. Long Beach, Calif., May 8, 1937; s. Joseph Shelby and Mary Juanita (Fowler) D.; B.S., U. Oreg., 1958; M.D., U. Calif., Irvine, 1962; m. Carolyn Kay Olson, Oct. 23, 1971; children—Shannon, Lisa, Christopher, Kevin. Intern, Sacred Heart Gen. Hosp., Eugene, Oreg., 1962-63; resident in ob-gyn Kaiser Found. Hosp., Oakland, Calif., 1965-67; practice medicine specializing in ob-gyn, Fairfield, Calif., 1967-74, Oreg. McLean Clinic, Oregon City, 1974-75; asst. dir. clin. pharmacology Abbott Labs., 1975-76; asso. dir. clin. pharmacology, then dir. clin. research Wallace Labs., 1976-79; v.p. med. affairs Boots Pharms., Inc., 1979-80; pres. Verex Labs., Inc., Englewood, Colo., 1980-82, pres., chief exec. officer, chmn., 1982—; asst. prof. family medicine and pharmacology La. State U. Med. Sch., 1979-81. Served as officer M.C., USAF, 1963-65. Fellow Am. Coll. Clin. Pharmacology, Am. Soc. Abdominal Surgeons, Royal Soc. Medicine, Internat. Coll. Physicians and Surgeons; mem. Am. Soc. Clin. Pharmacology and Therapeutics, AMA, N.Y. Acad. Sci., Am. Fertility Soc., AAAS, Western Soc. Ob-Gyn (a founder), Drug Info. Assn., Sigma Xi. Roman Catholic. Author articles in field, also poems, short stories. Address: 8925 E Nichols Ave PO Box 3817 Englewood CO 80112

DUNN, NANCY GAYLE, tax cons.; b. Portland, Oreg., June 6, 1940; d. Robert Herman and Ethel Wilhelmina (Lund) Richardson; student (scholar) Portland Art Mus., 1959; m. Gerald James Dunn, Sept. 12, 1966; 1 dau., Patricia Lynn. Mem. acctg. dept. staff Farwest Fed. Savs & Loan Assn., Portland, 1960-65; mgr. advt. Norwest Newspaper Co., Crescent, Calif., 1965; owner, pres. Nancy Dunn Tax Service, Portland, 1970—. Mem. Assn. Tax Cons. (nat. treas., pres. Portland chpt.). Republican. Roman Catholic. Club: Soroptimist (pres.). Home: 2204 NW 88th St Vancouver WA 98665 Office: 7537 N Richmond St Portland OR 97203

DUNN, RICHARD JOSEPH, investment counselor; b. Chgo., Apr. 5, 1924; s. Richard Joseph and Margaret Mary (Jennett) D.; A.B., Yale, 1948; LL.B., Harvard, 1951; M.B.A., Stanford, 1956; m. Marygrace Calhoun, Oct. 13, 1951; children—Richard, Marianne, Anthony, Gregory, Noelle. Admitted to Tex. bar, 1952; mem. firm Carrington, Gowen, Johnson, & Walker, Dallas, 1951-54; investment counselor Scudder, Stevens & Clark, San Francisco, 1956—, v.p., 1963-77, sr. v.p., 1977—, gen. partner, 1974—. Mem. Calif. Democratic Central Com., 1962, San Francisco County Dem. Central Com., 1963-66. Served with AUS, 1943-46. Decorated Purple Heart. Mem. San Francisco Security Analysts Soc. Club: Knights of Malta. Home: 530 Junipero Serra Blvd San Francisco CA 94127 Office: 101 California St San Francisco CA 94111

DUNN, S. THOMAS, consulting and publishing company executive; b. Rock Island, Ill., Aug. 27, 1940; s. Paul Thomas and Margaret

(Boultinghouse) Q.; B.S., Mo. Sch. Mines, 1962; M.S. Mech. Engring., Okla. State U., 1963, Ph.D., 1965; m. Rosemary Meehan, June 7, 1976; children—Paul, Bryan, Sussan, Angela. Instr. thermodynamics, grad. research asst. Okla. State U., 1963-64; project leader Inst. Basic Standards Methodology div. photometry and colorimetry sect. Nat. Bur. Standards, Washington, 1964-66; pres., majority owner Dunn Assocs., Inc., Silver Spring, Md., 1966-69; v.p., dir. Block Engring. Inc., Silver Spring, 1969-74; dir. Digilab, Inc. subs. Block Engring., Inc., Cambridge, Mass., 1969-74, pres., 1970-74; EOCOM Corp., Irvine, Calif., 1974-76; pres. Dunn Tech. Inc., Vista, Calif., 1976—; exec. dir. Lasers in Pub. User Group, 1979—. Mem. N.Y. Acad. Scis., AIM (pres.'s council 1974), Assn. Graphic Arts Cons., Graphic Arts Tech. Found., Inst. Graphic Communication (seminar chmn.), Optical Soc. Am., Printing Industries Am., Research and Engring. Council of Graphic Arts, Soc. Photo-Optical Instrumentation Engrs., Soc. Photog. Scientists and Engrs., Tech. Assn. Graphic Arts, AAAS, Am. Chem. Soc., ASME, ASTM, Inst. Environ. Scis., Instrumentation Soc. Am., Sci. Apparatus Makers Assn., Soc. Applied Spectroscopy, Phi Kappa Phi, Phi Tau Sigma, Tau Beta Pi, Kappa Mu Epsilon. Contbg. editor: Production News, 1976-79; what's new editor: Applied Spectroscopy, 1980—; contbr. numerous articles to profl. jours. Address: 1131 Beaumont Circle Vista CA 92083

DUNNETT, DENNIS GEORGE, state official; b. Auburn, Calif., Aug. 5, 1939; s. George DeHaven and Elizabeth Grace (Sullivan) D.; A.A. in Elec. Engring., Sierra Coll., 1959; A.B. in Econs., Sacramento State Coll., 1966. Engring. technician State of Calif., Marysville, 1961-62, data processing technician, Sacramento, 1962-67, EDP programmer and analyst, 1967-74, staff services mgr. and contract adminstr., 1974-76, hardware acquisition mgr., 1976—; instr. Am. River Coll., 1972; cons. to state personnel bd. on data processing testing, 1983. Mem. Data Processing Mgmt. Assn. (cert. in data processing, cert. in computer programming), Am. Mgmt. Assn., Calif. State U.-Sacramento Alumni Assn. (life), Assn. Computing Machinery, IEEE Computer Soc., Assn. Inst. for Certification of Computer Profls. Home: 8980 Bradshaw Rd Elk Grove CA 95624 Office: Box 160247 Sacramento CA 95816

DUNNIGAN, MARY ANN, former ednl. adminstr.; b. St. Maries, Idaho, Sept. 7, 1915; d. William Henry and Mary Ellen (Kelly) D.; B.A., Holy Names Coll., Spokane, 1942; M.A., Gonzaga U., Spokane, 1957; postgrad. U. Idaho, UCLA. Tchr. rural schs. Bonner County, 1936-41, elem. schs., 1941, 45-59, high sch., 1942, 45, coordinator elem. edn., 1959-78; prin. kindergarten Sch. Dist. 271, Coeur d'Alene, Idaho, 1978-81; tchr. extension classes U. Idaho; curriculum chmn. Gov.'s Conf. on Edn.; adv. council Head Start. Adv. council Council for Aging; mem. N. Idaho Mus., Community Council, Community Concerts, Community Theater, N. Idaho Booster Club, Mayor's Com. on Handicapped; mem. task force and diocesan bd. Catholic Edn. of Idaho, 1969-74. Named Citizen of Yr., N. Idaho Coll., 1974, Idaho Cath. Dau. of Year, 1968. Mem. Idaho Edn. Assn., NEA, Assn. Supervision and Curriculum Devel., Internat. Reading Assn., Nat. Council Tchrs. of Social Studies, Nat. Council Tchrs. of Math., Nat. Council Tchrs. of English, Kootenai County Ret. Tchrs. Assn. (pres. 1983-85), Delta Kappa Gamma. Club: Cath. Daus. Am. (state regent 1956-62). Home: 720 9th St Coeur d'Alene ID 83814 Office: 725 Hazel Ave Coeur d'Alene ID 83814

DUNSETH, WILLIAM BARKLEY, university administrator; b. McKeesport, Pa., July 26, 1918; s. William Walter and Ruth (Hershey) D.; B.A., Park Coll., 1942; M.B.A., U. Minn., 1947; m. Patricia A. Sullivan, Dec. 24, 1942; children—William Barkley, Katherine B. Head merchandising dept. Hall Bros., Kansas City, Mo., 1947-52; v.p. Park Coll., 1952-57; dir. devel. Hampden-Sydney Coll., 1957-59; dir. estate planning Pomona Coll., 1959-64; gen. sec. Calif. State Coll. System, 1964-68; exec. dir. U. Oreg. Devel. Fund, 1968-72; v.p., dir. estate planning Pomona Coll., Claremont, Calif., 1972-76, v.p., 1976-80, emeritus v.p., 1980—; exec. cons. Am. City Bur., Chgo., 1980—; mentor, sem. devel. officers tng. program Lilly Endowment, Inc., 1979—. Precinct chmn. 49th Republican Assembly Calif., 1961; mem. Claremont Planning Commn., 1962-64; adviser Pomona Valley Girl Scout councils, 1961-63; chmn. Pub. Solicitations Commn. Claremont, 1962-64; mem. cabinet Casa Colina Hosp., 1972-74; bd. dirs. Claremont chpt. ARC; vice chmn. Pomona Valley Health Plan, 1980—; adv. bd. So. Calif. Coll. Optometry, 1982—; bd. dirs. Friends of Claremont Colls., 1983—. Served with USNR, 1942-46. Mem. Navy League, U.S. Naval Inst., Am. Council Advancement and Support Edn. (commn. on taxation and philanthropy 1971-80), Am. Council Edn. (com. taxation), Nat. Soc. Fund Raising Execs. (dir. So. Calif. chpt.). Episcopalian. Clubs: Masons, Shriners, Rotary; Univ. Author: An Introduction to Annuity, Life Income and Bequest Programs, 1978. Home: 1845 Antioch Rd Claremont CA 91711

DUNTEN, MARY HELEN, association executive; b. Seattle, Apr. 17, 1932; d. Joseph Sylvester and Helen May (Steen) Ellerby; m. Caryl Wesley Dunten, May 24, 1958 (div.); 1 dau., Leslye Victoria. B.A. cum laude, Lewis and Clark Coll., 1954; postgrad. U. London, 1955-56; postgrad. summers U. Wash., 1955, Stanford U., 1957. Asst. pub. info. officer Ariz. State Employment Service, Phoenix, 1970-71; pub. info. specialist City of Phoenix, 1971-74; pub. info. officer Contra Costa County, 1974-79; pub. affairs officer Assn. Bay Area Govts., Berkeley, Calif., 1979-80, dir. pub. affairs, 1980—; instr. John F. Kennedy U., 1977-80. Recipient Communications award Nat. Assn. Regional Councils, 1980; Fulbright scholar, 1955-56. Mem. Pub. Relations Soc. Am. (accredited; hon. achievement award 1981), Nat. Assn. Govt. Communicators (Blue Pencil award 1978), Nat. Assn. County Info. Officers (excellence award 1978, 81), Internat. Assn. Bus. Communicators, San Francisco Pub. Relations Round Table, Media Aliance, Nat. Assn. Govt. Communicators (past nat. dir.), Nat. Assn. County Info. Officers (past pres.), Nat. Assn. Regional Councils (award of excellence 1980, 82). Unitarian. Home: 102 Ravenhill Rd Orinda CA 94563 Office: Hotel Claremont Berkeley CA 94705

DUNTON, JAMES KEGEBEIN, investment company executive; b. White Stone, Va., Jan. 18, 1938; s. Ammon G. and Carolyn Elizabeth (Kegebein) D.; m. Janet L. Jamison; m. 2d, Nancy C. Hilton; children—James Gresham, Robert Anson, Elizabeth Ann. B.A., U. Va., Charlottesville, 1959, M.B.A., 1962. Fin. analyst Capital Research Co., N.Y.C., 1962-63, Los Angeles, 1963-65, v.p., portfolio mgr., 1965-82, exec. v.p., 1982—; v.p. Capital Guardian Trust Co., Los Angeles, 1969-72; sr. v.p., vice chmn. The Investment Com., 1972-80. Treas., mem. vestry All Sts. Episcopal Ch., Pasadena. Served as officer, arty. U.S. Army, 1960. Mem. Los Angeles Soc. Fin. Analysts (dir., past pres.), SEC, Fin. Reporting Inst. Clubs: Valley Hunt, (Pasadena, Calif.); Univ. (Los Angeles). Home: 680 Burleigh Dr Pasadena CA 91105 Office: 333 S Hope Los Angeles CA 90071

DUPERON, DONALD FRANCIS, dentist, ednl. adminstr.; b. Regina, Sask., Can., Dec. 18, 1937; came to U.S., 1974; s. Francis and Eugenie (Dhuez) D.; D.D.S., U. Alta., Can., 1961; M.S., U. Man., Can., 1970; cert. Children's Hosp. of Winnipeg (Man., Can.); 1968; m. Donna Joy Hill, Aug. 20, 1960; children—Lori Anne, Mona Lee. Practice dentistry, Regina, 1961-67, Winnipeg, 1967-74; asst. prof. U. Man., Winnipeg, 1968-70, acting head children's dentistry, 1968-70, asso. prof., head sect. pediatric dentistry, 1970-74; chief of dentistry Children's Hosp. of Winnipeg, 1970-74; asso. prof. and head post-doctoral pediatric dentistry program UCLA, 1974—; adv. Area Health Edn. Center, UCLA, 1979—. HEW grantee, 1974-77. Mem. Man. Dental Assn., Internat. Assn. Dental Research, Calif. Soc. Pediatric Dentists, Can. Dental Assn., Can. Acad. Pedodontists, Royal Coll. Dentists Can., Coll. Dental Surgeons of Sask., Am. Amateur Karate Fedn. Contbr. articles on dental research to profl. publs. Home: 30169 Via Victoria Rancho Palos Verdes CA 90274 Office: Sch Dentistry UCLA Los Angeles CA 90024

DUPONT, L. MARTIN, manufacturing executive; b. Paia, Maui, Hawaii, Sept. 28, 1942; s. Lionel V. and Eva M. (Martin) DuP.; m. Kay Tinker, Aug. 8, 1963; m. Patrica Ann Marley, Apr. 16, 1982; children—Steven, Renee, Ginger, Jeff, Michelle, Tyler. B.S., U. Colo., 1964; M.B.A., U. Hawaii, 1973. Exec. v.p. Budget Rent A Car, Hawaii, 1969-70; pres. DuPont Industries Inc., Hawaii, 1970-76, Mgmt. Systems Inc., Hawaii, 1976-78, Atlantis Mfg. Corp., Boulder, Colo., 1978-82; chief exec. officer Atlantis Hi-Tech, Boulder, 1982—. Exec. in residence Colo. U. Bus. Sch. Chmn., March of Dimes; pres. Jaycees, Maui, Hawaii; pres. Democratic party Maui. Served to capt. U.S. Army, 1965-69. Decorated D.S.C., Silver Star, Bronze Star. Mem. Phi Beta Kappa, Phi Sigma Alpha. Roman Catholic. Inventor; author: The Atonement, 1983; Fitness at Any Age, 1981. Office: 1685 38th St Boulder CO 80301

DUPREE, JAMES ANDREW, speech therapist, educator, educational administrator, consultant; b. Shreveport, La., Feb. 6, 1947; s. Joseph Leon and Iris (Reddix) D.; m. Gwendolyn Ann Jackson, June 17, 1972; children—Opio, Adjua, Imani. B.S., Xavier U., New Orleans, 1969; M.A., Seattle U., 1976; Ed.D., U. Wash., 1983. Cert. sch. prin., sch. supt., Wash. Tchr. pub. schs., New Orleans, 1969-70, Tacoma, 1970-71; instr. U. Wash., 1971-73; tchr. pub. schs., Seattle, 1973-75, ednl. supr., 1975-77, sch. adminstr., 1977-79; exptl. alternative edn. supr. Lake Washington Pub. Schs., Kirkland, Wash., 1979-83, spl. program specialist, 1983—; cons. in field; career cons.; mem. Council Spl. Edn.; mem. Project Excel Task Force. Newton Smith Achievement scholar, 1965; NDEA fellow, 1971. Mem. Wash. Assn. Sch. Dirs., Nat. Assn. Black Sch. Adminstrs., Wash. Assn. Sch. Adminstrs., Black Educators Assn. (pres.), Seattle Prins. Assn. (exec. bd.), Mcpl. League, Council on Racial, Religious and Ethnic Harassment, NAACP, Seattle Urban League, Council World Affairs (host). Democrat. Roman Catholic. Clubs: Epicureans (New Orleans); Links of Seattle. Home: 12126 SE 240th St Kent WA 98031

DUPUY, HOWARD MOORE, JR., lawyer; b. Portland, Oreg., Mar. 15, 1929; s. Howard Moore and Lola (Dunham) D.; B.A., U. Portland, 1951; postgrad. Willamette U., Salem, Oreg., 1951; LL.B., Lewis and Clark Coll., 1956; m. Anne Irene Hanna, Aug. 26, 1950; children—Loanne Kay, Brent Moore. Admitted to Oreg. bar, 1956, since practiced in Portland; asso. Green, Richardson, Green & Griswold, 1956; partner Morton & Dupuy, 1957-67; partner Buell, Black & Dupuy, and predecessor firm, 1968—. Mem. fin. com. Oreg. Republican Central Com., 1962. Served with AUS, 1946-47. Mem. Am., Oreg., Multnomah County bar assns., Am. Arbitration Assn. (nat. panel arbitrators), Portland C. of C. Club: Aero of Oreg. (Portland). Home: 16116 NE Stanton St Portland OR 97230 Office: 421 SW Fifth Ave Suite 202 Portland OR 97204

DUQUETTE, ANTHONY MICHAEL, artist, designer; b. Los Angeles, June 11, 1920; s. Francis Flanders and Elsa (Fuhrer) D.; m. Elizabeth Johnstone, Feb. 14, 1949. Student Chouinard Art Inst., Art Inst. Chgo. Designer advt., theatre, film, Los Angeles, 1938—; pres. Anthony and Elizabeth Duquette Found., 1979—, Elsie de Wolfe Found., 1983—; one-man shows: Pavillon de Marson, Louvre, Paris, 1950, Los Angeles County Mus. Art, 1952, deYoung Meml. Mus., San Francisco, 1952, Santa Barbara Mus. Art, 1952, Los Angeles Mcpl. Art Gallery, 1972, Mus. Sci. and Industry, 1981; designer sets and costumes San Francisco Opera, 1954. Served with U.S. Army, World War II. Recipient Tony award for best costumes for original Broadway prodn. Camelot, 1969. Mem. Am. Soc. Interior Design, Internat. Soc. Interior Design. Office: 824 N Robertson Blvd Los Angeles CA 90069

DURALIA, PAUL MICHAEL, auditor; b. Pitts., Feb. 20, 1954; s. Emil Michael and Elizabeth Rachel (Trainor) D.; m. Michelle Joan Grainger, July 15, 1983; 1 son, Ryan Eugene. B.S. in Bus. Adminstrn., W.Va. U., 1978. Staff acct. Hall & Macher C.P.A.s, Riverside, Calif., 1978-80; with Kaiser Steel Corp., Fontana, Calif., 1980—, internal auditor, 1982—. Coach, referee Am. Youth Soccer Orgn., Redlands, Calif. Democrat. Roman Catholic. Lodge: Elks (Redlands).

DURAN, JUNE CLARK, publishing company executive; b. Los Angeles, June 10, 1919; d. Willis W. and Ethel M. (King) Clark; m. Frank M. Duran, Apr. 26, 1940; children—Timothy Clark, Patricia Ellen. Student Santa Monica Jr. Coll., 1936-37, UCLA, 1937-38; B.A., U. So. Calif., 1949; postgrad. U. Calif.-Berkeley, 1951-53; LL.B., LaSalle U. Personnel mgr., dir. ops. Calif. Test Bur., Los Angeles, 1950-65, asst. to gen. mgr., Monterey, Calif., 1965-66, asst. v.p., managing editor, 1966-68; asst. v.p. CTB/McGraw-Hill, Monterey, 1968—; mem. adv. com. Valley Nat. Bank. Pres. Clark Found.; trustee Community Hosp. Monterey Peninsula; bd. dirs. Alliance on Aging, 1971-82; mem. Monterey County Republican Central Com., 1963-78. Mem. Am. Personnel and Guidance Assn., Calif. Ednl. Research Assn., Calif. Assn. Measurement and Evaluation in Guidance, Copyright Soc. U.S.A., Monterey Peninsula C. of C. (dir. 1973-75). Office: CTB/McGraw-Hill 2500 Garden Rd Monterey CA 93940

DURAN, TOMAS LEONIDES, dentist; b. Trinidad, Colo., Sept. 21, 1945; s. Julian and Rosa Margarita (Cruz) D.; B.S. in Pharmacy, U. N.Mex., 1968; D.D.S., U. Mo., Kansas City, 1977; m. Isabelle Louise Sandoval, Apr. 13, 1968; 1 son, Tomas Andres. Pharmacist, Duran Central Pharmacy, Albuquerque, 1968-72; mgr. pharmacy Furr's, Inc., Albuquerque, 1972-73; part time pharmacist Skagg's Pharmacies, Inc., Independence, Mo., 1974-77; practice dentistry, Pueblo, Colo., 1977—. Mem. Acad. Gen. Dentistry, ADA, Colo. Dental Assn., Southeastern Colo. Dental Soc., Latino C. of C. of Pueblo (dir.), Nat. Chicano Democratic Caucus, Rho Chi. Mem. Ch. of Christ. Club: Kiwanis.

DURBIN, BETTY ANN, electronics co. ofcl.; b. San Mateo, Calif., May 27, 1939; 1 son, Arthur Dean. Assembler, Litton Industries, San Carolos, Calif., 1959, Advanced Tech. Labs., Mountain View, Calif., 1961-63; coil winder Daytron Inc., Mountain View, 1963-69, Stanford Applied Engring. Co., Santa Clara, Calif., 1969-71, Teledyne Co., Palo Alto, Calif., 1971-72; supr. coil winding Fall River Mills (Calif.) br. Mini-Magnetics Co., Inc., 1979—. Home: 3939 Bidwell Dr 505-22 Fremont CA 94538

DURHAM, ALVIN FRANKLIN, SR., minister; b. Roseburg, Oreg., Oct. 25, 1915; s. Daniel Omer and Roxie Leota (Pringle) D.; A.B., Ky. Christian Coll., 1942; postgrad. S.E. Mo State U., 1949-50, Platte Valley Bible Coll., 1957-58, Los Angeles Valley Coll., 1970-72, San Fernando Adult Sch., 1969-70; D.D., Internat. Bible Inst. and Sem. (Orlando, Fla.), 1980; m. Mavis Madeline Rasnick, May 29, 1942; children—Deanna Genevieve Durham Dyer, Alvin Franklin, Mary Elizabeth Durham Purdy. Ordained to ministry Christian Ch., 1939; pastor chs., S. Portsmouth, Ky., Springfield, Ky., Hickman, Ky., Pine Grove, W. Va., Fredericktown, Mo., Rockwell City, Iowa, Lewistown, Mont., Minatare, Nebr., Amity, Oreg., Elsinore, Calif., Farmington, N. Mex., Los Osos, Calif., 1940-66; minister First Christian Ch., San Fernando, Calif., 1966-82; tchr., prin. high sch., Minelamotte, Mo., 1949-51; prof. Platte Valley Bible Coll., Scottsbluff, Nebr., 1958-59; chaplain Iowa Reformatory for Women, 1952-55, CAP, 1955-76. Bd. dirs. Atascadero (Calif.) Christian Home. Mem. Smithsonian Assos. Republican. Clubs: Lions, Young Men's Bus., Masons. Home: 12960 Dronefield Sylmar CA 91342 Office: PO Box 549 San Fernando CA 91341

DURHAM, RICHARD LYLE, educational administrator; b. Carlton, Oreg. May 28, 1928; s. Ivan Everett and Hazel Emmaline (Roy) D.; m. Ruth Ernestine Fields, Apr. 30, 1930; children—Joanne Jenkins, Richard Jr., James E., Christine Ruth. B.A., Oreg. State U., 1957, M.A., 1960. Cert. secondary sch. adminstr., Calif. Tchr., counselor, adult sch. adminstr. Grant Joint Union High Sch. Dist., Sacramento, 1957-70; adult sch. dir., vocat. edn. coordinator Manteca (Calif.) Unified Sch. Dist., 1970-74; prin. East Union High Sch., Manteca, 1974—. Chmn. Park and Recreation Dist. North Highland; treas. Little League, North Highland. Served in USMC, 1946-47, 1951-53. Decorated Purple Heart; NSF grantee, 1962. Mem. Assn. Calif. Sch. Adminstrs., Calif. Pupil Personnel Assn. (officer), Calif. Indsl. Edn. Assn., Jaycees (Citizen of Yr.), Epsilon Pi Tau (trustee, laureate citation), Phi Delta Kappa, Oreg. State Alumni Assn. (treas. chpt.). Republican. Methodist. Club: Rotary. Home: 17748 S Austin Rd Manteca CA 95336 Office: 1700 N Union Rd Manteca CA 95336

DURHAM, STEVEN FORREST, advertising executive; b. Ithaca, N.Y., Oct. 10, 1946; s. Forrest and Ethel Margaret (Needham) D.; m. Sharon Lynn Parker, Dec. 30, 1977. B.A. in Geology, Hofstra U., 1969; M.A. in Geography, U. S.C., 1971; M.B.A., Harvard U., 1975. Instr. in geology and geography Hofstra U., 1971-73; research asst. Harvard U. Grad. Sch. Bus., 1975-76; asst. product mgr. Gen. Mills, Inc., Mpls., 1976-78; account exec. J. Walter Thompson Co, San Francisco, 1978-79; v.p. mktg. E.T.G., Inc., San Francisco, 1979-81; account supr. Allen and Dorward Advt., San Francisco, 1981-82, McCann-Erickson, Inc., San Francisco, 1982—. Mem. No. Calif. Harvard Bus. Sch. Assn. Clubs: Calhoun Beach (Mpls.); San Francisco Tennis. Home: 5968 Johnston Dr Oakland CA 94611 Office: 201 California St San Francisco CA 94111

DURKEE, RICHARD CURTIS, life ins. co. exec.; b. Nyack, N.Y., Jan. 22, 1930; s. Paul Curtis and Elizabeth (Ganung) D.; B.S., U. Rochester, 1951; m. Carmeleta Mary Reichl, May 22, 1952; children—Robert Curtis, Barbara Suzanne. With Transam. Occidental Life Ins. Co. 1951—, dir. tng. and manpower devel., 1971-73, asst. v.p., 1973-75, 2d v.p. personnel and organizational devel., 1975-80, 2d v.p. orgnl. devel., 1980—. Trustee group ins. trust Am. Heart Assn., Dallas, 1979-84, bd. dirs., 1981-83; chmn. bd. Am. Heart Assn., Los Angeles, 1980-81; adv. Gov.'s Office for Citizen Initiative and Voluntary Action, 1978-82; chmn. Kellogg-United Way Tng. Ctr., 1983—; bd. dirs. United Way Los Angeles, 1983—. Recipient Vol. of Yr. award City of Los Angeles, 1977; Heart of Gold award Am. Heart Assn., 1983. Fellow Life Mgmt. Inst. Home: 133 E Arthur Ave Arcadia CA 91006 Office: 1150 S Olive St Los Angeles CA 90015

DURKIN, JOHN S., airline company executive; b. Monticello, N.Y., Oct. 16, 1945; s. John A. and Marion (Cross) D.; m. L. Joan Ruof, June 29, 1968; children—John, Janeen. B.A., Mich. State U., 1967. C.P.A., Ohio. Auditor Touche Ross & Co., Cleve., 1967-68, Arthur Andersen & Co., Cin., 1970-71; v.p. Kanter Corp., Cin., 1971-75; pres. Econ. Data Inc., Cin., 1975-81; v.p., chief fin. officer Conair Inc., Salt Lake City, 1981—. Fin. advisor Cin. Assn. Children with Learning Disabilities, 1977. Served with AUS, 1968-70. Mem. Ohio Soc. C.P.A.s. Republican. Episcopalian. Clubs: Cin. Athletic, Bankers. Home: 824 East 3950 South Salt Lake City UT 84107

DURO, HENRY WILLIAM, Indian tribal council official; b. San Bernardino, Calif., Feb. 24, 1950; s. Micheal and Jane (Morongo) D.; m. Mary Ellen Wilkes, Dec. 10, 1971; children—Christopher, Gregory. Chmn. San Manuel Indian Reservation, Highland, Calif. Democrat. Roman Catholic. Implemented edn. programs and tribal devel.; founder med. facility on reservation. Office: 5771 N Victoria Ave Highland CA 92346

DURÓN, MARY SALINAS, banker; b. Los Angeles, Apr. 30, 1952; d. Jose Sanchez Salinas and Lupe Martinez; m. Armando Durón, Dec. 18, 1954. B.A., Loyola Marymount U., 1975; M.B.A., UCLA, 1978. Instr., SER-Jobs for Progress, Los Angeles, 1976; intern First Interstate Bank, Los Angeles, 1977-78, multi-nat. trainee, 1978-79, comml. loan officer, 1979-81, asst. v.p., mgr. Hispanic Projects, 1981—. Teaching cons. Jr. Achievement; active Los Angeles Olympic Cultural Affairs Adv. Commn., Mexican Am. Polit. Assn., Hispanic Women's Council, Comisión Femenil; pres. Loyola Marymount Mexican Am. Alumni Assn. Recipient Cert. of Achievement, YWCA Los Angeles, 1981. Mem. Hispanic Bankers Assn. (founding; past sec., program chair). Democrat. Roman Catholic. Office: First Interstate Bank 707 Wilshire Blvd Los Angeles CA 90017

DURRANT, DAVID RICHARD, farmer; b. Provo, Utah, Mar. 31, 1932; s. Clarence Henry and Evelyn Marguerite (Hinckley) D.; student pub. schs., Utah and Idaho; m. Lydia Ann Gordon, July 1, 1953; children—Kenneth Lynn, Richard Keith, Bruce Gordon, Marianne, Elizabeth June, Debora Kay. Dry bean and grain mcht. Big D Ranch, Inc., Meridian, Idaho, 1961-66, pres., gen. mgr., 1963—. Served with U.S. Army, 1953-55. Mem. Dairymen's Creamery Assn. Mem. Ch. Jesus Christ of Latter-day Saints. Home: 7590 S Ten Mile Rd Meridian ID 83642

DURRANT, DEAN OBORN, podiatrist; b. Tooele, Utah, Dec. 1, 1929; s. Rendell Porter and Emily (Oborn) D.; B.A., City Coll. San Francisco, 1955; B.S., Calif. Coll. Podiatric Medicine, 1956-57; D.Podiatric Medicine, 1960; m. Dian Overson, Apr. 10, 1953; children—Kathrine, Calleen, Russell Dean, Joyce, Suzanne, Ronda, LaDean. Gen. practice podiatry, Vallejo, Calif., 1960—; chief podiatry staff Broadway Hosp., Vallejo, 1978—. Mem., sec. Solano County Comprehensive Health Planning Council, 1974-75; trustee Calif. Coll. Podiatric Medicine, 1974-75; councilor Boy Scouts Am., 1963-64; bd. dirs. Vallejo Symphony Assn., 1968-72. Served with USN, 1953-55. Mem. Calif. Podiatric Assn. (pres. 1974-75), Am. Podiatry Assn. (commr. Region 12 1970-79), Redwood Empire Soc. Democrat. Mem. Ch. Jesus Christ Latter-day Saints. Clubs: Masons, Shriners. Home: 1325 Hestia Way Napa CA 94558 Office: 530 Oregon St Vallejo CA 94590

DURRENBERGER, J. E., engineer; b. Greenville, N.J., Sept. 8, 1916; s. Edward E. and Ida Phillipine (Mirz) D.; B.S. in M.E., N.Mex. State U., 1951; m. Esther Helen Milner, June 7, 1949; m. 2d Martha Ann Miller, Nov. 6, 1965. Photo-optical instrumentation engr. U.S. Army White Sands Missile Range, N.Mex., 1951-80, sr. gen. engr., 1960—. Served with U.S. Army, 1942-47. Registered profl. engr., N.Mex. Fellow Soc. Photo-Optical Instrumentation Engrs. (life; nat. sec. 1982, historian 1983; Pezzuto award); mem. ASME, Am. Def. Preparedness Assn., Astron. Soc. Las Cruces (sec. 1982-83), Astron. Soc. Pacific, Pi Tau Sigma. Asso. editor Optical Engineering, 1974-80. Home: PO Box 1655 Las Cruces NM 88004

DURRETT, JOHN CHARLES, aerospace corporation executive; b. Fort Worth, Feb. 5, 1939; s. John H. and H. Beatrice (Burkhart) D.; B.S., U. Kans., 1962; M.S., Air Force Inst. Tech., 1963; Ph.D., U. Colo., 1970; m. Leilani Mary Gresham, July 31, 1976; children by previous marriage—Michelle Rene, John Edward. Commd. 2d lt. USAF, 1962, advanced through grades to lt. col., 1978; flight test engr. Edwards AFB, Calif., 1963-67; supervising engr. Air Force Flight Dynamics Lab., Wright-Paterson AFB, Ohio, 1970-73; asso. prof. astronautics USAF Acad., Colo., 1973-77; space test program spacecraft program mgr. Space and Missile Systems Orgn., Los Angeles, 1977-79, dep. dir. space test program office, space div., Los Angeles, 1979-80, dir. space sensor test directorate, space div., 1980-82, ret., 1982; dep. program mgr. Def. Systems, Martin Marietta Aerospace Corp., Denver, 1983—. Decorated Meritorious Service medal with oak leaf cluster, Air Force Commendation medal with 2 oak leaf clusters. NASA summer faculty fellow Stanford U., 1975. Mem. AIAA, Am. Astron. Soc. Club: Toastmasters (Calif. area gov. 1966-67). Home: 8149 S Yukon St Littleton CO 80123 Office: Martin Marietta Aerospace Mail Stop S 4011 PO Box 179 Denver CO 80201

DURRETT, ROBERT DUANE, univ. adminstr.; b. Melrose, N.Mex., July 25, 1939; s. Melrose, N.Mex., July 25, 1939; s. Walter Edward and Lucy Bell (Ward) D.; B.A., Eastern N.Mex. U., Portales, 1964, M.B.A., 1971, Ed.S., 1982; m. Carolyn Jean McCoy, July 12, 1963; children—Derrell Duane, Debbie Lyn. Credit adjustor Central Bank and Trust Co., Denver, 1965-66; asst. mgr. Western Mobile Homes, Inc., Denver, 1966-67; credit mgr. Woolco Dept. Stores, Houston, 1968-69; dir. community services, asst. to pres. Eastern N.Mex. U., 1969-76, dir. univ. personnel services, 1976—; cons., lectr. in field. Mem. Portales City Council, 1978—; exec. com. Conquistador council Boy Scouts Am., 1978—, also scoutmaster. Served with U.S.NG, 1958-69. Mem. Coll. and Univ. Personnel Assn. (pres. N.Mex. chpt. 1976, chair-elect S.W. region 1983-84), Roosevelt C. of C. Republican. Methodist. Club: Portales Kiwanis (pres. 1976). Home: 801 W 19th St Portales NM 88130 Office: Station 21 Eastern New Mex Univ Portales NM 88130

DUSENBURY, DAVID ALLAN, police officer; b. Alhambra, Calif., Mar. 20, 1940; s. Jack Hamlin and Mildred Leigh (Galloway) D.; A.A., Compton Coll., 1967; B.S., Calif. State U., Los Angeles, 1970, M.S., 1976; m. Nancy Nugent Dusenbury, July 16, 1966; children—Debra Ann, David Alan. With Lynwood (Calif.) Police Dept., 1961-68; with Long Beach (Calif.) Police Dept., 1968—, police sergeant, 1976—, police lt., 1981; instr. Long Beach City Coll. Served with U.S. Army, 1963-65. Mem. Am. Soc. Pub. Adminstrn., Mensa. Republican. Office: 400 W Broadway Long Beach CA 90802

DUSHKIND, DONALD STANFORD, forensic psychologist, family mediator; b. N.Y.C., Jan. 24, 1926; s. Michael Herbert and Hannah (Gordon) D.; m. Winifred Joan Saphir; children—Paul Richard, James Alan, Laura Susan; m. Luise Friedman Bennett. B.S.S. with honors, CCNY, 1945; M.A., State U. Iowa, 1946; Ph.D., NYU, 1959. Lic. marriage, family, child counselor, Calif., 1964; lic. clin. social worker, 1969; lic. psychologist, 1976. Instr., U. Wis.-Madison, 1946-47; youth parole worker N.Y. State Tng. Sch. for Boys, N.Y.C., 1948-49, 51-56; lectr. Ind. U., Marion, 1949-50; psychiat. social worker Hudson River State Hosp., Poughkeepsie, N.Y., 1950-51; pvt. practice psychology and marriage counseling, Plainview, N.Y., San Diego, San Francisco, 1956—; arbitrator, family mediator, alienist. Exam. commr. Calif. Bd. Behavioral Sci. Examiners, 1976; exam. commr. Calif. Psychology Exam. Com., 1977. Mem. Am. Psychol. Assn., Am. Assn. Marriage and Family Therapy, Calif. Assn. Marriage and Family Therapists, Alpha Kappa Delta, Psi Chi, Pi Gamma Mu. Democrat. Contbr. articles to profl. jours. Home: 120 San Gabriel Dr Fairfax CA 94930 Offices: 3589 Brook St Lafayette CA 94549 also 10 Millwood St Mill Valley CA 94940 also 2226 California St San Francisco CA 94115

DUSZYNSKI, DONALD WALTER, biologist, educator; b. Chgo., July Galveston, 1943; s. Walter Mitchell and Martha Mary (Woronowicz) D.; m. Suzanne Lynn Gordon, Nov. 29, 1980; 1 son, Derek Walter. Asst. prof. biology U. N.Mex., Albuquerque, 1970-74, assoc. prof., 1974-79, prof., 1979—, chmn. dept., 1982—; sr. research scientist physiology U. Tex. Med. Sch., Houston, 1976-77; vis. assoc. prof. microbiology U. Tex. Med. Br., Galveston, 1977; vis. research scholar Kyoto U. (Japan), 1981; conf. presenter; jour. reviewer. Research grantee; NSF-Ford Found fellow, 1967; NIH-USPHS fellow, 1967-70. Mem. Am. Inst. Biol. Scis., Am. Micros. Soc., Am. Soc. Parasitologists, Brit. Soc. Parasitologists, Helminthological Soc. Wash., Rocky Mountain Conf. Parasitologists (pres. 1979-80), Southwestern Assn. Parasitologists (pres. 1979-80), Soc. Protozoologists, Wildlife Disease Assn., Sigma Xi, Phi Kappa Phi. Adv. editor Jour. Protozoology, 1974—; contbr. articles profl. jours. Office: Dept Biology U NMex Albuquerque NM 87131

DUTRO, CLAUD EDWARD, foodservice distributing company executive; b. Hugo, Colo., May 21, 1942; s. George H. and Alta L. Dutro. B.S., U. Colo., 1973, M.B.A., 1978; m. Karen L., Oct. 14, 1962; children—Susan L., Linda J. Vice pres. Associated Collection Bur., Denver, 1962-64; pres. Continental Coll. Corp., Denver, 1964-72; acct. Robert Parent & Assocs., Lakewood, Colo., 1973-74; pres. Carson's, Inc., Denver, 1974—. Served with USAF, 1968-69. C.P.A., Colo. Fellow Nat. Inst. Credit Mgmt.; mem. Foodservice Equipment Distbrs. Assn. (dir.), Rocky Mountain Credit Mgmt. Assn., Denver C. of C. Republican. Methodist. Clubs: Rotary, Masons, Shriners (Denver). Home: 7145 E Louisiana Ave Denver CO 80224 Office: 1301 Wazee St Denver CO 80204

DUTRO, KENNETH ROBERT, psychologist, cons.; b. Fullerton, Calif., Oct. 5, 1943; s. Jack William and Marjorie Wanda (Graham) D.; married June 13, 1964; children—Elizabeth, Kenneth. Ed.D., U. No. Colo., Greeley, 1973; lic. psychologist, Calif., 1979. Tchr., Hayward, Calif., 1965-67; rehab. counselor, Woodward, Iowa and Carson City, Nev., 1968-70; counseling psychologist VA, Denver, 1971-73, Washington, 1973-74, Miami, Fla., 1974-75, Hot Springs, S.D., 1975-77, Loma Linda, Calif., 1977—; asst. prof. psychiatry Loma Linda U., 1978—. Rehab. Services Adminstrn. grantees, 1967-68, 1970-71. Mem. Am. Psychol. Assn., Am. Personnel and Guidance Assn. Democrat. Seventh-Day Adventist. Home: 418 Arrowview Dr Redlands CA 92373 Office: VA Hosp Loma Linda CA 92357

DUTTON, DENNIS LEE, computer consultant; b. Independence, Mo., Sept. 20, 1950; s. Clifford and Ruby Flora (Paylor) D.; 1 dau., Fonda Marie. B.S. in Math., S.E. Mo. U., 1974, A.S. in Computer Sci., 1974. System analyst, computer programmer Quik Serv Systems, Kansas City, Mo., 1974-76, Recordata West, Inc., Los Angeles, 1976-77, Eastern Wash. U., Cheney, 1977-78, Stephens Nelsen Computer Ctr., Spokane, Wash., 1978-83; cons., 1983—. Assoc. adv. Explorers Post 135, Boy Scouts Am. Served with USN, 1970-72. Mem. Associated Systems Mgrs., Alpha Iota Delta. Mormon. Home: 717 W 15th St Apt D Spokane WA 99203

DUTTON, PAULINE MAE, fine arts librarian; b. Detroit, July 15; d. Thoralf Andreas and Esther Ruth (Clyde) Tandberg; B.A. in Art, Calif. State U., Fullerton, 1967; M.S. in Library Sci., U. So. Calif., 1971; m. Richard Hawkins Dutton, June 21, 1969; 1 dau., Nancy. Elem. tchr., Anaheim, Calif., 1967-68, Corona, Calif., 1968-69; fine arts librarian Pasadena (Calif.) Public Library, 1971-80; art cons., researcher, 1981—. Mem. Pasadena Librarians Assn. (sec. 1978, treas. 1979-80), Calif. Library Assn., Calif. Soc. Librarians, Art Librarians of N. Am., Nat. Assn. Female Execs., Am. Film Inst., Gilbert and Sullivan Soc., Alpha Sigma Phi. Club: Toastmistress (local pres. 1974).

DUTTON, ROBERT WENDELL, food mfg. co. exec.; b. Marion, Ohio: s. William Ervin and Mary Juanita (Manley) D.; B.A. in Edn., Kent State U., 1960; M.B.A., Mich. State U., 1963; m. Cynthia Lynn Ledbetter, Sept. 1, 1976: children—Christopher, Jeri, Johanna, Robin, Andrew. With H.J. Heinz Co. Inc., Columbus, Ohio, Harrisburg, Pa., Phila., New Orleans and Pitts., 1960-73; dir. sales/mktg. Collins Foods Internat., Los Angeles, 1973-74; v.p. sales and mktg. J. Hungerford Smith Co., Modesto, Calif., 1974-80; with R. Dutton Mgmt. Consultants, 1980-83; mng. ptnr., exec. v.p., sec. Danco Foods Inc., Modesto, Calif., 1983—. Served with USMC, 1954-56. Mem. Am. Mgmt. Assn., Nat. Restaurant Assn., Instl. Food Mfrs. Assn. Republican. Home: 2324 Candlewood Pl Riverbank CA 95367 Office: Danco Foods Inc 2416 Nickerson Dr Modesto CA 95351

DUTTON, WILLIAM HAROLD, communications educator, consultant; b. St. Joseph, Mo., Aug. 23, 1947; s. Paul Vernon and Rosa Lee (Sanko) D.; m. Jeanette Claire Justus, Dec. 22, 1968; m. 2d, Diana Lynn Nunnery, May 15, 1981. B.A., U. Mo.-Columbia, 1969; M.A., SUNY-Buffalo, 1972, Ph.D., 1974. Mem. faculty U. South Fla., Tampa, 1973-74, U. Calif.-Irvine, 1974-78, San Diego State U., 1978-79; assoc. prof. Annenberg Sch. Communications, U. So. Calif., Los Angeles, 1980—; cons. computing and communication tech. Mem. Am. Polit. Sci. Assn., Internat. Communication Assn., Acad. Polit. Sci., Internat. Teleconf. Assn. (dir.). Mem. Christian Ch. (Disciples of Christ). Author: The Management of Information Systems, 1981; Computers and Politics, 1982; Modeling as Negotiating, 1983. Home: 225 Homer St Manhattan Beach CA 90266 Office: Annenberg Sch U So Calif Los Angeles CA 90089

DUVALL, BETTY JEAN, educator; b. Ft. Benton, Mont., Jan. 31, 1932; d. Ernest Charles and Thelma Louise (Brown) Schultz; m. Richard W. Duvall, Dec. 17, 1955; children—Debbie Ripsom, Denise Wolff, Carla, Tracee. B.S., Eastern Mont. Coll., 1967; M.S., No. Mont. Coll., 1976; postgrad. Mont. State U., 1982—. Cert. elem. tchr., Mont. Tchr., Great Falls, Mont., 1964—, now curriculum coordinator; adj. prof. Western Mont. Coll., Seattle State U.; cons. to sch. dists. Mem. NEA, Mont. Ednl. Assn., Great Falls Ednl. Assn., Assn. Suprs. and Curriculum Dirs., Internat. Reading Assn., Soc. Scribes, Soc. Italic Handwriting. Author: Can Do, 1976; Duvall Method of Handwriting, 1981; Learn to Write Italic Style, 1981; The Formal Italic Hand, 1981. Home and Office: 514 Skyline Dr Great Falls MT 59404

DUVALL, GEORGE CHENNELL, ret. mfg. co. exec.; b. Davenport, Iowa, July 14, 1909; s. George William and Pearl (Chennell) D.; student Augustana Coll., 1928; m. Joyce Scott Wooster, Apr. 3, 1971; children by previous marriage—Frederick E. W., Diana E. W., Deborah Jane; children—John B. Wooster, Sharon W. Rowbury. Pilot, United Airlines, 1936-38, Trans World Airlines, 1938-69; pres., dir. Chick Master Incubator Corp., Cleve., 1963-68, chmn., 1968-74; chmn. CMG Corp., Shaker Heights, Ohio, 1974-76; chmn., dir. C.M. Textile Co., 1967-79; dir. ITB Mgmt. Corp., Boston, Chronogram Corp., Greenwich, Conn. Home: PO Box 726 Litchfield Park AZ 85340

DUVE, JOHN LARRY, univ. adminstr.; b. Pullman, Wash., Sept. 14, 1949; s. John Eugene and Ada (Popkema) D.; B.S., U. Nebr., 1972; m. Catherine L. Cramer Bushing, Oct. 1, 1977. With prodn. dept. M & M/Mars Co., Chgo., 1969-70; staff Zenith Radio Corp., Chgo., 1970; shift comdr. Univ. Police Dept., U. Nebr., Lincoln, 1971-74, asst. to dir., 1974-78, parking adminstr. bus. and fin., 1978-80; dir. parking and transp. systems U. Calif., Irvine and Med. Center, 1980—; mem. chancellor's adv. com. on status of handicapped persons and disabled vets. U. Calif., 1980—, also exec. dir. parking and transp. adv. com.; pvt. cons. parking and transp. systems mgmt., 1976—. Mem. City of Lincoln Carpool Resource Com., 1976-80; exec. sec. U. Nebr.-Lincoln Parking Adv. Com., 1974-80; mem. Irvine Transp. Corridor Adv. Bd., 1981—; mem. Orange County Transp. Commn., 1982—. Mem. Instl. and Mcpl. Parking Congress, Internat. Assn. Coll. and Univ. Security Dirs., Am. Mgmt. Assn., Nat. Assn. Vanpool Operations, Triangle Fraternity. Congregationalist. Home: 43 Esplanade Irvine CA 92715 Office: Parking and Transp Services Office U Calif Irvine CA 92717

DVORCHAK, STEPHEN ROBERT, operations analyst; b. Wood River, Ill., Feb. 10, 1934; s. Stephen Joseph and Rae Joan (Hanz) D.; m. Tertia Lea Tilley, Aug. 25, 1966; children—Justine Gaele, Jason Christopher. B.S. in A.E., Parks Coll., St. Louis U., 1954; M.S.B.A., Calif. State U., 1973. Aerodynamicist, McDonnell Aircraft Corp., St. Louis, 1954; commd. 2d lt. U.S. Air Force, 1954, advanced through grades to lt. col., 1971; ret., 1979; ops. analyst Veda, Inc., Las Vegas, 1979—. Decorated D.F.C., Air medal with 16 oak leaf clusters. Mem. Aircraft Owners and Pilots Assn., Soaring Soc. Am., Air Force Assn., Mil. Ops. Research Soc. Republican. Roman Catholic. Club: Order of Daedalians. Office: 3100 W Sahara Ave Suite 207 Las Vegas NV 89102

DWORSKY, WILLIAM ARTHUR, gynecologist; b. Iron Mountain, Mich., May 12, 1933; s. Paul and Lillian (Rigler) D.; B.A., U. Calif., 1955, M.D., 1958; m. Dorothy Ann Sanders, July 5, 1959; children—Philip Brian, Andrea Sanders. Intern, Los Angeles County Gen. Hosp., 1958-59; resident in obstetrics and gynecology Margaret Hague Maternity Hosp., Jersey City, 1961-64, U. N.C., 1964-65; staff physician Permanente Med. Group, Santa Clara, Calif., 1965-73; practice medicine specializing in gynecology, Palo Alto, Calif., 1973—; clin. asst. prof. obstetrics and gynecology Stanford. Bd. dirs. Univ.-Crescent Park Assn., Palo Alto, 1968-76, Calif. Youth Symphony Assn., 1974-78. Served as capt. USAF, 1959-61. Diplomate Am. Bd. Obstetrics and Gynecology. Fellow Am. Coll. Obstetricians and Gynecologists; mem. Am. Soc. Gynecologic Laparoscopists, Peninsula Gynecol. Soc., Shufelt Obstetrics and Gynecology Soc., Sacres Obstetrical Soc., Calif. Assn. Obstetricians and Gynecologists. Republican. Jewish. Clubs: Palo Alto Golf, Stanford Faculty. Office: 609 Cowper St Palo Alto CA 94301

DWYER, RICHARD MICHAEL, physician; b. Louisiana, Mo., Feb. 4, 1943; s. Thomas L. and Winifred (Brennan) D.; M.D., St. Louis U.; m. Marcia V. 1968; children—Sean, Kelly, Brennan. Rotating intern St. Johns Mercy Hosp., St. Louis, 1968-69; resident in internal medicine Los Angeles County Hosp.-U. So. Calif., 1971-73, fellow in gastroenterology, 1973-75; practice medicine specializing in gastroenterology, Los Angeles, 1979—; asst. clin. prof. medicine U. So. Calif., Los Angeles, 1975-76, sr. research scientist for lasers in medicine Ctr. for Laser Studies, 1975-81; mem. staff Harbor Gen. Hosp., Torrance, Calif., also asst. chief gastroenterology, head of endoscopy, 1975-79; asst. prof. medicine UCLA, 1975-79. Served to lt. comdr. USNR, 1969-71. Diplomate Am. Bd. Internal Medicine. Mem. Am. Gastroent. Assn., So. Calif. Soc. Gastroenterology (Rorer award 1974), Am. Soc. Gastrointestinal Endoscopy, So. Calif. Soc. Endoscopy, Am. Fedn. Clin. Research, ACP, AMA, Laser Surg. Soc., N.Y. Acad. Sci., Internat. Surg. Soc. (sec. 1982, 83), Am. Soc. Lasers in Medicine and Surgery (dir. 1982, 83, 84). Contbr. articles on laser applications in med. therapy to profl. jours. physician; b. Louisiana, Mo., Feb. 4, 1943; s. Thomas L. and Winifred (Brennan) D.; M.D., St. Louis U.; m. Marcia V. 1968; children—Sean, Kelly, Brennan. Rotating intern St. Johns Mercy Hosp., St. Louis, 1968-69; resident in internal medicine Los Angeles County Hosp.-U. So. Calif., 1971-73, fellow in gastroenterology, 1973-75; practice medicine specializing in gastroenterology, Los Angeles, 1979—; asst. clin. prof. medicine U. So. Calif., Los Angeles, 1975-76, sr. research scientist for lasers in medicine Ctr. for Laser Studies, 1975-81; mem. staff Harbor Gen. Hosp., Torrance, Calif., also asst. chief gastroenterology, head of endoscopy, 1975-79; asst. prof. medicine UCLA, 1975-79. Served to lt. comdr. USNR, 1969-71. Diplomate Am. Bd. Internal Medicine. Mem. Am. Gastroent. Assn., So. Calif. Soc. Gastroenterology (Rorer award 1974), Am. Soc. Gastrointestinal Endoscopy, So. Calif. Soc. Endoscopy, Am. Fedn. Clin. Research, ACP, AMA, Laser Surg. Soc., N.Y. Acad. Sci., Internat. Surg. Soc. (sec. 1982, 83), Am. Soc. Lasers in Medicine and Surgery (dir. 1982, 83, 84). Contbr. articles on laser applications in med. therapy to profl. jours. Office: 1300 N Vermont Ave Los Angeles CA 90027

DWYER, ROBERT FRANKLIN, II, arts administrator; b. Lake City, Fla., Dec. 7, 1943; s. Robert Franklin and Maxine Delores (Stenberg) D.; children—Erin Adair, Robert Franklin III. A.B., U. Calif.-Berkeley, 1967; M.T.S., Harvard U. Div. Sch., 1969; cert in arts mgmt., U. Chgo., 1981. Pub. affairs dir. Sta. KYDO-TV 3, Salem, Oreg., 1969-74; dir. mktg. Specialists Internat., Reno, Nev., 1974-77; dir. devel. Sierra Arts Found., Reno, 1977—; bd. dirs. Nev. Alliance for Arts, 1979—, v.p., 1980; cons. in field. Named Arts Adminstr. of Yr., Arts Mgmt. mag., 1982. Mem. Am. Council on Arts, Assn. Coll., Univ. and Community Arts Adminstrs., Nat. Assembly Community Arts Agys. Editor: Snow Peach, 1980; producer, writer TV documentary: Art Works, 1981.

DYCHE, DELBERT CARL, ednl. adminstr.; b. Waynoka, Okla., May 25, 1942; s. Carl Mervin and Marietta (West) D.; B.S., N.W. OKla. State U., 1964; M.A., N.Mex. State U., 1969; m. Susan Colby Higley, Mar. 28, 1967; children—Susan Elisabeth, Kristin Luise. Tchr., Las Cruces (N.Mex.) Public Schs., 1964-66; tchr. Dept. Def. Sch., London, 1966-68; prin., public schs., Roswell, N.Mex., 1970-72, curriculum dir., 1973-75; prin. White Sands Missle Range Sch., N.Mex., 1976-78; prin. University Hills Elem. Sch., Las Cruces, 1978-81; dir. elem. curriculum Las Cruces, 1981—; mem. State Adv. Com. on Early Childhood Edn., 1974-76. Bd. dirs. Chaves County United Way, 1973, mem. budget com., 1974; bd. dirs. Am. Cancer Soc., 1974; mem. Bd. Episcopal Schs., Diocese of Rio Grande. EPDA fellow, 1969. Mem. N.Mex. Assn. Supervision and Curriculum Devel. (pres.), Assn. Supervision and Curriculum Devel. (dir.), N.Mex. Sch. Adminstrs. Assn. (dir.), Phi Delta Kappa. Republican. Episcopalian. Club: Rotary. Home: 813 Raleigh Rd Las Cruces NM 88005 Office: 301 W Amador St Las Cruces NM 88005

DYE, DONALD FRANCIS, biologist, chem. co. exec.; b. Sacramento, Apr. 28, 1928; s. Oakley F. and Anna (Becker) D.; A.A., Hartnell Coll., 1950; B.A., San Jose State Coll., 1952; m. Anne M. Dye, Sept. 18, 1975; 1 dau., Joanne E. Research entomologist Stauffer Chem. Co., 1952-55, supr. entomology group, 1955-57, field research rep., 1957-64, product devel. specialist, 1964-65; supr. product registration Chevron Chem. Co., Richmond, Calif., 1965-70, regulatory and environmental specialist, 1970—, coordinator regulatory affairs, 1974—. Served with USNR, 1945-47. Decorated USAF Assn. medal. Mem. Entomology Soc. Am., Am. Registry Profl. Entomologists, Nat. Agrl. Chem. Assn. (regulatory adv. com. 1966—, codex alimentarius 1967—), Beta Beta Beta. Home: 1964 Montclair Ct Walnut Creek CA 94596 Office: 940 Hensley St Richmond CA 94804

DYER, ALAN GORDON, educator, educational administrator, consultant; b. San Diego, Mar. 30, 1941; s. Robert Beakley and Velma Ann (Griffin) D.; m. Beverly Anne Stipe, May 27, 1961; children—Dale Alan, Donna Diane. B.A. in Sociology, Calif. State U.-San Bernardino, 1968; M.A. in Edn., Pepperdine U., 1975. Adult edn. and community coll. life teaching and adminstrv. credentials, Calif. Child social worker Good Samaritan Boys' Home, Corona, Calif., 1968-69; tchr. manpower devel. tng. program San Hidalgo Inst., San Bernardino, 1971-74; adult edn. instr. San Bernardino Adult Sch., 1974—; high sch. equivalency instr., lead tchr. supr. Rialto (Calif.) Adult Sch., 1974—; instr. in English, Upward Bound Program, Calif. State Coll.-San Bernardino, 1978—; cons. adult edn. community services; dir. ednl. services Merrill Community Services, Fontana, Calif. Sec./treas. Corona Jaycees, 1973-74; elder Ch. of Jesus Christ of Latter-day Saints, Rialto, Calif.. Served with USNR, 1959-68. Decorated Meritorious Service medal. Recipient Ednl. Excellence award Program Dir. and Students of Upward Bound Program, Calif. State Coll.-San Bernardino, 1981. Mem. Assn. Calif. Sch. Adminstrs., Calif. Council Adult Edn., Am. Social. Assn., Alumni Calif. State Coll.-San Bernardino (life), Phi Delta Kappa. Democrat. Home: 19256 Arbeth St Rialto CA 92376 Office: Merrill Community Services 16846 Merrill Ave Suite 209 Fontana CA 92335

DYER, DENZEL LEROY, chemist; b. McCool Jct., Nebr., Oct. 12, 1929; s. Perry Raymond and Ester Mae (Seng) D.; m. J. Helen Sanchez, Aug. 18, 1952; children—Dale, Alan, Keith. B.S., York Coll., 1950; M.S., U. Nebr., 1953, Ph.D., 1955. Biochemist, Dow Chem. Co., Midland, Mich., 1955-59; assoc. research scientist Martin-Marietta, Denver, Colo., 1959-64; prin. scientist Northrop Corp., Hawthorne, Calif., 1964-69; pres. Dyer Labs., Torrance, Calif., 1969—; dir. mktg. and quality assurance Shankman Labs., Los Angeles, 1975—; sr. lectr. biol. scis. U.So. Calif., Los Angeles, 1967-71. Served to capt. USAR, 1948-67, ret. Fellow Am. Inst. Chemists; mem. Am. Acad. Forensic Scis., AAAS, Am. Chem. Soc., Am. Soc. Microbiology, Am. Soc. Quality Control, ASTM, Assn. Ofcl. Analytical Chemists, Biol. Photog. Assn., Cons. Chemists Assn. Republican. Methodist. Patentee microbiol. detection and identification system. Home: 6008 Flambeau Rd Rancho Palos Verdes CA 90274 Office: 2675 Skypark Dr Suite 311 Torrance CA 90505

DYER, DION GARY, lawyer; b. Greenville, S.C., June 4, 1943; s. Louis and Beverley C. (Lloyd) D.; B.A. in Physics, U. Calif., 1966, J.D., 1972; m. Judith Ann Collins, Dec. 20, 1970; children—Edward A.W., Joshua Patrick. Asst. to pres. Adams Properties, Inc., San Francisco, 1967-70; admitted to Calif. bar, 1972; practiced in San Diego, 1975—, mem. firm Dyer & Henrich, 1982—; atty. Crocker Nat. Bank, San Francisco, 1973-75; dir. Budget Computer Systems, Inc., San Diego, 1976-81, Aluminum Equipment, Inc., Los Angeles, 1976-81. Mem. San Diego Computer Soc. (dir. 1982—), ABA, State Bar Calif., San Diego County Bar Assn. Club: Kearny Mesa Rotary. Contbg. editor Calif. Real Estate Law and Practice. Office: 1850 5th Ave San Diego CA 92101

DYER, GREGORY CLARK, lawyer; b. Stanford, Calif., May 29, 1947; s. Allen Clayton and Mary Louise (Sutter) D.; A.B., Stanford U., 1970; J.D., 1971; m. Karyne Lee Clough, June 28, 1980; Admitted to Calif. bar, U.S. Dist. Ct. bar, U.S. Circuit Ct. bar, all 1972; individual practice civil law, Mill Valley, Calif., 1972—; team leader Rotary study exchange to Pakistan, 1981. Bd dirs. Legal Aid Soc. Marin County, 1979-82. Mem. Marin County Bar Assn. (dir. 1980-82), Calif. State Bar, Am. Bar Assn. Republican. Clubs: Rotary, (past sec., dir., chmn. dist., group study exchange com.), Scott Valley Swim and Tennis (past dir.). Office: 16 Buena Vista Ave Mill Valley CA 94941

DYER, WILLIAM PRESTON, seed company executive; b. Manor, Tex., Aug. 19, 1930; s. William and Arvilla Minerva (Malone) D.; m. Arlene Nell Olson, Oct. 25, 1950; children—Lana Kay (Mrs. Robert Williams), Denise Arlene (Mrs.Michael Butler). A.A., City Coll., San Francisco, 1953; student U. Minn., 1953-54, Acad. Acctg., 1954-55. Office mgr. A. Cederstrand & Co., Mpls., 1954-56; mgr. br. div. acctg. John Morrell & Co., Sioux Falls, S.D., 1956-60; asst. treas. Shelter Equipment Corp., Denver, 1960-62; acctg. mgr. Seedtec Internat., Inc. (formerly Pacific Oilseeds, Inc.), San Francisco, 1962-68, office mgr., Woodland, Calif., 1968-76, v.p., treas., 1976—, dir., 1972—; dir. Pacific Seeds Internat., WAC Seed, Inc. Served with USN, 1948-52. Mem. Calif. Seed Assn., Pacific Seedsmen's Assn., Am. Legion, Woodland C. of C. Republican. Lutheran. Clubs: Rancho Murieta Country, Woodland

Lions. Home: 1609 Spruce Dr Woodland CA 95695 Office: PO Box 2210 Woodland CA 95695

DYGERT, HAROLD PAUL, JR., physician; b. Rochester, N.Y., June 21, 1919; s. Harold Paul and Elsie Viola (Howe) D.; B.A., U. Rochester, 1941; postgrad. Alfred U., 1942-43; M.D., Syracuse U., 1950; m. Helen Adelaine Nelson, Apr. 22, 1944; children—Harold Paul III, William Nelson, Peter Howe. Intern, Receiving Hosp., Detroit, 1950-51, resident internal medicine, 1951-53, chief resident, 1953-54; instr. medicine Wayne U. Coll. Medicine, Detroit, 1954-55; mem. staff VA Hosp., Vancouver, Wash., 1955-59; practice medicine specializing in cardiology-internal medicine, Vancouver, 1959—; chmn. Health Care Consortium, 1974—. Pres., Wash. State Med. Ednl. and Research Found., 1971-73. Bd. dirs. Wash.-Alaska Regional Med. Program, 1966-72. Served with AUS, 1943. Diplomate Am. Bd. Internal Medicine. Fellow A.C.P., Am. Coll. Cardiology; mem. AMA (del. 1976-77), Am. Fedn. Clin. Research, Wash. State Med. Assn. (pres. 1973-74), Portland Heart Club (pres. 1975-77), Wash. State Soc. Internal Medicine (trustee 1976-80). Home: 8407 SE Evergreen Hwy Vancouver WA 98664 Office: 2102 E McLoughlin Blvd Vancouver WA 98661

DYKSTRA, DAVID CHARLES, accountant, management consultant, author; b. Des Moines, July 10, 1941; s. Orville Linden and Ermina (Dunn) D.; B.S.Ch.E., U. Calif., Berkeley, 1963; M.B.A., Harvard U., 1966; m. Ello Paimre, Nov. 20, 1971; children—Suzanne, Karin, David S. Corp. controller Recreation Environments, Newport Beach, Calif., 1970-71, Hydro Conduit Corp., Newport Beach., 1971-78; v.p. fin. and adminstrn. Tree-Sweet Products, Santa Ana, Calif., 1978-80; pres., owner Dykstra Cons., Newport Beach, 1980—; pres. Easy Data Corp., 1981—; pub. Easy Data Computer Comparisons, 1982—. Chmn. 40th Congressional Dist. Tax Reform Immediately, 1977-80; mem. nat. com. Republican Party; vice-chmn. Orange County Calif. Rep. Assembly, 1979-80; v.p., dir. Corona Del Mar Rep. Assembly, 1980. C.P.A., Calif. Mem. Am. Inst. C.P.A.s, Am. Mgmt. Assn., Calif. Soc. C.P.A.s, Assn. Computer Users, Ind. Computer Consultants Assn., Internat. Platform Assn., Orange County C. of C., Newport Beach C. of C., Town Hall. Mem. Universal Life Ch. Clubs: Rotary Internat., John Wayne Tennis, Lido Sailing. Author: Manager's Guide to Business Computer Terms, 1981; Computers for Profit, 1983; contbr. articles to profl. jours. Home: 1724 Port Ashley Pl Newport Beach CA 92660 Office: 1600 Dove St Newport Beach CA 92660

DYMALLY, MERVYN MALCOLM, congressman; b. Cedros, Trinidad, W. Indies, May 12, 1926; came to U.S., 1946, naturalized, 1954; s. Hamid A. and Andreid S. (Richardson) D.; B.A., Calif. State U.-Los Angeles, 1951; M.A., Calif. State U.-Sacramento, 1969; Ph.D., U.S. Internat. U., San Diego, 1978; J.D. (hon.), Calif. Law Coll., 1976, Lincoln U., Sacramento, 1975; LL.D. (hon.), U. West Los Angeles, 1970, Calif. Coll. Law, 1976, City U., Los Angeles, 1976; m. Alice M. Gueno, Dec. 28, 1968; children—Mark, Lyn. Mem. Calif. Assembly, 1962-67, Calif. Senate, 1967-75; lt. gov. Calif., 1975-79; pres. Mervyn M. Dymally Co., Inc., Sacramento, 1979-81; mem. 97th-98th Congresses from 31st Dist. of Calif.; lectr. Whittier (Calif.) Coll.; adj. prof. Golden State U., San Francisco. Chmn. Nat. Conf. Black Elected Ofcls., 1969-77; Mem. AAUP, Am. Politics Assn., Am. Acad. Polit. Sci., Am. Acad. Polit. and Social Sci., Nat. Conf. Black Elected Ofcls. (co-chmn.), Urban Affairs Inst. (pres.), ACLU, NAACP, Urban League, Arab Am. Affairs Council, Phi Kappa Phi. Democrat. Episcopalian. Author: The Black Politician: His Struggle for Power, 1971; editor: The Black Politician, 1969. Home: 223 S Acacia St 206 Compton CA 90220 Office: 1717 Longworth House Office Bldg Washington DC 20515

DYSON, ELIZABETH INEZ BURGAY, mcht.; b. Charleston, S.C., Oct. 10, 1929; d. Hamilton Kendrick and Bernice Vicki (Mizzell) Burgay; student public schs., Charleston; m. William James Dyson, Mar. 21, 1949; children—Vicki Lou Dyson Johnson, Donald Rodney, William Hap, Kenneth Lucky. Waitress, Charleston, 1948, Barstow, Calif., 1949; secretarial position Barstow Marine Base, 1948; salesman Stanley Products Co., Vernon, Calif., 1949-56, owner, operator Dyson's Custom Upholstery, Boron, Calif., 1957—, Dyson's Shoes and Upholstery, Boron, 1959—, Dyson's Collection Agy., Boron, 1963—, Dyson's Safety Shoe Store, Bakersfield, Calif., 1982—. Mem. Boron Bus. Men's Assn. (pres. 1967-69), C. of C. (sec. 1965-81). Democrat. Episcopalian. Home: Box 181 Tehachapi CA 93561 Office: 27012 20 Mule Team Rd Boron CA 93516 also 2345 Fruitvale #3 Bakersfield CA 93308

DYSON, RICHARD SAMUEL, public sch. adminstr.; b. Anderson, Ind., Feb. 12, 1947; s. Robert Bonner and Naomi Ruth (Cade) D., B.A. in Polit.Sci., Ind. U., 1969; postgrad. Harvard U., 1973; m. Kristen Keith, Aug. 21, 1976; children—Jeffrey Brantford Keith, Jonathan Richard Blackledge. Adminstr. employee services RCA Alascom, Inc., 1975-77; mktg. account exec. Totem Ocean Trailer Express, Inc., 1978-79; personnel adminstr. Anchorage Sch. Dist., 1979—. Chmn. public edn. com. Anchorage unit Am. Cancer Soc., 1976, bd. dirs. for Alaska, 1978—; chmn. pacesetter fundraising drive United Way Alascom, 1976; chmn. Bike-O-Thon for Anchorage, Am. Diabetes Assn., 1979, 80, bd. dirs. for Alaska, 1979—. Served with USAR, 1969-72. Recipient award Alaska Press Club, 1977; Merit award Am. Cancer Soc., 1978; Outstanding Service award Am. Diabetes Assn., 1979, 80. Mem. Am. Soc. Personnel Adminstrs., Pacific N.W. Personnel Mgmt. Assn., Alaska Assn. Sch. Bus. Ofcls., Anchorage Personnel Assn. (treas. 1980-81), Ind. U. Alumni Assn., Sigma Phi Epsilon. Episcopalian. Club: Rotary (treas. Anchorage 1978, chmn. public relations 1980). Home: 5060 Vi St Anchorage AK 99507 Office: 4600 DeBarr Ave Box 6-614 Anchorage AK 99502

EACHO, ROSA LEE, business executive; b. Elk River, Idaho, Dec. 27, 1931; d. Quinto and Lily Esther (Harlan) Paolini; m. Richard Gerald Eacho, Oct. 20, 1950 (div.); children—Rex, Roxanne Paolini, Rochelle Carroll, Rebecca. Sec., Salewoman Farmers Ins., Wenatchee, Wash.; owner Boatique Ltd., Seattle, Danish Waffle Sundae. Republican. Presbyterian Office: 7001 Seaview Ave NW Seattle WA 98117

EADES, LINNEA ERMA, educator, violinist; b. Las Vegas, Aug. 9, 1938; d. Waldo C. and Margarite (Brockenauer) Higbee; m. Arthur E. Eades, Aug. 21, 1960; children—Robert, Carole. B.S., UCLA, 1960. Cert. tchr., Calif. Tchr. home econs. Mt. Gleason Jr. High Sch., Sunland, Calif.; mem. San Fernando Valley Symphony Orch., 1965—, Canejo Symphony Orch., 1981—, Burbank Symphony, Highland Park Symphony, Westside Symphony, Met. Symphony, Pepperdine Symphony Orch. Burbank Tchr. Assn. scholar, 1956; Am. Legion awardee, 1953. Mem. United Tchrs. Los Angeles, Mu Phi Epsilon, Omicron Nu. Democrat. Mem. Ch. Religious Science. Home: 7036 Keokuk Ave Canoga Park CA 91306 Office: Mt Gleason Jr High Sch 19065 Mt Gleason Ave Sunland CA 91040

EADES, LUIS ERIC, artist, educator; b. Madrid, June 25, 1923; s. Alwyn Turley and Luisa (Olmedo) E.; student Bath (Eng.) Sch. Art, 1940-42, London U. Slade Sch., 1947-48, Nat. Poly. Inst. Mex., 1948-49; B.A. summa cum laude, U. Ky., 1952; came to U.S., 1949, naturalized, 1967; m. Ursula Jean Lambert, Dec. 27, 1957; children—Peter Luis, Helen Elisabeth. Instr., then asst. prof., U. Tex., 1954-61; faculty fine arts dept. U. Colo., Boulder, 1961—, prof., 1970—; exhibited one-man shows: Carlin Galleries, Fort Worth, 1968, 71, 74, 77, 80; Janet Nessler Gallery, N.Y.C., 1960, 64, Carson/Sapiro Gallery, Denver, 1979, 83; group shows include: Mus Modern Art, N.Y.C., 1962, A.F.A., N.Y.C., 1970; represented in permanent collections: Whitney Mus. Am. Art, N.Y.C., Dallas Mus. Fine Arts. Served with Brit. Intelligence Corps, 1943-45. U. Tex. research grantee, 1960, U. Colo. grantee, 1966, 72, 78, 83. Mem. Phi Beta Kappa. Roman Catholic. Office: Fine Arts Dept U Colo Boulder CO 80309

EADINGTON, WILLIAM RICHARD, economist; b. Fullerton, Calif., Jan. 1, 1946; s. Thomas James and Mary Elizabeth (Bastanchury) E.; m. Margaret Ann Dean, Feb. 3, 1968; children—Diana, Michael. B.S. in Econs., Santa Clara (Calif.) U., 1967; M.A. in Econs., Claremont (Calif.) Grad. Sch., 1970, Ph.D. 1973. Asst. prof. econs. U. Nev., Reno, 1969-74, assoc. prof., 1974-81, prof., 1981—, chmn. dept., 1976-77; 78-80, vis. prof., W. Ger., 1977-78, London Sch. Econs., 1978. Mem. Nat. Council Compulsive Gambling, Am. Econ. Assn., Western Regional Sci. Assn., Western Social Sci. Assn. office: Dept Econs U Nevada Reno NV 89557

EAGAN, PAMELA ANN, pharmacist, educator, trainer; b. Dubuque, Iowa, Aug. 21, 1949; d. Lawrence J. and Kathleen M. (Higgins) E. B.A. in English, Clarke Coll., 1971; B.S. in Pharmacy, Drake U., 1976; M.S. in Pharmacy Mgmt., U. Iowa, 1981, M.A. in Edn., 1981. Registered pharmacist. English instr., Dubuque, Iowa, 1971-73; pharmacist Mercy Med. Ctr., Iowa City, Iowa, 1977-81, Mercy Health Care Ctr., Des Moines, 1977-81; research asst. U. Iowa, Coll. Edn. and Coll. Pharmacy, 1977-81; assoc. dir., tng. specialist Community Pharmacy Enhancement Project, U. So. Calif., Los Angeles, 1981—. Mem. Am. Soc. Hosp. Pharmacists, Women's Health Network, Am. Soc. Tng. and Devel., Women in Mgmt. Los Angeles, World Future Soc., Sierra Club. Producer videotape programs in field. Office: 1985 Zonal Ave Los Angeles CA 90033

EAGEN, ISAAC BRENT, clergyman; b. Upland, Calif., Dec. 14, 1929; s. James O. and Stella E. (Powell) E. B.A., St. Francis Sem., 1951; M.A., Loyola-Marymount U., 1961; D.H.L. (hon.), U. San Diego, 1980. Ordained priest Roman Catholic Ch., 1956, rev. monsignor, 1969; assoc. pastor St. Joseph Cathedral, 1956; assoc. pastor Holy Rosary Ch., 1956-59; asst. prof. U. San Diego, 1960-65; prof. Mercy Coll. Nursing, San Diego, 1962-64, dir. sch. relations, 1965-67; chancellor Diocese of San Diego, 1968—; pastor Mission San Diego de Alcala, 1971—; pres. Cathedral Plaza Corp., San Diego, 1971—; bd. dirs. Diocese San Diego Edn. and Welfare Corp., 1968—; pres. Guadalupe Plaza Corp., San Diego, 1979—. Trustee, U. San Diego, 1968—; pres. Community Welfare Council, 1970; mem. Mayor's Crime Control Commn., 1981. Named Headliner of Year, San Diego Press Club, 1975, Brotherhood award NCCJ, 1971. Mem. Canon Law Soc. Am., Navy League U.S., Scholia, Phi Kappa Theta. Clubs: Circumnavigators, La Jolla Beach and Tennis, Kona Kai. Home: 10818 San Diego Mission Rd San Diego CA 92108 Office: PO Box 80428 San Diego CA 92138

EAGLE, JOHN MILTON, steel company executive; b. West Chester, Ohio, Sept. 25, 1917; s. Raymond Walter and Addie (Sloane) E.; grad. high sch., 1936; m. Marjorie Marie Jones, Mar. 25, 1941; 1 son, John Michael. Pipe fitter Armco Steel, Middletown, Ohio, 1936-42; pattern maker Vulcan Pipe Co., Los Angeles, 1946-47; welding foreman Pipe Fabricating & Supply Co., Santa Fe Springs, Calif., 1947-48, shop supt., 1948-52, plant mgr., 1952-54, gen. mgr., 1954-58, pres., 1958—, owner, 1960—; dir. Snap on Clamp, Apple Valley View Mutual Water Corp. Trustee Americanism Ednl. League; mem. Energy Exchange of Greater Los Angeles. Served with USNR, 1943-46. Mem. Am. Welding Soc. (life), Pacific Coast Electric Assn. Methodist. Mason. Clubs: Los Angeles Engineers (pres. 1968-69), Petroleum (dir.). Address: 16002 Arbela Dr Whittier CA 90603

EAGLE, ROBERT EDWARD, political science educator, consultant; b. Helena, Mont., July 3, 1941; s. Henry C. and Dorotha Dee (Hutt) E.; m. Carolyn Spangler, June 21, 1964; children—Amy, Ann. B.S., Mont. State U., 1963; M.A., Am. U., 1965, Ph.D., 1967. Prof. polit. sci. Ohio U., Athens, 1967-71, U. Mont., Missoula, 1971—; cons. developing simulations, computer assisted instrn. Edn. dir. Athens Citizens for Fair Housing, 1968-70. Mem. Am. Polit. Sci. Assn., Western Polit. Sci. Assn., Assn. Arid Lands Studies. Democrat. Methodist. Author: Student Creativity in Classroom Simulations, 1971; The Politics of Water Resources in Montana, 1979; Economic Development and Environmental Problems in China and Tanzania, 1981.

EAKIN, RICHARD MARSHALL, zoology educator; b. Florence, Colo., May 5, 1910; s. Marshall and Mary (Jack) E.; m. Mary Mulford, Aug. 8, 1935 (dec.); children—David Marshall, Dottie A.; m. 2d, Barbara A. Nichols, May 15, 1982. A.B., U. Calif.-Berkeley, 1931, Ph.D., 1935. Instr. to prof. zoology U. Calif.-Berkeley, 1936-77, emeritus prof., 1977—, chmn. dept., 1942-48, 52-57, asst. dean Coll. Letters and Scis., 1939-42, chmn. Miller Inst. Research in Basic Sci., 1961-67; vis. prof. biology Tougaloo Coll., 1978-79, Talladega Coll., Fisk U., 1981. Guggenhem fellow, 1953, 56; NRC fellow, 1935-36; NSF sr. fellow, 1957; recipient Walker prize, First Sr. citation for Disting. Teaching, U. Calif.-Berkeley, 1977; Associated Students award for Disting. Teaching, 1968, Disting. Research in Biology award Electron Microscope Soc., 1982. Fellow Calif. Acad. Scis.; mem. Am. Soc. Zoologists (pres. 1975), Western Soc. Naturalists (pres. 1949), AAAS, Electron Microscope Soc. Am., Am. Soc. Cell Biology, Soc. Developmental Biology. Author: The Third Eye; Great Scientists Speak Again; Vertebrate Embryology; contbr. articles to profl. jours.; assoc. editor Jour. Ultrastructure Research, 1982; Zoomorphology, 1982. Home: 1515 Oxford St Berkeley CA 94709 Office: Dept Zoology U Calif Berkeley CA 94720

EAKINS, PAMELA, sociologist; b. Denver, Mar. 12, 1953; d. George H. and V. Joyce (Tannlund) E.; m. Bernhard M. Haisch, July 29, 1977; children—Katherine Stuart, Christopher Taylor. B.A., U. Colo., 1975, M.A., 1977, Ph.D., 1980. Instr. U. Colo., Boulder, 1975-77, 78-79; affiliated scholar Ctr. Research on Women, Stanford U., Calif., 1982—; vis. sociologist Netherlands Nat. Ctr. Research and Devel. in Adult Edn., Amersfoort, 1977-78. Bd. dirs. Birth Place Maternity Ctr. Mem. Am. Sociol. Assn., Soc. Study Social Problems, Western Social Sci. Assn. (Women's Studies div. coordinator), Pacific Sociol. Assn., Sociologists for Women in Soc. (sec. Colo. chpt. 1979, treas. Bay area chpt. 1982). Author: Mothers in Transition, 1982; contbr. articles to profl. publs. Office: Ctr for Research on Women Stanford U Stanford CA 94305

EALES, JOHN RAY, former edn. cons.; b. Rushville, Ill., Nov. 3, 1910; s. Charles L. and Edith (Bogue) E.; B.A., Washington U., St. Louis, 1934; M.A., Northwestern U., 1946; Ed.D., UCLA, 1956; m. Edna Elizabeth Neal, Dec. 26, 1938; children—Meredith (Mrs. Mark J. Henderson), April (Mrs. G.L. Germany). Tchr., Litchfield (Ill.) Jr. High Sch., 1937-38; teaching prin. J.D. Colt Elem. Sch., Litchfield, 1938-39; tchr. Mo. Mil. Acad., Mexico, 1939-43, 45-46; prin. Nichols Jr. High Sch., Evanston, Ill., 1947-48; cons. secondary edn. Los Angeles County Schs., Calif., 1948-56, Calif. Dept. Edn., Sacramento, 1956-78; tchr. various colls., summers 1953-62. Mem. Accrediting Commn. Secondary Schs. Western Assn. Schs. and Colls. Served with USAAF, 1943-45. Mem. Tau Kappa Epsilon, Phi Delta Kappa. Mason, Elk. Author: (with M.K. Strasser, C.Z. Zaun, M.E. Mushlitz) When You Take The Wheel, 1961; (with M.K. Strasser, J.E. Aaron, R.C. Bohn) Fundamentals of Safety Education, 1964; (M.K. Strasser, J.E. Aaron) Driver Education, 1969. Home: 8012 Maybelline Way Sacramento CA 95823

EANEMAN, JAMES MICHAEL, public utility mgr.; b. Oakland, Calif., June 19, 1945; s. Robert Gilbert and Margaret (Mahoney) E.; m. Margaret Ann McCrea, Dec. 4, 1982. B.S. in Econs. and History, Chico State Coll., 1968; M.B.A. in Mgmt., Pepperdine U., 1980. With Pacific Gas & Electric Co., 1968—, analyst, corp. gen. office, customer services dept., 1972-74, customer services specialist San Jose div., 1974-77, field mktg. supr. San Jose div., 1977-78, dist. customer services supr., 1978-79, area mgr., Berkeley, 1979-82, project mgr. Corp. Gen. Office, 1982-83, No. San Mateo County dist. mgr., Daly City, Calif., 1983—. Bd. dirs. Berkeley Youth Employment Project, Berkeley-Albany YMCA, Center Ind. Living; bd. dirs., mem. exec. com., chmn. personnel com. ARC; pres. Jackson St Homeowners Assn.; mem. Mayor's Energy Adv. Com. Mem. Pacific Coast Electric Assn., Pacific Coast Gas Assn., Am. Mgmt. Assn., Berkeley Pvt. Industry Council (vice chmn.), Berkeley-Albany Industries Assn. (treas.), Berkeley C. of C. (v.p., Pres.'s award 1981, pres. 1981-82). Republican. Roman Catholic. Clubs: Berkeley Breakfast (dir. 1982—), Berkeley Rotary (program chmn. 1981-82), Commonwealth of Calif. Home: 517 Jackson St Albany CA 94706 Office: 450 Eastmoor Ave Daly City CA 94015

EARDLEY, RICHARD ROY, mayor Boise (Idaho); b. Denver, Dec. 23, 1928; s. Walter B. and Pearl (Wessels) E.; student Eastern Oreg. Coll., 1947-48; m. Patricia L. Engum, May 28, 1950; children—Rick, Randall, Ronald. Reporter, Democrat Herald, Baker, Oreg., 1951-52; news dir. KBKR Radio, Baker, 1952-55; sports editor Ida. Statesman, Boise, 1955-59; news dir. KBOI Radio-TV, Boise, 1959-73; mem. Boise City Council, 1970-74, mayor Boise, 1974—. Office: Office of Mayor City Hall PO Box 500 Boise ID 83701*

EARGLE, JOHN MORGAN, electroacoustical cons.; b. Tulsa, Jan. 6, 1931; s. Robert Gray and Josephine Virginia (Tennison) E.; student N. Tex. State Coll., 1948-50; B.Mus., Eastman Sch. Music, 1953; M.Mus., U. Mich., 1954; B.S. in Elec. Engring., U. Tex., 1962; M.Engring., Cooper Union U., 1970. Adminstr. mfg., rec. RCA Records Co., N.Y.C., 1962-69; chief engr. Mercury Records Co., N.Y.C., 1969-71; dir. comml. sound products Altec Corp., Anaheim, Calif., 1971-74; mem. firm JME Assos., electroacoustical cons., Hollywood, Calif., 1974-76, 82—; sr. dir. product devel. and application James B. Lansing Sound, Inc., Northridge, Calif., 1977—. Lectr. rec. seminars Brigham Young U., Provo, Utah, 1970-71, Eastman Sch. Music, Rochester, N.Y., 1971-72, Aspen Music Festival Audio Inst., 1979-80, 82, Eastman Sch. Music Rec. Inst., 1980—. Served with AUS, 1954-56. Fellow Audio Engring. Soc. (editorial bd. Jour. 1970- , pres. 1974-75); mem. IEEE (sr.), Audio Engring. Soc. (hon.), Acoustical Soc. Am., Soc. Motion Picture and TV Engrs., Tau Beta Pi, Eta Kappa Nu. Author: Sound Recording, 1976, 2d edit., 1980; The Microphone Handbook, 1982; contbr. articles to profl. jours. Home: 7034 Macapa Dr Los Angeles CA 90068 Office: 8500 Balboa Blvd Northridge CA 91329

EARL, ELLEN DOROTHEA, ret. retail corp. exec.; b. Joplin, Mo., Aug. 31, 1913; d. Jacob Leo and Lula Myrtle (Woolsey) Sturmer; A.A., S.W. Bapt. Coll., Bolivar, Mo., 1932; postgrad. Central Mo. Tchrs. Coll., 1933; m. Joseph Earl, Aug. 3, 1935; 1 dau., Emily Earl Campbell. Gen. office worker Quality Cone Co., Joplin, 1933-34, ARC, Joplin, 1935-38; stenographer H & L Block Co., San Francisco, 1938-39; sec. to mgr. Westvaco Chem. Co., Newark, Calif., 1941-44; partner, sec.-treas. Furniture Exchange, San Jose, Calif., 1944-46; partner, sec.-treas. Valley Supply Co., Shady Cove, Oreg., 1947-50; with No. Comml. Co., Seattle, 1951-75, corporate sec., to 1975, ret., 1975. Mem. Nat. Secs. Assn., Seattle C. of C. Republican. Baptist. Home: 7336 36th Ave SW Seattle WA 98126

EARLE, FRED A., III, owner tennis club; b. Modesto, Calif., Jan. 9, 1934; s. Fred Antipas and Lois (Wilson) E.; student Modesto Jr. Coll., 1951-53; B.S., UCLA, 1955, M.S., 1956, gen. secondary teaching credential, 1956; cert. master hypnotist; m. Vicki-Van Dallas, May 23, 1974; children—Kathliene Ann, David Owen, Jeffrey Dallas. Tchr., Roosevelt High Sch., Fresno, 1955-56; owner Modesto Racquet Club (Calif.), 1957-74, owner, mgr., head tennis profl., 1973- ; operator summer tennis camp for tournament jrs. in Japan, 1978—, speaker. Past pres. Meml. Hosp. Found. Mem. Mgrs. and Owners Assn. No. Calif. (founding mem., past pres.), U.S. Profl. Tennis Assn. (sec.; master profl.), Profl. Tennis Instrs. (past pres.), Profl. Tennis Registry, Sigma Nu (past pres.). Republican. Episcopalian. Clubs: Rotary (Modesto); Stanislaus Fly Fishermen (past pres.). Home: 1507 Patterson Rd Modesto CA 95355 Office: 200 Norwegian Ave Modesto CA 95355

EARLE, SYLVIA ALICE, biologist; b. Gibbstown, N.J.; d. Lewis R. and Alice F. (Richie) E.; A.A., St. Petersburg Jr. Coll., 1953; B.S., Fla. State U., 1955; M.A., Duke U., 1956, Ph.D., 1966; student U. Fla., 1959-60; children—Elizabeth Mead, Richie Mead, Gale Mead. Asst. in botany Fla. State U., 1952-55; herbarium asst. Duke U., 1956-57; fisheries biologist U.S. Fish and Wildlife Service, Beaufort, N.C., 1957; herbarium asst. U. Fla., 1959-60; instr. zoology St. Petersburg (Fla.) Jr. Coll., 1963-64; research assoc. Cape Haze Marine Lab., 1965-66, resident dir., 1966-67; marine botanist on NSF research vessel Anton Bruun, 1964-66; research scholar Radcliffe Inst., Cambridge, Mass., 1967-69; research fellow, scholar Farlow Herbarium, Harvard U., Cambridge, 1967—; curator, research biologist Calif. Acad. Scis., 1976—; v.p., dir. Deep Ocean Tech. Inc. and Deep Ocean Engring. Inc., 1981—; cons. Smithsonian-Link Man-In-Sea Project, Bahamas, 1968, Scientist-in-the-Sea Project, Panama City, Fla., 1972; coordinator and lectr. UCLA Extension Div., 1971-79; research assoc. botany Nat. History Mus. of Los Angeles County, 1970-75; research asso. in botany U. Calif., Berkeley, 1967—; mem. U.S.-Japan Panel on Diving Physiology and Tech., 1976—; mem. Nat. Adv. Com. on Oceans and Atmosphere, 1980—. Bd. dirs. Undersea Industries, Inc., 1978-80; trustee Ocean Trust Found., 1976—, World Wildlife Fund U.S., 1976-82, Environ. Defense Fund, 1974-81, Charles A. Lindbergh Fund, 1980—; trustee World Wildlife Fund Internat., 1977-82, mem. council, 1983—. Decorated Order of Golden Ark (Netherlands); named hon. citizen City of Chgo., 1970; Woman of Yr., Los Angeles Times, 1970, Scientist of Yr., Calif. Mus. Sci. and Industry, 1981; recipient Meritorious Service award Los Angeles County Mus. of Natural History, 1970, Conservation Service award U.S. Dept. Interior, 1970, Boston Sea Rovers award, 1972, Our World Underwater award Chgo., 1978. Fellow Calif. Acad. Scis.; mem. Internat. Phycol. Soc. Am. (sec. 1975-80), Soc. Southwestern Naturalists, Phycological Soc. Am., Am. Inst. Biol. Scis., Oceanic Soc. (trustee 1982—), Am. Soc. Ichtyologists and Herpetologists, Internat. Soc. Plant Taxonomists, Ecol. Soc. Am., AAAS, Soc. Radcliffe Fellows, New Eng. Bot. Club, Brit. Phycol. Soc., Explorers Club (Lowell Thomas award 1980). Contbr. numerous articles on marine botany and ecology to sci. jours. Office: California Acad of Sciences San Francisco CA 94118

EARLEY, JUDITH KAYE, psychotherapist; b. Iowa City, Iowa, Mar. 31, 1944; d. Clarence J. and Ethel M. (Hart) Reinhart. B.A., U. Iowa, 1966; M.A. Loyola Marymount U., 1979. Pvt. practice marriage and family therapy, Pasadena, Calif., 1980—; instr. assertiveness tng. Calif. State U.-Los Angeles. Mem. Am. Personnel and Guidance Assn., Calif. Assn. Marriage and Family Therapists, Psi Chi.

EARLS, WANDA IDRIS, savings and loan executive; b. Galveston, Tex., Apr. 18, 1937; d. Lorenzo Dolphus and Virgie (Landers) Clem; m. Roger Allan Pond, July 3, 1955; children—Allan, Deanna; m. Mack Lee Earls, Oct. 31, 1977. Student Bakersfield Coll., 1955, 62, West Hills Coll., 1975. Cashier, Beneficial Fin., 1955-59; with United Calif. Bank, Bakersfield, 1961-68; note dept. supr. Nat. Bank Agr., Bakersfield, 1968-72; br. mgr., v.p. Guarantee Savs. and Loan Assn., Bakersfield, 1973—. Mem. Coalinga C. of C. (pres. 1977-78), Greater Bakersfield C. of C. (v.p. 1983—), Women's Div. C. of C. (pres. 1983-84). Republican.

Baptist. Home: 3530 Adanac St Bakersfield CA 93309 Office: Guarantee Savs Loan 2525 Oswell St Bakersfield CA 93306

EARLY, JAMES MICHAEL, engineering manager; b. Syracuse, N.Y., July 25, 1922; s. Frank J. and Rhoda (Gray) E.; m. Mary Agnes Valentine, Dec. 28, 1948; children—Mary Beth, Kathleen, Joan, Rhoda, Maureen, Rosemary, James, Margaret Mary. B.S., N.Y. Coll. of Forestry, Syracuse, 1943; M.S., Ohio State U., Columbus, 1948, Ph.D., 1951. Instr., research assoc. Ohio State U., Columbus, 1946-1951; dir. lab. Bell Telephone Labs., Murray Hill, N.J., 1951-1964, dir. lab. Allentown, Pa., 1964-69; research and devel. dir. Fairchild Camera and Instrument Corp., Palo Alto, Calif., 1969—; mem., then chmn. Adv. Group on Electron Devices, Dept. Def., 1962-82. Served with U.S. Army, 1943-45. Recipient Outstanding Alumnus award Ohio State U., 1967; J.J. Ebers award Electron Device Soc., IEEE, 1979. Fellow IEEE; mem. AAAS, Am. Phys. Soc., Electrochem. Soc., Internat. Platform Assn. Roman Catholic. Clubs: Palo Alto (Calif.) Yacht. Patentee fundamental bipolar transistor structure, 1952. Home: 740 Center Dr Palo Alto CA 94301 Office: 4001 Miranda Ave Palo Alto CA 94304

EARLY, JOHN OAK, extension economist; b. Dublin, Ohio, Oct. 25, 1925; s. Wenzel Oak and Evelyn Ruth (Mason) E.; m. Martha May Swisher, Dec. 20, 1947; 1 son, Adrian Bruce. B.S. (Agr. scholar), Ohio State U., 1950, Ph.D., 1971; M.S., Colo. State U., 1956. Mgr. S. Lane Farms, Utica Ohio, 1951-54; research asst. Colo. State U., Ft. Collins, 1954-56; researcher Rath Packing Co., Waterloo, Iowa, 1956-61; commodity analyst Swift & Co., Chgo., 1961-65; research assoc. and tech. adv. Ohio State U., Columbus, 1965-71; extension economist U. Idaho, Moscow, 1971-82, N.Mex. State U., Las Cruces, 1982—. Mem. AAUP (pres. Idaho chpt. 1979-81), Am. Agr. Econs. Assn., Western Agr. Econs. Assn., Alpha Zeta, Gamma Sigma Delta, Epsilon Sigma Phi. Contbr. articles to profl. jours. Home: 180 Hoagland Rd Las Cruces NM 88005 Office: Box 3AE Coll of Agr New Mexico State U Las Cruces NM 88003

EARNEST, ELBERT EDGAR, insurance executive; b. Mena, Ark., Feb. 23, 1914; s. James Franklin and Roxanna (Maggard) E.; B.A., U. N.Mex., 1939, M.A., 1950; m. Altha Love Wright, Dec. 22, 1935; children—James W., Stephen E., David A., Kathleen A. Techr., Cedarvale (N.Mex.) Schs., 1935-37; Vaughn (N.Mex.) Schs., 1939-41; Hot Springs (N.Mex.) Schs., 1941-42; Espanola (N.Mex.) Schs., 1945-55, also dir. testing and guidance; assembler Lockheed Aircraft Corp., Burbank, Calif., 1942-45; owner, mgr. Elbert E. Earnest Agy., Santa Fe, N.Mex., 1955—. Chmn., Espanola Pediatric Found., 1953-54. Mem. N.Mex. Edn. Assn. (chmn. dist. 1949), Common Cause, N.Mex. Interch. Agy., Phi Kappa Phi. Democrat. United Methodist. Clubs: Toastmaster's Club of Espanola, Espanola Kiwanis, Santa Fe Kiwanis (mem. legion of honor). Home: 140 E Lupita Rd Santa Fe NM 87501 Office: 54 1/2 E San Francisco St Santa Fe NM 87501

EARNEST, OLEN JON, motion picture co. exec.; b. Ft. Smith, Ark., Nov. 20, 1937; s. Olen Jewel and Madge Pauline (Tate) E.; B.A. (Univ. scholar), Wichita State U., 1955, postgrad. (Guidance Center fellow), 1959; postgrad. (Acad. scholar, Univ. fellow) Washington U., St. Louis, 1959-64. Trainee in clin. psychology VA, St. Louis, 1959-64; asst. prof. psychology Wichita State U., 1964-68; dir. entertainment research ASI Mktg. Research Co., Los Angeles, 1969-74, 75-76; mgr. prime time comedy programming ABC TV, Los Angeles, 1974; current programming exec. Paramount TV, Los Angeles, 1975; dir. worldwide mktg. studies 20th Century-Fox Pictures, Los Angeles, 1976-80; v.p. mktg. research MCA/Universal, Universal City, Calif., 1980—; mem. faculty mktg. warfare conf. Advanced Mgmt. Research Internat., 1977-78. Mem. Sigma Phi Epsilon. Office: 100 Universal City Plaza Universal City CA 91608

EARP, THOMAS EARL, electronic engr.; b. Lennox, Calif., May 23, 1945; s. Thomas H. and Juanita V. (Odell) E.; A.A., Orange Coast Coll., 1968; m. Josefina Bello, Nov. 9, 1969; children—Frederick Louis, James Albert, Thomas Virgil. Staff photog. lab., Orange County (Calif.) Sch. Dist., 1964-67, teaching asst. engring. dept., 1967-68; head, receiving dept. R.A. Fischer and Co., Glendale, Calif., 1970-71, quality control dept., 1971-72; with Northrop Corp., Hawthorne, Calif., 1972—, electronic engr. flight simulation computer lab., 1972—. Mem. adv. panel Electronics Internat. Asso. fellow Brit. Interplanetary Soc., AAAS; mem. N.Y. Acad. Scis., Nat. Space Inst. Republican. Home: 1033 1/2 E Glenoakes St Glendale CA 91206 Office: 3901 W Broadway St Hawthorne CA 90250

EASA, SAID MOHAMED, civil engineer; b. Menofiah, Egypt, Jan. 28, 1949; came to U.S., 1978; s. Mohamed Hasanean and Monirah Elwahab E.; B.S. in Civil Engring. with honors and distinction, Cairo U., 1972; M.E. in Civil Engring. (Univ. fellow), McMaster U. (Can.), 1976; Ph.D. in Civil Engring., U. Calif., Berkeley, 1981. Instr., Cairo U., 1972-74; research engr. McMaster U., Hamilton, Ont., 1976-78; research asst. Inst. Transp. Studies, U. Calif., Berkeley, 1978-81, teaching asst., 1980-81; assoc. prof. civil engring. Lakehead U., Thunder Bay, Ont., Can., 1982—. Mem. Transp. Research Bd. (com. on traffic flow theory 1980—), Inst. Transp. Engrs. (pres. Berkeley Student chpt. 1980-81, Western U.S. and Can. Student Paper Competition winner 1979, 81). Contbr. articles to profl. jours.; prin. author models for analyzing freeway ops., downtown and residential areas, port ops.; developed graphic techniques for traffic flow ops. Office: Dept Civil Engring Lakehead U Thunder Bay ON P7B 5E1 Canada

EASLEY, GEORGE WASHINGTON, construction executive; b. Williamson, W.Va., Mar. 14, 1933; s. George Washington and Isabel Ritchie (Saville) E.; student U. Richmond, 1952-56; children—Bridget Bland, Kathy Clark, Saville Woodson, Marie Alexis, Isabell Roxanne, George Washington, Laura Dean. Hwy. engr. Va. Dept. Hwys., Richmond, 1956-62; dep. city mgr. City of Anchorage, 1962-68; prin. assoc. Wilbur Smith & Assos., Cons. Engrs., Los Angeles, 1969-70; commr. pub. works State of Alaska, Juneau, 1971-74; exec. v.p. Burgess Internat. Constrn. Co., Anchorage, 1974, pres., 1975; pres., chmn. bd. George W. Easley Co., Anchorage, 1976—; chmn. bd. Central Services, Inc. DBA Yellow Cab of Anchorage, 1982—; dir. Totem Ocean Trailer Express, Inc., Life Ins. Co. Alaska, Star Internat. Mem. New Capital Site Planning Commn. State of Alaska, 1981—; bd. dirs. Jr. Achievement, 1980—. Recipient commendations City of Anchorage, 1966, Greater Anchorage, Inc., 1969, Ketchikan C. of C., 1973, Alaska State Legis., 1974, Gov. of Alaska, 1974; named Outstanding Young Man, Anchorage Jaycees, 1964; Gold Pan award Anchorage C. of C., 1969, 77; registered profl. engr., Calif. Mem. Alaska C. of C. (dir. 1978—, 1980-82, chmn. 1982-83), Anchorage C. of C. (sec.-treas. 1976, v.p. 1977, pres.-elect 1978, pres. 1979-80, dir. 1982-85), Hwy. Users Fedn. Alaska (dir. 1972—, treas. 1974—), Orgn. Mgmt. of Alaska's Resources (past dir.), Pacific N.W. Waterways Assn. (v.p.), Am. Pub. Works Assn., Anchorage Transp. Commn. (past chmn.), Associated Gen. Contractors (dir. Alaska chpt. 1978—, chpt. treas. 1980-81, sec. 1981, v.p. 1982, nat. metric com., nat. edn. com.), Am. Mil. Engrs. (v.p. Alaska chpt. 1978), Inst. Mcpl. Engrs., Inst. Traffic Engrs., Internat. Orgn. Masters, Mates and Pilots (hon.), Petroleum Club Anchorage, Pvt. Industry Council Alaska (dir. 1978—), Common Sense for Alaska (past pres.), Commonwealth North (charter). Democrat. Presbyterian. Clubs: Tower, Rotary. Home: 333 M St #210 Anchorage AK 99501 Office: 310 K St Suite 507 Anchorage AK 99501

EASON, ERNEST DAY, consulting mechanical engineer; b. Denver, Apr. 10, 1949; s. Maurice Verne and Elma Iris Eason; m. Laurie Parker, Aug. 23, 1969. B.S. with spl. honors in Engring. Design and Econ. Evaluation, U. Colo., 1971; M.Eng. in Mech. Engring., U. Toronto (Can.), 1972; Ph.D. in Mech. Engring., U. Calif.-Berkeley, 1975. Registered profl. engr., Calif. Mem. tech. staff Sandia Labs., Livermore, Calif., 1976-79; mgr. mech. engring, Failure Analysis Assocs., Palo Alto, Calif., 1979—. Prin. trombonist Ohlone Community Band, 1979—. Recipient Pres.'s award as outstanding mem. jr. class U. Colo., 1970; Nat. Honor Soc. scholar, 1967; Nat. Merit scholar, 1967-71, Adolf Coors Co. scholar, 1967-71; NSF grad. fellow, 1971-74. Mem. ASME, Mathematical Programming Soc., Tau Beta Pi (past chpt. v.p.), Sigma Xi. Contbr. articles to profl. jours. and books. Office: 2225 E Bayshore Rd Palo Alto CA 94303

EASON, HAROLD VERNE, electronics engr.; b. Denver, June 18, 1944; s. Maurice Verne and Elma Iris (Cunningham) E.; B.S. in Elec. Engring. (Rio Grande scholar), U. Colo., 1966, M.B.A. in Mgmt. Sci., 1976; m. Diann Lee Imes, June 17, 1967; children—Michelle Belle, Jennifer Shawn. Engring. asst. Denver & Rio Grande Western R.R., Denver, 1966-71, asst. signal supr., Helper, Utah, 1971-73, centralized traffic control and electronics engr., Denver, 1973, asst. signal supr., 1973-74, engring. draftsman, 1974-76, chief draftsman, 1976-77, cost analyst, 1977-78, mgr. budgets and econ. analysis, 1979—; pres. Eason Service System, Inc., Commerce City, Colo., 1963—, B&E Stamp Co., Inc., Estes Park, Colo., 1978—. Mem. trumpet-trio Kiwanis Stars-of-Tomorrow, 1961; mem. Price Community Band, 1971-72; 1st trumpet Carbon County Chamber Orch., 1971, 72; mem. Denver Concert Band, 1977—; mem. Swing Inc., 1980—; sustaining mem. Colo. R.R. Hist. Found. Mem. IEEE, Nat. Rifle Assn., Nat. Wildlife Fedn., Nat. Geographic Soc., Amateur Trapshooting Assn., Am. Mus. Natural History, Mobile Post Office Soc., Am. Topical Assn., Am. Philatelic Soc., Cost Analysis Orgn. of Assn. Am. RRs, U. Colo. Alumni Assn., Durant Family Registry, Alpha Phi Omega (life), Kappa Kappa Psi (life), Sigma Iota Epsilon. Republican. Methodist. Mason (32 deg.). Clubs: Helper Gun (life); Oldsmobile of America (Fairfield, Conn.); Mercedes Benz of Am. (Colorado Springs, Colo.); Nash Car of America (Kenosha, Wis.); Model A Ford of America (Pomona, Calif.); Model A Ford of Colo. (sec. Denver 1971, v.p. 1977, pres. 1978); Milestone Car Soc. (Pacific Palisades, Calif.); Contemporary Hist. Vehicle Assn. (Cerritos, Calif.); Model A Restorers (Dearborn, Mich.). Home: 680 Poppy Way Broomfield CO 80020 Office: PO Box 5482 Denver CO 80217

EASTHAM, GEORGE MCCORD, educator, economist, consultant; b. Colon, Panama, Oct. 11, 1939; s. George Marion and Voncille (McCord) E.; m. Phyllis Cameron, Nov. 9, 1961; children—Patricia, Andrew, Kathleen, David. A.B., Chico State Coll., 1961; M.A., U. Calif.-Santa Barbara, 1966; Ph.D., Claremont Grad. Sch., 1978. Mem. faculty Calif. State Poly. U., San Luis Obispo, 1966—, acting head econs. dept., 1978-79, dept. head, 1979—; research assoc. Claremont Grad. Sch., 1970-72; cons. in field. Pres. San Luis Obispo Parents for Music 1974-76; bd. dirs. San Luis Obispo County Band, 1980—. Gen. Electric Found. fellow, 1968; Lincoln Found. fellow, 1970-72; named Father of Yr., San Luis Obispo Assn., 1974. Mem. Am. Econ. Assn., Western Econ. Assn., Atlantic Econ. Soc. Contbr. articles to profl. jours. Office: Econs Dept Calif State Poly U San Luis Obispo CA 93407

EASTON, FREDDIE LEE, psychologist; b. Lake Charles, La., Feb. 28, 1948; s. Arthur Jetson and Margie Lean (Kiel) E.; m. Rosemary Bradford, July 17, 1970; 1 son, Matthew Joshua. A.A., Los Angeles City Coll., 1969; B.A., Calif. State Coll., 1971; A.M., U. Ill., 1974, Ph.D., 1976. Adminstrv. teaching asst. dept. psychology U. Ill.-Urbana, 1972-73, research asst., 1973-74, teaching asst., 1974-75; psychology intern Danville (Ill.) VA Hosp., 1975-76; clin. psychologist Central City Community Mental Health Ctr., Los Angeles, 1976-77, U. Calif.-San Diego, 1980-81; chief clinic, supervising clin. psychologist Desert Community Mental Health Ctr., Blythe, Calif., 1981—. Served to lt. Med. Service Corps, USNR, 1977-80. USPHS fellow, 1971-75. Lic. clin. psychologist, Calif. Mem. Am. Psychol. Assn., Calif. Psychol. Assn., Assn. Black Psychologists, NAACP. Democrat. Author: The Effects of Social Class/Race on Mental Illness Diagnosis, 1974; The Effects of Social Class, Race and Behavioral Information on Labeling and Academic Expectancy of Children, 1976. Office: 244 E Hobsonway Blythe CA 92225

EASTON, ROBERT OLNEY, author, environmentalist; b. San Francisco, July 4, 1915; s. Robert Eastman and Ethel (Olney) E.; student Phillips Acad., Andover, Mass., 1932-33, Stanford, 1933-34; S.B., Harvard, 1938; M.A., U. Calif.-Santa Barbara, 1960; m. Jane Faust, Sept. 24, 1940; children—Joan (Mrs. Gilbert W. Lentz), Katherine (Mrs. Armand J. Renga), Ellen (Mrs. Gregory W. Brumfiel), Jane. Helped establish Sisquoc Condor Refuge, 1st sanctuary for Calif. Condor, 1937; assoc. editor Coast mag., San Francisco, Calif., 1939-40; freelance writer, 1942—; co-pub., editor Dispatch, Lampasas, Tex., 1946-50; co-owner, mgr. KHIT (now KCYL) radio sta., Lampasas, 1948-50; instr. English, Santa Barbara (Calif.) City Coll., 1960-65; cons. writing, pub. U.S. Naval Civil Engring. Lab., Port Hueneme, Calif., 1961-69; head citizens' com. establishment San Rafael Wilderness Area, Los Padres Nat. Forest, Calif., 1964-68; author: The Happy Man, 1943; (with Mackenzie Brown) Lord of Beasts, 1961; (with Jay Monaghan, others) The Book of the American West, 1963; (with Dick Smith) California Condor, 1964; The Hearing, 1964; Max Brand—The Big Westerner, 1970; Black Tide—The Santa Barbara Oil Spill and Its Consequences, 1972; Guns, Gold and Caravans, 1978; China Caravans, 1982; This Promised Land, 1982; editor Max Brand's Best Stories, 1967; Bullying the Moqui, 1968; contbr. numerous articles to popular mags., tech. jours., numerous stories to fiction, nonfiction anthologies. Co-chmn. Com. for Santa Barbara, 1972-76; pres. Santa Barbara Citizens for Environ. Def., 1975—; trustee Santa Barbara Mus. Natural History, 1972-75 Santa Barbara Community Environ. Council, 1973—. Served from pvt. to lt. AUS, 1942-46; ETO. Decorated Combat Inf. Badge, others; recipient Recipient Honor award Calif. Conservation Council, 1973. Mem. Explorers Club, Sierra Club, Nat. Audubon Soc., Wilderness Soc. Address: 2222 Las Canoas Rd Santa Barbara CA 93105

EATHER, KENNETH FREDERICK, physician; b. Eureka, Nev., June 2, 1921; s. Fred John and Josephine (Jeffries) E.; B.S., U. Nev., 1942; M.D., U. Pa., 1945; m. Elizabeth Ann Worthington, July 27, 1946; children—Katherine, Julie, Bruce, Paul. Intern, Geisinger Meml. Hosp., Danville, Pa., 1945-46; resident in anesthesiology Hosp. U. Pa., Phila., 1946-48; practice medicine specializing in anesthesiology Children's Anesthesia, Inc., Seattle, pres., 1970; dir. anesthesia Children's Orthopedic Hosp. and Med. Center, 1955-75, attending anesthesiologist, 1975—; clin. asso. prof. anesthesiology U. Wash. Sch. Medicine, Seattle, 1967—. Staff, Care-Medico mission to Algiers, 1963; bd. dirs. Conbela, mental rehab. center, 1979-81. Served with AUS, 1943-45, to capt. M.C., 1953-55. Diplomate Am. Bd. Anesthesiologists. Fellow Am. Coll. Anesthesiologists (bd. govs. 1960-66), Am. Acad. Pediatrics (affiliate); mem. Am., Wash. med. assns., King County Med. Soc., Am., Wash. (pres. 1957) socs. anesthesiologists, Wash. State Fedn. Anesthesiologists (pres. 1975), Biennial Western Conf. Anesthesiology (bd. govs. 1956-59), Phi Kappa Phi, Phi Chi, Alpha Tau Omega. Presbyn. (elder). Club: Variety. Contbr. numerous articles to med. jours. Home: 3005 W Mansell St Seattle WA 98199 Office: 720 Olive Way Seattle WA 98101

EATON, DEBRA (MRS. CONRAD ERNST PRUSAK), research psychologist; b. Hanover, N.H., Dec. 8, 1954; d. Herbert Howe and Mary Jean (Wilson) Eaton; m. Conrad Ernst Prusak, May 30, 1981. A.B. with honors in Psychology, U. Calif.-Berkeley, 1976; M.A., NYU, 1978, 19—, Ph.D. in Social and Personality Psychology, 1980. NIMH post-doctoral fellow U. Calif.-Berkeley, 1980-81, research psychologist, 1981—. Recipient George Zimbardo Meml. Fund award for excellence in scholarship and research, 1980. Mem. Am. Psychol. Assn., Western Psychol. Assn., Phi Beta Kappa. Contbr. articles to profl. jours. Office: Dept Psychology 3210 Tolman Hall U Calif Berkeley CA 94720

EATON, F. HOMER, corporation executive; b. Honolulu, Sept. 10, 1934; s. F. Homer and Z. M. (Lindemann) E.; m. Evelyn Jenney, Aug. 1, 1959; children—Rebecca Ann, Barbara True. B.S.E., Princeton U., 1956; M.B.A., Harvard U., 1962. Various positions, Castle & Cooke, Honolulu, Philippines, Honduras and Guatamala, 1962-77, v.p., gen. mgr. salmon, San Francisco, 1977-79, v.p., gen. mgr. tuna, 1979-81, exec. v.p., 1981—. Served to lt. USN, 1956-60. Office: 50 California St San Francisco CA 94111

EATON, GEORGE DANIEL, sales representative; b. Orange, N.J., July 4, 1922; s. John and Helen Martha (Demery) E.; m. Adeline Elizabeth Belenski, June 6, 1945; children—Michael, Thomas, Mark, Timothy. Student Kent State U., 1945, NYU, 1950. Asst. to v.p. Jersey Central Lines, Jersey City, 1941-48; purchasing dir. Turbine Equip. Co., Mountainside, N.J., 1948-56; sales rep., dist. mgr., regional mgr., sr. sales rep. Crane Co., N.Y.C. and San Francisco, 1956—. Pres. West End Democratic Club, Edison, N.J., 1954. Served in USMC, 1942-46. Mem. Am. Water Works Assn., Water and Wastes, Pub. Works Assn. Democrat. Roman Catholic.

EATON, LYNDA LOU, med. diagnostic co. exec.; b. Nevada, Mo., Aug. 31, 1946; d. Ira and Anna Mae (Welch) E.; m. John C. Carlisle, Dec. 1980. B.S. in Chemistry, Central Mo. State U., 1968; M.B.A., Pepperdine U., 1981. Blood bank supr. St. Luke's Hosp., Kansas City, Mo., 1968-71; acting blood bank supr. Hoag Meml. Hosp., Newport Beach, Calif., 1971-72; blood bank supr. City of Hope Nat. Med. Center, Duarte, Calif., 1975-77; mgr. Immuno-Sci., Inc., Orange, Calif., 1977-83, Ortho Diagnostic Systems Inc., Irvine, Calif., 1983—. Mem. Am. Soc. Clin. Pathology (med. technologist, specialist in blood banking), Am. Assn. Blood Banks. Republican. Home: 6 Palos Irvine CA 92715 Office: Ortho Diagnostic Systems 17392 Daimler Irvine CA 92714

EATON, MARTHA BACHER, psychologist; b. Ithaca, N.Y., Dec. 17, 1935; d. Robert Fox and Jean (Dow) Bacher; m. Aubrey Mac Eaton, Sep. 18, 1965 (div.). B.S., Pa. State U., 1957, M.S., 1959; Ph.D., U. Chgo., 1967. Nat. Register Health Service Providers in Psychology; lic. psychologist, Calif. Intern and psychometrist Counseling and Psychotherapy Research Ctr., U. Chgo., 1961-63, research coordinator, 1962-65, staff psychotherapist and editor Ctr. papers, 1963-65; Cause II staff mem. and trainer U. Chgo. Extension, 1965; research designer Charles F. Read Zone Ctr., Chgo., 1966; instr. DePaul U., Chgo., 1966-67, asst. prof., 1967-68, lectr., 1968-69; pvt. practice psychotherapy, 1969—; cons.; participant profl. confs. Mem. Am. Psychol. Assn., Calif. Psychol. Assn., Assn. Humanistic Psychology (research com., 1972-79), Assn. Past Life Research and Therapy (dir. 1980-82), Ctr. for Healing Arts, Women's Inst. and Health Ctr., Calif. Scholarship Fedn. Contbr. articles to profl. jours. Office: 407 E Gilbert Suite 1 San Bernadino CA 92404

EATON, MARY KATHERINE GIRTON (MRS. BURT ELLIOTT EATON), librarian; b. St. Paul, Mar. 9, 1924; d. John Francis and Mary Ahleen (Peck) G.; B.A., U. Minn., 1944; M.S., U. Oreg., 1952, M.L.S., 1968; postgrad. St. Paul Coll. Law, 1948-50; m. Burt Elliott Eaton, Oct. 18, 1947; children—John, Marilee, David. Reporter, Bakersfield (Calif.) Californian, 1945-46; women's editor Rochester (Minn.) Post-Bull., 1946-47; with chancellor's office Oreg. State System Higher Edn., 1952-53; library devel. cons. Oreg. State Library, 1968-70; asso. prof. U. Oreg. Library, Eugene, 1970—, mem. U. Oreg. Faculty Senate, 1980-82, 83—, pres., 1981-82; mem. Oreg. Interinstl. Faculty Senate, 1981—, pres., 1983-84. Cons., Lane County Library Adv. Council (Oreg.), 1968-76, 81—, chmn., 1981—; mem. Oreg. State Adv. Council on Libraries, 1972-73. Nat. bd. Camp Fire Girls, Inc., 1966-70, regional chmn., 1966-70, mem. council bd. Lane County, 1958-68, council pres., 1966-68; mem. Lane County Mental Health Clinic Adv. Bd., 1974—, chmn., 1972-74, 79-80; bd. chmn. Women's Transitional Living Center, Inc., 1972-74, Lane County Comprehensive Mental Health Planning Bd., 1975-81, 82—; mem. Oreg. Adv. Council in Mental Health, 1977—, chmn., 1981—. Named Outstanding Woman of Year, Eugene Jaycettes, 1956, Eugene Woman of Year, 1974; recipient Luther Gulick award, Camp Fire Girls, 1967, Ernest Thompson Seaton award, 1960, Hiitena award, 1972; named fellowship Eugene br. AAUW, 1970, Oreg. div., 1977. Mem. Oreg. League Women Voters (chpt. pres. 1963-65, mem. state bd. 1965-71), AAUW (br. pres. 1962-63, state bd. 1963-67, state legislature chmn. 1971-73, 1st v.p. 1973-75, state pres. 1975-77, nat. bd. 1976-80, nat. exec. v.p. 1981—, pres. legal advocacy fund 1981—), ALA, Pacific N.W., Oreg. Library Assn. (pres. 1973-74), Spl. Libraries Assn., Council Planning Librarians (pres. 1978-79), AAUP (treas. Oreg. chpt. 1977-78, v.p. 1979-80, pres. 1980-81), Assn. Oreg. Faculties (dir. 1981—, state v.p. 1983—), Sigma Kappa, Beta Phi Mu. Presbyn. (elder 1966-72). Editor: Taxes, Services and You, 1970, Oregon Library News, 1969-72, Council Planning Librarians Proc., 1976-77; AAUW Legislative History and Policy Notes, 1981. Home: 1631 E 24th Ave Eugene OR 97403 Office: Box 3177 Univ Oreg Eugene OR 97403

EATON, ROBERT E., city official; b. Sacramento, Sept. 3, 1935; s. Robert E. and Lillian (Larson) E.; m. Joanna Delano, Jan. 25, 1958; children—Robert, Thomas, David, Richard; B.A., Chico State U., 1958. Acct. W. B. Nystrom, C.P.A., Redding, Calif., 1958-59, Armour & Co., Dixon, Calif., 1959-61; dir. fin. Vacaville (Calif.), 1961—. Mem. Mcpl. Fin. Officers Assn. U.S., Mcpl. Fin. Officers Assn. Can., Calif. Soc. Mcpl. fin. Officers. Democrat. Methodist. Home: 530 Coventry Ct Vacaville CA 95688 Office: 650 Merchant St Vacaville CA 95688

EAVES, GARY WAYNE, mfg. co. exec.; b. Louisville, Miss., Nov. 4, 1946; s. Andrew Clinton and Grace (Boykin) E.; B.S., Miss. State U., 1968; Ph.D., U. Miss., 1974; m. Martha Kay Littlejohn, Apr. 4, 1969; children—Martha Grace, Emily Dianne, Gary Wayne. Chemist, Ariz. Chem., Panama City, Fla., 1969-71; toxicologist Miss. State Crime Lab., Jackson, 1971-74; toxicologist NIH, Bethesda, Md., 1974; product mgr. Finnigan Corp., Sunnyvale, Calif., 1974-77; product sales Litton Industries, Jackson, 1977-79; product mgr. Amsco Instrument Co., Santa Barbara, Calif., 1979-80; pres. Case Instruments, Ventura, Calif., 1980—. Mem. Am. Chem. Soc., Am. Mgmt. Assn., Sigma Xi. Democrat. Baptist. Contbr. articles to profl. jours. Patentee in field. Home: 221 Crown Hill Ct Ventura CA 93003 Office: 5528B Everglades Ventura CA 93003

EAVES, RONALD WELDON, computer scientist, educator; b. Beaumont, Calif., Aug. 28, 1937; s. Riley Weldon and Ruth (Marshall) E.; B.A., San Jose State U., 1959, M.A., 1962; Ph.D., U. Calif., Los Angeles, 1976; m. Betty L. Kurtz; children—Christopher, David, Erin, Terri, Sherene, Rebecca. Tchr. math jr. high sch., San Jose, Calif., 1960-62; tchr. sci. Fullerton Jr. Coll., 1962-65; systems engr. Honeywell, Inc., Los Angeles, 1965-68; prof. computer info. systems Calif. State Poly. U., Pomona, 1968—, assoc. dean sch. Bus. Adminstrn., 1983—. chmn. dept., 1972-76; prin. lectr. computing sci. Hong Kong Poly., 1979-80. Asst. treas. Hosp. Chaplains Ministry of Am., Inc., Fullerton, 1968-78.

NSF fellow, 1973; cert. data processor. Mem. Assn. Computing Machinery, EDP Auditors Assn. Office: 3801 W Temple Ave Pomona CA 91768

EBBELER, DONALD HERMAN, economist, research analyst; b. Lafayette, Ind., June 17, 1942; s. Donald Herman and Ethel Irene (Timmons) E.; m. Mary Ann McDonald, Oct. 24, 1970; children—Jennifer Valerie, Jonathan Wesley, Rebecca Jill. B.S.E.E., Purdue U., 1964, M.S.E.E., 1965, M.S. in Econs., 1969, Ph.D. in Econs., 1970. Research engr. Gen. Motors Corp., Santa Barbara, Calif., 1965-67; asst. prof. econs. Ga. Inst. Tech., Atlanta, 1970-71; asst. prof. Claremont (Calif.) Grad. Sch., 1971-73, assoc. prof., 1973-76; vis. assoc. prof. U. Iowa, Iowa City, 1976-77; economist So. Calif. Edison, Rosemead, 1978-80; sr. research analyst Jet Propulsion Lab., Pasadena, Calif., 1980—. NFS fellow, 1964-65; NDEA fellow, 1968-69; Krannert fellow, 1969-70. Mem. Econometric Soc., Am. Econ. Assn., Am. Statis. Assn. Contr. articles to profl. jours. Home: 2273 Bethel Ct Claremont CA 91711 Office: Jet Propulsion Lab 4800 Oak Grove Dr Pasadena CA 91109

EBEL, JOHN EDWARD, psychologist, educator; b. Hillsboro, Kans., July 19, 1935; s. A.R. and Esther (Hiebert) E.; A.A. in Edn., Reedley (Calif.) Coll., 1955; B.A. in Psychology, Tabor Coll., Hillsboro, 1957; M.A. in Counseling and Psychology, Fresno (Calif.) State Coll., 1960; Ph.D. in Ednl. Psychology, Lawrence (Calif.) U., 1978; married. Tchr., counselor Washington Union High Sch., Fresno, 1958-65; dir. guidance and psychology Tehachapi (Calif.) Unified Sch. Dist., 1965-68; coordinator guidance and testing Kern County (Calif.) Supt. Schs. Office, Bakersfield, 1968-71; psychologist Antelope Valley Union High Sch. Dist., Lancaster, Calif., 1971—; exec. dir. A.V. Behavioral Sci. Center, Lancaster, 1979—. Mem. Calif., Nat. assns. sch. psychologists, Calif. State Marriage Counselors Assn., Council for Exceptional Children (pres.), Nat. Council on Alcoholism (pres. Antelope Valley chpt., Lancaster 1980—). Author: D.E.S. Reading Scales., (with others) L.I.F.E. (Life Inventory Factors Evaluation). Certified as tchr., sch. psychologist, adminstr., Calif.; Licensed as Marriage, Family and Child Counselor, edn. psychologist, Calif. Office: 45024 3d St E Lancaster CA 93534 also 44000 Fenner Ave Lancaster CA 93534

EBERHARD, CHRISTINE LUCILLE, public relations executive; b. Fremont, Ohio, Jan. 12, 1951; d. Richard Lesley and Elva Lucille (Ransom) E. Student U. Am., Cholula, Mex. 1972-73; B.A. in Internat. Studies, Ohio State U. 1973. Account exec. News-Times Pub. Co., Anaheim, Calif. 1975-77; asst. dir. pub. relations and devel. Hawthorne Community Hosp. 1977-80; dir. pub. relations Presbyterian Intercommunity Hosp., Whittier, Calif. 1980-82; pres. CommuniQuest, Manhattan Beach, Calif., 1982—. Bd. dirs. Los Angeles South Bay-Harbor Industry Edn. Council 1978-81. Serving with USAR 1973—. Mem. Res. Officers Assn. (Outstanding Jr. Officer 1983), So. Calif. Soc. Hosp. Pub. Relations, Publicity Club Los Angeles, Internat. Assn. Bus. Communicators, Manhattan Beach C. of C., Los Angeles Area C. of C. Home: 115 1/2 31st St Hermosa Beach CA 90254 Office: 500 S Sepulveda 207 Manhattan Beach CA 90266

EBERHARDT, CLIFFORD ERIE, education specialist; b. Portland, Oreg., May 28, 1932; s. Ernest and Dorothy (Jackson) E.; m. Dorothy Mae Engel, Aug. 10, 1958; children—Ellen, Paul. B.S., Western Oreg. State Coll., 1953; M. Ed., U. Oreg., 1957; postgrad. Stanford U., 1962-63; D.Ed., Oreg. State U., 1972. Tchr. elem. schs., Oakridge and Portland, 1955-62; sch. administr. Lewis and Clark Sch., Astoria, Oreg., 1966-69; specialist for sex equity and linguistically different Oreg. Dept. Edn., Salem, 1971—. Vice pres. Cascade Area council Boy Scouts Am. Served with U.S. Army. Mem. Assn. for Supervision and Curriculum Devel., Am. Assn. Sch. Adminstrs., Am. Ednl. Research Assn., Phi Delta Kappa. Presbyterian. Home: 4585 Graber NE Salem OR 97305 Office: 700 Pringle Pkwy SE Salem OR 97310

EBERHARDT, LESTER LEE, quantitative ecologist; b. Valley City, N.D., Oct. 15, 1923; s. Lester W. and Gladys M. E.; m. Shirley L. Sage, Jan. 4, 1944; children—Laurie L. Eberhardt Birchill, Lester E., Lynn R. B.S. in Edn., N.D. State U., 1947; Ph.D. in Wildlife, Mich. State U., 1961. Cert. wildlife biologist. Ecologist, Mich. Dept. Conservation, 1953-61, U. Calif.-Berkeley, 1961-62, Gen. Electric Co., Richland, Wash., 1962-65, Battelle Meml. Inst.; ecologist Pacific N.W. Lab., Richland, 1965—, sr. staff scientist; mem. sci. adv. com. U.S. Marine Corps, 1975—. Served with U.S. Army, 1943-46. Mem. Ecol. Soc. Am., AAAS, Wildlife Soc., Biomed. Soc., Brit. Ecol. Soc., Am. Statis. Assn., Sigma Xi. Methodist. Contbr. numerous articles to profl. jours. Home: 2528 W Klamath Ave Kennewick WA 99336 Office: Battelle Meml Inst Richland WA

EBERT, BRUCE WALTER, psychologist; b. Elgin, Ill., Aug. 31, 1951; s. Donald Claude and Catherine (Hickey) E.; m. Pamela Pfitzer, July 11, 1981; children—Brent, Andrea. B.S., So. Ill. U., 1973; M.A., Sangamon State U., 1974; Ph.D., Calif. Sch. Profl. Psychology, 1979. Lic. psychologist, lic. marriage and family counselor, cert. community coll. tchr., cert. community coll. counselor, Calif. Intern, Midwest Inst. Psychodrama, Springfield, Ill., 1973-74; research asst. So. Ill. U., Carbondale, 1971-73, Med. Sch., 1973-74; program coordinator Merced (Calif.) Bridge Agy., 1974-82; commd. capt. U.S. Air Force, 1982; clin. psychologist U.S. Air Force Biomed. Sci. Corp. at USAF Regional Hosp., Eglin AFB, Calif., 1982—; instr. in ednl. psychology U. San Francisco, 1980-82. Mem. campaign com. Democratic Party, Merced. State of Calif. grantee, 1974-82; Merced County Mental Health grantee, 1974-82; Calif. Dept. Drug Abuse grantee, 1978, 79, 80, 81; Calif. Office Criminal Justice Planning, grantee, 1979, 80, 81. Mem. Am. Psychol. Assn., Assn. Air Force Psychologists, Calif. Coalition Rape Crisis Centers (founding), Mercy County Mental Health. Roman Catholic. Club: Eglin AFB Officers. Home: 2627 Saratoga Ct Merced CA 95340 Office: USAF Regional Hosp Eglin AFB CA

EBERT, ROBERT BALDWIN, safety engr.; b. Milw., Oct. 22, 1912; s. Walter R. and Elsie A. (Koepsel) E.; engring. degree U. Wis., 1934; architecture degree Harvard U., 1936; safety engring. degree N.Y. U., 1970; postgrad U. Chgo., 1970, Northwestern U., 1973; m. Charlotte King, Dec. 24, 1960; children—Anthony, Nancy, Michael, Timoth, Judith, Elisabeth. Asst. safety engr. Milw. Bd. Fire & Casualty Underwriters, 1940-44; chief photographer Honolulu Star-Bull., 1946-51; safety engr. State of Hawaii, 1951-61; chief safety U.S. Air Force, Hickam AFB, Hawaii, 1961-83; pres. Internat. Safety Cons., Honolulu, 1981—; pres. Pacific Prodns., Honolulu, 1981—; lectr. U. Hawaii. Taliesin fellow, 1932. Registered profl. engr., Hawaii; cert. safety mgr., master level; cert. safety profl. Mem. Am. Soc. Safety Engrs., Nat. Soc. Profl. Engrs., Vets. of Safety, Systems Safety Soc., Nat. Safety Mgmt. Soc. Republican. Lutheran. Clubs: Honolulu Press, Hawaii Swiss Soc. Author: Hawaii Foremen in Industry, 1956; Safety in Alaskan Schools, 1967. Home: 2710 Harbor Sq 700 Richards St Honolulu HI 96813 Office: PO Box 2881 Honolulu HI 96802

EBERTOWSKI, J. ROBERT, consciousness programmer; b. Milw., May 27, 1945; s. Robert Alexander and Dorothy Ann (Duray) E.; B.A., U. N.D., 1969; M.A., W. Ga. Coll., 1970. Advt. sales coordinator Davisons Dept. Stores, Atlanta, 1970-72; advt. dir. Massey Jr. Coll., Atlanta, 1972-74; sales communications designer, instr. Ga. State U., Atlanta, 1974-75; charter sales adminstr. World Airways, Inc., Oakland, Calif., 1975-76; dir. Barbizon Internat., San Francisco, 1975-76; founder, consciousness programmer Reality Cheque, San Francisco, 1976—; founder, pres. Channelled Communications, San Francisco, 1980—; v.p., treas., dir. Mustika-Hawaii, Honolulu, 1980—; sales rep. Inter-Continental Travel, San Francisco, 1982—. Recipient Nat. Editorial award, 1974. Democrat. Author: The Daemonic Aspects of Religion, 1970. Home: 2962 Clay St #4 San Francisco CA 94115 Office: 1772 Vallejo St San Francisco CA

EBLEN, JAMES HAMILTON, real estate broker, developer; b. Henderson, Ky., Oct. 2, 1929; s. Oscar Hamilton and Janet Reid (Brown) E.; A.A., Orange Coast Coll., 1971; student Lumbleau Real Estate Sch., 1968-71; grad. Realtors Inst., 1978; m. Velma Rawlings, Dec. 13, 1952; 1 son, Paul Hamilton. Salesman, Tarbell Realtors, Fountain Valley, Calif., 1968-70, sales mgr., Garden Grove, Calif., 1971; owner Eblen Real Estate, Fountain Valley, 1972; sales mgr. Percy Goodwin Co., Fountain Valley, 1973; owner Leadership Real Estate, Huntington Beach, Calif., 1973-74; mgr. Tobin Realty Sales, Huntington Beach, 1975-76; mng. partner E & E Devel. Co., San Jose, Calif., 1976-80; pres. Eblen Industries Inc., San Jose, Calif., 1979—. Co-chmn. Citizens Against New Taxes, 1975. Mem. Am. Security Council, Calif. Assn. Realtors (32d dist. chmn. legis. com., mem. polit. affairs lecture staff 1975-76), Huntington Beach-Fountain Valley Bd. Realtors (v.p. 1975, Realtor of Year 1975). Club: U.S. Senatorial. Office: 2355 Oakland Rd San Jose CA 95131

ECKE, BETTY TSENG YU-HO, artist, educator; b. Peking, China, Nov. 29, 1924. B.A., U. Peking, 1942; M.A., U. Hawaii, 1966; Ph.D., Inst. Fine Arts, NYU, 1972. Works exhibited in permanent collections: Honolulu Acad. Arts, Walker Art Ctr., Mpls., Nat. Mus. Modern Art, Stockholm, Mus. Cermuschi, Paris, Stanford (Calif.) Art Gallery; commns.: mural St. Katharine's Ch., Kaui, Hawaii, 1957; mural Manoa Chinese Pavilion, Honolulu, 1968; group shows: U. Ill.-Urbana, 1958, 61, 65, Carnegie Inst. Painting and Sculpture Internat., Pitts., 1961, 65, Kunstverein, Munich and Frankfort, Ger., Walker Art Ctr., San Francisco Mus. Art., others; instr. studio art Honolulu Acad. Art, 1950-63, cons. Chinese art, 1953—; assoc. prof. Chinese art history U. Hawaii, 1963-66; Fulbright visitor Chinese art history Acad. Bildenden Kunste and Univ., 1966-67; program chmn. art history U. Hawaii, also prof. art, 1973—. Recipient Am. Artists Western States award Stanford Art Gallery; NYU Founders Day award for outstanding scholarship, 1972. Mem. Honolulu Acad. Art, Am. Coll. Art Assn., Asian Soc., Asian and Pacific Art Assn. Hawaii (organizer 1972). Contbr. articles to profl. jours.; author: Some Contemporary Elements in Chinese Classic Pictorial Art, 1965, 71; Chinese Calligraphy; illustrator: The Analects of Confucious, 1970. Office: U Hawaii at Manoa Dept Art Honolulu HI 96822*

ECKERT, GEORGE ARTHUR, JR., stage dir.; b. Phila., Feb. 23, 1927; s. George Arthur and Alice Catherine (Watson) E. A.B., Brown U., 1950; postgrad. U.S. Army Command and Gen. Staff Coll., 1972. Prodn. stage mgr. Paper Mill Playhouse, Millburn, N.J., 1953-55, Griffith & Prince, N.Y.C., 1955-59, David Merrick, N.Y.C., 1960, 61, 65, Los Angeles Civic Light Opera, 1961-63, Los Angeles Greek Theatre Assn., 1966, 70, 71, Dome Prodns., Los Angeles, 1974—; dir. Starlight Musicals, Indpls., 1957, 58, Damn Yankees Australian Co., 1958, Circle Arts Theatre, San Diego, 1961, Valley Music Theatre, Los Angeles, 1964, 65, 66 and indsl. shows for Ford, 1963, Falstaff Brewing, 1964, Marathon Oil, 1964, Internat. Paper, 1969 and Exxon, 1971; asst. to Gene Kelly, 20th Century Fox Studios, 1966-69; spl. project officer Office of Sec. Army, 1972, 77-80. Served with AUS, 1945-46; to col., USAR, 1949-80. Decorated Legion of Merit, Meritorious Service medal. Mem. Soc. Stage Dirs. and Choreographers, Directors Guild Am., Actors Equity Assn., AFTRA, Am. Guild Mus. Artists, Acad. TV Arts and Scis., Soc. of Cincinnati, Soc. Mayflower Descs., SAR, Mil. Order World Wars, Res. Officers Assn. Republican. Episcopalian. Clubs: Army and Navy (Washington); The Lambs (N.Y.C.). Address: 1253 N Havenhurst Dr Hollywood CA 90046

ECKERT, JERRY BRUCE, agricultural development economics educator, consultant; b. Columbus, Ohio, Mar. 29, 1939; s. Phil S. and Eva L. (Moon) E.; m. Sue Taylor Radtke, June 29, 1963; children—Erin Lynn, William Scott; m. 2d, Betty Jo Fishburn Doss, May 21, 1977. B.S. with honors, U. Ariz., 1962; M.S., Stanford U., 1963; Ph.D., Mich. State U., 1970. Program specialist agrl. planning Ford Found., Pakistan, 1968-72; asst. prof. Colo. State U., 1972-77, assoc. prof., 1977-84, prof. agrl. devel. econs., 1984—; mem. Pakistan Water Mgmt. Team, 1972-76; co-dir. Lesotho Agrl. Sector Analysis Project, 1977-82; dir. Gambian Mixed Farming Project, 1980—; cons. fgn. govts., FAO, USAID, Brookings Instn., Agrl. Devel. Council. Vice pres., treas. Islamabad Internat. Sch. Bd., 1972-75; bd. dirs. Lesotho Internat. Sch. Served to 1st lt., USAF, 1963-65; Vietnam. Decorated Air Force Commendation Medal; recipient All-Pakistan Best Research award, 1974; Best Interdisciplinary Research award Colo. State U., 1978. Mem. Am. Agrl. Econs. Assn., Internat. Assn. Agrl. Econs., Am. Soc. Agronomy, Crop Sci. Soc. Am., Gamma Sigma Delta, Alpha Zeta. Author: contract and cons. reports; contbr. articles to profl. jours. Office: Agrl and Natural Resource Econs Dept Colorado State University Fort Collins CO 80523

ECKERT, ROBERT LEE, aeronautical engineer; b. Denver, Apr. 9, 1922; s. Bert Marvin and Marie E.; student aero. engring. Aero Tech. Inst., 1940-42; m. Rose McGahan, Mar. 4, 1944; children—Ron, Darla. Welding and engring. positions various cos., Los Angeles, 1946-52; with N. Am. space ops. Rockwell Internat., Downey, Calif., 1952—, engr. supr. environ. control system, 1969-75, research engr., environ. control system, space shuttle program, 1975—; cons. in field. Served with USAAF, 1943-46. Recipient Tech. Utilization award NASA, 1968, 69, 71. Republican. Mem. Grace Brethren Ch. Patentee cyrogentic, pneumatic, mech. devices. Home: 11231 Foster Rd Los Alamitos CA 90720 Office: 12214 Lakewood Blvd Downey CA 91720

ECKERT, ROSS DOUD, economist, educator, consultant; b. Los Angeles, Nov. 11, 1941; s. Chester Harold and Lillian B. (Doud) E.; m. Enid Fairclough, Nov. 15, 1975. B.A., UCLA, 1963, M.A., 1964, Ph.D., 1968. Asst. prof. econs. U. So. Calif., 1969-74, assoc. prof., 1974-80; prof. econs. Claremont McKenna Coll., 1980—, chmn. dept. econs., 1980—; economist TEMPO Ctr. Advanced Studies, Gen. Electric Corp., Santa Barbara, Calif.; vis. research fellow Hoover Inst., Stanford U., 1974-75; cons. govt. agys. Woodrow Wilson Nat. fellow, 1963-64. Mem. Am. Econ. Assn., Western Econ. Assn., Phi Beta Kappa. Author several books; contbr. articles to profl. jours. Office: Dept Econs Bauer Ctr Claremont McKenna Coll Claremont CA 91711

ECKHARDT, JOHN ROBERT, water resources engineer, civil engineer; b. Greeley, Colo., Sept. 21, 1948; s. Robert Arthur and Elsie Pearl (Miller) E.; m. Trudy Christine Pritchard, June 21, 1969; children—Heidi Lynn, Heather Johnn. B.S. in Civil Engring. with high distinction, Colo. State U., 1970, M.S. in Civil Engring., 1976. Registered profl. engr., Colo. Design engr. Standard Oil Co. Calif., San Francisco, 1970-71; design, resident, project engr. NHPQ, Greeley, 1971-74; water resources engr. Engrs. Office, State of Colo., Denver, 1976, with No. Colo. Water Conservancy Dist., Loveland, 1976—, div. head engring. and computer services, 1980—; guest lectr. in field; life mem. U.S. Com. on Irrigation, Drainage and Flood Control. Active Girl Scouts U.S.A., 1976—, Monroe Elem. Sch. PTO, Loveland. Edward B. House scholar Colo. State U., 1969. Mem. ASCE, Am. Water Works Assn., Kappa Mu Epsilon, Chi Epsilon, Sigma Tau, Phi Kappa Phi. Lutheran. Club: Loveland Swim. Home: 1637 Pinyon Ct Loveland CO 80537 Office: No Colo Water Conservancy Dist PO Box 679 Loveland CO 80537

ECKHARDT, WILLIAM BOYDEN, credit union exec.; b. Bellefonte, Pa., Aug. 31, 1949; s. Boyden and Maxine Alice (Young) E.; B.S. in Bus. Adminstrn., Oreg. State U., 1971. Adminstrv. officer Alaska U.S.A. Fed. Credit Union, Anchorage, 1971-72, ops. mgr., 1972-74, asst. gen. mgr., 1974-79, gen. mgr., 1979—; chmn. Alaska Option Services Corp.; dir. Alaska League Services Corp. Mem. Credit Union Execs. Soc. (pres. Alaska council 1975—), Alaska Credit Union League (pres. Anchorage chpt. 1979-81), Credit Union Nat. Assn. (alt. dir.). Club: Elks. Home: SRA Box 4216 Anchorage AK 99502 Office: Mail Pouch 6613 777 Juneau St Anchorage AK 99502

ECKLE, THOMAS KEITH, psychologist; b. Pitts., Dec. 25, 1939; s. Jacob H. and Willa C. (Jarrett) E.; student Modesto (Calif.) Jr. Coll., 1959; B.A., Calif. State U., Stanislaus, 1972, M.S., 1976; m. Cathrin Rodgers, Aug. 15, 1979; 1 son, Joshua. Instr. psychology Modesto Jr. Coll., 1972—; cons. human sexuality. Served with AUS, 1962-65. Mem. Am. Psychol. Assn., NEA, Calif. Tchrs. Assn., sex Edn. and Information Council U.S., Yosemite Faculty Assn., Am. Assn. Sex Educators, Counselors and Therapists. Author: Explorations in Human Sexual Behavior, in progress; cons. editor, advisor: Human Sexuality Readings, 1976—. Home: 3716 Corte Madera Ave Modesto CA 95350 Office: Modesto Jr College College Ave Modesto CA 95350

ECKS, JOHN ALFRED, psychiatrist; b. Milw., May 31, 1935; s. Alfred William and Elizabeth Bernadette (Kupecky) E.; M.D., Marquette U., 1960; children—Michael, Margaret, Elizabeth, Victoria. Intern, Milw. County Gen. Hosp.; resident in psychiatry Ill. State Psychiat. Inst., Chgo., 1962-64; dir. program devel. DuPage County Mental Health Clinic, Wheaton, Ill., 1965-68; chief inpatient services San Diego County Mental Health Dept., 1968-71; practice medicine specializing in psychiatry, Coronado, Calif., 1970—; asst. clin. prof. psychiatry Sch. Medicine, U. Calif., San Diego; mem. staffs Univ., Mercy, Harbor View, Vista Hill, Coronado, Scripps hosps.; mem. adv. bd. San Diego County Mental Health Dept., 1973-76. Fellow Am. Psychiat. Assn.; mem. AMA, Calif. Med. Assn., San Diego County Med. Soc., Mem. San Diego Psychiat. Soc. (pres. 1973-74), Alpha Sigma Nu. Home: 930 J Ave Coronado CA 92118 Office: 1023 5th St Coronado CA 92118

ECKSTEIN, CHARLES RICHARD, anesthesiologist; b. Shullsburg, Wis., Jan. 29, 1934; s. Wilbur LeRoy and Catherine Eva (Sarff) E.; m. Anna Mae Irwin, Feb. 6, 1960; children—David, James, Diane. B.S, U. Wis., 1956, M.D., 1959. Diplomate Am. Bd. Anesthesiology. Intern St. Luke's Hosp., Denver, 1959-60; resident in anesthesiology U. Minn., 1960-62; mem. staff Grossmont Hosp. Served to lt., M.C., USN, 1962-64. Fellow Am. Coll. Anesthesiologists; mem. Calif. Soc. Anesthesiologists, Calif. League Anesthesiologists, Am. Soc. Anesthesiologists. Office: 10815 Melva Rd La Mesa CA 92041

ECONOMAKOS, LAURA LUVERNE, accountant; b. Denver, Nov. 18, 1951; d. George Edward and Florence Effie (Washburn) Laffen; m. Daniel Loveland, June, 1970; m. 2d, Ronald Economakos (dec.). B.S. in Acctg., U. Colo.-Denver, 1979. C.P.A., Colo. With Halliburton, Hunter & Assocs., Denver, 1979; with Touche Ross & Co., Denver, 1980-81; pvt. practice pub. acctg., Denver, 1982—. Mem. Colo. Soc. C.P.A.s. Home and Office: 2796 S Lowell Blvd Denver CO 80236

EDABURN TAYLOR, SHARON LEE, museum director; b. Lennox, Calif., Aug. 31, 1946; d. Hugh and Laura Bernice (Caldwell) E.; m. Gregory Alan Taylor, Dec. 31, 1982. A.A., Am. River Coll., 1966; B.A., Sacramento State Coll., 1970, M.A., Calif. State U.-Sacramento, 1982. Dispatcher, Citrus Heights (Calif.) Fire Dept., 1966-70; dispatcher Reno Police Dept., 1972-75; firefighter U.S. Forest Service, Bridgeport, Calif., 1976; interpretive specialist Calif. State R.R. Mus., Sacramento, 1977-78; mus. dir., curator Churchill County Mus. and Archive, Fellon, Nev., 1978—; guest lectr. U. Nev., Reno and Las Vegas, 1978—; dir. Churchill County Oral History Project, 1979—. Chmn., Carson City Dist. Bur. Land Mgmt. Citizens Adv. Council, 1980-82. Mem. Soc. Indsl. Archeology, Am. Assn. State and Local History, Conf. Intermountain Archivists, Nev. Archaeol. Assn. (treas.), Nev. Council Profl. Archaeologists (treas.), Nev. Natural History Assn. (dir.). Democrat. Mem. Unity Ch. Office: 1050 S Maine St Fallon NV 89406

EDAMURA, FRED YOSHIHIRO, chemist; b. Vancouver, B.C., Can., Jan. 25, 1939; s. Tomegoro and Setsuko (Iwasaki) E.; B.S., U. Alt., 1960; M.S., Johns Hopkins U., 1962, Ph.D., 1966; m. Marian S. Gorsuch, Aug. 11, 1962; children—Stuart, Wendy, Michael, Diana. Chemist, Dow Chem. Co., Midland, Mich., 1965-72, research specialist, Walnut Creek, Calif., 1972-74, project mgr., Pittsburg, Calif., 1974-79, group leader, 1979-82, research mgr. analysis dept., 1982—. Mem. Am. Chem. Soc., Sigma Xi. Baptist. Patentee in agrl. fungicides and herbicides. Home: 3891 Logan Ct Concord CA 94519 Office: Dow Chem Co Western Div Research and Devel PO Box 1398 Pittsburg CA 94565

EDDE, HOWARD JASPER, cons. engring. co. exec.; b. Page City, Kans., Dec. 14, 1937; s. Gilbert H. and Jennie M. (Foulke) E.; B.S.C.E., Kans. State U., 1959; M.S.C.E., U. Kans., 1961; Ph.D., U. Tex., 1967; m. Marilyn Ann Scheleen, Sept. 5, 1961; children—Michael, Heather, Sonja. Civil engr. Kans. Hwy. Commn., 1959-60; research engr. Marley Co., Kansas City, Kans., 1961-62; field engr. Nat. Council for Stream Improvement, Balt., 1962-64, 67-70; project engr. Roy F. Weston Inc., West Chester, Pa., 1966-67; v.p., mgr. environ. services EKONO OY, Helsinki, 1970-72, Seattle, 1972-74; pres. Howard Edde, Inc., cons. engrs., Bellevue, Wash., 1974—; prof. dept. civil engring. U. Wash., Seattle, 1972-83. Diplomate Am. Acad. Environ. Engrs.; registered profl. engr., Wash., Md., Tex., Va., N.C., Pa., Alaska. Fellow ASCE TAPPI (chmn. water quality com.), Water Pollution Control Fedn. Lutheran. Club: Neptune Sailing (pres. 1979-81). Contbr. numerous articles on waste water treatment and environ. engring. to profl. jours.; developer aerated lagoon wastewater treatment process. Home: 3001 164th Pl NE Bellevue WA 98008 Office: 15436 NE Bellevue-Redmond Rd Suite 201 Redmond WA 98052

EDDINGS, JERRY, real estate broker; b. Mountain Home, Ark., Mar. 31, 1907; s. George W. and Dora Belle (Roe) E.; m. Carrie Ethel Turner, Feb. 28, 1963; 1 dau., Marcella Eddings Spoutz. Student Okla. Comml. Coll., Shawnee, 1924, LaSalle Extension U., 1930-32, Internat. Corr. Schs., 1929-30. Employed in Okla. oil fields, 1923-25; owner, operator filling sta. and garage, Cromwell, Okla., 1926-27; mgr. N.A.P.A. Auto Parks, Seminole, Okla., 1928; salesman Burroughs Adding Machine Co., 1929-32; carload salesman Morton Salt Co., 1932-37; mgr. br. automobile dealership, Hawthorne, Calif., 1938-40; owner automobile agy., Hawthorne, 1940-42; owner, operator Eddings Bros. Auto Parts, 1942-52; used car dealer, Los Angeles, 1952-53; salesman Heidelberg Printing Press, 1954-57; gen. sales man. Madera Ranchos subdiv., Madera, Calif., 1958-62; real estate broker, prin. Jerry Eddings Realtors, Madera, 1962—; owner, operator motels in Fresno, Calif., 1972—; owner, operator Permotile Roofs, 1977-80. Mem. Fresno Bd. Realtors, Madera Bd. Realtors, Madera C. of C. Republican. Mem. Ch. of Religious Science. Club: Exchange (pres. 1969-70) (Fresno). Office: 10648 Hwy 41 Madera CA 93637

EDDY, GLADYS LOUISE, educator; b. Castle Rock, Colo., Dec. 25, 1915; d. William Adam and Jessie Louise (Cozens) Shellabarger; m. Willard O. Eddy, Aug. 21, 1938; children—Sandra Carol, William Radford. B.S. in Bus. Adminstrn., U. Denver, 1937. Asst. dept. rural and vocat. edn. Colo. State U., Ft. Collins, 1937-42, sec. to pres., 1945-46, instr. coll. bus., 1957-62, 67-79, asst. prof., 1979—; instr. U.S Army Air

Force Clerical Sch., Ft. Collins, 1945-46; tchr. adult and summer schs. Poudre R-1 Sch. Dist., Ft. Collins, 1953-63; cons., lectr. bus. edn. and office mgmt. Mem. Ft. Collins Parks and Recreation Commn., 1963-77, LWV, 1952-60, Poudre R-1 Sch. Dist. Bd. Edn., 1971-83, Nat. Adv. Council Vocat. Edn., 1982-84. Named Colo. State U. Panhellenic Assn. Prof. of Year, 1962, Colo. State U. Outstanding Woman Tchr., 1973, Outstanding Woman of Larimer County, 1974; recipient intermountain sect. U.S. Tennis Assn. Hyram Cannon award, 1970, Colo. Park and Recreation Soc. award for outstanding service, 1977. Mem. Colo. State U. Women's Assn. (pres. 1955-56), Colo. Assn. Sch. Bds. (dir., pres. 1979), Nat. Sch. Bds. Assn. (del. assembly 1979, 80), Colo. Tennis Assn. (dir. 1972-76, Bud Robineau award 1975), AAUW, Mortar Bd. (sect. coordinator 1973-82, nat. dir. programming), Delta Kappa Gamma, Phi Chi Theta, Kappa Kelta Pi, Sigma Kappa. Republican. Episcopalian. Clubs: Ft. Collins Country, Order Eastern Star. Home: 509 Remington Fort Collins CO 80524 Office: 109 C Clark Bldg Colo State U Fort Collins CO 80523

EDELSTEIN, RONALD A(LAN), educational psychologist; b. Toledo, May 16, 1952; s. Irvin L. and Jeanett (Levine) E. B.A. in Polit. Sci., U. Calif.-Berkeley, 1974; M.A. in Ednl. Psychology, UCLA, 1976, Ed.D. in Ednl. Psychology, 1981. Tchr., Los Angeles Unified Sch. Dist., 1975-78; researcher UCLA Psychol. and Counseling Services, 1977-78; asst. prof. family medicine Charles Drew Med. Sch., 1978—. Mem. Am. Psychol. Assn., Am. Ednl. Research Assn. Home: 3457 Greenfield Los Angeles CA 90034

EDELSTEIN, ROSE MARIE, nurse educator, consultant; b. Drake, N.D., Mar. 3, 1935; d. Francis Jerome and Myrtle Josephine (Merbach) Hublou; m. Harry George Edelstein, June 22, 1957; children—Julie, Lori, Lynn, Toni Anne. B.S. in Nursing, St. Teresa's Coll., 1956; M.A. in Edn., Holy Names Coll., 1977; Ed.D., U. San Francisco, 1982; cert. public health nurse U. Calif., Berkeley, 1972. Dir., clin. supr. San Francisco Sch. for Health Professions, 1971-74, Rancho Arroyo Sch. of Vocat. Nursing, Sacramento, 1974-75; intensive care nurse Kaiser-Permanente Hosp., San Rafael, Calif., 1976-77; dir. inservice edn. Ross Hosp., Calif., 1977-78; asso. dir. nursing nursing edn. St. Francis Meml. Hosp., San Francisco, 1978—; cons. in field; instr. CPR. Served to maj. USAR Med. Res. Mem. Calif. Nurses Assn., Am. Heart Assn., Sigma Theta Tau. Roman Catholic. Author: (with Jane F. Lee) Acupuncture Atlas, 1974; The Influence of Motivator and Hygiene Factors in Job Changes by Graduate Registered Nurses, 1977; Effects of Two Educational Methods Upon Retention of Knowledge in Pharmacology, 1981. Home: 10 Grande Paseo San Rafael CA 94903 Office: 900 Hyde St San Francisco CA 94109

EDEN, RAYMOND LER, assn. exec.; b. Lee, Ill., July 19, 1925; s. S. Bennie and Hannah (Edwards) E.; B.S., No. Ill. U., 1950 with high honors; postgrad. Northwestern U., 1950, N.Y. U., 1955, U. Chgo., 1961, U. So. Calif., 1973; m. Ellen M. Mercer, Aug. 17, 1945; 1 son, Steven M. Exec. sec. Crippled Children's Center, Peoria, Ill., 1953-59; exec. dir. Crippled Children's Service, Milw., 1959-62, Ill. Heart Assn., Springfield, 1962-66, Calif. Heart Assn., San Francisco, 1966-69; adminstr. San Mateo (Calif.) Med. Clinic, 1969-70; exec. v.p. Am. Heart Assn., Los Angeles, 1970—. Chmn. objectives com. Calif. Regional Med. Program, 1968-73; v.p. Comprehensive Health Planning Agy., 1973-75; bd. dirs. UCLA Unicamp, 1974-76, Comprehensive Health Planning Council of Los Angeles County, 1975-77; mem. adv. com. UCLA Profl. Designation program for Voluntary Agy. Execs., 1972-74; faculty Center for Non-Profit Mgmt., 1978-82; pres. Council on Vol. Health Agys., Los Angeles, 1976-79, Los Angeles CPR Consortium, 1979-81; mem. Cardiac Care com. State of Calif., 1980-83; treas., chmn. fin. com. Little Co. of Mary Hosp., Torrance, 1977-81; chmn. South Bay (Los Angeles) Com. for Pres. Ford, 1976; mem. Atty. Gen.'s Task Force on Solicitations, 1977; chmn. Younger for Gov. Com., South Bay, 1978; chmn. bd. trustees Neighborhood Ch., Palos Verdes Estates, Calif., 1975; mem. Claremont Grad. Sch. Exec. Program adv. council, 1979-82; mem. clean air com., Los Angeles Area C. of C., 1980-82. Served with U.S. Army, 1944-46. Decorated Purple Heart, Bronze Star. Soc. Heart Assn. Profl. Staff fellow, 1980-81, 82-83; Alpha Gamma Delta Fellow award, 1955. Mem. Soc. Heart Assn. Profl. Staff (pres. 1981-82), Nat. Assn. Social Workers, Acad. Cert. Social Workers, So. Calif. Assn. Execs., Los Angeles Area C. of C., Sigma Alpha Eta. Republican. Clubs: Rotary, California, Masons, Shriners. Home: 30317 Via Cambron Rancho Palos Verdes Estates CA 90274 Office: 2405 W 8th St Los Angeles CA 90057

EDENS, GARY DENTON, broadcast company executive; b. Asheville, N.C., Jan. 6, 1942; s. James Edwin and Pauline Amanda (New) E.; m. Hannah Suellen Walter, Aug. 21, 1965; children—Ashley Elizabeth, Emily Blair. B.S., U. N.C., 1964. Account exec. PAMS Prodns., Dallas, 1965-67; account exec. Sta. WKIX, Raleigh, N.C., 1967-69; gen. mgr. Sta. KOY, Phoenix, 1970-81; sr. v.p. Harte-Hanks Radio, Inc., Phoenix, 1978-81, pres., chief exec. officer, 1981—; dir. Gt. Western Bank & Trust Ariz. Bd. dirs. Valley Big Bros., 1972—, Ariz. State U. Found., 1979—, COMPAS, 1979—, Men's Arts Council, 1975-78. Named One of Three Outstanding Young Men, Phoenix Jaycees, 1973. Mem. Phoenix Execs. Club (pres. 1976), Nat. Radio Broadcasters Assn. (dir. 1981—), Radio Advt. Bur. (dir. 1981—). Republican. Methodist. Clubs: Phoenix Country, Univ. Phoenix. Office: 840 N Central Ave Phoenix AZ 85004

EDGAR, BRYAN CYRUS, dentist; b. Kamloops, B.C., Can., Apr. 19, 1950; came to U.S., 1957, naturalized, 1968; s. Arthur Osmund and Laura Belle (Lapsley) E.; m. Linda Carol Johansen, June 23, 1973; 1 son, David. B.S. with distinction in Zoology, U. Wash., 1972, D.D.S., 1976. Gen. practice resident Irwin Army Hosp., Ft. Riley, Kans., 1976-77; dentist Madigan Army Med. Ctr., 1977-80; pvt. practice dentistry, Federal Way, Wash., 1979-81; pres. Bryan C. Edgar, D.D.S., P.S., Federal Way, 1981—; bus. and entrepreneurship cons.; owner Profl. Devel. Systems. Served with Dental Corps, U.S. Army, 1976-80. Mem. Bible Study Fellowship, Am. Med. Joggers Assn., Acad. Gen. Dentistry, ADA, Am. Acad. Periodontology, Seattle-King County Dental Soc., Wash. State Dental Assn., Pacific N.W. Study Club (sec.). Office: 2315 SW 320th St Federal Way WA 98003

EDGAR, JAMES MACMILLAN, JR., management consultant; b. N.Y.C., Nov. 7, 1936; s. James Macmillan Edgar and Lilyan (McCann) E.; B. Chem. Engring., Cornell U., 1959, M.B.A. with distinction, 1960; m. Judith Frances Storey, June 28, 1958; children—Suzanne Lynn, James Macmillan, Gordon Stuart. New product rep. E.I. duPont Nemours, Wilmington, Del., 1960-63, mktg. services rep., 1963-64; with Touche Ross & Co., 1964-78, mgr., Detroit, 1966-68, partner, 1968-71, partner in charge, mgmt. services ops. for No. Calif. and Hawaii, San Francisco, 1971-78, partner Western regional mgmt. services, 1978; prin. Edgar, Dunn & Co., Inc., San Francisco, 1978—; mem. San Francisco Mayor's Fin. Adv. Com., 1976—, mem. exec. com., 1978—, chmn. revenue study com., 1981—; chmn. city budget com. San Francisco C. of C., 1976-79. Recipient Award of Merit for outstanding public service City and County of San Francisco, 1978; Honor award for outstanding contbns. to profl. mgmt. Grad. Sch. Bus. and Public Adminstrn., Cornell U., 1978. C.P.A., cert. mgmt. cons. Mem. Assn. Corp. Growth (v.p. membership San Francisco chpt. 1979-81, v.p. programs 1981-82, pres. 1982-83, nat. bd. dirs. 1983—), Am. Inst. C.P.A.s, Calif. Soc. C.P.A.s, Am. Mktg. Assn., Inst. Mgmt. Cons. (regional v.p. 1973-80, dir. 1975-77, bd. v.p. 1977-80). Clubs: Univ., Meadow (fin. com. 1980—), Commonwealth of San Francisco. Patentee nonwoven fabrics. Home: 10 Buckeye Way Kentfield CA 94904 Office: One Market Plaza San Francisco CA 94105

EDGAR, THOMAS EVERETT, psychology educator; b. Kelso, Wash., Jan. 30, 1925; s. Clyde Howard and Opal Dora (Buckingham) E.; 1 son, Thomas A. B.S., Wash. State U., 1950, B.Ed., 1953; M.A., U. Wyo., 1965, Ed.D. in Counselor Edn., 1965; postgrad. Alfred Adler Inst., Chgo., 1974-75. Lic. psychologist, Idaho. Tchr. English, Clover Park High Sch., Washington, 1950-58, Univ. Place High Sch., Washington, 1959-62; dir. Bur. Ednl. Research, assoc. prof. ednl. psychology SUNY-Albany, 1965-66; assoc. prof. Idaho State U., 1966, chmn. dept. edn., 1967-68, prof. counselor edn., 1967—, dir. Family Edn. Ctr., 1975—; cons.; vice chmn. Nat. Bd. Cert. Counselors, 1982—. Chmn. Counselor Licensure Polit. Com., 1981-82. Served to sgt. U.S. Army, 1941-43; Fulbright Hayes sr. lectr., 1967-68; NDEA doctoral fellow, 1962-65; Ednl. Leaders fellow N.W. Regional Ednl. and Research Lab., 1980-81. Mem. Idaho Soc. Individual Psychology, Am. Personnel and Guidance Assn., Assn. Counselor Edn. and Supervision, N.Am. Soc. Adlerian Psychology (nat. treas. 1979-80), Idaho Personnel and Guidance Assn. (pres. 1981-82, Disting. Service award 1973-74). Cons. editor Counselor Edn. and Supervision, 1976-78, The Individual Psychologist, 1980-82; mem. editorial bd. Jour. Individual Psychology, 1982—; contbr. articles to profl. jours. Home: 419 S Garfield St Apt 3 Pocatello ID 83204 Office: Box 8225 Idaho State U Pocatello ID 83209

EDGE, JERRY THOMAS, turbine company official; b. Roseboro, N.C., Jan 17, 1941; s. Shelton Britt and Ella C. (Bunnell) E.; m. Ulrike Macy, Sept. 10, 1966; children—Russell, Melissa, Christina. B.S., U. N.C., 1966; M.B.A., Ga. State U., 1969; postgrad. George Washington U., 1971-76. Track supr. So. Ry., Ga., 1966-68, recruiter, 1969-70, compensation analyst, 1970-73, mgr. salary adminstrn., 1973-76; dir. compensation Morrison, Inc., 1976-79; mgr. salaried personnel Solar Turbines, Inc., San Diego, 1979-82, mgr. employee relations, 1982—; instr. San Diego State U., Am. Compensation Assn.; dir. Telesec Temporaries, Inc. Former mem. bd. dirs. Goodwill Industries; mem. pension com. Urban League. Served with USAF, 1958-62. Mem. Am. Compensation Assn. (life mem.; cert. compensation profl., chmn. bd. 1982), Am. Soc. Personnel Adminstrn. Republican. Presbyterian (elder). Home: 2210 Levante St Carlsbad CA 92008 Office: 2200 Pacific Hwy San Diego CA 92138

EDGINGTON, CLO EARL, govt. ofcl.; b. Findlay, Ohio, Nov. 20, 1938; s. Clo Earl and Mary Elizabeth (Fellabaum) E.; student U.S. Mil. Acad., 1956-59; B.A. in History, U. San Diego, 1970, M.A. in History, 1975; M.P.A., San Diego State U., 1974; m. Lucille Carolyn Edgington, June 5, 1965; children—Chris Eileen, Clo Earl, Laura Elizabeth. With County of San Diego, 1970-81, personnel and tng. adminstr. dept. health services, 1975-81; asst. dir. personnel Port of San Diego, 1981—; adj. prof. mgmt. Nat. U. San Diego, 1978—. Served with USN, 1961-65. Mem. Am. Soc. Personnel Adminstrn., Am. Soc. Tng. and Devel., Am. Mgmt. Assn., Personnel Mgmt. Assn. San Diego. Republican. Presbyterian. Home: 3811 Garden Ln San Diego CA 92106 Office: 3165 Pacific Hwy San Diego CA 92101

EDLUND, LAWRENCE RONALD, insurance company executive, realtor; b. Auburn, Wash., Jan. 11, 1942; s. John Victor and Pauline Slyvia E.; m. Kathleen Marie Taylor, Dec. 26, 1970; children—Jennifer Dyan, Philip Lawrence. B.A. in Bus. Adminstrn., U. Puget Sound, 1964. C.P.A., Wash.; lic. Realtor, Wash.; lic. massage therapist, Wash. Acct., Johnson, Paulson & Stolz (now Ernst & Whinney), Tacoma, 1965-66; acctg. supr. Weyerhaeuser Co., Tacoma, 1966-70; acctg. mgr. Mut. of Enumclaw Ins. Co. (Wash.), 1970-81, acct., treas., controller, 1981—. Bd. dirs., treas. Luth. Community Services. Mem. Am. Inst. C.P.A.s, Wash. Soc. C.P.A.s, Ins. Acctg. Statis. Assn. (past chpt. pres.), Sigma Alpha Epsilon, Alpha Kappa Psi (past pres.). Home: 505 103d St S Tacoma WA 98444 Office: Mutual of Enumclaw 1460 Wells St Enumclaw WA 98022

EDMISTON, JOSEPH TASKER, state ofcl.; b. Monterey Park, Calif., Oct. 27, 1948; s. Tasker Lee and Beula Viola (Bates) E.; A.A., East Los Angeles Coll., 1968; A.B., U. So. Calif., 1970. Mgr. of ct. process Roy Rottner & Associates, Hollywood, Calif., 1970-73; So. Calif Coastal coordinator Sierra Club, Los Angeles, 1973-76, energy coordinator, Sacramento, Calif., 1976-77; dir. State of Calif. Santa Monica Mountains Land Acquisition Program, 1979-80; exec. dir. Santa Monica Mountains Comprehensive Planning Commn., Los Angeles, 1977-79; exec. dir. Santa Monica Mountains Conservancy, State of Calif., 1980—. Pres. Associated Students, East Los Angeles Coll., 1968. Recipient Weldon Heald Conservation award Sierra Club, 1970. Mem. Marine Tech. Soc. (dir. Los Angeles region sect. 1975-77), Coastal Soc., Phi Rho Pi, Delta Sigma Rho, Tau Kappa Alpha. Democrat. Home: 24 Brooks Ave Venice CA 90291 Office: 107 S Broadway Los Angeles CA 90012

EDMONDS, CHARLES HENRY, publisher; b. Lakewood, Ohio, Sept. 4, 1919; s. Howard H. and Mary Frances (Galena) E.; student Woodbury Bus. Coll., 1939-40; m. Ruth Audrey Windfelder, Nov. 4, 1938; children—Joan Dickey, Charles Henry, Carolyn Anne, Dianne Marie. Owner, Shoreline Transp. Co., Los Angeles, 1946-58; mgr. transp. Purity Food Stores, Burlingame, Calif., 1958-61; supr. Calif. Motor Express, San Jose, 1961-64; account exec. Don Wright Assos., Oakland, Calif., 1964-65; sales mgr. Western U.S., Shippers Guide Co., Chgo., 1965-70; pub. No. Calif. Retailer, San Jose, 1970—. Recipient journalism awards various orgns. Republican. Roman Catholic. Contbr. articles to profl. jours. Home: 1442 Sierra Creek Way San Jose CA 95132

EDMONDS, IVY GORDON, author; b. Frost, Tex., Feb. 15, 1917; s. Ivy Gordon and Delia Louella (Shumate) E.; student pub. schs.; m. Reiko Mimura, July 12, 1956; 1 dau., Annette. Freelance writer; author books including: Ooka the Wise, 1961; The Bounty's Boy, 1963; Joel of the Hanging Gardens, 1966; Trickster Tales, 1966; Taiwan—the Other China, 1971; The Magic Man, 1972; Mao's Long March, 1973; Motorcycling for Beginners, 1973; Micronesia, 1974; Pakistan, Land of Mystery, Tragedy and Courage, 1974; Automotive Tuneups for Beginners, 1974; Ethiopia, 1975; The Magic Makers, 1976; The Shah of Iran, 1976; Allah's Oil: Mid-East Petroleum, 1976; Second Sight, 1977; Motorcycle Racing for Beginners, 1977; Islam, 1977; Buddhism, 1978; The Mysteries of Troy, 1977; Big U Universal in the Silent Days, 1977; D.D. Home, 1978; Bicycle Motocross, 1979; Girls Who Talked to Ghosts, 1979; The Magic Brothers, 1979; (with William H. Gebhardt) Broadcasting for Beginners, 1980; (with Reiko Mimura) The Oscar Directors, 1980; The Mysteries of Homer's Greeks, 1981; The Kings of Black Magic, 1981; Funny Car Racing for Beginners, 1982; author textbooks: (with Ronald Gonzales) Understanding Your Car, 1975, Introduction to Welding, 1975; pub. relations mgr. Northrop Corp., Anaheim, Calif., 1968-79, indsl. editor, Hawthorne, Calif., 1979—. Served with USAAF, 1940-45, USAF, 1946-63. Decorated D.F.C., Air medals, Bronze Star. Mem. Authors' Guild, Authors' League Am. Home: 5801 Shirl St Cypress CA 90630 Office: Northrop Corp 500 E Orangethorpe St Anaheim CA 92801

EDMONDSON, WILLIAM BRAXTON, editor, publisher; b. Clayton, Mo., Sept. 21, 1906; s. John Caswell and Almeda Jane (Williams) E.; student coll., marine tech. schs.; m. Lillian Anna Cuddy, Dec. 13, 1942; 1 son, William Braxton II. Enlisted in U.S. Marine Corps, 1928, advanced through grades to chief warrant officer, 1961; assigned aviation intelligence and ops., 1943-52, utilities officer, 1952-65, ret., 1965; editor, pub. Solar Energy Digest, San Diego, 1973—. Mem. ASME, Internat. Solar Energy Soc. (past dir. Am. sect.), Am. Soc. Heating, Refrigerating and Air Conditioning Engrs., AAAS. Democrat. Baptist. Club: Marine Officers. Asso. editor The Leatherneck, semi-ofcl. jour. U.S. Marine Corps, 1930-32. Patentee in field. Office: PO Box 17776 San Diego CA 92117

EDMONSON, JACK WILLIS EVERETT, physicist; b. Big Sandy, Tex., Apr. 15, 1923; s. Charles Lake and Winnie (Gore) E.; B.S., Tex. Coll. Arts and Industries, 1947, M.S., 1951; m. Mattie Sue Deville, Nov. 17, 1951; children—Jacqueline Sue, Jack Willis Everett, Beverly Jo, Charles Edward, David Ray, Mary Ann, Robert Don, Richard Deville. With geophys. dept. Shell Oil Co., Houston, Corpus Christi, 1947-51; asso. P.E. Narvarte, geophys. cons., San Antonio, 1951-67; now physicist, computer programming Naval Torpedo Sta., Keyport, Wash. Served with USAAF, 1943-46. Mem. Soc. Exploration Geophysicists, Am. Geophys. Union, IEEE, Geophys. Soc. S. Tex. (past pres.). Democrat. Home: 26715 Canalta Way NW Poulsbo WA 98370 Office: Research and Engring Dept Naval Torpedo Sta Keyport WA 98345

EDMUND, RUDOLPH WILLIAM, coll. adminstr.; b. Lockridge, Iowa, Mar. 9, 1910; s. Amos Daniel and Minnie Elizabeth (Odean) E.; A.B., Augustana Coll., 1934; M.S., State U. Iowa, 1938, Ph.D., 1940; D.Sc. (hon.), Calif. Luth. Coll., 1980; m. Doris Irene Swanson, June 8, 1939; children—Diane (Mrs. Jack Griffin), Janice (Mrs. Steven Smith), Linda (Mrs. David Kuntzman). Instr. Coe Coll., 1939-40; geologist Shell Oil Co., Tulsa, 1940-45, Globe Oil & Refining Co., Oklahoma City, 1945-48, 51-53; prof. Augustana Coll., 1948-51, 61-69; v.p. Sohio Petroleum Co., Oklahoma City, 1953-60; v.p. acad. affairs Calif. Luth. Coll., Thousand Oaks, 1969-74, dir. life long learning, prof. geology, 1974-80, emeritus, 1980—; partner Harris & Edmund Geol. Cons., Oklahoma City, 1945-46. Active in restructuring grad. record exam. in geology Ednl. Testing Service, 1968-72. Bd. dirs. Augustana Research Found., 1962-69; mem. adv. bd. Sch. Engring., Okla. State U., 1954-60; bd. dirs. Davenport Pub. Mus., 1964-69, vice chmn., 1968; bd. regents Calif. Luth. Coll., 1982—. Recipient outstanding service award Augustana Coll., 1960. Fellow Geol. Soc. Am., Am. Assn. Petroleum Geologists, AAAS; mem. Nat. Assn. Geology Tchrs. (pres. Central sect. 1967), Soc. Exploration Geophysicists, Phi Beta Kappa, Sigma Xi, Omicron Delta Kappa. Lutheran. Author: Structural Geology and Physiography of the Northern End of the Teton Range, Wyoming, 1951; (with E. Goebel) Subsurface Waste Disposal Potential in Salina Basin of Kansas, 1968; Sharing God's Gifts, 1978. Contbr. articles profl. jours. Home: La Serena Retirement Village 3575 N Moorpark Rd Thousand Oaks CA 91360

EDMUNDS, DON L., computer systems and services executive; b. Allen, Kans., May 11, 1936; s. William and Pearl Blanche (Olds) E.; m. Barbara Ga. Allen, Sept. 16, 1956; children—Kimberly, Grant. B.S., Emporia State U., 1959. Tchr. pub. schs., 1959-61; procedures engr. Denver div. Martin Marietta Corp., 1961-65, unit head engring. procedures, 1966-72; project mgr. engring. systems devel. Martin Marietta Data Systems Co., Englewood, Colo., 1972-75, product mgr., 1975-78, dir. info. system applications, comml. div., 1978—. Past chmn. park and recreation commn. City of Littleton (Colo.); past chmn. Littleton Bd. Adjustment; chmn. 1969 capital needs com. City of Littleton; campaign magr. various candidates for local offices, 1969-74. Mem. Am. Def. Preparedness Assn. Contbr. articles to profl. jours.

EDMUNDS, FRANKLIN MIDDLETON, optometrist, consultant; b. Cedar City, Utah, Apr. 28, 1950; s. Paul K. and Ella (Middleton) E.; m. Kathleen Oldham, Aug. 20, 1975; children—Staci, Theresa, Niccole, Tiffany. B.S., Brigham Young U., 1977; B.S., So. Calif. Coll. Optometry, 1979, O.D., 1981. Lic. optometrist, Utah, Calif., Idaho. Pres. Frank M. Edmunds, O.D., P.C., Orem, Utah, 1981—; cons. optical firms. Elder, Ch. of Jesus Christ of Latter-Day Saints, missionary, 1969-71. Recipient Outstanding Pub. Employee award Utah Pub. Employees Assn., 1977; Knight-Henry Meml. award sect. children's visual care and guidance Optometric Extension Program Found., 1981. Mem. Am. Optometric Assn., Utah Optometric Assn. Republican. Home: 823 E 600 N Orem UT 84057 Office: PO Box 1468 Orem UT 84057

EDSALL, KENNETH RICHARD, utility executive, lawyer; b. Des Moines, Dec. 6, 1926; s. Irving K. and Irene (Wupper) E.; m. Arlene Wilson, Feb. 15, 1975; children—Diane Fuller, Claudia Anne. Student U. Kans., U. Wyo., 1944-45; A.B., U. Wichita, 1949; LL.B., U. So. Calif., 1956. Bar: Calif. 1957. Atty various utility cos., Calif., 1957-65; asst. gen. counsel Pacific Lighting Service Co., Los Angeles, 1965-67, assoc. gen. counsel, 1967-71, assoc. gen. counsel Pacific Lighting Corp. (parent co.), 1971-72, v.p., sec., gen. counsel, 1975—. Served with U.S. Army, 1944-46. Mem. Am. Gas Assn. (legal com.), Pacific Coast Gas Assn. (legal adv. com.), Interstate Natural Gas Assn. (legal com.), ABA, Am. Soc. Corp. Secs., Conf. Pub. Utility Counsel, Fed. Energy Bar Assn., Los Angeles County Bar Assn. (corp. law dept. sect.), State Bar Calif. (bus. law sect.), Phi Alpha Delta. Club: Jonathan (Los Angeles). Office: 810 S Flower St Los Angeles CA 90017

EDUALINO, EMILIO QUIAL, educator; b. Agutaya, Palawan, Philippines, May 13, 1917; s. Telesforo Saldivia and Agapita (Quial) E.; came to U.S., 1979; Elem. tchr. cert. Philippine Normal Coll., Manila, 1935; B.S. in Edn., Far Eastern U., Manila, 1948; M.A., U. Mich., 1956, Ph.D., 1958. Tchr. then elem. sch. adminstr. various schs., Philippines, 1935-46; curriculum writer Dept. Edn., Manila, 1946-48; instr. edn. Philippine Normal Coll., Manila, 1948-48, master tchr., 1949-53, supr. student tching., 1953-55, dir. field units, prof. edn., 1957-64; primary edn. expert UNESCO, Guyana, S.Am., 1964-66, tchr. edn. expert Afghanistan, 1969-74, chief tech. adviser, Sierra Leone, 1974-79; prof. edn., chmn. dept. elem. edn. U. of the East, Manila,, 1966-69; tchr. St. Mary's Elem. Sch., Los Angeles, 1979—; cons.; mem. U.S. Edn. Found. selection com., Manila. Philippine Govt. travel fellow, 1948-49; U.S. Edn. Found. grantee, 1955-57. Mem. Childhood Edn. Internat., NEA, Nat. Soc. Study of Edn., Assn. Supervision and Curriculum Devel., Phi Delta Kappa. Roman Catholic. Clubs: Michigan (San Gabriel, Calif.); Michigan Alumni (Ann Arbor). Author: (with others) Integration as Practiced in the Philippine Normal College, 1952; also children's songs and reading materials; contbr. articles to profl. jours. Home: 2950 Manhattan Ave Glendale CA 91214 Office: 406 Saint Louis St Los Angeles CA 90033

EDWARDS, BARBARA RENE, university official; b. Cottage Grove, Oreg., Aug. 17, 1947; d. Ellis Roy and Irene Antoinette (Welding) E.; B.A., U. Oreg., 1969, M.A., 1974. Asst. editor alumni publs., editor faculty/staff Bull., U. Oreg., Eugene, 1972-75, editor alumni publs., 1975—, asst. v.p., 1979—, acting v.p., 1983—, guest lectr., 1976—; judge Council for Advancement and Support Edn., 1980—. Office rep. United Way, 1978—; active Fairmount Neighborhood Assn., Friends Eugene Public Library. Recipient citation award Council Advancement and Support Edn., 1978, Exceptional Achievement award, 1979, 1981, Spl. Merit award, 1980. Mem. Women in Communication, Women in Adminstrn., Oreg. Communicators Assn. (award of excellence 1979), Kappa Tau Alpha. Home: 1785 E 19th Ave Eugene OR 97403 Office: 154 Susan Campbell Hall U Oreg Eugene OR 97403

EDWARDS, BRUCE JACK, designer, consultant; b. Salt Lake City, May 6, 1951; s. Jack Grant and Mary Voyn (Griffith) E.; m. Joyce Edwards, April 3, 1974; children—Rochelle, Nicholas, Christel. B.F.A., Brigham Young U., 1977. Design intern Level Two Design Co., Salt Lake City, 1976; design cons. Greenhouse Design Studio, Salt Lake City,

1977-79; pres., owner B.J. Edwards Environments, Salt Lake City, 1977—; mgr. interior design and space planning Ch. of Jesus Christ of Latter Day Saints; design cons. Boy Scouts Am.; educator, lectr.; stage set designer Murray City Theatre, Osmond Studios, 1976. Council commr. Boy Scouts Am. Mem. Am. Soc. Interior Designers (pres. Utah chpt.). Republican. Contbr. articles in field to publs. Office: LDS Ch Hdqrs Salt Lake City UT 84150

EDWARDS, CARL VAUGHN, cons. engr.; b. Boise, Idaho, May 1, 1938; s. Lafell Hamblin and Marjorie Katherine (Justesen) E.; B.S., U. Idaho, 1964; m. Dalice Diane Schraft, Sept. 11, 1961; children—Carla, Sandrea, Hunter, Melinda. With U.S. Forest Service, Yreka, Calif., 1956-63, area engr., 1961-63; project engr. Morrison Knudsen Co., Boise, 1964-72; owner Edwards, Howard & Martens, Inc., cons. engrs., Twin Falls, Grangeville and Sun Valley, Idaho, 1972—; v.p. E M H Investments; engr. Idaho County, City of Grangeville. Am. Legion scholar, 1956, Carl Ramond Grey scholar, 1956. Mem. Nat., Idaho socs. profl. engrs., Am. Soc. Cons. Engrs., Cons. Engrs. Idaho. Elk. Home: 238 E South St Grangeville ID 83530 Office: 1139 Falls Ave E Twin Falls ID 83301 also 238 E South St Grangeville ID 83530 also Westside Office Bldg 5th and 1st Ave Ketchum ID 83340

EDWARDS, CHARLES RICHARD, printing equipment and supplies co. exec.; b. S. Bend, Ind., July 16, 1931; s. Bernard Stuart and Mary Irene (Chamberlaine) E.; student pub. schs.; m. Joanne Wood, Dec. 15, 1950; children—Timothy Stuart, Terry Lynne, David Bryan. Pressman, Toastmasters Internat., Santa Ana, Calif., 1954-60; with 3M Co., 1960-69, Salesman, Western U.S. tech. service and nat. market mgr., St. Paul, 1966-69; chief exec. officer, sec., chief fin. officer, co-owner Graphic Arts Supplies, Inc., Orange, Calif., 1969—; instr., cons. in field. Bd. dirs., treas. #1 Network, Inc., Chgo., 1982—. Served with USAF, 1950-54; Korea. Mem. Nat. Assn. Lithographic Clubs (chpt. co-founder, officer, dir.), Nat. Assn. Printing House Craftsmen (past chpt. pres., regional officer). Republican. Club: Toastmasters. Home: 7221 Judson Ave Westminster CA 92683 Office: 1636 W Collins Ave Orange CA 92667

EDWARDS, DANIEL PAUL, lawyer; b. Enid, Okla., Apr. 15, 1940; s. Daniel Paul and Joye Virginia (Van Horn) E.; B.A., U. Okla., 1962; J.D., Harvard, 1965; m. Virginia Lee Kidd, Mar. 27, 1976; children—David Paul, Ann Marie, Austin Daniel. Admitted to Colo. bar, 1965; practiced in Colorado Springs, 1965—, pres. London Investments, Ltd., lectr. in bus. law Colo. Coll., 1976—. Pres., Springs Area Beautiful Assn., 1978. Mem. ABA, Colo., El Paso County bar assns., Harvard Law Sch. Assn. (treas. Colo. bd. govs.), Phi Beta Kappa, Phi Delta Theta. Republican. Presbyterian. Clubs: Garden of Gods, Broadmoor Golf, El Paso, Cheyenne Mountain Country (Colorado Springs). Home: 5 Cheyenne Mountain Blvd Colorado Springs CO 80906 Office: 10 Boulder Crescent Suite 200 Colorado Springs CO 80903

EDWARDS, DON, congressman; b. San Jose, Calif., Jan. 6, 1915; grad. Stanford U., 1936, Stanford Law Sch., 1938; children—Leonard Perry II, Thomas Charles, Samuel Dyer, Bruce Haven, William Don. Admitted to Calif. bar; spl. agt. FBI, 1940-41; mem. 88th-97th congresses from 10th Dist. Calif. Served with USN, 1942-45. Democrat. Office: House Office Bldg Washington DC 20515

EDWARDS, (FLOYD) KENNETH, journalist, educator, mgmt. cons.; b. Salina, Kans., Sept. 29, 1917; s. Floyd Altamus and Grace Frances (Miller) E.; A.B., Fort Hays State U., 1940; M.S., 1970; m. Virginia Marie Lewark, Sept. 10, 1970, children—Elaine Patricia, Diana, Kenneth, John Michael, Melody, Daniel J. Ins. sales exec., Denver, 1947-50; reporter Sterling (Colo.) Daily Jour., 1950, editor, 1950-52; editor Waverly (Iowa) Newspapers, 1953-55; editor, pub. Edina (Minn.) Courier Newspapers, 1955-56; v.p., editor Mpls. Suburban Newspapers, Hopkins, Minn., 1956-65; editor, gen. mgr. Valley of the Sun Newspapers, Tempe, Ariz., 1968; instr. Mankato (Minn.) State U., 1970-72, asst. prof., 1972-73, assoc. prof. U. Ala., 1973-80, prof., 1980, vis. prof. communications U. Portland (Oreg.), 1981—; cons. on newspaper mgmt., videotex ops. Pres. Calhoun-Harriet Home Owners Assn., Mpls., 1958-60; bd. dirs. Hennepin County Assn. for Mental Health, 1959-60, S.W. Activities Council, 1960-61, S.W. High Sch. PTA, Mpls., 1960-61. Served with USN, World War II. Grantee Ford Found., 1976, U. Ala., 1977. Recipient awards for community service and editorial writing. Mem. Inst. Newspaper Controllers and Fin. Officers, Am. Mgmt. Assn., Assn. for Edn. in Journalism, Soc. Profl. Journalists, Nat. Conf. of Editorial Writers. Contbr. articles to profl. jours., chpts. to books; author newspaper profit planning and management manual. Home: 12960 SW Scout Dr Beaverton OR 97005 Office: 19576 SW 90th Ct Tualatin OR 97062

EDWARDS, GERALD WALTER, accountant, consultant; b. San Rafael, Calif., June 7, 1950; s. Fred Walter and Shirley Ann (Moore) E.; m. Nancy Sue Crowe, June 24, 1972; children—Shawn Michael, Christopher David. B.S., Calif. State U.-Northridge; postgrad. U. So. Calif., 1974-76. C.P.A., Calif., Ohio. Auditor, Blue Cross, Calif., 1972-73; with Ernst & Whinney, Cleve. and Los Angeles, 1974-82; founder Edwards & Co. (Edwards & Louis, 1982), pres., chmn. bd., 1982—; lectr. UCLA 1974-76; pub. speaker. Trustee, Delta Found. Mem. Am. Inst. C.P.A.s, Calif. Soc. C.P.A.s, Fedn. Am. Hosps., Hosp. Fin. Mgmt. Assn. Republican. Club: Racquet South Pasadena. Home: 4713 Vineta Ave La Canada CA 91011 Office: Edwards & Louis 87 N Raymond Ave 9th Floor Pasadena CA 91101

EDWARDS, JAMES RICHARD, lawyer; b. Long Beach, Calif., Apr. 14, 1951; s. Nelson James and Dorothy June (Harris) E.; m. Susan E. Winston, Mar. 17, 1973. B.S., Colo. State U., 1973; J.D., U. San Diego, 1977. Bar: Calif. 1977. Atty., Downtown Sr. tr., San Diego, 1977-78, Getty Oil Co., Los Angeles, 1978-80; atty. Logicon, Inc., Torrance, Calif., 1980—, sec., 1982—, gen. counsel, 1981—. Recipient championship medals U.S. Parachute Assn., 1977, 79, 80. Mem. ABA, Am. Corp. Counsel Assn., Am. Soc. Corp. Secs., State Bar Calif., Los Angeles County Bar Assn. Office: 3701 Skypark Dr Torrance CA 90505

EDWARDS, JAUNA CARPENTER, public accountant, city treasurer, educator; b. Childress, Tex., Mar. 16, 1935; d. Carl and Mildred (O'Daniel) C Carpenter; m. Carl M. Hall, Feb. 10, 1952; 1 son, Hal; m. 2d, John M. Edwards, Feb. 14, 1963; children—Nelta M., Bryant T. A.A., Tanana Valley Community Coll., 1982; student U. Alaska, 1977-83. Sec. to logistics mgr. RCA Service Co. at BMEWS, Clear, Alaska, 1961-62, sec. to sta. mgr. NASA Sta., Fairbanks, Alaska, 1962-64; pub. acct., Clear, 1966-83; city treas., Anderson, Alaska, 1968-83; treas. Tri-Valley Investment Corp., 1977-83. Chmn., Anderson Community Sch. Com. Mem. Nat. Soc. Pub. Accts., Alaska Soc. Ind. Accts., Clear Bus. and Profl. Women's Club. Democrat. Episcopalian. Home: 107 Aspen St Anderson AK 99704 Office: PO Box 174 Clear AK 99704

EDWARDS, JO BETH, university official, graphic designer; b. Deming, N.Mex., Sept. 28, 1952; d. Joe M. and Verna Jeanne (Renfro) Stell; m. Gary Robert Edwards, Jan. 6, 1973 (div.); children—Jennifer Leigh, Jeremy Todd. B.S., Eastern N.Mex. U., 1975, M.Ed., 1980. Apprentice illustrator Art Gorrell & Assocs., AIA, Carlsbad, N.Mex., 1975; graphic designer Adsociates/Mastertype, Albuquerque, 1975-77; graphic designer Eastern N.Mex. U.-Portales, 1980-81, media coordinator, Clovis, 1981—. Mem. Assn. for Supervision and Curriculum Devel., Assn. Ednl. Communication and Tech., Phi Delta Kappa. Republican. Mem. New Covenant Ch. Office: Eastern N Mex U 417 Schepps Blvd Clovis NM 88101

EDWARDS, JOHN THOMAS, public relations, advertising agency executive; b. Biloxi, Miss., Sept. 13, 1944; s. William Thomas and Martha E. (Eistetter) E.; B.J., U. Mont., 1966; M.A., U. Colo., 1976, postgrad., 1972—. Ranger, Yellowstone Nat. Park, 1966; pub. relations dir. U.S. Nordic Ski Team, 1972-75; account exec. William Kostka Assos., Denver, 1972-75; pres. John Edwards Assos., Denver, 1976—, also former pub. Colo. Newsfilm, Colo. Country Weekly newspaper, Stapleton Innerline newspaper, The Denver People newspaper; dir. Prime Property Cons.'s; U.S. press rep. World Nordic Ski Championships. Served to capt. USAF, 1967-71, to maj. Wyo. Air N.G., 1971—. Licensed real estate salesman, Colo. Mem. Pub. Relations Soc. Am. (accredited), Arnold Air Soc., Denver Advt. Fedn., Nat. Free Lance Photographers Assn., Nat. Press Photographers Assn., Radio/TV News Dirs. Assn., N.G. Assn., Wyo. N.G. Assn., U.S. Ski Assn., Rocky Mountain Ski Writers, Nat. Aviation/Space Writers Assn., Aurora C. of C., Denver Press Club, Porsche Club Am., Sigma Delta Chi, Sigma Chi. Republican. Episcopalian. Home: 2325 S Linden Ct Apt 301N Denver CO 80222 Office: 300 Greenwood Pl 5340 S Quebec Englewood CO 80111

EDWARDS, KEITH JOHN, psychology educator, consultant; b. Milw., June 26, 1944; s. Glenn George and Mary Helen (Hilmer) E.; m. Virginia Ruth Smith, Aug. 6, 1966; children—Jonathan, Rebecca, David. B.E., U. Wis.-Whitewater, 1966; M.A., N.Mex. State U., 1969, Ph.D., 1969. Asst. research prof. Rutgers U., New Brunswick, N.J., 1969-70; assoc. research scientist Johns Hopkins U., Balt.; prof. psychology, dir. research Rosemead Sch. Psychology, Biola U., La Mirada, Calif., 1973—; cons. in field. Exxon Found. grantee, 1978. Mem. Am. Psychol. Assn., Christian Assn. Psychol. Studies. Baptist. Author: Team Learning, 1978; contbr. articles to prof. jours. Office: 13800 Biola Ave LaMirada CA 90639

EDWARDS, LAMARR CLINTON, safety/security services adminstr.; b. San Bernardino, Calif., Apr. 19, 1949; s. Shelby Clinton and Myrtle W. (Carter) E.; A.A., San Bernardino Valley Coll., 1969; postgrad. Calif. State Coll., San Bernardino, 1974-76; grad. Internat. Safety Acad., Atlanta, 1975; m. Joanne Virginia Shuris, Nov. 16, 1969; children—Rebecca, Aubrey. Patrol officer campus police Loma Linda (Calif.) U., 1969-71, investigator, 1971-72, sgt., 1973-75, protection services coordinator Med. Center, 1975-77, dir. safety/security, 1977—, lectr. Sch. Hosp. Adminstrn., 1980—; dir. safety/security Loma Linda Community Hosp., 1972-73. Cert. protection profl. Mem. Adventist Loss Control Assn. (pres. 1978-80), So. Calif. Hosp. Safety Council, Am. Soc. Safety Engrs., Am. Soc. Indsl. Security, Nat. Assn. Chiefs of Police, Internat. Assn. Hosp. Security, Nat. Fire Protection Assn. Adventist. Office: Loma Linda U Loma Linda CA 92354

EDWARDS, MARIE BABARE, psychologist; b. Tacoma; d. Nick and Mary (Mardesich) Babare; B.A., Stanford, 1948, M.A., 1949; m. Tilden Hampton Edwards (div.); 1 son, Tilden Hampton Edwards III. Counselor guidance center U. So. Calif., Los Angeles, 1950-52; project coordinator So. Calif. Soc. Mental Hygiene, 1952-54; pub. speaker Welfare Fedn. Los Angeles, 1953-57; field rep. Los Angeles County Assn. Mental Health, 1957-58; intern. psychologist U. Calif. at Los Angeles, 1958-60; pvt. practice, human relations tng., counselor tng., condr. personal devel. seminars, also teaching Challenge of Being Single workshops at univs. Calif., U. So. Calif., Los Angeles, U. B.C. (Can.), others, 1970—. Mem. Am., Western, Calif., Los Angeles County psychol. assns., A.A.A.S., Nat. Acad. Religion and Mental Health, Soc. Advancement Mgmt., So. Calif. Soc. Clin. Hypnosis, Group Psychotherapy Assn. So. Calif., Assn. for Humanistic Psychology, Internat. Platform Assn. Author: (with Eleanor Hoover) The Challenge of Being Single, 1974. Office: 6100 Buckingham Pkwy Culver City CA 90230

EDWARDS, MICHAEL RUSS, marketing analyst; b. Duncan, Okla., July 24, 1935; s. Marshall James Edwards and Emma Elizabeth Persson; A.A., Casper Coll. (Wyo.), 1970; B.S., U. Wyo., 1974. With Mid-Continent Supply Co., Ft. Worth, 1974-82, mktg. systems analyst, Ft. Worth and Houston, 1977-79, pricing and inventory control specialist, Farmington, N.Mex., 1979-82; mktg. analyst Casper, Wyo., 1982—. Served with USAF, 1957-60. Mem. Am. Mktg. Assn., Am. Mgmt. Assn., U. Wyo. Alumni Assn., Ducks Unltd. Democrat. Presbyterian. Address: 1724 N Grass Creek Rd Casper WY 82604

EDWARDS, NOMA JAY, communications consultant, editor; b. Sikeston, Mo., Mar. 14, 1945; d. Harold Courtney and Phoebe Doris (Eaton-Billington) De Hart; student U. Wash., 1963-65, B.A. in Sociology, 1979; student San Jose U., 1966-68; m. D. Craig Edwards, Oct. 2, 1965; children—Jeffery Scott, Rebecca Dorae. Mem. exec. bd. Bellevue First Methodist United Methodist Women, 1969—; social worker Arden Nursing Home, Seattle, 1971-72; dir. vol. services Bellevue (Wash.) Probation Dept., 1979-80; book editor Snohomish Pub. Co., Bellevue, 1980—; cons. communications, Bellevue, 1979—. Mem. Bellevue Probation Citizen Adv. Bd.; vol. Vols. in Probation, City of Bellevue, 1977—; active PTA. Mem. AAUW (exec. bd.), LWV, Sororia Alumnae, Alpha Phi Alumnae. Democrat. Home: 10223 SE 13th Pl Bellevue WA 98004

EDWARDS, NORMAN WAYNE, civil engr.; b. Grand Haven, Mich., Jan. 25, 1942; s. George Gleason and Annetta Ann (Kramer) E.; B.C.E., U. Mich., 1964, M.C.E., 1965, Ph.D., 1969; 1 dau., Cary Ann. Design engr. Pitts. Des Moines Steel Co., Pitts., 1965-67, engring. mgr., 1970-73; ind. cons., Ann Arbor, Mich., 1967-69; dir. engring. NUTECH, San Jose, Calif., 1974-80, v.p. engring., 1980-82, pres NUTECH Internat., 1982—. NDEA fellow, 1968, 69; named Outstanding Civil Engr. of Year, U. Mich., 1964. Registered profl. engr., Pa., Calif. Mem. ASCE, ASME (boiler and pressure vessel com.), Sigma Xi, Tau Beta Pi, Chi Epsilon, Phi Kappa Phi. Patentee in field (4). Home: 17469 Hoot Owl Way Mogan Hill CA 95037 Office: 145 Martinvale Ln San Jose CA 95119

EDWARDS, PATRICIA BURR, leisure consultant; b. Oakland, Calif., Feb. 19, 1918; d. Myron Carlos and Claire Idelle (Laingor) Burr; A.B., U. So. Calif., 1939, M.S. in Edn., 1981; m. Jackson Edwards, Nov. 14, 1942; children—Jill Edwards Forman, Jan. Founder, sole owner, mgr. Constructive Leisure, Los Angeles, 1968—; counselor/cons. leisure, work and leisure fields; lectr.; tchr.; writer. Former vol. cultural family and child welfare, sports, polit. orgns. Recipient various community and orgn. awards. Mem. AAHPER and Dance, and Dance, Adult Edn. Assn., Am. Personnel and Guidance Assn., Calif. Personnel and Guidance Assn., Vol. Action of Los Angeles, Nat. Recreation and Park Assn., Internat. Soc. for Pre-Retirement Planners, Jr. League Los Angeles, Trojan League, Delta Gamma. Author: You've Got To Find Happiness; It Won't Find You, 1971; Leisure Counseling Techniques; Individual and Group Counseling Step-by-Step, 1975, 3d edit., 1980; writer other leisure counseling materials, 1968—; contbr. chpts. to books. Office: 511 N La Cienega Blvd Los Angeles CA 90048

EDWARDS, PATRICK JAMES, cons. co. exec.; b. Boise, Idaho, Mar. 30, 1941; s. Forren Joseph and Helen Patricia (Turner) E.; B.A., Boise State U., 1967; m. Janice Mae Paynter, Apr. 24, 1965; children—Kelly Marie, Michael Andrew. With Boise Cascade Corp., 1967-82, employee relations mgr., Chgo., 1974-78, gen. mgr., Miami, Fla., 1978-79, mgr. profl. and exec. staffing, Boise, 1979-82; owner human resources mgmt. cons. co., personal growth co., 1982—. Mem. Boise Comprehensive Health Planning Rev. Com., 1971. Served with U.S. Army, 1960-63. Mem. Am. Soc. Personnel Adminstrn., Am. Compensation Assn., Greater Boise C. of C. Home: 3440 Columbine Boise ID 83704 Office: Fairview Profl Center 4812 Fairview Boise ID 83706

EDWARDS, PHYLLIS RUTH, educational administrator; b. Needles, Calif., Nov. 7, 1944; d. Ross Allen and Ruth Margaret (Willis) E.; m. Hugh Alexander Patterson, Aug. 30, 1966 (div.); 1 son, Ross Alexander. B.A., Wheaton Coll., 1966; M. Ed., Boston U., 1975. Cert. secondary tchr., supr., adminstr. Calif. Cashier Merrill, Lynch, Pierce, Fenner & Smith, Boston, 1966-67; tchr. program coordinator Boston Pub. Schs., 1967-72; tchr., dept. chmn., curriculum devel. team mem. Wayland (Mass.) Pub. Schs., 1972-77; tchr., project dir. Oakland (Calif.) Unified Sch. Dist., 1977-81; prin., project dir. Greenfield (Calif.) Union Sch. Dist., 1981—. Mem. Calif. Fedn. Tchrs., Assn. Calif. Sch. Adminstrs., Assn. for Supervision and Curriculum Devel. Lutheran. Club: Greenfield Women's. Contbr. ednl. materials to pub. sch. publs.

EDWARDS, RALPH M., librarian; b. Shelley, Idaho, Apr. 17, 1933; s. Edward William and Maude Estella (Munsee) E.; m. Winifred Wylie, Dec. 25, 1969; children—Dylan, Nathan, Stephen. B.A., U. Wash., 1957, M.L.S., 1960; D.L.S. (fellow), U. Calif.-Berkeley, 1971. Librarian N.Y. Pub. Library, 1960-61, U. Ill., 1962-63; head regional library Portland (Oreg.) Pub. Library, 1964-67; mem. faculty Sch. Librarianship, Western Mich. U., Kalamazoo, 1970-74; library adminstrv. intern Council Library Resources, U. Mich., 1974-75; chief central research library Dallas Pub. Library, 1975-81; city librarian Phoenix Pub. Library, 1981—; cons. Council Library Resources, Washington, 1979-80. Mem. ALA, Assn. Coll. and Research Libraries, Ariz. Library Assn. Author: The Role of the Beginning Librarian in University Libraries, 1975. Home: 4839 E Mulberry Dr Phoenix AZ 85018 Office: 12 E McDowell Rd Phoenix AZ 85004

EDWARDS, SARAH ANNE, clin. social worker; b. Tulsa, Jan. 7, 1943; d. Clyde Elton and Virginia Elizabeth Glandon; B.A. with distinction, U. Mo., Kansas City, 1965; M.S.W., U. Kans., 1974; m. Paul Robert Edwards, Apr. 24, 1965; 1 son, Jon Scott. Community rep. OEO, Kansas City Regional Office, 1966-68; social service/parent involvement specialist, program rev. and resource specialist Office Child Devel., HEW, Kansas City, Kans., 1968-73, dir. tng. social services dept., children's rehab. unit U. Affiliated Facility, U. Kans. Med. Ctr., Kansas City, 1975-76; co-dir. Cathexis Inst. S., Glendale, Calif., 1976-77; pvt. practice psychotherapy, tng. and cons. personal, interpersonal, organizational behavior, Sierra Madre, Calif, 1973—; founder, dir. tng., lead therapist Matrix, Kansas City, Mo., 1975-76; founder, sponsor Creative Transactions, Kansas City, Mo., 1977—, dir. tng. Public Affairs Assistance, Kansas City, Mo., 1974-76; staff therapist Las Virgines Med. Ctr., Woodland Hills, Calif., 1977-78, Rockhurst Coll. Counselling Center, Kansas City, Mo., 1975, U. Kans. Psychol. Clinic, Lawrence, 1973; lectr. Project Head Start, Kans. State Tchrs. Coll., Pittsburg, 1972; teaching asst. undergrad. social work U. Kans. Sch. Social Welfare, 1973-74; instr. psychology dept. Pepperdine U., 1978; pres. Home Enterprises Unltd.; instr. bus. and mgmt. UCLA Extension; systems operator CompuServe Info. Service; nat. spokesperson Epson Am.; producer for cable TV, In The Neighborhood. Mem. adv. com. UCLA Extension Entrepreneurial Program; mem. adv. com. on instructional TV prodn. Los Angeles Community Colls., co-founder Assn. for Electronic Cottagers. Mem. Am. Soc. for Tng. and Devel. (dir. Los Angeles chpt. 1980—), Internat. Transactional Analysis Assn., Nat. Assn. Social Workers, Acad. Cert. Social Workers, Nat. Conf. for Family Relations, So. Calif. Psychotherapy Assn. Contbr. articles to profl. jours. Office: 677 Canyon Crest Dr Sierra Madre CA 91024

EDWARDS, SPENCER PENROSE, JR., school adminstr.; b. Idaho Falls, Ida., Jan. 19, 1918; s. Spencer Penrose and Edna Frances (Henderson) E.; m. Elizabeth Lee Boykin, Oct. 10, 1943; children—Mary Elizabeth, Robin Lee, Libby Ann, Megan Frances, Cader C., Alexandra. A.B., UCLA, 1940; M.A., U. Chgo., 1956; M.Div., Ch. Div. Sch. of Pacific, 1965. Commd. 2d lt. U.S. Army, 1940, advanced through grades to col., 1961; ret., 1962; head fgn. lang. dept. Harvard Sch., North Hollywood, Calif., 1965-70; pres. Tex. Mil. Inst., San Antonio, 1970-71; headmaster Flintridge Prep Sch., La Canada Flintridge, Calif., 1971-73, Gooden Sch., Sierra Madre, Calif., 1975—; ordained priest Episcopal Ch., 1965; priest-in-charge various chs. in Los Angeles area, 1975-82. Active Sierra Madre Community Hosp. Assn., Sierra Madre Cemetery Assn. Decorated Silver Star, Bronze Star with 3 oak leaf clusters, Army Commendation medal. Mem. Assn. U.S. Army, Ret. Officers Assn., Evang. and Cath. Mission, Prayer Book Soc., Delta Chi. Republican. Home: 576 Elm St Sierra Madre CA 91024 Office: 192 N Baldwin Ave Sierra Madre CA 91024

EDWARDS, SUSAN STABNAU, counselor, educator, consultant; b. York, Pa., Nov. 7, 1947; d. Fred C. and Eva Jane (Rothrock) Stabnau. B.S. in Edn., Shippensburg (Pa.) State Coll.; M.A. in Edn., Ariz. State U., 1971, M.C. in Counseling, 1975, Ph.D. in Counseling Psychology, 1983. Sch. counselor Tempe (Ariz.) Elem. Schs., 1971-76; psychology intern Ariz. Guidance Ctr., Phoenix, 1976-78; staff counselor Comprehensive Counseling and Mental Health, Phoenix, 1978-80; clin. supervisor New Ariz. Family, Phoenix, 1980-81; employee counselor Motorola, Inc., Phoenix, 1981-82; dir. Profl. Network Assocs., Phoenix, 1983—; tchr. counseling dept. Mesa Community Coll. Recipient Outstanding Program award Ariz. Personnel Guidance Assn., 1975-76. Mem. Am. Psychol. Assn., Am. Personnel and Guidance Assn., Pi Lambda Theta. Contbr. articles to profl. jours. Home: 1409 E Secretariat St Tempe AZ 85284 Office: 2333 N 3d St Phoenix AZ 85004

EDWARDS, WARD, psychologist, researcher; b. Morristown, N.J., Apr. 5, 1927; s. Corwin D. and Janet W. (Ferriss) E.; m. Ruth Page, Aug. 2, 1948 (div.); children—Tara, Page; m. 2d, Silvia Callegari, Dec. 12, 1970. B.A., Swarthmore Coll., 1947; M.A., Harvard U., 1950, Ph.D., 1952. Diplomate Am. Bd. Profl. Psychology, 1971. Instr., Bklyn. Coll., 1947-48, Johns Hopkins U., 1951-54; research psychologist Air Force Personnel and Tng. Research Ctr., Denver, 1954-56, San Antonio, 1956-58; asst. prof. to prof. U. Mich., 1958-73, dir. Engring. Psychology Lab., 1963-73, asso. dir. Hwy. Safety Research Inst., 1970-73; prof. psychology and indsl. systems engring. and dir. Social Sci. Research Inst., Los Angeles, 1973—; cons. Served with USN, 1945-46. Recipient Franklin V. Taylor award Soc. Engring. Psychologists, 1978. Mem. Am. Psychol. Assn., Soc. Med. Decision Making, Ops. Research Soc. Am., Am. Inst. Decision Scis. Author: (with A. Tversky) Decision Making, 1967; (with J.R. Newman) Multiattribute Evaluation, 1982; contbr. articles to profl. jours. Office: Social Sci Research Inst U So Calif Univ Park MC-1111 Los Angeles CA 90028

EDWARDS, WAYNE A., educational administrator; b. Putnam, Conn., Dec. 26, 1934; s. Dorian Arthur and Celia Evangeline (Gallup) E.; m. Esther Sylvia Balwit, June 4, 1955; children—Valerie Dinsdale, Kevin, Lynette, Karen Kerns. B.A. in Sociology and Psychology, Eastern Nazarene Coll., Quincy, Mass., 1959; M.A. in Edn., Holy Names Coll., Oakland, Calif., 1968; postgrad. in Bus. Adminstrn., Valley Christ U., 1982. Sci. instr. Eastern Nazarene Coll., 1955-58; instr. Oakland Pub. Schs., 1959-77, adminstrv. v.p. ednl. services, 1965-70; councilor, field rep. Calif. Tchrs. Assn., 1975-78; ptnr. Super Scoop Ice Cream Parlor, 1977-80; founder, owner, supt. Wayne Edwards Learning Ctrs., Calif., 1965—; pres. Evang. Released Time, Inc. Recipient award Calif. Assn. Neurologically Handicapped Children, 1970. Mem. NEA, Calif. Reading Assn., Assn. Christian Schs. Internat., C. of C. Republican. Mem. Assembly of God Ch. Club: Gideons Internat. Home: PO Box 424 Pinole CA 94564 Office: 2242 Morello Ave Pleasant Hill CA 94523

EFRON, BRADLEY, statistics educator, consultant; b. St. Paul, May 24, 1938; s. Miles Jack and Esther (Kaufman) E.; m. Gael Guerin (div.); 1 son, Miles James. B.S. in Math., Calif. Inst. Tech., 1960; Ph.D. in Stats., Stanford U., 1964. Asst. to assoc. prof. stats. Stanford (Calif.) U., 1965-72, prof., 1972—, chmn. dept. stats., 1976-79, chmn. maths. scis., 1982—; cons. stats. to corps. Macarthur Found. fellowship grantee, 1983. Fellow Inst. Math. Stats. (Wald and Rietz lectr. 1977, 81), Am. Stat. Assn. (Outstanding Statistician of Yr. Chgo. chpt. 1981); mem. Internat. Statis. Assn. Democrat. Author: Bootstrap Methods, 1982; co-author: Biostatistics Casebook, 1980. Office: Dept Stats Sequoia Hall Stanford CA 94305

EFTING, GAIL K., management consultant; b. Albuquerque, Oct. 21, 1948; d. Gardner L. and Lois H. K.; m. James Howard Efting, Feb. 4, 1983. Student Universidad De Salamanca, Spain, 1970; grad. with honors Am. Bankers Assn. Nat. Compliance Sch., 1980; B.A. in Mgmt., St. Mary's Coll., Moraga, Calif., 1983. Mgr. loan adjustment dept. Valley Nat. Bank, Salinas, Calif., 1978, compliance officer, 1978-80; compliance officer The Hibernia Bank, San Francisco, 1980-82; pres. Compliance Mgmt. Info. Services, Inc., Sunnyvale, Calif., 1982—. Instr., Am. Bankers Assn. Grad. Compliance Sch., 1982, 83, Consumer Bankers Assn., Calif. Bankers Assn.; lectr. Recipient cert. of appreciation Consumer Credit Assn., 1982. Mem. Am. Mgmt. Assn., Nat. Assn. Female Execs., Calif. Bankers Assn. Republican. Contbr. articles to profl. jours. Office: 527 S Frances St Sunnyvale CA 94086

EGBERT, BARBARA MAYER, pathologist; b. Cumberland, Md., Aug. 30, 1942; d. Robert Hillis and Thelma (Rehner) Mayer; B.S. in Zoology magna cum laude with honors (hon. Woodrow Wilson fellow), Duke U., 1964; M.D., Yale U., 1968; m. Peter Roy Egbert, Nov. 5, 1966; children—Susan, Tim, Emily. Intern, Yale-New Haven Hosp., 1968-69; instr. biology U. S.C., 1969-71; resident in pathology West Haven (Conn.) Vets. Hosp., 1971-73; resident, then chief resident in pathology Stanford U. Hosp., 1973-75; staff pathologist Palo Alto (Calif.) VA Hosp., 1975—; clin. asst. prof. Stanford U. Med. Sch., 1975—, dermatopathology U. Calif., San Francisco, 1980—. Diplomate Am. Bd. Pathology, Am. Bd. Dermatopathology. Mem. S. Bay Path. Soc., Am. Soc. Dermatopathology, Phi Beta Kappa. Contbr. to med. jours. Address: VA Hosp Lab Service Palo Alto CA 94304

EGERMEIER, ROBERT PAUL, engineer, lawyer; b. Oklahoma City, Dec. 25, 1927; s. Paul Fred and Dorothy Laura (Kluber) E.; m. Virginia T. Kotte, Mar. 2, 1952; children—John Carl, Paul William. B.S., Okla. U., Norman, 1951; M.S., N.Mex. State U., Las Cruces, 1957; LL.B., LaSalle Inst., Chgo., 1976. Lic. profl. engr., N.Mex., Calif., Tex., Utah. Project engr. U.S. Army Ordnance Corps, White Sands Missile Range (N.Mex.), 1951-53; asst. physicist N.Mex. State U., Las Cruces, 1953-57, asst. prof. mech. engring., 1957-62; dept. mgr. Aerospace Corp., San Bernardino, Calif., 1962-66; mgr. ordnance and mil. avionics RCA, Van Nuys, Calif., 1967-69; sr. scientist Hughes Aircraft Co., Canoga Park, Calif., 1969-80, sr. scientist tech. devel., missile devel. div., 1981—; admitted to Calif. bar, 1977, U.S. Supreme Ct. bar, 1982; registered patent atty. U.S. Patent and Trademark Office, 1979; individual practice law, Canoga Park, 1978—, mem. firm Alberi & Radke, 1979-80. Lay reader Episcopal Ch., warden and vestryman, 1953-55, 57-60, 68-75. Served with U.S. Army, 1951-52. Mem. AIAA, ASME, IEEE, AAAS, Am. Bar Assn., Los Angeles Patent Law Assn., Los Angeles County Bar Assn., Am. Def. Preparedness Assn., Assn. Old Crows, Sigma Xi, Sigma Pi, Sigma Pi Tau Sigma, Phi Kappa Tau. Democrat. Contbr. to Ethical Problems in Engineering, 1965. Home: 22354 Malden St Canoga Park CA 91304

EGGER, MICHAEL ARNOLD, optometrist; b. Portland, Oreg., June 6, 1953; s. Arthur and Catherine (Hanken) E.; m. Becky Ellen Green, July 20, 1974; children—Stephanie Catherine, Melissa Lena, Erika Karen. B.S. cum laude, Pacific U., 1975, D.Optometry with distinction, 1977. Lic. optometrist, Oreg. Pvt. practice optometry, Oregon City, Oreg., 1977—; mem. staff Pacific U. Coll. Optometry, 1979-80; lectr. Pacific U., Portland State U.; clin. assoc. Optometric Extension Program. Mem. Am. Optometric Assn. (optometric recognition awards for continuing edn. 1981-83), Oreg. Optometric Assn. (Outstanding Young Optometrist of Yr. award 1981), Portland Met. Optometric Soc. (pres. 1982-83), N.W. Oreg. Health Systems, N.W. Rafting Assn. Republican. Lodge: Oregon City Optimist (v.p. 1983-84). Home: 15116 S Henrici Rd Oregon City OR 97045 Office: 1017 Molalla Ave Suite 2 Oregon City OR 97045

EGGERS, ALFRED JOHN, JR., research company executive; b. Omaha, June 24, 1922; s. Alfred John and Golden May (Myers) E.; m. Elizabeth Ann Hills, Sept. 9, 1950; children—Alfred John, Philip Norman. A.B., U. Omaha, 1944; M.S., Stanford U., 1949, Ph.D., 1956. Research scientist Ames (Calif.) Research Ctr., NASA, 1944-59, chief vehicle environ. div., 1959-63, asst. dir. dir., 1963-64, dep. assoc. adminstr. advanced research and tech., Washington, 1964-68, asst. adminstr. for policy, 1968-71; asst. dir. research applications NSF, Washington, 1971-77; dir. Lockheed Palo Alto (Calif.) Research Lab., 1977-79; mem. U.S. Air Force Sci. Adv. Bd., 1958-72; Hunsaker prof. MIT, Cambridge, 1969-71; founder, dir. AIAA, 1963-66; pres. RANN, INC., Palo Alto, Calif., 1979—; Minta Martin lectr., 1970; chmn. bd. A.J. Eggers & Co., 1981—; mem. Aerospace Engring. Bd., Nat. Acad. Engring., 1972-76; 1st chmn. Geothermal Energy Coordination Mgmt. Project, 1974-75. Vice-chmn. Sch. Community Devel. Com., Los Altos, Calif., 1963-64; chmn. troop coms. Boy Scouts Am., Arlington, Va., 1968-77; chmn. safety com. ARC, Arlington, 1976-77. Served to lt. (j.g.) USN, 1943-46. Recipient Arthur S. Fleming award U.S. Jaycees, 1956; TOYM award, 1957; Outstanding Alumni award U. Omaha, 1958; Sylvanus Reed award AIAA, 1962; H.J. Allen award ARC, 1969; Exceptional Service medal NASA, 1971; Disting. Service award NSF, 1975; Pres.'s Disting. Service award, 1977; commendation Nat. Sci. Bd., 1977. Fellow AIAA, Am. Astronautical Soc., AAAS; mem. Nat. Acad. Engring., Tau Beta Pi, Sigma Xi. Republican. Club: Washington Golf and Country (Arlington). Contbr. over 50 articles on advanced aerospace and renewable energy technologies to profl. jours.; inventor supersonic and hypersonic wind tunnel concepts, ballistic and lifting reentry vehicle concepts applied in Inter-Continental Ballistic Missile, Apollo and Space Shuttle devel. Home: 23 Fair Oaks Ln Atherton CA 94025 Office: 260 Sheridan Ave Palo Alto CA 94306

EGGERS, LARRY ALAN, tax and fin. planning co. exec.; b. Maryville, Tenn., Oct. 15, 1941; s. Robert Carroll and Pearl Etta Glen (Jenkins) E.; A.S. in Edn. (High Scholastic scholar), Ricks Coll., 1965; B.S. in Bus. Adminstrn., U. Redlands, 1979; m. Ruth Ann Pearson, Apr. 4, 1963; children—Laurie Ann, Mark, David, Robert, Amber, April, Jason, Michelle. With toll transmission dept. Am. Telephone Co., Long Lines, Pocatello, Idaho, 1965-66; operations engr. Lockheed Co., Sunnyvale, Calif., 1966-72; owner, gen. mgr. Eggers Tax Service, San Jose, Calif., 1968-78, editor The ETS Taxpayer, 1972-78; v.p. Mighty-Mite Computer Systems, Inc., San Jose, 1975—, chmn. bd., 1975—; gen. partner E.T.S. Real Estate Partnership, San Jose, 1978—; pres. E.T.S. & Assocs., Inc., San Jose, 1978—; tax and fin. cons. Active Better Bus. Bur. Lic. real estate broker, life and disability agt., securities agt., former securities agt. Mem. Nat. Assn. Tax Cons., Calif. Assn. Realtors, Nat. Assn. Realtors, Internat. Assn. Fin. Planners, San Jose Real Estate Bd. Mormon. Author: Basic Federal Income Tax Training Course, 1971, 72, 73; Copyrighted Tax Questionaire Booklet, 1974, 80, 82; programming cons. income tax software for mini-computers, acctg. software for mini-computers. Home: 700 Dartmouth Pl Gilroy CA 95020 Office: 7174 Santa Teresa Blvd Suite A-2 San Jose CA 95139

EGGERS, TED, corporate president, advertising consultant; b. Sikeston, Mo., Oct. 6, 1929; s. Arthur Edwin and Opal (Elkins) E.; m. Ramona Jean Prillman, May 5, 1950 (div.); children—Chris, Paul, Larry. Student U. Ventura Calif. Coll., 1959-60, Md., 1961-62, Western Wash. State Coll., 1962-63. Cert. radio mktg. cons. Enlisted U.S. Air Force, 1946, supr. armed forces radio stas., 1947, supr. TV Spl. services, 1966, ret., 1966; chief vault teller Bank of Wash., Tacoma, 1969; radio and sales mgr., Sumner and Hoquiam, Wash., 1970-81; pres. TLC Specialities Corp., Aberdeen, Wash., 1981—; advt. cons. Pres. Aberdeen Rain Fair, 1976; active Kiwanis. Decorated Air Force commendation medal with Oak Leaf. Mem. Nat. Speciality Wholesalers Assn., Am. Entrepenuers Assn., Wash. State Fairs Assn. Republican.

EGGERT, ROBERT JOHN, economist; b. Little Rock, Dec. 11, 1913; s. John and Eleanora (Fritz) Lapp; B.S., U. Ill.-Urbana, 1935, M.S., 1936; doctoral candidate in philosophy U. Minn., 1938; m. Elizabeth Bauer, Nov. 28, 1935; children—Robert John, Richard F., James E. Research analyst Bur. Agrl. Econs., U.S. Dept. Agr., Urbana, 1935; prin. mktg. specialist War Meat Bd., Chgo., 1943; research analyst U. Ill., 1935-36, U. Minn., 1936-38; asst. prof. econs. Kans. State Coll., 1938-41; asst. dir. mktg. Am. Meat Inst., Chgo., 1941-43, economist, assoc. dir., 1943-50; mgr. dept. mktg. research Ford div. Ford Motor Co., Dearborn, Mich., 1951-53, mgr. program planning, 1953-54, mgr. bus. research, 1954-57, mgr. mktg. research mktg. staff, 1957-61, mgr. mktg. research Ford div., 1961-64, mgr. internat. mktg. research mktg. staff, 1964-65, mgr. overseas mktg. research planning, 1965-66, mgr. mktg. research Lincoln-Mercury div., 1966-67; dir. agribus. programs Mich. State U., 1967-68; staff v.p. econ. and mktg. research RCA, N.Y.C., 1968-73, staff v.p., chief economist, 1974-76; pres., chief economist Eggert Econ. Enterprises, Inc., Sedona, Ariz., 1976—; lectr. mktg. U. Chgo., 1947-49; adj. prof. bus. forecasting No. Ariz. U., 1976—; mem. econ. adv. bd. U.S. Dept. Commerce, 1969-71, mem. census adv. com., 1975-78; mem. panel econ. advisers Congressional Budget Office, 1975-76; mem. Ariz. Econ. Estimates Commn., 1978—. Recipient Econ. Forecast award Chgo. chpt. Am. Statis. Assn., 1950, 60, 68; Seer of Yr. award Harvard Bus. Sch. Indsl. Econs., 1973. Mem. Council Internat. Mktg. Research and Planning Dirs. (chmn. 1965-66), Am. Mktg. Assn. (dir., v.p. 1949-50, pres. Chgo. chpt. 1947-48, v.p. mktg. mgmt. div. 1972-73, nat. pres. 1974-75), Am. Statis. Assn. (chmn. bus. and econ. stats. sect. 1957—, pres. Chgo. chpt. 1948-49), Fed. Stats. Users Conf. (chmn. trustees 1960-61), Conf. Bus. Economists (chmn. 1973-74), Nat. Assn. Bus. Economists (council 1969-72), Ariz. Econ. Roundtable, Am. Farm. Econs. Assn., Am. Econs. Assn., Am. Quarter Horse Assn. (dir. 1966-73), Alpha Zeta. Republican. Congregationalist. Club: Poco Diablo Country. Contbr. articles to profl. jours.; lit. editor monthly Blue Chip Econ. Indicators; editor monthly Blue Chip Fin. Forecasts; co-editor monthly Blue Chip Econ. Worldscan. Home: Schnebly Hill Rd PO Box 1569 Sedona AZ 86336 Office: Sedonan-South Bldg Suite E Jordon Rd PO Box 1569 Sedona AZ 86336

EGNER, VICTOR CARL, investment broker; b. Jamestown, N.D., Feb. 10, 1944; s. Carl Otto and Fern Henrietta (Barth) E.; B.A. in Psychology and Econs., Baylor U., Waco, Tex., 1967; m. Pamelle Augspurger, Sept. 27, 1968. With Sperry-Univac, Mpls., 1967-70, 71-78; mgr. computer software devel. div. Weismantal Assos., St. Paul, 1970-71; engaged in investing, 1978—; v.p. investments Dean Witter Reynolds, Las Vegas, Nev., 1981—. Served with Army N.G., 1967-73. Mem. Nat. Assn. Securities Dealers. Libertarian. Methodist. Club: Elks. Co-designer computer operating systems. Home: 1020 E Desert Inn Suite 1207 Las Vegas NV 89109 Office: 300 S 4th St Las Vegas NV 89101

EHARDT, JOSEPH LAWRENCE, office automation cons. co. exec.; b. Oak Park, Ill., June 6, 1944; s. John and Mildred Elaine (Bitner) E.; m. Lela Merrette McMillian, Mar. 11, 1967. Programmer R&S Inc., San Francisco, 1966; mgr. utility program devel. Edmap Industries Inc., Walnut Creek, Calif., 1966-67; mgr. UNIX computer center Stanford Research Inst., Menlo Park, Calif., 1967-77; owner, pres. J.L. Ehardt & Assos., Milpitas, Calif., 1977—; lectr. U.S., Can., U.K. Mem. Assn. for Computing Machinery. Contbg. editor: The Seybold Report on Office Systems, 1979—. Office: PO Box 811 Milpitas CA 95035

EHEMANN, FREDERICK DANIEL, JR., water technician; b. Delaware County, Pa., Oct. 27, 1952; s. Frederick Daniel and Helen Belle (Pokorny) E. B.A. in Biology, W.Va. U., 1974, postgrad., 1975; postgrad. Austin Peay State U., Clarksville, Tenn., 1977. Cert. water treatment operator, Calif., wastewater treatment plant operator, Calif. Maintenance and operator trainee Sphere Mgmt. Inc., Federal Way, Wash., 1981; water plant technician Boeing Service Inc., Ft. Irwin, Calif., 1981—. Served with U.S. Army, 1976-80. Mem. Am. Water Works Assn. Presbyterian. Clubs: High Desert Bicycle, Elks (Barstow, Calif.). Home: 220 Hutchison St Apt A Barstow CA 92311 Office: 384 O & M Branch Fort Irwin CA 92310

EHLERS, ELEANOR MAY COLLIER (MRS. FREDERICK BURTON EHLERS), civic worker; b. Klamath Falls, Oreg., Apr. 23, 1920; d. Alfred Douglas and Ethel (Foster) Collier; B.A., U. Oreg., 1941; secondary tchr. credential Stanford U., 1942; m. Frederick Burton Ehlers, June 26, 1943; children—Frederic Douglas, Charles Collier. Tchr., Salinas Union High Sch., 1942-43; pvt. piano tchr., Klamath Falls, 1958—. Mem. Child Guidance Adv. Council Klamath Falls, 1956-60; mem. adv. com. Boys and Girls Aid Soc. Klamath Falls, 1965—; mem. Gov.'s Adv. Com. Arts and Humanities, 1966-67; mem. regional adv. com. Oreg. Arts Commn.; bd. dirs. Friends of Mus. U. Oreg., 1966-69, Arts in Oreg., 1966-68, Klamath County Colls. for Oreg.'s Future, 1968—; chpt. pres. Am. Field Service, 1962-63; mem. Gov.'s Com. Governance of Community Colls., 1967; bd. mem. Community Concert Assn., Klamath Falls, 1950-78, pres., 1966-76; established Women's Guild at Presbyn. Intercommunity Hosp., 1965; chmn. adv. com. for nursing Oreg. Tech. Inst., 1971—; trustee Presbyn. Intercommunity Hosp., Klamath Falls, sec. bd. trustees, 1962-65, 76—, mem. bldg. com. 1962-67, mem. planning com., chmn. edn. and research com. hosp. bd., 1967—; bd. dirs. Favell Mus. Western Art, 1971—. Named Woman of Month, Klamath Herald News, 1965; Quota Club Woman of Achievement for Klamath County, 1981; recipient Greatest Service award Oreg. Tech. Inst., 1971; Pioneer award U. Oreg., 1981. Mem. AAUW (local pres. 1955-56, local grant honoree 1970), Klamath Art Assn., Nat., Oreg. music tchrs. assns., PEO (state officer 1968-75, nat. com. 1975-77, trustee program for continuing edn. 1977—), Pi Beta Phi, Mu Phi Epsilon, Pi Lambda Theta. Presbyn. Address: 1338 Pacific Terr Klamath Falls OR 97601

EHLERS, FREDERICK DOUGLAS, real estate developer; b. San Francisco, Aug. 18, 1945; s. Frederick Burton and Eleanor (Collier) E.; B.B.A., U. Oreg., 1967; children—Claire Collier, Janet Victoria. Vice-pres. Swan Lake Moulding Co., Klamath Falls, Oreg., 1971—; real estate developer, 1978—; mng. ptnr. Jefferson Sq. Mall, Klamath Falls, 1979—. Prin. oboe, bd. dirs. Plum Ridge Symphony; mem. Klamath County Republican Central Com.; bd. dirs. Klamath Falls YMCA. Served with AUS, 1967-71. Decorated Bronze Star, Air medal with five oak leaf clusters. Mem. Internat. Council Shopping Ctrs., Klamath County Econ. Devel. Assn., Nat. Retail Hardware Assn., Nat. Bldg. Materials Assn., Western Bldg. Materials Assn. Republican. Presbyterian. Home: Sunset Beach Rd Klamath Falls OR 97601 Office: Box 5148 Klamath Falls OR 97601

EHLERS, JOHN PAUL, safety director; b. Chgo., July 4, 1954; s. Mason Charles and Dorothy Louise (Metz) E.; m. Angela Beate, Dec. 20, 1975. B.S. in Phys. Ed., Valparaise U., 1976. Safety dir. Crude Co., Casper, Wyo., 1980—. Served as capt. USMC, 1976-80. Recipient Safety Supr. of Yr. award Wyo. Trucking Assn., 1981. Mem. Am. Soc. Safety Engrs. (sec. 1980, v.p. 1981). Republican. Lutheran. Clubs: Masons, Toastmasters (pres. 1983).

EHLERS, KENNETH WARREN, physicist; b. Dix, Nebr., Aug. 3, 1922; s. Walter Richard and Clara (Sievers) E.; B.S., U. Colo., 1943; postgrad. Okla. A&M Coll., 1943-44, MIT, 1945; m. Marion Catherine Ward, Mar. 4, 1947; 1 son, Gary Walter. Head electronic aids dept. Landing Aids Exptl. Sta., Arcata, Calif., 1946-50; sr. physicist Lawrence Berkeley Lab., U. Calif., Berkeley, 1950—; cons. Brobeck Industries, Berkeley, 1961—, Avco Corp., Tulsa, 1962-65, Applied Radiation Corp., 1962-65, Cyclotron Corp., Berkeley, 1965—, New Eng. Nuclear. Served with USNR, 1942-46. Mem. Am. Phys. Soc., Am. Vacuum Soc., AAAS. Methodist. Contbr. articles to profl. jours.; editorial bd. Rev. Sci. Instruments, 1966—; inventor in field. Home: 3129 Via Larga Alamo CA 94507 Office: U Calif Lawrence Berkeley Lab Bldg 4 Berkeley CA 94720

EHLERS, WAYNE HENRY, state legislator, librarian; b. Bellingham, Wash., Nov. 25, 1938; s. Fritz and Maxine (Teller) E.; children—Jeffrey Spencer, Marcus Evans. B.A., B.S., Western Wash. U., 1960; M.A., U. Denver, 1967. Tchr., Tacoma, Wash., 1960-61, Sedro-Woolley, Wash., 1961-64, Lake Stevens, Wash., 1964-66, Franklin-Pierce Schs., Tacoma, 1967—; prof. Pacific Lutheran U., 1968-81; mem. Wash. Ho. of Reps., 1973—, minority leader, 1981-83, speaker, 1983—. Served with USMCR, 1955-56. Named Legislator of Yr., State VFW, 1977, Newsmaker of Tomorrow, Pierce County, 1983; recipient Disting. Alumni award Western Wash. U., 1979. Mem. NEA, Wash. Edn. Assn. Democrat.

EHORN, RALPH WILLARD, photographer; b. Red Bluff, Calif., Mar. 21, 1934; s. Samuel Fraley and Gertrude (Willard) E.; m. V. Joanne Hagan, Mar. 2, 1963; children—David, Tanya. A.A., Shasta Community Coll., 1955. Photographer, owner Ehorn's Natural Photography, Red Bluff, 1956—; one-man show: Humboldt Savs. & Loan, Red Bluff, 1982. Served with Calif. N.G., 1952-60. Mem. Profl. Photographers Am., Profl. Photographers N. Valley (pres.), Profl. Photographers Calif. Republican. Studio: 714 Main St Red Bluff CA 96080

EHRLICH, CAROLYN, nurse; b. Meadville, Pa., June 8, 1943; m. Ira B. Ehrlich. Diploma Meadville City Hosp. Sch. Nursing, 1964; B.S. in Nursing magna cum laude, Ariz. State U., 1972, M.S. in Nursing summa cum laude, 1973. R.N., Ariz. Staff nurse Meadville City Hosp., 1964-65; supr. critical care areas John F. Kennedy Meml. Hosp., Lake Worth, Fla., 1965-67; preceptor instr. coronary care project U. Wash., Seattle, 1967-68; nursing coordinator coronary care coordination project, co-dir. sub-regional coronary care edn. project Wash./Alaska Regional Med. Program, Seattle, 1968-69, coronary care cons., 1969; inservice educator for critical care areas Doctors Hosp., Phoenix, 1969-70; staff nurse St. Joseph's Hosp., Phoenix, 1971-72; dir., cardiovascular nurse specialist program Ariz. Heart Inst., Phoenix, 1973-76; dir. clin. nursing, critical care service Good Samaritan Hosp., Phoenix, 1976-80, sr. dir. nursing inpatient service, 1980-82; med.-legal cons. Jennings, Strauss & Salmon, 1983—. Coronary Care Edn. Project grantee, 1968; recipient Outstanding Performance award John F. Kennedy Meml. Hosp., 1967. Mem. Am. Assn. Critical Care Nurses (pres. chpt. 1972, nat. treas. 1973-75, chmn. numerous coms. 1973-78, nat. pres.-elect 1976, nat. pres. 1977, past pres. cert. bd. 1978, chmn. cert. com. 1973-78, liaison com. 1977, rep. to assns.; life), Am. Heart Assn. Ariz. Affiliate (nurse edn. com. 1973-76), Am. Soc. Nursing Service Adminstrs. (assoc.), Ariz. Nurses in Mgmt., Assn. Operating Room Nurses (cert. council, dir. 1978), Nat. League Nursing, Soc. Critical Care Medicine (nominating com. 1978, edn. com. 1978). Contbr. numerous articles to profl. jours.; editorial bd. Jour. Critical Care. Home: 2510 E Montebello Phoenix AZ 85016

EHRLICH, IRA BERT, cardiologist; b. Chgo., Oct. 30, 1938; s. Joe C. and Corinne (Freed) E.; B.A., Stanford U., 1960; M.D., Harvard, 1964; m. Carolyn; children—David, Diana. Intern, resident in internal medicine U. Calif. Los Angeles Med. Center, 1964-67; fellow cardiology U. Calif., San Francisco Med. Center, 1967-69; pvt. practice specializing in cardiology, Phoenix, 1969—; chmn. dept. medicine St. Joseph's Hosp., 1976—, dir. coronary care unit, 1974—. Fellow Am. Coll. Cardiology, A.C.P.; mem. Am. Heart Assn. (past pres. Ariz. affiliate and Maricopa County div.), Maricopa County Med. Soc., Ariz. Med. Assn., AMA. Republican. Jewish. Club: Moon Valley Country. Home: 2510 E Montebello Phoenix AZ 85016 Office: 222 W Thomas Rd Phoenix AZ 85013

EHRLICH, PAUL RALPH, biologist, educator; b. Phila., May 29, 1932; s. William and Ruth (Rosenberg) E.; A.B., U. Pa., 1953; M.A., U. Kans., 1955, Ph.D., 1957; m. Anne Fitzhugh Howland, Dec. 18, 1954; 1 dau., Lisa Marie. Research asso. U. Kans., Lawrence, 1958-59; asst. prof. biol. scis. Stanford U., 1959-62, asso. prof., 1962-66, prof., 1966—, Bing prof. population studies, 1976—, dir. grad. study dept. biol. scis., 1966-69, 1974-76; cons. Behavioral Research Labs., 1963-67; adviser in biol. scis. McGraw Hill Book Co., N.Y.C., 1966-75, cons. editor in population biology, 1966—. Fellow AAAS, Calif. Acad. Scis.; mem. Am. Acad. Arts and Scis., Soc. Study Evolution, Soc. Systematic Zoology, Am. Soc. Naturalists, Lepidopterists Soc., Am. Mus. Natural History (hon. life mem.). Author: How to Know the Butterflies, 1961; Process of Evolution, 1963; Principles of Modern Biology, 1968; Population Bomb, 1968, 2d edit., 1971; Population, Resources, Environment: Issues in Human Ecology, 1970, 2d edit., 1972; How to be a Survivor, 1971; Global Ecology: Readings Toward a Rational Strategy for Man, 1971; Man and the Ecosphere, 1971; Introductory Biology, 1973; Human Ecology: Problems and Solutions, 1973; Ark II: Social Response to Environmental Imperatives, 1974; The End of Affluence: A Blueprint for the Future, 1974; Biology and Society, 1976; Race Bomb, 1977; Ecoscience: Population, Resources, Environment, 1977; Insect Biology, 1978; The Golden Door: International Migration, Mexico and the U.S., 1979; Extinction: The Causes and Consequences on the Disappearance of Species, 1981; contbr. articles to profl. jours. Address: Biological Scis Stanford U Stanford CA 94305

EHRMAN, KENNETH ALFRED, lawyer; b. San Francisco, May 21, 1917; s. Alexis Leon and Elizabeth Arnold (Bissinger) E.; B.S., Harvard U., 1938; postgrad. U. Paris, 1938-39; LL.B., Lasalle U., 1960; m. Jean Ransohoff Colyer, Oct. 12, 1946; children—Michael James, David Alexis, Keith Arnold. With Internat. News Service, Paris, 1939-40; writer San Francisco Call-Bull., 1941, 46-51; admitted to Calif. bar, 1961; practiced in Monterey, Calif., 1961—; mem. firms Kenneth A. Ehrman, 1961-68, Ehrman, Flavin & Morris, 1968—; legal cons. Monterey Peninsula Coll., 1964—, Monterey Parking Authority, 1961-62; counsel Monterey Peninsula Found., 1972—; dir., counsel Human Interaction Research Inst., Los Angeles, 1962—; instr. U. So. Calif. Inst. Tax Adminstrn., part-time 1972-73; speaker U. So. Calif. Tax Inst., 1974, 79, 82. Served to capt. AUS, 1941-46, 51-52. Mem. State Bar Calif. (com. taxation 1971-74, mem. exec. com. tax sect. 1975-79, co-chmn. tax sect. 1977-78, chmn. property, sales and local tax com.

1976-77), Monterey County Bar Assn. (chmn. lawyers reference service com. and fee guide com. 1964-65), Am. Arbitration Assn. (panel 1962—). Author: (with Sean Flavin) Taxing California Property, 1967, 2d edit., 1979; contbr. articles to profl. publs. Home: 28 Sylvan Rd Monterey CA 93940 Office: 400 Camino El Estero Monterey CA 93940

EHRSAM, ELDON EDWARD, operations research analyst, real estate broker, securities representative; b. Bern, Kans., July 8, 1936; s. Loyd and Elma Elizabeth (Bauman) E.; B.S., Washburn U., Topeka, 1962; M.S., U. So. Calif., 1969; m. Clara Louise Schwartz, Nov. 20, 1957; children—Elizabeth Sue, Jeffrey Edward, John Eldon, Brian Loyd. Physicist, Naval Ordnance Lab., Corona, Calif., 1962-65; electronic engr. Hdqrs. AF Western Test Range, Vandenberg AFB, Calif., 1965-68; project mgr. Hdqrs. Space and Missile Test Center, Vandenberg AFB, 1968-73, telemetry systems mgr., 1973-76, ops. research analyst, 1976—; broker assoc. Real Properties Investments, Solvang, Calif., 1981—; securities rep. Vestcap Securities Corp., Solvang, 1982—. Asst. scoutmaster Boy Scouts Am. Cert. in computer tech. U. Calif., Santa Barbara, 1972; lic. real estate broker, Calif. Mem. AIAA, Internat. Platform Assn., Nat. Assn. Securities Dealers, Nat. Assn. Realtors, Real Estate Securities and Syndication Inst., Sigma Pi Sigma. Club: Masons, Elks. Home: 3087 Fairlea Rd Santa Ynez CA 93460 Office: Hq Space and Missile Test Center Code XREA Vandenberg Air Force Base CA 93437

EICHELBERGER, TED DAVID, real estate adminstr., developer; b. Dayton, Ohio, Feb. 24, 1930; s. Perle T. and Eleanor L. (Winters) E.; student Northwestern U., 1948-50, grad. Sch. Mortgage Banking, 1961; B.A. in Music, Ohio State U., 1952, postgrad. commerce, law, 1952-56; m. Martha May Burton, June 3, 1950; children—Jane (Mrs. Alan Baron), Martha Lynn, Ted David. Casualty adjuster Allstate Ins. Co., 1956-58; credit and loan adminstr. Security Pacific Bank, 1958-64; v.p. Citizens Nat. Co., 1961-64; realtor, San Bernardino, Calif., 1964—; v.p. Auto Coach Corp., San Bernardino, 1964-80. Bd. dirs. San Bernardino Bd. Realtors, 1965-68, mem. com. profl. standards, 1967-70, 72-78; bd. dirs. San Bernardino Symphony Assn., 1969-71. Mem. Town Hall Calif. Club: Bermuda Dunes Racquet. Home: 2395 Willow Dr San Bernardino CA 92404 Office: 80-975 Indio Blvd Indio CA 92201 Mailing Address: PO Box 476 Highland CA 92346

EICHENHOLTZ, MARC JEFFREY, computer consultant; b. N.Y.C. Aug. 7, 1951; s. Leonard Lester and Norma Emma (Markowitz) E. B.S. in Computer Sci., B.E. in Elec. Engring., SUNY-Stonybrook, 1974; M.B.A., Pepperdine U., 1981. Applications cons. Tymshare, 1974-75, sr. systems analyst, Cupertino, Calif., 1975-77, project leader, Mountain View, Calif., 1977-79; product mgr. DMC Systems Inc., Santa Clara, Clara, 1979-80; prin. Practical Solutions, Cupertino, 1980—. Mem. Am. Mgmt. Assn., S-100 Bus Assn. for Computing Machinery, NOW. Jewish. Author Billmaster (computer software), 1980. Office: Practical Solutions 175 N Central Ave Valley Stream NY 11580

EICHNER, BARBARA GAIL, home economist; b. Roseburg, Oreg., Oct. 11, 1946; d. Raymond E. and Regina (Steiner) Miller; m. Eugene P. Eichner, Sept. 6, 1969 (div.). B.S. in Home Econs., Oreg. State U.-Corvallis, 1968, M.Ed. in Adult Edn., 1972. Extension home economist Wash. State U., Skamania County, 1969-70, Oreg. State U., Harney County, 1972-73, U. Alaska, Anchorage, 1973—; panel speaker Arco Gas & Oil Contemporary Consumer Issues, 1981; judge Sheraton Anchorage Dream Dinner Contest, 1981-82, Alaska Airlines Dessert Classic, 1980-82. Treas., v.p. Conflict Resolution Ctr. Bd., Anchorage, mem. Community Housing Relations Bd., Anchorage. Mem. Am. Home Econs. Assn., Alaska Home Econ. Assn., Anchorage Home Econs. Assn., Internat. Farm Youth Exchange Assn., Internat. Fedn. Home Econs., Assn. Women in Devel., Nat. Assn. Extension Home Economists, Phi Kappa Phi. Episcopalian. Home: 3101 Delta Dr Anchorage AK 99502 Office: 2651 Providence Ave Anchorage AK 99508

EICHSTAEDT, ROBERT, physicist, inventor; b. Pasadena, Calif., Nov. 28, 1946; s. Howard M. and Elnora (Jellen) E.; B.S. in Physics, U. Calif., Berkeley, 1964, M.S. in Math., 1968, PH.D. in Physics, 1972. Dir. research physics dept. Calif. Acad. Scis., San Francisco; dir. Krypton Corp., Emeryville, Calif. L.E. Funt fellow, 1978. Mem. AAAS. Author: Suspensory Plates and Discs, 1977. Home: 3456 Baker St San Francisco CA 94122 Office: California Acad of Sciences Golden Gate Park San Francisco CA 94118

EIDAM, GREGORY RALPH, mech. engr.; b. Elyria, Ohio, Mar. 3, 1948; s. Henry Frank and Clara (Pniewski) E.; B.S., Central New Eng. Coll., 1975; m. Christine Coleman, June 13, 1970; children—Gregory Ralph, Shannon L., Meggan R., Curtiss S. Mech. engr. Stone & Webster Engring. Corp., Boston, 1974-75; design engr. Aerojet Nuclear Corp., Idaho Falls, Idaho, 1975-76; project engr. E G & G Idaho, Idaho Falls, 1976-78, mgmt. specialist, 1978-79, sr. project engr. assigned temporarily to Three Mile Island as mgr. radiation and environment project for Dept. Energy, NRC, GPU and EPRI Info. and Examination Program, 1979-81, sr. project engr. assigned to Three Mile Island in reactor evaluation program for Dept. Energy, 1981—. Active Boy Scouts Am., 1962—. Served with USN, 1968-74. Republican. Contbr. articles in field to profl. jours. Office: PO Box 1625 Idaho Falls ID 83415

EIDE, BARBY FAIRBANKS, author, profl. speaker, tng. specialist; b. Utica, N.Y., Aug. 26, 1938; d. Ben F. Swider and Sally M. (Bawol) George; student San Francisco City Coll., 1972-75; cert. in biofeedback tng. and stress mgmt. Menninger Found., Topeka, 1977; cert. instr. devel. program Wash. State Community Coll., 1979; m. Leroy M. Eide, Feb. 17, 1978. Owner, Barby Eide & Assos., personal and profl. devel. programs Spokane, 1979—. Mem. Am. Soc. Assn. Execs., Am. Soc. Tng. and Devel., Nat. Speakers Assn. Contbr. chpts. to books in field. Office: PO Box 8524 Spokane WA 99203

EIE, LEIF DAGFINN, airline exec.; b. Flekkefjord, Norway, July 12, 1929; s. Lars and Aagot Dagmar (Olsen) E.; came to U.S., 1952, naturalized, 1954; grad. Ringard Realskole, 1946, Flekkefjord Bus. Coll., 1947; student Non Commd. Officer Sch., 1953, Heilbron, Germany Studies Program, 1954-55; m. Patricia MacKean, June 21, 1957; children—Lisa Britt, Christian. Store mgr. Horjen's Bookstore, Norway, 1944-46; acct. Tonnesen's Paint Store, Norway, 1947-48; band leader, Norway, 1948-49; ventriloquist, singer, actor, Norway, 1950-52; with Scandinavian Airlines, 1952—, area mgr., Seattle, 1964—; founder Travel Com., 1960; condr. various travel seminars; bd. dirs. Wash. State Trade Commn., 1973-75, Seattle Vis. Bur., 1977-79. Founder Bergen-Seattle Sister City, 1967, Tashkent/Seattle Sister City, 1976, Ski for Light, cross-country ski for blind, Seattle, 1975; founder Norwegian Am. C. of C., 1968; founder, chmn. Swedish Am. C. of C., 1977; regent-at-large Pacific Luth. U., 1980-83. Served with Norwegian Air Force, 1948, U.S. Army, 1953-55. Decorated St. Olva medal (Norway); Order No. Star (Sweden); recipient Am. Spirit Honor medal 1953; Disting. Service award Pacific Luth. U., 1977; Readers Digest award, 1969; subject of Wash. State Senate Resolution, 1972; named Goodwill Ambassador, Wash. State, 1973. Mem. Seattle C. of C., Norwegian C. of C. Swedish C. of C., Danish C. of C., Seattle-King County Conv. and Vis. Bur., Nordic Council. Lutheran. Clubs: Swedish, Danish, Norwegian Comml., Sons of Norway. Recordings of Scandinavian folk songs; research on effects of electrolyses on humans. Office: 2727 Rainier Bank Tower Seattle WA 98101

EIFLER, CARL FREDERICK, ret. psychologist; b. Los Angeles, June 27, 1906; s. Carl Frederick and Pauline (Engelbert) E.; Ph.D., Ill. Inst. Tech., 1962; B.D., Jackson Coll.; m. Margaret Christine Aaberg, June 30, 1963; 1 son, Carl Henry; 1 stepson, Byron Hisey. Insp., U.S. Bur. Customs, 1928-35, chief insp., 1936-37, dep. collector, 1937-56; bus. mgr. Jackson Coll., Honolulu, 1954-56, instr., 1955-56; grad. asst. instr., research asst. Ill. Inst. Tech., Chgo., 1959-62; psychologist Monterey County Mental Health Services, Salinas, Calif., 1964-73. Served with U.S. Army, 1922-23, 40-47; col. ret. Decorated Combat Infantryman's Badge, Legion of Merit with 2 oak leaf clusters, Bronze Star medal, Air medal, Purple Heart. Mem. Am., Western States, Calif., Monterey County psychol. assns., AAUP, Res. Officers Assn. (Hawaii pres. 1947), Assn. Former Intelligence Officers (bd. govs., Western coordinator), Pearl Harbor Survivors, 101 Assn., Assn. U.S. Army, Vets. of OSS (western v.p.), Am. Law Enforcement Officers Assn., Nat. Intelligence Study Center, Security and Intelligence Fund, Ret. Officers Assn., Psi Chi. Clubs: Masons, KT, Shriners, Elks, Nat. Sojourners. Contbg. author Psychon. Sci., vol. 20, 1970; co-author: The Deadliest Colonel; author: Jesus Said. Home: 22700 Picador Dr Salinas CA 93908

EIGNER, MICHAEL, TV station executive; b. May 13, 1945; s. Ernst and Hana E.; M.B.A., CCNY, 1967; m. Linda Eigner, Nov. 9, 1969; children—Alyson Sara, Dana Beth. Account exec. Ted Bates Advt., N.Y.C., 1967-70; sales account exec Telerep Inc., N.Y.C., 1970-72, Petry TV Inc., N.Y.C., 1972-74; nat. sales mgr. Sta. KTLA-TV, Los Angeles, 1974-77, v.p., gen. sales mgr., 1977—. Office: 5800 Sunset Blvd Hollywood CA 90028

EIKENBERRY, KENNETH OTTO, lawyer, state ofcl.; b. Wenatchee, Wash., June 29, 1932; s. Otto Kenneth and Florence Estelle Eikenberry; B.A. in Polit. Sci., Wash. State U., 1954; LL.B., U. Wash., 1959; m. Beverly Jane Hall, Dec. 21, 1963. Admitted to Wash. bar, 1959; spl. agt. FBI, 1960-62; dep. pros. atty. King County, Seattle, 1962-67; with firm Clinton, Andersen, Fleck & Glein, Seattle, 1967-73; staff atty. King County Council, 1974-77; chmn. Wash. Republican Com., 1977-80; atty. gen. State of Wash., 1981—; judge pro tem Seattle Mcpl. Ct., 1979-80. Chmn. King County Rep. Conv., 1974, 78; mem. Wash. Ho. of Reps., 1970-74. Served with AUS, 1954-56. Named Legislator of Yr., Young Ams. for Freedom/Wash. Conservative Union, 1974, Rep. Man of Yr., Young Men's Rep. Club King County, 1979. Mem. ABA, Wash. Bar Assn., King County Bar Assn., Soc. Former Spl. Agts. FBI, Delta Theta Phi, Alpha Tau Omega. Clubs: Elks, Olympia Goose and Duck. Office: Temple of Justice Olympia WA 98504*

EILAND, MICHAEL DENT, army officer; b. Pasadena, Calif., Mar. 4, 1940; s. Julian Dent and Mary Kay (Thiele) E.; m. 2d, Chan Ve Hoang, Jan. 15, 1973; children—Daniel, Jonathan. B.S., U.S. Mil. Acad., 1961; M.A., Georgetown U., 1969, postgrad., 1976-83. Commd. 2d lt. U.S. Army 1961; advanced through grades to col., 1983; with Green Berets, Southeast Asia, 1966-74, asst. for econ. policy and analysis to Asst. Sec. Def., Washington, 1975-77, polit. mil. advisor to asst. sec. State for East Asia and Pacific Affairs Washington, 1977-79, dir. refugee and relief program U.S. Embassy, Bangkok, Thailand, 1980—. Decorated Bronze Star, Air medal, Republic Vietnam Cross of Gallantry, Honor medal. Mem. Am. Econ. Assn., Asia Soc., Assn. U.S. Army, Assn. Asian Studies. Club: Fgn. Correspondents (Bangkok). Contbr. articles to profl. jours. Home: 2011 Garfield Rd San Diego CA 92110 Office: American Embassy Bangkok Thailand

EILAND, MURRAY LEE, JR., psychiatrist; b. Taft, Calif., Sept. 9, 1936; s. Murray Lee and Francis Lenore (Perrigo) E.; B.A. with honors, U. Calif. at Berkeley, 1958; M.D., U. Calif. at San Francisco, 1961; m. Astrid Esther Hilweg, Nov. 19, 1966; 1 son, Murray Lee III. Intern USPHS Hosp., S.I., N.Y., 1961-62; resident Langley Porter Neuropsychiat. Inst., San Francisco, 1962-65; psychiatrist Napa State Hosp., Imola, Calif., 1965—, program dir., 1971—. Dir. Oriental Rug Co. Berkeley, Inc. Mem. A.M.A., Am. Psychiat. Assn., Phi Beta Kappa. Author: Oriental Rugs, A Comprehensive Guide, 1973; Oriental Rugs From Western Collections, 1973; Chinese and Exotic Rugs, 1979, We're Off to See The Wizard, 1980. Home: 199 Hillcrest Rd Berkeley CA 94705 Office: Napa State Hosp Imola CA 94558

EILERS, ELIZABETH ANNE, flight attendant, counselor; b. Saranac Lake, N.Y., Nov. 18, 1951; d. H.D. and Elizabeth T. (Carroll) Eilers. B.S. Mo. State U.-Warrensberg, 1974; M.A. U. Colo., 1982. Flight attendant, United Airlines, 1976—; counselor, U. Colo. Women's Ctr., 1982—; counselor, Auraria Higher Edn. Ctr., 1981—; counselor U. Colo.-Denver, 1980-82; cons., workshop leader. Mem. Am. Personnel and Guidance Assn., Colo. Personnel and Guidance Assn., Am. Mental Health Counselors Assn., Colo. Mental Health Assn., Nat. Assn. Social Workers, Psi Chi.

EILS, RICHARD GEORGE, retail store chain executive; b. Milw., 1937. Student U. Wis., 1960. Pres., dir. Thrifty Corp., Los Angeles, Borun Books, Discount Drug Stores, Thrifty Realty Co.; vice chmn., dir. Crown Books; dir. Newman Importing Co., United Merchandising Corp. Office: Thrifty Corp 5051 Rodeo Rd Los Angeles CA 90016*

EINHORN, DAVID RICHARD, fin. corp. ofcl.; b. N.Y.C., May 26, 1951; s. Norman Albert and Phyllis (Dolowitch) E.; B.S. in Acctg., Rider Coll., 1973; m. Peggy Ann Monegan, Aug. 7, 1976 (div.); children—Steven David, Michelle Peggy. Staff auditor Touche Ross and Co., Newark, 1973, sr. auditor, Los Angeles, 1973-78; asst. dir. systems audits Beneficial Standard Corp., Los Angeles, 1978, asst. dir. internal audit/systems audits, 1979, dir. internal audit, 1980-81; controller Exec. Life Ins. Co., Beverly Hills, Calif., 1979-80; mgr. West Coast corp. audit CIGNA Corp., Los Angeles, 1982—. C.P.A., cert. info. systems auditor. Mem. Am. Inst. C.P.A.s, Calif. Soc. C.P.A.s, EDP Auditors Assn., Inst. Internal Auditors. Republican. Jewish. Club: Jaycees. Home: 3416 Manning Ave Apt 1611 Los Angeles CA 90064 Office: 3807 Wilshire Blvd Los Angeles CA 90010

EISELE, MILTON DOUGLAS, viticulturist; b. N.Y.C., Apr. 2, 1910; s. Charles Francis and Helen Agnes (Dolan) E.; B.A., U. Calif.-Berkeley, 1933; grad. San Francisco Stock Exchange Inst., 1938; m. Barbara Lois Morgan, July 26, 1941; children—Helen Frances Eisele Osthimer, Barbara Glennis, William Douglas. Investment cashier Wells Fargo Bank, San Francisco, 1934-39; coordinator cement sales Permanente Corp., 1940-41, constrn. supt., 1941-43; mgr. refractory div. Kaiser Aluminum, 1943-47, mgr. regional sales, Chgo., 1947-50, mgr. foil div., 1950-55, mgr. prodn., 1955-60, mgr. market and prodn. devel., 1960-65, mgr. investments, 1966-71; ret., 1971; owner, operator Eisele Vineyards, Napa Valley, Calif., 1969—. Pres., bd. dirs. Napa Valley Found., 1981—; bd. dirs., past chmn. Vintage Hall, Inc., 1973—; bd. dirs., past pres. Napa Valley Heritage Fund, 1973—; past pres., bd. dirs. Upper Napa Valley Assocs., 1976-80; mem. adv. council Napa County Land Trust, 1976—. Mem. Am. Soc. Enologists, Napa Valley Grape Growers Assn. (dir.), Calif. Wine Grapes Growers Assn. (dir., past sec.), Kappa Alpha Order. Republican. Episcopalian (vestryman, sr. warden 1966-69). Club: Commonwealth (San Francisco). Home and Office: 2155 Pickett Rd Calistoga CA 94515

EISELE, RONALD MICHAEL, wastwater superintendent; b. Harvey, Ill., Aug. 8, 1955; s. Stanley John Siervga and Joy Ann Eisele; m. Cassy Lee, May 18, 1979; children—Jodi Lynn, Jerry Joe, Ronald Michael. A.A. in Law Enforcement, Northland Pioneer Coll., 1980; postgrad. in wastwater Pima Community Coll., 1978-83, No. Ariz. U., 1981-82. With Holbrook (Ariz.) Water Dept., 1977—, foreman, 1980-82, supt., mcpl. lab. dir., 1983—; assoc. faculty Northland Pioneer Coll. Served with AUS, 1976. Mem. Ariz. Water and Pollution Control Assn., Water Pollution Control Fedn., Am. Water Works Assn. Republican. Roman Catholic. Club: Elks. Home: 914 E Florida Holbrook AZ 86025 Office: PO Box 70 Holbrook AZ 86025

EISELEIN, EDDIE BILL, applied anthropologist; b. Pensacola, Fla., Dec. 31, 1942; s. Adolf E. and Jean (MacKenzie) E.; m. Judith Doonan, Apr. 30, 1978. B.A., U. Mont., 1965, M.A., U. Ariz., 1967, Ph.D., 1969. Research dir. Sta. KUAT-TV/AM/FM, Tucson, 1969-80; assoc. prof. Radio-TV U. Ariz., Tucson, 1971-80; research dir. A & A Research, Kalispell, Mont., 1980—; co-owner, mgr. Kalispell Litho Lab, 1980—. Career fellow Corp. Pub. Broadcasting, 1970-71; recipient Best of West award radio prodn. Western Ednl. Soc. Telecommunications, 1971; Ariz. Sch. Bell award radio programming Ariz. Ednl. Assn., 1973. Mem. Am. Assn. Pub. Opinion Research. Buddhist. Author: Broadcast Communications Research Materials, 1978; An Introduction to Communication Theory, 1978; FIESTA: Minority Television Programming, 1974, Minority Broadcasting, 1977; Native American Media and Information Needs, 1982. Home: 23 Konley Kalispell MT 59901 Office: A & A Research PO Box 919 Kalispell MT 59901

EISEN, JERRY M., management consultant; b. Bklyn., July 2, 1934; s. Benjamin and Tillie (Katzoff) E.; A.B., Bklyn. Coll., 1956; M.B.A., CCNY, 1959; Ph.D., Ariz. State U., 1977; m. Janet Mery Severance, June 18, 1977; children—Gwen Diane, Eileen Marci. Asst. dir. indsl. relations The O'Malley Cos., Phoenix, 1959-65; sr. v.p. indsl. relations Ramada Inns, Inc., Phoenix, 1965-79; pres. Human Resource Center, Inc., Phoenix, 1979—; instr. mgmt. grad. div. U. Phoenix; disting. vis. lectr. hospitality mgmt. U. Wis., 1975-76; instr. U. Phoenix Grad. Program; condr. workshops and seminars in personnel adminstrn., labor and indsl. relations; mgmt. cons. human resources. Bd. dirs. Kivel Geriatric Ctr.; mem. City of Phoenix Human Relations Commn. Mem. Am. Soc. Personnel Adminstrn. (accredited exec. personnel), Am. Mgmt. Assn., Am. Soc. Tng. Dirs., Am. Soc. Personnel Adminstrn., Ariz. Indsl. Editors Assn. (pres. 1965-66), Internat. Council Indsl. Editors, World Affairs Council, Am. Hotel and Motel Assn. (vice-chmn. employee relations com. 1976-80), Ariz. Indsl. Relations Assn., Ariz. Adult Edn. Assn. (bd. dirs.), Phoenix Personnel Mgmt. Assn. (pres. 1968-69), Am. Soc. Profl. Cons., Council Personnel Officers, Internat. Hospitality Mgmt. Soc. (dir.), Met. Phoenix C. of C. (bd. dirs. Small Bus. Council). Jewish. Home: 2101 E Pasadena Ave Phoenix AZ 85016 Office: 3150 N 24th St Suite 201 Phoenix AZ 85016

EISENBERG, LAWRENCE HENRY, lawyer; b. Los Angeles, Jan. 16, 1936; A.A., Los Angeles City Coll., 1958; B.S. in Pub. Accounting, U. So. Calif., 1962, J.D., 1966, children—Aron Scott, Karen Ann. Auditor, GAO, Los Angeles, 1962-63; admitted to Calif. bar, 1966, U.S. Supreme Ct. bar, 1970; assoc. firm Ward & Heyler, Beverly Hills and Century City, Calif., 1966-71; individual practice law, Sherman Oaks, Calif., 1971-78, Encino, Calif., 1978—; examiner Calif. State Bar, 1970-72, mem. local adminstrv. com., 1972-74, mem. appellate cts. com., 1982—; judge pro tempore Los Angeles and Beverly Hills municipal cts., 1972—; examiner Los Angeles Police Dept. oral selection unit, 1973-79. Bd. dirs. Legion Lex, U. So. Calif. Law Center support group, 1970-80. Mem. Am., Calif., Los Angeles County, Beverly Hills (gov.), San Fernando Valley bar assns., Calif. Acad. Appellate Lawyers, Digital Equipment Computers Users Soc., Phi Alpha Delta. Office: 17141 Nance St Encino CA 91316 Tel (213) 788-0354

EISENBERG, NANCY HOPE, psychology educator; b. Cin., Mar. 12, 1950; d. Stanley Cooper and Marion (Rosenberg) E.; B.A., U. Mich., 1972; M.A., U. Calif.-Berkeley, 1975, Ph.D., 1976. Lectr., Sch. Social Work, U. Calif.-Berkeley, 1975-76, research psychologist Inst. Human Devel., 1976; asst. prof. psychology Ariz. State U., Tempe, 1976-80, assoc. prof., 1980—. NIMH grantee, 1978-79, Child Devel. Found. grantee, 1982, Ariz. State U. grantee, 1977, 79. Mem. Am. Psychol. Assn., Soc. for Research in Child Devel. Author: (with P. Mussem) Roots of Caring, Sharing and Helping, 1977; editor: The Development of Prosocial Behavior, 1982. Contbr. articles to profl. jours. Office: Dept Psychology Ariz State Univ Tempe AZ 85287

EISENMAN, DAVID ALAN, educator; b. Los Angeles, June 20, 1936; s. Herman and Cecilia (Budne) E.; A.A., Los Angeles City Coll., 1956; B.A., Los Angeles State Coll., 1958; M.S., U. So. Calif., 1959; m. Marilyn R. Miller, June 15, 1958; children—Marla, Dana, Gregory. Spl. edn. tchr., counselor Los Angeles City Schs., 1959-62; ednl. therapist, cons. ednl. therapist Marianne Frostig Center Ednl. Therapy, 1962-72, founder, exec. dir. Mardan Sch. Ednl. Therapy, Costa Mesa, Calif., 1963—. Mem. state task force Hunt for Handicapped in Calif., 1972; govtl. appointee Calif. Block Grant Com., 1982. Mem. Jaycees (mem. exec. bd. Westchester 1961-62), Calif. Assn. Neurologically Handicapped Children (Man of Yr. 1963-64), Council for Adminstrs. Spl. Edn., Council for Exceptional Children, Am. Assn. on Mental Deficiency, Calif. Assn. Pvt. Spl. Edn. Schs. (pres. 1973-75). Office: 695 W 19th St Costa Mesa CA 92627

EISENSHTAT, SIDNEY, architect; b. New Haven, June 6, 1914; s. Morris and Ella (Sobole) E.; B.Arch., U. So. Calif., 1935; m. Alice Brenner, Dec. 19, 1937; children—Carole Eisenshtat Oken, Abby (Mrs. Michael Robyn). Prin., Sidney Eisenshtat, A.I.A., Architect, & Assos., Beverly Hills, Calif., 1941—. Cons., Hechal Shlomo, Israel; mem. architects panel Union Am. Hebrew Congregations. Bd. dirs. Internat. Tech. Coop. Centre, Tel Aviv, Israel; chmn. bd. dirs. Beth Jacob Congregation. Recipient honor award A.I.A., 1960, 1966, award Nat. Sch. Adminstrs., 1966. Mem. Bur. Jewish Edn. (vice-chmn. 1971-77), Jewish Fedn. Council (vice-chmn. planning dept. 1971-72). Prin. archtl. works include B'nai David Synagogue, Detroit, 1967, Union Bank Bldg., 1960, Friars Club, 1961, Temple Mt. Sinai, El Paso, Tex., 1962, House of the Book, Brandeis, Calif., 1972, Executive Life Bldg., Beverly Hills, Calif., 1966, Marlton Sch. for Deaf, Los Angeles, 1968, Amelia Gray Bldg. (City of Beverly Hills award), 1974, Knox Presbyn. Ch. (Los Angeles Beautiful award), 1975, U. Judaism, Los Angeles, 1977, Nazareno Gabrielli (City of Beverly Hills award), 1978, Hughes Aircraft Satellite Testing and Computer Center, El Segundo, Calif., Wells Fargo Bldg. (City of Beverly Hills award). Home: 2736 Motor Ave Los Angeles CA 90064 Office: 144 S Beverly Dr Beverly Hills CA 90212

EISENSTADT, MELVIN MORTIMER, mechanical engineer; b. N.Y.C., Feb. 1, 1931; s. Abraham and May (Sheriff) E.; B.S. in Mech. Engring., U. Fla., 1952; Ph.D., U. Ariz., 1965; J.D., U. N.Mex., 1976; m. Pauline Doreen Bauman, Nov. 20, 1960; children—Todd, Keith. Engr. N.Am. Aviation Co., Los Angeles, 1955-56; engr. Fairchild Engine & Aircraft Co., Manhattan Beach, Calif., 1956-57; sr. engr. Martin Co., Orlando, Fla., 1959-61; assoc. prof. mech. engring. U. P.R., Mayagues, 1970-73; asst. prof. mech. engring. U. Calif.-Santa Barbara, 1965-60; practice law, 1976-77, 81—; pres. Soltrax, Inc., 1977-78, Mel Eisenstadt & Assocs., Inc., 1978-81; judge Mcpl. Ct. of Corrales (N.Mex.), 1980—; cons. in field. Served as 1st. lt. USAF, 1952-54. NSF fellow, 1970, NASA fellow, 1971; N.Mex. State grantee, 1974-75. Mem. ASME, Nat., N.Mex. socs. profl. engrs., Am. Phys. Soc., N.Mex. Solar Energy Assn., N.Mex., Am. bar assns., Am. Trial Lawyers Assn., Sigma Tau. Author: Introduction to Mechanical Properties of Materials, 1971; contbg. author: Legal Aspects of Solar Energy, 1981. Contbr. articles to sci., engring., legal jours. Home: PO Box 658 Corrales NM 87048 Office: 3325 Candelara NE Albuquerque NM 87107

EISNER, ALAN M., social service supervisor; b. Steubenville, Ohio, Mar. 30, 1938; s. Arthur and Teressa Shirley (Weis) E.; B.S.J., Ohio U., 1960; M.S.W., U. Pitts., 1970; m. Rhonda Koff, July 4, 1976; 2 daus., Rachel Beth, Victoria Renee. Editor, Am. Jewish Outlook, Pitts., 1960-61; adminstrv. asst. Montefiore Hosp., Pitts., 1967-69; psychiat. social worker Met. State Hosp., Norwalk, Calif., 1970-73, Continuing Care Services br. State of Calif., Los Angeles, 1973-77; social service cons. health facilities licensing Calif. Dept. Social Services, Los Angeles, 1978-80, supr., 1980—; mem. Calif. Bd. Behavior Sci. Examiners; bd. dirs. Jefferson County Mental Health and Guidance Center, 1963-64; mem. Ohio Community Action Council, 1964. Served with AUS, 1961, 62-63. Lic. clin. social worker, Calif. Mem. Nat. Assn. Social Work, Acad. Cert. Social Workers, Sigma Delta Chi. Jewish. Home: 7238 Leescott Ave Van Nuys CA 91406 Office: Room 6016 107 S Broadway Los Angeles CA 90012

EISNER, RONALD RICHARD, physician; b. Bklyn., Mar. 21, 1933; s. Meyer Alan and Mae (Eisner) E.; B.S., Coll. William and Mary, 1954; M.D., Chgo. Med. Sch., 1958. Intern, Michael Reese Hosp., Chgo., 1958-59, resident, 1959-61; practice medicine specializing in anesthesiology, Phila., 1961-72, Oakland, Calif., 1972—; attending anesthesiologist Albert Einstein Med. Center, Phila., 1961-72; clin. asst. prof. anesthesiology Temple U. Sch. Medicine, 1966-67, clin. asst. prof. Sch. Dentistry, 1971-72; staff anesthesiologist Kaiser Found. Hosp., Oakland, 1972—. Diplomate Pan Am. Med. Assn., Am. Bd. Anesthesiology; Nat. Bd. Med. Examiners; fellow Am. Coll. Anesthesiology; mem. A.M.A. Home: 645 Stockton St San Francisco CA 94108 Office: Kaiser Found Hosp Oakland CA 94611

EISNITZ, MARK FREDERICK, psychologist; b. N.Y.C., Oct. 24, 1944; s. Jerome M. and Doris J. (Mellenhoff) E.; B.S., Bowling Green State U., 1965; M.A., Queens Coll., 1968; Ph.D., New Sch. Social Research, 1973. Sr. counsellor Morris J. Bernstein Inst., Beth Israel Med. Center, 1967-69; psychotherapist Bklyn. Center for Counselling and Psychotherapy, 1969-70; instr. psychology Manhattan Community Coll. of CCNY, 1969-72; asso. dir. Behavioral Consultants, Inc., Syosset, N.Y., 1973-75, also asst. prof. psychology Nassau Community Coll., Garden City, N.Y., 1972-75; pvt. practice psychotherapy with adults, Los Angeles, 1975-80, Santa Rosa and Sebastopol, Calif., 1980—; med. staff Palm Drive Hosp., Community Hosp. of Sonoma County, Brookwood Hosp., 1980—; dir. Milton H. Erickson Inst., Sebastopol, 1980—; cons. humanistic edn. program Plainview-Old Bethpage Sch. Dist., N.Y., 1973-75; dir. hotline crisis intervention program div. adolescent medicine Children's Hosp., Los Angeles, 1975-77; asst. prof. psychology Nassau Community Coll., Garden City, N.Y., 1972-75; assoc. dir. Behavioral Cons., Inc., Syosset, N.Y., 1973-75; instr. movement therapy dept. Immaculate Heart Coll., Los Angeles, 1977-79; adj. faculty U. San Francisco, 1980—, Profl. Sch. Humanistic Studies, 1980—; asso. clin. prof. div. family and community medicine U. Calif., San Francisco, 1980—; behavioral sci. Cons. Family Practice Ctr., Community Hosp., 1980—, also Cons. hemodialysis unit, 1980—; ora exam. Commr. Calif. Psychology Examining Com., 1980—; host KFTY-TV Forum 50 Stress program, 1981—, guest on Good Afternoon Show, 1981—; mental health cons. Los Angeles Job Corps, 1978-82; guest faculty Macomber oncology nursing edn. program Los Angeles County-U. So. Calif. Sch. Medicine Comprehensive Cancer Center, 1978-82; guest speaker various profl. groups. Lic. psychologist, N.Y., Calif.; Am. Cancer Soc. grantee, 1977. Mem. Am., Western, Calif., Los Angeles County psychol. assns., Soc. Adolescent Medicine, Calif. Assn. Youth Service Counselors, Center for Improvement Child Caring, Redwood Psychol. Soc. Office: Z Milton H Erickson Inst 450 Pitt Ave Sebastopol CA 95472

EITNER, GERALD GEORGE, food co. exec.; b. Salt Lake City, Aug. 14, 1929; s. Albert George and Carla Joanna (Kreipl) E.; student U. Utah, 1951-53; m. Shirley Diane Frahm, June 11, 1966; children—Jeri Lavon, Dawna Jean, Debbie Lee. Salesman, Clover Club Foods Co., Kaysville, Utah, 1954-59, dist. sales mgr., 1959-64, advt. and sales promotion mgr., 1964-73, div. mgr., 1973-81, gen. mgr. personnel devel., 1981—. Bd. dirs. Multiple Sclerosis Soc. Utah, 1976-77, Utah Travel Council; ex-officio dir. Golden Spike Empire-Travel Region. Served with USMC, 1946-48, 50-52. Recipient Distinguished Salesman award Sales & Mktg. Execs. Club, 1957; Distinguished Sales Mgrs. award, 1965; Compton Advt. Edn. award Am. Advt. Fedn., 1976. Mem. Utah Advt. Fedn. (pres. 1975, dir. 1976—), Mfrs. Reps. Club (dir., v.p. 1981, pres. 1982), Am. Advt. Fedn. (chmn. public relations com. 1981-82), Sales and Mktg. Execs., Salt Lake Area C. of C. Republican. Mormon. Club: Elks. Designer solicitation programs. Home: 4585 Orchard Ave Odgen UT 84403 Office: PO Box 228 Kaysville UT 84037

EITNER, LORENZ EDWIN ALFRED, art historian, educator; b. Brunn, Czechoslovakia, Aug. 27, 1919; s. Wilhelm and Katherina (Thonet) E.; came to U.S., 1935, naturalized, 1943; A.B., Duke, 1940; M.F.A., Princeton, 1948, Ph.D., 1952; m. Trudi von Kathrein, Oct. 26, 1946; children—Christy, Kathy, Claudia. Research unit head Nuremberg War Crimes Trial, 1946-47; from instr. to prof. art U. Minn., 1949-63; Hooker prof., chmn. dept. art, dir. mus. Stanford, 1963—; organized exbhn. works of Gericault for museums of Los Angeles, Detroit and Phila., 1971-72. Mem. Regional Arts Council San Francisco Bay Area. Served as officer OSS, AUS, 1943-46. Fulbright grantee, Belgium, 1952-53; Guggenheim fellow, Munich, Germany, 1956-57. Mem. Coll. Art Assn. Am. (dir., past v.p.), Phi Beta Kappa. Author: The Flabellum of Tournus, 1944; Gericault Sketchbooks in the Chicago Art Institute, 1960; Introduction to Art, 1961; Neo-Classicism and Romanticism, 1965; Géricault's Raft of the Medusa, 1972; co-author: The Arts in Higher Education, 1966; also articles. Home: 684 Mirada Stanford CA 94305 Office: Dept Art Stanford Univ Cummings Art Bldg 101 Stanford CA 94305*

EKELUND, JOHN JOSEPH, college president; b. Washington, Jan. 19, 1928; s. Kenneth Oscar and Marjorie (Buscher) E.; B.S., U.S. Naval Acad., 1949; M.S. in Systems Analysis, U. Rochester (N.Y.), 1969; m. Lynn Marie Schumacher, May 3, 1952; children—John Joseph, Christopher P., Terri L., Peter L., Tracy A., Patricia M., C. Kent. Commd. ensign U.S. Navy, 1949, advanced through grades to rear adm., 1976; service in Korea and Vietnam; chief staff Naval Forces, Vietnam, 1972-73; comdr. guided missile cruiser U.S.S. Albany, 1973-75; dean Naval War Coll., 1975-76; dep. dir. naval edn. and tng. Office Chief Naval Ops., Washington, 1976-77; nat. intelligence officer CIA, 1977-78; comdr. U.S. South Atlantic Force, 1978-80; supt. Naval Postgrad. Sch., Monterey, Calif., 1980-83; ret., 1983; pres. Calif. Maritime Acad., Vallejo, 1983—. Decorated Legion of Merit, Meritorious Service medal, Joint Commendation medal. Mem. U.S. Naval Acad. Alumni Assn., U.S. Naval Inst. Devel. math. treatment of modern submarine torpedo fire control, 1956. Office: Calif Maritime Acad PO Box 1392 Vallejo CA 94590

EKLUND, PAUL NELSON, real estate developer; b. San Diego, May 17, 1943; s. Paul John and Elizabeth (McLean) E.; B.S. in Civil Engring., Oreg. State U., 1966, B.S. in Applied Math, 1966. Partner, E & R Constrn. Co., Boulder, Colo., 1971; partner Timber Builders, Inc., Dillon, Colo., 1972, pres., Boulder, 1973-79; v.p. La-Grade-Eklund, Ltd., Boulder, from 1978, now pres. Served to lt. USNR, 1966-70. Mem. ASCE, Colo. Assn. Home Builders. Republican. Office: 777 29th St Boulder CO 80303

ELA, PATRICK HOBSON, museum director, consultant, educator; b. Oakland, Calif., June 20, 1948; s. Benjamin W., Jr., and Jeanette (Lamoreau) E. B.A., Occidental Coll., 1970; postgrad. in Art History, UCLA, 1970-71, M.B.A., 1973. Curator Gemini Graphics Edits., Ltd., Los Angeles, 1970-71; edn. intern Alta Pinakothek, Munich, W.Ger., 1972; asst. dir. Kohler Arts Ctr., Sheboygan, Wis., 1973-74; edn. specialist Los Angeles County Mus. Art, 1974-75; adminstrv. dir. Craft and Folk Art Mus., Los Angeles, 1975-82, exec. dir., 1982—; instr. Occidental Coll., Calif. State U.-Fullerton; mem. faculty mus. studies program John F. Kennedy U. Vice pres., pres. alumni bd. govs. Occidental Coll., 1979-80; bd. dirs. R.M. Schindler House. Mem. Calif. Assn. Mus. (founding bd. 1980-81). Mem. United Ch. of Christ. Club: Hajii Baba Soc. (Washington). Contbr. articles to profl. publs., pamphlet to symposium. Office: 5814 Wilshire Blvd Los Angeles CA 90036

EL-BAYOUMY, LOTFI EL-SAY, engineer; b. Fayoum, Egypt, Jan. 18, 1942; came to U.S., 1966; s. El-Sayed I. and Naggeya F. (El-Zainy) El-B.; m. Shahira A. El-Masry, Aug. 17, 1973; children—Sharif L., Khalid L., Dena L. B.S.c, Cairo U., 1964, M.Sc., 1967; Ph.D., NYU, 1970. Asst. prof., NYU, Bronx, N.Y., 1969-70; prin. engr. Dathar Corp., Ramsey, N.J., 1970-72; advanced vibration analyst Pratt & Whitney Aircraft, East Hartford, Conn., 1972-74; group engr. Sundstrand Corp., Rockford, Ill., 1975-80; mem. tech. staff Western Gear Co., Industry, Calif., 1980—; cons. engr. Long Beach Found., NASA, Hiller Aircraft, 1981—; assoc. prof. Calif. State U.-Long Beach, 1981—. Recipient Service award Sundstrand Corp., 1980. Mem. Am. Acad. Mechanics, AIAA, Nat. Mgmt. Assn., Assn. Egyptian Am. Scholars. Republican. Contbr. articles to profl. jours. Office: 14724 E Proctor Ave Industry CA 91744

ELCHERT, KENNETH CLARENCE, aerospace engineer; b. Delaware, Ohio, Aug. 3, 1949; s. Franklin Clarence and Marie Margaret (Lonsway) E.; B.A. in Math. and Physics, St. Joseph Coll., Rensselaer, Ind., 1971; B.S. in Aero./Astron. Engring., Ohio State U., 1973; m. Celia Berumen, Oct. 27, 1979; 1 son, John Kenneth. With Rockwell Internat. Co., 1974—, lead engr. separation analysis space shuttle program, Downey, Calif., 1980—. Recipient NASA Spl. award 1978, First Shuttle Flight Achievement award, 1981. Mem. AIAA, Nat. Space Inst. Roman Catholic. Home: 353 E Carter Dr Glendora CA 91740 Office: 12214 S Lakewood Blvd Downey CA 90241

ELDER, DOUGLAS SHIELDS, data processing consultant; b. Parker, Pa., Sept. 10, 1949; s. Joseph Clinton and Mary Charolette (Elliot) E.; B.S. in Math., Grove City (Pa.) Coll., 1972. Programmer trainee ATT, 1973-74; programmer, analyst Rockwell Internat., Pitts., 1974-76; cons. Informatics, Inc., 1976-78, Bank of Am., San Francisco, 1978-79; pres., data processing cons. Mega Systems Services, Los Angeles, 1979—. Republican. Methodist. Club: Masons. Office: Mega Systems Services 3712 Barham Blvd C109 Los Angeles CA 90068

ELDER, HAZEL GASSMAN, market research co. exec.; b. Freeport, Il., Aug. 17, 1915; d. Oliver August and Leona Gertrude (Pahl) Gassman; m. Billy J. Elder, Nov. 29, 1946. Mktg. research interviewer, San Diego, 1961-64; pres. Hazel Elder Enterprises, Inc., La Mesa, Calif., 1966—; v.p. sec., treas. Billy J. Elder Constrn. Co., Inc., Spring Valley, Calif., 1973—. Mem. San Diego C. of C. (research com. 1971), La Mesa C. of C., Market Research Assn. (awards chmn. 1972-73), Am. Mktg. Assn. (sec., 1968-70). Home: 9396 Crest Dr Spring Valley CA 92077 Office: 7700 University Ave La Mesa CA 92041

ELDREDGE, EDDA ROGERS, securities transfer co. exec.; b. Deseret, Utah, Feb. 15, 1915; d. James Noah and Alice (Critchley) Rogers; student Henager Bus. Coll., 1930-31, U. Utah, 1932-35; m. Frank Aubrey Eldredge, Sept. 5, 1936; children—Frank A., Noah R., Alice Lou, Julie, Joseph U. With Gen. Petroleum Corp., 1945-55; mgr. land dept. Utah So. Oil Co., 1955-62, asst. sec., 1956-62; pres., dir. Edda R. Eldredge & Co., Inc., Salt Lake City, 1967—; pres., dir. Bonneville Petroleum Corp., 1974—. Republican. Mormon. Office: 315 Newhouse Bldg 10 Exchange Pl Salt Lake City UT 84111

ELDREDGE, FRANK AUBREY, II, geneticist; b. Salt Lake City, Jan. 8, 1940; s. Frank Aubrey and Esther Edda (Rogers) E.; student U. Utah, 1958-60, B.A., 1965, M.S., 1969, Ph.D., 1972; m. Birgitta Veronica Osterberg, Dec. 19, 1963; children—John William, Jennifer, Christine, Emilie. Teaching asso. U. Utah, Salt Lake City, 1971; asso. prof. biology dept. Central Mich. U., Mt. Pleasant, 1972—, mem. coms. acad. senate. Active troop com. Lake Huron council Boy Scouts Am., 1973—. NIH genetics tng. fellow, 1967-72; faculty research and creative endeavors grantee, 1973-75, 77-79. Mem. Am. Genetic Assn., AAAS, Bot. Soc. Am., Smithsonian Asso., Sigma Xi, Beta Beta Beta, Phi Sigma, Phi Eta Sigma. Republican. Mormon. Club: Amateur Radio. Researcher in plant cytogenetics and evolution; contbr. writings to publ. in field. Home: 1205 Cedar Ridge Rd Sandy UT 84070 Office: Medical Resources Inc 315 Newhouse Bldg Salt Lake City UT 84111

ELECCION, MARCELINO, advertising executive, lecturer, artist; b. N.Y.C., Aug. 22, 1936; s. Marcelino G. and Margaret J. (Krcha) E.; B.A., NYU, 1961; postgrad. Courant Inst. Math. Scis., 1962-64; m. Naomi E. Kor, Jan. 5, 1978; children—Mark Eaton, Jordan Kai. Electromech. draftsman Coll. Engring., NYU, Bronx, 1954-57, chief designer dept. elec. engring., 1957-60, tech. editor lab. for electrosci. research, 1960-62, editor publs. Sch. Engring. and Scis., 1962-67; asst. editor IEEE Spectrum, N.Y.C., 1967-69, assoc. editor, 1969-70, staff writer, 1970-76, contbg. editor, 1976—; dir. adminstrn. Internat. Bur. Protection and Investigation, Ltd., N.Y.C., 1976-78; account exec., creative dir. Paul Purdom & Co., pub. relations, San Francisco, 1978-81, creative dir., 1981—; cons. tech. artist, 1953—; music orchestration cons., 1956-70; cons. Ency. Britannica, 1969-70, Time-Life Books, 1973; spl. guest lectr. Napa Coll., 1979—. Recipient Mayor's commendation award N.Y.C., 1971. Mem. IEEE (sr.), N.Y. Acad. Scis., Am. Math. Soc., AAAS, Optical Soc. Am., Smithsonian Assocs., Am. Numis. Assn., Nat. Geog. Soc., U.S. Judo Fedn., Athletic Congress, AAU. Fedn. Home: PO Box 26102 San Francisco CA 94126

ELEM, GARY ALLEN, psychologist, educator; b. Maywood, Calif., Aug. 2, 1949; s. Frank and Charlotte L. Elem; m. Linda F. Grimshaw, Dec. 17, 1977. B.A., UCLA, 1973; M.A., Calif. Poly State U., 1978; Ph.D., U.S. Internat. U., 1983. Property mgr., securite cons. RLS Assocs., 1969-76; counselor, testing officer Calif. Poly State U., San Luis Obispo, 1978-82, instr. edn., 1980-82, instr. psychology, 1982-83; pvt. practice cons., San Luis Obispo, 1973-83; staff psychologist Calif. Dept. Corrections, San Luis Obispo, 1977—; county and state workshop coordinator, 1973-83. Active Am. Lung Assn., Am. Heart Assn., Calif. Poly State U. Kennedy Library Assocs., UCLA Alumni Assn., Calif. Poly State U. Alumni Assn. Mem. Am. Psychol. Assn., Am. Personnel Guidance Assn., Mensa, Am. Soc. Clin. Hypnosis, Calif. Central Coastal Hypnosis Soc., San Luis Obispo County Psychol. Assn. (pres. 1983-84). Home: 3860 Higuera St Apt 158 San Luis Obispo CA 93401 Office: Calif Men's Colony PO Box AF San Luis Obispo CA 93409

ELGIN, RON A., advertising executive; b. Milw., Sept. 15, 1941; s. Carl J. and Vivien E. (Phillips) E.; m. Bonni K. Visintainer, Dec. 3, 1968; 1 dau., Alison. B.A. in Advt., U. Wash., 1965. Copywriter, Cole & Weber, Inc., Seattle, 1965-66, account exec., 1969-73, v.p., 1973-77, sr. v.p., gen. mgr., 1977-81; pres. Elgin/Kirkland/Syferd, 1981—; chmn. John Hornall Design Works, 1982—. Served to 1st lt., 1966-69. Decorated Commendation medal. Mem. Mktg. Communications Execs. Internat. (pres. Seattle chpt.), Seattle Advt. Fedn. Republican. Home: 17749 Bothell Way NE Seattle WA 98155 Office: 200 W Mercer #100 Seattle WA 98119

ELGUIN-BÖDY, GITA, psychologist; b. Santiago, Chile; came to U.S., 1968; d. Serafin Elguin and Regina Urizar de Elguin; B.S. in Biology, U. Chile, Santiago, Psy.D., 1964; Ph.D. in Counseling Psychology (Chancellor's Patent Fund grantee, NIMH fellow), U. Calif.-Berkeley, 1976; student Taoist Found., San Francisco, 1983, Nat. Assn. Cert. Bach Remedy Counselors, 1983; m. Bart Bödy, Oct. 23, 1971. Clin. psychologist Barros Luco-Trudeau Gen. Hosp., Santiago, 1964-65; co-founder, co-dir. Lab. for Parapsychol. Research, Psychiat. Clinic, U. Chile, Santiago, 1965-68; research fellow Found. Research on Nature of Man, Durham, N.C., 1968; researcher psychol. correlates of EEG-Alpha rhythms U. Calif., Berkeley, 1972-76; originator holistic method of psychotherapy Psychotherapy for a Crowd of One, 1978; co-founder, exec. dir. Holistic Health Assocs. (multidisciplinary health clinic), Montclair, Oakland, Calif., 1979—; lectr. holistic health Piedmont (Calif.) Adult Sch., 1979-80; hostess Holistic Perspective, Sta. KALW-FM, Nat. Public Radio, 1980; co-organizer task force to modify psychology licensing exam. in Calif., 1981. Lic. clin. psychologist, Chile, Calif. Mem. Am. Psychol. Assn., Assn. Advancement Psychology, Alameda County Psychol. Assn., Montclair Health Profls. Assn. (founder, pres. 1983), Sierra Club, U. Calif. Alumni Assn. Contbr. articles in clin. psychology and holistic health to profl. jours. Office: Montclair Profl Bldg Suite 203 2080 Mountain Blvd Oakland CA 94611

ELI, JOHNNIE CARL, JR., dentist; b. Austin, Tex., Feb. 27, 1930; s. Johnnie C. and Nan (Hope) E.; student U. Houston, 1953, D.D.S., Loma Linda U., 1960; m. E. Ruth Melnechuk, Sept. 6, 1953; children—Jenell Diane, Bradley Allen. Embossing pressman Cargill Printing Co., Houston, 1947-49; practice gen. dentistry San Bernardino, Calif.; pres. Protective Care Systems, Inc., Redlands, Calif., 1976-79; real estate cons., 1978—. Mem. nat. adv. bd. Am. Security Council, 1976—. Served with M.C., U.S. Army, 1951-53. Mem. Acad. of Gen. Dentistry, ADA, Calif. Dental Assn., Tri-County Dental Assn., Nat. Assn. of Seventh-Day Adventist Dentists (chpt. pres. 1974-75), Loma Linda U. Dental Alumni Assn. (dir. 1962-67, pres. 1981). Democrat. Mem. Seventh-Day Adventist Ch. Office: PO Box 5902 W San Bernardino CA 92412

ELIAS, THEODORE JOSEPH, ret. chem. engr.; b. Des Moines, June 13, 1914; s. Mitchell S. and Cecelia M. (Korey) E.; B.S., Iowa State U., 1942; m. Ann Marie Kouri, Nov. 26, 1946; children—Amy Louise, Donna Marie, Theodore J., Woodrow Mark. Engr., Chem. Equipment Co., Los Angeles, 1945-48, Technicolor Inc., Hollywood, Calif., 1948-57, Los Angeles County, 1957-63, State of Calif., Los Angeles, 1963-68; chem. engr. Los Angeles County, Los Angeles, 1968-77, ret., 1977; div. chief occupational health and safety Los Angeles County, 1970-77; cons. Nat. Insts. Occupational Safety and Health. Served with U.S. Army, 1942-46. Decorated Purple Heart, Silver Star, Bronze Star medal; diplomate Environ. Engrs. Mem. Am. Conf. Govtl. Indsl. Hygienists (chpt. pres. 1975-76), Am. Indsl. Hygiene Assn. (chpt. pres. 1977-78), Am. Legion, VFW, Calif. Profl. Engrs. Republican. Roman Catholic. Club: Elks. Inventor in field. Home: 4943 Densmore St Encino CA 91436

ELIASON, RICHARD I., state senator; b. Seattle, Oct. 14, 1925; m. Betty Eliason; 5 children. Student pub. schs. Formerly fisherman, pipefitter; mem. Alaska Ho. of Reps., 1968-80, Alaska State Senate, 1980—. Mayor, mem. Sitka City Council; mem. Pub. Utility Bd.; assemblyman Greater Sitka Borough. Served with USNR, 1943-46. Office: Alaska State Senate Juneau AK 99811*

ELIJAH, GERALD EUGENE, county ofcl.; b. Wood River, Nebr., Oct. 4, 1930; s. Harold Bent and Leola Linda (Burmood) E.; B.A., State U. Iowa, 1952, postgrad., 1952-55, 55-56; cert. public sector labor mgmt. relations UCLA, 1973. Asst. circulations mgr. Dover Publs., N.Y.C., 1957-59; group ins. adjustor Travelers Ins. Co., Los Angeles, 1960-62; with Los Angeles County, 1962—, dep. dist. dir. welfare, 1967-72, dist. dir., 1972—. Vol., Los Angeles Music Center Dance Assos. Mem. Indsl. Relations Research Assn., Inst. Indsl. Relations Assn., County Welfare Dirs. Assn., Los Angeles County Mgmt. Assn., Los Angeles County Employees Assn., Am. Mgmt. Assn., Am. Arbitration Assn. Republican. Congregationalist. Home: 2529 Ivanhoe Dr Los Angeles CA 90039 Office: 14545 Lanark St Panorama City CA 91402

ELIZALDE, PATRICIA ELAINE ALLEN, social services administrator; b. Flint, Mich., Sept. 5, 1954; d. Valgene and Cecile Lorene (Bell) A.; m. Francisco Xavier Elizalde, Jr., Jan. 1, 1980. B.A. in Psychology, U. Mich., 1977; M.A. in Ednl. Adminstrn., Central Mich. U., 1978. Probation officer Vol. Services of Genesee County, Flint, 1976-77; caseworker Youth Service Bur., Genesee County, Flint, 1976-77, CERCA Ctr., Flint, 1977; coordinator ctr. for student orgns. Central Mich. U., Mt. Pleasant, 1977-78, intern Office Admissions, 1978; counselor youth employment and tng. program Flint Bd. Edn., 1978-81; dir. Foster Grandparent Program, Cheyenne, Wyo., 1981—. Recipient cert. of appreciation Genesee County Probate Ct., 1976, Lansing Dist. Recruiting Command, 1981, Denver Dist. Recruiting Command, 1983; cert. of achievement La Raza adv. com. to Mich. Bd. Edn., 1978; cert. of recognition Student Assn. Central Mich. U., 1978. Mem. Am. Coll. Personnel Assn., Assn. Chicanos for Coll. Admissions, Bus. and Profl. Womens Assn., U. Mich. Alumni Assn., Central Mich. U. Alumni Assn. Democrat. Baptist. Home: 2533 E 9th St Cheyenne WY 82001 Office: 1603 Capitol Ave Cheyenne WY 82001

ELKIND-SAVATSKY, PAMELA DEE, sociology educator, consultant, researcher; b. Worcester, Mass., July 27, 1943; d. George and Rose (Silver) Elkind; m. Gordon Allen Savatsky, July 4, 1964; children—Rhonda T., Stacey H. A.B. in Sociology, Boston U., 1965, M.A., 1972; Ph.D., Northeastern U., 1979. Instr. sociology Boston U., 1970-72; lectr. sociology U. N.H., 1972-73; design critic M.Arch. Thesis Program, Harvard U., 1973-74; sr. faculty mem. Boston Archtl. Ctr., 1968-75; adj. asst. prof. Northeastern U., 1979; vis. prof. sociology and social anthropology Clark U., 1980-81, Dartmouth Coll., 1981; assoc. prof. sociology Eastern Wash. U., 1982—; vis. prof. Worcester Poly. Inst., 1975-76; lectr. Rural Am., Washington, 1978-80; sr. assoc. Harbridge House, Boston, 1978-79; research assoc. Tufts U. Med. Sch., 1976-78; pres. Social Assessment Services, Sudbury, Mass., 1976-78; dir. social scis. research dept. Environ. Research & Tech., Inc., 1973-76; research assoc. Boston Coll., 1972-73; cons. Framingham (Mass.) Redevel. Authority, 1970; research asst. Boston U., 1968-70. Pres. Assabet Valley Arts Ctr. Assn., 1980-81, Hudson Council on Youth, 1980; cons. Portuguese Parents Area Com., 1979. Recipient Profl. Merit award Eastern Wash. U., 1982, 83, cert. of appreciation EPA, 1981; postdoctoral research fellow, 1979; research fellow Tufts U., 1976-77. Mem. Am. Sociol. Assn., Eastern Sociol. Soc., Mass. Sociol. Soc., Groves Conf. Marriage and the Family, Rural Sociol. Soc., Sociologists for Women in Soc., Wash. State Sociol. Assn., Pacific Sociol. Assn., Western Social Sci. Assn., Research Soc. Am. Contbr. articles to profl. jours. Office: Patterson Hall 3103 Cheney WA 99004

ELKINS, WILLIAM DAVID, elec. engr.; b. Albany, Oreg., Dec. 9, 1920; s. Glen A. and Edith E. (Hackleman) E.; student U. Oreg., 1938-39, Oreg. State U., 1978-81; m. Contance E. Riddell, Dec. 18, 1942; children—W. David, Margaret Rae, John Glen. Installer-repairman Pacific Tel. & Tel., 1940-42, 46, 48-53; founding partner Abar Radio and TV, cable TV, Eugene, Oreg., 1953-66, mgr., chief engr., 1960-64; dur.

tech. ops. Liberty Communications, Inc., cable TV systems, Eugene, 1966-77, dir. safety and tng., 1977-78; cons. profl. engr., Eugene, 1978—; bd. dirs. Nat. Alliance Businessmen, Eugene, 1974-75. Served to capt. AUS, 1942-46, 47-48. Registered profl. engr., Oreg. Mem. Nat. Soc. Profl. Engrs., IEEE, Soc. Cable TV Engrs. Republican. Congregationalist. Clubs: Lions, Elks. Address: 1769 W 23d Ave Eugene OR 97405

ELKORT, MARTIN EDWARD, assn. exec.; b. N.Y.C., Apr. 18, 1929; s. Lewis George and Esther Dorothy (Kronenberg) E.; student Cooper Union, 1948-52; m. Edythe Esther Spiel, Feb. 28, 1953; children—Stefani, Daniel, Alicia. Cons., Communications Cons., Santa Monica, Calif., 1964-67; dir. mktg. Computer Scis. Corp., El Segundo, Calif., 1967-68; dir. Alaskaland, Fairbanks, 1968-69; exec. v.p. Am. Sightseeing Assn., N.Y.C., 1970-73; founder, pres. Internat. Reception Operators, Beverly Hills, Calif., 1975—; v.p. The Travel Co., Beverly Hills; tchr. coll. night sch., Watts, Calif., 1975-78; exhibited photographs in group shows; represented in permanent collection Mus. Modern Art, N.Y.C. Bd. dirs. Los Angeles Eilat Sister City Com., 1960-63; scoutmaster Beverly Hills Boy Scouts, 1960-63; v.p. Western U.S.A. region Soc. for Advancement Travel for Handicapped, 1977—. Recipient Alaska Press Club awards, 1968, cert. of appreciation Central Air Def. Force, 1958; cert. instr., Calif. Community Colls.; cert. in mktg. Am. Mgmt. Assn. Mem. Discover Am. Travel Orgns. (internat. com.), N. Am. Travel Assn. (co-founder 1980), Nat. Council Travel Industry Assn., Africa Travel Assn. (co-founder, regional dir.), Caribbean Travel Assn., Pacific Area Travel Assn., Travel Trade Research Assn., Mensa. Home: 357 S Palm Dr Beverly Hills CA 90212

ELLARD, TIMOTHY DANIEL, marketing research executive; b. Salem, Mass., Dec. 20, 1934; s. Daniel J. and Anna M. (Byrne) E.; m. Mary Patricia Amend, July 11, 1959; children—Marcia Ann, Daniel Joseph, Michael Patrick. A.B., Harvard U., 1956; M.B.A., U. Pa., 1958. Brand mgr. Procter & Gamble Co., Cin., 1961-64; with Opinion Research Corp., Princeton, N.J., 1964-82, San Francisco, 1982—, sr. v.p., 1969—. Served to 1st lt. USAR, 1958-61. Mem. Am. Mktg. Assn., Am. Assn. Pub. Opinion Research, Travel and Tourism Research Assn. Home: 139 Wildwood Ave Piedmont CA 94610 Office: Opinion Research Corp Four Embarcadero Ctr San Francisco CA 94111

ELLENBERG, ALEXANDER HYMAN, plastic surgeon; b. Stockton, Calif., Oct. 13, 1933; s. Morris and Gertrude (Barron) E.; A.B., U. Calif.-Berkeley, 1955; M.D., U. Calif.-Francisco, 1958; m. Maureen Aronow, Nov. 25, 1934; children—Steven, Gary. Intern, Los Angeles County Hosp., Los Angeles, 1958-59; resident U. Calif., San Francisco, 1959-61, resident plastic surgery, 1963-65; surgeon Am. Hosp., Paris, 1961-63; practice medicine specializing in plastic surgery, San Jose, Calif., 1965—; mem. staff Good Samaritan Hosp., chief plastic surgery, 1979-83; mem. staff San Jose, O'Connor, Los Gatos Community hosps., all San Jose; faculty plastic surgery Stanford U., 1965—. Bd. dirs. Jewish Community Fedn. San Jose, 1966—; bd. dirs. San Jose Museum Art, 1977—, v.p., 1979-82, pres., 1982—. Served with AUS, 1961-63. Diplomate Am. Bd. Plastic Surgery. Fellow A.C.S.; mem. AMA, Calif., Santa Clara County med. assns., Am. Soc. Plastic and Reconstructive Surgery, Calif. Soc. Plastic Surgery (exec. council 1982—), Am. Soc. Aesthetic Plastic Surgery, Am. Cleft Palate Assn. Contbr. articles to profl. jours. Office: 2550 Samaritan Dr San Jose CA 95124

ELLINGSON, JOHN ROSTAD, real estate co. exec.; b. Portland, Oreg., Dec. 21, 1938; s. George Irving and Mildred Florence (Edwall) E.; B.S., Lewis and Clark Coll., 1960; M.S., Ariz. State U., 1962; m. JoAnn Adair, Nov. 25, 1960; children—Janna Marie, Jennifer Joy. Sales engr. Aluminum Co. Am., Pitts., 1962-65; product mgr. Omark Industries, Portland, 1965-68; franchise dir. Pay 'N Pak Stores, Longview, Wash., 1968-69; Western sales mgr. Lark div. Hanna Industries, Portland, 1970-71; real estate salesman Mayfair Realty, Portland, 1972-76; owner John R. Ellingson, Realtors, Portland, 1976—; instr. Mt. Hood Community Coll., 1973-75, Portland Community Coll., 1974-77. Served with N.G., 1955-58. Bd. dirs. Indochinese Cultural and Service Ctr., 1979-83. Mem. Portland Bd. Realtors, Home Builders of Portland. Office: John R Ellingson Realtors Suite 208 6420 SW Macadam Ave Portland OR 97201

ELLINGWOOD, ROBERT EDWARD, mayor, real estate cons.; b. Los Angeles, Jan. 2, 1927; s. Karr William and Elizabeth Mary (Davis) E.; m. Naomi Jean Whitman, Oct. 8, 1947; children—Robert, Raymond, Rhonda, Richard; m. 2d, Mary Helen Newsam, Feb. 14, 1972; 1 stepson, John Yaple. Student Chaffey Coll., 1946-47. Cert. community coll. tchr., Calif.; cert. property mgr. Inst. Real Estate Mgmt. Agt., Prudential Ins. Co., Ontario, Calif., 1952-55, Farmers Ins., Ontario, 1955-62; salesman Hazen Realty, Upland, Calif., 1962-65, Cucamonga Realty, 1965-70; broker Ellingwood Realty, Ontario, 1970—; mayor City of Ontario, 1978—. Assoc. mem. Calif. State Republican Central Com., 1982. Served with USNR, 1944-48, to capt. U.S. Army, 1948-52. Named Citizen of Yr., West San Bernardino County, 1982. Mem. West San Bernardino County Bd. Realtors (Realtor of Yr. 1978, hon. dir. for life 1981), Calif. Assn. Realtors (state dir.), Calif. League of Cities (del.), Ontario C. of C. (dir.), Am. Legion. Clubs: Ontario Lions (hon.), Ontario Elks. Office: 303 East B St Ontario CA 91764

ELLION, M. EDMUND, aerospace co. exec.; b. Boston, Jan. 20, 1923; s. Michael N. and Beatrice Elizabeth (Patterson) E.; B.S., Northeastern U., 1944; M.S., Harvard U., 1947; Ph.D. in Engring. and Physics (inst. scholar), Calif. Inst. Tech., 1953; m. Dolores Diana Ralph, July 3, 1954; children—Laurie Ann, Thomas Michael. Engring. cons., Arcadia, Calif., 1953-57; exec. dir. Nat. Engring. Sci. Co., Pasadena, Calif., 1957-60; pres. Dynamic Sci. Corp., Pasadena, 1960-64; mgr. tech. devel. and asst. div. mgr. Hughes Aircraft Co., Los Angeles, 1964—; lectr. Calif. Inst. Tech., UCLA. Served to lt. (j.g.) USNR, 1943-46. Mem. AIAA (assoc. fellow), IEEE (sr.). Republican. Patentee in field. Home: 2152 Highland Oaks Dr Arcadia CA 91006 Office: 1950 E Imperial Hwy El Segundo CA 90245

ELLIOT, CHARLES LOTHROP, geophysical engineer; b. Northampton, Mass., Nov. 15, 1928; s. William Samuel and Eleanore Eunice (Lothrop) E.; m. Helen McMahon, Sept. 17, 1954; children—James D., Denise E., Colin D. B.S. in Mining Engring. with honors, Mich. Tech. U., 1954, M.S. in Geophysics, 1955. Registered profl. engr., Ariz. Geophys. engr. Newmont Exploration Ltd., 1955-64; research geophysicist Kennecott Exploration Services, Denver and Salt Lake City, 1964-66; owner, operator Elliot Geophys. Co., Inc., Tucson, 1966-82, pres. 1982—; cons. in field. Served with USN, 1946-49. Mem. Soc. Exploration Geophysicists, European Assoc. Exploration Geophysicists, AIME. Patentee electromagnetic instrument for geophys. exploration. Office: 4653 E Pima St Tucson AZ 85712

ELLIOT, FLORIAN CLAUSEN, foundation executive; b. San Francisco, Nov. 24, 1928; d. Henry Christian and Irene (McDonald) Clause; m. Gerald S. Thede, Feb. 22, 1951; children—Jeffrey C., Eric C. (dec.); m. William J. Elliot Aug. 24, 1972 (dec.). Student Mills Coll., 1947-48, U. Calif., 1948-49. Staff, Wells Fargo Bank, San Francisco, 1962-65; legal sec. Clausen and Clausen, 1965-67; adminstrv. asst. U. Calif.-Berkeley, 1969-72; coordinator Calif. Scottish Rite Found., San Francisco, 1974—. Republican. Unitarian. Club: Commonwealth (San Francisco). Office: Scottish Rite Foundation 234 Van Ness Ave San Francisco CA 94102

ELLIOT, JEFFREY M., educator; b. Los Angeles, June 14, 1947; s. Gene and Harriet (Sobsey) E. B.A., U. So. Calif., 1969, M.A., 1970; D. Arts in history, Carnegie-Mellon U., 1976; Ed.D., Laurence U., 1976; D.Arts in Govt., Claremont Grad. Sch., 1978; cert. in grantsmanship Grantsmanship Tng. Center, 1980. Research asst. U. So. Calif., 1969-70; instr. polit. sci. Glendale Coll., 1970-72; instr. polit. sci. Cerritos Coll., 1970-72; asst. prof. history and polit. sci. U. Alaska-Anchorage Community Coll., 1973-74; asst. prof. history and polit. sci., dean curriculum Miami-Dade Community Coll., 1974-76; asst. prof. polit. sci. Va. Wesleyan Coll., Norfolk, 1978-79; sr. curriculum specialist Edn. Devel. Center, Newton, Mass., 1979-81; assoc. prof. polit. sci. N.C. Central U., Durham, 1981—; assoc. editor Community Coll. Social Sci. Jour., 1974-80; Mem. community services adv. council Miami (Fla.) Community Services, 1974-76; mem. Mayor's Adv. Com., Los Angeles, 1971-72; speechwriter, research asst., campaign strategist, U.S. Sen. Howard W. Cannon, Nev., 1969-82; cons. Calif. Clean Environment Act, 1970-72. Recipient Fair Enterprise Medallion award, 1965; Outstanding Polit. Sci. Scholar citation, 1970; Outstanding Tchr. award, 1971; Outstanding Am. Educator citation, 1975; Disting. Service Through Community Effort award, 1976. Mem. Community Coll. Social Sci. Assn. (dir. 1970-77, pres. 1975-77), So. Assn. Colls. and Schs. (accreditation team 1974-76), AAUP, Am. Polit. Sci. Assn., Assn. Supervision and Curriculum Devel., Nat. Council for Social Studies, Rocky Mountain Social Sci. Assn., Am. Hist. Assn., Pi Sigma Alpha, Phi Delta Kappa. Author 36 books including: Keys to Economic Understanding, 1976; Science Fiction Voices, 1979; Literary Voices, 1980; Fantasy Voices, 1981; If Kennedy Had Lived, 1981; Analytical Congressional Directory, 1981; Deathman Pass Me By, 1982; If Kennedy Had Lived, 1982; Stanton A. Coblentz: Adventures of a Freelance, 1982; George Zebrowski: Perfecting Visions, Slaying Cynics, 1982; Pulp Voices, 1983; Tempest in a Teapot: The Falkland Islands War, 1983; The Presidential-Congressional Political Dictionary, 1984; others. Contbr. 425 articles and revs. to profl. and popular jours.; contbg. editor Negro History Bull., 1976-80, West Coast Writers' Conspiracy, 1978-80. Home: 2762 McConnell Dr Los Angeles CA 90064 Office: Dept Polit Sci NC Central U Durham NC 27707

ELLIOT, JOHN WILLIAM, agriculture science educator; b. Nome, Alaska, Mar. 3, 1925; s. John Jacob and Harriet Caroline (Snodgrass) E.; B.S. in Agr., B.Edn., Wash. State U., 1950, M.S. in Agrl. Edn., 1969; m. Marilyn Margaret Smith, Aug. 18, 1950; children—Margaret, Jack, Marie, Yvonne, Patricia, Theresa, Laura, Cheryl, William. Tchr. vocat. agr. Pub. Schs. Prescott (Wash.), 1950-53, Reardan (Wash.), 1953-66, Cheney (Wash.), 1966-68; instr. adult farm mgmt. Spokane Community Coll., 1968-72, instr. agribus., 1972—, chmn. agr. dept., 1977-80. Mem. Reardan Town Council, 1954-58. Served with U.S. Army, 1944-46. Decorated Bronze Star; recipient Community Service award Lions Club, 1960; Nat. Hon. Am. Farmer, Future Farmers Am., 1964; Geigy award, 1973; Faculty Mem. of Yr., Spokane Community Coll., 1979. Mem. NEA, Assn. Higher Edn. (mem. state bd., unit pres. 1979-80), Wash. Edn. Assn., Am. Vocat. Assn., Wash. Vocat. Assn. (pres. 1968-69, exec. sec. 1972-76; Pres.'s award 1976), Nat. Vocat. Agrl. Tchrs. Assn., Wash. Vocat. Agrl. Tchrs. Assn. (pres. 1967-68, exec. sect. 1976-79). Home: Box 144 Rt 2 Cheney WA 99004 Office: Spokane Community Coll N 1810 Greene Spokane WA 99207

ELLIOTT, ALICIA ANN, speech pathologist; b. Burbank, Calif., Feb. 12, 1948; d. Elmer P. and Patricia A. (Worley) E.; A.A., Ventura Community Coll., 1971, B.A., Calif. State U., Long Beach, 1973, M.A. (fellow), 1974; M.A., 1980; postgrad. (fellow) UCLA. Tchr. various pvt. schs., Simi Valley, Calif., 1966-68; aphasia specialist Los Angeles County Supt. Schs., 1975—, specialist for educationally handicapped and autistic, 1978—; lang./speech specialist, 1979—; instr. dept. ednl. psychology Calif. State U., Long Beach, 1978, alternative clin. tchr., 1977-83; pvt. edn. cons., 1981—; now asst. prof. Calif. State U., Los Angeles. Pres., Simi Valley Young Democrats, 1965-67. Recipient Faithful Service award Long Beach Unified Sch. Dist., 1972, Outstanding Service award Calif. State Univ., 1974, Individual Achievement award Nat. Soc. Autistic Children, 1979. Mem. Am. Speech and Hearing Assn., Calif. Speech and Hearing Assn., Nat. Soc. for Autistic Children, Phi Lambda Theta, Phi Delta Kappa. Mem. Brethren Ch. Home: 19149 Keswick Reseda CA 91335 Office: Los Angeles County Supt Schools Office Downey Education Center Imperial Hwy Downey CA 90242

ELLIOTT, DAVID ANDREW, mining geologist; b. Lewiston, Maine, Jan. 12, 1935; s. James Andrew and Marcia Lilla (Prince) E.; m. Sandra Dianne Higgins, May 2, 1936; children—Harold James, Richard Andrew. B.A. in Geology, U. Maine-Orono, 1956; student Alexander Hamilton Inst. 1966. Registered geologist, Calif. Mining geologist Bunker Hill Co., Kellogg, Idaho, 1956-62; geologist, mining mgr. Western ops. Interpace Corp., Hayward, Calif., 1962-75, environ. and regulatory affairs mgr., 1975-81; mgr. environ. regulatory affairs Western div. N.Am. Refractories Co., Ione, Calif., 1981—. Mem. Am. Inst. Profl. Geologists (cert. profl. geologist), Calif. Mining Assn. (past pres. 1982), Am. Inst. Mining Engrs. (past chmn. sect.). Democrat. Clubs: Tower Park Yacht (dir., commodore 1982-83), Weber Point Yacht. Home: 107 Dahlia Ave Sacramento CA 95828 Office: PO Box 785 Ione CA 95640

ELLIOTT, GORDON RAY, non profit organization executive; b. Winnipeg, Man., Can., July 31, 1916; s. Frank George and Ethel Maud (Johnson) E.; m. Shirley Anderson, Nov. 2, 1950; 1 dau. Student U. So. Calif., Southwestern U.; grad. Am. Inst. Banking, 1936; LL.B., Pacific Coast Sch. Law, 1940. With Security First Nat. Bank (now Security Pacific Bank), Los Angeles, 1934-41; budget analyst VA, San Francisco, 1946-47, asst. to dir., Los Angeles, 1947-56, dir., Albuquerque, 1957-58, Phila., 1958-62, dir. VA for Europe, Am. embassy, Rome, 1962-65, dir. regional office, attache vets. affairs, Am. embassy, Manila, 1965-67, dir. No. Calif. Regional Office, San Francisco, 1967-70, So. Calif. Regional Office, Los Angeles, 1970-73, spl. asst. to adminstr. vets. affairs, Washington, 1974-75; gen. mgr. DAV Charities of Greater Los Angeles, Inc., 1981—; bd. chmn. Vets. on Job, Inc.; dir., past pres. Purple Heart Vets. Rehab. Services, Inc.; pres. Valley Hunt Investors, Inc.; mem. adv. com. Calif. Dept. Rehab., Calif. Vets. Employment Com., Pres. Commn. on Employment of Handicapped; mem. exec. adv. council Congl. Medal of Honor Soc., 1976. Co-chmn. Calif. Vets. for Reagan and Bush Com. for 1980 nat. election; mem. Pres.-elect Reagan Transition Team, 1980. Recipient Civil Servant of Yr. Silver Helmet award Am. Vets. of World War II, Korea, Vietnam, 1972; Nat. Disting. Service award Mil. Order of Purple Heart, 1974; Mem. Fed. Bar Assn., Res. Officers Assn., DAV, Am. Legion, VFW, Amvets. Lutheran. Clubs: Masons, Shriners, Rotary, Town Hall, Overseas Press. Office: 731-A S Garfield Ave Alhambra CA 91801

ELLIOTT, GUY RUPERT BETTS, chemist; b. Mpls., Nov. 22, 1921; s. Guy Rupert Betts and Helen Virginia (Hough) E.; B.S., Mont. State Coll., 1943; Ph.D., U. Calif. at Berkeley, 1952; m. Gloria Lee Dority, Nov. 3, 1956; children—Nancy Ann, Stephen Henry, Russell Dority. Chemist Oak Ridge Nat. Lab., 1946-48, U. Calif. Radiation Lab., Berkeley, 1948-52, Nat. Bur. Standards, Washington, 1952-55; chemist-metallurgist Argonne (Ill.) Nat. Lab., 1955-56; staff Los Alamos Sci. Lab., 1956-82; adj. vis. prof. metallurgy U. Utah, 1970-76; pres. Los Alamos Cons., 1972—, E-Cubed, 1980. Mem. Los Alamos County (N.Mex.) Bd. Commrs., 1969-70. Served with AUS, 1943-46. Mem. Am. Chem. Soc., Electrochem. Soc., AIME, Chem. Soc. (London), AAAS. Contbr. numerous articles to sci. jours. Patentee direct electrochem. generators, coal processing, geothermal energy utilization, natural gas recovery, uranium processing. Home and Office: 133 La Senda Rd Los Alamos NM 87544

ELLIOTT, HARRY LLOYD, newspaper editor; b. Kansas City, Mo., Apr. 13, 1933; s. Harry Houlette and Justin Vera (Manuel) E.; m. Judith Lee Coons, Aug. 30, 1958; children—Sheryl Lynn, Cynthia Carol, John Darren. B.S. in Journalism, U. Kans., 1956. Reporter, photographer Lawrence (Kans.) Daily Journal-World, 1956-60; reporter, photographer, copy editor Sacramento Bee, 1960-63; editor Grants Pass (Oreg.) Daily Courier, 1963—. Rotary Group Study Exchange fellow, Australia, 1967; AP Photography, Sports regional competition 1st place winner, 1959. Mem. AP Mng. Editors Soc., Oreg. AP Mng. Editors (v.p., chmn. U. Oreg. press conf. 1976), Soc. Newspaper Designers. Republican. Episcopalian. Club: Rotary (Grants Pass).

ELLIOTT, HENRY HOWARD, chemical engineer; b. Stuttgart, Germany, July 15, 1925; came to U.S., 1944, naturalized, 1945; student Stanford U., 1944, San Francisco City Coll., 1947-48; B.S., Oreg. State U., 1951; postgrad. U. So. Calif., 1955-58; m. Carolyn S. Wakefield, Sept. 3, 1947; children—Catherine, Barbara, Stephen. Filtration engr. Dicalite div. Gt. Lakes Carbon Corp., Torrance, Calif., 1953-55; research project engr. Kerr McGee, Whittier, Calif., 1956-70; staff research engr. Kaiser Aluminum Chem. Co., Pleasanton, Calif., 1970-72; sr. chem. engr. Gen. Electric Co., Pleasanton, Calif., 1972-82; mgr. research and devel. Emcotek, Visalia, Calif., 1982—; cons. Stauffer Chem. Co., 1972. Served with U.S. Army, 1945-47; PTO; with USAF, 1951-53; Korea. Registered profl. engr., Calif. Mem. Am. Inst. Chem. Engrs. (chmn. career guidance com. No. Calif. sect. 1973-75, chmn. sect. directory com. 1978-80, mem. sect. exec. com. 1976-77). Inventor Elliott Retort Process, 1958; patentee rare earth, phosphate ore chlorination. Office: Emcotek Corp 8220 Doe Ave Visalia CA 93291

ELLIOTT, JAMES HEYER, mus. dir.; b. Medford, Oreg., Feb. 19, 1924; s. Bert R. and Marguerite E. (Heyer) E.; B.A., Willamette U., 1947; D.F.A, 1978; M.A., Harvard, 1949; m. Judith Ann Algar, Apr. 23, 1966 (div. 1979); children—Arabel Joan, Jakob Maxwell. Art critic N.Y. Herald Tribune, European edit., Paris, 1952-53; curator Walker Art Center, Mpls., 1953-55, acting dir., 1955-56; asst. chief curator, curator modern art Los Angeles County Mus. Art, Los Angeles, 1956-63, chief curator, 1963-66; dir. Wadsworth Atheneum, Hartford, Conn., 1966-76; dir. Univ. Art Mus., Berkeley, Calif., 1976—; adj. prof. Hunter Coll., N.Y.C., 1968, U. Calif., Berkeley, 1976—. Commr., Conn. Commn. on Arts, 1970-76; fellow Trumbull Coll., Yale U., 1971-75; bd. dirs. San Francisco Art Inst., 1980—. Served with USNR, 1943-46. James Rogers Rich fellow Harvard U., 1949-50; Fulbright grantee, 1951-52. Mem. Coll. Arts Assn., Internat. Council Museums, Am. Assn. Museums, Assn. Art Mus. Dirs. (sec., trustee), Artists Space (bd. dirs. 1980—). Club: The Arts (Berkeley, Calif.). Author: Bonnard and His Environment, 1964. Office: 2625 Durant Ave Berkeley CA 94720

ELLIOTT, JOHN E., educator, economist; b. Los Angeles, Oct. 22, 1931; s. James Edgar and Jessie (Metcalf) E.; B.A., Occidental Coll., 1952; M.A., Harvard U., Ph.D., 1956; m. Barbara Ann Hall, Feb. 21, 1952; m. 2d, Elda Rose Lazzara, Dec. 22, 1975; children—John, Nina, Richard, Lisa, James. Intr., U. So. Calif., Los Angeles, 1956-59, asst. prof., 1959-61, assoc. prof., 1961-66, prof., 1966—. Recipient Albert S. Raubenheimer Disting. Faculty award U. So. Calif., 1980, Pres.'s Assoc. award for excellence in teaching, 1981, Social Scis. Div. award for disting. teaching, 1981. Mem. Am. Econ. Assn., Western Econ. Assn., Assn. for Evolutionary Econs., Assn. for Social Econs., Atlantic Econ. Assn., Union for Radical Polit. Econs., Southwestern Social Sci. Assn., AAUP. Democrat. Author: Comparative Economic Systems, 1973; Competing Philosophies in American Political Economics, 1975; Economic Issues and Policies, 1975; Economics: A Student Guide and Resource Book, 1978; Marx and Engels on Economics, Politics, and Society, 1981. Office: Dept Economics Univ Southern Calif Los Angeles CA 90089

ELLIOTT, KATHLEEN MARIE, nurse, administrator; b. San Diego, Aug. 1, 1945; d. Howard O'Dell and Mary Elizabeth (Steging) Carr; m. Richard Wayne Elliott, Apr. 16, 1966; children—Aaron Louis, Brian Scott. Grad. Knapp Coll. Nursing, 1966, B.S. with departmental honor in Health Sci., Chapman Coll., 1982. R.N.; cert. tchr. designated subjects, Calif. Nurse Atascadero (Calif.) State Hosp., 1966-76; nurse III, hosp. supr. El Paso de Robles Sch., Calif. Dept. Youth Authority, 1976-78; mgr. Planned Parenthood Clinic, Fresno, Calif., 1978-79; staff nurse Fresno (Calif.) Community Hosp., 1979-80; rehab. nurse, dir. staff devel. Sierra Meadows Convalescent Hosp., Oakhurst, Calif., 1980-82, dir. nursing services, asst. to adminstr. Med. Services, 1983—; instr. Yosemite High Sch. nurses aide program. Mem. Central Valley In-Service Educators, Calif. Soc. Nursing Service Adminstrs., Calif. Assn. Health Care Educators. Democrat. Home: 39313 John West Rd Oakhurst CA 93644 Office: 40131 Hwy 49 Oakhurst CA 93644

ELLIOTT, LLOYD FLOREN, microbiologist, researcher; b. Clear Lake, S.D., July 5, 1937; s. Floren T. and Nellie A. (Hofman) E.; m. Lorna J. Wiesner, June 8, 1958; children—Paul L., Dawn M. B.S., S.D. State U., 1959; M.S., Kans. State U., 1961; Ph.D., Oreg. State U., 1965. Researcher Agrl. Research Service, USDA. Irrigated Agr. Research and Extension Ctr., Prosser, Wash., 1965-69, U. Nebr., Lincoln, 1969-75, microbiologist Wash. State U., Pullman, 1975—. Cert. Disting. Fgn. Scientist Agrl. Research Service, 1981; Underwood fellow, 1982. Fellow Am. Soc. Agronomy, Soil Sci. Soc. Am.; mem. Am. Soc. Microbiology, Sigma Xi. Republican. Lutheran. Contbr. numerous papers on animal waste mgmt., crop residue decomposition, nutrient cycling, plant rhizosphere. Home: 300 Bellevue St Pullman WA 99163 Office: US Dept Agr ARS 215 Johnson Hall Wash State U Pullman WA 99164

ELLIOTT, MYRTLE EVELYN KEENER, educator; b. Annawan, Ill., Apr. 11, 1898; d. John William and Mary (Baldwin) Keener; A.B., Cornell Coll., 1921; M.A., Columbia, 1926; postgrad. summers U. Iowa, 1928, Ohio State U., 1930, 31, U. Chgo., 1933, San Francisco State Coll., 1949, Fresno State Coll., 1958, 59, 61; m. Leo Louis Elliott, Aug. 19, 1935 (dec. 1948); children—Mary Ellen (Mrs. Jack Agan), Winona (Mrs. Herbert C. Sample), James, Joan. Tchr. pub. high schs., Panora, Iowa, 1921-23, Dewitt, Iowa, 1923-25; head English dept., dean girls, Kemmerer, Wyo., 1926-29; dean girls and English, Pendleton, Oreg., 1929-30; tchr., Ely, Nev., 1930-31; girls' adviser boarding schs. U.S. Indian Service, 1931-35; tchr. Latin and English, Cut Bank, Mont., 1944-46; tchr. older educable retarded children for Kern County Supt. Schs., Bakersfield, Calif., 1949-68; pvt. remedial work with children and adults. Recipient Alumni Merit award Cornell Coll., 1977. Fellow Am. Assn. Mental Deficiency; mem. Council for Exceptional Children, Internat. Reading Assn., NEA, Calif. Tchrs. Assn., Calif. Ret. Tchrs. Assn., Nat. (hon. life mem.), Calif. (hon. life mem.) congresses parents and tchrs., Catholic Daus. Am., Columbia Tchrs. Coll. Alumni Assn. (past local chmn.), Cornell Coll. Alumni Assn. (sec. Central Valley group 1958—), AAUW, Phi Beta Kappa. Home: 2709 4th St Bakersfield CA 93304

ELLIOTT, ROBERT BURNETT, coal co. mgr.; b. Roseburg, Oreg., Sept. 26, 1925; s. Archie Eli and Blanche Marie (Burnett) E.; student U. Oreg., 1945-47; m. Frances LeNore Moore, Jan. 11, 1947; children—Kathryn Lynn, Susan Lee, Robert Eugene. Mgr. motion picture theatres, 1947-53; with Hanna Mining Co., Riddle, Oreg., 1956-77, supr. inventory control, until 1977; purchasing agt. Colowyo Coal Co., Meeker, Colo., 1977-80, purchasing mgr., 1980—. Commr., Meeker Housing Authority, 1980—. Served with U.S. Army, 1944-45. Mem. Nat. Assn. Purchasing Mgmt., Am. Prodn. and Inventory Control Soc. Republican. Episcopalian. Clubs: Lions, Masons, Shriners, Moose (internat. officer 1971-78, mem. supreme council (internat. bd. dirs.) 1982—). Home: 879 7th St Meeker CO 81641 Office: 5731 State Hwy 13 Meeker CO 81641

ELLIOTT, ROGER HARLEY, state senator; b. Seattle, May 11, 1931; s. Roger Frederick and Geneva Ina (Jones) E.; B.B.A., U. Wash., 1954; m. Grace Marie DeWit, Apr. 17, 1959; children—Diane, Roger F., Wayne, Elizabeth. Pvt. practice acctg., Columbia Falls, Mont., 1955-78; mem. Mont. Senate, 1980—; dir. Glacier Nat. Bank. Mayor, City of Columbia Falls, 1967-71. Mem. Am. Inst. C.P.A.s, Mont. Soc. C.P.A.s. Republican. Presbyterian. Clubs: Lions, Masons, Shriners.

ELLIOTT, RUTH NICHOLS, training and organizational development specialist, consultant; b. Los Angeles, Apr. 15, 1948; d. John and Lodie Mae (Cherry) King; m. Ernest Nichols, Sept. 20, 1965; 1 son, Ernest; m. Alexander William Elliott, Sept. 22, 1979. Mgmt. certs. UCLA, 1980, Profl. designation in personnel mgmt., human resources and organizational devel.; postgrad. in orgnl. devel. Pepperdine U., 1983—. Tng. specialist Los Angeles County Dept. Mental Health, 1966-76; cons. organizational devel. Dobbs' Assocs., Los Angeles, 1976-78; pres., cons. organizational devel., Elliott-Elliott & Assocs., Pasadena, Calif., 1978-82; tng. specialist Info. Services div. TRW, Orange, Calif., 1982—; mem. faculty Pasadena City Coll., Calif. State U.-Los Angeles; cons. organizational and career devel. Mem. Black Women's Network, Organizational Devel. Network, Am. Soc. Tng. and Devel., Bus. and Profl. Women's Club. Republican. Baptist. Implemented 1st career devel. program used in pub. ednl. sector in Calif. Home: 7 Raven Hill Dr Pomona CA 91766 Office: Info Services Div TRW 505 City Pkwy W Orange CA 92668

ELLIS, BETTY RUTH, educator; b. Cin., Jan. 14, 1943; d. Clarence and Dorothy Regina (Copeland) Weaver; student Ohio U., 1960-61, Wilberforce U., 1961-62; B.S.Ed., U. Cin., 1973, M.S.Ed., 1978; children—Cassandra, Aaron. Reading resource tchr. Cin. Public Schs., 1973-76; tchr. Oceanside (Calif.) Unified Sch. Dist., 1976—. Mem. Calif. Tchrs. Assn., NEA, Internat. Reading Assn., Assn. Sch. Curriculum Devel., Assn. Calif. Sch. Adminstrs., Greater San Diego Reading Assn., Kappa Delta Pi. Democrat. Methodist. Home: 4367 Caminito Del Diamante San Diego CA 92121 Office: 940 Capistrano Dr Oceanside CA 92054

ELLIS, ELDON EUGENE, physician; b. Washington, Ind., July 2, 1922; s. Osman Polson and Ina Lucretia (Cochran) E.; B.A., U. Rochester, 1964, M.D., 1949; m. Irene Clay, June 26, 1948 (dec. 1968); m. 2d, Priscilla Dean Strong, Sept. 20, 1969; children—Paul Addison, Kathe Lynn, Jonathan Clay, Sharon Anne, Eldon Eugene, Rebecca Deborah. Intern surgery Stanford U. Hosp., San Francisco, 1949-50, resident and fellow in surgery, 1950-52, 55; Schilling fellow in pathology San Francisco Gen. Hosp., 1955; partner Redwood Med. Clinic, Redwood City, Calif., 1955—; dir. Sequoia Hosp., Redwood City, 1974-82; asst. clin. prof. surgery Stanford U., 1970-80. Served with USNR, 1942-46, 50-52. Mem. San Mateo County (pres. 1961-63), Calif. (pres. 1965-66), Am. (v.p. 1974-75) heart assns., San Mateo Med. Soc. (pres. 1969-70), San Mateo County Comprehensive Health Planning Council (v.p. 1969-70), Calif., Am. med. assns., San Mateo, Stanford surg. socs., Am. Coll. Chest Physicians, Calif. Thoracic Soc., Cardiovascular Council. Republican. Mem. Peninsula Covenant Ch. Club: Commonwealth. Home: 3621 Farm Hill Blvd Redwood City CA 94061 Office: 2900 Whipple Ave Redwood City CA 94062

ELLIS, GARLAND STEPHEN, electronics engr.; b. Richmond, Va., June 30, 1953; s. Garland Cecil and Mary (Fair) E.; B.S. in Elec. Engring., Va. Poly. Inst. and State U., 1974; M.S. in Elec. Engring., Fla. Inst. Tech., 1978; m. Debra Jean Ellis; children—Garland Stephen, Daniel Allen. System test engr. NASA, Kennedy Space Center, Fla., 1974-76; design engr. Sperry Flight Systems, Phoenix, 1976-79; staff engr. INTEL Comml. Systems, Phoenix 1979—. Mem. IEEE. Home: 14222 N 44th Dr Glendale AZ 85306 Office: 2402 W Beardsly Rd Phoenix AZ 85027

ELLIS, GEORGE EDWIN, JR., chem. engr.; b. Beaumont, Tex., Apr. 14, 1921; s. George Edwin and Julia (Ryan) E.; B.S. in Chem. Engring., U. Tex., 1948; M.S., U. So. Calif., 1958, M.B.A., 1965, M.S. in Mech. Engring., 1968, M.S. in Mgmt. Sci., 1971, Engr. in Indsl. and Systems Engring., 1979. Research chem. engr. Tex. Co., Port Arthur, Tex., 1948-51, Long Beach, Calif., Houston, 1952-53, Space and Information div. N.Am. Aviation Co., Downey, Calif., 1959-61, Magna Corp., Anaheim, Calif., 1961-62; chem. process engr. AiResearch Mfg. Co., Los Angeles, 1953-57, 57-59; chem. engr. Petroleum Combustion & Engring. Co., Santa Monica, Calif., 1957, Jacobs Engring. Co., Pasadena, Calif., 1957, Sesler & Assos., Los Angeles, 1959; research specialist Marquardt Corp., Van Nuys, Calif., 1962-67; sr. project engr. Conductron Corp., Northridge, 1967-68; information systems asst. Los Angeles Dept. Water and Power, 1969—. Instr. thermodynamics U. So. Calif., Los Angeles, 1957. Served with USAAF, 1943-45. Mem. Am. Chem. Soc., Am. Soc. for Metals, Am. Inst. Chem. Engrs., ASME, Am. Electroplaters Soc., Am. Inst. Indsl. Engrs., Am. Mktg. Assn., Ops. Research Soc. Am., Am. Prodn. and Inventory Control Soc., Am. Assn. Cost Engrs., Nat. Assn. Accts., Pi Tau Sigma, Phi Lambda Upsilon, Alpha Pi Mu. Home: 1344 W 20th St San Pedro CA 90731 Office: Dept Water and Power Los Angeles CA 90012

ELLIS, GEORGE RICHARD, museum administrator; b. Birmingham, Ala., Dec. 9, 1937; s. Richard Paul and Dorsie (Gibbs) E.; m. Nancy Lee Endersen, Aug. 27, 1975; 1 son, Joshua Richard. B.A., U. Chgo., 1959, M.F.A., 1961; postgrad. UCLA, 1971. Art supr. Jefferson County Schs., Birmingham, Ala., 1962-64; asst. dir. Birmingham Mus. Art, 1964-66; asst. dir. UCLA Mus. Cultural History, 1971-80, assoc. dir., 1980-81; dir. Honolulu Acad. Arts, 1981—. Served with USMCR, 1960-65. U. Chgo. scholar, 1955-59, 60-61; Kress Found. fellow, 1971; recipient Ralph Altman award UCLA, 1968, Outstanding Achievement award, 1980. Mem. Assn. Art Mus. Dirs., Am. Assn. Mus. Club: Pacific (Honolulu). Contbr. writings to publs. in field. Office: 900 S Beretania St Honolulu HI 96814

ELLIS, HENRY CARLTON, psychologist, educator; b. New Bern, N.C., Oct. 23, 1927; s. Henry Alford and Frances Lee (Mays) E.; B.S., Coll. William and Mary, 1951; M.A., Emory U., 1952; Ph.D. (Van Blarcom fellow), Washington U., 1958; m. Florence Pettyjohn, Aug. 24, 1957; children—Joan, Diane Elizabeth, John Weldon. Asst. prof. psychology U. N.Mex., 1957-62, assoc. prof., 1962-67, prof., 1967—, chmn. dept. psychology, 1975—; v.p. Gen. Programmed Teaching Corp., 1960-62; mem. vis. faculty Washington U., 1963-67; vis. prof. psychology U. Calif.-Berkeley, 1971, U. Hawaii, 1977; disting. vis. prof. U.S. Air Force Med. Center, Lackland AFB, Tex., 1978; chmn. Nat. Council Grad. Depts. Psychology, 1977-79, mem. exec. bd., 1976-81. Served with USAAF, 1946-47. Fellow Am. Psychol. Assn. (mem. edn. and tng. bd., council of reps., exec. bd. Div. Exptl. Psychology 1982-85), AAAS; mem. Psychonomic Soc., Cognitive Scis. Soc., Southwestern Psychol. Assn. (pres. 1977-78), Rocky Mountain Psychol. Assn. (pres. 1968-69), Sigma Xi, Phi Kappa Phi. Methodist. Clubs: Albuquerque Tennis, Twenty-One. Author: The Transfer of Learning, 1965; Fundamentals of Human Learning and Cognition, 1972; Fundamentals of Human Learning, Memory and Cognition, 1978; (with Bennett, Daniels and Rickert) Psychology of Learning and Memory, 1979; Fundamentals of Human Memory and Cognition, 1983; mem. editorial bd. Jour. Exptl. Psychology, 1967-74, Jour. Exptl. Psychology: Human Learning and Memory, 1974-76; Perception and Psychophysics, 1971-78; contbr. articles in field to profl. jours. Office: Dept Psychology U N Mex

ELLIS, JAMES GEORGE, retail exec.; b. Tacoma, Jan. 9, 1947; s. George James and Carol Christine (Webb) E.; B.B.A., U. N.Mex., 1968; M.B.A., Harvard, 1970. Asst. to v.p. ops. Broadway Dept. Stores, Los Angeles, 1970-73, buyer housewares, 1973-76, buyer mens sportswear, 1976-77, div. mdse. mgr. young men's div., 1977-79; div. mdse. mgr. Hub Distbg. Co., Ontario, Calif., 1979-81; v.p. men's div. Broadway Dept. Stores, Los Angeles, 1981-83; pres. E.R. Fredericks Co., Inc., San Diego, 1983—; mem. faculty Grad. Sch. Bus. Adminstrn., U. So. Calif., 1971—. Named Prof. of Yr., 1974, Outstanding Young Exec. Los Angeles C. of C., 1978. Mem. Housewares Club So. Calif. (sec.), Harvard Assn. So. Calif., Blue Key. Home: 1695 Caminito Aliviado La Jolla CA 92037 Office: 4090A Morena Blvd San Diego CA 92117

ELLIS, JAMES LEONARD, state senator, businessman; b. Tulsa, Oct. 28, 1928; s. Gaylord Harold and Faye (Proper) E.; m. Barbara Ella Gilligan, 1955; children—Gay Anne, Jon Thomas, Merrilee, James Clayton. Student Colo. State U., 1946-48, Western State Coll., 1948-49; B.A. in Polit. Sci., U.S. Naval Postgrad. Sch., 1965. Propr. Pacific Car Leasing, pres. Pacific Car Rental, San Diego, Calif., 1970—; mem. Calif. State Assembly, 1976-80, Calif. State Senate, 1981—. Mem. San Diego City Council, 1973-76. Served to comdr., U.S. Navy, 1949-70. Decorated 2 D.F.C.'s, 11 Air Medals, 3 Navy Commendation Medals, Bronze Star. Mem. El Cajon C. of C., VFW, Am. Legion, Mil. Order World Wars. Republican. Baptist. Club: Rotary. Home: 2755 Navajo Rd El Cajon CA 92020 Office: California State Senate Sacramento CA 95814*

ELLIS, JOHN W., utility company executive; b. Seattle, Sept. 14, 1928; s. Floyd E. and Hazel (Reed) R.; B.S., U. Wash., 1952, J.D., 1953; m. Doris Stearns, Sept. 1, 1953; children—Thomas R., John Barbara, Jim. Admitted to Wash. State bar, 1953; with firm Perkins, Coie, Stone, Olsen & Williams, Seattle, 1953-70; with Puget Sound Power & Light Co., Bellevue, Wash., 1970—, exec. v.p., 1973-76, pres., chief exec. officer, 1976, also dir.; chmn. bd. Fed. Res. Bank of San Francisco, Seattle br.; dir. Wash. Mut. Savs. Bank, Seattle, SAFECO Corp.; mem. Wash. Gov's. Spl. Com. Energy Curtailment, 1973-74. Pres. Bellevue Boys' Club, 1969-71; mem. exec. dirs. Seattle-King County Boys' Club, 1972-75; bd. dirs. Overlake Hosp., Bellevue, 1974—, United Way King County, 1977—, Seattle Sci. Found., 1977—, Seattle Sailing Found., Edison Electric Inst., 1978—, Evergreen Safety Council, 1981, Assn. Wash. Bus., 1980-81. Served with AUS, 1950-52. Mem. Am., Wash., King County (Wash.) bar assns., Nat. Assn. Elec. Cos. (dir. 1977-79), Edison Electric Inst. (dir. 1978-80), Assn. Edison Illuminating Cos. (exec. com. 1979-81), Seattle C. of C. (dir. 1980—), Phi Gamma Delta, Phi Delta Phi. Clubs: Rainier (sec. 1972), Seattle Yacht, Corinthian Yacht (Seattle); Meydenbauer Bay Yacht (Bellevue). Home: 901 SE Shoreland Dr Bellevue WA 98004 Office: Puget Power Bldg Bellevue WA 98009

ELLIS, KAREN ELLA, educator; b. La Grande, Oreg., May 10, 1950; d. Ellis Eddington and Gladys Vera (Smith) McGee; m. Lynn F. Ellis, June 14, 1975; children—Megan Marie, Matthew David. B.A. in Elem. Edn., Boise State U., 1972, M.A. in Spl. Edn., 1979. Tchr. learning disabilities resource room New Plymouth Joint Sch. Dist., 1972-73; tchr. learning disabilities resource room Payette Joint Sch. Dist., diagnostician project SELECT, 1974-75; cons. tchr. in learning disabilities Boise Ind. Sch. Dist., 1975-76, cons. tchr. in learning disabilities and gifted/talented, 1976-78, cons. tchr. in spl. edn., 1978—. Active Mental Health Assn., Hotline, Inc., Citizens Crisis Coalition, Idaho Fair Share, Snake River Alliance, Idaho Youth Theatre. Recipient Disting. Young Woman of Yr. award Boise Jaycettes, 1982, Idaho Jaycettes, 1983. Mem. NEA, Idaho Edn. Assn. (dir. 1983—), Boise Edn. Assn. (pres. 1982—), Nat. Council Urban Edn. Assn., World Future Soc., Council for Exceptional Children (pres. chpt. 1978-79), Assn. Supervision and Curriculum Devel. Unitarian. Contbr. articles to profl. jours. Office: 1207 Fort St Boise ID 83702

ELLIS, LEE, newspaper mag. pub. co. exec.; b. Medford, Mass., Mar. 12, 1924; s. Lewis Leeds and Charlotte Frances (Brough) E.; m. Sharon Kay Barnhouse, Aug. 19, 1972. Child actor, dancer, stage, radio, movies, Keith-Albee Circuit, Eastern U.S., 1927-37; announcer, producer, writer, various radio stas. and CBS, Boston and Miami, Fla., 1946-50; TV dir. ABC; mem. TV faculty Sch. Journalism U. Mo., Columbia, 1950-55; mgr. Sta. KFSD/KFSD-TV, San Diego, 1955-60, GM Imperial Broadcasting System, 1960-62; v.p., dir. advt., Media-Agencies-Clients, Los Angeles, 1962-66; v.p., dir. newspaper relations, Family Weekly, N.Y.C., 1966—; lectr. gen. semantics and communications Idaho State U., Utah State U., San Diego State U. Served with USN, 1941-44; PTO. Mem. San Diego Press Club. Republican. Methodist. Home: 84-250 Indio Springs Dr Box 104 Indio CA 92201

ELLIS, LELAND ROBBINS, urologist; b. Rockford, Ill., Jan. 30, 1935; s. Ernest Henry and Wilma Fern (Robbins) E.; B.S. summa cum laude, Purdue U., 1956; M.D. with honors, U. Ill., 1960; m. Charlotte Eve Anderson, Dec. 27, 1964; children—Allison, Lisa, Emilie. Intern Cook County Hosp., Chgo., 1960-61; resident in urology U. Oreg. Med. Sch., Portland, 1964-68; practice medicine specializing in urology, Seattle, 1968—; pres. Bellevue Urology Assos. Inc. (Wash.), 1969—; clin. asst. prof. urology U. Wash., Seattle, 1970—; attending surgeon Children's Hosp. Med. Center, Seattle, 1969—; chief-of-staff Overlake Meml. Hosp., 1981-82. Mem. citizens adv. com. Overlake Meml. Hosp., 1974-76, trustee, 1980—; pres. King County Urol. Com., 1975-78; trustee Eastside YMCA, 1975-79, Overlake Found., 1982-83. Served to maj. M.C., USAF, 1961-64. Fellow Am. Acad. Pediatrics; mem. Am. Urol. Assn., Am. Urol. Assn. Western (exec. com. 1980-82), Northwest Urol. Soc. (membership chmn. 1979—), ACS, Soc. Pediatric Urology, Seattle Surg. Soc., Bellevue C. of C. (econ. resources com.), AMA, Soc. Internat. d'Urologie, Sigma Alpha Epsilon, Alpha Omega Alpha. Republican. Episcopalian. Clubs: Bellevue Rotary (sgt. at arms 1974-75, youth exchange chmn. Dist. 503, 1977-81, pres. 1981-82), Overlake Country, Bellevue Athletic (Bellevue); Swinomish Gun. Home: 7625 Overlake Dr W Medina WA 98039 Office: 1201 116th Ave NE Bellevue WA 98004

ELLIS, MARCIA B., public relations associate; b. Nashua, N.H., Oct. 21, 1942; d. Robert and Lorraine (Bond) Polhemus; m. David Winston Ellis, Dec. 1, 1961; children—Jocelyn, Jim, Erik. B.A. in Theatre, Ariz. State U., 1980. Freelance writer, theatre critic Westsider, Phoenix, 1979-81; artistic dir. CAS/West Masquemakers, Phoenix, 1965-81; artistic dir. Phoenix Little Theatre, 1983; assoc. Buchen, Snell & Co., Phoenix, 1981—. Bd. dirs. Valley Leadership, exec. com. Candidate Selection Com., 1981-82; bd. dirs. Phoenix Little Theatre, chmn. by-laws com., co-chmn. fund-raising com.; mem. Republican Caucus; bd. dirs. Cultural Arts Soc./West, 1978-81; mem. Task Force for Hosp. Bed Needs Assessment, Central Ariz. Health Systems Assn., 1982. Mem. Pub. Relations Soc. Am. Republican. Club: Goodyear Golf and Country (Litchfield Park, Ariz.).

ELLIS, MICHAEL THOMAS, electronics company executive; b. Baldock, Hertfordshire, Eng., Nov. 8, 1942; came to U.S., 1968, naturalized, 1978; s. Thomas Andrew and Ceridwen (Jones) E.; B.Sc. with honors, No. Poly. U., London, 1965; postgrad. City U., London, 1965-66; M.S. in Mgmt. Engring., L.I.U., 1972; m. Janet Eileen Piper, Aug. 28, 1965; children—Damon Michael, Claire Janette. Student scholar W. H. Sanders Ltd., Stevenage, Eng., 1961-66; activity mgr. Brit. Aircraft Corp., Stevenage, 1966-68; program mgr. PRD Electronics, Syosset, N.Y., 1968-75; exec. v.p. ATE Assocs., Westlake, Calif., 1975—; founding mem., bd. dirs. Automatic Test Equipment Assn., 76-77; task chmn. industry ad hoc automatic test equipment com. for U.S. Navy, 1975-77; mem. industry-joint services automatic test equipment project, 1978—; tech. program coordinator Autotestcon, 1978; mem. Internat. Atlas Com., 1970—; cons. U.S. Mil., electronics/aerospace corps.; extensive lectr. U.S. and Europe; participant profl. confs. Sci. Research Council grantee City U., London, 1966; recipient certs. of appreciation, U.S. Navy, 1971, U.S. Army, 1972; Award of Excellence, Soc. Tech. Communications, 1975. Mem. Inst. Elec. Engrs., Inst. Physics. U.S. editorial corr. Test mag., 1978—; bd. advisors Electronics Test mag.; mem. tech. adv. bd Test and Measurement World mag.; author numerous tech. papers on test automation topics.

ELLIS, ROBERT LANE, marketing analyst and consultant; b. Port Hueneme, Calif., Aug. 21, 1955; s. John Robert and Elane Lavon (Harless) E. B.S. in Bus. Adminstrn. and Mktg., San Jose State U., 1977; M.B.A., Pepperdine U., 1982. Applications engr. Peterbilt Motors Co., Newark, Calif., 1979-81, parts mktg. analyst, 1981—. Republican. Home: 916 Concord St Pleasonton CA 94566 Office: Peterbilt Motors Co 38801 Cherry St Newark CA 94560

ELLIS, ROBERTA FAY, home economist, psychologist; b. Hemet, Calif., Nov. 18, 1932; d. John Henderson and Etta Mae (Owens) Virden; divorced; children—Colleen, Lantz. B.S. in Home Econs., U. Calif.-Davis, 1954; M.S. with distinction in Psychology, Calif. State Coll.-Stanislaus, 1980. Cert. secondary tchr. Calif. Home economist, 4-H advisor Solano County, Calif., 1956-60; 4-H advisor San Bernardino, Calif., 1968-70, Stanislaus County, Modesto, Calif., 1970—. Recipient commendation U. Calif., 1974; U. Calif. coop. extension fellow, 1980. Mem. Nat. 4-H Assn., Calif. 4-H Assn., Calif. Assn. Extension Home Economists, Nat. Assn. Extension Home Economists. Lutheran. Club: Soroptimist (Modesto). Office: 733 County Center III Court Modesto CA 95355

ELLIS, RONALD JAMES, systems developer, consultant, educator; b. Los Angeles, Mar. 13, 1952; s. Don R. and Cades A. (LeVay) E.; m. Pamela L. Newton, Nov. 1, 1974. B.A., Calif. State U.-Fullerton, 1974; M.B.A., U. So. Calif., 1978. Lifetime cert. community coll. instr., Calif. Adminstr., Bechtel Power Corp., Norwalk, Calif., 1974-77; data engr. Ralph M. Parsons Co., Pasadena, Calif., 1977-79; sr. account rep. Comshare, Inc., Los Angeles, 1979, client service mgr., 1979-81; systems/evaluation cons. ARCO Marine, Inc. subs. Atlantic Richfield, Los Angeles, 1981-82; mgr. systems devel. ARCO Transp. Co. div., Los Angeles, 1982—; cons.; instr. Coastline Community Coll. Scoutmaster, 1973—, vice chmn. Los Amigos dist. Boy Scouts Am., recipient Scoutmasters key, 1976, award of merit, 1977, Commr's. Key, 1977, Silver Beaver award, 1983; exec. bd. Orange County chpt. Nat. Eagle Scout Assn.; v.p. adminstrn. So. Calif. Lutheran Assn. Scouters; co. advisor Jr. Achievement; active United Way. Mem. Planning Execs. Inst. (v.p. Los Angeles chpt.), Data Processing Mgmt. Assn., Assn. M.B.A. Execs., Beta Gamma Sigma. Club: Toastmasters (past club pres.). Developed more than 20 different tng. courses promoting use of computers and computer systems by non-EDP profls. Home: 1668 W Norwood Ct Brea CA 92621 Office: 515 S Flower St Los Angeles CA 90071

ELLIS, TED ELLSWORTH, banker; b. Rexburg, Idaho, Aug. 1, 1927; s. Ted R. and Zella (Ellsworth) E.; student Ricks Coll., 1947, U. Wash., 1963; m. Margaret Lewis, Oct. 8, 1947; children—Nancy C. Ellis Chopko, Jolynn Ellis Woodworth, Patricia Ann. With First Security Bank of Idaho, 1947-77, sr. v.p., dir., 1972-77; exec. v.p., chief adminstrv. officer Idaho Bank and Trust Co., Pocatello, 1977-82, pres., chief exec. officer, Boise, 1982—. Bd. dirs. Bannock County ARC, 1965, Salvation Army, 1973—, Boy Scouts Am., 1976—, Jr. Achievement, 1977—, Idaho State Civic Symphony, 1977-78, YMCA, 1974—, Boise State U. Found.; pres. Pocatello Downtown Devel. Corp., 1970—; vice chmn. Assoc. Taxpayers Idaho, Idaho Council on Econ. Edn.; mem. Boise Mayor's Com. on Hiring Handicapped. Served with USNR, 1945-46. Mem. Pocatello C. of C. (pres. 1969-70, dir.). Club: Pocatello Rotary (pres. 1973-74). Home: 3675 Gramarcy Ln Boise ID 83703 Office: Box 2557 Boise ID 83701

ELLIS, WAYNE ELMO, bldg. materials co. exec.; b. Puxico, Mo., Apr. 13, 1915; s. Roscoe Clinton and Carrie Elizabeth (Palmer) E.; A.A., Bakersfield Jr. Coll., 1935; B.A., San Jose State U., 1938; m. Helen Flora Rice, Aug. 2, 1940; children—Helen Kuulei, Wayne Richard, Michael Lewis. Tchr., Dept. Pub. Instruction, Lihue, Kauai, Hawaii, 1938-42; owner, operator Lihue Hotel, 1942-46; mgr. Hale Kauai, Ltd., Lihue, 1945-50, pres., 1950—; dir. InterIsland Resorts; pres. Puhi Enterprises, Inc.; commr. Dept. Pub. Instrn. Ter. Hawaii, 1945-53; statehood commr. Ter. Hawaii, 1953-59; mem. adv. council for 7 western states SBA, 1955-56; mem. U.S. Army Adv. Council, 1965-78. Clubs: Rotary, Yacht, Masons, Shriners (Kauai). Home: PO Box 1749 Lihue HI 96766

ELLIS, WILLIAM DONALDSON, hotel executive; b. Buenos Aires, Argentina, Aug. 4, 1932; s. Richard Marion and Clara (Carey) E.; came to U.S., 1941; student U. Wash., 1955-57; m. Catherine Dixon, Oct. 29, 1966; 1 son, William David. Corporate auditor Westin Hotel Co., Seattle, 1951-58, regional controller, Portland, Oreg., 1963-65; controller Hotel Benson, Portland, 1958-63; controller, asst. sec. Century Plaza Hotel, Los Angeles, 1965-71; v.p., controller Westin Hotel Co., Seattle, 1971—. Area finance chmn. Boy Scouts Am., 1964; bd. dirs. United Air Lines Employees Credit Union, 1975—, chmn. bd., 1982; adv. bd. Social Devel. of Youth, vice chmn., 1983; adv. bd. Nat. Bus. League, 1982—; mem. hospitality adv. council Johnson & Wales Coll., 1982—; mem. project bus. com. Jr. Achievement, 1982—; bd. dirs. Pvt. Initiative for Pub. Edn., 1983—. Served with USNR, 1949-58. Mem. Internat. Assn. Hospitality Accts. (pres. 1972-73), Hotel-Motel Accts. Assn. So. Calif. (pres. 1967, chmn. pub. relations com. 1975—). Republican. Methodist. Club: Kiwanis (pres. 1968-71). Home: 3740 NE 149th Pl Seattle WA 98155 Office: Westin Hotel Co 2001 6th Ave Seattle WA 98121

ELLISON, CAROLE ANN, training consultant; b. San Francisco, Oct. 4, 1946; d. Jack Dwight Ellison and Jeanne Sinclair Lederer; m. Rodrigo Nunez Izquierdo, Aug. 13, 1978; 1 son, Nicholas Ellison Izquierdo. B.A. in Edn., U. Ariz., 1968. Tchr. elem. sch., Calif., Orient, Europe, 1968-74; officer for affirmative action Human Rights Commn., San Francisco, 1975-77; tng. cons. San Francisco Community Coll., Fed. Office Personnel Mgmt., San Francisco, Mare Island Naval Sta., Vallejo, Calif., U. San Francisco, 1977—, Calif. Dept. Indsl. Relations, San Francisco. Mem. Am. Soc. Tng. and Devel., Nat. Speakers Assn. Democrat. Office: Dept Indsl Relations Tng Office 525 Golden Gate Ave 7th Floor San Francisco CA 94102

ELLISON, PETER KEMP, banker, former state legislator; b. Cin., Sept. 21, 1942; s. Harris A. and Jane (Weber) E.; B.A., U. Cin., 1965; J.D., U. Utah, 1968; m. Elizabeth Sloan, Sept. 8, 1967; children—Ann Elizabeth, Rebecca Adams, Karen Sloan, Daniel Peter, David Christian. Sr. v.p., sr. trust officer Zions First Nat. Bank, Salt Lake City, 1975—; chmn. bd. Wycoff Trucking Co., 1976-80; dir. First Nat. Bank, Layton, Utah, Ellison Ranching Co.; mem. Utah Ho. of Reps. from 23d Dist., 1972-76; mem. adv. council fin. aid to students U.S. Dept. Edn. Chmn., Utah Citizens Adv. Council on Liquor Control. Mem. Am., Utah, Salt Lake County bar assns. Republican. Mormon. Home: 2438 Cardinal Way Salt Lake City UT 84121 Office: 1 Main St Lake City UT 84111

ELLISON, THOMAS GRIFFITTS (GRIFF), communications co. exec.; b. Portsmouth, Va., May 24, 1946; s. Thomas Ballard and Virginia (Griffitts) E.; B.S., in Commerce, U. Va., 1971; m. Pamela Noggle. Bus. mgr., asso. editor The Progressive mag., 1971-73; asso. pub. Harper's mag., 1974-76; pub. Bookletter, 1975-76; mem. press and advance staff Carter presdl. campaign, 1976; mem. presdl. transition staff, 1976; spl. asst. communications Dept. Commerce, 1977; advance staff White House, 1977-79; dep. dir. public affairs Dept. State, 1977-78; v.p. public and govtl. affairs Export-Import Bank U.S., Washington, 1978-80; mng. partner Energy and Communications Group, Denver, 1980-82; pres. Ellison Communications, Santa Fe, 1982; dir. Los Caballos de Santa Fe, Western Heritage Realty; ptnr. Ellison Quarter Horses. Nat. coordinator Vietnam Vets. Against the War, 1968-71; founder, chmn. U.S. Com. for Diversity of Press, 1971-73. Served with USMC, 1966-68; Vietnam. Mem. Public Relations Soc. Am., Colo. Export Council, Colo. Public Affairs Council, N.Mex. Advt. Fedn., Sigma Chi, Delta Sigma Phi. Clubs: Nat. Press, Denver Press. Home: 4 Vista Grande Santa Fe NM 87501 Office: One Hacienda Santa Fe NM 87501

ELLISOR, WILBURN LEE, association executive; b. Independence, Kans., Aug. 26, 1932; s. William Payne and Mary (Baty) E.; m. Ann L. Chester, Jan. 2, 1953; children—Conni L., Kristen A., William C., Susan K., Carol B. B.A., U. Wichita, 1955; grad. U.S. Army Command and Gen. Staff Coll., 1976. Program dir. Eastside br. YMCA, Wichita, Kans., 1953-56; exec. dir. Westside YMCA, Wichita, 1956-57; program dir. San Angelo (Tex.) YMCA, 1958-59, Abilene (Tex.) YMCA, 1960-64; exec. dir. Jefferson County YMCA, Lakewood, Colo., 1964-70; v.p. ops. YMCA Met. Denver, 1970—. Serving with F.A., USAR, 1955—. Recipient Disting. Service award Jaycees, Denver, 1969. Mem. Assn. Profl. Dirs. YMCA USA, N.G. Assn., Denver C. of C., Am. Camping Assn., ARC, Boy Scouts Am., Acad. Cert. Profl. Dirs., Sigma Tau Gamma, Alpha Phi Omega. Democrat. Mem. Evangelical Covenant Ch. Clubs: Kiwanis (program chmn. Denver); Optimists (pres. 1959, life). Office: 25 E 16th Ave Denver CO 80202

ELLS, RHEA S., interior designer; b. Chgo., Mar. 15, 1924; d. Joseph J. and Rose Marie Riha; m. Elliott G. Ells, May 12, 1945; children—Michael, Tracey, Rand, Peter. Grad. U. N.Mex., 1945. Designer, Mandel Bros., Chgo., 1945; prin. Rhea Ells Interior Design, Chgo., 1948; designer John Dempsey Interiors, Westwood, Calif., 1954; owner Rhea Ells Interior Design, Manhattan Beach, 1960—, co-owner The Design Co., Manhattan Beach, 1980—; founder, co-chmn. Sandpiper Design House, 1975; cons. in field. Recipient Sandpiper of Yr. award. Mem. Am. Soc. Interior Designers (assoc.), Internat. Soc. Interior Designers. Roman Catholic. Clubs: Sandpipers. Contbr. design work to profl. jours. Address: Rhea Ells Interior Design 701 25th St Manhattan Beach CA 90266

ELLSWORTH, FRANK L., college president; b. Wooster, Ohio, May 20, 1943; s. Clayton Sumner and Frances (Fuller) E.; B.A., Western Res. Coll., 1965; M.Ed., Pa. State U., 1967; M.A., Columbia U., 1969; Ph.D., U. Chgo., 1976; 1 dau., Kirstin Lynne. Asst. dir. devel. Columbia Law Sch., 1968-70; dir. spl. projects, prof. lit. Sarah Lawrence Coll., N.Y., 1971; asst. dean Law Sch., U. Chgo., 1971-79, instr. social sci. collegiate div., 1975-79; pres. Pitzer Coll., Claremont, Calif., 1979—, also prof. polit. sci., 1979—. Mem. vis. coms. Western Res. Coll.; bd. dirs. Ind. Colls. So. Calif.; bd. fellows Claremont Univ. Center; bd. dirs. Los Angeles Ballet. Recipient Disting. Young Alumnus award Case Western Res. U., 1981. Mem. Am. Hist. Assn., Friends Huntington Library, History Edn. Soc., Council for Advancement of Secondary Edn., Young Pres.'s Orgn. Clubs: Arts (Chgo.); University (Los Angeles and Claremont); Zamorano (Los Angeles); Town Hall of Calif. Author: Law on the Midway, 1977; contbr. articles to profl. jours. Office: 1050 Mills Ave Claremont CA 91711

ELLSWORTH, RICHARD GERMAN, psychologist; b. Provo, Utah, June 23, 1950; s. Richard Grant and Betty Lola (Midgley) E.; B.S., Brigham Young U., 1974, M.A., 1975; Ph.D., U. Rochester (N.Y.), 1979; postgrad. UCLA, 1980-83; Ph.D., Internat. Coll., 1983; m. Carol Emily Osborne, May 23, 1970; children—Rebecca Ruth, Spencer German, Rachel Pricilla. Lexicographer, Automated Lang. Processing, Brigham Young U., 1976; instr. U. Rochester, 1976-77; research assoc. Nat. Tech. Inst. for Deaf, Rochester, 1977; instr. West Valley Coll., Saratoga, Calif., 1979-80, San Jose (Calif.) City Coll., 1980; psycholinquist UCLA, 1980-81; psychologist Daniel Freeman Meml. Hosp., Inglewood, Calif., 1981—; cons. LDS Social Services Calif. Agy., 1981—. Scoutmaster, Boy Scouts Am., 1976-79. UCLA Med. Sch. fellow in psychiatry, 1980-81. Mem. Am. Psychol. Assn., Linguistic Soc. Am., Am. Soc. Clin. Hypnosis, Psi Chi. Mem. Ch. Jesus Christ of Latter-day Saints. Contbr. articles to profl. jours. Office: Daniel Freman Meml Hosp Dept Psycho-Social Services 333 N Prairie Ave Inglewood CA 90301 also 7220 Rosemead Blvd Suite 204 San Gabriel CA 91775

ELLSWORTH, ROBERT LEE, electronics co. exec.; b. Harvey, Ill., Dec. 29, 1945; s. Rawleigh Milton and Pearl Sarah (Buchmeier) E.; student La. State U., 1964-66, U. Wash., 1968-73; m. Jean A. Linsey, Mar. 17, 1978. With Blake Moffitt & Towne, Seattle, 1973-76; br. mgr. Western Paper Co., Tacoma, 1977-79; mgr. Hayes Tech., Seattle, 1979, owner, 1980-81; dir. Datacom Northwest, Seattle, 1981—. Mem. Electronics Reps. Assn. Republican. Club: Gig Harbor Yacht. Patentee in field. Home: PO Box 653 Gig Harbor WA 98335 Office: 11300 25th Ave NE Seattle WA 98125

ELLSWORTH, SUSAN, media cons.; b. Los Angeles, May 7, 1946; d. Theodore R. and Jeanne E.; A.A. in Library Media Tech. magna cum laude, Los Angeles Valley Coll., 1976; postgrad. UCLA extension; 1 dau., Alexandra Susan Hall. Media technician Sunkist Growers, Sherman Oaks, Calif., 1976; audiovisual coordinator St. Joseph Med. Center, Burbank, Calif., 1977; adminstrv. cons., founder, dir. Media Resource Service, Los Angeles, 1977—. Mem. Defenders Wildlife, Nat. Entrepreneurs Assn., Nat. Assn. Exec. Females, Calif. Hist. Soc. Vol. columnist Media Digest, 1978; researcher, author, pub. booklet The Handbook of Motion Picture Film Care, 1978. Home: 9043 Burroughs Rd Los Angeles CA 90046 Office: 1015 Gayley Ave Suite 172 Los Angeles CA 90025

ELMENDORF, BYRON LEE, parks and recreation administrator; b. Evansville, Ind., Oct. 8, 1944; s. Albert Henry and Nancy Laura (Carter) E.; m. Becky Ann Barnes, Aug. 20, 1967; children—Tyson, Amy. B.S., Ind. State U., 1966; M.S., No. Mich. U., 1972; Cert. adminstr., Wash. Parks and Recreation Assn., 1974, Nat. Parks and Recreation Assn., 1979. Recreation supr., Flagstaff, Ariz., 1969-71; supt. recreation, Vancouver, Wash., 1972-75, asst. dir. parks and recreation, 1976-78; dir. parks and recreation, Bellingham, Wash., 1978—; tchr., lectr. Mem. Bellingham Design Rev. Com., 1978—, mem. Visitors' and Conv. Bd.; mem. citizens adv. com. Bellingham Sch. Dist.; chmn. bd. Sehome Hill Arboretum, 1980-82; mem. exec. bd. Campus Christian Ministry; mem. adv. bd. Wash. State Trails, 1980—. Served with USMCR, 1966-69; Vietnam. Mott Found. fellow, 1971. Mem. Nat. Recreation and Park Assn., Wash. Recreation and Park Assn., Nat. Community Edn. Assn., Internat. Park Maintenance Assn. Presbyterian (elder, trustee). Clubs: Bellingham Bay Rotary, Bellingham Yacht. Home: 401 Morey Dr Bellingham WA 98225 Office: 210 Lottie St Bellingham WA 98225

ELMER, CARLOS HALL, author, photographer; b. Washington, July 22, 1920; s. Charles Percival and Dorothy Winslow (Hall) E.; A.B., U. Calif. at Los Angeles, 1947; m. Wilma Virginia Hudson, Jan. 29, 1943; children—Frank Hudson, Elizabeth Anne. Supr. photog. and presentations function U.S. Naval Ordnance Test Sta., China Lake, Calif., 1947-57; sales engr. Traid Corp., photog. instrumentation, Encino, 1957-65; author, 1939—; pub. Carlos H. Elmer, Scottsdale, 1967—. U.S. del. Internat. Com. High Speed Photog. Congresses, 1971-75, chmn. 9th Congress, Denver, 1970; mem. Brookings Instn. Seminar on the Alternative Futures, Scottsdale, Ariz., 1971-72. Served to capt. AUS, 1942-46. Fellow Soc. Motion Picture and TV Engrs. (v.p. photo instrumentation 1970-71); mem. Soc. Photo-Optical Instrumentation Engrs., Theta Xi. Presbyn. Author: London Bridge in Pictures, 1971, Carlos Elmer's Arizona, 1967, The Glorious Seasons of Arizona, 1971; Arizona in Color, 1973; Mohave County, Ariz., U.S.A., 1974; Grand Canyon Country, 1975; Colorful Northern Arizona, 1977; Hoover Dam, Lake Mead, and Lake Mohave, 1978. Author and photographer for Arizona Highways, mag., 1940—. Office: PO Box 4005 Scottsdale AZ 85261

ELMORE, HUGH EVAN, accountant; b. Missoula, Mont., Feb. 26, 1936; s. Harold Frank and Goldie Fern (Scheibal) E.; m. Joan Elaine Miller, June 20, 1959; children—Deborah Fern, David Frank. B.S. in Acctg., U. Mont., 1963. C.P.A., Mont. Pvt. practice acctg., Missoula, 1964-73; staff acct. Dobbins, DeGuire & Tucker P.C., Missoula, 1973-75, dir., 1975—. Bd. dirs. Opportunity Found. Workshop, 1964-81, Missoula Children's Theatre, 1982—, U. Mont. Athletic Assn., 1983. Served with USAF, 1954-58. Mem. Am. Inst. C.P.A.s, Mont. Soc. C.P.A.s. Club: Elks. Office: Dobbins DeGuire & Tucker 3819 Stephens St Missoula MT 59801

ELMORE, KATHLEEN ANN MARIE, food company executive; b. Indpls., Sept. 9, 1952; s. Martin Alfred and Florence Cecilia (Miara) E.; B.S., Purdue U., 1974; M.B.A., Central State U., Okla., 1978. Regional merchandiser Castle & Cooke Foods, Inc., Indpls., 1975, divisional merchandiser, New Orleans, 1975-76, asst. dist. sales mgr., Dallas, 1976, dist. sales mgr., Oklahoma City, 1976-77; mgr. field mktg. projects Pizza Hut div. Pepsi Co., Inc., Wichita, Kans., mgr. market research, 1979-81; mgr. sales planning Stokely-Van Camp Inc., Indpls., 1981-83; asst. product mgr. for seafoods Star-Kist Foods Inc. div. Heinz Inc., Terminal Island, Calif., 1983—. Ind. State scholar, 1970-74; Am. Bus. Women's Assn. scholar, 1971-73; Purdue U. Centennial grantee, 1974. Mem. Assn. M.B.A. Execs.

ELMSTROM, GEORGE P., optometrist, writer; b. Salem, Mass., Dec. 11, 1925; s. George and Emily Irene (Wedgwood) E.; grad. So. Calif. Coll. Optometry, 1951; m. Nancy DePaul, Apr. 29, 1973; children—Pamela, Beverly, Robert. Pvt. practice optometry, El Segundo, Calif., 1951—; mem. staff So. Calif. Coll. Optometry, 1951—; book cons. Med. Econs. Books, 1970—; instrument and forensic editor Jour. Am. Optical Assn.; comml. airplane and balloon pilot, 1968—. Served with U.S. Army, World War II. Decorated Bronze Star; named Writer of Year, Calif. Optometric Assn., 1957, Man of Year, El Segundo, 1956; recipient spl. citation Nat. Eye Found., 1955. Fellow Am. Acad. Optometry, AAAS, Southwest Contact Lens Soc., Disting. Service Found. of Optometry, Internat. Acad. Preventive Medicine; mem. Am. Optometric Assn., Assn. for Research in Vision, Am. Soc. Ultrasonography, Am. Pub. Health Assn., Optometric Editors Assn., Assn. Research in Vision, Internat. Soc. Ophthalmic Ultrasound, Profl. Airshow Pilots Assn., Flying Optometrists Assn. Am., Beta Sigma Kappa, So. Calif. Coll. Optometry Alumni (pres. 1955-56). Author: Optometric Practice Management, 1963; Legal Aspects of Contact Lens Practice, 1966, Advanced Management for Optometrists, 1974, Modernized Management, 1981; mgmt. editor Optometric Monthly, 1973. Home: 15 63d Ave Playa Del Rey CA 90291 Office: 502 Main El Segundo CA 90245

ELSBERND, MARK A., industrial engineer; b. Cin., July 18, 1956; s. Ralph Albert and Ruth Christine (Stauber) A. Elsbernd; student Joliet Jr. Coll., 1974-75, U. Dayton, 1976-78. Indsl. engring. clk. Monarch Marking, Inc., 1978; facilities engr. Dataproducts Corp., Woodland Hills, Calif., 1978-80, sr. indsl. engr., 1980—. Winner hon. mention for Office Bldg. of Yr., 1980. Mem. Am. Inst. Indsl. Engrs., Am. Inst. Plant Engrs. Democrat. Roman Catholic. Home: 20326 Saticoy St Apt 19 Canoga Park CA 91306 Office: Dataproducts Corp 6250 Canoga Ave Woodland Hills CA 91365

ELSING, WILLIAM TADDES, lawyer; b. Bisbee, Ariz., May 8, 1910; s. Morris J. and Celestine (Marks) E.; student Stanford, 1928, U. Calif.-Berkeley, 1929; J.D., U. Ariz., 1933. Admitted to Ariz. bar, 1933, Cal. bar, 1946; practiced in Prescott, 1933-38, Phoenix, 1938—. Chmn. bd. govs. Ariz. Dept. Mineral Resources, 1969-76. Served with CIC, AUS, 1942-45. Mem. ABA (chmn. hard minerals com. sect. natural resources law 1965), Calif., Ariz., Maricopa County (bd. dirs. 1965-67) bar assns., Soc. Mining Engrs., Am. Inst. Mining, Metall. and Petroleum Engrs., AAAS, Phi Delta Phi. Republican. Presbyn. Home: 6545 N 13th St Phoenix AZ 85014 Office: Suite 1010 34 W Monroe St Phoenix AZ 85003

ELSNER, WILLIAM HENRY, museum curator; b. LaGrange, Ind., Oct. 8, 1917; s. Fred Harold and Hildagarde Marie (Heiner) E.; B.A., Eastern Wash. Coll. Edn., 1938; postgrad. Oriental studies U. Calif. at Berkeley, 1949-52; m. Margaret Lindsay, Aug. 27, 1949. Pub. sch. tchr., Wash., Calif., 1938-42, 52-55; mem. staff Fine Arts Mus. San Francisco, 1955-77, curator painting and sculpture, 1974-77, curator emeritus, 1977—. Served with AUS, 1942-46. Mem. San Francisco Press Clubs. Author bulls., mus. catalogues. Home: 795 Sutter St San Francisco CA 94109 Office: Fine Arts Mus Golden Gate Park San Francisco CA 94118

ELSOM, SUSAN DOUGLAS, clinical psychologist; b. Seattle, Oct. 20, 1943; d. James Harvey and Anne Scott (Douglas) E. B.S. in Chemistry, Mary Washington Coll., U. Va., 1965; M.A. in Clin. Psychology, Lone Mountain Coll., San Francisco, 1974; Ph.D. in Clin. Psychology, Pacific Grad. Sch. Psychology, Palo Alto, Calif., 1980. Lic. psychologist, Calif., 1982, marriage, family, and child counselor, Calif., 1975. Research technologist dept. biochemistry U. Wash., Seattle, 1965-69; research asst. dept. pediatrics Stanford U., 1969-71; family therapist Children's Counseling Ctr., Catholic Social Service, Santa Clara, Calif., 1972-76, pvt. practice, Palo Alto, Calif., 1976-81; clin. psychology predoctoral intern Children's Health Council, Palo Alto, 1977-78; clin. psychologist Fairoaks Mental Health Ctr., Sunnyvale, Calif., 1980-81; pvt. practice clin. psychology, Fremont, Calif., 1982—. Mem. Am. Psychol. Assn., Calif. Psychol. Assn., Alameda County Psychol. Assn., Am. Assn. Marriage and Family Therapy, Assn. Transpersonal Psychology, Western Psychol. Assn. Office: 1999 Mowry Ave Suite 2-C Fremont CA 94538

ELVIDGE, VIVIAN PATRICIA, museum director; b. Okanogan, Wash., Jan. 6, 1940; d. Floyd Kenneth and Martha Grace (Hinshaw) Byrd; m. Robert Fred Elvidge, Dec. 26, 1962; 1 dau., Janice April. A.B., Bellevue Community Coll., 1974; B.A. cum laude in Anthropology, U. Wash., 1977, M.A. cum laude in Anthropology, 1980. Vol. coordinator Marymoor Mus., Redmond, Wash., 1979; curator, 1978-80, dir., 1980—. Mem. Am. Assn. Mus., Wash. Mus. Assn., Am. Assn. State and Local History, Phi Beta Kappa. Methodist. Author: Redmond Historic Tour Guide, 1981; Report on Collections, Marymoor Museum: Lace Collection, 1979; Indian Artifacts, 1978. Home: 17511 Avondale Rd Woodinville WA 98072 Office: PO Box 162 6046 W Lake Sammamish Pkwy Redmond WA 98052

ELY, JOHN THOMAS ANDERSON, research physicist; b. San Francisco, June 24, 1923; s. John Thomas Anderson and Ruth (Mallery) E.; B.A., Eastern Wash. State Coll., 1952; M.S., U. Wash., 1959, Ph.D., 1969. Commd. 2d lt. USAF, 1944, advanced through grades to col., 1965, ret., 1968, pilot conventional and jet aircraft, 1947-67; cosmic ray physicist, research faculty U. Wash., Seattle, 1969—. Lectr. physics Northeastern U., 1963-65, U. Wash., 1970—; sci. cons., 1969—. Mem. Am. Phys. Soc., Sigma Xi. Club: Swedish. Contbr. articles to profl. publs. Designed experiments flown on 5 satellites; research in physics of viruses; mutagenic burden of sea-level cosmic radiation as a factor in aging and cancer; immune response in viral and neoplastic diseases; explained tumor tolerance, other immune suppression of hyperglycemia. Office: U Wash Physics Dept Seattle WA 98195

ELY, MELVIN DAVID, electrical engineer; b. Ponca City, Okla., Mar. 20, 1931; s. John Melvin and Pauline Lucille (Pray) E.; A.S., No. Okla. Jr. Coll., 1951; B.S. in Elec. Engring., Okla. State U., 1954; M.B.A., Calif. Western U., 1967; m. Ruth Irene Pollock, Dec. 27, 1957; children—David James, John Richard, Elizabeth Ann. Elec. engr. RCA Victor, Camden, N.J., 1954-55; electronic design engr. Stromberg Carlson, San Diego, 1958-60; sr. systems testengr. Gen. Dynamics Astronautics, San Diego, 1960-65; research and devel. program mgr. U.S. Naval Electronic Labs., San Diego, 1965-69; head engring. dept., head program and planning dept. Naval Electronic Systems Engring. Ctr., San Diego, 1969-81, exec. dir. Naval Edn. and Tng. Support Ctr., San Diego, 1981—; owner, mgr. Kairos Enterprises, San Diego, 1981—. Elder, 1st Presbyterian Ch., San Diego, 1969—; chmn. citizens adv. com. Pub. Schs. San Diego, 1971-72. Served with USNR, 1955-58. Mem. IEEE, San Diego Computer Soc. Republican. Registered profl. engr., Okla. Home: 3814 Del Mar Ave San Diego CA 92106 Office: Naval Edn and Tng Support Center Pacific San Diego CA 92132

ELY, PARRY HAINES, dermatologist; b. Washington, Sept. 19, 1945; s. Northcutt and Marica (McCann) E.; B.A., Stanford U., 1967; M.D., U. So. Calif., 1971; m. Elizabeth Magee, June 20, 1969; children—Sims, Rebecca Jennings. Intern, U. So. Calif./Los Angeles County Hosp., 1971-72, resident in dermatology, 1972-75, chief resident, 1975; clin. instr. dermatology U. Calif., Davis, 1975-79, asso. clin. prof. dermatology, 1979—; practice medicine, specializing in dermatology, Roseville, Calif., 1975—; mem. staff Roseville Community Hosp. Bd. dirs. Am. Cancer Soc., Placer County, 1977-78. Served to lt. comdr. USNR, 1968-81. Winner, Nelson Paul Anderson Essay Contest, Pacific Dermatologic Assn., 1979. Fellow Am. Acad. Dermatology; mem. AMA, Calif. Med. Assn., Soc. Investigative Dermatology, Am. Soc. Dermatologic Surgery, Internat. Soc. Dermatoennui Research (pres. 1980-81), Soc. Internat. Tropical Dermatology, Sacramento Valley Dermatologic Soc., Alpha Delta Phi. Mem. Soc. of Friends. Contbr. articles to profl. jours. Office: 730 Sunrise Ave Roseville CA 95678

ELY, PAUL C., JR., electronics company executive; b. McKeesport, Pa., Feb. 18, 1932; s. Paul C. and Jean C. Ely; B.S. in Engring. Physics, Lehigh U., 1953; M.S. in Elec. Engring., Stanford U., 1964; m. Barbara Sheiry, Apr. 3, 1953; children—Paul C., Glenn. Research and devel. engr. Sperry Rand Corp., Great Neck, N.Y. and Clearwater, Fla., 1953-62; research and devel. sect. mgr., engring. mgr. microwave div. Hewlett-Packard Co., Palo Alto, Calif., 1962-73, gen. mgr. data systems div., 1973-74, gen. mgr. computer group, 1974-76, v.p., 1976-80, exec. v.p., 1980—. Chmn., Cupertino United Fund, 1976, Bay Area Sci. Fair, 1969; men. Calif. Econ. Devel. Commn., 1976. Mem. IEEE. Office: 3000 Hanover Palo Alto CA 94034

ELY, WALTER RALEIGH, JR., judge; b. Baird, Tex., June 24, 1913; s. Walter Raleigh and Lucy Ann (McCoy) E.; A.B., U. Tex., 1935, LL.B., 1935; LL.M., U. So. Calif., 1949, LL.D., 1973; m. Billie Bernice Gambill, Oct. 27, 1937; 1 son, William Raleigh; m. 2d, Ruby Ilene Walters, Sept. 18, 1945, 1945. Admitted to Tex. bar, 1935, Calif. bar, 1945; gen. practice, Abilene, Tex., 1935-39; asst. atty. gen. Tex., 1939-40; judge U.S. Ct. Appeals, 9th Circuit, 1964—, now sr. judge. Mem. exec. com. Calif. Conf. State Bar Dels., 1957-60; spl. counsel U.S. Senate, 1955. Bd. dirs. Los Angeles County Bar Found., Travel Program for Fgn. Diplomats. Served with USMCR, 1941-44. Decorated Silver Star medal. Fellow Am. Coll. Trial Lawyers; mem. Am., Tex. bar founds., Am. (ho. of dels. 1961-64), Los Angeles County (pres. 1962) bar assns., Marine Corps Res. Officers Assn. (hon. life), VFW, Order of Coif, Phi Delta Phi, Delta Kappa Epsilon. Methodist. Mason (Shriner, K.T.). Clubs: Los Angeles Athletic, Chancery (Los Angeles); Lakeside Golf of Hollywood; Navy Golf Course (Los Alamitos, Calif.). Contbr. articles to profl. jours. Office: 1621 US Courthouse 312 N Spring St Los Angeles CA 90012

EMAN, EVELYN (EVELYN EMAN DELMAR), communications exec.; b. N.Y.C., Dec. 31, 1949; d. John and Gay (Simon) Eman; m. Lawrence E. Delmar. Student NYU, 1975-76, Baruch Coll., 1981-82. Asst. mgr. Vanderbilt Athletic Club, N.Y.C., 1967-68; pub. relations mgr. DEC Enterprises, Inc., N.Y.C., 1968-73; exec. interviewer Dun & Bradstreet, Inc., N.Y.C., 1974; pub. relations rep. Parsons & Whittemore, Inc., N.Y.C., 1974-77; corp. mgr. pub. relations NEC Am., Inc., Melville, N.Y., 1977-82; pres. Perception, Colorado Springs, Colo., 1982—. Recipient cert. of merit Publicity Club N.Y., 1977. Mem. Colorado Springs Conv. and Visitors Bur., Women's Exchange Network Colorado Springs, Internat. Assn. Bus. Communicators, Internat. Platform Assn., Pub. Relations Soc. Am., Women in Communications. Composer: Face Another Day, 1973; Songbird, 1973; There's the Man, 1973; Hey Mister, 1974; In the Morning, 1974: It's Never Been Like This, 1974; contbr. editor PR Essay, 1976-77; editor: Women's Exchange Network Newsletter, 1983—; contbr. articles to mags. Office: 559 E Pikes Peak Ave Suite 307 Colorado Springs CO 80903

EMBLER, KATHLEEN JUNE, software engr.; b. Johnstown, Pa., Feb. 9, 1948; d. LeRoy J. and Eleanor M. (Johnston) Stein; children—Jennifer Lee, Jonathan David. B.A., U. Calif.-Riverside, 1970; M. Computer Sci., U. So. Calif., 1974. Mem. tech. staff Hughes Aircraft, Fullerton, Calif., 1970—, now sect. head. Hughes masters fellow. Mem. Assn. Computing Machinery, Phi Beta Kappa, Pi Mu Epsilon. Office: 1901 W Malvern St PO Box 3310 68/L215 Fullerton CA 92634

EMCH, ARNOLD F(REDERICK), mgmt. cons.; b. Manhattan, Kans., Nov. 3, 1899; s. Arnold and Hilda (Walters) E.; A.B., U. Ill., 1925, A.M., 1926; postgrad. U. Chgo., 1930; Ph.D., Harvard, 1934; m. Minna Libman (dec. 1958); m. 2d, Eleanore Merckens, June 30, 1960; children—Arnold Devere, Frederick Bolebec. Pres., Emch Constrn. Co., Wichita, Kans., 1920-22; regional dir. Tamblyn & Brown Co., Chgo., 1926-29; exec. dir. Chgo. Hosp. Council, 1936-39; asso. dir. Am. Hosp. Assn., 1939-42, U. Chgo. Inst. for Hosp. Adminstrn., 1939-42; mgr. Booz, Allen & Hamilton, mgmt. cons., Chgo., 1942-48, partner, 1948-60, ret., cons. corp., 1960—; pvt., personal mgmt. cons. vol. instns. and agys.; pres. North End Water Co., Colo., 1964-67, sec.-treas., 1967-75, treas., 1975—; dir., mgmt. cons. Calif.-Time Petroleum Corp., 1967-70; pres. Glory Ranch Arabian Stables, 1966-75; sec.-treas. Eagle Rock Ranches Devel., 1971—. Served in A.E.F., France, 1918-19; comdr. USNR, mgmt. cons. Navy Surgeon Gen., 1942-45, hon. cons., 1945—. Trustee William Alanson White Psychiat. Found., Washington, 1945-56, v.p., 1947, pres. 1948-52; dir. Washington Sch. Psychiatry, 1946-56, Mental Health Soc. Greater Chgo., 1958-59, Council on Hosp. Planning and Resources Devel. State Colo., 1961—. Mem. Am. Philos. Assn., AAAS, Shakespearean Authorship Soc., English Cocker Spaniel Club of Am., Chi Psi. Clubs: Harvard, University (Chgo.); Colo. Arabian Horse. Author: Uncommon Letters to a Son; Life, Love and Logic; Crowded

Years. Contbr. articles to profl. jours. Address: Glory Ranch Devil's Gulch Rd Estes Park CO 80517

EMERICH, BRIAN A., architect; b. Milw., Jan. 19, 1951; s. Charles A. and Virginia Emerich; B.Arch., U. Colo., 1972; postgrad. U. Alaska, 1977. Architect, chmn. bd. Alternative Design and Constrn., Inc., Juneau, Alaska, 1977—; pres. Emerich Enterprises, 1975—; prin., chmn. bd. Emerich & Assocs., architects; lectr. for Alaska Energy Dept. on insulation and solar tech.; lectr. U. Alaska; design rev. bd. City and Borough of Junea. cons. in field. Bd. dirs. A.W.A.R.E. Mem. AIA (pres. Southeast Alaska chpt. 1982 bd. dirs. Alaska state chpt. 1983, legis. lobbyist), Nat. Fedn. Ind. Businessmen, U.S. C. of C., Aircraft Owners and Pilots Assn. Research on solar energy, fish rearing and hatcheries. Office: 369 S Franklin St Juneau AK 99801

EMERSON, MICHAEL STEPHEN, communications corp. exec.; b. Hollywood, Calif., Sept. 10, 1947; s. Frank Perry and Ann Constance (Durkin) E.; B.A., UCLA, 1970; A.A., Santa Monica Coll., 1968; m. Christina Aerenlund, July 20, 1973; children—Christopher Michael, Maria Theresa. Dir. mktg. Dobard Industries, Los Angeles, 1973; dir. mktg. Am. Sound Corp., N. Hollywood, Calif., 1976, gen. mgr., 1977; pres. Media Americana, Santa Monica, Calif., 1979—; Host, nationally syndicated radio program Face to Face, 1979—; pub. relations cons.; lectr. in field. Mem. creative cons. bd. City of Hope Nat. Med. Center. Served with USAR. Recipient Pub. Service Broadcasters award, 1977, 78; Lions award, 1976; Kiwanis award, 1977, others. Mem. Communications Inst. Am. (govs. 1973—), Los Angeles County Mus. Art, Nat. Artists and Lectrs. Guild, World Affairs Council. Roman Catholic. Clubs: Calif. Yacht, Riviera Country, Los Angeles Athletic. Developer econ. method of sound recording making possible mass prodn. of audio-visual ednl. material.

EMERSON, PETER MICHAEL, administrator, family and marriage counselor; b. Portland, Oreg., Feb. 16, 1956; s. George and Rayola (Jones) E. B.S. in Psychology, Brigham Young U., 1980; M.Counseling, Idaho State U., 1982. Cert. Nat. Bd. Cert. Counselors. Dist. mgr. Bremerton Sun Pub. Co., Wash., 1972-77; customer service clk. Puget Sound Power & Light Co., Bremerton, summers 1978-80; counselor Cedar Valley Boys Home, Fairfield, Utah, 1978-79; dir. drug abuse prevention Blackfoot (Idaho) Sch. Dist. #55, 1980; dir. Trio Programs Upward Bound and Spl. Services, So. Utah State Coll., Cedar City, 1980—; dir. parent edn. program, Blackfoot; crisis intervention instr. So. Utah State Coll.; counselor for terminally ill Hospice of So. Utah. Mem. Idaho Soc. Individual Psychology (sec. 1980-81), Am. Personnel and Guidance Assn., Am. Assn. Marriage and Family Therapists, Assn. Counselor Edn. and Supervision. Mormon. Home: 142 S 800 W Cedar City UT 84720 Office: PO Box 375 SUS Cedar City UT 84720

EMERSON, SHIRLEY ARMSTRONG, marriage and family therapist; b. Houston, Dec. 29, 1930; d. Riley Clark and Neola (Pinckney) Armstrong; m. David Winthrop Emerson, Sept. 4, 1954; children—Richard, Eris, Ellen. B.A., Rice U., 1953; M.A., U. Mich., 1966, Ph.D., 1977. Counselor, Schoolcraft Coll., Livonia, Mich., 1975-81; pvt. practice therapy, Dearborn, Mich., 1978-81; dir. Operation Bridge Family Counseling Ctr., Las Vegas, 1982—; cons. Talbert Halfway House, Juvenile Ct.; prof. counseling, U. Nev.-Las Vegas. Horace H. Rackham research grantee, 1976. Mem. Am. Personnel and Guidance Assn., Nev. Personnel and Guidance Assn., Am. Assn. Marriage and Family Therapists, Nev. Assn. Marriage and Family Therapists, AAUW. Contbr. articles to profl. jours. Office: Operation Bridge Counseling Ctr 1712 Bearden Dr Las Vegas NV 89106

EMERT, VICTOR, radio station manager, clergyman; b. Dallas, June 16, 1938; s. Jess William and Ouida Mae (Duckett) E.; B.F.A., U. Tex., Austin, 1963; m. Joyce Elaine Rogers, July 7, 1965; children—Creagan Shrake, Ben Shrake. Chief announcer Sta. KUT-FM, U. Tex., 1960-63, prodn. mgr., 1962-63; program dir. Sta. KAZZ-FM, Austin, 1961-62; writer, producer, announcer Sta. WRVR-FM, N.Y.C., 1964-65; producer, announcer Sta. KHFM-FM, Albuquerque, 1966-72; dir. Drug Addicts Recovery Enterprises, Albuquerque, 1972-78; gen. mgr. Sta. KLYT-FM, Albuquerque, 1978—; pres. Victor Prodns., Inc., 1981—; ordained to ministry Evangelical Ch. Alliance, 1977; pastor Flock of God Fellowship, Albuquerque, 1980—; bd. dirs. Christian Broadcasting Acad., Inc. Vice pres. N.Mex. Art League, 1966; bd. dirs. Suicide Prevention and Crisis Control Center, 1967-70, Drug Addicts Recovery Enterprises, 1972—, Rio Grande Christian Community 1982—; pres. DARE New Life Ctr., 1982—; dir. New Life Theatre, Albuquerque, 1973-78. Served with U.S. N.G., 1963. Named Outstanding Writer, U. Tex. Radio/TV, 1962, Broadcaster of Yr., Sta. KLYT-FM, Gospel Music Assn., 1980; recipient Maj. Armstrong award Nat. Assn. FM Broadcasters, 1969. radio station manager, clergyman; b. Dallas, June 16, 1938; s. Jess William and Ouida Mae (Duckett) E.; B.F.A., U. Tex., Austin, 1963; m. Joyce Elaine Rogers, July 7, 1965; children—Creagan Shrake, Ben Shrake. Chief announcer Sta. KUT-FM, U. Tex., 1960-63, prodn. mgr., 1962-63; program dir. Sta. KAZZ-FM, Austin, 1961-62; writer, producer, announcer Sta. WRVR-FM, N.Y.C., 1964-65; producer, announcer Sta. KHFM-FM, Albuquerque, 1966-72; dir. Drug Addicts Recovery Enterprises, Albuquerque, 1972-78; gen. mgr. Sta. KLYT-FM, Albuquerque, 1978—; pres. Victor Prodns., Inc., 1981—; ordained to ministry Evangelical Ch. Alliance, 1977; pastor Flock of God Fellowship, Albuquerque, 1980—; bd. dirs. Christian Broadcasting Acad., Inc. Vice pres. N.Mex. Art League, 1966; bd. dirs. Suicide Prevention and Crisis Control Center, 1967-70, Drug Addicts Recovery Enterprises, 1972—, Rio Grande Christian Community 1982—; pres. DARE New Life Ctr., 1982—; dir. New Life Theatre, Albuquerque, 1973-78. Served with U.S. N.G., 1963. Named Outstanding Writer, U. Tex. Radio/TV, 1962, Broadcaster of Yr., Sta. KLYT-FM, Gospel Music Assn., 1980; recipient Maj. Armstrong award Nat. Assn. FM Broadcasters, 1969. Office: 3107 Eubank NE #19 Albuquerque NM 87111

EMERY, BETTY JO, cosmetology executive, fund-raiser; b. Culver City, Calif., Oct. 27, 1947; s. Phil Sheridan and Thelma Ione (Bernett) Emery; m Warren Lee Reavis Dec. 31, 1971 (div.) Student Bartmore Beauty Coll., Mesa Coll., U.Calif.-Irvine, 1979-81. Owner, operator Gene's of LaJolla (Calif.), 1968-70, The Hair Garden, LaJolla, 1974-78, Hairs to Ya! Dana Point, Calif., 1979—; treas., dir. fins., fund-raiser Pacific Ocean Found., Dana Point. Recipient Resolution of Commendation Orange County (Calif.) Suprs., 1982. Mem. Assn. Female Execs. Republican. Episcopalian. Office: 34213 Coast Hwy Suite C & D Dana Point CA 92629

EMERY, HENRY ALFRED, information company executive; b. Northfield, N.H., Feb. 9, 1926; s. Henry A. and Ruth (Trask) E.; B.A., U. Maine, 1950; M.B.A., U. Denver, 1966; Petroleum Engr., Colo. Sch. Mines, 1956; m. Barbara Sadwith, June 10, 1971; children—Trask, Timothy, Ptarmigan. With Mobil Pipeline Co., 1950-53, Portland Montreal Pipeline Co., 1956-59; maintenance design engr., planning supr., engring. supt., project mgr. Pub. Service Co. Colo., 1959-72; pres. Computer Graphics Co., Denver, 1972-78; div. mgr. Kellogg Corp., Littleton, Colo., 1978-82; pres. Universal Info. Inc., Englewood, Colo., 1982—. Registered profl. engr., Colo. Mem. Assn. Systems Mgmt., Rocky Mountain Ski Instrs. Assn., Profl. Ski Instrs. Am., Tau Beta Pi. Democrat. Home: 5680 S Big Canon Dr Englewood CO 80111 Office: 6767 S Spruce 140 Englewood CO 80112

EMERY, PAUL WHITE, II, business executive; b. Jamestown, N.Y., June 21, 1941; s. Paul W. and Caroline Elizabeth (Allard) E.; m. Sheridan Clark, Oct. 5, 1962; children—Elizabeth, Valerie, Paula. B.S., U. Tenn., 1962; M.B.A., U. Md., 1964. Lic. real estate broker, Calif. Mgr. fin. forecasts Ford Motor Co., Dearborn, Mich., 1964-68; mgr. fin. analysis IBM, Harrison, N.Y., 1968-71; v.p. fin., div. gen. mgr. Bardon Corp., Danbury, Conn., 1971-72; v.p. fin., dir. Xynetics, Santa Clara, Calif., 1972-73; prin. Paul Emery Assocs., Irvine, Calif., 1973-79; chmn., chief exec. officer Airmac Tech. Systems Inc., Irvine, 1979—; dir. Videometrix, Tankinetics. Dir., coach Little League Baseball, 1969-72, Bobby Sox Softball, 1976-80; ruling elder Presbyterian Ch. of Master. Mem. Nat. Acctg. Assn., U. Tenn. Alumni Assn., Phi Kappa Phi, Beta Gamma Sigma. Republican. Contbr. articles to profl. publs. Office: 15091 Bake Pkwy Irvine CA 92714

EMETT, ROBERT LYNN, ins. co. exec.; b. Oxnard, Calif., Aug. 9, 1927; s. Edward Llewellyn and Isabel (Vaughan) E.; B.A., Claremont Men's Coll., 1950; children—Robert Charles, Lindy Louise, James Stewart, Michael S. Underwriter, Swett & Crawford, 1950; account exec. Emett & Chandler, 1951-54, office mgr., 1954-57, San Francisco mgr., 1957-60, Los Angeles dir., 1957-60, v.p., gen. mgr., 1961-62, pres., 1962-68; pres. Emett & Chandler Cos., Inc., Los Angeles, 1968-73, chmn. bd., 1973—; dir. Emett & Chandler, Risk Mgmt. Inc., R.L. Kautz Co., Pinehurst Mgmt. Co., Ltd., Transworld Ins. Co., Ltd.; underwriting mem. Lloyds of London. Bd. dirs. YMCA of Greater Los Angeles, Calif. Congressional Recognition Project; trustee Claremont McKenna Coll., Honnold Library Soc.; finance chmn. Calif. Republican State Central Com., 1977-79. Served with USNR, 1945-46; PTO; served as 1st lt. USAF, 1951-59. Mem. Music Center for Performing Arts (founder), Claremont Men's Coll. Alumni Assn. (dir., pres. 1963-64), Chief Execs. Forum, World Bus. Council (dir.). Home: 25 Bay Island Balboa CA 92662 Office: 1800 Ave of Stars Century City Los Angeles CA 90067

EMETT, SHARON ELIZABETH, educator; b. Great Falls, Mont., June 12, 1938; d. Truce W. and Isabel V. (Rogers) E. B.A., U. Mont., 1960; postgrad. Oxford U., 1977, U. Amsterdam, 1974, 75, 82, numerous other colls. and univs. Elem. tchr. Great Falls (Mont.) Pub. Schs., 1960—. Sustaining mem. Republican Nat. Com.; mem. Presdl. Task Force; active Nat. Fedn. Rep. Women, Cascade County Rep. Women; vol. Mont. Deaconess Med. Ctr. Mem. Great Falls Edn. Assn. (sec. 1967-72), Northcentral Dist. Dept. Classroom Tchrs. (pres. 1966-70). Clubs: Daus. of the Nile, Eastern Star, White Shrine of Jerusalem. Home: 700 3d Ave S Great Falls MT 59405 Office: 2204 Fox Farm Rd Great Falls MT 59404

EMMELUTH, BRUCE PALMER, investment banker; venture capitalist; b. Los Angeles, Nov. 30, 1940; s. William J. and Elizabeth L. (Palmer) E.; m. Cheryl Elaine Miller, June 22, 1963; children—William J. II, Bruce Palmer, Carrie E. Sr. investment analyst, comml. and indsl. loan dept. Prudential Ins. Co. Am., Los Angeles, 1965-70; with Seidler, Amdec Securities, Inc., Los Angeles, 1970—, sr. v.p., mgr. corp. fin. dept., 1976—, dir., 1974—; pres., dir. SAS Captial Corp., Venture capital subs. Seidler Amdec Securities; dir. Denar Corp., Motherhood Maternity Shops, Inc.; allied mem. N.Y. Stock Exchange, Inc. Past. bd. dirs. UCLA Grad. Sch. Mgmt. Served with Army NG, 1965-71. Mem. Assn. for Corp. Growth (pres. Los Angeles chpt. 1979-80), Beta Gamma Sigma. Republican. Presbyterian. Club: Jonathan. Home: 17274 Avenida de la Herradura Pacific Palisades CA 90272 Office: Seidler Amdec Securities Inc 515 S Figueroa St Los Angeles CA 90071

EMMERICH, EUGENE WILLIAM, metallurgical engineering executive; b. Utica, N.Y., June 27, 1930; s. Eugene William and Helen Messina (Rogers) E.; m. Nancy Mariea Tector, Jan. 30, 1954 (div.); m. Theresa Eileen Surridge, Aug. 16, 1975. B.Metall. Engring., Rensselaer Poly. Inst., 1955, M.Metall. Engring., 1959, D.Engring. Sci., 1961. Cons. in engring., throughout U.S., 1973-75; v.p. mktg. GE/Calma Corp., Sunnyvale, Calif., 1976-78; v.p. corp. devel. Heizer Corp., Chgo., 1979-80; pres. Cadtrak Corp., Sunnyvale, 1981—. Served to capt. AUS, 1951-53. Rotary scholar, 1948-49; Allegheny-Ludlum fellow, 1959-60. Mem. AIME. Club: Union League (Chgo.). Home: 1012 Windjammer Circle Foster City CA 94404 Office: 823 Kifer Rd Sunnyvale CA 94086

EMMET, THOMAS ADDIS, JR., college administrator, consultant; b. Detroit, July 26, 1930; s. Thomas Addis and Leona Margaret (Schneider) E.; m. Anne Marie Baker, Mar. 3, 1972; children—Lynn, Anthony, William Novitsky. Ph.B., U. Detroit, 1952, M.Ed.. 1954; Ed.S., Ed.D., U. Mich., 1963. Asst. dean U. Detroit, 1953-57, dean men, 1957-64, dean evening coll. arts and scis., 1964-66, asst. prof. higher edn., 1964-67; asst. exec. v.p. Marquette U., 1966-67, adj. prof. higher edn. Wayne State U., Detroit, 1968-70; spl. asst. to pres., prof. edn. Regis Coll., Denver, 1972—; pres. higher edn. exec. assos. div. McGraw Hill, 1967-72; pres. Thomas A. Emmet & Assos., 1972—. Cons. collective negotiations in higher edn. Edn. Commn. of States, 1971—; cons. higher edn. Opinion Research Corp.; dir. leadership seminars, sr. adviser Am. Council on Edn., 1979—. Staff dir. Mich. State Senate Student Unrest Com., 1968-69; exec. sec. Conf. Jesuit Student Personnel Adminstrs., 1956-64; sec. Council Student Personnel Assns. in Higher Edn., 1966-69. Recipient Bernard Webster Reed award, 1963. Mem. Adult Student Personnel Assn. (v.p. 1961-64), Nat. Assn. Student Personnel Adminstrs. (editor Jour. 1962-63), Phi Kappa Phi, Alpha Sigma Nu, Alpha Sigma Lambda, Phi Delta Kappa, Phi Eta Sigma. Editor: The Academic Department and Division Chairman, 1972; Collective Bargaining in Postsecondary Institutions: The Impact on the Campus and the State, 1974; asso. editor Coll. and Univ. Bus., 1969-71. Home: 3941 E Orchard Rd Littleton CO 80121 Office: 50th St and Lowell Blvd Denver CO 80221

EMMETT, JOAN MARIE, English as second language specialist, consultant; b. Bonners Ferry, Idaho, Feb. 28, 1929; d. Joseph Augustus and Jean Elizabeth (Hughes) Rabdau; m. James Edward Emmett, Dec. 26, 1955 (div.); 1 son, Joseph Thomas. B.S. in Edn., Eastern Ore. Coll., 1951; M.Ed., U. Wash., 1975. Tchr. Tacoma Pub. Schs., 1952-64; tchr. No. Marianas, Saipan, Micronesia, 1964-66, lang. specialist, 1964-69; English specialist, Ponape, 1969-74; reading specialist Truk State, Micronesia, 1977-80; U. instr. Coll. Micronesia, Ponape, 1977-82; instr. U. Hawaii, 1980-82; lang. cons. for Marshall Islands, Palau and Federated States of Micronesia. NSF fellow Birmingham-So. U., 1962; NDEA fellow U. Guam, 1965; NDEA fellow UCLA, 1966. Mem. Internat. Reading Assn., Nat. Council Tchrs. English, Nat. Council Tchrs. Math., Assn. for Supervision and Curriculum Devel. Democrat. Roman Catholic. Author grammar lessons. Home and office: 5802 South M St Tacoma WA 98408

EMMETT, JOHN WILLIAM, JR., educator; b. Cheyenne, Wyo., Sept. 19, 1953; s. John William and Carol Mae (Shaw) E.; B.S., U. Wyo., 1977; m. Catherine Jean Graham, June 11, 1977; 1 dau., Abigail Rae. Coordinator mktg./distributive edn. program Lander (Wyo.) Valley High Sch., 1977—; mem. faculty Riverton Central Wyo. Coll., 1978-79; cons. in field. Ex-officio mem. bd. dirs. Wyo. State Winter Fair, 1977—. Named to Distributive Edn. Hall of Fame, 1977; recipient DECA's Outstanding Service award, State of Wyo., 1976, 77, 78, 79, 80. Mem. Wyo. Vocat. Assn. (exec. bd. 1978-79), Wyo. Assn. Distributive Edn. Tchrs. (pres. 1978, chmn. bd. 1979), Wyo. Assn. DECA. Club: Elks. Contbr. articles to profl. jours. Home: 790 Welch St Lander WY 82520 Office: 1000 Main St Lander WY 82520

EMMONS, MICHAEL LINDSAY, psychologist, consultant, lecturer; b. Lawrenceville, Ill., Sept. 30, 1938; s. Robert Lawrence and Ethel Lois (Bruner) E.; m. Kay Lynn Seagle, Aug. 7, 1965; children—Brent, Scott. B.S., Ill. State U., Normal, 1963, M.S., 1964; Ph.D., U. Wyo., 1968. Cert. counseling psychologist, Calif. Psychol. tchr./counselor Palatine (Ill.) High Sch., 1964-66; counseling psychologist Calif. Poly. State U., San Luis Obispo, 1968-77; v.p. Impact Pubs., Inc., San Luis Obispo, 1970-81; pvt. practice psychology, 1977-81; counseling psychologist/co-dir. The Holos Ctr., San Luis Obispo, 1978-80; counseling psychologist, spiritual psychologist Mustard Seed Found., San Luis Obispo, 1982—; psychol. cons. Impact Cons., San Luis Obispo. Served with USN, 1956-59. Mem. Am. Psychol. Assn. United Methodist. Author: The Inner Source, 1978; (with Robert E. Alberti) Your Perfect Right, 1970, 4th edit., 1982; Stand Up, Speak Out Talk Back!, 1975; (with David R. Richardson) The Assertive Christian, 1981. Home: 1764 Mountain View Los Osos CA 93402 Office: 1422 Monterey Bldg A Suite 200 San Luis Obispo CA 93401

EMMONS, ROBERT JOHN, educator; b. Trenton, Sept. 18, 1934; s. Charles John and Ruth Marie (Heilhecker) E.; A.B. in Econs., U. Mich., 1956, M.B.A., 1960, J.D., 1964; m. Christine Bebb; children—Bradley Thomas, Cathy Lynne, Christopher Robert. V.p. Baskin-Robbins Co., Burbank, Calif., 1964-68; pres. United Rent-All, Los Angeles, 1968-69, Master Host Internat., Los Angeles, 1969-71; prof. Grad. Sch. Bus., U. So. Calif., 1971—; pres. Inst. Mgmt. and Mktg. Studies, Los Angeles, 1973—; dir. Thriftimart, Fotomat, Opcon Industries, Lockwood Tech., Inc., Intersil Co., Probe Systems Co. Mem. Am., European mktg. assns., Am. Econ. Assn., Beta Gamma Sigma, Pi Kappa Alpha. Clubs: Calif. Yacht (Los Angeles), St. Petersburg (Fla.) Yacht. Author: The American Franchise Revolution, 1970; (poetry) Other Places, Other Times, 1974; (poetry) Love and Other Minor Tragedies, 1980. Home: 13900 Tahiti Way Marina del Rey CA 90291 Office: 400 Hoffman Hall Univ So Calif Los Angeles CA 90007

EMORY, NATHAN JEAN, oil company executive; b. Walla Walla, Wash., Apr. 29, 1922; s. Ralph J. and Mary Uneda (Warren) Sitts; A.B. in Math., U. Calif., 1945; m. Fritzi May Schneider, Nov. 28, 1970; children—Susan, David, Steven. Econ. analyst Standard Oil of Calif., 1945-61; analyst, v.p. Model, Roland & Co., 1964-71; pres. Taurus Oil Co., Denver, 1976-80; pres. Corsican Corp., Denver, 1980—; dir. Taurus Oil Co. Active Nat. Ski Patrol. Republican. Presbyterian. Clubs: Denver, Denver Petroleum, Bay Area Ski Assn. (pres. 1946-47), Masons, Shriners. Office: 718 17th St Suite 2200 Denver CO 80202

EMPEREUR, JAMES LESTER, educator, priest; b. Tigerton, Wis., Dec. 21, 1933; s. Frank and Margaret (Nero) E.; A.B., St. Louis U., 1958, Ph.L., 1959; S.T.L. Woodstock Coll., 1966; Ph.D., Grad. Theol. Union, 1972. Ordained priest Roman Cath. Ch., 1965; tchr. secondary schs., 1956-62; mem. faculty Georgetown U., Washington, 1966; with Campus Ministry, Normal, Ill., 1967; mem. faculty Sch. Applied Theology, Berkeley, Calif., 1969-81; editor Modern Liturgy, San Jose, Calif., 1973-83; founder Inst. for Spirituality and Worship, 1973; assoc. prof. liturgical and systematic theology Jesuit Sch. Theology, Berkeley, 1972—. Mem. N.Am. Acad. Liturgy, Liturgical Conf., Am. Acad. Religion, Cath. Theol. Soc., Societas Liturgica. Democrat. Author: Prophetic Anointing: God's Call to the Sick, the Elderly, and the Dying, 1982; contbr. articles to profl. jours. Office: 1735 LeRoy Ave Berkeley CA 94709

EMPEY, DONALD WARNE, dep. supt. schs.; b. McMinnville, Oreg., Feb. 8, 1932; s. Ernest Warne and Anna May (Alsman) E.; B.A., Willamette U., 1954; M.A., Stanford, 1955; Ed.D., U. Oreg., 1964; m. Mary Catherine Reeh, July 14, 1956; children—Elizabeth, Margaret, Jennifer. Tchr. history, Salem, Ore., 1955-58; asst. prin. Bend (Oreg.) Sr. High Sch., 1958-61, prin., 1961-63; dir. instructional services Arcadia (Calif.) Unified Sch. Dist., 1964-68; dep. supt. Lake Washington Sch. Dist., Kirkland, Wash., 1968-69, supt., 1969-76; dep. supt. Glendale (Calif.) Unified Sch. Dist., 1976—. Instr. U. Oreg., 1967-68; vis. lectr. Claremont (Calif.) Grad. Sch., 1966-68. Bd. dirs. Coop. Wash. Edn. Centers, 1972-75, Glendale Camp Fire Girls, 1979-82, Verdugo council Boy Scouts Am., 1982—; v.p. chpt. Am. Field Service, 1982. Served with USNR, 1950-54. Danforth/NASE fellow, 1976. Mem. Am., Calif. assns. sch. adminstrs., King County Sch. Supts. Assn. (pres. 1975-76), Willamette U. Alumni Assn. (dir. 1972-76), Pi Gamma Mu, Phi Delta Kappa. Presbyterian (elder 1981). Mason, Kiwanian (dir. Glendale/Gateway chpt. 1979—). Contbr. articles to profl. jours. Office: 223 N Jackson St Glendale CA 91206

EMPEY, GENE F., real estate exec.; b. Hood River, Oreg., July 13, 1923; B.S. in Animal Husbandry, Oreg. State U., 1949; masters degree in tech. journalism Iowa State U., 1950; m. Janet Halladay, Dec. 27, 1950; children—Stephen Bruce, Michael Guy. Publs. dir. U. Nev., Reno, 1950-55; mgr. Zephyr Cove Lodge Hotel, Lake Tahoe, Nev., 1955-65; owner Empey Co., real estate agy., Carson City and Tahoe, Nev., 1964—. Mem. Nev. Planning Bd., 1959-72, chmn., 1961-66; mem. Nev. Tax Commn., 1982—. Served to capt., inf. U.S. Army, 1943-47; PTO. G.R.I. (grad. Realtors Inst.). Mem. Nat. Assn. Realtors, (cert. comml. investment mem.; pres. Nev. chpt. 3 times), Tahoe Douglas C. of C. (pres. 1962, dir.), Carson City C. of C., Carson-Tahoe-Douglas Bd. Realtors. Republican. Clubs: Capital City, Rotary, Heavenly Valley Ski (pres. 1968). Home: PO Box 707 Zephyr Cove NV 89448 Office: 512 S Curry St Carson City NV 89701

ENDERUD, WILBUR DONALD, JR., data processing cons.; b. Pueblo, Colo., Nov. 4, 1945; s. Wilbur Donald and Loretta Faye (Jackson) E.; B.A. in Math., San Diego State U., 1967; M.B.A., Calif. State U., Long Beach, 1972; children—Cynthia. From programmer to project leader Mattel, Inc., Hawthorne, Calif., 1967-72; dir. mgmt. info. systems Audio-Magnetics Corp., Gardena, Calif., 1972-75; founder, 1975, since owner, prin. cons. Don Enderud & Assos. (now Mgmt. Info. Solutions, Inc.), Diamond Bar, Calif.; founding partner New Century Leasing, Diamond Bar, 1978—. Served with USAF, 1968-69; Vietnam. Decorated Army Commendation medal. Mem. Assn. Computing Machinery, Aircraft Owners and Pilots Assn. Republican. Lutheran. Home: 2811 Shadow Canyon Dr Diamond Bar Huntington Beach CA 91765 Office: PO Box 4237 Diamond Bar CA 91765

ENDLER, HENRY CHARLES, vocational education administrator, consultant; b. Akron, Ohio, Mar. 20, 1934; s. Henry Cleveland and Margaret Ione (Hartle) E.; m. Mary Elizabeth Howard, Dec. 26, 1964; children—Dawn Lynn, Charles Paul, Matthew Todd. A.A., Coll. of Canyons, 1972; B.A., U. Redlands, 1974, postgrad., 1979-81. Clear life teaching and supervisory credentials, Calif. Community Coll. System. Dist. service mgr. Internat. Auto Sales Inc., New Orleans, 1962-63; service orgn. mgr. Volkswagen Pacific, Inc., Culver City, Calif., 1963-65; service mgr. Hillcrest Cadillac, Beverly Hills, Calif., 1965-67; service mgr./leasing mgr. Wilkins Pontiac, Van Nuys, Calif., 1967-70; asst. dean of instrn. Coll. of Canyons, Valencia, Calif., 1970-80; dir. trades and techs. Chemeketa Community Coll., Salem, Oreg., 1980—; cons. risk mgmt. and loss control; tng. counselor Nat. Rifle Assn. Served with USAF, 1951-62; mem. USAR. Mem. Am. Vocat. Assn., Oreg. Vocat. Assn., Nat. Council Instrl. Adminstrs., Oreg. Community Coll. Vocat. Adminstrs., Oreg. Vocat. Tech. Tchrs. Assn., Salem Area C. of C. Club: Four Corners Rod and Gun. Office: PO Box 14007 Salem OR 97309

ENDO, EDWIN YOSHIO, optometrist; b. Maui, Hawaii, Nov. 30, 1953; s. Rikio and Oyen (Kikuchi) E. B.S. in Biol. Sci., U. Hawaii, 1976;

B.S., O.D., So. Calif. Coll. Optometry. Lic. optometrist, Hawaii, Calif. Intern, Optometric Ctr. of Fullerton (Calif.), 1978, Optometric Ctr. Los Angeles, 1979, Long Beach (Calif.) Naval Health Ctr., 1979, VA Hosp. Los Angeles, 1980, Silas B. Hayes Med. Hosp., Monterey, Calif., 1980; pvt. practice optometry, Honolulu, 1980—; sch. vision cons.; clin. investigator contact lens materials and designs. Mem. Hawaii Optometric Assn., Calif. Optometric Assn., Am. Optometric Assn., Optometric Extension Program Found., Honolulu Japanese Jaycees (Com. Chmn. of Quarter award 1982, Bronze Key award 1982, Recruiter award 1982, Jaycee of Quarter award 1981). Inventor Optometric Nearpoint Chart, 1978. Home: 1524 Pensacola St Apt 301 Honolulu HI 96822 Office: 98-1238 Kaahumanu St Suite 301 Pearl City HI 96782

ENDRIZZI, JOHN EDWIN, plant geneticist, educator; b. Wilberton, Okla., July 28, 1923; s. Lui and Maria Christina (Carignano) E.; m. Yvonne V. Barbot, June 6, 1955; children—Colette, George, Regina, Carisa, Karena. B.S., Tex. A&M U., 1948, M.S., 1949; Ph.D., U. Md., 1955. Asst. prof. Tex. A&M U. College Station, 1955-63; prof. plant genetics U. Ariz., Tucson, 1963—, dept. head, 1963-71. Served with AUS, 1943-46. Nichlson grad. fellow, 1949-50; DuPont grad. fellow, 1951-52; Johnson Research grantee, 1958-61; NSF research grantee, 1977-79; recipient Cotton Genetics award, 1969. Mem. Genetics Soc. Am., Am. Genetics Assn., Genetics Soc. Can., Am. Inst. Biol. Sci., AAAS, Ariz. Acad. Sci., Sigma Xi, Gamma Sigma Delta. Contbr. numerous articles to profl. publs. Home: 2335 E 9th St Tucson AZ 85719 Office: Plant Sci Dept U Ariz Tucson AZ 85721

ENDRUSICK, ROSE MARIE, educator; b. Creighton, Pa., Feb. 11, 1929; d. Paul Anthony and Ann Catherine Fricioni; m. Stanley Endrusick, June 19, 1950; children—Ann, Scott. B.S., Drexel Inst. Tech., 1950; M.A., Calif. State U.-Los Angeles, 1970; cert. Culinary Inst. Am., 1973. Tchr. home econs., Springdale, Pa., 1950-53, Glendale, Calif., 1953-55, Arcadia (Calif.) Unified Sch. Dist., 1955-83; designer antique doll clothes. Named Outstanding Tchr. in Arcadia, So. Calif. Industry-Edn. Council, 1968. Mem. Am. Home Econs. Assn., Calif. Tchrs. Assn., NEA, Arcadia/San Gabriel PTA (hon. life), Doll Collectors Gallery Calif. (v.p. 1981-83). Republican. Roman Catholic. Office: 301 S 1st Ave Arcadia CA 91006

ENFIELD, MORRIS CONRAD, JR., computer systems executive; b. Harlingen, Tex., Oct. 28, 1938; s. Morris Conrad and Eunice Irene (Hodge) E.; B.A., Rice U., Houston, 1960; postgrad. Southwestern Med. Sch., Dallas, 1961-62; M.S. in Computer Scis., U. Tex., 1968; M.B.A., So. Meth. U., 1977; m. Nancy Susan Lewis, June 11, 1972. Ops. mgr. Computer Center, U. Tex., Austin, 1962-68; sr. systems analyst SDC, Santa Monica, Calif., 1968-69; project mgr. Computer Scis. Corp., San Diego and Netherlands, 1969-73; systems cons. Control Data Corp., San Diego, 1973-75; computer systems mgr. Univ. Computing Co., Dallas, 1975-77; computer systems specialist Rockwell Internat. Co., Dallas, 1977-79; advanced systems mgr. for secure operating systems NCR Corp., Systems Engring. Scripps Ranch, San Diego, 1979—; instr. Sch. Bus. and Computer Sci., U. Tex., Dallas, 1977—. Fellow in molecular cytology U. Tex., Austin, 1962-64; fellow Argonne (Ill.) Nat. Lab., 1964. Mem. AAAS, IEEE, Assn. Computing Machinery, N.Y. Acad. Scis., Am. Heart Assn., U. Tex. Alumni Assn., So. Meth. U. M.B.A. Assn. Author tech. papers. Home: PO Box 26805 San Diego CA 92126 Office: 9900 Old Grove Rd San Diego CA 92131

ENG, BENJAMIN, JR., elec. engr.; b. Seattle, Dec. 15, 1942; s. Benjamin and Elsie (Lew) E., B.S. in Elec. Engring., U. Wash., 1965, B.S. in Indsl. Engring., 1969; student Vocational Corr. Sch., Nat. Radio Inst., 1961, 65. Staff engr. John Fluke Mfg. Co., Everett, Wash., 1969—. Served to 1st lt. AUS, 1966-68; Vietnam. Registered profl. engr., Wash. Mem. Nat. Radio Inst. Alumni Assn., IEEE, Armed Forces Communications and Electronics Assn., U. Wash. Alumni Assn. Home: 13215 Hwy 99 S Everett WA 98204 Office: PO Box C9090 Everett WA 98206

ENG, HOWARD JUNE, pharmacist; b. Tucson, Dec. 15, 1949; s. Moon Chau and June Hi (Wey) E.; B.S. in Zoology, U. Ariz., 1971, B.S. in Pharmacy, 1974, M.S. in Pharm. Scis., 1978; postgrad. U. Tex. Sch. Public Health, 1980—. Pharmacy intern Carl Hayden Community Hosp., Tucson, 1972-74; relief pharmacist Walgreen Drug Co., Tucson, 1974-76; asst. to dean Coll. Pharmacy, U. Ariz., Tucson, 1974-80; mem. group health of Ariz. Pharmacy Therapeutics Com., 1975-80. Recipient Upjohn Award, 1974. Mem. Am. Pharm. Assn. (chpt. faculty adviser 1974-80, regional faculty adviser, nat. adv. com. 1976-78), Am. Public Health Assn., Kappa Psi. Home: 4766 S 6th Ave Tucson AZ 85714

ENGEL, ALBERT E., electronics co. exec.; b. Chgo., Jan. 24, 1929; s. Otto and Anna Agneda (Andrich) E.; B.S.E.E., U. So. Miss., 1957, M.S.E.E., 1959; m. Donna Rae Warntjes, July 21, 1979; stepchildren—Michael Alan, Kevin Eugene, Karen Yvonne. With Aerojet Gen. Corp., Azusa, Calif., 1962-72, engring. mgr., 1972-76; pres., chmn. bd. Def. Systems, Inc., Marina Del Rey, Calif., 1976-79; pres., chmn. bd. Angel & Co., Inc., San Luis Obispo, Calif., 1979—; sr. systems engr. Def. and Space Systems TRW, Redondo Beach, Calif.; spl. cons. govt. and industry. Served with USAF, 1948-52. Mem. AIAA, Am. Mgmt. Assn., IEEE, Am. Astronautical Soc. (sr.). Republican. Roman Catholic. Clubs: Elks, Moose, Eagles. Home: PO Drawer 1550 Hawthorne CA 90250 Office: TRW 1 Space Park Redondo Beach CA 90278

ENGEL, EMILY JO, school counselor; b. Columbus Tex., Sept. 15, 1938; d. William A. and Jeanette D. (Hastedt) Flachmeier; m. Lars Norlick Engel, Dec. 28, 1957; children—Jan Kristin, Karen Gale. B.S. in Edn., U. Tex.-Austin, 1959, M.Ed., 1966. Social sci. staff asst. U. Tex.-Austin, summers 1962-63; tchr. Lamar Jr. High Sch., Austin, 1960-62; counselor Pearce Jr. High Sch., 1963-64, Cumbres Jr. High Sch., Los Alamos, 1967—; workshop leader devel. guidance program, pub. relations for sch. guidance services. Treas. No. Central N.Mex. Health Planning Council, 1979-70; active Los Alamos Choral Soc. Mem. NEA, Am. Personnel and Guidance Assn., N.Mex. Personnel and Guidance Assn., Am. Sch. Counselors Assn., N.Mex. Sch. Counselors Assn., Los Alamos Edn. Soc., LWV (past sec.), Delta Kappa Gamma, Alpha Omicron Pi. Republican. Methodist. Home: 1210 Myrtle St Los Alamos NM 87544 Office: Cumbres Jr High School 2101 Cumbres Dr Los Alamos NM 87544

ENGEL, JOANNE BOYER, psychologist; b. Meadville, Pa., Mar. 15, 1944; d. Edward Charles and Wanda Ann (Chasco) Boyer; m. Harold N. Engel, Mar. 12, 1971; children—Cynthia, Keith Nichols. B.S., Pa. State U., 1965; M.Ed., U. Sydney (Australia), 1972; M.Sc., Iowa State U., 1978, Ph.D., 1979. Tchr. Pub. Schs. Broomall/Wallingford (Pa.), 1965-69; instr. U. Sydney, 1969-71; instr., dir. Child Research Ctr., Auburn (Ala.) U., 1971-75; faculty Iowa State U., Ames, 1975-79; asst. prof. Oreg. State U., Corvallis, 1979-81; asst. prof., chmn. dept. edn. Willamette U., Salem, Oreg., 1981—. Referee, Am. Youth Soccer Orgn., 1980-82. Ala. Dept. Social Services grantee, 1979. Mem. Am. Ednl. Research Assn., Am. Psychol. Assn., Confedn. Oreg. Sch. Adminstrs., Oreg. Sch. Execs. Assn., N.W. Women in Edn. Adminstrn., Oreg. Women's Polit. Caucus, Phi Delta Kappa, Kappa Delta Pi. Presbyterian. Contbr. articles to profl. jours. Home: 2855 NW Skyline Dr Corvallis OR 97330 Office: Edn Dept Willamette Univ Salem OR 97301

ENGEL, JOHN WILLIAM, family therapist, educator; b. Effingham, Ill., Mar. 17, 1946; s. Edwin Voris and Anastasia Agnes (Fischenich) E.; m. Barbara Jo Schiltgen, Nov. 22, 1975; children—Theresa Nani, Patricia Ann. B.S., St. John's U., 1968; Ph.D. (NDEA fellow), Rehab. Services Act (trainee), U. Minn., 1978. Instr. family social sci. U. Minn., St. Paul, 1970-79; asst. prof. human devel. U. Hawaii, Honolulu, 1979—; pvt. practice marriage and family therapy, 1975—; family therapist East Communities Youth Service Bur., St. Paul, 1975-77, dir., 1978-79. Dayton-Hudson Found. grantee, 1978; U. Hawaii Found. grantee, 1981-82. Mem. Am. Assn. Sex Educators, Counselors and Therapists (cert. counselor), Hawaii Assn. Marriage Family Therapists (pres.), Am. Home Econs. Assn., Am. Psychol. Assn., Nat. Council Family Relations. Author: Dynamics of Marriage and Parenthood, 1976; Human Sexual Behavior, 1976, 79; Changing Attitudes Towards the Dual Work, Home Roles of Women, 1978; Changes in Male-Female Relationships and Family Life in the People's Republic of China, 1982.

ENGEL, LEONARD LORNE, public transp. mgmt. exec.; b. Medicine Hat, Alta., Can., May 5, 1946; came to U.S., 1952, naturalized, 1965; s. John F. and Bertha K. (Biffart) E.; student Sacramento State Coll., 1964-66; B.A. in Social Sci., Calif. State Coll.-Turlock, 1972; postgrad. in urban planning Calif. State U.-Fresno, 1972-74; m. Cheryl Sue Baumback, Mar. 28, 1970; 2 daus., Thea Nicole, Sarai Sae-Hee. Comml. broadcaster, Lodi, Calif., 1970-72; planner Stanislaus Area Assn. Govts., Modesto, Calif., 1972-74; assoc. transp. planner Ada Council Govts., Boise, Idaho, 1974; prin. transp. planner Idaho Transp. Dept., Boise, 1974-76; v.p., Boise resident mgr. McDonald Transit Assocs., Ft. Worth, 1976-77; gen. mgr. Boise Urban Stages, 1976—; pres., gen. mgr. Transit West Services, Inc.; gen. mgr. Sno Coach; mem. Gov.'s AMTRAK Adv. Com., 1974-75. Pres.'s mem. Boise Music Week, 1978. Served with USAF, 1966-72. Recipient Cert. of Appreciation, City of Boise, 1977, Cert. of Merit Idaho Advt. Fedn., 1978, 82. Mem. Am. Public Transit Assn. (dir.), Greater Boise C. of C. Democrat. Mem. Christian and Missionary Alliance. Office: PO Box 9016 3113 Airport Way Boise ID 83707

ENGEL, VICTOR BOYNTON, construction industry company executive; b. Keokuk, Iowa, Jan. 29, 1914; s. Martin T. and Gertrude (Boynton) E.; A.A, Calif. Concordia Coll., 1935; various bus. and mil. schs.; B.A., U. Calif. at Berkeley, 1949; certificate Acad. Internat. Law, Hague, Netherlands, 1951; M.A., Grad. Inst. Internat. Studies and U. Geneva, Switzerland, 1952; m. Dorothea Ann Messner, Mar. 18, 1944. Prof. constl. law, U.S. history U. Geneva, 1950-52; exec. mgr. Assn. Plumbing and Heating Contractors of Contra Costa County, Richmond, Calif., 1952-54; exec. dir. Contra Costa Builders Exchange, Concord, Calif., 1954—; pres. Constrn. Mgmt. Services, Inc., Metro-Mgmt. Services, Inc. Pres., Internat. Builders Exchange Execs., U.S., Can., 1962-63; chmn. Builders Exchange Council, 1971-72; pres. Builders Exchanges Constrn. Industry Conf., 1969-70. Mem. Contra Costa County Devel. Assn., Contra Costa Taxpayers Assn., Bay Area Coalition for Transp. Served with AUS, 1941-46. Recipient Dan Patrick award of merit Internat. Builders Exchange Execs., 1983. Mem. World Affairs Council No. Calif., Calif. Alumni Assn., Am. Soc. Assn. Execs., No. Calif. Soc. Assn. Execs., Assn. des Anciens l'Inst. Geneva. Rotarian. Clubs: Commonwealth (San Francisco); Concord Century, Toastmasters (Concord). Author: Significant Developments in American Society, 1952. Editor: Constrn. Weekly, 1954—. Home: 10 Gran Via Alamo CA 94507 Office: 2490 Salvio St Concord CA 94520

ENGELBART, RICHARD CHARLES, ins. co. exec.; b. Ft. Dodge, Iowa, Mar. 15, 1929; s. Walter Lawrence and Marie (Becher) E.; student Ft. Dodge Jr. Coll., 1947-49; B.S.C., U. Iowa, 1952; postgrad. Drake U., 1953-54; m. Lucille E. Wertz, Oct. 3, 1953; 1 son, Richard Scott. Group adminstr., claims auditor Bankers Life Co., Des Moines, 1952-58; with HBA Life Ins. Co., Phoenix, 1958—, treas., 1965—, v.p., 1971—, also dir. Mem. Ins. Accounting and Statis. Assn., Life Office Mgmt. Assn. (fellow 1963). Home: 6816 E Vernon Ave Scottsdale AZ 85257 Office: 1st and Willetta Sts Phoenix AZ 85001

ENGELBECK, RANALD MARSHALL, air force officer; b. Des Moines, Iowa, Jan. 30, 1933; s. Ranald Beyer and Florence (Marshall) E.; m. Veronica Terisa Bogenrief, June 15, 1978; children by previous marriage—Ranald Marshall, George Essex. B.S.C., State U. Iowa, 1955; M.S., Air Force Inst. Tech., 1966; postgrad. Indsl. Coll. Armed Forces, 1974-75. Commd. officer U.S. Air Force, 1955, advanced through grades to col., 1973; chief programs div. AF Div., Republic of Viet Nam, 1973-74; comdr. Tinker AFB, Okla., 1975-78; dir. maintenance Oklahoma City Air Logistics Ctr., 1978-79; comdr. Logistics Support Group, Saudi Arabia, 1978-80; vice comdr. Air Force Contract Mgmt. Div., Albuquerque, 1980—. Active Boy Scouts Am., 1966-73. Decorated Legion of Merit with oak leaf cluster. Mem. Soc. Logistics Engrs., Indsl. Coll. Armed Forces Alumni Assn. Home: 2206 22d Dr Kirtland AFB NM 87116 Office: AFCMD/CV Kirtland AFB NM 87117

ENGELS, REMI CARLOS, engineer; b. Ghent, Belgium, Apr. 5, 1948; s. Juliaan and Martha Augusta (Pattijn) E.; m. Jennifer Beth Wendell, Jan. 17, 1980. B.S. in Math. U. Ghent (Belgium), 1968, M.S., 1971, profl. teaching degree, 1972; Ph.D. in Engring. Sci. and Mechanics, Va. Poly. Inst. and State U., 1977. Prof. math. Normal Sch. Ghent, 1971-73, Royal Sch. Cadets, Brussels, 1973-74; instr. engring. sci. and mechanics Va. Poly. Inst. and State U., Blacksburg, 1974-78, asst. prof., 1978-80; sr. engr. structural mechanics Martin Marietta Aerospace, Denver, 1980-82, staff engr., 1982—. Recipient New Technology award NASA, 1981; New Technology award Martin Marietta, 1981, Author of Yr. award, 1981. Mem. AIAA, Phi Beta Kappa, Sigma Xi. Contbr. articles to profl. jours. Office: D 6072 Martin Marietta Aerospace PO Box 179 Denver CO 80201

ENGELS, ROBERT VALENTINE, postmaster; b. Chgo., Aug. 16, 1922; s. Henry Charles and Rose (Hensel) E.; student Mont. State U., 1948-49, Modern Bus. Coll., Missoula, Mont., 1955-56; m. Leoba Henscheid Kaphammer, May 14, 1971; stepchildren—Robert Kaphammer, Susan Kaphammer, Linda Kaphammer McCartney, James Kaphammer, Karl Kaphammer, Patricia Kaphammer Dellwo. Warehouse foreman W.P. Fuller & Co., Missoula, 1949-52; operator heavy equipment Anaconda Co., Bonner, Mont., 1954-56; car clk. Chgo., Milw. & St. Paul R.R., Missoula, 1956-59; clk. U.S. P.O., Missoula, 1959-74; postmaster, Corvallis, Mont., 1974-75, Ronan, Mont., 1975—. County chmn. A.R.C., fund drive chmn., 1967-71; mem. Northwest Mont. Areawide Health Planning Council, 1970-71. Alt. del. Republican nat. conv., 1952; treas. Mont. State Young Reps., 1950-54; chmn. Missoula Young Reps., 1949-50. Served with USAAF, 1942-46. Recipient awards U.S. Postal Service, 1967—. Mem. Aircraft Owners and Pilots Assn., Antique Airplane Assn., Nat. League Postmasters, Nat. Assn. Postmasters, Am. Legion, Internat. Platform Assn. Christian Scientist. Mason (Shriner, K.T.), Elk. Home: PO Box 548 Ronan MT 59864 Office: US Post Office Ronan MT 59864

ENGELSEN, EDWARD GEORGE, economist, banker; b. Portland, Oreg., Oct. 29, 1922; s. Olaf Johan and Jennie F. (Johnson) E.; B.S., Linfield Coll., 1943; B. Internat. Mgmt., Am. Grad. Sch. Internat. Mgmt., 1947; m. Celeste Victoria Hidalgo, Nov. 7, 1948. With internat. div. Bank of Calif., N.A., San Francisco, 1947—, internat. economist, 1959—, editor quar. mag., 1967-76. Served to lt. (j.g.) USNR, 1942-46; PTO. Mem. Am. Econ. Assn., Nat. Fgn. Trade Council, World Affairs Council No. Cal., Theta Chi. Office: 400 California St San Francisco CA 94104

ENGEN, RICHARD BRUCE, librarian; b. Aberdeen, Wash., Nov. 23, 1927; s. Laurie H. and Esther (Howenstine) E.; B.S., Northwestern U., 1952; M.L.S., U. Wash., 1953; m. Rebecca L. Bartels, July 13, 1975; children—Kristen, Paul, Kyle, Tobin. Br. librarian, exec. asst., supt. brs. Seattle Pub. Library, 1953-60; dir. Columbia River Regional Library Demonstration, Wenatchee, Wash., 1960; reference asst. Evanston (Ill.) Pub. Library, 1960-61; county librarian Inyo-Mono counties, Calif., 1962-63; head field services div. Oreg. State Library, 1963-67; dir. Alaska Div. State Libraries and Museums, Juneau, 1968—. Exec. bd. Pacific N.W. Bibliog. Center, 1971—, v.p., 1972, 73. Served with AUS, 1946-48. Mem. ALA (councilor 1970-74), Alaska, Oreg. (pres. 1966-67), Pacific N.W. (sec. 1967-68) library assns., Western Council of State Libraries (pres. 1981-82). Home: PO Box 1782 Juneau AK 99802 Office: Pouch G Juneau AK 99811

ENGLAND, RULON HAROLD, hosp. materials mgr.; b. Burley, Idaho, June 23, 1921; s. Carlos Smith and Ethel Mary (Egan) E.; m. Mary Lou Bates, Feb. 11, 1966; children—Gary, Dennis, Kelly, Barbara, Larry, Brian Val, James H., William P. Office mgr., asst. mgr. Idaho Creameries, Idaho Falls, 1946-50; sales rep., hosp. sales coordinator Intermountain Surg. Supply Co., Boise, Idaho, 1950-78; materiels mgr. Caldwell (Idaho) Meml. Hosp., 1978—. Served with USN, 1942-46. Mem. Nat. Assn. Hosp. Purchasing and Materiels Mgmt., Assn. Western Hosps. Purchasing Mgmt., Materiels Mgmt. Assn. Idaho (pres. 1980-83), Million Dollar Sales Club. Republican. Methodist. Clubs: Masons, Order Eastern Star, Shriners. Home: Terrace Lakes Garden Valley ID 83622 Office: 1717 Arlington St Caldwell ID 83605

ENGLANDER, HARVEY ALAN, advertising and public relations executive, political consultant; b. N.Y.C., May 21, 1950; s. Nathen Greenberg and Sylvia (Fischler) E.; m. Susan Kramer, Sept. 20, 1975; m. 2d, Sandy Gilbert, Apr. 2, 1978; children—Adam, Joshua. A.A., Los Angeles City Coll., 1970; B.A., UCLA, 1972. Vice-pres. Cerrell Assocs., Los Angeles, 1972-78; pub. relations dir. Jewish Fedn. Los Angeles, 1977-78; v.p. Butcher-Forde Cons., Newport Beach, Calif., 1978-80; pres. The Englander Group, Newport Beach, 1980—; lectr. in field. Pres. Calif. Fedn. Young Democrats, 1973-74; former v.p. Jewish Fedn. Orange County; chmn. new leadership dir. Am. Friends of Tel Aviv U. Recipient U.S. Youth Council Mission to Europe award, 1973; Resolution of Commendation, Calif. Assembly, 1974. Mem. Am. Assn. Polit. Cons. Democrat. Jewish. Office: Suite 970 One Newport Pl Newport Beach CA 92660

ENGLE, DUANE RAYMOND, architect; b. Abilene, Kans., Sept. 2, 1936; s. Raymond E. and Pauline Gertrude (Long) E.; B.Arch. with honors (Shaver scholar 1958; AIA student medal 1959), Kans. State U., 1959; m. Marian Elizabeth Joy, Nov. 23, 1963 (div. June 1973); children—Margaret Elizabeth, David Raymond; m. 2d, Joan Tenhoor Vermaire, May 15, 1976 (div. Apr. 1980). Architect, Linder Wright & White, Denver, 1959-63, Wheeler and Lewis, Denver, 1963; owner D.R. Engle, architect, Colorado Springs, Colo., 1963-64; architect, W.A. Miller, Colorado Springs, 1964-66; partner firm Miller and Engle, architects, Colorado Springs, 1966-70; pres. Engle Assos., Inc., Architecture and Planning, Colorado Springs, 1970—. Mem. Colorado Springs Symphony Council, sec., 1973—; bd. dirs. Planned Parenthood Colorado Springs, 1974-76, pres., 1975; bd. dirs. Rocky Mountain Planned Parenthood, 1975-76; bd. dirs., sec.-treas. Energy Resource Center of Pikes Peak Region, 1980—. Weigel scholar, 1958. Mem. AIA (treas. Colo. So. chpt. 1972-73, v.p. 1974, pres. 1975, Western Mountain rep. to AIA com. on architecture for commerce and industry 1976-81), Colo. Soc. Architects (dir. 1975-78). Lutheran (ch. council 1979-82). Clubs: Sertoma Internat. (dir. 1972-73), Colorado Springs Country, Rocky Mountain. Home: 2607 Fairmount St Colorado Springs CO 80909 Office: 1715 N Weber St Colorado Springs CO 80907

ENGLE, GEORGE STANLEY, JR., oil company executive, oil producer; b. St. Louis, Nov. 3, 1942; s. George Stanley and Dorothy Jeanette (Rogers) E.; m. Susan Bea Philips, Dec. 12, 1973 (div. 1980); children—Anne Marie, George Stanley III, Robert Charles. B.S. in Econs., U. Pa., 1964; M.B.A. in Mgmt., U. Miami, 1966; grad. Realtors Inst. La., 1979. Ind. oil producer, 1968—; pres. Baham Inn, Inc., 1973-76, Contemporary Renovations, Inc., New Orleans, 1978-82; regional landman McMoran-Freeport Oil Co., Denver, 1982-83, acting land mgr., 1983—; dir. Contemporary Renovations, Inc., New Orleans. Sec., Upper Keys Jaycees, Tavernier, Fla., 1976-78. Recipient award of Friendship, City of Miami, 1971; named Ky. col., 1981. Mem. Okla. City Assn. Petroleum Landmen, Denver Assn. Petroleum Landmen, Am. Assn. Petroleum Landmen. Republican. Methodist. Clubs: Coral Reef Yacht (Miami, Fla.); Brown Palace (Denver); Mt. Kenya Safari. Author: Growing Outward, 1981. Home: 1065 Lafayette St Unit 1 Denver CO 80218 Office: 1860 Larimer St Suite 290 Denver CO 80202

ENGLE, RAPHAEL, graphic designer; b. Calgary, Alta., Can., June 6, 1934; s. Ely and Lilian (Belkin) E.; B.Profl. Art, Art Center Coll. Design, Los Angeles, 1959; M.A., U. Calif., Los Angeles, 1973; m. Anne Mary Jiry, Mar. 24, 1960; children—Elysa, Shaena. Designer, Porter & Goodman, Los Angeles, 1959-60; cons. McCann-Erickson, Los Angeles, 1960-63; pres. Ray Engle Assos., graphic design and visual communications, Los Angeles, 1963—; mem. faculty Art Center Coll. Design, 1960—, Calif. State U., Northridge, 1979—. adv. bd. Noland Paper Co. Adv. bd. Los Angeles Employment Rev. Bd.; adv. bd. Los Angeles Trade Tech. Recipient Design awards N.Y. Art Dirs. Club, Type Dirs. Club, 20th Century Design, Dept. Commerce, Cannes Film Festival. Mem. Soc. Art Center Alumni Assn. (pres. 1967), Am. Inst. Graphic Arts (awards), Internat. Center Typographic Arts (awards). Clubs: Marina City, Pacific Mariners Yacht. Home: 4726 La Villa Marina Marina del Rey CA 90291 Office: 626 S Kenmore St Los Angeles CA 90005

ENGLE, RAYMOND EDWIN, lawyer; b. Chgo., Mar. 8, 1927; s. Robert Henry and Faerie Josephine (Mallory) E.; student U. Chgo., 1942-45; B.S. with distinction, U.S. Naval Acad., 1950; J.D., Stanford U., 1978; m. Claire Louise Wallach, July 31, 1955; children—Andrew Tobias, Timothy Grant, Robert Benedict. Enlisted U.S. Navy, 1945, commd. ensign, 1950, advanced through grades to capt., 1970; line officer in cruiser, Korean conflict; entered submarine service, 1952; mem. first crew USS Nautilus, 1954-56; comdg. officer submarines USS Seadragon, USS U.S. Grant, 1965-69; in charge tng. and readiness Pacific Submarines Force, 1969-70; dep. dir. Pacific, Def. Advanced Research Project Agy., 1973-75; ret., 1975; admitted to Hawaii bar, 1978, Fed. bar, 1978; asso. firm Hoddick, Reinwald, O'Connor & Marrick, Honolulu, 1978-81; individual practice, 1981—; chmn. Guam Consol. Recreation Program. Mem. Guam Bd. Edn., 1970-73; mem. exec. bd. Aloha council Boy Scouts Am., 1971-75, 79—, mem. Western Region leadership com., 1976—, leader World Scout Jamboree, 1975, 83, Silver Beaver award, 1982; trustee, chmn. bd. Central Union Ch., 1979-82. Decorated Meritorious Service medal, Air medal, Joint Service Commendation medal, Navy Commendation medal; Order of Chamorri (Guam). Mem. Am. Bar Assn., Bar Assn. Hawaii, Assn. Trial Lawyers Am., Maritime Law Assn. U.S., U.S. Naval Inst., Nat. Rifle Assn. Republican. Congregationalist. Club: Pacific (Honolulu). Mem. Nat. Collegiate Championship Rifle team, 1948; mem. All-Am. Rifle team, 1948, 50; significant research on under ice navigation leading to 1st trans-polar submarine trip. Home: 3600 Kawelolani Pl Honolulu HI 96816 Office: Law Office Raymond Engle 126 Queen St Suite 306 Honolulu HI 96813

ENGLE, RICHARD MINOR, assn. exec.; b. Oklahoma City, Dec. 21, 1937; s. Alan David and Opal Louise E.; A.A., Howard County Jr. Coll., 1958; B.A., Tex. Wesleyan Coll., 1960; M.S. (Mott fellow), George Williams Coll., 1961; m. Sylvia Gay, Feb. 6, 1960; children—Cynthia

Gay, Patrice Lynnett. Youth dir. San Antonio YMCA, 1962-65; br. dir. Oklahoma City YMCA, 1965-70; mng. dir. Snow Mountain Ranch, Colo. YMCA of the Rockies, Granby, 1970—; bd. dirs., paraprofl. Mental Health Center. Ruling elder Presbyn. Ch., 1974-76; commr. Gen. Assembly, Presbyn. Ch., 1973; commr. 1978 Synod; mem. Grand County Regional Planning Commn. Recipient Disting. Service award U.S. Jaycees, 1964; named an Outstanding Young Man Am., 1969. Mem. Internat. Assn. Conf. Dirs., Assn. Profl. Dirs. (dir., treas. Western Colo. Health Systems Agy., mem. Commn. on White Racism 1968), Grand County Alcohol Council. Republican. Club: Kiwanis (pres. 1974, lt. gov. 1976). Contbr. articles on fitness and communication to profl. jours. Home: Box 558 Granby CO 80446 Office: Snow Mountain Ranch Box 558 Granby CO 80446

ENGLER, DARLENE JO, ins. co. mgr.; b. Crested Butte, Colo., May 24, 1938; d. Joseph Nelson and Cecelia Evelyn (Tezak) Schafer; A.A., Fullerton Coll., 1958; m. Richard F. Engler, Sept. 1, 1967. Adminstrv. asst. Sherwin Elec. Co., Los Angeles, 1966-67; acctg. supr. Caldwell-Miller, Inc., Inglewood, Calif., 1967-71; office mgr. Nat. Certified, Inc., Whittier, Calif., 1971-77; mktg. coordinator IRM Ins. Brokers, Tustin, Calif., 1977-78; ins. agt., broker, 1973—; fin. mgr. Quinlan Ins. Inc., Newport Beach, Calif., 1978-80; ops. mgr., chief fin. officer Paul Muench Co., Orange, Calif., 1980—, also chief fin. officer, dir. Paul Muench Assos. Treas. Venture Club of Anaheim (Calif.), 1963-64; active Whittier Republican Women's Fedn. Mem. Soc. C.P.C.U.s, Ins. Women Orange County, Western Ins. Info. Speakers Bur., Orange Empire Soc. Roman Catholic. Club: Hacienda Golf. Home: 740 S Mariposa Dr LaHabra CA 90631 Office: Paul Muench Co 1400 E Katella Orange CA 92667

ENGLER, GEORGE NICHOLS, educator, bus. fin. cons.; b. Los Angeles, Sept. 27, 1944; s. James George and Esther (Nichols) E.; B.S. in Bus., U. So. Calif., 1965; M.B.A., UCLA, 1966, Ph.D. in Bus., 1969; m. Suzanne J. Knudson, June 11, 1967; 1 dau., Cristina Noel. Asst. prof. fin. Calif. State U.-Long Beach, 1968-69; asst. prof. fin. U. So. Calif., Los Angeles, 1969-75, also pres. Century Fin. Mgmt., Inc., Los Angeles, 1973-75; prof. fin., chmn. dept. fin. and business law Calif. State U.-Los Angeles, 1975-81, dir. grad. programs Sch. of Bus. and Econs., 1980—; cons. Keplar Galen & Assos., Inc., N.J., 1977-79. Mem. Am. Fin. Assn., Western Fin. Assn., Fin. Mgmt. Assn. Democrat. Christian Scientist. Author: Business Financial Management, rev. ed., 1978; Managerial Finance: Cases and Readings, 1973; (with John Boquist) Cases in Managerial Finance, 1982; contbr. articles to profl. bus. jours. Office: Dept Fin Sch Business Calif State U 5151 State University Dr Los Angeles CA 90032

ENGLERT, ROBERT DIXON, diversified industry co. exec.; b. Portland, Oreg., Feb. 11, 1920; s. Robert L. and Blanche (Dixon) E.; B.S., U. Portland, 1942; B.S., Oreg. State U., 1944, M.S., 1944; Ph.D., U. Colo., 1949; m. Patricia Duff Englert, Feb. 12, 1954; children—Janice, Jolene, Nancy. Organic chemist So. Calif. Labs. Stanford Research Inst., 1949-55, exec. dir., 1955-70; div. v.p. Dresser Industries Inc., Irvine, Calif., 1970—. Mem. exec. com. West Coast sect. Air Pollution Control Assn., 1972-75; mem. Emergency Action Com. Los Angeles County Air Pollution Control Dist., 1960-65. Served with USNR, 1944-46. USPHS fellow, 1946-47; U. Colo. Chem. Found. fellow, 1948-49. Mem. Am. Chem. Soc., Research Soc. Am., Air Pollution Control Assn., Calif. Acad. Sci., Sigma Xi, Phi Lambda Upsilon. Clubs: Balboa Bay. Patentee insecticides, chem-treatment cotton fabrics, pollution control hardware. Home: 1312 Sandcastle Dr Corona Del Mar CA 92625 Office: 1702 McGaw Ave Irvine CA 92713

ENGLISH, CAROL O'BRIEN, research consulting co. exec.; b. St. Louis; d. John Joseph and Natalie Therese (Walewski) O'Brien; B.A. cum laude, Mundelein Coll., M.A.T., St. Louis U.; Ph.D. in Modern European History; m. Robert Erwin English, Nov. 28, 1970; children—Gail, Edwin, Catherine, Dom. Tchr., Our Lady of Peace High Sch., St. Paul, Cathedral High Sch., Chgo., Assumption High Sch., Davenport, Iowa; tchr. adult edn. Moline (Ill.) Public High Sch.; dir. Neighborhood Youth Corps, OEO, Muscatine, Iowa, 1969; v.p. Internat. Indsl. Cons., Inc., Denver, 1974—. Mem. Am. Hist. Assn., Soc. Spanish and Portuguese Hist. Studies, Cath. Hist. Assn. Roman Catholic. Home: 9920 W 34th Dr Wheat Ridge CO 80033

ENGLISH, CAROLYN SUE, service research and development company executive; b. Rockford, Ill., July 1, 1953; d. Willis B. and M. Sue (Holder) English. Student Okla. Christian Coll., 1973, U. N.Mex., 1976. Staff sec. NASA Tech. Application Ctr., Albuquerque, 1975-77, dept. sec., office mgr., 1977-79, dept. mgr. publs., documents, 1979-83; mgr. tech. transfer Global Resources & Assocs., Albuquerque, 1983—. Recipient certs. for mgmt. performance. Office: PO Box 40478 Albuquerque NM 87196

ENGLISH, CHARLES ROYAL, lawyer; b. Santa Monica, Calif., Apr. 9, 1938; s. Charles James and Antoinette Frieda (Schindler) E.; m. Marylyn English, Sept. 6, 1969; children—Mitchell Lloyd, Charles James, Julia Catherine. A.A., Santa Monica City Coll., 1958; B.S., UCLA, 1961, LL.B., 1965. Bar: Calif. 1966. Sole practice, Santa Monica, Calif., 1967; staff Los Angeles County Pub. Defender's Office, 1967-78; ptnr. Lafaille, Chaleff & English, Santa Monica, 1978-82; Chaleff & English, 1982—. Served with USAR, 1961-67. Mem. Santa Monica Bar Assn., State Bar Calif., ABA, Criminal Cts. Bar Assn., Bur. Automotive Repair, Los Angeles County Bar Assn., Los Angeles County Pub. Defender's Assn. (treas. 1971-73, 76-78, v.p. 1973-75, trustee 1980-83, pres. 1976-77), UCLA Law Alumni Assn. (pres. 1980). Office: 1337 Ocean Ave Garden Suite Santa Monica CA 90401

ENGLISH, DEIRDRE ELENA, editor, author; b. Washington, May 4, 1948; d. Maurice and Fanita B. English; B.A., Sarah Lawrence Coll., 1970; M.S.W., SUNY-Stony Brook, 1975. Founding mem. Am. Studies Program, SUNY, Old Westbury, 1970; lectr. SUNY and U. Calif.-Santa Cruz, 1970-77; sr. editor Mother Jones Mag., San Francisco, 1978-81, exec. editor, 1981—; coll. lectr., 1972—. Co-author: For Her Own Good: 150 Years of the Experts' Advice to Women, 1978. Office: Mother Jones Magazine 1663 Mission St San Francisco CA 94103

ENGLISH, FORREST KAY, marketing company executive; b. Phila., Apr. 7, 1927; s. Matthew Radcliffe and Sarah Dorothy (Weil) E.; B.S.E.E., Rensselaer Poly. Inst., 1951; M.B.A., U. So. Calif., 1957-64; m. Marilyn Louise Webb, Apr. 27, 1957; children—Forrest Edward, Scott Webb. Mgr. Western sales Link Aviation, Los Angeles, 1952-59; sales mgr. Perkin Elmer Corp., Los Angeles, 1960-64; nat. sales mgr. Datex div. Conrac Corp., 1965-70; founder, pres. Calif. Electronic Mktg., Inc., Santa Ana, 1970—. Mem. Villa Park (Calif.) Planning Commn., 1972-74; chmn. Villa Park Beautification Com., 1971-72; mem. Orange County Central Republican Com., 1981-82. Recipient Civic award Villa Park, 1977. Mem. Electronic Reps. Assn., Orange County Sales Club. Home: 10261 Westwood Dr Villa Park CA 92667 Office: 1905 E 17th St Santa Ana CA 92701

ENGLISH, GERALD ALAN, chemist; b. Chester, Pa., Sept. 17, 1946; s. Richard Nelson and Paulina (Yedinak) E.; B.A., LaSalle Coll., 1968; M.S., Purdue U., 1972, Ph.D., 1974. Analytical chemist, coal chemist Energy Systems Group, Rockwell Internat., Canoga Park, Calif., 1974-81; nuclear chemist for nuclear plant ops. Pacific Gas and Electric Co., San Francisco, 1981—. Mem. Am. Chem. Soc., Am. Phys. Soc., Sigma Xi, Alpha Chi Sigma, Phi Lambda Upsilon. Office: 77 Beale St San Francisco CA 94106

ENGLISH, MANUEL LEON, univ. pres.; b. Carthage, Tex., Nov. 14, 1936; s. Ellis Miller and Joy Opal (Lawhorn) E.; B.A., U. Nebr., 1966; M.A., U. Okla., 1968; Ph.D., U. Manchester, 1972; m. Jeanette Marie Haenni, July 31, 1962; children—Eschelle, Monrae, Nigel, Melanie. Adminstr., Schick Shadel Hosp., Seattle, 1977-79; adj. prof. U. Tex., San Antonio, 1974-77; prof. mgmt. and internat. bus. U. Puget Sound, Tacoma, 1979-81; pres. Seattle Internat. U., 1981—; cons. in field; chmn. bd. Internat. Profl. Mgmt. Corp. Mem. community adv. bd. Schick Shadel Hosp., Seattle, 1980. Served to capt. USAF, 1966-75. Mem. Am. Mgmt. Assn., Acad. Internat. Bus., Acad. Mgmt., Acad. Med. Adminstrs., Am. Coll. Hosp. Adminstrs., Internat. Hosp. Fedn. Club: Elks. Contbr. articles to profl. jours. Home: 1270 Fairview Dr Tacoma WA 98465 Office: Office of Pres Seattle Internat U 33919 9th Ave S Federal Way WA 98003

ENGLISH, RAYMOND HERMAN, architect; b. Grants Pass, Oreg., May 31, 1940; s. William Herman and Sarah May (Heald) E.; B.A. in Environ. Design, U. Wash., 1971. Mem. team designing and constructing factory system to mfr. low income housing units (UN Pilot Housing Project), Govt. of Morocco, 1970; VISTA vol., Balt., 1972-74; archtl. apprentice various offices, Balt., 1974-78; owner, pres. Pavilion, Inc., archtl., real estate devel., gen. contracting firm, Seattle, 1978—; design cons. Author (article) "Double Dome", 1971. Served with USMC, 1959-63. Discoverer new polyhedron. Home and office: 4411 SW 100th St Seattle WA 98146

ENGLUND, KEITH EVERT, association executive; b. Rexburg, Idaho, Mar. 16, 1926; s. Constantine E. and Cathrine G. (Ronnenkamp) E.; m. Maxine Stoddard, June 8, 1948; children—Wade, Brad, Celia, Didri, Ryan, Valrie, Dane, Tad. Student Ricks Coll., 1946-51; B.S., Brigham Young U., 1951. Personnel supt. Hercules Powder Co., Magna, Utah, 1957-67; personnel dir. Honeywell, Inc., Seattle, 1967-71; dir. gen. services Rocket Research Corp., Richmond, Wash., 1971-76; mgr. Inland Empire chpt. Nat Elec. Contractors Assn., Spokane, Wash., 1976—; cons. labor and indsl. relations. Chmn. precinct com. Republican party, 1980—. Served with U.S. Army, 1944-46. Mem. Am. Soc. Tng. and Devel., Am. Soc. Personnel Adminstrn., Western Elec. Mfg. Assn. Mormon. Club: Rotary. Office: Nat Elec Contractors Assn 1715 N Atlantic Ave Spokane WA 99205

ENGLUND, ROBERT THEODORE, growing, packing and shipping company executive; b. McIntosh, Minn., Apr. 18, 1911; s. Godfred Theodore and Elizabeth (Conkey) E.; B.S., UCLA, 1936; postgrad. Princeton U., 1936; m. Constance Maurine Roberts, Aug. 21, 1937; children—Paul Willard, Pamela (Mrs. Thomas Cole), Theodora Alice (Mrs. J. Crewson). With Calif. Dept. Agr., 1936-37; with sales dept. Am. Fruit Growers, 1938-41; pres., owner R. T. Englund Co., Salinas, Calif., 1946—; pres. R.T. Englund Equipment Corp., Salinas, 1962-79; gen. partner, mgr. Bonanza Ranches of Ariz., 1965-81; pres. Mohave Copper Corp., 1959-70; dir. Pioneer Bank of Ariz., 1967-69; dir., v.p. Monterey County Ice & Devel. Co., 1953-69. Trustee, UCLA Found., 1973-79; mem. U.S. Congl. Adv. Bd., 1983—; chmn.'s advisor Am. Security Council Found., 1983—. Served to lt. (j.g.) USNR, 1944-46. Mem. Ariz. Acad., N.A.M. (mktg. and research com. 1960-78), Salinas C. of C. (dir. 1958-59), Council of Calif. Growers, Vegetable Growers Assn. of Central Ariz. (dir. 1962-63). Republican. Club: Phoenix Country. Lodge: Masons. growing, packing and shipping company executive; b. McIntosh, Minn., Apr. 18, 1911; s. Godfred Theodore and Elizabeth (Conkey) E.; B.S., UCLA, 1936; postgrad. Princeton U., 1936; m. Constance Maurine Roberts, Aug. 21, 1937; children—Paul Willard, Pamela (Mrs. Thomas Cole), Theodora Alice (Mrs. J. Crewson). With Calif. Dept. Agr., 1936-37; with sales dept. Am. Fruit Growers, 1938-41; pres., owner R. T. Englund Co., Salinas, Calif., 1946—; pres. R.T. Englund Equipment Corp., Salinas, 1962-79; gen. partner, mgr. Bonanza Ranches of Ariz., 1965-81; pres. Mohave Copper Corp., 1959-70; dir. Pioneer Bank of Ariz., 1967-69; dir., v.p. Monterey County Ice & Devel. Co., 1953-69. Trustee, UCLA Found., 1973-79; mem. U.S. Congl. Adv. Bd. 1983—; chmn.'s advisor Am. Security Council Found., 1983—. Served to lt. (j.g.) USNR, 1944-46. Mem. Ariz. Acad., N.A.M. (mktg. and research com. 1960-78), Salinas C. of C. (dir. 1958-59), Council of Calif. Growers, Vegetable Growers Assn. of Central Ariz. (dir. 1962-63). Republican. Club: Phoenix Country. Lodge: Masons. Home: 41 Casa Blanca Estates Scottsdale AZ 85253 Office: PO Box 1705 Scottsdale AZ 85252

ENGSTROM, ERIC GUSTAF, interior design executive; b. Plymouth, Mass., July 9, 1942; s. Walder Julius and Victoria Sarah (Brewer) E.; m. Jacqueline Suzanne Del Savio, Apr. 19, 1969; children—Lars-Eric, Kate Pratumtip. B.F.A., Rhode Island Sch. of Design, 1964; postgrad. Southeastern Mass. U., 1967-69. Cert. interior designer. Exhibits designer Plimoth Plantation Mus., Plymouth, Mass., 1964-69; designer Johnson-Hotvedt & Assocs., Boston, 1969-71; designer, owner Engstrom Design, Boston, 1971-73; assoc., dir. Interior and Graphic Design Architects Hawaii Ltd., Honolulu, 1973-78; designer Wudtke Watson Davis, San Francisco, 1978-79; pres. WME Interior Architecture, San Francisco, 1979-81; v.p., dir. design Wudtke Watson Davis & Engstrom, San Francisco, 1981—; guest lectr. Hotel Sch. Cornell U., Ithaca, N.Y., 1981; lectr. U. Hawaii, 1977-78. Mem. Town of Fairfax Design Rev. Bd., 1982; mem. Planning Commn. Town of Fairfax, 1981—. Recipient 1st place award, Chain Restaurants, 1981; 1st place award Fast-Food Restaurants, 1981; design awards Restaurant Hospitality mag. Mem. Am. Soc. Interior Designers (project design award 1980), Inst. Bus. Designers, Marin Soc. of Artists (fine arts awards), AIA (assoc.). Club: Outrigger Canoe (Honolulu). Projects published in profl. mags. Office: 200 Green St San Francisco CA 94111

ENNIS, RUTH M., Realtor; b. Toledo, Feb. 27, 1913; d. Charles Newton and Ethel J. (Wagoner) Detwiler; student pub. schs., Toledo; m. Arthur Waldo Holly, Jan. 19, 1935 (div.); 1 dau., Barbara Ann (Mrs. Lawrence J. Novak); m. 2d, Harry E. Beddoe, Sept. 29, 1948 (div. 1967); 1 son, Thomas Weston; m. 3d, Wilbur John Ennis, Feb. 14, 1974. Real estate broker Chas. N. Detwiler, realtor, Huntington Park, Calif., 1942-48, Harry E. Beddoe, realtor, Huntington Park and Downey, Calif., 1948-67; escrow officer Universal Escrow Co., Huntington Park, 1944, Advance Escrow Co., 1945-47; v.p. Beddoe Investments, 1957-68, Golden State Hawaiian Corp., 1964, now pres.; exec. v.p. Hawaiian Home Developers, to 1973. Precinct capt. Rep. Party, Buena Park, Calif., 1960, area chmn., 1962-72. Mem. Calif. Real Estate Assn., Ainaloa (Hawaii) Community Assn. (dir. 1966-78). Club: Hilo Yacht. Home: 421 Avenida Adobe Escondido CA 92025 Office: 120 Pauahi St Suite 308 Hilo HI 96720

ENOCH, JAY MARTIN, visual scientist, educator; b. N.Y.C., Apr. 20, 1929; s. Jerome Dee and Stella Sarah (Nathan) E.; m. Rebekah Ann Feiss, June 24, 1951; children—Harold Owen, Barbara Diane, Ann Allison. B.S. in Optics and Optometry, Columbia U., 1950; postgrad. Inst. Optics, U. Rochester, 1953; Ph.D. in Physiol. Optics, Ohio State U., 1956. Asst. prof. physiol. optics Ohio State U., Columbus, 1956-58, assoc. supr. Mapping and Charting Research Lab., 1957-59; fellow Nat. Phys. Lab., Teddington, Eng., 1959-60; research instr. dept. ophthalmology Washington U. Sch. Medicine, St. Louis, 1958-59, research asst. prof., 1959-64, research assoc. prof., 1965-70, research prof., 1970-74, research prof. dept. psychology, 1970-74; fellow Barnes Hosp., St. Louis, 1960-64, cons. in ophthalmology, 1964-74; grad. research prof. ophthalmology and psychology U. Fla. Coll. Medicine, Gainesville, from 1974, dir. Ctr. for Sensory Studies, from 1976, grad. research profl. physics, from 1979; mem. nat. adv. eye council Nat. Eye Inst., NIH, 1975-77; mem. exec. com., com. on vision Nat. Acad. Sci.-NRC, 1971-74; mem. U.S. nat. com. of Internat. Commn. for Optics, NRC, 1976—; mem. nat. sci. adv. bd. Retinitis Pigmentosa Found., 1977—; U.S. rep. Internat Perimetric Soc., 1974—; trustee Illuminating Engrs. Research Inst., 1978—. Served to 2d lt. U.S. Army, 1951-52. Recipient career devel. award NIH, 1963-73. Fellow AAAS, Am. Acad. Optometry (Glenn A. Fry award, 1972, Charles F. Prentice medal 1974), Optical Soc. Am. (chmn. vision tech. 1974-76), Am. Acad. Ophthalmology (assoc.); mem. Assn. for Research in Vision and Ophthalmology (pres., chmn. bd. trustees 1972-73, Francis I. Proctor medal 1977), Internat. Strabismological Assn., Internat. Soc. for Clin. Electro-retinography, Biophys. Soc., Psychonomic Soc., Am. Soc. for Photobiology, AAUP, Am. Psychol. Assn., Contact Lens Soc. U. K., Sigma Xi. Mem. editorial bd. Vision Research, 1974—, Internat. Ophthalmology, 1977—; assoc. editor Sight-Saving Rev., 1974—, Sensory Processes, 1974—; contbr. numerous articles on visual sci., receptor optics, perimetry, contact lenses and infant vision to sci. jours., also chpts. to med. books. Address: 54 Shirey Dr Moraga CA 94556

ENOWITZ, EVAN, coll. adminstr.; b. Hoboken, N.J., Aug. 14, 1947; s. Morton and Laura (Sklarew) E.; B.S., Pratt Inst., 1969; M.A., New Sch. Social Research, 1974. Group personnel mgr. Restaurant Assos. Industries, N.Y.C., 1969-72; asst. prof. Middlesex County Coll., Edison, N.J., 1972-77; cons. Windows on the World Restaurant, 1977; coordinator food service mgmt. instrnl. program, instr. Grossmont Coll., El Cajon, Calif., 1978—; adj. prof. Temple U., Phila., 1976-77, U. Calif. San Diego, La Jolla, 1981—. Mem. Council on Hotel, Restaurant and Instnl. Educators, Soc. Wine Educators. Home: 8008 El Capitan Dr LaMesa CA 92041 Office: 8800 Grossmont College Dr El Cajon CA 92026

ENRIGHT, JAMES THOMAS, biology educator; b. Baker, Oreg., Nov. 23, 1932; s. Paul Robert and Kathryn Elizabeth (Higgins) E.; m. Roswitha Hauenschild, Dec. 23, 1968; children—Phillip, Paul, Kenneth, Patrick. B.A., UCLA, 1957, M.A., 1959, Ph.D., 1961. Postdoctoral fellow Max-Planck-Institut, 1961-63; asst. prof. UCLA, 1963-66; assoc. prof., prof. behavioral physiology Scripps Instn. Oceanography, U. Calif., San Diego, La Jolla, 1966—. Served with U.S. Army, 1954-56. NSF predoctoral fellow, 1959-61, postdoctoral fellow, 1961-63; Fulbright fellow, 1978-79; recipient Alexander von Humboldt Prize, 1981-82. Fellow AAAS; mem. Am. Soc. Naturalists, Sigma Xi. Author: The Timing of Sleep and Wakefulness, 1980; contbr. articles to sci. jours. Office: Scripps Inst Oceanography La Jolla CA 92093

ENRIGHT, PAUL FRANCIS, sales executive; b. Rock Rapids, Iowa, Aug. 7, 1940; s. Michael William and Dorothy Evelyn (Bendinger) E.; m. Patricia Ann Martin, Aug. 24, 1969; children—Theresa, Michelle, Paul. B.A., Mich. State U., 1962. Salesman, then sales mgr. Maxwell House, Denver, 1968-73, Mead Johnson, Dallas, 1973-75; mktg. exec., Coca Cola Co. Foods div., Houston, 1975-78, dir. sales ops., 1978-80; v.p. mktg. and sales Celestial Seasonings, Boulder, Colo., 1980—. Served to capt. U.S. Army. Decorate Air medal with oak leaf clusters, Viet Nam Service award. Club: Flatirons (Boulder). Home: 5306 Gallatin Pl Boulder CO 80303 Office: Celestial Seasonings 1780 55th St Boulder CO 80301

ENRIGHT, WILLIAM BENNER, judge; b. N.Y.C., July 12, 1925; s. Arthur Joseph and Anna Beatrice (Plante) E.; A.B., Dartmouth, 1947; LL.B., Loyola U. at Los Angeles, 1950; m. Bette Lou Card, Apr. 13, 1951; children—Kevin A., Kimberly A., Kerry K. Admitted to Calif. bar, 1951; dep. dist. atty. San Diego County, 1951-54; partner Enright, Levitt, Knutson & Tobin, San Diego, 1954-72; judge U.S. Dist. Ct. So. Dist. Calif., San Diego, 1972—. Mem. adv. bd. Joint Legis. Com. for Revision of Penal Code, 1970-72, Calif. Bd. Legal Specialization, 1970-72; mem. Judicial Council, 1972. Bd. dirs. Defenders, Inc., 1965-72, pres., 1972. Served as ensign USNR, 1943-46. Diplomate Am. Bd. Trial Advocates. Fellow Am. Coll. Trial Lawyers, Am. Bar Found.; mem. Am., San Diego County (dir. 1963-65, pres. 1965) bar assns., State Bar Calif. (gov. 1967-70, v.p. 1970, exec. com. law in a free soc. 1970—), Dartmouth Club San Diego, Am. Bar Assn., Am. Judicature Soc., Alpha Sigma Nu, Phi Delta Phi. Rotarian. Recipient Honor award San Diego County Bar, 1970, Extraordinary Service to Legal Professions award Mcpl. Ct. San Diego Judicial Dist., 1971. Office: 940 Front St San Diego CA 92101

ENSELE, KENNETH WILLIAM, ret. electronic engr.; b. Grenada, Calif., Sept. 12, 1920; s. William and Mary Alice (Cooley) E.; student U. Calif. at Berkeley, 1945-49; m. Doris Mary Work, Jan. 1, 1941; 1 dau., Carolyn (Mrs. Gerald Raymond Carver). Electronics engr. Mare Island Naval Shipyards, Vallejo, Calif., 1949-71, design engr. for USN on Nautilus, Groton, Conn., 1953-54, USN Underwater Labs., New London, Conn. and San Diego, Hoffman Labs., Los Angeles, 1960-63, head communications and antennae design div. Mare Island Naval Shipyard, 1963-71; ret., 1971. Lic. comml. pilot, ground sch. instr. Napa County Airport; rec. engr. U. Calif. at Berkeley, Standard Oil Co., others, 1958-60; profl. musician, music tchr.; free lance photographer for advertisers. Participant, Music Educators Nat. Conf., Salt Lake City, 1959; charter mem. Symphony League. Served with USNR, 1941-45; PTO. Mem. Musicians Union, Am. Theatre Organ Soc., Quarter Century Wireless Assn., Am. Radio Relay League. Home: 85320 Edenvale Rd Pleasant Hill OR 97455

ENSIGN, LINDA SUE, educational counselor, consultant; b. Bonham, Tex., Nov. 18, 1942; d. Don W. and Pearline U. (Warnett) Packwood; children—Eric, Erin. B.A. in Sociology, Seattle Pacific Coll., 1965, M.Ed. in Guidance and Counseling, 1968; postgrad. U.S. Internat. U., 1972-75. Cert. adminstrv. counseling. Elem. tchr., Seattle, 1966-68, elem. sch. counselor, 1970-76; coordinator elem. counselors, 1977-78, counselor Alternative High Sch., 1979-81; head counselor Chief Sealth High Sch., Seattle, 1982—; tng. cons. in communication skills and group process. Mem. Seattle Tchrs. Assn., Am. Personnel and Guidance Assn., Wash. Sch. Counselors Assn. Congregationalist. Home: 4803 Gilman W Seattle WA 98199 Office: Chief Sealth High Sch Seattle WA 98136

ENSTICE, WAYNE EDWARD, artist, educator, art critic; b. Irvington, N.J., Dec. 16, 1943; s. Jon Franklin and Eleanor Frances Enstice; B.F.A., Pratt Inst., 1965; M.A., U. N.Mex., 1969; m. Marie Frances Geditz, Aug. 28, 1967; children—Timothy Jon, Kirsten Anne, Nicolas Brett. Mem. faculty dept. art U. Ariz., Tucson, 1970—, assoc. prof., 1978—. One-man shows of drawings and/or mixed-media work include: R. Mutt Galleries, Los Angeles, 1974, Limner Gallery, Phoenix, 1975, U. Ark. Art Gallery, Fayetteville, 1979; group shows include: Calif. Mus. of Sci. and Industry, Los Angeles, 1975, Yuma (Ariz.) Art Mus., 1976, Phoenix Art Mus., 1977, La Fonda Gallery, Santa Fe, N.Mex., 1977, Tucson Mus. Art, 1978, Bonfoey Gallery, Tucson, 1978, Springfield (Utah) Mus. Art, 1979, The Kioski Mus., Hermosillo, Mexico, 1979, Alternative Mus., N.Y.C., 1983, U. Houston, 1983; represented in permanent collections: Yuma Art Mus., Tucson Mus. Art, U. N.C., Chapel Hill, Ariz. Commn. on the Arts and Humanities, Phoenix. Recipient Juror's Prize, Phoenix Art Mus., 1977; Roswell Mus. and Art Ctr. artists-in-residency grantee, 1984-85. Author various articles and essays. Office: U Ariz Dept Art Tucson AZ 85721

ENSTROM, JAMES EUGENE, cancer epidemiologist; b. Alhambra, Calif., June 20, 1943; s. Elmer Melvin, Jr. and Klea Elizabeth (Bissell) E.; B.S., Harvey Mudd Coll., Claremont, Calif., 1965; M.S., Stanford U., 1967, Ph.D. in Physics, 1970; M.P.H., UCLA, 1976; m. Marta Eugenia Villanea, Sept. 3, 1978. Research asso. Stanford Linear Accelerator

Center, 1970-71; research physicist, cons. Lawrence Berkeley Lab., U. Calif., 1971-75; Celeste Durand Rogers cancer research fellow Sch. Pub. Health, UCLA, 1973-75, Nat. Cancer Inst. postdoctoral trainee, 1975-76, cancer epidemiology researcher, 1976-81, asso. research prof., 1981—, program dir. for cancer control epidemiology Jonsson Comprehensive Cancer Center, 1978—, mem. dean's council, 1976—; cons. epidemiologist Linus Pauling Inst. Sci. and Medicine, 1976—; cons. physicist Rand Corp., 1969-73, R&D Assos., 1971-75. NSF predoctoral trainee, 1965-66; grantee Am. Cancer Soc., 1973—, Nat. Cancer Inst., 1979—; Preventive Oncology Acad. award, 1981—. Fellow Am. Coll. Epidemiology; mem. Soc. Epidemiologic Research, Am. Heart Assn., Am. Pub. Health Assn., Am. Phys. Soc., AAAS, N.Y. Acad. Scis., Galileo Soc. Author papers in field. Office: Sch Pub Health U Calif Los Angeles CA 90024

ENTIN, KENNETH, educator, polit. scientist; b. N.Y.C., Dec. 7, 1944; s. Phillip and Hannah (Goodman) E.; B.A., CCNY, 1966; M.A. (NDEA fellow), N.Y.U., 1968, Ph.D. in Polit. Sci., 1971; m. Marilyn Sue Kahan, June 10, 1967. Instr. polit. sci. N.Y.U., N.Y.C., 1969; asst. prof. polit. sci. Calif. State Coll., Stanislaus, 1971-74, assoc. prof., 1974-78, prof., 1978—, chmn. dept. polit. and public adminstrn., 1982—; dir. Inst. Pub. and Govtl. Affairs, 1973—. Mem. adv. com. Emanuel Hosp. Mental Health, Turlock, Calif., 1972-74; mem. City Turlock Citizens Com. on Future, 1973-74, Citizens Com. Stanislaus Area Assn. Govts., 1974-82, Stanislaus County Planning Commn., 1982—. NSF trainee, 1970; Nat. Security Edn. Sem. fellow, 1972; Danforth Found. asso. Mem. Am., Western polit. sci. assns., Am. Soc. Public Adminstrn. Author: (with Barbara P. Greene) Government and the Consumer: The California Model, 1973. Contbr. articles to profl. jours. Home: 635 Camellia St Turlock CA 95380 Office: 800 Monte Vista Ave Turlock CA 95380

ENYEART, JAMES L., art historian, educator, administrator; b. Auburn, Wash., Jan. 13, 1943; s. Lyle F. and Emma A. (Ham) E.; m. Roxanne Malone, Sept. 7, 1964; children—Mara, Sasha, Megan. B.F.A., Kansas City Art Inst., 1965; M.F.A. with honors, U. Kans., 1972. Dir., Albrecht Gallery of Art, St. Joseph, Mo., 1967-68; curator photography Mus. Art, U. Kans., 1968-76, asst. prof. art, 1969-75, assoc. prof. art, 1976; exec. dir. Friends of Photography, Carmel, Calif., 1976-77; dir. Ctr. Creative Photography, Tucson, 1977—; cons. collection mgmt. and appraisal. OAS fellow, U. Chile, Santiago, 1966-67; profl. mus. fellow, 1975; hon. research fellow, U. Exeter (Eng.), 1974; Nat. Endowment Arts grantee, 1973-83. 1973, 1974, 1975. Mem. Nat. Soc. for Photo. Edn. Office: 843 E University Blvd Tucson AZ 85719

EPPERLY, KERMIT LOWELL, college dean, accountant; b. Piqua, Ohio, June 23, 1928; s. Kelly Hamilton and Edna Myrtle E.; m. Betty Lee Freebairn, Apr. 13, 1974. A.A., Long Beach (Calif.) City Coll., 1949; B.S., UCLA, 1951; M.A., Calif. State U., 1956. Teaching credential, Calif.; supervision credential, Calif. Pvt. practice acctg., Long Beach, 1950—; tchr. Long Beach Poly. High Sch., 1954-62, chmn. dept. bus., 1962-67; assoc. prof. bus. Long Beach City Coll., 1967-78, dean of bus., 1978—. Served with U.S. Army, 1952-54. Mem. Am. Vocat. Assn., Assn. Calif. Community Coll. Adminstrs., Calif. Assn. Community Colls. (articulation council), Calif Bus. Edn. Assn., Long Beach City Coll. Mgrs. Assn., Long Beach City Coll. Adminstrs. Assn. (pres. 1982-83), Sales and Mktg. Execs. Internat., Phi Delta Kappa. Republican. Methodist. Club: Long Beach City Coll. Faculty. Author: Calculation Machines, 1973, 5th edit., 1983.

EPPERSON, ERIC ROBERT, food co. mgr.; b. Oregon City, Oreg., Dec. 10, 1949; s. Robert Max and Margaret Joan (Crawford) E.; B.S., Brigham Young U., 1973, M.Acctg., 1974; M.B.A., Golden Gate U., 1977, J.D., 1981; m. Lyla Gene Harris, Aug. 21, 1969; 1 dau., Marcie. Instr. acctg. Brigham Young U., Provo, Utah, 1973-74; supr. domestic taxation Bechtel Corp., San Francisco, 1974-78; supr. internat. taxation Bechtel Power Corp., San Francisco, 1978-80; mgr. internat. tax planning Del Monte Corp., San Francisco, 1980-82, mgr. internat. taxes, 1982—. Eagle Scout, 1965; scoutmaster, Boy Scouts Am., Provo, 1971-73, troop committeeman, 1973-74; mem. IRS Vol. Income Tax Assistance Program, 1972-75; pres. Mut. Improvement Assn., Ch. Jesus Christ of Latter-day Saints, 1972-74, pres. Sunday sch., 1977-79, tchr., 1974-80, ward clk., 1980-83, bishopric, 1983—. Mem. Am. Acctg. Assn., Tax Assn. Am., Am. Bar Assn., Beta Alpha Psi. Republican. Clubs: Commonwealth, Masters of Accountancy Brigham Young U. Author: (with T. Gilbert) Interfacing of the Securities and Exchange Commission with the Accounting Profession: 1968 to 1973, 1974. Office: One Market Plaza San Francisco CA 94105

EPPERSON, VAUGHN ELMO, civil engr.; b. Provo, Utah, July 20, 1917; s. Lawrence Theophilus and Mary Loretta (Pritchett) E.; B.S., U. Utah, 1953; m. Margaret Ann Stewart Hewlett, Mar. 4, 1946; children—Margaret Ann, Vaughn Hewlett, David Hewlett, Katherine (Mrs. Franz S. Amussen), Lawrence Stewart. With Pritchett Bros. Constrn. Co., Provo, 1949-50; road design engr. Utah State Road Commn., Salt Lake City, 1951-53, bridge design engr., 1953-54; design engr. Kennecott Copper Corp., Salt Lake City, 1954-60, office engr., 1960-62, sr. engr., 1962, assigned concentrator plant engr., 1969-73, assigned concentrator project engr., 1973-78; cons. engr. Vaughn Epperson Enging. Service, Salt Lake City, 1978—; project engr. Newbery-State Inc., Salt Lake City, 1980. Scoutmaster Troop 190, Salt Lake City, 1949-51. Served to capt. AUS, 1941-45; maj. N.G., 1951; col. Utah State Guard, 1952-70. Decorated Army Commendation medal; recipient Service award Boy Scouts Am., 1949; Community Service award United Fund, 1961; Service award VA Hosp., Salt Lake City, 1977. Mem. ASCE, Am. Soc. Mil. Engrs., Sons of Utah Pioneers. Republican. Mem. Ch. of Jesus Christ of Latter Day Saints. Home: 1537 Laird Ave Salt Lake City UT 84105 also PO Box 39 RFD Kamas UT 84036 Office: PO Box 8769 Salt Lake City UT 84108

EPPINETTE, SHIRLEY LYNN, educator, journalist; b. New Orleans; d. Woodie Trevillion and Thelma Elizabeth (Axline) E.; A.A. (Journalism Alumni Assn. scholar), East Los Angeles, Coll., 1967; B.A. (Arthur J. Baum journalism scholar), Calif. State U., Los Angeles, 1969, postgrad., 1969-70; postgrad. U. Santa Clara, 1981, U. So. Calif., 1982, Chapman Coll., 1983. Elem. tchr. Covina-Valley Unified Sch. Dist., 1970-74, San Gabriel (Calif.) Sch. Dist., 1974-75, Alhambra (Calif.) City Sch. Dist., 1976-78, Los Angeles City Unified Sch. Dist., 1978—; rewrite editor, staff writer San Gabriel Valley Newspaper Publs., 1975-76; mem. membership adv. group Automobile Club So. Calif. Recipient TAP award Alhambra-San Gabriel dist. Soroptimist Club, 1975; Calif. State PTA scholar, 1981. Mem. NEA, Calif. Tchrs. Assn., United Tchrs. Los Angeles, Women in Communications, Nat. Press Women, AAUW (com. internat. relations 1977-78, chmn. ednl. com. 1978-79), Humane Soc. U.S., Nat. Rifle Assn., Sigma Delta Chi. Club: Pacific Coast Press. Home: 1717 S 8th St Alhambra CA 91803

EPSTEIN, BEE JEFFRIE, management consultant; b. Tubingen, Germany, July 14, 1937; d. Paul F. and Milly (Stern) Singer; m. Leonard J. Epstein, June 10, 1959 (div. 1982); children—Bettina, Nicole, Seth. Student Reed Coll., 1954-57; B.A., U. Calif.-Berkeley, 1958; M.A., Goddard Coll., 1976; Ph.D., Internat. Coll., 1982. Mem. faculty Monterey (Calif.) Peninsula Coll., 1975—; mem. faculty extension U. Calif.-Santa Cruz, 1978-80, Golden Gate U., 1981; adj. faculty U. Alaska, 1981—; pres. Bee Epstein Assocs., Carmel, Calif.; pres. Success Tours, Inc., Carmel, 1981—; instr. Calif. Fire Acad., 1981-82, Am. Inst. Banking, 1979-81. Monterey Peninsula Coll. grantee, 1976. Mem. Monterey Peninsula C. of C., Nat. Assn. Female Execs., Peninsula Profl. Womens Network, Calif. Tchrs. Assn., Women in Communication, Soc. Tng. and Devel. Nat. Speakers Assn. Democrat. Jewish. Office: Box 221383 Carmel CA 93922

EPSTEIN, IRVING, design engineer, inventor; b. Seattle, May 16, 1917; s. Samuel Ella and Sophie Esther (Broches) E.; m. Irene Ainsburg, Oct. 7, 1947; children—Lawrence Jay, Ronald Ellis, David Alan. Student Seattle Pub. Schs. Machinist apprentice, 1936-40; toolmaker U.S. Govt., 1940-45; machine shop foreman Machinery Exchange, 1945-48; master machinist Sternoff's Metal Corp., 1948-55; dir. engring. Wash. Chain Supply, Inc., Seattle, 1955-77; engring. cons. Donaldson, Lufkin & Jenrette; inventor; patentee U.S., Can. and Gt. Britain (11). Scoutmaster Boy Scouts Am.; active Big Bros. Home: 4216 Shoreclub Dr Mercer Island WA 98040 Office: 2901 Utah Ave S Seattle WA 98124

EPSTEIN, JACOB DAVID, lawyer; b. Louisville, May 9, 1951; J.D., Vanderbilt U., 1978; B.A., Eckerd Coll., 1975; m. Cindy Renzoni, June 19, 1982. Bar: Pa. 1978, Calif. 1980; ptnr. Lowenthal & Epstein, Phila., 1978-79; sole practice, Phila. and San Diego, 1979-81; ptnr. Epstein & Treadwell, San Diego, 1981-82; sole practice, taxation law and real estate, LaJolla, Calif., 1982—; cons. City of Phila., 1980; dir., officer Marseilles Corp., Dover, Del., 1980-81. Del. Tenn. Constl. Conv., 1977. Mem. Phila. Bar Assn., Calif. Bar Assn., San Diego County Bar Assn., ABA, San Diego Bd. Realtors, Calif. Assn. Realtors, Nat. Assn. Realtors. Republican. Jewish. Address: 5568 Linda Rosa Ave La Jolla CA 92037

EPSTEIN, MICHELLE PAULETTE, librarian; b. Los Angeles, Oct. 3, 1951; d. Cyrus Jerry and Margot (Hollander) E.; B.A., UCLA, 1973; M.S.L.S., U. So. Calif., 1975, M.P.A., 1978. Reference and circulation librarian Southwestern U., Los Angeles, 1976-80; law librarian Rifkind & Sterling, Inc., Beverly Hills, Calif., 1980-81; coordinator library services Western Ctr. on Law and Poverty, Inc., 1982—. Mem. So. Calif. Assn. Law Librarians, Am. Assn. Law Librarians, UCLA Alumni Assn., U. So. Calif. Library Sch. Alumni Assn. Democrat. Jewish. Home: 4752 Kraft Ave North Hollywood CA 91602 Office: 3535 W 6th St Los Angeles CA 90020

EPSTEIN, ROBERT MICHAEL, advt. agy. exec.; b. Albuquerque, Feb. 22, 1944; s. Sam K. and Sadye K. Epstein; B.B.A., U. N.Mex., 1965, M.B.A., 1967; children—Barry, Stacey. Pres., Epstein Enterprises, Inc., Albuquerque, 1973—. Bd. dirs. Albuquerque Little Theater, Albuquerque Internat. Balloon Fiesta. Mem. Am., N.Mex. advt. fedns., Greater Albuquerque C. of C. (bd. dirs.). Office: 6020 San Academy Blvd NE Albuquerque NM 87109

EPSTEIN, ROBERT STANLEY, lawyer; b. Omaha, Oct. 24, 1941; s. Sidney Louis and Gertrude D. (Robinson) E.; B.S., Northwestern U., 1963; J.D., Stanford, 1966; m. Catherine Aubale, 1978; 1 son, Stephen Aubale. Bar: Calif. 1966. Law clk. Justices Paul Peek and Raymond Sullivan, Calif. Supreme Ct., 1966-67; practice law, San Francisco; lectr. Golden Gate Law Sch., Washburn Law Sch.; arbitrator Nat. Assn. Securities Dealers. Bd. dirs., gen. counsel The Guardsmen. Mem. Assn. Internationale des Etudiants en Sciences Economiques et Commerciales-U.S. Alumni (bd. dirs.), Phi Epsilon Pi. Clubs: Univ., Mchts. Exchange (San Francisco). Editorial bd. Stanford Law Rev., 1964-66. Home: One 18th Ave San Francisco CA 94121 Office: 155 Sansome St Suite 700 San Francisco CA 94104

EPSTEIN, STANLEY WILLIAM, aviation company executive; b. Norfolk, Va., Oct. 30, 1922; s. Benjamin and Florence Epstein; m. Sara Strumfman, Dec. 3, 1950; children—Ben, Doritte. Student Coll. William and Mary, 1939, U. So. Calif., 1952. With Norfolk Airport Co., 1939-45; purchasing agt. Southland Aero Supply, Norfolk, 1945-46; gen. mgr., v.p. Am. Airmotive, Miami, Fla., 1946-52; pres. Anglo Am. Aviation Co., North Hollywood, Calif., 1952—, Doram Mgmt. Corp., North Hollywood, 1974—; counselor Calif. World Trade Commn. Recipient Stanley T. Olafson bronze plaque award Los Angeles area C. of C., 1978. Mem. Export Mgrs. Assn. Calif. (hon. life mem.; Export Merit award 1975, Above and Beyond award 1978), Brit. Am. C. of C., Fgn. Trade Assn., French-Am. C. of C., Dist. Export Council. Clubs: Los Angeles Athletic, Masons, Shriners.

EPTING, MARION AUSTIN, educator, artist; b. Forrest, Miss., Jan. 28, 1940. A.A., Los Angeles City Coll.; M.F.A., Los Angeles County Art Inst., 1969. Group shows include San Diego Fine Arts Soc., 1969, Seattle Art Mus., 1969, Oakland Art Mus., 1973, Western Assn. Art Mus., 1973-75; represented in permanent collections: Oakland Mus., Calif., Seattle Art Mus., Library Congress, Washington, Auchebach Found., De Young Mus., San Francisco, Whitney Mus., N.Y.C.; commns. include Lakeside Studios, Mich., 1972-74; assoc. prof. art Calif. State U.-Chico, 1969—. Recipient Best of Show award San Diego Fine Arts Guild, 1969; 1st Place Graphics award Calif Expo, Del Mar, 1969. Office: California State University Dept Art Chico CA 95929*

ERB, GEORGE FREDERICK, interior designer; b. Gothenburg, Nebr., Nov. 3, 1915; s. Ed and Edyth Charlotte (Loostrom) E. Student UCLA, 1934-36. Interior designer Barker Bros., Los Angeles, 1936-77; ret. 1977; cons. in field. Served to maj. USAF, 1943-45. Decorated Presdl. citation with oak leaf cluster. Mem. Am. Soc. Interior Designers. Republican. Methodist. Home and office: 8405 Dory Dr Mariners Cove Huntington Beach CA 92646

ERBURU, ROBERT F., newspaper executive, lawyer; b. Ventura, Calif., Sept. 27, 1930; s. Michael Peter and Kathryn (Sarzotti) E.; m. Lois Stone, July 31, 1943; children—Susan Kit, Lisa Ann. B.A., U. So. Calif., 1952; J.D., Harvard U., 1955. Assoc. Gibson, Dunn & Crutcher, Los Angeles, 1955-61; gen. counsel, sec. Times Mirror, Los Angeles, 1961, v.p., 1965-69, dir., 1968—, sr. v.p., 1969-74, pres., 1974—, chief operating officer, 1980, chief exec. officer, 1981—; dir. Tejon Ranch Co. Bd. dirs. YMCA Met. Los Angeles, 1973—, vice chmn., 1976—; bd. dirs. Ind. Colls. So. Calif., 1973—, chmn., 1976-77; trustee Marlborough Sch., 1974—, pres., 1979-81; bd. dirs., v.p. Times Mirror Found.; bd. visitors Grad. Sch. Mgmt., UCLA, 1974—, bd. overseers, 1976-81, trustee, 1981—; trustee Huntington Library, Art Gallery and Bot. Gardens, 1980—, William and Flora Hewlett Found., Pfaffinger Found.; bd. dirs. Council Fgn. Relations, Carrie Estelle Doheny Found., 1981—, Fletcher Jones Found., 1982—. Recipient Human Relations award Am. Jewish Com., 1977; Brotherhood award So. Calif. Region, NCCJ, 1979. Mem. ABA, U.S. C. of C. (bd. dirs. 1974—, treas. 1980—), Los Angeles Area C. of C. (bd. dirs. 1977-82), Central City Assn. (bd. dirs.), U. So. Calif. Journalism Alumni Assn. (bd. dirs.), Sigma Delta Chi. Office: Times Mirror Co Times Mirror Sq Los Angeles CA 90053

ERDI, GEORGE, electronics design engr.; b. Budapest, Hungary, July 1, 1939; came to U.S., 1965, naturalized, 1971; s. Mor and Edith (Menczer) E.; B.S., McGill U., Montreal, 1965; M.S., U. Calif., Berkeley, 1966; m. Maria Gerzon, Aug. 25, 1970; 1 son, Gabriel. Design engr. Fairchild Semicondr. Research and Devel. Labs., Palo Alto, Calif., 1966-69; project mgr. Precision Monolithics, Inc., Santa Clara, Calif., 1969-79, staff v.p. design, 1979-81; co-founder Linear Technology Co., 1981; program com. Internat. Solid State Circuits Conf., 1980, 81, 82. Named Master of Precision Linear Integrated Circuits, Electronics Mag., 1977. Sr. mem. IEEE. Guest editor IEEE Jour. Solid State Circuits, 1981; contbr. articles on integrated circuits to tech. jours. Patentee in field. Home: 2 Longspur Portola Valley CA 94025

ERDLE, PHILIP JOHN, business executive; b. Bethlehem, Pa., Sept. 17, 1930; s. Louis Jacob and Elizabeth Mary (Costigan) E.; m. Carolyn Mary Knies, June 14, 1952; children—Patricia Quinnell, William, Ann Holzer, Terry, Margaret. B.S., U.S. Milit. Acad., 1952; M.S. in Mech. Engring., U. Mich., 1960; Ph.D. in Civil Engring., U. Colo., 1964. Commd. 2nd lt. U.S. Air Force, 1952, advanced through grades to brig. gen., 1979; prof., vice dean U.S. Air Force Acad., Colo., 1964-79; ret., 1979; mgr. tng. and edn. Bechtel Corp., Saudi Arabia, 1979-81, dir. human resources devel., San Francisco, 1981-82; pres. Nat. Edn. Internat., Newport Beach, Calif., 1982—; ednl. cons. Royal Commn. for Jubail and Yanbu, Saudi, Arabia. Decorated Legion of Merit, DFC, Air medal, Meritorious Service medal. Mem. Am. Soc. Engring. Edn., Am. Soc. Tng. and Devel. Contbr. articles to profl. publs. Home: 720 Dillon Dr Colorado Springs CO 80908 Office: 4361 Birch St Newport Beach CA 92660

ERDMANN, JOACHIM CHRISTIAN, physicist; b. Danzig, June 5, 1928; s. Franz Werner and Maria Magdalena (Schreiber) E.; doctorate Tech. U. Braunschweig (Germany), 1958; m. Ursula Maria Wedemeyer, Aug. 24, 1957; children—Michael Andreas, Thomas Christian, Maria Martha Dorothea. Physicist, Osram Labs., Augsburg, Germany, 1954-60; sr. research scientist Boeing Sci. Research Labs., Seattle, 1960-72; sr. research scientist Boeing Aerospace Co., Seattle, 1972-73; prin. engr. Boeing Comml. Airplane Co., Seattle, 1973-81, sr. prin. engr., 1981—; vis. prof. Max Planck Inst. for Metals Research, Stuttgart, Germany, 1968-69; lectr. Tech. U. Stuttgart, 1968-69; pres. Optologics Inc., Seattle, 1973—. Mem. Am. Phys. Soc., Optical Soc. Am., Soc. Photo Optical Instrumentation Engrs. Author: Heat Conduction in Crystals, 1969. Contbr. articles to profl. jours. Research in cryogenics, statis. physics and opto electronics. Home: 11245 12th Ave S Seattle WA 98168 Office: PO Box 3707 Seattle WA 98124

ERICKSEN, DONALD ELROY, marriage and family counselor; b. Fresno, Calif., Nov. 8, 1922; s. Laurence A. and Mary A. (May) E.; m. Jo Ann Joy, Apr. 7, 1963; 1 dau., Patricia; stepchildren—Richard, Judith. M.A., Loma Linda U., 1965; M.A., Chapman Coll., 1981. Cert. life elem. and secondary tchr., Calif. Food processor Loma Linda (Calif.) Foods, 1943-48; self-employed salesman, 1948-52; precision honer Ace Bushings, Riverside, Calif., 1955-56; tchr. Newport-Mesa (Calif.) Unified Sch. Dist., 1958-83; marriage, family and child counselor, Orange County, Calif., 1983—. Recipient Valley Forge Tchrs. Freedom Found. award, 1972, Newport Mesa Educators Assn. Educators award, 1973-74. Mem. Calif. Assn. Marriage and Family Therapists, Newport Mesa PTA (hon. life), Am. Personnel and Guidance Assn., Nat. Fedn. of Blind. Republican. Seventh-day Adventist.

ERICKSON, A. RONALD, marketing and advertising executive; b. N.Y.C., Aug. 21, 1942; s. Alfred Lear and Tullia Virginia (Pase) E.; m. Elisabeth Racek, Aug. 21, 1980. B.A., Wagner Coll., 1965; B.A. in Internat. Mgmt., M.B.A., Thunderbird Grad. Sch., 1970. Lic. real estate broker, Colo. Account exec. SSC&B Inc., N.Y.C., 1972-74; v.p. acctg. services NCK Sports, N.Y.C., 1976; v.p., account supr. Norman Craig & Kummel, N.Y.C., 1974-76; pres., owner Erickson, Fuller & Assocs., Advt., Aspen, Colo., 1977—; Lectr. in mktg. Colo. Mountain Coll., Aspen, 1979—. Trustee Grass Roots TV 12; bd. dirs. Aspen Winternat./World Cup, former v.p., dep. dir. registration. Served to lt. USN, 1965-69. Decorated Bronze Star, Air medal. Mem. Roaring Fork Assn., Advt. Agys. Club: Elks (Aspen). Office: 330 E Main St Aspen CO 81611

ERICKSON, CHARLES JOHN, anthropologist; b. Chgo., Sept. 4, 1931; s. Charles Gustave and Alice (Wackenfeldt) E.; A.B., U. Chgo., 1952, A.M., 1954; m. Roberta Ann Moose, Jan. 6, 1953; children—Kristina Lynn, Kirsten Leigh, Karin Lisa Ellen. Asso. social scientist Rand Corp., Santa Monica, Calif., 1954-56; human engr. Northrop Corp., Hawthorne, Calif., 1956-59; human factors specialist Systems Devel. Corp., Santa Monica, 1959-60; systems analyst Stanford Research Inst., Menlo Park, Calif., 1960-62; supr. Apollo life systems, space div. N.Am. Aviation, Downey, Calif., 1962-64, systems engr. crew equipment; 1964-65; dir. health systems, autonetics div. N.Am. Rockwell, Anaheim, Calif., 1965-70; dir. health program systems center Indian Health Service, Tucson, 1970-80, dep. dir. Office of Research and Devel., 1980-81, acting dir., 1981—. Cons. Thailand Peace Corps Tng. Program, Calif. State Coll., Los Angeles, 1969; cons. rural health improvement ministry of Health, Arab Republic of Egypt, 1978, 79. Chmn. systems panel Los Angeles Mental Health Assn., 1969-70. Bd. dirs. Los Angeles Comprehensive Health Planning, 1969-70, Health Planning Council of Pima County, Ariz., 1973-76; mem. governing body Health Systems Agy. So. Ariz., 1976-79. Recipient Superior Service award Health Services Adminstrn. HEW, 1974; citation Dept. HHS, 1983. Fellow Soc. Applied Anthropology; mem. AAAS, Am. Anthrop. Assn., Soc. Gen. Systems Research, Human Factors Soc. (pres. Los Angeles chpt. 1969-70). Asso. editor Southwest Gen. Systems Bulletin, 1973-74. Contbr. articles to profl. jours. Home: 5570 N Camino Miraval Tucson AZ 85718 Office: PO Box 11340 Tucson AZ 85734

ERICKSON, DON, mayor Cheyenne (Wyo.); b. Chgo., Jan. 15, 1937; s. Lyden L. and Irene E. (Reich) E.; B.S., U. Ill., 1960, M.Ed., 1969; M.P.H., U. N.C., 1965; m. Jacqueline S. Jones; children—Cori Kerstin, Carie Lynn, Darryl Scott, Darren Thomas, Caryn Marie. Dir. health edn. and community services Wyo. Dept. Public Health, Cheyenne, until 1967; dir. ednl. devel. Mountain States Regional Med. Program, Cheyenne, 1967-73, Wyo. dir., 1973-76; mayor City of Cheyenne, 1976—; former mem. task force on urban growth U.S. Conf. Mayors; mem. human resources steering com., mem. fin. and goals com. Nat. League Cities; chmn. Cheyenne Area Devel. Com., 1979—; chmn. policy com. Cheyenne Area Transp. Planning Process. Former mem. Model Cities Bd., Wyo. Gov.'s Hwy. Safety Council, Spl. Sch. Dist. Adv. Com. on Policy Revisions; pres. Wyo. Heart Assn. Mem. Wyo. Assn. Municipalities. Roman Catholic. Office: 2101 O'Neil Ave Cheyenne WY 82001

ERICKSON, FRANK, artist; b. Salt Lake City, Dec. 29, 1922; s. Frank Washington and Sylvia (Parker) E.; B.F.A., U. Utah, 1949, M.F.A., 1950; m. Gloria Jean Schell, May 21, 1946; children—Frank Schell, Steven Edward, Gloria Gaye. Tchr. Alpine Sch. Dist., 1950, Salt Lake Sch. Dist., 1952-53; med. illustrator U. Utah, 1954; dir. art Stewart Sch., 1955-65; tchr. Granite Sch. Dist., Salt Lake City, 1966-74; artist in residence Phranque's Gallery of Fine Art, Salt Lake City, 1974—; lectr. oil painting, condr. workshops, Utah, Idaho, Nev., Ariz.; works represented in Wind River Valley Nat. Exhibit, DuBois, Wyo., 1979, 80, Western Art Show and Auction, Rapid City, S.D., 1980, Kalispell (Mont.) Art Auction, 1979, 80, 81, 82, Sun Valley Art Auction, 1980, 81, 82, All Media '80 Juried Exhibit, Houston, Western and Wildlife Art Invitational, Sioux City, Iowa, 1982, C.M. Russell Art Auction, Gt. Falls, Mont., 1983. Served with USN, 1942-46. Recipient Utah Bicentennial art award, 1976; Wind River Valley Nat. Exhibit awards, 1979, 80. Mem. Wind River Valley Artists Guild, Sedona Center for the Arts Guild. Author: The Lexicon of Color Mixing, 1981. Home: 2796 S 2000 E Salt Lake City UT 84109 Office: 2735 S 2000 E Salt Lake City UT 84109

ERICKSON, GERALD ARTHUR, research and cons. co. exec.; b. Ft. Lewis, Wash., May 31, 1943; s. Arthur and Lillian Margaret (Brockman) E.; B.S. in Physics, U. Wash., 1965, M.S. in Physics, 1967, Ph.D., 1971; M.B.A., U. Wash., 1978; m. Juel Helen Souers, June 15, 1968. Research asso. Imperial Coll., London, 1971-72; cons. scientist Math. Scis. N.W., Seattle, 1973-77; co-founder, v.p., prin. scientist Infometrix, Inc., Seattle,

1978—, pres., 1980—; cons. Monsanto Co., 1978-80. Mem. Am. Phys. Soc., Air Pollution Control Assn., AAAS, Chemometrics Soc., U. Wash. Grad. Sch. Bus. Alumni Assn. (v.p. 1980-81). Clubs: NW Fly Anglers, Wash. State Hi-Lakers. Home: 2325 NE 103d Seattle WA 98125 Office: 939 NE 43d #202 Seattle WA 98105

ERICKSON, LAWRENCE WILHELM, university dean, educator; b. Huron, S.D., Aug. 5, 1915; s. Hilding M. and Hildur M. (Johnson) E.; B.S., UCLA, 1942, M.S., 1945, Ed.D., 1955; children—Michael, Jeffrey Sellwood. With Wohl Shoe Co., Huron, 1931-32, Armour & Co., various cities, 1932-35, Chgo. & Northwestern Ry., 1935-38; tchr. Beverly Hills (Cal.) High Sch., 1943-44; faculty U. San Francisco, 1949-50, Columbia U., N.Y.C., 1952-58; faculty UCLA, 1945—, prof. edn., 1967—, asst. dean, 1967—. Cons. to various businesses, industries and ednl. instns. Mem. Nat. Assn. for Bus. Tchr. Edn. (pres. 1971-73), Western, Cal. bus. edn. assns. Author: The Secretary's Book, 1955; 20th Century Typewriting, 4th to 9th edit., 1952-67; Typing Our Language, 1970; Clerical Office Typing, 1972; Century 21 Typewriting, 1972, 77, 82; Typewriting —Learning and Instruction, 1979; Basic Information Keyboarding Skills, 1982; Basic Keyboarding and Typewriting Applications, 1983. Coordinating editor Nat. Assn. Bus. Tchr. Edn. Rev., 1973—. Home: 16954 Strawberry Dr Encino CA 91436 Office: 405 Hilgard Ave Los Angeles CA 90024

ERICKSON, LINDA MAY, educator; b. Corry, Pa., Feb. 16, 1948; d. Emery Ernest and Bernetha May (Couse) Elmquist; m. Orlin Meredith Erickson, May 30, 1970. B.A., U. Ariz., 1970, M.A., 1972; M.S., Calif. State U.-Hayward, 1983. Teaching asst. U. Ariz., Tucson, 1970-72, adminstrv. asst., 1971-72; tchr. English, Moreau High Sch., 1973—, chmn. English dept., 1975-82, dir. curriculum, 1980—, prin. summer sch., 1980—. John Paddy Tucker meml. scholar, 1960. Mem. Assn. Supervision and Curriculum Devel., Nat. Council Tchrs. English, Nat. Cath. Edn. Assn., Assn. Calif. Sch. Adminstrs., Phi Beta Kappa, Phi Kappa Phi, Phi Delta Kappa.

ERICKSON, PAUL, educator; b. Pittsburg, Kans., June 3, 1926; s. Paul and Mabel Elizabeth (Gumersell) E.; B.A., Ariz. State U., 1949; M.A., Stanford, 1951; Ed.D., U. So. Calif., 1964; m. Marilyn J. Stevenson, Aug. 22, 1953; children—Erick Edward, Michael Kristian. Tchr., Mammoth, Ariz., 1949-52, Bad-Nauheim, Germany, 1952-53; counselor Catalina Jr. High Sch., Tucson, 1953-56; tchr., counselor Pacific Beach Jr. High Sch., San Diego, 1956-60; practicum supr. U. So. Calif., Los Angeles, 1960-63; faculty San Diego State U., 1963—, now prof. dept. secondary edn., dir. Clin. Tng. Center, 1969-70. Bd. dirs. Episcopal Community Service, 1971-80; trustee All Saints Sch., 1970—. Served with AUS, 1945-46. Mem. Nat. Vocat. Guidance Assn., Am., Western psychol. assns., N.E.A., Am. Personnel and Guidance Assn., Am. Psychol. Assn. Home: 6610 Sunny Brae Dr San Diego CA 92119

ERICKSON, RICHARD CARL, psychologist, educator; b. Seattle, Oct. 28, 1937; s. Richard Carl and Winona Elizabeth (Dinges) E.; m. Joyce Quiring, Sept. 12, 1958; children—Diana Laureen, David Mark, Jonathan. Student Seattle Pacific Coll., 1955-56; B.S. in Psychology, U. Wash., 1959, Ph.D., 1969; M.Div., Fuller Theol. Sem., 1962. Ordained to ministry United Presbyn. Ch. of U.S.; intern Olympic Ctr., Bremerton, Wash., 1968-69; psychologist mental hygiene clinic, Seattle VA Hosp., 1969-70, day hosp. unit, 1970-74, rehab. medicine service, 1974-78; instr. dept. psychiatry and behavioral scis. U. Wash. Med Sch., 1971-73, asst. prof., 1973-77, assoc. prof., 1977-78; psychologist inpatient psychiatry Portland (Oreg.) VA Med. Ctr., 1979—; assoc. prof. dept. med. psychology Oreg. Health Scis. U., 1979—. Mem. Am. Psychol. Assn., Assn. Advancement Psychology. Contbr. articles to profl. jours. Home: 2211 NE 30 Portland OR 97212 Office: 3710 SW US Veterans Hospital Rd Portland OR 97201

ERICKSON, ROSE MARY, interior designer, space analyst; b. Orlando, Fla., Feb. 24, 1943; d. Kenneth La Verne Barnes and Viola Matilda-Irene (Evans) B.; m. Dennis Ray Erickson, Aug. 15, 1940. B.F.A. cum laude in Interior Design, U. Wash., 1971, B.S. cum laude in Art, 1971. Cert. interior designer Nat. Council Interior Design Qualifications. Space analyst SAFECO Corp., Seattle, 1972-75; project dir., mktg. dir., SpaceMgmt. Group Co., Seattle, 1975-77; prin., cons. Basics. Co., Seattle, 1977-81; dir. design Innerspace, Cholla Bus. Interiors Co., Phoenix, 1981-82; prin., v.p. bus. devel. Basicomp, Inc., Mesa, Ariz., 1981—; cons. to bus. Lambda Rho hon. scholar, 1968; Tri-Delt scholar, 1969. Mem. Am. Soc. Interior Designers (past v.p. Seattle chpt.), Inst. Bus. Designers. Lutheran. Club: Cottonwood Country (Sun Lakes, Ariz.). Contbr. copy right computer software programs in field, 1979-82. Office: 1345 E Main Suite 209 Mesa AZ 85203

ERICKSON, ROY DENMAN, artist, interior designer, corp. exec.; b. Lincoln, Nebr., Dec. 24, 1922; s. Edwin Emmanual and Hildur (Helstrom) E.; student U. Nebr., 1940-41, Pomona Coll., 1941-42, Art Center Sch., 1942, Chouinard Art Inst., 1945-47; m. Sammye Jean Williams, Nov. 1, 1946; children—Eric Edwin, Bradford Alan. Prof. art U. Wis., 1947-49; art educator Chouinard Art Inst., Los Angeles, 1949-57; prin. Eric Hand Prints, El Segundo, Calif., 1947-60; dir. contract sales and design Sagar Assos., Los Angeles, 1960-63; pres. Erickson Assos. Inc., Alhambra, Calif., 1963—; cons. on design projects. active Luth. Ch. Served as pilot USNR, 1942-46. Decorated Air medal with four oak leaf clusters, D.F.C. with oak leaf cluster; recipient Gold Nugget award for best office, 1979. Mem. Am. Soc. Interior Designers (award 1976), Soc. Calligraphers, Am. Inst. Designers. Club: Chess. Works include Mary Kay Cosmetics office tower, Dallas, 1977, major hotels, Guatemala, 1976, P.R., 1979, N.Y.C., 1976, Boca Raton, Fla., 1980, Inn on the Beach, Long Boat Key, Fla., Tampa (Fla.) Airport Hilton; contbr. articles to profl. publs. Home: 328 Bellefontaine Pasadena CA 91105 Office: 1112 S Garfield Alhambra CA 91801

ERICKSON, STANLEY WILLIAM, accountant, consultant; b. Joliet, Ill., Dec. 20, 1913; s. Felix Emanuel and Tojny Elizabeth (Hagman) E.; m. Dorothy Marie Johnson, Sept. 3, 1939; children—Robert, William, Carol, Cheryl. B.S. in Acctg., U. Idaho, 1938. C.P.A., Idaho. Acct., Idaho State U., Pocatello, 1939-41, IRS, Lewiston, Moscow and Pocatello, Idaho, 1942-43, 47; acct. M.T. Deaton & Co., C.P.A.s, Pocatello, 1947—, pres., 1967-82, now cons.; planning com. Idaho State Tax Inst., 1958—; mem. Idaho State Bd. Accountancy, 1974-79, chmn., 1979. Mem. Pocatello C. of C. Served to 1st lt., inf., AUS, 1943-46. Mem. Idaho Soc. C.P.A.s (pres. 1957-58), Am. Inst. C.P.A.s (dir. 1957-58, Idaho mem. Region II trial bd. 1982-85). Republican. Methodist. Clubs: Pocatello Rotary (treas.), Pocatello Golf and Country (treas.), Masons (knight comdr. Ct. of Honor, mem. supreme council). Office: 425 E Benton St PO Box 4670 Pocatello ID 83201

ERICKSON, WILLIAM H., justice Colo. Supreme Ct.; b. Denver, May 11, 1924; s. Arthur Xavier and Virginia (Hurt) E.; Petroleum Engr., Colo. Sch. Mines, 1947; J.D., U. Va., 1950; m. Doris Rogers, Dec. 24; children—Barbara Ann, Virginia Lee, Stephen Arthur, William Taylor. Admitted to Colo. bar, 1950; practiced in Denver, 1950-71; asso. justice Supreme Ct. Colo., Denver, 1971—, now dep. chief justice. Chmn., President's Nat. Commn. for Rev. Fed. and State Laws Relating to Wiretapping and Electronic Surveillance; mem. cts. task force Nat. Adv. Commn. on Criminal Justice Standards and Goals; mem. Adv. Com. on Revision Uniform Rules of Criminal Procedure; formerly bd. dirs. Nat. Jud. Coll.; bd. dirs. Pretrial Services Resources Center; mem. sec. com. Commn. on Accreditation of Law Enforcement Agys.; hon. adviser Nat. Edn. Inst. Fellow Am. Bar Found., Am. Coll. Trial Lawyers, Internat. Acad. Trial Lawyers (past dir., sec.-treas.), Internat. Soc. Barristers (pres. 1971); mem. Am. (jud. mem. at Large, bd. govs. 1975-79, mem. action commn. on ct. cost and delay rules and calendar, past chmn. council sect. criminal justice, criminal justice sect. del. to Ho. of Dels., state del. to Ho. of Dels. 1976—, chmn. spl. com. on adminstrn. criminal justice 1973-74, former chmn. com. to implement standards for criminal justice, mem. fed. rules Com. 1969-79), Colo. (gov. 1968-72, founder, past chmn. criminal law sect., past chmn. negligence sect.), Denver (trustee, pres. 1968-69) bar assns., Am. Law Inst. (council), Am. Judicature Soc. (past dir.), Practising Law Inst. (nat. adv. council), Inst. Jud. Adminstrn. (adv. com. for promulgation juvenile justice standards), Nat. Legal Aid and Defender Assn. (past Colo. dir.), Nat. Assn. Def. Lawyers in Criminal Cases (past dir.), Scribes (pres. 1978, dir.), Order of Coif. Home: 10 Martin Ln Englewood CO 80110 Office: 2 E 14th Ave Denver CO 80203

ERICSSON, LLOYD BAYLES, lawyer; b. Salina, Kans., Aug. 12, 1939; s. Herman Lloyd and Theodore (Van Tassell) E.; B.A., U. Kans., 1962; LL.B. cum laude, U. Va., 1965; children—John Douglas, Patrick Lloyd. Bar: Va. 1965, Oreg. 1965, Wash. 1978, Alaska 1980, U.S. Supreme Ct. 1971; assoc. Martin Bischoff Templeton Biggs & Ericson, Portland, Oreg., 1965-68, ptnr., 1968-75, sr. ptnr., 1975—. Mem. Oreg. Bar Assn., Wash. Bar Assn., Alaska Bar Assn., Lawyer/Pilots Bar Assn. (pres. 1978-80), Order of Coif. Republican. Episcopalian. Club: Columbia Aviation Country. Editor Lawyer Pilots Bar Assn. Jour., 1967-80. Home: 70 Madrona Beach Dr Port Townsend WA 98368 Office: 2908 1st Interstate Tower Portland OR 97201

ERIKSEN, STEVEN E., optometrist; b. Portland, Oreg., Mar. 26, 1949; s. Robert W. and Laura P. E.; m. Barbara Willing, Dec. 28, 1970; children—Jennifer Elaine, Michael Donald. Student U. Oreg., 1967-69; B.S., Pacific U., 1971, O.D., 1973. Lic. optometrist, Oreg., Wash. Practice Optometry, Redmond Vision Clinic, Wash., 1975—; cons. Group Health Coop. of Puget Sound. Served optometry service, U.S. Army, 1973-75. Mem. Am. Optometric Assn., Wash. Optometric Assn., King County Optometric Assn., Redmond C. of C. (v.p., dir.). Republican. Roman Catholic. Clubs: Redmond Kiwanis, Jaycees. Home: 4518 164th Ct Redmond WA 98052 Office: Redmond Vision Clinic 15660 Redmond Way Redmond WA 98052

ERLANDER, STIG ROBERT, biochemist, nutritionist, educator; b. Mpls., May 24, 1928; s. Erland Hartvig and Elvira (Andersson) E.; B.A., U. Minn., 1951; postgrad. Drexel Inst. Tech., 1951-52; Ph.D., Iowa State U., 1956; m. Leatrice Gloria Kurtyka, June 20, 1952; children—Stig Paul (dec.), Linnea Justina, Mark Gottfrid. NIH fellow Purdue U., Lafayette, Ind., 1957-59; prin. chemist No. Regional Research Lab., U.S. Dept. Agr., 1959-66; prof. chemistry and biol. scis. Ambassador Coll., Pasadena, Calif., 1966-74, chmn. dept. chemistry; prof. U. Pasadena, 1975-78; clin. nutritionist, asso. W.D. Currier, M.D., Inc., Pasadena, 1976-77; lectr., nutritional cons., propr. Erlanders Pathway to Health, Inc., 1977—; lectr. Los Angeles Chiropractic Coll., 1979-80, Pacific States U., 1979-81; host weekly radio and TV programs on nutrition. Served with USN, 1946-48, 51-52. Mem. Am. Chem. Soc., N.Y. Acad. Scis., AAAS, Am. Assn. Cereal Chemists, Sigma Xi, Pi Mu Epsilon, Phi Lambda Upsilon. Contbr. articles to tech. jours.; pub. jour. A Diet to End Diseases; producer Catalogue of Natural Products. Developed new method for determining bonds in polymers, new model for DNA, diet for healing various diseases. Office: 2279 N Lake Ave Altadena CA 91001

ERLINGER, LARY KENT, executive search company executive, management consultant; b. Bonne Terre, Mo., Oct. 18, 1942; s. James Herman and Bertha Corine (Chrismer) E. B.A., St. Louis U., 1967; postgrad. U. Mo., 1968. Gen. mgr. Osage Enterprises, Lake of the Ozarks, Mo., 1969-70; pres. Kent Security, St. Louis, 1970-76; gen. mgr. Chadwick Jewelers, Dallas, 1976-78; mng. ptnr. Erlinger Assocs., El Cajon, Calif., 1978—; mktg. cons. to corps. Recipient numerous achievement awards, letters of commendation from numerous chief exec. officers of Fortune 500 cos. Methodist. Office: 2548 Fletcher Pkwy El Cajon CA 92020

ERNST, CHADWICK ELLSWORTH, III, fastener co. exec.; b. Oakland, Calif., Mar. 19, 1933; s. Archibald Ellsworth and Beatrice Jessie (Ort) E.; B.A., U. Calif. at Berkeley, 1958. Gen. mgr. Cee Merchandise Co., Oakland, Calif., 1948-67; asst. to pres. F.W. Aurich & Co., Inc., Seattle, 1967-68; exec. v.p., gen. mgr. Aimsco Inc., Seattle, 1969—; dir. Cheler Corp., Seattle; pub. Mail Order World, Mail Order Roundup. Active CD, Berkeley, 1955-62. Mem. Internat. Mail Dealers Assn., Mfrs. Agts. Nat. Assn., Nat. Assn. Credit Mgmt., Am. Soc. Notaries, Small Bus. Assn. Presbyterian. Clubs: Swedish, Lake of the Woods Country. Author several self-help books. Home: 3669 W Viewmont Way W West Seattle WA 98199 also 6 Lake of Woods Gig Harbor WA 98335 Office: 4024 22d Ave W Seattle WA 98199

ERSKINE, JANICE MARIE, psychologist, educator; b. San Antonio, Feb. 11, 1935; d. John Elmer and Elizabeth Florence (Lanier) E.; m. Andrew James Karoly, Aug. 22, 1966 (div.). B.A., Baylor U., 1956, M.A., 1957; Ph.D., U. Mich., 1963. Research scientist Am. Inst. Research, Pitts., 1962-65; asst. prof. Humboldt State U., Arcata, Calif., 1965-71, assoc. prof. psychology, 1971-76, prof., 1976—, chmn. div. of interdisciplinary studies and spl. programs, 1976-80; assoc. acad. planning div. edn. programs and resources. Office of Chancellor, Calif. State U., 1981—, mem. acad. senate, 1975-80; cons. Environ. Cons., Arcata, 1972-76; Trustee Mattole Ctr. for Sci. and Edn. 1980-82; mem. Citizens Adv. Comm. for Humboldt Bay Harbor and Recreation Dist., 1975-77; mem. state planning com. Nat. Identification Program, Am. Council Edn., 1980—. USPHS trainee U. Mich., 1958-60; NSF fellow, 1970, 71-72; adminstrv. fellow Calif. State U. and Colls., 1980-81. Mem. Am. Psychol. Assn., Western Psychol. Assn., Congress of Faculty Assns. (state del. 1974-76), Am. Primatological Soc., Internat. Primatological Soc. Democrat. Home: 333 1st St Apt H106 Seal Beach CA 90740 Office: Ednl Programs and Resources 400 Golden Shore Long Beach CA 90802

ERVIN, RICHARD MICHAEL, advertising executive; b. Los Angeles, Oct. 22, 1947; s. Richard Herman and Geraldine M. (Hannum) E.; m. Joan C. Boardman, May 12, 1970; children—Jesse M., Jody M. B.S., Woodbury U., 1969. Art dir. Studio 2, 1969-72, Burns Typesetting Service, 1972-74, Palko Advt., 1974-76; creative dir. Taylor-Foltz Denardo, 1976-79; v.p., creative dir. Taylor-Daniels, 1979-81; owner, pres. Ervin Advt. & Design, Seal Beach, Calif., 1981—; lectr. in field. Recipient Orange County civic commendation, 1983; Art Ctr. Coll. of Design cert. of merit, 1981; Tool of Trade Show 5 cert. of excellence, 1980; award of excellence Aladdin Litho, 1982, others. Mem. Orange County Art Dirs. Assn., Western States Advt. Assn., Seal Beach Bus. Assn., Calif. Water Pollution Control Assn., Long Beach C. of C., Huntington Beach C. of C., Art Dirs. Club of Los Angeles. Club: Sierra. Office: 829 Ocean Ave Seal Beach CA 90740

ERVINE-CARR, C. YVONNE, educator; b. Seattle, June 10, 1946; d. Charles Woodrow and Christene Rosett (Griffin) Ervin; 1 son David Anthony. B.A. in Speech and English, U. Washington, 1969, M.Ed. in Curriculum and Instrn., 1971. Part-time instr. humanities div. Seattle Central Community Coll., 1977—; part time instr. English U. Wash., Seattle, 1979—; owner, cons. Effective Communication Skills, Seattle, 1980—; cons. Tng. and Devel. Dept., City of Seattle, 1981; tchr. English, Seattle Pub. Schs., 1971—. Mem. Profl. and Managerial Network, Am. Soc. for Tng. and Devel., Council on Black Am. Affairs, Nat. Assn. of Female Execs., Black Profl. Educators, AAUW, Urban League, NAACP, Nat. Council of Negro Women, Delta Kappa Gamma. Baptist. Office: PO Box 18965 Seattle WA 98118

ERWIN, DOUGLAS GEORGE, banker; b. Bklyn., Oct. 15, 1938; s. Frank Joseph and Phyllis Mae (Lofthouse) E.; student Penn Yan Acad., 1956; m. Judy E. Forman, Dec. 19, 1981; children by previous marriage—Kelley Anne, Patrick. With State Mut. Savs. Bank, Tacoma, 1961—, exec. v.p., 1970-72, trustee, 1972—, pres., chief exec. officer, 1976—. Bd. advs. Tacoma Gen. Hosp.; bd. dirs. YMCA; bd. dirs., past gen. chmn. United Way; bd. dirs. Pantages Theater. Served with U.S. Army Res., 1956-63. Cert. rev. appraiser. Mem. Mut. Savs. Banks Assn. Wash. (past pres.), Savs. League Tacoma (past pres.), Am. Savs. Inst. (past pres.), Wash. Savs. League, Soc. Fin. Officers (past pres.), Homebuilders Assn. Greater Tacoma, Tacoma Bd. Realtors, Am. Inst. Banking, Tacoma C. of C. Roman Catholic. Clubs: Tacoma Country and Golf, Fircrest Golf, Lions, Tacoma, Wash. Athletic. Home: 4420 Sunset Beach Rd W Tacoma WA 98467 Office: 955 Tacoma Ave S Tacoma WA 98466

ERWIN, JENNY LIND, education specialist, consultant; b. Maryville, Tenn., Sept. 10, 1946; d. Roland Edward and Virginia Verle (Vassey) Jett; m. William Shafer Erwin, Jr., May 25, 1968 (div.); 1 son: Douglas Roland. B.S. in Edn., Maryville Coll., 1968; M.A. with honors in Counseling, No. Ariz. U., 1977. Cert. elem. tchr., counselor and adminstr., Ariz. Tchr., Prestonia Elem. Sch., Louisville, 1968-70, Green Valley Sch., New Albany, Ind., 1970-72; owner, mgr. Flagstaff Newcomer Service (Ariz.), 1972-74; career co-ordinator Flagstaff Pub. Schs., 1972-80; project supr. Coconino County Ednl. Services, Flagstaff, 1980-81; specialist Ariz. Ctr. Vocat. Edn., Dept. Edn., Phoenix, 1981—; cons. in field. Co-dir. Camp Viola, La Grange, Ga., summer 1968; bd. dirs. Flagstaff Library, 1976-78, Big Sisters No. Ariz., 1978-81; bd. advs. Women's Shelter, 1980-81. Ariz. Dept. Edn. grantee, 1979-80. Mem. Ariz. Personnel and Guidance Assn., No. Ariz. Guidance Assn. (pres. 1979-80), Am. Personnel and Guidance Assn., Ariz. Vocat. Assn., Am. Vocat. Assn., Vocat. Edn. Equity Council. Democrat. Mem. Trinity Bible Ch. Club: Toastmasters Internat. Capitol (membership award, service award 1982). Editor, publisher Connections, 1981—; author ednl. handbooks and slide tapes. Office: Ariz Dept Edn 1535 W Jefferson Ave Phoenix AZ 85007

ERWIN, JOHN WINTON, geophysicist; b. Chgo., Mar. 7, 1924; s. John C. and Jeanie (Winton) E.; B.S., Mich. Coll. Mining and Tech., 1949; M.S., Colo. Sch. of Mines, 1954; m. Patricia Jane Young, Apr. 15, 1946; children—James W., Thomas P., John A., Susan M., Debra Ann. Asst. geophysicist Phelps-Dodge Corp., Tyrone, N.Mex., 1950; with U.S. Geol. Survey, Denver, 1951; geologist Anaconda Co., Salt Lake City, 1952; research physicist Dow Chem. Co., Midland, Mich., 1953-54; regional geophysicist ASARCO, Salt Lake City, 1954-61; devel. engr. Hercules Co., Salt Lake City, 1961-64; geophysicist Nev. Bur. of Mines and Geology, U. Nev., Reno, 1964—, prof. geophysics, 1964—; cons. to maj. mining and oil cos. in various western states and Can., 1964—. Served with USMC, 1943-46. Registered profl. engr., Nev.; registered geophysicist, Calif. Mem. Am., Can. insts. mining engrs., Soc. Exploration Geophysicists, European Assn. Exploration Geophysicists, Geol. Soc. Nev., Sgima Xi. Clubs: Masons, Tahoe Yacht. Contbr. maps, gravity and paleomagnetic studies to profl. publs. Home: 2685 Everett Dr Reno NV 89503 Office: Nevada Bur of Mines and Geology Univ of Nevada Reno NV 89507

ESCALANTE, ROEL, material management executive; b. Los Angeles, July 16, 1937; s. Angel and Maria (Arellanos) E.; m. Rita Carolyn Egger, July 9, 1960 (div.); 1 son, Anthony Miles. A.A., Valley Jr. Coll., 1959. Asst. purchasing agt. Colony Paint & Chem. Co., Los Angeles, 1964-67; buyer Traid Corp., Los Angeles, 1967-69; asst. purchasing mgr. Walt Disney Prodns., Burbank, Calif., 1969-76; dir. purchasing MCA, Inc., Universal City, Calif., 1976-79, corp. dir. material, div. v.p., 1979—. Mem. Los Aneles Purchasing Mgmt. Assn., Am. Mgmt. Assn., Nat. Assn. Purchasing Mgmt. (cert.), So. Calif. Regional Purchasing Council. Republican. Roman Catholic. Home: PO Box 8836 Universal City CA 91608 Office: MCA Inc 100 Universal City Plaza Universal City CA 91608

ESCANDON, RALPH, foreign language educator; b. Barranquilla, Colombia, May 21, 1928; s. Antonio and Leonor (Hernandez) E.; came to U.S., 1953, naturalized, 1961; B.A., Union Coll., 1957; M.A., U. Nebr., 1960; Ph.D., Interamerica U., Mexico, 1968; m. Lena Moore, June 6, 1955; 1 son, Willie Rafael. Instr. Spanish, U. Nebr., Lincoln, 1958-60, asst. prof., 1966-67; asst. prof. Creighton U., Omaha, 1960-62; prin. Cali (Colombia) Jr. Acad., 1962-66; assoc. prof. modern lang. dept. Pacific Union Coll., Angwin, Calif., 1968—, chmn. dept., 1977-81. Mem. Adventist Lang. Tchrs. Assn., MLA, Phi Sigma Iota. Republican. Adventist. Author 24 books in English, Spanish and French, including Curiosidades matemáticas, 1965; senderos de victoria, 1977; Smoke and Ashes, 1973; Spanish for Medical Personnel, 1979; On the Brink of the Whirlpool, 1979; contbr. articles in field to profl. jours., denom. mags. Home: 280 Washburn St Angwin CA 94508 Office: Pacific Union College Dept Foreign Languages Angwin CA 94508

ESHAGIAN, JOSEPH, ophthalmologist; b. Iran, Mar. 15, 1951; s. Ebrahim and Touran (Monasebian) E.; B.S. with honors, U. Mich., 1971; M.D., SUNY, Syracuse, 1975. Intern, U. Mich. Hosp., Ann Arbor, 1975-76; resident in ophthalmology U. Iowa Hosp., Iowa City, 1976-79, asso. dept. ophthalmology, 1979; practice medicine specializing in ophthalmology, Los Angeles, 1981—; fellow in oculoplastic and reconstructive surgery Jules Stein Eye Inst., UCLA Med. Center, 1980-81. Diplomate Am. Bd. Ophthalmology and Otolaryngology. Mem. Am. Acad. Neurology, Assn. Research in Vision and Ophthalmology, Nat. Assn. Residents and Interns, Iowa Med. Soc., Am. Assn. Ophthalmology, Contact Lens Assn. Ophthalmologists, Med. Eye Services Calif., Am. Acad. Ophthalmology, AMA, Calif. Med. Assn., Los Angeles County Med. Assn., Am. Soc. Contemporary Ophthalmology, Internat. Glaucoma Congress. Contbr. articles to med. jours. Office: 1200 N Vermont Ave Los Angeles CA 90029 also 1200 N Vermont Ave Los Angeles CA 90029

ESKRIDGE, ROBERT LEE, internat. mktg. cons. firm exec.; b. St. Louis, Nov. 12, 1948; s. Robert Lee and Dolores C. Eskridge; B.A., U. Santa Clara, 1970; M.B.A., U. So. Calif., 1972; m. Constance Kevin Menke, May 28, 1977. Pub., Beach Peoples Easy Reader, Hermosa Beach, Calif., 1972-74; mem. advt. dept. Procter & Gamble Co., Cin., 1974-75; asso. camp dir. Camp Bloomfield, Malibu, Calif., 1972-76; v.p. Mktg. InterContinental, Redondo Beach, Calif., 1976-82; exec. v.p. Growth Mgmt. Center, Palos Verdes Estates, 1982—; dir. Radio and TV News Bur., U. Santa Clara, 1973. Mem. adv. bd. Found. for Jr. Blind, 1978—; chmn. bd. dirs. Celebration Found., 1979-80; UCLA Community Service Commn. cons., 1980. Recipient Optimists Internat. Youth Achievement award, 1976. Mem. So. Calif. Corporate Planners Assn., Am. Soc. for Tng. and Devel., Am. Camping Assn. (cert. camp dir. 1975—, dir. ecol. tng. 1980—), So. Calif. Camping Assn. (dir., ecology chmn. 1977-79). Roman Catholic. Home: 517 S Francisca St Redondo Beach CA 90277 Office: Growth Mgmt Center 796 Via Delmonte Palos Verdes Estates CA 90274

ESPARZA, MOCTESUMA DIAZ, film producer; b. Los Angeles, Mar. 12, 1949; s. Francisco Chavez and Ester (Diaz) E.; B.A., UCLA,

1971, M.F.A., 1973; m. Esperanza Vasquez, July 24, 1977; children—Tonatiuh, Tonantzin, Tenoch. Producer documentary unit Sta. KNBC, Los Angeles, 1972; producer bilingual TV prodn. TV, Villa Allegre, Pub. Broadcasting Service, 1973-74; pres. Moctesuma Esparza Prodns., Inc., Los Angeles, 1974—, Buenavision Telecommunications, Inc., Los Angeles, 1976—; lectr. Stanford U., Univ. So. Calif., UCLA, Yale, U. Calif., San Diego, U. N.Mex., 1971—. Mem. Los Angeles Bicentennial com.; mem. jury Golden Harp Film Festival, Ireland, 1981. Recipient awards including Emmy, 1974; Ohio State award Ohio State Telecommunications Dept., 1976; Cine Golden Eagle, Am. Film Festival, 1977; Clarion award Woman in Film, 1976; Ruben Salazar Communications award Nat. Council La Raza, 1980; nominee Acad. award, 1977. Mem. Writers Guild Am., Acad. TV Arts and Scis., Pub. Advt. Council (dir.), Presdl. Commn. Scholars. Office: 2036 Lemoyne St Los Angeles CA 90026

ESPEY, WILLIAM MALLONEE, psychiatrist; b. Trinidad, Colo., June 3, 1938; s. James Gill and Virginia Alta (Mallonee) E.; student Va. Mil. Inst., 1956-57; B.A., U. Colo., 1960, M.D., 1964; m. Marianne Fort, June 30, 1961 (div. June 1980); children—Lisa Anne, William Todd. Intern, USAF Hosp., Travis AFB, Calif., 1964-65; resident psychiatry U. Colo. Sch. Medicine, Denver, 1968-72, Denver Psychoanalytic Inst., 1972-75; practice medicine specializing in psychiatry, Denver, 1972—; mem. staff Bethesda, Mt. Airy, VA hosps., Denver; asst. clin. prof. dept. psychiatry U. Colo., Denver, 1972—, teaching fellow, 1971-72. Served to capt. USAF, 1963-68. Mem. Am. Psychiat. Assn., Colo. Psychiat. Soc., Colo., Denver med. socs. Home: 1050 S Monaco Apt 51 Denver CO 80224 Office: 4900 E Cherry Creek Dr S Denver CO 80222

ESPOSITO, LESLIE VINCENT, JR., educational administrator; b. Los Angeles, Apr. 22, 1944; s. Leslie Vincent and Philomena Christina (Di Carlo) E. B.A., St. John's Coll., Ventura, Calif., 1967; M.S. in Edn. and Sch. Adminstrn., Mt. St. Mary's Coll., 1984. Tchr. religion Mary Star of the Sea High Sch., San Pedro, Calif., 1975-76; tchr., dept. head, adminstr. Santa Clara High Sch., Oxnard, Calif., 1980-81; prin. Daniel Murphy High Sch., Los Angeles, 1982—. Mem. Nat. Catholic Ednl. Assn., Am. Assn. Sch. Adminstrs. Republican. Club: Optimists. Office: 241 S Detroit St Los Angeles CA 90036

ESPOSITO, VINCENT JOSEPH, aerospace co. mgr.; b. Honolulu, Sept. 16, 1934; s. Vincent Joseph and Eleanor (Vinyard) E.; B.S. in Engring. (Disting. Grad. award), U.S. Mil. Acad., 1956; M.A. in Astronomy, U. Calif., 1962; m. Kathleen Angela Hoernig; children—Vincent J., Karen, Bruce. Commd. lt. U.S. Army, 1956, advanced through grades to capt., 1961; with 65th Engr. Bn., Hawaii, 1957-60, 8th U.S. Army, Korea, 1962-63, Army Map Service, Washington, 1963-65, resigned, 1965; research scientist Bellcomm Inc., Washington, 1965-67; research engr. to asso. adminstr. Nat. Hwy. Traffic Safety Adminstrn. U.S. Dept. Transp., Washington, 1967-76; dir. transp. programs U.S. Dept. Energy, Washington, 1976-79; mgr. advanced systems devel. TRW Automotive, Los Angeles, 1979-81; gen. mgr. Irvin Industries, Inc., Gardena, Calif., 1981—. Recipient Adminstrs. award, Dept. Transp., 1976. Mem. Soc. Automotive Engrs., IEEE (sr.), AIAA, West Point Soc. Los Angeles (pres.), Phi Kappa Phi, Sigma Xi. Patentee automotive safety devices. Home: 3503 Heroic Dr Rancho Palos Verdes CA 90274 Office: 15001 S Figueroa St Gardena CA 90248

ESRAELIAN, PETER, savings and loan executive; b. Fresno, Calif., Nov. 12, 1932; s. Setrak and Anna (Vahanian) E.; A.A., Reedley Coll., 1952; B.A. in Bus., U. Calif.-Fresno, 1954; m. Dee Neece Mary Kandarian, Oct. 23, 1960; children—Jeffrey, Stacey, Randall. Sales rep. Ford Motor Co., Fresno, 1955-59; underwriter N.Y. Life Ins. Co., Fresno, 1959-65; finance officer, city clk. City of Selma, Calif., 1965-78; asst. v.p. Guarantee Savs. & Loan Assn., Selma, 1978—. Mem. policy adv. com. Fresno County Council Govts., 1968-78; vocat. edn. adv. com. Fresno County, 1971-72; chmn. Selma Centennial Jubilee Com., 1980; mem. City of Selma Econ. Devel. Commn., 1983; trustee Selma Hosp. Dist. Found., 1982. Named Citizen of Year, Selma, 1968; grand marshall Selma Ann. Marching Band Festival, 1974. Mem. Selma Dist. C. of C. (pres. 1965-67), Fresno County Assn. chambers commerce (pres. 1969), League Calif. Cities (Blue Ribbon Task Force 1977), Triple X frat. Clubs: Rotary (pres. 1977-78), 20-30 (Selma). Home: 2135 Huntsman St Selma CA 93662 Office: 2121 High St Selma CA 93662

ESSERT, GENE GORDON, psychiatrist; b. Riga, Latvia, Nov. 26, 1917; s. Wladimir Vlyanovitch and Sarah Johanna (Bernhardt) E.; came to U.S., 1960, naturalized, 1965; B.A. in Psychology, U. Western Ont., London, Can., 1953, M.A., 1954, M.D., 1959; children—Karin Rubin, Ruth Essert Carlson, Jane. Intern, Hotel Dieu Hosp., Windsor, Ont., 1959-60; resident psychiatry Wayne State U. Lafayette Clinic, Detroit, 1960-62, Oreg. State Hosp., Salem, 1962-63; pvt. practice, Portland, Oreg., 1963-73, La Mesa, Calif., 1973—; mem. staff Grossmont, Alvarado, El Cajon Valley, Sharp hosps. Instr., U. Oreg. Med. Sch., 1963-67. Bd. dirs. Portland Mental Health Assn.; adv. com., bd. dirs. Concordia Coll., Portland, 1966-71. Fellow Royal Soc. Health; mem. Am. Security Council (nat. adv. bd.), Internat. Platform Assn. Author functioning efficiency evaluation scale, 1971. Home: 620 W Solana Circle Unit 2F Solana Beach CA 92075 Office: 10201 Mission Gorge Rd Suite D Santee CA 92071

ESSEX, HARRY, writer; b. N.Y.C., Nov. 29, 1915; s. Wolfe Wilhelm and Sarah (Bratter) E.; B.B.A., St. Johns U., 1936; m. Lee Berman, June 22, 1945; 1 son, David. Writer, Columbia Studio, 1945-48, RKO, 1949-51, Universal, 1951-56, MGM, 1960-62, United Artists, 1962-68; scenarist films including The Lonely Man, 1956, The Amigos, 1974, Man and Boy, 1973, Sons of Katie Elder, 1964, He Walked by Night, 1948, It Came From Outer Space, 1953; playwright Broadway prodns. Something for Nothing, 1954, Neighborhood Affair, 1960, One for the Dame, 1961, Twilight, 1980; owner, head writer Target the Corruptors, 1961-62; author novels I Put My Right Foot In, 1954, Man and Boy, 1971, Marina, 1981; writer for Untouchable series. Playhouse 90, others; scriptwriter, story editor Warner Bros., 1974—; writer NBC Movie of Week, 1974—. Served with AUS, 1942-44. Recipient Venice Festival award for motion picture He Walked by Night, 1949; Theatre Guild award for playwriting, 1940. Mem. Dramatists League, Writers Guild Am. West, Acad. Motion Picture Arts and Scis. Home: 9303 Readcrest Dr Beverly Hills CA 90210

ESSINGTON, EDWARD HERBERT, soil scientist; b. Santa Barbara, Calif., Feb. 19, 1937; s. Benner Heber and Joannina Catherina (Vercillino) E. m. Betty Joan Dacus, Sept. 15, 1957; children—Michael Edward, Laura Diane. B.S., Calif. Poly. Coll.-San Luis Obispo, 1958; M.S., UCLA, 1964. Soil scientist UCLA, 1957-64; geochemist Teleydne Isotopes, Palo Alto, Calif., 1964-71, Las Vegas, 1971-72; soil scientist Los Alamos Nat. Lab., 1972—. Mem. Soil Sci. Soc., Health Physics Soc., AAAS. Club: Tennis Los Alamos (v.p.). Home: 118 Balboa Dr Los Alamos NM 87544 Office: PO Box 1663 MS-K495 Los Alamos NM 87545

ESSINGTON, JAMES GIBSON, communications engr.; b. Huey, Ill., Mar. 1, 1926; s. James Gibson and Ruby Edith (Donaldson) E.; student Utah State Agrl. Coll., 1943; student various spl. and corr. courses; m. Lorene Genevieve Burnett, Aug. 20, 1950. Field engr. Philco Corp., Phila., 1950-57; owner J & W, Albuquerque, 1957-59; electronics technician Pub. Service Co. N.Mex., Albuquerque, 1958-60, acting communications engr., 1960-67, supt. communications and relay dept., 1962-81, supr. insps., 1981-83; ret., 1983; owner Essington Locksmith, 1975—; mil. occupational specialty ednl. evaluator Am. Council Edn., 1975—. Served with AUS, 1944-46. Mem. IEEE, Rocky Mountain Utilities Telecommunications Council (chmn. 1965-66, 73-75), N.Mex. Coop. Interference Com. (mem. steering com. 1964-69, 75-79). Research on wide band carrier coupling applications. Home: 9225 Las Camas Rd NE Albuquerque NM 87111

ESTES, JAMES PAUL, ins. co. exec.; b. Fullerton, Calif., Oct. 28, 1946; s. Paul Herbert and Dorthy Jane (Fairweather) E.; B.A., Calif. State U., 1968, M.B.A., 1973; m. Denise Finley, June 7, 1968; 1 dau., Jill. Ops. div. supr. Allstate Ins. Co., Santa Ana, Calif., 1971-73; ops. mgr. Nat. Auto and Casualty Ins. Co., Los Angeles, 1973-75; mktg. specialist Metro. Property & Casualty, Orange, Calif., 1975-77; asst. v.p. Nat. Am. Ins. Co., Los Angeles, 1977-78; v.p./sec. Baccala & Shoop Ins. Services, Los Angeles, 1978-81; Sec. Nat. Excess Ins. Co., Los Angeles, 1981—; pres. Oxford Fin. Corp., Diversified Life Ins. Co., Los Angeles. Served to lt., USN, 1968-71. Mem. Adminstrv. Mgmt. Soc., Am. Mgmt. Soc., Chartered Property and Casualty Underwriters Assn. (chartered property and casualty underwriter), Assn. C.L.U.'s (C.L.U.), Soc. Ins. Research. Home: 730 Stillwater Ln Anaheim Hills CA 92807 Office: 101 Lincoln Way Monterey Park CA 91754

ESTLOW, EDWARD WALKER, newspaper exec.; b. Snyder, Colo., Mar. 20, 1920; s. Edward G.W. and Mary Rachel (McConnel) E.; A.B., U. Denver, 1942, student law, 1946-49; m. Charlotte Ann Schroder, Mar. 27, 1943; children—Susan Lyday, Nancy Hawes, Sally Baier, Mary Erculiani. Gen. mgr. Lovington (N.Mex.) Press, 1949-52; account exec. Rocky Mountain News, Denver, 1952-55, personnel mgr., 1955-64, now pres.; bus. mgr. Denver Pub. Co., 1964-70; asst. gen. bus. mgr. Scripps-Howard Newspapers, N.Y.C., 1970-72, v.p., gen. mgr., 1972-76, pres., 1976—; officer or dir. Denver Pub. Co., Albuquerque Pub. Co., Newspaper Printing Corp., El Paso, Tex., Ft. Worth Press, Knoxville News Sentinel, Memphis Pub. Co., Birmingham Post-Herald, E.W. Scripps Co., Cin. Pres., Mile High Red Cross, Denver, 1965-66; trustee U. Denver, 1977—; bd. dirs. Jr. Achievement, Denver, Better Bus. Bur., Denver. Served to capt. USAAF, 1942-45. Mem. U. Denver Alumni (pres. 1973—). Office: 400 W Colfax Ave Denver CO 80204*

ESTRADA, ISABEL VICTORIA, obstetrician, gynecologist; b. San Juan, P.R., Nov. 17, 1918; d. Serafin and Elisa (Molinari) Estrada; student, U. P.R., 1938; M.D., Marquette U.; children—Kenneth Wayne, Lisa Darlene. Intern St. Joseph's Hosp., Milw.; gen. practice medicine Santurce, P.R., 1943-50; resident St. Luke's Hosp., New Bedford, Mass., 1950-51; fellow in ob-gyn pathology Free Hosp. Med. Women, Brookline, Mass., 1952; resident Mt. Sinai Hosp., Milw., 1952-54; USPHS fellow, Rio Piedras, P.R., 1956-62; practice medicine specializing in ob-gyn, Whittier, Calif. Pres. pro tem Hispanic Republican Women Los Angeles County. Recipient Los Angeles Med. Woman of Yr. award Am. Med. Women's Assn., 1966; Cert. of Appreciation of Vol. Service Am. Coll. Obstetricians and Gynecologists and Indian Health Service, 1981; Pope John XXIII award Italian Cath. Fedn., Shiprock, N.Mex., 1982; diplomate Am. Bd. Ob-Gyn Fellow Am. Coll. Obstetricians and Gynecologists, ACS, Los Angeles Ob-Gyn Soc.; mem. Gynecol. Urological Soc., Los Angeles County Med. Women (pres. 1968), Calif. Hispanic Drs. Assn., P.R. Med. Soc., P.R. Ob-Gyn Soc., Assn. Marquette Univ. Women (dir. 1954-56), Flying Drs. of Mercy, Am. Med. Women's Assn., N.Y. Acad. Scis., AAAS, Women's Overseas Service League, Marquette U. Med. Alumni Assn. (bd. dirs. Los Angeles County), La Mirada Bus. and Profl. Women (Merit award 1983), Marquette U. Alumni Assn. (Merit award 1983), Baker-Channing Soc., Alpha Sigma Nu, Gamma Pi Epsilon. Home: 1309 Dorothea Rd La Habra Heights CA 90631 Office: 1201 W Lambert Rd La Habra CA 90631

ETCHART, MARK S., state senator, rancher; b. Glasgow, Mont., Aug. 31, 1923; s. John and Catherine (Urquilux) E.; m. Delores Stroble, 1949; children—Colette, Kathy, Brian, Diane, Denise. Student St. Thomas Coll., St. Paul, 1940-41, Carroll Coll., Helena, Mont., 1941-42; B.S. in Animal Industry, Mont. State U., 1951. Ptnr., Etchart Ranch, 1943—; dir. Buggy Creek State Grazing Dist., 1964—, pres. Glasgow Irrigation Dist., 1966; mem. Mont. Ho. of Reps. from Valley County, 1961-65, from Dist. 5B, 1957-59; mem. Mont. State Senate, 1975—. Del Mont. Constl. Conv., chmn. gen. govt. com., 1972. Served with U.S. Navy, 1945-46. Mem. Mont. Pilots Assn., Am. Legion, Nat. Water Resources Assn., Alpha Zeta, Lambda Chi Alpha. Clubs: Elks, K.C. Roman Catholic. Republican. Home: Box 229 Glasgow MT 59230 Office: Montana State Senate Helena MT 59620*

ETCHESON, DENISE ELENE, architect; b. Iowa City, Iowa, May 17, 1950; d. Warren Wade and Marianne (Newgent) E.; B.A. in Environ. Design, U. Wash., 1973, cert. in Urban Design, 1977, M.Arch., 1977. Planner, designer Temel Muhendislik A.S., Istanbul, Turkey, 1974; project designer Astra Zarina Assos., Seattle, 1973-74, 76-77; project designer, constrn. coodinator G.R. Bartholick Architect/Planner, Seattle, 1975, 78; airport planning mgr. TRA Airport Cons., Seattle, 1978—; lectr. U. Wash., 1977. Mem. City of Seattle Pike Pl. Market Hist. Commn., 1975—, vice chmn., 1977-79, chmn., 1979-81, mem. Landmarks Preservation Bd., 1976-77. Recipient U. Wash. Archtl. Found. award, 1975. Mem. Am. Planning Assn., Historic Seattle Preservation and Devel. Authority, Nat. Trust Historic Preservation, Internat. Council Monuments and Sites. Club: Washington Athletic. Home: 3146 Portage Bay Pl E Seattle WA 98102 Office: 215 Columbia St Seattle WA 98104

ETHELL, DONALD EUGENE, publisher; b. Rockbridge, Ill., Dec. 25, 1927; s. Lester and Bernice (Scott) E.; student U. N.Mex., 1967-68, Calif. State U., 1971; m. Pauline Cecil, Mar. 11, 1948; children—Linda, Donald Ellsworth, James Lester. Editorial dir. Publs. Engrs., Hollywood, Calif., 1969-70; owner, pres. D.E.E. & Assos. Publs., Northridge, Calif., 1970—; pres. Abonnir Advt., Northridge, Los Angeles, 1973-76. Served to lt. comdr. USN, 1945-69; 5000 flight hours. Mem. Soc. Logistics Engrs. (pres. 1973), AIAA, Soc. Tech. Communications, Advt. Club Los Angeles (council), Beverly Hills Navy League Council, Fleet Res. Assn., Am. Legion, VFW, San Fernando Valley Public Relations Council. Democrat. Methodist. Clubs: Lions, Elks. Office: 8904 Reseda Blvd Northridge CA 91325

ETTENBERG, AARON, psychobiologist; b. Montreal, Que., Can., Oct. 12, 1953; came to U.S., 1980; s. Bernard and Rosa (Shaffer) E.; B.A., Concordia U., 1975; M.A., McGill U., 1977, Ph.D., 1980; m. Ina Dale Greenspon, Aug. 26, 1978. Research scientist A.V. Davis Center for Behavioral Neurobiology, The Salk Inst., San Diego, Calif., 1980-82; asst. prof. dept. psychology U. Calif., Santa Barbara, 1982—; guest lectr. U. Calif., San Diego, 1980-82. Recipient J.W. Bridges Medal for Psychology, 1975; Nat. Research Council fellow, 1976-79, Que. provincial fellow, 1976, 78, 79, Med. Research Council Can. fellow, 1980, 81. Mem. Am. Psychol. Assn., Soc. Neuroscis., Canadian Psychol. Assn. Contbr. articles in field to profl. jours. Office: Dept Psychology U Calif Santa Barbara CA 93106

ETTER, DELORES MARIA, elec. engr., educator; b. Denver, Sept. 25, 1947; d. Murvin Lee and Janice Van Camp; student Okla. State U., 1965-67; student U. Tex., Arlington, 1968; B.S., Wright State U., 1970, M.S., 1972; Ph.D., U. N.Mex., 1979; m. Jerry Richard Etter, Sept. 9, 1967; 1 dau., Amy Marie. Lectr., elec. engring.-computer engring. dept. U. N.Mex., 1973-77, program dir. Coll. Engring., 1977-79, asst. prof. elec. engring.-computer engring., 1979-82, asso. prof., 1982—; research faculty asso. Sandia Labs., summers 1978, 79; cons. computer engring., signal processing. Faculty advisor student chpt. Soc. Women Engrs., 1979, 80, 81; asst. leader Chaparral council Girl Scouts U.S.A., 1979—. NSF grantee, 1981. Mem. IEEE, AAAS, Am. Soc. Engring. Edn., Sigma Xi, Tau Beta Pi, Eta Kappa Nu. Phi Kappa Phi. Republican. Contbr. articles to tech. jours. Office: Elec Engring/Computer Engring Dept U New Mexico

ETTINGER, STEPHEN JOEL, veterinarian; b. Queens, N.Y., Feb. 28, 1941; s. Samuel and Charlotte (Adler) E.; D.V.M., Cornell U., 1964; children—Nicole Lynn, Andrew David. Intern, med. resident Animal Med. Ctr., N.Y.C., NIH postdoctoral fellow in cardiology, 1966-68, mem. staff, 1968-71; veterinarian Berkeley (Calif.) Vet. Med. Group, 1971-79; veterinarian, internal medicine and cardiology Calif. Animal Hosp., Los Angeles, 1979—; sci. cons. Hills Pet Products, Topeka, Kans.; clin. prof. vet. medicine U. Calif., Davis, until 1980. Pres. Berkeley Vet. Research Found. Recipient Bourgelet award as Internat. Vet. of Yr., London, 1980; diplomate Am. Coll. Vet. Internal Medicine. Fellow Am. Coll. Cardiology, Am. Coll. Vet. Pharmacology; mem. Acad. Vet. Cardiology (pres. 1975-77), Am. Coll. Vet. Internal Medicine (bd. regents 1975-78, pres. splty. of cardiology 1974-78). Author: Canine Cardiology, 1970. Editor: A Textbook of Veterinary Internal Medicine, 1975, 2d edit., 1983. Contbr. articles to profl. jours. Office: 1736 S Sepulveda Blvd Los Angeles CA 90025

ETTL, DOROTHY ANNE, home economist; b. Marysville, Calif., Apr. 19, 1943; d. Walter Joseph and Celia Marie (Hill) E. B.S., U. Calif.-Davis, 1964; M.S., Tex. Tech. U., 1969; postgrad. U. Hawaii, summer 1970, Chadron State Coll., summer 1971; Ph.D., U. Minn., 1976. Niobrara County extension home economist U. Wyo., Lusk, 1964-67; asst. prof. home econs. Calif. State U.-Chico, 1969-73; extension clothing specialist Wash. State U., Pullman, 1976—. Mem. Assn. Faculty Women Wash. State U., Am. Home Econs. Assn., Wash. Home Econs. Assn., Pullman Home Econs. Assn., Assn. Coll. Profs. Textiles and Clothing, Epsilon Sigma Phi, Omicron Nu, Phi Upsilon Omicron. Columnist, Lusk Herald, 1964-67. Office: 301 F Ag Phase II Wash State U Pullman WA 99164

EU, MARCH KONG FONG, state ofcl.; b. Oakdale, Calif., Mar. 29, 1927; d. Yuen and Shiu (Shee) Kong; student Salinas Jr. Coll.; B.S., U. Calif., Berkeley; M.Ed., Mills Coll., 1951; Ed.D., Stanford, 1956; postgrad. Columbia U., Calif. State Coll., Hayward; m. Henry Eu; children by previous marriage—Matthew Kipling Fong, Marchesa Suyin Fong You; stepchildren—Henry, Adeline, Yvonne, Conroy, Alaric. Chmn. div. dental hygiene U. Calif. Med. Center, San Francisco; dental hygienist Oakland (Calif.) Pub. Schs.; supr. dental health edn. Alameda County (Calif.) Schs.; lectr. health edn. Mills Coll., Oakland; mem. Calif. Assembly, 1966-74, chmn. com. on employment and public employees, 1973-74, chmn. select com. on agr., foods and nutrition, 1973-74; sec. of state Calif., Sacramentao, 1975—. Spl. cons. Bur. Intergroup Relations, Calif. Dept. Edn.; endl., legislative cons. Mem. Alameda County Bd. Edn., 1956-66, pres., 1961-62, legis. adv., 1963; mem. budget panel Bay Area United Fund Crusade, Oakland Econ. Devel. Council, Citizens Com. Housing, Council Social Planning, Calif. Econ. Devel. Commn., Calif. Interagency Council Family Planning, Fair Oaks Bus. and Profl. Women's Club; edn. chmn., mem. council social planning dir. Baymont Dist. Community Council, Oakland Area; charter pres., hon. life mem. Howard Elementary Sch. PTA; charter pres. Chinese Young Ladies Soc. Oakland; mem., vice chmn. adv. com. Youth Study Centers and Ford Found. Interagency Project, 1962-63; chmn. Alameda County Mother's March, 1971-72; mem. adv. Compensatory Edn. Commn., Adv. Commn. Status of Women; mem. exec. com. Calif. Democratic Central Com., mem. central com., 1963-70; asst. sec., del. Dem. Nat. Conv., 1968; dir. 8th Congl. Dist. Dem. Council, 1963; v.p. Dems. of 8th Congl. Dist., 1963; dir. Key Women for Kennedy, 1963; women's vice chmn. No. Calif. Johnson for Pres., 1964. Bd. dirs. Oakland YWCA, 1965. Recipient ann. award for outstanding achievement Eastbay Intercultural Fellowship, 1959; Phoebe Apperson Hearst Distinguished Bay Area Woman of Year award, 1967; Merit citation Calif. Assn. Adult Edn. Adminstrs., 1970, also numerous awards for outstanding leadership, public and legis. service, and contbns. to fields of public health and edn.; cert. in health and devel. edn., gen. secondary edn., jr. coll. edn., secondary adminstrn. and supervision, State of Calif. Mem. Am. (life, pres. 1956-57), No. Calif. (life) dental hygienists assns., Oakland League Women Voters, AAUW (area rep. in edn. Oakland br.), Calif. Tchrs. Assn. (mem. study panel Profl. Standards Commn. 1965), Calif., Alameda County (pres. 1965) sch. bds. assns., Nat. Women's Polit. Caucus, Delta Kappa Gamma. Office: Sec State 1230 J St Sacramento CA 95814*

EUELL, JULIAN THOMAS, museum administrator; b. N.Y.C., May 23, 1929; s. Thomas Bass and Helen Lillian (Adams) E.; m. Dolores Lolita Brown; children—Julian Thomas Jr., Juliette, Dana, Denise, Simeon, Miles; m. 2d, Barbara Jean Tiggs, Mar. 5, 1967. B.S. in Sociology, N.Y.U.; postgrad. Columbia U., Julliard Sch. Music, George Washington U. Counselor, Essex County Youth House, Neward, N.Y., 1956-59; profl. jazz musician, 1959-62; dir. arts and culture dept. HARYOU-ACT, Inc., 1962-66; cons. N.Y.C. Anti-Poverty Com., 1966, Nat. Found. of Arts and Humanities, Washington, 1966, Whitney Mus. Am. Art, N.Y.C., 1966-67; dir. arts program and adolescent services Einstein Coll. Medicine, 1967-70; program mgr., cons. Smithsonian Instn., Washington, 1968-73, asst. sec. for pub. service, 1973-82; dir. The Oakland (Calif.) Mus., 1982—. Bd. dirs. NAACP Legal Def. and Ednl. Fund; mem. exec. com. Reading is Fundamental; mem. jazz panel Nat. Endowment for the Arts; mem. music panel D.C. Commn. on Arts and Humanities. Served with AUS, 1947-48. Recipient Martin Luther King award. Mem. Am. Fedn. Musicians, Fgn. Student Service Council, Nat. Trust Historic Preservation, Am. Assn. Museums, Internat. Council Museums. Democrat. Club: Rotary (Oakland). Contbr. articles to profl. jours. Office: 1000 Oak St Oakland CA 94607

EUSTAQUIO, AURORA CORTEZ, multicultural educator; b. Manila, Philippines, Nov. 20, 1938; s. Cosme Domingo Cortez and Macaria Lagman Mascarenas-Cortez; m. Nereo Guanlao Pecson, May 12, 1928; children—Arner, Nereo Cortez, Ma Aurita; m. 2d, Ildefonso Landicho Eustaquio, May 7, 1945; 1 son, Joseph Cortez. M.A., MLQ U., 1966; M.Ed., U. Nev.-Reno, 1973. Elem. head tchr., asst. prin. Philippine Schs., 1964-66; librarian, ESL instr. Heald Coll., San Francisco, 1966-69; elem. sch. tchr. St. Albert Parochial Sch., Reno, 1969-70; sch. tchr., reading specialist Washoe Sch. Dist., Reno, 1970-75; dir. Sun Valley Children's Ctr., Sparks, Nev., 1974-78; coordinator adult basic edn., Truckee Meadows Community Coll., Reno, 1977—. Chmn. No. Nev. Literacy Council, 1978—; Nev. state rep., communications com. Laubach Literacy Action, N.Y.C., 1980—. Recipient Plaque, 1981; U.S. Dept. Edn. scholar U. San Francisco, 1982-83. Mem. Internat. Reading Assn., Bus. and Profl. Women's Club, Adult Basic Edn. Assn. Mountain Plains, Women for Good Govt., Nev. Assn. Community Edn. (pres. 1983, plaque for outstanding work in community edn. 1981). Republican. Roman Catholic. Co-author: American Citizenship Handbood, 1981, revised edit., 1982.

EUSTIS, JOHN MORRIS, III, police officer, lawyer; b. Sacramento, July 31, 1936; s. John Morris, Jr. and Genevieve Claire (Pausback) E.; A.A., Sacramento City Coll., 1964; student McGeorge Sch. Law, U. of Pacific, 1964-68; m. Sandra Kay Gallagher, Nov. 1, 1961; children—Patrick Casey, Steven Matthew, Joseph Raymond. Dep. sheriff, Sacramento County, 1959-74; admitted to Calif. bar, 1970; practice law, Sacramento, 1974—. Police legal adviser, legis. advisor Sacramento

Sheriff's Dept., 1970-74, also chmn. professionalization and ethics com.; adviser Calif. Peace Officers Assn. Project dir. Calif. Uniform Warrant Study. Served with USAF, 1955-58. Mem. Calif. Peace Officers Assn. (mem. law and legis. coms., vice chmn. membership com. 1970-74), Calif. State Sheriffs Assn., Footprinters Internat. Assn. Republican. Roman Catholic. Home: PO Box 13392 Sacramento CA 95813 Office: 1000 Fulton Ave 58 Sacramento CA 95825

EVANS, BARBARA MALKIN, marketing executive; b. N.Y.C.; d. Samuel and Edna (Gurner) Hirsch; m. Fred J. Evans, July 5, 1974; children—Theodore Andrew, Samantha Noelle. B.A., Boston U., 1961; postgrad. Carnegie Mellon U., 1962. Assoc. creative dir. Ogilvy & Mather, Inc., N.Y.C., 1964-67; creative mgr. Avon Products, Inc., N.Y.C., 1970-73; founder, pres. Ideas Unltd., Inc., Los Angeles, 1975-79; creative dir. Vidal Sassoon, Inc., Los Angeles, 1980—. Recipient Gold and Silver medal N.Y. Internat. Film Festival, 1965. Mem. Speakers Bur., Pub. Relations Soc. Am., Fashion Group (dir., chmn. pub. relations com.), Publicity Club Los Angeles, Art Dirs. Club. Clubs: Sand and Sea, Marina City. Sand and Sea (Santa Monica); Marina City (Marina del Rey). Home: PO Box 69407 Beverly Hills CA 90069 Office: 2049 Century Park E Suite 3800 Los Angeles CA 90067

EVANS, BILL (JAMES WILLIAM), dancer, choreographer, educator, arts adminstr.; b. Lehi, Utah, Apr. 11, 1940; s. William Ferdinand and Lila (Snape) E.; B.A. in English, U. Utah, 1963, M.F.A., 1970; dance student various pvt. dance schs. and studios; m. Aug. 27, 1962 (div. 1965); 1 dau., Thais. Profl. ballet dancer, Salt Lake City, N.Y.C., Chgo., 1965-67; mem., choreographer, artistic coordinator Utah Repertory Dance Theatre, U. Utah, 1967-75; founder, artistic dir. Bill Evans Dance Co., Salt Lake City, 1975-76, Seattle, 1976—; founder, tchr., artistic dir. Bill Evans Dance/Seattle Sch., 1977—; founder Seattle Summer Inst. and Festival of Dance, 1977—; free-lance dancer, 1969—, including Berlin Ballet, 1969, Jacob's Pillow Dance Festival, Lee, Mass., 1973, Harvard U., 1973, 74; choreographer numerous works for various ballet and modern dance cos., 1967—; dance/movement specialist Artist-in-Schs. program Nat. Endowment for Arts; guest prof. dance U. Wash., 1979-81; Am. Arts Alliance rep. before House and Senate appropriations coms., 1979. Served as officer U.S. Army, 1963-65. Recipient various choreographic awards, including from Nat. Endowment for Arts, 1972-75, 77, 78. Western States Arts Found., 1975, Utah Bicentennial Com., 1976; Guggenheim fellow, 1976-77; recipient Teaching Plaudit award Nat. Dance Assn., 1981. Mem. Dancers, Inc. (adv. bd.). Creator Evans technique for tng. body. Home: 1221 Minor Ave #1010 Seattle WA 98101 Office: 704 19th Ave E Seattle WA 98112

EVANS, DANIEL DONALD, hydrology educator, consultant; b. Oak Hill, Ohio, Aug. 13, 1920; s. Thomas H. and Mary Jane (Jenkins) E.; m. Frances Louise Merdink, Jan. 26, 1923; children—Robert Keith, Thomas George, Roger Alan, Susan Mary Evans Fisher. B.S., Ohio State U., 1947; M.S., Iowa State U., 1949, Ph.D., 1952. Research assoc., asst. prof. Iowa State U., Ames, 1950-53; assoc. prof. hydrology Oreg. State U., Corvallis, 1953-60, prof., 1960-63; prof. hydrology and water resources U. Ariz., Tucson, 1963—; cons. Govt. Kenya, 1960-62; pvt. practice water resources consulting. Served with U.S. Army, 1942-45. Fellow Soil Sci. Soc. Am., Am. Soc. Agronomy, Am. Water Resources Assn.; mem. Am. Geophys. Union, Internat. Assn. Hydrogeologists, AAAS, Sigma Xi, Gamma Sigma Delta. Presbyterian. Contbr. chpts. to books and articles to profl. jours. Home: 5845 N Mina Vista Tucson AZ 85718 Office: Dept Water Resources U Ariz Tucson AZ 85721

EVANS, DAVID CANNON, computer company executive; b. Salt Lake City, Feb. 24, 1924; s. David Woolley and Beatrice (Cannon) E.; m. Joy Frewin, Mar. 21, 1947; children—Gayle Scheidel, Susan Foote, David F., Anne Brown, Peter F., Douglas F., Katherine. B.S., U. Utah, 1949, Ph.D. in Physics, 1953. With computer div. Bendix Corp., 1962-66, dir. engring. research and devel.; mem. faculty ele. engring. and computer sci. U. Calif.-Berkeley, 1962-65; mem. faculty, chmn. dept. computer sci. U. Utah; co-founder, pres. Evans & Sutherland Computer Corp., Salt Lake City, 1968—, chmn. bd., dir.; dir. Comml. Security Bank, VLSI Tech. Inc. Served with U.S. Army, 1942-45. Named to Computer Hall of Fame. Fellow IEEE; mem. Nat. Acad. Engring. Republican. Mormon. Office: PO Box 8700 Salt Lake City UT 84108

EVANS, DON ALAN, hospital administrator; b. Jerome, Ariz., June 22, 1948; s. Rulon C. and Berniece (Ensign) E.; m. Susan Dahl, June 3, 1972; children—Emily, Austin, Adrienne, Alan. B.B.A., Ariz. State U., 1972; M.S. in Health Adminstrn., U. Colo., 1974. Dir. hosp. and clin. services Nat. Jewish Hosp. and Research Center, Denver, 1974-80; asst. adminstr. LDS Hosp., Salt Lake City, 1980—. Mem. Am. Coll. Hosp. Adminstrs., Pi Kappa Delta, Beta Gamma Sigma. Republican. Mem. Ch. Jesus Christ of Latter-day Saints. Home: 1163 E 1900 S Bountiful UT 84010 Office: 325 8th Ave Salt Lake City UT 84143

EVANS, ELLIS DALE, educator, psychologist; b. Topeka, Nov. 6, 1934; s. Ellis Meredith and Ruth Alice (Burchinal) E.; B.Music Edn., U. Kans., 1956; M.S. in Edn., Ind. U., 1962, Ed.D., 1964; m. Cynthia Ann McClure, Dec. 23, 1961; children—Jennifer Ann, Alicia Ruth. Tchr., Shawnee Mission, Kans., 1957; field rep. Delta Upsilon, 1960-61; research asst., teaching asso. Ind. U., 1961-64; mem. faculty U. Wash., 1964—, prof. ednl. psychology, 1971—; spl. instr. Shoreline Community Coll., Seattle, 1973-75; cons. editor Charles Merrill Pub. Co.; cons. in field. Active local music orgns., Shoreline Schs. Served to capt. USAF, 1957-60. Fellow U.S. Office Edn., 1970-71. Mem. Western Psychol. Assn., Am. Ednl. Research Assn., Nat. Assn. Edn. Young Children, Nat. Soc. for Study of Edn., Soc. for Research in Child Devel., Phi Delta Kappa, Omicron Delta Kappa, Delta Upsilon. Author: Development and Classroom Learning, 1973; Children and Youth: Psychosocial Development, 1973, rev. edit., 1978; Contemporary Influences in Early Childhood Education, 1975; The Transition to Teaching, 1976; also articles. Home: 19045 46th St NE Seattle WA 98155

EVANS, ERSEL ARTHUR, manufacturing company executive; b. Trenton, Nebr., July 17, 1922; s. Arthur E. and Mattie Agnes (Perkins) E.; B.A., Reed Coll., 1947; Ph.D. (Research Corp. Am. fellow, DuPont fellow), Oreg. State U., 1951; m. Patricia A. Powers, Oct. 11, 1945; children—Debra Lynn (dec.). Paul Arthur. Sr. engr. nuclear fuel devel. Gen. Electric Co., Richland, Wash., 1951-55, mgr. ceramic fuels group, 1956-64, mgr. plutonium fuels devel. Vallecitos Lab., Pleasanton, Calif., 1964-67; mgr. fuels and materials dept. Battelle Meml. Inst., Richland, 1967-70; mgr. fuels and materials dept. Westinghouse Electric Corp., Richland, Wash., 1970-71, mgr. materials tech. dept., 1971-73, mgr. materials dept., 1973-76; v.p. Westinghouse Hanford Co., 1977—; assoc. dir. Hanford Engring. Devel. Lab., Richland, 1972-76, tech. dir., Tech. Mgmt. Center, Reactor Fuels and Materials, 1979-80, Applied Systems Devel., 1980—. Bd. dirs. ARC; mem. coop. research com. dept. chemistry U. Wash., 1974—; mem. fusion adv. panel Congressional Fusion Adv. Panel, 1978—; mem. Tech. Assistance and Adv. Group for Three Mile Island. Bd. dirs. Mid-Columbia Mental Health Center; mem. vis. com. U. Wash. Coll. Engring. Served with USNR, 1943-45. Recipient Westinghouse Order of Merit, 1975; registered profl. engr., Calif. Fellow Am. Nuclear Soc. (Spl. Merit award 1964 Exceptional Service award 1980), Am. Inst. Chem. Engrs., Am. Soc. for Metals, Am. Ceramic Soc.; mem. Nat. Acad. Engring., Phi Kappa Phi. Contbr. articles to profl. jours., books. Patentee in field. Home: 2033 Weiskopf Ct Richland WA 99352 Office: Westinghouse Hanford Co PO Box 1970 Richland WA 99352

EVANS, FRED J., plastic extrusion co. exec.; b. Chgo., June 27, 1937; s. Sam J. and Ethel (Weiss) Levin; B.S.C., DePaul U., Chgo., 1958; J.D., Northwestern U., 1961; m. Barbara Hirsch, July 5, 1973; children—Jennifer Jill, John Abraham, Theodore Andrew, Samantha Noelle. Admitted to Ill. bar, 1961; pres. No. Life Ins. Co., Seattle, 1971-73, N.Y. Services, Inc., 1973-78; exec. v.p. Am. Custom Coachworks, 1978-80; pres. J.W. Carroll & Sons, Inc., Carson, Calif., 1980-82, Kennedy, Fitzgerald, Inc., Los Angeles, 1982—. Served with USAF, 1962-66. Democrat. Jewish. Clubs: Marina City, Sand and Sea. Home: PO Box 69407 Los Angeles CA 90069 Office: 6222 Wilshire Blvd Los Angeles CA 90048

EVANS, GARY WILLIAM, social ecology educator; b. Summit, N.J., Nov. 22, 1948; s. Roger and Mary (Conover) E. A.B. with high honors, Colgate U., 1971; M.S., U. Mass., 1973, Ph.D. in Psychology, 1975. With VISTA, 1968-69; co-founder, dir. Vol. Bur., draft counselor, co-founder, counselor Drug Crisis Clinic, Colgate U., 1969-71, resident advisor, 1969-70, head resident advisor, 1970-71; assoc. dir. undergrad. affairs Program in Social Ecology, U. Calif.-Irvine, 1979-81, asst. prof. social ecology, 1975-80, assoc. prof., 1980—; research asst. psychology Colgate U., 1969-71; research assoc. Inst. Man and Environ., U. Mass., 1971-73, instr. psychology and Bklyn. Career Opportunities Program, 1973-75; conf. presenter. Univ. scholar, 1966-71; George Cobb fellow, 1970; recipient Disting. Teaching Asst. award U. Mass., 1974; NSF dissertation yr. fellow, 1974-75; Regents Jr. Faculty fellow U. Calif., 1977; recipient Fulbright award Council Internat. Exchange of Scholars, U. Poona (India), 1981-82; recipient numerous research and ednl. grants. Fellow Am. Psychol. Assn. Editorial rev. bd. Rep. Research in Social Psychology, 1973-75, Man-Environ. Systems, 1975—, Environ. Psychology and Nonverbal Behavior, 1976-79, Jour. Population and Environ., 1981—; ad hoc reviewer NSF, NIH, numerous jours.; contbr. articles profl. jours. Office: Program in Social Ecology U Calif Irvine CA 92717

EVANS, HANNAH IMOGENE, psychologist; b. Richmond, Va., Nov. 6, 1945; d. Charles and Ruth (Powell) E.; B.A., U. Vt., 1967; M.S., Pa. State U., 1970, Ph.D., 1972; M.P.A., U. Colo., Denver, 1981; m. Robert F. McKenzie, July 12, 1975. Clin. psychology intern, psychol. cons. II, Denver Dept. Health and Hosps., 1972-77; adj. faculty U. Colo., Denver, summer 1978; resource counselor Regional Transp. Dist., 1978-79; pvt. practice psychotherapy, Denver, 1976—. Mem. community adv. bd. Sch. Profl. Psychology, U. Denver; mem. grievance com. Colo. Supreme Ct., 1982—; mem. transp. group Project Colo., 1982—; mem. Gov.'s Front Range Task Force, 1980-81; bd. dirs. Denver Sexual Assault Council, 1974-80; founding bd. Colo. Center Women and Work, 1979-81; mem. Women's Forum of Colo., 1979—, selection com., 1980—. USPHS fellow, 1968-70; named one of Faces of Colo., Colo. mag., 1976. Mem. Am. Psychol. Assn., Colo. Psychol. Assn., Colo. Women Psychologists, Rocky Mountain Road Runners. Club: Phiddipides Track. Contbr. articles to profl. jours. and popular mags. Office: 60 Kearney St Denver CO 80220

EVANS, JERRY LEE, state supt. edn.; b. Cascade, Idaho, Sept. 6, 1931; s. Ivan Lee and Verna Luella E.; B.S. Ed., U. Idaho, 1953; M.S., Oreg. State U., 1961; m. Phyllis Norene LaVoy, Apr. 13, 1952; children—Andrew Lee, Catherine Marie, Vicki Susan. Tchr., coach high sch., 1953-54; tchr., prin. high sch., 1956-60; supt. Sch. Dist. 422, Cascade, Idaho and Sch. Dist. 132, Caldwell, Idaho, 1960-75; dep. supt. public instrn. Idaho State Dept. Edn., Boise, 1975-78, supt. public instrn., 1979—; mem. Idaho Land Bd., Edn. Commn. of the States. Served with USAF, 1954-56. Mem. Council Chief State Sch. Officers, Am. Assn. Sch. Adminstrs. Republican. Club: Masons. Office: Len B Jordan Office Bldg Dept Edn Idaho Boise ID 83720

EVANS, JOHN JOSEPH, mgmt. cons.; b. St. Louis, Mar. 1, 1940; s. Roy Joseph and Henrietta Frances (Schweizer) E.; B.A., Centenary Coll., 1962; postgrad. Syracuse U., 1969, U. Wis., 1971, Harvard U. Bus. Sch., 1971-73; M.B.A., Pepperdine U., 1972; m. Jennie Trees Nutt, Dec. 19, 1962 (div.); children—Todd, Karlyn, Jane, Mark. Pres., chief exec. officer Evans Distbg. Cos., La., 1962-72; pres. Evans & Co., 1968—; gen. mgr. Agmet, Inc., La. Wire & Cable, 1976-77; mgr. Qwip Systems div. Exxon Enterprises, Los Angeles, 1977-78; adj. prof. Centenary Coll. Bd. dirs. La. Real Estate Trust, Caddo Parish Red Cross, Mental Health Assn.; trustee Grad. Sch. Sales Mgmt. and Mktg.; pres. La. Real Estate Investment Trust; pres. North La. Mental Health Hosp. Bd. Mem. Nat. Beer Wholesalers' Assn. (adv. dir.), Sales and Mktg. Execs. of Shreveport (pres.), SW Sales and Mktg. Execs. Council (pres.), Young Pres.' Orgn., Conf. Bd., Aspen Inst., Sales and Mktg. Execs. Internat., Am. Soc. Tng. and Devel., Am. Soc. Personnel Adminstrn., Personnel and Indsl. Relations Assn. (vice chmn. 1982—), Syracuse U. Grad. Sch. Sales Mgmt. and Mktg. Alumni Assn. (pres. 1974-75, trustee 1975—), Westlake Village C. of C. (v.p. 1981), Pi Sigma Epsilon. Republican. Episcopalian. Clubs: Shreveport Country, Century (Fort Worth); North Ranch Country, Pierremont Oaks Tennis, Cotillion, Shreveport; Ariz. (Phoenix). Office: CPI Box 26260 San Diego CA 92126

EVANS, JOHN THORNLEY, lawyer; b. Salt Lake City, Mar. 14, 1938; s. Richard L. and Alice (Thornley) E. J.D., U. Utah, 1965. Bar: Utah 1965. Law clk. to chief justice Utah Supreme Ct., 1964-65; dep. atty. Salt Lake County, 1965-66; asst. atty. gen. State of Utah, Salt Lake City, 1968-73; ptnr. Clyde & Pratt, Salt Lake City, 1968-80; sole practice, Salt Lake City, 1980—; registered rep. Security Nat. Investment Corp., Salt Lake City, 1980—; speaker, lectr. numerous seminars, convs. law enforcement, legal groups. Active Greater Salt Lake council Boy Scouts Am., 1967—, Explorer post adv., 1967-69, neighborhood commr., 1969-71, chmn. fund drive, 1982, 83. Republican conv. del. Salt Lake County, 1968, 74, State of Utah, 1978. Served as staff sgt. M.C., U.S. Army, 1961-62. Mem. ABA, Utah State Bar (exec. com. Young Lawyers sect. 1965-67, chmn. condemnation sect. 1973-74), Nat. Assn. Securities Dealers, Salt Lake County Bar Assn., Phi Delta Phi. Home: 1032 Douglas Salt Lake City UT 84105 Office: Security Nat Investment Corp 455 E 400 S Suite 103 Salt Lake City UT 84111

EVANS, JOHN VICTOR, gov. Idaho; b. Malad City, Idaho, Jan. 18, 1925; s. David Lloyd and Margaret (Thomas) E.; B. Bus. and Econs., Stanford U., 1951; m. Lola Daniels, 1945; children—David L., John Victor, Martha Anne, Susan Dee, Thomas Daniels. Mem. Idaho Senate, 1953-59, 67-74, majority leader, 1957-59, minority ldr., 69-74; mayor City of Malad City, 1960-66; lt. gov. State of Idaho, 1975-76, gov., 1977—; chmn. Western Gov.'s Conf., 1978—; past v.p., dir. J.N. Ireland Bank, Malad City; past v.p. Bear River Water Users; past pres. Deep Creek Irrigation Co., Oneida R.C. & D. Served with inf., AUS, 1944-46; PTO. Recipient Disting. Service award for meritorious service during legis. career Assn. Idaho Cities, 1974. Mem. Nat. Govs. Assn. (chmn. nuclear power subcom., Co-chmn. agrl. subcom. on rangeland mgmt., mem. exec. com), Am. Legion (vice chmn. nat. disting. guests com. 1977—), Western Gov.'s Conf. (vice chmn. 1977—), VFW, Farm Bur. Democrat. Mormon. Clubs: Masons; Eagles; Kiwanis. Office: Statehouse Boise ID 83720*

EVANS, JUNIUS ANTHONY, physician; b. Festus, Mo., Aug. 13, 1911; s. George James and Daisy (Keiser) E.; A.B. in Chemistry, U. Tex., 1937, B.S. in Pharmacy, 1939, M.D., 1943; m. Josephine Van Zandt, Nov. 28, 1936; children—Martha Ellen (Mrs. Metarelis), Mary Daisy (Mrs. Everhart), Junius Anthony Jr. Intern U.S. Marine Hosp., New Orleans, 1943-44; resident No. Mich. Tb San., Gaylord, Mich., USPHS, Washington, 1945-46, U. Ark., VA Hosps. Little Rock and North Little Rock, 1960-62; career officer USPHS, 1943-47; pvt. practice medicine, Las Vegas, N.Mex., 1947-60; specializing in dermatology, Roswell, N.Mex., 1962—; formerly chief of staff Las Vegas, St. Anthony hosps. (both Las Vegas); staff mem. St. Mary's Hosp.; chief of staff Eastern N.Mex. Med. Center, Roswell, 1968-69; clin. asso. dermatology U. N.Mex., 1974—. Served from ensign to lt. USCG, 1943-46; capt. Res. Mem. Chaves County, N.Mex. (councillor 1956-59, mem. pub. relations com. 1963-73, chmn. pub. relations com. 1963-64, ho. of dels. 1969—, mem. liaison com. to allied professions 1972-74) med. socs., Am., N.Mex. (pres. 1958) thoracic socs., Am. Acad. Dermatology, N.Mex. Tb Assn. (dir. 1950-62), Am. Acad. Tb Physicians, Am. Cancer Soc. (v.p. 1970, chmn. service com. N.Mex. div. 1965-70), Chaves County Cancer Soc. (dir. 1965-79), Am. Council Med. Staffs (regional dir. S.W. area 1972—, pres. N.Mex. council 1972-74), Assn. Am. Physicians and Surgeons, N.Mex. (dir.), Chaves County (pres. 1970-71) heart assns., S.W. Dermatol Soc. (pres. 1966-67), N.Mex. Dermatol. Soc., Rho Chi, Theta Kappa Psi. Mason (Shriner), Rotarian. Home: 2200 Palomar Dr Roswell NM 88201 Office: 207 N Union St PO Box 1226 Roswell NM 88201

EVANS, KAREN LOUISE, editor; b. Boulder, June 28, 1947; d. Calvin Edmond and Louise Wigton E.; m. Edward Klamm, June 13, 1980. B.A., U. Colo., 1964. Staff writer, asst. editor Scholastic Mags., N.Y.C., 1965-67; stringer Newsweek mag., San Francisco, 1967-69, Hong Kong, 1969-72; spl. programs coordinator Foremost-McKesson, San Francisco, 1972-75; sr. editor San Francisco mag., 1975-76; asso. editor Outside mag., San Francisco, 1976-77; feature writer San Francisco Chronicle, 1978; sr. editor, editor Rocky Mountain mag., Denver, 1979-80; editor spl. sects. Santa Fe Reporter, 1980-81; contbr. Denver Post, 1982-83; sr. editor New Mexico mag., 1983—. Recipient 2d pl. award newspaper supplements Nat. Newspaper Assn., 1981. Mem. Nat. Fedn. Press Women (2d place award lifestyle sects. 1980), N.Mex. Press Women (1st place award lifestyle sects. 1981, 2d place award page makeup 1981, 1st place award spl. supplements, 1981). Author: The Hong Kong Shopper, 1972. Home: 110 W Houghton St Santa Fe NM 87501 Office: Bataan Meml Bldg Santa Fe NM 87503

EVANS, LAWRENCE JACK, JR., lawyer; b. Oakland, Calif., Apr. 4, 1921; s. Lawrence Jack and Eva May (Dickinson) E.; diplomate Near East Sch. Theology, 1950; M.A., Am. U. Beirut, 1951; Ph.D., Brantridge Forest Sch., Sussex, Eng., 1968; J.D., Ariz. State U., 1971; grad. Nat. Jud. Coll., 1974; m. Marjorie Hisken, Dec. 23, 1944; children—Daryl S. Kleweno, Richard L., Shirley J. Coursey, Donald B. Served as enlisted man U.S. Navy, 1938-41, U.S. Army, 1942-44; commd. 2d lt. U.S. Army, 1944, advanced through grades to lt. col., 1962; mem. Airborne Command Post Study Group, Joint Chiefs of Staff, 1967; ops. staff officer J-3 USEUCOM, 1965-68; ret., 1968; admitted to Ariz. bar, 1971; individual practice law, cons. Near and Middle Eastern affairs, Tempe, Ariz., 1971-72, 76-77; chief hearing officer Ariz. Corp. Commn., Phoenix, 1972-76; v.p., dir. Trojan Investment & Devel. Co., Inc., 1972-75. Chmn. legal and legis. com. Mayor's Com. to Employ Handicapped, Phoenix, 1971-75; active Tempe Leadership Conf., 1971-75, Ariz. Tax Conf., 1971-75; mem. adminstrv. law com., labor mgmt. relations com., unauthorized practice of law com. Ariz. State Bar; chmn. Citizens Against Corruption in Govt.; v.p., bd. dirs. Tempe Republican Men's Club, 1971-72; mem. Princeton Council Fgn. and Internat. Studies. Decorated Silver Star, Legion of Merit, Bronze Star, Purple Heart; named Outstanding Adminstrv. Law Judge for State Service for U.S., 1974. Mem. Nat. Rifle Assn. (life), Ranger Bns. Assn. World War II (life), U.S. Army Airborne Ranger Assn. (life), Mil. Order Purple Heart (life), Phi Delta Phi, Delta Theta Phi. Episcopalian. Club: Masons (32 deg.), KT. Author: Legal Aspects of Land Tenure in the Republic of Lebanon, 1951; (with Helen Miller Davis) International Constitutional Law, Electoral Laws and Treaties of the Near and Middle East, 1951; contbr. articles to mags., chpts. to books. Home: 539 E Erie Dr Tempe AZ 85282

EVANS, LEONARD ALBERT, educator; b. Ogden, Utah, July 11, 1932; s. George H. and Mathilda D. (Brockley) E.; B.S., U. Utah, 1957; M.S., U. Wis., 1959, Ph.D., 1961. Teaching and research asst. dept. psychology U. Wis., Madison, 1957-61; human factors specialist Gen. Electric Co., Syracuse, N.Y., 1961-64; specialist research N. Am. Aviation, Inc., Columbus, Ohio, 1964-67; mem. faculty dept. psychology Ohio State U., Columbus, 1965-66; mem. tech. staff N. Am. Rockwell Corp., Anaheim, Calif., 1967-70; asst. prof. med. edn. U. So. Calif. Sch. Medicine, Los Angeles, 1970-77, asso. prof. clin. med. edn., 1977—, coordinator instructional devel., 1975—; cons. Am. Heart Assn., Nat. Med. Ctr., Dallas, 1972—, Am. Cancer Soc., Los Angeles, 1978—. Served with USAF, 1950-53. Recipient Dart award U. So. Calif., 1975. Mem. Am. Psychol. Assn., Health Scis. Communication Assn., Sigma Xi, Phi Kappa Phi. Contbr. chpts to books, articles on med. edn. to profl. jours. Home: 1489 Poppy Peak Dr Pasadena CA 91105 Office: 1975 Zonal Ave Los Angeles CA 90033

EVANS, LOUISE, psychologist; b. San Antonio; d. Henry Daniel and Adela (Pariser) Evans; B.S. (Evansville, Ind., Central High Sch. PTA scholar 1945, Univ. scholar 1945), Northwestern U., 1949; M.S. in Psychology, Purdue U., 1952, Ph.D. in Clin. Psychology, 1955; m. Thomas Ross Gambrell, Feb. 23, 1960. Teaching asst. Purdue U., 1950-51; intern in clin. psychology, Menninger Found.-Topeka (Kans.) State Hosp., 1952-53; staff psychologist Kankakee (Ill.) State Hosp., 1954; USPHS-Menninger Found. postdoctoral fellow in child clin. psychology Menninger Clinic, Topeka, 1955-56; head child guidance clinic, staff psychologist Kings County (N.Y.) Hosp., Bklyn., 1957-58; instr. in med. psychology, dir. Barnes Hosp. Psychology Clinic, Washington U. Sch. Medicine, St. Louis, 1959; cons. Episcopal City Mission, St. Louis, 1959; pvt. practice clin. psychology, Fullerton, Calif., 1960—; psychol. cons. Fullerton Community Hosp., 1961—; staff cons. in clin. psychology Martin Luther Hosp., Anaheim, Calif., 1963—; lectr. in field; real estate developer; citrus grower. Recipient award Yuma County (Ariz.) Head Start Program, 1972. Diplomate in clin. psychology Am. Bd. Profl. Psychology. Fellow Internat. Council Psychologists (sec. 1962-64, 73-76, dir. 1977-79), Am. Psychol. Assn. (cons. div., mem.-at-large exec. bd. 1976-79), Royal Soc. Health, AAAS, Am. Orthopsychiat. Assn.; mem. Internat. Platform Assn., AAUP, Calif., Orange County (Calif.) (chmn. com. on ethics 1961-62), Los Angeles County psychol. assns., Orange County (pres. 1964-65), Los Angeles (exec. bd. 1966-67) socs. clin. psychologists, Am. Acad. Polit. Social Sci., Am. Pub. Health Assn., World Fedn. Mental Health, Am. Judicature Soc., Alumni Assn. Menninger Sch. Psychiatry, Center for Study of Presidency, Purdue U. Alumni Assn. (1 of 5 1st Citizenship awards 1975), Sigma Xi, Pi Sigma Phi. Office: 127 W Commonwealth Ave Fullerton CA 92632

EVANS, LYNETTE EILEEN, newspaper editor; b. Everett, Wash., Apr. 26, 1941; d. Delmer H. and Georgia Mary (Johnson) Buse; B.A., U. Wash., 1963; postgrad. U. Nev., Las Vegas, 1967-68; m. John Basil Evans, Nov. 10, 1962. Sch. tchr., Everett, Wash., 1963-64; police officer, Everett, Wash., 1964-65, teaching asst. U. Nev., Las Vegas, 1967-68; reporter, women's news editor Everett (Wash.) Herald, 1969-74; dir. Learning Center Tulalip Indian Tribes, 1974-75; Sunday mag. editor Las Vegas (Nev.) Sun, 1976; news dir. Foster's Daily Democrat, Dover, N.H., 1977-79; pub. Lake Tahoe News, South Lake Tahoe, Calif., 1979-83; mng. editor San Francisco Progress, 1983—; v.p. Buse Media, Inc., Everett, Wash. Mem. South Lake Tahoe Theatre Co. Guild, 1980—. Recipient State Writing awards Wash. Press Women, 1972. Mem. NOW, Nat. Newspaper Assn., Sigma Delta Chi, South Lake Tahoe C. of C. (dir. 1981-85). Author: (with George Burley) Roche

Harbor: A Saga in the San Juans, 1972. Home: 243 Byxbee San Francisco CA 94132 Office: 851 Howard San Francisco CA 94103

EVANS, MARGARET NIELSEN, technical editor; b. St. Paul, Mar. 7, 1926; d. Martin Karesgaard and Pearl Vivian (Mercer) Nielsen; m. Charles Deane Evans, Aug. 28, 1956; children—Paul, Eric; stepchildren—Richard, Mary Barbara. B.A. cum laude, U. Minn., 1948; postgrad. Iowa State U., 1955. Publs. editor, Inst. Agr., U. Minn., 1949-52; extension publs. editor Wash. State U., Pullman, 1952-56; assoc. editor Alaska Mag., Anchorage, 1972-74; tech. editor, Bur. of Land Mgmt., U.S. Dept. Interior, Alaska State Office, Anchorage, 1974-82; tech. editor, partner Peregrine Ventures, Anchorage, 1982—. Mem. Soc. Tech. Communication (founding moderator Greater Anchorage br.), Alaska Press Women, Sierra Club. Democrat. Unitarian. Club: Nordic Ski. Home and office: 6020 Trappers Trail Rd Box 110727 Anchorage AK 99511

EVANS, MARJORIE WOODARD, lawyer, scientist; b. Denver, Mar. 15, 1921; d. Raymond George and Mary (Garvin) Woodard; m. George W. Evans, Jan. 30, 1943 (dec.); children—George, Anne. A.B., U. Colo. 1942; Ph.D., U. Calif.-Berkeley, 1945; J.D., Stanford U., 1972. Bar: Calif. 1972. Scientist, Calif. Research Corp., Richmond, 1945-46; scientist, cons. N.Y. U., Princeton U., 1947-51; scientist Armour Research Found., Chgo., 1952-53; scientist, dir. lab. Stanford Research Inst., Menlo Park, Calif., 1953-69; dir. Poulter Lab., 1966-68, exec. dir. phys. sci., 1968-69; partner Evans Assos., Los Altos Hills, Calif., 1969-72; dir. Natomas Co., Rainier Bancorp., Rainier Nat. Bank; atty. and corporate cons. specializing in banking, and tech. Mem. Calif. Air Resources Bd., 1976-81; dir., chmn. program com. 12th Internat. Symposium on Combustion Inst., 1968-80; vice chmn. bd. regents U. Santa Clara, chmn. bd. visitors Sch. Law, 1980-82; bd. visitors, exec. com. Stanford U. Law Sch. Recipient Phoebe Hearst Distinguished Woman award, 1967, George Norlin award U. Colo., 1972, Centennial Alumnus award, 1976. Fellow AIAA; mem. Am. Bar Assn., Am. Chem. Soc., Am. Phys. Soc., Phi Beta Kappa, Sigma Xi, Delta Delta Delta. Contbr. numerous articles to sci. jours. Office: 2600 El Camino Real Suite 506 Palo Alto CA 94306

EVANS, MARY BURNETT, paralegal administrator; b. Munich, Germany, Jan. 11, 1948; d. William Howard and Martha Louise (Forbes) Burnett; m. Robert K. Evans, Nov. 16, 1974 (div.). B.F.A., U. N.Mex., 1971, grad. paralegal tng. course, 1975. With Burnett Ins. Agy., Inc., 1966-72; paralegal Threet & King, Albuquerque, 1972, specialist in civil litigation, 1972-82, exec. adminstr. mgmt., profl. mktg. and devel., 1982—. Vol. Bernalillo County Mental Health Ctr., 1980-81, mem. steering com., 1981—; mem. N.Mex. Council Crime and Delinquency. Mem. ABA, Legal Assts. N.Mex., Nat. Paralegal Assn., Nat. Legal Adminstrs. Assn., N.Mex. Legal Adminstrs. Assn., Albuquerque Symphony Women's Assn., Albuquerque Opera Guild, Friends of Art. Republican.

EVANS, MICHELE BEAL, educator; b. Salem, Oreg., Feb. 19, 1949; d. Paul Bellamy and Donna Lou (Hearing) Beal; student Willamette U., 1967-69; B.A., NYU, 1972; M.A., U. Madrid, 1973; teaching cert. Oreg. Coll. Edn., 1977; adminstrv. cert. Portland State U., 1983; m. Michael John Evans, Mar. 30, 1973. Bilingual aide Bush Elem. Sch., Salem, Oreg., 1974-76, bilingual tchr., 1976-78; secondary bilingual resource tchr. Salem Public Schs., 1978-80, bilingual program asst. Newcomer Center, 1980—; cons. in field, 1978—. Mem. Assn. Supervision and Curriculum Devel., Oreg. Assn. Bilingual Edn. (editor newsletter, 1978-79, corr. sec. 1980-82), NEA, Oreg. Edn. Assn., Salem Edn. Assn., Nat. Assn. Asian-Am. and Pacific Edn., Am. Assn. Tchrs. Spanish and Portuguese, Tchrs. of English to Speakers of Other Langs. Home: 11264 Summit Loop S E Turner OR 97392 Office: Salem Bd Edn 2825 Commercial St S E Salem OR 97302

EVANS, OAKLEY SPENCER, department stores executive; b. Springville, Utah, May 14, 1913; s. Shirl O. and Blanche Oakley (Graves) E.; A.B. summa cum laude in Bus. Adminstrn., Brigham Young U., 1935; m. Mabel Wilson, Sept. 14, 1935; children—Antoinette Evans Clark, Wendy Evans Ruppel, Christine, Julie Ann Evans Webster, Elizabeth. With J.C. Penney & Co., 1935-72, v.p., dir. corp. devel., dir., 1968-72, pres., dir., chmn. exec. com., mem. retirement com. Zion's Co-op Merc. Instn., Salt Lake City, 1973—; pres. Mormon Tabernacle Choir; dir., mem. exec. com. U & I Inc.; dir. Deseret Book Co., 1st Security Corp. Mem. nat. bd. advisers U. Utah Coll. Bus.; hon. bd. dirs. Better Bus. Bur. Salt Lake City; mem. Utah Am. Revolution Bicentennial Com.; mem. nat. adv. bd. Utah Symphony Orch. Mem. Nat. Retail Mchts. Assn. (dir.), Utah Retail Mchts. Assn. (pres.), Utah Taxpayers Assn. (dir., exec. com.), Salt Lake Area C. of C. (bd. govs.), Newcomen Soc. N. Am. Mormon. Clubs: Rotary, Country of Salt Lake, Alta, Timpanogos. Office: Tabernacle Choir 50 E North Temple St Salt Lake City UT 84150 Office: ZCMI 2200 S 900 W Salt Lake City UT 84137

EVANS, PAULINE (DAVIDSON), physicist; b. Bklyn., Mar. 24, 1922; d. John A. and Hannah (Brandt) Davidson; B.A., Hofstra Coll., 1942; postgrad. N.Y. U., 1943, 46-47, Cornell U., 1946, Syracuse U., 1947-50; m. Melbourne Griffith Evans, Sept. 6, 1950; children—Lynn Janet Evans Hannemann, Brian Griffith. Jr. physicist Signal Corps Ground Signal Service, Eatontown, N.J., 1942-43; physicist Kellex Corp. (Manhattan Project), N.Y.C., 1944; faculty dept. physics Queens Coll., N.Y.C., 1944-47; teaching asst. Syracuse U., 1947-50; instr. Wheaton Coll., Norton, Mass., 1952; physicist Nat. Bur. Standards, Washington, 1954-55; instr. physics U. Ala., 1955, U. N.Mex., 1955, 57-58; staff mem. Sandia Corp., Albuquerque, 1956-57; physicist Naval Nuclear Ordnance Evaluation Unit, Kirtland AFB, N.Mex., 1958-60; programmer Teaching Machines, Inc., Albuquerque, 1961; mem. faculty dept. physics Coll. St. Joseph on the Rio Grande (name changed to U. Albuquerque 1966), 1961—, assoc. prof., 1965—, chmn. dept., 1961—. Mem. Am. Phys. Soc., Am. Assn. Physics Tchrs., Fedn. Am. Scientists, AAUP, Sigma Pi Sigma, Sigma Delta Epsilon. Patentee in field. Home: 5801 Coors Rd SW Albuquerque NM 87105 Office: Dept Physics Univ of Albuquerque Albuquerque NM 87140

EVANS, RICHARD TAYLOR, missile research, engineering educator; b. Denver, July 2, 1940; s. Lawrence Taylor and Geraldine Edline (Shoemaker) E.; m. Mary Wilma Kalmar, Apr. 10, 1965; children—Christine Michelle, Richard Gregory; A.B., Columbia U., N.Y.C., 1962; B.S.E.E., U. Colo.-Boulder, 1964; M.S.E.E., Air Force Inst. Tech., Dayton, Ohio, 1969; Ph.D. in Aero. Engring., U. Tex.-Austin, 1980. Served to lt. col., USAF, 1965—; missile launch control officer, Malmstram AFB, Mont., 1965-69; guidance and control system project officer, Minuteman II & III, Norton AFB, Calif., 1969-74; Tech. Mgr., MX Guidance System On-site, C.S. Draper Lab, Mass., 1974-76; deputy dir. aerospace-mechanics sci. F. J. Seiler Research Lab, U.S. Air Force Academy, 1979—, instr., 1981—; instr. engring. U. Colo.-Colorado Springs, 1981—. Decorated 3 Commendation Medals, Combat Readiness. Cubmaster, Pack 65, Colorado Springs, 1982—. Mem. AIAA, Air Force Assn., Armed Forces Communications and Electronics Assn. Republican. Presbyterian. Contbr. articles to profl. jours. Home: 1740 Applewood Ridge Ct Colorado Springs CO 80907 Office: FJSRL/NH USAF Academy CO 80840

EVANS, ROBIN WAYNE, physicist; b. Lakeview, Oreg., Mar. 15, 1949; s. Robert K. and Doris K. (Kennedy) Whitlock; B.A. in Physics and Math. (Sr. Physics award 1972), Calif. State U., Sacramento, 1972; M.A. in Physics, U. Calif., Davis, 1974, Ph.D. in Physics, 1982. Teaching asst. U. Calif., Davis, 1972-80; mem. tech. staff Aerospace Corp., El Segundo, Calif., 1975-76, Eutek, Inc., Sacramento, 1976; instr. physics Calif. State U., Sacramento, 1979—. Mem. Sigma Xi, Sigma Pi Sigma. Office: Physics Dept Calif State U 6000 J St Sacramento CA 95819

EVANS, RUSSELL POPEJOY, accountant, tax consultant; b. Marshfield, Mo., Dec. 11, 1915; s. Roy Campbell and Harriet Lucille (Popejoy) E.; student Heald's Bus. Sch., 1954-55, Golden Gate U., 1955-58; m. Bertha Mae Gentry, June 22, 1946; children—Janice Marie (Mrs. Arthur H. Longo), Howard Keith. Partner, Jimmy & Russ Mobil Service, San Francisco, 1947-54, mgr., accountant, 1956-58; jr. accountant McNeil & Libby, San Francisco, 1955; owner Mission Bus. Service, San Francisco, 1959—. Served with USNR, 1943-46; PTO. Accredited in accountancy and taxation Accreditation Council for Accountancy; enrolled to practice before IRS. Mem. Nat. Soc. Pub. Accts., Soc. Calif. Accts. Address: 118 Tocoloma Ave San Francisco CA 94134

EVANS, SANDRA, educational administrator, nurse; b. Caldwell, Idaho, Jan. 10, 1947; d. Bill A. and Marjorie R. (Massie) E.; m. A. Jerry Davis, June 25, 1983. B.S. in Nursing, Idaho State U., 1971, M.A.Ed. in Curriculum/Supervision, 1979. R.N., Idaho. Staff nurse Peter Bent Brigham Hosp., Boston, 1971-74; staff nurse, inservice dir. St. Anthony Community Hosp., Pocatello, Idaho, 1974-76; media center coordinator dept. nursing Idaho State U., 1976-79; supr. health occupations edn. Idaho Div. Vocat. Edn., Boise, 1979—; asst. dir. Idaho Vocat. Indsl. Clubs Am. Mem. Idaho Nurses Assn., Am. Nurses Assn., Idaho, Pub. Employees Assn., Idaho Vocat. Assn., Am. Vocat. Assn., Idaho Health Occupations Edn. Assn., Alpha Omicron Pi. Office: 650 W State St Boise ID 83720

EVANS, TED DAVID, psychologist; b. Los Angeles, Aug. 25, 1947; s. Nat R. and Ann M. Evans; B.A. in Psychology, U. So. Calif., 1969; Ph.D. in Psychology, M.A. in Theology, Fuller Theol. Sem., 1975; m. Ava Kamens, Sept. 8, 1974. Pvt. practice clin. psychology, 1975—; asst. prof. psychology Pepperdine U., 1975-77; asst. clin. prof. psychology UCLA-Neuropsychiat. Inst., 1977—; Woodrow Wilson fellow, 1976. Mem. Am. Psychol. Assn., Calif. Psychol. Assn., Western Psychol. Assn. Democrat. Jewish. Contbg. editor: Family in Mourning, 1977; contbr. articles to psychol. jours. Office: 11645 Wilshire Blvd Los Angeles CA 90025

EVANS, THOMAS EDGAR, JR., title ins. agy. exec.; b. Toronto, Ohio, Apr. 17, 1940; s. Thomas Edgar and Sarah Ellen (Bauer) E.; B.A., Mt. Union Coll., 1963; m. Cynthia Lee Johnson, Feb. 23; children—Thomas Edgar, Douglas, Melinda, Jennifer. Tchr. Lodi, Ohio, 1963-64; salesman Simpson-Evans Realty, Steubenville, Ohio, 1964-65, Shadron Realty, Tucson, 1965-67; real estate broker, co-owner Double E Realty, Tucson, 1967-69; escrow officer, br. mgr., asst. county mgr., v.p. Ariz. Title Ins., Tucson, 1969-80; pres. Commonwealth Land Title Agy., Tucson, 1980-82, also dir.; pres. Fidelity Nat. Title Agy., 1982—. Named Boss of Year, El Chaparral chpt. Am. Bus. Women's Assn., 1977. Mem. So. Ariz. Escrow Assn., So. Ariz. Mortgage Bankers Assn., Ariz. Mktg. Bankers Assn., Young Businessmen's Assn. Tucson, Tucson Bd. Realtors, Ariz. Assn. Real Estate Exchangors (bd. dirs. 1968-69), So. Ariz. Homebuilders Assn., Blue Key, Sigma Nu. Republican. Methodist. Clubs: Old Pueblo Courthouse, Centre Court, Elks, Pima Jaycees (dir. 1966), Sertoma (charter pres., chmn. bd. Midtown sect. 1968-70); Tucson Real Estate Exchangors (pres. 1968). Home: 5142 E Camino Faja Tucson AZ 85718 Office: 4903 E Broadway Suite 100 Tucson AZ 85711

EVANS, TRICIA WARD, vocational education administrator; b. Franklin Lakes, N.J., Nov. 20, 1947; d. Lloyd William and Avis Louise (Nagle) Ward; div.; children—Eric Ward, Pamela Ward. B.A. in Pub. Adminstrn., U. La Verne (Calif.), 1979; postgrad. Calif. State U.-Long Beach, 1981-83. Cert. vocat. educator, Calif. Sales mgr., tech. rep. Ford Motor Co. and Gen. Motors Corp., Manila, Philippines, 1968-75; with personnel dept. Orange County (Calif.), 1975-76; adminstr. Los Angeles County Regional Occupational Program, 1982—; instr. Cerritos Community Coll. Chmn. employer adv. group Calif. Employment Devel. Dept.; chmn. adv. group Regional Adult Vocat. Edn. Council; mem. bus. edn. adv. bd. Cerritos Coll. Recipient Pub. Service award State of Calif., 1979, 80. Mem. Calif. Assn. Regional Occupational Programs, NOW, Nat. Assn. Female Execs., Cerritos C. of C. (chmn. women's council). Democrat. Unitarian. Office: 15415 S Pioneer Blvd Norwalk CA 90650

EVANS, WAYNE CANNON, advertising and public relations executive; b. Salt Lake City, Aug. 26, 1931; s. David Woolley and Beatrice (Cannon) E.; m. Vella Sydne Neil, Aug. 30, 1956, children—Laurel Evans Galli, Nancy, Patricia, Wayne Neil. B.A., U. Utah, 1957, M.S. in Journalism, 1959. Corp. sec., v.p., dir., account exec. David W. Evans, Inc., Salt Lake City, 1965—; dir. 1st Thrift & Loan Corp. Mem. Salt Lake City Sch. Bd., 1973—, pres., 1979-80, 83, 84; mem. Salt Lake County Parks and Recreation Bd., 1973—, pres., 1974, 78, 82, 83; mem. Salt Lake County Arts adv. Bd., 1982; bd. dirs. Family Counseling Ctr., 1982—. Served with U.S. Army, 1954-55. Mem. Pub. Relations Soc. Am. (accredited). Republican. Mormon. Club: Phoenix Rotary. Home: 1246 Gilmer Dr Salt Lake City UT 84105 Office: 110 Social Hall Ave Salt Lake City UT 84111

EVANS, WILLIAM THOMAS, physician; b. Denver, Aug. 21, 1941; s. Alfred Lincoln and Marian Audrey (Biggs) E.; student Whitman Coll., 1959-60, U. Vienna (Austria), 1961-62; B.A., U. Colo., 1963; M.D., Baylor U., 1967; grad. Chinese Coll. U.K.; Licentiate Acupuncture, Oxford, Eng., 1976; m. Lucy Fales. Intern, Mary Fletcher Hosp., Burlington, Vt.; physician Villages of Kodiak Island and Lake Iliamna, 1968-70; founder, dir. emergency dept. St. Elizabeth Hosp., Yakima, Wash., 1970-75; practice medicine specializing in health care, practice traditional acupuncture, Denver; founder, dir. Colo. Back Sch., Denver, 1979—; Friends of Earth del. Limits to Medicine Congress, 1975. Organizer, Protest Poison in Our Presence run, Colo., 1977; initiated Colo. Sun Day, 1978. Served to lt. comdr. Indian Health Service, USPHS, 1968-70. Mem. Rocky Mountain Traumatological Soc., Denver County Med. Soc., Colo. Med. Soc., Am. Coll. Emergency Physicians (treas. Wash. 1974), Am. Coll. Sports Medicine, Traditional Acupuncture Soc. Office: 2045 Franklin B-3 Denver CO 80205

EVANS, WINTHROP SHATTUCK, airline captain, lawyer; b. Santa Monica, Calif., June 21, 1939; s. Clifford E. and Luella (Wyble) E.; m. Carlene D. Buschena, June 26, 1965; children—Theresa, Shalene, Shanna, Michelle. A.A., Fullerton Coll., 1969; B.A., Calif. State U.-Fullerton, 1973; J.D., Western State U., Fullerton, 1980. Bar: Calif. 1980. Enlisted in U.S. Navy, 1957, commd. ensign, 1961, advanced through grades to lt. comdr., 1969; served with U.S. Naval Reserve, 1965-76, ret. lt. comdr., 1976; airline capt. Am. Airlines, Los Angeles, 1965—; sole practice law, Placentia, Calif., 1980—; substitute tchr. Western State U. Mem. Calif. Bar Assn., Orange County Bar Assn., Aircraft Owners and Pilots Assn. Republican. Roman Catholic. Office: PO Box 532 Placentia CA 92670

EVARTS, HAL GEORGE, JR., author; b. Hutchinson, Kans., Feb. 8, 1915; s. Hal George and Sylvia (Abraham) E.; B.A., Stanford U., 1936; m. Dorothea Van Dusen Abbott, June 28, 1942; children—Virginia Leland, William Abbott, John Van Dusen. Reporter, Evening Tribune, San Diego, 1935, Call Bull., San Francisco, 1939; reporter, writer Occidental Pub. Co., San Francisco, 1938; writer N.Y. Herald Tribune, European edit., Paris, 1939-40; author novels, including: Treasure River, 1964; The Talking Mountain, 1966; Smugglers' Road, 1968; Mission to Tibet, 1970; The Pegleg Mystery, 1972; Bigfoot, 1973; author biographies: Jedediah Smith, 1958; Jim Clyman, 1959; author anthology: Fugitive's Canyon, 1955; contbr. numerous short stories to nat. mags., including Saturday Evening Post, Esquire, Collier's, Am., This Week; tchr. creative writing at workshops. Served with inf. U.S. Army, 1943-45. Recipient Charlie May Simon award for children's lit. Ark. State Sch. Council, 1976, Spl. award Mystery Writers Am., 1964, 68. Mem. Western Writers Am. (v.p. 1959-60, Spl. award 1973), Zeta Psi. Home and Office: 6625 Muirlands Dr La Jolla CA 92037

EVENS, ROBLEY DUNGLISON, retired army officer, former county official; b. Pasco, Wash., July 16, 1909; s. Silas Monroe and Emma (Pays) E.; B.A. in Bus. Adminstrn., Wash. State U., 1932; postgrad Sch. Social Work, U. Calif., 1963-64; m. Edythe Mae Greene, June 7, 1931 (dec. Sept. 1979); children—Marian Louise Evens Oppenlander, Roberta Diane Evens Crownover; m. 2d, Ruth Hamilton Airey, June 1980. With Pacific Power & Light Co., Yakima County, Wash., 1933-41; apptd. 2d lt. Inf., U.S. Army Res., 1932, advanced through grades to capt., entered active duty, 1941, advanced through grades to col., 1957; comdg. officer various facilities, Ft. Buchanan, San Juan, P.R., 1944-46, U.S. Army Forces, Aruba-Curacao, 1946; service in Dutch Guiana, 1946-47, Istanbul, Turkey, 1952-53; prof. mil. sci. and tactics U. Oreg., Eugene, 1953-56; asst. chief of staff G-I, Hdqrs. U.S. Army, Pacific, 1959-61, ret., 1961; supr. social services County of Sonoma, Calif., 1961-71. Bd. dirs. Sonoma County Taxpayers Assn., 1971-80. Decorated Army Commendation medal. Mem. Ret. Officers Assn., Nat. Assn. Uniformed Services. Club: Masons. Home: 6445 Mesa Oaks Circle Santa Rosa CA 95405

EVENSON, FLAVIS RICHARDS (MRS. PATTEE EVENSON), music cons., author, music supr. pub. schs.; b. Spirit Lake, Iowa, June 3, 1918; d. Ralph Raymond and Anna Sophia (Moe) Richards; B.S. in Music, Cornell Coll., Mt. Vernon, Iowa, 1940; M.A., Columbia U., 1945, profl. diploma, 1946; postgrad. U. Innsbruck (Austria), 1949; m. Pattee Evenson, Mar. 23, 1951. Tchr., supr. music Washington and Waterloo, Iowa, 1940-44; tchr. music, Long Beach, Calif., 1946; asst. prof. music San Francisco State Coll., 1946-51; coordinator music pub. schs. San Diego County, 1951-55; supr. music Los Angeles City Schs., 1955-76; author Curriculum Publ. Cons., Los Angeles Philharm. Symphonies for Youth, 1968-76; adviser Calif. Arts Commn., 1972-73. Recipient Los Angeles Unified Sch. Dist. Merit award. Lydia Roberts fellow, 1944-46. Mem. Music Educators Nat. Conf., Council Dist. Suprs. Los Angeles City Schs. (past pres.), Delta Kappa Gamma. Republican. Methodist. Author: The Study of Music in the Elementary School—A Conceptual Approach, 1967; The Magic of Music, Teacher's Manuals, 1969. Contbr. articles to profl. jours. Home: 3622 Terra Granada Apt 1A Walnut Creek CA 94595

EVERETT, CARL NICHOLAS, management consultant; b. Ardmore, Okla., June 4, 1926; s. Elmer Edwards and Cecile (Jones) E.; B.S., Columbia U., 1948; M.B.A. with distinction, Harvard U., 1951; m. Susan Blessing Lindstrom, Oct. 1975; children by previous marriages—Carl N., Karen Lee, E. Anthony. With Benton and Bowles, N.Y.C., 1951-54, asso. account exec. Gen. Foods Corp., asst. account exec. Hellmanns and Best Foods Mayonnaise; with Campbell Mithun, Mpls., 1954-56, sr. account exec. Pillsbury Mills, account exec. Pillsbury Refrigerated Products; with McCann Erickson, N.Y.C., 1956-62, bottle sales account exec. Coca Cola Co., sr. account exec. Esso Standard Oil, accounts supr. Westinghouse Electric Corp., account dir. Liggett and Myers Tobacco, mem. mktg. plans bd. and mktg. and advt. cons. Coca Cola Co.; sr. v.p., dir. Western region ops. Barrington & Co., N.Y.C., 1962-64; founder, pres. Everett Assos., Inc., mktg. and mgmt. cons., N.Y.C., 1964-74; founder, pres. Everett Corp., Scottsdale, Ariz., 1974—; cons. Chrysler Corp., Pepsico Inc., Michelin Tire Corp., Gen. Electric Corp., Can. Dry Corp., Allied Van Lines, Continental Airlines; co-founder, dir. Precision Investment Co., Denver, 1977—, dir. V&S Tooling Co., Boulder, Colo., 1977—; mng. partner Wilmot Properties, Tucson, 1979—. Served with USNR, 1944-46. Mem. Am. Mgmt. Assn., Smithsonian Assos., Sigma Alpha Epsilon. Unitarian. Clubs: Harvard Business School (dir. Ariz.), Safari International (dir.), Campfire. Patentee in field. Home: 6733 N 60th St Paradise Valley AZ 85253 Office: Everett Corp 4300 N Miller Rd Suite 110 Scottsdale AZ 85251

EVERETT, ELBERT KYLE, mktg. exec.; b. Knoxville, Tenn., June 17, 1946; s. David Abraham and Lois (Hill) E.; student E. Tenn. U., 1965-67; m. Jane Harville, June 13, 1967; 1 dau., Evelyn Anne. Sales rep. Met. Life Ins. Co., Knoxville, 1968-70, Creative Displays, Knoxville, 1970-73; market mgr. central and No. Calif., Nat. Advt. Co. subs. 3M Co., Stockton, 1973-80, western dist. mgr., 1981—; advt. cons. athletic dept. Fresno State Coll.; lectr. outdoor advt. and mktg. Fresno City Coll. Mem. subcom. on tourism State of Nev.; cons. Stockton Civic Theater. Served with AUS, 1964. Recipient cert. of recognition U.S. Treasury Dept., 1977, 78; recognition award for best design Advt. Age, 1974; 2 recognition awards Outdoor Advt. Assn. Am., 1973; cert. of appreciation United Way, 1978. Mem. U. Pacific Athletic Found., Stockton C. of C., Fresno C. of C., Advt. Club Sacramento, Advt. Club Fresno, Phi Sigma Kappa. Presbyterian. Home: 6432 N Benedict Ave Fresno CA 93711 Office: 1816 S Van Ness Ave Fresno CA 93777

EVERETT, HOWARD CHESTON, civil engineer; b. Pelahatchee, Miss., Feb. 12, 1909; s. Looney Newton and Loretta Adela (Moore) E.; m. Maude Evelyn Rockefeller, May 29, 1929; 1 son, Howard Cheston (dec.). B.Sc. in Civil Engring., U. Houston, 1950, postgrad., 1950-52; postgrad. U. Calif.-San Francisco, 1960-61, Coll. San Mateo, 1959-60. Registered profl. engr. Tex., Calif., Colo. Numerous engring. positions with United Gas and other companies in petroleum industry Tex., La., 1928-45; asst. prof., civil engring. U. Houston, 1950-51; pres. Everett-Heinen Corp., Houston, 1948-50; pres. Fairfield Park Corp., Houston, 1951-52; chief draftsman, structural engr. Holly Sugar Corp., San Mateo, Calif. and Colorado Springs, Colo., 1955-74; chief engr. Schloss & Shubart, Denver, 1974-80; instr. engring. Menlo (Calif.) Coll., 1960-63; cons. and lectr. in field. Mem. Colo. Soc. Profl. Engrs., Tau Beta Pi, Phi Kappa Phi. Lodges: Masons, Shriners. Engring. research and devel. of new machinery for waste water and sewage treatment, 1979-80.

EVERETT, LORNE GORDON, hydrologist; b. Thunder Bay, Ont., Can., Jan. 1, 1943; s. Leonard Reese and Ethel Violet (McCollum) E.; B.Sc., Lakehead U., 1966; B.Sc., U. Ariz., 1968, M.S., 1969, Ph.D., 1972; m. Jennifer Mae Hawkins, July 5, 1962; children—Stephen Edward, Jennifer Lauren. Asst. prof. dept. hydrology and water resources U. Ariz., Tucson, 1972-74; dir. Colo. River Investigation Center, Tucson, 1972-74; mgr. natural resources program Gen. Electric-Tempo Center for Advanced Studies, Santa Barbara, Calif., 1974-81, mgr. water resources program, 1974-78; mgr. natural resources program Kaman Tempo, 1980—; dir. Codecu Internat., Inc.; cons. Henningson, Durham & Richardson, Bell Engring., Coll. Engring., Logan, Utah. Bd. dirs. Get Oil Out, Inc., 1974—; bd. dirs. Sci. and Engring. Council, 1982. Mem. Internat. Water Resources Assn., ASCE, Am. Water Resources Assn., Nat. Water Well Assn., Am. Soc. Clin. Pathologists, Am. Med. Lab. Assn., Nat. Assn. Underwater Instrs., Sigma Xi, Beta Beta Beta. Mem. United Ch. of Christ. Club: Santa Barbara Tennis Patrons. Author: Establishment of Water Quality Monitoring Programs; Groundwater Monitoring of Western Coal Mining; contbr. 70 articles to profl. jours. Office: 816 State St Santa Barbara CA 93102

EVERETT, RICKY JOE, interior designer; b. Los Angeles, Nov. 16, 1948; s. Paul Alford and Helen Fae (Saunders) E.; B.A., Brigham Young

U., 1972. Sales mgr. Zion's Upholstering, Provo, Utah, 1972-74; exec. dir. House of Lords, Provo, 1974-76; pres. Rick Everett Designs, Provo, 1976—. J. Winter Smith scholar, 1966-67. Mem. Calif. Scholastic Fedn. Mormon. Clubs: Alpine Country, Elks. Home: 2942 Marrcrest W Provo UT 84604

EVERHART, GEORGE DAVID, III, information resources representative; b. York, Pa., Aug. 30, 1943; s. George David and Dorothy Louise (Schriver) E.; B.S., Am. U., 1972, cert. in mgmt. info. systems, 1974; m. Marina Glenda Blouse, Oct. 30, 1965 (div. 1976); m. 2d, Kathleen Ann McGowan, May 19, 1977; children—George David, Stacy Ann; 1 stepson, Rick Rutherford Instr., Dept. Def. Computer Inst., Washington, 1965-69; supervisory computer specialist U.S. Army Surgeon Gen., Fort Detrick, Md., 1969-74; sr. computer specialist HEW, Rockville, Md., 1975; info. resources rep. GSA, U.S. Naval Undersea Warfare Engring. Sta., Keyport, Wash., 1976—; instr. mgmt. Olympic Coll., City U. Seattle; instr. data processing George Washington U.; cons. Interracial Council for Bus. Opportunities, Washington. Commr. Port of Brownsville (Wash.), 1981—. Served with USN, 1963-67. Recipient Outstanding Performance awards, 1968, 71, 74, 82. Clubs: Brownsville Yacht. Editor: College Readings, Inc., 1969. Home: PO Box 34 Keyport WA 98345 Office: US Naval Undersea Warfare Engring Sta Keyport WA 98345

EVERINGHAM, HARRY TOWNER, orgn. exec., editor; b. Memphis, Aug. 14, 1908; s. William Kirby and Ida Pauline (Towner) E.; student Christian Brothers Coll., Memphis, 1919-20, Northwestern U., 1936-39; m. Margaret Sophia Johnson, May 1, 1934; children—Martha (Mrs. George F. Meister, Jr.), Barbara (Mrs. Lawrence H. Miller), Richard Kirby. Radio writer, producer Miles Labs., Murine Co., Henry C. Lytton & Co., 1934-41; film producer, speaker Employers Assn. Chgo., 1942; pub. relations dir. Ingalls-Shepherd div. Wyman-Gordon Co., editor Forging Ahead, Harvey, Ill., 1942-45; editor, pub. The Fact Finder, Chgo., 1942-65, Phoenix, 1965—; nat. pres., trustee We The People, 1955—; pres., trustee Free Enterprise Fedn., 1955—. Former v.p. Greater Chgo. Churchmen; founder Publicity Club Chgo., 1942. Club: Arizona Breakfast (founder, pres. 1969—). Editor, pub. U.S.A.-Beyond the Crossroads, 1952; The Best-Kept Secrets of Our Enemy Within, 1963; Free Enterprise, 1955-76; The American Patriot, 1976—. Home: 6630 E Monterosa St Scottsdale AZ 85251 also Box A Scottsdale AZ 85252 Office: 2422 E Indian School Rd Phoenix AZ 85016

EVERINGHAM, MELVIN ALBERT, coll. pres.; b. Ainsworth, Nebr., Dec. 12, 1918; s. Albert B. and Mable Mae E.; B.S., Wayne State Coll., 1942; M.A., U. Nebr., 1950, Ed.D., 1957; m. Lucille Mildred Williams, June 9, 1949; children—Susan Marie, Cheryl Ann. With Nebr. Dept. Edn., 1950-57; asst. supt. schs. Sidney, Nebr., 1957-59; supt. schs. Beatrice, Nebr., 1959-61, Ottumwa, Iowa, 1961-65; pres. Indian Hills Community Coll., Ottumwa, 1965-73; v.p. Central Ariz. Coll., Coolidge, 1973-76, pres., 1976—. Pres., Town Hall, Casa Grande, 1976-77. Served with USN, 1942-46, 50-52. Maude Craven scholar, 1942. Mem. Am. Assn. Community and Jr. Colls., North Central Assn. (evaluator). Republican. Presbyterian. Club: Rotary. Office: Woodruff and Overfield Rd Coolidge AZ 85228

EVERINGTON, CAROLINE TIPPENS, educator; b. Nashville, Mar. 14, 1950; d. Clark Balckman and Martha Elizabeth (Lane) Tippens; m. Richard Michael Everington, Feb. 14, 1971 (div.); 1 son, Dorian Clark. B.S. in Elem. and Spl. Edn., George Peabody Coll. Tchrs., 1976, M.S. in Spl. Edn., 1977. Cert. tchr. spl. edn., N.Mex. Tchr., Nashville, 1976; cons. Merci-Homes, Nashville, 1977; grad. research asst., practicum supr. Peabody Coll., Nashville, 1977; tchr. pub. schs., Los Lunas, N.Mex., 1977-81, curriculum specialist, 1981-82, methods and materials specialist adult edn., 1982—; mem. State Adopted Textbook Com., chmn. multi-handicapped; instr. dept. continuing U. N.Mex. Bur. Edn. Handicapped fellow, 1976-77; recipient State N.Mex. Exemplary Performance award, 1982. Mem. Assn. Severely Handicapped, Assn. Supervision and Curriculum Devel., Kappa Delta Epsilon, Kappa Delta Phi. Co-author: Los Lunas Curriculum System, 1981; (with Jones, Heckert, Worley and Thomas) The Los Lunas Curriculum System, 1980, The Los Lunas Educational Assessment for the Severely Profoundly Handicapped, 1979. Home: 929 11th NW Albuquerque NM 87102 Office: Los Lunas Hosp and Tng Sch PO Box 1269 Los Lunas NM 87031

EVERS, BARBARA JO, savings and loan company executive, consultant; b. Portland, Oreg., Jan. 22, 1949; d. Marvin Allen and Dorothy Geneva (Berry) Emerson; Student Mills Coll., 1967-69; B.S. summa cum laude in Mgmt., Woodbury U., 1979; A.A. with honors in Real Estate, Fullerton Coll., 1980, cert. in Escrow, 1982; cert. Mortgage Banking, Cypress Coll., 1980. Loan servicing analyst then loan adminstrn. supr. Coldwell Banker Mgmt. Corp., Los Angeles, 1976-78; mktg. services mgr., document control mgr. then systems devel. mgr. Standard Precision, Inc., Santa Fe Springs, Calif., 1978-80; project adminstr., procedure design and publs. mgr., then deposit ops. adminstrn. mgr. Home Fed. Savings & Loan Assn., San Diego, 1980—; career counselor; organizational systems cons. Mem. Ops. Research Soc. Am., Women in Mgmt., Nat. Assn. Female Execs., Am. Soc. Profl. Exec. Women, Project Mgmt. Inst., Inst. Mgmt. Scis., Soc. Tech. Communications, San Diego Symphony Assn., San Diego Repertory Theater, Alpha Gamma Sigma, Phi Gamma Kappa (Key award 1979). Home: 1650 8th Ave San Diego CA 92101 Office: 5545 Morehouse Dr San Diego CA 92121

EVERSON, DOUGLAS ALVIN, accountant; b. Eugene, Oreg., Jan. 22, 1952; s. Alvin Carl and Gloria Myrtle (Grove) E.; B.S., Oreg. State U., 1975. Acct., Gene C. Jerome, C.P.A., Hillsboro, Oreg., 1975-76; acct. Valley Bookkeeping Service, Dallas, Oreg., 1976-77, owner, partner, 1978—; tchr. Chemeketa Community Coll., Dallas, 1978—. Treas., Polk County Fair, 1978—. Lic. tax cons., Oreg.; enrolled to practice before IRS. Mem. adv. com. Chemeketa Community Coll. Mem. Salem Jaycees. (treas. 1981-82, community devel. v.p. 1982-83, individual devel. v.p. 1983-84), Oreg. Jaycees (treas. 1983-84). Oreg. Assn. Public Accts., Assn. Tax Cons., Nat. Assn. Tax Cons. Club: Elks. Home: 975 Espana St N Salem OR 97303 Office: 127 SW Walnut St Dallas OR 97338

EVERSON, WILLIAM OLIVER, poet; b. Sacramento, Sept. 10, 1912; s. Louis Waldemar and Francelia Marie (Herber) E.; student Fresno State Coll., 1931, 34-35; m. Susanna Rickson, Dec. 13, 1969; 1 son, Jude. With Civilian Conservation Corps, 1933-34; head syrupmaker Selma plant Libby, McNeil & Libby, 1936-42; with Civilian Public Service, 1943-46; dir. Fine Arts Group, Waldport, Oreg., 1944-46; with U. Calif. Press, 1947-49, Catholic Worker Movement, 1950-51, Dominican Order, Province of West, 1951-69; poet-in-residence Kresge Coll., U. Calif., Santa Cruz, 1951-81; master printer Lime Kiln Press, U. Calif., Santa Cruz; author: (verse) The Residual Years, Poems, 1934-48, 1968, Man-Fate, 1974, The Veritable Years, Poems, 1949-1966, 1978, The Masks of Drought, 1980; (prose) Robinson Jeffers Fragments of an Older Fury, 1967, Archetype West, 1976, Earth Poetry, Selected Essays and Interviews, 1980. Guggenheim fellow, 1949; Pulitzer Prize nominee, 1959; recipient Silver medal Commonwealth Club of Calif., 1967; Shelley Meml. award, 1978; Book of Yr. award MLA Conf. on Christianity and Lit., 1978; Nat. Endowment Arts grantee, 1981. Home: 312 Swanton Rd Davenport CA 95017

EVRIGENIS, JOHN BASIL, obstetrician, gynecologist; b. Athens, Greece, Feb. 23, 1929; s. Basil J. and Maria G. (Soteriou) E.; came to U.S., naturalized, 1951; B.S., U. Athens, 1947, M.D., 1951; m. Sophia M. Goritsan, June 22, 1952; children—Mary Ellen, Debbie, Gregory, John Basil. Intern, Providence Hosp., Portland, Oreg., 1951-52; resident in gen. practice Providence Hosp. and affiliated U. Oreg. Hosps., Portland, 1952-53; resident in obstetrics and gynecology Emanuel Hosp., Portland, 1953-56; pvt. practice medicine, specializing in obstetrics and gynecology, Sacramento, 1956—; mem. staffs Sutter, Mercy, Am. River, Meth. hosps., Sacramento Med. Center; asst. clin. prof. obstetrics and gynecology U. Calif., Davis Med. Sch. Mem. Sacramento County Med. Soc., Calif., Am., Panama med. assns., Am. Fertility Soc., Pacific Coast Fertility Soc., No. Calif. Obstetrics-Gynecology Soc. (pres. 1975-76), So. Calif. Obstetrics-Gynecology Assembly, Royal Soc. Health, Royal Soc. Medicine, Am. Assn. Gynecologists and Laparoscopists, AAUP. Eastern Orthodox. Clubs: Sutter, Del Paso Country, Comstock, Lions, Elks, Masons, Ahera. obstetrician, gynecologist; b. Athens, Greece, Feb. 23, 1929; s. Basil J. and Maria G. (Soteriou) E.; came to U.S., naturalized, 1951; B.S., U. Athens, 1947, M.D., 1951; m. Sophia M. Goritsan, June 22, 1952; children—Mary Ellen, Debbie, Gregory, John Basil. Intern, Providence Hosp., Portland, Oreg., 1951-52; resident in gen. practice Providence Hosp. and affiliated U. Oreg. Hosps., Portland, 1952-53; resident in obstetrics and gynecology Emanuel Hosp., Portland, 1953-56; pvt. practice medicine, specializing in obstetrics and gynecology, Sacramento, 1956—; mem. staffs Sutter, Mercy, Am. River, Meth. hosps., Sacramento Med. Center; asst. clin. prof. obstetrics and gynecology U. Calif., Davis Med. Sch. Mem. Sacramento County Med. Soc., Calif., Am., Panama med. assns., Am. Fertility Soc., Pacific Coast Fertility Soc., No. Calif. Obstetrics-Gynecology Soc. (pres. 1975-76), So. Calif. Obstetrics-Gynecology Assembly, Royal Soc. Health, Royal Soc. Medicine, Am. Assn. Gynecologists and Laparoscopists, AAUP. Eastern Orthodox. Clubs: Sutter, Del Paso Country, Comstock, Lions, Elks, Masons, Ahera. Home: 3615 Winding Creek Rd Sacramento CA 95825 Office: 3939 L St Sacramento CA 95819

EWALD, ROBERTA GRANT, artist, travel service co. exec., art gallery exec.; b. Mpls., Aug. 25; d. Oscar and Hannah Theolinda (Johannson) Grant; student Calif. Sch. of Arts, 194S-46; m. Henry C. Ewald, Sept. 7, 1946; 1 son, Grant. Public acct. Ernst & Ernst, San Francisco, 1943-44, Harris Kerr Forster, San Francisco, 1944-46; owner, operator Travelers' Art Gallery, Roberta's Art Gallery, 1973—, Travel Services, South San Francisco, Calif. Bd. dirs. Art Guild Pacifica (Calif.), 1960-64, pres., 1963-64; bd. dirs. Pacifica Spindrift Players, 1978—, dir. children's choirs, 1968-73; mem. Pacifica Arts & Heritage, Art-Rise of San Bruno. Recipient various art exhibit awards. Mem. Pacific Area Travel Assn., Am. Soc. Travel Agts., San Francisco Conservatory Music. Author, lead, producer musical The Wanderers, 1979; sponsor various art functions; numerous appearances with theatrical groups, 1938—. Office: 757 Kains St San Bruno CA 94066 also 345-9 Baden St San Francisco CA 94080

EWAN, JAMES, elec. engr.; b. Chengtu, China, Jan. 9, 1949; s. Nelson and Lucy (Wu) E. B.S., UCLA, 1971, M.S., 1973. Chief engr. United Detector Technology, Santa Monica, 1969-73; mem. tech. staff Hughes Research Labs., Malibu, Calif., 1974-81; research engr. Aerospace Corp., El Segundo, 1981—. Hughes fellow, 1976-78. Contbr. articles to profl. jours. Office: 2350 E El Segundo Blvd El Segundo CA 90245

EWAN, MARION, optometrist; b. Hong Kong, Apr. 19, 1952; came to U.S., 1959, naturalized, 1962; d. Nelson and Lucy (Wu) E. B.A. in Psychobiology, UCLA, 1973; O.D., So. Calif. Coll. Optometry, 1977. Lic. optometrist, Calif. Optometrist Joseph Mulach Eye Ctr., Long Beach, Calif., 1977-81, cons. contact lenses, 1981—; pvt. practice optometry specializing in contact lenses, Los Angeles, 1982—. Mem. Am. Optometric Assn., Calif. Optometric Assn., South Bay Optometric Soc. (pres. 1980-81). Clin. study on extended-wear soft contact lenses, 1981. Office: 8737 Beverly Blvd Suite 401 Los Angeles CA 90048

EWING, CLIFFORD EDWARD, TV exec.; b. Casper, Wyo., July 3, 1926; s. Edward M. and Sylvia (Ericksen) E.; student Pacific Luth. Coll., 1946-48; m. Audrey Marie Wilber, Sept. 1, 1951. Announcer KVOC, Casper, Wyo., 1946-48, news editor, 1948-51; announcer KOOK, Billings, Mont., 1951-53, program dir., 1953-56, prodn. dir. KOOK-TV, 1956-59, operations dir., 1959-61, gen. mgr., 1961-66; gen. mgr. KOOK Radio and TV, 1966-69, KRTV, Great Falls, Mont., 1969—. Publicity dir. Billings United Neighbors, 1964, 65, v.p., 1966, mem. exec. bd., 1966-67; mem. pres.'s. com. Coll. Gt. Falls, 1972-75; mem. C.M. Russell Mus. Bd. dirs. United Fund Cascade County, Gt. Falls Symphony Assn. Served with USNR, 1944-46. Mem. Mont., Rocky Mountain broadcasters assns., Gt. Falls C. of C., Advt. Club, Gt. Falls Lutheran. Elk, Rotarian. Club: Meadowlark Country. Home: 1100 Adobe Dr Great Falls MT 59404 Office: KRTV PO Box 1331 Great Falls MT 59403

EWING, COLEMAN CLAY, architect; b. San Antonio, Oct. 11, 1944; s. William Thomas and Ina Fay (Talley) E.; student San Antonio Jr. Coll., 1963-65; B.S., U. Houston, 1970; m. Marjorie Glennda Sewell, Aug. 28, 1965; children—Christopher Coleman, Michelle InaMarie. Customer engr. IBM Co, Houston, Tex., 1965-67; draftsman Morton Levy, Houston, 1967-71, Roland Johnson, Denver, 1971-72, DMJM Phillips, Denver, 1972-73, Wheeler/Lewis, Denver, 1973-75, Frank Lundquist, Denver, 1975-76, Oliver, Hellegren, Denver, 1976-77; prin. Ewing Architect & Assocs., Denver, 1977-80; pres. Ewing Gorman Archtl. Group, Denver, 1980-81, also dir.; pres. Ewing Archtl. Group, P.C., 1981—. Republican. Mem. Ch. of Christ. Office: Ewing Architectural Group PC 6634 S Clarkson St Suite B Littleton CO 80221

EWING, DAVID RUSSELL, physician; b. Berkeley, Calif., Dec. 13, 1931; s. Russell Charles and Susan M. (Sawyer) E.; student U. Ariz., 1949-50, 54-56; M.D., Tulane U., 1960; m. Terry Lee Petersen Evans, Feb. 18, 1978; 1 son, Eric; children by previous marriage—Julie, Jennifer, Benjamin, Justin, Joshua, David. Intern, Orange (Calif.) County Gen. Hosp., 1960-61, resident 1961-62; practice medicine specializing in family practice, Yorba Linda, Calif., 1962-77, Afton, Wyo., 1977—; mem. staff Star Valley Hosp., Afton. Served with USN, 1951-54. Diplomate Am. Bd. Family Practice. Fellow Am. Acad. Family Physicians; mem. AMA, Wyo. Med. Soc. Republican. Mormon. Home: Fairview WY 83119 Office: Star Valley Hosp PO Box 978 Afton WY 83110

EWING, EDGAR LOUIS, educator, artist; b. Hartington, Nebr., Jan. 17, 1913. Grad. Art. Inst. Chgo., 1935, student Boris Anisfeld; two yrs. European travel, study. One-man shows: Greek Nat. Gallery, 1973, Mcpl. Gallery, Los Angeles, 1974, Fisher Gallery, U. So. Calif., 1978; 20 years Retrospective, Palm Springs Desert Mus., 1976-77; group shows include: Sao Paulo (Brazil) Mus. Art Internat., Carnegie Mus. Internat., Pitts., Art Inst. Chgo., Met. Mus. Art, N.Y.C., Pa. Acad. Fine Arts, Phila., represented in permanent collections at Richmond (Va.) Mus. Fine Arts, Los Angeles County Mus. Art, Santa Barbara Mus., De Young Mem. Mus., San Francisco, Nat. Gallery, Athens; instr. painting Art Inst. Chgo., 1937-43, prof. fine arts U. So. Calif., 1946-78, emeritus prof., 1978—; Mellon prof. painting Carnegie Mellon U., 1968-69. Recipient Samuel Goldwyn award Los Angeles County Mus. Art, 1957; Los Angeles Library Assn. award, 1976; Floresheim award Art Inst. Chgo., 1937-43. Mem. AAUP, Nat. Watercolor Soc. (pres.), Los Angeles Mus. Assn. Home: Office: University Southern Calif Dept Art University Park Los Angeles CA 90007

EWING, MARY ARNOLD HENGY, lawyer; b. Shreveport, La., Feb. 21, 1948; d. George and Christine (Cocek) Hengy; m. R. Craig Ewing. B.A., U. Colo., 1972; J.D., U. Denver, 1975. Bar: Colo. 1975, U.S. Supreme Ct. 1979. Law clk. Johnson and Mahoney, P.C., Denver, 1972-75, assoc., 1975-80; ptnr. Branney & Hillyard, Englewood, Colo., 1980-82, Branney, Hillyard, Ewing & Barnes, 1982—; asst. prof. law U. Denver Coll. Law, 1977-78, part-time prof., 1978—; judge continuing legal edn. Course in Trial Advocacy, 1979, 80; guest lectr. local colls. and univs. Chmn., Denver County Task Force, Health and Hosp., 1976-77; treas. 1st. Congressional Dist. Central Com., 1976-77; v.p. Young Republican League of Denver, 1975, pres., 1976; mem. govt. relations com. Jr. Symphony Guild, 1978—. Mem. ABA, Colo. Bar Assn., Denver Bar Assn. (vice chmn. new lawyers assistance com. 1977), Internat. Platform Assn., Mountain States Combined Tng. Assn., Rocky Mountain Dressage Soc. (sec. High Plains chpt. 1979, 80), Am. Trial Lawyers Assn., Colo. Trial Lawyers Assn. (chmn. interprofl. com. 1980, bd. dirs. 1982), U. Denver Coll. Law Alumni Council, Kappa Beta Pi (pres. 1977-78). Club: Toastmasters Internat. Home: 816 W Quarry Rd Littleton CO 80124 Office: 3333 S Bannock St Suite 1000 Englewood CO 80110

EWING, RUSSELL CHARLES, II, physician; b. Tucson, Aug. 16, 1941; s. Russell Charles and Sue M. (Sawyer) E.; B.S., U. Ariz., 1963; M.D., George Washington U., 1967; m. Louise Anne Wendt, Jan. 29, 1977; children—John Charles, Susan Lenore. Intern, Los Angeles County-U. So. Calif. Med. Center, Los Angeles, 1967-68; gen practice medicine and surgery, Yorba Linda, Calif. and Placentia, Calif., 1970—; mem. staff St. Judes Hosp., Fullerton, Calif., 1970—; mem. staff Placentia Linda Community Hosp., 1972—, vice chief staff, 1977-78, chief staff, 1978-80; sec., dir. Yorba Linda (Calif.) Med. Clinic, Inc., 1974—; dir. Placentia Linda Savs. & Loan Assn. (Calif.). Bd. dirs. Yorba Linda YMCA, 1973—, pres., 1973-74, 81; bd. dirs. Placentia Linda Community Hosp., 1974-81. Served with USN, 1968-70. Diplomate Am. Bd. Family Practice. Fellow Am. Acad. Family Practice; mem. AMA, Calif. Med. Assn. (house of del. 1978—), Orange County Med. Assn. Republican. Episcopalian. Home: 9212 Smoketree Lane Villa Park CA 92667 Office: 4900 Prospect Yorba Linda CA 92686

EXTON, EILEEN, physician; b. Braddock, Pa., Jan. 14, 1950; d. Edward Albert and Margaret Helen (Winkenbach) Exton; B.S. cum laude, U. Pitts., 1971, M.D., 1975; student George Washington U. Sch. Medicine, 1971-73. Resident family practice Shadyside Hosp., Pitts., 1975-78; family practitioner Kaiser-Permanente, Lahaina, Hawaii, 1978—; clin. asst. prof. U. Hawaii, Manoa, 1979—; clin. assoc. UCLA Sch. Medicine, 1979—; mem. staffs Maui Meml. Hosp., Kaiser Found. Hosp. Vol. physician Pitts. Free Clinic, 1977-78; pres. Shadyside Housestaff Assn., Pitts., 1977-78; flutist Maui Symphony Orch., 1979—; clinician Hawaii Planned Parenthood, Lahaina, Hawaii, 1978-79. Diplomate Am. Bd. Family Practice. Fellow Am. Acad. Family Physicians; mem. Hawaii Acad. Family Physicians, Maui County Med. Soc., Hawaii Med. Assn. Office: 910 Wainee St Lahaina HI 96761

EXUM, FRANK ALLEN, petroleum geologist; b. Tulsa, Aug. 30, 1930; s. Frank Martin and Florence Edith (Young) E.; B.A. in Geology, U. Calif. at Los Angeles, 1956, M.A. (Gen. Petroleum Corp. fellow), 1957; m. Patricia Jean Conroy, Feb. 27, 1960; children—Susan Elizabeth, Robert Allen. Geologist, Harrington, Marsh & Wagner, Amarillo, Tex., 1955; geologist Marathon Oil Co., Los Angeles, 1957-62, advanced geologist Denver Research Center, 1962-71, sr. geologist, Casper, Wyo.. 1971-77, area exploration supr., 1977-81; regional exploration mgr. ENSTAR Petroleum, Inc., Denver, 1981—. Served with USMCR, 1952-54. Fellow Geol. Soc. Am.; mem. Am. Assn. Petroleum Geologists (exec. com. Pacific sect. 1961, A.I. Levorsen award 1968), Am. Inst. Profl. Geologists (chmn. com. state sect. affairs 1970, v.p. Wyo. sect. 1975), Soc. Econ. Paleontologists and Mineralogists (Best Paper award nat. conv. 1968), Rocky Mountain Assn. Geologists, Wyo. Geol. Assn. (1st v.p. 1981, co-editor Guidebook 1975), Sigma Xi. Contbr. articles to profl. jours. Editor: Pacific Petroleum Geologist, 1961. Home: 3928 S Jasmine St Denver CO 80237 Office: 1125 17th St Suite 2040 Denver CO 80202

EYBERG, SHEILA MAXINE, clinical psychologist; b. Omaha, Dec. 31, 1944; d. Clarence George and Geraldine Elizabeth (Gilbert) E.; B.A., U. Omaha, 1967; M.A., U. Oreg., 1970, Ph.D., 1972. Intern in med. psychology Oreg. Health Scis. U., Portland, 1971-72, postdoctoral resident, 1972-74, asst. prof. med. psychology, 1974-81, assoc. prof., 1981—, coordinator child psychology outpatient clinic, 1982—; cons., workshop leader psychol. assessment and treatment of children Curry County Mental Health Clinic, Gold Beach, Oreg., 1973; psychol. cons. North Clackamas Sch. Dist., Portland, 1974-75; psychol. cons. Summer Speech and Lang. Clinic, Portland Center for Hearing and Speech, 1974-75; psychol. cons. Parent-Child Services, Inc., Portland, 1976; mem. asso. profl. staff Woodland Park Psychiat. Hosp., Portland, 1977-80, mem. neuropsychiat. com., 1977-80; leader workshops U. Wash., Seattle, 1980—. Lic. psychologist, Oreg. Mem. Am. Psychol. Assn. (sec.-treas. child psychology sect.), Soc. Pediatric Psychology (pres. elect), Western Psychol. Assn., Oreg. Psychol. Assn. (com. sci. and profl. ethics 1980—), Assn. Advancement of Behavior Therapy, Oreg. Acad. Profl. Psychologists, Nat. Register of Health Service Providers, Alpha Lambda Delta, Phi Kappa Phi, Psi Chi. Contbr. numerous articles to profl. jours. editorial bd. Journal of Pediatric Psychology, 1977—Jour. Clin. Child Psychology, 1982—; editorial cons. Behavior Therapy, 1978; Behavior Modification, 1981, Child Devel., 1981. Home: 31 Greenridge Ct Lake Oswego OR 97034 Office: 3181 SW Sam Jackson Park Rd Portland OR 97201

EYE, CHARLES THOMAS, lawyer; b. Lindsay, Okla., July 17, 1934; s. Walter Weldon and Eugenia Cleo (Hinton) E.; A.A., Chaffey Coll., 1969; J.D., Pepperdine U., 1973; m. Leona Fae Gilley, Nov. 8, 1953; children—Lawrence Wendell, Cheryl Lynn, Nancy Ann, Christian Thomas. Admitted to Calif. bar, 1973, U.S. Supreme Ct. bar, 1977; draftsman U.S. Army Corps of Engrs., Los Angeles, 1953-54, Calif. Inst. Tech. Jet Propulsion Lab., Pasadena, 1953-55; mech. designer Amtec Engring. Co., Anaheim, 1955-60; design engr., Ontario, Calif., 1960-73; dir., atty. Pomona (Calif.) Legal Aid Soc., 1973-77; dep. exec. dir. Legal Services Program for Pasadena, San Gabriel & Pomona Valleys, Pasadena, 1976-77; owner, exec. dir. Legal Clinic of Charles Thomas Eye, Upland, Calif., 1977—; adj. prof. bus. law Chaffey Coll., Alta Loma, Calif., 1974—; dir., lectr. LaVerne (Calif.) Law Center Clin. Program, 1976-77. Res. dep. sheriff San Bernardino County, 1959-69. Named Social Sci. Div. honor student of yr., Chaffey Coll., 1969; recipient Am. Jurisprudence award in Family Law, Pepperdine Law Sch., 1970. Mem. Am. Bar Assn., Calif. State Bar-Legal Services Div., Calif. Trial Lawyers Assn., Phi Alpha Delta, Alpha Gamma Sigma. Republican. Presbyterian. Contbr. articles to profl. jours. Home: 1455 W 4th St Ontario CA 91762 Office: 1152 N Mountain Ave Suite 215 Upland CA 91786

EYRE, MARYBELLE MURDOCK, government official; b. Beaver, Utah, Mar. 3, 1933; d. Charles Edward and Alverta Luciel (Bakes)

Murdock; m. Garold F. Eyre, June 2, 1950; children—Kendal G., Lori Eyre Rasmussen, Rodney S. Student U. Utah, So. Utah State Coll. Ptnr., bookkeeper cattle ranch, 1950—; town clk., sec., bookkeeper Irrigation Co., Minersville, Utah, 1956-71; sec. Soil Conservation Service, U.S. Dept. Agr., Minersville, 1956-71, county office asst. Farmers Home Adminstrn., Beaver, Utah, 1971-76, asst. county supr. Salt Lake City, 1976-79, county supr., Cedar City, Utah, 1979—. Sec. Republican County Com., 1960. Recipient Cert. Merit for outstanding service in county offices Farmers Home Adminstrn. Mem. Nat. Orgn. County Supervisors (v.p.), Am. Legion Aux. (pres. 1974), Nat. Assn. Female Execs. Mormon. Club: Literary (pres. 1975).

EZELL, ANNETTE SCHRAM, educator; b. West Frankfort, Ill., June 19, 1940; d. Woodrow C. and Rosa (Franich) Schram; student Evansville Coll., 1957, Protestant Deaconess Hosp. Sch. Nursing, 1957-59, Ind. U., 1959; B.S. in Nursing, U. Nev., 1962, M.S. in Physiology, 1967; Ed.D. in Pub. Adminstrn., Brigham Young U., 1977; divorced; children—Michael L., Rona Maria. Staff nurse Washoe Med. Center, Reno, 1962; teaching asst. U. Nev., Reno, 1962-63, instr., 1963-64, 1965-67, asst. prof. nursing, 1967-71; curriculum specialist U. Nev. Med. Sch., 1971-72, project mgr. Fed. Grant Intercampus Nursing Edn. Project, 1969-71, asso. prof. nursing, curriculum specialist rural nurse practitioner program, 1971-73; staff asso. Mountain States Regional Med. Program, 1974-75; ednl. cons. Nev. Dept. Edn., 1975-77; asso. dean acad. affairs Coll. Nursing, U. Utah, 1977-80, prof. and dir. doctoral program in nursing edn. adminstrn., 1981—, acting dean Coll. of Nursing, 1981-82; prof., dept. head Coll. Human Devel. Pa. State U., 1982—; cons. nursing edn., orgn. behavior, research methology; adviser to various research and ednl. bds. Mem. Am. Utah nurses assns., AAAS, Am. Acad. Arts and Scis., AAUP, Am. Nurses Found., Nat. League Nursing, Assn. for Humanistic Psychology, Phi Kappa Phi, Sigma Xi. Contbr. to publs. Home: 603 Old Farm Ln State College PA 16801 Office: Coll Human Devel Pa State U University Park PA 16802

EZELLE, ROBERT EUGENE, govt. ofcl.; b. Mattoon, Ill., Dec. 5, 1927; s. Zonner Robert and Nina Leora (Smith) E.; student U. So. Calif., 1947-49, U. Bonn, 1954-56, U. Munich, 1956-57; Ph.D., U. Vienna, 1960; M.B.A., Stanford U., 1977; Dr. h.c., Nat. U., 1981; m. Lesly Marion Hopkins, Apr. 30, 1955; children—Robert, Lesley, John, Paul. Instr., Bonn, Munich and Vienna, 1954-60; dir. lang. sch., San Mateo, Calif., 1960-61; joined U.S. Fgn. Service, 1961; internat. relations officer State Dept., Washington, 1961-62; staff asst. Fgn. Service Inst., 1962-63; assigned Hong Kong, 1963-65, Bern, Switzerland, 1965-69, Naples, Italy, 1969-72; chief consular affairs sect. Am. embassy, Bonn, 1972-75; internat. relations officer State Dept., Washington, 1975-76; assigned to Grad. Sch. Bus., Stanford U., 1976-77; dep. consul. gen. Am. embassy, London, 1977-80; consul gen. Am. consulate, Tijuana, Mex., 1980—. Served with USAF, 1949-53. Home: PO Box 1358 San Ysidro CA 92073

EZZARD, MARTHA MCELVEEN, state senator, lawyer, journalist; b. Atlanta, Nov. 8, 1938; B.A. in Journalism, U. Ga., 1960; M.A. in Journalism, U. Mo., 1968; J.D., U. Denver Coll. Law; m. John Ezzard; children—Shelly, Lisa, John. Journalist, Atlanta newspapers, NBC News; tchr. English, Littleton High Sch.; press aide to Govs. John Love and John Vanderhoof; mem. Colo. Ho. of Reps., 1978-80; mem. Colo. Senate from 20th dist., 1980—; mem. firm Bader & Cox, Denver; bd. dirs. United Bank of Littleton, Women's Forum, Jud. Inst. Recipient Outstanding Senator award Colo. Legis. Com., 1980. Mem. Phi Beta Kappa. Republican. Office: 1660 17th St Denver CO 80202

FAALAND, HALVDAN GERHARD KEYSER, gynecologist; b. Bklyn., Sept. 22, 1916; s. Karl Tobias and Harriet Elise Bergljot (Keyser) F.; student U. Oslo (Norway), 1936-37; student N.Y. U., 1938; M.D., L.I. Coll. Medicine, Bklyn., 1943; m. May Heartness, Apr. 4, 1943; children—Bruce Harold, Barbara Jeanette (Mrs. Charles D. Christopher), Carl Norman. Intern, Norwegian Hosp., Bklyn., 1943-44, resident, 1946-48, practice medicine specializing in obstetrics, gynecology, Bklyn., 1948-50; commd. lt. comdr., M.C., USN, 1950, advanced through grades to capt., 1957; resident Naval Hosp., St. Albans, N.Y., 1953-54; chief obstetrics, gynecology Naval hosps., Jacksonville, Fla., 1954-57, Naples, Italy, 1957-59, Newport, R.I., 1959-62, Guam, 1962-64; chief obstetrics, gynecology Marine Corps Supply Center, Barstow, Calif., 1964-67; chief outpatient service Naval Hosp., San Diego, 1967-69; ret., 1969; gynecologist Napa State Hosp., Imola, Calif., 1969-80; ret., 1980. Served to lt. USNR, 1944-46. Diplomate Am. Bd. Obstetrics and Gynecology. Fellow Am. Coll. Obstetricians Gynecologists, A.C.S.; mem. Calif. Med. Assn., Napa County Med. Soc., Norsemen's Fedn. Victory Lodge, Sons Norway. Home: 102 Woodland Dr Napa CA 94558

FAAS, LARRY ANDREW, educator; b. Iowa City, Sept. 25, 1936; s. Merlin Andrew and Verla Lavonne (Cheney) F.; B.S., Iowa State U., 1959; M.A., U. No. Colo., 1961; Ed.D., Utah State U., 1967; m. Patricia Middleton, Dec. 18, 1962; children—Anna Rachel, Eric Andrew, Audra Beth. Instr. vocat. agr. English Valley Community Schs., North English, Iowa, 1959-60; sch. psychologist Tri-County Spl. Edn., Decorah, Iowa, 1961-63, dir. spl. edn. edn., 1963-65; asst. prof., dir. spl. edn. U. Nev., 1966-67; asst. prof. edn. Ariz. State U., Tempe, 1967-70, asso. prof. edn., 1970-75, prof., 1975—. Mem. Council Exceptional Children, Phi Delta Kappa. Author: The Emotionally Disturbed Child, 1970; Learning Disabilities, 1972; Learning Disabilities: A Competency Based Approach, 1976, 2d edit., 1981; Children with Learning Problems: A Handbook for Teachers, 1980. Home: 519 E Del Rio Dr Tempe AZ 85282

FABE, DANA ANDERSON, lawyer, public defender; b. Cin.; d. George and Mary (VanAntwerp) Fabe; m. Randall Gene Simpson, Jan. 1, 1983. B.A., Cornell U., 1973; J.D., Northeastern U., 1976. Bar: Alaska, 1977, U.S. Supreme Ct., 1981; law clk. Hon. Edmond Burke, Alaska Sup. Ct., Anchorage, 1976-77; staff atty. Alaska Pub. Defender Agy., 1977-81, chief pub. defender, 1981—. Mem. Anchorage Assn. Women Attys. Office: Office of the Public Defender 900 W 5th St Suite 200 Anchorage AK 99501

FABER, GEORGE, radio, TV exec.; b. Mpls., June 17, 1921; s. William Maurice and Lowell Ella (Whiteman) F.; student Wis. Coll. Music, Northwestern U.; m. Marjorie Knodel, June 2, 1945; children—Kathie Diane, Michael William, Patricia Dawn. Writer, announcer, actor Sta. WHBL, Sheboygan, Wis., 1937-39; prodn. mgr. Sta. WMFD, Wilmington, N.C., 1939-41; columnist and author Behind the Mike series, Cape Fear Pub. Co., Wilmington, 1940-41; news editor NBC, Chgo., 1943-46; news editor, writer CBS, 1946—; now internat. dir. Viacom Enterprises (formerly CBS Enterprises); dir. Callahan and Assos. Chmn. internat. com. Hollywood Mus. Mem. Hollywood Radio-TV Club, Internat. Photo Journalists (hon. life), Sigma Delta Chi. Home: 10760 Cushdon Ave Los Angeles CA 90064 Office: Viacom Enterprises 10900 Wilshire Blvd Los Angeles CA 90024

FABER, MARSHALL LEE, producer; b. Washington, Aug. 20, 1917; s. Marshall Lee and Margaret (Shaw) F.; grad. high sch.; m. Martha Mogan, Aug. 29, 1941; children—Margaret Louise, Marshall Lee, Marianne Lucretia. Owner, operator Bus. Films, indsl. comml., ednl. motion pictures, Washington, 1934-46; film prodn., Phoenix, 1947-50; with KPHO, Phoenix, 1950-53, McClatchy Broadcasting Co., Sacramento, Fresno, Calif., 1953-55, KBTV, Denver, 1955-63; producer Marshall L. Faber Prodns., motion pictures, Denver, 1963—; tech. rep. Western Cine, Denver-Hollywood, 1975-78; tech. cons. Canon 35 Hearing, Colo. Supreme Ct., 1957; cons. Fedn. Rocky Mountain States Satellite Project, 1973; cons. cadre Ariz. Dept. Edn., 1975—, also to producers of feature films, 1974—; sculptor silver miniatures. Recipient citations Du Pont Found., 1955, Inst. Edn. by Radio, Ohio State U., 1961, Advt. Fedn. Am. 9th dist., 1960, ABC TV Network, 1960; recipient 1st pl. awards TV Radio Mirror, 1960, Omaha Art Dirs., 1958, Broadcast Music Inc., Am. Assn. State and Local History 1960, Cine Golden Eagle, 1964; recipient 4 Chris awards Columbus Film Festival, 1964, Ednl. Film Library Assn. award, 1965, Ad Club award, 1966, Am. Assn. Indsl. Advertisers awards, 1966, 68, award of Excellence Sunset Mag. Travel Film Festival, 1971, award for excellence in editing U.S. TV Comml̲s. Festival, Chgo., 1971, bronze medal Internat. Film and TV Festival of N.Y., 1971, commendation award Denver sect. Soc. Motion Picture and TV Engrs., 1972, award Nat. Ednl. Film Festival, 1972. Mem. Soc. Motion Picture and TV Engrs. (life, chmn. Denver sect. 1971), Soc. Photog. Scientists and Engrs. (bd. govs. 1967-69), Internat. Photographers Motion Picture Industry. Episcopalian. Author: Making Money With Low Budget Features, 1977; pioneer in design TV and film camera booth for use in courtroom photography, 1957, Fasdraw timer, 1958; designer teaching machines, audio visual machines for teaching machines, audio visual machines for spl. adaption; mfr. F8 projector. Address: 6412 E Desert Cove Scottsdale AZ 85254

FABIAN, KAREN MARJORIE, home economics consultant; b. Mpls., Oct. 17, 1935; d. Theodore T. and Margaret Marie (O'Halloran) Karlquist; m. Joseph Charles Fabian, Oct. 25, 1958; children—Michael J., Susan Lynn. B.S. in Household Equipment, Iowa State U., 1957; postgrad. Colo. State U., U. Colo., U. No. Colo. Student trainee Betty Crocker Kitchens, Mpls., 1956; home economist Ind.-Mich. Electric Co., Ft. Wayne, Ind., 1957-58, Fairmont Foods, Denver, 1960, Pub. Service Co. of Colo., Denver, 1960-64; home service advisor Emily Griffith Opportunity Sch., Denver, 1964-71, mem. homemaking adv. bd., 1964-74; high altitude food and microwave cons., 1970—. Pres. Denver Jr. Symphony Guild, 1973-74; mem. scholarship auction com. Colo. Acad. Mem. Colo. Home Econs. Assn. (pres. 1965), Colo. Home Economists in Bus. (chmn. 1964), Am. Home Economists Assn., Nat. Home Economists in Bus., Inst. Food Technologists, Internat. microwave Power Inst., Achievement Rewards for Coll. Scientists (dir. Denver chpt.). Mem. Congregational Ch. Club: Lakewood Country. Contbr. articles to homemaking jours. Home and office: 7177 W 8th Ave Denver CO 80215

FABRIS, GRACIO, research scientist, educator; b. Dubrovnik, Yugoslavia, Nov. 18, 1941; s. Ivan and Filomena (Sablic) F.; m. Neda Saravanja, Nov. 4, 1967; children—Drazen, Nicole. Degree in Mech. Engring., U. Sarajevo, 1965; M.S. in Mech. Aerospace Engring., Ill. Inst. Tech., 1971, Ph.D., 1974. Research assoc R&D Ctr. for Thermal and Nuclear Energy, Energoinvest Corp., Sarajevo, 1965-67; instr. U. Sarajevo, 1967-69; research teaching asst. Ill. Inst. Tech., 1969-74; asst. mech. engr. Argonne Nat. Lab., 1974-79, mech. engr., 1977-79; sr. scientist Combustion Dynamics and Propulsion Tech. div. Sci-Applications Inc., Canoga Park, Calif., 1979-81; sr. engr. scientist aerodynamics McDonnell Douglas Corp., Long Beach, Calif., 1981—; lectr. Calif. State U.-Los Angeles. Recipient 1st award for sci. work, Univ. Sarajevo, 1964. Assoc. fellow AIAA; mem. ASME, Am. Physical Soc., Sigma Xi. Contbr. articles to profl. jours. Office: 3855 Lakewood Blvd Long Beach CA 90846

FABRY, JOSEPH BENEDIKT, author, editor, logotherapist; b. Vienna, Austria, Nov. 6, 1909; s. Ernst and Irma B.; m. Judith Lieban, Nov. 2, 1940; children—Wendy Banks, Claire Bradley, Richard. J.D., U. Vienna, 1934. Writer, Office of War Info. (now Voice of Am.), 1943-48; editor agrl. publs. U. Calif.-Berkeley, 1948-72; dir. Inst. Logotherapy, 1977—; editor Internat. Forum for Logotherapy, 1979—. Mem. Calif. Writers Club. Unitarian. Author: The Pursuit of Meaning, 1968; Logtherapy in Action, 1979; Swingshift, 1982; transl.: Johann Nestroy, Three Comedies, 1967, Willy Haas: Bert Brecht, 1970, Heinrich Heine: Poems, 1973, Bert Brecht: Schweyk in World War II, 1974; Karl Kraus: Last Days of Mankind, 1974. Address: 315 Carmel Ave El Cerrito CA 94530

FACINELLI, JIM WALTER, educator; b. Lander, Wyo., Aug. 5, 1939; s. James E. and Marie I. (Presgrove) F.; m. Colleen A. Mitchum, Feb. 13, 1962; children—Beth M., Jimbob. B.S., U. Wyo., 1961; M.Ed., Colo. State U., 1970. Range conservationist Bur. Land Mgmt., 1958-61; tchr. agr. Fremont County Vocat. High Sch., Lander, Wyo., 1961-64; tchr. agr. Cody (Wyo.) High Sch., 1964—, chmn. vocat. edn. dept., 1982-83. Bd. dirs. Cody Stampede, 1970—, Cody Nite Rodeo, 1970—; dir. design and constrn. Cody Stampede Park Facility, 1977; mem. Park County Republican Com. Served with Army N.G., 1957-62, U.S. Army, 1961-62. Recipient Hon. Am. Farmer degree Nat. Future Farmers of Am. Assn., 1978. Mem. Nat. Vocat. Agrl. Tchrs. Assn. (Nat. Agribus. Career Exploration award 1976), Wyo. Vocat. Agr. Tchrs. Assn. (pres. 1975, Nat. Sound Off for Agr. award 1980), Am. Vocat. Assn., Wyo. Vocat. Assn., NEA, Wyo. Edn. Assn., Cody Edn. Assn., Am. Quarter Horse Assn., Wyo. Quarter Horse Racing Assn., Intermountain Quarter Horse Assn., Methodist. Club: Elks (Elk of Yr. 1969). Home: 11 Sunset Rim Cody WY 82414 Office: Cody Senior High Sch 1225 10th St Cody WY 82414

FACKERELL, TERRELL DAVID, plumbing contractor; b. Colorado Springs, Apr. 6, 1938; s. Alvin Perry and Frances Isabell (Gaines) F.; student Lee Coll., 1970-71; m. Donna Louise Brashears, May 24, 1973; children—Stephen, Erik, Kevin. Office mgr. Community Produce, Boston, 1962-67; counselor alcoholics Sacred Heart Center, Detroit, 1968-70; with Roto Rooter, Kansas City, Mo., 1973-75, Marysville, Calif., 1975-76; owner N. Valley Sewer & Drain, Williams, Calif., 1976—. Mem. Commn. on Juvenile Delinquency and Drug Abuse, Colusa County, Calif., 1979-80; mem. Tree Com. Williams, 1976-79; active Williams Civic Assn., 1976-79; pres. Williams Recreation Commn. Served with USN, 1955-61. Mem. C. of C. Republican. Clubs: Lions, Moose. Home: Hill Rd Williams CA 95987 Office: PO Box 643 Williams CA 95987

FACTOR, ALAN JAY, TV, film producer; b. Chgo.; s. John Jacob and Rella (Cohen) F.; B.F.A., Northwestern U.; student Art Inst. Chgo., Goodman Theatre; m. Phyllis Ezrach, Feb. 25, 1961; children—Mitchell, Daniel, Robert, Angela, Steven. Vice pres. Calumet Agy., 1953-60; story editor Karzmar Prodn., 1961-62; prodn. exec. Fox Prodns., 1962-63, Screen Gems, 1963-64; pres. Bedford Prodns., Hollywood, Calif., 1965-75, Factor-Newland Prodns., 1975—; dir. Bewitched, The Next Step Beyond, People Need People, El Rosario Story, Spl. Olympics, commls., others; producer Something Evil, Siege, Terror on the Beach, A Sensitive, Passionate Man, Overboard, The Suicide's Wife, The Next Step Beyond, Angel City, The Five of Me, others. Pres., Beverly Hills Charitable Found., 1964; v.p. Eddie Cantor Charitable Found., 1970; mem. spl. adv. com. TV Acad. Awards, 1974; bd. dirs., v.p. Am. Nat. Theatre and Acad. Served with Armed Forces Radio Service, 1950-52. Recipient Masada award State Israel, 1973. Mem. Producer Guild Am., Dirs. Guild Am., Screen Actors Guild, Actors Equity Assn., Hollywood Radio and TV Soc. (dir., v.p.), Tau Delta Phi. Mem. B'nai B'rith (past pres.). Home: 817 N Roxbury Dr Beverly Hills CA 90210

FADDEN, DELMAR MCLEAN, elec. engr.; b. Seattle, Nov. 10, 1941; s. Gene Scott and Alice Elizabeth (McLean) F.; B.S., U. Wash., 1963, M.S., 1975; m. Sandra Myrene Callahan, June 22, 1963; children—Donna McLean, Lawrence Gene. With Boeing Co., Seattle, 1969—, site mgr. terminal configured vehicle program NASA Langley Research Center, 1974-77, mgr. 757/767 flight deck integration, Seattle, 1977—. Served with USAF, 1963-69. Decorated Air medal. Mem. Human Factors Soc., IEEE, AIAA. Republican. Clubs: Mountaineers, Am. Alpine. Patentee in field. Home: 14901 NE 147th Pl Woodinville WA 98072 Office: Boeing Co PO Box 3707 Seattle WA 98124

FADELEY, EDWARD NORMAN, state senator, lawyer; b. Williamsville, Mo., Dec. 13, 1929; s. Robert Sylvester and Nelle (Norman) F.; m. Nancie Newell Peacocke, 1953; children—Charles Norman, Shira Nannette. A.B., U. Mo., 1951; J.D., U. Oreg., 1957. Sec.-treas. Oreg. Research Inst., Inc., 1960-76; chmn. uniform laws com. Oreg. State Bar, 1963-65; presiding chmn. state conv. Oreg. State Bar, 1962; mem. Oreg. Ho. of Reps. from Lane County, 1961-63, Oreg. State Senate, 1963—, asst. majority leader, chmn. disclosure of influences on govt. com., 1964-66, mem. steering com. Com. to Repeal Death Penalty, chmn. environ. and energy com., 1977-79, mem. ways and means com., 1976-79, now chmn. Precinct committeeman Democratic Party, Eugene, 1956—, area chmn., 1958-64; permanent chmn. Dem. State Platform Com., 1964-66; chmn. Oreg. Dem. Party, 1967-68; del. Dem. Nat. Conv., 1968; nominee for U.S. Congress, 1968; chmn. Oreg. Legis. Counsel Com., 1971-73; chmn. law and justice com. Nat. Legis. Conf., 1977-78. Served to lt. (j.g.), U.S. Navy, 1947-54; ETO. Nominee as Disting. Jr. Citizen, Eugene, 1963, 64; recipient 1st Pioneer award U. Oreg., 1980, Oreg. Civil Rights award, 1977. Mem. Am. Acad. Polit. and Social Sci., Am. Judicature Soc., C. of C., ACLU. Methodist. Club: Metropolitan Civic. Contbr. articles to profl. jours. Home: 260 Sunset Dr Eugene OR 97403 Office: Oregon State Senate Salem OR 97310*

FADEM, JOYCE A., professional association executive, political science consultant; b. Los Angeles, Feb. 25, 1932; d. Arthur J. and Regina T. (Goodman) Abrams; m. Jerrold Alam Fadem, June 17, 1951 (div.); children—Cheryl, Judith. B.A. with highest honors in Polit. Sci., UCLA, 1952, M.A., 1961. Cert. secondary tchr., Calif. Tchr. pub. schs., Los Angeles, 1953-57, 59-60; tng. tchr. UCLA Tchr. Tng. Program, 1955-57, 59-60, project writer UCLA Sch. Edn., 1960-61, instr., 1963; cons. Calif. Dept. Edn., 1964-69; faculty Immaculater Heart Coll., 1967-69, Social sci. dept. Los Angeles City Coll., 1961-69; instr. U.S. Internat. U., 1971-72; polit. edn. exec. Calif. Tchrs. Assn., 1969-78, polit. affairs dir., 1978—. Chmn. Democratic State Central Com. Campaign Conf., 1968; coordinator Educators for Alan Cranston, 1968, 80; vol. coordinator 1974 U.S. Senate election; state sec. Calif. Dem. Council, 1963-67; active Los Angeles Dem. County Central Com., 1966-76, Calif. Dem. State Central Com., 1960-64, 66-76; alt. del. Dem. Nat. Conv., 1964, 68, 74; active Mayor's Mgmt. Adv. com., 1974-75, Los Angeles City Bicentennial commn., 1975-76, adv. com. Joint Com. State Legislation Revision Election Code, 1975-77; commr. Los Angeles City Housing Authority, 1974—; chmn. 1976-77; bd. govs. State Bar Calif., 1976-81. Mem. Nat. Council Social Studies, Law in Free Soc. (exec. com.), Women's Trusteeship. Jewish. Co-author: A Program to Improve Teaching about the Bill of Rights, 1962; contbr. articles to profl. jours. Office: 3737 W Century Blvd Suite 400 Los Angeles CA 90045

FAFARMAN, DAVID S., structural engr., systems analyst; b. Bklyn., Jan. 30, 1944; s. Alfred and Mildred F.; B.S. in Computer Sci., SUNY, 1977; m. Melissa Jean Thomas, Dec. 30, 1970; children—Ethan, Aaron. With Bridge Div. City of Los Angeles, 1966-73, Ralph M. Parsons Co., 1973-77, Boeing Computer Services Co., 1977-78; with EDS Nuclear Inc., 1978-80; research engr. Cygna Energy Services (formerly Earthquake Engring. Systems, Inc.), San Francisco, 80—, speaker engring., software. Registered structural engr., Calif. Mem. Am. Concrete Inst., ASCE. Author various computer programs. Office: 101 California St San Francisco CA 94111

FAGAL, RUTH ELLEN, educator; b. Everett, Mass., July 27, 1924; d. Alexander Thomson and Esther Inga (Wehner) Smith; B.A., Atlantic Union Coll., 1945; M.A.T., Andrews U., 1964; Ph.D., U. Calif., Riverside, 1977; m. Harold E. Fagal, Oct. 15, 1944; children—Carolyn, Marilyn. Sci. tchr. Miami (Fla.) Jackson High Sch., 1959-63, Benton Harbor (Mich.) Jr. High Sch., 1963-64; tchr. chemistry Norte Vista High Sch., Riverside, Calif., 1964—, chmn. sci. dept. 1967—; classroom instrnl. resource tchr.; chmn. policy bd. Inland Empire region 13 Tchr. Edn. and Computer Ctr. Mem. Nat. Sci. Tchrs. Assn., Assn. Supervision and Curriculum Devel. Republican. Seventh-day Adventist. Club: Loma Linda Univ. Women's. Home: 11845 Claycroft Ln Riverside CA 92505 Office: 6585 Crest Ave Riverside CA 92503

FAGAN, JACK CALVIN, physician; b. Chgo., July 4, 1937; s. Howard and Selma (Kaufman) F.; student Loyola U. Chgo., 1954-57; B.S., U. Ill., 1959, M.D., 1961; m. Veronica Hope Levin; children—Cynthia, Melissa, Jeffrey, Andrew, Lisa. Intern Jackson Meml. Hosp., Miami, Fla., 1961-62; resident Northwestern U. Hosp., Chgo., 1962-66; otorhinolaryngologist So. Calif. Permanente Med. Group, Van Nuys, 1969—. Served to capt. USAF, 1966-68. Diplomate Am. Bd. Otolaryngology. Fellow A.C.S., Am. Acad. Otolaryngology and Ophthalmology, Am. Acad. Facial Plastic and Reconstructive Surgery; mem. A.M.A., Tau Delta Phi, Phi Delta Epsilon. Office: 10401 Balboa Blvd Granada Hills CA 91344

FAGAN, WILLIAM LAWRENCE, plant engineer, hospital official; b. Middletown, Conn., Feb. 15, 1927; s. William Robert and Margaret Gonsega (Drennan) F.; m. Catherine Victoria Graham, Feb. 14, 1949; children—William R., Deborah, Jennifer, Jeffrey; m. 2d, Dorothy May Fluke, Jan. 10, 1973. Cert. in air conditioning and refrigeration Conn. State Tech. Inst., Hartford, 1948. Adminstrv. engr. Bay State Med. Ctr., Springfield, Mass., 1967-74, St. Luke's Episcopal Hosp., Houston, 1974-75; asst. adminstr. Alexandria (Va.) Hosp., 1975-77; dir. plant engring. Cedars-Sinai Med. Center, Los Angeles, 1977-81; dir. facilities devel. and constrn. Hoag Meml. Hosp., Newport Beach, Calif., 1981—. Served to chief warrant officer U.S. Army, 1945-67. Mem. Am. Soc. Hosp. Engrs., Am. Inst. Plant Engrs. (cert. plant engr., sr. mem.; Plant Engr. of Yr. award 1973), Calif. Hosp. Engrs. Soc., Am. Legion, Nat. Rifle Assn. Roman Catholic. Club: Industry Hills (Calif.) Golf. Contbr. chpt. to Handbook for Hospital Engineers, 1974.

FAGEN, RICHARD REES, political scientist; b. Chgo., Mar. 1, 1933; s. Abel E. and Mildred E. (Rees) F.; children—Sharon, Ruth, Elizabeth, Michael. B.A. in English Lit., Yale U., 1954; M.A. in Journalism, Stanford U., 1959, Ph.D. in Polit. Sci., 1962. Asst. prof. polit. sci. Stanford U., 1962-66, assoc. prof., 1966-70, prof., 1970—, Gildred prof. Latin Am. studies, 1981—; vis. prof. El Colegio de Mexico, Mexico City, 1965-66; resident cons. Ford Found., Santiago, Chile, 1972-73; fellow Ctr. for Advanced Study in Behavioral Scis., 1970-71; chmn. com. on Latin Am., Social Sci. Research Council, 1981-83. Served with U.S. Army, 1954-56. NSF sr. postdoctoral fellow, 1970-71; Rockefeller Found. fellow, 1977-79; Ford Found. fellow, 1965-67. Mem. Latin Am. Studies Assn. (pres. 1975). Author several books including: Rich and Poor Nations in the World Economy, 1978; Capitalism and the State in U.S.-Latin American Relations, 1979; The Nicaraguan Revolution,

1981; The Future of Central America: Policy Choices for the U.S. and Mexico, 1983. Office: Dept Polit Sci Stanford U Stanford CA 94305

FAGOT, ROBERT FREDERICK, psychologist, educator; b. Nicaragua, July 4, 1921; s. Fred Clark and Ruby M. (Howorka) F.; m. Beverly I. Fields, Apr. 1, 1961; children—Brian Kevin, Clark Albert. B.S. MIT, 1946; Ph.D., Stanford U., 1956. Asst. prof. psychology U. Oreg., Eugene, 1956-61, assoc. prof., 1962-66, prof., 1966—, acting head dept., 1966-67, head, 1968-80. Served with USNR, 1942-46. Fellow Netherlands Inst. Advanced Study, 1972-73; USPHS spl. fellow U. Calif., 1962-63. Mem. Am. Psychol. Assn., Psychonomic Soc., Psychometric Soc., Am. Statis. Assn., Sigma Xi (pres. chpt. 1965). Contbr. articles to profl. publs. including Behavioral Sci., Psychometrika, Jour. Exptl. Psychology, Perception and Psychophysics, Bull. Psychonomic Soc., Jour. Math. Psychology. Home: 680 W 35th Pl Eugene OR 97405 Office: Dept Psychology Straub Hall Univ Oreg Eugene OR 97403

FAHRENBACH, HILDEGARD B., optometrist; b. San Francisco, Apr. 12, 1934; d. Hans C. and Irma (Borgwart) Brodersen; m. Wolf-Henrich Fahrenbach, Aug. 10, 1955, (div.). B.S., Portland State U., 1975; postgrad. U. Wash., 1976; O.D., Pacific U., 1980. Fellow, Pacific U. Coll. Optometry, 1980-81; optometrist Kaiser-Permanente Med. Ctr., 1980; ptnr. Jacobs and Fahrenbach, Aloha, Oreg., 1981—; clin. instr. Pacific U. Coll. Optometry, 1982—. Mem. Am. Optometric Assn., Portland Met. Optometric Soc., Oreg. Optometric Assn., Beta Sigma Kappa. Republican. Clubs: Soroptimists Internat., Mazamas. Office: 17455 SW Farmington Rd Suite 31A Aloha OR 97007

FAHRENKOPF, FRANK JOSEPH, JR., lawyer; b. Bklyn., Aug. 28, 1939; s. Frank J. and Rose (Freeman) F.; B.A., U. Nev., 1962; J.D., U. Calif. at Berkeley, 1965; m. Mary Ethel Bandoni, Aug. 25, 1962; children—Allison Marie, Leslie Ann, Amy Michelle. Admitted to Nev. bar, 1965, D.C. bar, 1983; asso. atty. Breen & Young, Reno, Nev., 1965-67; partner, atty. Sanford, Sanford, Fahrenkopf & Mousel, Reno, 1967-75, Fahrenkopf, Mortimer, Sourwine, Mousel & Sloane, Reno, 1976—. Criminal law instr. U. Nev., 1967—; panelist reporter Citizens Conf. on Nev. Cts., 1968; mem. Nev. Bd. Bar Examiners, 1971—; judge pro tem Reno Municipal Ct., 1972—. Lectr. Nat. Jud. Coll., Reno, 1974—. Chmn. lawyers' div. United Fund, 1969-70. Chmn. Nev. Republican Com., 1975—, gen. counsel, 1972-75; No. Nev. co-chmn. Com. for Re-election of Pres., 1972; mem. exec. bd. Nev. Rep. Central Com., 1972—; mem. exec. bd. Washoe County Rep. Central Com., 1969—; nat. committeeman Nev. Young Rep., 1969-73; mem. Rep. Nat. Com., 1975—, chmn., 1983—; del. Rep. Nat. Conv., 1972, 76; chmn. Western State's Rep. Chairmens Assn., 1978—; chmn. bd. dirs. Nev. Cancer Soc., Washoe County Legal Aid Soc., Babe Ruth Baseball League, Nev. Opera Guild, Reno YWCA, Sierra Sage council Camp Fire Girls, 1974-76. Served with AUS, 1957. Recipient Distinguished Service award U.S. Jr. C. of C., 1973. Mem. Am. Judicature Soc., Comml. Law League Am., Am. Bar Assn., Am., No. Nev. (v.p. 1969) trial lawyers assns., State Bar Nev., Washoe County Bar Assn. (pres. 1973-74), Execs. Assn. Reno (dir. 1973-74), Barristers' Club Nev. (v.p. 1969-73), Republican State Chairmen's Assn. (nat. chmn. 1981-83), Nat. Assn. Gaming Attys. (pres. 1983—), Alpha Tau Omega. Home: 1040 LaRue Ave Reno NV 89509 Office: PO Box 460 Reno NV 89504

FAIGIN, LARRY BERNARD, real estate executive, lawyer; b. Cleve., Nov. 10, 1942; s. Leonard A. and Ethyl (Wax) F.; A.B., Western Res. U., 1965, J.D., 1968; m. Pamela Heishman Cornwall, Oct. 7, 1979. Admitted to Ohio bar, 1968, N.Y. bar, 1969, Ga. bar, 1972, Calif. bar, 1977; With firm Willkie Farr & Gallagher, N.Y.C., 1968-72, Alston, Miller & Gaines, Atlanta, 1972-75; v.p., gen. counsel Shapell Industries, Inc., Beverly Hills, Calif., 1976-80, sr. v.p., 1980—, gen. counsel, 1980-82 dir. 1980—, vice chmn., 1983; of counsel firm Hurt, Richardson, Garner, Todd & Cadenhead, Atlanta, 1979-81; dir. First Nat. Bank of Beverly Hills (Calif.); lectr. Yale U. Law Sch., spring 1973, fall 1974. Bd. dirs. Friends of Beta Falasha Community in Ethiopia, 1970-73; mem. vis. com. Case Western Res. U. Law Sch., 1979-81. Dewit scholar, 1966; Alumni scholar, 1967. Mem. Am. (mem. com. civil and criminal procedure anti-trust sect.), N.Y. State, Ga., Atlanta, Calif., Los Angeles County, Beverly Hills bar assn., Assn. Bar City, N.Y., Los Angeles Olympics Citizens Comm., 1980; Governor's Comm. on Affordable Housing (author of Comms. Interim Report to Governor, 1980—), Alpha Epsilon Pi, Phi Alpha Delta. Club: Ansley Golf (Atlanta). Office: 8383 Wilshire Blvd Ste 700 Beverly Hills CA 90211

FAIRBANKS, EUGENE FOX, physician; b. Eugene, Oreg., Mar. 20, 1921; s. Avard Tennyson and Beatrice Maude (Fox) F.; A.B., U. Mich., 1942, M.D., 1945; m. Florence Marie Sundwall, Dec. 19, 1944; children—Eugene Sundwall, Suzanne (Mrs. Dan Weller), Lenore (Mrs. John Frodsham), Mary Annette, Marcus Allen, Peter Nathan, Christopher Neil, Laura Diane, John Leo, Virginia Louise. Intern, Wayne County Gen. Hosp., Eloise, Mich., 1945-46; resident anesthesiology U. Utah., 1948; practice gen. medicine, Kennewick, Wash., 1949-57; resident anesthesiology Mason Clinic, Seattle, 1958; practice medicine specializing in anesthesiology and gen. medicine, Bellingham, Wash., 1959—; clin. asso. anesthesiology faculty U. Wash. Med. Sch., 1965-74. Served to capt. M.C., AUS, 1946-48. Diplomate Am. Bd. Anesthesiology, Am. Bd. Family Practice. Mem. AMA, Am. Soc. Anesthesiologists, Am. Acad. Gen. Practice, AAAS. Author: (with Charles J. Flora) The Sound And The Sea, A Guide to Northwestern Neritic Invertebrate Zoology, 1966; A Sculptor's Testimony in Bronze and Stone, The Sacred Sculpture of Avard T. Fairbanks. Home: 815 17th St Bellingham WA 98225 Office: Herald Bldg Bellingham WA 98225

FAIRBANKS, ROBERT MILTON, television advertising sales; b. San Francisco, July 24, 1939; s. Milton Roy and Elizabeth Mary (Natusch) F.; m. Patricia Anne Gilkeson, Jan. 19, 1952; children—Richard, William, Elizabeth. B.A. in English, U. San Francisco, 1951. Promotion, research Sta. KCBS, San Francisco, 1951-54; research dir. Sta. KNX, Los Angeles, 1954-56; research & local sales Sta. KNXT-TV, Los Angeles, 1956-60, gen. sales mgr., 1970-73; nat. sales CBS-TV, San Francisco, 1961, Chgo., 1962-65, N.Y.C., 1966-68, dir. sta. services, N.Y.C., 1969; retail sales mgr. Sta. KABC, Los Angeles, 1975; v.p. (western sales) Television Bur. Advt., Los Angeles, 1976—; mem. faculty U. So. Calif., UCLA; lectr. Bd. mem. Advt. Industry Emergency Fund Los Angeles, 1975; bd. dirs., past pres. Cath. Press Council So. Calif., 1979. Served to 1st lt. USNG, 1951-61. Mem. Hollywood Radio & TV Soc., Alpha Sigma Nu (pres.). Clubs: Los Angeles Tennis. Home: 2631 Nichols Canyon Rd Los Angeles CA 90046 Office: 6380 Wilshire Blvd Los Angeles CA 90048

FAIRCHILD, ARVID PERSHING, travel agy. exec.; b. Turlock, Calif., Jan. 6, 1925; s. Clarence Frank and Maybelle (Dunagan) F.; B.S. in Civil Engring., U. Miami (Fla.), 1955; m. Grace M. Stewart, June 20, 1943; children—Jack W., Jeenne A. Fairchild Cook. Dir. ops. Interocean Airways, Luxembourg, 1961-63; flight instr. United Airlines, 1963-64; check pilot Japan Air Lines, 1964-74; pres., chmn. bd. Island Air Tours, Kilohana World Travel (formerly Scenic Island Travel), Honolulu, 1974—; v.p. Horizon Airlines/Trans Nat. Airlines; v.p. Pacific Air Express; dir. ops. UN airlift for Congo, 1962; capt. Seaboard Western Airlines, 1955-62. Served with USN, 1940-53. Decorated Air medal (3), Purple Heart, Army Disting. Service medal with oak leaf clusters. Mem. Nat. Assn. Businessmen. Republican. Presbyterian. Clubs: Masons, Shriners, Order Eastern Star. Author: Instrument Flight Technique; also articles in aviation publs. Home: 927 Prospect St Apt 1504 Honolulu HI 96822 Office: 1012 Piikoi St Honolulu HI 96814

FAIRCHILD, ELIZABETH MAGDALENE, ret. oil co. ofcl.; b. Springfield, Mo., Sept. 11, 1916; d. Adolph and Maude Elizabeth (Suttle) Lohr; B.A., UCLA, 1936; m. Ennis Payne Fairchild, Mar. 27, 1937; children—Ennis Payne, James B., Michael W. Mem. data processing staff Douglas Aircraft Co., Santa Monica, Calif., 1937-41; supr. data processing Wilmington (Calif.) Boat Works, 1952-55, Hazelton Wholesale Hardware Co., Compton, Calif., 1955-59, Calif. Marine Packing Co., Terminal Island, Calif., 1959-71; mgr. data processing UCO Oil Co., Irvine, Calif., 1973-82. Mem. Am. Mgmt. Assn., Univac User's Group, Data Processing Mmgt. Assn., Long Beach Symphony Guild. Republican. Christian Scientist. Home: 2800 Cedar Ave Long Beach CA 90806

FAIRCHILD, ROGER LEE, state senator, beverage company executive; b. Weiser, Idaho, Jan. 19, 1953; s. Virgil Roy and Olive Mae (Coffman) F.; student Coll. of Idaho, 1971-73. Pres., Payette Cider Co., Fruitland, Idaho, 1973—, pres., 1978—; mem. Idaho Senate, 1980—. Mem. C. of C. (dir. 1979—).

FAIRCHILD, THOMAS NEWMAN, psychologist, educator; b. Burley, Idaho, Nov. 21, 1947; s. Loyal Bryant and Bernyce Elizabeth (Rudolph) F.; m. Carolyn Ardria Yoder, Oct. 1, 1966 (div.); children—David Brian, Brandi Michelle, Nicole Kathryn; m. 2d, Ellen Lorett; 1 son, Joshua Thomas. B.S. in Psychology, U. Idaho, 1969, M.Ed. in Guidance and Counseling, 1971, Specialist D., 1972; Ph.D. in Sch. Psychology, U. Iowa, 1974. Cert. sch. counselor, psychologist, Idaho. Counselor, sch. psychologist Walla Walla Community Sch. Dist. (Wash.), 1971; sch. psychologist Cedar Rapids Community Schs. (Iowa), 1971-74; counselor educator, sch. psychologist trainer Coll. Edn., U. Idaho, Moscow, 1974—, chm. dept. guidance and counseling, 1978—; cons. in field. Mem. Rocky Mountain Assn. for Counselor Edn. Supervision (sec. treas.), Nat. Assn. Sch. Psychologists (accountability com.), Am. Personnel and Guidance Assn., Am. Psychology Assn., Council Exceptional Children, Assn. for Counselor Edn. and Supervision (resources and research com.), Idaho Assn. for Counselor Edn. and Supervision, Idaho Personnel and Guidance Assn., Idaho Sch. Psychologists Assn., Idaho Stateline Guidance Assn., Phi Delta Kappa. Co-author: (with A. Lee Parks) How to Survive Educator Burnout, 1981; editor: Accountability for School Psychologists: Selected Readings, 1977; Mainstreaming Series, 1976—; mem. editorial bd. Psychology in the Schools, 1976—, Sch. Psychology Rev., 1978-81; contbr. to profl. jours. and filmstrips. Home: 714 S Sherwood PO Box 8748 Moscow ID 83843 Office: Coll Education U Idaho Moscow ID 83843

FAIRCHILD, THOMAS WILLIAM, counselor, therapist; b. Aberdeen, Wash., Apr. 10, 1943; s. Wesley and Jean Elizabeth (Cox) F.; B.A. in Ethnic Study, Human Services, W. Wash. State Coll., 1975; degree in Society and Justice, U. Wash., 1977. Counselor, Women's Treatment Center, Purdy, Wash., 1970-74, Seattle Crisis Clinic, 1974-75; pvt. practice counseler-therapist, Seattle, 1975—; cons. in tng. and personal dynamics. Mem. Democratic Precinct Com., Person, Seattle, 1975-78; chmn. law and justice com. Thurston County, Olympia, 1972-75. Recipient outstanding jaycee of yr. award Olympia Jaycees, 1972. Mem. Nat. Assn. Vols. in Criminal Justice, Nat. Council on Crime and Delinquency, ACLU. Democrat. Unitarian. Club: Unitarian Singles. Address: 3212 21st W Seattle WA 98199

FAIRFIELD, THEODORE CORBIN, civil engr.; b. Modesto, Calif., June 20, 1935; s. Corbin Francis and Meta Cecilia (Johansen) F.; A.A., Modesto Jr. Coll., 1954; B.S., San Jose State U., 1959; m. Evelyn Gail Ewin. Aug. 13, 1971; children—Terri L. (Mrs. Brian Anderson), Connie L. (Mrs. Jeff Ganz). Civil engr. City of San Jose (Calif.), 1957-59, Town of Los Gatos (Calif.), 1959; civil engr., v.p. Mackay & Somps, San Jose, 1960-78; cons. civil engr., Pleasanton, Calif., 1978—. Pres. M & S Environ. Center, 1974-77; park commr. City of Pleasanton, 1966-68; bd. dirs. Valley Meml. Hosp., Livermore, Calif., 1970-79. Served with AUS, 1954-56. Fellow ASCE, Calif. Council Civil Engrs. and Land Surveyors (pres. 1977), Asso. Bldg. Industry (dir. E. Bay div. 1971-76), Pleasanton C. of C. (dir. 1969-72). Clubs: Rotary (pres. Pleasanton 1967-68), Masons. Home: 2333 Woodthrush Way Pleasanton CA 94566 Office: PO Box 1148 Pleasanton CA 94566

FAIRHURST, STANLEY JAMES, university administrator; b. Seattle, Feb. 17, 1929; s. Cyril J. and Catherine Lucy (Costello) F.; m. Mary W. Olson, Oct. 11, 1956; children—Mary, Vincent, Ann, Kathryn, Victoria, Kenneth, Laura. B.A., Gonzaga U., 1952, M.A., 1955. Vice pres., Fairhurst Lumber Cos., San Rafael, Calif., 1955-62, also dir.; pres. Star & Crescent Towboat Co., San Diego, 1963-68; v.p. Dillingham Corp., Maritime Services, Honolulu, 1969-75; v.p. bus. and fin. Gonzaga U., 1975—; guest lectr. in field. Bd. dirs. various charitable orgns. Mem. Nat. Assn. Coll. and Univ. Bus. Officers, Western Assn. Coll. and Univs. Bus. Officers, Assn. Jesuit Coll. and Univ. Bus. Officers. Republican. Contbr. articles to Modern Schoolman. Home: N 7523 Fox Point Dr Spokane WA 99208 Office: E 502 Boone Spokane WA 99258

FAIRWEATHER, PAUL DOUGLAS, clin. psychologist; b. Bottineau, N.D., July 22, 1919; s. William and Vera Eleanor (Turner) F.; B.S., U. So. Calif., 1948, M.S., 1949, Ph.D., 1960; B.Div., Fuller Theol. Sem., 1953; m. Nelle Bryles, Feb. 16, 1947; children—Paul Douglas, Pamela Dianne; m. 2d, Marguerite Cardinalli, Aug. 22, 1980; 1 son, Mathan Sergio. Ordained to ministry Am. Baptist Ch., 1957; minister, Oakridge, Oreg., 1953-56; counseling psychologist U. So. Calif., 1958-60; minister of counseling and edn. Calvary Bapt. Ch., Pasadena, Calif., 1958-60; prof. psychology, dean students Calif. Bapt. Sem., Covina, 1958-60; prof. psychology Fuller Theol. Sem., Pasadena, 1961-64, prof. clin. psychology Fuller Sch. Psychology, 1964-68; dir. counseling psychologists Fairweather-Bade Assocs., Glendale, Arcadia and Monrovia, Calif., 1968-80; pvt. practice psychology, Arcadia and Laguna Niguel, Calif., 1978—; cons.; owner, operator Fairweather Farms, Santa Barbara, Calif., 1970—. Bd. dirs. Verdugo Found. Human Growth, Glendale, Center for Human Intimacy, 1981—. Served to lt. USAAF, 1943-47. Decorated Air medal with oak leaf cluster, D.F.C. Mem. Am., Calif. psychol. assns., Pasadena Clin. Psychol. Assn., Soc. Clin. Hypnosis, Am. Personnel and Guidance Assn., Am. Assn. Pastoral Counselors, Am. Soc. Advancement Psychology, Phi Delta Kappa. Author: Symbolic Regression Psychology. Home: 1210 Vista Cantora San Clemente CA 92672 Office: 30131 Town Center Dr Laguna Niguel CA 92677

FAISON, EDMUND WINSTON JORDAN, business educator; b. Rocky Mt., N.C., Oct. 13, 1926; s. Nathan Marcus and Margery Lucille (Jordan) F.; A.B. in Psychology, George Washington U., 1948, M.A., 1950, Ph.D., 1956; m. Lois Harger Parker; children—Charles, Dorothy Anne, Barbara Jeane. Research asst. NRC, Washington, 1948-49; mgr. exptl. lab. Needham, Louis and Brorby, Chgo., 1955-56; account exec. Leo Burnett Co., Chgo., 1957-58; v.p. Market Facts Inc., Chgo., 1959; pres. Visual Research Internat., Zurich, Switzerland, 1960-61; adviser AID, Dept. State, Latin Am., 1963-68; prof. bus. adminstrn. U. Hawaii, Honolulu, 1968—, chmn. mktg. dept., 1975-81; chmn. bd. East-West Research and Design Inc.; vis. prof. Aoyama Gakuin U., Japan, 1973, London Grad Sch. Bus. Studies, 1974-75. Served with USN, 1944-46; USAF, 1950-54. Mem. Am. Psychol. Assn., Soc. Consumer Behavior, Am. Marketing Assn. (pres. Honolulu chapter 1973-74), Acad. Mktg. Sci., Acad. Mgmt., Am. Acad. Advt., Am. Assn. for Pub. Opinion, Sales and Mktg. Execs. Internat., Advt. Research Found., Honolulu Advt. Fedn., Honolulu Acad. Arts, All-Industry Packaging Assn. (chmn. 1961), European Packaging Fedn. (U.S. Rep., 1961), Sigma Xi, Pi Sigma Epsilon. Clubs: Kaneohe Yacht, Oahu Country, Pacific. Author: Advertising: A Behavioral Approach for Managers; editorial bd. Jour. of Mktg., 1958-63. Contbr. articles to profl. jours. Home: Box 1207 Kailua HI 96734 Office: 146-103 Hekili St Kailua HI 96734 also U Hawaii Honolulu HI 96822

FAISS, WILBUR, state senator; b. Centralia, Ill., Oct. 14, 1911; m. Theresa Watts; children—Robert, Donald, Ronald. Ed. Brown's Univ. of Bus., Chillicothe, Mo. Mem. Nev. State Senate, 1977—. Adv. bd. Nev. Youth Agy., 1974-76; sec. Eldorado Valley Adv. Group. Mem. So. Nev. Teamster Retirees. Democrat. Clubs: Clark County Srs. Golf, YMCA Men's Health. Lodge: North Las Vegas Lions. Office: Nevada State Senate Legislative Bldg Carson City NV 89701*

FAIT, LINDA, educator; b. Tooele, Utah, Oct. 22, 1945; d. Joseph A. Vicevich and Lucille Murray Fait; B.S., Utah State U., 1967, M.Ed., 1971; Ed.S., Brigham Young U., 1980, Ed.D., 1982. Tchr., asst. prin. Granite Sch. Dist., Salt Lake City, 1967—; sec. EEO officer, Mather AFB, 1969. Mem. leadership and tng. staffs Ch. Jesus Christ Latter-day Saints. Mem. Granite Edn. Assn., Utah Edn. Assn., NEA, Delta Kappa Gamma, Delta Delta Delta.

FAIT-COLOMBO, JAMI LUCILLE, real estate syndication/construction company executive; b. Inglewood, Calif., Mar. 18, 1950; d. Benjamin and Lillian (Aquino) Ybarra; m. Paul J. Colombo, 1983. Bus. adminstrn. student Calif. State U. Asst. mgr. H.F.C., Long Beach, Calif., 1967-70; constrn. liaison First Interstate Bank/Restaurant Adventures, Garden Grove, Calif., 1970-73; mgr. spl. assignments Thomas Temporaries, Irvine, Calif., 1973-78; with Hughes Investments, Newport Beach, Calif., 1978-81; regional mgr. The Heritage Group, Beverly Hills, Calif., 1981-82; constrn. mgr. Ralphs Grocery Co., Compton, Calif., 1982—; cons. BFS-The Property Doctor, 1982—. Mem. Nat. Assn. Female Execs., Apt. Owners, Mgrs. Assn., Bldg. Owners and Mgrs. Assn. Club: Long Beach Civic Light Opera. Office: PO Box 54143 Los Angeles CA 90055

FAITH, CHARLES ALBERT, III, ins. co. exec.; b. Rahway, N.J., Jan. 31, 1952; s. Charles Albert and Jessiemay (Aycock) F. B.A., U.S. Internat. U., 1974. Counselor, Model Ex-Offenders, San Diego, 1974-75; loss control rep. Continental Ins. Co., San Francisco, 1976-77; Fireman's Fund Ins. Co., San Diego, 1977-80; comml. ins. broker Bromac, San Diego, 1980—. Mem. Profl. Ins. Agts. Assn., Am. Soc. Safety Engrs. Home: 2041 Alta View Dr San Diego CA 92139 Office: 1817 Morena Blvd #E San Diego CA 92110

FAJARDO, RAOUL JOSE, physicist; b. Santiago, Cuba, Feb. 17, 1919; s. Albert Hilarion and Elena (Real) F.; came to U.S., 1936, naturalized, 1944; B.A., Stanford U., 1950, M.A., 1951; postgrad. U. Santa Clara, 1958. Asst. instr. Spanish, Stanford U., 1948-51; vis. prof. comparative religions U. Oriente and U. Havana, Cuba, 1951-52; specifications engr. Lockheed MSD, Sunnyvale and Palo Alto, Calif., 1958-59; tech. writer Philco Corp., Palo Alto, 1961-62; prof. physics and electronics Pasadena (Calif.) City Coll., 1962—; project engr. Scott Aviation. cons. flute acoustics. Pres. Human Resonance Assn. Served with USAAF, 1942-46. Recipient medal for Disting. Services to Music, 1975. Mem. Stanford Alumni Assn. Author: The Sound of the Flute, 1981; Creative Constitution of the Universe, 1982; Romantic Adventure, 1983. Patentee in field. Home and Office: PO Box 80711 San Marino CA 91108-8711

FAKHRY, REBECCA JONES, health care executive; b. Long Beach, Calif., Oct. 29, 1953; d. Donald A. and Selma B. (Barry) Jones; m. Ahmed M. Fakhry, May 7, 1978. B.A., U. Hawaii, 1975; M.A., UCLA, 1977. Curriculum devel. specialist UCLA project in Cairo, Egypt, 1977-79; curriculum dir. Cambria Adult Sch., Los Angeles, 1979; mgr. employment support services Nat. Med. Enterprises, Los Angeles, 1979—. Am. Field Service Internat. scholar, Jogjakarta, Indonesia, 1971; Intra-U. Consortium on Indonesian Abroad scholar, Malang, 1976. Mem. UCLA Alumni Assn., Nat. Assn. Female Execs., Am. Field Service Alumni. Democrat. Contbr. articles to profl. jours. Home: 5230 Carmelynn St Torrance CA 90503 Office: 2901 28th St Santa Monica CA 90405

FAKLER, THOMAS LOUIS, computer cons.; b. Winona, Minn., Dec. 30, 1948; s. Emil Louis and Marjorie (Ferguson) F.; m. Dianne Marie Toebe, Mar. 21, 1978. B.A., Winona State U., 1970; M.S., U. So. Calif., 1982. Commd. officer U.S. Air Force, 1971, advanced through grades to capt.; ret., 1981; sr. cons. Price Waterhouse, Anchorage, Alaska, 1980—; adj. lectr. Anchorage Community Coll., 1982-83. Decorated Air medal with oak leaf cluster. Mem. Data Processing Mgmt. Assn., Assn. for Systems Mgmt. Home: 8211 Pioneer Dr Anchorage AK 99504 Office: Price Waterhouse 101 W Benson Blvd Suite 500 Anchorage AK 99503

FALCIONI, JOSEPH GEORGE, mfg. engr.; b. Jessup, Pa., July 12, 1922; s. Vincent and Elizabeth (Brancaleoni) F.; B.S. in Mech. and Civil Engring., Ind. Inst. Tech., 1954; m. Mary Margaret Haggstrom, Apr. 23, 1949; children—Melanie, Cynthia, Deborah, Kristina. Designer, Boeing Airplane Co., Seattle, 1954-56, mfg. research and devel. engr., Everett, Wash., 1958—; plant maintenance engr. Kaiser Aluminum Co., Tacoma, 1956-58. Served to capt. USAF, 1943-50. Roman Catholic. Home: 1812 70th Ave E Tacoma WA 98424 Office: Boeing Airplane Co Everett WA

FALCONE, PATRICIA JEANNE LALIM, ret. educator, pvt. investor; b. Montevideo, Minn., Oct. 12; d. Clarence I. and Eva (Corneliusen) Lalim; B.S. (Silver Key for leadership), U. Minn., 1956; M.S., U. Wis., Madison, 1958, Ph.D. (fellowship, U. scholar), 1962; m. Alfonso Benjamin Falcone, Oct. 22; children—Christopher Laurence Lalim, Steven Benjamin Lalim. Instr., Sch. Family Resources and Consumer Sci., U. Wis., Madison, 1965-66; pvt. investor, Fresno, 1968—; contbr. to Wis. Improvement Program Conf., Betty Crocker Search for Am. Homemaker of Tomorrow, Space and Equipment Workshop, Conf. Gateway to the Future, U. Wis. Vice-pres., Fresno Parents for the Gifted; mem. Ruth Gibson Sch. Site Council. Mem. Am. Home Econs. Assn., AAUW, Norwegian-Am. Hist. Assn., Am. Scandinavian Found., Med. Aux. of Fresno County Med. Soc., Calif. Assn. for Gifted, Calif. Home Econs. Assn., Fresno Arts Ctr., Met. Mus. Fresno, Omicron Nu, Pi Lambda Theta, Phi Delta Gamma. Clubs: Sons of Norway, The Valdres Samband. Contbr. ednl. articles to profl. jours. and newspapers; lectr. ednl. groups. Office: 2240 E Illinois St Fresno CA 93701

FALERO, FRANK, JR., educator, economist; b. N.Y.C., Dec. 22, 1937; s. Frank and Lydia Del Castillo (Camis) F.; B.A. in History, U. So. Fla., 1964; M.S. in Econs., Fla. State U., 1965, Ph.D., 1967; children—Lisa Ann, Sara Francine. Asst. prof. Va. Poly. Inst. and State U., Blacksburg, 1967-72; prof. econs. and fin. Calif. State Coll., Bakersfield, 1972—; v.p. fin. Am. Wind Energy Systems. Fulbright vis. prof., Lima, Peru, 1968-69; cons. AID, 1970-72. Trustee Calif. Council Econ. Edn.; bd. dirs. Center for Econ. Edn. Served with AUS, 1955-58. NDEA IV fellow, 1964-67. Fellow Royal Econ. Soc.; mem. Am. Econs. Assn., N.Am. Econs. Studies Assn. Author: Monetary History of Honduras, 1950-68, 1972; Elementos Básicos de Econometria, 1969. Home: 2316 Gosford Rd Apt U Bakersfield CA 93309

FALICK, ABRAHAM JOHNSON, economist, corporate executive; b. Chgo., Oct. 11, 1920, s. Simon and Ellen Martina (Johnson) F.; m. Carolyn Weber, Aug. 12, 1916; 1 dau., Leslie Carol Koplof. B.A. in Econs., Ind. U., 1947; M.B.A. in Bus. Econs., U. Chgo., 1951; M.A. in Econ. Geography, UCLA, 1967, Ph.D., 1970; cert. planner. Vice pres. mktg. Webb Linn Printing Co., Chgo., 1948-56; pres. Falick Assos., Los Angeles, 1960-67; planning economist Los Angeles City Planning Dept., 1967-75; sec.-treas. Navigator Press, Inc., Los Angeles, 1975-81, pres., 1982—. Chmn. Coalition for Rapid Transit, Los Angeles. Served to lt. comdr. USNR, 1940-67; PTO. Mem. Am. Econ. Assn., Nat. Assn. Bus. Economists, Assn. Am. Geographers, Am. Planning Assn., Am. Inst. Cert. Planners. Office: 1636 W 8th St Suite 111 Los Angeles CA 90017

FALK, EUGENE L., newspaper exec.; b. Smith Center, Kans., May 10, 1943; s. Lester S. and Esther Belle (Hatfield) F.; B.S. in Elec. Engring. and Journalism (L.C. Paddock fellow), U. Colo., 1967; M.B.A., Rochester Inst. Tech., 1971; m. Joanne Krys, Jan. 20, 1968; children—Laura Rae, Shannon Lynn. Asst. prodn. dir. Wall St. Jour., N.Y.C., 1967-69, Gannett Newspapers, Rochester, N.Y., 1969-71; dir. systems and engring. Harte-Hanks Newspapers, San Antonio, 1971-73; with Knight-Ridder Newspapers, 1973—, asst. dir. prodn. Ridder Publs., Denver, 1973-75, prodn. dir. Wichita (Kans.) Eagle-Beacon, 1975-76, dir. ops. San Jose (Calif.) Mercury-News, 1976—; lectr. Am. Press Inst., 1977-78. Mem. Am. Newspaper Prodn. Assn., Western Newspaper Pubs. Assn. (dir.). Republican. Clubs: San Jose W. Rotary, Courtside Tennis, La Rinconado Country. Home: 212 Brooke Acres Los Gatos CA 95030

FALKENBERG, WILLIAM STEVENS, architect, contractor; b. Kansas City, Mo., July 21, 1927; s. John Joseph and Maraba Elizabeth (Stevens) F.; B.S. in Archtl. Engring., U. Colo., 1949; m. Janis Patton Hubner, Apr. 13, 1951; children—Ruth Elizabeth, Christopher Joseph, Charles Stevens. Pres., Falkenberg Constrn. Co., Denver, 1951-71; broker Hogan & Stevenson Realty, Denver, 1971-74; pres. Falkenberg Constrn. Co., 1974—. Chmn. constrn. Archdiocesan Housing Com., Inc.; chmn. restoration 9th St. Hist. Park; chmn. bldg. com. Four Mile House Hist. Park; chmn. Rocky Mountain Better Bus. Bur., 1965-67; pres. Denver Friends of Folk Music, 1966. Served to lt. (j.g.) USNR, 1945-51. Mem. AIA (bd. dirs. Denver chpt. 1978-81, treas. 1981), Home Builders Assn. Met. Denver, Serra Internat. (pres. 1971, dist. gov. 1973), Delta Tau Delta. Clubs: Denver Athletics, Cactus, Equestrian Order of Holy Sepulchre. Home: 430 Marion St Denver CO 80218 Office: 430 Marion St Denver CO 80218

FALLIS, RICHARD MONROE, chem. co. exec.; b. Gallup, N.Mex., May 16, 1934; s. John Fred and Bess May (Reed) F.; B.S., U. N.Mex., 1959; postgrad. U. So. Calif., 1959-61; grad. Advanced Mgmt. Program, Harvard, 1975; m. Carol Anne Martin, Aug. 29, 1959; children—Paul Richard, Mark Christopher, Keith Martin. Chemist Internat. Chem. and Nuclear Corp., Industry, Calif., 1960-63, lab. dir., 1963-67, pres. Chem. and Radioisotope div., Irvine, Calif., 1967-73, ops. officer Arco div., Geneva, 1973-76, pres. ICN Med. Labs. div., 1976-78, corp. devel. staff ICN Pharms., 1978-80, v.p. mfg. Viratek subs., 1980—. Served with AUS, 1954-56. Mem. Am. Chem. Soc., Sigma Chi. Presbyn. (deacon). Home: 1825 Wedgewood Upland CA 91786 Office: 222 N Vincent Covina CA 91722

FALLON, MARY PATRICIA, counselor; b. Kansas City, Mo., Sept. 15, 1953; d. Joseph John and Ethel Mary (Schwartz) Fallon; m. Daniel Louis Coleman, July 26, 1975; B.A. in Psychology and Human Devel., U. Kans.-Lawrence, 1974; M.A. in Counseling, W. Va. U.-Morgantown, 1976; Ph.D. in Ednl. Psychology, U. Wash.-Seattle, 1983. Play therapist U. Kans. Med. Ctr., Lawrence, 1971-75; fellow in genetics counseling W. Va. U. Med. Ctr., Morgantown, 1976; elem. sch. counselor, Winston-Salem, N.C., 1977-80, supr. for new counselors, 1978 80; counselor U. Wash. Counseling Ctr., Seattle, 1980—; cons. on women and eating disorders U. Wash., 1982-83; cons. family styles project UCLA, 1982. Active Sierra Club, chmn. Ednl. Psychology Student Caucus, 1981-83. Mem. Am. Psychol. Assn., Am. Personnel and Guidance Assn., Assn. for Counselor Educators and Suprs., Assn. for Women in Psychology, Phi Beta Kappa, Pi Lambda Theta. Contbr. numerous articles to profl. jours. Office; Counseling Ctr 401 Schmitz Hall PB 05 University of Washington Seattle WA 98195

FALSONE, ANNE MARIE MCMAHON, state ofcl.; b. N.Y.C., May 20, 1937; d. Thomas Henry and Betty May (Stansel) McMahon; B.S., Memphis State U., 1956, M.A., 1968; M.L.S., George Peabody Coll., Vanderbilt U., 1969; m. James H. Kennedy. Head librarian White Station Jr./Sr. High Sch., Memphis, 1966-71; asst. head history dept. Memphis Public Library, 1971-72; cons. sch. libraries Colo. State Library, 1972-75; supr. state sch. library programs Colo. Dept. Edn., Denver, 1975-76, asst. commr. Office Library Services, 1976-82, asst. commr. library and adult services, 1982—; trustee Bibliog. Center Research; mem. Colo. Gov.'s Commn. on Public Telecommunications. Mem. ALA, Colo. Library Assn., Colo. Ednl. Media Assn., Chief Officers of State Library Agys., Western Council State Libraries, Colo. Assn. Sch. Execs., Phi Alpha Theta, Beta Phi Mu, Alpha Lambda Delta, Alpha Delta Pi. Home: 1551 Larimer Apt 805 Denver CO 80202 Office: 1362 Lincoln St Denver CO 80203

FANCHER, DOUGLAS BURTON, psychologist; b. Birmingham, Ala., Oct. 20, 1934; s. Odess Burton and Winnie Wilma (Weathers) F.; A.B., Birmingham So. Coll., 1960; M.S., U. So. Miss., 1967, Ph.D., 1970. Psychology intern Milw. Child Psychiatric Clinic, 1970-71; clin. psychologist VA Hosp., Ft. Lyon, Colo., 1971-77; cons. Colo. Boys' Ranch, La Junta, 1974-76; cons., tester Arkvah Sch. for Handicapped, La Junta, 1974-76; pvt. practice psychology, Ft. Lyon, 1974-76; cons. psychologist Swartzlander & Heyer Inc., Denver, 1977, E. Grand Sch. Dist., Granby, Colo., 1979. Served to lt. (j.g.) USN, 1960-64. U. So. Miss. fellow, 1966-70; lic. psychologist, Colo. Mem. Am. Psychol. Assn., Rocky Mountain Psychol. Assn., Colo. Psychol. Assn. Contbr. articles to profl. jours. Home: E Carriage Rd Fraser CO 80442

FANCHER, DOUGLAS GRANT, internat. co. exec.; b. Chgo., Feb. 19, 1942; s. Wesley Vernon and Lavinia Mary (Pertile) F.; B.A., Southwestern at Memphis, 1964; M.A., Memphis State U., 1965; M.B.A., U. Calif. at Berkeley, 1969; m. Paula Jean Conser, Nov. 25, 1966; children—Christian Anne Poole, Justin Grant. Asst. acctg. mgr. Time Inc., N.Y.C., 1969-71; controller Compucar Fin. Corp., Palo Alto, Calif., 1971-74; dir. acctg. ITEL Corp., San Francisco, 1974-76; controller, treas. Asia Devel. Corp., Oakland, Calif., 1976-78, pres., 1978-81; pres., chief exec. officer Greenwich Corp., 1980—, also subs. Assoc. Containers Ltd., Sri Lanka. Mem. Sausalito (Calif.) Sch. Dist. Bd. Edn., 1971-82; elder Sausalito Presbyn. Ch., 1968—; pres., bd. dirs. Marin Community Playhouse, 1983—; mem. Sausalito Planning Commn., 1983—. Mem. Omicron Delta Kappa, Alpha Tau Omega. Democrat. Office: 215 Caledonia St Sausalito CA 94965

FANCIULLO, JOSEPH MATTHEW, JR., auditor, appraiser; b. Omaha, Nov. 1, 1946; s. Joseph Matthew and Marie Josephine (Gulizia) F. B.S. in Acctg., Calif. State U.-Fresno, 1968. C.P.A.; cert. appraiser, cert. community coll. tchr., Calif. Pvt. practice acctg., Fresno, Calif., 1980; auditor-appraiser Office of Assessor, County of Fresno, 1969—; instr. acctg. Fresno City Coll.; grad. asst. Dale Carnegie course, 1981. Organizing com. Fresno Met. Mus., 1983. Mem. Am. Inst. C.P.A.s, Calif. Soc. C.P.A.s, Soc. Calif. Accts., Soc. Auditor-Appraisers (William Littledale Meml. award 1978, past pres. award 1980, accredited, nat. pres. 1979-80), Calif. State U.-Fresno Alumni Assn. Democrat. Roman Catholic. Club: Elks. Home: 4446 E Terrace Ave Fresno CA 93703 Office: Hall of Records PO Box 1146 Fresno CA 93715

FANDRICH, LAMONT H., controller; b. Bismarck, N.D., Oct. 10, 1951; s. Roy and Lucille Clara F.; B.A. cum laude in Bus. Adminstrn., Minot (N.D.) State Coll., 1973. Acctg. supr. Collins Foods Internat., 1977; gen. ledger supr. Sambos, 1977-1979; asst. controller Amfac Garden Products, 1979-81; controller Amfac Nurseries Select, Fallbrook, Calif., 1981—. Served with USMC, 1973-76. Mem. Am. Inst. C.P.A.s, Nat. Assn. Accts. Office: 2500 Rainbow Valley Blvd Fallbrook CA 92028

FANE, GERARD JOSEPH, lawyer; b. N.Y.C., Jan. 16, 1935; s. Gerard Joseph and Anna Marie (Hassett) F.; m. Lucetta Anne Dunn, Jan. 12, 1980; children—Christine, Anna, Gerard J. III, Edward. B.A., Fordham U., 1956; J.D., Western State Coll. of Law, 1975. Bar: Calif. 1976. Sole practice, Santa Ana, Calif., 1977-82; sr. ptnr. Dunn & Fane, Santa Ana, 1982—. Mem. ABA, Calif. State Bar, Orange County Bar Assn., Orange County Estate Planning Council. Democrat. Roman Catholic. Office: Dunn & Fane 837 N Ross St Suite 100 Santa Ana CA 92701

FANELLI, LEE RYDER, savings and loan executive; b. Dorchester, Mass., Sept. 10, 1946; d. Paul Anthony and Virginia Estelle (Noonan) R.; m. Joseph Anthony Fanelli, Jr. Mar. 21, 1970; 1 dau., Holly Ryder. Cert. Burdett Coll., 1966; student Boise State U., 1972-74. Sec. to Congressman James R. Grover, Jr., Washington, 1966-67; legal sec. Bradford Ross, Ross, Marsh & Foster, Washington, 1967-71, 75-76; sec. to pres. Intermountain Gas Co., Boise, Idaho, 1971-75; sec. to pres. N.Mex. Fed. Savs. & Loan, Albuquerque, 1976-77, asst. v.p. personnel, 1977-81; v.p. personnel, individual retirement account adminstrn., 1981—. Campaign worker Democratic Party of N.Mex., 1977-80. Recipient cert. of appreciation N.Mex. Employment Security Dept., 1979, 80. Mem. Internat. Soc. Cert. Employee Benefit Specialists (charter), Am. Soc. Personnel Adminstrn., N.Mex. Personnel Assn., Am. Soc. for Tng. and Devel., Am. Compensation Assn. Office: New Mexico Fed Savs and Loan Assn 2900 Louisiana Blvd NE Albuquerque NM 87110

FANESTIL, DARRELL D(EAN), physician, educator; b. Great Bend, Kans., Oct. 31, 1933; s. Carl Leonard and Esther (Fail) F.; B.A., U. Kans., 1955, M.D., 1958; m. Dorthy Ann Smith, Aug. 14, 1955; children—Bradley, John, Jane, Katherine. Intern, Los Angeles Gen. Hosp., 1958; fellow Lahey Clinic, Boston, 1959, Scripps Clinic and Research Found., La Jolla, Calif., 1960-62, U. Calif. at San Francisco, 1964-66; asst. prof. Kans. U. Med. Sch., 1966-68, asso. prof., 1968-70; asso. prof. U. Calif. at San Diego, 1970-72, prof., 1972—, mem. staff Univ. Hosp. San Diego; established investigator Am. Heart Assn., 1966-71. Served with USPHS, 1962-64. Markle scholar in acad. medicine, 1966-71. Mem. Am. Soc. Nephrology, Am. Physiol. Soc., Am. Fedn. Clin. Research, Am. Soc. Clin. Investigation. Home: 8491 Cliffridge Ln La Jolla CA 92037 Office: U Calif San Diego La Jolla CA 92093

FANG, JEFFREY MING-SHAN, research economist; b. Tainan, Taiwan, Sept. 15, 1940; came to U.S. 1963, naturalized 1975; s. Nau Sou and Tau Tsai F.; m. Yu-Mei Lu, Jan. 1, 1970; children—Eric Y., Karen Y., Gary Y. B.A. in Econs. Nat. Taiwan U. 1962, M.A. U. Wash. 1965, Ph.D. 1969. Lectr. econs. Western Washington U., Bellingham 1968-69, asst. prof. 1969-75; staff economist Dept. Energy State of Oreg., Salem 1975-79; sr. research economist Battelle Pacific Northwest Labs., Richland, Wash. 1979—. Served with Republic of China Army 1962-63. Mem. Am. Econ. Assn., Western Econ. Assn. Republican. Contbr. in field. Home: 3705 S Dennis St Kennewick WA 99336 Office: Battelle Blvd Richland WA 99352

FANNIN, THOMAS A., administrator, safety officer, b. Boise, Idaho, Nov. 9, 1936; s. John T. and Helen L. (Ottwood) F.; m. Sharon Koontz, Apr. 8, 1955 (div.); children—Gregory, Constance, Mark, Angela, Kevin; m. 2d, Jocelyn Shaw, Feb. 22, 1975. Student Boise Jr. Coll., 1956-60; B.A., Boise State U., 1980. Cert. Safety profl. With E.W. Little Co., Boise, 1962—, supt., 1962-78, safety officer, 1962-83, owner, 1980-82, v.p./gen. mgr., 1982—; dir. safety com. AGC, 1978-80. Active C. of C., ARC. Mem. Am. Soc. Safety Engrs., ASHRAE. Methodist. Club: Elks. Home: 2212 Division Boise ID 83706 Office: 315 S 11th Boise ID 83702

FANNING, JOHN WOOD, association executive; b. Grand Rapids, Mich., Jan 17, 1932; s. Francis Burke and Audrey (Young) F.; m. Hannah Call, Dec. 20, 1958; children—Audrey, David, Mary. B.S., U. Ill., 1953. Dist. exec. Boy Scouts Am., Des Plaines, Ill., 1955-60, Kermit and Odessa, Tex., 1960-67, Lawton, Okla., 1967-69, field dir., Tulsa, 1969-73, scout exec., Pikeville, Ky., 1973-79, Lake Charles, La., 1979-82, dir. support services Gt. Salt Lake council, Salt Lake City, 1982—. Recipient Virgil honor, Order of Arrow, Bronze Pelican award Boy Scouts Am. Mem. Sigma Pi. Republican. Mormon. Club: Rotary. Home: 1564 Winward Dr Salt Lake City UT 84117 Office: 525 Foothill Dr Salt Lake City UT 84113

FANNING, KATHERINE WOODRUFF, newspaper co. exec.; b. Chgo., Oct. 18, 1927; d. Frederick William and Katherine Bower (Miller) Woodruff; B.A., Smith Coll., 1949; LL.D., (hon.), Colby Coll., 1979; m. Marshall Field, Jr., May 12, 1950 (div. 1963); children—Frederick Woodruff, Katherine Woodruff, Barbara Woodruff; m. 2d, Lawrence S. Fanning, Sept. 13, 1966. With Anchorage Daily News, 1965—, editor, pub., 1972—, v.p., 1979—. Mem. Anchorage Urban Beautification Commn., 1968-71, Alaska Ednl. Broadcasting Commn., 1971—; dir. Alaska Repertory Theater, 1975—; pres. Greater Anchorage Community Chest, 1973-74. Recipient Elijah Parish Lovejoy award Colby Coll., 1979; Smith Coll. medal, 1980; medal of honor U. Mo. Journalism Sch., 1980. Mem. Am. Soc. Newspaper Editors (dir. 1981—), Anchorage C. of C. (dir.). Club: Anchorage Press. Office: Pouch 6616 Anchorage AK 99502

FANTUZZO, JOHN WILLIAM, clinical child psychologist, psychology educator; b. Rochester, N.Y., Aug. 23, 1952; s. John and Josephine Helen (Carey) F.; m. Christine Else, July 1, 1978; children—Lia, Cara. B.A., Marietta Coll., 1974; M.A., Fuller Theol. Sem., 1977; Ph.D. in Clin. Psychology, Fuller Grad. Sch. Psychology, 1979; postgrad. in clin. psychology U. So. Calif. Med. Sch., 1978-79; postgrad. in child psychology, Harvard U. Med. Sch., 1979-80; lic. psychologist, Calif. Dir., Covenant House, Pasadena, Calif., 1980-82; asst. prof. psychology Fuller Grad. Sch., Pasadena, 1982—, dir. child Devel. Center, 1982—. Recipient Fuller Grad. Sch. Lee Edward Travis award, 1976. Mem. Am. Psychol. Assn., Assn. for Advancement Behavior Therapy, Phi Delta Kappa. Republican. Contbr. articles to profl. jours. Home: 1519 Locust Pasadena CA 91106 Office: 190 N Oakland Pasadena CA 91101

FARACO, WILLIAM GEORGE, JR., designer; b. Glen Cove, N.Y., July 16, 1927; s. William George and Hildegard F.; m. Marylou Fisher, Dec. 27, 1958; children—Marguerite, Juliette. B.A., U. Calif., Berkeley, 1951. Owner, pres. Faraco Design, Saratoga, Calif., 1970—. Served with USMC, 1945-46. Mem. Indsl. Designers Am., Internat. Bus. Designers.

FARAH, TAWFIC ELIAS, polit. scientist; b. Nazareth, Palestine, Aug. 12, 1946; came to U.S., 1965, naturalized, 1975; s. Elias Tawfic and Itaf Fahim F.; B.A., Calif. State U., Fresno, 1970, M.A. summa cum laude, 1971; Ph.D., U. Nebr., 1975; m. Linda Maxwell, Apr. 24, 1969; children—Omar Lee, Aliya Jane. Market researcher Xerox Corp., Lincoln, Nebr., 1974-75; asst. prof. polit. sci. Kuwait U., 1975-79, pres. Middle East Research Group, 1979—; vis. asso. prof. UCLA, summers 1978-83, fellow Center for Internat. and Strategic Affairs, 1980-81; Fulbright scholar, 1983. Mem. Am. Polit. Sci. Assn., Middle East Studies Assn. Greek Orthodox. Co-author: Research Methods in the Social Sciences, 1977; A Dictionary of Social Analysis, 1980; author: Aspects of Modernization and Consociationalism: Lebanon as an Exploratory Test Case, 1975, 77; co-editor: Palestinians Without Palestine: Socialization of Palestinian Children, 1979; editor Political Behavior in the Arab States, 1983; editor Jour. Arab Affairs, 1981—. Home: 4379 N 7th St Fresno CA 93726 Office: 2611 N Fresno St Fresno CA 93703

FARAHNIK, LEON DERRICK, manufacturing company executive; b. N.Y.C., Aug. 27, 1953; s. Habib and Nona (Jacobson) F.; B.S. in Bus. Mgmt., U. So. Calif., 1976. Founder, Plasti Pak, Tehran, Iran, 1976; founder, pres. Hilex Poly Co., Inc., Vernon, Calif., 1979—. Mem. Calif. Film Extruders Assn. Republican. Jewish. Office: 5015 Hampton St Los Angeles CA 90058

FARAONE, FRANK RAYMOND, public relations consultant; b. San Francisco, Oct. 19, 1927; s. Frank and Josephine (Lauritano) F. B.S. in Commerce, U. Santa Clara, 1951. Pub. relations regional mgr. Gen. Motors Corp., San Francisco, 1955-58, Dallas, 1958-60, Cleve., 1960-65, N.Y.C., 1965-70, Chgo., 1970-72, media relations dir., Detroit, 1972-75, Washington, 1975-81; cons. in pub. relations, Mill Valley, Calif., 1982—; vis. instr. pub. relations Santa Clara Bus. Sch., 1979. Served with U.S. Army, 1946-48. Mem. Nat. Press Club, Pub. Relations Soc. Am. (accredited; Golden Scroll award 1976), San Francisco Press Club. Republican. Roman Catholic. Club: Harbor Point (Mill Valley).

FARBER, ALLAN DAVID, psychologist; b. Boston, Apr. 2, 1947; s. Irving Lewis and Ruth Lea F.; B.A., Northeastern U., 1971; Ph.D. in Psychology, U. Colo., 1976. Staff psychologist Shasta County Mental Health Services, Redding, Calif., 1976-77, chief of psychology, dir. tng., 1977-78; pvt. practice psychology, cons., Redding, 1978—; founder Being in Life Workshops. Served with USNR, 1965-67. NIMH fellow, 1971-74. Mem. Am. Psychol. Assn., Am. Soc. Clin. Hypnosis, Soc. Clin. and Exptl. Hypnosis, Soc. Descriptive Psychology. Contbr. to Advances in Descriptive Psychology, Vol. 1. Office: 280 Hemsted St Suite K Redding CA 96002

FARBER, GERALDINE OSSMAN, civic worker; b. Salt Lake City, May 4, 1929; d. Lawrence N. and Janet (Perkins) Ossman; student Vassar Coll., 1947-49, U. Liege (Belgium), 1951-53, U. Utah, 1955; m. John Val Browning, July 19, 1949 (div. June 1964); 1 son, John Allen; m. 2d, Seymour M. Farber, June 5, 1973. Tchrs. aid spl. programs elem. schs., Ogden, Utah, Los Altos and Woodside, Calif., 1962-70; cons. Glasrock Products, Inc., 1979-80. Bd. dirs. Am. Field Service, Ogden, 1960-64, Utah Ballet, Ogden, 1963-64, Christmas Bur., Palo Alto and Los Altos, 1964-66, Jr. League Palo Alto, 1966-69. Community Com. for Internat. Students, Stanford, 1965-67; dir. Ednl. TV Fgn. Student Series, Ogden, 1963-64; bd. dirs. Vol. Bur. No. Santa Clara County (Calif.), 1965-68, exec. v.p., 1967-68; vol. parentis in locus, tubercular refugee children Caritas Catholique, Liege, 1952-55; ways and means chmn. San Francisco Ballet Assn. Aux., 1970, pres., 1974-75, trustee assn., 1974-75; co-founder, pres. bd. dirs. Archives for Performing Arts, 1975-76; bd. dirs. Am. Conservatory Theater, 1975-82; mem. Calif. Public Broadcasting Commn., 1975—. Mem. exec. com. Paul N. McCloskey, Jr. congl. campaign Republican party, San Mateo, Calif., 1967; vol., asst. media buyer campaign Supt. Public Instrn. Calif., 1970, mem. exec. planning com. and nat. adv. bd. John Muir Med. Film Festival, 1979—. Recipient awards of Merit City and County San Francisco, Vol. Bur. No. Santa Clara County. Club: San Francisco Peninsula Vassar Alumnae (pres. 1968-70). Editor Teilhard de Chardin: In Quest of the Perfection of Man, 1973. Home and Office: 26303 Esperanza Dr Los Altos Hills CA 94022

FARBER, MARGIE POMFRET, systems analyst; b. Fayetteville, Ark., Mar. 11, 1944; d. James E. and Marguerite H. (Humphreys) Pomfret; m. Peter D. Farber, Dec. 28, 1968. B.A., U. Ark., 1966; postgrad. NYU, San Francisco State U. Programmer trainee IBM, Gaithersburg, Md., 1966-68; programmer, analyst Boeing Co., Seattle, 1968-69, Weyerhaeuser, Tacoma, Wash., 1969-70, CPC Internat., Englewood Cliffs, N.J., 1970-73; systems mgr. Morgan Bank, N.Y.C., 1973-80, Crocker Nat. Bank, San Francisco, 1980—. Mem. Assn. Systems Mgmt.

FARFEL, ARTHUR BERYL, cardiologist; b. Portsmouth, Va., Jan. 30, 1936; s. Paul and Olga F.; B.S. in Chemistry, U. Richmond (Va.), 1956; M.D. (A.D. Williams scholar), Med. Coll. Va., 1960; children—Marc, Melissa, Michael. Intern New Eng. Center Hospital, Boston, 1960-61; resident in medicine Boston City Hosp., 1961-62, sr. med. resident, 1962-63; fellow in cardiology VA Hospital, West Roxbury, Mass., 1963-64; vis. physician Children's Hospital Cardiology Clinic, 1963-64; practice medicine specializing in cardiology, Washington, 1966-67, Burbank, Calif., 1967—; mem. staff St. Joseph Med. Center, Burbank, 1967—; clin. instr. medicine U. Calif., 1967-69; instr. coronary care training program U. So. Calif., 1968-71, clin. asso. prof. medicine, 1971—. Bd. dirs. Los Angeles County Am. Heart Assn., 1972-74, chmn. Burbank/Glendale div., 1971-72. Served to capt. U.S. Army, 1964-66. Recipient Ryland award, 1956; Strauss Prize, 1957. Fellow Am. Coll. Chest Physicians, Am. Coll. Physicians (asso.), Am. Coll. Cardiology, Am. Heart Assn.; Mem. AMA, Calif. Med. Assn., Phi Beta Kappa, Gamma Sigma Epsilon, Alpha Omega Alpha, Sigma Zeta. Contbr. articles to med. jours. Office: 2701 W Alameda Ave Burbank CA 91505

FARGO, CHARLES GORDON, aerospace company executive; b. Wausau, Wis., Jan. 11, 1929; s. Roman Claude and Helen Margaret (Flanagan) F.; B.S. cum laude in Civil Engring., Mont. State U., 1952; M.S. in Engring. Mechanics, Cornell U., 1954; m. Elizabeth Anne Bruce, June 23, 1948; children—Robert C., Kathleen A., Michael D., Timothy P., Theresa M. Instr., Mont. State U., Bozeman, 1950-52, Cornell U., Ithaca, N.Y., 1952-54; engr. D.F. Gunder Assocs., Ithaca, 1952-54; with Rocketdyne div. Rockwell Internat., Canoga Park, Calif., 1954—, v.p. engring. and test, 1979—. Served with USMC, 1946-48. Fellow Inst. Advancement Engring., AIAA (assoc.); mem. ASCE, Sigma Xi, Tau Beta Pi, Phi Kappa Phi. Office: 6633 Canoga Ave Canoga Park CA 91304

FARINHA, MARCELLA A., union ofcl.; b. Osceola, Iowa, Aug. 29, 1929; d. Raymond E. and Iva (True) Brown; m. Phil Farinha, July 22, 1950; children—Michael (dec.), Jan. Student U. Calif.-Berkeley, 1948, 49, Chabot Jr. Coll., 1976. Sec. to sr. union rep. Local 29, Office and Profl. Employees Union, AFL-CIO, 1959-73, sec.-treas., 1979—, health welfare trustee, mem. com. on polit. edn; del. Alameda County Central Labor Council; cons. labor mgmt. to grad. students. Active Workers

Compensation; mem. Voice of Electorate, Democratic Party. Recipient Salute to Women of Labor award Calif. Senate, 1983. Mem. Internat. Found. Employee Benefit Plans. Office: Office Profl Employees Union Local 29 1475 Powell St Emeryville CA 94608

FARIS, DE LENA CAROL, floral designer, consultant, educator; b. Dublin, Erath, Tex., Oct. 14, 1950; d. Lottie Webster and Helen Ruth (Clack) F. Student, U. of Ams., 1968-69, U. N.Mex., 1969-70. Propr. floral bus., Albuquerque, 1970-74; co-owner Plantation Flower Shop, Albuquerque, 1974—; designer and commentator convs., U.S.A., Can.; instr. floral design classes; exhibited in Brandywine Gallery, Albuquerque, 1983. Mem. Am. Inst. Floral Designers, Knud Neilsen Design Team, Soc. Am. Florists. Republican. Baptist. Contbr. to Profl. Floral Design mag. Office: The Plantation 5901 Wyoming NE Albuquerque NM 87109

FARISS, BRUCE LINDSAY, endocrinologist, army officer; b. Allisonia, Va., July 22, 1934; s. Alven Pierce and Hetty Jo (Lindsay) F.; B.S., Roanoke Coll., 1957; M.D., U. Va., 1961; m. Cheryl Louise Tomasie, Jan. 18, 1975; children—Bruce Lindsay, Melissa, Margaret, Susan, Henry, Sarah Jane, Caroline Intern in medicine U. Va. Hosp., 1961-62; commd. capt. M.C. U.S. Army, 1962, advanced through grades to col., 1976; gen. med. officer, Ft. Monroe, Va., 1962-63; resident in internal medicine Brooke Gen. Hosp., Ft. Sam Houston, Tex., 1963-66; fellow in endocrinology U. Calif.-San Francisco, 1966-68; chief, endocrine service Madigan Gen. Hosp., Tacoma, Wash., 1968-71, chief clin. research service, 1968-76, asst. chief dept. medicine, 1972-73, dir. endocrine fellowship program, 1971-76, chief dept. clin. investigation, 1979—, dir. endocrine-metabolism fellowship tng. program, 1979—; cons. internal medicine MEDCOM Europe, 1976-79; cons. endocrinology to surgeon gen. U.S. Army, 1979—. Diplomate Am. Bd. Internal Medicine, Am. Bd. Endocrinology; decorated Legion of Merit; recipient Meritorious Service award Office of Surgeon Gen. Army, 1977. Fellow ACP; mem. Am. Fedn. Clin. Research, Endocrine Soc. (ednl. com. 1980-83), Am. Diabetes Assn., Alpha Omega Alpha. Contbr. articles to med. jours. Home: 10124 Cedrona St SW Tacoma WA 98498 Office: Dept Clin Investigation PO Box 99 Madigan Gen Hosp Tacoma WA 98431

FARLEY, D. (DONALD) GRAY, business exec.; b. Phila., Dec. 6, 1939; s. Donald Gray and Margaretta (Eickhoff) F.; B.S., U.S. Naval Acad., 1961; m. Clora Lee Paiso, Mar. 23, 1963; children—Jennifer, Julie, Jeffrey. Sales engr. Ingersol Rand Co., Los Angeles, 1965-66; nat. sales mgr. Chgo. Pneumatic Tool Co., 1967-68; pres. Continental Air Tools, Cerritos, Calif., 1976—, FTL Enterprise, Cypress, Calif., 1981—. Served from ensign to lt. USN, 1961-65. Mem. C. of C., Jaycees. Republican. Clubs: Kiwanis, Toastmasters. Patentee in field. Home: 4597 Chelsea St Cypress CA 90630 Office: 11447 Beach St Cypress CA 90701

FARLEY, FRANK FREDERIC, environmental consultant; b. Perrysburg, Ohio, Oct. 9, 1912; s. Frank Eugene and Mary (Shiple) F.; A.B., St. John's U., 1934; M.S., U. Detroit, 1936; Ph.D., Iowa State U., 1941; m. Maureen O'Neil, Aug. 28, 1941; children—Jeanne (Mrs. Bruce Rodgers), George Farley, Anne (Mrs. Thomas Kleehammer). Instr., U. Detroit, 1941-42; sr. research chemist Shell Oil Co., Wood River, Ill., 1942-43, group leader, 1943-46, chief research chemist, 1946-53, chief research chemist, Martinez, Calif., 1953-61, research dir., 1961-64, rep. West Coast environ. affairs, San Francisco, 1972-77; head dept. Shell Devel. Co., Emeryville, Calif., 1964-71, environ. conservation rep., 1971-72; cons. Environ. Affairs, Inc., 1978—. Mem. Air Pollution Control Assn., Water Pollution Control Fedn., Bay Area Council, Bay Area League Indsl. Assns., Western Oil and Gas Assn., Calif. Mfrs. Assn., Am. Chem. Soc., Am. Petroleum Inst., Friends of Earth, World Affairs Council. K.C., Rotarian. Club: Commonwealth. Contbr. articles to sci., tech. jours. Home and Office: 26 Monte Ave Piedmont CA 94611

FARLEY, GOSCOE OSCAR, retired state superior court judge; b. Wheatland, Ind., July 9, 1906; s. Otha and Edna E. (Berry) F.; m. Sue Holland, Feb. 14, 1975. J.D., Hastings Coll. Law U. Calif.-San Francisco, 1937; LL.D. (hon.), U. Pacific, 1967. Bar: Calif. 1937. Atty. Prudential Ins. Co., San Francisco, 1938-45; sec. com. bar examiners State Bar Calif., 1945-61; legis. rep. State Bar Calif., 1953-61; exec. dir. joint judiciary com. on adminstrn. justice Calif. Legislature, 1957-58; Los Angeles mcpl. ct. judge, 1961-64; judge Superior Ct., 1964-75. Pres., Conf. Calif. Judges, 1969-70. Mem. Phi Beta Kappa. Club: Calif. Horsemen (pres. 1977-78). Home: 30105 Cabrillo Ave Temecula CA 92390

FARLEY, HALE RALPH, electronic manufacturing company sales executive; b. Lick Creek, W.Va., Aug. 11, 1935; s. Wilbur Burnice and Annie May (Brown) F.; m. Imogene Croy, June 1, 1957; children—Beverly Farley McCann, Cynthia, Chris. A.S. in Electronic Tech., Central Tech. Inst., 1963; B.S., U. N.Mex., 1976, C.S.E.E., 1975; B.A. in Mgmt., St. Mary's Coll., 1982. Instrumentation engr. Sandia Lab., Albuquerque, 1963-73; mktg. mgr. Tektronix, Beaverton, Oreg., 1973-75, master salesman, Santa Clara, Calif., 1976-82; sales rep. Lecroy Research Systems Inc., Livermore, Calif., 1982—; condr. in-plant seminars; presenter paper 3d Internat. Electro-Optic Conf., Tokyo, 1980. Served with USAF, 1954-57. Mem. Nat. Manpower Council. Republican. Methodist. Home: 909 Roxanne St Livermore CA 94550 Office: 2133 Research Dr Livermore CA 94550

FARLEY, JOHN MELVIN, psychologist, educator; b. Sioux City, Iowa, Oct. 20, 1948; s. Melvin W. and M. Irene (Reid) F.; M. Jacqueline L. Treadwell, Aug. 10, 1973; children—Jennifer Lee, Karen M. B.S. in Psychology, Wash. State U., 1973; B.S. in Edn., U. Idaho, 1973, Specialist in Guidance and Counseling, 1979, Ph.D. in Guidance and Counseling, 1979; M.Ed. in Guidance and Counseling, Eastern Wash. U. 1976. Lic. psychologist, Idaho, Wash; registered psychologist, Australia. Tchr., counselor Scope program North Central High Sch., Spokane, Wash., 1973-74; psychologist State of Victoria, Melbourne, Australia, 1976-78; assoc. dir. Idaho Sch. Testing Service, U. Idaho, Moscow, 1979-80, affiliate prof. guidance and counseling Coeur d'Alene Graduate Ctr.; clin. psychologist Mental Health Dept., State of Utah, St. George and Kanab, 1980-81; clin. psychologist Bur. Mental Health, State of Idaho, Coeur d'Alene, 1981—; pvt. practice, Coeur d'Alene, 1981—; Eastern Wash. U. fellow. Fellow Idaho Psychol. Assn.; mem. Am. Psychol. Assn., Inland Empire Soc. Profl. Psychologist, Idaho Sch. Psychologists Assn., Phi Delta Kappa. Clubs: Elks, Coeur d'Alene, Idaho. Home: 409 Park Dr Coeur d'Alene ID 83814 Office: Region 1 Mental Health Services 2195 Ironwood Ct Coeur d'Alene ID 83814 also 2110 Ironwood Parkway Suite 208 Coeur d'Alene ID 83814

FARLEY, LEON ALEX, executive search consultant; b. London, May 6, 1935; s. George Alexander and Kathleen Mary (Thompson) F.; m. Patricia Ann, Aug. 9, 1960; children—Kathleen, Kerry, Patrick, Erin. B.A. in English lit., UCLA, 1956, J.D., 1959. Contract adminstr. Hughes Aircraft, Los Angeles, 1959-63; contracts mgr. Ford Aerospace, Newport Beach, Calif., 1963-67, fin. mgr. Palo Alto, Calif., 1967-69; v.p. ITT, aerospace division, Sylmar, Calif., 1970-72, Korn Ferry Internat., Los Angeles, 1972-76; pres., mng. partner Leon A. Farley Assos., San Francisco, 1976—. Trustee Reed Union Sch. Dist., 1977-81, chmn. 1980, Mem. Assn. Exec. Search Cons. (pres.). Democrat. Club: Southern Calif. Rugby Union (pres. 1964-66). Office: 468 Jackson St San Francisco CA 94111

FARLEY, ROBERT DAY, regional government official; b. Jackson, Mich., Feb. 15, 1936; s. Robert Day and Kathryn Louise (Blackmore) F.; A.A., Jackson Community Coll., 1956; B.A. with honors in Polit. Sci., Mich. State U., 1958; M.P.A., U. Colo., 1981; m. Judy Ann Aldrich, Feb. 20, 1954; children—Christopher, Kathy, Robin. Asst. city assessor City of East Lansing (Mich.), 1958; city mgr. City of Corunna (Mich.), 1958-59, City of Hudson (Mich.), 1959-62; asst. dir. Suprs. Inter-County Com., Detroit, 1962-66; dir. intergovtl. relations Met. Fund, Inc., Detroit, 1966-68; dep. exec. dir. S.E. Mich. Council of Govts., Detroit, 1968-70; exec. dir. Denver Regional Council of Govts., 1970—; disting. public exec. in residence U. Denver, 1978; vis. lectr. L.B. Johnson Sch. Public Affairs, U. Tex., Austin, 1978. Mem. adv. com. for social planning dept. Mile High United Way, 1971-73, policy com. Regional Emergency Med. Care, 1973; mem. mayor's manpower com. City and County of Denver, 1971-72, Mayor's Com. on Youth Problems, 1973, Mayor's Com. on the Platte Valley, 1971-73; bd. govs. Metro Denver Urban Coalition, 1971-79; mem. capital improvements adv. com. Denver Water Bd., 1973; mem. policy bd. Urban Obs. of Denver, 1971—; mem. intergovtl. personnel adv. com. State of Colo., 1977-82; mem. adv. council Grad. Sch. Public Affairs, U. Colo., 1978-82; mem. community adv. com. Jr. League Denver, 1979—; mem. adv. panel on urban impacts Charles F. Kettering Found., Dayton, Ohio, 1980. Recipient award for outstanding contbn. in meeting urban problems Denver Fed. Exec. Bd., 1976. Mem. Am. Inst. Planners (asso.), Nat. Assn. Regional Councils (staff dirs. adv. com. 1972-79, 81—, tng. adv. com. 1978, dir. 1972-75, Walter A. Scheiber Regional Leadership award 1978), Am. Planning Assn. (task force on met. and regional planning 1974), Internat. City Mgmt. Assn. (com. regionalism policy 1973, com. growth mgmt. 1973-76, L.P. Cookingham award 1978), Acad. Profl. com. on regionalism 1973), Denver (policy steering com. 1973-74) chambers commerce, Am. Soc. Pub. Adminstrn., Nat. League of Cities (mem. solid waste adv. com. 1973-74), Colo. Assn. Regional Councils (dir. 1977—, sec. bd. 1977), Denver Regional Council Govts. (transp. com. 1977—), Colo. Council of Chs. (met. ch. community service bd. 1973-79). Office: 2480 W 26th Ave Suite 200B Denver CO 80211

FARLEY, THOMAS T., lawyer, former state legislator; b. Pueblo, Colo., Nov. 10, 1934; s. John Bacon and Mary Magdelan (Tancred) F.; m. Kathleen M. Murphy, May 14, 1960; children—John Baron, Michael Murphy, Kelly Kathleen, Anne Michele. B.S., U. Santa Clara, 1956; LL.B., U. Colo., 1959. Bar: Colo. 1959, U.S. Dist. Ct. (10th dist.) Colo. 1959. Ptnr., Peterson & Fonda, P.C., Pueblo, 1969—; mem. Colo. Ho. of Reps., 1965-75, minority leader, 1967-75; dir. United Bank of Pueblo, New Era Cellular Communications. Bd. dirs. Mile High Kennel Club; chmn. Colo. Wildlife Commn., 1975-79; trustee Colo. State U., U. So. Colo., Ft. Lewis Coll., Cannon City Abbey Sch. for Boys. Mem. ABA (pub. utilities, health sects.), Colo. Bar Assn., Pueblo Bar Assn., U. Colo. Sch. Law Alumni Assn. (bd. dirs). Democrat. Roman Catholic. Clubs: Rotary, Elks, KC 553, Garden of Gods (Colorado Springs); University (Denver).

FARM, GERALD E., artist; b. Grand Island, Nebr., Mar. 8, 1935; s. Paul W.R. and Ruth A. F.; m. Sharon R. Darling, Aug. 9, 1959; children—Kirk G., Kim K. B.A. in Art, Nebr. State Coll., 1961. Tchr. Loveland (Colo.) High Sch., 1961-62; art dir. Hewlett Packard Co., Loveland, 1962-68; freelance artist, Farmington, N.Mex., 1968—. Mem. Farmington Sch. Bd., N.Mex., 1975-81; mem. San Juan Coll. Bd., Farmington, 1975-81, pres., 1977. Mem. artists Equity Assn., Profl. Artists of the Rockies. Art works featured in Southwest Art mag., June 1974, Feb. 1979. Home: 5609 Foothills Dr Farmington NM 87401

FARMER, JANENE ELIZABETH, artist, educator; b. Albuquerque, Oct. 16, 1946; d. Charles John Watt and Regina M. (Brown) Kruger; m. Frank Urban Farmer, May, 1972 (div.) B.A. in Art, San Diego State U., 1969. Owner, operator Iron Walrus Pottery, 1972-79; designer ceramic murals, Coronado, Calif., 1979—; executed commns. for clients in U.S.A., Can., Japan and Mex.; pvt. tchr. pottery; mem. faculty U. Calif.-San Diego; substitute tchr. Calif. community colls.; design cons. Mem. Coronado Arts and Humanities Council; resident artist U. Calif.-San Diego. Recipient grant Calif. Arts Council, 1980-81. Mem. Am. Soc. Interior Design (affiliate). Roman Catholic.

FARMER, LEE R., insurance executive; b. Alliance, Nebr., Feb. 23, 1924; s. Lee R. and Berenice (Ellis) F.; student U. Nebr., 1941-43, 46-47, U. Minn., 1948; m. Constance Audrey Lang, Sept. 18, 1954; children—Diana Lee, Lee R. III, Stuart Lang. Spl. rep. Minn. Hosp. Service Assn., St. Paul, 1948-50, dist. mgr., Duluth, 1950-55; regional mgr. Continental Casualty Co., Chgo., 1955-56, supt. group div., 1956-59, asst. v.p., 1959-61, v.p., chief operating officer of gen. group div. and ind. plans div., 1961-65; exec. v.p. Nat. Ben Franklin Life Ins. Corp. and Nat. Ben Franklin Ins. Co. affiliates of Continental Ins. Co., Chgo., 1965-68; pres. Lee R. Farmer & Assos., Inc., Hinsdale, Ill. 1969-70; exec v.p. Continental Life & Accident Co., 1971-74; pres. Profl. Adminstrs., Inc., 1974—. Served as lt. (j.g.) USNR, 1943-45. Mem. Sigma Nu. Methodist. Clubs: Masons (32 deg.), Hillcrest Country. Home: 209 E Curling Dr Boise ID 83702 Office: Box 1722 Boise ID 83701

FARNER, DONALD SANKEY, zoophysiology educator; b. Waumandee, Wis., May 2, 1915; s. John and Lillian O. (Sankey) F.; B.S., Hamline U., St. Paul, 1937, D.Sc. (hon.), 1962; M.A., U. Wis., 1939, Ph.D., 1941; m. Dorothy S. Copps, Dec. 21, 1940; children—Carla M., Donald C. Instr. zoology U. Wis., 1941-43; asst. prof. U. Kans., 1946-47; mem. faculty Wash. State U., 1947-65, prof. zoophysiology, 1952-65, dean Grad. Sch., 1960-64; prof. zoophysiology U. Wash., Seattle, 1965—, chmn. dept. zoology, 1966—. Served with USNR, 1943-46; capt. Res. ret. Fulbright fellow, 1954; Guggenheim fellow, 1959; sr. scientist Alexander von Humboldt Found., 1978. Mem. Am. Physiol. Soc., Am. Soc. Zoologists, Am. Inst. Biol. Scis., Am. Chem. Soc., Am. Ornithol. Union, Soc. Systematic Zoology, Internat. Union Biol. Scis. (pres. 1967-73), Am. Soc. Naturalists, Cooper Ornithol. Soc., German Ornithol. Soc., Ornitologiska Foreningen (Finland), Soc. Endocrinology, Explorers Club, Phi Beta Kappa, Sigma Xi, Phi Kappa Phi, Phi Sigma, Gamma Alpha, Omicron Delta Kappa. Methodist. Club: Cosmos (Washington). Author books, papers, revs. in avian biology. Home: 4533 W Laurel Dr Seattle WA 98105 Office: Dept Zoology Univ Wash Seattle WA 98195

FARNUM, DAVID KINGSFORD, environmental microbiologist, engineering company executive; b. Polson, Mont., Aug. 21, 1951; s. Donald D. and Lois K. (Kingsford) F.; m. Peggy L. Quamen, Aug. 27, 1977; 1 son, Matthew D. A.A. in Water/Wastewater Tech., Community Coll. Denver, 1978; B.S. in Environ. Microbiology, Mont. State U., 1974. Cert. vocat. tchr., Colo. Chemist/A-operator City of Bozeman (Mont.), 1974-76; coordinator, instr. Nat. Pollution Discharge Elimination System grant program Community Coll. Denver, Golden, Colo., 1976-78; adminstrv. mgr. Tri-Cons. Inc., Lakewood, Colo., 1978-82; mgr. bus. ops. Sellards & Grigg Inc., Lakewood, 1982—; instr. water/wastewater dept. Community Coll. Denver; cons. lab. devel. for wastewater facilities. Mem. Am. Water Works Assn., Rocky Mt. Water Pollution Control Assn. (membership com.). Republican. Lutheran. Club: Ducks Unlimited (Denver). Home: 9093 W Stetson Pl Littleton CO 80123 Office: Sellards & Grigg Inc One Union Sq 143 Union Blvd Suite 280 Lakewood CO 80228

FARON, JOHN FRANK, engineerig executive; b Chgo., Aug. 27, 1933; s. John Theordore and Mary Rose (Szczecina) F.; m. Martha Darling, Nov. 2, 1957; children—Kathleen, Susan, Sandra, Edward. Student Ohio State U., 1951-53, U. So. Calif., 1962, Fresno State U., 1967-69; A.B., U.S. Naval Postgrad. Sch., 1971; postgrad. George Washington U., 1972; M.A., Calif. State U.-Dominguez Hills, 1982. Commd. ensign U.S. Navy, 1955; advanced through grades to comdr., 1968; pilot, 1953-78; intelligence officer, 1955-59; flight instr., 1959-61; combat pilot, Vietnam, 1962-64; aviation maintenance officer USS Hancock, 1964-66; dept. head tech. tng. Attack Squadron 125, 1966-69; exec. sec. to chief naval ops. sub-com. command, control and communication, 1971-73; chmn. ops. sub-group R-2508 enhancement program, mgr. USN portion 56M radar enhancement program, test pilot, 1973-78; ret., 1978. sr. engring. tech. writer, Comarco Engring. Inc., Ridgecrest, Calif., 1978-80; head systems effectiveness engring. group, sr. staff cons. PRC Ridgecrest Engring. Co., 1980—. Decorated Navy Commendation medal, 1973. Mem. AIAA, Nat. Air Racing Group, U.S. Air Racing Assn. (hon.), Am. Legion, Delta Chi. Republican. Roman Catholic. Clubs: China Lake Men's Golf, So. Calif. Golf Assn., Calif. Golf Assn. Home: 618 Scott St Ridgecrest CA 93555 Office: 543 Graaf St Ridgecrest CA 93555

FAROOQI, MOHAMMAD ABDUL RAUF, agronomist; b. Karnal, India, Aug. 1, 1944; came to U.S., 1977; s. Ali and Samadya Murtaza; B.Sc. in Agr., Sind (Pakistan) U., 1965, M.Sc. in Agrl. Chemistry, 1967; Ph.D., Colo. State U., 1982; married; children—Mohammad Omar, Yumna, Sarah. Research asst. dept. chemistry Agr. Coll. Tandojam (Pakistan), 1965-68; jr. research officer in soil and reclamation Water and Power Devel. Authority Pakistan, Lahore, 1968-75; sr. sci. officer Irrigation Drainage and Flood Control Research Council, Lahore, 1975-77; grad. research asst. U.S.-Pakistan Water Mgmt. Research Program, dept. agronomy Colo. State U., 1977-80, 81, 82; panelist UN Case Study in Irrigated Waterlogging, UNESCO, 1976-77. Sec., Mona Sports Club, Bhalwal; Sargodha, Pakistan, 1974-75. Mem. Am. Soc. Agronomy, Crop Sci. Soc. Am., Soil Sci. Soc. Am., Soil Sci. Soc. Pakistan, Pakistan Assn. Advancement Sci. Moslem. Author various profl. publs.; editor English sect. Agr. Coll. Mag., 1961-62. Office: Agronomy Dept Colo State U Fort Collins CO 80523

FARQUHAR, PETER HENRY, marketing educator; b. Boston, May 7, 1947; s. Henry Adamson and Alice May (Grant) F.; m. Andrea Pyne, June 7, 1969; children—Thomas, Michelle, David. B.S. magna cum laude, Tufts. U., 1969; M.S., Cornell U., 1972, Ph.D., 1974. Lectr., Cornell U., Ithaca, N.Y., 1971-73; assoc. mathematician Rand Corp., Santa Monica, Calif., 1974-75; asst. prof. Northwestern U., Evanston, Ill., 1975-78, Harvard U., Boston, 1978-80; assoc. prof. adminstrn. and agrl. econs. Grad. Sch. Adminstrn., U. Calif.-Davis, 1980—. Mem. Bd. Edn., Sch. Dist. 67, Morton Grove, Ill., 1977-78. Recipient award of Merit, Ill. Assn. Sch. Bds., 1978. Mem. Ops. Research Soc. Am., Inst. Mgmt. Sci., Am. Statis. Assn., Am. Mktg. Assn., Psychometric Soc., Phi Kappa Phi. Assoc. editor Ops. Research, 1979—, Large Scale Systems, 1982—; contbr. articles on decision analysis to various profl. jours. Office: Grad Sch Administration U Calif Davis CA 95616

FARQUHARSON, PATILU, sch. psychologist; b. Luray, Kans., July 25, 1925; d. Hugh Everton and Roberta (Albach) Farquharson. Student Garden City Jr. Coll., 1940-42, Ft. Hays (Kans.) State Coll., 1942-44; B.A., U. Calif. at Berkeley, 1945; M.S. in Clin. Psychology, Purdue U., 1948; postgrad. U. Kans., 1952-53; Ph.D. in Clin. Psychology, U. Denver, 1956. Tchr. Mound Valley (Kans.) High Sch., 1945-46; psychometrist Purdue U. Guidance Center, 1946-48; clin. psychologist Mendocino State Hosp., Talmage, Calif., 1948-51, State Hosp. for Epileptics, Parsons, Kans., 1951-52; intern Menorah Med. Center, Kansas City, Mo., 1953-54; asst. dir. Psychol. Services for Children, U. Denver, 1955-56, asst. prof., 1956-60; dist. sch. psychologist Elk Grove (Calif.) Unified Sch. Dist., 1960-83; ret., 1983; supr. interns in sch psychology U. Calif.-Davis, 1982-83; guest. lectr. Sacramento State Coll., 1962—; mem. Bd. Behavioral Sci. Examiners, 1970-76. Bd. dirs. Family Service Agy., Sacramento. Diplomate Am. Bd. Examiners in Profl. Psychology. Mem. Am. (local arrangement chmn.), Western, Sacramento Valley (past dir.) psychol. assns., Calif. (sec. 1965-66), Sacramento Area assns. sch. psychologists, NEA, Calif., Elk Grove tchrs. assns., Calif. Assn. Neurologically Handicapped Children, Soroptimists (v.p. Sacramento South 1968-69, pres. 1969-70, dir. 1970—). Home: PO Box 485 Garden Valley CA 95633

FARR, LEE EDWARD, physician; b. Albuquerque, Oct. 13, 1907; s. Edward and Mabel (Heyn) F.; B.S., Yale, 1929, M.D., 1933; m. Anne Ritter, Dec. 28, 1936; children—Charles E., Susan A., Frances A. Asst. pediatrics Sch. Medicine, Yale U., 1933-34; asst. medicine Hosp. of Rockefeller Inst. Med. Research, 1934-37, asso. medicine, 1937-40; dir. research Alfred I. duPont Inst. of Nemours Found., Wilmington, Del., 1940-49; vis. asso. prof. pediatrics Sch. Medicine, U. Pa., 1940-49; med. dir., physician-in-chief hosp. Brookhaven Nat. Lab., 1948-62; prof. nuclear medicine U. Tex. Postgrad. Med. Sch., 1962-64, prof. nuclear and environ. medicine Grad. Sch. Bio-Med. Scis., U. Tex. at Houston, 1965-68; chief sect. nuclear medicine U. Tex.-M.D. Anderson Hosp. and Tumor Inst., 1962-67, cons., 1967-68; prof. environ. health U. Tex. Sch. Pub. Health, Houston, 1967-68; head disaster health services Calif. Dept. Health, 1968, chief emergency health services unit, 1968-70, chief bur. emergency med. services, 1970-73; chmn. bd. dirs. Sequoia Assos., San Francisco, 1972-75. Lippitt lectr. Marquette U., 1941; Sommers Meml. lectr. U. Oreg. Sch. Med., Portland, 1960; Gordon Wilson lectr. Am. Clin. and Climatol. Assn., 1956; Sigma Xi nat. lectr., 1952-53. Mem. adv. com. on naval med. research NRC, 1953-68, adv. com. on atomic bomb, 1953-68, chmn. 1954-68, adv. com. on medicine and surgery, 1955-56, exec. com., 1962-65; Naval Research Mission to Formosa, 1953; tech. adviser U.S. delegation to Geneva Internat. Conf. for Peaceful Uses Atomic Energy, 1955; mem. N.Y. Adv. Com. Atomic Energy, 1956-59; mem. AMA Com. Nuclear Medicine, 1963-66; mem. com. med. isotopes NASA Manned Spacecraft Center, 1966-68; mem. expert adv. panel radiation WHO, 1957-79; mem. Calif. Gov.'s Ad Hoc Com. Emergency Health Service, 1968-69; mem. sci. adv. bd. Gorgas Meml. Inst., 1967-72; mem. Naval Res. Adv. Com., 1970-78, numerous other sci. adv. bds., panels; cons. TRW Systems, Inc., 1966-70, Consol. Petroleum Co., Beverly Hills, Calif., 1946-70. Mem. alumni bd. Yale, 1962-65, mem. alumni fund, 1966-76. Served as lt. comdr. M.C., USNR, 1942-46; capt. (M.C.) USNR, ret. Recipient Mead Johnson award for pediatric research, 1940; decorated Gold Cross Order of Phoenix, Greece; Order of Merit, West Germany; named community leader in Am., 1969. Diplomate Nat. Bd. Med. Examiners, Am. Bd. Pediatrics. Fellow AAAS, Royal Soc. Arts, Am. Acad. Pediatrics, N.Y. Acad. Scis., Royal Soc. Health, Am. Coll. Nuclear Medicine (disting. fellow); mem. Soc. Pediatric Research, Soc. Exptl. Biology and Medicine, Harvey Soc., Am. Pediatric Soc., Soc. Exptl. Pathology, Am. Soc. Clin. Investigation, Radiation Research Soc., A.M.A. (mem. council on sci. assembly 1960-70, chmn. 1968-70), Houston C. of C. (chmn. subcom. on quality in living 1966-68), Med. Soc. Athens (Greece) (hon.), Alameda County Med. Assn., Sigma Xi, Alpha Omega Alpha, Phi Sigma Kappa, Nu Sigma Nu, Alpha Chi Sigma. Club: Commonwealth (San Francisco). Author articles on nuclear medicine, nuclear reactors, protein metabolism, emergency med. services organizational support, radioactive and chem. environ. contaminants, environ. noise in homes. Home: 2502 Saklan Indian Dr Apt 2 Walnut Creek CA 94595

FARR, SHELDON GRANT, fin. exec.; b. Marmarth, N.D., Sept. 30, 1918; s. Herman LuVerne and Grayce Laura (Rinderneck) F.; B.A., U. N.D., 1942; M.B.A., U. Chgo., 1947; m. Helen Balich Farr, Nov. 22,

1944; children—Grant, Sheila, Pamela. Project acct. Howard S. Wright & Co., 1948-52; controller Don Williams & Co., 1952-53, Kromona Mines Corp., Seattle, 1954-55; fin. mgr. The Boeing Co., Seattle, 1956-70; owner Farr Enterprises, Kirkland, Wash., 1970—. Mem. Citizens Adv. Council, P.T.A.; mem. Sch. Bd., 1952-61, pres., 1956-57; cubmaster, scoutmaster Boy Scouts Am., 1954-61; active Mcpl. League Seattle-King County. Served with USMCR, 1942-45. Decorated Air medal. Mem. Common Cause. Home and Office: 8923 NE 127th St Kirkland WA 98033

FARR, WILLIAM FOREST, physician; b. Seattle, Mar. 5, 1935; s. Forest Willard and Dorothea Marian (Blair) F.; B.S. cum laude, Willamette U., 1956; M.D., U. Oreg., 1960; m. Ellen Nora Stewart, Aug. 5, 1961; children—Margaret, Kathleen, Elizabeth. Intern, U.S. Naval Hosp., Oakland, Calif., 1960-61; resident in ophthalmology U. Oreg. Med. Sch., 1965-68; practice medicine specializing in ophthalmology, Tigard, Oreg., 1968—; mem. staff Physicians and Surgeons, Good Samaritan, St. Vincent's, Meridian Park hosps., Portland, Oreg., Newberg (Oreg.) Hosp.; asst. clin. prof. U. Oreg., 1968—. Served to lt. USN, 1961-64, to capt. MC, USNR. Diplomate Am. Bd. Ophthalmology. Fellow Am. Acad. Ophthalmology; mem. AMA, Am. Assn. Ophthalmology, Oreg. Acad. Ophthalmology, Pacific Coast Oto-Ophthalmolog. Soc., Oreg. Med. Assn., Beta Theta Pi, Alpha Omega Alpha. Republican. Clubs: Willamette Sailing (commodore 1980), Mazamas, Nat. Trust for Scotland, St. Andrews Soc. Oreg. Home: 1844 SW Dolph St Portland OR 97219 Office: 11737 SW 88th St Tigard OR 97223

FARRAR, DONALD EUGENE, mutual fund executive; b. Seattle, Dec. 15, 1931; s. Joseph Lester and Ruth Emily (Close) F.; m. Joan Fowler Drew, July 29, 1974; children—Donald E., John M., Peter H., Cordelia G.; stepchildren—Terri J., Walter M., Jason J.W. A.B. magna cum laude, Harvard U., 1954, M.A. in Econs., 1961, Ph.D., 1961. Instr. econs. U. Wis.-Madison, 1959-61, asst. prof., 1961-62; economist Inst. Naval Studies, Cambridge, Mass., 1962-63; asst. prof. fin. MIT, 1963-66, assoc. prof., 1966-68; assoc. prof. fin. Columbia U., 1968; dir. Instn. Investor Study, SEC, Washington, 1969-71; sr. fellow U. Pa., Phila., 1971; sr. research assoc. Nat. Bur. Econ. Research, Cambridge, 1972; prof. fin. UCLA, 1973-76; prof. fin. U. Utah, Salt Lake City, 1976-81; exec. v.p. Benham Mgmt. Corp., Palo Alto, Calif., 1981—; dir. Mattel, Inc., Mattel Found., Capital Preservation Fund Internat., Benham Mgmt. Corp., Permanent Portfolio Fund, Inc.; cons. in field. Served to lt. U.S. Army, 1955-56. IBM fellow, 1955; Ford Found. fellow, 1967. Mem. Western Fin. Assn. (dir. 1978-81, pres. 1980). Clubs: Harvard of San Francisco; Commonwealth of Calif. Author: The Investment Decision Under Uncertainty, 1962; (with others) Managerial Economics, 1970, Institutional Investor Study Report of the Securities & Exchange Commission, 8 vols., 1971; editor: Explorations in Economic Research, 1974-75; (with others) Readings in Investments, 1980. Home: 14575 DeBell Dr Los Altos Hills CA 94022 Office: 755 Page Mill Rd Palo Alto CA 94304

FARRAR, ELAINE WILLARDSON, artist; b. Los Angeles, Feb. 27, 1929; d. Eldon and Gladys Elsie (Larsen) Willardson; B.A., Ariz. State U., 1967, M.A., 1969; children—Steve, Mark, Gregory, Jan Leslie, Monty, Susan. Tchr., Camelback Desert Sch., Paradise Valley, Ariz., 1966-69; mem. faculty Yavapai Coll., Prescott, Ariz., 1970—, chmn. dept. art, 1973-78, instr. art in watercolor and oil and acrylic painting and intaglio, 1971—; one-man shows include: R.P. Moffat's, Scottsdale, Ariz., 1969, Art Center, Battle Creek, Mich., 1969, Nat. Gallery, Oslo, 1978, The Woodpeddler, Costa Mesa, Calif., 1979; group shows include Prescott Fine Arts Assn., 1982, Juried Am. Watercolorists, Adirondacks, N.Y., 1982; works rep. local and state exhibits; supt. fine arts dept. County Fair; com. mem., hanging chmn. Scholastic Art Awards. Mem. Mountain Artists Guild (past pres.), Nat. League Am. Pen Women (treas. Prescott br.), NEA, Ariz. Edn. Assn., Nat. Art Edn. Assn., Ariz. Coll. and Univ. Faculty Assn., AAUW, Verde Valley Art Assn., Kappa Delta Pi. Republican. Mormon. Home: 635 Copper Basin Rd Prescott AZ 86301 Office: Yavapai College Art Dept 1100 E Sheldon Rd Prescott AZ 86301

FARRAR, JAMES PAUL, electrical engineer; b. Albuquerque, May 29, 1937; s. Clyde William and Lina Mae (Hudson) F.; B.S., U. N.Mex., 1960; M.B.A., Pepperdine U., 1981; m. Marilyn Austa Johnson, June 21, 1958; children—Paul Frederick, Jamie Austa, Kimberly Sue. Design engr. E.G.&G., Las Vegas, Nev., 1960-63; project engr. Motorola, Inc., Scottsdale, Ariz., 1963-66; sr. engr. Collins Radio Co., Dallas, 1966-68; research fellow NIH, 1968-70; project mgr. TRW, Colorado Springs, Colo., 1970-74; project mgr. Ford Aerospace and Communications Corp., 1974-79; programming services mgr. GenRad, Inc., Santa Clara, Calif., 1979-80, tech. support mgr., Phoenix, 1980-81, dir. product support, 1982—; mem. sr. faculty U. Phoenix, 1981—; adj. faculty Ottawa U. Mem. Am. Mgmt. Assn., Assn. Field Service Mgrs., IEEE. Republican. Roman Catholic. Home: 6243 E Gelding Dr Scottsdale AZ 85254 Office: 4620 N 16th St Phoenix AZ 85016

FARRAR, JOHN EDSON, II, business executive, public relations consultant; b. Williamsport, Pa., Oct. 9, 1938; s. John Edson and Ruth (Price) F.; B.A. in Psychology, Pasadena Coll., 1963; postgrad. U. Calgary (Alta.), 1967, pub. relations certificate; postgrad. Claremont Grad. Sch., 1963-64, U. Calif. at Riverside, 1968-71; m. Judith Elizabeth Brodie, Jan. 23, 1965; 1 son, John Edson III. Evaluating social services dir. Head Start dental research project Loma Linda (Calif.) U. Sch. Dentistry, 1966-67; coordinator Head Start, Riverside County Econ. Opportunity Bd., Riverside, Calif., 1967; dir. community relations San Bernardino County Welfare and Probation Depts., San Bernardino, Calif., 1968-73; publicity and promotions coordinator in charge tourism and indsl. devel. Econ. Devel. Dept. San Bernardino County, 1973; dir. pub. relations Middle East, Boeing Comml. Airplane Co., Seattle, 1973-75; dir. pub. relations Northwest Hosp., Seattle, 1975-77; owner Craig & Farrar Pub. Relations and Advt., 1977-80; exec. v.p. Environ. Research and Devel. Corp., Seattle, 1980-82; owner Aamco Transmissions of Bremerton (Calif.), 1982—; lectr. pub. relations San Bernardino State Coll., Riverside U., Calif. State Coll., San Bernardino, Chaffee Coll.; chmn. dept. pub. relations and advt. City Coll., Seattle; instr. pub. relations U. Wash.; pub. relations cons. to pvt. bus., govt. Pres. bd. dirs. Frazee Community Center, 1970-71; bd. dirs., pub. relations chmn. Chief Seattle council Boy Scouts Am., promotions chmn. for camping in Southwestern U.S.; exec. bd. Seattle-King County Visitors and Conv. Bur. Mem. Pub. Relations Soc. Am. (chpt. pres. 1971, 72, dist. chmn. govt. sect.), Calif. Social Workers Orgn. (v.p. 1970-71), Soc. for Internat. Devel., Nat. Pub. Relations Council Health and Welfare Services, Internat. Pub. Relations Assn., U.S.-Arab C. of C. Rotarian. Home: PO Box 603 Mercer Island WA 98040 Office: 299 S National Ave Bremerton WA 98310

FARR-CANNON, VIVIAN MARIE, educator, musician; b. Colorado Springs, Colo., Sept. 17, 1946; d. Ruben Henry and Vivian Lee (Richardson) Farr; m. Edward Cannon, Dec. 29, 1976 (div.); children—Angela Renee, Aelaina Joy, Daphine Devon McChriston. B.A., Adams State Coll., 1972, M.A., 1978. Clk.-typist, supr., travel co-ordinator various firms, 1964-70; tchr. Martin Luther King Elem. Sch., Widefield, Colo., Florence Sabin Jr. High Sch., Colorado Springs, 1977-80; work experience and study coordinator-tchr. Doherty High Sch., Colorado Springs, 1980-83; career edn. specialist Colorado Springs Sch. Dist., 1983—; youth cons., dir. church youth group, 1972—. Ednl. chmn. El Paso County Black Caucus; mem. John Adams PTA. Mem. Black Educators Dist. Eleven, Colo. Springs Tchrs. Assn., NEA, Am. Edn. Assn., Colo. Vocat. Assn., NAACP, Alpha Kappa Alpha. Democrat. Baptist. Club: Eastern Star. Developed first career exploration activity for minority students in Colo. Springs, Feb. 1983. Home: 4513 Harwood Rd Colorado Springs CO 80916 Office: Diagnostic and Spl Learning Ctr 917 E Moreno St Colorado Springs CO 80903

FARRELL, FRANCIS XAVIER, executive search company executive; b. N.Y.C., Sept. 6, 1941; s. Francis Xavier and Helen Mary (Delaney) F.; A.B. in English Lit., St. Michael's Coll., Winooski, Vt., 1962; m. Kathy Kimbell, Sept. 16, 1978; children—Catherine, Oona, Ian, Miguel. Salesman, IBM, N.Y.C., 1965-69; sales mgr. N.Am. Phillips Co., N.Y.C., 1969-71; ind. mktg. cons., Los Angeles, 1971-73; search cons. EDP World, Ic., Beverly Hills, Calif., 1973-74; partner CDF Internat., exec. search, Marina del Rey, Calif., 1975-78; founder, 1978, since v.p. Farrell Assocs., Marina del Rey.

FARRELL, JAMES PATRICK, hospital executive; b. San Diego, Feb. 12, 1948; s. George W. and Doris M. (Dixon) F.; m. Bonnie Birdseye, July 31, 1973; children—Christine, Shelley, Karissa. B.S., U. Utah, 1972, M.S. in Bus. Adminstrn. Indsl. Relations, 1974. Coordinator job evaluation Salt Lake City Sch. Dist., 1973-74; research fellow, teaching asst. Coll. Bus., U. Utah, Salt Lake City, 1974; dir. personnel Meth. Hosp., Madison, Wis., 1975-77; v.p. personnel services Meth. Med. Ctr. of Ill., Peoria, 1977-80; v.p. human resources Sutter Community Hosp., Sacramento, 1980—. Vice pres. profl. devel. Sacramento Personnel Assn.; bd. dirs., programs chmn. Sacramento Urban League; mem. Peoria Urban League; founder Employee Adv. Com., Madison, Wis.; mem. task force Nat. Council Community Hosps., Washington. Served with USN, 1967-68. Recipient award Central Ill. Hosp. Personnel Mgmt. Assn., 1978. Mem. Am. Soc. Personnel Adminstrn., Am. Compensation Assn., Calif. Hosp. Assn. (legis. task force).

FARRELL, KATHY, mgmt. cons. firm exec.; b. Washington, Sept. 11, 1943; d. Jack M. and Maxine (Bascue) Kimbell; B.A., U. Va., 1965; postgrad. Pepperdine U., 1978; m. Frank Farrell, Sept. 16, 1978. Tech. writer Wang, Boston, 1969; systems analyst Fin. Info. Co., Los Angeles, 1970; with Xerox Computer Services, Los Angeles, 1971-77, mktg. staff specialist, 1976-77; mktg. staff specialist Computer Scis. Corp., El Segundo, Calif., 1977-78; owner Farrell Assos., Marina Del Rey, Calif., 1978-82; owner The Human Energy Co., 1982—. Mem. Am. Soc. Tng. and Devel. (dir. spl. div. Los Angeles chpt.), Women in Bus. (dir. Los Angeles), OD Network, Am. Mktg. Assn. Home and office: 4324 Promenade Way 114 Marina del Rey CA 90291

FARRELL, PAUL HARRY, lawyer; b. Cambridge, Mass., Sept. 14, 1927; s. Harry Gordon and Frances Rose (Fay) F.; m. Blanche Church, Oct. 24, 1948; children—James, John, Joan, Peter, William. Student Duke U., 1946-49; A.B., U. Pitts., 1950; J.D., Harvard U., 1954. Bar: Mass. 1954, Ohio 1974, Calif. 1981. Assoc., Goodwin, Procter & Hoar, Boston, 1954-63; atty. United Fruit Co., Boston, 1963-65; asst. v.p. United Fruit Europa, The Hague, 1965-67; pres. United Fruit, S.A., Paris, 1967-68; asst. gen. counsel United Brands Co., N.Y.C. and Boston, 1968-73; sr. v.p., gen. counsel Buckeye Internat. Inc., Columbus, Ohio, 1973-79; v.p., gen. counsel, sec. Clorox Co., Oakland, Calif., 1979—. Mem. adminstrn. and legal processes adv. com. Mills Coll., Oakland. Served with USNR, 1945-48. Mem. ABA, San Francisco Bar Assn. Republican. Clubs: Harvard (N.Y.C.); Bankers (San Francisco). Home: 56 Ironship Plaza San Francisco CA 94111 Office: Clorox Co 1221 Broadway Oakland CA 94612

FARRELL, SCOTT DOUGLAS, optometrist; b. Ogden, Utah, Jan. 21, 1951; s. Glen L. and Norma (Cross) F.; m. Janis Johnson, Feb. 20, 1946; children—David Lauren. Student Weber State Coll., 1969-70; B.A. cum laude in Psychology, Spanish, U. Utah, 1975; B.S. in Visual Sci., So. Calif. Coll. Optometry, 1977, O.D., 1979. Lic. optometrist, Utah. Pvt. practice optometry specializing in contact lenses and pediatric vision care, Roy, Utah, 1979—. State senatorial campaign worker, Republican Party, 1982. Western Interstate Commn. for Higher Edn. scholar, 1975-79. Mem. Utah Optometric Assn., Am. Optometric Assn., Optometric Extension Program, Roy C. of C. (bd. dirs. 1981—). Mormon. Club: Lions (1st v.p. 1981—). Contbr. articles to newspapers and vision related publs. Home: 568 E 3300 N North Ogden UT 84404 Office: Herefordshire Med Bldg 1845 W 4400 South Roy UT 84067

FARRELL, THOMAS GEORGE, lawyer; b. Pitts., Aug. 6, 1931; s. Thomas Joseph and Christine Geddes (Burnett) F.; B.A., Pa. State U., 1954; J.D., Southwestern U., Los Angeles, 1970; m. Suzanne Marion Kellogg, Feb. 18, 1967; children—Colleen Suzanne, Sean Thomas. Mem. congl. staff James G. Fulton, 1957-58; negotiator Navy Dept., 1959-62; adminstr. Rockwell Internat. Co., Los Angeles, 1962-64; announcer, engr. Sta. KFMU-FM, Los Angeles, 1964-65; missionary Mormon Ch., 1964-65; contracting officer Def. Contract Adminstrn. Services Region, Los Angeles, 1966-71, asst. counsel, 1972; admitted to Calif. bar, 1971; resident counsel Rand Corp., Santa Monica, Calif., 1973-75; atty. adviser USAF Space div., Los Angeles, 1975—; prof. law Woodbury U., Los Angeles, 1974-79; guest lectr. UCLA. Served to lt. (j.g.) USNR, 1954-57. Mem. State Bar Calif., Nat. Contract Mgmt. Assn., Classical Assn., Soc. Histoire du Droit, Tech. Mktg. Soc. Am., Am. Legion, Phi Alpha Delta, Chi Phi. Republican. Home: 2329 231st St Torrance CA 90501 Office: Hdqrs USAF Space Div Los Angeles Air Force Sta PO Box 92960 Worldway Postal Center Los Angeles CA 90009

FARRELL, THOMAS JOSEPH, ins. co. exec.; b. Butte, Mont., June 10, 1926; s. Bartholomew J. and Lavina H. (Collins) F.; student U. San Francisco, 1949; grad. Life Ins. Agy. Mgmt. Assn., 1960; m. Evelyn Irene Southam, July 29, 1951; children—Brien J., Susan M., Leslie A., Jerome T. Partner, Affiliated-Gen. Ins. Adjusters, Santa Rosa, Calif., 1949-54; agt. Lincoln Nat. Life Ins. Co., Santa Rosa, 1954-57, supr., 1957-59, gen. agt., 1959-74; pres. Thomas J. Farrell & Assos., 1974-76, 7 Flags Ins. Mktg. Corp., 1976-81, Farrell-Dranginis & Assos., 1981—; pres., dir. Lincoln Nat. Bank, Santa Rosa, San Rafael; pres. Redwood Empire Estate Planning Council, 1981-82, Sonoma County Council for Retarded Children, 1956—, City Santa Rosa Traffic and Parking Commn., 1963; pres., nat. dir. United Cerebral Palsy Assn., 1954-55; chmn. Santa Rosa Community Relations Commn., 1973-76; pres. Sonoma County Young Republicans, 1953; past dir. Sonoma County Fair and Expn., Inc.; bd. dirs. Sonoma County Family Service Agy., Eldridge Found., North Bay Regional Center for Developmentally Disabled; trustee Sonoma State Hosp. Mentally Retarded Children; mem. Pres.'s Com. Mental Retardation. Recipient cert. Nat. Assn. Retarded Children, 1962; C.L.U. Mem. Sonoma County Life Underwriters (pres. 1956), Nat. Assn. Life Underwriters, Redwood Empire Assn. C.L.U.s (pres. 1974—), Gen. Agts. and Mgrs. Assn., Japanese-Am. Citizens League, Jaycees (Outstanding Young Man of Year 1961, v.p. 1955), Santa Rosa C. of C. (dir. 1974-75), Calif. PTA (hon. life). Clubs: Commonwealth, Press (San Francisco); Rotary (Santa Rosa). Home: 963 Wyoming Dr Santa Rosa CA 95405 Office: 747 Mendocino Ave Santa Rosa CA 95401

FARRELL, TRACEY KARSTEN, advertising and communications executive; b. Oklahoma City, Mar. 21, 1953; d. Harold John and Jayne Frances (Gourley) Karsten; B.A., Mt. Holyoke Coll., 1975; m. Glenn Michael Farrell, June 3, 1975. With East/West Network, Los Angeles, 1977-79, asso. editor, 1979; mng. editor San Francisco mag., 1979, editor, corp. officer, 1979-81; supr. advt. and communications Levi Strauss Internat., Levi Strauss & Co., 1981-82; mgr. sales promotion Levi Strauss U.S.A., 1982—. Mem. Market St. Devel. Project, San Francisco, 1980—. Mem. Am. Soc. Mag. Editors, City and Regional Mag. Assn., Mag. Pubs. Assn., Mt. Holyoke Coll. Alumnae Assn. Office: 1155 Battery St San Francisco CA 94106

FARRELLY, JANET, insurance agent; b. Arlington, Mass., Oct. 11, 1928; d. Philip and Constance Franklin; m. Richard Lloyd Farrelly, Aug. 17, 1928; children—Andrew Benes, Nicholas Benes, Richard. B.A., Harvard U., 1950. Formerly head art dept. Northampton Sch. for Girls; with Mut. of Omaha, Loveland, Colo., 1975—, agt., 1983—. Mem. Nat. Life Underwriters. Office: C Roderich Dist Office Mut of Omaha Greeley CO 80631

FARRER, REX DALE, elec. engr.; b. Salt Lake City, June 11, 1930; s. Royal Irvine and Hazel Lorinda (Arrowsmith) F.; B.A., Brigham Young U., 1952; B.S. in E.E., U. Utah, 1959, postgrad., 1964-67; postgrad. Stevens Henager Bus. Coll., 1974, U. Calif. ext., 1974, U. Utah, 1976. Salesman, Daynes Music Co., 1953-54; with Gen. Electric Co., 1954-55, 1955-58; with Sperry Univac, Salt Lake City, 1959-71, prin. engr., 1968-71; real estate agt., United Homes Inc., Salt Lake City, 1971-72, Weissman Realtors, Salt Lake City, 1972-74; prin., broker Farrer Real Estate, Salt Lake City, 1974-79; sr. elec. engr. Boeing Aircraft Co., Wichita, Kans., 1979, Martin-Marietta Corp., Vandenberg AFB, Calif., 1979—. Tchr. Sunday sch., elder Ch. Jesus Christ of Latter-day Saints. Served with USAF, 1952-53. Mem. IEEE, Eta Kappa Nu. Home: 634 Roskilde Rd Solvang CA 93463

FARRINGTON, NANCY, nurse, home health care consultant; b. Orange, N.J., Feb. 11, 1944; d. Edward Walker and Nancy (Weyers) Wilkins; m. Albert Garry Luini, Aug. 12, 1967; m. 2d Clyde Jesse Farrington, July 26, 1973; 1 son, Ian Walker, B.S. in Nursing, SUNY, 1966. R.N., Alaska 1971. Nurse, tchr., Buffalo, New Haven, Calgary, Alta., Puyallup, Wash., and Anchorage, 1966-75; rehab. cons., Anchorage, 1975; regional dir. Alaska Homemaker-Home Health Aide Program, Anchorage. 1975-76, program dir., dir. ops., 1979-82; supr. of nurses Hope Cottages, Inc., Anchorage, 1977; dir. Alaska Nurses Registry, Anchorage, 1977-79; ptnr. Health and Rehab. System of Alaska, Anchorage, 1982—. Past chmn. Alaska Chpt., Nat. Multiple Sclerosis Soc., den mother Cub Scouts. Recipient service award Multiple Sclerosis Soc. Mem. Nat. Home Caring Council (past chmn. exec. council), Alaska Rehab. Assn. (chmn.), Am. Personnel Guidance Assn. Home: SRA Box 372V Anchorage AK 99507 Office: Health Rehab System 626 F St Suite 102 Anchorage AK 99501

FARRINGTON, WILLIAM BENFORD, geophysicist; b. N.Y.C., Mar. 10, 1921; s. Harold Phillips and Edith C. (Aitken) F.; B.C.E., Cornell U., 1947, M.S., 1949; Ph.D., Mass. Inst. Tech., 1953; m. Frances A. Garratt, 1949 (div. 1955); children—William Benford, Phyllis Ashley, Timothy Colfax; m. 2d, Gertrude E. Eby, Jan. 3, 1979. Radio engr. Naval Research Labs., 1942-43; dir. Read Standard Corp., 1948-55; plant engr. Hope's Windows, Inc., 1950-51; instr. geology, geophysics U. Mass., 1953-54; research geophysicist Humble Oil & Refining Co., 1954-56; lectr. U. Houston, 1955-56; sr. investment analyst Continental Research Corp., N.Y.C., 1956-61; pres., dir. Farrington Engring. Corp., 1958-67; v.p. Empire Resources Corp., 1961-62; asst. v.p. Empire Trust Co., 1962-64; sr. partner Farrington & Light Assos., 1967-82; sr. asso. Farrington Assos., 1982—; sr. cons. (geophys.) Trident Engring. Corp.; dir. Commonwealth Gas Co., N.Y. Lectr., U. Calif. at Los Angeles; sci. dir. Select Com. on Govt. Research, U.S. Ho. of Reps, 1964-65. Chmn. crusade Am. Cancer Soc., Jamestown, N.Y., 1951. Fellow AAAS, Fin. Analysts Fedn.; mem. Am. Assn. Petroleum Geologists, Am. Astronautical Soc., Am. Geophys. Union, Am. Inst. Mining, Metall. and Petroleum Engrs., Am. Petroleum Inst., Am. Inst. Aeros. and Astronautics, Los Angeles Soc. Financial Analysts, Geol. Soc. Am., Seismol. Soc. Am., Soc. Exploration Geophysicsts, N.Y. Soc. Security Analysts, Sigma Xi. Episcopalian. Contbr. articles to profl. jours. Address: 1565 Skyline Dr Laguna Beach CA 92651

FARRIS, DOROTHY COLE, information systems company manager; b. Binghamton, N.Y., June 1, 1951; d. Eudelmar Edgar and Arlouine Louise (Dunham) Cole; m. William Howard Farris, Oct. 13, 1979. A.A.S. in Math., Rochester (N.Y.) Inst. Tech., 1973. B.S. in Bus. Adminstrn., 1973. Sales rep. IBM, Rochester, N.Y., 1973-76, analyst, comml. analysis, 1976-80; mktg. mgr. Exxon Office Systems, Costa Mesa, Calif., 1980-82, regional program mgr., 1982, br. mgr., 1982—. Mem. Nat. Assn. Female Execs., Huntington Beach C. of C. Office: 695 Town Center Dr Suite 1440 Costa Mesa CA 92626

FARRIS, JEROME, judge; b. Birmingham, Ala., Mar. 4, 1930; s. William J. and Elizabeth (White) F.; B.S., Morehouse Coll., 1951, LL.D. (hon.), 1978; M.S.W. Atlanta U., 1955; J.D., U. Wash., 1958; m. Jean Shy, June 27, 1957; children—Juli Elizabeth, Janelle Marie. Admitted to Wash. State bar, 1958; mem. firm Weyer, Roderick, Schroeter and Sterne, Seattle, 1958-63, Schroeter, Farris, Bangs and Horowitz, Seattle, 1963-65, Farris, Bangs and Horowitz, 1965-69; judge Wash. State Ct. Appeals, Seattle, 1969-79, U.S. Ct. Appeals 9th circuit, Seattle, 1979—; lectr. U. Wash. Law Sch. and Sch. Social Work, 1976—; mem. faculty Nat. Coll. State Judiciary, U. Nev., 1973; adv. bd. Nat. Center for State Cts. Appellate Justice Project, 1978—; founder First Union Nat. Bank, Seattle, 1965, dir., 1965-69. Del., White House Conf. on Children and Youth, 1970; mem. King County (Wash.) Youth Commn., 1969-70; mem. King County Mental Health-Mental Retardation Bd., 1967-69; mem. vis. com. U. Wash. Sch. Social Work, 1977—; mem. U. Wash. Law Sch. Found., 1978—; past bd. dirs. Seattle United Way. Served with Signal Corps, U.S. Army, 1952-53. Recipient Disting. Service award Seattle Jaycees, 1965. Mem. Am. Bar Assn. (exec. com. appellate judges conf. 1978—, chmn. conf. 1982-83), Washington Council Crime and Delinquency (chmn. 1970-72), State-Fed. Jud. Council State of Wash. (vice chmn. 1977—). Home: 1908 34th Ave S Seattle WA 98144 Office: 912 US Courthouse Seattle WA 98104

FARRIS, MARTHA IRENE, city official; b. Champaign, Ill., July 19, 1934; d. Glenn Clair and Maurine (Slater) Ruckman; m. Richard Louis Farris, Sept. 14, 1958; children—Jon, Jan, Jil; B.S., U. Ill., Champaign, 1957; Supr. girls and womens activities, dir. spl. events and pub. relations, supr. youth activities City of Oceanside, Calif., 1960-75, acting recreation supt., 1975-77, recreation supt., 1977—, intergovtl. and community relations specialist, 1982—. Mem. Bus. and Profl. Women, AAUW, Oceanside C. of C., Calif. Women in Govt., Mcpl. Mgmt. Assts. So. Calif., Assn. Vol. Adminstrn., Calif. Park and Recreation Soc., Nat. Recreation and Park Assn., So. Calif. Mcpl. Athletic Fedn., Chi Kappa Rho. Rep. Home: 1004 Morse St Oceanside CA 92054 Office: 321 N Nevada St Oceanside CA 92054

FARRIS, MARTIN T., economist, educator; b. Spokane, Wash., Nov. 5, 1925; s. Jacob B. and Edith S. (Gunderson) F.; m. Rhoda H. Harrington, Aug. 20, 1948; children—Christine A. Farris Zenobi, Diana Lynn Farris, Elizabeth, M. Theodore II. B.A. U. Mont., 1949, M.A., 1950; Ph.D. Ohio State U., 1957. Graduate asst. U. Mont., 1949-50; asst. in Econs. Ohio State U. 1950-51, asst. instr. 1953-55, instr. 1955-57; asst. prof. Ariz. State U., 1957-59, assoc. prof., 1959-62. chmn. dept. econs 1967-69, prof. transp. and public utility econs., 1962—; vis. prof. U. Hawaii, 1969-70, vis. scholar, 1979. Republican precinct committeeman. Served with U.S. Army, 1944-46. Decorated 2 battle stars, Philippine Liberation Metal; recipient Transp. Man of the Yr. award, 1972; Outstanding Faculty Achievement award Ariz. State U. Alumni Assn., 1978; Outstanding Faculty Researcher award Coll. Bus., Ariz. State U., 1982. Mem. Am. Econ. Assn., Western Econ. Assn., Am. Soc. Traffic and Transp. Assn., ICC Practitioners, Transp. Research Forum, Traffic Clubs Internat., Phi Kappa Phi, Omicron Delta Epsilon, Sigma Phi Epsilon, Delta Nu Alpha, Beta Gamma Sigma. Republican. Episcopalian. Club: Phoenix Traffic. Author (with Roy Sampson), Domestic Transportation; Practice, Theory and Policy, 1979; (with Roy Sampson) Public Utilities: Regulation, Management and Ownership, 1973; (with Paul McElhiney) Modern Transportation, 1973; (with Grant Davis and Jack Holder), Management of Transportation Carriers, 1975; (with Forrest Hardine) Passenger Transportation, 1976; (with Dave Bess) U.S. Maritime: History and Prospects, 1981; also contr. to profl. jours. in field. Home: 6108 E Vernon Scottsdale AZ 85257 Office: Coll Bus Adminstrv Ariz State U Tempe AZ 85287

FARRIS, WILLIAM EDWARD, communications educator; b. Columbus, Ohio, May 12, 1936; s. Ralph Edward and Remah J. (Monroe) F.; m. Joyce Alene Leaman; 1 dau., Nancy Jolene. B.S. in Edn., Ashland (Ohio) Coll., 1958; M.Ed., Kent State U., 1966. Cert. tchr. secondary, post-secondary. Tchr. high schs., Mansfield, Ohio, 1958-77; tchr. mktg. communications Mansfield Bus. Coll., 1974-77; coordinator retail mgmt. No. Central Tech. Coll., Mansfield, 1968-69; dir. news and sports Sta. WFCO-TV, Mansfield, 1971-73; free-lance communications cons., Mansfield, 1974-77; tchr. radio, TV broadcasting Career Devel. Ctr., Longmont, Colo., 1979—; tchr. bus. mgmt. Community Coll.-N. campus, Denver, 1981—. Bd. dirs. Mansfield Playhouse. Mem. NEA, Colo. Edn. Assn., Nat. Bus. Edn. Assn., Colo. Vocat. Assn., Am. Vocat. Assn., Colo. Educators Bus., St. Vrain Valley (Colo.) Edn. Assn., Jaycees (past sec.) (Ashland, Ohio); Triumph Registrar Am./Ohio. Republican. Lutheran. Wrote one-act play used in curricular devel. theatre of the absurd.

FARROW, BERNARD EDWARD, psychologist, educator; b. Monticello, N.Y., July 6, 1936; s. Saul and Ruth (Finkelstein) F.; B.S., SUNY-Oswego, 1961; M.A., No. Ariz. U., Flagstaff, 1971; m. Arlene Mendelson, May 30, 1960; children—Scott Andrew, Randy Mark. Tchr., Brentwood (N.Y.) Pub. Schs., 1961-62, Roslyn (N.Y.) Pub. Schs., 1962-66, Half Hollow Hills Pub. Schs., Huntington, N.Y., 1966-67; tchr. Clark County Schs., Las Vegas, Nev., 1968-72, counselor, 1978-79; adj. prof. Nova U., Fort Lauderdale, Fla., 1978—; instr. Park Coll., Nellis AFB, Las Vegas, Nev., 1979—; prof. Embry Riddle Aero. U., Nellis AFB, Las Vegas, 1978—; pvt. practice psychology, Las Vegas, 1979—; psychologist State Nev., Nev. Indsl. Commn., State Indsl. Ins. System, 1979—; spl. investigator child custody div. 8th Jud. Dist. Ct., 1979-80. Mem. Town Bd., Mount Charleston, Nev., 1980—, chmn., 1981—; team couple World Wide Marriage Encounter, 1982—; precinct chmn. Nev. Democratic Party, 1982; mem. Nev. Speakers Bur., 1983—. Served with USN, 1954-57. Mem. Am. Personnel and Guidance Assn., Am. Fedn. Tchrs., Rehab. Counselors Assn., Am. Psychol. Assn., Soc. Behavioral Medicine, Nev. Adlerian Soc., Nev. State Counselors Assn., Nev. Mental Health Counselors Assn. (county rep.), Nev. Psychol. Assn.

FARWELL, HERMON WALDO, JR., educator, speech communicator; b. Englewood, N.J., Oct. 24, 1918; s. Hermon Waldo and Elizabeth (Whitcomb) F.; A.B., Columbia, 1940; M.A., Pa. State U., 1964; m. Martha Carey Matthews, Jan. 3, 1942; children—Gardner Whitcomb, Linda Margaret (Mrs. Richard Hammer). Mil. service, 1940-66, advanced through grades to maj. U.S. Air Force; ret., 1966; instr. aerial photography Escola Tecnica de Aviação, Brazil, 1946-48; faculty U. So. Colo., Pueblo, 1966-83, assoc. prof., chmn. dept. speech communications, from 1969, now prof. emeritus; cons., tchr. parliamentary procedure. Mem. Speech Communication Assn., Am. Inst. Parliamentarians (nat. dir. 1977-84), Commn. on Am. Parliamentary Practice (chmn. 1976), Ret. Officers Assn. Author: The Majority Rules-A Manual of Procedures for Most Groups; Parliamentary Motions; editor: The Parliamentary Jour. Home: 65 MacAlester Rd Pueblo CO 81001

FARWELL, SIGRID OLAFSON, consulting and apparel company executive; b. Ithaca, N.Y., June 4, 1933; d. Peter and Harriette Elizabeth (Smith) O.; m. Theodore Austin Farwell, July 11, 1954; children—Karin Farwell Swanson, Peter, Eric. B.A., Cornell U., 1955; M.A., U. Colo., 1978. Owner, mgr. Farwell Ballet Sch., Littleton, N.H., 1962-69; inservice coordinator N.W. Colo. Bd. Coop. Services, 1973-74; theatre dir. Platt Jr. High Sch. and Fairview High Sch., Boulder Valley Schs., Boulder, Colo., 1975-79; pres. Sigrid Farwell & Assocs. Inc., Boulder, 1979-82, BDF Reflections Inc., Boulder, 1982—; pub. speaker; cons. speaking, personal devel. Mem. Am. Soc. Tng. and Devel., Nat. Speakers Assn., Nat. Assn. Female Execs. Playwright: The Child of Fear, 1975. Home: 7363 Cortez Ln Boulder CO 80303 Office: 1035 Pearl St Boulder CO 80302

FASAL, PAUL, physician, leprologist; b. Vienna, Austria, Oct. 9, 1904; came to U.S., 1941; s. Hugo and Betty (Pollak von Rudin) F.; M.D., U. Vienna, 1929; m. Elfriede Hitzler, Sept. 6, 1936; children—Maria (Mrs. Forrest H. Faulconer), John. Resident dept. dermatology U. Vienna Med. Sch., 1929-34; chief dept. dermatology Wiedner Krankenhaus, Vienna, 1935-37; research assoc. in tropical medicine Inst. for Med. Research, Kuala Lumpur, Malaya, 1938-41; assoc. clin. prof. dermatology U. Calif. at San Francisco, 1950-78, emeritus, 1978—; chief leprosy service USPHS Hosp., San Francisco, 1960-78; cons. dermatopathology Letterman Gen. Hosp., 1949-78; cons. on leprosy State of Calif., 1954-78; cons. USPHS Hosp., Carville, La., 1964-78; mem. leprosy panel U.S.-Japan Coop. Sci. Program, 1965-70; participant Internat. Congresses Leprosy and Dermatology, Hungary, U.S., Germany, Japan, Italy, Eng., Norway; cons. emeritus U.S. Army Health Services Command, San Francisco, 1978. Recipient Ehrenzeichen, German Red Cross, 1936; Outstanding Civilian Service medal U.S. Army, 1970, Disting. Service award HEW, 1972. Diplomate Am. Bd. Dermatology. Mem. Internat. Leprosy Assn., Soc. Tropical Dermatology, Pacific Dermatologic Assn. (hon.), Am. Acad. Dermatology, Austrian (hon.), San Francisco (past pres.) dermatol. socs., Assn. Mil. Dermatologists, Soc. Physicians Vienna (hon.). Contbr. over 80 papers, articles in field to profl. publs. Home: 2 Fallon Pl Apt 36 San Francisco CA 94133

FASSETT, GORDON WADSWORTH, water resource engineering company executive; b. Summit, N.J., Nov. 3, 1952; s. James W. and Jean (Fowler) F.; m. Cindy Bernd, May 20, 1975; 1 son, Scott F. B.S. in Civil Engring., U. Wyo., 1974. Registered profl. engr., Colo., Wyo., S.D. Water resource engr. water dept. City of Denver, 1975-79; project engr., mgr. Leonard Rice Cons. Water Engrs., Denver, 1979—, v.p., 1982—. Mem. Nat. Soc. Profl. Engrs., Am. Water Works Assn., Cons. Engrs. Council, Colo. Profl. Engrs. Republican. Office: Leonard Rice Cons Water Engrs 2695 Alcott St Denver CO 80211

FASSETT, JAMES ERNEST, geologist; b. Dearborn, Mich., May 1, 1933; s. Ernest E. and Mary (Sleiva) F.; B.S., Wayne State U., 1959, M.S. in Geology, 1964; m. Sarah Lynn Sheafe, June 13, 1970; children by previous marriage—Melissa Jo, Douglas Paul, Leslie Ann; step-children—Susan Lynne, Tracy Anne Badsgard. Geologist U.S. Geol. Survey, Washington, 1960, Farmington, N.Mex., 1961—, dist. geologist Farmington dist., 1967-79, dep. conservation mgr. Resource Evaluation, Albuquerque, 1980-82, chief br. Eastern tech. reports, geol. div., Reston, Va., 1983—. Cons. to Time-Life Wilderness Series, 1973-74; instr. geology N.Mex. State U., San Juan br., Farmington, 1975—; cons. Harper and Rowe, Pubs., Inc., 1977. Chairperson San Juan County (N.Mex.) Human Rights Com., 1974—; bd. dirs. San Juan Legal Aid, 1977—, Totah Council on Alcoholism, 1978—. Served with AUS, 1953-55. Recipient Superior Performance award Interior dept., 1963, 81; A.I. Levorson award Am. Assn. Petroleum Geologists, 1969, also continuing edn. lectr., 1977—. Fellow Geol. Soc. Am.; mem. Am. Assn. Petroleum Geologists (ho. of dels.), Soc. Econ. Paleontologists and Mineralogists, Am. Inst. Profl. Geologists (cert.), N.Mex. (v.p. 1975—, pres. 1976), Four Corners (pres. 1973, hon. life), Farmington (pres. 1966) geol. socs. Contbr. articles on geology of N.Mex., Colo., Ariz., Utah, to profl. publs.; also geol. quadrangle maps and bulls. on stratigraphy and coal resources of Southwest; editor several geol. guidebooks. Home: 2310 Teodoro NW Albuquerque NM 87107 Office: 505 Marquette St NW Suite 815 Albuquerque NM 87102

FASSETT, WILLIAM EDMOND, pharmacist, educator; b. Torrance, Calif., Nov. 8, 1945; s. Minard Webster and Ruth Georgia (Eyer) F.; B.S. in Pharmacy, U. Wash., 1969; M.B.A., U. Puget Sound, 1983; m. Sharon Elaine Johnson, Aug. 6, 1966; children—Mark Edward, David William. Pharmacist, nursing home cons. Ostrom Enterprises, Inc., Kenmore, Wash., 1969-71; profl. services rep. Upjohn Co., Portland, Oreg., 1971-78, hosp. specialist, 1978-79; mgr. Inglewood Drug, Bothell, Wash., 1979-80; lectr., coordinator profl. experience programs Sch. Pharmacy, U. Wash., Seattle, 1980—; v.p. Wash. Pharmacy Cons. Inc., Bellevue, 1982—. Mem. social action div. Involved Northshore Communities, 1970; chmn. adv. bd. INC Spot Community House, 1972, sec. bd. dirs., 1974. Bd. dirs., chmn. bd. Earn Youth Employment Service, 1969; bd. dirs. Thurston-Mason County (Wash.) chpt. ARC, 1976-79, vice-chmn., 1978. Mem. Am., Wash. State (bd. mgrs. 1975-78), East King County (pres. 1974, 81) pharm. assns., Am. Assn. Colls. Pharmacy, U. Wash. Sch. Pharmacy Alumni Assn. (trustee, editor Alumni News 1977-79, pres. 1979-80), Kappa Psi, Rho Chi. Club: Kiwanis (pres. 1975). Home: 16204-197 NE Woodinville WA 98072 Office: Sch Pharmacy SC-69 U Wash Seattle WA 98195

FASSLER, JOSEPH K., food service executive; b. N.Y.C., Jan. 26, 1942; s. Charles and Sallie (Hirshhorn) F.; m. Carey K. Larson, June 6, 1981. B.S., Okla. State U., 1963. With Greyhound Food Mgmt. Inc., Phoenix, 1963—, dist. mgr., 1973-75, v.p., 1976-79, exec. v.p., 1980-81, pres., chief operating officer, 1982—; lectr. Sponsor, contbr. Boys Brotherhood Republic, 1963—. Served with USMC, 1964. Recipient Outstanding Alumni award N.Y.C. Community Coll., 1972, Okla. State U., 1983. Mem. Soc. Foodservice Mgmt., Nat. Restaurant Assn., Internat. Foodservice Mfrs. Assn. Office: Greyhound Tower 3103 Phoenix AZ 85077

FAST, DOUGLAS ELLIS, real estate mgmt. and investment exec.; b. Dayton, Ohio, Dec. 20, 1941; s. Ellis Valentine and Mable Viola (Pellar) F.; B.B.A., U. N.Mex., 1969; m. Mary Marjorie Putney, Aug. 19, 1967; children—Douglas Ellis, Deanna Marie. Auditor Peat, Marwick, Mitchell & Co., Albuquerque, 1968-71; controller Med. Resources, Colorado Springs, 1971-73, treas., 1973-76, exec. v.p., 1976-77, also dir.; v.p., gen. mgr. U.S. ops. Hillcrest Investments Ltd., Acadia Investments, Inc., Denver, 1978-80; pres., chief exec. officer Remad, Inc., Denver, 1980—; dir. Colonial Columns, Colorado Springs Life Center, Terrace Gardens, Minnequa Medicenter. Mem. Pikes Peak Council Boy Scouts Am. Mem. Am. Inst. C.P.A.s, Colo. Soc. C.P.A.s, N.Mex. Soc. C.P.A.s, Nat. Assn. Accts., Sigma Phi Epsilon. Clubs: Colorado Springs Racquet, Garden of the Gods, Elks. Home: 5689 S Hillside St Englewood CO 80111 Office: 8000 E Prentice Ave Englewood CO 80111

FAST, PHILIP EUGENE, psychologist; b. Wichita, Kans., Sept. 10, 1945; s. Chester Kelly and Marjorie Ellen (Krueger) F.; B.A. in Psychology, Emporia State U., 1968, M.S. in Counseling Psychology, 1969; postgrad. sch. psychology cert. program Utah State U., 1973; postgrad. spl. edn. cert. program Weber State Coll., 1981; m. Phyllis Elaine Clayton, Feb. 14, 1969; children—Douglas Craig, David Thomas. Research asst. Wichita Guidance Center, summer 1968; psychology intern Public Schs. Topeka, 1969-70; sch. psychologist KI-COM Coop. Services, Greensberg, Kans., 1970-71; psychol. cons. Public Schs. Lincoln County (Wyo.), 1971-73, sch. psychology intern, spring 1973; clin. psychology summer intern Wyo. State Hosp., Evanston, 1972; sch. psychologist Public Schs. Davis County (Utah), 1973—, psychology internship coordinator, 1975-80, chmn. research rev. com., 1980—; marriage and family counseling summer trainee Davis County Mental Health Center, 1975; part-time pvt. practice marriage and family counseling, 1975—; part-time juvenile drug counselor Davis County Mental Health Center, 1978—; adj. prof. spl. edn. Weber State Coll., 1979-81; instr. off-campus in-service classes Brigham Young U., 1983—; sch. psychology tng. program evaluator Nat. Council Accreditation in Tchr. Edn., 1980—. Mem. Am. Psychol. Assn. (asso.), Nat. Assn. Sch. Psychologists (charter mem.; certificate recognition for profl. leadership 1974, Wyo. del. 1971-73, Utah alt. del. 1979-81), NEA, Utah Assn. Sch. Psychologists (dir. 1979-80). Contbr. articles to profl. jours. Home: 995 North 390 West Sunset UT 84015 Office: Dept Spl Edn Davis Sch System 20 N Main St Farmington UT 84025

FAST, RAYMOND GARRY, educational administrator; b. Saskatoon, Sask., Can., Jan. 17, 1936; s. Bernhard Harold and Mary Ethyl (Thiessen) F.; m. Helen Marion Lane, Sept. 10, 1960; children—Lori-Lynn, Raymond Garry. B.Ed., U. Sask., 1960; M.Ed., U. Alta., 1964; Ph.D., Pa. State U., 1968. Supt. schs. dept. edn. Govt. Alta., Edmonton, 1964-66, exec. asst. provincial bd. post-secondary edn., 1968-69, asst. dep. minister program services br. dept. advanced edn., 1973; dir. instructional services Alta. Colls. Commn., Edmonton, 1969-72; adminstr. Red Deer (Alta.) Coll., 1972-73; dir. edn. Saskatoon Bd. Edn., 1974—. Mem. Saskatoon Bd. Trade, 1974—. Kellogg fellow, 1960. Mem. Am. Assn. Sch. Adminstrs., Can. Edn. Assn., Can. Assn. Sch. Adminstrs., League of Ednl. Adminstrs., Dirs. and Supts. Sask., Phi Delta Kappa. Author: Some Perceptions of Education in Western Europe, 1970; Red Deer College: The Critical Years, 1974. Home: 146 Columbia Dr Saskatoon SK S7K 1E9 Canada Office: 405 3d Ave S Saskatoon SK S7K 1M7 Canada

FASY, ALAN PAUL, data processing company executive; b. Oakland, Calif., Oct. 19, 1946; s. Joseph Emile and Alice Mary (Gervais) F.; m. Marilyn Ida Hogenson, July 12, 1980; children—Terry, Shauna. Programmer clin. lab. Swedish Hosp., Seattle, 1970-72; programmer II, U. Wash., 1973-74; pres. Stellar Systems, Inc., bus. computer systems, Tacoma, Wash., 1975—; v.p. tech., med. computer systems Med. Computer Alliance, Bainbridge Island, Wash., 1983—. Mem. Data Processing Mgmt. Assn. Mormon. Office: 219 Madison Ave S Bainbridge WA 98110

FATT, HELENE VAN DYK, biology, genetics and optometry educator; b. Haarlem, Netherlands, Nov. 1, 1919; d. Louis and Emma (Polak) Van Dyk; came to U.S., 1939; m. Irving Fatt, Dec. 26, 1942; 1 dau., Lois Emily Fatt White. A.B., UCLA, 1943; M.A., U. Calif.-Berkeley, 1961, Ph.D., 1966. Lectr. nutritional scis. U. Calif.-Berkeley, 1966-68; instr. biology Santa Rosa (Calif.) Jr. Coll., 1968-69; assoc. prof. dept. biology Coll. of Marin, Kentfield, Calif., 1970-76; prof., 1976—; lectr. Sch. Optometry U. Calif.-Berkeley, 1979-83; mem. San Francisco Bay Area Sci. Adv. Bd. Nat. Retinitis Pigmentosa Found., 1980—. USPHS fellow, 1964-66; Moorfield's Eye Hosp. studentship, London, 1976-77. Mem. AAAS, Nat. Assn. Biology Tchrs., Hastings Inst. for Ethics, ACLU, Sigma Xi. Unitarian. Co-author: Genetics for Primary Eye Care Practitioners, 1983; contbr. articles to profl. jours. Home: 1891 San Antonio Ave Berkeley CA 94707 Office: Dept Biology Coll of Marin Kentfield CA 94904

FATTU, EMIL, metallurgist; b. Kellogg, Idaho, Jan. 9, 1917; s. Nicholas and Dorothy (Mannet) F.; A.A., Itasca Jr. Coll., 1935; B.Chemistry with distinction, U. Minn., 1938; m. Hazel Hattie Waldrip, Oct. 30, 1943; children—Emil, Charles Victor, Dale Robert, Arlene Mae, Barbara Kay. Metall. chemist Bunker Hill Co., Kellogg, Idaho, 1938-50, instrument engr., 1950-60, research engr., 1960-77, metallurgist, 1977—. Named Man of Yr., Kellogg Jr. C. of C. 1947; Engr. of Yr., Am. Soc. Metals, 1973. Mem. Am. Chem. Soc. (chmn. Inland Empire sect. 1969), Am. Soc. Metals (chpt. chmn. 1973). Congregationalist. Home: 611 Hill St Kellogg ID 83837 Office: PO Box 29 Kellogg ID 83837

FATZINGER, LLOYD ARTHUR, rehabilitation services administrator; b. Lehighton, Pa., Sept. 18, 1921; s. James A. and Cora E. (Steigerwalt) F.; m. Mary Rose Walender, June 3, 1973; children—Pamela J. Fatzinger Williamson, Karen Krotzer Murtaugh, Brenda Fatzinger Krotzer. A.B., Moravian Coll., 1946; postgrad. in history Lehigh U., 1946-47; M.Ed. in Counseling, U. Ariz., 1974. Cert. rehab. counsel Commn. on Rehab. Counseling. Enlisted U.S. Army; ret., 1965; engring. writer Bell Aerospace, Tucson, 1965-70, Lockheed Electronics, Tucson, 1970-73; counselor, evaluator Devereux Found., Santa Barbara, Calif., 1974-79; dir. rehab. services Crawford Rehab. Services, San Luis Obisop, Calif., 1979—. Mem. Nat. Rehab. Assn., Nat. Rehab. Counseling Assn., Am. Rehab. Counselors Assn., Calif. Personnel and Guidance Assn., Calif. Rehab. Counselors Assn., Nat. Vocat. Guidance Assn., Am. Personnel and Guidance Assn. Republican. Lutheran. Clubs: Kiwanis. Office: Crawford Rehab Services 864 OSOS Suite B San Luis Obispo CA 93401

FAUCETT, JUSTIN (JAY) MARTYR, building materials corporate executive, builder, developer; b. Bell, Calif., Apr. 15, 1933; s. Phillip Henry and Vera Effie (Henshaw) F.; m. Norma Jean Lunsford; June 6, 1950; children—John Allen, Karen Elaine, Cheryl Lynn. Diploma in higher acctg., Kaiser Bus. Coll., 1956; B.A., Chapman Coll., 1958; Th.M., Claremont (Calif.) Sch. Theology, 1973. Pub. acct., Huntington Park, Calif., 1956-58; with So. Calif. Conf. United Meth. Ch., Los Angeles, 1958-68; credit mgr. I.C.N. Pharms., Irvine, Calif., 1968-69; asst. controller Islander Motor Homes, Santa Ana, Calif., 1970; controller, then treas. La Habra Products, Inc., Anaheim, Calif., 1970-83, chief fin. officer, 1983—. Served to corp., U.S. Army, 1953-55. Profl. devel., manuscript dir., v.p. Orange County chapter Nat. Acctg. Assn. Office: PO Box 3639 Anaheim CA 92803

FAUCHER, DARLENE, advt. and public relations exec.; b. Bell, Calif., June 3, 1944; d. Duane Orr and Maxine Brady (Schmitt) Taylor; student San Diego State U., 1962-65; Stewardess, Pacific S.W. Airlines, 1965-66, saleswoman, 1966-70; chmn. bd., pres. Faucher & Meenan Advt. and Public Relations, San Diego, 1970—, My Handy Tool Store; v.p. Gardner & Faucher Advt. and Public Relations, San Diego, 1979—; owner Taylor Advt., Costa Mesa, Calif. Mem. alumni bd. San Diego State U.; bd. dirs. Bayside Settlement House, 1978-80, Jr. Achievement; mem. chancellors assos. U. Calif., San Diego; mem. Campership Council. Recipient Graphic Achievement award Fox River Paper Corp., 1974-75; Graphic Excellence award Strathmore Paper Co., 1976; La Jolla Town Council Beautification award, 1976; named Business Leader of Day, KSON, 1976. Mem. Internat. Assn. Bus. Communicators, Am. Mktg. Assn., Public Relations Soc., Am., Small Businesswomen Owners Assn. (pres. 1978-80), Politically Organized Women. advt. and public relations exec.; b. Bell, Calif., June 3, 1944; d. Duane Orr and Maxine Brady (Schmitt) Taylor; student San Diego State U., 1962-65; Stewardess, Pacific S.W. Airlines, 1965-66, saleswoman, 1966-70; chmn. bd., pres. Faucher & Meenan Advt. and Public Relations, San Diego, 1970—, My Handy Tool Store; v.p. Gardner & Faucher Advt. and Public Relations, San Diego, 1979—; owner Taylor Advt., Costa Mesa, Calif. Mem. alumni bd. San Diego State U.; bd. dirs. Bayside Settlement House, 1978-80, Jr. Achievement; mem. chancellors assos. U. Calif., San Diego; mem. Campership Council. Recipient Graphic Achievement award Fox River Paper Corp., 1974-75; Graphic Excellence award Strathmore Paper Co., 1976; La Jolla Town Council Beautification award, 1976; named Business Leader of Day, KSON, 1976. Mem. Internat. Assn. Bus. Communicators, Am. Mktg. Assn., Public Relations Soc., Am., Small Businesswomen Owners Assn. (pres. 1978-80), Politically Organized Women. Home: 33522 Seagull Ct Dana Point CA 92629 Office: 432 F St Suite 400 San Diego CA 92101

FAULCONER, KAY ANNE, cons. exec.; b. Shelbyville, Ind., Aug. 19, 1945; d. Clark Jacks and Charlotte (Tindall) Keenan; B.A. in English, Calif. State U., Northridge, 1968; M.B.A., Pepperdine U., 1975, M.A. in Communications, 1976; m. James Faulconer; children—Kevin Lee, Melissa Lynne. Pres., Kay Faulconer & Assos., Oxnard, Calif., 1977—; instr. Oxnard Coll., U. LaVerne. Former pres., founder Oxnard Friends of Library; former exec. bd. Ventura County March of Dimes; mem. PTA; officer, bd. dirs. Oxnard Girls Club. Named Businesswoman of Yr., Ventura Bus. and Profl. Women's Club, 1976; Woman of Achievement, Oxnard Bus. and Profl. Women's Club, 1973, recipient Career Woman award, 1974; Mark Hopkins award for excellence in teaching Oxnard Coll., 1982. Mem. Am. Soc. Tng. and Devel., Am. Assn. Women in Community and Jr. Colls., Ventura County Profl. Women's Network. Club: Oxnard Jr. Monday (past pres., hon. life). Home and Office: 601 Janetwood Dr Oxnard CA 93030

FAULCONER, THOMAS PLEASANT, ret. engring. exec.; b. San Diego, Apr. 7, 1912; s. Thomas Nichols and Margaret (Adams) F.; B.S. in M.E., U. Calif., 1940; m. Barbara Dauchy, May 1, 1936 (dec.); m. 2d, Lillian Mathis, Feb. 14, 1965; children—Marion Dauchy, Katharine, Ann. Engr., Consol. Aircraft Corp., San Diego, 1936-38, engr. charge landing gear design, 1940-41, dir. edn., 1941-43, asst. dir. indsl. relations, 1943-46, asst. chief engr. flying automobile, 1946-49; mgr. indsl. relations Solar Aircraft Corp., San Diego, 1949-53; pres. Jet Air Engring. Corp., San Diego, 1953-55; mil. relations rep. Convair div. Gen Dynamics Corp., 1958-59; pres Rick-Faulconer Engring. Corp., 1957-59, Thomas Faulconer Co., Inc., 1959-71, Geo. E. Barney Co., Inc., San Diego, 1959-62; Faulconer Bros. Inc., 1962-69; owner, licensor Caliputer Engring. & Sci. Instruments Co., 1962-69. Mem. engring. adv. council U. Calif., 1946-70. Served as lt. USCGR, 1943-45. Asso. fellow AIAA; mem. San Diego C. of C. (edn. and aviation com. 1946-47), San Diego County Industries Assn. (dir. 1946-48), San Diego Maritime Mus., San Diego Aerospace Mus., U.S. Naval Inst., Mensa. Clubs: San Diego Yacht, Rotary of Point Loma (dir. 1946-56, pres. 1954). Author: Introduction to Aircraft Design; How to Make Money in California Real Estate, 1962; A New Concept of the Theory of Virtual Mass; High Altitude, High Speed Interceptor Study; editor, illustrator: Preparing for Aviation; contbr. to tech. mags., profl. jours.; patentee sliderule, caliper. Home: 1354 Clove St San Diego CA 92106

FAULKNER, ADELE LLOYD, interior designer, color cons.; b. Los Angeles, Dec. 26, 1913; d. Lloyd Lawrence and Coralynn (DeVoe) Lloyd; grad. Woodbury Coll., 1932; m. 2d, William Carl Quinn, Dec. 22, 1963; 1 son by previous marriage, Lloyd Nelson Faulkner. Pres., Adele Faulkner & Assos., Inc.; syndicated columnist Copley News; dir. Los Angeles Community Design Center, 1972-76; tchr. UCLA extension, U. Calif.-Irvine; mem. adv. council, bd. visitors Fider Nat. Accrediting Body for Univs. Teaching Interior Design. Fellow Am. Soc. Interior Designers (twice past chpt. pres., v.p. nat. bd. govs., nat. sec. 1972-73, regional v.p. 1973-75, Nat. Design award 1968, 69), Home Fashions League; mem. Internat. Women in Design (award of merit 1980), Profl. Women for So. Calif. Symphony. Office: PO Box 112 North Hollywood CA 91603

FAULKNER, DEXTER HAROLD, executive editor; b. Grand Island, Nebr., Sept. 10, 1937; s. Jack L. and Wanetta May (Howland) F.; student U. Calif.-Fresno, 1956-58, Ambassador Coll., 1958-60; m. Shirley Ann Hume, Jan. 11, 1959; children—Nathan Timothy, Matthew Benjamin. Mng. editor Good News mag. and Worldwide News internat. div. Ambassador Coll., Sydney, Australia, 1960-66, news research asst. dir. Ambassador Coll. Editorial, Pasadena, Calif., 1966-71, regional editor Plain Truth mag., Washington, 1971-75, asst. mng. editor, Pasadena, 1975-78, mng. editor, 1980-82, exec. editor, 1982—, mng. editor Good News mag., Worldwide News-Tabloid, 1978—, Youth/83 mag., 1980—; instr. mass communications Ambassador Coll., 1980—; columnist Just One More Thing . . ., By the Way. Mem. Inst. Journalists (London), Profl. Photographers Am. Inc., Bur. Freelance Photographers (London), Nat. Press Club, World Affairs Council (Los Angeles), Internat. Assn. Bus. Communicators, Nat. Press Photographers Assn., Am. Mgmt. Assn., Sigma Delta Chi. Mem. Worldwide Ch. God. Contbr. articles, photos on internat. relations, social issues to Plain Truth mag., Good News mag., Worldwide News Publs., 1970—. Home: 7859 Wentworth St Sunland CA 91040 Office: 300 W Green St Pasadena CA 91123

FAULKNER, DOROTHY WHOWELL, speech/lang. pathologist; b. Johnstown, Colo., May 9, 1924; d. Harry Owen and Ruth Theresa (Foley) Whowell; B.A., U. Denver, 1946; M.A., U. No. Colo., Greeley, 1968; m. Earl Junior Faulkner, June 5, 1947; children—Lisa Kaye Faulkner Shultz, David Scott. Speech and lang. pathologist Sch. Dist. 6, Greeley Public Schs., 1945—. Grantee gen. semantics U. Chgo., 1964; grantee speech and audiology Colo. State U., 1965. Mem. NEA, Colo. Edn. Assn., Am. Speech and Hearing Assn., Colo. Speech and Hearing Assn., Greeley Tchrs. Assn., Alpha Delta Kappa, Zeta Phi Eta, Delta Zeta. Republican. Congregationalist. Club: P.E.O. Address: 2175 Buena Vista Dr Greeley CO 80631

FAULKNER, FRANK DAVID, mathematician, educator; b. Humansville, Mo., Apr. 6, 1915; s. Marion Alexander and Bertha Ellanora (Pfandler) F.; m. Theresa Alice Hellmer (dec.); children—Frank David Jr., Harold G., Mary Kirk, William M., Robert G., Andrew W. B.S., Kans. State Tchrs. Coll., Emporia, 1940; M.S., Kans. State U., Manhattan, 1942; Ph.D., U. Mich., 1969. Engr., U.S. Rubber Co., Detroit, 1942-43; instr. U. Mich., 1943-44, research mathematician, 1946-50; asst. prof. to prof. math. Naval Postgrad. Sch., Monterey, Calif., 1950-81, Disting. prof., 1971-81, Dist. prof. emeritus, 1981—; cons. in field. Mem. Am. Math. Soc., Math. Assn. Am. Club: Moose. Contbr. articles on numerical methods in optimal control and partial differential equations to profl. jours. Home: PO Box 3835 Carmel CA 93921 Office: Dept Math Naval Postgrad Sch Monterey CA 93940

FAULKNER, LARRY REID, consulting engineer; b. Denver, Dec. 20, 1936; s. Frederick William and Wilma Louise (Reid) F.; m. Vera Ruth Lockard, June 21, 1963; children—Larry Reid Jr., Laura Lockard. Profl. degree in geol. engring. Colo. Sch. of Mines, 1959. Cert. profl. engr. and land surveyor, Colo. Engr., U.S. Army C.E., 1959-60; cons. engr. Meurer-Serafini & Meurer, 1960-64, 1972-73, T.V. Garel, 1964-66, Wright-McLaughlin Engrs., Denver, 1966-68; design engr. J. M. Bush Co., Denver, 1969-71; pres., prodn. engr. Faulkner-Kellogg & Assocs., Inc., Lakewood, Colo., 1973—. Mem. Am. Arbitration Assn., Colo. Air Quality Hearings Bd., Colo. Cons. Engrs. Council, Am. Pub. Works Assn. Republican. Presbyterian. Clubs: Rolling Hills Country, Elks. Home: 2501 Beech Ct Golden CO 80401 Office: 7190 W 14th Ave Lakewood CO 80215

FAULKNER, MAURICE ERVIN, educator, musician; b. Fort Scott, Kans., Feb. 2, 1912; s. Ervin Philetus and Minnie Mae (Munday) F.; B.S. in Music, Fort Hays State Coll., 1932; postgrad. Interlochen, U. Mich., summer 1933; M.A., Columbia, 1936; Ph.D., Stanford, 1956; m. Ellen Marie Stradal, May 24, 1934 (div. 1951); children—Katherine Sydney, Barbara Ellen; m. 2d, Suzanne Sommerville, Oct. 18, 1958. Instr. music, pub. schs., Quinter, Kans., 1932-36; instr. instrumental music pub. schs., Clay Center, Kans., 1936-37; asst. in music Columbia U., summers 1934-40; asst. prof. San Jose State Coll., 1937-40; asst. prof., assoc. prof. U. Calif., Goleta, 1940-60, prof. music, 1960— chmn. dept., 1950-54; vis. prof. U. Tex., summer 1947; music critic Santa Barbara Star, 1951-56; research musicologist Inst. for Environ. Stress, U. Calif., Santa Barbara, 1968—, prof. emeritus, 1979—; condr. Santa Barbara Symphony Orch., 1941-44, All-Calif. High Sch. Symphony Orch., 1941-73; guest condr. Korean Symphony, 1945-46; condr., mus. dir. Santa Barbara Fiesta Bowl Mus. Show, 1951-53; condr., Kern Co. Honor Band of Calif., music cons., adjudicator Calif., Nev. festivals; free lance music, drama, art critic for Mus. Courier, Sat. Rev., Christian Sci. Monitor; research asso. Inst. for Environ. Stress, 1968—. Chmn., Santa Barbara Mayor's Adv. Com. on Arts, 1966-69. Served from lt. (j.g.) to lt. USNR, 1944-46. Recipient Max Reinhardt Meml. medal for Outstanding Service to Salzburg Festival on 50th Anniversary, Salzburg Golden Service medal, 1981. Fellow Internat. Inst. Arts and Letters (life); mem. Music Acad. West (pres., dir. 1949-82, pres. emeritus, 1954—), So. Calif. Sch. Band and Orch. Assn. (hon. life, v.p. 1955), Musicians Union (hon. life), Nat. Music Educators Conf., Phi Mu Alpha, Phi Delta Kappa. Presbyn. Mason. Brass clinic editor Instrumentalist, 1964—. Contbr. articles to profl. jours. Ann. tours European music festivals, as adviser, critic. Home: Box 572 Goleta CA 93116

FAULKNER, SEWELL FORD, realtor; b. Keene, N.H., Sept. 25, 1924; s. John Charles and Hazel Helen (Ford) F.; A.B., Harvard, 1949; M.B.A., 1951; m. June Dayton Finn, Jan. 10, 1951 (div.); children—Patricia Anne, Bradford William, Sandra Ford, Jonathan Dayton, Winthrop Sewell; m. 2d, Constance Mae Durvin, Mar. 15, 1969 (div.); children—Sarah Elizabeth, Elizabeth Jane. Product mgr. Congoleum Nairn, Inc., Kearny, N.J., 1951-55; salesman, broker pres. Jack White Co. real estate, Anchorage, 1956—; dir. Life Ins. Co. Alaska. Mem. Anchorage City Council, 1962-65, Greater Anchorage Area Borough Assembly, 1964-65, Anchorage Area Charter Commn., 1969-70. Pres., Alaska World Affairs Council, 1967-68; treas. Alyeska Property Owners, Inc., 1973-75, pres., 1977-78; pres. Downtown Anchorage Assn., 1974-75; mem. Girdwood Bd. Suprs. Served with USAAF, 1943-45. Mem. Anchorage Area C. of C. (dir. 1973-74), Urban Land Inst., Bldg. Owners and Mgrs. Assn., Nat. Inst. Real Estate Brokers. Clubs: Alaska Notch, Anchorage Petroleum. Home: Mt Alyeska Girdwood AK 99587 Office: 3201 C St Anchorage AK 99503

FAUQUIER, ROBERT VIRGIL, civil engr.; b. Blond, La., June 21, 1929; s. Joseph Breaux and Elizabeth Bertha Louise (Jung) F.; B.S.C.E., U. Mo., 1961; m. Jo Ann Merideth, June 12, 1955; children—Roberta Lea, Deborah Ann. Project engr. Ben C. Gerwick, Inc., Petaluma, Calif., 1961-62; project engr., gen. supt. Dondlinger & Sons Constrn. Co., Wichita, Kans., 1962-63; project engr., project mgr. Santa Fe-Pomeroy Inc., San Francisco, 1963-74; adminstrv. mgr. H.F. Lauritzen, Inc., Antioch, Calif., 1974-75; project engr., sr. estimator Bechtel, Inc., San Francisco, 1975—. Served with U.S. Navy, 1950-54; Korea. Registered profl. engr., Calif., Mo. Mem. Mo. Soc. Profl. Engrs., Calif. Soc. Profl. Engrs., Nat. Soc. Profl. Engrs., ASCE, Am. Soc. Mil. Engrs. Republican. Lutheran. Home: 34 Deer Park Ave San Rafael CA 94901 Office: 50 Beale St San Francisco CA 94105

FAUSETT, JEFFREY RAY, accountant, controller; b. Ogden, Utah, Sept. 7, 1952; s. Walter Ray and Florence Emma (Carroll) F.; m. Carol Anne Spackman, June 9, 1972; children—Adam, Lindsey. B.S. in Acctg., Brigham Young U., 1978, M.S. in Acctg., 1978. Sr. acct. Arthur Young & Co., Salt Lake City, 1978-80; controller Rocky Mountain Helicopters, Inc., Provo, Utah, 1980—. Active Young Republicans of Utah. Served with U.S. Army, 1972-76. Mem. Utah Soc. C.P.A.s, Am. Inst. C.P.A.s. Mem. Church of Jesus Christ of Latter-day Saints.

FAUSKIN, GARY NEALE, physician, psychotherapist; b. Fargo, N.D., Dec. 11, 1931; s. Arthur Oliver and Lauretta A. (Krueger) F.; B.S., N.D. State Coll., 1953; B.S., U. N.D., 1958; M.D., U. Tex., 1960; m. Lana Lea Halstead, Jan. 14, 1979; children—Michael, James, Laura, Jean, Eric, Jeff. Intern, Cedars of Lebanon Hosp., Los Angeles, 1960-61, resident in pediatrics, 1961-63; medicine specializing in pediatrics, Torrance, Calif., 1966—; clin. prof. pediatrics UCLA, 1966—; mem. staff Harbor Gen. Hosp., Torrance; chief pediatrics South Bay Hosp., Redondo Beach, Calif. Mem. bd. edn. Redondo Beach City Schs., 1970. Served to 1st lt. USAF, 1954-56. Recipient Mosby Med. Book Scholarship award, 1958. Mem. AMA, Calif. Med. Assn., Los Angeles County Med. Assn., Los Angeles Pediatrics Soc. Home: 616 S Gertruda St Redondo Beach CA 90277 Office: 21350 Hawthorne Blvd #258 Torrance CA 90503

FAVERTY, JAMES B(ENNETT), optometrist; b. Neenah, Wis., Aug. 28, 1952; s. Harold E. and Patricia A. Faverty; m. Lorraine M. Hewitt, July 30, 1983. B.S., U. Fla., 1976; O.D., So. Coll. Optometry, 1980. Lic. optometrist, Calif., N.Y., Wash. Resident in optometry SUNY-Manhattan, 1980-81, asst. clin. instr., 1980-81; assoc. in optometry practice, San Anselmo, Calif., 1981-82; pvt. practice optometry specializing in preventive and therapeutic care for refractive and binocular anomalies, Mill Valley, Calif., 1982—; cons. contact lens; Nat. Nikon scholar, 1977. Mem. Am. Optometric Assn., Calif. Optometric Assn., Optometric Extension Program, San Anselmo C. of C. Research in vision. Office: 393 Miller Ave Suite 42 Mill Valley CA 94941

FAWCETT, F(RANK) CONGER, lawyer; b. Newton, Mass., Apr. 16, 1934; s. William Vaughn Moody and Barbara (Conger) F.; A.B. cum laude, Harvard, 1956, J.D., 1962; m. Margaret Rose Goldsmith, June 26, 1963; children—Peter Leon, Katharine Conger. Admitted to Calif. bar, 1963, U.S. Supreme Ct. bar, 1966; asso. firm Graham, James & Rolph (now Graham & James), San Francisco, 1962-68, partner, 1969—; dir., sec. Gavilan Vineyards, Inc., 1969—. Mem. Indigent Criminal Appellant Panel, 1963-70, San Francisco Bar Legal Assistance Panel, 1963-68, San Francisco Lawyer's Com. for Urban Affairs, 1973—; sec., dir. Marin Friends, Am. Conservatory Theatre, 1967-68; active fund raising Calif. Theatre Found., 1967-69; class area agt. Harvard Coll. Fund, 1971—, Harvard Law Sch. Fund, 1975—; bd. dirs., treas. New Games Found., 1974-75, San Francisco Legal Aid Soc., 1975—. Served from ensign to lt. (j.g.) USNR, 1956-59. Mem. Am., Calif., San Francisco bar assns., Maritime Law Assn. Clubs: Commonwealth (Calif.); Merchants Exchange, University (San Francisco); Tiburon Peninsula. Home: 100 Elinor Ave Mill Valley CA 94941 Office: 1 Maritime Plaza San Francisco CA 94111

FAWCETT, STANLEY ANTHONY, educator; b. McGill, Nev., Jan. 29, 1932; s. Edward Eardley and Ada Ruth (Bruno) F.; B.S., No. Ariz. U., 1965, M.A., 1966, Ed.S., 1967; postgrad. Oreg. State U., 1968-69; Ph.D., U. No. Colo., 1974; m. Francine Gayle Luwe, Aug. 23, 1957; children—Stancine Brenda, Stanley Edward, Ronald Shawn. Ops. mgr. Bonanza Airlines, Inc., Reno, Nev., 1955-64; asst. prof. econs. U. Wis., Whitewater, 1966-72; asso. prof. mgmt., chmn. dept. econs. and mgmt. Eastern Mont. Coll., Billings, 1976—. Served with USAF, 1951-55. Mem. Nat. Assn. Bus. Economists, Am. Soc. Traffic and Transp., Assn. ICC Practitioners, Travel Research Assn., Soc. Logistics Engrs. Republican. Mormon. Contbr. articles to profl. jours. Home: 821 Nutter Blvd Billings MT 59105 Office: Eastern Montana College Dept Economics and Management Billings MT 59101

FAWZY, FAWZY IBRAHIM, psychiatrist, medical educator; b. Cairo, June 17, 1942; came to U.S., 1972, naturalized, 1978; married; 2 children. Student English Mission Coll., Cairo, 1960-62; P.N.S. with honors, Cairo U., 1962-63, M.B., B.Ch., 1968. Rotating intern Cairo U., 1968-69; sr. house officer in psychiatry Bexley (Kent, Eng.) Hosp., 1969-70; registrar in psychol. medicine, dept. psychiatry St. Olave's Hosp., London, 1970-71, 3d yr. registrar dept. psychol. medicine St. Olave's Hosp., Guys Group of Hosps., U. London, 1971-72; resident I, Brentwood VA Hosp., Los Angeles, 1972-73, resident II in psychiatry UCLA Sch. Medicine, 1973-74, resident III in psychiatry, 1974-75, chief resident, consultation-liaison service, 1974-75, post-residency fellow, consultation-liaison service, dept. psychiatry, 1975-76, assoc. dir. service, 1976-79, chief service, 1979—, asst. prof. in residence, 1976—, staff psychiatrist Neuropsychiat. Inst., 1976—, asst. dir. Lab. for Study Life-Threatening Behavior, 1976-80; chief consultation-liason service, staff psychiatrist Brentwood VA Med. Center, Los Angeles, 1978—; mem. UCLA Jonsson Comprehensive Cancer Center. Cons., Community Cancer Control Los Angeles, Am. Cancer Soc., Leukemia Soc., Los Angeles, Vis. Nurses' Assn., Los Angeles. Calif. Dept. Alcohol and Drug Program, 1977-80; NIMH Psychiatry Edn. Br. grantee, 1980-83. Mem. Egyptian Med. Syndicate, Royal Coll. Psychiatrists (Eng. affiliate), Am. Psychiat. Assn., Am. Psychosomatic Soc., So. Calif. Psychiat. Soc. (chmn. sect. on consultation-liaison psychiatry 1979-80), Assn. Dirs. Med. Student Edn. in Psychiatry. Contbr. articles, chpts. to profl. publs.; author: (with others) Current Themes in Psychiatry III, 1982; editor: (with others) Contemporary Models in Liaison Psychiatry, 1978. Office: UCLA Neuropsychiat Inst 760 Westwood Plaza Los Angeles CA 90024

FAY, ABBOTT EASTMAN, JR., educator; b. Scottsbluff, Nebr., July 19, 1926; s. Abbott Eastman and Ethel (Lambert) F.; B.A., Colo. State Coll., 1949, M.A., 1953; postgrad., U. Denver, 1961-63, Western State U., 1963; m. Joan D. Richardson, Nov. 26, 1953; children—Rand, Diana, Collin. Tchr. Leadville (Colo.) Pub. Schs., 1950-52, elem. prin., 1952-54; prin. Leadville Jr. High Sch., 1954-55; pub. info. dir., instr. history Mesa Coll., Grand Junction, Colo., 1955-64; asst. prof. history Western State Coll. Colo., Gunnison, 1964-76, assoc. prof. history, 1976-82, assoc. prof. emeritus, 1982—; fellow Hamline U. Inst. Asian Studies, 1975, 79; propr. Mountaintop Books, Paonia, Colo. Bd. dirs. Colo. Asso. Univ. Press; founder, coordinator Nat. Energy Conservation Challenge; project reviewer Nat. Endowment Humanities, Colo. Hist. Soc. Served with AUS, 1944-46. Named Top Prof., Western State Coll., 1969, 70, 71. Mem. Western Writers Am., Rocky Mountain Social Sci. Assn. (sec. 1961-63), Am. Hist. Assn., Assn. Asian Studies, Western History Assn., Western State Coll. Alumni Assn. (pres. 1971-73), Internat. Platform Assn., Am. Legion (Outstanding Historian award 1981), Phi Alpha Theta, Phi Kappa Delta, Delta Kappa Pi. Club: Kiwanis. Author: Mountain Academia, 1968; Writing Good History Research Papers, 1980. Contbr. articles to profl. jours.; freelance writer popular mags. Home: 1750 Hwy 133 Paonia CO 81428

FAY, RICHARD JAMES, mechanical engineer, executive, educator; b. St. Joseph, Mo., Apr. 26, 1935; s. Frank James and Marie Jewell (Senger) F.; m. Marilyn Louis Kelsey, Dec. 22, 1962; B.S.M.E., U. Denver, 1959, M.S.M.E., 1970; Registered profl. engr., Colo., Nebr. Design engr. Denver Fire Clay Co., 1957-60; design, project engr. Silver Engring. Works; research engr., lectr. mech. engring. Colo. Sch. Mines, 1963-74, asst. prof., 1974-75, founder, pres. Fay Engring. Corp., 1971—. Served with Colo. N.G., 1962. Mem. Soc. Automotive Engrs. (past chmn. Colo. sect.), ASME (past chmn. Colo. sect.; coll. relations chmn. region). Contbr. articles to profl. jours.; patentee in field. Office: 516 Acoma St Denver CO 80204

FAY, ROBERT LEE, elec. engr.; b. Akron, Ohio, Dec. 13, 1941; s. Robert A. and Flora H. (Allison) F.; B.Sc. in Engring., Calif. State U., Northridge, 1966; m. Gretchen Eileen Kleine, July 11, 1964; children—Brian Howard, Melissa Suzanne. Elec. engring. design engr. Lockheed Calif. Co., Burbank, 1966-68; sr. engr. Litton Data Systems, Van Nuys, Calif., 1968-72; mgr. avionics design and analysis Ventura div. Northrop Corp., Newbury Park, Calif., 1972—, also project engr. microprocessor based systems; cons. digital circuit design, systems concepts, 1967—. Recipient company patent award, 1971. Mem. IEEE, Northrop Ventura Mgmt. Club. Home: 1130 LaGrange St Newbury Park CA 91320 Office: 1515 Rancho Conejo Newbury Park CA 91320

FAZIO, JOHN PETER, statistician; b. Portland, Oreg., Feb. 22, 1952; s. Jack Frank and Maria Nativita (Rebagliati) F. B.S. in Math., Oreg. State U., 1974, M.S. in Stats., 1975. Statistician Texaco Research Labs., Port Arthur, Tex., 1975-77; sr. process control engr. Corning Glass Works, N.Y., 1977-78; ops. research analyst U.S. Army C.E., Portland, Oreg., 1979-82; statistician Bonneville Power Adminstrn., Portland, 1982—; cons. in field. Mem. Am. Soc. Quality Control, Am. Statis. Assn., Jaycees. Roman Catholic. Clubs: Toastmasters Internat. (Essayons ednl. v.p. 1980), KC (Portland). Developer statis. and problem-solving methods; contbr. to model to assist in planning for Northwest's energy future.

FAZIO, STEVE, educator; b. Phoenix, Sept. 2, 1916; s. Steve and Angie (Perazzo) F.; B.S., U. Ariz., 1940, M.S., 1951; m. Mary Ellen Howe, Sept. 12, 1940; children—Mary Jean (Mrs. David Wilford), Steven A. Insp., Ariz. Commn. Agr. and Horticulture, Phoenix, 1940-42; prof. horticulture U. Ariz., Tucson, 1942—, head dept., 1964-71. Named Outstanding Prof. of Yr., U. Ariz. Coll. Agr., 1962; recipient U. Ariz. Found. Creative Teaching award, 1973, Faculty Achievement award U. Ariz. Alumni Assn., 1977; Faculty Recognition award Tucson Trade Bur., 1973. Mem. Internat. Plant Propagators Soc. (dir. 1967-69, 79-80, pres. Western region) Am. Soc. Hort. Sci. (L.M. Ware teaching award 1973). Home: 3554 E Calle Alarcon Tucson AZ 85716

FAZIO, VICTOR H., congressman; b. Winchester, Mass., Oct. 11, 1942; s. Victor Herbert and Betty V. (Freeman) F.; B.A. in History, Union Coll., 1965; postgrad. (Coro Found. fellow), Calif. State U., Sacramento; children—Dana Elizabeth, Anne Noel. Dir., Office of Assembly Majority Cons., 1971-72, 75; asst. to speaker Calif. Assembly, 1973, mem., 1975-78; mem. 98th Congresses from 4th Dist. Calif. Former v.p. Planning and Conservation League; mem. Sacramento County Charter and Planning Commns., Sacramento Citizens for a Better Govt.; mem. Democratic State and County Central Coms. Club: Comstock Founder, Calif. Jour., 1970. Office: 421 Cannon House Office Bldg Washington DC 20515

FEARN, CLARENCE HAVEN, clin. psychologist; b. Chattanooga, July 9, 1943; s. Clarence Haven and Mary Hue (Gregory) F.; B.S., Tenn. State U., 1965; M.A., Fisk U., 1970; Ph.D., Purdue U., 1973; m. Donna Rae Floyd, June 7, 1969; 1 son, Ayo Jafari. Intern, Camarillo (Calif.) State Hosp., 1973-74, research asso. clin. research unit, 1974; instr. LaVerne Coll., 1974, Mt. San Antonio Coll., Walnut, Calif., 1974-78; prof. psychology Calif. Poly. State U., Pomona, 1978—, Chaffey Coll., Alta Loma, Calif., 1978-79; dir. partial hospitalization Tri-City Community Mental Health Center. Served with AUS, 1962-65. Decorated Army Commendation medal. Fels Found fellow, 1968-70; Woodrow Wilson/Martin Luther King fellow, 1970-72. Mem. Assn. Advancement Behavior Therapy, AAAS, N.Y. Acad. Scis., Congress Faculty Assns., Nat. Audubon Soc. Club: Sierra. Home: 255 Roberts St Pomona CA 91767 Office: 1149 N Garey Ave Pomona CA 91767

FEARN, DEAN HENRY, statistics educator; b. Portland, Oreg., June 8, 1943; s. Clyde Henry and Sylvia Adele (Dahl) F.; m. Gloria June Wilber; children—Neal, Justin. B.S., U. Wash., 1965; M.A., Western Wash. U., 1967; Ph.D., U. Calif.-Davis, 1971. Sr. mathematician Aerojet Gen., Inc., Sacramento, 1970-71, prof. stats. dept. Calif. State U.-Hayward, 1971—. Mem. Inst. Math. Stats., Am. Statis. Assn., Am. Math. Soc. Contbr. articles to profl. jours. Home: 3255 Sunnybrook Ct Hayward CA 94541 Office: Stats Dept Calif State U Hayward CA 94542

FEARN, LEIF, education educator, consultant; b. Pottstown, Pa., Dec. 23, 1939; s. Bruce and Jeanne (Cooley) F.; m. Colleen Rosemary Fahey, June 27, 1938; children—Bridget, Eric. B.S., Shippensburg State Coll., 1961; M.A., Ariz. State U., 1962, Ed.D., 1969. Dir. lang. arts Navajo Tribe, 1965-66; asst. prof. elem. edn. San Diego State U., 1967-74, prof. spl. edn., 1975-83, prof. edn., 1983—; cons., pub. speaker. Mem. Nat. Council Tchrs. English, Assn. Supervision and Curriculum Devel., Nat. Assn. for Gifted. Author: Ways to Have Fun with My Mind, 1975; Teaching for Thinking, 1980; First I Think, 1981; The Writing Kabyn, 1981; Developmental Writing, 1983; Direct Services in Gifted Education, 1980; Literature and Story Writing, 1981; (novel) The Fear, 1983; contbr. articles to profl. jours. Home: 5987 Baja Dr San Diego CA 92115 Office: San Diego State U 5402 College Ave San Diego CA 92182

FEASTER, RICHARD VERNON, metall. and ceramic engr.; b. Los Angeles, May 6, 1934; s. Vernon and Muriel Aileen (Seymour) F.; B.S. in Ceramic Engring. (Gladding McBean and Co. scholar 1952-56), U. Wash., Seattle, 1956; M.S. in Metall. Engring., U. Okla., 1968; m. Janice K. Peterson, Feb. 5, 1956; children—Lisa, Debra, Richelle. Commd. 2d lt. USAF, 1956, advanced through grades to col., 1978; combat pilot, Vietnam; ret., 1979; program mgr. Large Optics Demonstration Expt., Lockheed Missiles & Space Co., Palo Alto, Calif., 1979—. Chmn. adminstrv. bd. St. Paul's United Meth. Ch., Albuquerque, 1976-78. Decorated Legion of Merit, D.F.C., Air Force Commendation medal, Air medal; recipient Air Force Research and Devel. award, 1974. Mem. Air Force Assn. Republican. Club: Masons. Author papers in field. Office: 3251 Hanover St Palo Alto CA 94304

FECHTEL, EDWARD RAY, lawyer, educator; b. Pocatello, Idaho, Apr. 20, 1926; s. Edward Joseph and Frances Lucille (Myers) F.; m. Jewell Reagan, Apr. 7, 1950 (div.); children—Scot Gerald, Mark Edward, Kim. B.A. in Bus., Idaho State U., 1949; J.D., U. Oreg., 1967; M.B.A. in Fin., 1968. Bar: Oreg. 1967, U.S. Dist. Ct. Oreg. 1967, U.S. Ct. Appeals (9th cir.) 1968. Sales rep. Genesco, 1950-59; gen. mdse. mgr. Wilson Wells Co., Pocatello, 1960-64; ptnr. Husband, Johnson & Fechtel, Eugene, Oreg., 1967—; prof. bus. law U. Oreg.; lectr. Oreg. State Bar. Bd. dirs. Legal Aid Soc., Lane County, Oreg., Oreg. Citizens for Fair Land Planning. Served with USN, 1944-46. Mem. ABA, Oreg. State Bar Assn., Phi Alpha Delta. Republican. Home: 1852 Happy Ln Apt 19 Eugene OR 97401 Office: 72 W Broadway St Suite 225 Eugene OR 97401

FEDERHAR, DAVID BERNARD, psychologist; b. Tucson, Apr. 4, 1951; s. Richard Harvey and Doris F.; B.A., U. Ariz., 1972, M.A., 1975, Ph.D., 1983; m. Kristin Pedersen, Aug. 3, 1974; children—Lars, Peter. Grad. teaching asst., instr. psychology U. Ariz., 1972-75; autism program cons. Tucson Unified Sch. Dist., 1975-77, sch. psychologist, 1977—, neuropsychologist, 1978—; mem. assoc. faculty Pima Community Coll., 1977—, Embry-Riddle Aero. U., 1982—, Park Coll., 1983—; cons. in field. Mem. Am Psychol. Assn., Ariz. State Psychol. Assn., So. Ariz. Psychol. Assn. (v.p. 1978-80, sec. 1979-80), Nat. Assn. Sch. Psychologists. Contbr. articles to profl. jours. Home: 7580 E La Cienega Dr Tucson AZ 85715 Office: Tucson Unified Sch Dist I Region II Robinson School Tucson AZ 85716

FEDERICI, WILLIAM R., state supreme court justice; b. Cimarron, N.Mex., July 15, 1917; B.A., U. N.Mex., 1939; J.D., U. Colo., 1941; m. Elsie, Mar. 20, 1945; children—Linda Federici Stevens, Richard, Larry, Gina. Admitted to N.Mex. bar, 1941; began practice law, Santa Fe, 1941; with Atty. Gen.'s Office, 1942, 46-48; justice N.Mex. Supreme Ct., 1977—. Served with aircraft arty. U.S. Army, 1942-46. Mem. State Bar N.Mex., First Jud. Dist. Bar Assn., ABA, vets. orgns. Democrat. Roman Catholic. Club: Elks. Office: Supreme Ct NMex 327 Don Gaspar Ave Santa Fe NM 87503*

FEDERICO, PAT-ANTHONY, research psychologist; b. Newark, Mar. 4, 1942; s. Pasquale and Vincenza (Caramanna) F.; m. Suzanne Marie Boudreaux, Nov. 24, 1967. B.A. cum laude in Math. and Philosophy, U. St. Thomas, Houston, 1965; M.S. in Gen. Exptl. Psychology, Tulane U., 1967, Ph.D. in Gen. Exptl. Psychology, 1969. Research psychologist, U.S. Air Force Human Resources Lab., Denver, 1969-72; sr. research psychologist U.S. Navy Personnel Research and Devel. Center, San Diego, 1972—; honorarium faculty U. Colo., Denver, 1969-71; lectr. dept. psychology San Diego State U., 1972, 77. Served to capt. USAF, 1969-72. NDEA fellow, 1966-69; NSF presdl. intern in sci. and engring., 1972-73. Mem. Human Factors Soc. (exec. dir., pres., sec.-treas. San Diego chpt.), Cognitive Sci. Soc., Psychonomic Soc., Am. Ednl. Research Assn. Sr. author: Management Information Systems and Organizational Behavior, 1980. Co-editor Aptitude, Learning and Instruction: Vol. 1, Cognitive Process Analyses of Aptitude, Vol. 2, Cognitive Process Analyses of Learning and Problem Solving, 1980. Contbr. articles to profl. jours. Home: 4493 Pescadero Ave San Diego CA 92107 Office: Navy Personnel Research and Development Center San Diego CA 92152

FEENEY, ROBERT HICKMAN, advertising executive; b. Beacon, N.Y., Oct. 8, 1930; s. John Patrick and Frances Winifred (Flynn) F.; B.A., Siena Coll., 1953; m. Ann Philippa, Oct. 6, 1956; children—Michael, Kathryn, Matthew, Roberta. Reporter, Poughkeepsie (N.Y.) Jour., 1953-55; dir.publicity Prentice-Hall Inc., N.Y.C., 1955-57; asst. dir. advt. pub. relations H.K. Porter Co., Inc., 1958-59; v.p., account supr. G.M. Basford Co., N.Y.C., 1959-62; exec. v.p. Turner & Feeney Inc., N.Y.C., 1962-70; v.p., dir. advt. Johns Manville Sales Corp., Denver, 1971-82; dir. corp. advt. Manville Corp., 1983—; chmn. advt. and public relations com. Asphalt Roofing Mfrs. Assn.; chmn. adv. bd. 1982—; Mineral Insulation Mfrs. Assn. Chmn. adv. bd. Denver Cath. Register; bd. dirs. Colo. Hearing and Speech Center, 1975-81. Mem. Denver Advt. Fedn. (dir.), Siena Coll. Alumni Assn. (pres.). Roman Catholic. Home: 5812 S Laurel Pl Littleton CO 80123 Office: Ken-Caryl Ranch Denver CO 80217

FEES, LARRY J., wood products company executive; b. Lebanon, Pa., Aug. 3, 1940; s. John D. and Louella (Dishong) F.; B.A., Pa. State U., 1962. Owner, Annville News Agy. (Pa.), 1968-72; controller Fire Systems div. Chemetron Corp. Chgo., 1972-77; treas. Networks Electronic Corp., Chatsworth, Calif., 1977-78; pres. United Wood Products Co., Inglewood, Calif., 1978—. Lutheran. Office: 20691 Horizon Ln Huntington Beach CA 92646

FEHR, J. WILL, newspaper editor; b. Long Beach, Calif., Mar. 8, 1926; s. John and Evelyn (James) F.; B.A. in English, U. Utah, 1951; m. Cynthia Moore, Sept. 4, 1951; children—Michael John, Martha Ann. Reporter, Deseret News, Salt Lake City, 1953-55, med. writer 1957-62; writer Calif. Med. Assn., Los Angeles, 1957-59; city editor Salt Lake Tribune, Salt Lake City, 1964-79, mng. editor, 1979-80, editor, 1981—. Served to 1st lt. USAF, 1951-53. Mem. Am. Assn. Newspaper Editors, Sigma Delta Chi (past pres. Utah Headliners chpt.), Sigma Chi. Club: Ft. Douglas Hidden Valley Country. Home: 468 13th Ave Salt Lake City UT 84103 Office: 143 S Main St Salt Lake City UT 84110

FEHR, LOLA MAE, nurse, assn. exec.; b. Hastings, Nebr., Sept. 29, 1936; d. Leland Rader and Edith Gertrude (Wunderlich) Gaymon; diploma St. Lukes Sch. Nursing, Denver, 1958; B.S. in Nursing, U. Denver, 1959; M.S., U. Colo., 1975; m. Harry Eugene Fehr, Aug. 15, 1972; children—Dawn Marie, Cheryl Lynn, Michael Paul. Staff nurse St. Luke's Hosp., Denver, 1959, head nurse, 1959-60; dir. christian edn. First United Methodist Ch., Greeley, Colo., 1966-71; staff nurse Weld County Hosp., Greeley, 1970-72, dir. inservice edn., 1972-76, dir. nursing, 1976-80; exec. dir. Colo. Nurses Assn., 1980—. Mem. Am. Nurses Assn., Colo. Nurses Assn. (Profl. Nurse of Yr. award 1979), Am. Hosp. Assn., Phi Beta Kappa, Sigma Theta Tau. Congregationalist. Club: Greeley Chorale. Home: 1321 15th St Greeley CO 80631 Office: 5453 E Evans Pl Denver CO 80222

FEHRMAN, CHERIE CHRISTINA, interior designer, writer; b. London, Apr. 13, 1945; came to U.S., 1958, naturalized, 1971; d. James Albert and Lucia Allen; B.A. in English and Creative Writing, San Francisco State U., 1969; postgrad. U. Calif., Berkeley, m. Kenneth R. Fehrman, Apr. 7, 1967. Sr. savs. officer Citizens Savs. & Loan, San Francisco, 1969, asst. br. mgr., to 1974; v.p. Kenneth R. Fehrman Interior Design, Ltd., San Francisco, 1976—; free-lance writer, fiction and non-fiction, San Francisco, 1974—; author: The Complete School Handbook, 1981; The School Encyclopedic Dictionary; Nomadic Interiors; Soft Machine; (novels) Disc, 1980; Fanatic; Einstein, Christ and David Bowie; Friends and Other Fantasies; The Dream Machine; contbr. articles to antique mags.; tchr. design seminars. Mem. Internat. Soc. Interior Designers (dir.), Authors Guild. Democrat. Home and Office: 4112 California St San Francisco CA 94118

FEHRMAN, KENNETH R., interior designer, educator; b. San Antonio, Oct. 24, 1941; s. Oscar and Ruth (McVey) F.; m. Cherie Fehrman, April 7, 1967. B.A., San Francisco State U., 1966, M.A., 1969; doctorate candidate U. San Francisco, cert. tchr. Calif., 1968. Co-founder, Calif. Design Sch., San Francisco, 1980-81; instr. Rudulph Schaeffer Sch. of Design, San Francisco, 1978-80; ptnr., designer Kenneth/Scott Designs, San Francisco, 1978-80; pres. Kenneth Fehrman Interior Design Ltd., 1976—; asst. prof. interior design San Francisco State U., 1980—. Mem. Internat. Soc. Interior Designers (pres. N. Calif. chpt. 1980-82), Am. Soc. Interior Designers Fiber sculptures exhibited San Francisco Mus. of Modern Art; contbr. designs to publs. Office: 4112 California St San Francisco CA 94118

FEIDELSON, MARC, advertising executive; b. N.Y.C., Aug. 20, 1939; s. Robert and Ceil Feidelson; m. Linda Sarnoff, June 11, 1964; children—Lee, Pamela. B.S. in Bus. Adminstrn., Boston U., 1961; M.A. in Psychology, CUNY, 1966. Media research analyst CBS-TV, N.Y.C., 1964-65; sr. media research analyst Ted Bates Advt., N.Y.C., 1966-67; media research dir. Benton & Bowles Advt., N.Y.C., 1967-70; media mgr. RCA Corp., N.Y.C., 1970-72; dir. advt. services Hunt-Wesson Foods, Fullerton, Calif., 1973-79; sr. v.p., media dir. Dailey & Assocs. Advt., Los Angeles, 1979—; guest lectr. UCLA. Mem. Hollywood Radio and TV Soc., Los Angeles Media Dirs. Council (pres. 1981-82). Jewish. Guest editor Media Decisions mag., Apr. 1983. Office: 3055 Wilshire Blvd Los Angeles CA 90010

FEIG, KONNILYN GAY, university dean; b. Raymond, Minn., Sept. 24, 1936; d. Herbert Cecil, Jr., and Mildred (Weyer) F. Student Concordia Coll., Moorhead, Minn.; B.S. in Bus. Adminstrn., U. Mont., 1958, B.A. in History, 1959, M.A. in History, 1963; Ph.D. in History, U. Wash., 1970. Asst. dir. women's affairs and student affairs, instr. history Whitman Coll., 1962-67; teaching fellow history U. Wash., 1967-68; Office of Edn. fellow, Washington, 1968-69; assoc. dean of students U. Pitts., 1969-70, dir. spl. programs, 1970-72; dean Coll. Arts and Scis., assoc. prof. history U. Maine-Portland, Gorham, 1972-77; v.p. adminstrn. San Francisco State U., 1977-82, dean univ. and strategic planning, 1982—; cons. Ford Found., Office of Edn. Bd. dirs., mem. exec. com. Holocaust Library and Research Ctr. San Francisco; mem. Mayor's Holocaust Meml. Commn. on San Francisco; exec. com. Calif. Concerns; mem. Friends of San Francisco Commn. on Status of Women; dir. People Speaking; rep. Am. Council Edn. Nat. Identification Project; mem. Am. Friends of Hebrew U. Mem. Am. Assn. Univ. Adminstrs., Nat. Women's Polit. Caucus, World Future Soc., Am. Hist. Assn., AAUP, Calif. State U. Assn. Vice Pres.' for Adminstrn and Fin. (chmn. 1980-82), Mensa, Phi Kappa Phi, Phi Alpha Theta, Beta Gamma Sigma. Clubs: Commonwealth (San Francisco); San Francisco Press. Author: Hitler's Death Camps: The Sanity of Madness, 1981; contbr. articles to profl. jours.

FEIL, LINDA MAE, tax preparer; b. Dallas, Oreg., Apr. 9, 1948; d. Fred Henry and Ruth Irene (Hoffman) F. A.A., West Valley Community Coll., 1975; student Golden Gate U. Ctr. for Tax Studies, 1975, Menlo Coll. Sch. Bus. Adminstrn., 1978. Enrolled agt. IRS. Income tax preparer, office mgr. H & R Block, Inc., Santa Clara, Calif., 1972-74, asst. area mgr., 1974-76; propr. L.M. Feil Tax Service, Santa Clara, 1976-80; ptnr. Tennyson Tax Service, Santa Clara, 1980-81; owner McKeany-Feil Tax Service, San Jose, Calif., 1981-83, Feil Tax Service, San Jose, 1983—. Tchr. Mem. Nat. Soc. Enrolled Agts. (chpt. v.p. 1983—), Calif. Soc. Enrolled Agts. Republican. Christian. Home: 220 Richfield Dr 1 San Jose CA 95129 Office: McKeany-Feil Tax Service 4300 Stevens Creek Blvd 129 San Jose CA 95129

FEIN, EILEEN YARVITX, insurance brokerage executive; b. Los Angeles, Apr. 23, 1949; d. Samuel and Adlynn (McKnight) Yarvitz. Student Los Angeles Valley Jr. Coll., 1966-67, Pierce Jr. Coll., 1968-69. Cert. continuing edn. profl. designation; cert. employee benefit specialist. Adminstrv. aide Los Angeles County Employees Assn., 1970-72; program specialist Econ. & Youth Opportunities Agy., 1972-74; adminstrv. asst. Ins. Planning Assocs., 1974; account exec. Gannon Mgmt. Assocs., 1974-75; agt. Ind. Group Ins., Santa Ana, Calif., 1975-76; adminstr. Airport Med. Group, Irvine, Calif., 1975-76; mktg. rep. The Doctors Co., Santa Monica, Calif., 1977; adminstr. Tepper Med. Group, Alhambra, Calif., 1978; ind. group ins. specialist, Mendocino, Calif., 1978-79; dir. ins. services Hosp. Council So. Calif., Los Angeles, 1979-81; v.p. employee benefits BMF Mktg. Ins. Services, Inc., Los Angeles, 1981—. Recipient Econ. and Youth Opportunities Assn. Community Activity award, 1971. Mem. Employee Benefit Planning Assn., Employee Benefit Specialists Soc. Republican. Jewish. Originator: Creative Health Plan Design, Calif., 1981. Office: BMF Mktg Ins Services Inc 3200 Wilshire Blvd Los Angeles CA 90010

FEIN, MARA HECHT, apparel company marketing executive; b. N.Y.C., Jan. 10, 1952; d. Jacob and Edith (Gordon) Hecht; m. Harvey Allan Fein, Feb. 18, 1978. B.A. in English, Northwestern U., 1974; M.B.A. in Mktg., U. So. Calif., 1981. Project mgr. U. So. Calif., Los Angeles, 1980-81; mktg. mgr. Tomboy Co., Los Angeles, 1981-82, dir. mktg., 1982—. Active atty. gen. campaign State of Calif., 1978. Mem. U. So. Calif. M.B.A. Assn., U. So. Calif. Alumni Assn., Northwestern U. Alumni Club, Beta Gamma Sigma. Office: Tomboy 343 E Jefferson Blvd Los Angeles CA 90011

FEIN, WILLIAM, ophthalmologist; b. N.Y.C., Nov. 27, 1933; s. Samuel and Beatrice (Lipschitz) F.; B.S., CCNY, 1954; M.D., U. Calif., Irvine, 1962; m. Bonnie Fern Aaronson, Dec. 15, 1963; children—Stephanie Paula, Adam Irving, Gregory Andrew. Intern, Los Angeles County Gen. Hosp., 1962-63, resident in ophthalmology, 1963-66; instr. U. Calif. Med. Sch., Irvine, 1966-69; mem. faculty U. So. Calif. Med. Sch., 1969—, asso. prof. ophthalmology, 1979—; attending physician Cedars-Sinai Med. Center, Los Angeles, 1966—, chief ophthalmology clinic service, 1979—, chmn. div. ophthalmology, 1981—; attending physician Los Angeles County-U. So. Calif. Med. Center, 1969—; chmn. dept. ophthalmology Midway Hosp., 1975-78. Diplomate Am. Bd. Ophthalmology. Mem. Am. Acad. Ophthalmology, Am. Soc. Ophthalmic Plastic and Reconstructive Surgery, AMA, Calif. Med. Assn., Los Angeles Med. Soc. Contbr. articles to med. publs. Address: 415 N Crescent Dr Beverly Hills CA 90210

FEINAUER, LYMAN RICHARD, JR., neonatologist; b. Salt Lake City, Mar. 4, 1943; s. Lyman Richard, Sr., and Lorraine (Barrett) F.; B.Sc. in Chem. Engring., U. Utah, 1965, M.Sc. in Chem. Engring., 1969, M.Sc. in Fin., 1967; M.D., U. Utah, 1971; m. Karen L. Barnett, Sept. 9, 1972; children—Jonathan Richard, Christian Frederick, Richard Benjamin, Joshua James. Cons., Jet Propulsion Lab., 1965-70; intern Los Angeles County/U. So. Calif. Med. Center, 1971-72, resident in pediatrics, 1972-73, fellow neonatology, 1974; partner Salt Lake Clinic, Salt Lake City, 1975-81, also partner Pension Fund and Investment Council, 1975—; asso. clin. prof. pediatrics U. Utah, 1974—; clin. investigator Eli Lilly & Co., 1979—; pres. JCRJ Investments; dir. newborn intensive care Latter Day Saints Hosp. Served with USAR, 1960-68. Diplomate Am. Bd. Pediatrics, Am. Bd. Med. Examiners. NASA fellow, 1965-67. Fellow Sigma Xi, Am. Acad. Pediatrics, Chem. Soc. (London), Am. Chem. Soc., Am. Fedn. Clin. Research, Am. Soc. Microbiology; mem. AMA, Utah Med. Soc., Intermountain Pediatric Soc., Los Angeles Pediatric Soc., Utah Acad. Arts, Scis. and Letters. Contbr. articles to med. and sci. jours. Office: 857 E 200 S Suite 203 Salt Lake City UT 84102

FEINBERG, RICHARD ALAN, clinical psychologist; b. Oakland, Calif., Aug. 12, 1947; s. Jack and Raechel Sacks (Hoff) F. B.A., Calif. State U.-Hayward, 1969; M.A. in Clin. Psychology, Mich. State U., 1972, Ph.D., 1979; Nat. Register of Health Service Providers in Psychology, 1980. Instr., Merritt Coll., Oakland, 1975-76; clin. psychologist Highland Gen. Hosp., Oakland, 1976-79; asso. Lafayette Center Counseling and Edn., 1978-79; clin. psychologist Tri-City Mental Health Center, Fremont, Calif., 1979-81, dir., 1981—; pvt. practice clin. psychology, 1976—; participant profl. conf. USPHS fellow, 1969-71. Mem. Am. Psychol. Assn., Calif. Psychol. Assn. Jewish. Office: 38930 Blacow Rd Suite F Fremont CA 94536

FEINSTEIN, DIANNE, mayor San Francisco; b. San Francisco, June 22, 1933; d. Leon and Betty (Rosenburg) Goldman; B.S., Stanford U., 1955; m. Bertram Feinstein, Nov. 11, 1962; 1 dau., Katherine Anne. Intern in pub. affairs Coro Found., San Francisco, 1955-56; asst. to Calif. Indsl. Welfare Commn., Los Angeles and San Francisco, 1956-57; mem. vice-chmn. Calif. Women's Bd. Terms and Parole, Los Angeles and San Francisco, 1962-66; chmn. San Francisco City and County Adv. Com. for Adult Detention, San Francisco, 1967-69; supr. City and County of San Francisco, 1969-79; mayor San Francisco, 1979—; pres. San Francisco City and County Bd. Suprs., 1970-72, 74-76, mem. Mayor's Comm. on Crime, 1967-69; chmn. Environ. Mgmt. Task Force, Assn. Bay Govts., 1976-78. Mem. exec. com., del. gen. assembly Assn. Bay Area Govts., 1970, 74, 76, 78; bd. govs. Bay Area Council, 1972-73; mem. Bay Conservation and Devel. Commn., 1973-78; chmn. bd. regents Lone Mountain Coll., 1972-75. Recipient Women of Achievement award, Bus. and Profl. Women's Clubs of San Francisco, 1970, Disting. Woman award San Francisco Examiner, 1970; Coro award, 1979; Scopus award for Outstanding Pub. Service, 1981. Mem. Multi-Culture Inst. (dir.), San Francisco. Tomorrow, Bay Area Urban League, Planning and Conservation League, Friends of Earth, Chinese Culture Found., N. Central Coast Regional Commn., Sierra Club. Clubs: Propeller, Commonwealth. Office: 200 City Hall San Francisco CA 94102

FEIST, F. MICHAEL, personnel service co. exec.; b. Vancouver, Wash., Sept. 3, 1949; s. Frank Paul and Marlene Marie F.; B.S., Portland State U., 1975; Salesman Riback and Navaroo Interiors, Vancouver, Wash., 1967-69, Vancouver Furniture Co., 1969-74; sales rep. Paper Cybernetics, Culver City, Calif., 1974-75; pres., owner Devonshire Personnel Service, Inc., Garden Grove, Calif., 1976—. Mem. Am. Employment Assn. Republican. Home: 18303 Mt Kristina Fountain Valley CA 92708 Office: 12900 Garden Grove Blvd. #202 Garden Grove CA 92643

FEIST, RAYMOND FRANK, JR., lawyer; b. Coronado, Calif., June 27, 1946; s. Raymond Frank and Marjorie Lee (Major) F.; m. Barbara Ruth Cornell, June 20, 1970; children—Laura Virginia, Raymond Scott. B.A., U. Calif.-Santa Barbara, 1968; J.D., Calif. Western Sch. Law, 1975. Bar: Calif. 1975. Assoc. Feist Vetter Knauf & Loy, Oceanside, Calif., 1975-78, ptnr., 1979—. Served USN, 1968-72. Decorated Air medal. Mem. ABA, Bar Assn. State of Calif., San Diego County Bar Assn., North San Diego Bar Assn., Phi Delta Phi, Phi Delta Theta. Republican. Office: Feist Vetter Knauf & Loy 810 Mission Ave Suite 300 Oceanside CA 92054

FELANDO, SANDRA SANFORD, interior designer; b. Fort Worth, Dec. 4, 1934; d. John Richard and Virginia (Campbell) Sanford; m. Wayne Schmad, Sept., 1956 (div.); m. 2d, Lawrence Joseph Felando, May 1963 (div.); 1 son, John August. Student interior design U. Wash., 1956; Designer, Arthur Morgan & Assocs., Seattle, 1956-57; with passenger accommodation dept. Boeing Aircraft, Seattle, 1957-58; dir. design Curt Wagner, Inc., Redondo Beach, Calif., 1959-76; pres. Sandra Felando, ASID, Redondo Beach, 1976—. Mem. Am. Soc. Interior Designers (sec. Los Angeles chpt. 1979, treas. 1983, dir. 1971-74, 77, 78, 82). Democrat. Episcopalian. Contbr. articles on design installations to various periodicals. Office: 1719 S Catalina Ave Redondo Beach CA 90277

FELCHLIN, MARY KATHLEEN, banker; b. Cleve., Feb. 16, 1951; d. Ernest J. and Margaret Jane (McKenna) Conroy. m. J. Timothy Felchlin, Sept. 8, 1979. B.A., U. Calif.-Berkeley, 1973; M.B.A., U. So. Calif., 1977. Mortgage banker, Mason McDuffie Investment Co., Berkeley, 1974-75; inter Gilbraltar Savs. & Loan Assn., Beverly Hills, summer 1976; account officer Wells Fargo Bank, Los Angeles, 1977-79; v.p. Citicorp Real Estate, Los Angeles, 1979—. Wittenberg fellow, 1975-76; Commerce Assos. fellow, 1976-77. Mem. Am. Mgmt. Assn. Home: 8960 Wonderland Ave Los Angeles CA 90046 Office: 444 S Flower St 21st Floor Los Angeles CA 90071

FELDMAN, AVNER IRWIN, neurosurgeon; b. N.Y.C., Mar. 9, 1927; s. Joseph O. and Lillian (Markowitz) F.; B.S., N.Y. U., 1947; M.D., State U. Coll. Medicine, N.Y.C., 1950; m. Helene West, July 21, 1975; children by previous marriage—Sheri, David. Intern, Beth Israel Hosp., N.Y.C., 1950-51; asst. resident in gen. surgery Maimonides Hosp., Bklyn., 1951-52, in neurology Mt. Sinai Hosp., N.Y.C., 1952; resident neurosurgery Beth Israel Hosp., 1953, Bronx Municipal Hosp., N.Y.C., 1955-56; resident Montefiore Hosp., N.Y.C., 1956-57, chief resident, 1957-58; pvt. practice specializing in neurosurgery, Inglewood, Calif., 1959—; asst. clin. prof. neurol. surgery U. Calif. (Los Angeles) Med. Center. Served with USAF, 1953-55. Diplomate Nat. Bd. Med. Examiners, Am. Bd. Neurosurgery. Recipient William S. Linder Surg. prize, 1950. Fellow A.C.S.; mem. Am. Assn. Neurol. Surgeons, Congress Neurol. Surgeons, So. Calif. Neurosurg. Soc., Los Angeles Soc. Neurology and Psychiatry, A.M.A., Calif., Los Angeles County med. assns., Alpha Omega Alpha. Home: 8900 Burton Way Beverly Hills CA 90211 Office: 323 N Prairie Ave Inglewood CA 90301

FELDMAN, BURTON LEON, insurance company executive; b. Bklyn., Sept. 9, 1946; s. Samuel and Dorothy F.; m. Noanna Loyce Dix, Nov. 8, 1969; 1 dau., Andrea Eden. B.A. in Psychology, Bklyn. Coll., 1966. Rehab. adminstr. Occidental Life Ins. Co., Los Angeles, 1969-78; asst. sec., dir. rehab. Mission Ins. Co., Los Angeles, 1978—; cons. Neurol. Learning Ctr., South Pasadena, Calif.; tng. programs in ins. rehab. Casa Colina Hosp., Pomona, Calif., Craig Rehab. Hosp., Englewood, Colo. Mem. Mayor's Com. for Employment of the Handicapped, Los Angeles, 1976-80; mem. blue ribbon ins. com. Nat. Head Injury Found., 1981—. Mem. Nat. Rehab. Assn. (pres. Pacific region and a So. Calif. chpt. 1979-80), Nat. Rehab. Counselors Assn., Calif. Assn. Rehab. Profls., Nat. Assn. Rehab. Profls. in the Pvt. Sector, Nat. Rehab. Adminstrs. Assn., Ins. Rehab. Study Group. Clubs: Indian Palms Country (Indio, Calif.); Channel Island Shores Marina (Oxnard, Calif.). Office: 2600 Wilshire Blvd Los Angeles CA 90051

FELDMAN, DONALD JORDAN, psychiatrist; b. Chgo., Aug. 27, 1940; s. Ben and Bernice (Wexler) F.; B.S., U. Ill., 1961, M.D., 1965; m. Diane C. Bender, June 14, 1964; children—Bradley, Heidi, Corey. Intern, Cook County Hosp., Chgo., 1965-66; resident Ill. State Psychiat. Inst., 1966-69; dir. Psychiat. Outpatient Services, San Bernardino County, Calif., 1971-72; practice medicine specializing in psychiatry, San Bernardino, 1972—. Asst. prof. Loma Linda U., 1971—. Trustee San Bernardino Community Hosp. Served to maj. AUS, 1969-71. Mem. Am. Psychiat. Assn., Am., Calif. med. assns., San Bernardino County Med. Soc. Office: 399 E Highland Ave San Bernardino CA 92404

FELDMAN, HARVEY WOLF, sociologist, ethnographer, educator, social worker; b. Pitts., July 1, 1929; s. Charles and Fannie (Enoch) F.; B.A., U. Pitts., 1953; M.S.W., Columbia U., 1957; Ph.D., Brandeis U., 1970. Research asso. Brandeis U., 1967-72; fellow Drug Abuse Council, Washington, 1972-73; asso. prof. Sch. Social Service, St. Louis U., 1974-76; sr. research asso. URSA Inst., San Francisco; project dir. Youth Environ. Study, 1980—; v.p. Central Intake Drug Prevention Project, San Francisco. Served with U.S. Army, 1953-55. ETO. NIMH grantee, 1964-66. Mem. Am. Sociol Assn., Soc. for Study Social Problems, Nat. Assn. Social Workers, Nat. Assn. Ethnography and Social Policy (sec./treas.), Western Mastiff Fanciers, Mastiff Club Am. Sr. editor: Angel Dust: An Ethnographic Study of PCP Users, 1979. Office: 1779 Haight St San Francisco CA 94117

FELDMAN, IRA S., accountant; b. N.Y.C., June 18, 1943; s. Meyer and Esther F.; m. Susan Haber, May 31, 1965; children—Lisa, Jason, Amy. B.S. in Bus. Adminstrn., U. Ariz., 1965; M.B.A., Ariz. State U., 1970. C.P.A., Calif., Ariz. Acct., Peat, Marwick, Mitchell & Co., Los Angeles and Phoenix, 1965-70; ptnr. Laventhol & Horwath, Phoenix, 1970-76; mng. dir. Toback & Co., P.C., Phoenix, 1976—. Pres., Madison Meadows Owners Assn.; bd. dirs. DeGrazia Art and Cultural Found. Mem. Am. Inst. C.P.A.s, Ariz. Inst. C.P.A.s, Phoenix Tax Workshop (dir.). Contbr. articles to profl. jours. Office: 3550 N Central Ave #500 Phoenix AZ 85012

FELDMAN, NATHANIEL EDWARD, elec. engr.; b. New London, Conn., Oct. 7, 1925; s. Morris and Frieda (Felenberg) F.; B.S. in E.E., U. Calif., Berkeley, 1948, M.S. in E.E., 1950; m. Clara Klein, Oct. 20, 1946; children—Ellis, Phillip, David, Pamela. Asst. elec. engr. U. Calif., Berkeley, 1949-50, engr. Radiation Lab., 1951-54; instr. fire control radar Hughes Aircraft Co., Culver City, Calif., 1955; leader advanced devel. engring. RCA, West Los Angeles, 1956-60; systems analysis engr. RAND Corp., Santa Monica, Calif., 1960-78; chief scientist systems research operation Sci. Applications, Inc., Century City, Calif., 1978-81; systems dir. Advanced Communications Office, Communications Div.,

Aerospace Corp., El Segundo, Calif., 1981-83, sr. staff mem., 1983—; cons. Advanced Research Project Agy., U.S. Dept. Def., 1965—; lectr. telecommunications Harvard Summer Inst., 1972, U. Calif., San Diego, 1973, U. Colo., 1973. Served with USAAF, 1945-47. Assoc. fellow AIAA (chmn. tech. com. on communications systems 1970-72); mem. Tau Beta Pi, Eta Kappa Nu, Sigma Xi. Co-author: Communication Satellites for the '70's: Technology, 1971; Communication Satellites for the '70s: Systems, 1971. Editorial bd. Microwave Jour., 1966-78. Contbr. articles to profl. jours. Home: 10294 Cresta Dr Los Angeles CA 90064 Office: Mail Station M5/690 PO Box 92957 Los Angeles CA 90009

FELDMAN, STANLEY GEORGE, judge; b. N.Y.C., Mar. 9, 1933; s. Meyer and Esther Betty (Golden) F.; student UCLA, 1950-51; LL.B., U. Ariz., 1956; m. Norma Arambula; 1 dau., Elizabeth L. Admitted to Ariz. Bar, 1956; practiced in Tucson, 1956—; partner firm Miller, Pitt & Feldman, 1968-82; justice Supreme Ct. of Ariz., 1982—; lectr. Coll. Law, U. Ariz., 1965-76, adj. prof., 1976—. Bd. dirs. Tucson Jewish Community Council. Mem. Am. Bd. Trial Advocates (past pres. So. Ariz. chpt.), ABA, Ariz. (pres. 1974-75, bd. govs. 1967-76), Pima County (past pres.) bar assns., Am. Trial Lawyers Assn. (dir. chpt. 1967-76). Democrat. Jewish. Office: 111 S Church Ave Tucson AZ 85701

FELICIANO, MARTHA ANNE, city recreational dir.; b. Stuttgart, Germany, Aug. 20, 1949; came to U.S., 1952, naturalized, 1953; d. Elbert Richard and Suzanne Elizabeth (Jungblut) Winter; m. Michael Alen Feliciano, Sept. 19, 1970; A.A., Monterey Peninsula Coll., 1970. Baton, ballet tchr., recreation leader, pre-sch. tchr. City of Monterey, 1967-72; program specialist City of Seaside, Calif., 1972-77, asst. dir. parks and recreation, 1977-80, dir. recreational services, 1980—. Mem. Calif. Parks and Recreation Soc.

FELICITA, JAMES THOMAS, aerospace co. exec.; b. Syracuse, N.Y., May 21, 1947; s. Anthony Nicholas and Ada (Beech) F.; A.B., Cornell U., 1969; postgrad. Harvard U., 1969, U. So. Calif., 1970, UCLA, 1975-77. Contracting officer U.S. Naval Regional Contracting Office, Long Beach, Calif., 1974-80; sr. contract negotiator space and communications group Hughes Aircraft Co., El Segundo, Calif., 1980-81, head NASA contracts, 1981—. Recipient cost savs. commendation Pres. Gerald R. Ford, 1976. Mem. Nat. Contract Mgmt. Assn., Cornell Alumni Assn. So. Calif., Planetary Soc. Republican. Club: Nat. Space. Home: 8541 Kelso Dr Huntington Beach CA 92646 Office: 909 N Sepulveda Blvd Los Angeles CA 90245

FELIX, JOHN HENRY, investments exec.; b. Honolulu, June 14, 1930; s. Henry and Melinda (Pacheco) F.; student Chaminade Coll., 1947, San Mateo Coll., 1950; grad. Advanced Mgmt. Program, Stanford, 1967, Harvard 1971; Ph.D., Walden U., 1975; m. Patricia Berry, children—Laura Marie, Melinda Susan, John Morgan, Jayne Sherry, Annette Sherry. Asst. to pres. AFL-CIO Unity House, 1955-57; exec. v.p. Hotel Operating Co. of Hawaii, 1957-60; v.p. Music Polynesia, Inc.; asst. to Gov. of Hawaii, 1960-62; pres. LaRonde Restaurants, Inc., 1962—, Hotel Assos., Inc.; dir., mem. exec. com., chmn. personnel com. Hawaii Nat. Bank; pres., chmn. exec. com. Hawaiian Meml. Park. Chmn. ARC, 1961-63, 72; del. League Red Cross Socs.; chmn. Gov.'s Jobs for Vets. Task Force, 1971-76, Honolulu Redevel. Agy., 1971, 72, Honolulu City and County Planning Com., 1959; chmn. Bd. Water Supply, 1973-75; chmn. Honolulu City County Bd. Parks Recreation; mem. City and County Honolulu Police Commn., 1979; pres. bd. Hawaii Public Radio, 1979; bd. govs. ARC, also chmn. Pacific div.; nat. trustee March of Dimes Birth Defects Found. Served with AUS, 1952-54. Named Young Man of Year, Hawaii Jr. C. of C., 1959, Distinguished Service award Sales and Marketing Execs. Hawaii, 1968, Harriman award distinguished vol. service A.R.C., 1975, others. Mem. Young Pres.'s Orgn., Hawaii Restaurant Assn. (pres. 1967), Air Force Assn. (pres. Hawaii), C. of C. of Hawaii (life), Nat. Eagle Scout Assn. (life), CAP-U.S. Air Force Aux. (comdr. Hawaii Wing 1980). Club: Waikiki Rotary (Honolulu). Home: 4731 Kahala Ave Honolulu HI 96816 Office: 1330 Maunakea St Honolulu HI 96817

FELLIN, OCTAVIA ANTOINETTE, librarian; b. Santa Monica, Calif.; d. Otto P. and Librada (Montoya) F.; student U. N.Mex., 1937-39; B.A., U. Denver, 1941; B.A. in L.S., Rosary Coll., 1942. Asst. librarian, instr. library sci. St. Mary-of-Woods Coll., Terre Haute, Ind., 1942-44; librarian U.S. Army, Bruns Gen. Hosp., Santa Fe, 1944-46, Gallup (N.Mex.) Public Library, 1947—; post librarian Camp McQuaide, Calif., 1947; free lance writer mags., newspapers, 1950—; library cons.; N.Mex. del. White House Pre-Conf. on Libraries and Info. Services, 1978; dir. Nat. Library Week for N.Mex., 1959. Vice-pres., publicity dir. Gallup Community Concerts Assn., 1957-78; organizer Gt. Decision Discussion groups, 1963—; mem. Gallup St. Naming Com., 1958-59, Aging Com., 1964-68; chmn. Gallup Mus. Indian Arts and Crafts, 1964-78; mem. publicity com. Gallup Inter-Tribal Indian Ceremonial Assn., 1966-68; mem. Gov's. Com. 100 on Aging, 1967-70; N.Mex. Humanities Council, 1979; mem. U. N.Mex.-Gallup Campus Community Edn. Adv. Council, 1981—; N.Mex. organizing chmn. McKinley Hosp. Aux.; mem. N.Mex. Library Adv. Council, 1971-75, vice chmn., 1974-75; chmn. adv. com. Gallup Sr. Citizens, 1971-73; mem. steering com. Gallup Diocese Bicentennial, 1975-78, chmn. hist. com., 1975; chmn. Trick or Treat for UNICEF, Gallup, 1972-77; chmn. pledge campaign Rancho del Nino San Huberto, Empalme, Mexico; bd. dirs. Gallup Opera Guild, 1970-74; bd. dirs., sec., organizer Gallup Area Arts Council, 1970-78; mem. N.Mex. Humanities Council, 1979, Gallup Centennial Com., 1980-81; mem. Cathedral Parish Council, 1980—, v.p., 1981; pres. McKinley Gen. Hosp. Aux., 1983. Recipient Dorothy Canfield Fisher $1,000 Library award, 1961; Outstanding Community Service award for mus. service Gallup C. of C., 1969, 70, Outstanding Citizen award, 1974, Benemerenti medal Pope Paul VI, 1977. Mem. ALA, N.Mex. Library Assn. (v.p., sec., chmn. hist. materials com. 1964-66, salary and tenure com., nat. coordinator N.Mex. legislative com., chmn. com. to extend library services 1969-73, Librarian of Yr. award 1975, chmn. local and regional history roundtable 1978, Community Achievement award 1983), AAUW (v.p., co-organizer Gallup br., N.Mex. nominating com. 1967—, chmn. fellowships and centennial fund Gallup br., chmn. com. on women), Plateau Scis. Soc., N.Mex. Folklore Soc. (v.p. 1964-65, pres. 1965-66), N.Mex. Hist. Soc. (dir. 1979—), Gallup Hist. Soc., Gallup Film Soc. (co-organizer, v.p. 1950-58), LWV (v.p. 1953-56), NAACP, Gallup C. of C. (organizing chmn. women's div. 1972, v.p. 1972-73), N.Mex. Women's Polit. Caucus, N.Mex. Mcpl. League (pres. librarian's div. 1979—), Alpha Delta Kappa (hon.). Roman Catholic (Cathedral Guild, Confraternity Christian Doctrine Bd. 1962-64, Cursillo in Christianity Movement, mem. of U.S. Cath. Bishop's Adv. Council 1969-74; corr. sec. Latin Am. Mission Program 1972-75, sec. Diocese of Gallup Pastoral Council 1972-73, corr. sec. liturgical commn. Diocese of Gallup 1977). Author: Yahweh the Voice that Beautifies the Land. Home: 513 E Mesa Ave Gallup NM 87301 Office: 115 W Hill St Gallup NM 87301

FELLOWS, FRANCIS JAMES, safety adminstr.; b. Cleve., Apr. 5, 1925; s. Cornelius Francis and Amanda Esther (Smith) F.; B.S., Ariz. State U., 1971; student Cleve. State U., 1946-54; m. Marjorie Ann Myers, Sept. 16, 1950; children—Kevin, Karen, Gary, Gail, Marjorie, Raymond, Bernice, Francis James, Brendan, Roberta, David. Designer, Internat. Aviation, Cleve., 1947-49; engring. checker Electro-Motive div. Gen. Motors Corp., Cleve., 1949-54; facility-safety engr. AiResearch Mfg. Co., Phoenix, 1955-67, safety adminstr., 1967—. Bd. dirs. Maricopa County Traffic Survival Sch., Maricopa County chpt. ARC. Served with USAAF, 1943-46. Mem. Ariz. Safety Assn. (exec. com., dir.), S.W. Safety Congress Assn., Inc. (chmn. bd. 1975-76), Asso. Safety Engrs. Ariz. (pres. 1973-74), Am. Indsl. Hygiene Assn. (treas. Ariz. sect. 1977-78), Am. Soc. Safety Engrs. Club: Ariz. Yacht. Office: 402 S 36th St Phoenix AZ 85010

FELLOWS, GEORGE HARVEY, city manager; b. Ft. Dodge, Iowa, Sept. 22, 1920; s. William Harvey and Ellen (Saville) F.; B.C.E., Iowa State Coll., 1944; m. Bertha Jean Abbe, July 4, 1944; children—Jonathon Allen, Thomas Lee, Georganne. City engr., Spencer, Iowa, 1947-49; asst. city engr., Waterloo, Iowa, 1949-53; dir. pub. service, Greeley, Colo., 1953-57; dir. pub. works, Pueblo, Colo., 1957-59, city mgr., 1959-66; city mgr. Colorado Springs, 1966—. Exec. com. Pueblo Single Fund and Red Cross, 1961-65; sec. Red Cross, 1965; dir. Goodwill, 1964-65, Pueblo YMCA. Mem. Citizens Adv. Council U. Colo., El Paso Community, Coll. Served as ensign USNR, 1944-46. Mem. Internat. Assn. City Mgrs., Pueblo, Colorado Springs chambers commerce. Presbyn. Elk, Kiwanian, Mason. Home: 3134 San Luis Dr Colorado Springs CO 80909 Office: City Adminstrn Bldg Colorado Springs CO 80902

FELMLEE, ROBERT W., farmer; b. Alamosa, Colo., Apr. 23, 1932; s. William W. and Alice M. (Woodward) F.; m. Betty Ann Rush, Dec. 11, 1959; children—James W., Pamela J. B.A., Colo. State Coll. Edn., Greeley, 1954. Farmer, Center, Colo., 1957—; dir., sec. Marshall Produce Co., Center, 1972—; mem. bd. Nat. Potato Bd. Mem. Center Consol. Schs. Bd. Edn., 1972-79, pres., 1972-79; chmn. Saguache County Republican Com. Mem. Nat. Potato Council (steering com.), Colo. Assn. Sch. Bds. (regional v.p.). Methodist. Club: Masons (past master). Address: 2405 County Rd 49 Center CO 81125

FELSHAW, JULIE ANN, business educator; b. Ft. Defiance, Ark., Sept. 8, 1954; d. George Morris and Mary Alice (Moss) Felshaw. B.S. in Bus. Edn., Brigham Young U., 1977. Bus. educator Jordan Sch. Dist., Salt Lake City, 1979-83, North Summit Sch. Dist., Coalville, Utah, 1978-79; legal sec. Voshell & Wright, Idaho Falls, Utah, 1977; tchr. bus. edn. Jordan High Sch., Sandy, Utah, 1983—; sec. Brigham Young U., 1976; advisor Future Bus. Leaders Am. Mem. Utah Bus. Edn. Assn. (state officer 1982), Nat. Bus. Edn. Assn., Am. Vocat. Assn. Republican. Mormon. Home: 426A Creekside Circle Salt Lake City UT 84107 Office: Jordan High Sch 9351 S State St Sandy UT 84070

FELTER, JACK LAWDER, optometrist; b. Dayton, Ohio, Dec. 23, 1926; s. Alph and Mae Elizabeth (Lawder) F.; m. Ann L. Fischer, June 4, 1949; children—Nancy, Jeffrey. Student U. Dayton, 1950-52; O.D., Ohio State U., 1956. Pvt. practice optometry, Albuquerque, 1956—; sec., pres. N.Mex. Bd. Examiners in Optometry, 1962-69. Served with USN, 1942-44. Fellow Am. Acad. Optometry; mem. Am. Optometric Assn., N.Mex. Optometric Assn. (pres.-elect, past pres., N.Mex. Optometrist of Yr. 1976), Better Vision Inst., Am. Optometric Found., Pub. Health Assn., Epsilon Psi Epsilon. Republican. Club: Masons.

FELTER, JAMES DICKSON, interior designer; b. Dayton, Ohio, Jan. 20, 1942; s. James Richard and Bertha Louise (Schubert) F.; children—David James, Anne Marie. B.A. in Art, Midland Coll., Fremont, Nebr., 1964; postgrad. U. N.Mex., 1965. Asst. mgr., head designer Design Interiors, Inc., Albuquerque, 1968-70; pres., prin. Environ., Inc., Albuquerque, 1970-75; mgr. design dept. N.Mex. Office Furniture, Albuquerque, 1975-79; pres. James D. Felter & Assocs. Ltd., Albuquerque, 1979—. Works include: interior for Rust Tractor, Albuquerque, 1977, interior for Rio Grande Title Co., 1973. Bd. dirs. Santa Fe Opera, Albuquerque chpt. Mem. Am. Soc. Interior Designers (1st pl. award for comml. interiors 1972), Inst. Bus. Designers. Home: 6223 Rio Hondo Dr NE Albuquerque NM 87109

FELTER, JAMES WARREN, painter, curator; b. Bainbridge, N.Y., Aug. 25, 1943. B.F.A., U. South Fla., 1964; student U. Wash. Group shows include: Musee d'Art et d'Histoire, Geneva, Switzerland, 1976, Mus. Modern Art, Sao Paulo, Brazil, 1976, 37th Venice (Italy) Biennale, 1976, Moderna Galerija, Liubljana, 1976, Pratt Graphics Ctr., N.Y.C.; represented in permanent collections: City of Vancouver (B.C., Can.), B.C. Provincial Collection, Manawatu Art Gallery, N.Z., Mildura Arts Centre, Australia, Musee d'Art et d'Histoire, Geneva; commns. include Trademark, OCEPA-Ecuadorian Handcrafts, Quito, 1965, Seattle Opera Assn., 1967, Simon Fraser Univ. Arts Centre, Burnaby, B.C., 1970, 72; dir. Galeria de Oceps, Quito, Ecuador, 1965-66; curator-dir. exhbn. Simon Fraser U., 1970—, Simon Fraser Gallery, Burnaby; vis. artist Escuela de Bellas Artes, Univ. Ctr., Ecuador, 1966. Can. Council grantee, 1979. Mem. Community Arts Council Vancouver (dir.), Western Can. Art Assn. (chmn. 1975-76, 78-80), Can. Museum Assn., Home: Office: Simon Fraser University Simon Fraser Gallery Room 3004 Academic Quadrangle Burnaby BC V5A 156 Canada

FELTON, GARY SPENCER, clin. psychologist, educator; b. San Francisco, Mar. 8, 1940; s. Jean Spencer and Janet Elizabeth (Birnbaum) F.; B.A. (George F. Baker scholar 1957-61), Grinnell Coll., 1961; M.S. (Neuropsychiat. Clin. Psychiat. fellow 1963), San Francisco State U., 1966; Ph.D. (USPHS fellow 1966-68, State of Calif. fellow 1968-70), U. So. Calif., 1970; m. Lynn Ellen Sandell, Mar. 21, 1970; children—Colin Spencer, Megan Ariana. Asst. counselor, instr. psychology Counseling Center, Calif. State U., San Francisco, 1965-66; counseling psychologist Orthopaedic Hosp., Los Angeles, 1967-69; psychology intern Los Angeles County, U. So. Calif. Med. Center, 1968-69; instr. psychology, coordinator of counseling services, co-dir. research programs Student-Devel. Center, Mount St. Mary's Coll., Los Angeles, 1969-71; dir. Ctr. for Interpersonal Studies, Los Angeles, 1969—; psychotherapist, pvt. individual and group practice, Los Angeles, 1969—; coordinator Human Services Worker Tng. Program, Brentwood VA Hosp., Los Angeles, 1971-72; field placement coordinator, instr. psychology Calif. Sch. Profl. Psychology, Los Angeles, 1971-72; coordinator child health care worker tng. program Children's Hosp. Los Angeles, 1972-75; adj. prof. psychology, clin. program cons. Los Angeles City Coll., 1972—; instr. psychology Los Angeles City Coll., 1972-74, dir. spl. edn. programs, 1974—, asso. prof. psychology, 1976-81, mem. community adv. com. human relations worker tng. program, 1972—; program and community cons. Harbor Coll.; cons. Ednl. Devel. Center, Claremont, Calif., 1973-81. Bd. dirs. Pub. Advt. Council of Los Angeles, 1977-80. Mem. Am., Western, Calif., Los Angeles County psychol. assns., Soc. Pediatric Psychology, Los Angeles Soc. Clin. Psychologists, Group Psychotherapy Assn. So. Calif. (bd. mem. 1972-75, dir. publs. 1972-75), Am. Humanist Assn., Assn. for Humanistic Psychology, Am. Name Soc. Author: Up from Underachievement, 1977; The Record Collector's International Dictionary, 1980; editorial bd. Coll. Student Jour., 1972-81; contbr. articles to profl. jours. Home: 2739 Forrester Dr Los Angeles CA 90064 Office: Suite 22 11941 Wilshire Blvd Los Angeles CA 90025

FENDERSON, ALBION PRENTICE, marketing executive; b. Wilkinsburg, Pa., Apr. 21, 1914; s. Albion P. and Elizabeth J. (Harris) F.; m. Lynne Gage Mar. 21, 1975; children—Jeremy, Kelley and Christopher. Student, Carnegie Inst. Tech., 1930-34; B.S., George Washington U., 1941. Dir. coll. orgns. Am. Liberty League, 1934-46; mgr. research and statistics Distilled Spirits Inst., 1936-41; asst. to dir. Alcohol div. War Prodn. Bd., 1941-42; chief alcohol procurement and storage Def. Supplies Corp., 1942-43; asst. to pres. Fleischman Distilling Co., 1944, Publicker Industries, 1944-51; v.p. United Distillers, 1951-52; exec. v.p. E & J Gallo Winery, Modesto, Calif., 1952—. Mem. Beta Theta Pi, Omicron Delta Kappa, Tau Beta Pi. Home: 221 El Rio Dr Modesto CA 95354 Office: PO Box 1130 Modesto CA 95353

FENDERSON, RICHARD A(DNEY), JR., advertising executive; b. N.Y.C., June 8, 1938; s. Richard A. and Teva Belle (Spinks) F. B.S. in Chemistry, St. John's U., 1956; postgrad. in bus. adminstrn. NYU, CCNY. Copywriter, Cunningham & Walsh, N.Y.C., 1961-64, creative supr., 1973-75; copy contact McCann-Erickson, N.Y.C., 1964-66; sr. copywriter J.M. Mathes, N.Y.C., 1966-67; copy supr. Ketchum, Macleod & Grove, N.Y.C., 1967-70; creative supr. Foote, Cone & Belding, N.Y.C., 1970-73; v.p., creative dir. N.W. Ayer, San Francisco, 1975-82; sr. v.p., dir. creative services Bozell & Jacobs, Palo Alto, Calif., 1982—. Recipient profl. awards including: Saturday Rev. Corp. Advt., 1970, N.C.B.A. award, 1977, A.A.F. Silver award, 1978, Time Mag. Power of Print award, 1978, Harry McMahon's 100 Best TV, 1978, Cara, 1980, N.Y. Art Dirs., 1980, CLIO, 1980. Office: 819 Lyon St San Francisco CA 94115

FENG, JAMES SHUMIN, geographer, photogrammetrist; b. Siangtan, Hunan Province, China, May 4, 1922; s. Cheng Liang and Cheng Tai F.; B.A., Nat. Chengchi U., Nanking, China; M.A., U. Wash. 1951; m. Tsin Lee Tsai, Oct. 27, 1962 (dec. Nov. 1973); children—Debbie Lee, Nancy Ann. Geographer U.S. Geol. Survey, Menlo Park, Calif., 1952—; lectr. geography De Anza Coll., Cupertino, Calif., 1968—, Foothill Coll., Los Altos Hills, Calif., 1965—. Mem. Assn. Am. Geographers, Am. Soc. Photogrammetry, Calif. Council Geography Edn., Assn. Pacific Coast Geographers, Am. Congress Surveying and Mapping. Contbr. articles on Chinese polit. and econ. geography to profl. publs. Home: 21965 Hyannisport Dr Cupertino CA 95014 Office: US Geol Survey 345 Middlefield Rd Menlo Park CA 94025

FENG, LILLIAN WAN-MING LEI, nurse, nursing home adminstr.; b. Canton, China, May 5, 1923; came to U.S., 1968, naturalized, 1973; d. Chin Chang and Sui Ching (Chen) Lei; R.N., Turner Sch. Nursing, Canton, China, 1946; B.S. in Health Care Adminstrn., Central Mich. U., 1976, M.A., 1979; m. Ping Tien Feng, June 3, 1950; children—Paul, Lucy, May, Howard. Asst. head nurse, nursing instr. Turner Nursing Sch. of Hacket Hosp., Canton, China, 1946-47; head nurse, instr. Hoihow (China) Am. Presbyn. Hosp. and Nursing Sch., 1947-50; instr. Tb nursing, head nurse Taiwan Tb Control Center, 1950-56, supr., 1956-66; clin. head nurse U.S. Naval Med. Research Unit No. 2, Taiwan, China, 1966-67; asst. adminstr. Palolo Chinese Care Home, Honolulu, 1968—. U.S.A. Internat. Corp. Adminstrn. grantee, 1958. Mem. Hawaii Nurses Assn., Am. Nurses Assn., Nat. League for Nursing, Hawaii Pacific Gerontol. Soc., Acupuncture Sci. Research Found. Hawaii, Am. Health Care Assn., Central Mich. U. Alumni Assn., Hawaii Long Term Care Assn. Address: 2459 10th Ave Honolulu HI 96816

FENIMORE, GEORGE WILEY, diversified manufacturing executive; b. Bertrand, Mo., Jan. 15, 1921; s. George Wiley and Florence March (Bush) F.; m. Benetta Brevoort Lindsey, Oct. 27, 1949; children—Lindsey C., Marian H., George Wiley III. B.S. in Fin. and Bus. Adminstrn., Northwestern U., 1941; J.D., Harvard U., 1947; postgrad. U.S. Air Force Statis. Sch., 1944, UCLA Exec. Program, 1954-55. Bar: Mich. 1948. Asst. to dir. planning Ford Motor Co., 1947-48; exec. asst. to v.p. and gen. mgr. Hughes Aircraft Co., 1948-53; adminstrv. mgr. tech. products Packard Bell Electronics, 1954-55; with TRW, Inc., 1955-64, v.p., gen. mgr. TRW Internat., 1959-64; v.p. internat. ops. Bunker Radio Corp., 1964-65; dir. pub. affairs Litton Industries, Inc., Beverly Hills, Calif., 1964-66, corp. sec., 1966 , sr. v.p., 1981—. Past chmn. bd. trustees Southwestern U. Sch. Law; dir., chmn. edn. com., past pres. Beverly Hills C. of C.; dir., past pres. Beverly Hills YMCA.; past dir. Pacific Region Nat. Council; bd. dirs., past pres. Mandeville Canyon Assn. Served to maj. USAFR, 1955-76. Recipient Citizen of Yr. award Beverly Hills Lions Club, 1976, Beverly Hills C. of C., 1979. Mem. Am. Soc. Corp. Secs. (past pres. Los Angeles Regional Group, past nat. dir.). Presbyterian. Clubs: Beverly Hills Men's, Shriners, Beverly Hills Rotary (dir., past pres.). Home: 13107 Chalon Rd Los Angeles CA 90049 Office: 360 N Crescent Dr Beverly Hills CA 90210

FENN, GEORGE S., agricultural technology company executive; b. Chgo., July 20, 1924; s. Louis J. and Lola M. Fenn; m. Marjorie Frances Goodman, Sept. 1, 1945; children—Elizabeth, Louise, Martha, George W. B.S., Calif. Inst. Tech., 1945, M.S., 1946. Lectr. engring. UCLA, 1947-50; gen. mgr. missile guidance div. Northrop Aircraft, Inc., 1946-54; dir. research labs. Magnavox Co., 1954-59; founder, chmn., pres. FMA, Inc., Los Angeles, 1959-67, pres. Fenn & Co., Cottage Grove, Oreg., 1982—; dir. FMA, Inc., Los Angeles, 1959-67, ETI, SA, Brussels, 1961-69, Precision Standards Corp., Santa Ana, Calif., 1967-71, Hensway, Inc., Corvallis, Oreg., 1977-79, Novar Corp., Santa Clara, Calif., 1970-74. Served with U.S. Army, 1943-45. Recipient Spl. Achievement award Inst. Navigation, 1950. Mem. IEEE, Am. Forage and Grassland Council, Soc. Automotive Engrs., Soc. Motion Picture and TV Engrs. Home: Box 8 Henderer Rd Elkton OR 97436 Office: 1445-D N Gateway Blvd Cottage Grove OR 97424

FENNELL, TERRESA ANN, counselor, consultant; b. Norfolk, Va., Feb. 18, 1955; d. Robert Wallace and Patricia Louise (Riley) Fennell; m. Duncan Marshall, Nov. 11, 1978 (div.). B.A. in Spanish, Erskine Coll., 1976; M.A. in Counseling Psychology, U. Pacific, 1982. Registered marriage, family, child counselor intern, Calif. Counselor Valley Community Counseling Services, Stockton, Calif., 1981—. Mem. council San Joaquin County Sexual Abuse Treatment Providers. Mem. Assn. Measurement and Evaluation in Guidance, Am. Mental Health Counselors Assn., Am. Personnel and Guidance Assn., Nat. Vocat. Guidance Assn., Assn. Religious and Value Issues in Counseling, Assn. Specialists in Group Work. Democrat. Presbyterian. Home: 1176 Rosemarie Ln Apt 171 Stockton CA 95207 Office: 845 N California St Stockton CA 95202

FENOLIO, RONALD LAWRENCE, lawyer; b. Antioch, Calif., Feb. 25, 1943; s. Lawrence and Lola (Jacuzzi) F.; B.S. in Bus. Adminstrn., U. Calif., Berkeley, 1964; J.D., U. Calif., San Francisco, 1967; LL.M. in Taxation, N.Y. U., 1970. Admitted to Calif. bar, 1968; asst. to gen. counsel N.Y. U., 1967-68; asso. firm Miller, Starr & Regalia, Oakland, Calif., 1968-70; partner firm Rosenblum, Fenolio, Parish, Jack & Bacigalupi, San Francisco, 1970-79, vice chmn., sec., 1977-79, of counsel, 1979-80; gen. partner, co-developer Veedercrest Vinyards, Napa and Emeryville, Calif.; instr. real estate law and taxation Merritt Coll., Oakland, 1969-70, Contra Costa Coll., San Pablo, Calif., 1969-71, San Francisco City Coll., 1971-77; lectr. in field; dir. Electra N.W. Resources, Pacific N.W. Resources, Westcap Fin. Group (chmn.); charter sec. Am. Real Estate Investment Trust. Pres., Calif. Republican League, San Francisco, 1972-73. Mem. Am., San Francisco bar assns., State Bar Calif., Italian-Am. Bar Assn. No. Calif. (co-founder, charter sec. 1978-79, pres. 1979-80, dir. 1978—), Barristers Club San Francisco, Nat. Assn. Realtors (ad hoc com. on edn.), Calif. Assn. Realtors (chmn. legal and regulatory com.), Sigma Phi Epsilon (dist. gov. 1968-70, mem. nat. leadership com. 1975-81, nat. ritual com. 1969-75, nat. ednl. found. 1980-82), Alpha Kappa Psi, Phi Alpha Delta. Clubs: Commonwealth, Olympic, Bachelors (San Francisco). Home: 1181 Chestnut St San Francisco CA 94113 Office: 165 Octavia St San Francisco CA 94102

FENSTERMAKER, PERRY MOLAN, educator; b. Burley, Idaho, Nov. 10, 1926; s. Francis Molan and Jessie Eileen (Fuller) F.; B.A., Idaho State Coll., 1959, M.A. in Edn., 1965; postgrad. U. Idaho, 1962-63, Calif. State U., San Bernardino, 1969, U. Calif., Riverside,

1969-70, Calif. State U., Los Angeles, 1971, Whittier Coll., 1971; m. Neta McLean, May 28, 1949; children—Teresa Rae, Francis Mark, Scott McLean, Jared Luke, Connie Eileen, Bryan Edward. Tchr., Aberdeen, Idaho, 1953-56, Pocatello, Idaho, 1957-63, Thomas Jefferson Sch., Indio, Calif., 1963-71; asst. prin. Palm Desert Middle Sch., Indio, 1971-78, tchr. math., 1978—, tchr. computer literacy, 1982—; Calif. textbook evaluator, 1970—; owner, operator Perry M. Fenstermaker & Assos., Tax Preparers, Fence's Swap Shop, The Yarn Barn. Merit badge counselor Boy Scouts Am., 1950-76, camp dir., 1960-61, Eagle bd. chmn., 1968-71. Served with USMCR, 1944-46, 50-51, 67. Decorated Purple Heart. Mem. Nat. Tchrs. Assn. (life), Calif. Tchrs. Assn., Nat. Tchrs. Math., Calif. Tchrs. Math., Assn. for Supervision and Curriculum Devel., Am. Philatelic Soc., Coachella Valley Mineral Soc. (pres.), Indio C. of C. Republican. Mormon. Editor: Mathematics Game Book, 1970; Mathematics Curriculum Guide, 1982. Co-discoverer of Crystal Ice Cave, 1956. Home: 82 357 Oleander St Indio CA 92201

FENTON, DONALD MASON, chemist; b. Los Angeles, May 23, 1929; s. Charles Y. and Dorothy M. (Mason) F.; B.S., U. Calif. at Los Angeles, 1952, Ph.D., 1958; m. Margaret M. Keehler, Apr. 24, 1953; children—James Michael, Douglas Charles. Chemist, Rohm & Haas Co., Phila., 1958-61; sr. research chemist Union Oil Co. Calif., Brea, 1962-67, research asso., 1967-72, sr. research asso., 1972-82, mgr. planning devel., 1982—; tech. cons. AMSCO div., 1967-73. Served with AUS, 1953-55. Mem. Am. Chem. Soc., Alpha Chi Sigma (chpt. pres. 1953), Sigma Xi. Club: Toastmaster (pres. Brea 1973). Patentee in field. Home: 2861 Alden Pl Anaheim CA 92806 Office: PO Box 76 Brea CA 92621

FENTON, MARY, writing and design consultant, public relations counselor; b. Butte, Mont., Dec 26, 1920; d. Samuel J. and Anna (Sagar) Bukvich; m. Ray William Fenton, Apr. 20, 1946; children—Neil, Bruce, Ross, Janis Fenton Kollar. B.A. in Journalism, U. Mont.-Missoula, 1943. Reporter/photographer Gt. Falls (Mont.) Tribune, 1943-46; Mont. supr. Am. Research Bur., Washington, 1961; Mont. corr., supr. corrs. Fairchild Publs., N.Y.C., 1956-64; assoc. editor Mont. Rural Electric News, 1967-75; community coordinator, communications cons. Program for Advanced Children's Edn., Great Falls Pub. Schs., 1971-74; ptnr. Fenton & Fenton, Pub. Relations Assocs., Helena, Mont., 1960—; coordinator, facilitator Mont. Career Edn. Policy Forums, Inst. Ednl. Leadership, George Washington U., Washington, 1977; coordinator Mont. Bd. Pub. Edn. Ad Hoc Com. on Hearing Impaired, 1978; cons. N.W. Connection (U.S. Office Edn. Career Edn. Project), Portland, Oreg., 1979-80; field researcher Parental Involvement Project, System Devel. Corp., Santa Monica, Calif., 1980—; writing cons. State of Wash. and State of Mont., U. Mont. Law Sch., IFG Leasing, VA; design cons. Great Falls Tribune, U. Mont. Sch. Journalism; records mgmt. cons. State of Mont., Ft. Belknap Tribal Council. Bd. dirs. Mont. Multiple Sclerosis Soc., 1964; fund raising cons. Great Falls Symphony Guild, 1968-74; citizens' com. C.M. Russell High Sch., Great Falls, 1969; chmn. Community Council, gifted children's program Great Falls Pub. Schs., 1971; mem. Mont. Blue Ribbon Commn. on Post-Secondary Edn., 1973-75; bd. dirs. Gt. Falls Voluntary Action Com., 1972-73; judge Mont. high sch. speech tournaments, 1972-74. Mem. Pub. Relations Soc. Am. (cert.), Counselors Acad. of Pub. Relations Soc. Am., Soc. Newspaper Design, Nat. Electric Coop. Editorial Assn. (emeritus). Club: Meadow Lark Country. Contbr. articles to nat. profl. and popular publs. Home and Office: 2855 West Shore Dr Helena MT 59601

FENTON, RAY WILLIAM, writing and design consultant; b. San Diego, June 25, 1921; s. Virgil Ray and Georgia Elizabeth (Shaw) F.; m. Mary Bukvich, Apr. 20, 1946; children—Neil, Bruce, Ross, Janis Kollar. B.A., U. Mont., 1943. Instr., Sch. Journalism U. Mont., 1946-48; editor Great Falls (Mont.) Tribune Leader, 1948-60; exec. dir., ptnr. Pub. Relations Assocs., Great Falls, 1960-80; ptnr., design writing cons., Fenton & Fenton, Helena, Mont., 1980—. Active Mont. council Boy Scouts Am., 1960-80; mem. adv. com. ARC Mont. Served with USMCR, 1942-62. Decorated Bronze Star, Purple Heart (3); recipient Meritorious Service award Mont. Grain Growers Assn., 1978; Editorial Excellence award Mont. Assn. Conservation Dists., 1979; Disting. Service award Boy Scouts Am., 1970. Mem. Pub. Relations Soc. Am. (accredited), Press Club Great Falls (pres.), Great Falls Newspaper Guild (pres.). Club: Meadow Lark Country. Contbr. articles to profl. jours.

FENTON, TERRY LYNN, art gallery director, art critic, landscape painter; b. Regina, Sask., Can., July 1, 1940; s. John Albert and Gertrude Irene (Hirons) F.; m. Sheila Ann Cowle, Dec. 1, 1962; 1 son, Mark. B.A., U. Sask., 1962. Asst. to dir. Mackenzie Gallery, Regina, 1965-71; dir. Edmonton (Alta., Can.) Art Gallery, 1972—. Mem. Can. Mus. Assn., Can. Art Mus. Dirs. Assn.

FENTRESS, CURTIS WORTH, architect; b. Greensboro, N.C., Oct. 26, 1947; s. Paul Worth and Hazel Izula (Terrel) F.; B.Arch., N.C. State U., 1972. Sr. designer I.M. Pei & Partners, N.Y.C., 1972-77; project designer Kohn Pedersen Fox Assos., N.Y.C., 1977-80; prin. C.W. Fentress & Assos., Denver, 1980—. Mem. Downtown Denver, Inc., 1981—. Recipient Alpha Rho Chi medal, 1972; named Young Profl. of the Yr., Bldg. Design and Constrn., 1980; Graham Found. travelling fellow, 1970-71. Mem. AIA, N.Y. Bldg. Congress, N.Y. Assn. Architects, Nat. Council Archtl. Registration Bds., Archtl. League of N.Y., Phi Kappa Phi. Office: 511 16 St Suite 600 Denver CO 80202

FENWICK, DAVID BROOKE, church school principal; b. Portland, Oreg., Feb. 6, 1929; s. David Lee and Mae Evangel (Brooke) F.; m. Nellie Grace Zook, Sept. 16, 1950; children—Steven Mark, Deonna Marie, Jonathan Brooke, Sam Ana Danel. B.A. in Secondary Edn., Cascade Coll., 1952; M. Ed. in Guidance and Counseling, Seattle Pacific U., 1969. Ordained deacon Oreg. Conf. Free Meth. Ch., 1950, elder Pacific Coast Latin Am. Conf. Free Methodist Ch., 1961. Spanish tchr. Cascade Coll., Pacific Bible Coll., 1950-51, George Fox Coll., 1952-54; pastor West Lynn (Oreg.) Free Meth. Ch., 1950-54; prin. East Los Angeles Light and Life Christian Sch., 1954—, assoc. chapel pastor; v.p. Free Meth. Urban Fellowship. Mem. Am. Personnel and Guidance Assn., Am. Sch. Counselor Assn., Assn. Christian Schs. Internat. Republican. Office: 207 Dacotah St Los Angeles CA 90063

FERCHO, GORDON E., univ. admnstr.; b. Lehr, N.D., Mar. 16, 1933; s. Gottleib J. and Sophia M. (Weisz) F.; B.A. in Bus. Adminstrn., Sacramento State U., 1957; m. Ruby R. Harlan, June 25, 1955; children—Debra Lynne, Dennis Alan, David Wayne. Auditor, Calif. Dept. Fin., Sacramento, 1957-59, acctg. systems analyst, 1961-66, 67-72; acctg. officer Calif. State Controller's Office, Sacramento, 1959-61; fin. specialist Public Adminstrn. Services, Recife, Brazil, 1966-67; asso. v.p., dir. bus. affairs Calif. State U., Chico, 1972—. Deacon, Esplanade Baptist Ch., Chico, 1973, trustee, 1973-76, tchr., 1972, dir. music, 1977; bd. dirs. Calif Bapt. Found., Fresno, 1973-77, pres., 1977; trustee Golden Gate Bapt. Sem., 1982—. Served with U.S. Army, 1952-55; Korea. Mem. Nat. Assn. Coll. and Univ. Bus. Officers, Western Assn. Coll. and Univ. Bus. Officers. Office: Calif State U Bus Affairs Office Chico CA 95929

FERDON, FRED DAVID, aircraft maintenance educator, engineering consultant; b. Cin., May 30, 1938; s. Ebes David and Mini Flora (Fortson) F.; m. Jane O. Grimm, Aug. 30, 1958; children—Tammy, David. B.S. in Engring, Miami U., Oxford, Ohio 1960; M.A. in Edn., Calif. State U.-Los Angeles, 1969; Postgrad. Northrop U., UCLA 1965-66. Certified tchr., Calif. Sr. test engr. SSP Products, Burbank, Calif., 1961-65; tchr. drafting Cleveland High Sch. Reseda, Calif., 1971-81, Lincoln High Sch. Los Angeles, 1965-71; flight status coordinator, prof. Los Angeles Airport Coll. Ctr., 1981-83; cons. Rockwell Aerospace, Downey Space Shuttle, Shuttle Engine Rocketdyne, N.Am. B-1 Bomber, Lockheed Aircraft Tng. Recipient award of merit Aircraft Distbrs. Mgrs. Assn., 1974, Los Angeles Indsl. Educators, 1970. Mem. Calif. Indsl. Edn. Assn., Calif. Aerospace Assn., Exptl. Aircraft Assn (local chpt. pres. 1976-77), Baptist. Club: Coll. Senate Sec. (Los Angeles). Office: 9700 S Sepulveda Blvd Los Angeles CA 90045

FEREBEE, DAVID MORGAN, III, civil engineer; b. New Orleans, June 28, 1945; s. D.M. Tex and Alice Ruth (Sturman) F.; m. Nancy Lee Banes, July 2, 1971; children—Devin, Kurtis. B.S. in Civil Engring. Tech., Met. State Coll., 19—. Registered land surveyor, Colo., N.Mex.; cert. assoc. engring. technologist Nat. Soc. Profl. Engrs. Engring. technician U.S. Forest Service, Delores, Colo., 1968-69; survey instrumentman Ernst Engring. Co., Durango, Colo., 1969-70; party chief Clark Thomas Engring. Co., Durango, 1970-71; survey instrumentman, party chief Denver Water Bd., 1971-75; asst. civil engr. Denver Water Dept., 1975—; chmn. Rocky Mountain Surveying and Mapping Edn. Com., 1982—. Chmn. Pack 511 Cub Scouts Am., Broomfield, Colo., 1981-82, Webelos leader, 1981—. Mem. Profl. Land Surveyors Colo., Am. Congress Surveying and Mapping (reporter, editor Colo. sect. 1982, sec., treas. Colo. sect. 1983), Am. Soc. Cert. Engring. Technicians, Am. Water Works Assn. Presbyterian. Contbr. articles in field to profl. jours. Home: 14618 Benton St Broomfield CO 80020 Office: Denver Water Dept 1600 W 12th Ave Denver CO 80254

FERGERSTROM, ERNEST JOHN, ret. city ofcl.; b. Waipunalei, Hawaii, Nov. 8, 1917; s. John C. and Gloria (Silva) F.; student Honolulu Bus. Coll., 1942-43, FBI Nat. Acad., 1966, Honolulu Community Coll., 1967-68, Hawaii Community Coll., 1970-72, U. Hawaii, 1972; m. Florence A. Garcia, Jan. 28, 1950; children—Dale Alan, Ann Louise, Fay Marie. Field supr. Laupahoehoe Sugar Co., 1937-40; with Hawaii County Police Dept., Hilo, 1945-76, chief of police, 1970-76. Mem. supervisory bd. Hawaii Law Enforcement and Juvenile Delinquency Planning Agy., 1970-76. Mem. State Hwy. Safety Council, 1970-76; mem. council of Pacific, Girl Scouts U.S.A., 1970—; mem. exec. bd. Aloha council Boy Scouts Am., 1970—, vice chmn. Pukahi dist., Hilo, 1980—; bd. dirs. Hawaii County Biddy Boxing Commn., 1972-76; mem. sch. adv. bd. St. Joseph High Sch., Hilo, 1972-75; vice chmn. Hawaii County Republican Com., 1980. Served with USNR, 1940-45. Recipient award of merit 3d Circuit Ct., 1950, County Chmn.'s award for Distinguished County Service County Hawaii, 1965, Father of Yr. award County of Hawaii, 1966. Mem. Internat. Assn. Chiefs of Police, Hawaii Law Enforcement Ofcls. Assn. (treas. 1971-72, pres. 1973-74), Hawaii Nat. Acad. Assos. (pres. 1970-71), Am. Legion. Roman Catholic. Home: 1593 Wailuku Dr Hilo HI 96720

FERGUSON, BEN EARL, financial planning consultant; b. Palmer, Tex., Aug. 20, 1937; s. Burton E. and Eddie Faye (Scarborough) F.; m. Susan Rachel Paul, Feb. 22, 1958; children—Lisa, David Benjamin, Rachel; m. 2d, Nancey Lee, Dec. 30, 1982. B.S. in Bus. Adminstrn., San Jose State U., 1962; M.Th., Dallas Theol. Sem., 1966. CLU, Am. Coll., 1980; cert. fin. planner, Coll. Fin. Planning. Ordained to interdenominational ministry, 1966. Pastor Sunnyside Bapt. Ch., Hanford, Calif., 1968-75; asst. mgr. Conn. Gen. Fin. Services, San Jose, Calif., 1975-80; dist. mgr. Mfrs. Fin. Services, Santa Clara, Calif., 1980-82; pvt. practice fin. planning cons., San Jose, Calif., 1982—. Served with USN, 1956-58. Mem. Am. Soc. CLU, San Jose Life Underwriters, Am. Assn. Life Underwriters, Santa Clara County Estate Planning Council, Inst. Cert. Fin. Planners. Author: God I've Got a Problem, 1974; The Shaping of a Man of Faith, 1980.

FERGUSON, CAROL A., manufacturing company executive; b. Cleve., Jan. 23, 1946; d. John M. and Catherine (Yusko) Haydu; m. Robert Ferguson, July 26, 1980. Student, St. Louis U., 1964-65; B.A., U. Dayton, 1968; M.B.A., West Coast U., 1980. Cert. prodn. inventory mgr. Asst. office mgr. Fry Cons., Los Angeles, 1968-69; supr. MacDonald's, Los Angeles, 1969-70; fin. analyst Xerox Corp., Los Angeles, 1970-72; self-employed distbr. home care products, Los Angeles, 1972-76; mktg. analyst R & G Sloane, Sun Valley, 1976-78, indsl. engr., 1978-79, mgr. indsl. engring., 1979-80, mgr. mfg. control, 1980—. Vol. Los Angeles Bur. Consumer Affairs, 1976. Mem. Am. Prodn. and Inventory Control Soc.

FERGUSON, EVELYN CLAIRE, educational administrator, consultant; b. Simcoe, Ontario, Can., Oct. 22, 1915; d. Charles Herbert and Leeta Belva (Wood) Fick; came to U.S., 1942; m. Ernest Wayne Ferguson, June 12, 1941 (dec.); children—Donald Wayne, Alan Wood. A.A., Bakersfield Coll., 1964; B.A. with honors (scholar), Fresno State Coll., 1966; M.A., Fresno State U., 1970. Cert. reading specialist, Calif. Elem. tchr., 1966-68; Miller-Unruh reading specialist, 1968-72; adj. lectr. Calif. State Coll.-Bakersfield, 1971-72, coordinator early childhood program, 1972-73, spl. programs coordinator, 1973-74, dir. Calif. Demonstration Program in Reading, 1974—; cons., presenter regional, state confs., program writing. Past pres. Wayside PTA, 1955-56, Bakersfield Council PTA, 1957-58, South High Sch. PTA, 1959-60; past sec., area dir. 7th Dist. PTA, 1958-60; past pres. Kern Council Internat. Reading Assn., 1978-79, dir. 1972—. Mem. Reading Specialists Calif., Internat. Reading Assn. (mem. exec. bd. Kern Council), Fresno Area Reading Council, Assn. Calif. Sch. Adminstrs., Nat. Council Tchrs. English, Assn. Supervision and Curriculum Devel., AAUW, PTA (hon. life), Delta Kappa Gamma (exec. bd.). Democrat. Episcopalian. Office: 1109 Pacheco Rd Bakersfield CA 93307

FERGUSON, FRANK R., state senator; b. Kotzebue, Alaska, July 14, 1939; s. Warren J. and Minnie (Gallahorn) F.; m. Sophie A. Kagoona, Jan. 5, 1970; children—Duane, Charlene, Cheree, Crystal. With Community and Regional Affairs Agy.; with Northwest Native Assn.; former mem. Alaska Ho. of Reps.; now mem. Alaska Senate; pres. Alaska Fedn. Natives. Served with mil., 1962-65.

FERGUSON, HUGH MILTON, mgmt. cons.; b. Tacoma, Nov. 11, 1934; s. Robert Woods and Charlotte Evelyn (Hemmings) F.; B.S., Seattle U., 1956; M.B.A., George Washington U., 1963; m. Rose Marie Davis, Nov. 28, 1959; children—Kathleen Marie, Karen Michele, Robert Michael. Cons. data systems CEIR, Arlington, Va., 1961-63, Tech. Ops. Research Co., Washington, 1963-64; mgr. systems and programming Western Pacific R.R. Co., San Francisco, 1964-70; mgmt. cons. Ernst & Whinney, C.P.A.s, San Francisco, 1970-80; pres., dir. Amicon Corp., San Francisco, 1980—; mem. fin. mgmt. adv. bd. San Francisco Unified Sch. Dist., 1977-78. Served as officer USNR, 1957-61; comdr. Res. C.P.A., Calif.; cert. data processor, data processing auditor. Mem. Am. Inst. C.P.A.s, Assn. Systems Mgmt., Calif. Soc. C.P.A.s, Res. Officers Assn., Naval Res. Assn., U.S. Navy League, Soc. Mayflower Descs. Republican. Roman Catholic. Clubs: San Francisco Comml., Presidio Golf, Home: 3320 Bowmore Ct Walnut Creek CA 94598 Office: 101 Gregory Ln Pleasant Hill CA 94523

FERGUSON, JOHN BECKER, architect; b. State College, Pa., July 24, 1915; s. John Arden and Susan (Becker) F.; B.S., Pa. State U., 1937; m. Kathleen Shannon, Oct. 31, 1943; children—John Arden, Thomas Burton, Laura Jane. Archtl. detailer Davidson Enamel Co., Lima, Ohio, 1939-40; constrn. engr. Vega Aircraft Corp., Burbank, Calif., 1940-43; ambulance driver Am. Field Service, India and Burma, 1943-45; archtl. engr. Henry F. Withey, Architect, Sherman Oaks, Calif., 1945-47; structural engr. Davis & Ferguson, Architects, Van Nuys, Calif., 1947-59; prin. John B. Ferguson, AIA, Van Nuys, 1959-60; partner Ferguson & Hutchison, 1961-62; prin. John B. Ferguson & Assos., Tarzana, Calif., 1963—; cons. Land Engring. Co., Van Nuys, 1959—. Mem. Tarzana C. of C., Constrn. Specifications Inst., AIA, Structural Engrs. So. Calif. Republican. Baptist. Home: 20513 Eccles St Canoga Park CA 91306 Office: 18340 Ventura Blvd Tarzana CA 91356

FERGUSON, JOYCE EILEEN, educational administrator; b. Denver, Jan. 18, 1936; d. Lester Ernest and Helen Marian (Winkler) Conover; children—Kevin Leslie, Richard Scott, Bryan David, Gary Allen. Student U. Colo., 1978-79. With accounts payable dept. Gates Rubber Co., Denver, 1953-55; teller new accounts, savs. and loan depts. Aurora Nat. Bank (Colo.), 1970-75; clk. typist purchasing dept. Joint Sch. Dist. 28J of Adams and Arapahoe Counties, Aurora, 1977-79, sr. buyer, 1979-83, supr. purchasing services, 1983—. Pres. Virginia Court PTA, Aurora, 1968; chmn. coop. purchasing Rocky Mountain Sch. Study Council, 1981-83, chmn. by-law revision com., 1981. Mem. Assn. Sch. Bus. Ofcls. (vice chmn. purchasing research com. 1982—), Nat. Assn. Purchasing Mgrs., Epsilon Sigma Alpha. Contbr. articles to profl. publs. Home: 14601 E Caspian Pl Aurora CO 80014 Office: 1085 Peoria St Aurora CO 90011

FERGUSON, KEITH MCDOWELL, electrical engineer; b. Corpus Christi, Tex., Oct. 6, 1940; s. Elmer Leroy and Carol Rushmore (McDowell) F.; m. Margaret E. Shank, June 27, 1982. B.S., M.I.T., 1962, M.S., 1964, E.E., 1965. Project mgr. Hewlett Packard Co., Santa Clara, Calif., 1965—. Bd. dirs. WTBS Found., Cambridge, Mass., 1961-62. Mem. IEEE, Sierra Club, Sigma Xi (asso.), Tau Beta Pi, Eta Kappa Nu. Libertarian. Methodist. Patentee in electronics. Home: 3060 Mel-Chester Dr San Jose CA 95132 Office: 5301 Stevens Creek Blvd Santa Clara CA 95050

FERGUSON, LARRY NEIL, psychologist; b. Hillsdale, Mich., June 24, 1944; s. Neil W. and Laura B. (Schultz) F.; m. Rosalinda Iglesia, June 7, 1969; children—Gregory-Paul, Tiffany-Lin. B.A., Calif. State U.-Northridge, 1967; M. Div., Conservative Bapt. Theol. Sem., 1970; Ph.D. in Psychology, Fuller Theol. Sem., 1975. Lic. psychologist, Calif. Asst. dir. Family Counseling Ctr., Van Nuys, Calif., 1975-80; psychologist, Des Plantes Psychiat. Clinic, Reseda, Calif., 1977-80; clin. dir. Link Care Ctr., Fresno, Calif., 1980—; lectr. in field. Past pres. So. Calif. Interfaith Coalition on Aging. Mem. Am. Psychol. Assn., Calif. State Psychol. Assn., Western Psychol. Assn., Gerontol. Soc., Christian Assn. Psychol. Studies (sec.-treas. Western region, internat. v.p. 1981-83, pres. 1983-85). Democrat. Baptist. Contbr. articles to religious publs. Home: 642 E Fremont St Fresno CA 93710 Office: 1734 W Shaw St Fresno CA 93711

FERGUSON, LLOYD NOEL, chemist; b. Oakland, Calif., Feb. 19, 1918; s. Noel Swithin and Gwendolyn Louise Ferguson; B.S., U. Calif., Berkeley, 1940, Ph.D., 1943; D.Sc. (hon.), Howard U., 1970, Coe Coll., 1979; m. Charlotte Welch, Jan. 2, 1944; children—Lloyd Noel, Stephen Bruce, Lisa Annette. Research asst. Nat. Def. project U. Calif., Berkeley, 1941-44; asst. prof. A&T Coll., Greensboro, N.C., 1944-45; mem. faculty Howard U., 1945-65, head dept. chemistry, 1958-65; mem. faculty Calif. State U., Los Angeles, 1965—, prof. chemistry, 1958—, chmn. dept., 1968-71; vis. prof. U. Oreg., Eugene, summers 1958, 60, 63; mem. bd. sci. counselors Nat. Inst. Environ. and Health Scis., 1979-83; mem.-at-large div. chemistry Nat. Acad. Scis.-NRC, 1970-73; mem. various other govt. coms. Recipient award Oakland (Calif.) Museum Assn., 1973; award Mfg. Chemists Assn., 1974; Outstanding Prof. award Calif. State U., Los Angeles, 1974; Disting. Am. medallion Am. Found. Negro Affairs, 1976; Outstanding Teaching award Nat. Orgn. Black Chemists and Chem. Engrs., 1979; Outstanding Prof. award Calif. State U. Trustees, 1981; NSF fellow, 1961-62, Guggenheim Found. fellow, 1953-54. Fellow AAAS; mem. Am. Chem. Soc. (chmn. div. chem. edn. 1980—; Chem. Edn. award 1978), AAUP, Sigma Xi, Phi Kappa Phi. Author: Electron Structures of Organic Molecules, 1952, Textbook of Organic Chemistry, 2d edit., 1965, The Modern Structural Theory of Organic Chemistry, 1963, Organic Chemistry—A Science and an Art, 1972, Highlights of Alicyclic Chemistry, Vol. 1, 1972, Vol. 2, 1977, Structural Organic Chemistry, 1975; also numerous articles. Home: 4221 S Cloverdale Ave Los Angeles CA 90008 Office: 5151 State University Dr Los Angeles CA 90032

FERGUSON, RICHARD LEE, franchise company executive, corporate director; b. Bloomsburg, Pa., Jan. 5, 1927; s. William James and Genevieve Grace (Speary) F.; m. Clara Margaret Hutton, June 6, 1946; m. 2d, Jacqueline Marie Nelson, Jan. 8, 1966; children—Richard William, John Bradley, Fred Howard, Deborah Marie, Randal Owen, Scott Eric. Student in Bus. Adminstrn, Rider Coll., 1949. Propr. snack foods distbn. co., 1950-61; food broker, 1961-72; chief exec. officer, chmn. The Badgemant Internat. Ltd., San Juan Capistrano, Calif., 1972—; dir. Page Products, South Coast Inc. Served with U.S. Navy, 1943-46. Mem. Internat. Franchise Assn. Republican. Methodist. Clubs: Masons, Elks, Reciprocity Am. (co-founder). Office: 31877 Del Obispo Suite 105 San Juan Capistrano CA 92675

FERGUSON, ROBERT BRUCE, JR., mortgage banker; b. Middleboro, Ky., June 1, 1934; s. Robert Bruce and Nelle Sue (Walker) F.; m. Shirley Ann Vickers, Dec. 17, 1955; children—David Keith, Kenneth Scott, Lori Lynne. A.A., Lees McRae Coll.; B.S. in Bus. Adminstrn., U. N.C.-Chapel Hill. Cert. Mortgage Banker, Mortgage Bankers Assn. Am. Asst. v.p. Cameron-Brown Co., Raleigh, N.C., 1959-64; v.p. Wachovia Mortgage Co., Winston-Salem, N.C., 1964-72; pres. Mercantile Mortgage Co., St. Louis, Mo., 1972-77; pres. Security Pacific Mortgage Co., Denver, 1977—, chmn., 1977—. Active Denver United Way. Served with U.S. Army, 1954-57. Mem. Colo. Mortgage Bankers Assn. (past pres.), Mortgage Bankers Am. (assoc. gov.). Republican. Methodist. Clubs: Denver Rotary, Cherry Hills Country, Denver. Office: 2460 W 26th Ave Denver CO 80211

FERGUSON, ROGER NEPHI, franchise bus. exec.; b. Ocean Park, Calif.; s. Robert Byron and Fawn Bernice (Christensen) F.; student Brigham Young U., Provo, Utah, 1952; m. Sybil Rae Clarke, 1952; children—Debra Kay, Michael David, Wade Clarke, Lois Christine, Julie Xarissa. Pres., Diet Center, Inc., Rexburg, Idaho, franchises, U.S., Can., 1972; owner, chmn. bd. Dietology Sch., Diet Center Inn, Feruson's Pharms. Labs., Audio-Visual Studio, Diet Center Shipping and Receiving Co., Diet Center Print Shop; dir. Internar. Livestock, Inc., Sybils, Inc., Ferguson and Assos.; co-owner Big Grassy, potato ranch, Ferguson Farms; regional mgr. Bio-Chem. Farm Products Co.; pres. local Insulators in Indsl. Trade, 1960-62. Recipient award Rick's Coll. Boosters Club, 1977-81. Mem. U.S. C. of C., Rexburg C. of C. Mormon. Club: Rexburg Golf Assn. (bd. dirs. 1981). Office: Diet Center Inc 220 W 2d St S Rexburg ID 83440

FERGUSON, WAYNE SANDER, sch. supt.; b. Ogden, Utah, Apr. 26, 1926; s. George Cochran and Charlotte (Sander) F.; B.S., Brigham Young U., 1950, M.Ed., 1953; Ed.D., U. So. Calif., 1960; m. Dorothy Jean Curtis, Dec. 19, 1952; children—George Ray, April Lynne, Susan Gaye. Math. tchrs. Tooele County Sch. Dist., Utah, 1950-53; prin. Dugway (Utah) Elem. and High Schs., 1953-55; asst. supt. bus. services Mt. Eden Sch. Dist., Hayward, Calif., 1956-61, asst. supt. instructional services, 1961-63; supt. Orland (Calif.) public schs., 1963-72, Palmdale (Calif.) Sch. Dist., 1972-75, Fremont (Calif.) Unified Sch. Dist., 1975—; instr. San Jose State U., part-time, 1978-80. Served with USN, 1944-46. Mem. Am. Assn. Sch. Adminstrs., Assn. Calif. Sch. Adminstr., Phi Kappa Phi, Phi Delta Kappa, Delta Epsilon. Republican. Mormon.

Lodge: Kiwanis (pres. 1980-81, H. gov. div. 40 Calif.-Nev.-Hawaii 1983-84). Home: 2620 Forrest Ct Fremont CA 94536 Office: 40775 Fremont Blvd Fremont CA 94538

FERGUSSON, ROBERT GEORGE, ret. army officer, corp. exec.; b. Chgo., May 20, 1911; s. Archibald Campbell and Anne (Sheehan) F.; student Beloit Coll., 1929-32; B.S., U.S. Mil. Acad., 1936; grad. Army War Coll., Naval War Coll.; M.A. in Internat. Relations, Boston U., 1959; m. Charlotte Lawrence, Nov. 18, 1937; 1 son, Robert Lawrence. (dec.). Commd. 2d lt. U.S. Army, 1936, advanced through grades to maj. gen., 1962; ret., 1970; mem. gen. staff 7th Inf. Div., 1943-45; assigned hdqrs. Pacific Base Command, then Hawaii, 1945-46; instr. Command and Gen. Staff Coll., Ft. Leavenworth, Kan., 1946-48; chief dissemination br. intelligence div. Dept. Army, Washington, 1948-49; assigned 8th Inf. Regt., 4th Div., Ft. Ord, 1949, Hdqrs. 8th Army, Korea, 1950-51; chief S.E. Asia br. fgn. mil. affairs Office Sec. Def., Washington, 1952-54; dep. chief staff Hdqrs. U.S. Army Pacific, 1954-55; comdg. officer 14th Inf. Regt., Hawaii, 1955-57; chief army adv. group Naval War Coll., Newport, R.I., 1957-61; asst. div. comdr. 24th Inf. Div., Augsburg, Germany, 1961-62; chief staff Hdqrs. Central Army Group (NATO), Heidelberg, Germany, 1962-65; comdg. gen. U.S. Army Tng. Center, Inf., Ft. Ord, Monterey, Cal., 1965-67; comdr. U.S. Forces, Berlin, 1967-70; corporate group v.p. Dart Industries, 1970-78, cons., 1978—. Decorated D.S.M., Legion of Merit with oak leaf cluster, Bronze Star with 3 oak leaf clusters, Purple Heart (U.S.); officer Legion of Honor (France); knight comdr. Cross with badge and star Order of Merit (Fed. Republic Germany). Mem. Beta Theta Pi. Clubs: Cypress Point (Pebble Beach); Old Capitol (Monterey). Home: Box 1515 Pebble Beach CA 93953

FERICANO, PAUL FRANCIS, poet, writer, satirist; b. San Francisco, Jan. 16, 1951; s. Frank Paul and Josephine Angelina (Anello) F.; student San Francisco State U., U. Calif.-Berkeley, Calif. State U.-Hayward, Stanford U., U. Calif.-Santa Barbara, Sacramento State U., 1969-76; m. Katherine Judeen Daly, Oct. 14, 1972. Mng. editor Crow's Nest mag., San Francisco, 1973-76; editor The West Conscious Rev., Millbrae, Calif., 1974-77; pub. Scarecrow Books, Millbrae, 1974-78, Poor Souls Press, Millbrae, 1978—; dir. The Creative Response Outlet for Writers, 1973-78; asst. field coordinator Calif. Poets-in-the Schs. San Mateo County, 1977-78; chmn. Millbrae Arts Commn., 1976-77. Recipient commendation City of Millbrae, 1977; Howitzer prize, 1982. Author: Beneath the Smoke Rings, 1976; Cancer Quiz, 1977; Loading the Revolver with Real Bullets, 1977; The Condition of Poetry in the Modern World, A Stoogist Manifesto, 1980; Sinatra, Sinatra, 1982; Commercial Break, 1982; poetry and prose to numerous mags., 1970—. Home and Office: PO Box 236 Millbrae CA 94030

FERNANDEZ, ALFRED PETER, college district administrator; b. San Diego, July 26, 1934; s. Alfonso R. and Pola (Pickering) F.; B.A., UCLA, 1957, M.A., 1959; Ph.D., U. So. Calif., 1976; m. Dolores Russell, May 1, 1952; children—Christina, Virginia, Pamela, Steven. Asso. engring. geologist Calif. Div. Hwys., Los Angeles, 1960-62; asso. prof. geology Chaffey Coll. Dist., Alta Loma, Calif., 1962-69; admission officer Calif. State U., Los Angeles, 1969-71; asso. dean continuing edn. Santa Monica (Calif.) Coll., 1971-74; dean instruction Ventura (Calif.) Coll., 1974-80; pres. Los Angeles Mission Coll., San Fernando, Calif., 1980-82; chancellor Ventura County (Calif.) Community Coll. Dist., 1982—. Mem. Chancellor's Adv. Com. on Gen. Edn., 1982—; mem. council Ventura County Ednl. Tng. Adminstrn., 1975-78; trustee Neighborhood Youth Assn.; div. vice chmn. United Way. Mem. Assn. Calif. Community Coll. Adminstrs., So. Calif. Community Coll. Chief Exec. Officers Assn., Assn. Mexican-Am. Educators, Calif. Tchrs. Assn., Assn. Engring. Geologists, Calif. Coll. and Univ. Faculty Assn., Indsl. Assn. San Fernando Valley, Mexican-Am. Polit. Assn. Pomona (chmn.), UCLA Alumni Assn., San Fernando C. of C., Sylmar C. of C. Democrat. Roman Catholic. Home: 981 Scenic Way Dr Ventura CA 93003 Office: 71 Day Rd Ventura CA 93003

FERNANDEZ, DELIA MARIE, public realtions director; b. Los Angeles, May 24, 1952; d. Charles A. and Eva M. (McGee) F. B.A. in Brit. and Am. Lit., Scripps Coll., 1974; M.B.A., Calif. State U.-Long Beach, 1982. Teacher's aide Aviation High Sch., Manhattan Beach, Calif., 1974-76; intern planning dept. Solano County Econ. Opportunity Council, summer 1976; policies and procedures adminstr. TRW Info. Services Div., Orange, Calif., 1976-78, consumer affairs specialist, 1979-80, consumer affairs mgr., 1980-81, dir. pub. affairs, 1981—. Bd. dirs. TRW Systems Credit Union; mem. adv. com. Women's Transitional Living Ctr. Mem. Internat. Assn. Bus. Communicators, Pub. Relations Soc. Am. Office: TRW Info Services One City Blvd West Suite 920 Orange CA 92668

FERNANDEZ, JOSE LUIS, JR., photo finishing company executive; b. Puebla, Mexico, Aug. 24, 1946; s. Jose Luis and Maria Eugenia (de Fernandez) F. m. Maria Eugenia Carmelo Bernal, June 7, 1974; 1 son, Jose Luis Fernandez Carmelo. Student Universidad Iberco Anjelicana, 1964-66. Salesman, Jimmy Process Co., Mex., 1968, gen. mgr., 1969-72; gen. mgr. Nippon Photo Supply de Mexico, S.A., 1972-76; exec. v.p., gen. mgr. Sufoto S.A. de C.V., Baja California, Mex., 1976—. Mem. Sales and Mktg. Execs. Ensenada. Roman Catholic. Home: Calle Arenas #283 Ensenada Baja California Mexico Office: Calle Ryerson #55 Ensenada Baja California Mexico

FERRANT, SUSAN LOUISE, psychotherapist, consultant; b. N.Y.C., May 13, 1947; d. Wilbur J. and Elizabeth A. (Hartman) F. B.A. in Stats., U. Rochester, 1969; M.A. in Psychology, Calif. State U.-Northridge, 1979. Lic. marriage and family therapist, Calif. Systems engr. IBM, Rochester, N.Y., 1970-71; cons. programmer, analyst, Los Angeles, 1972-74; sr. systems analyst Xerox Computer Graphics, Los Angeles, 1978-80; dir. restaurant systems Sambo's Restaurants, Santa Barbara, Calif., 1978-80; pvt. practice psychotherapy, Santa Barbara and Los Angeles, 1980—; bus. cons.; writer, speaker on women in bus., women and work issues. Recipient Service award Xerox Computer Graphics, 1976. Mem. Calif. Assn. Marriage and Family Therapists (dir. chpt.), Nat. Assn. Female Execs., Associated Network Exec. Women (dir.), S. Coast Bus. Network. Am. Psychol. Assn., Calif. Psychol. Assn. Home: 3710 San Remo Dr Santa Barbara CA 93105 Office: 22 W Micheltorena St Santa Barbara CA 93101 also 1514 N Crescent Heights Los Angeles CA 90046

FERRANTE, MICHAEL JOHN, research chemist; b. N.Y.C., Feb. 1, 1930; s. Joseph and Faustina (Mongelli) F.; B.A. in Chemistry, B.A. in Edn., Eastern Wash. Coll., 1952; m. Carol Francis Gerkey, June 18, 1953; children—Debora Lynn, Joseph Michael, Jean Marie. Shift chemist Longview Fibre Co. (Wash.), 1955-56; research chemist chem. processing U.S. Bur. Mines, Albany, Oreg., 1956-69, research chemist thermodynamics, 1969—. Mem. Albany Parks Com., 1964-69. Served with AUS, 1953-55. Mem. Am. Inst. Chem. Engrs., Am. Legion, Sigma Xi. Democrat. Roman Catholic. Club: Elks. Author research papers. Home: 1235 Chestnut St Albany OR 97321

FERRANTI, LINDA FAY, insurance agency accounting manager; b. LaGrande, Oreg., Jan. 20, 1953; d. Norman H. and Fay Pauline (Andrews) Schroth; m. Richard John Ferranti. Student Blue Mountain Community Coll., 1971-72; B.A. in Retail Merchandising, Puget Sound U., 1975. Grad. Aetna Life & Casualty Sales Course, 1975. Mktg. rep. Aetna Life & Casualty Co., Portland, Oreg., 1975-76, underwriter, Hartford, Conn., 1976-77; acctg. mgr. Schroth Ins. Agy., Hermiston, Oreg., 1979—. Active Nat. Congl. Com., Nat. Republican Senatorial Com., Umatilla County Reps., Rep. Presdl. Task Force. Mem. Alpha Phi (Inspirational award 1975). Episcopalian. Home: 720 View Dr Hermiston OR 97838 Office: Schroth Ins Agency 411 Main St Hermiston OR 97838

FERRANTI, PHILIP RALPH, educator, counselor; b. Columbus, Ohio, Dec. 3, 1945; s. William and Irene (Vince) F. B.A., Divine Word Coll., 1967; M.Ed., U. San Diego, 1972. Migrant edn. resource tchr. Desert Sands Sch. Dist., Indio, Calif., 1972-74; instr. Coll. of the Desert, Palm Desert, Calif., 1975—; counselor Turnoff, Inc., Desert Hot Springs, Calif., 1975—; presenter Transformation Seminars, Palm Desert, Calif., 1980—. Served with U.S. Army 1968-70. Recipient Desert Mental Health Assn. Hayman-Vaile award in mental health, 1979-80. Mem. Am. Soc. Trainers and Developers. Roman Catholic. Author: In Search of a Feeling, 1979; Overcoming Our Obsessions, 1978. Home: 42-720 Virginia Ave Palm Desert CA 92260 Office: 71 175 Aurora Ave Desert Hot Springs CA 92240

FERRARI, EILEEN STEWART, hotel executive; b. Fairfield, Calif., Apr. 27, 1950; d. Albert and Margaret Donohue (Mulroney) F. B.A. in Fine Arts, U. Mont., 1973. Buyer, mgr. Farm Gift Shop, Vallejo, Calif., 1973-75; asst. food mgr. Red Top Coffee Shop, Vallejo, 1973-75; asst. food, beverage mgr. Holiday Hotel and Casino, Reno, 1974-77, dir. sales, 1977-80, dir. sales and mktg., 1980-82, gen. mgr. hotel ops. and sales, 1982—, also dir.; mem. Ad Hoc Com. to Develop of Tourism. Vice-pres. Riverside Living Assn., 1982—; bd. dirs. Jr. League Reno, 1982—; mem. Com. to Aid Abused Women. Mem. No. Nev. Hotel Motel Assn., Hotel Sales Mgmt. Assn., (nat., Nev. chpts.), NOW, Nat. Assn. Female Execs., Whale Protection Soc., Planned Parenthood, Animal Protection Agy., Sierra Club, Defenders of Wildlife, World Wildlife Fund, Kappa Kappa Gamma. Club: Reno Press and Va. (pres. 1983—). Author of various books, handbooks, booklets related to hotel and food ops. Home: 1246 Riverside Dr Reno NV 89503 Office: PO Box 2700 Reno NV 89505

FERRARI, JOSEPH, restaurateur; b. Rome, Sept. 11, 1926; s. Victor and Rose (Saporito) F.; student pub. schs., Rome; m. Josette Courniaud, Feb. 6, 1960; children—Phillip, Nadia. Busboy, waiter, bartender, capt., maitre d'manager, Rome, Stockholm, Rio de Janeiro, Paris, London, N.Y.C., San Francisco, Los Angeles, 1950-70; ship steward, 1952, butler Brazilian Legation, Italion legation, Brit. embassy, Stockholm, 1950-54; ptnr. restaurants in Eng., 1957-58, London, 1954-60; owner, mgr. Casina Valadier Restaurant, San Diego, 1975—; tchr. basic French and Italian cooking, 1975—. Mem. San Diego Conv. and Visitors Bur.; bd. dirs. Calif. Ballet. Served with Italian Army, 1947-48. Recipient Silver award of merit So. Calif. Restaurant Writers, 1978, 79, 80, 81, 82; Excellence in Dining award United Airlines mag., 1978, 79, 80. Mem. Nat. Restaurant Assn., San Diego C. of C. Republican. Roman Catholic. Office: 4445 Lamont St San Diego CA 92109

FERRARO, EDWARD JAMES, city manager; b. McKees Rocks, Pa., Sept. 12, 1928; s. Frederick and Catherine (Hughmanic) F.; m. Karen Virginia Isaac, Apr. 12, 1973; children—Vincent, Michael. B.A. in Polit. Sci., UCLA, 1956, M.A. in Pub. Adminstrn., 1958. Adminstrv. trainee, then adminstrv. analyst Chief Adminstrs. Office, Los Angeles County, 1957-59; city adminstr., Lawndale, Calif., 1960-62; asst. city mgr., Torrance, Calif., 1962-64, city mgr., 1964—; exec. dir. City of Torrance Redevel. Agy.; asst. prof. Ctr. Pub. Policy and Adminstrn., Calif. State U.-Long Beach; guest lectr. in field. Served with U.S. Army, 1951-53. Mem. Internat. City Mgmt. Assn., Nat. Council Urban Econ. Devel., Calif. Assn. Local Econ. Devel., Am. Soc. Pub. Adminstrn. (Clarence A. Dykstra award Los Angeles chpt. 1980), Am. Acad. Polit. and Social Sci. (dir.), Calif. Assn. Pub. Adminstrn. Edn., South Bay City Mgrs. Assn. (past pres.), League Calif. Cities. Contbr. articles to profl. jours. Office: 3031 Torrance Blvd Torrance CA 90503

FERREIRA, BEATRIZ VALADEZ, lawyer; b. Scottsbluff, Nebr., June 16, 1947; d. Genevevo and Priscilla (Jimenez) Valadez; 1 son, Juan Roberto Miguel. B.A. in Sociology, N.Mex. State U., 1970; M.S. in Edn., U. So. Calif., Heidelberg, W.Ger., 1974; J.D., U. N.Mex., 1980. Bar: N.Mex. 1982. Adult edn. coordinator N.Mex. State U., Las Cruces, 1976-77; research asst. U. N.Mex. Law Sch., 1978-79; coordinator Farmworkers' Legal Rights Ctr., Las Cruces, 1979; atty. U.S. Dept. Transp., Washington, 1980-81; ptnr. Saenz, Ganzales and Ferreira, Las Cruces, 1981—. Mem. ABA, N.Mex. Bar Assn., Nat. Assn. Criminal Def. Lawyers, Judicature Soc., IMAGE (Hispanic profl. assn.). Contbr. articles to profl. jours. Office: Saenz Gonzalez and Ferreira 300 E Griggs St Las Cruces NM 88001

FERREIRA, JACKIE WILMA, company product manager; b. Ont., Can., Oct. 20, 1954; d. William and Margaret Jane (Hunter) Waddell; m. Ronald C. Ferreira, Apr. 16, 1977. Cert. in bus. mgmt. U. Calif.-Hayward, 1983. Adminstrv. asst. Wells Fargo Bank, Oakland, Calif., 1972-75, Mason McDuffe Investment Corp., Berkeley, Calif., 1975-76, Sargent Industries, Oakland, 1976-77; order adminstr. Humphrey Instruments Inc., San Leandro, Calif., 1977-80, product specialist, 1980-82, tng. mgr., 1981-83, product mgr., 1983—. Named Maid of Oakland, 1972; recipient Service Recognition award Humphrey Instruments Inc., 1979. Mem. Am. Soc. Tng. and Devel., Women in Info. Processing. Editor Wheelbarrow Johnny mag., 1976-78. Office: Humphrey Instruments Inc 3081 Teagarden St San Leandro CA 94577

FERRER, RAFAEL GEORGE, lawyer; b. Spokane, Wash., Aug. 27, 1930; s. Rafael Guilermo and Lucia O. (Button) F.; student Whitworth Coll. 1948-50; B.A., Wash. State Coll., 1954; J.D., U. Wash., 1959; m. Barbara Ann Gould, Aug. 8, 1954; children—Rafael Gregory, Douglas Paul. Tchr., Yakima High Sch., 1954-56; admitted to Wash. bar, 1959, since practiced in Seattle; asso. Montgomery, Purdue, Blankinship & Austin, 1959-63, partner, 1963—; dir. Tyee Industries, Inc., Brodie/Dohrmann Inc., Ala Jabima Ltd., Pilot-King Corp., others. Chmn., Shoreline YMCA, 1981-82, Shoreline dist., Boy Scouts Am., 1970-73. Served with USAF, 1951-52. Mem. Seattle C. of C., Am. Trial Lawyers Assn., Wash. Trial Lawyers Assn., Am., Wash., Seattle-King County bar assns., Richmond Highlands Athletic Assn. (founder, sec.). Conglist. Home: 17707 17th NW Seattle WA 98177 Office: Norton Bldg Seattle WA 98104

FERRIN, ALLAN HOGATE, architect; b. N.Y.C., Oct. 24, 1951; s. Allan Wheeler and Barbara (Hogate) F.; student Princeton U., 1969-71; B.A. in Chinese, U. Wis., 1973; M.Arch., U. N.Mex., 1975; m. Barbara Lorayne Weaver, May 1, 1976; 1 dau., Leigh Elizabeth. Architect, Mitchell Assos., Albuquerque, 1976-77, Jorge De La Torre, Albuquerque, 1977-78, John Graham & Co., Seattle, 1978-79; project mgr. Charles Kober Assos., Seattle, 1979—; exhbn. of sculpture New West Gallery, Albuquerque, 1976-78. Mem. AIA. Office: 1100 Olive Way Seattle WA 98101

FERRIN, GAIL LUCILLE, educator; b. Baker, Oreg., Dec. 26, 1948; d. Kenneth James and Florence Ruth (Summers) Kofford; m. John Ralph Ferrin, July 6, 1979; 1 dau., Christine Anne. B.S. in Home Econs. Edn., Oreg. State U., 1971. Teaching cert. Utah. Tchr. home econs. Prineville (Oreg.) Jr. High Sch., 1971-73, Woods Cross (Utah) High Sch., 1977—; welfare services missionary Ch. of Jesus Christ of Latter-day Saints, Cali, Colombia, 1975-76. Union Pacific scholar, 1967. Mem. NEA, Utah Edn. Assn., Davis Edn. Assn., Omicron Nu. Office: Woods Cross High Sch 2200 S 600 W Woods Cross UT 84087

FERRIS, STEPHEN DAVID, biochemist; b. Ithaca, N.Y. Feb. 27, 1951; s. Spencer David and Margaret (Bailer) F.; B.S. in Biology, Cornell U., 1973; Ph.D. in Cell Biology, U. Ill., Urbana, 1978. Researcher, Oak Ridge Nat. Lab., 1972; grad. teaching asst. U. Ill., 1973-77, NIH postdoctoral researcher regulation and evolution gene expression in tetraploid fishes, 1978; Miller fellow evolution animal mitochondrial DNA, U. Calif., Berkeley, 1979—. Mem. Am. Soc. Zoologists, Soc. Study Evolution, Sigma Xi. Author papers in field. Home: 6715 1/2 Portola St El Cerrito CA 94530 Office: Dept Biochemistry U Calif Berkeley CA 94720

FERRIS, YVONNE MARIE, manufacturing company executive, statistician; b. East St. Louis, Ill., June 6, 1934; d. Clarence Raymond and Frankye Elizabeth (Bradberry) Clark; m. Livingston Polk Ferris II, July 5, 1967. B.S., Iowa State U., 1956; postgrad. Rochester Inst. Tech., 1962, U. Colo., 1964-66. Statistician, Rockwell Internat., Golden, Colo., 1956-63, sr. statistician, 1963-73, mgr. stats. lab., 1973-75, mgr. stats. and nuclear material control, 1975-77, mgr. stats. and systems analysis, 1979—; group leader safeguards IAEA, Vienna, Austria, 1977-79; chmn. Measurement Control Task Force; mem. speakers bur.; chmn. Standard N15.46, Measurement Control. com. Am. Nat. Standards Inst. Counselor Rocky Flats Personal Assistance Program; mem. Expts. in Friendship; active local programs emotionally disturbed and mentally retarded adults. Recipient Cost Improvement Suggestion awards Rockwell Internat., 1971-73, named Engr. of Yr., 1982. Mem. Inst. Nuclear Materials Mgmt. (vice-chmn., cert. safeguards specialist), Am. Statis. Soc. (adv. com. nuclear regulatory research), Am. Soc. Quality Control, Nat. Mgmt. Assn., LWV, Altrusa Internat. (past pres.). Contbr. articles to profl. jours. Office: Rockwell Internat PO Box 464 Golden CO 80401

FERRY, JOSEPH HOWARD, hospital administrator; b. Bklyn., Dec. 9, 1917; s. Joseph Aloysius and Louis Dorothy (Pfuhl) F.; m. Elizabeth Patricia McKeon, Oct., 1944; m. Elsie Mae Trovillion, Dec. 31, 1946; children—Karen Ferry McCreery, Michael J., Stephen T., Susan A. Student Fordham U., 1938-40; B.S. in Pub. Adminstrn., U. So. Calif., 1957. Trainee Chase Nat. Bank, N.Y.C., 1935-42; with VA, 1946—, fiscal officer trainee to asst. fiscal officer, Los Angeles and Van Nuys, Calif., 1946-50, asst. fiscal officer, fiscal officer, Long Beach, Calif., 1950-64, asst. hosp. dir. trainee, West Los Angeles, Calif., 1964-65, asst. hosp. dir., Vancouver, Wash., 1965-68, hosp. adminstrn. specialist VA Central Office, Washington, 1968-70, exec. asst. to assoc. dep. chief med. dir. for field ops., 1970-72, med. ctr. dir., Roseburg, Oreg., 1972-79, Livermore, Calif., 1979-81, dir. VA Med. Ctr., Portland, Oreg., 1981—; mem. steering com. Portland Fed. Exec. Bd., mem. State Health Coordinating Com. Oreg. Served to 1st lt. USAAF, 1942-44. Decorated Purple Heart. Republican. Roman Catholic. Office: 3710 US Veterans Hospital Rd Box 1034 Portland OR 97207

FERRY, MILES YEOMAN, state senator Utah; b. Brigham City, Utah, Sept. 22, 1932; s. John Yeoman and Alta (Cheney) F.; B.S., Utah State U.; m. Suzanne Call, May 19, 1952; children—John, Jane (Mrs. Dave Stewart), Ben, Helen, Sue, Nora. Rancher, Corinne, Utah, 1952—; mem. Utah Ho. of Reps. from Box Elder Dist., 1965-66; mem. Utah Senate from 24th Dist., 1967—, minority whip, 1975-76, minority leader, 1977-79, pres., 1979-84, chmn. legis. mgmt. com., 1979-80; chmn. state and fed. relations Council State Govts., also mem. exec. com. and governing bd.; exec. com. Nat. Conf. State Legislators, v.p., 1981, pres.-elect, 1982-83. Pres., Brigham Jr. C. of C., 1956-61; v.p. Utah C. of C., 1960-61; pres. Farm Bur., 1958-59; active Lake Bonniville council Boy Scouts Am. Bd. dirs. Box Elder chpt. ARC. Recipient award of merit Utah Vocat. Assn., 1981. Named Outstanding Young Man of Year, Brigham City Jr. C. of C., 1957; Outstanding Nat. Dir., U.S. Jaycees, 1962; Outstanding Young Man in Utah, Utah Jr. C. of C., 1961; Hon. State Farmer, Future Farmers Am., 1975; Alumnus of Yr., Utah State U., 1981. Mem. Sons Utah Pioneers, Phi Kappa Phi. Republican. Mormon (high council 1971-76). Address: Box 70 Corinne UT 84307

FERRY, PAMELA DENIECE, utility official, lobbyist; b. Wichita, Kans., Feb. 6, 1953; d. George Edward and Maxine Fay (Lofton) Seaman; m. Henry J. Ferry, Jr., Oct. 27, 1979. B.A. in Econ., San Diego State U., 1975, postgrad., 1983—. Research asst. San Diego Econ. Devel. Corp., 1974-75, loan mgmt. trainee San Diego Fed. Savs. & Loan, 1975-77; econ. analyst San Diego Gas & Electric Co., 1979-80, regulatory affairs rep., 1980-82, sr. regulatory affairs rep., 1982—; mem., chmn. Citizens for Good Govt. polit. action com. San Diego Gas & Electric Co. Chmn., Smoketree Condos Neighborhood Watch, San Diego; ednl. chmn. San Diego Republican Businesswomen, LWV. Chapman Coll. World Campus Afloat scholar, 1974. Republican. Mem. Christian Ch. Editor San Diego Econ. Devel. Corp. Bus. Index, 1975. Home: 9905 Aviary Dr San Diego CA 92131 Office: PO Box 1831 San Diego CA 92112

FERTIG, TED BRIAN O'DAY, producer, pub. relations and assn. exec.; b. Miami, May 18, 1937; s. Peter John and Frances Marie (Aswell) F.; A.B., 1960; M.B.A., 1969. Mem. profl. staff Congress U.S., Washington, 1965; dir. mem. relations Nat. Bellas Hess, Inc., Kansas City, 1963-69; mgr. employment/manpower planning Capitol Industries, Inc., 1969-70; pres. Mgmt. Cons. Group, Hollywood, Calif., 1970—, Fertig, Toler & Dumond, Hollywood, 1973; sr. partner Nascency Prodns., Hollywood and Sacramento, 1971—; exec. dir. Soc. Calif. Accts., 1974-83, Ednl. Found., Inc., 1975-80. Pres., Hollywood Community Concert Assn., 1971-72; exec. dir. Hollywood Walk of Fame, 1971-74; sec.-treas. Save the Sign, 1972-73; producer, Santa Claus Lane Parade of Stars, Hollywood, 1971-73; dir. Old Eagle Theatre, Sacramento, Sacramento Film Festival. Trustee, finance chmn. Los Angeles Free Clinics, 1970-71; mem. Calif. Commn. on Personal Privacy. Served with AUS, 1960-62. Cert. assn. exec. Mem. Pub. Relations Soc. Am., Am. C. of C. Execs., Am. Soc. Assn. Execs., Sacramento Soc. Assn. Execs. (pres. 1980). Author: A Family Night to Remember, 1971; Los Ninos Cantores de Mendoza, 1972; (with Paul Yoder) Salute to Milwaukee, 1965. Home: 715 Regatta Dr Sacramento CA 95833 Office: 2131 Capitol Ave PO Box 1610.82 Sacramento CA 95816

FERY, JOHN BRENT, forest products co. exec.; b. Bellingham, Wash., Feb. 16, 1930; s. Carl Salvatore and Margaret (Hauck) F.; B.B.A., U. Wash., 1953; M.B.A., Stanford U., 1955; m. Delores L. Carlo, Aug. 22, 1953; children—John Brent, Bruce Todd, Michael Nicholas. Asst. to pres. Western Draft Corp., 1955-56, prodn. mgr., 1956-57; with Boise Cascade Corp. (Idaho), 1957—, v.p., 1960-67, exec. v.p., 1967-72, pres., 1972-78, chief exec. officer, 1972—, also dir.; dir. Idaho First Nat. Bank, Union Pacific Corp., Albertsons, Inc. Trustee St. Alphonsus Hosp. Served with USN, 1950-51. Recipient Ernest Arbuckle award Stanford U. Sch. Bus., 1980. Mem. Am. Paper Inst. (chmn.). Clubs: Arid, Hillcrest County, Links, Arlington, Elks. Office: 1 Jefferson Square Boise ID 83728

FESHBACH, NORMA DEITCH, educator; b. N.Y.C., Sept. 5, 1926; d. Samuel and Lena R. (Katz) Deitch; m. Seymour Feshbach, Aug. 16, 1947; children—Jonathan Stephen, Laura Elizabeth, Andrew David. B.S. cum laude, CCNY, 1947, M.S., 1949; Ph.D. (USPHS fellow), U. Pa., 1956. Tchr., Betsy Ross Nursery Sch., Yale U., 1947-48; clin. psychologist Yale U. Med. Sch., 1948; lectr. Jr. Coll. Phys. Therapy, New Haven, 1948-49; teaching asst. dept. psychology Yale U., 1948-51; research asst. George Washington U., Washington, 1951-52; psychology intern Phila. Gen. Hosp., 1955-56; assoc., lectr. dept. psychology, U. Pa., Phila., 1956-57, research assoc., 1959-61; clin./research cons. Youth Services, Inc., Phila., 1955-61; vis. asst. prof. Stanford (Calif.) U., 1961-62; lectr.

dept. psychology U. Calif.-Berkeley, 1962-63; research assoc. Inst. Behavioral Sci., U. Colo., Boulder, 1963-64; research psychologist UCLA, 1964-65, clin. psychologist UCLA, 1964-65, clin. psychologist II, lectr., Neuropsychiat. Inst., 1965, program dir. Ctr. for Study of Evaluation, 1966-69, co-dir. Bush Found. Tng. Program in Child Devel. and Social Policy, 1978—, dir. Program in Early Childhood and Devel. Studies, 1968-80, prof. dept. psychology, Grad Sch. Edn., 1965—; dir. NIMH Tng. Program in Early Childhood and Devel. Studies, 1972—; cons. in field. Recipient James McKeen Cattell Fund Sabbatical award, 1980-81; Townsend medal, Disting. Alumnus award CCNY, 1982; named Women of Yr., Hadassa, Los Angeles, 1973. Fellow Am. Psychol. Assn; mem. Assn. for Advancement Psychology (trustee), AAAS, AAUP, Am. Bd. Profl. Psychologists, Am. Ednl. Research Assn., Calif. Assn. for Edn. Young Children, Calif. Ednl. Research Assn., Calif. Profs. of Early Childhood Edn., Calif. Psychol. Assn. (Disting. Sci. Achievement award 1983), Internat. Assn. Applied Psychology, Internat. Soc. for Research on Aggression, Internat. Soc. Study of Behavioral Devel., Nat. Assn. for Edn. Young Children, Nat. Register of Health Service Providers in Psychology, Nat. Soc. Study of Edn., Soc. for Research in Child Devel., Soc. for Psychol. Study of Social Issues (exec. council), Western Psychol. Assn. (pres. 1980), Sigma Xi, Delta Phi Upsilon. Co-author: Learning to Care, 1983. Contbr. numerous articles to profl. jours. Office: Grad Sch Edn UCLA Los Angeles CA 90024

FESSLER, EDWARD ANTHONY, naval officer, lawyer; b. Sheboygan, Wis., Oct. 14, 1944; s. Jacob Anthony and Lucile Alice (Flaccus) F.; B.A., Northwestern U., 1967, J.D., 1970; LL.M., George Washington U., 1978; m. Sherrie Lynn Monte, Aug. 17, 1968. Bar: Wis. 1970, U.S. Supreme Ct. 1973, Calif. 1976, Hawaii 1983. Law clk. Gruhle, Fessler & Van de Water, Sheboygan, Wis., 1970; commd. officer US Navy, 1970, advanced through grades to comdr. JAGC, 1980; asst. staff judge advocate Comdr. Naval Forces Marianas, Guam, Marianas Islands, 1971-73; staff judge advocate U.S. Naval Communications Sta., San Miguel, Philippines; force judge advocate, comdr. U.S. Naval Support Force Antarctica, Operation Deep Freeze, 1975-77; head security assistance br. internat. law div. Office Judge Advocate Gen., Dept. Navy, Washington, 1978-81; asst. fleet judge advocate internat. law, staff, comdr.-in-chief U.S. Pacific Fleet, Pearl Harbor, Hawaii, 1981—; guest lectr. Defense Inst. Security Assistance Mgmt., 1979-80. Mem. vestry St. Mark's Episcopal Ch., 1979-81; chmn. Boy Scout com. U.S. Naval Communication Sta., San Miguel, Philippines, 1973-75; legal adviser Apra Harbor Sports Divers Assn., U.S. Naval Sta., Guam, Marianas Islands, 1972-73; fed. coordinator Com. to Preserve Huntley Meadows Park, Alexandria, Va. Mem. Fed. Bar Assn., ABA, Law of Sea Inst., Pac-Asian Affairs Council, Hawaii Law of Sea Assn., State Bar Wis., Calif. State Bar Assn., Calif. Trial Lawyers Assn., Hawaii Bar Assn. Republican. Episcopalian. Club: Hono Canoe (dir.). Author: Directed Energy Weapons-A Juridicial Analysis, 1978. Home and Office: CINCPACFLT Box 03J Pearl Harbor HI 96860

FESTE, KAREN ANN, political science educator, consultant; b. Mpls., Jan. 4, 1944; d. Chris and Ruth (Vold) F.; m. Roger A. Hanson, Sept. 23, 1966; 1 dau., Kristina. B.A., Concordia Coll., 1965; postgrad. U. Oslo (Norway), 1966; M.A., U. Minn., 1969, Ph.D., 1973; postgrad. U. Strathclyde (Scotland), 1973, U. Mich., 1976. Asst. prof. polit. sci. U. Denver, 1972-76, assoc. prof., 1976—; CACI, Inc., Washington, 1980; cons. to Egyptian Govt. Mem. Am. Polit. Sci. Assn., Internat. Studies Assn. Democrat. Author: The Arab Israeli Conflict, 1977. Home: 720 S Milwaukee St Denver CO 80209 Office: Grad Sch Internat Studies U Denver Denver CO 80208

FETTES, JOSEPH JOHN, JR., farmer, rancher; b. Antonito, Colo., Oct. 31, 1914; s. Joseph John and Sarah Rosalie (Shores) F.; student pub. schs.; m. Inza Maun Smith, June 14, 1940; children—Joseph John, III, Karen Viola Fettes Jacks, Rosalie Fern Fettes Garrett. Store clk., truck driver, sheet metal worker, 1931-43; farm mgr., 1943-51, salesman, 1951-59; farmer, rancher, 1959—; owner, operator Fettes Farms, Romeo, Colo., 1958—; dir. Conejos County Farm Bur., Western Farm Bur. Life Ins. Co.; v.p. Colo. Farm Bur., Colo. Farm Bur. Mut. Ins. Co.; voting del. Am. Farm Bur. Mayor, police magistrate, justice of peace, Romeo, 1945-51; sec. Sch. Bd., 1945-51; Republican precinct chmn., 1970-78; chmn. Conejos County Rep. Com., 1978-83; vice chmn. Conejos County Planning Commn., 1971-78, chmn., 1978-83; mem. adv. bd. Bur. Land Mgmt. Canon City Dist., 1983—. Served with USN, 1934-38. Presbyterian. Home: 937 2d St Romeo CO 81148

FETTIS, HENRY E., mathematician; b. East Orange, N.J., May 17, 1915; s. Arthur Erskine and Christine (Gall) F.; A.B., Wittenberg Coll., 1939; M.S., Ohio State U., 1952; m. Earline L. Klapper, Aug. 15, 1959. Mathematician, Aircraft Lab., Wright Patterson AFB, Ohio, 1943-50, Aero-space Research Lab., Wright-Patterson AFB, 1950-72, cons., 1972-73; cons. mathematics, Mountain View, Calif., 1973—; NSF fellow Stanford U., 1960-61. Mem. Soc. Indsl., Applied Mathematics, Spl. Interest Group on Numerical Analysis, Am. Acad. Mechanics, Assn. Computing Machinery, Math. Assn. Am., AIAA. Author govt. pub. tables of math. functions, 1964-72; contbr. numerous articles to math. and aeronautical jours., 1949—; co-editor: Theory of Incomplete Cylindrical Functions, English version, 1969; reviewer Math. Revs., Computing Revs. Home: 1885 California St Apt 62 Mountain View CA 94041

FETTO, JOHNNY ANTHONY (SEVEN), entertainment executive, actor, producer, realtor; b. Bklyn., Feb. 23, 1926; s. John A. and Marie (Cianci) F.; m. Edith Patricia Piselli, Oct. 8, 1949; children—John A. Jr., Laura. Grad. Lumbleau Sch. Real Estate Agts., 1961, Lumbleau Sch. Real Estate Brokers, 1963. Constrn. supt. S.S. Silbarblatt Corp., N.Y.C., 1946-50; film, TV actor, 1950—; founder, owner, chmn. bd. Johnny Seven Enterprises, Granada Hills, Calif., 1965—; founder Lone Star Realty (name changed to J-Seven Realty, 1977), 1967, now chmn. bd.; chmn. bd. Johnny Seven Prodns., John Seven Music Co. Hon. police chief City of Granada Hills, 1976, hon. fire chief, 1977. Served with U.S. Army, 1944-46. Decorated Purple Heart; recipient Los Angeles city council humanitarian award for documentary film, 1966, Las Vegas Internat. Film Festival best picture in category award, 1980. Mem. Screen Actor's Guild, AFTRA, Actor's Equity Assn., Calif. Assn. Realtors, San Fernando Valley Bd. Realtors. Roman Catholic. Club: Knollwood Country (Granada Hills). Home: 11213 McLennan Ave Granada Hills CA 91344 Office: 11024 Balboa Blvd Granada Hills CA 91344

FETZ, MARGOT, information systems analyst; b. Evanston, Ill., Nov. 10, 1935; d. Wesley and Mary (Slater) Hardenbergh; m. James Lawrence Talbot, Nov. 15, 1957 (div.); children—Katrin, Gretchen, Susan. Student U. Ill., 1953-55; A.B., U. Calif.-Berkeley, 1958; postgrad. South Australian Sch. Art, Adelaide, 1965, Lakehead U., 1967-68, U. Mont., 1975; cert. in archives and record mgmt. adminstrn. Western Wash. U., 1979; postgrad. Seattle U. Librarian, Lakehead U., Thunder Bay, Ont., Can., 1968-70; dept. head U. Mont. Library, Missoula, 1973-76; exec. asst. Soc. Photo-Optical Instrumentation Engrs., Bellingham, Wash., 1977-78; cons., Seattle, 1979—; analyst Wash. Mut. Savs. Bank, Seattle, 1981-82; info. systems analyst Alpac Corp., Seattle, 1982—. Chmn. County Park Feasibility Com., Missoula, 1973-74; vice-chmn. Missoula Local Govt. Study Commn., 1974-76, chmn. drafting com.; bd. dirs. Musica Viva Internat., Bellingham, 1979-81, Missoula Farmers Market, 1973-76. Mem. Assn. Records Mgrs. and Adminstrs., Assn. Systems Mgmt., Soc. Am. Archivists, Assn. Systems Mgmt. Club: Mountaineers (Seattle). Author: Bibliography of Sir Douglas Manson, 1958; Wash. State Dept. Civil Def. Archival Inventory, 1950-72, 1979; The Mount Vernon Pittman Papers, 1886-1897 (micropubl.), 1979. Home: 215 Valley St Seattle WA 98109 Office: Alpac Corp 2300 26th Ave S Seattle WA 98144

FEUCHT, DONALD LEE, solar energy research ofcl., elec. engr.; b. Akron, Ohio, Aug. 25, 1933; s. Henry G. and Dorothy F. (Kroeger) F.; B.S., Valparaiso U., 1955; M.S., Carnegie Inst. Tech., 1956, Ph.D., 1961; m. Janet Wingerd, Aug. 16, 1958; children—Lynn Janet, Paul Henry. Electronics engr. Convair Co., San Diego, 1956; instr. elec. engring. Carnegie-Mellon U. (formerly Carnegie Inst. Tech.), Pitts., 1958-61, asst. prof., 1961-65, asso. prof., 1965-69, prof., 1969-77, asso. dean, 1973-77; chief advanced materials research and devel. Dept. Energy, Washington, 1977-78; mgr. photovoltaic program office Solar Energy Research Inst., Golden, Colo., 1978-79, mgr. photovotaics div., 1979-80, dep. dir., 1981—; cons. Power Components Inc., Scottsdale, Pa., 1965-67, PPG Industries, Pitts., 1967-69, Essex Internat., Pitts., 1967-74. Recipient Disting. Alumnus award Valparaiso U., 1979. Fellow IEEE (treas. Pitts. 1965-66, chmn. group electron devices 1962-63); mem. Am. Phys. Soc., Electrochem. Soc., Am. Vacuum Soc., Sigma Xi, Phi Kappa Phi, Tau Beta Pi, Theta Chi. Author: (with A.G. Milnes) Heterojunctions and Metal Semiconductor Junctions, 1972; contbr. articles to profl. jours.; patentee method for making semiconductors for solar cells. Home: 8102 W 22d Way Lakewood CO 80215 Office: SERI 1617 Cole Blvd Golden CO 80401

FEULNER, PATRICIA NANCY, sociology educator; b. Queens, N.Y., July 9, 1946; d. George John and Laura Lottie (Sablynski) F.; B.A., Fordham U., 1968; M.A., Ohio State U., 1969, Ph.D., 1973; m. David R. Schlegel, Oct. 20, 1979. Asst. prof. sociology N.E. Mo. State U., Kirksville, 1971-72, Ohio State U., Lima, 1973-75; assoc. prof. sociology U. San Diego, 1975-83, prof., 1983—, chmn. dept. anthropology and sociology, 1980-83; community cons.; coordinator Univ. of the Third Age. Bd. dirs. Sr. Adult Services of San Diego; sec. San Diego Regional Consortium on Aging. Danforth asso., 1981—. Mem. Am. Sociol. Assn., Western Gerontol. Soc. Author: Women in Professions: A Social-Psychological Study, 1979. Home: 4915 Foothill Blvd San Diego CA 92109 Office: U San Diego Dept Anthropology and Sociology Alcala Park San Diego CA 92110

FEWELL, ANNE, artist, writer; b. Little Rock, Mar. 26, 1939; d. R.B. and Willimette (Bland) Fewell. B.A., Kansas City Art Inst., 1962. Exhibited in group shows: Anaheim (Calif.) Conv. Ctr., 1976, Calif. Mus. Sci. and Industry, 1979, Los Angeles Celebrity Ctr., 1979, Contemporary Showcase, Los Angeles, 1979; represented in numerous pvt. collections; author/illustrator: The First Spirit of Christmas as Told by Merrywinkle, 1981. Winner, Ann. Art. Competition, Ark., 1953, 54, W.Va., 1970; Eyes and Ears Found. award, Los Angeles, 1979.

FEYNMAN, RICHARD PHILLIPS, physics educator; b. N.Y.C., May 11, 1918; s. Melville Arthur and Lucille (Phillips) F.; B.S., Mass. Inst. Tech., 1939; Ph.D., Princeton, 1942. Staff atomic bomb project Princeton, 1942-43, Los Alamos, 1943-45; assoc. prof. theoretical physics Cornell U., 1945-50; prof. theoretical physics Calif. Inst. Tech., 1950—, Richard Chase Tolman prof., 1959—. Recipient Einstein award, 1954; Nobel prize in physics, 1965; Oersted medal, 1972; Niels Bohr Internat. Gold medal, 1973. Mem. Am. Phys. Soc., AAAS, Royal Soc. (fgn. mem.), Pi Lambda Phi. Contbr. theory of quantum electrodynamics, beta decay and liquid helium. Address: Physics Dept Calif Inst Technology Pasadena CA 91125*

FIBISH, ALAN BURTON, principal; b. San Francisco; s. Solomon A. and Minnie (Nadler) F.; m. Carole Jean Nyman, Sept. 3, 1950; children—Earl, Elaine, Marla. A.B., U. Calif.-Berkeley, 1952, Ed.D., 1971; M.A., San Francisco State U., 1957. Tchr. sci. George Washington High Sch., San Francisco, 1953-63; instr., head sci. dept. Wilson High Sch., San Francisco, 1963-68; asst. prin. several high schs., San Francisco, 1968-75; adj. assoc. prof. edn. San Francisco State U., 1970-71; prin. Lincoln High Sch., San Francisco, 1975-79, Lowell High Sch., San Francisco, 1979—. Vice-pres., bd. dirs. Homewood Terrace Residential Care Agy., 1972-78. Mem. Assn. Supervision and Curriculum Devel., San Francisco Sch. Adminstrs. Assn. Democrat. Jewish (past v.p., dir. temple). Office: 1101 Eucalyptus Dr San Francisco CA 94132

FICK, GERALD DENNIS, telephone utility executive; b. Fargo, N.D., Nov. 23, 1939; s. Walter Albert and Edna Laura Louise (Schleske) F.; m. Anita Olson, Apr. 16, 1960; children—Jeffrey, Pamela, Mark; m. 2d, Charlotte Williams, Feb. 14, 1981. With Continental Telephone Service Corp., Bakersfield, Calif., 1967—, chief acct., 1968-72, gen. acctg. mgr., 1972-75, asst. controller, gen. acctg. mgr., 1975, asst. v.p., budget dir., 1975-76, v.p. fin., 1976; v.p., treas., dir. Continental Telephone Co. Calif., Continental Telephone N.W., Inc., Continental Telephone of Tex., Continental Telephone Co. of West. Glacier State Telephone Co., Juneau and Douglas Telephone Co. Bd. dirs. Calif. Taxpayers Assn., 1979—; bd. dirs., treas. United Way Kern County, 1980—. Served in Army N.G., 1956-64. Mem. Nat. Assn. Accts., Ind. Telephone Pioneer Assn. Republican. Club: Bakersfield Country. Home: 5917 Azalea Bakersfield CA 93306 Office: PO Box 5246 Bakersfield CA 93388

FIDEL, JOSEPH A., state senator, real estate broker; b. Bibo, N.Mex., Oct. 14, 1923; s. Abdoo Habeeb and Latiffe (Hanosh) F.; student public schs., San Fidel and Santa Fe, N.Mex.; m. Aurora Baca, Oct. 14, 1949; children—Barbara, Donna, Marcia, Annamarie, Mary Lee, Mark. Ins. and real estate agt., Grants, N.Mex., 1945—; councilman City of Grants, 1954-60; county assessor, 1950-54, 62-66; sch. bd. mem., 1959-71; mem. N.Mex. Senate, 1972—; dir. Western Investors Inc., Bank Holding Co. Mem. Nat. Bd. Realtors, Ind. Ins. Agts. Assn. Democrat. Roman Catholic. Clubs: KC, Elks (Grants). Office: 825 E Santa Fe Ave Grants NM 87020

FIDLAR, MARION MOORE, ret. geologist; b. Vincennes, Ind., June 7, 1909; s. Orville F. and Clara M. (Moore) F.; A.B., Ind. U., 1934, M.A., 1936, Ph.D., 1942; m. Martha E. Thorn, May 9, 1937. Asst. geologist Ind. State Geol. Survey, summers 1932-35; asst. state geologist, state gas supr. Ind. Div. Geology, 1936-38; dist. geologist Ohio Oil Co., 1938-43; sr. geologist Mountain Fuel Supply Co., Rock Springs, Wyo., 1943-45, chief geologist, 1945-51, mgr. exploration div., 1951-54, v.p., 1954-58, bd. dirs., 1956-77, exec. v.p., Salt Lake City, 1958-62, pres., 1962-72, chmn., 1972-76, chief exec. officer, 1962-74; chmn. Entrada Industries, Inc., 1971-76, pres., 1971-74, dir., 1971-82; dir. Wexpro Co., Interstate Brick Co., Rock Springs Nat. Bank. Bd. dirs. St. Mark's Hosp. Fellow Geol. Soc. Am.; mem. Am. Assn. Petroleum Geologists, Pacific Coast Gas Assn. (pres. 1967-68), Pro-Utah (pres. 1968-70), Rocky Mountain, Intermountain assns. geologists, C. of C. (pres. 1963-64), AIME, Ind. Acad. Sci., Wyo. Geol. Assn., U.S. C. of C. (dir. 1969-77), Phi Beta Kappa, Sigma Xi, Sigma Gamma Epsilon. Rotarian. Clubs: Salt Lake City Country, Alta. Contbr. tech. articles to profl. jours. Home: 1040 Vista View Dr Salt Lake City UT 84108

FIEDLER, BOBBI, congressman; b. Santa Monica, Calif., Apr. 22, 1937; children—Lisa, Randy. Student Santa Monica City Coll., Santa Monica Tech. Sch.; LL.D. (hon.), West Coast Coll. Law, 1979. Owner, operator 2 pharmacies; mem. 97th-98th Congresses from Calif. Mem. Los Angeles Bd. Edn., 1977; cofounder antibusing orgn. BUSTOP; mem. Republican Women's Fedn.; mem. sponsor's bd. B'nai B'rith Youth Orgn.; active Hadassah, Bus. and Profl. Women's Assn. Named Outstanding Freshman of 97th Congress; recipient Anita S. Perlman award B'nai B'rith; named twice by Van Nuys Daily News as one of 10 most prominent people in San Fernando Valley, as one of most prominent people in So. Calif., Los Angeles Herald Examiner; honored for community work by Calif. Senate, Calif. Assembly, Los Angeles City Council, various chambers of commerce and service orgns. Republican. Office: 1607 Longworth House Office Bldg Washington DC 20515*

FIEDLER, DIANE MARIE, family economist; b. Mobridge, S.D., Dec. 7, 1947; d. J. Herman and Emma (Stangl) Fiedler; m. Michael Allan Smith, May 31, 1980. B.S. in Home Econs., S.D. State U., 1970; M.S. in Family Environment, Iowa State U., 1977. Mdse. asst. Carson Pirie Scott & Co., Chgo., 1969-70; asst. home agt. Rosebud Indian Reservation, Mission, S.D., 1971; extension home economist, Todd County, Long Prairie, Minn., 1972-76; grad. asst. family environment dept. Iowa State U., Ames, 1975-77; extension family resource mgmt. specialist, U. Wyo., Laramie, 1977—; coordinator family resource mgmt. specialist-western region, USDA. Del. Internat. Farm Yough Exchange, Norway, 1970. Metric Edn. grantee, HEW, 1978. Mem. Am. Home Econs. Assn., Wyo. Home Econs. Assn., Am. Council Consumer Interests, Wyo. Resident Extension Assn., Internat. 4-H Youth Exchange Alumni, Omicron Nu, Phi Upsilon Omicron. Lutheran. Home: Box 4034 University Station Laramie WY 82071 Office: Box 3354 University Station Laramie WY 82071

FIELD, ALEXANDER JAMES, educator; b. Boston, Apr. 17, 1949; s. Mark George and Anne (Murray) F.; m. Valerie N. Wolk, Aug. 8, 1982. A.B. magna cum laude, Harvard U., 1970; M.Sc. in Econs., London Sch. Econs., 1971; Ph.D., U. Calif.-Berkeley, 1974. Asst. prof. econs. Stanford (Calif.) U., 1974-82; mem. Inst. for Advanced Study, Princeton (N.J.), 1979-80; assoc. prof. econs. U. Santa Clara (Calif.), 1982—. NSF fellow, 1970-73; Nevins prize, 1975. Mem. Am. Econ. Assn., Econ. History Assn., Phi Beta Kappa. Democrat. Asso. editor Jour. Econ. Lit., 1981—; contbr. articles to profl. jours. Home: 3762 Redwood Circle Palo Alto CA 94306 Office: Dept Econs U Santa Clara Santa Clara CA 95053

FIELD, ANTHONY WAYNE, III, real estate exec.; b. East Hampton, N.Y., May 31, 1926; s. Anthony Wayne and Laura Edith (Walters) F.; B.S., Syracuse U., 1950; m. Patricia Ann Beck, June 23, 1956; children—Kathleen (Mrs. Jerry Lewis), Laura, Linda, Nancy, Anthony IV, Michael. With Sunbeam Corp., Chgo., 1955-59; dist. mgr. outboard motor and boat sales McCulloch Corp., Mpls., 1959-61; sr. sci. computer programmer-analyst Wolf Research & Devel. Corp., West Concord, Mass., 1961-67; data processing mgr. Holly Sugar Corp., Colorado Springs, Colo., 1967-69; pres., chief exec. officer Computerama, Inc., Colorado Springs, 1969-74, Mountain States Computer Corp., Colorado Springs, 1971—; owner, broker Mountain States Realty, 1978-82; pres., broker Arrowhead Properties, Ltd., 1981—; pres. Mountain States Realty Investment Corp., 1982—. Mem. N.Y.C. Aux. Police, 1951-53; mem. Civil Air Patrol, 1943—, officer, 1951—. Served with U.S. Army, 1943-46. Decorated Purple Heart. Mem. Data Processing Mgmt. Assn., Assn. Computing Machinery (chpt. chmn. 1969-70), Aircraft Owners and Pilots Assn. Republican. Club: Optimist (v.p. 1970-71) (Colorado Springs). Home: 2602 Summit Dr Colorado Springs CO 80909 Office: 2500 N Circle Dr Colorado Springs CO 80909

FIELD, CHARLES WILLIAM, JR., elec. engr.; b. Hollywood, Calif., Jan. 6, 1942; s. Charles William and Mary Elizabeth (Beedle) F.; A.A., Long Beach City Coll., 1963; B.S., Calif. State U. at Long Beach, 1964; M.S., George Washington U., 1967; m. Mary Elizabeth Cole, June 25, 1966 (div. Sept. 1972); 1 dau., Mary Waddell; m. 2d, Joan Marie Woodbury, Oct. 20, 1979. Draftsman, Autonetics, Anaheim, Calif., 1961; asso. engr. N.Am. Aviation, Downey, Calif., 1963-64; sr. engr. Raytheon Co., Goleta, Calif., 1967-79; sr. project engr. Delco Electronics Co., Goleta, Calif., 1980—. Served to lt. (j.g.) USNR, 1964-67. Recipient Letter of Appreciation, Nat. Security Agy., 1967. Home: 148 San Milano Dr Goleta CA 93117 Office: 6767 Hollister Ave Goleta CA 93117

FIELD, REBECCA ANN, psychologist; b. Denver, Dec. 18, 1934; d. Herbert P. and Marjorie (Sharp) F.; m. Kenneth Gordon, Sept. 5, 1959; children—David B., Robert W. B.A., No. Colo. State U., 1957; M.A., Calif. Inst. Integral Studies, 1977, Ph.D., 1981. Camp counselor Girl Scouts U.S.A., Colorado Springs, Colo., 1955, Flint, Mich., 1956; tchr. Anchorage Pub. Schs., 1957-58, Markham (Ill.) Pub. Schs., 1959-65; sr. citizens coordinator W. Valley Coll., Saratoga, Calif., 1977; home social worker Odd Fellows Home, Saratoga, 1977-78; psychol. counselor, Los Gatos, Calif., 1981—; cons., lectr. in field. Recipient 1st prize Sri Aurobindo Centennial Essay Contest, 1973; Kern Found. grantee, 1979-81. Mem. Assn. Transpersonal Psychology, Am. Futurist Assn., Nat. Speakers Assn., W. Valley Republican Women, San Jose C. of C., Alpha Psi Omega. Clubs: Toastmasters (pres.), The Seekers Quest (dir.), Rebekah. Contbr. articles to profl. jours. Address: 105 Vista del Campo Los Gatos CA 95030

FIELD, THOMAS WALTER, JR., supermarket chain executive; b. Alhambra, Calif., Nov. 2, 1933; s. Thomas Walter and Pietje (Slagveld) F.; student Stanford U., 1951-53; m. Ruth Inez Oxley, Apr. 10, 1959; children—Julie, Sherry, Cynthia, Thomas Walter, III, James. Vice pres. retail ops. Alpha Beta Co., La Habra, Calif., 1972-73, sr. v.p., 1973-75, exec. v.p., 1975-76, pres., chief exec. officer, 1976-81; pres. Am. Stores Co., 1981—, also chief operating officer. Bd. dirs. La Habra Boys' Club. Mem. Calif. Retailers Assn. (dir.), Automobile Club So. Calif. (adv. bd.). Republican. Office: Am Stores Co 709 E South Temple Salt Lake City UT 84127*

FIELDEN, C. FRANKLIN, III, educator; b. Gulfport, Miss., Aug. 4, 1946; s. C. Franklin and Georgia Freeman F.; student Claremont Men's Coll., 1964-65; A.B., Colo. Coll., 1970; M.S., George Peabody Coll. Tchrs., 1976, Ed.S., 1979. Tutor Proyecto El Guacio, San Sebastian, P.R., 1967-68; asst. tchr. GET-SET Project, Colorado Springs, Colo., 1969-70, co-tchr., 1970-75, asst. dir., 1972-75; tutor Early Childhood Edn. Project, Nashville, 1975-76; public policy intern Donner-Belmont Child Care Center, Nashville, 1976-77; asst. to urban minister Nashville Presbytery, 1977; intern to prin. Steele Elem. Sch., Colorado Springs, 1977-78, tchr., 1978—; lectr. Arapahoe Community Coll., Littleton, Colo., 1981—; instr. Met. State Coll., Denver, 1981—; cons. Jubail Human Resources Devel. Inst., Saudi Arabia, 1982. Mem. governing bd. GET-SET Project, 1969-79; mem. Nashville Children's Issues Task Force, 1976-77; mem. Tenn. United Meth. Task Force on Children and Youth, 1976-77; mem. ad hoc bd. trustees Tenn. United Meth. Agy. on Children and Youth, 1976-77; mem. So. Regional Edn. Bd. Task Force on Parent-Caregiver Relationships, 1976-77; mem. day care com. Colo. Commn. Children and their Families, 1981-82; mem. El Paso County Sch. Dist. #11 Staff Devel. Coordinating Council, 1982—. Recipient Arts/Bus./Edn. award, 1983; NIMH fellow, 1976. Mem. Assn. Supervision and Curriculum Devel., Nat. Assn. Edn. Young Children, Colo. Assn. Edn. Young Children (legis. com. 1979—, governing bd. 1980—, exec. com. 1980—, sec. 1980—, research conf. chmn. 1982), Pikes Peak Assn. Edn. Young Children, Am. Film Inst., Colorado Springs Fine Arts Center, Huguenot Soc. London, Nat. Trust Historic Preservation, Phi Delta Kappa. Presbyterian. Club: Country of Colo. Home: PO Box 7766 Colorado Springs CO 80933 Office: 1720 N Weber Colorado Springs CO 80907

FIELDEN, GEORGIA FREEMAN, interior designer; b. Alexandria, La., Aug. 3, 1919; d. John D. and Landis (Barton) Freeman; m. Clarence

Franklin Fielden Jr., July 16, 1942; children—Clarence Franklin III, Landis Michaux. Student fine arts Ward-Belmont, 1932-37, Blue Mountain Coll., 1937-38; B.S., George Peabody Coll., 1941; postgrad. N.Y. Sch. Interior Design, 1953. Head dept. arts and crafts Camp Bon Air, Sparta, Tenn., 1939-42; asst. instr. fine arts demonstration sch., Peabody Coll., 1940-41; instr. fine arts Jackson (Miss.) Pub. Schs., 1941-42; lectr., interior designer, Colorado Springs, Colo., 1952-67; design cons., Denver, 1968—. Mem. AAUW, Am. Inst. Interior Designers (sec., 1959-60), Am. Soc. Interior Designers, English Speaking Union, Huguenot Soc. London, Huguenot Soc. Founders Manakin Colony of Va., Constrn. Specifications Inst., DAR, Illuminating Engring. Soc. (asso.), Denver Art Mus., Nat. Trust Hist. Preservation, Nat. Soc. Lit. and Arts, Internat. Platform Assn., PEO, Nat. Geneal. Soc., Nat. Home Fashion League. Presbyterian. Clubs: Rotary Ann, Soroptimists. Contbr. articles to profl. jours. Office: 518 Seventeeth Suite 260 Denver CO 80202

FIELDS, DARWIN DALE, environmental health and safety engineer; b. Jeffersonville, Ind., Sept. 20, 1948; s. Aaron and Lillian (Morgan) F.; m. Ramona Ann Moore, Aug. 20, 1977 (div.). B.S. in Bus. Mgmt., Ind. U., 1970; M.S. in Fin., U. Ariz., 1978; cert. Safety Profl. Lectr. hazard control tech. Ind. U., Bloomington, 1974-77; safety supr. Douglas Reduction Works, Phelps Dodge Corp., Douglas, Ariz., 1978-79; environ. health and safety engr. Hughes Aircraft Co., Tucson, 1979—. Served with U.S. Army, 1970-72. Mem. Am. Soc. Safety Engrs., (pres. chpt.). Home: 8301 E Louise Tucson AZ 85730 Office: Hughes Aircraft Co PO Box 11337 Tucson AZ 85734

FIELDS, JOYCE M., fin. exec.; b. Indpls., July 24, 1947; d. Martin Douglas and Edith (Gold) Garfield; B.B.A. with distinction, U. Mich., 1969; 1 dau., Jessica. Portfolio analyst Merrill Lynch, Pierce, Fenner & Smith, N.Y.C., 1969-70; securities analyst Shearson, Hayden Stone, N.Y.C., 1971-72; asst. to treas. Knapp King-Size Corp., Brockton, Mass., 1973-75; asst. treas. The Times Mirror Co., Los Angeles, 1975—. Mem. Los Angeles Soc. Fin. Analysts. Office: The Times Mirror Co Times Mirror Sq Los Angeles CA 90053

FIELDS, LEE ARTHUR, manufacturing company executive; b. Greenwood, La., May 27, 1932; s. George and Mary (Birdsong) F.; student Long Beach City Coll., 1966-68; m. Velma Myles, Aug. 5, 1953 (div.); children—Patricia, Gwendolyn, Brenda, Geanell, Lee Arthur, Belinda, DeAndria, Leah Megan; m. 2d, Syvilla Armstrong Pettiford, May 4, 1982. Nurses aide VA, Shreveport, La., 1956-60; urol. asst. VA, Long Beach, Calif., 1960-75, hemodialysis technician, 1975-78; owner, mgr. craft products mfg. bus., Long Beach, 1979—; owner, dir. nursing facility for handicapped. Active Nat. Republican Congressional Com., Norman Rockwell Mus. Soc., PTA, NAACP; mem. Rep. Presdl. Task Force. Served with U.S. Army, 1951-54. Decorated Purple Heart. Recipient cert. of recognition Nat. Rep. Congressional Com., 1980; various service awards VA. Mem. Nat. Fedn. Ind. Bus., Nat. Urol. Assn., Long Beach Area C. of C., Calhoun Collectors' Soc. Home: 2041 Caspian Ave Long Beach CA 90810 Office: 1819 W Anaheim St Long Beach CA 90813

FIELDS, RICHARD STANLEY, anesthesiologist; b. Cleve., July 17, 1937; s. Stanley D. and Nanette K. (Kraft) F.; B.S. in Chemistry, Yale U., 1955; M.D., Albany (N.Y.) Med. Coll., 1963; J.D., Pepperdine U., Malibu, Calif., 1978; m. Carol B. Smurl, July 16, 1960; children—Katherine D., Jacqueline M., Richard Stanley. Intern, then resident in anesthesiology Los Angeles County Gen. Hosp., 1963-66; practice medicine specializing in anesthesiology, Orange, Calif., 1968—; mem. staff St. Joseph Hosp., Orange, Children's Hosp. of Orange County (Calif.); admitted to Calif. bar, 1978; asso. firm Ronald L.M. Goldman, Inc., Marina del Rey, Calif., 1978—. Served as officer M.C., USAR, 1966-68. Mem. AMA, Am. Soc. Anesthesiologists, Am. Bar Assn., Calif. Med. Assn., Calif. Soc. Anesthesiologists, Orange County Med. Assn. Office: 12440 Firestone Blvd Norwalk CA 90650 also 13737 Fiji Way Marina del Rey CA 90291

FIERHELLER, GEORGE ALFRED, communications company executive; b. Toronto, Ont., Can., Apr. 26, 1933; s. Harold Parsons and Ruth Hathaway (Bauld) F.; B.A., U. Toronto, 1955; LL.D., Concordia U.; m. Glenna E. Fletcher, Apr. 17, 1957; children—Vicki Elaine, Lori Ann. With IBM, Toronto, 1955-68, account mgr., 1962-65, mktg. mgr., 1966-68; founder, pres. Systems Dimensions Ltd., Ottawa, Ont., 1968-79; pres., chief exec. officer Premier Cablesystems Ltd., Vancouver, B.C., Can., 1979—; dir. B.C. Systems Corp., Extendicare Inc., GBC Capital Ltd., Dominion Scottish Investments, Oakwood Petroleums Ltd., Calgary. Gen. chmn. United Appeal Campaign Ottawa, 1972; chmn. campaign Carleton U., 1975-77, also chmn. bd. govs., 1977-79; mem. adv. com. Norman Paterson Sch. Internat. Affairs; bd. dirs., v.p. United Way Ottawa, 1975-79, Opera Ottawa, 1970-71; trustee, mem. exec. com. Nat. Arts Centre, 1973-79; trustee Royal Ottawa Hosp., 1978-79; bd. dirs. Vancouver Opera; bd. govs. Simon Fraser U., Vancouver, 1981—; chmn. United Way campaign, Vancouver, 1981; trustee Vancouver Gen. Hosp. Found., 1981—; chmn. B.C. Council of 80's, 1980-83; mem. Vancouver Centennial Commn., 1983—. Mem. Can. Info. Processing Soc. (pres., 1970-71), Young Pres. Orgn., Conf. Bd., Can. Assn. Data Processing Service Orgns. (sec.-treas., dir. 1971-73), Cert. Certification of Computer Profls. (founding com.). Clubs: Shaughnessy Golf and Country, Vancouver Lawn Tennis, Vancouver, Rideau. Contbr. articles to profl. jours. Home: 4184 Musqueam Dr Vancouver BC V6N 3R7 Canada Office: 1818 Cornwall Ave Vancouver BC V6J 1C7 Canada

FIFE, WILLIAM ARTHUR, airline pilot; b. Corning, Iowa, Dec. 19, 1919; s. Lavern Harvey and Grace Lenore (VanHouten) F.; student U. Iowa, 1939-41, United Air Lines Flight Sch., 1945; m. Mildred Gwendolyn Mercer, Dec. 24, 1943; children—Claire Louise, Cheryl Liane, Gregory William. First officer United Air Lines, Denver, 1945-52, capt., 1952-80, ret., 1980, sr. 1st officer, Airline Pilots Assn. rep., 1946-47. Bd. dirs. Broadmore Civic Assn., Littleton, Colo., 1953-55. Served to 1st lt. USAAF, 1942-45. Decorated D.F.C., Air medal with five oak leaf clusters. Mem. Airline Pilots Assn., Nat. Wildlife Assn. Democrat. Methodist (finance officer 1955-65). Club: Colo. Hunting and Fishing. Home: 5081 W Rowland Ave Littleton CO 80123

FIGEL, WALTER, JR., air force officer; b. Passaic, N.J., Aug. 24, 1941; s. Walter and Anna (Ruschak) F.; B.A. in Chemistry, U. Pa., 1964; M.S. in Aerospace Engring., Air Force Inst. Tech., 1969; Ph.D. in Bus. Adminstrn., U. Nebr., 1977; m. Darlene Dayton, Apr. 17, 1971; children—Scott, Walter Andrew. Commd. 2d lt. U.S. Air Force, 1965, advanced through grades to lt. col., 1980—; minuteman combat comdr. Malmstrom AFB, 1965-69; systems analyst Offutt AFB, 1969-75; Dept. Def. automatic data processing staff officer Def. Communications Agy., Washington, 1975-78; chief program mgmt. div. NORAD Combat Ops. Ctr., Colorado Springs, Colo., 1978-79, dir. ADP resources, 1979-80, chief space resource and ADP tech. support div., 1980-82; comdr. 6002 Computer Services Squadron, Hickam AFB, Hawaii, 1982—; adj. prof. Va. Poly. Inst., Washington, 1977-78, U. Colo., Colorado Springs, 1978-82, U. Hawaii, Honolulu, 1982—; cons. ALFI Assocs., Inc., Reston, Va., 1977-80. Chmn., Cub Scouts pack 1970, Boy Scouts Am., Reston, 1976-78. Decorated Meritorious Service medal (2), Joint Service Commendation medal, Air Force Commendation medal (2). Mem. Armed Forces Communications and Electronics Assn. (v.p. 1977-78, 80-81, founding chpt. officer 1977; Regional V.P. Honor award 1977), Inst. Mgmt. Scis., Ops. Research Soc. Am., Am. Radio Relay League, Assn. Computing Machinery, AIAA, Am. Philatelic Soc., Beta Gamma Sigma. Club: Masons. Home: 94-455 Kapakapa Way Mililani Town HI 96789 Office: 6002 Computer Services Squadron Hickam AFB HI 96853

FILCHAK, JOHN ADAM JAMES, chemist; b. New Buffalo, Mich., Nov. 1, 1925; s. John and Eva Victoria (Nickolin) F.; B.S., U. Puget Sound, 1950; m. Linda Melitta Krieger, Apr. 25, 1964; children—George, Gaylen, Lucinda. Chemist, Fed. Supply Service, GSA, Seattle, 1950-60, chief research and testing br., Seattle and Auburn, Wash., 1961-71, regional dir. quality assurance div., Auburn, 1971-82; cons. coating engr. Daniel G. Jarvie & Assos., Seattle, 1982—; instr. Highline Community Coll., Seattle, evenings 1966-70; mem. adv. com. paint procurement Wash. Dept. Purchasing, 1960—. Pres., Messiah Luth. Ch., Auburn, 1971-74, chmn. fin. com. Served with AUS, 1944-46. Named Man of Year, Seattle Fed. Exec. Bd., 1966; Fellow Am. Soc. Quality Control (past pres. Seattle), Pacific N.W. Soc. Coatings Tech. (past pres., rep.), Fedn. Socs. Coating Tech. (dir., chmn. fedn. specification com.). Clubs: Moose, Elks. Home: 1505 23d St SE Auburn WA 98002 Office: 4540 8th Ave NE #801 Seattle WA 98105

FILEP, ROBERT THOMAS, business exec.; b. New Brunswick, N.J., Dec. 2, 1931; s. John Kossuth and Irma Antonio (Matyus) F.; B.S., Rutgers U., 1953; M.A., Columbia, 1957; Ph.D., U. So. Calif., 1966; m. Francis Tudor Moxley, Aug. 8, 1964; children—Felicia Allison, Ian Robert. Tchr. sci., coach Teaneck (N.J.) High Sch., 1953-56; asst. dir. admissions Rensselaer Poly. Inst., Troy, N.Y., 1957-59; dir. admissions and aid Mills Coll. of Edn., N.Y.C., 1959-61; sec. corp., dir. info. and training div. Center for Programmed Instruction Inst. Ednl. Tech., Columbia U., 1961-63; asso. investigator cinema research U. So. Calif., 1963-65; human factors scientist System Devel. Corp., Santa Monica, Calif., 1965-67; v.p., dir. studies Inst. Ednl. Devel., El Segundo, Calif., 1967-72; asso. commr., dir. Nat. Center for Ednl. Tech., U.S. Office of Edn., HEW, 1972-73; prof. communications and edn., dir. University-Wide Learning Systems Center, U. So. Calif., Los Angeles, 1974-79; pres. Communications 21 Corp., Redondo Beach, Calif., 1979—. Mem. Mayor's Commn. on Cable TV; bd. dirs. English-Speaking Union, Los Angeles. Served with USAF, 1953-55. Fulbright-Hays lectr., India, 1975. Mem. Nat. Soc. Performance and Instruction (past pres.), Ednl. Media Council (past pres.), Am. Psychol. Assn., Internat. Inst. Communications, AIAA, AAAS, Chi Phi. Editor: Prospectives in Programming, 1963. Contbg. editor Ednl. Communications Tech. Jour., 1964—; contbr. chpts. to books, articles to profl. jours. Home: 3104 Palos Verdes Dr N Palos Verdes Estates CA 90274 Office: 1611 S Pacific Coast Hwy Suite 206 Redondo Beach CA 90277

FILIPEK, LORRAINE HENRIETTA, research geochemist; b. Dearborn, Mich., Oct. 27, 1947; d. Henry Joseph and Sophie Patricia (Slaga) F.; m. Allen Lee Eavy, Oct. 24, 1974; m. 2d, Stacy Walters, Feb. 24, 1979. B.S. U. Mich., 1969; M.A., Johns Hopkins U., 1974; Ph.D., U. Mich., 1979. NRC post doctoral research assoc. U.S. Geol. Survey, Denver, 1979-80, research chemist, 1980—. Balt. Gas and Electric fellow, 1972-73; Gilman fellow, 1973-74; Scott Turner fellow, summer 1977; Rackman predoctoral fellow, 1978-79; Continuing Edn. Women scholar, 1977-78; Sigma Xi Student Research grantee, 1977-78; Geol. Soc. Am. Student Research grantee, 1977-78. Mem. Geol. Soc. Am., Geochem. Soc., Assn. Exploration Geochemists, Denver Regional Econ. Geologists Soc., Assn. Women Geoscientists, Nat. Assn. Female Execs., NOW, Sigma Xi, Tau Beta Pi. Contbr. numerous articles to profl. jours. Office: US Geol Survey Fed Ctr MS955 Denver CO 80225

FILLENWORTH, PEGGY ANN MYHRE, utility company executive, sailboat dealer; b. Minot, N.D., June 10, 1951; d. Clayton Wallace and Arlene Betty (Ostrom) Myhre; m. John C. Fillenworth, Aug. 24, 1974 (dec.). B.S. with honors in Home Econs., Mont. State U., 1973. Tchr. home econs. pub. schs., Absavokee, Mont., 1973-74; drapery cons. Missoula Mont. Mercantile, 1975; sec., receptionist Culbertson, Inc. Missoula, 1976; activities coordinator Glendive (Mont.) Community Nursing Home, 1976-79; consumer relations rep. Mont. Dakota Utilities, Glendive, 1979—; sec. Energy Adv. Bd.; lectr. in field. Mem. Glendive Community Hosp. Long Range Planning Com.; pres. adv. bd. Ret. Sr. Vol. Program, 1983; mem. eastern adv. bd. Energy Share Mont., 1983. Named Young Career Women of Yr. Glendive Bus. and Profl. Womans Club, 1981. Mem. Am. Home Econs. Assn., Big Sky Home Economists in Bus. (pres.), Mont. Home Economists Assn., Beta Sigma Phi (Alpha Iota chpt. pres. 1980, Girl Yr., Woman Yr. 1980, 81). Lutheran. Columnist local newspapers, 1980-83. Home: 104 Juniper St Hillcrest Subdiv Glendive MT 59330 Office: Montana Dakota Utilities Box 201 Glendive MT 59330

FILOSA, GARY FAIRMONT RANDOLPH DE MARCO, II, financier; b. Wilder, Vt., Feb. 22, 1931; s. Gary F.R. and Rosaline (Falzarano) F.; grad. Mt. Hermon Sch., 1950; Ph.B., U. Chgo., 1954; B.A., U. Americas, 1967; M.A., Calif. Western U., 1968; Ph.D., U.S. Internat. U., 1970; m. Edith Wilson du Motier Schoenberg, Nov. 24, 1953 (div.); children—Marc Christian Bazire III, Gary Fairmont Randolph De Marco III. Account exec., editor house publs. Robertson, Buckley & Gotsch, Inc., Chgo., 1953-54; account exec., copywriter Fuller, Smith & Ross, Inc., N.Y.C., 1954-55; editor Apparel Arts mag., Esquire, Inc., N.Y.C., 1955-56; pres., chmn. bd. Filosa Publs., N.Y.C., 1956-61, pub. Teenage, Teenlife, Talent, Campus Personalities, Stardust, Mystery Digest, Rock and Roll Roundup, Rustic Rhythm mags., N.Y.C., 1956-60; pres. Montclair Sch., 1958-60; exec. asst. to Benjamin A. Javits, 1961-62; dean adminstrn. Postgrad. Center for Mental Health, N.Y.C., 1962-64; dir. Filosa Films Internat., 1964-67; v.p. acad. affairs World Acad., San Francisco, 1967-68; asst. headmaster, instr. Latin, San Miguel Sch., 1968-69; assoc. prof. philosophy Art Coll., San Francisco, 1969-70; v.p. acad. affairs, dean of faculty Internat. Inst., Phoenix, 1968-73; pres. Universite Universelle, 1970-73; v.p. acad. affairs, dean Summer Sch., Internat. Community Coll., Los Angeles, 1970-72; chmn. bd., pres. Am. Assn. Social Directories, 1970-78; surfing coach U. Calif.-Irvine, 1975-78, Coastline Community Coll., Fountain Valley, Calif., 1976-79; chmn. Social Directory of Calif., 1967-78; producer TV series Surfing USA, 1980-83. Chmn. Pubs. for John F. Kennedy, 1960, Educators for Reelection of Ivy Baker Priest, 1970; mem. exec. com. Brown for Gov. Calif., 1974. Served with AUS, 1954-55. Recipient DAR Citizenship award, 1959. Mem. Am. Surfing Assn. (founder, pres. 1974—), Internat. Amateur Surfing Fedn. (founder, pres. 1974), Internat. Fedn. Profl. Surfers (founder, pres. 1977), Internat. Council for Advancement of Surfing (founder, pres. 1977—), Alumni Assn. U. Americas (pres. 1967-70, dir.), United Shareowners Am., World Affairs Council San Francisco, Am. Acad. Polit. Sci., Sigma Omicron Lambda. Democrat. Episcopalian. Clubs: Mt. Kenya Safari (Nairobi); Chapultepec (Mexico City); KonaKai (San Diego); Commonwealth, Sierra (San Francisco); Embajadores (U. of Americas, Puebla, Mexico); Los Angeles Athletic, Town Hall (Los Angeles). Author: Technology Enters 21st Century, 1966; (with Peter Duchin) Feather Light (musical), 1968; No Public Funds for Nonpublic Schools, 1968; Creative Function of the College President, 1969; The Surfer's Almanac, 1977. Contbr. articles to profl. publs. including World Book, Sci. Digest, Fgn. Affairs Quar. Office: Box 1315 Beverly Hills CA 90213

FINCH, JEANNETTE MARION, ednl. adminstr.; b. Seattle, June 17, 1921; d. Joseph Harold and Rina (Hansen) F.; student Northwest Coll., Seattle, 1941-44; B.A., Seattle Pacific Coll., 1971; M.A., U. Calif., Riverside, 1973; Ph.D., Laurence U., Santa Barbara, 1983, Tchr., Children's Home, Rupaidia, India, 1946-48; asst. registrar Northwest Coll., Seattle, 1949-52; tchr. Wolfe County (Ky.) Schs., 1954-58; tchr. Paramount Park Sch., Seattle, 1960-61, Garden Grove (Calif.) Day Sch., 1961-62, Kahnack Acad., Glendale, Calif., 1962-64, San Bernardino (Calif.) County Schs., 1968-73; co-founder, dir. Teen Valley Ranch, Redlands, Calif., 1964—; founder, adminstr. Creative Ednl. Center, Redlands, 1974—. Mem. Assn. Suprs. and Curriculum Developers, Council Exceptional Children, Calif. Assn. Neurologically Handicapped Children, AAUW. Home: Route 2 Box 120 Redlands CA 92373 Office: PO Box 1192 Redlands CA 92373

FINCH, THOMAS WESLEY, corrosion engineer; b. Alhambra, Calif., Dec. 17, 1946; s. Charles Phillip and Marian Louisa (Bushey) F.; m. Jinx L. Heath, Apr. 1979. Student Colo. Sch. Mines, 1964-68. Assayer, prospector Raymond P. Heon, Inc., Idaho Springs, Colo., 1968; corrosion engr. Cathodic Protection Service, Denver, 1973-80, area mgr., Lafayette, La., 1980-81; area mgr. Corrintec/USA, Farmington, N.Mex., 1981—. Served with C.E., U.S. Army, 1968-72. Mem. Nat. Assn. Corrosion Engrs., Soc. Am. Mil. Engrs., U.S. Ski Assn., Am. Security Council (nat. adv. bd. 1978—), Kappa Sigma. Republican. Lutheran. Home: 2629 Cliffside Farmington NM 89401 Office: PO Box 388 Farmington NM 87401

FINE, CLAIRE, medical executive search company executive; b. Hammond, Ind., Oct. 19, 1942; d. Theodore I. and Gilda (Mallah) Grossman; m. Michael David Fine, Mar. 31, 1974; 1 son, Daniel Jonas. B.A. in Psychology, CUNY, 1964; postgrad. U. Md., 1967-68; postgrad. in medicine George Washington U., 1968-69. Sec.-technician dept. neurology Cornell U. Med. Sch., 1965; counselor Beth Israel Hosp., N.Y.C., 1966; research technician Children's Hosp. Washington, 1967-68; sr. project coordinator med. follow-up agy. Nat. Acad. Scis., Washington, 1969-73; account exec. V.I.P. Agy., Los Angeles, 1974-77; pres., Med. Search Assocs., Reseda, Calif., 1978—. Jewish.

FINE, DONALD EMERSON, real estate company executive; b. Dayton, Ohio, Sept. 14, 1936; s. John Emerson and Louise Jane (Thayer) F.; B.S., U. Dayton, 1958; m. Edith Hope, Dec. 28, 1965; children—Michael Scott, Gregory Stuart. Bank examiner U.S. Treasury, Los Angeles, 1961-62; tchr. Mira Costa High Sch., Manhattan Beach, Calif., 1965-68; economist Metlox Mfg. Co., Manhattan Beach, 1967-73; pres. Lomas Santa Fe Realty, Solana Beach, Calif., 1977—. Bd. dirs. Encinitas Sch. Facilities Corp., 1979—; bd. dirs. United Way, North San Diego County, 1977—, campaign chmn., 1980. Recipient Spl. United Way award, 1980. Mem. Calif. Assn. Realtors (state dir. 1979), San Dieguito Bd. Realtors (dir. 1980-81). Republican. Episcopalian. Clubs: Rotary (dir.), Univ., Theta Chi. Home: PO Box 62 Del Mar CA 92014 Office: 265 Santa Helena Suite 101 Solana Beach CA 92075

FINE, KENNETH, psychotherapist, marriage and family counselor, stress/time management consultant; b. Phila., May 9, 1949; s. Bernard and Harriet (Brier) F. B.A. in Exptl. Psychology, Fla. Atlantic U., 1979; M.A. in Clin. Psychology, Antioch U., Los Angeles, 1980; Ph.D. in Clin. Psychology, U. Humanistic Studies, 1982. Cert. stress mgmt. trainer; lic. marriage and family counselor, Nev. Electronic music instr. Lebanon Valley Coll., Annville, Pa., 1974-76; substance abuse counselor Do It Now Found., Hollywood, Calif., 1978-80; alcoholism counselor Comprehensive Care Corp., North Las Vegas (Nev.) Hosp., 1980-82; prof. psychology Univ. Humanistic Studies, Las Vegas, 1982-83; pvt. practice psychotherapy, stress/time mgmt. cons. bus. and industry, Las Vegas, 1982—; writer, producer, host holistic health show Sta. KUNV, Las Vegas; lectr., condr. workshops on stress and biofeedback. Mem. Nat. Assn. Psychotherapists, Am. Personnel and Guidance Assn., Am. Mental Health Counselors Assn., Biofeedback Soc. Am. Developed Calif. Projective Music Test, Los Angeles, 1980; producer, dir. film A Record Is Born, 1979; author booklet: Unstressing, 1983; contbr. articles to publs. Office: 3790 Paradise Rd Suite 250 Las Vegas NV 89109

FINE, RICHARD ISAAC, lawyer; b. Milw., Jan. 22, 1940; s. Jack and Frieda Fine; m. Mary Ellen Olman, Nov. 25, 1982. B.S., U. Wis., 1961; J.D., U. Chgo., 1964; Ph.D. in Internat. Law, London Sch. Econs. and Polit. Sci., 1967. Admitted to Ill. bar, 1964, D.C. bar, 1972, Calif. bar, 1973, U.S. Supreme Ct. bar, 1972; trial atty. antitrust div. Dept. Justice, 1968-72; chief antitrust div. Los Angeles City Atty.'s Office, 1973-74, spl. counsel govt. efficiency com., 1973-74, individual practice, Los Angeles, 1974—, prof. (N.Y.) Syracuse U. Law Sch. overseas program, summers 1970-72; antitrust adv. bd. Bur. Nat. Affairs-Antitrust, 1980—. Mem. Am. Bar Assn. (chmn. coms.), Am. Soc. Internat. Law, Am. Fgn. Law Assn., Internat. Law Assn., Brit. Inst. Internat. and Comparative Law, World Peace Through Law Center, State Bar Calif. (chmn. com. and sect. antitrust and trade regulation law 1978—), Los Angeles County Bar Assn. (chmn. antitrust com. and sect. 1977-80), Ill. Bar Assn., Phi Delta Phi. Contbr. numerous articles to profl. jours. Home: 5331 Horizon Dr Malibu CA 90265 Office: 10100 Santa Monica Blvd Suite 250 Los Angeles CA 90067

FINE, VIRGINIA OWENS, psychologist, educator; b. Great Falls, Mont., Apr. 18, 1921; d. Jesse Thomas and Helen (Hanner) Owens; m. Robert Day Kemble, Oct. 29, 1944; children—Stephen Brooks, Brian Sanford, David Boyce, Marcia Jean, Janet Kemble Onopa; m. 2d, Jules Fine, July 6, 1969; stepchildren—Joan Fine Hudson, Amy, Sylvia. B.A., Okla. State U., 1943; M.Ed., U. Hawaii, 1964, Ph.D., 1975. Lic. psychologist, Hawaii. Research staff U. Hawaii, 1963-69, counselor Lab. Sch., 1969-71, counselor intern, Counseling and Testing Center, 1971-73, lectr., 1968-71, 77; therapist Human Resources Devel. Center, Honolulu, 1974-78; pvt. practice psychology, Honolulu, 1978—; lectr. extensions Pepperdine U., 1975-80, Antioch U., 19—. Mem. AAUW, Am. Psychol. Assn., Hawaii Psychol. Assn., Am. Personnel and Guidance Assn., Western Psychol. Assn., Hawaii Personnel and Guidance Assn., Assn. Humanistic Psychology (pres. chpt. 1981-83), Orthopsychiatic Assn., Nat. Assn. Family Relations, Kappa Alpha Theta. Democrat. Unitarian. Contbr. articles to profl. jours. Home: 1042 Maunauili Loop Kailua HI 96734 Office: 615 Piikoi St 1404 Honolulu HI 96814

FINEMAN, KENNETH ROBERT, clin. psychologist, social services adminstr.; b. Los Angeles, July 11, 1943; s. Maurice and Gertrude (Jacobson) F.; B.A., UCLA, 1965, M.A. (fellow), 1967, Ph.D. (Newman fellow), 1972; m. Doreen Binette Moss, Jan. 19, 1968; children—Lorin Brooke, Carolyn Michelle, Intern in clin. psychology Los Angeles Child Achievement Center, Sherman Oaks, Calif., 1967-71; asst. dir. child and adolescent psychiat. unit Long Beach (Calif.) Neuropsychiat. Inst., 1971-72; postdoctoral intern clin. psychology Neuropsychiat. Med. Group, Huntington Beach, Calif., 1972-73; dir. psychol. services Family and Child Mental Health Center, Huntington Beach, 1973—; asst. clin. prof. med. psychology U. Calif., Irvine, 1973—; cons. and supr. Coast Community Coll. System, 1972—; cons. to U.S. Fire Adminstrn., 1977—, various hosps., sch. dists., TV stations, 1972—; program dir. children's mental health unit Huntington Intercommunity Hosp., 1973-81; faculty supr. Calif. Sch. Profl. Psychology, Los Angeles campus, 1975—. Diplomate Am. Bd. Profl. Psychology, Am. Bd. Clin. Feedback, Am. Acad. Behavioral Medicine. Mem. Calif. State Psychol. Assn. (dir. 1978-79, clin. div. 1976-78, chmn. fire services and arson prevention com. 1976—), Orange County Psychol. Assn. (pres. 1979), Am. Psychol. Assn., Am. Soc. Clin. Hypnosis, Internat. Neuropsychology Soc., Fedn. Am. Scientists, Am. Assn. Mental Deficiency, Assn. Advancement of Psychology (chief field rep. Calif. 1977—), Nat. Acad. Neuropsychologists, AAAS, Am. Assn. Biofeedback Clinicians, Orange County Soc. Clin. Hypnosis (treas. 1978, dir. 1978-81), Calif. Assn. Clin. Hypnosis Socs. (bd. govs. 1980, pres. 1982), Am. Law-Psychology Soc. Author: Counseling and Interviewing the Juvenile Firesetter, Vols. I, II, 1982; contbr. chpts. to books, articles to profl. jours.; editor The Profl.

Psychologist, 1974-78; asso. editor Am. Jour. Clin. Biofeedback, 1978—. Office: Huntington Med Towers 17822 Beach Blvd Suite 437 Huntington Beach CA 92647

FINGER, PHILLIP REID, college administrator; b. St. Joseph, Mo., Feb. 9, 1941; s. Henry Reid and Norma Laura (Van Buskirk) F.; B.A., U. Wash., 1963; M.B.A., Central Mo. U., 1974; m. Dorothy Ann Lund, Sept. 4, 1977; 1 son, Derek Reid. Sr. personnel asst. Seattle City Light, 1969-72; media technician III, Bellevue (Wash.) Community Coll., 1976-77, fin. aid supr., 1977-78, asst. dir.-fin. aid, 1978-79; asst. dir. fin. aid N. Seattle Community Coll., 1979-81; dir. fin. aid Yakima Valley Community Coll., 1981—. Served in USAF, 1964-68; Vietnam. Mem. Wash. Fin. Aid Assn. (pres.-elect), Wash. Community Coll. Fin. Aid Assn. (exec. com.). Presbyterian and Catholic. Office: 16th and Nob Hill Blvd Yakima WA 98907

FINK, JAMES WILLIAM, engineering/manufacturing executive; b. Los Angeles, Sept. 11, 1939; s. Frederick G. and Alma Irene (Eslick) F.; m. Linda Reavis, Apr. 22, 1967; children—Christi, Kevin, Andrew. B.A., Azusa Pacific U., 1961; postgrad. Calif. State U.-Los Angeles, Calif. State U.-Fullerton, 1962-63. Various mgmt. positions Revell, Inc., Venice, Calif., 1965-77, dir. internat. materials control, 1977-78, v.p. corp. materials mgmt., 1978-79, v.p. engring., 1979—, dir. Revell Engring., Ltd., Hong Kong, 1980—, corp. sec., 1982—; officer all Revell subs.; lectr. MBA program Azusa Pacific U. Mem. Am. Prodn. and Inventory Control Soc., Nat. Assn. Purchasing Mgmt., Internat. Material Mgmt. Soc., Am. Soc. Quality Control, Fgn. Trade Assn. So. Calif. Republican. Office: 4223 Glencoe Ave Venice CA 90291

FINK, JOHN PHILLIP, psychologist; b. Seattle, Wash., May 6, 1942; s. John (stepfather) and Irma Ferne (Ray) Raney; m. Susan Marie Siron, July 11, 1964; children—Randy, Danny. B.S. in Edn., U. Idaho, 1964, M.S. in Psychology, 1967; Ed.D. in Counseling, U. N. Colo., 1977. Lic. psychologist, Idaho. Psychologist, Children's Hosp., Denver, 1967-69; mental health coordinator, 1976-77; sch. psychologist Jefferson County (Colo.) Schs., 1970-73, Coeur d'Alene Sch., Idaho, 1978—; cons. in field. Bd. dirs. jr. tackle football, Coeur d'Alene; Mem. Am. Psychol. Assn., Idaho. Psychol. Assn., Idaho Sch. Psychologists Assn., Nat. Assn. Sch. Psychologists. Lutheran. Club: Avondale Golf (Haydenlk). Home: 11260 Strahorn Rd Hayden Lake ID 83835 Office: 311 N 10th St Coeur d'Alene ID

FINK, PATRICK TERRY, bioenvironmental engineer; b. Newark, Mar. 11, 1950; s. Edward Joseph and Margaret Mary (Augustin) F.; B.S. in Civil Engring., Newark Coll. Engring., 1972, M.S. (teaching fellow), 1974; m. Diane E. Ramer, Dec. 29, 1974; children—Christopher, Kimberly. Civil engr. Austin Co., Roselle, N.J., 1973-75; commd. 2d lt. USAF, 1975, advanced through grades to capt., 1977; chief bioenviron. engring. USAF Hosp., Beale AFB, Calif., 1978-81; chief bioenviron. engring. services USAF Clinic, Andersen AFB, Guam, 1981—. Little League coach, Panama City, Fla., 1975. Decorated Air Force Commendation medal; recipient Jr. Bioenviron. Engr. of Yr., 1980. Mem. ASCE, Soc. Am. Mil. Engrs., Water Pollution Control Fedn., Am. Council Govtl. Indsl. Hygieneists, Tau Kappa Epsilon. Roman Catholic. Author tech. reports. Home: 8 Golden Shower Ln FPO San Francisco CA 96630 Office: USAF Clin/SGPB Anderson AFB Guam APO San Francisco CA 96334

FINKE, RONALD ALAN, psychologist; b. Columbus, Ohio, June 10, 1950; s. Phillipp William and Sally (Watson) F. B.S. cum laude in Physics, U. Tex., Austin, 1972, B.A. magna cum laude in Psychology, 1974; M.A. in Exptl. Psychology, U. N.H., 1976; Ph.D. in Exptl. Psychol., MIT, 1979. Teaching research asst. dept. psychology, U.N.H., Durham, 1974-76; inst. staff scholar dept. psychology MIT, Boston, 1976-77, teaching asst., 1977-78, Spencer found. predoctoral fellow, 1978-79; NSF postdoctoral fellow, lectr. dept. psychology Cornell U., 1979-80; Sloan found. fellow in cognitive sci. Stanford U., 1980-81; asst. prof. dept. psychology U. Calif.-Davis, 1981—. Mem. AAAS, Am. Psychol. Assn., Western Psychol. Assn., Psychonomic Soc., Phi Beta Kappa. Contbr. articles to profl. jours. Home: 3000 Cowell Apt 279 Davis CA 95616 Office: Dept Psychology U Calif Davis CA 95616

FINKELMAN, SOL, accountant; b. Warsaw, Poland, Feb. 6, 1918; s. Sam and Rose (Sapirstein) F.; came to U.S., 1923, naturalized, 1929; B.B.A., Coll. City N.Y., 1947; m. Luisa Anne Knecht, Nov. 2, 1976; children by previous marriage—Lawrence Frederick, Cynthia Lois, Richard David, Rhonda Diane, Nancy Lynne. Departmental coordinator Ludwig Baumann & Co., N.Y.C., 1936-42; sr. accountant Isaac Benwitt & Co., N.Y.C., 1946-51; partner Morris Kawin & Co., Beverly Hills, Calif., 1951-56; prin., partner Sol Finkelman & Co., Beverly Hills, 1956—; trustee pension plans, several wills. Served as fin. and lang. specialist AUS, 1943-46. Mem. Am. Inst. C.P.A.s, N.Y. State, Calif. socs. C.P.A.s. Contbr. articles to profl. jours.

FINKELSTEIN, SHELDON SY, educational administrator; b. N.Y.C., Nov. 3, 1955; s. Lou and Selma (Wolinskes) F. B.A. in Psychology and Sociology (Scholar), U. Mich., 1977, B.A. with distinction in Edn., 1978, M.A. in Guidance and Counseling, 1979. Resident dir. U. Mich., Ann Arbor, 1977-79; residence hall dir. Bowling Green (Ohio) State U., 1979-81; area coordinator Office Residence Life, No. Ariz. U., Flagstaff, 1981—, counselor, staff supr. and trainer, adminstr. student and profl. devel.; workshop presenter. Vol. instr. ARC, 1976-82. Mem. Am. Personnel and Guidance Assn., Am. Coll. Personnel Assn., Pi Lambda Theta. Office: Box 5784 No Ariz U Flagstaff AZ 86011

FINKLE, LOUIS, dentist; b. Winnipeg, Man., Can., June 25, 1912; s. Ben and Bessie (Averbach) F.; student U. Man., 1929-31; D.D.S., U. Minn., 1934; m. Mona Margaret Rosenblatt, Mar. 28, 1943; children—Brenda Marilyn Finkle Christopher, Robert, Sandra Anne Finkle Massaro, Harley Sheldon. Came to U.S., 1945, naturalized, 1957. Postgrad. Mayo Clinic, Rochester, Minn., 1934-35, Winnipeg Gen. Hosp., 1935-38; pvt. practice dentistry, Winnipeg, 1938-61; mem. attending staff Winnipeg Gen. Hosp., 1938-61; pvt. practice dentistry, Burbank, Calif., 1961—; mem. active attending staff St. Joseph's Hosp., Encino Hosp., Los Angeles-U. So. Calif. Med. Center, Cedars Sinai Lebanon Hosp.; periodontal surgeon Los Angeles Gen. Hosp.-U. So. Calif. Med. Center; dir. grad. study in oral implantology U. Calif. at Los Angeles, 1972—; examiner Am. Acad. Oral Implantology. Served to capt. RCAF, 1942-45. Fellow Royal Soc. Health (London, Eng.); mem. Internat. Acad. Orthodontics, So. Calif. Soc. Clin. Hypnosis, Am., Calif., So. Calif., San Fernando Valley, Man. dental assns., Am. Acad. Oral Implantology (admission and credential bd. examiners), Am. Acad. Implant Prosthodontics, Inst. Dental Research (chmn. West Coast). Home: 16115 Meadowcrest Rd Sherman Oaks CA 91403 Office: 3005 W Magnolia Blvd Burbank CA 91505

FINKNER, MORRIS DALE, statistician, educator, consultant; b. Akron, Colo., Feb. 11, 1921; s. Adolph Gustav and Atha Iona (Roszell) F.; m. Mary Ella Berry, Sept. 3, 1949; children—Ronald Wayne, Dale Gordon. B.S., Colo. State U., 1943; M.S., Kans. State U., 1947; Ph.D., N.C. State U., 1952. Asst. prof. Miss. State U., Mississippi State, 1947-49; biometrician U.S. Dept. Agr., Beltsville, Md., 1956-57; asst. prof. N.Mex. State U., Las Cruces, 1952-55, assoc. prof., 1958-64, prof., 1964-70, dir. and dept. head, 1970—. Served to capt. U.S. Army, 1943-46. Recipient Disting. Service award Coll. Agr. and Home Econs., 1968; 100% Dist. Govs. award Lions Club Internat., 1977. Mem. Am. Statis. Assn., Biometric Soc., Am. Soc. Agronomy, Crop Sci. Soc., Sigma Xi, Gamma Sigma Delta, Alpha Zeta. Democrat. Methodist. Club: Las Cruces Sunrise Lions (pres. 1968-69, 78-79, dist. gov. 1976-77). Contbr. articles to profl. jours. Home: 1802 Half Moon Dr Las Cruces NM 88005 Office: Box 3130 Las Cruces NM 88003

FINKNER, RALPH EUGENE, agronomist, educator; b. Akron, Colo., Mar. 24, 1925; s. A. Ed G. and Atha Iona (Roszell) F.; m. Daisy Laurene Hale, June 11, 1950; children—Twila Rene Hendrix, Lisa Gay Templeman, Lyle Gene. B.S., Colo. State U., 1950; M.S., Iowa State U., 1951, Ph.D., 1953. Biol. aid Hort. Expt. Sta., Cheyenne, Wyo., 1949; grad. asst. Iowa State U., Ames, 1950-53; plant breeder, chief plant breeder, mgr. research sta., dir. agrl. research Am. Crystal Sugar Co., Rocky Ford, Colo., 1953-66; supt. Plains Br. Sta., prof. agronomy N.Mex. State U., Clovis, 1966—; agronomist U.S. AID Paraguay, 1970, Turkey, 1971; leader Major Cereals Improvement Design Team, Egypt, 1978-79; agronomist, Egypt, 1982. Served with USN, 1945-46, USNR, 1946-50. Mem. Am. Soc. Agronomy, Am. Soc. Sugar Beet Technologists (dir. 1960-61, 66-67), Am. Crop Sci. Soc., Western Soc. Crop Sci., Am. Peanut Research and Edn. Assn. Inc., Sigma Xi (pres. 1968-69, sec. 1974-75), Alpha Zeta (treas. 1948-49), Beta Beta Beta, Sigma Gamma Delta. Methodist. Club: Rotary. Author numerous papers for tech. jours. Home: Route 2 Box 211 Clovis NM 88101 Office: Star Route Box 77 Clovis NM 88101

FINLEY, ALLEN BROWN, religious organization administrator; b. Albermarle, Va., Nov. 11, 1929; s. William Walter and Melissa (Hoover) F.; m. Ruth Ann Goodwin, Aug. 14, 1953; children—Ruth Naomi, Catherine Ann, Gayla Melissa. B.A., Bob Jones U., Greenville, S.C., 1952; M.A., Calif. Grad. Sch. Theology, 1981. Ordained to ministry Evangelical Ch. Alliance, 1952; missionary Gospel Fellowship Assn., 1952-53; Phila. office dir. Internat. Students, Inc., 1953-54; West Coast dir. Internat. Students, Inc., 1954-60; gen. dir. Christian Nats. Evangelism Commn., San Jose, Calif., 1960-76, internat. pres., 1976—; editor World Report, 1960-72; dir. Fellowship Bible Inst. Commn., 1969—, Evang. Ch. Alliance, 1958—; del. World Congress Evangelism, Berlin, 1966; del. Lausanne Com. for World Evangelization, 1974, Thailand, 1980, Internat. Conf. Itinerant Evangelists, Amsterdam, 1983; elder Berkeley First Presbyn. Ch., 1957-60, Westminster Presbyn. Ch., San Jose, Calif., 1968—; pastor Setzer's Gap Presbyn. Ch., Lenoir, N.C., 1950-52, Beattie Meml. Presbyn. Ch., Lenoir, 1950-52; mem. internat. bd. dirs. CNEC, 1976—; cons. U.S. Ctr. for World Mission, Pasadena, Calif., 1978—; bd. dirs. CNEC Council, Sydney, Australia; mem. Council Advs. Presbyns. United for Mission Advance, No. Calif.; bd. dirs. ENI Mission, Sinoe, Liberia, 1972-80, Evang. Ch. Alliance, Ill., 1955—; mem. N.Am. bd. reference Nairobi Evang. Grad. Sch. Theology; mem. bd. reference Chinese for Christ Theol. Sem. Club: Commonwealth. Author: Assisting Third World Church Ministries, Vol. II, No. 3, 1980; Mission: A World-Family Affair, 1981; editor CNEC Communique, 1960-72. Home: 1290 S Baywood Ave San Jose CA 95128 Office: 1470 N 4th St San Jose CA 95115

FINLEY, LEWIS MERREN, financial planner; b. Reubens, Idaho, Nov. 29, 1929; s. John Emory and Charlotte (Priest) F.; student public schs., Spokane; m. Virginia Ruth Spousta, Feb. 23, 1957; children—Ellen Annette, Charlotte Louise. With Household Finance Co., Portland, Oreg. and Seattle, 1953-56; with Doug Gerow Finance, Portland, 1956-61; pres. Family Fin. Planners Inc., Portland, 1961—; realtor Peoples Choice Realty, Inc., Milwaukie, Oreg., 1977-82; prin. Lewis M. Finley, Real Estate Broker, Inc., Portland, 1982—. Standing trustee Chpt. 13, Fed. Bankruptcy Ct., Dist. of Oreg., 1979-80. Served with U.S. Army, 1951-53. Mem. Oreg. Assn. Credit Counselors (past pres.), Northwest Assn. Credit Counselors (past treas.), Am. Assn. Credit Counselors (v.p.), Authors Guild. Republican. Methodist. Clubs: Masons (past worshipful master), Shriners. Author: The Complete Guide to Getting Yourself Out of Debt, 1975. Home: 3015 SE Riviere Dr Milwaukie OR 97222 Office: 1924 NE Broadway Portland OR 97232

FINLINSON, FRED WHEELER, lawyer, state senator; b. Murray, Utah, June 27, 1942; s. Fred Lyman and Luella (Wheeler) F.; m. Jeanne Braithwaite, June 13, 1967; children—Scott, Michelle, Laurie Ann, Jami, Robert. B.S. in Acctg., U. Utah, 1967, J.D., 1969. Bar: Utah 1969. Ski instr. Alf Engen Ski Sch., Alta, Utah, 1967-75; law clk. Utah Supreme Ct., 1968; asst. atty. gen. State of Utah, 1969; ptnr. Finlinson & Finlinson, Salt Lake City, 1971—; mem. Utah Senate, Salt Lake City, 1973—, minority whip, 1977-78, majority leader, 1979-80, chmn. energy and natural resources com., 1979-84, chmn. reapportionment com. 1980-82, chmn. water devel. task force, 1982, chmn. oil and gas policy task force, 1983. Exec. dir. Utah Republican Party, 1969-72; v.p. Nat. Rep. Legislators' Assn., 1981-82, pres., 1983-84; del. to various state and Salt Lake County Rep. convs., 1964—. Mem. ABA, Utah Bar Assn., Salt Lake County Bar Assn., Am. Judicature Soc., Nat. Conf. State Legislatures, Natural Resources and Energy (vice chmn. 1980-81, chmn. 1983-84). Home: 720 Shiloh Way Murray UT 84107 Office: 721 Kearns Bldg Salt Lake City UT 84101

FINN, GERALD ROBERT PATRICK, educator; b. Wayne, Nebr., Oct. 31, 1944; s. John Hugh and Frances Acyntha (Verzani) F.; A.A., Pasadena City Coll., 1964; B.A., Pasadena Coll., 1974; M.A., Loyola Marymount U., 1980; m. Sharon Ann Friesen, Apr. 4, 1970. Engr., Consol. Electro Dynamics, Monrovia, Calif., 1965-68. Hoffman Electronics, El Monte, Calif., 1968-69; studio technician Pasadena City Coll., 1969—, prof. communications dept., 1974—. Mem. Am. Soc. Lighting Dirs., Soc. Motion Picture and Television Engrs., Nat. Assn. Ednl. Broadcasters. Home: 1735 Midwick Dr Altadena CA 91001 Office: 1570 E Colorado Blvd Pasadena CA 91106

FINN, SARA SHIELS, public relations consultant; b. Cin., July 12; d. Paul Vincent and Freda K. (Kohstall) Shiels; m. Thomas Finn, Nov. 11, 1952; children—Shawn, Paula, Anne-Marie, Sara Louise. B.A. in English, Maryville Coll., 1950. Reporter La Jolla (Calif.) Jour.; advt. and pub. relations rep. San Diego Mag., 1964-71; dir. pub. relations U. San Diego, 1971—; lectr. and cons. Pres. Nat. Assn. Alumnae of Sacred Heart, 1979-81; active San Diego Mus. Art. Inducted into Equestrian Order Holy Sepulchre induction, 1982. Mem. Pub. Relations Soc. Am. (accredited), Pub. Relations Club San Diego, San Diego Press Club (charter mem.), Council Advancement and Support Edn., San Diego C. of C. Roman Catholic. Office: U San Diego Alcala Park San Diego CA 92110

FINNEGAN, JOAN CORÉE, water utility official; b. Oakland, Calif., Apr. 5, 1934; d. Arthur Wallace and Virginia Corée (Dandy) Jensen; m. Robert Harold Finnegan, Aug. 19, 1951; children—Sherrill Corée Finnegan Edmondson, Brenda Mae. Student Santa Ana Jr. Coll., 1951-57, Orange Coast Coll., 1959-62. Bookkeeper Reed's TeWinkle Hardware, Costa Mesa, Calif., 1960-62; cashier, acct., adminstv. sec. Mesa Consol. Water Dist. (formerly Costa Mesa County Water Dist.), Costa Mesa, 1962—, office mgr., 1974—, auditor, officer of dist., 1974-82. Mem. Costa Mesa Crime Prevention Com., 1980-81, Orange County Grand Jury Assn.; life mem. Women of Ch., Newport Harbor Luth. Ch.; bd. dirs. YMCA Newport Beach. Named City of Costa Mesa Woman of Yr., C. of C., 1980; Woman of Yr., Costa Mesa Jr. Women's Club, 1958, Water Dist. Employees' Assn., various years. Mem. Orange County Water Assn. (dir.), Ind. Spl. Dists. Orange County (sec.-treas.), Am. Water Works Assn., Assn. Calif. Water (fin. com., alt. mem. Joint Powers Inst. Agy.), Am. Bus. Women's Assn. (charter Newport Beach; Woman of Yr. award 1973). Republican. Home: 258 Sherwood St Costa Mesa CA 92627 Office: 1965 Placentia Ave Costa Mesa CA 92627

FINNIE, C(LARENCE) HERB(ERT), JR., aerospace co. ofcl.; b. San Marcos, Tex., Feb. 22, 1930; s. Clarence Herbert and Robbie Mary (Hinkle) F.; B.S., S.W. Tex. State U., 1951; M.A., U. Calif. at Berkeley, 1955; M.B.A., U. Santa Clara, 1968; m. Bruna Rebecchi, June 28, 1955; children—Elisa Gene, John Herbert, Mary Lea, Ann Catherine. With Lockheed Missiles & Space Co., Inc., Sunnyvale, Calif., 1958—, supr. computer programming, systems analyst, mgr. software design and devel., advanced system sr. staff engr. Served to capt. USAF, 1951-58. Mem. Assn. Computing Machinery, Nat. Mgmt. Assn., Assn. Old Crows, Alpha Chi, Beta Gamma Sigma, Phi Mu Alpha Sinfonia. Roman Catholic. Designed and developed first generally used compiler prepared for a digital electronic computer, 1952. Home: 1582 Lewiston Dr Sunnyvale CA 94087 Office: PO Box 504 Sunnyvale CA 94086

FINNIE, PHILLIP POWELL, aerospace engr.; b. Memphis, Dec. 21, 1933; s. Phillip and Daisy L. (Green) F.; B.S.C.E., Howard U., 1956; postgrad. U. Calif., Los Angeles, U. So. Calif.; M.B.A., Pepperdine U., 1979; m. Mary Bebe Clark, Sept. 14, 1968. Stress analyst N.Am. Aviation Corp., Los Angeles, 1956-59; dynamicist RCA, Van Nuys, Calif., 1959-62, Aerojet Gen. Corp., Azusa, Calif., 1962-64, Philco-Ford Corp., Newport Beach, Calif., 1964-67; dynamicist, analyst of radar observables, TRW Inc., Redondo Beach, Calif., 1967—. Mem. Republican Nat. Com. Mem. AIAA, Air Force Assn. Baptist. Home: 20102 Dalfsen Ave Carson CA 90746

FINOCCHIARO, MAURICE ANTHONY, philosophy educator; b. Floridia, Italy, June 13, 1942; s. Biagio and Jane (Mudano) F.; came to U.S., 1957; m. Ramona K. Thomason, Dec. 11, 1966. B.S., MIT, 1964; Ph.D., U. Calif., 1969. Asst. prof. philosophy U. Nev., Las Vegas, 1970-74, assoc. prof., 1974-77, prof., 1977—. Recipient Barrick Disting. Scholar award U. Nev., 1981-82; Nat. Endowment Humanities fellow, 1983-84; NSF grantee, 1976-77. Mem. Am. Philos. Assn., Philosophy of Sci. Assn., History of Sci. Soc., Soc. for Social Study Sci., Am. Polit. Sci. Assn., Am. Soc. Polit. and Legal Philosophy. Author: History of Science as Explanation, 1973; Galileo and the Art of Reasoning, 1980. Office: Dept Philosophy U Nev Las Vegas NV 89154

FINOCCHIO, ALBERTO, elec. designer; b. Rosario, Argentina, Dec. 19, 1940; s. Jose and Emilia (Valvassori) F.; came to U.S., 1966; degree in electricity, Indsl. Sch., Rosario, 1960; m. Josefa Settecase, Nov. 5, 1970. Designer, water and elec. energy, City of Rosario, 1963-65; draftsman C.F. Braun & Co., Alhambra, Calif., 1966-68, 71-73; designer Cities Service Oil Co., Argentina, 1969-70, So. Calif. Edison Co., Rosemead, 1974—. Home: 956 Palo Alto Dr Arcadia CA 91006 Office: 2244 Walnut Grove Ave Rosemead CA 91770

FIORE, EDITH ANNE, clinical psychologist, author; b. Scarsdale, N.Y., Sept. 13, 1930; d. Frank Fiore and Edith (Gobel) Holbert; children—Gail de Nava, Dana Fiore Heintz, Leslie Anne Luxenberg; M.A. in Psychology, U. Md., 1965; Ph.D., U. Miami, 1969. Staff psychologist Children's Psychiat. Ctr., Miami, Fla.; pvt. practice psychology, Miami, 1970-72, pvt. practice clin. psychology, hypnotherapy, Saratoga, Calif., 1973—; lectr. trainer hypnoanalytic therapy. Mem. Am. Psychol. Assn., Am. Soc. Hypnosis, Internat. Soc. Hypnosis. Author: You Have Been Here Before, 1979. Office: 20688 4th St Saratoga CA 95070

FIORINO, JOHN WAYNE, podiatrist; b. Charleroi, Pa., Sept. 30, 1946; s. Anthony Raymond and Mary Louise (Caramela) F.; student Nassau Coll., 1969-70; B.A. in Biology, U. Buffalo, 1972; Dr. Podiatric Medicine, Ohio Coll. Podiatric Medicine, 1978. Salesman, E. J. Korvettes, Carle Place, N.Y., 1962-65; orderly Nassau Hosp., Mineola, N.Y., 1965-66; operating room technician-trainee heart-lung machine L.I. Jewish-Hillside Med. Center, New Hyde Park, N.Y., 1967-69; pharmacy technician Feinmel's Pharmacy, Roslyn Heights, N.Y., 1969-70; mgr., asst. buyer Fortunoffs, Westbury, N.Y., 1972-73; bd. certified perfusionist L.I. Jewish-Hillside Med. Center, New Hyde Park, N.Y., 1973-74; clin. instr. cardiopulmonary tech. Stony Brook (N.Y.) Univ., 1973-74; operating room technician Cleve. Met. Hosp., 1975; lab. technician Univ. Hosp., Cleve., 1976-78; surg. resident Mesa (Ariz.) Gen. Hosp., 1978-79, staff podiatrist, 1979—; pvt. practice podiatry, Mesa, 1979—; staff podiatrist Sacaton (Ariz.) Hosp., 1979—, podiatrist U.S. Govt. Nat. Inst., Sacaton, 1980—, Indian Health Services, Sacaton, 1980—. Served with USN, 1966-67. Mem. Am. Podiatry Assn., Ariz. Podiatry Assn., Acad. Ambulatory Foot Surgery, Mut. Assn. Profls., Pi Delta, Alpha Gamma Kappa. Home: 603 S 34th St Mesa AZ 85204 Office: 5520 E Main St Mesa AZ 85205

FIORITO, BASIL ANTHONY, marriage and family therapist, educator; b. N.Y.C., Oct. 8, 1945; s. Basil Anthony and Crace Z. (Marotta) F.; m. Laura Cornelia Lehmann, Sept. 2, 1978; 1 son, Nicholas Matthew. B.A. magna cum laude, Marist Coll., 1968; M.S., NYU, 1970; Ph.D., Syracuse U., 1977. Lic. marriage, family, child counselor, Calif., 1979. Teaching asst. NYU, N.Y.C., 1968-70; sci. tchr. Pearl River (N.Y.) High Sch., 1970-73; marriage and family counselor Onondaga Pastoral Counseling Ctr., Syracuse, N.Y., 1975-77; asst. prof. Calif. Poly State U., San Luis Obispo, 1977-81, assoc. prof., 1981—. Adv. bd. Nat. Family Life Edn. Network, 1982—; exec. bd. County Women's Shelter Program, 1982; active County Council for Protection of Children, 1979—. Syracuse U. fellow, 1973-76. Mem. Nat. Council Family Relations, Am. Assn. Marriage and Family Therapy; Am. Personnel and Guidance Assn. Club: Elks. Office: Child Devel Dept Calif Poly State U San Luis Obispo CA 93407

FIRFIRES, NICHOLAS SAMUEL, painter; b. Santa Barbara, Calif., Nov. 10, 1917; s. Michael Nicolas and Ethel (Kimes) F.; student Art Center Sch., Los Angeles, 1937-39, Otis Art Inst., Los Angeles, 1939-40; m. Maxine Jones, Aug. 11, 1969. Freelance mag. and book illustrator, 1946-58; one man shows: Cowie Gallery, Los Angeles, 1960-61, Maxwell Gallery, San Francisco, 1962-63, Biltmore Gallery, Los Angeles, 1965, 66, 67, Denver Art Gallery, 1965, 66, 68, Saks Gallery, Denver, 1970, Huntington Sheraton Gallery, Pasadena, Calif., 1974-76; numerous group shows; represented in permanent collections: Riveredge Found. Mus., Calgary, Can., Santa Barbara (Calif.) Hist. Mus., S.W. Mus., Los Angeles, U. Wyo. Mus., Laramie. Served with U.S. Army, 1941-45. Decorated Bronze Star. Mem. Cowboy Artists Am. Club: Rancheros Visitadores. Home and Studio: 1330 Pepper Ln Santa Barbara CA 93108

FIRSCHEIN, WILLIAM, architect, planner; b. N.Y.C., May 24, 1930; s. Harry and Ruth (Tambor) F. Student Ciudadella Art Sch., Mexico City, 1962; cert. welding and metal fabrication Ort Vocat. Sch., Jerusalem, 1967; student Lafayette Coll., Easton, Pa., 1974-75; B.A., U. N.Mex., 1952, M.A., 1958; M.Arch., UCLA, 1981. Painter, graphic artist, Calif., Mexico, Italy, Greece, Israel, 1958-68; indsl. designer Diamond Chem. Co., Glen Gardner, N.J., 1973; sculptor, N.Y.C., Carrara, Italy, 1968-79; mem. faculty N.Y. Inst. Tech., 1965-72, Lafayette Coll., 1973-76; lectr. UCLA Extension Div., 1978-81, instr., 1981; preservation cons. Historic Easton, Inc. (Pa.), 1978, Nat. Trust Historic Preservation Restoration Workshop, Lyndhurst, Tarrytown, N.Y., 1978, El Pueblo de Los Angeles State Park, 1979, Banning House Mus., 1981, Sierra Club, 1983 archtl. designer FHNS Assocs., Los Angeles, 1979-80; designer, draftsman M. Bernstein AIA, Los Angeles, 1980; archtl. designer Built Environments, Los Angeles, 1980-81; preservation cons. Com. for Simon Rodia's Towers in Watts, Los

Angeles, 1979-81; project planning analyst devel. and maintenance div. dept. small craft harbors County of Los Angeles, Marina del Rey, Calif., 1980—; project coordinator Le Sopha Group revitalization project, 1983—; prin. Concept Marine Assocs., 1982—; speaker profl. confs.; cons. and lectr. in field. Bd. dirs. Historic Easton, Inc., Com. for Simon Rodia's Towers in Watts. Recipient Painting Prizes, Mus. N.Mex., 1958, Roswell Art Mus., 1959; Purchase Prizes, Dallas Art Mus., 1959, 60; awards sculpture Hunterdon Art Center, 1977, Lackawanna Arts Council, 1978; Huntington Hartford Found. fellow, 1966; MacDowell Colony fellow, 1968; Yaddo Found. fellow, 1969; Lafayette Coll. faculty research grantee, 1975; Nat. Trust for Historic Preservation cons. service grantee, 1980. Mem. Assn. Preservation Tech., Preservation Action, Nat. Trust Historic Preservation. Contbr. articles to profl. publs. Office: 29 Stowe Ln Menlo Park CA 94025

FIRTH, LORRAINE ANN, savings and loan executive; b. Cleve., Oct. 31, 1951; d. Edward Raymond and Trudy S. (Longley) Charvat; B.S.B.A., U. Ariz., 1974; m. Richard William Firth, Nov. 21, 1973; children—Heather Ann, Ian Andrew. Program mgr., Jr. Achievement, Tucson, 1969-72; acctg. clk. Home Fed. Savs. & Loan Assn., Tucson, 1972-75, accountant, 1975-78, investment mgr., 1978—, asst. v.p., 1978—. Mem. Fin. Mgrs. Soc. (pres. Ariz. chpt.), Inst. Fin. Edn., Am. Soc. Women Accts. (pres. Tucson chpt.). Author: (with others) Hedging with Financial Futures, 1980. Office: 32 N Stone Ave Tucson AZ 85701

FISCH, EDWARD CARL, corporate executive; b. N.Y.C., Aug. 10, 1943; s. Leonard and Fimi (Podell) F.; m. Susan Carol Greenburg, Aug. 6, 1967; 1 son, Jeremy Lawrence. B.A., U. Pa., 1965; J.D., U. Pitts., 1968; LL.M., Harvard U., 1970. Bar: Calif. Law clerk for Hon. Lawrence Bilder, Jersey City, 1968-69; assoc. atty. Goodis, Greenfield, Narin & Mann, Phila., 1970-71; staff atty. SEC, Washington, 1971-72; spl. counsel N.Y. Stock Exchange, N.Y.C., 1972-73; sr. v.p., gen. counsel Birr, Wilson & Co., Inc., San Francisco, 1973—. Home: 1060 Longridge Oakland CA 94610 Office: 155 Sansome St San Francisco CA 94104

FISCHBEIN, ERNEST, financial executive; b. Bklyn., June 7, 1928; s. Samuel and Dorothy (Rubenstein) F.; m. Joyce Diamond, June 25, 1950; children—Mark David, Paul Michael. B.A., Bklyn. Coll., 1949, M.A., 1953. Instr., Bklyn. Coll., 1949-52; commd. officer, U.S. Navy, 1952, advanced through grades to comdr., 1974, ret., 1974; mgr. Monterey Savs. 1974-82; mgr. Home Fed. Savs., Monterey, Calif., 1982—; instr. real estate fin. Monterey Peninsula Coll., 1983. Mem. hosp. aux. Monterey Community Hosp., Carmel, Calif., 1982; pres. Congregation Beth Israel, Monterey, 1981; bd. dirs. Suicide Prevention, Monterey County, 1979. Named Disting. Pres., Kiwanis, 1977-78; named trustee for life Congregation Beth Israel, 1977. Mem. Inst. Fin. Edn. (pres. 1978), Phi Delta Kappa. Club: Kiwanis (lt. gov. 1979). Contbr. articles to profl. jours.

FISCHER, EDWARD PRESTON, surgical oncologist; b. Lima, Ohio, June 6, 1939; s. Edward B. and Evelyn E. (Fiester) F.; B.S., Wheaton Coll., 1961; M.D., Baylor U., 1965. Intern, USAF Med Corps, Scott AFB, Ill., 1965-66; resident Baylor Coll. Medicine, Houston, 1970-72, research asst., 1970-71, asst. in surgery, 1971-72; resident in gen. surgery Kern Med. Center, Bakersfield, Calif., 1972-75; Am. Cancer Soc. fellow in surg. oncology M.D. Anderson Hosp. and Tumor Inst., 1975-76; practice medicine, specializing in surg. oncology, Bakersfield, 1976—; clin. instr. Baylor U., 1971-72, Kern Med. Center, 1972-75, cons. surgeon, 1976—; liaison asso. Commn. on Cancer, Am. Cancer Soc., 1977—, div. rep., chmn. profl. edn. com. Kern unit, 1978—, pres. Kern County unit, 1983-84; active staff Mercy Hosp., Bakersfield, 1977—; active staff San Joaquin Hosp., 1976—; med. staff Greater Bakersfield Mem. Hosp., 1978—; cons. surgeon Delano Community Hosp., 1978—; cons. surgeon John C. Freemont Hosp., Mariposa, Calif., 1979—; asst. clin. prof. dept. surgery U. Calif., San Diego, 1978—. Served with USAF, 1965-70. Named Intern of Yr., Radiology and Diagnosis, USAF Hosp., Scott AFB, 1966; recipient Physicians Achievement award AMA, 1972, 76-78; Physicians Achievement award Calif. Med. Assn., 1975-76; Research Edn. Service fellow, 1975-76; U. Tex. System Cancer Center fellow, 1975-76; diplomate Tex. Bd. Med. Examiners, Calif. Bd. Med. Examiners, Am. Bd. Surgery. Fellow ACS, Am. Coll. Angiology; mem. Am. Trauma Soc. (founding), Aircraft Owners and Pilots Assn., Kern County Med. Soc. (editor bull. 1977-78). Clubs: Rotary, Bakersfield Racquet. Contbr. articles to profl. jours. Home: 4300 Flintridge Bakersfield CA 93306 Office: 4001 Union Ave Bakersfield CA 93305

FISCHER, FRED WALTER, physicist, engineer, educator; b. Zwickau, Germany, June 26, 1922; s. Fritz and Louiska (Richter) F.; B.S. in Mech. Engring., Columbia U., 1949, M.S., 1950; M.S. in Physics, U. Wash., 1957; Dr.Engr. in Elec. Engring., Tech. U. Munich, 1966; m. Yongja Kim, Oct. 1, 1970. Analyst, Boeing Co., Seattle, Munich, Bonn, W. Ger., 1950—; instr. North Seattle Community Coll., 1973—. Served with AUS, 1943-46. Boeing scholar, Max Planck Inst. Plasma Physics, Munich, 1964-65. Mem. Sigma Xi (life). Office: North Seattle Community Coll 9600 College Way N Seattle WA 98103

FISCHER, JEANETTE LUCILLE STOCKETT (MRS. RICHARD ALLEN FISCHER), occupational therapist; b. Albert Lea, Minn., Nov. 13, 1937; d. Stewart Joseph and Bessie Lucille (Junk) Stockett; B.S. in Occupational Therapy, Washington U., St. Louis, 1960; postgrad. Webster Coll., m. Richard Allen Fischer, Oct. 22, 1960; children—Richard Arnold, Robert Andrew. Occupational therapy aide St. Louis State Hosp., 1958-59; dir. occupational therapy Alexian Bros. Hosp., St. Louis, 1960-62. Americana Healthcare Center, Florissant, Mo., 1975-80; coordinator occupational therapy, phys. medicine dept. St. Mary's Health Center, 1980-81; dir. occupational therapy dept. Fullerton (Calif.) Care Convalescent Hosp., 1981—. Clinic vol. aide ARC, 1971-73; treas. Midland Valley Estates Improvement Assn., 1966-68, 69-70, v.p., 1971-72, pres., 1972-73, bd. dirs., 1974-81, treas., 1972-73; treas., Marion PTA, carnival chmn., 1968-69, v.p., 1969-71, picnic chmn., 1969-73; sch. talent show dir. Boy Scouts Am., 1971-72; mem. St. Louis Civic Ballet, 1973-78; mem. Sta. KETC-TV Ednl. TV, 1971-78; sec.-receptionist Michael Simms Acad. Dance, St. Louis, 1974-76. Mem. Am., Mo. (public relations chmn. 1965. program chmn. 1979, pres. 1980-81), Calif. (v.p. Orange County chpt. 1983-84) occupational therapy assns., World Fedn. Occupational Therapy, Orange County Dirs. Forum, Los Angeles Occupational Therapy Dirs. Forum, Internat. Platform Assn., Met. Ballet St. Louis Dance Concert Soc., Humane Soc. Mo., Alpha Xi Delta. Lutheran. Home: 4217 Elder Ave Seal Beach CA 90740 Office: 2222 N Harbor Blvd Fullerton CA 92635

FISCHER, JOEL, educator; b. Chgo., Apr. 22, 1939; s. Sam and Ruth (Feiges) F.; B.S., U. Ill., 1961, M.S.W., 1964; D.S.W., U. Calif.-Berkeley, 1970; m. Ursula R. Seeberger, June 14, 1964; children—Lisa, Nicole. Prof., Sch. Social Work, U. Hawaii, Honolulu, 1970—; vis. prof. George Warren Brown Sch. Social Work, Washington U., St. Louis, 1977, U. Wis. Sch. Social Welfare, Milw., 1978-79, U. Natal (South Africa), 1982; cons. various orgns. and univs. Served with U.S. Army, 1958. Mem. Nat. Assn. Social Workers, Council Social Work Edn., Acad. Cert. Social Workers, Nat. Conf. Social Welfare, AAUP. Democrat. Author: (with Harvey L. Gochros) Planned Behavior Change: Behavior Modication in Social Work, 1975; Handbook of Behavior Therapy with Sexual Problems, Vol I, 1977; Vol. II, 1977; Analyzing Research, 1975; Interpersonal Helping: Emerging Approaches for Social Work Practice, 1973; The Effectiveness of Social Casework, 1976; Fundamentals of Social Work Practice, 1982; Effective Casework Practice: An Eclectic Approach, 1978; (with Martin Bloom) Evaluating Practice: A Guide for the Helping Professions, 1982; (with Harvey L. Gochros) Treat Yourself to a Better Sex Life, 1980; contbr. articles to profl. jours. Home: 2328 Seaview Ave Honolulu HI 96822 Office: 2500 Campus Rd U Hawaii Honolulu HI 96822

FISCHER, MARGARET ELEANOR, psychologist, educator; d. John T. and Mary (Worden) F.; B.S. cum laude in Psychology, Seton Hall U., 1958; postgrad. U. Paris, 1958, Carl G. Jung Inst., Switzerland, 1958-59, NYU, 1959-60, U. Md., 1960-63; M.A. magna cum laude in Ednl. Psychology, San Diego State U., 1966; postgrad. (NDEA grantee), U. Alaska, 1965; Ph.D. cum laude in Psychology and Spl. Edn., U. Wash., 1970. Resident counselor Children's Center, N.Y.C., 1959-60; tchr. Am. Dependents' Schs., Okinawa, Germany, Turkey, France, 1960-64; tchr. English as fgn. lang. Jean Giraudoux Lycée, Chateauroux, France, 1963-64; tchr. English and French, Sweetwater Sch. Dist., Chula Vista, Calif., 1964-66; asst. to editor Rev. of Ednl. Research Jour., Seattle, 1967-68; psychologist vocat. rehab. program Edmonds Sch. Dist., Lynnwood, Wash., 1968-70, Charles Denny Youth Center, Everett, Wash., 1969-71; instr. psychology Seattle Community Coll., 1971; asst. prof. dept. social scis., humanities and edn. Purdue U., Lafayette, Ind., 1971-72; lang. evaluation specialist Def. Lang. Inst., Monterey, Calif., 1972; research psychologist U. Calif., San Francisco, 1972; asst. prof. psychology U. Calif., Santa Cruz, 1973, Mass. State Colls., 1973-76; pvt. practice psychology, Mass., 1976-78; psychologist N.Y. State Dept. Mental Hygiene, 1978, Alaska div. mental health Harborview Developmental Center, Valdez, 1978-79; lic. psychologist Alaska Psychiat. Inst., Anchorage, 1979—. Recipient Internat. Travel award Purdue U., 1972, Scholarly Support award Mass. State Coll., 1974, 75, 76; lic. pvt. pilot. Mem. Am. Psychol. Assn., Internat. Council Psychologists (area chmn. Alaska 1979-81), Interam. Soc. Psychologists, DAR, Alaska 99's, Mensa. Contbr. articles to psychol. jours. Home: Star Route 7401-F Anchorage AK 99516 Office: Alaska Psychiat Inst 2900 Providence Dr Anchorage AK 99504

FISCHER, MERLIN ERNEST, food processing co. exec.; b. Oregon City, Oreg., Aug. 24, 1937; s. Ernest August and Thelma Muriel (DeBok) F.; B.S., Oreg. State U., 1959; m. Vivian S. Worley, June 2, 1962; children—Scott, Heidi, Erik. Mgr. quality control Ore-Ida Foods, Burley, Idaho, 1960-62; quality control supr. brands buying div. Safeway Stores, Oakland, Calif., 1962-66; v.p., gen. mgr. Kerr Concentrates, Inc., div. Internat. Flavors and Fragrances, Salem, Oreg., 1966—. Mem. Inst. Food Technologists. Clubs: Multnomah Athletic, Old Guard Soc., Rotary. Home: 979 Mistletoe Loop Salem OR 97303 Office: 2340 Hyacinth NE Salem OR 97303

FISCHER, VIC, state senator, businessman; b. Berlin, May 5, 1924. Ed. U. Wis., MIT, Harvard U. Businessman, planning and econ. devel.; mem. Alaska Ho. of Reps., 1957-58, Alaska State Senate, 1980—. Del. Alaska Constl. Conv., 1955-58; asst. dir. Alaska State Housing Authority, 1957-61; dir. Inst. Social, Econ. and Govt. Research of U. Alaska, 1966-76; mem. Alaska Growth Policy Council, 1975-76. Served with C.E., U.S. Army, World War II. Democrat. Office: Alaska State Senate Juneau AK 99811*

FISCHER, VIRGINIA RIGG, educator, poet; b. Alderson, W.Va.; A.B., Coll. William and Mary; M.A., Northwestern U.; postgrad. W.Va. U., Va. Poly. Inst. and U.; m. Monroe C. Fischer. Chmn. dept. theatre arts Lander Coll., Greenwood, S.C.; hosp. recreation worker ARC, Ft. Campbell, Ky. and Ft. Jackson, Columbia, S.C.; costume designer, radio dir., dept. theatre arts Va. Commonwealth U., Richmond; instr. English dept. Va. Poly. Inst. and U., Blacksburg; costume designer Dock St. Theatre, Charleston, S.C.; founder Blacksburg Thursday Contemporary Book Club. Recipient 1st place prize Nev. Bicentennial Poetry Contest. Mem. Nat. League Am. Pen Women, DAR (state motion picture chmn.), AAUW, Nat. Writers Club, Assn., World Poetry Soc. Intercontinental, Acad. Am. Poets, Delta Delta Delta, Theta Alpha Phi, Alpha Psi Omega, Zeta Phi Eta. Republican. Methodist. Clubs: Mesquite, Las Vegas Rep. Women's. Contbr. poetry to various publs.

FISCHER, VOLKER, research farm manager; b. Wertheim/Main, W.Ger., Sept. 8, 1942; came to U.S., 1978; M.S. in Agr., U. Goettingen (W.Ger.), 1967; Ph.D. summa cum laude in Plant Genetics, Free U. Berlin, 1972. Research assoc. Estación Experimental La Mayora, Malaga, Spain, 1972-73; staff agrl. div. research and devel. of Schering, Berlin, 1974-77; mgr. research farm BASF Wyandotte Corp., Dinuba, Calif., 1978—. Research in herbicides, insecticides, plant growth regulators. Office: PO Box 758 Dinuba CA 93618

FISCH-SWANSON, ELAINE, educator; b. N.Y.C., June 21, 1936; d. Abraham and Ruth Fisch; B.S., N.Y. U., 1966, M.A. (grantee), 1967; Ph.D. (fellow), U. Calif., Berkeley/ San Francisco State U., 1977; credential ednl. adminstrn. U. San Francisco, 1974; m. Roy George Swanson, Aug. 1, 1978; stepchildren—Mark Swanson, Matthew John Swanson, Suzanne Swanson. Tchr., Expt. Children's Center, Bank St. Coll., N.Y.C., 1958-61; tchr. N.Y.C. Public Sch. System, 1967-68; tchr. spl. edn. Alum Rock Sch. Dist., San Jose, Calif., 1968-70; clin. supr., dept. spl. edn. U. Mich., summer 1968; spl. educator Min Quong Sch. for Seriously Distburbed, Los Gatos, Calif., 1970-71; dir. spl. educators Free U., Los Gatos, 1970-71; cons., tchr., evaluator San Francisco Unified Sch. Dist., 1971-78; asst. prof. edn. U. San Francisco, 1977-78, St. Mary's Coll., Moraga, Calif., 1978—; mem. Calif. Dept. Spl. Edn. presch. children task force, 1979. Mem. Calif. League Handicapped (dir. 1978-79), Assn. Supervision and Curriculum Devel., Calif. Council Edn. Tchrs., Council Exceptional Children, Calif. Tchrs. Assn., Calif. Assn. Neurologically Handicapped, Phi Delta Kappa. Home: 2379 Glendale Circle Antioch CA 94509 Office: Dept Edn St Marys Coll Calif Box K Moraga CA 94575

FISH, RUBY MAE BERTRAM (MRS. FREDERICK GOODRICH FISH), civic worker; b. Sheridan, Wyo., July 24, 1918; d. Ryan Lawrence and Ruby (Beckwith) Bertram; R.N., St. Luke's Hosp., 1936; postgrad. Washington U., St. Louis, 1941; m. Frederick Goodrich Fish, Apr. 12, 1942; children—Bertram Frederick, Lisbeth Ann Fish Kalstein. Staff nurse Huntington Meml. Hosp., Pasadena, Calif., 1941-42; dr.'s office nurse, Denver, 1943-44; travel cons. Buckingham Travel Agy., Aurora, Colo., 1976—. Bd. dirs. Jefferson County Easter Seal Soc., 1949—, pres., 1952-53, 56-57, 66-67; pres. Colo. Easter Seal Soc., 1960-61; bd. dirs. Nat. Easter Seal Soc., 1968-69, sec. ho. of dels., 1976-77; bd. dirs. Assistance League Denver, 1968-70, 75-76, People to People for Handicapped; mem. Pres.'s Com. on Employing Handicapped, 1976—; active Rehab. Internat. of U.S.A., 1972—, Rehab. Internat., 1960—; mem. Denver chpt. Freedom Found. at Valley Forge. Mem. Dau. of Nile-El Mejedel. Home: 4646 Bow Mar Dr Littleton CO 80123 Office: 1387 Joliet St Aurora CO 80012

FISH, VICTOR J., radiation oncologist; b. Zolkiew, Poland, July 24, 1919; s. Ignatius and Claire (Schaechter) F.; came to U.S., 1951, naturalized, 1956; student John Casimir U., Lwow, Poland, 1937-45; M.D., U. Wroclaw, Poland, 1946; children—Allen Paul, Eva Rene, Clark Edgar. Intern, St. Bernard's Hosp., Chgo., 1951-52; resident Mt. Sinai, Cook County hosps., Chgo., 1952-55; attending in radiation therapy Cook County Hosp., 1955-57, Cedars of Lebanon Hosp., Los Angeles, 1960-62; dir. radiation therapy Palo Alto (Calif.) Med. Clinic, 1962—; clin. asso. prof. radiation therapy Stanford Med. Sch.; asso. physician Lawrence Radiation Lab., U. Calif., Berkeley, 1964-71. Served to maj. M.C., AUS, 1957-60. Fellow Am. Coll. Radiology; mem. Central Soc. Nuclear Medicine (charter), Radiol. Soc. N.Am., Am. Soc. Therapeutic Radiologists, Am. Cancer Soc. (dir. Santa Clara County). Office: 300 Homer Ave Palo Alto CA 94301

FISHBEIN, HAROLD JACOB, lawyer, association executive; b. Indpls., Nov. 23, 1898; s. Benjamin and Fannie (Gluck) F.; Ph.B., U. Chgo., 1918; LL.B., Chgo., Kent Coll. Law, 1927; postgrad. Pa. State U., 1942; m. Elise G. Pinkus, Aug. 6, 1921 (dec. Apr. 1983); children—Elise (Mrs. Henry D. Friedman) (dec. 1972), Stephan M. Admitted to Ill. bar, 1927; exec. dir. Nat. Assn. Bottle Dealers, 1931-42; field dir. ARC, 1942-45; dir. UNRRA, 1945-47, Internat. Refugee Orgn., 1947-48; exec. dir. Pa. Retail Florists, 1956-60; exec. dir. Am. Assn. for Maternal and Child Health, Los Altos, Calif., 1968—. Served with U.S. Army, 1918-19. Mem. Am. Arbitration Assn., Phi Beta Kappa. Address: 233 Prospect P-209 La Jolla CA 92037

FISHBEIN, STEVEN CARL, lawyer; b. Sacramento, Aug. 4, 1949; s. Jerry J. and Eleanor (Stepper) F.; B.S., U. Ariz., 1971, J.D., 1974. Bar: Ariz. 1974, Calif. 1975. Practice, Sacramento and Los Angeles; chief legis. and adminstrv. asst. to Calif. assemblyman and senator, 1977; legis. coordinator Calif. Dept. Consumer Affairs, 1978-81. Chmn., Sacramento Jewish Community Relations Council, 1980-83; vice chmn. Jewish Pub. Affairs Com. Calif., 1982—. Mem. ABA, Israel-Am. C. of C. (dir.), Sacramento Area Commerce and Trade Orgn. Office: Suite 1510 555 Capitol Mall Sacramento CA 95814

FISHBURN, WILLIAM ROBERT, psychologist; b. Freeport, Ill., Sept. 1, 1933; s. Robert Kenneth and Lauretta Phyllis (Heiserman) F.; B.S., U. Ill., 1960; M.Ed., U. Mo., 1963; Ed.D., U. Ariz., 1967; m. Miriam Jean Burns, Nov. 27, 1952; children—Sarah Elynn, John William, Peter Thomas, Joseph Paul. Pvt. practice psychology, Albuquerque, 1967—; asst. prof. Ind. U., Bloomington, 1967-69; asso. prof. U. N.Mex., 1969-73, prof., 1973—; chmn. psychology sect. Presbyn. Hosp. Center, Albuquerque, 1980-83. Chmn., N.Mex. Psychologists for Responsible Govt., 1982—. Served with USAF, 1953-57. Fellow Am. Group Psychotherapy Assn., N.Mex. Psychol. Assn. (pres. 1980-81, Meritorious Service award 1977); mem. Rocky Mountain Psychol. Assn. Cons. editor: Jour. Sex Edn. and Therapy, 1982—; Contbr. articles to profl. jours. Home: 3821 Shenandoah Pl NE Albuquerque NM 87111 Office: 4017 Mesa Vista U NMex Albuquerque NM 87131

FISHCO, DANIEL T., educator; b. Bayonne, N.J., Oct. 7, 1936; s. William and Fannie (Sweet) F.; B.A., Jersey City State Coll., 1962, M.A., 1964; Ed.D., Lehigh U., 1966; children—Ilene Beth, William David, Sherisse Hawkins; m. Vivian V. Hawkins, Aug. 9, 1974. Asst.-asso. prof. reading So. Ill. U., Carbondale, 1966-73; prof. reading Western Ill. U., Macomb, 1973-77; dir. Instl. Devel. Programs, Yavapai Coll., Prescott, Ariz., 1977—. Chmn. adv. com. Right to Read State of Ill., 1974-77. Served with AUS, 1956-58. Mem. Coll. Reading Assn. (pres. 1971-73), Am. Assn. Community and Jr. Colls., Nat. Council Resources Devel., Nat. Council Staff Programs and Orgnl. Devel., Internat. Reading Assn., Phi Delta Kappa. Revs. editor Reading World. Home: 1130 Deerfield Rd Prescott AZ 86301

FISHEL, CHARLES VINTON, management consultant, lawyer; b. Washington, June 6, 1938; s. Vinton Crews and Helen (Mayo) F.; m. Agnes Janelle, Sept. 10, 1960; children—Lindley Scott, Michelle Denise. A.B., U. Kans., 1959, J.D., 1963. Bar: Mo. 1963. Asst. tax atty. Williams Bros. Pipeline Co., Kansas City, Mo., 1963-65; asst. tax counsel Peter Kiewit Sons, Inc., Omaha, 1965-69; tax counsel Carnation Co., Los Angeles, 1969-71; mgr. tax planning and research Teledyne, Inc., Los Angeles, 1971-72, mgr. internat. taxes and reporting, 1972-74; mgr. taxes/risk mgmt., customs, treasury Intel Corp., Santa Clara, Calif., 1974-80; pres. ImaginAction, Inc., Santa Clara, Calif., 1980—; lectr. Grad. Sch. Internat. Mgmt., Golden Gate U., others. Mem. exec. adv. com. Internat. High Tech. Mgmt., Golden Gate U. Mem. ABA (com. fgn. activities U.S. taxpayers of sect. taxation; com. internat. taxation, com. pvt. internat. law of sect. internat. and comparative law), Tax Execs. Inst. (past chpt. chmn. continuing edn., chmn. com. internat. taxation; Los Angeles chpt. chmn. com. internat. ops. and taxation), Calif. C.P.A. Found. (adv. coms. risk mgmt., industry, internat. tax and corp. tax), Calif. Bar Assn. (com. fgn. income of sect. taxation). Democrat. Quaker. Assoc. editor Economics; Fgn. Intelligence Report, 1980-83; contbr. articles to profl. jours. Office: 1333 Lawrence Expy Suite 150 Santa Clara CA 95051

FISHELSON-HOLSTINE, HOLLIS LISA, statistician, computer educator, consultant; b. Mineola N.Y., June 9, 1953; d. Morton Paul and Dorothy (Seidman) Fishelson; m. Charles Morris Holstine, Mar. 19, 1978. B.S., Cornell U., 1975; M.S., Oreg. State U., 1981. Statis. cons. oceanography dept. Oreg. State U., Corvallis, 1980, Computer Ctr., 1980-81; statis. cons. EPA, Corvallis, 1981; computer programmer U.S. Forest Service, Sitka, Alaska, 1982-83; instr. Sitka Community Coll., 1983—; cons. Rec. sec. Sitka Health Edn. for Families, 1981-82. Oreg. State U. grantee, 1980; U.S. Forest Service grantee, 1982. Mem. Biometric Soc., Am. Statis. Assn., Alaska Assn. Computers in Edn., Caucus for Women in Stats., Bus. Profl. Women Sitka (sec.), Sigma Xi, Phi Kappa Phi. Democrat. Home: PO Box 2681 Sitka AK 99835 Office: Sitka Community Coll PO Box 490 Sitka AK 99835

FISHER, ALICE EVELYN, univ. ofcl; b. Eldon, Iowa, July 14, 1919; d. John and Olive (Randall) Fisher; student U. Mo., 1937-39; B.A., Parsons Coll., 1940. Wire chief S.W. Daily Times, Liberal, Kans., 1944-45; editor Forum, Eldon, 1947-49; sta. mgr., sec.-treas. KBIZ, KTVO-TV, Ottumwa, Iowa, 1950-57; exec. dir. Ottumwa Community Chest, 1957-63; publs. mgr. U. Calif. Extension, Riverside, 1964—. County chmn. Am. Cancer Soc., 1956-57; mem. communications com. San Gorgonio council Girl Scouts U.S.A., 1974-82, chmn., 1978-81, bd. dirs., 1978-81; sec. Animal Relief League, 1955-63; v.p Ottumwa Community Players, 1957; mem. pub. relations com. San Bernardino YWCA. Recipient Best Acting Female in Minor Role award Ottumwa Community Players, 1959; Pub. Relations Practice certificate U. Calif., 1973. Mem. Pub. Relations Soc. Am. (Most Outstanding Contbn. to Pub. Edn. award Calif. Inland Empire chpt. 1973, 79, 80, 81, award of excellence for outstanding contbn. to pub. relations 1982, sec. 1973-75, pres. 1975-76, bd. dirs. 1973—, del. assembly 1980-81, chmn. profl. devel. 1977—), AAUW (Iowa State editor 1957), World Affairs Council, Alpha Chi Omega. Republican. Baptist. Clubs: Soroptimist (assembly del.) Eastern Star. Home: 2900 Pecos Way Riverside CA 92506 Office: 1161 Adminstrn Bldg U Calif Riverside CA 92521

FISHER, ANTHONY CLINTON, economics educator; b. Washington, Dec. 19, 1940; s. Solomon and Evelyn (Schuster) F.; m. Sirkka-Liisa Simpson, June 25, 1971; 1 son, John Olaf. B.A., Columbia U., 1962, Ph.D., 1968. Asst. prof. Brown U., Providence, 1967-71; research assoc. Resources for the Future, 1971-73; assoc. prof. U. Md., College Park, 1973-77; prof. energy and resources, econs. and agrl. and resource econs., U. Calif., Berkeley, 1977—. Mem. Assn. Environ. and Resource Economists (dir.), Am. Council for an Energy Efficient Economy (dir.), Am. Econs. Assn. Author: The Economics of Natural Environments, 1975; Economic and Fiscal Impacts of Coal Development, 1978; Resource and Environmental Economics, 1981; contbr. articles to profl. jours. Office: Energy and Resources Group Univ Calif Berkeley CA 94720

FISHER, BARBARA E., lawyer; b. Duluth, Minn., Apr. 14, 1938; d. Max and Sara Lee (Ginsburg) Edelstein; m. H. Kenneth Fisher, July 24,

1964; children—Hugh Edward, Joshua Benjamin, Michael Bernard. A.B., Wellesley Coll., 1960; J.D., NYU, 1963, LL.M. in Taxation, 1966. Bar: N.Y. 1963, Calif. 1966, Wash. 1970, Ariz. 1973. Law clk. U.S. Dist. Ct. So. Dist. N.Y., 1963-64; atty. N.Y. Legal Aid Soc., 1964-66, San Francisco Neighborhood Legal Asst. Found., 1966-69; asst. dir. legal services Region 9, OEO, 1969-70, dir. legal services Region 10, 1970-72; dir. Ariz. Pub. Law Assocs., Tucson, 1973-75; chief Tucson Office, Ariz. Atty. Gen., Tucson, 1976-79; mng. atty. Little, Fisher, Bromley & Siegel, P.C., Tucson, 1979—; law tchr. U. Ariz., 1973—. Bd. dirs. Legal Aid; mem. Ariz. Opera Co., Friends of Tucson Pub. Library, Pima Council on Aging, Widowed to Widowed. Mem. Ariz. Bar Assn., Pima County Bar Assn., Calif. Bar Assn., Ariz. Women Lawyers Assn., Queen's Bench. Contbr. articles to profl. jours. Home: 101 N Sahuara Ave Tucson AZ 85711 Office: Little Fisher Bromley & Siegel PC 177 N Church Ave Suite 1000 Tucson AZ 85701

FISHER, BENJAMIN PAUL, architect; b. El Paso, Tex., Apr. 26, 1952; s. Robert S. and Ann Gordon (Clise) F.; m. Margaret Anne Long, July 31, 1976. B.A. with distinction, Stanford U., 1974; M.B.A., U. Calif.-Berkeley, 1983. Registered architect, Calif.; lic. gen. contractor, Calif. Owner, Benjamin P. Fisher Gen. Contractor, San Francisco, 1976-78; project architect Knudson Assos., Boulder, Colo., 1978-79, L. Gale Abels Assos., Boulder, 1979-80; staff Daniel, Mann, Johnson, Mendenhahl, Denver, 1980-81; owner, prin. Fisher Assocs., Architects, Berkeley, Calif., 1981—. Sailing instr. Stanford U., 1973, 74; past pres. No. Calif. Intercollegiate Yacht Racing Assn.; past bd. dirs. Pacific Coast Intercollegiate Yacht Racing Assn. Mem. Stanford Alumni Assn., Tau Beta Pi. Republican. Home and Office: 2440 Cedar St Berkeley CA 94708

FISHER, BRYAN KENDALL, data processing manager; b. Liberal, Kans., June 1, 1952; s. Charles Keith and Alma Ruth (Funk) F.; m. Connie Joy Houston, December 1, 1979; children—Jessica Christine, Joshua Bryan. B.S. in Bus. Adminstrn. and Info. Systems, Colo. State U., 1975. Programmer, analyst Alascom Inc., Anchorage, 1975-80; systems analyst Motznik Computer Services Inc., Anchorage, 1980-81; mgr. mgmt. adv. services Price Waterhouse, Anchorage, 1981—; guest instr. Anchorage Community Coll. Active United Way. Mem. Data Processing Mgmt. Assn., Assn. Systems Mgmt. (charter mem. Anchorage chpt.). Episcopalian. Office: Price Waterhouse 101 W Benson Blvd Suite 500 Anchorage AK 99503

FISHER, DAVID ALEXANDER, lawyer; b. Pasadena, June 25, 1951; s. Joseph S. and Elizabeth (Jensen) F. B.A., U. Calif., San Diego, 1973; J.D., Western State U., 1976; postgrad. diploma in taxation U. San Diego, 1982. Bar: Calif. 1977. Long, Fisher & Miller, San Diego. Mem. ABA, San Diego Bar Assn., Real Estate and Securities Inst., Nat. Assn. Realtors, Internat. Assn. Fin. Planners. Club: San Diego Mission Bay Boat and Ski. Contbr. articles to profl. jours. Office: 2515 Camino Del Rio S Suite 238 San Diego CA 92108

FISHER, DONALD BOYD, plant physiologist; b. Phila., Oct. 14, 1935; s. Alexander Metcalf and Catherine (Boyd) F.; B.S. in Botany, U. Wash., 1957; M.S. in Botany, U. Wis., 1961; Ph.D. in Biochemistry/Biophysics, Iowa State U., 1965; m. Rita Campbell, June 8, 1963; children—Jennifer, Gregory. NIH postdoctoral fellow dept. botany U. Calif.-Berkeley, 1965-67, research assoc., 1967-68; asst. prof. botany U. Ga., 1968-72, assoc. prof., 1972-78; prof. botany Wash. State U., Pullman, 1978—. Served to lt. (j.g.) USN, 1957-59. NSF grantee, 1970-83; U.S. Dept. Agr. grantee, 1980—. Mem. Am. Assn. Plant Physiologists, AAAS, Am. Inst. Biol. Scis. Contbr. articles to profl. jours., chpts. to books. Office: Dept Botany Wash State Univ Pullman WA 99164

FISHER, ELIZABETH (BETTY) CHRISTENSEN, photo-journalist, public relations exec.; b. Salt Lake City, May 9, 1919; d. Orsen Reuben and Anna Katherine (Felix) Christensen; student U. Utah, 1938-39, L.D.S. Bus. Coll., 1940-41; m. Etsil Robert Fisher, Apr. 23, 1943 (dec. 1981); children—Edward Robert, Ellen Fisher Trickler, Colleen Fisher Newey, Randall Etsil, Garth Newell (dec.). Corr., Deseret News, Salt Lake City, 1951-60; asst. editor, photographer Weekly Reflex, Kaysville, Utah, 1961-63; asst. editor Br. Clearings, First Security Bank, Salt Lake City, 1962-64; corr. Salt Lake Tribune, 1963-64; photo-journalist Magna (Utah) Times, 1963-64; courthouse reporter Davis County Clipper, 1961-64; editor, columnist Weekly Reflex, 1964-69; freelance photo-journalist, freelance public relations exec., editor, 1969—; editor Utah Women Speak, 1979—; condr. workshops, lectr. in field. Mem. Davis County Fair Bd., 1952-80, Davis County Indsl. Commn., 1958-61; leader 4-H Clubs, 1947-61; publicity and promotion chmn. Davis County Fair, 1975-80; pub. info. chmn. Davis S. unit Am. Cancer Soc., 1974-81, mem. pub. info. bd. Utah div., 1976-80. Recipient 4 public info. awards Am. Cancer Soc.; 18 awards Utah Press Assn. Mem. Nat. Fedn. Press Women (7 press awards), Utah Press Women (pres. 1958-60, 2d v.p. 1965-66, rec. sec. 1971-72, 1st v.p. 1968-69, now historian; 70 press awards; Utah Woman of Achievement award 1981), Utah Assn. Indsl. Editors (awards), Utah Assn. Women, Internat. Platform Assn. Mormon. Asst. editor: My Farmington, 1975; editor Utah Women Speak, 1979—; editor indsl. brochures, jours.; contbr. articles, features and photos to mags. and newspapers. Address: 375 North 200 East PO Box 396 Farmington UT 84025

FISHER, FOREST FRANCIS RUTLEY, aeronautical engineer; b. Hertsfordshire, Eng., Nov. 9, 1934; came to U.S., 1964, naturalized, 1977; s. Francis Edwin and Violet Olivia (Rutley) F.; m. Gillian Barbara Trengove, Apr. 23, 1962; children—Forest Francis William, Nigel Norman Francis. B.A. in Math. with honors, Cambridge (Eng.) U., 1958, M.A. in Math. with honors, 1961; B.A. in Elec. Engring., Southall U., London, 1960; B.A. in Mech. Engring., Brunnel U., London, 1962; M.S. in Elec. Engring., U. Calif.-Irvine, 1970, Ph.D. in Info. Theory, 1974. Mgmt. trainee aircraft elec. systems Rotax Ltd., London, 1958-62; optical and radar systems engr. EMI Ltd., London, 1962-64; mem. advanced research group Boeing Co., Huntsville, Ala., 1964-66; sr. specialist engr. in optical and radar systems Aeronutronic div. Ford Aerospace and Communications Co., Newport Beach, Calif., 1966—; lectr. U. Calif., Irvine. Served with RAF, 1953-55. Mem. Inst. Elec. Engrs. (Eng.), Nat. Mgmt. Assn. Clubs: Hurlingham (London); Palisades Tennis, Balboa Bay (Newport Beach). Patentee in field. Home: 1417 Antigua Way Newport Beach CA 92660 Office: Aeronutronic Div Ford Aerospace and Communications Co Ford Rd Newport Beach CA 92660

FISHER, FREDERICK HENDRICK, oceanographer; b. Aberdeen, Wash., Dec. 30, 1926; s. Severe and Astrid (Kristofferson) F.; midshipman U.S. Naval Acad., 1945-47; B.S., U. Wash., 1949, Ph.D., 1957; m. Julie Gay Saund, June 17, 1955; children—Bruce Allen, Mark Edward, Keith Russell, Glen Michael. Research fellow acoustics Harvard, 1957-58; research physicist, research oceanographer Marine Phys. Lab., Scripps Instn. Oceanography, La Jolla, Calif., 1958—, asso. dir., 1975—; dir. research Havens Industries, San Diego, 1963-64; prof., chmn. dept. physics U. R.I., Kingston, 1970-71. Mem. San Diego County Democratic Central Com., 1956-57, 60-62; NCAA nat. tennis doubles champion, 1949. Served with USNR, 1945. Fellow Acoustical Soc. Am. (assoc. editor jour. 1969-76, v.p. 1980-81, pres. 1983-84), Explorers Club; mem. IEEE (sr.), Am. Chem. Soc., U.S. Naval Inst., Sigma Xi, AAAS, Pi Mu Epsilon. Club: Seattle Tennis. Co-designer research platform FLIP, 1960-62. Home: 3726 Charles St San Diego CA 92106 Office: U Calif Marine Phys Lab Scripps Institution Oceanography La Jolla CA 92093

FISHER, GORDON GERARD, optometrist; b. Dickinson, N.D., July 16, 1921; s. I. G. and Olga A. (Zdrahl) F.; m. Mildred L. Parker, Apr. 30, 1944; children—Gerard, Jeffrey, Jonathan, Laurie. O.D., No. Ill. Coll. Optometry, 1947. Practice optometry, Polson, Mont., 1947—. Mem. Polson City Council, 1960-81. Served to cpl., inf. U.S. Army, 1943-46. Mem. Am. Optometric Assn., Mont. Optometric Assn. Republican. Roman Catholic. Clubs: Rotary, Elks. Home: 414 6th Ave W Polson MT 59860 Office: 405 Main St Polson MT 59860

FISHER, H. RUSSELL, pathologist; b. Phila., May 4, 1905; s. Harry Wilford and Mary Ellen (Glass) F.; B.S., Hahnemann Coll. of Sci., 1926, M.D., Hahnemann Med. Coll., 1928; fellow U. Vienna, 1939; m. Virginia I. Moore, Sept. 19, 1931 (dec. 1979); children—Harry Russell, John G., Mary Ellen. Intern, Hahnemann Hosp., Phila., 1928-29, resident, 1929-32; prof. pathology Hahnemann Med. Coll., 1939-46; prof. pathology So. Calif. Sch. Medicine, 1946-72, emeritas, 1973—; practice medicine specializing in pathology; mem. staffs Moore White Clinic, Los Angeles, 1946-53, Eye & Ear Hosp., Los Angeles, 1953-72; dir. lab. Huntington Meml. Hosp., Pasadena, Calif., 1953-56, Meml. Hosp., Glendale, 1960-72; dir. lab. Santa Fe Hosp., Los Angeles, 1956-81, research asso., 1981—; mem. Com. on Internat. Council of Socs. of Pathology, Nat. Acad. Sci., 1967—. Served to comdr. USN, 1943-46. Named Alumnus of Yr., Hahnemann Med. Coll., 1972. Mem. AMA, Internat. Acad. Pathologists, Am. Soc. Clin. Pathologists, Calif. Soc. Pathologists, Los Angeles County Med. Assn., Calif. Med. Assn., Coll. Am. Pathologists (v.p. 1963-65) Republican. Lutheran. Club: Kiwanis. Contbr. articles in field to profl. jours. Home and Office: 1920 Melwood Dr Glendale CA 91207

FISHER, HOWARD NORTON, radio broadcast executive, producer; b. Chgo., Dec. 16, 1928; s. Jacob and Adele (Gershon) F.; m. Edith Reimer, Jan. 8, 1950; children—Jody, Richard; m. 2d Sylvia Ruth Guenther, Feb. 14, 1971; children—Debra, Rhonda, Cyndi, Tamra. Student Northwestern U., 1948, Columbia U., 1949. Radio announcer, sportscaster, newscaster Sta. WHOT, South Bend, Ind., 1950, Sta. WASK, Lafayette, Ind., 1951-53, Sta. WARL, Arlington, Va. and Washington, 1953; with sales and mgmt. Sta. WLSE, Wallace, N.C., 1953-56, Sta. KFMA, Davenport, Iowa, 1956-61, Sta. WEEF, Highland Park, Ill., 1961-65; sales and mgmt. positions Sta. WPRO, Riverside, Calif., 1965—, pres., gen. mgr., 1970—; pres., gen. mgr. Stas. KPRD and KZNA, Barstow, Calif., 1981—; news and spl. reporter Voice of Am., Washington, 1954; co-owner Am. Race Broadcasters subs. Am. Radio Broadcasters; exec. producer. Bds. dirs. Salvation Army, ARC, Loma Linda Faculty, U. Calif., Riverside; past pres. Am. Cancer Soc.; mem. adv. com. Riverside City Coll. Recipient various awards Calif. State Senate, Calif. State Legislature. Mem. So. Calif. Broadcasters Assn. (bd. dirs.), Inland Empire Broadcasters Assn. (past pres.), Greater Riverside C. of C. (past pres.). Club: Rotary.

FISHER, JOEL MARSHALL, polit. scientist, legal recruiter; b. Chgo., June 24, 1935; s. Dan and Nell (Kolvin) F.; A.B., U. So. Calif., 1955; LL.B., M.A., U. Calif., Berkeley; Ph.D. in Govt., Claremont Grad. Sch., 1968; m. Linda Joyce Buss, 1970; children—Sara Melinda, Matthew Nicholas. Orgn. dir. Republican Citizens Com. of U.S., Washington, 1964-65; dir. arts and scis., state legis. divs. Rep. Nat. Com., Washington, 1968-69; asst. dep. counsel to Pres. U.S., White House, 1969-70; dep. asst. sec. econ. and social affairs U.S. Dept. State, Washington, 1969-71; vis. prof. comparative and internat. law Loyola U. Sch. Law, Los Angeles, 1972-73; asso. prof. polit. sci. Calif. State U., Fullerton, 1966-68, 71-73; dir. World Bus. Inst., Center for Internat. Bus., Pepperdine U., Los Angeles, 1974-75; prof. constl. law Southwestern U. Sch. Law, Los Angeles, 1974-76; dir. World Trade Inst., Los Angeles, 1976—; prof. internat. law, asst. dean Whittier Coll. Sch. Law, Los Angeles, 1977-80; prin. Ziskind, Greene & Assos., Atty. Placement, 1980—; ofcl. visitor The European Communities, 1974, 76; mem. U.S. dels. UN Confs., 1969-71; chmn. Strategy for Peace Conf. Panel on U.S. and UN, 1972—; coordinator Series on the Contemporary Am. Presidency, 1972-73; cons. Interconti, Inc., 1975-76, Robert Taft Inst., 1977—, World Trade Inst. N.Y., 1977—, Woodstock Prodns., 1978—, Curtis Hoxter & Co., N.Y.C., 1978—. Mem. steering com. Calif. Com. for Reelection of Pres., 1972; nat. chmn. Community Leaders for Ford, 1976; trustee Rep. Assos., 1978—; vestryman St. Michael and All Angels Ch. Nobel Found. fellow, 1958, Falk fellow, 1961-62, Am. Polit. Sci. Assn. State fellow, 1970-73. Mem. Am. Soc. Internat. Law, Am. Polit. Sci. Assn., Fgn. Law Assn. So. Calif., Calif. Ctr. for Edn. in Pub. Affairs, Brit.-Am. C. of C., German-Am. C. of C. Co-author 2 books; contbr. articles on polit. sci. to profl. publs. Home: 4963 Bluebell Ave N Hollywood CA 91607 Office: 8912 Burton Way Beverly Hills CA 90211

FISHER, JOHN SERGIO, architect, educator; b. Milano, Italy, May 7, 1934; s. Albert Darius and Elsa Maria (Weinstock) F.; came to U.S., 1939, naturalized, 1952; B.Arch., Carnegie Inst. Tech., 1958; Finnish Inst.Tech., 1959; M.Arch., Carnegie Inst. Tech., 1961; m. Bonnie Jean McIntosh, Jan. 28, 1962; children—Ava, Carina, Matt. Asst. prof. dept. architecture U. Calif., Berkeley, 1963-69; partner Fisher/Jackson Assos., Architects/Urban Designers, Berkeley, N.Y.C., 1964-67; pres. Fisher/Jackson Assos., Inc., Architecture/Systems Development/Urban Planning, Berkeley, Calif., 1967-72; dean Sch. Architecture, Syracuse (N.Y.) U., 1972-75; pres. John Sergio Fisher AIA & Assos., Inc., Studio City and Oakland, Calif., 1976—; adj. lectr. dept. architecture Calif. Poly. Inst., Pomona, fall 1975, Sch. Architecture and Urban Planning, UCLA, 1979, 80, 82; hearing examiner Calif. Bd. Archtl. Examiners. Shelter analyst, instr. Office of CD, 1962; mem. Com. on Aging, Berkeley, 1966-69; chmn. Fisher Housing Systems, 1977-79; trustee Los Angeles Actors Theatre, 1979—. Fulbright grantee, 1958; HUD Urban Devel. Action grantee, 1979. Mem. AIA (Spl. Design award 1969), Design Methods Group, Internat. Solar Energy Soc., Inst. Urban Planning, Nat. Trust Historic Preservation. Democrat. Patentee in field. Office: 11536 Ventura Blvd Studio City CA 91604

FISHER, JOHN WILLIAM, water conditioning specialist; b. Lincoln, Nebr., Nov. 11, 1930; s. James Weller and Ruth (Harper) F.; m. Donna Julia Klinck, July 7, 1953 (div.); children—James Weller, Darien Faye, Barratt Harper, Robert Hoyt. A.A., Santa Rosa Jr. Coll., 1951; B.S., U. Calif., 1954. Cert. water specialist. Ptnr. James Fisher and Son, Santa Rosa, Calif., 1951—, pres. James Fisher & Son, Inc., 1966—; v.p. Culligan Water Conditioning of Santa Rosa, 1966-78, pres., 1978—; bd. dirs., sec. Culligan Soft Water Service Operators, Inc., 1955-57. Paul Harris fellow, 1966. Mem. Am. Water Works Assn., Pacific Water Quality Assn., Water Quality Assn., C. of C. Santa Rosa (dirs.). Republican. Clubs: Rotary (pres.), Santa Rosa Golf and Country (past pres.), Barbfish Lodge. Home: 134 Country Club Dr Santa Rosa CA 95401 Office: 1236 Cleveland Ave Santa Rosa CA 95401

FISHER, KENNETH L., sculptor; b. Tacoma, Apr. 28, 1944; s. Henry John and Anna Mary (Trafford) F. B.S., U. Oreg., 1968, B.F.A., 1969, M.F.A., 1971. Cert. univ. level tchr., Calif. Group shows include: Idaho State U. (1st Place award), 1982, Del Mar Coll., (Joseph A. Cain Meml. Purchase award in sculpture), Corpus Christi, Tex., 1982, Goldsboro's 3d Ann. Juried Exhbn., N.C., 1982, Fine Arts League 14th Nat. Art Show, (1st Place award), Colo., 1982, Franklin Sq. Gallery (M. Brumbacher, Inc. Bronze medallion), N.C., 1982, J. K. Ralston Museum (1st and 2d Place awards), Mont., 1982, Oreg. State U. (Honor award), 1983, Hill Country Arts Found. 11th Ann. Exhbn. (1st Place award in sculpture), Tex., 1983; represented in numerous pvt. collections. Mem. Portland Art Assn.

FISHER, LAVERNE AUGUST, business executive, consultant, band leader; b. Pullman, Wash., June 6, 1920; s. William Alfonse and AnnaBelle Rose (Menglekamp) F.; m. Nora Kathleen Creed, Aug. 7, 1941; 1 son, Arthur William. Student Spokane pub. schs. Band leader, Spokane, Wash., 1937-77; owner restaurant, Spokane, 1950-62, taverns, Spokane, 1962-83; pres. Securities Tng. Inst., Inc., Spokane, 1983—; pres. Your Place, Inc., My Place, Inc.; cons. to small bus. Mem. corps of execs. SBA.; pres. Spokane Valley Tavern Assn. Recipient ACE award of yr. SBA, 1982. Mem. Nat. Assn. Securities Schs. (past dir.). Clubs: Spokane Comml. Travelers, Athletic Round Table (dir.), Moose, KC. Office: 6415 E Broadway Spokane WA 99206

FISHER, LAWRENCE W., public relations company executive; b. Los Angeles, June 5, 1938; s. Gilbert W. and Augusta (Gelsheimer) F.; A.B. magna cum laude, U. So. Calif., 1960; m. Elizabeth Sheridan Burke, July 16, 1966; children—Lawrence Timothy, Lara Elizabeth. Legislative asst. Speaker Assembly, Calif. Legislature, 1960-62; exec. dir. Democratic State Central Com., 1962-66; pres. Braun & Co., Los Angeles, 1966—. Dir. Los Angeles Conv. Center. Mem. Town Hall, Phi Beta Kappa, Sigma Delta Chi. Home: 767 Via de la Paz Pacific Palisades CA 90272 Office: 3055 Wilshire Blvd Los Angeles CA 90010

FISHER, LINDA JOYCE, airframe manufacturing company project coordinator; b. Mpls., Sept. 1, 1943; d. Maynard M. and Arline I. (Hanson) Buss; m. Joel M. Fisher, Aug. 29, 1970; children—Sara Melinda, Matthew Nicholas. A.B., Stanford U., 1965; M.A. (fellow), U. Tex., 1966. Staff mem. Legis. Liaison Office VA, Washington, 1966-68; manpower specialist U.S. Dept. Labor, Washington and Los Angeles, 1968-74; project coordinator Lockheed-Calif. Co., Burbank, 1979—. Recipient Outstanding Performance award U.S. Dept. Labor, 1969. Mem. Nat. Mgmt. Assn., Stanford Profl. Women Los Angeles County, Stanford Alumni Orgn. Episcopalian. Office: Lockheed-Calif Co D/86-20 PO Box 551 Burbank CA 91520

FISHER, LOUIS MCLANE, JR., engring. company executive; b. Balt., July 25, 1938; s. Louis McLane and Betty Taylor (Griswold) F.; B.A. magna cum laude, Hampden-Sydney Coll., 1961; postgrad. U. Va., 1961-62; M.B.A., U. Oreg., 1963; m. Sue Jane Roderick, Jan. 2, 1977; children—Kathy, Mark, Matthew, Andy; stepchildren—Rolf (dec.), Sonja, Kirsten. Exec. trainee First Nat. Bank Oreg., Portland, 1963, investment analyst, 1964; owner, mgr. Bus. Services, Corvallis, Oreg., 1964-65; adminstrv. mgr. CH2M Hill Corvallis, 1965-70, treas., 1970-75, exec. v.p., 1975—; guest lectr. Oreg. State U.; dir. Open Door Inc. Bd. dirs. Corvallis Arts Center. Fellow Profl. Services Mgmt. Assn. (dir. 1975-78, pres. 1976-77); mem. Corvallis Area C. of C. (dir., v.p. 1971), Am. Mgmt. Assn., Am. Cons. Engrs. Council, Assn. M.B.A. Execs., Fin. Execs. Inst., Soc. Mktg. Profl. Services, Denver C. of C. Republican. Episcopalian. Clubs: Metropolitan, Colo. Racquet. Contbr. articles to profl. jours. Home: 9637 E Lake Ave Englewood CO 80111 Office: 5995 S Syracuse PO Box 22508 Denver CO 80222

FISHER, PAUL CARY, economist, business executive; b. Lebanon, Kans., Oct. 10, 1913; s. Carey A. and Alice (Bales) F.; B.S., Kans. State U., 1939; Children—Terry Lynn, Paul Cary, Jr., Caroleen, Pomm, Marteen, Morgan, Scott. Asst. to pres. Aetna Ball Bearing Mfg. Co., Chgo., 1942-45; pres., owner Fisher Pen Co., Boulder City, 1948—; inventor Pressurized Ball Pen, 1965, The Fisher Space Pen, 1968. Named Nevada's Small Bus. Person of Yr., SBA, 1980. Democrat. Methodist. Club: Rotary. Author: Road to Freedom, 1960; Tax Reform—America at the Brink, 1968. Home and office: 711 Yucca St Boulder City NV 89005

FISHER, RICHARD FORREST, educator; b. Champaign, Ill., May 15, 1941; s. Richard Forrest and Hannah Elizabeth (Ponath) F.; B.A., B.S. in Forestry, U. Ill., 1964; Ph.D., Cornell U., 1968; m. Karen Dangerfield, Sept. 4, 1959; children—William, Marilu, Kevin. Asst. prof. U. Ill., 1968-72; assoc. prof. faculty of forestry U. Toronto (Ont., Can.), 1972-77; prof. forest soils Sch. Forest Resources, U. Fla., 1977-82; prof., head dept. forest resources Coll. Natural Resources, Utah State U., 1982—. Mem. Soil Sci. Soc. Am., Soc. Am. Foresters, AAAS, Am. Inst. Biol. Scis., Sigma Xi. Democrat. Presbyterian. Contbr. numerous articles to profl. jours. Home: 1573 East 1260 North Logan UT 84321 Office: Coll Natural Resources UMC 52 Utah State Univ Logan UT 84322

FISHER, RICHARD LESLIE, state management analyst; b. Sacramento, Calif., Jan. 22, 1948; s. Leslie Davis and Mildred Lavon (Sommers) F.; A.A., Sacramento City Coll., 1970; B.A. in Econs., Calif. State U.-Sacramento, 1972; postgrad. McGeorge Sch. Law, U. of Pacific, 1972-73; m. Carol Ann Richardson, Aug. 14, 1971; children—Lee James, Kari Ann, Kevin Richard, Robin Marissa, Andrew Michael. Office services supr. Bur. Criminal Identification, Calif. Dept. Justice, Sacramento, 1971-73; field rep. State Tchrs. Retirement System, Sacramento, 1973-75, asst. sec. mgr., membership reporting, 1975-76, deptl. coordinator mandatory state programs, 1976-79, mgr. tax sheltered annuity program, 1979-80, budget officer, mgr. adminstrv. services, 1980-81; mgr. budget, fiscal and bus. services, mgmt. info. and analysis Calif. State Personnel Bd., 1981—; cons. community facility site selection City of Pleasant Hill. Res. dep. Sacramento County Sheriffs Dept., 1975-79; active Boy Scouts Am., 1976—; chmn. citizens adv. com. on middle schs. Elverta Joint Elem. Sch. Dist. Mem. Nat. Micrographics Assn. Republican. Mem. Ch. Jesus Christ of Latter-day Saints. state management analyst; b. Sacramento, Calif., Jan. 22, 1948; s. Leslie Davis and Mildred Lavon (Sommers) F.; A.A., Sacramento City Coll., 1970; B.A. in Econs., Calif. State U.-Sacramento, 1972; postgrad. McGeorge Sch. Law, U. of Pacific, 1972-73; m. Carol Ann Richardson, Aug. 14, 1971; children—Lee James, Kari Ann, Kevin Richard, Robin Marissa, Andrew Michael. Office services supr. Bur. Criminal Identification, Calif. Dept. Justice, Sacramento, 1971-73; field rep. State Tchrs. Retirement System, Sacramento, 1973-75, asst. sec. mgr., membership reporting, 1975-76, deptl. coordinator mandatory state programs, 1976-79, mgr. tax sheltered annuity program, 1979-80, budget officer, mgr. adminstrv. services, 1980-81; mgr. budget, fiscal and bus. services, mgmt. info. and analysis Calif. State Personnel Bd., 1981—; cons. community facility site selection City of Pleasant Hill. Res. dep. Sacramento County Sheriffs Dept., 1975-79; active Boy Scouts Am., 1976—; chmn. citizens adv. com. on middle schs. Elverta Joint Elem. Sch. Dist. Mem. Nat. Micrographics Assn. Republican. Mem. Ch. Jesus Christ of Latter-day Saints. Home: 308W Los Garcias Ln Elverta CA 95626 Office: 801 Capitol Mall Sacramento CA 95814

FISHER, ROBERT FRANCIS, architect; b. Cin., July 9, 1921; s. Robert Howard and Faye (Maple) F.; B.Arch., U. Mich., 1946; B.S. in Civil Engring., Oreg. State U., 1944; postgrad. U. Calif., Berkeley, 1965; m. Mary Angeline Marchese, Apr. 8, 1944; children—Beth, Ingrid, Cary. Draftsman, architect Pietro Belluschi, Portland, Oreg., 1946-48; ind. practice architecture, Grants Pass, Oreg., 1948—; exhibited archtl. work and watercolors Rogue Art Gallery, Medford, 1966, Josephine County Library, 1955; constrn. mgmt. cons. for comml. projects, Oreg., Wash., Calif., Utah, Tex.; seismology collaborator Nat. Earthquake Info. Service. County chmn. Great Decision Study Groups, 1958-64; chmn. Grants Pass Planning Com., 1960-67, mem., 1954-77; v.p. Josephine County council Boy Scouts Am., 1955. Served with AUS, 1942-45. Decorated Bronze Star (2); registered architect, Oreg., Calif., Iowa; certified Nat. Council Archtl. Registration Bds. Mem. AIA (pres. So. Oreg. chpt. 1968, v.p. 1967, sec. 1966, treas. 1965), Constrn. Specifications Inst., Tau Sigma Delta, Phi Kappa Phi. Archtl. works include: U.S. Post Office, Grants Pass, 1967; North Jr. High Sch., Grants Pass, 1966;

Forest Glen Sr. Residence, Canyonville, 1962; Grants Pass Shopping Center, 1970; Champion Products plant, Burlington, Iowa, 1972; Rogue Community Coll., Grants Pass, 1971-74; Pacific Power & Light Co. bldg., Grants Pass, 1972; Grants Pass Profl. Plaza, 1973; Apostolic Faith Ch., Eureka, Calif., 1974; Royale Gardens Nursing Home, Grants Pass, 1974; Sutherlin (Oreg.) High Sch., 1974; Mormon chs., Etna, Calif., 1977, Central Point, Oreg., 1977, Grants Pass, Oreg., 1976, Myrtle Creek, Oreg., 1974, Cave Junction, Oreg., 1972, 79, Grants Pass Stake Center, 1980. Address: 131 NE B St Grants Pass OR 97526

FISHER, WAYNE H., business executive; b. Los Angeles, Dec. 27, 1920; s. Wayne Holmes and Lucille (Bartlett) F.; B.A., Pomona Coll., 1942; J.A., Harvard U., 1943; M.B.A., Stanford, 1946; m. Theo Frisbee, May 26, 1942; children—William Noble, Robert Gregory, Elizabeth Helen. With Owl Drug Co., Los Angeles, from 1947, pres., 1960-62; with Lucky Stores, Inc., 1962—, exec. v.p., 1968-71, pres., 1971-80, chmn., 1974—, chief exec. officer until 1980, also dir.; dir. Transam. Corp., 1979—, Denny's, Inc., 1980—, Standard Brands Paint Co., 1980—. Mem. bd. govs. and exec. com. Food Employers Council of Calif., 1963-80; past pres., past mem. bd. dirs. and adv. com. Western Assn. Food Chains, Inc., 1965-69; bd. dirs., mem. exec. com. Food Mktg. Inst., 1974-80; mgmt. chmn. Joint Labor Mgmt. Com., 1978-80. Bd. dirs. Bay Area Council, 1972-79; mem. adv. council Stanford Grad. Sch. Bus., 1973-79; bd. govs., mem. long-range planning com. San Francisco Symphony Assn., 1975-80; trustee Pomona Coll., 1978—. Address: Lucky Stores Inc 6300 Clark Ave Dublin CA 94566

FISHER, WILLIAM BRADFORD, computer systems company executive, educator, consultant; b. Newton, Mass., Feb. 24, 1941; s. Francis Perkins and Marion Ruth (House) F.; m. Elizabeth Marie England, Nov. 22, 1962; children—Bradford, Wendy, Katherine. B.A., Middlebury Coll., 1963; M.A.T., Harvard U., 1965, cert. advanced study, 1972, Ed.D., 1974. Lic. prin., supt., Mass. Tchr. history Belmont (Mass.) High Sch., 1967-69; asst. prin. Burlington (Vt.) High Sch., 1969-71; ednl. cons. Westinghouse Learning Corp., Waltham, Mass., 1971-73; prin. Hamilton-Wenham High Sch., Hamilton, Mass., 1973-74; supt. Hamilton-Wenham Regional Sch. Dist., 1974-81; dir. basics div. WICAT Systems, Orem, Utah, 1981—; dir., chmn. Cape Anne Collaborative, 1975-81; pres. North Shore Supts. Roundtable, 1980-81; cons. Strategic Info., Waltham, Mass., 1980-81; Utah Bd. Edn. Adv. Com. Computers in Edn., 1982 ; chmn. Mass. Basic Skills Adv. Commn., 1977-81, chmn. Mass. Assessment Adv. Com., 1977-79. Served to 1st lt. U.S. Army, 1965-67. Decorated Bronze Star; Mott fellow, 1971. Mem. Mass. Assn. Sch. Supts., Assn. Supervision and Curriculum Devel., Am. Assn. Sch. Adminstrs. Home: 1888 S Main St Orem UT 84057 Office: 1875 S State St Orem UT 84057

FISHER-BYNER, SALLY JEAN, messenger service executive; b. Dayton, Ohio, June 19, 1949; d. Russell Eugene and Kathleen Virginia (Browne) Fisher; m. John Thomas Byner, May 21, 1982. B.A., U. Ky., 1972. Owner, mgr. Malibu Messenger Service (Calif.), 1980—. Mem. Malibu C. of C. Republican. Christian.

FISHKIN, GERALD LOREN, psychologist, educator; b. Bronx, N.Y., Aug. 16, 1944. A.A., El Camino Jr. Coll., Torrance, Calif., 1965; B.A., Calif. State Coll., Long Beach, 1967; M.S., Brigham Young U., 1969; Ph.D., U.S. Internat. U., 1978. Research asst. psychology dept. Calif. State Coll., Long Beach, 1965-66, dir. research-counseling and testing dept., asst. prof. ednl. psychology, 1969-70, cons. to police officers standards and tng. workshops Center for Criminal Justice, 1975—; clin. psychometrist VA Hosp., Long Beach, 1966-68; clin. intern Brigham Young U. Counseling Center, Provo, Utah, 1968-69; pvt. practice psychology, Long Beach, 1970—; cons. psychologist Long Beach Meml. Hosp., 1970-74; founder, coordinator dept. spl. edn. Long Beach City Coll., 1971-77, instr. applied psychology for law enforcement, dept. adminstrn. of justice, 1972—, assoc. prof. and psychologist, 1978—; pvt. clin. practice, 1978 ; cons. Long Beach Police Dept., 1975; dir. Community Rehab. Industries, Inc. Mem. Mayor's Com. for Employment Handicapped, Long Beach; bd. dirs. Long Beach Retarded Children's Found. Mem. NEA, Calif. Tchrs. Assn., Harbor Soc. Clin. Hypnosis, Am. Psychol. Assn., Calif. Assn. Marriage and Family Therapists, Calif. Community and Jr. Coll. Assn. (Task Force on Post-Secondary Ednl. Programs for Developmentally Disabled), Brit. Psychol. Soc. (fgn. affiliate), Long Beach Police Officers Assn. (hon.), Phi Delta Kappa. Office: 5199 E Pacific Coast Hwy Suite 304 N Long Beach CA 90804

FISHMAN, MAX, electrical engineer; b. Haverhill, Mass., Apr. 30, 1921; s. Nathan and Tillie (Blecher) F.; m. Zehava Itzhaki, Sept. 14, 1950; children—Ronit Pearl, Ethan N., Deena B., Jonathan N. B.Sc., Carnegie Inst. Tech., 1942, M.Sc., 1943, D.Sc., 1948. Registered profl. engr., Calif., Israel. Electronic engr. Transducer div. AM & F, Boston, 1950-52, Convair, San Diego, 1952-54; sr. engr. Ultrasonic Corp., Cambridge, Mass., 1954-55; sr. scientist Lockheed, Sunnyvale, Calif., 1955-59; sr. engr. SRI, Menlo Park, Calif., 1959-61; mem. tech. staff Stanford Linear Accelerator Center, 1961-70; staff cons. Israel Electo Optical Lab., 1970-79; vis. prof. Calif. State U.-Sacramento, 1979-81; dir. research and devel. Jones Futura Found., Fair Oaks, Calif., 1981—; mem. summer faculty Lawrence Livermore Lab. Served to lt. (j.g.), USNR, 1944-46; PTO. Buhl fellow in elec. engring., 1943-44; recipient Kaplan prize, 1973. Mem. IEEE, Sigma Xi. Republican. Jewish. Contbr. articles profl. jours. Home: 84 Cadillac Dr 81 Sacramento CA 95825 Office: 9700 Fair Oaks Blvd Fair Oaks CA 95628

FISK, CHARLES CARROLL, consulting engineer; b. St. Croix Falls, Wis., Jan. 7, 1918; s. Harry Abner and Emma (Anderson) F.; B.S. in Agr., U. Wis., 1941, B.S. in Civil Engring., 1942; Profl. Cert. Meterology U. Chgo., 1943; m. Micki Rennie, June 3, 1942; children—Terren Allen, Cherie Lyn, Lucinda Louise, Carolee Marie. Hydraulic engr. U.S. Bur. Reclamation, Denver, 1946-50, asst. chief river operations, Loveland, Colo., 1950-55; water supply engr. Denver Water Bd., 1955-61; cons. engr. water supply, water rights, hydrology, Denver, 1961—; editor Colo. Water Congress Newsletter, 1957-63; editor, pub., owner Western Water Newsletter, 1961-62. Served with USAAF, 1942-46. Decorated Bronze Star medal. Fellow ASCE. Home and Office: PO Box 830 Fraser CO 80442

FISK, EDWARD RAY, civil engr., author, educator; b. Oshkosh, Wis., July 19, 1924; s. Ray Edward and Grace O. (Meyer) Barnes; student Marquette U., 1949, Fresno (Calif.) State Coll., 1954, UCLA, 1957-58; B.S., M.B.A., Calif.-Western U.; m. Oct. 28, 1950; children—Jacqueline Mary (Mrs. John Joseph Stamp), Edward Ray II, William John, Robert Paul. Engr., Calif. Div. Hwys., 1952-55; engr. Bechtel Corp., Vernon, Calif., 1955-59; project mgr. Toups Engring Co., Santa Ana, Calif., 1959-61; dept. head Perliter & Soring, Los Angeles, 1961-64; Western rep. Wire Reinforcement Inst., Washington, 1964-65; cons. engr., Anaheim, Calif., 1965; asso. engr. Met. Water Dist. So. Calif., 1966-68; chief specification engr. Koebig & Koebig, Inc., Los Angeles, 1968-71; mgr. constrn. services VTN Consol., Inc., Irvine, Calif., 1971-78; pres. E.R. Fisk Constrn., Orange, Calif., 1978-81; corp. dir. constrn. mgmt. James M. Montgomery Cons. Engrs., Inc., Pasadena, Calif., 1981-83; v.p. Lawrence, Fisk & McFarland, Inc., Santa Barbara and Orange, 1983—; adj. prof. engring. Orange Coast Coll., Costa Mesa, Calif., 1957-78, Calif. Poly. State U., Pomona, 1974; lectr. U. Calif., Berkeley, internationally for ASCE Continuing Edn.; former mem. Calif. Bd. Registered Constrn. Insps. Served with USN, 1942-43, USAF, 1951-52. Registered profl. engr., Ariz., Calif., Colo., Fla., Idaho, La., Mont., Nev., Oreg., Utah, Wash., Wyo.; lic. land surveyor, Oreg., Idaho; lic. gen. engring. contractor, Calif.; cert. abritator Calif. Constrn. Contract Arbitration Com. Fellow ASCE (chmn. exec. com. constrn. div.; former chmn. nat. com. inspection 1978—); mem. Orange County Engring. Council (former pres.), Calif. Soc. Profl. Engrs. (past pres. Orange County), Am. Arbitration Assn. (nat. panel), U.S. Com. Large Dams, Order Founders and Patriots Am. (past gov. Calif.), Soc. Colonial Wars, S.R. (past dir.), Engring. Edn. Found. (trustee), Tau Beta Pi. Republican. Author: Machine Methods of Survey Computing, 1958; Construction Project Administration, 1978, 82; Construction Engineers Form Book, 1981. Contbr. articles on constrn., tech., hist. and geneal. subjects to publs. Columnist, Engr. of So. Calif. mag., 1971-73. Home: PO Box 6448 Orange CA 92667 Office: 314 E Carrillo St Suite 1 Santa Barbara CA 93101

FITCH, DORINNE GRIFFIN, accounting firm official; b. Inglewood, Calif., May 28, 1956; d. Donald Dexter and Joan Alvina (Marsh) Griffin; m. Donald Charles Fitch, Apr. 19, 1980. B.S. in Gerontology, U. So. Calif., 1978. Recreation dir. Palmcrest Retirement Villas, Long Beach, Calif., 1978-79; asst. dir. alumni spl. events, U. So. Calif. Alumni House, Los Angeles, 1979-80; dir. community relations Lesley, Thomas, Schwarz & Postma, C.P.A.s, Newport Beach, Calif., 1980-81, Ernst & Whinney C.P.A.s, Newport Beach, 1981—. Mem. benefit com. Providence Speech & Hearing Ctr.; bd. dirs. Newport C. of C. Dolphins. Recipient White Orchid award Newport C. of C.; 1st prize newsletter contest Nat. Assn. Accts., 1982. Mem. Nat. Assn. Accts., Pub. Relations Soc. Am., Am. Bus. Women's Assn., U. So. Calif. Town & Gown Jrs., Kappa Kappa Gamma. Republican. Lutheran. Contrb. articles to profl. jours. Office: 4000 MacArthur Blvd Ste 800 Newport Beach CA 92660

FITCH, FRANK, alternative criminal justice project adminstr.; b. Honolulu, Feb. 13, 1943; s. Frank Wallace and Francis (Gunnerson) F.; student U. Colo., 1960-63, San Francisco City Coll., 1970-73. Office mgr. public relations firm, Los Angeles, 1971-73; exec. dir. Gay Community of Concern, Stanford, Calif., 1973-76; dep. dir. San Francisco Pretrial Diversion Project, 1976—; cons. computer bus. systems; polit. cons. Founding sec. Market St. Mchts. Assn., San Francisco, 1975-76, Golden Gate Bus. Assn., San Francisco, 1976-77; pres. Soc. Individual Rights, San Francisco, 1975-76; mem. San Francisco Sheriff's Adv. Com., 1976—; chmn. San Francisco Human Rights Advs., 1977-78; mem. San Francisco Fire Safety Task Force, 1977—; co-chmn. Gay Caucus, Calif. Democratic Council, 1977-79; del. Nat. Dem. Mid-term Conf., Memphis, 1978; pres. Eureka Valley Promotion Assn., San Francisco, 1977-78, 81-82, Alice B. Toklas Dem. Club, San Francisco, 1977-79; treas. San Francisco Charter Commn., 1978—; mem. Calif. State Dem. Central Com., 1978—; controller Calif. Dem. Council, 1978-81, treas., 1981—; chmn. affirmative action adv. com. San Francisco Civil Service Dept., 1978—; treas. Castro St. Fair. Recipient cert. Calif. State Assembly, 1979. Mem. Nat. Assn. Pretrial Services, Calif. Assn. Pretrial Services, ACLU, Nat. Gay Task Force, NOW, Nat. Women's Polit. Caucus, Gay Rights Nat. Lobby, Calif. Human Rights Advs., Nat. Orgn. for Repeal Marijuana Laws. Author: Ending Discrimination Against Lesbians and Gay Men, 1976. Home: 2347a Market St San Francisco CA 94114 Office: 685 6th St San Francisco CA 94103

FITCH, JOHN RICHARD, newspaper executive; b. Newark, Ohio, June 1, 1938; s. John Clyde and Mildred Josephine (Nethers) F.; children—Joanne Elizabeth, Troy Alan, Victoria Dianne, Vallerie Jo. Student Baylor U., 1958-59, Imperial Valley Coll., 1960-64. Advt. salesman Associated Desert Newspapers Inc., El Centro, Calif., 1960-64, advt. mgr., 1964-65, bus. mgr., 1965-66, gen. mgr., 1966-69, editor, pub., 1969-76, pres., 1978—. Pres. El Centro C. of C., 1970; chmn. Imperial County Grand Jury, 1976-77; chmn. El Centro Community Hosp. bond drive, 1976. Served with USAF, 1956-60. Mem. Calif. Newspaper Pubs. Assn. (chmn. govtl. affairs com.). Republican. Baptist. Club: Kiwanis (pres. 1970-71, lt. gov. 1982) (El Centro). Home: 903 W McCabe Rd El Centro CA 92243 Office: 205 N 8th St PO Box 251 El Centro CA 92244

FITCH, SANFORD, technical manufacturing company executive; b. N.Y.C., Sept. 3, 1940; s. Lucius William and Zona Gale (Stevenson) F.; B.S., Stanford, 1962, M.B.A., 1968; m. Susan Cardot Vastine, Sept. 13, 1969; children—Brian, Melissa. Mgr. financial planning Raychem Corp., Menlo Park, Calif., 1968-69; mgr. finance and adminstrn., also sec. corp. Chemelex Inc., Redwood City, Calif., 1969-76; v.p. fin. Telecommunications Tech. Inc., Sunnyvale, Calif., 1977-78; v.p. fin., sec., treas. Durango Systems Inc., San Jose, Calif., 1978-82, v.p., gen. mgr. ins. div., 1982—. Served with USN, 1962-66; Vietnam. Mem. Fin. Execs. Inst. (dir.). Office: 3003 N 1st St San Jose CA

FITCH, STEPHEN HENRY, aircraft company manager; b. Los Angeles, Aug. 19, 1925; s. Stephen Bertram and Lilian Edith Olive (Weeks) F.; B.S. in Applied Physics, UCLA, 1949; M.B.A., U. Utah, 1977; m. Joan Louise LaFehr, Aug. 10, 1945; children—Caryn Louise, Stephen Michael, Mark Thomas, Robin Ann, Timothy Andrew, Susan Elizabeth. With Nat. Bur. Standards, Washington, 1949-50, Naval Radiol. Def. Lab., San Francisco, 1950-51, Calif. Research & Devel. Corp., Livermore, 1952-54, Broadview Research & Devel. Corp., Burlingame, Calif., 1954-55; supr. radiation instrumentation Atomics Internat. div. Rockwell Internat., Canoga Park, Calif., 1955-66, nuclear hardness tech. dir., Rockwell Anaheim, Calif., 1966-73, nuclear hardness lead engr., Hill AFB, Utah, 1973-79, radiation project engr., Anaheim, 1979—; cons. environ. engring./mgmt. Served with U.S. Army, 1943-46; ETO. Lic. nuclear reactor operator; registered profl. engr., Calif. Mem. Am. Nuclear Soc., Am. Soc. Quality Control, Nat. Mgmt. Assn., IEEE, AIAA. Republican. Episcopalian. Contbr. articles on nuclear hardness assurance, nuclear reactor safety devices, X-ray film dosimetry to profl. jours. Home: 6923 Rutgers Dr Anaheim CA 92807 Office: 3370 Miraloma Ave Anaheim CA 92803

FITZGERALD, JOHN CHARLES, JR., investment banker; b. Sacramento, May 23, 1941; s. John Charles and Geraldine Edith (McNabb) F.; B.S., Calif. State U. at Sacramento, 1964; M.B.A., Cornell U., 1966; m. Mildred Ann Kilpatrick, June 26, 1965; children—Geraldine Kathrine, Erec John. Dir. corp. planning Bekins Co., Los Angeles, 1966-73; mgr. corp. planning Ridder Publs., Inc., Los Angeles, 1973-75; chief fin. officer City of Inglewood (Calif.), 1975-77; treas./controller Inglewood Redevel. Agy., 1975-77, Inglewood Housing Authority, 1975-77; v.p. municipal fin. White, Weld & Co., Inc., Los Angeles, 1977-78; v.p. pub. fin. Paine Webber Jackson & Curtis, Los Angeles, 1978-79; v.p., mgr. western region, municipal fin. dept. Merrill Lynch White Weld Capital Markets Group, 1979-82, mng. dir. western region mcpl. fin. dept., 1982—; instr. fin./adminstrn. El Camino Coll., Torrance, Calif., 1977—. Bd. dirs., exec. com., chmn. bd. Los Angeles chpt. Am. Heart Assn., 1977—. Bd. dirs., mem. fin. com. Daniel Freeman Hosp., Inglewood, Calif., 1980—. Mem. Fin. Execs. Inst., Municipal Fin. Officers Assn., Calif. Soc. Municipal Fin. Officers, League Calif. Cities, So. Calif. Corp. Planners Assn. (past pres.), Beta Gamma Sigma. Republican. Clubs: Rotary, Jonathan. Office: 707 Wilshire Blvd Los Angeles CA 90017

FITZGERALD, JUDY, advertising company executive; b. N.Y.C., Nov. 3, 1941; d. Harry A. and Evelyn I. (Radnoff) Brolin; m. John E. Fitzgerald, Oct. 8, 1971. B.S., C.W. Post Coll., 1962. With Needham Harper Steers, 1970-73, Rosenfeld Sirowitz, Lawson/West, 1973-74; with BBDO/West, 1975-81, v.p., 1979-81; copywriter Benton & Bowles Inc, Los Angeles, 1981—, v.p., copy chief, 1981—; tchr. copy class Advt. Ctr., Los Angeles, 1980-81. Recipient awards Am. Advt. Fedn., Art Dirs. Club, Copy Club. Clubs: Copy, Creative. Office: Benton & Bowles Inc Suite 1200 3435 Wilshire Blvd Los Angeles CA 90010

FITZGERALD, LAURIE ANN, human resource and organizational development consultant; b. Kalamazoo, Apr. 8, 1950; d. William Nolen F. and Olga Hunchak (Zajac) F.; children—A. Nikolai, Katye M. B.S., Western Mich. U.-Kalamazoo, 1972; M.Ed., U. Ariz.-Tucson, 1977. Conf. coordinator Western Mich. U.-Kalamazoo, 1968-72; spl. edn. coordinator Tucson Pub. Schs., 1973-75; owner, mgr. Salon de Te Bar/Restaurant, Torreguadiaro, Spain, 1975-77; sr. cons., dir. The Denver Consultancy Co., 1978—; mem. faculty Regis Coll., U. Phoenix-Colo. Div. Faculty scholar Western Mich. U., 1968-72. Mem. Orgn. Devel. Network, Am. Soc. Tng. and Devel., Nat. Assn. Orgn. Devel. Profls., NOW. Author: Installing Quality Circles: A Strategic Approach, 1982. Office: The Denver Cons Co PO Box 18003 Denver CO 80218

FITZGERALD, PATRICIA ANN, motivational and mgmt. cons. co. exec.; b. Dallas, Sept. 16, 1937; d. Thomas O'Neil and Minerva Hannah (Gilliland) Anderson; student Sawyer Bus. Coll., 1955, Phoenix City Coll., 1960-66, Brigham Young U., Hawaii, 1979, U. Calif., Irvine, 1979, UCLA, 1979-80; m. Gerald William Fitzgerald, Mar. 6, 1976; children by previous marriage—Vicki Lee Jones Duncan, Gregg Ronald Jones, Randall Thomas Jones, Lori Lynn Jones Newman. Service rep. So. Calif. Gas Co., 1956-60, Ariz. Public Service, 1961; sales rep. Shaw Walker Co., 1967-68; sales mgr. Selective Office Service, 1968-69; communications cons., mktg. mgr. Pacific Telephone Co., Orange, Calif., 1970-80; pres. Fitzgerald & Assos., Anaheim Hills, Calif., 1979—; cons. in field. Recipient awards of appreciation Personnel and Indsl. Relations Assn., Brooks Coll., Pacific Telephone. Mem. Orange County C. of C., Los Angeles C. of C., Newport-Harbor C. of C., Am. Soc. Tng. and Devel. (appreciation award), Am. Mktg. Assn. (dir.), Women in Mgmt. (appreciation award), Nat. Speakers Assn., Relief Soc. Republican. Mormon. Contbr. articles to newspapers, Long Beach and Los Angeles; various appearances ednl. TV, Orange County. Home and Office: 980 Calle Venado Anaheim Hills CA 92807

FITZGERALD, RONALD EUGENE, safety and health manager; b. Lynwood, Calif., Nov. 10, 1946; s. Lewis David and Josephine Alice (Gieleghem) F.; m. Robyn Michelle Carnes, June 12, 1971; children—Edward C., Katherine A. B.S. in Mech. Engring., Northrop U., Inglewood, Calif., 1968; B.A. in Bus. Adminstrn., Park Coll., Alamogordo, N.Mex., 1977; M.S. in Systems Mgmt., U. So. Calif., 1979. Engr., Safety Office, Holloman AFB, N.Mex., 1975-77; systems safety engr. Sacramento Air Logistics Center, McClellan AFB, 1977-1981, chief occupational safety div., 1980-81, chief tech. safety div., 1981—. Coach, Roseville Youth Soccer League. Served to capt. USAF, 1968-75. Decorated Purple Heart, Air medal. Mem. Field Fed. Safety and Health Com., System Safety Soc., Am. Soc. Safety Engrs. Republican. Roman Catholic. Home: 405 Lyndhurst Ave Roseville CA 95678 Office: SM-ALC/SE Bldg 250HH McClellan AFB CA 95652

FITZ-HENLEY, NORMAN HOWARD, physician; b. Port-au-Prince, Haiti, Sept. 25, 1931; came to U.S., 1961, naturalized, 1968; s. Randolph and Doris (Campbell) Fitz-Henley; student CCNY, 1967; M.D., George Washington U., 1971; m. Gem Smellie, July 16, 1958; children—Onyl Grace, Garnell Dean, John Aldwyn, Orville Jay. Ofcl. verbatim ct. reporter Supreme Ct. Kingston, Jamaica, 1951-61; freelance ct. reporter Beekman's Reporting Service, N.Y.C., 1962-67; intern D.C. Gen. Hosp., George Washington U. Service, Washington, 1971-72, resident in internal medicine, U. Calif., San Diego, 1972-75; practice medicine specializing in internal medicine, El Centro, Calif., 1975—; chmn. dept. medicine El Centro Community Hosp., 1977; dir. Valley Ind. Bank, El Centro. Active non-denominational religious evang. affairs. Life fellow Royal Soc. Arts (London); mem. AMA, Calif. Med. Assn., Am. Heart Assn., Imperial County Med. Soc., Calif. Heart Assn. (dir., pres. Imperial Valley div.), Imperial Valley Heart Assn. (pres.), Alpha Sigma Lambda. Co-inventor Fitz-Henley's All-Curve System of Shorthand, 1962. Home: 659 W Main Rd El Centro CA 92243 Office: 1745 S Imperial Ave El Centro CA 92243

FITZHUGH, GILBERT WRIGHT, ret. life ins. co. exec.; b. Bklyn., July 8, 1909; s. Herbert W. and Ethel (Gilbert) F.; B.S., Princeton, 1930; LL.D., Carroll Coll., 1966; m. Lea Van Ingh, June 17, 1933; children—Gilbert Van Ingh, Lea Armistead. With Met. Life Ins. Co., 1930-73, various positions actuarial and group divs., 1930-58, asst. gen. mgr. Canadian head office, 1946-47, v.p. charge planning and devel., N.Y.C., 1958-60, v.p., gen. mgr. for Can., 1960-61, exec. v.p., N.Y.C., 1962, pres., 1963-66, chmn. bd., 1966-73, also chief exec. officer, 1963-73. Chmn., Pres.'s Blue Ribbon Def. Panel, 1969-70. Trustee Calif. Inst. Tech. Fellow Soc. Actuaries, Casualty Actuarial Soc.; mem. Am. Acad. Actuaries. Clubs: Princeton (N.Y.C.); Adirondack Mountain (Lake Placid, N.Y.); Pacific Union (San Francisco); Cuyamaca (San Diego); Pauma Valley (Calif.) Country. Home: Box 682 Pauma Valley CA 92061

FITZHUGH, MARTHA MILLICENT, real estate agent; b. Pittsylvania County, Va., Sept. 22, 1939; d. William Chesley Elmo and Nancye Lee (Hudson) Rorer; m. Gary Lowell Fitxhugh, June 15, 1968 (div.); children—Richard Anthony Bolling, James Henry Bolling, III. Clk., Naval Ops. Base, Norfolk, Va., 1963-64; procuring clk. Panorama Properties, Oak Harbor, Wash., 1975-77; real estate agt. Oak Bay Realty, Oak Harbor, 1977-79; real estate agt. North Island Realty, Inc., Oak Harbor, 1980—; Sec. Oak Harbor Area Council, 1977. Recipient Cert. of Appreciation Navy League U.S., 1977. Mem. Nat. Bd. of Realtors, Whidbey Island Bd. Realtors (pres. 1981), Farm Land Inst., Navy League. Republican. Baptist. Club: Officers Wives (pres. 1975) (Whidbey Island). Contbr. articles to newspapers. Home: PO Box 692 Oak Harbor WA 98277 Office: 1442 Midway Blvd Oak Harbor WA 98277

FITZPATRICK, RICHARD EDWARD, physician; b. Atlanta, July 21, 1944; s. James Robert and Elizabeth Frances (Fuller) F.; A.B., Princeton U., 1966; M.D., Emory U., 1970; m. Cheryl Annelle Palmer, Jan. 14, 1969; children—Cheryl Palmer, Elizabeth Billie, Richard Edward. Intern, U. So. Calif.-Los Angeles County Med. Center, 1970-71; practice gen. medicine, Gardena, Calif., 1974-75; resident in dermatology UCLA Med. Center, 1975-78; pvt. practice medicine, specializing in dermatology, La Jolla, Calif., 1978—; mem. staff Scripps Meml. Hosp., La Jolla and Encinitas, Calif., Tri-City Hosp., Oceanside, Calif.; cons. Am. Cancer Soc., 1978—, U. Calif., San Diego, 1980—. Bd. dirs. Am. Cancer Soc., 1980—; trustee Rancho Santa Fe Youth, 1980—. Served with USN, 1971-74. Diplomate Am. Bd. Dermatology. Fellow Am. Acad. Dermatology; mem. Internat. Soc. Dermatol. Surgery, Am. Soc. Dermatol. Surgery, Soc. Investigative Dermatology, San Diego Dermatol. Soc., Alpha Omega Alpha. Presbyterian. Author chpt. in Pediatric Infectious Diseases, 1980; contbr. articles to profl. jours. Home: Mimulus Box 1296 Rancho Santa Fe CA 92067 Office: 850 Prospect St La Jolla CA 92037

FITZPATRICK, WILLIAM RANDOLPH, JR., accountant, real estate developer and consultant; b. Elkhart, Ind., June 10, 1951; s. William Randolph and Jeanette (Fairfield) E.; m. Ellen Ross, Dec.30, 1972; 1 dau., Whitney. B.S., Ariz. State U., 1974. C.P.A., Ariz. Staff acct. Walmsley Fitzpatrick & Kelly, Phoenix, 1973-77, ptnr., 1977—, sr. mng. ptnr., 1980—. Mem. exec. council Boys Clubs Phoenix; mem. Thunderbirds, the spl. events com. Phoenix C. of C. Mem. Am. Inst. C.P.A.s, Ariz. Soc. C.P.A.s, Sigma Alpha Epsilon (pres. Ariz. Beta chpt. 1972). Republican. Club: Rotary (Phoenix).

FITZSIMMONS, CHARLES KENNETH, govt. ofcl.; b. Colfax, Wash., Apr. 20, 1940; s. Kenneth Ellsworth and Lulu Elizabeth (Fyhrie) F.; m. Donna Jean Steckler, Dec. 2, 1972. student Mexico City Coll., 1961; B.S. In Physics, Wash. State U., 1963; M.S. in Radiol. Health, Oreg. State U., 1971. With USPHS, Las Vegas, 1963-65; designer, operator airborne air quality monitoring systems EPA, Las Vegas, 1973-80, program mgr., 1981—. Recipient Bronze medal EPA, 1974. Mem. Air Pollution Control Assn., So. Nev. Bluegrass Music Soc. Contbr. articles profl. jours. Office: Box 15027 Las Vegas NV 89114

FITZSIMMONS, EDMUND FOSTER, investment advisor; b. South Portland, Maine, Nov. 14, 1921; s. John Joseph and Minerva Lillian (Griffin) F.; student Tufts Coll., 1938-39, U. Hawaii, 1941, U. Pa., 1976; children—Mary Elaine, John Edmund. Pres., E.F. Fitzsimmons Ltd., Honolulu, 1945-72; pres. Real Estate, Inc., Realtors, Constrn. Systems, Inc., Honolulu, 1972-76; pres. Foster Assos., Inc., Honolulu, 1976—. Chmn., Contractors Lic. Bd., State of Hawaii, 1964-71; chmn. Gov.'s Com. on Housing, 1961-64; chmn. Com. for Housing the Aged, 1961-64; chmn. ARC Fund Drive, 1966-67, chpt. chmn., 1969. Registered investment advisor. Mem. Home Builders Assn. Hawaii (past pres.), Nat. Assn. Home Builders (dir.), Gen. Contractors Assn. Hawaii, Nat. Assn. State Contractors Lic. Bds., Internat. Found. Employee Benefit Plans Assn. Club: Volcano Golf and Country. Office: PO Box 2994 Honolulu HI 96802

FITZSIMONS, PATRICK S., chief of police; b. N.Y.C., Apr. 16, 1930; s. Patrick Joseph and Mary (Brabazon) F.; B.S., Fordham U., 1954, J.D., 1972; m. Olga Parker, Aug. 18, 1959. Successively dir. tng., comdr. Manhattan South, asst. chief for programs and policies N.Y.C. Police Dept.; now chief of police City of Seattle; adj. prof. John Jay Coll.; mem. Wash. State Gov.'s Council on Criminal Justice; mem. Wash. State Bd. on Law Enforcement Tng. and Standards; bd. dirs. Nat. Criminal Info. Center; fellow in criminal justice Harvard U. Law Sch., 1972-73. Bd. dirs. Chief Seattle council Boy Scouts Am. Served to 1st lt. USMC, 1953-56. Recipient award for outstanding nat. contbn. to advancement criminal justice Am. Soc. Public Adminstrn., 1975. Mem. Police Execs. Research Forum (dir.), Fordham Law Alumni Assn., Harvard Law Sch. Assn. Clubs: Wash. Athletic, 101. Dir. prodn. of texts and manuals for N.Y.C. Police Acad. Office: Office of Chief of Police 610 3d Ave Seattle WA 98104

FITZWATER, BONNIE, editor; b. Watonga, Okla., Nov. 16, 1923; d. Clarence Eugene and Evelyn Ellen (Funk) Fitzwater; B.A. magna cum laude, U. Okla., 1945; M.A., Northwestern U., 1947. Announcer, scriptwriter, control operator radio sta. WNAD, 1941-45; dormitory counselor Northwestern U., Evanston, Ill., 1945-46, teaching asst., psychology dept., 1945-47; asst. to dir. personnel, indsl. relations dept. Atlantic Refining Co., Dallas, 1947-48; dir. social activities So. Meth. U., 1948-50, dir. student activities, 1950-57, dean women, 1957-61; asst. dean women Stanford, 1961-62, asso. dean, 1962-65; pubs.'s rep. Wadsworth Pub. Co., Belmont, Calif., 1966-67, spl. projects editor Brooks/Cole div., 1967-75; sociology-anthropology editor Brooks/Cole Pub. Co., 1975-78; free-lance editor, 1978—. Mem. Am. Sociol. Assn., Am. Anthrop. Assn., P.E.O., Nat., Tex., Calif. assns. women deans and counselors, Phi Beta Kappa, Sigma Xi, Kappa Alpha Theta, Alpha Lambda Delta, Mortar Bd. Presbyn. Home: 11140 Monarch Ln Apt L Pacific Grove CA 93950 also 721 N Noble St Watonga OK 73772

FJORDBOTTEN, EDWIN LEROY, government official; b. Claresholm, Alta., Can., Nov. 4, 1938; s. Artun Edwin and Belinda Janet (Enbysk) F.; m. Deanne Marie Perchinsky, Nov. 16, 1962; children—Tracy, Karine. Grad. Camrose Luth. Coll., 1956. Farmer nr. Granum, Alta., Can., 1960-83; mem. Alta. Legis. Assembly, Edmonton, 1979—, minister of agr., 1982—. Progressive Conservative, Lutheran. Office: Legislature Bldg Room 418 Edmonton AB T5K 2B6 Canada

FLACCO, PAUL RICHARD, economics educator; b. Washington, Feb. 19, 1950; s. Richard Anthony and Sidonie Marianne (Alemann) F.; m. Margaret Sue Woodley, June 23, 1972 (div.); 1 dau., April Margaret. A.B., U. Calif.-Santa Cruz, 1975, M.S., Oreg. State U., 1977, Ph.D., U. Oreg., 1980. Research asst. Oreg. State U., 1975-77; grad. teaching fellow U. Oreg., 1977-80; asst. prof. econs. Claremont McKenna Coll. and Claremont Grad. Sch., 1980—. Calif. State scholar 1973-75, Eric England Meml. scholar 1977-78. Mem. Am. Econs. Assn., Western Econs. Assn., So. Econs. Assn. Democrat. Author: A Generalized Theory of Markets: The Demand and Supply of Heterogeneous Commodities, 1980. Home: 150 W Foothill Blvd 11B Pomona CA 91767 Office: 314 Bauer Center Claremont McKenna College Claremont CA 91711

FLACH, VICTOR H., designer, educator; b. Portland, Oreg., May 31, 1929; s. Victor H. and Eva M. (Huget) F.; student Vanport Coll., 1950-51; B.S., U. Oreg., 1952, M.F.A., 1957; postgrad. U. Pitts., 1959-65. Teaching fellow and asst. curator Henry Clay Frick Fine Arts Dept. and Gallery, U. Pitts., 1959-63; docent, Frank Lloyd Wright's Fallingwater, Western Pa. Conservancy, 1963-64; prof. art, design, painting, theory and history, dept. art, U. Wyo., Laramie, 1965—; participant R. Buckminster Fuller Geodesic Prototype Projects, 1953, 59; interviewer Heritage series PBS-TV, 1966; cons. Nat. Symposium on Role of Studio Arts in Higher Edn., U. Oreg., 1967; participant various TV programs including Arts in Practice series, 1971-77; designer multi-wall murals U. Oreg., Eugene, 1952, Rainbow Club, 1954, Clear Lake Sch., Eugene, 1956, Sci. Center, U. Wyo., Laramie, 1967; one-man and group shows of paintings, photographs, exptl. films and drawings, 1949—. Served with U.S. Army, 1953-55. Author and editor: IJH-TBIW20 Poems, 1949; 12 New Painters, 1953; IN/SERT Active Anthology for the Creative, 1955-62; Gloss of the Four Universal Forms, 1959; The Anatomy of the Canvas, 1961; The Eye's Mind, 1964; By These Presents, 1975; The Stage, 1978; The Indigenous Image, 1978; Contra/Verses Selected Poems, 1980; Contextualist Manifesto, 1982; contbr. poems, articles and photographs to lit. jours., 1949—. Office: Dept of Art University of Wyoming Laramie WY 82071

FLACHSBART, PETER GEORGE, educator; b. St. Louis, Apr. 15, 1944; s. Bernard Ernst and Florence Lillian (Trapp) F.; B.S., Wash. U., St. Louis, 1966; M.S., Northwestern U., 1968, Ph.D., 1971; m. Carol Emiko Minn, July 24, 1976. Sr. research asso. U. So. Calif., Los Angeles, 1971-72; lectr. Inst. Urban & Environ. Mgmt., Calif. State U., Dominguez Hills, 1972-73, asst. prof. public adminstrn., 1973-76; asst. prof. civil engring. Stanford (Calif.) U., 1976-80; asst. prof. urban and regional planning U. Hawaii at Manoa, Honolulu, 1980—. Served to capt. U.S. Army, 1966-74. NDEA fellow 1968. Mem. Am. Inst. Cert. Planners, Am. Planning Assn., Urban Land Inst., Sigma Xi. Lutheran. Club: Kuhio Surf. Contbr. articles in field to profl. jours. Home: 966 Honokahua Place Honolulu HI 96825 Office: University Hawaii Porteus Hall 107A 2424 Maile Way Honolulu HI 96822

FLACK, J(OHN) ERNEST, engineering educator; b. Ft. Collins, Colo., Jan. 28, 1929; s. John Ernest and Marie (Schaefer) F.; m. Joan Myrlee; children—Mark, Janice Flack Brekke, Paul. B.S. in Civil Engring., Colo. State U., 1950; M.S., U. Iowa, 1954; Ph.D., Stanford U., 1965. Profl. engr., Colo. Field engr. C-B Engring. Co., Denver, 1950-51; engr. Calif. Div. Water Resources, Sacramento, 1954-55; instr. to prof. dept. civil engring. U. Colo., Boulder, 1955—; vis. prof. New South Wales Inst. Tech., Sydney, Australia, 1980, Ga. Inst. Tech., Atlanta, 1968-69; researcher. Served to 1st lt. USAF, 1951-53. NSF fellow, 1962-63; Engring. Found. fellow, 1978-79. Fellow ASCE; mem. Am. Water Works Assn. (Acad. Achievement award 1965), Am. Water Resources Assn., Am. Geophys. Union, AAAS, Sigma Xi. Democrat. Roman Catholic. Contbr. articles to profl. publs. Home: 4190 Eutaw Dr Boulder CO 80303 Office: Campus Box 428 Univ Colo Boulder CO 80309

FLAGG, CHARLES JUNIOR, computer services company official, graphic arts consultant; b. Phoenixville, Pa., Apr. 2, 1947; s. Charles L. and Vera M. (Collins) F.; m. Kathleen A. Hughes, Jan. 17, 1952; 1 dau., Jennifer L. B.A., Chapman Coll., 1974; M.F.A. (scholar), Claremont Grad. Sch., 1975. Graphic artist Chapman Coll., Orange, Calif., 1973-74; project coordinator Burk's Advt., San Bernardino, Calif., 1974-75; pub. info. coordinator San Bernardino County (Calif.), San Bernardino, 1975-79; mktg. presentations coordinator Ford Aerospace & Communications Corp., Newport Beach, Calif., 1979-81; advt. and pub. relations mgr. Tymshare-Unitax, Inc., Anaheim, Calif., 1981—. Bd. dirs. Arrowhead Allied Arts Council, San Bernardino, 1976-77. Served with USAF, 1966-70; Vietnam. Decorated Air Force Commendation medal with one oak leaf cluster. Mem. Advt. Club Los Angeles, Pub. Relations Soc. Am., Riverside-San Bernardino Counties Advt. Fedn. (founder, pres. 1978-79), Am. Advt. Fedn. (Dist. 15 dir.), Twin Counties Press Club (dir.). Exhibited in group shows: Phila. Mus. Art, 1972, C.I.P. Palais Des Congres, Paris, 1975. Office: Unitax Inc 639 N Euclid Ave Anaheim CA 92801

FLAGG, DENIS ANTHONY, economist educator; b. Santa Monica, Calif., Sept. 24, 1920; s. Edwin Harvey and Gladys Patricia (Hanst) F.; m. Virginia Cookins, June 16, 1950; children—Bruce Denis, Kenneth Warren, Denis Timothy. A.B., Harvard U., 1942; postgrad. UCLA, 1946-47; Ph.D., U. Calif.-Berkeley, 1954. Teaching asst. econs. U. Calif.-Berkeley, 1949-52, assoc. in econs., 1954-55; asst. prof. econs. San Diego State U., 1955-61, assoc. prof., 1961-65, prof., 1965—. Served to capt. U.S. Army, 1942-46. Mem. Am. Econs. Assn. Contbr. articles to profl. jours.

FLAGG, MORGAN, service, constrn. and agr. co. exec.; b. Oakland, Calif., Mar. 13, 1926; s. A.J. and Mabel R. (Yeagel) F.; ed. pub. schs.; m. Claire E. Barker, Dec. 2, 1950; children—Lawrence J., Janine A., Brian E., James M., John P., Lori R. (dec.), Kerri L. (dec.), Mary Claire. Asst. sec. Calif. Senate, Sacramento, 1947-49; in real estate sales and devel., San Francisco, 1948-54; pres. Lindero Investment Co., Inc., Oakland, San Luis Obispo, Calif., 1954-64, Hacienda Convalescent Hosp. Inc., Monterey, Calif., 1963-68; chmn., pres. Flagg Industries Inc. (formerly Calif. Health Care Inc.), Van Nuys, Calif., 1968-73, chmn., 1973—; v.p. Hawaii Koi Corp., Glenwood, 1973-81, pres., 1981—; mng. partner Lakewood Assos., Monterey, North Point Prodn., Monterey; pres., dir. Glenwood Water Co. Mem. Calif. Commn. on Housing and Community Devel., 1965-68; chmn. finance com. Monterey Am. Revolution Bicentennial, 1976. Alternate del. Democratic Nat. Conv., 1964, del., 1972; chmn. Monterey County Dem. Central Com., 1967-69; candidate U.S. Congress, 1973. Chmn. bd. dirs. Flagg Family Found.; trustee Robert Louis Stevenson Sch., 1971-76; 1st v.p. Monterey Peninsula Mus. Art. Served with USAAF, 1944-45. Episcopalian. Club: Beach and Tennis (Pebble Beach, Calif.). Home: PO Box 1281 Pebble Beach CA 93953 Office: PO Box 3230 Monterey CA 93940

FLAGG, VIRGINIA GOOKINS, economist, educator; b. Denver, May 4, 1926; d. Robert Pierre and Eva Sophia (Cannon) G.; m. Denis Anthony Flagg, June 16, 1950; children—Bruce Denis, Kennth Warren, Denis Timothy. A.B. in Physics, UCLA, 1947; Ph.D. in Econs., U. Calif.-Berkeley, 1955. Lectr. econs. U. Calif.-San Diego, 1956-58, 66-65; lectr. econs. San Diego State U. 1967—. Mem. Quality of Life Bd., San Diego, 1974-75. Fed. Sea grantee, 1974-76. Mem. Western Econ. Assn., Am. Econ. Assns. Contbr. articles to profl. jours. Office: Dept Econs San Diego State Univ San Diego CA 92182

FLAGLER, WILLIAM LAWRENCE, publisher; b. Oakland, Calif., June 13, 1922; s. Albert William and Violet Dorthy (Marris) F.; B.A., San Francisco State U., 1951; degree in Library Sci., San Jose State U., 1963; m. Ruth Greiner Gilbert, Aug. 23, 1970; children by previous marriage—Vickie, David, Michael; stepchildren—Denise Gilbert, Ethan Gilbert. Pres., LaRu Enterprises, San Jose, Calif., 1975—. Active Boy Scouts Am. Served with U.S. Army, World War II. Republican. Club: Masons. Office: PO Box 10460 San Jose CA 95157

FLAHERTY, JOHN JOSEPH, publisher; b. Seattle, Nov. 5, 1942; s. James Ellis and Katherine (Morgenroth) F.; m. Linda M. Nyman, Aug. 9, 1942; children—Sean, Erin, Megin. Student Whitman Coll., 1960-63; B.A. in Econs., U. Wash., 1965. With sales and mktg. depts. News-Jour., Inc., Seattle, 1964-68, v.p., 1968-78, pres., dir., 1978—; pres., dir. Capitol Hill Times, Inc., Seattle, 1976—, Active Press Inc., Seattle, 1978—, Flaherty Newspapers Inc., Seattle, 1980—. Mem. Wash. Newspaper Pubs. Assn. (bd. dirs.), Rainier C. of C., Capitol Hill C. of C. (pres. 1974-75), Univ. C. of C. Roman Catholic. Club: Athletic (Bellevue, Wash.). Club: Rotary (Rainier). Office: 2720 S Hanford St Seattle WA 98144

FLAIM, SILVIO JOSEPH, economist, consultant; b. Augusta, Ga., Feb. 19, 1952; s. Rudolph Alfred and Bernice Marie (Haddock) F.; m. Mary Louise Prosser, May 25, 1974; children—Amanda Leigh, Michael Joseph. B.S. in Agrl. Econs., U. Mo., Columbia, 1973, M.S., 1974; Ph.D. in Resource Econs., Cornell U., 1978. Teaching and research asst., U. Mo., Cornell U., 1970-77; econ. cons., AID, Nicaragua, 1973; sr. economist Solar Energy Research Inst., Golden, Colo., 1977-81; sr. economist, Amoco Prodn. Co., Denver, 1981—; cons. on Renewable Energy Applications in Agr. Mem. Am. Agrl. Econs. Assn., Am. Econs. Assn., Western Econs. Assn. Contbr. articles to profl. jours. Home: 12236 Powhatan Trail Conifer CO 80433 Office: 17th and Broadway Denver CO 80202

FLAKE, CHAD JOHN, coll. librarian; b. Snowflake, Ariz., Dec. 28, 1929; s. John T. and Carrie (Lindsey) F.; B.A., Brigham Young U., 1953; M.A., Denver U., 1955. Reference librarian Brigham Young U., Provo, Utah, 1953-54, documents librarian, 1955-56, curator spl. collections, asst. prof. library sci., 1956-72, asso. prof., curator spl. collections, 1972—. Mem. Am. Utah (past pres.) library assns., Utah (v.p.), Western hist. socs., Utah Westerners, Beta Phi Mu. Co-author: The Brescia Danti. Editor: Mormon Americana; Bibliography of Mormonism, 1830-1930. Contbr. articles to profl. publs. Home: 80 N 2d E Provo UT 84601

FLAMAND, EUGENE DAVID, electronic supply co. exec.; b. Blackfeet Indian Reservation, Browning, Mont., May 6, 1951; s. Leo V. and Patricia L. Flamand; B.S. in Elec. Engring., Mont. State U., 1975; m. Nancy Flamand, Feb. 19, 1983; 1 son by previous marriage, Terry. Engring. technician Forestry Sci. Lab., Bozeman, Mont., 1971-73, Mountain Bell Telephone Co., Helena, Mont., summer 1973, Mont. Power Co., Butte, summer 1974; singer and guitarist Schmidlap Bros. Band, Bozeman, 1971-75; elec. engr. U.S. Bur. of Reclamation, Billings, Mont., 1975; pres. Flamand Electronic Supply Co., Inc., Belgrade, Mont., 1976-78, Spirit Lake, Idaho, 1978-82; pres. A-I Electronics, Inc., 1982—; solo guitarist and singer, Bozeman, Mont., 1975, 78. Mem. Kappa Sigma. Democrat. Club: Jaycees. Home and office: PO Box 458 3d and Vermont Sts Spirit Lake ID 83869

FLAMER, MARY JEAN, advertising executive; b. Orange, N.J., Mar. 2, 1950; d. Vincent Carl and Jean Niven (Breingan) Cuccinello; m. Michael Abraham Flamer, June 7, 1981. B.A. in Theatre Arts, U. Bridgeport, 1972. Media buyer Batten, Barton, Durstine & Osborne Advt., N.Y.C., 1973-75; media supr. Ted Bates Advt., N.Y.C., 1975-78; media dir. Fotomat Corp., San Diego, 1978-81; v.p., dir. network TV and radio Western Internat. Media, Los Angeles, 1982-83; account exec. nat. sales CBS-FM, Los Angeles, 1983—; instr. UCLA. Mem. Holy Spirit Cenacle House. Office: 6121 Sunset Blvd Los Angeles CA 90028

FLAMM, BRYCE C., insurance company executive, state senator; b. Billings, Mont., Oct. 9, 1927; s. George William and Mabel (Stauffer) F.; m. Uleah Chlarson, May 1, 1927; children—Ronald, Jeffrey, Sheri, Sheila, Kenneth, Nyla, Richard. B.S. in Acctg., Utah State U. C.L.U. Ptnr., Skancky Market, 1949-50, Dunkley Music, 1950-56; salesman, gen. mgr. N.Y. Life Ins. Co., 1956-70; pres. Fin. Cons. Am., Ogden, Utah, 1970—; mem. Utah State Senate, 1980—. Mem. North Ogden City Council, 1964-72. Served with AUS, 1945-46. Mem. Million Dollar Roundtable, Nat. Assn. Life Underwriters, Am. Soc. C.L.U.'s, Life Ins. Agy. Mgrs. Assn. Republican. Mormon. Club: Kiwanis. Home: 3951 N 550 West Ogden UT 84404 Office: Box 1670 727 24th St Ogden UT 84402

FLAMSON, RICHARD J., III, banker; b. 1929. B.A. in Econs. and Bus. Adminstrn., Claremont Men's Coll., 1951; grad. Sch. Banking U. Wash., 1962. With Security Pacific Nat. Bank, Los Angeles, 1955—, v.p., 1962, se. v.p., 1969, exec. v.p. and mem. mgmt. com., 1970, vice chmn. bd., 1973, pres. and chief exec. officer, 1978, chmn. bd. and chief exec. officer, 1980—, also dir.; chmn. bd., chief exec. officer and dir. Security Pacific Corp., officer and or dir. subs. cos.; pres. and dir. Los Angeles Central City Assn.; dir. Northrop Corp., Santa Fe Industries Inc., Kaufman and Broad. Bd. dirs. So. Calif. Vistors Council; trustee Claremont Men's Coll.; chmn. Central City Assn. Served to 1st lt. U.S. Army, 1951-53. Office: Security Pacific Nat Bank 333 S Hope Los Angeles CA 90071*

FLANAGAN, BRIDGET ANNE, public relations executive; b. Merced, Calif., Nov. 10, 1949; d. John Thomas and Roberta Gail (Haun) F.; A.A. in Liberal Arts, Foothill Jr. Coll., 1969; B.S. in Sociology, U. Calif.-Fresno, 1973. Apprentice food clk. Safeway Stores, Inc., Merced, Calif., 1969-71, retail food clk., 1971-73, retail food clk./journeyman food clk., Fresno, 1971-76; employee relations mgr./trainee, Sacramento, 1976-78, retail interviewer, employee relations supv., 1978-79, pub. relations mgr. trainee, Oakland, Calif., 1979, pub. relations mgr., Portland, Oreg., 1979—; internat. flight attendant Trans-Internat. Airlines, Oakland, Calif., 1973-75; dir. Inter-Agy. Food Bank, Portland; dir., exec. sec. Oreg. Food Share, 1979—. Mem. Portland Mayor's Traffic Safety Commn., 1981—; mem. Oreg. Gov's Council on Sports, Health and Fitness. Recipient Presdl. commendation Pres.'s Council on Sports and Fitness, 1982. Mem. Pub. Relations Roundtable, Pub. Relations Soc. Am., Soc. Consumer Affairs Roundtable. Republican. Office: Safeway Stores Inc Portland Div PO Box 523 Clackamas OR 97015

FLANAGAN, LEWIS LEE, seed co. exec.; b. Abasarokee, Mont., Feb. 23, 1929; s. Lewis J. and Ida (Kitchen) F.; B.A., Mont. State Coll., 1950; postgrad. Wash. State U., 1962; m. Ruth Hamilton, Nov. 11, 1951; children—Rickey S., Michael K., Terrance D., Janice M. Pvt. agrl. cons., Billings, Mont., 1955-62; asst. mgr. Western Farmers Inc., Moses Lake, Wash., 1962-65; area mgr. Pacific Supply Coops., Walla Walla, 1965-70; Western regional mgr. Velsicol Corp., Chgo., 1970-76; chief exec. officer, gen. mgr. Ramsey Seed Inc. div. DeKalb AgResearch, Manteca, Calif., 1976—. Mem. Walla Walla (Wash.) County Republican Central Com., 1965-70. Served with AUS, 1951-55. Mem. Manteca, Walla Walla (chmn. agr. 1968-69) chambers commerce, Weed Sci. Soc. Am., Western Soc. Weed Sci., Calif. Seed Assn., Pacific Seedsmen, Am. Seed Trade Assn., Western Seedsmen. Republican. Clubs: Masons, Eastgate Lions (officer 1966-70), Spring Creek Country. Home: 435 Palomino Ct Manteca CA 95336 Office: 205 Stockton St Manteca CA 95336

FLANAGAN, VERNON DALE, agricultural engineer; b. Junction City, Oreg., Oct. 10, 1924; s. Charles Bartlett and Clara Alice (Rutherford) F. B.S. in Agrl. Engring., Oreg. State U., 1953. From jr. engr. to engring. mgr. factory services Aurora Vertiline Pump Co., Industry, Calif., 1953-74; service mgr. Penco div. Hudson Engring. Co., 1974-78; chief engr. Valley Pump Co. div. Valley Industries, Inc., Lubbock, Tex., 1978-81; chief engr. Nat. Pump Co., Glendale, Ariz., 1982—. Mem. Am. Soc. Agrl. Engrs., Am. Water Works Assn., Tau Beta Pi. Republican. Club: Masons. Home: PO Box 2414 Glendale AZ 85311 Office: PO Box 1599 Glendale AZ 85311

FLANDERS, STEPHEN L(AWRENCE), stockbroker, investor; b. Boston, July 10, 1942; s. Royal Call and Mildred Grace (O'Brien) F.; m. Robin Lee Lord, Nov. 20, 1963 (div. 1969); 1 son, Bradford; m. 2d, Barbara Ann Randol, Apr. 1, 1971 (div. 1977); children— William Brett, Krystal; m. 3d, Linda Lorraine Skodack, Dec. 1, 1979. B.S. in Bus. Adminstrn. and Econs., U. Denver, 1967; postgrad. Babson Inst., Harvard U., Boston U., C.W. Post Coll. Stockbroker, McDonnell & Co., Denver, 1966-69; mgr. spl. services, stockbroker Wall St. West, Inc., Englewood, Colo., 1982—; chmn. bd. Denver Penny Stocks, Inc.; lectr., cons. Pres. Heather Ridge Homeowners Assn., 1978-79. Named Salesman of Yr., Townsend, Bauerle, Inc., 1981; winner Stockbrokers Bull and Bear Ski Race, Winter Park, Colo., 1983. Mem. N.Y. Stock Exchange, Nat. Assn. Securities Dealers, Profl. Ski Patrol Assn. Republican. Roman Catholic. Club: Heather Ridge Country (treas., dir. pub. relations 1978-81). Contbr. articles to newspapers and trade mags. Home: 2192 S Victor St Aurora CO 80014 Office: 5340 S Quebec St 100 Englewood CO 80111

FLANIGAN, JOYCE MARY, educational administrator; b. Springfield, Mass., Mar. 5, 1937; d. Mark Harold and Mary Elizabeth (Beasley) Kelliher; children—Paul, Pamela, Robert, Cynthia. B.A., Coll. Our Lady at the Elms, 1965; M.A., Calif. State U.-Sacramento, 1975. Tchr., Mass., 1957-67; tchr. high sch. math., Vacaville, Calif., 1967-74, high sch. dean students, 1974-75, elem. prin., 1975-79; asst. supt. curriculum and instrn., Gilroy, Calif., 1979—; instr. Grad. Sch., U. San Francisco, 1983. Mem. Assn. Supervision and Curriculum Devel., Assn. Calif. Sch. Adminstrs., Gilroy C. of C. bd. dirs. Gilroy Community Theatre, South Valley Symphony. Home: 767 Carla Way Gilroy CA 95020 Office: 7663 Church St Gilroy CA 95020

FLATE, RONALD ALLEN, lawyer; b. Cleve., Nov. 26, 1937; B.S., U. Wis., 1960; J.D., Calif. Western Sch. Law, 1966. Admitted to Calif. bar, 1967, U.S. Supreme Ct. bar, 1974; atty.-agt. IRS, Los Angeles, 1966-68; supervisory atty. SBA, Los Angeles, 1971-72; sr. partner firm Ronald A. Flate, Los Angeles, 1968-71, 72—; judge pro tem Los Angeles Mcpl. Ct., 1977—; owner Ron Realty; chmn. bd., chief exec. officer F&H Metals Co., Ariz. Mem. Am., Calif., Los Angeles (mem. coms. tax, real estate, probate, bus. corp.) bar assns., Nat. Assn. Realtors, Los Angeles Bd. Realtors, Phi Delta Phi. Contbr. articles to legal jours.; lectr. bus. assns., civic orgns. Office: 4929 Wilshire Blvd #700 Los Angeles CA 90010 Tel (213) 933-7141

FLATLEY, MARIE ELIZABETH, business educator; b. Davenport, Iowa, Oct. 22, 1947; d. Robert E. and Mary L. (Meersman) F. B.B.A., U. Iowa, 1969, M.A., 1971, Ph.D., 1979. Tchr. bus. Atkinson (Ill.) High Sch., 1969-76; instr. Blackhawk Coll., Moline, Ill., 1975-78; grad. asst. U. Iowa, Iowa City, 1976-79; prof. info. systems San Diego State U., 1979—. Recipient Outstanding Teaching Asst. award U. Iowa, 1977; named Tchr. of Yr., San Diego State U. Latter Day Saints Student Assn., 1981. Mem. Am. Bus. Communication Assn., Nat. Bus. Edn. Assn., San

Diego Computer Soc., Delta Pi Epsilon. Republican. Roman Catholic. Contbr. articles to profl. jours.; author: Filing Systems for Information Management. Office: San Diego State U Coll of Bus San Diego CA 92182

FLAVIN, MICHAEL AUSTIN, telecommunications executive; b. N.Y.C., Nov. 27, 1932; s. Nell Flavin; m. Lois Tooley, Aug. 20, 1955; children—Suzanne, Michael, Mark, Mary Beth. B.S.E.E., U. Conn., 1954; M.S.E.E., Columbia U., 1960. Supr. Bell Labs., Indpls., 1954-65, dept. head, 1965-71, dir., Whippany, N.J., 1971-74, dir., Murray Hill, N.J., 1974-75, dir. Allentown, Pa., 1975-79, assoc. exec. dir., Indian Hill, Ill., exec. dir., Denver, 1979—. Home: 6914 Frying Pan Rd Boulder CO 80301 Office: 11900 N Pecos St Denver CO 80234

FLAY, BRIAN RICHARD, health sciences researcher and educator; b. Hamilton, N.Z., Feb. 1, 1947; s. William Trevor and Elsie (Emett) F.; m. Michele J. Shanberg, Oct. 30, 1978. Engring. student Canterbury (N.Z.) U. 1967-68; B.Social Sci. in Stas. and Pyschology, Waikato U., N.Z., 1972, M.Social Sci. in Pyschology, 1973, Ph.D. in Social Psychology, 1976; postgrad. London Sch. Econs. and Polit. Sci., 1973-74. Part-time instr. stas. Waikato Tech. Inst., 1970-75; part-time lectr. psychology dept. Waikato U., 1972-76; vis. asst. prof. Northwestern U., Evanston, Ill., 1977-78; asst. prof. health studies dept. U. Waterloo (Ont., Can.), assoc. chmn. grad. affairs, 1979-80; asst. prof. U. So. Calif. Sch. Pharmacy, asst. dir. health behavior research inst., 1980—, adj. asst. prof. Annenberg Sch. Communication, 1982—. Mem. Am. Psychol. Assn., Am. Pub. Health Assn., Brit. Psychol. Soc., Canadian Evaluation Soc. (charter), Canadian Health Edn. Soc., Evaluation Research Soc., Internat. Union Health Edn., N.Z. Psychol. Soc., Soc. Psychol. Study Social Issues, Soc. Behavioral Medicine. Contbr. articles to profl. jours. Office: Health Behavior Research Inst U So Calif 1985 Zonal Ave Los Angeles 90033

FLECKNER, ALAN NORMAN, physician; b. N.Y.C., May 3, 1934; s. Paul Richard and Martha (Feldman) F.; B.S., Fordham U., 1956; M.D., Jefferson Med. Coll., 1960; M.P.H., Harvard U., 1969; m. Ann McGranachan, Mar. 29, 1976; children by previous marriage—David, Marcia, Brett; stepchildren—Patricia Minard, Charles Minard, Donna Minard. Intern, Fitzsimmons Gen. Hosp., Denver, 1960-61; resident in ob-gyn Boston City Hosp., 1964-67, med. dir. maternal-infant care project, 1967-69; practice medicine, specializing in ob-gyn, Billerica, Mass., 1968-80; instr. ob-gyn Boston U. Sch. Medicine, 1967-70; clin. instr. Tufts U. Med. Sch., Boston, 1976-80; adj. asso. prof. health scis. Lowell (Mass.) U., 1973-80; v.p. Middlesex (Mass.) Gyn Ob-Inc., 1969-80; dir. ambulatory care dept. St. Joseph Hosp., Lowell, 1977-80; chief emergency med. services San Bernardino County (Calif.) Med. Ctr., 1980-83. Mem. Nashoba Assoc. Bd. Health, 1973-74; med. chmn. Westford Bd. Health, 1973-74; chmn. Lowell Emergency Med. Services Com. 1978-80. Served to col. USAF, 1959-64; Vietnam; mem. Res. Decorated Meritorious Service medal, Air Force Commendation medal, others; recipient Outstanding Aerosapace Medicine Physician award USAFR, 1975; Res. Flight Surgeon of Yr., Soc. Air Force Flight Surgeons, 1976. Diplomate Am. Bd. Ob-Gyn. Fellow Am. Coll. Obstetricians and Gynecologists, Am. Coll. Preventive Medicine; mem. AMA, Am. Coll. Emergency Physicians, Am. Occupational Medicine Assn., Assn. Mil. Surgeons, Air Force Assn., Res. Officers Assn., Calif. Med. Assn., Riverside County Med. Soc., Aerospace Med. Assn. Editor: Programmed Guide to Sex Education, 1969. Office: 41591 E Florida Ave Hemet CA 92343

FLEENOR, ELISA FALLARIA, nursing adminstr.; b. Lucena City, Philippines, Sept. 1, 1934; d. Pablo and Gliceria Alido (Alido) Fallaria; came to U.S., 1966, naturalized, 1970; R.N., Philippine Union Coll., 1959; B.S.N., Ariz. State U., 1982; m. George Herbert Fleenor, June 10, 1967. Pvt. duty nurse, Manila, Philippines, 1959-62; clin. nursing instr. St. Francis Xavier Hosp., Manila, 1963-66; pub. health nurse Govt. of Guam, Agana, 1966-68; instr. midwifery U. Cartagena, Colombia, S. Am., 1969-71; staff nurse VA Hosp., Phoenix, 1971-73; instr. pub. health nursing Keren, Ethiopia, Africa, 1973-74; nursing supr. Ebeye Field Hosp., Trust Ter. of the Pacific Islands, Marshall Islands, 1976-77; dir. nursing Ponape Hosp., Eastern Caroline Islands, 1977-79; staff nurse VA Hosp., Phoenix, 1979-82; nursing supr. Sonora (Calif.) Community Hosp., 1982—. Mem. Am., Philippine (pres. 1967-68), Guam, Calif. nursing assns., Hawaii Pub. Health Assn. Home: 20227 Gibbs Dr Sonora CA 95370

FLEENOR, GEORGE HERBERT, hospital administrator; b. Ardmore, Okla., Sept. 8, 1922; s. William D. and Allie F. (Dickson) F.; m. Elisa Fallaria, June 10, 1967. B.S., Union Coll., 1949; M.P.H., U. Hawaii, 1969. Hosp. adminstr. Gen. Conf. Seventh-Day Adventist, Colombia and Mex., 1949-60; hosp. adminstr. Am. Hosp. Mgmt. Co., Los Angeles, 1960-66; hosp. adminstr. Govt. of Guam, 1966-69; project adminstr. Project Hope, Colombia, 1969-71; hosp. adminstr. Valley View and Mesa Gen. Hosps., Phoenix, 1971-73; project adminstr. Project Concern-Ethiopia, 1973-74; adminstr. Health Maintenance Assocs., Phoenix, 1974-75; hosp. adminstr. Kwajalein Army Missile Range, Marshall Islands, 1975-77; hosp. adminstr., Trust Terr. of the Pacific Islands, Siapan and Mariana Islands, 1977-79; pres. Valley Prosthetics, Inc., Tempe, Ariz, 1979-82; adminstr. Sonora (Calif.) Med. Group, Inc., 1982—. Mem. Am. Coll. Hosp. Adminstrs., Am. Acad. Med. Adminstrs., Am. Pub. Health Assn., Am. Hosp. Assn., Med. Group Mgmt. Assn. Home: 20227 Gibbs Dr Sonora CA 95370

FLEER, KEITH GEORGE, motion picture executive; b. Bklyn., Feb. 28, 1943; s. Samuel Robert and Sophia M. (Scherer) F.; B.A. in Govt., Am. U., 1964, J.D., 1967. Admitted to N.Y. bar, 1968, D.C. bar, 1968, Calif. bar, 1976; asst. dir. athletics Fordham U., 1967-68; assoc. firm Gettinger, Gettinger & Manheimer, N.Y.C., 1968-72, Kaye, Scholer, Fierman, Hays & Handler, N.Y.C., 1972-75; sr. counsel Avco-Embassy Pictures, Hollywood, Calif., 1976; asso. firm Schiff, Hirsch & Schreiber, Beverly Hills, Calif., 1977; sr. v.p. bus. and legal affairs Melvin Simon Prodn., Inc., Beverly Hills, 1978-81; exec. v.p. Simon, Reeves, Landsburg Prodns., Beverly Hills, 1982—; guest lectr. U. West Los Angeles Law Sch., 1979-80; legis. counsel N.Y. State Assemblyman, 1969-70. Recipient Bruce Hughes award Am. U., 1964, Alumni award Am. U. Law Sch., 1967, Stafford H. Cassell award, 1979. Mem. Am. Bar Assn., Beverly Hills Bar Assn., Los Angeles Copyright Soc. (trustee 1983—). Bus. editor Am. U. Law Rev., 1966-67. Office: 260 S Beverly Dr Beverly Hills CA 90212

FLEISCHER, MORTON HERSCHIL, fin. co. exec.; b. Dallas, Dec. 27, 1936; s. Max and Rose (Peskind) F.; B.S. in Bus. Adminstrn., Washington U., St. Louis, 1958; m. Essie Dorothy Steinfeld, Sept. 1, 1962; children—Roslyn Jeri, Jeffrey Miles. Exec. v.p. Ozark Nat. Life Ins. Co., LaFayette, La., 1965-67; partner Fleischer & Fogel, Phoenix, 1968-72; pres., dir. PFO Fin. Corp., Los Angeles, 1972-74; pres. AVR Properties, Inc., Phoenix, 1974—; owner M.H. Fleischer & Assos., Phoenix, 1975—; pres., treas. Franchise Fin. Corp. Am., 1980—; dir. TDA Industries, Inc., N.Y.C. Served with AUS, 1959. Republican. Jewish. Home: 5104 N 42d Pl Phoenix AZ 95018 Office: 3443 N Central Ave Suite 419 Phoenix AZ 85012

FLEISCHMANN, ERNEST MARTIN, orchestra administrator, music festival director; b. Frankfurt, Germany, Dec. 7, 1924; s. Gustav and Antonia Fleischmann; student U. Witwatersrand, 1940-45; m. Elsa Leviseur, 1953; children—Stephanie, Martin, Jessica. Mus.B., U. Cape Town, 1954; postgrad. S.African Coll. Music, 1954-56. Debut as condr. Johannesburg Symphony Orch., 1942; asst. condr. South African Nat. Opera, 1948-51, Cape Town U. Opera, 1950-54; condr. South African Coll. Music Choir, 1950-52, Labia Grand Opera Co., 1953-55; music organizer Van Riebeck Festival, Cape Town, 1952; dir. music and drama Johannesburg Festival, 1956; gen. sec. London Symphony Orch., 1959-67; dir. for Europe, CBS Records, 1967-69; exec. dir. Los Angeles Philharmonic Orch., 1969—; gen. dir. Hollywood Bowl, 1969—. Mem. French Govt. Commn. on Reform of Paris Opera, 1967-68; mem. steering com. U.S. Nat. Commn., UNESCO Conf. on Future of Arts, 1975; bd. dirs. Assn. Calif. Symphony Orchs. Calif. Confedn. Arts; co-chmn. music policy and festivals panels Nat. Endowment for Arts; mem. exec. com. Am. Symphony Orch. League. Recipient John Steinway award for disting. service to music, 1979; President's spl. award Assn. Calif. Symphony Orchs., 1980. Contbr. to Music and Musicians, 1961-66, High Fidelity, 1968. Address: 135 N Grand Ave Los Angeles CA 90012

FLEMING, DONOVAN ERNEST, JR., psychologist, researcher; b. Ogden, Utah, Aug. 16, 1932; s. Donovan Ernest and Isabell (Bramwell) F.; m. Mary Ruth Hacking, Sept. 1, 1955; children—Clark, Karen, Greg, Suzanne, David, Allen. Student Weber State Coll., 1950-52; B.S., Brigham Young U., 1956, M.S. 1957; Ph.D., Wash. State U., 1962. Lic. psychologist, Utah. Research psychologist VA Med. Center, Salt Lake City, 1961-64; chief Psychol. Research Labs., VA Med. Ctr., Phoenix, 1964-71; prof. psychology Brigham Young U., 1971—, chmn. dept. psychology, 1977—; cons. Utah Valley Hosp. High-Risk Infant Nursery. Vice pres. Utah Nat. Parks council Boy Scouts Am., 1981—. Served with USN, 1952-54. Recipient Carl G. Maeser Research award Brigham Young U. Alumni Assn., 1978, Silver Beaver award Utah Nat. Parks council Boy Scouts Am., 1981. Mem. Am. Psychol. Assn., Utah Psychol. Assn. (pres. 1978-79), Am. Physiol. Soc., Soc. Neurosci., Psychonomic Soc. Mormon. Contbr. numerous articles to profl. jours.; author profl. papers. Home: 477 S 850 E Orem UT 84057 Office: 1082 SWKT Brigham Young U Provo UT 84602

FLEMING, GEORGE, telephone company executive, state senator; b. Dallas, June 29, 1938; m. Tina Bradley, Mar. 2; children—Sonja, Yemi. B.A. in Bus. Adminstrn., U. Wash. Football player Oakland Raiders, 1961, Winnipeg Blue Bombers, 1963-65; examiner fgn. corps. Wash. Sec. of State, Olympia, 1965-66; employment asst. Wash.-Idaho area Pacific Northwest Bell, Seattle, 1966-70, communication cons. Seattle area, 1970-73, personnel supr. Wash.-Idaho area, 1973-75, mgr. econ. devel. Wash.-Idaho area, 1975—; mem. Wash. State Senate, 1980—; mem. Am. Indsl. Devel. Council; mem., past pres. Pacific Northwest Indsl. Devel. Council; mem. Econ. Devel. Council Puget Sound, Nat. Council for Urban Devel. Bd. dirs. Randolph Carter; mem. Gov.'s Council on Tourism and Devel.; mem. adv. bd. Urban, Racial, Rural and Disadvantaged Edn. Named to All Big-Five Conf. Football Team, 1960, All Stars Coast Football Team, 1960, U. Wash. Husky Hall of Fame, 1980; numerous other awards for pub. service. Mem. Nat. Conf. State Legislatures (fiscal adv. com.), Puget Sound C. of C. (bus. adv. com.), Econ. Devel. Execs. Wash. (dir.), NAACP. Democrat. Baptist. Club: Masons. Home: 1100 Lake Washington Blvd Seattle WA 98144 Office: 1600 Bell Plaza Bldg Room 1804 Seattle WA 98199

FLEMING, M(ARY) PATRICIA, utility company official; b. Louisville, Sept. 26, 1937; d. Anthony and Addie Lang (Caldwell) F. B.S., La. State U., 1968. Asst. dir. info. Harvard U. Bus. Sch., Boston, 1970-76; nuclear info. rep. San Diego Gas & Electric Co., 1976-77, mem. fin. pub. relations staff, 1977-79, govtl. affairs rep., 1979—, assigned to Com. for Energy Awareness, Washington, 1980. Mem. Pub. Relations Soc. Am. (accredited), Am. Nuclear Soc., San Diego Voice of Energy, San Diego Gas and Electric Mgmt. Forum, Republican Assocs. San Diego, San Diego Symphony Assn., San Diego Mus. Art, Zeta Tua Alpha. Roman Catholic. Club: Rep. Bus. and Profl. (San Diego). Home: 3172-G Via Alicante La Jolla CA 92037 Office: PO Box 1831 San Diego CA 92112

FLEMING, PATRICIA ANN, psychologist; b. Cheyenne, Wyo., Aug. 23, 1929; d. Patrick William and Flo M. (Barnes) Dinneen; m. George Robert Fleming, June 16, 1952; children—Dawn, Ray, Grant, Patrick. B.A. cum laude, U. Wyo., 1951, M.A., 1951; Ed.D., U. No. Colo., 1971. Lic. psychologist Wyo. Dean of girls Laramie County Sch. Dist. #1, Cheyenne, Wyo., 1951-52; county dir. welfare, Bowman, N.D., 1952-54; psychologist Ednl. Diagnostic and Planning, Dist. #1, Cheyenne, 1966-69, Chaplin Ctr., Cheyenne, 1971-73; dir. Ednl. Resource Ctr., Cheyenne, 1974-78; psychologist (part-time) Fleming Assocs., Cheyenne, 1978—; instr. Chapman Coll., Warren AFB, Cheyenne; cons. Stride Learning Ctr., Laramie County Sch. Dist. Bd. dirs. Wyo. Children's Soc., Mountain View Towers, Child Protection Team; active Women's Civic League. Mem. Am. Psychol. Assn., Wyo. Psychol. Assn., Council for Exceptional Children, Am. Personnel and Guidance Assn., Phi Beta Kappa, Phi Delta Kappa, Kappa Kappa Gamma. Democrat. Roman Catholic. Author: Wyoming Young Children, 1979; Move, Grow, Learn, 1979. Home: 303 W 8th Ave Cheyenne WY 82001 Office: Fleming Assocs 1805 E 19th St Cheyenne WY 82001

FLEMING, PATRICK EDWARD, business exec.; b. Blackfoot, Idaho, Aug. 15, 1940; s. David Elihue and June Arlena (Edwards) F.; student Highline Community Coll., 1968-70; m. Jeanne Alberta Bainbridge, Dec. 24, 1972; children—Leesa Anne, Jill Leanne, David Eric, Erin Lynn. Quality control technician Donor Sci. Corp., Concord, Calif., 1959; electronic repair technician Automotive Equipment Repair Service, Inc., Oakland, Calif., 1960; prodn. engr. Smith Corona Marchant Co., Albany, Calif., 1960; engring. staff cons. Pacific N.W. Bell Telephone Co., Seattle, 1967-80; exec. v.p. Security Record Systems, Inc., Olympia, Wash., 1980—. Precinct committeeman, del. Wash. Republican Conv., 1968-70; leadership and speak up counselor Firlands Correctional Center, Seattle. Served with USN, 1960-67; Vietnam. Mem. IEEE, Jaycees Internat., Wash. Jaycees (pres. 1975-76, region dir. 1976-77, Outstanding Local Pres. award 1976), Nat. Small Bus. Assn., Airplane Owners and Pilots Assn., Western Farmer- Assn. Mormon. Clubs: Olympia Evergreen Gun, Elks, Toastmasters (pres. local chpt. 1970, area gov. 1971, Area Speaker award 1970, Disting. Service award 1971). Author chpt. history Kirkland Jaycees (Wash. State Henry GiessenBier award 1976). Office: Rowe Six Bldg 5 4224 6th Ave SE Lacey WA 98503

FLEMING, WILLIAM HENRY, medical instrument manufacturing company executive; b. Kansas City, Mo., Dec. 14, 1946; s. Philip George and Josephine Anna Fleming; m. Suzanne Gayle, Apr. 22, 1972; children—David K., Kathryn A. B.A., Calif. State U.-Hayward, 1971, M.B.A., 1973; Ph.D., Calif. Western U., 1981. Asst. quality assurance mgr. Flintkote Co., 1971-73; mgr. wafer fab prodn. Nat. Semicondr. Co., 1973-76; shift supr. Intel Corp., 1977-78; mgr. mfg. Instromedix, Inc., Beaverton, Oreg., 1978-79; v.p., gen. mgr. Cardiac Resuscitator Corp., Lake Oswego, Oreg., 1980-81; pres. Life Sci. Instrumentation, Inc., Portland, Oreg., 1981—; cons. med. device quality assurance, 1977—. Served with USN, 1966-68. Decorated Air medal with 2 gold stars. Mem. ASTM, Assn. for Advancement of Med. Instruments. Republican. Roman Catholic. Patentee surg. back plate electrode. Office: 10150 SW Nimbus Ave Suite E-7 Portland OR 97223

FLEMINGS, HAROLD LLOYD, trade association executive; b. Detroit, Mar. 1, 1938; s. James and Anne Mae (Brown) F.; m. Geraldine Roland, Aug. 11, 1956; children—Antonio, Paris, Angelo, Rachele. Wayne State U., 1964; postgrad., U. Mich., 1966. Reporter, Mich. Chronicle Newspaper, Detroit, 1960—; tech. asst. and hosp. attendant Wayne County Gen. Hosp., Eloise, Mich., 1961-64; tchr. Detroit Pub. Schs., 1964-67; life underwriter Equitable Life Assurance Soc. Am., Detroit, 1967-69; customer relations rep. Blue Cross-Blue Shield, Mt. Pleasant, Mich., 1969-74, mktg. trainer, Detroit, 1974-78, profl. achievement program instr., 1978-81; v.p. Service Holding, Ltd., Orange, Calif., 1981-83; health care plan mgr. New World Maintenance Assn., Inc., Orange, 1980-82, pres., 1982-83; exec. Ind. Operators Assn., 1983—; writer Detroit Set Mag., 1964. Lay speaker Mich. Cancer Found., 1963-64; bd. dirs. Career Devel. Ctr., Detroit, 1968. Mem. Am. Soc. Tng. and Devel. (award 1976), Mich. Soc. Instructional Tech. Jehovah's Witness. Home: 1442 Blossom Ln Anaheim CA 92805 Office: PO Box 367 Anaheim CA 92805

FLEMMING, JOAN ANTOINETTE, business executive; b. Tulsa, Apr. 27, 1921; d. Homer Virgil and Ida Buelah (Arnold) F.; B.S., U. Tulsa, 1942. Sales mgr. Avon Products Co., Portland, Oreg., 1957-59; accountant P.I.E. Truck Transp. Co., Walnut Creek, Calif., 1959-69; supr. acctg. Western Temp. Services Co., San Francisco, 1969-75; mgr. acctg. ADP Collision Estimating Services, Hayward, Calif., 1975-80, mgr. billing and collecting, 1980—. Mem. Tulsa Art Assn., Tulsa Symphony Orch. Mem. Phi Mu (v.p. 1942), Alpha Rho Tau, Beta Sigma Phi (pres. 1955-56). Democrat. Mem. Christian Ch. (Disciples of Christ). Club: Pilot Internat. Home: 430 Taylor Ave Alameda CA 94501 Office: 2380 W Winton Hayward CA 94545

FLEMMING, PAUL EUGENE, JR., accountant; b. Norfolk, Va., Aug. 12, 1948; s. Paul Eugene and Marjorie Ruth (Rudiger) F.; B.S. in Bus. Adminstrn., U. Nev., 1970; m. Barbara Ann Bateman, June 13, 1970; children—Jeffrey Paul, Allison Marie. Acct., Lear Motors, Stead, Nev., 1971; sr. acct. Washoe County Sch. Dist., Reno, Nev.; acctg. instr. Truckee Meadows Community Coll., Reno, 1975-81. Served with U.S. Army, 1970-71. Home: 4330 Toro Ct Reno NV 89502

FLEMMING, WALLACE EDWARD, hospital administrator; b. Minneota, Minn., Sept. 27, 1938; s. Arthur E. and Mary L. F.; m. Margie Smith, June 25, 1960; children—Theresa, Michael. Student St. Thomas Coll., St. Paul, 1956-57; B.S. in Bus. Adminstrn., Creighton U., 1960. C.P.A., Calif. Acct., Honeywell Inc., Mpls., 1960-64; dir. fin. Golden Valley Health Ctr., Mpls., 1964-74; sr. auditor R.G. Engelhart & Co., C.P.A.s, Burnsville, Minn., 1974-77; adminstr. Sacred Heart Hosp., Hanford, Calif., 1977—; mem. adminstrs. bd. So. Calif. Blue Cross. Mem. Am. Coll. Hosp. Adminstrs., Am. Acad. Hosp. Adminstrs., Soc. Calif. Accts., Hosp. Fin. Mgmt. Assn. (William G. Follmer award 1980), Am. Inst. C.P.A.s, Soc. Calif. C.P.A.s, Calif. Hosp. Assn. (bd. dirs. central council), Hanford C. of C. (dir. 1979-82), Tulare-Kings Hosp. Conf. (pres. 1978). Roman Catholic. Club: Kiwanis. Office: Sacred Heart Hospital 1025 N Douty St Hanford CA 93230

FLENNIKEN, JOHN CALVIN, power and light co. exec.; b. Portland, Oreg., Oct. 1, 1944; s. John Calvin and Rosemary Winefred F.; B.S., Portland State U., 1968, M.S.T., 1973; postgrad. Brown U., 1973; m. Susan P. Sage, Aug. 26, 1967; children—Gregory Michael, Zachary Robert. Research technician Kruger Labs., Portland, Oreg., 1965-68; chemistry tchr. Portland Public Schs., 1968-80; energy cons. Energy & Man's Environment, Inc., Portland, 1976-80; tech. tng. and devel. supr. Pacific Power & Light Co., Portland, 1980—; cons. The Coll. Bd., 1975-80. Recipient Worthington award Multnomah Jr. Coll., 1962; NSF grantee, 1970, 73. Mem. Nat. Sci. Tchrs. Assn., Am. Soc. Tng. and Devel., AAAS. Author: Precipitation, Steam Flow and Water Supply, 1975; Water Content of Snow-Using Radio-Isotope Techniques, 1975; Critical Thinking About Energy Consumption, 1979; Energy Flows Through Natural Systems, 1979; Underground Cable and Fault Locating Handbook, 1980. Office: 920 SW 6th Ave Portland OR 97204

FLETCHER, ALLEN, stage director; b. San Francisco, July 19, 1922; s. Allen and Jessica Laurestine (Dinsmoor) F.; B.A., Stanford U., 1947, M.A., 1949; postgrad. Yale Univ., Bristol Old Vic Theatre Sch., London Acad. Music; m. Anne Lawder, Dec. 20, 1955; children—John Crandall, Julia Kathryn. Instr., then asst. prof. drama Carnegie-Mellon Inst., Pitts., 1951-59; stage dir. N.Y.C. Opera, 1959-65; dir. plays Oreg. Shakespeare Festival, 1948-49, 1950-52, 1953-54, 1956, San Diego Shakespeare Festival, 1955, 57-64, 72, Assn. Producing Artists, 1959-61; artistic dir. Am. Shakespeare Festival, 1961-65, Seattle Repertory Theatre, 1965-70; resident dir., conservatory dir. Am. Conservatory Theatre, San Francisco, 1965—; guest dir. Pacific Conservatory Performing Arts. Served with U.S. Army, 1942-46. Fulbright scholar, 1957-58; Ford Found. grantee, 1959-60. Mem. Soc. Stage Dirs. and Choreographers, Inc., Actors Equity Assn., Am. Guild Mus. Artists, Ibsen Soc. Am. Episcopalian. Club: Marines Memorial (San Francisco). Translator plays by Ibsen. Office: Am Conservatory Theatre 450 Geary St San Francisco CA 94102

FLETCHER, DONALD WARREN, microbiologist, university administrator; b. Phoenix, June 8, 1929; s. Donald Warren and Ruth Marie (Staton) F.; children—Lisa Marie Nicholas, Timothy Warren Fletcher. B.S., Oreg. State U., 1957, M.S., 1953; Ph.D., Wash. State U., 1956. Instr. Wash. State U., 1956-59; asst., then assoc. prof. San Francisco State U., 1959-67; dean sch. arts and scis., U. Bridgeport (Conn.), 1969-70; assoc. dean sch. natural scis., San Francisco State U., 1970-74; assoc. state univ. dean, Office of Chancellor, Calif. State U.-Long Beach, 1975—; dir. Ctr. Advanced Med. Tech., 1968-69. Served with USNR, 1950-54. Fellow USPHS, 1954; NSF Insts., 1960, AAAS, 1967; Fulbright fellow, 1966, 1967. Mem. Am. Soc. Microbiology, Soc. Gen. Microbiology, AAAS, Am. Inst. Biol. Scis., Newcomen Soc., Sigma Xi, Phi Kappa Phi, Theta Xi. Author: Laboratory Manual of General Microbiology, 1962. Contbr. articles to profl. jours. Home: 12200 Mentecito St Apt K 204 Seal Beach CA 90740 Office: 400 Golden Shore Suite 306 Long Beach CA 90802

FLETCHER, DONNA LYNNE, association executive; b. Johnson City, N.Y., Aug. 12, 1952; d. Donald Curtis and Elizabeth (Belden) F. B.A. in Pub. Affairs, George Washington U., 1974. Legis. asst. Nat. Fedn. Business and Profl. Women's Clubs Inc., Washington, 1974-75; asst. to exec. dir. No. Calif. Service League, San Francisco, 1976-78; asst. to program funding dir. Sierra Club, San Francisco, 1978-79, dir. gen. giving, 1979—. Bd. dirs. Gray Panthers met. group, Washington, 1974-75. Mem. Nat. Soc. Fundraising Execs. Democrat. Office: 530 Bush St San Francisco CA 94117

FLETCHER, HOMER LEE, librarian; b. Salem, Ind., May 11, 1928; s. Floyd M. and Hazel (Barnett) F.; B.A., Ind. U., 1953; M.S. in L.S., U. Ill., 1954; m. Jacquelyn Ann Blanton, Feb. 7, 1950; children—Deborah Lynn, Randall Brian, David Lee. Librarian, Milw. Pub. Library, 1954-56; head librarian Ashland (Ohio) Pub. Library, 1956-59; city librarian Arcadia (Calif.) Pub. Library, 1959-65; city librarian Vallejo (Calif.) Pub. Library, 1965-70; city librarian San Jose, Calif., 1970—. Pres. S. Solano chpt. Calif. Assn. Neurologically Handicapped Children, 1968-69. Served with USAF, 1946-49. Mem. Am. (intellectual freedom com. 1967-72), Calif. (pres. pub. libraries sect. 1967) library assns., Phi Beta Kappa. Democrat. Mem. Christian Ch. (Disciples of Christ) (elder, chmn. congregation 1978-79). Rotarian. Contbr. articles to profl. jours. Office: 180 W San Carlos St San Jose CA 95113*

FLETCHER, JOHN DEXTER, research psychologist; b. Providence, Dec. 9, 1940; s. John Dexter and Agnes (McClelland) F.; m. Sheila Gates, June 17, 1968; children—Scott Dexter, Jeffrey Quinn, Brian Whitford. B.A. in English, U. Ariz., 1965; M.S. in Computer Sci., Stanford U., 1973, Ph.D. in Ednl. Psychology, 1973. Research assoc.

Stanford (Calif.) U., 1969-73; asst. prof. computer sci., psychology U. Ill., Chgo., 1973-74; research psychologist, supr. U.S. Navy Personnel Research and Devel. Ctr., San Diego, 1974-78; program mgr. Def. Advanced Research Projects Agy., Arlington, Va., 1978-80; coordinator tng. research and devel. U.S. Army Research Inst., Alexandria, Va., 1980-81; dir. Wicat Edn. Inst., Provo, Utah, 1981—; mem. Apple Edn. Found. adv. com.; mem. adv. bd. Def. Sci. Panel on Tng. and Tng. Tech. Webelos leader Nat. Capital Area council Cub Scouts Am., 1980-81; troop com. mem. Utah Nat. Parks council Boy Scouts Am., 1981-82; asst. soccer coach Utah Youth Soccer Assn., Orem, Utah, 1981-82. Mem. AAAS, Am. Edn. Research Assn., Am. Psychol. Assn., Assn. Computing Machinery, Assn. Devel. Computer-Based Instrn. Systems. Developer procedures and devices for computer-assisted reading instrn.; contbr. numerous articles and papers in field to profl. jours. Home: 586 W 440 South St Orem UT 84057 Office: Wicat Edn Inst 931 E 300 North Provo UT 84601

FLETCHER, JOHN FORBES, chem./nuclear engr.; b. Vancouver, Wash., Dec. 12, 1923; s. Charles V. and Estella F. (Forbes) F.; B.S. in Ch.E., Wash. State U., 1948, M.S. in Ch.E., 1951; m. Jessie Louise Towne, June 12, 1948; children—Marcia Lee Fletcher Moreno, Linda Kay Fletcher Woodall, Cheryl Anne Fletcher Brandt. Engr., sr. engr. Gen. Elec. Co., Richland, Wash., 1950-64; sr. devel. engr. Battelle-N.W., Richland, 1965-70, staff engr., 1982—; mgr. environ. and econ. analysis Westinghouse Hanford Co., Richland, 1970-82. Mem. ad hoc adv. coms. Wash. Dept. Ecology, 1971-73, 76—. Served with AUS, 1943-46. Registered profl. engr., Calif., Wash. Mem. Am. Nuclear Soc., Am. Inst. Chem. Engrs., Am. Chem. Soc. Republican. Episcopalian. Club: Richland Rod and Gun (pres. 1971). Contbr. articles profl. jours. Patentee in field. Home: 112 W 28th Ave Kennewick WA 99336 Office: PO Box 999 Richland WA 99352

FLETCHER, ROBERT DAWSON, meteorologist; b. Lampacitos, Mexico, Feb. 11, 1912; s. Edmond McC. and Grace (Dawson) F.; B.S. in Mech. Engring., Calif. Inst. Tech., 1933, M.S. in M.E. (Aero), 1934, M.S. in Meteorology, 1935; D.Sc. in Meteorology, Mass. Inst. Tech., 1941; m. Elsie Walser, June 1, 1935; children—Robert Dawson, John E. Meteorologist Am. Airlines, Inc., 1935-39; instr. meteorology U. Calif. at Los Angeles, 1940- 42; meteorologist U.S. Weather Bur., 1940-50, supervising forecaster, 1941-46, chief hydrometeorol. sect., 1946-50; with USAF Air Weather Service, 1950—, cons., 1950-52, dir. sci. services, 1952-64, dir. aerospace scis., 1964-71, chief scientist, 1971-72; cons. in meteorology, 1972—. Tech. cons. OSRD, 1944, USAAF in CBI and Caribbean, 1944-45; U.S. del. World Meteorological Orgn. (UN), 1952—; USAF and NRC del., Manila, 1952, Bangkok, 1957, NASA adv. group aero. research and devel. NATO Conf. Polar Meteorology, Oslo, Norway, 1956, Australian Conf. Tropical Storms, Brisbane, 1956; mem. meteorology panel U.S. Nat. Com. on Internat. Geophys. Year, 1955-64; liaison rep. com. on high altitude rocket and balloon research Nat. Acad. Scis., 1963—, mem. panel on edn., 1963—. Pres. Bannockburn (Md.) Citizens Assn., 1951-52. Recipient USAF decoration for exceptional civilian service, 1962, 72; Robert M. Losey award Am. Inst. Aeros. and Astronautics, 1969; Charles Franklin Brooks award Am. Meteorol. Soc., 1970. Fellow Am. Meteorol. Soc. (pres. 1956-57, councillor 1972—); asso. fellow Am. Inst. Aeros. and Astronautics (chmn. tech. com. on atmospheric environment 1964-65); mem. Am. Geophys. Union, Royal Meteorol. Soc., Sigma Xi. Contbr. articles to profl. jours. Home: Tubac Valley Country Club Estates PO Box 2461 Tubac AZ 85640

FLETCHER, STEVEN ANTHONY, environmental engineer, industrial hygienist, chemist, safety engineer; b. Osaka, Japan, Dec. 29, 1951; s. Clarence Leonard and Kazuyo (Okamoto) F.; m. Emma Faye Tutt, Mar. 17, 1973; 1 dau., Lauren Aiko. B.A. in Chemistry (pres.'s scholar), So. Ill. U., Carbondale, 1973. Cert. indsl. hygienist Am. Bd. Indsl Hygiene. Chemist, Ralston Purina Co., St. Louis, 1973-74, Azcon Corp., Cripple Creek, Colo., 1974-75; indsl. hygienist Colo. Dept. Health, Denver, 1975-78; safety mgr. Assoc. Grocers, Denver, 1978-79; envirnon. engr. Western Electric Co., Denver, 1980—. Mem. Am. Indsl. Hygiene Assn., Am. Acad. Indsl. Hygiene, Air Pollution Control Assn. Home: 2455 S Deframe St Lakewood CO 80228 Office: 1200 W 120th Ave Denver CO 80234

FLICK, ROBERT JAMES (BOB ROBERTS), broadcasting exec.; b. Butte, Mont., Sept. 9, 1952; s. Raymond P. and Marie B. Flick; diploma Brown Inst. Broadcasting, Mpls., 1973. Journeyman, Bert's Car Triming, Butte, 1969-73; with Sta. KOPR, Butte, 1974, Sta. KBOW, Butte, 1974-75; with Sta. KXLF, Butte, 1975—, program dir., music dir., 1976-80; program dir., music dir. Sta. KQUY-FM, Butte, 1982—; music cons., 1977—. Mem. Nat. Assn. Broadcasters, Mont. Assn. Broadcasters, Nat. St. Rod Assn., United Comml. Travellers, Butte Jaycees. Club: Butte Elks. Home: 428 Colorado St Butte MT 59701 Office: KQUY-FM 3219 Harrison Ave PO Box 3788 Butte MT 59701

FLICK, THOMAS JOHN, environ. affairs and safety coordinator; b. Jefferson City, Mo., Feb. 15, 1955; s. Joseph Anthony and Corine Margaret (Huhnman) F.; B.S. in Graphic Art, Central Mo. State U., 1977, M.S. in Indsl. Safety, 1979; m. Amy Louise Farmer, May 31, 1980. Dist. environ. affairs and safety coordinator Getty Oil Co., Denver, 1978—; instr. Nat. Safety Council def. driving, ARC, 1980-81. Mem. Am. Soc. Safety Engrs., Rocky Mountain Petroleum Safety Assn., Colo. Soc. Safety Engrs., Theta Chi. Republican. Roman Catholic. Home: 9900 W Walden Ave Littleton CO 80127 Office: 1670 Broadway Denver CO 80202

FLICKINGER, ROBERT LEE, real estate executive; b. Waukegan, Ill., June 4, 1943; s. Robert John and Elizabeth C. (Miller) F.; student New Bedford Inst., 1963-65, numerous trade schs.; m. Deborah E. Mallory, June 27, 1981; children by previous marriage—Sheri Dawn, Robert Lee. Research and devel. engr. Photon, Inc., Wilmington, Mass., 1966-70; dir. spl. applications Automix, Inc., Bellevue, Wash., 1970-75; pres. Currency Brokers, Inc., Orange, Calif., 1975—; real estate investor low-income housing, Los Angeles. Served with USAF, 1962-66. Mem. Newport Harbor C. of C. Clubs: Balboa Bay, Hollywood Turf. Designer electronic designs graphic arts industry. Office: 840 Newport Center Dr #675 Newport Beach CA 92660

FLINN, GALEN VAUGHN, air monitoring instrumentation specialist; b. Reno, Nev., Apr. 22, 1950; s. Gordon Roland and Pauline Christine (Guthmiller) F.; B.S., U. Nev., 1972; postgrad., 1972-73; m. Gloria C. Eastwood, May 1, 1977; children—Conyne, Dale, David. Announcer, Sta. KSRN-FM, Reno, 1969-75; profl. tech. photographer, owner C.O.I.N. Photo, Carson City, Nev., 1970-79; farm project foreman, main sta. U. Nev., Reno, 1972-73; stage hand, stage mgr. John Ascuaga's Nuggett, Sparks, Nev., 1972-74; process foreman U.S. Platinum Refineries, Sparks, Nev., 1974-75; environ. mgmt. specialist State of Nev. Air Monitoring, Carson City, 1975-81; monitoring systems devel. cons. Syrian Meteorol. Dept. Monitoring Project, Damascus, 1980—; v.p. customer services Telos Labs, Inc., indsl. toxicological monitoring systems, 1981—; cons. in field. Mem. Am. Radio Relay League, Airplane Owners and Pilots Assn., Alpha Zeta. Republican. Club: Toastmasters. Home: 4141 Stoneridge Dr Tracy CA 95376 Office: 4480A Enterprise St Fremont CA 94538

FLINN, ROBERTA JEANNE, swimming pool company executive; b. Twin Falls, Idaho, Dec. 19, 1947; d. Richard H. and Ruth (Johnson) F. Student Colo. State U., 1966-67. Ptnr., Aqua-Star Pools & Spas, Boise, Idaho, 1978—, mng. ptnr., 1981-83; ops. mgr. Polly Pools, Inc., Canby, Oreg., 1983—. Mem. Nat. Assn. Female Execs., Nat. Appaloosa Horse Club. Republican. Mem. Christian Ch. Office: 158 SW First St Canby OR 97013

FLINT, GREGORY SCOTT, social work administrator; b. Los Angeles, July 13, 1953; s. Bennie Charles and Jean (Collier) F.; m. Claudia Lee Breslow, June 1, 1974; children—Amy Michele, Jennifer Leigh. B.A., U. Redlands, 1975; M.S.W., San Diego State U., 1978. Lic. clin. social worker, Calif. Student social worker Redlands (Calif.) Welfare Dept., 1974-75; child care worker Am. Boys Ranch, Beaumont, Calif., 1975-76; social work intern Vis. Nurse Assn., San Diego, 1976-77, Donald N. Sharp Meml. Hosp., San Diego, 1977; clin. social worker St. Mary Med. Ctr., Long Beach, Calif., 1978-81, dir. clin. social work, 1981—. Active area 54 patient service and rehab. com. Am. Cancer Soc., program planning and devel. com. Sr. Care Action Network. Mem. Nat. Assn. Social Workers, Nat. Soc. Hosp. Social Work Dirs., So. Calif. Soc. Hosp. Social Work Dirs., Long Beach Area Med. Social Service Orgn. Democrat. Home: 14381 Shirley St Westminster CA 92683 Office: 1050 Linden Ave PO Box 887 Long Beach CA 90801

FLINT, LOU JEAN, state education official; b. Ogden, Utah, July 11, 1934; d. Elmer Blood and Ella D. (Adams) F.; children—Dirk Kershaw Brown, Kristie Susan Brown Felix, Flint Kershaw Brown. B.S., Weber State Coll., 1968; M.Ed., U. Utah, 1974, Ed.S, 1981. Cert. early childhood and elem. edn., Utah Bd. Edn., 1968, edn. adminstrn., 1981. Master tchr. Muir Elem., Davis Sch. Dist., Farmington, Utah, 1968-77; edn. specialist Dist. I, Dept. Def., Eng., Scotland, Norway, Denmark, Holland, Belgium, 1977-79; ednl. cons. Office Higher Edn. State of Utah, Utah System Approach to Individualized Learning, Tex., S.C., Fla., Utah, 1979—; dir. spl. projects Office Commr. Higher Edn. State of Utah, Salt Lake City, 1982—; mem. Equity Vocat. Edn. Bd.; mem. Women and Bus. Conf. Bd. Active fund raising Sta. KUED. Named Exemplary Tchr., Utah State Bd. Edn., 1970-77; Outstanding Educator, London Central High Sch., 1979; recipient award Appreciation, Gov. Matheson, 1983. Mem. AAUW, Am. Council Edn. (Nat. Identification Program 1982), Consortium Women in Higher Edn., Nat. Assn. Edn. Young Children, Utah Assn. Edn. Young Children (past pres.), Utah Jaycee Aux. (past pres. Centerville), Phi Delta Kappa, Delta Kappa Gamma. Mormon. Author: The Comprehensive Community College, 1980; others. Office: 807 E S Temple St Suite 204 Salt Lake City UT 84110

FLINT, ROBERT THOMAS, psychologist; b. Los Angeles, Sept. 16, 1935; s. Thomas and Louise (Jones) F.; m. Winifred LaVonne, Aug. 29, 1955 (div.); m. 2d Gayla Kaibel, May 21, 1972; children—Jerretta Villines, Sean Flint, Kathleen Flint, Deirdre Flint. B.A., San Francisco State Coll., 1961, M.A., 1963; Ph.D. (USPHS fellow), U. Minn., 1970. Lic. cons. psychologist, Minn.; lic. psychologist, Calif. Research psychologist Am. Rehab. Found., Mpls., 1966-68; instr. Student Counseling Bur., U. Minn., 1968-70, asst. prof., 1970-74, assoc. prof., 1974-77; v.p. Judson Family Ctr., Mpls., 1977-80; chief psychol. services Ashby Med. Group, Berkeley, Calif., 1980—; cons. law enforcement, 1968—; pvt. practice psychotherapy; trainer psychotherapists; forensic psychologist; tchr. in field; founder Minn. Health Careers Council, 1965; sec., bd. dirs. Central Contra Costa County (Calif.) Rape Crisis Service, 1982-83. Served with USN, 1954-58. Mem. Am. Psychol. Assn., Calif. Psychol. Assn., Nat. Coalition Against Sexual Assault, No. Calif. Soc. Clin. Hypnosis (sec.), Internat. Assn. Chiefs of Police (assoc.). Democrat. Contbr. articles on psychology as related to occupational therapy, dental hygiene, nursing, dentistry and law enforcement to profl. jours.; script writer, cons. tng. films for law enforcement on psychology of crime victims, especially sexual assault victims. Home: 3630 Sun View Ct Concord CA 94520 Office: 2305 Ashby Ave Berkeley CA 94705

FLOM, TERRENCE EDSEL, electronics company official; b. Moose Lake, Minn., Sept. 21, 1940; s. Andrew Felix and Olga (Koskey) F.; B.E.E., Ga. Inst. Tech., 1964. Electronic engr. computers Control Data Corp., Mpls., 1964-67; electronic engr. laser radar Xerox, Pasadena, Calif., 1967-68; electronic engr. laser radar and communications ITT, Van Nuys, Calif., 1968-75; sect. head laser communications GTE, Mountain View, Calif., 1975-78, dept. mgr. electro-optics systems engring., 1978-82, mgr. electro-optics tech. devel., 1982—. Mem. Optical Soc. Am., Laser Inst. Am. Contbr. articles to profl. publs. Home: 873 Balboa Ln Foster City CA 94404 Office: Box 7188 Mountain View CA 94039

FLOOD, JAMES TYRRELL, broadcasting executive, public relations consultant; b. Los Angeles, Oct. 5, 1934; s. James Joseph and Teresa (Rielly) F.; m. Bonnie Carolyn Lutz, Mar. 25, 1966; children—Hilary C., Sean L. B.A. in Sociology, U. Calif.-Santa Barbara, 1956; M.A. in Communications, Calif. State U.-Chico, 1981. Cons. pub. relations, Beverly Hills, Calif., 1964-72; account exec. Birr, Wilson & Co., Inc., Paradise, Calif., 1972-76; pub. relations cons. Medic Alert Found. Internat., Paradise, 1976-83; owner, mgr. Sta. KRIJ-FM, Paradise, 1983—; instr. Calif. State Sch. Communications, Chico, 1982—; cons. Nat. Assn. Visually Handicapped, 1983—. Calif. media cons. Carter/ Mondale campaign, 1976; mem. Calif. Democratic party fin. com., 1982-83. Served with USNR, 1956-58. Mem. Pub. Relations Soc. Am. Club: Rotary (Paradise).

FLOOR, EMANUEL ANDREW, land devel. exec.; b. Salt Lake City, Dec. 3, 1935; s. Andrew W. and Marie A. (Trakas) F.; B.S., U. Utah, 1957; m. Nan Hansen, June 6, 1964; children—David Emanuel, Gina Marie, Michael Patrick. Pres., dir. Triad Utah, 1975—; v.p., dir. Triad Am., Salt Lake City; dir. Tracy Collins Bank. Pres. Salt Lake Internat. Council; dir. Utah Travel Council, 1964-66; dir. instl. devel. Utah State U., Logan, 1966-68; vol. program cons. ARC, 1950-66; chmn. Western Gov.'s Travel Council, 1966-69; bd. dirs. Catholic Charities, Salt Lake City, Utah Symphony, Pine Canyon Ranch for Boys. Mem. Salt Lake Area C. of C. (vice chmn., dir.), Pi Kappa Alpha. Clubs: University, Ambassador, Ft. Douglas. Home: 2205 Country Club Dr Salt Lake City UT 84109 Office: Suite 500 Lakeside Plaza I 5225 Wiley Post Way Salt Lake City UT 84116

FLOR, LOY LORENZ, chemist, corrosion engr.; b. Luther, Okla., Apr. 25, 1919; s. Alfred Charles and Nellie M. (Wilkinson) F.; B.A. in Chemistry, San Diego State Coll., 1941; m. Virginia Louise Pace, Oct. 1, 1946; children—Charles R., Scott R., Gerald C., Donna Jeanne, Cynthia Gail. With Helix Water Dist., La Mesa, Calif., 1947—, chief chemist, 1963—, supr. water quality, 1963—, supr. corrosion control dept., 1956—. Served to 1st. lt. USAAF, 1941-45. Registered profl. engr., Calif. Mem. Am. Chem. Soc. (chmn. San Diego sect. 1965—), Am. Water Works Assn. (chmn. water quality div. Calif. sect. 1965—), Nat. Assn. Corrosion Engrs. (chmn. western region 1970). Republican. Presbyterian. Club: Masons. Office: RM Levy Treatment Plant 9550 Lake Jennings Park Rd Lakeside CA 92040

FLORA, EDWARD BENJAMIN, research co. exec.; b. Phillipsburg, Ohio, June 23, 1929; s. Russell Thomas and Elizabeth Lucille (Hollinger) F.; B.S., Carnegie Mellon U., 1951, M.S., 1953; m. Dolores G. Havrilla, May 3, 1952; children—Christopher D., Stephanie A., Christine M. Project engr. Columbia U. Nevis Cyclotron Lab., Irvington, N.Y., 1953-58; sr. engr. Dalmo Victor Co., Belmont, Calif., 1958-63; with Anamet Labs., Inc., Berkeley, Calif., 1963—, v.p., 1963-82, pres., 1982—, mgr. aerospace structures info. and analysis center, 1972—. Mem. bd. edn. St. Gregory's Sch., San Mateo, Calif., 1971-72. Registered profl. engr., Calif., Ohio. Mem. ASME, Am. Ceramic Soc., Soc. Automotive Engrs., Soc. for Exptl. Stress Analysis, Sigma Xi. Home: 1292 Laurel Hill Dr San Mateo CA 94402 Office: 100 Industrial Rd San Carlos CA 94070

FLORA, ERIC S., computer scientist; b. Los Angeles, Nov. 3, 1951; s. LaVere Paul and Ople (Shirley) F.; B.A. cum laude, LaVerne Coll., 1973; M.S., Tex. A&M U., 1975. Software engr. TRW, Redondo Beach, Calif., 1975-78; systems engr. Northrop Electronics, Hawthorne, Calif., 1978-80; group supr. software engring. Magnavox Advanced Products and Systems Co., Torrance, Calif., 1980-82; project engr., sect. head TRW, Redondo Beach, Calif., 1982—. Leader, Am. Youth Hostels; trip leader Sierra Club; instr. basic mountaineering course. Mem. IEEE, Assn. Computing Machinery, Nat. Mgmt. Assn., U.S. Ski Assn. Home: 531 S Helberta Ave Redondo Beach CA 90277 Office: 1 Space Park Redondo Beach CA 90278

FLORA, JOHN WILLIAM, nuclear cons.; b. Missoula, Mont., June 16, 1926; s. Joel Hubert and Gladys Augusta (Rooth) F.; B.S., U. Denver, 1948; m. Ruth JoAnne Aspinall, June 15, 1952; children—Pamela JoAnne, Paula Marie, Patricia Ann, Shawn William, Physicist, Gen. Electric Co., Richland, Wash., 1948-52, Calif. Research & Devel. Corp., Livermore, 1952-54; group leader reactor safety Atomics Internat., Canoga Park, Calif., 1954-62; sr. reactor inspector Denver office, Regulatory Operations, U.S. AEC, Denver, 1962-70, dir., 1970-73; nuclear cons., 1974—. Served with USAAF, 1944-45. Recipient Spl. Achievement award U.S. AEC, 1970. Mem. A.A.A.S., Am. Nuclear Soc. (pres. Colo. 1964-65), Sigma Pi Sigma, Phi Beta Kappa. Methodist. Patentee in field. Home: 3076 S High St Denver CO 80210

FLORY, PAUL JOHN, chemist, educator; b. Sterling, Ill., June 19, 1910; s. Ezra and Martha (Brumbaugh) F.; B.S., Manchester Coll., 1931, Sc.D. (hon.), 1950; M.S., Ohio State U., 1931, Ph.D., 1934, Sc.D., 1970; m. Emily Catharine Tabor, Mar. 7, 1936; children—Susan, Melinda, Paul J. Engaged in research on synthetic fibers, synthetic rubber and other polymeric substances, DuPont Exptl. Sta., Wilmington, Del., 1934-38, U. Cin., 1938-40, Standard Oil Devel. Co., Elizabeth, N.J., 1940-43; dir. fundamental research Goodyear Tire & Rubber Co., Akron, O., 1943-48; prof. chemistry, Cornell U., 1948-57; exec. dir. research Mellon Inst., Pitts., 1956-61; J.G. Jackson-C.J. Wood prof. chemistry Stanford U., 1961—. Recipient Sullivant medal Ohio State U., 1945; Baekeland award Am. Chem. Soc., 1947; George Fisher Baker non-resident lectureship in chemistry Cornell U., 1948; Peter Debye award in phys. chemistry Am. Chem. Soc., 1968, Gibbs medal, 1973, Priestley medal, 1974; Cresson medal Franklin Inst., 1971; Nobel prize for chemistry, 1974, Nat. medal of sci., 1974. Fellow AAAS; mem. Am. Chem. Soc., Nat. Acad. Scis., Am. Acad. Arts and Scis., Am. Phys. Soc., Am. Philos. Soc. Author: Principles of Polymer Chemistry and of Statistical Mechanics of Chain Molecules. Contbr. to sci. publs. Pioneered research on constitution and properties of substances composed of giant molecules (rubbers, plastics, fibers, films, proteins, etc.). Home: 210 Golden Oak Dr Portola Valley CA 94025 Office: Stanford U Stanford CA 94305

FLOURNOY, NANCY, biostatistician, consultant, researcher, rancher; b. Long Beach, Calif., May 4, 1947; d. Carr Irvine and Elizabeth (Blincoe) F.; m. Leonard Bradley Hearne, Aug. 28, 1978. Ph.D. in Biostats., U. Wash., 1982. Statistician, Regional Med. Programs, Calif., 1969-70; assoc. mem. profl. staff S.W. Regional Lab for Ednl. Research and Devel., Calif., 1971-73; biostatistician div. clin. scis. Fred Hutchinson Cancer Research Ctr., Seattle, 1973—. Mem. Am. Statis. Assn., Inst. Math. Stats., Biometric Soc., Wash. Cattleman's Assn., Fedn. Bus. and Profl. Women. Republican. Contbr. to profl. publs. Home: 13001 271st Ave SE Monroe WA 98272 Office: Fred Hutchinson Cancer Research Center 1124 Columbia St Seattle WA 98104

FLOWERDAY, JOHN CECIL, ednl. adminstr.; b. Coquille, Oreg., July 25, 1944; s. Cecil Sidney and Estella Minnie (Shipp) F.; m. Susan Bower Loggan, Apr. 17, 1970; children—Julie Anne, Sarah Lynn, Timothy John. B.S., Oreg. State U., 1974; M.A., Valley Christian U., 1983, postgrad. in edn., 1983—. Cert. tchr., Oreg.; ordained Minister Assembly of God Ch., 1979. Computer programmer Data Enterprises, Ltd., Portland, Oreg., 1969-70; asst. supr. Planer Mill, Thomas Lumber Co., Klamath Falls, Oreg., 1974-79; prin. Klamath (Oreg.) Christian Acad., 1979—, chief adminstr. Klamath Inst. Ministry and Valley Christian U., Klamath, 1979—. Served with AUS, 1964-68. Mem. Assn. Christian Schs. Internat. Republican. Home: 1330 Tamera Dr Klamath Falls OR 97601 Office: 235 S Laguna St Klamath Falls OR 97601

FLOWERS, GERALD DUANE, school administrator; b. Minot, N.D., Mar. 19, 1932; s. Harvey J. and Marie A. (Owens) F.; B. Gen. Studies, U. Nebr., Omaha, 1968; M.A. in Edn., Monterey Inst. Fgn. Studies, 1973; m. Tokiko Takahashi, June 10, 1965; children—Pamela Terisa, Victoria Marie. Enlisted U.S. Army, 1950, advanced through grades to lt. col., 1968; served as engr., Japan, 1950-52; tank corps comdr., 1952-58; comdg. officer and communications officer, Japan, Okinawa, Republic of China, Thailand, U.S.A., 1959-72; ret., 1972; vice prin. Palma High Sch., Salinas, Calif., 1973—; tchr. U.S. citizenship preparation class Monterey Adult Sch., 1973—; edn. counselor Army Edn. Center, Ft. Ord, 1969-72. Supt. religious edn. Ch. of the Oaks, Del Rey Oaks, Calif., 1981, ch. moderator, 1982-83. Decorated Legion of Merit, Meritorious Service medal, Army Commendation medal (3). Mem. Assn. Supervision and Curriculum Devel, Ret. Officers Assn., Japanese Am. Citizens League, Western Cath. Edn. Assn. (secondary commn. mem.), Am. Legion, D.A.V. Democrat. school administrator; b. Minot, N.D., Mar. 19, 1932; s. Harvey J. and Marie A. (Owens) F.; B. Gen. Studies, U. Nebr., Omaha, 1968; M.A. in Edn., Monterey Inst. Fgn. Studies, 1973; m. Tokiko Takahashi, June 10, 1965; children—Pamela Terisa, Victoria Marie. Enlisted U.S. Army, 1950, advanced through grades to lt. col., 1968; served as engr., Japan, 1950-52; tank corps comdr., 1952-58; comdg. officer and communications officer, Japan, Okinawa, Republic of China, Thailand, U.S.A., 1959-72; ret., 1972; vice prin. Palma High Sch., Salinas, Calif., 1973—; tchr. U.S. citizenship preparation class Monterey Adult Sch., 1973—; edn. counselor Army Edn. Center, Ft. Ord, 1969-72. Supt. religious edn. Ch. of the Oaks, Del Rey Oaks, Calif., 1981, ch. moderator, 1982-83. Decorated Legion of Merit, Meritorious Service medal, Army Commendation medal (3). Mem. Assn. Supervision and Curriculum Devel, Ret. Officers Assn., Japanese Am. Citizens League, Western Cath. Edn. Assn. (secondary commn. mem.), Am. Legion, D.A.V. Democrat. Office: 919 Iverson St Salinas CA 93901

FLOYD, MARY ALICE, counselor, educator; b. Fairhope, Ala., Feb. 27, 1928; d. Walter S. and Nell Palmer; student San Francisco U., 1945-47; B.A., Ala. U., 1949; postgrad. Tulane U., 1951-52, San Jose State U., 1958, U. Calif., Santa Barbara, 1966-72; M.A., U. So. Ala., 1969; m. Gerald L. Floyd, Mar. 22, 1952; 1 son, Jonathan Curran. Guidance cons. and coordinator Careers for Women project Santa Barbara (Calif.) Sch. Dist., 1973-74; counselor terminally ill Life Acceptance unit Pinecrest Hosp., Santa Barbara, 1973-77; counselor-dir. Women's Center, Santa Barbara City Coll., 1977-78; tchr. adult edn., Santa Barbara, 1972—, pvt. practice cons., counseling; cons., coordinator Alienated Youth Program, 1971; mem. faculty U. Calif. at Santa Barbara Extension, 1976. Mem. Am. Personnel and Guidance Assn., Nat. Vocat. Guidance Assn., Calif. Personnel and Guidance Assn., Calif. Coll. Personnel Assn., AAUW, South Coast Bus. Network. Democrat. Unitarian. Office: 310 W Padre St Santa Barbara CA 93101

FLOYD, WILLIAM L., state senator, farmer, real estate developer; m. Shirley Floyd; 5 children. Student Teton Valley and Boise pub. schs.; grad. in Bus. Adminstrn. and Econs., U. Idaho. Active in potato growing and shipping, farming, ranching, homebuilding, real estate; mem. Idaho State Senate. Served with USN. Republican. Office: Idaho State Senate Boise ID 83720*

FLUETSCH, PETER JAY, ins. co. exec.; b. Merced, Calif., Nov. 17, 1934; s. John Jay and Helen Katherine (Shaffer) F.; A.A., Menlo Coll.; m. Mary Catherine Bacciarini, Nov. 10, 1957; children—Kathleen, John, Christine, Jeanette, Douglas. Partner, Fluetsch Ins. Agy., Merced, 1960-67, v.p., 1967-80; pres. Fluetsch & Busey Ins., 1980—. Pres., Merced-Mariposa bd. Am. Cancer Soc. Central Calif. Bd. Rev.; active Yosemite Area council Boy Scouts Am., pres., 1976-78, area v.p. Western region com., 1980-83, recipient Silver Beaver award, 1967; v.p. Merced United Way, 1976-79, pres., 1979—. Served with Calif. N.G. Mem. Merced Mariposa Ind. Ins. Agts. (past pres.), Merced County Life Underwriters Assn. (pres.) Calif., Merced City (past pres.), Merced County chambers commerce. Democrat. Club: Merced Boosters, Merced Trade (past pres.) Kiwanis (past dist. lt. gov., past. pres.) Elks, Masons. Home: 1012 Wyoming Dr Merced CA 95340 Office: 725 W 18th St Merced CA 95340

FLUHARTY, JESSE ERNEST, judge; b. San Antonio, July 25, 1916; s. Jesse Ernest and Gwendolyn (Elder) F.; student Calif. State U., San Diego, 1935-36, Art Ctr. Sch. Design Los Angeles, 1938-39; J.D. with distinction, U. Pacific, 1951; grad. Nat. Judicial Coll. Adminstrv. Law; m. Ernestine Gertrude Corlies, Oct. 25, 1945; 1 son, Stephen. Bar: Calif. 1951. Sole practice law, Sacramento, 1951-60; presiding workers' compensation judge, Stockton, Calif., 1960-67, Los Angeles, 1967-81, Long Beach, Calif., 1982—; instr. para-legal studies Pasadena City Coll. Pres., Family Service Agy., Sacramento, 1958, 59, Community Council Stockton and San Joaquin County, 1965, Service Club Council Los Angeles, 1973-74, Glendale Hills Coordinating Council, 1976-78, Chevy Chase Estates Assn., 1971-77; chmn. San Joaquin County Recreation and Park Commn., 1963-67. Served with U.S. Army, 1943-45. Decorated Bronze Star, Philippine Liberation medal; recipient Meritorious citation Calif. Recreation Soc., 1967. Mem. Calif. State Bar, Los Angeles County Bar Assn., Glendale Bar Assn., Am. Judicature Soc. Republican. Congregationalist. Clubs: Lions (pres. Los Angeles 1971-72), Lawyers (pres. Los Angeles County, Judge of Yr. 1982), Chevy Chase Country, Masons, Shriners. Home: 3330 Emerald Isle Dr Glendale CA 91206 Office: 245 W Broadway Long Beach CA 90802

FLUKE, JOHN MAURICE, electronic test equipment manufacturing company executive; b. Tacoma, Dec. 14, 1911; s. Lee and Lynda Pearl (Epley) F.; B.E.E., U. Wash., Seattle, 1935; M.S. (scholar), MIT, 1936; LL.D. (hon.), Gonzaga U., 1982; m. Lyla Adair Schram, June 5, 1937; children—Virginia Lee Fluke Gabelein, John Maurice, David L. Engr., Gen. Electric Co., 1936-40; founder John Fluke Mfg. Co. Inc., Seattle, 1948, pres., 1948-71, chmn. bd., chief exec. officer, 1971—; chmn. bd., chief exec. officer John Fluke Internat. Co., 1966—; dir. Peoples Nat. Bank Wash., Gen. Telephone Co. N.W.; leader Wash. Trade Mission to Orient, 1965; pres. Wash. Research Council, 1961-73; mem. exec. bd. Seattle King County Safety Council, 1962-63; chmn. bd., hon. life mem. Seattle Area Indsl. Council, 1962-66; mem. exec. com. Assn. Wash. Bus., 1966-78; mem. Pres.'s blue ribbon panel Dept. Def., 1969-70, chmn. electronic test equipment task force, 1974-78; mem. trade mission to Eng. and Scotland, 1964; civilian aide to Sec. Army, 1974; mem. Snohomish County Econ. Devel. Council, 1972-73; chmn. Wash. State Export Council, 1982—. Bd. dirs. Doctors Hosp., Seattle, 1969-73, Seattle Hist. Soc., 1974-79, Seattle Found., 1970—; v.p. bd. dirs. Seattle Symphony, 1969—; chmn. vis. com. U. Wash. Coll. Elec. Engring., 1976—; trustee Pacific Sci. Center, Seattle, 1971-78; bd. dirs. Econ. Devel. Council Puget Sound, 1976—; chmn. personnel dir. selection com. City of Seattle, 1969; chmn. endowment fund Seattle Symphony, 1967, 77-79; mem. corp. vis. com., dept. elec. engring. and computer sci. MIT, 1976, recipient Corp. Leadership award, 1976; pres. chmn. bd. Seattle Jr. Achievement, 1973-78, nat. dir., regional chmn., 1975-78, mem. field adv. commn., 1977-78, chmn. emeritus, 1976-78, recipient Gold Leadership award, 1981; mem. planning and devel. com. Salvation Army, 1976; mem. ann. fund bd. U. Wash., 1975-78; trustee Mus. Flight Found., 1983—. Served with USNR, 1940-46. Decorated Legion of Merit; recipient Charles A. Coffin award Gen. Electric Co., 1940; Howard Vollum Sci. and Tech. award Reed Coll., 1976; Man of Yr. award Mountlake Terr. C. of C.-State Adv. Council, 1966; named Small Bus. Man of Year, 1966; First Citizen of Seattle, 1979; registered profl. engr., Wash. Fellow IEEE (engring. edn. and accreditation com. 1971-72, Regional Pub. Service award 1967, Industrialist of Yr. award 1966); mem. Am. Electronics Assn. (chmn. Wash. council tech. advancement 1983—), Am. Security Council, Instrument Soc. Am. (hon.), Seattle C. of C. (pres. 1965-66, life mem.), Tau Beta Pi (pres. 1934-35). Republican. Lutheran. Clubs: Rainier, Seattle Golf, Rotary (Vocat. Service award) (Seattle). Patentee in field. Home: 1206 NW Culbertson Dr Seattle WA 98177 Office: Box C-9090 Everett WA 98206

FLUKE, LYLA ADAIR, publisher; b. Maddock, N.D.; d. Olaf John and Anne Marie (Rodberg) Schram; B.S. in Zoology and Physiology, U. Wash., Seattle, 1934, teaching diploma, 1935; m. John M. Fluke, June 5, 1937; children—Virginia Fluke Gabelein, John M., David Lynd. High sch. tchr., 1935-37; tutor Seattle schs., 1974-75; pub. Portage quar. jour. of Seattle Hist. Soc., 1980—. Founder, N.W. chpt. Myasthenia Gravis Found., 1953-63; obtained N.W. artifacts for destroyer tender Puget Sound, 1966; mem. Seattle Mayor's Com. for Seattle Beautiful, 1968-69; sponsor Seattle World's Fair, 1962; charter mem. Seattle Youth Symphony Aux., 1974; active Cascade Symphony; mem. U.S. Congl. Adv. Bd. Fellow Seattle Pacific U., 1972—. Mem. Wash. Trust for Historic Preservation, Nat. Trust for Historic Preservation, English Speaking Union, Northwest Ornamental Hort. Soc., Smithsonian Assocs., Nat. Assn. Parliamentarians (charter mem., pres. N.W. unit 1961), Wash. Parliamentarians Assn. (charter), IEEE Aux. (chpt. charter mem., past pres.), Seattle C. of C. (women's div.), Seattle Symphony Women's Assn. (life mem.; sec. 1970), Hist. Soc. Seattle and King County (exec. com. 1975-78), pres. women's mus. league 1975-78, pres. Moritz Thomsen Guild of Hist. Soc., 1978-80. Republican. Lutheran. Clubs: Women's U., Rainier, Seattle Golf. Author articles on history. Address: 1206 NW Culbertson Dr Seattle WA 98177

FLUKEN, DONALD VICTOR, micro-computer co. exec.; b. Denver, Aug. 30, 1941; s. Harry McLeod and Pauline Marie (Wolf) F.; B.A. in Econs., U. Wash., 1964, M.A. in Econs., 1965; m. Linda Ann LaRue, Mar. 27, 1976; children—Christine Ann, Andrew Donald, Alexander Douglas. Research asst. U. Wash., 1962-64, teaching asst., 1964-65; fin. analyst Ford Motor Co., Oakwood, Mich., 1965-67; adminstr. internat. fin. Bell & Howell Co., Lincolnwood, Ill., 1967-70; asst. treas. Levi Strauss & Co., San Francisco, 1970-71; mgr. internat. fin. Varian Assocs., Inc., Palo Alto, Calif., 1971-77; treas. Measurex Corp., Cupertino, Calif., 1977-81; v.p. fin. and adminstrn. Micropro Internat. Corp., San Rafael, Calif., 1981—. Mgmt. adviser Jr. Achievement. Mem. Am. Mgmt. Assn., Fin. Execs. Inst., Nat. Fgn. Trade Assn., Bus. Internat. Republican. Home: Two Sutton Ln Novato CA 94947 Office: 33 San Pablo Rd San Rafael CA 94903

FLY, CLAUDE LEE, soil and water resource development consultant; b. Fulbright, Tex., June 23, 1905; s. Anderson Bureaugard and Emmeline Josephine (Lowery) F.; m. Miriam Rector, Aug. 21, 1927; children—Maurita Fly Kane, John M. B.S. in Soils and Chemistry, Okla. State U., 1927, M.S. in Soils and Chemistry, 1928; Ph.D. in Soil Chemistry and Plant Physiology, Iowa State U., 1931. Head sci. dept., prof. chemistry Panhandle State Coll., Goodwell, Okla., 1931-35; soil scientist, asst. regional adminstr. soil surveys Dept. of Agr. Soil Conservation Service, 1935-52; chief agronomist Morrison-Knudsen, also Internat. Engring. Co., 1952-58; asst. adminstr., project leader Agrl. Research Service, USDA, 1958-63; pres. Claude L. Fly & Assocs., Ft. Collins, Colo., 1963—; cons.; dir. Lower Lower Brule Farm Corp. Nat. adv. bd. Am. Security Council; mem. U.S. Def. Com.; mem. Ams. Against Union Control of Govt., Am. Legis. Exchange Council, Action Adv. Council, Conservative Caucus, Nat. Right to Work Com., Nat. Taxpayers Union, Citizens for Representation, Nat. Congl. Club, Republicans of Colo., Rep. Nat. Com., Rep. Presdl. Task Force, U.S. Senatorial Club, Nat. Fedn. Decency, Salvation Army. Named hon. mayor City of Oklahoma City, 1972; recipient Gold medal of Good Citizenship, SAR, 1972, Disting. Service to Agr. award Gamma Sigma Delta, 1972, Alumni Ambassadors Hall of Fame award Panhandle State Coll., 1974, 4-H Alumni award Nat. and Colo. 4-H, 1976, Disting. Service awards, Am. Soc. Agrl. Cons., 1971, 81. Fellow Soil Conservation Soc. Am. (citation Kans. chpt. 1972), Am. Inst. Chemists; mem. Am. Soc. Agrl. Cons. (pres. 1975), Am. Soc. Agrl. Engrs., Internat. Soc. Soil Sci., Am. Soc. Agronomy (hon. life), Soil Sci. Soc. Am., Sigma Xi, Phi Lambda Upsilon, Gamma Sigma Delta, Alpha Chi Sigma. Methodist. Club: Lions. Author: No Hope But God, 1971; contbr. numerous articles to profl. jours. Home and Office: 415 S Howes St Apt 1107 Fort Collins CO 80521

FLYNN, CHARLES TERRENCE, city adminstrator; b. Los Angeles, July 14, 1936; s. David James and Georganna Mary (Gfroerer) F.; m. Susan Muir Hanna, Mar. 19, 1959; children—Michael Hanna, Allison Muir and Maureen Sheridan (twins). B.A. in Pub. Adminstrn. summa cum laude, San Jose State U., 1961. Asst. to city mgr. City of San Leandro (Calif.), 1961-63; research asst. League Calif. Cities, Berkeley, 1963-66; city mgr. City of LaMesa (Calif.), 1966-72; pub. works dir. City of San Diego, 1972-74, gen. services dir., 1974—; grad. lectr. personnel adminstrn. San Diego State U., 1975. Mem. Calif. Commn. Peace Officer Standards and Tng., 1971-73; chmn. mgmt. com. Comprehensive Planning Orgn. San Diego County, 1971-72, San Diego County Criminal Justice Planning Council, 1970-71. Served with USNR, 1955-57. HUD grantee, 1978. Mem. Internat. City Mgmt. Assn., Am. Pub. Works Assn. Democrat.

FLYNN, CYNTHIA BULLOCK, sociologist; b. Seattle, Dec. 21, 1945; Kenneth W. and Helen M. (Woodley) Bullock; m. James H. Flynn, Apr. 12, 1968; stepchildren—Cecelia Jean, Patrick, Theresa, Margaret. B.A. in Sociology, U. Wash., 1968; M.A. in Sociology, U. N.C., 1970, Ph.D., 1974. Instr. to asst. prof. sociology SUNY-Geneseo, 1972-75; asst. to assoc. prof. sociology U. Kans., Lawrence, 1975-79; research assoc. Inst. Social & Environ. Studies, Lawrence, 1976-79; pres. Social Impact Research, Inc., Seattle, 1979—. Reed Coll. scholar, 1963-65, Alumni scholar, 1966-67; Woodrow Wilson fellow, 1968; Ednl. Opportunity grantee U. Wash., 1967-68. Mem. Am. Sociol. Assn., Population Assn. Am., Internat. Assn. Impact Assessment, Pacific Sociol. Assn., Network Exec. Women (pres.), Jr. League. Author: The Social and Economic Effects of the Proposed Ski Development at Early Winters, 1981; The Effects of Proposed Chicago Bridge & Iron Facility at Cherry Point on Socioeconomic Characteristics, 1980; The Social and Economic Effects of Accident at Three Mile Island, 1980. Home: 1329 NE 63d St Seattle WA 98115 Office: 4020 E Madison St Suite 300 Seattle WA 98112

FLYNN, J(OHN) JAY, law enforcement ofcl.; b. San Francisco, Jan. 24, 1930; s. John Joseph and Bernice (Tosney) F.; A.A., City Coll. San Francisco, 1959; student San Francisco State Coll., 1959-63; grad. FBI Nat. Acad., 1975; m. Sarah Nell Huff, Nov. 15, 1952; 1 son, John Logan. State traffic sgt. Calif. Hwy. Patrol, Redwood City, 1956-68, lt., 1968-73, comdr., Lakeport, 1973—. Tchr., Coll. San Mateo, Canada Coll. Chmn. Personnel Bd. City of Daly City, Calif., 1972, 73; chmn. Lake County Traffic Advisory Bd. Served with USMC, 1948-52. Mem. Calif. Assn. Hwy. Patrolmen (pres. 1963-64, dir. 1960-72), Calif. State Employees Assn., Californians for Modern Hwys. (dir. 1964—), Redwood Empire Assn. (exec. bd., chmn. Lake County), Lake County Peace Officers Assn. (sec.-treas.), Navy League, FBI Nat. Acad. Assos. Republican. Roman Catholic. Clubs: Commonwealth of California (San Francisco); North County Civic (San Mateo County); Mountain Lions (pres. 1981-82). Home: Trinity Rd Box 305 Cobb CA 95426 Office: 525 Main St Lakeport CA 95453

FLYNN, KATHLEEN FRANKLYN, educator; b. Cleve., Jan. 28, 1941; d. Frank and Emma (Skolaris) Pretnar; m. John Michael Flynn Jr., Aug. 8, 1964; children—Monica Allene, John Michael. B.S., Ohio State U., 1963; student Calif. State U.-Northridge, 1972-78; M.S., U. Oreg., 1982. Cert. reading specialist, cert. English and journalism tchr., Calif., Oreg. English and journalism tchr. Cleve. Pub. Schs., 1963-65; substitute tchr. Los Angeles Pub. Schs., 1972-77; reading specialist Chaminade Prep. Sch., Chatsworth, Calif., 1977-78, Coquille (Oreg.) Sch. Dist., 1979—; cons., adv. special edn., gifted programs. Pres. Friends of Library, Coquille, 1981—, Coquille Jr. Women's Club, 1980-81; sec. Coquille Edn. Assn., 1981—; mem. Long-Range Planning Com. Coquille Schs., 1983, Spl. Edn. Com., 1979—. Mem. Internat. Reading Assn., Assn. for Curriculum and Supervision Devel., Delta Kappa Gamma. Republican. Contbg. author: Reflections, 1980; presenter on dyslexia Coos County Edn. Service Dist., 1983. Home: 1505 N Johnson Coquille OR 97423 Office: Coquille School Dist 1366 N Gould Coquille OR 97423

FLYNN, PATRICIA CHRISTINE, writer, management consultant; b. Providence. Mar. 27, 1953; d. William and Eileen (Nolan) F.; B.S. in Mgmt., Pepperdine U., 1979; 1 dau., April Eileen. Mgr. with Atlantic Richfield Co., Los Angeles, 1974-81, Hydril Co., Los Angeles, 1982; mgmt. cons., Long Beach, Calif., 1982—. Mem. Mayor's Com. to Employ Handicapped, Los Angeles; mem. vol. teaching staff Terminal Island Fed. Correction Inst. Mem. Am. Mgmt. Assn. Office: 345 Wisconsin Ave Long Beach CA 90814

FLYNT, LARRY CLAXTON, publisher; b. Magoffin County, Ky., Nov. 1, 1942; s. Larry Claxton and Edith (Arnett) F.; student public schs., Saylersville, Ky.; m. Althea Leasure, Aug. 21, 1976; children—Tonya, Lisa, Teresa, Larry Claxton, III. Factory worker Gen. Motors, Dayton, Ohio, 1958, 64-65; owner, operator Hustler Club, Dayton, Columbus, Toledo, Akron and Cleve., 1970-74; owner, pub. Hustler, Chic mags., Los Angeles, 1974—; owner, operator Flynt Distbg. Co., Los Angeles, 1976—. Served with U.S. Army, 1958, USN, 1959-64. Mem. Am. Atheists. Anarchist. Office: 2029 Century Park E Suite 3800 Los Angeles CA 90067

FOCH, NINA, actress, educator; b. Leyden, Netherlands, Apr. 20, 1924; d. Dirk and Consuelo (Flowerton) F.; came to U.S., 1928, naturalized, 1933; grad. Lincoln Sch., N.Y.C., 1939; m. James Lipton, June 6, 1954; m. 2d, Dennis R. Brite, Nov. 27, 1959; 1 son, Schuyler Dirk; m. 3d, Michael Dewell, Oct. 31, 1967. Appeared in motion pictures: Nine Girls, 1944, Return of the Vampire, 1944, Shadows in the Night, 1944, Cry of the Werewolf, 1944, Escape in the Fog, 1945, A Song to Remember, 1945, My Name is Julia Ross, 1945, I Love A Mystery, 1945, Johnny O'Clock, 1947, The Guilt of Janet Ames, 1947, The Dark Past, 1948, The Undercover Man, 1949, Johnny Allegro, 1949, An American in Paris, 1951, Scaramouche, 1952, Young Man with Ideas, 1952, Sombrero, 1953, Fast Company, 1953, Executive Suite, 1954 (Acad. award nominee for supporting performance 1954), Four Guns to the Border, 1954, You're Never Too Young, 1955, Illegal, 1955, The Ten Commandments, 1956, Three Brave Men, 1957, Cash McCall, 1959, Spartacus, 1960, Such Good Friends, 1971, Salty, 1973, Mahogany, 1976, Jennifer, 1978; Broadway plays include: John Loves Mary, 1947, Twelfth Night, 1949, A Phoenix Too Frequent, 1950, King Lear, 1950, Second String, 1960; appeared with Am. Shakespeare Festival in Taming of the Shrew and Measure for Measure, 1956; appeared with San Francisco Ballet and Opera in The Seven Deadly Sins, 1966, also many regional theatre productions, including Seattle Repertory Theatre in All Over, 1972, The Seagull, 1973; actress TV, 1947—, including Playhouse 90, Studio One, Pulitzer Playhouse, Playwrights 56, Producers Show Case, Naked City, Kraft Suspense Theatre, Route 66, Arrest and Trial, Burke's Law, The Trailmaster, Dr. Kildare, The Outer Limits, The Steve Allen Show, Gunsmoke, McCloud, Mod Squad, I Spy, Columbo, Barnaby Jones, Lou Grant (Emmy nominee best supporting actress 1980), Hawaii Five-O, The Name of the Game, The Wonderful World of Disney, also many other series, network spls. and films for TV; TV panelist and guest on numerous shows, including The Tonight Show, Dick Cavett Show, Merv Griffin Show, Mike Douglas Show, Dinah Shore Show; TV moderator Let's Take Sides, 1957-59; asso. dir. film The Diary of Anne Frank, 1959; dir. nat. tour and Broadway prodn. Tonight at 8:30, 1966-67; asso. producer re-opening Ford's Theatre, Washington, 1968; adj. prof. U. So. Calif., 1966-68; artist-in-residence U. N.C., 1966, Ohio State U., 1967, Calif. Tech. Inst., 1969-70; mem. sr. faculty Am. Film Inst., 1973-77; founder, tchr. Nina Foch Studio, Hollywood, Calif., 1973—; adj. prof. U. So. Calif., 1978-80; a founder, actress Los Angeles Theatre Group, 1960-65; bd. dirs. Nat. Repertory Theatre, 1967-75. Hon. chmn. Los Angeles chpt. Am. Cancer Soc., 1970. Mem. Acad. Motion Picture Arts and Scis. (exec. com. for fgn. film award 1973—, mem. student award com. 1978—), Hollywood Acad. TV Arts and Scis. (gov. 1976-77). Address: PO Box 1884 Beverly Hills CA 90213

FODEN, SUSAN HALL, computer specialist; b. Summit, N.J., Dec. 15, 1952; d. Edward Bennington and Barbara Louise (Jones) Hall; m. Athol Martin Foden, Oct. 2, 1982. Systems rep. II, Sperry Univac, San Francisco, support analyst, 1981; programmer analyst Tri-Valley Growers, 1981-82, tech. support specialist, 1982—; v.p. Specific Solutions, Novato, Calif., 1983—. Mem. Assn. for Computing Machinery. Democrat. Unitarian Universalist. Home: 1898 Anthony Ct Mountain View CA 94040 Office: 100 California St San Francisco CA 94111

FOGARETTE, LOUIS P., manufacturing company executive; b. Chgo., Jan. 29, 1925; s. Louis Phillip and Jennie (Prete) F.; B.A., Wabash Coll., 1948; postgrad Stanford U., 1951-54. Chemist, W.P. Fuller Co., San Francisco, 1948-49; asst. chief chemist Nat. Industries, Los Angeles, 1950-60; tech. writer N.Am. Aviation Corp., Downey, Calif., 1961-64, sr. project staff engr. parent co. N.Am. Rockwell, 1965-69; supr. subcontractor configuration mgmt. Litton Ship Systems, Los Angeles, 1969-72; v.p. Stic-Adhesive Products Co., Los Angeles, 1972—; head configuration mgmt. program office Hughes Aircraft Co., Los Angeles, 1974-82, dept. configuration mgr., 1982—; tech. cons. Tannenbaum & Assocs., Ft. Lauderdale, Fla., 1975-82. Served to lt. USNR, 1943-46. Home: 8254 Telegraph Rd Downey CA 90240 Office: Hughes Aircraft Co Long Beach CA

FOLBERG, HAROLD JAY, lawyer; b. East St. Louis, Ill., July 7, 1941; s. Louis and Matilda (Ross) F.; B.A., San Francisco State U., 1963; J.D., U. Calif., Berkeley, 1968; children—Lisa, Rachel, Ross. Admitted to Oreg. bar, 1968; asso. law firm Rives & Schwab, Portland, Oreg., 1968-69; dir. Legal Aid Service, Portland, 1970-72; exec. dir. Assn. Family and Conciliation Cts., Portland, 1974-80; prof. law Lewis and Clark Law Sch., 1972—; clin. asst. prof. child psychiatry U. Oreg. Med. Sch., 1976—; judge pro-tem Oreg. Trial Cts., 1974—. Mem. Oreg. State Bar Assn. (chmn. family and juvenile law sect. 1979-80), Am. Bd. Trial Advocates, Legal Aid Service Multnomah Bar Assn. (chmn. 1973-76), Internat. Soc. Family Law, ABA (chmn. mediation and arbitration com. family law sect. 1980—), Assn. Family and Conciliation Cts. (pres.-elect 1983-84). Contbr. articles to profl. jours. Office: 10015 SW Terwilliger St Portland OR 97219

FOLEN, RAYMOND ALEXANDER, psychologist; b. Phila., Nov. 9, 1950; s. Victor Alexander and Barbara Louise (Rossi) F.; B.A., LaSalle Coll., 1972; M.Ed., U. Hawaii, 1974, Ph.D., 1978; m. Allene Eim Fong Chun, Aug. 11, 1979. Counselor, Honolulu Community Coll., 1978-79; pvt. practice psychology, Honolulu and Aiea, Hawaii, 1978—; v.p. Hawaii Behavioral Sci. Services, Honolulu, 1980-82; clin. psychologist State of Hawaii Mental Health Div., 1980—; pres. Psychol. Resources Hawaii, Aiea, 1982—; asst. clin. prof. dept. psychology U. Hawaii, 1982—. Chmn. psychologist's sect. Aloha United Way, 1978-79. East-West Center grantee, 1975-78. Diplomate Am. Acad. Behavioral Medicine. Mem. Nat. Register Health Service Providers in Psy-chology, Am. Assn. Marriage and Family Therapists, Am. Psychol. Assn., Am. Personnel and Guidance Assn., Hawaii Psychol. Assn. (sec. 1981, pres. 1983), Hawaii Personnel and Guidance Assn., Assn. Psychol. Type (regional v.p.), Hawaii Council Family Relations (corr. sec. 1979). Home: 98-1699B Kaahumanu St Aiea HI 96701 Office: 98-211 Pali Momi St Suite 820 Aiea HI 96801

FOLEY, CRAY LYMAN, mechanical engineer; b. Tulsa, Apr. 15, 1927; s. Lyndon Lyman and Margaret Clark (Cray) F.; student U. Tulsa, 1945-46, 47-48; B.S., Okla. State U., 1951, M.S., 1957; m. Paula Ann Vincent, Nov. 30, 1957; children—Kelly Ann, Jill, Cray, Seth. Jr. research engr. Lockheed Aircraft Corp., Burbank, Calif., 1951-52; engr. Sperry Gyroscope Co., Great Neck, N.Y., 1953-57; advanced systems staff engr. Lockheed Missile & Space Co., Sunnyvale, Calif., 1957-82, sr. staff engr., 1982—. Pres. Homeowners Assn., 1964-66; Cub Scout com. chmn. Santa Clara County council Boy Scouts Am., 1971-72. Mem. Nat., Okla. socs. profl. engrs., Soc. Automotive Engrs., Am. Def. Preparedness Assn., Lockheed Mgmt. Assn., Okla. State U. Alumni Assn., Lambda Chi Alpha. Republican. Home: 7090 Galli Dr San Jose CA 95129 Office: PO Box 504 Sunnyvale CA 94088

FOLEY, DANIEL EDMUND, real estate devel. exec.; b. St. Paul, Mar. 1, 1926; s. Edward and Gerry (Fitzgarld) F.; student U. Minn., 1941-43; m. Paula Evans, Apr. 1, 1946; children—Daniel, Margaret, Paula, David, Deane. Chmn. bd. Realty Partners Ltd., Los Angeles. Served with AUS, 1943-46. Home: 1255 S Oak Knoll Pasadena CA 91005 Office: 523 W 6th St Los Angeles CA 90014

FOLEY, JUDITH ANN, educational administrator; b. Steubenville, Ohio, Sept. 1, 1936; d. Joseph and Katherine Ann (Pavich) Moses; m. John Paul Foley, Dec. 27, 1958; children—Katherine, John, Sean, Judith. B.S. in Edn., Ohio U., 1958; M.A. in Adminstrn., Pacific Coll., 1980; postgrad. Brigham Young U., 1982. Cert. tchr., adminstr., Calif. Jr. high sch. tchr. phys. edn., math., coach Madera (Calif.) Unified Sch. Dist., 1958-60, sr. high sch. tchr., coach, 1960-62, elem. tchr., 1963-64, 72-80, reading specialist, 1971-72, acting elem. prin., 1980; chmn. phys. edn. dept., coach Dos Palos Joint Union High Sch., 1963-64; prin. Chowchilla (Calif.) Elem. Sch., 1980—; master tchr. Calif. State U.-Fresno, 1980-81; instr. Merced City Coll., 1980-81; lectr. curriculum resource, phys. fitness. PTA scholar, 1978. Mem. Assn. Calif. Sch. Adminstrs. (project leadership scholarship 1981), AAUW, Assn. for Supervision and Curriculum Devel. Mem. Serbian Eastern Orthodox Ch. Clubs: Serbian Mother's (Fresno). Home: 228 Granada Dr Madera CA 93637

FOLEY, MARY REGINA RYAN, management consultant; b. Madison, Wis., Sept. 26, 1941; d. Louis August and Marian Jane (O'Connell) Maier; A.B., Marquette U., 1963; M.S.W. (U.S. Children's Bur. scholar), St. Louis U., 1965; m. Henry A. Foley, Aug. 21, 1982; children from previous marriage—Christopher John Matek, Monica Marie Matek, Maria Regina Matek. Med. social worker Milwaukee County Gen. Hosp., 1965-67; cons. dept. sociology Marquette U., 1969-71; research asst. Mental Health Planning Com. Milwaukee County, 1971-73; field rep. Nat. Found. March of Dimes, 1976-77; dir. community services Orange County Health Planning Council, Tustin, Calif., 1977-82; mgmt. cons. Foley & Ryan Assocs., 1982—; cons. Western Center Health Planning, San Francisco, 1978—. Chmn., Tustin Traffic Commn., 1976-77; del. Wis. Democratic Conf., 1971; mem. citizens adv. com. Sta. KOCE-TV; mem. adv. com. Calif. Health Tng. Center, Family Service Assn. Orange County, United Cerebral Palsy Assn.; mem. coms. United Way, Orange County unit Am. Cancer Soc., 1978—, Vol. Action Center, 1981— host, interviewer KOCM Community Forum Program, 1979—. Mem. Am. Public Health Assn. (governing council 1981—), Am. Health Planning Assn., Roman Catholic. Club: Jr. League of Phoenix. Home: 4605 E Palo Verde Dr Phoenix AZ 85018 Office: 202 Fashion Ln Suite 219 Tustin CA 92680

FOLEY, ROBERT JORDAN, marketing consultant; b. West Hartford, Conn., Oct. 8, 1922; s. Maurice Hugh and Mary (Hannon) F.; B.S., Georgetown Sch. Fgn. Service, 1946; LL.B. (hon.), U. Del., 1957; m. Lois Nichol; children—Elizabeth, Robert Jordan; 1 stepson, Ford Englehart. Sales, sales promotion, mktg., mgmt. positions Bristol Myers Corp., N.Y.C., 1966-67, Am. Home Products Co., N.Y.C., 1969-70; exec. v.p. Grocery Mfrs. Am., N.Y.C., 1967-69; pres. Robert J. Foley & Assocs. Inc., Atherton, Calif., 1969—. Served to 1st lt. USAF, 1943-45. Recipient several food industry awards. Mem. Food Merchandising Ednl. Council (founder 1968—). Republican. Clubs: San Francisco Merchandising Execs. (pres. 1972-73), Olympic, Sharon Heights Golf, Shinnelock Hills Golf, Siwanoy Golf, Indian Creek Golf. Home: 35 Stockbridge Ave Atherton CA 94025 Office: Robert J Foley & Assos Inc 1135 Industrial Way Reno NV

FOLEY, THOMAS STEPHEN, congressman; b. Spokane, Wash., Mar. 6, 1929; s. Ralph E. and Helen Marie (Higgins) F.; student Gonzaga U., 1947-50; B.A., U. Wash., 1951, LL.B., 1957. Admitted to Wash. bar; dep. pros. atty. Spokane County, Spokane, 1958-60; asst. atty. gen. State of Wash., Olympia, 1960-61; spl. counsel interior and insular affairs com. U.S. Senate, Washington, 1961-64; mem. 89th to 98th congresses from 5th Dist. Wash., majority whip, vice chmn. Com. Agr. Mem. Phi Delta Phi. Home: 2219 California St NW Washington DC 20008 Office: House Office Bldg Washington DC 20515

FOLKMAN, SUSAN KLEPPNER, research psychologist, educator; b. N.Y.C., Mar. 19, 1938; d. Otto and Beatrice (Taub) Kleppner; m. David H. Folkman, June 22, 1958; children—Louis, Sarah, Karen, Jeffrey. B.A., Brandeis U., 1959; M.Ed., U. Mo., 1974; Ph.D., U. Calif.-Berkeley, 1979. Asst. research psychologist dept. psychology U. Calif.-Berkeley, 1979—; dir. Berkeley Stress and Coping Project. Mem. Am. Psychol. Assn. Contbr. numerous articles to profl. jours. Office: Dept Psychology U Calif-Berkeley CA 94720

FOLLETT, RONALD FRANCIS, soil scientist; b. Laramie, Wyo., June 26, 1939; s. Roy L. and Frances E. (Hunter) F.; m. Dorothy M. Spangle, Jan. 1, 1967; children—William, Jennifer, Michael. B.S., Colo. State U., 1961, M.S., 1963; Ph.D., Purdue U., 1966; postgrad. Cornell U., 1975-76. Research scientist Agrl. Research Services, U.S. Dept. Agr., Mandan, N.D., 1968-75, Ithaca, N.Y., 1975-76, nat. research program leader for soil fertility and plant nutrition, Beltsville, Md., 1976-82, nat. program leader for soil productivity and environ. quality research, Ft. Collins, Colo., 1982—. Served to capt., arty. U.S. Army, 1961-76; to maj. Res., 1975—. Mem. Am. Soc. Agronomy, Soil Sci. Soc. Am., Soil Conservation Soc. Am., Alpha Zeta, Sigma Xi, Tri Beta, Scabbard & Blade. Presbyterian. Contbr. numerous articles to profl. jours. Office: Exec Plaza Bldg #130 2625 Redwing Rd Fort Collins CO 80526

FOLLETT, ROY HUNTER, soil science educator; b. Cowdrey, Colo., Feb. 27, 1935; s. Roy L. and Frances E. (Hunter) F.; m. Barbara Ann Delehoy, June 28, 1959; children—Kevin, Karen. B.S., Colo. State U., 1957, M.S., 1963, Ph.D., 1969. Cert. profl. agronomist. Soil scientist Soil Conservation Service, Ft. Collins, Colo., 1963-64; jr. agronomist Colo. State U., Ft. Collins, 1964-70, prof., 1981—; asst. prof. Ohio State U., Columbus, 1970-74; assoc. prof. Kans. State U., Manhattan, 1974-81. Served as lt. U.S. Army, 1957-58. Fellow Soil Conservation Soc. Am.; mem. Am. Soc. Agronomy, Alpha Zeta, Epsilon Sigma Phi, Sigma Xi. Author: Fertilizers and Soil Amendments, 1981; Our Soils and Their Management, 1983; numerous articles. Home: 1040 Clubview Rd Ft Collins CO 80524 Office: Agronomy Dept Colo State Univ Ft Collins CO 80526

FOLLETTE, ANNE L., aerospace engineer; b. San Francisco, Sept. 27, 1950; d. William T. and Wilma (Carlson) F.; m. Jorge Armando Verdi D'Eguia, July 4, 1970 (div.). A.A., Coll. Marin, 1977; B.A. in Math. with honors, Mills Coll., 1979. Sr. computer operator Bank of Am. Internat. Services, San Francisco, 1972-74; mathematician Pacific Missile Test Ctr., Pt. Mugu, Calif., 1979-80; engr. Grumman Aerospace Corp., Pt. Mugu, 1979—. Vice chmn. Marina West Neighborhood Council, 1982—; mem. NOW. Aurelia Henry Reinhart scholar, 1978-79; recipient Project Sterling award Grumman Aerospace Corp., 1982. Mem. Nat. Assn. Female Execs., Soc. Women Engrs. (chmn. career guidance com. and speaker Ventura County sect.), Assn. Old Crows, Mills Coll. Alumni, Alpha Gamma Sigma (life). Office: Grumman Aerospace Corp PO Box 42232 Pt Mugu CA 93042

FOLLICK, EDWIN DUANE, chiropractor, educational administrator; b. Glendale, Calif., Feb. 4, 1935; s. Edwin Fulfford and Esther Agnes (Catherwood) F.; B.A., Calif. State U., Los Angeles, 1956, M.A., 1961; M.A., Pepperdine U., 1957, M.P.A., 1977; Ph.D., D.Theol., St. Andrews, London, 1958; M.S. in L.S., U. So. Calif., 1963, M.Ed., 1964, Adv.M.Ed., 1969; LL.B., Blackstone Law Sch., 1966, J.D., 1967; D.C., Cleveland Chiropractic Coll., Los Angeles, 1972; Ph.D., Academia Theatina, Pescara, 1978. Tchr., library adminstr. Los Angeles City Schs., 1957-68; law librarian Glendale U. Coll. of Law, 1968-69; coll. librarian Cleveland Chiropractic Coll., Los Angeles, 1969-74, dir. edn. and admissions, 1974—, prof. jurisprudence, 1975—, dean student affairs, 1976—; assoc. prof. Grad. Sch. Bus. and Pub. Adminstrn., Newport U., 1982—; extern prof. St. Andrews, London, 1961; dir. W. Valley Chiropractic Health Centre, 1972—. Served as chaplains asst. U.S. Army, 1958-60. Decorated cavaliere Internat. Order Legion of Honor of Immacolata (Italy); knight of Malta, Sovereign Order St. John of Jerusalem, numerous others. Mem. ALA, NEA, Am. Assn. Sch. Librarians, Assn. Coll. and Research Librarians, Am. Assn. Law Librarians, Nat. Geog. Soc., Phi Delta Kappa, Sigma Chi Psi, Delta Tau Alpha. Democrat. Episcopalian. Contbr. articles to profl. jours. Home: 7022 Owensmouth Ave Canoga Park CA 91303 Office: 590 N Vermont Ave Los Angeles CA 90004

FOLSOM, BOBBY LEE, educator; b. Lindsay, Okla., July 10, 1928; s. Robinson B. and Elizabeth (Davis) F.; m. Ruth V. Brown, 1946; children—Bobby Lee, Shirley Christine. Student, Okla. State U., 1948-49, East Central State U., 1954-56; B.S. in Edn., No. Ariz. U., 1957, M.A. in End. and Adminstrn., 1980. Tchr., prin. Flagstaff (Ariz.) pub. schs., 1957-67, Chinle (Ariz.) pub. schs., 1967-68; reading specialist Prairie Grove (Ark.) pub. sch., 1968-69; reading specialist Title III Sequoyah County Diagnostic and Remedial Ctr., Sallisaw, Okla., 1969-71; career specialist Okla. State Dept., Stillwater, 1971-72; prin. Roland (Okla.) pub. schs., 1972-73; prin. Chinle pub. schs., 1973-78, asst. supt., 1978—; cons. Devel. Vocat. Curriculum, Okla. State Dept. Edn. Organized Boy Scout of Am. troops at Navajo Reservation, Leupp, Ariz. and Red Mesa Sch., Teec Nos Pos, Ariz., scoutmaster, 1957-63, 75-78. Served to cpl. U.S. Army, 1946-48, 50-51. Okla. State Dept. Edn. grantee, 1972. Mem. Nat. Assn. Secondary Sch. Adminstrs., Assn. Supervision and Curriculum, Phi Delta Kappa. Democrat. Christian. Club: Masons. Developed learning programs for bilingual Navajo studies; diagnosing and developing learning programs for remedial students.

FOLTZ, MELVYN LEROY, counselor; b. Barstow, Calif., July 21, 1940; s. Raymond Edwin and Ethel Gertrude (Wright) F.; student N.W. Christian Coll., Eugene, Oreg., 1959-60; B.S., U. Oreg., 1964, M.S., 1966; m. Mary Jane Gabriel, June 20, 1964 (dec. Jan. 1971); 1 dau., Melody. Vocat. rehab. counselor Oreg. Div. Vocat. Rehab., Eugene, 1965-66, Calif. Dept. Rehab., Vallejo, 1966-71, Napa, 1971-77, Fairfield, 1977-79; pvt. practice counseling, specializing in hypnosis, Napa, 1980—; pvt. practice group co-counseling, 1976. Mem. Health Manpower Com., 1973-75, Napa County Comprehensive Health Planning Council, 1975, Napa County Manpower Planning Council, 1974-77; founder, pres. Napa New Age Enterprises; alt. mem. Napa County Democratic Central Com., 1976; bd. dirs. Napa County chpt. Am. Cancer Soc., 1978-80. Lic. marriage, family and child counselor, Calif. Mem. San Francisco Acad. Hypnosis, Am. Soc. for Psychical Research, Am. Personnel and Guidance Assn., No. Calif. Soc. Clin. Hypnosis. Democrat. Club: Single Parents (founder, pres. 1973-79). Home: 1698 San Vicente Napa CA 94558 Office: 2025 Redwood Rd Suite 6A Napa CA 94558

FOLTZ, ROBERT EMMERT, sales cons. co. exec.; b. Polo, Ill., Oct. 11, 1910; s. Daniel Stauffer and Clara Mae (Landis) F.; M.B.A., Brown U., 1940; m. Belva Luella Magill, June 16, 1933; children—Janet, Ronald, Carol, Diane. Cost accountant Lawrence Bros. Inc., Sterling, Ill., 1930-45, sales mgr., 1946-50, v.p. sales, 1951-72, sales cons., 1973—. Mem. standing com. Nat. Bur. Standards, U.S. Dept. Commerce; trustee Moody Bible Inst., Chgo., 1966—; elder Christian and Missionary Alliance Ch. Fellow Internat. Biog. Assn.; mem. Builders Hardware Mfrs. Assn., Am. Inst. Mgmt., Internat. Platform Assn. Club: Rotary. Patentee builders hardware (20). Home: PO Box 2126 Sedona AZ 86336

FONG, ANNABELLE CHING, univ. ofcl.; b. Honolulu, June 9, 1926; d. Foo Lin and Annie (Ling) Ching; B.A., Bowling Green State U., 1947; M.A., Columbia U. Tchrs.'s Coll., 1950; postgrad. U. Hawaii, Honolulu, 1966-69 children—Robert, Brenda, Roanne, Bruce. Extension agt., U. Hawaii, 1947-48; home economist, 1950-53; dir. Ednl. Guidance and Opportunities program U.S. Office Edn., Hawaii, 1966-70; trio project dir. U. Hawaii Consortium, 1970-74, dir. fin. aids, 1974—, acting dean of students, 1980-81, instr. dept. ednl. psychology 1968-69, mem. statewide articulation com., 1972-74. Mem. tech. adv. com. Concentrated Employment Program, 1968; mem. exec. com. Western Regional Coll. Bd., 1970-74, chmn., 1973; trustee Coll. Bd., 1976-80; mem. Com. for Handicapped, 1971-73; mem. Task Force Equal Ednl. Opportunity, 1972; spl. asst. to dep. commr. Bur. Higher Edn., Washington, 1979-80. chmn. Minority Aid Panel Coll. Scholarship Service, 1970-73. Bd. govs. U. br. YMCA, 1968-72. Mem. Am. (Francis E. Clark award 1973-74), Hawaii (pres.) personnel and guidance assns., Asso. Chinese U. Women (pres. 1969), Western Assn. Student Fin. Aid Aminstrs. (sec. exec. com. 1976-77, 1981-82). Home: 6370 Hawaii Kai Dr 55 Honolulu HI 96825 Office: U Hawaii Honolulu HI 96822

FONG, JOHN RICHARD, chemist; b. Pitts., May 25, 1950; s. Ban Sue and Yung Kwai (Wong) F.; B.S. in Chemistry, U. Calif., Berkeley, 1972. Sr. chemist, personal care products devel. Shaklee Corp., Hayward, Calif., 1973-78; mgr. research and product devel. Neutrogena Dermatologics, Los Angeles, 1978—. Mem. Soc. Cosmetic Chemists, Am. Soc. Quality Control, Am. Mgmt. Assn. Office: 5755 W 96th St Los Angeles CA 90045

FONG, RANDALL HUNG WAH, college admissions counselor; b. Honolulu, Dec. 30, 1955; s. Richard Kam Hoy and Arlene Kam Chin F. B.A. in Psychology, U. Hawaii, 1978; M.Ed. in Counseling, U. San Diego, 1980. Ednl. asst. Hawaii Sch. for Blind and Deaf, Honolulu, 1980; resident counselor, Hawaii Assn. Retarded Citizens, Honolulu; admissions counselor, Hawaii Loa Coll., Kaneohe, 1980—. Active Leeward Oahu Jaycees (recipient several awards) 1982—. Mem. Hawaii Personnel and Guidance Assn., Am. Personnel and Guidance Assn., Pacific Assn. Collegiate Registrars and Admissions Counselors. Democrat. Episcopalian. Office: Admissions Dept Hawaii Loa College 45 045 Kamehameha Hwy Kaneohe HI 96744

FONG, WILLIAM LIM, pharmacist; b. China, Feb. 2, 1948; s. Richard Gew and Lai Heung (Yee) F.; B.A., U. Calif.-Berkeley, 1970; Pharm.D., U. Calif. at San Francisco, 1975; m. Gail Ann Chong, Aug. 15, 1971; children—Gregory, Joanna. Lab. research asso. VA Hosp., San Francisco, 1970-72; postdoctoral resident in clin. pharmacy U. Calif. at San Francisco Med. Center, 1975-76; pharmacist Children's Hosp. at Stanford, Palo Alto, Calif., 1976-78, satellite pharmacist, Stanford U. Med. Center, 1978—. Women's Aux. Calif. Pharm. Assn. scholar, 1974-75. Mem. Am. Soc. Hosp. Pharmacists, Am., Calif. pharm. assns., Rho Pi Phi. Democrat. Club: Foster City Tennis. Contbr. articles to profl. jours. Office: Stanford U Med Center Stanford CA 94305

FONSHILL, IRA WILLIAM, III, real estate and securities broker; b. Balt., May 16, 1930; s. Ira William and Irma Marie (Gardner) F.; B.S., N.Y. U., 1955; M.B.A., U. Wash., 1957; grad. Realtors Inst.; m. Pamela W. Leavitt, June 1, 1955; children—Ira William, Susan B., Peter B., Pamela H. Indsl. engr. aerospace div. Boeing Co., Seattle, 1956-59; long range planner Monsanto Co., N.Y.C., 1960-65; fin. long range planner Boise Cascade Corp. (Idaho), 1965-70; officer Devco, Inc., Boise, 1971—; pres.-broker Intermountain Realty Assocs., Boise, 1974—; propr. Fonshill & Co., Boise, 1977—; gen. partner Boise Geothermal, Ltd.; v.p., sec.-treas. DLB, Inc. Active bus. div. United Way, Boise, 1977-78. Served with USAF, 1950-54. Cert. residential specialist, comml. investment mem., specialist in real estate securities. Mem. Nat., Ida., Boise bds. Realtors, Realtors Nat. Mktg. Inst., Real Estate Securities and Syndication Inst. (pres. Idaho chpt. 1980-82), Nat. Assn. Securities Dealers, Am. Mktg. Assn., N.W. Investment Soc. (vice chmn. 1978-79), Fedn. Internationale des Professions Immobilieres. Republican. Lutheran. Home: 200 Coston St Boise ID 83702 Office: 331 W Idaho St PO Box 1228 Boise ID 83701

FONSWORTH, BENNETT YOUNG, school district superintendant; b. Houston, Nov. 19, 1929; s. Bennett Young Fonsworth; B.A., San Francisco State U., 1966, M.A., 1968; postgrad U. San Francisco; children—Leslie, Michael, Stephen, Sandra, Philip. Med. technologist Kaiser Hosp., 1956-60; tchr. dept. sci. Franklin Jr. High Sch., San Francisco, 1960-66, dept. chmn., 1966-67; tchr. dept. sci. Everett Jr. High Sch., San Francisco, 1966-67; attendance supr. San Francisco Unified Sch. Dist., 1967-68, supr. personnel services, 1968-69, asst. prin. guidance and counseling, 1969-70, asst. prin. curriculum, 1970-71, prin., 1971-73, supr. secondary div., 1973-75, asst. supt., 1975-78, area supt., 1978—; pres. BD Cons. Firm. Served with USN, 1954. Mem. Urban Sch. Adminstrs., Phi Delta Kappa. Club: Golden Gaters Golf. Office: 4545 Anza St San Francisco CA 94121

FONTAINE, VALERIE ANNE, executive recruiter, lawyer; b. Honolulu, May 17, 1955; d. Warren Tremlett Chaffey and Dorine Marks Foster; m. Michael Fontaine, Apr. 17, 1980; 1 dau., Genevieve Brianne. A.B. in Polit. Sci. magna cum laude, UCLA, 1976; J.D., U. Calif.-San Francisco, 1979. Bar: Calif. 1979, U.S. Dist. Ct. (cen. dist.) Calif. 1979, Law clk. to justice Calif. Ct. Appeals, 1979; litigation asst. O'Melveny & Myers, Los Angeles, 1979-81; exec. recruiter-legal Lee, Jackson & Bowe, Beverly Hills, Calif., 1981—; also founder, cons. Presence: Exec. Image & Career Consultation, Beverly Hills, 1980—; speaker. Sustaining mem. Chancellor's Circle of UCLA; active Jewish Marriage Encounter; program sponsor Sta. KCET; mem. Hastings Alumni Assn. Mem. State Bar Calif., Phi Beta Kappa, Phi Alpha Delta, Pi Sigma Alpha. Democrat. Office: 270 N Canon Dr Suite 103 Beverly Hills CA 90210

FONTES, BONNIE FAHERTY, health care adminstr.; b. Amarillo, Tex., Sept. 6, 1943; d. Frank Fredrick and Helen Gladys (King) Faherty; children—Nancy T. Montoya, Lisa Y. Montoya, Patrick M. Student Regina Sch. Nursing, Albuquerque, 1960; A.A., Los Angeles S.W. Coll., 1970; B.S. in Nursing, Calif. State U.-Long Beach, 1974; M.P.H., UCLA, 1976, M.Nursing, 1975. R.N., Calif. Cons., tchr., lobbyist, expert witness in health care, Los Angeles, 1964—. Profl. nursing rep. Los Angeles Health Systems Agy., 1980-82. Mem. Calif. Democratic Com., 1970—. Mem. Am. Nurses Assn., Calif. Nurses Assn (v.p. 1977-79), Am. Pub. Health Assn., Sigma Theta Tau. Democrat. Roman Catholic. Address: 750 S Spaulding Ave #313 Los Angeles CA 90036

FOOTE, CHRISTOPHER, chemist, educator; b. Hartford, Conn., June 5, 1935; s. William J. and Dorothy (Bennett) F.; B.S. magna cum laude, Yale U., 1957; A.M., Harvard U., 1959, Ph.D. (NSF fellow), 1961; children—Jonathan, Thomas. Instr., UCLA, 1961-62, asst. prof., 1962-66, asso. prof., 1966-69, prof., 1969—, chmn. dept. chemistry, 1975-81; cons. Proctor & Gamble Co., 1969—; Pfister lectr. MIT, 1972. Guggenheim fellow, 1967-68. Mem. Am. Chem. Soc. (Leo Hendrick Baekeland medal N.J. sect. 1975; councillor 1981—), Am. Soc. Photobiology, (councillor 1979-81), AAAS, Chem. Soc. London, European Photochemistry Assn., Gesellschaft Deutscher Chemiker, Sigma Xi, Phi Beta Kappa, Phi Lambda Upsilon. Contbr. numerous articles on organic chemistry to sci. jours.; editorial bd. Photobiology Jour., 1970-73, Jour. Am. Chem. Soc., 1977-80, Chem. Revs., 1979-82. Home: 766 Malcolm Ave Los Angeles CA 90024 Office: Dept Chemistry UCLA Los Angeles CA 90024

FOOTE, SHERRY LEE, administrative assistant; b. San Bernardino, Calif., July 12, 1947; d. Chuck Howard and Norma Joyce (Rodgers) Pennington; children—Natalie Lynn, Mandy Leigh. Grad. Palmdale (Calif.) High School, 1965, Lumbleau Real Estate Sch., Calif. Designers Guild, C. of C. Inst. Mem. traffic div. Newhall (Calif.) Mcpl. Ct., 1965-69; clerical supr. Los Angeles County Dept. Pub. Social Services, 1969-72; mgr. Palmdale C. of C., 1978-80; now asst. to Los Angeles County supr.; cons. interior design. Mem. Alpha Charter Guild of Antelope Valley Hosp., Antelope Valley Bd. of Trade, Antelope Valley Domestic Violence Ctr., Palmdale C. of C., Lancaster (Calif.) C. of C. Home: 38736 Yucca Tree Palmdale CA 93550 Office: 1040 W Ave J Suite 217 Lancaster CA 93534

FOOTMAN, GORDON ELLIOTT, ednl. adminstr.; b. Los Angeles, Oct. 10, 1927; s. Arthur Leland and Meta Fay (Neal) F.; B.A., Occidental Coll., 1951, M.S., 1954; Ed.D., U. So. Calif., 1972; m. Virginia Rose, Aug. 7, 1954; children—Virginia, Patricia, John. Tchr., Arcadia, Calif., 1952, Glendale, Calif., 1956; psychologist Burbank (Calif.) Schs., 1956-64, supr., 1964-70, dir. pupil personnel services, 1970-72; dir. div. ednl. measurement, evaluation and research Office Los Angeles County Supt. Schs., Downey, Calif., 1972—. Lectr. ednl. psychology U. So. Calif., 1972-75, asst. prof. ednl. psychology, 1976—. Pres. Council for Exceptional Children, 1969-70; pres. Burbank Coordinating Council, 1969-70; mem. Burbank Family Service Bd., 1971-72. Served with AUS, 1945-47. Mem. Am. Edn. Research Assn., Am. Personnel and Guidance Assn. (senator 1983—), Calif. Personnel and Guidance Assn. (pres.), Calif. Assn. Sch. Psychologists and Psychometrists, Nat., Calif. (monograph editor 1977—) assns. pupil personnel adminstrs., Calif. Assn. Counselor Educators and Suprs. (trustee), Calif. Assn. Sch. Adminstrs., Calif. Soc. Ednl. Program Auditors and Evaluators (sec. 1975-76, v.p. 1976-77, pres.), Calif. Assn. Measurement and Evaluation in Guidance (sec. 1976, pres.), Council Exceptional Children (pres. Foothill chpt. 1969-70), Phi Beta Kappa, Phi Alpha Theta, Psi Chi. Republican. Presbyn. Home: 1259 Sherwood Rd San Marino CA 91108 Office: 9300 E Imperial Hwy Downey CA 90242

FORAKER-THOMPSON, JANE, criminology educator, researcher; b. Alhambra, Calif., Oct. 23, 1937; d. Field and Margaret Hall (Foraker) Thompson; m. Laurence E. Lynn, Aug. 24, 1958; m. Edwin W. Stockly, July 29, 1979; children—Stephen, Daniel, Diana, Julia Lynn. Student U. N.Mex., 1955-56; B.A., U. Calif.-Berkeley, 1959, M.A., 1965; postgrad. Stanford U., 1970-74, U. Leiden (Netherlands), summer 1973. A founder, active Stanford/Soledad Teaching Project, 1971-74; criminal justice specialist Bernalillo County Mental Health Ctr., Albuquerque, 1974-75; chief planner N.Mex. State Police, Santa Fe, 1975-78; project mgr. N.Mex. restitution project N.Mex. Criminal Justice Dept., Santa Fe, 1978-80; pres. Innovation, Devel., Inc., human services cons., Santa Fe, 1980-81; asst. prof. criminal justice Boise State U., 1981—; mem. N.Mex. Task Force on Victims of Sex Crimes, 1974-81, pres., 1978-80; chairwoman N.Mex. Gov.'s Task Force on Family Policy, 1979-80; first pres., chairwoman bd. Alternatives, Inc., treatment program for offenders, 1974-75; mem. ABA Jail Incapacitation and Prisons Com., 1982-83; mem. planning com. workshop leader N.W. Regional New Call to Pacemaking Conf., 1983; mem. N.Mex. Council Community Mental Health Services, 1974-81, mem. exec. com., 1979-80; mem. adv. bd. Albuquerque Rape Crisis Ctr., 1974-75; mem. adv. bd. N.Mex. Bar Assn. Com. Criminal Justice System, 1975; mem. adv. bd. Idaho Inter-Faith Peace Fellowship, 1981—; pres. Citizens for Prison Change, Inc., N.Mex., 1980-81. Mem. Western Assn. Sociologists and Anthropologists, Am. Polit. Sci. Assn., Am. Soc. Pub. Adminstrn., ABA, Nat. Orgn. Victim Assistance, Acad. Criminal Justice Scis., Am. Soc. Criminology, Internat. Soc. Law Enforcement and Criminal Justice Instrs., Snake River Alliance. Quaker. Contbr. articles to profl. jours. Office: Dept Anthropology Sociology and Criminal Justice Boise State U Boise ID 83725

FORAN, DOUGLAS JAMES, computer software company public relations manager; b. Seattle, Sept. 14, 1953; s. Francis Bernard and Patricia Ann (Storer) F. B.A. in French and Spanish (scholar), Lewis and Clark Coll., 1974. Lead singer and keyboardist Ovation, 1971-77; translator Portland, Oreg., 1975; singer, pianist Club Mediterranee, Pompadour, France, 1976; bilingual adminstrv. asst. IMPACT, Inc., Portland, 1978; editorial asst. The Update, Timberline Systems, Beaverton, Oreg., 1978-80, editor, 1980-81; conf. coordinator, 1979—, advt., pub. relations mgr., 1981—. Mktg. cons. St. Cecilia Parish, Beaverton, Oreg.; active Right to Life Oreg. Recipient Marketing award Timberline Systems, 1979. Composer In Your Pride, Colibri, piano/vocal compositions. Office: 7180 SW Fir Loop Portland OR 97223

FORAN, JAMES KEITH, computer services co. exec.; b. Mpls., Dec. 19, 1943; s. Harold and Martha Marie (Wilson) Stevens; A.A., Diablo Valley Coll., 1965; B.S., Calif. State U., 1968; m. Sylvia Carolyn Nilsen, Dec. 11, 1965; children—Perry Keith, Kevin James, Robin Wendy. Asst. mgr. Franklin Credit Union, Oakland, Calif., 1968-69; sales and tng. rep., edp ops. mgr., sr. mktg. and tng. mgr. League Data Processing

Service, Pomona, Calif., 1969-74; sales mgr., br. mgr., so. Calif. regional ops. mgr. U.S. Data Corp., Los Angeles, 1974-79; Western regional mktg. mgr. System Devel. Corp., Santa Monica, 1979-80, nat. sales mgr., 1980-82, dir. mktg. and Sales, 1982—. Named to Burroughs Worldwide Legion of Honor, 1981. Mem. Am. Mgmt. Assn., So. Calif. Microfilm Assn. Congregationalist. Home: 23937 Sapphire Canyon Rd Diamond Bar CA 91765 Office: System Development Corp 2500 Colorado Ave Santa Monica CA 90406

FORAN, JOHN FRANCIS, state senator; b. San Francisco, July 11, 1930; s. James Edward and Kathleen (Egan) F.; m. Constanza G. Ilacqua, 1958; children—David John, Mary Carmel, Thomas Edward, Kathleen Joia. B.S., U. San Francisco, 1956, LL.B., 1959. Mem. Calif. State Assembly, 1963-76, Calif. State Senate from Dist. 6, 1976—. Mem. Calif. Transp. Bd.; intergovt. relations com., task force com. on commerce and transp. Council State Govts. Served to cpl., U.S. Army, 1951-54; Korea. Decorated Purple Heart. Mem. Lawyers Club San Francisco, DAV, VFW, Ancient Order Hibernians, Sons of Italy. Democrat. Roman Catholic. Home: 15 Southgate Ave Room 238 Daly City CA 94015 Office: California State Senate Sacramento CA 95814*

FORBES, BERTHA CATHERINE, librarian, media specialist; b. Florence, Ariz., Mar. 4, 1927; d. Alfred James and Annette Marie (Gino) Brandenburg; B.A. in Edn., Ariz. State Coll., Tempe, 1947; M.A. in Audio-Visual Edn., Ariz. State U., 1976; m. Walter Barrington Forbes, June 1, 1947; children—Michael J., Lynn L., Gail M., Drew L., Bradley W. Tchr., librarian Washington Sch. Dist. 6, 1947-48; tchr. Friendly Corner Farm Labor Sch., Eloy, Ariz., 1950-52; cataloging asst. Matthews Library, Ariz. State U., 1957-58; tech. librarian Goodyear Aircraft Corp., 1958-62; librarian Ariz. State Hosp. Med. Library, 1962-63, Monroe Elem. Sch., Phoenix Elem. Sch., 1963-67; tchr. Wilson Elem. Sch., Phoenix, 1967-69; librarian Cholla Elem. Sch., Phoenix, 1969-70; media specialist/librarian Shea Middle Sch., Phoenix, 1970-82, Sunrise Middle Sch., Paradise Valley, Phoenix, 1982—. Active, CAP Search and Rescue, 1965-68; co-chmn. Republican campaign for state sch. supt., 1974. NDEA grantee, 1965. Mem. NEA, Ariz. Edn. Assn., Paradise Valley Edn. Assn., Ariz. Ednl. Media Assn. Office: 4960 E Acoma St Scottsdale AZ 85254

FORBES, KENNETH ALBERT FAUCHER, urol. surgeon; b. Waterford, N.Y., Apr. 28, 1922; s. Joseph Frederick and Adelle Frances (Robitaille) F.; B.S. cum laude, U. Notre Dame, 1943; M.D., St. Louis U., 1947; m. Eileen Ruth Gibbons, Aug. 4, 1956; children—Michael, Diane, Kenneth E., Thomas, Maureen, Daniel. Intern, St. Louis U. Hosp., 1947-48; resident in urol. surgery VA Hosp., Washington U., St. Louis U. schs., medicine, St. Louis, 1948-52; fellow West Roxbury (Harvard) VA Hosp., Boston, 1955; asst. chief urology VA Hosp., East Orange, N.J., 1955-58; practice medicine specializing in urology, Green Bay, Wis., 1958-78, Long Beach, Calif., 1978—; mem. cons. staff Fairview State Hosp., U. Calif. Med. Center, Irvine, VA Hosp., Long Beach; asst. clin. prof. surgery U. Calif., Irvine, 1978—. Served with USNR, 1944-46; capt. U.S. Army, 1952-54. Diplomate Am. Bd. Urology. Fellow A.C.S., Internat. Coll. Surgeons; mem. AMA, Calif. Med. Assn., Orange County Med. Assn., Am. Urol. Assn., AAAS, Royal Soc. Medicine (London), N.Y. Acad. Scis., Urologists Corr. Club, Orange County Urol. Soc., Phi Beta Pi. Republican. Roman Catholic. Clubs: Notre Dame (Los Angeles); Newport Sailing. Contbr. articles to profl. jours. Home: 5447 Oleta Turn Long Beach CA 90815 Office: 5901 E 7th St Long Beach CA 90822

FORBES, LEONARD, engineering educator; b. Grande Prairie, Alta., Can., Feb. 21, 1940; came to U.S., 1966; s. Frank and Katie (Tschetter) F.; B.Sc. with distinction in Engring. Physics, U. Alta., 1962; M.S. in E.E., U. Ill., 1963, Ph.D., 1970. Staff engr. IBM, Fishkill, N.Y. and Manassas, Va., 1970-72; IBM vis. prof. Howard U., Washington, 1972; asst. prof. U. Ark., Fayetteville, 1972-75; assoc. prof. U. Calif.-Davis, 1976-82; with Hewlett-Packard Labs., Palo Alto, Calif., 1978; cons. to Telex Computer Products, D.H. Baldwin, Hewlett Packard, Fairchild. Served with Royal Can. Air Force, 1963-66. Mem. IEEE, AAUP. Contbr. articles to profl. jours. Home: 537 Mountain View Ave Santa Rosa CA 95401 Office: Dept Elec Engring Oreg State U Corvallis OR 97331

FORD, ALAN B(RENT), lawyer, real estate developer; b. Provo, Utah, July 16, 1951; s. Lloyd A. and AnnaLee (Baird) F.; m. Nichole Pace, Dec. 28, 1975; children—Bradley Alan, Stacy. B.S., San Jose State U., 1975; M.B.A., U. Santa Clara, 1976, J.D., 1979; LL.M. in Taxation, NYU, 1980. Bar. Calif. 1979, Utah 1980. Assoc., Ray, Quinney & Nebeker, Salt Lake City, 1980-82; gen. ptnr. Winget, Vicchrilli & Ford, Salt Lake City, 1982—. Mem. ABA, Calif. Bar Assn., Utah Bar Assn.

FORD, BOB JOE, mgmt. cons. co. exec.; b. Noel, Mo., Sept. 26, 1938; s. Arthur David, Lois Ruth (Taylor) F.; B.S., Mo. U., 1962; M.B.A., Harvard, 1970; m. Mary Ann Smith, June 6, 1962; children—David, Larry. Dir. data processing OCS Co., Springfield, Mo., 1962-68; mgmt. cons. Pilkerton Internat., Anaheim, Calif., 1968-72, pres., 1972—; dir. Eon Co. Served with U.S. Navy, 1958-61. Recipient Dumont award, 1974. Mem. Orange County Execs. Internat. Author: How Computers Can Help or Hurt Your Company Profits, 1974; How to Acquire a Business With Its Own Assets, 1975. Home: 18091 Mark Circle Villa Park CA 92667 Office: Box 6372 Anaheim CA 92806

FORD, CHARLES, elementary school principal administrator; city official; b. Patterson, La., June 5, 1936; s. Charles Ford and Maxie Monica (Columbus) Reels; m. Doris Jefferies, June 27, 1976; children—Bryan, Gwendolyn, Monica. B.A., Dillard U., 1960; M.Ed., U. Ariz., 1966; Ed.D., Atlanta U., 1976. Secondary cert., elem. prin. cert., supt. cert., all Ariz. Tchr. Tucson Pub. Schs., 1964-67, vis. tchr., 1967-69; ednl. specialist Model Cities Program, Tucson, 1970; prin. Reynolds Elem. Sch., Tucson, 1970-74, 76—; mem. Tucson City Council, 1979—, vice mayor, 1982; tchr. bus. adminstrn. Pima Community Coll.; condr. workshops on phys. edn. in elem. schs., alcohol and drug abuse, self-concept devel. Served with U.S. Army, 1956-58. Recipient Lugman award Am. Muslim Mission, 1981; Outstanding Service to Community award Tucson Urban League, 1983; Outstanding Citizen award Elks Club, 1982; Ford fellow, 1974; named hon. admissions counselor U.S. Naval Acad., 1978. Mem. Nat. Assn. Elem. Sch. Prins., Council of Black Educators, Am. Assn. for Sch. Curriculum Devel., Urban League, NAACP, Phi Delta Kappa, Kappa Alpha Psi. Democrat. Methodist. Clubs: Optimis, Masons (Tucson). Home: 5912 E 26th St Tucson AZ 85711 Office: Reynolds Elementary School 7450 E Stella Rd Tucson AZ 85730

FORD, CLARENCE QUENTIN, mechanical engineer, educator; b. Glenwood, N.Mex., Aug. 6, 1923; s. Clarence Noel and Elsie May (Jones) F.; B.S., U.S. Mcht. Marine Acad., 1944; B.S. in Mech. Engring., N.Mex. State U., 1949; M.S., U. Mo., 1950; Ph.D., Mich. State U., 1959; m. Ruth Madge McKinney, June 11, 1950; children—Glenn Mac, Dabney Ann. Instr., U. Mo., 1949-50; instr. Wash. State U., 1950-53, asst. prof., 1953-56; instr. Mich. State U., 1956-59; prof. N.Mex. State U., Las Cruces, 1959—, head dept. mech. engring., 1960-70, assoc. dean engring., 1974-80, 81—, dean engring., 1980-81; prin. Ford & Assocs.; dir. Sun Country Savs. Bank; mem. N.Mex. Bd. Registration Profl. Engrs. and Land Surveyors, chmn. 1980-81. Served to lt. USNR, 1942-46. Fellow AAAS; mem. ASME, Am. Soc. Engring. Edn., Nat. Council Engring. Examiners, N.Mex. Soc. Profl. Engrs. (Outstanding Engr. 1964), Sigma Xi, Phi Kappa Phi, Pi Tau Sigma, Tau Beta Pi, Pi Mu Epsilon. Presbyterian. Clubs: Masons, Kiwanis. Editor: Space Technology and Earth Problems, Vol. 23 Sci. and Tech. Series, 1969. Home: 1985 Crescent St Las Cruces NM 88005

FORD, DAVID LYNN, farmer; b. Del Norte, Colo., May 1, 1948; s. William Howard and Lenore Rowena (Dantice) F.; B.A., Adams State Coll., 1971; m. Vickie Irene Harney, Mar. 15, 1969; children—Ernest David, Rebecca Lynn. Owner, operator farm Center, Colo., 1971—. Adv. bd. Colo. State U. Extension Service, 1973—, also mem. Dean's Adv. Bd. Agrl. Coll.; asso. dir. Monte Vista Prodn. Credit Assn., 1974—; mem. San Luis Valley Potato Adminstrv. Com., 1977-81, vice chmn., 1980-81; mem. agrl. adv. bd. Adams State Coll., 1978-81. Mem. Rio Grande Arts Council, Creede Theatre Guild. Mem. Colo. Cert. Potato Growers Assn. (v.p. 1975-76, pres. 1977-78), Nat. Potato Council (contbg.). Methodist. Clubs: Model Aeros., Elks (Monte Vista, Colo.). Home and office: 50501 County Rd C Center CO 81125

FORD, ELIZABETH BLOOMER (MRS. GERALD R. FORD), wife of 38th Pres. U.S.; b. Chgo., Apr. 8, 1918; d. William Stephenson and Hortence (Neahr) Bloomer; student Bennington Sch. Dance, 1936-38; LL.D. (hon.), U. Mich., 1976; m. William Warren, 1942 (div. 1947); m. 2d, Gerald R. Ford (38th Pres. U.S.), Oct. 15, 1948; children—Michael Gerald, John Gardner, Steven Meigs, Susan Elizabeth. Dancer, Martha Graham Concert Group, N.Y.C., 1939-41; model John Powers Agy., N.Y.C., 1939-41; fashion dir. Herpolsheimer's Dept. Store, Grand Rapids, Mich., 1943-48; dance instr., Grand Rapids, 1932-48. Formerly active Cub Scouts Am.; formerly program chmn. Alexandria (Va.) Cancer Fund Drive; mem. Nat. Commn. on Observance of Internat. Women's Year, 1977; trustee Eisenhower Med. Center, Palm Desert, Calif.; mem. adv. bd. Rosalind Russell Med. Research Fund; hon. chairperson Palm Springs Desert Mus.; hon. bd. dirs. The Lambs, Inc., Libertyville, Ill.; co-chmn. Betty Ford Center Com.; hon. mem. Golden Circle of Patrons of Center Theatre of Performing Arts. Recipient Disting. Woman of Year award Nat. Art Assn., 1975; Silver Anniversary Humanitarian award Phila. Assn. Retarded Children, 1975; Rita V. Tishman Human Relations award Women's div. Anti-Defamation League, 1975; Silver Spirit of Life award Los Angeles City of Hope Nat. Med. Center, 1976; Centennial award McCall's mag., 1976; Media award Phila., 1976; Parson's award N.Y. Parson's Sch. Design, 1976; Woman of Year, Ladies Home Jour., 1976; Alfred P. Sloan, Jr., Meml. award, 1977; USO Woman of Year, 1977. Author: (autobiography) The Times of My Life, 1979. Home: PO Box 927 Rancho Mirage CA 92270*

FORD, GERALD L., industrial relations executive, psychologist; b. Council Bluffs, Iowa, May 21, 1929; s. Walter Louis and Bonnie (Clay) F.; children—Allison, Ann. B.A., State U. Iowa, 1952; M.A., Case-Western Res. U., 1958. Dir. employee relations Gilette Co., Chgo., 1960-66; cons., East Aurora, N.Y., 1967-69; mgr. employee relations Fisher-Price Toys, East Aurora, 1970-78; v.p. indsl. relations Continental Graphics, Los Angeles, 1979—. Mem. Am. Psychol. Assn., Soc. Indsl. and Orgnl. Psychology. Office: 101 S LaBrea Los Angeles CA 90036

FORD, GERALD RUDOLPH, JR., former President of U.S.; b. Omaha, July 14, 1913; s. Gerald R. and Dorothy (Gardner) F.; A.B., U. Mich., 1935; LL.B., Yale U., 1941; LL.D. (hon.), Mich. State U., Aquinas Coll., Spring Arbor Coll., Albion Coll., Grand Valley State Coll., Belmont Abby Coll., Western Mich. U.; m. Elizabeth Bloomer, Oct. 15, 1948; children—Michael Gerald, John G., Steven M., Susan Elizabeth. Admitted to Mich. bar, 1941, practiced in Grand Rapids, 1941-49; asso. firm Butterfield, Amberg, Law & Buchen, Grand Rapids, 1946-51; mem. firm Amberg, Law, Buchen & Fallon, 1951-59, Buchen & Ford, after 1960; mem. 81st to 93d congresses from 5th Mich. Dist., mem. appropriations com., minority leader, 1965-73; vice pres. U.S., 1973-74, Pres. U.S., 1974-77; dir. Santa Fe Internat., GK Techs., Shearson Loeb Rhoades, Pebble Beach Corp., Tiger Internat., Amax Inc. Served to lt. comdr. USN, 1942-46. Recipient 1948 Grand Rapids Jr. C. of C. Distinguished Service award; Distinguished Service award as one of ten outstanding young men in U.S., U.S. Jr. C. of C., 1950, Sports Illus. Silver Anniversary All-Am. award, 1959, Congl. Distinguished Service award Am. Polit. Sci. Assn., 1961; George Washington award Am. Good Govt. Soc., 1966; Gold Medal award Nat. Football Found., 1972. Mem. Am., Mich., Grand Rapids bar assns., Delta Kappa Epsilon, Phi Delta Phi. Author: A Time to Heal: The Autobiography of Gerald R. Ford, 1979; Global Stability, 1982. Republican. Episcopalian. Mason. Clubs: University, Peninsular (Kent County). Co-author: Portrait of the Assassin. *

FORD, HERBERT PAUL, journalism educator, clergyman; b. San Benito, Tex., Aug. 27, 1927; s. Jack and Bertha Louise (Graybill) F.; m. Anita Alice Cavagnaro, Sept. 7, 1952; children—Jana Marie Ford Harder, Cynthia Rae, Alyssa Ann. B.A., Pacific Union Coll., Angwin, Calif., 1954; M.A., Calif. State U.-Northridge, 1975. Ordained to ministry Seventh-day Adventist Ch., 1967; pub. relations dir., religious liberty and indsl. relations dir. So. Calif. Conf. Seventh-day Adventists, Glendale, Calif., 1954-57, pub. relations dir., 1959-63; asst. pub. relations dir. Gen. Conf. Seventh-day Adventists, Washington, 1957-59, also asst. editor mag.; pub. relations dir. Pacific Union Conf. Seventh-day Adventists, Glendale, 1963-69; pub. relations dir. Voice of Prophecy, Glendale, 1969-74; asst. prof. journalism Pacific Union Coll., 1974-78, assoc. prof., 1978—, chmn. communications div., 1976-81, 82-83, v.p. pub. relations devel., recruitment, 1981-82; dir. corp. communications Adventist Health System-West, Glendale, 1983—; instr. journalism Potomac U., Takoma Park, Md., 1958; editorial cons. Insight Mag., Washington. Served with USAF, 1946-49, 50-51. Decorated Commendation medal. Mem. Assn. Edn. in Journalism and Mass Communication, Pub. Relations Soc. Am., Internat. Assn. Bus. Communications, Kappa Tau Alpha, Sigma Delta Chi. Author: Wind High, Sand Deep, 1965, Flee The Captor, 1966; Vlucht Naar de Vrijheid, 1967; No Guns on Their Shoulders, 1968; Crimson Coats and Kimonos, 1968; Affair of The Heart, 1970; Rudo the Reckless Russian, 1970; For The Love of China, 1971; Pitcairn, 1972; The Miscellany of Pitcairn's Island, 1980. Home: 531 Sunset Dr Angwin CA 94508 Office: Communication Dept Pacific Union Coll Angwin CA 94508

FORD, JAMES WILLIAM, real estate broker; b. Oregon City, Ore., Dec. 13, 1929; s. Paul William and Alma Loretta (Woodrum) F.; m. Eileen Laura Dean, Dec. 26, 1953; children—Pamela M., Debra L., Jeffery W. B.A., San Francisco State Coll., 1962; M.A., Boston U., 1971. Commd. U.S. Army, 1953, advanced through grades to lt. col., ret., 1973; personnel mgr./labor relations Kaiser Steel Corp., Napa, Calif., 1973-76; real estate broker Napa Valley Properties, Napa, 1976-83; prin. James W. Ford, Realtor, Napa, 1983—; instr. real estate Napa Valley Coll., 1979—. Decorated Legion of Merit, Air medal. Named Realtor of Yr., Napa County Bd. Realtors, 1981, 82. Mem. Calif. Assn. Realtors (state dir., regional v.p.), Napa County Bd. Realtors (pres.), Nat. Assn. Realtors, Res. Officers Assn., Aircraft Owners and Pilots Assn., Napa C. of C. Republican. Roman Catholic. Club: Rotary (pres. 1982-83).

FORE, EILEEN MARIE, magazine exec.; b. N.Y.C., Mar. 14, 1940; d. John L. and Lillian J. Sullivan; A.A., Ventura (Calif.) Coll., 1980; m. Gerald E. Fore; children—Donna, Roy, Gale, Kathy, Jeri, Shaw. Artist, Pro Art, music pubs., Westbury, N.Y., 1959-68; artist Crane Cams, Hollandale, Fla., 1968-70; advt. artist, L.I., 1970-76; art dir. Simco Media Co., automotive and gun mag. pubs., Ventura, 1974-81; art dir. Haynes Publs., Newbury Park, Calif., 1981—. Mem. steering com. Concerned Parents Against Drug Abuse Program, Ventura. Mem. Ventura County Bicycle Club, So. Calif. Motorcycle Assn. Republican. Home: 361 Plumas Ave Ventura CA 93004 Office: 861 Lawrence Dr Newbury Park CA 91320

FORER, LUCILLE KREMITH, psychologist; b. Springfield, Ill., Sept. 30; d. William Frederick and JoAnn Marie (Teubner) Kremith; m. Bertram Robin Forer, Sept. 27, 1941; children—Stephen Keith, William Robert. M.A., U. So. Calif., 1942, Ph.D., 1953. Lic. psychologist, Calif. Personnel officer, adminstrv. officer, Office of Adminstr. OPA, Washington, 1942-45; asst. prof. psychology Calif. State U.-Los Angeles, 1953-58; pvt. practice clin. psychology, Los Angeles and Malibu, Calif., 1953—. Bd. dirs. Malibu Library. Fellow Soc. Personality Assessment; mem. Los Angeles County Psychol. Assn., Calif. State Psychol. Assn., Am. Psychol. Assn., Internat. Council Psychologists, AAUW, Malibu Writing Group (chmn.), Writing Group Santa Monica (chmn.), LWV. Republican. Lutheran. Author: Birth Order and Life Roles, 1969; The Birth Order Factor, 1976, paperback edit., 1977. Home: 19854 Pacific Coast Hwy Malibu CA 90265

FORESTER, RUSSELL, artist; b. Salmon, Idaho, May 21, 1920; s. Alvin R. and Mary (Isley) F.; student Inst. Design, Chgo., 1950; m. Marie-Christine Meynet, Feb. 2, 1968; 1 dau., Lynn. Prin., Russell Forester Architect, Inc., 1948-72; free lance artist, 1972—; group shows include: LaJolla Mus. Contemporary Art, Guggenheim Mus., N.Y.C., Everson Mus. Art, Syracuse, N.Y.; represented in permanent collections; Guggenheim Mus., Cedars-Sinai Med. Center, Los Angeles, McCrory Corp., N.Y.C., 1st Nat. Bank of Chgo. Mem. AIA, Artists Equity.

FORHAN, WILLIAM EDWARD, accountant; b. Butte, Mont., Mar. 20, 1947; s. Rudi and Alice (Mehrens) F.; m. Carol Lynn Johnson, Nov. 25, 1967; children—David John, Michael Scott. B.S. in Bus. Adminstrn., U. Mont., 1969. C.P.A., Mont. Staff acct. Krausman & Assocs., Englewood, Colo., 1972-74; controller, I.T.T. Auto. Distbrs., Colo.-Utah ops., 1974-78, Iowa-Ill. ops., 1978-80; controller Billings (Mont.) Gazette, 1980—. Sec.-treas. community adv. bd. Sch. Bus. and Econs., Eastern Mont. Coll., 1981-83. Served to 1st lt. U.S. Army, 1969-72. Mem. Inst. Newspaper Controllers, and Fin. Officers. Republican. Episcopalian. Office: 401 N Broadway Billings MT 59101

FORKEL, CURT EMIL, mech. engr.; b. Cameron, Tex., Oct. 26, 1922; s. Curt Emil and Mary Louise (Baade) F.; B.S., U. Tex., 1944; postgrad. U. Denver, 1946; postgrad. U. Tex., 1947; M.S., U. Idaho, 1969; m. Chloe Tidwell, Oct. 30, 1943; children—Kaye Forkel Bentzen, Mary Candace Forkel Wilkinson, Ruth Ann. Draftsman, N.Am. Aviation Co., Dallas, 1943-44; instr. U. Tex. at Austin, 1944-45; instr. U. N.Mex., 1945-46; instr. U. Denver, 1946-47, asst. prof., 1947-48; metall. engr. Phillips Petroleum Co., Bartlesville, Okla., 1948-60, design group supr., Borger, Tex., 1960-63, design group supr., Idaho Falls, Idaho, 1963-69; design group supr. Idaho Nuclear Corp., Idaho Falls. 1969-70; design group supr. Aerojet Nuclear Co., Idaho Falls, 1970-76; sr. project engr. EG&G Idaho, Inc., Idaho Falls, 1976-77, br. mgr. design rev. and cost estimating, 1977, design sect. supr., 1977-78, br. mgr. engring. support for nuclear energy programs, 1978-80, supr. design for nuclear energy programs, 1980-81, sr. program specialist, 1981—. Republican precinct committeeman, 1963-64. Registered profl. engr., Okla. Mem. ASME, Phi Eta Sigma, Pi Tau Sigma. So. Baptist. Patentee in field. Home: 2306 Koro Ave Idaho Falls ID 83401 Office: PO Box 1625 Idaho Falls ID 83415

FORKERT, CLIFFORD ARTHUR, civil engr.; b. Verona, N.D., Oct. 16, 1916; s. Arthur Louis and Bessie (Delamater) F.; grad. N.D. State Coll., 1940; postgrad. M.I.T.; m. Betty Jo Erickson, July 1, 1940; children—Terry Lynn Forkert Williamson, Michael, Debra. Hwy. engr., N.D., Tex., 1937-40; hydraulic engr. Internat. Boundary Commn. Tex. on Rio Grande and Tributaries, 1940-43; constrn., topographic and cons. engr., Calif. 1946—; now civil engr., prin. Clifford A. Forkert, Civil Engr.; pres. Calif. Poly. Pomona Assos. Served as capt. USMCR, 1943-46. Registered civil engr. Calif., Oreg., Ariz., profl. engr., Nev., lic. land surveyor, Nev. Fellow Am. Congress and Mapping (life); mem. ASCE (life), Land Surveyors Assn. Calif. (dir.), Alumni Assn. N.D. State Coll. Home: 20021 Skimmer Ln Huntington Beach CA 92646 Office: 22311 Brookhurst St Huntington Beach CA 92646

FORMAN, BARRY JOEL, electrical engineer; b. Phila., Sept. 19, 1938; s. Nathan Victor and Celia (Sklarz) F.; B.S., UCLA, 1960, M.S., 1962. Mem. tech. staff Hughes Aircraft Co., Culver City, Calif., 1961-73, project engr., El Segundo, Calif., 1973-78, sr. tech. staff asst., 1978-79, sr. staff engr., 1980—; sec. Bet Acta, Inc., 1979-80. Mem. IEEE, Mensa. Republican. Jewish. Patentee in field. Home: 4250 Via Marina 61 Marina del Rey CA 90291 Office: Hughes Aircraft Co PO Box 92919 Los Angeles CA 90292

FORMAN, SANFORD, mgmt. co. exec.; b. Bronx, Sept. 22, 1932; s. Louis and Rose (Fenster) F.; B.S., Fairleigh Dickinson U., 1962; student Am. Traffic Acad., 1958; m. Marilyn Resnick, Aug. 29, 1954; children—Suzanne Myrna, Jody Lynn. Mgr. traffic ops. W. T. Grant Co., Los Angeles and N.Y.C., 1958-69; gen. traffic mgr. Mattel, Inc., Hawthorne, Calif. 1969-79; v.p. A.Cesana & Assos., Inc., Torrance, Calif., 1979—; faculty Golden West Coll., 1978, Los Angeles Unified Sch. Dist., 1976-79; cons. Served with USAF, 1951-55. Decorated Purple Heart, D.S.M. Mem. Toy Mfrs. Assn. (chmn. transp. steering com. 1976-79, chmn. So. div. Western traffic conf. 1967-69, 74-76), Am. Soc. Traffic and Transp. (cert.), Jewish War Vets. Jewish. Home: 496 Palos Verdes Blvd Redondo Beach CA 90277 Office: 21535 Hawthorne Blvd Torrance CA 90503

FORMEISTER, RICHARD BRUNO, electronics engr.; b. Chgo., Jan. 14, 1946; s. Bruno and June Patricia (Kelly) F.; B.S. in Elec. Engring., U. Ill., 1968; M.S. in Engring., Ariz. State U., 1978; m. Jonille Denise Fay, July 20, 1968 (div. Apr. 1980); 1 dau., Tiffany Rose. Insp., communications products div. Motorola Co., Chgo., 1965-66; test analyzer Warwick Electronics Inc., Niles, Ill., 1966, 67; with Sperry Flight Systems, Phoenix, 1968—, head engring. sect., 1979—. Mem. Eta Kappa Nu. Republican. Roman Catholic. Patentee in field. Home: 6407 W Yucca St Glendale AZ 85304 Office: 5353 W Bell Rd Glendale AZ 85308

FORMHALS, ROBERT WILLARD YATES (SANGUSZKO), ret. ednl. adminstr.; b. Los Angeles, June 14, 1919; s. Carl Wright and Muriel (Yates) (Sanguszko) Formhals; LL.B., J.D., Welch Coll. Law, Los Angeles, 1943; cert. pub. adminstrn. Sacramento State Coll., 1959; D.C.L., Sheffield Coll., 1965; m. Elaine Mary Peters, Apr. 4, 1947; 1 son, Robert Arthur Clinton. Personnel mgr. Warman Steel Casting Co., Vernon, Calif., 1943-47; dep. labor commr. Calif., 1948; adminstrv. asst. to state architect Calif., 1948-59; No. Calif. mgr. William L. Aldrich Co., 1960-61; exec. sec.-treas. Calif. Sch. Bds. Assn., 1961-67; dir. bd. policies services Ednl. Service Bur., 1967; pres. Assos. Mgmt. Service, 1967-70; mcpl. employee relations officer City of San Jose (Calif.), 1970-74; program mgr. West Valley Coll., Saratoga, Calif., 1975-76, also instr. labor relations and mgmt., 1972-75; dir. employer-employee relations Conejo Valley Unified Sch. Dist., 1976-81. Commr. Calif. Commn. Sch. Dist. Orgn., 1961-64; chmn. Gov. Calif. Edn. and Tng. Adv. Com. Civil Def., also mem. Calif. Disaster Council, 1961-67; personnel commr. Pleasant Valley Sch. Dist., 1979-81, trustee, 1981—; exec. vice chmn. Young Democrats Calif., 1941-44; mem. Nat. Com. Dems. for Dewey, 1944; Calif. chmn. Dems. for Knowland, 1946; vice chmn. Sacramento County Com. for Nixon, 1960. Chmn. bd. Pacific Maritime Acad.,

1950-52; trustee St. John Found., 1972—. Served with AUS, 1943-44. Created knight by King Peter II of Yugoslavia; decorated grand officer White Eagle, grand officer Crown (Yugoslavia); grand master, grand cross St. John Jerusalem; grand cross Constantine the Gt.; knight comdr. St. Laszlo (Hungary). Mem. Am. Soc. Safety Engrs. (past nat. exec. bd.), Am. Arbitration Assn. (nat. labor panel), Am. Legion, SAR (pres. Palo Alto chpt., pres. Patton chpt., state exec. sec. 1978-79, state pres. 1979-80 nat. trustee 1980-81, nat. v.p. gen. 1981-82), KP, Eagles. Clubs: Commonwealth (San Francisco); Severance (Los Angeles). Author: Handbook of Armed Forces of the World, 1948; Book of Precedence, 1965; White Cross, 1980; also articles. Address: 5609 E Willow View Dr Camarillo CA 93010

FORNBERG, BENGT, mathematics researcher, educator; b. Halmstad, Sweden, June 8, 1946; s. Bertil and Eva (Friese) F.; m. Jennifer Margaret Horne, Apr. 9, 1974; children—Pelle, Lisa, Anders. Ph.D., Uppsala U., 1972. Fellow, CERN, Geneva, 1972-74; Bateman researcher inst. dept. applied math. Calif. Inst. Tech., Pasadena, 1974-75, asst. prof., 1975-80, assoc. prof., 1980—; Guggenheim fellow, sr. visitor Cambridge (Eng.) U., 1981-82. Office: 217-50 Calif Inst Tech Pasadena CA 91125

FORNESS, STEVEN ROBERT, ednl. psychologist; b. Denver, May 13, 1939; s. Robert E. and Rejeana C. (Houck) F.; B.A. in English, U. No. Colo., 1963, M.A. in Ednl. Psychology, 1964; Ed.D., Spl. Edn., UCLA, 1968. Tchr., Santa Maria (Calif.) High Sch., 1964-66; counselor Sch. Edn. U. Calif. at Los Angeles, 1966-68, spl. educator Neuropsychiat. Inst., 1968—, prof. dept. psychiatry, 1972—; prin. Neuropsychiat. Inst. Inpatient Sch., 1977—. Western coordinator, Consortum Spl. Edn., 1970—. Fulbright scholar Ministry of Edn., Portugal, 1976. Mem. Am. Assn. Mental Deficiency, Council Exceptional Children. Specialist in classroom observation tech. early identification of handicapped children. Author over 100 publs. including (with Frank Hewett) Education of Exceptional Learners, 3d edit., 1984. Home: 11901 Sunset Blvd Los Angeles CA 90049 Office: Dept Psychiatry UCLA 760 Westwood Plaza Los Angeles CA 90024

FORNIA, DOROTHY LOUISE, educator; b. Youngstown, Ohio, Feb. 14, 1918; d. Joseph Victor and Margaret Alice F.; B.Sc. in Edn., Ohio State U., 1941, M.A., 1944; Ed.D., U. So. Calif. Tchr. health and phys. edn. Xenia (Ohio) Public Schs., 1941-43; asst. prof. health and phys. edn. Wilmington Coll., Ohio, 1944-45, Ohio Wesleyan U., 1946-47, Bowling Green (Ohio) State U., 1947-53; teaching asst. U. So. Calif., 1953-56; asst. prof. Calif. State U., Long Beach, 1955-59, asso. prof., 1959-64, prof., dir. gerontology program Sch. Applied Arts and Scis., 1964—. Bd. dirs. Sr. Care Action Network, Long Beach. Fellow Am. Sch. Health Assn.; mem. Calif. Employees Assn., Calif. Tchrs. Assn., NEA, Calif. Assn. Health, Phys. Edn. and Recreation, AAHPER, Calif. Council Gerontology and Geriatrics, Western Soc. Phys. Edn. Coll. Women, Calif. Women in Higher Edn. (v.p.). Presbyterian. Home: 6941 Driscoll St Long Beach CA 90815 Office: Calif State U 1250 Bellflower Blvd Long Beach CA 90840

FORREST, GARY GRAN, psychologist, consultant, author; b. New Castle, Pa., Dec. 1, 1943; s. Granville Hamilton and Florence Ruth (Cox) F.; m. Sandra G. Della-Giustina, Dec. 28, 1974; children—Sarah Ellen, Allison Giustina. B.A. (Coll. scholar), Westminster Coll., 1965; M.Ed. (Vocat. Rehab. Assn. stipendee), U. Mo.-Columbia, 1967; Ed.D. (Univ. higher edn. grantee), U. N.D., 1970; diploma U. Okla., Norman, 1971. Lic. clin. psychologist, Colo.; diplomate in profl. psychotherapy Internat. Acad. Profl. Counselors and Psychotherapists. Clin. dir. alcohol rehab. program, dept. psychiatry Alcohol and Drug Rehab. Ctr., Ft. Gordon, Ga., 1971-73, ctr. clin. dir., 1973-76; instr. dept. psychology Augusta Coll., 1971-73; mem. dept. psychiatry Community Mental Health Ctr., Med. Coll. Ga., 1973; vis. prof. psychology, counseling and guidance U. No. Colo., 1975-81; exec. dir. Psychotherapy Assocs. and Inst. for Addictive Behavioral Change, Colorado Springs, Colo., 1976—; cons. psychologist alcohol services div. Pikes Peak Mental Health Ctr., Colorado Springs, 1982-83. Mem. adv. bd. Nat. Council on Alcoholism, Colorado Springs, 1975—; bd. dirs. Riegel Ctr., Penrose Community Hosp., Colorado Springs, 1980—. Recipient Nat. Service award Nat. Council Alcoholism, 1981. Mem. Am. Psychol. Assn., Colo. Psychol. Assn., Am. Personnel and Guidance Assn., Nat. Register Health Service Providers in Psychology, Assn. for Advancement Profl. Psychology, Phi Delta Kappa, Delta Tau Delta. Republican. Methodist. Author books, the most recent being: Confrontation in Psychotherapy With Alcoholics, 1982; Alcoholism and Human Sexuality, 1982; How to Cope with a Teenage Drinker, 1983; Alcoholism, Narcissism and Psychopathology, 1983. Home: 935 War Eagle Dr N Colorado Springs CO 80919 Office: 3208 N Academy Blvd Suite 160 Colorado Springs CO 80907

FORREST, JAMES TAYLOR, mus. dir.; b. New Castle, Ind., Sept. 22, 1921; s. Jesse E. and Katie M. (Lee) F.; student Hanover Coll., 1938-39, Ind. U., 1941; B.S. with honors, U. Wis., 1948, M.S., 1949, postgrad., 1949-50; m. Suzanne de Borhegyi, 1979; children—Mary Christine, Barbara Lee. Research asso. SAC, USAF, 1950-53; curator state mus.'s Colo. Hist. Soc., Denver, 1953-55; dir. Gilcrease Inst. Am. History and Art, Tulsa, 1955-61; dir. Fine Arts, Mus. N.Mex., Santa Fe, 1961-62; dir. Mus. N.Mex., 1962-64; dir. Bradford Brinton Meml. Ranch, Big Horn, Wyo., 1964—; prof. art U. Wyo., dir. univ. art mus., 1968—; instr. Sheridan Coll., 1969—; cons. Cowboy Hall of Fame, exhibits at Grand Teton Lodge, 1954-55. Bd. dirs. Wyo. Council on Arts, 1967, chmn., 1971—. Project dir. Civic Responsibility Center, Sheridan, 1966-67. Served with USAAF, 1942-45; CBI. Mem. Am. Assn. Museums (council, sec. 1979-82), Santa Fe Westerners (acting pres. 1962-63), Omaha Historians Council (pres.), Am. Assn. State and Local History, Colo.-Wyo. Assn. Museums (past chmn.), Mountain-Plains Mus. Assn. (council, pres. 1980-81), Western Assn. Art Museums sect. Am. Assn. Museums. Author: History of New Mexico, 1971; Bill Gollings—The Man and His Art, 1979. Editor: The American Scene, 1958-61. Contbr. articles to profl. jours. Home: 2035 Spring Creek Dr Laramie WY 82070 Office: PO Box 3138 Laramie WY 82070

FORREST, WILLIAM EDWIN, mountaineer; b. Glendale, Calif., Oct. 20, 1939; s. Fredrick Wayne and Bernice E. (Finningsmeir) F. B.A. with distinction in English, Ariz. State U., 1965. Cert. secondary tchr. Ariz., Colo. Owner, pres. Forrest Mountaineering, Denver, 1968—. Trustee Colo. Outward Bound Sch. Served with U.S. Army, 1959-62. Contbr. articles to mountain climbing mags; designer mountain equipment; patentee in field; first ascent of Uli Biaho (Pakistan), 1979. Home and Office: 1517 Platte St Denver CO 80202

FORREST, WILLIAM GEORGE, engineering executive; b. Hamilton, Ont., Can., May 10, 1927; s. Alexander William and Pauline Emma (Dove) F.; m. Janice Kanaline Putnam, Oct. 15, 1970; 2d m. Elvira Palacio, June 17, 1978; children—Janine, Leslie, Maggie, Joann, Michelle, William. B.A., Hamilton Tech. Inst., 1945. Tool designer Robertson Irwin, Hamilton, 1947-52; lead tool designer Can. Westinghouse, Hamilton, 1952-59; lead designer, lead tool designer Master Mech. Design, Toronto, 1959-60; die design lead, tool and plant engring. mgr. Leach Relay, Los Angeles, 1960—; instr. in field. Mem. Soc. Mfg. Engrs., Delta Collegiate. Home: 3741 Catalina Ct Chino CA 91710 Office: Leach Relay 5915 Avalon Blvd Los Angeles CA 90003

FORRESTER, ALVIN THEODORE, physics educator; b. Bklyn., Apr. 13, 1918; s. Joseph David and Rose M. (Kissen) Finkelstein; m. Joy Levin, June 28, 1948 (dec. 1954); children—Bruce H., Cheri J.; m. 2d June D. Berg, Oct. 5, 1958 (div. 1973); children—William C., Susan J. B.A., Cornell U., 1938, M.A., 1939, Ph.D., 1942. Research assoc. radiation lab. U. Calif.-Berkeley, 1942-45; physicist RCA Labs., Princeton, N.J., 1945-46; asst. prof. physics U. So. Calif., Los Angeles, 1946-51, assoc. prof., 1951-54; physicist Westinghouse Research Labs., Pitts., 1954-58; propulsion specialist Rocketdyne, Canoga Park, Calif., 1958-59; dept. mgr. Electro-Optical Systems, Pasadena, Calif., 1959-65; prof. physics U. Calif.-Irvine, 1965-67; prof. physics and engring. UCLA, 1967—; vis. prof. astronomy U. Utrecht (Holland), 1971; vacation assoc. Culham (Eng.) Lab., 1974; vis. prof. physics Technion, Haifa, Israel, 1977. Recipient AIAA Research award, 1962; Office Naval Research grantee, 1948-54; Army Research Office grantee, 1966-69; NSF grantee, 1970-76; AEC grantee, 1976-77; Dept. Energy grantee, 1978-82, others. Fellow IEEE, Am. Phys. Soc.; mem. AIAA, AAAS, Am. Assn. Physics Tchrs., AAUP, Union Concerned Scientists, Fedn. Am. Scientists, Sierra Club, Sigma Xi. Democrat. Patentee in field; contbr. articles to profl. jours. Home: 11525 Ohio Ave Apt 4 Los Angeles CA 90025 Office: UCLA Room 7731 Boelter Hall Los Angeles CA 90024

FORSEN, HAROLD KAY, engineering executive; b. St. Joseph, Mo., Sept. 19, 1932; s. Allen Kay and Mabel Evelyn (Buehler) F.; m. Betty Ann Webb, May 25, 1952; children—John Allen, Ronald Karl, Sandra Kay. A.A., Compton Jr. Coll., 1956; B.S., Calif. Inst. Tech., 1958, M.S., 1959; Ph.D., U. Calif., Berkeley, 1965. Research assoc. Gen. Atomic, San Diego, Calif., 1959-62; research assoc., elec. engr., U. Calif.-Berkeley, 1962-65; assoc. prof. nuclear engring. U. Wis., Madison, 1965-69, prof., 1969-73, dir. Phys. Scis. Lab., 1970-72; mgr. engring. Exxon Nuclear Co., Bellevue, Wash., 1973-75, v.p., dir., 1975-80, exec. in charge laser enrichment, 1981; exec. v.p. Jersey Nuclear-Avco Isotopes, Inc., 1975-80, pres., 1981, dir., 1975-81; mgr. engring. and materials, Bechtel Group, Inc., San Francisco, 1981—, dep. mgr. research and engring., 1983—; mem. fusion power reactor sr. rev. com. Dept. of Energy, 1977, magnetic fusion adv. com., 1982—; chmn. U.S. del. of AEC on Ion Sources to Soviet Union, 1972; cons. Oak Ridge Nat. Lab., 1969-72, Argonne Nat. Lab., 1970-72, Exxon Nuclear Co., 1970-73, Battelle N.W. Lab., 1971-72; mem. sci. and tech. adv. com. Argonne Nat. Lab., 1983—; mem. fusion energy adv. com. Oak Ridge Nat. Lab., 1977—. Vice pres. bd. trustees Pacific Sci. Ctr. Found., 1977, pres., 1978-80, chmn., 1981; mem. deans vis. com. Coll. Engring., U. Wash., 1981—. Served with USAF, 1951-55. Mem. Am. Nuclear Soc. (Arthur H. Compton award 1972, chmn. tec. group controlled nuclear fusion 1973), IEEE (sr.), Am. Phys. Soc., Sigma Xi. Contbr. articles to tech. jours. Patentee fusion and laser isotope separation. Home: 255 Tim Ct Danville CA 94526 Office: Bechtel Group Inc PO Box 3965 San Francisco CA 94119

FORSIAK, WALTER WILLIAM, television executive; b. Detroit, Apr. 30, 1935; s. John J. and Patricia (Jurek) F.; m. Ella Eggers, July 27, 1963; children—Erica, Christa. B.S. in Bus. Adminstrn., Wayne State U., 1957. Advt. sales McGraw-Hill Pub. Co., various locations, 1957-83; v.p. Bus. Times, Inc., TV show, 1983—. Bd. dirs. Switzer Ctr. Ednl. Therapy, 1979-81. Served in USAFR, 1958-64. Mem. San Francisco Advt. Club, Los Angeles Advt. Club. Roman Catholic. Clubs: Chuck Wagon Trail Riders of N.Mex.; The Guardsmen (San Francisco). Office: 49 Gold St San Francisco CA 94111

FORSMAN, CHARLES STANLEY (CHUCK), educator, artist; b. Nampa, Idaho, May 5, 1944. B.A., U. Calif.-Davis, 1967, M.F.A., 1971; student Skowhegan Sch. Painting and Sculpture, 1970. One-man shows: Tibor De Nagy Gallery, N.Y.C., 1973, 75, 77, 79, Watson De Nagy Gallery, Houston, 1976, St. Charles Gallery, Denver, 1978, Wichita Art Mus., 1981; group shows include: Am. Acad. Arts and Letters, N.Y.C., 1974, 79, Denver Art Mus., 1975, 78, 81, Indpls. Mus. Art, 1976, Flint (Mich.) Inst. Arts, 1977, Sheldon Mem. Art Gallery, U. Nebr., Lincoln, Whitney Mus. Am. Art, Fairfield, Colo., 1981; represented in permanent collections at Phoenix Art Mus., Marion Koogler McNay Art Inst., San Antonio, Grinnell (Iowa) Coll., Wichita Art Mus., Denver Art Mus.; asst. instr. painting and sculpture U. Calif.-Davis, 1970-71; instr. U. Colo., Boulder, 1971-75, asst. prof., 1975-79, assoc. prof., 1979—. Nat. Endowment Arts grantee, 1979; faculty fellow U. Colo., Boulder, 1979. Office: University of Colorado Dept of Art Boulder CO 80309

FORSTE, NORMAN LEE, cons.; b. Carthage, Mo., Aug. 18, 1935; s. John Edward and Lula Mae (Martin) F.; A.A., Am. River coll., 1961; B.A., Calif. State U., 1964, M.A., 1971; M.B.A., Golden Gate U., 1973; Ph.D., in higher edn. U. Wash., 1983; m. Catherine Jean Culver, July 20, 1958; children—Patricia, Diana, John II, Karl. Adminstrv. analyst State of Calif., Sacramento, 1962-64, sr. data processing systems analyst, 1966-67, supr. info. systems devel., 1967-68; sr. adminstrv. analyst County of Sacramento (Calif.), 1964-66, dir. systems and data processing dept., 1968-74; dir. adminstrv. data processing div. U. Wash., Seattle, 1974-76; mgr. mgmt. adv. services Deloitte Haskins & Sells, 1976-81, dir. mgmt. adv. services, 1981—; instr. mgmt. scis. program U. Calif. at Davis, 1968; professorial lectr. mgmt. info. systems Golden Gate U., Sacramento, 1971-74, 79—; instr. info. systems Calif. State U.-Sacramento, 1982-83; instr. systems analysis and introduction to data processing Am. River Coll., Sacramento, 1968-71. Mem. curriculum adv. com. for data processing Am. River Coll., Sacramento, 1969-74, mem. com. to evaluate vocational and tech. edn. program for accreditation, 1972-73. Served with USAF, 1954-57, 62. Mem. Am. Soc. Pub. Adminstrn. (dir. 1969-71), Data Processing Mgmt. Assn. (chpt. pres. 1968-69), Methods and Procedure Assn. (pres. 1969), Calif. Assn. County Data Processors (1st v.p. 1973-74), Air Force Res. Officers Assn. (chpt. v.p. 1971-74, 79-82), Air Force Calif. Dept. Res. Officers Assn. (jr. v.p. 1971). Home: 5401 Valhalla Dr Carmichael CA 95608 Office: 1425 River Park Dr Suite 500 Sacramento CA 95815

FORSYTH, JOSEPH, librarian; b. County Durham, Eng., Aug. 15, 1942; s. James Frederick and Maisie (Appleby) F.; came to Can., 1966; Asso. of Library Assn., Newcastle (Eng.) Sch. Librarianship, 1963; M.A. in L.S., U. London, 1976, Fellow of Library Assn., 1971; m. Kay Frances Appleby, Oct. 3, 1964; children—Julian Alastair, Andrew Stuart. Library asst. Durham County Library, 1960-62; coll. librarian Easington (Eng.) Tech. Coll., 1962-63; regional librarian North Riding County (Eng.) Library, 1964-66; reference librarian Calgary (Alta., Can.) Public Library, 1966-70; library devel. officer Govt. Alta., Edmonton, 1970-77; dir. library services Alta. Dept. Culture, Edmonton, 1977—. Mem. ALA, Edmonton Library Assn., Library Assn. Alta., Can. Library Assn., Library Assn. Gt. Britain, Internat. and Comparative Librarianship Group of Library Assns. Anglican. Author: Government Publications Relating to Alberta, 1972. Home: 15211 83d Ave Edmonton AB T5R 3TS Canada Office: 16214 114th Ave Edmonton AB T5M 2Z5 Canada

FORSYTH, RAYMOND ARTHUR, civil engr.; b. Reno, Mar. 13, 1928; s. Harold Raymond and Fay Exona (Highfill) F.; B.S., Calif. State U., San Jose, 1952; M.C.E., Auburn U., 1958; m. Mary Ellen Wagner, July 9, 1950; children—Lynne, Gail, Alison, Ellen. Jr. engr., asst. engr. Calif. Div. Hwys., San Francisco, 1952-54; assoc. engr., sr. supervising, prin. engr. Calif. Dept. Transp., Sacramento, 1961-83, chief geotech. br., 1972-79, chief soil mechanics and pavement br., 1979-83, chief Transp. Lab., 1983—; cons., lectr. in field. Served with USAF, 1954-56. Fellow ASCE (pres. Sacramento sect., chmn. Calif. council 1980-81); mem. Transp. Research Bd. (chmn. embankments and earth slopes com. 1976-82, chmn. soil mechanics sect. 1982—), ASTM. Contbr. articles to profl. publs. Home: 5017 Pasadena Ave Sacramento CA 95841

FORSYTHE, SANDRA JOHNSON, educator; b. Woodbury, N.J., June 27, 1942; d. Herbert Halston and Elizabeth Ann (Jones) Johnson; m. Dale William Forsythe, June 18, 1966; children—Michael Glenn, John David. B.A., Hanover Coll., 1964; M.E., U. Mont., 1976; Ed.D., U. Ark., 1981. Cert. tchr., Alaska, Calif. Tchr. social studies and English, Garden Grove (Calif.) Jr. High Sch., 1964-66; specialized supr. Parents' Coop. Sch., Jeddah, Saudi Arabia, 1970-75, reading cons., 1976-80, lang. arts cons., 1980-81; asst. prof. edn. Alaska Pacific U., Anchorage, 1981—. Mem. Internat. Reading Assn., Nat. Council Tchrs. English, Western Coll. Reading Assn., Phi Delta Kappa. Democrat. Office: 4101 University Dr Anchorage AK 99508

FORTE, VINCENT FERDINANDO, investment banker; b. Boston, July 19, 1950; s. Saverio Vincent and Annunziata (Siesto) F.; m. Amelia Shill Besson, June 18, 1977; children—Anthony Vincent, Marisa Siesto. B.A., John Hopkins U., 1972; M.B.A., Stanford U., 1975, M.S., Med. Sch., 1975. Research assoc. Calif. Hosp. Assn., Sacramento, 1975; sr. asso. Amherst Assos., Inc., Walnut Creek, Calif., 1976-78; sr. v.p. Blyth Eastman Paine Webber Health Care Funding, Inc., San Francisco, 1978—; vis. lectr. U. Calif.-Berkeley, UCLA, Golden Gate U. HEW scholar, 1973-75; Ford Found. scholar, 1973-75. Mem. Hosp. Fin. Mgmt. Assn. No. Calif. (div.), Municipal Bond Forum. Roman Catholic. Office: Blyth Eastman Paine Webber Health Care Funding Inc 555 California St 43d Floor San Francisco CA 94104

FORTENBACH, CHARLES DANIEL, aeronautical engineer; b. Memphis, Nov. 16, 1956; s. Robert Charles and Helen Elizabeth (Utzinger) F. B.Aerospace Engring., Ga. Inst. Tech., 1978; M.S., Stanford U., 1980. Assoc. engr. Gen. Dynamics, Fort Worth, 1977, 78; sr. research engr. Lockheed Missiles and Space Co., Sunnyvale, Calif., 1980—. Mem. AIAA, Assn. Unmanned Vehicle Systems. Home: 507 Bernardo St Apt I Sunnyvale CA 94086 Office: PO Box 504 0/54-52 B592 Sunnyvale CA 94086

FORTH, KEVIN BERNARD, beverage distbg. co. exec.; b. Adams, Mass., Dec. 4, 1949; s. Michael Charles and Catherine Cecilia (McAndrews) F.; A.B., Holy Cross Coll., 1971; M.B.A., N.Y. U., 1973; m. Alice Jane Farnum, Sept. 14, 1974; children—Melissa, Brian. Div. rep. Anheuser-Busch, Inc., Boston, 1973-74, dist. sales mgr., Los Angeles, 1974-76, asst. to dir. mktg. staff, St. Louis, 1976-77; v.p. Straub Distbg. Co., Inc., Orange, Calif., 1977-81, pres., 1981—, also dir. Benjamin Levy fellow, 1971-73. Adv. bd. Rancho Santiago Community Coll. Dist.; dir. Santa Ana Youth Boxing; mem. Orange County Council, Nat. Council on Alcoholism; mem. Titan Athletic Found., Calif. State U. at Fullerton, Arms Found., Olympia Brewing Co. Wholesaler Forum. Mem. Assn. MBA Execs., Calif. Beer Wholesalers Assn. (dir., exec. com., v.p.), Nat. Beer Wholesalers Assn., Industry Environ. Council, Beta Gamma Sigma, Holy Cross Alumni Assn. Roman Catholic. Clubs: Lincoln, Silver Circle, Sports Car Am. Home: Yorba Linda CA 92686 Office: 410 W Grove Ave Orange CA 92667

FORTHMANN, ANDREW KEATING, lawyer; b. Los Angeles, Aug. 27, 1910; s. John A. and Elvira (Keating) F.; A.B., U. So. Calif., 1933, M.A., 1934, LL.B., 1939; m. Gertrude Ingli, Apr. 26, 1947; children—Andrea Marie, Andrew Keating, Christopher, DruAnne, Angele. Admitted to Calif. bar, 1946; with firm Dockweiler & Dockweiler, Los Angeles, 1946; with Los Angeles Soap Co., 1942, chmn. bd., 1956, also dir.; with White King Soap Co., Los Angeles, 1947, pres., 1955, also dir.; pres., dir. Calif. Rendering Co., 1947-62, chmn. bd., 1962-66; v.p., sec. Forthmann Estate Co., 1950-74, pres., 1974. Served from 1st lt. to capt. USAAF, 1942-46. Decorated knight comdr. Equestrian Order of Holy Sepulchre of Jerusalem. Mem. Am., Calif., Los Angeles bar assns., Soap and Detergent Assn. (v.p. Western div. 1954-58, 61-65, nat. pres. 1958-61), So. Calif. Wine and Food Soc. Clubs: Los Angeles Country, California (Los Angeles), Chevaliers du Tastevin. Home: 913 N Roxbury Dr Beverly Hills CA 90210 Office: PO Box 2198 TA Los Angeles CA 90051

FORWARD, ROBERT L(ULL), physicist, consultant; b. Geneva, N.Y., Aug. 15, 1932; s. Robert Torrey and Mildred (Lull) F.; m. Martha Neil Dodson, Aug. 29, 1954; children—Robert Dodson, Mary Lois, Julie Elizabeth, Eve Laurel. B.S. in Physics, U. Md., Ph.D., 1965; M.S. in Applied Physics, UCLA, 1958. With Hughes Aircraft Co., 1956—, assoc. mgr., theoretical studies dept., 1966-67; mgr. exploratory studies dept., 1967-74, sr. scientist, 1974—; popular sci. writer and lecturer. Served to capt. USAF, 1954-56. Hughes Masters and Doctoral fellow, 1956-62. Fellow AIAA (assoc.), Brit. Interplanetary Soc.; mem. Am. Phys. Soc., Am. Geophys. Union, IEEE (sr. mem.), Am. Astronautical Soc. (sr.), Sigma Xi, Sigma Pi Sigma. Author, science fiction: Dragon's Egg, 1981; Rocheworld, 1983; contbr. articles to profl. jours. Builder 1st gravitational radiation antenna; patentee in field. Home: 34 Carriage Sq Oxnard CA 93030 Office: Hughes Research 3011 Malibu Canyon Rd Malibu CA 90265

FORWOOD, MARGARET RANDALL, editor; b. Chgo.; d. Roy Oscar and Clara Edwards Randall; student U. Chgo.; grad. Goodman Sch. Theatre, Chgo.; m. Harris McAlpine Forwood. Actress summer stock and on Broadway, Paramount Studios; mem. editorial staff Let's Live Mag., Los Angeles, 1975-78; asso. editor Bestways Mag., Carson City, Nev., 1978-83; writer hist. articles Port Townsend (Wash.) Leader, 1967-69, contbr. to Irving Wallace's People's Almanac, 1978. Mem. Actors Equity, Actors Fund Am. (life).

FOSCANTE, RAYMOND EUGENE, chemical company executive; b. N.Y.C., Mar. 24, 1942; s. Carl Francis and Hazel Frances (Stapleton) F.; m. Elaine Marguerite Perry, Dec. 5 1964; children—James R., Aimee R. B.S., Manhattan Coll., 1962; M.S., Seton Hall U., 1965, Ph.D., 1966; J.D., U. Mo., 1975. Sr. research chemist, head organic and polymer chemistry sect. Midwest Research Inst., Kansas City, Mo., 1971-75; dir. corp. research and devel. Ameron Inc., Brea, Calif., 1975-81, v.p. internat. tech. ops., 1981—. Served to capt. USAF, 1966-69, to maj. USAFR, 1970-75. Mem. Am. Chem. Soc., N.Y. Acad. Scis., Research Soc. Am. Republican. Contbr. articles to profl. jours; patentee in field. Home: 20547 Manzanita Ave Yorba Linda CA 92686 Office: 201 N Berry St Brea CA 92621

FOSSEEN, NEAL RANDOLPH, banker, mayor; b. Yakima, Wash., Nov. 27, 1908; s. Arthur Benjamin and Florence (Neal) F.; A.B., U. Wash., 1930; LL.D., Whitworth Coll., 1967; m. Helen Witherspoon, Sept. 26, 1936; children—Neal Randolph, William Roger. Laborer, Wash. Brick, Lime & Sewer Pipe Co., 1923-32, v.p., 1932-38; pres. Wash. Brick & Lime Co., 1938; chmn. bd. emeritus Old Nat. Bancorp., dir., 1959-78; pres. 420 Investment Co. Mayor, City of Spokane, 1960-67, mayor emeritus, 1967—. Past chmn. adv. bd. Wash. State Inst. Tech.; emeritus mem. adv. bd. Wash. State Coll. Engring., U. Wash. Grad. Sch. Bus.; hon. trustee St. Luke's Hosp.; hon. regent, past chmn. Gonzaga U.; bd. dirs. Pacific Sci. Found., 1970-73, Deaconess Hosp. Found., Mountain States Legal Found. Served as lt. col. USMCR, 1942-45; now col. Res. (ret.). Recipient USMC Non Sibi, Sed Patriae award, Boy Scouts Am. Disting. Eagle, Silver Beaver, Silver Antelope awards; named hon. citizen of Nishinomiya (Japan). Mem. Assn. Wash. Bus. (past pres.), Spokane-Nishinomiya Sister City Soc. (pres. 1968-78, pres. emeritus, 1978—), N.W. Srs. Golf Assn. (gov.). Clubs: Balboa Club de Mazatlan (Mexico); Spokane, Spokane Country, University. Home: W

1002 Riverside St Spokane WA 99201 Office: Old Nat Bank Bldg Spokane WA 99201

FOSTER, ARTHUR LEE, psychologist; b. Seattle, May 7, 1926; s. Robert Kinsman and Myrta (Annis) F.; B.S., Wash. State U., 1951; M.S., U. Houston, 1954, Ph.D., 1956; m. Margaret Eleanor Slater, Aug. 15, 1953; children—Nancy Carol, Gregory Allen, Margo Michelle. Psychologist dept. neuropsychiatry Parkland Hosp., Dallas, 1955; sr. psychologist Utah State Hosp., 1956-58; chief psychologist Santa Clara County, Calif., 1959-62; pvt. practice psychology, Los Gatos, Calif., 1963-75; dir. Phoenix Inst., Los Gatos, 1976—; vis. lectr. U. Santa Clara. Served with USAF, 1944-46. Mem. Am. Psychol. Assn., Calif. Psychol. Assn. Developer The Sexual Compatibility Test, 1974; columnist, writer in field; contbr. articles to profl. jours. Office: 248 Blossom Hill Rd Los Gatos CA 95030

FOSTER, CHARLES THOMAS, elementary educator; b. Fremont, Ohio, Apr. 17, 1921; s. Charles Lincoln and Lucy Elizabeth (Rooney) F.; m. Evelyn May Foster, Jan. 1, 1942; children—Charles Thomas, Stephanie. B.G.E., U. Nebr., 1964; M.A., Chapman Coll., 1974. Cert. elem., secondary, and coll. tchr., Calif. Asst. to sales mgr. Henkel Clauss Co., Fremont, Ohio, 1945-50; commd. U.S. Air Force, 1950, advanced through grades to lt. col., 1964, ret., 1967; tchr. Los Padres Elem. Sch., Lompoc, Calif., 1968—. Mem. exec. bd. PTA, 1974-75; mem. site com. Calif. Sch. Improvement Program, 1974-75; mem. instructional evaluation panel Curriculum Devel. & Supplemental Materials Commn. of Calif. State Bd. Edn., 1978-79. Served to capt., U.S. Army, 1942-45. Decorated Bronze Star, Army Commendation medal, Air Force Commendation medal with two oak leaf clusters; Recipient Hon. Service award PTA. Mem. Air Force Assn., Ret. Officers Assn. (scholarship com. 1979-83), PTA. Republican. Lutheran. Clubs: Officers, Thousand Trails, Elks. Home: 2155 Fallen Leaf Dr Santa Maria CA 93455 Office: Los Padres Elem Sch Mountain View Blvd Lompoc CA 93436

FOSTER, DALE GIBSON, surgeon; b. Los Angeles, Jan. 22, 1920; s. Chester Fremont and Augusta Belle (White) F.; student U. Calif. at Los Angeles, 1937-40; A.B. summa cum laude, U. Calif. at Berkeley, 1941; M.D., U. Calif. at San Francisco, 1943; m. Florence Barford, July 20, 1941; children—Dennis George, Judith Anne (Mrs. Jerry Hendrix). Intern, Los Angeles County Gen. Hosp., 1943-44, Johns Hopkins Hosp., 1946-47; asst. resident in gen. surgery Johns Hopkins Hosp., 1947-48, U. Calif. at San Francisco Hosp., 1948-49; resident in surgery San Francisco City, County Hosp., 1950-51, City of Hope Med. Center, Duarte, Calif., 1958-59, asst. oncologic, gen. surgery, 1962-63; attending physician Los Angeles County Gen. Hosp., 1963-66; chief surgery, med. dir. Sakbayeme Hosp., EDEA, Cameroun, West Africa, 1952-71; surgeon So. Calif. Permanente Med. Group Kaiser Found. Hosp., Bellflower, Calif., 1965-67, 1971—; asst. clin. prof. surgery U. Calif. at Irvine, 1966-73. Served to capt. M.C., AUS, 1944-46. Recipient Gold Headed Cane award U. Calif. at San Francisco, 1943. Diplomate Am. Bd. Surgery. Fellow A.C.S., Internat. Coll. Surgeons, Ordre Nationale Des Medecins, Ordre Des Medecins Du Cameroun; mem. A.M.A., Howard C. Naffziger Surg. Soc., Christian Med. Soc., Am. Sci. Affiliation, Phi Beta Kappa, Sigma Xi, Alpha Omega Alpha, Alpha Gamma Omega. Republican. Presbyn. (ruling elder). Club: Pine Mountain (Frazier Park, Cal.). Contbr. to med. books, articles to profl. jours., religious mags. Home: 1223 S Gaymont St Anaheim CA 92804 Office: 9100 E Rosecrans Ave Bellflower CA 90706

FOSTER, DAVID RAMSEY, former soap company executive; b. London, Eng., May 24, 1920 (parents Am. citizens); s. Robert Bagley and Josephine (Ramsey) F.; student econs. Gonville and Caius Coll., Cambridge (Eng.) U., 1938; m. Anne Firth, Aug. 2, 1957; children—Sarah, Victoria. With Colgate-Palmolive Co. and affiliates, 1946-79, v.p., gen. mgr. Europe, Colgate Palmolive Internat., 1961-65, v.p., gen. mgr. household products div. parent co., N.Y.C., 1965-68, exec. v.p., 1968-70, pres., 1970-75, chief exec. officer, 1971-79, chmn., 1975-79. Trustee, Woman's Sport Found., San Francisco; founding sponsor World Golf Hall of Fame; bd. govs. Desert Hosp., Palm Springs. Served as lt. comdr. Royal Naval Vol. Res., 1940-46. Decorated Disting. Service Order, D.S.C. with bar, Mentioned in Despatches (2); recipient numerous awards. Mem. Soc. Mayflower Descs. Clubs: Am. (London); Hawks (Cambridge U.); Royal Ancient Golf (St. Andrews, Scotland); Royal St. Georges Golf, Royal Cinque Ports Golf (life), Sunningdale Golf, Swinley Forest Golf (U.K.); Sankaty Head Golf; Racquet and Tennis (N.Y.C.) Baltusrol Golf, Mission Hills Country. Contbr. to Exec. Golfer. Home: 540 Desert West Dr Rancho Mirage CA 92270 also High Time Wauwinet Nantucket MA 02554

FOSTER, DONALD ISLE, art dealer; b. Seattle, July 9, 1925; s. Harry Ralph and Vera (Isle) F.; A.B., Stanford U., 1947, M.B.A., 1949. Dir. exhbns. Seattle World's Fair, 1960-64; gen. mgr. Seattle Repertory Theatre, Seattle, 1964-70; project dir. Ford Found., N.Y.C., 1970-73, cons. div. humanities and arts, 1970-74; art dealer, owner Foster/White Gallery, Seattle, 1973—. Founding mem. Seattle Arts Commn., 1971; bd. dirs. Seattle Repertory Theatre, Seattle Symphony Orch. Served with U.S. Army, 1943. Club: Rainier (Seattle). Home: 1915 10th Ave E Seattle WA 98102 Office: Foster/White Gallery 311 1/2 Occidental St S Seattle WA 98104

FOSTER, DUDLEY EDWARDS, JR., musician, educator; b. Orange, N.J., Oct. 5, 1935; s. Dudley Edwards and Margaret (DePoy) F.; student Occidental Coll., 1953-56; A.B., UCLA, 1957, M.A., 1958; postgrad. U. So. Calif., 1961-73. Lectr. music Immaculate Heart Coll., Los Angeles, 1960-63; dir. music Holy Faith Episcopal Ch., Inglewood, Calif., 1964-67; lectr. music Calif. State U., Los Angeles, 1968-71; assoc. prof. music Los Angeles Mission Coll., 1975-83, prof., 1983—, also chmn. dept. music, 1977—; dir. music First Lutheran Ch., Los Angeles, 1968-72; organist, pianist, harpsichordist; numerous recitals; composer O Sacrum Convivium for Trumpet and Organ, 1973, Passacaglia for Brass Instruments, 1969, Introduction, Arioso & Fugue for Cello and Piano, 1974. Fellow Trinity Coll. Music, London, 1960. Mem. Am. Guild Organists, Am. Musicol. Soc., Town Hall Calif., Los Angeles Coll. Tchrs. Assn. (pres. Mission Coll. chpt. 1976-77, v.p., exec. com. 1982—), Mediaeval Acad. Am. Republican. Anglican. Office: Dept Music Los Angeles Mission Coll 1101 San Fernando Rd San Fernando CA 91340

FOSTER, HAROLD DOUGLAS, geographer, educator; b. Tunstall, Eng., Jan. 9, 1943; s. Arthur Frederick and Alison Skirving (Pratt) F.; B.Sc., U. London, 1964, Ph.D., 1968; m. Lorelei Ann Hairsine, July 22, 1964. Asst. prof. U. Victoria, B.C., Can., 1968-72, assoc. prof. geography, 1972-81, prof., 1981—; cons. UN, Ont. and B.C. Provincial Govt., Canadian Fed. Govt. Mem. Canadian (chmn. Western div. 1969-70), Am. assns. geographers, Inst. Brit. Geographers, Geog. Assn., Am. Geophys. Union, N.Y. Acad. Scis. Club: Explorers. Editor: Western Geog. Series, 1969—; The Geographer and Society; Resources, Recreation and Research; Geographica; Victoria: Physical Environment and Development; Images of Canadian Futures; Analysis of the United States Experience in Modifying Land Use to Conserve Energy; United States Policies to Accelerate the Growth of Solar Manufacturing; Solar Home Heating in Canada: Problems and Prospects; Disaster Planning: The Preservation of Life and Property. Author numerous articles on applied phys. geography, solar energy, disaster planning and conservation. Home: 2625 Burdick Ave Victoria BC V8R 3L8 Canada

FOSTER, JEANETTE YVONNE, writer, photographer; b. Bethesda, Md., Apr. 28, 1951; d. Mark Coleman and Chris (Silveria) F. B.A. in Communication and Pub. Policy, U. Calif.-Berkeley, 1972. Free-lance writer-photographer, 1974—; contbr. articles, photos to numerous mags. including Time, Rolling Stone, Esquire, Runner's World, Women's Sports; contbr. photos to Los Angeles Times, AP, ABC-TV news and sports, others; media coordinator Ironman Triathlon. Recipient Young Career Women of Yr. award Bus. and Profl. Women, 1979. Home and Office: PO Box 448 Haiku HI 96708

FOSTER, KEITH LEROY, museum curator; b. Bell, Calif., Mar. 2, 1942; s. Hugh Foster and Myrna G. (Kelley) Foster McCracken; m. Christina D. Goodale, Mar. 21, 1980; children—Brian Daniel, Stephen Andrew. B.A., Calif. State Poly. U.-Pomona, 1974; M.A., U Calif.-Riverside, 1982. Hist. curator Rancho Los Cerritos Mus. and Library, City of Long Beach (Calif.), 1976-82, Rancho Los Alamitos Mus., City of Long Beach, 1977-82; assoc. dir. historic sites div. Long Beach Dept. Library/Mus. Services, City of Long Beach, 1977—. Served with UNSR, 1961-67. Mem. Am. Assn. State and Local History, Am. Assn. Museums, Western Museums Conf. Democrat. Office: 6400 Bixby Hill Rd Long Beach CA 90815

FOSTER, MARY FRAZER (LECRON), anthropologist; b. Des Moines, Feb. 1, 1914; d. James and Helen (Cowles) LeCron; B.A., Northwestern U., 1936; Ph.D., U. Calif., Berkeley, 1965; m. George McClelland Foster, Jan. 6, 1938; children—Jeremy, Melissa Foster Bowerman. Research asso. dept. anthropology U. Calif., Berkeley, 1955-57, 75—; lectr. in anthropology Calif. State U., Hayward, 1966-75; mem. faculty Fromm Inst. Lifelong Learning, U. San Francisco, 1980. Fellow Am. Anthropol. Assn.; mem. Linguistic Soc. Am., Internat. Linguistic Assn., Southwestern Anthrop. Assn., AAAS, Soc. Woman Geographers. Democrat. Author: (with George M. Foster) Sierra Popoluca Speech, 1948; The Tarascan Language, 1969; editor: (with Stanley H. Brandes) Symbol As Sense: New Approaches to the Analysis of Meaning, 1980. Home: 790 San Luis Rd Berkeley CA 94707

FOSTER, NORMAN HOLLAND, geologist; b. Iowa City, Iowa, Oct. 2, 1934; s. Holland and Dora Lucinda (Ransom) F.; B.A., U. Iowa, 1957, M.S., 1960; Ph.D., U. Kans., 1963; m. Janet Lee Grecian, Mar. 25, 1956; children—Kimberly Ann, Stephen Norman. Instr. geology U. Iowa, 1958-60, U. Kans., 1960-62; sr. geologist, geol. specialist, exploration team supr. Sinclair Oil Corp. and Atlantic Richfield Co., Casper, Wyo., also Denver, 1962-69; dist. geologist Trend Exploration Ltd., 1969-72, v.p., 1972-74; v.p. exploration geology Filon Exploration, Denver, 1974-79, dir., 1977-79; ind. geologist, 1979—; guest lectr. geology Colo. Sch. Mines, 1972—, U. Colo., 1972—, U. Iowa, 1975—, U. Kans., 1975—. Served to capt., inf. AUS, 1957. Recipient Haworth Distinguished Alumni award dept. geology U. Kans., 1977. Fellow Geol. Soc. Am.; mem. Am. Assn. Petroleum Geologists (mem. ho. of dels. 1972-75, 79—, disting. lectr. 1976-77, pres. Rocky Mountain sect. 1979-80, nat. treas. 1982-84, A.I. Levorsen award 1980), Rocky Mountain Assn. Geologists (sec. 1970, 1st. v.p. 1974, pres. 1977, best paper award 1975, Explorer of Yr. award 1980, Disting. Service award 1981), Soc. Econ. Paleontologists and Mineralogists, Am. Inst. Profl. Geologists, Colo. Sci. Soc., Houston Geol. Soc., Sigma Xi, Sigma Gamma Epsilon. Republican. Presbyn. Asso. editor Guidebook to Geology and Energy Resources of Piceance Basin, Colorado, 1974. Asso. editor Mountain Geologist, 1967-68, 71—, editor, 1968-70. Contbr. papers on geology to profl. publs.

FOSTER, PATRICIA WHITE, printing company executive; b. Philadelphia, Miss., Nov. 4, 1940; d. Archie D. and Evalena (Agent) White; m. Cecil Winthrop Foster, Dec. 24, 1975; 1 dau., Robin Renee. Student U.S.C. Owner, operator R & R Liquor Store, Columbia, S.C., 1972-73, co-owner, mgr. Foster Printing Co., Denver, 1976—. Troop leader Girl Scouts U.S.A.; vol. Charity Hosp. children's wing; campaign worker Republican Party; active fund drives Nat. Cancer Soc., Nat. Heart Assn.; dir. Teens Acting Group; church sch. tchr. Baptist. Office: 1400 Grove St Denver CO 80204

FOSTER, PAUL D., surgeon; b. Cedar Rapids, Ia., Jan. 12, 1934; s. Caryll S. and Hermina (Dorweiler) F.; B.A., U. Ia., 1955, M.D., 1958; m. Sara L. Mavis, Aug. 27, 1957; children—Gregory, Michael. Intern, San Bernardino (Calif.) County Hosp., 1958-59; resident in surgery U. Ia., Iowa City, 1959-63; cons. in surgery VA Hosp.- White City, Ore., 1968—, practice medicine, specializing in surgery, Medford, Ore., 1965—; asst. clin. prof. surgery U. Ore. Med. Sch., Portland, 1973—; mem. staff Providence Hosp., Medford, Ore., 1966—, chief of staff, 1977—; mem. staff Rogue Valley Meml. Hosp., Medford, Oreg., 1966—; dir., treas. Rogue Valley Physicians Service, 1975-76, v.p., 1977, pres., 1978. Served with M.C., USAF, 1963-65. Decorated Air Force Commendation Medal; diplomate Am. Bd. Surgery. Fellow A.C.S. (sec.-treas. Oreg. chpt. 1967-71, pres. 1973-74; mem. AMA, Oreg. Med. Assn., Portland Surg. Soc., Jackson County Med. Soc. (pres. 1980), Phi Beta Kappa, Alpha Omega Alpha. Home: 6069 Hughes Rd Medford OR 97501 Office: 1025 E Main St Medford OR 97501

FOSTER, RICHARD MICHAEL, agricultural education educator; b. Council Bluffs, Iowa, Oct. 11, 1950; s. Richard Edward and Helen Jane (Mass) F.; m. Cheryl Kaye Barry, May 30, 1970. B.S. in Agrl. Edn., Iowa State U., 1972, M.S., 1974, Ph.D., 1978. Tchr. vocat. agr. Guttenberg (Iowa) High Sch., 1972-74, Clarinda (Iowa) High Sch., 1974-76; instr. agrl. edn. Iowa State U., Ames, 1976-78; asst. prof. agrl. edn. U. Idaho, Moscow, 1978-82, assoc. prof., 1982-83; assoc. prof. agrl. edn. U. Nebr., Lincoln, 1983—; assessor internat. agrl. needs, Taiwan, Philippines, Indonesia, Thailand; trustee Idaho Future Farmers Am. Found.; cons. Nat. Future Farmers Am. Bd. Dirs.; ednl. evaluator sch. dists. in Idaho. Recipient Disting. Service award Idaho Future Farmers Am. Assn., 1983, Hon. State Farmer degree, 1982; Outstanding Counselor award Coll. Agr., U. Idaho, 1983. Mem. Am. Assn. Tchr. Educators in Agr., Am. Vocat. Edn. Research Assn., Nat. Vocat. Agr. Tchrs. Assn., Am. Vocat. Assn., Idaho Vocat. Assn., Gamma Sigma Delta, Phi Delta Kappa. Methodist. Author curriculum and instructional materials; contbr. articles to profl. jours. Office: 305 Ag Hall U Nebr Lincoln NE 68503

FOSTER, ROBERT LEE, retired aerospace company executive, realtor; b. Murphysboro, Ill., Feb. 7, 1922; s. Moses Franklin and Ethel Gladys (Hendrickson) F.; m. Antoinette Tomlin Hayne, June 12, 1950 (div. 1981); children—Robert Lee, Jr., Sarah Amanda, William Ashley. Student, Tulane U., 1939-40; student Washington U., St. Louis, 1940; B.S. in Elec. Engring., Ga. Inst. Tech., 1952. With McDonnell Aircraft Co., St. Louis, 1953, sr. engr., F101 Fighter Airplane, 1953-57; group engr. advanced design, Project Mercury, Cape Kennedy, Fla., 1958-59, sr. group engr., 1959-60, engring. mgr., 1960-65, ops. mgr. Project Gemini, 1965-67; base mgr. McDonnell Astronautics Co., Vandenberg AFB, Calif., 1967-68; dep. dir. McDonnell Douglas Thor-Delta project, Vandenberg Test Center, 1968, dir. test center, 1969-74, guidance systems mgr., Huntington Beach, Calif., 1975-79. Served with U.S. Army, 1942-43, to capt., 1943-50, to maj., NG, 1950-59. Decorated Am. Campaign medal, European African Middle Eastern Campaign medal with two battle stars, WW II Victory medal. Mem. Nat. Mgmt. Assn., Phi Kappa Phi. Republican. Presbyterian. Club: Rotary of Santa Ynez Valley (Solvang, Calif.) Home: 2831 Quail Valley Rd Solvang CA 93463 Office: 435 1st St Suite 23 Solvang CA 93463

FOSTER, RODNEY PATRICK, personnel executive; b. San Antonio, Apr. 30, 1951; s. Cecil Glenn and Margaret Mary (Frazar) F.; m. Lynell Porritt, June 6, 1974; children—Alisa, Paul, Melinda. B.A. cum laude, Brighan Young U., 1974. Missionary to Norway, 1970-72; adminstrv. asst. First Presidency's Office, Mormon Ch., Salt Lake City, 1974-80, mgr. tng. and pre-dedication services, Temple Dept., 1980—. Mem. Am. Soc. Tng. and Devel. Republican. Office: 50 E North Temple Salt Lake City UT 84150

FOSTER, WILLIAM WEST, real estate appraising and consulting company executive; b. Fredericksburg, Va., Apr. 23, 1941; s. Clayton Holliday and Jane Bradley (West) F.; m. Carolyn Burns, June 18, 1966; children—Valerie Ann, Courtney Burns. B.S. in Gen. Bus., Colo. State U., Ft. Collins, 1964, M.S. in Econs., 1968. Accredited rural appraiser Am. Soc. Farm Mgrs. and Rural Appraisers. Pres., Foster Tire Ctr., Inc., Fredericksburg, 1968-75; owner Foster Valuation Co., Greeley, Colo., 1976—. Served to capt. U.S. Army, 1965-67. Colo. State U. grantee, 1968. Mem. Am. Inst. Real Estate Appraisers (dir. Colo. chpt. 22, nat. chmn. rural property com. div. course adminstrn.), Am. Soc. Real Estate Appraisers. Republican. Congregationalist. Clubs: Rotary, Weld County Ducks Unltd. (past. chmn. com.). Home: 2508 W 20th St Rd Greeley CO 80631 Office: 1750 25th Ave Suite 303 Greeley CO 80631

FOSTER-ROSS, CONNIE SUE, public relations specialist; b. Topeka, May 7, 1947; d. Norlan Wilson and Ruth Eileen (Leech) Foster; m. David Eugene Ross, June 9, 1968; 1 son, Sean David. B.A. summa cum laude in English, Washburn U., 1969; postgrad. U. Kans., 1970-71. Tchr. Topeka Pub. Schs., 1969-71; reporter Copley Pub., Wheaton, Ill., 1977-78; coordinator Read-a-thon, Ill. Multiple Sclerosis Soc., Chgo., 1978-79; dir. communications Salt Lake Area C. of C., 1981-82; dir. investor communications Gulf Energy Corp., Salt Lake City, 1982—. Mem. exec. bd. Salt Lake City Sch. Vols.; chmn. Salt Lake Adopt-a-Sch. Program; mem. Utah Commn. Ednl. Excellence. Mem. Internat. Assn. Bus. Communicators, Pub. Relations Soc. Am., Utah Council Econ. Edn. (bd. dirs.). Methodist. Office: 505 E 200 South Salt Lake City UT 84111

FOUAD, MOHAMED TAHER AHMED, pharms. lab. exec.; b. Cairo, Sept. 21, 1921; s. Ahmed Fouad El-Sharif and Zakia Noor; came to U.S., 1961, naturalized, 1976; B.V.Sc., Cairo U., 1946; M.Sc., Reading U. (Eng.), 1952; Ph.D., Cornell U., 1964; m. Karen S. Peck, Feb. 29, 1968; children—Gameil Taher, Karima Karen, Rheda Omar. Lectr., Cairo U., 1952-54; head research Cairo Vet. Research Inst., 1954-61; research asst. Cornell U., Ithaca, N.Y., 1961-64; postdoctoral fellow Kans. U. Med. Center, Kansas City, 1964-67; with nat. labs. Am. Hoechst, Kansas City, Kans., 1967-70; v.p. Intermountain Labs., Inc., founder Kelatron Pharm. Div., Ogden, Utah, 1974—; founder, pres., chmn. bd. Biotron Labs., Inc., Odgen, 1979—. Mem. Soc. Microbiology (Eng.), AVMA, Am. Soc. Microbiology, AAAS, Internat. Coll. Applied Nutrition (sec.-treas.), N.Y. Acad. Scis. Contbr. sci. articles to Am., Brit., Egyptian and German profl. jours.; assoc. editor Jour. Applied Nutrition, 1976-79, editor-in-chief, 1979—; inventor parainfluenza vaccine, 1970; developer new technique of preparing mineral chelates, 1971, 79. Home: 2594 E Pinewood Ln Layton UT 84041 Office: 750N 1250W Centerville UT 84014

FOULDS, JON MARQUIS, city public works executive; b. San Antonio, Aug. 2, 1938; s. Emmett Lee and N. Margaret (Terry) F.; m. Joyce Annette Huber, Sept. 1, 1961 (div.); 1 son, Charles Edward. B.S., Southwest Tex. State U., 1960, M.A., 1961; M.S. N.Mex. State U., 1970. Registered profl. engr., N.Mex., Del., Pa. Mem. faculty chemistry dept. U. Tex.-El Paso, 1963-66; civil engr. various cons. firms, 1971-81; dir. City of Alamogordo (N.Mex.) Dept. Pub. Works, 1981—. Named col., a.d.c. staff N.Mex. Gov. Mem. Am. Water Works Assn., Am. Pub. Works Assn., Alamogordo C. of C., Alpha Chi. Democrat. Baptist. Contbr. chem. abstracts to profl. lit. Office: City of Alamogordo Dept Pub Works 511 10th St Alamogordo NM 88310

FOUNTAIN, FREEMAN PERCIVAL, physician; b. Hawley, Minn., Apr. 16, 1921; s. Percival Freeman and Chloie May (Ritteman) F.; B.A., Stanford, 1943; B.S., U. N.D., 1949; M.D., U. Colo., 1951, M.S., 1956; m. Jerrlyn McGraw, June 10, 1951; children—Diana, David, Daniel. Intern, Fitzsimmons Army Hosp., Denver, 1951-52; resident in phys. medicine and rehab. U. Colo. Med. Center, 1953-56; practice medicine specializing in phys. medicine and rehab., 1977—; asst. prof. phys. medicine and rehab. U. Louisville, 1956-58, U. Colo., 1958-60; med. dir. dept. rehab. medicine Lovelace Clinic, Albuquerque, 1960-66; asso. med. dir. Rehab. Inst. Phoenix, 1966-70. Served with USNR, 1942-46; USAR, 1951-53. Certified Am. Bd. Physical Medicine and Rehab., Am. Assn. Electromyography and Electrodiagnosis; diplomate Nat. Bd. Med. Examiners. Fellow Am. Acad. Phys. Medicine and Rehab., Am. Congress Rehab. Medicine, Coll. Sports Medicine. Lutheran. Contbr. articles to med. jours. Home: 11618 N Sundown Ave Scottsdale AZ 85260 Office: 7331 E Osborn Dr Scottsdale AZ 85251

FOUNTAIN, STEVEN SCOTT, orthopedic surgeon; b. Hutchinson, Kans., Apr. 25, 1940; s. Gerald Leon and Maybelle Marjorie (Sallee) F.; B.A., U. Kans., 1962; M.D., U. Kans. Sch. Medicine, 1966; m. Marcia Lynn Harmon, Aug. 26, 1962; children—Stephanie Renee, Dionee Michele. Intern, Bethany Hosp., Kansas City, Kans., 1966-79; resident Univ. Calif. Hosp., San Francisco, 1971-74; hon. lectr. orthopedic surgery, Hong Kong, 1974-75; asst. chief orthopedic surger Santa Clara Valley Med. Center, San Jose, Calif., 1975-79, chief dept. orthopedic surgery, 1979—; asst. prof. surgery Stanford Univ. Med. Center, Palo Alto, Calif., 1975—; co-dir. No. Calif. Spinal Injury Center, San Jose, 1979-80; mem staff Los Gatos Community, Good Samaritan, El Camino hosps., cons. orthopedic surgery VA Hosp., Palo Alto, 1975—. Served with M.C., U.S. Army, 1967-70. Postgrad. fellow Am. sect. Internat. Coll. Surgeons, Fellow A.C.S.; mem. Am. Acad. Orthopedic Surgeons, AMA, Calif. Med. Assn., Santa Clara County Med. Soc., Santa Clara Valley Orthopedic Club, Am. Spinal Injury Assn. Contbr. articles to profl. jours. Office: 777 Pollard Rd Suite 14 Los Gatos CA 95030

FOUNTAINE, BEECHER CASSELLS, real estate co. exec.; b. Atlanta, Feb. 28, 1927; d. Thomas Beecher and Bertha M. (Jackson) Travis; cert. Aristo Bus. Coll., N.Y.C., 1950; student Freedman's Hosp. Sch. Nursing, 1961-63; B.S., D.C. Tchrs. Coll., 1968, postgrad. 1969; now student N.Y. Sch. Interior Design; m. Shepard Fountaine, Jr., May 20, 1972. Ednl. media specialist D.C. Public Schs., 1968-69; dir. health careers program Nat. Med. Assn., 1969-72; cons. Office of Health Manpower HEW, NIH, 1972-74; realtor asso., pres. Bee Tee Enterprises, Sacramento, 1974—; del. White House Conf. on Poverty; mem. Pres. Com. on Health Edn., White House Conf. on the Aged. Mem. AAUW, Council Adminstrv. Women in Edn., Calif. Assn. Realtors, Sacramento Bd. Realtors, Nat. Urban League, NAACP, Nat. Med. Assn., A-Capitol Med. Soc., Nat. Council Negro Women, Sacramento Symphony League, Alpha Kappa Alpha. Author: Health Careers Guide. Democrat. Methodist. Clubs: Sacramento Democratics Womens, Nat. Democratic Womens, Links, Comstock. Office: 2720 Capitol Ave Suite 200 Sacramento CA 95816

FOURNIER, R(AYMOND) E(MILE) KEITH, geneticist; b. Attleboro, Mass., July 26, 1949; s. Roland Emile and Marguerite Claire (Fortier) F. B.S. in Chemistry, Providence Coll., 1971; Ph.D. in Biochemistry, Princeton U., 1974. Research fellow biology and human genetics Yale U., 1975-78; asst. prof. dept. microbiology and Comprehensive Cancer Center, U. So. Calif., 1978—; adj. faculty W. Alton Jones Cell Sci. Center, Lake Placid, N.Y. Recipient faculty research award Am. Cancer Soc., 1980; Leukemia Soc. Am. fellow, 1975-77; NIH Research grantee, 1979—; R.E. Goldberg Meml. cancer research grantee, 1980. Mem. AAAS, Sigma Xi. Contbr. articles to sci. jours. Office: Norris Cancer Research Inst 1441 Eastlake Ave Los Angeles CA 90031

FOUSHI, NINA ROSE, pharmacist; b. Chicago Heights, Ill., May 8, 1935; d. George G. and Mary Elizabeth (Cuda) F.; B.S. in Pharmacy, U. Ill., 1958. Chief pharmacist South Suburban Hosp., Hazel Crest, Ill., 1960-68; clin. pharmacist Maricopa Med. Center, Phoenix, 1969-76, chief pharmacist, 1976—. Recipient Appreciation award, South Suburban Pharmacy Assn., 1964. Mem. Am., Ill. pharmacy assns., Am. Soc. Hosp. Pharmacists, Ariz. Soc. Hosp. Pharmacists, Chgo. Retail Druggists Assn., Fedn. Internat. Pharmaceutique, Lambda Kappa Sigma, Phoenix Fine Arts Assn. Roman Catholic. Home: 3334 E Turney Ave Phoenix AZ 85018 Office: 2601 E Roosevelt St Phoenix AZ 85008

FOWLER, BETTY JANMAE, dance co. dir., editor; b. Chgo., May 23, 1925; d. Harry and Mary (Jacques) Markin; student Art Inst., Chgo., 1937-39, Stratton Bus. Coll., Chgo., 1942-43, Columbia U., 1945-47; 1 dau., Sherry Mareth Connors. Mem. public relations dept. Girl Scouts U.S.A., N.Y.C., 1961-63; adminstrv. asst. to editor-in-chief Scholastic Mags., N.Y.C., 1963-68; adminstrv. dir. Leonard Fowler Dancers, Fowler Sch. Classical Ballet, Inc., N.Y.C., 1959-78, tchr. ballet, 1959-61; editor Bulletin, Kiwanis weekly publ., Spokane, Wash., 1978-82, also adminstrv. sec. Kiwanis Club; instr. Spokane Falls Community Coll., 1978. Cert. metabolic technician Internat. Health Inst. Address: N 7105 G St Spokane WA 99208

FOWLER, CHARLES WINSOR, large mammal population dynamicist; b. Loup City, Nebr., Apr. 21, 1941; s. Ervon Winsor and Merna Dorothy (Kee) F.; B.A., Hastings (Nebr.) Coll., 1963; M.S., U. Wash.-Seattle, 1966, Ph.D., 1973; m. Jean Forsyth, June 10, 1967; 1 dau., Catherine Marie. Instr., San Jose (Calif.) State U., 1966-67; with Peace Corps, prof. La Universidad Javeriana, Bogota, Columbia, 1967-69; research asst. prof. Utah State U., Logan, 1973-79; mgr. for seal research program Nat. Marine Mammal Lab., Seattle, 1979—; cons. FAO (Africa), U.S. Marine Mammal Commn.; prin. investigator for prodn. Internat. Conf. on Population Dynamics of Large Mammals, 1978. Mem. Ecol. Soc. Am., AAAS, Am. Inst. Biol. Scis. Unitarian. Editor: (with T.D. Smith) Dynamics of Large Mammal Populations, 1982. Contbr. numerous articles and papers to profl. jours. Office: Nat Marine Mammal Lab Bldg 32 7600 Sand Point Way NE Seattle WA 98115

FOWLER, DONALD OWEN, architect; b. Honolulu, Dec. 31, 1931; s. Owen George and Adele Irene (Seabury) F.; m. Gloria Hmurcik, Aug. 2, 1980; 1 son, Nicholas Seabury. B.A. in Architecture, U. Calif., Berkeley, 1961. Architect, John Carl Warnecke & Assos., Hawaii, 1961-65, Donald O. Fowler, AIA, & Assos., Hawaii, 1965-75; urban designer City and County of Honolulu, 1975-80; sr. architect, engr. Hawaiian Telephone G.T.E., Honolulu, 1980—; urban design cons. Registered architect, Hawaii, Calif. Mem. AIA, Phi Gamma Delta. Democrat. Clubs: Outrigger Canoe, Honolulu, Winged Helmet. Home: 4629 Kolohala St Honolulu HI 96816

FOWLER, GEORGE ANDERSON, retired physician; b. Colorado Springs, Apr. 19, 1914; s. George Anderson and Gladys (McConnell) F.; student Downside Sch., nr. Bath, Eng., 1927-32; B.A., Princeton, 1936; M.D. Columbia, 1940; m. Diana Athansia Skouras, June 28, 1944 (dec. Aug. 14, 1982); children—George Anderson, Amanda Skouras Fowler Stimson, Elizabeth Ann. Intern, St. Luke's Hosp., N.Y.C., 1940-41, resident, 1941-47; in pvt. med. practice, Sharon, Conn., 1947-75; mem. surg. staff Sharon Hosp.; surgeon Sharon Clinic. Advisory bd. Sharon office Colonial Bank & Trust Co., Waterbury, Conn. Mem. bd. edn., Sharon, 1952—, mem. bd. finance, 1963-75. Diplomate Am. Bd. Surgery. Fellow A.C.S.; mem. Conn. Soc. Bd. Surgeons, New Eng. Surg. Soc. Democrat. Roman Catholic. Home: Casa Crosselle 803 Camino Atalaya Santa Fe NM 87501

FOWLER, HEDLEY STEWART PETE, mining engineer; b. Nelson, B.C., Can., June 18, 1911; s. Samuel Stewart and Frances Elizabeth (Hedley) F.; m. Catherine Moore, June 23, 1939; children—Kenneth Stewart, Helen Frances Fowler Neville. B.Applied Sci., U. B.C., 1933; postgrad. extension U. Denver, U. Calif.-Berkeley. Mining engr. Cominco Ltd., B.C., Ont., S. Am., 1933-46; gen. supt. Pacific Lime Co., B.C., 1946-48; prodn. mgr. Denver Equipment Co., Colo., 1948-50; gen. supt. to chief site investigator Kaiser Aluminum Co. and Kaiser Engrs., Calif., Nev., India, Ghana, 1951-60; chief engr., dir. research and devel. Mountain Copper Co., Martinez, Calif., 1961-68; chief metallurgist Phillips Petroleum Co., Martinez, 1968-70; partner, exec. job counselor Bernard Haldane Assos., San Francisco, 1971-74; cons. mining and metal. engr., Oakland, Calif., 1974—. Dir., CD, Roseland, B.C., 1941-43; chmn. career guidance com. San Francisco Bay Area Engring. Council, 1973-77. Mem. AIME (rep. to Nat. Council Engring. Examiners, past chmn. San Francisco sect.), Mining and Metall. Soc. Am., ASCE, Canadian Inst. Mining and Metallurgy (life), Nat. Soc. Profl. Engrs., Engrs. Club San Francisco. Republican. Congregationalist. Address: 6633 Colton Blvd Oakland CA 94611

FOWLER, JOHN CHARLES, naval officer, psychologist; b. Hackensack, N.J., June 3, 1945; s. Sterling Edwin and Elizabeth Lou (Hatton) F.; B.A., Hampden-Sydney (Va.) Coll., 1975; M.Ed., James Madison U., Harrisonburg, Va., 1976; Ph.D., U.S. Internat. U., 1980; m. Marie Therese Ann Herndon, July 29, 1972; children—Courtney Marie, Douglas Edwin. Served with U.S. Navy, Vietnam, 1969; psychologist Piedmont Geriatric Hosp., Burkeville, Va., 1976-78; commd. lt. (j.g.) U.S. Navy, 1978, advanced to lt., 1979; clin. psychologist, asst. chief psychologist Naval Drug Rehab. Center, Naval Air Sta., MiraMar, San Diego, 1978-81; clin. psychologist, instr. psychology U.S. Naval Acad., Annapolis, 1981—; instr. psychology Southside Va. Community Coll., Keysville, 1976-78. Decorated Bronze Star, Purple Heart (U.S.); Cross of Gallantry (Vietnam). Fellow Md. Psychol. Assn.; mem. Am. Psychol. Assn. Lutheran. Club: Masons. Home: 123 Groh Ln Annapolis MD 21402 Office: US Naval Acad Annapolis MD 21402

FOWLER, LESLIE R., insurance company executive, state senator; b. St. Louis, June 21, 1924; s. Leslie H. and Sarah Golda (Jarrett) F.; B.S. in Bus., U. Colo., 1948 C.L.U., Am. Coll. Life Underwriters, 1954; m. Wilma Jane Ladegard, Nov. 5, 1945; children—Nancy L. Fowler Denton, Mark L., Martin J. With Northwestern Mut. Life Ins. Co., Boulder, Colo., 1949—, dist. agt., 1951—; mem. Colo. Ho. of Reps., 1966-68; mem. Colo. Senate, 1969—; dir. First Nat. Bank, Boulder. Mem. council City of Boulder, 1966-68; lay leader First Methodist Ch. Boulder. Served with U.S. Navy. Named to Colo. State Golf Hall of Fame. Republican. Clubs: Optimists, Masons, Elks. Office: PO Box 36 Boulder CO 80306

FOWLER, LUMMIE JAMES, record mfg. co. exec.; b. Waterford, Miss.; s. Walter and Lela (Moore) F.; student Los Angeles Conservatory of Music and Arts, U. Chgo. Extension Conservatory, Eubanks Conservatory. Song composer and music pub.; producer comml. mus. recs. Lummtone Records, Los Angeles. Served with USN. Mem. Broadcast Music, Am. Fedn. Musicians. Composer: I Lost My Love in the Big City; Finding a Sweetheart; You Don't Have To; numerous others. Address: PO Box 11121 Los Angeles CA 90011

FOWLER, NATHANIEL EUGENE, ophthalmologist; b. Rochester, N.Y., Dec. 19, 1922; s. John Denison and Lettie (Oliver) F.; student U. Wis., summers 1940, 41, U. Mich., 1940-43; M.D., U. Rochester, 1946; postgrad. Northwestern U., 1947-48; m. Norma Pammenter, Dec. 27, 1944; children—Leigh Pammenter, James Nathaniel, Richard Edward. Intern Genesee Hosp., Rochester, N.Y., 1946-47; commd. lt. (j.g.), M.C., USN, 1946, advanced through grades to lt. comdr., 1956; chief eye, ear, nose throat dept. U.S. Naval Hosp., Key West, Fla., 1948-51, 54-56; resident in ophthalmology U.S. Naval Hosp., Bethesda, Md., 1951-53; sr. med. officer in U.S.S. Baltimore, 1953-54; practice medicine specializing in ophthalmology, Casper, Wyo., 1956—; chief of staff Natrona County (Wyo.) Meml. Hosp., 1964-66. Trustee Natrona County Sch. Bd., 1963-70, pres., 1967-68; mem. Natrona County Commn., 1971-82, chmn., 1980. Diplomate Am. Bd. Ophthalmology. Fellow ACS, Am. Acad. Ophthalmology; mem. Casper C. of C. (dir. 1962-64), Natrona County Med. Soc. (pres. 1959), AMA, Pan Am. Med. Assn., Pan Am. Assn. Ophthalmology, Wyo. Sch. Bds. Assn., N.Am. Yacht Racing Union. Clubs: Elks, Lions (dir. 1961-64), Masons, Shriners, Casper Mountain Ski, Casper Boat (commodore 1960-62), Nat. Ski Patrol. Home: 3338 Monte Vista Dr Casper WY 82601 Office: Wyo Bldg Casper WY 82601

FOWLKES, NELSON J., medical institution executive; b. Chattanooga, Dec. 26, 1934; s. Edward B. and Dorothy (Nelson) F.; B.S., Central State U., 1957; M.S., U. Tenn., 1970; postgrad. U. Calif.-Long Beach, 1976—; M.P.A., Calif. State U., 1982; m. Peggy Jackson, Aug. 25, 1957; children—Errol A., Janet L., Nelson Joseph. Commd. 2d lt. U.S. Army, 1958, advanced through grades to lt. col., 1978, ret., 1978; adminstrv. asst. St. Agnes Med. Center, Fresno, Calif., 1975-76, lab. mgr., 1978-80, health planner, 1980-82, asst. dir. health planning strategies, 1982—; adminstrv. asst. Mich. Biomed. Lab., Flint, 1976-78. Decorated Army Commendation medal. Mem. Am. Mgmt. Assn., Am. Assn. Clin. Chemistry, Am. Soc. Hosp. Planning, Omega Psi Phi. Methodist. Club: Optimist. Home: 524 W Vartikian Fresno CA 93704 Office: St Agnes Medical Center 1303 E Herndon Ave Fresno CA 93710

FOX, ALLEN ROBERT, consulting engineer; b. Fond du Lac, Wis., Nov. 30, 1946; s. Lawrence and Catherine F.; m. Shirley Jean Renninger, July 20, 1974. B.S., U. Wis., 1969, M.S., 1971, Ph.D., 1973. Lic. land surveyor, Wis.; registered profl. engr., Colo. Engring. aide City of Fond du Lac, 1965; engr. City of Lake Mills (Wis.), 1966-68; engr.-in-tng. Dept. Hwys., State of Wis., 1966-68; assoc. engr. Lakeland Engrs., Madison, Wis., 1969-74; v.p. engring. Dismuke & Dismuke, Inc., Steamboat Springs, Colo., 1974—. Aring Equipment Co. scholar, 1967, U. Wis. fellow, 1968. Mem. ASCE, Am. Water Works Assn., Water Pollution Control Fedn.

FOX, DALE JOSEPH, data processing exec.; b. Youngstown, Ohio, Nov. 7, 1933; s. Franklin Bowman and Ruthella (Geesaman) F.; B.S., Pepperdine U., 1955; M.B.A., U. So. Calif., 1962; m. Carol Dee Campbell, June 11, 1955 (div. 1974); 1 son, Christian Dale; m. 2d, Mildred Joann O'Neill, Mar. 12, 1977; children—Tracey Ann, Shelley Elisabeth, Kathleen Joann, Shannon Leigh, Erin Ruth. Chief mktg. adminstrn. Autonetics, Downey, Calif., 1959-64; asst. lab. mgr. TRW, Inc., Redondo Beach, Calif., 1964-68, sr. adminstr., 1972—; computer center mgr. Xerox Corp., El Segundo, Calif., 1968-71. Data processing cons., Los Angeles, 1971-72. Mem. Com. to elect Richard M. Nixon, 1968. Served with USCGR, 1956-59. Recipient Individual Performance award Data Processing Mgmt. Assn., 1972. Mem. Data Processing Mgmt. Assn. (dir. 1971-72), Assn. Computing Machinery, Res. Officers Assn. Republican. Lutheran. Clubs: Masons, Shriners. Home: 4315 Piedmont Mesa Dr Claremont CA 91711 Office: 1 Space Park Redondo Beach CA 90278

FOX, DENAMAE DAWSON, college administrator; b. Denver, Dec. 29, 1924; d. William Thomas and Ethel May (McGaffey) Dawson; B.A., U. Colo., 1964, M.A., 1967, Ph.D., 1972; postgrad. San Jose City Coll., 1976, U. Del., 1977; m. Wayne Odell Fox, Mar. 15, 1947; children—Dana Wayne, Julie Kay. Grad. teaching asso. U. Colo., 1972; vis. prof. U. N.D., 1972-74; asst. prof. communications U. Hartford, 1972-74; tng. coordinator Aurora (Colo.) Dept. Police, 1975-78; dir. Aurora Extension of Columbia Coll., 1978—. Pres., Westminister LWV, 1957; treas. Colo. LWV, lobbyist, 1959. Mem. Am. Soc. Tng. and Devel. (pres. 1979-80), Speech Communication Assn., Internat. Communication Assn. Democrat. Methodist. Home: 13850 E Marina Dr 207 Aurora CO 80014 Office: 2600 S Parker Rd Suite 240 Aurora CO 80014

FOX, JANE ISAACS, advertising executive; b. N.Y.C., Sept. 18, 1953; d. Abner H. and Mildred H. Isaacs; m. James Warren Fox, June 17, 1979; B.A., Wellesley Coll., 1975; M.B.A., U. Pa., 1977. Asst. brand mgr. Procter & Gamble, Cin., 1977-81; account supr. Ross Roy, Detroit, 1981; product mgr. Carnation Co., Los Angeles, 1981-82; account supr. Dailey & Assocs., Los Angeles, 1982—. Club: Los Angeles Wellesley (dir. 1982—). Office: Dailey & Associates 3055 Wilshire Blvd Los Angeles CA 90010

FOX, JOHN WILLIAM, sociology educator; b. Sept. 15, 1944; s. William Michael and Agnes (Best) F.; m. Patricia Grace Snowden, Jan. 24, 1970; children—David Nathan, Sarah Bordeaux. B.S., Mich. State U., 1967; M.A., Western Mich. U., 1973, Ph.D., 1976. Instr. Western Mich. U., Kalamazoo, 1974-75; research fellow U. Wis., Madison, 1975-77; asst. prof. sociology U. No. Colo., Greeley, 1977-82, assoc. prof., 1982—; cons., researcher in field. Served U.S. Army, 1969-70. Decorated Bronze Star. Mem. Am. Sociol. Assn. Democrat. Roman Catholic. Contbr. articles in field to profl. jours. Home: 1905 11th Ave Greeley CO 80631 Office: Dept Sociology U Northern CO Greeley CO 80639

FOX, JOSEPH MARLIN, bank executive, insurance executive; b. Longford, Kans., July 23, 1915; s. Hurley Wellington and Eva Kathryn (Marty) F.; m. Mildred Maxine Randall, Aug. 25, 1946; children—Lynette, Jonathan. B.A., U. Colo., 1937. With Fowler (Colo.) State Bank, 1937—, v.p., cashier, dir., 1945-54, pres., dir., 1955—; co-owner Fox Agy., Fowler. Treas. bd. edn. Sch. Dist. 26 Otero County, Colo., 1945—; treas. Local Rodeo Assn.; active Ark. Valley Fair Assn., Colo. Arkansas Valley, Inc.; regional chmn. for banks Colo. 4-H Club Found., 1964; mem. 16th Jud. Dist. Nominating Commn. for Judges, 1967; dist. chmn. Rocky Mountain council Boy Scouts Am. Served with U.S. Army, 1941-44. Mem. Am. Bankers Assn., Colo. Bankers Assn., Ind. Bankers Am., Bank Adminstrn. Inst., Ark. Valley Clearing House Assn. (pres.), Am. Legion (local service officer). Democrat. Methodist. Clubs: Pueblo (Colo.) Country, Lions. Home: 3308 Rd KK 75/100 Fowler CO 81039 Office: 201 Main St Fowler CO 81039

FOX, ROBERT AUGUST, food company executive; b. Norristown, Pa., Apr. 24, 1937; s. August Emil and Elizabeth Martha (Deimling) F.; m. Linda Lee Carnesale, Sept. 19, 1964; children—Lee Elizabeth, Christina Carolyn. B.A. with high honors, Colgate U., 1959; M.B.A. cum laude, Harvard U., 1964. Unit sales mgr. Procter & Gamble, 1959-62; gen. sales mgr. T.J. Lipton, 1964-69; v.p. mktg. Can. Dry Corp., 1969-72; pres., chief exec. officer, dir. Can. Dry Internat., 1972-75; exec. v.p., dir. Hunt-Wesson Foods, Inc., 1975-78; pres., chief exec. officer, dir. R.J. Reynolds Tobacco Corp., 1980-82; pres., chief operating officer, dir. Del Monte Corp., San Francisco, 1982-83, pres., chief exec. officer, dir., 1983—; dir. New Perspective Fund, Growth Fund Am., Income Fund Am., Am. Balanced Fund. Mem. San Francisco C. of C., Colgate U. Alumni Assn. Club: Olympic (San Francisco). Office: 1 Market Plaza PO Box 3575 San Francisco CA 94119

FOX, ROBERT LEE, soil science educator; b. Clark, Mo., May 26, 1923; s. John Victor and Verna Ann (Ward) F.; m. Ruby Irene Tullock, Jan. 30, 1948; children—Ronald, Debra, Bruce, Alan, Sharon. B.S. in Agr., U. Mo., 1948, M.A. in Soils, 1950, Ph.D. in Soils, 1955. Asst. prof. agronomy U. Nebr., Lincoln, 1950-56, assoc. prof., 1958-61; assoc. prof. agronomy U. Ankara (Turkey), 1956-58; prof. soil sci. U. Hawaii, Honolulu, 1961—; vis. prof. soil sci. N.C. State U., Raleigh, 1967; soil scientist Internat. Inst. Tropical Agr., Ibadan, Nigeria, 1974; NRC sr. sci. fellow Ruakura Agrl. Research Ctr., Hamilton, N.Z., 1981; prof. Coll. Tropical Agrl., soil scientist Hawaii Inst. Tropical Agr. Deacon, Kailua Baptist Ch. Served to lt. USN, 1943-46. Mem. Soil Sci. Soc. Am., Am. Soc. Agronomy, Internat. Soil Sci. Soc. Republican. Contbr. articles to profl. jours. and books.

FOX, SALLY LORRAIN, travel counselor; b. Olwein, Iowa, May 15, 1952; d. Arthur Lindy and Betty Jean (Daisy) Frey; m. Ryan L. Fox, Aug. 15, 1971; 1 dau., Stephanie Lynn. Grad., Humboldt Inst., Mpls. Counselor, AAA World Wide Travel, Cedar Rapids, Iowa, 1971-74, Big Country Travel, Montrose, Colo., 1974-76; pres., mgr. Montrose (Colo.) World Travel, 1976—. Mem. Montrose C. of C. (dir. 1976-81). Republican. Presbyterian. Club: Altrusa of Montrose (pres. 1983-84).

FOX, STUART IRA, physiologist; b. Bklyn., June 21, 1945; s. Sam and Bess Fox; B.A., UCLA, 1967; M.A., Calif. State U.-Los Angeles, 1967; postgrad., U. Calif.-Santa Barbara, 1969; Ph.D., U. So. Calif., 1978; m. Ellen Diane Fox; 1 dau., Laura Elizabeth. Research assoc. Children's Hosp. Los Angeles, 1972; prof. physiology Los Angeles City Coll., 1972—, Calif. State U.-Northridge, 1979; cons. William C. Brown Co. Pubs., 1976—; project dir. NSF. Named Outstanding Tchr. Los Angeles City Coll., 1978. Mem. AAAS, So. Calif. Acad. Sci., Am. Physiol. Soc., Sigma Xi. Author: Laboratory Guide to Human Physiology, 2d edit., 1980, 3d edit., 1984; Textbook of Human Physiology, 1984; Computer-Assisted Instruction in Human Physiology, 1979. Home: 10525 Encino Ave Granada Hills CA 91344 Office: Los Angeles City Coll 855 N Vermont Los Angeles CA 90036

FOX, WILLIAM WALTER, business consultant; b. Fort Morgan, Colo., Oct. 3, 1921; s. Eugene and Cora Irene (Gerkin) F.; B.Mech. Engring., U. Va., 1943; postgrad. Exec. Program UCLA, 1959, Stanford U., 1970; m. Mary Gregg Rea, July 15, 1943; children—William Walter, Arthur Gregg, James Henry. With Convair div. Gen. Dyamics, 1939-72; chief engr., San Diego, 1960-62; founder, dir. U.S. Fin., San Diego, 1962-77, pres., 1975-77; bus. cons., San Diego, 1977—. Served with U.S. Army, 1945-46. Mem. Inst. Aero. Scis. Home: 1264 Santa Barbara St San Diego CA 92107 Office: Peninsula Ctr Suite 107 3065 Rosecrans Pl San Diego CA 92110

FOXWORTHY, LAUREL RAE, ophthalmologist; b. Veedersburg, Ind., Feb. 2, 1913; d. Francis Marion and Fannie (Patton) Foxworthy; B.S., Ind. U., 1935, M.D., 1939; m. Frank Edgar Adley, Apr. 25, 1946 (div. 1953). Intern Ind. U. Hosp., Indpls., 1939-40; fellow in ophthalmology Mayo Clinic, Rochester, Minn., 1940-44; practice ophthalmology, Seattle, 1944—; mem. staff Swedish, Children's Orthopedic hosps. Active precinct worker Rep. party. Diplomate Am. Acad. Ophthalmology. Mem. Pacific Coast Ophthalmology and Otolaryngology Soc., Puget Sound Soc. Ophthalmology and Otolaryngology. Methodist. Clubs: Seattle Tennis, Broadmoor. Home: 1660 Shenandoah Dr E Seattle WA 98101 Office: 509 Olive Way Seattle WA 98101

FOY, ROBERT WILLARD, moving company executive; b. San Francisco, Sept. 18, 1936; s. Willard C. and Anita Louise (McKenna) F.; m. Barbara L. Barron, Oct. 21, 1967; children—Matthew S., Peter A. B.S. with distinction, San Jose State U., 1959. With Continental Group, Inc., 1961-64; with Pacific Storage Co. agts. for Bekins Van Lines, Stockton, Calif., 1964—, pres., 1977—, also dir.; dir., sec. Wagner Corp.; pres. Movers & Investors, Inc., Sunnyvale, Calif., 1980-81; dir., sec. Reid Travel Assocs., Inc., Stockton, 1975—. Chmn., Stockton Parole Adv. Com. Calif., 1965-66; vol. United Crusade, 1962—; bd. dirs. San Joaquin County United Way, 1964-71, trustee, 1980—, pres., 1969-70; bd. dirs. Calif. United Way, 1970-71, Boys Club, 1965-67, Better Bus. Bur. San Joaquin County, 1965-67, Calif. Water Service Co., 1977—; mem. San Joaquin County Grand Jury, 1969-70; mem. Stockton Unified Sch. Dist.'s Citizens Com. to Study Year-Round-Sch., 1965-66, State of Calif. Atty. Gen.'s Vol. Adv. Com., 1963-67; mem. community forward together com. U. Pacific, 1975—, mem. search com. for dean Sch. Bus. and Pub. Administrn., 1978, mem. adv. bd., 1979—, co-chmn. San Joaquin Adv. Council for univ. fund raising campaign, 1981—; commr. Stockton Port Dist., 1970-73, chmn. bd. commrs., 1973; mem. transp. policy bd. San Joaquin County Council Govts., 1972-73; 1st v.p. San Joaquin Employers Council, 1975-81, pres., 1981-83; fundraising co-chmn. A Safe Place for Battered Women, 1981-82; charter mem. Pioneer Mus. Club, 1980—; mem. 14th Congl. Dist. Mil. Acad. Selection Com., 1979—, San Jose State U. Spartan Found., 1978—. Served to capt. USAR, 1959-67. Mem. Nat. Def. Transp. Assn., Am. Soc. for Pub. Adminstrn. (com. on relations with bus. and industry 1977-78), Greater Stockton C. of C. (exec. com. 1973-77, sr. v.p. 1975-76, pres. 1976-77), Calif. Moving and Storage Assn. (pres. 1978-79), Nat. Furniture Warehousemen's Assn. (bd. dirs. 1980—), San Jose State U. Alumni Assn., San Jose State U. Sch. Bus. Alumni Assn. (Disting. Alumnus award 1981). Episcopalian. Clubs: West Lane Tennis, Downtown Lions (bd. dirs. 1970-73), Yosemite (sec.-treas. 1982-83, v.p. 1983-84). Home: 933 W Monterey Ave Stockton CA 95204 Office: Pacific Storage Co PO Box 334 517 N Hunter St Stockton CA 95201

FRADKIN, DAVID BARRY, aeronautical engineer; b. Washington, Aug. 14, 1941; s. William Stanley and Gertrude (Hoffeld) F.; B.S. cum laude, U. Md., 1963; M.S. in Aerospace Engring. (Guggenheim fellow), Princeton, 1965, Ph.D. in Aerospace and Mech. Sci. (AEC fellow), 1973; m. Stacey A. Fradkin, Dec. 30, 1979; children—Sheryl Lynn, Jonathan Matthew, Jesse Dor. Staff mem., research scientist advanced laser systems Los Alamos (N.Mex.) Scientific Lab., 1965-74, asst. group leader applied photochemistry div., 1974-77, alt. group leader, 1977-78, group leader, 1978—. Bd. dirs. Los Alamos Jewish Center, 1972-74, 78—, religious chmn., 1972-74. Mem. AIAA, Am. Chem. Soc., AAAS, N.Y. Acad. Sci., Sigma Xi, Omicron Delta Kappa, Tau Beta Pi. Club: Rio Grande Valley Sports Car. Contbr. articles to profl. jours. Home: 162 Chamisa Los Alamos NM 87544 Office: Los Alamos Nat Lab Box 1663 Los Alamos NM 87544

FRAGER, HAROLD DEAN, executive search consultant; b. Oxford, Ind., Dec. 5, 1926; s. Chester Elmer and Estella May (Nagle) F.; m. Evelyn Rose Dienhart, May 13, 1950; children—Douglas Allen, Bradley Dean, Kevin Scott, Trina Lynn. B.S. in Bus., Purdue U., 1951; M.B.A., Am. Grad. U., 1981; postgrad. Butler U., 1955, Calif. Maritime Acad., 1976-77. Cert. profl. contracts mgr. Acct., Aluminum Co. Am., Lafayette, Ind., 1944-47; acct. Gen. Telephone Co. Ind., Lafayette, 1949-54; project engr. Ind. Bell Telephone Co., Indpls., 1954-59; sr. engr. Kellogg Switchboard & Supply Co., Chgo., 1959-61; project mgr. Techo Corp., Emeryville, Calif., 1962-63, corp. dir., 1964-79, mgr. contracts adminstrn., 1964-65, v.p., 1965-67, sr. v.p., 1967-79; exec. v.p., gen. mgr.

Murphy Pacific Marine Salvage Co., Emeryville, 1973-79, corp. dir., 1973-79, corp. dir. Murphy Pacific Marine Salvage Co. Liberia Inc., 1975-79; pres., owner Frager Co. Inc., San Rafael, Calif., 1979—; dir., owner Sanford Rose Assocs. of San Francisco & Marin, San Rafael, 1982—; corp. dir. Caribtow Ltd., Kingston, Jamaica, 1975-79. Served with U.S. Army, 1945-46. PTO. Recipient Pres.'s Missile Sites Labor Commn. cert. of merit, 1963. Mem. Nat. Contracts Mgmt. Assn., Am. Arbitration Assn. (panel), Air Force Assn., Am. Ordnance Assn. Lodges: Masons, Shriners, Elks. Home: 380 Via La Cumbre Greenbrae CA 94904

FRAGER, ROBERT DAVID, psychologist, inst. exec.; b. N.Y.C., June 20, 1940; s. Solomon and Doris (Levin) F.; m. Lya Hirth, Aug. 24, 1968 (div.); children—Ariel, Edward. B.A., Reed Coll., 1961; Ph.D., Harvard U., 1967. Lic. psychologist, Calif. Vis. lectr. in psychology U. Calif.-Berkeley, 1968-69; asst. prof. psychology U. Calif.-Santa Cruz, 1969-75; founder, pres. Calif. Inst. Transpersonal Psychology, Menlo Park, 1975—; cons. inter-personal communications and stress mgmt. to civic and bus. orgns. Bd. dirs. New Dimensions Found., 1978—. Mem. Am. Psychol. Assn., Assn. Transpersonal Psychology (pres. 1982—). Author: (with J. Fadiman) Personality and Personal Growth, 1976. Home: 1235 Laurel St #101 Menlo Park CA 94025 Office: 250 Oak Grove Ave Menlo Park CA 94025

FRAGNER, BERWYN N., human relations exec.; b. Uniontown, Pa., Aug. 5, 1927; s. Rudolph and Rose (Lebowitz) F.; B.A. with distinction, U. Del., 1950; M.A., Harvard U., 1952; m. Marcia Ruth Salkind, June 11, 1950; children—Robin Beth, Matthew Charles, Lisa Rachel. Vice pres. Royer & Roger, Inc., N.Y.C., 1952-62; dir. Western div. Goodway Printing Co., Los Angeles, 1962; v.p., dir. indsl. relations TRW Def. and Space Systems Group, Redondo Beach, Calif., 1963-77, v.p. human relations TRW Systems and Energy, 1977-81, TRW Electronics and Def., 1981—; adv. bd. 1st Women's Bank of Calif. Chmn. Los Angeles City Pvt. Industry Council, 1979-81; chmn. Los Angeles County Pvt. Industry Council, 1983—; mem. Calif. Ednl. Mgmt. and Evaluation Commn., 1974-82; chmn. bd. trustees Calif. Acad. Decathalon, 1980-81; mem. bus. execs. adv. com. So. Calif. Research Council, 1979—; USAR mem. Res. Forces Policy Bd., U.S. Dept. Def., 1981—; alt. mem.-at-large Army Res. Forces Policy Com., U.S. Dept. Army, 1979-82. Bd. dirs. Ind. Colls. So. Calif., 1982—, bd. councillors U. So. Calif. Sch. Pharmacy, 1982—. Served with AUS, 1944-47. Decorated Disting. Service Medal, Meritorious Service medal with 2 oak leaf clusters; recipient Presdl. citation for community service, 1981. Mem. Assn. U.S. Army, Res. Officers Assn., Sr. Army Res. Comdrs. Assn., Internat. Assn. Applied Social Scientists (cert.). Clubs: Army and Navy (Washington); Los Angeles Athletic. Contbr. to New World of Managing Human Resources, 1979. Office: One Space Park E2 11092 Redondo Beach CA 90278

FRAHMANN, DENNIS GEORGE, business machine company manager; b Medford, Wis., June 25, 1953; s. George Henry and Aini (Siimarla) F.; B.A. in Philosophy and English, Ripon Coll., 1974; M.S. in Journalism, Columbia U., 1975; postgrad. U. Minn., 1979-80. Freelance tech. writer, Mpls., 1975-77; instructional developer Control Data Corp., Mpls., 1977-78, instructional design cons., 1978-79; instructional designer Xerox Bus. Systems div. Xerox Corp., Los Angeles, 1980-81, mgr. customer edn. Xerox Office Products, 1981-82, mgr. product info. Xerox Office Systems, El Segundo, Calif., 1982—. Mem. adv. com. Mcpl. Elections Com. Los Angeles, 1982—; bd. dirs. Ripon Coll. Alumni, 1977-80. Nat. Merit scholar, 1971; Wis. Honor scholar, 1971; Aid Assn. for Lutherans All Coll. scholar, 1971; Scripps-Howard scholar, 1974; Johnson Found. fellow, 1971-74. Mem. Am. Soc. Tng. and Devel. Contbr. articles to popular mags.; contbg. editor Mpls.-St. Paul mag., 1977-81. Home: 5280 Village Green Los Angeles CA 90016 Office: Xerox Office Systems 830 S Nash St Suite NI 03 El Segundo CA 90245

FRAKES, ANNA JAY, psychological counselor, consultant; b. Woods County, Okla., Nov. 30, 1939; d. Dale and Marie (Fulton) Holmes; m. Lee Wayne Frakes, July 14, 1970; children—Samuel, Kim Erlich, Mark, Suzanne. B.A. in Clin. Psychology, Pepperdine U., 1974, M.A. in Clin. Psychology, 1976. Psychology instr. Rogue Community Coll., Grants Pass, Oreg., 1976-79; mental health therapist Josephine County (Oreg.) Mental Health Dept., 1979-81; pvt. practice Anna Jay Frakes Counseling Service Inc., Grants Pass, 1976—; condr. workshops, presentations for local, state orgns., colls. Charter mem., pres. bd. dirs. Josephine County (Oreg.) Women's Crisis Support Team; elder Bethany Presbyterian Ch.; organizer Planned Parenthood for Josephine County; mental health rep. Josephine-Jackson Counties Health Council. Mem. Oreg. Profl. Guidance Assn. (pres.-elect Mental Health Div.), Am. Assn. Exec. Women, Exec. Woman's Group (organizer), AAUW.

FRAKES, ROD V., plant geneticist, educator; b. Ontario, Oreg., July 20, 1930; s. Wylie and Pearl (Richardson) F.; m. Ruby L. Morey, Nov. 27, 1952; children—Laura Ann, Cody Joe. B.S., Oreg. State U., 1956, M.S., 1957; Ph.D., Purdue U., 1960. Instr. dept. agronomy Purdue U., 1959-60; asst. prof. dept. crop sci. Oreg. State U., 1960-64, assoc. prof., 1964-69, prof., 1969—, assoc. dean research, 1981—. Served with USCG, 1950-53. Name Pacific Seedsmen's Assn. Man of Year, 1972; recipient Oreg. State U. Elizabeth P. Ritchie Disting. Prof. award, 1980. Fellow Am. Soc. Agronomy; mem. Crop Sci. Soc. Am., AAAS, Nat. Council Univ. Research Adminstrs. Author numerous papers and abstracts, contbr. to books in field. Home: 2625 NW Linnan Circle Corvallis OR 97330 Office: Research Office Oreg State U Corvallis OR 97331

FRALEY, ANTHONY DUANE, cash register co. exec.; b. Munisung, Mich., Jan. 29, 1941; s. John Clyde and Eva Tumbilesi (Stigall) F.; certs. of completion Nat. Cash Register Service Sch., 1965, Sharp Electronics Service Sch., 1977; m. Patricia Ann Barnett, May 30, 1981. Service technician Nat. Cash Register Co., Long Beach, Calif., 1963-68; service mgr. Santa Monica (Calif.) Cash Register Co., 1968-70; part owner A.D. Cash Register Co., Reseda, Calif., 1970-72, owner, gen. mgr., 1972—. Served with USN, 1959-63. Mem. Ind. Cash Register Dealers Assn., Reseda C. of C. (dir. 1978, pres. 1981). Roman Catholic. Clubs: Cerritos Bahia Yacht (commodore 1977), Elks, Rotary (dir. 1980, pres. 1984). Office: 7243 Reseda Blvd Reseda CA 91335

FRALEY, DOUGLAS DONALD, coop. exec.; b. Klamath Falls, Oreg., Oct. 31, 1942; s. Donald Vincent and Charlene Elizabeth (Fraley) Lutz; asso. degree in surveying tech. Oreg. Tech. Inst., 1964; m. Carol Ann Ross, June 2, 1967; children—Robert G., William F., Tina M., Douglas L. With U.S. Forest Service, Chiloquin, Oreg., 1963, Klamath County Engr.'s Office, Klamath Falls, 1964-65, 66-70, U.S. Bur. Public Roads, Portland, Oreg., 1965-66, EPA, Portland, 1971-73; with Oreg. Dept. Environ. Quality, Portland, 1973-79, mgr. oil spill response program, spl. investigator for air quality enforcement, 1979; mgr. Clean Rivers Coop., Portland, 1979—. Served with USNG, 1964-70. Democrat. Baptist. Clubs: Eagles. Home: 5075 SW Freeman Ct Portland OR 97219 Office: 2416 N Marine Dr Portland OR 97217

FRAME, ANNE PARSONS, civic worker; b. Berkeley, Calif., Jan. 3, 1904; d. Reginald Hascall and Maude (Bemis) Parsons; A.B., Mills Coll., 1924; postgrad. Columbia, 1924-25; m. Frederic D. Tootell, Apr. 3, 1926 (div. July 1935); children—Geoffrey H., Natalie (Mrs. Oliver); m. 2d, Jasper Ewing Brady (dec. Dec. 1944); 1 son, Hugh Parsons; m. 3d, Howard Andres Frame, Mar. 29, 1948. Dir. Parsons, Hart & Co., Seattle, Hillcrest Orchard Co., Seattle. Mem. bd. mgmt. Palo Alto br. A.R.C., 1955-61; bd. dirs. Children's Health Council, Palo Alto, Calif., 1953-63, 64-76, pres., 1954-58; sponsor Nat. Recreation Assn., 1942-66, trustee, 1948-66; sponsor Nat. Recreation and Park Assn., 1966—, trustee, 1966-73; trustee Nat. Recreation Found., 1964—; 1st v.p. Children's Hosp. at Stanford Sr. Aux., 1965-67, bd. dirs. Hosp., 1967-81; former mem. adv. com. Holbrook-Palmer Park; trustee Mills Coll., 1952-62; bd. dirs. Holbrook-Palmer Recreation Park Found., 1968—; bd. govs. San Francisco Symphony Assn., to 1979; mem. Atherton (Calif.) Park and Recreation Commn., 1968-81. Mem. LWV, Bowne House Hist. Soc., San Mateo County, Seattle, Chgo., Calif. hist. socs., Calif. Heritage Council, San Francisco Mus. Art, Seattle Art Mus., Museum Soc., Nat. Trust for Historic Preservation, Nat. Soc. Colonial Dames Am. Episcopalian. Clubs: Sunset, Tennis (Seattle); Woodside-Atherton Garden (dir. 1966-68); Francisca (San Francisco).

FRAME, GEORGE JACK, sales engineer, mining consultant; b. Amarillo, Tex., Aug. 20, 1922; s. George and Daisey (Morrow) F.; m. Margaret Matheny, Mar, 3, 1943; children—Robert L., Charles R. Student Eastern N.Mex. U., 1950. Sr. rep. Douglas Aircraft and Rockwell Internat., N.Y., Pa., 1951-68; export mgr. Western Gear Co., Los Angeles, 1968-70; sales engr. Rubbercraft Corp., Torrance, Calif., 1970-73; sales engr., internat. trade rep. GF Indsl., Albuquerque, 1973—; mining cons. Served with USAAF, 1942-45. Decorated Bronze star (11). Mem. Ch. of Christ.

FRAME, ROBERT AARON, painter, art educator; b. San Fernando, Calif., July 31, 1924; s. Joseph Aaron and Isabel (Jardine) F.; m. Barbara Ann Routh, Apr. 23, 1977; children—Christopher, Erin, Diana. B.A., Pomona Coll., 1948; M.F.A., Claremont Coll., 1951. Instr. San Diego State Coll., 1954-55, Pasadena (Calif.) City Coll., 1956-60, Otis Art Inst., Los Angeles, 1958-63; prof. Santa Barbara (Calif.) City Coll., 1966—; numerous one-man shows in N.Y.C., Los Angeles, Scottsdale, Ariz. and San Francisco. Served with USNR, World War II, 1944-46. Guggenheim fellow 1957-58. Mem. Artist Equity. Address: 2102 Edgewater Way Santa Barbara CA 93109

FRAME, TED RONALD, lawyer; b. Milw., June 27, 1929; s. Morris and Jean (Lee) F.; student UCLA, 1946-49; A.B., Stanford U., 1950, LL.B., 1952; m. Lois Elaine Pilgrim, Aug. 15, 1954; children—Kent, Lori, Nancy, Owen. Bar: Calif. 1953. Gen. law practice, Coalinga, Calif., 1953—; sr. ptnr. Frame & Courtney, 1965—, agribus. and related concerns. Trustee, Baker Mus. Mem. ABA, Calif. Bar Assn., Fresno County Bar Assn., Coalinga C. of C. (past pres.). Clubs: Masons, Shriners, Elks. Home: 1222 Nevada St Coalinga CA 93210 Office: 201 Washington St Coalinga CA 93210

FRANCE, JOHN LYONS, air force officer; b. Forest City, Mo., Sept. 11, 1933; s. Calvert Glen and Gertrude May (Lyons) F.; B.A. in English, U. Denver, 1963, J.D., 1966; m. Carole Jean Denton, Sept. 16, 1961; children—Allison Lisa, Amy Denton. Commd. 2d lt. USAF, advanced through grades to brig. gen.; now adj. gen., State Colo., Denver; flight leader Colo. Air N.G., later squadron comdr., group comdr., wing comdr. Mem. Air Res. Forces Policy Com.; mem. Tactical Air Command Res. Forces Policy Counil. Decorated D.F.C., Air medal with ten oak leaf clusters. Mem. ABA, Colo. Bar Assn., Air Force Assn. Office: 300 Logan St Denver CO 80203

FRANCE, RICHARD S., ballet co. exec.; b. Chgo., Jan. 6, 1930; s. Eugene and Suzanne (France) Schweizer; studied under masters Aubrey Hitchins, Anthony Tudor, Igor Schwitzoff, Edward Caton and Richard Thomas of Ballet Theatre; protege of Anton Dolin; 1 son, Sean France. Dancer Chgo. Civil Ballet Co., Markova-Dolin Co., Am. Ballet Co.; partner Alexandra Danilova, Zizi Jeanmarie; actor/dancer/singer on Broadway in What Makes Sammy Run, Pal Joey (also London prodn.), Oklahoma, Wish You Were Here, Kiss Me Kate, Carnival, Girls Against the Boys, Annie Get Your Gun, Show Boat, Fiorello, Seventeen; dir. Casa Mañana Theatre, Ft. Worth, Tex., Starlight Theatre, Kansas City, Mo., St. Louis Mcpl. Opera Co., Tucson Civic Ballet, until 1974; now dir. Tucson Met. Ballet Co.; owner, tchr. France Acad. Dance, Tucson. Choreographer, The Legends of Supersition Mountain, in collaboration with composer Brandson Smith, Les Patineurs, Peter and the Wolf, Gaite Parisienne, Graduation Ball, The Nutcracker, Swan Lake, Act II, Les Sylphides. Office: PO Box 17053 Tucson AZ 85731

FRANCE, SHERROD W(ELLS), banker; b. Rawlins, Wyo., Apr. 3, 1947; s. John W. and Marie W. France; B.S. in Bus. Adminstrn., U. Wyo., 1971; grad. Colo. Sch. Banking, 1978; m. Janet K. DeWitt, Feb. 20, 1971; children—Dawn Robin, Copper Wells, Jon Bryce. Corp. pilot George B. Storer, Wyo. and Fla., 1971; auditor, comptroller, then asst. v.p. Jackson (Wyo.) State Bank, 1972-76; cashier, then v.p. Rawlins Nat. Bank, 1976-78, asst. trust officer, dir., 1978—, pres., 1979—. Mem. Am. Bankers Assn. (adv. bd. community bankers div. 1979-81, govt. relations council 1982—), Wyo. Bankers Assn. (exec. council 1981-83), Nat. Fedn. Ind. Bus., Rawlins C. of C., Airplane Owners and Pilots Assn., U. Wyo. Alumni Assn. (dir., pres. 1981), Sigma Chi. Republican. Presbyterian. Clubs: Rotary (dir. 1981), Elks (exalted ruler 1975). Address: Box 607 Rawlins WY 82301

FRANCIS, ALUN, orchestral and operatic conductor, composer; b. Kidderminster, Eng., Sept. 29, 1943; s. Emlyn and Eluned (Peters) F.; m. Pamela Hope Fong, Nov. 19, 1982. Assoc. Royal Manchester Coll. Music, 1963. Music dir. Ulster (U.K.) Orch., 1966-76, Tehran (Iran) Opera, 1976-77; condr. over 50 orchs. world wide; regular condr. Royal Philharmonic and Philharmonia Hungerica; music dir. Northwest Chamber Orch., Seattle; composer orchestral, vocal, chamber music, film scores. Recipient Leon Grindon Prize for composition, Royal Manchester Coll. Music, 1963. Mem. Composers Guild Gt. Brit. Office: 119 S Main 2d Floor Seattle WA 98104

FRANCIS, CHARLES SYLVESTER LAMBERT, city ofcl.; b. Kingston, Jamaica, Sec. 13, 1943; s. Claude Sylvester and Barbara Pauline (Alexander) F.; student Reedley Coll., 1964-66; B.S., Calif. State U., Fresno, 1970, M.City and Regional Planning, 1973; m. Wilma Jean Smith, July 22, 1966; children—Charles Sylvester Lambert II, Mikel Colan, Erica Nicole, Aaron Christopher. Indsl. engr. Pitts. Plate Glass Industries, Fresno, 1969-70; program devel. planner City of Fresno, 1972-73, adminstrv. analyst, 1973-77; dep. dir. planning and ops. Fresno Employment and Tng. Commn., 1977—; instr. Calif. State U., Fresno, 1970—. Legis. liaison Black Polit. Council, 1976-78; bd. dirs. Central Valley YMCA, 1973-76; active PTA. Served with U.S. Navy, 1960-64. Mem. Nat. Assn. Planners, Am. Planning Assn., Am. Soc. Planning Ofcls., Internat. City Mgrs. Assn., Alpha Phi Alpha. Democrat. Baptist. Clubs: West Fresno Y's Men's, West Fresno Tennis Found. Home: 190 S Valentine St Fresno CA 93706 Office: 1404 L St Fresno CA 93721

FRANCIS, FREDRIC MICHAEL, redevelopment administrator; b. Tucson, Ariz., Mar. 17, 1942; s. Wildon John and Carol Jane (Horn) F.; m. Joan Carol Whitlock, Dec. 18, 1965; children—Linda Michelle, Michael Sean, Devan Tomas. B.S., U. Ariz., 1967. Adminstrv. and budget analyst City Adminstrv. Office, City of Los Angeles, 1967-68, exec. asst. to adminstr., owner participation officer, chief real estate devel., dir. real estate, sr. project mgr., program mgr. downtown projects Community Redevel. Agy., 1968-78, dep. adminstr., 1978—. Bd. dirs. Angelus Plaza Elderly Housing Devel. Served with U.S. Army, 1960-61. Recipient Cert. of Recognition, Retirement Housing Found., 1981. Mem. Nat. Assn. Housing and Redevel. Ofcls., Urban Land Inst. Office: 345 S Spring St Suite 800 Los Angeles CA 90013

FRANCIS, GARY BRENT, architect; b. Los Angeles, Aug. 20, 1953; s. Robert N. and Ruth M. (Gothberg) F.; B.S. in Architecture, Calif. Poly. State U., San Luis Obispo, 1976. Pres., Gary B. Francis, Inc., Archtl. Design and Devel., Park City, Utah, 1979—, chief designer, 1979—. Office: PO Box 2129 Park City UT 84060

FRANCIS, JAMES EDWARD, hospital pharmacist; b. Old Town, Maine, Apr. 20, 1950; s. Leslie Joseph and Rose Marie (Bishop) F.; m. Geraldine Ann Boner, Sept. 6, 1975; children—Jennifer Ellen, Elizabeth Ann. B.S. in Pharmacy, U. Wash, 1973; M.S. in Hosp. Pharmacy, Ohio State U., 1976. Registered pharmacist, Wash., Ill. Utah. Asst. dir. pharmacy, Lutheran Gen. Hosp., Park Ridge, Ill., 1976-81; dir. pharmacy, McKay-Dee Hosp. Ctr. Ogden, Utah, 1981—. Mem. Am. Soc. Hosp. Pharmacists, Utah Soc. Hosp. Pharmacists, Rho Chi Honor Soc. Roman Catholic. Club: Elks. Home: 795 Ridgeview Dr S Ogden UT 84403 Office: 3939 Harrison Blvd Ogden UT 84409

FRANCIS, JOANNE R(UTH), advertising executive; b. Manitowoc, Wis., Aug. 20, 1931; d. Lawrence William and Laura Louise (Wollensack) Robertson; m. James K. Francis, Mar. 20, 1970 (div.). Broadcast supr. Mathisson & Assocs., Milw., 1964-70, D'Arcy MacManus & Masius, Chgo., 1972-76, Foote Cone & Belding, Los Angeles, 1976-78; media supr. Dailey & Assocs., Los Angeles, 1978—. Named Time Buyer of Yr., Chgo. Broadcast Reps. Assn., 1974. Republican. Roman Catholic. Office: 3055 Wilshire Blvd Los Angeles CA 90010

FRANCIS, MARC BARUCH, pediatrician; b. Rochester, N.Y., Mar. 3, 1934; s. Nathan and Beverly (Salsburg) F.; A.B., U. Rochester, 1955; M.D., N.Y. U., 1959; m. Janet Irene Harding, Sept. 21, 1960; children—Josephine, Teresa, Jacqueline, Wallace. Intern, Los Angeles County Harbor Gen. Hosp., 1959-60; resident in pediatrics Children's Hosp. of Los Angeles, 1960-62; practice medicine specializing in pediatrics, Salt Lake City, 1962-65; clin. instr. pediatrics U. Utah Med. Sch., 1962-70; chief dept. pediatrics Cottonwood Hosp., 1963-65; partner dept. pediatrics Permanente Med. Group Inc., Napa, Calif., 1971—, chief dept., 1982—. Served to capt. M.C., USAF, 1966-68. Diplomate Am. Bd. Pediatrics. Fellow Am. Acad. Pediatrics; mem. Calif. Med. Assn., Napa County Med. Soc. Clubs: N.Y. U., U. Rochester Alumni. Office: 3284 Jefferson St Napa CA 94558

FRANCIS, SONDRA MARLAE, marketing manager, consultant; b. Mitchell, S.D., Feb. 9, 1939; d. Duane L. Smith; m. Warren B. Francis, Apr. 5, 1976; children—Mike, Garvin, Lisa. B.S., UCLA, 1965. Owner, operator Sunny Tour & Travel, Hollywood, Calif., 1965-67; controller Pacific Homes Corp., Los Angeles, 1965-71; dir. Am. Heart Assn., Los Angeles, 1968-71; mktg. mgr. Xerox Corp., South San Francisco, Calif., 1978-80, regional mgr. European mktg. dept., 1980-82, mgr. retail store, Sunnyvale, Calif., 1982—. Mem. Peninsula Women's Orgn. Home: 145 W 43d Ave San Mateo CA 94403 Office: Xerox Corp 542 N Lawrence Exp Sunnyvale CA 94086

FRANCIS, WINIFRED ANN, investment adviser; b. N.Y.C., Jan. 14, 1944; d. Tudor R. and Elfreda (Woods) Finch; B.A. in Internat. Affairs and Econs., U. Colo., 1966; M.A. in Econs. (scholarship 1967-69), Denver U., 1969; m. Jack Francis, June 21, 1970. Securities analyst Financial Programs Co., Denver, 1966-70, sales liaison, securities analyst, editor Dain Kalman Quail, Mpls., 1971-72; securities analyst, instl. sales Meis & Co., Colorado Springs, 1972-74; supervisory analyst Boettcher & Co., Denver, 1974-76; partner Foster, Francis & Assos., registered investment advisers, Colorado Springs, 1976-78; partner Wini Francis & Assos., Colorado Springs, 1979—; speaker in field. Chartered fin. analyst. Mem. Colo. Assn. Investment Advisers, Colorado Springs Estate Planning Council, Inst. Chartered Fin. Analysts, Fin. Analysts Fedn., Denver Soc. Security Analysts, Colo. Assn. Bus. Economists, Women Bus. Owners Colorado Springs (founder). Office: Mining Exchange Bldg Colorado Springs CO 80903

FRANCISCO, WAYNE M(ARKLAND), petroleum mktg. co. exec.; b. Cin., June 14, 1943; s. George Lewis and Helen M. (Markland) F.; student Ohio State U., 1962-63; B.S. in Mktg. and Acctg., U. Cin., 1967; div.; children—Diana Lynn, W. Michael; m. Inez Francisco. Unit sales mgr. Procter & Gamble, Cin., 1967-69; mktg. mgr. Nat. Mktg. Inc., Cin., 1969-70; pres. Retail Petroleum Marketers, Inc., Cin., 1970-72, chmn. bd., chief exec. officer, Phoenix, 1972—; pres., chief exec. officer Cassia Petroleum Corp., Vancouver, B.C., Can., 1980-81. Mem. Phoenix Bd. Appeals, 1978-80. Recipient Top Performer award Phoenix dist. Shell Oil Co., 1979, 80. Mem. Petroleum Retailers Ariz. (pres. 1977-79), Nat. Congress Petroleum Retailers (adv. bd.), Nat. Inst. Automotive Service Excellence (cert.), Studebaker Drivers Club (regional dir.), Avanti Owners Assn. (nat. dir.). Republican. Office: 3201 E Shea Blvd Phoenix AZ 85028

FRANCO, JORGE, physician; b. Ica, Peru, June 9, 1929; s. Fortunato and Sabina (Cabrera) F.; B.S., San Marcos U., 1947, M.D., 1955; m. Mary Loretta Jones, Sept. 19, 1957; children—Mary Pat, Lori, Ann Marie, Raymond Joseph, Stephen Michael. Came to U.S., 1955. Intern, Bon Secours Hosp., Balt., 1955-56; fellow medicine Stanford Med. Sch., 1956-58, asst. clin. prof. nuclear medicine, 1969-76, assoc. clin. prof., 1976—; resident pathology O'Connor Hosp., San Jose, Calif., 1958-62, assoc. pathologist, 1963—, chief clin. pathology, dir. nuclear medicine, 1968—. Diplomate Am. Bd. Pathology, Am. Bd. Nuclear Medicine. Mem. Am. Fedn. Clin. Research, Am. Soc. Clin. Pathologists, Am. Soc. Hematology, Am. Assn. Blood Banks, Soc. Nuclear Medicine, Am. Inst. Ultrasonics in Medicine, AMA, Calif. Med. Assn., Calif. Soc. Pathologists, Am. Thermographic Soc., Calif. Acad. Medicine, N.Y. Acad. Scis. Contbr. articles to profl. jours.; also clin. and lab. research. Home: 1259 Central Ave San Jose CA 95128 Office: O'Connor Hosp Tumor Center San Jose CA 95128

FRANCO, JUAN N., counselor, consultant, educator; b. Ft. Hancock, Tex., Mar. 22, 1949; s. Ruben A. and Benita (Yglecias) F.; m. Elisa Urquidez, Aug. 14, 1976; children—Juan, Jaime, Fabian. B.S. in Math., Sul Ross State U., 1970; postgrad. U. Tex., 1971; Ph.D. in Counseling Ednl. Psychology, N. Mex. State U., 1975. Statistician Project Bravo Community Action Program, El Paso, Tex., 1974-75; prof. N. Mex. State U., Las Cruces, 1975-81, acting dept. head, 1981—, cons. social work dept., 1981; cons. Open Door Ctr., Las Cruces, 1978-79; program evaluation cons., Southwest Community Mental Health Ctr., Las Cruces, 1978-79; program evaluation cons. Dist. 6 Area Mental Health, Roswell, N. Mex., 1979. Sec. Mesilla Valley Psychologist, 1980—; bd. dirs., vice chmn. Children in Need of Supervision, 1980—; bd. dirs. Dona Ana Mental Health Assn., 1977-82; mem. Chicano adv. com., 1976-77, Chicano scholarship com., 1976-77. NIMH fellow, 1971-74. Mem. Am. Psychol. Assn., Am. Personnel and Guidance Assn. (editorial bd. jour.), Evaluation Research Soc., Evaluation Network, N. Mex. Psychol. Assn. Roman Catholic. Contbr. numerous articles to profl. jours. Home: Box 3436 Las Cruces NM 88003 Office: Box 3AC N Mex State U Las Cruces NM 88003

FRANCOM, ALFRED STERLING, public relations executive, advertising and marketing consultant; b. Salt Lake City, Aug. 17, 1941; s. Joseph Stephen and Alice Myrtle Solomon F.; m. Matha LaRee Peck, Nov. 18, 1965; children—Jamie Lynn, Wade S., Brandon T. B.S. U. Utah, Salt Lake City, 1969, M.S., 1971; comml. notes teller Continental

Bank & Trust Salt Lake City, 1964-70; asst. comptroller Murray First Thrift & Loan, Salt Lake City, 1966-67; teaching asst. U. Utah, 1971-72; resource analyst Div. Water Resources, State of Utah, 1972-73; grants adminstr. Salt Lake City Corp., 1972-73; instr. Church Coll. N.Z., 1973-75; pres., account exec. Francom Advt., Inc., 1976—. Served with U.S. Army, 1960-66. Mem. Utah Assn. Advt. Agys., Phi Kappa Phi. Republican. Mormon. Office: 5282 S 320 W Suite D-100 Murray UT 84107

FRANDEN, BLANCHE M., nursing educator; b. N.Y.C., June 9, 1923; d. Samuel and Rebekah (Stern) Randall; m. Robert Jacob Franden, Aug. 20, 1950; children—Richard Jules, Peter Herb, Daniel Ethan. Grad. Mass. Meml. Hosp. Sch. Nursing (now U. Hosp.), 1945; B.Vocat. Edn., Calif. State U.-Los Angeles, 1980. Registered nurse, Calif. dir. student health Mass. Meml. Hosp., Boston, 1947-49; staff nurse various hosps., N.Y., Calif., 1949—; instr. Rio Hondo Community Coll., Whittier, Calif., 1981—, Baldwin Park Unified Sch. Dist. Adult Sch. (Calif.), 1983, East San Gabriel Valley Regional Occupational Program, West Covina, Calif., 1973—; CPR instr.-trainer; mem. CPR com. Am. Heart Assn. Mem. Calif. Assn. Regional Occupational Programs/Ctrs., Calif. Assn. Career Health Educators, Am. Vocat. Assn., AAUW, Women's Au. VFW. Democrat. Jewish. Author student manual. Home: 15111 Mystic St Whittier CA 90604 Office: East San Gabriel Valley Regional Occupation Program 1717 W Merced West Covina CA 91791

FRANDSEN, WALTER JAMES, engring., mgmt. cons.; b. Hammond, Ind., Jan. 1, 1936; s. Walter N. and Edna (Smith) F.; B.S., in Chem. Engring., U. Utah, 1957, M.B.A., 1959; Ph.D. in Behavioral Scis., U.S. Internat. U., 1969; m. Wanda Lorene Cluff, June 13, 1964; children—Deborah Lynn, Walter James. Research analyst Tide Water Oil Co., Avon, Calif., 1956; project engr. Utah Power & Light Co., Salt Lake City, 1957; chem. process engr. Bur. Mines, Salt Lake City, 1958; engring. project coordinator Sperry Utah Engring. Co., Salt Lake City, 1959-61; sr. liaison engr., supr. tech. tng. and devel. Hercules Inc., Bacchus, Utah, 1961-63; cons. engring., mgmt. Gen. Atomic, a Gulf & Royal Dutch/Shell Co., San Diego, 1963-81; cons. Solarturbines, Inc., 1981—; human resources cons.; speaker in field; mem. staff San Diego Community Colls., 1969—, U. Calif. at San Diego Extension, 1969—, Nat. U., 1975—; asst. prof. bus. adminstrn. San Diego State U., 1972—; prof. bus. adminstrn. U. San Diego, 1981—. Active Boy Scouts Am. Served with USCGR, 1960. Registered profl. engr., Calif. Mem. Am. Psychol. Assn., Acad. Mgmt., Am. Soc. for Tng. and Devel. (chpt. pres. 1967), Am. Soc. Personnel Adminstrn., U.S. Internat. U. Doctoral Soc., Am. Inst. Chem. Engrs., Personnel Mgmt. Assn. San Diego. Mormon. Research, publs. on strategic planning, strategic mgmt. and enhancing organizational and individual performance, effectiveness. Home: 500 Camino De Orchida Encinitas CA 92024 Office: 2200 Pacific Hwy San Diego CA 92138

FRANGADAKIS, MICHAEL, real estate executive; b. San Francisco, Apr. 15, 1947; s. Manos and Helen (Rutzakis) F.; m. Elizabeth Ruth Casassa, Sept. 6, 1981; 1 dau., Eleni Sharon. B.A., San Jose U., 1976; M.B.A., U. Phoenix, 1983. Cert. appraiser Calif. Broker, owner Frangadakis and Friends, Cupertino, Calif., 1978—.

FRANK, ANTHONY MELCHIOR, financial executive; b. Berlin, May 21, 1931; s. Lothar and Elisabeth (Roth) F.; m. Gay Palmer, Oct. 16, 1954; children—Tracy, Randall. B.A., Dartmouth Coll., 1953, M.B.A., 1954; postgrad. in fin. U. Vienna, 1956. Asst. to pres., bond portfolio mgr. Glendale Fed. Savs. & Loan Assn. (Calif.), 1958-61; v.p., treas. Far West Fin. Corp., Los Angeles, 1962; adminstrv. v.p., v.p. savs. 1st Charter Fin. Corp., Beverly Hills, Calif., 1962-66; pres. State Mut. Savs. & Loan Assn., Los Angeles, 1966-68, Titan Group, Inc., N.Y.C. and Los Angeles, 1968-70, INA Properties, Inc., 1970-71; pres. Citizens Savs. & Loan Assn., San Francisco, 1971-73, vice chmn., chief exec. officer, 1973-74; pres., chmn. bd., chief exec. officer United Fin. Corp., San Francisco, 1974—; vice chmn., industry dir. Fed. Home Loan Bank of San Francisco, 1972-77, dir., 1983—; chmn. bd. Calif. Housing Fin. Agy., 1978—; pres. Calif. Savs. and Loan League, 1977; dir. Allianz Ins. Co. Am., Golden West Homes, Kaiser Cement Corp., Leisure Tech. Corp., Nat. Steel Corp.; dir., trustee, treas. Blue Shield of Calif. Del. Calif. Democratic Conv., 1968. Served with AUS, 1954-56. Mem. Greater San Francisco C. of C. (dir.), Bankers Club, Young Pres.' Orgn. Clubs: Dartmouth of No. Calif., University (Los Angeles).

FRANK, BARTON, music educator; b. Phila., Oct. 5, 1926; s. Adam and Anne (Goldblum) F.; student Curtis Inst. Music, 1943-46; B.A., U. Tulsa, 1956, M.A., 1957; m. Janet Luciel Harold, Dec. 24, 1972; children—Marcus, Adrienne, Leora, Eamon. Asso. prin. cellist Nat. Symphony, Washington, 1947-48; prin. cellist Vancouver (B.C.) Symphony, 1948-51, Longines Symphonette, N.Y.C., 1952-53, Tulsa Symphony, 1953-57, New Orleans Symphony, 1957-65; faculty U. Tulsa, 1953-57; faculty, dir. symphony Wash. State U., Pullman, 1965-69; faculty Western Wash. State Coll., Bellingham, 1969—, prof. music, mus. dir., condr. Bellingham-Western Symphony, 1969—. Dir. N.W. Concert Assn., 1970—; several concert tours U.S., Can., Mexico, including solo appearances with maj. symphonies; guest condr. with various orgns. Mem. Music Educators Nat. Conf., Am. Fedn. Musicians, Am. Fedn. Tchrs. Home: 506 Boulevard Bellingham WA 98225

FRANK, DELBERT, SR., Indian tribal councilman, natural resources manager; b. Warm Springs Reservation, Oreg., Sept. 9, 1923; s. Charles Huss and Myrtle (Yahtin) F.; m. Rosiland St. Claire, Oct. 15, 1973; children—Priscilla, Myrna, Lillian, Malene, Carol Dee, Delbert, Charles; m. 2d, Velma Charley, Sept. 5, 1980. Student schs. Warm Springs, Oreg. Cattle breeder; baker, cook Warm Springs (Oreg.) Indian Boarding Sch.; served as tribal credit Warm Springs Tribal Council, mem. tribal council, 1956—, researcher for reservation Oreg. State U.; mem. Oreg. State Water Bd.; mem. numerous state coms. mem. Scenic Water Commn., Oreg. Scenic Rivers Commn. Mem. Oreg. Deschutes River Task Force; minister Indian Shaker Ch. Served with USN, 1942-46. Recipient service award as tribal councilman, 1983, awards for establishment of tribal welfare orgns., 1983. Mem. Affiliated Tribes Northwest (Oreg., Wash., Idaho, pres.), Columbia River Alliance Orgn., Oreg. Wildlife Fedn. (dir. Dist. 6). Responsible for founding Northwest Portland Area Indian Health Bd. and Columbia Inter-Tribal Fish Commn. Office: Tribal Office Warm Springs OR 97761

FRANK, ELAINE KOENIGSDORF, lawyer; b. Kansas City, Mo.; d. Henry and Dorothy Belle (Levin) Koenigsdorf; cert. Lindenwood Coll., 1937; student McKay's Bus. Coll., 1948; LL.B., Southwestern U., 1957; children—Babette Frank Naslund, Robert Nelson. Legal sec., Los Angeles, 1948-57; admitted to Calif. bar, 1958; research atty. Los Angeles Superior Ct., 1958-59; atty. Belli, Ashe & Gerry, San Francisco, 1959; research atty. Calif. Supreme Ct.-Calif. Jud. Council, 1959-60; practiced in Los Altos, 1961—; atty.-editor Commerce Clearing House, San Francisco, 1961-62; staff atty. Continuing Edn. of Bar, U. Calif., Berkeley, 1963-75; corp. counsel, dir. legal econs. Capital Diversified Internat. Ltd., 1977—. Mem. curriculum guide com. Calif. Community Colls., 1973-74; mem. adv. com. legal forms Jud. Council, 1974-78. Mem. Santa Clara County Bar Assn., Am. Fedn. Tchrs., Alumni Assn. Southwestern U., Harry S. Truman Library Inst., Am. Judicature Soc., State Bar Calif. (recorder com. on probate and trust law 1970-77), Internat. Platform Assn., So. Poverty Law Center, Santa Clara County Women Lawyers, Themis Soc., Iota Tau Tau. Editor, co-author: California Civil Writs, 1970; author/editor: California Civil Court Forms, 1972; mem. editorial bd. Calif. Edn. of Bar, 1963-74. Home: 1405 Montclaire Pl Los Altos CA 94022 Office: 1405 Montclaire Pl Los Altos CA 94022

FRANK, ELLIOT STEVEN, software engineer; b. New Brunswick, N.J., Aug. 31, 1949; s. Henry J. and Bernice M. (Kantor) F. B.A., Columbia U., 1971. Systems engr. Software Ag N.A., Reston, Va., 1974-75; sr. systems engr. Informatics Inc., N.Y.C., 1976-77; sr. systems programmer Amdahl Corp., Sunnyvale, Calif., 1978-79, mgr. teleprocessing, 1980-82, prin. engr., 1982—. Mem. Assn. Computing Machinery. Office: 1250 E Arques Ave Sunnyvale CA 94086

FRANK, ERIC LUDWIG, indsl. mgmt. cons.; b. Munich, Bavaria, Nov. 4, 1910; s. Benno and Ida (Wanger) F.; came to U.S., 1939, naturalized, 1943; M.S. in Indsl. Engring., Aachen (Germany) Tech. Inst., 1931; M.A. in Econs., Munich (Germany) U., 1933; m. Eva Reeves Frank, Feb. 21, 1946; children—Eric Ludwig, Nancy D. (Mrs. Birt L. Duncan), Carole A., Wendy L. (Mrs. Gary M. Archibald). Chief exec. B&S Frank, Munich, 1933-38; economist War Assets Adminstrn., Seattle, 1945-48; indsl. specialist U.S. Army, Oakland, 1948-51; mgmt. cons. U.S. Air Force, Pleasanton, Calif., 1951-53; indsl. engr. U.S. Army, Herlong, Calif., 1953-55; chief indsl. engr. U.S. Navy, Honolulu, 1955-57; indsl. mgmt. cons. U.S. Navy, Seal Beach, Calif., 1957-75; faculty Orange Coast Coll., 1960-61; del. Calif. Legis. Council Profl. Engrs., 1972. Mem. Manpower Adv. Council of Contra Costa, Calif., County, 1978—; counselor Service Corps Ret. Execs. (SCORE). trustee Engring. Edn. Found., 1967-75. Served to lt. col. AUS, 1940-45; ETO. Decorated Purple Heart, Bronze Star medal, 5 Battle Stars. Registered profl. engr., Calif. Mem. Calif. Soc. Profl. Engrs. (chpt. dir. 1970-71, chmn. legis. affairs, dir. Mt. Diablo chpt. 1978—, pres. 1981-82), Am. Inst. Indsl. Engrs. (chpt. dir. 1969-70, regional chmn. community affairs), Orange County Engring. Council (pres. 1966-67, dir. 1968-74, Am. Arbitration Assn. (panel). Home: 42 Tam O'Shanter Alamo CA 94507

FRANK, FRED JAMES, ret. army officer, educator; b. Jersey City, Mar. 20, 1919; s. George and Anna (Frances (Fischer) F.; B.S., St. Johns U., 1940; postgrad U. Queensland, 1943, Fordham U., 1940; M.A., N.Y.U., 1949; Edn. Specialist, N.Mex. State U., 1974; m. Dorothea Vernice Plaut, July 13, 1942; children—Dorothea Pamela, Robert George, Barbara Karen. Commd. 2nd lt. U.S. Army, 1942, advanced through grades to lt. col., 1958; asso. prof. mil. sci. Northeastern U., Boston, 1954-58; dep. chief mission, communications adviser to cmdg. gen. Imperial Iranian Gendarmerie, Tehran, 1961-65; dir. communications, later dep. for logistics White Sands Missile Range, N.Mex., 1965-67; ret., 1967; supr. quality control Zia Co., NASA, Las Cruces, N.Mex., 1967-69; tchr. journalism, head English dept. Las Cruces (N.Mex.) High Sch., 19—; instr. summer journalism workshops N.Mex. State U., 1973-76. Decorated Bronze Star. Mem. Journalism Edn. Assn. (dir. Rocky Mountain), Armed Forces Communications Electronics Assn. (past pres. chapters), Am. Def. Preparedness Assn. (past pres. White Sands), Nat. Assn. Profl. Educators, U.S. Naval Inst., Phi Delta Kappa (past pres. N.Mex. State U. chpt., nat. del.). Democrat. Roman Catholic. Clubs: Las Cruces, Country (dir.), Lancers, Elks. Editor, Epee, 1974—; contbr. articles to profl. jours., poetry to Nat. Poetry Anthology, N.Y. English Jour. Home: 1800 Altura Ave Las Cruces NM 88001 Office: 1755 El Paseo St Las Cruces NM 88001

FRANK, GERALD WENDEL, business executive; b. Portland, Oreg., Sept. 21, 1923; s. Aaron M. and Ruth (Rosenfeld) F.; student Stanford U., 1941-43; B.A. with honors, Cambridge U., 1948, M.A., 1953; D.Bus. Adminstrn. (hon.), Greenville Coll., 1971; LL.D. (hon.), Pacific U., 1983. With Meier & Frank Co., Portland, 1948-53, mgr., Salem, Oreg., 1953-65; v.p. Meier & Frank Co., Inc., 1958-65; pres. Frank Investment Co.; spl. asst. to Senator Mark Hatfield, 1966-72, adminstrv. asst., 1973—, gen. chmn. Mark Hatfield for U.S. Senate Com., 1966, 72, 78; mem. Culver Commn. on Operation U.S. Senate, 1976, mem. mgmt. com., 1977-79; dir. U.S. Nat. Bank of Oreg., Standard Ins. Co., Am. Fed. Savs. & Loan Assn. Pres., Cascade area council Boy Scouts Am., 1960-61, mem. Western regional com., 1957—, mem. at large Nat. council; chmn. Citizens Conf. for Govtl. Cooperation, Mid-Willamette Valley of Oreg., 1958-59; bd. dirs. Portland Rose Festival Assn., 1954—, Jr. Achievement of Portland, 1953—; bd. dirs. Salem United Fund, 1956-62, 63—, pres., 1965-67; pres. Marion Polk County United Good Neighbors, 1965-67. Mem. Gov.'s adv. com. Oreg. Dept. Planning and Devel., 1957-73, chmn. 1959-66; trustee, gov., chmn. devel. com. Willamette U.; trustee Salem YWCA; v.p. Oreg. Grad. Study and Research Center, 1963-69; mem. bd. control Salem Gen. Hosp., 1955-61; bd. overseers Oreg. Health Scis. U.; mem. adv. bd. Mt. Angel Sem.; adv. bd. Salvation Army, Salem, mem. nat. adv. council; bd. dirs. Campfire Girls. Served with F.A., AUS, 1943-46; ETO. Named Jr. 1st Citizen of Salem, 1957; Silver Beaver award Boy Scouts, 1963; Sr. First Citizen of Salem, 1964; Pacific N.W. Service to Mankind award Sertoma Internat., 1967; Ernest Thompson Seton award Camp Fire, 1980; Disting. Service award Western Oreg. State Coll., 1980-81. Mem. Nat. Retail Mchts. Assn. (dir. 1959, v.p. 1960), Oreg. Hist. Soc. (dir. 1960-68), Salem Area C. of C. (pres. 1965-67), Am. Legion. Lodges: Elks, Rotary. Clubs: Multnomah Athletic, Illahe, Arlington, Waverley. Home: 3250 Crestview Dr Salem OR 97302 Office: 475 Cottage NE PO Box 2225 Salem OR 97308

FRANK, HELMUT JACK, economist, educator; b. Koblenz, Germany, June 6, 1922; s. Arthur A and Anna T (Sternberg) F.; m. Annemarie Bartknecht Dec. 30, 1961 (div.); 1 son, Thomas. B.S. in Econs., Columbia U., 1948, M.A., 1950, Ph.D., 1961. Economist, W.J. Levy Cons., N.Y.C., 1950-56; instr., Princeton U., 1958-59; asst. prof., U. Ariz., 1961-63, assoc. prof., 1963-67, prof., 1967—, dir. econ. and bus. research 1978-80; research economist, U. Denver Research Inst., 1967-68; cons., energy econs. Active Tucson-Pima Met. Energy Commn., 1980—. Served with U.S. Army 1943-45. Mem. Am. Econs. Assn., Western Econs. Assn., Internat. Assn. Energy Economists, AAAS, Ariz. Econ. Round Table. Author: Crude Oil Prices In The Middle East, 1966; (with John Lichtblau) Outlook For World Crude Oil Prices Into The 21st Century, 1978; editor: Arizona's Energy Future, 1982; The Energy Jour., 1980—. Home: 810 N Camino Santiago No 20 Tucson AZ 85745 Office: Dept of Economics U Ariz Tucson AZ 85721

FRANK, ROBERT GREGG, life insurance company executive; b. Chgo., Feb. 22, 1918; s. George Charles and Estelle (Cosgrove) F.; B.S. in Finance, U. Okla., 1939; m. Patricia Walsh Shoaf, Dec. 14, 1942; children—Robert Gregg, Stephen Cosgrove, Jon Lindsay. With Equitable Life Assurance Soc., 1939-41; stockbroker Brailsford & Co., Chgo., 1945-47; regional v.p. Hugh W. Long & Co., mut. fund underwriter, Los Angeles, 1947—, chmn. sales adv. bd., 1963-66, exec. v.p. Western states, 1966-73; exec. v.p. Anchor Corp., 1973-77; pres., dir. Anchor Nat. Fin. Services, Phoenix, 1974-82, Anchor Nat. Life Ins. Co., Phoenix, 1976-83; dir. Washington Nat. Corp. Served to lt. col., AUS, 1941-45. Decorated Bronze Star medal with cluster. Mem. Phi Kappa Sigma. Republican. Roman Catholic. Clubs: Plaza; Country of Colo.; Garden of Gods; Camelback Country. Home: 4317 N 70th St Scottsdale AZ 85251 Office: Anchor Nat Plaza Camelback at E 22d St Phoenix AZ 85016

FRANK, SANDERS THALHEIMER, physician; b. Middletown, Conn., May 11, 1938; s. Harry S. and Pauline (Thalheimer) F.; B.A., Amherst Coll., 1959; M.D., N.Y. Med. Coll., 1963; m. Marta Santoyo, Jan. 7, 1981; children by previous marriage—Geoffrey Brooks, Susan Kimberly, Jonathan Blair, Adam. Intern, Sinai Hosp., Balt., 1963-64; resident Wilford Hall Med. Center, San Antonio, 1965-68; practice medicine, specializing in pulmonary disease, Monterey Park, Calif., 1971—; dir. respiratory care Garfield Hosp., Monterey Park, 1974—, Beverly Hosp., Montebello, Calif., 1975-78; asso. prof. medicine U. So. Calif., Los Angeles, 1972—. Served to maj. USAF, 1964-71. Decorated USAF Commendation medal; recipient Philip Hench award for demonstrating relationship of rheumatoid arthritis to lung disease, 1968; award of merit Los Angeles County Heart Assn., 1974. Fellow Royal Soc. Medicine (London), Am. Coll. Chest Physicians, A.C.P.; mem. Am. Thoracic Soc., Calif. Thoracic Soc., Nat. Assn. Dirs. Respiratory Care, Respiratory Care Assembly Calif., Alpha Omega Alpha. Contbr. articles in field to med. jours. Recorded relationship of ear-lobe crease to coronary artery disease, 1973. Home: 891 E Grandview Sierra Madre CA 91024 Office: 500 N Garfield Ave Monterey Park CA 91754

FRANK, STUART BARRY, optometrist; b. N.Y.C., July 10, 1951; s. Morty Lawrence and Harriet (Stackel) F.; m. Keiko Helen Inouye, Sept. 6, 1980. B.A. with honors, U. Calif.-San Diego, 1973; postgrad. Calif. State U.-Fullerton, 1973-76; O.D., New Eng. Coll. Optometry, 1980. Lic. optometrist, Hawaii, Calif., Wash., N.Y., Mass. Resident in rehabilitative optometry VA Med. Ctr., Northport, N.Y., 1980-81; primary care optometrist Community Health Plan of Suffolk, Hauppauge, N.Y., 1980-81; assoc. Dr. Sheldon Golden, O.D., Whittier, Calif., 1981—; asst. clin. instr. optometry Coll. Optometry, State U. N.Y., 1980-81. Mem. Am. Pub. Health Assn., Rio Hondo Optometric Soc., Calif. Optometric Assn., Am. Optometric Assn., Nat. Geog. Soc., Beta Sigma Kappa.

FRANK, THOMAS, interior designer; b. Salt Lake City, Nov. 23, 1937; s. Simon and Suzanne (Seller) F.; B.F.A., U. Utah, 1963. Owner, Thomas Frank Interior Designs/Constrn., Salt Lake City, 1962—; instr. design and textiles Latter-day Saints Jr. Coll., Salt Lake City, 1964—; profl. adviser U. Utah Interior Design Curriculum Devel. Program, 1978; mem. profl. adv. council Utah State Bldg Bd., 1978. Exec. v.p. Salt Lake City Art Center, 1977-80; spl. adv. Children's Center, 1970—; co-chmn. spl. events Utah div. Am. Cancer Soc., 1978. Recipient awards U. Utah, 1962, Utah Designers Craftsman Guild, 1962, State Fair Fine Arts, 1962; Honor award Utah Soc. AIA, 1982. Fellow Inst. Profl. Designers, Am. Soc. Interior Designers (nat. publicity chmn. 1978, nat. chmn. energy conservation com. 1980-83, edn. com. 1981, membership retention com. 1981-83, nat. bd. dirs. 1977-82, nat. regional v.p. 1980). Jewish. Home: 2360 Oakhills Dr Salt Lake City UT 84121 Office: 1321 E 3300 S Salt Lake City UT 84106

FRANKE, WILLIAM AUGUSTUS, corp. exec.; b. Bryan, Tex., Apr. 15, 1937; s. Louis John and Frances (Hanna) F.; B.A., Stanford, 1959, LL.B., 1961; m. Carolyn D. Walker, July 16, 1977; children—Catherine Anne, Paige Estelle, Brian Hanna, David Parker, Rebecca Ann Walker. Admitted to Wash. bar, 1961; asso. firm MacGillivray, Jones, Clark & Schiffner, Spokane, 1962-67, partner, 1967-70; v.p., sec., corporate counsel S.W. Forest Industries, Phoenix, 1970-72, sr. v.p., sec., 1972-73, exec. v.p., asst. chief exec. officer, 1973-75, pres., 1975—, chief operating officer, 1977-78, chief exec. officer, 1978—, also dir. subs. cos.; dir. Phelps Dodge Corp., ABS Industries, Valley Nat. Bank. Trustee, Combined Health Resources, Inc.; mem. dean's council Stanford U. Law Sch. Served to capt. U.S. Army, 1961-62. Mem. Am., Wash., Spokane County bar assns., Am. Paper Inst. (dir.), Young Presidents Orgn. Episcopalian. Clubs: Stanford, Arizona, Paradise Valley Country, Phoenix Country (Phoenix), Plaza. Home: 7701 N Saguaro Dr Paradise Valley AZ 85253 Office: 6225 N 24th St Phoenix AZ 85016

FRANKEL, ARTHUR M., architect; b. Bklyn., Oct. 1, 1935; s. Samuel and Sadie (Schoenfeld) F.; B.Arch., Pratt Inst., Bklyn., 1959; m. Sandra Weiner, Nov. 12, 1961; children—Dana Lynn, Amy Denise. Staff architect Lloyd Morgan, N.Y.C., 1962-63, Fellheimer & Wagner, N.Y.C., and Emery Roth & Sons, N.Y.C., 1963-64, Fred G. Frost, Jr., N.Y.C., 1964-66, Philip Johnson, Ed Larabee Barnes, 1966-67, Roy Rosenbaum, 1969-72; territorial architect Met. Life Ins. Co., San Mateo, Calif., 1972—. Served to lt. (j.g.), USNR, 1959-62. Registered architect, N.Y., Calif.; lic. Nat. Council Archtl. Registration Bds. Office: 2855 Campus Dr San Mateo CA 94403

FRANKEL, A(RTHUR) STEVEN, clin. psychologist; b. N.Y.C., Aug. 13, 1942; s. Henry Samuel and Lillian (Krasoff) F.; B.A. in Psychology, U. Vt., 1964; Ph.D. in Clin. Psychology, Ind. U., 1968; m. Rita Irene Krauss, Aug. 20, 1967; 1 dau., Hali Samantha. Mem. faculty U. So. Calif., 1968—, clin. prof. psychology, 1980—, dir. Ph.D. program, 1971-76; cons. Del Amo Hosp., Torrance, Calif., Brotman Meml. Hosp., Culver City, Calif., South Bay Human Services Ctr., 1981—. Recipient Outstanding Tchr. award U. So. Calif., 1971. Diplomate Am. Bd. Profl. Psychology. Mem. Am. Psychol. Assn., Assn. Advancement Behavior Therapy, Calif. Psychol. Assn. (bd. dirs. 1982—), So. Calif. Soc. Clin. and Exptl. Hypnosis, Los Angeles County Psychol. Assn., Sigma Xi. Author: Inside Psychotherapy, 1971; also articles, chpts. in books. Home: 2805 Via Rivera Palos Verdes Estates CA 90274 Office: 927 Deep Valley St Suite 200 Rolling Hills Estates CA 90274

FRANKEL, DEXTRA L., educator, artist; b. Los Angeles, Nov. 28, 1924. Student Long Beach State Coll. Group shows include Los Angeles County Mus. Art, 1959, 62, 66, Cin. Art Mus., Newport Harbor Art Mus., Newport Beach, Calif., Butler Inst. Am. Art, Youngstown, Ohio, Calif. Palace of Legion of Honor, San Francisco, Denver Art Mus., Seattle Art Mus., Portland (Oreg.) Art Mus., San Francisco Mus. Art, H.M. deYoung Mus., San Francisco, Smithsonian Inst.; represented in permanent collections at Phila. Free Library, La Jolla (Calif.) Art Mus., St. Paul Art Ctr., Pacific View Meml. Park, Corona Del Mar, Calif., Kennecott Copper Co., Salt Lake City; from asst. prof. to assoc. prof. art Calif. State U.-Fullerton, 1964-79, prof., 1979—, dir. art gallery, curator and designer exhbns., 1967—. U.S. del. World Craft Council Conf., Mexico, 1976; trustee Western Assn. Art Mus., San Francisco, 1979-82. Recipient Design award Soc. Typographic Arts Union Bank Hist. Mus., 1981; Nat. Endowment Arts grantee, 1975, 1977-82. Mem. Am. Assn. Museums, Am. Craft Council (trustee 1975-78), Art Mus. Assn. Office: Calif State University Dept Art Fullerton CA 92634

FRANKEL, EDWARD IRWIN, fin. exec.; b. Bklyn., Aug. 26, 1941; s. Paul and Anna (Pasmowitz) F.; student N.Y. U., 1962-66; certificate N.Y. Inst. Fin., 1962; m. Ann Ruth Weinstein, Apr. 5, 1964; children—Jennifer Lynn, Rachel Gale. Partner, Baerwald & DeBoer, mems. N.Y. Stock Exchange, N.Y.C., 1966-70; instl. account exec. Frederick & Co., N.Y.C., 1970-72; v.p., regional mgr. Variable Annuity Life Ins. Co., Los Angeles, 1972-76; dir., chmn. F&M Assos. Ltd., Torrance, Calif., 1976—; chmn. United Econ. Services, Inc., dir. C.F.O., F & M Agy. Inc., CFO United Econ. Services Inc. Mem. Ins. Com., Palos Verdes Estates; trustee South Bay Hosp. Found.; bd. dirs. Temple Menorah. Mem. Nat. Securities Dealers Assn., Nat., Los Angeles (chmn. legis. com., 1976-77) assns. life underwriters., Palos Verdes Community Arts Assn. Clubs: Palos Verdes Breakfast, Townhall (Los Angeles).

FRANKEL, FREDERICK DAVID, psychologist; b. N.Y.C., Feb. 26, 1946; s. Jack Jacob and Beatrice (Trus) F.; B.A., SUNY, Stony Brook, 1967; Ph.D., U. Calif.-Irvine, 1971; m. Lucinda Frankel. Research asst. SUNY, Stony Brook, 1966-67, U. Calif.-Irvine, 1967-68, teaching asst., 1968-69; research asst. Rockefeller U., 1969-71; research psychologist UCLA, 1972-76, adj. asst. prof., 1976-80, assoc. prof.-in-residence, 1980—, behavioral cons. Neuropsychiat. Inst. Sch., 1972—, tng. dir. Clin. Research Ctr., 1980—, dir. Parent Tng. Clinic, 1983—. Social Sci.

Research Council fellow, 1971; Maternal and Child Health postdoctoral fellow, 1972-73. Mem. Am. Psychol. Assn., Am. Assn. Mental Deficiency. Contbr. articles to profl. jours. Office: 760 Westwood Plaza Los Angeles CA 90074

FRANKEL, JEFFREY, economist, educator, consultant; b. San Francisco, Nov. 5, 1952; s. Jack Earle and Donna (Lyons) F. B.A., Swarthmore Coll., 1974; Ph.D., MIT, 1978. Asst. prof., U. Mich., Ann Arbor, 1975-79; acting assoc. prof. U. Calif.-Berkeley, 1979—; econ. cons. Bank of Portugal, Lisbon, 1976; vis. asst. prof. Yale U., 1980; vis. scholar Fed. Res. Bd., Washington, 1981; internat. policy economist Council Econ. Advisers, 1983-84. NSF grantee, 1980-82, 83-85. Mem. Am. Econ. Assn. Sierra Club (econs. com.). Contbr. articles to profl. jours. Home: 8 Mosswood Rd Berkeley CA 94704 Office: Dept of Econs U Calif Berkeley CA 94720

FRANKENSTEIN, JOHN, educator, consultant; b. San Francisco, Jan. 27, 1940; s. Alfred Victor and Sylvia (Lent) F.; m. Veronica Li, July 1, 1967; children—Karen Wielan, Paul. B.A., Stanford U., 1961; M.A., San Francisco State U., 1967; diploma in internat. relations Johns Hopkins Sch. Advanced Internat. Studies European Ctr., Bologna, Italy, 1976; Ph.D. in Polit. Sci., MIT, 1983. Lectr. U. Hawaii, 1967-68; fgn. service officer USIA, assigned to Senegal, Belgium, Taiwan, Hong Kong, Italy, 1968-77; research asst. MIT Ctr. for Internat. Studies, 1977-78, instr., grad. asst., 1978-81; instr. Northeastern U., Brandeis U., 1978-81; lectr. Asian studies U. Mass., 1981-82; asst. prof. Am. Grad. Sch. Internat. Mgmt., Glendale Ariz., 1982—. Served with USN 1961-63. Mem. Am. Polit. Sci. Assn., Asian Studies Assn., Internat. Studies Assn., Phoenix Com. Foreign Relations. Office: Am Graduate School of International Studies Glendale AZ 85306

FRANKIE, GORDON WILLIAM, entomology educator; b. Albany, Calif., Mar. 29, 1940; s. Anthony and Eleanor (Grasso) F.; m. Jutta Kirsch, Jan. 1969. B.S. in Entomology, U. Calif.-Berkeley, 1963; Ph.D. in Entomology, 1968. Tchr., researcher Texas A.&M. U., 1970-76; prof. U. Calif.-Berkeley, 1976—. NSF grantee, 1968-82; EPA grantee, 1973-76, 78-79. Mem. AAAS, Entomol. Soc. Am., Ecol. Soc. Am., Assn., Assn. Tropical Biology, Am. Inst. Biol. Scis. Editor: (with C.S. Koehler) Perspectives in Urban Entomology, 1978, Urban Entomology: Interdisciplinary Perspectives, 1983. Contbr. articles to profl. jours.

FRANKLIN, CHARLES ELLSWORTH, social worker, educator; b. Washington, Apr. 1, 1947; s. William McHenry and Alicelia (Hoskins) F.; m. Cynthia Jean Beattie, Nov. 22, 1975; children—Nathan Charles, Andrew Warner. B.A. in Psychology and Sociology, Earlham Coll., 1969; M.S.W., U. Wash., 1973; Ph.D. in Sociology, U. Colo., 1981. Trainee Eastern State Hosp., Medical Lake, Wash., 1972-73; therapist Bethesda Mental Health Ctr., Denver, 1973—; ptnr. Colo. Discourse Cons.; assoc. Arvada Psychol. and Family Service; pvt. practice specializing in psychotherapy, Denver; research assoc. TOSCO Found., Boulder, Colo., 1977-78; assoc. Greenwood Psychotherapy and Counseling Assocs., Englewood, Colo., 1979-81. Contbr. articles to profl. publs. Vol., Am. Friends Service Com., 1966-71. Recipient Amigos de las Americas Service award, 1976, 78. Mem. Am. Sociol. Assn., Nat. Assn. Social Workers, Acad. Cert. Social Workers. Home: 1918 Cherry St Denver CO 80220 Office: 360 S Monroe St Suite 280 Denver CO 80209

FRANKLIN, DOUGLAS RICHARD, agricultural economist, educator; b. Albuquerque, Apr. 23, 1953; s. Robert Ayers and Mary Elena (Davis) F.; m. Kathryn Franklin, Aug. 17, 1974; children—Rachel Marie, Matthew Richard. B.A. in Econs., U. N.Mex., 1975, M.A. in Econs., 1978; Ph.D. in Econs., Utah State U., 1982. Research asst. econs. U. N.Mex., 1976-77; research asst. dept. econs. Utah Water Research Lab., Utah State U., 1979-81; vis. asst. prof. div. agrl. econs. U. Wyo., 1981—. Mem. Am. Agrl. Econs. Assn., Am. Econs. Assn., Assn. Environ. and Resources Economists, Western Agrl. Econs. Assn., Omicron Delta Epsilon. Contbr. articles to profl. jours. Office: Division of Agricultural Economics PO Box 3354 University Station University of Wyoming Laramie WY 82071

FRANKLIN, IRL LEON, educator, former air force officer; b. Hutchinson, Kans., Sept. 29, 1934; s. Clifford Oscar and Carol Renetta (Rollins) F.; m. Ella Mae Barno, Sept. 2, 1956; 1 dau., Susan Renee. B.S., Kans. State U., 1956; M.S., U. So. Calif., 1970. Cert. counselor schs., Nev. Commd. 2d lt. U.S. Air Force, 1956, advanced through grades to lt. col., 1973, served as pilot, U.S., Republic of South Vietnam, W.Ger., 1956-79, staff officer U.S. Air Force Ops. Hdqrs., 1974-79, ret., 1979; counselor Winnemucca (Nev.) Jr. High Sch., 1979—; dist. microcomputer coordinator, faculty No. Nev. Community Coll. Decorated Silver Star, Air Medal with 13 oak leaf clusters. Mem. NEA, Nev. Ednl. Assn., Am. Personnel and Guidance Assn., Air Force Assn. Democrat. Methodist. Office: Box 712 Winnemucca NV 89445

FRANKLIN, MATTHEW JAMES, construction and pipe manufacturing executive; b. Salt Lake City, June 7, 1928; s. James Matthew and Bernice Ella (Simpson) F.; Annalee Simpson, July 25, 1952; children—Susan, Charlene Franklin Romano, Diane. B.C.E., U. Santa Clara, 1952. Registered profl. engr., Calif. Project engr. Morrison-Knudson Co., Inc., Los Angeles, 1952-59; v.p. Cen-Vi-Ro Pipe Corp., Shafter, Calif., 1959-71; pvt. practice tech. cons., Shafter, 1971-76; project engr. Ameron Inc., Fontana, Calif., 1976-80; pres. Ameron-Price Co., Fontana, Calif., 1980—. Served with U.S. Army, 1946-48. Mem. ASCE. Republican. Club: Masons. Patentee various pipe mfg. processes and equipment. Home: 15304 Pintura Dr Hacienda Heights CA 91745 Office: Ameron-Price Co 13189 Slover Ave Fontana CA 92335

FRANKLIN, MELVIN RAY, JR., psychologist; b. Norfolk, Va., Mar. 23, 1947; s. Melvin Ray and Mary Catherine (Bennett) F.; m. Melissa J. Ard, Aug. 10, 1977; 1 son, Matthew Edward. B.A., So. Meth. U., 1969, M.A., 1970; Ph.D. in Ednl. Psychology, U. Ariz., 1978. Asst. dir. admissions So. Meth. U., Dallas, 1970-73; grad. assoc. in teaching U. Ariz., Tucson, 1973-74; sch. psychologist Amphitheater Sch. Dist., Tucson, 1974—; adj. clin. asst. prof. U. Ariz., 1980—; pvt. practice psychology, Tucson, 1979—; cons. U. Ariz. Med. Sch., Merrill Pub. Co., 1980—. Mem. Am. Psychol. Assn., Nat. Assn. Sch. Psychologists, Phi Delta Kappa, Psi Chi. Republican. Methodist. Club: Rotary. Contbr. articles to profl. jours. Home: 8118 N Gibraltar Dr Tucson AZ 85704 Office: 701 W Wetmore Rd Tucson AZ 85705

FRANKLIN, MICHAEL HAROLD, orgn. exec.; b. Los Angeles, Dec. 25, 1923; s. A.B., U. Calif. at Los Angeles, 1948; LL.B., U. So. Calif., 1951; children—Barbara, John, James, Robert. Admitted to Calif. bar, 1951; practiced law, Los Angeles, 1951-52; pvt. practice, 1951-52; atty. CBS, 1952-54; atty. Paramount Pictures Corp., 1954-58; exec. dir. Writers Guild Am. West, Inc., 1958-78; nat. exec. dir. Dirs. Guild Am., 1978—. Mem. Fed. Cable Adv. Commn. Served with C.E., AUS, 1942-46. Mem. ACLU, Los Angeles Copyright Soc., Order of Coif. Office: 7950 Sunset Blvd Los Angeles CA 90046

FRANKLIN, WILLIAM WARREN, utilities co. exec.; b. Chgo., May 17, 1915; s. Howard Brace and Natalie (Purdy) F.; B.S. in Mech. Engring., U. Cal. at Berkeley, 1939; m. Mary Ellen Gerard, Jan. 6, 1940; children—Barbara Inez (Mrs. John Paul Binaski), Patricia Ellen, Richard G. With So. Calif. Water Co., 1939—, exec. v.p., Los Angeles, 1969-71, pres., 1971-80, pres., chief exec. officer, 1980-82, chmn. bd., 1982—, also dir. Chmn., Los Angeles County Water Appeals Bd. Served to lt. col. AUS, 1941-46. Registered profl. engr., Calif. Mem. Am. Legion, Los Angeles C. of C. (vice chmn. water and energy commn. 1969—), Calif. Water Assn. (past pres.). Elk. Club: Jonathan (Los Angeles). Home: 312 Avenida Atezada Redondo Beach CA 90277 Office: 3625 W 6th St Lost Angeles CA 90020

FRANKS, STEPHEN FIELD, lawyer; b. Biltmore, N.C., June 12, 1930; s. Thomas Hendricks and Margaret (Field) F.; A.B., Duke, 1952; LL.B., U. N.C., 1955, J.D., 1969; m. Mary Elizabeth Volbeda, Apr. 28, 1962; children—Stephen Bruce, Andrea Carol, Craig Thomas. Admitted to N.C. bar, 1956, Calif. bar, 1964; practiced in Asheville, N.C., 1960-61, San Francisco, 1962-64; dep. city atty., San Bernardino, Calif., 1964-66, fed. aid coordinator, 1966-68; legis. adviser, San Bernardino County, 1969-80. Mem. Sacramento County Bd. Edn., 1974-78, chmn., 1977-78; mem. San Juan Unified Sch. Bd., 1978—, chmn., 1979; mem. Sacramento County Democratic Central Com., 1976-79; bd. dirs. Sacramento County Mental Health Assn., pres., 1978-79. Served to lt. USNR, 1956-60, now comdr. ret. Res. Mem. State Bar N.C., State Bar Calif., Amvets, Phi Alpha Delta. Episcopalian. Elk. Clubs: Comstock; Glen Oaks (Carmichael, Calif.). 95608 Office: 127 S Main St Hendersonville NC 28739

FRANSCELL, GEORGE J., lawyer; b. Los Angeles, Mar. 31, 1933; s. Joseph Peter and Myrtle May (Diltz) F.; m. Billie Marie te Groen, Sept. 9, 1961; children—Thomas, Michael, Michelle. B.B.A., Loyola U., 1955; J.D., UCLA, 1958. Advocate, Am. Bd. Trial Advs. Bar: Calif. 1959; with Los Angeles City Attys.' Office, 1959-73, prin. asst. city atty., until 1973; assoc., then ptnr. Dryden, Harrington & Swartz, Los Angeles, 1973-79; ptnr. Citkin, Collins, Kolts & Franscell, Los Angeles, 1979—; nat. lectr., cons. on police misconduct and civil and criminal culpability. Mem. ABA, Calif. Bar Assn., Los Angeles County Bar Assn., Assn. Trial Lawyers Am., Calif. Peace Officers Assn., Internat. Assn. Chiefs of Police. Office: 550 S Hill St Suite 1300 Los Angeles CA 90013

FRANTZ, BONNIE LEE, college administrator; b. Sugar City, Colo., May 9, 1923; d. Emmons and Lillie Phyrne (Demits) Ringle; student Barnes Bus. Sch., 1943-44; student Otero Jr. Coll., 1960-61, Colo. State U., 1963, 65; m. Galen E. Frantz, Nov. 28, 1947; children—Maybelle, Paulette Jo, James Earl, Joy Lee. Sec. to supt. Rocky Ford Sch. Dist., Colo., 1958-61; clk.-typist Colo. State U. Extension Service, Ft. Collins, 1961; exec. sec. Colo. State U. Research Found., Ft. Collins, 1961-64, overseas br. in Enugu, Nigeria, 1964-66; prin. clk. internat. edn. office Colo. State U., Ft. Collins, 1966-70, adminstrv. asst., 1970-75, adminstrv. officer, Coll. Profl. Studies, 1975-83, asst. to dean, 1983—, rep. to statewide steering com. for classified staff, 1974-76; mem. Colo. State U. Classified Personnel Council, 1973-77; pres. Statewide Liaison Council Classified Personnel Staff, 1976-80. Recipient Outstanding award Colo. State U., 1973, Outstanding Achievement award, 1978; Disting. Service award Coll. Profl. Studies, 1980. Mem. Colo. Assn. Pub. Employees (dir. 1969-77, v.p. 1972-73). Republican. Methodist. Club: Order Eastern Star. Home: 1425 Lakeshore Dr Fort Collins CO 80525 Office: Colo State U Coll Professional Studies Fort Collins CO 80523

FRANTZ, JOHN CORYDON, librarian; b. Seneca Falls, N.Y., Aug. 25, 1926; s. John Clark and Cora May (Gilbert) F.; A.B., Syracuse (N.Y.) U., 1950, B.S., 1951, M.S., 1952; m. Vivien May Rowan, Dec. 31, 1947; children—Sheila Heather, Keith Hunter, Jay Corydon. Cons., Wis. State Library, 1954-58; dir. Green Bay (Wis.) Pub. Library, 1958-61; dir. pub. library grants U.S. Office Edn., 1961-67; dir. Bklyn. Pub. Library, 1967-70; dir. Nat. Book Com., 1970-75; exec. chmn. Pahlavi Nat. Library, Tehran, Iran, 1975-77; librarian San Francisco Pub. Library, 1977—; bd. dirs. Reading is Fundamental, Bookmobile Services Trust, Am. Reading Council, Metro Research Libraries Council. Served with U.S. Army, 1945-47. Mem. Am., N.Y. State, Calif. library assns. Club: Coffee House (N.Y.C.). Home: 1390 Market St San Francisco CA 94102 Office: Public Library Civic Center San Francisco CA 94102

FRANTZ, THEODORE CLAUDE, fisheries biologist; b. Reno, Jan. 27, 1922; s. Theodore and Alma Natalia (Swanson) F.; B.S. in Biology, U. Nev., 1951. Researcher stream and lake surveys Nev. Dept. Wildlife, 1951-58, mgr. fisheries Eastern Nev., 1958-60, researcher interstate fisheries study, Lake Tahoe, Nev., 1960-65, mgr. fisheries Western Nev., Smith, 1965—. Mem. Lake Tahoe Basin Environ. Coms., 1970-72; mem. tech. resource team Lake Tahoe Regional Planning Agy., 1982—. Served with USNR, 1942-45. Recipient Nev. Fish and Game Fisheries Project, 1964, Shikar Safari Internat. award, 1981; commended by Lake Tahoe Area Council, 1972. Mem. Am. Fisheries Soc., Wildlife Soc. Contbr. articles on fisheries research to tech. jours. Home and office: PO Box 50 Smith NV 89430

FRANZ, KAY BURTA, nutrition educator; b. Walkermine, Calif., Oct. 30, 1936; d. John Cahoon and Eva (Burton) F. B.S., U. Calif.-Berkeley, 1958, Ph.D., 1978; M.S., Brigham Young U., 1968. Instr. nutrition Brigham Young U., Provo, Utah, 1968-78, asst. prof., 1978-83, assoc. prof., 1983—. Mem. Am. Dietetic Assn., Inst. Food Technologists, Am. Coll. Nutrition. Mem. Ch. of Jesus Christ of Latter-day Saints. Office: Dept Food Science and Nutrition Brigham Young Univ Provo UT 84602

FRANZEN, ALAN TRAHERN, foundation executive; b. Redwood City, Calif., Oct. 31, 1956; s. Walter Forrest and Nancy Najera (Collins) F. A.B., U. Calif.-San Diego; 1978; A.M., U. Calif.-Davis, 1980. Office mgr., research asst. Dolby Assocs., Los Altos, Calif., 1981-83; project mgr. lang. of data project San Jose State U. Found., 1983—; cons. orthographics, linguistic software. Mem. Am. Statis. Assn., AAAS. Republican. Congregationalist. Office: 885 N San Antonio Rd Suite T Los Altos CA 94022

FRANZINI, LOUIS RALPH, clinical psychologist, educator, business consultant; b. Beaver Falls, Pa., Aug. 11, 1941; s. Louis Ralph and Martha Lavina (Householder) F.; m. Dolores Ann Napiecek, Aug. 8, 1964; children—Mary Lou, Jeremy. B.S., U. Pitts., 1963; M.A., U. Toledo, 1965; Ph.D., U. Pitts., 1968. Lic. psychologist, Calif., Pa. Postdoctoral fellow SUNY-Stony Brook, 1968-69; prof. psychology, San Diego State U., 1969—; condr. bus. mgt. seminars. Mem. Am. Psychol. Assn., Western Pshychol. Assn., Assn. Advancement of Behavior Therapy. Office: Dept Psychology San Diego State U San Diego CA 92182

FRASER, ELEANOR RUTH, physician; b. Woodlake, Calif., May 31, 1927; d. Morton William and Dorothy (Harding) Fraser; B.A., Pomona Coll., 1949; M.D., Stanford, 1954. Intern, Los Angeles County Hosp., 1953-54, resident in radiology, 1954-57; radiologist Hoag Meml. Hosp., Newport, Calif., 1957-58, St. Joseph Hosp., Orange, Calif., 1957-61; practice medicine specializing in radiology, Anaheim, Calif., 1961-78; radiologist Antelope Valley Hosp. Med. Center, Lancaster, Calif., 1978—. Diplomate Am. Bd. Radiology. Mem. A.M.A., Pan-Am. Med. Assn., A.A.A.S., Pomona Coll. Assos., Laguna Beach Art Assn., Phi Beta Kappa. Republican. Presbyn. Clubs: Balboa Bay (Newport Beach); Crystallaire Country (Llano, Calif.). Home: 1035 Lakeview Palmdale CA Office: 1600 W Ave J Lancaster CA 93534

FRASER, JOHN PRESTON, lawyer, water agency executive; b. Mendocino City, Calif., Dec. 7, 1932; s. Melville and Mildred (Ferguson) F.; m. Joan Deiter, Nov. 18, 1978; children—Kenneth John, Kathleen Marie, James Michael, Diana Elizabeth. A.A., Santa Rosa Jr. Coll., 1953; A.B., San Francisco State Coll., 1958; J.D., Golden Gate Law Sch., 1964. Bar: Calif. 1964. Atty. Calif. State Automobile Assn., San Francisco, 1958-70; exec. dir., gen. counsel Assn. Calif. Water Agys., Sacramento, 1970—. Served with U.S. Army, 1953-55. Mem. ABA, Calif. State Bar Assn., Am. Water Works Assn., Nat. Water Resources Assn., Western States Water Council, Am. Soc. Assn. Execs., Interstate Conf. Water Problems, Am. Water Coalition. Club: Commonwealth. Home: PO Box 708 El Dorado CA 95623 Office: Assn Calif Water Agys 1127 11th St Sacramento CA 95814

FRASER, ROBERT HENRY, marketing executive; b. Washington, Apr. 30, 1939; s. Havelock F. and Dorothy (Cassel) F. B.A., U. Ky., 1962; B.A. in Bus., Mich. State U., 1963. Dir. advt. John R. Thompson Co., Chgo., 1963-69; v.p. David W. Evans Advt., Los Angeles, 1969-76; v.p. mktg. Lyon's Restaurants, Inc., Foster City, Calif., 1976—. Republican. Presbyterian. Office: 1165 Triton Dr Foster City CA 94404

FRASIER, C(ARL) DOUGLAS, JR., security specialist; b. Sparta, Tenn., July 12, 1943; s. Carl Douglas and Roetta Marie (Fowler) F.; student Wright State U., 1965, U. Dayton, 1968; B.A. in Bus., Antioch Coll., 1975; M.B.A.; m. Linda Ann Cheatam, June 24, 1967; children—Phillip Tyler, Brian Douglas. Dir. ops. Liberal Markets, Inc., Dayton, Ohio, 1970-75; exec. v.p. C.W.C., Inc., Findlay, Ohio, 1975-76; dir. security Dillon Cos., Grand Junction, Colo., 1976-80; pres., chief exec. officer Frasier & Assos., Ltd., Grand Junction, 1977—; cons. exec. protection to corp. dirs. Hon. trainee Dayton Police Acad.; mem. U.S. Congl. Adv. Bd. Served with U.S. Army, 1963-65. Mem. Am. Soc. Indsl. Security, Assn. Fed. Investigators, Am. Def. Preparedness Assn. Republican. Mem. Assembly of God. Home: PO Box 2251 Grand Junction CO 81502 Office: 1204 N 7th St Grand Junction CO 81501

FRAUSE, ROBERT DONALD, public relations/communications executive, professional fund raiser; b. Seattle, Nov. 25, 1945; s. Henry J. and Sophie V. (Kopkas) F.; m. Susan Kay Bjorn, Feb. 5, 1951; 1 son, Max Bjorn. B.A. in Journalism, Seattle U., 1967. Accredited Pub. Relations, Pub. Relations Soc. Am., 1979. Dir. pub. relations, advt. Sunvan Internat., 1971-72; sr. account exec./dir. account service Hill and Knowlton Inc., Seattle, 1972-78; dir. communications and devel. Seattle Univ., 1978-81; dep. dir. Econ. Devel. Council of Puget Sound, Seattle, 1981—. Mem. City Council, City of Langely (Wash.), 1980-81; bd. dirs. Wash. div. Am. Cancer Soc., 1977—. Served to capt. U.S. Army, 1967-71. Decorated DSM; recipient Gold Quill award Internat. Assn. Bus. Communicators, 1982, Totem award Pub. Relations Soc. Am., 1982. Mem. Pub. Relations Soc. Am. (pres. Puget Sound chpt.), Northwest Devel. Assn. Roman Catholic. Club: Wash. Athletic (Seattle). Home: 848 Saratoga Rd Langley WA 98260 Office: Economic Development Council of Puget Sound 1218 3d Ave Suite 1900 Seattle WA 98101

FRAVEL, CYNTHIA MARIE, psychotherapist; b. Alexandria, Va., Aug. 10, 1950; d. Ralph Edwin and Marie (Devine) F. B.A., Old Dominion U., 1973; M.A. in Counseling, Pepperdine U., 1978. Therapist, Partial Care Adolescent Program, Alexandria, 1975-78, Child and Family Team, Ft. Collins, Colo., 1978—, Family Cons., Ft. Collins, 1982—; familty therapy and parenting workshops. Mem. Am. Personnel and Guidance Assn. Office: PO Box 1190 Fort Collins CO 80522 also 141 S College Fort Collins CO 80521

FRAYN, ROBERT MORT, printing and publishing company executive; b. Faulkton, S.D., May 3, 1906; s. Newton James and Margaret (Waterman) F.; m. Helen Elvira Carlson, Oct. 17, 1930; children—Suzanne, Robert Mort. B.A., U. Wash., 1929. With Frayn Printing Co./Book Pub. Co., Seattle, 1930—, owner, 1942—, pres., chief exec. officer, 1960—, chmn. bd., 1970—; former dir. Lincoln Mut. Bank, Braniff Internat.; mem. Wash. State Ho. of Reps., 1945-55, speaker, 1953. Chmn. Wash. Republican Party, 1951, 60; mem. Rep. Nat. Com., 1951-60; mem. bd. regents U. Wash., 1970-82, pres., 1975—; bd. dirs. Virginia Mason Hosp., 1946-60, U. Hosp., 1977-82; mem. Nat. Adv. Com. on Careers. Recipient Alumni Activity award U. Wash., 1977. Mem. Alumni Assn. U. Wash. Congregationalist. Clubs: Wash. Athletic, Univ., Seattle Golf, Thunderbird Golf, Rotary. Home: 1628 Windermere Dr E Seattle WA 98112 Office: 2318 Western Ave Seattle WA 98121

FRAZER, CHARLES FREDRIC, journalist, educator; b. Portland, Oreg., Jan. 21, 1946; s. Fredric Robert and Doris Edna (Mabie) F.; A.B., Rutgers U., 1968; M.A., Fairfield U., 1974; Ph.D., U. Ill., 1976; m. Kathleen Ann Rooney, June 1, 1968. Advt. editor Eastman Kodak Co., Rochester, N.Y., 1968-70; account exec. Young & Rubicam, Inc., Detroit, 1970-73; instr. U. Ill., Urbana, 1973-74; asst. prof. communications U. Wash., 1975-82; assoc. prof. journalism U. Colo., 1982—. Direct Mail/Mktg. fellow, 1978; Ad Age Creative Workshop Educator fellow, 1978. Mem. Am. Acad. Advt. (chmn. pedagogic com. on advt. social effects and social responsibility), Am. Advt. Fedn. (ednl. bd. 1977—, vice-chmn. ednl. bd. 1979-80, chmn. ednl. bd. 1980-81), Puget Sound Advt. Fedn. (dir. 1979-82), Assn. Edn. in Journalism (exec. com. div. advt. 1978-81, program chmn. advt. div. 1979-80, head advt. div. 1980-81). Unitarian. Club: Mountaineers. Bd. dirs. Jour. Advt., 1981—. Office: U Colo Sch Journalism Box 287 Boulder CO 80309

FRAZER, CLOYCE CLEMON, educator; b. Warren, Ark., Jan. 2, 1919; s. Charles Columbus and Maude Mae (Jones) F.; m. Beverley Jane Mundorff, Apr. 10, 1942. B.A., Calif. State U.-San Jose, 1952, M.A., Calif. State U.-Sacramento, 1961. Cert. spl. secondary life diploma in indsl. arts, 1959, gen. secondary life diploma, 1960, standard teaching credentials life, 1971, services, 1971 (all Calif.); FAA comml. pilot lic. with flight instr. cert., 1949, aircraft and power plant lic., 1948. Aircraft mechanic, flight instr., Oakland, Calif., 1946-50; tchr. Folsom (Calif.) Unified Sch. Dist., 1953-54, Sacramento City Unified Sch. Dist., 1954-63; tchr. San Mateo (Calif.) Union High Sch. Dist., 1963—, dept. head, 1963-73, program evaluator, 1976-77. Pres., Crestmoor High Sch. Faculty Assn., 1965-66, Calif. Aerospace Edn. Assn., 1978-79. Served to major USAF, 1941-79. Recipient honorable mention for sculpture San Mateo County Fair and Floral Fiesta, 1967. Mem. NEA, Calif. Tchrs. Assn., Calif. Aerospace Edn. Assn., Calif. Assn. Vocat. Edn., Calif. Indsl. Edn. Assn., Vocat. Edn. Assn., Am. Craft Council, Aircraft Owners and Pilots Assn., Exptl. Aircraft Assn. (Individual Achievement award 1983), Epsilon Pi Tau. Democrat. Club: Caterpillar. Contbr. articles to profl. jours; co-author curriculum materials. Office: San Mateo Union High School 650 N Delaware St San Mateo CA 94401

FRAZIER, LAKE JENKINS, ret. lawyer; b. nr. Danville, Pa., Dec. 11, 1898; s. Daniel Edward and Sarah Jane (Herr) F.; student Lafayette Coll., U. Va.; LL.M., J.D., Georgetown U.; m. Helen P. Holshue, Aug. 27, 1921; children—Virginia Louise (Mrs. Kermit Shotts), Lake Jenkins. Admitted to Va. bar, 1922, N.Mex., 1927, U.S. Supreme Ct. bar, 1945; police judge, juvenile and domestic relations ct. judge, Winchester, Va., 1923-26; probate judge, Roswell, N.Mex., 1931-32; asst. dist. atty. Roswell, 1933-39; mem. firm Frazier, Cusack & Schnedar, Roswell, 1940-77, ret., 1977; pres. Ruidoso State Bank, 1954-61; mayor Roswell, 1948-52, 60-64. Pres., N.Mex. Mcpl. League, 1950-51. Vice chmn. N.Mex. Democratic State Com., 1954-56; chmn. adv. bd. St. Mary's Hosp., Roswell, 1954-72; mem. A.A.A. Adv. Bd., 1954-74, N.Mex. Lung Assn. Bd., 1958-74. Mem. Va., N.Mex., Chaves County (past pres.), Am. bar assns., Internat. Assn. Ins. Counsel, Fedn. Ins. Counsel, Am. Legion (past comdr.), DAV (past dept. comdr.), SAR, Delta Theta Phi. Episcopalian. Clubs: Masons, Shriners, Elks, Kiwanis (past pres.). Address: Brentwood Rd Roswell NM 88201

FRAZIER, LARRY PAUL, psychologist; b. Waco, Tex., Oct. 28, 1947; s. Gerald Hill and Nettie Ruth Gant F.; m. Sharon Toddy Bowden, Feb.

1, 1978; 1 dau., Erin. B.S., North Tex. State U., 1972, M.Counseling, 1973; Ph.D., Tex. A&M U., 1976. Lic. psychologist, Tex., Ariz. Instr. edn. psychology dept. Tex. A&M U., College Station, 1974-76; asst. prof. psychology, psychologist Counseling Ctr., Sam Houston State U., Huntsville, Tex., 1976-77; chief psychologist Southern Highlands Mental Health Ctr., Princeton, W.Va., 1978; psychologist Lamar U., Beaumont, Tex., 1978-79; clin. supr. Mental Health-Mental Retardation of Southeast Tex., Beaumont, 1979-80; supervising psychologist Youth and Family Services, So. Ariz. Mental Health Ctr., Tucson, 1980—; pvt. practice, psychology, 1982—. Bd. dirs. Greater Council Tucson on Children, Youth and Families, 1981—; steering com. Divorce Recovery Program Tucson, 1981-83. Tex. A&M U. grad. fellow, 1973-74. Mem. Am. Psychol. Assn., Am. Assn. for Marriage and Family Therapy. Episcopalian. Home: 3833 Sunny Shadows Pl Tucson AZ 85741 Office: Youth and Family Services So Ariz Mental Health Ctr 1930 E 6th St Tucson AZ 85719

FRAZIER, LELAND SCOTT, clin. psychologist; b. Berkeley, Calif., Nov. 27, 1945; s. Leland and Mary (Partridge) F.; B.S., Harvard U., 1967, M.S., 1970; M.S. (World Council fellow), U. France, 1971; D.Phil. (Roothbert fellow), St. John's Coll., Oxford (Eng.) U., 1978; 1 son, Joshua Leland. Legis. intern U.S. Senate, 1970; prof. U. Bénin, West Africa, 1971-73; vis. lectr. Reading U., Eng., 1974-78; pvt. practice clin. psychology, Beverly Hills, Calif., 1978—; lectr. UCLA. Mem. Am. Psychol. Assn., Calif. Psychol. Assn., Am. Philos. Assn., Am. Acad. Religion. Democrat. Presbyterian. Author: T.S. Eliot: A Psychological Perspective, 1978. Office: 416 N Bedford Dr Suite 301 Beverly Hills CA 90210

FRAZIER, ROSYLAND RENA, health foundation administrator; b. Los Angeles, Mar. 13, 1955; d. Obert and Monter B. (Williams) F. B.A. in Sociology, Pitzer Coll., 1976, M.S. in Pub. Health, 1978; student U. N.C.-Chapel Hill, 1976-78. Adminstrv. asst. San Francisco Gen. Hosp. Med. Ctr., 1977; coordinator paraprofl. tng. Los Angeles Free Clinic, 1978-79; co-clinic adminstr., dir. med. service Valley Free Clinic, North Hollywood, Calif., 1979-82; project dir. maternal and child health Watts Health Found., Inc., Los Angeles, 1983—. Active Perinatal Adv. Council, Los Angeles Communities. Mem. Am. Mgmt. Assn., Nat. Assn. Female Execs. Methodist. Office: 10300 Compton Ave Los Angeles CA 90002

FREDERICK, (LEONARD) HARLAND, educator, TV moderator; b. San Francisco, Aug. 22, 1905; s. Leonard Berens and Adeline Isabel (Harland) F.; A.B., U. Calif. at Berkeley, 1932, postgrad., 1932-36; postgrad. U. San Francisco, 1948; D.D. (hon.), Am. Fellowship Ch., 1978; children—Allen Harland, John Howland, Ann Hester (Mrs. William E. Bradley), Jane Wardwell. Library bur. Remington Rand, San Francisco, 1926-30; lectr. polit. sci. U. Calif. extension div., 1933-57; dean Dodd Sch., Berkeley, Calif., 1941; news analyst radio stas. KLX and KSFO, Oakland, Calif. and San Francisco, 1944-48; examiner NLRB San Francisco, 1948-52; news analyst TV interview program KPIX, San Francisco, 1954-57; tchr. speech, world affairs, English for fgn. born, comparative lit., history San Francisco Community Coll., 1945-81; dir. summer sessions Berkeley Hills Nursery Sch., 1954-65. Organizer East Bay Regional Park, 1933; personnel dir. cashiers Golden Gate Internat. Expn., San Francisco, 1940; founder mem. World Affairs Council San Francisco, 1944, dir., 1944-47; dir. Internat. Center, 1945-46; radio del. UN Conf. Internal Orgn., San Francisco, 1945; moderator Town Hall sta. KSFO, San Francisco, 1945-46; pres. Bay Area San Francisco Calif. Council Adult Edn., 1947-51; sec., exec. bd. athletes Pacific Assn. AAU, San Francisco, 1966-76, mem. bd. mgrs., 1966-81, sec., 1982—, bd. govs., nat. bd. athletics, 1966—, nat. bd. dirs., 1982—; chmn. Met. Referral Service, San Francisco, 1972-82; del. Calif. Democratic Conv., 1940; mem. heptathlon (pentathlon) com. Track and Field Assn., 1978—; mem. Athletic Congress, Inc. U.S.A., 1979—; mem. Geary Road Center Council, 1982-83; sec. Pacific Assn., AAU, 1982—; mem. South Main Center Council (Consumer Coop. of Berkeley), 1981-82. Mem. Radio Writers Guild (dir. 1944), Pi Sigma Alpha, Delta Sigma Rho, Delta Chi. Unitarian. Columnist; contbr. articles to newspapers and mags. Address: 46 Berkeley Ave Orinda CA 94563 Office: 2200 Central Ave Suite 208 Alameda CA 94501

FREDERICKS, DALE EDWARD, lawyer; b. Springfield, Ill., Mar. 12, 1943; s. John E. and H. Louise Fredericks; B.S. with honors, Bradley U., Peoria, Ill., 1965; J.D., U. Ill., 1968; m. Jean Schmidt, June 8, 1968; children—Michael, Amy. Admitted to D.C. bar, 1969, Calif. bar, 1971; pvt. practice, San Francisco, 1972—; partner firm Sedgwick, Detert, Moran & Arnold, 1978—. Served to capt. USMC, 1968-72. Mem. Internat. Bar Assn., Am. Bar Assn., D.C. Bar Assn., San Francisco Bar Assn. Club: World Trade (San Francisco). Address: 111 Pine St San Francisco CA 94111

FREDRICKS, CONRAD BRADLEY, lawyer; b. Helena, Mont., Apr. 10, 1934; s. William Henry and Mabel Elizabeth (DeKay) F.; m. Patricia C. Pettichord, June 3, 1967; children—Bradley Earl, William Conrad. B.S. in Chemistry, Mont. State U., Bozeman, 1955; J.D., U. Mont., Missoula, 1962. Bar: Mont. 1962. Chemist, then asst. to chief chemist Anaconda Aluminum Co., Columbia Falls, Mont., 1955-59; assoc., then partner firm Loble, Picotte & Fredricks, and predecessor, Helena, 1962-67; individual practice, Helena, 1967-68; partner firm Josephson & Fredricks, Big Timber, Mont., 1968—; county atty. Sweet Grass County, 1971-74, 78-82; mem. Mont. Criminal Law Commn. Mem. Gov. Mont. Air Pollution Adv. Com.; chmn. Sweet Grass County Republican Central Com., 1969—; exec. com. Mont. Rep. Party, 1976-81; alt. del. Rep. Nat. Conv., 1976; legal counsel Mont. Young Republicans, 1965-66. Served with USAR, 1955-64. Mem. ABA, Mont. Bar Assn. (past pres. young lawyers sect.), Mont. Trial Lawyers Assn., Park-Sweet Grass Bar Assn., South Central Peace Officers Assn. (pres. 1982), Alpha Chi Sigma, Phi Delta Phi. Clubs: Big Timber Lions (sec., past pres.), Shriners, Elks. Home: 901 Hooper St Big Timber MT 59011 Office: 115 W 2d Ave Big Timber MT 59011

FREDRICKS, ROBERT EMMETT, internist, hospital executive; b. Jamestown, N.D., Apr. 21, 1925; s. Robert Emmett and Agnes Alice (Sullivan) F.; m. Shirley Jean Welk, Sept. 11, 1954; children—Laura Jeanne, Robert Emmett III, David Neal, Jonathan Paul, Lisa Virginia. B.S., U.S. Naval Acad., 1946; postgrad. George Washington U., 1948-50; M.D., Marquette U., 1954. Diplomate Am. Bd. Internal Medicine, Nat. Bd. Med. Examiners. Intern, resident in medicine Georgetown U. Hosp., Washington, 1954-56; resident in medicine, fellow in hematology Boston City Hosp., 1956-58; research fellow, instr. medicine UCLA, 1958-60, asst. clin. prof., 1965—; practice medicine specializing in internal medicine and hematology, Los Angeles, 1960-70; sr. v.p. med. affairs, med. dir. St. John's Hosp. and Health Center, Santa Monica, Calif., 1971—; dir. Teleklew Inc.; mem. task force on health systems agys. Los Angeles County Bd. Suprs., 1975-76. Served to lt. (j.g.) USN, 1946-50. Recipient Thomas Linacre award Nat. Fedn. Catholic Physicians and Guilds, 1968. Fellow ACP; mem. Am. Acad. Med. Dirs. (dir. 1981—), Hosp. Council So. Calif. (dir. 1976-82), Cath. Health Assn. U.S. (trustee 1981—), Am. Coll. Physician Execs., Calif. Hosp. Assn. (trustee 1978-81), Calif. Med. Assn., Los Angeles County Med. Assn., U.S. Naval Acad. Alumni Assn. Roman Catholic. Club: Rotary (Santa Monica). Contbr. articles to med. jours. Office: 1328 22d St Santa Monica CA 90404

FREDRICKSON, EDWARD JAMES, dentist; b. Chgo., Apr. 20, 1921; s. Edward J. and Loretta F. Fredrickson; student Cornell U., 1939-42; D.D.S., Northwestern U., 1945; m. Joann Higgins, Feb. 15, 1947; children—W. Timm, Kevin E., Kamma L., Edward Burke. Resident in dental surgery Billings Hosp., U. Chgo., 1947; practice dentistry specializing in prosthodontics, Spokane, Wash., 1948—; vis. lectr. Gonzaga U., Wash. State U., Eastern State U., U. Wash., Seattle. Served to lt. USNR, 1945-47. Fellow Internat. Coll. Dentists; mem. ADA (Nat. Honor award 1958), Am. Prosthodontic Soc. (past pres.), Am. Acad. Maxillofacial Prosthodontics (past pres.), Pacific Coast Prosthodontic Soc., Spokane C. of C. (exec. council 1975). Clubs: City, Spokane Country, Racquet (Spokane). Author articles in field. Home: S 2415 Crestline St Spokane WA 99203 Office: W 105 8th Ave Spokane WA 99204

FREDRICKSON, JOEL SCOTT, systems analyst; b. Houston, July 21, 1956; s. Howard Roy and Vilyn Elaine (Erb) F. B.S. with distinction in Resource Systems Engring., U. Colo., Colorado Springs, 1979. Assoc. programmer computer services Texaco U.S.A., Houston, 1978-80, programmer, computer services, 1980, analyst, planning and fin., 1980; systems analyst, research service Farmbank Services, Denver, 1980—. Mem. Am. Statis. Assn. Office: Farmbank Services 12000 E 47th Ave 2d Floor Denver CO 80234

FREDRICKSON, VANCE O., insurance company executive; b. McIntosh, Minn., Sept. 27, 1928; s. Almer M. and Norah E. (Hefte) F.; m. Elois D. Osen, June 9, 1950; children—Kathryn, Paul. C.P.C.U., 1962; C.L.U., 1977. Underwriter Mut. of Enumclaw (Wash.), 1955-57, underwriting supr., 1957-67, v.p. underwriting, 1967-68, exec. v.p., gen. mgr., 1968-81, pres., dir., 1981—. Mem. Wash. Ins. Council (bd. dirs., past pres.), Enumclaw C. of C., Soc. C.P.C.U., Soc. C.L.U. Lutheran. Office: 1460 Wells St Enumclaw WA 98022

FREDRIKSEN, RICHARD LEE, forest scientist; b. Spokane, Wash., Feb. 20, 1930; s. Chester S. and Doris G. (Lewis) F.; m. Constance K., Sept. 20, 1952 (dec.); children—Erik, Janet (dec). B.S. in Forest Mgmt., U. Wis., 1954, M.S. in Forest Soils and Silviculture, 1961; Ph.D. in Forest Soils, Oreg. State U., 1976. Teaching asst. silviculture, plant taxonomy, plant pathology U. Wash., Seattle, 1954-56; researcher Weyerhaeuser Co., Centralia, Wash., 1959-60; researcher scientist, forester, soil scientist U.S. Forest Service, Corvallis, Oreg., 1960. Bd. dirs. local Issac Walton League. Mem. Am. Soc. Agronomy. Office: 3200 Jefferson Way Corvallis OR 97331

FREE, WILLIAM ALBERT, educational counselor; b. Muskogee, Okla., July 6, 1929; s. Jack and Esther Elizabeth (Eckenrode) F.; m. Mary Lou Skelton, Aug. 25, 1953; children—Janna, Scott, Joel. B.A., Pepperdine U., 1951, M.A., 1958. Tchr., counselor Middleton (Idaho) High Sch., 1958—; pilot, officer Idaho Air N.G., Boise, 1958-78, asst. adj. gen., 1978—. Bd. dirs. Columbia Christian Coll., Portland, Oreg.; mem. Planning and Zoning Commn., Caldwell, Idaho. Served with USAF, 1951-56; served to brig. gen. Air N.G., 1958—. Mem. Am. Personnel and Guidance Assn., Am. Sch. Counselors Assn., Assn. for Supervision and Curriculum Devel., Air Force Assn. Mem. Ch. of Christ. Home: 523 East Easy Caldwell ID 83605 Office: Middleton High Sch Middleton ID 83644

FREED, PETER QUENTIN, amusement park executive; b. Salt Lake City, Jan. 8, 1921; s. Lester David and Jasmine (Young) F.; B.A. with honors, U. Utah, 1947; children—David Wicker, Michael Stahle, Howard Eldred, Anne, Kristen, Jennifer. Pres., Freed Corp., 1952-74; v.p., sec., Freed Co., 1952-74; exec. v.p. Amusement Service, Salt Lake City, 1947—; v.p. Terrace Co., Salt Lake City, from 1952; exec. v.p. Patio Gardens, Farmington, Utah, from 1956; v.p. Westworld Corp., Salt Lake City, from 1974, Pioneer Village Campground, Farmington, from 1975; dir. Pioneer Village, Farmington; pres. Lagoon Corp., Salt Lake City, 1974—. Mem. Union Sta. Theatre Bd. Served with USNR, 1942-45. Mem. Nat. Assn. Amusement Parks, Utah Mus. Assn. Republican. Christian Scientist. Clubs: Salt Lake Tennis, New Yorker. Home: 642 Aloha Rd Salt Lake City UT 84103 Office: Box N Farmington UT 84025

FREEDMAN, LAWRENCE DAVID, physician; b. N.Y.C., Mar. 8, 1934; s. Joe and Helen Rebecca (Racer) F.; B.A., Hobart Coll., 1954; M.D., U. Chgo., 1959; m. Carole Plaut, June 14, 1959; children—Eric, Jill, Gail. Intern, Los Angeles County Hosp., 1960; gen. practice medicine, La Mirada, Calif., 1963—; chief of staff La Mirada Community Hosp.; asst. prof. dept. family practice U. Calif., Irvine. Served as capt. 82d Airborne Div., U.S. Army, 1961-62. Diplomate Am. Bd. Family Practice. Fellow Am. Acad. Family Practice; mem. AMA, Calif. Los Angeles County med. assns. Contbr. articles profl. jours. and newspapers. Patentee med. instruments. Home: 2019 Yacht Resolute Newport Beach CA 92660

FREEDMAN, MARVIN, county ofcl.; b. Albany, N.Y., Jan. 8, 1924; B.A., U. So. Calif., 1951, M.S.W., 1953; postgrad. studies in social welfare adminstrn. U. Chgo.; m. Nancy Ordway; children—Robert, Alan, Stuart. Child welfare services worker San Bernardino County Welfare Dept., 1953-55; rehab. counsellor Bur. Vocat. Rehab., Calif. Dept. Edn., Van Nuys, 1955-57; asst. prof. U. So. Calif., 1957-61; asst. dean Sch. Social Service Adminstrn., U. Chgo., 1961-63; from tng. dir. to asst. dir. Dept. Pub. Social Services, County of Los Angeles, 1963-71; dir. Dept. Social Welfare, Sacramento County, 1971-73; legis. rep. County of Los Angeles, 1973—. Office: Suite 350 11th and L Bldg Sacramento CA 95814

FREEDMAN, MERVIN BURTON, psychologist, educator; b. Bklyn., Mar. 6, 1920; s. Eli and Rose Gladys (Weithorn) F.; B.S., CCNY, 1940; Ph.D., U. Calif., Berkeley, 1950; m. Marjorie Irene Ellingson, Feb. 16, 1952; children—Eric, Kristin, Rolf, Anne Marie. Research asst. U. Calif., San Francisco, 1950-51, lectr. dept. psychology, Berkeley, 1951-53; research assoc. Mary Conover Mellon Found. for Advancement of Edn. Vassar Coll., 1953-58, dir., 1958-60; asst. dean undergrad. edn. Stanford U., 1962-65; chmn. dept. psychology San Francisco State U., 1965-68, prof. psychology, 1968—; dean. Grad. Sch. The Wright Inst., Berkeley, 1969-79; cons. in field. V.p. Am.-Scandinavian Found., 1969-72. Served with AUS, 1941-45. Decorated Bronze Star. Center for Advanced Study in Behavioral Sci. fellow, 1960-61; Fulbright fellow, 1961-62. Fellow Am. Psychol. Assn.; mem. Internat. Soc. Polit. Psychology, Western Psychol. Assn. Author: The College Experience, 1967, Search for Relevance, 1969, Academic Culture and Faculty Development, 1979; Human Development in Social Settings, 1983; editor: Stress and Campus Response, 1968; Agony and Promise, 1969; consulting editor: Sociology of Education, 1968-73; asso. editor: Political Psychology, 1978—; contbr. articles to profl. jours. Home: 866 Spruce St Berkeley CA 94707 Office: 1600 Holloway Ave San Francisco CA 94132

FREEHILL, MAURICE F., educational psychology educator; b. Chgo., Nov. 29, 1915; s. Pat and Anna (Dillon) F.; m. Kay M. Cronan, Nov. 3, 1924; 1 son, Bernard J. B.Ed., U. Alta. (Can.), 1945; M.A., Stanford U., 1947, Ed.D., 1948. Cert. tchr., Alta. Tchr., then prin., Alta., 1937-45; prof. ednl. psychology Western Wash. U., Bellingham, 1948-62, U. Wash., Seattle, 1962—. Ellwyn Morey fellow, Australia. Author: Gifted Children, Their Psychology and Education, 1981; editor: Disturbed and Troubled Children, 1973; contbr. numerous articles to profl. jours. Home: 5600 S Tara Dr Freeland WA 98249 Office: U Wash Seattle WA 98195

FREEL, MARLIN JAMES, manufacturing executive; b. Glendive, Mont., Feb. 27, 1924; s. Amos F. and Beatrice (Polen) F.; children—Michael, Cynthia. B.S., U. So. Calif., 1948; postgrad. Woodbury Coll., 1955, UCLA, 1973, LaVerne U. Law, 1974. Pres., Sproco Mfg. Inc., 1949-58; v.p. Tasker Instruments, 1958-63, mgr. contracts TRW Systems Group, 1964-68, Litton Data Systems, 1968-72; legal asst. Ingram, Baker & Griffiths Law Office, Covina, Calif., 1972-78; pres. Ricon Corp., Sun Valley, Calif., 1978—; cons. govt. contracts, pres. Ricon Inernat. Inc. Chmn. Park and Recreation Dept. City of San Dimas (Calif.), 1979—; PTA sch. bd. rep. Bonita Sch. Dist.; scoutmaster Boy Scouts Am., Troop 106, Pomona, Calif. Served with USN, 1942-46. Co-inventor wheelchair lift, 1982. Office: Ricon Corp 11684 Tuxford St Sun Valley CA 91352

FREELAND, ROBERT FREDERICK, librarian; b. Flint, Mich., Dec. 20, 1919; s. Ralph V. and Susan Barbara (Goetz) F.; B.S., Eastern Mich. U., 1942; M.S., U. So. Calif., 1948, postgrad., 1949; postgrad. UCLA, 1960, U. Mich., 1950-52, Calif. State U., 1956-58; Litt.D. (hon.), Linda Vista Bible Coll., 1973; m. June Voshel, June 18, 1948; children—Susan Beth (Mrs. Kenneth S. Visser), Kent Richard. Music supr. Consol. Schs. Warren (Mich.), 1946-47; music dir. Carson City (Mich.) Pub. Schs., 1948-49; librarian, audio-visual coordinator Ford Found., Edison Inst., Greenfield Village, Dearborn, Mich., 1950-52; librarian, audio-visual coordinator Helix High Sch. Library, 1952-76; librarian, prof. library sci. Linda Vista Bible Coll., 1976—; guest prof. Calif. State U., San Diego, 1963-66, U. Calif.-San Diego, 1969-71, Linda Vista Bible Coll., El Cajon, Calif., 1970-72; lectr. San Diego City Coll., 1954-65, Grossmont Coll., El Cajon, 1966-68; librarian San Diego City Coll., 1953-54, San Diego County Library, 1955-56, San Diego Pub. Library, 1968—; scholar Freedoms Found., Valley Forge, Pa., 1976-80. Served with USAAF, 1942-46. Recipient leadership award Grossmont Union High Sch. Dist., La Mesa, Calif., 1970, 71, 72. Mem. NEA (life), ALA, Assn. for Ednl. Communication and Tech., Western Ednl. Soc. for Telecommunications, Calif. Tchrs. Assn., Music Library Assn. So. Calif. (adviser exec. bd.), Calif. Library Assn. (pres. Palomar chpt. 1972-73), Sch. Library Assn. Calif. (treas. 1956-58), Calif. Media and Library Educators (charter mem.), Am. Legion (Americanism chmn. 22d dist. San Diego County, chmn. oratorical contest com. La Mesa post), Ret. Officers Assn., San Diego Aero Space Mus., San Diego Mus. Art. Mem. Christian Ref. Ch. (former deacon and elder, librarian 1969-72). Book and audio-visual aids rev. editor Sch. Musician, Director and Teacher, 1950—. Home: 4800 Williamsburg Lane Apt 223 La Mesa CA 92041 Office: 7323 University Ave La Mesa CA 92041

FREEMAN, ALLAN EDWARD, mktg. cons.; b. Bklyn., May 8, 1937; s. William and Frances (Levy) F.; B.A., Dartmouth Coll., 1958; postgrad. Columbia U., 1960; m. Barbara Jacobs, June 26, 1960; children—Joanne, Richard, Marc. Jr. research analyst Newspaper Advt. Bur., 1960-61; sr. analyst J. Walter Thompson Co., 1961-63; sr. analyst Gardner Advt., 1963-65; asso. research dir. Gen. Foods Corp., White Plains, N.Y., 1965-68; v.p. sales Market Facts, Inc., N.Y.C., 1969-71, Crossley Surveys, N.Y.C., 1971-73; asso. research dir. Bristol Myers, N.Y.C., 1973-75; v.p. market research 20th Century Fox Film Corp., Los Angeles, 1976-77; v.p. advt. and publicity planning Warner Bros., Burbank, Calif., 1977-80; pres. Allan Freeman Mktg. and Research Assos., 1980—; guest lectr. U. Calif., Los Angeles, U. So. Calif., Calif. State U., Long Beach. Jewish.

FREEMAN, DONNA RHEA, small business owner; b. Waldron, Ark., Apr. 18, 1937; d. Oliver Raymond and Lura Edna (Doyle) Cook; m. Clarence Lee Freeman, Jan. 24, 1954; children—Scott, Kevin, Steven, Melissa, Melinda. Student Humphrey's Bus. Coll., Stockton, Calif., U. So. Calif. Sec., Bodega Bay Sch. (Calif.), 1973-75; staff aquaculture dept. U. Calif. Bodega Marine Lab., 1976-77; real estate assoc., 1978-82; co-owner Accident and Crime Scene Reproductions, 1981—; ptnr. Freeman's Union 76 Service, Bodega Bay, 1983—. Pres., Bodega Bay C. of C., 1979-81, dir., 1982-83; vice-chmn. Shoreline Trust Ednl. Program Services, 1981—; bd. dirs. Bodega Bay Area Rescue, 1973-74; chmn. Bodega Bay Fisherman's Festival, 1973, 74, 83; alt. Democratic Central Com., 1982; mem. local bd. SSS, 1982—. Mem. Bodega Bay Fisherman's Aux., Bodega Bay Community Assn., Bodega Bay Grange. Home: 1060 Bay View St Bodega Bay CA 94923

FREEMAN, EUGENE, author, emeritus educator; b. N.Y.C., Feb. 16, 1906; s. Alexander Samuel and Rose (Weinstock) F.; A.B., UCLA, 1926; Ph.D. (Univ. fellow), U. Chgo., 1937; O.D., No. Ill. Coll. Optometry, 1934; D.Optometric Sci. (hon.), Chgo. Coll. Optometry, 1949; m. Ann Sternberg, Nov. 2, 1930; children—James Montague, Thomas Parry. Asst. prof. to asso. prof. No. Ill. Coll. Optometry, 1933-39, prof., chmn. div. humanities, 1939-43; asst. prof. philosophy Ill. Inst. Tech., Chgo., 1947-53; v.p. Chgo. Coll. Optometry, 1949-56; free lance editor, 1956-59; dir. philosophy div., editor Monist (internat. quar. philosophy jour.), Hegeler Inst., 1959—; assoc. prof. philosophy San Jose (Calif.) State U., 1964-65, chmn. dept. philosophy, 1965-68, prof., 1965-73, prof. emeritus, 1973—. Recipient Distinguished Service Found. award, 1952; Omega Epsilon Phi Nat. award, 1951; Nat. Gold medal Beta Sigma Kappa, 1952. Mem. Am. Philos. Assn., Peirce Soc., Am. Metaphys. Soc. Rotarian. Author: Categories of Charles Peirce, 1934; (with I. Borish) Manual of Accreditation, 1942. Editor: (with D. Appel) Great Ideas of Plato, 1952, reprinted as Wisdom and Ideas of Plato, 6th printing, 1973; (with J. Owens) Wisdom and Ideas of St. Thomas Aquinas, 1968; (with W. Reese) Process and Divinity, 1967; (with W. Sellars) Basic Issues in the Philosophy of Time, 1971; (with M. Mandelbaum) Spinoza: Essays in Interpretation, 1975; The Abdication of Philosophy: Philosophy and the Public Good, 1976; editor: Spirit, Being, and Self: Studies in Indian Thought, 1981; The Relevance of Charles Peirce, 1983. Editorial adv. bd. Library of Living Philosophers, Philosophia, Folia Humanistica. Address: 15401 Blackberry Hill Rd PO Box 1908 Los Gatos CA 95031

FREEMAN, GRACE CLAUDIA, accountant; b. Buenos Aires, Argentina, Oct. 23, 1954; came to U.S., 1957, naturalized, 1963; d. Hugh Rubin and Nilda Nieves (Fernandez) Getty; 1 son, Lance Alexander. Student acctg. U. No. Colo., 1971-72; student U. Ga., 1972-74, Colo. State U., 1974. Head of fin. Young's West, Inc., Ft. Collins, Colo., 1972-74; with Hewlett Packard Co., Loveland, Colo., 1975-76; partner, sr. acct. Dickson's Acctg. Service, Ft. Collins, 1977-79; owner, mgr. G & L Assos., Ft. Collins, 1979—; lectr., cons. in field; pvt. acct. Internat. Project: Contemporary Crafts of the Ams., 1974-75; profl. acct. for Internat. Artists, 1977—. Recipient Cert. Excellence, Clarke County Sch. Dist. Mem. Nat. Soc. Public Accts., Gamma Eta Pi. Asso. editor Illiad Mag., 1972. Home: 718 E Laurel St Fort Collins CO 80524 Office: 420 S Howes St Suite 105 Fort Collins CO 80521

FREEMAN, HENRY WILLIAM, accountant; b. Ainsworth, Nebr., Dec. 4, 1945; s. William Chester and Maxine June (Schroder) F.; B.A., Chadron (Nebr.) State Coll., 1972; M.Acctg., Utah State U., 1974; m. Elaine I. Kuhnel, Mar. 11, 1967; children—Leah A., Lora L. Staff acct. Peat, Marwick, Mitchell & Co., Omaha, 1974-76, supr., Anchorage, 1976-78; owner, operator Henry W. Freeman, C.P.A., Anchorage, 1978—. Served to capt. U.S. Army, 1966-70. Mem. Alaska Soc. C.P.A.s, Nebr. Soc. C.P.A.s, Alaska Sport Fishermen's Assn. (dir.). Office: 4335 Laurel St Suite 300 Anchorage AK 99504

FREEMAN, HERBERT JAMES, educational administrator; b. Raleigh, N.C., May 14, 1941; s. Hurley Lee and Annie Lee (Upchurch) F.; m. Ollie Faye Mack, Aug. 23, 1965 (div.). B.A., Shaw U., 1963; M.A., U. Nev., 1978. Cert. elem. tchr., spl. edn. tchr., elem. prins., Elem. tchr.,

1963-65, 70-72; spl. edn. tchr. emotionally disturbed, 1965-70; program specialist Clark County Sch. Dist., Las Vegas, Nev., 1972-79, adminstrv. asst., 1979-80; prin. Rex Bell Elem. Sch., Las Vegas, 1980—; mem. Nev. State Bd. for Child Care. Choir dir. Zion United Methodist Ch., 1977—, So. Nev. Mass Meth. Chs.; registrar voter registration. Named Boss of Yr., Clark County Assn. Office Personnel, 1982. Mem. Assn. Supervision and Curriculum Devel., Nat. Alliance Black Sch. Educators, Clark County Elem. Prins. Assn., Clark County Assn. Sch. Adminstrs., NAACP, Phi Delta Kappa, Kappa Alpha Psi. Democrat. Home: 1101 Sharon Rd Las Vegas NV 89106 Office: 2900 Wilmington Way Las Vegas NV 89102

FREEMAN, HOWARD E., sociologist, educator; b. N.Y.C., May 28, 1929; s. Herbert M. and Rose H. Freeman; m. Marian A. Solomon, Feb. 2, 1979; children—Seth Richard, Lisa Jill. B.A., NYU, 1948, M.A. in Sociology, 1950, Ph.D. in Sociology, 1956; postgrad. Columbia U., 1950, Wash. State U., 1951-52, U. N.C., 1952-53. Statistician, O'Brien-Sherwood Assocs., N.Y.C., 1950-51; research asst. Wash. Pub. Opinion Lab., Pullman, 1951-52; lectr. in sociology CCNY, also asst. study dir. NYU, 1953-55; asst. social scientist Rand Corp., 1955-56; research assoc. in sociology Harvard U. Sch. Pub. Health, 1956-62; assoc. prof. social research Florence Heller Grad. Sch. Advanced Studies in Social Welfare, Brandeis U., 1960-63, prof., 1963-66, 67-69, dir. Research Ctr., 1960-66, Morse prof. urban studies, 1969-72; vis. prof. sociology U. Wis., 1966-67, U. Colo., summer 1967; social sci. adviser for Mexico, Central Am., and Caribbean, Ford Found., 1972-74; prof. sociology UCLA, 1974—, dir. Inst. Social Sci., 1974-81; lectr. Clark U., 1956-57, Boston U., 1957-65; vis. prof. Ctr. for Survey Research and Methodology, Mannheim, W. Ger., 1982; research adviser Inst. Nutrition of Central Am. and Panama, Pan Am. Health Orgn., Guatemala City, Guatemala, 1965—; sociologist Russell Sage Found., N.Y.C., 1967-72, cons. sociologist, 1974-77; sr. research adviser Robert Wood Johnson Found., Princeton, N.J., 1976—; mem. planning com. Bd. Health Services, U.S. Mexico Border Health Assn., 1981—; mem. rev. com. Mass. Comprehensive Health Planning Program, 1968-72. Served with USAF, 1952-53. Co-recipient Hofheimer prize Am. Psychiat. Assn., 1963-67. Mem. Soc. for Study Social Problems (chmn. com. permanent orgn. 1957-59), Am. Sociol. Assn. (mem. council Med. Sociology Sect. 1965-66, chmn. sect. 1966-67, chmn. com. on sects. 1967-69, chmn. com. on profl. opportunities in applied sociology 1979-81, chmn. com. on applied sociology 1982-83). Co-author books, including: Evaluation: A Systematic Approach, 2d edit., 1982; Applied Sociology, 1983. Contbr. numerous chpts., articles to profl. publs.; editor Prentice-Hall Series in Social Policy, 1970-76; assoc. editor Am. Sociol. Rev., 1962-66, Social Problems, 1962-66, Jour. Health and Social Behavior, 1966-69; cons. editor Community Mental Health Jour., 1964-80; editor Jour. Health and Social Behavior, 1962-72; referee Am. Jour. Pub. Health, 1974—; editorial adv. bd. Man and Medicine: Jour. of Values and Ethics in Health Care, 1975-80, Evaluation Studies Rev. Anns., 1976—, New Directions for Program Evaluation, 1981—; co-editor Evaluation Rev., 1976—; editorial bd. Values and Ethics in Health Care, 1977—, Annals Pub. Adminstrn., 1979—. Office: Dept Sociology UCLA Los Angeles CA 90024

FREEMAN, JAMES THOMAS, psychologist; b. Oklahoma City, June 22, 1925; s. Thomas Wyatt and Ann Burger (Williamson) F.; B.A., U. Okla., 1950, M.S., 1950; Ph.D., Northwestern U., 1953; m. Donna Jean Stambaugh, Nov. 28, 1947; children—Douglas, Kathryn, Scott. Asst. prof., asso. prof. psychology Iowa State U., Ames, 1953-59; ops. analyst U.S. Air Force, 1959-62; supr. Honeywell, Covina, Calif., 1962-64; psychologist, Life Scis. N. Am. Aviation, Downey, Calif., 1964-66; prof. psychology, dir. Inst. Research, Calif. State U., San Bernardino, 1967-71; staff psychology services U.S. Dept. Justice, San Pedro, Calif., 1982—; pvt. practice psychology, Long Beach, Calif., 1975—; cons. Behavior Mgmt. Assos. Served with USAAF, 1943-45. Lic. psychologist, Calif.; diplomate Am. Bd. Forensic Psychology. Mem. Am. Psychol. Assn., Calif. State Psychol. Assn., Western Psychol. Assn., Orange County Psychol. Assn., Long Beach Psychol. Assn. (pres.), Nat. Register Health Providers in Psychology, Acad. Forensic Psychology. Democrat. Contbr. articles to profl. jours. Home: 11275 Linda Way Los Alamitos CA 90720 Office: 5199 E Pacific Coast Hwy 200 Long Beach CA 90804

FREEMAN, MALLORY BRUCE, art dealer; b. Tulsa, Jan. 9, 1938; s. Milton Bruster and Mary Shannon (Brummett) F.; student Union Coll., Lincoln, Nebr., 1957-58; B.A., U. Tulsa, 1961. Dir. Tortue Gallery, Santa Monica, Calif., 1972—; curator exhbns. Chmn. Hist. Site Com., Santa Monica, 1974—. Mem. Art Dealers Assn. So. Cal., Am. Guild Musical Artists. Home: 1519 6th St Santa Monica CA 90404 Office: 2917 Santa Monica Blvd Santa Monica CA 90404

FREEMAN, PAUL DOUGLAS, symphony conductor; b. Richmond, Va., Jan. 2, 1936; s. Louis H. and Louise (Willis) F.; m. Cornelia Perry; 1 son, Douglas Cornel. Mus. B., Eastman Sch. Music, 1956, Mus. M., 1957, Ph.D., 1963. Dir. Hochstein Music Sch., Rochester, N.Y., 1960-66; founder, condr. Faculty-Community Orch., music dir. Opera Theatre, Rochester, 1961-66; dir. San Francisco Community Music Ctr., 1966-68; condr. San Francisco Conservatory Orch., 1966-67; music dir. San Francisco Little Symphony, 1967-68; assoc. condr. Dallas Symphony, 1968-70; condr.-in-residence Detroit Symphony Orch., 1970-79; condr., Music dir. Victoria (B.C., Can.) Symphony, 1979—; music dir. Saginaw Symphony; artistic dir. Delta Festival Music and Art, 1977-79; numerous guest appearances with maj. orchs. in U.S. and Europe; rec. artist Columbia Records, Vox Records, Orion Records. First v.p. Nat. Guild Community Music Schs., 1964-66; bd. dirs. N.Y. State Opera League, 1963-66, Detroit Community Music Sch.; music adv. com. San Francisco chpt. Young Audiences; mem. Calif. Framework Com. for Arts and Humanities, 1967-68. Fulbright scholar Hochshule für Musik, Berlin, W. Ger., 1957-59; recipient Dimitri Mitropolous Internat. Condr.'s Competition prize, 1967; Festival of Two Worlds Spoleto award, 1968. Office: Victoria Symphony 631 Superior St Victoria BC V8V 1V1 Canada

FREEMAN, PHILIP CONRAD, JR., computer systems co. exec.; b. Santa Barbara, Calif., Jan. 1, 1937; s. Philip and Mabel (Linville) F.; student Ventura (Calif.) Jr. Coll., 1955-57; B.S. in Bus. Adminstrn, U. So. Calif., 1960, M.B.A., 1964; m. Virginia Ann Bramham, June 14, 1959; children—Jon Allen, Kym Michelle. Pres., F.A.C.T., Inc., Los Angeles, 1968-71; v.p., western regional mgr. Intercontinental Computer Inc., Los Angeles, 1971-73; exec. v.p. Kimberly Devel., Inc., Los Angeles, 1973-75; v.p., gen. mgr. Met. Computer Center, Glendale, Calif., 1975-82; pres., chmn. bd. Data Select Systems Inc., Woodland Hills, Calif., 1982—; pres., dir. Golden Coin Data Systems, Inc., San Francisco, 1982—; asst. treas., asst. sec. Forest Lawn Co., Glendale, 1978-82; dir. Mad Computer, Inc., Santa Clara, Calif. Bd. dirs., treas. Hidden Hills (Calif.) Homeowners Assn., 1976-81; pres. Bill Bryant So. Calif. Jr. Golf Assn., 1979-80; ptnr. Manzanita City Devel., Solano County, Calif. Mem. Calif. Savings and Loan League, Nat. Mortgage Bankers Assn., U.S. Savs. and Loan League, Am. Bankers Assn. Republican. Presbyterian. Clubs: Calabasas Park (Calif.) Country, Hidden Hills Horseman Assn., Calif. Poly Rodeo Boosters, Hidden Hills Vaulting Assn., Hidden Hills Tennis Assn. Home: 24333 Long Valley Rd Hidden Hills CA 91302 Office: 6400 Canoga Ave Suite 320 Woodland Hills CA 91367

FREEMAN, RALPH CARTER, accountant, cons.; b. LaGrange, Ga., Mar. 6, 1937; s. Ralph Carter and Alice (Cordell) F.; B.B.A., Emory U., 1959; grad. Chaminade Tax Inst., 1967; m. Nancy Lynn Brown, Apr. 8, 1977; children by previous marriage—Ralph Carter III, Allyson Louise, Stephens Cordell, LeAnna Torbert. Staff auditor Pannell, Kerr, Forster & Co., C.P.A.s, Atlanta, 1959-62, partner, Honolulu and Atlanta, 1967-71; partner Freeman & Noll, Accts. and Auditors, Ga., 1962-66, Touche Ross & Co., C.P.A.s, Honolulu, Am. Samoa, 1972-75; partner Freeman & Co., C.P.A.s Honolulu, 1975—; pres., dir. FP Investments Inc., fin. cons., investors, Honolulu, 1976—, Rivercrest Agribus., Inc., agrl. investments, Ga., Mont., 1977—, FPI Comml., Inc., comml. property investors, 1977—; organizer Peoples Bank LaGrange, 1965; sec.-treas., dir. Freeman Enterprises, Inc., Ga., 1963—; pres., dir. Trapper Peak Recreation Inc., Mont., 1977—. Hawaii chmn. Emory U. merit program, 1968. C.P.A., Ga., Hawaii, Mont. Mem. Ga., Hawaii, Mont. socs. C.P.A.s, Am. Inst. C.P.A.s, Inst. Mgmt. Cons., Nat. Assn. Security Dealers, Hawaii C. of C., Aircraft Owners and Pilots Assn., Hawaii Visitors Bur. Methodist. Kiwanian (treas., dir. 1965-66). Mem. Sigma Alpha Epsilon. Home: 235 Kulamanu Pl Honolulu HI 96816 also 1957 E Broadway Missoula MT 59801 also 208 Gordon St LaGrange GA Office: 745 Fort St Suite 1414 Honolulu HI 96813 also 101 E Broadway Suite 201 Missoula Mt 59801 also 201 W Depot St LaGrange GA

FREEMAN, RAYMOND CECIL, energy consultant; b. Moscow, Minn., Aug. 5, 1908; s. Cecil Loomis and Jeannette Alice May (Bennett) F.; m. Marguerite G. Clough, July 15, 1933; 1 son, Raymond Cecil. B.E.E., U. Minn., 1929; postgrad. in bus. adminstrn. Boston U., 1932-33. Registered profl. engr., Calif., Mass. With Gen. Electric Co., 1929-73, mgr. engring. Nuclear Energy div., Schenectady, N.Y. and San Jose, Calif., 1955-57, Washington rep., 1957-61, mgr. sales, N.Y.C., 1961-73; pres. Separative Work Unit Corp., Stamford, Conn., 1973-75, dir., 1973—; pres., dir. Freeman Cons., Inc., Santa Barbara, Calif., 1976—; dir. SISCO, Gaithersburg, Md. Mem. IEEE (life), Am. Nuclear Soc., Atomic Indsl. Forum. Patentee welding machine. Home: 1048 Las Alturas Rd Santa Barbara CA 93103 Office: 311 E Carrillo St Santa Barbara CA 93101

FREEMAN, ROXANN THOMAS, health care company executive; b. Providence, Apr. 15, 1950; d. James Edward and Priscilla Yvonne (Henry) Thomas; m. Charles Wallace Freeman, Oct. 7, 1970; 1 son, Charles Wallace, Jr. B.A., U. Ill.-Chgo., 1972; M.A.T., U. Chgo., 1973. Tchr., instr. Van Vlissingen Sch., Chgo., 1972-73, Austin Middle II Sch., Chgo., 1973-76; tng. specialist City Colls. Chgo., Cook County Hosp., 1976-77; dir. tng. and devel. Sears Bank & Trust Co., Chgo., 1977-79; mgr. tng., personnel planning and devel. V. Mueller div. Am. Hosp. Supply Corp., Niles, Ill., 1979-80, Western area personnel mgr. Am. Hosp. Supply div., Irvine, Calif., 1981—; bank rep. Am. Inst. Banking, 1977-79. Bd. dirs. Afro Am. Community/Family Services, Chgo., 1977-79. Mem. Am. Soc. Tng. and Devel., NAACP (dir. DuPage County chpt. 1977-79), Nat. Soc. Performance and Instrn., Alpha Kappa Alpha. Baptist. Home: 54 Beechwood Dr Urvine CA 92714 Office: 17201 Redhill Ave Irvine CA 92714

FREEMAN, SHIRLEY JEAN, communications company executive; b. Richmond, Calif., Feb. 11, 1949; d. John Joseph and Genevieve Laura (Muncy) Rubick; student Contra Costa Coll., 1967; grad. Heald Bus. Coll., 1977; m. Lake L. Freeman, Dec. 31, 1972. Pres., Community Communications Corp., Concord, Calif., 1971—, Intrastate Agy., Concord, Calif., 1975—; mem. exec. bd. Diablo Direct Mail & Printing Co., Concord, Calif. Mem. Status of Women Com., City of Concord, 1980-81; mem. Mt. Diablo Hosp. Found. Mem. Todos Santos Bus. and Profl. Women (pres.), NOW, Concord Pavilion Assocs., Concord C. of C., Tel. Answering Services of Calif., Nat. Assn. Female Execs., Concord Hist. Soc., Direct Mail Media Assn. Club: Concord Athletic League. Home: 1656 Liana Ln Concord CA 94519 Office: 3112 Clayton Rd Concord CA 94519

FREEMAN, VAL LEROY, geologist; b. Long Beach, Calif., June 25, 1926; s. Cecil LeRoy and Marjorie (Austin) F.; B.S., U. Calif. at Berkeley, 1949, M.S., 1952; m. June Ione Ashlock, Sept. 26, 1959 (div. June 1962); 1 dau., Jill Annette Freeman Mishenar; m. 2d, Elizabeth Joann Sabia, Sept. 4, 1964 (div. Oct. 1972); 1 dau., Rebecca Sue; 1 stepson, Jeffrey David. Geologist, U.S. Geol. Survey, 1949—, Fairbanks, Alaska, 1955-57, Denver, 1957-70, 74—, Flagstaff, Ariz., 1970-74, now dep. chief coal resources br. Served with USNR, 1943-45. Fellow Geol. Soc. Am.; mem. Soc. Econ. Paleontologists and Mineralogists, A.A.A.S. Contbr. articles to profl. jours. Research in coal resources of Western Colo. Home: 1409 Utah St B Golden CO 80401 Office: MS 972 US Geol Survey Fed Center Box 25046 Denver CO 80225

FREESTED, WILLIS CARL, elec. engr.; b. Mpls., July 22, 1936; s. Carl Willis and Alice Irene (Loken) F.; B.S. with distinction, U. Minn., 1958, B.Mech. Engring., 1960; M.S., Purdue U., 1965. Engr., Gen. Electric Co., Schenectady, 1960-62, Gen. Dynamics Co., San Diego, 1962-63; research scientist Martin Marrietta Co., Denver, 1965-68; engr., scientist McDonnell-Douglas Co., Huntington Beach, Calif., 1968-72; research specialist Lockheed, Sunnyvale, Calif., 1972—. Registered profl. engr., Calif. Mem. IEEE, AIAA, Pi Tau Sigma. Republican. Presbyn. Mason. Home: 1367 Zurich Terr Sunnyvale CA 94087 Office: POB 504 Sunnyvale CA 94088

FREIMARK, ROBERT MATTHEW, artist, educator; b. Doster, Mich., Jan. 27, 1922; s. Alvin Otto and Nora Esther (Shinaver) F.; B.Ed., U. Toledo, 1950; M.F.A., Cranbrook Acad. Art, 1951; m. Mary Carvin; 1 son, Matisse Jon; m. 2d, Lillian Thilarik; 1 dau., Christine Gay. Instr. art Ohio U., Athens, 1955-59; artist-in-residence Des Moines (Ia.) Art Center, 1959-63; vis. prof. Harvard U., Cambridge, Mass., 1972-73; faculty San Jose (Calif.) State U., 1964—, prof. art, 19—; lectr. in field; one-man shows in Toledo (Ohio) Mus., Des Moines (Iowa) Art Center, also Europe, Mex., Can.; exhibited in group shows at Library of Congress, Smithsonian Instn., Chgo. Art Inst., Cranbook Mus. Art, others. represented in permanent collects at Brit. Mus., Bibliotheque Nationale, Paris, Nat. Gallery Art, Prague, Boston Mus. Fine Arts, Los Angeles County Mus. Olympic Flame tapestry executed for Olympic Games, Moscow, 1980. Served with USN, 1939-46. Ford Found. fellow, 1965; Western Interstate Commn. for Higher Edn. grantee, 1967; Calif. State Coll. System spl. creative leave, 1967. Mem. Am. Craftsmen, Am. Fedn. of the Arts. Home: Route 2 PO Box 539A Morgan Hill CA 95037 Office: Dept Art San Jose State Univ San Jose CA 95192

FREITAS, BEATRICE B(OTTY), opera theatre artistic director, musician, educator; b. Youngstown, Ohio, Aug. 28, 1938; d. John and Pauline (Esterhay) Botty; m. Lewis P. Freitas, Nov. 30, 1963; children—Roslyn K., John B. B.A., Oberlin Coll., 1958; M.Mus., Boston U., 1959; spl. student Juilliard Sch. Music, 1959-62. Artistic dir. Hawaii Opera Theatre, Honolulu; pianist, organist, harpsichordist, tchr. Recipient Outstanding Achievement in Area of Arts award YMCA, 1983.

FREIXAS, CLAUDIO JESUS, educator; b. Havana, Cuba, June 28, 1916; s. Joaquin Maria and Maria Antonia (de los Reyes) de Freixas; came to U.S., 1962, naturalized, 1971; LL.D., U. Havana, 1941; m. Margarita Marta Martinez, Nov. 4, 1949; children—Claudio, Antonio, Margarita Marta, Joaquin Emilio. Admitted to Cuban bar, 1941; partner Freixas Law Office, Havana, 1941-62; counselor at law Cuban Ministry Edn., 1944-46, Cuban Ministry Pub. Works, 1946-52; instr. Spanish, Lewis and Clark Coll., Portland, Oreg., 1963, Warner Pacific Coll., Portland, 1963-64, YWCA, Portland, 1963-64; mem. faculty Humboldt State U., Arcata, Calif., 1965—, asso. prof. Spanish, 1972-79, prof., 1979—; Spanish lang. coordinator Peace Corps Chile Fishing Coops. Tng. Program, 1966. Mem. Calif. Fgn. Lang. Tchrs. Assn. (dir. 1974-75, 77-78), Calif. N. Coast Fgn. Lang. Assn. (past pres.), Am. Assn. Tchrs. Spanish and Portuguese, Calif. Employees Assn. Translator, author introduction: Transls. Poems of Five Modernist Spanish-American Poets, 1975; Afro-Cuban Poetry-De Oshún a Yemayá, 1978; author: (poetry) Polarizaciones, 1978. Home: 971 Bayside Rd Arcata CA 95521 Office: Humboldt State Univ Arcata CA 95521

FRELIGH, EDITH ADELE, college administrator, consultant; b. Upper Volta, French West Africa, Mar. 5, 1925; d. Paul Elton and Mabel Katherine (Ray) F. B.A., U. Wash., 1949, M.A., 1950; Ed.D., UCLA, 1973. Instr. English and music Skagit Valley Coll., Mt. Vernon, Wash., 1950-56; instr., div. chmn. Am. River Coll., Sacramento, 1957-64, dean instrn., 1962-64; assoc. prof. English, Orange Coast Coll., Costa Mesa, Calif., 1964-66; div. chmn., dean acad. adminstrn., dean mgmt. and personnel Golden West Coll., Huntington Beach, Calif., 1966-79; vice-chancellor ednl. services and personnel State Ctr. Community Coll. Dist., Fresno, Calif., 1979—. Mem. Community Council. Mem. Assn. Calif. Community Coll. Adminstrs. (personnel com.), UCLA Alumni Assn., UCLA Doctoral Alumni Assn., Pi Lambda Theta. Democrat. Episcopalian. Contbr. articles to profl. jours. Office: 1525 E Weldon Ave Fresno CA 93704

FRENCH, C. L., shipbuilding executive; b. New Haven, Oct. 13, 1925; s. Clarence L. and Eleanor V. (Curry) F.; m. Jean Sprague, June 29, 1946; children—Craig Thomas, Brian Keith, Alan Scott. B.S. Tufts U., 1945, B.S.M.E., 1947. Engr. Bethlehem Steel Corp., 1947-56; staff engr., asst. supt. Kaiser Steel Corp., 1956-64; supervising engr. Bechtel Corp., 1964-67; project coordinator Nat. Steel and Shipbldg. Co., San Diego, successively chief metals engr., mgr. engring., dir. engr., v.p. engring., exec. v.p., gen. mgr., 1967-77, pres., chief operating officer, 1977—. Bd. dirs. San Diego United Way. Served to lt. USN, 1943-53. Mem. Am. Bur. Shipping, Am. Soc. Naval Engrs., ASTM, Maritime Transp. Research Bd., Nat. Research Council, Navy League U.S., Shipbuilders Council Am. (past chmn. bd.), Soc. Naval Architects and Marine Engrs. (pres.), U.S. Naval Inst., Webb Inst. Naval Architecture (trustee), Pres.' Roundtable of San Diego (past chmn.). Office: 28th St and Harbor Dr San Diego CA 92138

FRENCH, FRANCES ELIZABETH, broadcasting co. exec.; b. Los Angeles, Sept. 16, 1947; d. William Baxter and Frances Olin (Porter) French; A.A., Glendale (Calif.) Community Coll., 1975; 1 son, George Joseph Zawalonka, Jr. Video tape scheduling coordinator NBC, Burbank, Calif., 1967-72, unit mgr., 1976-81, sr. unit mgr., 1982—; prodn. coordinator KNBC, Burbank, 1972-74, supr. film editing, 1974-75, unit mgr., 1975-76; chief fin. officer, dir. Zawa & Son, Inc., 1980—. Mem. Am. Women in Radio and TV (bd. dirs.), LWV, NOW, DAR, Delta Theta Tau. Republican. Episcopalian. Office: 3000 W Alameda St Burbank CA 91523

FRENCH, GEORGINE LOUISE, guidance counselor; b. Lancaster, Pa., May 15, 1934; d. Richard Franklin and Elizabeth Georgine (Driesbach) Beacham; B.A., Calif. State U., San Bernardino, 1967; M.S., No. Ill. U., 1973; D.D., Am. Ministerial Assn., 1978; m. Barrie J. French, Feb. 4, 1956; children—Joel B., John D., James D., Jeffrey D. Personnel counselor Sages Dept. Store, San Bernardino, 1965-66; asst. bookkeeper Bank Calif., San Bernardino, 1964-65; tchr. Livermore (Calif.) Sch. Dist., 1968-69; guidance counselor Bur. Indian Affairs, Tuba City, Ariz., 1974-80, Sherman Indian High Sch., Riverside, Calif., 1980-82, Ft. Douglas Edn. Ctr., U.S. Army, Salt. Lake City, 1982—; extension tchr. Navajo Community Coll., Yavapai Jr. Coll.; personnel counselor USNR; ordained to ministry Am. Ministerial Assn., 1979. Served with USAF, 1954-56. Cert. guidance counselor, secondary tchr. Mem. Am. Personnel and Guidance Assn., Home: PO Box 8734 Salt Lake City UT 84108 Office: Army Edn Ctr Fort Douglas UT 84113

FRENSDORFF, WESLEY, bishop; b. Hanover, Germany, July 22, 1926; s. Rudolph August and Erma Margarete (Asch) F.; B.A., Columbia U., 1940; S.T.D., Gen. Theol. Sem., N.Y.C., 1951; m. Dolores C. Stoker, Nov. 1, 1953; 5 children. Ordained deacon Episcopal Ch., 1951, priest, 1951, vicar St. Mary Virgin Ch., Winnemucca, Nev., St. Andrew's Ch., Battle Mountain, Nev., St. Anne's Ch., McDermitt, Nev., 1951-54; rector St. Paul's Ch., Elko, Nev. and vicar St. Barnabas and St. Luke Ch., Wells, Nev., and St. Martin's Ch., Upper Skagit Valley, Nev. and Community Ch., Newhalem, Wash., 1959-62; dean St. Mark's Canthedral, Salt Lake City, 1962-72; bishop Diocese of Nev., Reno, 1972—; dir. North Pacific and Western parish tng. program Episcopal Ch., 1959-64, trustee Gen. Theol. Sem., 1965-74; priest in charge St. Francis Ch., Managua, Nicarague, 1968-69. Address: 2930 W 7th St Reno NV 89503*

FRERICHS, JOHN SILVER, manufacturing and quality control executive; b. Lincoln, Nebr., Jan. 18, 1927; s. Edward Abraham and Elsie (Silver) F.; m. Shirley May Stocker, Mar. 17, 1951; children—Stacey, Edward. B.S., U.S. Naval Acad., 1950; M.B.A., Portland (Oreg.) State U., 1975. Registered profl. engr., Calif. Mgr. quality engring. Burroughs Corp., Pasadena, Calif., 1956-63; quality control supr. N. Am. Aviation Co., Autonetics, Calif., 1963-66; quality assurance mgr. Ford Industries, Portland, 1966-70; mfg. mgr. Powerdyne Co., Tualatin, Oreg., 1970-73; quality assurance mgr. Allis-Chalmers Co., Tigard, Oreg., 1974-76; gen. mgr., treas., dir. Timber Products Insp. Co., Portland, 1976-81; mgmt. cons. Melden Co., Lake Oswego, Oreg., 1981-82; mgr. procurement quality control Tektronix, Beaverton, Oreg.; 1982—. Mem. dist. com. local Boy Scouts Am., 1969-75. Served as officer U.S. Navy, 1950-56; Korea. Mem. Am. Soc. Quality Control. Republican. Presbyterian. Address: 13730 SW Cameo Ct Lake Oswego OR 97034

FRESCHI, RICHARD ALBERT, med. supply co. exec.; b. Oakland, Calif., Feb. 11, 1937; s. Albert P. and Marie F.; student U. Calif. at Berkeley, 1955-57; B.S., Armstrong Coll., Berkeley, 1959; m. Joy Sylvia Ritter, Feb. 26, 1961; children—Paula J., Lisa M. Salesman, Don Baxter Inc. div. Am. Hosp. Supply Co., Glendale, Calif., 1962-65, Western area mgr. Coverters div., Santa Ana, Calif., 1965-71; founder, pres. Sentinel Disposables Co., Los Angeles, 1971-74; v.p. mktg. Plasta-Medic div. Bergen Brunswig Corp., Los Angeles, 1974-78, gen. mgr., 1978-80; pres. Plasta-Medic div. Hadley Industries, Inc., v.p. Hadley Industries, Inc., 1980-82; pres. Jordan/Plasta Medic, Romalite Corp., Union Plastics Calif., 1982-1983; v.p. Jordan Group, 1982-83; pres. Paulisa Inc., Reno, Nev., 1983—. Mem. Health Industries Mfrs. Assn., Assn. Micro Biol. Media Mfrs., Am. Surg. Trade Assn., Soc. Plastics Industry, Native Sons Golden West, Kappa Sigma Kappa, Alpha Sigma Rho. Club: Elks. Home: 10151 Phelan Dr Villa Park CA 92667 Office: EPCO A Paulisa Co 130 Woodland Ave PO Box 6509 Reno NV 89513

FRESTON, NORMA PATRICIA, energy company manager; b. Brigham City, Utah, July 2, 1939; d. Lawrence and Norma Josephine (Wight) Robinson; 1 son, Mitchel. B.S., Weber State Coll., 1966; M.A., Utah State U., 1968; M.S., U. Tex., 1971; Ph.D. in Indsl. Psychology, U. Utah, 1978. Tchr., counselor Utah State Welfare Program, Ogden, 1964-66; assessment counselor Women's Resource Ctr., U. Utah, Salt Lake City, 1971, program specialist women's programs Div. Continuing Edn., 1972-74, dir. acad. programming, 1974-77; asst. dir. manpower planning and devel. Mountain Fuel Supply Co., Salt Lake City, 1977-80, mgr. personnel services corp. div., 1980—. Adv. bd. Grad. Sch. Social Work, U. Utah; re-entry program Utah Tech. Coll., Westminster Coll. Recipient Silver Medal award, 1981. Mem. Am. Soc. Personnel

Adminstrs., Am. Psychol. Assn., Am. Soc. Tng. and Devel. (Argyle-Linberg award 1978, 79). Mormon. Club: Zonta. Author research papers in field. Office: Corp Div Mountain Fuel Supply Co 180 E 100 S Salt Lake City UT 84139

FRETWELL, DAVID HERBERT, tech. educator; b. Lacombe, Alta., Can., Nov. 23, 1942; s. Geoffrey A. and Ivy M. Fretwell; B.Ed., U. Alta., 1968; M.Ed., Oreg. State U., 1968, Ph.D., 1972; m. Janet Ruby Hicks, Apr. 1944; children—Terra Michelle, Shannon Lee. Instr. indsl. edn. Alta., 1963-69; asst. prof. Calif. Poly. U., 1969-71; manpower planner State of Oreg., 1972-74; adviser tech. edn., Kenya, 1974-76; asst. dir. Portland Job Corps Ctr., 1977-78; exec. sec. Oreg. Occupational Info. Coordinating Com., 1978-80; coordinator, instr. Tng. Inst., Saudi Arabia, 1980—; cons. in field. Mem. Am. Vocat. Assn., Am. Indsl. Arts Assn., Am. Vocat. Edn. Research Assn., Council Indsl. Edn. Tchrs., Soc. Automotive Engrs., Phi Kappa Phi. Contbr. articles to profl. jours. Home: 7488 Acorn Hill Crescent SE Salem OR 97301 Office: USREP/JECOR APO New York NY 09036

FREUDENBERGER, OTTO LEWIS, aeronautical engineer; b. St. Petersburg, Fla., May 8, 1930; s. Norman Leslie and Elizabeth Maria (Otto) F.; B.S.C.E., Clemson U., 1953; M.S.E.A., So. Meth. U., 1964; m. Judith Diane Burroughs, June 29, 1972; children—Karl Lewis, Curt Leslie. Successively aero. engr., project engr., program mgr., mgr. advanced systems Chance Vought Corp., Dallas, 1956-72; mgr. advanced systems Electronics Group, Rockwell Internat., Anaheim, Calif., 1972-74; dir. engring. Celesco Industries, Costa Mesa, Calif., 1974-75; engring. cons., 1975-77; mgr. strategic planning Northrop Corp. Aircraft Group, Pico Rivera, Calif., 1977—; mem. Critical Tech. Expert Group, Info. Issues of the 80's Study Group, Office Sec. of Def.; conf. speaker U.S. and Abroad; lectr. Served with USAF, 1953-57. Registered profl. engr., Calif. Mem. Tech. Mktg. Soc. Am. (founding chmn. Los Angeles chpt.). Republican. Episcopalian. Home: 18761 Haven Ln Yorba Linda CA 92686 Office: 8900 E Washington Blvd Pico Rivera CA 90660

FREUDENBURG, WILLIAM R., sociologist, educator; b. Norfolk, Nebr., Nov. 2, 1951; s. Eldon G. and Betty M. (Davis) F. B.A., U. Nebr., 1974; M.A., Yale U., 1976, M.Phil., 1977, Ph.D., 1979. Research assoc. Yale U., New Haven, 1975-77; asst. prof. sociology and rural sociology, Wash. State U., Pullman, 1978-83, assoc. prof. rural sociology, 1983—; researcher, cons. in field. Hawksworth scholar, 1970-72; Nat. Merit scholar, 1970-74; Nebr. Regents Scholar, 1970-74; NSF grad. fellow, 1975-79. Mem. Am. Sociol. Assn. (council, sect. on environ. sociology 1980—), Internat. Assn. for Impact Assessment, Rural Sociol. Soc. (chmn. natural resources research group 1982—), AAAS (Rural Sociol. Soc. rep. 1979—), Soc. for Applied Anthropology, Wash. State Sociol. Assn., Phi Beta Kappa, Phi Eta Sigma. Contbr. articles to profl. publs. including Am. Sociologist, Pacific Sociol. Rev., Am. Jour. Sociology, Rural Sociology. Office: 27 Wilson Hall Wash State Univ Pullman WA 99164

FREY, DAVID LYNN, management company executive; b. Cumberland, Md., Jan. 24, 1950; s. Christian Miller and Betty Ruth F.; m. LeAnn Marie Adams, Nov. 14, 1981. B.A., Calif. State U.-Fresno, 1978, M.A. in Indsl. Edn., 1978. Chmn. dept. indsl. edn. Elk Grove (Calif.) Unified Sch. Dist., 1974-78; project mgr., edn. div. Singer Careers Systems, San Francisco, 1978-81; dir. ednl. services Mgmt. & Tng. Corp., Reno, Nev., 1981—. Mem. Am. Vocat. Assn., Nev. Vocat. Assn. Democrat. Home: 11845 Overland Rd Reno NV 89506 Office: PO Box 60009 Reno NV 89506

FREY, WILLIAM CARL, bishop; b. Waco, Tex., Feb. 26, 1930; s. Harry Frederick and Ethel (Oliver) F.; B.A., U. Colo., 1952; Th.M., Phila. Divinity Sch., 1955, D.D. (hon.), 1970; m. Barbara Louise Martin, June 12, 1952; children—Paul, Mark, Matthew, Peter, Susannah. Ordained to ministry Episcopal Ch.; vicar Timberline Circuit (Colo.) Missions, 1955-58; rector Trinity-on-the-Hill Ch., Los Alamos, 1958-62; missionary priest Episcopal Ch., Costa Rica, 1962-67, bishop, 1967; bishop Diocese of Guatemala, 1967-72; chaplain U. Ark., Fayetteville, 1972; bishop Diocese of Colo., Denver, 1972—. Contbr. articles to religious mags. Office: PO Box 18M Capitol Hill Sta Denver CO 80218*

FRICK, OSCAR LIONEL, physician; b. N.Y.C., Mar. 12, 1923; s. Oscar and Elizabeth (Ringger) F.; A.B., Cornell U., 1944, M.D., 1946; M. Med. Sci., U. Pa., 1960; Ph.D., Stanford, 1964; m. Mary Hubbard, Sept. 2, 1954. Intern, Babies Hosp., Columbia Coll. Phys. and Surg., N.Y.C., 1946-47; resident Children's Hosp., Buffalo, 1950-51; pvt. practice, specializing in pediatrics, Huntington, N.Y., 1951-58; fellow allergy immunology Royal Victoria Hosp., Montreal, Que., Can., 1958-59; fellow allergy U. Calif. at San Francisco, 1959-60, asst. prof. pediatrics, 1964-67, asso. prof., 1967-72, prof., 1972—, dir. allergy tng. program, 1964—; fellow immunology Inst. d'Immunobiologie, Hospital Broussais, Paris, France, 1960-62. Served with M.C. USNR, 1947-49. Diplomate Am. Bd. Allergy and Immunology (chmn. 1967-72). Mem. Am. Assn. Immunologists, Am. Acad. Pediatrics (chmn. allergy sect. 1971-72), Am. Acad. Allergy (exec. com. 1972—, pres. 1977-78), Internat. Assn. Allergologists (exec. com. 1970-73), Am. Pediatric Soc., Mason. Contbr. articles, papers to profl. publs. Home: 370 Parnassus Ave San Francisco CA 94117

FRICKE, ALMA BLAKE, assn. exec.; b. Somerville, Tex., June 3, 1916; d. Edward Henry and Alice Mae (Warren) Lott; student Tex. Woman's U., 1938-39, N. Tex. State U., 1939-41; m. Frederick John Fricke, Apr. 16, 1941; children—Frederick John, Alice June Fricke Missall. Organizing regent Charles Dibrell chpt. DAR, 1963, chpt. regent, 1963-65, state librarian N.Mex., 1965-67, state treas., 1969-71, dist. dir., 1971-73, state vice-regent, 1971-73, state regent, 1973-75, v.p. gen., 1976-78. Mem. adv. bd. Kate Duncan Smith Sch., Grant, Ala., 1977-80. Recipient medal of appreciation, SAR, 1976. Mem. Soc. Lees of Va., Order First Families of Miss., Washington Family Descs., Colonial Dames XII Century, Daus. Am. Colonists (state vice regent), Daus. Am. Revolution, Daus. Republic of Tex., UDC, Jamestowne Soc. (life), Nat. Huguenots Soc., Alumni Assn. Tex. Woman's U. Republican. Episcopalian. Home: 4214 Avenida La Resolana NE Albuquerque NM 87110

FRIDAY, WILLETTE J., pharmaceutical company official; b. Waukegan, Ill., Aug. 3, 1951; d. William B. and Marlys L (Green) Braasch; m. Timothy J. Friday, Aug. 22, 1981; 1 dau., Claire Marlys. B.A. in Theatre Arts, U. Minn., 1973. Copywriter, May Co., Los Angeles, 1975-76; copy supr. Maher, Kaump and Co., Los Angeles, 1976-79; dir. advt. Mead Johnson and Co., Evansville, Ind., 1979-81; creative dir. Allergan Pharms., Irvine, Calif., 1981—. Recipient filmmaking grant U. Minn., 1972. Mem. Orange County Advt. Fedn., Med. Mktg. Assn. Home: 5889 E Trapper Trail Anaheim CA 92807 Office: Allergan Pharmeceuticals 2525 DuPont Dr Irvine CA 92713

FRIED, BERNARD, bus. exec.; b. Bklyn., Dec. 9, 1928; s. Charles and Sylvia (Reznov) F.; m. Joan Ann Gillis, June 16, 1956; children—Debi Elise, Dana Lynn. B.B.A., CCNY, 1950; LL.B., Bklyn. Law Sch., 1953, J.D., 1963. Bar: N.Y. 1953, Calif. 1976, D.C. 1976, U.S. Supreme Ct. 1963; cert. profl. contracts mgr. Contracts mgr. Bendix Corp., Towson, Md., 1958-60; contracts and bus. mgr. Martin Co., Balt., 1960-64; contracts mgr. Bunker-Ramo Corp., Westlake Village, Calif., 1964-65; v.p., gen. counsel, sec. System Devel. Corp., Santa Monica, Calif., 1965—; dir. Aquilla BST Ltd., Montreal, Que., Can., Mechanics Research Inc., Los Angeles, Systems Mgmt. and Engring. Corp., Los Angeles, Flitchport Ltd., London. Lectr. contract law. Pres. Cromwell Valley Civic Improvement Assn., 1962-63; mem. bd. advisers Computer Law Inst. of U. So. Calif. Law Sch.; mem. bd. advisors govt. contract law program Northrup U. Sch. Law. Served to lt. Supply Corp, USNR, 1953-57. Fellow Nat. Contract Mgmt. Assn. (chmn. 17th and 20th ann. symposia), mem. Am. Arbitration Assn. (arbitrator), Nat. Security Indsl. Assn., ABA, Fed. Bar Assn., Calif. Bar Assn., D.C. Bar Assn., Santa Monica Bay Bar Assn., Los Angeles County Bar Assn., Computer Law Assn., AIAA, Beta Delta Mu. Mem. bd. advisers Fed. Contracts Report; contbr. articles to profl. jours. Home: 1851 Calle Yucca Thousand Oaks CA 91360 Office: 2500 Colorado Ave Santa Monica CA 90406

FRIED, ELAINE JUNE, business exec.; b. Los Angeles, Oct. 19, 1943; grad. Pasadena (Calif.) High Sch., 1963; various coll. courses; m. Howard I. Fried, Aug. 7, 1966; children—Donna Marie, Randall Jay. Agt., office mgr. Howard I. Fried Agy., Alhambra, Calif., 1975—; v.p. Sea Hill, Inc., Pasadena, Calif., 1973—. Publicity chmn., unit telephone chmn. San Gabriel Valley (Calif.) unit Am. Diabetes Assn.; publicity chmn. San Gabriel Valley region Women's Am. Orgn. for Rehab. Tng. (ORT); chmn. spl. events publicity Temple Beth Torah, Alhambra; bd. dirs., public relations com. vis. Nurses Assn., Pasadena and San Gabriel Valley, Recipient Vol. award So. Calif. affiliate Am. Diabetes Assn., 1974-77. Clubs: B'nai B'rith Women, Hadassah, Temple Beth Torah Sisterhood. Speaker on psycho-social aspects of diabetes.

FRIED, GERALD SAMUEL, marketing executive, consultant; b. N.Y.C., July 24, 1943; s. Walter and Gladys Elaine (Krausz) F.; m. Annette Gail Furst; children—Amy, David. B.S. in Indsl. Engring., Pa. State U., 1965; M.B.A., U. Chgo., 1967. Mktg. exec. H.J. Heinz Co., Pitts., 1967-72, Ralston Purina Co., St. Louis, 1972-78, Banquet Foods Co., St. Louis, 1978-80, Mattel Inc., Los Angeles, 1980-82; co-founder, exec. Mktg. Advancements Inc., Huntington Beach, Calif., 1982—; cons. small cos. Mem. Am. Mktg. Assn. Republican. Jewish. Home: 6732 Crista Palma Dr Huntington Beach CA 92647

FRIED, HOWARD LEE, artist, educator; b. Cleve., June 14, 1946; s. Julius E. and Rose (Krasovicz) F.; div.; 1 son, Paul K. Student, Syracuse U., 1967; B.F.A., San Francisco Art Inst., 1968; M.F.A., U. Calif.-Davis, 1970. One-man shows: Reese Palley Gallery, San Francisco, 1970, 72, N.Y.C., 1971, U. Santa Clara Mus., 1972, San Francisco Art Inst., 1972, N.S. Coll. Art and Design, Halifax, 1972, San Francisco Mus. Modern Art, 1977, Mus. Modern Art, N.Y.C., 1979, Univ. Art Mus., Berkeley, Calif., 1982, 83, Artist's Space, N.Y.C., 1983, others; group shows: Kunsthalle, Dusseldorf, W.Ger., 1971, Friedrecianum, Kassel, West Germany, 1972, Everson Mus. Art, Syracuse, N.Y., 1973, Kunsthalle, Cologne, W.Ger., 1974, Inst. Contemporary Art, Phila., 1975, Whitney Mus. of Am. Art, N.Y.C., 1977, 79, 81, San Francisco Mus. Modern Art, 1979, Stedelijk Mus., Amsterdam, Netherlands, 1982, others; chmn. performance/video dept. San Francisco Art Inst. Mem. artists com. San Francisco Art Inst., 1971-82, chmn., 1976-78, trustee, 1971-82. Nat. Endowment for the Arts fellow, 1975-80. Subject of articles in various art publs. Home: 16 Rose St San Francisco CA 94102

FRIED, NORMAN ZANDER, paint manufacturing corporation executive; b. Chgo., Sept. 18, 1920; s. Philip Edward and Fannie (Grezenda) F.; m. Zelda Elaine Lasky, Feb. 4, 1944; children—Leslie Fried Rice, Gayle Fried Friedlander, Kenneth. B.Ed., No. Ill. U., 1942; postgrad. U. Colo., 1972-74, Air War Coll., 1974-75. Tchr., high sch., 1942; freelance advt. artist, 1946-55; owner Norman Fried Advt. Agy., 1955-66; advt./pub. relations dir. KWAL Paints, Inc., Denver, 1966—, v.p. communication, 1974—; lectr. advt., pub. relations U. Denver, U. Colo., 1956-72. Vice pres. Mile Hi council Girl Scouts U.S.A., 1980-82; active Denver Area council Boys Scouts Am., 1958—; v.p. Colo. USO, 1976-77. Served to lt. col. USAAF, 1942-46. Mem. Pub. Relations Soc. Am., Nat. Paint and Coatings Assn. (communication com. 1970—), Sigma Delta Chi, Alpha Delta Sigma, Denver C. of C. Clubs: Denver Press; Pinery Country (Parker, Colo.). Contbr. articles to profl. jours.

FRIEDL, RICK, coll. pres.; b. Berwyn, Ill., Aug. 31, 1947; s. Raymond J. and Ione L. (Anderson) F.; B.A., Calif. State U., Northridge, 1969; M.A. (Calif. State Grad. fellow 1970-72), UCLA, 1976; M.A., U. So. Calif., 1979; Ph.D., U. Central Calif., 1982; m. Diane Marie Guillies, Sept. 2, 1977; children—Richard, Angela, Ryan. Dept. mgr. Calif. Dept. Indsl. Relations, 1973-78; mem. faculty dept. polit. sci. U. So. Calif., 1978-80; pres. Beverly Hills (Calif.) City Coll., 1981—; bd. dirs. Calif. State U., Northridge, 1979. Mem. Am. Polit. Sci. Assn., Latin Am. Studies Assn., Acad. Polit. Sci., Pacific Coast Council Latin Am. Studies. Author: The Political Economy of Cuban Dependency, 1981. Home: PO Box 449 Beverly Hills CA 90213 Office: 8306 Wilshire Blvd Suite 177 Beverly Hills CA 90211

FRIEDLAND, DAVID LEE, indsl. psychologist; b. Long Beach, Calif., Nov. 10, 1941; s. Bernard Paul and Bernice Friedland; B.A., Calif. State U., Long Beach, 1964, M.A., 1972; Ph.D., U. So. Calif., 1975; m. Lilli Rebhun, Feb. 22, 1969; children—Jered Michael, Elana. Personnel research analyst County of Los Angeles, 1967-72; dir. personnel research City of Los Angeles, 1972-80; dir. mgmt. services Friedland Psychol. Assocs., Los Angeles, 1980—. Mem. tech. adv. com. on testing Calif. Fair Employment and Housing Commn. Mem. Internat. Personnel Mgmt. Assn., Internat. Personnel Mgmt. Assn. Assessment Council (dir.), Los Angeles County Psychol. Assn. (dir.), Am. Psychol. Assn., Calif. Psychol. Assn., Personnel Testing Council Los Angeles (pres. elect), West Los Angeles C. of C. Office: 2080 Century Park E Suite 204 Los Angeles CA 90067

FRIEDLAND, LILLI, clinical psychologist; b. Badgastein, Austria, Feb. 24, 1947; came to U.S., 1950, naturalized, 1956; d. Joseph and Marie (Bierkenhejm) Rebhun; B.A., U. Oreg., 1966; Ph.D., U. So. Calif. 1975; m. David Lee Friedland, Feb. 22, 1969; children—Jered, Elana. Research asst. Research Service Bur., Los Angeles, 1968-70; cons. to Council of Jewish Fedn., N.Y.C., 1969-70; research analyst Los Angeles Mental Health Dept., 1970-73; chief planning div. Office of Alcohol Abuse and Alcoholism, Los Angeles County, 1973-74, chief program and system evaluation, 1973-74; chief drug abuse planning Los Angeles County Dept. Health Services, 1973-76; dir. family devel. program Suicide Prevention Center, Los Angeles, 1975-77; pres. Friedland Psychol. Assos., Inc., Beverly Hills, Calif., 1975—; cons. to pvt. secondary schs., Calif., 1973—; condr. workshops. Chairperson Developmental Disabilities Area Bd., Calif., 1977-79, Program Planning and Evaluation Com. Area Bd., 1975-77; exec. com., community service com., mem. program planning and budgeting com., community relations com. Jewish Fedn. Council, 1981—. Recipient certs. of appreciation Bd. Suprs. Los Angeles County, 1980, Los Angeles County Narcotics and Dangerous Drugs Commn., 1975. Mem. Am. Psychol. Assn., Calif. Psychol. Assn., Los Angeles Psychol. Assn. (mem. profl. conduct com. 1979—), Los Angeles County Psychol. Assn. (dir. 1980—), Los Angeles County Clin. Psychol. Assn. (dir. 1980—), Women in Bus., Hadassah. Republican. Jewish. Home: 1216 Daniels Dr Los Angeles CA 90035 Office: 2080 Century Park E Suite 204 Los Angeles CA 90067

FRIEDLAND, ROGER OWEN, sociology educator; b. N.Y.C., June 20, 1947; s. Harry and Helen F.; m. Debra, July 12, 1981. B.A., U. Calif.-Berkeley, 1969; M.S., U. Wis.-Madison, 1971, Ph.D. in Sociology, 1977. Lectr. U. Calif.-Santa Cruz, 1977; asst. prof. sociology U. Calif.-Santa Barbara, 1978-81, assoc. prof., 1982—; Fulbright prof. Hebrew U., Jerusalem, 1983; leader Hillel Leadership Seminar, Jerusalem; cons. Nat. Acad. Scis.; reviewer Nat. Sci. Found. German Marshall fellow, 1978. Mem. Am. Sociol. Assn., Am. Polit. Sci. Assn. Democrat. Jewish. Author: Power and Crisis in the City, 1983; contbr. articles on sociology to profl. jours.; mem. editoral bd. Urban Policy Analysis, Internat. Jour. Health Services. Office: Dept Sociology U Calif Santa Barbara CA 93106

FRIEDMAN, ARNOLD PHINEAS, physician, cons.; b. Portland, Oreg., Aug. 25, 1909; s. Carl and Lena (Levy) F.; B.A., U. So. Calif., 1932, M.A., 1934; M.D., U. Oreg., 1939; m. Sara Fritz, July 10, 1939; 1 dau., Carol L. Friedman Ludwig. Intern, Los Angeles County Hosp., 1939-40, resident in neurology, 1940-42; asst. physician Boston Psychopathol. Hosp., 1942-43; fellow in neurology Harvard U. Med. Sch., 1943-44; research asso. Boston City Hosp., 1943-44; head injury project Office Sci. Research and Devel., 1943-44; practice medicine specializing in neurology, N.Y.C., 1944; attending physician div. neurology Montefiore Hosp., N.Y.C., 1949-73; attending neurologist Neurol. Inst., Presbyn. Hosp., N.Y.C., 1971-73; prof. neurology Health Scis. Center U. Ariz., Tucson, 1971-75; cons. Neurol. Assos. of Tucson, 1975—. Recipient Lucy G. Moses award Columbia-Presbyn. Hosp., 1973; diplomate Am. Bd. Psychiatry and Neurology (dir. 1964, pres. 1971). Fellow Am. Acad. Neurology (trustee 1958-59), Am. Psychiat. Assn. (life, Rush silver medal 1969), Am. Coll. Physicians and Surgeons; mem. AMA (chmn. sect. nervous and mental diseases, sect. 63/64, Billings silver medal 1959, outstanding exhibit award, 1968 cert. of appreciation 1977-78), Am. Neurol. Assn. (sr., chmn./sec. research group on headache and migraine 1967-80), Am. Assn. for Study of Headache (disting. clinician award 1976, pres. 1978-80), Nat. Migraine Found. (chmn. 1980-82). Contbr. articles to profl. publs. Home: 3250 N Sabino Vista Circle Tucson AZ 85715 Office: 5402 E Grant Rd B-9 Tucson AZ 85712

FRIEDMAN, DOTTIE JUDITH, retail clothing store exec.; b. N.Y.C., June 5, 1938; d. Max and Hannah (Levy) Shlafer; student Salt Lake City public schs.; divorced; children—Elisabeth, Tracy. Engaged in retail clothing bus., 1963—; v.p., chief exec. officer Contempo Casuals, Los Angeles, 1979—; cons. Broadway Hale Corp., 1980. Named Retail Woman of Yr., Cedars-Sinai Hosp., 1980. Mem. Fashion Group. Address: 1104 Sunset Vale Los Angeles CA 90069

FRIEDMAN, MILTON, economist, author; b. Bklyn., July 31, 1912; s. Jeno Saul and Sarah Ethel (Landau) F.; A.B., Rutgers U., 1932, LL.D., 1968; A.M., U. Chgo., 1933; Ph.D., Columbia U., 1946; LL.D., St. Paul's (Rikkyo) U., 1963, Kalamazoo Coll., 1968, Lehigh U., 1969, Loyola U., 1971, U. N.H., 1975, Harvard U., 1979, Brigham Young U., 1980, Dartmouth U., 1980, Gonzaga U., 1981; Sc.D., Rochester U., 1971; L.H.D., Rockford Coll., 1969, Roosevelt U., 1975, Hebrew Union Coll., Los Angeles, 1981; Litt.D., Bethany Coll., 1971; Ph.D. (hon.), Hebrew U., Jerusalem, 1977; m. Rose Director, June 25, 1938; children—Janet, David. Assoc. economist Nat. Resources Com., Washington, 1935-37; mem. research staff Nat. Bur. Econ. Research, N.Y., 1937-45, 48-81; vis. prof. econs. U. Wis., 1940-41; prin. economist, tax research div. U.S. Treasury Dept., 1941-43, assoc. dir. research, statis. research group, war research div. Columbia U., 1943-45; assoc. prof. econs. and stats. U. Minn., 1945-46; assoc. prof. econs. U. Chgo., 1946-48, prof. econs., 1948-62, Paul Snowden Russell Disting. Service prof. econs., 1962-82, Paul Snowden Russell Disting. Service prof. emeritus, 1983—; Fulbright lectr. Cambridge U., 1953-54; vis. Wesley Clair Mitchell Research prof. econs. Columbia U., 1964-65; fellow Center for Advanced Study in Behavioral Sci., 1957-58. Mem. Pres.'s Commn. All-Volunteer Army, 1969-70, Pres.'s Commn. on White House Fellows, 1971-74; vis. scholar Fed. Res. Bank, San Francisco, 1977; sr. research fellow Hoover Instn., Stanford U., 1977—. Recipient John Bates Clark medal Am. Econ. Assn., 1951; Nobel prize in econs., 1976; Pvt. Enterprise Exemplar medal Freedoms Found., 1978; named Chicagoan of Year, Chgo. Press Club, 1972; Educator of Year, Chgo. United Jewish Fund, 1973. Fellow Inst. Math. Stats., Am. Statis. Assn., Econometric Soc.; mem. Nat. Acad. Scis., Am. Econ. Assn. (exec. com. 1955-57, pres. 1967), Am. Enterprise Inst. (adv. bd.), Royal Econ. Soc., Western Econ. Assn. (v.p., 1982-83, pres. 1984-85), Am. Philos. Soc., Mont Pelerin Soc. (dir. 1958-61, pres. 1970-72). Club: Quadrangle. Author: Taxing to Prevent Inflation (with Carl Shoup and Ruth P. Mack), 1943; Income from Independent Professional Practice (with Simon S. Kuznets), 1946; Sampling Inspection (with Harold A. Freeman, Frederick Mosteller, W. Allen Wallis), 1948; Essays in Positive Economics, 1953; A Theory of the Consumption Function, 1957; A Program for Monetary Stability, 1959; Price Theory, 1962; (with Rose D. Friedman) Capitalism and Freedom, 1962, Free To Choose, 1980; (with Anna J. Schwartz) A Monetary History of the United States, 1867-1960, 1963; Inflation: Causes and Consequences, 1963; (with Anna J. Schwartz) The Great Contraction, 1965, Monetary Statistics of the United States, 1970, Monetary Trends in the United States and the United Kingdom, 1982; (with Robert Roosa) The Balance of Payments: Free vs. Fixed Exchange Rates, 1967; Dollars and Deficits, 1968; The Optimum Quantity of Money and Other Essays, 1969; (with Walter W. Heller) Monetary vs. Fiscal Policy, 1969; A Theoretical Framework for Monetary Analysis, 1972; (with Wilbur J. Cohen) Social Security, 1972; An Economist's Protest, 1972; There Is No Such Thing As A Free Lunch, 1975; Price Theory, 1976; (with Robert J. Gordon et al) Milton Friedman's Monetary Framework, 1974; (with William R. Allen) Bright Promises, Dismal Performance: An Economist's Protest, 1983; editor: Studies in the Quantity Theory of Money, 1956; bd. editors Am. Econ. Rev., 1951-53, Econometrica, 1957-69; columnist Newsweek mag., 1966—, contbg. editor, 1971—; contbr. articles to profl. jours. Office: Hoover Instn Stanford U Stanford CA 94305

FRIEDMAN, MYRON ALBERT, financial management consultant; b. Cleve., June 2, 1934; s. Louis J. and Betty Helen (Wilcox) F.; m. Carol Morton; children—Dana Lee Picard, Laurie Lyn. B.S. in Acctg., Miami U., Oxford, Ohio, 1956. C.P.A., Ohio, Calif. Staff Alexander Grant & Co., Cin., 1956-64, mgr., 1964-67, ptnr., 1967-79; pres. Myron A. Friedman & Co., Palos Verdes Estates, Calif., 1979—. Bd. dirs. Cystic Fibrosis Found., Los Angeles, 1973-82, pres., 1978-80; bd. dirs. Palos Verdes Community Arts Assn., 1983, treas., 1983. Mem. Am. Inst. C.P.A.s, Calif. Soc. C.P.A.s, Planning Execs. Inst. (pres. Los Angeles 1979-80, v.p., 1980-83), So. Calif. Corporate Planners Assn. (pres. 1982-83), N. Am. Soc. Corporate Planners (dir. 1982-83).

FRIEDMANN, PERETZ PETER, educator, aero. engr.; b. Timisoara, Rumania, Nov. 18, 1938; s. Mauritius and Elisabeth (Gross) F.; came to U.S., 1969, naturalized, 1977; D.Sc., Mass. Inst. Tech., 1972; m. Esther Sarfati, Dec. 8, 1964. Engring. officer Israel Def. Force, 1961-65; sr. engr. Israel Aircraft Industries, Ben Gurion Airport, Israel, 1965-69; research asst. dept. aeros. and astronautics Mass. Inst. Tech., Cambridge, 1969-72; asst. prof. mechanics and structures dept. U. Calif., Los Angeles, 1972-77, asso. prof., 1977-80, prof., 1980—. Recipient grants NASA, NSF. Asso. fellow Am. Inst. Aeros. and Astronautics; mem. ASME, AM. Helicopter Soc., Sigma Xi. Jewish. Editor-in-chief: Vertica-Internat. Jour. Rotorcraft and Powered Lift Aircraft; contbr. numerous articles to profl. jours. Home: 221 N Bowling Green Way Los Angeles CA 90049 Office: Dept Mechanics and Structures Univ Calif Los Angeles CA 90024

FRIEDRICH, MIKE, publishing agent; b. Oakland, Calif., Mar. 27, 1949; s. Paul Michael and Barbara Jean (Warren) F. B.A. in English, U. Santa Clara, 1971. Writer, DC Comics, N.Y.C., 1967-71, Marvel Comics, N.Y.C., 1971-76, mgr. direct sales, 1980-82; editor, publisher Star*Reach Prodns., Berkeley, Calif., 1974-80, publishing agt., 1982—.

Recipient Inkpot award San Diego Comic Conv. Com., 1981. Mem. Comic Art Profl. Soc. Democrat. Pub. numerous comic books including: Parsifal, 1978; Cody Starbuck, 1978; Star*Reach Greatest Hits, 1979. Address: PO Box 2328 Berkeley CA 94702

FRIEDRICH, PHILIP, kitchen appliance manufacturing company executive; b. Fullerton, Calif., 1941. Grad. Calif. State U.-Fullerton, 1964. Pres. Thermador/Waste King div. Norris Industries Inc., Los Angeles, 1967—. Mem. Am. Mgmt. Assn., Calif. Elec. Alliance. Office: Thermador/Waste King Co 5119 District Blvd Los Angeles CA 90040*

FRIEND, GEORGE EUGENE, safety executive, pilot; b. Elk River, Idaho, Aug. 15, 1926; s. Clarence Melford and Edith Richmond (Lillard) F.; m. Lucille Marie Payne, May 15, 1948; children—Eileen, Bruce. Student Aero Industries Tech. Inst., 1947-48, U. Calif., 1948, Colo. Sch. Mines, 1980. Maintenance supr. Potlatch Timber Protective Assn., Elk River, Idaho, 1948-56; purchasing agt./pilot/v.p. Hall Logging Co., Elk River and Spokane, Wash., 1956-71; safety dir./chief pilot N.A. Degerstrom, Inc., Spokane, 1971—; instr. indsl. first aid classes and CPR. Served with USAAF, 1944-45. Mem. Nat. Assn. Purchasing Agts., Am. Soc. Safety Engrs., Assoc. Gen. Contractors (chmn. accident prevention com. Inland Empire chpt.). Lutheran. Club: Masons. Home: E 10806 21st Ave Spokane WA 99206 Office: N 3303 Sullivan Rd Spokane WA 99216

FRIES, CHARLES WILLIAM, film producer. B.A., Ohio State U. Prodn. controller Ziv TV Programs, Inc., 1952-60; v.p., exec. prodn. mgr. Columbia Pictures TV; various positions to v.p. prodn. adminstrn. theatrical div. Screen Gems, 1960-70; exec. v.p., ind. producer Metromedia Producers Corp., 1970-74; pres. Charles Fries Prodns., Inc., Studio City, Calif., 1974—; adv. com. Am. Film Inst.; dir. Film Industry Workshops; past chmn. steering com. Caucus of Producers, Writers and Dirs.; contbr. Cinema Circulus of U. So. Calif. Cinema Sch. Recipient Cine Golden Eagle, Humanitas awards, Christopher awards and Eddy awards for various prodns. Mem. Alliance TV Film Producers (past pres.), Acad. Motion Picture Arts and Scis. (gov.), Producers Guild Am.

FRIES, HERLUF BECK, rancher, investor; b. Fresno, Calif., Apr. 1, 1915; s. Christian Peterson and Emma (Beck) F.; student pub. schs.; m. Geraldine Wood, Aug. 17, 1954; children—Donna, Doug, Jean, Benta. Farmer, rancher, Oakhurst, Calif., 1980-83; cons. Fgn. Farming Corp., Fidanam, Lugano, Switzerland, 1977-80; state pres. Calif. Young Farmers, 1948. Recipient Calif. State Farmer degree Future Farmers Am., 1949. Mem. Fresno County Farm Bur. (dir.). Republican. Lutheran. Address: 49526 Meadowwood St Oakhurst CA 93644

FRIESE, ROBERT CHARLES, lawyer; b. Chgo., Apr. 29, 1943; s. Earl Matthew and Laura Barbara (Mayer) F.; A.B. in Internat. Relations, Stanford U., 1964; J.D., Northwestern U., 1970. Admitted to Calif. bar, 1972; dir. Tutor Applied Linguistics Center, Geneva, Switzerland, 1964-66; atty. Bronson, Bronson & McKinnon, San Francisco, 1970-71, SEC, San Francisco, 1971-75; atty., partner Shartsis, Friese & Ginsburg, San Francisco, 1975—; dir., co-founder Internat. Plant Research Inst., Inc., San Carlos, Calif., 1978—. Chmn. Bd. Suprs. Task Force on Noise Control, 1972—; chmn. San Franciscans for Cleaner City, 1977; exec. dir. Nob Hill Neighbors, 1972-81; bd. dirs. Nob Hill Assn., 1976-78, Calif. Heritage Council, 1977-78. Mem. Am. Bar Assn., Calif. Bar Assn., Bar Assn. San Francisco, Lawyers Club of San Francisco, Mensa, Calif. Hist. Soc. Clubs: Commonwealth; Swiss-American Friendship League (chmn.). Office: 255 California St Suite 900 San Francisco CA 94111

FRIETZSCHE, ARTHUR H., educator; b. San Francisco, July 22, 1922; s. Clarence Harrell and Anna (Johnson) F., A.A., San Francisco Jr. Coll., 1942; B.A., U. Calif. at Berkeley, 1944, M.A., 1945, Ph.D., 1949. Lectr. English, U. Calif. at Berkeley, 1949-51; supr. tech. publs. Hanford Atomic Works, Richland, Wash., 1952-56; asst. prof. English, Utah State U., Logan, 1956-59, asso. prof., 1959-65; asst. prof. English, Calif. Poly. State U., San Luis Obispo, 1965-67, asso. prof., 1967-72, prof., 1972—. Mem. Modern Lang. Assn. Am., Am. Soc. for Engring. Edn., Soc. for Tech. Communications. Author: The Monstrous Clever Young Man: the Novelist Disraeli and His Heroes, 1959; Disraeli's Religion, 1961. Contbr. articles to profl. jours. Home: PO Box 83 San Luis Obispo CA 93406

FRIIS, HELENE ELIZABETH, architect, sculptress; b. Stuttgart, W.Ger., 1948; came to U.S., 1950, naturalized, 1967; d. Kasimerz and Anastasia Rogalski; B.F.A., Ft. Wright Coll. Holy Names, 1967; B.A. in Edn., Wash. State U., 1970, B. Archtl. Studies, 1971, B.Arch., 1972; m. Terry E. Friis, June 13, 1973; 1 dau., Angela Dominique. One-woman shows; Avant Guard Gallery, Spokane, 1965-66, Spokane Pub. Library, 1964, Ft. Wright Coll. Holy Names, 1967, Boston U., 1968, U. Idaho, 1968, Wash. State U., 1970; represented in permanent collections: HEF Design, Architects and Planners, 3D Devel., Inc., Rogalski Collection; instr. fine arts Spokane Sch. Dist., 1969; assoc. architect, designer, planner GFG & Assocs., Spokane, 1972-74; founder, owner, prin. HEF Design Architects & Planners, Spokane, 1975-82, dir. mktg., 1975—; founder, v.p. 3D Devel., Inc., Spokane, 1982—, artist in residence Boston U., 1967-68. Mem. AIA, Council Ednl. Facilities Planners, Urban Land Inst., Nat. Trust Historic Preservation. Roman Catholic. Club: Spokane Bus. Office: W 1520 3d Ave Suite 301 Spokane WA 99204

FRISBEE, DON CALVIN, utility co. exec.; b. San Francisco, Dec. 13, 1923; s. Ira Nobles and Helen (Sheets) F.; grad. Pomona Coll., 1947; M.B.A., Harvard U., 1949; m. Emilie Ford, Feb. 5, 1946; children—Ann, Robert, Peter, Dean. With First Nat. Bank of Oreg., Portland, 1949-52; adminstrv. asst. Pacific Power & Light Co., Portland, 1953-56, asst. treas., 1956-58, treas., 1958-60, v.p., 1960-65, exec. v.p., 1965-66, pres., from 1966, chmn. bd., 1973—; dir. First Nat. Bank of Oreg., Standard Ins. Co., Oreg. Portland Cement, Lucky Stores, Inc. Gen. campaign chmn. United of Columbia Willamette, 1969-70, pres., 1972; mem. adv. bd. Columbia Pacific council Boy Scouts Am.; trustee Reed Coll., Whitman Coll. Served with arty. U.S. Army, 1943-46. Mem. Edison Electric Inst., Com. for Econ. Devel. (trustee). Republican. Unitarian. Clubs: Univ., Arlington, City, Multnomah Athletic, Racquet. Office: 920 SW 6th Ave Portland OR 97204*

FRISCH, ROBERT ARNOLD, fin. planning co. exec.; b. Schenectady, N.Y., July 22, 1922; s. Harry and Ann (Hirschmann) F.; B.S., Western Mich. U., 1947; postgrad. Wharton Sch. Bus., 1956-57; m. Leona A. Abbey, Sept. 9, 1951; children—Dana R., Randi. Vice pres. Halsey, Bache & Co., 1971-73; founder, chief exec. officer ESOT Group, Inc., Los Angeles, 1973—; lectr. corporate finance and devel., fringe benefits, exec. benefit planning; qualified mgr. N.Y. Stock Exchange, 1971-73; fin. cons. Active Boy Scouts Am. Served with USAF, 1943-46. Mem. Am. Mgmt. Assn. (chmn. employee stock ownership plan seminars), Am. Soc. C.L.U.'s (pres. 1968-69), Nat. Assn. Security Dealers (prin.). Author: The Magic of ESOT: The Fabulous New Instrument of Corporate Finance, 1975; Triumph of Esop, 1977; Esops for the Eighties. Home: Encino CA 91316 Office: 3701 Wilshire Blvd Los Angeles CA 90010

FRISCHE, RICHARD HENRY, geophysicist; b. Anthony, Kans., June 4, 1931; s. Carl Alfred and Harriet (Ross) F.; A.B. in Physics, Miami U., 1954; M.S. in Earth Sci., N.Mex. Tech. U., 1956; postgrad. Calif. Inst. Tech., 1957-59; m. Lupe Maureen Messinger, Aug. 1, 1954 (div. 1979); children—Scott Richard, Leland Ross, Stuart Vinson. Grad. asst. N.Mex. Tech. U., Socorro, 1954-57, Calif. Inst. Tech., Pasadena, 1957-59, Scripps Inst. Oceanography, La Jolla, Calif., 1959-60; engr. Sperry Flight Systems, Phoenix, 1960—, now Sr. staff engr. Mem. troop council Boy Scouts Am., 1969-70, cub scout den leader, 1973-74. Mem. Am. Geophys. Union, Am. Vacuum Soc., Sigma Xi, Beta Theta Pi. Patentee in field. Home: 2223 W Bluefield Ave Phoenix AZ 85023 Office: 21111 N 19 Ave Phoenix AZ 85036

FRISCH-KALVARI, CONNIE FURNISS, gerontologist, psychologist; administrator; b. San Francisco, Dec. 26, 1945; d. Wilford Orland and Phyllis (Dean) Furniss; m. Lewis Edward Frisch, June 26, 1970; m. 2d, Moshe Kalvari, May 10, 1982. B.A. magna cum laude in Internat. Relations-Middle Eastern Studies, U. Utah, 1969; postgrad. (NDEA fellow) Pa. State U., 1969; M.L.A. with honors in Psychology, Johns Hopkins U., 1975; postgrad. NYU, 1975; doctoral candidate U. Md., 1976—. Cert. rehab. counselor. Adminstrv. asst., head corr. relations dept. 1st Nat. Bank Md., Balt., 1969-70; counselor IV gerontology/prosthetic orthopedic dept. State of Md. Vocat. Rehab., Johns Hopkins Hosp., Balt., 1970-78; instr. dept. psychology Essex Community Coll., Balt., 1977-78; dir. mental health and aging program U. Utah, Salt Lake City, 1978-82; dir. diversion program Project Turn, Utah State Dept Corrections, Salt Lake City, 1982—; group therapist, psychol. cons. Victims of Huntington's Chorea, Salt Lake City, 1982—; instr., cons. Legis. chmn. Kingsville (Md.) Civic Assn., 1976; active Utah State Women's Polit. Caucus; dist. vice chmn. and chmn. Democratic party, Salt Lake City, 1980-81, 81-82; reader Utah State Library for Blind; active Crisis Drug Ctr., U. Utah, Rape Crisis Ctr., Balt., Hadassah, Congregation Kol Ami Sisterhood; tchrs. aide Holladay Children's Ctr. Emotionally Disturbed Children, Salt Lake City; vol. Utah Assn. Retarded Citizens, Utah Spl. Olympics, 1982; guardian ad litem Utah State Juvenile Ct., 1982; cons. psychologist Utah Assn. Retarded Citizens, 1982; nat. steering com. Nat. Action Forum Older Women; health action com. Washington chpt. Gray Panthers; active Kidney Found Md., Utah Diabetes Assn. NIMH grantee, 1979-80, 80-81; Utah State Devel. Disabilities Council grantee, 1981-82; Castle Found. grantee, 1981-82. Mem. Western Gerontol. Soc. (nat. chmn. mental health and aging program planning com. 1979-80, 80-81), Nat. Gerontol. Soc., Nat. Rehab. Counseling Assn., Internat. Transactional Analysis Assn., Am. Orthopsychiat. Assn., Nat. Council on Aging, Am. Acad. Polit. and Social Sci., Women's Studies Student Assn., Nat. Rehab. Assn., Nat. Assn. Retarded Citizens, Utah Assn. Retarded Citizens, Nat. Fedn. for Blind, Utah Fedn. for Blind, Assn. Anthropology and Gerontology Edn., Am. Personnel and Guidance Assn., Am. Mental Health Counseling Assn., Am. Assn. Mental Deficiency, Forum on Death Edn. and Counseling (nat. sec. 1980-81, 81-82), Phi Kappa Phi, Pi Sigma Alpha, Lambda Delta, Kappa Alpha Theta. Jewish. Club: Johns Hopkins U. Alumni. Author: (with Roberts Grace Setzer) Bibliography/Filmography: Ethnicity and Aging, 1982; editor: (with Roberta Grace Setzer) Occasional Papers in Mental Health and Aging, 1981; producer mental health and aging video tape series, 1979. Home: 118 S St Salt Lake City UT 84103 Office: Project Turn 255 E 400 S Salt Lake City UT 84111

FRISHMAN, RUTH I., lawyer, housing consultant; b. Pitts., Aug. 9, 1946; d. Isadore L. and Vyvyan K. (Mathews) F.; m. Mamoru Mac Suzuki, June 9, 1979. A.B., U. Calif.-Berkeley, 1971; J.D., Golden Gate U., 1979. Bar: Calif. Sole practice, San Francisco, 1979—; cons. property mgmt.; commr. Alameda County Housing Authority, 1978—, Community Devel. Adv. Commn., Emeryville, Calif., 1976-78; instr. U. Calif., U. San Francisco. Bd. dirs. No. Calif. Assn. Non-Profit Housing, Berkeley, Mid-Peninsula Coalition Housing Fund, Palo Alto; Mem. Nat. Assn. Housing and Redevel. Ofcls. (nat. commrs. com.). Democrat. Contbr. articles to profl. jours. Office: 44 Montgomery St San Francisco CA 94104

FRISK, JACK EUGENE, recreational vehicle mfg. co. exec.; b. Nampa, Idaho, Jan. 22, 1942; s. Steinert Paul and Evelyn Mildred (Letner) F., m. Sharon Rose Caviness, Aug. 3, 1959; 1 dau., Toni. With Ideal of Idaho, Inc., Caldwell, purchasing mgr., 1969-75, gen. mgr., sec.-treas., 1975-82; dir. mktg. Traveleze Industries, Sun Valley, Calif., 1982—. Mem. adv. bd. Ctr. for Employment Tng. Mem. Recreational Vehicle Industry Assn. Episcopalian. Club: Optimists. Home: 2527 Marisa Pl Simi Valley CA 93065 Office: 11473 Penrose St Sun Valley CA 91352

FRITSCH, ROBERT WILLIAM, architect; b. Spokane, Wash., Nov. 2, 1914; s. Joseph William and Jeanettg Blanche (Baker) F.; student Lewis & Clark Coll., 1933-35; m. Dorothy Marie Hansen, May 1, 1938; children— Frederick Norman, Douglas Michael. With various archtl. firms, Portland, Oreg., 1935-41; with Willamette Iron & Steel, Portland, 1943-46; pvt. practice Whittier & Fritsch, Architects, Portland, 1946-59, Robert William Fritsch, Architect, Portland, 1959-64; archtl. cons. Oreg. State Bd. Higher Edn., Office of Facilities Planning, Eugene, 1964—; faculty in brick masonry Portland Apprenticeship Sch., 1962-64. Mem. Plumbing Code Bd. Appeals, City of Portland, 1954-63; mem. Housing Code Rewrite Com., Portland, 1952; chmn. campaign com. for public accommodations law, Portland, 1950; Republican precinct committeeman, 1945-49. Recipient Cert. of Appreciation, Portland chpt. AIA, 1957, 64, Southwestern chpt., 1975; Cert. of Merit and Appreciation, Constrn. Specifications Inst., 1972, 74, Tech. Excellence award, 1971, Region Dirs. citation, 1975, 80. Mem. AIA, Constrn. Specifications Inst. Republican. Presbyterian. Clubs: City (Portland), Urban League. Home: 1475 Queens Way Eugene OR 97401

FRITSINGER, CHARLES ALVIN, SR., fin. co. exec.; b. Superior, Nebr., Mar. 3, 1924; s. George A. and Charlotte (Kirby) F.; ed. high sch. Englewood, Colo.; m. Louise McAdoo, Aug. 12, 1945; children—Charles, Connie, Cynthia, Craig. Pres. Investment Constrn. Co., 1945-56, 1st Western Trust Co., 1956-58; trustee govt. leased bldgs., Western States, 1958-69; gen. partner Am. Syndicated Properties Co., Phoenix, 1969-78; pres. Internat. Trust Center, Phoenix, 1972-77, The Vault Inc., Scottsdale, Ariz., 1977—. Chmn. Colo. Indsl. Com., 1953; bd. dirs. Investment Research and Ednl. Found. Served with U.S. Army, 1943-44. Republican. Clubs: Balboa Bay, Sertoma (pres. club 1952-53, Colo. gov. 1954), Elks, DAV. Editor: Who Owns The Wealth of America?, 1966. Home: 7770 E Camelback Rd Scottsdale AZ 85251 Office: PO Box 2041 Scottsdale AZ 85252

FRITTS, HAROLD CLARK, dendochronology educator, researcher; b. Rochester, N.Y., Dec. 17, 1928; s. Edwin Coulthard and Ava Lee (Washburn) F.; m. Barbara Smith, June 11, 1955 (dec.); children—Marcia L., Paul T.; m. 2d, Miriam Colson, July 19, 1982. A.B., Oberlin Coll., 1951; M.S., Ohio State U., 1953, Ph.D. in Botany, 1956; asst. prof. botany Eastern Ill. U., 1956-60; asst. prof. dendochronology U. Ariz., Tucson, 1960-64, assoc. prof., 1964-69, prof., 1969—; dir., founder Internat. Tree-Ring Data Bank, 1975—; NSF faculty. Mem. local sch. bd., 1971-72. Recipient Am. Meteorol. Soc. award for outstanding achievement in bioclimatology, 1982; NATO fellow Advanced Study Inst. on Climatic Variability, Sicily, 1980; Guggenheim fellow, 1968-69; NSF grantee, 1963-84. Mem. Am. Assn. Quaternary Environment (council 1978-82, adv. com. paleoclimatology), Ecol. Soc. Am., AAAS, Am. Inst. Biol. Scis., Tree-Ring Soc., Am. Meteorol. Soc., Am. Quaternary Assn. Author: Tree Rings and Climate, 1976; contbr. articles to profl. jours. Home: 5703 N Lady Ln Tucson AZ 85704 Office: U Ariz Bldg 58 Tucson AZ 85721

FRITZ, ETHEL MAE HENDRICKSON, writer; b. Gibbon, Nebr., Feb. 4, 1925; d. Walter Earl and Alice Hazel (Mickish) Hendrickson; B.S., Iowa State U., 1949; m. C. Wayne Fritz, Feb. 25, 1950; children—Linda Sue, Krista Jane. Dist. home economist Internat. Harvester Co., Des Moines, 1949-50; writer Wallace's Farmer mag., Des Moines, 1960-64; free-lance writer, 1960—. Flower show judge, 1957—. Mem. Women in Communications (pres. Phoenix chpt. 1979-80), Am. Home Econs. Assn., Am. Soc. Profl. and Exec. Women, AAUW, S.W. Writers Conf., P.E.O., Ariz. Authors Assn., Phi Upsilon Omicron, Kappa Delta.

FRITZ, RENE EUGENE, JR., manufacturing company exective; b. Prineville, Oreg., Feb. 24, 1943; s. Rene and Ruth (Munson) F.; B.S. in Bus. Adminstrn. and Mech. Engring., Oreg. State U., 1965; m. Sharyn Ann Fife, June 27, 1964; children—Rene Scott, Lanz Eugene, Shay Steven, Case McGerrett. Sales mgr. Renal Corp., Albany, Oreg., 1962-65, Albany Machine & Supply, 1965-66; pres. Albany Internat. Industries, 1966—, Rene Internat., Inc., Albany, 1966—, Wood Yield Tech. Corp., Albany, 1972—, Automation Controls Internat., Albany, 1975—, Albany Internat. Maintenance & Service, 1976; chmn. Albany Titanium Inc., 1981—; dir. Sunne Maskiner, Stockholm, Home Fed. Savs. & Loan Assn., Albany. Mem. Young Pres.'s Orgn. (sec.-treas. 1978, membership chmn. 1979), Forest Products Research Soc., World Trade Council (Oreg. pres. 1982), High Tech. Inst. (Oreg. co-chmn. 1983). Republican. Presbyterian. Clubs: Elks, Rotary. Office: 840 SW 30th St Albany OR 97321

FRITZ, RONNIE EUGENE, mfg. co. purchasing agent; b. Detroit, May 25, 1938; s. Eugene Joseph and Amalie (Fingerlein) F.; B.S., Mich. State U., 1963; B.B.A., U. North Fla., 1977; m. Jacquelyn Dague, Sept. 5, 1964; children—Jeannette Loban, Robert Dague, Darryl McKennan. Conservation forester Union Camp Corp., McRae, Ga., 1967-68, tng. coordinator, Savannah, Ga., 1969, asst. mgr. indsl. relations, Montgomery, Ala., 1969-73, indsl. relations mgr., Green Cove Springs, Fla., 1973-75; Safety and tng. mgr. Ga. Ports Authority, Savannah, 1977-79; tng./devel. supr. FMC Corp., Pocatello, Idaho, 1979-82, sr. purchasing agt., 1982—; cons./dir. Mink Creek Irrigation Coop. Squadron comdr. U.S. Power Squadrons, 1973; flotilla comdr. USCG Aux., 1974-75, div. vice-capt., 1976, div. capt., 1977; exec. bd. Tendoy Area council Boy Scouts Am., 1980—. Served with U.S. Army, 1964-67. Decorated Bronze Star, Air medal with 5 oak leaf clusters; scouters award Boy Scouts Am., 1963; lic. profl. forester, Ala. Mem. Soc. Am. Foresters, Am. Soc. Tng. and Devel. (pres. S.E. Idaho chpt. 1981), Nat. Assn. Purchasing Mgrs. (dir. Idaho chpt. 1983). Presbyterian. Club: Rotary (pres. Green Cove Springs chpt. 1976). Home: 421 Mink Creek Rd Pocatello ID 83204 Office: Box 4111 Pocatello ID 83202

FRITZ, RUSSELL RALPH, association executive; b. Van Nuys, Calif., Jan. 27, 1942; s. Russell Roland and Betty (Howell) F.; m. Jacqueline Blake, May 1, 1963; children—Douglas, April. B.Sociology, Fla. Christian Coll., 1972, M.Sociology, 1974; Th.D., Maranatha Sem., 1977; D.D. (hon.), Coll. Christianity, 1979. With Packard Bell Electronics, 1963-68; Salvation Army officer, 1968—, community relations and devel. dir., Denver, 1979—. Mem. Mayor's Commn. on Handicapped, Eugene, Oreg., 1974-76; chmn. Chalan Council of Social Agys., 1977-78. Served with U.S. Army, 1960-63. Decorated Legion of Merit, Bronze Star, Purple Heart with oakleaf cluster, others. Mem. Colo. Press Assn., Religious Pub. Relations Council. Clubs: Kiwanis, Masons. Contbr. articles to profl. jours. Office: PO Box 2369 Denver CO 80201

FRITZ, WILLIAM JOSEPH, lobbyist, cons.; b. Colorado Springs, Colo., May 21, 1931; s. Henry and Joan Regina (Cvaniga) F.; B.A. in Bus. Adminstrn. and Banking, Colo. Coll., 1955; children—William Joseph, Heidi Illis, Brooke Edward. Mgmt. trainee Firestone Tire & Rubber Co., Memphis and Seattle, 1955-56; indsl. relations and mgmt. devel. supr. Boeing Co., Seattle, 1956-59, govt. relations mgr., 1959-68, govt. and bus. relations mgr., 1968-72; congressional relations mgr. ITT, Washington, 1968; pres. Public Affairs Assocs., Inc., Seattle, 1972—, Silent Communication Systems, Inc., Seattle, 1979—; lectr. condr. seminars. Vice pres. Community Club, 1956-57; precinct committeeman, 1957-64; alt. del. at large Rep. Nat. Conv., 1964; bd. dirs. Campfire Girls, 1960; Little League Coach, 1966-67; asst. scoutmaster Chief Seattle council Boy Scouts Am., 1966-67; mem. com. Pacific Sci. Ctr.; mem. gov.'s adv. com. on salmon and steelhead, 1973; mem. comml. vessel safety com. NOAA, 1973-74. Served with USMC, 1951-52. Recipient certs. of appreciation Kiwanis, Rotary, Jr. Achievement, United Good Neighbors, Campfire Girls, Boy Scouts Am., others. Mem. Assn. Wash. Bus., Nat. Fedn. Ind. Bus., Seattle C. of C., The Third House, Wash. State Assn. of Deaf, NAM (bus. /industry polit. action com.), U.S. Power Squadrons (Seattle), Boat Owners Assn. U.S., Phi Gamma Delta. Republican. Roman Catholic. Contbr. articles to profl. jour. Home and Office: 2600 Fairview Ave E Dock 11 Seattle WA 98102

FRITZE, JAMES RONALD, lawyer; b. Chgo., July 23, 1947; s. William P. and Margaret Louise Fritze; m. Sheila Kay Boos, June 17, 1972; children—Elizabeth Ann, Julia Louise. B.A., Wis. State U., 1969; J.D., U. Ill., 1972. Bar: Ill. 1973, U.S. Dist. Ct. (cen. dist.) Ill. 1978 Colo. 1982, Colo. 1982. Asst. state's atty. Iroquois Co., Ill., 1972-74, asst. pub. defender, 1976, state's atty., 1976-80; sole practice, Watseka, Ill., 1974-76, 81; asst. county atty., Eagle County, Colo., 1982—; mem. Nat. Conf. Republican County Ofcls. Pres. Iroquois County Young Reps., 1974-76, dep. dist. gov. Ill., 1975; active Indian Trails Dist. Boy Scouts Am., 1977-78, exec. bd. dirs. Piankeshaw council, 1978-79. Recipient Outstanding Service to Law Enforcement award Iroquois County Law Enforcement Assn., 1976. Mem. Ill. Bar Assn., Colo. Bar Assn., Continental Divide Bar Assn., Nat. Dist. Attys. Assn., Colo. Family Support Council. Lutheran. Club: Lions. Home: 101 Shorthorn Dr Eagle CO 81631 Office: Asst County Atty Office 550 S Broadway St Eagle CO 81631

FRITZEN, DAVID WILLIAM, publisher; b. Fresno, Calif., June 17, 1944; s. Vernon Linden and Lorene Elizabeth (Jackson) F.; B.A., Calif. State U., Fresno, 1971, postgrad., 1971-72; m. Andrea K. Fish, Dec. 28, 1968; children—Krista Nicole, Cassandra. Founder, pub. Uniques (renamed Unique Homes 1980), Santa Barbara, Calif., 1973-80; founder, editor-in-chief, pub. Santa Barbara mag., 1975—; founder, pub. Islands mag., 1981—, Showboats mag., 1982—; pres. The Calif. Press, Inc., Santa Barbara, 1976—; cons. Ziff Davis Pub Co., N.Y.C., 1980-81. Served with AUS, 1968-70. Recipient Best City, Met. or State Mag. award Western Publs. Assn., 1978, 80. Mem. Santa Barbara C. of C., Western Publs. Assn. Office: 123 W Padre St Santa Barbara CA 93017

FROEHLICH, DODY (JEANNINE), industrial chemicals company executive; b. Denver, Aug. 20, 1935; d. Douglas James and Ruth Snowden (Johnston) Izett; m. Fred Froehlich, Oct. 26, 1934. Student U. Colo., 1953-54, Colo. State U., 1955-56. GS-5 and div. sec. Air Res. Records Ctr., Denver, 1954-55; stewardess various airlines, N.Y.C. and San Francisco, 1957-61; asst. to fashion salon dir. Gump's, San

Francisco, 1961-62; sec. Z.W. Wong, Esq., San Francisco, 1961-62; exec. sec., asst. David Nelson Pub. Relations Co., San Francisco, 1962-65; sec. to mayor San Francisco, 1965-68; reservationist, then mgr. Silver Tree Inn & Eldorado Lodges, then asst. mgr. Crestwood Condominiums, Snowmass-at-Aspen, Colo., 1968-78; owner, pres. D. Froehlich Indsl. Co., Anchorage, 1978—. Mem. Anchorage Mayor's Adv. Bd. Animal Control, 1979—; mem. Alaska State Bd. Veterinary Examiners, 1981—. Recipient Dog World award Alaska Kennel Club, 1979; winner Top Alaskan Showdog Kennel Rev. System, 1978, 80, 82. Mem. Am. Dog Owners Assn. (dir.), Alaska Kennel Club, CARE Alaska (founding), Puget Sound Norwegian Elkhound Assn., Norwegian Elkhound Assn. Am. (dir.). Episcopalian. Home and Office: PO Box 110849 Anchorage AK 99511

FROHNEN, RICHARD GENE, educator; b. Omaha, Mar. 26, 1930; s. William P. and Florence E. (Rogers) F.; student U. Nebr., Omaha, Mo. Valley Coll., 1948-52; B.A., Calif. State Coll., 1954; M.S., UCLA 1961; Ed.D., Brigham Young U., 1976; grad. Army War Coll., 1982 m. Harlene Grace LeTourneau, July 4, 1958; children—Karl Edward, Eric Eugene. Bus. mgr. athletics and sports publicity dir. U. Nebr., Omaha, 1951-52; pub. relations dir. First Congl. Ch. Los Angeles, 1953-54, 58-59; writer Los Angeles Mirror News, 1959; gen. assignment reporter, religion editor Los Angeles Times, 1959-61; prof. journalism, dean men Eastern Mont. Coll., Billings, 1961-65; N.W. editor, editorial writer Spokesman-Review, Spokane, 1965-67, also editor Sunday mag.; prof. journalism U. Nev., Reno, 1967-79; exec. dir. devel. Coll. of Desert/Copper Mountain Coll., 1982—; pub. relations officer Sch. Med. Scis. U. Nev., 1969-75; adj. prof. mgmt. U. Redlands (Calif.), 1979—; cons. pub. relations. Mem. exec. bd. Nev. area council Boy Scouts Am., 1968-76, council commr., 1973-74, v.p., 1975-76, recipient Silver Beaver award, 1974; founder, mng. dir. Gt. Western Expdns., 1958—. Served to 1st lt. USMC, 1954-58; now col. Res. Mem. Assn. Edn. Journalism, Am. Legion, Res. Officers Assn. U.S., Marine Corps Assn., Marine Corps Res. Officers Assn., Am. Humanics Found., Internat. Platform Assn., Nat. Soc. Fund Raising Execs., Planning Execs. Inst., Internat. Communication Assn., Religion Newswriters Assn., Navy League, Semper Fidelis Soc., Kappa Tau Alpha, Alpha Phi Omega, Sigma Delta Chi (sec.-treas. chpt.). Episcopalian. Kiwanian, Lion, Rotarian. Office: PO Box C Twentynine Palms CA 92277

FROHNMAYER, DAVID BRADEN, state atty. gen.; b. Medford, Oreg., July 9, 1940; s. Otto J. and Marabel Fisher (Braden) F.; A.B. magna cum laude, Harvard Coll., 1962; B.A., Oxford U., 1964, M.A., 1971; J.D., U. Calif., Berkeley, 1967; m. Lynn Diane Johnson, Dec. 30, 1970; children—Kirsten, Mark, Kathryn. Cons., Civil Rights div. U.S. Dept. Justice, Washington, 1973-74; admitted to Calif. bar, 1967, Oreg. bar, 1971; assoc. firm Pillsbury, Madison & Sutro, San Francisco, 1967-69; asst. to U.S. Sec. HEW, Washington, 1969-70; mem. Oreg. Ho. of Reps., 1975-81; atty. gen. State of Oreg., Salem, 1981—; prof. law, spl. asst. to pres. U. Oreg., Eugene, 1971-80. Recipient award Samuel Pool Weaver Constl. Law Essay Competition, Am. Bar Found., 1972, 74; Ross Essay Competition, Am. Bar Assn. Jour., 1980; named Eugene Jr. First Citizen, 1974; Rhodes scholar, 1962-64. Mem. Phi Beta Kappa, Order of Coif. Home: 2875 Baker Blvd Eugene OR 97403 Office: 100 State Justice Bldg Salem OR 97310

FROHOW, NORRIS ANDREW, charity organization administrator; b. Oklahoma City, Dec. 14, 1935; s. Milo Aldelbert and Esther Meriam (Williams) F.; B.A. in Sociology, Fresno State Coll.; 1958; M.S.Ed. in Vocat. Rehab. Counseling, Los Angeles State Coll., 1961. Adminstr. Pilgrim Sch., Los Angeles, 1961-78; pvt. rehab. counselor D.S. Assocs., San Luis Obispo, Calif., 1978-79; dir. Kern County unit Goodwill Industries of So. Calif., Bakersfield, 1979—. U.S. Govt. grantee, 1959. Mem. Nat. Assn. Rehab. Adminstrs., Nat. Rehab. Assn., Bakersfield C. of C. Republican. Lutheran. Home: 4301 Isla Verde St Apt A Bakersfield CA 93301 Office: PO Box 3552 Bakersfield CA 93385

FROMM, HANNA, educational administrator; b. Nuremberg, W.Ger., Dec. 20, 1913; d. David and Meta (Stiebel) Gruenbaum; m. Alfred Fromm, July 4, 1936; children—David, Caroline Fromm Lurie. Grad. in choreography and music Folkwang Sch. Dancing and Music, Essen, Gemany, 1934; D.Pub. Service (hon.), U. San Francisco, 1979. Served with ARC, World War II; exec. dir. Fromm Inst. Lifelong Learning, U. San Francisco, 1975—. Co-founder Music in the Vineyards, Saratoga, Calif.; former dir. Young Audiences, Community Music Ctr., Legal Aid to Elderly; coordinating com. geriatric curriculum U. Calif.-San Francisco; dir. Nat. Council on Aging. Mem. Gerontology Soc. Am. Jewish. Club: Met. (San Francisco). Home: 850 El Camino del Mar San Francisco CA 94121 Office: 538 University Center 2130 Fulton St San Francisco CA 94117

FRONK, WILLIAM JOSEPH, machinery company executive; b. Spring Green, Wis., Apr. 14, 1925; s. Joseph Edward and Irene (Caspers) F.; B.B.A., U. Wis., 1950; m. Jeanne Gillon, Apr. 18, 1953; children—James, Nancy, Robert. With Haskins & Sells, C.P.A.'s, Chgo., 1950-54, Ford Motor Co., Dearborn, Mich., 1954-66; pres., dir. Hyster Co., Portland, Oreg., 1966—; dir. Esco Corp., Orbanco. Trustee, Linfield Coll. Served with AUS, 1943-46. C.P.A., Wis. Mem. Am. Inst. C.P.A.'s, Fin. Execs. Inst., Beta Alpha Psi, Alpha Kappa Psi, Sigma Phi Epsilon. Clubs: Arlington (dir.), Waverly Country (Portland). Office: Hyster Co PO Box 2902 Portland OR 97208

FRONKE, ROBERT EUGENE, auditor; b. Kansas City, Mo., Nov. 2, 1926; s. Joseph L. and Rose (Ernst) F.; m. Martha Schulze, Dec. 5, 1952; children—Michael, Alan, Mark, Janice, Matthew. A.B., U. Ga., 1956; M.B.A., Stanford U., 1959. C.P.A., Calif. Acct., mgmt. cons. Windes & McClaughry, Long Beach, Calif., 1964-67; v.p., treas. H.B. Grubbs & Co., Long Beach, 1967-69; exec. v.p. Kit Mfg. Co., Long Beach, 1969-75; city auditor City of Long Beach, 1976—; adj. prof. Sch. Bus. and Mgmt., Pepperdine U., 1976—. Chmn. bd. mgmt. Long Beach YMCA, 1974—; trustee St. Mary's Hosp. Found., 1980—; bd. dirs. Goodwill Industries, 1980—; exec. bd. Long Beach Area council Boy Scouts Am., 1983—. Served to comdr. USN, 1946-64. Mem. Am. Inst. C.P.A.s, Calif. Soc. C.P.A.s, Mcpl. Fin. Officers Assn. Democrat. Roman Catholic. Club: Rotary. Home: 116 Paloma Ave Long Beach CA 90803 Office: 333 W Ocean Blvd Long Beach CA 90802

FRONTIERE-ROSENBLUM, GEORGIA, professional football team executive; m. Carroll Rosemblum, July 7, 1966 (dec.); children—Dale Carroll, Lucia. Pres. Los Angeles Rams, NFL, 1979—. Bd. dirs. Los Angeles Boys and Girls Club, Los Angeles Orphanage Guild, Los Angeles Blind Youth Found. Named Headliner of Yr., Los Angeles Press Club, 1981. Office: Los Angeles Rams 2327 W Lincoln Ave Anaheim CA 92801*

FROST, ARETA HURLEY, community college administrator; b. Seattle, June 10, 1938; d. Jesse Raymond and Carolyn Lee (Green) Hurley; B.A. magna cum laude in Speech and Hearing Pathology, U. Wash., 1960; various profl. courses and seminars; m. June 11, 1960 (div. 1971); children—John, Jeff, Chris. Speech and hearing pathologist, Seattle, Spokane and Everett, Wash., also N.J., 1960-71; communications-public relations dir. Mayor's Office, City of Everett, 1971-73; mktg. cons., tng. instr. Gen. Telephone Co., Everett, 1973-75; account exec. Investor's Diversified Services, Seattle, 1975; exec. recruiter, mgr. Seattle office Acme Personnel, Inc., Seattle, 1976-78; mktg. mgr. Home Savs. & Loan Assn., Burien, Wash., 1978—, asst. v.p., 1979-80; asst. v.p. mktg. Umpqua Savs. & Loan Assn., Roseburg, Oreg., 1980-83; community relations dir. Umpqua Community Coll., Roseburg, 1983—; host radio show What's Up With Business, 1982. Del., White House Conf., 1960; chmn. U. Wash. 10-Yr. Reunion, 1970; v.p., bd. dirs. Central Douglas County United Way, 1981-83, pres., 1983—. Mem. Roseburg C. of C. (pres. Greeters 1982; bd. dirs. 1982—), Roseburg Downtown Assn., U.S. League Savs. and Loans, Wash. Savs. League, Mortar Bd. (alumnae bd.), Phi Beta Kappa. Contbr. articles to profl. publs. Home: 1818 NE Todd Roseburg OR 97470 Office: Umpqua Savs & Loan Assn 445 SE Main St Roseburg OR 97470

FROST, BRENT HIXSON, finance executive; b. Glendale, Calif., Oct. 26, 1945; s. Donald Ernest and Elizabeth B. (Hixson) F.; m. Janet Susan Wright, Aug. 1, 1969; children—Todd, Ryan, Jared, Darren, Chanel. B.S. cum laude, Brigham Young U., 1969. C.P.A., Calif., 1973. Staff acct., tax mgr. Peat, Marwick, Mitchell & Co., Los Angeles, 1969-78; v.p., dir. taxes Fin. Corp. Am., Los Angeles, 1978—; v.p., dir. taxes Am. Savs. & Loan, 1978—. Missionary, Ch. of Jesus Christ of Latter-day Saints, Eng., 1965-67, pres. Elders Quorum, Glendale, Calif., 1973-80; Cub Scout leader Boy Scouts Am., La Canada, Calif., 1980—. Mem. Calif. League Savs. Instns., Am. Inst. C.P.A.s, Calif. Soc. C.P.A.s. Republican. Office: 6420 Wilshire Blvd Suite 1500 Los Angeles CA 90048

FROST, COLLETTE LIZOTTE, electronics company executive; b. Palo Alto, Calif., Feb. 22, 1955; d. William Vincent and Lolita (Anzar) Lizotte; m. James Edward Frost, Sept. 4, 1976; children—David, Megan. Student Foothill Jr. Coll., 1973-76; B.A. in Psychology, U. Calif.-Davis, 1976-78. Buyer, Hewlett Packard Co. Palo Alto, 1978—.

FROST, GORDON TUCKER, lumber co. exec.; b. San Diego, May 15, 1915; s. Albert Abel and Jessie (Tucker) F.; A.B., Stanford U., 1938; postgrad. (Tarver Interfrat. scholar), Heidelberg (Ger.) U., 1939; m. Adeline Jeanne Lehman, July 25, 1940; children—Alison Frost Gildred, Gordon Tucker, Susan duLaux Frost Ahlering. With Frost Hardwood Lumber Co., San Diego, 1940—, pres., 1961—; dir. San Diego Beach Co., San Diego Trust & Savs. Bank. Served as officer USCGR, 1940-46. Mem. Nat. Hardwood Lumber Assn. (past dir.), Nat. Wholesale Hardwood Distbrs. Assn. (past pres.), Pacific Coast Wholesale Hardwood Distbrs. Assn. (past pres.), Maritime Mus. Assn. San Diego (past pres.). Clubs: San Diego Yacht (staff commodore), San Diego Rotary (past pres.). Office: 347 W Market St San Diego CA 92101

FROST, JOHN ROOT, indsl. and mfg. engr.; b. Oakland, Calif., Sept. 29, 1906; s. George Booth and Ruth (Godfrey) R.; student San Francisco Sch. Bus., 1933-34, San Francisco Sch. Law, 1934-37; spl. postgrad. U. Calif. at Berkely, 1936-50; m. Esther M. Foster, June 19, 1932; children—Lisa E. (Mrs. Robert L. Smythe) (dec.), John Hunnicutt. With Calif. & Hawaiian Sugar Co., Crockett, Calif., 1932-70; developer curricula, organizer Engring. Sch., John F. Kennedy U., Martinez, Calif., 1967-70, adminstrv. v.p., 1970-73, dean. Sch. Engring., 1968-70; vis. prof. dept. indsl. sci. Korea Advanced Inst. Sci., Seoul, 1973-75; exec. dir. Productivity Council of S.W. (Calif. State U. at Los Angeles and Am. Inst. Indsl. Engrs.), 1977—; expert examiner Calif. State Bd. Registration for Profl. Engrs., 1968-70; pvt. cons. indsl. engring., 1969—; mem. Internat. Exec. Service Corps, 1969—. Active Boy Scouts Am., ARC. Named Indsl. Engr. of Year, Am. Inst. Indsl. Engrs., San Francisco and Oakland, Calif., 1968. Registered profl. engr., Calif. Fellow Am. Inst. Indsl. Engrs. (pres. 1946-47, chmn. edn. com. 1948-53); mem. Nat., Calif. socs. profl. engrs., Soc. Mfg. Engrs., Korean Inst. Indsl. Engrs. (hon.), Alpha Pi Mu (hon.). Club: Commonwealth. Contbr. articles to profl. jours. Address: 3173 Buckingham Rd Glendale CA 91206

FROST, OTIS LAMONT, JR., insurance company executive; b. Wynnewood, Okla., May 26, 1917; s. Otis L. and Viola (Knight) F.; B.A., Vanderbilt U., 1938; J.D., U. Calif.-Berkeley, 1941; LL.M., U. So. Calif., 1947; m. Nelle Edwards, June 14, 1942; 1 son, Otis Lamont, III. Admitted to Calif. bar, 1947; agt. IRS, Treasury Dept., Los Angeles, 1946-48; with Transam. Occidental Life Ins. Co., Los Angeles, 1948—, v.p., 1965-75, exec. v.p., gen. counsel, 1975—, also dir.; v.p. Transam. Corp., Los Angeles, 1968-73; sr. v.p., gen. counsel dir. Transam. Ins. Corp., Los Angeles, 1969—; dir. Direct Mktg. Internat. Ltd., 1975—; dir., gen. counsel Occidental Internat. Enterprises, 1975—; dir., v.p., gen. counsel Transam. Assurance Co., 1981—; gen. counsel Transam. Life Ins. and Annuity Co., 1977—, dir., 1981—. Mem. Calif. Constn. Revision Commn., 1967—; bd. dirs., treas. Coro Found., Los Angeles; bd. dirs. Los Angeles Taxpayers Assn. Served to lt. USNR, 1941-46. Mem. Assn. Calif. Life Ins. Cos. (dir. 1961—; chmn. exec. com. 1977—), Health Ins. Assn. Am. (Calif. State chmn., mem. govt. relations com.), Calif. Ins. Fedn. (v.p., dir. 1960—), Nat. Assn. Ins. Commrs., Assn. Life Ins. Counsel (bd. govs.), Am. Council Life Ins. (Calif. v.p., mem. legis. com.), Am., Calif. State, Los Angeles County bar assns., Los Angeles Area C. of C., Calif. C. of C. Home: 2740 Monte Mar Terr Los Angeles CA 90064 Office: Transam Occidental Life Ins Co 1150 S Olive St Los Angeles CA 90015

FROST, ROBERT L., training and development administrator; b. Glendale, Calif., July 25, 1947; s. Robert A. and Nancy M. (Price) F. B.A. in Psychology, Calif. State U.-Northridge, 1969. Cert. adult edn. tchr. in life and mgmt., Calif., 1976. Probation officer Los Angeles County, 1969-72; benefit systems cons. State Compensation Ins. Fund, Los Angeles, 1972-76; personnel devel. specialist Kaiser-Permanente, Los Angeles, 1976-81; mgr. human resource devel. Union Bank, Los Angeles, 1981—; cons. in field. Mem. Am. Soc. Tng. and Devel., Westwood Inst. Psychodrama, Gustav Mahler Soc. Author: The Psychological Contract in a Medical Center Environment, 1979. Home: 4428 Van Noord Studio City CA 91606 Office: 605 W Olympic 5th Floor Los Angeles CA 90015

FROST, RONALD ALDEN, psychologist, educator, consultant; b. Chgo., Aug. 14, 1935; s. Worlie Howard and Mildren Linnea (Alden) F.; m. Chalma René Spoonemore, Aug. 25, 1957; children—Susan L. McKinnon, Christopher L. B.S. in Psychology, Ariz. State Coll., 1958; M.A., Ariz. State U., 1965, Ph.D. in Counseling Psychology, 1972. Cert. Ariz. State Bd. Psychol. Examiners. Youth dir. Phoenix YMCA, 1959-63; dir. psychol. services Dysart (Ariz.) Schs., 1963-66; dir. counseling, prof. psychology, staff devel. co-ordinator Glendale (Ariz.) Coll., 1966—; dir. Counseling Inst., Ariz. State U., 1973-77; pvt. practice Adlerian Assocs. Arizona, 1973—; cons. adult basic edn. programs. Bd. dirs. Community Mental Health; pres. ch. council; chmn. personnel bd., del. Synod Convs. Served to lt. USAF, Ariz. Air N.G., 1950-66. NDEA fellow, 1965, 66. Am. Personnel and Guidance Assn., Nat. Vocat. Guidance Assn., Mem. Nat. Council Staff, Program and Orgnl. Devel., Assn. Ednl. Data Systems, Phi Delta Kappa. Republican. Lutheran. Contbr. papers to profl. confs. and jours. Office: 6000 W Olive Ave Glendale AZ 85302

FROST, STANLEY FREDERICK, mgr. hunting lodge; b. Toronto, Ont., Can., Nov. 1, 1924; came to U.S., 1929, naturalized, 1944; s. Paul Liston and Mable (Roberts) F.; student Munger Trade Sch., Detroit, 1938-39; m. Marta Anna Klein, Aug. 22, 1949; children—Konstanza, Karen, Cathy, Candace. Technician, Huffman TV, Los Angeles, 1952-53; owner, mgr. Alaskan TV, Domestic Appliace Service, Frost Refrigeration Service, Anchorage and Palmer, Alaska, 1954-67; owner, mgr. Farewell Lake Lodge, Via McGrath, Alaska, 1970—; pres. Frost Guide Service, Inc., 1964-81. Mem. adv. com. to guide licensing and control bd. State of Alaska, 1979-81; bd. dirs. Citizens for Mgmt. Alaskan Lands, 1976-77. Served with AUS, 1943-46; ETO. Registered big game guide, Alaska. Mem. Alaska Profl. Hunters Assn. (dir., past pres.), Safari Club Internat. (dir.), Internat. Profl. Hunters Assn., NRA (life), Game Conservation Internat., Alaska Sportsmen Club. Republican. Editor: Alaska Profl. Hunter mag., 1978—. Home: SRA Box 2395-C Hillside Dr Anchorage AK 99507 Office: Farewell Lake Lodge Via McGrath AK 99627

FROST, WILLIAM, English educator; b. N.Y.C., June 8, 1917; s. John William and Christina (Gurlitz) F.; m. Marjorie Hayes Pangburn, Aug. 5, 1942; children—Marjorie Augusta Frost McCracken, Christina Emily, Clifford William. A.B., Bowdoin Coll., 1938, D.Litt. (hon.), 1980; M.A., Columbia U., 1942; Ph.D., Yale U., 1946. Instr., Carnegie Inst. Tech., 1942-44; instr. Yale U., 1946-47, vis. assoc. prof., 1958-59; asst. prof. Wesleyan U., 1947-51; asst. prof. U. Calif., Santa Barbara, 1951-55, assoc. prof., 1955-58, 59-61, acting chmn. dept. English, 1965-66, chmn., 1974-79, prof. English, 1961—, co-editor Works of John Dryden, Vol. IV, 1974. Bd. dirs. Friends of Santa Barbara Pub. Library. Guggenheim fellow, 1959, 79-80, Am. Council Learned Socs. fellow, 1966-67, Nat. Endowment for Humanities fellow, 1972-73; Am. Philos. soc. grantee, 1982-83. Mem. MLA, Philol. Assn. of Pacific Coast, Medieval Acad. Am., Calif. State Employees Assn., Phi Beta Kappa. Club: Elizabethan (Yale U.). Author: Fulke Greville's Caelica: An Evaluation, 1942; Dryden and the Art of Translation, 1955-69; Dryden and Future Shock, 1976; editor, co-editor, assoc. editor: English Masterpieces, 1950, 61; Selected Works of Dryden, 1953, 71; Pope's Homer, 1967; Dryden's Juvenal and Persius and Other Poems, 1974; contbr. articles on Chaucer, Shakespeare, Pope, Persius, others to publs. Office: English Dept Univ Calif Santa Barbara CA 93106

FROSTAD, WAYNE ALAN, orthodontist; b. North Bend, Oreg., Aug. 21, 1933; s. S.P. and Lillian E. (Strom) F.; B.S., Oreg. State U., 1958; D.M.D., U. Oreg., 1962; M.S., U. Man. (Can.), 1970; m. Jo Ann Woods, June 13, 1959; children—Kristi Jo, Kip Alan. Gen. practice dentistry, Medford, Oreg., 1962-69; practice orthodontics, Medford, 1969—; v.p., treas. Oreg. Dental Service. Bd. dirs., sec.-treas., v.p. Providence Hosp., Medford, 1972—; bd. dirs. Easter Seal Soc. Oreg., 1974-78, Medford Community Action, 1970-71, Providence Hosp Found., 1978—. Served with AUS, 1954-56. Research grantee Med. Research Council Can., 1968-69. Mem. Am., Oreg. (trustee 1977-81, exec. com. 1980-81), Can. (asso.), So. Oreg. (pres. 1976) dental socs., Am. Soc. Dentistry Children (Achievement award 1962, C.V. Mosby Acad. Achievement award 1962), Am. Assn. Orthodontics. Republican. Episcopalian. Clubs: Rotary (dist. youth exchange officer 1978—), Univ., Elks. Home: 306 Medford Heights Ln Medford OR 97401 Office: 801 E Main St Medford OR 97501

FRUCHTHENDLER, SAUL IRA, advertising company executive, author; b. Tucson, Feb. 11, 1947; s. Jacob Carl and Jean (Abend) F. Student U. Ariz., 1965-66, NYU, 1966-68. With Daniel & Charles Advt. Co., 1968-70, Foote Cone & Belding Co., 1970; creative dir. McCann Erickson Co., Pacific Basin, 1970-72; with Young & Rubicam Co., Los Angeles, 1977-80; ptnr., pres. Louis & Saul, Inc., Santa Monica, Calif., 1980—; guest lectr. Sch. Entrepreneur and Venture Mgmt., U. So. Calif. Mem. Am. Heart Assn., Jewish Fedn. Mem. Los Angeles Advt. Club, Advt. Club N.Y., Am. Assn. Advt. Agys., Western States Advt. Agy. Assn. Democrat. Jewish. Club: Marquesas, University. Author: The Debates of Clarence Darrow, 1973; Nobody Loves Me, 1975; The C.A.I., 1976; others. Office: Louis & Saul Inc 506 Santa Monica Blvd Santa Monica CA 90401

FRUMKIN, GENE, author, educator; b. N.Y.C., Jan. 29, 1928; s. Samuel and Sarah (Blackman) F.; B.A. in English, U. Calif. at Los Angeles, 1951; m. Lydia Samuels, July 3, 1955 (div.); children—Celena, Paul. Exec. editor Calif. Apparel News, Los Angeles, 1952-66; asst. prof. English, U. N.Mex., Albuquerque, 1967-71, asso. prof., 1971—. Mem. Rio Grande Writers Assn., AAUP. Author: The Hawk and the Lizard, 1963; The Rainbow-Walker, 1968; Dostoevsky and Other Nature Poems, 1972; Locust Cry: Poems 1958-65, 1973; The Mystic Writing-Pad, 1977; Loops, 1979; Clouds and Red Earth, 1982; co-editor San Marcos Rev., 1976—; The Indian Rio Grande: Recent Poems from 3 Cultures (anthology), 1977; editor: Coastlines Lit. Mag., 1958-62, N.Mex. Quar., 1969. Home: 3721 Mesa Verde NE Albuquerque NM 87110

FRUMKIN, KENNETH, army officer, physician; b. Hazleton, Pa., Mar. 11, 1947; s. Joseph Benjamin and Lillian (Cohen) F.; m. Bernardine Jane Yamulla, July 29, 1969. B.A., Franklin and Marshall Coll., 1969; M.A., McGill U., 1970, Ph.D., 1972; M.D., Hahnemann Med. Coll., 1978. Diplomate Am. Bd. Emergency Medicine. Commd. 2d lt. U.S. Army, 1970, advanced through grades to maj., 1981; research psychologist U.S. Army Biomed. Lab., Edgewood Arsenal, Md., 1972-74; intern Letterman Army Med. Ctr., San Francisco, 1978-79; resident in emergency medicine Brooke Army Med. Ctr., Fort Sam Houston, 1979-81; staff physician dept. emergency medicine Madigan Army Med. Ctr., Tacoma, Wash., 1981-83, chief dept. emergency medicine, 1983—. Mem. AMA, Am. Coll. Emergency Physicians, Am. Psychol. Assn., Eastern Psychol. Assn., Alpha Omega Alpha. Office: Box 849 Madigan Army Med Center Tacoma WA 98431

FRUSH, JAMES CARROLL, JR., health services cons.; b. San Francisco, Oct. 18, 1930; s. James Carroll and Edna Mae (Perry) F.; B.A., Stanford, 1953; postgrad. U. Calif. at San Francisco, 1957-58; m. Patricia Anne Blake, Oct. 29, 1960 (div. 1977); children—Michael, Gloria; m. 2d, Carolyn Fetter Bell, Aug. 23, 1978. Partner, James C. Frush Co. San Francisco, 1960-70; v.p., dir. research Retirement Residence, Inc., San Francisco, 1964-70, pres., 1970—; pres. Nat. Retirement Residence, San Francisco, 1971—, Casa Dorinda Corp., 1971—; lectr. Pres., Marin Shakespeare Festival, 1971-73, James C. Frush Found., 1972-78. Bd. dirs. San Francisco Sr. Center, 1973-78. Mem. Gerontol. Soc., Informational Film Producers Am., Internat. Hosp. Assn., Am. Geriatrics Soc., Assn. for Anthropology and Gerontology, Stanford Alumni Assn. Author (with Benson Eschenbach): The Retirement Residence: An Analysis of the Architecture and Management of Life Care Housing, 1968. Contbr. articles to profl. jours.; producer ednl. films. Office: care T Pimsleur 2155 Union St San Francisco CA 94123 also 1004 Sea Cliff N Daphne AL 36526

FRY, HENRY JOSEPH, aero. engr.; b. Scranton, Pa., June 25, 1926; s. Henry James and Ann Agnes (Gibbons) F.; B.Aero. Engring., Cath. U. Am., 1951; D.D. (hon.), Universal Life Ch., Modesto, Calif., 1977. Group supr. Erco Mfg. Co., Riverdale, Md., 1951-55; prin. mech. engr. Melpar, Inc., Falls Church, Va., 1956-62; engring. specialist Apollo spacecraft atennas N.Am. Aviation, Downey, Calif., 1962-69; cons. engr., 1969-72; sr. engr. Hughes Aircraft Co., Culver City, Calif.,

1972—. Served with U.S. Army, 1944-46. Decorated Bronze Star. Recipient various design engring. awards. Mem. Inst. Aero. Scis., Inventors Workshop Internat., USCG Aux. (flotilla comdr.), Calif. Rifle and Pistol Assn. (life), Nat. Rifle Assn. Contbr. polit. articles to newspaper; patentee radar antenna. Home: 1030 S Verde St Anaheim CA 92805 Office: Centinella and Teale Streets Culver City CA 90230

FRY, LINCOLN J., sociologist-researcher, administrator-consultant; b. San Francisco, Feb. 12, 1937; s. Orville Otto and Emma Louise (Scott) F.; m. Beryl R. Fry, Sept. 14, 1968. B.A., San Francisco State U., 1964; M.A., Calif. State U.-Los Angeles, 1968; Ph.D. in Sociology, U. So. Calif., 1972. Lic. marriage, family and child counselor, Calif. Research specialist II Camarillo Neuropsychiat. Inst., UCLA, 1971-74; project dir. Model Evaluation Project, Ventura Regional Planning Bd. (Calif.), 1974-77; assoc. prof. urban studies Howard U., Washington, 1977-78; research assoc. U. So. Calif., Los Angeles, 1978-80; vis. prof. Stockholm U., (Sweden), 1982; dir. sponsored research, Title III coordinator Loyola Marymount U., Los Angeles, 1982—; cons. to numerous agys. Served with USMC, 1954-57. Grantee Nat. Inst. Drug Abuse, Calif. State Bar Bd. Legal Specialization, Nat. Inst. Law Enforcement and Criminal Justice. Mem. Am. Sociol. Assn., So. Sociol. Assn., Soc. for Study Social Problems, Am. Soc. Criminology, Acad. Criminal Justice Scis. Republican. Author numerous publs.; contbr. articles to profl. jours. Home: 20757 Keswick Canoga Park CA 91306 Office: Loyola Marymount U W 80th St and Loyola Blvd Los Angeles CA 90045

FRY, MAXWELL JOHN, economist, educator; b. Maidenhead, U.K., Feb. 12, 1944; came to U.S., 1974; s. Thomas Maxwell and Jeanne Mary (Kislingbury) F.; m. Celia Gordon, June 17, 1972; children—Benjamin N., Zoe Logan. B.Sc., London Sch. Econs., 1965, Ph.D., 1970; M.A., UCLA, 1966. Lectr., Morley Coll., 1966-67, Middle East Tech. U., Ankara, Turkey, 1967-69; lectr. fin. econs. City U. London, 1969-74; prof. econs. U. Hawaii, Honolulu, 1974-81; vis. prof. Bogazici U., Istanbul, 1977-79, UCLA, 1981—; prof. econs. U. Calif.-Irvine, 1981—; cons. in field. Contbr. articles to profl. jours. Author: Finance and Development Planning in Turkey, 1972; The Afghan Economy, 1974; Money and Banking in Turkey, 1979; American Money and Banking, 1984. Home: 3085 Nestall Rd Laguna Beach CA 92651 Office: Sch of Social Scis Univ Calif Irvine CA 92717

FRYE, JUDITH ELEEN MINOR (MRS. VERNON LESTER FRYE), editor trade mag.; b. Seattle; d. George Edward and Eleen G. (Hartelius) Minor; student U. Cal. at Los Angeles, evenings 1947-48, U. So. Calif., 1948-53; m. Vernon Lester Frye, Apr. 1, 1954. Accountant, office mgr. Colony Wholesale Liquor, Culver City, Calif., 1947-48; credit mgr. Western Dist. Co., Culver City, 1948-53; partner in restaurants, Palm Springs, Los Angeles, 1948, partner in date ranch, La Quinta, Calif., 1949-53; partner, owner Imperial Printing, Huntington Beach, Calif., 1955—; editor New Era Laundry and Cleaning Lines, Huntington Beach, 1962—. Mem. Laundry and Cleaning Allied Trades Assn., Laundry and Dry Cleaning Suppliers Assn., Calif. Coin-op Assn. (exec. dir. 1975—; Cooperation award 1971, Dedicated Service award 1976), Nat. Automatic Laundry and Cleaning Council (Leadership award 1977), Women in Laundry/Drycleaning (past pres.; Outstanding Service award 1977). Office: 22031 Bushard St Huntington Beach CA 92646

FRYE, THOMAS LEE, JR., architect; b. Charles Town, W.Va., Oct. 9, 1947; s. Thomas Lee and Alice Mohler F.; B.Arch., U. Wash., 1970; m. Valerie Jean Hinkle, Sept. 11, 1976. Acoustician, Towne, Richards & Chaudiere, Seattle 1970-73; project architect El Baylis Assoc., Bellevue, Wash., 1973-74, project and group mgr. Kramer, Chin & Mayo, Inc., Seattle and Portland, Oreg., 1974-82; pvt. practice, Vancouver, Wash., 1982—. Bd. dirs. Enological Soc. Pacific NW, 1978—, program chmn., 1978-80; bd. dirs. Seattle Day Nursery Assn., 1980-82. Mem. AIA, Nat. Soc. Historic Preservation, Smithsonian Assoc., Napa Valley Wine Library Assn., Oreg. Winegrowers Assn. Club: Western Wash. Amateur Winemakers Assn. Prin. archtl. works include Olympia Wastewater Treatment Plant, Manchester Fisheries Research Lab., Carpenter Meml. Library, Bremerton (Wash.) Ferry Terminal, Hinman Winery expansion. Home: 5906 NE 79th Ave Vancouver WA 98662 Ofice: 518 Main St Vancouver WA 98662

FRYE, VERNON LESTER, publisher; b. Niagara Falls, N.Y., Sept. 5, 1915; s. Reinhart B. and Cora B. (Carl) F.; student U. Calif. at Los Angeles, 1947-50; m. Judith Eleen Minor, Apr. 1, 1954. Accountant, McLaren, Goode & West, C.P.A.'s, Los Angeles, 1950-51; br. chief accountant Philco Corp., Los Angeles, 1951-54; chief accounting officer Centinela Valley Union High Sch. Dist., Hawthorne, Calif., 1955-60; partner Imperial Printing Co., Los Angeles, 1955-68; pub. New Era Mag., Los Angeles, 1962—. Served with AUS, 1941-45; ETO. Mem. Laundry and Drycleaning Allied Trade Assn., Nat. Automatic Laundry and Cleaning Council, Nat. Automatic Coin Laundry Equipment Operators, Huntington Beach C. of C. Office: 22031 Bushard St Huntington Beach CA 92646

FRYER, ROBERT SHERWOOD, theatrical producer; b. Washington, Nov. 18, 1920; s. Harold and Ruth (Reade) F.; B.A., Western Res. U., 1943. Asst. to mng. dir. Theatre Inc., 1946, casting dir., 1946-48; asst. to exec. CBS, 1949-51, casting dir., 1951-52; Broadway producer Wonderful Town, 1953; co-producer By the Beautiful Sea, 1954; The Desk Set, 1955, Shangri-La, 1956, Auntie Mame, 1956, Redhead, 1959, There Was a Little Girl, 1960, Advise and Consent, 1960, A Passage To India, 1962, Hot Spot, 1963, Roar Like a Dove, 1964, Sweet Charity, 1966, Mame, 1966, Chicago, 1975, The Norman Conquests, 1976, On the Twentieth Century, 1977, Sweeney Todd, 1978, Merrily We Roll Along, 1981, A Doll's Life, 1982, Noises Off, 1983, A Sense of Humor, 1983, Brighton Beach Memoirs, 1983; co-producer films The Boston Strangler, The Prime of Miss Jean Brodie, Myra Breckenridge, Travels with My Aunt, Mame, Abdication, 1973, Great Expectations, 1974, Voyage of the Damned, 1976, The Boys from Brazil, 1978, The Shining, 1979; artistic dir. Center Theatre Group, 1 Ahmanson Theatre Los Angeles, 1971—. Mem. Pres.'s Task Force Arts and Humanities, 1981, Pres.'s Com. Arts and Humanities, 1982—. Served as capt. AUS, 1941-46; maj. Res. Decorated Legion of Merit. Rockefeller Found. fellow. Mem. Episcopal Actors Guild (v.p.), League of N.Y. Theatres (bd. govs.). Author: Professional Theatrical Management New York City, 1947. Home: 8800 Thrasher Ave Los Angeles CA 90069 also 425 E 58th St New York NY 10022 Office: 135 N Grand Ave Los Angeles CA 90012

FRYM, JANET CAROLYN (KOPF), travel executive; b. San Francisco, Oct. 30, 1946; d. Richard Kenneth Carmoney and Nancy Ruth (Doud) Carmoney Kopf; m. Dale Roderic Oates, June, 1967 (div.); m. 2d, Roy Wertheimer Frym, Dec. 24, 1972 (div.). Student Sonoma State Coll., 1964-65, Heald's Bus. Coll., 1965-66. Travel agt. Small World Travel, Mill Valley, Calif., 1964-66, mgr., 1967-70, sole owner, 1970-75; travel agt., asst. mgr. Santa Rosa (Calif.) Travel, 1966-67; outside sales agt. Blue Marble Travel, Novato, Calif., 1976-77; co-owner Enterprises Unlimited, Riverside/Orange County, Calif., 1977-80; mgr. Traveltime, Inc., Laguna Hills, Calif., 1980-83; gen. mgr. Bay Travel, Inc., Corona Del Mar, Calif., 1983—; adv. bd., formation bd. Marin Savs. and Loan, Mill Valley, 1974—. Recipient multiple sales achievement awards, airlines, cruise lines, 1970-75. Mem. Orange County Travellarians, Nat. Assn. Female Execs. Republican. Presbyterian. Club: Orange County Sabre (v.p.). Home: 2115 Arbutus Pl Newport Beach CA 92660 Office: 2435 E Coast Hwy Corona Del Mar CA 92625

FRYMIRE, WILLIAM LOREN, soil scientist, computer programmer; b. Wallace, Idaho, July 8, 1948; s. William Walter and Christy Ann (Thatcher) F.; B.S. in Edn., U. Idaho, 1972; M.S. in Soil Sci., 1980; m. Martha Fae Needham, Aug. 12, 1974. Biol. and forestry technician U.S. Forest Service, Sandpoint, Idaho, summers 1966-74; tchr. sci. and math, secondary public schs., Idaho and Wyo., 1972-76; grad. asst. in soils U. Idaho, 1978-80; soil scientist Bur. Land Mgmt., Idaho Falls, Idaho, 1980-81; computer programmer/analyst Exxon, Idaho Falls, Idaho, 1982—. Asst. treas. Trinity Bapt. Ch., Moscow, Idaho, 1979-80. Served with U.S. NG., 1972-79. NSF grantee, summer 1975. Mem. Am. Registry Cert. Profls. in Agronomy Crops and Soils (soil scientist in tng.), Am. Soc. Agronomy, Soil Sci. Soc. Am., Gamma Sigma Delta, Phi Sigma. Baptist. Clubs: Alpine Ski, Idaho Falls Apple Users. Home: 1895 Avalon St Idaho Falls ID 83402 Office: INEL CPP 637 Idaho Falls ID 83401

FU, FREDERIC C.L., mechanical engineer, consultant; b. Jeho, China, Sept. 12, 1943; s. K.T. and Shisaye (Yamamoto) F.; divorced; 1 dau., Janet. Ph.D., U. Calif.-San Diego, 1972. Vis. scholar in research Northwestern U., Evanston, Ill., 1972-73; cons. Pratt & Whitney Aircraft Co., Hartford, Conn., 1973-74; sr. engring. specialist Boeing Co., Seattle, 1974—. Mem. AIAA, ASME. Presbyterian (deacon). Contbr. articles to profl. jours. Office: PO Box 3707 Seattle WA 98124

FUCHS, JACOB, chemistry educator; b. N.Y.C., May 7, 1923; s. Alexander and Irma (Radocy) F.; B.A. in Chemistry, N.Y.U., 1944; M.S. in Chemistry, U. Ill., 1947, Ph.D. in Chemistry, 1950; m. Rose Lochansky, June 15, 1946; children—Tara Ellen, Gary Allan. Postdoctoral research asst. U. Ill. at Urbana, 1950-52; asst. prof. chemistry Ariz. State U. at Tempe, 1952-56, asso. prof. chemistry, 1956-59, prof. chemistry, 1959—, exec. officer dept., 1961-75, dir. ann. summer programs in applied molecular spectroscopy, modern indsl. spectroscopy, 1956—; vis. prof. chemistry U. Colo. at Boulder, 1965 (summer). Prin. tympanist Phoenix Symphony Orch., 1952-79. Served with AUS, 1944-45. Fellow Am. Inst. Chemists; mem. Ariz. Acad. Sci., Am. Chem. Soc., Soc. Applied Spectroscopy, Sigma Xi, Phi Kappa Phi, Phi Lambda Upsilon, Pi Mu Epsilon, Research in X-ray spectroscopy and X-ray diffraction. Office: Dept Chemistry Ariz State Univ Tempe AZ 85287

FUDIM, OWEN KENNETH, psychologist; b. N.Y.C., Sept. 20, 1950; s. Jack and Sylvia Rhoda F.; m. Dale Sheila, Mar. 1, 1981. M.A., UCLA, 1973, Ph.D., 1979. Lic. psychologist, Calif. Psychologist VA Hosp., Brentwood, Calif., 1975-76, Long Beach, Calif., 1976-77; postdoctoral scholar UCLA, 1979-81; pvt. practice psychology, Pleasant Hill, Calif., 1981-83; mem. Contra Costa County Children and Adolescent Task Force. Calif. State scholar; NIMH fellow. Mem. Calif. State Psychol. Assn., Am. Psychol. Assn., Contra Costa County Psychol. Assn. (sec.-elect).

FUGATE, IVAN DEE, lawyer, banker; b. Blackwell, Okla., Dec. 9, 1928; s. Hugh D. and Iva (Holmes) F.; A.B., Kans. State U.-Pittsburg, 1949; LL.B., U. Denver, 1952, J.D., 1970; children—Vickie Michelle, Roberta Jean, Douglas Bennett, Thomas Philip; m. Lois Unita Rossow, June 3, 1966. Admitted to Colo. bar, 1952; exec. sec., mgr. Colo. Jr. C. of C., 1950-52; individual practice law, Denver, 1954—; chmn. bd., pres. Western Nat. Bank Denver; dir. Kit Carson State Bank (Colo.); pres., chmn. exec. com. North Valley Bank, Thornton, Colo.; sec.-treas. Citizens Investment Co.; sec. 1st Nat. Bank Burlington, Colo.; dir., mem. exec. com. Midtown Nat. Bank, Pueblo, Colo.; chmn. bd., pres. Green Mt. Bank, Lakewood, Colo., 1975—; chmn. bd. Ind. State Bank Colo., 1978—; owner farms, ranches, Kans., Colo.; instr. U. Denver Coll. Law, 1955-60; mem. faculty 36th Assembly for Bank Dirs. Mem. Colo. State Treas.'s Com. Investment State Funds, 1975—. Treas., Republican Assos. Colo., 1959-61, trustee, 1959-64. Served to 1st lt. AUS, 1952-54. Mem. Am., Colo., Denver (trustee 1962-65) bar assns., Colo. Bankers Assn. (dir.), Ind. Bankers Colo. (founder, chmn. bd. 1973—), Ind. Bankers Assn. Am. (mem. fed. legis. com. 1974-75, mem. exec. council and adminstrv. com. 1976—, pres. 1978—), Denver Law Club, Colo. Cattlemen Assn., Phi Alpha Delta. Methodist. Clubs: 26, Denver Athletic, Petroleum (Denver); Lakewood (Colo.) Country; Commerce (Dallas); Pueblo Birdwatchers. Home: 12015 W 26th Ave Lakewood CO 80215 Office: 5350 S DTC Pkwy Bldg 52 Englewood CO 80111

FUGELSANG, KENNETH C., enologist; b. Fresno, Calif., Dec. 13, 1946; s. P. and Ardith F.; B.A. cum laude, Calif. State U., Fresno, 1969, M.A. cum laude, 1972; postgrad. U. Calif.; m. Ann L. Panzarella, Dec. 18, 1971. Enologist, food scientist Calif. State U., Fresno, 1971—, lectr. in enology, 1973—; wine cons., v.p. analytical services Bacchus Lab., Fresno. Mem. Am. Soc. Enologists and Viticulturists, Am. Soc. Wine Educators, Phi Kappa Phi. Author: The Winemakers Guide, 1978; Wine Analysis and Production, 1981; contbr. articles to profl. jours. Office: Calif State U Dept Enology and Food Sci Fresno CA 93710

FUHLRODT, NORMAN THEODORE, ret. ins. co. exec.; b. Wisner, Nebr., Apr. 24, 1910; s. Albert F. and Lena (Schafersman) F.; student Midland Coll., 1926-28; A.B., U. Nebr., 1930; M.A., U. Mich., 1936; m. Clarice W. Livermore, Aug. 23, 1933; 1 son, Douglas B. Tchr., athletic coach high schs., Sargent, Nebr., 1930-32, West Point, Nebr., 1932-35; with Central Life Assurance Co., Des Moines, 1936-74, pres., chief exec. officer, 1964-72, chmn. bd., chief exec. officer, 1972-74, also dir. Named Monroe St. Jour. Alumnus of Month, U. Mich. Grad Sch. Bus. Adminstrn. Gen. chmn. Greater Des Moines United campaign United Community Service, 1969-70. Former bd. dirs. Des Moines Center Sci. and Industry. Fellow Soc. Actuaries. Home: 6230 Via Regla San Diego CA 92122

FUHRMAN, HOWARD DAVID, real estate syndication company executive; b. Bklyn., Sept. 4, 1944; s. Saul and Bertha (Friedheim) F.; m. Laura Ann Marer, Mar. 19, 1967; children—Gregory, Scott, Karen. B.S. in Bus. Adminstrn., UCLA, 1966; M.S. in Fin., Calif. State U.-Long Beach, 1972. C.P.A., Calif.; life time teaching credential Calif. Community Colls. Acct., Kenneth Leventhal & Co., Los Angeles, 1969-79; v.p., controller Lesny Devel. Co., Beverly Hills, Calif., 1979-82; v.p. fin. The Heritage Group, Santa Monica, 1982—. Past pres. Ladera Heights (Calif.) Civic Assn. Served with U.S. Army, 1967-69. Mem. Am. Inst. C.P.A.s, Calif. Soc. C.P.A.s, Los Angeles C.P.A.s.

FUHRMAN, ROBERT ALEXANDER, aerospace company executive; b. Detroit, Feb. 23, 1925; s. Alexander A. and Elva (Brown) F.; m. Nan McCormick, Sept. 16, 1949; children—Lee Anne, Richard, William. B.S., U. Mich., 1945; M.S., U. Md., 1952; postgrad. Stanford U., 1964, U. Calif.-San Diego, 1958. Project engr. Naval Air Test Ctr., Patuxent River, Md., 1946-53; chief tech. engring. Ryan Aero. Co., San Diego, 1953-58; v.p., asst. gen. mgr. missile systems div. Lockheed Missiles & Space Co., Sunnyvale, Calif., 1958-69, v.p., gen. mgr., 1969, exec. v.p., 1973-76, pres., 1976—, chmn., 1979—, also dir.; pres. Lockheed Ga. Co., Marietta, 1970-71, Lockheed Calif. Co., Burbank, 1971-73; dir. Bank of West; chmn. bd. Ventura Mfg. Co., 1970-71. Adv. bd. Stanford U. Sch. Engring.; mem. Def. Sci. Bd.; chmn. Task Force on Indsl. Responsiveness, 1980; mem. adv. com. Ala. Space and Rocket Ctr.; chmn. bd. dirs. DIALOG, ctr.; Bay Area Council; mem. FBM Steering Task Group, 1966-70; mem. exec. com. San Jose Mgmt. Task Force; mem. adv. bd. Sch. Bus., U. Santa Clara County, 1975—; bd. dirs. Atlanta Jr. Achievement. Served to ensign USNR, 1944-46. Recipient Silver Knight award Nat. Mgmt. Assn., 1969, John J. Montgomery award, 1964; award Soc. Mfg. Engrs., 1973. Fellow AIAA (dir.-at-large, Von Karman 1978); mem. Nat. Acad. Engring., Am. Astronautical Soc. (sr.), Nat. Aeros. Assn., Ga. C. of C. (dir.), Am. Def. Preparedness Assn. (dir., exec. com.), Navy League U.S. (life), Air Force Assn., Assn. U.S. Army, Soc. Am. Value Engrs. (hon.), Beta Gamma Sigma. Club: Cosmos (Washington). Office: 1111 Lockheed Sunnyvale CA 94086

FUJII, GERTRUDE SUGIOKA, educator; b. Hollister, Calif., Feb. 10, 1918; d. Seijiro and Kameno (Takeda) Sugioka; B.A., UCLA, 1961, M.A., 1962; Ph.D., U. So. Calif., 1970; m. George S. Fujii, Sept. 9, 1945. Adminstrv. asst. So. Calif. Council Protestant Chs., 1947-52; tchr. English, Los Angeles Unified Dist., 1962-66; asst. prof. English, Los Angeles Valley Coll., 1966-68, asso. prof., 1968-69, prof., 1969—, chmn. dept. English, 1970-76; vis. lectr. UCLA, 1980—; chmn. English div. State Chancellor's Com. on Basic Skills; mem. intersegmental com. on writing Calif. Postsecondary Com., Sacramento; pres. English Council Calif. Two-Yr. Colls., 1976-80; dir. Wilnor Corp., Los Angeles. Sec. bd. dirs. Div. Higher Edn., Disciples of Christ (nat.), St. Louis; pres. congregation and bd. adminstrn. Wilshire Christian Ch. Recipient Outstanding Service award Los Angeles Community Coll. Dist., 1979. Mem. MLA, Assn. Governing Bds. Univs. and Colls., Philol. Assn. Pacific Coast, Am. Studies Assn., NEA, Nat. Council Tchrs. English, Phi Delta Gamma. Club: Altrusa (Los Angeles). Contbr. articles to profl. jours.; editorial adv. bd. Teaching English in the Two-Year Coll., 1980—; contbg. writer Chronicle of Higher Edn. Office: 5800 Fulton Ave Van Nuys CA 91401

FUJII, KIYO, pharmacist; b. Portland, Oreg., July 1, 1921; s. Kanji and Mitoyo (Kurata) F.; student U. Wash., 1939-42; B.S., St. Louis Coll. Pharmacy, 1943. Pharmacist, C.F. Knight Drug, St. Louis, 1943-48, Sargent Drug, Chgo., 1950-52, Mt. Sinai Hosp., Chgo., 1953-54, Campus Pharmacy, Los Angeles, 1973—; chief pharmacist Evang. Hosp., Chgo., 1948-49, Am. Hosp. Clinic, Los Angeles, 1958-60. Mem. Am., Calif. pharm. assns., Am. Soc. Hosp. Pharmacists, St. Louis Coll. Pharmacy Alumni Assn., Rho Chi, Sigma Epsilon Sigma. Democrat. Presbyterian. Home: 7913 Kentwood Ave Los Angeles CA 90045 Office: 3611 S Vermont Ave Los Angeles CA 90007

FUJII, KOZO, research scientist, educator; b. Kofu, Yamomashi, Japan, Oct. 17, 1951; s. Yoshio and Tomie (Odagiri) F.; m. Yashimi Hirai, July 8, 1974; 1 son, Kotaro. B.S. in Engring., U. Tokyo, 1974, M.S., 1977, Ph.D., 1980. Research assoc. Japan Soc. Promotion Sci., Inst. Space and Astronautical Sci. 1980-81; NRC postdoctoral research assoc. NASA Ames Research Ctr., Moffett Field, Calif., 1981—; instr. math. and physics, Japan. Mem. AIAA; Japan Soc. Aeros. and Astronautics, Japan Soc. Mech. Engrs. Clubs: Snowman Ski (dir. 1978-81). Contbr. articles to profl. jours. Office: NASA Ames Research Ctr 202A-14 Moffett Field CA 94035

FUJII, WESLEY MOTONORI (MORT), magnetic recording and profl. audio products co. exec.; b. Sacramento, July 29, 1929; s. Riuye and Moto (Fujimoto) F.; student Sacramento Coll., 1947-48, Am. TV, 1948-49; B.S. in E.E., Ill. Inst. Tech., 1952; m. Asako Marianne Matsuo, July 5, 1953; children—Darlene Gale, Russell Scott. Engr. broadcast audio RCA, Camden, N.J., 1952-55; engr. tape recorders Ampex Corp., Redwood City, Calif., 1955-59; mgr. audio custom engring., 1959-60, audio engring. mgr., 1962-67; v.p. Foster Investment Service, Menlo Park, Calif., 1960-62, Bell Sound Studios, N.Y.C., 1967-68, Electro Sound, Inc., Sunnyvale, Calif., 1968-75; pres. Cetec Gauss, Sun Valley, Calif., 1975—. Audio Engring. Soc. fellow, 1965. Mem. I.E.E.E., Soc. Motion Picture and TV Engrs., Tau Beta Pi, Eta Kappa Nu (corr. sec. 1951), Rho Epsilon. Patentee in field. Home: 18843 Tulsa St Northridge CA 91326 Office: 9130 Glenoaks Blvd Sun Valley CA 91352

FUJIKI, SUMIKO, psychiat. nurse; b. Devil's Slide, Utah, Feb. 21, 1926; d. Jusaburo and Shigeyo (Nishimura) F.; R.N., Thomas D. Dee Meml. Hosp., Ogden, Utah, 1948; A.S., Weber Jr. Coll., 1948; B.S. in Nursing Edn., U. Utah, 1949; M.S. in Nursing, Washington U., St. Louis, 1954; Ph.D. in Cultural Found. of Edn., U. Utah, 1976. Instr., Thomas D. Dee Meml. Hosp. Sch. Nursing, 1949-52; instr. psychiat. nursing Washington U., 1953-55; asst. prof. to assoc. prof. psychiat-mental health nursing U. Utah, 1957-78, head grad. program in psychiat.-mental health nursing, 1957-76; vis. assoc. prof. UCLA, 1978-80; assoc. prof. nursing U. Colo., Denver, 1980—; assoc. prof. nursing U. Utah, 1967-80; mem. rev. com.; cons., visitor psychiat. nursing edn. NIMH, 1975-78; mem. Bd. Ethnic Nurses for Advancement of Health Care, 1978—; family and marriage counselor; counselor Helpline, 1978-80. Bd. dirs. Asian Pacific Devel. Ctr., Denver, 1980—. Mem. Am. Nurses Assn., Nat. League Nursing, Asian Human Services Assn., Japanese-Am. Citizenship League (bd. dirs. Salt Lake City 1978), Sigma Theta Tau. Home: 645 S Alton Way Denver CO 80231 Office: 4200 E 9th Ave Denver CO 80262

FUJIMOTO, AKIRA, engr., ret. county ofcl.; b. Honolulu, June 12, 1925; s. Eiji and Yukiyo (Miyagi) F.; B.S., U. Hawaii, 1950; m. Hazel Sayoko Furutani, Mar. 24, 1951; children—Terrance B. H., Kyle W. T. Jr. civil engr. Dept. Pub. Works, County of Hawaii, Hilo, 1950-52, civil engr., 1952-57, bur. head plans and surveys, 1957-61; asst. mgr.-engr. Dept. Water Supply, County of Hawaii, Hilo, 1961-68, mgr.-engr., 1968-79; resident engr. R.M. Towill Corp., 1980—. Served with U.S. Army, 1945-47. Registered profl. engr., Hawaii. Named Hawaii Engr. of the Year, Hawaii Soc. Profl. Engrs., 1976. Mem. ASCE, Hawaii Water Works Assn., Nat. Soc. Profl. Engrs., Hawaii Soc. Profl. Engrs., Am. Water Works Assn. (George W. Fuller award Hawaii sect. 1982). Buddhist. Clubs: Young Buddhist Assn., 442d Vets of Hawaii. Home: 152 Hoonanea St Hilo HI 96720

FUJINAKA, MILES SHOJI, optometrist; b. Aiea, Hawaii, Dec. 1, 1950; s. Yoshimitsu and Yoshie (Kusuda) F. B.A., U. So. Calif., 1972, B.S., 1974; O.D., Pa. Coll. Optometry, 1976. Lic. optometrist Hawaii. With Optical Suppliers Inc., extern Joseph C. Wilson Health Ctr., Rochester, N.Y., 1976; assoc. Dr. Roger C. Ede, Hawaii, 1977-78; pvt. practice optometry, Aiea, Hawaii, 1978—. Queen pageant chmn. Cherry Blossom Festival, 1981, awards com. chmn., 1982, advisor to awards com., 1983. Recipient Honolulu Japanese Jr. C. of C. Bronze Key, 1981, Silver Key, 1982. Mem. Am. Optometric Assn., Hawaii Optometric Assn. (treas. 1978-79, bd. dirs. 1981-82), First Study Club Optometrists (treas. 1982, sec. 1983). Club: Honolulu. Office: 98-211 Pali Momi St Suite 803 Aiea HI 96701

FUJIYAMA, WALLACE SACHIO, lawyer; b. Honolulu, Aug. 8, 1925; s. George S. and Cornelia (Matsumoto) F.; student U. Hawaii, 1943-44,

49-50; LL.B., U. Cin., 1953; m. Mildred H. Morita, Jan. 24, 1959; children—Rodney, Susan, Keith. Admitted to Hawaii bar, 1954; dep. atty. gen. Hawaii, 1954-56; examiner, atty. Hawaii Employment Relations Bd., 1956-59; individual practice law, 1956—, Honolulu, 1959—; partner Fujiyama, Duffy & Fujiyama; chmn. bd. Honolulu Corp.; dir. First Hawaiian Bank, Mid Pacific Airlines. Mem. Hawaii Statehood Commn., 1957-59, Stadium Authority, 1982—; mem. nat. platform com. from Hawaii, Rep. Nat. Conv., 1956; bd. regents U. Hawaii, 1974-82, chmn., 1975-79. Served with Transp. Corps, AUS, 1946. Recipient Cin. Ct. Index award, 1953. Mem. Am. Arbitration Assn. (mediator), Am., Hawaii (pres.) bar assns., Hawaii Trial Lawyers Assn. (pres.), Internat. Savs. and Loan Assn. (sec., dir. 1979-82), Order of Coif, Phi Alpha Delta. Club: Honolulu Internat. Country (dir.). Asso. editor U. Cin. Law Rev. Home: 1803 Laukahi St Honolulu HI 96821 Office: Suite 2650 Pacific Trade Center 190 S King St Honolulu HI 96813

FUKUDA, NOBUKO, educator; b. Honolulu, Feb. 27, 1921; d. Kazuki and Kaneyo (Ozaki) Kosaki; B.E., U. Hawaii, 1943, 5th yr. diploma, 1943; M.A., Mich. State U., 1961; Ph.D., Claremont Grad. Sch., 1975; m. Robert Toshiyuki Fukuda, June 30, 1945; children—Lois, Mona. Tchr., Molokai High Sch., Hoolehua, Hawaii, 1943-45; tchr. Hilo (Hawaii) High Sch., 1950-58, registrar, 1958-60; vice prin. Hilo Union Sch., 1961-63, Kalanianaole Sch., Papai Kou, Hawaii, 1963-65; lectr. in edn. U. Hawaii, Hilo, 1963-65, specialist in edn., 1965-72, asso. prof., 1972-77, prof., 1977-79, now emeritus, chmn. div. social scis. and edn., 1976-79; assessment officer Peace Corps Projects in Hilo; cons. Hawaii Dept. Edn.; organizer, chmn. Big Island sect. World Educators Conf., 1976. Mem. planning commn. Hawaii County, 1963-64, chmn. planning commn., 1968-69, mem. 2d charter commn., 1965-66, mem. bd. appeals, 1966-69; acad. humanist to housing project Internat. Longshoremen Warehousemen Union Local 142, 1975, values edn., 1976, mental health project, 1978. Recipient commendation NEA, 1966; Community Found. scholarship grantee, 1960-61; NDEA Guidance Inst. grantee, 1960-61; U. Hawaii grantee 1966-67, 67-68, travel grantee, 1975. Mem. Council Anthropology and Edn., Nat. Council Social Studies Edn., Assn. Supervision and Curriculum Devel., Assn. Tchr. Educators, AAUP, Delta Kappa Gamma. Democrat. Buddhist. Contbr. articles to profl. jours. Home: 50 E Palai St Hilo HI 96720 Office: 1400 Kapiolani St Hilo HI 96720

FUKUNAGA, GEORGE JOJI, corporate executive; b. Waialua, Oahu, Hawaii, Apr. 13, 1924; s. Peter H. and Ruth (Hamamura) F.; B.A., U. Hawaii, 1948; certificate Advanced Mgmt. Program Harvard U. Hawaii, 1955; m. Alice M. Tagawa, Aug. 5, 1950; 1 son, Mark H. Adminstrv. asst., dir. Service Motor Co., Ltd. (named changed to Servco Pacific Inc. 1969), Honolulu, 1948-50, v.p., 1952-60, pres., 1960—; chmn., dir. 10 subsidiaries of Service Fin., Ltd. (name now Servco Financial Corp.), 1960—, Servco Services Corp., Am. Ins. Agy. Inc., Servco Internat. Corp., Servco Securities Corp., Servco Investment Corp., Hawaiiana Advt. Agy., Pacific Internat. Co. Inc. (Guam), Pacific Fin. Corp. (Guam), Pacific Motors Corp. (Guam); dir. Am. Trust of Hawaii Inc., Island Ins. Ltd., Hawaiian Pacific Resorts, Inc. Bd. govs. Iolani Sch.; trustee Fukunaga Scholarship Found.; trustee Hawaii Pacific Coll.; mem. State of Hawaii Post-Secondary Edn. Commn.; bd. dirs. Boy Scouts Am., Goodwill Industries; bd. govs. U. Hawaii Found. Served to 2d lt. AUS, 1945-47, to 1st lt., 1950-52. Mem. Hawaii (v.p. 1970, 83, dir. 1970-75), Honolulu Japanese (pres. 1969, dir. 1963—) chambers commerce, Hawaii Employers Council (dir.), Better Bus. Bur. (v.p. 1963-66, dir. 1977—), Hawaii Econ. Study Club (pres. 1962), Hawaii-Japan Econ. Council, U.S.-Japan Soc., Oriental Importers Assn. Methodist. Clubs: Pacific, Plaza (dir.), 200 Rotary, Deputies. Office: Suite 500 900 Fort St Mall Honolulu HI 96813

FUKUSHIMA, BARBARA NAOMI, accountant; b. Honolulu, Apr. 5, 1948; d. Harry Kazuo and Misayo (Kawasaki) Murakoshi; B.A., U. Hawaii, 1970; postgrad. Oreg. State U., 1971, 73, U. Oreg., 1972; m. Dennis Hiroshi Fukushima, Mar. 23, 1974; 1 son, Dennis Hiroshi. Intern, Coopers & Lybrand, Honolulu, 1974; auditor Haskins & Sells, Kahului, Hawaii, 1974-77; pres. Book Doors, Inc., Pukalani, 1977—; pres. Barbara N. Fukushima C.P.A., Inc., Wailuku. 1979—; sec. treas. Target Pest Control, Inc., Wailuku, 1979—; internal auditor, acct. Maui Land & Pineapple Co., Inc., Kahului, 1977-80; auditor Hyatt Regency Maui, Kaanapali, 1980-81; partner D & B Internat., Pukalani, 1980—. Recipient Phi Beta Kappa Book award, 1969. Mem. Am. Inst. C.P.A.s, Hawaii Soc. C.P.A.s, Nat. Assn. Accts., Am. Womens Soc. C.P.A.s, Hawaii Assn. Public Accts., Bus. and Profl. Women's Club. Tenrikyo. Home: 200 Aliiolani St Pukalani HI 96788 Office: 270 Hookahi St Suite 210F Wailuku HI 96793

FUKUTA, NORIHIKO, atmospheric scientist; b. Tokoname, Japan, May 11, 1931; s. Teizo and Haru (Takeuchi) F.; came to U.S., 1966; B.S., Nagoya U., 1954, M.S., 1956, Ph.D., 1959; m. Yoko Kuriyama, Mar. 3, 1966. Prof. environ. engring. U. Denver, 1968-75, adj. prof. physics, 1976-77, head atmospheric engring. lab. Denver Research Inst., 1968-74, head cloud physics div., 1974-77; prof. meteorology U. Utah, 1977—; cons. in field. Huffsmith awardee U. Denver, 1971; recipient medal of Honor, Leningrad State U., 1980. Mem. Am. (Editor's award 1974), Japanese meteorol. socs., Am. Phys. Soc., Am. Geophys. Union, Weather Modification Assn., Sigma Xi. Asso. editor Jour. Atmospheric Scis., 1976—, Jour. Applied Meteorology, 1972-79. Contbr. articles to profl. publs. atmospheric scis., 1954—. Home: 931 E Capitol Blvd Salt Lake City UT 84103 Office: Dept Meteorology U Utah Salt Lake City UT 84112

FULCO, ARMAND JOHN, biochemist; b. Los Angeles, Apr. 3, 1932; s. Herman J. and Clelia Marie (DeFeo) F.; B.S. in Chemistry, UCLA, 1957, Ph.D. in Physiol. Chemistry, 1960; m. Virginia Loy Hungerford, June 18, 1955; children—William James, Lisa Marie, Linda Susan, Suzanne Yvonne. Research fellow dept. chemistry Harvard U., Cambridge, Mass., 1961-63; prin. investigator Lab. of Biomed. and Environ. Scis., UCLA, 1963—, asst. prof. dept. biol. chemistry, 1965-70, asso. prof., 1970-76, prof., 1976—; cons. biochemist VA, Los Angeles, 1968—. Served with U.S. Army, 1952-54. Mem. Am. Chem. Soc., Am. Soc. Biol. Chemists, Am. Oil Chemists Soc., AAAS, Harvard Chemists Assn., Am. Soc. Microbiologists, Sigma Xi. Author: (with J.F. Mead) The Unsaturated and Polyunsaturated Fatty Acids in Health and Disease, 1976; contbr. over 60 articles on research in biochemistry to sci. jours. Home: 3000 Stoner Ave Los Angeles CA 90066 Office: Warren Hall Univ Calif 900 Veteran Ave Los Angeles CA 90024

FULGHUM, BRICE ELWIN, cons.; b. Fredonia, Kans., Aug. 27, 1919; s. Byron Harmon and Myrtle (Broderick) F.; student U. Kansas City, San Francisco State Coll.; m. Virginia L. Fulghum; 1 dau., Linda Lee Fulghum McDonald. Asst. to sales mgr. Gas Service Co., Kansas City, Mo., 1939-41, sales mgr. Ace Auto Rental & Sales Co., Kansas City, 1945-48; asst. mgr. Owl Drug Co., San Francisco, 1948-50; mgr. Pacific Mut. Life Ins. Co., 1950-61; v.p. Gordon H. Edwards Co., 1961-64; v.p. Federated Life Ins. Co. Calif., 1964-66; gen. mgr. Los Angeles Fulghum agy. Pacific Mut. Life Ins. Co., 1966-71; v.p. Hendrie Bonding & Ins. Corp., Huntington Beach, Calif., 1976-77; chmn. bd. PGA Ins. Services, Inc., Torrance, Calif., 1976-77; cons. Am. Health Profiles, Inc., Nashville; sr. fin. cons. Shearson Hayden Stone Inc., Newport Beach, Calif., 1977-79; cons. Penn Gen. Agys., Los Angeles and Employee Benefit Cons.'s, Santa Ana, Calif., 1979—; cons. Assn. Calif. State U. Profs., Profl. Sponsoring Fund, 1979—. Chmn. Cancer drive; active Community Chest, Am. Heart Assn. Served with Q.M.C., U.S. Army, 1941-43. C.L.U. Mem. Am. Soc. C.L.U.s (Golden Key Soc.), Leading Life Ins. Producers No. Calif. (life mem., pres. 1955), San Francisco Peninsula (charter), Los Angeles-San Fernando Valley (life) estate planning councils, Orange County Life Underwriters Assn. Republican. Clubs: Commonwealth, El Niguel Country. Mem. editorial advisory bd. Western Underwriter. Contbr. articles to ins. publs. Home: 30561 N Hampton Rd Laguna Niguel CA 92667 Office: 1055 N Main St Suite 420 Santa Ana CA 92701

FULKS, ROBERT GRADY, computer exec.; b. Kansas City, Mo., Apr. 8, 1936; s. Hilburne Grady and Dora Elouise (Johnson) F.; children—Stephanie, Scott Grady. B.S.E.E., M.I.T., 1958, M.S.E.E., 1959. Engr., chief engr. v.p. engring. and product mktg. Genrad, Inc. (formerly Gen. Radio Co.), Concord, Mass., 1959-73; pres. Mirco Systems, Inc., 1973-75, Omnicomp, Inc., Phoenix, 1975-80, gen. mgr. advanced tech div. (formerly Omnicomp, Inc.) Genrad, Inc., Phoenix, 1980—, also v.p. parent co.; dir. Ci US Sigma Ltd., Fareham, Eng., Texco Corp., Phoenix, Custom Data Mgmt. Inc., Phoenix, Markwood, Inc., Phoenix, Office Tech. Ltd., Boston. Former bd. dirs., chmn. fin. com. Concord (Mass.) C. of C. Mem. IEEE, Assn. Computing Machinery, Sigma Xi. Contbr. articles tech. jours. Patentee in field. Office: 4620 N 16th St Phoenix AZ 85016

FULL, ROY PERRY, geologist; b. Portland, Oreg., Oct. 25, 1913; s. Oscar E. and Anna (Edstrom) F.; B.S., U. Idaho, 1942, Geol. Engr., 1955; m. Helene Picq, Oct. 20, 1945; 1 dau., Mariette H. Mining engr. Sunshine Mining Co., Kellogg, Idaho, 1942-43; geologist U.S. Geol. Survey, Spokane, Wash., 1943-46; cons. geologist Shenon & Full, Spokane, 1946-48, Salt Lake City, 1952-66; cons. geologist, Salt Lake City, 1966—; asso. prof. mining U. Utah, 1949-52. Mem. Soc. Econ. Geologists, Soc. Mining Engrs., Geol. Soc. Am., Mining and Metall. Soc. Am., Utah Mining Assn. Club: Gyro (Salt Lake City). Home: 660 Terrace Hills Dr Salt Lake City UT 84103

FULLBRIGHT, JAMES ROLLIN, constrn. co. exec.; b. Troy, Kans., Nov. 27, 1922; s. John Barney and Anna Leonora (Steanson) F.; student Coll. Idaho, 1940-41, U. Seattle, 1943-44; m. Lillian Jacqueline Tweeddale, Feb. 27, 1971; children—Steven Gene, Christine, Jodi Rae. With Morrison Knudsen Co., Inc., Boise, Idaho, 1950—, mgr. quality assurance, 1976-79, chief estimator Indsl. and Mining div., 1979—; dir. Simpson Steel Fabricators & Erectors, Salt Lake City. Served with USMC, 1942-43. Mem. ASTM, Smithsonian Instn. Lutheran. Home: 3009 Kootenai Boise ID 83705 Office: PO Box 7808 Boise ID 83729

FULLER, ASHLEY ELLISON, fin. cons.; b. Merced, Calif., May 13, 1930; s. Walter Simmons and Mary Roselle (Stafford) F.; B.A., Calif. State U., 1957; m. Patricia Josephine Dennis, June 23, 1951; children—Patricia, Peggy, Paulette, Jonathan. Acct., Del Monte Corp., San Francisco and Honolulu, 1957-64; ops. acctg. mgr. Levi Strauss & Co., San Francisco, 1964-71; cons., gen. mgr. Fuller Assocs., Hayward, Calif., 1971—; lectr. in field. Served with USN, 1950-54. Lic. pvt. pilot. Mem. San Leandro C. of C. (dir. 1973-76), Nat. Assn. Accts., Nat. Soc. Pub. Accts., Nat. Assn. Enrolled Agts., Calif. Soc. Enrolled Agts., Internat. Platform Assn. Republican. Mem. Assemblies of God Ch. Contbr. articles in field to profl. jours. Office: 26046 Eden Landing Rd Suite 4 Hayward CA 94545

FULLER, CYNTHIA DIANE, banking automation company regional manager; b. Sagami, Japan, Dec. 13, 1958; d. Richard Glen and Margaret Anne (Moran) Fuller. Student U. San Francisco, 1976-77, San Francisco State U., 1978. Specialist, automated teller machine dept. Calif. Can. Bank, San Francisco, 1978, asst. to data control officer, 1978-79, officer electronic banking, 1979-80, coordinator automated teller machine dept., 1980-81; account cons. Docutel/Olivetti Corp., San Francisco, 1981, sr. account cons., 1981-83, regional support mgr. tech. and mktg. support personnel, 1983—; coordinator Automated Teller Machine Mgmt. Seminars. Sustaining mem. Republican Nat. Com. Recipient Achievement award Bank Am., 1976. Mem. Nat. Assn. Female Execs. Roman Catholic. Club: Republican Women's (San Francisco). Office: Docutel/Olivetti Corp 3541 Investment Blvd Suite 1 Hayward CA 94545

FULLER, DONALD PAUL, maritime labor official; b. San Francisco, July 26, 1936; s. Donald George and Ethel (Langer) F.; student Dobies Sch. Navigation, 1960-66, Coll. San Mateo, 1964-66; grad. U. San Francisco Labor-Mgmt. Sch., 1971; m. Coral Lei Hagain, Jan. 27, 1958; children—Donald, Scott, Christopher, Grant, Sarah. Tugboat deckhand, 1958, tugboat mate, 1961, tugboat master, 1963-66, ships pilot, 1966-69; agt. Masters, Mates and Pilots Union, San Francisco, 1969—; ofcl. San Mateo County Harbor Police, 1974—, commr., 1975—. Cons. to maritime and aviation law firms. Mem. Calif. Atty. Gen.'s Adv. Council, Comdg. Adm.'s Sea Lane Task Force Com.; citizen adv. rules com. Calif. Assembly, 1982. Mem. Sch. Bd. Adv. Council Cabrillo Dist., 1965-67; pres. San Mateo County Spl. Dists. Assn., 1976-78, dir., 1978—; pres. Point Montara Firemens Assn., 1966. Philhistorian judge U. San Francisco, 1970—. Served with USMCR, 1953-55. Mem. Internat. Orgn. Masters, Mates and Pilots (agt. San Francisco br., sec.-treas. West Coast and Pacific region, internat. master at arms, legis. adv. Calif., organizer, rep. Shoreside and Govt. divs., sec.-treas. internat. ballot com., liaison to Labor Dept.), Internat. Longshoremen's Assn. (Sergeant-at-arms, sec. organizing/strike team), N.Y. Detectives Endowment Assn. Clubs: Marines Meml. (San Francisco); Royal Racquet (Burlingame, Calif.). Contbr. articles profl. jours. Home: 2815 Hillside Dr Burlingame CA 94010 Office: Masters Mates and Pilots Pier 9 San Francisco CA 94111

FULLER, DONALD WILLIAM, computer co. exec.; b. Portsmouth, Eng., July 2, 1931; s. Richard and Irene (Fitzgerald) F.; m. Celia Raymond, Aug. 5, 1955 (div.); m. 2d, Doris Ann Roberts, Aug. 29, 1982; children—Traci, Andrew, D.J., Alex. B.S., Kings Coll., 1953, M.S., 1955. Project engr. indsl. control, Systems Div., Beckman Instruments, Fullerton, Calif., 1958-59; mgr. computer devel. engring. Packard Bell, West Los Angeles, Calif., 1959-61; v.p. engring. Redcor Corp., Canoga Park, Calif., 1961-66, v.p. engring. and mktg., v.p., gen. mgr., 1966-67, pres., chief exec. officer, 1968—; mem. adv. bd. So. Calif. Nat. Bank; dir. Tecstor, Inc., Digidyne Corp. Served with British Royal Navy, 1946-51. Mem. Indsl. League Orange County, Am. Electronics Assn.

FULLER, GARY RAY, vocational educator; b. North Bend, Oreg., Sept. 16, 1940; s. Medford C. and Elsie K. F.; m. Nicole M. Sipe, Aug. 11, 1963; children—Trisha LeAnn, Krista LeVon. B.S. in Bus. Adminstrn., Linfield Coll., 1962, M.Ed., 1964; Ed.D., Oreg. State U., 1976. Type A teaching cert., Alaska. Tchr., Dallas (Oreg.) Sr. High Sch., 1963-68; asst. program supr. Oreg. Dept. Edn., Salem, 1968-69; program supr. Alaska Dept. Edn., Juneau, 1969-72, program mgr., 1976-82; vocat. dir. U. Alaska—Juneau, 1972-73; assoc. prof. vocat. tchr. edn., 1982—. EPDA fellow, 1972-74. Mem. Am. Soc. Pub. Adminstrn., Am. Soc. Tng. and Devel., Am. Vocat. Assn. (life), Alaska Vocat. Assn. (charter mem., pres. 1983-84, Phi Delta Kappa (pres. S.E. chpt. 1979), Gastineau Aeromodler Soc. (pres. 1979), Acad. Model Aeronautics (v.p. region XI Alaska). Contbr. articles to profl. jours. Home: 3050 Riverwood Dr Juneau AK 99801

FULLER, GEORGE ASHER, economist; b. Muscatine, Iowa, Feb. 8, 1909; s. Frank Asher and Minnie (Lane) F.; B.S., Iowa State U., 1934; M.B.A., U. Iowa, 1939, Ph.D., 1952; student U. Colo., 1934, Harvard U., 1958, Danforth fellow, 1958; m. Raili Alli Laitinen, Nov., 1962; children—Anne (Mrs. Bernard Taverne), Frank George, Dan Alan. Mgmt. trainee Internat. Trade, Dodge & Seymour Ltd., N.Y.C., 1935-37; asst. export mgr. Ecko Products Corp., Chgo., 1937-38; traffic, personnel and econ. controls adminstr. United Air Lines, Washington, 1944-45, Chgo., 1945-46, Los Angeles, 1946-48; ind. analyst WPB, Washington, 1942-43; sr. economist to asst. chief air staff U.S. Air Force, Pentagon, Washington, 1943-44; lectr. U.S. Dept. Agr. Grad. Sch., Washington, 1944-45, UCLA, 1947-48; asso. prof. U. So. Calif., 1948-50; asso. prof. U. Utah, 1950-53, prof., 1953-77, prof. emeritus, 1977—; prof. Westminster Coll., 1977—; vis. prof. U. Iowa, 1951, U. N.C., 1959; Fulbright vis. prof. Swedish Sch. Economics, Helsinki Sch. Economics, 1960-61; mem. econ. group to USSR, 1968. Mem. Am. Econ. Assn., AAUP, Smithsonian Assos., Beta Gamma Sigma, Pi Kappa Alpha. Clubs: Aztec, Snowbird. Home: 953 Military Dr Salt Lake City UT 84108 Office: Dept Economics Westminster Coll Salt Lake City UT 84105

FULLER, KEITH RAYMUND, media executive; b. Portland, Oreg., Jan. 23, 1926; s. Harold S. and Anna E. (Meagher) F.; m. Dorothy E. Stokes, Oct. 30, 1944; children—Michael K., Kelley K. B.A., U. Portland, 1949; student U. Minn., 1950-51. Labor relations asst. McClatchy Newspapers Inc., Sacramento, 1951-58, indsl. relations mgr., 1958-63, indsl relations dir., 1963-70, dir. employee relations, 1970-75, dir., 1975—; bd. dirs. Western Newspapers Indsl. Relations Bur., 1978—. Served with USN, 1944-46. Mem. Am. Newspaper Pubs. Assn. (vice chmn. labor and personnel). Republican. Roman Catholic. Clubs: Sutter (Sacramento), Sierra View Country (Roseville, Calif.), Elks (Carmichael, Calif.). Office: PO Box 15779 21 and Q Sts Sacramento CA 95852

FULLER, KENNETH ROLLER, architect; b. Denver, Mar. 7, 1913; s. Robert K. and Nelle G. (Roller) F.; student U. Colo., 1932-35, U. Denver, 1936; postgrad. U. Ill., 1937; m. Gertrude A. Heid, June 16, 1938; children—Robert K., Richard H. Chief archtl. draftsman Robert K. Fuller, 1937-41; architect-engr. U.S. Engrs., 1942-46; tchr. U. Colo., Denver, 1947-48; partner Fuller, Fuller & Fuller, Denver, 1949-64; pres. Fuller & Fuller, Denver, 1965-69; prin. Fuller Fuller & Assos., Denver, 1969—. Bd. dirs. Park Hill Improvement Assn., 1966—; mem. adv. council Rocky Mountain area Am. Arbitration Assn., 1968—; sec.-treas., permanent corp. trustee Ednl. Fund, Colo. Soc. Architects, 1966—. Recipient Disting. Service award Colo. Soc. Architects, 1970, Outstanding Service cert., 1974, Combined Service award, 1980; Honor award for Disting. Service, U. Colo., 1983. Mem. AIA, Sigma Chi. Republican. Presbyterian. Club: Lions (dir. 1964-66, 76-77). Home: 1932 Hudson St Denver CO 80220 Office: 508 Colorado Bldg 1615 California St Denver CO 80202

FULLER, M(ARY) CHRISTINE, personnel coordinator, management consultant; b. Ogden, Utah, Aug. 28, 1947; d. Ralph M. and Gladys Eola (Peavey) Fuller; A.A., Southwestern Coll., Chula Vista, Calif., 1972, A.A. in Photography, 1983; B.A., San Diego State U., 1974; M.P.A. in Finance and Personnel, San Diego State U., 1981; m. Mark Adam Ardagna, Jan. 29, 1972. Program dir., student adv., asst. to chmn. dept. phys. edn., San Diego State U., 1975-79; founder, chmn. South Bay Cons., Chula Vista, Calif., 1978—; program and tng. coordinator United Way San Diego County, 1980—; spl. cons. to many civic orgns.; exhibited pictures Mus. Photographic Art, San Diego, 1983. Vice pres. devel. San Diego Civic Light Opera Assn./Starlight Women, 1980—; docent, editor, mem. Mus. Photographic Art, San Diego. Served with U.S. Army, 1968-70. Mem. Nat. Assn. Female Execs., Am. Assn. Pub. Adminstrs., Nat. Assn. Student Personnel Adminstrs., Am. Mgmt. Assn. Author: History of Student Activities: 1642-1900, 1978; California Dreams: A Collection of Poems, 1982. Home and Office: 781 Ada St Chula Vista CA 92011

FULLER, MARY FALVEY, management consultant; b. Detroit, Oct. 28, 1941; d. Lawrence C. and Mathilde G. Falvey; m. James W. Fuller, Aug. 22, 1981. B.A. with honors in Econs., Cornell U., 1963; M.B.A., Harvard U., 1967. Systems engr. IBM Corp., N.Y.C., 1963-65; mgmt. cons. McKinsey & Co., Inc., N.Y.C., 1967-75; v.p. Citibank, N.A., N.Y.C., 1975-78, head asset servicing div., 1977-78; sr. v.p., dir., head adminstrn. div., mem. exec. com., mem. operating com. Blyth Eastman Dillon & Co., Inc., N.Y.C., 1978-80; pres. M.C. Falvey Assocs., Inc., N.Y.C., 1980-81; v.p. fin. Shaklee Corp., San Francisco, 1981-82; pres., dir. Falvey Autos, Inc., Troy, Mich., 1978—. Mem. Com. for N.Y. Philharmonic, 1975-77; mem. 1979 Adv. Council on Social Security, 1979-80, Pres. Reagan's Transition Task Force on Social Security, 1979-80, Nat. Commn. on Social Security Reform, 1982—, Human Resources Financing Council, 1980—; mem. adminstrn. and legal processes adv. council Mills Coll., 1982—; trustee San Francisco Performances, 1982—. Harvard Bus. Sch. grantee, 1965-67. Republican. Episcopalian. Club: Recess (N.Y.C.). Home and Office: 2584 Filbert St San Francisco CA 94123

FULLER, MARY (MARY FULLER MCCHESNEY), sculptor, writer; b. Wichita, Kans., Oct. 20, 1922; d. Edward Emery and Karen Mabel (Rassmussen) F.; m. Robert Pearson McChesney, Dec. 17, 1949. A.A., U. Calif.-Berkeley, 1941. Exhibited sculpture at Syracuse (N.Y.) Mus., San Francisco Mus., Oakland (Calif.) Mus., Labaudt Gallery, Bolles Gallery, Rotunda Gallery, Kroebar Gallery, Hobbs Gallery, Both-Up Gallery, Choice Inc., San Francisco Art Festivals (merit award 1971), Calif. State U.-Sonoma, Santa Rosa (Calif.) Civic Ctr., San Francisco Women's Art Ctr., U. Oaxaca (Mex.); numerous commns. include: sculpture San Francisco Gen. Hosp., carved animals Children's Sculpture Park, Salinas, Calif., concrete falcon Andrew Hill High Sch., San Jose, Calif., Temko lions, Berkeley, Ellen Anderson lion, Berkeley, Sun, Moon, Stars and Rain, Anshen-Mays Gallery, Sausalito, Calif., children's sculpture Portsmouth Sq., San Francisco, West Side Pumping Sta. sculpture, San Francisco, others; research Archives Am. Art, San Francisco, 1964-65; staff writer Current Mag., San Francisco, 1975-76; assoc. editor News Front Mag., Petaluma, Calif., 1977-79. Ford Found. fellow, 1965-66; Nat. Endowment Arts critics' grantee, 1975. Author: A Period of Exploration (art book), 1973; (under pseudonym Joe Rayter) The Victim Was Important (mystery novel), 1954; Asking for Trouble (mystery novel), 1955; Stab in the Dark (mystery novel), 1955, French edit., 1971. Contbr. articles, short stories, poems to profl. and popular lit. Home and Office: 2955 Sonoma Mountain Rd Petaluma CA 94952

FULLER, PATRICK JON, manufacturing executive; b. Hopkinsville, Ky., Apr. 28, 1942; s. Luther Thomas and Patrica Genevieve (Murphy) F.; m. Catherine Sue Cummings, June 1, 1973; children—Andrea Jenine, Jessica Rhea. B.A., B.S., Western Ky. U., 1964-68; M.B.A., U. Fla., 1970. Various mgmt. positions Kaiser Roth, Woodbury, Tenn., 1971-74, Genesco, Nashville, 1974-76; dir. engring. Levi Strauss & Co., San Francisco, 1976—; cons. Bd. dirs. Mental Health Assn. Contra Costa County. Club: Elks. Office: Levi Straus & Co Levi Plaza LS/4 San Francisco CA 94106

FULLER, ROBERT KENNETH, architect, urban designer; b. Denver, Oct. 6, 1942; s. Kenneth Roller and Gertrude Ailene (Heid) F.; B.Arch., U. Colo., 1967; M.Arch. and Urban Design, Washington U., St. Louis, 1973; m. Virginia Louise Elkin, Aug. 23, 1969; children—Kimberly Kirsten, Kelsey Christa. Archtl. designer Fuller & Fuller, Denver; architect/planner Urban Research and Design Center, St. Louis, 1970-72; architect/urban designer Fuller, Fuller & Assos., Denver, 1972—; prin. works include Skyline Urban Renewal project, Denver, 1969, Pattonsburg New Town project, St. Louis, 1972; del. Aspen Design Conf. 1966. Sec., Cherry Creek Improvement Assn.; bd. dirs.

Greater Cherry Creek Steering Com., Capitol Hill United Neighborhoods; pres. Denver East Central Civic Assn. Served with USMCR, 1964-70. Recipient Indsl. Arts award Ford Found., 1960; traveling scholar to Gt. Britain, Colo. chpt. AIA, 1972. Mem. Phi Gamma Delta, Delta Phi Delta. Home: 2244 E 4th Ave Denver CO 80206 Office: 3320 E 2d Ave Denver CO 80206

FULLER, WILLIAM HOLTON, state senator, business executive; b. Sandpoint, Idaho, Dec. 28, 1913; s. William Eugene and Nellie (Holton) F.; divorced, 1976; children—Christopher M. Martin, Robin R., Eric D., Carol J. Fuller Schwab, Mark E., William Bruce. Student U. Puget Sound, 1931-32. Pres., mgr. Fuller Market Basket, Inc., Chehalis, Wash., 1971—; former mem. Wash. Ho. of Reps.; now mem. Wash. State Senate. Dir. Dist. 302 Sch. Bd., Chehalis, from 1975. Served with USNR, 1942-45. Mem. Chehalis Indsl. Commn. (dir.), C. of C. (pres.), Am. Legion. Republican. Club: Toastmasters (pres.). Home: 330 Brockway St Chehalis WA 98532 Office: Washington State Senate Olympia WA 98504*

FULLER, WILLIAM WADE, agronomist; b. San Angelo, Tex., May 24, 1931; s. Melbourne Wade and Mary May (Strong) F.; m. Gloria June Jones, June 7, 1952; children—Micheal Wade, William Kurt. B.A., U. Okla., 1954; M.S., Okla. State U., 1960, Ph.D., 1972. Cert. profl. agronomist. Soil conservationist, Okla., 1960-66; supt. Eastern Okla. Pasture Resources Sta., Okla. State U., Muskogee, 1966-70, grad. resources asst. dept. agronomy, Stillwater, 1970-72; asst. prof., forage agronomist Southeast Kans. Exptl. Sta., Kans. State U.-Mound Valley, 1972-74; environ. specialist watershed planning staff U.S. Dept. Agriculture Soil Conservation Service Claremore, Okla., 1974-80, state agronomist/plant materials specialist, Albuquerque, 1980—. Served to col. USAR, 1953-83. Recipient special achievement award, 1962. superior service award, 1965, cert. of merit, 1979, 1983 (all U.S. Dept. Agriculture Soil Conservation Service). Mem. Am. Soc. Agronomy, Crop Sci. Soc. Am., Soil Conservation Soc. Am., Res. Officers Assn. Republican. Methodist. Patentee experimental forage plot harvester, 1971; author numerous publs. Home: 6000 Unitas Lane NW Albuquerque NM 87114 Office: USDA-SCS Fed Bldg 6th & Gold PO Box 2007 Albuquerque NM 87103

FULLERTON, GAIL JACKSON, university president; b. Lincoln, Nebr., Apr. 29, 1927; d. Earl Warren and Gladys Bernice (Marshall) Jackson; m. Stanley Fullerton, Mar. 27, 1967; children by previous marriage—Gregory Putney, Cynde Putney. A.B., U. Nebr., 1949, A.M., 1950; Ph.D., U. Oreg., 1954. Lectr. sociology Drake U., Des Moines, 1955-57; asst. prof. Fla. State U., Tallahassee, 1957-60; prof. sociology San Jose (Calif.) State U., 1963-72, dean, 1972-76, exec. v.p., 1977-78, pres., 1978—. Bd. dirs. San Jose Symphony, 1979—, Associated Western Univs., Inc., 1981—; bd. govs. NCCJ of Santa Clara County, 1981—; trustee Nat. Commn. Coop. Edn., 1982—. Carnegie fellow, 1950-51; Doherty fellow, 1951-52. Mem. AAAS, Internat. Sociol. Assn., Am. Sociol. Assn., Western Coll. Assn. (v.p. 1980-82, pres. 1982—), Western Assn. Schs. and Colls. (sr. accrediting com. 1982—), San Jose C. of C. (dir. 1978—). Author: Survival in Marriage, 1972, 2d edit., 1977; (with others) The Adjusted American, 1964. Home: 226 Wave Crest Ave Santa Cruz CA 95060 Office: Office of Pres San Jose State U Washington Sq San Jose CA 95192

FULLING, KATHARINE PAINTER, educator, writer; b. Dodge City, Kans., Aug. 6; d. William George and Carrie (Lopp) Painter; B.A., Northwestern U., 1943; M.A., Columbia U., 1947; postgrad. Vassar Coll., 1948, San Marcos U., Lima, Peru, 1948-49, (fellow) Inst. Internat. Edn., U. Madrid, Spain, 1952-53; m. Virgil H. Fulling, Sept. 24, 1948. Asst. dir. Casa Panamericana, Mills Coll., 1944; asst. to dir. Fine Arts Dept., Columbia U., N.Y.C., 1945-47; tchr. public schs. Port Washington, L.I., N.Y., 1953-55; lectr. Global Edn., UN, N.Y.C., 1953-56; public relations dir. Nat. League Am. Pen Women, Washington, 1958-60, Non-Govtl. Orgns. rep. United Women of the Ams., UN, N.Y.C., 1959-62; lectr. Asia and Africa Halls, Smithsonian Inst., Washington, 1965-69; lectr. Folger Shakespeare Library, Washington, 1969-73; art reviewer Wyo., Denver Art Mus., 1974—. Mem. Wyo. Council for Humanities, 1979-80. Mem. Asia Soc., Inter-Am. Center, AAUW, Nat. League Am. Pen Women, LWV (pres. 1967-69), Mark Twain Soc. (hon. mem.), Sigma Alpha Iota. Author: The Cradle of American Art, 1948; Mantillas and Silver Spurs, 1952; contbr., columnist numerous jours. and mags.

FULLMER, DANIEL WARREN, educator; b. Spoon River, Ill., Dec. 12, 1922; s. Daniel Floyd and Sarah Louisa (Essex) F.; B.S., Western Ill. U., 1947, M.S., 1952; Ph.D., U. Denver, 1955; m. Janet Saito, June 1980; children—Daniel William, Mark Warren. Mem. faculty U. Oreg., 1955-66; prof. psychology Oreg. System of Higher Edn., 1958-66; faculty dept. edn. U. Hawaii, Honolulu, 1966—, now prof.; pvt. practice psychol. counseling, Honolulu, 1974—. Served with USNR, 1944-46. Mem. Am. Psychol. Assn., Am. Personnel and Guidance Assn. Methodist. Office: 1750 Kalakaua Ave Suite 809 Honolulu HI 96826

FULTON, ALFRED MILLER, physician; b. Coraopolis, Pa., Sept. 29, 1914; s. Alfred Miller and Lua Matilda (Bane) F.; B.A., Carleton Coll., 1936; M.B., U. Minn., 1940, M.D., 1941; m. Ruth Florence Rossman, Mar. 18, 1941; children—Martha Fulton Murphy, Victoria Fulton Blackford, Keith Fulton Warne, Angus Bane. Intern, Trinity Hosp., Minot, N.D., 1940-41; resident in internal medicine Northwest Clinic, Minot, 1941-42; fellow in internal medicine Lahey Clinic, Boston, 1947-48; internist Billings (Mont.) Clinic, 1948-78; mem. staff Billings Deaconess, St. Vincent's Hosps. (both Billings); dir. Security Bank, N.A., Billings. Trustee, Billings Deaconess Hosp., 1980—. Served to capt. M.C., USAAF, 1942-46. Diplomate Am. Bd. Internal Medicine. Fellow A.C.P.; mem. Mont. Med. Assn. (pres. 1967-68, med. adv. 1979), Mont Found. for Med. Care (v.p. 1975—), Billings C. of C. (pres. 1966-67), U.S. C. of C. (dir. 1971-76), Am. Soc. Internal Medicine, AMA. Republican. Home: 3120 W MacDonald Dr Billings MT 59102 Office: Box 2555 Billings MT 59103

FULTON, DOROTHEA LEA, banker; b. Los Angeles, Apr. 6, 1921; d. William Clarence and Theodora Jane (Peck) Lea; student U. of Redlands, 1942; m. James S. Fulton, Aug. 9, 1941; children—Charles Thomas, William Howard, David Edwin. With So. Calif. Gas Co., 1941-43; right-of-way agent Coachella div. All-Am. Canal, Colorado River project Bur. of Reclamation, U.S. Govt., 1951-54; escrow clerk Bank of Am., Indio, Calif., 1954-56, escrow officer, 1956-73, loan officer, Lake Arrowhead, Calif., 1973-74, mgr. office Running Springs, Calif., 1974-77, sr. escrow officer Big Bear Lake, Calif., 1977-82; instr. Coll. of the Desert, 1965-73, San Bernardino Valley Coll., 1978—; treas. Strawberry Flats Land Exchange Corp., 1962-70; treas. Strawberry Flats Owner's Assn., 1970-76, dir., 1979—. Chmn., Running Springs Area Winterfest, 1975; youth dir. First Bapt. Ch., Thermal, Calif., 1958-71, youth dir. Desert Assn., 1971-73; dir. music Twin Peaks Community Ch., 1974—. Cert. sr. escrow officer. Mem. Riverside County, Desert, San Bernardino County, High Desert, Calif. State escrow assns., Nat. Assn. Bank Women, Running Springs Area C. of C. (Citizen of the Yr. 1974-75, chamber pres. 1975-76), Running Springs Woman's Club (Woman of Yr. 1976). Clubs: Am. Field Service, Worthwhile of Twin Peaks.

FULTON, LEN, publisher; b. Lowell, Mass., May 15, 1934; s. Claude E. and Louise E. (Vaillant) F.; A.A., U. Maine, 1957; B.A., U. Wyo., 1961; postgrad. U. Calif.-Berkeley, 1961-63; 1 son, Timothy. Pub., Tourist Topic, Kennebunkport, Me., Weekly News, Freeport, Maine, 1957-59; biostatistician Calif. Dept. Public Health, Berkeley, 1962-68; editor, pub. Dustbooks, Paradise, Calif., 1963—; chmn. Com. of Small Mag. Editors and Pubs., 1968-71, 73; cons. small presses ALA; mem. lit. adv. panel Nat. Endowment Arts, 1976. Calif. Arts Commn. panelist, 1975; bd. dirs. Paradise Irrigation Dist., 1979-82, chmn., 1981; supr. 5th Supervisional Dist., Butte County, Calif., 1982—; mem. Butte County Arts Commn., 1982—. Served with AUS, 1953-55. NEA grantee, 1959-61; coordinating Council Lit. Mags. grantee, 1970-73; Nat. Endowment for Arts grantee, 1974, 75. Mem. PEN. Author: The Grassman, 1974; Dark Other Adam Dreaming, 1975; (with Ellen Ferber) American Odyssey, 1975. Home: PO Box 1056 Paradise CA 95969

FULTON, NORMAN ROBERT, home entertainment co. exec.; b. Los Angeles, Dec. 16, 1935; s. Robert John and Fritzi Marie (Wacker) F.; A.A., Santa Monica Coll., 1958; B.S., U. So. Calif., 1960; m. Nancy Butler, July 6, 1966; children—Robert B., Patricia M. Asst. v.p. Raphael Glass Co., Los Angeles, 1960-65; credit adminstr. Zellerbach Paper Co., Los Angeles, 1966-68; gen. credit mgr. Carrier Transicold Co., Montebello, Calif., 1968-70, Virco Mfg. Co., Los Angeles, 1970-72, Superscope, Inc., Chatsworth, Calif., 1972-79; asst. v.p. credit and adminstrn. Inkel Corp., Carson, Calif., 1980-82; corp. credit mgr. Gen. Consumer Electronics, Santa Monica, Calif., 1982—. Served with AUS, 1955-57. Fellow Nat. Inst. Credit; mem. Credit Mgrs. So. Calif., Nat. Notary Assn. Home: 24609 Plover Way Malibu CA 90265

FULTON, THOMAS DARNALL, social services administrator; b. Denver, Mar. 4, 1948; s. Robert Carroll and Helen (Lahey) F.; B.A., DePauw U., 1971; M.A., Calif. State U.-Fresno, 1976. Evaluations asst. Fresno County Mental Health Dept. (Calif.), 1975; VISTA vol., Fresno and Concord, Calif., 1976-78; adminstrv. dir. No. Calif. Family Ctr. Walnut Creek, 1978—; researcher on family systems. Mem. Children's and Adolescents' Task Force, Contra Costa Mental Health Dept. L.J. and Mary C. Skaggs Found. grantee, 1981. Mem. Am. Psychol. Assn., Contra Costa Childrens' Coalition. Home: 2118 Ramona Dr Pleasant Hill CA 94523 Office: No Calif Family Center 1621 N Broadway Walnut Creek CA 94596

FULWOOD, WILMA DARLENE, curriculum and instruction adminstr.; b. Portsmouth, Ohio, June 22, 1935; d. Elbert Victor and Vergie Belle (Fraley) Barker; m. Hilliard Wesley Fulwood, Aug. 17, 1957; children—Robert Dean, Deena Marie, Kimberli Lynn, Timothy Wesley. B.S. in Edn., Olivet Nazarene Coll., 1957; M.A.T., Oakland U., 1968. Cert. adminstr., Idaho. Classroom, reading tchr. various schs., 1960-72; prof. dept. edn. Northwest Nazarene Coll., Nampa, Idaho, 1972-73; curriculum assoc. Dist. 4J, Eugene, Oreg., 1973-75; kindergarten dir., summer migrant program dir. Dist. 131, Nampa, 1975-78, elem. prin., 1978-82, dir. curriculum and instruction, 1982—; cons. tchrs., adminstrs., tchr. staff supervision. Active ch. Recipient Internat. Reading Assn. Commendation award Phi Delta Lambda. Mem. Assn. Supervision and Curriculum Devel., Idaho Assn. Elem. Sch. Prins. Nat. Assn. Elem. Sch. Prins., Internat. Reading Assn., Valley Reading Council, Nat. Council Tchrs. English, Nampa C. of C. (mem. edn. com.), Phi Delta Kappa. Protestant-Nazarene. Club: Soroptimists. Home: 4519 Lake Ridge Rd Nampa ID 83651 Office: School District 131 619 S Canyon St Nampa ID 83651

FUNABIKI, DEAN, psychologist; b. San Jose, Calif., Jan. 14, 1951; s. Mason and Grace (Okagaki) F.; m. Ruth Patterson, Aug. 25, 1977. A.B., Stanford U., 1973; Ph.D., SUNY-Stony Brook, 1977. Lic. clin. psychologist, Calif. Psychology intern Palo Alto VA Med. Ctr., Calif., 1977; asst. prof. psychology and basic med. sci., Wash. State U., Pullman, 1977-82; clin. psychologist, Edward A. Dreyfus, Ph.D. and Assocs., Santa Monica, Calif., 1982—, dir. psychol. services Gateways Hosp., Los Angeles, 1982—. Mem. Am. Psychol. Assn., Soc. Behavioral Medicine, Assn. Advancement Behavior Therapy, Western Psychol. Assn., Sigma Xi. Contbr. articles to sci. publs. Office: 1421 Santa Monica CA 90401

FUNASAKI, GARY ISAMU, elec. engr.; b. Kahuku, Hawaii, Dec. 13, 1950; s. Makoto and Judy Kimiko (Wakumoto) F.; B.S., U. Hawaii, 1972. Elec. engr. Nakamura, Kawahata & Assocs., Honolulu, 1973-78; elec. engr. fed. govt., Pearl Harbor, Hawaii, 1978-79; v.p. Ronald N.S. Ho & Assocs., Inc., Honolulu, 1979—. Fedn. asst. treas. Young Buddhist Assn., 1978—, state councillor, 1978—. Named outstanding teenage boy State of Hawaii, 1968; registered profl. engr. Mem. Eta Kappa Nu. Office: 1251 S King St Suite B Honolulu HI 96814

FUNFSTUCK, HORST, instrument co. exec.; b. Hamburg, West Germany, May 28, 1930; s. Albert and Erna Louise (Kuhl) F.; state diploma Molln Tech. Sch., 1951; diploma in engring. Escuelas Int de Bogota (Colombia), 1956; postgrad. U. Calif. at Los Angeles, intermittently 1958-70; m. Margot Parbs, Sept. 24, 1955; 1 son, Albert. Prof. electronics U. Bogota (Colombia), 1955-56; lectr. electronics and physics Naval Acad., Cartagena, Colombia, 1956-58; project coordinator Magnetic Research Corp., Hawthorne, Calif., 1959-62; sr. research and devel. project engr. Statham Instruments, Inc., Oxnard, 1962, chief engr., med., 1964-71, dir. operations, 1971-73; v.p. engring. and mfg. Pacesetter Systems, Inc., Sylmar, Calif., 1973-74; sr. group v.p. Optical Radiation Corp., Azusa, Calif., 1974—. Mem. Fernsehtechnische Gesellschaft (founding mem.), Internat. Inst. Med. and Biol. Engring., Assn. Advancement Med. Instrumentation, I.E.E.E., Am. Mgmt. Assn. Contbr. articles to profl. jours. Patentee in field. Home: 408 Valley Vista Dr PO Camarillo CA 93010 Office: 6352 N Irwindale Ave Azusa CA 91702

FUNK, ALBERT GAIL, chemist; b. Sterling, Utah, Feb. 18, 1925; s. Charles Buckley and Emily Sarah (Johnson) F.; student Snow Coll., 1949-50; B.S., Brigham Young U., 1952; Ph.D., U. Utah, 1957, postgrad. (fellow), 1957-58; m. Arla Wangsgard, Aug. 15, 1963; children—Christine, David Richard, Matthew John, Michael Paul. Research scientist Thiokol Chem. Corp., Brigham City, Utah, 1958-59; asst. research prof. U. Utah, 1959-64; research scientist IRECO Chems., Salt Lake City, 1964-68, asst. research and devel. dir., 1968-71, dir. research and devel., 1971-80, dir. research and product devel., 1980-81, asst. v.p. research and devel., 1981—; prin. investigator Cook Assos., Salt Lake City, 1974—. Del., Republican Nat. Conv., 1964, Rep. State Conv., 1964, 78, 80. Served with U.S. Army, 1945-47. Mem. Soc. Explosives Engrs., Nat. Def. Preparedness Assn., Sigma Xi. Mormon. Patentee in field. Home: 1265 E 1 S Salt Lake City UT 84102 Office: 3000 W 8600 S West Jordan UT 84084

FUNK, BILLY LEE, educator; b. Worthington, Mo., Sept. 27, 1927; s. Ralph W. and Dorothy O. (Lewis) F.; m. Jacqueline Carr, Nov. 25, 1948; children—David, Dale. B.A., Western State Coll., 1950, M.A., 1956, Ed.S., 1961; Ph.D., Walden U., 1973. Elem. and jr. high prin., Pagosa Springs, Colo., 1956-58; dir. instrn. Moffat County Schs., Craig, Colo., 1958-66, Colo. Edn. Assn., 1967-68; elem. prin., Boulder, Colo., 1968-69, Littleton (Colo.) Pub. Schs., 1969—. Served with U.S. Army, 1946-47. Mem. Nat. Assn. Elem. Sch. Prins., Assn. Supervision and Curriculum Devel., Colo. Assn. Sch. Execs., Phi Delta Kappa. Democrat. Unitarian. Home: 6671 S Cherokee St Littleton CO 80120 Office: 7455 S Elati St Littleton CO 80120

FUNK, KAARON WAHLBERG, psychotherapist; b. San Francisco, Sept. 12, 1949; d. Richard and Mary Ruth (Seamon) W.; m. Michael Harold Funk, Feb. 28, 1982; 1 son, Hal. B.A. in English Lit., Wellesley Coll., 1971; M.Ed. in Sch. Psychology, Boston U., 1972; Ph.D. U. Ariz., 1982. Dir. Indian Affirmative Action Program, Civil Rights Div., Dept. Law, State of Ariz., 1972-74, psychology assoc., Dept. Corrections, 1974-78; staff therapist Terros Inc., Phoenix, 1979; dir. Dove of Peace Counseling Ctr., 1982—. Mem. Am. Personnel and Guidance Assn. Lutheran. Contbr. articles to profl. jours.

FUNK, MILTON ALBERT, real estate broker; b. Cantonement, Okla., Oct. 12, 1918; s. John Anton and Cornelia Elizabeth (Schwake) F.; certificate in real estate U. Calif. at Los Angeles, 1960; m. Earline Myrtle Burkholder, Feb. 15, 1937; children—DeAnne (Mrs. Nickolas Kiralla), Gary Milton. Owner, Realty Sales & Exchange Co., South Gate, Calif., 1961—; sec.-treas. Apt. Investments, Inc., South Gate, 1961—; dir. Apple Valley View Water Assn. Mem. redevel. agy. com. City of South Gate, 1974-79. Served with arty. AUS, 1944-46; PTO. Mem. Calif. Assn. Realtors (regional v.p. 1969, dir.), S.E. Bd. Realtors (pres. 1966, dir. 1980), Los Angeles County Apt. Assn. (dir., sec.), Laguna Shores Owners Assn. (pres.), V.F.W., Downey, South Gate chambers commerce. Home: 11714 Bellflower Blvd Downey CA 90242 Office: 3947 Tweedy Blvd South Gate CA 90280

FUNK, WILLIAM HENRY, ecology educator; b. Ephraim, Utah, June 10, 1933; s. William George and Henrietta (Hackwell) F.; B.S. in Biol. Sci., U. Utah, 1955, M.S. in Zoology, 1963, Ph.D. in Zoology (USPHS trainee), 1966; m. Ruth Sherry Mellor, Sept. 19, 1964; 1 dau., Cynthia Lynn. Tchr. sci., math. Salt Lake City schs., 1957-60; research asst. U. Utah, Salt Lake City, 1961-63; head sci. dept. N.W. Jr. High Sch., Salt Lake City, 1961-63; mem. faculty Wash. State U., Pullman, 1966—, assoc. prof. civil engring., 1971-75, prof., 1975—, chmn. environ. sci. program, 1979-81, dir. Environ. Research Center, 1980-83; dir. State of Wash. Water Research Ctr., 1981—; cons. Harstad Engrs., Seattle, 1971-72, Boise Cascade Corp., Seattle, 1971-72, U.S. Army Corps Engrs., Walla Walla, Wash., 1970-74, ORB Corp., Renton, Wash., 1972-73, State Wash. Dept. Ecology, Olympia, 1971-72, U.S. Civil Service, Seattle and Chgo., 1972—. Served with USNR, 1955-57. NSF Summer Inst. grantee, 1961, Office Water Resources Research grantee, 1971-72, 73-76; EPA grantee, 1980-83. Mem. Naval Res. Officers Assn. (chpt. pres. 1969), Res. Officers Assn. (U.S. Naval Acad. info. officer 1973-76), Pacific N.W. Pollution Control Assn. (editor 1969-77), Water Pollution Control Fedn. (Arthur S. Bedell award Pacific N.W. Assn. 1976, nat. dir. 1978-81), Am. Soc. Limnology and Oceanography, Am. Microscopical Soc., Northwest Sci. Assn., Sigma Xi, Phi Sigma. Author publs. on water pollution control and lake restoration. Home: SW 330 Kimball Ct Pullman WA 99163

FUNKHOUSER, ROBERT BRANE, advertising executive; b. Hagerstown, Md., Oct. 25, 1926; s. Elmer Newton and Nellie Evelyn (Spielman) F.; m. Margaret Ann Crissman; children—Lisë K., Robert B. Jr., Kristen N. B.A., Dartmouth Coll., 1950. Asst. account exec. McCann-Erikson, N.Y.C., 1951-52; account exec. Ketchum, MacLeod & Grove, Inc., Pitts., 1953-57; v.p., account supr. Batten Barton Durstine & Osborn, Pitts., 1957-70, v.p., regional mgr., Los Angeles, 1970-74; v.p. advt. and pub. relations Carnation Co., Los Angeles, 1974—; instr. account mgmt. Inst. Advanced Advt. Studies, Los Angeles. Bd. dirs. Los Angeles chpt. ARC. Served with AC, U.S. Army, 1945-46. Mem. Am. Advt. Fedn. (dir., Bell Ringer award 1983), Ad Council, Assn. Nat. Advertisers, Nat. Advt. Rev. Bd., Advt. Edn. Found., Audit Bur. of Circulations. Republican. Presbyterian. Club: Los Angeles Country. Home: 2346 Mandeville Canyon Rd Los Angeles CA 90049 Office: 5045 Wilshire Blvd Los Angeles CA 90036

FUOG, RENE MAX, environ. engr.; b. Zurich, Switzerland, Apr. 28, 1942; came to U.S., 1965; s. Max A. and Greti (Schurch) F.; civil engring. draftsman, trade sch., Zurich, 1961, B.S. in Civil Engring., Tech. Coll., Winterthur, Switzerland, 1965. Jr. engr., then engr. Somer, Zurich, 1965; asst. engr. Gibbs & Hill, N.Y.C., 1966-68; project engr. Metcalf & Eddy, Palo Alto, Calif., 1968-78; project mgr. Creegan & D'Angelo, San Jose, Calif., 1978—, head environ. dept., 1978—, mgr. Lake Tahoe (Nev.) Office, 1981—. Served with Swiss Army, 1963-65. Registered profl. engr., Calif., Nev.; registered engr., Switzerland. Mem. ASCE, Am. Soils Conservation Service, Calif. Water Pollution Control Fedn. Office: Creegan & D'Angelo 1046 W Taylor St San Jose CA 95126

FUREDY, JOHN PETER, insurance company executive; b. Yugoslavia, May 2, 1910; came to U.S., 1941, naturalized, 1943; s. Jaco and Jenny (Schrank) F.; student Pazmany Peter U., Budapest, 1929-30; grad. Life Ins. Agts. Mgmt. Assn. Sch. Mgmt., 1955; m. Lila Anne Moore, Mar. 31, 1978. Vice pres., dir. life agys. Beneficial Standard Life Ins. Co., Los Angeles, 1950-58; pres., chmn. bd. Nat. Security Ins. Agy., Inc., Los Angeles, 1958—; pres. T.W.A. Ins. Agy., Los Angeles, 1979—. Served with U.S. Army, 1943. Mem. Life Ins. Agts. Mgmt. Assn. (research com., ins. co. com.), Gen. Agts. Mgmt. Corp. (charter), Life Underwriters Assn., Fgn. Affairs Council. Club: TownHouse. Home: 8364 Mulholland Dr Los Angeles CA 90046 Office: 3660 Wilshire Blvd Penthouse E Los Angeles CA 90010

FURGURSON, L. CLIF, JR., advertising executive; b. High Point, N.C., Oct. 5, 1921; s. L. C. and Lillie (Leonard) F.; m. Katherine McGuire Williams, Aug. 11, 1945; children—Jill E., Kip, James. B.A. in Journalism and Advt., Fresno, (Calif.) State Coll., 1948. With McClatchy Newspapers, Fresno, 1945-53; pres. Clif Furgurson Advt., 1953—; chmn. bd. Hume Printing, Fresno, 1960—. Served with USAAF, 1942-45. Republican. Home: 2133 W Alluvial Fresno CA 93711 Office: 700 Van Ness Fresno CA 93721

FURIA, THOMAS EDWARD, chemist; b. N.Y.C., May 5, 1934; s. Andrea and Francesca (Taussi) F.; B.S., N.Y.U., 1956; m. Olga M. Pollono, July 28, 1956; children—Andrew, Lawrence, Marie. Tech. mgr. Ciba-Geigy, Ardsley, N.Y., 1956-73; dir. food scis., dir. comml. devel. Dynapol, Palo Alto, Calif., 1973-80; sr. cons. SRI Internat., 1980—; pres. Intechmark Corp., N.Y.C., 1972—; pub. Food Ingredient Directory, 1968—; dir. CFS Corp. Served with U.S. Army, 1956-58. Recipient Bausch and Lomb chemistry award, 1952. Mem. N.Y. Acad. Scis., Am. Oil Chemists' Soc. (Bond award 1975, 76), Am. Chem. Soc., AAAS, Inst. Food Technologists, Am. Soc. Enologists, Am. Soc. Microbiologists, Alpha Phi Delta, Phi Tau Alpha. Author/editor: Handbook Food Additives, 1968—, Handbook Flavor Ingredients, 1970—, Critical Rev. in Food Sci. and Nutrition, 1973—; ; Current Aspects of Food Colorants, 1977, Regulatory Status of Direct Food Additives, 1980—; contbr. to sci. publs. on antimicrobial agts., sequestrants and polymeric food additives; patentee antimicrobial agts., biotech., bioengring., food and agrl. industries, sequestrants, dyes and antioxidants. Office: PO Box 11201 Palo Alto CA 94306

FURLEY, NANCY LYNN, data processing trainer; b. Texas City, Tex., July 26, 1954; d. Willard Russell and Carol Lee (Glasser) Furley. B.A. in Psychology, U. Tex., 1975. Cert. social worker, Tex. Computer operator Geotronics, Austin, Tex., 1978-79; dir. service bur., trainer AIS Data Systems, Austin, 1979-80; data processing trainer western div. Times Mirror Cable TV, Laguna Niguel, Calif., 1980-83, Cable Data, Sacramento, 1983—. Mem. Am. Soc. Tng. and Devel. Home: 6347 Nachez Way Sacramento CA 95610 Office: 11020 Sun Center Sacramento CA 95670

FURLONG, ALEXANDRA DABOVICH, psychologist; b. Chgo., Oct. 19, 1947; d. Thomas Christopher and Natalie Shaw (Holmes) Dabovich; B.A., U. Mich., 1968; M.A., U. Iowa., 1972, Ph.D., 1980; m. Robert McCann Furlong, Jan. 3, 1970; children—Michael, Timothy, Paul.

Reporter, writer City News Bur., Chgo., 1968-70; reporter Rock Island (Ill.) Argus, 1970; tchr., coordinator autism program Child Psychiatry Service, U. Iowa, 1973-79; psychologist youth and family services unit West Yavapai Guidance Clinic, Prescott, Ariz., 1979—. Mem. Am. Psychol. Assn. Address: 507 Frederick Prescott AZ 86301

FURLOW, WILLIAM LAWRENCE, mfg. co. exec.; b. Castroville, Tex., July 19, 1944; s. William E. and Mary Ellen Griffin F.; student U. Ky., 1962-64; 1 son, Christopher Randolf. With Voi-Shan Mfg. Co., Culver City, Calif., 1965-68; materials coordinator Hughes Aircraft, Culver City, 1969-70; with Everest and Jennings, Inc., Los Angeles, 1970-72; supr. Audio Magnetics Corp., Compton, Calif., 1973-74; supr. Am. Safety Corp., Pacoima, Calif., 1975-76; buyer Perma-Bilt Industries, Torrance, Calif., 1976-78; gen. mgr. Cweco & Saferall, Inc., Gardena, Calif., 1979-82, Excelco, Redondo Beach, Calif., 1983—. Republican. Methodist. Office: 305 N Broadway 7 Redondo Beach CA 90277

FURMAN, DEANE PHILIP, parasitologist; b. Richardton, N.D., June 4, 1915; s. Raymond Walter and Estelle Mae (O'Harrow) F.; B.S., U. Calif.-Berkeley, 1937; Ph.D., U. Calif.-Davis, 1942; m. Katherine McKeehan, Dec. 17, 1938; children—Philip Deane, Bryan Dale, Lynne Anne Furman Ladwig. Entomologist, USPHS, 1946; mem. faculty U. Calif.-Berkeley, 1946—, prof. parasitology, 1960-82, entomologist, 1960-82, emeritus prof. parasitology and entomologist, 1982—, chmn. div. parasitology, 1963-72, chmn. div. entomology and parasitology, 1973-75, chmn. interdisciplinary grad. group parasitology, 1969-82; mem. fellowship rev. panel NIH, 1963-66; trustee Alameda County Mosquito Abatement Dist., 1961-64. Served to maj. AUS, 1942-46. Decorated Bronze Star; NIH spl. fellow, 1964-65. Fellow AAAS; mem. Entomol. Soc. Am., Am. Soc. Parasitologists, Am. Soc. Tropical Medicine and Hygiene, Wildlife Disease Assn., Acarological Soc. Am. (chmn. 1962-63), N. Calif. Parasitologists Assn. (pres. 1973-74), Pacific Coast Entomol. Soc. Author manuals, papers in field, chpts. in books; mem. editorial bds. profl. jours. Home: 235 Lake Dr Berkeley CA 94708 Office: Dept Entomology Univ Calif Berkeley CA 94720

FURMAN, ERIC BERTRAM, pediatric anesthesiologist; b. Johannesburg, South Africa, Nov. 27, 1934; came to U.S., 1965, naturalized, 1976; s. Solomon and Milly (Dinkin) F.; M.B., B.Ch., U. Witwatersrand, Johannesburg, 1958; m. June Elizabeth Abrams, Dec. 16, 1958; children—Terrence, Joanne Peta, Nicola Millicent. Intern in family practice, resident in anesthesiology U. Witwatersrand Hosps., Johannesburg, 1964; fellow in pediatric anesthesia Hosp. Sick Children, Toronto, 1965; fellow in anesthesiology, then instr. U. Vt. Hosps., 1965-68; dir. pediatric anesthesia Mass. Gen. Hosp., Boston, instr. anesthesia Harvard U. Med. Sch., Boston, 1968-71; prin. anesthesist Children's Hosp., Johannesburg, 1972-74; dir. anesthesia Children's Orthopedic Hosp. and Med. Center, Seattle, clin. asso. prof. anesthesia and pediatrics U. Wash. Med. Sch., Seattle, 1974—. Trustee, Bush Sch., Seattle, 1977—, v.p., 1978. Recipient African Oxygen Gold medal in anesthesia, 1963. Mem. Am. Soc. Anesthesiologists (chmn. com. pediatric practice 1978-81), Am. Acad. Pediatrics (chmn. sect. anesthesia 1980—), AMA, Wash. Med. Soc., Wash. Soc. Anesthesiologists. Jewish. Author articles in field; editor: International Anesthesia Clinics, 1975. Home: 4416 54th St NE Seattle WA 98105 Office: Children's Orthopedic Hosp and Med Center Seattle WA 98105

FURMAN, EVELYN E. LIVINGSTON, retail executive; b. Albert Lea, Minn., Apr. 17, 1913; s. Henry Clarence and Florence Eliza (Ayars) Livingston; student Milton (Wis.) Coll., 1932-33, U. Colo., 1960; m. Gordon Howard Furman, Apr. 8, 1934 (div.); 1 dau., Sharon P. Furman Martin. Owner, operator Furman's Store, Leadville, Colo., 1937—; owner, mgr. Evelyn E. Furman Mining Co., 1967—, Evelyn E. Furman Rentals, 1945—; tour guide Tabor Opera House Museum, Leadville, 1955-65, mgr., operator, tour guide, 1965—. Mem. Nat. Writers Club, Cloud City Garden Club (past pres.), Leadville C. of C., St. Andrews Soc. Colo. Clubs: Bus. and Profl. Women's (past pres.) (Leadville), Order of Eagles (past pres. Leadville aux.). Author: Leadville Crystal Carnival 1896, 1962; Tabor Opera House, A Captivating History, 1972; Silver Dollar Tabor, 1982. Address: 815 Harrison Ave Leadville CO 80461

FURNIVAL, GEORGE MITCHELL, petroleum and mining consultant; b. Winnipeg, Man., Can., July 25, 1908; s. William George and Grace Una (Rothwell) F.; B.Sc., U. Man., 1929; M.A., Queens U., 1933; Ph.D., MIT, 1935; m. Marion Marguerite Fraser, Mar. 8, 1937; children—William George, Sharon (Mrs. John M. Roscoe), Patricia M., Bruce A. Field geologist in Man., Ont., N.W.T., and Que., 1928-36; asst. mine supt. Cline Lake Gold Mines, Ltd., 1936-39; geologist Geol. Survey Can., No. and Southwestern Sask., 1939-42; sr. geologist Standard Oil Co. of Calif. (Chevron Standard, Ltd.), Calgary, Alta., 1942-44, asst. to chief geologist, 1944-45, field supt. So. Alta., 1945-46, mgr. land and legal dept., 1948-50, v.p. land and legal, dir., 1950-52, v.p. legal, crude oil sales, govt. relations, dir., 1952-55; dir. mines Dept. Mines and Natural Resources, Man., 1946-48; pres., dir. Dominion Oil, Ltd., Trinidad and Tobago, 1952-60; v.p. exploration, dir. Calif. Exploration Co. (Chevron Overseas Petroleum, Inc.), San Francisco, 1955-63; staff asst. land to v.p. exploration and land Standard Oil Co. of Calif., 1961-63; chmn. bd., mng. dir. West Australian Petroleum Pty., Ltd., Perth, 1963-70; v.p., dir. Newport Ventures, Ltd., Calgary, 1971-72; v.p. ops., dir., mem. exec. com. Brascan Resources, Ltd., Calgary, 1973-75, sr. v.p., dir., 1975-77, sr. cons., 1977-78; pres., chief exec. officer, dir. Western Mines Ltd., 1978-80, exec. v.p., gen. mgr. mining div. Westmin Resources Ltd., also dir., mem. exec. com., 1981-82; dir. Western Mines Inc., 1978-82; pres., acting gen. mgr. Coalition Mining, Ltd.; petroleum and mining cons., 1982—; pres., dir. Lathwell Resources Ltd., 1983—; dir. Cretaceous Pipe Line Co., Ltd., Austen & Butta Pty., Ltd., Western Coal Holdings, Inc.; del. Interprovincial Mines Ministers Conf., several years; sec. Winnipeg Conf., 1947. Elected to Order of Can., 1982. Fellow Royal Soc. Can., Geol. Soc. Am., Geol. Soc. Can.; mem. Am. Assn. Petroleum Geologists, Engring. Inst. Can. (hon. life), Canadian Inst. Mining and Metallurgy (hon. life mem., past br. chmn., dist. councillor, v.p., Distinguished Service award 1974, Selwyn G. Blaylock gold medal 1979), Australian Petroleum Exploration Assn. (hon. life mem., chmn. com. West Australian petroleum legislation, councillor, state chmn. for Western Australia), Australian Am. Assn. in Western Australia (councillor), Australian Geol. Soc., Soc. Econ. Geologists. Clubs: Calgary Golf and Country, Calgary Petroleum, Ranchmen's. Contbr. sci. articles to profl. jours. Home: 1315 Baldwin Crescent SW Calgary AB T2V 2B7 Canada

FURR, COLEMAN, coll. adminstr.; b. Lincoln, Nebr., Feb. 22, 1925; s. Archie and Mattie (Houghton) F.; B.S., U. Nebr., 1950; m. Lois Stewart, July, 1952; children—Jean Elizabeth, Lisa Martin, Kevin Clark, Colette Marie, Martina. Buyer, Archie Furr Co., Lincoln, 1946-51; dir. ops. S&W Foods, San Francisco, 1951-59; computer cons. Govt. of P.R., 1959-61; pres. Union Distbg. Co., San Diego, 1961-62; founder, pres. Coleman Coll., San Diego, 1963—. Served with AUS, 1943-46. Mem. Assn. Ind. Colls. and Schs. (chmn. accrediting commn. 1977), Inst. Certification Computer Profls. (founder), Data Processing Mgmt. Assn., Automation I Assn. Republican. Unitarian. Home: 6014 Sierra View Way San Diego CA 92120 Office: 2384 San Diego Ave San Diego CA 92110

FURST, EMANUEL F., biomedical engineer; b. N.Y.C., Jan. 25, 1942; s. Alexander and Jennie I. (Obletz) F.; m. Miriam F., June 30, 1963; children—Bety Robyn, Jonathan Paul. B.E.E., Clarkson Coll., 1962; M.S.E.E., Columbia U., 1963; Ph.D. (NIH predoctoral fellow), Worcester Poly. Inst., 1969. Registered profl. engr., cert. clin. engr., Ariz. Asst. prof. electronic engring. Calif. State Poly. U., San Luis Obispo, 1963-66; devel. engr. Electronics Research Labs., Hewlett Packard, Palo Alto, Calif., 1969-72; asst. prof. elec. engring. U. Ariz., Tucson, 1972-77; dir. biomed. engring. Ariz. Health Scis. Ctr., U. Ariz., Tucson, 1972—; cons. med. instrumentation. W.K. Kellogg found. grantee, 1974. Mem. Assn. Advancement Med. Instrumentation (dir.), IEEE, Am. Soc. Hosp. Engrs. Editorial bd. IEEE Trans. Biomed. Engring.; contbr. articles profl. jours. Office: 1501 N Campbell Ave Tucson AZ 85724

FURTH, ALAN COWAN, business executive, lawyer; b. Oakland, Calif., Sept. 16, 1922; s. Victor L. and Valance (Cowan) F.; A.B., U. Calif. at Berkeley, 1944, LL.B., 1949; grad. Advanced Mgmt. Program, Harvard U., 1959; m. Virginia Robinson, Aug. 18, 1946; children—Andrew Robinson, Alison Anne. Admitted to Calif. bar, U.S. Supreme Ct. bar; with S.P. Co., 1950—, gen. counsel, from 1963, v.p., 1966, exec. v.p. law, 1976-79, pres., 1979—, also dir. and mem. exec. com.; dir., mem. exec. com. So. Pacific Transp. Co., St. Louis Southwestern Ry. Co.; chmn., chief exec. officer So. Pacific Communications Co., from 1981; dir. So. Pacific Land Co., Indsl. Indemnity Co., Ticor, Fed. Res. Bank of San Francisco. Trustee, Pomona Coll., Claremont, Calif., Merritt Hosp., Oakland, Calif.; trustee Pacific Legal Found., The Anna Head Sch.; bd. dirs. U. Calif. at Berkeley Found. Served to capt. USMCR, 1944-46, 51-52. Mem. Am. Bar Assn., Calif. State Bar Assn. Clubs: Bohemian, Pacific-Union, San Francisco Golf (San Francisco); Met., Burning Tree (Washington). Office: So Pacific Co One Market Plaza San Francisco CA 94105

FURU, KAREN LEE, nurse, counselor; b. Ft. Riley, Kans., May 3, 1950; d. Jack Alvin and Mabel Lee (Zirk) Stanturf; m. Robert Llaird Furu, June 30, 1971; children—Robert B., Sandra R. Student Idaho State U., 1968-70, U. Idaho, 1970; grad. Walter Reed Army Inst. Nursing, 1972; B.S.N., U. Md., 1972; M.Ed. in Counseling and Guidance, Mont. State U., 1981, postgrad., 1981-82. R.N., Idaho, 1972, Mont., 1973. Chief nurse U.S. Army Res. 396th Sta. Hosp., Helena, Mont., 1973—; asst. dir. nursing Hillcrest Retirement Ctr., Bozeman, Mont., 1974-77; staff nurse, team leader/supr. Bozeman Deaconess Hosp., 1977—; tchr., cons. Mont. Law Enforcement Acad., Bozeman. Den leader Cub Scouts, Boy Scouts Am., 1981. Served in U.S. Army, 1968-72, with Army Nurse Corps, 1972-73; to maj. USAR, 1973—. Decorated Army Commendation medal. Mem. Am. Nurses Assn., Mont. Nurses Assn., Res. Officers Assn., Mil. Surgeons U.S., Am. Personnel and Guidance Assn., Mont. Personnel and Guidance Assn., Pub. Offenders Counselors Assn., Alpha Omicron Pi (pres.; honored alumnus 1982). Democrat. Presbyterian. Clubs: United Presbyterian Women, Order Eastern Star. Home: 1145 S Cedarview Ave Bozeman MT 59715 Office: 396th Sta Hosp 501 Euclid St Helena MT 59601

FURUIKE, ALVIN NORIO, physician, educator; b. Honolulu, Mar. 21, 1949; s. Takeo and Setsuyo (Tsukamoto) F.; B.A. in Zoology, U. Hawaii, 1970, postgrad, 1970-72; M.D., UCLA, 1974. Intern, Queen's Med. Center, Honolulu, 1974-75; resident U. Hawaii, 1975-78; fellow in pulmonary disease UCLA, 1978—; instr. medicine U. Hawaii, 1978-81, asst. prof., 1981—. Diplomate Am. Bd. Internal Medicine, subsplty. of Pulmonary Diseases. Fellow Am. Coll. Chest Physicians; mem. Am. Thoracic Soc., Calif. Thoracic Soc., Hawaii Thoracic Soc., Hawaii Heart Assn., ACP. Home: 1044-D Green St Honolulu HI 96822 Office: 321 N Kuakini St Suite 310 Honoulu HI 96817

FURUKAWA, DAVID HIROSHI, consulting chemical engineer; b. San Pedro, Calif., Mar. 26, 1938; s. James T. and Frances F. (Kamei) F.; B.S.Ch.E., U. Colo., 1960; m. Natchi Natsumi Matsunami, June 21, 1964; children—Douglas, Ross, Gregg, Derek, Ryan. Desalting sect. head Bur. Reclamation, Denver, 1960-69; mgr. research and devel. Havens Internat., San Diego, 1969-71; mgr. comml. devel. Calgon Corp., Pitts., 1971-73, UOP, Inc., San Diego, 1973-75; cons. Furukawa & Assos., Poway, Calif., 1975-78; prin. chem. engr. Boyle Engring. Corp., San Diego, 1978-81; dir. mktg. Resources Cons. Co., San Diego, 1981-83; dir. mktg. Filmtec Corp., San Diego, 1983—; cons. on reverse osmosis, ultrafiltration, desalination and water pollution control. Recipient Meritorious Service award U.S. Govt., 1968. Mem. Am. Inst. Chem. Engrs., Water Pollution Control Fedn., Internat. Desalination and Environ. Assn., Water Supply Improvement Assn. (dir.), Am. Water Works Assn., Am. Chem. Soc. Patentee in field. Home: 13511 Willow Run Rd Poway CA 92064 Office: 9747 Business Park Ave Diego CA 92131

FURUKAWA, RONALD EIJI, optometrist, educator, consultant; b. Tokyo, Apr. 4, 1949; s. James Tsugio and Eiko (Ogawa) F.; came to U.S., 1967; m. Sheila Flynn, Aug. 15, 1976; 1 dau., Erin Keiko. B.S. in Bio-Engring., U. Calif.-Berkeley, 1972, B.S. with honors in Optometry, 1974, O.D., 1976. Lic. optometrist, Calif., Colo. Assoc. pvt. practice optometry, Tracy, Calif., 1976-78; clin. instr. U. Calif. Sch. Optometry, Berkeley, 1976-81, now asst. clin. prof.; pvt. practice optometry, Fairfield, Calif., 1978—; cons. Mem. Japanese-Am. Citizen's League. Recipient Howard Kohn award U. Calif., 1976. Mem. Am. Optometric Assn., Calif. Optometric Assn., North Bay Optometric Soc., Fairfield C. of C., Mensa. Office: 2560 N Texas St Suite F Fairfield CA 94533

FURUKAWA, SHIRO BRUCE, computer programmer; b. Pasadena, Calif., June 7, 1953; s. Shiro and Matsuko (Miyamoto) F.; B.S. in Biol. Scis. (Edmondson fellow in pathology), U. So. Calif., 1975. Research technician U. So. Calif. Med. Center, Los Angeles, 1973-74, supervising research technician, 1975-76; research chemist Rancho Los Amigos Hosp., Downey, Calif., 1976-79, phlebotomist, 1979-80, asst. data systems analyst, 1980-81; computer programmer Hughes Aircraft Corp., Fullerton, Calif., 1981-83; data processing mgr. Irwin Industries Inc./Westinghouse, 1983—. Mem. So. Calif. Data Point Users Group, Assn. M.B.A. Execs., Pacific Slopes Biochem. Soc. Republican. Contbr. writings to profl. publs. in field. Home: 633 Taylor #11 Montebello CA 90640 Office: PO Box 3310 Fullerton CA 92634

FURUMOTO, HOWARD HOOSAKU, veterinarian; b. Ninole, Hawaii, July 13, 1921; s. Kuniji and Kiyo (Sorakubo) F.; B.S., Kan. State U., 1947, M.S., 1948, D.V.M., 1950; Ph.D. (fellow), U. Ill., 1966; M. Viola Gilbertine Ferris, Jan. 13, 1946; children—William, Wesley, Alice, David, Nancy, James, Edward. Intern, Angell Meml. Animal Hosp., Boston, 1950-51; asst. prof. Kans. State U., Manhattan, 1951-52; veterinarian Care Animal Hosp., Honolulu, 1952-62, pres., dir., 1969-82; dir. vet. medicine Atlas Chem. Co., Wilmington, Del., 1966-67; assoc. prof., researcher U. Hawaii, Honolulu, 1967-68; vis. prof. dept. vet. pathobiology U. Minn., 1978-79; chmn. Hawaii State Bd. Vet. Examiners, 1971-78; vet. chmn. for Hawaii, Morris Animal Found., 1974—. Served with M.I., AUS, 1941-46. Decorated Bronze Star. Mem. Am. Soc. Tropical Medicine and Hygiene, Honolulu Vet. Soc. (pres. 1957-58), Hawaii Vet. Assn. (pres. 1972-74), Am. Animal Hosp. Assn. (area dir. 1974—Vet. of Yr., Far West region 1981, Charles E. Bild Practitioner of Yr. award 1981), N.Y. Acad. Sci., Alpha Zeta, Phi Zeta, Gamma Sigma Delta. Methodist. Rotarian (dir. 1960-63, pres. 1963). Home: 4433 Aukai Ave Honolulu HI 96816 Office: 1135 Kapahulu Ave Honolulu HI 96816

FUSCALDO, ANTONIO FRANK, educational administrator; b. Greenwich, Conn., Feb. 8, 1919; s. Joseph Mario and Anna Maria (Columbo) F.; m. Marie V. Green, Nov. 5, 1982. B.B.A., Pace Coll., 1948; M.A., U. Ariz., 1965, M.Ed., 1970; postgrad. Ariz. State U., 1965-68, Cochise Coll., 1965-67, U. Nev., 1974, Phoenix Coll., 1981, N.Y.C. Fashion Mdse. Workshop, 1981. Practice acctg., Cos Cob, Conn., 1948-58; comptroller Superior Elec. Industries, Hollywood, Fla., 1958-59; asst. sales mgr. PESCO, Ft. Lauderdale, Fla., 1959-62, v.p., 1962-63; tchr. adult edn., distributive edn. tchr.-coordinator pub. schs., Douglas, Ariz., 1965-67; distributive edn. tchr. coordinator Pueblo High Sch., Tucson, 1967—. Mem. Tucson Distributive Edn. Adv. Com. Served with USAAF, 1942-45. Recipient Ariz Kidney Found. award Pima County Chpt., 1972; Distributive Edn. Dir. award Ariz. Dept. Edn., 1972; cert. of appreciation Future Bus. Leaders Am., 1983; Service award Ariz. Dept. Edn., 1983; Outstanding Service award Tucson Mktg./Distributive Educators, 1983; others. Mem. Ariz. Assn. Distributive Edn. Tchrs. (pres. 1972-73), Nat. Assn. Distributive Edn. Tchrs. (chmn. com. pub. relations 1970-71), Tucson Distributive Edn. Tchr-Coordinators Assn., Tucson Bus. Edn. Assn., Ariz. Bus. Edn. Assn., Nat. Bus. Edn. Assn., Douglas Bus. Edn. Assn., Distributive Edn. Clubs Am. (dir. chpt.), Council Distributive Tchr. Educators Assn., Am. Vocat. Assn., Ariz. State Vocat. Assn. (dir. 1970-72), Nat. Soc. Pub. Accts., Am. Legion, Beta Alpha Psi. Clubs: Elks, Lions, Eagles/Moose, Ariz. Diamond, Ariz./Nat. DECA. Contbr. articles to profl. jour. Home: 2510 W Calle Tonala Tucson AZ 85745 Office: 3500 S 12th Ave Tucson AZ 85713

FUSSELMAN, ELTON CARL, educator; b. Hominy, Okla., July 19, 1925; s. Carl Clinton and Ethel F.; m. Paulin Martin, Nov. 9, 1925. A.A., Casper Coll., 1950; B.Distributive Edn., Colo. State U., 1963; M.S., U. Wyo., 1972. With Prudential Ins. Co., 1952-57, State Farm Ins. Agy., 1957-62; tchr. mktg. and distributive edn. Natrona County Dist. #1, Casper, Wyo., 1963—, chmn. dept. Natrona County High Sch. Served with USN, 1943-46; CBI. Mem. NEA (life), Wyo. Edn. Assn., Am. Vocat. Assn., Wyo. Vocat. Assn., Nat. Assn. Distributive Edn. Tchrs., Wyo. Distributive Edn. Tchrs., Natrona County Classroom Tchrs. Assn., Wyo. Assn. Distributive Edn. Clubs, Natrona County Vocat. Conf., Am. Legion. Office: 930 S Elm St Natrona County High Sch Casper WY 82601

FUTER, RUDOLPH ERNST, equipment mfg. co. exec.; b. San Francisco, Feb. 22, 1917; s. Otto and Else Fuetterer; B.S., U. Calif., Berkeley, 1938; 1 son, Gary R. Originator airfilm accumulating for high speed packaging ops. for food, paper products; owner, pres. Engrs. Assos. Inc., Berkeley, 1953-67; owner, pres. Jetveyors, Inc., Oakland, Calif., 1967-71; pres., owner Futerized Systems, Inc., Hayward, Calif., 1971—. Registered profl. engr., Calif. Mem. ASME, Calif. Soc. Profl. Engrs. Patentee in field of airveying. Office: 100 Berry Ave Hayward CA 94544

FYE, RODNEY WAYNE, real estate company executive; b. Sutherland, Nebr., Aug. 3, 1928; s. Elmer Theodore and Pearl Gertrude (Combs) F. Grad. Chillicothe Bus. Coll., 1948; B.S., Brigham Young U., 1959; M.A., San Francisco State U., 1964; secondary teaching cert. U. Utah, 1962. Clk., Union Pacific R.R. Co., Utah, 1948-57; sec. to pres. Hughes Tool Co., Los Angeles, 1958-59; tchr. Granite Dist. High Schs., Salt Lake City, 1960-63; adminstr. Millcreek Terrace Nursing Home, Salt Lake City, 1962-63; instr. Reading Dynamics, No. Calif., 1967-75; owner, mgr. Keycount Properties, San Francisco, 1975-79; v.p. Casa Loma Properties, Inc., San Francisco, 1979—; v.p. Pan Am. Investments, Inc., St. Thomas, V.I., 1980—. Pres., San Francisco Safety Council, 1980-82; pres.-elect Safety Council of San Francisco/San Mateo Counties, 1983—. Mormon. Author: (musical comedy) Gandy, 1959; (dramatization) Absinthe & Wormwood, 1964; contbr. articles to mags. Office: PO Box 15308 San Francisco CA 94115

GABALDON, J. LEROY, psychotherapist; b. Albuquerque, Feb. 2, 1947; s. Joe P. and Molly S. (Sanchez) G. B.S. in Acctg. and Econs., U. Albuquerque, 1968; M.A. in Counseling, U. N.Mex., 1977; Ph.D., Fielding Inst., 1980. Tax auditor State of N.Mex., Albuquerque, 1968-78; family/adolescent therapist Youth Devel. Inc., Albuquerque, 1978-79; marriage/couple therapist in pvt. practice, Albuquerque, 1978-80; research assoc. U. N.Mex., Albuquerque, 1980-81; psychotherapist, med. social services Hospice-St. Joseph's Hosp., Albuquerque, 1982—; cons. U. N.Mex. Child Coop., 1980—. Mem. Am. Psychol. Assn., AAAS, Am. Anthrop. Assn., Am. Studies Assn., Internat. Transactional Analysis Assn., N.Y. Acad. Scis., Am. Group Psychotherapy Assn., S.W. Group Psychotherapy Assn. Author: The Patterns of an Age: The Psychological Writings of Theodora M. Abel, 1980.

GABALLA, HELMI A., mechanical engineer; b. Cairo, Egypt, June 20, 1928; s. Abdel-Malik Gaballa Rizkala and Martha Estaphanos Khalil; m. Mary H. Papadimitriou, June 12, 1949; 1 dau., Martha H. Culpepper Walters. B.S.M.E.; M.S.M.E., U. Beverly Hills. Field service engr. Internat. Harvester Tractor and Engring. Co., Cairo, 1952-65; project mech. engr. Kuwait Nat. Petroleum Co., Shoaiba, 1965-68; sr. mech. engr. Lang Engring. Co., Ferkessi-Dougo, Republic Ivory Coast, 1969-73; project mech. engr. J.F. Pritchard Co., Hassi R'Mel, Algeria, 1973-76; sr. maintenance engr. Inst. de Petroquimica, Moron, Venezuela, 1976-77; sr. field engr. Pullman Kellogg Inc., Bethioua, Algeria, Plaquemine, La., 1977-79; field product service engr. Dresser Clark Co., Olean, N.Y., 1979-80; sr. machinery engr. C.F. Braun Co., Alhambra, Calif., 1980-81; group supr. Davy McKee Corp., San Mateo, Calif., 1982—; cons. in field. Recipient cert. of achievement Def. Civil Preparedness of Houston, 1974. Mem. Nat. Soc. Profl. Engrs., Calif. Soc. Profl. Engrs., ASME, Am. Soc. Safety Engrs., Inst. Gen. Technician Engrs. (U.K.). Patentee in field.

GABBERT, CLAYTON RONALD, orthopedic surgeon; b. Ogden, Utah, Aug. 28, 1933; s. Clay and Helene (Nielson) G.; A.S., Weber State Coll., 1953; B.S., U. Utah, 1955, M.D., 1958; m. Kayla Kerr, Sept. 16, 1955; children—Wendy Lynn, Sheri Lolene, Ronald Leon, Nancy Helene. Intern, Thomas D. Dee Meml. Hosp., Ogden, 1958-59, resident gen. surgery, 1959-60; resident orthopedic surgery Mayo Clinic, 1960-63; practice medicine specializing in orthopedic suregery, Ogden, 1963—; mem. staff McKay-Dee Hosp., St. Benedicts Hosp. Served with USPHS, 1957-59. Recipient Mosby Book award for Scholastic Excellence, 1956. Diplomate Am. Bd. Orthopedic Surgery. Mem. AMA, Utah Med. Assn., Weber County Med. Soc., Am. Acad. Orthopedic Surgery, Western Orthopedic Assn. Home: 1815 Ross Dr Ogden UT 84403 Office: 3905 Harrison Blvd Ogden UT 84403

GABBITA, KASI VISWANATH, agricultural researcher, consultant; b. Machilipatnam, India, July 26, 1943; came to U.S., 1980; s. Soma Sundaram and Vara (Lakshmi) G.; m. Geetha Viswanath, June 22, 1972; children—Soma Kiran, Siva Ranjani. B.S. in Botany, Zoology and Chemistry, Andhra U., Waltair, India, 1961; M.S. in Soil Sci. and Argl. Chemistry, Indian Agrl. Research Inst., New Delhi, 1963; Ph.D., Indian Inst. Sci., Bangalore, 1972. Sr. research asst. Indian Inst. Sci., Bangalore, 1970-78; tech dir. CIERS Research & Consultancy Pvt. Ltd., Bangalore, 1978-80; project assoc. U. Wis.-Milw., 1980-81; asst. research engr. Nat. Ctr. Intermedia Transport Research, UCLA, 1981—; cons. in field. Recipient award Bangalore Water Supply and Sewerage Bd., 1975, Ramineni Ranga Rao Transport Contractors, 1976, AMCO Batteries, 1977; Indian Ministry Food and Agr. merit scholar, 1962-63; Council Sci. and Indsl. Research grantee, 1963-65; Indian Dept. Atomic Energy grantee, 1965-68. Mem. Am. Soc. Agronomy, Internat. Assn. Humic Substances. Contbr. articles on soil sci., water, wastewater, indsl. waste treatment, land treatment of wastes and environ. impact to profl. jours. Home: 1610 Preuss Rd Apt 6 Los Angeles CA 90035 Office: 5531 Boelter Hall UCLA Los Angeles CA 90024

GABEL, PETER SCUDDER, public relations executive; b. Meriden, Conn., Feb. 7, 1930; s. Cuthbert Charles and Margaret Miller (Scudder) G.; m. Thelma Lurene Stewart, Aug. 28, 1956; children—Duane A., Sharon S. B.A., Wesleyan U., 1952; M.S.W., U. Denver, 1955; Ed.D., U. Colo., 1971. Camping and youth dir. YMCA, Pueblo, Colo., 1955-58; youth program dir. YMCA, Wichita, Kans., 1958-59; sales rep. Hoflund Graphics, Denver, 1959-62; Adminstrv. dir. Cheley Colo. Camps, Denver and Estes Park, Colo., 1962-79; dir. pub. relations YMCA of Met. Denver, 1980—; part-time tchr. Met. State Coll., Denver, U. Colo., Boulder, 1972-79. Bd. dirs. Wellshire Samaritan Counseling Ctr., Inc., Denver. Mem. Pub. Relations Soc. Am. (chmn. communications workshop Colo. chpt. 1983), Am. Camping Assn. (cert., bd. dirs. Rocky Mountain sect.). Contbr. articles to profl. jours. Home: 1574 S Fillmore St Denver CO 80210 Office: YMCA 25 E 16th Ave Denver CO 80202

GABERSON, HOWARD AXEL, mech. engr.; b. Detroit, Apr. 11, 1931; s. Axel Rudolph and Lillian (Quatherine) G.; B.S.M.E., U. Mich., 1955; M.S., MIT, 1957, Ph.D., 1967; m. Dale Virginia Maitland, Apr. 27, 1969. Stress analysis engr. Raytheon Co., Wayland, Mass., 1957-59; asst. prof. mech. engring. Lowell (mass.) Tech. Inst., 1959-60; asst. prof. Boston U., 1960-64; asso. prof. mech. engring. U. Hawaii, 1967-68; shock and vibration research research mech. engr. Naval Civil Engring. Lab., Port Hueneme, Calif., 1968—. NSF fellow, 1964; Wilfred Lewis fellow, 1966. Mem. Am. Acad. Mechanics, ASME (chpt. pres. 1973, 80), Soc. Exptl. Stress Analysis, Soc. Automotive Engrs., Nat. Soc. Profl. Engrs., Inst. Noise Control Engrs., U. Mich. Alumni Assn., MIT Alumni Assn., UCLA Alumni Assn., Rare Bird Preservation Soc. (pres. 1980-81), West Valley Bird Soc., Ventura County Bird Soc., Am. Fedn. Aviculture, Aviculture Soc. Am., Bromeliad Soc., Alpha Sigma Phi, Sigma Xi, Tau Beta Pi, Pi Tau Sigma. Patentee in field. Home: 234 Corsicana Dr Oxnard CA 93030 Office: US Naval Civil Engring Lab Port Hueneme CA 93043

GABIER, WELLES, state education official; b. Traverse City, Mich., Dec. 26, 1941; s. Otto and Fayvella Gabier. B.A., Central Mich. U., 1964, M.A. in Polit. Sci., 1966; postgrad. No. Colo. U., Adam State Coll., U. Alaska. Secondary teaching cert., Alaska. Tchr., Kalkaska (Mich.) Pub. Schs., 1966, Oakridge High Sch., Muskegan, Mich., 1966-67; vocat. counselor Colo. Dept. of Employment, Pueblo, 1968-70; state counseling supr. Employment Security Div., Alaska Dept. Labor, Juneau, 1970-73, adminstrv. officer to dir. employment security div., 1973-75; staff devel. specialist Alaska Dept. Health and Social Service, Juneau, 1975-76; owner, operator truck farm, Woodville, Miss., 1976-78; coordinator Alaska Occupational Info. Coordinating Com./Alaska Career Info. System, Alaska Dept. Edn., Juneau, 1978—. Mem. Am. Personnel and Guidance Assn., Alaska Adult Edn. Assn., Alaska State Counselors Assn., Alaska State Vocat. Assn., Am. Vocat. Assn., Assn. Computer-Based Systems for Career Info. (dir.), Alaska Conservation Council, Alaska Native Brotherhood, Alaska Public Employees Assn., Audubon Soc., Nat. Rifle Assn., Territorial Sportsmen, S.E. Alaska Conservation Council. Democrat. Club: Sierra. Office: Alaska Department of Education Pouch F Juneau AK 99811

GABLE, RALPH KIRKLAND, psychologist; b. Canton, Ohio, Mar. 21, 1934; s. Harry C. and Mary (Blackburn) Schwitzgebel; student Heidelberg Coll., 1952-54; B.S., Ohio State U., 1956; Ed.D., Harvard U., 1962, J.D., 1970, m. Colleen Nooter Ryan, Dec. 28, 1963, children—Eric, Sandra. Lectr. social relations Harvard U., 1968-71; asst. prof. Law-Medicine Inst., Boston U., 1966-69, asst. prof. dept. psychiatry Harvard U., 1975-78; prof. psychology Calif. Luth. Coll., Thousand Oaks, 1978; mem. Workshop on Behavioral Research and Secret Service, Nat. Acad. Scis., 1981; cons. NIMH. NIMH grantee, 1972-76. Author: Legal Aspects of the Enforced Treatment of Offenders, 1979; Street Corner Research, 1963; Law and Psychological Practice, 1980. Home: 515 Fargo St Thousand Oaks CA 91360 Office: California Lutheran College Thousand Oaks CA 91360

GABLE, ROBERT S., psychology educator; b. Canton, Ohio, Mar. 21, 1934; s. Harry C. and Mary (Blackburn) Schwitzgebel. B.A., Heidelberg Coll., 1954; Ed.D., Harvard U., 1964; Ph.D., Brandeis U., 1964; LL.D. (hon.), San Fernando Valley Coll. Law, 1982. Asst. prof. UCLA, 1964-68; asst. prof. Claremont (Calif.) Grad. Sch., 1968-75, assoc. prof., 1975-83, prof., 1983—, dir. life sci. research group. Mem. Am. Psychol. Assn. Author: (with Schwitzgebel) Law and Psychological Practice, 1980. Office: Psychology Dept Claremont Grad Sch Claremont CA 91711

GABLEHOUSE, REUBEN HAROLD, aerospace exec.; b. Berthoud, Colo., Aug. 31, 1923; s. Daniel Henry and Mollie Emma (Henry) G.; m. Genevieve Margaret Willburn, June 19, 1949; children—Timothy, Daniel, Nancy, Kelly. B.S.E.E., B.S. in Bus., U. Colo.-Boulder, 1951; M.S.E.E., U. N.Mex.-Albuquerque, 1956. Registered profl. engr., Colo. Electronics engr. instrumentation design Chance-Vought, 1951-52; staff mem. instrumentation devel. Sandia Corp., 1952-60; project dir. to pres. Ball Aerospace Systems Div., Boulder, Colo., 1960—. Bd. dirs. Fiske Planetarium; vice chmn. Boulder United Way, 1983. Served to 2d lt. AUS, 1943-46. Mem. AIAA, Am. Astron. Soc. Methodist. Home: 1840 Forest Ave Boulder CO 80302 Office: 1600 Commerce St Boulder CO 80303

GABLEHOUSE, TIMOTHY REUBEN, lawyer; b. Boulder, Colo., May 13, 1951; s. Reuben H. and Genevieve M. (Willburn) G.; m. Barbara Lynn Dorough, June 23, 1973; children—Brian, Kristin, Andrew. B.A. in Environ. Biology, U. Colo., 1973, J.D., 1975; M.B.A., U. Denver, 1981. Bar: Colo. 1976. Assoc. Geddes, McDougal and McHugh, Colorado Springs, Colo., 1976-77; regulatory analyst Adolph Coors Co., Golden Colo., 1977-78, regulatory affairs coordinator, 1978-79, new product devel. mgr. 1979-82, regulatory affairs mgr., 1982—. Mem. Commn. for Prevention of Sexual Assault, City of Arvada (Colo.), 1982—. Mem. ABA, Colo. Bar Assn., Environ. Law Inst., Am. Corp. Counsel Assn. Methodist. Republican. Club: Jaycees. Office: Adolph Coors Co Mail Number 344 Golden CO 80401

GABRIEL, BARBARA JAMIESON, educator; b. Pasadena, Calif., Jan. 21, 1929; d. Hamer Hershal and Hazel (Kendall) Jamieson; m. Albert Lawrence Gabriel, June 28, 1947; children—Sam Winston, Bryn Patricia Petersen. B.A. magna cum laude, Calif. State U.-Long Beach, 1971, M.A. in Ednl. Adminstrn., 1982. Cert. tchr., sch. adminstr., Calif. Bilingual tchr. Parkview Sch., 1973-78, minimum essential tchr., 1978-80; instructional materials specialist Mountain View Sch. Dist., Long Beach, Calif., 1980—. Mem. State Book Rev. Com., 1979, Four Dist. Task Force, 1979; supporting mem. Aero-Space Mus., Globe Theatre. Mem. Internat. Reading Assn., Assn. Supervision and Curriculum Devel., NEA, Calif. Tchrs. Assn., San Diego Zool. Soc., Phi Kappa Phi, Kappa Delta Pi, Phi Delta Kappa. Clubs: Alamitos Bay Yacht, (Long Beach, Calif.). Office: 2850 N Mountain View Rd El Monte CA 91732

GABRIEL, BILLIE LUCILLE BURKLE, computer company executive; b. Poteau, Okla., Mar. 1; d. Nick Angelo and Pearl Audry (McDonald) Burkle; m. Kenneth L. Gabriel, Nov. 1, 1963 (div. Apr. 1967). B.S., Memphis State U. Lic. real estate salesperson. Mgr. fin. and adminstrn., dir. Calif. Data Processors/Data 100 Corp., Santa Ana, Calif., 1971-75; cons. computer industry, Orange County, Calif., 1976-79; v.p., gen. mgr. Isotronix, Inc., Santa Ana, 1980-81; pres., owner Gabriel Computer Products, Newport Beach, Calif., 1981—. Author: Hostility Between the Sexes, 1976. Founder, bd. dirs. Com. for Ednl. Excellence, Newport Beach, 1983; bd. dirs., v.p. Braille Inst. Aux., Newport Beach, 1981-83. Recipient cert. of commendation Balboa Dist./U.S. Power Squadron, Newport Beach, 1981. Mem. Am. Mgmt. Assn. (Cert. of excellence 1973), Western Electronic Mfrs. Assn., Mchts. and Mfrs. Clubs: Odyssean Yacht (founder, commodore Newport Beach 1981-83), Balboa Power Squadron (chmn. various coms. 1966—), Balboa Bay. Home: 2888 Bayshore Dr Newport Beach CA 92663

GABRIEL, EBERHARD JOHN, lawyer; b. Bucharest, Rumania, Mar. 22, 1942; s. William and Margaret (Eberhart) Krzyzewski; B.A. in English, St. Joseph's Coll. (Ind.), 1963; J.D., Georgetown U., 1966; m. Janice Josephine Jedrzejewski, Oct. 17, 1941; children—John, Stephanie, Christopher. Bar: Md. 1966. Staff atty. Fgn. Claims Settlement Commn., Washington, 1966-68; corp. atty. Govt. Employees Ins. Co., Washington, 1968-70; sr. v.p., gen. counsel Govt. Employees Fin. Corp. and subs., Denver, 1970—; sec.-treas., dir. Indsl. Bank Savs. Guaranty Corp. Colo., 1973—. Trustee, Lakewood Polit. Action Com., 1978—; sr. v.p. fund raising Lakewood on Parade, 1980, chmn. bd. govs., 1982; vice chmn. fin. div. United Way Metro Denver, 1982. Mem. ABA, Md. Bar Assn., Fellows St. Joseph's Coll., Georgetown U. Alumni Assn., Nat. Consumer Fin. Assn. (lectr. 1974-81, mem. law forum 1974—, mem. law com. 1978-82, dist. chmn. congl. action com. 1979—), Lakewood C. of C. (dir. 1974-78, 79-80, 82—, chmn. civic affairs council 1975-76, chmn. govtl. action council 1980-81, chmn. local govt. task force S. Jeffco council 1981-82, vice chmn., mem. exec. com. 1982—), Indsl. Bankers Assn. Colo. (chmn. legis. com. 1980—, chmn. polit. action com. 1981—), Phi Alpha Delta. Democrat. Roman Catholic. Club: Pinehurst Country (Denver). Office: 7551 W Alameda Ave PO Box 5555 Denver CO 80217

GABRIEL, HERMAN WILLIAM, ecologist; b. Wilmington, Del., Dec. 21, 1933; s. Hermann William and Ruth Gertrude (Hickman) G. B.S. in Forest and Wildlife Conservation (state scholar 1952, 53), Va. Poly. Inst., Blacksburg, 1956; postgrad. Mich. State U., 1956, Utah State U., Logan, 1960-61; Ph.D. in Wildlife Mgmt., U. Mont.-Missoula, 1976. Mich. State U. research asst., 1956; forester U.S. Forest Service, Ogden, Utah, 1958-61, Teton Nat. Forest, Jackson, Wyo., 1961-66; forestry officer UN FAO, Quito, Ecuador, 1966-67; teaching assoc. U. Mont. Sch. Forestry, 1968-71; chief environ. sect. Alaska Dist. U.S. Army C.E., 1971-74; chief Biol. Resources Br., Bur. Land Mgmt., Alaska State Office, 1975-78, leader spl. studies group, 1978—. Served with U.S. Army, 1956-58. Recipient Spl. Achievement award Bur. Land Mgmt., 1980. Mem. Wildlife Soc., Soc. Am. Foresters, Alaska Acad. Engring. and Sci., AAAS, Ecol. Soc. Am., Anchorage Audubon Soc. (sec.). Contbr. several sci. papers and articles on wildlife to jours. and mags, numerous photographs on wildlife to Audubon and other publs. Home: 2900 Wesleyan Drive Anchorage AK 99504 Office: USDI Bur Land Mgmt 701 C St Box 13 Anchorage AK 99513

GABRIEL, WILLIAM JOHN, advertising and public relations executive; b. Cleve., Mar. 5, 1927; s. William John and Esther May (Snyder) G.; m. Janet R. Mackey, Apr. 23, 1953 (div. Feb. 1976); children—Robin L., Kathi A.; m. 2d, Linda Scott McGraw, June 27, 1977. B.J., U. Mo., 1950. Owner, Gabriel Advt. Agy., Cleve., 1956-58; v.p. Baisch, Blake & Gabriel, Inc., Cleve., 1959-75; v.p. Hang Ten Internat., San Diego, 1975-77; sales, pub. relations and advt. cons., San Diego, 1978; cons. Cedar St. Inc., div. John Burnham & Co., San Diego, 1979—; co-founder, corp. sec. Card-Pak, Inc., Cleve., 1965-73. Vice pres. Lake Erie Jr. Nature and Sci. Center, Bay Village, Ohio, 1969-73. Served with USCGR, 1944-45. Mem. Nat. Assn. Real Estate Editors (assoc.), U Mo. Alumni Assn., QEBH, Surfsong Owners' Assn. (pres. 1979-80), Kappa Sigma, Alpha Delta Sigma. Republican. Methodist. Clubs: U.S. Lawn Tennis Assn., Press of San Diego, Breakfast of San Diego (pres. 1981), San Diego Advt. Tennis Assn., Mo. Alumni of San Diego, Mustang Owners of San Diego. Home: Surfsong 205-M S Helix Ave Solana Beach CA 92075 Office: Cedar St Inc Box 2910 San Diego CA 92112

GABRIELE, GUY FRANK, advertising executive; b. Schenectady, Feb. 27, 1954; s. Edward and Angelina Julia (Fusco) G.; m. Joyce Marie Valentino, Dec. 10, 1981. B.B.A., Siena Coll., 1977, M.B.A., Rensselaer Poly. Inst., 1980. Asst. to pres. Urbach, Kahn & Werlin, P.C., Albany, N.Y., 1978-80; mktg. mgr. Calwest Systems Inc., Santa Barbara, Calif., 1980; v.p., gen. mgr. Komar Mktg. Communications, Inc., Santa Barbara, 1980—; instr. U. Calif.-Santa Barbara, 1982—; mktg. cons. SBA. Mem. Am. Advt. Fedn., Greater Santa Barbara Ad Club. Republican. Roman Catholic. Office: Komar Mktg Communications Inc 1436 Chapala St Santa Barbara CA 93101

GABRIELE, SHERRY LEE SOSKIN, accountant; b. Cleve., Jan. 1, 1943; d. Zelman and Molly (Miller) Soskin; B.S., UCLA, 1964; M.Bus. Taxation, U. So. Calif., 1976. Acct. various firms, Calif., 1960-69; acct. Wolf and Co., Los Angeles, 1969-75, mgr., 1969-73, partner in charge tax dept., 1973-75; pvt. practice acctg. specializing in tax planning and compliance, Los Angeles, 1975—; substitute instr. acctg. UCLA, 1965-66. C.P.A., Calif. Mem. Am. Inst. C.P.A.s, Calif. Soc. C.P.A.s, Am. Women's Soc. C.P.A.s, Calif. Scholarship Soc. (seal bearer life mem.). Contbr. articles to profl. publs. Office: 5567 Reseda Blvd Suite 218 Tarzana CA 91356

GABRIELSEN, PAUL THOMAS, clergyman, educational administrator; b. Bonners Ferry, Idaho, Aug. 1, 1929; s. Gabriel and Edna C. (Roen) G.; m. Karen Elaine Johnk, July 18, 1954; children—Virginia, Stephen. B.A., Concordia Coll., 1952; B. Th., Luther Theol. Sem., 1956; M.A., U. Chgo., 1960; Ph.D., U.S. Internat. U., 1975; postgrad. U. Minn., 1960-62, Bibl. Sem. N.Y., 1952. Ordained to ministry, 1958; pastor North Cape Evang. Luth. Ch., 1958-60; chaplain Augsburg Coll., Mpls., 1960-61; dir. counseling Golden Valley Luth. Coll., Mpls., 1960-70; dir. advancement Luth. Bible Inst., Seattle, 1976-79, dir. planned giving, 1979—; ptnr. Capital Growth Planning, 1970-73; owner Kairos Fin., San Diego, 1973-76; writer bd. publ. Am. Luth. Ch., 1965. Mem. Am. Assn. Pastoral Counselors, Am. Coll. Student Personnel Assn., Nat. Vocat. Guidance Assn., Internat. Assn. Fin. Planners, Nat. Assn. Security Dealers, Nat. Assn. Charitable Estate Counselors, Calif. Real Estate Brokers, Author: Tests of True Christianity, 1966; Why Doesn't God?, 1965. Office: Luth Bible Inst Providence Heights Issaquah WA 98027

GAEDE, CARL DEAN, architectural planner, designer; b. Newton, Kans., May 31, 1936; s. John E. and Anna Marie (Reiss) G.; student Bethany Nazarene Coll., 1954-56; B.S. in Archtl. Engring., B.Arch. magna cum laude, Kans. State U., Manhattan, 1960; m. Dawn Arlene Dube, Apr. 6, 1968; children—Peter Austin, Katrina Marie. Project designer A. Quincy Jones/Frederick E. Emmons, Architects, Los Angeles, 1962-64, Skidmore Owings and Merrill, Architects and Engrs., San Francisco, 1965-68, Daniel Mann Johnson and Mendenhall, Architects and Engrs., Los Angeles, 1969-72; pvt. practice architecture, Pasadena, Calif., 1973—; pres. Gaede, Alcorn & Assos., architects and planning cons., Pasadena and LaJolla, Calif., 1976—; faculty Calif. State Poly. U., Pomona, 1972-73; lectr. in field. Served with AUS, 1960-62. Mem. AIA (chpt. bd. dirs. 1981—, sec. 1982, v.p. 1983), Tournament of Roses Assn., Phi Kappa Phi, Tau Sigma Delta. Mem. Ch. of Nazarene (dir.). Club: Univ. (Pasadena). Home: 980 Roxbury Dr Pasadena CA 91104 Office: 255 S Marengo Ave Pasadena CA 91101

GAEDEKE, RALPH MORTIMER, business administration educator; b. Nadrau, Germany, May, 25, 1941, came to U.S. 1953. s. Horst Friederich and Margot Hanna (Boltz) G.; m. Johanna Vivian House, June 19, 1965; children—Jolene R., Michael C. B.A., U. Washington, 1964, M.A., 1965, Ph.D., 1969. Instr. U. Sask. (Can.), 1965-66, U. Wash., 1967-69; assoc. prof. Calif. State U. Sacramento, 1969-71, U. Alaska, Anchorage, 1971-73; prof. bus. adminstrn. U. Sacramento, 1974—; also cons. Scholar study tour grantee W.Ger., 1977. Mem. Am. Mktg. Assn. (pres. Sacramento chpt. 1974-75), Acad. Internat. Bus., Delta Sigma Pi. Author: Marketing: Principles and Applications, 1983; co-author: Marketing Management: Cases and Readings, Small Business Management; Small Business Management: Operations & Profiles; Marketing in Private and Public Non-Profit Organizations; Consumerism. Home: 237 Hartnell Pl Sacramento CA 95825 Office: 6000 J St Sacramento CA 95819

GAER, ERIC WILLIAM, marketing executive; b. Bklyn., June 21, 1948; s. Joseph and Rena (Weiss) G.; m. Tamara Hess, Sept. 21, 1975; 1 son, Christopher Scott. B.A. in Mass Communications, Calif. State U.-Northridge, 1970. Sales mgr. West Los Angeles Music Inc., 1970-73; dir. advt. and promotion Acoustic Control Corp., Van Nuys, Calif., 1973-74; pres. Gaer & Assocs. Inc., Westlake Village, Calif., 1974-78, Eric Gaer Co., Woodland Hills, Calif., 1978—. Served with U.S. Army, 1969-72. Mem. Western States Advt. Agys. Assn., Nat. Acad. Recording Arts and Scis. Club: Warner Center (Woodland Hills). Contbr. profl. articles to jours. Home: 22420 Sentar Rd Woodland Hills CA 91364

GAFFIN, GERALD LEE, clinical psychologist; b. Youngstown, Ohio, Sept. 28, 1953; s. Arthur Sam and Joan (Gold) G. B.A. with honors in Psychology, Oberlin Coll., 1975; M.A., Mich. State U., 1979, Ph.D., 1981. Lic. psychologist, Calif. Childcare worker Walker Home and Sch., Needham, Mass., 1974, 75-76, 77-79; intern in psychology Kaiser Permanente Mental Health Ctr., Los Angeles, 1980-81; staff psychologist Hathaway Home for Children, Pacoima, Calif., 1981; staff psychologist San Fernando Valley Child Guidance Clinic, Northridge, Calif., 1981—; clin. asst. prof. Fuller Theol. Sem. Grad. Sch. Psychology. Recipient Jerome Davis award Oberlin Coll., 1974-75; NIMH trainee, 1976-77, 77-78; Mich. Dept. Mental Health grantee, 1980. Mem. Soc. Psychotherapy Research, Am. Psychol. Assn., Sigma Xi. Office: San Fernando Valley Child Guidance Clinic 9650 Zelzah Ave Northridge CA 91325

GAFFNEY, DAVID LAWRENCE, business executive; b. San Francisco, Aug. 10, 1937; s. Lawrence and Irene G.; B.B.A., Armstrong Coll., 1962; M.S. in Mgmt., Calif. State U., Northridge, 1973. Corp. tng. specialist Safeway Stores, Oakland, Calif., 1955-65; dir. adminstrn. A&W Internat., subs. United Brands, Santa Monica, Calif., 1965-71; dir. indsl. relations Arden Mayfair Inc., Commerce, Calif., 1971-74, Internat. Foodservice, Century City, Calif., 1974-77; corp. employee resources mgr. Nissan Motor Corp. U.S.A. (Datsun), Carson, Calif., 1977-82; dir. adminstrn. Nissan Motor Acceptance Corp. (Datsun), 1982—; exec. search cons., Encino, Calif., 1975—; instr. bus. U. Redlands and Calif. State U., 1976—. Mem. Personnel and Indsl. Relations Assn. (dir., exec. com., dist. chmn., position referral chmn.), Am. Soc. Personnel Adminstrn., Am. Soc. Tng. and Devel., Los Angeles Area C. of C., Calif. State U. at Northridge Alumni Assn. Armstrong Coll. Alumni Assn. (pres. 1977-78). Republican. Roman Catholic. Club: Kiwanis (dir. Woodland Hills 1978-82). Home: 21695 Yucatan Ave Woodland Hills CA 91364 Office: 18455 S Figueroa St Carson CA 90248 also PO Box 191 Gardena CA 90247

GAFFNEY, DIANE LEE, employee benefits cons.; b. Laramie, Wyo., July 12, 1952; d. Harold Max and Margaret Adella (Vincent) G.; A.A., Pasadena (Calif.) City Coll., 1972; B.S. in Mgmt., San Diego State U., 1977. Fin. asst. Cabrillo Med. Center, San Diego, 1974-76, personnel mgr., 1976-78, personnel services adminstr., 1978-80; asst. adminstr., profl. services, 1980-81; owner, pres. Health Care Profls., 1981-82; pension benefits analyst Johnson & Higgins of Calif., 1983—. Bd. dirs. Pres' Council of San Diego. Mem. Globe Guilders, Jr. League, Am. Hosp. Assn., Calif. Hosp. Assn., Nat. Kidney Found. Office: 110 West A St Suite 1170 San Diego CA 92101

GAGE, DELWYN ORIN, state senator, accountant, oil producer; b. Calvin, N.D., Nov. 28, 1930; s. Orin Mann and Beatrice Blanche (Bell) G.; m. Sarah Marlene Brenchley, Jan. 3, 1953; children—Scott, Paul Shelley, Jerri, Mark, Connie. Student Brigham Young U. Acct., R.E. Svare, Shelby, Mont., 1956-59; acctg. ptnr. with Paul W. Wolk, Cut Bank, Mont., 1960-64; pvt. practice acctg. practice, Cut Bank, 1964—; mem. Mont. Senate, 1982—; thoroughbred owner. Served with USMC, 1951-52. Named Jaycee Boss of Yr. Mem. C. of C. Mormon. Club: Elks.

GAGRAT, MANI, educator; b. Kanpur, India; d. Sorabji H. and Tehimina (Dalal) G.; came to U.S., 1972; B.A., Christ Ch. Coll., 1965, M. Degree, 1967; Ph.D., Indian Inst. Tech., 1970; m. Joseph Huang, Mar. 21, 1975. Vis. prof. U. Colo., Boulder, 1972-74, Marquette U., Milw., 1974-75; instr. math. Met. State Coll., Denver, 1975-76, Los Angeles Harbor Coll., Wilmington, Calif., 1976—. Recipient Chancellor's Gold medal Christ Ch. Coll., 1966-67. Mem. Am. Math. Soc. Author: Symmetric Generalised Topological Structures, 1976.

GAINES, FRANCIS PENDLETON, JR., university dean; b. State College, Miss., Sept. 7, 1918; s. Francis Pendleton and Sadie (Robert) G.; grad. Woodberry Forest Prep. Sch., 1935; student Washington and Lee U., 1935-37; A.B. summa cum laude, U. Ariz., 1942; M.A., U. Va., 1946, Ph.D. (DuPont fellow), 1950; L.H.D., Coll. Artesia, 1968; m. Dorothy Ruth Bloomhardt, Oct. 10, 1942; children—Francis Pendleton III, Paul Randolph, Sallie du Vergne; m. 2d, Marjorie Anne Hurt, Mar. 25, 1975. Engr. on Mississippi River, War Dept., 1937-39; dean of men, asst. to pres. Birmingham So. Coll., 1946-48; supt. Gulf Coast Mil. Acad., 1948; dir. pub. relations and devel. U. Houston, 1950; dean students So. Meth. U., 1951-52; pres. Wofford Coll., 1952-57; v.p. Piedmont Nat. Bank, Spartanburg, S.C., 1957-58; dir. research study Fund for Advancement Edn., 1958-59; dean continuing edn. and summer session U. Ariz., Tucson, 1959-73, dean adminstrn., 1973—, also prof. ednl. adminstrn.; sec. Assn. Summer Session Deans and Dirs., 1961-62. Pres. Conf. Ch.-related Colls. South, 1956-57; ofcl. del. to jurisdictional, gen. and world confs. Meth. Ch., 1956; mem. Council for Basic Edn.; mem. Woodrow Wilson Regional Selection com.; treas. S.C. Found. Ind. Colls.; citizens adv. council U.S. Senate Com. to P.O. and Civil Service; adv. com. Robert A. Taft Inst. Govt.; mem. Ariz. Civil War Centennial Commn. Served as capt. AUS, War Dept., Gen. Staff, M.I., 1942-45. Named S.C. Young Man of Year, Jaycees, 1954; Outstanding Faculty Mem., U. Ariz., 1971; recipient Ariz. award, 1971. Fellow Nat. Univ. Extension Assn.; mem. U. Ariz. Alumni Assn. (dir. 1967—), Newcomen Soc., Washington and Lee Alumni (pres. Tucson chpt. 1981—), Phi Beta Kappa, Omicron Delta Kappa, Phi Kappa Phi, Pi Delta Epsilon, Phi Kappa Sigma, Raven Soc. Methodist. Club: Davis-Monthan Officers (Tucson). Editorial bd. Spartanburg Herald-Jour.; contbr. articles to profl. jours. Home: 3919 E Cooper St Tucson AZ 85711 Office: Slonake Alumni Bldg Room 112 U Ariz Tucson AZ 85721

GAINEY, HAROLD FRANKLIN, electronics company executive; b. Aynor, S.C., Aug. 20, 1937; s. Corbett Lewis and Mary Edna (Thompson) G.; B.S. in Elec. Engring., U. Fla., 1960; m. Nora Gainey; children—Alan, Robert, Patricia, Shawn, Nickolas. Engr., Bell Telephone Labs., Whippany, N.J., 1960-61; flight test engr. GD Astronautics Co., Omaha, Cheyenne, Wyo., 1961-62; mem. tech. staff Hughes Aircraft Co., El Segundo, Los Angeles, Calif., 1962-68; founder, v.p. Electronic Systems and Programming, Inc., Hawthorne, Calif., 1968-76, pres., chmn. bd., 1976-81, pres., 1981—also dir. Served with U.S. Army, 1957. Mem. Wilmington Jr. C. of C., Hawthorne C. of C. Home: 4856 W 134th

Pl Hawthorne CA 90250 Office: 12832 Chadron Ave Hawthorne CA 90250

GAITHER, DOROTHY JAMES, ednl. adminstr.; d. Quinton and Agnes (Belton) James; B.S., William Paterson Coll., 1953; M.S., Mt. St. Mary's Coll., Los Angeles, 1973; m. Frank T. Gaither, Oct. 26, 1962 (dec.); 1 son, Thomas Frank. Tchr. public schs., Bergenfield, N.J., 1953-58; with Los Angeles Unified Sch. Dist., 1958—, reading specialist, 1966-70, cons., 1970-72, dir. STAR program, 1972-75, asst. prin., 1975-77, prin., 1977-80, asst. dir. ESAA, 1980—. Mem. Calif. Tchr. Preparation and Licensing Commn. Adv. Bd., 1977-78. Mem. Nat. Assn. Elem. Sch. Prins., Assn. Elem. Sch. Adminstrs., Assn. Calif. Sch. Adminstrs., Nat. Assn. Supervision and Curriculum Devel., Council Black Adminstrs., Nat. Council Negro Women, Links, Inc., Delta Kappa Gamma. Mem. Ch. of Christian Fellowship. Office: 450 N Grand Ave Los Angeles CA 90012

GALATI, MICHAEL ANTHONY, insurance executive; b. N.Y.C., Aug. 1, 1930; s. Peter and Helen (Minando) G.; m. Gloria Katherine Duncan, Apr. 17, 1971; children—Peter, Christine, Michael. B.A., Ariz. State U., 1956. Claims adjuster Aetna Casualty Ins. Co., N.Y.C., 1948-55; exec. asst. Glens Falls (N.Y.) Ins. Co., 1955-70; asst. v.p. Gt. Am. Ins. Co., Los Angeles and Cin., 1970-75; pres. Miken Assocs., Inc., Sedona, Ariz., 1975—. Served with USAF, 1951-52. Mem. Pacific Claims Exec. Assn., N.Y. Claims Men's Assn. Club: Rotary, Elks, Kiwanis. Home: PO Box 1561 Sedona AZ 86336 Office: Southwest Bank Bldg Sedona AZ 86336

GALATI, ROSE ANN, accountant; b. Burbank, Calif., June 16, 1954; d. Alan Whitney and Betty Jane (Eddy) Rucker; m. James Galati, Aug. 12, 1971; 1 son Christopher. A.A., Moorpark Coll., 1975; B.S. in Acctg., Calif. State U.-Northridge, 1977. C.P.A., Calif. Acctg. positions, Thousand Oaks, Calif., 1980—; pvt. practice acctg., Thousand Oaks, 1982—. Active Speakers Bur. Conejo Valley. Mem. C. of C. Conejo Valley (chmn. profl. com.). Office: 100 E Thousand Oaks Blvd Suite 236 Thousand Oaks CA 91360

GALBRAITH, ALLAN LEE, lawyer; b. Las Cruces, N.Mex., Feb. 16, 1955; s. Graeme C. and Joanne (Brack) G.; m. Lorena Gail Boyd, May 28, 1982. B.S. in Bus., U. Idaho, 1977, J.D., 1980. Bar: Wash. 1980; C.P.A., Wash.. Staff acct. Boyd Olafson & Co., C.P.A.s, Yakima, Wash., 1980-82; assoc. Carlson & Drewelow, P.S., Wenatchee, Wash., 1982—; instr. bus. law City U., Yakima, Wash. Dir. Chelan-Douglas County Community Action Council, Wenatchee. Mem. ABA, Wash. Bar Assn., Wash. Soc. C.P.A.s, Wenatchee Area C. of C. Club: Rotary (Wenatchee).

GALE, ANDREW ROBERT, software development corporation executive; b. Los Angeles, June 23, 1942; s. Myron and Clarice (Sitomer) G.; m. Hanuska Branicka, Sept. 18, 1972. B.A., North Tex. U., 1964; M.A., New Sch. Social Research, 1966. Asst. dir. program evaluation Jersey City Job Corps, 1966-68; project mgr. M.I.S. RCA Corp., N.Y.C., 1968-72; mgr. major systems mktg. and support Internat. Computers Ltd., London, 1972-74; ptnr. Systems Devel. Internat., London, 1974-77; pres. SDI: Industry Systems, Los Angeles, 1977—; dir. I.T.M. Corp., Travel Cons. Internat. Fellow Brit. Computer Soc.; mem. Internat. Fedn. Info. Processing, Data Processing Mgmt. Assn., Assn. Iron and Steel Engrs., Am. Mgmt. Assn., Soc. Mfg. Engrs. (sr.), Commonwealth Soc. Office: 1543 W Olympic Blvd Suite 306 Los Angeles CA 90015

GALE, DANIEL BAILEY, architect; b. St. Louis, Nov. 6, 1933; s. Leone Caryll and Gladys (Wotowa) G.; student Brown U., 1951-53, Ecole Des Beaux Arts, Paris, 1954-55; B.Arch., Washington U., 1957; m. Nancy Susan Miller, June 15, 1957; children—Caroline Hamilton, Rebecca Fletcher, Daniel Bailey With Gale & Cannon, Architects and Planners, Hellmuth, Obata & Kassabaum, Inc., Architects, St. Louis, and exec. v.p. corp. devel., dir. HOK, Inc., St. Louis, 1961-79; ptnr. Heneghan and Gale, architects and planners, Aspen, Colo., 1967-69; gen. ptnr. Gale, Hornberger & Worstell, Architects, San Francisco, 1979-83; pres., chief exec. officer Gale, Kober Assocs., San Francisco, Los Angeles, Seattle, Phoenix, Dallas, Chgo., Honolulu, N.Y.C. and London, 1983—. Recipient Henry Adams prize Washington U., 1957, also sophmore and final honors. Mem. AIA, Singapore Inst. Architects. Home: 13 Peninsula Rd Belvedere CA 94920 Office: 170 Maiden Ln San Francisco CA 94108

GALE, GLEN DONALD, television executive, educator, lecturer; b. Salt Lake City, Aug. 23, 1933; s. Glen Franklin and Doris (Raddon) G.; m. Doris Jean Chipman, June 24, 1954; children—Michael, Pamela, Christine. B.A., U. Utah, 1958, M.A., 1960, postgrad., 1976-82. Editor, Utah Power & Light Co., 1958-61; U. Utah, 1961-65, instr., 1966-71; instr. Weber State Coll., 1965-66; mng. editor Olympus Pub. Co., 1971-76; dir. Public Affairs KSL Radio and Television, 1977—. Served with U.S. Army, 1954-56. Recipient 1st place award editorial comment Radio/Television News Dirs. Assn., 1979, 80; Service to Journalism award, U. Utah, 1982. Mem. Soc. Profl. Journalists, Nat. Broadcast Editorial Assn., Public Relations Soc. fellow, 1969. Mormon. Co-author: Career Education in the High School, 1977; Your Child's Career, 1977. Office: 55 N 3d W Salt Lake City UT 84101

GALE, HOYT RODNEY, paleontologist, author; b. Boston, Aug. 1, 1904; s. Hoyt Stoddard and Almira Louise (Miller) G.; A.B. magna cum laude, Harvard U., 1926; Ph.D. in Geology and Paleontology, Stanford U., 1929; M.A. in Econs., UCLA, 1936; m. Violet Jane Ransome, Aug. 4, 1929 (dec. 1933); m. 2d, Marian Blewitt, June 20, 1940; children—Laurence Stanley, Carole Lorraine; m. 3d, Barbara Rolens, Aug. 5, 1952; m. 4th, Alta Ireland Yetter, Feb. 9, 1980. Geologist, Gulf Oil Corp., 1930; asst. geologist, spl. agt. U.S. Gen. Land Office and Bur. Land Mgmt., 1931-33; tchr. Pasadena (Calif.) Jr. Coll., 1938-44; vis. lectr. U. So. Calif., 1944-47; asso. prof. Pasadena City Coll., 1947-70; sci. research and writing, 1970—; cons. geologist. Mem. Paleontol. Soc., Am. Assn. Petroleum Geologists, Am. Econ. Assn., Sierra Club. Republican. Congregationalist. Club: B & B Square Dance. Author: (with U.S. Grant IV) Pliocene and Pleistocene Mollusca of California, 1931; The Natural Path to Genuine Lasting Happiness, 1976. Home: 823 St Clair St Costa Mesa CA 92626 Office: 669 Sturtevant Dr Sierra Madre CA 91024

GALE, LARRIE ELDON, instructional scientist; b. Salt Lake City, Feb. 16, 1942; s. Eldon and Reha Myrl (Higginson) G.; m. Nell Velasco, Sept. 11, 1964; children—Eldon, Donald, Sean, Taña, Tamra, Kim. B.A., San Diego State U., 1967, M.A., 1970; Ph.D., U. Wash., 1973. Instr., San Diego State U., 1968-70; adminstr. U. Utah, Salt Lake City, 1970-72, researcher, 1972-73; adminstr. U. Tex., San Antonio, 1973-78; researcher David O. McKay Inst., Brigham Young U., Provo, 1978—; cons. Dept. Def., Govt. Bolivia, Govt. Mexico, Def. Lang. Inst. Leader, Ch. Jesus Christ Latter-day Saints, 1975-78, Pleasant Grove, Utah, 1979—. Recipient grants SONY, Atari, Tex. Instruments, BBC, Dept. Def., and others. Mem. Soc. Intercultural Edn., Tng. and Research, Assn. Ednl. Communications and Tech., Phi Kappa Phi, Sigma Delta Pi, Alpha Mu Gamma. Republican. Co-author, designer computer programs, videodiscs. Office: 113 KMB Brigham Young U Provo UT 84602

GALEENER, FRANK LEE, physicist; b. Long Beach, Calif., July 31, 1936; s. Floras Frank and Daisy Elizabeth (Lee) G.; S.B., M.I.T., 1958, S.M. (Woodrow Wilson fellow), 1962; Ph.D. in Physics, Purdue U., 1970; m. Janet Louise Trask, June 7, 1959. Physicist, Lincoln Lab., M.I.T., 1959-61, Nat. Magnet Lab., 1961-64; scientist Xerox Palo Alto (Calif.) Research Center, 1970-73, mgr. semicondr. research, 1973-77, prin. scientist, 1977—; mem. com. on recommendations U.S. Army Basic Sci. Research, 1976-79; co-chmn. adv. panel amorphous materials Dept. of Energy Div. Materials Sci., 1980; adv. panel solid state physics Office of Naval Research, 1980. Mem. Am. Phys. Soc. (program com. ann. meeting 1981, 82), Am. Ceramic Soc., Optical Soc. Am., Sigma Xi, Sigma Pi Sigma. Editor: (with G. Lucovsky) Structure and Excitations of Amorphous Solids, 1976; (with G. Lucovsky and S.T. Pantelides) The Physics of MOS Insulators, 1980. Home: 4035 Orme St Palo Alto CA 94306 Office: 3333 Coyote Hill Rd Palo Alto CA 94304

GALEF, ANDREW GEOFFREY, executive; b. Yonkers, N.Y., Nov. 3, 1932; s. Gabriel and Anne (Fruchter) G.; m. Suzanne Jane Cohen, June 26, 1954 (div. Feb. 1964); children—Stephanie, Marjorie, Michael; m. 2d, Billie Ruth Medlin, Nov. 7, 1964; children—Phyllis, Catherine. B.A., Amherst Coll., 1954; M.B.A., Harvard U., 1958. Vice pres. Kamkap, Inc., 1958-61; pres. Zeigler-Harris Corp., 1961-63; exec. v.p. Fullview Industries, 1964-65; cons. Mordy & Co., 1966-67; prin. Grisanti & Galef, Inc., Encino, Calif., 1968—; pres. The Spectrum Group, Inc., Encino, 1978—; chmn., chief exec. officer Aviall, Inc., Dallas, 1979—, Century Electric, Inc., St. Louis, 1983—; dir. Mid-Atlantic Coca Cola Bottling Co., Cin. Coca Cola Bottling Co., Exide Corp., Pacific Homes, Inc. Served to capt. USAF, 1954-56. Clubs: Woodland Hills (Calif.) Country; Sunrise Country (Rancho Mirage, Calif.). Office: 16000 Ventura Blvd Encino CA 91436

GALEY, DAVID WINLOCK, business exec.; b. Shawnee, Okla., Aug. 23, 1929; s. Harry Winlock and Bernice Bridget (Henley) G.; B.S. in Archtl. Engring., U. Okla., 1952; m. Alice Roberta Johnston, June 17, 1967; children—Brian, Deborah, Sandra, Jane, Theresa, Dan. Structural designer Douglas Aircraft Co., Tulsa, 1952-57; engring. program mgr. Rohr Industries, Chula Vista, Calif., 1957-68; owner Devel. Tech. Co., Riverside, Calif., 1968-71; chief engr. Hunter Engring., Riverside, 1971-72; owner, gen. mgr. Computer Center, Riverside, 1977-79; pres. Docktor Pet Center, Riverside, 1973—; instr. engring. Yuba Evening Coll., 1954-55. Vice chmn. Environ. Protection Commn., Riverside, 1977-79. Served with C.E. U.S. Army, 1952-54, with USCG, 1958-60. Mem. Tyler Mall Mchts. Assn. (pres.). Republican. Club: Kiwanis. Home: 10280 Balmoral Ct Riverside CA 92503 Office: 3517 Tyler Mall Riverside CA 92503

GALICK, ARTHUR, physician; b. N.Y.C., Nov. 13, 1939; 2 children. Student SUNY, Binghamton, 1956-58; B.A., CUNY, 1961; M.D., N.Y. Med. Coll., 1965. Med. intern Downstate Med. Ctr. State N.Y., 1965-66; resident N.Y. Med. Coll., 1966-69, fellow in cardiology, 1969-70; fellow in cardiology Pacific Med. Ctr., San Francisco, 1972-73; practice medicine specializing in clin. and lab. cardiovascular disease, 1972—; dir. Cardiology Lab., Huntington Intercommunity Hosp., 1972-76, dir. critical care, 1976-77, chief staff, 1981; asst. clin. prof. medicine cardiology div. U. Calif.-Irvine. Diplomate Am. Bd. Internat Medicine. Fellow ACP, Am. Coll. Cardiology, Council Clin. Cardiology; mem. AMA, Orange County Med. Assn. Served with USN, 1970-72. Home: 17752 Beach Blvd Huntington Beach CA 92647

GALIN, RICHARD SAFIR, psychiatrist; b. Milw., Sept. 27, 1940; s. Benjamin Philip and Marion (Safir) G.; B.A., U. Wis., 1962; M.D., Harvard, 1966. Intern, UCLA Med. Center, 1966-67; resident psychiatry Langley Porter Neuropsychiat. Inst., San Francisco, 1967-70; staff psychiatrist student mental health service UCLA 1974—. Served with USNR, 1962-70. Recipient Physicians Recognition award AMA. Diplomate Nat. Bd. Med. Examiners, Am. Bd. Psychiatry and Neurology. Mem. Am. Psychiat. Assn., So. Calif. Psychiat. Soc., Phi Beta Kappa, Eta Sigma Phi, Phi Eta Sigma. Contbr. articles to profl. jours. Home: PO Box 24655 Los Angeles CA 90024 Office: U Calif Center for Health Scis Los Angeles CA 90024

GALL, ERIC PAPINEAU, physician; b. Boston, May 24, 1940; s. Edward Alfred and Phyllis Hortense (Rivard) G.; A.B., U. Pa., 1962, M.D., 1966; m. Katherine Elizabeth Theiss, Apr. 20, 1968; children—Gretchen Theiss, Michael Edward. Intern, U. Cin., 1966-67, resident in internal medicine, 1967-68; resident in internal medicine Hosp. U. Pa., 1970-71; fellow in rheumatology, research trainee rheumatic diseases, Hosp. U. Pa., Phila. VA Hosp., 1971-73; chief rheumatology service Tucson VA Hosp., 1973-78; asst. prof. internal medicine U. Ariz. Med. Sch., 1973-78, assoc. prof., 1978-83, prof. internal medicine, 1983—, prof. surgery (orthopedics), family and community medicine, 1983—, chief rheumatology, allergy and immunology sect., dept. internal medicine, 1983—; cons. U.S. VA Hosp., Tucson, Social Security Disability Bur. of Hearings and Appeals. Bd. dirs. So. Ariz. Arthritis Found., 1975—, chmn. med. and sci. com., 1977-79; nat. ho. of dels. Nat. Arthritis Found., 1980—, trustee, 1981—, vice-chmn., 1982-83. Served with M.C., U.S. Army, 1968-70: Vietnam. Decorated Bronze Star. Diplomate Am. Bd. Internal Medicine. Fellow ACP; mem. Am. Rheumatism Assn., Arthritis Health Profls. Assn. (2d v.p. 1980-81, v.p. 1981-82, pres. 1982-83), N.Y. Acad. Sci., Assn. Am. Med. Colls., Am. Fedn. Clin. Research, Ariz. Acad. Arthritis Health Profls., Alpha Omega Alpha, Alpha Epsilon Delta. Contbr. articles to profl. jours. Office: Clinical Immunology Section Arizona Health Sciences Center Tucson AZ 85724

GALL, MEREDITH DAMIEN, education educator, author; b. New Britain, Conn., Feb. 18, 1942; s. Theodore A. and Ray (Ehrlich) G.; m. Joyce Pershing, June 12, 1968; 1 son, Jonathan. A.B., Harvard U., 1963, Ed.M., 1963; Ph.D., U. Calif., Berkeley, 1968. Sr. research assoc. Far West Lab. for Ednl. Research and Devel., San Francisco, 1968-75; assoc. prof. edn. U. Oreg., 1975-79, prof., 1980—. Mem. Am. Ednl. Research Assn., Am. Psychol. Assn., Assn. Supervision and Curriculum Devel., Phi Delta Kappa (Dist. I Meritorious award 1978). Author: (with K. A. Acheson) Techniques in the Clinical Supervision of Teachers, 1980; Handbook for Evaluating and Selecting Curriculum Materials, 1981; (with Borg) Educational Research: An Introduction, 4th edit., 1983; editor: (with B.A. Ward) Critical Issues in Educational Psychology, 1974; cons. editor Jour. Ednl. Research. Office: U Oreg Coll Edn Eugene OR 97403

GALLAGHER, DENNIS JOSEPH, state senator, educator; b. Denver, July 1, 1939; s. William Joseph and Ellen Philomena (Flaherty) G.; B.A., Regis Coll., 1961; M.A., Cath. U. Am., 1968; postgrad. (Eagleton fellow) Rutgers U., 1972; m. Joanne Ruth Froling, July 8, 1973; 1 dau., Meaghan Kathleen. With locals of Internat. Assn. Theatrical and Stage Employees, Denver and Washington, 1956-63; tchr. St. John's Coll. High Sch., Washington, 1964-66, Heights Study Center, Washington, 1965-67, Regis Coll., 1967; mem. Colo. Ho. of Reps from 4th Dist., 1970-74; mem. Colo. Senate, 1974—. Mem. Platte Area Reclamation Com., 1973—; mem. Denver Anti-Crime Council, 1976-77; trustee Denver Art Mus.; bd. dirs. Cath. Community Services; mem. Colo. Commn. on Aging; mem. Colo. State Adv. Council on Career Edn. Mem. Colo. Fedn. Tchrs. (pres. local 1333, 1972-74). Democrat. Roman Catholic. Club: Irish Fellowship. Home: 2511 W 32d Ave Denver CO 80211 Office: Dept Communication Regis Coll W 50th Ave and Lowell Blvd Denver CO 80221

GALLAGHER, DOLORES ELIZABETH RUEBECK, psychologist; b. N.Y.C., Aug. 7, 1944; d. Joseph and Elizabeth (Goehringer) Ruebeck; B.S., Fordham Coll., 1965; M.A., Duquesne U., 1967; Ph.D. in Psychology, U. So. Calif., 1979; m. William Gallagher, Aug. 27, 1966 (dec. 1979); m. 2d, Larry W. Thompson, Dec. 12, 1981. Rehab. psychologist Fedn. of Handicapped, N.Y.C., 1967-72; staff psychologist Altoona (Pa.) Hosp. Community Mental Health Center, 1972-74; clin. psychologist Los Angeles County Dept. Personnel, Occupational Health Service, 1974-75, cons. psychologist, 1976-79; clin. psychology intern UCLA Neuropsychiat. Inst., 1977-78; dir. Adult Counseling Center, Andrus Gerontology Center, U. So. Calif., 1978-80, sr. staff assoc. Inst. for Policy and Program Devel., 1981—; coordinator interdisciplinary team tng. program in geriatrics Palo Alto VA Hosp., 1981—; social sci. research assoc. Stanford U. Sch. Medicine, 1981—; tng. cons. Rancho Los Amigos Hosp., Downey, Calif., VA Hosp., Palo Alto, Calif. NIMH fellow, 1975-77. Mem. Am., Western psychol. assns., Nat., Western gerontol. socs. Democrat. Contbr. chpts. to books, articles to profl. jours. Home: 355 Los Altos Ave Los Altos CA 94022 Office: GRECC Palo Alto VA Hosp 3801 Miranda Ave Palo Alto CA 94304

GALLAGHER, DONALD MCNAUGHTON, surgeon; b. Rossford, Ohio, Mar. 25, 1922; s. Joseph and Gertrude (McNaughton) G.; student U. Toledo, 1940-43; M.D., Washington U., St. Louis, 1946; m. Elizabeth Harlow, Nov. 4, 1944; children—Mary (Mrs. Warren Brown), Lon, Donald McNaughton, Dennis, Anne, Joan, Robert, Nancy. Intern DePaul Hosp., St. Louis, 1946-47, Brooke Gen. Hosp., Ft. Sam Houston, Tex., 1947-48; resident in surgery St. Louis VA Hosp., 1949-52; preceptee Dr. Robert A. Scarborough, San Francisco, colon and rectal surgery, 1952-54; practice medicine specializing in surgery, San Francisco, 1952—; clin. instr. Stanford Sch. Medicine, 1952-72; asso. clin. prof. surgery U. Calif. Med. Center, 1974—; chief staff St. Mary's Hosp., San Francisco, 1971-73; mem. exec. com. Children's Hosp. and Adult Med. Center, San Francisco, 1974-78. Chmn. San Francisco Com. to Establish Enterostomal Therapy Center, 1969; bd. dirs. Bay Area Health Facilities Planning Assn., 1966-70, St. Mary Hosp. and Med. Center, San Francisco, 1980—. Named papal Knight St. Gregory. Diplomate Am. Bd. Colon and Rectal Surgery (bd. pres. 1972-74). Fellow A.C.S. (gov. 1970-76, chmn. bd. govs. 1975-76, v.p. 1978), Am. Soc. Colon and Rectal Surgeons (council 1973-75, pres. 1978); mem. San Francisco Med. Soc. (dir. 1962-65, del. 1964-68), Calif. Med. Assn., Pacific Coast Surg. Assn., San Francisco Surg. Soc., No. Calif. Proctologic Soc. (pres. 1969-70). Asso. editor Jour. Diseases of Colon and Rectum, 1968-78. Cons. Calif. Adv. Hosp. Council, 1969-71. Contbr. articles to profl. publs. Home: 728 Eucalyptus Dr Novato CA Office: 3838 California St San Francisco CA 94118

GALLAGHER, MARIAN GOULD, law librarian, law educator; b. Everett, Wash., Aug. 29, 1914; d. John Hughes and Grace (Smith) Gould; student Whitman Coll., 1931-32; A.B., U. Wash., 1935, LL.B., 1937, B.L.S., 1939; m. D. Wayne Gallagher, Oct. 1, 1942 (dec. 1953). Asst. law librarian U. Wash., 1937-39, law librarian, and asst. prof. law, 1944-48, law librarian, asso. prof. law, 1948-53, prof. law, 1953-81, prof. emeritus, 1981—; law librarian instr. law U. Utah, 1939-44; vis. prof. law, disting. law librarian U. Calif., Hastings, 1982. Mem. Gov.'s Commn. on Status of Women, 1964-71, Pres.'s Nat. Adv. Commn. Libraries, 1967-68; adv. com. White House Conf. Library and Info. Services, 1977-80. Recipient Disting. Service Citation award Am. Assn. Law Libraries, 1966; Disting. Alumnus award U. Wash. Sch. Librarianship, 1970, Disting. Service citation, 1980; Alumna of Merit citation Whitman Coll., 1981. Fellow Am. Bar Found.; mem. Am. Assn. Law Libraries (pres. 1954-55), Am., Wash., Seattle-King County (sec. 1960-61) bar assns., Mortar Bd., P.E.O., Order of Coif, Delta Delta Delta, Phi Delta Delta. Presbyterian. Home: 1000 8th Ave Seattle WA 98104

GALLAGHER, NANCY ELIZABETH, tax consultant; b. Ontario, Oreg., June 27, 1950; d. Martin P. and Dorothy Ann (Bush) G.; 1 dau., Susan. Lic. tax cons., lic. tax preparer. Tax preparer H.R. Block, Eugene, Oreg., 1974-76; tax cons. Scheer & Stewart, Eugene, 1976-77; ptnr. Gallagher & Gleason, Eugene, 1977-79, Gallagher, Gleason & Raven, 1979—; instr. Lane Community Coll., H.R. Block. Bd. dirs., pres. Aslan House, Eugene, 1982-83; bd. dirs. Unity Sch., 1978-83, Alliance for Career Advancement, 1980, Lane Community Coll. Bus. Assistance Ctr., 1983. Mem. Assn. Tax Cons. (pres. 1977-79, nat. v.p. 1981-82, Above and Beyond award 1978, 79), Oreg. Assn. Tax Cons. (sec.). Republican. Episcopalian. Editor Oreg. Assn. Tax Cons. Newsletter; contbr. articles on taxes and tax law changes to profl. jours. Home: 995 Waverly Eugene OR 97401 Office: 1745 Coburg Rd #2 Eugene OR 97401

GALLAGHER, WILLIAM JOSEPH, stock broker; b. Mt. Vernon, N.Y., Aug. 5, 1924; s. Joseph William and Mary Bobbie (Menagh) G.; student N.Y. U., 1941-42, Pasadena Theatre Arts Coll., 1951-52, U. So. Calif., 1959-61, U. Calif. Grad. Sch. Bus. Adminstrn., Los Angeles, 1964-65; m. Ethel Elizabeth Caucci, Oct. 19, 1947; children—John W., William Joseph, T. Clayton, Craig, Pamela, Damian, Robert. Sales mgr. Royal Distbrs., 1947-50, Bellmar Sales & Mktg. Co., 1950-54; resident mgr. Marache, Dofflemyre Co., Pasadena, 1954-68, Merrill, Luther, Kalis & Co., Pasadena, 1968-73; v.p., resident mgr. Sterling West, Inc., Pasadena, 1973-76; pres. Gallagher, Gliksman, Boylan, Robbins, Keegan & Dow, Inc., Pasadena, 1977—; pres., dir. Pasadena Mgmt. Co., Inc. Bd. dirs. Radiol. Atomic Def. Emergency Force Group, Los Angeles County, 1968-70, Vis. Nurses Assn. Pasadena-San Gabriel Valley. Served with USMCR, 1942-46; PTO. Mem. Officers Assn. Calif. State Mil. Res. (chmn. bd.), 2d Marine Div. Assn. (pres. 1970, dir. Semper Fi council Los Angeles County), Officers Assn. Calif. N.G. Res. (pres. 1969, 81), Am. Legion (v.p. 1949), Bus. and Profl. Mens Assn. Los Angeles, Pasadena Bond Club, Pasadena C. of C. Clubs: Optimist (pres. 1959) (Pasadena); Vaquero (pres. 1981) (Glendale); Bond (Los Angeles). Home: 2627 Hermosita Dr Glendale CA 91208 Office: 747 E Green St Pasadena CA 91101

GALLATIN, JUDITH ESTELLE, psychologist, author, researcher; b. Grand Rapids, Mich., Feb. 15, 1942; Marcus Laniado and Marilyn (Gittlen) Gallatin; m. Charles Everett Helppie, Jan. 2, 1975; stepchildren—Charles, Bruce, Kathleen; B.A., U. Mich., Ann Arbor, 1962, M.A., 1963, Ph.D., 1967. Lic. psychologist, Mich. Research assoc. U. Strathclyde (Eng.), 1968; asst. prof. to prof. Eastern Mich. U., 1968-77; author-researcher, 1977—; cons., Ford Found., 1975; reviewer, NSF, 1979—. Mem. Portland chpt. Com. on Fgn. Relations. USPHS research fellow, 1963-66; teaching fellow, U. Mich., 1966-67; project dir. U.S. Office of Edn. Grant, 1970-72. Mem. Am. Psychol. Assn., Western Psychol. Assn., Soc. Research Child Devel., Am. Orthopsychiat. Assn., Phi Beta Kappa. Club: Portland City. Author: Adolescence and Individuality: A Conceptual Approach to Adolescent Psychology (1975); Abnormal Psychology: Concepts, Issues, Trends (1982); co-author: Understanding Adolescence (1976); Handbook of Adolescent Psychology 1980; contbr. articles to jours.

GALLAUGHER, LESLIE CARTER, banker; b. Seattle, Mar. 7, 1938; s. Leslie Paul and Vera Juanita (Carter) G.; B.A. in Bus. Adminstrn., U. Wash., 1960; M.B.A., Golden Gate U., San Francisco, 1969; m. Mary Virginia Williams, Sept. 11, 1965; children—Michael Scott, Scott Carter, Kevin Patrick. Trust ops. clk. Bank of Calif., Seattle, 1962-64; sr. investment officer trust investment dept. Bank Am., San Francisco, 1964-78; investment officer personal investment mgmt. group Wells Fargo Bank, San Francisco, 1978-79; sr. investment officer Office of Treas., U. Calif., Berkeley, 1979—. Served with Wash. N.G., 1962. Chartered fin. analyst. Mem. Security Analysts San Francisco, Fin. Analyst Fedn., U. Wash. Alumni Assn. Home: 3104 Perra Way Walnut Creek CA 94598 Office: 2200 University Ave Room 615 Berkeley CA 94720

GALLAWAY, MARTHINE SOLARES, artist; b. Oakland, Calif., June 15, 1913; d. Hector Lorillard and Alma A. (Steffensen) Solares; B.A., U. Nev., 1934; postgrad. Positano (Italy) Art Sch., 1961; m. Howard M. Gallaway, June 14, 1936; children—Heather, Bruce, Brian, Kent, Kirk. Painter in glazes on ceramic tile; muralist; represented in numerous pvt. and public locations; chmn. San Carlos Art Commn., 1973. Mem. San Carlos City Hall Bldg. Com., 1967, San Carlos Library Bldg. Com., 1959-63. Fellow AAUW (pres. San Carlos br. 1958); mem. Am. Soc. Interior Designers, Zeta Tau Alpha, Cap and Scroll. Club: Univ. (Palo Alto). Commd. by Piedmont (Calif.) Community Ch. to execute 8 tile panels for courtyard fountain, 1964; murals pictured in nat. publs. including House & Garden Decorating Guide, 1966-67, 70, House Beautiful Decoration Guide, House Beautiful, American Home, Interior Planning & Design, Designers West Showcase Houses; developer original glazes, ceramic mural art form techniques. Home and Office: 1400 Native Sons Rd Woodside CA 94062

GALLEGO-GARCÍA, JOSÉ MIGUEL, analytical chemist, laboratory executive, educator; b. Mexicali, Baja California, Mexico, Nov. 5, 1955; came to U.S., 1981, naturalized, 1983; s. Waldemar Gallego-Muñóz and Josefina García-Baker; m. Leticia Osuna Torronteguí, Jan. 21, 1981. Chemist (Univ. Spl. scholar), Universidad Autónoma de Guadalajara (Mex.), 1977; certs. various edn. courses. Analytical chemist and supr. State Water Commn., Tijuana, Baja California, 1978-79; chief instrumental analytical chemist Química Orgánica de México, S.A., Mexicali, 1979-81; owner, mgr. Laboratorios Industriales y Servicios Técnicos, S.A., Tijuana, 1981—; prof. lasers applied to chemistry Universidad Autónoma de Guadalajara, 1976, prof. chemistry and physics, 1977-78; prof. BASIC programming in chemistry, instrumental analysis, algebra, numerical analysis Universidad Autónoma de Baja California, Tijuana, 1981—. Served with Mexican Army, 1973-74. Recipient cert. for outstanding programmable calculator programs in area of chemistry Profl. Program Exchange of Tex. Instruments, Inc., 1977. Mem. Exptl. Sci. Soc. Tijuana (pres. 1972-73), Mexican Chem. Soc., Am. Chem. Soc. Roman Catholic. Contbr. articles to profl. jours., especially on programmable calculator programs of properties of water, radiochemistry, thermochemistry and analytical problems; editor Universidad Autónoma de Guadalajara Chem. Newsletter, 1974-77. Home: 1844 D Ave National City CA 92050 Office: Popocatepetl Number 700 Fraccionamiento La Sierra Tijuana Baja California Mexico

GALLEGOS, ANNE YVONNE, special education educator, grants assistant project director; b. St. Joseph, Mo., Oct. 8, 1946; d. Chester Rex and Sara Coe (Higbee) Steffey; m. Robert Levi Gallegos, Aug. 19, 1979; children—Michael Lee, Amy Rebecca, Heather Anne. Student U. Md., 1964-67; B.S. in Elem. and Secondary Edn., N.Mex. State U., 1969, M.A.T., 1979, Ed.D. in Spl. Edn., 1979. Pub. sch. cert. history, English, library sci., spl. edn., adminstrn. High sch. tchr. Las Cruces (N.Mex.) Pub. Schs., 1969-74; program mgr. Open Door Ctr. for Disabled Children and Adults, Las Cruces, 1974-77; grad. asst. N.Mex. State U., Las Cruces, 1977-78, coordinator projects, Coll. Human and Community Services, asst. prof. spl. edn., Dept. Ednl. Specialties, asst. dir. Women's Ednl. Equity Act Project; coordinator, presenter profl. workshops and confs. in field, U.S. Mex. Mem. Assn. for Children with Learning Disabilities, (pres. N.Mex. chpt. 1979), Assn. for Retarded Citizens (bd. dirs. Las Cruces chpt. 1978-79), Assn. for Supervision and Curriculum Devel., Council for Exceptional Children (pres.-elect Las Cruces chpt. 1980), Nat. Assn. Bilingual Edn., N.Mex. Assn. Bilingual Edn., Epsilon Sigma Alpha, Phi Delta Kappa, Phi Kappa Phi. Democrat. Episcopalian. Recipient, participant various grants. Contbr. articles to profl. publs. Home: 2640 Ardis Las Cruces NM 88001 Office: Box 3AC New Mexico State Univ Las Cruces NM 88003

GALLENBECK, EDITH DARLENE, rehabilitation counselor, consultant; b. Denver, Sept. 3, 1932; d. Orval Fredrick and Darlene Faye (Simon) Johnston; m. William Glen Gallenbeck, Jan. 27, 1977; B.A. in Sociology, U. Colo., 1973; M.A. in Rehab. Counseling, U. No. Colo., 1977; postgrad. Columbia Pacific U. Cert. rehab. counselor. Counselor Wyo. State Penitentiary, Rawlens, 1975-76; counselor NW affiliate Western Regional Mental Health Ctr., Craig, Colo., 1977; program dir. Colorado Springs (Colo.) Life Care Ctr., 1978-79; pvt. practice personal growth counseling, Colorado Springs, 1979-80; sr. rehab. specialist Internat. Rehab. Assocs., Englewood, Colo., 1980—; cons. individuals, orgns., agys. Mem. Citizens Choice, 1982-83; mem. Republican Nat. Com., 1982-83. Mem. Nat. Rehab. Assn., Nat. Assn. Female Execs., Adminstrv. Mgmt. Soc., Am. Soc. Tng. and Devel. Republican. Home: 3105 Monica Dr W Colorado Springs CO 80916 Office: Internat Rehab Assocs 5500 S Syracuse St Suite 267 Englewood CO 80111

GALLETTA, JOSEPH LEO, physician; b. Bessemer, Pa., Dec. 21, 1935; s. John and Grace (Galletta) G.; student U. Pitts., 1953-56; M.D., U. Santo Tomas, Manila, Philippines, 1962; m. Teresita Suarez Soler, Feb. 19, 1961; children—John II, Angela, Eric, Christopher, Robert Francis, Michael Angelo. Intern, St. Elizabeth Hosp., Youngstown, Ohio, 1963-64; family practice medicine, 29 Palms, Calif., 1967-77, Hemet, Calif., 1977—; chief of staff 29 Palms Community Hosp., 1970-71, 73-76; vice chief of staff Hi-Desert Med. Center, Joshua Tree, Calif., 1976-77; chmn. dept. family practice Hemet Valley Hosp., 1981-83; pres. Flexisplint, Inc.; founding mem. Hemet Hospice; former cons. Morongo Basin Mental Health Assn. Hot Line. Hon. mem. 29 Palms Sheriff's Search and Rescue, 1971-77. Bd. dirs. 29 Palms Community Hosp. Dist., Morongo Unified Sch. Dist. Served with M.C. USN, 1964-67. Diplomate Am. Bd. Family Practice. Founding fellow West Coast div. Am. Geriatric Soc.; fellow Am. Acad. Family Practice; mem. AMA, Calif. Med. Assn., Am. Holistic Med. Assn. (charter), Calif. Soc. Treatment Alcoholism and Drug Dependencies, Riverside County Med. Assn., Am. Acad. Family Practice, Calif. Acad. Family Practice. Roman Catholic. Elk. Established St. Anthonys Charity Clinic, Philippines, 1965; inventor Flexisplint armboards. Home: 27691 Pochea Trail Hemet CA 92343 Office: 850 E Latham Ave Suite B Hemet CA 92343

GALLI, DARRELL JOSEPH, mgmt. cons.; b. Ft. Bragg, Calif., Nov. 10, 1948; s. Joseph Germain and Esther Edith (Happajoki) G.; B.A., San Francisco State U., 1975; M.B.A., Golden Gate U., 1980, postgrad., 1980-81; m. Rondus Miller, Apr. 23, 1977 (div. 1981); 1 dau., Troyan Hulda. With Pacific Gas & Electric Co., Santa Cruz, Calif., 1972-73; with Calif. Western R.R., Ft. Bragg, 1975-77, Sheldon Oil Co., Suisun, Calif, 1978-80; mgr. House of Rondus, Suisun, 1974-79; mgmt. cons., Suisun City, 1979—; instr. Solano Coll., 1979-81, Golden Gate U., 1981; mem. faculty U. Md. European div., Heidelberg, W.Ger., 1982—; coordinator Small Bus. Mgmt. Seminar, 1980. Asst. coordinator Sr. Citizens Survey for Solano Coll. and Sr. Citizens Center, 1980. Served with U.S. Army, 1969-71. Lic. Calif. real estate agt. Mem. Am. Assn. M.B.A. Execs., World Trade Assn., Bay Area Elec. R.R. Assn. Republican. Episcopalian. Club: Odd Fellows. Home: 321 Morrow St Fort Bragg CA 95437 Office: U Md Heidelberg W Ger APO New York NY 09102

GALLI, ROBERT JOSEPH, former sheriff; b. Elko, Nev., Dec. 2, 1927; s. Pete and Rose (Moderilli) G.; B.A. in Law Enforcement Adminstrn., San Jose State Coll., 1952; postgrad. Provost Marshal Gen. Sch., 1953, FBI nat. Acad., 1957; m. Marilyn Jeane Tavernia, Aug. 3, 1952; children—Robert M., Annette L., Gregory J. With Elko County Sheriff's Dept., 1950, Nev. Hwy. Patrol, 1953-55; chief of police, Sparks, Nev., 1955-60, 63-71; police adviser U.S. State Dept., Bangkok, Thailand, 1960-62; dir. personnel and mgmt. Sparks Nugget Inc., 1962-63; sheriff, Washoe County, Reno, Nev., 1971-83; div. bus. devel. Summit Engring. Corp., 1983—; dir. security Nat. Gov.'s Conf., 1973; former instr., U. Nev., former Provost Marshal Gen. Center. Vice chmn. Nev. State Commn. on Crime, Delinquency and Corrections, 1969—; chmn. Washoe County Allocation Com., 1971; former mem. Gov.'s Com. on Pub. Defender; mem. Com. on Detention and Corrections, 1971; spl. adviser on drugs to Pres. of A.M.A.; former chmn. adv. bd. U. Nev.; mem. exec. bd. Nev. Area Boy Scouts Am.; Nev. rep. Nat. Project SEARCH. Bd. dirs. Teenage Opportunity Program, 1969, Reno Redevel. Salvation Army, Washoe County Council on Alcoholism. Served to sgt. AUS, 1946, 1st lt., 1952. Recipient outstanding community service award Greater Reno-Sparks C. of C., 1969, civic service award Fraternal Order of Eagles, 1958; Nat. Law Enforcement Commendation medal SAR; Humanitarian award NCCJ. Mem. Western Nev. Peace Officers Assn. (dir.), Internat. Assn. Chiefs of Police, Nat. Sheriffs Assn., FBI Nat. Acad. Assos. (past pres. Utah-Nev. chpt.), Am. Legion, San Jose State Coll., U. Nev. alumni assns., Alpha Tau Omega, Chi Pi Sigma. Roman Catholic. Clubs: Reno Executive, Prospectors, Elks. Home: 920 York Way Sparks NV 89431 Office: 248 Winter St Suite 1 Reno NV 89503

GALLI, STANLEY WALTER, artist; b. San Francisco, Jan. 18, 1912; s. Ismene and Laura (Frediani) G.; m. Frances Margaret Salvato; children—Timothy, Thomas. Student San Francisco Sch. Fine Arts, 1936-38, Art Ctr. Sch., 1939. Illustrator, ptnr. Patterson & Hall, San Francisco, 1945-48; illustrator Saturday Evening Post, 1954-68, True Mag., 1954-68, McCalls Mag., 1964-68; advt. illustrator corps., also Readers' Digest, 1950-78; designer 23 U.S. postage stamps; art faculty San Francisco City Coll., 1967-74; cons., advt. designer Weyerhauser Co., 1952-68; one-man shows Nut Tree, 1972, Foremost McKesson Corp Hdqrs., 1974, Crocker Art Mus., Sacramento, 1980, Robert Mondavi Winery, 1981, Charles Semma Frye Art Mus., Seattle, 1983; two-man show Palm Springs Desert Mus., 1978; represented in permanent collections various corps., Palm Springs Desert Mus., N.Y. Soc. Illustrators Hall of Fame, U.S. Postal Service Archives. Recipient numerous awards for advt. and fiction illustration, stamp designs, others. Mem. N.Y. Soc. Illustrators, Soc. Animal Artists, San Francisco Soc. Illustrators. Address: PO Box 66 Kentfield CA 94904

GALLIATH, ANDRE PAUL, ceramic engineer, educator; b. Rheinfelden, Switzerland, April 19, 1943; s. Robert Emile and Martha (De Angeli) G.; m. Marion Rinko, Dec. 10, 1966; children—Lisa Lillian, Nicole Simone, Adam Paul. B.S. in Ceramic Engring., Rutgers U., 1965, Ph.D., 1969. Research scientist Interpace Corp., Los Angeles, 1969-72; v.p. and gen. mgr. Johanson Dielectrics, Burbank, Calif., 1972-79; pres. Novacap Inc., Burbank, 1980—; ptnr. Ceramic Correspondence Inst., Saugus, Calif. Mem. ceramic tech. adv. com. Los Angeles Trade Tech. Coll., 1980. Recipient Service Award So. Calif. sect. Nat. Inst. Ceramic Engrs., 1972. Mem. Am. Ceramic Soc., Nat. Inst. Ceramic Engrs. Republican. Office: 1811 N Keystone Burbank CA 91504

GALLIN, JOEL GARY, food company executive; b. Boston, Oct. 4, 1936; s. Henry Daniel and Rose (Shaler) G.; m. Ingrid Goldstein, Dec. 30, 1956; children—Deborah, Lisa, Stacy. B.A. in Biochemistry, U. Calif.-Berkeley, 1958. Asst. research pharmacologist Cutter Lab., Berkeley, 1958-61; quality control mgr. Hunt-Wesson Foods, Hayward, Calif., 1961-67, quality assurance technologist, Fullerton, 1969-71, mgr. research and devel. project planning, 1971-72, quality assurance mgr., 1972-78, dir. quality assurance, 1978—; assoc. divisional dir. quality assurance Gen. Foods, Chgo., 1967-69; instr. Chapman Coll. Served with USCGR, 1954-62. Mem. Inst. Food Technologists. Author (with R.J. Moshy) Factors Affecting Quality-Consumer, Cost and Government, 1980. Office: Hunt-Wesson Foods 1645 W Valencia Dr Fullerton CA 92633

GALLINGTON, ROGER WAYNE, engineer, former air force officer; b. Balt., Dec. 12, 1937; s. Ralph Ora and Mary Katherine (Roales) G.; m. Alice Louise Moreau, June 10, 1961; children—Steven, Elizabeth, Katherine. B.S. in Mech. Engring., U. Ill., Urbana, 1960, M.S. in Mech. Engring., 1961, Ph.D. in Aero. and Astronautical Engring., 1969. Cert. comml. pilot; cert. flight instr. Commd. 2d lt. U.S. Air Force, 1960, advanced through grades to lt. col., 1977; mech. engr. Missile Site Activation, Little Rock, 1961-64; research assoc. Frank J. Seiler Research Lab., U.S. Air Force Acad., 1967-71, assoc. prof., 1971-75, 78-81; br. chief advanced vehicles, Naval Ship Research and Devel. Ctr., Bethesda, Md., 1975-78; ret., 1981; sr. staff engr. Martin Marietta Aerospace Co., Denver, 1981—; Street and sewer commr., Monument, Colo., 1982—. Mem. AIAA, Instrument Soc. Am. Presbyterian. Contbr. articles to profl. jours. Home: PO Box 38 Monument CO 80132 Office: Martin Marictta Acrospacc Co PO Box 179 Dcnvcr CO 80201

GALLISON, H(AROLD) BAILEY, hospital public relations exec.; b. Orange, N.J., Apr. 6, 1924; s. Harold Hobron and Stella Camille (Holm) G.; m. Janet Caralee Frazier, June 23, 1951; children—Claudia Jean, Harold Bailey II. B.A., U. Mo., 1948. Exec. dir. La Jolla (Calif.) Town Council, 1953-63; mktg. dir. Security Pacific Bank, San Diego, 1963-70; dir. pub. relations Mercy Hosp. and Med. Ctr., San Diego, 1970—. Bd. dirs., past pres. La Jolla Civic Center Corp.; bd. dirs. La Jolla Youth, Inc., treas., 1969-74; mem. team selection com. Holiday Bowl Assn.; bd. dirs. Muir Coll. Parents Council, U. Calif., San Diego, San Diego County Boys Club Found.; mem. adv. council Sr. Aides Project San Diego; chmn. citizens adv. council La Jolla High Sch., 1974-76; former com. mem. Andy Williams San Diego Open; coach boys baseball and flag football programs; co-chmn. beach area San Diego Padres Baseball Action Com. Served with USN, 1943-46. Mem. Nat. Soc. Fund Raisers (vice chmn. San Diego chpt. 1972), Am. Soc. for Hosp. Pub. Relations Dirs., So. Calif. Soc. for Hosp. Pub. Relations Dirs., Calif. Hosp. Assn. (news info. com.), San Diego C. of C. (chmn. sports com. 1969-73), U. Mo. Alumni Assn. (nat. dir., pres. San Diego chpt. 1960-75), San Diego Pub. Relations Club (pres. 1972, Pub. Relations Man of Yr. award 1973), U.S. Navy League, Am. Legion, Phi Kappa Psi. Republican. Presbyterian. Clubs: La Jolla Beach and Tennis, La Jolla Kiwanis (pres. 1960, lt. gov. dist. 21, Calif.-Nev.-Hawaii dist. 1962); San Diego Press (charter); Columns (U. Mo.). Home: 7940 Avenida Alamar La Jolla CA 92037 Office: 4077 7th Ave San Diego CA 92103

GALLIVAN, JOHN WILLIAM, publisher; b. Salt Lake City, June 28, 1915; s. Daniel and Frances (Wilson) G.; B.A., U. Notre Dame, 1937; m. Grace Mary Ivers, June 30, 1938; children—Gay, John, William, Michael D., Timothy. With Salt Lake Tribune, 1937—, promotion mgr., 1942-48, asst. pub., 1948-60, pub., 1960—; pres. Kearns-Tribune Corp., 1960—; v.p., dir. Telemation, Inc., 1963—, Tele-Communications, Inc., 1965—; pres. Silver King Mining Co., 1960—. Pres. Utah Symphony, 1964-65; exec. com. Pro-Utah, 1964—. Mem. Sigma Delta Chi. Clubs: Nat. Press (Washington); Alta, Salt Lake Country, Rotary (Salt Lake City). Home: 17 S 12th E Salt Lake City UT 84102 Office: care Newspaper Agy Corp 143 S Main St PO Box 838 Salt Lake City UT 84110*

GALLIVAN, LAURA LYN, former association executive; b. Piggott, Ark., Oct. 30, 1949; d. Richard Lynn and Edith Mae (Bain) Gower; m. Patrick John Gallivan, Apr. 8, 1980. Student Rock Valley Coll., 1968, So. Ill. U., 1969. Flight attendant N.W. Orient Airlines, Mpls.-St. Paul, 1970-72; employment cons. Exec. Staffing, Inc., Washington, 1972-73; cosmetologist Lord & Taylor, Washington, 1973-74; rep. NASCO Inc., Springfield, Tenn., 1974-76; promotion dir. Signal Hills Shopping Ctr., West St. Paul, Minn., 1976-79; dir. Downtown Council, St. Paul Area C. of C., 1979-82; part-time instr. Inver Hills Community Coll., Inver Grove Heights, Minn., 1978-82; mem. adv. com. small bus. mgmt. program., 1979-82; Mary Kay beauty cons., 1981-82. Bd. dirs. Downtown Community Devel. Council, St. Paul, 1980-82, St. Paul Winter Carnival Assn., 1979-82, Carriage Hill Mchts. Assn., 1980-82, Lowertown Community Council, 1979-82, Mem. Am. C. of C. Execs., Tchrs. Retirement Assn., Delta Zeta. Clubs: North Oaks Golf, St. Paul Athletic. Address: 72645 Hedgehog Palm Desert CA 92260

GALLOWAY, TERRY RANDOLPH, chem. engr.; b. Oakland, Calif., Sept. 25, 1940; s. Quince Rudolph and Janis Bonnie (Webster) G. B.S., U. Calif., Berkeley, 1962, M.S., 1963; Ph.D., Calif. Inst. Tech., 1967. Group leader, supr. Shell Devel. Co., Emeryville, Calif., 1967-75; asst. dir. San. Engring. Research Lab., lectr. environ. engring. U. Calif., Berkeley, 1972-75; sect. leader U. Calif. Lawrence Livermore Nat. Lab., 1975-82; mgr. Advanced Energy Conversion div. Mittelhauser Corp., Hercules, Calif., 1982—. engring. lectr. U. Calif., Berkeley, 1973-75. Vice chmn. San Leandro Bicentennial Com., 1976; pres. Casa Peralta Found., 1971-75; chmn. Oakland Pub. Sch. Earthquake Safety Com., 1972—; guest investigator Chabot Obs. and Sci. Center, 1968—. Fluor Found. fellow, 1964-67; Richfield Oil fellow, 1962-63. Mem. Am. Inst. Chem. Engrs., AAAS, Calif. Acad. Scis., Astron. Soc. Pacific, East Bay Astron. Soc., San Leandro Hist. Soc., Water Pollution Control Fedn., Sierra Club, Sigma Xi, Tower and Flame. Research and numerous publs. on thermophysical and transport properties of hydrocarbons, turbulent heat and mass transfer to cylinders and spheres, solar energy, fusion energy, thermochem. hydrogen, methanol, others. chem. engr.; b. Oakland, Calif., Sept. 25, 1940; s. Quince Rudolph and Janis Bonnie (Webster) G. B.S., U. Calif., Berkeley, 1962, M.S., 1963; Ph.D., Calif. Inst. Tech., 1967. Group leader, supr. Shell Devel. Co., Emeryville, Calif., 1967-75; asst. dir. San. Engring. Research Lab., lectr. environ. engring. U. Calif., Berkeley, 1972-75; sect. leader U. Calif. Lawrence Livermore Nat. Lab., 1975-82; mgr. Advanced Energy Conversion div. Mittelhauser Corp., Hercules, Calif., 1982—. engring. lectr. U. Calif., Berkeley, 1973-75. Vice chmn. San Leandro Bicentennial Com., 1976; pres. Casa Peralta Found., 1971-75; chmn. Oakland Pub. Sch. Earthquake Safety Com., 1972—; guest investigator Chabot Obs. and Sci. Center, 1968—. Fluor Found. fellow, 1964-67; Richfield Oil fellow, 1962-63. Mem. Am. Inst. Chem. Engrs., AAAS, Calif. Acad. Scis., Astron. Soc. Pacific, East Bay Astron. Soc., San Leandro Hist. Soc., Water Pollution Control Fedn., Sierra Club, Sigma Xi, Tower and Flame. Research and numerous publs. on thermophysical and transport properties of hydrocarbons, turbulent heat and mass transfer to cylinders and spheres, solar energy, fusion energy, thermochem. hydrogen, methanol, others. Home: 6833 Charing Cross Rd Berkeley CA 94705 Office: 560 Railroad Ave Hercules CA 94547

GALLUP, STAN, assn. exec.; b. Chamita, N.Mex., May 27, 1922; s. Arthur Hicks and Margaret Jane (Standley) G.; student U. N.Mex., 1940-42, Purdue U., 1942-43; m. Sue K. Knox, Jan. 26, 1942; 1 son, Gary Joe. Advt. dir. Las Cruces (N.Mex.) Sun News, 1946-54; part owner-mgr. radio sta. KGFL, Roswell, N.Mex., 1954-68; info. officer N.Mex. Mil. Inst., Roswell, 1968-70; exec. dir. Chaves County chpt. ARC, Roswell, 1970-71; dir. pub. relations and info. Santa Fe Downs Race Track, 1971-73; exec. dir., sec.-treas. Golden Gloves Assn. Am., Inc., 1964—. Pres. various athletic booster clubs; chmn. for Las Cruces and Roswell Recreation and Athletic Commn., 1947—. Served with USAAF, 1942-45; CBI; mem. ret. Res. Mem. Nat. Sportscasters and Sportswriters, N.Mex. Sportswriters Assn., VFW. Home: 8801 Princess Jeanne St NE Albuquerque NM 87112 Office: 9000 Menaul NE Albuquerque NM 87112

GALST, LESTER ROY, Realtor; b. Milw., Sept. 9, 1918; s. Joseph and Bertha (Slabodkin) G.; student U. Wis., 1936, Washington and Lee U., 1943; m. Madeline Serota, Jan. 31, 1965; children from previous marriage—Lynne Galst Aitken, Mildred Jo, Joel. Actor, dancer various studios, Hollywood, Calif., 1938-41, 46; owner Expcotation Shops, retail chain, Phoenix, 1947-63; buyer Bon Marche group Allied Stores Corp., Seattle, 1966-68; owner, broker Londonderry Realty, Gallery of Homes, Lake Havasu City, Ariz., 1968-80, Les Galst & Assos., Realtors, Lake Havasu City, 1980—, Ticket of Ariz., Scottsdale, 1981, Les Galst, Realtor, 1982—. Mem. bus. adv. council Mohave Community Coll., Lake Havasu City, 1974-75. Bd. dirs. Lake Havasu Assn. for Retarded and Handicapped, v.p., 1976, pres., 1977-78; bd. dirs. Lake Havasu Community Devel. Corp., 1979-81. Served to 1st lt. Signal Corps, AUS, 1941-45. Mem. Lake Havasu City C. of C. (pres. 1972), Mohave County Bd. Realtors (pres. 1974), Lake Havasu Bd. Realtors (hon. life mem.; pres. 1974-75, Realtor of Yr. 1975), Nat. Assn. Realtors (dir. 1981-83), Ariz. Assn. Realtors (exec. com. 1975-82, dir., 2d v.p. 1978, 1st v.p. 1979, pres. 1980, treas. 1982). Clubs: Elks, Masons. Home: 5566 N 76th Pl Scottsdale AZ 85253 Office: 5566 N 76th Pl Scottsdale AZ 85253

GALTON, SIDNEY ALAN, adminsistrative law judge; b. Portland, Oreg., Jan. 9, 1947; s. Herbert B. and Ida Mae G.; m. Cynthia Weintraub Weber, Aug. 6, 1970 (div. Dec. 1980); children—Amy Louise, Allen Weintraub. A.B. in German, Polit. Sci., Stanford U., 1969; J.D., U. Calif.-Berkeley, 1972. Bar: Oreg. 1972. Ptnr., Galton, Popick & Scott, Portland, 1972-81; adminstrv. law judge Oreg. Workers Compensation Bd., Salem and Portland, 1982—; attys.' fee arbitrator Oreg. State Bar, 1977, 78, 81; judge Northwestern Regional Moot Ct. Competition, 1977. Chmn. adv. com. Bridlemile Elem. Local Sch., Portland, 1978-80. Recipient Florence-Virginia K. Wilson scholar, 1969-70. Mem. Oreg. State Bar Assn., Multnomah Bar Assn., Oreg. Workers Compensation Attys. Assn. (pres. 1976-78). Democrat. Jewish. Rev. editor: Ecology Law Quar., U. Calif., 1971-72; contbr. in field. Office: 1201 SW 12th Ave Portland OR 97205

GALVAN, SABINO, public school business officer; b. Kyle, Tex., Oct. 27, 1934; s. Paul R. and Mary A. Galvan; student Trinity U., 1954; A.A., Sacramento Community Coll., 1960; B.S., Sacramento State U., 1967; m. Jo Ana K., June 12, 1981; children by previous marriage—Gregory P., Jeanette K.; stepchildren—Jimmy, Peggy, Donna, Steve, Todd. Auditor trainee dept. fin. State of Calif., Sacramento, 1962; tax examiner IRS, Sacramento, 1962-63; auditor-appraiser Sacramento County Assessor's Office, 1963-64; acct. Sacramento County Office Edn., 1965-67, adminstrv. asst., 1967-68; chief acct. San Juan Unified Sch. Dist., Carmichael, Calif., 1968-76, sr. fin. analyst, 1976-78, asst. dir. fin., 1978-80, dir. acctg. services, 1980—, chmn. payroll task force, 1977-78. Troop treas. Golden Empire council Boy Scouts Am., 1968-69, chmn. membership com., 1969-70; bd. dirs. Superior Calif. Sch. Employees Credit Union, 1977—, chmn. nominating com., 1979, chmn. planning com., 1979-80. Served with USAF, 1954-58. Mem. Calif. Assn. Sch. Bus. Ofcls. (dir. 1972-73, 75-76, pres. 1976-77, chmn. acctg. research and devel. com. 1980—), Assn. Calif. Sch. Adminstrs. (dir. 1982-83), San Juan Adminstrs. Assn. (dir. 1979—, pres. 1982-83), Assn. Calif. Sch. Adminstrs. Region III (v.p. programs), Calif. Assn. Purchasing Officers. Democrat. Home: 8215 Scarlet Oak Circle Citrus Heights CA 95610 Office: 3738 Walnut Ave Carmichael CA 95608

GALVIN, DENNIS MICHAEL, elec. engr.; b. Buffalo, Sept. 4, 1938; s. Edward Joseph and Margaret Ruth (Smiley) G.; B.S., Mich. State U., 1961; Social Welfare certificate, U. Calif., Irvine, 1973; m. Mary Edith Dakers, Dec. 16, 1960; children—Mary Margaret, Thomas Lee, Bonnie Jean. Engr., Lockheed Calif. Co., Burbank, 1961-62; sr. engr. research Rockwell Internat., Downey, Calif., 1962—; cons. community day care centers. Pres., chmn. bd. Orange Ch. Service Com., 1968-71; bd. dirs. Santa Ana/Tustin United Fund, Inc., Parent Involvement Council. Recipient Urban Service award Office Econ. Opportunity, 1968. Mem. I.E.E.E., Delta Chi. Methodist. Contbr. articles profl. jours. Home: 1134

E Darby St Orange CA 92665 Office: 12214 Lakewood Blvd Downey CA 90241

GALVIN, GEORGE TIMOTHY, marketing executive; b. Joliet, Ill., Jan. 3, 1951; s. George Charles and Mary Margaret (Meade) G. B.A., U. Calif.-Irvine, 1973; M.P.A., U. So. Calif., 1975. Asst. cruise dir. Bahama Cruise Lines, 1975; research asst. Ultra Systems Inc., 1975-76; sales mgr. Walker & Lee Real Estate, Anaheim, Calif., 1976-78; dir. sales and mktg. Taylor Woodrow Homes, Newport Beach, Calif., 1978—. Bd. dirs. Newport Harbor Art Mus. Mem. Inst. Residential Mktg., So. Calif. Sales and Mktg. Council (pres. 1983). Republican. Roman Catholic. Office: 1600 Dove St Suite 225 Newport Beach CA 92660

GAMAL, IRWIN (IRV) BERT, management consultant; b. Bklyn., Aug. 1, 1943; s. Murray H. and Rose (Jones) G.; A.A., Cerritos (Calif.) Coll., 1965; B.A., Calif. State U.-Long Beach, 1967, M.A., 1972; m. Karen Ann Sawko, Aug. 24, 1974. Regional zone mgr. ARC, Los Angeles, 1973-75; personnel rep. Vornado, Inc., Whittier, Calif., 1975, W. coast tng. mgr., 1975-77; dir. mgmt. devel. Wienerschnitzel, Internat., Newport Beach, Calif., 1977-81; v.p. Arrindell Assocs., Newport Beach, Calif., 1981; internal cons. Fluor Corp., Irvine, Calif., 1981—; instr., mem. mgmt. and supervisory adv. com. Coastline Community Coll., Fountain Valley, Calif.; lectr. Cerritos Coll., Norwalk, Calif., Saddleback Coll., Mission Viejo, Calif.; instr. U. Phoenix, Irvine. Vice pres. Center for Human Resources, Newport Beach Calif., 1980—. Recipient ARC Commendation for Outstanding Service, 1975; Disting. Service award LaCanada (Calif.) Sch. Dist., 1982, Mgmt. Inst. of Coastline Community Coll., 1983. Mem. Am. Soc. Tng. and Devel. (dir. 1978), Home: 28075 Klamath Ct Laguna Niguel CA 92677 Office: 3333 Michelson Dr Irvine CA 92730

GAMAN, RACHEL SIMMI, social worker; b. Chgo., July 14, 1949; d. Garrison George and Aldythe Phyllis (Wood) G.; 1 adopted dau., Ronda Renee. Student Mount San Antonio Coll., 1967-69, Calif. State U.-Fullerton, 1969-70; B.S., Calif. Poly. U., 1973; M.S.W., U. So. Calif., 1975. Lic. clin. social worker, Calif. Dir. social rehab. Met. Psychiat. Services, Los Angeles, 1975-76; dir. rehab. services Continuity of Care Home Health Agy., Los Angeles, 1976; med. social worker Kern Med. Center, Bakersfield, Calif., 1976-78; coordinator geriatric services Kern View Community Mental Health Center, Bakersfield, 1978-80; dir. social services Greater Bakersfield Meml. Hosp., 1980—; tchr. U. Calif. Santa Barbara Extension Program, 1976-80, Chapman Coll., Bakersfield Coll., 1978-82; cons. Hilltop Convalescent Hosp., Colonial Convalescent Hosp., 1979—, Park View Julian Convalescent Hosp., 1980-83, Park View Real Convalescent Hosp., 1980-83, Westchester Rehab. Agy., 1981—, Rosewood Health Facility, 1982—; pvt. practice psychotherapy, Bakersfield, 1979—. Mem. Nat. Assn. Social Workers, Am. Cancer Soc. (service com., profl. edn. com.), Med. Social Workers Kern County, Direct Alcohol Service Com. Democrat. Jewish. Club: Quota. Home: 4305 Garnsey Ln Bakersfield CA 93309 Office: 420 34th St Bakersfield CA 93301

GAMBELL, LEONA MARIE, psychologist; b. Hedrick, Iowa, Sept. 17, 1922; d. Ralph E. and Elizabeth (Zihlman) Gambell. B.A., Drake U., 1955; M.A., Drake U., 1956; Ph.D., Ariz. State U., 1973. Cert. clin. psychologist, sch. psychologist. Prof. psychology Doane Coll., 1954-56, Nebr. Wesleyan U., 1956-63, Nebr. State U., 1962-67, Phoenix Coll., 1967-73; cons. sch. psychologist Phoenix Pub. Schs., 1967—, Pinal County (Ariz.) Schs., 1973-78, Mesa (Ariz.) Pub. schs., 1978—; pvt. practice clin. psychology, Scottsdale, Ariz., 1967—; cons. in field. Mem. Am. Psychol. Assn., Ariz. Psychol. Assn., Maricopa County Psychol. Assn., Ariz. Sch. Psychologists Assn., Psi Chi. Democrat. Lutheran. Address: PO Box 2437 Scottsdale AZ 85252

GAMBER, LYNDEN LORRAINE, photographer; b. Longford, Kans., Feb. 21, 1917; s. Reuben Hayes and Mattie (Wiltse) G.; student Winona Sch. Profl. Photography; M.Photography, 1967; m. Mildred Arlene Bevan, July 4, 1937; 1 dau., Lynda Kathleen (Mrs. James Alton Bewley). Reporter, news editor, photographer Abilene (Kans.) Daily Chronicle, 1936-39; photographer Dodge City (Kans.) Globe, 1940-42; photographer, platemaker Warrensburg (Mo.) Star-Jour., 1942-45; owner Gamber Studio, Curtis, Nebr., 1945-55, Gamber's Aurora Photographers, Aurora, Colo., 1955-83. Recipient Photographer of Yr. award Profl. Photographers Greater Denver, 1960; (with wife) Nat. award Profl. Photographers Am., 1975. Mem. Profl. Photographers Colo., Profl. Photographers Am., Am. Soc. Photographers, Rocky Mountain Profl. Photographers Assn. (dir. 1957-63, pres. 1963-64), Photographers Greater Denver (pres. 1959-60, dir.), Aurora C. of C. (dir. 1972-74). Mason, Rotarian (pres. 1950-51). Home: 502 N Lima St Aurora CO 80010

GAMBLE, BARBARA JEAN, dietitian; b. Garden City, Kans., June 6, 1950; d. Joe P. and Anna M. (Burgardt) Dreiling; B.S. in Dietetics and Instl. Mgmt., Kans. State U., 1972; m. Don L. Gamble, Dec. 14, 1973; 1 dau., Angelene. Dietitian, Cinderella Nursing Home, Lamar, Colo., 1972-74, cons. dietitian, 1974—; dietitian Prowers Med. Center, Lamar, 1974—; cons. Holly Nursing Center, 1975—, SE Colo. Hosp., Springfield, 1978—; v.p. Wood-Gamble Funeral Home, Inc. Mem. Am. Dietetic Assn., Colo. Dietetic Assn., Cons. Dietitians in Health Care Facilities, Am. Legion Aux., Cath. Daus. Am., St. Frances Altar Soc., Beta Sigma Phi. Club: Eagles. Home: 402 Willow Valley Lamar CO 81052 Office: S Memorial Dr Lamar CO 81052

GAMBLE, DOUGLAS S., wholesale and retail foods company executive; b. 1925. Grad. Williams Coll.; postgrad. Stanford U. With Pacific Gamble Robinson Co., Inc., Kirkland, Wash., 1949—, v.p. distbg. brs., 1965, pres., chief exec. officer, dir., 1974—. Office: Pacific Gamble Robinson Co Inc 10829 NE 68th St Kirkland WA 98033*

GAMBLE, GEOFFREY L., educator, linguist; b. Kentfield, Calif., June 10, 1942; s. Thomas B. and Rosemary (Sechrist) G.; m. R. Janette Brisendine, Aug. 1963 (div.); children—Jennifer C., Lara J. B.A., Fresno (Calif.) State Coll., 1965; M.A., with distinction, Calif. State U., Fresno, 1971; Ph.D., U. Calif.-Berkeley, 1975. Research assoc. Survey of Calif. Indian Langs., Berkeley, 1971-73; teaching asst. dept. linguistics U. Calif.-Berkeley, 1972-75; linguistic cons. Head Start Program, Visalia, Calif., 1973-75; postdoctoral fellow Smithsonian Instn., Washington, 1975-76, cons. Harrington microfilm project, 1975—; linguistic cons. Hesquiat Lang. Program, 1978, Makah Lang. Program, 1978—; cons., evaluator Music and Culture of the Northwest project NEA, 1979-81; asst. prof. Wash. State U., Pullman, 1976-81, assoc. prof., 1981—, dir. gen. studies-linguistics, 1981—, chmn. dept. anthropology, 1982—. Grantee Shell Found., 1979, E.O. Holland, 1979, Nat. Endowment for Arts, 1978, Newhouse Found., 1971-72, Am. Philos. Soc., 1971. Mem. Am. Anthrop. Assn., Linguistic Soc. Am., Nat. Soc. Classical Guitar, Southwest Anthrop. Assn., AAAS, Sigma Xi, Phi Kappa Phi. Contbr. articles to profl. jours. Office: Dept Anthropology Wash State Univ Pullman WA 99164

GAMBLE, LARRY WARD, broadcasting co. exec.; b. Postville, Iowa, Feb. 1, 1943; s. Adrian W. and Arlene I. (Sanger) G.; A.A., Modesto Jr. Coll., 1964; B.A., Fresno State Coll., 1966; M.A., Calif. State U., Fresno, 1968; postgrad. Western Mich. U., 1973-74; cert. N.Y. Sch. Interior Design, 1975; m. Sylvia Ann Sprouls, June 11, 1964; children—Robert Lawrence, Johannes Sanger. Asst. prof. performing arts Kalamazoo (Mich.) Coll., 1969-74; asst. prof. design Coll. Santa Fe (N.Mex.), 1974-75; advt. account exec. Bob Eurich Enterprises, Fresno, Calif., 1975-76; advt. account exec. Sta. KMJ-TV, Fresno, 1976-81; chmn. Golden Oak Advt. Awards, 1979-80; treas. Calif. Sierra Corp.; dir. mktg. Pappas Teleprodns., Fresno, 1981—. Chmn., Clovis City Council Downtown Steering Com., 1979—. Ford Found. grantee, 1974. Mem. Am. Advt. Fedn. (bd. govs. dist. 14 1983-84, Silver medal 1983), AAUP, Fresno Advt. Fedn. (exec. bd. 1978—), Kings/Tulare Advt. Assn. (pres., 1979-80), Internat. Alliance Theatre and Stage Employees. Presbyterian. Home: 2179 Rall Ave Clovis CA 93612 Office: 5111 E McKinley Fresno CA 93727

GAMBLE, MICHAEL IRVING, aerospace co. exec.; b. Everett, Wash., Dec. 19, 1935; s. Paul I. and Margaret (Isacson) G.; B.S. in Physics, U. Wash., 1957; m. Charlotte A. Albrecht, Dec. 20, 1957; children—Michael Scott, Paula Michel. Asso. engr. applied physics staff Boeing Co., 1956-59, research engr. physics tech. dept., 1959-62; mgr. environ. physics dept. AVCO Corp., Tulsa Div., 1962-65, mgr. engring. instrument div., 1965-66, mgr. program devel., 1966-69, area marketing mgr. space applications, govt. products group, Los Angeles, 1970-72, area marketing mgr., govt. products group, Albuquerque, 1972-73; laser systems mgr. Boeing Aerospace Co., Seattle, 1974-79, dep. program mgr. designating optical tracker, 1979-81, mgr. ballistic missile def., 1981—. Served to capt. AUS, 1953-62. Asso. fellow Am. Inst. Aeros. and Astronautics; mem. Phi Kappa Psi. Club: National Space. Home: 13915 SE 241st St Kent WA 98031 Office: PO Box 3999 Seattle WA 98124

GAMBLE, THOMAS WILLIAM, electrical engineer; b. Poplar Bluff, Mo., May 15, 1937; s. William Woodrow and Georgia Irene (Perry) G.; children—Leslie Louise, William Edwin. B.S.E.E., Chico State Coll., 1961. Registered profl. engr., Calif. With U.S. Bur. Reclamation, 1961—, ops. and maintenance chief Folsom (Calif.) Field Div., 1965-68, Shasta Field Div., Redding, Calif., 1968-74, power ops. mgr. Colo. River Storage Project, Page, Ariz., 1974—; dir. All Field Insulation Co., Albuquerque. Mem. personnel bd. City of Page, 1979—. Club: Rotary. Home: PO Box 485 Page AZ 86040 Office: PO Box 1477 Page AZ 86040

GAMBOA, GEORGE CHARLES, oral surgeon; b. King City, Calif., Dec. 17, 1923; s. George Angel and Martha Ann (Baker) G.; pre-dental certificate Pacific Union Coll., 1943; D.D.S., U. Pacific, 1946; M.S., U. Minn., 1953; A.B., U. So. Calif., 1958; Ed.D., U. So. Calif., 1976; m. Winona Mae Collins, July 16, 1946; children—Cheryl Jan Gamboa Williams, Jon Charles, Judith Merlene Gamboa Hiscox. Fellow oral surgery Mayo Found., 1950-53; tchr. grad. program oral surgery U. So. Calif., Los Angeles, 1954—; assoc. prof. Loma Linda (Calif.) U., 1958—, chmn. dept. oral surgery, 1960-63; pvt. practice oral surgery, San Gabriel, Calif., 1955—. chmn. first aid com. West San Gabriel chpt. ARC. Diplomate Am. Bd. Oral and Maxillofacial Surgery. Fellow Am. Coll. Oral and Maxillofacial Surgeons, Am. Assn. Oral and Maxillofacial Surgeons; mem. Internat. Assn. Oral Surgeons, So. Calif. Soc. Oral and Maxillofacial Surgeons, Western Soc. Oral and Maxillofacial Surgeons, Am. Acad. Dental Radiology, Marsh Robinson Acad. Oral Surgeons, So. Calif. Acad. Oral Pathology, Profl. Staff Assn. Los Angeles County-U. So. Calif. Med. Center (exec. com. 1976—), Am. Cancer Soc. (profl. edn. subcom. 1977—), Xi Psi Phi, Omicron Kappa Upsilon, Delta Epsilon. Seventh-day Adventist. Home: 1102 Loganrita Ave Arcadia CA 91006 Office: 132 S Mission Dr San Gabriel CA 91776

GAMMILL, DARRYL CURTIS, financier; b. Milw., Jan. 20, 1950; s. Lawrence H. and Eunice G. (Birkett) G.; B.S., U. Colo., 1973; m. Maureen Mulcahy, Sept. 16, 1972; children—Rebecca, Bridgett, Maureen, Bryann. Stockbroker, Douglas, Stanat, Inc., Denver, 1974; dir. research Pittman Co., Denver, 1975; option specialist B.J. Leonard & Co., Denver, 1976; v.p. research, corp. fin. Neidiger, Tucker Bruner, Denver, 1977—; chmn., pres., chief exec. officer G.S. Omni Corp., 1979-82; chmn., chief exec. officer G.O.R.K. Corp.; mng. partner G.S. Leasing; pres., dir. Valudyne, Inc., 1973-79; pres. Chalton Investment Services; chmn., pres. Fusion Mgmt. Corp., 1981-83; dir. Am. Frontier, Search Natural Resoures; chmn. Applied Fusion Research & Tech. Corp.; gen. partner Fusion Ltd. Trustee Gammill Found.; v.p., bd. dirs. Opera Colo. Mem. Fin. Analysts Fedn., Nat. Assn. Security Dealers, Denver Soc. Security Analysts, Nat. Energy Assn. (nat. chmn.). Clubs: Optimists, Elks. Contbr. articles to profl. jours. Home: 9770 W Frost Pl Littleton CO 80123

GAMO, HIDEYA, electrical engineering educator; b. Ueda, Japan, Apr. 1, 1924; s. Toshioki and Shizuko (Kuwano) G.; B.S., U. Tokyo, 1946, D.Sc. in Physics, 1958; m. Yasko Ejima, Nov. 11, 1955; children—Yuriko, Kay. Came to U.S., 1958. Research asst. physics U. Tokyo, 1946-49, research asso., lectr., 1949-58; cons. physicist T. J. Watson Research Center, IBM Corp., 1958-59, research physicist, 1959-63; vis. prof. elec. engring. U. Rochester (N.Y.), 1963-64, prof. elec. engring. 1964-68; prof. elec. engring. U. Calif. at Irvine, 1968—, chmn. electronics engring. group 1971-75, chmn. bd. studies elec. engring. program, 1972-74; adv. com. elec., computer and systems engring. div. NSF, 1979-81. Fellow Soc. Photo-Optical Instrumentation Engrs., Optical Soc. Am.; mem. IEEE (sr.), AAAS, Am. Phys. Soc., Optical Soc. So. Calif. (program chmn. 1979-80, councillor 1980-82), Phys. Soc. Japan, Japan Soc. Applied Physics (overseas editor Japanese Jour. Applied Physics 1982—), Laser Soc. Japan (overseas editor Rev. Laser Engring.), Inst. Electronics and Communications Engrs. Japan, Sigma Xi, Eta Kappa Nu. Congregationalist. Home: 3812 Inlet Isle Dr Corona del Mar CA 92625 Office: Elec Engineering Univ Calif Irvine CA 92717

GAMWELL, CECIL CALVERT, IV, writer, producer; b. N.Y.C., Nov. 24, 1949; s. Cecil Calvert and Arlene Marie (Bickford) G.; B.A., Colgate U., 1971. Writer, GAC Corp., Miami, 1972; copy chief Gabel Advt., Denver, 1973; head writer Frontier Airlines, Frye-Sills/Young & Rubicam Advt., Denver, 1974; freelance writer and producer, Aurora, Colo., 1975—; strategic mktg. cons. Adolph Coors Co., Golden, Colo., Huskey Oil Co., Denver, Mountain Bell Telephone, Denver, Storage Technology Corp., Louisville, Colo.; tchr. advt. Colo. U. Recipient Denver Ad Fedn. NIKE award for Creative Excellence, 1973; Grand Alfie and Alfie awards for creative excellence Advt.'s Best, 1977, 78, 80, 82, 83. Mem. Denver Art Dirs. Club (dir. public relations 1973-75; Creative award 1975, 3 Honor awards, award of Excellence 1980), Colgate U. Alumni Assn., Phi Kappa Psi. Presbyterian. Club: Aurora Athletic. Founder, editor: Hamilton (N.Y.) Shopper's Guide, 1971. Contbr. articles to Denver mag. Home and Office: 13961 E Oxford Pl Aurora CO 80014

GAN, MICHAEL L., photographer; b. San Francisco, Nov. 16, 1955; s. Daniel L. and June Gan; m. Janice D. Lussier, Sept. 15, 1979; A.B., U. Calif.-Davis, 1978. Owner, operator Gan Photography, 1980—. Recipient all-state coll. photojournalism award, 1976. Mem. Profl. Photographers Am. (awards 1979, 80), Profl. Photographers Greater Bay Area. Club: Rotary Internat. Office: 7057 Village Pkwy Dublin CA 94568

GANAS, PERRY SPIROS, physicist; b. Brisbane, Australia, June 20, 1937; s. Arthur and Lula (Grivas) G.; came to U.S., 1968, permanent resident, 1975; B.S., U. Queensland (Australia), 1960; Ph.D., U. Sydney, 1968. Postdoctoral research asso., instr. U. Fla., 1968-70, vis. asst. research prof., 1972, vis. asso. prof. physics, 1978, vis. asso. research prof., 1979-80; prof. physics Calif. State U., Los Angeles, 1970—; referee Phys. Rev., Phys. Rev. Letters. Mem. Congress of Faculty Assns., AAUP, Am. Phys. Soc., Sigma Xi. Contbr. articles to profl. jours. Home: 11790 Radio Dr Los Angeles CA 90064 Office: Physics Dept Calif State U Los Angeles CA 90032

GANDARA, DAVID RAYMOND, physician; b. Tyler, Tex., June 18, 1947; s. Raymond R. and Catherine (Cates) G.; B.A., U. Tex., Austin, 1969; M.D., U. Tex. Med. Br., Galveston, 1973; m. Lonita Hersh, Dec. 18, 1971. Intern, Madigan Med. Center, Tacoma, 1973-74, resident in internal medicine, 1974-76; in hematology/oncology Letterman Med. Center, 1976-77; commd. 2d. lt., M.C., U.S. Army, 1971, advanced through grades to lt. col. 1981, staff hematologist/oncologist Letterman Army Med. Center, Presidio of San Francisco, 1977-79, chief hematology/oncology service, 1979—; prin. investigator Nat. Surg. Adjuvant Breast project, 1978—, clin. investigator No. Calif. Oncology Group, 1978—, dir. granulocyte support and plasmapheresis project at med. center, 1978—. Fellow ACP; mem. AMA, Alpha Omega Alpha. Researcher hematologic malignancy. Home: 210 San Leandro San Francisco CA 94127 Office: Dept Hematology/Oncology Letterman Army Med Center Presidio of San Francisco CA 94129

GANDHI, OM PARKASH, electrical engineer; b. Multan, Pakistan, Sept. 23, 1934; came to U.S., 1967, naturalized, 1975; s. Gopal Das and Devi Bai (Patney) G.; B.S. with honors, Delhi (India) U., 1952; M.S.E., U. Mich., 1957, Sc.D., 1961; m. Santosh Nayar, Oct. 28, 1963; children—Rajesh Timmy, Monica, Lena. Research specialist Philco Corp., Blue Bell, Pa., 1960-62; asst. dir. Central Electronics Engring. Research Inst., Pilani, Rajasthan, India, 1962-65, dep. dir., 1965-67; prof. elec. engring., research prof. bioengring. U. Utah, 1967—; cons. U.S. Army Med. Research and Devel. Command, Washington, 1973-77; cons. to industry; mem. Internat. URSI Commn. B, 1976—; panel on PAVE PAWS Radar, Nat. Acad. Sci., 1978-79; mem. study sect. on diagnostic radiology NIH, 1978-81. Recipient Disting. Research award U. Utah, 1979-80. Fellow IEEE (Tech. Achievement award Utah sect. 1975); mem. Bioelectromagnetics Soc. (dir. 1979-82). Author: Microwave Engineering and Applications, 1981; editor Procs. of IEEE Spl. Issue, 1980; contbr. articles on biol. effects and med. applications of electromagnetic energy, microwave semicondr. devices and microwave tubes to profl. jours. Office: Dept Electrical Engineering U Utah Salt Lake City UT 84112

GANDSEY, LOUIS JOHN, oil company executive; b. Greybull, Wyo., May 19, 1921; s. John Wellington and Leonora (McLaughlin) G.; A.A., Compton Jr. Coll., 1941; B.S., U. Calif. at Berkeley, 1943; M.Engring., UCLA, 1958; m. Mary Louise Alviso, Nov. 10, 1945; children—Mary M., Catherine K., John P., Michael J., Laurie A. With Richfield Oil Corp., Los Angeles, 1943-65, process engr., processing foreman, sr. foreman, mfg. coordinator, 1943-61, project leader process computer control, 1961-63, light oil operating supt., 1963-64, asst. refinery supt., 1964-65; mgr. planning Richfield div. Atlantic Richfield Co., Los Angeles, 1966-68, mgr. evaluation products div., Los Angeles, 1968-69, mgr. supply and transp., Chgo., 1969-71, mgr. planning and mgmt. sci., N.Y.C., 1971, mgr. supply and transp., Los Angeles, 1971-72, mgr. coordination and supply, 1972-75, mgr. domestic crude, 1975-77; v.p. refining Lunday-Thagard Oil Co., South Gate, Calif., 1977-82; petroleum cons., 1982—; instr. chem. and petroleum tech. Los Angeles Harbor Coll., 1960-65. Active Boy Scouts of Am. Served with C.E., AUS, 1944-45. Mem. Am. Chem. Soc., AAAS, Pacific Energy Assn. Contbr. articles to profl. jours. Home: Route 1 Box 16A Templeton CA 93465

GANG, MARTIN, JR., instl. food service co. exec.; b. Los Angeles, Jan. 13, 1940; s. Martin and Josephine (Tripplett) G.; B.A. in Bus. Adminstrn., U. Hawaii, 1965; m. Jeanne L. Kelso, Mar. 9, 1974; children—Deborah, Steven. Div. ops. mgr. Burke Concrete, San Francisco, 1967-74; dist. sales mgr. Internat. Food Service Co., San Diego, 1975-79; gen. sales mgr. Klauber Wangenheim Co., San Diego, 1979-80; dist. sales mgr. Interstate Restaurant Supply, Los Angeles, 1980-82; gen. slaes mgr. W.S. Enterprises, Escondido, Calif., 1982—. Chmn., First Spl. Olympics, San Diego, 1969. Served with USN, 1958-67. Named Key Man of Yr., San Diego Jr. C. of C., 1968; Man of Yr., San Diego Assn. Retarded Children, 1969. Mem. Internat. Food Service Execs. Assn. (asso., adv. to bd. dirs.), Chefs de cuisine (asso.), Mensa. Democrat. Clubs: Good Fellows (San Diego); Elks (trustee and mgr. club), Am. Legion. Contbr. poems to Mensa mag., 1979. Home: 15028 Amso St Poway CA 92064

GANN, RONALD ORION, consulting firm executive, economist; b. Birmington, Ala., Nov. 23, 1942; s. Orion Mastus and Martha Jeanette (Edwards) G.; m. Gael Sisson, Mar. 27, 1964; children—Kelly Lee, Ronald Christian. B.A., U. Ala., 1963; M.A., Calif. State U.-Long Beach, 1965; Ph.D., Northwestern U., 1979; J.D., Southwestern U., Calif., 1983. C.L.U., 1980. With sales dept. Mass. Mut. Life Ins., Reno and Sacramento, 1968-72; pres., chief exec. officer First Interstate Cons., Los Angeles, San Francisco and Reno, 1972—.

GANNON, GERALD EDWARD, mathematics educator; b. Topeka, Kans., June 3, 1941; s. Thomas Paul and Ramona Regina (Downey) G.; m. Marie Daralyn Rosebaugh, Aug. 17, 1963; children—Jeffrey H., Joseph T., Jason E. B.S. in Edn., Rockhurst Coll., 1963; M.A. in Math. (NSF fellow), Kans. State Tchrs. Coll., 1967; postgrad. U. Mo., Kansas City, 1968-69; Ed.D. in Math. Edn., U. No. Colo., 1972. Tchr., Coach Kaupaun High Sch., Wichita, Kans., 1963-65; tchr., head basketball coach Miege High Sch., Shawnee Mission, Kans., 1965-68; asst. prof. math. Winona (Minn.) State Coll., 1972-73; asst. prof. math. Calif. State U., Fullerton, 1973-77, assoc. prof., 1977-82, prof., 1982—. Mem. Nat. Council Tchrs. of Math., Calif. Math. Council, Orange County Math Assn. (pres. 1976), United Profs. Calif., AAUP, Phi Delta Kappa, Lambda Sigma Tau, Pi Mu Epsilon. Home: 2025 E Nutwood Ave Fullerton CA 92631 Office: Dept Math Calif State U Fullerton CA 92634

GANOPOLE, GERALD, consulting geologist; b. Portland, Oreg., June 11, 1921; s. Joseph and Clara (Portnoy) G.; children—Denise Susan, Deidre Ellen Lissa Caryl. B.A., UCLA, 1948. Registered geologist, Calif.; lic. profl. geologist, Alaska. Dist. geologist Seaboard Oil Co., Bakersfield, Calif., 1948-58; Alaskan exploration rep. Texaco Inc., Anchorage, 1959-62; cons. geologist privately owned firm, 1962—; pres. Alaska Exploration Corp., 1964—. Served to lt. col. USAF. Mem. Am. Inst. Profl Geologists, Am. Assn. Petroleum Geologists. Office: Box 4-1261 Anchorage AK 99509

GANS, SHELDON PHILLIP, urban mgmt. cons.; b. Boston, Jan. 11, 1932; s. Nathan N. and Rose Shirley (Grossman) G.; B.Arch., U. Fla., 1954; M.Urban Planning, M.I.T., 1960; m. Shirley Slater, Oct. 24, 1957; children—Gregory, Jeffrey, Jason. Pvt. practice architecture, Miami, Fla., 1958; teaching asst. M.I.T., Cambridge, 1959-60; urban planner San Diego, 1960-64; founder, Marshall Kaplan Gans & Kahn (now MKGK Inc.), San Francisco, 1965, sr. partner, 1965-78; pres., MKGK Inc., 1978—. Contbr. articles to profl. jours. Home: 293 Bay View Ave Belvedere CA 94920 Office: 1095 Market St Suite 300 San Francisco CA 94103

GANT, DARYAL TILLMAN, research orgn. adminstr.; b. Blair, Okla., Nov. 14, 1933; s. Fount Tillman and Maggie Pearl (Farmer) G.; B.S., UCLA, 1956, M.B.A., 1957; m. Mary Clara West, Oct. 26, 1956; children—Brenda, Tracey. Prodn. control planner Beckman Instruments, 1957-58; engring. planner Douglas Aircraft, 1958-60; mgr. adminstrn. Pneumo Dynamics, Inc., 1960-62; mgr. procurement div. Jet Propulsion Lab., Pasadena, Calif., 1962—. Served with U.S. Army, 1956-57; lt. col. USAR ret. Recipient exceptional service medal NASA. Fellow Nat. Contract Mgmt. Assn. (pres. San Gabriel Valley chpt.

1977-78); mem. Res. Officers Assn., Am. Def. Preparedness Assn., Beta Gamma Sigma, Lambda Chi Alpha. Home: 2425 Cross St La Crescenta CA 91214 Office: 4800 Oak Grove Dr Pasadena CA 91103

GANT, JOSEPH ERWIN, chemist, state senator; b. Altamahaw, N.C., Feb. 4, 1912; s. Joseph Erwin and Mary (Banner) G.; B.S., U. N.C., 1934; m. Opal Martin, Feb. 11, 1938; children—Joseph Erwin III, Mary Martin. With U.S. Potash Co., Carlsbad, N.Mex., 1934-56, U.S. Borax & Chem. Co., Carlsbad, 1956-67; chmn. N.Mex. Bd. Eddy Commrs., 1967-68; mem. N.Mex. Senate, 1969—, mem. judiciary com., 1969-72, rules com., 1973—, chmn. conservation com., 1973—, chmn. majority caucus, 1973—, also vice chmn. legis. univ. study com., 1971-75, mem. local govt. com., 1974-75, chmn. legis. higher edn. admissions standards com., 1976-77, legis. energy com., 1976-77, mem. legis. council, 1978—, chmn. joint interim radioactive waste consultation com., 1979; dir. Glen Raven (N.C.) Mills, Inc. Pub. mem. N.Mex. State Investment Council, 1959-60; v.p. N.M. Assn. Counties, 1969; dir. Southeastern N.Mex. Econ. Devel. Dist.; mem. Southwestern Regional Energy Council, 1975—; mem. nat. resources task force intergovtl. com. Nat. Conf. State Legislatures, 1973-77; mem. state-fed. relations energy com., 1977—; mem. Roswell Dist. Land Use Com., Bur. Land Mgmt., 1978-82, N.Mex. Water Resources Adv. Com., 1982—; chmn., Eddy County Democratic Party, 1948—; mem. N.Mex. Dem. Exec. Com., 1953-54. Mem. Am. Chem. Soc., Alpha Tau Omega. Episcopalian. Elk. Home: 602 Riverside Dr PO Box 909 Carlsbad NM 88220 Office: State Capitol Santa Fe NM 87503

GANTZ, NANCY ROLLINS, nurse; b. Buffalo Center, Iowa, Mar. 7, 1949; d. Troy Gaylord and Mary (Emerson) Rollins; diploma in Nursing, Good Samaritan Hosp. and Med. Center, Portland, Oreg., 1973. m. Aug. 1981. Nurse ICU, Good Samaritan Hosp., 1973-75; charge nurse Crestview Convalescent Hosp., Portland, 1975; dir. nursing services Roderick Enterprises, Inc., Portland, 1976-78, Holgate Center, Portland, 1978-80; nursing cons. in field of adminstrn., 1980—; mem. task force Oreg. State Health Div. Rules and Regulations Revision for Long Term Health Facilities and Hosps., 1978-79. Mem. Am. Nurses Assn., Oreg. Nurses Assn., Nat. League Nursing, Am. Heart Assn., Oreg. Heart Assn., Geriatric Nurses Assn. Oreg. (founder, charter pres.), Clackamus Assn. Retarded Citizens. Adventist. Home and Office: 3682 SE Roanoke Ct Hillsboro OR 97123

GARAMENDI, JOHN R., state legislator; m. Patricia Garamendi; 5 children. Grad., U. Calif.-Berkeley; M.B.A., Harvard U. Rancher nr. Calaveras County, Calif.; former mem. Calif. Assembly, now mem. Calif. Senate, mem. fin. elections, local govt., natural resources and wildlife coms., also majority leader. Served with Peace Corps. Office: 31 E Channel St Room 408 Stockton CA 95202

GARAMI, EDWARD STEWART, aircraft systems engineer; b. Budapest, Hungary, July 15, 1932; came to U.S., 1957, naturalized, 1962; s. Tibor Bela and Ethel Vanessa (Chmelik) G.; Dipl. Ing. and B.Sc. in Mech. Engring., Tech. U. Budapest, 1956; cert. bus. mgmt. for tech. personnel UCLA, 1975; m. Elisa Munguia, May 27, 1960; children—Alan, Glenn, Jeffrey. Engring. draftsman Sylvania Electric Products, Inc., Ann Arbor, Mich., 1957-58; designer Barton Instrument Corp., Monterey Park, Calif., 1958-64; engr. Inca Engring. Corp., San Gabriel, Calif., 1964-65; engr. Aircraft Group, Northrop Corp., Hawthorne, Calif., 1966-69; sr. engr., 1969-74, engring. specialist, 1974-79, sr. tech. specialist, 1979-82, advanced systems dir., 1982—. Registered profl. engr. in control system engring., Calif. Mem. IEEE, Soc. Info. Display. Republican. Roman Catholic. Home: 932 W 37th St San Pedro CA 90731 Office: One Northrop Ave Hawthorne CA 90250

GARBER, HENRY ANDREW, ret. city ofcl.; b. Hamburg, Calif., Sept. 20, 1922; s. Henry Andrew and Laurel A. (Johnston) G.; B.S. in Mech. Engring., U. Calif. at Berkeley, 1944, certificate in pub. adminstrn., 1966; m. Barbara A. Freeman, Oct. 9, 1960. Valuation engr., Victor E. Roth & Asso. (name later changed to Tait Appraisal Co.), appraisal and cons. engrs., San Francisco, 1947-52, owner, mgr., 1952-55, div. mgr., 1955-58; chief dep. assessor City of Berkeley, Calif., 1958-65, city assessor-collector-treas., 1965-66, asst. dir. finance, 1966-70; dir. finance, 1970-73. Cons. legal sect. Calif. Div. Hwys., 1961-71; cons. Real Estate Research Corp., San Francisco, 1962-73; lectr. appraising taxation U. Calif. Extension Sch. at Berkeley, 1962-63. Trustee Herrick Hosp., 1961—; treas. Herrick Found., 1976—; bd. dirs. Berkeley chpt. ARC, treas. Berkeley-West Contra Costa chpt. ARC; mem. exec. com. Boy Scouts Am.; treas. Berkeley Municipal Employees Credit Union, 1965-78; bd. dirs. Berkeley-Sakai Assn. Served with USNR, 1944-46. Fellow Constrn. Surveyors Inst., Am. Soc. Appraisers, Soc. Valuers and Auctioneers Gt. Britain; mem. Am. Arbitration Assn. (nat. panel arbitrators), Internat. Assn. Assessing Officers, Municipal Finance Officers U.S., Calif. Municipal Treas. Assn., Calif. Credit Union League (dir. 1973-81). Clubs: Masons, Shriners, Commonwealth, Rotary (treas.), Elks. Home: 385 Ocean View Ave Berkeley CA 94707

GARBER, JANICE WINTER, advertising executive; b. N.Y.C., July 25, 1950; d. Irving and Frances (Edelman) Winter; m. Dale Wayne Garber, Nov. 30, 1978. B.A., Queens Coll., 1979. Prodn. asst. P & F Graphics, N.Y.C., 1969-73; guest service mgr. Sheraton Corp., N.Y.C., 1973-76; advt. mgr. Am. Specialty Corp., N.Y.C., 1976-79; mng. editor VPO Industry News, 1979; advt. mgr. B & M Automotive Products, 1979-80; advt. mgr. Toyota Indsl. Trucks, U.S.A., Inc., Carson, Calif., 1980—.

GARBER, MORRIS JOSEPH, statistical consultant, computer programmer; b. N.Y.C., Nov. 6, 1912; s. Isidor and Ethel (Shevack) G.; m. Gloria Ruth Routman, Sept. 4, 1943; children—David I., Diana L. Garber McCarthy. B.S. in Zoology, Columbia U., 1929; Ph.D. in Genetics, Tex. A&M U., 1951. Asst. prof. genetics Tex. A&M U., College Station, 1947-56; prof. statistics, biometrician U. Calif., Riverside, 1956-80, emeritus, 1980—; statistician, head statis. lab. Inst. Tropical Agr., 1974-76; cons. research planning and statistics Inter-Am. Inst. Agrl. Scis., Brazilian Enterprise for Agrl. Research, and Nat. Ctr. Research in Rice and Beans, 1980-81. Served M.C., AUS, 1941-45. Fellow AAAS, Tex. Acad. Sci.; mem. Am. Genetics Assn., Am. Statis. Assn., Assn. Computing Machinery, Biometric Soc., Sigma Xi. Democrat. Jewish. Club: B'nai B'rith. Home: 3504 Bryce Way Riverside CA 92506 Office: Univ Calif Riverside Dept Stats Riverside CA 92621

GARCIA, DAVID MARTIN, bank executive; b. Montebello, Calif., Aug. 23, 1956; s. Nick and Laura (Frontino) G.; m. Laura Velez, Apr. 23, 1983. B.A. in Pub. Relations, U. So. Calif., 1978. Spl. project participant Carnation Co., 1978; dir. Student News Bur. U. So. Calif., Los Angeles, 1978; pub. relations rep. TigerAir, Inc., Los Angeles, 1978; asst. pub. info. officer Bank Am., Los Angeles, 1978-80, pub. info. officer, 1980-82, sr. pub. info officer, 1982—. Vol., ARC, Pasadena (Calif.) chpt., 1980—; pub. relations mgr. Amaranth Prodns., 1980-81; mem. Pasadena Scholarship Com. Ams. Mexican Descent, 1982; mem. Altadena Mountain Rescue Team, Res. Forces Bur., Los Angeles County Sheriff's Dept. Named Outstanding Grad. USC, 1978; mem. Outstanding Squad, U. So. Calif. Trojan Marching Band, 1978; acad. honors Los Angeles County Sheriff's Acad., 1982. Mem. Pub. Relations Soc. Am. Publicity Club Los Angeles, Pub. Relations Soc. (Los Angeles chpt.), U. So. Calif. Alumni Assn., U. So. Calif. Mexican Am. Alumni Assn., Nat. Assn. Latino Elected and Apptd. Officials, Nat. Rifle Assn., Skull and Dagger (men's honor soc.). Republican. Roman Catholic. Office: Bank of America 555 S Flower St Los Angeles CA 90071

GARCIA, F. CHRIS, coll. dean, political science educator, public opinion researcher; b. Albuquerque, Apr. 15, 1940; s. Flaviano P. and Crucita A. G.; m. Sandra D.; children—Elaine L., Tanya C. B.A., U. N.Mex., 1961, M.A. in Govt., 1964; Ph.D. in Polit. Sci., U. Calif.-Davis, 1970. Asst. prof. polit. sci. U. N.Mex., Albuquerque, 1970-74, assoc. prof., 1974-78, prof. polit. sci., 1978—, asst. dir. div. govt. research, 1970-72, assoc. dean coll. arts and scis., 1975-80, dean coll. arts and scis., 1980—; pres. Zia Research Assocs., Inc., Albuquerque, 1973—. Served with N.Mex. Air NG, 1957-63. Mem. Western Polit. Sci. Assn. (pres. 1977-78), Am. Polit. Sci. Assn., Am. Assn. Pub. Opinion Research, Council of Colls. of Arts and Sci., Phi Kappa Phi. Democrat. Roman Catholic. Author: Political Socialization of Chicano Children, 1973; La Causa Política: A Chicano Politics Reader, 1974; The Chicano Political Experience, 1977; State and Local Government in New Mexico, 1979; New Mexico Government, 1976, 1981. Home: 1409 Snowdrop Pl NE Albuquerque NM 87112 Office: U New Mex Ortega Hall 201 Albuquerque NM 87131

GARCIA, GARY STEPHEN, photo copier technician; b. S.I., Sept. 28, 1941; s. Stephen and Jane Ellen (Steele) G.; student S.I. Community Coll., 1959-60, U. Tenn., 1960-61, Palomar Coll., 1975-76; m. Charlotte Lynnette Cripps, Sept. 14, 1974; children—Brenda, Danny, Stephen. Tech. rep. Nat. Cash Register Co., N.Y.C., 1963-69, San Diego, 1969-70; sr. tech. rep., tech. support rep. Xerox Corp., San Diego, 1972—; mktg. dir. Genuine Products Internat.; owner apt. bldg., 1972—. Committeeman Cub Scouts Escondido council Boy Scouts Am., 1977. Served with USAF, 1960-64. Recipient recognition and appreciation Allied Vets., 1976, recognition of excellence 1st quarter Xerox Corp., 1978; named Jaycee of Month, Calif. Jaycees, 1973, to Par Club, 1975. Mem. Armed Forces Benefit and Aid Assn., San Diego Apt. Assn., U.S., Escondido (Calif.) (parade chmn. and del. 1969-77) jaycees, Am. Legion (sgt. at arms and dir. local chpt. 1975-77). Home: Escondido CA also Idyllwild CA Office: 404 Camino del Rio S San Diego CA 92108

GARCIA, HECTOR THOMAS, accountant; b. San Juan Bautista, Calif., Oct. 28, 1926; s. Tomás Jose Garcia y Espinosa and Aurelia María Esparza y Terrazas; B.S., U. Calif.-Berkeley, 1950; M.B.A., U. Santa Clara, 1966; M.S., Golden Gate U., San Francisco, 1978; m. Leah Adele Mumm, Nov. 3, 1951; children—Thomas R., Carolyn A., Daniel C., Susan L. Cost acct. Bethlehem Steel Corp., South San Francisco, Calif., 1951-54; supr. cost acctg. Western Gear Corp., Belmont, Calif., 1954-56; supr. microwave cost acctg. Varian Assos., Palo Alto, Calif., 1956-62; sr. budget analyst Lockheed Missiles & Space Co., Sunnyvale, Calif., 1962-66; supr. auditing Calif. Dept. Finance, Sacramento, 1966-70; chief acct. San Jose State U., 1971-72; prin. acct. U. Calif., Berkeley, 1972-80; chief auditor U. Calif., Davis, 1980—. Served with inf. U.S. Army, 1944-46; PTO, ETO. C.P.A., Calif. Mem. Am. Inst. C.P.A.s. Calif. Soc. C.P.A.s. Inst. Internal Auditors (cert.). Home: 630 Cleveland St Davis CA 95616 Office: Internal Audit Office Room 5415 Chem Annex Bldg U Calif Davis CA 95616

GARCIA, JOHN, psychology educator; b. Santa Rosa, Calif., June 12, 1917; s. Benigno and Sara (Casanovas y Unamuno) G.; m. Dorthy Inez Robertson, July 18, 1943; children—Roderick, Ben David, John Everett. A.A. Santa Rosa Jr. Coll., 1943; A.B., U. Calif.-Berkeley, 1948; M.A., 1949, Ph.D., 1965. Teaching asst. dept. psychology U. Calif. Berkley, 1949-51; psychologist U.S. Naval Radiol. Def. Lab., San Francisco, 1951-58; tchr. biol. sci. Oakland (Calif.) Pub. Schs., 1958-59; asst. prof. psychology Calif. State Coll., Long Beach, 1959-65; lectr. psychology surgery dept. Harvard Med. Sch., Boston, 1965-68; assoc. biologist Neurosurg. Services, Mass. Gen. Hosp., Boston, 1965-68; prof. psychology SUNY, Stony Brook, 1968-71, chmn. dept. psychology, 1971-72; prof. U. Utah, Salt Lake City, 1972-73; prof. psychology and psychiatry UCLA, 1973—; cons. and lectr. in field. Served with U.S. Army AC, 1942-46. Recipient Disting. Lectr. U. Ill. Mem. Soc. Explt. Psychologists (Howard Crosby Warren medal), Am. Psychol. Assn. (Disting. Sci. Contbns. award), Western Psychol. Assn., Soc. for Neurosci., Phi Beta Kappa (hon.). Contbr. numerous chpts. to books and articles to profl. jours.

GARCIA, MARTHA ELAINE, legal secretary; b. Silver City, N.Mex., June 10, 1955; d. G. Rawley and Shirley E. (Leach) Jackson, m. Ronald Joseph Garcia, Sept. 12, 1975; 1 son, Houston Bradley. Student N.Mex. State U. Cert. profl. legal sec. Nat. Assn. Legal Secs. Legal sec. Pickett and Bates (name changed to Pickett, Bates & Holmes), Las Cruces, N.Mex., 1974—, now also office mgr. Mem. Dona Ana County Legal Secs. Assn. Office: 500 N Church St PO Box 1239 Las Cruces NM 88004

GARCIA, MARTI, interior designer; b. Marrakech, French Morrocco, Sept. 28, 1942; d. Meyer and Sabine (Corcos) Sabbah; m. Othon Reyes Garcia, Aug. 4, 1963; children—Anthony Martin, Mark Othon. B.P.A. cum laude in Interior Design, Woodbury Coll., Los Angeles, 1962. Interior designer Robinsons, Los Angeles, 1972-74, Bullocks, Santa Ana, 1975-77; prin. Interiors By Marti, Huntington Beach, Calif., 1977—. Mem. Am. Soc. Interior Designers (dir.). Office: Interiors by Marti 8841 Dorsett Dr Huntington Beach CA 92646

GARCIA, MERLE L(LOYD), tribal governor; b. Acoma, N.Mex., Nov. 3, 1926; s. Frank L. and Sanatana (Vicente) G.; m. Jenny Vallo, Feb. 12, 1957; children—Arlene, Norma Torivio-Viola. Student schs., Albuquerque. Store mgr. Acoma Pueblo, N.Mex., 1957-73, lt. gov., 1974-75, gov., 1975-76, 82—; chmn. So. Pueblos Govs. Council, 1983; mem. exec. com. All Indian Pueblo Council, 1982, 83; mem. exec. bd. Council of Energy Resource Tribes, 1982, 83; mem. exec. bd. Nat. Tribal Chairmen Assn. Republican. Office: PO Box 309 Acomita NM 87034

GARCIA-BORRAS, THOMAS, oil co. exec.; b. Barcelona, Spain, Feb. 2, 1926; came to U.S., 1955, naturalized, 1961; s. Thomas and Teresa (Borras-Jarque) Garcia-Julian; M.S., Nat. U. Mex., 1950; postgrad. Rice U., 1955-56; m. Alia Castellanos Lima, Apr. 30, 1952; children—Erik, Angelica, Laureen, Cliff. Chief chemist Petroleos Mexicanos, Veracruz, Mex., 1950-55; research engr. Monsanto, Texas City, Tex., 1956-60; pilot plant mgr. Cabot and Foster Grant Co., 1960-69; engring. mgr. Signal Chem. Co., Houston, 1969-71; mgmt. and engring. cons., Covina, Calif., 1971-73; project mgr. Occidental Petroleum Co., Irvine, Calif., 1973-79; fleet and indsl. mgr. internat. ops. Wynn Oil Co., Fullerton, Calif., 1979—. Mem. Internat. Mktg. Assn., Am. Inst. Chem. Engrs., Am. Chem. Soc. Author: Manual for Improving Boiler and Furnace Performance, 1983; contbr. articles to profl. jours. Home: 1430 E Adams Park Dr Covina CA 91724 Office: 2600 E Notwood Ave Fullerton CA 92631

GARCIA-BUNUEL, LUIS, neurologist; b. Madrid, Spain, Feb. 24, 1931; s. Pedro Garcia and Concepcion Bunuel; came to U.S., 1956, naturalized, 1965; B.A., Universidad de Zaragoza, 1949, B.S., 1949, M.D., 1955; m. Virginia M. Hile, June 30, 1960. Intern, Universidad De Zaragoza Hosp. Clinico, 1955-56 resident in neurology Georgetown U., Washington, 1956-59; NIH fellow in neurochemistry dept. pharmacology, Washington U., St. Louis, 1959-61; practice medicine specializing in neurology St. Louis, 1959-61; instr. neurology Jefferson Med. Coll., Phila., 1961-64, asst. prof. neurology, 1964-67; asst. prof. neurology U. N.Mex., Albuquerque, 1967-72; chief neurology service VA Hosp. Portland, Oreg., 1972; asso. prof. neurology, U. Oreg. Health Center, 1972—. Diplomate Am. Bd. Neurology and Psychiatry. Fellow Am. Acad. Neurology; mem. AAAS, Am. Soc. Neurochemistry, Oreg. Neuropsychiat. Soc., Portland Myasthenia Gravis Assn. (med. adv. bd.), Sigma Xi, Phi Kappa Phi. Contbr. articles to profl jours. Home: 2933 NW 53d Dr Portland OR 97210 Office: VA Hosp Sam Jackson Park Portland OR 97207

GARDENSWARTZ, LEAH ELLEN, mgmt. cons. co. exec.; b. Denver, May 12, 1943; d. Nathan William and Rosyne Miriam (Bloom) G. B.A., U. Colo., 1965; M.A., Calif. Luth. Coll., 1977; Ph.D., U.S. Internat. U., 1981. Tchr., Los Angeles Sch. Dist., 1965-77, various positions, 1977-80; cons., trainer, ptnr. Tng. and Cons. Assocs., Marina Del Rey, Calif., 1980—. Mem. Am. Soc. Tng. and Devel., Calif. Women Bus. Owners, Nat. Assn. Female Execs. Democrat. Jewish. Contbr. articles to profl. jours. Address: 4550 Via Marina Suite 106 Marina Del Rey CA 90291

GARDINER, GLENN NAYSMYTHE, sch. adminstr.; b. Los Angeles, Apr. 6, 1908; s. John N. and Blanche (Putnam) G.; B.A., U. Oreg., 1931; student UCLA, 1932-42; M.A., Long Beach State Coll., 1951; m. Rachel Reynolds, Aug. 18, 1934 (dec. Aug. 1972); children—Kenneth N., Kathryn (Mrs. Kenneth C. Brown), John R., Susan (Mrs. Ronald D. Broome); m. 2d, Ruth Frances Tiedje, Mar. 21, 1976. Supervising prin. Bremerhaven Am. Sch., Bremerhaven, W.Ger., 1958-60; adult edn. curriculum coordinator Los Angeles City Schs., 1962-68; chief adviser East African Literacy Center, Nairobi, Kenya, 1968-70; adult sch. prin. Manual Arts Community Adult Sch., Los Angeles, 1970-71; adult sch. prin. Van Nuys Community Adult Sch., Van Nuys, Calif., 1971-73; coordinator div. career-continuing edn. Los Angeles Unified Schs., 1973—; lectr. audio visual edn. Long Beach State Coll., 1951-53; lectr. lectr. radio edn. U. Calif. at Los Angeles, 1944-47; TV edn. U. So. Calif., 1947-49. 54th Assembly committeeman Democratic party, 1973-74. Mem. Los Angeles Adult Prin.'s Assn. (pres. 1972-73), San Pedro Coordinating Council, Phi Delta Kappa, Theta Chi. Clubs: Toastmaster (pres. 1959-60), Kiwanis. Educational editor Oxford Book Co. Inc., N.Y.C., 1970-73. Home: 29500 Heathercliff Rd Apt 80 Malibu CA 90265

GARDNER, BARBARA ELAINE, programmer analyst; b. Sandia Base, N.Mex., Sept. 5, 1950; d. Orville Kenneth and Gladys (Hancock) G.; B.S., U. Colo., M.B.A., 1978. Instr. adult basic edn., Independence, Iowa, 1971; merit grad. asst. U. Colo., Boulder, 1976, 77, 78, grad. adminstr. simulated production game, 1977, grad. teaching asst., 1976-77, research asst. to Bur. Econ. Research, 1977, computer lab. advisor, statis. tutor, 1977-78, instr. prodn. mgmt., 1980-81; devel. programmer IBM, Boulder, 1979—. Organizer, coordinator legal aid program Welfare Rights Orgn.; protective payee and conservator Social Service Dept.; worker Drug Councils, Planned Parenthood, Probation Office, Council on Alcoholism, 1970-72. Mem. Am. Prodn. and Inventory Control Soc., Sigma Iota Epsilon, Beta Gamma Sigma. Home: 209 29th St Boulder CO 80303 Office: IBM 3131 28th St Boulder CO 80303

GARDNER, DAVID PIERPONT, university president; b. Berkeley, Calif., Mar. 24, 1933; s. Reed S. and Margaret (Pierpont) G.; m. Elizabeth Fuhriman, June 27, 1958; children—Karen, Shari, Lisa, Marci. B.S., Brigham Young U., 1955; M.A., U. Calif.-Berkeley, 1959, Ph.D., 1966. Calif. Alumni Found. dir. U. Calif.-Berkeley, 1962-64; asst. chancellor U. Calif.-Santa Barbara, 1966-69; vice chancellor, exec. asst., also assoc. prof. higher edn. U. Calif.-Santa Barbara, 1969-71; v.p. U. Calif. System, Berkeley, 1971-73; pres. U. Utah, Salt Lake City, 1973-83, prof. higher edn., 1973-83; pres. U. Calif.-Berkeley, 1983—; vis. fellow Clare Hall, Cambridge U., 1979, assoc., 1979—; dir. Utah Power & Light Co., Salt Lake City, First Security Corp., Denver and Rio Grande Western RR Co. Mem. pres.' council Nat. Assn. State Univs. and Landgrant Colls., 1973—, Western Athletic Conf., 1973—; bd. dirs. Am. Council on Edn., 1977-80, chmn. bd. trustees Tanner Lectures on Human Values, Salt Lake City, 1978—; mem. Nat. Commn. on Student Fin. Assistance, 1981—; chmn. Nat. Commn. on Excellence in Edn., 1981—; chmn. George S. and Dolores Doré Eccles Found. Mem. Am. Assn. for Higher Edn., AAUP, Phi Kappa Phi, Phi Beta Kappa. Clubs. Rotary, Alta, Timpanogos, Ft. Douglas, Century Assn. Author: The California Oath Controversy. 1967. Home: 714 University Hall 2200 University Ave Berkeley CA 94720

GARDNER, DOROTHY GRACE, artist, writer, arts and crafts shop executive; b. Salt Lake City, July 9, 1921; d. William Amasa and Dorothy Harriet (Marsh) Lyman; m. Fay Rosklin Sutton, Aug. 14, 1939 (div. 1958); children—Steven, Sierra, Daniel, Paul, Michael (dec.); m. 2d, LaMar Bushman, Jan. 15, 1965 (div. 1972); m. 3d, Donald Rex, Sept. 7, 1973. Student, Art Instrn., Inc., 1954-56, U. Utah, 1969-72, Ririe Sch. Music, 1973-74. Cert. choral dir. Clk., Paris Co., 1941-42; welder Everett Pacific Shipyard, 1943-45; substitute tchr., Salt Lake City, 1954-57, 69-72, Emery County, Utah, 1975-76, Carbon County (Utah) High Sch., 1977-83; pres., councillor drama and speech, music dir. Young Women's Mut. Improvement Assn., Salt Lake City, 1957-74, Lynndyl, Utah, 1974-78, Spring Glen, Utah, 1980-82; one-women shows: Ricks Coll., Rexburg, Idaho, Springfield Mus. Art, Utah State Fair, 1967-68, others; group shows include: Utah State Capitol, Salt Lake City, 1969, Daus. of Utah Pioneers, 1970-74, also Salt Lake City pub. schs. and malls, others; owner, mgr. GG's Creations, Helper, Utah, 1982—; newspaper corr. Green Sheet, Murray, Utah, Sun Adv., Price, Utah, Emery County Progress, Millard County Chronicle. Legis. reporter Utah State Women's Legis. Council, 1974-74; chmn. dist. Republican party, 1968-72, election judge, 1972-74; pres. Ch. of Jesus Christ of Latter-day Saints Relief Soc., Eldredge Ward; 1964-68, tchr. Sunday Sch., 1957-83, counsellor, 1957-64. Recipient Leadership awards Ch. of Jesus Christ of Latter-day Saints, 1957-73; art awards Utah State Fair, Salt Lake County Fair, Millard County Fair, Emery County Fair, Intermountain Soc. Artists, others. Mem. Sand and Sage Art Group, Intermountain Soc. Artists, Daus. Utah Pioneers. Club: Eagles Aux. (chaplain 1977-81).

GARDNER, GRACE GAIL, psychologist; b. N.Y.C., Dec. 14, 1938; d. Ledyard D. and Grace Fuller (Cowles) G. B.A., Smith Coll., 1960; Ph.D., Columbia U., 1966. Lic. clin. psychologist, Colo. Instr. psychology in pediatrics Cornell U. Med. Sch., N.Y.C., 1967-70; asst. prof. clin. psychology U. Colo. Med. Sch., Denver, 1970-76, assoc. prof. clin. psychology, 1976—, dir. tng. clin. psychology, 1982—; lectr. in field. Fellow Am. Psychol. Assn., Soc. Clin. and Exptl. Hypnosis (exec. sec.). Author: (with Karen Olness) Hypnosis and Hypnotherapy with Children, 1981. Contbr. articles to profl. jours. Home: 955 Eudora St Apt 1503 Denver CO 80220 Office: Box C231 U Colo Med School 4200 E 9th Ave Denver CO 80262

GARDNER, MARCELLA LYNN, marketing manager; b. Centralia, Ill., July 16, 1954; d. Joe Marshall and Ernestine (Vaughn) Gardner. B.A. in Bus. Adminstrn. and Communication, U. Pacific, 1976; M.B.A., U. Wash., 1978. Systems engr. trainee IBM, Seattle, 1977-78; mktg. engr. customer relations Hewlett-Packard Co., Cupertino, Calif., 1978, mktg. engr. sales devel., major account program, bus. devel. group, 1979-81, mktg. engr. third party program, 1981-82, mktg. program mgr., 1982—; prin. Lynn Gardner & Assocs. Advisor Jr. Achievement, Santa Clara County (Calif.), 1979-81. Mem. Nat. Assn. Female Execs., Nat. Assn. M.B.A.s, Internat. Fedn. Female Execs., Delta Sigma Theta. Democrat. Office: Hewlett Packard Co 19447 Pruneridge Ave Cupertino CA 95104

GARDNER, MARY BERTHA HOEFT CHADWICK, retired postmaster; b. Vernal, Utah, June 13, 1914; d. Edward and Hazel (Burgess) Hoeft; B.S. in Elem. Edn., Utah State U., 1950; m. Rulon Chadwick, Sept. 3, 1935 (div. July 1949); children—Mary Jo Chadwick Wight, Adriana Chadwick Forsgren; m. Leon D. Gardner, July 14, 1951 (dec. May 1974). Bookkeeper, Model Dairy, 1935-49; Weber Central Dairy,

1949-51, Bishops Storehouse, 1950-51; sch. tchr., Ogden, Utah, 1950-51; clk. Post Office, Honeyville, Utah, 1956-72, postmaster, 1972-81. Pres., Relief Soc. Ch. Jesus Ch. of Latter-day Saints, mem. stake bd. relief soc., mem. stake bd. Sunday sch., mem. stake bd. mut. improvement assn. orgn. Mem. Nat. League Postmasters (exec. v.p. state br., editor newsletter), Nat. Assn. Postmasters, AAUW (treas.), Daus. Utah Pioneers, Bus. and Profl. Women's Club (treas. Brigham City). Home: 8440 N Hwy 69 Honeyville UT 84314

GARDNER, NORD ARLING, management consultant; b. Afton, Wyo., Aug. 10, 1923; s. Arling A. and Ruth (Lee) G.; B.A., U. Wyo., 1945; M.S., Calif. State U., Hayward, 1972, M.P.A., 1975; postgrad. U. Chgo., U. Mich., U. Calif.-Berkeley; m. Thora Marie Stephen, Mar. 24, 1945; children—Randall Nord, Scott Stephen, Craig Robert, Laurie Lee. Commd. 2d lt. U.S. Army, 1942, advanced through grades to lt. col., 1964; ret., 1966; personnel analyst Univ. Hosp., U. Calif.-San Diego, 1946-48; coordinator manpower devel. U. Calif.-Berkeley, 1968-75; univ. tng. officer San Francisco State U., 1975-80, personnel mgr., 1976-80; exec. dir. CRDC Maintenance Tng. Corp., non-profit community effort, San Francisco; pres., dir. Sandor Assos. Mgmt. Cons., Pleasant Hill, Calif.; instr. Japanese, psychology, supervisory courses, 1977-78. Adv. council San Francisco Community Coll. Dist. Decorated Army Commendation medal. Mem. Ret. Officers Assn., Am. Soc. Tng. and Devel., No. Calif. Human Resources Council. Am. Assn. Univ. Adminstrs., Internat. Personnel Mgrs. Assn., Internat. Platform Assn., Coll. and Univ. Personnel Assn. (West Coast rep.). Republican. Clubs: Commonwealth of Calif., U. Calif.-Berkeley Faculty, Univ. (San Francisco). Author: To Gather Stones, 1978. Home: 2995 Bonnie Ln Pleasant Hill CA 94523 Office: 615 Grant Ave 4th Floor San Francisco CA 94108

GARDNER, RICK MICHAEL, psychologist, educator, researcher; b. Fresno, Calif., Aug. 10, 1943; s. Joseph Howard and Edna Mae (Shull) Jensen; m. Elizabeth Ann Gardner, June 3, 1967; children—Michael, Lisa. B.A., Humboldt State U., 1965; M.A., U. Nev.-Reno, 1967, Ph.D., 1969. Asst. prof. psychology U. So. Colo., 1969-74, assoc. prof., 1974-78, prof., 1978—, asst. v.p. for research, 1981-82, chmn. dept. psychology and mental health, 1982—; cons. on numerous state and federally funded research grants. NIMH grantee, 1981—. Mem. AAAS, Am. Psychol. Assn., Rocky Mountain Psychol. Assn., Sigma Xi. Author: Behavioral Objective Unit Workbook for Introductory Psychology, 1975; Exercises for General Psychology, 1980; contbr. articles on psychology to profl. jours. Home: 10 Hastings Dr Pueblo CO 81001 Office: Dept Psychology U So Colo Pueblo CO 81001

GARDNER, ROBERT DEAN, advertising and pubic relations executive, television producer; b. Little Falls, Minn., July 29, 1939; s. Charles George and Tecla Matilda (Gwost) G.; m. Sherry Nadine Karr, Aug. 18, 1963 (div. Oct. 1977); children—Christopher Dean, David Charles. Student San Diego City Coll., 1958-59; B.S., San Diego State U., 1963. Photojournalist, film editor Sta. XETV, ABC, San Diego, 1959-62; photojournalist, dir./producer, cinematographer Sta. KFMB-VT, CBS, San Diego, 1962-78; pres. Gardner & Assocs., Inc., advt. and pub. relations, San Diego, 1978—. Bd. dirs. Bayside Settlement House. Recipient John Swett award Calif. Tchrs. Assn., 1965; Sylvania award, 1967; silver medal N.Y. Film Critics, 1967; best video tape of 1978, AP, 1978; Internat. Broadcasting award Hollywood Radio and TV Soc., 1979; award of merit Communicating Arts Group, 1980; Andy award Advt. Club N.Y., 1980; Homburg award San Diego Advt. Club, 1981, 82. Mem. Nat. Acad. TV and Sics. (Emmy awards 1976, 77, 78, 80, 81, 82, gov.), Soc. Motion Picture and TV Engrs., Sigma Delta Chi, Alpha Epsilon Rho. Democrat. Roman Catholic. Office: 432 P St Suite 409 San Diego CA 92101

GARDNER, ROBERT KAHN, advertising agency executive; b. Oklahoma City, Okla., Mar. 22, 1943; s. Irvin Bassist and Barbara Clara (Kahn) G.; m. Gretchen Demmler Schenck, Sept. 16, 1979; children—Mollie Elizabeth, Besse Bassist. B.A., U. Pa., 1964, M.B.A., 1967. Creative group supr. J. Walter Thompson Co., N.Y.C., 1967-72, v.p., creative dir., San Francisco div., 1974-76; chief speechwriter Cost of Living Council, Washington, 1972-73, Office of Mgmt. and Budget, Washington, 1973-74; assoc. creative dir. Pres. Ford Election Campaign, Washington, 1976-77; pres., creative dir. Gardner Communications, Inc., San Francisco, 1977—. Bd. dirs. Wharton Sch. Grad. Club of No. Calif., Guardsmen. Republican. Jewish. Clubs: Burlingame Country, Concordia-Argonaut, Mask and Wig. Author: Gardner's Guide to San Francisco, 1964-70; Gardner's Guide to Atlanta, 1972; also music and lyrics to numerous advt. jingles (4 Clio awards). Office: Gardner Communications Inc 153 Kearny St San Francisco CA 94108

GARDNER, ROBERT LEE, physicist; b. Monroe, N.C., Dec. 23, 1946; s. Leon Elmore and Vera Madgeline (Coleman) G.; B.S. in Physics, Clemson (S.C.) U., 1968; M.S. in Engring. Physics, Air Force Inst. Tech., 1973; Ph.D. in Physics, U. Colo., 1980; m. Linda Lee Marksbury, Aug. 23, 1975. Group leader discharge physics Mission Research Corp., Albuquerque, 1980—. Served as officer USAF, 1969-76. Decorated Air Force Commendation medal. Mem. IEEE, Am. Geophys. Union. Republican. Contbr. articles to profl. jours. Home: 2812 Dallas NE Albuquerque NM 87110 Office: 1720 Randolph Rd SE Albuquerque NM 87106

GARDNER, ROBERT PAUL, JR., home entertainment hardware manufacturer; b. Hannibal, Mo., Dec. 7, 1937; s. Robert Paul and Leona Bell (Boullear) G.; m. Mary Jane Couch, Aug. 31, 1957; children—Pamela, Rob, Greg, Beth. B.S., N.E. Mo. State U., 1959. Various Positions Western Pub. Co., Inc., Racine, Wis., 1959-73; pres. Success Methods, Inc., Santa Ana, Calif., 1973-74; v.p. sales and mktg. Wham-o Mfg. Co., San Gabriel, Calif., 1974-82; v.p. mktg. Starpath Corp., Santa Clara, Calif., 1982—; exec.-in-residence N.E. Mo. State U., 1981; guest lectr. Long Beach State U. Bd. dirs. Tustin Jr. All-Am. Football. Mem. Am. Mgmt. Assn., Phi Sigma Epsilon. Roman Catholic. Club: KC. Pub.: Moving Ahead, 1974. Home: 1271 Tropicana Ln Santa Ana CA 92705 Office: 2005 De La Cruz Blvd Santa Clara CA 95050

GARDNER, WALTER HALE, soil science educator, researcher, consultant; b. Beaver, Utah, Feb. 24, 1917; s. Willard and Rebecca Viola (Hale) G.; Barbara Brown, Aug. 11, 1948; children—Jeanne G. Gardner Minert, Marolyn G. Gardner Mortensen, Janet, Laurie Gardner Boyce, Willard. B.S., Utah State U., 1939, M.S., 1947, Ph.D., 1950; postgrad. Cornell U., 1940-41. Cert. profl. soil scientist. Prof. soils Wash. State U., Pullman, 1950-82, prof. emeritus, 1982—; with IAEA, Vienna, Austria, 1971-72. Served to lt. col. USAF, 1941-46, USAFR, 1946-77. Guggenhein fellow, 1963-64. Mem. Soil Sci. Soc. Am. (pres. 1983), Am. Soc. Agronomy, Western Soil Sci. Soc. (pres. 1967), AAAS (mem. exec. com. Pacific div. 1981-85), Am. Inst. Planners, Am. Soc. Planning Ofcls. Mormon. Author: (with L.D. Baver and W.R. Gardner) Soil Physics, 1972; editor Jour. Soil Sci. Soc. Am., 1966-69; contbr. numerous profl. papers to chpts. books, encys. Home: NE 1505 Upper Dr Pullman WA 99163 Office: Dept Agronomy and Soils Wash State U Pullman WA 99164

GARDUQUE, THEODORE ELTON, architect; b. Honolulu, Jan. 1, 1951; s. Gabriel and Mabel (Amor) G.; B.Arch., U. Oreg., 1973; M.Arch., Cornell U., 1975; Project designer, architect Architects Hawaii Ltd., Honolulu, 1974-77, dir. interiors and graphics, 1977-78; dir. design and planning Kapalua LandCo. Ltd., Maui, 1978-80; prin. T.E. Garduque, Architect, 1980; asso. Architects Hawaii Ltd., Honolulu, 1981-82; prin. Wudtke Watson Davis Engstrom Garduque, Honolulu, 1982—; art dir. Hawaii Architect Mag., 1976-78; instr. U. Oreg., 1972-73, Cornell U., 1974-75. N.Y. State Urban Research grantee, 1974-75. Mem. AIA (treas. Hawaii), Graphic Designers Assn., Planners Architect Landscape Architects Maui (v.p. 1979), Urban Design Inst., Chi Psi. Episcopalian. Club: Oahu Athletic. Home: 1980 Aamaka Pl Pearl City HI 96782 Office: 1188 Bishop St Suite 607 Honolulu HI 96813

GAREY, DONALD LEE, pipeline exec.; b. Ft. Worth, Sept. 9, 1931; s. Leo James and Jessie (McNatt) G.; B.S. in Geol. Engring., Tex. A. and M. U., 1953; m. Elizabeth Patricia Martin, Aug. 1, 1953; children—Deborah Anne, Elizabeth Laird. Reservoir geologist Gulf Oil Corp., 1953-54, sr. geologist, 1956-65; v.p., mng. dir. Indsl. Devel. Corp. Lea County, Hobbs, N.Mex., 1965-72, dir., 1972—, pres., 1978—; v.p., dir. Minerals, Inc., Hobbs, 1966-72, pres., dir., 1972—, chief exec. officer, 1978—; mng. dir. Hobbs Indsl. Found. Corp., 1965-72, dir., 1965-76; v.p. Llano, Inc., 1972-74, exec. v.p., chief operating officer, 1974-75, pres., 1975—, chief exec. officer, 1978—, also dir.; pres., chief exec. officer, dir. Pollution Control, Inc., 1969-81; pres., dir. NMESCO Fuels, Inc., 1982—; dir. Liberty Nat. Bank; cons. geologist, geol. engr., Hobbs, 1965-72. Chmn., Hobbs Manpower Devel. Tng. Adv. Com., 1965-72; mem. Hobbs Adv. Com. for Mental Health, 1965-67; chmn. N.Mex. Mapping Adv. Com., 1968-69; mem. Hobbs adv. bd. Salvation Army, 1967-78, chmn., 1970-72; mem. exec. bd. Conquistador council Boy Scouts Am., Hobbs, 1965-75; vice chmn. N.Mex. Gov.'s Com. for Econ. Devel., 1968-70; bd. regents Coll. Southwest, 1982—. Served to capt. USAF, 1954-56. Registered profl. engr., Tex. Mem. Am. Inst. Profl. Geologists, Am. Assn. Petroleum Geologists, AIME, N.Mex., Roswell geol. socs., N.Mex. Amigos. Club: Rotary. Home: 315 E Alto Dr Hobbs NM 88240 Office: Broadmoor Bldg PO Box 1320 Hobbs NM 88240

GAREY, PAT MARTIN, artist; b. State College, Miss., Nov. 11, 1932; d. Verey G. and Eva (Jones) Martin; B.S., Tex. Woman's U., 1953; M.F.A., Tex. Tech. U., 1973; m. Donald L. Garey, Aug. 1, 1953; children—Deborah Anne Furst, Rick Furst, Elizabeth Laird. Display advt. artist Anchorage Daily Times, 1954-55; prodn. mgr. Cox Advt. Agy., Roswell, N.Mex., 1959-62; graphic artist, painter, ceramic sculptor, Hobbs, N.Mex., 1962—; instr. art Coll. of Southwest, 1967-70, 74; artist-in-the-schs. program HEW Emergency Sch. Aid Act Project, 1974—; pres. Llano Estacado Art Assn., 1968; one woman shows include: N.Mex. Jr. Coll., 1968, 81, Cross Gallery, Ft. Worth, 1972, Coll. of Southwest, 1973, Sangre de Cristo Art Center, Pueblo, Colo., 1980; group shows include: 13th Ann. Tex. Fine Arts Assn., 1968, Roswell Mus. and Art Center, 1969, Laguna Gloria Mus., Austin, Tex. (Tex. Fine Arts Assn. award), 1969, N.Mex. State Fair, 1969, Mus. of Southwest, Midland, Tex., 1972, N.Mex. State U., 1975, Okla. Art Center, Oklahoma City, 1975, Little Rock Art Center, 1977, El Paso Mus. Art, 1978, Armory for the Arts Exhbn., Mus. Fine Arts, Santa Fe, 1980, U. Tex., 1981, 82, Front Room Gallery, Dallas, 1983, Sylvia Ullman's Am. Crafts, Cleve., 1983. Recipient 1st place award Llano Estacado Art Assn., 1982. Mem. Delta Phi Delta, Chi Omega. Methodist. Address: 315 E Alto St Hobbs NM 88240

GARFEIN, CAROLYN HERSH, marketing research executive; b. Bklyn., Mar. 20, 1943; d. Isaac and Esther (Cohen) Hersh; m. John D. Garfein, May 30, 1970; children—Matthew, Joanna. B.A., Cornell U., 1963; M.B.A., Calif. State U., 1981. Research analyst Eric Marder Assocs., N.Y.C., 1963-65; mgr. program research, NBC, N.Y.C., 1965-67, Burbank Calif., 1967-69; mktg. research and promotions mgr. Knott's Berry Farm, Buena Park, Calif., 1974-77, v.p. Yankelovich, Shelly & White, Newport Beach, Calif., 1977-78; Houlahan/Parker Mktg. Research, Whittier, Calif., 1979—; part-time faculty mem. Chapman Coll., Orange, Calif. Mem. AAUW (nat. com. women 1982-84, Calif. State Div. budget dir. 1980-82, exec. com. mem.), Am. Mktg. Assn. Home: 8391 Circle Westminster CA 92683 Office: Houlahan/Parker Mktg Research 15851 E Whittier Blvd Whittier CA 90603

GARFIELD, ALEC SAMUEL, tribal government official; b. Tule River Indian Reservation, Mar. 3, 1939; s. William James and Jennie Frances (Vera) G.; m. Cypriana Louise Franco, Aug. 22, 1959; children—Joseph, Karen Ann; m. 2d, Janet Sue Crabtree, Nov. 28, 1980. Mem. council Tule River Indian Reservation, Porterville, Calif., 1969—, chmn., 1970-83, also mgr. dept. reservation devel.; pres. Rohnert Park Radio, Inc., 1982—; pres. Calif. Tribal Chmn.'s Assn., 1976-80; area v.p. Nat. Congress Am. Indians, 1974. Bd. dirs. Calif. Indian Legal Services, Oakland, 1974. Served with USN, 1957-61. Democrat. Roman Catholic. Office: PO Box 589 Porterville CA 93258

GARFINKLE, ELLEN M., clinical psychologist; b. Boston, Oct. 21, 1948; d. Harold A. and Jeanne L. (Newman) G.; B.S. in Social Sci., New Sch. Social Research, N.Y.C., 1971; M.A., Calif. Sch. Profl. Psychology, Berkeley, 1976, Ph.D. in Clin. Psychology, 1978. Presch. tchr. Univ. Plaza Nursery Sch., N.Y.C., 1970-71, Corlears Sch., N.Y.C., 1971-72; counselor Planned Parenthood, San Francisco, 1973-74; therapist Women's Ctr. for Creative Counseling, San Francisco, 1974-75; psychology intern Sunset Mental Health Ctr., San Francisco, 1975-76, N.E. Community Mental Health, San Francisco, 1976-77, City of Berkeley Mental Health Dept. Family, Youth and Children's Ctr., 1977-78; psychol. asst. to Carol Tuttle, San Francisco and Edith Kasin, Berkeley, 1977—; psychol. cons. Albany Children's Ctr., 1978-81, Counseling Ctr., U. Calif., Berkeley, 1977, Contra Costa County Hosp., Martinez, Calif., 1979, Operation Concern, San Francisco, 1979. Nat. Inst. Alcoholism and Alcohol Abuse grantee, 1976-77. Mem. Am. Psychol. Assn., Calif. Psychol. Assn., Assn. Gay Psychologists, Assn. Women in Psychology, Psychotherapy Inst. Berkeley. Contbr. articles to profl. jours. Office: 1905 Berkeley Way Berkeley CA 94704

GARGANTA, NARCISO MERIOLES, librarian; b. Masbate, Philippines, Sept. 18, 1932; s. Francisco Legaspi and Leonor (Merioles) G. B.L.S., Arellano U., 1956; M.L.S., Pratt Inst., 1971; cert. profl. pub. librarian N.Y. Dir. tech. library United Drug Co., Inc., United Labs. Inc., Manila, Philippines, 1960-67; serials librarian Norris Med. Library, U. So. Calif. Med. Ctr., 1967-68; med. librarian Milton Helpern Library Legal Medicine, N.Y.C., 1970-72; curriculum devel. specialist RCA Resource Ctr., N.Y.C., 1972-77; asst. librarian VA Med. Ctr., Brentwood, Calif., 1978-79; dir. med. library Burbank (Calif.) Community Hosp., 1979—. Mem. Med. Library Assn., Am. Soc. Info. Sci., Med. Group So. Calif. and Ariz., N.Y.C. Geneal. Soc. Mng. editor Philippine Library Jour., 1959, Internat. Microform Jour. of Legal Medicine, 1970. Home: 4914 York Blvd Los Angeles CA 90042

GARGER, STEPHEN JOSEPH, educator, educational consultant; b. N.Y.C., May 26, 1949; s. Joseph Stephen and Mary Elizabeth (Repko) G.; m. Leigh Anne Bell. B.S. in Acctg., Manhattan Coll., 1970; M.A. in Religious Studies, Ottawa U., 1976; Ed.D., Seattle U., 1982. Cert. elem. and secondary tchr., sch. adminstr., Wash. Acct., Arthur Young & Co., N.Y.C., 1970; chmn. dept. religion LaSalle Acad., N.Y.C., 1971-73, Loyola High Sch., Missoula, Mont., 1975-77; chmn. dept. religion, acad. v.p. O'Dea High Sch., Seattle, 1977—; adolescent learning cons., Seattle, 1983—; adj. faculty St. Martin's Coll., Lacey, Wash., Seattle U. Named Outstanding Young Educator, Missoula Jaycees, 1976. Mem. Assn. for Supervision and Curriculum Devel., Am. Psychol. Assn., Am. Acad. Religion, Phi Delta Kappa. Roman Catholic. Club: Ft. Steilacoom Running (Tacoma, Wash.). Home: 508 E Harrison St Seattle WA 98102

GARLOUGH, WILLIAM GLENN, marketing exec.; b. Syracuse, N.Y., Mar. 27, 1924; s. Henry James and Gladys (Killam) G.; B.E.E., Clarkson Coll. Tech., 1949; m. Charlotte M. Tanzer, June 15, 1947; children—Jennifer, William, Robert. With Knowlton Bros., Watertown, N.Y., 1949-67, mgr. mfg. services, 1966-67; v.p. planning, equipment systems div. Vare Corp., Englewood Cliffs, N.J., 1967-69; mgr. mktg. Valley Mould div. Microdot Inc., Hubbard, Ohio, 1969-70; dir. corp. devel. Microdot Inc., Greenwich, Conn., 1970-73, v.p. corp. devel., 1973-76, v.p. adminstrn., 1976-77, v.p. corp. devel., 1977-78; v.p. corp. devel. Am. Bldg. Maintenance Industries, San Francisco, 1979-83; pres. The Change Agts., Walnut Creek, Calif., 1983—. Mem. citizens adv. com. to Watertown Bd. Edn., 1957. Bd. dirs. Watertown Community Chest, 1958-61. Served with USMCR, 1942-46. Mem. Am. Mgmt. Assn., Mensa, Am. Mktg. Assn., TAPPI, Assn. Corp. Growth, Lincoln League (pres. 1958), Am. Contract Bridge League (life master), Clarkson Alumni Assn. (Watertown sect. pres. 1955), Tau Beta Pi. Presbyterian (ruling elder). Clubs: Olympic; No. N.Y. Contract (pres. 1959), No. N.Y. Transp. Home: 2557 Via Verde Walnut Creek CA 94598 Office: 1990 N California Blvd Walnut Creek CA 94596

GARMAN, GLEN DALE, clinical psychologist; b. Minerva, Ohio, May 12, 1922; s. Frederick Glenn and Helen Effie (Hoopes) G.; m. Florence E. Hoffman, Mar. 13, 1965; children—Patricia Lois, Glen Craig, Sherri Lea. B.A., U. Mich., 1949, M.A., 1951, Ph.D., 1954. Lic. psychologist, Calif., 1967; Nat. Register of Health Service Providers in Psychology, 1979. Staff psychologist VA Hosp., Salt Lake City, 1954-60; chief psychologist, Mental Hygiene Clinic, VA, San Diego, 1960-65; staff psychologist Community Mental Health Ctr., San Diego, 1965-68; pvt. practice clin. psychology, 1968—; lectr. San Diego State U., 1966-69, Calif. Sch. Profl. Psychology, 1976; instr. Ala. A&M, San Diego Extension Program, 1982—; cons. Episcopal Community Services, San Diego, 1968, Imperial County Health Dept., 1969. Bd. dirs. Calif. Psychology Health Plan, 1977—, pres., 1974-80. Served to 2d lt. USAAF, 1943-46. Fellow Acad. San Diego Psychologists (pres. 1969); mem. San Diego County Psychologists Assn. (pres. 1964), Calif. State Psychologists Assn., Western Psychologists Assn., Am. Psychologists Assn. Home: 6478 Caminito Estrellado San Diego CA 92120

GARMHAUSEN, WINONA MARIE, educator; b. Ft. Wayne, Ind., Jan. 21, 1930; d. Frederick and Viola M. Kunz; B.S. in Edn., Ohio No. U., 1961; M.F.A., Bowling Green State U., 1964; Ph.D. in Am. Studies, U. N.Mex., 1982; m. Allen F. Anderson, Jan. 10, 1979; children by previous marriage—Jacqueline, Jeffrey, Jan, Jill. Chmn., art dept. Shawnee Schs., Lima, Ohio, 1964-65; instr. Ohio State U., Lima, 1965-72; mem. Ohio Arts Commn., 1972; arts specialist State Dept. of Edn., Santa Fe, N.Mex., 1974-76; dir. Visual Arts div. Coll. of Santa Fe, 1976-81; arts cons., prof. Highlands U., Las Vegas, N.Mex., 1981—; asst. curator Allen County Mus., Lima, 1964-67. Mem. N.Mex. Gov.'s Commn. on Pub. Broadcasting Mem. N.Mex. Art Edn. Assn., Nat. Art Edn. Assn., N.Mex. Alliance for Arts Edn. (exec. com.), AAUP, Coll. Art Assn. Contbr. articles on Ohio courthouse architecture and native Am. edn. to profl. jours. Home: Route 9 Box 90K Santa Fe NM 87501 Office: Highlands Univ Las Vegas NM 87701

GARN, EDWIN JACOB, U.S. Senator; b. Richfield, Utah, Oct. 12, 1932; s. Jacob Edwin and Fern (Christensen) G.; B.S., U. Utah, 1955; m. Hazel Rhae Thompson, Feb. 2, 1957 (dec. 1976); children—Jacob Wayne, Susan Rhae, Ellen Marie, Jeffrey Paul; m. Kathleen Brewerton, Apr. 8, 1977; 1 stepson, Brook Bingham; children—Jennifer Kathleen, Matthew Spencer. Spl. agt. John Hancock Mut. Life Ins. Co., Salt Lake City, 1960-61; asst. mgr. Home Life Ins. Co. N.Y., Salt Lake City, 1961-66; gen. agt. Mut. Trust Life Ins. Co., Salt Lake City, 1966-68; city commr. Salt Lake City, 1968-72; mayor Salt Lake City, 1971-74; U.S. Senator from Utah, 1974—, mem. Armed Services Com., 1974-78, Select Com. on Intelligence, 1976—, Appropriations Com., 1978—, chmn. Banking, Housing and Urban Affairs Com., 1981—, chmn. Appropriations Subcom., Housing and Urban Devel., 1981—. Mem. adv. bd. Salvation Army; sec. Republican Conf., 1978—. Served to lt. (s.g.) USNR, 1956-60. Recipient Tom McCoy award Utah League Cities and Towns, 1972; Watchdog of Treas. cert., VFW; Am. Conservative Union Statesman award N.G. Assn. U.S., USNR. Mem. Utah League Cities and Towns (pres. 1971-72, dir. 1968—), Nat. League Cities (2d v.p. 1972-73, 1st v.p. 1973-74, hon. pres. 1975—, dir. 1972—), Sigma Chi. Mem. Ch. Jesus Christ Latter-day Saints. Club: Kiwanis. Author: A Changing America—Conservatives View the '80's from the U.S. Senate, 1980. Home: 7707 Bridle Path Ln McLean VA 22101 Office: 5207 Dirksen Bldg Washington DC 20510

GARNAND, GARY LEE, produce mktg. co. exec.; b. Twin Falls, Idaho, Oct. 28, 1946; s. Vay Ross and Maxine Sadie (Campbell) G.; B.S., U. Idaho, 1970; m. Lori Allgaier, June 28, 1975; children—Stacy, Kristen. Asst. sales mgr. Chef Reddy Foods Co., Othello, Wash., 1970-71; pres. Garnand Mktg., Inc., Firth, Idaho, 1971—, also dir.; lectr. in field; pres., chmn. bd. Garnand Produce Co. Bd. dirs. Tri-County Big Bros.-Big Sisters, Moses Lake, Wash., pres., 1980-81; mem. Grant County Community Action Bd., 1978-80. Mem. Produce Mktg. Assn. (dir. ins. bd. 1975—, food-service and fgn. trade coms.), United Fresh Fruit and Vegetable Assn. (bd. dirs. onion div.), Am. Mktg. Assn., Sigma Alpha Epsilon (dist. pres. 1974-76, 78-82). Republican. Lutheran. Clubs: Masons, Rotary (dir. Moses Lake, pres. 1982-83), Elks, Toastmasters. Home: 559 Edgewater Ln Moses Lake WA 98837 Office: 406 Country Club Dr Route 3 Jerome ID 83338

GARNER, DAVID L., marketing executive; b. Rupert, Ida., July 1, 1947; s. Leland J. and Maxine (Call) G.; m. Rita Goodman, Aug. 26, 1969; children—Alecia, Krista, Michael, Shauna. B.S., Brigham Young U., 1980. Cons., asst. sales mgr. communications dept. Central Telephone Co., Las Vegas, Nev., 1973-78; area sales mgr. Continental Telephone, Tremonton, Utah, 1978-82, adminstr. mktg., Phoenix, 1983—. Served with USAR, 1970-76. Named Salesman of the Year, Continental Telephone, 1981, Area Sales Mgr. of the Year, 1982; Pres.'s award for managerial excellence, 1982. Republican. Mem. Ch. of Jesus Christ of Latter Day Saints.

GARNER, GIROLAMA THOMASINA, educational administrator, educator; b. Muskegon, Mich., Sept, 15, 1923; d. John and Martha Ann (Thomas) Funaro; student Muskegon Jr. Coll., 1941; B.A., Western Mich. U., 1944, M.A. in Counseling and Guidance, 1958; Ed.D., U. Ariz., 1973; m. Charles Donald Garner, Sept. 16, 1944 (dec.); 1 dau., Linda Jeannette Garner Blake. Elem. tchr., Muskegon and Tucson, 1947-77; counselor Erickson Elem. Sch., Tucson, 1978-79; prin. Hudlow Elem. Sch., Tucson, 1979—, adj. prof. U. Ariz., 1973—, Pima Community Coll., 1981—; mem. Ariz. Com. Tchr. Evaluation and Cert., 1976-78; del. NEA convs. Active ARC, Crippled Children's Soc., UNESCO, DAV Aux., Rincon Renegades; bd. dirs. Hudlow Community Sch., 1973-76. Recipient Apple award for teaching excellence Pima Community Coll., 1982. Mem. Nat. Assn. Sci. Tchrs., Tucson Edn. Assn., Ariz. Edn. Assn., NEA, Assn. Supervision and Curriculum Devel., AAUW, Delta Kappa Gamma, Kappa Rho Sigma, Kappa Delta Pi. Democrat. Christian Scientist. Home: 6922 E Baker St Tucson AZ 85710 Office: 502 N Caribe St Tucson AZ 85710

GARNER, LAVAL FRANCIS, pharmacist; b. Hyrum, Utah, May 20, 1933; s. William Francis and Anna LaRue (Jensen) G.; B.S., U. Utah, 1959; m. Rose Epsie Emily Parks, Feb. 2, 1961; children—Heidi Ann, Troy Val, David Parks, Jana Janell, Laura Lynn, Jared Jens, Karl Edmun, Bryce William. Pharmacist, West Fullerton, Calif., 1959-60; v.p. Hacienda Gardens Drug Corp., San Jose, Calif., 1960-67, pres., 1967—; pres. Key Rexal Drugs, San Jose and Campbell, Calif.; partner G & C Reflections, San Jose, 1976-79. Missionary, Ch. Jesus Christ of Latter-day Saints, Norway, 1954-56. Served with U.S. Army, 1958-59. Mem. Am., Utah, Calif. (del. 1978-82, mem. govt. affairs com. 1980-82), Santa Clara County (dir. 1976—, pres. 1980) pharm. assns., Nat. Assn. Retail Druggists. Republican. Writer prose pub. in poster form and as plaques, 1976. Office: 3065 Meridian Ave San Jose CA 95124

GARNER, MARGARET MARY, microcomputer firm executive; b. Syracuse, N.Y., July 3, 1951; d. John Joseph and Joyce Irene (Pelletier) Galuski; m. Dariel D. Garner, Sept. 29, 1960. B.A. in Math., U. N.C., 1973. Lic. real estate agt., Calif. Ops. supr. regional service center Allstate Ins. Co., Charlotte, N.C., 1973; mgr. Mut. of N.Y. Ins., Fresno, Calif., 1975-77; owner ORBA Fin. Services, Visalia, Calif., 1977-79; real estate agt. Century 21 Realty, Visalia, 1978-80; co-founder, corp. sec. Merlin Info. Systems Inc., San Diego, 1979—; sec./treas. Merlin Info., San Diego, 1981—; cons. microcomputers Transylvania U., Lexington, Ky. Named Salesperson of month, Century 21, 1978, 79, 80. Mem. Phi Mu. Democrat. Roman Catholic. Developer microcomputer software for banking industry. Office: PO Box 178510 San Diego CA 92117

GARNES, MARLENE CAROL, systems analyst; b. Portland, Oreg., Oct. 21, 1944; d. Johnie and Florence (Alwell) Garnes; student Ga. State U., 1976-78, Grove St. Coll., Oakland, Calif., 1971; 1 dau., Marlo. Mgmt. analyst City of Atlanta, 1974-78; mgmt. cons. Parametrics, Inc., Washington, 1978; analyst/programmer Security Nat. Bank, Concord, Calif., 1978-80; EDP auditor Crocker Nat. Bank, San Francisco, 1980-82; systems analyst Wells Fargo Bank, San Francisco, 1982—. Served with USNR, 1979—. Mem. Black Assn. Data Processing Profls. (dir.). Office: 425 Market St 28th Floor San Francisco CA 94163

GARNIER, JOHN EDWARD, materials research scientist; b. Milw., Oct. 29, 1947; s. Robert Charles and Catherine (Sulich) G.; B.S., Marquette U., 1970, M.S., 1972, Ph.D., 1974. Vice-pres., treas. Energy Transducers Ltd., Milw., 1971-73; sr. research scientist Battelle N.W. Labs., Richland, Wash., 1974—. Program coordinator Council on Aging, 1975-76. NSF grantee, 1971. Mem. Am. Ceramic Soc., AAAS, Tau Beta Pi, Pi Tau Sigma, Pi Sigma Epsilon. Roman Catholic. Contbr. articles to profl. jours. Home: 26004 Vaca Rd Kennewick WA 99336 Office: Battelle NW Labs Richland WA 99352

GARON, SHIELA ROSALYN, sch. counselor; b. Colo., Mar. 12, 1942; d. Bernard I. and Helene P. Garon; B.A. in English, U. Colo., 1964; M.A. in Counseling and Guidance, Denver U., 1968; M.A. in Ednl. Adminstrn., Loyola Marymount U., Los Angeles, 1979. Tchr., Englewood, Colo., 1965-68; counselor WIN program State of Colo., 1968-69, State of Calif. Vocat. Rehab., 1971, Los Angeles Unified Sch. Dist., 1972—; adminstr. week-end seminars Beverly Hills Adult Sch., 1981-82. Mem. NEA, Calif. Edn. Assn. Office: 450 N Grand St Los Angeles CA 90002

GAROUTTE, BILL CHARLES, neurophysiologist; b. Absarokee, Mont., Mar. 15, 1921; s. Bernard Clark and Anna (Kosir) G.; student San Diego State Coll., 1939-42; A.B., U. Calif.-Berkeley, 1943, M.D., 1945, Ph.D., 1954; m. Sally Jeter, July 18, 1948; children—Brian, Susanna, David, Katherine. With U. Calif. Med. Sch., San Francisco, 1949—, successively lectr., instr., asst. prof., assoc. prof. anatomy and neurology, 1949-66, prof. anatomy and neurology, 1966—; vis. asst. prof. U. Indonesia Faculty of Medicine, Djakarta, 1956-57; staff electroencephalography and electromyography U. Calif.-San Francisco, 1953-71; vis. investigator Brain Research Inst. U. Tokyo (Japan), 1963. Served as lt. (j.g.) M.C., USNR, 1946-47. Fulbright scholar, London, 1950-51. Mem. Western Inst. on Epilepsy (pres. 1962), Am. Assn. Anatomists, Am. Acad. Neurology, Am., Western (pres. 1961-62) electroencephalography socs., Hist. Soc. Pa., San Francisco Neurol. Soc. (pres. 1969-70), Am. Assn. Electromyography and Electrodiagnosis. Research on elec. activity of the central nervous system. Author: Survey of Functional Neuroanatomy, 1981. Home: 105 Molino Ave Mill Valley CA 94941 Office: U Calif San Francisco CA 94143

GARRA, RAYMOND HAMILTON, mktg. exec.; b. Chgo., Apr. 2, 1934; s. Raymond Hamilton and Dorothy (Gardner) G.; student Duke, 1951-53; B.A., U. Calif. at Los Angeles, 1956; m. Sandra Beatrice Pheasant, Dec. 27, 1962 (div. May, 1970); children—Terese Helene, Raymond Hamilton III. Gen. mgr. fine paper div. Noland Paper Co., Inc., Buena Park, Calif., 1959-67; v.p. sales Western Lithograph Co., Inc., Los Angeles, 1967-71; pres. Los Angeles Lithograph Co., 1971-73; pres. World Sports Mktg., Inc., also Westaire Properties, Inc., and Miss Calif. Teen-ager, Inc., 1974—. Mem. Republican State Central Com., 1966-67; exec. bd. U. Calif., Irvine Sports Assos. Served with USCGR, 1956-59; lt. comdr. Res. Recipient Sports Family of Year award, 1975. Mem. Nat. Coronado 25 Assn. (pres. 1969-70; Yachtsman of Year award 1971), Buena Park C. of C. (sec. 1967), Mensa (founder Orange County Soc. 1964), Phi Kappa Psi. Mason. Clubs: Balboa Bay, Bahia Corinthian Yacht, Newport Bayview Yacht (1st commodore 1980). mktg. exec.; b. Chgo., Apr. 2, 1934; s. Raymond Hamilton and Dorothy (Gardner) G.; student Duke, 1951-53; B.A., U. Calif. at Los Angeles, 1956; m. Sandra Beatrice Pheasant, Dec. 27, 1962 (div. May, 1970); children—Terese Helene, Raymond Hamilton III. Gen. mgr. fine paper div. Noland Paper Co., Inc., Buena Park, Calif., 1959-67; v.p. sales Western Lithograph Co., Inc., Los Angeles, 1967-71; pres. Los Angeles Lithograph Co., Inc., 1971-73; pres. World Sports Mktg., Inc., also Westaire Properties, Inc., and Miss Calif. Teen-ager, Inc., 1974—. Mem. Republican State Central Com., 1966-67; exec. bd. U. Calif., Irvine Sports Assos. Served with USCGR, 1956-59; lt. comdr. Res. Recipient Sports Family of Year award, 1975. Mem. Nat. Coronado 25 Assn. (pres. 1969-70; Yachtsman of Year award 1971), Buena Park C. of C. (sec. 1967), Mensa (founder Orange County Soc. 1964), Phi Kappa Psi. Mason. Clubs: Balboa Bay, Bahia Corinthian Yacht, Newport Bayview Yacht (1st commodore 1980). Home: 405 Dahlia Ave Corona del Mar CA 92625

GARRETSON, OWEN LOREN, oil refining co. exec., engr.; b. Salem, Iowa, Feb. 24, 1912; s. Sumner Dilts and Florence (White) G.; student Iowa Wesleyan Coll., 1930-32; B.S., Iowa State U., 1937; m. Erma Mary Smith, Jan. 23, 1932; children—John A., Owen Don, Susan Marie, Leon T. Engr. Bailey Meter Co., Cleve., 1937, St. Louis, 1937-38; engr., dist. mgr., Phillips Petroleum Co., Bartlesville, Okla., 1938-39, engr., dist. mgr., Amarillo, Tex., 1939-40, engr., dist. mgr., Detroit, 1940-41, mgr., asst. mgr., 1941-42, mgr. product supply and transp. div., Bartlesville, 1942-44, mgr. engring., devel. div., 1944-46; mgr. spl. products engring., devel. div., 1946-47; pres., dir. Gen. Tank and Steel Corp., Roswell, N.Mex., United Farm Chem. Co.; pres., dir. Garretson Equipment Co., Mt. Pleasant, Iowa; v.p., dir. Valley Industries, Inc., Mt. Pleasant; pres., dir. Garretson Carburetion of Tex., Inc., Lubbock,; v.p., dir. Sacra Gas Co. of Roswell, 1957-58; exec. v.p., dir. Arrow Gas Co., Roswell, and affiliated corps., N.Mex., Tex. and Utah, 1958-60; asst. to pres. Nat. Propane Corp., New Hyde Park, N.Y.; chmn. bd., dir. Plateau, Inc., oil refining, Farmington, N.Mex., 1978-83; chmn. bd. Southwest Motels, Inc., Farmington; organizing dir. Farmington Nat. Bank, 1964; dir., cons. Suburban Propane Gas Corp., Morristown, N.J., 1973-83. Mem., past pres. Farmington Indsl. Devel. Service. Mem. N.Mex. Liquefied Petroleum Gas Commn., 1955-78, chmn., 1956-58; mem. Iowa Gov.'s Trade Commn. to No. Europe, 1970, Iowa Trade Mission to Europe, 1979; chmn. Internat. LP-Gas Engine Fuel Symposium, Detroit, 1970; mem. com. on natural gas/liquefied natural gas Internat. Petroleum Expn. and Congress, 1970-71. Mem. Nat. Council on Crime and Delinquency. Recipient Merit award Iowa Wesleyan Coll. Alumni Assn., 1968. Registered profl. engr., Okla., N.Mex., Iowa, Mo. Mem. Nat. Liquefied Petroleum Gas Assn. (dir., Disting. Service award 1979), Am. Petroleum Inst., Nat. Petroleum Refiner's Assn. (dir., pres.), Ind. Refiners Assn. Am., Agrl. Ammonia Inst. Memphis (dir.), N.Mex. Liquefied Petroleum Gas Assn. (pres., dir.), ASME, Ind. Petroleum Assn. Am., N.Mex. Acad. Sci., Nat. Soc. Profl. Engrs., Am. Soc. Agrl. Engrs., Am. Soc. Automotive Engrs., N.Mex. Amigos, Am. Inst. Chem. Engrs., Newcomen Soc. N.Am., Soc. Indsl. Archeology, Ancient Gassers, 25-Year Club Petroleum Industry, Phi Delta Theta, Tau Beta Pi. Mason, Rotarian. Author articles in field; 40 patents issued in several fields. Home: 500 E LaPlata St Farmington NM 87401 Office: PO Box 108 Farmington NM 87401

GARRETT, A. MILTON, educator; b. Maryville, Mo., Aug. 23, 1937; s. Arthur M. and Laurene B. Garrett; B.A., U. No. Colo., 1963, M.A., 1965; Ed.D., Tex. A&M U., 1971; m. Jane Ann Schultz, Nov. 29, 1963; children—Kristin Kay, Charles Peter David. Tchr., indsl. coop. tng. coordinator Gt. Falls (Mont.) High Sch., 1965-68; archtl. draftsman, Gt. Falls, 1966; asst. prof. secondary and adult tchr. edn. U. N.Mex., Albuquerque, 1971—, dir. Sci. and Engring. Fair, 1975—, asst. dean continuing edn., 1975-78, asso. dir. personnel dept., mgr. mgmt. devel. and tng. div., 1978—; pres., owner Garrett Mgmt. Services; past dir. Coronado Credit Union. Bd. dirs. Albuquerque Internat. Balloon Festival, 1979-82, Amiguetos Children's Day Care Center, Albuquerque, 1980-82; vice chmn., then chmn. Albuquerque Transit Adv. Bd., 1978-81. Served with USNR, 1958-59. NDEA fellow, 1967; named Outstanding Tchr. in Mont., 1966. Mem. Am. Soc. Tng. and Devel., NEA (life), Am. Indsl. Arts Assn. (life), Am. Vocat. Assn. (life), Mountain Plains Adult Edn. Assn., N.Mex. Coll. and Univ. Personnel Assn., Nat. Tng. and Devel. Council, Coll. and Univ. Personnel Assn., N.Mex. Vocat. Assn., Gen. Contractors N.Mex., Albuquerque C. of C., Phi Delta Kappa, Delta Phi Delta. Democrat. Methodist. Club: Elks. Author curriculum materials. Home: 9117 Atkinson Pl NE Albuquerque NM 87112 Office: U New Mex Albuquerque NM 87131

GARRETT, DUANE W., commercial photographer; b. San Pedro, Calif., July 8, 1925; s. Lawrence L. and Mildred (Larsen) G.; m. Marney L. Dunbar, July 3, 1948; children—Virginia, Robert, Roger, Carol; attended Ray Sch. Photography, Chgo., 1948-49; Progressive Sch. Photography, New Haven, 1949-50. Photographer, Statesman Newspaper Boise, Idaho 1949-53; photographer, ptnr. Bach Photography, Boise, 1953-66; owner, operator Garrett Photography, 1966—. Served with USN, 1942-46. Mem. Profl. Photographers Assn. Am., Profl. Photographers Assn. Idaho, Idaho Preservation Soc., Communicator's Guild. Baptist. Club: Rotary. Home: Route 1 Gardena ID 83629 Office: 714 West State St Boise ID 83702

GARRETT, EDWARD O'BANION, advertising agency executive; b. Long Beach, Calif., June 19, 1951; s. Frank O'Banion and Marie Louise (Goodman) G. B.B.A., U. Notre Dame, 1973; M.A., Mich. State U., 1976. Asst. media planner Campbell-Mithun Advt. Co., Chgo., 1976-77; ops. supr. Ackerley Airport Advt. Co., Seattle, 1981—. Club: Notre Dame of Western Wash. Office: Ackerley Airport Advt Co 3601 6th Ave S Seattle WA 98134

GARRETT, GEORGE ALVIN, cons. nuclear energy; b. Sardis, Miss., Nov. 29, 1910; s. Weedie Andrew and Laverna Ann (Harmon) G.; B.A. with spl. distinction, U. Miss., 1931; M.A., Rice U., 1933, Ph.D., 1935; certificate Inst. Mgmt. Sch. Bus. Northwestern U., 1967; m. Olle Louise Low, Sept. 5, 1934; 1 dau., Patricia Lynn. Teaching fellow, mathematics, Rice U., Houston, 1931-35; geophysicist Independent Exploration Co., Houston, 1935-42, staff mem. radiation lab. Mass. Inst. Tech., Cambridge, 1942-45; head, analysis and design dept. Union Carbide Corp. Nuclear Div., Oak Ridge, 1946-54, supt. ops. analysis div., 1954-62, planning cons., 1969-72; dir. info. processing Lockheed Missiles & Space Co., Sunnyvale, Calif., 1962-69; sr. scientist Bechtel Corp., San Francisco, 1972-77; asst. prof. elec. engring. U. Tenn., 1949-50; cons. CIA, Washington, 1963-65. Patentee radar scanning system. Home: 830 Stanford Ave Menlo Park CA 94025

GARRETT, JERRY WAYNE, engineering consultant; b. Gorman, Tex., July 24, 1940; s. William D. and Allene Bell (Rodgers) G.; B.S. in Elec. Engring., U. Tex., 1963; m. Carolyn Sue Pye, June 2, 1962; children—Laura Denise, Alissa Renée Jenny Elizabeth. Assoc. engr. Westinghouse Elec. Corp., Balt., 1963-65; engr. Shell Pipeline Corp., Houston, 1965-68; mgr. ops. and maintenance Santa Clara Valley (Calif.) Water Dist., San Jose, 1968-81; pres. Western Control Cons., San Jose, 1981—. Registered profl. engr., Calif., Wash., Oreg., Ohio, N. Mex. Mem. IEEE, Am. Water Works Assn., Instrument Soc. Am. (dir. water and wastewater industries div.). Office: 3150 Almaden Expressway San Jose CA 95118

GARRETT, JOYCE LYNN, teacher educator; b. Prineville, Oreg., Oct. 17, 1946; d. James Edward and Bettye Jeanne (Forbes) G. B.A., U. Oreg., 1968, M.S., 1973, M.A., 1981, Ph.D., 1982; B.S., Oreg. State U., 1970. Tchr., Lincoln County Sch. Dist., Newport, Oreg., 1970-76; tchr. Eugene (Oreg.) Sch. Dist. 4-J, 1976-77; dir. spl. edn. Creswell (Oreg.) Pub. Schs., 1978-80; asst. prof. elem. edn. Weber State Coll., Ogden, Utah, 1982—; cons. coll. depts. edn. Mem. Sch. Bd. Adv. Bd. Ogden City Sch. Dist., 1983—; exec. bd. sec., chmn. water safety, instr. water safety and 1st aid ARC Lincoln County; camp dir. 4-H, 1970-74, club leader, 1970-76. Weber State Coll. grantee, 1983. Mem. Am. Ednl. Research Assn., Council Exceptional Children, Nat. Council Tchrs. English, AAUW, Phi Delta Kappa. Contbr. articles to profl. jours. Office: 3750 Harrison Blvd Ogden UT 84408

GARRETT, NORMAN LAWRENCE, psychologist; b. Atlantic City, Dec. 28, 1924; s. Frank B. and Sadie (Rapport) G.; married; children—Gayle, Betsy. A.A., UCLA, 1947, B.A., 1949; M.A., Calif. State U.-Los Angeles, 1954; Ed.D., U. So. Calif., 1971; lic. psychologist, Calif. Personnel officer City of Pasadena (Calif.), 1951-53; recruitment and placement officer, salary analyst, tng. coordinator Los Angeles Dept. Water and Power, 1953-64; prof. psychology Los Angeles City Coll., 1956—; asst. dean, prof. psychology West Los Angeles Coll., 1969-78; asst. prof., coordinator, counselor, asst. to dean Pierce Coll., 1961-69; cons. to bus. and govt. Recipient Gold Key UCLA, 1947-49; Chancellor's award Los Angeles Community Coll. Dist., 1973. Mem. Am. Psychol. Assn., AAAS, Acad. Polit. and Social Sci., Fedn. Community Coordinating Councils (pres., exec. bd. 1970—), Coll. Fed. Council (chmn. and mem. exec. bd. 1970—). Served with U.S. Army, 1943-44. Author: Human Relations, 1953; Line Patrolman Handbook, 1957; Recruitment of College Teachers, 1970; Salary Determination, 1971; Recruitment of Accountants and Auditors, 1979; Attitude and Opinion Measurement, 1980. Office: Los Angeles City Coll 855 N Vermont Ave Los Angeles CA 90029

GARRETT, STEPHEN GEORGE, museum dir.; b. Ashtead, Eng., Dec. 26, 1922; s. Howard George and Ida (King-Harman) G.; came to U.S., 1973; M.A., Trinity Coll., Cambridge (Eng.) U., 1950; m. Petronella Jones, 1952; children—Carey, Georgia; m. 2d, Jean Mackintosh, 1964; children—Rebecca, Jason. Pvt. archtl. practice, London, 1952-73; dep. dir. J. Paul Getty Mus., Malibu, Calif., 1973-77, dir., trustee, 1977—; Lectr. architecture Poly. Central, London, 1965-73. Served with Brit. Navy, 1941-46. Mem. Assn. Mus. Dirs.; asso. Royal Inst. Brit. Architects. Author booklets, articles in architecture and design projects. Address: J Paul Getty Museum 17985 Pacific Coast Hwy Malibu CA 90265

GARRIGUES, JOHN SHARPLESS, geophysicist; b. East Orange, N.J., Apr. 30, 1941; s. Henry Haydock and Elizabeth (Russell) G.; m. Vivien Monica Sexton, June 30, 1979; 1 son, John-Paul Henry. B.S.C. in Math., N.Mex. Tech. U., 1963; postgrad. in math., Purdue U., 1963-64. Seismologist, Geosource, Middle East, 1965-71; geophysicist, London, 1971-79; sr. geophysicist Marathon Oil Co., Casper, Wyo., 1979—. Mem. Union Concerned Scientists, Soc. Exploration Geophysicists, AAAS, Am. Geophys. Union, European Assn. Exploration Geophysicists. Club: Casper Petroleum. Office: PO Box 2659 Casper WY 82602

GARRIS, KAREN ANN, equal employment opportunity counselor; b. Pasadena, Calif., Sept. 6, 1956; d. Willie Franklyn and Helen Elizabeth (Walker) G.; Student, San Francisco State U., 1974-76; B.S., Tuskegee Inst., 1979. Animal caretaker, Los Angeles, 1970-74; library asst., San Francisco, 1974-77; forestry technician, Glendora, Calif., 1977; Capine research asst. Tuskegee Inst., 1976-79; forestry technician, Hillsboro, Ga., 1979; agrl. commodity grader, Chico, Calif., 1979-80; agrl. commodity grader poultry, Modesto, Calif., from 1980. Mem. Nat. Assn. Female Execs., Orgn. Profl. Employees Dept. Agr. Democrat. Baptist. Club: TheSpa Fitness. Home: 11125 S Van Ness Ave Inglewood CA 90303

GARRISON, JEAN ANN, communications educator; b. Riverside, Calif., Feb. 20, 1947; d. Alan P. and Constance (Norwood) Ratliff. B.A., U. Calif.-Berkeley, 1968; M.A., San Francisco State U., 1970; postgrad. U. Tex., Calif. Inst. Integral Studies. Cert. jr. coll. tchr. Eligibility worker Santa Barbara (Calif.) Dept. Welfare, 1970-72; instr. bus., speech, pub. speaking Santa Barbara City Coll., Brooks Photographic Inst., 1973-74; asst. prof. speech communications Del Mar Coll., Corpus Christi, Tex., 1974-81; edn. coordinator I.S.E., San Francisco, 1982; adminstr., communications cons. Sch. Exptl. Ecology, Berkeley, Calif., 1983—; instr. Mgmt. Supervision Contra Costa Coll.; guest lectr. J.F.K. U., Calif. Inst. Transpersonal Psychology. Mem. NOW, Tarot Symposium Planning Com., Stownes & Gold Bus. Network, Sierra Club. Mem. Teaching Inner Christ Ch. Contbr. to poetry mag. Home: 126B Chenery San Francisco CA 94131 Office: 2140 Shattuck Berkeley CA 94704

GARRISON, PHILIP WAYNE, aerospace engineer; b. York, Ala., Apr. 24, 1944; s. James Philip and Margaret Elizabeth (Bennett) G.; m. Sandra Deloris Henderson, Dec. 21, 1963; 1 dau., Shelley Dore; m. 2d, Sharon Lee Hudson, Dec. 21, 1973; children—Kimberly Vohn Sutphen, Melanie Page Sutphen. B.S. in Aerospace Engring., Auburn U., 1965; M.S. in Aeros., Calif. Inst. Tech., 1968. Mem. engring. staff propulsion systems McDonnell Douglas Astronautics Co., Huntington Beach, Calif. and Kennedy Space Ctr., Fla., 1966-76; mem. devel. staff fast reactor safety Oak Ridge Nat. Lab., 1976-80; tech. supr. propulsion systems Jet Propulsion Lab., Pasadena, Calif., 1980—. Mem. AIAA, Omicron Delta Kappa, Tau Beta Pi, Sigma Gamma Tau, Phi Kappa Phi. Contbr. articles to profl. jours. Home: 2124 Bogie Dr La Verne CA 91750 Office: 4800 Oak Grove Dr M/S 125/218 Pasadena CA 91103

GARRISON, SUSAN ELOISE, hosp. adminstr.; b. San Rafael, Calif., Jan. 11, 1946; d. Dwight C. and Laura E. (Frazier) Birch; B.A. summa cum laude, U. Calif., Berkeley, 1968, M.P.H., 1975. Social planning cons. Alameda and San Francisco counties, 1968-72; adminstrv. asst. Children's Hosp. Med. Center No. Calif., 1974-75; asst. adminstr. Kaiser Found. Hosp., West Los Angeles, Calif., 1975-76, hosp. adminstr., 1977-79; med. center adminstr. Canyon Gen. Hosp., a Kaiser Found. hosp., and So. Calif. Permanente Med. Group facilities, Orange County, Calif., 1979—. Mem. Am. Coll. Hosp. Adminstrs., Hosp. Council So. Calif. (chmn. com. on budget and fin. 1979-80). Anaheim C. of C., Orange County Health Planning Council (Facilities rev. com., dir.), U. Calif.-Berkeley Hosp. Adminstrn. Alumni Assn. (pres. elect), Phi Beta Kappa. Office: 441 Lakeview Ave Anaheim CA 92807

GARRISON, THOMAS SMITH, editor; b. Bakersfield, Calif., Jan. 18, 1952; s. Tom and Nell Louise (Chinnis) G.; m. Lorraine Denise Irwin, June 24, 1972; m. 2d, Deborah Ann Looker, Mar. 8, 1982. B.A. magna cum laude in Polit. Sci., Calif. State Coll.-Bakersfield, 1974; M.A. in Polit. Sci., U. Calif.-Davis, 1976; C. Phil. in Polit. Sci., U. Calif.-Santa Barbara, 1982. Cert. tchr., Calif. Instr. Allan Hancock Community Coll., Santa Maria, Calif., 1977; mng. editor Current World Leaders Internat. Acad. at Santa Barbara, 1981—. coordinator The Gathering Place, Santa Barbara, 1981. Trustee Santa Barbara Peace Fund Escrow Account, 1982—. Unitarian. Universalist scholar, 1972; Pelletier Found. scholar, 1972, 73; U. Calif.-Santa Barbara grantee, 1978, Acad. Senate Patent Fund grantee, 1979. Mem. Am. Polit. Sci. Assn., War Resisters League. Socialist. Office: 2074 Alameda Padre Serra Santa Barbara CA 93103

GARRITY, RODMAN FOX, psychologist, educator; b. Los Angeles, June 10, 1922; s. Lawrence Hitchcock and Margery Fox (Pugh) G.; student Los Angeles City Coll., 1946-47; B.A., Calif. State U. at Los Angeles, 1950; M.A., So. Methodist U., Dallas, 1955; Ed.D., U. So. Calif., 1963; m. Juanita Daphne Mullan, Mar. 5, 1948; children—Diana Daphne, Ronald Fox. Tchr. elementary sch. Palmdale (Calif.) Sch. Dist., 1952-54; psychologist, prin. Redondo Beach (Calif.) City Schs., 1954-60; asst. dir. ednl. placement, lectr., ednl. adviser U. So. Calif., 1960-62; asso. prof., coordinator credentials programs Calif. State Poly. U., Pomona, 1962-66, chmn. social sci. dept., 1966-68, dir. tchr. preparation center, 1968-71, coordinator grad. program, 1971-73, prof. tchr. preparation center, 1968—; cons. psychologist, lectr. in field. Pres. Redondo Beach Coordinating Council, 1958-60; mem. univ. rep. Calif. Faculty Assns., 1974-76. Served with Engr. Combat Bn., AUS, 1942-45. Mem. Prins. Assn. Redondo Beach (chmn. 1958-60), Nat. Congress Parents and Tchrs. (hon. life), Am. Psychol. Assn., Calif. Tchrs. Assn. Democrat. Office: Calif State Poly U Pomona CA 91768

GARROD, PETER VINCE, agricultural economics educator; b. Saratoga, Calif., Aug. 12, 1943; s. Vince S. and Jane W. (Whiteman) G.; m. Nora W. Garrod, Feb. 20, 1979. B.S. U. Calif., Davis 1965, M.S. U. Calif., Berkeley 1966, Ph.D. 1971. Cons., Ford Found., Chile 1969-71; prof. agrl. econs. U. Hawaii 1972—, grad. chmn. 1982—. Mem. Am. Econ. Assn., Am. Agrl. Econs. Assn., Western Agrl. Econs. Assn., Am. Assn. Econometrics. Contbr. articles to profl. jours. Home: 46024 Puulena #613 Kaneohe HI 96744 Office: 2545 The Mall Honolulu HI 96822

GARSD, ARMANDO, biostatistician, ecologist; b. Buenos Aires, Jan. 6, 1945; s. Miguel and Lina Rosa (Jacovobsky) G.; m. Marta Susana (García-Barrio), May 25, 1974; 1 dau., Jasmine Serena. Diploma in biology U. Buenos Aires, 1970; M.S. in Ecology, U. Calif.-Davis, 1975, Ph.D. in Ecology, 1979. Biomathematician, Lab. Energy-Related Health Research, U. Calif., Davis, 1979-81, sr. statistician Remote Sensing Research Program, Space Scis. Lab., Berkeley, 1981, quantitative analyst Marine Rev. Com., Santa Barbara, 1981—, adj. asst. prof. math., 1982; tchr., lectr. U. Buenos Aires, 1070-74. Fulbright grantee, 1974-75; recipient U. Calif, Davis disting. scholar award, 1976-78. Fellow Royal Statis. Soc., mem. Am. Statis. Assn., Ecol. Soc. Am., Internat. Statis. Inst., Bermoulli Soc. Math. Stats. and Probability. Contbr. numerous articles to sci. jours. Office: Dept Math U Calif 6505 South Hall Santa Barbara CA 93106

GARSIDE, JAYNE GILLETTE, psychology educator; b. Salt Lake City, Aug. 12, 1936; d. Willard Lester and Rowena (Speirs) Gillette; m. A. LaMoyne Garside, Sept. 14, 1956; children—Bradford LaMoyne, Scott LaMoyne, Dawn Kawehiomahina. B.A., Brigham Young U., 1958,

M.A., 1960, Ph.D., 1965. Tchr. Springville (Utah) Sr. High Sch., 1958-60, Henderson (Nev.) Jr. High Sch., 1960-61; sch. psychometrist, psychologist, counselor cons. Clark County Sch. Dist., Las Vegas, Nev., 1961-62; prof. psychology Hawaii campus Brigham Young U., Laie, 1963—, also dir. instl. research. Psychol. cons., 1963-72, coordinator advisement and testing, 1975—; mem. Hawaii Mental Health Coalition. Chmn., Windward Adv. Council. Mem. Hawaii Personnel and Guidance Assn. (newsletter editor 1969-70, publicity chmn. 1969-70), Hawaii Psychol. Assn. (exec. com.), Humanistic Psychology Assn. Hawaii, Hawaii Acad. Sci., Am. Personnel and Guidance Assn., Hawaii Sch. Counselors Assn., Mensa (Hawaii proctor). Home: 55-439 Naniloa Loop Laie HI 96762 Office: Hawaii Campus Brigham Young Univ Laie HI 96762

GARSTANG, ROY HENRY, astrophysics educator; b. Southport, Eng., Sept. 18, 1925; s. Percy Brocklehurst and Eunice (Gledhill) G.; B.A., U. Cambridge, 1946, MA., 1950, Ph.D., 1954, Sc.D., 1983; m. Ann Clemence Hawk, Aug. 11, 1959; children—Jennifer Katherine, Susan Veronica. Came to U.S., 1964. Research asso. U. Chgo., 1951-52; lectr. astronomy U. Coll., London, Eng., 1952-60; reader astronomy U. London, 1960-64, asst. dir. Obs., 1959-64; prof. astrophysics U. Colo., 1964—. Chmn. Joint Inst. for Lab. Astrophysics, 1966-67; cons. Nat. Bur. Standards, 1964-73; v.p. commn. 14 Internat. Astron. Union, 1970-73, pres., 1973-76; Erskine vis. fellow U. Canterbury (New Zealand), 1971; vis. prof. U. Calif. at Santa Cruz, 1971; Fellow Am. Phys. Soc., AAAS, Optical Soc. Am., Brit. Inst. Physics, Royal Astron. Soc.; mem. Am. Astron. Soc., Royal Soc. Scis. Liege, Belgium (corr.). Editor: Observatory, 1953-60. Contbr. numerous articles to tech. jours. Research on atomic physics and astrophys. applications. Home: 830 8th St Boulder CO 80302 Office: Joint Inst for Lab Astrophysics U Colo Boulder CO 80309

GARTHE, EDMUND CONRAD, ret. state ofcl.; b. Dover, N.J., May 4, 1912; s. August and Maria Magdalene (Langendorfer) G.; C.E., Rensselaer Poly. Inst., 1933; M.P.H. (Rockefeller Found. fellow), U. Mich., 1948; m. Clara Elizabeth Earhart, May 10, 1936 (dec. Aug. 1982); children—Nancy (Mrs. Garry Griesser), Karen (Mrs. Joseph Moore), Edmund Carlton; m. Elizabeth Esther Scott, Mar. 8, 1983. Surveyor, U.S. Geol. Survey, various locations, 1933-36; commd. officer USPHS, 1936, advanced through grades to col., 1952; ret., 1960; regional engr., 1946-48, 53-60; chief Interstate Carrier br. USPHS, Washington, 1948-53; asst. dir. div. environ. health Ky. Dept. Health, 1960-65; asst. commr. for environ. health services Ariz. Dept. Health Services, Phoenix, 1965-74, planning engr. div. environ. health services, 1974-77; lectr. Ariz. State U., Tempe, 1966. Mem. Gov.'s Commn. on Ariz. Environment, 1965-81; mem. Nat. Indian Health Adv. Com., 1967-72. Registered profl. engr., Ariz. Fellow Am. Acad. Environ. Engrs.; mem. Ariz. Pub. Health Assn., Loyal Order of Boar, Tau Beta Pi, Delta Omega. Contbr. tech. articles on pollution to profl. jours. Inventor, patentee tire changer. Home: PO Box 1454 Payson AZ 85541

GARTMAN, GAYLORD EARL, purchasing executive; b. Poynette, Wis., Mar. 14, 1943; s. Wilmer F. and Emma K. (Brandt) G.; m. Judy E. Wells, June 25, 1966; children—Larissa Sue, Heather Jeanne. B.A., Northwestern Coll., 1965; B.D., Wis. Evang. Luth. Sem., 1969; diploma World Evangelism Sch. of Ministry, 1979. Head frozen foods Kroger Foods, Milw., 1968-69; ordained to ministry, Luth. Ch., 1969; pastor Our Saviour Luth. Ch., Sault Ste. Marie, Ont., Can., 1969-75; jr. order desk exec. Soo Mill & Lumber, Sault Ste. Marie, 1975-78; high sch. adminstr. Poynette (Wis.) Christian Sch., 1979-81; purchasing/personnel officer Hineni Ministries, San Francisco, 1981—; parochial sch. cost cons. Liaison to Interfaith Immigration Com., Sault Ste. Marie, 1976-78; coordinator newspaper religion editorials and pub. relations editor Sault Daily Star, 1973-78; mem. ch. council and paraochial bd. edn. St. John's Luth. Ch., 1982. Recipient Citizenship award City of Poynette, 1961. Republican. Mem. Nat. Model R.R. Assn. Home: 236 Ripley St San Francisco CA 94110 Office: 60 Haight St San Francisco CA 94102

GARVIN, WILLIAM HORTON, civil engineering firm exec.; b. Newton, N.C., Feb. 25, 1948; s. Noel Eugene and Sara (Horton) G.; m. Susan Teresa McGhie, Apr. 15, 1978. B.S., Clemson U., 1970; M.S., Mont. State U., 1978. Registered profl. engr., Mont., Wyo. With Mont. Dept. Health, Helena, 1972-76; pres. Garvin Engring. Co., Helena, 1976—; cons. energy conservation, water and sewer fields, 1976—. Active Big Bros. and Sisters, 1972-80. Served with USMC, 1970-72. J.E. Sirrine scholar, 1967; recipient Carolinas Architects and Engrs. award, 1968. Mem. Am. Water Works Assn., Alt. Energy Resource Orgn. Presbyterian. Home: 2028 Missoula Ave Helena MT 59601 Office: Garvin Engring Co 1539 Gallitan St Helena MT 59601

GARWOOD, VICTOR PAUL, speech pathologist, educator, cons.; b. Detroit, Sept. 13, 1917; s. Paul J. Schultz and Helen E. Garwood Schultz; m. Dorothy O., Mar. 13, 1942; children—Don P., Martha H. B.A., U. Mich., 1939, M.S., 1948, Ph.D. (Univ. scholar), 1952; lic. psychologist, speech pathologist, audiologist, Calif. Prodn. mgr. Bohn Aluminum & Brass Corp., 1942-46; teaching fellow U. Mich., 1948-50; instr. U. So. Calif., 1950-52, asst. prof., 1952-55, assoc. prof., 1955-58, prof. communication arts and scis., speech sci. and tech., otolaryngology, 1958—, chmn. grad. program in communicative disorders, 1968-72; spl. cons. speech-hearing and hearing aids Dept. Health Services, Los Angeles Field Office, 1967—; postdoctoral research fellow Nat. Inst. Neurol. Diseases and Blindness, NIH, 1957-58, spl. research fellow, 1961-64. Mem. Am. Psychol. Assn, Acoustical Soc. Am., Am. Speech and Hearing Assn., Psychonomic Soc., Acad. Rehabilitative Audiology, Sigma Xi. Contbr. articles to profl. jours. Home: 1240 Chautauqua Blvd Pacific Palisades CA 90272 Office: Kerckhoff Hall U So Calif 734 W Adams Blvd Los Angeles CA 90007

GARY, JAMES FREDERICK, business executive; b. Chgo., Dec. 28, 1920; s. Rex Inglis and Mary Naomi (Roller) G.; B.S., Haverford (Pa.) Coll., 1942; m. Helen Elizabeth Gellert, Sept. 3, 1947; children—David Frederick, John William, James Scott, Mary Anne. With Wash. Energy Co., and predecessors, Seattle, 1947-67, v.p., 1956-67, pres. Pacific Resources Inc., and predecessor, Honolulu, 1967-79, chmn., chief exec. officer, 1979—, also dir.; dir. Hawaiian Ind. Refinery, Inc., Gasco, Inc., Bancorp., Hawaii Inc., Bank of Hawaii, Brewer Pacific Agronomics Co., Castle & Cooke, Inc., Wash. Energy Co., Seattle, Airborne Freight Corp., Seattle, GDC, Inc., Chgo.; dir. Research Corp. of U. Hawaii, 1971-77, chmn., 1974-77. Pres. Chief Seattle council Boy Scouts Am., 1966-67, Aloha council, 1973-74, mem. Nat. council, 1964—, v.p. western region, 1978—, mem. exec. bd.; regent U. Hawaii, 1982—; chmn. Aloha United Way, 1978, pres., 1979, chmn., pres., 1980, dir., officer or trustee Oahu Devel. Conf., Hawaii Employers Council, Hawaii Loa Coll., Friends of East-West Center, Honolulu Symphony Soc. Served to capt. AUS, 1942-46. Recipient Distinguished Eagle award Boy Scouts Am., 1972, Silver Beaver award, 1966, Silver Antelope award, 1976. Mem. Am. (dir. 1970-71), Pacific (pres. 1974; Basford trophy 1960) gas assns., Nat. LP-Gas Assn. (dir. 1967-70), Hawaii C. of C. (chmn. 1979), Inst. Gas Tech., Chgo. (trustee 1975—), Nat. Petroleum Council, Hawaii Dist. Export Council, Japan-Calif. Assn., Japan-Hawaii Econ. Council, Pacific Basin Econ. Council, Japan-Am. Soc. Honolulu, Pacific Forum. Episcopalian. Clubs: Pacific Union (San Francisco); Rotary, Oahu Country, Waialae Country, Outrigger Canoe, Pacific, Plaza (Honolulu); Seattle Tennis, Wash. Athletic (Seattle). Office: Pacific Resources Inc PO Box 3379 Honolulu HI 96842

GARY, KATHLEEN NOLAND, pharmaceutical and life sciences company executive; b. Long Beach, Calif., July 3, 1945; d. Richard Lee and Grace Irene (Vincent) Noland. B.A. in Journalism, U. Wash., 1967. Assoc. editor Kaiser Aluminum News Kaiser Aluminum and Chem. Corp., Oakland, Calif., 1968-73, dir. communications Kaiser Engrs., Oakland, 1973-75, Kaiser Industries Corp., Oakland, 1975-77, v.p. pub. affairs Kaiser Steel Corp. Oakland, 1977-81; corp. v.p. pub. affairs and communications Syntex Corp., Palo Alto, Calif., 1981—. Mem. Calif. Adv. Council on Econ. Devel.; treas. Calif. Health Products Info. Council; mem. Mayor's Bus. Adv. Council, City of San Jose (Calif.). Mem. Pharm. Mfrs. Assn., Calif. Mfrs. Assn. (dir.), Pub. Relations Soc. Am., World Affairs Council, Palo Alto C. of C. Author: (with Don Fabun) Dimensions of Change, 1972, Children of Change, 1970.

GARY, RICHARD NEEL, steel company executive; b. Los Angeles, May 27, 1943; s. Gordon Neel and Kathryn Ann (Bell) G.; A.B. in Econs., U. Calif.-Berkeley, 1965, J.D., 1968; children—Mary Kathryn, John Carleton. Admitted to Calif. bar, 1968; asso. firm Hill, Farrer & Burrill, Los Angeles, 1969-72, Thelen, Marrin, Johnson & Bridges, San Francisco, 1972-78; with Kaiser Steel Corp., Oakland, Calif., 1978—, v.p., gen. counsel, sec., 1980-82, exec. v.p., 1982-83, pres., 1983—. Mem. ABA, State Bar Calif. Office: Kaiser Steel Corp 9400 Cherry Ave Fontana CA 92335

GASKILL, HERBERT LEO, accountant; b. Seattle, July 1, 1923; s. Leo Dell and Vesta Rathbone (Dahlen) G.; m. Margaret Helen Jenkins, Mar. 1, 1944 (div.); children—Margaret V., Herbert Leo. B.S. and M.S. in Chem. Engring., U. Wash., 1949, M.B.A., 1976. C.P.A., Wash. Asst. prof. dental materials, exec. officer dept. dental materials Sch. Dentistry, U. Wash., 1950-56; ops. analyst The Boeing Co., Seattle, 1958-71, mktg. cons. govt. programs, 1972-74; pvt. practice acctg., Seattle, 1976-80; hazardous waste adminstr. The Boeing Co., Seattle, 1980—. Active Seattle Art Mus., Pacific Northwest Aviation Hist. Found. Served to lt. (j.g.) USNR, 1941-46. TAPPI fellow, 1956; U. Wash. Engring. Expt. Sta. fellow, 1957. Mem. Wash. Soc. C.P.A.s. Contbr. articles to profl. jours.

GASPARD, MARCUS STUART, state senator, accountant; b. Puyallup, Wash., Apr. 19, 1948; s. Gordon Stuart and Joanne (Johnston) G.; m. Jo Anne Crouch, 1973. B.B.A., U. Oreg., 1970; student law, U. Puget Sound, 1972—. Accountant; mem. Wash. State Ho. of Reps., 1973-77, Wash. State Senate, 1977—. Adminstrv. asst., research analyst Senate Com. and Regulatory Agys. Com., Legis. Interim Com. Banking, Ins. and Utility Regulation, 1971-72. Mem. Sigma Phi Epsilon. Democrat. Home: 8220 191st St Ave E Sumner WA 98390 Office: Washington State Senate Olympia WA 98504*

GASPARI, RUSSELL ARTHUR, electronic engr., educator; b. Redding, Calif., Jan. 15, 1941; s. Richard Anthony and Elena Adelaide (Biancalana) G.; B.S., U. Calif., Berkeley, 1963; M.S., San Diego State Coll., 1965; Ph.D., U. Calif., Los Angeles, 1970; m. Carole Anne Sterni, Feb. 20, 1965; children—Heather Elizabeth, Catherine Annette. Electronic engr. astronoautics div. Gen. Dynamics, San Diego, 1963-65; instr. engring. No. Ariz. U., Flagstaff, 1965-67; engring. specialist data systems div. Litton Systems, Van Nuys, Calif., 1968-71; sr. staff scientist microwave applications group Chatsworth, Calif., 1971-72; vis. prof. engring. Calif. State U., San Diego, 1972-73; sr. scientist Hughes Space & Communications Group, Los Angeles, 1973—. Litton fellow, 1969-70. Registered profl. engr., Calif. Mem. IEEE (sr. mem., officer, Outstanding Engr. award San Diego computer chpt. 1973, outstanding engr. award Los Angeles Harbor Sect. 1980, mgr. winter communications conf.). Patentee in field. Home: 6656 W 87th Pl Los Angeles CA 90045 Office: Mail Station S12/W315 PO Box 92919 Los Angeles CA 90009

GASSAWAY, ALEXANDER RAMSEY, geographer, educator; b. Cairo, Ill., Jan. 22, 1924; s. Crosby Mitchell and Helen Stephanie (Rapp) G.; certificate Meteorology and Polar Geography, U. Oslo, Norway, 1948; B.A. with honors in Geography, U. Va., 1950; M.S. in Geography, George Washington U., 1957; Ph.D. in Geography (grad. fellow), Clark U., 1971; m. Carolyn Grace Hoecker, July 29, 1941; children—David Ramsey, Jon Peter. Staff Army map service, Map Intelligence div. U.S. C.E., Washington, 1950-52, engr. Strategic Intelligence div., 1952-56, supr., 1954-56, sect. chief Phys. Geographic Research, Western Hemisphere, 1954-56; asst. prof. geography George Washington U., Washington, 1962-66; asso. prof. geography Portland (Oreg.) State U., 1966-76, prof., 1976—; prof., vis. lectr. Lewis and Clark Coll., 1978—; cons. U.S. Dept. Agr., 1968, Harper and Row Co., 1970, Oreg. Milk Stablzn. Bd., 1973-74, Ministry Edn., Norway, 1969. Served with USAAF, 1943-45. Nat. Acad. Scis. grantee, Norway, 1958-60. Mem. Assn. Am. Geographers, Assn. Pacific Coast Geographers, Oreg. Comprehensive Health Planning Assn. (mem. Physician Index com. 1974-76), Oreg. Acad. Scis. (mem. exec. com. 1974-75), Phi Beta Kappa (sec. George Washington U. 1964-66), Sigma Xi, Pi Gamma Mu, Theta Chi. Author: The Food Geography of Finnmark Fylke, Northernmost Norway, 1971; Factors Affecting the Sufficiency of Food Supply of an Arctic Area Undergoing an Economic Development Program: 1946-65, 1971; contbr. articles to profl. jours. Home: 2135 SW Boundary St Portland OR 97201

GASSNER, JULIUS STEPHEN, history, political science educator; b. N.Y.C., Sept. 22, 1915; s. Julius and Barbara (Arlitsch) G.; m. Renee Marie Gardere Staring, Feb. 13, 1943; children—Jules L., Stephen T., John C., Elizabeth M., Martin C., Thomas A. A.B., St. Peter's Coll., 1937; M.A., Fordham U., 1940. Instr. politics Coll. St. Thomas, St. Paul, 1947-52; asst. prof. history U. Southwestern La., Lafayette, 1952-57; asst. prof. history, politics U. Albuquerque, 1957-61, assoc. prof., 1961-73, prof., 1973—; cons. to Choice; abstracter Am. Bibliog. Ctr. Served with U.S. Army, 1942-46. Mem. AAUP, Am. Polit. Sci. Assn., Am. Judicature Soc., Hakluyt Soc., Assn. U.S. Army, Ret. Officers Assn. Democrat. Roman Catholic. Translator: Voyages and Adventures of La Perouse, 1969. Home: Drawer G Corrales NM 87048 Office: U Albuquerque St Jospeh Pl NW Albuquerque NM 87140

GAST, MONTE W., media executive; b. Dec. 21, 1947; s. Rudi Kurt and Reli Victoria Gast; B.A. in Journalism, Humboldt State U., 1969; M.Journalism, UCLA, 1971. Writer, editor Tarcher Pub., Los Angeles, 1971-72; reporter KRLA Radio, Pasadena, Calif., 1972-74; account exec. KMET Radio, Los Angeles, 1974-75; sales mgr. KWST Radio, Los Angeles, 1975-77, gen. mgr., 1977-79; pres. JAM Advt., Culver City, Calif., 1980-82; pres. Monte Gast & Assocs., Malibu, Calif., 1982—. Recipient Gold medal Internat. Film and TV Festival N.Y.C., 1981, Silver medal, 1982. Author: Getting the Best of L.A., 1972.

GASTELUM, SYLVIA ROCHIN, union official; b. Nogales, Ariz., Aug. 13, 1937; d. Mario L. and Maria Jesus (Puchi) Rochin; m. James J. Gastelum, Sept. 16, 1957; children—Anthony James, Therese Marie, Sandra Rosina. Student Flagstaff Coll., 1955-57. Main cashier Capins Mdse., 1955-56; sec. Schrader Ins. Agy., 1956; rep. Avon Corp., 1955-58; sec. to dir. Walt Disney Prodns., Burbank, Calif., 1958-59; U.S. postal clk., Nogales, Ariz., 1960—, postmaster service, Tumacacori, Ariz., 1979—; sec. Local #658, Am. Postal Workers Union, 1980—. Leader 4-H, 1969-79. C.C. Cheshire Scholar, 1955. Mem. Am. Bus. Women's Assn. (membership chair), Gamma Chi Beta, Better Govt. Assn. Republican. Roman Catholic. Club: Newman (Flagstaff). Office: Morley Ave Nogales AZ 85621

GATCH, LINDA JEAN, shopping mall executive; b. Chehalis, Wash., Jan. 26, 1950; d. Henry Joseph and Betty Jean (Hall) Gatch; m. Don Richard LaCombe, Mar. 21, 1981; B.F.A., Pacific Luth. U., 1972. Asst. promotional mgr. Sta. KOMO-TV, Seattle, 1972-73; advt. account exec. J/D/M, Seattle, 1973; advt. account exec., retail copywriter Nordstrom, 1974-75; advt. account exec. Kelly, Nason, Inc., 1975; comml. dir. Sta. KING, 1976, TV producer/technician, 1976-80; account mgr. Kraft Smith Pub. Relations, 1981; asst. gen. mgr., advt./mktg. dir. Alderwood Mall, Lynnwood, Wash., 1981—. Mem. Nat. Acad. TV Arts and Scis., Seattle Ad Club. Office: Alderwood Mall 3000 184th St SW Suite 127 Lynnwood WA 98036

GATEKA, FREDRICK ALAN, engineering executive; b. Chickasha, Okla., Aug. 15, 1929; s. Floyd Fredrick and Odla Irene (Caldwell) G.; m. Helen Jo Bolton, Jan. 28, 1958; children—Renee, Stephen. B.S.E.E., Okla. State U., 1955. Field engr. Western Electric Co., Long Beach, Calif., Fort Walton Beach, Fla., Whippany, N.J., 1955-60; mem. tech. staff Bell Telephone Labs., Reading, Pa., Whippany, N.J., 1960-67; v.p. engring. Semtech Corp, Newbury Park, Calif., 1967—. Republican. Mem. Christian Ch. Club: Rotary Internat. Patentee semiconductor magnetron modulator. Office: 652 Mitchel Rd Newbury Park CA 91320

GATES, ALLEN BENSON, engineering executive; b. Westwood, Calif., Feb. 6, 1940; s. St. Clair and Dora Lavaun (Morey) G.; m. Betsy A. Ankers, July 4, 1960 (div.); children—Allison, Tod, Jeffrey. B.S.M.E., U. Nev., 1961, M.S.M.E., 1963; Ph.D. in Systems Mgmt., Case Western Res. U., 1967; M.S., MIT, 1977; with Naval Weapons Ctr., China Lake, Calif., 1962-78; Sidewinder program mgr. Ford Aerospace & Communications Corp., Newport Beach, Calif., 1978-80, long-range planning mgr., thermal imaging program mgr., v.p., tech. affairs Detroit office, 1980-81, dir. advanced development operation, 1981—. Served with U.S. Army, 1963-66. Recipient Naval Weapons Ctr. Tech. Dirs. award, 1974, fellow, 1966-68; Sloan fellow, 1976-77. Mem. Assn. U.S. Army, AIAA, Nat. Security Indsl. Assn. Republican. Protestant. Club: Rotary. Home: 33032 Driftwood Ct San Juan Capistrano CA 92675 Office: Ford Aerospace and Communications Corp Aeronutronic Div Ford Road Newport Beach CA 92660

GATES, CAROL JOYCE, nurse; b. Ericson, Nebr., Mar. 28, 1933; d. William David and Violet Genice (Benson) Bingham; R.N., Bishop Meml. Hosp., 1953; B.S., U. Nebr., Omaha, 1957; M.N. (Public Health Nursing fellow, 1965-67), UCLA, 1967; m. Gerald F. Gates, children—Chris Anne, Gail Ellen. Staff nurse, head nurse, relief supr. VA Hosps., Los Angeles, Omaha, Denver, Bklyn., 1953-65; tech. dir. Comprenetics Co., Los Angeles, 1968-69; asst. prof. Sch. Nursing, U. Colo., Denver, 1970-74; chief nursing service VA Med. Center, Hampton, Va., 1974-79; chief nursing service VA Med. Center, Salt Lake City, 1979-81; dep. assoc. dir. nursing VA Med. Center, Long Beach, Calif., 1981—; asso. prof. nursing dept. nursing Old Dominion U., Hampton Inst., U. Utah. Mem. Am. Nurses Assn., Nat. League for Nursing. Home: 6261 Cheyenne Dr Westminster CA 92683

GATES, CHARLES CASSIUS, rubber company executive; b. Morrison, Colo., May 27, 1921; s. Charles Cassius and Hazel LaDora (Rhoads) G.; m. June Snowcroft Swaner, Nov. 26, 1943; children—Diane, John Swaner. Student MIT, 1939-41; B.S., Stanford U., 1943; D.Engring. (hon.), Mich. Tech. U., 1975. With Copolymer Corp., Baton Rouge, La., 1943-46; with Gates Rubber Co., Denver, 1946—, v.p., 1951-58, exec. v.p., 1958-61, pres., chmn. bd. 1961-82; chmn. bd., pres., Gates Corp., 1982-83, chmn. bd., chief exec. officer, 1983—; chmn. bd. Gates Learjet Corp., Wichita, Kans.; dir. Fed. Res. Bank of Kansas City, Hamilton Bros. Petroleum Corp., Denver, Robinson Brick & Tile Co., Denver. Pres., Trustee Gates Found., Denver Mus. Natural History. Recipient Community Leadership and Service Award Nat. Jewish Hosp., 1974; named Mgmt. Man of Yr., Nat. Mgmt. Assn., 1965. Mem. NAM (bd. dirs.), Rubber Mfrs. Assn. (bd. dirs.), Colo. Assn. Commerce and Industry. Clubs: Conquistadores del Cielo, Denver Country, Cherry Hills Country, Denver, Outrigger Canoe, Waialae Country, Boon and Crockett, Club Ltd., Country of Colo., Roundup Riders of Rockies, Shikar-Safari Internat., Augusta Nat. Golf, Castle Pines Golf. Home: 444 S University Blvd Denver CO 80209 Office: 900 S Broadway Denver CO 80209

GATES, DARYL F., city chief of police; b. Glendale, Calif., Aug. 30, 1926. B.S. in Pub. Adminstrn., grad. Managerial Policy Inst. and exec. program, grad. summer exec. program Grad. Sch. Bus. adminstrn., U. So. Calif. With Los Angeles Police Dept., 1949—, dep. chief, 1968-69, asst. chief, 1969-78, chief, 1978—; bd. councilors U. So. Calif. Inst. Safety and Systems Mgmt.; mem. Los Angeles C. of C. Ad Hoc Juvenile Justice and Law and Justice Exec. Coms.; mem. exec. com. Council for Peace and Equality in Edn.; past adv./author Nat. Adv. Commn. on Civil Disorder; mem. country-wide Criminal Justice Coordination Com. Bd. dirs. Los Angeles chpt. YMCA; mem. adv. bd. Children's Village. Served with USN, World War II. Mem. Calif. Peace Officers Assn. (exec. and law com., legis. com.), Internat. Police Assn., Calif. Police Chiefs Assn., Internat. Assn. Chiefs Police (editorial cons.), Criminal Justice Group (acting chmn.), Women's Peace Officers Assn. Calif. Lodge: Rotary (Los Angeles). Office: Los Angeles Police Dept PO Box 30158 Los Angeles CA 90020*

GATES, DAVE LOWRY, JR., university offical; b. Houston, Jan. 6, 1942; s. Dave Lowry and Frances Elizabeth (Lyles) G.; m. Judith Gates; children—Caton Merrill, Ian David; stepchildren—Ramey, Bob. B.S. magna cum laude, U. Houston, 1962; M.A., U. So. Calif., 1966; LL.D., U. Tex.-San Antonio, 1969; Ph.D., Tex. A&M U., 1973. Prof. Alvin Jr. Coll., 1963-65; asst. to pres. Sam Houston State U., 1967-70; asst. to pres. U. Tex.-San Antonio, 1970-72; asst. provost U. Houston, Clear Lake City, 1973-76; v.p. for mgmt. Tex. Woman's U., Denton, Tex., 1976-77, v.p. for acad. affairs, 1977-79; v.p. for internal affairs U.S. Internat. U., San Diego, 1980—; mem. nat. bd. advisors Am. Inst. Fgn. Study. Democrat. Home: 10673 Canyon Lake Dr San Diego CA 92131 Office: 10455 Pomerado Rd San Diego CA 92131

GATES, GLODEAN KENT KERKMANN, broadcasting executive; b. St. Louis, May 6, 1934; d. H. Warren and Glodean (Warthen) Kerkmann; m. Armand H. Hemon, May 25, 1957 (div.); children—Angela Hemon Baker, Charles; m. 2d, Philip W. Gates, May 22, 1976. Student U. Mich., 1955-56; B.A., UCLA, 1958. Tchr. Pub. Schs. Lancaster (Calif.), 1965-69; sales rep. Sta. KBVM-AM, Lancaster, 1967-69; account exec. Sta. KOTE-FM, Lancaster, 1970-71, sales mgr., 1971-73; gen. sales mgr. Sta. KOTE-FM, Sta. KKZZ-AM, Lancaster, 1973, v.p., gen. mgr. Lancaster-Palmdale Broadcasting Co., Lancaster, 1974-77; regional affairs dir. Sta. KFWB News 98, Westinghouse Broadcasting & Cable, Inc., Los Angeles, 1978—; guest lectr. broadcasting UCLA Extension. Mem. communications, exec. heart health coms. Los Angeles affiliate Am. Heart Assn.; bd. dirs. Hollywood Human Services, Recipient Martin R. Gainsbrugh citation Econ. News Broadcasters Assn., 1981; citation Disting. Service, Am. Heart Assn., 1981; Community Service award United Way, 1980; Achievement award Credit Counselors Los Angeles, 1982; Champion Media award for Econ. Understanding, Amos Tuck Sch. Bus., Dartmouth Coll., 1982. Mem. Pub. Relations Soc. Am., Pub. Info. Radio and TV Edn. Soc., So. Calif. Broadcasters Assn. Pub. Affairs Dirs., Women's Council Greater Los Angeles C. of C. (dir. 1979-80), Women in Pub. Affairs, Coro Found. Assocs., UCLA Alumni Club (life), Nat. Assn. Broadcasters (chmn. small market radio com.), Pi Beta Phi. Office: 6230 Yucca St Hollywood CA 90028

GATES, JERRY DELMAR, educational psychologist; b. Des Moines, June 20, 1943; s. Delmar Eugene and Madeline Violet (Martin) G.; m. Janis Knickerbocker, Sept. 4, 1965; children—Jason, Eric, Justin; m. 2d, Julie Nyquist, June 12, 1982. B.A. in Psychology and History, Tex. Christian U., 1968, M.A. Counseling Psychology, 1970; Ph.D. in Ednl. Psychology, U. Nebr., 1976. Dir. research and evaluation, clin. edn. ctr. U. Tenn., Chattanooga, 1973-76; ednl. specialist Michael Reese Hosp. and Med. Ctr., Chgo., 1976-82; project dir. diabetes research and tng. ctr. U. Chgo, 1977-82; dir. edn. and tng. internat. div. Nat. Med. Enterprises, 1982—; lectr. div. research med. edn., U. So. Calif., Los Angeles, 1982—. Contbr. numerous publs. and reports to profl. jours. and handbooks. Office: National Medical Enterprises 2901 28th St PO Box 2140 Santa Monica CA 90406

GATES, KAREN ELAYNE, educator; b. Fort Worth, Apr. 17, 1953; d. John Frederick and Ernestine Stanislaus (Hawkins) G.; m. Johnnie V. Lee, July 28, 1947 (div.). B.A., SUNY, 1975; M.A., San Diego State U., 1981. Cert. teaching, adminstrv. services, reading specialist, adult edn., Calif. Securities clk. Bankers Trust Co., N.Y.C., 1974-75; tchr. Ithaca (N.Y.) City Schs., 1975-76; ESAA math resource tchr. Wake County (N.C.) Sch. Dist., 1976-77; mgmt. trainee Allstate Ins. Co., Rancho Bernardo, Calif., 1977; tchr. elem. grades San Diego Unified Sch. Dist., 1977-81, project resource tchr., 1981-83; tchr. adult edn., reading; community tutor. Active Internat. Coed Y's Men's Assn., 1982-83, YWCA, 1981-83; coordinator Ann. Spelling Bee, 1981-83; sch. coordinator Heart Assn.'s Jump Rope for Heart, 1981-83; coach, coordinator YMCA basketball. Recipient Jackie Robinson award Coed Y's Men's Club, 1982; Brothers United award San Diego Fire Fighters, Inc., 1983; award Am. Heart Assn., 1981, Ronald B. Oakes Boys Club, 1982. Mem. San Diego Tchrs. Assn., Internat. Reading Assn., Assn. Supervision and Curriculum Devel., Calif. Assn. Phys. Edn., Health and Dance, PTA. Home: 2546 A St San Diego CA 92102 Office: 1098 S 49th St San Diego CA 92113

GATES, MAHLON EUGENE, research institute executive; former army officer; b. Tyrone, Pa., Aug. 21, 1919; s. Samuel Clayton and Elsie (Nieweg) G.; m. Patricia Lawrence, Dec. 19, 1942; children—Pamela Townley, Lawrence Alan; m. 2d, Esther Boone, July 4, 1972. B.S., U.S. Mil. Acad., 1942; M.S., U. Ill., 1948; student Command and Gen. Staff Coll., 1957, Army War Coll., 1962, Advanced Mgmt. Program, Harvard U., 1965. Commd. 2d lt., U.S. Army, 1942, advanced through grades to brig. gen., 1966; area engr. Gulf Dist., Iran, 1960-61; chief engr. br., officer personnel directorate Dept. of Army, 1963-65; gen. staff Dept. of Army, 1965-66; comdg. gen. Cam Ranh Bay, Vietnam, 1966-67; dir. constrn., Vietnam, 1967; dir., dep. dir. research, devel. and engring. Army Material Command, Washington, 1969-72; ret., 1972; mgr. Nev. ops. office Dept. of Energy, Las Vegas, 1972-82; sr. v.p. ops. S.W. Research Inst., San Antonio, 1982—. Former pres. Boulder Dam area council Boy Scouts Am.; chmn. adv. bd. Clark County Community Coll.; trustee Nev. Devel. Authority; bd. dirs. Greater Las Vegas C. of C., United Way So. Nev. Decorated Disting. Service medal, Legion of Merit, Bronze Star, Air medal (U.S.), Disting. Service Order 1st Class (Vietnam); recipient Meritorious Service award Energy Research and Devel. Adminstrn.; named Meritorious Exec., Dept. of Energy, 1980; recipient Outstanding Service medal, Sec. of Energy, James Edwards, 1981; Disting. Career award Sec. of Energy, Don Hodel. Republican. Home: 210 Country Wood San Antonio TX 78216 Office: PO Drawer 28510 San Antonio TX 78284

GATROUSIS, CHRISTOPHER, research instn. chemist; b. Norwich, Conn., Oct. 8, 1928; s. George John and Irene (Romeliotou) G.; B.S., De Paul U., 1956; M.S., U. Chgo., 1960; Ph.D., Clark U., 1965; m. Patricia O'Brien, May 16, 1951; 1 son, John F. Research asso. Argonne (Ill.) Nat. Lab., 1956-61; asst. scientist Woods Hole (Mass.) Oceanographic Inst., 1964-66; chemist Lawrence Radiation Lab., Livermore, Calif., 1966-71; chemist Lawrence Livermore Lab., 1971-72, asst. div. leader, 1972-73, asso. div. leader, 1973-74, dep. div. leader, 1974-77, div. leader, 1977—. Chmn. Livermore Beautification Com., 1969-71; chmn. Livermore Design Rev. Study Com., 1970-71. Served with USMCR, 1950-52. AEC grantee, 1972-73. Mem. Am. Phys. Soc., Am. Chem. Soc. Author (with C.E. Crouthamel), Chapt. 4, Applied Gamma Ray Spectrometry, 1960; (with R.R. Heinrich and C.E. Crouthamel) Progress in Nuclear Energy, 1961. Researcher in nuclear chemistry. Home: 5179 Diane Ln Livermore CA 94550 Office: Lawrence Livermore Laboratory Livermore CA 94550

GATZKE, DONALD ALLEN, coll. pres.; b. Huron, S.D., Nov. 16, 1942; s. Alvin Earl and Mabel Irene (Hinemann) G.; B.A. in B.A., Dakota Wesleyan U., 1964; M.A. in Counseling Psychology (pres.'s scholar 1967-69), U. Mont., 1969; Ph.D., U. Mo.-Columbia, 1973. Dir. bus. placement Dakota Wesleyan U., Mitchell, S.D., 1963-64; adminstrv. asst. Bur. Land Mgmt., Dept. Interior, Fairbanks, Alaska, 1964-65; regional mgr. univ. trust div. Girard Life Ins. Co. Am., Aberdeen, S.D., 1965-67; counselor Upward Bound Project Talent, HEW, Missoula, Mont., 1967-69; indsl. and ednl. cons., 1967—; psychologist St. Paul Pub. Schs., 1970-71; adminstrv. intern student affairs U. Mo.-Columbia, 1971-72; acting and asst. dean Central Meth. Coll., Fayette, Mo., 1972-73; dir. work/service, dir. internships, dir. summer term and evening programs, dir. continuing edn., asst. to dean for program devel. Coe Coll., Cedar Rapids, Iowa, 1973-75; founder, pres. N.W. Community Coll., U. Alaska, Nome, 1975-79; campus pres. U. N.Mex., Gallup, 1979-81; pres. Flathead Valley Community Coll., Kalispell, Mont., 1981—. Mem. exec. bd. United Way. Recipient disting. service award Bur. Land Mgmt., Dept. Interior, 1965. Mem. Adult Edn. Assn. U.S.A., Mont. Assn. Community Coll. Adminstrs., Am. Assn. Community and Jr. Colls., Am. Assn. Higher Edn., Am. Assn. Univ. Adminstrs., Am. Personnel and Guidance Assn., Assn. Continuing Higher Edn., Mont. Personnel and Guidance Assn., Assn. Counselor Edn. and Supervision, Mo. Personnel and Guidance Assn. (charter), Nat. Assn. Student Personnel Adminstrs., N.W. Adult Edn. Assn., McKinley County C. of C. (exec. bd.), Kappa Delta Pi. Clubs: Kiwanis (pres. 1962), Rotary (exec. bd.). Nat. editorial bd. The Record, Kappa Delta Pi Edn. Jour., 1972-74. Office: 256 Lake Blaine Dr Kalispell MT 59901

GAUGER, DAVID CHARLES, creative art designer, lecturer; b. Santa Maria, Calif., Sept. 4, 1950; s. Alexander David and Florence E. (Smith) G. B.S. with gt. distinction, in Graphic Design, San Jose State U., 1968-74. Designer Osborn & Assocs. Advt., Los Gatos Calif, 1969; art dir. Creative House Advt., Campbell, Calif., 1969-72; owner, art dir. Gauger Sparks Design Studio, San Jose, Calif., 1972-73; designer Sam Smidt Assocs., Palo Alto, Calif., 1973, SSR/Swiss Student Travel Office, Geneva, Switzerland, 1974; owner, creative dir., Gauger Sparks Silva, Inc., San Francisco, 1974—; lectr. graphic design, advanced visual communication, San Jose (Calif.) State U., 1978—. One-man show: Gauger Sparks Silva, San Francisco, 1980; two-man shows: San Jose State U., 1971, 72; group shows: San Jose State U. (3), 1972-73, Word Works Gallery, San Jose, 1979; numerous shows and exhbns. in illustration, painting, graphic design, environ. sculpture. Recipient ITCA Five award Internat. Typographic Composition Assn., 1973; Murphy award, San Jose Advt. Club, 1981, NFM Merchandising gold award, 1982. Mem. Am. Inst. Graphic Arts, San Francisco Soc. Communication Arts. Office: 129 Hyde St San Francisco CA 94102

GAULDEN, EDMUND COLON, physician; b. San Juan, P.R., Dec. 27, 1921; s. Edmund Dimas Colon and Zelia Gaulden Lewis; B.S., MIT, 1946; M.D., Columbia U., 1950; children—Edmund Louis, Robert Lee, Elaine Catherine, Thomas John, James Eric, Cindy, Gabrielle; m. 2d, Teresa Lucchese; 1 son, Frank Hewitt. Intern Bellevue Hosp., 1950-51; resident, 1951-52, VA Hosp., Bronx, N.Y., 1952-53, Homer Folks Hosp., Oneonta, N.Y., 1953-54; chief chest sect. VA Hosp., Portland, Oreg., 1954-57; individual practice medicine, Branford, Conn., 1957-59; asso. med. dir. Jbroerig, 1959-62; clin. instr. medicine U. Oreg., 1954-57, Yale U., 1957-62; now practice internal medicine and cardiology; chmn. dept. medicine Santa Ana Community Hosp., 1968-70, dir. coronary care unit, 1968-72; chief cardiology and cardiopulmonary lab. Canyon Gen. Hosp., 1974-80; attending staff cardiology U. Calif. at Irvine Hosp.; asst. clin. prof. medicine U. Calif. at Irvine. Chmn. bd. dirs. Canyon Gen. Hosp., 1974-77. Served from pvt. to 1st lt., CWS, 1943-46. Diplomate Am. Bd. Internal Medicine. Fellow Am. Coll. Cardiology, Council Clin. Cardiology Am. Heart Assn., Internat. Coll. Angiology, Coll. Chest Physicians, ACP, Am. Soc. Echocardiography; mem. Conn. Med. Soc., AMA, Calif., Orange County med. assns., Med. Dirs. Assn., Orange County Soc. Internal Medicine, S.R. Author: A Biography of Hemeterio Colon Warrens, 1977; The Enigma of Jedediah Hewitt Lewis, 1977. Home: 11161 Limetree St Santa Ana CA 92705 Office: 17541 Irvine Blvd Tustin CA 92680

GAUSTAD, EDWIN SCOTT, historian; b. Rowley, Iowa, Nov. 14, 1923; s. Sverre and Norma (McEachron) G.; B.A., Baylor U., 1947; M.A., Brown U., 1948, Ph.D., 1951; m. Helen Virginia Morgan, Dec. 19, 1946; children—Susan, Glen Scott, Peggy Lynn. Instr., Brown U., 1951-52, Am. Council Learned Socs. scholar in residence, 1952-53; dean Shorter Coll., 1953-57; prof. humanities U. Redlands, 1957-65; asso. prof. history U. Calif., Riverside, 1965-67, prof., 1968—. Served to 1st lt., AC, U.S. Army, 1943-45. Decorated Air medal; Am. Council Learned Socs. grantee, 1952-53, 1972-73; Am. Philos. Soc. grantee, 1972-73. Mem. Am. Hist. Assn., Am. Acad. Religion, Am. Soc. Ch. History (pres.), Phi Beta Kappa. Democrat. Baptist. Author: The Great Awakening in New England, 1957; Historical Atlas of Religion in America, 1962, 2d rev. edit., 1976; A Religious History of America, 1966, 2d rev. edit., 1974; Dissent in American Religion, 1973; Baptist Piety: The Last Will and Testimony of Obadiah Holmes, 1978; George Berkeley in America, 1979; editor books, most recent being: Documentary History of Religion in America, 2 Vols., 1982, 83; contbr. articles to profl. publs.; editor Arno Press, 1970-79; editorial council Jour. Ch. and State, 1970—. Office: Dept History U Calif Riverside CA 92521

GAUTHIER, MARJORIE ANN, educator; b. Franklin, N.H.; d. Ernest J. and Beatrice E. (Sorette) G. B.A. in Humanities, Mt. St. Mary Coll., 1960; M.Ed., Boston Coll., 1969. Life teaching credential, Calif. Tchr. elem. schs. Diocese of Manchester (N.H.), 1960-70; prin. elem. sch. Archdiocese Los Angeles, 1970-74; tchr. Paramount (Calif.) Unified Sch. Dist., 1974-79, 81—; tchr. Dept. Def. Dependent Schs., Worms, Ger., 1979-81. Spl. minister of Eucharist, master catechist, lay missionary Roman Catholic Diocese Orange (Calif.). Mem. Assn. Supervision and Curriculum Devel., Calif. Reading Assn., Calif. Council Social Studies, Calif. Tchrs. Assn., Paramount Tchrs. Assn. (dir. 1982—), NEA, PTA, Sierra Club, Peace and Justice Ctr. So. Calif. Democrat. Home: 4900-84 E Chapman Ave Orange CA 92669

GAVIN, DELANE MICHAEL, broadcasting exec.; b. Pierre, S.D., Oct. 6, 1935; s. Daniel Everett and Evelyn Agnes (Michaelson) G.; B.A. in Journalism, San Francisco State Coll., 1962; M.A. in Journalism, UCLA, 1971; M.B.A. in Organizational Behavior, U. So. Calif., 1982; m. Paula Ethel Handelman, Feb. 22, 1969. With San Francisco Examiner, 1961-62; corr. A.P., San Francisco, Reno and Las Vegas, 1962-64; reporter Las Vegas Rev.-Jour. Sun, 1964-65; editor suburban sect. Los Angeles Times, 1965-66; writer, producer CBS News, KNXT-TV, Hollywood, Calif., 1966-68; writer, reporter, dir., producer NBC News, KNBC-TV, Burbank, 1968-78; med. producer ABC News, KABC-TV, Hollywood, 1978—; instr. Sch. of Communications, U. So. Calif. Served with USNR, 1955-57. Recipient Christopher awards (2), 1973, 76; Golden Mike award Radio and TV Assn., 1968-70, 72, 74, 75. Mem. Acad. TV Arts and Scis. (bd. govs.; Emmy award 1968-69, 70, 72-73, 73-74), Dirs. Guild Am., Writers Guild Am., AFTRA, Nat. Assn. Broadcast Engrs. and Technicians, Wire Service Guild, Am. Newspaper Guild, Sigma Delta Chi. Club: Deadline (N.Y.C.). Home: 4660 Willis Ave Sherman Oaks CA 91403 Office: 4151 Prospect Ave Hollywood CA 90027

GAWTHROP, ALFRED, retired mining company executive; b. Wilmington, Del., Nov. 27, 1912; s. Alfred H. and Arabella (McGill) G.; student Westminster Sch., 1928-31; B.S. in Engring., Princeton, 1935; m. Elizabeth Baum, Sept. 7, 1936; children—Gertrude Gail Gawthrop Lumpkin, Alfred, Elizabeth Linda. Engr., E.I. DuPont de Nemours & Co., Inc., Parlin, N.J., 1935-41, Remington Arms Co., Lowell, Mass., 1941-43; area supr. Manhattan Project, Hanford, Wash., 1943-45; chief engr. Internat. Packers Co. Ltd., Chgo., 1945-49; v.p. Del Monte Properties Co. (name changed to Pebble Beach Co., 1977), 1969-70, chmn., chief exec. officer, 1970-76, chmn. exec. com., 1976-77, dir., mem. exec. com.; pres. Wedron Silica div., Chgo., also Chgo. Brick Co., 1949-60, Am. Brick Co., 1966-69; dir. Sioux City Iron Co. (Iowa), Baum Realty Co., Omaha. Alderman, Lake Forest, Ill., 1957-65. Mem. Nat. Indsl. San. Assn. (treas. 1964-65, pres. 1968-70), Am. Inst. Mining Engrs., Am. Ceramic Soc. Clubs: University (Chgo.); Onwentsia (Lake Forest, Ill.); Pacific-Union (San Francisco); Cypress Point (Pebble Beach, Calif.). Home: Box 941 Pebble Beach CA 93953

GAY, HOWARD PAUL, electronics engr.; b. Detroit, Feb. 8, 1947; s. Alfred Bernard and Gladys Velma (Howard) G.; B.S. in Elec. Engring., Mich. Tech. U., 1970; M.S. in Elec. Engring./ Computer Sci., U. Santa Clara, 1978; m. Diane Rose Maykowski, Aug. 13, 1971 (dec.); 1 son, Jeffrey Alan. Project Engr. Underwriters Labs., Chgo., 1970-72; sr. engr. Hallicrafters Corp., Rolling Meadows, Ill., 1972-73; project engr. Spectra Physics Corp., Mountain View, Calif., 1973-78; sr. project engr. Honeywell Corp., Seattle, 1978-79; pres., founder Memory Tech Corp., Redmond, Wash., 1979—; v.p. engring., dir. Cyberdata Corp., Monterey, Calif. Registered engr.-in-tng., Ill. Mem. IEEE. Lutheran. Research on micro-computers, disk memory storage controllers, memory systems and integrated circuits, laser storage systems, robotics and software for microprocessor control systems. Home: 6225 NE 129th St Kirkland WA 98033 Office: 2611 Garden Rd Monterey CA 93940

GAY, JORDANA (ROBYN), internal. corp. negotiator; b. Los Angeles; d. H. Bruce Humberstone and Gay Robinson; student (scholar) UCLA, 1970-72; student seminars Interpol, Paris, Scotland Yard, London, 1973-74. Mem. internal affairs staff IWTG, European holding co., Los Angeles, 1974-77; asst. dir. corp. and indsl. counter-espionage unit Teltec Investigations, Inc., Beverly Hills, Calif., 1977-80; partner, dir. Elective Info. Cons.'s, West Los Angeles, 1980—; chmn. Espace camouflage Intenat., 1981—; condr. seminars for legal bus., consumer affairs groups. Co-chairwoman Women's Def. League Los Angeles, 1978-79; vol. legal aid investigations Los Angeles County, 1980—; founder, dir. Paralegal Hotline, 1980—. Fellow Internat. Acad. Criminology; mem. Nat. Crime Prevention Assn., Am. Fedn. Investigators, Beverly Hills C. of C. (mem. crime council), Nat. Assn. Chiefs of Police. Office: 1414 Greenfield Ave Suite 306 West Los Angeles CA 90025

GAYNOR, BARBARA LYNNE, special education administrator; b. Cleve., Nov. 14, 1953; d. Joseph and Elaine (Bauer) G. B.A. in Psychology, UCLA, 1975; M.S. in Spl. Edn., Calif. State U. Cert. resource specialist Calif. Research and teaching asst. dept. psychology UCLA, 1975, clinician Speech and Communication Disorders Clinic, 1975-76; aide Fernald Sch. for Learning Disabilities, 1975; tchr. Comprehensive Activities Program, S. Central Regional Ctr. for Developmentally Disabled, 1976; grad. asst. dept. spl. edn. Calif. State U.-Los Angeles, 1976-77; student tchr. Culver City (Calif.) Unified Sch. Dist., 1977, Monebello (Calif.) Unified Sch. Dist., 1977; tchr. South Pasadena (Calif.) Unified Sch. Dist., 1977-78; tchr. Hacienda-La Puente (Calif.) Unified Sch. Dist., 1979-80, resource specialist, 1980-81, curriculum cons., 1980-81; prin. Marianne Frostig Ctr. of Ednl. Therapy, Pasadena, Calif., 1981—. Recipient Owl award for outstanding achievement Frostig Ctr., 1981. Mem. Council for Exceptional Children (past pres.), Calif. Assn. for Neurologically Handicapped Children—, Nat. Tchrs. Assn., Calif. Tchrs. Assn., Calif. Assn. Ednl. Therapists, Assn. Calif. Sch. Adminstrs., Assn. for Supervision and Curriculum Devel., Calif. Adminstrs. in Spl. Edn., Calif. Assn. Pvt. Spl. Edn. Schs. (del.). Chairperson sensory motor devel. workshop; developer of programs in spl. edn.

GAYNOR, EMIL, aerospace executive; b. N.Y.C., June 3, 1923; s. Morris and Frieda Sophie (Chuchem), G.; B.E.E. cum laude, Poly. Inst. Bklyn., 1950, M.E.E., 1953; postgrad. U. Pa., 1956-59; m. Rose Ruth Greenfield, Jan. 25, 1944; children—Joanne Sue, Jon Michael. With research and devel. Am. Dist. Telegraph Co., N.Y.C., 1950-52, Fairchild Guided Missiles, 1952-55; mgr. advance programs RCA Missile and Radar, Moorestown, N.J., 1955-62; dir. advance info. systems N.Am. Aviation, space div., Downey, Calif., 1962-66; v.p. plans and programs System Devel. Corp., Santa Monica, Calif., 1966-73; mgr. program devel. Systems and Energy, Group, TRW Inc., Redondo Beach, Calif., 1973-80, dir. advanced programs Def. Systems Group, Electronics and Def., 1982—; lab. instr. Poly. Inst. Bklyn., 1950. Dist. commr. Boy Scouts Am., 1955-58; mem. Pres.'s Peace Commn., 1966. Served with AUS, 1943-46. Mem. IEEE, Am. Mgmt. Assn., AAAS, AIAA, Assn. U.S. Army, Air Force Assn., Armed Forces Mgmt. Assn., Nat. Security Indsl. Assn. (chmn. C3 com.), Sigma Xi, Tau Beta Pi, Eta Kappa Nu. Club: Corsair Yacht (Los Angeles). Patentee in field. Home: 121 Cottonwood Circle Rolling Hills Estates CA 90274 Office: One Space Park Redondo Beach CA 90278

GAYNOR, JOSEPH, chemical engineer; b. N.Y.C., Nov. 15, 1925; s. Morris and Rebecca (Schnapper) G.; m. Elaine Bauer, Aug. 1, 1951; children—Barbara Lynne, Martin Scott, Paul David, Andrew Douglas. B.Ch.E., Poly. Inst. Bklyn., 1950, M.S., Case-Western Res. U., 1952, Ph.D., 1955. Research asst. Case Inst., Cleve., 1952-55; with Gen. Engring. Labs., Gen. Electric Co., Schenectady, N.Y., 1955-66, sect. mgr., 1962-65; group v.p. research Bell & Howell Co., 1966-72; mgr. comml. devel. group Horizons Research, Inc., Cleve., 1972-73; pres. Innovative Tech. Assocs., Sierra Madre, Calif., 1973—; participant internat. congresses, 1970, 81. Served with U.S. Army, 1944-46. Fellow AAAS, Am. Inst. Chem. Engrs.; mem. Am. Chem. Soc., Soc. Photog. Scientists and Engrs. (sr., chmn. bus. graphics tech. sect.), Am. Soc. Photobiology, Sigma Xi, Tau Beta Pi, Phi Lambda Upsilon, Alpha Chi Sigma. Editor: Advances in Non-Impact Printing Technologies, 1983; Patentee in field. Home: 1407 Oaklawn Pl Arcadia CA 91006 Office: PO Box 637 Sierra Madre CA 91024

GAZZANO, EDWARD MARCO, personnel director; b. San Francisco, Apr. 18, 1946; s. Marco Peter and Alda Alberta (Ferretti) G.; m. Catherine C. Ortelle, Feb. 24, 1968; children—Victoria, Melissa. B.A., U. San Francisco, 1968. Underwriter, Safeco. Ins. Co., Burlingame, Calif., 1970-71; personnel officer, San Francisco Health Dept., 1971-77, personnel dir., 1978—. Served to 1st lt. U.S. Army, 1968-70. Decorated Bronze Star. Mem. Am. Mgmt. Assn., Mcpl. Execs. Assn. Republican. Roman Catholic. Home: 1185 Debbie Hill Rd Cotati CA 94928 Office: 101 Grove St Suite 212 San Francisco CA 94102

GDOWSKI, SANDRA, software engring. co. exec.; b. Utica, N.Y., Nov. 3, 1953; d. Michael and Frances (Carzo) G.; B.A., U. Calif., San Diego, 1975; postgrad. in elec. engring. U. So. Calif., 1978-81. Programmer analyst Tech. Service Corp., Santa Monica, Calif., 1975-79; software design engr. TRW, Def. and Space Systems Group, Redondo Beach, Calif., 1979-80; mgr. advanced tech. The BDM Corp., Hawthorne, Calif., 1980—. Mem. Nat. Assn. Female Execs., Armed Forces Communications and Electronics Assn., Am. Mgmt. Assn., Am. Soc. Profl. and Exec. Women. Office: 5155 Rosecrans Ave Hawthorne CA 90250

GEARHART, GLENN LLOYD, investment firm exec.; b. Lottsville, Pa., May 10, 1945; s. Lloyd J. and Pear E. Gearhart; B.S. in Elec. Engring., Tri-State U., 1967; M.S. in Systems Engring., West Coast U., 1969; J.D., Western State U., 1978; m. Sharon Marie Manti, 1970; children—Steve, Shauna, Kevin. Bar: Calif. 1978; lic. real estate broker, Calif., Tex. Owner, gen. ptnr. Sungrowth Investments, Huntington Beach, Calif., 1981. Mem. ABA, Calif. Bar Assn. Republican. Author: Wealth Tree, 1979. Office: Sungrowth Investments 1120 Pacific Coast Hwy Huntington Beach CA 92648

GEBEYEHOU, SLOUM, nuclear engineer; b. Addis Ababa, Ethiopia, Jan. 20, 1940; came to U.S., 1969; s. Gebre Tsadik and Bekeletch Wolde (Yohannes) G.; m. Helen Branchcomb, Apr. 14, 1972; children—Menelik, Tewodros. Student, Haile Sellasie U., Ethiopia, 1960-65; M. in Civil Engring., San Jose State U., 1975; Constrn. engr. Salcost, Ethiopia, 1966-69, sr. design engr., 1969-78; gas engr., project control engr. Pacific Gas Transmission, Alaskan Pipeline, 1978-82; project mgmt. engr. Pacific Gas & Electric Co., Diablo Canyon (Calif.) nuclear plant, 1982—. Home: 1118 Rainier Ave Pacifica CA 94044 Office: 77 Beale St Room 1427 San Francisco CA 94105

GEBHARD, DAVID, museum director, architectural historian; b. Cannon Falls, Minn., July 21, 1927; s. Walter J. and Ann (Olson) G.; B.A., U. Minn., 1949, M.A., 1951, Ph.D., 1957; m. Patricia Peeke, July 7, 1954; children—Ellen Jean, Tyra Ann. Curator, instr. art U. N.Mex., 1953-55; dir. Roswell (N.Mex.) Mus., 1955-61; prof. art curator archtl. drawing collection U. Calif. at Santa Barbara, 1961—; field research in archeology, summers 1949-57; Fulbright prof. Tech. U. Istanbul, Turkey, 1960-61; cons. hist. preservation, 1970—. Vice pres. Citizens Planning Assn. Santa Barbara County, Inc., 1970—; co-chmn. Historic Landmark Commn., Santa Barbara, 1973—; mem. Montecito Archtl. Bd., 1980—. Bd. dirs. Regional Plan Assn. So. Calif., Western Found. Served with AUS, 1945-47. Research grantee NSF, NEA, Nat. Endowment Humanities; Nat. Park Service grantee; Ford found. grantee study Turkish architecture, 1965; Guggenheim fellow, 1981-82. Mem. AIA (hon.), Soc. Am. Archaeology, Am. Anthrop. Assn., Coll. Art Assn., Soc. Archtl. Historians (pres. 1979-82, bd. dirs. 1982—). Author: Prehistoric Cave Paintings of the Diablo Region of Texas, 1960; A Guide to the Architecture of Purcell and Elmslie, 1960; A Guide to Architecture in Southern California, 1964; R.M. Schindler: Architect; Architecture in California, 1868-1968, 1968; Kem Weber and the Moderene, 1969; The Richfield Building 1928-1968, 1969; Charles F.A. Voysey, Architect, 1970; co-author: Lloyd Wright, Architect, 1972; A Guide to Architecture in San Francisco and Northern California, 1973; Indian Art of the Northern Plains, 1974; Los Angeles in the 30's; Bay Area Houses, 1976; A Guide to Architecture in Los Angeles and Southern California, 1977; A Guide to Architecture in Minnesota, 1977; 200 Years of American Architectural Drawing, 1977; A View of California Architecture 1960-1976, 1977; Picturesque California Homes, 1978; The Architecture of Samuel and J.C. Newsom, 1878-1908, 1978; The Architecture of Gregory Ain, 1980; (with others) California Crazy, 1980, Tulsa Art Deco, 1980; Josef Hoffman, Design Classic, 1982; Santa Barbara: The Creation of a New Spain in America, 1982; contbr. articles to profl.

jours. Home: 895 E Mountain Dr Santa Barbara CA 93103 Office: Archtl Drawing Collection U Calif Santa Barbara CA 93106

GEBO, EMMA MARIE, home economics educator, administrator; b. Billings, Mont., Jan. 1, 1945; d. Waino August and Vera H. (Luoma) Joki; m. David Ray Gebo, Apr. 18, 1942; children—Lorri Dawn, Paul Adrien, Robyn Jeanette. B.S. in Home Econs., Mont. State U., 1966; M.A. in Edn., U. Mont., 1971. Cert. secondary tchr., Idaho. Substitute tchr. pub. schs., Idaho, Mont., 1967-74; adult educator Fashion Fabrics, Pocatello, Idaho, 1975-76; instr. consumer econs. dept. Idaho State U., Pocatello, 1975-79, asst. prof. consumer econs., 1979—, dept. chmn., 1980—; corp. officer Super Save Drug, Inc., Pocatello; researcher, cons. Idaho Assn. Future Homemakers Am. Mem. Idaho Assn. Future Homemakers Am. (hon.), Am. Home Econs. Assn., Idaho Home Econs. Assn. (pres-elect 1982-83), Am. Vocat. Assn., Idaho Vocat. Assn., Nat. Council Adminstrs. Home Econs., Assn. Coll. Profs. Textile and Clothing, Idaho State U. Profl. Women, Home Econs. Edn. Assn., Assn. Tchr. Educators, Pocatello C. of C., Kappa Omicron Phi, Phi Upsilon Omicron. Methodist. Contbr. articles to profl. jours. Home: 2409 S Fairway Pocatello ID 83201 Office: Campus PO Box 8081 Idaho State U Pocatello ID 83209

GEE, HENRY KIM, san. engr.; b. Reno, Jan. 31, 1931; s. Yum and Shee (Leong) G.; B.S., U. Calif. at Berkeley, 1953, M.S., 1958; B.S., U. Hawaii, 1980; m. Juanita Luevano, May 6, 1949; children—Richard, Marilyn, Virginia, Henry. Research asst. san. engring. research lab. U. Calif. at Berkeley, 1952-58, research asso., 1958-71; research asso. Water Resources Research Center, U. Hawaii, Honolulu, 1971—; cons. in field. Mem. Water Pollution Control Fedn., Sigma Xi, Gamma Sigma Delta. Researcher algae. Home: 537 Kekupua St Honolulu HI 96825 Office: 2540 Dole St Honolulu HI 96822

GEER, WILLIAM RODNEY, public information specialist; b. McComb, Miss., Nov. 3, 1947; s. William Upshaw and Jo Elaine (Welborn) G.; m. Maria R. Garcia, June 6, 1970; 1 dau., Anna Caitlin. B.A. in Journalism, U. N.Mex., 1969. Gen. assignment reporter Albuquerque Tribune, 1969-70; radio-TV-film mgr., news bur. mgr. U. N.Mex., Albuquerque, 1971-76; pub. info. specialist Sandia Nat. Labs., Albuquerque, 1976—; judge Nat. Fedn. Press Women State Competition, 1977-78. Mem. N.Mex. Council on Crime Delinquency. Recipient 1st place awards Am. Coll. Pub. Relations Assn., 1972, 74. Mem. Pub. Relations Soc. Am. Republican. Episcopalian. Home: 816 Turner NE Albuquerque NM 87123 Office: Div 3161 Sandia Nat Labs Albuquerque NM 87123

GEERY, MICHAEL JAMES, electronics co. exec.; b. Missoula, Mont., July 15, 1937; s. Glenn Leroy and Rhye (Ward) G.; B.S. in Aero. Engring., Northrop U., 1960; m. Michelle A. Decrow, July 9, 1983; children—Laura Lynn, Patricia, Melanie, Angela, Jeffrey, Jill, Holly, Michelle, Laura. Electronic design engr. N. Am. Aviation, Los Angeles, 1960-62; electronic project engr. Lockheed Electronics, Los Angeles, 1962-64; biomed. electronic design engr. Space Labs Inc., Chattsworth, Calif., 1964-65; mktg. staff exec. TRW, Los Angeles, 1965-73; western area mgr. Gales Energy Products Co., Los Angeles, 1973-78; chief exec. officer Xenotronix Inc., Valencia, Calif., 1978—; cons. Mem. Ch. of Scientology. Home: 27179 Sena Ct Valencia CA 91355 Office: 25520 Ave Stanford #305 Valencia CA 91355

GEESMAN, JOHN LEONARD, investment banker; b. Long Beach, Calif., May 6, 1951; s. James W. and Junne Geesman; B.A. cum laude, Yale U., 1973; J.D., U. Calif., Berkeley, 1976. Admitted to Calif. bar, 1977; legis. adv. San Francisco Consumer Action, 1974-75; energy staff counsel Calif. Citizen Action Group, Sacramento, 1976-78; exec. dir. Calif. Energy Commn., Sacramento, 1979-83; pub. fin. specialist First Boston Corp., 1983—; vis. fellow Found. Nat. Progress, San Francisco, 1976-77; founding bd. mem., corp. sec. The Solar Center. Mem. campaign staff Tom Bradley for Mayor of Los Angeles, 1973, George Moscone for Mayor of San Francisco, 1975. Co-author: Deceptive Packaging: A Close Look at the California Department of Consumer Affairs, 1974. Office: 101 California St San Francisco CA

GEETING, DAVID BRIAN, advertising executive; b. San Francisco, Dec. 21, 1940; s. Baxter Melson and Corinne (Nelson) G., B.A. in Communications, Stanford U., 1962, M.A., 1964. Asst. dir. ALN Prodns., San Francisco, 1964-67; TV producer Campbell Ewald Advt., Detroit, 1967-69; supervising producer D'Arcy, MacManus Advt., Detroit, 1969-72; exec. producer Leo Burnett Advt., Chgo., 1972-79, Foote, Cone & Belding/Honig, Los Angeles, 1979—. Bd. dirs. Chamber Music Plus. Mem. Western Region Agy. Producers (pres.), Acad. TV Arts & Scis. Republican. Episcopalian. Clubs: Bayview Yacht, Columbia Yacht. Office: Foote, Cone & Belding/Honig 2727 E W 6th St Los Angeles CA 90057

GEETING, DAVID G., pharmaceutical executive, clinical researcher; b. Muncie, Ind., Mar. 8, 1943; s. Gilbert E. and E. Ann (Rice) G.; m. Elaine K. Miller, July 26, 1964. B.S., Ball State U., 1965, M.A. (NSF stipend 1967), 1968; Ph.D., Independent U. Australia, 1974; M.B.A., Pepperdine U., 1982. Tchr., coach Ind. Pub. Secondary Schs., 1965-69; with Miles Labs., Inc., Elkhart, Ind., 1969-75; clin. researcher Westwood Pharms., Buffalo, 1975-78; dir. clin. affairs Barnes-Hind/Hydrocurve, Revlon Health Care Group, Sunnyvale, Calif. 1978—. Mem. Elem. Sch. Site Improvement Council, 1979-82; elder Presbyn. Ch., 1980. Mem. AAAS, Am. Inst. Biol. Sci., Am. Acad. Dermatology, Soc. Clin. Research. Presbyterian. Contbr. articles in field to profl. jours. Home: 5685 Abington Dr Newark CA 94560 Office: 895 Kifer Rd Sunnyvale CA 94086

GEFFNER, DAVID LEWIS, endocrinologist; b. N.Y.C., Mar. 21, 1942; s. Samuel Benjamin and Jean (Domb) G.; B.A. with honors, N.Y. U., 1962, postgrad. in biology, 1962-63; M.D., Georgetown U., 1967; m. Patricia June Fischer, June 7, 1970; 1 dau., Laura Simpson. Intern, VA Hosp., Bklyn., 1967-68; resident in internal medicine Cornell Cooperating Hosps., N.Y.C., 1968-71; clin. fellow in medicine Cornell U. Coll. Medicine, 1969-72; fellow in admitting and diagnostic service Meml. Hosp. for Cancer and Allied Diseases, 1971-72; research fellow in endocrinology, USPHS grantee N.Y. Hosp., N.Y.C., 1971-72; fellow in endocrinology Wadsworth VA Hosp., Los Angeles, UCLA, 1972-73, asst. chief dept. endocrinology, 1973-74; practice internal medicine specializing in endocrinology and metabolism, Los Angeles, 1974—; mem. staff UCLA Hosp., Cedars-Sinai Med. Center, Ross-Loos Med. Center, Queen of Angels Hosp., St. Vincent's Med. Center; research asst., head biology group, epidemiology sect. Sloan-Kettering Inst., N.Y.C., 1965; asst. prof. dept. medicine U. Calif. Sch. Medicine, Los Angeles, 1973-74, asst. clin. prof., 1974-81, asso. clin. prof., 1981—; chmn. continuing med. edn. Ross-Loos Med. Center, Los Angeles, 1974-82, chief endocrinology INA and Ross-Loos Health Plans, 1981—; cons. endocrinology Wadsworth VA Hosp., 1975—. Mem. steering com., chmn. legis.-jud. com. Santa Monicans Against Crime. Diplomate Am. Bd. Internal Medicine, Nat. Bd. Med. Examiners. Mem. Am. Cancer Soc. (asso.), Assn. Mil. Surgeons U.S., Am. Diabetes Assn., Endocrine Soc., AAAS, ACP, N.Y. Acad. Scis., St. George Soc., Beta Lambda Sigma, Phi Delta Epsilon. Contbr. articles in field to med. jours. and books; polit. columnist Ind. Jour., Santa Monica, Calif. Office: 1711 Temple St Los Angeles CA 90026

GEHLAR, PAUL MARK, food processing executive; b. Salem, Oreg., July 30, 1950; s. Mark Gale and Paula Irma (Trommlitz) G. B.A., Linfield Coll., 1975. With Oreg. Fruit Products Co., Salem, 1962—, dir., 1974—, treas., 1978-80, pres., gen. mgr., 1980—; dir. Northwest Packers Indsl. Relations Assn., 1981—, vice chmn., 1983—; dir. Northwest Food Processors Assn., 1982—; dir. Capital Improvement Inc., Salem, 1973—, pres., 1974—. Mem. Am. Bonanza Soc., Western Bonanza Soc., Aircraft Owners and Pilots Assn., Oreg. Pilots Assn. Lic. private pilot, Oreg. Home: PO Box 5398 Salem OR 97304 Office: PO Box 5283 Salem OR 97304

GEHLER, TERRI MARIE, educator, wholesale products distributor; b. New Britain, Conn., Mar. 31, 1937; d. Catello A. and Marie T. (Motta) Gioia; B.S., Central Conn. State Coll., 1959; M.A., U. Colo., Boulder, 1974, Ph.D., 1979; m. Robert Ray Gehler, June 12, 1962; children—Richard Ray, Debra Lynn. Tchr., West Hartford, Conn., 1959-61, Am. Dependent Schs., Verdun, France, 1961-64, Aurora (Colo.) Pub. Schs., 1966-75; prin. Altura Elem. Sch., Aurora, 1975-78, Yale Elem. Sch., Aurora, 1978-82; owner D. Terobick Enterprises, a Shaklee Co., 1982—. Mem. ch. council, chmn. parish edn. bd., chmn. presch. bd. St. Mark's Lutheran Ch. Recipient Sustained Superior Performance award U.S. Army Dependent Schs., 1962; named Aurora Young Educator of Year, Jaycees, 1972. Mem. Colo. Assn. Sch. Execs., Nat. Assn. Elem. Sch. Prins., Assn. Supervision and Curriculum Devel., AAUW, U. Colo. Alumni Assn., Phi Delta Kappa. Home: 11878 Park East Rd Aurora CO 80010

GEHRIG, ALLEN JOHN PETER, bank exec.; b. N.Y.C., Nov. 4, 1944; B.A., U. N.Mex., 1968; M.P.A., Golden Gate U., 1980, M.B.A., 1983. Vice-pres., comml. loan officer First Enterprise Bank, San Francisco. Pres., San Francisco Spl. Olympics, 1977-81, chmn. bd., 1981-82; state treas. Calif. Spl. Olympics, 1982—; trustee St. Francis Hook and Ladder Soc., San Francisco, 1981—. Recipient cert. of commendation U.S. Senator S.I. Hayakawa, 1978, 81; KABL Citizen of Day, 1978; joint resolution of commendation Calif. State Legislature, 1979; San Francisco Mayoral Proclamation of Commendation, 1979; letter of commendation U.S. Senator Alan Cranston, 1979, 81; cert. of appreciation Joseph P. Kennedy Jr. Found., 1979; plaque of appreciation San Francisco Spl. Olympics, 1980; President's award for social service Wells Fargo Bank, 1981, Outstanding Vol. award, 1981; resolution San Francisco Bd. Suprs., 1979; communications award Easter Seals Soc. San Francisco, 1979; San Francisco Vol. Activist award Bay Area Vol. Bur. and Macy's Calif., 1981; recognition of valuable contbn. to community through vol. service cert. No. Calif. Council Vol. Burs., 1981; Nat Commendation for vol. service in the community Pres. Reagan; award of merit City and County of San Francisco, 1981; resolution Bd. Suprs. City and County of San Francisco, 1981; San Francisco mayor's commendation for public services, 1981; commendation resolution Calif. Spl. Olympics, 1981; resolution Calif. Senate, 1981; letter of commendation Eunice Kennedy Shriver/Spl. Olympics, Inc., Washington, 1981. Mem. San Francisco Jaycees (pres. 1977-79, chmn. bd. 1979-80, Mem. of Yr. 1978, Officer of Yr. 1978, Disting. Service award 1979). Club: Commonwealth of Calif. Roman Catholic. Home: 1550 Bay St Apt 340 San Francisco CA 94123 Office: First Enterprise Bank 65 Post St San Francisco CA 94104

GEHRING, GEORGE JOSEPH, JR., dentist; b. Kenosha, Wis., May 24, 1931; s. George J. and Lucille (Martin) G.; D.D.S., Marquette U., 1955; m. Ann D. Carrigan, Aug. 2, 1982; children—Michael, Scott. Individual practice dentistry, Long Beach, Calif., 1958—. Chmn. bd. Long Beach affiliate Calif. Heart Assn.; mem. Long Beach Grand Prix com. of 300. Served with USNR, 1955-58. Mem. Harbor Dental Soc. (dir.), Delta Sigma Delta. Club: Rotary. Home: 14202 Cedar Ave Long Beach CA 90807 Office: 532 E 29th St Long Beach CA 90806

GEHRY, FRANK OWEN, architect; b. Toronto, Ont., Can., Feb. 28, 1929; s. Irving and Thelma (Caplan) G.; B.Arch., U. So. Calif., 1954; postgrad. Grad. Sch. Design, Harvard U., 1956-57; m. Berta Isabel Aguilera, Sept. 11, 1975; children—Leslie, Brina, Alejandro, Samuel. Archtl. designer Victor Gruen Asso., Los Angeles, 1953-54, planning, design and project dir., 1958-61; archtl. designer and planner Hideo Sasaki, landscape architect, Boston, 1957; archtl. designer Pereira & Luckman, architects, Los Angeles, 1957-58; project designer and planner Andre Remondet, architect, Paris, France, 1961-62; prin. Frank O. Gehry & Assos., Venice, Calif., 1962—; asst. prof. U. So. Calif., 1972-73; instr. So. Calif. Inst. Architecture, 1975-76; vis. critic UCLA, 1977; Wm. Bishop chair Yale U., 1979; design critic Harvard U., 1980-81; exhibited at Museum Modern Art, N.Y.C., Palais du Louvre, Paris, France, Contemporary Arts Mus., Houston, La Jolla (Calif.) Mus. Contemporary Art, Cooper Hewitt Muse., N.Y.C., San Francisco Mus. Modern Art, Biennale Venezia, Italy, 1980, others. Trustee Found. for Research in Hereditary Disease. Fellow AIA (merit awards, honor awards). Inventor cardboard furniture. Office: Frank O Gehry & Assocs 11 Brooks Ave Venice CA 90291

GEIGER, ADRIANNE HAWK, banking executive, consultant; b. Fostoria, Ohio, Sept. 27, 1932; d. William McClure and Hettie Elizabeth (Ash) Hawk; m. William John Geiger, Mar. 17, 1951; children—Gwynn Geiger Mannes, Christianne Geiger Gobrecht, William Gregory, John Ash. B.A., Ohio State U., 1953; M.P.A., U. So. Calif., 1974, Ph.D., 1977. Concert violinist, violinist numerous orchs. including: Toledo Symphony, Pacific Strings, Orange County Symphony, Orange Coast Community Symphony, 1953-73; coordinator ednl. programs Internat. Pub. Adminstrn. Ctr., U. So. Calif., Los Angeles, 1974-75; cons. United Way, Orange County, Calif., 1975-76; mem. faculty M.P.A. program U. Dayton, Wright State U., Dayton, Ohio, 1976-79; orgn. devel. cons. Owens-Ill. Inc., Toledo, 1979-80, mgr. human resource systems, 1980-82; v.p., mgr. human resource planning, exec. devel. First Interstate Bancorp., Los Angeles, 1983—; mem. adv. bd. Pub. Adminstrn. Tng. Ctr., Washington, 1980. Bd. dirs. Community Chest, Toledo, 1976-82, mem. exec. allocations com., chairperson child and family subcom., 1981-82; v.p., bd. dirs. Community Mental Health Ctr., Toledo, 1976-77; state del. Orange County chpt. Nat. Women's Polit. Caucus, 1974-76. Recipient Euterpr Award for service in music, Orange County, 1974. Mem. Am. Soc. Tng. and Devel., Am. Soc. Pub. Adminstrn. (co-chairperson sect. profl. devel. 1980-81), Human Resource Planning Soc., Family Service Assn. Am. (nat. bd. dirs., planning and ops. com., Western regional council), Orange County Family Service Assn. (pres. bd. dirs. 1974-76). Office: First Interstate Bancorp 707 Wilshire Blvd Los Angeles CA 90017

GEIGER, ALLEN RICHARD, research physicist; b. Sayre, Pa., Dec. 31, 1951; s. Richard A. and Francis M. (Aumick) G.; B.S. in Physics, N.Mex. State U., 1975. Research aid N.Mex. State U., Las Cruces, 1975-76; research physicist Deep Space Systems, Las Cruces, 1977-79; chmn. bd. G.E.I., Las Cruces, 1979-81; research physicist Atmospheric Sci. Lab., White Sands Missile Range, N.Mex., 1980—; cons. to petroleum industry, 1981—. Mem. U.S. Naval Inst. (asso.), World Space Found. (charter), Planetary Soc. (charter). Republican. Patentee in field. Home: PO Box 2425 Las Cruces NM 88004 Office: Atmospheric Sciences Laboratory White Sands Missile Range NM 88002

GEIGER, HAROLD JOSEPH, III, statistician; b. Denver, Dec. 15, 1952; s. William McDade and Beverly Ann (Clayborne) G.; B.S., So. Oreg. Coll., 1977; M.S., Oreg. State U., 1980. Research asst. Oreg. State U., 1979-80; math. statistian U.S. Dept. Agriculture, Madison, Wis. 1980-82; biometrician Alaskan Dept. Fish Game, Juneau, Alaska, 1982—. AAAS, Am. Statis. Assn., Am. Fisheries Soc. Republican. Home: 3555 Mendonhall Loop 16 Juneau AK 99801 Office: 230 S Franklin Juneau AK 99801

GEIKEN, ALAN RICHARD, agrl. engr.; b. Toledo, Aug. 24, 1923; s. Martin Herman and Herta Regina G.; student St. Ambrose Coll., 1946; B.S. in Engring., Iowa State U., 1950. Engr., corp. sec. Hot Spot Detector, Inc., Des Moines, 1950-53, sales engr., asst. gen. mgr., 1953-60; prin. Alan Geiken Co., grain-storage cons., San Francisco, 1960—. Served with USAAF, 1943-45. Mem. Am. Soc. Agrl. Engrs., Calif. Warehousemen's Assn., Calif. Grain and Feed Assn., Grain Elevator and Processing Soc., Internat. Platform Assn. Lutheran. Grain-storage cons. in Madrid, Moscow, Stockholm, London, Mexico; developer electronic grain-storage temperature system. Office: PO Box 214 255 Sacramento CA 95821

GEISER, KARL FREDERICK, ret. lawyer; b. New Hampton, Iowa, June 6, 1903; s. Mathias Edgar and Belle (Rowe) G.; student Oberlin Coll., 1921-22; A.B., State U. Iowa, 1925, J.D., 1927; m. Jane Schoentgen, June 6, 1928; children—Karl Frederick, Gretel (Mrs. George E. Stephens, Jr.). Admitted to Iowa bar, 1927, U.S. Supreme Ct. bar, 1974, Calif. bar, 1946; partner firm Geiser, Donohue & Geiser, New Hampton, Iowa, 1927-29; exec. v.p. E. H. Lougee, Inc., 1929-30; partner Tinley, Mitchell, Ross, Everest & Geiser, Council Bluffs, Iowa, 1930-42; individual practice, Beverly Hills, Calif., 1946-78. Served from lt. to comdr. USNR, 1942-45. Mem. Am., Iowa State, Calif. State bar assns., Los Angeles Bar Assn., Order of Coif, Phi Delta Phi, Sigma Alpha Epsilon. Republican. Home: 12919 Montana Ave Apt 103 Los Angeles CA 90049

GEIST, CHARLES RUH, psychologist; b. Pasadena, Calif., Oct. 29, 1946; s. Charles E. and Doris V. (Ruh) G.; B.S., U. San Diego, 1968; M.A., U. Mont., 1973, Ph.D., 1975; m. Enid Marci Vick, Dec. 20, 1975; children—Thorin Aiden, Dain Ahren, Tamar Ariel. Research asst. dept. psychology U. Mont., Missoula, 1973-74; asst. prof. psychology U. Alaska, Fairbanks, 1974-78, affiliate prof. Inst. Marine Sci., 1975—, research asso. Center Alcohol and Addiction Studies, Anchorage, Alaska, 1978—; asso. prof. psychology, 1978—; psychol. asso. Fairbanks Psychiat. and Psychol. Clinic, 1978—; panelist on alcohol and alcoholism Sta. KFAR, 1978-79. Recipient Outstanding Young Educator award North Star Jr. C. of C., 1978. Mem. Am. Psychol. Assn., Am. Inst. Biol. Scis., Western Psychol. Assn., Animal Behavior Soc., Am. Soc. Primatologists, Am. Forestry Assn., AAAS, Nat. Geog. Soc., Nat. Audubon Soc., Oceanic Soc., San Diego Soc. Natural History, N.Y. Acad. Scis., Psi Chi, Sigma Xi. Democrat. Contbr. articles on behavioral biology and exptl. psychology to profl. jours. Club: KC. Home: 1 1/2 Summit Dr Star Route Box 40022 Fairbanks AK 99701 Office: Dept Psychology U Alaska Gruening Bldg 314 Chandalar Ave Fairbanks AK 99701

GEIST, HAROLD, educator, clin. psychologist; b. Pitts., July 22, 1916; s. Alexander and Edna (Liebhaber) G.; A.B., Cornell U., 1936; A.M., Columbia, 1937; Ph.D., Stanford, 1951. Ednl. and vocat. adviser Community Service Center, Paterson, N.J., 1946; asso. advisement and guidance officer VA, Washington, 1946-47; psychologist, Vallejo, Calif., 1947-48; chief clin. psychologist Mare Island (Calif.) Naval Hosp., 1951-53; pvt. practice, Berkeley, Calif., 1953—; mem. faculty U. Calif. at Berkeley, 1951-54; vis. prof. U. P.R., summers 1955-58; lectr. San Francisco State U., 1966—; staff psychologist Gladman Meml. Hosp. and Found., Oakland, Cal., 1970—; psychologist Episcopal Homes Found., 1969—; sr. clin. psychologist Napa State Hosp., Imola, Calif., 1966-74. Mem. psychol. panel Alameda and San Francisco County Welfare Dept., 1968—; mem. panel div. disability determination Calif. Dept. Health, 1969—; expert cons. Bur. Hearing and Appeals, Social Security Adminstrn., HEW, 1969—. Served with AUS, 1942-46. Fellow Internat. Council Psychologists; mem. Am., Western, Calif. psychol. assns., AAAS, Am. Personnel and Guidance Assn., Interam. Soc. Psychology, Nat. Gerontological Soc. Author: The Etiology of Idiopathic Epilepsy, 1962; The Psychological Aspects of Diabetes, 1964; A Child Goes to the Hospital, 1965; The Psychological Aspects of Rheumatoid Arthritis, 1966; The Psychological Aspects of Retirement, 1968; The Psychological Aspects of the Aging Process, 1968; From Eminently Disadvantaged to Eminence, 1973; Tennis Psychology, 1975; Emotional Aspects of Heart Disease, 1976; Emotional Aspects of Migraine, 1980; Bahian Adventure, 1982; also articles. Home: 2255 Hearst Ave Berkeley CA 94709

GEIST, JERRY DOUGLAS, utility executive; b. Raton, N.Mex., May 23, 1934; s. Jacob D. and Jessie Kathleen (Wadley) G.; m. Sharon Ludell Kaemper, June 9, 1956; children—Douglas, Bruce, Robert. B.E.E., U. Colo., 1956. Registered profl. engr. With Pub. Service Co. N.Mex., Albuquerque, 1970—, v.p. engring. and ops., 1970-71, v.p. corp. affairs, 1971-73, exec. v.p., 1973-76, pres., 1976—, chmn., 1982—; dir. Associated Elec. & Gas Ins. Ltd., Bank Securities, Edison Electric Inc. Dir. Resources for the Future, SW Community Health Services; mem. Western Regional Council, former chmn. Served with USN, 1952-59. Mem. Albuquerque C. of C. Clubs: Four Hills Country, Albuquerque Country, Tanoan Country, Petroleum.

GEIST, WILLIAM SIDNEY, SR., architectural engineer; b. Spokane, Wash., Dec. 8, 1936; s. Walter Louise and Helen Lee (Donovan) G.; m. Sharon Joyce Schaffert, Mar. 12, 1961 (div. Mar. 1975); children—William Sidney, Christina Lee, Timothy Patrick. B.S. in Architecture, Wash. State U., 1960. Facilities engr. Sylvania Electronics Co., Mountain View, Calif., 1960-66; engr. planning dept. Boeing Co. Seattle Facilities, 1966-69; engr. bldgs. Pacific N.W. Bell Telephone Co., Seattle, 1969—; photographer. Chmn. Wash. State Big Game Council, 1974-78, treas., 1976-77; sec. Pacific N.W. Bell Community Relations Team, Seattle, 1978-82; mem. Nat. Republican Congl. Com., 1981—. Served with USNR, 1953-63. Mem. Constrn. Specifications Inst. (chmn. membership 1981-82). Lutheran.

GELB, LAWRENCE NASON, mental health specialist; b. N.Y.C., Jan. 30, 1952; s. Richard Lee and Phyllis (Nason) G.; grad. Phillips Acad., 1969; B.A. magna cum laude, Harvard U., 1973; M.S., U. Calif., Berkeley, 1977; D.M.H., U. Calif., San Francisco, 1980. Clinician, Mental Health Police Project, Berkeley, Calif., 1979-80; asst. clin. prof. dept. psychiatry Sch. Medicine, U. Calif., San Francisco, 1981—; mental health coordinator Total Health Care Program, Permanente Med. Group, Oakland, Calif., 1980—. Mem. Doctor of Mental Health Assn. (exec. com.), Am. Orthopsychiat. Assn., Langley Porter Psychiat. Inst. Alumni-Faculty Assn., A. K. Rice Inst. Club: Telegraph Hill. Home: 2562 Pine St San Francisco CA 94115 Office: Total Health Care Program 3772 Howe St Oakland CA 94611

GELBART, MORRIS, psychologist; b. Wiesbaden, Germany, June 10, 1948; s. Harry and Zelda (Awendstern) G.; m. Deborah Gelbart, June 6, 1971; 1 child, Jamie Allison. B.A., Bklyn. Coll., 1969; M.S., CCNY, 1974; Ph.D., U. So. Calif., 1979. Lic. clin. psychologist, Calif. Psychologist Los Angeles Sherrif's Dept., 1976; chief psychologist, dir. pain mgmt. program Bay Harbor Rehab. Ctr., Torrance, Calif., 1977; pvt. practice clin. psychology, Redondo Beach, Calif., 1976—; clin. dir. pain program Torrance Meml. Hosp., 1979—; pres. So. Calif. Network, Inc. alcohol rehab. program; cons. in field. N.Y. State regents scholar, 1965-69. Mem. Am. Psychol. Assn., Calif. State Psychol. Assn., Am. Pain Soc., Los Angeles Pain Soc. Office: 324 S Pacific Coast Hwy Redondo Beach CA 90277

GELBER, MARTIN BENJAMIN, architect, educator; b. Los Angeles, Dec. 19, 1936; s. Albert Hart and Diana Mae (Weinberg) G.; A.A., Los Angeles City Coll., 1959; B.Arch., U. So. Calif., 1963; m. Michela Gunn, Jan. 22, 1970. Project designer Adrian Wilson & Assocs., Los Angeles, 1962-63; assoc., project designer Kamnitzer, Marks & Partners, 1963-66; prin. Martin B. Gelber AIA & Assocs., 1966-73, 76—, Gelber/Ostrick & Assocs., 1973-76, Martin B. Gelber, AIA & Assocs., 1976—; prof. Los Angeles Pierce Coll., Woodland Hills, Calif., 1960—; vis. critic U. So. Calif. Sch. Architecture, 1982-83. Mem. Com. to Save the Dodge House, 1965-70; archtl. bd. examiner State of Calif. Bd. dirs. Los Angeles Free Clinic, 1973—. Served with USNR, 1955-63. Laurel MacDonald fellow, 1962-63; recipient Illuminating Engring. award U. So. Calif., 1962; merit award for design So. Calif. chpt. AIA, 1976, Los Angeles chpt., 1982; Ceramic Tile Inst. award, 1980, 81. Mem. AIA (edn. com. 1971-72, nat. hist. preservation com. 1971-72, chmn. edn. com. So. Calif. chpt., dir. Los Angeles chpt. 1980, dir. Calif. chpt. 1980, budget com., v.p., pres.-elect Los Angeles chpt. 1983-85), Friends of Gamble House, Archtl. Panel of Los Angeles (speaker com. 1965-68), U. So. Calif. Archtl. League, Archtl. Guild (bd. dirs.), Architects/Designers/Planners for Social Responsibility (bd. advs.), Sertoma Club. Mem. B'nai B'rith. Author articles in field. Home: 12268 Canna Rd Los Angeles CA 90049 Office: 1424 4th St 502 Santa Monica CA 90401

GELBERG, JEFF STEVEN, author, copywriter; b. Los Angeles, Dec. 2, 1955; s. Irving and Ann G. Student, Los Angeles Valley Coll., 1973-75, UCLA, 1975-78. Co. mgr. Tony Urbano Prodns., 1974; assoc. producer Cunningham & Walsh, 1975-76; jr. copywriter Chickering/Howell, 1976; sr. copywriter Wells, Rich, Greene, Los Angeles, 1978-80; sr. copywriter Grey Advt., Inc., Los Angeles, 1980—; creative dir. Jeff Gelberg/Neal Gill Prodns.; mem. Clio awards judging com., 1981-83. Recipient One Show Merit award Creative Club N.Y., 1981; Andy award of merit Advt. Club N.Y., 1982. Mem. Screen Actors Guild, Am. Fedn. TV and Radio Artists. Democrat. Author: Into the 27th Year, 1980; Take Three, Breaking into Hollywood, 1981; What Would You Do If I Sang Out of Tune, 1982.

GELBKE, WILLIAM DUNLEA, property mgmt. co. exec.; b. Ecuador, July 13, 1939; s. Arthur W. and Matilde (Velez) de G.; B.A. in Econs., U. of the Americas, 1962; M.B.A., Am. Grad. Sch. Internat. Mgmt., Phoenix, 1964. Gen. Mgr. Plasticos Reforma, S.A., Mexico City, 1964-67; mktg. exec. IBM Corp., Los Angeles, 1967-71; pres., chmn. bd. Western Properties, Inc. Served to col. U.S. NG, 1967-71. Mem. Soc. Plastics Engr., Beverly Hills Bd. Realtors, Delta Phi Epsilon. Club: Internat. Marketing and Finance. Republican. Home: 2300 Brentford Rd San Marino CA 91108 Office: PO Box 99215 San Francisco CA 94109

GELD, ISIDORE, corrosion engr.; b. N.Y.C., Feb. 2, 1917; B.S. in Chemistry, CCNY, 1939; postgrad. Bklyn. Poly. Inst., 1963-65; m. Rose Freda Prasow, Feb. 4, 1945; children—Helen, Howard. Analytical chemist Naval Applied Sci. Lab., Bklyn., 1947-57, corrosion specialist, 1957-70; corrosion specialist N.Y.C. Bd. Water Supply, 1970-76; corrosion engr. Rohr Marine Inc., San Diego, Calif., 1978; cons. corrosion engring., San Diego, 1976—; freelance sci./tech. Russian translator Plenum Press, 1978—; tech. adviser for U.S. Navy film, 1966. Recipient U.S. Navy Cert. of Merit, 1969. Registered profl. engr., Calif. Mem. Nat. Assn. Corrosion Engrs., Am. Chem. Soc., Am. Translators Assn., Sigma Xi. Contbr. articles on corrosion to profl. jours. and manuals in field; translator (Russian text) Theory of Corrosion and Protection of Metals (N. Tomashov), 1966; contbr. abstracts of Russian lang. articles on corrosion to profl. jours.; patentee in field. Address: 8854 Heraldry St San Diego CA 92123

GELERIS, IRWIN PAUL, physician; b. Lithuania, July 24, 1923; naturalized U.S. citizen, 1951; s. Leon and Anna Geleris; M.D., U. Turin (Italy), 1949; m. Marilyn Rothschild, Aug. 12, 1951; children—Andrew M., Joseph A. Intern, Alexidn Bros. Hosp., Elizabeth, N.J., 1950-51; resident in pathology, instr. pathology N.Y. Med. Coll., N.Y.C., 1951-55; served as sr. surgeon, chief pathology service USPHS hosps., Chgo., San Francisco, 1955-57; chief pathologist, dir. labs. Glendora (Calif.) Community Hosp., 1958 , W. Covina (Calif.) Hosp., 1959 , San Dimas (Calif.) Community Hosp., 1971—, Foothill Presbyn. Hosp., Glendora, 1972—; assoc. clin. prof. pathology UCLA Med. Sch.; pres. Anna Meml. Cancer Found. Adv. bd. Citrus Coll., Glendora; pres. Citrus Coll. Found., Azusa. Diplomate Am. Bd. Pathology. Fellow Am. Soc. Clin. Pathologists, Am. Coll. Pathologists; mem. Am. Cancer Soc. (pres. NE Los Angeles unit 1977-78), Am. Coll. Nuclear Physicians, Am. Coll. Nuclear Medicine, Am. Pubic Health Assn., Am. Assn. Blood Banks, Am. Soc. Cytology, N.Y. Acad. Sci., AAAS, Soc. Nuclear Medicine. Club: Town Hall (Los Angeles). Office: 210 S Grand Ave Glendora CA 91740

GELFAND, MARTIN HARRY, sales exec.; b. Newark, June 19, 1937; s. Jules and Sally (Zuckerman) G.; B.S. in Scis., Am. U., Washington, 1959; student U. San Fernando Valley Coll Law., 1967-68; children—David, Marc. Sales exec. United Mchts. and Mfrs., N.Y.C., 1961-63, Warner-Lambert Co., Morris Plains, N.J., 1963-79; sales exec., nat. sales mgr. Barnes-Hind Pharms. div. Revlon, Sunnyvale, Calif., 1979-82; dir. sales for spl. markets Mattel Toys, Hawthorne, Calif., 1982—. Fund raiser Diabetes Assn., Muscular Dystrophy; active Boy Scouts Am. of Santa Clara. Served with AUS, 1959-61. Recipient E.H. Bobst award, 1971; named Key Account Div. Man of Yr., Warner-Lambert Co., 1975, 77. Mem. Nat. Wholesale Druggists Assn. (nat. health and beauty aids adv. panel), Nat. Assn. Chain Drug Stores, Gen. Mdse. Distbn. Council, Nat. Assn. Service Merchandisers, Nat. Coll. Store Assn., Nat. Food Brokers Assn. Jewish. Club: Santa Monica Bay Yacht. Author: Guide to Effective Merchandising, 1979. Home: 610 N Guadalupe Ave Redondo Beach CA 92077 Office: 5150 Rosecrans Ave Hawthorne CA 90250

GELLERT, ROBERT WILLIAM, chemist; b. Budapest, Hungary, May 25, 1947; s. Jeno and Matild (Vajda) G.; student Los Angeles City Coll., 1969-71; B.S. summa cum laude, U. So. Calif., 1973; Ph.D., 1980; m. Karen Resh, Jan. 2, 1970; 1 dau., Tami. Asst. lab. dir., lectr. U. So. Calif., Los Angeles, 1979-80; research assoc. Calif. State U., Northridge, 1980—. Mem. AAAS Am. Chem. Soc., N.Y. Acad. Sci., All Am. Karate Fedn., Sigma Xi. Democrat. Home: 8054 Matilija Ave Panorama City CA 91402 Office: 18111 Nordhoff St Northridge CA 91330

GELL-MANN, MURRAY, theoretical physicist; b. N.Y.C., Sept. 15, 1929; s. Arthur and Pauline (Reichstein) Gell-M.; B.S., Yale, 1948; Ph.D., Mass. Inst. Tech., 1951; m. J. Margaret Dow, Apr. 19, 1955; children—Elizabeth, Nicholas. Mem. Inst. for Advanced Study, 1951; instr. U. Chgo., 1952-53, asst. prof., 1953-54, asso. prof., 1954, research dispersion relations, developed strangeness theory; asso. prof. Calif. Inst. Tech., Pasadena, 1955-56, prof., 1956—, now R.A. Millikan prof. physics. Mem. Pres.'s Sci. Adv. Com., 1969-72. Regent Smithsonian Instn., 1974—. NSF post doctoral fellow, vis. prof. Coll. de France and U. Paris, 1959-60. Recipient Dannie Heineman prize Am. Phys. Soc., 1959; E.O. Lawrence Meml. award AEC, 1966; Franklin medal, 1967; Carty medal Nat. Acad. Scis., 1968; Research Corp. award, 1969; Nobel prize in physics, 1969. Fellow Am. Phys. Soc.; mem. Nat. Acad. Scis., Am. Acad. Arts and Scis. Club: Cosmos. Author: (with Y. Neeman) Eightfold Way. Research theory of weak interactions, developed eightfold was theory and Quark scheme. Office: Dept Physics Calif Inst Tech Pasadena CA 91125*

GELWICKS, LOUIS EDWIN, gerontologist, architect, planner; b. Flushing, N.Y., Sept. 9, 1928; s. Louis Edwin and Virginia (Laggren) G.; B.A., Princeton, 1951; diploma U. Stockholm, 1957; M.Arch. (U. So. Calif. Gerontology Center 1st Inst. fellow), U. So. Calif., 1967; m. Jeanne Marie Hill, June 11, 1955; children—James John, Elizabeth. Designer F.G. Frost Assos., N.Y.C., 1955-56; v.p., dir. Rex Whitaker Allen & Assos., San Francisco, 1957-66; architect, planning cons., also prof. architecture U. So. Calif., Los Angeles, 1967-70; partner Gelwicks & Walls, Architects, 1969-76; research asso. Gerontology Center, 1967-73; pres. Gerontological Planning Assos., 1972—. Served to lt. USNR, 1951-55. Fellow Gerontol. Soc., AIA (chmn. hosp. and health com.). Club: Bohemian (San Francisco). Author: Planning Housing Environments for the Elderly, 1974. Architect: St. Francis Meml. Hosp., San Francisco. Home: 3041 Queensbury Dr Los Angeles CA 90064

GENG, SHU, agronomist, biometrician; b. China, Sept. 3, 1942; came to U.S., 1965, naturalized, 1976; s. M. C. and S. Q. (Hou) G.; Ph.D., Kans. State U., 1972; m. Hai-Yen Wong, June 30, 1968; children—Elvin H., Joy J. Biostatistician, agrl. research and devel. div. Upjohn Co., Kalamazoo, 1972-76; asst. prof. agronomy and range sci. U. Calif., Davis, 1976-78, asso. prof., 1978—, asso. biometrician, 1978—; cons. biostats. Mem. Crop Sci. Soc. Am., Am. Soc. Agronomy, Biometric Soc., Am. Statis. Assn., AAAS. Mem. Christian Ch. Contbr. articles to profl. jours. Office: Dept Agronomy and Range Sci U Calif Davis CA 95616

GENGERELLI, CARMEN NOGUERO, educator; b. Barcelona, Spain, Sept. 9, 1912; d. Ramon Noguero and Pilar Cierco de Noguero; came to U.S., 1936, naturalized, 1946; B.A., U. Barcelona, 1936; M.A., U. Calif., Los Angeles, 1942; m. Joseph A. Gengerelli, Aug. 27, 1942; children—Carmen, Joseph G., Grenat. Instr. Spanish, Interam. Tng. Center, Washington, 1942-44; lectr. fgn. langs., chmn. dept. Los Angeles Sch. Dist., 1955-63; asso. prof. fgn. langs. Los Angeles Pierce Coll., Los Angeles, 1963-77, prof., 1977-79, emeritus, 1979—; vol. tchr. Mem. NEA, Calif., Los Angeles Coll. Tchrs. assns., Sigma Delta Pi, Alpha Mu Gamma. Roman Catholic. Club: Calif. Art. Author; Vamos a Mexico con Pepe y Ramon, 1971; (poetry) Reliquias de mi rincón, 1980. Home: 2001 Linda Flora Dr Los Angeles CA 90024

GENOVA, ALDO JOHN, architect; b. Italy, June 11, 1922; came to U.S., 1937, naturalized, 1944; s. Efisio Salvino and Pierina (Fiamma) G.; student U. So. Calif., 1937; m. Doris Natalie Banino, Apr. 8; children Dennis, Charles. Architect, Victor Gruen Assos., Los Angeles, 1972-74, William L. Pereira Assos., Los Angeles, 1974-75; pres. Genova Assos., Santa Monica, Calif., 1975—; prin. works include shopping centers, office bldgs., recreational devels. Served with AUS, 1943-46. Recipient 1st prize downtown redevel. All-Am. Cities, 1978. Mem. AIA. Democrat. Roman Catholic. Home: 1948 Holmby Ave Los Angeles CA 90025 Office: 3340 Ocean Park Blvd Santa Monica CA 90405

GENRICH, JOHN HOWARD, pediatrician; b. Buffalo, Oct. 11, 1941; s. John Harold and Marcia Howard (Merkel) G.; B.A., Johns Hopkins U., 1963; M.D., Hahnemann Med. Coll., Phila., 1969; m. Karen Linda Shepherd, Aug. 5, 1967; children—Toby John, Allison Hughson, Peter Howard, Jay Harold. Intern, then resident in pediatrics Children's Meml. Hosp., Oklahoma City, 1969-71; resident in pediatrics Walter Reed Army Med. Center, Washington, 1972-73; practice medicine specializing in pediatrics, Colorado Springs, Colo., 1975—; mem. staff Penrose Hosp., Meml. Hosp., St. Francis Hosp. Served with USAF, 1971-75. Decorated Air Force Commendation medal. Diplomate Am. Bd. Pediatrics. Conservative. Lutheran. Address: 625 N Cascade Ave Colorado Springs CO 80903

GENTA, BARRY THOMAS, real estate broker; b. Rexburg, Idaho, Aug. 10, 1944; s. Norman Thomas and Ellen Ann G.; grad. in automotive tech., Ricks Coll., 1965; m. Sandra Nalder, Sept. 13, 1969; children—Travis William, Shurron, Broc Thomas. Quality control insp. Aerojet Nuclear, Idaho Falls, Idaho, 1966-74; real estate asso. broker Reese Realty, Rexburg, 1974-80; broker Dietrich-Genta Realty, Rexburg, 1980—, lectr. on real estate Ricks Coll. Mem. Upper Valley Bd. Realtors (pres. 1977-78, Realtor of Yr. 1978). Mormon. Club: Kiwanis. Office: 117 E Main St Rexburg ID 83440

GENTILE, DOMINICK EDWARD, nephrologist; b. Asbury Park, N.J., Jan. 12, 1932; s. Louis C. and Madeline (DelBene) G.; B.S., U. Notre Dame, 1953; M.D., Georgetown U., 1957; m. Zora Kingson, Nov. 15, 1958; children—Susan, David, Mary, Thomas, Jason. Intern, Detroit Receiving Hosp., 1957-58; resident in internal medicine VA Hosp., Washington, 1958; instr. U. Louisville, 1964-65, asst. prof. medicine, 1965-68, asso. pediatrics, 1967-68; asst. prof. biophysics and medicine Mt. Sinai Sch. Medicine, N.Y.C., 1968-69; asst. prof. to asso. prof. medicine U. Calif., Irvine, 1969-73, clin. asso. prof., 1973-77, clin. prof., 1977—; dir. hemodialysis center St. Joseph Hosp., Orange, Calif., 1972—, chmn. dept. medicine, 1976-77, v.p. med. staff, 1982-83; chmn. sci. adv. council Kidney Found. So. Calif., 1976—. USPHS postdoctoral research fellow, 1960-62; recipient research career devel. award NIH, 1965-68. Diplomate Am. Bd. Internal Medicine. Fellow ACP; mem. Biophys. Soc., N.Y. Acad. Scis., Am. Fedn. Clin. Research, Am. Soc. Artificial Internal Organs, Am. Soc. Nephrology. Roman Catholic. Contbr. articles to profl. jours. nephrologist; b. Asbury Park, N.J., Jan. 12, 1932; s. Louis C. and Madeline (DelBene) G.; B.S., U. Notre Dame, 1953; M.D., Georgetown U., 1957; m. Zora Kingson, Nov. 15, 1958; children—Susan, David, Mary, Thomas, Jason. Intern, Detroit Receiving Hosp., 1957-58; resident in internal medicine VA Hosp., Washington, 1958; instr. U. Louisville, 1964-65, asst. prof. medicine, 1965-68, asso. pediatrics, 1967-68; asst. prof. biophysics and medicine Mt. Sinai Sch. Medicine, N.Y.C., 1968-69; asst. prof. to asso. prof. medicine U. Calif., Irvine, 1969-73, clin. asso. prof., 1973-77, clin. prof., 1977—; dir. hemodialysis center St. Joseph Hosp., Orange, Calif., 1972—, chmn. dept. medicine, 1976-77, v.p. med. staff, 1982-83; chmn. sci. adv. council Kidney Found. So. Calif., 1976—. USPHS postdoctoral research fellow, 1960-62; recipient research career devel. award NIH, 1965-68. Diplomate Am. Bd. Internal Medicine. Fellow ACP; mem. Biophys. Soc., N.Y. Acad. Scis., Am. Fedn. Clin. Research, Am. Soc. Artificial Internal Organs, Am. Soc. Nephrology. Roman Catholic. Contbr. articles to profl. jours. Home: 5125 Altoona Ln Irvine CA 92715 Office: 1310 W Stewart Dr Orange CA 92068

GENTRY, JAMES WILLIAM, state ofcl.; b. Danville, Ill., Aug. 14, 1926; s. Carl Lloyd and Leone (Isham) G.; A.B., Fresno State Coll., 1948; M.J., U. Calif., Berkeley, 1956; m. Dorothie Shirley Hechtlinger, Mar. 18, 1967; 1 stepdau., Susan (Mrs. Leonard Mushkin). Field rep. Congressman B.W. Gearhart, Fresno, Calif., 1948, Assemblyman Wm. W. Hansen, Fresno, 1950, sec., 1953-56; exec. asst. Calif. Pharm. Assn., Los Angeles, 1956-69, editor, pub. jour., 1956-69; pub. relations dir. PAID Prescriptions, 1963-64; dir. pub. info. comprehensive Health Planning Council, Los Angeles County, 1969; asst. adminstr., dir. pub. info. So. Calif. Comprehensive Health Planning Council, 1969-71, acting adminstr., 1971-72; exec. sec. Calif. State Health Planning Council, 1972-73, Calif. Adv. Health Council, 1973—, Calif. Health Care Commn., 1973-75; acting public info. officer Calif. Office Statewide Health Planning and Devel., 1978-79; interim dir. Calif. Office Statewide Health Planning and Devel., 1983; mem. Los Angeles Civil Service Police Interview Bd., 1967-72; asst. sgt.-at-arms Calif. State Assembly, 1950; exec. sec. Calif. Assembly Interim Com. on Livestock and Dairies, 1954-56; mem. adv. bd. Am. Security Council; mem. Calif. Health Planning Law Revision Commn.; former mem. Calif. Bldg. Safety Bd. Mem. Fresno County Republican Central Com., 1950. Served to col. AUS, 1949-50, 50-53; Korea. Decorated Legion of Merit, Bronze Star medal, Commendation Ribbon with metal pendant; recipient pub. awards Western Soc. Bus. Publns. Assn., 1964-67. Mem. Am. Assn. Comprehensive Health Planning, Pub. Relations Soc. Am., Ret. Officers Assn., Allied Drug Travelers So. Calif., Los Angeles Press Club, Mil. Police Assn., Res. Officers Assn. (life), Assn. U.S. Army, Pi Gamma Mu, Phi Alpha Delta. Sigma Delta Chi. Editor: Better Health, 1963-67; Orientation Conf. Comprehensive Health Planning, 1969; Commentary, 1969-71. Editorial adv. Pharm. Services for Nursing Homes: A Procedural Manual, 1966. Editor: Program and Funding, 1972; Substance Abuse, 1972. Home: 902 Commons Dr Sacramento CA 95825 Office: 1600 9th St Sacramento CA 95814

GENTRY, MICHAEL LEE, electronic engr.; b. Durant, Okla., Sept. 20, 1942; s. G.P. and Lucille Elizabeth (Tomlin) G.; B.S. in Elec. Engring., Okla. State U., 1964; M.S. in Nuclear Engring., M.I.T., 1966; Ph.D., U. Ariz., 1971; grad. U.S. Army War Coll., 1983; m. Lois Jean Jones, June 11, 1968; children—Christopher Michael, Cynthia Lee. Asso. engr. Boeing Co., 1964-65; electronic engr. Tex. Instruments, Inc., 1966-67, CIA, 1971-73; tech. dir., supr. electronic engring. U.S. Army, Ft. Huachuca, Ariz., 1973—; instr. Cochise Coll., Sierra Vista, Ariz., 1974—; grad. teaching asst. U. Ariz., 1970-71. NSF fellow, 1965-66; NDEA fellow, 1967-70. Mem. Armed Forces Communications Electronics Assn. Author papers, articles. Home: 1648 Crestwood Dr Sierra Vista AZ 85635 Office: USA Communications Command CCC-TAD Fort Huachuca AZ 85613

GENUIT, DAVID WALTER, podiatrist; b. Stockton, Calif., May 12, 1949; s. Walter M. and Betty A. (Behney) G.; B.S., U. Calif., Davis, 1971; B.S., Calif. Podiatric Medicine, 1973, D.P.M., 1975. Practice podiatry, Bremerton, Wash., 1975—; instr. Edmonds Community Coll., Lynnwood, Wash.; clinician Waldo Clinic, Seattle; pres. podiatry staff Waldo Gen. Hosp., 1980-81; med. adviser Olympic Mountain Rescue. Mem. Wash. State Podiatry Assn. (v.p. 1978-79), Am. Acad. Podiatric Sports Medicine, Am. Coll. Sports Medicine, Am. Pub. Health Assn., Am. Podiatry Assn., Nat. Assn. Search and Rescue, Am. Assn. Trauma Specialists. Home: 1903 Shorewood Dr Bremerton WA 98310 Office: 1935 Wheaton Way Bremerton WA 98310

GENZ, GEORGE FRANCIS, vocational education administrator, consultant; b. Rosemount, Minn., Dec. 1, 1939; s. Carl Frederick and Mathilda Marian (Beaudette) G. B.S., St. Cloud State U., 1963; M.Ed., U. Nev., 1976; E.Ed., Oreg. State U., 1978. Dir. pub. relations Bishop Gorman High Sch., Las Vegas, Nev., 1967-71; asst. dir. So. Nev. Tng. Ctr., Las Vegas, 1972-74; dir. CETA Programs Clark County Community Coll., Las Vegas, 1974-76; asst. dir. S.E. Regional Resource Ctr., Juneau, Alaska, 1981—; pres. Gebia Dons, Inc. Recipient Ednl. Profl. Devel. award, U.S. Office of Edn., 1976-77, 1977-78. Mem. Am. Soc. Personnel Adminstrn., Am. Correctional Assn., Am. Vocat. Assn., Alaska Vocat. Assn., Phi Delta Kappa, Tau Kappa Epsilon. Democrat.

GEORGE, FRANK BLAINE, ednl. adminstr.; b. Santa Monica, Calif., 1914; s. Anthony Edward G.; B.S., U. Calif., Los Angeles, 1937; M.A. in Edn., Calif. State U., Long Beach, 1954; Ed.D., U. So. Calif., 1965; m. Donna Dee White, 1969; children—Diane, Vicki. Advt. mgr. Hadley Pub. Co., Los Angeles, 1937-39; tchr., pub. schs. Glendale, Calif., 1947-49; instr. Long Beach City Coll., 1949-52; supr. Long Beach Unified Sch. Dist., 1952-67, dir. instructional resources, 1967-83. Pres., Travelers Aid Soc., Long Beach. Served to comdr. USN, 1939-47. Mem. Nat. Assn. Ednl. Broadcasters, Assn. Ednl. Communications and Tech., Assn. Calif. Sch. Adminstrs., Calif. Assn. Ednl. Media and Tech., Ret. Officers Assn. Republican. Episcopalian. Clubs: Rotary, Elks, Commonwealth of Calif. Home: 17178 Courtney Ln Huntington Beach CA 92649

GEORGE, G. WORTH, retirement center adminstr.; b. Goshen, Ind., Apr. 7, 1933; s. Gilbert W. and Alfie (Jasper) G.; B.A., Manchester Coll., 1955; M.Div., Bethany Theol. Sem., 1958; postgrad. U. Chgo., 1958-61; M.P.A., Calif. State U., Fullerton, 1983; health care facilities mgmt. cert. UCLA Sch. Public Health, 1977; m. Mary Lou Smith, Nov. 24, 1956; children—Diane, Lawrence, Lynda. Lic. marriage and family counselor, nursing home adminstr. Ordained to ministry United Ch. of Christ, 1960; hosp. chaplain, instr. Bethany Hosp. and Sem., Chgo., 1957-60; minister Morgan Park Congl. Ch., Chgo., 1960-62; asso. minister Bryn Mawr Community Ch., Chgo., 1962-66; sr. minister Ch. of the Oaks, Thousand Oaks, Calif., 1966-72; exec. dir. Pilgrim Place, Claremont, Calif., 1973—; faculty Center for Non-Profit Mgmt., Los Angeles. Bd. dirs. Pomona Valley Counseling and Growth Centers, 1977-79; vice chmn. bd. dirs. Pomona Valley Community Services, 1976-78, United Way Task Force on Aging. Profl. designation in pub. relations. Fellow Am. Coll. Health Care Adminstrs.; mem. Assn. Homes for the Aging (pres. 1979-80), Am. Soc. Tng. and Devel., Am. Assn. Public Adminstrn., Nat. Speakers Assn., Nat. Soc. Fund Raising Execs., Assn. Voluntary Action Scholars, World Future Soc., Non Profit Mgmt. Assn., Western Gerontol. Soc., Internat. Soc. Pre-Retirement Planners. Club: Univ. (Claremont). Office: 660 Avery Rd Claremont CA 91711

GEORGE, HAROLD MILES, real estate corporation executive; b. Wichita, Kans., Oct. 26, 1953; s. Miles Wiley and Lois Emily (Windiate) G.; m. Stephanie Suzanne Clay, June 20, 1981. A.B. summa cum laude, Princeton U., 1974. Dir. research methodology Decision Making Info., Santa Ana, Calif., 1976-80; dir. research Century 21 Real Estate Corp., Irvine, Calif., 1980—. Mem. Am. Statis. Assn., Am. Econ. Assn., Am. Mktg. Assn. Office: Century 21 Real Estate Corp PO Box 19564 Irvine CA 92713

GEORGE, MARY SHANNON (MRS. FLAVE JOSEPH GEORGE), state senator; b. Seattle, May 27, 1916; d. William Day and Agnes (Lovejoy) Shannon; B.A. cum laude, U. Wash., 1937; postgrad. U. Mich., 1937, Columbia, 1938; m. Flave Joseph George, Apr. 25, 1946; children—Flave Joseph, Karen George Van Hook, Christy, Shannon (Mrs. Fred M. Lowrey). Prodn. asst., asst. news editor Pathe News, N.Y.C., 1938-42; fgn. editions staff Readers Digest, Pleasantville, N.Y., 1942-46; columnist Caracas (Venezuela) Daily Jour., 1953-60; mem. Honolulu City Council, 1969-74; mem. Hawaii State Senate, 1974—; chmn. transp. com., 1981-82. Mem. Nat. Air Quality Adv. Bd., 1974-75; vice chmn. Hawaii Ethics Commn., 1968; co-founder Citizens Com. on the Constl. Conv., 1968. Chmn. Hawaii Conf. Elected Republicans, 1972-73, 83—; vice chmn. Rep. Nat. Conv. Platform Com., 1976, co-chmn., 1980; bd. dirs. Hawaii Med. Services Assn. Named Woman of Year, Honolulu Press Club, 1969, Hawaii Fedn. Bus. and Profl. Women, 1970, Citizen of Yr., Honolulu Fed. Exec. Bd., 1974, 76; recipient Brotherhood award Jewish Men's Clubs Hawaii, 1973. Mem. League of Women Voters of Honolulu (pres. 1966-67, 67-68), Hawaii Planned Parenthood Assn. (dir. 1970-72, 79—), Phi Beta Kappa, Kappa Alpha Theta, Mensa. Republican. Episcopalian. Author: A Is for Abrazo, 1961. Home: 782-G N Kalaheo Ave Kailua HI 96734 Office: Hawaii State Senate Capitol Bldg Honolulu HI 96813

GEORGE, PETER T., orthodontist; b. Akron, Ohio; s. Tony and Paraskeva (Ogrenova) G.; B.S. Kent State U., 1952; D.D.S., Ohio State U., 1956; cert. in orthodontics Columbia U., 1962; m. Wendy Houston Mawhinney; children—Barton Herrin, Tryan Franklin. Pvt. practice orthodontics, Honolulu, 1962—; cleft palate cons. Hawaii Bur. Crippled Children, 1963—; asst. prof. Med. Sch., U. Hawaii, Honolulu, 1970—. Mem. Hawaii Gov.'s Phys. Fitness Com., 1962-68; mem. Honolulu Mayor's Health Council, 1967-72; mem. med. com. Internat. Weightlifting Fedn., 1980-84. Served to capt. Dental Corps, U.S. Army, 1956-60.

Olympic Gold medallist in weightlifting, Helsinki, 1952, Silver medallist, London, 1948, Melbourne, 1956; six times world champion; recipient Disting. Service award Hawaiian AAU, 1968; Gold medal Internat. Weightlifting Fedn., 1976; named to Helms Hall of Fame, 1966. Diplomate Am. Bd. Orthodontics. Fellow Am. Coll. Dentistry, Internat. Coll. Dentistry; mem. Hawaii Amateur Athletic Union (pres. 1964-65), U.S. Olympians (pres. Hawaii chpt. 1963-67), Am. Assn. Orthodontists, Honolulu Dental Soc. (pres. 1967-68), Hawaii Dental Assn. (pres. 1978), Hawaii Soc. Orthodontists (pres. 1972). Editor Hawaii State Dental Jour., 1965-67. Home: 920 Ward Ave Honolulu HI 96814 Office: 1441 Kapiolani Blvd Room 520 Honolulu HI 96814

GEORGE, ROBERT HENRY, educator; b. St. Louis, Sept. 7, 1941; s. Cletis O'Dell and Lois America (Hardwick) G.; m. Marilyn Jean Taylor, May 24, 1942; children—Sheryl, Craig. Student Harris Tchrs. Coll., 1962-63, U. Md., 1967; B.S., U. Colo.-Colo. Springs, 1971, M.A., 1977. Cert. profl. tchr. Type B, Colo. Tchr. English and social studies Washington Irving Jr. High Sch., Colorado Springs, Colo., 1971—, wrestling coach, 1973—. Served to sgt. USAF, 1964-68. Mem. NEA (life), Colo. Edn. Assn., Colorado Springs Tchrs. Assn., Nat. Council Social Studies, Colo. Council Social Studies, Assn. Supervision and Curriculum Devel. Democrat. Mem. N.E. Bible Chapel. Home: 672 Bridger Dr Colorado Springs CO 80909 Office: Washington Irving Jr High Sch 1702 N Murray Blvd Colorado Springs CO 80909

GEORGE, RONALD MICHAEL, senior financial adviser, consultant, publisher, market analyst; b. Endicott, N.Y., Sept. 27, 1951; s. Vincent Ambrose and Christine Ann (Nasoni) G.; m. Elissa Gail Schultz, June 26, 1983. A.S., Broome Community Coll., 1971; B.S. in Organic Chemistry, U. Miami (Fla.), 1974; postgrad. in Econs., Wharton Sch. Fin., U. Pa., 1974-75. Commodity trading adviser, commodity pool operator. Sole propr. R.M. George Bus./Estate Fin. Advisers, Binghamton, N.Y., 1974-77, v.p. Trafalgar Fin. Corp., Los Angeles, 1978-80; pres. Fin. Services Internat., La Jolla, Calif., 1980-81; pres. S.W. Advisers Group, Inc., San Diego, Beverly Hills, Calif. and N.Y.C., 1982—; instr. C.P.A.s continuing edn. program; lectr. in field. Mem. Ind. Fin. Planners Assn., Nat. Assn. Securities Broker Dealers, Commodities Futures Trading Commn. Libertarian. Club: La Costa Country. Author and pub. —$— Hard Money Econ. Newsletter, The Atlas Newsletter. Office: 6563 Riverdale St San Diego CA 92120

GEORGE, SUSAN ELIZABETH, county government administrator; b. Ft. Benning, Ga., Nov. 24, 1951; d. Robert Houston and Marie (Borrell) G.; m. David Blake Robison, Aug. 28, 1970 (div. 1979). B.S. in Bus. Adminstrn., San Jose State U., 1974; M.P.A., Golden Gate U., 1978. Internal auditor County of Santa Clara (Calif.), 1973-77, sr. mgmt. analyst Office of Mgmt. and Budget, 1977-78, budget dir., 1978-82, asst. county adminstr., San Joaquin County (Calif.), 1982—. Mem. Nat. Women's Polit. Caucus, 1978—; sec. bd. dirs. Big Bros./Big Sisters of San Joaquin County, 1982—; mem. Gov.'s Govt. Efficiency Team, 1983. Mem. Am. Soc. Pub. Adminstrn. (chpt. council advisor), Mcpl. Fin. Officers Assn. Am. Democrat.

GEORGE, WALLACE ERBY, JR., air force officer; b. Columbia, S.C., Mar. 28, 1940; s. Wallace Erby and Emily L. (Blair) G.; m. Eleanor Shull, Oct. 15, 1960; children—Tara L., Wallace S., Krista L., Patrick M. B.S. in Bus. Adminstrn., U. S.C., 1963; M.A. in Edn., Boston U., 1976. Commd. 2d lt. U.S. Air Force, 1963, advanced through grades to lt. col., 1983, chief of supply, Luke AFB, Ariz., 1983—. Decorated Bronze Star medal. Mem. Air Force Assn.

GEORGE, WESTON WILLIAM, JR., marketing executive, writer; b. Hutchinson, Kans., Mar. 21, 1935; s. Weston William and Frances Marie (Craven) G.; m. Jennie Lee, June 15, 1957; children—Denise Diane, James Weston, Robert Walter. B.F.A., U. Kans.-Lawrence, 1957. Designer, Franz Wagner Assocs., Chgo., 1963-64; sr. designer Warwick Electronics, Chgo., 1964-66; product devel. mgr. Hubbard Sci., Northbrook, Ill., 1966-73; dir. product devel. Creative Publs., Mountain View, Calif., 1973-74; mktg. services mgr. MedaSonics, Inc., Mountain View, Calif., 1975—; writer ednl. materials. Founder, pres. North Shore Ecology Center, Highland Park, Ill., 1972. Served to 1st lt. USAF, 1958-60. Mem. Internat. Customer Service Assn. Author: Kites for All Seasons, 1978; contbr. articles to mags.

GEORGE, WILFRED RAYMOND, investment co. exec.; b. Grinnell, Iowa, Apr. 1, 1928; s. Raymond Lawrence and Doris Durey G.; B.S., U. Iowa, 1950; M.B.A., Harvard U., 1955; Ph.D., Golden Gate U., 1979; m. Katherine Shaughnessy, Aug. 14, 1971; children—Winifred Doris, Katheryn Gwen, Engr., Westinghouse Electric Co., Pitts., 1950-51; budget supr., sales, employment adminstr. Lockheed Missile and Space Div., Sunnyvale, Calif., 1955-59; account exec. Hooker and Fay, Inc., Redwood City, Calif., 1959-63; with Shearson Hammill & Co., Menlo Park, Calif., 1963; with Bache Halsey Stuart Shields, Inc., San Francisco, 1964—, vice pres. investments, 1972—. Instr. investments Golden Gate U. Served with USNR, 1951-52. Mem. St. Andrews Soc. (trustee), Brit. Benevolent Soc. (trustee), Securities Analysts of San Francisco, Tech. Securities Analysts of San Francisco, Nat. Assn. Bus. Economists, San Francisco Bond Club. Republican. Author: The Profit Box System of Forecasting Stock Prices, 1976; Tight Money Timing, 1982; Certified Stockbroker, 1966. Patentee paper-grate, 1975. Home: 16 Bonita Ave Piedmont CA 94611 Office: 350 California St San Francisco CA 94104

GEORGE, WILLIAM RAY, nuclear power research co. exec.; b. St. Anthony, Idaho, Aug. 27, 1940; s. David Elmer and Elsie Ruth (Howell) G.; cert. in electronics Idaho State U.; B.S., Weber State Coll., 1965; m. Cherie Lee Singleton, Sept. 2, 1961; children—Heather Sue, Jon Eric. Electronic technician FAA, Helena, Mont., 1961-63; reactor instrument technician Idaho Nuclear Corp., Idaho Nat. Engring. Lab., Idaho Falls, 1965-69, reactor ops. engr. Aerojet Nuclear Corp., 1969-73, reactor ops. tng. supr., 1974-75, reactor ops. shift supr., 1975-77; reactor ops. instrument and data systems supr. E G & G Corp., 1977—; reactor ops. supr. Gen. Electric Co., San Jose, Calif., 1973-74. Lutheran. Author: Nuclear Power—A Basic Understanding, 1982. Home: 6200 Marbrisa Ln Idaho Falls ID 83401 Office: E G & G PO Box 1625 Idaho Falls ID 83415

GERBER, DONALD LINDAHL, mgmt. cons.; b. N.Y.C., June 16, 1930; s. Stephen Ward and Hilma Louise (Lindahl) G.; ed. San Francisco Jr. Coll., Stanford U., Pacific Western U.; B.S.I.E.; M.B.A. Developer Adminstrv. System for Profl. Projects, Task Analysis Programs; v.p. Mgmt. Research Found. Registered profl. engr., Calif. Mem. Assn. Internal Mgmt. Consultants, Assn. Systems Mgmt., Nat. Soc. Profl. Engrs., Internat. Soc. Gen. Semantics, Nat. Micrographics Assn., Mensa. Club: Commonwealth. Home: 160 Caldecott Ln Apt 214 Oakland CA 94618 Office: 44 Montgomery St Suite 300 San Francisco CA 94104

GERBERDING, WILLIAM PASSAVANT, college administrator; b. Fargo, N.D., Sept. 9, 1929; s. William Passavant and Esther Elizabeth Ann (Habighorst) G.; B.A., Macalester Coll., 1951; M.A., U. Chgo., 1956, Ph.D., 1959; m. Ruth Alice Albrecht, Mar. 25, 1952; children—David Michael, Steven Henry, Elizabeth Ann, John Martin. Congl. fellow Am. Polit. Sci. Assn., Washington, 1958-59; instr. Colgate U., Hamilton, N.Y., 1959-60; research asst. Senator E.J. McCarthy, Washington, 1960-61; staff Rep. Frank Thompson, Jr., Washington, 1961; faculty UCLA, 1961-72, prof., chmn. dept. polit. sci., 1970-72; dean faculty, v.p. for acad. affairs Occidental Coll., Los Angeles, 1972-75; exec. vice chancellor UCLA, 1975-77; chancellor U. Ill., Urbana-Champaign, 1978-79; pres. U. Wash., Seattle, 1979—; dir. Wash. Mut. Savs. Bank, Seattle, Pacific N.W. Bell, Seattle, Safeco Corp.; cons. Def. Dept., 1962, Calif. Assembly, 1965. Trustee, Macalester Coll., 1980-83. Served with USN, 1951-55. Mem. Am. Polit. Sci. Assn. Recipient Distinguished Teaching award UCLA, 1966; Ford Found. grantee, 1967-68. Author: United States Foreign Policy: Perspectives and Analysis, 1966; co-editor, contbg. author; The Radical Left: The Abuse of Discontent, 1970. Address: 808 36th Ave E Seattle WA 98112

GERBERICK, DAHL ANTHONY, data processing executive; b. Los Angeles, June 14, 1945; s. Dahl Irwin and Dolores Elaine (Gussette) G.; B.S. in Engring., Loyola U., Los Angeles, 1969; M.B.A., Calif. Poly. U., Pomona, 1980; m. Stella Marie Pontrelli, Apr. 30, 1966; children—Christina Marie, Anthony Dahl, Theresa Marie. Programmer analyst dept. water and power City of Los Angeles, 1967-70, project leader, systems analyst, 1970-72; project mgr. General Dynamics Corp., Pomona, Calif., 1972-73; EDP cons. So. Calif. Edison Co., Rosemead, Calif., 1973-78; mgr. requirements planning Xerox Computer Services, Los Angeles, 1978-80, mgr. mgmt. services, 1980-82; mgr. mgmt. info. systems Gould Electronics, El Monte, Calif., 1982—; lectr. in field. Recipient Disting. Achievement award Supt. Los Angeles City Schs., 1971, 72; Outstanding Mem. award Assn. for Computing Machinery, 1973; Cert. of Appreciation, Inst. Internal Auditors, 1975, 77, 78; cert. info. systems auditor EDP Auditors Found. Mem. Assn. for Computing Machinery (chmn. chpt. ombudsman com. 1971-75; chmn. ombudsman com. privacy and security 1974-76; nat. chmn. ombudsman com. 1975-78, chmn. Los Angeles chpt. 1979, Appreciation award 1980), EDP Auditors Assn., Data Processing Mgrs. Assn. Democrat. Roman Catholic. Author: Privacy, Security and the Information Processing Industry, 1976. Home: 1174 Flintlock Rd Diamond Bar CA 91765 Office: 4323 Arden Dr El Monte CA 91731

GERBINO, KENNETH JOSEPH, investment adviser; b. N.Y.C., July 8, 1945; s. Joseph Charles and Lisette Diana (Attard) G. B.S. in Bus., Ithaca Coll., 1967; M.B.A., Syracuse U., 1968. Fin. analyst Litton Industries, Van Nuys, Calif., 1968-70, Republic Corp., Los Angeles, 1970-71; asst. v.p. mktg. Capital Records Club, Thousand Oaks, Calif., 1971; exec. v.p. Axioms Prodns., Los Angeles, 1972-73; fin. and investment adviser, prin. Ken Gerbino & Co., Beverly Hills, Calif., 1973—; editor, pub. Ken Gerbino Commentary, investment letter, 1973—; econ. lectr.; chmn. Am. Econ. Council. Mem. Internat. Investment Letter Assn. Contbr. articles to econ. research jours. Office: 9595 Wilshire Blvd Suite 200 Suite 206 Beverly Hills CA 90212

GERBODE, FRANK LEVEN ALBERT, surgeon, educator; b. Placerville, Cal., Feb. 3, 1907; s. Frank A. and Anna Mary (Leven) G.; B.A. cum laude in Physiology, Stanford, 1932, M.D., 1936; M.D. (hon.), U. Thessaloniki (Greece), 1964, U. Uppsala (Sweden), 1965, M.Surgery (hon.), Nat. U. of Ireland, 1961; children—Maryanna Gerbode Shaw, Frank Albert, Penelope Ann, John Philip. Intern, Highland Hosp., Oakland, Calif., 1935-36; asst. in pathology U. Munich (Germany), 1936-37; asst. resident in surgery Stanford U. Hosps., 1937-38, 38-39, asst. in surg. research, 1938, resident in surgery, 1939-40; practice medicine specializing in surgery, San Francisco, 1945—; instr. surgery Stanford Med. Sch., 1940-42, asst. clin. prof. surgery, 1947-50, asso. clin. prof., 1950-54, asso. prof., 1954-59, clin. prof., 1959-71, clin. prof. emeritus, 1971—; asso. in surgery St. Bartholomew's Hosp., London, 1949; cons. Letterman Army Hosp., San Francisco, 1949—; surg. cons. of U.S. Army, Korea and Japan, 1952, NIH, Bethesda, Md., 1955-72; cons. staff Children's Hosp., San Francisco, 1947—; guest prof. surgery Royal North Shore Hosp., Sydney, Australia, 1953, St. Thomas's Hosp., London, Eng., 1958, Free U. of West Berlin (Germany), 1960, U. of New South Wales, Sydney, 1963, U. Heidelberg (Germany), 1964, Duke, Durham, N.C., 1973, U. Alta. (Can.), Edmonton, 1974; chief dept. cardiovascular surgery Insts. Med. Scis., Pacific Med. Center, San Francisco, 1959-80; dir. Heart Research Inst., San Francisco, 1959—; lectr., surgeon Karolinska Hosp., Stockholm, Sweden, 1964; clin. prof. surgery U. Calif. Med. Sch., San Francisco, 1964-76, Stanford Med. Sch., 1971—; mem. surgery tng. com., USPHS, NIH, 1966-67. Mem.-at-large San Francisco Bay Area council Boy Scouts Am., 1971—. Served from maj. to lt. col., M.C., AUS, 1942-45; ETO, MTO. Recipient U.S. Army Disting. Civilian Service award, 1979; named knight Brit. Order St. John of Jerusalem, 1979. Diplomate Am. Bd. Surgery, Am. Bd. Thoracic Surgery (founding mem. 1951). Fellow Royal Coll. Surgeons (Eng.) (hon.), Royal Coll Surgeons (Edinburgh) (hon.); mem. Am. Coll. Cardiology, A.C.S., Am., Calif., San Francisco heart assns., A.M.A., Calif., Pan Am. med. assns., Am., Pacific Coast, Pan Pacific (pres. 1966-69), Western surg. assns., Am., Calif. thoracic socs., Calif., Hollywood acads. medicine, Calif. Acad. Sci., Excelsior, So. surg. socs., Halsted Soc., James IV Assn. Surgery, Internat. Soc. Cardiovascular Surgery (pres. N.Am. chpt. 1961-62), Internat. Soc. Surgery (pres. N.Am. chpt. 1971-74, pres. congress 1973-75, pres. 1975-77), Royal Soc. Health, Am. Assn. Thoracic Surgery (pres. 1972-73), Samson Thoracic Surg. Soc., Soc. Thoracic Surgeons, Soc. Univ. Surgeons, Soc. Vascular Surgery (pres. 1958-59), Soc. Clin. Surgery, San Francisco Med. Soc., AAAS, Deutsche Gesselschaft für Chirurgie, Soc. Thoracic and Cardiovascular Surgeons of Gt. Britain and Ireland, Societá Italiana di Chirurgia, Societè de Chirurgie Thoracique de Lange Francaise, 38th Parallel Med. Soc. (Korea), Sigma Xi, Alpha Omega Alpha. Clubs: St. Francis Yacht, Stanford, Pacific-Union, Bohemian, Chit Chat (San Francisco); University (N.Y.C.). Home: 2560 Divisadero St San Francisco CA 94115 Office: Pacific Medical Center PO Box 7999 San Francisco CA 94120

GERDES, RANDY DUANE, management training administrator; b. Caldwell, Idaho, July 8, 1952; s. Duane Theodore and Jeanne Mary (martin) G.; m. Mary Frances Sims, May 3, 1956; m. Deborah Louise Johnson, Nov. 17, 1952. B.A., Boise State U., 1980; M.A., Ariz. State U., 1982. Supr. Idaho 1st Nat. Bank, Boise, 1972-76; youth minister Christian Communion Ch., Boise, 1976-78; loan adjuster Idaho 1st Nat. Bank, Boise, 1978-80; S.W. mgr. Communications Skills, Inc., Mesa, Ariz., 1980-82; performance cons. Wilson Learning Inc., Scottsdale, Ariz., 1982; tng. adminstr. Salt River Project, Phoenix, 1982—. Mem. Am. Soc. Tng. and Devel., Internat. Assn. Bus. Communicators, World Future Soc. Republican. Home: 12836 S Pai St Phoenix AZ 85044 Office: PO Box 1980 Phoenix AZ 85001

GERDTS, DONALD DUANE, TV sta. mgr.; b. Janesville, Minn., Oct. 18, 1932; s. Ernest William and Gertrude Louise (Bartsch) G.; B.S., Mankato (Minn.) State U., 1957; postgrad. UCLA, 1958-59; M.A., Calif. State U., Fullerton, 1970; m. Marilyn June Anderegg, June 15, 1957; children—James, Paul, Julie. Chmn. fine arts El Rancho High Sch., Pico Rivera, Calif., 1959-66; sr. producer, dir. ITV Center, Santa Ana, Calif., 1967-70; dir. prodn. Sta. KOCE-TV, Huntington Beach, Calif., 1971-75, asst. sta mgr., exec. producer, 1976-78, exec. v.p., sta. mgr., 1978—; exec. producer Bill Alexander's Magic of Oil Painting TV series; lectr. in field. Served with USMC, 1951-54. Recipient Emmy award (2) Acad. TV Arts and Scis., 1978, 1979. Mem. Acad. TV Arts and Scis. Conglist. Exec. producer 12 ednl. television series used by 800 colls. and univs., also 21 documentary films for Pub. Broadcasting Service. Office: 15751 Gothard St Huntington Beach CA 92647

GEREND, ROBERT PAUL, real estate company executive; b. Memphis, Feb. 7, 1938; s. Joseph J. and Herta Frieda (Mueller) G.; B.S. in Mech. Engring. with honors, U. Wis., 1961; M.S., Seattle U., 1968. Unit chief Boeing Co., Seattle, 1961-77; pres. Pace Corp., Bellevue, Wash., 1977—, Pace Securities Corp., 1979—; realtor, broker; nat. lectr. on real estate; comml. flight instr. Mem. Real Estate Securities and Syndication Inst. (past pres. Wash. chpt.), Nat. Assn. Fin. Cons., Nat. Assn. Home Builders, President's Assn. Republican. Author real estate newsletter, papers on aircraft propulsion and noise. Home: 14877 SE 50th St Bellevue WA 98006 Office: Pace Corp 16301 NE 8th St Suite 251 Bellevue WA 98008

GERHART, JUDITH ANN, college dean; b. Indpls., Apr. 6, 1946; d. Elmer H. and Ruth E. (Geier) Cox. Student Ind. U., 1965-67; B.S., DePaul U., 1969, M.Ed., 1972; Ed.D., Nova U., 1976. Tchr. Bremen High Sch., Midlothian, Ill., 1969-71, Central YMCA Community Coll., Chgo., 1969-71, Thornton High Sch., Lansing, Ill., 1970-71; instr. secretarial sci. Oakton Community Coll., Morton Grove, Ill., 1971-72, asst. prof. secretarial sci. program, 1972-78, asso. prof. office systems tech. and word processing, 1978-8, chmn. dept. office systems tech. and word processing, 1972-81, coordinator coll.-wide faculty and staff devel. program, 1980-81; vocat. dean Oxnard (Calif.) Coll., 1981-83; dean admissions Moorpark Coll. (Calif.), 1983—; coordinator Midwest cluster Inst. Higher Edn., Nova U., Ft. Lauderdale, Fla., 1976-80; condr. word processing and communications workshops, 1974—. Named Young Career Woman of Yr., Bus. and Profl. Women's Assn., 1975 Soroptimist Woman of Yr., 1983. Mem. Am. Assn. Higher Edn., Am. Vocat. Assn., Ill. Vocat. Assn., Am. Mgmt. Soc., Am. Soc. Tng. and Devel., Council of Women, Internat. Word Processing Assn., Nat. Secretaries Assn., Nat. Bus. Edn. Assn., Ill. Bus. Edn. Assn., Nat. Council for Resource Devel. Delta Pi Epsilon, Kappa Delta Pi. Republican. Mem. Christian Ch. Home: 2158 Lathan Camarillo CA 93010 Office: 7025 Campus Dr Moorpark CA 93032

GERKEN, WALTER BLAND, ins. co. exec.; b. N.Y.C., Aug. 14, 1922; s. Walter Adam and Virginia (Bland) G.; B.A., Wesleyan U., 1948; M. Pub. Adminstrn., Maxwell Sch. Citizenship and Pub. Affairs, Syracuse, 1958; m. Darlene Stolt, Sept. 6, 1952; children—Walter C., Ellen M., Beth L., Daniel J., Andrew P., David A. Supr. budget and adminstrv. analysis Wis., Madison, 1950-54; mgr. investments Northwestern Mut. Life Ins. Co., Milw., 1954-67; v.p. finance Pacific Mut. Life Ins. Co., Los Angeles, 1967-69, exec. v.p., 1969-72, pres., 1972-75, chmn. bd., 1975—, also dir.; dir. Whittaker Corp., Carter Hawley Hale Stores, So. Calif. Edison Co., Times Mirror Co. Bd. dirs. Los Angeles World Affairs Council; trustee Occidental Coll., Los Angeles; trustee emeritus Wesleyan U., Middletown, Conn. Served to capt. USAAF, 1942-46. Decorated D.F.C., Air medal. Mem. Am. Council Life Ins. (chmn. 1981). Clubs: California, Stock Exchange (Los Angeles); Pacific Union (San Francisco); Balboa Bay (Newport Beach, Calif.); Dairymen's Country (Boulder Junction, Wis.); Metropolitan (Washington). Office: 700 Newport Center Dr Newport Beach CA 92660

GERKING, SHELBY D., econs. educator; b. Bloomington, Ind., Dec. 1, 1946; s. Shelby D. and Louisa B. Gerking; m. Janet Lynn, Sept. 1, 1967; 1 son, Shelby Evan. A.B. Ind. U. 1968, M.B.A. U. Wash. 1970, A.M. Ind. U. 1972, Ph.D. 1975. Asst. prof. econs. Ariz. State U. 1974-78; vis. asst. prof. Ind. U. 1977-78; assoc. prof. U. Wyo. 1978-82, prof. 1982—, dir. Inst. Policy Research, 1980—; vice chmn. research program com. Consortium on Energy Impacts, Boulder, Colo. Mem. Am. Econ. Assn., Regional Sci. Assn. Contbr. in field. Office: Institute for Policy Research PO Box 3925 University of Wyoming Laramie WY 82071

GERLACH, KINGSLEY SNOW, newspaper advertising executive; b. N.Y.C., Nov. 17, 1943; s. Harry J. and Helene S. (Roauer) G.; m. Donna M. Tice, Aug. 16, 1980; 1 dau., Jennifer Marie. B.A., Bloomfield Coll., 1965. Grocery mgr. Handy Andy Food Stores, San Antonio, 1970-74; retail advt. account exec. Express/News, San Antonio, 1974; nat. advt. mgr., 1974-78, retail advt. mgr., 1979-80; nat. advt. account exec. N.Y. Post, N.Y.C., 1978-79; nat. advt. mgr. San Francisco Chronicle/Examiner, 1980—. Served with USAF, 1966-70. Decorated D.S.M. Mem. Calif. Newspaper Advt. Execs., Internat. Newspaper Advt. and Mktg. Execs. Clubs: San Francisco Advt., San Francisco Press. Home: Apt 309 370 N Civic Dr Walnut Creek CA 94596 Office: San Francisco Chronicle/Examiner 925 Mission St San Francisco CA 94103

GERLACH, THURLO THOMPSON, elec. engr.; b. Sparta, Ill., Oct. 30, 1916; s. Kenneth Frederick and Golda M. (Thompson) G.; B.S. in Elec. Engring., Tri State Coll., 1937; postgrad., Command and Staff Coll., 1952; m. Ellen Marie Kuhn, July 14, 1946. Dist. and area engr., Ill. Power Co., Centralia, 1937-40, Sparta, 1940-41, Granite City, 1946-48; elec. engr. U.S. Bur. Standards, Washington, 1948-50, Fed. Power Commn., Washington, 1953-56, U.S. Bur. Reclamation, Billings, Mont., 1956-77; cons., 1977—. Mem. U.S. Com. Large Dams, 1967—. Served with USAF, 1941-46, 51-53; CBI; maj. Res. Registered profl. engr. Ill., Mont. Mem. Nat. Soc. Profl. Engrs., IEEE. Methodist. Clubs: Masons, Shriners, Elks. Home and office: 533 Park Ln Billings MT 59102

GERMAIN, ANNE CROFT, newspaper editor, publisher; b. Helena, Mont., Feb. 14; d. George Noel and Mary Alice (Blaisdell) Middlemas; student U. Mont., 1947-51, U. Calif., 1954-56; m. Richard L. Croft, 1949; children—Laren V. Croft Brill, Wendy A.; m. 2d, Richard K. Germain, 1957. Editor, photographer, writer Los Gatos (Calif.) Times-Observer, 1958-61, Sta. KSBW-AM-TV, Salinas, Calif., 1962-64; editor, feature writer San Jose (Calif.) Mercury, 1961-62; asst. to pub., book editor Monterey (Calif.) Peninsula Herald, 1965-70, editor, columnist, 1970—; founding pres. Town and Country Press, Monterey, 1975—. Mem. Newspaper Guild, ACLU (dir.). Author: Pebble Beach: The Way It Was, 1976. Office: Box 271 Monterey CA 93940

GERMANY-BRIDGES, BOBBYE, special education specialist; b. Burnet, Tex., Aug. 12, 1934; d. Gene and Kathleen (Fisher) Germany; children—Kerry Dune, Byron, Nancy, Rachael. M.Ed., Tex. U., 1956; M.S., East Carolina U., 1977; B.A., B.S., U.S. Air Force Pacific Coast Staff Coll., 1980; M.B.A., Western N.Mex. U., 1982. Cert. ednl. adminstr., tchr. Asst. dir. in-service tng. Caswell Ctr., Kinston, N.C., 1966-70; dept. head, community services liaison Greene County Schs., Snow Hill, N.C., 1970-77; program specialist spl. edn. Gallup (N.Mex.) McKinley County Schs., 1977—; staff devel. coordinator McKinley Manor (Hill-Haven Corp.), Gallup, 1977—; aerospace edn. officer CAP, Gallup, 1977-84; time mgmt. cons. pvt. industry. Named Outstanding Tchr., Greene County, 1972, 74, 77. Mem. Nat. Tchrs. Assn., Aerospace Educators Assn., Council for Exceptional Children, Assn. Supervisors and Adminstrs., N.Mex. Council Computers Edn. Democrat. Office: Edn Devel Center 1100 E Aztec Ave Gallup NM 87301

GERMERAAD, DONALD POUND, aerospace company executive, consultant; b. Billings, Mont., July 18, 1921; s. John Henry and Jane

Holland (Blake) G.; m. Esther Pietrina, Mar. 6, 1946; children—Paul Blake, Ann Germeraad Swain. B.S. with honors in Aero. Engring., MIT, 1950; M.S. in systems Mgmt., U. So. Calif., 1971. Airline transport pilot cert., airframe and propulsion cert. FAA; profl. mgr. cert. Nat. Mgmt. Assn. Chief engring. test pilot Convair, Gen. Dynamics Co., San Diego, 1947-62, chief crew performance, astronautics, 1962-66; mgr. ocean systems advanced programs Lockheed Missiles & Space Co., Inc., Sunnyvale, Calif., 1966-69, dir. test ops. spacecraft program, 1969-72, program mgr. high speed ships, 1972-76, dir.-mgr. ocean systems program devel., 1976 ; cons.; acrospace lectr. Stanford U., Palo Alto, Calif. Pres. Tollgate Homeowners Assn., Saratoga, Calif., 1980-81; chmn. bd. deacons Saratoga Federated Ch., 1981-82. Served to capt. AC, USN, 1941-46. Recipient aviation award San Diego C. of C., 1961; Man of Yr. award Gen. Dynamics Co., 1961. Fellow Soc. Exptl. Test Pilots; assoc. fellow AIAA, Royal Aero. Soc.; mem. Survival and Flight Equipment Assn. (hon. life). Republican. Club: Naval Officers (Moffett Field, Calif.). Office: Lockheed Missiles & Space Company Inc 1111 Lockheed Way Orgn 57-70 Bldg 568 Sunnyvale CA 94086

GERNERT, JAMES EDWARD, urologist; b. Wilkinsburg, Pa., June 12, 1933; s. Carl William and Helen Martha (Weber) G.; B.S., U. Pitts., 1955, M.D., 1959. Intern Santa Barbara (Calif.) County Hosp., 1959-60; resident in urology Long Beach (Calif.) VA Hosp., 1960-64; practice medicine specializing in urology, Long Beach, 1964-67, Los Angeles, 1967—; staff urologist Long Beach VA Hosp., 1964-67, Kaiser Found. Hosp., Los Angeles, 1967-70, chmn. sect. urology Hollywood Presbyn. Med. Center, Los Angeles, 1978—; mem. staff Hosp. of the Good Samaritan, Los Angeles, Queen of Angels Hosp., Los Angeles, St. Vincent's Hosp., Los Angeles. Bd. dirs. The Original Men's Twelve Step House, Los Angeles, chmn., 1971-80. Diplomate Am. Bd. Urology. Fellow A.C.S.; mem. Am., Calif., Los Angeles med. assns., Am. Urol. Assn. (merit award 1964), Hollywood Acad. Medicine (sec.-treas. 1980, council 1981-82, v.p. 1983, pres. 1984), Los Angeles Urol. Soc., Mensa. Republican. Conglist. Club: Century (U. Pitts.). Home: 1723 Rotary Dr Los Angeles CA 90026 Office: 7080 Hollywood Blvd Los Angeles CA 90028

GERNERT, WILLIAM EDGAR, real estate executive, retired air force officer; b. Bowling Green, Ohio, May 21, 1917; s. William Henry and Lillian Leon (Forrest) G.; m. Mary Alice Hawley, May 30, 1942; children—William Edgar III, Deborah Janssen, Peggy Lane, Mary Beth Emry. B.A., Bowling Green State U., 1938; B.S. in Civil Engring., U.S. Mil. Acad., 1942; M.B.A., Ohio State U., 1948; grad. Indsl. Coll. Armed Forces, 1962. Commd. Col. U.S. Air Force, 1955, advanced through grades to brig. gen., 1967; B-24 squadron comdr., Pacific Theater, 1944-45; chief advanced planning Armed Forces Nuclear Weapons Program, Albuquerque, 1951-53; dir. research and devel. Def. Atomic Support Agy., N.Mex., 1962-63; dir. nuclear safety U.S. Air Force, Kirtland AFB, N.Mex., 1965-67, ret. 1970; self-employed broker and real estate appraiser, Colorado Springs, Colo., 1972—; dir. Central Bank Colorado Springs; instr. real estate fin. and real estate appraising U. Colo., Colorado Springs, 1974-81. Decorated Legion of Merit with 3 clusters, DFC, Air medal with 4 clusters, Purple Heart. Sr. mem. Nat. Assn. Rev. Appraisers. Republican. Lutheran. Club: East Side Rotary (past pres.) (Colorado Springs). Home and Office: 14440-A Club Villa Pl Colorado Springs CO 80908

GERNON, WILLIAM HALL, surgeon; b. Urbana, Ill., Mar. 26, 1938; s. John Hall and Lydia Angeline (Pauk) G.; m. Norma Andrea Schmidt, Feb. 23, 1940; children—John Hall, Stephen Monroe, William Gregory, Thomas Jefferson. B.S., U. Chgo., 1959, M.D., 1963. Commd. capt. U.S. Army, 1964, advanced through grades to col., 1978, resident otolaryngology Walter Reed Army Med. Ctr., 1965-69, chief otolaryngology U.S. Army Hosp., West Point, N.Y., 1969-72, 5th Gen. Hosp., Stuttgart, Germany, 1972-75, asst. chief otolaryngology Madigan Army Med. Ctr., Tacoma, 1975—; clin. asst. prof. U. Wash., Seattle, 1982—. Decorated Army Commendation medal. Mem. ACS, Am. Acad. Otolaryngology, Am. Acad. Facial Plastic and Reconstructive Surgeons. Roman Catholic. Office: PO Box 87 Madigan Army Med Ctr Tacoma WA 98431

GEROULD, GARY LEE, TV Sportscaster, motor sports publicist; b. Bay City, Mich., June 30, 1940; s. Charles Henry and Zaida Alice (Parks) G.; B.A., Anderson Coll., 1962; m. Marlene Kay Chesterman, Sept. 5, 1961; children—Beth Lynne, Robert Charles. Newscaster, sports dir. Sta. WMDN, Midland, Mich., 1962-63; news and sports dir. Sta. KHSL, Chico, Calif., 1963 65; sports dir. Sta. KHSL-TV, Chico, Calif., 1963-65, sports dir. Sta. KCRA-TV, Sacramento, 1965-77, news anchorman, 1970-74; publicity dir. West Capital Raceway, Sacramento, 1977-79; motor sports editor Sacramento mag., 1977-79; sports commentator NBC-TV Network, MRN Broadcasting Co.; sports commentator KRAK Radio; publicity dir. Silver Dollar Speedway, Chico, Placerville (Calif.) Speedway; TV comml. spokesman. Bd. dirs. Pocket Little League, 1979-80. Mem. U.S. Auto Club Nat. Championship Radio Network, No. Calif. Motor Sports Press Assn., Kennedy Am. Legion Baseball Boosters Assn. (dir.). Contbg. writer Nat. Speed Sport News, Western Racing News, Racing Wheels. Home: 6 Spray Ct Sacramento CA 95831

GERRINGER-BUSENBARK, ELIZABETH JACQUELINE, systems analyst; b. Edmund, Wis., Jan. 7, 1934; d. Clyde Elroy and Matilda Evangeline Knapp; student San Francisco State Coll., 1953-54, Biscayne Acad. Music, Miami, Fla., 1955, Los Angeles City Coll., 1960-62, Santa Monica (Calif.) Jr. Coll., 1963, London Art Coll., 1979, others; Ph.D., Cambridge (Eng.) U., 1979; m. Roe Devon Gerringer-Busenbark, Sept. 30, 1968 (dec. Dec. 1972). Actress, Actors Workshop San Francisco, 1959, 65, Theatre of Arts Beverly Hills (Calif.), 1963, also radio; cons. and systems analyst for banks, ins. cos., acctg. and govt. agys.; artist, singer. Pres., Originals by Elizabeth, also Environ. Improvement, San Francisco, 1973—; ordained minister, 1978. Author: The Virgin Twenty, 1967; Happening-Impact-Mald, 1971; Seven Day Rainbow, 1972; Zachary's Adversaries, 1974; Fifteen from Iowa, 1977; Bart's White Elephant, 1978; Skid Row Minister, 1978; Points in Time, 1979; Special Appointment, 1979; Happenings, 1980. Address: PO Box 1640 7th and Mission Sta San Francisco CA 94101

GERSTLE, MARK LEWIS, III, public relations professional, writer; b. San Franicsco, Feb. 12, 1919; s. Mark Lewis Jr. and Marion (Mercier) G.; m. Elizabeth Bunker, Apr. 30, 1922; children—Judith Gerstle Mayhew, M. Philip. Student pvt. schs., Lawrenceville, N.J. Prodn. mgr. Sta. KLX-AM-FM, 1947-52; pub. relations mgr. San Francisco Internat. Airport, 1952-59; press sec. to mayor, San Francisco, 1959-63; exec. asst. to Bishop James Pike, San Francisco, 1963-64; dir. info. Episcopal Diocese of Washington, 1966-71; ptnr. Freeman & Gerstle, San Francisco, 1964-66; pub. and press relations rep. Calif. State Automobile Assn., San Francisco, 1971—. Served with O.S.S., U.S. Army, 1940-45. Mem. Pub. Relations Soc. Am., San Francisco Bay Area Publicity Club (past pres.). Office: Calif State Automobile Assn 150 Van Ness Ave San Francisco CA 94102

GERSTMAN, JUDITH ANNE, nurse; b. Cin., Sept. 23, 1948; d. Alford William and Mary Margaret (Stix) G.; Asso. Sci. with honors, U. Cin., 1970, B.S.N., 1972. Typist, proofreader, bookkeeper Milford (Ohio) Advertiser, 1965-67; receptionist Joseph P. Hunt, oral surgeon, Milford, 1965-66; student nurse aide, staff nurse Cin. Gen. Hosp., 1969-72; commd. 2d lt., Nurse Corps, U.S. Army, 1971, advanced through grades to capt., 1975, resigned, 1978; head nurse gen. practice clinic/emergency room Walson Army Hosp., Ft. Dix, N.J., 1977-78; commd. lt. USPHS, 1978, advanced through grades to lt. comdr., 1980; staff nurse surg. unit Gallup (N.Mex.) Indian Med. Center, 1978-79, charge nurse emergency room/ambulatory care dept., 1979-80; asst. head nurse, charge nurse emergency room/outpatient dept. Phoenix Indian Med. Center, 1980—. Mem. Am. Nurses Assn., USPHS Commd. Officers Assn., Emergency Dept. Nurses Assn., Tau Beta Sigma (life). Mem. Ch. Jesus Christ of Latter-day Saints. Home: 1540 E Colter St #1 Phoenix AZ 85014 Office: 4212 N 16 St Phoenix AZ 85016

GERTNER, MICHAEL JAY, lawyer; b. N.Y.C., Mar. 16, 1939; s. Aaron and Blanche (Javer) G.; B.S., U. Pa., 1960; J.D., Columbia U., 1964; LL.M., N.Y. U., 1965; m. Judy Landau Hurwitz, Oct. 18, 1970; 1 son, Gregory Scott; stepchildren—Michael Hurwitz, Mitchell Hurwitz. With Charles S. Krantz & Co., C.P.A.'s, N.Y.C., 1957-65; admitted to N.Y. bar, 1965, Calif. bar, 1966; practiced in Newport Beach, 1965—; mem. Howser, Gertner & Brown and predecessor firm, 1965—; lectr., instr. Orange Coast Coll., Costa Mesa, Calif., 1968—, Golden West Coll., Huntington Beach, 1971—, Calif. Continuing Edn. of the Bar, 1972—. C.P.A., Calif. Mem. Am. Inst. C.P.A.'s, Calif. Soc. C.P.A.'s, Am. Inst. Atty.-C.P.A.'s, Am., N.Y., Orange County (chmn. tax com. 1969-71, chmn. probate and trust law sect. 1975-76) bar assns., State Bar Calif., Orange County Estate Planning Council (pres. 1980). Club: Exchange (pres. Newport Harbor 1978-79). Home: 3051 Capri Ln Costa Mesa CA 92626

GERWITZ, PAUL FRANK, indsl. engr.; b. Machias, N.Y., Mar. 31, 1929; s. Lawrence Henry and Margaret Elizabeth (Benz) G.; B.S., Iowa State Coll., 1956; M. Engring., U. Calif. at Los Angeles, 1970; M. Betty Lou Einspahr, Aug. 2, 1952; children—Douglas, Paula, David. Design, project engr. Bourns, Inc., Riverside, Calif., 1956-60; engring. mgr. Spectrol Electronics Corp., design and mfr. precision patentiometers, dials and mechanisms, City of Industry, Calif., 1960—. Served with USAF, 1948-52. Registered profl. engr., Calif. Mem. Am. Soc. Profl. Engrs. Roman Catholic. Club: Toastmasters (pres. 1966) (West Covina, Calif.). Home: 3424 Sunset Hill Dr West Covina CA 91791 Office: 17070 E Gale Ave City of Industry CA 91745

GESSEL, STANLEY PAUL, soil science educator; b. Providence, Utah, Oct. 14, 1916; s. Gottlieb and Esther (Heyrend) G.; B.S., Utah State Agr. Coll., 1939; Ph.D., U. Calif.-Berkeley, 1950; m. Beverly Ann Pfieffer, June 29, 1974; children—Susan, Paula, Patti, Pamela, Michael. Instr., Coll. Forest Resources, U. Wash., Seattle, 1948-50, asst. prof., 1950-56, assoc. prof., 1956-60, prof. forest soils, 1960—, assoc. dean, 1965-82, dir. spl. programs, 1982—; cons. soil, water and forestry problems. Mem. Lake City Citizens Adv. Group. Served to capt. USAAF, 1942-45. Recipient citation N.W. Sci. Assn.; named hon. alumnus Foresters Alumni Assn. U. Wash., 1976. Fellow AAAS, Soil Sci and Agronomy Soc. Am., Soc. Am. Foresters; mem. Internat. Forestry Assn., Tropical Forestry Soc., Internat. Union Forest Research Orgns. Contbr. numerous articles to sci. publs., chpts. to books. Home: 8521 Latona St NE Seattle WA 98115 Office: Coll Forest Resources Univ Wash Seattle WA 98195

GESSERT, EDWARD CYRUS, JR., ret. electronic mfg. co. exec.; b. Roswell, N.Mex., Jan. 18, 1919, s. Edward C. and Phyllis Lee (Nisbet) G.; student Westminster Coll. (Utah), 1935-37; B.S., U. Colo., 1940; m. Ruth E. Gatzke, Sept. 1, 1951; children—Phyllis, Paul. Engr., Am. Tel. & Tel. Co., Phila., N.Y.C., Denver, Albuquerque, Kansas City, 1940-57; engr. Lenkurt Electric Co., San Carlos, Calif., 1957-60; engr., quality control mgr., v.p. Farinon Electric Co., San Carlos, 1960-75, ret. Served to maj. Signal Corps, AUS, 1942-46. Home: 14130 Sontag Hill Rd Grass Valley CA 95945

GETREU, SANFORD, city planner; b. Cleve., Mar. 9, 1930; s. Isadore and Tillie (Kuchinsky) G.; B.A. in Architecture, Ohio State U., 1952; M.A. in Regional Planning, Cornell U., 1955; m. Gara Eileen Smith, Dec. 8, 1952 (div. Feb. 1983); children—David Bruce, Gary Benjamin, Allen Dana. Resident planner Mackesey & Reps., consultants, Rome, N.Y., 1955-56; planning dir., Rome, 1956-57; dir. gen. planning, Syracuse, N.Y., 1957-59, dep. commr. planning, 1959-62, commr. planning, 1962-65; planning dir. San Jose, Calif., 1965-74; urban planning cons., 1974 . Vis. lectr., critic Cornell U., 1960-65, Syracuse U., 1962-65, Stanford, 1965—, San Jose State Coll., 1965—, Santa Clara U., Calif. State Poly. Coll., DeAnza Coll., San Jose City Coll., U. Calif. at Berkeley; pres. planning dept. League of Calif. Cities, 1973-74; advisor State of Calif. Office of Planning and Research. Past bd. dirs. Theater Guild, San Jose, Triton Mus., San Jose. Mem. Am. Soc. Cons. Planners, Am. Planning Assn., Am. Inst. Cert. Planners, Bay Area Planning Dirs. Assn. (v.p. 1965-74, mem. exec. com. 1973-74), Assn. Bay Area Govts. (regional planning com. 1967-74). Club: Rotary. Home: 1724 Hudson Dr San Jose CA 95124 Office: 925 Regent St San Jose CA 95110

GETZ, GEORGE FULMER, JR., business executive; b. Chgo., Jan. 4, 1908; s. George Fulmer and Susan Daniel (Rankin) G.; student Choate Sch.; m. Olive Cox Atwater, Jan. 17, 1933 (dec. Sept. 1980); children—George F. III (dec.), Bert Atwater. Trainee Eureka Coal & Dock Co., 3 years; chmn., chief exec. officer Globe Corp.; chmn. bd. Getz Coal Co., 1939-48, pres., 1948-53, Servisoft, Inc., Rockford, Ill., 1960-61; trustee Bankers Life Nebr., Lincoln; dir. Chgo. Nat. League Ball Club, 1940-72, Santa Fe Industries, A.T. & S.F. Ry., 1955-80, United Rep. Fund, Ill. (gov. 1956). Pres., bd. dirs. Nat. Hist. Fire Found., Arthur R. Metz Found., Globe Found.; bd. dirs. Ind. U. Found., Getz Found., Jr. Achievement Chgo., Ariz. Zool. Soc., Phoenix, 1966-81; trustee Chgo. Zool. Soc., Grand Central Art Galleries, N.Y.C., 1982—; bd. dirs. Ch. of Holy Communion Found., Inc., 1961-71; former v.p. fin. and treas. Nat. Safety Council; v.p. Geneva Lake Water Safety Com., Inc., 1954-66; mem. citizens bd. U. Chgo., 1956-71; mem. All Chicago Citizens Com., 1956; dir. Antarctic Assocs., 1956; mem. Ill. State com. Crusade for Freedom, Inc., 1957-58; bd. dirs. Kemah Camping Ground, Lake Geneva, Wis., 1957; trustee Am. Grad. Sch. Internat. Mgmt.; mem. Nat. Republican Fin. Com., 1976; mem. western region panel Pres.' Commn. on White House Fellowships, 1982, 83. Mem. Chgo. Assn. Commerce and Industry. Episcopalian. Clubs: Chgo., Tavern, Yacht (Chgo.); Economic, Los Rancheros Visitadores (Santa Barbara, Calif.); Paradise Valley Country, Valley Field Riding and Polo (Scottsdale, Ariz.); Kiva (Phoenix); Balboa (Mazatlan, Mexico); Circumnavigators. Home: 120 Mountain Shadows West Scottsdale AZ 85253 Office: Globe Corp 3634 Civic Center Plaza Scottsdale AZ 85251 also 16555 W Hwy 120 Libertyville IL 60048

GEVINS, ALAN STUART, neuroscientist; b. N.Y.C., Feb. 4, 1946; s. Michael S. and Rose (Master) G.; B.S., M.I.T., 1967; postgrad., Calif. Inst. Asian Studies, 1968-71. Sr. systems analyst Berkeley (Calif.) Sci. Labs., 1968-69; sr. ops. analyst Langley Porter Neuropsychiat. Inst., San Francisco, 1971-72; dir. EEG systems lab. U. Calif. Med. Sch., San Francisco, 1972-81, chief scientist, pres., 1981—; regents prof. U. Calif.; cons. in field. NIMH grantee, 1978-80; Nat. Inst. Neurol. Diseases grantee, 1981—; Office Naval Research grantee, 1980—; Air Force Office Sci. Research grantee, 1981—; Air Force Sch. Aerospace Medicine grantee, 1981—. Mem. AAAS, Soc. Biol. Psychiatry, Am. Epilepsy Soc., IEEE, Soc. Neurosci., Psychophilosophy Soc., Am. EEG Soc., N.Y. Acad. Scis. Contbr. articles in field to profl. jours. Office: 1855 Folsom San Francisco CA 94103

GEVIRTZMAN, ROBERT JOSEPH, management consultant; b. N.Y.C., Jan. 26, 1935; s. Abe and Ida Pauline (Waxler) G.; m. Selma Beatrice Milecofsky, Sept. 2, 1954; children—Debra, Tracy, Susan. B.B.A., CCNY, 1956; M.B.A., NYU, 1957. Systems analyst Sandia Labs., Albuquerque, 1958-61, Gen. Precision Co., Pleasantville, N.Y., 1961-63; systems specialist Gen. Foods Co., White Plains, N.Y., 1963-65; cons. S.D. Leidesdorf, N.Y.C., 1965-67; prin. Peat, Marwick, Mitchell & Co., Albuquerque, 1967—. Mem. fin. com. Albuquerque United Way, 1981-83; fin. com. Temple Albert, Albuquerque, 1981—. Mem. Assn. Systems Mgmt., Greater Albuquerque C. of C., Sandia Heights Civic Assn., Data Processing Mgmt. Assn. (cert. 1963), GUIDE. Democrat. Clubs: Albuquerque Petroleum, Tanoan Country. Contbr. articles in field to profl. jours.

GEWECKE, ROGER LELAND, stockbroker; b. Evanton, Wyo., Apr. 6, 1937; s. Clifford George and Edna Marie (Smith) G.; B.S., U. So. Calif., 1959, M.B.A., 1967; m. Barbara Marie Bilafer, June 27, 1959; children—Roger Leland, Robert, Ellen, Stephen. With Bateman Eichler Hill Richard, Los Angeles, 1960—, v.p., 1974—; tchr. courses in field. Mem. Los Angeles Soc. Fin. Analysts (pres. 1971-72). Clubs: Los Angeles Athletic; Arcadia Rotary. Home: 603 Vaquero Rd Arcadia CA 91006 Office: 277 Solake Ave Pasadena CA 91101

GEWERTER, HAROLD PHILLIP, lawyer; b. Los Angeles, Oct. 1, 1953; s. Fred and Henrietta G.; B.A. with honors (Calif. State scholar), U. So. Calif., 1975, M.S. in Edn., 1977; J.D., Southwestern U. Sch. Law, 1979; m. Karen Livingston, 1981. Tutor counselor, exptl. admissions program, U. So. Calif., Los Angeles, 1971-73, dir. community affairs Sta. KUSC, 1972-74; co-founder, developer, joint ednl. project. Dist. team leader IRS Vol. Income Tax Assistance Program, 1977-78; law clk. to judge 8th Jud. Dist., Las Vegas, 1979; practice law, Las Vegas, 1979—; mem. firm Apple, Zervas & Gewerter, Las Vegas; profl. faculty U. Nev., 1979—. Recipient award for profls. in taxation UCLA, 1979. Mem. Phi Alpha Delta. Address: 6221 Shadywood Dr Las Vegas NV 89102

GEYER, PHILLIP LLEYELLYN, newspaper marketing executive; b. Kingston, Pa., Jan. 6, 1933; s. William Eugene and Isabel (Llewellyn) G.; m. Barbara Ann Sullivan, Dec. 17, 1952; m. Vivian Ailene Shewalter, Nov. 8, 1962; m. Ruth Conn, Aug. 14, 1970; children—Maureen Ann, William James, Stephen Phillip, Cheryl Lynn, Phillip Llewellyn. B.S.J.M., U. Fla., 1963. Chief news bur. Gannett Newspapers, Rochester, N.Y., 1965-66; dir. pub. service Gannett Fla. Newspapers, Cocoa, 1966-68; dir. promotion and research Corpus Christi (Tex.) Caller-Times, 1968-69, dir. promotion and research Dallas Times Herald, 1969-70; promotion dir. San Francisco Newspaper Agy., agt. S.E. Chronicle/San Francisco Examiner, 1970-82, dir. mktg. services, 1982—. Served with USN, 1951-55; Korea. Recipient award Editor & Pub. mag. (8), 1969-82; CLIO award (2), 1977; Cannes Film Festival award, 1977; Atlanta Ad Club award, 1976; N.Y. Internat. Film Festival award, 1976, 79; Cable Car award San Francisco Ad Club, 1976. Mem. San Francisco So. Communication Arts, Internat. Newspaper Promotion Assn. (internat. dir. 1977-81, pres. West region 1975-76), San Francisco Advt. Club (pres.), Sigma Delat Chi (pres. Cape Kennedy chpt. 1966-68). Club: Peninsula Golf and Country (San Mateo, Calif.). Office: 925 Mission St San Francisco CA 94013

GHILARDI, LINNEA PHILLIP, educator; b. Chgo., Jan. 30, 1945; d. William George and Doris (Bartelt) Phillip; B.A., Northwestern U., 1966, M.A., 1967; postgrad. Northeastern Ill. U., 1975-77; m. Lawrence L. Ghilardi, Dec. 22, 1967 (div. Sept. 1980); m. 2d, Steven A. Armstrong, Nov. 25, 1981. Tchr. math. Jackson Jr. High Sch., Villa Park, Ill., 1967-68; tech. editor Bell Telephone Labs., Naperville, Ill., 1968-70; public relations writer Western Electric Co., Rolling Meadows, Ill., 1970-72; tchr. social studies Glenbrook North High Sch., Northbrook, Ill., 1972-78, also instr. history DeLourdes Coll., Des Plaines, Ill., 1971-72, chmn. dept. social studies Helena (Mont.) High Sch., 1978—; cons. Ginn Pub. Co. Fulbright fellow, China, summer 1982. Mem. Mont. Council Social Studies, Nat. Council Social Studies, Assn. Supervision and Curriculum Devel., Alpha Delta Kappa, Delta Kappa Gamma, Phi Delta Kappa. Mem. Baha'i Faith. Editor Mont. Council Social Studies Newsletter, 1979—; contbr. to Exploring World Cultures, 1980. Home: Box 72 Gruber Estates Clancy MT 59634 Office: 1300 Billings Ave Helena MT 59601

GHOLSTON, HELEN ALBERTA, educator; b. Lawrence, Mass., May 13, 1923; d. Albert Clinton and Helen Gertrude (Mitchell) McIlwain; B.A. in English with distinction, San Diego State U., 1976, M.A. in Edn., 1980; m. Andrew J. Gholston, Apr. 25, 1944; children—Andrea, Juanita, Corale, Wendy, Michael, Andrew J. Microfilm operator San Diego City Civil Service, 1957-58; engaged in real estate, 1961-70; tutor EEO program San Diego Community Colls., 1971-75; tchr. San Diego city schs., 1977—, tchr. English, Abraham Lincoln Sr. High Sch., 1979—, chmn. dept., 1980-82, mem. textbook com. San Diego city schs. Mem. Nat. Council Tchrs. English, Assn. Supervision and Curriculum Devel., Nat. Council Negro Women, Am. Bus. Women's Assn. San Diego State U. Alumni Assn., Browning Soc. Baptist. Author articles, Curriculum materials. Home: 5322 Hilltop Dr San Diego CA 92114 Office: Lincoln High Sch 150 S 49th St San Diego CA 92113

GHORMLEY, JOHN HARNED, bldg. contractor; b. Greenfield, Iowa, Aug. 11, 1936; s. Clarence E. and Dorothy (Harned) G.; student Purdue U., 1954; B.S., U. Wis., 1959; m. Anne Doran, May 25, 1960; children—Dorothy Lynne, Rebecca Anne. Assoc. engr. Douglas Aircraft Co., El Segundo, Calif., 1959; civil engring. assoc. City of Torrance, Calif., 1959-62; dir. pub. works-city engr. City of Gardena, Calif., 1962-66, adminstrv. officer, 1966-70; cons. civil engring. practice, Gardena, 1962-66; ptnr. Benner and Ghormley, Santa Paula, Calif., 1970-75; v.p. Ervin, Ghormley, Johnson & Assocs., Los Angeles, 1975-77; pres. Bonita Homes, Inc., 1977—. Adviser, Boy Scout Splty. Explorer Post, 1968-70; bd. mgrs. Gardena Valley YMCA; pres. South County Econ. Devel. Assn. Recipient award for outstanding service Gardena Valley C. of C., 1968. Registered profl. engr., Calif., Fla., Ind. Mem. Sigma Phi. Republican. Presbyterian. Clubs: Masons, Ojai Optimist (pres. 1976), Kiwanis. Home: 980 Branch Mill Rd PO Box 356 Arroyo Grande CA 93420 Office: 1203 Pike Ln PO Drawer B Oceano CA 93445

GHORMLEY, WILLIAM JAMES, civil engr.; b. Fredericktown, Mo., Nov. 26, 1939; s. Clarence Emmett and Dorothy L. (Harned) G.; B.S. in Civil Engr., Wis. State Coll. and Inst. Tech., 1964; m. Karen Jean Bidlingmaier, Jan. 25, 1964; children—Laura Lee, Pamela Jean, Sharon Marie. Chief subdiv. engring. Ventura County (Calif.), 1969-71; prin. Benner and Ghormley Engrs., Santa Paula, Calif., 1971-75, Ervin, Ghormley, Johnson & Assos., Civil Engrs., Camarillo, Calif., 1975-79; owner William J. Ghormley, Cons. Civil Engrs., Ventura, 1979—; dist. engr. Carpinteria San. Dist., 1976-79, Meiners Oaks County Water Dist., 1979—, Ventura River County Water Dist., 1981—. Served with USAR. Registered profl. engr., Calif., Ariz. Mem. ASCE (pres. Santa Barbara-Ventura br. 1972-73), Am. Public Works Assn., Am. Water Works Assn., TriCounties Water Assn., Council Cons. Engrs. of Ventura County (sec.-treas., dir. 1979—, pres. 1981), Sigma Phi. Home: 412 Del Norte Rd Ojai CA 93023 Office: 1587 Morse Ave Ventura CA 93003

GHOSH, SUBIR, statistical researcher and educator; b. Calcutta, India, Aug. 26, 1950; s. Subimal and Padmarenu (Guha); m. Susnata Roy, Apr. 27, 1978; 1 dau., Malancha. M.S. in Stats., Calcutta U., 1970; Ph.D. in Stats., Colo. State U., 1976. Mem. Faculty Indian Statis. Inst., Calcutta, 1976-80; asst. prof. dept. stats. U., Calif.-Riverside, 1980—; researcher; cons. Recipient S.S. Bose Gold medal 1968; U. Calcutta Gold medal 1970. Mem. Am. Statis. Assn., Inst. Math. Stats., Biometric Socs. Contbr. articles to profl. jours. Office: Dept Stats U Calif Riverside CA 92507

GIACOPELLI, JOSEPH A., podiatrist; b. N.Y.C., Feb. 2, 1952; s. James J. and Doris Giacopelli; B.S. in Biology, St. John's U., 1973; D.P.M., Ill. Coll. Podiatric Medicine, 1977. Pvt. practice podiatric medicine and surgery Pico Rivera (Calif.) Podiatrists Group, West Covina (Calif.) Podiatrists Group; on staff French, Beverly, Downey Community, Pico Rivera Community, Lincoln Community, Queen of the Valley, West Covina hosps. Podiatric cons. for Walk-a-thon March of Dimes, 1978-79. Diplomate Am. Bd. Podiatric Examiners. Mem. Am. Podiatry Assn., Calif. Podiatry Assn., Pub. Health Assn., Los Angeles County Podiatry Assn., Assn. Podiatric Pneumo Plesthysmography, Am. Hosp. Podiatrists, Durlacher Honor Soc. Office: 1212 S Glendora West Covina CA 91790 also 8715 Washington Blvd Pico Rivera CA 90660

GIALANELLA, PHILIP THOMAS, publishing co. exec.; b. Binghamton, N.Y., June 6, 1930; s. Felix and Frances (Demuro) G.; B.A., Harpur Coll., 1952; M.A., SUNY, 1955; m. Marie Amelia Davis, May 1, 1953; 1 son, Thomas Davis. Promotion dir. Evening Press and Sta. WINR-TV, Binghamton, 1957-62; v.p., gen. mgr. Daily Advance, Dover, N.J., 1962-66; v.p. Hartford (Conn.) Times, 1966-70; pres., pub. Newburgh (N.Y.) News, 1970-71; exec. v.p. Hawaii Newspaper Agy., Honolulu, 1971-73, pres., 1974—, also dir.; pub. Honolulu Star-Bull., 1975—; pres. Gannett S.W. and Pacific Newspaper Group; v.p., dir. Gannett Pacific Corp.; sec., asst. treas. Newspaper Printing Corp., Newspaper Realty Corp., El Paso, Tex.; dir. Tucson Newspaper Inc., Guam Publs., Capital Investment Co., AP Assn. Calif., Ariz., Hawaii and Nev. Bd. dirs. Honolulu Symphony, Pacific Asian Affairs Council, Aloha United Way; pres. Hawaii Newspaper Agy. Found. Bd. govs. Pacific Asian Affairs Council. Served with AUS, 1952-54. Mem. Am. Newspaper Pubs. Assn. Hawaii Pubs. Assn. Hawaii-Japan Econ. Council (dir.), Nat. Alliance Businessmen (exec. com.). Roman Catholic. Office: 605 Kapiolani Blvd PO Box 3350 Honolulu HI 96801

GIAMBRONE, ANDREA, advertising executive; b. Bklyn., Sept. 27, 1943; d. Andrew and Theresa (Maida) Vetrano. Student NYU, 1960-63. Copywriter, Compton Advt., Los Angeles, 1965-67; copy supr. Kelly Advt., Los Angeles, 1967-69; sr. writer to v.p., copy dir. to sr. v.p., creative dir. Eisaman, Johns & Laws Advt., Los Angeles, 1969—. Guest lectr. UCLA, Santa Monica City Coll., Fashion Inst.; assoc. writer Suzanne Somers' USO TV spls., 1981, 82; career counsellor Calif. State U.-Northridge. Recipient Lulu award Los Angeles Advt. Women; Best in the West award Western States Advt. Assn., 1968, 69, 70, 71, 72, 73, 74, 75; Belding award Belding Awards Com., 1975, 80; award Internat. Mktg. Assn., 1976. Mem. Fashion Group, Los Angeles Creative Club, Los Angeles County Mus. Art, Acad. TV Arts and Scis., Women For, NOW. 1976. Office: Eisaman Johns & Laws Advt 6255 Sunset Blvd 14th Floor Los Angeles CA 90078

GIAMPICCOLO, JAMES STEPHEN, electronic components mfg. co. exec.; b. N.Y.C., Sept. 9, 1920; s. Carmelo and Carmela (Ruggiero) G.; B.Aero. Engring., N.Y. U., 1941; postgrad. N.Y. U., Poly. Inst. Bklyn.; m. Theresa Speciale, Aug. 6, 1944; children—James S., Louise, Laura. Numerous engring. positions, 1941-50; sales engr., eastern tech. rep., spl. programs mgr. Cinch Mfg. Co., Chgo., 1950-68; founder, pres., chmn. bd. Jolo Industries, Inc., Garden Grove, Calif., 1968—. Mem. Electronic Connector Study Group, Alpha Phi Delta. Roman Catholic. Home: 10432 Brightwood Dr Santa Ana CA 92705 Office: 13921 Nautilus Dr Garden Grove CA 92643

GIANELLA, VINCENT P(AUL), cons. geologist, educator; b. Marysville, Calif., Feb. 9, 1886; s. Vincenzo and Mary (Hagan) G.; B.S., Oreg. State U., 1910; M.S., U. Nev., 1920; Ph.D., Columbia, 1937; m. Catherine Thiele, June 27, 1917 (dec.); children—Faith Mary (dec.), Catherine (Mrs. Robert Callahan) (dec.), Vincent P. With mines, ore mills and smelters, Juneau, Alaska, Tonopah, Nev., Douglas, Ariz., 1911-18; cons. geologist 1918—; faculty U. Nev., Reno, 1923-52, prof. emeritus geology, 1952—. Recipient Distinguished Nevadan award U. Nev., 1962; Bronze Bust installed MacKay Sch. Mines, U. Nev., 1973; Am. Fedn. Mineral. Socs. Scholarship Found. plaque, 1975. Fellow Geol. Soc. Am., AAAS; mem. Soc. Econ. Geologists, Seismological Soc. Am., Am. Inst. Mining Engrs. Rotarian. Contbr. articles to profl. jours. Home: 175 Temple Dr Auburn CA 95603

GIANNOTTI, GENE CARMEN, electronics company executive; b. San Francisco, Apr. 22, 1931; s. Fil and Julia (Basile) G.; B.S., U. Santa Clara, 1952; m. Joyce Darlene Baerwald, Aug. 12, 1952; children—Anthony Philip, Christopher Paul, Maria Elizabeth. Registered rep. Sutro & Co., San Francisco, 1954-57; project coordinator Ampex Corp., Redwood City, Calif., 1957-61; logistics group supr. Philco-Ford, Palo Alto, Calif., 1961-64; br. mgr. Statis. Tabulating Corp., San Jose, Calif., 1964-65; systems asso. Bay Area Rapid Transit, San Francisco, 1965-67; project leader GTE Sylvania, Mountain View, Calif., 1967-74, computer services dept. mgr., 1974-80; data center dir. GTE Data Services, 1980-82; dir. mgmt. info. systems Measurex Corp., 1982—. Served with AUS, 1952-54. Decorated Commendation medal. Mem. Data Processing Mgmt. Assn. (chpt. pres. 1971-72). Club: Toastmasters Internat. (chpt. pres. 1978). Home: 1615 Stanford Ave Menlo Park CA 94025 Office: 1 Results Way Cupertino CA 95014

GIBB, JACK REX, psychologist, consultant; b. Magrath, Alta., Can., Dec. 20, 1914; s. John Lye and Ada Laura (Dyer) G.; m. Lorraine Miller, Dec. 29, 1951; children—Lawrence Henry, Blair Bradford, John Randolph. A.B. (fellow), Brigham Young U., 1936, M.A., 1937; Ph.D. (fellow), Stanford U., 1943. Diplomate Am. Bd. Profl. Psychology, 1970. Asst. prof. psychology Brigham Young U., Provo, Utah, 1937-46; prof. psychology Mich. State U., Lansing, 1946-49, U. Colo., Boulder, 1949-56; fellow Fels Group Dynamics Ctr., Newark, Del., 1956-64, Western Behavioral Scis. Inst., 1964-67; cons., 1952—; pvt. practice psychology, 1952—; pres. TORI Assocs., dir. TORI profl. intern program. Served with U.S. Army, 1943-46. Ford Found. fellow, 1951-52; recipient Sigma Xi research award, 1937. Mem. Am. Psychol. Assn., Assn. Humanistic Psychology, Am. Sociol. Assn. Democrat. Mormon. Contbr. articles to profl. jours. Home and Office: 8475 La Jolla Scenic Dr N La Jolla CA 92037

GIBB, RICHARD DEAN, univ. pres.; b. Smithshire, Ill., Dec. 6, 1928; s. Edward Dale and Anna Marie (Anderson) G.; student Western Ill. U., 1947-50; B.S., U. Ill., 1951, M.E., 1955; Ph.D., Mich. State U., 1958; m. Betty G. Epperson, Dec. 22, 1951; children—Richie William, Connie Marie. Faculty agrl. econs. Western Ill. U., Macomb, 1958-68, prof., 1965-68, adminstrv. asst. to pres., 1964-67, dean adminstrn., 1967-68, acting coordinator internat. programs, 1964-67, dean adminstrn., 1967-68, acting coordinator internat. programs, 1964-65; S.D. commr. for higher edn., Pierre, 1968-74; Ind. commr. for higher edn., Indpls., 1974-77; pres. U. Idaho, 1977—. Served with AUS, 1952-53. Mem. Am. Assn. Higher Edn., Statewide Higher Edn. Assn., Am. Agrl. Econs. Assn., Delta Sigma Phi. Home: 1026 Nez Perce Dr Moscow ID 83843 Office: Office of the President U Ida Moscow ID 83843

GIBBONS, BENJAMIN FRANKLIN, safety engineer; b. Wilmington, Del., Mar. 29, 1953; s. Donald Merritt and Elizabeth Jane (Weyl) G.; m. Rosemarie Yoshiko Markgraf, Aug. 2, 1980. B.A. in Psychology, Ind. U., 1979; M.S. in Indsl., Organizational Psychology, Purdue U., 1983. Sr. med. technician, instr. Dept. Def., Ft. Harrison, Ind., 1978-81; sr. med. instr. Ind. Vocat. Sch., Indpls., 1977-80; sr. safety engr. Hosp. Shared Service of Colo., State of Colo., Denver, 1981—; cons. in field. Instr. CPR, Am. Heart Assn., ARC, 1975—. Served with U.S. Army, 1972-78. Recipient cert. Patriotic Civilian Service, U.S. Army, 1981; Service award ARC, 1978. Mem. Am. Psychol. Assn., Am. Soc. Safety Engrs., Colo. Hosp. Assn., Colo. Hosp. Safety Assn. Republican. Home: 1305 S Joplin St Aurora CO 80017 Office: 333 E 19th Ave Denver CO 80203

GIBBONS, GEORGE EDWARD, range conservationist; b. Phoenix, Aug. 16, 1940; s. Charles Agustus and Velda Olea (Wiltbank) G.; m. Linda Carter, Sept. 2, 1965; children—Karyn, Maverick, Jonna, Sherra, Carter, Casey, Trym, Heath, Brock, Vince. A.A., Eastern Ariz. Coll., 1960; B.S., Brigham Young U., 1965; postgrad. N. Mex. State U., Las Cruces, 1967. County exec. dir. agr. stblzn. and conservation service U.S. Dept. Agr., Clayton, N. Mex., 1968-75; range conservationist U.S. Forest Service, Luna, N. Mex., 1975—, EEO counselor, 1978—. Active Boy Scouts Am., 1952-58, Clayton (N. Mex.) Jr. C. of C., 1970-75; bd. dirs. Res. Ind. Sch. Dist. N. Mex., 1975—; bishop Ch. of Jesus Christ of Latter-day Saints (N. Mex.), 1978—. Mem. N. Mex. Assn. County Office Employees (pres. 1973-74), Nat. Rifle Assn., Lamba Delta Sigma. Republican. Club: Stockman's. Home: PO Box 90 Luna NM 87824 Office: PO Box 91 Luna NM 87824

GIBBONS, JERRY LEE, advertising executive; b. Coalinga, Calif., Feb. 10, 1936; s. James A. and Hazel Bernice (Drummond) G.; m. Alba Valdez, Feb. 22, 1963; children—Jeffery Scott, Cristin Lyn, Trisha Leigh. B.A., San Jose State Coll., 1958. Trainee Young & Rubicam, San Francisco, 1957; account exec. McCann Erickson, San Francisco, 1960-63; asst. to pres. Western Outdoor Markets, San Francisco, 1964; v.p., sales mgr. Naegele Outdoor Advt., Oakland, Calif., 1965-67; account exec. Blair Radio, San Francisco, 1968, Campbell-Ewald, San Francisco, 1969; v.p., account supr. Dailey & Assocs., San Francisco, 1970-71; co-founder, pres. Pritikin & Gibbons Communications, San Francisco, 1971-73; pres. Ayer/Pritikin & Gibbons, San Francisco, 1973-81; pres. Doyle Dane Bernbach, San Francisco, 1981—. Bd. dirs. Oakland Symphony. Served with AUS, 1958-60. Mem. San Francisco Soc. Communicating Arts (past pres.), San Francisco Ad Club (pres.), Sales & Mktg. Assn. San Francisco (past dir.). Presbyterian. Home: 1767 Woodhaven Way Oakland CA 94611 Office: Doyle Dane Bernbach 425 Bush St San Francisco CA 94108

GIBBS, JACQUELINE, mathematics educator, businesswoman; b. Newnan, Ga., Mar. 13, 1942; d. George W. and Isma Lee (Howard) Gibbs; B.S. in Math. and Sci., Tenn. A&I U., 1962; M.A. in Adminstrn. and Supervision, Calif. State U.-Hayward, 1973. Math. tchr., Kansas City, Kans., 1962-67, Berkeley (Calif.) Unified Sch. Dist., 1967-69, Peralta Coll., Oakland, Calif., 1973—; owner, operator Gibbs Bookkeeping and Tax Service, Oakland, Calif., 1970—; co-pres. Digital Acctg. Inc., 1983—; cons., leader tax planning seminars. Chmn. Berkeley Tchrs. Negotiating Com., 1974, founder girls' club West Campus Berkeley High Sch., asst. dir. Right-to-Read Program, 1974. Named Outstanding Secondary Tchr. Berkeley; recipient award Pearl S. Buck Found., 1976, cert. leadership devel. Cornell U., 1977. Mem. Nat. Assn. Accts., Nat. Assn. Enrolled Agts., Bay Area Women Entrepreneurs, Oakland Mcht. Assn., Nat. Assn. Tax Cons. Nat. Notary Assn., Calif. Assn. Enrolled Agts., Nat. Council Negro Women (life). Office: Digital Accounting Inc 436 14th St Suite 150 Oakland CA 94612

GIBBS, JEWELLE TAYLOR, psychologist, educator; b. Stratford, Conn., Nov. 4, 1933; d. Julian Augustus and Margaret Pauline (Morris) Taylor; m. James Lowell Gibbs, Jr., Aug. 25, 1956; children—Geoffrey Taylor, Lowell Dabney. A.B. cum laude, Radcliffe Coll., 1955; postgrad. Harvard-Radcliffe Program in Bus. Adminstrn., 1959; M.S.W., U. Calif., Berkeley, 1970, Ph.D., 1980. Jr. mgmt. asst. U.S. Dept. Labor, Washington, 1955-56; market research coordinator Pillsbury Co., Mpls., 1959-61; clin. social worker Stanford (Calif.) U. Student Health Service, 1970-74, 78-79, research assoc. dept. psychiatry, 1971-73; asst. prof. Sch. Social Welfare, U. Calif.-Berkeley, 1979—. Bd. regents U. Santa Clara (Calif.), 1980-84. Mem. Minn. State Commn. on Status of Women, 1963-65; co-chairperson Minn. Women's Com. for Civil Rights, 1963-65. NIMH fellow, 1979; Soroptimist Internat. grantee, 1978-79. Fellow Am. Orthopsychiat. Assn.; mem. Am. Psychol. Assn., Nat. Assn. Social Workers, Western Psychol. Assn. Democrat. Mem. editorial bd. Am. Jour. Orthopsychiatry, 1980—; bd. publs. Nat. Assn. Social Workers, 1980-82; contbr. chpts. to books, articles to profl. jours. Office: Haviland Hall Sch Social Welfare U Calif Berkeley CA 94720

GIBBS, RANDALL LEE, pharmacist; b. Los Angeles, Jan. 19, 1947; s. Don Fredric Gibbs and Sheryn (Kimball) Gibbs Hughes; m. Valerie Mary Cayongcong, June 4, 1983. B.S. in Pharmacy, U. Pacific, 1970. Staff pharmacist Red Cross Drugstore, Coos Bay, Oreg., 1976-77; dir. pharmacy services Tracy (Calif.) Community Meml. Hosp., 1977-82; owner Mark Twain Pharmacy, Altaville, Calif., 1982—. Served to capt. USAF, 1971-76. Mem. Central Valley Soc. Hosp. Pharmacists, Am. Soc. Hosp. Pharmacists, Calif. Soc. Hosp. Pharmacists, Am. Pharm. Assn., Calif. Pharm. Assn., Alaska Prospectors Soc., Sierra Club. Home: PO Box 850 Altaville CA 95221 Office: Mark Twain Pharmacy 362 N Main St Altaville CA 95221

GIBBS, THOMAS GLYNN, architect; b. Athens, Tex., Sept. 21, 1948; s. Billy Jack and Martha June (Bement) G., student Tex. Tech. U., 1967-73, B. Arch., 1975; student N. Tex. State U., 1975; m. Johanna Kathleen O'Neill, July 26, 1975. Project architect Harwood K. Smith & Ptnr., Dallas, 1973-78; head of prodn. Fowler/Ferguson/Kingston/Ruben Architects, Rexburg, Idaho 1978-79, head field supervision, 1979-82, pres., 1982—; sec., ptnr.-in-charge Gotham Enterprises, Salt Lake City, 1982—. Scoutmaster, Boy Scouts Am., Salt Lake City, 1978-79. Registered architect, Tex.; cert. fallout shelter analyst. Mem. Rexburg C. of C. Alpha Tau Omega. Democrat. Mormon. Home: 235 W 400 S Rexburg ID 83440 Office: 350 S 400 E #300 Salt Lake City UT 84121

GIBLETT, PHYLIS LEE WALZ, educator; b. Denver, July 17, 1945; d. Henry and Leah (Pabst) Walz; B.S.B.A. (Estelle Hunter scholar 1963, Denver Classroom Tchr.'s scholar 1963, Outstanding Bus. Edn. Student scholar 1967), U. Denver, 1967, M.B.A., 1969; m. Thomas Giblett, May 31, 1975; children—Leann Ruth, Douglas Henry. Tchr. bus. Aurora (Colo.) Central High Sch., Aurora Public Schs., 1967-80, 82—, on leave, 1980-82, chmn. bus. dept., 1972-79; evening tchr. S.E. Met. Bd. Coop Services, 1967-68, post secondary/adult classes Aurora Public Schs., 1972-75, Community Coll. Denver, North Campus, 1973; mem. Dist. Tchr. Adv. Com., 1975-79; adviser chpt. Future Bus. Leaders Am., 1976-78; mem. Colo. Curriculum Specialist Com., 1976-77. Named Miss Future Bus. Tchr., Phi Beta Lambda of Colo., 1965. Mem. Nat. Mountain-Plains (participant leadership conf. 1977), Colo. (pres. 1976-77) bus. edn. assns., Colo. Educators for/About Bus., Am., Colo. vocat. assns., NEA, Colo., Aurora edn. assns., Delta Pi Epsilon (pres.-elect Eta chpt. 1978, pres. 1980-81). Republican. Lutheran.

GIBSON, ARTHUR CHARLES, biologist, educator; b. Bronx, N.Y., Oct. 16, 1947; s. Richard Goodwin and Rosalie (Reinhardt) G.; m. Linda Lee Corey, Aug. 15, 1970; children—Heather Elizabeth, Erin Kathryn. B.A. in Botany, Miami U., 1969; Ph.D. in Botany, Claremont (Calif.) Grad. Sch., 1973. Asst. prof. U. Ariz., Tucson, 1973-79, assoc. prof., 1979-80; assoc. prof. UCLA, 1980—, also dir. Mildred E. Mathias Bot. Garden. Mem. Bot. Soc. Am., Am. Assn. Plant Taxonomists, Soc. Systematic Zoologists, Ecol. Soc. Am. Author: (with J.H. Brown) Biogeography, 1983; contbr. articles to profl. jours. Office: Dept Biology UCLA Los Angeles CA 90024

GIBSON, BARBARA JOHNSON, electronics company executive, financial administrator; b. Southbridge, Mass., July 19, 1954; d. Robert Barrows and Jan (Huey) Johnson. B.A. in Psychology, U. Denver, 1975; M.B.A. in Fin., 1978; postgrad. Golden Gate U., 1983—. Asst. dir. Johnson McFarlane Dormitory, U. Denver, 1972-75; asst. to v.p. fin., mktg. First Capitol Mortgage Co., Englewood, Colo., 1978-79; area mgr. Adolph Coors Co., 1979-81; sr. fin. adminstr. Applied Tech. div. Litton Industries, Sunnyvale, Calif., 1982—; part-time counselor personnel fin. planning. Mem. Inst. Cert. Fin. Planners.

GIBSON, BILL NEIL, JR., advertising agency executive; b. Olney, Ill., Sept. 21, 1956; s. Bill Neil and Barbara Rose (Larkin) G.; m. Cynthia Renee Bromley, June 4, 1977. B.S. in Journalism, So. Ill. U.-Carbondale, 1978. With advt. dept. Champion Labs., Inc., West Salem, Ill., 1978-79; writer Barnhart Advt., Denver, 1979-81; owner Bill Gibson Advt., Denver, 1981—. Elected del. Democratic Nat. Conv., 1976. Baptist. Home: 4490 E 118th Pl Northglenn CO 80233 Office: PO Box 33234 Northglenn CO 80233

GIBSON, BRUCE, executive recruiter; b. Hartford, Sept. 24, 1940; s. Nelson and Helen Mary (Janek) G.; B.S., UCLA, 1964; m. Barbara Anne Bares, Nov. 25, 1961; children—William, Robert, Leslie. Vice pres. Hergenrather, Gibson, Hanrahan & Assocs., Los Angeles, 1969-71; founder, sr. v.p. N.W. Gibson Assocs., Los Angeles, 1971-80; pres., chmn. Gibson & Co., Los Angeles, 1980—. Roman Catholic. Office: PO Box 7000-318 Palos Verdes CA 90274

GIBSON, DAVID, educator; b. Galt, Ont., Can., Apr. 6, 1926; s. John William and Martha (Sweeney) G.; B.A., U. Toronto, 1950, M.A., 1952, Ph.D., 1960; m. Kathleen May Sudbury, Sept. 9, 1961; children—Martha, Jennifer, Judith, Peter, John. Chief psychologist Rideau Hosp. Sch., Ontario, Can., 1952-62; prof. U. Calgary (Alta., Can.), dir., exec. v.p. Vocat. and Rehab. Research Inst., 1965-70. Served with Canadian Army, 1944-46. Fellow Am. Assn. Mental Deficiency; mem. Am. Psychol. Assn., Council for Exceptional Children, Psychologists Assn. Alta. (past pres.), Canadian Psychol. Assn. (past pres.). Editor: Canadian Psychol. Rev. Home: 2411 Usher Rd Calgary AB Canada

GIBSON, DAVID JAMES, physician; b. Cin., May 1, 1945; s. James David and Elizabeth (Shaw) G.; A.B., Asbury Coll., 1967; M.D., U. Ky., 1971. Med. intern Ind. U. Med. Center, Indpls., 1971-72, med. resident, 1972-73; research fellow Harvard Med. Sch. Robert B. Brigham Hosp., Boston, 1973-75; clin. asso. prof. medicine La. State U., New Orleans, 1975; practice medicine specializing in rheumatology and internal medicine, Santa Barbara, Calif., 1977—; attending physician Keesler Air Force Med. Center, Biloxi, Miss., 1975-77; physician, dept. medicine, div. rheumatology Santa Barbara Med. Found. Clinic, 1977—; clin. asst. prof. medicine UCLA, 1977—; Bd. dirs. Arthritis Found., 1977—, mem. med. and sci. com. So. Calif. chpt., 1979—; trustee Meml. Rehab. Hosp., Santa Barbara, 1978—; bd. dirs. Health Force Inc. Served to maj., M.C., USAF, 1975-77. Diplomate Am. Bd. Internal Medicine. Mem. Calif. Med. Assn., Santa Barbara Soc. Internal Medicine (v.p.), Santa Barbara County Med. Soc., New Eng. Rheumatism Soc., So. Calif. Rheumatism Soc., Am. Rheumatism Assn., Soc. of Air Force Physicians, AAAS. Contbr. articles on rheumatology to med. jours. Home: 1129 Las Olas Ave Santa Barbara CA 93109 Office: 215 Pesetas Ln Santa Barbara CA 93102

GIBSON, EDWARD FERGUS, physicist, educator; b. Colorado Springs, Colo., Apr. 2, 1937; s. George Merrick and Elsie Ida (Schnurr) G.; B.A., U. Colo., 1959, M.A., 1964, Ph.D., 1966; m. Harriette Graham DuShane, June 1, 1963; children—Sascha, Graham, Clark, Eileen. Physicist, Nat. Bur. Standards, Boulder, Colo., 1958-64; research asst., research asso. U. Colo., Boulder, 1964-66; postdoctoral research asso. U. Oreg., Eugene, 1966-68; scientist-in-residence Naval Radiol. Def. Lab., San Francisco, 1968-69; prof. physics, Calif. State U., Sacramento, 1969—, dept. chmn., 1979—; cons. on alternative energy sources Calif. Energy Commn., 1977-78; cons. computer assisted instrn. Control Data Corp., 1981—. Associated Western Univs. fellow, 1971, 72, 73. Mem. Am. Phys. Soc., Phi Beta Kappa, Sigma Xi, Sigma Pi Sigma. Home: 527 Blackwood St Sacramento CA 95815 Office: Dept Physics Calif State U Sacramento 6000 J St Sacramento CA 95819

GIBSON, ELISABETH JANE, principal; b. Salina, Kans., Apr. 28, 1937; d. Cloyce Wesley and Margaret Mae (Yost) Kasson; m. William Douglas Miles, Jr., Aug. 20, 1959; m. Harry Benton Gibson, Jr., July 1, 1970. A.B., Colo. State Coll., 1954-57; M.A. (fellow), San Francisco State Coll., 1967-68; Ed.D., U. No. Colo., 1978; postgrad. U. Denver, 1982. Cert. tchr., prin., Colo. Tchr. elem. schs., Santa Paula, Calif., 1957-58, Salina, Kans., 1958-63, Goose Bay, Labrador, 1963-64, Jefferson County, Colo., 1965-66, Topeka, 1966-67; diagnostic tchr. Cen. Kans. Diagnostic Remedial Edn. Ctr., Salina, 1968-70; instr. Loretto Heights Coll., Denver, 1970-72; co-owner Ednl. Cons. Enterprises, Inc., Greeley, Colo., 1974-77; resource coordinator Region VIII Resource Access Project Head Start Mile High Consortium, Denver, 1976-77; exec. dir. Colo. Fedn. Council Exceptional Children, Denver, 1976-77; asst. prof. Met. State Coll., Denver, 1979; dir. spl. edn. Northeast Colo. Bd. Coop. Edn. Services, Haxtun, Colo., 1979-82; prin. elem. jr. high sch., Elizabeth, Colo., 1982—; cons. Montana Dept. Edn., 1978-79, Love Pub. Co., 1976-78, Colo. Dept. Inst., 1974-75; pres. Found. Exceptional Children, 1980-81; pres. bd. dirs. Northeast Colo. Services Handicapped, 1981-82; bd. dirs. Dept. Ednl. Specialists, Colo. Assn. Sch. Execs., 1982-84; mem. Colo. Title IV Adv. Council, 1980-82. Mem. Colo. Dept. Edn. Data Acquisition Reporting and Utilization Com., 1983, Denver City County Commn. for Disabled, 1978-81; chmn. regional edn. com. 1970 White House Conf. Children and Youth. Recipient Ann. Service award Colo. Fedn. Council Exceptional Children, 1981. Mem. Colo. Assn. Retarded Citizens, Assn. Supervision Curriculum Devel., Nat. Assn. Elem. Sch. Prins., Kappa Delta Pi, Pi Lambda Theta, Phi Delta Kappa. Republican. Methodist. Club: Order Eastern Star. Author: (with H. Padzensky) Goal Guide: A minicourse in writing goals and behavioral objectives for special education, 1975; (with H. Padzensky and S. Sporn) Assaying Student Behavior: A minicourse in student assessment techniques, 1974. Contbr. articles to profl. jours. Home: 2443 S Colorado Blvd Denver CO 80222 Office: Elizabeth School PO Box 490 Elizabeth CO 80107

GIBSON, GEORGE, artist; b. Edinburgh, Scotland, Oct. 16, 1904; s. George and Elizabeth L. (Gilchrist) G.; student Edinburgh Sch. Art, Glasgow Sch. Art, Chouinard Art Inst., Los Angeles; pupil William E. Glover, F. Tolles Chamberlain; m. Alice C. Milligan, June 4, 1937; 1 dau., Jean. Came to U.S., 1930, naturalized, 1938. Scenic art dir., head scenic art dept. Metro-Goldwyn-Mayer Studios, 1934-69. One-man shows include: Chabot Galleries, Los Angeles, 1950, Long Beach, Calif., 1950, Laguna Beach (Calif.). Art Assn., 1951, Santa Barbara Mus. Art, 1952, Santa Monica Library Art Gallery, 1958, St. Mary's Coll., 1958, A. Huney Gallery, 1982; exhibited Am. Watercolor Soc. anns., 1945-72, Calif. Watercolor Soc. anns. and travelling shows, All Cities Art Festival annuals, 1970, 72, also galleries, museums in U.S.; represented in permanent collections San Diego Mus., Newport Union High Sch., Los Angeles County Mus., Santa Paula C. of C., Laguna Beach Art Gallery. Recipient 1st prize Santa Paula Ann., 1946, 63, 72, City Los Angeles Ann., 1947, 49, Santa Cruz Ann., 1948, 50, Ariz. State Fair, 1948, Montgomery (Ala.) Exhbn., 1949, Westwood Art Assn. Ann., 1951, Calif. Watercolor Soc. 32d Ann., 1953, Newport Beach 6th Ann., 1953; also numerous 2d and 3d prizes, hon. mentions. Served with USMCR, World War II. Asso. NAD (watercolor award 1959); mem. Am. (Verda McCracken award 1972), Calif. (pres. 1950-51) watercolor socs., Acad. Motion Picture Arts and Scis. Home: 1449 Santa Maria Ave Los Osos CA 93402 Office: care A Huney Gallery 3746 6th Ave San Diego CA 92103

GIBSON, HARRY LEE, information systems educator, consultant; b. Shirley, Mo., Dec. 18, 1932; s. James Harrison and Eula Faye (Johnson) G.; m. Anita Sue Gremore, Jan. 11, 1955; children—Steven, Grant, Suzanne, Paul, Craig, Alisa. B.S., S.W. Mo. State U., 1956; M.S., U. Wyo., 1961; Ph.D., U. Iowa, 1964. Assoc. prof. bus. Ga. State U., Atlanta, 1963-66; prof. info. systems Colo. State U., Ft. Collins. 1966—; mem. staff USDA Computer Ctr., 1979—. Served with U.S. Army, 1953-55. Grantee U.S. Air Force Office Sci. Research, 1972-74, U.S. Dept. Justice Law Enforcement Assistance Adminstrn. Mem. Assn. Ednl. Data Systems, Am. Bus. Communications Assn. Baptist. Co-author: Introduction to Computers and Information Systems, 1983. Home: 4926 E Ridge Fort Collins CO 80526 Office: Colo State U B-344 Clark Bldg CIS Dept Fort Collins CO 80523

GIBSON, JAMES ANDREW, management consultant; b. San Francisco, Sept. 22, 1948; s. Robert Ross and Lucile (Elvin) G.; m. Char Eleen Maass, 1971 (div.). B.S. in Agrl. Econs. with high honors U. Calif. 1971, Ph.D. in Resource Econs., Iowa State U. 1976. Prin. agrl. economist Harza Engring. Co., Chgo. 1976-78; prin. Arthur Young & Co., Sacramento 1978—. Bd. dirs. Capitol City Ballet, Sacramento, YMCA Sacramento. Contbr. articles to profl. jours. Home: 15 Noah Ct Sacramento CA 95831 Office: 555 Capitol Mall Suite 1490 Sacramento CA 95814

GIBSON, JAMES EDWARD, coll. dean; b. Harrison, Ark., Aug. 12, 1929; s. James M. and Beula (Fernside) G.; B.S., S.W. Mo. State Coll., 1953; M.A., Colo. State Coll., 1955; Ed.D., U. Ariz., 1961; m. Mary Sue Smith, Mar. 25, 1951. Tchr., Tucson High Sch., 1955-57; asst. dean continuing edn. and summer sessions U. Ariz., Tucson, 1957-60, placement dir., 1960-63, alumni dir., 1963-67; pres. Coll. Artesia (N.Mex.), 1968-73; exec. dean Pima Coll., Tucson, 1973—; cons. S.W. Co-op. Edn. Lab., 1968—. Bd. dirs. Cerebral Palsy Assn. Ariz.; pres. Artesia Airport Authority, after 1968; bd. dirs. Amphitheater Sch., Sunday Evening Forum. Served with AUS, 1950-53. Mem. Flying Farmers Assn. Ariz. (adv. bd.), Phi Delta Kappa. Clubs: Masons, Artesia Country, Univ. (Phoenix) (dir.). Contbr. articles to profl. jours., newspapers. Home: 1627 Entrada Tercera Tucson AZ 85718

GIBSON, JAMES I., state senator, civil engineer; b. Golden, Colo., Mar. 22, 1925; m. Audrey Brinley; children—James Brinley, David Scott, Robin Lee Hales, Terry Lynn Walker, Cynthia Rae, Holly Jo. Student U. Kans., U. Colo., U.S. Naval Acad., B.S., U.S. Naval Acad., postgrad., B.C.E., M.C.E., Rensselaer Poly. Inst. Registered profl. engr., Nev., Ariz. Vice pres., dir. Pacific Engring. and Prodn. Co. of Nev., Henderson; mem. Nev. Assembly, 1959-66, Nev. Senate, 1967—, maj. leader, 1977-81. Mem. Western Interstate Com. Workmen's Compensation, 1959-60, Joint Interregional Conf. Water Problems, 1959-60, Higher Edn. Adv. Com., 1967-70; v.p. Western Conf. Council State Govts., 1967-68, pres., 1968-69, exec. bd., 1970-79, bd. govs., 1968-79; v.p. Boulder Dam Area council Boy Scouts Am., 1965-70, treas., 1970, exec. bd., 1970-80; exec. com. Nat. Conf. State Legislatures, 1977-79; pres. Lake Mead stake Ch. of Jesus Christ of Latter-day Saints, regional rep., 1973-80. Served with USN, World War II and Korea. Mem. Am. Inst. Plant Engrs. Democrat. Home: 806 Park Ln Henderson NV 89015 Office: State Senate Legislative Bldg Carson City NV 89701*

GIBSON, KIRK RUSHMORE, research engineer; b. Nashville, Feb. 11, 1946; s. Charles Kirker and Helen Margaret (Marvel) G.; m. Sara Louise Lohse, Dec. 12, 1971; 1 son, Joshua Charles. B.S., Stanford U., 1968; post grad., U. Calif., Berkeley, 1968-69. Research engr. Chevron Research Co., Richmond, Calif., 1969-81; sr. research engr., 1981—. Mem. Am. Inst. Chem. Engrs., Am. Chem. Soc. Methodist. Contbr. articles to profl. jours; patentee of numerous petroleum processing devices. Office: 576 Standard Ave Richmond CA 94802

GIBSON, MELVIN ROY, educator; b. St. Paul, Nebr., June 11, 1920; s. John and Jennie Irene (Harvey) G.; B.S., U. Nebr., 1942, M.S., 1947; Ph.D., U. Ill., 1949. Asst. prof. pharmacognosy Wash. State U., Pullman, 1949-52, asso. prof., 1952-55, prof., 1955—; sr. vis. fellow OECD, Royal Pharm. Inst., Stockholm, also U. Leiden, Holland, 1962. Served as arty. officer AUS, 1942-46. Decorated Bronze Star, Purple Heart; recipient Nat. Kappa Psi citation for service, 1961; Rufus A. Lyman award; founder, charter mem. Am. Diplomates in Pharmacy. Fellow AAAS, Soc. Public Health Edn.; asso. fellow Am. Coll. Apothecaries; mem. N.Y. Acad. Sci., Am. Pharm. Assn., Am. Soc. Pharmacognosy (pres. 1964-65), Am. Assn. Coll. Pharmacy (exec. com. 1961-63, dir. 1977-79, chmn. council of faculties 1975-76, pres. 1979-80), U.S. Pharmacopeia (revision com. 1970-75), Am. Found. Pharm. Edn. (life; vice-chmn. bd. 1982-83, exec. com. 1981, 82, 83, dir. 1979—), AAUP, Acad. Pharm. Sci., Am. Public Health Assn., Fed. Internat. Pharm., Am. Inst. History of Pharmacy, Am. Acad. Polit. and Social Sci., Sigma Xi, Kappa Psi, Rho Chi, Phi Kappa Phi, Omicron Delta Kappa. Democrat. Presbyterian. Club: Spokane. Editor Am. Jour. Pharm. Edn., 1956-61; editorial bd., co-author: Remington's Pharm. Sci., 1970, 75, 80, 85; editor, co-author Studies of a Pharm. Curriculum, 1967; author over 100 articles. Home: SE 625 Spring St Pullman WA 99163 Office: Coll Pharmacy Wash State U Pullman WA 99164

GIBSON, PAUL RAYMOND, international trade and investment development consultant; b. Cathay, Calif., Apr. 10, 1924; s. Otto and Louella (Vestal) G.; m. Janice Elizabeth Carter, Dec. 19, 1952; children—Scott C., Paula S. B.S. in Internat. Commerce, Georgetown U., 1956. Export mgr. Asia Philip Morris Co., San Francisco, 1952-54; founder, v.p., gen. mgr. McGregor and Werner Internat. div., Washington, 1954-62, v.p., dir. McGregor and Werner, Inc., 1955-62; v.p. fin. Parsons & Whittemore, Inc., N.Y.C., 1962-65; founder, pres. Paul R. Gibson and Assocs., Washington, 1965-70; mng. dir. Black Clawson Pacific Co., Sydney, Australia, 1970-72; pres. Envirotech Asia Pacific, Sydney, 1972-74, pres. Envirotech Internat., Menlo Park, Calif., 1975-80; founder, pres. INTERACT, Burlingame, Calif., 1980—; dir. Emico K.C.P., Ltd., India, Projects Internat. Corp., Mountain States Mineral Enterprises, Odino Valperga Italeuropa S.p.A., Italy, Intered; mem. Pecten Coal Pipeline Project Exec. Com., 1983—. Mem. Pacific Basin Econ. Council Exec. Com., vice chmn. govt. liaison U.S. Sect., 1976—; mem. SRI Internat.-Internat. Assocs. Program, 1976—; mem. Japan-Calif. Assn. 1976—; trustee World Affairs Council No. Calif., 1978—; mem. San Francisco Com. Foreign Relations, 1980—; bd. dirs. Action for World Devel., 1981—; vice chmn. San Francisco Dist. Export Council, 1982—; mem. adv. council Bus. and Social Policy Program, U. Calif.-Berkeley Bus. Sch., 1982—. Served to sgt. USMC, 1941-45. Mem. U.S. C. of C. (mem. internat. policy com., chmn. internat. forum Western region 1980—, chmn. Asia-Pacific council Am. C. of C. 1974, mem. adv. com. 1975—). Clubs: Internat. (Washington); Am. Nat. (Sydney, Australia). Home: 801 Irwin Dr Hillsborough CA 94010 Office: 1350 Old Bayshore Hwy Suite 750 Burlingame CA 94010

GIBSON, ROBERT LEE, food company executive; b. Anaheim, Calif., Feb. 14, 1919; s. Robert Lee and Dorothy (Morrison) G.; B.S., U. Calif., 1940; M.S., MIT, 1955; m. Charlotte Lowe, June 1, 1940; children—Anne, Carol, Robert, Ellen, Thomas. With Libby, McNeill & Libby, 1940-67, v.p., gen. mgr. West Coast div., San Francisco, 1958-62, dir., 1961-67, pres., Chgo., 1962-67; pres. Calif. Canners and Growers Coop., 1967—. Trustee Nutrition Found., Golden Gate U., San Francisco. Served as 2d lt. CIC, AUS, World War II. Mem. Soc. Sloan Fellows, Theta Delta Chi. Office: Calif Canners & Growers 3100 Ferry Bldg San Francisco CA 94106

GIBSON, ROY BERRETT, educator; b. North Ogden, Utah, Feb. 17, 1924; s. John William and Hazel (Berrett) G.; B.F.A., U. Utah, 1949; m. Bena Le Bowring, Mar. 22, 1948; children—Robert Barrett, Kathy Danielle, Cory Denise, Wendy Jo, Laurie Lee, Susan Kaye. Comml. announcer sta. KTVT-TV, Salt Lake City, 1952-57; newscaster KDYL Radio, Salt Lake City, 1957; news dir. KTVT-TV, 1958-62, KCPX-TV, Salt Lake City, 1962-72; guest lectr. U. Utah Sch. Journalism, 1968-72, vis. prof., 1972-73, asso. prof. communication, 1973—. Served with AUS, 1943-46. Mem. Radio-TV News Dirs. Assn., Assn. Edn. in Journalism, Nat. Broadcast Editorial Assn., Sigma Delta Chi (chpt. pres. 1965, regional dir. 1970-72). Club: Exchange (pres. Salt Lake City 1968-69). Home: 561 Northmont Way Salt Lake City UT 84103

GIBSON, WILLIAM G., accountant; b. Salt Lake City, Aug. 22, 1946; s. William M. and Katherine T. Lupas; m. Christine Scothern, Feb. 15, 1974. B.S. in Acctg., U. Pacific, 1970; LL.B., La Salle U., 1974; C.P.A., Utah. Area dir. Person-Wolinsky C.P.A. Rev. Course, Salt Lake City, 1979-81; gen. ptnr., mgr. Gibson Investment Fund., 1980—; owner William Gibson, C.P.A.s, 1979—; tchr. Bryman Sch.; fin. cons. Mem. Am. Inst. C.P.A.s. Contbr. articles to profl. jours. Office: 455 S 3d E Salt Lake City UT 84111

GICLAS, HENRY LEE, astronomer; b. Flagstaff, Ariz., Dec. 9, 1910; s. Eli and Hedwig Herminna (Leissling) G.; B.S., U. Ariz., 1937; postgrad. U. Calif. at Berkeley, 1939-40; Ph.D. (hon.), No. Ariz. U., 1980; m. Bernice Francis Kent, May 23, 1936; 1 son, Henry Lee. Research asst. Lowell Obs., Flagstaff, Ariz., 1931-44, astronomer, 1944-79, exec. sec., 1952-75; adj. prof. Ohio State U., Columbus, 1968-79, No. Ariz. U., 1972—. Mem. Flagstaff Freeholder's Com., 1959; exec. v.p. Raymond Ednl. Found., 1971-77, pres., 1977—. Fellow AAAS; mem. Am. Astron. Soc., Ariz. Acad. Sci., Astron. Soc. Pacific (dir. 1959-61), No. Ariz. Pioneers Hist. Soc. (pres. 1972-80), Internat. Astron. Union. Elk. Clubs: Coconino Country (pres. 1962), Continental Country (adv. bd. 1972-75). Home: 120 E Elm Ave Flagstaff AZ 86001 Office: Lowell Obs Flagstaff AZ 86002

GIDDINGS, CRANDALL BLAND, physician, specialist nuclear medicine; b. Weiser, Idaho, Dec. 28, 1915; s. Luther E. and Berniece Chipman (Crandall) G.; B.S., Brigham Young U., 1938; M.S., U. Cin., 1939, Ph.D., 1943, M.D., 1947; m. Elizabeth Ann Kiefer, Aug. 14, 1952 (dec. 1971), children—Luther Val, Thomas Crandall; m. 2d, Lucile Layton, Aug. 24, 1973. Asst. in chemistry Brigham Young U., Provo, Utah, 1934-38; instr. and research asst. in biol. chemistry U. Cin., 1938-44; intern Swedish Hosp., Seattle, 1947-48; resident pathology U. Utah, 1948-49; instr. clin. pathology and nuclear medicine La. State U., New Orleans, 1949-53; dir. labs. and nuclear pathology Idaho Falls (Idaho) Hosp., 1955-65; practice nuclear medicine with office and hosps. in Scottsdale, Tempe, Chandler, and Mesa, Ariz. Dir. Sch. Med. Tech., Idaho Falls, 1955-66; clin. instr. Idaho State and Ricks colls., 1955-66; research cons. Utah State U., Logan, 1955-66; asst. coroner Bonneville County, Idaho, 1955-61; pres., Eastern Idaho Tumor Bd., Idaho Falls, 1959-61; mem. com. Alcohol and Drugs, Nat. Safety Council, Chgo., 1958-75. Bd. dirs. Idaho Falls Symphony; cellist Mesa Symphony Orch., 1961—, pres., 1965—; Scottsdale Community Orch.; co-founder, bd. mem., cellist Ariz. Cello Soc., 1969, now v.p.; pres. Mesa Fine Arts Assn., 1967-68; bd. dirs. Ariz. Cello Soc.; mem. Phoenix Chamber Music Soc.; founder, pres. Mesa Symphony Orchestra Assn., 1973—. Served to lt. AUS, 1943; to capt. USAF, 1953-55. Named Ariz. Artist of Year (music), 1972. Diplomate Am. Bd. Pathology, Am. Bd. Nuclear Medicine. Fellow Coll. Am. Pathologists, Am. Coll. Nuclear Physicians (charter), Am. Coll. Nuclear Medicine (charter mem., Disting. fellow), Am. Coll. Med. Imaging (charter), Am. Acad., Forensic Sci.; mem. Am., Ariz. med. assns., Nat. Bd. Med. Examiners, Soc. Nuclear Medicine (charter), Ariz. Safety Council, Idaho Acad. Sci., Ariz. Nuclear Medicine Physicians (pres. 1976-78), Am. Cancer Soc., Idaho Falls C. of C., Mesa C. of C., Utah Geneal. Soc., Ariz. Geneal. Soc. (founding mem.), Assn. Profl. Genealogists, Alpha Kappa Kappa. Republican. Mormon. Home: 1820 E Jensen St Mesa AZ 85203 Office: 500 W 10th Pl Mesa AZ 85201

GIDDINGS, KAREN LOUISE, distributing company executive; b. Modesto, Calif., Jan. 29, 1960; d. George Warren and Marianne (Corson) G. B.A. in Pub. Adminstrn., Applied Arts and Scis., San Diego State U., 1982. Brands promotion coordinator Mesa Distributing Co., Inc., San Diego, 1982, asst. mgr. brands promotion, 1983—. Active Young Republicans. Recipient Outstanding Achievement award Miller Brewing Co., 1982. Mem. Am. Mktg. Assn., Nat. Assn. Female Execs. Alpha Chi Omega. Methodist. Club: P.E.O. Home: 6670 Bell Bluff San Diego CA 92119 Office: Mesa Distributing Co 7598 Trade St San Diego CA 92121

GIDDINGS, MANYA KOSHKO, aircraft service executive; b. Kansas City, Kans., Sept. 21, 1922; d. Stefan and Mehelena (Zybko) Koshko; m. Edwin Wight Giddings, July 12, 1948 (dec.); 1 son, David. A.A., Cerritos Coll., 1967; B.A., Calif. State U.-Fullerton, 1970. Sec. aircraft mfg. co., 1941-48; co-founder, owner, pres. Elsinore Aerospace Services, Inc., Downey, Calif., 1971—, pres., chmn. bd., dir. subs. Random Access Micro Ctr. Mem. adv. bd. Downey Community Hosp. Mem. Nat. Bus. Aircraft Assn., Air Transp. Assn., Assistance League. Republican. Roman Catholic. Club: Aero.

GIDNEY, JOHN ARCHIBALD, acct.; b. Buffalo, Apr. 19, 1920; s. Ray Millard and Jean Ellison (Brock) G.; A.B., Dartmouth Coll., 1941; B.B.A., Western Reserve U., 1948; m. Margaret J. Dempster, Aug. 4, 1945 (div. Oct. 1962); 1 dau., Martha J.; m. Frances A. Merrell, Dec. 4, 1962. With Haskins & Sells, Cleve., Pitts., Buffalo, 1945-62, partner, 1959-62; partner Paulus & Gidney, C.P.A., 1963-72; pvt. practice accounting, Reno, 1972-73; pres. John A. Gidney Ltd., Reno, 1973-80, Gidney, Quinn & Summers, Ltd., 1980-81; pres. John A. Gidney Ltd., 1981—; tchr. acctg. Cleve. Coll., Western Res. U., 1951-54; pres. Estate Planning Council, Reno, 1976-77; chmn. Mountain States Conf. C.P.A.s, 1978-82. Bd. dirs., treas. Fairway Villas Condominium Assn., 1971-78, Nev. Opera Guild, 1974-78; bd. dirs., treas. Unitarian Fellowship, Reno, Nev., 1975-76. Served with AUS, 1942-45. C.P.A., Ohio, Pa., N.Y., Calif., Utah, N.C., Nev. Mem. Am. Inst. C.P.A.s (council 1976, 79-82), Nev. Soc. C.P.A.s, (pres. 1976-77), Beta Alpha Psi. Clubs: Hidden Valley Country (dir., treas. 1976-78, pres. 1979), Prospectors (Reno, Nev.). Home: 2670 Tamarisk Dr Reno NV 89502 Office: 1 East 1st St No 900 Reno NV 89501

GIEDT, BRUCE ALAN, paper company executive; b. Fargo, N.D., May 7, 1937; s. Alexander and Alice Mildren (Roonaldson) G.; m. Suzanna Tae Abbott, Apr. 30, 1963; m. 2d, Gail Ann Platt, May 8, 1981; children—Alex, Jeffrey, Marybeth. B.A., U. Wash., 1959; M.B.A., Harvard U., 1965. Regional sales mgr., mill mgr., dir. mktg., gen. sales mgr., gen. mgr. then v.p. service products bus. units, Crown Zellerbach Corp., San Francisco, 1965—; pres. Champion Paper Distbrs., Inc./Champion Container, Riverside, Calif., 1981—. Served to capt. USAF, 1959-63. Evans Scholar, Western Golf Assn., 1967. Mem. Am. Paper Inst. (past com. chmn.), Riverside C. of C. (exec. com., econ. devel. com.). Republican. Lutheran. Clubs: Victoria, Elks (Riverside). Author: The Future of Commercial Arbitration, 1965. Office: 1180 Spring St Riverside CA 92507

GIEM, ROSS NYE, JR., physician-surgeon; b. Corvallis, Oreg., May 23, 1923; s. Ross Nye and Goldie Marie (Falk) G.; children—John, David, Paul, James, Ross Nye III Matthew, Julie. Student U. Redlands, Walla Walla Coll.; B.A., M.D., Loma Linda U.; Intern, Sacramento Gen. Hosp., 1952-53; resident in Ob-Gyn, Kern County Gen. Hosp., Bakersfield, Calif., 1956-57, in gen. surgery, 1957-61; practice medicine specializing in gen. surgery, Sullivan, Mo., 1961-70; staff emergency dept. Hollywood Presbyn. Med. Center, 1971-73, Meml. Hosp., Belleville, Ill., 1973—, St. Luke Hosp., Pasadena, Calif., 1973—; instr. emergency physicians, nurses, paramedics, emergency med. technicians, 1973—. Served with AUS, 1943-46. Diplomate Am. Bd. Surgery. Fellow A.C.S.; mem. AMA, Ill. Med. Assn., Pan Am. Med. Assn., Pan Pacific Surg. Assn., Royal Coll. Physicians (Eng.).

GIENGER, RONALD JOHN, dairy rancher; b. Tillamook, Oreg., May 7, 1940; s. John Ernest and Bernadine Bernetta (Surbaugh) G.; B.S., U. Oreg., 1962; B.F.T., Thunderbird Grad. Sch. Internat. Mgmt., Phoenix, 1963; m. Marianne Johnson, Aug. 10, 1980. Second v.p. internat. div. Chase Manhattan Bank, N.A., N.Y., S.Am. and Caribbean, 1963-74; engaged in dairy ranching, Tillamook, 1974—. Mem. adminstrv. bd. dirs. Tillamook County Community Counseling Services, 1978—; mem. Tillamook County Fair Bd. Mem. Oreg. Farm Bur., Oreg. Dairyman's Assn., Aircraft Owners and Pilots Assn., Sigma Chi (life). Republican. Mem. United Ch. Christ. Clubs: Tillamook Kiwanis (pres. 1982-83, President's award 1980, 81), Elks. Address: 3030 Fitzpatrick Rd Tillamook OR 97141

GIESCHEN, VICTOR WOODWARD, internist, medical educator; b. Milw., May 17, 1931; s. Victor A. and Mildred (Woodward) G.; m. Barbara Lee Eglin, June 11, 1955; children—Susan, Bonnie, Kevin, Larry, Jennifer. B.S., U. Wis., 1952, M.D., 1955. Intern, Med. Coll. Va., 1955-56; resident in internal medicine Los Angeles County Gen. Hosp., 1956-59; fellow in endocrinology U. So. Calif., 1961-62; practice medicine specializing in internal medicine, Thousand Oaks, Calif., 1962—; pres. Lombard Med. Group Inc., Thousand Oaks, 1962—; mem. staff Los Robles Regional Med. Ctr., Thousand Oaks, Westlake Hosp., Westlake Village, Calif. Served to lt. comdr. USN, 1959-61. Mem. AMA, Phi Beta Kappa, Alpha Omega Alpha, Sigma Sigma, Nu Sigma Nu. Republican. Lutheran. Club: Rotary. Office: Lombard Med Group 2230 Lynn Rd Thousand Oaks CA 91360

GIESE, JOHN DAVID, mechanical engineer; b. Cairo, Ill., May 23, 1937; s. John Rossi and Edith Virginia (Herb) G.; A.B., Harvard, 1959; m. Filomena Bonamis, Apr. 14, 1968; children—Christopher, Ligia. Mech. engr. White Sands (N.Mex.) Missile Range, 1964-66, Pacific Pumping Co., Oakland, Calif., 1966-67; asst. devel. engr. mech. engring. dept. U. Calif., Berkeley, 1967-70; mech. engr. Mepaco div. Chemetron, Oakland, 1970—, now chief engr. Served with AUS, 1961-66. Mem. ASME. Democrat. Club: Mensa. Home: 67 Kingston Rd Kensington CA 94707 Office: PO Drawer 7025 Oakland CA 94601

GIESE, JOHN HUGO, educator, farmer; b. Faulkton, S.D., Dec. 27, 1926; s. Edward William and Esther Fredia (Klein) G.; m. Mary Lou Neilan, Sept. 27, 1952; children—Daniel John, Susan Rachelle, Douglas Edward. B.S., No. State Coll., Aberdeen, S.D., 1961, M.S., 1968; postgrad. No. Ill. U., U. Mont., Miss. State U., U. Wyo., Mont.-State U. Tchr. Bowdle (S.D.) Pub. Sch., 1961-64; tchr. Missoula County (Mont.) High Sch., 1964-68, dir. adult edn., 1968-72, dir. fed. programs, 1972-80; asst. dir. Missoula (Mont.) Vocat. Tech. Ctr., 1980—; cons. N.W. Regional Lab. Served with U.S. Army, 1945-46. Named Outstanding Young Farmer, Faulk County, S.D., 1956; Outstanding Indsl. Arts Tchr., Mont., 1967. Mem. Am. Vocat. Assn., Mont. Vocat. Assn., Mont. Council Local Adminstrs., Epsilon Pi Tau. Methodist. Office: 909 South Ave W Missoula MT 59801

GIESEKE, MARGARET GARLAND, rehabilitation counselor; b. Philipsburg, Pa., Oct. 26, 1951; d. Don Fredrick and Barbara Garland (Brown) G. B.A., Coll. William and Mary, 1973; M.S., U. Ariz., 1981. Cert. community coll. instr., interpreter II, Ariz. Counselor Counseling Ctr. Hearing Impaired, Phoenix, 1981-82, counselor/coordinator, 1982; vocat. rehab. counselor III, Phoenix, 1982—; instr. Glendale (Ariz.) Community Coll., 1982; cons. Phoenix Dept. Corrections Adobe Mountain Sch. Mem. Mayor's Com. on Employment of Handicapped, Ariz. Adv. Com. on Deaf-Blind Persons. Mem. Am. Personnel and Guidance Assn., Am. Mental Health Counselors Assn., Am. Rehab. Assn. Democrat. Presbyterian. Home: 7123 W Granada Phoenix AZ 85035 Office: 1313 N 2d St Suite 26 Phoenix AZ 85004

GIET, GEORGE ROBERT, librarian; b. N.Y.C., Oct. 11, 1898; s. Daniel Nathanial and Laurina (Calyo) G.; A.B., Columbia, 1921, E.E., 1923; m. Cary Ellis, July 14, 1928. With Am. Tel. & Tel. Co., N.Y.C., 1923-25; prof. radio engring. U.S. Naval Postgrad. Sch., Annapolis, Md., 1925-42, prof. electronics engring., 1946-51, prof. electronics engring., Monterey, Calif., 1952-65, chmn. dept. electronics engring., 1954-62. Librarian, Allan Knight Maritime Museum Library, Monterey, 1970—, mem. ops. bd., 1973—. Served to comdr. USNR, 1942-46; capt. Res. ret. Named fellow U.S. Naval Postgrad. Sch. Faculty, 1962; first recipient Distinguished Prof. award U.S. Naval Postgrad. Sch., 1966. Mem. IEEE (life, sr. mem.), Am. Soc. Engring. Edn., Monterey History and Art Assn., Nat. Ret. Officers Assn., Mil. Order World Wars, Navy League U.S., Tau Beta Pi. Clubs: Monterey Peninsula Country, Ft. Ord Officers, Naval Postgrad. Officers and Faculty, Marines Meml. Home: 24702 Upper Trail Carmel CA 93923 Office: 550 Calle Principal Monterey CA 93940

GIETZ, ROBERT HAMILTON, highway engineer; b. Laramie, Wyo., Sept. 6, 1935; s. Robert George and Bessie Belle (McBride) G.; m. Wilma Lorene Murry, Apr. 13, 1955; children—Mark, Dale, Robert, Kirk. B.S.C.E., U. Wyo., Laramie, 1961, M.S.C.E., 1965. Registered profl. engr., Wash. Jr. engr. J. T. Banner and Assocs., Laramie, 1962-65; asst. research engr. U. Wyo., 1965-67; hwy. engr., project insp., project engr., dist. materials engr. Wash. Dept. of Transp., Spokane, 1967-78, spl. project engr., testing and quality control engr., Olympia, 1978—. Served with U.S. Army, 1955-56, 61-62. Lutheran. Home: 3515 Hawthorne Tumwater WA 98501 Office: PO Box 167 Olympia WA 98504

GIFFIN, MARGARET ETHEL (PEGGY), management consultant; b. Cleve., Aug. 27, 1949; d. Arch Kenneth and Jeanne (Eggleton) G.; B.A. in Psychology, U. Pacific, Stockton, Calif., 1971; M.A. in Psychology, Calif. State U., Long Beach, 1973; Psychometrist, Auto Club So. Calif., Los Angeles, 1973-74; dir. EEO Compliance Services div. Psychol. Services, Inc., Los Angeles, 1975—; researcher Social Sci. Research Inst., U. So. Calif., Los Angeles, 1981; mem. tech. adv. com. on testing Calif.

Fair Employment and Housing Commn., 1974—, mem. steering com., 1978—. Mem. Internat. Personnel Mgmt. Assn. Assessment Council, Am. Psychol. Assn., Western Psychol. Assn., Personnel Testing Council So. Calif. (pres. 1980, bd. dirs. 1981). Club: Athletic (Los Angeles). Home: 330 S Westmoreland Ave Los Angeles CA 90020 Office: 3450 Wilshire Blvd Suite 1200 Los Angeles CA 90010

GIFFORD, JOHN ALAN, newspaper executive; b. East Orange, N.J., Sept. 5, 1952; s. Jack S. and Helen (Leonard) G.; m. Kathy Renee DeFord, Sept. 9, 1979; 1 son, Jarad Alan. B.A., Wash. State U., 1974. Salesman Walla Walla (Wash.) Union-Bull., 1974-78, advt. mgr., 1978—; tchr. advt. Walla Walla Coll., winter 1980, 82. Pres., Allied Arts, 1981-82; bd. dirs. Historic Preservation Found., 1979-80; coach Youth Basketball, 1979-82, Youth Soccer, 1980; active YMCA. Named Salesperson of Yr., Walla Walla Union-Bull., 1976. Mem. Internat. Newspaper Advt. and Mktg. Execs., Pacific N.W. Newspaper Advt. Execs. Assn., Assn. Newspaper Classified Advt. Mgrs., Walla Walla C. of C. Presbyterian. Clubs: Walla Walla Country, Walla Walla Downtown Lions (pres. 1980-81). Home: 1715 Sunset St Walla Walla WA 99362 Office: Walla Walla Union-Bull PO Box 1358 Walla Walla WA 99362

GIGNAC, JUDITH ANN, county official; b. Detroit, Mar. 21, 1939; d. Durward Arthur and Gertrude Marian (Maneck) DuPont; student Broward Bus. Coll., 1957-58, U. Colo., 1967-69, Cochise Coll., 1975-76; m. Paul Ross Gignac, Sept. 12, 1964; children—Beth Andrea, Christopher Ross. Data processor Kettelle & Assocs., Colorado Springs, Colo., 1968-69; computer programmer RCA Ballistic Missile Early Warning Systems, Colorado Springs, 1962-68; mem. Cochise County Bd. Suprs., Bisbee, Ariz., 1977—, chmn., 1978-79; dir. Bank of Cochise. Past mem. council govt. affairs Ariz. Hosp. Assn., 1979-80; v.p. Sierra Vista (Ariz.) Indsl. Devel. Authority, 1976-78; chmn. Safford Dist. Pub. Land Adv. Council, 1980-82; founder Women's Resource Network, 1982; chmn. Southeastern Ariz. Emergency Med. Service Regional Council, 1982—; pres. Thunder Mountain Republican Women, 1972-74; treas. Ariz. Rep. State Com., 1976-77; chmn. Cochise County Rep. Com., 1972-75; sub-com. chmn. Nat. Rep. Platform Com., 1980; del. White House briefing on econ. recovery program, 1981; founder series of seminars Women as Leaders, 1981; chmn. S.E. Ariz. Emergency Med. Services Regional Council, 1982—; mem. adv. com. U. Ariz. Rural Health Office, 1983—; lay leader Sierra Vista United Meth. Ch., 1982-83, v.p. bd. trustees, 1983—. Named Lady of Yr., Sierra Vista chpt. Beta Sigma Phi, 1978, Woman in Action, AAUW, 1975; Leadership-Communications award Area 3 Toastmasters Internat., 1982. Mem. Am. Soc. Pub. Adminstrn., Ariz. Assn. Ind. Developers, Ariz. Acad., U.S. Border Cities, Counties and States (dir.), Southeastern Ariz. Govt. Orgn. (dir.), Ariz. Assn. Counties, Assn. for Laissez-Faire (dir. 1978—, pres. 1978-80), Federally Employed Women, Ariz. Consumer Council (dir. 1983—), Thunder Mountain Republican Women, Sierra Vista C. of C., Bisbee C. of C., Bus. and Profl. Women Club (Woman of Yr., Huachuca chpt. 1974-75). Home: 565 Raymond Dr Sierra Vista AZ 85635 Office: PO Box 225 Bisbee AZ 85603

GILB, ROBERT FRANK, accounting firm executive, consultant; b. Los Angeles, Jan. 16, 1946; s. Charles F. and Elizabeth Y. (Molino) G.; m. Kathryn L. Oertel, Nov. 6, 1971 (div.); children—Stephanie M., Michael S. A.A., Harbor Jr. Coll., 1966; B.S., Calif. State U.-Long Beach, 1968. C.P.A., Calif., Wash. With Arthur Andersen & Co., 1968—, ptnr., Seattle, 1979—; asst. to spl. master U.S. Dist. Ct. for Dist. Alaska. Active Jr. Achievement, Seattle, United Way, Seattle. Mem. Nat. Assn. Accts., Am. Inst. C.P.A.s, Wash. Soc. C.P.A.s, Am. Electronics Assn., Seattle C. of C. Republican. Episcopalian. Clubs: Harbor, Rainier (Seattle). Contbr. in field. Office: 801 Norton Bldg Seattle WA 98104

GILBERT, ALMA MAGGIORE, broadcast executive; b. Canton, Ohio; d. Vincent D. and Florence A. (Manack) Maggiore; m. Richard B. Gilbert; 1 son, Gary Richard. Student Mt. Marie Acad., Canton, Ohio. Stockholder, dir., sec. Ariz. Aircasters, Inc., Scottsdale, 1955-58, Scottsdale Broadcasting Co., 1956-58; stockholder, dir., sec. and program dir. KPOK-AM, Scottsdale, 1956-58; stockholder, dir., v.p., sec. KYND Radio Corp., 1959-66; stockholder, dir., v.p., sec., program dir. KYND-AM, Tempe, Ariz., 1960-66; stockholder, dir., v.p., sec. Aircasters, Inc., Scottsdale, 1966-82, Ariz. Communications Corp., 1968-82; stockholder, dir., v.p., sec., program dir. KXTC-FM, Phoenix and Glendale, Ariz., 1970-78; pres., stockholder, dir. Am. Aircasting Corp. and KQST-FM, Sedona, Ariz. Mem. Sedona Arts Ctr., Sedona Friends of the Library, Keep Sedona Beautiful. Mem. Broadcast Pioneers, Sedona-Oak Creek Canyon C. of C.

GILBERT, CAROL BIRNBAUM, engineering supervisor, career consultant, speaker; b. San Francisco, Jan. 19, 1939; d. Charles Hall and Evelyn Dorritt (Bloom) Birnbaum; m. David Irvin Gilbert, Oct. 25, 1959; 1 dau., Valerie Jean. A.A., U. Calif.-Berkeley, 1958; B.A. in Sociology, Calif. State U.-San Jose, 1972. Tchr. Santa Clara County, Calif., 1973-78; software technician Measurex Corp., Cupertino, Calif., 1978-79, prodn. tng. adminstr., 1979-81, tng. supr., 1981—; career transition cons., pub. speaker. Mem. Pride's Crossing Homeowner's Assn. Mem. Am. Soc. Tng. and Devel., AAUW, Delta Phi Epsilon Alumnae Assn. Home: 12667 Cambridge Dr Saratoga CA 95070 Office: Measurex Way #1 Results Way Cupertino CA 95014

GILBERT, GAYLE, nursing administrator; b. Crescent City, Calif., Aug. 18, 1937; d. Francis and Martha (Newcomer) Bandy; children—Cathy, Karyn, Scott. B.M. cum laude, Linfield Coll., 1980; R.N., St. Luke's Hosp., 1959. Nurse, nursing supr. various no. Calif. hosps., 1959-72; dir. inservice edn., dir. nursing San Luis Obispo (Calif.) Gen. Hosp., 1972-77; sr. health care cons. Stanford Research Inst., Menlo Park, Calif., 1975; profl. recruiter Sacred Heart Gen. Hosp., Eugene, Oreg., 1978-80, assoc. dir. nursing service, 1980—. Chmn. profl. edn. Am. Cancer Soc., Friends of Hospice, Am. Heart Assn. Mem. Am. Nurses Assn., Calif. Nurses Assn., Am. Soc. Nursing Adminstrs., Oreg. Soc. Nursing Adminstrn. Democrat. Unitarian.

GILBERT, GEORGE RONALD, management educator, consultant; b. Phila., Nov. 12, 1939; s. J. Ralph and Miriam (Wagner) G.; m. Janet Abercrombie, Sept. 30, 1962; children—Jennifer Lynn, Stephen A. Student U. Oreg., 1962, Calif. State Coll.-Fresno, 1967; M. Pub. Adminstrn., U. So. Calif., 1971, Ph.D, 1973. Adminstr., Lockheed Co., 1962-65; dir. War on Poverty, 1967-69; dir. research U. So. Calif., 1969-73, asst. prof., 1973-74; prof. Fed. Exec. Inst. Charlottesville, Va., 1974-77, Fla. Internat. U., Miami, 1977-83; prof., dir. exec. programs U. Colo., Denver, 1983—; bus., govt. cons. Named Outstanding Disting. Lectr., U. No. Calif., 1979. Mem. Acad. of Mgmt., Am. Soc. Pub. Adminstrn., Am. Soc. Personnel Adminstrn., Phi Kappa Phi. Author: Evaluation Management, 1979; Making and Managing Policy, 1984; contbr. articles and chptrs. to profl. jours. Home: 182 S Holman Way Golden CO 80401 Office: Univ Colo 1055 Wazee St Denver CO 80202

GILBERT, HEATHER CAMPBELL, bus. services co. exec.; b. Mt. Vernon, N.Y., Nov. 20, 1944; d. Ronald Ogston and Mary Lodivia (Campbell) G. B.S. in Math. (Nat. Merit scholar), Stanford U., 1967; M.S. in Computer Sci. (NSF fellow), U. Wis., 1969. With Burroughs Corp., 1969-82, sr. mgmt. systems analyst, Detroit, 1975-77, mgr. mgmt. systems activity, Pasadena, Calif., 1977-82; mgr. software product mgmt. Lolean Data Mgmt. Inc., Covina, Calif., 1982-83, dir. mktg., 1983—. Mem. Assn. Computing Machinery, Am. Product and Inventory Control Soc., Women in Cable, AAUW, Stanford U. Alumni Assn. (life), Stanford Profl. Women Los Angeles County (pres. 1982-83), Nat. Assn. Female Execs., Town Hall. Club: So. Calif. Cable. Home: 2020 Dacian Dr Walnut CA 91789 Office: 529 S 2d Ave Covina CA 91723

GILBERT, JOAN EVELYN, management information systems manager, consultant; b. Glendale, Calif., Dec. 29, 1943; d. William Theodore and Gladys (Lovett) Bergmann; m. James Carroll Gilbert, Aug. 18, 1962 (div.); children—Tracey Leigh, David Mark. Student Valley Bus. Coll., 1961, Santa Ana Coll., 1975-78. Cert. community coll. tchr., cert. notary public, both Calif. Sec., office mgr. Santa Ana (Calif.) Coll., 1973-80; pvt. practice secretarial/acctg. firm, Santa Ana, 1980-81; mgmt. info. systems analyst/mgr. First Alliance Mortgage Co., Santa Ana, 1981—; bus. cons.; designer profl. brochures. Mem. Nat. Assn. Female Execs. Democrat. Office: 2700 N Main St 12th Floor Santa Ana CA 92701

GILBERT, MARJORIE JEAN, stockmarket advisor, artist; b. Englewood, Colo., Dec. 27, 1936; d. Lonzo E. and Dorothy Imogene (Fowler) Cox; m. Donald L. Gilbert, Sept. 4, 1955; children—David Lee, Daniel Leigh, Dawna Lea. Owner, v.p. Escondido Foods, 1960-82, also freelance writer, 1975-80; artist, 1976—; investment counselor, 1980—; organizer investment clubs; tchr. classes on stock market. Area chmn. San Diego Light Opera Assn.; mem. San Diego Zool. Soc. Named Escondido Mother of Yr., 1966. Mem. Nat. Assn. Investment Clubs (pres. San Diego council). Republican. Methodist. Club: Toastmasters. Home and Office: 1603 Skyhawk Rd Escondido CA 92025

GILBERT, NEIL ROBIN, educator; b. N.Y.C., Sept. 18, 1940; s. Allan and Ida G.; B.A., Bklyn. Coll., 1962; M.S.W., U. Pitts., 1965; Ph.D., 1968; m. Barbara Feinstein, June 2, 1963; children—Evan, Jesse. Caseworker, Interdepartmental Service Center, N.Y.C., 1963; dir. research and planning Mayor's Com. on Human Resources, Inc., Pitts., 1967-69; sr. research fellow UN Research Inst. for Social Devel., Geneva, 1974-75; prof. social welfare U. Calif., Berkeley, 1969—. Sr. Fulbright research fellow, London, 1981. Mem. Nat. Assn. Social Workers, Internat. Sociol. Assn., Gerontol. Soc. Author: Clients or Constituents, 1970; (with Harry Specht) Dimensions of Social Welfare, 1974; Planning for Social Welfare, 1976; Dynamics of Community Planning, 1978; Capitalism and the Welfare State, 1983; mem. editorial bd. Social Work, 1975-79; editor social work and social welfare series Prentice-Hall, Inc., social services series Praeger. Office: Sch Social Welfare U Calif Berkeley CA 94720

GILBERT, RICHARD GENE, research plant pathologist, research microbiologist; b. Holdenville, Okla., Dec. 3, 1935; s. Myron Lee and Martha Viola (Cates) G.; m. Sharon Lee Smith, Sept. 7, 1959 (div.); children—Mark Dean, Jill Susanne; m. 2d, Sallie Arambula, July 22, 1978 (div.). B.S. in Phys. and Biol. Scis. (scholar), Colo. State U., 1961, M.S. in Plant Pathology (NDEA fellow), 1963, Ph.D. in Plant Pathology, 1964. Research asst. plant pathology dept. U. Calif., Berkeley, 1964; research microbiologist U.S. Soils Lab. U.S. Dept. Agr., Beltsville, Md., 1965-70; research microbiologist U.S. Water Conservation Lab., Phoenix, 1970-82; research plant pathologist Irrigated Agrl. Research and Extension Ctr., Prosser, Wash., 1982—. With U.S. Army, 1954-57. Recipient Unit award U.S. Dept. Agr., 1973. Mem. Am. Phytopathological Soc., Am. Soc. Agronomy, Soil Sci. Soc. Am., Phi Theta Kappa, Phi Kappa Phi, Sigma Xi. Unity. Club: Kiwanis (Grandview). Contbr. numerous research publs. to tech. jours. Home: 623 E 3rd St Grandview WA 98930 Office: IAREC PO Box 30 Prosser WA 99350

GILBERT, ROBERT WOLFE, lawyer; b. N.Y.C., Nov. 12, 1920; s. L. Wolfe and Katherine (Oestreicher) G.; A.B. with highest honors in Polit. Sci., UCLA, 1941; J.D. (Pres.'s scholar 1941-43, State Legislators' scholar 1942), U. Calif., Berkeley, 1943; m. Beatrice R. Frutman, Dec. 25, 1946; children—Frank Richard, Jack Alfred. Admitted to Calif. bar, 1944; pres. firm Gilbert, Cooke & Sackman, partner predecessors, Beverly Hills, 1944—; West Coast legal counsel numerous AFL-CIO labor unions, various talent guilds in entertainment field, 1944—. Commr. Housing Authority, Los Angeles, 1953-63; dir. Calif. Housing Council, 1955-63; mem. Mayors Council Internat. Visitors; mem. Los Angeles County Democratic Central Com., 1948-53; pres. Hollywood Dem. Club, 1964-73. Mem. Internat. Bar Assn., Inter-Am. Bar Assn., ABA, Am. (co-chmn. internat. labor law com. 1977-80) Fed. Bar Assn., Am. Judicature Soc., World Affairs Council, Nat. Lawyers Club, Order of Coif, Pi Sigma Alpha. Contbr. law jours.; editor-in-chief Calif. Law Rev., 1942-43. Home: 7981 Hollywood Blvd Los Angeles CA 90046 Office: 400 S Beverly Dr Beverly Hills CA 90212

GILBERT, WALLY, publishing executive; b. Los Angeles, Apr. 30, 1940; s. Walter Eugene and Carolyn B. (May) G.; m. Leah Banen, Sept. 10, 1964; children—David, Jeff. B.S. in Mktg. and Advt., U. Ariz., 1963. Asst. mgr. Browne's Travel, Tucson, 1963-68; with adv. sales dept. Sunset Mag., Los Angeles, 1968-74; western sales mgr. Progressive Architecture, Los Angeles, 1974-77; dir. mktg. Morgan-Grampian Pub., Irvine, Calif., 1977—, also assoc. pub. Mem. Los Angeles Advt. Club, Mag. Reps. Assn., Orange County Advt. Fedn. Home: 19411 Sierra Noche Rd Irvine CA 92715 Office: 2041 Business Center Dr Suite 206 Irvine CA 92715

GILBERT, WILLIAM ALLAN, agronomist, consultant; b. Batavia, N.Y., Sept. 6, 1954; s. Reed Davies and Frances (Owens) G.; m. Lucinda Russell, June 2, 1973; children—Seth, Jesse. B.S., Cornell U., 1976; M.S., Colo. State U., 1978. Research asst. agronomic research Colo. State U., 1976-78; asst. scientist, room control supr. Castle & Cooke Inc., East Windsor, Conn., 1978-80; cons. agronomist Inter-Am. Labs., Ft. Collins, Colo., 1980-82; owner Applied Agronomics, Ft. Collins, 1982—. Gt. Western Sugar Co. grantee Colo. State U., 1976-78. Mem. Am. Soc. Agronomy, Crop Sci. Soc. Am., Soil Sci. Soc. Am. Democrat. Contbr. articles to profl. jours.

GILBERTSON, ELIZABETH MCNUTT, therapist, chemical dependency counselor; b. Oconomowoc, Wis., July 6, 1943; d. Emil Wicks and Cedilia Mary (Allen) McNutt; m. David L. Gilbertson, July 3, 1981; children—John, Kristen, Eric. M.A. in Human Ecology, Mich. State U., 1973; M.S. in Health Care Adminstrn., Trinity U., 1982. Child devel. specialist World of Childhood Program, E.W. Sparrow Hosp., Lansing, Mich., 1970-72; dir. social services Central Mont. Hosp. and Nursing Home, Lewistown, 1977-81; obesity and related eating disorders therapist Shodair Children's Hosp., Helena, Mont., 1981—. Mem. Mental Health Assn. Mont. (bd. dirs. 1979—), Anorexia Nervosa and Related Eating Disorders, Inc., Am. Anorexia Nervosa Assn. Roman Catholic. Office: Shodair Children's Hosp 840 Helena Ave Helena MT 59601

GILBERTSON, OSWALD IRVING, marketing executive; b. Bklyn., Mar. 23, 1927; s. Olaf and Ingeborg (Aase) Gabrielsen; m. Magnhild Hompland, Sept. 11, 1954; children—Jan Ivar, Eric Olaf. Electrotechnician, Sorlandets Tekniske Skole, Norway, 1947; B.S. in Elec. Engring., Stockholms Tekniska Institut, Stockholm, Sweden, 1956. Planning engr. test equipment design and devel. Western Electric Co., Inc., Kearny, N.J., 1957-61, planning engr. new prodn., 1963-67, engring. supr. test equipment, 1963-67, engring. supr. submarine repeaters and equalizers, 1967-69; engring. mgr. communication cables ITT Corp., Oslo, Norway, 1969-71, mktg. mgr. for ITT's Norwegian co., Standard Telefon og Kabelfabrik A/S, 1971—, div. mgr. Eswa Heating Systems. Hon. Norwegian consul, 1981. Served with AUS, 1948-52. Registered profl. engr., Vt. Mem. IEEE, Norwegian Soc. Profl. Engrs., Soc. Norwegian Am. Engrs., Sons of Norway. Patentee in field. Home: 6240 Brynwood Ct San Diego CA 92120 Office: Standard Telefon OG Kabelfabrik A/S 591 Camino de la Reina Suite 500 San Diego CA 92108

GILBREATH, MARILYN KAY, optometrist; b. Kokomo, Ind., Feb. 1, 1955; d. Dexter and Ramona Joyce (Price) Gilbreath. B.A. in Biology, Indiana U., 1978, O.D., 1982. Licensed optometrist, Calif. Intern Indpls. (Ind.) Optometry Clinic, 1981, VA Hosp., Huntington, W.Va., 1982, VA Hosp., Wilkes-Barre, PA., 1982; resident in rehabilitative optometry VA Outpatient Clinic, Los Angeles, 1982-83. Mem. Low Vision Consultants Calif., Am. Optometric Assn. Lutheran. Office: 425 S Hill St MDP 112 C Los Angeles CA 90013

GILCHRIST, ROGER LARRY, health physicist, nuclear engr.; b. Pontiac, Mich., Oct. 9, 1948; s. Maurice LeRoy and Juanita Mae (Young) G.; B.S.E.E., U. Tenn., Chattanooga, 1975; M.S. in Nuclear Engring. and Health Physics, Tex. A&M U., 1977; m. Christine Miller, Apr. 28, 1973 (dec.); 1 dau., Stacy Gail. Engr., Hensley-Schmidt Cons. Engrs., Chattanooga, 1973-74; power elec. engr. TVA, Chattanooga, 1974-75; research asst. Tex. A&M U., College Station, 1975-77; sr. research scientist Battelle Pacific N.W. Labs., Richland, Wash., 1977—; cons. Internat. Atomic Energy Agy., Atomic Indsl. Forum; lectr. various univs.; public speaker. Served with USMC, 1967-71. Profl. engr. asso. Mem. Nuclear Engring. and Radiation Soc., Health Physics Soc., Am. Nuclear Soc., Sigma Pi Sigma, Pi Mu Epsilon. Home: 1119 Saddle Way Richland WA 99352 Office: PO Box 999 Richland WA 99352

GILCHRIST, WILLIAM RODNEY, city planner; b. Atlantic, Iowa, Oct. 25, 1931; s. Gerald Warren and Margaret (Workman) G.; student Dana Coll., Blair, Nebr., 1949-51; B.S., Iowa State U., 1955; m. Joanne Griffone, Oct. 25, 1958; children—Gary John, Greg, Ginger. Jr., asst. planner San Diego City Planning Dept., 1957-61, assoc. planner transp. and traffic engring. sect. City of San Diego, 1961-63; prin. planner Harstad Assocs., Planning and Engring. Cons., Seattle, 1963-65; dir. S.W. Snohomish County Joint Planning Council, Edmonds, Wash., 1965-66; dir. planning and bldg. div. City of Idaho Falls (Idaho), 1966-72; dir. Bonneville Council Govts., Idaho Falls, 1972-78; dir. planning and bldg. div. City of Idaho Falls, 1978—. Active Boy Scouts Am. Served with U.S. Army, 1955-57. Mem. Idaho Planner Assn. (bd. dirs. 1975-76), Assn. Planning Ofcls., Am. Planning Assn., Am. Inst. Cert. Planners, Am. Inst. Planners. Episcopalian. Club: Kiwanis. Home: 520 Vassar Way Idaho Falls ID 83401 Office: 620 Park Ave Idaho Falls ID 83401

GILD, ANTHONY MAX, retail and real estate leasing cons.; b. Cape Town, S. Africa, July 31, 1943; s. Percy and Eve (Kuritzky) G.; came to U.S., 1977; student Mktg. Mgmt. Program, Harvard Bus. Sch., 1970; m. Renee Ketz, Jan. 31, 1972; children—Paula and Lisa (twins). Store mgr. OK Bazaars, Johannesburg, S. Africa, 1968-70, dir. merchandising, 1971-75, v.p. mktg., 1975-77; mgr. mktg. planning Fedmart Corp., San Diego, 1977-79; pres. Anthony M. Gild and Assocs., retailing cons., San Diego, 1979—; guest lectr. retail mktg. San Diego (Calif.) State U., 1978; lectr. Internat. Council Shopping Ctrs., Nat. Retail Mchts. Assn. Mem. Am. Mktg. Assn. (dir. San Diego chpt. 1978-79), San Diego Research Council. Club: Rotary. Home: 2856 Sugarman Way La Jolla CA 92037 Office: PO Box 1836 La Jolla CA 92038

GILE, JANICE ANN, educator; b. Richland, Wash., Jan. 16, 1948; d. John Alexander and Sarah Helen (Grant) G.; A.A., Columbia Basin Coll., 1968; B.A. in Edn., Eastern Wash. State Coll., 1970, M.A. in Edn., 1979. Tchr. Keene-Riverview Regular Kindergarten, Prosser, Wash., 1970-75, Bilingual Title VII Kindergarten, Keene-Riverview Elem. Sch., Prosser, 1975-81; tchr. first grade Whitstran Elem. Sch., Prosser, 1981—; Title I summer migrant tchr., Prosser, 1971, 80, 81; Title I remedial summer math. program tchr., Prosser, 1973; participant workshop, summer 1974, Bilingual-Bicultural Inst., summer 1977. Co-leader Bluebirds, 1972-73; mem. choir Luth. Ch., 1970—. Mem. NEA, Wash. Edn. Assn., Prosser Edn. Assn. (sec., 1972-74, bldg. rep., 1971-72, 82-83, negotiator, 1977-78), Assn. for Supervision and Curriculum Devel., Phi Delta Kappa, Alpha Delta Kappa. Home: 1026 Hemlock Prosser WA 99350 Office: 832 Park Ave Prosser WA 99350

GILES, JEAN HALL, corp. exec.; b. Dallas, Mar. 30, 1908; d. C. D. and Ida (McIntyre) Overton; m. Alonzo Russell Hall, II, Jan. 23, 1923 (dec.); children—Marjorie (Mrs. Kenneth C. Hodges, Jr.), Alonzo Russell III; m. 2d, Harry E. Giles, Apr. 24, 1928 (div. 1937); 1 dau., Janice Ruth; 1 adopted dau., Marjean Giles. Capt., comdg. officer S.W. Los Angeles Women's Ambulance and Def. Corps., 1941-43; maj., nat. exec. officer Women's Ambulance and Def. Corps, 1944-45; capt., dir. field ops. Communications Corps of the U.S. Nat. Staff, 1951-52; dir. Recipe of the Month Club. Active Children's Hosp. Benefit, 1946; coordinator War Chest Motor Corps, 1943-44; dir. Los Angeles Area War Chest Vol. Corps and Motor Corps, 1945-46; realtor Los Angeles Real Estate Exchange, 1948—; also partner Tech. Contractors, Los Angeles. Bd. dirs. Tchr. Remembrance Day Found. Inc. Mem. Los Angeles C. of C. (women's div.), A.I.M., Los Angeles Art Assn., Hist. Soc. So. Calif., Opera Guild So. Calif., Assistance League So. Calif., Needlework Guild Am. (sect. pres. Los Angeles), First Century Families Calif., Internat. Platform Assn. Clubs: Athletic, Town Hall, The Garden (Los Angles); Pacific Coast. Office: Box 36474 Wilshire-LaBrea Station Los Angeles CA 90036

GILES, TERRI BECHTOLD, nurse; b. Forks, Wash., Oct. 20, 1952; d. Henry Harold and Marjorie Ellen (Klahn) Bechtold; m. Joel Giles, Aug. 28, 1982. B.S. in Nursing, U. Wash., 1974. Registered nurse; cert. in med./surg. nursing Am. Nurses Assn./Wash. State Bd. Nursing. Charge nurse U. Wash. Hosp., Seattle, 1974-75; staff and charge nurse Forks (Wash.) Community Hosp., 1976-77; staff nurse Surg ICU/Cardiovascular ICU, Stanford (Calif.) U. Hosp., 1977-79; asst. dir. nursing Forks Community Hosp., Forks, 1979-82, acting dir. nursing, 1982-83; acting dir. nursing Mark Reed Meml. Hosp., McCleary, Wash., 1981-82; cert. cardiopulmonary resuscitation instr. Am. Heart Assn. Mem. Am. Assn. Critical Care Nurses (cert.), Puget Sound Assn. Critical Care Nurses. Office: RR Box 3575 Forks WA 98331

GILFILLAN, S. COLUM, social scientist; b. St. Paul, Apr. 5, 1889; s. Joseph Alexander and Harriet Woodbridge (Cook) G.; A.B., U. Pa., 1910; A.M., Columbia U., 1920, Ph.D., 1935; m. Louise H. Wenzel, Sept. 15, 1922 (dec. 1971); children—Barbara (Mrs. John C. Crowley); Marjorie. Faculty U. of South, Sewanee, Tenn., 1923-26; instr. sociology Grinnell (Iowa) Coll., 1926-28; faculty Purdue U., Lafayette, Ind., 1936-37; curator social sci. and ships Mus. Sci. and Industry, Chgo., 1929-30; research on prediction, and social sci. aspects of invention U. Chgo., 1930-63. Served with U.S. Army, 1917-19. Mem. Atlantic Union, Shakespeare Oxford Soc. (v.p.), Phi Beta Kappa. Author: The Sociology of Invention, 1935; Inventing the Ship, 1935; Invention and the Patent System, 1964; Supplement to the Sociology of Invention, 1971; Rome's Ruin by Lead Poison, 1982. Home: 615 Linda Vista Pasadena CA 91105

GILHOOLY, DAVID JAMES, III, artist; b. Auburn, Calif., Apr. 15, 1943; s. David James and Gladys Catherine (Schulte) G.; m. Camille Margot Chang, Aug. 22, 1983; children—David James, Andrea Elizabeth, Abigail Margaret, Peter Rodney. B.A., U. Calif.-Davis, 1965, M.A., 1967. Exhibited in numerous one-man shows, including: San Francisco Museum Art, 1967, M. H. deYoung Meml. Mus., San Francisco, 1968, Martha Jackson Gallery, N.Y.C., 1971, Matrix Gallery, Wadsworth Athenuem, Hartford, Conn., 1976, Mus. Contemporary Art, Chgo., 1976, Vancouver (B.C., Can.), Art Gallery, 1976, ARCO Ctr. for Visual Arts, Los Angeles, 1977, Mus. Contemporary Craft, N.Y.C., 1977; numerous group shows, including: U. Calif.-Berkeley Art Mus. and Inst. Contemporary Art, Boston, 1967, Whitney Mus. Am. Art, N.Y.C., 1970, 74, 81, Musee d'art de la Ville Paris, 1973, Chgo. Art Inst., 1975, San Francisco Mus. Art and Nat. Collection of Fine Art, Washington, 1976-77, Stedelijk Mus., Amsterdam, Netherlands, 1979; represented in permanent collections, including: S. Bronfman Collection of Can. Art, Montreal, Que., San Francisco Mus. Art, Phila. Mus. Art, Vancouver Art Gallery, Art Gallery Greater Victoria (B.C.), Albright-Knox Art Gallery, Buffalo, San Antonio Mus. Art, Oakland (Calif.) Mus. Art, Stedelijk Mus., Stanford U., Palo Alto, Calif., City of Seattle, Australian Nat. Gallery, Canberra, Govt. Can., Calgary, Alta., Whitney Mus. Am. Art, Eugene (Oreg.) Ctr. Performing Arts; San Jose (Calif.) State Coll., 1967-69; U. Sask., (Can.), Saskatoon, 1969-71; York U., Toronto, Ont., Can., 1971-75, 76-77; U. Calif.-Davis, summer 1971, 1975-76; Calif. State U.-Sacramento, summers 1978-79; lectr. in field. Can. Council grantee, 1975, 78. Mem. Royal Can. Acad. Republican. Mem. Ch. of Scientology. Office: 400 Iris Davis CA 95616

GILL, GAIL STOORZA, pub. relations exec.; b. Yoakum, Tex., Aug. 28, 1943; d. Roy Otto and Ruby Pauline (Ray) Blankenship; student N.Tex. State U., Denton, 1961-63. Stewardess, Central Airlines, Ft. Worth, 1963; advt. and account exec. Phillips-Ramsey Advt., San Diego, Calif., 1963-68; dir. advt. Rancho Bernardo, San Diego, 1968-72; dir. corporate communications Avco Community Developers, 1972-74; pres. The Gail Stoorza Co., San Diego, 1974—; dir. Sun Savs. and Loan Assn. Mem. public affairs adv. com. Children's Hosp. and Health Center. Named One of San Diego's Ten Outstanding Young Citizens, 1979, Profl. of Yr., Pub. Relations Club of San Diego, 1981. Mem. Pub. Relations Soc. Am. (accredited), San Diego C. of C. (dir., vice chmn. exec. com.), Nat. Assn. Home Builders (residential mktg. com.), La Jolla Mus. Contemporary Art, Chancellor Assocs. of U. Calif.-San Diego, San Diego Press Club. Home: 727 Gage Dr San Diego CA 92106 Office: Central Fed Tower 225 Broadway Suite 1309 San Diego CA 92101

GILL, GENE, painter, printmaker; b. Memphis, June 18, 1933; s. Edward Morris and Zelma Pauline (Mondy) G.; student Memphis State U., 1951-53, Chgo. Art Inst., 1956-57; B.F.A., Chouinard Art Inst., 1962. Exhibited in one-man shows at Comara Gallery, 1970, 71, 74; exhibited in group shows at Los Angeles County Mus. Art, 1973, 81, Palm Springs Desert Mus., 1973, Loyola U., 1973, Laguna Beach Art Mus., 1972, 77, San Diego Fine Arts Gallery, 1971, Scripps Coll., 1971, Occidental Coll., 1971; works represented in collections at Los Angeles County Mus. Art, Palm Springs Desert Mus., Atlantic Richfield Corp., Northrop Corp., others, also numerous pvt. collections. Served with USNR, 1954-58. Recipient several purchase awards. Mem. Los Angeles Art Assn. Home: 2430 Cascadia Dr Glendale CA 91206

GILL, GEORGE WILHELM, anthropologist; b. Sterling, Kans., June 28, 1941; s. George Laurance and Florence Louise (Jones) G.; B.A. in Zoology with honors (NSF grantee), U. Kans., 1963, M.Phil. Anthropology (NDEA fellow, NSF dissertation research grantee), 1970, Ph.D. in Anthropology, 1971; m. Pamela Jo Mills, July 26, 1975; children—George Scott, John Ashton, Jennifer Florence, Bryce Thomas. Mem. faculty U. Wyo., Laramie, 1971—, asso. prof. anthropology, 1978—; forensic anthropologist law enforcement agencies, 1972—; sci. leader Easter Island Anthrop. Expdn., 1981. Served to capt. U.S. Army, 1963-67. Research grantee U. Wyo., 1972, 78, 82, Nat. Geog. Soc., 1980, Center for Field Research, 1980; diplomate Am. Bd. Forensic Anthropology. Mem. Am. Assn. Phys. Anthropologists, Am. Acad. Forensic Scis., Human Biology Council, Soc. Study Social Biology, Human Biology Council, Current Anthropology (asso.), Plains Conf., Wyo. Archael. Soc., Sigma Xi. Republican. Unitarian. Author articles, chpts. in books. Home: Howe Rd Laramie WY 82070 Office: Dept Anthropology Univ Wyo Laramie WY 82071

GILL, JAMES LEONARD, water resources official; b. Milw., Apr. 27, 1940; s. Leonard William and Edna Rae G.; m. Lynette Lewis Ward, June 29, 1963; m. 2d, Nancy Jane Simms, Sept. 7, 1968; children—Jay, Julie, David, Stephen. B.Arch., U. N. Mex., 1962. Urban planner Planning Dept. City of Albuquerque, 1960-69, water resources planner, 1970-76; asst. dir. Aubuquerque Water Resources Dept., 1976—. Active Middle Rio Grande Flood Control Assn. Mem. Am. Water Works Assn., Water Pollution Control Assn. Republican. Roman Catholic. Author profl. writings in field. Home: 3207 Texas St NE Albuquerque NM 87110 Office: 505 Marquette NW Suite 911 Albuquerque NM 87103

GILL, JEANETTE THERESA HARPENAU, bus. systems co. exec.; b. Tell City, Ind., Mar. 24, 1937; d. Francis L. and Frances Harpenau; B.S., Ind. State U., 1959; m. John Thomas Gill, Dec. 30, 1961. Tchr. math. Cln. Pub. Schs., 1959-60; engring. technician Gen. Electric Co., Cin., 1960-61; engr. Space div. N.Am. Aviation, Downey, Calif., 1962-66, Nortronics div. Northrop Corp., Anaheim, Calif., 1966-68; sr. applications programmer Collins Radio, Newport Beach, Calif., 1968-69; sr. programmer analyst MDM div. Control Data Corp., Santa Ana, Calif., 1969-71; lead programmer, applications programming mgr., standard systems programming mgr., mgr. customer programming AM Documentor div. AM Internat., Inc., Santa Ana, 1971—. Office: 2921 S Daimler St Santa Ana CA 92711

GILL, JOHN STILLMAN, clergyman, educator; b. San Diego, Jan. 2, 1917; s. Louis John and Mildred Elizabeth (Stillman) G.; B.A., Calif. State U., San Diego, 1938; M.A., UCLA, 1961; D.D., Ch. Div. Sch. of Pacific, 1978. Instr. math. and history Bonita (Calif.) Sch., 1940-42; instr. history Harvard Sch., Studio City, Calif., 1942—, chaplain, 1947-78, sr. chaplain, 1978—; ordained deacon Episcopal Ch., 1945, priest, 1947; examining chaplain Diocese of Los Angeles, 1951-74, chaplain to Bishop of Los Angeles, 1973—; hon. canon St. Paul's Cathedral, Los Angeles, 1977—. Mem. Mayor's Advisory Com., Los Angeles, 1964-72. Recipient Hon. Arms Elizabeth II, 1952; bailiff, prelate Order of Knights Hospitaler St. John of Jerusalem, chaplain Order of St. Lazarus. Mem. Am. Philatelic Soc., Hist. Soc. Gt. Britain, Calif. Hist. Soc., Heraldry Soc. Gt. Britain, Order St. Dunstan, Kappa Delta Pi, Lambda Delta Lambda. Designer stained-glass windows St. Saviour's Chapel, Harvard Sch., 1962. Office: Box 1037 Studio City CA 91604

GILL, LYNN EDWARD, marketing and logistics educator, distribution executive; b. Traverse City, Mich., June 28, 1939; s. Willard David and Elizabeth Aurella (Putman) G.; m. Patricia Joan Berry, June 7, 1963; m. 2d, Sharon Joy Bradshaw, Sept. 3, 1973; children—Kristin Joy, Juli Anna, Alexander Putnam. B.S., Mich. State U., 1962; M.B.A., U. So. Calif., 1965; Ph.D. in Bus. Orgn., Ohio State U., 1968. Packaging and transp. engr. N.Am. Aviation Co., Downey, Calif., 1962-64; asst. prof. mktg. and logistics U. So. Calif., 1968-72, research dir., 1969-72, assoc. prof., 1972—; vis. research prof. Nat. Cheng Kung U., Taiwan, 1974-75; pres. So. Calif. Cons., 1968—; chmn. and sec. treas. Gill Distbn. Ctrs., 1979—; pres. Interdis Corp., 1979—. Pres. Pa. Symphony Assn., Palos Verdes Peninsula, Calif., 1980-82, bd. dirs., 1982—. NDEA fellow, 1965-68; NRC grantee, 1974-75, Nat. Assn. Purchasing Mgmt. grantee, 1967-68. Mem. Nat. Council Distbn. Mgmt. (regional pres.), Beta Gamma Sigma, Phi Lambda Tau, Sigma Chi, Alpha Phi Omega, Alpha Kappa Psi (hon.), Delta Nu Alpha. Clubs: Palos Verdes Breakfast, Palo Verdes Tennis. Contbr. articles to profl. jours. Home: 3305 Via Palomino Palos Verdes Estates CA 90274 Office: 2575 El Presidro St Carson CA 90810

GILL, SANDRA LEE, mgmt. cons.; b. Mt. Clemens, Mich., June 23, 1948; d. Richard Sullivan and Evalena (Sherrill) Gill; B.A., Mich. State U., 1970, M.A., 1974; postgrad. U. Wis., 1976-82; m. Andre L. Delbecq, July 1, 1977. Tchr. deaf/blind Mich. Sch. for Blind, 1969-71; project coordinator Mich. Services to Deaf/Blind Children, Mich. Dept. Edn., Lansing, 1971-75; project coordinator Center for Evaluation Research and Program Devel., U. Wis., Madison, 1977-79; orgn. devel. specialist Kaiser Permanente Med. Care Program, 1979-81; coordinator orgn. devel. O'Connor Hosp., San Jose, Calif., 1981-82; pres. Performance Mgmt. Resources, Inc.; mgmt. cons., 1974—. Mem. Acad. Mgmt., Policy Studies Orgn., Evaluation Research Soc., AAUW, Phi Kappa Phi, Kappa Delta Pi, Omicron Nu. Roman Catholic. Office: PMR Inc PO Box 556 Santa Clara CA 95052

GILL, STEPHEN PASCHALL, physicist; b. Balt., Nov. 13, 1938; s. Robert Lee and Charlotte (Olmsted) G.; B.S., M.I.T., 1960; M.A., Harvard U., 1961, Ph.D., 1964; m. Margaret Ann Gaskins, Dec. 21, 1961; children—Elizabeth Olmsted, Richard Paschall. Cons. hypersonic aerodynamics Raytheon Corp., Bedford, Mass., 1963-64; research physicist Stanford Research Inst., Menlo Park, Calif., 1964-65, head high energy gasdynamics, 1965-68; head high energy gasdynamics Physics Internat. Co., San Leandro, Calif., 1968-70, mgr. shock dynamics dept., 1970-72; founder, pres. Artec Assos., Inc., Hayward, 1972-77, chief scientist, chmn. bd. dirs., 1977—; founder, pres. Votan Corp., 1979-81, chief scientist, chmn. bd. dirs., 1981—. Mem. San Francisco Symphony Assn., San Francisco Mus. Art. Mem. Am. Phys. Soc., AAAS, IEEE, AIAA, Am. Math. Soc., Soc. Indsl. and Applied Math., M.I.T. Alumni Assn., Sigma Xi, Delta Kappa Epsilon. Republican. Episcopalian. Clubs: M.I.T., Harvard (San Francisco). Home: 32 Flood Circle Atherton CA 94025 Office: 26046 Eden Landing Rd Hayward CA 94545

GILLA, MARILYN JEUNE, university personnel development specialist; b. Aurora, Ill., Jan. 12, 1940; d. John and Mary Gilla. B.S. in Edn., No. Ill. U., 1965, M.S. in Edn., 1973. Cert. tchr. Ill., Calif. Bus. edn. tchr., Ill. and Calif., 1965-73; exec. legal asst. John J. Ford & Co., San Francisco, 1971-72; staff devel. specialist Personnel Dept. Stanford (Calif.) U., 1973—; cons. in field of career counseling. Mem. Bay Area Personnel Assn. (v.p. 1979-80), Am. Soc. Tng. and Devel., Delta Pi Epsilon, Sigma Sigma Sigma. Roman Catholic. Office: Stanford U Personnel Dept Old Pavilion Stanford CA 94305

GILLAND, BRUCE, guidance counselor, education officer; b. Marion, Ky., Mar. 8, 1933; s. Roy T. and Francis A. (Horning) G.; m. Anita D. Hendrickson, Jan. 31, 1959; children—Cynthia Ann, Brent Stuart, Kristi Faye. B.Gen. Sci., Rollins Coll., 1973, B.S., 1976; B.A., SUNY-N.Y.C., 1977; M.A., Calif. State U. Consortium-Sacramento, 1979. Enlisted U.S. Air Force, 1950; ret., 1974; guidance counselor U.S. Army, Korea, 1977-78, U.S. Air Force, Malstrom AFB, Mont., 1979, edn. officer, Sunnyvale AFS, Calif., 1980-81, guidance counselor, Travis AFB, Calif., 1982—. Mem. Am. Personnel and Guidance Assn., Nat. Vocat. Guidance Assn., Am. Vocat. Assn., Am. Mgmt. Assn. Republican. Baptist. Club: DAV. Office: 60th ABG/DPE Travis AFB CA 94535

GILLARD, ELIZABETH BARTLETT, educator; b. Vernal, Utah, June 21, 1923; d. Charles Owen and Caroline Mabel (Jones) Bartlett; m. Don C. Hall, June 1, 1945 (dec.); m. 2d Hyrum Earl Carlson, June 12, 1956; m. 3d, Virgil Roy Gillard, July 1, 1960; 1 dau., Jean Hall Chiovaro. B.S., Brigham Young U., 1950; stenographical cert. LDS Bus. Coll., Salt Lake City, 1944; postgrad. U. Utah, Utah State U., Brigham Young U. Gen. secondary edn. teaching cert., Utah. Bookkeeper, Lyman Gas & Oil Co., Vernal, Utah, 1942; dep. county clk., Vernal, 1943-44; mem. steno pool RFC, Salt Lake City, 1944-45; sec. Alterra High Sch., Roosevelt, Utah, 1947-48; tchr. bus. Twin Falls (Idaho) Bus. Coll., 1950-51, Parowan (Utah) High Sch., 1951-54, Cyprus High Sch., Magna, Utah, 1954-59, Wasatch Jr. High Sch., Salt Lake City, 1959-63, Skyline High Sch., Salt Lake City, 1963-81; tchr. bus., chmn. dept. Taylorsville High Sch., Salt Lake City, 1981—; mem. Utah Bus. and Office Edn. Adv. Bd., 1977-80; bd. dirs. Utah Future Bus. Leaders Am., 1978-81. Recipient Scroll of Honor, Sal Ute chpt. Nat. Secs. Internat., 1969; named Outstanding Tchr., Utah Bus. Edn. Newsletter, 1975, Bus. Tchr. of Yr., Delta Pi Epsilon, 1983. Mem. Internat. Soc. Bus. Edn., Nat. Bus. Edn. Assn., Western Bus. Edn. Assn. (sec. 1979-80), NEA, Utah Bus. Edn. Assn. (pres. 1976-77, research award 1980), Granite Edn. Assn., Classroom Educators of Bus. and office Edn., Am. Vocat. Assn., Utah Vocat. Assn. (Bus. Educator of Yr. 1976, mem. exec. bd. 1975-77), Profl. Secs. Internat. Mormon. Home: 3784 S 3145 E Salt Lake City UT 84109 Office: Taylorsville High Sch 5225 S Redwood Rd Salt Lake City UT 84107

GILLENWATERS, THEODORE ROOSEVELT, investment advisor, lawyer; b. Maryhill, Wash., Apr. 21, 1903; s. Joseph Warren and Annie (Van Hoy) G.; B.S., U. Oreg., 1925; LL.D. (hon.), Kenyon Coll., Gambier, Ohio, 1942; m. Elizabeth Ramsby, June 29, 1929; children—Elizabeth Ann, Edgar Martin, Jayne Eileen. Admitted to Oreg. bar, 1927, Calif. bar, 1936, U.S. Supreme Ct. bar, 1942; dep. dist. atty. Klamath County (Oreg.), 1927-29, dist. atty., 1930-34; individual practice law, 1934-35; corp. counsel Reiber Elec. Corp., Los Angeles, 1936-41, O'Keefe & Merritt, 1946-48, Dr. Irving P. Krick, 1949, Water Resources Devel. Corp., 1949; trustee, officer Oceanic Research Inst., 1963; sr. partner Newport 1st Investment Services, Newport Beach, Calif., 1975-81; sec., dir. Helionetics, Inc., Irvine, Calif., 1980—; dir. Dynametron. Mem. Calif. Commn. Navigation and Ocean Devel., 1969; advisor marine affairs Calif. and Alaska Govs., 1967. Served to col., USAAF, 1941-48. Decorated Legion of Merit. Mem. Oreg. Dist. Attys. Assn. (life), Am. Legion (past post comdr., life), Marine Tech. Soc., Air Force Assn., Res. Officers Assn., Orange County Philharm. Soc., Western Pension Conf. Republican. Episcopalian. Clubs: Univ. (Los Angeles); Balboa Bay, Irvine Coast Country, Masons, Shriners, Elks Rotary (charter mem. Newport Sunrise). Bd. dirs. Oceanic Jour. and Oceanic Index, 1964-82; mem. sea grant adv. panel U. So. Calif., 1969-81. Home: 1070 Granville Dr Newport Beach CA 92660 Office: Suite 104 567 San Nicholas Dr Newport Beach CA 92660

GILLES, TERE JOSEPH, journalist; b. Billings, Mont., Nov. 23, 1948; s. Joseph Elroy and Jeanne Elanora (Ketchum) G.; student U. Mont., 1967-70; m. Margarita Valdez Hernandez, Mar. 1, 1980; 1 dau., Argentina Monica. Reporter, Western Livestock Reporter, Billings, Mont., 1971-73, feature editor, 1980-81; mgr. Spring Creek Charolais Ranch, Laurel, Mont., 1973-82; founding mem. Missoula (Mont.) Borrowed Times newspaper, 1972; asst. to pub. Billings (Mont.) Farm & Ranch Forum, 1976-80; founder UMP Pub., Laurel, 1976; reporter/editor Billings Agri-News, 1980-81; editor energy mag. The Roustabout, Shelby, Mont., 1981-82; mng. editor the Record Stockman, Denver, 1982—; newsman, sportscaster KSEN/KZIN Radio, Shelby, 1981—. Recipient Grand award Mont. Press Assn., 1972. Mem. Am.-Internat. Charlolais Assn., Mont. Charolais Assn., Mont. Grain Growers Assn., Livestock Publs. Council. Editor, writer: When Tillage Begins, 1977. Office: 4877 National Western Dr Denver CO 80216

GILLESPIE, BARBARA OLGA, educational administrator; b. Sonora, Calif., Apr. 4, 1935; d. Palmer Allen and Olga Bertha (Stillman) Wells; A.B., with honors in Music, San Jose State U., 1957, M.A. in Edn., 1975; Ed.D. in Sch. Mgmt., U. La Verne, 1980; m. Sherman Gillespie, June 16, 1968. Tchr. vocal music, Alum Rock and San Jose (Calif.) Unified Sch. Dist., 1957-60; instr. secondary edn. San Jose State U., 1963-69; English and reading cons., instructional team leader East Side Union High Sch. Dist., San Jose, 1960-80; secondary curriculum coordinator Morgan Hill (Calif.) Unified Sch. Dist., 1980-83; prin. Live Oak High Sch., 1983—; cons. Am. Book Co.; mem. policy bd. San Jose State and East Side Union High Sch. Dist., 1973-76. Named outstanding profl. educator East Side Union Teachers Assn., 1966. Mem. Assn. for Supervision and Curriculum Devel., Calif. Curriculum Forum, Am. Ednl. Research Assn., Nat. Council Tchrs. of English (mem. Talent Bank), Calif. Assn. Tchrs. of English, Assn. of Tchr. Educators, Calif. Council on Edn. of Tchrs., Assn. Calif. Sch. Adminstrs., Delta Kappa Gamma (pres. San Jose chpt., 1970-72, state officer, 1977-78, scholar, 1978), Phi Delta Kappa. Republican. Presbyterian. Clubs: Order Eastern Star, Rainbow for Girls (life), Theta Rho (life), Order Job's Daughters (life). Author materials in field, workbooks, programmed texts, publs. Home: 6248 Blauer Ln San Jose CA 95135 Office: 17810 Monterey St Morgan Hill CA 95037

GILLESPIE, DAIR LINDSAY, sociology educator; b. Lafayette, La., Feb. 24, 1940; d. Mosby James and Elsie Belle (Abbott) Lindsay; m. Clayton W. Gillespie Sr., June 4, 1960 (div.); children—Clayton Wayne Jr., Copper. B.A. magna cum laude, U. Houston, 1966, M.A. with honors, 1968; Ph.D., U. Calif.-Berkeley, 1978. Instr. sociology Univ. St. Thomas, Houston, 1967-68, U. Houston, 1968; teaching asst. U. Calif., Berkeley, 1968-77; asst. prof. sociology U. Utah, Salt Lake City, 1978—, mem. women's studies coordinating com. NSF trainee U. Houston, 1967-68, U. Calif.-Berkeley, 1968-72; NIMH trainee U. Calif.-Berkeley, 1973-75. Mem. Am. Sociol. Assn., Pacific Sociol. Assn., Internat. Sociol. Assn., Nat. Women's Studies Assn., ACLU. Contbr. articles to profl. jours. Home: 760 1st Ave Salt Lake City UT 84103 Office: Dept Sociology University of Utah Salt Lake City UT 84112

GILLESPIE, DOUGLAS GRANT, food supplement mfr.; b. Tulsa, Sept. 19, 1946; s. Francis Aiken and Martha Allen (Grant) G.; B.A., Diablo Valley Coll., 1967; postgrad. San Francisco State Coll., 1967-68; children—Jo Ann, Alexander; m. 2d, Melinda Ann Sellers, Apr. 9, 1977. Sales clk. Sports Unltd., Orinda, Calif., 1964-67; loan officer, mgr. United Calif. Bank, Oakland, 1967-69; pres., chief exec. officer Natura 1 Formulas, Inc., Hayward, Calif., 1970-81; pres., chief exec. officer Doug Gillespie & Assocs., Inc., Hayward, Calif. Pres. Nat. Protein Council, 1978—. Mem. Inst. Food Technologists, Council for Responsible Nutrition. Nat. Small Bus. Assn. Home: 11 Vista Del Mar Orinda CA 94563 Office: 2125 American Ave Hayward CA 94545

GILLESPIE, MICHAEL GORDON, exploration co. exec.; b. Great Falls, Mont., Sept. 12, 1945; s. Elmer W. and Ruth E. (Rosedale) G.; B.S., U. Mont., 1969; 1 son, Eric Sean. Safety dir. Boulder River Sch. and Hosp., Boulder, Mont., 1969-74, Employees Benefit Inst. Co., Portland, Oreg., 1974; safety cons. Zidell Exploration Co., Portland, 1974—, asst. safety dir., 1973—. Cardiopulmonary resuscitation, 1st aid instr. ARC, 1971, Jefferson County chpt. chmn., 1970-74; pres. Boulder River Sch. and Hosp. Fire Dept. and Ambulance, 1969-77. Mem. Assn. Vol. Firemen, Assn. Rescue and Ambulance. Author: Boulder River School and Hospital Fire Emergency and Disaster Manual, 1971, Boulder River School and Hospital Employees Safety Manual, 1972, Safe Workers Manual, 1978. Home: 10238 NE Morris Ct Portland OR 97220 Office: Zidell Exploration Co 3121 SW Moody St Portland OR 97201

GILLESPIE, ROBERT WILLIAM, geotechnical engr.; b. Beverly, Mass., Jan. 31, 1946; s. William and Anne Eilene (Sutherland) G.; A.A.S., Franklin Inst., Boston, 1967; B.S.C.E. with honors, Northeastern U., 1972; M.S.C.E., M.I.T., 1973; m. Phyllis B. Tanzella, Oct. 6, 1967; children—Amanda Marie, Joshua Robert. Structural designer R.J. Donovan, Inc., Winchester, Mass., 1969-72; soils engr. Ardaman & Assocs., Orlando, Fla., 1973-74; project engr. J.V. Lowney & Assos., Palo Alto, Calif., 1974-76; area mgr. No. Testing Labs., Inc., Great Falls, Mont., 1976-81, dir., 1980-81; pres. Geotech. Group, P.C., Gt. Falls, Mont., 1981—. Served with USMC, 1967-69; Vietnam. Registered profl. engr., Fla., Calif., Colo., Mont., Wyo., N.D., S.D. Mem. ASCE, Nat. Soc. Profl. Engrs., Tau Beta Pi, Chi Epsilon. Republican. Congregationalist. Office: PO Box 1741 Great Falls MT 59403

GILLETT, CARLENE TONI, physiologist; b. Salt Lake City, Aug. 7, 1947; d. Anthony J. and Anita Marie (Castellano) Carpino; student U. Utah; m. Larry J. Gillett, Oct. 4, 1969. Research technician dept. physiology lab. U. Utah, Salt Lake City, 1965—; cons. design and fabrication of ion-selective microelectrodes for determinations of intracellular pH, sodium, potassium and chloride activities. Home: 6386 S 1820 W West Jordan UT 84084 Office: Dept Physiology Univ Utah Salt Lake City UT 84108

GILLETTE, ERIC ALLISON, computer scientist, consultant; b. Rochester, N.Y., May 4, 1935; s. George A. and Mildred (Lockwood) G. B.A., Alfred U., 1958; M.B.A., Syracuse U., 1960. Computer systems analyst Ford Motor Co., Dearborn, Mich., 1960-67; project mgr. Bell & Howell, Lincolnwood, Ill., 1967-69; comml. systems mgr. G.D. Searle, Skokie, Ill., 1969-74; internal cons. Fed. Res. Bank of Chgo., 1974-78; sr. systems info. specialist Computer Scis. Corp., El Segundo, Calif., 1978—; assoc. prof. Calif. State U., Dominguez Hills. Mem. Assn. Systems Mgmt., Am. Prodn. Inventory Control Soc. Office: 650 N Sepulveda Blvd Suite E 340 El Segundo CA 90245

GILLETTE, FRANKIE JACOBS, former govt. ofcl.; b. Norfolk, Va., Apr. 1, 1925; d. Frank Walter and Natalie (Taylor) Jacobs; B.S., Hampton Inst., 1946; M.S.W., Howard U., 1948; postgrad. Merrill-Palmer Inst.; m. Maxwell C. Gillette, June 19, 1976. Supr., Ada S. McKinley Community House, Chgo., 1950-53; dir. Concerted Services Project, Pittsburg, Calif., 1964-65; program coordinator staff devel. programs U. Calif. at Berkeley, 1965-68; spl. programs coordinator, div. chief OEO, San Francisco, 1968-73, spl. program coordinator U.S. Community Services Adminstrn., 1973-82; asso. prof. Sch. Social Work, Sacramento State U., 1967; cons. ARC, others; dir. Time Savs. & Loan Assn. Mem. Calif. Commn. U.S. Commn. on Civil Rights, 1970—; mem. Calif. Gov.'s Commn. on Personal Privacy, 1981. Named Alumnus of Year, Hampton Inst., 1966. Mem. Nat. Assn. Social Workers, Nat. Council Negro Women, Nat. Assn. Negro Bus. and Profl. Women's Clubs (pres. 1983—), ACLU (San Francisco dir. 1970-72), Delta Sigma Theta. Home: 85 Cleary Ct San Francisco CA 94109

GILLETTE, GARY LYNN, constrn. exec.; b. Lewisville, Idaho, Apr. 8, 1935; s. Samuel and Valear (Thompson) G.; m. Nellie Rose Wright, May 6, 1954; m. 2d, Jeweldean Mitchell, July 30, 1970; children—Gary

Lynn Jr., Tamara Hodge. Supt. Carl E. Nelson Constrn. Co., Logan, Utah, 1948-66; gen. mgr. Boise (Idaho) Paving and Asphalt Co., 1966—; dir. Rock Contractors, G2C Syscom Inc. Mem. Mayor's Hire the Handicapped Com., Idaho Pub. Works Licensing Bd.; mem. Rep. Presdl. Task Force, 1981-82. Mem. Boise State U. Bronco Athletic Assn. (life), Nat. Asphalt Pavement Assn. (Idaho gov.), Associated Gen. Contractors (sec., treas. 1980-81). Clubs: Terrace Lakes Country (Crouch, Idaho); Hillcrest Country, Elks (Boise). Home: 3025 El Rio Dr Meridian ID 83642 Office: 2190 S Cole Rd Boise ID 83709

GILLETTE, KATHLEEN ANN, poet, hosp. ofcl.; b. Denver, June 17, 1947; d. S.W. and Jeanette J. Schoendaller; student Coe Coll., Cedar Rapids, Iowa, 1965-66, U. Colo., Denver, 1966-67. Adminstr. EKG dept. U. Colo. Health Scis. Center, 1979—; author 10 short stories, 1975—, 84 poems; books include: My People, The Colors of My Life, 1976; numerous poetry readings, U.S., 1978—; instr. poetry for prisoners; co-editor Foothills Art Flyer, 1978. Named Poet of Yr., Nat. Poetry Pubs. Assn., 1974; winner competitions Colo. Poetry Soc., 1978-80, 1st place Encore Nat. Contest, 1978. Mem. Nat. League Am. Pen Women (sec. Denver br. 1977-80), Colo. Poetry Soc. (2d v.p. 1980-83), Foothills Art Center, Nat. Fedn. Poetry Socs., Am. Assn. Med. Assts. Home: 5611 E 13th Ave Denver CO 80220

GILLETTE, OMNI LARRY, structures scientist; b. Tooele, Utah, June 4, 1927; s. Samuel Lindberg and Zelpha Ursula (Jones) G.; B.S. in Naval Sci., U. Utah, 1949, B.S. in Mech. Engring., 1952; m. Mary Alice Flygare, Nov. 25, 1949; children—John, Richard, Julie, Robert, Wendy, Jeffrey, Scott, Carolyn. Sr. structural engr. N.Am. Aviation, Los Angeles, 1955-58, supr. structural testing lab., 1958-62; mgr. instrument and automation depts. Utah Research & Devel. Co., Salt Lake City, 1962-64; project mgr. Hughes Aircraft Co., Los Angeles, 1964—; v.p. Armont Motor Vu Theatres, Inc., 1965—, Trolley Theatres, Inc., 1973—; instr. exptl. mechanics U. Calif. at Los Angeles, 1966-68. Active Boy Scouts Am. Served to lt. j.g., USN, 1945-46, 49-52. Mem. Soc. Exptl. Stress Analysis. Contbr. articles to profl. jours. Home: 28929 Briarhurst Dr Rancho Palos Verdes CA 90274 Office: Bldg 366 M/S 626 PO Box 92919 Los Angeles CA 90009

GILLEY, GEORGE CLAYTON, computer researcher, educator, inventor; b. San Jose, Calif., Mar. 28, 1934; s. William B. and Victoria Josephine (Dobish) G.; m. Janet Wanda Dorr, June 21, 1953; children—Debra Kay, Caryn Wanda, Steven Dean. B.S. in Aero. Engring., Northrop U., 1955; M.S. in Info. Systems, UCLA, 1967, Ph.D. in Computer Engring. (dissertation fellow), 1970. Guided missile systems engr. Northrop Corp., Hawthorne, Calif., 1955-60, missile weapon system project engr., 1960-62, satellite network research leader, 1962-63, spaceflight ops. mgr., 1963-64; multi-mission space flight ops. developer Jet Propulsion Lab., Pasadena, Calif., 1964-69, autonomous-fault-tolerant spacecraft researcher, 1969-72, planetary robotics researcher, 1972-75, advanced computer systems researcher, 1975-78; mgr. fault tolerant computer devel. Aerospace Corp., El Segundo, Calif., 1978-80, dir. Autonomy and Survivability Tech. Office, 1980—; teaching fellow UCLA, 1966, mem. faculty, 1967-72; mem. faculty Loyola-Marymount Coll., 1972-75; cons. on data processing systems; organizer profl. confs.; study dir. on autonomous spacecraft maintenance Air Force Office Sci. Research, summer 1980. Youth dir. North Redondo Chapel; mem. bd. Sounds of Grace. Mem. IEEE (tech. com. fault tolerant computing), ACM, AIAA, Internat. Fedn. Info. Processing (working group reliable computing). Republican. Contbr. articles to profl. jours.; patentee fault tolerant memory, virtual memory system. Home: 21730 Redbeam Ave Torrance CA 90503 Office: PO Box 92957 Los Angeles CA 90009

GILLIAM, EARL BEN, federal judge; b. Clovis, N.Mex., Aug. 17, 1931; s. James Earl and Lula Mae Gilliam; m. Barbara Jean Gilliam, Dec. 6, 1956; children—Earl Kenneth, Derrick James. B.A., Calif. State U.-San Diego, 1953; J.D., Hastings Coll. Law, 1957. Bar: Calif. 1957. Dep. dist. atty., San Diego, 1957-62; judge San Diego Mcpl. Ct., 1963-74; judge Superior Ct. Calif., San Diego County, 1975—; prof. law Western State Coll. Law, 1968—. Commr. gen. San Diego's 200th Anniversary. Name Jaycee's Young Man of Yr., 1965. Democrat. Office: U S Courthouse 940 Front St San Diego CA 92189

GILLIAM, JACKSON E., bishop; b. Heppner, Oreg., June 20, 1920; s. Edwin Earle and Mary (Perry) G.; A.B., Whitman Coll., 1942; B.D., Va. Sem., 1948, S.T.M., 1949, D.D., 1969; m. Margaret Kathleen Hindley, Aug. 11, 1943; children—Anne Meredith, Margaret Carol, John Howard. Ordained to ministry Protestant Episcopal Ch. as deacon, 1948, priest, 1949; vicar St. John's Ch., Hermiston, Oreg., 1949-53; canon St. Mark's Cathedral, Mpls., 1953-55; rector Ch. of Incarnation, Gt. Falls, Mont., 1955-68; bishop Diocese Mont., 1968—; dep. gen. convs., 1952, 61, 64, 67; pres. 6th Province Episcopal Ch., 1965-67. Vice chmn. ARC, Cascade County, Mont., 1965-66; mem. Mont. Council Alcoholism, 1964-65, Nat. Council Alcoholism, Gov. Adv. Bd. Chaplaincy, 1964-66; pres. Mont. Council Chs., 1967—. Bd. dirs. St. Peter's Hosp., Helena. Served to 1st lt. AUS, 1943-45. Decorated companion Order Cross of Nails. Mem. Tau Kappa Epsilon. Republican. Rotarian. Home: 1100 LeGrande Cannon Blvd Helena MT 59601 Office: 515 N Park Ave Helena MT 59601

GILLIAM, PAULETTE MARIE, communications executive; b. Houston, July 21, 1947; d. Bert James and Marie Hester (Hardcastle) Gilliam; m. Richard Raymond Peterson, Aug. 28, 1970 (div.). B.S. in Broadcasting, U. Tex., 1969; M.A. in Communications, Ariz. State U.-Tempe, 1977. Producer TV programs, Tyler, Tex., 1969, Austin, Tex., 1970, Pitts., 1970-72; devel. dir. KAET-TV, Phoenix, 1973; lectr. Ariz. State U., 1974-75; dir. field services Cactus-Pine council Girl Scouts U.S.A., Phoenix, 1977-78; exec. dir. Consortium for Learning in Ariz. through Mediated Instrn., Phoenix, 1978-79; pub. affairs cons Fed. Emergency Mgmt. Agy., Washington, 1978-83, Ariz. Div. Emergency Services, 1978-82; chief info. and edn. div. Ariz. Game and Fish Dept., Phoenix, 1982—; mem. Gov.'s Adv. Council for Emergency Edn. and Tng., 1980-82. Recipient (with others) Peabody award, 1972; Gold Medal award Nat. Assn. Ednl. Broadcasters, 1973; Nat. Promotion award Corp. for Pub. Broadcasting, 1974; Superior Service award Fed. Emergency Mgmt. Agy., 1980; HEW grantee, 1979. Mem. Internat. TV Assn., Assn. for Conservation Info., Alpha Epsilon Rho (sec. 1968-69, faculty advisor 1974-75). Contbg. editor The Family Game, 1972; producer TV series: The Turned-On Crisis, 1971, The Family Game, 1972, Womankind, 1976. Home: 10430-1 N 10th Pl Phoenix AZ 85020 Office: 2222 W Greenway Rd Phoenix AZ 85023

GILLILAND, PAUL MICHAEL, farm exec., city ofcl.; b. Brewer, Maine, Dec. 10, 1932; s. William Lester and Lucile (Cartmell) G.; B.S. in Chemistry, Purdue U., 1958, M.A. in English, 1964; M.A. in L.S., Ind. U., 1966; cert. Advanced Study, U. Chgo., 1969; m. Lorraine Elizabeth Amidei, June 2, 1962; children—Laura Christine, William Dean. Research chemist DeSoto Chem. Coatings, Chgo., 1961-62; librarian Purdue U., 1962-66; asst. prof. library sci. McGill U., Montreal, Can., 1969-71; sec.-treas. Gilliland Farms, Inc., Harrington, Wash., 1971—; mayor City of Harrington, 1980—; mem. Wash. State Library Commn., 1978—; del. Wash. Gov.'s Conf. Library and Info. Service. Committeeman, Wash. State Democratic Com., 1977—. Served with U.S. Army, 1952-55. Mem. ALA, Am. Chem. Soc., AAAS, Wash. Library Assn., Wash. Assn. Wheat Growers, Air Force Assn., Nat. Trust Historic Preservation, Beta Phi Mu. Mem. Ch. of Christ. Home and Office: PO Box 421 Harrington WA 99134

GILLIN, PHILIP HOWARD, lawyer; b. Council Bluffs, Iowa, Apr. 11, 1937; s. Nathan E. and Louise (Herzoff) G.; student U. Ariz., 1955-57, U. Calif., San Francisco, 1957-59; J.D., U Santa Clara, 1960; m. Joycelyn Hall, Apr. 1, 1976; children—Jamie Lynn, Julia Ann. Andrea Leigh. Admitted to Calif. bar, 1961; mem. firm Gillin & Scott, Hollywood, Calif., 1959-60; individual practice law, Hollywood, 1970-75; mem. firm Gillin, Gottesman & Menes, Los Angeles, 1975—; tchr. real estate law Calif. Continuing Edn. for the Bar; pres. Church Lane Music Inc., Berkeley Square Music Inc.; pres. Scott Gillin Ltd. Chmn. March of Dimes, Sherman Oaks, 1964-69. Mem. Am. (nat. sec. student assn. 1958-59), Hollywood (dir. 1963-66, sec. 1967-68, pres. 1971) bar assns., Century City Bar Assn., Calif. Copywright Conf. Office: 1901 Ave of Stars #1240 Century City CA 90067

GILLINGS, MARK DALE, constrn. co. exec.; b. Madison, Wis., Feb. 3, 1951; s. Dale Nelson and Joanne Katherine Gillings; B.S., U. Wis., Stout, 1973. Estimator, Waldinger Corp., Des Moines, 1974-77, project estimator, Richland, Wash., 1977-78, contract adminstr., 1978-79, asst. project mgr., 1979-80, project mgr., 1981—. Mem. Am. Mgmt. Assn., Sigma Tau Gamma. Office: Box 1430 Richland WA 99352

GILLIS, CHRISTINE DIEST-LORGION, stockbroker; b. San Francisco; d. Evert Jan and Christine Helen (Radcliffe) Diest-Lorgion; B.S. in Bus. Adminstrn., U. Calif.; M.S., U. So. Calif., 1968; children—Suzanne and Barbara (twins). Account exec. Winslow, Cohu & Stetson Inc., N.Y.C., 1963-64, Paine, Webber, Jackson & Curtis, N.Y.C., 1964-65; sr. investment exec. Shearson, Hammill, Beverly Hills, Calif., 1966-72; cert. fin. planner E.F. Hutton & Co., Glendale, Calif., 1972—; instr. investment classes UCLA, U. So. Calif. Sec., dir., mem. bd. govs. Town Hall of Calif., 1975-80. Cert., Inst. Cert. Fin. Planners. Mem. Women Stockbrokers Assn. (founder, pres.), Women of Wall St. West (founder, pres.), AAUW (life mem., founder Palos Verdes br., trustee Nat. Edn. Fellowship Found.), Bus. and Profl. Women's Club, Navy League (life mem.), Phi Chi Theta (life). Home: 1495 Pegfair Estates Dr Pasadena CA 91103

GILLISS, MARCUS RONALD, psychiatrist, med. adminstr.; b. Modesto, Calif., June 15, 1915; s. Antoine Berry and Flora Augusta (Cooper) G.; A.B., Humboldt State Coll., 1953; M.D., George Washington U., 1957; m. Marjorie June Carlson, Feb. 28, 1948; children—Carolyn Anne (Mrs. Billy Thompson), Marcus Ronald. Intern St. Elizabeth's Hosp., Washington, 1957-58; psychiat. resident Cleve. Psychiat. Inst., 1958-63; chief psychiat. service Hawthornden State Hosp., Macedonia, Ohio, 1960-61; resident psychiatrist Cleve. Psychiat. Inst., 1962-63; sr. psychiatrist, asst. supt., asso. med. dir. Office Program Rev. Stockton (Calif.) State Hosp., 1963-80; cons. Superior Ct., 1965-70, Social Security Regional Office, 1980-83; pvt. practice psychiat. cons., 1983—; asst. clin. prof. psychiatry U. Calif., Davis, 1972-76. Served with AUS, 1945-47. Fellow Am. Psychiat. Assn., Royal Soc. Health; mem. Central Calif. Psychiat. Soc., Pan Am. Med. Assn., World Fedn. Mental Health, Nat. Geog. Soc. Home: 37 W Pine St Stockton CA 95204 Office: 37 W Pine St Stockton CA 95204

GILLIT, HAROLD GENE, mech. engr.; b. Lyford, Tex., Apr. 16, 1932; s. Donald Lee and Hazel Beatrice (Bradford) G.; student Tex. Western Coll., El Paso, 1951-53; B.S.M.E., U. N.Mex., 1956; m. Frances Anne Young, Jan. 28, 1956; children—Bruce, Helen, Steven. Engr., El Paso Natural Gas Co., Jal, N.Mex., 1956-62; design engr. ACF Industries, Albuquerque, 1962-64; sr. design engr. Stearns-Roger Co., Denver, 1964-67; sr. engr., chief div. engr. El Paso Natural Gas Co., Salt Lake City, 1968-74; project engr. NW Pipeline Corp., Salt Lake City, 1974-77, chief engr., 1977—. Served with U.S. Army, 1956-58. Registered profl. engr. N.Mex. Mem. Am. Gas Assn. Mem. Bible Ch. Home: 1410 E 4080 S Salt Lake City UT 84117 Office: NW Pipeline Corp PO Box 1526 Salt Lake City UT 84110

GILLMAR, STANLEY FRANK, lawyer; b. Honolulu, Aug. 17, 1935; s. Stanley Eric and Ruth (Scudder) G.; divorced; children—Sara Tamsin, Amy Katherine. A.B. cum laude with high honors, Brown U., 1957; LL.B., Harvard U., 1963. Bar: Calif. 1963. Ptnr. Graham & James, San Francisco, 1970—. Sec., Calif. Council Internat. Trade, 1973—; mem. Mayor San Francisco Adv. Council Econ. Devel., 1976—, Title IX Loan Bd., 1982—. Served with USNR, 1957-60. Mem. ABA, Calif. State Bar, Bar Assn. San Francisco. Clubs: Bankers (San Francisco); Villa Taverna, Inverness Yacht. Co-author: How To Be An Importer and Pay For Your World Travels, 1979; co-pub. Travelers Guide to Importing, 1980. Office: 300 One Maritime Plaza San Francisco CA 94111

GILLO, MARTIN WALDEMAR, semiconductor co. exec.; b. Leipzig, Germany, Mar. 23, 1945; s. Waldemar Karl and Irmgard Elisabeth (Meinke) G.; B.A., U. Hamburg, 1969; M.A. in Psychology, U. Kans., 1970, Ph.D. in Psychology, 1973; m. Gail E. Godfrey, Dec. 28, 1972; children—Susan Elisabeth, Karen Eileen. Asst. prof. psychology U. Wash., Seattle, 1972-74; mgmt. cons. Hay Assos., Phila., Frankfurt, Germany, San Francisco, 1974-80; dir. compensation and benefits Advanced MicroDevices, Sunnyvale, Calif., 1980—. Fulbright scholar, 1969. Mem. Am. Psychol. Assn. Lutheran. Home: 12 Shenandoah Way Pacifica CA 94044 Office: 901 Thompson Pl Sunnyvale CA 94086

GILLOW, GEORGE BRACEY, elec. engr.; b. Potrerillos, Chile, Oct. 27, 1945; s. Joseph Robert and Annie Rachel (Taylor) G.; came to U.S., 1957; B.S. in Elec. Engring., San Diego State U., 1970, M.S. in Elec. Engring., 1973; m. Pamela Jean Kennedy, Sept. 24, 1982. Project leader, design central processing units for computer, advanced devel. dept. Data Processing div. NCR Corp., San Diego, 1970-78; group mgr., design of large central processing units for computer Nat. Semi-condr. Corp., San Diego, 1978-80; with JRS Industries, San Diego, 1980-82; mgr. engring. DDG Corp., San Diego, 1982—; v.p. Digidyne Corp., San Diego, 1983—; instr. Southwestern Coll., evenings, 1974, 75. Chmn. Environ. Control Commn. Chula Vista, 1975-78, chmn. Hist. Sites Bd., 1975-78; mem. Chula Vista City Council, 1978—, vice mayor, 1979-80. Mem. Tau Beta Pi. Democrat. Home: 250 Camino Del Cerro Grande Bonita CA 92002 Office: 8650 Balboa Ave San Diego CA 92123

GILMAN, DON, state senator, businessman, mayor; b. Long Creek, Oreg., Apr. 20, 1934; m. Nikki Gilman; 2 children. M.S. in Edn., U. Oreg. Kenai Peninsula Borough mayor; small businessman; mem. Alaska State Senate, 1980—. Co-chmn. Alaska Coastal Policy Council; dir. Alaska Mcpl. League; asst. dir. Alaska Skill Ctr. Served with JAGC, U.S. Army. Mem. Am. Petroleum Inst. Office: Alaska State Senate Juneau AK 99811*

GILMAN, ELISA AMBROSINA, fin. exec.; b. Locarno, Switzerland, Sept. 1, 1929; came to U.S., 1930, naturalized, 1947; d. Mario A. and Ida Elisa (Fantoni) Ferrari; B.S., N.Y. Inst. Fin., 1955; children—Gary R. Freeman, Sandra K. Kanahele. With Paine Webber, Santa Barbara, Calif., 1953-55; cashier/broker Shearson Hammil, Santa Barbara, 1955-69; stockbroker, sr. investment exec. Reynolds Securities, Santa Barbara, 1970-79, v.p., 1976; account exec., v.p. Dean Witter Reynolds, Santa Barbara, 1979—; cons. Com. for Status Am. Women, 1974—. Mem. grants com. Dir. Relief Found., 1980. Republican. Club: Coral Casino. Home: 5100 Camino Floral Santa Barbara CA 93111 Office: 200 E Carrillo St Santa Barbara CA 93101

GILMAN, RICHARD CARLETON, college president; b. Cambridge, Mass., July 28, 1923; s. George Phillips Brooks and Karen Elise (Theller) G.; B.A., Dartmouth, 1944; student New Coll., U. London (Eng.), 1947-48; Ph.D. (Borden Parker Bowne fellow Philosophy, 1949-50), Boston U., 1952, LL.D., 1969; LL.D., Pomona Coll., 1966, U. So. Calif., 1968, Coll. Ida., 1968; m. Lucille Young, Aug. 28, 1948 (dec. June 1978); children—Marsha, Bradley Morris, Brian Potter, Blair Tucker. Teaching fellow religion Dartmouth, 1948; mem. faculty Colby Coll., 1950-56, asso. prof. philosophy, 1955-56; exec. dir. Nat. Council Religion Higher Edn., New Haven, 1956-60; dean coll., prof. philosophy Carleton Coll., 1960-65; pres. Occidental Coll., 1965—; counselor, exec. asst. to U.S. sec. Edn., 1979-80; mem. Intergovtl. Council on Edn., 1980-82. Bd. dirs. Los Angeles World Affairs Council, Assn. Ind. Calif. Colls. and Univs., Council Postsecondary Edn.; pres. Ind. Colls. So. Calif.; past bd. dirs. Am. Council on Edn., Assn. Am. Colls., Nat. Assn. Ind. Colls. and Univs., Council Fin. Aid to Edn., Calif. Museum Found.; Served with USNR, 1944-46. Fellow Soc. Religion Higher Edn., Newcomen Soc., Calif. C. of C. (dir.); mem. Phi Beta Kappa. Presbyterian. Clubs: University (N.Y.C.); California, Twilight, 100 (Los Angeles). Home: 1852 Campus Rd Los Angeles CA 90041 Office: 1600 Campus Rd Los Angeles CA 90041

GILMARTIN, AMY JEAN, biology educator, administrator; b. Red Bluff Calif., Oct. 15, 1932; d. Ruy Herbert and Margaret Helena (Harvey) Finch; m. Malvern Gilmartin Jr., June 8, 1954 (div.); children—Malvern III, Dale Moana, Sheila Ann, Ian Harvey. A.B., Pomona Coll., 1954; M.S., U. Hawaii, 1956, Ph.D., 1968. Research asst. Hawaii Agr. Expt. Sta., 1954-56; curatorial asst., teaching asst. U. B.C., Vancouver, 1957-59, research asst. forest genetics, 1960; prof. U. Guayquil (Ecuador), 1961-63; vis. researcher San Diego Natural History Mus., 1965; research assoc. in flora N.Am., Smithsonian Instn., Washington, 1969-70; instr. biology Monterey (Calif.) Peninsula Coll., 1970-75; dir. Ownbey Herbarium, Pullman, Wash., 1975—; asst. prof. botany Wash. State U., 1975-79, assoc. prof. 1979-83, prof., 1983—; cons. Active ACLU in coordination with Natural Heritage and Nature Conservancy, State of Wash. AAUW predoctoral fellow, 1968, 83; sr. Fulbright fellow, 1982; NSF grantee, 1971-82; Am. Philos. Soc. research grantee, 1967. Mem. Guayquil Natural History Soc., nat. and internat. bot. and zool. socs. Democrat. Presbyterian. Author: Bromeliads of Ecuador, 1972; mem. editorial bd. Taxon, 1975-77, Madrono, 1982-84. Home: SE 425 Hill St Pullman WA 99163 Office: Dept Biology Wash State U Pullman WA 99164

GILMORE, ALLAN EMORY, govt. ofcl., chemist; b. Riverside, Calif., Apr. 7, 1924; s. Elvin E. and Emma Martha (Picker) G.; m. Betty Jo Hoskinson, Jan. 2, 1943; children—William Allan, Robert Donald, David Ernest. Student Riverside Jr. Coll., 1942-43, The Citadel, 1943-44, Loughborough Tech. Coll. (Eng.), 1945-46; A.B., U. Calif., Berkeley, 1948. Chief chemist Western Gulf Oil Co., Bakersfield, Calif., 1948-53; narcotic chemist-inspector State of Calif., Sacramento, 1953-56, criminalist, 1956-67; crime lab. dir. Sacramento County, 1967-81; cons. Calif. Forensic Lab., Foster City, 1981—; part-time instr. Sierra Coll., Rocklin, Calif., 1972-76; instr. Sacramento City Coll., 1981—; Served with AUS, 1943-46. Decorated Bronze Star; Office of Traffic Safety grantee, 1970. Mem. Nat. Assn. Crime Lab. Dirs., Calif. Assn. Criminalists (life), Criminalists Mgmt. Assn., Internat. Assn. Toxicologists, Internat. Assn. Arson Investigators, Calif. Peace Officers Assn. (life), N.W. Forensic Soc., Nat. Assn. Clock and Watch Collectors. Club: Masons. Contbr. articles to profl. jours. Home and Office: 7635 Bar Du Ln Sacramento CA 95829

GILMORE, DARLA MARIE, computer company executive; b. Mpls., June 27, 1948; d. Billy P. and LaVina (Whitcomb) Rife; m. Robert Barry Gilmore, June 22, 1973. Student Saddleback Community Coll. Cert. realtor, Ohio. Bookkeeper Internat. Hotel Coonstrn. and Mgmt., San Diego, 1974-76; asst. to controller Continental Properties, San Diego, 1976-77; project fin. mgr. Ajay Devel. Corp., Centerville, Ohio, 1977-79; asst. to controller McCombs Corp., Irvine, Calif., 1979-80; sec.-treas., chmn. bd. Capricorn Computing, Inc., Mission Viejo, Calif., 1980—; cons. acct. Wild West Stores, Inc., Costa Mesa, Calif. Mem. Nat. Assn. Accts., Nat. Bd. Realtors. Republican. Office: 23866 Via Calzada Mission Viejo CA 92691

GILROY, JOHN JOSEPH, university administrator; b. Phila., Nov. 30, 1935; s. John Joseph and Josephine B. (Kernan) G.; m. Helene L. (Maushardt), June 10, 1972; children—Jeremy, Kristen. B.A., LaSalle Coll., 1957, M.A., 1958; M.A., Middlebury Coll., 1967; Ph.D., U. Pitts., 1972. Secondary sch. tchr., Phila., 1958-67; secondary sch. prin. South Hills Catholic Sch., Pitts., 1967-69; coordinator secondary edn. Point Park Coll., Pitts., 1969-73; assoc. dean, coordinator grad. studies SUNY-Oswego, 1973-82; dean Sch. Edn., Seattle U., 1982—. Bd. dirs. Oswego County Sheltered Workshop, 1979-82; v.p. Oswego County Assn. Retarded Children, 1978-82; bd. dirs. Oswego County Community Services Bd., 1979-82. Am. Assn. Tchrs. French scholar, 1964. Mem. Am. Assn. Colls. Tchrs. Edn. (chief instl. rep.), Assn. Supervision and Curriculum Devel., Phi Delta Kappa. Roman Catholic. Contbr. articles to profl. jours. Home: 1000 Greenwood Blvd Issaquah WA 98027 Office: Sch Edn Seattle U Seattle WA 98122

GILSON, ARNOLD LESLIE, engring. co. exec.; b. Perrysburg, Ohio, Apr. 10, 1931; s. Leslie Clair and Velma Lillian (Hennen) G.; B.S. in Mech. Engring., U. Toledo, 1962; m. Phyllis Mary Seiling, Sept. 15, 1951 (dec. May 1982); children—David, Jeffrey, Luann, Suzanne. Engr., Miller, Tillman & Zamis engrs., Toledo, 1962-67, regional mgr., Phoenix br., 1967-69; owner, mgr. A B S Tech. Services, Phoenix, 1969—. Served with U.S. Army, 1952; Korea. Decorated Bronze Star. Mem. Nat. Mil. Intelligence Assn. Republican. Roman Catholic. Commd. extraordinary minister, 1975. Patentee in several fields. Home: 8226 E Meadowbrook Ave Scottsdale AZ 85251 Office: PO Box 2440 Scottsdale AZ 85252

GILSON, THOMAS QUINLEVAN, labor arbitrator, industrial relations and management educator; b. Summit, N.J., June 27, 1916; s. Herbert Clark and Elinor Reading (Gebhardt) G.; m. Marie Jacques, Feb. 11, 1939; children—Marie, Thomas Q., William R. B.A. in Econs., Princeton U., 1938; M.A. magna cum laude (Woodrow Wilson scholar), Columbia U., 1942; Ph.D., MIT. 1954. Asst. prof. Clark U., Worcester, Mass., 1946-50; research assoc. Harvard U., 1950-52; prof., chmn. dept. mgmt. Rutgers U., 1952-64; prof. indsl. relations and mgmt. U. Hawaii, Honolulu, 1964—, assoc. dean academic affairs, 1975-81; labor arbitrator, cons. in field. Mem. Hawaii Personnel Assn., Am. Soc. Public Adminstrn. (chmn. Hawaii chpt.), Nat. Acad. Arbitration, Indsl. Relations Research Assn., Am. Psychol. Assn., Am. Arbitrators Assn., Phi Delta Kappa, Phi Beta Kappa. Contbr. articles to profl. jours. Home: 2033 Nuuanu Ave PH 27A Honolulu HI 96817 Office: 2404 Maile Way CBA U Hawaii Honolulu HI 96822

GIMBEL, GILBERT WILLIAM, accountant, lawyer; b. Hazelton, N.D., Oct. 28, 1937; s. Milbert Walter and Myrtle May (Beseler) G.; student Jamestown Coll., 1955-57; B.S. in Bus. Adminstrn. magna cum laude, U. N.D., 1959, LL.B., 1962; m. Lynda Marie Holdren, May 19, 1979; children—John William, Robert Karl, LaVone Alice. Auditor, GAO, Washington, 1961; instr. U. Nebr., 1962-63; admitted to N.D. bar, 1962, Oreg. bar, 1973; pvt. practice pub. accounting, Omaha, 1964-65, Corvallis, Oreg., 1966-69, Hillsboro, Oreg., 1969—; instr. Portland Community Coll. C.P.A., Oreg. Mem. Hillsboro C. of C. Oreg. Soc. C.P.A.s, Oreg. State Bar, Phi Delta Phi, Sigma Nu, Beta Gamma Sigma (award 1959), Beta Alpha Psi. Republican. Lutheran. Rotarian. Author: (with Glen A. Mumey) An Analysis of North Dakota Trust Funds, 1960. Home: 532 NE Birchwood Terr Hillsboro OR 97123 Office: 238 SE 2d Ave Hillsboro OR 97123

GIMELLI, REBECCA DOUGLASS, psychology counselor, therapist, consultant; b. N.Y.C., Aug. 6, 1945; d. Lathrop Smith and Dorothy (Howe) Douglass; m. Juan Emilio Gimelli, May 1, 1975; children—Noa Catalina, Terra Ana. B.A., Wheaton (Mass.) Coll., 1967; postgrad. U. Florence (Italy), 1968-69; M.A., Gonzaga U., 1982. Asst. tchr. Montessori Sch., Coeur d'Alene, Idaho, 1977-78; counselor Cath. Family Services, Spokane, Wash., 1981-82; psychol. technician Pinecrest Psychiat. Ctr., Coeur d'Alene, 1983—; pvt. practice as counselor in psychology, Coeur d'Alene, 1982—. Active Coeur d'Alene Council for Youth, Panhandle Child Sexual Abuse Network, North Idaho Substance Abuse Network. Mem. Am. Personnel and Guidance Assn. Club: 1254 Athletic (Coeur d'Alene). Office: 627 Government Way Coeur d'Alene ID 83814

GIMMESTAD, MICHAEL JON, psychology educator; b. Mnpls., Oct. 23, 1943; s. Walter A. and Leona M. (Dorf) G.; m. Effie L. Gryting, June 19, 1965; children—Chad, Wendy, Cory. B.A. in Math., St. Olaf Coll., 1965; M.S. in Counseling, Ind. U., 1967; Ph.D. in Counseling Psychology, U. Minn., 1970. Tchr. Robbinsdale (Minn.) pub. schs., 1965-66; counselor U. Minn., Mpls., 1967-70; assoc. prof., chmn. dept. counseling, health, rehab. Fla. State U., Tallahassee, 1970-77; prof., chmn. dept. psychology U. No. Colo., Greeley, 1977—. Mem. Am. Psychol. Assn., Am. Personnel and Guidance Assn. Office: U No Colo Greeley CO 80639

GINEPRA, ALFRED LEON, JR., pub. relations exec.; b. Boston, July 30, 1933; s. Alfred Leon and Ruth Dorothy (Burns) G.; A.B., Columbia U., 1955, M.B.A., 1963, postgrad. in law, 1955-56; student law Stanford U., 1958-59, U. Calif., Los Angeles, 1969; m. Joan Marie Mariner, June 27, 1959; children—Joanne Ruth, Lawrence Paul. Analyst, Dun & Bradstreet, Inc., 1959-61; editor E.I. duPont de Nemours & Co., 1963; govtl. affairs rep. Gen. Telephone Co., 1963-69; pub. relations supr. Carnation Co., Los Angeles, 1969-78; public relations mgr. Korean Airlines, 1978-79; public relations dir. USO, 1979—; asst. prof. Calif. State U., Northridge, 1975; sr. lectr. U. Calif., Los Angeles, 1973—; lectr. Pacific States U., 1980—. Bd. dirs., exec. com. Am. Heart Assn., Los Angeles ARC. Served with AUS, 1956-58. Mem. Public Relations Soc. Am., Los Angeles Soc. Public Relations Counselors (pres. 1976), Los Angeles Area C. of C., Calif. C. of C., NAM, Los Angeles Pub. Affairs Officers Assn., Northridge Hosp. Found., San Fernando (pres. 1974), Century City (pres. 1975) pub. relations roundtables, Psi Upsilon, Phi Delta Phi. Republican. Congregationalist. Clubs: Olympic (San Francisco); Columbia Univ., Los Angeles Rugby, Old Blue, N.Y. Rugby (life), UCLA Public Relations (founder 1981), Masons (32 deg.), Toastmasters. All-Am. scholastic football player, 1954; mem. Columbia Coll. Centennial All-Star football team, 1870-1970. Home: 843 11th St 4 Santa Monica CA 90403 Office: 1641 N Ivar Ave Hollywood CA 90028

GINGRICH, JAMES EARL, chemical engineering executive; b. Lafayette, Ind., Oct. 21, 1930; s. Earl and Olive (Sense) G.; B.S. in Chem. Engring., Oreg. State U., 1953; m. Joan M. Craig, Mar. 7, 1953; children—James E., Jeffrey, Jodi, Jon. Engr., Alcoa, Wenatchee, Wash., 1953-55; chem. engr. Mobil Oil Co., Vernon, Calif., 1955-56; project engr. Atomics Internat., Canoga Park, Calif., 1956-66; mgr. Gen. Electric, Pleasanton, Calif., 1966-74; v.p. Terradex Corp., Walnut Creek, Calif., 1974—; cons., lectr. in field. Recipient award for outstanding tech. paper Am. Nuclear Soc., 1973. Mem. Am. Inst. Chem. Engrs., Am. Nuclear Soc., Can. Inst. Mining and Metallurgy. Republican. Presbyterian. Contbr. articles to profl. jours. Office: 460 N Wiget Ln Walnut Creek CA 94598

GINZTON, EDWARD LEONARD, electronics manufacturing company executive; b. Dnepropetrovsk, Ukraine, Dec. 27, 1915; s. Leonard Louis and Natalia P. (Philipova) G. (parents Am. citizens); m. Artemas Alma McCann; June 16, 1939; children—Anne, Leonard, Nancy, David. B.S., U. Calif.-Berkeley, 1936, M.S., 1937; E.E., Stanford U., 1938, Ph.D., 1940. Research assoc. Stanford U., Palo Alto, Calif., 1938-40, asst. prof. applied physics, elec. engring., 1946-47, assoc. prof., 1947-50, prof., 1951-68, dir. Microwave Lab., 1949-59, dir. Project M Stanford Linear Accelerator Ctr., 1957-60, univ. del. to China, 1978; research engr. Sperry Gyroscope Co., N.Y.C., 1940-46; dir. Varian Assocs., Palo Alto, Calif., 1948—, chmn. bd., 1959—, chief exec. officer, 1959-72, pres., 1964-68; mem. sci. and ednl. adv. com. Lawrence Berkeley Lab. 1972-80; mem. No. Calif. Adv. Bd. Union Bank, 1973-81. Co-chmn. Stanford Mid-Peninsula Urban Coalition, 1968-72, mem. exec. com., 1968-74; bd. dirs. Mid-Peninsula Housing Devel. Corp., 1970—, Stanford U. Hosp., 1975-80; trustee Stanford U., 1977—. Named Calif. Mfr. of Yr., Calif. Mgmt. Assn., 1974. Fellow IEEE (Morris Liebmann Meml. prize 1958, medal of honor 1969); mem. Nat. Acad. Scis., Am. Acad. Arts and Scis., Nat. Acad. Engring. (council 1974-80), Sigma Xi, Eta Kappa Nu, Tau Beta Pi. Club: Palo Alto. Contbr. articles to tech. jours. Patentee in field. Home: 28014 Natoma Rd Los Altos Hills CA 94022 Office: Varian Assocs Inc 611 Hansen Way Palo Alto CA 94303

GIOMI, THELMA ANNE, psychologist; b. Albuquerque, Feb. 26, 1947; d. James E. and Esma A. (Snyder) G. B.A., U. N.Mex., 1969, M.A., 1972, Ph.D., 1974. Psychometrician, Albuquerque Pub. Schs., 1969-72; instr. child psychology U. N.Mex., 1973-74; intern Pitts. Child Guidance Ctr., 1974-75; dir. psychology and staff tng., staff psychologist U. N.Mex., 1975-81, asst. prof. psychiatry and psychology, 1975-81, adj. prof. dept. psychology, 1979—; pvt. practice clin. psychology, Albuquerque, 1981—; cons. to sch. programs, women's groups; tchr. cognitive and family therapy. Mem. Youth Work Alliance, Rio Grande Writers Assn. NIMH research grantee, 1968-69; U. N.Mex. grantee, 1972-74. Mem. Am. Psychol. Assn., AAAS, Nat. Register Health Care Providers, N.Mex. Psychol. Assn., Phi Beta Kappa, Phi Kappa Phi. Home: 713 Manzano NE Albuquerque NM 87110 Office: 406 San Mateo Blvd NE Suite 8-B Albuquerque NM 87108

GIPSON, JAMES HAMMOND, investment advisor; b. Los Angeles, Oct. 1, 1942; s. James R. and Mary Jean (Hammond) G.; m. Janice Quinn, Jan., 1983. B.A., UCLA, 1963, M.A., 1964; M.B.A., Harvard U., 1973. Mgmt. cons. McKinsey & Co., 1967-69; analyst Los Angeles Times Mirror, 1970-71; v.p. Source Capital, 1971-73, sr. v.p., 1973-78; sr. v.p. Batterymarch Fin., 1978-80; pres. Pacific Fin. Research, Beverly Hills, Calif., 1980—. Served to lt. USNR, 1964-67. Mem. Harvard Bus. Sch. Assn., Fin. Analysts Fedn. Republican. Club: Harvard. Contbr. articles to Washington Post, Boston Globe, Pensions and Investments, Jour. Portfolio Mgmt. Home: 909 Stone Canyon Rd Bel Air CA 90077 Office: 9401 Wilshire Blvd Suite 1175 Beverly Hills CA 90212

GIPSTEIN, ROBERT MALCOLM, internist; b. Springfield, Mass., Mar. 29, 1936; s. Benjamin Louis and Dorothy Ida (Weitzman) G.; B.A. with honors and distinction in creative writing, Wesleyan U., 1957; M.D., Tufts U., 1961; m. Gwynne Jewel Zacks, June 3, 1961; 1 son, Jason. Intern, Seton Hall (Jersey City Med. Center), 1961-62; med. resident Long Beach (Calif.) VA Hosp., 1962-63, Wadsworth VA Hosp., Los Angeles, 1963-64; sr. resident in metabolism Wadsworth VA Hosp., Los Angeles, 1964-65, attending physician, 1968—; research fellow in metabolism N.C. Meml. Hosp., Chapel Hill, 1965-66; practice medicine specializing in internal medicine and nephrology, Los Angeles, 1968—; attending physician Los Angeles County U. So. Calif. Med. Center, Los Angeles, 1968-75, asso. in medicine, 1964-65; clin. instr. medicine UCLA Center Health Sci., 1968-74, asst. clin. prof. medicine, 1975-83, asso. clin. prof., 1983—; attending physician Harbor Gen. Hosp., 1974—; sr. staff physician, chief nephrology, dir. hemodialysis and plasmapheresis units Santa Monica (Calif.) Hosp.; sr. staff physician, dir. hemodialysis unit St. John's Hosp., Santa Monica; research asso. medicine U. N.C., 1965-66; sci. adv. council So. Calif. Kidney Found., 1969—. Mgr. W. Los Angeles Little League, 1975, 76. Served with M.C. to capt., U.S. Army, 1966-68. Diplomate Am. Bd. Internal Medicine, Am. Bd. Nephrology. Fellow ACP; mem. Am. Soc. Nephrology, Internat. Soc. Nephrology, Los Angeles County Soc. Internal Medicine, Am. Soc. Internal Medicine, Los Angeles County Med. Assn., Calif. Med. Assn., AMA (Physicians Recognition award 1974-77, 77-80, 81-84), AAAS, N.Y. Acad. Scis., Smithsonian Instn. Assos. Contbr. articles to profl. jours. Home: 1367 Brinkley Ave Los Angeles CA 90049 Office: 11860 Wilshire Blvd Los Angeles CA 90025

GIRARD, ALEXANDER H(AYDEN), architect; b. N.Y.C., May 24, 1907; s. Carlo Matteo and Lezlie (Cutler) G.; grad. Royal Inst. Brit. Architects, 1929, Royal Sch. Architecture, Rome, Italy, 1931, N.Y.U., 1935; m. Susan Needham, Mar. 1936; children—Sansi, Marshall. Worked archtl. offices, Florence, Rome, London, Paris, N.Y.C.; practice of architecture, Florence, 1930-32, N.Y.C., 1932-37, Detroit, 1937, Santa Fe, 1953—; works exhibited Barcelona, Florence, London, N.Y.C., Detroit, Walker Art Center, Rochester Mus., Cranbrook Acad., Museum of Modern Art, Cooper Union, Mus. Internat. Folk Art, Santa Fe, Nelson Gallery, Atkins Mus., Kansas City, Mo.; outstanding works include part of Italian exhibit Internat. Exhbn., Barcelona, 1929, offices Ford Motor Co., Dearborn, Mich., 1943, cafeteria Lincoln Motor Co., Detroit, 1946, pvt. residences, Mich., 1962, offices Irwin Mgmt., Columbus, Ind., 1972-73; established Girard Found., 1961; dir. Gen. For Modern Living Exhbn. Detroit Inst. Arts, 1949; color cons. Gen. Motors Research Center, Detroit, 1951-52; now dir. fabric div. Herman Miller Furniture Co.; designer Design for Use traveling show, Mus. Modern Arts, 1950, Herman Miller Furniture Co. exhibit Furniture Mus., Grand Rapids, Mich., 1951, spl. fabric collection, catalog, 1952. Good Design exhbn., Mdse. Mart Chgo., 1952, 53; Herman Miller Showroom, San Francisco, 1958; La Fonda del Sol Restaurant, N.Y.C., 1959-60; Herman Miller Textile and Objects Shop, N.Y.C.; other exhbns. in home furnishings, textile and ornamental arts Mus. Modern Art, 1954, 55, contbr. fabric designs to Am. Fabrics Exhbn., 1956; exhbn. table settings Georg Jensen, Inc., N.Y.C., 1955, 56. Juror Good Design exhibit Mdse. Mart, Chgo., 1950, Internat. Fabric Competition, Greensboro, N.C., 1952, Craftsman of N.Mex., 1962, Craft Guild, San Antonio, 1962, Own Your Own Exhibit, Denver Art Mus., 1963; interiors St. John's Coll., Santa Fe, 1963; 3-dimensional mural John Deere & Co., Moline, Ill., 1964; redesign visual airline aspects Braniff Internat.; L'Etoile restaurant, N.Y.C., 1966; The Compound restaurant, Santa Fe, 1966; color cons. Golden Gateway Redevel. project, 1964; color cons. San Francisco Civic Auditorium rehab., 1964; exhibited at John Deere Historic Site Mus., 1967, Hemis-Fair 68. Received Florence traveling scholarship Royal Inst. Brit. Architects, England, 1929, gold medal Barcelona Exhbn., 1929, fabric competition Museum Modern Art, N.Y.C., Trail Blazer award for Herman Miller Fabric Collection, Home Fashion League New York, 1952; medal of honor Archtl. League N.Y., 1965; diploma Royal Soc. Arts, 1966; Allied Professions medal A.I.A., 1966; Elsie de Wolfe award Am. Inst. Interior Designers, 1966; Burlington House award Burlington Industries, 1974; Gold medal Tau Sigma Delta, 1980. Registered architect, N.Y., Mich., Conn., N.Mex. Benjamin Franklin fellow Royal Soc. Arts London; mem. AIA, Archtl. Assn. London. Club: Archtl. League (silver medal for design La Fonda del Sol Restaurant 1962) (N.Y.C.). Author: (film, with Charles Eames) Day of the Dead, 1956; El Encanto de un Pueblo, 1968. Contbr. articles to trade and other publs. Address: PO Box 2168 Santa Fe NM 87501

GIRARD, STEPHEN A., steel and mining company executive; b. 1913; married. Student U. Wash. With various Kaiser cos. in mgmt.-heavy constrn. and shipbldg., 1938-59; pres. Kaiser Jeep Corp., 1959-67, sr. v.p., pres. group ops. Kaiser Industries Corp., parent co., 1967-72, 73-79, pres., chief exec. officer Kaiser Resources Ltd., also dir., 1972-73, vice chmn., then chmn. and chief exec. officer Kaiser Steel Corp., Fontana, Calif., 1979—, also dir.; dir. Am. Motors Corp. Office: Kaiser Steel Corp 9400 Cherry Ave Fontana CA 92335*

GIRARDI, LAURENCE LEONARD, graphic designer; b. Sewickly, Pa., Sept. 23, 1953; s. Leonard and Annabella Helen (Yurcak) G. A.A., Los Angeles Pierce Coll., 1975. Art dir. Wine World Mag., Van Nuys, Calif., 1975-76, La Rose Graphics, Van Nuys, 1976-77; pres. Girardi Design, Canoga Park, Calif., 1977-78, Grafica, Woodland Hills, Calif., 1978—; design cons. Fiberworks, Center for Textile Arts, Berkeley, Calif., 1981—. Recipient Community Recognition award Los Angeles Pierce Coll., 1980. Mem. Nat. Fedn. Ind. Bus., Graphic Artists Guild, Alpha Gamma Sigma. Republican. Roman Catholic. Office: 21044 Ventura Blvd Suite 202 Woodland Hills CA 91364

GIRAULT, LAWRENCE JOSEPH, aircraft engineer; b. Washington, Aug. 27, 1915; s. Alexandre Arsene and Elizabeth Jeanette (Pilcher) G.; m. Lenora Josephine Keahey, Jan. 19, 1946. Ground engr. Q.A.N.-T.A.S., Brisbane, Queensland, Australia, 1932-41; engring. test operator Commonwealth Aircraft, Port Melbourne, Australia, 1941-42; aircraft insp. Douglas Aircraft Corp., Park Ridge, Ill., 1944; design engr. Belmont Radio Corp., Chgo., 1944-45; engr.-in-charge liaison engring. dept. Aeronca Aircraft Corp., Middletown, Ohio, 1945-46; designer Waco Aircraft Corp., Troy, Ohio, 1946; self-employed airplane and power plant mechanic, Williams, Calif., 1946-47; asst. mech. engr. Phelps Dodge Corp., Ajo, Ariz., 1947-48; designer Fairchild Aircraft Corp., Hagerstown, Md., 1948-50; lead designer Chance Vought Aircraft Corp., Dallas, 1950-60; lead designer The Boeing Co., Renton, Wash., 1960-63, sr. engr., 1967-71; staff N.Mex. State U., Las Cruces, 1963-67; self-employed gen. aviation aircraft mechanics insp., Las Cruces, 1971—; broker O'Donnell Realty, Las Cruces, 1971-83. Served with USAAF, 1942-44. Lic. ground engr., Australia; lic. pilot; real estate broker, N.Mex.; lic. aircraft mechanic. Mem. U.S. Naval Inst. (life), Aircraft Owners and Pilots Assn. Republican. Adventist. Inventor main landing gear uplock, outer panel-wing and wing fold prototype, other inventions in field of aircraft mechanics. Home: Shoestring Ranch Airport 8110 Holman Rd Las Cruces NM 88001

GIROD, RAY ELTON, indsl. engr.; b. Salem, Oreg., July 1, 1932; s. Henry Arthur and Juanita (Hockett) G.; B.S., Oreg. State U., 1963; postgrad. Pacific Luth. U. Grad. Sch.; m. Loree Eleanor Sliffe, July 27, 1965. Indsl. engr. C. Brewer & Co., Ltd., Hilo, Hawaii, 1963-68, Interior Systems, Inc., Tacoma, 1969-71; sr. indsl. engr. Buffelen Woodworking Co., Tacoma, 1971-72; cost accounting price estimator Boeing Aerospace Co., Kent, Wash., 1973; sr. cost accountant Sundstrand Data Control Inc., Redmond, Wash., 1973-75; indsl. engr. Dept. Social and Health Services, State of Wash., Olympia, 1975-82; contracts adminstr. Bencorp, Inc., Tacoma, 1982—, also dir. Chmn. Hawaii State Republican Resolutions Com., 1966, state chmn. rules com., 1967; chmn. Hawaii County Rep. Com., 1968. Served with USAF, 1954-58. Registered profl. engr., Wash. Mem. Am. Inst. Indsl. Engrs., Ops. Research Soc. Am., Inst. Mgmt. Scis., Odd Fellow, Mason. Home: 8017 75th St SW Tacoma WA 98498

GIROUARD, WILLIAM FRANCIS, electronics co. exec.; b. Somerville, Mass., May 10, 1921; s. Dona William and Lauretta Catherine (Reidy) G.; student Oberlin Coll., 1943-44, A.B., 1947; B.S. in Indsl. Engring., cum laude, U. So. Calif., 1958, M.S., 1959; m. Rita Frances Phipps, Apr. 5, 1975; children—Kathleen M., Maureen L. Asst. headmaster Friends Acad., Mass., 1948-51, 53-55; asst. prof. U. So. Calif., Los Angeles, 1955-59; dir. indsl. engring. Librascope div. Singer Co., Glendale, Calif., 1960—; adj. asso. prof. U. So. Calif., also mem. adv. com.; expert examiner Calif. Bd. Engring. Examiners, 1967-69; chmn. com. for profl. registration of indsl. engrs., 1960-66. Served with USMC, 1942-45, to maj., 1951-53. Registered profl. engr., Calif.; recipient certificate of appreciation for public service, Calif., 1969. Fellow Am. Inst. Indsl. Engrs. (pres. Los Angeles chpt. 1964-65, nat. dir. profl. registration and standards 1966-76); mem. Sigma Xi, Pi Tau Sigma, Alpha Pi Mu, Tau Beta Pi, Phi Kappa Phi, Oberlin Coll. Alumni Assn., U. So. Calif. Alumni Assn. Republican. Roman Catholic. Contbr. articles to profl. publs. Home: 1649 Indiana Ave South Pasadena CA 91030 Office: 833 Sonora Ave Glendale CA 91201

GIRSH, FAYE JOAN, clinical and forensic psychologist, educator, cons., b. Phila., Pa., May 5, 1933; d. Jack and Rose (Rosenberg) G.; children—Mark, Claudia. B.A. in Psychology, Temple U., 1954; M.A. in Psychology, Boston U.; Ed.D. in Human Devel., Harvard U., 1962. Lic. psychologist, Calif., 1978, Ill., 1974, Ga., 1968. Research psychologist NIMH, Bethesda, Md., 1959-61; chmn., faculty psychology dept. Morehouse Coll., Atlanta, 1965-74; research assoc., assoc. prof. dept. psychiatry U. Chgo., 1974-78; psychologist Psychiatry and Law Ctr., San Diego, 1978-81; pvt. practice clin. and forensic psychology, San Diego, 1918—; cons. Trial Services, Inc. Bd. dirs. Pacific Forensic Inst., San Diego chpt. ACLU; adj. faculty Calif. Sch. Profl. Psychology. Nat. Inst. Drug Abuse grantee, 1972; Soc. Psychol. Study of Social Issues grantee, 1975. Mem. Am. Psychol. Assn., Calif. Psychol. Assn., Forensic Cons. Assn. (dir.), Psychol. Law Soc. Democrat. Jewish. Clubs: City, Harvard (dir.) (San Diego). Author: chpts. in books; contbr. articles to profl. jours. Home: 2600 Torrey Pines Rd A36 La Jolla CA 92037 Office: 401 W A St Suite 1200 San Diego CA 92101

GIRTCH, CLARENCE MARVIN, municipal official; b. White City, Kans., May 28, 1933; s. Clarence Joshua and Beulah Norma (Edwards) G.; m. Margaret S. Stansfield, Aug. 21, 1955; children—Charles Andrew, Jon Michael. B.S., U. Ill., 1956, M.S., 1957; postgrad. U. Calif.-San Francisco, 1960-62; Ed.D. in Exec. Devel., Ind. U., 1971. Registered recreator, cert. in adminstrn., Calif. Bd. Parks and Recreation Personnel. With Ford Found. Interagy. Project, City of Oakland (Calif.), 1959-62; recreation coordinator, assoc. dean of students U. Calif.-Santa Barbara, 1962-68; dep. dir. Indpls. Dept. Parks and Recreation, 1968-69, chief adminstrv. officer, 1969-75; dep. supt. Seattle Dept. Parks and Recreation, 1975-77, chief operating officer, 1975—; adj. prof. Cen. Wash. U. Bd. regents Pacific N.W. Maintenance Mgmt. Sch., 1976-81; pres. bd. trustees Univ. Unitarian Ch. of Seattle, Camp Conestoga, Inc., 1964—; mem. planning commn. Seattle Sch. Dist., 1979-81. Served with AUS, 1957-59. Named Profl. of Yr., Ind. Parks and Recreation Assn., 1973. Mem. Ind. Parks and Recreation Assn. (pres. 1974-75), Nat. Recreation and Park Assn. (council Gt. Lakes Dist. 1974-75), Nat. Sports Governing Bd., Am. Park and Recreation Soc. Club: Evergreen Aqua (v.p., dir.). Author series of monographs; contbr. numerous articles to profl. jours. Office: 210 Municipal Bldg 600 4th Ave Seattle WA 98104

GIRTON, LYDA GENE, psychologist; b. Lafayette, Ind., July 28, 1946; d. Charles Harold and Virginia Irene (Sheek) Girton Schneider; B.S., Ind. U., 1968, M.S. in Edn., 1971, Ed.D., 1973; m. H. Marshall Goldsmith, July 20, 1974. Tchr. English, Frankfort (Ind.) Sr. High Sch., 1968-70; tchr., research asst. Ind. U., 1971-73; psychol. counselor Loyola Marymount U., Los Angeles, 1973-75; asst. dir. counseling ctr., 1975-77, dir., 1977-81; also lectr. edn.; guest speaker; pvt. practice psychology, marriage, family and child counseling, 1976—. Leader assertion and stress seminars, 1975—. Recipient outstanding service award Loyola Marymount U. Student Body, 1974-75. Mem. Am. Personnel and Guidance Assn., Am. Psychol. Assn., Western Psychol. Assn., Am. Coll. Personnel Assn., Nat. Assn. Student Personnel Adminstrs., Calif. Women in Higher Edn., Calif. Assn. Marriage, Family and Child Therapists, Ind. U. Alumni Assn., Zeta Tau Alpha, Pi Lambda Theta. Contbr. articles to profl. jours. Has made TV appearances on assertiveness tng. and peer counseling. Home: 5505 Soledad Rd La Jolla CA 92037

GISCLON, JOHN MARSHALL, engineer; b. East Ely, Nev., Aug. 16, 1938; s. John Louis and Esther Lydia (Gehl) G.; m. Evelyn Frances Beeck, Dec. 12, 1965; children—John, Amy. B.S.M.E., U. Nev., 1961. Registered profl. engr. Power prodn. engr., tech. asst. Pacific Gas and Electric Co., Humboldt Bay, Eureka, Calif., 1966-68; engr. Westinghouse Electric Corp., Naval Reactors Facility, Idaho, 1968-70; power prodn. engr. Pacific Gas and Electric Co., Diablo Canyon, 1970-74, sr. power prodn. engr., 1974-79, power plant engr., 1979—. Served to lt. USNR, 1961-65. Mem. Am. Nuclear Soc., ASME, Sigma Tau. Republican. Lutheran. Home: 421 Woodland Dr Arroyo Grande CA 93420 Office: PO Box 56 Avila Beach CA 93424

GISH, NORMAN RICHARD, business executive; b. Eckville, Alta., Can., Oct. 13, 1935; s. Robert Bruce and Lillian (Foster) G.; B.A., U. Alta, 1957; LL.B., U. B.C., 1960; m. Joan Ann Thompson, Sept. 5, 1959; children—David Cole, Carolyn Nancy, Graeme Christopher. Asst. trade commr. Fgn. Trade Service of Canadian Govt., Ottawa, 1961-62, Hong Kong, 1962-65; asst. to v.p. and sec. B.C. Forest Products, Ltd., Vancouver, 1965-67, sec., 1967-72, gen. counsel, sec., 1972-74, v.p., 1974-76; chmn. B.C. Energy Commn., 1977-80; v.p. Turbo Resources Ltd., 1980-83, pres., chief exec. officer, 1983—. Mem. Law Soc. B.C., Canadian Bar Assn. Clubs: Canadian, Lawn Tennis (Vancouver), Glenmore Racquet (Calgary). Home: 8940 Bayridge Dr Calgary AB T2V 3M8 Canada Office: 1035 7th Ave SW Calgary AB T2P 3E9 Canada

GITHENS, JOHN HORACE, JR., physician, educator; b Woodbury, N.J., Jan. 2, 1922; s. John Horace and Gladys (Jones) G.; B.A., Swarthmore Coll., 1944; M.D., Temple U., 1945; m. Virginia R. Freeman, Mar. 29, 1945; children—James S., Wendy M. Intern, Abington (Pa.) Meml. Hosp., 1945-46; resident pediatrics Phila. Children's Hosp., 1948-50, U. Colo. Med. Center, 1950-51; from instr. to asso. prof. pediatrics U. Colo., 1951-60; asso. dir. gen. med. clinic Denver Gen. Hosp., 1952-57; asst. dir. Rheumatic Fever Diagnostic Clinic, Denver, 1951-53; dir. Colo. Sickle Cell Center, 1974—; prof. pediatrics, chmn. dept. U. Ky. Med. Center, 1960-63; prof. pediatrics U. Colo. Med. Center, Denver, 1963—, asso. dean U. Colo. Sch. Medicine, 1964-73, vice chmn. dept. pediatrics, 1973-74. Served to lt. (j.g.) USNR, 1946-48. Recipient Disting. Alumnus award Temple U., 1964; diplomate Am. Bd. Pediatrics; subcert. in pediatric hematology-oncology. Fellow Am. Acad. Pediatrics; mem. Soc. Pediatric Research, AMA, Western Soc. Pediatric Research (1st Ross award 1957), Transplantation Soc., Am. Pediatric Soc. Co-author: Teaching Comprehensive Medical Care: a Psychological Study of a Change in Medical Education, 1959. Contbr. articles to profl. jours. Office: 4200 E 9th Ave Denver CO 80262

GITTLESON, HOWARD, electronic production tools executive; b. Chgo., Nov. 22, 1928; s. Louis Lawrence and Jane (Goodkin) G. B.S., Calif. State U., 1972. With Erem Corp., Torrance, Calif., 1968-76, v.p. mktg., 1968-76; pres. Yale Sales Corp., Los Angeles, 1976-79, Vertron Internat., Inc., 1979—; chmn. United Barcode Technologies Inc.; cons. Intervend Industries, Inc., Los Angeles, 1965—. Served with Signal Corps, AUS, 1950-52. Sr. mem. Soc. Mfg. Engrs. Home: 2011 Stonewood Ct San Pedro CA 90732 Office: Vertron Internat Inc 20906 Higgins Ct Torrance CA 90291

GITZ, MITCHELL, govt. ofcl.; b. Phila., Mar. 16, 1946; s. Irving and Isabel (Fienman) G.; m. Virginia Ann Sublett, Nov. 21, 1981; children—Michael, Robert. A.S. in Elec. Engring., Philco Tech. Inst., 1966; B.A. in Bus. Adminstrn., Nat. U., 1976, M.B.A., 1978. Field engr. Burroughs Corp., Paoli, Pa., 1966-67; electronic warfare repairman U.S. Air Force, 1967-71; field engr. Raytheon Service Co., Burlington, Mass., 1971-72; equal opportunity officer U.S. Navy, San Diego, 1972—; owner/mgr. Gitz Electronics, 1975; pres. Fed. EEO Council San Diego County. Treas. Cub Scout Pack 1210, Boy Scouts Am., 1978—, scout leader, 1980—; chmn. sch. improvement com. Walker Sch., San Diego, 1981-83. Served with USAF, 1967-71; Vietnam. Mem. Federally Employed Women, Assn. Retarded Citizens San Diego. Club: Toastmasters. Home: 8628 Perseus Rd San Diego CA 92126 Office: 200 Catalina Blvd San Diego CA 92147

GIULINI, CARLO MARIA, conductor; b. Barletta, Italy, May 9, 1914; ed. Accademia Santa Cecilia, Rome, Chigiana Acad., Siena; married, 3 sons. Played viola, Santa Cecilia Orch., Augusteo Orch., Rome; debut as orchestral conductor, Rome, 1944; asst. condr. Rome Radio Orch., 1944-46, prin. condr., 1946-50; founder, prin. condr. Orch. of Radio Milan, 1950-54; debut as opera condr. Bergamo Festival, 1951; prin. conductor, La Scala, Milan, 1954-58; condr. symphony orchs. in Boston, Phila., N.Y.C., Los Angeles, Israel, Berlin, London, Vienna, Paris; condr. symphony orch., Chgo., prin. guest condr., 1969-72; condr. for music festivals in Edinburgh, London, Venice, Florence, Strasbourg, Prague, Aix-en-Provence; condr. opera Covent Garden, Prague Nat. Zurich, Amsterdam, Tel Aviv, Florence Maggio, Turin, Venice; prin. condr. Rome Opera; music dir. Los Angeles Philharmonic Orch., 1978—. Recipient Grammy award for best classical rec., 1971. Recs. for Deutsche Grammophon, RCA, Angel, London, EMI. Office: care Los Angeles Philharmonic 135 N Grand Los Angeles CA 90012

GIVAN, GUY V., ceramic engineer, sales rep.; b. Independence, Mo., Dec. 15, 1946; s. Victor Howell and Alice Elizabeth (Bradica) G.; m. Doris Jean Prindable, May 17, 1975; children—Gordon Victor, Gerald John, Geoff Matthew. B.S., U. Mo.-Rolla, 1969, M.S. in Ceramic Engring., 1970. Mgt. trainee, Gen. Steel, Granite City, Ill., 1966-67; research engr. Alcoa, East St. Louis, Ill., 1970-75; ceramic engr., Rocky Mountain Refractories, Salt Lake City, 1975—, sales rep. Mem. Am. Ceramic Soc., Am. Concrete Inst., Nat. Inst. Ceramic Engrs., Keramos. Clubs: Beehive Track, Salt Lake City Track. Contbr. articles to profl. jours. Home: 2522 Kenwood Salt Lake City UT 84106 Office: 2436 W Andrew Ave Salt Lake City UT 84104

GIVENS, HARRY V., constrn. equipment appraiser; b. Hanson, Ky., Mar. 2, 1918; s. Robert H. and Ruth (Walker) G.; student Austin Tech. Inst., 1938, U. So. Calif., 1940-41; m. Geraldine S. Wiebring, Apr. 17, 1937; 1 dau., Karen Kathryn (Mrs. David Nyeland). Sales engr. Smith Booth Usher Co., Los Angeles, 1938-41; gen. mgr. Edward F. Hale Co., San Francisco, 1941-45; owner Givens Indsl. Co., San Francisco, 1945-62; pres. Pacific Appraisal Co., San Carlos, Calif., 1948—. Served with USNR, 1945. Recipient Commendation award Office of Civilian Def., 1943. Fellow Constrn. Surveyors Inst.; mem. Am. Soc. Appraisers (sr.), Nat. Assn. Review Appraisers, Am. Arbitration Assn. (nat. panel). Originator Green Guide (handbook of new and used constrn. equipment values) used throughout constrn. industry, U.S. and fgn. countries, 1959—. Home: 1980 Eucalyptus Ave San Carlos CA 94070

GIVENS, RONALD DOUGLAS, mfg. co. exec.; b. Portland, Oreg., Nov. 11, 1942; s. Lawrence Myron and Meneta June (Bidgood) G.; B.B.A., Golden Gate U., 1966; m. Rosalie Scaglione, Aug. 2, 1964; children—Julie Michelle, Sean Douglas. Supervisory auditor Def. Contract Audit Agy., San Francisco, 1966-78; mgr. internal audit Guy F. Atkinson Co., South San Francisco, 1978-79; owner Ronald Givens & Assocs., Mgmt. Cons., San Jose, Calif., 1973—; prin., treas. Corso-Gray Instruments, Inc., Los Gatos, Calif., 1979—. Cert. internal auditor; cert. info. systems auditor. Mem. Assn. Govt. Accts., Nat. Contract Mgmt. Assn., Inst. Internal Auditors, EDP Auditors Found. Home: 1069 Phelps Ave San Jose CA 95117 Office: 120 Albright Way Los Gatos CA 95030

GIVON, BERND SHLOMO, testing co. exec., engring. cons.; b. Berlin, Sept. 28, 1932; s. Harry Meyer Lewis and Eva Ruth (Weissenberg); came to U.S., 1960; B.Sc. in Engring. with honors, U. London, 1960; M.S. in Mech. Engring., N.J. Inst. Tech., 1966; m. Hannah Gelman, Dec. 25, 1957; children—Eve Judith Givon Harow, Ilana Ruth Givon Nurkin. Research and devel. engr., air conditioning div. Worthington Corp., East Orange, N.J., 1960-62; asst. to v.p./mfg. Sonneborn div. Witco Chem. Co., N.Y.C., 1962-66; sales mgr., design engr. B-K Elec. Products, N.J., 1966-68; mgr. product evaluation div. U.S. Testing Co., Hoboken, N.J., 1968-70, v.p., mgr. Calif. div., Los Angeles, 1970—; mng. partner Ogden Terr., Forest Hills Assos., apt. bldgs.; adj. lectr. air conditioning N.J. Inst. Tech., 1962-64. Mem. CD, Maplewood, N.J., 1967-70. Chmn. western div. Am. Council Ind. Labs. Registered profl. engr., Calif., N.J. Mem. Nat. Soc. Profl. Engrs. (pres. Los Angeles chpt.), ASME, ASTM, Am. Mgmt. Assn., Inst. Engring. and Tech. Clubs: Los Angeles Athletic, B'nai Brith. Patentee in liquid refrigerants, heat exchange apparatus. Home: 106 N Poinsettia Pl Los Angeles CA 90036 Office: US Testing Co 5555 Telegraph Rd Los Angeles CA 90040

GLACEL, BARBARA PATE, educator, management consultant; b. Balt., Sept. 15, 1948; d. Jason Thomas Pate and Sarah Virginia (Forwood) Pate Wetter; m. Robert Allan Glacel, Dec. 21, 1969; children—Jennifer Warren, Sarah Allane, Ashley Virginia. A.B., Coll. William and Mary, 1970; M.A., U. Okla., 1973, Ph.D., 1978. Tchr. Harford County (Md.) Schs., 1970-71; tchr. Dept. Def. Schs., W.Ger., 1971-73; ednl. counselor U.S. Army, W.Ger., 1973-74; lectr. U. Md., W.Ger., 1973-74; adj. prof. Suffolk U., Boston, 1975-77, C.W. Post Ctr., L.I. U., John Jay Coll. Criminal Justice, N.Y.C., 1979-80, St. Thomas Aquinas Coll., N.Y.C., 1981; acad. adviser Central Mich. U. 1981-82; adj. prof. Anchorage Community Coll., 1982—; asst. prof. U. Alaska-Anchorage, 1983—; mgmt. cons. Barbara Glacel & Assocs., Anchorage, 1980—; ptnr. Pracel Prints, Williamsburg, Va., 1981—; dir. Chesapeake Broadcasting Corp. Md.; guest lectr. U.S. Mil. Acad. Chmn. 172d Inf. Brigade Family Council. AAUW grantee, 1977-78. Mem. Am. Soc. Tng. and Devel., Am. Soc. Pub. Adminstrn., Am. Polit. Sci. Assn. Pi Sigma Alpha. Author: Regional Transit Authorities, 1983. Address: 143B Juneau Ave Fort Richardson AK 99505

GLAD, DAIN STURGIS, aerospace engr.; b. Santa Monica, Calif., Sept. 17, 1932; s. Alma Emanuel and Maude La Verne (Morby) G.; B.S. in Engring., U. Calif. at Los Angeles, 1954; M.S. in Elec. Engring., U. So. Calif., 1963; m. Betty Alexandra Shainoff, Sept. 12, 1954 (dec. 1973); 1 dau., Dana Elizabeth; m. 2d, Carolyn Elizabeth Giffen, June 8, 1979. Electronic engr. Clary Corp., San Gabriel, Calif., 1957-58; with Aerojet Electro Systems Co., Azusa, Calif., 1958-72; with missile systems div. Rockwell Internat., Anaheim, Calif., 1973-75; with Aerojet Electrosystems, Azusa, 1975—. Served as ensign U.S. Navy, 1954-56; lt. j.g. Res., 1956-57. Registered profl. engr., Calif. Mem. IEEE, Calif. Soc. Profl. Engrs., Soc. Info. Display. Home: 1701 Marengo Ave South Pasadena CA 91030 Office: 1100 W Hollyvale St Azusa CA 91702

GLAD, EDWARD NEWMAN, lawyer; b. Polk, Nebr., June 30, 1919; s. Lewis Olaf and Esther Ruth (Newman) G.; student U. Omaha, 1938-41; J.D., U. Mich., 1948; m. Suzanne Watson Lockley, Nov. 7, 1953; children—Amy Lockley, Lisanne Watson, William Edward. Bar: N.Y. 1949, Calif. 1959, D.C. 1964. Assoc., Barnes, Richardson & Colburn, N.Y.C., 1948-59; sr. ptnr. Glad & Tuttle, Los Angeles, San Francisco, 1959-71, Glad, Tuttle & White, 1971-79, Glad & White, 1979-81, Glad, White & Ferguson, 1981—. Pres. Fgn. Trade Assn. So. Calif., 1965; v.p. Japan Am. Soc., 1969-73; pres. British-Am. C. of C., 1963-64, 70-72, Spain-U.S. C. of C., 1977-80. Trustee St George's Episcopal Nursery and Ungraded Sch., 1968-73; chmn. adv. council Calif. State World Trade Commn., 1983—. Served to lt. comdr. USNR, 1941-46; ETO, PTO. Decorated hon. officer Order Brit. Empire. Mem. State Bar Calif., Bar Assn. D.C., N.Y. State Bar. Club: Internat. of Los Angeles. Home: 519 Meadow Grove St Flintridge CA 91011 Office: 350 S Figueroa St Los Angeles CA 90071 also 625 Market St San Francisco CA 94105

GLAD, JOAN BOURNE, clin. psychologist; b. Salt Lake City, Apr. 24, 1918; d. Ernest LeRoy and Ethel Geneve (Rogers) Bourne; B.A., UCLA, 1955; Ph.D., U. Utah, 1965; m. Donald Davison Glad, Sept. 10, 1938; children—Dawn Joanne, Toni Ann, Sue Ellen, Roger Bruce. Chief psychologist Utah Dept. Health, Salt Lake City, 1959-65; dir. Child and Family Guidance Center, Primary Children's Hosp., Salt Lake City, 1965-68; dir. parent edn. Children's Hosp. of Orange County, Orange, Calif., 1968-75; adminstrv. coordinator Family Learning and Behavior Center, Santa Ana-Tustin Community Hosp., Santa Ana, Calif., 1975-77; dir. Glad Assos. Psychol. Services, Orange, Calif., 1977—; instr. psychology dept. Chapman Coll., 1971-74; guest lectr. Calif. Assn. Neurologically Handicapped Children, 1973-77, Fullerton Coll., Santa Ana Coll.; mem. Pres.'s Commn. on Handicapped Children, 1969. Mem. Assn. Holistic Health (founder). Republican. Mem. Ch. Jesus Christ of Latter-day Saints. Office: 1442 Irvine Blvd Tustin CA 92680

GLADISH, LEROY ELMER, publ. specialist; b. St. Paul, Mar. 15, 1924; s. John Joseph and Jeanette Emeline (Klug) G.; B.A. cum laude, U. Minn., 1957; m. Sharrell Joan Robertson, Feb. 2, 1960 (div., 1977). Account exec., copywriter Advt., Inc., Boulder, Colo., 1958-61; publ. specialist Western Interstate Commn. for Higher Edn., Boulder, 1961-76; exec. editor Colo. Quar., U. Colo., Boulder, 1977-80; editor, book coordinator Geol. Soc. Am., Boulder, 1980—; program cons. Boulder Civic Opera Assn.; promotion cons. Boulder Public Library Commn. Mayor, Gold Hill, Colo., 1962-63. Served with USN, 1942-48, 51-52. Recipient award of merit, Soc. Illustrators, 1979. Republican. Presbyterian. Home: 900 Hartford Dr Boulder CO 80303 Office: 3300 Penrose Pl Boulder CO 80301

GLADYSCHILD, KAREN JEAN, psychologist; b. Sandpoint, Idaho, Sept. 15, 1951; d. Rudolph and Gladys Mabel (Miller) Drovdahl. B.A. with honors, Mills Coll., 1972; M.S., San Jose State U., 1974; Ph.D., U. Miami, 1982. With Mailman Ctr. for Child Devel., Miami, Fla., 1977-78, Children's Psychiat. Ctr., Miami, 1978-79, Morrison Ctr. for Youth and Family Service, Portland, 1979-80; family therapist Edgefield Lodge, Inc., Troutdale, Oreg., 1980-82; psychology resident Portland, 1982—; tng. coordinator Project LUCK, N/NE Community Mental Health Ctr., Portland, 1982—; cons. in field. Sec.-treas. bd. Parent Child Services, Inc., Portland, 1979—; bd. dirs. Parents Anonymous, 1982—. Mills Coll. scholar, 1969-72. Mem. Am. Psychol. Assn. (assoc.), Assn. for Advancement Psychology, Oreg. Psychol. Assn., Western Psychol. Assn., Phi Beta Kappa. Contbr. articles to profl. jours. Home: 2835 NE 39th Ave Portland OR 97212 Office: 310 NE Oregon Portland OR 97232

GLASCOCK, RAY D., engring. services co. exec., office furniture and equipment co. exec.; b. Auxausse, Mo., Apr. 1, 1922; s. Joseph Ewing and Mildred Hazel (Thomas) G.; B.S., U. Ill., 1949, M.S., 1950; m. Martha G. Greene, Nov. 18, 1977; children—Barbara Joan (Mrs. Jerry Bourland), Donald Ray. Group leader Norair div. Northrop Corp., Hawthorne, Calif., 1951-59; sect. head communications div. Hughes Aircraft Co., Los Angeles, 1959-63; sect. head aeronutronic div. Philco Ford Corp., Newport Beach, Calif., 1964-65; owner/mgr. Engring. Corp. of Am.-Orange County, Anaheim, Calif., 1966—; owner Glascock Enterprises, Anaheim, 1976—. Served with U.S. Maritime Service, 1943-46. Mem. IEEE, Eta Kappa Nu. Home: 111 S Broadview St Anaheim CA 92804 Office: 210 A and B N Crescent Way Anaheim CA 92801

GLASER, DONALD A(RUTHUR), physicist; b. Cleve., Sept. 21, 1926; s. William Joseph Glaser; B.S., Case Inst. Tech., 1946, Sc.D., 1959; Ph.D., Calif. Inst. Tech., 1949. Prof. physics U. Mich., 1949-59; prof. physics U. Calif.-Berkeley, 1959—, prof. physics and molecular biology, 1964—. Recipient Henry Russel award U. Mich., 1955; Charles V. Boys prize Phys. Soc. London, 1958; Nobel prize in physics, 1960: NSF fellow, 1961; Guggenheim fellow, 1961-62. Fellow Am. Physics Soc. (prize 1959); mem. Nat. Acad. Scis., Sigma Xi, Tau Kappa Alpha, Theta Tau. Constructed 1st bubble chamber for visual demonstrations of movements of high-energy atomic particles; research on cosmic rays, bacterial evolution, control of biol. cell growth and division, automatic identification of bacteria species; automation of cell biology to study growth of somatic cells and effects of carcinogens, mutagens and teratogens. Office: Molecular Biology Dept U Calif Berkeley CA 94720*

GLASER, PAUL FRANKLYN, banker; b. N.Y.C., Apr. 17, 1926; s. Philip and Bertha G.; B.E.E., N.Y. U., 1949, M.E.E., 1953; m. Florence Hellman, June 1, 1947; children—Stephanie, Wendy. Chief engr. Am. Chronoscope Corp., 1949-55; dir. engring. Gruen Watch Co., 1955-58; project engr. Space Tech. Labs., 1958-60; v.p., gen. mgr. TRW Systems, 1960-73; chmn. Transaction Tech., Inc., also sr. v.p., mem. policy com., chmn. corp. tech. com. Citibank, Los Angeles, 1973—; former lectr. UCLA.; former chmn. space and mil. electronics symposiu. Mem. western region campaign cabinet United Way, 1977; spl. committeeman for commerce and industry United Crusade, 1965-68. Served with USNR, 1944-46. Mem. IEEE (sr.), Tau Beta Pi, Eta Kappa Nu. Contbr. articles on spacecraft communications and electronic funds transfer systems to profl. jours. Patentee automated teller terminal. Home: 5004 Timberlake Terr Culver City CA 90230 Office: 3100 Ocean Park Blvd Santa Monica CA 90405

GLASER, RUTH BONNIE, psychologist; b. Tenafly, N.J., May 11, 1937; d. John Henry and Ruth Louise (Ferris) Thompson; children—Louise Ferris, William Thompson. B.A., U. Calif.-Berkeley, 1970, M.A., 1975, Ph.D., 1976. Lic. psychologist, Calif. Mem. staff U. Calif.-Berkeley, 1976—, lectr., 1980—; pvt. practice psychology, Berkeley, 1976—. Bd. dirs. Ann Martin Children's Ctr. Mem. Am. Psychol. Assn., Kappa Mu Epsilon. Office: 917 The Alameda Berkeley CA 94707

GLASGOW, EDSEL RAY, mechanical engineer; b. Tulsa, Oct. 7, 1940; s. Clarence Ogden and Elizabeth Helen (McClung) G.; B.S.M.E., Purdue U., 1962; M.S.M.E. (Univ. fellow), Stanford U., 1964; M.B.A., U. So. Calif., 1970; m. Arlene Lynne Lundgren, July 9, 1965; children—Gayle, Glenn. Engr. propulsion div. Lockheed-Calif. Co., Burbank, 1963-74, 76—, group engr. 1978-81, dept. mgr., 1981-83, div. mgr., 1983—; chief engr. Ellco Engring., Inc., Compton, Calif., 1974-76. Mem. adv. com. Balboa Elem. Sch., Glendale, Calif. 1975-79, chmn., 1978; active YMCA Indian Guides, Glendale, 1976-79, Boy Scouts Am., 1982—; coach Little League, Glendale, 1979. Registered profl. engr., Calif. Mem. AIAA, Soc. Automotive Engrs. (engr. activity bd. 1982—, aerospace coordinating com. 1982—, chmn. aerospace propulsion activity 1982—), Stanford Alumni Assn., Glendale Symphony Orch. Assn., Lockheed Mgmt. Inst., Phi Kappa Phi, Beta Gamma Sigma, Phi Tau Sigma. Republican. Presbyterian. Author profl. reports, papers. Home: 1525 Irving Ave Glendale CA 91201 Office: 2555 N Hollywood Way Burbank CA 91520

GLASGOW, GERALD EDWARD, wine company executive; b. Flushing, N.Y., Aug. 18, 1941; s. Leland E. and Blanche A. G.; m. Joan M. Danti, June 26, 1964; children—Kimberly, Robert, Kristan. A.B., Dartmouth Coll., 1963, M.B.A., 1965. Product mgr. Armour Dial Co., Chgo., 1967-72, v.p. mktg., Phoenix, 1977-81; Acct. supr. Foote, Cone and Belding, Chgo., 1973-77; group mktg. dir. Ernest and Julio Gallo Winery, Modesto, Calif., 1981—. Served to 1st lt. AUS, 1965-67. Decorated Bronze Star. Republican. Home: 3521 Wycliffe Dr Modesto CA 95355 Office: PO Box 1130 Modesto CA 95353

GLASPY, MARIA FE, dietitian; b. Philippines, Mar. 20, 1945; came to U.S., 1967, naturalized, 1974; d. Wilfrido and Maria (Reyes) Simon; B.S. in Foods and Nutrition, Coll. of Holy Spirit, Manila, 1966; M.A. in Foods and Nutrition, Calif. State U., Los Angeles, 1971; m. Bruce Glaspy, Jan. 25, 1970; children—Kevin Bruce, Gary Jason. Staff dietitian David Brothman Meml. Hosp., Culver City, Calif., 1967-68; chief dietitian East Los Angeles Drs. Hosp., 1968-74; cons. dietitian Century Med., Inc., Los Angeles, 1968-74; dir. food services Greater El Monte (Calif.) Community Hosp., 1974—; cons. dietitian East Los Angeles Drs. Hosp. Mem. San Gabriel Valley Dist. Dietetic Assn., Calif. Dietetic Assn., Am. Dietetic Assn. Home: 23718 Sunset Crossing Rd Diamond Bar CA 91765 Office: 1701 Santa Anita Ave South El Monte CA 91733

GLASS, GARY BERTRAM, geologist, state official; b. Pitts., Mar. 6, 1940; s. George Addison and Beverly Martha (Gauding) G.; m. Charlotte Louise Fry, Sept. 2, 1962; children—Susan Lynne, Gary Bertram, William Charles. B.S. in Geology, Bucknell U., 1962; M.S. in Geology, Lehigh U., 1964; postgrad. U. Wyo.-Laramie, 1976-77. Cert. profl. geologist. Part time assoc. geologist Pa. Geol. Survey, Harrisburg, 1964; coal geologist, 1967-71; staff coal geologist Wyo. Geol. Survey, Laramie, 1971-78, dep. dir./coal specialist, 1978-81, state geologist, exec. dir., Laramie, 1981—; part time adj. lectr. dept. geology and geophysics U. Wyo., Laramie; commr. Wyo. Oil and Gas Conservation Commn., Casper. Served with C.E., U.S. Army, 1964-67. Decorated Bronze Star, Air medal. Mem. Assn. Am. State Geologists, Am. Inst. Profl. Geologists, Geol. Soc. Am. (sec. coal geology div. 1980-82), Soc. Econ. Paleontologists and Mineralogists, Soc. Mining Engrs. of AIME, Wyo. Geol. Assn., Am. Assn. Petroleum Geologists (energy minerals div.), Sigma Xi. Mem. editorial bd. Elsevier's Internat. Jour. Coal Geology. Office: Box 3008 University Station Laramie WY 82071

GLASS, HERBERT, magazine editor; b. Frankfurt alM, Germany, Apr. 17, 1934; s. Leon and Rose (Langmann) G.; came to U.S., 1941, naturalized, 1946; B.A. in English, Brandeis U., 1955; m. Susanne Joan Pleibel, July 9, 1965; 1 son, Alexander David. Asst. press dir. N.Y. Philharm., 1962-65; pub. relations dir. San Francisco Opera, 1965-67; editor-in-chief Performing Arts mag., Beverly Hills, Calif., 1967—; music critic (under name Fred Pleibel) Los Angeles Times, 1970—; programming dir. Los Angeles Chamber Orch., 1969-74; cons. for program devel. Sta. KUSC-FM (Nat. Public Radio), 1978—. Office: 9025 Wilshire Blvd Beverly Hills CA 90211

GLASS, JOHN FRANKLIN, sociologist, consultant; b. Berlin, Jan. 15, 1936; came to U.S., 1940, naturalized, 1945; s. Paul and Anni Lotte (Hoff) G.; m. Judith Chanin, Feb. 27, 1966; 1 son, Aaron. B.S. in Indsl. Adminstrn., U. Ill., 1958, M.A. in Labor and Indsl. Relations, 1962; Ph.D. in Sociology, UCLA, 1968. Lic. marriage and family counselor, Calif. Asst. prof. sociology Calif. State U.-Northridge, 1968-73; mem. faculty Calif. Sch. Profl. Psychology, 1972-76; cons. sociology, Studio City, Calif., 1976—; vis. asst. prof. Pitzer Coll., 1980-81; Served with U.S. Army, 1960-62. Mem. Clin. Sociology Assn. (co-founder 1978, 1st pres. 1978-80, sec.-treas. 1980—, dir. 1978—, Founders award 1982), Am. Sociol. Assn., Am. Assn. Marriage and Family Therapy. Editor: (with John R. Staude) Humanistic Society: Today's Challenge to Sociology, 1972. Home and Office: 4242 Wilkinson Ave Studio City CA 91604

GLASS, PAUL WILLIAM PARSONNET, accounting corporation executive; b. Newark, June 27, 1945; s. William Burton and Doris (Parsonnet) G.; m. Susan Volpe, Dec. 9, 1967; children—Andrew Parsonnet, William Shane, Joshua Michael. B.S. in Bus. Adminstrn., Boston U., 1967; postgrad. U. R.I.-Kingston, 1967-68. C.P.A., R.I., N.Y., Mass., Calif. Staff acct. Glass, Dittelman & Co., C.P.A.s, Providence, 1969; supr. Laventhal & Horwath, C.P.A.s, N.Y.C., 1969-73, audit mgr., Boston, 1973-77, continuing edn. faculty Am. Inst. C.P.A.s, 1976-77; ptnr. Glass, Karp, Warburg & Perera, C.P.A.s, Beverly Hills, Calif., 1977-80; ptnr., pres. Glass & Rosen, An Accountancy Corp., Encino, Calif., 1981—. Active Free Arts Clinic, Malibu, Calif. Served with Army N.G., 1968-74. Mem. Am. Inst. C.P.A.s, Calif. Soc. C.P.A.s, Mass. Soc. C.P.A.s, Boston U. Alumni Assn. Jewish. Club: B'nai B'rith (v.p., treas. Framingham, Mass. 1976-77). Co-designer computerized acctg. system for non-profit orgns., 1977.

GLASS, RICHARD LEE, pub. co. exec.; b. Overton, Tex., Sept. 25, 1934; s. John Richard and Zelma Lee (Howe) G.; B.A., Tex. Christian U., 1956; postgrad. U. Tex., Nacogdoches, 1957-58; m. Rosalie Annette Haley, Dec. 16, 1961; 1 son, Richard Lee. Tchr. public schs., Lufkin, Tex., 1956-60; sales rep. Steck-Vaughn Pub. Co., Austin, Tex., 1960-62, Charles E. Merrill Pub. Co., Columbus, Ohio, 1962-64; with Houghton Mifflin Pub. Co., 1964—, Calif. sales mgr., 1975-76, Western div. sales mgr., Palo Alto, Calif., 1976—; pres., dir. Haley-Kruger, Inc., Reedley, Calif., 1977-78. Mem. Calif. Council Tchrs. English, Nat. Council Tchrs. Math., Internat. Reading Assn., Assn. Curriculum and Devel., Nat. Council Tchrs. Social Studies, Council Basic Edn., Phi Delta Kappa. Democrat. Presbyterian. Clubs: Commonwealth, Cupertino Hills Swim and Racquet. Home: 11077 Linda Vista Dr Cupertino CA 95014 Office: 777 California Ave Palo Alto CA 94304

GLASS, THOMAS RANDALL HOOKER, state senator, businessman, consultant; b. Edgewood, Md., May 1, 1945; s. Sanford Ross and Eileen V. (See) G.; m. Tracy Griswold; children—David, Tracy Lyon. Student Union Coll.; B.A., Western Conn. Coll., 1968; postgrad. in bus. adminstrn., U. S.C., Harvard U., 1980. With Crested Butte (Colo.) Transit Corp., Gunnison Valley Ins., Mesa San. Supply Co., 1971-78; incorporator, dir. Crested Butte State Bank, until 1982; exec. dir. Northwest Colo. Council of Govts., 1978-82; v.p. Rocky Mountain Group, 1982—; now mem. Colo. Senate; sec. Colo. Passenger Tramway Safety Bd., 1977-83; dir. Club 20. Mem. city council, Crested Butte, mayor, 1974-78; pres. Dist. 10 Colo. Mcpl. League. Served with U.S. Army, 1968-70. Gates fellow, 1980; scholar John F. Kennedy Sch. Govt., Harvard U., 1980; named Outstanding Freshman Senator, Colo. Social Legislation Com., 1983. Democrat. Presbyterian. Club: Human Avalanche Missile Team (Crested Butte). Office: Senate Chambers State Capitol Denver CO 80203

GLASSCOCK, MICHAEL EMMANUEL, Realtor; b. N.Y.C., Feb. 26, 1913; s.Michael Emmanuel and Rosa Marie (Valerio) G.; B.S. in Speech, LL.B., Cumberland U., 1933; M.B.A., Calif. Western U., 1976, Ph.D. in Fin. and Real Estate, 1978; m. Martina Taylor, Feb. 18, 1932; children—Michael Emmanuel III, Patrick T. Rancher, Utopia, Tex., 1933-42; owner, operator Glasscock Aviation, also Glasscock Constrn., Corpus Christi, Tex., 1945-49; mktg. and research exec. Glasscock Assos. & Constrn. Co., San Antonio and Dallas, 1949-55; real estate investor, cons., fin. advisor, 1955-63; pres. Marmont Investment Properties, Los Angeles, 1963—; mem. faculty West Los Angeles Coll., 1976-78; instr. real estate appraisal continuing edn. div. U. So. Calif.;

adviser Smith County Bank, Carthage, Tenn.; appraiser; contbg. mem. Appraisers Info. Center. Served to comdr. USNR, 1942-45. Col., aide-de-camp Gov. Frank Clement of Tenn., 1965; certificate of appreciation Los Angeles Jaycees, 1978; cert. mortgage underwriter, constrn. estimator, rev. appraiser, fine arts appraiser, real estate broker; cert. tchr. Calif. Community Colls. Mem. Am. Soc. Fine Arts Appraisers, Nat. Assn. Realtors, Calif. Assn. Realtors (17th dist. chmn. of investment div. 1977-79, 17th dist. chmn. Real Estate Cert. Inst. div. 1977-78), Los Angeles Bd. Realtors, Beverly Hills Bd. Realtors, Nat. Assn. Rev. Appraisers, Calif. Inst. Real Estate (pres.), Am. Assn. Mortgage Underwriters, Nat. Inst. Investment Seminars (pres.), Navy League (life), Assn. Fed. Appraisers (cert.), Real Estate Cert. Inst. (cert.), Am. Soc. Profl. Estimators, Internat. Assn. Fin. Planners, Calif. Assn. Real Estate Tchrs., Sigma Delta Kappa. Roman Catholic. Clubs: Los Angeles Athletic, West Hollywood Rotary (dir.). Author: Real Estate Investments (textbook); Real Estate Investments, The Last Brass Ring; contbg. editor Apt. Owners/Builder Mag., 1976-78. Home and Office: 2622 29th St Santa Monica CA 90405

GLASSER, LEWIS, physician; b. Flushing, N.Y., Jan. 30, 1935; s. Frank B. and Hannah G. (Goodman) G.; A.B., Cornell U., 1956, M.D., 1960; m. Jane G. Coker, Nov. 14, 1975; children—Stefanie, Benjamin R., Carol Lynn. Intern, Columbia Presbyn. Med. Center, N.Y.C., 1960-61, resident in pathology, 1964-65; resident in pathology Emory U. Med. Sch., 1965-66; dir. clin. labs. Grady Meml. Hosp., Atlanta, 1966-71; asso. prof. pathology Emory U., 1969-71; asso. prof. clin. pathology, chief clin. chemistry U. Ala., Birmingham, 1971-73; asso. prof. pathology, chief hematopathology U. Ariz., Tucson, 1973-82, prof., 1982—. Served with U.S. Army, 1962-64. Mem. Am. Soc. Clin. Pathology, Am. Assn. Blood Banks, Soc. Cryobiology, AAAS, Phi Beta Kappa, Alpha Omega Alpha. Contbr. articles to med. jours. Home: 6621 E Via Cavalier Tucson AZ 85715 Office: 1501 N Campbell Tucson AZ 85724

GLASSMAN, JOEL A., artist, educator, video artist, photographer; b. N.Y.C., Sept. 10, 1946; s. Irving and Miriam (Lipstiz) G. B.F.A. U. N.Mex., 1969; postgrad. Parsons Sch. of Design, 1965-67; M.A., Hunter Coll., 1970. Sales rep. Gen. Electronics Systems, Inc., Berkeley, Calif.; artist, tchr. San Francisco Art Inst., 1982—; represented in permanent collections: San Francisco Mus. of Modern Art, Everson Mus., Los Angeles County Mus., Koln Kunsthall, Germany. Recipient Video award NEA, 1976, 78. Author: Video Anthology, 1977. Home: 2803 Cherry St Berkeley CA 94705 Office: 863 Florida St San Francisco CA 94110

GLASSMEYER, JAMES MILTON, aerospace engr., elec. engr.; b. Cin., Mar. 31, 1928; s. Howard Jerome and Ethel Marie (Niemann) G.; m. Anita Mary Tschida, Apr. 21, 1979. Student U. Cin., 1947-49; B.S. in E.E. with honors, U. Colo., Boulder, 1958, M.S. in Aero, Astron., M.I.T., 1960. Commd. 2d lt. U.S. Air Force, 1950, advanced through grades to lt. col., 1971; astron. engr. div. hdqrs. Air Force Space Systems, Los Angeles, 1960-64, Rocket Propulsion Lab., Edwards AFB, Calif., 1967-73; ret., 1973; pvt. practice aero. and astron. research and analysis, 1973—. Mem. AIAA, Air Force Assn., Planetary Soc., Ret. Officers Assn., Tau Beta Pi, Eta Kappa Nu, Sigma Tau, Sigma Gamma. Tau, Sigma Xi. Roman Catholic. Contbr. articles to jours. in field. Home: 5701 E Glenn St #66 Tucson AZ 85712

GLATHE, JOHN PARSONS, psychiatrist; b. Bklyn., Nov. 22, 1926; s. Henry Bernhard and Alice Elizabeth (Parsons) G.; A.B., Stanford U., 1949, M.D., 1953; divorced; children—Jeffrey, Susan, Caroline. Intern U. Mich. Hosp., 1952-53; fellow Mayo Found., 1955-60; staff psychiatrist Community Hosp., San Mateo, Calif., 1960-61; practice medicine specializing in psychiatry, Palo Alto, Calif., 1961—; mem. staff Stanford U. Med. Center; clin. asso. prof. Stanford U. Med. Sch., 1961—. Served with USAF, 1953-55. Fellow Am. Psychiat. Assn.; mem AMA, Biofeedback Research Soc., Soc. Med. Friends of Wine, Sigma Chi, Nu Sigma Nu. Address: 780 Welch Rd Palo Alto CA 94304

GLATT, MEREL MIRIAM, educator; b. Berlin, Germany, Oct. 31, 1935; d. Morris and Erna (Michaelis) Fishbaum; widow; children—Robert M., Stephen M. B.A. in Music, Calif. State U.-Los Angeles, 1974, M.S. in Counselor Edn., 1979. Lic. marriage, family and child counselor, Calif. Career counselor Montebello (Calif.) Unified Schs., 1980—; cons. Buena Vista Counseling and Learning Ctr., Duarte, Calif., 1979. Mem. Calif. Personnel and Guidance Assn., Calif. Assn. Work Experience Educators; Am. Personnel and Guidance Assn., AAUW, Calif. Assn. Marriage and Family Therapists; Monterey Park C. of C. Democrat. Unitarian. Author numerous articles and revs., also poems. Office: 1230 Vail Ave Montebello CA 90640

GLATZER, ROBERT ANTHONY, advertising executive; b. N.Y.C., May 19, 1932; s. Harold and Glenna (Beaber) G.; m. Paula Rosenfeld, Dec. 20, 1964; m. 2d, Mary Ann Murphy, Dec. 31, 1977; children—Gabriela, Jessica, Nicholas. B.A., Haverford Coll., 1954. Br. store dept. mgr. Bloomingdale's, N.Y.C., 1954-56; media buyer Ben Sackheim Advt., N.Y.C., 1956-59; producer TV commls. Ogilvy, Benson & Mather Advt., N.Y.C., 1959-62; dir. broadcast prodn. Carl Ally Advt., N.Y.C., 1962-63; owner Chronicle Prodns., N.Y.C., 1963-73; dir. Folklife Festival, Smithsonian Inst., Washington, 1973, Expo 74 Corp., Spokane, Wash., 1973-74; pres. Robert Glatzer Assocs., Spokane, 1974—; ptnr. Delany/Glatzer Advt., Spokane. Bd. dirs. Riverfront Arts Festival, 1977-78; bd. dirs. Comprehensive Health Planning Council, 1975-78, Spokane Quality of Life Council, 1976-82, Allied Arts of Spokane, 1976-80, Art Alliance Wash. State, 1977-81, Spokane chpt. ACLU, 1979-83. Recipient CINE Golden Eagle award (2). Mem. Dirs. Guild Am. Democrat. Jewish. Author: The New Advertising, 1970; co-scenarist Scorpio and other TV prodns. Office: W 905 Riverside Ave Spokane WA 99201

GLAUS, RONALD ARTHUR, psychologist; b. Portland, Oreg., May 23, 1943; s. Arthur William and Eva Leon (Johansen) G.; children—Deborah LeAnn, Lorene Rae, Shane Charlton. B.A., Portland State U., 1970; M.A., Pacific Luth. U., 1974; Ph.D., U. Oreg., 1979. Lic. psychologist, Wash., Oreg. Psychology technician VA Hosp., Tacoma, 1971-75; psychometrist asst. U. Oreg., Eugene, 1975-76; psychologist Polk County Mental Health Clinic, Dallas, Oreg., 1977—; instr. psychology Chemeketa Community Coll., 1980—. Social services chmn. West Salem Community Council, 1978-79. Served with U.S. Army 1962-65. Mem. Am. Psychol. Assn., Oreg. Psychol. Assn., Wash. State Psychol. Assn., Salem Psychol. Soc. Home: 938 Lynda Ln Salem OR 97304 Office: 635 Church St NE Salem OR 97301

GLAVIS, GEORGE OSCAR, design engr.; b. Alexandria, Va., May 26, 1939; s. Edward and Margot Gertrude (Jerike) G.; B.S., U.S. Naval Acad., 1961; M.S.E.E., USN Postgrad. Sch., 1968; M.B.A., Pepperdine U., 1977; m. Jeanne Noreen Cavanah; children—George Geoffrey, Katherine Anne, Ann Marie, Anthony Mathew. Commd. ensign U.S. Navy, 1961, advanced through grades to comdr.; served as repair officer USS Hawkins, Mayport, Fla., 1961-63, chief engr. supply dept. USS Blackwood, Phila., 1963-65; chief engr., ops. officer USS Wilson, San Diego, 1968-71; ret., 1971; communications mgr. Pacific Telephone Co., San Diego, 1971—, customer service engr., 1971-72, power systems engr., 1973-74, transmission design engr., 1975-76, bldg. design engr., 1977—; chmn. advisory com. Communications Explorer Post, San Diego, 1975-79. Judge, Greater San Diego County Sci. Fair, 1974—; adv. Jr. Achievement Program, 1972; coach Little League, 1974-76; mem. San Diego Council Noise Abatement Bd., 1980—. Registered profl. engr., Calif.; lic. F.C.C. Comml. Radio. Mem. IEEE, Nat. Soc. Profl. Engrs., Smithsonian Inst., AAAS, Soc. Am. Mil. Engrs., Am. Soc. Naval Engrs., U.S. Navy League (dir. 1979—), Calif. Soc. Profl. Engrs. (pres. San Diego 1978-79, state dir. 1980—). Republican. Lutheran. Clubs: San Diego High Twelve (treas. 1975-77), Antique Auto, Amateur Radio, Calif. Grand (area rep. 1976-79). Research in field. Home: 2893 Oak Hill Ln Julian CA 92036 Office: 525 B St San Diego CA 92101

GLAZER, BARBARA LOIS, psychotherapist; b. Bklyn., Mar. 8, 1936; d. Daniel S. and Isabelle (Bloomberg) Cassell; m. Robert L. Friedman, Aug. 12, 1956 (div.); children—Deborah McCandlish, Leslie, Diane; m. 2d, Morton S. Glazer, Aug. 21, 1977 (dec.). B.A. in Psychology, Calif. State U.-Sacramento, 1970, M.S. in Counseling, 1972. Lic. Marriage, family and child counselor, Calif.; cert. coll. counselor, instr., supr. Calif. Counselor Dos Rios Children's Ctr., N. Sacramento Sch. Dist., 1972-74; instr. Sacramento City Coll., 1974-78; program dir. client and staff services Community Interaction Program, Sacramento, 1975-82; pvt. practice in marriage, family, child therapy, Sacramento, 1978—; affiliated with Mental Health Inst. Sacramento, Pain Ctr. of Sacramento Inc. Pres. Juvenile Service Council, Sacramento, 1966-68. Named Woman of Yr., Nat. Council of Jewish Women, 1968. Mem. Am. Personnel and Guidance Assn., Am. Mental Health Counselors Assn., NOW, Hadassah, Orgn. Rehab. Therapy, Sacramento Traditional Jazz Soc. Democrat. Home: 6310 Eastmont Ct Carmichael CA 95608 Office: 755 46th St Sacramento CA 95819

GLEASON, CYNTHIA S., public relations company executive, public relations educator; b. Portage, Wis., Mar. 2, 1949; d. Walter E. and Arleen (Slette) G.; m. William J. Kostka, Jr., Apr. 6, 1974; children—Jennifer Kostka, William Kostka III. B.A. in Journalism, U. Wis., 1972. Intern, U. Wis.-Madison Med. Ctr. Office of Pub. Info., 1970, State of Wis. Dept. Natural Resources, Madison, 1971; writer-researcher, jr. account exec. William Kostka & Assocs., Denver, 1972—, sr. account exec., 1974-77, v.p., 1977-79, sr. v.p., 1979-81, exec. v.p., 1981—; instr. dept. journalism U. Colo. Bd. dirs. Juvenile Offenders In Need, Inc., Denver; active Guardians Ad Litem. Recipient Pub. Relations Person of Year award Southland Corp., 1976. Mem. Pub. Relations Soc. Am. (accredited; counselors acad.), Denver Press Club. Home: 13955 E Hamilton Dr Aurora CO 80014 Office: William Kostka & Assocs 1407 Larimer Sq Denver CO 80202

GLEASON, JOHN HAROLD, color trend analyst, color dir.; b. New Brunswick, N.J., Dec. 25, 1939; s. Harry Joseph and Gertrude Cecelia (Schwarz) G. Student Los Angeles City Coll., 1957-60; B.P.A. cum laude, Woodbury U., Los Angeles, 1963. Owner Key II Interiors, 1963-69; nat. product designer Textone, Inc., Los Angeles, 1969-70; mgr. product design, market design coordinator Evans Products Co., Portland, Oreg., 1970-74; design cons. Ga. Pacific Corp., Portland, Permaneer Corp., St. Louis, Dai Nippon, Tokyo, 1974-79; color dir. Ameritone Paint Corp., Long Beach, Calif., 1979—. Recipient 1st Place Nat. award Residential Design Competition, Nat. Soc. Interior Designers, 1973. Mem. Am. Soc. Interior Designers, Internat. Soc. Interior Designers, Color Assn. U.S. (chmn. Color Marketing Group), Internat. Soc. Color Council (del). Home: 7268 Franklin Ave #34 Los Angeles CA 90046 Office: PO Box 190 Long Beach CA 90801

GLEASON-JORDAN, IRENE O., ofcl. VA; b. Pala Maui, Hawaii, 1922; M.D., U. Calif. at San Francisco, 1951; children—Barbara, Edward, Colin. Intern Harbor Gen. Hosp., Torrance, Calif., 1951-52; resident pathology Bellevue Hosp., 1952-54; resident pathology VA Hosp., Los Angeles, 1954-56, staff pathologist, 1956-57, sr. staff pathologist, 1957-59, chief staff, 1959-67; chief staff pathologist VA Hosp., Long Beach, Calif., 1967-79; dir. labs. Lancaster (Calif.) Community Hosp., 1979—; asst. clin. prof. pathology UCLA, 1961-73, assoc. clin. prof. pathology, 1981—; asso. clin. prof. pathology U. Calif., Irvine, 1973-81; cons. Bur. Drugs, FDA, 1974-75; commr.-med. Calif. State Bd. Quality Assurance, 1978—. Diplomate Am. Bd. Pathology. Fellow Coll. Am. Pathologists; mem. Internat. Acad. Pathologists, AMA, Am. Orchid Soc. (chmn. research, trustee). Office: Lancaster Community Hosp 43830 N 10th St W Lancaster CA 93534

GLECKLER, DONNA MICHAEL, interior designer; b. Covington, Ky., Sept. 20, 1950; d. Frank and Margaret (Mersch) Michael; A.S., U. Cin., 1970; B.A., 1976; M.S.W., Ohio State U., 1978; B.A., San Francisco State U., 1981; m. Joseph David Gleckler, Dec. 4, 1972. Asst. designer Interior Adventures, San Francisco, 1980-81; prin. Donna Gleckler Interior Design, San Francisco, 1981—. Mem. Am. Soc. Interior Designers (assoc.), AIA (affiliate). Office: 42 Portola Dr San Francisco CA 94131

GLEIM, GEORGIE, retail jewel co. exec.; b. Palo Alto, Calif., May 30, 1951; d. Arthur Frederick and Marjorie (Wilson) G.; A.A., Foothill Jr. Coll., 1971; grad. Gemologist Inst. Am., 1978. Buyer, sec. corp. Gleim The Jeweler Inc., Johnson & Co. Inc., Palo Alto, 1971—. Cert. gemologist. Mem. Am. Gem Soc. (edn. com. 1974-78), Jewelers Exchange Group, Jewellers Research Group, Peninsula Execs. Assn. Office: Gleim The Jeweler Inc 322 University St Palo Alto CA 94301

GLENCHUR, THOMAS CHONG, surgeon; b. Coalinga, Calif., Mar. 28, 1924; s. Thomas L. and Lee Shee Glenchur; m. Blanche Lee, June 20, 1952; children—Kim, Thomas Lee, Paul, Katharine. A.A., U. Calif.-Berkeley, 1945; M.D., Stanford U., 1949. Intern, Stanford U. Hosp., 1951-52; resident in surgery VA Hosps., Iowa City and Des Moines and U. Iowa Hosps., 1952-56; practice medicine specializing in surgery, Fresno, Calif., 1957—. Mem. A.C.S. Republican. Roman Catholic. Address: 1735 N Fresno St Fresno CA 93703

GLENN, EDWARD STANLEY, structural engr.; b. Covington, Tenn., May 31, 1932; s. Sanford G.; student U. Tenn., 1958-65; m. Claudette Schulze, Aug. 20, 1977. Designer, Ellers & Reaves, Cons. Engrs., Phoenix, 1965-69; chief structural engr. Ramada Inns, Inc., Phoenix, 1969-74; owner, sr. structural engr. Glenn-Plummer Cons., Inc., Scottsdale, Ariz., 1974-78, Glenn Cons. Internat., Inc., Phoenix, 1978—; v.p. structural engring. Lufkin Constrn. Co., Phoenix, 1975—; chmn. bd. Glenn Smith Internat. Corp., Phoenix, 1981—. Served with U.S. Army, 1953-55. Recipient E award U.S. Jr. C. of C., Outstanding State Chmn. award Tenn. Jaycees. Mem. Structural Engrs. Assn. Ariz., Internat. Assn. Bridge and Structural Engrs., Am. Concrete Inst. Republican. Methodist. Office: 2701 E Thomas Rd Suite G Phoenix AZ 85016

GLENN, GUY CHARLES, physician; b. Parma, Ohio, May 13, 1930; s. Joseph Frank and Helen (Rupple) G.; B.S., Denison U., 1953; M.D., U. Cin., 1957; m. Lucia Ann Howarth, June 13, 1953; children—Kathryn Holly, Carolyn Helen, Cynthia Marie. Intern, Walter Reed Army Med. Center, Washington, 1957-58; resident in pathology Fitzsimons Army Med. Center, Denver, 1959-63; commd. 2d lt. U.S. Army, 1956, advanced through grades to col., 1977; demonstrator pathology Royal Army Med. Coll., London, Eng., 1970-72; chief dept. pathology Fitzsimons Army Med. Center, Denver, 1972-77; mem. governing bd. Mont. Health Systems Agy., 1978-82. Diplomate Am. Bd. Pathology. Mem. Coll. Am. Pathologists (chmn. chemistry resources com.), Am. Soc. Clin. Pathology, Soc. Med. Cons. to Armed Forces, Colo. Assn. Continuing Lab. Edn., Midland Empire Health Assn. (past pres.). Contbr. articles to profl. jours. Home: 3225 Jack Burke Ln Billings MT 59102 Office: St Vincent Hosp Billings MT 59106

GLENN, HUGH DAVID, physicist; b. Paw Paw, W.Va., Aug. 27, 1932; s. Hugh Shaw and Florence Ethel (Eckman) G.; B.S., Fairmont State Coll., 1953; H.P. (Orins fellow), U. Rochester, 1954; M.A., U. Calif., Berkeley, 1960; Ph.D., Wash. State U., 1966; m. Raili Mirja Kontunen, Feb. 6, 1971. Health physicist Oak Ridge Inst. Nuclear Studies, Rochester-Brookhaven, N.Y., 1953-54; physicist Nat. Bur. Standards, Washington, 1954-57, Boeing Co., Seattle, 1960-62, Lawrence Livermore (Calif.) Lab., 1966-70, Systems, Sci. and Software, LaJolla, Calif., 1971-74, Lawrence Livermore Lab., 1974—. Cert. health physicist. Mem. Sigma Xi. Republican. Presbyterian. Contbr. articles on plasma dynamics, high energy shock propagation, numerical code simulation, nuclear weapons research to sci. jours. Home: 4246 Drake Way Livermore CA 94550 Office: PO Box 808 Livermore CA 94550

GLENN, JAMES D., JR., lawyer; b. Oakley, Idaho, July 1, 1934; s. Vernal D. and Vilate H. Glenn; student U. Utah, 1952-57, J.D., 1960; m. Alice Rexine, Dec. 14, 1956; children—Sheilagh Ann Glenn Thornock, Michelle Glenn Larson, James D. III, Deirdre, David R., Alison. Asso. counsel Fed. Trade Commn., San Francisco, 1960-61; admitted to Utah bar, 1960, Calif. bar, 1961, Idaho bar, 1978; partner firm Ferguson & Vohland, 1961-63; partner firm Ferguson & Glenn, 1963-65; individual practice law, Oakland, Hayward and Fremont, Calif., 1965-77; partner firm Webb, Burton, Carlson, Pedersen & Paine, Twin Falls, Idaho, 1977—; sec. Virga Land Corp., Calif.; counsel Norton Enterprises, Inc., A & B Bean & Grain, Inc. Bd. dirs. So. Alameda County (Calif.) Legal Services Corp., 1969-73. Mem. Am. Judicature Soc., Idaho Trial Lawyers Assn., Phi Kappa Phi. Republican. Mormon. Office: 155 2d Ave N PO Box 1768 Twin Falls ID 83301

GLENN, KATHLEEN GLORIA, motivational sales training specialist; b. Monterey, Calif., Aug. 20, 1943; d. Antonino Jack and Josephine (Spataro) Constanza; 1 son, Bradley Stewart. B.A., San Jose State U., 1965. Owner, pres. Fashions Unltd., B. Steward Glenn Co., Fancy That, Monterey, Calif., 1965-74; Western regional mgr. Mary Quant Co., 1974-77; exec. account dir. Princess Marcella Borghese, No. Calif., 1977-80; dir. tng., pres. Sales Plus Co., San Jose, Calif., 1980—; exec. dir. You Deserve to Be Successful seminars for women, 1982—. Office: 137 Manton Dr San Jose CA 95123

GLENN, MARY WILLIE, hospital department administrator; b. Perry, Fla., Mar. 9, 1939; d. Willie Lee and Mary Ellis (Cook) Glanton; m. Jack G. Glenn, Oct. 2, 1955; children—Alfred, Bea Essie, Jacqueline, Julie, Janeith, Jeffery. A.A., Marysville Bus. Coll., 1965; student U. Calif.-Berkeley, 1970, U. San Cruz, 1980. Asst. dir. food service Rideout Hosp., Marysville, Calif., 1960-65, Alameda Hosp., Calif., 1965-70; dir. food service Parkland Hosp., San Leandro, Calif., 1970; dir. food service Children Hosp. Med. Ctr., Oakland, Calif., 1970-77, dir. gen. services, 1977-81; dir. environ. services Kaiser Hosp., Hayward, Calif., 1981—. Recipient awards in field. Mem. Nat. Assn. Female Execs., Nat. Exec. Housekeeper Assn. Buddhist. Home: 23840 Clayton St Hayward CA 94541 Office: 27400 Hesperian St Hayward CA 94541

GLENN, NANCY M., interior designer; b. San Diego, Oct. 24, 1945; d. Dolf E. and Gretchen S. (Saum) Muehleisen; m. Tyler B. Glenn, Jr., June 7, 1969. B.F.A., U. Colo., 1968. Interior designer Nancy Glenn Interiors, Palo Alto, Calif., 1968-72; gen. mgr. Borel Interiors, San Mateo, Calif., 1972-78; pres. owner Glenn Design Co., Sausalito, Calif., 1978—. Bd. dirs. World Runners, Designers Lighting Forum, Hunger Project. Mem. Am. Soc. Interior Designers, Film Inst. No. Calif. (sponser, fundraiser), Interior Bus. Designers. Republican. Methodist. Home: 44 Sunshine Ave Sausalito CA 94965 Office: Glenn Design Co 819 Bridgeway Sausalito CA 94965

GLENN, TREVOR DAVID, physician; b. Sharon, Pa., Jan. 29, 1934; s. James Dryden and Treva Irene (Hartman) G.; B.S., Temple U., 1955; M.D., Jefferson Med. Coll. Phila., 1959; m. Ann Shirlee Haas, Aug. 20, 1955; children—Susan, Trevor David II. Intern, Harrisburg (Pa.) Polyclinic Hosp., 1960, resident psychiatry N.J. State Hosp., Ancora, 1960-63, chief of service, 1963-65, asst. med. dir., 1965-67, dep. med. dir., 1967-68; practice of medicine specializing in forensic psychiatry, Fresno, Calif., 1968—; dir. Dept. Mental Health, Fresno County, 1970-74, acting health officer Dept. Pub. Health, 1973-74, dir. Dept. Health, 1974-78, air pollution control officer, 1974-78, mem. Children's Task Force, 1976—; pvt. practice psychiatry, Fresno; asst. prof. U. So. Calif., 1970; adj. prof. Fresno (Calif.) State Coll., 1971-72; mem. faculty UCLA, 1974-82; assoc. prof. psychiatry U. Calif., San Francisco, 1975—; prof. health sci. Calif. State U., Fresno, 1978-80; coordinator residency tng. VA Hosp., Fresno, 1980—, clin. psychiatrist, 1980-81, assoc. chief service, 1982—. Chmn. adminstrv. services com. Conf. Local Mental Health Dirs., 1972-73; pres. Calif. Conf. Local Mental Health Dirs., 1974-78; mem. Gov.'s Task Force Mental Health Funding, 1974-78. Bd. dirs., chmn. mental health services com. San Joaquin Valley Health Consortium, 1972-73, mem. exec. com., 1975-78; bd. dirs. comprehensive Health Planning Fresno County, 1975-78, Comprehensive Health Planning Central Calif., 1975-78. Diplomate Am. Bd. Psychiatry and Neurology. Fellow Am. Psychiat. Assn. (del. Area VI), A.C.P.; mem. Central Calif. Psychiat. Soc. (editor newsletter 1970-73, pres. 1974-75), Calif. Conf. Local Health Officers (sec. 1977-78), Fresno County Med. Soc. (gov. 1973), Fresno County Mental Health Assn. (bd. dirs.), AMA, County Suprs. Assn. Calif. (health policy task force medi-Calif.), Royal Soc. Health, Rho Chi (charter mem.), Kappa Psi, Theta Kappa Psi, Kappa Beta Phi. Home: 5072 N Van Ness Fresno CA 93711 Office: Gateway Centre 1960 N Gateway Blvd Suite 102 Fresno CA 93727

GLENN, WILLIAM HAMILTON, public works administrator, rancher; b. Miles City, Mont., July 5, 1910; s. William Jay and Emma C. (Svepke) G.; m. Laura Mae Aronhalt, Dec. 24, 1940; 1 son, Jay E. Student No. Mont. Coll., 1977. Class I water and wastewater cert., Mont. Foreman, S-1 Cattle Co., Miles City, 1932-34; rancher, Miles City, 1934—; water and wastewater supt. City of Chinook (Mont.), 1967—; cons. instr. coop. edn. Team roping champion Mont. No. Rodeo Cowboys Assn., 1967. Mem. Am. Water Works Assn., Pro Rodeo Cowboys Assn. Presbyterian. Club: Elks. Office: Dept Water and Wastewater Chinook MT 59523

GLENNEN, ROBERT EUGENE, JR., university president; b. Omaha, Mar. 31, 1933; s. Robert E. and LaVerda F. (Elledge) G.; m. Mary C. O'Brien, Apr. 17, 1958; children—Maureen, Bobby, Mary Colleen, Billy, Barry, Katie, Molly, Kerry. A.B., U. Portland, 1955, M.Ed., 1957; Ph.D., U. Notre Dame, 1962. Instr., coach, asst. prof. U. Portland (Oreg.), 1955-60; asst. prof., then assoc. prof. edn. Eastern Mont. Coll., Billings, 1962-65; assoc., prof., asst. dean, assoc. dean U. Notre Dame, 1965-72; prof., dean, then v.p. U. Nev., Las Vegas, 1972-80; pres., prof. Western N.Mex. U., Silver City, N.Mex., 1980—; cons. on student retention and advisement; vocat. cons. HEW. Ford Found. fellow, 1961-62; faculty in-service grantee, 1965. Past pres. Swanson PTA, South Bend, Ind.; dir. Pop Warner League, Las Vegas; senator Notre Dame Alumni Assn.; bd. dirs. Senior Citizens Orgn., Las Vegas, Nev. Welfare Bur., Las Vegas Aquatic Club; mem. Nat. Health Com. Recipient Coll. Student Jour. Model of Excellence award, 1983. Mem. Am. Personnel and Guidance Assn., Am. Assn. State Colls. and Univs., Am. Assn. Higher Edn., Nev. Personnel and Guidance Assn. (pres. 1979-80), Nat. Assn. Student Personnel Adminstrs., Assn. Counselor Educators and Suprs., Nat. Vocat. Guidance Assn., AAUP, Am. Psychol. Assn., Am. Coll. Student Personnel Assn., Silver City C. of C., Phi Kappa Phi, Phi Lamda Alpha, Phi Eta Sigma. Republican. Roman Catholic. Author textbook; contbr. articles to profl. jours. Home: 500 College Ave Silver City NM 88061 Office: PO Box 680 Silver City NM 88062

GLENNY, LYMAN ALBERT, political science educator; b. Trent, S.D., Jan. 26, 1918; s. Walter and Ann (Henning) G.; m. Carolyn Joy Ballou, Dec. 19, 1942 (div. Mar. 1977); children—Terence Alan, Celia Joy, Colleen Marie; m. 2d, Helen S. Thompson, June 14, 1978. B.S., U. Minn., 1947; M.A., U. Colo., 1948; Ph.D., State U. Iowa, 1950. Instr. polit. sci. U. Iowa, Iowa City, 1948-50, asst. prof., 1950-54, assoc. prof., 1954-58, prof., 1958-60; prof. Sacramento State Coll., 1960-62; assoc. dir. Ill. Bd. Higher Edn., Springfield, 1962-65, exec. dir., 1965-69; prof. higher edn. U. Calif.-Berkeley, 1968—, dir. Ctr. for Research and Devel. in Higher Edn., 1969-76; dir. Nebr. Study Adminstrn. Higher Edn., 1960. Served to capt. U.S. Army, 1941-46, 51-52. Mem. AAUP, Am. Assn. Higher Edn., Am. Soc. Pub. Adminstrn., Am. Inst. Research, State Higher Edn. Exec. Officers Assn., Western Polit. Sci. Assn. Author: Autonomy of Public Colleges, 1959; Coordinating Higher Education for the 70's, 1971; State Budgeting for Higher Education: Interagency Conflict and Consensus, 1976; Issues in Higher Education: A Six Nation Analysis, 1979; (with J. R. Kidder) State Tax Support of Higher Education: Revenue Appropriation Trends and Patterns, 1963-73, 1973; (with T. K. Dalglish) Public Universities, State Agencies, and the Law: Constitutional Autonomy in Decline, 1973; (with others) Presidents confront reality: From edifice complex to university with walls, 1975; (with Janet Ruyle) Trends in State Revenue Appropriations for Higher Education, 1968-78, 78; (with F. M. Bowen) Uncertainty in Public Higher Education, 1980; Quality and Accountability, 1981; also other publs. on state budgeting for higher edn. Editor: Statewide Planning for Post-Secondary Education, 1971. Contbr. articles, chpts. to profl. publs.; mem. editorial bd. Western Polit. Quar., 1959-62, research series Assn. Instl. Research, 1976. Home: 3123 Lippizaner Ln Walnut Creek CA 94598 Office: Tolman Hall U Calif Berkeley CA 94720

GLICK, BETTY JANE, accountant; b. Carlisle, Pa., Sept. 15, 1935; d. Benjamin Burns and Margaret Irene (Brinkerhoff) Bailey; student pub. schs., Carlisle; m. Carl Samuel Glick, Jr., Sept. 4, 1953; children—Elizabeth Rose, Carl Samuel III (dec.), John Robert, William Joseph. Sec., Bedford Shoe Co. div. G.R. Kinney Co., Carlisle, 1953-54, bookkeeper, 1956-57, lacer pre-fit room, 1959; accountant M.G. Riley, C.P.A., Kenai, Alaska, 1966-82. Program chmn. Kenai PTA, 1968-69, pres., 1969-70; mem. Kenai Planning & Zoning Adv. Com., 1974-76, chmn., 1976; mem. Kenai City Council, 1976-82, vice mayor, 1979-82; parliamentarian Kenai Peninsula Borough Planning & Zoning Com., 1976-77, vice chmn., 1977-81, chmn., 1981-82; mem. Kenai Peninsula Borough Assembly, 1982—; chmn. Jr. Achievement, Kenai, 1977-78, treas., 1978-81, chmn., 1981-82; bd. dirs., 1982-84; bd. dirs. Alaska Mcpl. League, 1980-81, 1st v.p., 1982-83, pres., 1983-84; bd. dirs. Cook Inlet Council Alcoholism, 1983. Named Citizen of Month, Kenai C. of C., 1977. Mem. Billiken Bus. and Profl. Women's Club (named Woman of Yr. 1978). Club: Peninsula Petroleum Wives. Home: PO Box 528 Highbush and E Aliak St Kenai AK 99611

GLICK, BETTY JOAN, university official; b. Ft. Leavenworth, Kans., Feb. 10, 1954; d. John Russell and Irene (Dybko) Glick. B.S. in Child Devel., Colo. State U., 1976; M.S. in Higher Edn., Iowa State U., 1979. Tchr. United Day Care Ctr., Ft. Collins, Colo., 1976-77; hall adviser Iowa State U., Ames, 1977-79; resident dir. U. Calif.-Davis, 1979-81; asst. dir. residence life Western Wash. U., Bellingham, 1981—. Recipient ednl., media grant, Assn. Coll. Univ. Housing Officers, 1983. Mem. Nat. Assn. Student Personnel Adminstrs., Am. Coll. Personnel Assn., Northwest Coll. Personnel Assn. Presbyterian.

GLICKMAN, DAVID (BUD) FURTH, personnel consultant; b. Oakland, Calif., Sept. 29, 1932. B.S. in Bus. Adminstrn., U. Calif.-Berkeley, 1955; m. Judith Reich, Mar. 26, 1969; children—Hillary, David. Sales mgr. Norton Simon Inc., Fullerton, Calif., 1955-66; propr. Bud Glickman & Assocs. Inc., San Francisco, 1967—. Democrat. Jewish. Office: 50 California St #2255 San Francisco CA 94111

GLINES, ALAN CLAIR EDWIN, space systems engineering manager; b. Independence, Kans., Jan. 1, 1943; s. Lewis Clair and Mary Ellen (Patty) G. B.S. in Elec. Engring., U. Kans., 1966 M.S. in Systems Mgmt., U. So. Calif., 1983. With NASA Johnson Space Ctr., Houston, 1966-79, asst. flight dir. mission control Apollo-Soyuz, 1974-75, astronaut rep. Space Shuttle Checkout, Palmdale, Calif., 1976-78; mgr. launch ops. Western Union Spacecom, Los Angeles, 1979; sub-project mgr. space systems TRW Space and Tech. Group, Redondo Beach, Calif., 1980—, also civic affairs spokesman. Recipient Presdl. Medal of Freedom for contbns. to NASA Apollo 13. Mem. Am. Space Found., Planetary Soc. Republican. Methodist. Home: 6740 Los Verdes Dr Rancho Palos Verdes CA 90274 Office: TRW 1 Space Park Redondo Beach CA 90278

GLINES, DON EUGENE, educational consultant; b. Sacramento, Calif., Nov. 25, 1930; s. Clarence E. and Helen V. (Jacobson) G.; m. Ruth V. Begneaud, Dec. 22, 1957; children—Laurie, Harlan. B.S., Springfield Coll., 1952; M.S., U. Oreg., 1956, Ph.D., 1960. Cert. tchr., adminstr., Calif. Various ednl. positions Calif., Oreg., Spain, W. Ger., Taiwan, Haiti, Ariz., Mo., S.D.; prof. Mankato (Minn.) State U., 1968-73; adminstr. Calif. State Dept. Edn., Sacramento, 1974-83; dir. Ednl. Futures Projects, Sacramento, 1983—; tchr. univ. courses; dir. workshops; lectr. in field; guest numerous talk shows. Mem. Cousteau Soc., Common Cause, Environ. Action, Global Futures Network. Served to lt. U.S. Army, 1952-54. Mem. Nat. Council Yr—Round Edn. (pres.), World Future Soc., Soc. Clin. Ecology, Am. Assn. Social Psychiatry, Phi Delta Kappa. Author: Implementing Different Schools, 1968; Creating Humane Schools, 1972; Educational Futures, 5 vols., 1980; (with others) Diagnosis and Treatment of Environmentally Induced Illness, 1983; Schooling to Learning, 1984. Contbr. articles to profl. jours. Home: 1501 3d St Sacramento CA 95814 Office: Ednl Futures Projects PO Box 2977 Sacramento CA 95812

GLISSON, FLOYD WRIGHT, II, food company executive; b. Akron, Ohio, Aug. 13, 1947; s. Floyd Wright and Audrey Mae (Hill) G.; m. Janice Talbert, Aug. 22, 1970; children—Tenley, Evan. B.S. in Acctg., U. Akron, 1969; M.B.A., U. Pitts., 1970. C.P.A., Colo. Staff Auditor Arthur Andersen & Co., Denver, 1970-71; controller More Combs & Burch, Denver, 1972-74; v.p., controller Armour-Dial Inc., Phoenix, 1974-80; v.p. fin. and planning Hunt-Wesson Foods Inc., Fullerton, Calif., 1980—. Mem. bus. adv. council Calif. State U.-Fullerton. D.G. Sisterson fellow, 1970. Office: 1645 W Valencia Fullerton CA 92634

GLODAVA, MILAGROS GARCIA, business service executive; b. Bauan, Batangas, Philippines, May 27, 1945, came to U.S., 1972, naturalized, 1976; d. Francisco Ramos and Rosalia Marialo (Coronel) Garcia; m. Mark Jeffrey Glodava, Jan. 29, 1972; children—Kirsten, Angela, Kevin Marc. B.S. in Edn., St. Paul Coll., Manila, 1969. Tchr. Mt. Carmel High Sch., Polillo, Quezon, P.I., 1969-72; bookkeeper First Nat. State Bank of N.J., Newark, 1972-74; pres. Glodava Bus. Services, Arvada, Colo., 1980—. Active in Filipino-Am. community affairs. Mem. Arvada C. of C., Nat. Assn. Female Execs., AAUW. Democrat. Roman Catholic. Author: In Search of a Dream, 1980. Home and Office: 7350 Braun Way Arvada CO 80005

GLOOR, RICHARD DETMORE, aerospace company executive; b. Louisville, Mar. 13, 1929; s. Richard Lauffer and Dorothy Mildred (Johnston) G.; m. Patti Virgina Bolton, June 12, 1954; children—Nancy Virginia, Diane Elizabeth. B.E.E., U. Louisville, 1951, M.E.E., 1970; M.S. in Elec. Engring., MIT, 1955. With TRW Inc., Redondo Beach, Calif., 1955—, dir. design integrity and productivity, space and tech. group. Served as lt. USN, 1951-54; Korea. Mem. AIAA, Aerospace Industries Assn. Am., Am. Productivity Mgmt. Assn., Assn. Profl. Genealogists, South Bay Cities Geneal. Soc., Sigma Xi, Theta Tau, Eta Kappa Nu. Methodist. Home: 4843 Blackhorse Rd Rancho Palos Verdes CA 90274 Office: TRW Space and Technology Group One Space Park Redondo Beach CA 90278

GLOSSER, JAMES WILLIAM, veterinarian; b. Helena, Mont., Aug. 2, 1931; s. Paul Joseph and Mildred (Greer) G.; m. Julie Marie Indorf, Sept. 20, 1951; children—John Louis, Theresa Anne Clark, Christopher Paul. B.S., Wash. State U., 1960, D.V.M., 1963; M.P.H., U. Minn., 1971. Lic. veterinarian, Mont., Wash. With Mont. Vet. Diagnostic Lab., Helena, 1951-59; owner vet. practice, Miles City, Mont., 1963-65; vet. epidemiologist USPHS Center for Disease Control, Atlanta, 1966-73; chief disease control animal health div. Mont. Dept. Livestock, Helena, 1974-77, adminstr. div., 1977—; state veterinarian State of Mont., 1978—; tech. advisor Nat. Cattlemen's Assn. Trustee, Dist. 1 Sch. Bd., Helena, 1979—. Served with USPHS, 1966-73. Recipient Superior Service award Dept. Agr., 1971; Gov.'s commendation Territory of Guam, 1968. Mem. Nat. Assn. State Pub. Health Veterinarians, Am. Vet. Med. Assn., USPHS Commd. Officers Assn., Soc. for Epidemiol. Research, Intermountain Vet. Med. Assn. (1st v.p., dir. 1979—), Western States Animal Health Assn., U.S. Animal Health Assn., Nat. Cattlemen's Assn., Mont. Vet. Med. Assn., Phi Zeta, Gamma Sigma Delta. Roman Catholic. Club: Kiwanis. Contbr. articles to profl. jours. Home: PO Box 586 Helena MT 59624 Office: Mont Dept Livestock Capitol Station Helena MT 59620

GLOVER, ALAN HARNEY, state senator; b. Carson City, Nev., June 10, 1949; s. John Nelson and Peggy (Harney) G. Student U. Nev.-Reno, 1968-72. Mem. Nev. State Assembly, from 1972; now mem. Nev. State Senate. Mem. Phi Delta Theta. Democrat. Roman Catholic. (Lodge); K.C. Home: 901 N Richmond Ave Carson City NV 89701 Office: Nevada State Senate Carson City NV 89710*

GLOVER, STEVEN MERRITT, optometrist; b. Roswell, N.Mex., Dec. 22, 1949; s. Victor Steven and Jean (Hanchey) G.; m. Sally J. Cammon, July 20, 1974; 1 son, Drew. B.S., U. N. Mex., 1973; O.D., So. Calif. Coll. Optometry, 1980. Pvt. practice optometry, Roswell, N. Mex. Served to lt. USN, 1973-76. Mem. Am. Optometric Assn., Coll. Optometrists in Vision Devel., Optometric Extension Program Found., Jaycees. Club: Kiwanis. Home: 406 W 5th St Roswell NM 88201 Office: 509 W Alameda St Roswell NM 88201

GLOVER, TERRENCE F., economist, educator; b. Farmington, Utah, June 12, 1940; s. Valence C. and Hattie (Solomon) G.; m. Barbara Ann Bybee, March 18, 1966; children—Julie Ann, Angela, Natalie, Sherene. B.S., Utah State U., 1965, M.S., 1966; Ph.D., Purdue U., 1971. Asst. prof. Ohio State U., Columbus, 1970-74; assoc. prof. Utah State U., Logan, 1975-78, prof. 1978—, dir. Econ. Research Inst., 1982—; dir. spl. projects, Strategic Info., Inc., Burlington, Mass., 1980-81; cons. Commodity Info. Inc., Lewis Asso.; economist Inland Econometrics Inc.; pres. T.F. Glover, Econ. Cons. Mem. Ohio Taxation Reform Group, 1973-74; mem. Platform Cons. Com. Ariz. State Repulican Party, 1982. Recipient Brazilian Ministry of Agr. Research award, 1974; U. Hokkaido grantee, 1976; Sears Roebuck scholar, 1958-60. Mem. Am. Econ. Assn., Am. Agrl. Econ. Assn., Western Agrl. Econ. Assn., Econometric Soc., Am. Statis. Assn., Nat. Assn. Bus. Economists. Mormon. Author: Feasibility of Siting Energy Facilities in Utah, 1981; Appropriate Technology-Utah Energy Facility Siting Study, 1981; Farm Growth in Brazil, 1975. Contbr. articles to profl. jours. Home: 1697 E 1460 N Logan UT 84321 Office: Dept Econs UMC 35 Utah State U Logan UT 84322

GLUCKSTERN, BYRNECE, domestic relations counselor; b. Bklyn., July 30, 1924; d. Herman H. and Selma (Weinstein) Horowitz; B.A., Bklyn. Coll., 1946; postgrad. Denver U., 1947-48, summers 1945, 46, 64, U. Colo., Denver, 1952-53, 69-70; m. Henry Gluckstern, Sept. 18, 1948; children—Mark, Susan, Jonathan. Part time tchr. Emily Griffith Opportunity Sch., Denver, 1957-63; caseworker Arapahoe County Dept. Social Services, Littleton, Colo., 1966-68; assoc. marriage counselor Arapahoe County Dist. Ct., Littleton, 1968-77, ct. marriage counselor, 1977-79, chief domestic relations counselor, 1979—; mediator Family Mediation Ctr., Boulder, Colo.; faculty, co-chmn. confs. in field; speaker community and profl. groups. Registered social worker, Colo. Mem. Assn. Family Conciliation Cts. (Colo. membership chmn., dir.), Interdisciplinary Com. on Child Custody (pres.), Nat. Council Family Relations, Colo. Assn. Public Employees. Democrat. Club: Pioneer Women. Contbr. chpts. to handbooks. Home: Denver CO Office: 5606 S Court Pl Littleton CO 80120

GLUSHIEN, ARTHUR SAMUEL, physician, educator; b. Bklyn., July 15, 1911; s. Isaac and Minnie (Hoffman) G.; m. Edith Risk, Dec. 25, 1938 (dec. July 1978); 1 son, Thomas Michael. B.S. cum laude, N.Y. U., 1930, M.D., 1936. Intern, Kings County Hosp., Bklyn., 1936-37, Ellis Hosp., Schenectady, 1937-38; physician VA Hosp., Pitts., 1939-44, cardiologist, 1944-55, chief med. service, 1955-59; pvt. practice medicine, Pitts., 1959-64; chief cardiology sect. VA Hosp., East Orange, N.J., 1964-74; pvt. practice medicine specializing in cardiology, San Diego, 1974-78; council Inst. Continued Learning U. Calif.-San Diego, 1978—; assoc. clin. prof. medicine U. Pitts. Sch. Medicine, 1952-64; asso. prof. medicine N.J. Coll. Medicine, 1965-74; chief staff Russellton Med. Group, 1959-64. Pres. Western Pa. Heart Assn., 1961-62. Served to maj. U.S. Army, 1944-46. Recipient Distinguished Service award Western Pa. Heart Assn., 1962; Superior Performance award East Orange VA Hosp., 1969. Diplomate Am. Bd. Internal Medicine. Fellow A.C.P., Am. Coll. Cardiology; mem. Am. Heart Assn., Phi Beta Kappa, Alpha Omega Alpha. Independent. Jewish. Contbr. articles to med. jours. Home: 6761 Caminito del Greco San Diego CA 92120

GLYNN, JAMES AUGUSTINE, sociology educator; b. Bklyn., Sept. 10, 1941; s. James Augustine and Muriel Marie (Lewis) G.; A.A., Foothill Coll., 1961; B.A., Calif. State U., 1964, M.A., 1966; m. Marie Janet Gates, Dec. 17, 1966; 1 son, David Sean. Faculty Bakersfield (Calif.) Coll., 1966—, prof. sociology, 1974—; asst. prof. sociology Calif. State Coll., Fresno, 1971-72, Chapman Coll., Orange, Calif., 1972. Founder, charter sec. Kern Community Coll. Fedn. of Tchrs., 1973-75. Mem. Am. Sociol. Assn., Calif. Tchrs. Assn., Calif. Fedn. Tchrs., Faculty Assn. of Calif. Community Colls., Community Coll. Social Sci. Assn. Democrat. Author: (with Elbert W. Stewart) Introduction to Sociology, 1971, 3d edit., 1979; Studying Sociology, 1979; contbg. author Visions of Wong, 1979; Writing Across the Curriculum Using Sociological Concepts, 1983; book reviewer for various pub. cos. Home: 2507 Rio Vista Bakersfield CA 93306

GMELCH, WALTER HOWARD, university official, educational administration educator; b. N.Y.C., May 18, 1947; s. George John and Edna B. Gmelch; m. Paula Lynn Cowgill, Dec. 28, 1969; children—Benjamin, Thomas. B.A., Stamford U., 1969; M.B.A., U. Calif.-Berkeley, 1971, Ph.D., 1975. UNESCO research scholar, New Delhi, India, 1971-72; assoc. dir. Field Tng. and Service and Bur., U. Oreg., 1975-78; pres. GTS Airfreight, San Francisco, 1978-80; assoc. prof. ednl. adminstrn. Wash. State U., Pullman, 1980—, assoc. dir. partnership for rural improvement, 1981-82, dir. cert., 1983—. Recipient Million Dollar award Pan Am. Airways, 1979, 80; Nat. Kellogg Found. fellow, 1983-86. Mem. Am. Ednl. Research Assn., Am. Assn. Sch. Adminstrs., Assn. Supervision and Curriculum Devel., Am. Soc. Tng. and Devel., Phi Delta Kappa (profl. devel. award 1981), Kappa Delta Pi. Clubs: World Trade, Rotary (San Francisco); Family (Pullman). Author: Beyond Stress to Effective Management, 1982; others; contbr. articles to profl. jours. Home: SW 640 Dawnview Ct Pullman WA 99163 Office: Coll Edn Wash State U Pullman WA 99164

GOAR, LELA JO, educator; b. Burnet, Tex., Nov. 8, 1939; d. Gordon Arlyn and Anne Mae (Bales) Glimp; m. Lane Keith Goar, June 28, 1963; children—Guy Alan, Carolyn Sue, Clay Todd. B.S., S.W. Tex. State U., San Marcos, 1961; M.S., Tex. Tech. U., 1965; postgrad Eastern N.Mex. U., 1968-82. Tchr. homemaking Bovina (Tex.) Pub. Sch., 1966; Clovis (N.Mex.) Mcpl. Schs., 1966—, Gattis Jr. High Sch., 1980—. Named Curry County Homemaker of Yr. Curry County Extension Council, 1978. Coordinator March of Dimes Walkathon, 1979-83. Mem. N.Mex. Vocat. Assn., N.Mex. Vocat. Home Econs. Tchrs. Assn., N.Mex. Edn. Assn., Clovis Edn. Assn., FHA/HERO Alumni Assn. Democrat. Methodist. Home: Star Rte Box 29 Clovis NM 88101 Office: 8th and Pile Sts Gattis Jr High Sch Clovis NM 88101

GOATES, DELBERT TOLTON, child psychiatrist; b. Logan, Utah, Apr. 14, 1932; s. Wallace Albert and Roma (Tolton) G.; B.S., U. Utah, 1953, M.D., 1962; postgrad. U. Nebr., 1965, 67; m. Claudia Tidwell, Sept. 15, 1960; children—Jeanette, Byron, Rebecca Lynn, Alan, Paul, Jonathan Phillip, Kendra Michelle, George Milton. Asst. prof. child psychiatry U. N.Mex., 1967-71, dir. children's services, 1967-71, asst. prof. pediatrics, 1969-71; intern Rochester (N.Y.) Gen. Hosp., 1962-63; resident Nebr. Psychiat. Inst., Omaha, 1963-67; practice medicine specializing in child psychiatry, Omaha, 1963-67, Albuquerque, 1967-71, Salt Lake City, 1971—; clin. dir. Children's Psychiat. Center, Primary Children's Med. Center, Salt Lake City, 1971-77. Pres., Magic Mini Maker Inc., Salt Lake City, 1972—; chmn. bd. Intermountain Polytex, Inc. Bd. dirs. Utah Cancer Soc., Great Salt Lake Mental Health. Served with M.C., AUS, 1953-55. Mem. A.M.A., Orthopsychiat. Assn., Am., Utah, Sioux psychiat. assns., Intermountain Acad. Child Psychiatry (pres. 1974-76), Pi Kappa Alpha, Phi Kappa Phi. Mem. Ch. of Jesus Christ of Latter-day Saints (bishop 1968-71). Home: 1275 Chandler Dr Salt Lake City UT 84103 Office: 77 S 700 E Suite 250 Salt Lake City UT 84102

GOBAR, ALFRED JULIAN, econ. cons. co. asso., educator; b. Lucerne Valley, Calif., July 12, 1932; s. Julian Smith and Hilda (Millbank) G.; B.A. in Econs., Whittier Coll., 1953, M.A. in History, 1955; postgrad. Claremont Grad. Sch., 1953-54; Ph.D. in Econs., U. So. Calif., 1963; m. Sally Ann Randall, June 17, 1957; children—Wendy Lee, Curtis Julian, Joseph Julian. Asst. pres. Microdot Inc., Pasadena, 1953-57; regional sales mgr. Sutorbilt Corp., Los Angeles, 1957-59; market research asso. Beckman Instrument Inc., Fullerton, 1959-64; sr. marketing cons. Western Mgmt. Consultants Inc., Phoenix, Los Angeles, 1964-66; partner, prin., chmn. bd. Darley/Gobar Assos., Inc., 1966-73; pres., chmn. bd. Alfred Gobar Assos., Inc., Brea, Calif., 1973—. Asst. prof. finance U. So. Calif., Los Angeles, 1963-64; asso. prof. bus. Calif. State U., Los Angeles, 1963-68, 70-79, asso. prof., Fullerton, 1968-69; marketing, financial adviser 1957—; pub. speaker seminars and convs. Contbr. articles to profl. publs. Home: 1100 W Valencia Mesa Dr Fullerton CA 92633 Office: 207 S Brea Blvd Brea CA 92621

GOBLE, JULIE SEAL, educator; b. Provo, Utah, May 1, 1945; d. Glenn T. and Zelma T. Seal; m. Edwin Goble, Jan. 28, 1967; children—Michelle, Jim. B.S. in Elem. Edn., Utah State U., 1968, M.Ed., 1981. Certified tchr., adminstr., supr., Utah. Tchr. West Point Elem. Sch., Davis County Schs., 1970-77, acting asst. prin., 1977-82; tchr. Fremont Elem. Sch., Sunset, Utah, 1982—; intern North Davis Jr. High Sch., winter, 1983, media coordinator, 1976-79. Faculty rep. PTA, 1976-79; tchr., organist, chorister Mormon Ch.; sec., treas. Ward Relief Soc. Mem. Assn. Suprs. Curriculum Devel., Davis Edn. Assn., Utah Edn. Assn., NEA, Phi Kappa Phi (Utah chpt.), Phi Delta Kappa (Ogden chpt.), Daus. of Utah Pioneers. Home: 364 S 3000 W Syracuse UT 84041 Office: Fremont Elem Sch 2525 N 160 W Sunset UT 84051

GOBRECHT, ROBERT WILLIAM, retail toy store exec.; b. Waukegan, Ill., July 8, 1923; s. Edwin Rudolph and Ruth Martha (Parmenter) G.; B.S., U. So. Calif.; m. Betty Barbara Cazel, Apr. 15, 1944; children—Janet Claire, Robert Edwin, Carol Ruth. Underwriter, Firemans Fund Ins. Co., Los Angeles, 1946-48; with exec. tng. program Sears Roebuck & Co., Calif. zone, 1948-60, operating supt., 1959-60; founder, owner, pres. Macabob Toys Co., Inc., Pasadena, Calif., 1961—; cons. to toy cos. and factories throughout U.S. and Far East. Dep. sheriff Los Angeles County; former pres. Los Angeles County Sheriff Rhythm Posse, 1973-75. Served with USAAF, 1941-45, USAF, 1951-54. Mem. Hobby Industry Am. Asso., So. Calif. Hobby Am. Assn., Nat. Retail Mchts. Assn., Nat. Bicycle Dealers Assn., Nat. Miniature Enthusiasts Assn., Family Motor Coach Assn. (nat. bd. dirs.), Hon. Order Ky. Cols. Republican. Presbyterian. Clubs: U. So. Calif. Trojan, Masons, Maestros. Home: 3575 Newhaven Rd Pasadena CA 91107 Office: Box 5577 2980 E Colorado Blvd Pasadena CA 91107

GODDARD, ALICE MARY, data processing exec.; b. Butte, Mont., Feb. 5, 1936; d. Frank Michael and Alice Mary (Curtis) Holly; B.S. in Accounting, U. Ariz., 1959; m. Volney Beckner Goddard, III, Apr. 6, 1963. Statistician, Boeing Airplane Co., Seattle, 1959; computer programmer Lockheed Aircraft Corp., Sunnyvale, Calif., 1959-62; computer programmer, sr. programmer, United Technologies Chem. Systems Div., Sunnyvale, 1963-66, mgr. adminstrv. computer programming, 1966-77, mgr. computer center, 1977—. Named Distinguished Woman of Year of San Francisco Peninsula, 1974. Mem. Beta Gamma Sigma, Alpha Xi Delta. Home: 558 Endicott Dr Sunnyvale CA 94087 Office: 1050 E Arques Ave Sunnyvale CA 94086

GODDARD, JERRY FRANK, business education instructor, counselor, consultant; b. Imperial, Nebr., July 4, 1939; s. Russell Jefferson and Ruth Irene (Skewes) G.; m. Carol Louise Gunderson; children—Caren Renee, John Russell. A.A., Graceland Coll., 1960; B.A., U. No. Colo., 1962; M.A., Colo. State U., 1969. Tchr., McCook, Nebr., 1962-67; asst. state advisor State Bd. Community Coll. and Occupational Edn., Denver, 1969-72; chmn. secretarial dept., instr. Aims Community Coll., Greeley, Colo., 1972—; cons.; counselor; nat. bd. dirs. Future Bus. Leaders Am.-Phi Beta Lambda. Active Republican Party. Recipient Presl. award Aims Community Coll., 1983. Mem. Colo. Educators Bus., Mountain-Plains Bus. Edn. Assn., Aims Coll. Edn. Assn., Am. Vocat. Assn., Colo. Vocat. Assn., Nat. Bus. Educators Assn., NEA, Colo. Edn. Assn., Delta Phi Epsilon. Mormon. Club: Jaycees (McCook, Nebr.).

GODEK, STEPHEN CHESTER, political scientist; b. Chgo., Mar. 4, 1950; s. Chester Joseph and Alice Margaret (Stelmasiak) G.; m. Merrilee Ann Sebela, May 14, 1953; children—Anthony Kokociuski, Timothy, Sarah. A.B. with honors and distinction, U. Ill.-Chgo., 1973, M.A., 1978, Ph.D. in Pub. Policy, 1983. Instr. U. Ill.-Chgo, 1977-81; lectr. Calif. State U.-Long Beach, 1981—; instr. Ill. Inst. Tech., 1980; analyst Select Joint Com. on Regulatory Agy. Reform, Ill. Gen. Assembly, 1980-81; referee Policy Studies Jour., Policy Studies Rev. Adviser Calif. State U. Students for Bradley for Gov., 1982. Mem. Am. Polit. Sci. Assn., Policy Studies Orgn., Midwest Assn. for Pub. Opinion Research, Pi Sigma Alpha. Democrat.

GODFREY, DOROTHY DOUD, home economist in business; b. Chattanooga; d. John Veeder and Georgie Louellen (Vest) Doud; m. Chester O. Godfrey, (div.); 1 dau., Jane Godfrey Rhinehart. B.S. in Foods and Nutrition, U. Tenn., 1948, postgrad., 1952. Central regional home economist Westinghouse Electric Corp., 1948-52, southeastern regional home economist, 1953-57; instr. foods and home mgmt. Ohio Wesleyan U., Delaware, 1952-53; home econs. dir. Rena Ware Distbrs., Opportunity, Wash., 1957-66, internat. home econs. dir., Bellevue, Wash., 1966—. Mem. Internat. Fedn. Home Econs., Am. Home Econs. Assn., Home Economists in Bus., Inst. Food Technologists, Nat. Assn. Parliamentarians, Chi Omega Alumnae, Phi Kappa Phi, Omicron Nu. Author Rena Ware use and care books, cookbooks, sales articles for profl. publs. Home: 3035 125th Ave NE Bellevue WA 98005 Office: 8383 158th Ave NW Box C-50 Redmond WA 98052

GODFREY, ERIK BRUCE, agricultural economist, educator, cons.; b. Idaho Falls, Idaho, Feb. 7, 1941; s. Charles E. and Claudia (Hansen) G.; m. Judy R. Matson, Aug. 30, 1963; children—Shauna, Karen, Ronald, Wendy. B.S., Utah State U., 1967, M.S., 1968; Ph.D., Oreg. State U., 1971. Research asst. Utah State U., Logan, 1966-67, assoc. prof., 1977—; teaching asst. Oreg. State U., 1969; asst. prof. U. Idaho, 1970-74, assoc. prof., 1974-77; cons. range econs. U.S. Forest Service, Bur. Land Mgmt., pvt. cos., 1974—; cons. pub. land policy N.W. Agrl. Devel. Project, 1979. Named Tchr. of Yr., Utah State U., Coll. Agrl., 1981; NDEA fellow, 1967-70. Mem. Am. Econs. Assn., Am. Agrl. Econs. Assn. (mem. com.), Western Agrl. Econs. Assn. (editorial council 1981—, bd. dirs. 1976-78), Soc. Range Mgmt. (pres. N. Idaho chpt., 1977), Xi Sigma Pi, Phi Kappa Phi, Sigma Xi, Omicron Delta Epsilon. Mormon. Contbr. articles to profl. jours. Office: Dept Econs Utah State U UMC 35 Logan UT 84322

GODFREY, JANA RHOADS, advertising art director, designer, consultant; b. Pocatello, Idaho, Feb. 27, 1954; d. Steve C. and Betty June (Olson) Rhoads; m. Jeffrey Keith Dudley, July 21, 1974 (div.); m. 2d, Emil William Godfrey, June 22, 1981; 1 son, Jason Rhoads. B.F.A. in Advt. Design, Utah State U., 1981. Dir. transition gallery Idaho State U., Pocatello, 1976-78; advt. dir., bus. mgr. Utah Statesman, Logan, 1978-80; art dir. Klein/Richardson Advt., Beverly Hills, Calif., 1981-82, Calif. Cable Systems, LaMirada, Calif., 1982; pres., owner, art dir. Good Godfree Prodns., Huntington Beach, Calif., 1982—. Active Republican Task Forces, 1982. Recipient gen. excellence in ad campaign award Rocky Mountain Collegiate Press Assn., 1980. Mem. Los Angeles Art Dirs. Club, Women in Design, Los Angeles Graphic Artists Guild. Episcopalian. Exhibitor: one woman show Idaho State U. 1981; several group shows. Home: 214 Portland Ave Apt 1 Huntington Beach CA 92648

GODFREY, PAUL GANNON, surgeon; b. Evanston, Ill., Feb. 14, 1944; s. Paul Rochette and Mary Frances (Gannon) G.; B.S. in Physics, M.I.T., 1966; M.D., U. Ill., 1970; m. Maureen Ann Kelly, June 7, 1969; 1 dau., Kelly Kristine. Diplomate Am. Bd. Surgery. Intern, Rush Presbyn.-St. Luke's Hosp., Chgo., 1970-71, resident in surgery, 1970-75; surg. asst. N.W. Community Hosp., Arlington Heights, Ill., 1975-76; gen. surgeon San Bernardino (Calif.) Med. Group, 1977—; attending staff St. Bernardine Community Hosp.; vol. tchr. dept. surgery San Bernardino County Med. Center. Fellow ACS; mem. AMA, Calif. Med. Assn., San Bernardino County Med. Soc., Tri-County Surg. Soc. Office: 1700 N Waterman Ave San Bernardino CA 92404

GODFREY, RICHARD GEORGE, real estate appraiser; b. Sharon, Pa., Dec. 18, 1927; s. Fay Morris and Elisabeth Marquerite (Stefanak) G.; B.A., Ripon Coll., 1949; m. Golda Fay Goss, Oct. 28, 1951; children—Deborah Jayne, Gayle Rogers, Bryan Edward. Vice-pres. 1st Thrift and Loan Assn., Albuquerque, 1959-61; pres. Richard G. Godfrey and Assos., Inc., Albuquerque, 1961—. Mem. Am. Inst. Real Estate Appraisers, Am. Right of Way Assn., Am. Soc. Real Estate Counselors (cert.). Baptist. Club: Elks. Home: 1700 Columbia Dr SE Albuquerque NM 87106 Office: 523 Louisiana Blvd SE Albuquerque NM 87108

GODFREY, WILLARD HORACE, JR., marketing executive; b. Salt Lake County, Utah, Jan. 10, 1938; s. Willard H. and Dona LaRue (Canning) G.; m. Ann Marie Doty, Aug. 18, 1962; children—Ben, Shawn, Kimberly Ann. Student, Colo. State U., 1956-58; B.S., Brigham Young U., 1963; M.S., U. Ariz., 1964, Ph.D., 1969. Asst. prof. econs. Central Wash. State U., Ellensburg, 1969-71; assoc. prof. mktg. Boise (Idaho) State U., 1971-75, prof., 1975-78; v.p. mktg. Murdock Internat., Provo, Utah, 1978 . Sr. v.p. ops. and fin. Fedn. Fly Fishers, 1981-83; pres. Fly Fishing Ctr. Internat., Inc., 1967-83. Mem. Pi Sigma Epsilon. Mormon. Contbr. articles in sports field to profl. jours.

GOEBEL, RUDIGER CARL, water bureau administrator; b. Bremen, Germany, Dec. 2, 1940; s. Herman and Katherine (Hofmann) G.; m. Michael Weber, Sept. 12, 1966; children—Craig, Cort. B.A. in Econs., Portland State Coll., 1968, M.A. in Econs., 1972. Instr. econs. Lewis and Clark Coll., Portland, Oreg., 1972-73; mgmt. analyst City of Portland, 1973-74, sr. mgmt. analyst, 1974-75, prin. mgmt. analyst, 1975-77, asst. water bur. mgr., 1977-79, adminstr., 1979—; trustee Assn. Met. Water Agencies. Chmn. Portland Energy Task Force; rep. for water utilities Senate Sub-Com. on Mining Minerals and Water Issues. Served with USN, 1958-62. NSF scholar, 1971-72. Mem. Am. Water Works Assn., Assn. Met. Water Agys. Democrat. Lutheran. Club: Lloyd Ctr. Racquetball. Home: 810 SW Broadway Dr #10 Portland OR 97201 Office: 1120 SW 5th Ave 6th Floor Portland OR 97204

GOELTZ, JUDITH LENZ, writer, publisher, real estate investor; b. Boscobel, Wis., Nov. 23, 1940; d. Sheridan Lee and Bernice Angeline (Graf) Lenz; m. Francis S. Goeltz, Dec. 7, 1968; step-children—Marshall Linc, Dianna, Shaun, Robert. B.S. in Spanish, U. Wis., 1962; postgrad. Adelphi U., U. San Francisco, Valencia, Spain. Cert. high sch. tchr., Wis., N.Y. Tchr. Spanish, Huntington, N.Y., 1962-65; flight attendant, purser Pan Am. Airways, 1965-70; tchr. pvt. schs., Salt Lake City, also salesperson Castleton's, 1971-72; mgr. organic farm, Fairview, Utah, 1973-78; pub., owner Tony B. Enterprises, San Francisco, 1979—; hostess radio show Sta. KEST, San Francisco, 1979-80. Mem. Bus. and Profl. Women, Nat. Assn. Female Execs., Nat. Speakers Assn., Marin Self-Pubs., Media Alliance, Com. Small Mag. Editors and Pubs., Nat. Writers Club, Orthomolecular Med. Soc., Internat. Acad. Nutritional Cons., Nat. Health Fedn., Ams. for Med. Freedom, AAUW, Phi Beta Kappa, Phi Kappa Phi, Sigma Delta Pi, Pi Lambda Theta, Eta Kappa Lambda. Author: Beginner's Natural Food Guide and Cookbook, 1975, Jet Stress; What It Is & How To Cope With It, 1980; contbr. articles to profl. jours. Home and office: 2168 Candelerd Santa Fe NM 87501

GOERLITZ, HARVEY THEODORE, ins. co. exec.; b. Oakland, Calif., Oct. 5, 1922; s. Harvey F. and Alma M. (Hoffman) G.; A.A., San Diego Jr. Coll., 1948; B.A. in Bus., San Diego State Coll. 1950; postgrad. Wharton Sch. U. Pa., 1977; m. Frances Virginia McNevin, May 3, 1946; children—Barbara Ann, Robert Harvey. With Farmers Ins. Group, 1950—, dir. life sales Farmers New World Life, also v.p., gen. mgr. Investors Guaranty Life Ins. Co., Mercer Island, Wash.; pres. Investors Guaranty Life Ins. Co.; now pres. Ohio State Life. Bd. dirs. Griffith Found. Served with USN, 1942-46. Mem. Columbus C. of C. Republican. Clubs: E Clampus Vitus, Masons, Order of the Arrow. Home: 4427 138th Ave SE Bellevue WA 98006 Office: 9611 Sunset Hwy Mercer Island WA 98040

GOETTLICH RIEMANN, WILHELMINA MARIA, chemist; b. Jaworow, Poland, June 25, 1934; d. Jan Stanislaw and Kazimiera Henryka (Smielowska) Goettlich; came to U.S., 1965, naturalized, 1971; B.S., Warsaw Agrl. U., 1955, M.S., 1957; Ph.D. in Chemistry, Gdansk Tech. U., 1977; m. Hans Riemann, Aug. 28, 1965. Research asst. Polish Milk Research Inst., Warsaw, 1957-62; asst. prof. Meat Research Inst., Warsaw, 1961-65; staff research asso. animal sci. U. Calif.-Davis, 1966-67, research asst. food sci., 1967-70, staff research asso. dept. nutrition, 1970-73; mem. Polish Patent Commn., 1963-65. Mem. Am. Dietetic Assn., Soc. Nutrition Edn., Am. Fedn. Tchrs, Vets. Faculty Wives, Food Tech. Club, Am. Vet. Assn. Aux.; asso. mem. Am. Home Econs. Assn., Sigma Xi; mem. N.Y. Acad. Sci., Smithsonian Instn., AAAS. Roman Catholic. Club: Toastmistresses (Davis). Author papers, abstracts in field.

GOETZ, THERESE ELIZABETH (MRS. R.J. LIPINSKI), organizational cons., psychology educator; b. Orange, N.J., Nov. 23, 1950; d. Henry and Mathilde (Cornely) G.; m. Ronald J. Lipinski, July 30, 1977; 1 dau., Valerie Anne. B.A. with honors, Douglass Coll. Rutgers U., 1972; M.A., U. Ill., Urbana, 1975, Ph.D., 1978. Cert. psychologist, N.Mex. Asst. prof. psychology U. N.Mex., 1977-81, part-time 1981—; organizational sr. cons. firm Therese E. Goetz & Assos., 1981—. U. Ill. fellow, summer 1974, 1976; NSF undergrad. research grantee, summer 1971; research grantee U. N.Mex., 1977-79. Mem. Am. Mgmt. Assn., Nat. Health Agys. N.Mex. (profl. adv. council), Am. Psychol. Assn., Am. Soc. Tng. and Devel., Profl. Orgn. for Women (exec. bd. 1980-82), N.Mex. Network for Women in Sci. and Engring. Roman Catholic. Contbr. articles to profl. jours. Office: 4800 Southern Ave SE Albuquerque NM 87108

GOETZEL, CLAUS GUENTER, metallurgical engineer; b. Berlin, July 14, 1913; s. Walter and Else (Baum) G.; m. Lilo Kallmann, Nov. 19, 1938; children—Rodney Gerard, Vivian Lynn. Dipl.-Ing., Technische Hochschule, Berlin, 1935; Ph.D., Columbia U., 1939. Registered profl. metall. engr., Calif. Research chemist, lab. head Hardy Metall. Co., 1936-39; tech. dir., works mgr. Am. Electro Metal Corp., 1939-47; v.p., dir. research Sintercast Corp. Am., 1947-57; adj. prof., sr. research scientist NYU, 1957-60; cons. scientist Lockheed Missiles & Space Co., 1960-78; metall. engring. cons., Portola Valley, Calif., 1978—; lectr., vis. scholar materials sci. dept. Stanford U., 1961—. Recipient U.S. Navy commendation, 1961; Alexander-von-Humboldt Sr. U.S. scientist award West Germany, 1978. Fellow Am. Soc. Metals, AIAA (assoc.); mem. AIME (life), Am. Powder Metall. Inst. (sr.), Metal Sci. Club N.Y. (life; past pres.), Metals Soc. (life) (London). Author: Treatise on Powder Metallurgy, 5 vols., 1949-63; contbr. articles to profl. publs.

GOETZMAN, RICHARD, consultant; b. Rochester, N.Y., Jan. 1, 1929; s. Walter K. and Angelyn (Brown) G.; B.S., U. N.Mex., 1958. Pres. Teletube Corp., Albuquerque, 1958-60; owner Richard Goetzman, pub. accounting, Albuquerque, 1960-62; gen. mgr., treas. Corrigan Communications, Inc., Santa Ana, Calif., 1962-64; controller Met. Savs. & Loan, Los Angeles, 1964-65; dir. finance and adminstrn. Litton Industries, Anaheim, Calif., 1965-67; pres. Goetzman & Assoc., Los Angeles, 1967—, PMM, Inc., 1978—; dir., treas. Unisafe, Inc., Anchorage, 1973—; dir. Unisafe, Ltd., London, Eng., 1974—; dir., treas. MacKinlay Winnacker McNeil & Assoc., Oakland, Calif., 1970—; dir. Schell, Inc., St. Petersburg, Fla., 1975—, Alan Nowell, Inc., Fullerton, Calif.; treas., dir. Action Leathercraft, Commerce, Calif., 1982—. Trustee U.S. Ski Ednl. Found., 1971—, treas. 1971-73; trustee Far West Ski Found., 1969-74, 76—, treas., 1976—. Served to capt. U.S. Army, 1951-54. Decorated Bronze Star. Recipient Man of Year award Far West Ski Assn., 1969; Founder's award So. Council of Far West Ski Assn., 1974. Mem. U.S. Ski Assn. (dir. 1968—, pres. 1974-76, chmn. bd. 1982—), Blegen award 1978, Man of Yr. award 1968), Far West Ski Assn. (pres. 1969-71, dir. 1967-73), Sigma Alpha Epsilon, Delta Sigma Pi. Home: 1750 E Ocean Blvd Long Beach CA 90802 Office: 3620 Long Beach Blvd Suite C-1 Long Beach CA 90807

GOFF, ROBERT DAVIS, retired driver and traffic educator; b. Sturgeon Bay, Wis., Mar. 3, 1917; s. Moulton Babcock and Agnes (Davis) G.; B.A., U. Wis., 1940; M.S., U. Utah, 1963; m. Margaret Woodburn Tuttle, June 16, 1942 (div. Apr. 1957); children—Beatrice Mowbray, Robert Lawrence, Cedric Tuttle, Roger Becker; m. 2d, Elizabeth Bassford, Jan. 1, 1980. Govt. hull insp. U.S. Maritime Commn., San Francisco, 1942-44; with small bus. firms, Calif. and Utah, 1947-56; lectr. on driver and traffic safety edn. U. Utah, 1957-63; partner Ind. Safety Services, Salt Lake City, 1963-66; instr. driver and traffic edn. Castle Valley and Kingman Job Corps Conservation Centers, 1966-68, U. Utah, 1968-82, ret., 1982; cons. safety; mem. interdisciplinary team cons. engrs., 1971-82; ret., 1982. Exec. sec. Utah Citizens Orgn. for Civil Rights, 1962-63. Mem. Utah Council Safety Suprs., Utah Indsl. Safety Soc., Am., Utah, Calif. driver edn. assns., Nat. Safety Council, ACLU, Common Cause (Utah bd.), Utah Peace Network (dir.), Utahns United Against Nuclear Arms Race (dir.), Am. Acad. Polit. and Social Sci., Pi Sigma Alpha. Democrat. Unitarian. Home: 1899 Sycamore Ln Salt Lake City UT 84117

GOFF, ROBERT E., business executive; b. Grant City, Mo., Sept. 8, 1935; s. Elvis G. and Gladys G. (Adams) G.; m. Donna Lee Peters, June 27, 1964; children—Laura L., Launa L. B.S., San Jose State U., 1972; M.B.A. U. Santa Clara, 1977; regional mgr. Signetics Corp., 1966-70, mktg. mgr., 1970-73; dir. mktg. Avantek Inc., 1973-78, v.p., gen. mgr., 1978—; dir. Datastream Communications Inc. Served with U.S. Army, 1958-60. Mem. IEEE, Assn. of Old Crows, Beta Gamma Sigma. Republican. Episcopalian. Clubs: Saratoga Country. Mem. editorial rev. bd. Jour. Electronics Def. Office: 3175 Bowers Ave Santa Clara CA 95051

GOGAN, HARRY LEO, technical manager; b. Buffalo, Apr. 6, 1922; s. Harold Steven and Anna Marie (Klimko) G.; student U. N.Mex., part-time 1951-61, U. Va., 1949-51; B.S. in Aero. Engring., U. Ala., 1948; M.P.A., Harvard U., 1964; postgrad. Fed. Exec. Inst., 1973; m. Joan Lorraine Althen, Dec. 27, 1947; children—Mary Jo, Eileen Ann, Susan Marie, Pamela Katherine. Design and devel. engr. USAF, 1951-53, aerodynamics devel engr., 1953-55, asst. chief tech. projects, 1955-59, chief long-range plans br., 1959-60, chief plans and programs div. 4900th Test Group, Air Force Spl. Weapons Center, Kirtland AFB, N.Mex., 1961-63, dir. tech. ops., 1964-67, tech. adviser, 1967-72, tech. dir. Air Force Spl. Weapons Center, 1972-76, tech. dir., Directorate Aerospace Studies, 1976-80; tech. dir. spl. systems BDM Corp., 1980—. Chmn. bd. Cath. Social Services, 1964-67. Served with USAAF, 1942-45. Decorated Purple Heart, Air medal; registered profl. engr., N.Mex. Fellow AIAA (assoc.); mem. Air Force Assn. (state pres. 1975), Rocky Mountain Sci. Council, Fed. Exec. League, Fed. Exec. Inst. Alumni Assn., Theta Tau, Tau Beta Pi. Democrat. Roman Catholic. Home: 2913 Charleston St NE Albuquerque NM 87110 Office: BDM Corp 1801 Randolph Rd SE Albuquerque NM 87106

GOGINENI, PRASADA RAO, aerodynamics engineer; b. Kesarapalli, India, May 14, 1944; s. Venkates Rao and Janaki Devi (Gondi) G.; m. Chandra Bala Jasti; children—Alvin, Brian. B.S. in Mech. Engring., Andhra U., Waltair, India, 1962-67; M.S. in Engring., Aeros., Indian Inst. of Sci., Bangalore, 1967-69; Ph.D. Va. Poly. Inst. and State U., Blacksburg, 1979. Aerodynamics engr. Indian Space Research Orgn., Trivandrum, India, 1970-75; staff engr. Acurex, Mountain View, Calif., 1979-80; sr. aerodynamics engr. Lockheed Missiles and Space Co., Sunnyvale, Calif. 1980—. Mem. AIAA. Republican. Clubs: Lera Flying. Contbr. articles to profl. jours. and co. reports. Home: 6681 Devonshire Dr San Jose CA 95129 Office: Lockheed Missiles and Space Co PO Box 504 Sunnyvale CA 94806

GOHEEN, AUSTIN CLEMENT, research plant pathologist; b. Bellingham, Wash., Apr. 22, 1917; s. Benjamin Frank and Melanie Charlotte (Clement) G.; children—Donald J., Thomas A., Andrew M., Susan M., David M. Student Western Wash. State Coll., Bellingham, 1936-38; B.S., U. Wash., 1947; Ph.D., Wash. State U.-Pullman, 1953. Research assoc. Rutgers U., 1950-54, Beltsville, Md., 1954-55, U. Calif.-Davis, 1956-82; research plant pathologist U.S. Dept. Agr., Agrl. Research Service, Davis, Calif., 1956—, adj. lectr., 1975—. Recipient Disting. Alumnus award Western Wash. State Coll., 1974; Ruth Allen award Am. Phytopath. Soc., 1974; Service award U.S. Dept. Agr., 1980. Mem. Am. Phytopath. Soc., Am. Soc. Enologists, Sigma Xi. Contbr. articles to profl. jours. Office: Dept Plant Pathology U Calif Davis CA 95616

GOHEEN, DAVID WADE, research chemist; b. Bellingham, Wash., June 23, 1920; s. Frank B. and Melanie Charlotte (Clement) G.; student W. Wash. U., 1937-39; B.S., U. Wash., 1942, Ph.D., 1951; m. Laura Elizabeth Smith, Nov. 27, 1943; children—Stephan Charles, Frank William. Research assoc. engring. research inst., U. Mich., Ann Arbor, 1951-52; chief chem. research sect., central research div. Crown Zellerbach Corp., Camas, Wash., 1952-55, sr. research chemist, 1955-78, project leader, pioneering research, 1978-82; v.p. E.M. Seidel Assocs., Vancouver, Wash., 1982—; mem. adv. panel Biomass Resources Inc.; vis. scientist U. Groningen (Netherlands), 1968-69. Served with USAAF, 1942-46. Mem. Am. Chem. Soc., TAPPI, Am. Rhododendron Soc. (Bronze medal 1976, bd. dirs.), Rhododendron Species Found. (dir., pres.). Presbyterian. Clubs: Kiwanis, Men's Garden. Author: Plant Collecting on Borneo, 1981; contbr. sects. to books, articles to publs.; patentee in organic and wood chemistry. Home: 2193 NE 3d St PO Box 826 Camas WA 98607 Office: Eugene M Seidel Assocs Shorewood West 6504 5545 E Evergreen Blvd Vancouver WA 98661

GOIN, JOHN MOREHEAD, plastic surgeon; b. Los Angeles, Mar. 29, 1929; s. Lowell Sidney, M.D., and Margaret Catherine (Morehead) G.; B.A. in Zoology, U. Calif., Los Angeles, 1951; M.D., St. Louis U., 1955; m. Marcia Stewart Kraft, M.D., Mar. 6, 1960; children—Suzanne Jennifer, Jessica Michele. Intern U. Calif. Med. Center, San Francisco, 1955-56, asst. resident in surgery, 1956-59, asst. resident to chief resident in plastic surgery, Los Angeles, 1959-62; fellow in plastic surgery Queen Victoria Hosp., East Grinstead, Sussex, Eng., 1961; pvt. practice specializing in plastic and reconstructive surgery, Los Angeles, 1962—; clin. prof. surgery U. So. Calif.; chief of plastic surgery Los Angeles County/U. So. Calif. Med. Center, 1971—; head div. plastic surgery Children's Hosp. of Los Angeles, 1976-79. Diplomate Am. Bd. Plastic Surgery (bd. dirs. 1980—). Fellow A.C.S.; mem. AMA, Calif. Soc. Plastic Surgeons (past pres.), Am. Soc. Plastic and Reconstructive Surgeons (sec. 1979-82, v.p. 1982—), Am. Soc. Aesthetic Plastic Surgery, Am. Assn. Plastic Surgeons, Pacific Coast Surg. Assn. Republican. Episcopalian. Contbr. articles profl. jours. Home: 2500 Park Oak Dr Los Angeles CA 90068 Office: 1245 Wilshire Blvd Los Angeles CA 90017

GOING, E. JACKSON, JR., civil engineering administrator; b. Houston, Feb. 22, 1928; s. E. Jackson and Mae A. (Courtney) G.; m. Audrey B. Pabst, Nov. 8, 1962; children—E. Jackson III, Michael B., Mary Eleanor. B.C.E., U. Santa Clara, 1949. Registered civil engr., Calif., Colo. Assoc., Leo W. Ruth, Jr., 1949-52; ptnr. Ruth & Going, San Jose, Calif., 1952-82, chmn. bd., treas., 1983—, also adv. dir. Regent emeritus U. Santa Clara; founding chmn. bd. regents Bellarmine Coll. Prep. Recipient Spirit of Life award City of Hope Hosp. and Med. Center, 1974, award San Jose area Anti-Defamation League Council B'nai B'rith, 1978. Mem. Am. Cons. Engrs. Council, Nat. Soc. Profl. Engrs., Cons. Engrs. Assn., Calif. Council Civil Engrs. and Land Surveyors, ASCE, Associated Civil Engrs. and Land Surveyors Santa Clara County. Republican. Roman Catholic. Club: St. Claire. Home: 820 Morse St San Jose CA 95126 Office: 919 The Alameda PO Box 26430 San Jose CA 95126

GOLD, BARRY MICHAEL, lawyer; b. Chgo., June 27, 1941; s. Allan and Bernice (Kappel) G.; m. Michelle Ann Zola, July 7, 1975; 1 dau., Ashley Kate. B.A., Calif. State U.-Northridge, 1963; M.A., UCLA, 1965, J.D., 1971. Bar: Calif. 1971. Theatrical pub. relations account exec. McFadden, Strauss, Eddy, Irwin, Los Angeles, 1963-68; spl. adviser Senator Eugene McCarthy Presdl. Campaign, 1968; assoc. Godfrey Isaac, Beverly Hills, Calif., 1971-73; ptnr., personnel mgr. Schwimmer & Gold, Beverly Hills, 1981—. Named Journalist of Yr. in Calif., Beta Phi Gamma, 1963. Mem. ABA, Beverly Hills Bar Assn., Screen Actors Guild. Office: 9808 Wilshire Blvd Suite 202 Beverly Hills CA 90212

GOLD, CAROL SAPIN, management consultant, author; b. N.Y.C., June 28; d. Cerf Saul and Muriel Louise (Fudin) Rosenberg; m. Joseph Bernard Weinstein, Dec. 26, 1976; children from previous marriage—Kevin Bart Sapin, Craig Paul Sapin, Courtney Byrens Sapin. B.A., U. Calif.-Berkeley, 1955. Asst. credit mgr. Union Oil Co., 1956; with U.S. Dept. State, 1964-66; mem. pub. relations dept. Braun & Co., Los Angeles, 1966-67; corporate dir. personnel tng. Gt. Western Fin. Corp., Los Angeles, 1967-70; pres. Carol Sapin Gold & Assos., Los Angeles, 1971—; dir. Cortex, Inc.; cons. Can. and Mex.; frequent guest radio and TV; producer tng. film Instant Replay, Power of Words. Mem. Sales and Mktg. Execs., Am. Soc. Tng. and Devel., Internat. Soc. Tng. and Devel., World Affairs Council, Nat. Platform Assn., Women in Bus. Author: Success Secrets; Solid Gold Customer Relations; contbr. articles to nat. mags. and profl. jours. Office: 701 Washington St Marina del Rey CA 90291

GOLD, FRANK JOEL, psychologist, educator; b. Bklyn., Mar. 9, 1942; s. Walter J. and Sara (Gurian) G.; B.A., Tarkio (Mo.) Coll., 1963; Ed.D. (Regents fellow), U. Nebr., 1970. Asst. prof. edn. U. Alaska, Fairbanks, 1970-75; psychologist, Fairbanks, 1971—; exec. dir., staff psychologist KILA, Inc., 1978—; chmn. continuing edn. com. Alaska Bd. Psychologist Examiners, 1973-77; dir. tutorial project U. Alaska-Fairbanks North Star Borough, 1971-75. Mem. classification com. Alaska Div. Corrections, 1973-81; co-dir. State Ombudsman Program for Regional Boarding Dormitories, 1972-73; mem. community adv. panel Greater Fairbanks Head Start Assn., Inc., 1973-78; program dir. Fairbanks Drug Treatment Center, 1974-78; mem. Fairbanks City Council, 1977-78; mem. City of Fairbanks Commn. on Health and Social Services, 1978-82; bd. dirs. Alaska State Mental Health Assn., 1977—. Recipient ann. Achievement award NAACP, 1973. Mem. Am., Alaska (ethics com. 1973-77) psychol. assns., Am. Personnel and Guidance Assn., Soc. Profs. Edn., John Dewey Soc., Phi Delta Kappa. Address: 3098 Airport Way Fairbanks AK 99701

GOLD, GINGER, educational, motivational speaker company executive, real estate firm executive; b. Los Angeles, Aug. 8, 1940; d. George Wilson and Maxine Merrill (Matthews) Campbell; m. J. W. Woodward, Dec. 3, 1960 (dec.); children—Pamela Gold Lukens, Steven, Daniel, Derek. Student, Idaho State U., 1974-75. Cert. med. asst., Calif. Owner, Transpeak-Speaker Mgmt. Service, Seattle, 1981-82; seminar dir., co-owner New Image Weight Mgmt., Seattle, 1981-82; area dir. Total Success Inc., Scottsdale, Ariz., 1982; exec. dir. Seattle Winners Circle, 1982—; real estate agt. Greenlake Properties, Inc., Seattle, 1982—; exec. v.p. Bus. with Style, Seattle, 1982—. Mem. Seattle C. of C. Home: 6717

11th Ave NW Seattle WA 98117 Office: Green Lake Properties Inc 7300 E Greenlake Dr N Seattle WA 98105

GOLD, JOSEPH, advertising executive; b. Gary, Ind., June 5, 1950; s. Morris and Lea Gold; m. Phyllis Levin, Jan. 2, 1972. B.A. in Journalism, U. Ariz., 1972. Gen. assignment reporter Ariz. Daily Star, Tucson, 1971-73; copywriter, prodn. dir., creative dir. various Tucson advt. agys., 1974-79; pres. Gold Images Inc. (formerly Eta Communications), Tucson, 1979—; mktg. instr. Pima Community Coll., Tucson. Bd. dirs., exec. com., edn. chmn. Community Orgn. Drug Abuse Control; bd. dirs. Ariz. Behavioral Health Network. Pulitzer prize nominee, 1971, 73; recipient Ariz. Press Club award, 1973. Democrat. Office: 2450 E Speedway Suite 6 Tucson AZ 85719

GOLD, RUSSELL STUART, psychologist; b. Chgo., Jan. 7, 1949; s. Irving Louis and Victoria (Saltzman) G.; B.A., U. Ill., 1970; M.A., Northwestern U., 1973; Ph.D., Calif. Sch. Profl. Psychology, San Diego, 1978. Intern, postdoctoral fellow Mercy Hosp. and Med. Center, San Diego, 1977-79; pvt. practice psychology, San Diego, 1979—. Mem. Am. Psychol. Assn., Calif. Psychol. Assn., Acad. San Diego Psychologists (pres.-elect), Council Exceptional Children. Office: 4060 4th Ave San Diego CA 92103

GOLD, STEVEN H., real estate cons.; b. Los Angeles, Apr. 30, 1940; s. Charles and Ann G.; M.B.A., UCLA, 1965; m. Carole Rowe, Jan. 28, 1962; children—Leslie, Randy. Sales mgr., Friden, Los Angeles, 1962-67; v.p. data processing Enterprises, Los Angeles, 1967-71; v.p. Sonnenblick Goldman Corp., Los Angeles, 1971-76; chmn. bd. Center Fin. Group, Inc., Los Angeles, 1976—; mem. adv. bd. real estate edn. UCLA, U. Calif.-San Diego. Served with AUS, 1957. Mem. Banking Inst. Am., Assn. Indsl. Realtors, Internat. Council Shopping Ctrs., Nat. Assn. Office Parks. Author: Creative Real Estate Finance, 1979; Condominium Conversion, 1978; Office and Industrial Condominiums, the Way of the Future, 1981. Office: 1888 Century Park E Los Angeles CA 90067

GOLD, STEVEN LOUIS, sheepskin outerwear manufacturer, tannery and raw skin trading company executive; b. N.Y.C., June 8, 1945; s. Louis Walter and Marjorie Ann (Goldman) G.; B.A., Ohio U., 1967; B. Fgn. Trade, Am. Grad. Sch. Internat. Mgmt., 1968; M.A. in Liberal Studies, New Sch. for Social Research, 1974; m. Anne Marie Scully, Aug. 9, 1974. With Young & Rubicam, N.Y.C., 1968-69; with Seligman & Latz, Inc., leased beauty salons, cosmetic, jewelry depts. in retail stores, N.Y.C., 1969-79, v.p., 1972-75, sr. v.p., 1975-79, exec. v.p. beauty div., 1975-79, also head San Francisco Office; pres., chief exec. officer, dir. Sawyer of Napa Inc. (Calif.), 1980—. Mem. Young Pres.'s Orgn. Office: PO Box 238 68 Coombs St Napa CA 94559

GOLD, THOMAS BARON, sociology educator; b. Cin., Mar. 7, 1948; s. Baron Herschel and Harriet Toby (Neurman) G.; m. Lucy Anne Harris, Aug. 10, 1980. B.A., Oberlin Coll., 1970; M.A., Harvard U., 1975, Ph.D., 1981; Cert. Advanced Study, Fudan U., Shanghai, China, 1980. Asst. prof. dept. sociology U. Calif.-Berkeley, 1981—, vice chmn. Ctr. Chinese Studies; interpreter escort in Chinese lang. U.S. Dept. State. Trustee Oberlin Shansi Meml. Assn. Oberlin Shansi Meml. Assn. fellow, 1970-73; Sheldon traveling fellow, Taiwan, South Korea, Japan, 1977-78; China exchange student, 1979-80. Mem. Assn. Asian Studies, Am. Sociol. Assn. Author: Selected Stories of Yang Ch'ing-ch'u, 1978; Youth in China Today: Obstacle to Economic Modernization?, 1981; China's Youth: Problems and Programs, 1982. Home: 645 Congo St San Francisco CA 94131 Office: U Calif 410 Barrows Hall Berkeley CA 94720

GOLDBERG, CARYN, psychotherapist; b. Jersey City, Jan. 12, 1954; d. Walter and Elayne (Schwartz) Goldberg. B.A., U. Colo., 1975; Ph.D., Calif. Sch. Profl. Psychology, 1980. Therapist, Fremont (Calif.) Youth Service Center, 1977-78, Vallejo (Calif.) Mental Health Center, 1978-80; pvt. practice psychotherapy, Denver, 1980—. Mem. Colo. Psychol. Assn., Am. Psychol. Assn., N.Am. Soc. for Adlerian Psychology. Jewish. Contbr. articles to profl. jours.

GOLDBERG, HERBERT, psychologist, educator; b. Berlin, Germany, July 14, 1937; s. Jacob and Ella (Nagler) G.; m. Lois Young; children—Amy, Elizabeth. B.A., CCNY, 1958; Ph.D., Adelphi U., 1963. Lic. psychologist, Calif. Faculty, Calif. State U.-Los Angeles, 1965—, prof., 1973—; pvt. practice psychotherapy. Mem. Am. Psychol. Assn., Am. Acad. Psychotherapists, Phi Beta Kappa. Jewish. Author: (with George Bach) Creative Aggression, 1974; The Hazards of Being Male, 1977; (with Robert T. Lewis) Money Madness, 1979; The New Male, 1979; The New Male-Female Relationships, 1983. Office: 1100 Glendon Ave Suite 903 Los Angeles CA 90024

GOLDBERG, LEE WINICKI, furniture co. exec.; b. Laredo, Tex., Nov. 20, 1932; d. Frank and Goldie (Ostrowiak) Winicki; student San Diego State U., 1951-52; m. Frank M. Goldberg, Aug. 17, 1952; children—Susan Arlene, Edward Lewis, Anne Carri. With United Furniture Co., Inc., San Diego, 1953—, corp. sec., dir., 1963—, dir. environ. interiors, 1970—; founder Drexel-Heritage store Edwards Interiors, subs. United Furniture, 1975; founding ptnr. v.p. FLJB Corp., 1976—. Den mother Boy Scouts Am., San Diego, 1965; vol. Am. Cancer Soc., San Diego, 1964-69; chmn. jr. matrons United Jewish Fedn., San Diego, 1958; del. So. Pacific Coast region Hadassah Conv., 1960, pres. Galilee group San Diego chpt., 1960-61; supporter Marc Chagall Nat. Mus., Nice, France, Smithsonian Instn., Los Angeles County Mus., La Jolla (Calif.) Mus. Contemporary Art. Recipient Hadassah Service award San Diego chpt., 1958-59. Mem. Nat. Home Furnishings Inst. Democrat. Jewish. Address: San Diego CA Office: 1231 Camino Del Rio S San Diego CA 92108

GOLDBERG, LESLIE DANIEL, advertising company executive; b. N.Y.C., Jan. 28, 1943; s. Mauri H. and Edythe (Charney) G.; m. Carole Karp, Sept. 24, 1964 (div. 1971); children—Elizabeth, Andrew. B.A., N.Y.U., 1964. Cert. radio mktg. cons., Radio Advt. Bur. Account exec. Sta. WVOX-AM-FM, New Rochelle, N.Y., 1964-65; account exec. Spot Time Sales, Inc., N.Y.C., 1965-66, Stone Reprs., N.Y.C., 1966-68; account exec. McGavren Guild, Inc., N.Y.C., 1968-69, asst. sales mgr., 1970-71, regional mgr., Detroit, 1971-74, exec. v.p., dir. Western div., Los Angeles, 1974—. Office: McGavren Guild Inc 6420 Wilshire Blvd Los Angeles CA 90048

GOLDBERG, MORRIS, physician; b. N.Y.C., Jan. 23, 1928; s. Saul and Lena (Schanberg) G.; B.S. in Chemistry cum laude, Poly. Inst. Bklyn., 1951; M.D., SUNY, Bklyn., 1956; m. Elaine Shaw, June 24, 1956; children—Alan Neil, Seth David, Nancy Beth. Intern, Jewish Hosp. Bklyn., 1956-57, resident, 1957-58, 61-62, renal fellow, 1958-59; practice medicine, specializing in internal medicine, N.Y.C., 1962-71, Phoenix, 1971—; instr. to asst. clin. prof. internal medicine State U. N.Y. Coll. Medicine, Bklyn., 1962-71; clin. investigator, metabolic research unit Jewish Hosp. Bklyn., 1962-71; cons. in field; mem. staff Phoenix Bapt., Maryvale Samaritan, Good Samaritan, St. Joseph's hosps. Served to capt. M.C., U.S. Army, 1959-61. Diplomate Am. Bd. Internal Medicine. Fellow ACP, Am. Coll. Angiology, Sigma Xi; mem. Am. Soc. Internal Medicine, AMA, Am. Coll. Nuclear Physicians, Internat. Soc. Internal Medicine, Am. Soc. Nephrology, Internat. Soc. Nephrology, 38th Parallel Med. Soc. S. Korea, Ariz., Maricopa County med. assns., N.Y. Acad. Sci., Phi Lambda Upsilon, Alpha Omega Alpha. Jewish. Contbr. articles to med. jours. Home: 24 E Wagonwheel Dr Phoenix AZ 85020 Office: 1728 W Glendale Ave Phoenix AZ 85021 also 4616 N 51st Ave Phoenix AZ 85031

GOLDBERG, RONALD RAY, architect, photographer; b. Bozeman, Mont., Apr. 21, 1936; s. Manley Omfred and Josephine Celia (Hyle) G. Children—Laurie L., Cynthia J., Britton R. B.S. in Architecture, Mont. State U., 1959. Lic. architect, Mont., Wyo., Alaska. Project architect CTA Architects/Engrs., 1961-79; pvt. practice architecture; architect Health Resources Development State of Alaska, Juneau, 1981—. Mem. Am. Soc. Hosp. Engring., Nat. Fire Protective Assn. Home: 9448 La Perouse Juneau AK 99801

GOLDBERG, STEPHEN ROBERT, biologist, educator; b. Bronx, N.Y., Mar. 4, 1941; s. Jack and Ruth (Maltzman) G.; divorced. B.A. in Biology, Boston U., 1962; M.S., U. Ariz., 1965, Ph.D. in Zoology, 1970. Asst. prof. biology Whittier (Calif.) Coll., 1970-77; assoc. prof., 1977—; research assoc. herpetology County Mus. Los Angeles, 1976—; instr. biology Lincoln Internat. Acad., Santiago, Chile, 1981-82. Recipient Nat. Marine Fishery Service award, 1979. Mem. Am. Inst. Biol. Scis., Am. Soc. Ichthyologists and Herpetologists, Sierra Club. Contbr. numerous articles on reproductive marine biology to profl. jours. Office: Biology Dept Whittier Coll Whittier CA 90608

GOLDBERG, VICTOR PAUL, economics educator; b. Washington, Nov. 26, 1941; s. Albert Isaac and Muriel Edna (Kallich) G.; m. Lee Ann Goldberg, Aug. 19, 1967; children—Marc, Todd. With dept. econs. U. Calif.-Davis, 1967—, now prof.; vis. fellow Pub. Choice Ctr., 1975-76, Inst. Advanced Study, 1978-79; vis. prof. law and econs. U. Calif.-Berkeley, 1977, U. Va., 1981. Mem. Am. Econ. Assn., Western Econ. Assn., Assn. Evolutionary Econs. Editorial bd. Jour. Econ. Issues, 1978-81; contbr. articles to profl. jours. Home: 2429 Creekhollow Ln Davis CA 95616 Office: Dept Econs U Calif Davis CA 95616

GOLDBERG, YALE FREDRIC, lawyer; b. Phila., Sept. 12, 1947; s. Bert and Bertha (Frankel) G. B.B.A., George Washington U., 1969, J.D. with honors, 1972, L.L.M. in Taxation, 1976. Bar: D.C., 1972, Pa. 1976, U.S. Supreme Ct. 1976, U.S. Tax Ct. 1976, Ariz. 1978; cert. legal specialist in taxation Ariz. Clk., U.S. Dept. Justice, Tax div., Washington, 1970-72, trial atty., 1972-77; assoc. Lewis & Roca, Phoenix, 1977-80, ptnr., 1980—; lectr., TV guest on legal issues. Asst. treas. Master Apprentice Program, Ariz., 1978—. Mem. ABA (chmn. payroll taxes subcom.), George Washington U. Alumni Assn., Phi Delta Phi. Contbr. articles to profl. jours. Home: 6221 N 29th Pl Phoenix AZ 85016 Office: 100 W Washington Suite 2200 Phoenix AZ 85003

GOLDBERGER, MARVIN L., univ. pres., physicist; b. Chgo., Oct. 22, 1922; s. Joseph and Mildred (Sedwitz) G.; B.S., Carnegie Inst. Tech., 1943; Ph.D., U. Chgo., 1948; m. Mildred Ginsburg, Nov. 25, 1945; children—Samuel M., Joel S. Research asso. Radiation Lab., U. Calif., 1948-49; research asso. M.I.T., 1949-50; asso. prof. U. Chgo., 1950-55, prof., 1955-57; Higgins prof. physics Princeton U., 1955-57, chmn. dept., 1970-76, Joseph Henry prof. physics, 1977-78; pres. Calif. Inst. Tech., Pasadena, 1978—; mem. Pres.'s Sci. Adv. Com., 1965-69; dir. Gen. Motors Corp., Haskell, Inc. Bd. dirs. Nat. Energy Found.; bd. govs. Weizmann Inst. Sci.; mem. Am. Com. East-West Accord, Com. Internat. Security Studies; chmn. Fedn. Am. Scientists, 1972-73. Fellow Am. Phys. Soc., Am. Acad. Arts and Scis.; mem. Nat. Acad. Scis., Am. Philos. Soc., Council Fgn. Relations. Clubs: Bohemian (San Francisco); Calif. (Los Angeles); Princeton (N.Y.C.). Office: Office of Pres Calif Inst Tech 1201 E California Blvd Pasadena CA 91125

GOLDBLATT, STEVEN MELVIN, electrical engineering educator, lawyer; b. Sacramento, Jan. 24, 1950; s. Walter Irving and Shirley Ann (Marcus) G.; B.S.E.E., U. Calif.-Berkeley, 1971; J.D., Golden Gate U., 1977. Bar: Calif. 1977. Sports editor Daily Californian, 1970-71; elec. engring. asst. Los Angeles Dept. Water and Power, 1971-74; contracts engr. Pacific Gas and Electric Co., San Francisco, 1974-77, quality control engr., 1977-78; asst. mgr., regional counsel Western Caissons Inc., Concord, Calif., 1978-79; sr. cons. Wagner-Hohns-Inglis, Inc., La Crescenta, Calif., 1979-80; asst. prof. dept. bldg. constrn. and contracting Purdue U., West Lafayette, Ind., 1980-82; assoc. prof. U Wash., Seattle, 1982, chmn. dept. bldg. constrn., 1982—. Mem. Am. Arbitration Assn., Am. Nuclear Soc., ABA, Calif. Bar Assn., Fed. Bar Assn., Fed. Energy Bar Assn., Am. Inst. Constructors, Assn. for Pub. Policy Analysis and Mgmt., IEEE, Nat. Soc. Profl. Engrs., ACLU, NAACP, Now, Sierra Club. Editor: So. Sierran, 1973-74. Office: 208 Gould Hall JO-24 U Wash Seattle WA 98105

GOLDEN, ALFRED LOWELL, writer, mktg. cons.; b. Pitts., May 28, 1909; s. Benjamin and Rose (Kendall) G.; B.A. in Psychology, U. Pitts., 1931, M.A. in Psychology, 1935; m. Dorothy Maret, May 26, 1934; children—Harvey Paul, Vickie Ann. Psychol. researcher Western State Penitentiary, Pitts., 1930-31, criminologist, 1934-43; head dept. criminology Allegheny County (Pa.) Prison, 1934-35; spl. investigator Allegheny County Quar. Sessions Ct., Pitts., 1935-36; screenwriter, playwright, freelance writer, N.Y.C., 1934—; dir., 1934-47; author plays: The Female of The Species, 1935; A Young Man's Fancy, 1947; Mimie Scheller, 1936; Lady Behave!, 1943; Collector's Item, 1951; screenplays: One Mile From Heaven, 1936; Born Reckless, 1937; The Hughes Mystery, 1977; asso. prof. speech and drama Duquesne U., 1938-41; tchr. public relations CCNY, 1945-46, New Sch. Social Research, 1947-49; prof. playwriting, lectr. UCLA, 1967-68; founder, dir. Blue Cross and Blue Shield, 1933-57; v.p. pub. relations Beneficial Standard Life Ins. Co.; pres. Mass Mktg. Council, Inc., Los Angeles, 1976-78, chmn., 1978—; founder, pres. Direct Mktg. Corp., Am., 1968-76; founder, pres., Direct Mktg. Internat., 1975-79. Mem. Dramatists Guild, Pub. Relations Soc. Am., Money Mgmt. Council (founder). Home: 217 S Rose St Burbank CA 91505 Office: 10850 Riverside Dr 400 North Hollywood CA 91602

GOLDEN, CONSTANCE JEAN, aerospace engineer; b. Highland Park, Ill., June 8, 1939; d. Herman William and Chrystle O'Linda (Tolley) Leuer; B.S., Beloit Coll., 1961; A.M., Harvard U., 1962; M.S., Stanford U., 1970; m. Charles Joseph Golden, June 13, 1962; 1 dau., Kerri Lynn. Scientist/engr. research and devel. div. Lockheed Missiles & Space Co., Sunnyvale, Calif., 1962-68, sr. scientist/engr. Lockheed Palo Alto Research Labs., 1968-74, mgr. planning requirements missile div., Sunnyvale, Calif., 1975-78; program mgr. manned space ops. Ford Aerospace and Communications Corp., Palo Alto, Calif., 1978-79, corp. strategy mgr., Detroit, 1980-81, mgr. mission ops., Sunnyvale, 1982—; mem. info. systems survivability subpanel Nat. Security Telecommunications Adv. Com.; mem. adv. council sci. and math. Mills Coll., 1976-80. Named Disting. Woman of Year, Lockheed, 1976; NSF fellow, 1961-62. Mem. AIAA (pub. policy com., space systems tech. panel 1982), Armed Forces Communications and Electronic Assn. (sect. dir.), Aero. and Astronautical Soc., Soc. Women Engrs. (past pres. sect., past nat. scholarship chmn.), Phi Beta Kappa. Club: Toastmasters (past pres.). Contbg. author: Second Careers for Women, 1975. Office: 1260 Crossman Ave Sunnyvale CA 94086

GOLDEN, JUDITH GREENE, artist, photography educator; b. Chgo., Nov. 29, 1934; d. Walter Cornell and Dorothie Dillon (Cissell) G.; m. David T. Golden, Jr., Sept. 10, 1955; children—David III, Lucinda Golden Rizzo. B.F.A., Sch. Art Inst. Chgo., 1973; M.F.A., U. Calif.-Davis, 1975. Lectr. UCLA, 1975-79, acting head photography program, 1978-79; lectr. U. Calif.-Davis, spring 1980, Calif. Coll. Arts and Crafts, Oakland, fall 1980; assoc. prof. photography U. Ariz., Tucson, 1981—; one-man shows U. Colo., 1976, U. Calif.-San Francisco, 1977, Sch. Art Inst. Chgo., 1977, Women's Bldg., Los Angeles, 1977, Orange Coast Coll., Costa Mesa, Calif., 1978, Portland Sch. Art (Mass.), 1978, G. Ray Hawkins Gallery, Los Angeles, 1978, Quay Gallery, San Francisco, 1979, 81, So. Ill. U., Carbondale, 1980, A. Nagel Galerie, Berlin, 1980, Colo. Mountain Coll., Breckenridge, 1982, Catskill Ctr. for Photography, Woodstock, N.Y., 1982, Ctr. for Creative Photography, Tucson, 1983; 2-man show San Francisco Mus. Modern Art, 1981; exhibited in numerous group shows in U.S. and fgn. countries, 1973—, including Portland Mus. Art (Maine), 1976, Fogg Mus. Art, Harvard U., Cambridge, Mass., 1977, Seattle Art Mus., 1977, Los Angeles Inst. Comtemporary Art, 1977, Oakland Mus., 1978, Santa Barbara Mus. Art (Calif.), 1978, 79, Los Angeles County Mus. Art, 1978, San Francisco Mus. Modern Art, 1979, 81, 82, 83, Arts Council Gt. Britain travelling exhbn., 1981, Centre National d'Art et de Culture Georges Pompidou, Paris, 1981, Contemporary Art Mus., Houston, 1982, Palos Verdes Art Ctr. (Calif.), 1982, also numerous univ. and coll. museums; represented in permanent collections San Francisco Mus. Modern Art, Mus. Modern Art, N.Y.C., Ctr. for Creative Photography, Fogg Mus. Art, Newport Harbor Mus. Art, Newport Beach, Calif., E.B. Crocker Art Gallery, Sacramento, George Eastman House, Rochester, N.Y., Frederick Wight Gallery, UCLA, Los Angeles County Mus. Art, Mpls. Inst. Arts, Oakland Mus., U. N.Mex. Art Mus., U. Calif.-Davis, U. Colo., Portland Mus. Art, also pvt. collections; presenter numerous workshops; lectr. numerous colls. and univs.; juror various shows. U. Calif.-Davis chancellor's grad. fellow, 1974, regent's grad. fellow, 1974-75; UCLA faculty research grantee, 1975-79, regent's faculty fellow for creative research, 1977; Nat. Endowment for Arts grantee, 1979, photographers fellow, 1979, artist-in-resident grantee So. Ill. U., 1980. Mem. San Francisco Camerawork, Soc. for Photog. Edn., Los Angeles Ct. for Photog. Studies (dir. 1977-79), Friends of Photography, Womens Caucus for Arts. Contbr. to profl. publs. Office: Art Dept U Ariz Tucson AZ 85721

GOLDEN, MORTON JAY, museum director; b. Bklyn., Apr. 11, 1929; s. Sam C. and Anna (Denmark) G.; m. Evelyn Lois Gould, Oct. 6, 1956; children—Caron, Linda, Jay. B.S., U. So. Calif., 1952. Dep. dir. Los Angeles County Mus. Art, 1972-82; dir. Palm Springs (Calif.) Desert Mus., 1982—; guest lectr. in arts mgmt. UCLA, in mus. mgmt. U. So. Calif. Served with USNR, 1946-51. Decorated Honor of Republic (Egypt), 1979; recipient Scroll of Merit, Los Angeles County Bd. Suprs., 1982; fellow Grad. Sch. Fine Arts, U. So. Calif., 1982-83. Mem. Am. Assn. Mus. Democrat. Jewish. Office: PO Box 2288 Palm Springs CA 92263

GOLDENBERG, IRENE TOBY, psychologist, educator; b. Memphis, Apr. 18, 1934; d. Morris and Isobel (Erenberg) Feinstein; B.A. in Psychology, U. Calif., Berkeley, 1956, Ed.D. in Ednl. Psychology, Los Angeles, 1969, M.A. in Guidance, Calif. State U., 1960; m. Herbert Goldenberg, Feb. 17, 1963; children—Philip, Erica, Karen. Tchr. pub. elementary schs. Los Angeles City Unified Sch. Dist., 1957-61; sch. psychometrist Pasadena City Coll., 1961-62, Pasadena (Calif.) City Unified Sch. Dist., 1962-64; psychol. cons. educationally handicapped program Alamitos Sch. Dist., 1964-66; dir. psychol. services Operation Head Start, Pasadena, 1965; sr. mental health cons. Head Start, Los Angeles Fedn. Settlements and Centers, 1966-67; sch. psychologist to spl. presch. program Dubnoff Sch. for Ednl. Therapy, North Hollywood, Calif., 1967-69; asst. prof. in residence, supr. psychology assessment lab. U. Calif. Los Angeles Neuropsychiat. Inst., 1969—, acting supr. outpatient child psychology div., 1971-72, asst. prof. in residence and supr. inpatient child psychology div., 1972-75, dir. psychol. services mental retardation and child psychiatry, 1975—; asst. prof. psychology Calif. State U., Los Angeles, summer 1969; adj. asso. prof. in residence Neuropsychiat. Inst., U. Calif., 1977—; lectr. in field; cons. Calif. Sch. Profl. Psychology. Diplomate Am. Bd. Profl. Psychology (mem. Western regional bd., nat. trustee 1981—). Mem. Am., Calif. psychol. assns., Am. Orthopsychiat. Assn. Democrat. Jewish. Co-author: Family Therapy: An Overview (named Book of Yr. Am. Jour. Nursing 1980), 1980; contbr. articles to profl. publs. Home: 869 Malcolm Ave Los Angeles CA 90024 Office: 760 Westwood Plaza Los Angeles CA 90024

GOLDETSKY, MARILYN, controller; b. Boston, Mar. 25, 1930; d. Morris and Pearl (Kastan) Nankas; B.A. in Acctg., U. Ariz., 1949; postgrad. Los Angeles Valley Coll., 1952—. Asst. to dir. grad. sch. Los Angeles Coll. of Chiropractic, Glendale, Calif., 1950-53; acting supr. Lee's Furniture, San Fernando, Calif., 1955-57; office mgr., acctg. supr. Valley Crest Landscape, North Hollywood, Calif., 1957-59; controller City of Hope, a Nat. Med. Center, Los Angeles, 1959-80; dir. fin. Simon Wiesenthal Center for Holocaust Studies, Yeshiva U., Los Angeles, 1980—, dir. adminstrn. and fin. univ. and Simm Wiesenthal Center, 1981—; tech. cons. City of Hope Med. Group, Inc., Los Angeles, Bd. dirs. City of Hope, Los Angeles. Recipient First Prize award San Fernando Valley Art Competition, 1977. Democrat. Jewish. Home: 6145 Whitsett Ave North Hollywood CA 91606 Office: 9760 W Pico Blvd Los Angeles CA 90035

GOLDFARB, BERNARD, design co. exec.; b. Chgo., Feb. 24, 1916; s. Louis and Rose (Orenstein) G.; ed. U. Chgo., Northwestern U., Loyola U., Chgo.; m. Florence Marjorie Karsh, Nov. 17, 1940; children—Linda Naomi, Iris Dorene. Accountant, Bernard Goldfarb & Assos., Chgo.; controller Mayflower Foods, Chgo.; gen. mgr., controller A.E. Goldfarb Assos., Northridge, Calif., 1969—. Fund raiser City of Hope Hosp., Los Angeles, 1969—, pres., 1973-74, 80-81, chmn. bd. aux., 1972-73, 79-80. Served with USNR, 1942-46. Club: Braemar Country (Tarzana, Calif.). Office: AE Goldfarb Assos 19434 Londelius St Northridge CA 91324

GOLDFARB, I. JAY, accountant; b. N.Y.C., Mar. 8, 1933; s. Joseph and Fay E. (Hirschhorn) G.; m. Arlene Storch, May 8, 1955; children—Meryl, David. B.A., Queen's Coll., CUNY, 1955. C.P.A., N.Y., Calif. Staff acct. T.D. Davidson & Co., N.Y.C., 1957-59; ptnr. Rashba & Pokart, N.Y.C., 1959-65; fin. v.p. Fabrics by Joyce, Inc., N.Y.C., 1965-66; ptnr. Clarence Rainess & Co., N.Y.C., 1966-71, Los Angeles, 1971-75; ptnr. Joseph Herbert & Co., Los Angeles, 1975-78; ptnr. Goldfarb, Whitman & Cohen, Los Angeles, 1978—. Exec. v.p., fund raising chmn. Professions and Fin. Assocs. City of Hope, Los Angeles, 1973, pres., 1974-75, v.p., dinner chmn., 1976-78; also bd. dirs., trustee City of Hope, 1983—; mem. professions, fin. div. United Jewish Welfare Fund, Los Angeles, 1978—; bd. dirs. Community Synagogue, Port Washington, N.Y., 1971—. Served to capt. USAF, 1955-57. Mem. Am. Inst. C.P.A.s, N.Y. State Soc. C.P.A.s, Calif. Soc. C.P.A.s. Club: Masons. Office: 12233 W Olympic Blvd Suite 210 Los Angeles CA 90064

GOLDFARB, ROBERT PAUL, neurological surgeon; b. St. Paul, July 17, 1936; s. Jack and Frances S. (Singer) G.; B.A. with distinction (Baird scholar), U. Ariz., 1958; M.D., Tulane U., 1962; m. Lesley Gail Zatz, Aug. 11, 1963; children—Jill, Pam. Intern, Michael Reese Hosp. and Med. Center, Chgo., 1962-63; resident gen. surgery Presbyn.-St. Luke's Hosp., 1963; resident neurol. surgery U. Ill. Research and Ednl. Hosps., Chgo., 1964-67; neurol. surgeon Neurol. Assos. Tucson, 1967—; asso. in neurology and neurosurgery U. Ariz. Coll. Medicine, Tucson, 1973, acting chief sect. neurosurgery, 1975—, adj. asso. prof. neurosurgery, 1978—; cons. neurosurgeon Davis-Monthan AFB Hosp., Tucson, 1967; chief neurosurgery St. Joseph's Hosp., 1970—; chief neurosurgery Tucson Med. Center, 1970—, chief of staff, 1978—; neurol. surgeon Western Neurosurgery, Ltd., 1980—. Pres. Crippled Children's Services, Tucson, 1973-75. Diplomate Am. Bd. Neurol. Surgery. Fellow ACS; mem. Congress Neurol. Surgeons, Ariz. Neurosurg. Soc. (pres. 1977), Rocky Mountain Neurol. Soc. (v.p. 1979), AMA, Am. Assn. Neurol. Surgeons, Internat. Med. Soc. Paraplegia, Phi Delta Epsilon, Zeta Beta Tau. Office: 5182 E Farness Dr Tucson AZ 85712

GOLDIE, RAY ROBERT, lawyer; b. Dayton, Ohio, Apr. 1, 1920; s. Albert S. and Lillian (Hayman) G.; student U. So. Calif., 1943-44, J.D., 1957; student San Bernardino Valley Coll., 1950-51; m. Dorothy Roberta Zafman, Dec. 2, 1941; children—Marilyn, Deanne, Dayle, Ron R. Elec. appliance dealer, 1944-54; teaching asst. U. So. Calif. Law Sch., 1956-57; admitted to Calif. bar, 1957; dep. atty. gen. State of Calif., 1957-58; individual practice, San Bernardino, 1958—. Pres., Trinity Acceptance Corp., 1948-53. Mem. World Peace Through Law Center, 1962—; regional dir. Legion Lex, U. So. Calif. Sch. Law, 1959-75; chmn. San Bernardino United Jewish Appeal, 1963; v.p. United Jewish Welfare Fund San Bernardino, 1964-66, Santa Anita Hosp., Lake Arrowhead, 1966-69. Bd. dirs. San Bernardino Med. Arts Corp. Served with AUS, 1942-43. Fellow Internat. Acad. Law and Sci.; mem. Am., San Bernardino County bar assns., State Bar Calif., Am. Judicature Soc., Am. Soc. Hosp. Attys., Calif. Trial Lawyers Assn. (v.p. chpt. 1965-67, pres. 1967-68), Am. Arbitration Assn. (nat. panel arbitrators), Order of Coif, Nu Beta Epsilon (pres. 1956-57). Club: Lake Arrowhead Country (pres. 1972-73, 80-81). Home: Hamiltair Dr Lake Arrowhead CA 92352 Office: 432 N Arrowhead Ave San Bernardino CA 92401

GOLDIN, ROBERT W., aerospace engineer; b. Phila., Nov. 7, 1919; s. Solomon and Marcia (Agrons) G.; B.S., U. Pa., 1941; M.S., Calif. Inst. Tech., 1942; children—Patricia Gail, Robert Wayne. Cartographic engr. U.S. Coast and Geodetic Survey, Washington, 1942-43; stress analyst Curtiss Wright Corp., Columbus, Ohio, 1943-44; group engr. applied loads, U.S. Navy, Washington, 1945-49; asst. chief engr. Bell Aerosystems Co., Niagara Falls, N.Y., 1950-60; cons. engr. Lockheed Missiles & Space Co., Sunnyvale, Calif., 1960—; flight safety counselor FAA; instr. Evening Sch., De Anza Coll.; cons. engr. Aircraft Owners and Pilots Assn. Air Safety Found. Served to lt. USN, 1944-46. Named Flight Instr. of Yr., grantee Aircraft Owners and Pilots Assn. Air Safety Found., 1971; recipient Group Achievement award NASA, 1979. Asso. fellow AIAA; mem. Soc. Automotive Engrs., Nat. Assn. Flight Instrs., Tau Beta Pi. Co-author: Aircraft Owners and Pilots Assn. Mountain Flying Course, 1971; patentee aircraft flight instruments. Home: 1372 Sydney Dr Sunnyvale CA 94087 Office: 1111 Lockheed Way Sunnyvale CA 94086

GOLDING, GEORGE EARL, journalist; b. Oakdale, Calif., Aug. 26, 1925; s. Herbert Victor and Elva M. (Leydecker) G.; A.A., Modesto Jr. Coll., 1950; B.A., San Francisco State Coll., 1959; m. Joyce Mary Buttner, July 15, 1948; children—Earlene Golding Brown, Brad Leslie, Dennis Lee, Frank Edwin, Charlton Kenneth, Daniel Duane. Advt. salesman Riverbank News, 1949; galley bank boy, cub reporter San Bernardino Sun, 1951; editor Gustine Standard, 1952; photographer-reporter Humboldt Times, 1952-56; reporter, asst. city editor San Mateo (Calif.) Times, 1956—; corr. UPI; contbg. writer, photographer Nat. Motorist mag., aviation writer, columnist Flight Log. Pub. relations adviser Powder Puff Derby start. 1972. Bd. dirs., sec. Amphlett Employees Fed. Credit Union. Served with U.S. Maritime Service, 1943, USAAF, 1944-46, AUS, 1951. Recipient John Swett award Calif. Tchrs. Assn., 1964; nominee McQuaid award Cath. Newsmen, 1965, 68; A.P. and Ency. Brit. photography awards, 1954-55, A.P. newswriting award, 1964. Mem. Am. Newspaper Guild, San Francisco-Oakland News Guild, Aviation/Space Writers Assn. (regional writing awards), Peninsula Press Club (founding dir., pres. 1976), San Mateo County Arts Council (charter), San Mateo Guild. Home: 1625 Ark St San Mateo CA 94403 Office: 1080 S Amphlett Blvd San Mateo CA 94402

GOLDMAN, EDWARD SUMNOR, wholesale executive; b. Boston, Dec. 11, 1924; s. Frank and Rose Lillian (Sydeman) G.; m. Elaine Beck, Sept. 2, 1945; children—Stephen M., Carol G. Maxym, Richard L. B.A. cum laude, Harvard U., 1946. With Central Electric Co., Denver, 1946—, sec., 1952-64, v.p., 1964-75, pres., 1975—. Served to ensign USNR, 1942-46. Democrat. Office: 500 Quivas St Denver CO 80204

GOLDMAN, EMANUEL, securities analyst; b. San Francisco, Feb. 23, 1938; s. Louis Joseph and Frances Miriam (Grant) G.; m. Diane Ryna Temkin; children—David Scott, Vicki Joy, Lori Michelle. B.A. cum laude, U. Calif.-Berkeley, 1960, M.A. cum laude, 1962; M.B.A. summa cum laude, Fairleigh Dickinson U., 1973. Nuclear physicist Gen. Electric Co., San Jose, Calif., 1962-63; physicist Lockheed Missiles and Space Co., Sunnyvale, Calif., 1963-69; dept. mgr. MB Assoc., San Ramon, Calif., 1969-70; sr. staff physicist Gen. Research Corp., Denville, N.J., 1970-73; research dir. Sanford C. Bernstein & Co., N.Y.C., 1973-83; analyst, ptnr. Montgomery Securities, San Francisco, 1983—. Mem. Phi Beta Kappa. Contbr. articles to jours. in field.

GOLDMAN, HERBERT PHILIP, psychiatrist; b. N.Y.C., Feb. 6, 1939; s. Eli and Paula (Wyle) G.; B.A., Duke U., 1960, M.D., 1964; m. Joan Gail Budd, May 2, 1965; 1 dau., Elizabeth. Intern, Brookdale Hosp. Center, N.Y.C., 1964-65; resident in psychiatry Duke U. Med. Center, Durham, N.C., 1965-68; psychiatrist East Los Angeles Mental Health, County of Los Angeles, 1970-71, regional chief Rio Hondo Mental Health, 1971-75; practice medicine specializing in psychiatry, San Gabriel, Calif., 1970—; pres. Hillcrest Guidance Clinic Med. Group, Inc. Served to maj. U.S. Army, 1968-70. Decorated Bronze Star. Diplomate Am. Bd. Psychiatry and Neurology. Mem. Am. Psychiat. Assn., So. Calif. Psychiat. Soc., Am. Soc. Clin. Hypnosis. Office: 201 S Mission Dr San Gabriel CA 91776

GOLDMAN, KENNETH LEWIS, accountant; b. Bklyn., May 4, 1952; s. Harold and Selma (Tracer) G.; m. Susan M. Guralnick, June 5, 1977; 1 dau., Stephanie. B.S., Calif. State U.-Northridge, 1973. C.P.A., Calif. Acct., Clarence Rainess & Co., C.P.A.s, Los Angeles, 1974-78; ptnr. Goldfarb, Whitman & Cohen, C.P.A.s, Los Angeles, 1979—. Mem., Professions and Fin. Assocs. of City of Hope. Mem. Am. Inst. C.P.A.s, Calif. Soc. C.P.A.s, Textile Profls. Club. Office: 12233 W Olympic Blvd Suite 210 Los Angeles CA 90064

GOLDMAN, MOISES JULIAN, systems control scientist; b. Mexico City, Mex., Sept. 6, 1949; came to U.S., 1968; s. Samuel and Hinda (Mondlak) G.; B.S. in Elec. Engring., U. Houston, 1971, M.S. in Elec. Engring., 1973; Ph.D. in Dynamic Systems Control, UCLA, 1976; m. Deloris May, Sept. 9, 1973; 1 son, Joshua Justin. Research engr. LAAD and B-1 divs. Rockwell Internat. Los Angeles, 1975-76; exec. v.p. Lakin Tire Inc., Los Angeles, 1977-78; prin. scientist Sci. Support Lab., U.S. Army Devel. Experimentation Command, BDM Corp., Ft. Ord, Calif., 1979-81; adj. prof. elec. engring., digital control systems, Navy Postgard. Sch., 1979-81; research specialist Lockheed Missiles and Space Co., 1981—. Research grantee NSF, 1971-73, U.S. Army, 1971-73, USAF, 1973-76. Mem. IEEE, AAAS, Inst. of Physics, Am. Mgmt. Assn., Sigma Xi, Tau Beta Pi, Eta Kappa Nu. Jewish. Contbr. articles to sci. jours.; expert on aggregation theory; developer techniques for modelling complex systems by simple models. Home: 25840 Rancho Alto Dr Carmel CA 93923 Office: PO Box 100 Fort Ord CA 93941

GOLDNER, JAMESON CHARLES, filmmaker, educator; b. Los Angeles, Feb. 22, 1938; s. Arthur M. and Golde (Holzman) G.; A.A., Glendale (Calif.) Coll., 1958; B.A., UCLA, 1960, M.A., 1962; m. Enulla Shamir, 1974; 1 dau., Naomi Anne. Dir. psychiat. tng. films UCLA, 1962; asso. dir. Motion Picture Center, Stanford, 1962; dir. film prodn. Lawrence Radiation Lab., U. Calif. at Berkeley, 1963; asst. prof. San Francisco State U., 1963—, dir. film curriculum, 1964-67, asst. prof. dept. film, 1967-78, assoc. prof., 1978-82, prof., 1982—; mem. summer faculty Swig Camp Inst. for Living Judaism, 1969-71; owner Jameson C. Goldner Films, 1965—; pres. Cinemassociates San Francisco, 1970—; vis. faculty Tel Aviv U., 1976-78; dir. Cinema Aleph Ltd., Israel. Vis. prof. Beitzvi Nat. Theatre Acad., Israel; chmn. Film As Art, short film competition San Francisco Internat. Film Festival, 1967-70; judge Calif. High Sch. Film Festival, 1970, Can. Coll. Festival, 1970, Foothill Ind. Filmmakers Festival, 1971; audiovisual cons. and producer OR & KOL, Ltd., Tel Aviv, 1976-78; cons., guest lectr. Nat. Iranian TV, 1972; cons. film study in pub. schs. Calif. Bd. Edn.; cons. film edn. Ministry of Edn. and Culture, Israel; writer, dir. Message for Chaim, film for Israel Nat. TV. Chmn. bd. Film Arts Found., San Francisco. Mem. Soc. Motion Picture and TV Engrs., Univ. Films Assn., Media Instrs. No. Calif., United Profs. Calif., Central Calif. Council Tchrs. English (v.p., program chmn. film commn. 1973—). Films include Aspects, Impressions of a Very Special Place, We Shall Not Do Nothing. Home: 1229 Diamond St San Francisco CA 94131 Office: Film Dept San Francisco State U 1600 Holloway St San Francisco CA 94132

GOLDSMITH, CLAUDE ORVILLE, oil company executive; b. Robinson, Ill., Aug. 10, 1932; s. Alonzo Fremont and Ona Cleo (Bean) G.; m. Shirley Ann Moore, Aug. 29, 1954; children—Christopher Kent, Gretchen Claudette. Student Eastern Ill. State U., 1950-51; B.S. in Bus. Adminstrn., Ohio State U., 1954, J.D., 1956. Bar: Ohio 1956. Acct., Marathon Oil Co., Findlay, Ohio, 1956-58, auditor, 1958-59, acctg. supr., 1960-61, chief acct., 1961-62, tax specialist, 1962-65; mgr. fin. reporting Atlantic Richfield Co., Phila., 1965-66, controller Internat. div., Los Angeles, 1966-68, asst. treas. fin., N.Y.C., 1969-71, treas., 1971-75, v.p. fin. and tax div., 1975-80, sr. v.p., chief fin. officer, Los Angeles, 1980—; dir. Mitsui Mfrs. Bank. Bd. dirs. Big Bros. Greater Los Angeles. Mem. Am. Petroleum Inst., Fin. Execs. Inst., Western Oil and Gas Assn. Republican. Mem. Christian Ch. Club: Jonathan (Los Angeles). Home: 1365 Hillcrest Ave Pasadena CA 91106 Office: 515 S Flower St Los Angeles CA 90071

GOLDSMITH, FRANK, executive, real estate developer, marina owner; b. Mulheim, W.Ger., Oct. 13, 1949; came to U.S., 1950, naturalized, 1954; s. Henry L. and Ellen H. (Baldeschwiler) G. B.S.E.E., CCNY, 1972. Master electrician, Colo. Electrician, Elec. Union, N.Y., 1972-74; electrician Aspen Highlands Ski Corp. (Colo.), 1974-76; propr. pres. Aspen Elec., Inc. (Colo.), 1976—; pres. Lake George Marina, Inc.; faculty Colo. Mountain Coll. Home: PO Box 3126 Aspen CO 81612 Office: Aspen Elec Inc 465 N Mill St Aspen CO 81611

GOLDSMITH, ISABELLE GAN, consulting nutritionist, lecturer; b. Chgo., Apr. 25, 1925; d. Louis and Anna (Tay) Gan; m. Paul Goldsmith, Aug. 9, 1947; children—Larry Bruce, Susan, Carole. Student Ill. Inst. Tech., 1943-45; B.S., U. Ill., 1947; cert. UCLA, 1972, U. Calif., 1964. Registered dietitian. Nutritionist Chgo. Health Dept., 1947-50, Pasadena (Calif.) Health Dept., 1962-64; nutrition parent interviewer Child Health Study, U. Calif.-Berkeley, 1965; nutrition cons. Villa Esperanza, Pasadena, 1968, Pasadena Vis. Nurses Assn., 1969-70, Pasadena City Sch. Head Start Program, 1965-66; nutrition supr. Community Planning Council Head Start Program, Pasadena, 1965-70; dir. Personal Achievement Assn., Pasadena, 1972-78; cons. nutritionist U. So. Calif. Sch. Medicine, 1979-82; pvt. practice cons. nutritionist, Los Angeles County, 1978—; cons. to planning com. Am. Heart Assn., 1979, Los Angeles Day Care and Devel. Council, 1979; task force on foods and nutrition of com. on aging Pasadena Community Council, 1965-70; mem. task force on hunger State of Calif., 1965-70; edn. dir. San Gabriel Valley Dial-A-Dietitian Project, 1961-66; mem. LWV, NOW, AAUW. Scholar, Ill. Inst. Tech., 1943. Mem. Am. Diabetes Assn., Am. Pub. Health Assn., Am. Home Econs. Assn., Greater Los Angeles Nutrition Council (treas. 1973-76), Soc. Nutrition Edn., Group Psychotherapy Assn. Club: Happy Hearts.

GOLDSMITH, MARTIN, aerospace engineer; b. Los Angeles, Nov. 21, 1929; s. Louis and Freda (Singer) G.; m. Shirley Elaine Solot, Feb. 24, 1961; children—Gregory, Joseph, Daniel; m. 2d, Brita Kristina Selden, Aug. 28, 1982. B.S., U. Calif.-Berkeley, 1951; Ph.D., Calif. Inst. Tech., 1955. Engr., Rand Corp., Santa Monica, Calif., 1955-61; group dir. Aerospace Corp., El Segundo, Calif., 1961-71; dep. dir. Environ. Quality Lab., Calif. Inst. Tech., Pasadena, 1971-76; mgr. ctr. for army studies and analysis Jet Propulsion Lab., Pasadena, 1976—; chmn. utility adv. commn. City of Pasadena, 1979-82; dir. Met. Water Dist. So. Calif., 1980—. Guggenheim Jet Propulsion fellow, 1952-54. Contbr. articles to tech. publs. Home: 215 N Grand Ave Pasadena CA 91103 Office: Jet Propulsion Lab 800 Oak Grove Dr Pasadena CA 91109

GOLDSTEIN, CHARLOTTE LEAH TAYLOR, writer, publishing executive; b. Phila., Feb. 8, 1923; d. Harry and Fanny (Goldberg) Taylor; m. S. Edward Goldstein, Feb. 28, 1942; children—Jeffrey-Allan, Sharon-Leigh, Charles-Terry, James-Stephen. Owner, Postal Instant Press, Los Angeles, 1971—, Printing Plant, Culver City, Calif., 1972—; owner, v.p. S/C Enterprises, Inc., Culver City, Calif., 1972—; dir. 1st Nat. Bank, Culver City. Mem. exec. com. Calif. J.F. Kennedy for Pres., 1960; co-organizer, Temple Beth Ami, Reseda, Calif., 1950; organizer Hadassah, Encino, 1954, B'nai Brith, West Los Angeles, 1964; chmn. Hollywood USO, 1954-64; adult tng. dir. Boy Scouts Am. Recipient Silver Bruin award Boy Scouts Am., 1965. Mem. Printing Industry Am. Republican. Clubs: Elks, Emblem, Jewish War Vets. Aux. Author: The American Flag, American Presidents, The Stars Cry, Sea and Sand, Time and Tide, Call An Ambulance, Tomorrow is for the Living, others; co-author, founding dir. nat. pioneer Stay-Well med. program for sr. citizens, 1966-71; co-founder So. Calif. Drug Control Program; bd. dirs. Doctor's Hosp. Mem. Life Found. Medicine and Law, J.W.V. Aux. Author 19 books. Home: 2136 Benedict Canyon Dr Beverly Hills CA 92010 Office: 9900 Washington Blvd Culver City CA 90230

GOLDSTEIN, DONALD AARON, engring. co. exec.; b. N.Y.C., May 11, 1934; s. Joachim and Anna G.; B.B.A., CCNY, 1955; M.S., Pa. State U., 1957, Ph.D., 1961; m. Audrey Pearl Buonocore, May 5, 1968; children—Carla, Seth, Liza. Dir. indsl. engring. electric boat div. Gen. Dynamics, Groton, Conn., 1973-76; mgmt. cons., Waterford, Conn., 1976-77; exec. v.p., gen. mgr. Health Physics Systems, Gainesville, Fla., 1979-80; dir. adminstrn. and personnel Quadrex Corp., Campbell, Calif., 1977-79, 80; pres. Project Assistance Corp., San Jose, Calif., 1981—. Mem. Am. Psychol. Assn. Contbr. articles in field to profl. jours. Home: 2261 Elkhorn Ct San Jose CA 95125 Office: 100 N Winchester Blvd San Jose CA 95128

GOLDSTEIN, FRED JEROME, clinical psychologist, educator; b. N.Y.C., Jan. 27, 1923; s. Abraham and Leah (Parkman) G.; m. Naomi M. Levens, Aug. 23, 1950 (div.); children—Marc, Joshua, Jonathan; m. 2d, Kathy Louise Robinson, Feb. 5, 1981. B.S., NYU, 1946; Ph.D., U. Calif.-Berkeley, 1953. Postdoctoral fellow Menninger Sch. Psychiatry, Topeka, Kans., and VA Mental Health Ctr., Los Angeles, 1954-55; teaching/research asst. U. Calif.-Berkeley, 1948-53; lectr., instr. U. So. Calif., Los Angeles, 1954-65; asst. prof. Los Angeles State Coll., 1965-67; instr. Calif. Sch. Profl. Psychology, 1969-73, 83—; supr. pre- and post-doctoral students in Psychiatry, Cedars-Sinai Med. Ctr., Los Angeles, 1960—; clin. psychologist Pinel Found. Hosp., Seattle, 1955-57, Los Angeles Psychiat. Service, 1957-60, Kaiser Permanente Found., So. Calif. Med. Group, 1960-63, Peterson-Guedel Family Ctr., Los Angeles, 1960-62; pvt. practice, clin. psychology, 1963—. Mem. Am. Psychol. Assn., Western Psychol. Assn., Calif. Psychol. Assn., Los Angeles County Psychol. Assn., Los Angeles Soc. Clin. Psychologists, Sigma Xi, Psi Chi. Contbr. articles to profl. jours. and papers at profl. meetings. Office: 337 S Beverly Dr Beverly Hills CA 90212

GOLDSTEIN, GEORGE STEPHEN, state official; b. N.Y.C., May 31, 1941; s. Arnold L. and Rae E. Goldstein; B.A., Fla. State U., 1963; M.A., U. Richmond, 1965; Ph.D., Colo. State U., 1969; m. Lynn M. Wackerly, Dec. 28, 1968. Instr., research assoc. Colo. State U., 1965-69; asst. prof. psychology Denison U., 1969-71; dir. psychol. services mental health programs Navajo Area Indian Health Service, 1971-73, dir. program devel. and evaluation, 1973-76; dir. programs and planning Dept. Hosps. and Instns., State N.Mex., 1976-77; sec. Hosps. and Instns. Dept., 1977-78; sec. for Health and Environ., State N.Mex., 1978—; assoc. mem. Grad. and Gen. Faculty dept. psychology Colo. State U., 1973—; clin. assoc. dept. psychiatry U. N.Mex. Sch. Medicine, Albuquerque, 1977—. Mem. exec. bd. Santa Fe Council for the Arts; mem. Com. for Orch. Santa Fe; bd. dirs. N.Mex. Health Resources. NIH, NIMH, NSF, Indian Health Service, Nat. Inst. Drug Abuse grantee. Mem. AAUP, Am. Psychol. Assn., Internat. Soc. Psycho-Therapy Research, Nat. Assn. State Mental Health Program Dirs., Assn. State and Territorial Health Ofcls. (chmn. Indian health com. 1980—, chmn. environ. health com. 1980—), U.S./Mexico Border Health Assn. (trustee governing council 1978—), Assn. Phys. Fitness in Bus. and Industry, World Fedn. Mental Health, Nat. Rehab. Assn., N.Mex. Rehab. Assn., N.Mex. Psychol. Assn., Nat. Environ. Health Assn., Am. Pub. Health Assn., Psi Chi. Contbr. articles to profl. jours. Office: Dept Health and Environ PO Box 968 Santa Fe NM 87503

GOLDSTEIN, HOWARD, illustrator, graphic designer; b. N.Y.C., Dec. 21, 1931; s. Fred Pilip and Kay (Oleck) G.; m. Susan Frye, Jan. 22, 1961; children—Lisa Fawn, Amanda Rose. B.A., CCNY, 1953, postgrad., 1956-57; postgrad. Hunter Coll., 1956-57. Pub. Decorator's Directory Greater N.Y., 1955-57; with Am. Visuals Corp., N.Y.C., 1957-58; artist, prodn. mgr. Petersen Publs., Los Angeles, 1958-59; art dir. Dave Beck & Co., Los Angeles, 1959-60, Datamation Inc., Los Angeles, 1961-63, Missile Systems Corp., Los Angeles, 1961-63, Revell Inc., Los Angeles, 1963-65, Howard Goldstein/Artist, Van Nuys, Calif., 1969-82; ptnr. The Howard Group Inc., Woodland Hills, Calif., 1981-82; pres. Howard Goldstein Design Inc., cons. in graphic art, Van Nuys, 1982—; mem. faculty Otis Inst. Parsons Sch. Design, Los Angeles. Mem. UCLA Alcohol Research Ctr. Com. Served with AUS, 1953-55. Recipient Western Publs. Assn. Eddie awards, 1975, 76, Maggie awards 1978, 80-83; over 50 awards for graphic design and illustration. Mem. Soc. Illustrators Los Angeles (pres. 1979-80), Graphic Artists Guild Los Angeles (co-founder, chmn. bd. 1980-81), Art Dirs. Los Angeles (bd. dirs.), Am. Inst. Graphic Arts. Jewish. Creator over 300 pub. illustrations, paintings and mag. covers, numerous metal sculptures and constrns.

GOLDSTEIN, HOWARD EDWARD, chemical engineer; b. White Plains, N.Y., June 28, 1937; s. Nathen and Matilda (Sussman) G.; children—David, Allen, Debra. B.S. in Chem. Engring., U. Ariz., 1961, M.S. in Chem. Engring., 1963. Grad asst. U. Ariz., Tucson, 1961-63; engr. Lockheed Missiles and Space Co., Sunnyvale, Calif., 1963-67, thermodynamics engr. Applied Space Products, Palo Alto, Calif., 1967-70, research scientist NASA Ames Research Ctr., Moffett Field, Calif., 1970-76, sect. head thermal protection materials sect., 1976—. Recipient NASA exceptional sci. achievement medal, 1976. Asso. fellow AIAA (thermo-physics com. 1978-81); mem. Am. Chem. Soc., AAAS, Soc. Advancement Materials and Processing Engring. Contbr. articles to profl. jours. Office: Bldg 234 Ames Research Center Moffett Field CA 94035

GOLDSTEIN, MARK KINGSTON LEVIN, chemist; b. Burlington, Vt., Mar. 22, 1941; s. Harold Meyer and Roberta Olga (Butterfield) Levin; B.S., U. Vt., 1964; Ph.D., U. Miami, 1971. Assoc. engr. The Boeing Co., Huntsville, Ala., 1966; nuclear engr. Lockheed, Plum Brook, Ohio, 1966-68; pres., founder Internat. Bus. and Research, Inc., Coral Gables, Fla., 1970-74; group leader Brookhaven Nat. Lab., Upton, N.Y., 1974-77; research asso. East-West Center, Honolulu, 1977-78; sr. tech. advisor JGC Corp., Yokohama, Japan, 1978-81; cons. Calif. Energy Conservation and Devel. Commn., 1971-82; founder, pres., chmn. bd. Quantum Group, Inc., La Jolla, Calif., 1982—; chmn. bd. Internat. Bus. and Research, 1972-74; dir. Executivo Magnatek, Ltd., Brasil. Mem. AAAS, Am. Chem. Soc., Am. Nuclear Soc., Am. C. of C. in Japan. Clubs: Hawaii Yacht, La Mariana Sailing. Contbr. articles to profl. jours. Address: 8110 El Paseo Grande #103 La Jolla CA 92037

GOLDSTEIN, NORMAN, dermatologist; b. Bklyn. July 14, 1934; s. Joseph H. and Bertha (Docteroff) G.; B.A., Columbia Coll., 1955; M.D., SUNY, 1959; m. Ramsay, Feb. 14, 1980; children—Richard, Heidi. Intern, Maimonides Hosp., N.Y.C., 1959-60; resident Skin and Cancer Hosp., 1960-61, Bellevue Hosp., 1961-62, N.Y. U. Postgrad. Center, 1962-63 (all N.Y.C.); partner Honolulu Med. Group, 1967-72; practice medicine specializing in dermatology, Honolulu, 1972—; asso. clin. prof. dermatology U. Hawaii Sch. Medicine, 1973—. Trustee, Hawaii Jewish Welfare Bd.; bd. dirs. Skin Cancer Found.; trustee Dermatol. Found. Recipient Henry Silver award Dermatol. Soc. Greater N.Y., 1963; Husik award N.Y. U., 1963; Spl. award Acad. Dermatologia Hawaiiana, 1971. Served with U.S. Army, 1960-67. Fellow Am. Acad. Dermatology (Silver award 1972), ACP, Royal Soc. Medicine; mem. Internat. Soc. Tropical Dermatologists (Hist. and Culture award), Soc. Investigative Dermatologists, Assn. Mil. Dermatologists, AAAS, Am. Soc. Photobiology, Environ. Health and Light Research Inst., Am. Assn. Clin. Oncology, Biol. Photog. Assn., Internat. Solar Energy Soc., Photog. Soc. Am., Health Sci. Communication Assn., Internat. Pigment Cell Soc., Am. Med. Writers Assn., Am. Coll. Cryosurgery, Internat. Soc. Dermatol. Surgery, Am. Soc. Preventive Oncology, Hawaii State Med. Assn. (mem. public affairs com.), Hawaii Dermatol. Soc. (sec.-pres.), Hawaii Public Health Assn., Pacific Dermatol. Assn., Pacific Health Research Inst., Honolulu County Med. Soc. (gov.), Nat. Wildlife Fedn., Am. Forestry Assn., C. of C. Jewish. Clubs: Outrigger Canoe, Rotary, Plaza, Honolulu, Chancellor's. Contbr. articles to profl. jours. Office: 1077 Bishop St Stuie 326 Honolulu HI 96813

GOLDSTEIN, SAMUEL JACK, pediatric psychologist, educator; b. Jersey City, May 13, 1952; s. Nathan and Sarah G.; m. Janet Hollis, Dec. 5, 1976. B.S., Bklyn. Poly. Inst., 1973; M.S., Montclair State Coll., 1976; Ph.D., U. Utah, 1980. Lic. psychologist, cert. sch. psychologist, both Utah; cert. sch. psychologist, N.Y. State, N.J. Clin. psychology intern Children's Ctr., Salt Lake City, 1978-79; sch. psychologist Jordon Resource Ctr., Salt Lake City, 1979-82; clin. dir. Neurology, Learning and Behavior Ctr., Salt Lake City, 1982—. Mem. Am. Psychol. Assn., Utah Sch. Psychologist Assn., Nat. Register Health Service Providers in Psychology. Office: 3950 S 700 E Suite 200 Salt Lake City UT 84107

GOLDSTEIN, STEVEN EDWARD, psychologist; b. Bronx, N.Y., Nov. 25, 1948; s. Maurice and Matilda (Weiss) G.; B.S. in Psychology, CCNY, 1970, M.S. in Sch. Psychology, 1971; Ed.D. in Sch. Psychology, U. No. Colo., 1977. Tchr., N.Y.C. Public Schs., 1970-71, 72-73, tchr., counselor, 1974; extern in sch. psychology N. Shore Child Guidance, 1972; sch. psychologist Denver Public Schs., 1975; asst. prof. psychology Northeastern Okla. State U., Tahlequah, 1976-78; coordinator inpatient, emergency services Winnemucca (Nev.) Mental Health Center, 1978-80; dir. Desert Devel. Ctr., Las Vegas, Nev., 1980-82; sr. psychologist Las Vegas Mental Health Ctr., 1982—; participant NSF seminar on biofeedback, 1977. Sec. grad. council CUNY, 1971; pres. grad. council in edn. CCNY, 1971. Cert. sch. psychologist, N.Y., Okla., Ariz., Calif. Mem. Am. Psychol. Assn., Nat. Assn. Sch. Psychologists, Biofeedback Soc. Nev. (membership dir. 1982—), Nev. Soc. Tng. and Devel. (bd. dirs. 1982—), Biofeedback Soc. Am. Presented papers to profl. confs. Office: 6161 W Charleston Blvd Las Vegas NV 89158

GOLDSTEIN-SAULTER, RITA, marital-family therapist; b. N.Y.C., Jan. 4, 1929; d. Joel Herbert and Pauline Birns; children—Michael Alan Goldstein, Robert Steven Goldstein; m. Leon Saulter, May 7, 1982. A.A., Santa Monica Coll., 1966; B.A., Calif. State U.-Northridge, 1970, M.A., 1974; postgrad. Profl. Sch. for Humanistic Studies, San Diego, 1980—. Cert. marriage family and child counselor, Calif. Group facilitator campus problems, reform, and innovations Hamilton High Sch., Los Angeles, 1969; dir. new counseling program So. Calif. Counseling Ctr., 1971-76; group facilitator city-wide conf. on youth and sr. citizens services Mayor Bradley's office, 1974; supr. mental health ctr. for young adults Beverlywood Board and Care, 1976; supr. families with battered children Anando Marga Family Unity Ctr., 1977; pvt. practice marital and family therapy, Beverly Hills and Van Nuys, Calif., 1974—. Recipient service awards So. Calif. Counseling Ctr., Calif. Assn. Marriage and Family Therapists, Group Psychotherapy Assn. of So. Calif., Mar Vista Optomist Club. Mem. Am. Psychol. Assn., Am. Assn. Marriage and Family Therapists, Nat. Council Family Relations, Assn. Humanistic Psychology, Los Angeles Mental Health Assn. Contbr. articles to profl. jours. Home: 13854 Vanowen St Van Nuys CA 91405 Office: 321 S Beverly Dr Suite F Beverly Hills CA 90212

GOLDSWORTHY, ROBERT JAMES, psychologist; b. Dover, N.J., July 11, 1952; s. Robert and Ann Marie (Lorenzo) G. B.S. in Psychology, U. N.Mex., 1974; M.A., Ariz. State U., 1978, Ph.D. in Psychology, 1980. Cert. psychologist, Ariz. Psychology intern Ariz. State Dept. Corrections, psychologist in tng. psychology clinic, Ariz. State U., Tempe, 1976-77; psychology intern Phoenix VA Med. Ctr., 1978-79; clin. dir. Brighton Sch. and Diagnostic Ctr., Phoenix, 1980-82; psychologist Maricopa Med. Ctr. Mental Health Annex, Phoenix, 1982—; instr. introductory psychology and psychology of adjustment Ariz. State U. Mem. Am. Psychol. Assn., Ariz. State Psychol. Assn. Republican. Contbr. articles to textbooks profl. jours. Home: 4540 E Belleview Apt 42 Phoenix AZ 85008 Office: Maricopa Med Ctr Mental Health Annex 2601 E Roosevelt Phoenix AZ 85008

GOLDWATER, BARRY MORRIS, senator; b. Phoenix, Jan. 1, 1909; s. Baron and Josephine (Williams) G.; student Staunton Mil. Acad., U. Ariz., 1928; m. Margaret Johnson, Sept. 22, 1934; children—Joanne Butler, Barry, Michael, Margaret (Mrs. R. Clay). With Goldwater's Inc., 1929—, pres. 1937-53; U.S. senator from Ariz., 1953-64, 1968—. Served as city councilman, Phoenix, 1949-52; adv. com. Indian affairs Dept. Interior, 1948-50; Republican candidate for Pres., 1964. Bd. dirs. Heard Mus., Mus. No. Ariz., St. Joseph's Hosp., Am. Grad. Sch. Indsl. Mgmt. Served as pilot USAAF, 1941-45; maj. gen. Res., ret.; col., chief staff air Ariz. N.G., 1945-52. Recipient award U.S. Jr. C. of C., 1937, Am. Good Govt. Soc. award, 1960, also Maxwell Kriendler award, Wright Bros. Meml. trophy, Assn. U.S. Army award, Aviation/Space Writers Pub. Service award, Frank Hawkes Meml. award; named Man of Year, Phoenix, 1949. Mem. Royal Photog. Soc. (asso.) Am. Legion, V.F.W., Sigma Chi, Eta Mu Pi. Mason (Shriner, 33 deg.), Elk. Author: Arizona Portraits (2 vols.), 1940; Journey Down the River of Canyons, 1940; Speeches of Henry Ashurst; The Conscience of A Conservative, 1960; Why Not Victory, 1962; The Face of Arizona, 1964; Where I Stand, 1964; People and Places, 1967; Delightful Journey, 1970; The Conscience of a Majority, 1970; The Coming Breakpoint, 1976; With No Apologies, 1979. Home: Phoenix AZ Office: US Senate Office Bldg Washington DC 20510

GOLDWYN, RALPH NORMAN, finance company executive; b. Chgo., Jan. 24, 1925; s. Herman and Rissie F. Goldwyn; B.S., UCLA, 1948; m. Joan J. Snyder, Dec. 24, 1954; children—Bob, Greg, Lisa. Partner, Arc Loan Co., Los Angeles, 1948-52; v.p. Arc Discount Co., Los Angeles, 1952-73; pres. Arc Investment Co., Los Angeles, 1952-73; partner First Factors, Los Angeles, 1960-78; pres. First Comml. Fin., Los Angeles, 1978—; dir. Roy J. Maier, Inc. Trustee UCLA Found. Served to lt. (j.g.) USN, 1943-46. Mem. UCLA Chancellor Assocs., Anti-Defamation League; U. Judaism Patrons Soc. Democrat. Clubs: Town Hall of Calif. (life), Brentwood Country, Los Angeles. Office: 1060 Crenshaw Blvd Los Angeles CA 90019

GOLITZ, LOREN EUGENE, dermatologist, pathologist, clinical administrator, educator; b. Pleasant Hill, Mo., Apr. 7, 1941; s. Ross Winston and Helen Francis (Schupp) G.; M.D., U. Mo., Columbia, 1966; m. Deborah Burd Frazier, June 18, 1966; children—Carrie Campbell, Matthew Ross. Intern, USPHS Hosp., San Francisco, 1966-67, med. resident, 1967-69; resident in dermatology USPHS Hosp., Staten Island, N.Y., 1969-71; dep. chief dermatology, 1972-73; vis. fellow dermatology Columbia-Presbyn. Med. Center, N.Y.C., 1971-72; asst. in dermatology Coll. Physicians Surgeons, Columbia, N.Y.C., 1972-73; Earl D. Osborne fellow dermal pathology Armed Forces Inst. Pathology, Washington, 1973-74; assoc. prof. dermatology pathology U. Colo. Med. Sch., Denver, 1974—; chief dermatology Denver Gen. Hosp., 1974—; attending physician dermatology Denver VA Hosp., 1974—; mem. nat. pathol. panel Mycosis Fungoides Coop. Group, 1975—; mem. Residency Rev. Com. for Dermatology, 1983—, Residency Rev. Com. for Dermatopathology, 1983—. Diplomate Am. Bd. Dermatology (dermatopathology test com. 1979—), Nat. Bd. Med. Examiners. Mem. Am. Acad. Dermatology (chmn. council on clin. and lab. services), Soc. Pediatric Dermatology (pres. 1981), Am. Soc. Dermatopathology (program com. 1979-81), Soc. Investigative Dermatology, Pacific Dermatol. Assn. (chmn. pathology com. 1979, exec. com. 1979—, sec.-treas. 1984), Noah Worcester Dermatol. Soc. (publs. com. 1980), Colo. Dermatol. Soc. (pres. 1978), Colo. Med. Soc., Denver Med. Soc., AMA (residency rev. com. for dermatology 1982—), Denver Soc. Dermatopathology (pres. 1978, chmn. edn. com. 1978—), Am. Dermatol. Assn. Editorial bd. Jour. Pediatric Dermatology, Current Issues in Dermatology. Contbr. articles to med. jours. Home: 11466 E Arkansas Ave Aurora CO 80012

GOLL, JIM F., printing exec.; b. Malta, Mont., Sept. 26, 1935; s. Christ R. and Ann (Andrews) G.; student U. Wash., 1958; m. Shirley Ann Winkel, June 18, 1954; children—J. Paul, Chris Michael. Campus mailing services mgr. U. Wash., Seattle, 1977-78, telecommunications mgr., 1978, mgr. dept. printing, 1971—. Mem. adv. bd. Conbella, Seattle, 1975-80; adv. cons. Job Corps, Seattle, 1976-78; mem. adv. com. Early Work Release, Wash. Correctional Insts., 1975-77. Named Seattle Printer of Yr., Printing House Craftsmen, 1976. Mem. In-Plant Printers (co-founder), Seattle Printing Craftsmen (pres. 1975-76). Address: G1 Communications DS10 U Wash Seattle WA 98195

GOLLOB, HARRY FRANK, psychologist; b. Newark, June 7, 1939; s. Joseph S. and Doris C. (Miller) G.; B.A., U. Denver, 1960; M.S., Yale U., 1962, Ph.D., 1965; m. Maureen M. Morris, Sept. 4, 1959; children—Steven P., David J., Kenneth J. Asst. prof. to asso. prof. U. Mich., Ann Arbor, 1965-69; research psychologist Mental Health Research Inst., Ann Arbor, 1965-69; prof. psychology U. Denver, 1969—; cons. statis. and EEO. Recipient fellowships and fed. research grants. Fellow Am. Psychol. Assn.; mem. Am. Statis. Assn., Soc. Multivariate Exptl. Psychologists, Psychometric Soc., AAAS, Soc. Exptl. Social Psychologists, Ednl. Statisticians. Editorial bd. Multivariate Behavioral Research, 1971—, Jour. Exptl. Social Psychology, 1974-80; contbr. articles to sci. jours. Home: 2558 E Cresthill Ave Littleton CO 80121 Office: Dept Psychology U Denver Denver CO 80208

GOLOWITZ, WILLIAM, transp. co. exec.; b. Akron, Ohio, Jan. 13, 1931; s. Fred and Stella (Wolfe) G.; student U.S. Armed Forces Inst., 1953; m. Sylvia Tan, Nov. 22, 1977. Gen. mgr. Smyth Hawaiian Van Lines, Honolulu and Smyth Internat. Van Lines, Japan, 1956-63; v.p. Worldwide Moving & Storage, Inc., Honolulu, 1963-64; regional mgr. Far East and S.E. Asia, Vanpac Carriers, Inc., 1965-76; mng. dir. Vanpac Internat. Pte., Ltd., Singapore, 1976—; dir./cons. Japan Van Lines, 1960-63; v.p. Livermore Van & Storage, Inc., 1963—. Served with USAF, 1948-54. Decorated Air medal. Recipient Nat. Def. Transp. Assn. Nat. award, 1959. Mem. Am. C. of C. of Japan and Philippines, Nat. Def. Transp. Assn., Internat. Execs. (Paris), Am. Bus. Council (Singapore), VFW. Republican. Episcopalian. Club: Am. Home: 10 Hooper Rd Singapore 0922 Singapore Office: 138 Bukit Timah Rd Singapore 0922 Singapore

GOLTZ, HAROLD ARTHUR, state senator, college administrator; b. Balaton, Minn., Aug. 13, 1924; s. Albert O. and Olga (Mitzner) G.; B.A., Macalester Coll., 1945; M.A., U. Minn., 1950; m. Marguerite Nauss, Mar. 20, 1948; 1 son, Jeffrey David. Asst. dir. student personnel Macalester Coll., 1947-57; dir. student activities Western Wash. State Coll., Bellingham, 1957-60, asst. to pres., 1960-65, dir. planning and devel., 1965—; mem. Wash. State Ho. of Reps., 1973-74; mem. Wash. Senate, 1975—, pres. pro tem, 1983—; v.p. Answers Inc., 1980—; ednl. facilities cons., 1964—; chmn. Wash. State Interinstl. Com. Phys. Plant Adminstrn., 1966—; v.p. Answers, Inc., 1981—. Bd. dirs. Friends of Mabel Zoe Wilson Library, Whatcom Mental Health Found.; trustee St. Luke's Hosp., Bellingham. Served with USAAF, 1945-46. Recipient Wash. State chpt. AIA honor award for client, 1964, Viking Union Nat. Housing and Urban Devel. Design award, 1964, 66, Wash. State Arts Commn. award, 1969; named Best New Legislator for 1973-75, Seattle Argus. Mem. ACLU (v.p. Whatcom County 1965—), Bellingham C. of C., Nat. Conf. State Legislators (chmn. com. on sci. and tech. 1980—), Am. Coll. and Univ. Pub. Relations Assn., Soc. Coll. and Univ. Planners. Home: 3003 Vallette St Bellingham WA 98225

GOLUBIC, THEODORE ROY, sculptor, designer, urban planner; b. Lorain, Ohio, Dec. 9, 1928; s. Ivan and Illonka (Safar) G.; m. Rose Andrina Ieraci-Golubic, Nov. 27, 1958; children—Vincivan, Theodore E., Victor, Georjia. Student Ohio State U., Columbus, 1947-48, Miami U., Oxford, Ohio, 1948-51; B.F.A. in Painting, Syracuse U., 1955; M.F.A. in Sculpture, U. Notre Dame, 1957. Asst. to Ivan Mestrovic, 1954-60; guest tchr. U. Notre Dame, 1959; urban planner redevel. dept., South Bend, Ind., 1960-65; sculpture cons., Rock of Ages Corp., 1965-67; instr. Central Mo. State U., 1969; instr. San Diego Sculptors' Guild, 1970-71; artist-in-resident Roswell (N.Mex.) Mus. and Art Ctr., 1971-72; sculptor, designer, 1972—; works include: Limestone relief sculpture Cathedral of the Nativity, Dubuque, Iowa, 4 dimensional sun environ. design, South Bend, Ind. Served in U.S. Army, 1951-53. Mem. Artists Equity Assn., Coll. Art Assn. Am., Internat. Sculpture Ctr. Contbr. articles to profl. jours.

GOLYN, RUDI FRANKLIN, advertising executive; b. San Francisco, Aug. 13, 1938; s. Robert H. and Mary (Mauber) G.; m. Joanne Bravacos, Jan. 10, 1965; children—Peter, Sarah. Student U. Colo., 1956-59; B.A. in Communications, San Jose State U., 1960. Writer, producer Young & Rubicam Co., N.Y.C., 1966-70; v.p., creative dir. McCaun Erickson, San Francisco, 1970-74; sr. v.p., creative dir. Kelly Nason-Univas, San Francisco, 1978-80; sr. v.p. mktg. communications Telelearning Systems, Inc., San Francisco, 1980—; ptnr. theatrical prodn. co., 1970-80. Recipient numerous advt., theatrical awards for creative excellence. Mem. Dramatists Guild N.Y.C. Theatrical prodns. include: Bleacher Bums, San Francisco, 1981; The Mouse Trap, San Francisco, 1977; Finn MacKool, N.Y.C., 1976; One Flew Over the Cuckoo's Nest, San Francisco, 1970, N.Y.C., 1971, Boston, 1972, Nat. Coll. Tour (longest running play in San Francisco), 1975. Home: 2 Chestnut St Ross CA 94957 Office: Telelearning Systems Inc 505 Beach St San Francisco CA 94113

GOLZE, ALFRED RUDOLF, civil engr.; b. Washington, July 6, 1905; s. Rudolph Leon and Blanche (Wenderoth) G.; B.S.C.E., U. Pa., 1930, C.E., 1940; m. Gladys Louise Whitney; children—Gretchen Wenderoth, Peter Wenderoth. Engr. subways, Phila., 1925-27; valuation engr. ICC, Washington, 1930-33; designing engr. U.S. Bur. Reclamation, Denver, 1933-35; supervising engr. in charge Civilian Conservation Camps on reclamation projects Bur. of Reclamation, Washington, 1936-43; budget examiner public works Bur. of Budget, San Francisco and Washington, 1943-45; asst. dir. operations and maintenance Bur. of Reclamation, 1945-47, dir. of programs and finance, 1947-53, chief, program coordination and finance div., 1953-58, asst. commr., 1958-61; chief engr. Calif. Dept. Water Resources, 1961-67, Sacramento, dep. dir., 1967-71; chief hydroelectric engr. Burns and Roe, Inc., Los Angeles, 1971-73, chief water resources engr., 1973-74; pvt. practice as cons. engr., 1975—; cons. Govt. Turkey, 1960, AID, Pakistan, 1964; mem. exec. com. U.S. Com. on Large Dams, 1969-74, chmn. com. model law on safety of dams, 1968-71; mem. exec. com. U.S. Com. on Irrigation, Drainage and Flood Control, 1967-72. Recipient Distingished Service award U.S. Dept. Interior, 1962; Toulmin medal Soc. Am. Mil. Engrs., 1964; Outstanding Service Engring. Profession award Engring. Council Sacramento Valley, 1966; Dir.'s Service award Calif. Dept. Water Resources, 1966; Dr. Robert Yarnall award Alumni Soc. U. Pa., 1979. Fellow ASCE (hon. mem.; pres. nat. capital sect. 1958-59, chmn. com. engring. edn. 1959-60, chmn. nat. water policy com. 1972-73, pres. Sacramento sect. 1968-69, mem. jury to select outstanding civil engring. achievement of 1979); mem. Fed. Govt. Accountants Assn. (Washington chpt. pres. 1960-61), Soc. Am. Mil. Engrs., Earthquake Engring. Research Inst., Sigma Xi (asso.), Tau Beta Pi, Sigma Tau, Chi Epsilon (hon. U. Colo. chpt.), Theta Xi (pres. Washington alumni 1956-57). Clubs: Cosmos (Washington); Commonwealth, Engineers (San Francisco). Author: Reclamation in the United States, 1952; Your Future in Civil Engineering, 1965; contbr. to Applied Sedimentation, 1950. Editor: Handbook of Dam Engineering, 1977. Contbr. numerous articles in engring. and other mags. Address: 1508 La Sierra Dr Sacramento CA 95825

GOLZE, RICHARD, life insurance company executive, estate planning consultant, lawyer; b. St. Louis, Dec. 5, 1922; s. Roscoe Conkling and Lillian Grace (Reimold) G.; m. Mary Frances Green, Feb. 9, 1925; children—Richard William, Janet E., Michael J. B.A., U. Ill., 1947, J.D., 1948. Bar: Wash. 1950, Hawaii 1977. With tax dept. C.M.St.P. & P. R.R., 1949-56; assoc. gen. counsel Safeco Life Ins. Co., Seattle, 1956-76; 2d v.p., dir. advanced sales Hawaiian Life Ins. Co., Honolulu, 1957—. Office: PO Box 3140 Honolulu HI 96802

GOMBERG, CHRISTOPHER, marriage, family and child counselor, consultant; b. Los Angeles, Jan. 27, 1952; s. Sy and Maxine (Cooper) G.; m. Lisa Cutler, Mar. 18, 1979. B.A. in Psychology, U. Vt., 1974; M.Ed. in Counseling and Guidance, 1977. Lic. marriage, family and child counselor, Calif. Research asst. dept. psychology U. Vt., 1970-73, research coordinator, co-therapist dept. psychiatry, 1974-77; group leader Project CRASH, Waterbury, Vt., 1971-74; coordinator Hunt Youth Ctr., Burlington, Vt., 1973-74; assoc. profl. staff SW Regional Labs., Los Alamitos, Calif., 1978-79; Curriculum analyst UCLA, 1978-80, staff research assoc. Alcohol Research Ctr., 1978-79, 80-82; counselor Kaiser Alcohol and Drug Program, Los Angeles, 1979—; cons. employee assistance program Mattell, Inc., Hawthorne, Calif.; pvt. practice marriage, family and child counseling, North Hollywood, Calif. Mem. Calif. Gov.'s Task Force on Alcohol, Drugs and Traffic Safety, 1981—, acting chmn. rehab., 1981; bd. dirs. Los Angeles chpt. Mothers Against Drunk Drivers, 1982—. Mem. Am. Psychol. Assn., Soc. Psychologists in Addictive Behaviors, Western Psychol. Assn., Am. Personnel and Guidance Assn. Democrat. Jewish. Contbr. articles to profl. publs. editorial referee Jour. Studies on Alcohol, 1977, 79, 81, Hazelden Found., 1982. Office: 4418 Vineland Blvd Suite 120 North Hollywood CA 91602

GOMEZ, ELAINE PAMELA, airline executive; b. Pitts., Dec. 28, 1943; d. Edward Vincent and Sara Ann (Kelly) Boraten; B.A., Okla. State U., 1965; M.S. in Bus., Armstrong Coll., 1977; m. Juan Gomez, Mar. 1, 1969. Flight attendant Pan Am. World Airways, San Francisco, 1966-69; supr. stewardesses United Airlines, San Francisco, 1969-72, inflight services chief, 1972-73, inflight services adminstrv. services mgr., 1973-77, adminstrv. services mgr. maintenance supply services, 1977-79, mgr. maintenance supply services, 1979—. Bd. dirs., treas. Women's Recovery Assn. San Mateo County. Mem. NOW, Am. Mgmt. Assn. Office: United Airlines San Francisco CA 94128

GOMEZ, HECTOR ERNESTO, public service company executive; b. Tijuana, Baja California, Mex., Sept. 21, 1955; s. Hector H. Gomez Martinez. B.S. in Bus. Adminstrn., U. Phoenix, 1982. Personnel mgr. Mex. ops. Badger Meter Corp., Nogales, Mex., 1980; tng. and devel. specialist Gen. Instrument Corp., Nogales, 1983—; indsl. relations mgr. combustibles S.A. State Utility Co. Mem. Nat. Geog. Soc. Club: Racquet of Nogales.

GOMEZ, JOHN, III, educator, former air force officer; b. San Jose, Calif., May 12, 1930; s. John and Erva Belle (Morris) G.; A.A. with honors, Skyline Coll., 1973; B.A. magna cum laude, San Francisco State U., 1976; m. Elizabeth Ellis Abney, Nov. 8, 1967; children—Charlotte Diane, John, Jennifer Anne. Commd. 2d lt. U.S. Air Force, 1949, advanced through grades to maj., 1974, ret., 1974; tchr. Tennyson High Sch., Hayward, Calif., 1979—. Decorated Bronze Star, Air medal (2), Air Force Commendation medal (2). Mem. Nat. Aerospace Edn. Assn., The Daedalians, Am. Aviation Hist. Soc., Air Force Hist. Soc., D.A.V., Epsilon Pi Tau, Phi Delta Kappa. Mem. Christian Ch. Contbr.: Herk: Hero of the Skies (J.E. Dabney), 1979. Home: 206 Escobar Pl San Ramon CA 94583 Office: 27035 Whitman St Hayward CA 94544

GOMEZ, KEVIN LAWRENCE JOHNSON, government official; b. Erie, Pa., Nov. 27, 1950; s. Arthur and Yvonne Mason (Johnson) G.; B.A., U. Colo., 1972; postgrad. U. Mich., 1974. Dir. Student Health Conf. of Southwest, HEW, 1972; asst. Colo. Senators Floyd Haskell and Gary Hart, U.S. Senate, 1975-80; state programs specialist Office of Surface Mining, U.S. Dept. Interior, Denver, 1980-82; legis. adv. Colo. Rural Legal Services, 1982—. Mem. Colo. adv. bd. Sickle Cell Anemia; asst. sec. Denver Democratic Central Com., 1975-79, sec., 1979-81; pres. Colo. Young Dems., 1974-76; del. Dem. Nat. Conv., 1980. bd. dirs. Denver Opportunities Industrialization Center; chmn. Denver Affirmative Action Com., 1975-77; v.p. Leadership Denver. Mem. NAACP, Denver C. of C. (Leadership Denver), Am. Assn. Blacks in Energy, Am. Polit. Sci. Assn., Am. Soc. Public Adminstrs. Episcopalian. Home: 2936 Colorado Blvd Denver CO 80207 Office: 2801 E Colfax Ave Denver CO 80206

GOMEZ, ROGER WILLIAM, chiropractor; b. Los Angeles, Apr. 22, 1946; s. William James and Marie E. G.; B.S., M. Stewart Internat. U., 1973; D.C., Cleveland Chiropractic Coll., Los Angeles, 1976; children—Tracy M., Chad E., April L., Travis J. Instr., Computer Learning Inst., Los Angeles, 1975-76; practice chiropractic medicine, No. Hollywood, Calif., 1976-78, Vista, Calif., 1978-80; chiropractor, Coachella Chiropractic Offices, San Bernardino, Calif., 1981—. Mem. Crime Prevention Commn., Vista, Calif., 1979-81; bd. dirs. Vista Bobby Sox, 1979-80; mem. Parker Research Found., 1980—. Served with U.S. Army, 1965-67. Diplomate Nat. Bd. Chiropractic Examiners. Mem. San Diego Chiropractic Soc. (dir.), Am. Chiropractic Assn., Calif. Chiropractic Assn., Riverside Chiropractic Soc., San Diego Computer Soc. Clubs: Optimist, Coachella Valley Rotary. Office: 1441 6th St Coachella CA 92236

GOMMI, JULIUS VERDIER, chemical engineer; b. L.I., N.Y., Mar. 9, 1940; s. Julius Washington and Alice Blanche (Verdier) G.; m. Loretta Rizzo, Dec. 2, 1961; children—Lorraine E., Michael J., Julie L. B.Chem. Engring., Poly. Inst. N.Y., 1961; M.S. in Mech. Engring., Rensselaer Poly. Inst., 1969. With Combustion Engring., Windsor, Conn., 1961-77, recovery systems sect. mgr., 1974-79; recovery cycle research mgr. Weyerhaeuser Co., Tacoma, 1977-79, process engring. specialist, 1979—. Served as 1st lt. U.S. Army, 1961-63. Mem. Am. Inst. Chem. Engrs., TAPPI (chmn. recovery boiler com. of steam and power). Contbr. papers and articles to profl. jours. Office: Corp Engring Weyerhaeuser Co Tacoma WA 98477

GOMOLSKI, JOSEPH RAYMOND, accountant; b. Chgo., Feb. 6, 1944; s. Harry Edward and Josephine L. (Bono) G.; B.S. in Econs., U. Ill., 1967; M.B.A., Loyola U., Chgo., 1968; postgrad. Denver U., 1975; m. Karen D. Kirkland, Jan. 1, 1980; children—Brian Joseph, Kevin Eric. Instr., U. Wis., Eau Claire, 1969-71; asst. controller Mountain Banks, Ltd., Colorado Springs, Colo., 1971-73; pvt. practice public acctg., Colorado Springs, 1973; honorarium prof. U. Colo., Colorado Springs. Dir., Colorado Springs Mcpl. Airport Adv. Bd., 1976-80. Fellow, U. Ky., 1971; recipient letter of recognition of public service City of Colorado Springs, 1980. Mem. Am. Inst. C.P.A.s, Colo. Soc. C.P.A.s (chmn. govtl. bd., trustee Edn. Found. 1973-79). Republican. Club: Rocky Mountain. Colo. editor Research Inst. Am. Home: 77 Saddle Mountain Rd Colorado Springs CO 80919 Office: 130 E Kiowa Suite 612 Colorado Springs CO 80903

GOMORY, PAUL LOUIS, JR., executive recruitment company executive; b. Darby, Pa., Jan. 5, 1948; s. Paul Louis and Margaret Mary (Burke) G.; B.A. in Econs. (Nat. Merit scholar), Amherst Coll., 1970; M.B.A., Stanford U., 1975. With IMF, Washington, 1967-68; staff asst. to Pres., White House, Washington, 1970-73; v.p. Kearns Internat., San Francisco, 1975-78; assoc. corp. fin. Weiss, Peck & Greer, San Francisco, 1978-80; sr. assoc. Korn/Ferry Internat., San Francisco, 1980-81, mng. assoc., 1981-82, v.p., 1983—. Bd. dirs. Bay Group, 1980—; chmn. bd. San Francisco Dance Theater, 1981—. Republican. Club: St. Francis Yacht (San Francisco). Patentee window insulation. Office: 600 Montgomery St 39th Floor San Francisco CA 94111

GONDER, ROBERT ANDRE, constrn. co. exec.; b. Sheridan, Wyo., Feb. 20, 1937; s. Robert Charles and Ruth (Morrison) G.; student No. Wyo. Community Coll., 1956-58; m. Carolina Mae Olheiser, June 3, 1961; children—Robert Edward, Carol Jean, Roger Wayne. With Hank's Auto Repair, Sheridan, Wyo., 1954-56, Fair's Home & Auto Supply, Sheridan, 1956-57, Storm Vulcan, Dallas, 1957-58, Weber Auto Body, Denver, 1958-59, Bob Jones Skyland Ford, Denver, 1959, Western Nuclear Mining & Constrn., Rawlins, Wyo., 1959-61, Gilpatrick Constrn. Co., Riverton, Wyo., 1961-62, Morningstar Dairy, Riverton, 1962-64, Vitro Minerals, Healy, Alaska, 1964, Yukon Equip., Anchorage, 1964-65, Bernard Stewart Excavating Co., Anchorage, 1965, No. Comml. Machinery, Anchorage, 1965-66, Steve Cooper Constrn. Co., Delta Junction, Alaska, 1966, Aspeotis Constrn. Co., Anchorage, 1967-71, Chris Berg, Inc., Anchorage, 1971, Studnix, Anchorage, 1971-72, Greater Anchorage Area Borough, 1972-75, Parker Drilling Co., 1980; real estate salesman ERA-Bowden Realty, Inc., 1980-82; real estate sales rep. Nova Real Estate, Inc., 1982—; builder, landlord and mgr. house and trailer rentals, Riverton, Wyo., 1963-64; owner, operator heavy equipment co., Anchorage 1971; builder, property mgr., developer Robert A. Gonder Enterprises and Gonder-Kelly Enterprises, Anchorage, 1968—. Mem. Ad hoc com. Alaska Landlord and Property Mgrs. Assn. to Anchorage Mcpl. Assembly, 1977. Mem. Am. Fedn. Bus., Whittier Boat Owners Assn., Coast Guard Aux., Internat. Union of Operating Engrs., United Fisherman of Alaska. Home and office: 1460 W 26 Ave Anchorage AK 99503

GONG, WILLIAM CHOY, pharmacist, educator; b. San Francisco, Aug. 22, 1948; s. Wilfred Young and Wing Kum (Shew) G.; B.A., San Jose State U., 1970; Pharm.D., U. So. Calif., 1974. Resident in clin. pharmacy Los Angeles County/U. So. Calif. Med. Ctr., 1975; lectr. pharmacy U. So. Calif., Los Angeles, 1974-75, asst. prof., 1975-81, assoc. prof., 1982—, coordinator clin. pharmacy residency program, 1978—, sect. leader ambulatory care and geriatric programs, 1979—; dir. clin. pharmacy services Los Angeles County Ambulatory Care Health Ctrs., East Los Angeles, 1975—. Contbr. articles to profl. jours., chpts. to books; editor newsletters. Mem. Am. Coll. Clin. Pharmacology, Am. Assn. Colls. Pharmacy, Am. Pub. Health Assn., Am. Pharm. Assn., Calif. Pharm. Assn., Am. Soc. Hosp. Pharmacists, Calif. Soc. Hosp. Pharmacists, U. So. Calif. Sch. Pharmacy Alumni Assn., Alpha Phi Omega, Rho Chi. Home: 218 N Marguerita Ave Alhambra CA 90801 Office: U So Calif 1985 Zonal Ave Los Angeles CA 90033

GONOS, BESSIE, nurse; b. Bell, Calif., July 16, 1926; d. John and Georgia (Kotichas) Gonos; R.N., Calif. Hosp. Sch. Nursing, 1950; B.S., U. So. Calif., 1950; M.S., Calif. State U., Los Angeles, 1978. With St. Francis Med. Center, Lynwood, Calif., 1950 , head nurse, 1951-56, supr., 1956-60, asso. dir., 1960-76, asst. adminstr. nursing services, 1976-79; sch. nurse, 1980; edn. instr. Dominguez Valley Hosp., Compton, Calif., 1980-83, asst. adminstrv. supr., 1983—. Bd. dirs., chmn. profl. edn. com. Long Beach Area Am. Cancer Soc. Mem. Calif. Nurses Assn., Am. Nurses Assn., Nat. League for Nursing, Am. Nurses Assn. Coll. Ob.-Gyn. Greek Orthodox. Clubs: Daughters of Penelope, Emblem, Philoptoches Soc. Home: 9824 Norlain Ave Downey CA 90240 Office: 3100 S Susana Rd Compton CA 90221

GONSALVES, CARLOS JOSEPH, clinical psychologist; b. Santa Clara, Calif., Sept. 22, 1935; s. Manuel Airea and Leanor G.; m. Carole Johnson, Dec. 11, 1971; children—Mark Joseph, Timothy David. B.A., San Luis Rey Coll., 1958; M.A., Fresno State U., 1972; Ph.D., Pacific Grad. Sch. Psychology, 1979. Lic. psychologist, Calif. Psychologist, Adult Day Treatment, San Jose, Calif., 1974-76; lectr. San Jose State U., 1976-79; clin. psychologist, Inpatient Psychiatry, Valley Med. Ctr., San Jose, 1979-80; clin. psychologist Central Community Mental Health, San Jose, 1980—; bd. dirs. Alum Rock Counseling Ctr., San Jose, 1973—; mem. adv. bd. Contact Teleministries, San Jose, 1980—. Mem. Am. Psychol Assn., Am. Orthopsychiat. Assn., Chicano Mental Health Assn. Democrat. Roman Catholic. Office: 2221 Enborg Ln San Jose CA 95128

GONZALES, ELOY HERNANDEZ, sch. adminstr.; b. Silver City, N.Mex., Oct. 18, 1949; s. Pete S. and Dolores (Hernandez) G.; B.A., N.Mex. Highlands U., 1972; M.A., Western N.Mex. U., 1978. Tchr., Unified Sch. Dist. #373, Newton, Kans., 1972-75, West Las Vegas (N.Mex.) Jr. High Sch., 1975-76; tchr. Silver Consol. Sch. Dist., Silver City, 1977-80, asst. prin. jr. high sch., 1980—. Mem. Assn. for Supervision and Curriculum Devel., NEA, N.Mex. Edn. Assn. Democrat. Roman Catholic. Home: 3725 Fran Dr Silver City NM 88061 Office: Bin 1060 Silver City NM 88061

GONZALES, LUCILLE CONTRERAS, ednl. adminstr.; b. Colton, Calif., Nov. 30, 1937; d. Antonio Colunga and Ramona (Arroyo) Contreras; A.A., San Bernardino Valley Coll., 1958; B.A., U. Calif., Santa Barbara, 1960; M.A., Claremont Grad. Sch., 1969; m. Enrique Gonzales, Aug. 27, 1960; children—Leticia Maria, Cecilia Maria. With Chino (Calif.) Public Schs., 1960—, bilingual classroom tchr., 1970-74, bilingual coordinator, 1974-76, coordinator consol. application-intergroup relations, 1976-78, supr. spl. projects, 1978, adminstr. spl. projects, 1978-82, dir. spl. projects, 1982—. Mem. Migrant Regional Exec. Bd.; mem. Bilingual Dirs. Task Force. Mem. Nat. Assn. Female Execs., San Bernardino County Assn. Compensatory Edn. Dirs., PEO, Assn. Secondary Spl. Projects, Assn. Calif. Sch. Adminstrs., Pi Lambda Theta, Delta Kappa Gamma. Office: 5130 Riverside Dr Chino CA 91710

GONZALES, PAUL DONALD, health care exec.; b. Los Angeles, Jan. 18, 1953; s. Jose H. and Marie L. (Pinard) G.; student Coll. Santa Fe, 1971, St. John's Coll., 1972; B.A., UCLA, 1973; diploma Coll. State Judiciary, U. Nev., 1977, Fed. Police Acad., 1977. Ct. judge San Ildefonso Indian Reservation, 1977-78; asst. dir. Santa Fe Service Unit, Indian Health Bd., 1979, dir. Home Health Care Agy., 1980—; sales mgr. Santa Fe Assos., 1979; cons. in field. Chmn., San Ildefonso Pueblo Elem. Sch. Bd., 1976-80; chmn. Indian edn. com. Pojoaque Valley Schs., 1976-81; mem. personnel selection com. 8 No. Indian Pueblo Council, 1977-78; mem. San Ildefonso Pueblo Tribal Council, 1976-78, 81—. All Indian Pueblo Council scholar, 1971-76. Mem. Am. Indian Ct. Judges Assn., Nat. Indian Edn. Assn., Nat. Congress Am. Indians, Am. Indian Planners Assn., Nat. Wildlife Fedn. Republican. Home: Route 5 Box 316 Santa Fe NM 87501 Office: Route 1 Box 117 BB Santa Fe NM 87501

GONZALES, RICHARD ROBERT, coll. counselor; b. Palo Alto, Calif., Jan. 12, 1945; s. Pedro and Virginia (Ramos) G.; A.A., Foothill Coll., 1966; B.A., San Jose (Calif.) State U., 1969; M.A., Calif. Poly. State U., San Luis Obispo, 1971; grad. Dept. Def. Equal Opportunity Mgmt. Inst. Counselor student activities Calif. Poly. State U., San Luis Obispo, 1969-71, instr. ethnic studies, 1970-71; counselor Ohlone Coll., Fremont, Calif., 1971-72, coordinator coll. readiness, 1971; counselor De Anza Coll., Cupertino, Calif., 1972-78, mem. community speakers bur., 1975-78; counselor Foothill Coll., Los Altos Hills, Calif., 1978—, mem. community speakers bur., 1978—. Mem. master plan com. Los Altos (Calif.) Sch. Dist., 1975-76; vol. worker, Chicano communities, Calif.; fellow Masters and Johnson Inst.; Served with Calif. Army N.G., now capt. Adj. Gen. Corps, USAR. Recipient Counselor of Year award Ohlone Coll., 1971-72; lic. marriage family child counselor, Calif. Mem. Am. Calif. personnel and guidance assns., Am. Coll. Personnel Assn., Calif. Assn. Marriage and Family Therapists, Calif. Community Coll. Counselor Assn., Res. Officers Assn., La Raza Faculty Assn. Cal. Community Colls., Phi Delta Kappa. Democrat. Roman Catholic. Office: Foothill Coll Los Altos Hills CA 94022

GONZALEZ, ALEXANDER, psychologist, educator; b. Los Angeles, Sept. 14, 1945; s. William and Altagracia (Medina) G.; m. Gloria Martinez, June 12, 1971; children—Alejandro, Michael. B.A., Pomona Coll., Claremont, Calif., 1972; postgrad. Harvard Law Sch., 1972-74; M.A., U. Calif.-Santa Cruz, 1977, Ph.D. in Psychology, 1979. Research asst. U. Calif.-Santa Cruz, 1970-72, acad. preceptor, 1975-78, fellow in psychology, 1975-79; assoc. prof. Calif. State U.-Fresno, 1979—; cons., participant profl. confs. Served with USAF, 1963-67. Ford Found. fellow, 1974-79; NRC fellow, 1982. Mem. Am. Psychol. Assn., Calif. Psychol. Assn., Internat. Assn. for Advancement of Cooperation in Edn., Phi Beta Kappa. Contbr. articles to profl. jours. and chpts. to books. Home: 181 N Karen Ave Clovis CA 93612 Office: Dept Psychology Calif State U Fresno CA 93740

GONZALEZ, MANUEL ESQUIVEL, cable TV co. exec.; b. Mexico City, Jan. 6, 1950; came to U.S., 1970; s. Manuel Gonzalez Vazquez and Lydia Esquivel Sanchez; B.F.A. (Outstanding Student scholar), San Francisco Art Inst., 1975; postgrad. in bus. adminstrn. U. Mexico City, 1968-70; postgrad. N.Y. U., 1975-77; m. Alaciel Haddad; children—Manuel Maiz, Rodrigo. Media-art therapist caring center for Children with Learning Disabilities, Berkeley, Calif., 1973-75; instr. in media Ohloney Coll., 1976; bilingual programming coordinator Hayward Cable TV (Calif.), 1974-77; programming dir. Fresno Cable TV (Calif.), 1978-81; scriptwriting intern with Molly Gregory, San Francisco, 1973; Cable TV apprentice Alt. Media Center, N.Y.C., 1975. Founding mem., media coordinator Everybody's Creative Arts Center, Oakland, Calif., 1976-78; coordinator, designer apprenticeship program for teenagers San Antonio Community Health Media Project, Oakland, Calif., 1977; bd. dirs. Community Service Channel Found., Calif., 1980-81. Artist-in-Residence grantee Calif. Arts Council, 1977; Nat. Endowment for Arts/Markle Found. grantee, 1975. Mem. Nat. Fedn. Local Cable Programmers (founding; treas. 1977-79), Bay Area Video Coalition (founding; treas. 1978), Nat. Cable TV Assn. (judge for Ace award 1979). Roman Catholic. Contbr. articles to profl. jours.; producer, dir., editor, animator Marine World documentary: Kifunyo, 1973. Home: 1105 East Terrace Fresno CA 93703

GOOCH, EVERETT JAMES, hospital administrator; b. LaCrosse, Wis., Mar. 5, 1948; s. Aubrey LaVoy and Violet Rose (Meyer) G.; m. Marcia Marie Erb, Sept. 13, 1973; children—Allison Joy, Erin Janell. B.S., Union Coll., 1971; M.S., U. Wis., 1976. Adminstrv. asst. Loma Linda (Calif.) U. Med. Ctr., 1976-77, asst. adminstr., 1978-80, v.p., 1980-82; pres. Loma Linda Community Hosp., 1982—; trustee ctr., hosp., Adventist Health Systems. Mem. Am. Coll. Hosp. Adminstrn. Republican. Seventh-day Adventist. Home: 22684 Minona Dr Grand Terrace CA 92324 Office: Loma Linda Community Hosp Loma Linda CA 92354

GOOCH, GEORGIA YVONNE, health care financial executive, consultant; b. Astoria, Oreg., Sept. 8, 1942; d. George William and Marianne Walker (Tichenor) Cooper; m. Ronald George Webb, June 19, 1960; m. 2d, David Edward Gooch, Sept. 18, 1965; children—Judith Webb, Steven Edward, Lyndal Margaret. B.A. in Bus. Adminstrn., Southwestern U., Phoenix, 1982. Cert. patient account mgr. Coordinator, Kaiser-Permanente Med Group, Oakland, Calif., 1961-65; vol./chmn., various U.S. Air Force Orgns., U.S., 1966-75; safety coordinator Del Monte Corp., Yuba City, Calif., 1975; patient account mgr. Stevens Meml. Hosp., Edmonds, Wash., 1979-81; dir. bus. services Valley Gen. Hosp., Renton, Wash., 1981—. Mem. Am. Guild Patient Account Mgmt., Health Care Fin. Mgmt. Assn., AAUW, Puget Sound Health Systems Agy. Author: Certified Patient Account Manager's Study Guide, 1981. Home: 10914 Circle Dr Bothell WA 98011 Office: 400 S 43d St Renton WA 98055

GOOD, DAVID EDWARD, safety engineer; b. Bloomington, Ill., Feb. 2, 1952; s. Sam Eugene and Kathy Joyce (Nevious) G.; children—Daniel, David. B.S. in Fire Protection and Safety Engring., Okla. State U., 1975, teaching cert. fire service tng. 1973; A.A.S. in Fire Sci., Coll. of DuPage, 1981; attended Internat. Loss Control Inst., Atlanta, 1982. Cert. firefighter, insp., Instr. Property claims adjuster, Home Ins. Co., Chgo., 1977-78; loss control engr., Hanover Ins. Co., Chgo., 1978-79, U.S. Fidelity & Guaranty, Chgo., 1979-81; corp. safety engr. Indsl. Hygiene Scis., Carnation, Los Angeles, 1981—. Served with USN, 1971-73, USAF, 1973-77. Mem. Am. Soc. Safety Engrs., Soc. Fire Protection Engrs., Nat. Fire Protection Assn. Republican. Roman Catholic. Home: 13004 Valleyheart Dr Apt 3 Studio City CA 91604 Office: 5045 Wilshire Blvd Los Angeles CA 90036

GOOD, SUSAN PAULINE, banker; b. Sanger, Calif., Aug. 17, 1953; d. Alfred Anton and Elsbeth Bates (Grimm) Good; m. David James Lehman, May 22, 1976. A.A. in Journalism, Reedley Coll., 1973; B.A. summa cum laude in Journalism, Calif. State U.-Fresno, 1975. Account asst. Elvin Bell Pub. Relations, Fresno, 1976-77; account exec. Meeker Advt. Co., Fresno, 1977-78; dir. advt. First Savs. and Loan, Fresno, 1978-81; br. promotions mgr. Central Savs., Fresno, 1981-82, br. mgr., asst. v.p., 1982—; part-time prof. advt. Calif. State U. Vice-chmn. Fresno County Democratic Central Com; past chmn. Fresno City-County Commn. Status of Women. Recipient Silver Medal award Fresno Advt. Fedn. and Am. Advt. Fedn., 1982. Mem. Fresno Advt. Fedn. (pres.), Inst. Fin. Edn., Calif. State U.-Fresno Alumni Assn. (past pres.). Roman Catholic. Home: 8630 E Herndon Clovis CA 93612 Office: Central Savings 1930 E Shields Fresno CA 93726

GOODACRE, GLENNA MAXEY, artist, sculptor; b. Lubbock, Tex., Aug. 28, 1939; d. Homer and Melba Maxey; B.A., Colo. Coll., 1961; postgrad. Art Students League, N.Y.C., 1967; m. Ronald William Goodacre, Sept. 9, 1961; children—Tim, Jill. Two-person show: Thomas Gilcrease Mus., Tulsa, 1982; group show: Peking, 1981. Recipient Gold medal Nat. Acad. Design, 1978; Silver medal Solon Borglum Exhbn., 1975; numerous awards Nat. Sculpture Soc. Fellow Nat. Sculpture Soc.; mem. Allied Artists Am., Nat. Acad. Western Art. Contbr. articles to art publs. Home: 313 Foxtail Ct Boulder CO 80303

GOODACRE, KENNETH ROBERT, real estate executive; b. San Antonio, Jan. 21, 1943; s. Robert Edward and Lorraine Allison G.; B.S., Ariz. State U., 1970; m. Cinda C. Poarch, Sept. 9, 1972; 1 stepson, Donald Ray Bouthillier. Asst. dir. property mgmt. O'Malley Investment Co., Phoenix, 1970; mgr. residential properties Del E. Webb Realty & Mgmt., Phoenix, 1970-76, gen. mgr. Dewguard div., 1974-76; pres., chief exec. officer, co-founder Camelback Mgmt. Co., Phoenix, 1976-82; v.p. Murdock Realty Services, Inc., 1982-83; pres., chief exec. officer Ventura Properties, Inc., 1982—. Mem. Ariz. Gov.'s Sports Council, 1978—; bd. dirs. Phoenix Symphony; mem. legal arbitration panel State Bar Ariz., 1979—. Served with AUS, 1966-68. Mem. Inst. Real Estate Mgmt. (cert. property mgr.), Phoenix Bd. Realtors, Am. Mgmt. Assn., Phoenix C. of C. Republican. Club: Guardian Angels Ariz. State U. Home: 5124 E Desert Park Ln Paradise Valley AZ 85253 Office: 2111 E Highland St Phoenix AZ 85016

GOODALE, SALLY MCCANN, Realtor; b. Alton, Ill., May 13, 1915; d. Irving Goff and Fannie LeRoy (Sands) McCann; B.A., Ariz. State U., 1973; m. Lawrence L. Larmore, July 16, 1937 (div. 1968); children—Antoinette, Lawrence L., Francis, Kathleen, Diana; m. 2d Tom Goodale, Dec. 1968 (div. 1976). Real estate saleswoman Harriet H. Neil, Real Estate, Palo Alto, Calif., 1945-55; realtor Robin Elverson, Houston, 1955-60; broker Sally Larmore Agency, Houston, 1960-70; owner-operator Sally Goodale, Realtor, Phoenix and Scottsdale, Ariz., 1970—; adv. Nat. Million Dollar Real Estate Club, pres. Nat. Women's Bd. Vice pres. nat. women's bd. Northwood Inst.; treas. Ariz. State U. Lyric Opera Theatre Guild. Cert. residential broker (C.R.B.); cert. residential specialist (C.R.S.). Mem. Internat. Real Estate Fedn. (dir.-chpt.), Scottsdale Bd. Realtors (chmn. polit. affairs com.), Scottsdale C. of C., Million Dollar Club, Farm and Land Brokers, Delta Zeta. Republican. Presbyterian. Home: 5925 E Calle Tuberia Phoenix AZ 85018 Office: 4419 N Scottsdalr Rd Scottsdale AZ 85251

GOODALL, JACKSON WALLACE, JR., restaurant executive; b. San Diego, Oct. 29, 1938; s. Jackson Wallace and Evelyn Violet (Koski) G.; B.S.I.M., San Diego State U., 1960; m. Mary E. Buckley, June 22, 1958; children—Kathy, Jeff, Suzy, Mindy. Ops. coordinator Foodmaker, Inc., San Diego, 1962-65, v.p. real estate, 1965-67, v.p. ops., 1967-70, pres., 1970-79, pres., chief exec. officer, 1979—; founder Grossmont Bank, La Mesa, Calif., 1972; dir. Grossmont Bank. Mem. Calif. State Bd. of Edn. Planning Commn., 1972-74; trustee San Diego State U., 1975-77; trustee San Diego Young Life Assn., 1972-79, nat. bd. dirs., 1975-79; bd. dirs. Metro YMCA; chmn. Easter Seals campaign, San Diego, 1982; co-chmn. Nat Bible Week, 1981; bd. dirs. Faith Chapel Ch., La Mesa, Youth for Christ, 1980—. Recipient distinguished alumni award, San Diego State U., 1975. Mem. Nat. Restaurant Assn., Am. Mgmt. Assn., San Diego C. of C. (dir. 1975-77), Sigma Alpha Epsilon. Republican. Club: Kadoo of N. Am. Office: Foodmaker Inc 9330 Balboa St San Diego CA 92041

GOODALL, LEONARD EDWIN, university president; b. Warrensburg, Mo., Mar. 16, 1937; s. Leonard Burton and Eula (Johnson) G.; B.A., Central Mo. State U., 1958; M.A., U. Mo., 1960; Ph.D. (Kendrick C. Babcock fellow), U. Ill., 1962; A.A. (hon., Schoolcraft Coll., 1977; m. Lois Marie Stubblefield, Aug. 16, 1959; children—Karia, Karen, Greg. Asst. prof. polit. sci., asst. dir. Bur. Govt. Research, Ariz. State U., Tempe, 1962-65, dir. Bur., 1965-67; asso. prof. polit. sci., asso. dean faculties U. Ill. at Chgo. Circle, 1968-69, vice chancellor, 1969-71; chancellor U. Mich., Dearborn, 1971-79; pres. U. Nev., Las Vegas, 1979—; cons. Ariz. Acad., Phoenix, 1964-67; dir. Peace Corps tng. program for Chile, 1965. Mem. univ. exec. com. United Fund, 1966-67; v.p. Met. Fund, Inc.; mem. Mich. Gov.'s Commn. Long Range Planning, 1973-75. Mem. Tempe Planning and Zoning Commn., 1965-67, New Detroit Com., 1972—; mem. Wayne County (Mich.) Planning Commn., 1973—, vice chmn., 1976-79. Served with AUS, 1959. Mem. Am. Polit. Sci. Assn., Am. Soc. Pub. Adminstrn., Western Govtl. Research Assn. (exec. council 1966-68), Dearborn C. of C. (dir. 1974-79), Phi Sigma Epsilon, Phi Kappa Phi. Club: Las Vegas Country. Author: The American Metropolis: Its Governments and Politics, 1968, rev. edit., 1975; Gearing Arizona's Communities to Orderly Growth, 1965; State Politics and Higher Education, 1976. Editor: Urban Politics in the Southwest, 1967. Office: Office of President U Nev Las Vegas NV 89154

GOODE, WILLIAM J., sociology educator; b. Houston, Aug. 30, 1917; s. William Josiah and Lilian Rosalie (Bare) G.; m. Mary Kannizzo, Dec. 22, 1937; m. Ruth Siegel, Nov. 10, 1950; children—Brian Erich, Barbara Nan Baldwin, Andrew Josiah. B.A. in Philosophy, U. Tex., 1938, M.A. in Philosophy, 1939; Ph.D. Sociology, Pa. State U., 1946. Instr. Pa. State U., 1941-43; asst. prof. Wayne State U., 1946-50; from research assoc. to prof. Columbia U., N.Y.C., 1952-77, Franklin H. Giddings prof. sociology, 1975-77; prof. sociology Stanford (Calif.) U., 1977—; vis. scholar Wolfson Coll., Oxford U., 1980; U.S. del. UN Conf. on Application Sci. and Tech. for Benefit Less Developed Areas, Geneva, 1961; UNESCO Internat. Seminar on Family, Yugoslvia, 1960, Tokyo, 1965, Paris, 1973, Belgium, 1982; mem. com. on scholarly communication with China, Nat. Acad. Arts and Scis. Served with USN, 1944-45. Guggenheim fellow, 1965-66, 83-84; NIMH sr. scientist career awardee, 1969-74; Fellow Nat. Acad. Arts and Scis.; mem. Am. Sociol. Assn. (past pres., MacIver prize 1965, Burgess award 1969), Eastern Sociol. Soc. (past pres.).

GOODELL, CAROL GUYTON, educational administrator, consultant; b. River Forest, Ill., Feb. 18, 1936; d. Robert Harmar and Margaret (Thomas) Guyton; m. William Dudley Goodell, Dec. 20, 1958; children—Douglas Sewall, Elizabeth Ormond. B.S., B.A., Ohio State U., 1958; M.A. in Ednl. Adminstrn., Stanford U., 1969, M.A. in Anthropology, 1974, Ph.D., 1979. Tchr., pub. schs., DeCoto, San Mateo, Hillsborough, Calif., 1958-67; pres. Real World Learning, Inc., San Carlos, Calif., 1968-72; co-ordinator Early Childhood Project, Mass. State Dept. Edn., Boston, 1977-79; dir. Nueva Learning Ctr., Hillsborough, Calif., 1979—. Quaker. Editor: The Changing Classroom, 1973, 75, 79.

GOODENOUGH, SAMUEL HENRY, biomedical engineer, consultant; b. Oakland, Calif., Sept. 8, 1919; s. Samuel Henry and Katherine Mary (Amet) G.; m. Frances Carolyn Johns, Oct. 12, 1940; 1 son, John S.; m. 2d, Kathleen Eula McIntyre, Sept. 15, 1961. Student U. Calif.-San Francisco, 1946-53. Registered engr., Ill., 1960. Sr. research engr. Cutter Lab., Berkeley, 1963-77; sr. project engr. Shiley Lab., Irvine, Calif., 1978-79; v.p. engring. Mitral Med. Internat., Inc., Irvine, 1979-82; biomed. engring. cons., 1982—. Mem. ASME, Assn. Advancement Med. Instrumentation, Soc. Mfg. Engrs. Democrat. Contbr. to profl. jours. Home and Office: 5040 Tierra Del Oro Carlsbad CA 92008

GOODER, HAROLD GLENN, design engineer; b. Fresno, Calif., Mar. 10, 1941; s. Paul Oliver and Helen Carrie (Hansen) G.; m. Janice Nadine Sommer, Aug. 19, 1961; children—Pamela Dawn, Laurie Dee, Paul Brian. A.A., Los Angeles Trade Tech. Coll., 1961. Design draftsman Mattel Inc., Hawthorne, Calif., 1962-63; designer spl. products group A.M.F., Santa Monica, Calif., 1963-69, design engr. tire equipment div., Santa Ana, Calif., 1969-71, sr. design engr. A.M.F. Voit Inc., Santa Ana, 1971—. Methodist. Clubs: Calif. Youth Soccer Assn., Masons. Home: 6881 Shannon Dr Huntington Beach CA 92647 Office: 3801 S Harbor St Santa Ana CA 92704

GOODFELLOW, JERRY FRANK, electronics engineer; b. Los Angeles, Feb. 18, 1939; s. Willard Frank and Lula (Bringhurst) G.; m. Lorraine Nellis Cross, Sept. 6, 1963; children—Craig Loren, Eric Frank, Paul Jerry, Jerit Devin. B.S.E.E., U. Nev., Las Vegas and Reno, 1970. Sr. draftsman Pan Am. World Airways, Inc., Jackass Flats, Nev., 1963-66; prodn. engr. Lynch Communications Systems Inc., Reno, 1970-73, systems test supr., 1973-76, applications engr., 1976-78, design engr., 1978-80, sr. systems engr., 1980—. Served with USN, 1958-62. Mem. Math. Assn. Am. Republican. Morman. Home: 3475 Kings Row Reno NV 89503 Office: 204 Edison Way Reno NV 89520

GOODHILL, VICTOR, otologist; b. Boston, Oct. 15, 1911; s. Morris L. and Molly (Cramer) G.; A.B., U. So. Calif., 1933, M.D., 1937; L.H.D. (honoris causa), U. Judaism, 1970, Jewish Theol. Sem. Am., 1970; m. Ruth Marcus, Dec. 6, 1936; children—Dean Kenneth, Barbara June. Intern, Cedars of Lebanon Hosp., Los Angeles, 1936-37; resident otolaryngology Children's Hosp., Los Angeles, 1937-38; now sr. attending otolaryngologist; ear research Washington U., St. Louis, 1938-39; practice medicine specializing in otology, Los Angeles, 1939—; prof. surgery (otology) UCLA; Joseph Toynbee Meml. lectr. Royal Coll. Surgeons (Eng.), 1976; Alumni lectr. in otology U. Oreg., 1976; chmn. bd. Hope for Hearing Research Found., UCLA; cons. otologist John Tracy Clinic. Chmn. bd. govs. U. Judaism; bd. overseers Jewish Theol. Sem. Am. Recipient Maimonides award of Wis., 1974. Fellow Am. Speech and Hearing Assn., Am. Laryngol. Rhinol., and Otol. Soc. (pres.

1970-71), Am. Otol. Soc. (pres. 1975-76, mem. council 1976), Am. Acoustical Soc., ACS (past gov.); mem. AAAS, Am. Acad. Ophthalmology and Otolaryngology (Wherry Meml. lectr. 1970), Am. Acad. Otolaryngology (pres. 1979), Los Angeles Acad. Medicine, Los Angeles Soc. Otolaryngology (past pres.), Pacific Coast Oto-Ophthal. Soc., Otosclerosis Study Group (past pres.), Société Française d'Oto-Laryngologie (fgn. corr.), Pan Am. Med. Assn., Oto-Rhino-Laryngol. Soc. Japan (hon.), Soc. Univ. Otolaryngologists, AMA (chmn. sect. on laryngology, rhinology and otology 1969, cons. on hearing loss Video Clinic), Otolaryngol. Soc. Australia (hon.), Phi Beta Kappa, Phi Kappa Phi, Alpha Omega Alpha. Author: Stapes Surgery for Otosclerosis, 1961; Ear Diseases, Deafness and Dizziness, 1979; (videotape) Beethoven: Triumph Over Silence, 1983; chpt. in Current Pediatric Therapy, 1968, Handbook of Trends in Diseases of the Ear, Nose and Throat, 1972, Otolaryngology Looseleaf Series, 1973, Human Communication and It's Disorders of the Nervous System, 1976; contbr. to sci. publs. Editorial bd. Annals. Otology, Rhinology and Laryngology. Office: 469 N Roxbury Dr Beverly Hills CA 90210

GOODHUE, NEIL BRUCE, real estate exec.; b. Oakland, Calif., June 7, 1954; s. Neil Ostrander and Mary Lee (Herd) G.; student Calif. State U., 1972-73; St. Mary's Coll., 1974; B.S., Lone Mountain Coll., 1975; m. Diane, Sept. 7, 1980. Properties mgr. Nat. Mgmt. Corp., Lafayette, Calif., 1972-73; pres. Bonanza Bldg., Inc., Lafayette, 1972-74; pres., pub. Claremont Press, Inc. (Calif.), 1971-74; pres. NBG Enterprises, Inc., Oakland, 1974-77; v.p. 1200 Lakeshore Inc., Oakland, 1976—; gen. partner Laketowers, 1979—; dir. Hill Castle Properties. Res. police officer City of Oakland, 1975-78; dir. Lafayette Youth Adult Council, Inc., 1971-73; mem. Oakland Mayor's task force on condominium conversion, 1979, rent control conditions, 1980; mem. Alameda County Commn. on Drug Abuse. Recipient award of merit No. Calif. Industry-Edn. Council, 1973, advt. award Future Bus. Leaders Am., 1973; accredited real estate mgr. Inst. Real Estate Mgmt. Mem. Bldg. Owners and Mgrs. Assn., Oakland C. of C., Oakland Mus. Assn. Democrat. Congregationalist. Clubs: Athenian-Nile, Commonwealth of Calif., San Francisco Press, Wash. Athletic, Oakland Athletic, Oakland Optimist, Highlands Country. Home: 170 Sandringham Rd Piedmont CA 94611 Office: 1200 Lakeshore Ave Oakland CA 94606

GOODIN, MAURICE E., petroleum consultant; b. Louisville, Sept. 30, 1913; s. Edward C. and Bertha (Vorhies) G.; student U. Colo., 1932-34; m. Shirlee Anderson, July 12, 1947; children—Phillip, Michael, Carl. With Petroleum Info. Corp., Denver, 1946—, pres., 1946-75, chmn. bd., 1975—, chmn. emeritus, 1978-80; chmn. bd. Petroleum Info. Exchange, Calgary, Alta., Can.; petroleum cons., 1982—. Commr. Denver Centennial Authority, 1957-59, Colo. Centennial Authority, 1958-59. Served to capt. USAAF, 1941-46. Mem. Rocky Mountain Oil and Gas Assn. (dir. 1949—), Am. Landmens Assn., Am. Petroleum Inst., Ind. Petroleum Assn. Am., Denver C. of C., (dir. 1958-61), Colo. Petroleum Council (dir. 1959—), Colo. Pioneer Oil Men. Clubs: Denver Cherry Hills Country (dir. 1959-62), Denver, Garden of Gods, Petroleum (pres. 1948, 55), Denver Athletic (Denver). Home: 3165 Floyd Dr Denver CO 80210 Office: Petro Inf Corp PO Box 2612 Denver CO 80201

GOODIN, WILLIAM CHARLES, publishing company executive; b. Louisville, Sept. 18, 1917; s. Edward C. and Bertha G. (Vorhies) G.; m. Emily E., Sept. 8, 1946; children—Sue Ellen, Charles W. B.A., U. Colo., 1941. Chmn. bd., chief exec. officer Petroleum Info. Corp. subs. A.C. Nielsen Co., Denver, 1946—. Past mem. Colo. Oil and Gas Conservation Comn.; bd. dirs. Swedish Med. Ctr. Found., U. Colo. Found. Served to 1st lt. U.S. Army, 1942-46. Recipient Betty McWhorter award, 1979. Mem. Rocky Mountain Oil and Gas Assn. (bd. dirs.), Denver Landmen Assn., Rocky Mountain Assn. Geologists, Soc. Petroleum Engrs. of AIME, Am. Assn. Petroleum Geologists, Rocky Mountain Petroleum Pioneers, Assn. Petroleum Writers, Denver Petroleum Club (past pres.). Presbyterian. Clubs: Denver Athletic, Cherry Hills Country, Children of God, Metropolitan, 25-Year Club of Petroleum Industry. Home: 11 Parkway Dr Englewood CO 80110 Office: 4100 E Dry Creek Rd Littleton CO 80122

GOODIN, WILLIAM REX, computer applications engineer; b. Bronxville, N.Y., 1947.; s. Rex Eugene and Rose Catherine (Buhlmann) G. B.A. in Math., San Jose State U., 1969; M.S. in Computer Sci., UCLA, 1971, Ph.D. in Engring., 1975, M.E. in Engring. Mgmt., 1982. Computer programmer System Devel. Corp., Santa Monica, Calif., 1969-71; teaching asst. Sch. Engring., UCLA, 1971-75; research fellow Environ. Quality Lab., Calif Inst. Tech., 1975-78; asst. dir. research and devel. Dames & Moore, Los Angeles, 1978-82; sr. staff engr. Radar Systems Group, Hughes Aircraft Co., Culver City, Calif., 1982—; cons. air pollution. Mem. Am. Meterol. Soc. (cert. 1982), Assn. Computing Machinery, Spl. Interest Group in Computer Graphics. Contbr. articles to profl. jours.

GOODKIN, SANFORD RONALD, real estate analyst; b. Passaic, N.J., Feb. 8, 1929; s. Robert and Lillian (Ellman) G. Pres., chmn. bd. The Goodkin Group, Sanford R. Goodkin Research Corp., Goodkin/Cowan, Inc., Goodwin/Criterion, Inc., Del Mar, Calif. and Santa Fe, 1957—; pub., writer The Goodkin Report, also real estate editor Calif. Bus. Mag.; contbg. editor, columnist writer column Real Estate Dynamics in Profl. Builder Mag.; syndicated columnist Winning in Real Estate 30 newspapers; cons. to industry; author Web Apt. Reporter; dir. Landmark Fin., Harvest Savs. and Loan; condr. realestate seminars; lectr. colls. and univs.; sr. fellow Hubert Humphrey Sch. Social Ecology, Ben Gurion U., Israel. Mem. San Diego County Housing Adv. Com.; founder, bd. govs. Ben-Gurion U., Negev, Israel; exec. bd. and internat. adv. bd. World Congress of Engrs. and Architects. Recipient Medal of Valor, State Israel, 1975, Max C. Tipton Meml. award for mktg. excellence, 1974; named one of West's most disting. citizens Sunset Mag., 1973. Mem. Urban Land Inst. (mem. council), Nat. Assn. Homebuilders (trustee sales and mktg. council), Inst. Residential Mktg. (trustee), Lambda Alpha. Author: The Goodkin Guide to Winning in Real Estate, 1977. Address: 1201 Camino Del Mar Del Mar CA 92014

GOODLEY, PAUL HARVEY, physician; b. Bklyn., Feb. 6, 1932; s. Israel Harry and Ruth (Reiter) G.; B.A. cum laude, U. So. Calif., 1955; M.D., U. Calif. at Los Angeles, 1959; m. Dolores Henrietta Ledfors, Apr. 2, 1955; children—Mark David, Pamela Susan, Diane Deborah, Caryn Lynn, Lisa Louise. Intern, Harbor Gen. Hosp., Torrance, Calif., 1959-60; gen. practice indsl. medicine, Torrance, 1960, Wilmington, Calif., 1961-72; resident phys. medicine and rehab. U. So. Calif.-Los Angeles County Med. Center, 1972-73, U. Calif. at Davis, 1974; practice medicine, specializing in phys. medicine and rehab., Los Angeles, 1975—; med. dir. rehab. center Glendale (Calif.) Adventist Med. Center, 1975-76; med. cons. orthopedic medicine U.S. VA, 1981-83; founder Pain Diagnostics and Rehab. Inst., Los Angeles, 1977, adj. prof. orthopedic medicine Coll. Osteo. Medicine of Pacific. Exam. physician Los Angeles County Sheriff's Dept., 1962-79; mem. Founders Club, Music Center Performing Arts. Recipient award of valor Los Angeles County Sheriffs' Dept., 1968. Diplomate Am. Bd. Phys. Medicine and Rehab., Am. Bd. Family Practice. Mem. AMA, Los Angeles County Med. Assn., Am. Assn. Electromyography and Electrodiagnosis, Am. Acad. Phys. Med. and Rehab. (chmn. com. musculoskeletal medicine), Internat. Rehab. Medicine Assn. (chmn. orthopedic medicine com.), Am. Congress Rehab. Medicine, Am. Assn. Orthopedic Medicine (co-founder, 1st pres.), Soc. Orthopedic Medicine, Internat. Assn. for Study of Pain, Am. Pain Soc., Am. Thermographic Soc., Nat. Rifle Assn. (life master; Gold medal Calif. Championships 1968), Phi Delta Epsilon. Inventor: Goodly polyaxial cervical traction system; co-inventor Goodley/Shemet lumbar lift. Home: 39 Strawberry Ln Rolling Hills Estates CA 90274 Office: Medical Square 2210 W 3d St Los Angeles CA 90057

GOODMAN, ARDEN PATRICIA, chemist, medical optical device company executive; b. N.Y.C., Aug. 16, 1949; d. Sheldon Stuart and Elizabeth Lillian (Weiss) Goodman; m. Joseph Theodore Gacsi, Dec. 26, 1976; children—Ted, Vickie. B.S. in Chemistry and Life Scis., U. Ill., 1971. Chemist, Ferro Corp., Huntington Beach, Calif., 1971-72, Beckman Instruments, Fullerton, Calif., 1972-73; research chemist Edwards Labs, div. AHSC, Irvine, Calif., 1974-80, mgr, quality assurance Am. Med. Optics div., 1980-81, mgr. quality assurance 1981—. Mem. Am. Soc. Quality Control, Am. Chem. Soc., Am. Horse Show Assn., Internat. Arabian Horse Assn. Contbr. articles on biochemistry and med. research to profl. jours. Office: 1402 E Alton Ave Irvine CA 92714

GOODMAN, GARY MICHAEL, statistician; b. Scotts Bluff, Neb., Feb. 20, 1945; s. Michael Thomas and Sybil Pauline (Bailey) G.; m. Nelda Jean Morris, June 7, 1969; 1 son, Gary Tyler. B.S., U. Wyo., 1972, M.B.A., 1982. Statistician, Crop & Livestock Reporting Service, U.S. Dept. Agr., Cheyenne, Wyo., 1972-73; plant operator Wycon Chem. Co., Cheyenne, 1973—. Cubscout leader Boy Scouts Am. Served with USN, 1963-67. Mem. Am. Statis. Assn. Mem. Congregational Ch. Office: PO Box 1287 Cheyenne WY 82003

GOODMAN, JOEL HARRY, JR., university administrator; b. Seattle, Apr. 18, 1944; s. Joel H. and Edith (Kullmann) G.; m. Barbara Guzofsky, May 8, 1976. B.A. with distinction, Stanford U., 1966; M.A.T., Harvard U., 1967; M.A., Stanford U., 1972, M.A., 1974; postgrad. U. Chgo., 1975-76. Asst. dir. admissions Stanford U., Palo Alto, Calif., 1972-74; mktg. services mgr. Bell & Howell Edn. Group, Chgo., 1974-80; dir. planning and devel. Western State U., Fullerton, Calif., 1980-83, dean of admissions, 1983—. Office: 1111 N State Coll Blvd Fullerton CA 92631

GOODMAN, JOHN KESTNER, investment company executive, rancher; b. Kansas City, Mo., Aug. 1, 1920; s. Barney and Sophia (Kestner) G.; m. Beatrice Gardiner Prescott, Apr. 1, 1948 (div. 1958); 1 dau., Lucy Prescott; m. 2d, Aline Lees Bragg, Aug. 6, 1966; 1 son, John K. II. Student U. of Pa., 1938-40; B.A. summa cum laude, Yale U., 1942. Owner, operator, H Bar A Ranch, Mammoth, Ariz., 1944-46; dir. Goodman Properties, Tucson, 1946—; ptnr. Ashton Goodman Properties, Tucson, 1948—; ptnr. Kittle, Goodman Hook Bar Ranch, Show Low, Ariz., 1955-66; founding dir. Catalina Savings and Loan Co., Tucson 1959-82; owner, dir. ranch, Australia, 1970—. Bd. dirs., Tucson Mus. of Art, 1968-83; pres. Friends of Western Art, 1982; mem. Ariz. Racing Commn, 1965—, chmn., 1982-83. Served with U.S. Army, 1942-43. Recipient Wrangler award, Best Western Art Book, Cowboy Hall of Fame, 1978. Mem. Nat. Assn. State Racing Commrs. (pres. 1979, exec. bd. mem. 1980—), U.S. Polo Assn. (del.), United Polo Assn. (gov.). Clubs: Mountain Oyster, Tucson Country, Los Charros del Desierto (Tucson); Jockey, Yale (N.Y.C.), Rancheros Visitadores (Santa Barbara, Calif.), Rolls Royce Owners (Mechanicsville, Pa.). Author: Ross Stefan-An Impressionistic Painter of the Southwest, 1977. Office: 283 N Stone Ave Tucson AZ 85701

GOODMAN, JOSEPH LEE, music industry executive; b. Los Angeles, Apr. 24, 1954; s. Ralph A. and Natalie Belle Goodman. B.A. in Polit. Sci., U. Hawaii, 1976, B.A. in Music, 1976. Owner, Goodman Music, North Hollywood, Calif., 1977—; promoter Profl. Keyboard Product Show. Active ACLU, Variety Clubs. Club: Lions. Office: 5311 Lankershim Blvd North Hollywood CA 91601

GOODMAN, MAXINE RUTH, newspaper publisher; b. Cambridge, Mass., Apr. 3, 1945; d. Herman and Shirley (Kneller) G.; B.A., U. Ariz., 1968. Tchr., Lake Hovasu Elem. Sch. (Ariz.), 1969-71; edn./art editor Scottsdale (Ariz.) Daily Progress, 1971-73; gen. assignment reporter Schenectady Gazette, 1973-75; free-lance journalist N.Y. Daily News, Christian Sci. Monitor, Travel/Holiday mag., Income Opportunities, Leisure, Ski, House Beautiful, 1975-79; co-pub., founder El Observador, San Jose, Calif., 1980—. Pres.' adv. trustee Santa Clara County Council Girl Scouts U.S., 1981-82; student affirmative action adv. bd. San Jose State U., 1983. Named Outstanding New Bus., Mexican-Am. C. of C., 1981. Mem. Mexican-Am. C. of C., Western Pubs. Assn., San Jose C. of C., Sigma Delta Chi. Office: 401 E Taylor St San Jose CA 95112

GOODMAN, SEYMOUR EVAN, computer science educator, researcher, consultant; b. Chgo., June 19, 1943; s. Paul S. and Shirley (Young) G.; m. Diane Margot Samuel, Dec. 18, 1966; children—Richard Michael, Steven Neal. B.S., Columbia U., 1965, M.S., 1966; Ph.D., Calif. Inst. Tech., 1970. Asst. prof. applied math. U. Va., Charlottesville, 1970-75, assoc. prof., 1975-81; vis. prof. applied math. and computer sci., Princeton (N.J.) U., 1977-79, research fellow, 1978-79; vis. scholar U. Chgo., 1979; prof. mgmt. info. systems U. Ariz., Tucson, 1981—; mem. adv. com. Internat. Trade Adminstrn., Dept. Commerce, 1979—; mem. adv. com. Def. Sci. Bd., Dept. Def., 1981—, Def. Intelligence Agy., 1983—; cons. govtl. agys. Danforth Assoc., 1977-82; Sesquicentennial Assoc. State of Va., 1977; NSF grantee, 1978-79, 83; numerous grant and research contracts Office Tech. Assessment, U.S. Congress, 1979-81, Los Alamos Nat. Lab., U.S. Air Force, Battelle Meml. Labs., IBM, Nat. Council for Soviet and East European Research. Mem. Assn. for Computing Machinery (nat. lectr. 1981-82, com. computing and pub. policy 1981-83), Am. Assn. for Advancement Slavic Studies, IEEE. Contbr. numerous articles to profl. jours. Office: Univ of Arizona MIS BPA Tucson AZ 85721

GOODMAN, STEVEN MARK, advertising executive; b. Bronx, N.Y., June 21, 1941; s. Al and Rose G.; m. Rachel Lancry, Apr. 15, 1978; 1 son, Harold. B.B.A. in Advt., CUNY, 1963, M.B.A. in Mktg. Mgmt., 1970. Product mgr. Union Carbide Corp., N.Y.C., 1964-68; sales promotion dir. Ketchum, MacLeod & Grove, N.Y.C., 1968-72; v.p., account supr. Ayer, Jorgensen & MacDonald, Los Angeles, 1972-77; sr. v.p. Molnar & Assocs., Los Angeles, 1977-82; pres., chief operating officer HSR Advt. & Mktg., Inc., Los Angeles, 1982—. Served with USAR, 1963-69. Mem. Advt. Club, Bus. and Profl. Advt. Assn., Sales and Mktg. Execs. Assn., Milline Club, Illuminators, So. Calif. Deli Council, Food Industry Sales Mgrs. Club. Home: 5545 Whitsett Ave Apt 5 North Hollywood CA 91607 Office: 15910 Ventura Blvd Suite 800 Encino CA 91436

GOODOVER, PAT MICHAEL, state senator; b. Sheridan, Wyo., Oct. 17, 1916; s. George and Anna (Barna) G.; grad. Radio-TV Inst., Kansas City, 1937; m. Erma Louise Nelson, June 30, 1941; children—Pat M., Joyann, Barbara Lynn. Radio announcer, engr. Sta. KGNF, North Platte, Nebr., 1937-38, Sta. KGIR, Butte, Mont., 1938-39; mgr. Sta. KRBM, 1939-40; asst. mgr. Sta. KGIR, 1940-41; radio cons., 1946-47; part owner, mgr. Sta. KXLL, Missoula, Mont., 1948-58; owner, mgr. Sta. KARR-KOPR-FM, Great Falls, Mont., 1958-73; cons. Sta. KARR, 1973-76; real estate broker, 1963—; mem. Mont. Senate, 1974—. Bd. dirs. Mont. Easter Seal Soc., 1973-76; vice chmn. Great Falls Internat. Airport Authority, 1973-75. Served with USAAF, 1942-46. Recipient Bronze star (3), Air Medal with clusters; named Outstanding Freshman Republican Senator, UPI, 1975. Mem. Outdoor Writers Assn. Mont. Broadcasters Assn. (past pres.). Republican. Presbyterian. Clubs: Lions (past pres.), Advt. Club of Great Falls (past pres.), Press Club of Missoula (past pres.), Bus. Builders (past pres.), Elks, Masons, Shriners, Royal Order Jesters.

GOODSON, GREGORY LESTER, state ofcl.; b. Tucson, Aug. 4, 1932; s. Samuel Lester and Mary Agnes (Mathiesen) G.; diploma police adminstrn. Northwestern U., 1965; B.S., Ariz. State U., 1971; children—Mary Katherine, Lisa Ann, Vikki Jeanette, Michael Robert. With Ariz. Hwy. Patrol, 1955—, adminstrv. asst. to chief, 1978-80, maj. Phoenix div. comdr., 1980—; chmn. traffic law enforcement com. Transp. Research Bd., Nat. Acad. Scis., 1970-76; instr. field div. Traffic Inst., Northwestern U., 1972—; mem. tech. asv. com. Ariz. Legis. Council Distbn. Hwy. User Revenues, 1974-76; cons. Inst. Police Traffic Mgmt., U. North Fla., 1980—. Pres., Cypress Gardens III Homeowners Assn., 1983—. Served with USNR, 1953-55; Korea. Dept. Justice fellow, 1970-71; grantee Automotive Safety Found., 1964-65. Mem. Internat. Assn. Chiefs of Police, Traffic Inst. Alumni Assn., Ariz. Adminstrs. Assn., Associated Hwy. Patrolmen Ariz., Fraternal Order Police, Ariz. Hist. Soc., Aircraft Owners and Pilots Assn., Nature Conservancy, Sierra Club. Democrat. Roman Catholic. Home: 3646 N 69th Ave Unit 21 Phoenix AZ 85033 Office: PO Box 6638 Phoenix AZ 85005

GOODSTEIN, LEONARD D(AVID), psychologist; b. N.Y.C., Jan. 11, 1927; s. Moses and Stella (Warshar) G.; m. Ruth Cecile Finhorn, Dec. 18, 1948; m. 2d., Jeanette Treat, Aug. 28, 1972; children—Richard Edward, Steven Michael. B.S. cum laude, CCNY, 1948; M.A., Columbia U., 1948, Ph.D., 1952. Lic. psychologist Calif.; diplomate in clin. psychology Am. Bd. Profl. Psychologists. Began as instr., advanced to prof. U. Iowa, Iowa City, 1951-64; prof. psychology U. Cin., 1964-74; prof. chmn. dept. psychology Ariz. State U., Tempe, 1974-80; pres. Univ. Assocs., Univ. Assocs. Grad. Sch., San Diego, 1980-83, chmn. bd. dirs., 1984—; cons., lectr. in field. Pres. bd. dirs. Codama, Phoenix, 1978-80. Fellow Am. Psychol. Assn., Internat. Assn. Applied Psychology; life mem. Am. Personnel Guidance Assn.; mem. Am. Soc. Tng. and Devel. Author: Consulting with Human Service Systems, 1978; Adjustment, Behavior and Personality (2d edition), 1979; Trends and Issues in OD, 1979; Understanding Abnormal Behavior, 1982; The 1982 Annual for Facilitators, Trainers and Consultants; Personality Assessment, 1982. Home: 16134 Ladera Pieda Poway CA 92064 Office: 8517 Production Ave San Diego CA 92121

GOODWILL, SIDNEY, retail apparel company executive; b. Montreal, Que., Can., Jan. 3, 1930; s. Harry and Helen Gutwillig; student public schs.; m. Lois Anne Goldstein, Apr. 2, 1956; children—Jonathan, Eric, Lisa, Gilbert. Buyer/mgr. Morrie Gold Inc., Montreal, 1950-57; pres. Surrey Shops Ltd., Montreal, 1957-72; exec. v.p. Holt, Renfrew & Co. Ltd., Montreal, 1972-79; pres./owner Bullock & Jones Inc., San Francisco, 1979—. Office: Bullock & Jones Inc 340 Post St San Francisco CA 94108

GOODWIN, CAROLYN CAMPER, public relations executive, consultant; b. Toledo, May 20, 1939; d. Earl Frederick and Edith Roberta (Bruehlman) Camper; 1 dau., Joan Helen. B.S. Bowling Green State U., 1961; postgrad. Baldwin-Wallace Coll., 1962-64, Ariz. State U., 1974-76; M.A., Kent State U., 1968. Tchr. English, Bay Village (Ohio) Schs., 1963-68, Maricopa County Community Coll., Phoenix, 1973-78; instr. English, Lorain County Community Coll., Elyria, Ohio, 1969-73; pub. info. dir. Am. Cancer Soc., Phoenix, 1979-81; pub. relations dir. Planned Parenthood of Central and No. Ariz., Phoenix, 1981—; cons. in field. Mem. Paradise Valley Bd. Edn., 1976-80. Mem. Pub. Relations Soc. Am., Women in Communications, Paradise Valley C. of C. Democrat. Unitarian. Office: Planned Parenthood Central and No Ariz 1301 S 7th Ave Phoenix AZ 85007

GOODWIN, FELIX LEE, retired educational administrator, former army officer; b. Lawrence, Kans., Nov. 24, 1919; s. Felix and Lucille Marie (Lee) G.; m. Esther Brown, Nov. 1, 1941; children—Cheryl Washington, Sylvia, Judith Barnes. B.S., U. Md., 1958; M.Pub. Adminstrn., U. Ariz., 1965; Ed.S., U. Ariz., 1974, Ed.D., 1979. Enlisted in U.S. Army, 1939, advanced through grades to lt. col., 1963; ret., 1969; asst. prof. army mil. sci. dept. U. Ariz., Tucson, 1968-69, asst. to pres., 1969-83. Chmn., Pima County Merit System Commn., 1977-82, Pima County Law Enforcement Merit Council, 1973-82; mem. Ariz. Bicentennial Commn., 1974-77, chmn., 1976-77. Decorated Legion of Merit, Army Commendation medal with oak leaf cluster; recipient cert. of Appreciation, City of Tucson, 1967, Pima County (Ariz.), 1975; Man of Yr. award Una Noche Plateada, Tucson, 1976; Leadership award Tucson Urban League, 1975; cert. of award IRS, 1981; others. Mem. Nat. Alliance Black Sch. Educators (life), NEA, Soc. Ethnic and Spl. Studies, Assn. U.S. Army, NAACP (life), Am. Legion, DAV, Nat. Rifle Assn., Phi Delta Kappa, Alpha Phi Alpha, Pi Lambda Theta, Alpha Delta Delta, Beta Gamma Sigma. Roman Catholic. Club: Kiwanis.

GOODWIN, FRANK EUGENE, physicist, communication systems executive; b. Hastings, Nebr., Sept. 7, 1927; s. Frank E. and Margaret M. (Kealy) G.; A.B. in Physics, UCLA, 1956, M.S., 1957; m. Gayle Marie Ferguson, Aug. 14, 1949; children—Glenda Clyde, Teresa Frances, Neal K. Mem. tech. staff Hughes Research Labs., Malibu, Calif., 1957-61, sr. staff engr., 1962-68, asst. mgr. quantum electronics dept., 1968-74, mgr. advanced systems dept., El Segundo, Calif., 1974-83; chief scientist TRW, Redondo Beach, Calif., 1983—. Pres., Sunset Mesa Home Owners Assn., 1965-66. Served with U.S. Army, 1953-55; Korea. Mem. IEEE, Am. Phys. Soc., Optical Soc. Am. Contbr. articles on microwave theory and techniques to profl. jours.; patentee electronic devices. Home: 13000 Mindanao Way Marina Del Rey CA 90291 Office: PO Box 902 Los Angeles CA 90245

GOODWIN, GLENN ALBERT, sociologist, educator; b. Buffalo, N.Y., Apr. 10, 1939; s. Ralph D. and Ruth D. (Zeaska) G.; B.A., SUNY, Buffalo, 1964; Ph.D. (NDEA Fellow), Tulane U., 1972. Instr. dept. sociology Tulane U., New Orleans, 1964-67; asst. prof. sociology Wayne State U., Detroit, 1967-69; vis. prof. sociology U. Bath (Eng.), 1974; vis. asso. prof. sociology Am. U. in Cairo, 1974-76, acting chmn. dept. sociology, 1976, vice-chmn. faculty, 1975-76; adj. prof. sociology U. Calif., San Francisco, 1979; prof. sociology Pitzer Coll., Claremont, Calif., 1969—. Named Most Outstanding Tchr. Dept. Sociology, Am. U. in Cairo, 1975-76. Mem. Am. Sociol. Assn., Pacific Sociol. Assn., Soc. Study of Social Problems. Contbr. articles on sociol. problems and theory to profl. jours.; contbr. revs. to sociol. publs. Home: 1425 Mural Dr Claremont CA 91711 Office: Pitzer College 1050 N Mills Ave Claremont CA 91711

GOODWIN, JOAN (NAOMI WISE), film critic; b. N.Y.C., Oct. 25, 1943; d. Sam and Rose (DeMars) Golomb; m. Michael B. Goodwin, June 30, 1963. B.A., U. of Mich., 1963; postgrad. Columbia U., 1963-64. Film critic San Francisco mag., 1981—; film critic, contbg. editor East Bay Express, Berkeley, Calif., 1978-82; sr. supr. San Francisco Dept. of Social Services, 1976, 82; asst. editor Assn. for Aid of Crippled Children, N.Y.C., 1966-68; assoc. editor ByLine Pub. Co., N.Y.C., 1965-66; guest lectr. San Francisco State U.; instr. City Coll. San Francisco. Judge, Palo Alto Film Festival, 1982, Northwestern Region Student Acad. Awards, 1981. Mem. ACLU, NOW, Nat. Abortion Rights Action League, Calif. Abortion Rights Action League, Friends of Family Planning, Gardens for All. Contbr. articles to San Francisco Mag., East Bay Express, Berkeley Monthly, Washington Post, Film Quar., Take One, KQED Focus, Rolling Stone and others.

GOODWIN, JOHN ROBERT, lawyer, educator; b. Morgantown, W.Va., Nov. 3, 1929; s. John Emory and Ruby Iona G.; m. Betty Lou Wilson, June 2, 1952; children—John R., Elizabeth Ann Paugh, Mark Edward, Luke Jackson, Matthew Emory. B.S., W.Va. U., 1952, J.D.,

1964. Bar: W.Va., U.S. Supreme Ct. Formerly city atty., county commr., spl. pros. atty., Morgantown; prof. bus. law W.Va. U.; now prof. hotel and casino law U. Nev., Las Vegas. Served with U.S. Army; Korea. Recipient Bancroft-Whitney award in Constl. Law. Democrat. Author: Twenty Feet From Glory; Business Law, 3d edit.; High Points of Legal History; Travel and Lodging Law; Desert Adventure; editor Hotel and Casino Letter; past editor Bus. Law Rev., Bus. Law Letter. Home: 241 Sands Ave Apt 201B Las Vegas NV 89109 Office: Beam Hall U Nev Las Vegas NV 89109

GOODWIN, MARTIN BRUNE, radiologist; b. Vancouver, B.C., Can., Aug. 8, 1921; came to U.S., 1948, naturalized, 1953; s. Ray Star and Emma Augusta (Brune) G.; B.S. in Agr., U. B.C., 1943; M.D., C.M., McGill U., Montreal, Que., 1948; m. Cathy Dennison, Mar. 7, 1980; children—Nancijane, Suzanne. Intern, Scott and White Hosp., Temple, Tex., 1948-49; resident Scott and White Clinic, Temple, 1949-52; instr. radiology U. Tex., 1952; practice medicine specializing in radiology, Clovis, N.Mex., 1955-75, 79—, pres. Med. Radiologists, Clovis, 1969—; chief radiology Clovis High Plains Hosp., 1979—, Roosevelt Gen. Hosp., Portales, N.Mex., 1955—; clin. prof. health Western Mich. U., 1976-77; clin. prof. medicine Eastern N.Mex. U., 1975-76. Chmn., bd. dirs. N.Mex. Health and Social Services Bd. Served to capt. M.C., U.S. Army, 1953-55; to col. M.C., USAF, 1975-79. Fellow Am. Coll. Radiology, AAAS; mem. N.Mex. Radiol. Soc., N.Mex. Thoracic Soc., Radiol. Soc. N.Am., Soc. Nuclear Medicine, Am. Coll. Nuclear Physicians, Am. Coll. Chest Physicians. Republican. Presbyterian. Clubs: Elks, Lions, Masons, Shriners. Home: 1121 Pile St Clovis NM 88101 Office: 1001 Pile St Clovis NM 88101

GOODWIN, SANDRA JEANETTE, business educator, employment services company executive; b. Dallas, Oct. 16, 1949; d. James Winford and Bertha May (Robinson) Goodwin; m. Lee Alton McCaslin, May 26, 1979. B.S., U. Nev.-Las Vegas, 1976, M.Ed., 1979. Sr. sec. Reynolds Elec. & Engring. Co. Inc., Las Vegas, Nev., 1969-73; legal sec. City Atty.'s Office, Las Vegas, 1973; sec. City of Las Vegas Met. Police Dept., 1973-74; instr. office adminstrn. and automation Clark County Community Coll., North Las Vegas, Nev., 1975—, coordinator bus. div., 1980-81, coordinator communications and arts div., 1981-82; owner, gen. mgr. Ace Word Processing and Employment Services, Las Vegas, 1981—; advisor Word Processing Assn.; mem. State of Nev. Personnel Oral Bd. Vol. Am. Cancer Soc. Recipient Faculty Excellence award Clark County Community Coll., 1983. Mem. Assn. Info Systems Profls., Nat. Bus. Educators Assn., Am. Vocat. Assn. Baptist. Home: 4510 E Cincinnati Ave Las Vegas NV 89104 Office: 3200 E Cheyenne Ave North Las Vegas NV 89030

GOODWIN, WILLIAM CHARLES, publisher; b. Louisville, Sept. 18, 1917; s. Edward C. and Bertha (Vorhies) G.; m. Emily E. Percefull, Sept. 8, 1946; children—Sue Ellen, Charles W. B.A., U. Colo., 1941. Pres. Petroleum Info. Corp. subs. A.C. Nielsen Co., Littleton, Colo., from 1946, now, chmn., chief exec. officer, also dir. parent co. Past mem. Colo. Oil and Gas Conservation Commn. Served to 2d lt., M.I., USAAF, 1942-44; to 1st lt., CIC, AUS, 1944-46. Recipient Betty McWhorter award, 1979. Mem. Rocky Mountain Oil and Gas Assn. (dir.), Denver Landmens Assn., Rocky Mountain Assn. Geologists, Soc. Petroleum Engrs. of AIME, Am. Assn. Petroleum Geologist, Rocky Mountain Petroleum Pioneers, Assn. Petroleum Writers. Presbyterian. Clubs: Denver Petroleum (past pres.), Denver Athletic, Cherry Hills Country (Denver); Garden of Gods (Colorado Springs, Colo.). Home: 11 Parkway Dr Englewood CO 80110 Office: 4100 E Dry Creek Rd Littleton CO 80122

GOOKIN, WILLIAM SCUDDER, engring. co. exec., hydrologist; b. Atlanta, Sept. 8, 1914; s. William Cleveland and Susie (Jaudon) G.; B.S., Pa. State U., 1937; m. Mildred Miriam Hartman, Sept. 4, 1937; children—William Scudder, Thomas Allen Jaudon. Engr., U.S. Geol. Survey, 1937-38, City of Tucson, 1938-39, Allison Steel Mfg. Co., 1939-40, U.S. Bur. Reclamation, 1940-53; dist. engr. San Carlos Irrigation and Drainage Dist., Coolidge, Ariz., 1953-58; chief engr. Ariz. Interstate Stream Commn., Phoenix, 1956-62; adminstr. Ariz. Power Authority, Phoenix, 1958-60; State water engr., Phoenix, 1962-68; pres. W.S. Gookin & Assocs., Cons. Engrs. Scottsdale, Ariz., 1968—; mem., sec. Ariz. Bd. Tech. Registration, 1979-82. Democratic precinct committeeman, 1977—, Dem. state committeeman, 1978—; packmaster Cub Scouts Am., 1949-53, asst. scoutmaster Boy Scouts Am., 1953-56. Mem. ASCE, Nat. Soc. Profl. Engrs., Ariz. Planners Assn., Ariz. Soc. Civil Engrs., Ariz. Soc. Profl. Engrs., Am. Congress Mapping and Surveying, Culver Legion of Honor, Chi Epsilon, Delta Tau Delta. Democrat. Episcopalian. Clubs: Masons (32 deg.), Shriners, Order Eastern Star. Home: 9 Casa Blanca Estates Scottsdale AZ 85253 Office: WS Gookin & Assos 4203 N Brown Ave Scottsdale AZ 85251

GOOKIN, WILLIAM SCUDDER, JR., cons. engr.; b. Phoenix, July 23, 1942; s. William Scudder and Mildred Mirriam (Hartman) G.; B.S., Ariz. State U., 1964, B.S.E., 1970; m. Victoria Martin Browne, June 10, 1965; children—William Browne, Edward Allen. With W.S. Gookin & Assos., Scottsdale, Ariz., 1965—, v.p., 1968—, also dir.; sec. Quadrangle Electro-Magnetics, Inc., 1982—. Vice pres. Scottsdale Boys Club Dad's Club, 1974; Democratic precinct and state committeeman, 1976; dist. chmn. Dem. Party, 1980; pres. Scottsdale Dem. Luncheon Club, 1980; lt. Maricopa County Sheriff's Adj. Posse, 1981—. Registered profl. engr., Ariz., Colo., N.Mex., Calif., Oreg., Utah, Kans.; registered land surveyor, Oreg. Mem. ASCE, Nat., Ariz. (pres.) socs. profl. engrs., Ariz. Soc. Civil Engrs., Ariz. Assn. Planners, Horseless Carriage Club Am, Kappa Sigma. Episcopalian. Home: 8620 E Mitchell Dr Scottsdale AZ 85251 Office: 4203 N Brown Ave Scottsdale AZ 85251

GOOLSBY, JE Y., advertising executive; b. Livingston, Tenn., Jan. 25, 1936; s. John Y. and Nina Elizabeth (Bullock) G.; m. Ingeborg F. Rabe, Oct. 30, 1969 (div. 1979); children—Ellen F., Desiree Monique, Cjaer Zorba; m. 2d, Christine F. Milkes, May 2, 1982. B.A., U. Calif.-Santa Barbara, 1963; postgrad. Santa Barbara Bus. Coll., 1963-64. Publs. mgr. Human Factor Research, Inc., Santa Barbara, 1965-70; art dir. KVZK-TV, Govt. Am. Samoa, Pago Pago, 1970-72; publs. mgr. U. Calif.-Santa Barbara, 1972-76; advt. mgr. Sloan Tech. Corp., Santa Barbara, 1981—. Served with U.S. Army, 1955-56. Recipient Best Archtl. Graphics award Am. Fedn. Advt., 1976, Best Trade Mag. Design award, 1976. Mem. Advt. Club Tri-County. Democrat. Unitarian.

GOOSMAN, JAMES EDWARD, computer systems engr.; b. Colorado Springs, Colo., Oct. 19, 1948; s. Michael John and Veda Mildred (Drysdale) G.; B.S. in Engring. Physics, Colo. Sch. Mines, 1970, M.S., 1974. Computer systems engr. Texaco Inc., Houston, 1970, Colo. Sch. Mines, Golden, 1971-74, Ensco Inc., Springfield, Va., 1974-78, Safetran Traffic Systems, Colorado Springs, Colo., 1978—; asso. Foster-Morrell Engring., Colorado Springs. Mem. Sigma Xi. Congregationalist. Home: 392 G W Rockrimmon Blvd Colorado Springs CO 80919 Office: 1485 Garden of the Gods Rd Colorado Springs CO 80907

GORANS, GERALD ELMER, accountant; b. Benson, Minn., Sept. 17, 1922; s. George W. and Gladys (Schnieder) G.; student Lower Columbia Jr. Coll., 1941-43, Whiteman Coll., 1943-44; B.A., U. Wash., 1947; m. Mildred Louise Stallard, July 19, 1944; 1 dau., Gretchen. Staff auditor Allen R. Smart & Co., 1947; auditor Touche, Niven, Bailey & Smart, 1947-57, partner, 1957-60; partner Touche, Ross, Bailey & Smart, 1960-69; partner Touche Ross & Co., 1969—, charge Seattle office, 1962-82, chmn. Seattle office, 1982—, coordinating partner Western region, sr. partner, 1977—, mem. policy group., 1964-69, also dir. Chmn. budget and fin. com., v.p. budget and fin. Seattle Worlds Fair; chmn. budget and fin. com. Century 21 Center, Inc.; head profl. div. United Good Neighbor Fund campaign, 1963, 64, advanced gifts div., 1965, bd. dirs., 1963-67, v.p., 1966, pres., 1967; adv. bd. Salvation Army, 1965-80, treas., 1974-80; chmn. fin. com. Bellevue Christian Sch.; mem., chmn. Alumni Fund, U. Wash., 1969-72; bd. dirs. Seattle Symphony Assn., N.W. Hosp. Found., 1977—, N.W. Hosp., 1980—; bd. dirs., treas. Citizens Council Against Crime, 1972-80, pres., 1975-77; treas. Against Ban on Nuclear Energy, 1976; trustee U. Wash. Pres.'s Club, 1980-83; chmn. fin. com., mem. exec. com., bd. dirs. Com. for Balanced Regional Transp., 1980—; bd. dirs., treas., exec. com. Scandinavia Today in Seattle, 1981-83; bd. dirs., treas. Inter-Hosps. Assocs., 1982—. Served from seaman to lt. (j.g.), USNR, 1943-45. Mem. Am. Inst. C.P.A.'s (chmn. com. on nat. def.), Wash. Soc. C.P.A.'s (dir. 1974-76), Nat. Office Mgmt. Assn. (past pres.), Seattle C. of C. (trustee, v.p. 1981—, 1st vice chmn. 1983—), Mayors Loaned Execs., Nat. Def. Exec. Res. Clubs: Harbor, Wash. Athletic (gov. 1971-77, pres. 1974-75), Rainier (treas. 1976-77), Greater Seattle (dir., commodore). Seattle Golf; Family (San Francisco). Home: 9013 NE 37th Pl Bellevue WA 98004 Office: 1111 3d Ave Seattle WA 98101

GORANSON, ULF GORAN, structural engineer; b. Stockholm, Apr. 21, 1937; s. John E. and Esther J. Goransson; m. Inger A. Gredin, Sept. 16, 1961; children—Pete T., Marie A. M.S. in Aero. Engring., Royal Inst. Tech., Stockholm, 1962, D. Engring. in Aircraft Structures, 1965. Lic. mech. engr. Wash. Researcher, Royal Inst. Tech., Stockholm, 1962-67; mgr. structural damage tech. staff Boeing Comml. Airplane Co., Seattle, 1967—. Served to 2d lt. Swedish Army, 1960. Assoc. fellow AIAA; mem. ASTM. Lutheran. Contbr. articles to tech. jours.

GORCHYNSKI, SYLVIA ANNE, psychologist; b. Yorkton, Sask., Can.; came to U.S., 1960; d. Stanley Walter and Stephanie Alice (Fedoruk) G.; B.Sc., R.N., U. Sask., 1959; cert. public health nursing, U. Calif., San Francisco, 1963, M.Sc. in Psychiat. Nursing (NIMH scholar), 1964, cert. nursing service adminstrn., 1965; Ph.D. in Personality and Social Psychology (USPHS scholar) Boston U., 1973. Nurse hosps. in Santa Barbara, Calif., 1960-62; instr. continuing edn. U. Calif., San Francisco, 1964-65; vis. lectr. Calif. State U., San Francisco, 1964-65; resident nursing service adminstrn. St. Mary's Hosp., San Francisco, 1964-65; clin. psychology intern Kaiser Hosp., San Francisco, 1970; asso. instr. Calif. State U., Bakersfield; Jungian pre-tng. analysis, 1973; clin. psychologist San Francisco Community Mental Health Services, research coordinator Center Spl. Problems, 1974-80; pvt. practice psychotherapy and consultation, San Francisco, 1975—; ind. cons. Arthur D. Little, Cambridge, Mass., 1973-76; cons. Research Triangle Inst., 1977—; mem. adv. com. San Francisco Vol. Bur., 1978-80. Mem. Am. Psychol. Assn., Assn. Women in Sci., Sigma Theta Tau. Club: Order Eastern Star. Author papers in field. Address: 2305 Van Ness Ave San Francisco CA 94109 also 435-10830 Jasper Ave Edmonton AB T5J 2B3 Canada

GORDINIER, GARY WAYNE, safety engineer; b. Fort Sill, Okla., Apr. 7, 1945; s. Billy Malcolm and Alma Marie (Kosler) G.; m. Charleen Susan Hassinger, Aug. 27, 1971; children—Warren Grant, Jon William. B.A. in Indsl. Edn., Ariz. State U., 1973. Sr. tech. rep. Home Ins. Co., Albuquerque, 1973-76; sr. loss control rep. Transamerica Ins. Co., Phoenix, Ariz., 1976-81; sr. tech. rep. Home Ins. Co., Albuquerque, 1981—; safety technician Ariz. Air N.G. Served with USN, Vietnam. Mem. Am. Soc. Safety Engrs. Republican. Methodist. Home: 1602 Virginia NE Albuquerque NM 87110 Office: 2500 Louisiana NE Albuquerque NM 87190

GORDON, ALAN LESLIE, physician; b. Chgo., June 12, 1931; s. Lee S. and Doree (Leslie) G.; B.S., U. Ill., 1952, M.B., 1953, M.S., 1955, M.D., 1955; m. Babs Schneider, Aug. 8, 1954; children—Leslie Gordon Tenzer, Todd, Jill, Peter. Intern, Cook County Hosp., Chgo., 1955-56; fellow in internal medicine Mayo Clinic, Rochester, Minn., 1958-61, asst. to staff, 1961-62; practice medicine specializing in internal medicine, Phoenix, 1962—; assoc. in medicine U. Ariz. Med. Coll., 1968-76; instr. coronary care nursing Phoenix Coll., 1967; mem. staff Good Samaritan, St. Joseph hosps. Phoenix; mem. exec. com. Maricopa County Hosp., Phoenix; cons. VA Hosp., Phoenix. Mem. Nat. Residency Rev. Com. for Internal Medicine, 1984—. Chmn. physicians United Fund Drive; reader, Recording for the Blind; mem. cardiovascular adv. bd. Indsl. Commn. Ariz.; mem. Pres. Fords Emergency Conf. on Swime Influenza; bd. dirs. Valley Big Brothers; trustee Maricopa Found. for Med. Care. Served with USN, 1956-58; China. Recipient Physicians Recognition award AMA, 1972, 75. 78, 81; A. Ashley Rousuck award Mayo Clinic; Borden Found. award. Diplomate Am. Bd. Internal Medicine. Fellow ACP (gov. for Ariz.); mem. Mayo Clinic Alimni Assn.(dir.), Ariz. Soc Internal Medicine (pres.), Ariz. Heart Assn. (pres.), Maricopa County Med. Soc. (dir.; v.p., pres.), Am. Heart Assn., Am. Soc. Internal Medicine, AMA, Ariz. Med. Assn, Aesculapian Soc., Alpha Omega Alpha, Pi Kappa Epsilon. Club: Arizona. Pioneer in inulobiose research. Home: 5823 37th Pl N Paradise Valley AZ 85253 Office: 2200 N 3d St Phoenix AZ 85004

GORDON, ELAINE TRAVIS, occupational therapist; b. Chgo., Aug. 11, 1932; d. James and Doris (Gittelsohn) Travis; m. Milton Paul Gordon, Jan. 1, 1955; children—David Bryan, Karen Rose, Nancy Lynn, Peter Wallace. B.S., Columbia U., 1955; M.A., NYU, 1957; Ph.D., Union Grad. Sch., San Francisco, 1977. Occupational therapist Hosp. for Joint Diseases, N.Y.C., 1955-57; faculty family life edn. Seattle Pub. Schs., 1959-67; counselor, therapist Self Discovery Service, Seattle, 1975—; pvt. practice marriage and family therapy, Seattle, 1978—; instr. Exptl. Coll., U. Wash., 1976—; allied health profl. staff Fairfax Hosp., 1981—; bd. dirs. Psychology Forum, 1980-81; governing bd. N.W. Neurol. Rehab., 1981—. King County Arts Commn. grantee, 1976. Mem. Am. Psychol. Assn., Am. Occupational Therapy Assn., Internat. Transactional Analysis Assn., Am. Personnel and Guidance Assn., Lake City C. of C., Women's Bus. Exchange. Home: 8255 45th Ave NE Seattle WA 98115 Office: Landmark Bldg 11000 Lake City Way NE Seattle WA 98125

GORDON, FRANK X., JR., judge; b. Chgo., Jan. 9, 1929; s. Frank X. and Lucille (Gburek) G.; B.A., Stanford U., 1951; LL.B., U. Ariz., 1954; m. Joan C. Gipe, Sept. 17, 1950; children—Frank X., Candace Gordon Lander. Admitted to Ariz. bar, 1954; assoc. firm Gordon & Gordon, Kingman, Ariz., 1954-62; atty. City of Kingman, 1955-57; judge Superior Ct. Mohave County (Ariz.), Kingman, 1962-75; justice Ariz. Supreme Ct., Phoenix, 1975—; mem. various coms. State Bar Ariz.; Ariz. rep. to Council for State Ct. Reps. for Nat. Center State Cts.; bd. visitors U. Ariz. Law Sch., 1972-75. Trustee, Chester H. Smith Meml. Scholarship Fund; past dir. and pres. Mohave County Mental Health Clinic, Inc.; past mem. Gov.'s Commn. Mental Health; state bd. dirs. Ariz. Heart Assn.; active Boulder Dam Area council Boy Scouts Am. Mem. ABA, Ariz., Maricopa County bar assns., Am. Judicature Soc., Mohave County C. of C. (past pres.). Democrat. Methodist. Clubs: Rotary, Elks. Office: Ariz Supreme Ct State Capitol Bldg Phoenix AZ 85007*

GORDON, FREDRICK JAMES, mechanical engineer, consultant; b. Calgary, Alta., Can., Apr. 16, 1944; s. George and Virginia Rosella (Plummer) G.; m. Sherryl Kay Ayers, June 12, 1964; children—Tisha, Bart, Brett; m. 2d, Pamela Marie Pyke, Mar. 21, 1976. B.S.M.E., U. Wash., 1968. Registered profl. engr., Wash., 1975, Calif., 1977, Alaska, 1982. Engr., Union Oil Co., Wilmington, Calif., 1968-73; project engr. Marmac Engring., Long Beach, Calif., 1973-74; project mgr. Harbinger, Inc., Bellingham, Wash., 1974-75; mgr. engring. Hallanger Engrs., Bellevue, Wash., 1975-82; project mgr. Coffman Engrs., Bellevue, 1982—. Mem. ASME, Instrument Soc. Am., TAPPI. Office: 1021 112th Ave NE Bellevue WA 98004

GORDON, GUY GILBERT, educator; b. Helix, Oreg., June 2, 1914; s. Marshall E. and Pearl Genevieve (Clay) G.; B.A., U. Wash., 1949, M.B.A., 1950; Ph.D., U. Calif. at Berkeley, 1957; m. Margaret Mary Dever, Feb. 19, 1938; children—Gay Gordon Newton, Diane Gordon Nett. Pres. Marine Research Corp., Tacoma, 1946-47; lectr. Sch. Bus. Adminstrn., U. Calif. at Berkeley, 1950-52; faculty U. Wash., Seattle, 1952—, prof. bus. adminstrn., 1962-77, prof. emeritus, 1977—; v.p. 2001 Mgmt. Services, Inc., 1981—; dir. Pan Pacific Group Ltd. Commr., sec., treas. Wash. Fryer Commn., Seattle, 1960-82; trustee U. Wash. YMCA, 1968-72, pres. 1970-71. Served with AUS, 1944-46. Ford Found. fellow, 1959-60; Sperry and Hutchinson grantee, 1961-62; U.S. Maritime Adminstrn. grantee, 1967-68; ACDA grantee, 1965-66. Mem. Am. Mktg. Assn. (nat. dir. 1962-64, pres. Puget Sound chpt. 1963-64), Am. Econ. Assn., Seattle Economists Club. Club: Useless Bay Golf and Country. Book review editor Jour. of Marketing, 1968-73. Home: 2061 E Shore Dr Freeland WA 98249 Office: U Wash Seattle WA 98195

GORDON, JACK FRANCIS, assn. exec.; b. Portland, Oreg., June 30, 1921; s. James Samuel and Mabel Ann (Ratchford) G.; grad. Seattle U., 1950, U. Wash., 1955; m. Roberta M. Gordon, May 1, 1948; children—John, Mary, Ann, Joseph. City editor Catholic NW Progress, Seattle, 1947-48; dir. pub. relations Seattle U., 1948-50, Greater Seattle, Inc., 1950-64; commr. employment security State of Wash., 1964-65; dir. spl. events Seattle Ctr., 1965; exec. v.p. Restaurant Assn. Wash., Seattle, 1966—, Wash. Lodging Assn., 1981—; spl. asst. to gov. Wash., 1973-74, spl. agt., 1980; v.p., bd. dirs. Wash. Trade Fair, 1950-78; mem. Seattle Human Rights Commn., 1966-79, Wash. Am. Bicentennial Commn., 1975-76; bd. dirs. Seattle-King County Conv. and Visitors Bur., 1976—; mem. Wash. State Personnel Appeals Bd., 1981-82. Pres., Providence Med. Found., 1980-81; bd. dirs. Seattle Youth Symphony Orch.; pres. Pacific Internat. Hospitality Indsl. Expn., 1982—. Served with USNR, World War II; maj. NG. Named Alumnus of Year, Seattle U., 1969, Newsmaker of Tomorrow, Time Mag., 1953. Mem. Am. Soc. Assn. Execs., AGVA, Seattle C. of C., Internat. Platform Assn., Am. Security Council, U.S. Security and Intelligence Fund, Musicians Assn., Am. Legion (past post comdr.). Roman Catholic. Clubs: Rainier, Wash. Athletic, Rotary, KC. (Seattle). Home: 6814 44th Pl NE Seattle WA 98115 Office: 722 Securities Bldg Seattle WA 98101

GORDON, JAN IRENE, financial consultant; b. Portland, Oreg., May 28, 1951; d. Lyle Henry and Juanita Jean (Hilton) Vandercook; m. Stephen Roger Gordon, Dec. 28, 1980; 1 dau., Jennifer Spring; m. Gary Richard Straight, Dec. 21, 1974. Student Portland State U., 1969-70, Ga. So. Coll., 1970-71, Portland State U., 1971-75; B.S., Portland State U., 1975. C.L.U. Sales staff Lincoln Nat. Life Ins. Co., San Jose, 1975-80; owner, mgr. Jan Straight & Assocs., San Mateo, Calif., 1980—; gen. mgr. Oreg. Handling Equipment Co., Portland, 1980—; staff photographer Friends of the Winemakers; founding mem. Friendly Acres Neighborhood Bd., Mem. Nat. Assn. Life Underwriters (chmn. Peninsula Polit. Action Com.), Calif. Assn. Life Underwriters, Peninsula Assn. Life Underwriters, Women Leaders Underwriters Conf., Internat. Assn. Fin. Planners. Republican. Christian-scientist.

GORDON, JERRY A., media specialist; b. Rochester, N.Y., Apr. 27, 1939; s. Philip R. and Grace G. (Itkin) G.; m. Susan G. Gerring, June 24, 1962; children—Julie, Lili. B.S. in Radio and TV, Ithaca Coll., 1962; M.S. in Ednl. Tech., Syracuse U., 1966; Ed.D. in Instructional Tech. and Curriculum Devel., SUNY-Buffalo, 1979. Media specialist, coordinator Tchr. Edn. Materials Ctr., State U. Coll., Fredonia, N.Y., 1966-69; assoc. prof., curriculum coordinator communication media Alfred (N.Y.) State Coll., 1969-82; dir. Instructional Media Resources Ctr., U. Calif.-Riverside, 1982—; cons. in field. Mem. Alfred Zoning Bd. Appeals, 1972-82. Mem. Assn. Ednl. Communications and Tech., Ednl. Media Assn. (pres.), Internat. TV Assn. (regional dir. ednl. relations). Democrat. Jewish. Contbr. numerous articles to profl. publs. Home: 5471 Via del Tecolote Riverside CA 92507 Office: U Calif Riverside CA 92721

GORDON, JOHN SHIELDS, JR., banker; b. Washington, Apr. 2, 1944; s. John Shields and Osa Marie (Beck) G.; m. Martha Fowler, Dec. 16, 1967; children—Susan Lynn Warme, Jane Kathleen Warme. B.S. summa cum laude, Calif. State U.-Los Angeles, 1970; postgrad. Pacific Coast Banking Sch., 1978. Asst. v.p. Bank Am., Los Angeles, 1970-74; v.p. Rainier Bank, Seattle, 1974-78; v.p., mgr., U.S./Can. internat. div. First Bank Mpls., 1978-80; v.p., mgr. credit and mktg. multinat. div. Peoples Nat. Bank, Seattle, 1980—; lectr. internat. bus. U. Wash., 1976-77. Served with USMC, 1964-67. Named Student of Yr., Sales and Mktg. Execs., 1969. Mem. Nat. Assn. Credit Mgmt., Bankers Assn. Fgn. Trade (export expansion com.), Seattle C. of C. Clubs: World Trade, Harbor (Seattle). Office: 1414 4th Ave Seattle WA 98111

GORDON, KENNETH STEVEN, psychologist, organizational consultant; b. L.I., N.Y., Oct. 24, 1951; s. Murray and Ruth (Klasson) G.; B.A., UCLA, M.B.A., Ph.D. Pres., Gordon Optical Design, Camarillo, Calif., Videoptics Internat. Co., Camarillo; v.p. Gordon Optical Supply, Camarillo; owner Simply Natural Health Foods, Pacific Coast Satellite, G.O. Sports; wine cons. cons. in field; dir. Nirkoda Dance Found., Los Angeles, 1976-80. Nat. Endowment for Arts grantee, 1979-80; recipient UCLA Grad. Sch. Mgmt. award, 1976; award Bd. Public Works, Los Angeles, 1977; Bicentennial award City of Los Angeles, 1977. Mem. Am. Psychol. Assn. (affiliate), Calif. Psychol. Assn., Assn. for Advancement Psychology, Gemological Inst. Am., UCLA Grad. Sch. Mgmt. Alumni Assn., Acad. Magical Arts, Soc. for Preservation of Variety Arts, Los Angeles Area Dance Alliance, Folk Dance Fedn. Calif., UCLA Alumni Assn., Los Angeles Area Dance Alliance, Folk Dance Fedn. Calif., UCLA Alumni Assn., Los Angeles Zoo Assn., Phi Gamma Mu. Developer, creater of eye catchers optical displays and accessories, video optics; patentee in field; developer, creator videoptics, video optical dispensing systems. Office: 4870 Adohr Ln Camarillo CA 93010

GORDON, LAURENCE, rehabilitation company executive; b. Peabody, Mass., Aug. 30, 1943; s. Abraham Lewis and Esther (Goldenberg) G.; m. Madelyn Marie Buonocore, Feb. 25, 1972; children—Rachel, Sarah. B.S. in Edn., State Coll. Salem, Mass., 1965, Ed.M., 1968; postgrad. Boston U., 1969-73. Tchr. Newburyport High Sch., (Mass.), 1965-68; counselor Mass. Rehab. Commn., 1968-72, supr., 1972, area mgr., 1973, regional dir., 1974, dir., 1975-78; mem. faculty dept. psychology Mass. Community Coll., Beverly, 1971-78; pvt. practice rehab. 1978-79; v.p. CRS Inc., Arcadia, Calif., 1978-82; v.p. Rehab Data, Inc.; pres. BIS, Inc., Northridge, Calif. Recipient service and leadership award State of Mass. Mem. Nat. Rehab. Counseling Assn. of Calif. (mem. bd. dirs.), Nat. Rehab. Assn. (cert. rehab. counselor). Home: 18336 San Fernando Mission Blvd Northridge CA 91326 Office: CRS Inc 41 W Santa Clara St Arcadia CA 91006

GORDON, LEONARD, sociology educator; b. Detroit, Dec. 6, 1935; s. Abraham and Sarah (Rosen) G.; m. Rena Joyce Feigelman, Dec. 25, 1955; children—Susan Melinda, Matthew Seth, Melissa Gail. B.A., Wayne State U., 1957, Ph.D., 1966; M.A., U. Mich., 1958. Mich. area dir. Am. Jewish Com., Detroit, 1964-67; asst. prof. sociology Ariz. State U., Tempe, 1967-70, assoc. prof., 1970-77, prof., 1977—, chmn. dept.

sociology, 1980—. NSF grantee, 1962; Rockefeller Found. grantee, 1970. Mem. Pacific Sociol. Assn. (pres. 1980), AAUP, Am. Sociol. Assn., Am. Jewish Com. Democrat. Author: A City in Racial Crisis, 1971; Sociology and American Social Issues, 1978; (with A.J. Mayer) Urban Life and the Struggle to Be Human, 1980.

GORDON, LOUIS EDWARD, hosp. adminstr.; b. Jackson, Mich., Dec. 18, 1929; s. George Edward and Anna Amelia (Hansmann) G.; B.A., Andrews U., 1952; M.A.(Schlitz fellow 1955-56), Mich. State U., 1957; m. Shirley Winifred Bishop, Nov. 14, 1954; children—Jan Alyce, Jill Annette, Traci Lynn. Asst. dir. Edward W. Sparrow Hosp., Lansing, Mich., 1955-61; adminstr. Battle Creek (Mich.) Sanitarium Hosp., 1961-67; hosp. dir. Liberian Nat. Med. Center, U.S. AID, 1967-72; chief party USPHS team, Liberia, West Africa, 1971-72; dir. Ind. Regional Med. Program, Ind. U. Sch. Medicine, Indpls., 1972-73; dir. Kino Community Hosp. and Dept. Hosps. and Nursing Homes of Pima County, Tucson, Ariz., 1973-78; pres. Bannock Meml. Hosp., Pocatello, Idaho, 1978—; mem. teaching faculty Idaho State U., Pocatello, 1979—; cons. hosp. orgn. and devel., 1967—. Commr., City of Battle Creek, Mich., 1965-67. Served with U.S. Army, 1952-54. Decorated, Govt. of Liberia; recipient Unity for Service award Nat. Exchange Club, 1967, Meritorious Honor award U.S. Dept. State/AID, 1972. Mem. Am. Coll. Hosp. Adminstrs., Am. Hosp. Assn., Am. Pub. Health Assn., Mountain States Shared Services Corp. (trustee), Idaho Hosp. Assn. (trustee), Idaho Health Systems Agy. (trustee, exec. com.), Idaho Health Services Consortium, Inc. (founder, chmn. bd. trustees). Clubs: Rotary, Masons, Elks. Home: 805 Cahina Way Pocatello ID 83201 Office: Bannock Regional Med Ctr Memorial Dr Pocatello ID 83201

GORDON, MARILYN LU, health care co. exec.; b. Los Angeles, July 11, 1954; d. Frank Ephraim and Seemah Kitty (Masliah) G.; B.A. in Health Services Adminstrn., Antioch U., 1977. Med. equipment and supply buyer Am. Med. Internat., Beverly Hills, Calif., 1972-73, computer coordinator, 1973-77, asst. to v.p. purchasing, 1977-80, dir. materials systems, 1980-82; pres. Medi-Genics, Inc., Sherman Oaks, Calif., 1982—; cons. in field. Mem. Am. Inst. Hosp. Cons., Internat. Materials Mgmt. Soc., Calif. Assn. Hosp. Purchasing Agts., Nat. Assn. Female Execs., AAUW. Office: 15445 Ventura Blvd Suite 10-309 Sherman Oaks CA 91413

GORDON, NORMAN WALLACE, physician; b. Elizabeth, N.J., June 18, 1915; s. Benjamin and Mary (Burstein) G.; B.A., U. Wis., Madison, 1936, M.A., 1937; M.D., N.Y. U., 1941; m. Evelyn Neumann, Sept. 22, 1942; children—Jonathan, Wendy, Stephen, Lance. Intern, Elizabeth Gen. Hosp., 1941-42; pvt. practice gen. and aviation medicine, Van Nuys, Calif., 1948—; sr. aviation med. examiner FAA; former chief of staff Encino Hosp., Riverside Hosp., Meml. Hosp of Panorama City. Mem. Pres.'s adv. bd. Calif. State U., Northridge, 1972—. Served as flight surgeon M.C., USAAF, 1942-46. Fellow Am. Acad. Family Practice; mem. AMA, Calif. Med. Assn., Los Angeles Med. Assn., Civil Aviation Med. Assn., Aerospace Med. Assn., Wis. Alumni Club of San Fernando (founder), Friends of Scandinavia (founder). Office: 14434 Gilmore St Van Nuys CA 91401

GORDON, ROBERT GIBSON, lawyer; b. Freeport, N.Y., Nov. 8, 1944; s. MacClellan Thompson and Dorothy (Gibson) G.; B.A. magna cum laude, Golden Gate U., 1972; J.D., U. Calif., San Francisco, 1975. Admitted to Calif. bar, 1976; tax atty. Bank of Am., San Francisco, 1976-77, asst. tax counsel, 1977, mgr. internat. services sect., 1977-82, tax counsel, 1982; internat. tax mgr. Price Waterhouse, San Francisco, 1983—; guest lectr. internat. tax Golden Gate U., San Francisco. Served with U.S. Army, 1968-70; Vietnam. Decorated Army Commendation medal. Mem. State Bar Calif., Am., San Francisco bar assns., San Francisco Internat. Trade Counsel, Golden Gate Audubon Soc. (1st v.p. 1978-79). Home: 851 Ashbury St San Francisco CA 94117 Office: 555 California St Suite 2200 San Francisco CA 94104

GORDON, ROSE MARIA ELIZABETH, counselor-therapist, consultant, lecturer; b. Camden, N.J., Aug. 27, 1931; d. Rocco and Mary Antonio Theresa (Sartarella) Locantore; m. Irving Gordon, Feb. 29, 1952 (div.); children—Rocky, Maia, Heidi, Aaron. B.S. in Secondary and Sociology, U. Nev.-Las Vegas, 1978, M.S. in Rehab. Counseling, 1981. Cert. substance abuse counselor, Nev. Counselor-therapist Verdun Trione, Ph.D., Las Vegas, Nev., 1971—, North Las Vegas Hosp. Care Unit, part-time 1975—; cons.-lectr. Raleigh Hills Hosp., Las Vegas, 1982—; cons. in field; expert witness in substance abuse; rape crisis counselor; vol. counselor-therapist Clark County Jail, Las Vegas, 1982—; founder, dir. August Found. Pres. Counselors-Community Action Against Rape. Mem. Am. Personnel and Guidance Assn., Am. Rehab. Counselors Assn., Nev. Rehab. Assn. Office: 3180 W Sahara Ave Suite C-21 Las Vegas NV 89102

GORDON, STEVEN VERN, computer mfg. co. exec.; b. Long Beach, Calif., Dec. 26, 1942; s. Vern Arthur and Edith Europha (Walker) G.; B.S. in Computer Sci., Brigham Young U., 1971; m. Ruth Christensen, Nov. 5, 1965; children—Andra, Amy, Boyce, Ariane, Alaney, Catherine. Computer operator Continental Bank, Salt Lake City, 1966-67; programmer, analyst, computer operator Brigham Young U., 1967-71; mgr. data processing Sav-on Drugs, Inc., Marina del Rey, Calif., 1971-73; mgr. data processing City of Downey (Calif.), 1973-77; sr. systems rep. Honeywell Info. Systems, 1977-80; systems engr. NCR Corp., 1980—; instr. data processing Cerritos Coll., Norwalk, Calif.; cons. in field. Served with U.S. Air Force Res., 1962. Mem. Data Processing Mgmt. Assn., So. Calif. Assn. Mcpl. Data Processing Dirs. Republican. Mormon. Home: 22771 S Ferguson Rd Beaver Creek OR 97004 Office: 3025 SW Corbett Portland OR 97201

GORDON, STUART MARSHALL, lawyer; b. Los Angeles, Dec. 25, 1940; s. Jack C. and Celia Anne (Stock) G.; A.B., U. Calif.-Berkeley, 1962; LL.B., U. Calif.-Boalt Hall Sch. Law, 1965, J.D., 1966; m. Elizabeth Ann Marsteller, Feb. 22, 1968; children—Thomas Edward, John Stuart. Admitted to Calif. bar, 1966; assoc. firm Sedgwick, Detert, Moran & Arnold, San Francisco, 1966-67; ptnr. Gordon & Rees and predecessor, San Francisco, 1967—; chmn. bd., chief exec. officer Marine World, Inc., 1979—; chief exec. officer, pres. G&G Mgmt. Co., Inc., 1980—; mem. Atty. Gen.'s. Adv. Com., 1971—; chmn. Juvenile Justice Commn. City and County of San Francisco, 1980—. Mem. aux. San Francisco Gen. Hosp., 1974-77. Bd. dirs. The Guardsmen San Francisco, 1971-74, San Francisco Boys Club, 1973-76; founder, trustee Golden Bear Athletic Found., 1970-74; bd. dels. U. Calif. Alumni Found., 1970-74. Mem. San Francisco Lawyers Club, Barristers Club, Internat. Assn. Ins. Counsel, Assn. Def. Counsel, ABA, Wine and Food Soc. of San Francisco. Clubs: University, Olympic, California Tennis, San Francisco Grid, Commonwealth of California, Bohemian (San Francisco). Home: 2524 Filbert St San Francisco CA 94123 Office: 601 Montgomery St San Francisco CA 94111

GORDON, WILLIAM EDWARD, physician; b. St. Louis, July 1, 1921; s. William Edward and Sylvia Christine (Calvin) G.; M.D., St. Louis U. Sch. Medicine, 1947; m. Julia Elizabeth Beile, Sept. 1, 1944; children—Deborah Lynn, William Edward, Timothy Edward. Intern, St. Louis City Hosp., 1947-48; resident psychiatry N.Y. State Hosp. System, 1948-49; resident, staff physician Wayne County (Mich.) Gen. Hosp., 1949-51; staff psychiatrist Mich. State Mental Health Clinic, Detroit, 1951-52; instr. psychiatry Wayne State U. Dept. Edn., 1952-54; cons. forensic psychiatry and medicine probation dept., cts., police agencies, juvenile facilities, Wayne County, Mich., Macomb County, Oakland County, Mich., 1952-68; cons. Mental div. Probate Ct., Wayne County, Mich., 1952-68; asst. supt. psychiat. services Calif. State Dept. Corrections, 1969-74; cons. Dist. Atty.'s Office, Probation Dept. and Superior Ct., San Luis Obispo County, Calif., 1972-76; asst. jail physician, 1973-76; dir. outpatient clinics San Luis Obispo County Health Dept., 1982—; program coordinator San Luis Obispo County Sexual Assault Reponse Team, 1981—; mem. Continuing Med. Edn. Com., San Luis Obispo, 1974-76; active child health disability prevention program, 1973-76, Child Abuse program, 1973-75; bd. dirs. Heart Assn., 1975-77; instr. Cardio pulmonary resuscitation, 1975-77; free-lance med. writer, 1978—. Served with USAF, 1955-57. Recipient award for service to community in support of law enforcement and crime prevention San Luis Obispo County Criminal Justice Adminstrs. Assn., 1976. Mem. Am., Calif. med. assns., San Luis Obispo County Med. Soc., Am. Psychiat. Assn., Wayne County Med. Soc., No. Calif. Psychiat. Soc. Home and Office: 9000 S River Rd Atascadero CA 93422

GORDON, WINTHROP O., lawyer; b. Worcester, Mass., Mar. 8, 1905; s. George Andrew and Lucy Walker (Southwick) G.; m. Thelma Gerrard, June 15, 1935; 1 dau., Sandra Deitz. LL.B., Harvard U., 1932. Bar: Calif., 1933, U.S. Supreme Ct. 1957. Individual practice law, Santa Ana, Calif. Mem. Orange County Bar Assn. Office: 900 N Broadway Santa Ana CA 92702

GOREHAM, JACQUELINE SUE WILLIAMS, home economics educator; b. Danville, Ill., Jan. 21, 1935; d. Logan A. and Edith Marie (Shelton) Williams; m. Donald James Goreham, Aug. 17, 1957; children—Elizabeth V., Andrew B. B.S. in Home Econs., Eastern Ill. U., 1957; postgrad. U. No. Colo., 1973-80, Colo. State U., 1981-83. Asst. home adviser U. Ill Extension Service, Kankakee, 1957-60; freelance home economist in Ill., Colo., 1961-71; tchr. home econs. York Jr. High Sch., Thornton, Colo., 1972-76; exec. dir. Dairy Council Greater Kansas City (Mo.), 1977-78; dept. head home econs. Northglenn (Colo.) Jr. High Sch., 1979—. Communications dir. Denver Area Friendship Force. Mem. Am. Home Econs. Assn., Colo. Home Econs. Assn. (state bd. dirs., membership chmn. 1981-82), Am. Vocat. Assn., Colo. Edn. Assn., AAUW, Delta Kappa Gamma, Kappa Omicron Phi, Sigma Sigma Sigma Alumni Denver (v.p. 1983). Republican. Presbyterian. Represented U.S. Treasury Savs. Bonds Div. as Mrs. U.S. Savs. Bonds, 1971-72; researched, tested recipes for Complete Fireplace Cookbook, 1982. Home: 8805 W 80th Dr Arvada CO 80005 Office: 1123 Muriel Dr Northglenn CO 80233

GORMEZANO, KEITH S., publisher; b. Madison, Wis., Nov. 22, 1955; s. Isadore and Miriam (Fox) G.; B.S., U. Iowa, 1977. Pub. relations dir. Hillel Found., Iowa City, Iowa, 1976-77; overseas rep. Le Beacon Presse, Iowa City, 1978, pub., chief exec. officer, Seattle, 1981—; pub. info. officer Op. City, 1979-80; chmn. Iowa City Young Ams. for Freedom, 1979- Improvement Found., Seattle, 1980-81; vol. VISTA, 1982-83; dir. ACJS, Inc. Vice chmn. Resource Conservation Commn., Iowa City, 1979-80; chmn. Iowa City Young Ams. for Freedom, 1979-81; pres. Downtown Neighborhood Assn., 1980-83; bd. dirs. Seattle Mental Health Inst., 1981; Mem. Mcpl. League, Com. of Small Mag. Editors and Pubs., Cityclub, NOW Sigma Delta Chi. Republican. Jewish. Club: Wash. Athletic. Editor, M'godolim, 1979-81, Le Beacon Rev., 1979-81; author (poetry) 36 Flavours, 1980. Home: 621 Holt Ave Iowa City IA 52240 Office: 2921 E Madison St Suite 7WWW Seattle WA 98112

GORRIE, MILDRED DUNN, savs. and loan exec., ednl. orgn. exec.; b. Waitsburg, Wash., Dec. 7, 1915; d. Harvey and Selena J. (Wagstaff) Hussey; student Seattle Secretarial Sch., 1935; m. Jack O. Gorrie, Dec. 6, 1969; children by previous marriage—Michael Dunn, Carol J. Dunn Caldwell. Various secretarial, fin., office mgmt. positions, Seattle area, 1935-68; dir. bus. and fin. Wash. State Nurses Assn., Seattle, 1968-78, ret., 1978; organizer Sound Savs. and Loan, Seattle, 1975—, treas., dir., 1976—; founder, partner World of Continuing Edn., Seattle, 1978—. Chmn. Gov.'s Commn. on Status of Women, 1960-63. Recipient Matrix Table award, Seattle chpt. Women in Communications, 1978. Clubs: Totem Bus. and Profl. Women, Quota (Seattle). Home: 7106 230th SW Mountlake Terrace WA 98043 Office: 1020 Lloyd Bldg Seattle WA 98101

GORSIC, BONNIE LOUISE, systems engineer; b. Hershey, Pa., Dec. 3, 1956; d. Joseph Sr. and Caroline (Eby) G. B.S. in Biology, Lock Haven State Coll., 1979. Assoc. analyst Computer Scis. Corp., Kennedy Space Ctr., Fla., 1979-80; engr. in charge MTS III, Rockwell Internat., Downey, Calif., 1981—. Mem. Nat. Assn. Female Execs., Nat. Space Inst., Long Beach Rowing Assn., Sierra Club. Office: 12214 Lakewood Blvd Suite FA 36 Downey CA 90241

GORSKI, JOSEPH JOHN, criminalist; b. Hazleton, Pa., July 11, 1946; s. Joseph and Agnes Rose (Mederos) G.; B.S., Pa. State U., 1968; M.S., Bloomsburg State Coll., 1975; m. Mary Ellen G. Patton, Sept. 2, 1968; 1 son, Joseph. Tchr., Carson Long Inst., New Bloomfield, Pa., 1968-70; criminalist Pa. State Police Crime Lab., 1970-76; supervising criminalist Eastern Wash. State Crime Lab., Spokane, 1976-81; mng. criminalist Wash. State Patrol Crime Lab., Kennewick, 1981—; pres., dir. Gorski Plastics, West, Inc., 1980-82; mem. edn. and tng. com. Gov.'s Developmental Disabilities Planning Council, 1978-79. Chmn., Guild Sch. Parent Group, Spokane, 1979-80; vol. coordinator Benton-Franklin County Guardian Ad Litem Program, Benton-Franklin County Juvenile Ct. Fellow Am. Acad. Forensic Sci.; mem. Wash. Assn. Retarded Citizens (legis. com. 1979-80), Internat. Assn. Arson Investigators, Mid-Atlantic Assn. Forensic Scientists (charter), N.W. Assn. Forensic Scientists. Democrat. Jewish. Club: Masons. Office: Wash State Patrol Crime Lab Rt 12 Box 12450 Kennewick WA 99336

GORSUCH, CAROL DOTY, communications/public relations exec.; b. Plainfield, N.J., July 3, 1943; d. Wilbur Aaron and Ellen Anna (Strom) Doty; B.A. in Journalism, Colo. State U., 1965; m. Keith Edward Gorsuch, Aug. 13, 1966; children—Kim Lynn, Mark David. Reporter, photographer Brighton (Colo.) Blade, 1965-66; asst. to dir. publs. Tacoma Public Schs., 1966-69; owner Gorsuch Communications-Public Relations/Publs., Tacoma, 1969—; asst. to dir. mktg. and pub. relations Met. Park Dist. Tacoma, 1983—; public info. officer City of Tacoma Human Relations Dept., 1977-81; instr. Ft. Steilacoom Community Coll., 1978, Tacoma Community Coll., 1981; mgmt. tng. instr. City of Tacoma Tng. and Devel. Dept.-Media Relations, 1981. Vol. instr. United Way of Pierce County/Mgmt. Assistance Program-Public Relations for Vol. Agys., 1981; bd. dirs. Sharing, 1976-82; bd. dirs. South Sound Women's Network, 1980-82, v.p. membership, 1980-81; chmn. City of Tacoma Beautification Com., 1977-78; co-chmn. public relations com. Jr. League Tacoma, 1978, asst. evening active chmn., 1979-80; chmn. City of Tacoma Human Relations Dept., United Way Campaign, 1978; co-chmn. City of Tacoma U.S. Savs. Bond Campaign, 1978; mem. City of Tacoma Legis. Analysis Com., 1980-81; press. sec., mktg. dir. Doug Sutherland for Mayor Campaign, 1981. Recipient Disting. Service citation Keep America Beautiful, 1977; named Pierce County Newsmaker of Tomorrow, 1983. Mem. Women in Communications (chpt. v.p. 1975-77), Internat. Assn. Bus. Communicators, Tacoma-Pierce County C. of C. (communications council 1981, chair visitor and conv. burs. emissaries com.), Colo. State U. Alumni Assn., Kappa Delta. Episcopalian. Home and Office: 7203 N 27th St Tacoma WA 98407

GORSUCH, NORMAN CLIFFORD, lawyer; b. Pitts., Oct. 3, 1942; s. Clifford Lee and Helen (Berzac) G.; A.B. cum laude, U. N.C., 1964; J.D., Columbia, 1967; m. Marjorie Jean Menzi, Sept. 10, 1966; children—Elizabeth, Keith, Jennifer, Deborah, David. Admitted to Alaska bar, 1968; asso. firm Ely, Guess & Rudd, Anchorage, 1967-70, mem., 1970-71, 75-82; dep. atty. gen. State of Alaska, Juneau, 1971-73, atty. gen. 1973-74, 82—. Mem. state exec. br. budget rev. com., 1971—; Alaska del. to legal com. Interstate Oil and Gas Compact Commn., 1971; mem. Joint Fed.-State Land Use Planning Commn. for Alaska, 1977-79; public mem. paperwork reduction com. Alaska Dept. Environ. Conservation, 1977; mem. subcom. pub. transp. Greater Anchorage Area Borough Zoning and Planning Commn., 1970-71; vice-chmn., v.p. bd. Chugach Rehab. Assn., 1970, pres., chmn., 1970-71; pres., Anchorage Young Democrats, 1968; mem. Bartlett Dem. Club, 1970-71. Mem. Am., Fed. (program chmn. Anchorage chpt. 1969-70), Anchorage, Juneau (pres. 1976-77) bar assns., Greater Anchorage C. of C. (chmn. pub. transp. com. Operation Breakthrough 1970), Am. Radio Relay League, Juneau C. of C. (2d v.p. 1980), Alaska State C. of C. (treas. 1980-81), Phi Beta Kappa. Methodist (mem. adminstrv. bd. 1969-70). Club: Rotary. Home: 411 Coleman Dr Juneau AK 99801 Office: Pouch K Juneau AK 99811

GORSUCH, RICHARD LEE, psychology educator, minister, consultant; b. Wayne, Mich., May 14, 1937; s. Culver C. and Velma L. (Poe) G.; m. Sylvia Sue Coalson, Aug. 18, 1961; children—Eric, Kay. B.A., Tex. Christian U., 1959; Ph.D., U. Ill., 1965; M.Div., Vanderbilt U., 1968. Ordained minister Christian Ch. (Disciples of Christ). Asst. prof. psychology Vanderbilt U., Nashville, Tenn., 1965-68, Peabody Coll., Nashville, 1968-73; Kennedy asst.-assoc. prof. psychology Tex. Christian U., Ft. Worth, 1973-75; assoc. prof. social work psychology U. Tex., Arlington, 1975-79; prof. psychology Grad. Sch. Psychology, Fuller Theol. Sem., Pasadena, Calif., 1979—; cons. in field. Author: Factor Analysis, 1973, 83; (with H.N. Maloney) Nature of Man: A Social Psychological Perspective, 1976. Editor Jour. for the Sci. Study of Religion, 1975-79. Home: 3367 Ellington Villa Altadena CA 91001 Office: 177 N Madison Pasadena CA 91101

GORTON, SLADE, senator; b. Chgo., Jan. 8, 1928; s. Thomas Slade and Ruth (Israel) G.; A.B., Dartmouth Coll., 1950; LL.B., Columbia U., 1953; m. Sally Jean Clark, June 28, 1958; children—Tod, Sarah, Rebecca. Bar: Wash. 1953. Practiced in Seattle, 1953-69; atty. gen. Wash., Olympia, 1969-81; now mem. U.S. Senate from Wash.; mem. Wash. Ho. of Reps., 1959-69, majority leader, 1967-69, mem. legis. council, 1961-69; chmn. Wash. Com. on Law and Justice, 1969-77. Found. mem. Pacific Sci. Center, Seattle. Served with AUS, 1946-47, to 1st lt. USAF, 1953-56; col. Res. Mem. Am., Wash. bar assns., Nat. Assn. Attys. Gen. (pres. 1976-77), Phi Beta Kappa. Clubs: Seattle Tennis, Washington Athletic (Seattle). Office: US Senate Washington DC 20510

GOSE, RICHARD VERNIE, lawyer; b. Hot Springs, S.D., Aug. 3, 1927; s. Vernie Oren and Mame Kristine (Thompson) G.; B.S., U. Wyo., 1950; M.S., Northwestern U., 1955; LL.B., George Washington U., 1967, J.D., 1968; children—Beverly Marie, Donald Paul, Celeste Marlene. Asso. prof. engring. U. Wyo., 1957-60; admitted to N.Mex. bar, 1967, U.S. Supreme Ct. bar, 1976, Wyo. bar, 1979; exec. asst. to U.S. Senator J.J. Hicky, 1960-62; cons. U.S. Senate Interior and Insular Affairs Com., 1961; mgr. EG&G Inc., Washington office, 1964-66; asst. atty. gen. State of N.Mex., Santa Fe, 1967-70; prin. Gose & Assos., Santa Fe, 1967—; individual practice law, Santa Fe, 1967-80, Casper, Wyo., 1980—; pres., chmn. Mountain Internat., Inc., 1976—. Co-chmn. Johnson for Pres., Wyo., 1960. Served with AUS, 1950-52. Registered profl. engr., Wyo., N.Mex.; lic. real estate broker, Wyo., N.Mex. Mem. 1st Jud. Dist. Bar Assn. N.Mex. (past pres.), 7th Jud. Dist. Bar Assn. Wyo., Phi Delta Theta, Pi Tau Sigma, Sigma Tau. Club: Masons. Home: 3920 S Oak St Casper WY 82601 Office: 200 American Bank Center PO Box 2722 Casper WY 82601

GOSHORN, JAMES WILLIAM, communications skills executive, consultant; b. Ft. Wayne, Ind., May 4, 1935; s. Glenn Estel and Beryl Florence (Wilson) G.; m. Joyce Carol Herendeen, Oct. 22, 1960; m. 2d Madelon E. Heatherington, Sept. 20, 1976; children—Bruce Alan, Joni Kay. B.A., Purdue U., 1960, M.A. in English, 1962; Ph.D. in English, U. N.Mex., 1971. Asst. prof. English, Adams State Coll., Alamosa, Colo., 1964-65; systems analyst Sandia Labs., Albuquerque, 1965-70; assoc. prof. English, Mont. State U., Bozeman, 1970-79; staff devel. rep. Aerospace Corp., El Segundo, Calif., 1979—; cons. Communications Mgmt. Assocs., Long Beach, Calif. Served with USAF, 1953-57. NEH grantee, Yale U., 1979. Mem. Am. Soc. Engring. Edn., Soc. Tech. Communications (pres. Los Angeles chpt. 1983-84), Calif. Assn. Faculty of Tech. Profl. Writing, Am. Soc. Tng. and Devel. Home: 2536 Golden Ave Long Beach CA 90806 Office: Aerospace Corp 2350 E El Segundo Ave El Segundo CA 90245

GOSLIN, IVAL VINTON, civil engineer; b. Pullman, Wash., May 7, 1911; s. Raymond L. and Zelma (Gustin) G.; m. Glenda Marcelyn Bridal, Mar. 2, 1963. Student U. Oreg., 1929-30; B.A., U. Utah, 1934, M.A., 1935; postgrad. U. Idaho, 1940-42; B.S. in C.E., Utah State U., 1944. From asst. to project engr. U.S. Geol. Survey, Logan, Utah, 1943-46; gen. mgr. Aberdeen-Springfield Canal Co., Abderdeen, Idaho, 1946-52; asst. chief engr. Upper Colorado River Commn., Grand Junction, Colo., 1953-55, acting sec., 1955, exec. dir., Salt Lake City, 1955-79; pvt. cons. civil engring., 1955—. Treas., Aberdeen Bd. Edn., 1948-52; v.p. Snake River Com. of 9; pres. Upper Snake River Valley Water Users Protective Assn., 1948-52; mem. Snake River Compact Commn., 1949-50; mem. Columbia River Basin Compact Commn., 1950-52; mem. Wyo. Reclamation Projects Survey Team, 1962-63; charter mem. adv. com. on Water Data for Pub. Use, U.S. Geol. Survey, 1965—; exec. dir. Colo. Water Resources and Power Devel. Authority, 1982—. Recipient Citizens award U.S. Dept. Interior, 1976; Water Leader of Yr. award Colo. Water Congress, 1981; Outstanding Pub. Service award Water for Colo., 1982, others. Mem. Water Resources Congress (chmn. 1981), ASCE, Nat. Rifle Assn., Beta Theta Pi. Clubs: Masons, (32 deg.), Shriners. Address: 340 Lorey Dr Grand Junction CO 81505

GOSS, BARRY ALAN, computer systems executive, consultant; b. Bronx, N.Y., Nov. 14, 1946; s. Milton and Marilyn (Klein) G.; m. Claire Maureen Wechsler; 1 son, Andrew Ian. B.E., SUNY-Stony Brook, 1968; M.S.M.E., U. Conn., Storrs, 1971, Ph.D. in Applied Mechanics, 1975. Sr. systems analyst Pratt & Whitney Aircraft, East Hartford, Conn., 1968-73; product devel. mgr. Olinski Co., Middletown, Conn., 1975; mgr. computer systems and product integration Gerber Systems Tech., South Windsor, Conn., 1975-80; v.p. systems div. Comsat Gen. Integrated Systems, Palo Alto, Calif., 1980-81, v.p. tech. planning, 1981-83; v.p. ops. NCA Corp., Sunnyvale, Calif., 1983—; cons. Congruent Concepts, Menlo Park, Calif. Mem. IEEE, ACM, ASME, AIAA, Computer and Automated Systems Assn., Phi Kappa Phi, Pi Tau Sigma, Tau Beta Pi. Contbr. articles to profl. jours.

GOSS, GEORGIA BULMAN, translator; b. N.Y.C., Dec. 1, 1939; d. James Cornelius and Marian Bright (McLaughlin) Bulman; m. Douglas Keith Goss, Dec. 21, 1957; children—Kristin Anne, David. B.A., U. Mich., 1961. Librarian, High Altitude Obs., Boulder, Colo., 1963-64, U.S. Bur. Standards, Boulder, 1964-65; cons. editor Spanish lang. pilots' tng. manual, 1981-82; freelance translator, Englewood, Colo., 1982—. Mem. Internat. Trade Assn. Colo., Nat. Assn. Female Execs., Phi Sigma Iota. Republican. Episcopalian. Home and Office: 5091 S Boston St Englewood CO 80111

GOSS, JAMES ARTHUR, botanist; b. Brigham City, Utah, May 19, 1924; s. Archie James and Mary Alberta (Pulsipher) G.; m. Lucille Woolley, Mar. 21, 1947; children—Lawrence Arthur, Raymond Lynn, Linda Lucille, Gerlad Lee, Liana Denise, Lori Jean. B.S., Utah State U., 1951; Ph.D., UCLA, 1957. Jr. plant physiologist Salinity Lab., U.S. Dept. Agr., Riverside, Calif., 1951-53; research asst. atomic energy project Sch. Medicine, UCLA, 1953-56; mem. faculty div. biology Kans. State U., Manhattan, 1956-76; livestock feed analyst Scott-Pro, Inc., Scott City, Kans., 1979-83; owner, analyst DAR Lab., Lamar, Colo., 1983—; lectr. throughout world. Mem. Bot. Soc. Am., Am. Chem. Soc., Am. Assn. Feed Microscopists, Am. Assn. Cereal Chemist, Sigma Xi, Gamma Sigma Delta. Mormon. Author: Physiology of Plants and Their Cells; contbr. articles to profl. jours., mags., newspapers; research on plant physiology and chemistry. Home: 405 S 3d St Lamar CO 81052

GOSS, JOHN RAY, agricultural engineer; b. Winona, Minn., May 30, 1923; s. Homer and Cora Emila (Sebo) G.; student U. Notre Dame, 1943-44, St. Olaf Coll., 1941-43; B.S., UCLA, 1952; M.S., U. Calif.-Davis, 1956; m. Patricia Louise Dunn, Aug. 10, 1947; children—John Randall, Patricia Anne, William Arlington, Nancy Louise. Mem. faculty agrl. engring. U. Calif.-Davis, 1956—, chmn. dept., 1968-73, acad. asst. to chancellor, 1963-66, prof., agrl. engr. Agrl. Expt. Sta., 1966—; agrl. engr. Coop. State Research Service, Dept. Agr., 1975-76; cons. NSF, 1976-77; mem. bd. patents U. Calif. Served to 1st lt. USMC, 1943-49. Registered profl. engr., Calif. Fellow Am. Soc. Agrl. Engrs. (Engr. of Yr. award Pacific region, pvt. research award); mem. AAAS, Am. Soc. Agrl. Engrs., Soc. Am. Foresters, Am. Soc. Engring. Edn., Nat. Soc. Profl. Engrs., Calif. Soc. Profl. Engrs., N.Y. Acad. Scis., Sigma Xi, Tau Beta Pi. Contbr. articles to profl. jours., chpts. to books. Home: 754 Plum Ln Davis CA 95616 Office: Dept Agrl Engring U Calif Davis CA 95616

GOTELLI, DOLPH EDWARD, designer, educator; b. Stockton, Calif., Feb. 9, 1942; s. Adolph Anthony and Catherine Adelle (Delucchi) G.; B.A., San Francisco State U., 1964; M.A., UCLA, 1967. Designer exhbns. Homage to Bag, Am. Crafts Mus., N.Y.C., 1976, Devils, Demons and Dragons, Los Angeles Craft and Folk Art Mus., 1976-77, Box Show, Meml. Union Art Gallery, U., Calif.-Davis, 1977, The Souvenir as Art, Meml. Union Art Gallery, 1980, World Crafts Council, 1980, Chevron Gallery, San Francisco, 1981-82; faculty U. Calif., Davis, 1970—, asso. prof. design, 1978—; guest curator, designer Santa Show, E.B. Crocker Art Mus., Sacramento, 1977-78; freelance designer, cons.; lectr. on fantasy in design, antique Christmas memorabilia. Served with USCGR, 1965. Mem. Am. Assn. Art Museums. Office: Dept Design U Calif Davis CA 95616

GOTO, KENJI, former hosp. adminstr. and cons.; b. Puako, Hawaii, Oct. 10, 1904; s. Unokichi and Yana (Inaba) G.; B.A. in Bus. and Econs., U. Hawaii, 1927, postgrad., 1930-31; m. Hagino Mikami, Feb. 23, 1935; children—Irving Ken, Alan Jiro. Salesman, Theodore H. Davies & Co., Honolulu, 1927-29; mgr. U. Goto Store, Kona, Hawaii, 1929-30; tchr. Konawaena High Sch., 1931-42; prin. Hookena Elementary Sch., 1942-43; supr. On-Job Tng. Program for Vets., Honolulu, 1947-48; adminstr. Kuakini Hosp. and Home, 1948-69, cons., 1970-73. Pres., Oahu Health Council, 1959-61; mem. Mayor's Adv. Com. on Community Renewal Program, 1964-65; vice chmn. Hawaii Adv. Council Hosp. and Med. Facilities, 1965-76; mem. Honolulu Com. on Aging, 1970-78, chmn., 1976-78; chmn. adv. com. Honolulu Heart Research Programs, 1964-77, state and Oahu chmn. Com. for Centennial Celebration of Japanese Immigration to Hawaii, 1967-68; chmn. Centennial Celebration Arrival of Govt.-contract Japanese Immigrants to Hawaii, 1983—; leader U.S. Army Pacific Friendship Mission to Japan, 1968; chmn. adv. com. Japan-Hawaii Cancer Study, 1971-77; mem. Crown Prince Akihito Scholarship Fund, 1972—, chmn., 1980—; treas., chmn. membership com. Japanese Immigrant Heritage Mus., 1975—; bd. dirs. Kuakini Med. Center, 1973-79; chmn. bd. Hawaii Sr. Services, Inc., 1977-79. Served with AUS, 1943-45. Named Hawaii Man of Year, 1970; recipient Outstanding Older Am. award for County of Honolulu, 1979. Mem. United Japanese Soc. Hawaii (pres. 1967-68, adviser 1969—), Am. Coll. Hosp. Adminstrs. (life), Hosp. Assn. Hawaii (pres. 1957, 67), Japan-Am. Soc. Honolulu (trustee 1976—), Teiko Kai (pres. chpt. 1978—). Home: 99-869 Lalawai Dr Alea HI 96701

GOTSHALL, DANIEL WARREN, biologist, state ofcl.; b. Springfield, Ill., Dec. 20, 1929; s. Robert W. and Louise Julia (Steele) G.; A.A., Modesto Jr. Coll., 1951; M.S., Humboldt State U., 1970; m. Cordia Ann Moreland, Apr. 12, 1952. Jr. aquatic biologist Calif. Dept. Fish and Game, Eureka, 1957-59, asst. marine biologist, Menlo Park, 1960-64, asso. marine biologist, Eureka, 1964-70, sr. research marine biologist, Monterey, 1971—; cons. on shrimp and market crab studies Alaska Dept. Fish and Game, 1969, Calif. State U. at Humboldt, 1969-70; cons. biol. studies Morro Bay Canal, Calif., 1970; research asso. in ichthyology Los Angeles Mus. Natural History, 1971—; vice chmn. Calif. Adv. Bd. on Underwater Parks and Reserves, 1974—; mem. Calif. Dept. Fish and Game Diving Safety Bd., 1970-80; asso. invertebrate Zoology Calif. Acad. Scis., 1975—; lectr. Pacific Sci. Congress, 1975. Served with USNR, 1952-54; Korea. Fellow Am. Inst. Fishery Research Biologists, Explorers Club; mem. Am. Fisheries Soc. (pres. Nev.-Calif. chpt. 1979). Author: Fishwatchers Guide to the Inshore Fishes of the Pacific Coast, 1977. Pacific Coast Subtidal Marine Invertebrates, 1979; Pacific Coast Inshore Fishes, 1981; Marine Animals of Baja California, 1982; contbr. articles on marine ecology and biology to sci. jours. Home: 1851 Don Ave Los Osos CA 93402 Office: PO Box 98 Avila CA 93424

GOTTFREDSON, DOUGLAS KING, clinical psychologist; b. Ely, Nev., Jan. 27, 1933; s. Raymon Ward and Melba Utahna (Riddle) G.; B.A., Brigham Young U., 1957, M.S., 1971, Ph.D., 1973; m. Janice Leone Walker, June 8, 1956; children—Mark, Vicki, Colette, Melanie, Karen. Psychologist, VA Med. Center, Ft. Lyon, Colo., 1973-77; chief psychiat. assessment unit VA Med. Center, Salt Lake City, 1977-82, psychologist biomed. and computer systems sect., 1982-83; psychologist Regional Info. Services Ctr., VA Med Region 5, 1983—; cons. VA, hosps.; asst. prof. U. Utah. Served with USAF, 1958-69. Decorated Air Force Commendation medal; recipient outstanding performance awards VA; HEW research grantee, 1973. Mem. Am. Psychol. Assn., Utah Psychol. Assn. Mormon. Author computer users manual. Home: 9932 S 2270 E Sandy UT 84092 Office: 500 Foothill Dr Salt Lake City UT 84148

GOTTLIEB, ALAN MERRILL, association executive; b. Los Angeles, May 2, 1947; s. Seymour and Sherry (Schutz) G.; m. Julie Hoy Versnel, July 27, 1979; 1 dau., Amy Jean. B.S. in Nuclear Engring., U. Tenn., 1971; postgrad. Georgetown U. Inst. Comparative Econ. and Polit. Systems. Nat. dir. Young Ams. for Freedom, Washington, 1971-72; nat. treas. Am. Conservative Union, Washington, 1971—; chmn. Citizens Com. for Right to Keep and Bear Arms, Bellevue, Wash., 1974—; pres. Ctr. Def. of Free Enterprise, Bellevue 1976—; pres. Second Amendment Found., Bellevue, 1974—. Served with U.S. Army, 1968-74. Recipient Good Citizenship award Citizens Home Protective Assn., 1978, Cicero award Nat. Assn. Federally Licensed Firearms Dealers, 1982. Mem. Direct Mail Mktg. Assn. Wash., Nat. Rifle Assn. Republican. Jewish. Author: The Gun Owners Political Action Manual, 1976; The Rights of Gun Owners, 1981.

GOTTLIEB, PETER, computer scientist; b. Cleve., Nov. 29, 1935; s. Morris and Edith (Chaikoff) G.; student U. Chgo., 1954; B.S., Calif. Inst. Tech., 1956; Ph.D., M.I.T., 1959; m. Laurie Geber, July 14, 1956; children—Michael, Gabrielle, James. Mem. tech. staff Hughes Research Labs., Malibu, Calif., 1959-64, Librascope, Inc., Glendale, 1964-66, Jet Propulsion Lab., Pasadena, 1966-73; dir. computer services Dames & Moore, Los Angeles, 1973-82; dept. mgr. TRW Systems, Redondo Beach, Calif., 1982—; vis. asst. prof. Calif. State U., Los Angeles, 1967; research asso. U. Calif., San Diego, 1962-63. Mem. IEEE, Sigma Xi. Author: Probably and Statistics, 1971. Home: 246 S Anita St Los Angeles CA 90049 Office: 445 S Figueroa Ave Los Angeles CA 90071

GOTTSCHALK, LOUIS AUGUST, psychiatrist; b. St. Louis, Aug. 26, 1916; s. Max W. and Kelmie (Mutrux) G.; A.B., Washington U., St. Louis, 1940, M.D., 1943; m. Helen Reller, July 24, 1944; children—Guy H., Claire A., Louise H., Susan E. Asst. in neuropsychiatry Washington U. Sch. Medicine, 1944-46; commd. asst. surgeon USPHS, 1946, advanced through grades to med. dir., 1960, instr. psychiatry S.W. Med. Coll., Dallas, 1947-48, research psychiatrist Nat. Inst. Mental Health, Bethesda, Md., 1950-53; coordinator research, research prof. psychiatry U. Cin. Coll. Medicine, 1953-67; attending psychiatrist Cin. Gen. Hosp., 1953-67; faculty Inst. Psychoanalysis, Chgo., 1957-67; chmn. research com. Hamilton County (Ohio) Diagnostic Center, 1958-67; cons. 1963-67; prof. dept. psychiatry and human behavior Coll. Medicine, U. Calif.-Irvine, 1967—, chmn. dept., 1967-78, prof. social sci., social ecology, 1969—, asst. dir. psychiat. services Med. Center, 1967-71, dir., 1971-77, dir. psychiat. consultation and liaison program Med. Ctr., 1978—; dir. psychiat. services Orange County Med. Ctr., 1972-79; Mem. clin. psychopharmacology study sect. NIMH, research rev. com. NIDA, Calif. Dept. Mental Hygiene, 1968-71. Recipient Franz Alexander Essay prize So. Cal. Psychoanalytic Inst., Los Angeles, 1973. Fellow AAAS, Am. Psychiat. Assn. (Founds. Fund Prize for psychiatry research 1978), Am. Coll. Neuropsychopharmacology, (coms.), Am. Coll. Psychiatrists; mem. Assn. Research Nervous and Mental Diseases, Am. Psychosomatic Soc., Cin. Soc. Neurology and Psychiatry (past pres.), Am. Psychoanalytic Assn., AMA, Orange County Med. Assn., So. Calif. Psychiat. Soc., Am. Assn. Child Psychoanalysts, So. Calif., Los Angeles psychoanalytic socs. and insts., Phi Beta Kappa, Sigma Xi, Alpha Omega Alpha. Author: (with G.C. Gleser) The Measurement of Psychological States through the Content Analysis of Verbal Behavior, 1969. Editor: Comparative Psycholinguistic Analysis of Two Psychotherapeutic Interviews, 1961; (with A.H. Auerbach) Methods of Research in Psychotherapy, 1966, How to Understand Your Own Dreams, 1975, Content Analysis of Verbal Behavior: Further Studies, 1979; Pharmacokinetics of Psychoactive Drugs: Further Studies, 1979; (with McGuire, Dinovo and others) Guide to the Investigating and Reporting of Drug Abuse Deaths, 1979, Drug Abuse Deaths in Nine Cities: A Survey Report, 1980; (with R. Cravey) Toxicological and Pathological Studies on Psychoactive Drug-Involved Deaths, 1980; others. Editorial bd. Research Communications in Psychology, Psychiatry, Psychiatry and Behavior, Am. Jour. Psychotherapy, Methods and Findings in Exptl. and Clin. Pharmacology. Contbr. numerous articles to tech. lit. Home: 4607 Perham Rd Corona Del Mar CA 92625 Office: Dept Psychiatry and Human Behavior College Medicine U Calif Irvine CA 92717

GOUGH, DENIS IAN, educator; b. Port Elizabeth, South Africa, June 20, 1922; B.Sc., Rhodes U. Coll., South Africa, 1943, M.Sc., 1947; Ph.D. in Geophysics, U. Witwatersrand, 1953; m. 1945; 2 children. Research officer geophysics South African Nat. Phys. Research Lab., 1947-55, sr. research officer, 1955-58; lectr. Univ. Coll. Rhodesia and Nyasaland, 1958-60, sr. lectr., 1961-63; asso. prof. geophysics Southwest Center Advanced Studies, Dallas, 1964-66; prof. U. Alta., 1966—. Fellow Royal Soc. Can., Royal Astron. Soc., Am. Geophys. Union; mem. Can. Geophys. Union (chmn. 1975-77). Address: Dept Physics U Alberta Edmonton AB T6G 2J1 Canada

GOUGH, ROBERT GEORGE, air force officer; b. Abington, Pa., Apr. 15, 1941; s. Harold B. and Ruth M. (Dupert) G.; m. Jean B. Craig, Apr. 6, 1963, 1 son, Steven R. B.S. in Chem. Engring., Lehigh U., 1962; M.B.A. with honors, U. Chgo., 1966; M.S., Stanford U., 1972, Ph.D., 1974. Commd. officer U.S. Air Force, 1963, advanced through grades to lt. col., 1983, asst. to dir. net assessment Immediate Office of Sec. of Def., Washington, 1976-79, chief Electronic Systems Div., Air Force Test and Evaluation Ctr., N.Mex., 1979—; adj. prof. mgmt., statistics and econs. U. Md., 1969-70, U. Colo., 1968, 75-76, George Washington U., 1976-79, N.Mex. Highland U., 1981—, U. N.Mex., 1982—; cons. in field. Bishop's warden, vestryman, treas. ch. bldg. com. Episcopal Ch., 1970—; bd. dirs. PTO, 1974-76. Mem. Am. Inst. Decision Sci. (v.p. 1976), Mil. Ops. Research Symposium (founding chmn. Decision Analysis Working Group), Alpha Iota Delta, Beta Gamma Sigma, Omicron Delta Epsilon. Contbr. articles to prof. jours. Home: 8912 Camino Osito NE Albuquerque NM 87111 Office: AFTEC/OAY Kirtland AFB NM 87117

GOUGH, WILLIAM CABOT, engr.; b. Jersey City, Aug. 22, 1930; s. William Lincoln and Lillian May (Mansmann) G.; B.S. in Engring., Princeton U., 1952, M.S. in Engring., 1953; postgrad. Harvard U., 1966-67; m. Marion Louise McConnell, Apr. 27, 1957; children—Barbara Louise, William Scott. Adminstrv. engr. civilian power program AEC, Washington, 1953-55, indsl. info. officer, 1958-60, tech. asst. for systems, plans and programs, div. controlled thermonuclear research, 1960-74; project engr. nuclear aircraft program U.S. Navy, Washington, 1955-58; program mgr. fusion power, new energy resources dept. Electric Power Research Inst., Palo Alto, Calif., 1974-77; sr. DOE/EPRI energy program coordinator, tech. dir. Office Program Assessment and Integration, U.S. Dept. Energy, San Francisco and Palo Alto, Calif., 1977-81, site mgr. Stanford U., Oakland and Stanford, Calif., 1981—; cons. in field. Served with USN, 1955-58. Registered profl. engr., Calif.; recipient Spl. Achievement Certificate, AEC, 1973. Mem. Am. Nuclear Soc. (Sec. exec. com. of controlled nuclear fusion div.), N.Y. Acad. Scis., Fedn. Am. Scientists, AAAS, World Future Soc., Common Cause, UN Assn. Contbr. articles, chpts. to tech. jours., texts. Home: 442 Knoll Dr Los Altos CA 94022 Office: Stanford Linear Accelerator Center PO Box 4349 Bin 8A Stanford CA 94305 also US Dept Energy 1333 Broadway Oakland CA 94612

GOULD, ARTHUR, real estate and energy devel. co. exec.; b. National City, Calif., Apr. 12, 1917; s. Arthur L. T. and Lilian (Whittemore) G.; B.A., Brigham Young U., 1940; m. Barbara Bunting, Apr. 23, 1955; children—Dianne, Arthur B., Frederick Earl, Brian Keith, Michael John; 1 stepson, Kenneth P. Bunting. Pres., Argo Co., Carlsbad, Calif. Served with U.S. Army, 1946. Office: Suite 138 Box 9000 Carlsbad CA 92008

GOULD, CHARLES LAVERNE, aerospace company executive; b. Winston, Mo., Oct. 26, 1933; s. Clem Seward and Nora Beatrice (Harris) G.; B.S.M.E., Iowa State U., 1956; Cert. of Bus., UCLA, 1966; Ph.D., Calif. Western U., 1978; children—Anita Christine, Katherine Marie. Aerospace engr. U.S. Air Force, Dayton, Ohio, 1960-62; with Rockwell Internat., Downey, Calif., 1962—, program engring. mgr. NASA programs, 1970-72, program engring. mgr. def. programs 1972-74, program mgr. space industrialization, 1976-78, program mgr. space shuttle utilization, 1980—. Chmn. bd. St. Mark's Meth. Ch., Anaheim, Calif., 1967, trustee, 1972-75; mem. bus. steering com. Reagan for Pres., 1980. Served with USAF, 1957-60. Recipient Sustained Superior Performance award USAF, 1962. Cert. profl. mgr., Calif. Asso. fellow AIAA; mem. Nat. Mgmt. Assn. Contbr. articles to profl. jours. Home: 1832 Sunset Ln Fullerton CA 92633 Office: 12214 Lakewood Blvd Downey CA 90241

GOULD, CLIO LAVERNE, electric utility and irrigation dist. exec.; b. Madison, S.D., Feb. 20, 1919; s. Howard Bennett and Moneta Kay (Herrick) G.; student Walla Walla Coll., 1948, U. Wash. Extension, 1954, U. Calif. at San Diego Extension, 1962, Capital Radio Engring. Inst. Corr., 1958-62; diploma elec. engring. Internat. Corr. Schs., 1958; m. Mildred May Newell, Apr. 13, 1942; children—George Marcus, Deanna May (Mrs. Terry L. Paxton). With astronautics div. Gen. Dynamics Corp., San Diego, 1957-66, sr. design engr. research and devel. Atlas and Centaur space vehicles, 1958-66; supt. power and pumping depts. Wellton Mohawk Irrigation & Drainage Dist., Wellton, Ariz., 1966-76, gen. mgr., 1976—. treas. Liga Internat., Inc., San Diego, 1964-65. Served with AUS, 1941-45; PTO. Recipient Performance award Gen. Dynamics Corp., 1963. Registered profl. engr., Ariz. Mem. IEEE (sr.), AIAA, Nat., Ariz. (pres. chpt. 1977-78) socs. profl. engrs., Photog. Soc. Am., Nat. Water Resources Assn., Ariz. State Reclamation Assn., Colorado River Water Users Assn. (bd. dirs. 1982—), Ariz. Agri-Bus. Council (exec. bd. 1980—, v.p. 1981). Republican. Seventh-day Adventist (elder 1956—, chmn. bldg. com. 1970-73). Home: Route 1 Box 4 Wellton AZ 85356 Office: Route 1 Box 19 Wellton AZ 85356

GOULD, DARLENE CARYL, communicologist; educator; b. Los Angeles, Apr. 28, 1939; d. Allen Charles and Loretta Catherine (Geary) Geer; B.A. with honors, San Diego State U., 1962, M.A., 1965; postgrad. Purdue U., 1965-66; m. Lowell Davies (dec.); 1 son, David Gould. Instr. speech and drama Bishop's Sch., La Jolla, Calif., 1961; speech pathologist, supr. chmn. speech pathology dept. Children's Health Center, San Diego, 1967-71; dir. speech and hearing clinic Naval Regional Med. Center, Balboa Naval Hosp., 1971-76; clinic coordinator, asst. prof. communicative disorders San Diego State U., 1976—; mem. prof. adv. bd. San Diego Speech and Hearing Neurosensory Center, 1971-74; cons. several San Diego county sch. dists., 1977-81. Mem. San Diego City Adv. Bd. on Women, 1981; bd. visitors Bishop's Sch., La Jolla, 1983; founder Old Globe Theatre. Lic. in speech pathology Calif. Bd. Med. Quality Assurance. Mem. Am. Speech Lang. and Hearing Assn. (cert. clin. competence in speech pathology; asst. book rev. editor), Alexander Graham Bell Assn. for Deaf, Mortar Bd. Alumni Assn. Contbr. articles to profl. and gen. interest publs.; asst. book rev. editor Am. Speech-Lang-Hearing Assn., 1981—. Office: San Diego State U San Diego CA 92182

GOULD, FRANK NELSON, JR., banker; b. Mpls., May 19, 1926; s. Frank Nelson and Ella (Exe) G.; B.A., Mont. State U., 1950; m. June Beach, Sept. 1, 1948; children—Howard, Gregory, Tracy. Asst. v.p. Metals Bank & Trust Co., Butte, Mont., 1950-60; with First Interstate Bank of Calif., Los Angeles, 1960—, sr. v.p., 1971—. Bd. dirs. Oakland Boys Club, 1978—, A Central Place, 1980—; mem. adv. council Family Companion Program of City of Oakland, 1979—; adv. bd. Nat. Alliance of Bus., 1974-80. Served with USN, 1944-46. Republican. Lutheran. Home: 409 Birchwood Dr Moraga CA 94556 Office: 1330 Broadway Oakland CA 94612

GOULD, GARY HOWARD, state senator, insurance agent; b. Dayton, Oreg., Apr. 1, 1938; s. Calvin J. and Alice Viola G.; student North Idaho Coll., 1957-59; B.A. in Govt., Idaho State U., 1965, M.A. in Edn., 1971; m. March Jean Gould, July 24, 1963; children—Susan Marie, Jon Calvin. Dir. fin. aids and scholarships Idaho State U., 1969-78, spl. asst. to v.p. for adminstrn., 1978-79, ins. agent, realtor Paul Smith Agy., Pocatello, Idaho, 1979—; mem. Idaho Ho. of Reps., 1977-80, Idaho Senate, 1980—. Precinct committeeman, Bannock County, Idaho, 1972-74; chmn. Democratic Central Com., 1974-77. Served with U.S. Army, 1959-61. Mem. Idaho Realtors Assn., Ind. Ins. Agts. Assn., Western Council State Legislators, Phi Delta Kappa. Roman Catholic. Clubs: Masons, Elks. Office: 541 S 7th St Pocatello ID 83201

GOULD, JONATHON PAUL, marketing executive; b. Queens, N.Y., Mar. 17, 1955; s. Leon Mark and Lucille S. G. B.A. in Econs., UCLA, 1977; M.B.A., U. Mich., 1981. Mem. police/fire selection unit City of Los Angeles, 1977-78; mgr. trainee Distgn. Center, Upjohn Co., Los Angeles, Calif., 1978-79; logistics anlayst Standard Brands, Inc., N.Y.C., 1980; product mgr. mass market Avery Consumer Products, Los Angeles, 1981—. Mem. Los Angeles Olympic Com.; mem. Citizen's Adv. Commn. Fencing. Recipient Sabre Gold medal Under 19 Pacific Coast Championships, 1964, Foil Bronze medal, 1964. Mem. Am. Mktg. Assn., Planning Execs. Inst., Am. Mgmt. Assn., So. Calif. Assn. Corporate Planners, Beta Gamma Sigma. Democrat. Jewish. Clubs: U.S. Fencing Assn.; Mori Fencing Acad. (Los Angeles). Home: 4452 Ensign Ave Apt 202 North Hollywood CA 91602 Office: 777 E Foothill Blvd Azusa CA 91702

GOULD, MAXINE LUBOW, oil and gas company official; b. Bridgeton, N.J., Feb. 28, 1942; d. Louis A. and Bernice L. (Goldberg) Lubow; B.S., Temple U., 1962, J.D., 1968; m. Sam C. Gould, June 17, 1962 (separated 1982); children—Jack, Herman, David. Head resident dept. student personnel Temple U., 1962-66; dir., treas. Hilltop Interest Program, Inc., Los Angeles, 1973-74; law clk. law firms, Los Angeles, 1975-77; with Buffalo Resources Corp., Los Angeles, 1978-82, corporate sec., 1979-82; corporate sec., securities prin. Buffalo Securities Corp., Los Angeles, 1979-82; contracts analyst Texaco, Inc., 1982—; corp. sec. LaMaur Devel. Corp., Los Angeles, 1979-82. Mem. Roscomare Valley Assn. Edn. Com., Bel Air, Calif., 1975-76; subcom. chmn. Roscomare Rd. Sch. Citizens Adv. Council, Bel Air; active various community drives. Recipient Joseph B. Wagner Oratory award B'nai B'rith, 1959, Voice of Democracy award, 1958-59, award Commentator Club, 1959. Mem. Nat. Assn. Female Execs. (network dir.), Calif. Women Lawyers, Women in Bus., Los Angeles Assn. Petroleum Landmen, Am. Assn. Petroleum Landmen, Toastmasters Internat. (adminstrv. v.p. Texaco chpt.), Phi Alpha Theta, Alpha Lambda Delta. Jewish. Home: 2501 Roscomare Rd Bel Air CA 90077

GOULD, NELSON AARON, aerospace engr.; b. New Bedford, Mass., June 22, 1931; s. William and Jennie (Rotman) Goldstein; m. Adele Ila Mennis, Jan. 30, 1960. B.S.Ch.E., Purdue U., 1959; courses in contract adminstrn. UCLA, 1964; courses in aerospace ops. mgmt. U. So. Calif., 1968; attended Coll. Armed Forces, 1975, Air Force Inst. Tech., 1978, Def. Systems Mgmt. Coll., 1980. Test engr. Rocketdyne div. NAA, Inc., 1959-60; chem. engr., Air Force plant rep. Office Rocketdyne Div., Air Force Contract Mgmt. Div., Air Force Systems Command, Dept. Air Force, 1961-69, supervisory aerospace engr., 1970-77, supervisory aerospace engr. Def. Contract Adminstrn. Office, 1978-82, Air Force Plant Rep. Office, also chief engring. and program support div., 1982—. Bd. govs. North Hollywood Terr. Homeowners Assn.; bd. dirs. Oaktree Homeowners Assn. Served with U.S. Army, 1953-56. Fellow ASTM (vice chmn. com. F-7 on aerospace industry methods, aerospace and aircraft 1978-83, award of merit 1978), Inst. Advancement Engring., Los Angeles Council Engrs. and Scientists; mem. AIAA, Am. Inst. Chem. Engrs., San Fernando Valley Engrs. Council (Engring. Merit award 1970), Planetary Soc., Air Force Assn., Am. Ordnance Assn. Democrat. Jewish. Club: Elks. Home: 2424 Stow St Simi Valley CA 93063 Office: 6633 Canoga Ave AA14 Canoga Park CA 91304

GOULD, RONALD BRUCE, accountant, auditor; b. Pasadena, Calif., Sept. 30, 1944; s. Fletcher Oliver and Bernita (Worrall) G.; B.S. with honors in Econs. and Stats., U. Calif.-Berkeley, 1966, M.B.A. with honors in Acctg. and Systems Theory, 1967; m. Christine Zakarian, Sept. 9, 1967; children—Ryan Berkeley, Dyana Lindsay. Cons., Touche, Ross & Co., Portland, Oreg., 1967-68, staff acct., 1972-75, audit supr., 1975-77, audit mgr., 1977-79, audit partner, 1980-81, dir. audit ops.,

1981—. Active Multiple Sclerosis Soc., Served to capt. U.S. Army, 1968-71. Mem. Am. Inst. C.P.A.s, Oreg. Soc. C.P.A.s, M.B.A. Execs., Planning Execs. Inst. (past pres., past sec., past dir., mem. chmn. Portland chpt., recipient outstanding achievement awards, 1975, 76), Big C Soc. (U. Calif.-Berkeley), Calif. Alumni Assn., Calif. Bus. Alumni Assn. Republican. Presbyterian. Home: 4970 Centerwood St Lake Oswego OR 97034 Office: One SW Columbia St Suite 1500 Portland OR 97258

GOULD, WILLIAM EBEN, mathematician; b. Orange, N.J., May 7, 1934; s. Eben Cassius and Margaret (Purple) G.; B.A., Rutgers U., 1956, M.S., 1958; M.A., Princeton U., 1964, Ph.D. (NSF fellow), 1966; Instr., Rutgers U., New Brunswick, N.J., 1961-62; instr. Washington Coll., Chestertown, Md., 1962-66; asso. prof. Bradley U., Peoria, Ill., 1966-69; asso. prof. math Calif. State U., Dominguez Hills, 1969-74, prof., 1974—. Mem. AAUP, Math. Assn. Am., Sigma Xi. Home: 12529 Sleepyhollow Ln Cerritos CA 90701 Office: Dept Math Calif State U Dominguez Hills Carson CA 90747

GOULD, WILLIAM RICHARD, utility exec., engr.; b. Provo, Utah, Oct. 31, 1919; s. William Gilbert and Pauline Eva (Faser) G.; B.S. in Mech. Engring., U. Utah, 1942; postgrad. Mass. Inst. Tech., U. Calif. at Los Angeles, U. Idaho; m. Erlyn Arvilla Johnson, Mar. 20, 1942; children—Erlyn Sharon, William Richard, Gilbert John, Wayne Raymond. With So. Calif. Edison Co., 1948—, mgr. engring., 1962-63, v.p. engring., constrn., planning, 1963-67, sr. v.p., 1967-73, exec. v.p., 1973-78, pres., 1978-80, chmn. bd., 1980—, also dir.; dir. Energy Services Inc., Mono Power Co., Electric Systems Co., Associated So. Investment Co. Chmn., Calif. Tech. Services Adv. Council; pres. U.S. nat. com. Internat. Congress Large Electric Systems; chmn. bd. Atomic Indsl. Forum. Mem. sci. and engring. com. U. Redlands; bd. councilors Sch. Engring., U. So. Calif., chmn. mgmt. com. WEST Assos.; mem. energy adv. bd. Calif. Inst. Tech.; mem. nat. regulatory commn., exec. com. Assembly Engring.; mem. nat. adv. bd. U. Utah; mem. adv. com. electric certificate program U. Calif. at Los Angeles; mem. adv. bd. Naval Postgrad. Sch. Trustee Long Beach Community Hosp.; bd. dirs. Electric Power Research Inst., Eyring Research Inst. Served to lt. USN, 1942-47. Registered profl. engr., Utah, Calif. Fellow ASME, Inst. Advanced Engring. (chmn. bd., Engr. of Year 1970); mem. Nat. Acad. Engring., Newcomen Soc. N.Am., Edison Electric Inst. (chmn. exec. adv. bd. policy com. on nuclear power, mem. policy com. on research), Pacific Coast Elec. Assn. (dir.), Los Angeles C. of C. Mem. Ch. of Jesus Christ of Latter Day Saints. Clubs: Lincoln, California. Office: 2244 Walnut Grove Ave Rosemead CA 91770*

GOULDING, MERRILL KEITH, consulting engineer; b. Erie, Pa., Jan. 21, 1933; s. Forest Clute and Felicita Clara (Johnson) G.; B.S., UCLA, 1968, Ph.D., 1979; children—Merrill, Robert, Nida, Gina. Asst. to v.p. Internat. Controls Corp., 1963-69; chmn. bd. Village Verde Corp., 1963-64; pres. Merrill K. Goulding & Assocs., Inc., Glendale, Calif., 1974—; chief exec. officer Coin Cop Electronics Co., 1975—. Bd. dirs. Rio Hondo Area Action Com., 1970; guiding counselor Inst. Cultural Affairs; past pres. Request Computer Users Group. Served with USMC, 1953. Registered profl. engr., N.Y. Calif., NY. Mem. ASME, IEEE, AIAA, Nat. Soc. Profl. Engrs., Calif. Soc. Profl. Engrs., Am. Soc. Metals, Constrn. Specifications Inst., Soc. Material and Process Engrs., Vols. in Tech. Assistance, Mensa. Republican. Clubs: Shriners, Calif. Yacht. Address: PO Box 33 Glendale CA 91209

GOULDS, PETER JOHN, art dealer; b. London, Oct. 5, 1948; s. Anthony John and Florence Mary Ann (Keenes) G.; m. Elizabeth Mary Temple, Jan. 1, 1975. Student Wathemstow Sch. Art (Eng.), 1965-67; B.A. with honors, Coventry Sch. Art (Eng.), 1970; H.D.D., Manchester (Eng.) Sch. Art, 1971; postgrad. (fellow of advanced studies) Manchester Poly., 1971-72; Cert. Soc. Typographic Designers. Lectr. Bolton Sch. Art, 1971; lectr. Leeds (Eng.) Sch. Art, 1972; lectr. UCLA, 1972-75; owner, dir. L.A. Louver Gallery and L.A. Louver Publs., Venice, Calif., 1975—. Recipient Lever hulme award, 1971; U. Calif. research grantee, 1972-75. Mem. Art Dealers Assn. So. Calif. Contbr. articles to profl. jours. Office: 55 N Venice Blvd Venice CA 90291

GOULDTHORPE, KENNETH ALFRED PERCIVAL, publisher; b. London, Jan. 7, 1928; s. Alfred Edward and Frances Elizabeth Finch (Callow) G.; came to U.S., 1951, naturalized, 1956; m. Judith Marion Cutts, Aug. 9, 1975. Student U. London, 1948-49, Bloomsbury Tech. Inst., 1949-50; diploma City and Guilds of London, 1949; student, Washington U., 1951-53. Staff photographer St. Louis Post-Dispatch, 1951-57, picture editor, 1955-57; nat. and fgn. corr. Life mag., Time, Inc., N.Y.C., 1957-65, regional editor Australia-New Zealand, 1966-68, editorial dir. Latin Am., 1969-70; editor Signature mag., N.Y.C., 1970-73; mng. editor Penthouse mag., N.Y.C., 1973-76, pub. cons., 1976-79; editor, exec. pub. Adventure Travel mag., Seattle, 1979-80; sr. ptnr. Pacific Pub. Assocs., Seattle, 1981—; tchr. design, editorial techniques Parsons Sch. Design, N.Y.C.; lectr., mem. seminar faculty Writer's Digest. Served with Royal Navy, 1946-48. Decorated Naval Medal and bar; recipient awards of excellence Nat. Press Photographers Assn., AP and UP, 1951-57; certs. excellence, Am. Inst. Graphic Arts, 1971, 72, 73, Communication Arts, 1980, 81; spl. award, N.Y. Soc. Publs. Designers, 1980. Mem. Western Publs. Assn. (Best Consumer Mag. award, Best Travel Mag. awards, 1980), Time/Life Alumni Soc., Sigma Delta Chi. Episcopalian. Nominated for Pulitzer Prize for coverage of Andrea Doria disaster, 1956; contbr. articles, photographs to nat. mags., books by Life mag. Home: 3049 NW Esplanade Seattle WA 98117

GOVINE, BARBARA FREUDENTHAL, transpersonal therapist, educator; b. Chgo., Mar. 19, 1933; d. James Hart and Margaret (Eisenstaedt) Freudenthal; children—Deborah Weiner Lillo, Richard Kenneth Weiner. B.S., UCLA, 1955; M.A., Pepperdine U., 1972. Cert. marriage, family and child counselor, Calif., clin. hypnosis practitioner, Calif. Activities therapist psychiat. unit Los Angeles County-U. So. Calif. Med. Ctr., 1964-65; social case worker dept. social services City of Los Angeles, 1965-69; social rehab. counselor Los Angeles County Dept. Mental Health, 1969-74; clin. movement therapist Brotman Mem. Hosp., Culver City, Calif., 1973-77; practice transpersonal counseling, 1972—; instr. dept. continuing edn. Humboldt State U. Bd. dirs. Full Circle Inc. The Good Health Co. Mem. Am. Dance Therapy Assn. (charter mem.), Assn. Humanistic Psychol., Am. Psychol. Assn. (assoc.). Contbr. chpt. to book articles to profl. jours. Home and office: 2870 Evergreen Ln Arcata CA 95521

GOWAN, JOHN CURTIS, educator; b. Boston, May 21, 1912; s. Harry J. and Edythe (Chute) G.; A.B., Harvard, 1933, Ed.M., 1935; Ed.D., U. Calif. at Los Angeles, 1952; m. Priscilla Buckwell, Sept. 30, 1934; children—John A., Priscilla Anne (Mrs. Lawrence Curry); m. 2d, May Seagoe, Oct. 10, 1953; m. 3d, Jane Thompson, Aug. 28, 1958. Registrar, New Hampton Sch., 1935-41; counselor Culver Mil. Acad., 1941-52; research educationist UCLA, 1952-53; asst. prof. Los Angeles State Coll., 1953-58; asso. prof., prof., chmn. dept. San Fernando Valley State Coll., Northridge, Calif., 1958—, also dir. Creativity Workshops. Fulbright lectr. U. Singapore, 1962-63; vis. prof. U. Hawaii, summers 1965-67, U. Canterbury, Christchurch, N.Z., 1970, Massey U., Palmerston, N.Z., 1975; chmn. bd. Thompson Constrn. Co., Indpls. Bd. dirs. Calif. Adv. Council of Ednl. Research. Fellow Am. Psychol. Assn.; mem. Assn. for Gifted (pres. 1972-73, exec. dir. 1975-79), Nat. Assn. for Gifted Children (citation of merit for disting. service to gifted children 1967, pres. 1974-75), Am. Ednl. Research Assn. Author: The Education and Guidance of the Ablest, 1964; The Guidance of Exceptional Children, 1965; The Disadvantaged and Potential Dropout, 1966; Creativity: Its Educational Implications, 1967, 81; Educating the Ablest, 1972; The Development of the Creative Individual, 1972; The Development of the Psychedelic Individual, 1974; Trance, Art and Creativity, 1975; Operations of Increasing Order, 1980. Home: 1426 Southwind Circle West Lake Village CA 91361

GOWDY, EUNICE JEAN, medical technologist; b. Fayetteville, N.C., Nov. 18, 1930; d. Bertie D. and Cassie D. Gowdy; diploma Sch. Med. Tech., Med. Coll. Va., 1953; B.S., Rocky Mountain Coll., Billings, Mont., 1971. Med. technologists hosps. in Va., Md. and Mont., 1953-62; chief med. technologist Billings (Mont.) Clinic, 1962-77; part-time med. technologist St. Vincent's Hosp., Billings, 1978—; bus. mgr. All Trails Riding Sch., also Ranch Kampground Am., Billings, 1977—; mem. adv. group Mont. PSRO, 1976-79, liaison adv. group to bd. dirs., 1976-79; mem. sub area council Mont. Health Systems Agy., 1978-80, mem. governing bd., 1980-83; cons. Nat. Health Fairs, 1979. Bd. dirs. Messiah United Methodist Ch., Billings, 1970, treas., 1970. Mem. Am. Soc. Med. Technicians (dir. 1974-77), Mont. Soc. Med. Technicians (pres. 1964-65, 71-72), Alpha Mu Tau. Republican. Club: Lake Hills Ladies Golf Assn. Author papers in field. Address: Pryor Star Route Billings MT 59101

GOWER, B. DEWAYNE, superintendent schools; b. Kendrick, Okla., Aug. 9, 1935; s. Barney E. and Florence G.; m. Frankie Delores Loe, Feb. 24, 1956; children—Sandra, Lisa. M.Ed., Eastern Wash. U., 1965; Ed.D., Wash. State U., 1974. Cert. tchr., prin., supt., Wash. Sch. prin. Pasco (Wash.) Sch. Dist., 1965-72; supt. schs. Lind (Wash.) Sch. Dist., 1973-74, Elma (Wash.) Sch. Dist., 1974-82, South Kitsap Schs., Port Orchard, Wash., 1982—. Mem. Republican. Nat. Com. Served with U.S. Army, 1956-60. Mem. Am. Assn. Sch. Adminstrs., Assn. Supervision and Curriculum Devel., Wash. Assn. Sch. Adminstrs., Wash. Assn. Supervision and Curriculum Devel., Phi Delta Kappa, Phi Kappa Phi. Mem. Ch. of Christ. Home: 5190 SE Burley-Olalla Rd Olalla WA 98359 Office: South Kitsap Schs 1962 Hoover Ave SE Port Orchard WA 98366

GOYER, ROBERT STANTON, communication educator; b. Kokomo, Ind., Oct. 7, 1923; s. Clarence V. and Genevieve M. (Sober) G.; m. Patricia Ann Stutz, Aug. 12, 1950; children—Karen, Susan, Linda, Amy. B.A., DePauw U., 1948; M.A., Miami U., Oxford, Ohio, 1950; Ph.D., Ohio State U., 1955. Instr. Miami U., Oxford, 1949-51; instr., asst. prof. Ohio State U., Columbus, 1955-58, research assoc., research cons. research found., 1956-63; asst. prof. Purdue U., Lafayette, Ind., 1958-60, assoc. prof., 1960-64, prof., 1964-66; prof. Ohio U., Athens, 1966-81, dir. ctr. communications studies, 1966-74, 79-81, assoc. dean grad. coll., 1978, dean grad. coll., acting dir. research, 1979, acting assoc. provost grad. and research programs, 1979; prof., chmn. dept. communication Ariz. State U., Tempe, 1981—; cons. in field. Served to 1st lt. U.S. Army, 1943-46, 52-53. Decorated Bronze Star. Fellow Internat. Communication Assn. (past pres.), AAAS; mem. Am. Psychol. Assn., Acad. Mgmt., Speech Communication Assn. Presbyterian. Author books; also contbr. articles to profl. jours. Home: 517 W Summit Pl Chandler AZ 85224 Office: Ariz State U Dept Communication Tempe AZ 85287

GRACE, JOHN WILLIAM, elec. co. exec.; b. Swissville, Pa., May 29, 1921; s. Joseph and Ruth Margaret (Bailey) G.; student Am. TV Inst. Tech., 1950; B.S. in Elec. Engring., Drexel U., 1960; m. Ruth Delores Schroeder, Nov. 25, 1950; children—Martha, Joan, Nancy, John William. Technician missiles and surface radar div. RCA, Moorestown, N.J., 1950-56, design engr., 1956-60, project engr., 1960-66; mgr. engring. and sci. exec. EG & G, Inc., Las Vegas, Nev., 1966-73, mgr. bus. devel. operational test and evaluation, Albuquerque, 1973-77; engring. mgr. Instrumentation div., Idaho Falls, Idaho, 1977-79, mgr. systems project office, 1979, mgr. instrumentation program office, 1979-82, mgr. engring. spl. products div., 1982—. Active Boy Scouts Am., 1969-71. Served with USNR, 1941-45. Mem. IEEE, Instrument Soc. Am. (dir. sci. instrumentation and research div.), Assn. Old Crows, Am. Legion (post adj. vice comdr. 1950). Episcopalian (pres. couples retreat 1969-70). Patentee contradirectional waveguide coupler. Home: 2900 S Valley View 154 Las Vegas NV 89102 Office: EG&G Spl Projects Div 2755E Desert Inn Las Vegas NV 89121

GRACE, THOMAS GLADSON, orthopedic surgeon; b. Portland, Oreg., Nov. 27, 1945; s. George Dewey and Esther Victoria (Petterson) G.; B.S. in Gen. Sci., U. Oreg., 1967; M.D., Tulane U., 1970; m. Mar. 29, 1969; children—Thomas Jonathon, Brian Braley. Straight surg. intern U. Tex., San Antonio, 1970-71; resident in surgery Tripler Army Med. Center, Honolulu, 1972-75; practice medicine specializing in orthopedic surgery, Albuquerque, 1976; asst. prof. orthopedic surgery U. N.Mex. Med. Center, Albuquerque, 1976—; practice medicine, specializing in orthopaedic surgery, 1980—; mem. staff Bernalillo County Med. Center, Presbyn. Med. Center, St. Joseph's Hosp., Anna Kaseman Hosp., Univ. Heights Hosp., Albuquerque VA Hosp.; cons. spinal surgery and pediatric orthopedics, mem. med. adv. bd. Carrie Tingley Hosp. for Crippled Children. Served with U.S. Army, 1971-76. Diplomate Am. Bd. Orthopedic Surgery. Mem. Soc. Mil. Orthopedic Surgeons, Am. Acad. Orthopedic Surgeons, N.Mex. Orthopedic Assn., Aloha Orthopedic Soc., Western Orthopedic Assn. (dir.), Am. Coll. Sports Medicine, Bernalillo County Med. Soc. (research and edn. dir. sports medicine com.). Office: 7000 Cutler NE Suite 3-25 Albuquerque NM 87110

GRADY, JACK ATTLEE, mgmt. cons.; b. Gary, Ind., Oct. 23, 1918; s. Emil and Grace (Mains) G.; B.A. in Bus. Adminstrn.; U. Mich., 1942; J.D., Ariz. State U., 1970; m. Jane LaBine, Apr. 27, 1946 (div.); children—Diane, Sharon, Timothy, Michael. Asst. state personnel dir. War Manpower Commn., Mich., 1942-44; indsl. relations staff Detroit Edison Co., 1944-47; asso. sec. Indsl. Council, Phoenix, 1947-52, 55-63; indsl. relations mgr. Fisher Contracting Co., Phoenix, 1952-55; pres. UniService, Inc., Phoenix, 1955—. Chmn. Ariz. Merit System bd., 1961-67; bd. dirs. YMCA, 1952-57, ARC, 1948-52 Salvation Army, 1960-67, Vis. Nurse Assn., 1963-67. Mem. Ariz. Gen. Contractor Assn. (chmn. labor negotiating com. 1948-63), U. Mich. Alumni Assn., Phoenix Personnel Mgmt. Assn. (pres. 1954-55), Ariz. Personnel Forum, Am. Bar Assn., Ariz. Bar Assn., Soc. Profl. Mgmt. Cons., Phoenix Personnel Mgmt. Assn., Phi Beta Kappa, Phi Kappa Phi, Phi Eta Sigma, Theta Chi. Clubs: Kiva, University, Arizona 100, Scottspark Country. Home: 137 E Coronado Apt 21 Phoenix AZ 85004 Office: Suite 333 33 E McDowell Rd Phoenix AZ 85004

GRADY, JOAN BUTTERWORTH, principal, educator; b. N.Y.C., May 4, 1929; d. Roderick Gerard and Pearl (Levy) Butterworth; m. George Howard Grady, Nov. 24, 1954; children—Alicia Lynn, Glen Andrew. B.A., Hunter Coll., 1951; M.A., Columbia U., 1953; Ph.D. U. Colo., 1976. Cert. prin., supt., Colo. Tchr. Graland Country Day Sch., Denver, 1954-56, St. Marys Acad., Englewood, Colo., 1963-75; dept. chmn., athletic dir., tchr. English, Cherry Creek Sch. Dist., Englewood, 1975-81; asst. prin. Laredo Middle Sch., 1981—, prin. Horizon Middle Sch., Aurora, Colo., 1981—; cons. Coll. Bd. Advanced Placement, adj. instr. U. No. Colo.; cons. various sch. dists.; mem. Commn. on Writing, Council for Basic Edn., 1977-79; participant Wingspread Conf. on Writing, 1979. Bd. dirs. Mile Hi council Girl Scouts U.S.A.; dir. Nat. Wider Opportunities. Recipient Disting. Service award Nat. Assn. Student Councils, 1980; Thanks Badge, Mile Hi council Girl Scouts U.S.A., 1976. Mem. Nat. Assn. Secondary Sch. Prins., Assn. for Curriculum and Devel., Colo. Assn. Middle Level Educators, Nat. Middle Sch. Assn., Am. Philatalic Soc., Am. Topical Assn. Republican. Episcopalian. Contbr. articles to profl. jours. Office: 3981 S Reservoir Rd Aurora CO 80013

GRAEBNER, LINDA S., marketing executive; b. Lakewood, Ohio, Mar. 28, 1950; d. Herman F. and Marilynn J. (Baumer) G.; m. Vincent L. Schantz, June 13, 1981. B.S., Purdue U., 1972; M.B.A., Stanford U., 1974. Cons. Griffenhagen Kroeger Inc., San Francisco, 1974-75; assoc. mgr. Booz, Allen & Hamilton, San Francisco, 1975-79; mgr. Bus. and Planning Crown Zellerbach Corp., San Francisco, 1979-82, dir. mktg., 1982—. Club: San Francico Bay. Office: 1 Bush St Suite 1700 San Francisco CA 94104

GRAESE, JUDITH A., costume designer, dance instructor, artist, illustrator; b. Loveland, Colo., Nov. 8, 1940; d. Erwin H. and Hildegarde C. (Spieler) G.; m. Chester Harold Budz II, May 30, 1976; student Augustana Coll., Sioux Falls, S.D., 1958-59; U. Colo., 1964-67. Window display designer, Neusteters, Denver, 1959-62, May Co., Denver, 1967-70; costumer, dancer, actress, designer, Third Eye Theater, Denver, 1968-73; instr. contemporary dance Kent-Denver Country Day Sch., 1968—; exhibited art in galleries throughout U.S., 1962—; co-founder, Colo. Contemporary Dance. Illustrator: The Treasure Is the Rose, 1973; The Song of Francis, 1973; The Fisherman and His Soul, 1983. Home: 2055 S Franklin Denver CO 80210

GRAF, DONALD FORREST, environ. engr.; b. Dec. 23, 1947; s. John Henry and Naomi Virginia (Forrest) F.; B.S. in Zoology, U. Wash., 1970, M.S. in Water Pollution Biology, 1971; m. Inga Valeria Steidl, Aug. 31, 1970. Govt. ecologist Govt. Am. Samoa, Pago Pago, 1971-75, asst. to gov., 1976-77; environ. scientist Dames & Moore Cons., Honolulu, 1977—. Dir., Territorial Hist. Preservation, 1972-74, Territorial Parks and Recreation; exec. dir. Am. Samoa Bicentenial Adminstrn., 1976. Mem. Am. Soc. C.E., Fed. Water Pollution Control Assn., Nat. Ski Patrol, Delta Tau Delta. Club: Pago Pago Yacht (commodore 1975). Contbr. articles to profl. jours. Home: 6219 Kawaihae Pl Honolulu HI 96825 Office: Suite 200 1144 10th Ave Honolulu HI 96816

GRAF, MICHAEL GEORGE, psychologist, administrator; b. Dallas, Feb. 28, 1948; s. J. George and Isabel (Klase) G. B.A. in Psychology, B.S. in Pub. Adminstrn., U. Oreg., 1970; M.A. in Clin. Psychology, Ariz. State U., 1974, Ph.D. in Clin. Psychology, 1977. Lic. clin. sch. psychologist Alaska. Intern U. Wash. Sch. Medicine, 1975, postdoctoral fellow, 1976; dir. Tanana Chiefs Mental Health Programs, Fairbanks, Alaska, 1977—; affiliate asst. prof. U. Alaska. Past mem. Statewide Health Coordinating Council; past pres. bd. dirs. Fairbank Youth Services. U. Oreg. tuition scholar, 1968; Ford Found. fellow, 1970; Ariz. State U. tuition scholar, 1972-74; DeMund Meml. scholar, 1975; NIMH trainee, 1975. Mem. Alaska Psychol. Assn. (past pres.); Am. Psychol. Assn., Western Psychol. Assn., Alaska Mental Health Program Dirs. Assn. (past pres.), Nat. Assn. Rural Mental Health Providers. Contbr. articles to profl. jours.

GRAF, OTTO WALTER, JR., biologist, educator; b. San Francisco, May 26, 1925; s. Otto Walter and Mildred Ilyne (Morrison) G.; m. Anne Marie Minaker, Mar. 7, 1953; children—Catherine, David, Paul, Lloyd, John, Walter, Matthew, Robert. A.B., San Francisco State Coll., 1952; M.A., U. San Francisco, 1979; postgrad. Stanford U., Duke U., U. Calif.-Berkely, Calif. State U.-Hayward. Secondary teaching credential, Calif. Profl. asst. San Francisco State Coll., 1950-51; film librarian, supr. student sect. Calif. Acad. Scis., 1954-62; instr. U. Calif.-Berkeley, 1956-61, Washington High Sch., Fremont, Calif. 1955—. Active Boy Scouts Am., Republican Party. Served with USN, 1943-46; to 1st lt., U.S. Army, 1951-54. Decorated Pacific Theatre ribbon, Am. Theatre ribbon, Korean ribbon, Presidential Unit citation, Presidential citation, Korean Merit citation; recipient Silver Beaver award, Boy Scouts Am., 1971; Outstanding Secondary Tchr. award, 1974; NSF grantee; Biol. Scis. Curriculum Studies grantee. Mem. Pan Pacific Entomol. Soc., Nat. Sci. Tchrs. Assn., Nat. Assn. Biology Tchrs., E. Africa Wild Life Soc., Internat. Wildlife Fedn., Nat. Wildlife Fedn. Roman Catholic. Author: Key to the Mosquitos of Korea, 1951, Flies of Medical and Veternary Importance of Japan & Korea, 1952; Nature Games for the Secondary School, 1979; designed trap for live mice in Korea. Home: 5151 Tenaya Ave Newark CA 94560 Office: Washington High Sch 38442 Fremont Blvd Fremont CA 94536

GRAFF, EVERETT EDWARD, hospital official; b. Lincoln, Nebr., Sept. 23, 1925; s. John Henry and Juliana (Gloucer) G.; m. Betty Louise Jameson, July 20, 1951; children—Gretchen Juliana, Valerie Lyn Graff Flannery, Courtney Jon Graff. Grad., Gen. Motors Inst. Tech., 1943; student U. Denver, 1947; B.A. summa cum laude, Park Coll., 1975; M.A., Central Mich. U., 1980. City clk., treas. City of York (Nebr.), 1949-51; prin. and sr. acct. W.D. Messenger & Co., C.P.A.s, 1951-53, 55-57; tax. acct. No. Natural Gas, 1953-55; controller Refinite Corp., 1957-59; asst. adminstr. adminstrv. services Nebr. Meth. Hosp., Omaha, 1959-70; chief fin. officer North Kansas City (Mo.) Meml. Hosp., 1971-76; asst. adminstr. for fin. St. Mary's Hosp. and Health Center, Tucson, 1976-78; asst. exec. dir. fin. Lawrence (Kans.) Meml. Hosp., 1978-80; asst. exec. dir. adminstrn. services Riverside (Calif.) Community Hosp and Med. Center, 1980-83; v.p. fin., treas. St. Joseph's Hosp. of Orange (Calif.), 1983—; dir. Trujillo Water Co., Riverside. Mem. Riverside Pub. Utilities Commn.; bd dirs. Riverside chpt. ARC. Served with USAAF, 1946-47. Mem. Am. Coll. Hosp. Adminstrs., Fin. Execs. Inst., Hosp. Fin. Mgmt. Assn. (past pres. Nebr. chpt., past mem. bd. dirs. Nebr. and Kansas City chpts., nat. dir. 1966-69, dir. So. Calif. chpt. 1981—, former mem. nat. inst. com., nominating com., past chmn. nat. data processing com., William G. Follmar Individual Achievement award 1968, Robert H. Reeves award 1974), Sigma Iota Epsilon. Republican. Presbyterian. Contbr. articles to profl. publs. Home: 1985 Longmont Riverside CA 92506 Office: 1100 W Stewart Dr Orange CA 92667

GRAFF, LLOYD LEE, advertising agency executive, writer, broadcast journalist; b. Dalton, Nebr., June 2, 1933; s. Raymond August and Alice Clara (Martin) G.; m. Elizabeth E. Wray, May 1, 1954; children—Sharon Lee Graff Crable, Steven Wray, Martin Joseph, Michael Edward. B.A. in Journalism and Drama, U. Nebr., 1956. Writer, performer, producer, dir. radio and TV sta., Iowa and Nebr., 1956-60; writer, account exec., gen. mgr. Bozell & Jacobs, Inc., Sioux City and Omaha, 1960-69; account supr. Standard Oil-McCann Eickson, Inc., San Francisco, 1969-75; dir. corp. communications Barnes Hind, div. Revlon, Inc., Sunnyvale, Calif., 1975-82; pres., owner The Agency Mktg. Communications, Inc., Palo Alto, Calif., 1982—; direct distbr. Amway Corp. Active Iowa Democratic Campaign Com., 1968-69, Pres.'s Council Youth Opportunity, 1968; chmn. first day of issue Post Office Dept., 1966; mem. mayor's com. on communications, Sioux City, 1964-68; cub master, com. chmn. Boy Scouts Am., 1965-75. Served with U.S. Army, 1954-56. Recipient spl. recognition Pres.'s Council on Youth Opportunity, 1968. Mem. Nat. Agrl. Mktg. Assn. (pres. 1970, 72), Med. Mktg. Assn. (v.p. 1978-79), Med. Writers Assn. Democrat. Roman Catholic. Club: KC (past grand knight). Home: 1170 Valcartier Dr Sunnyvale CA 94087 Office: 4151 Middlefield Rd Suite 209 Palo Alto CA 94303

GRAFTON, CLIVE LLEWELLYN, educator; b. Los Angeles, Apr. 24, 1930; s. Llewellyn Jerome and Lucille Marilla (Highett) G.; A.A., Compton Coll., 1950; B.A., Pepperdine U., 1956; M.S., U. So. Calif., 1958, Ed.D., 1968; m. Marilyn Joanne Dougless, Aug. 1, 1957. Instr., adminstrv. asst. Compton Coll., Calif., 1952-58; instr. Cerritos Coll.

(Calif.), 1958-61, dean men, 1961-65; dir. student activities U. So. Calif., Los Angeles, 1965-67, dir. spl. events, 1967-68, asst. dean students, 1968-69, asso. prof. higher edn., chmn. dept. higher and postsecondary edn., 1969—, assoc. dean Sch. Edn., 1981—. Served with USAF, 1950-52. Decorated Commendation medal. Named outstanding educator in Am., 1972. Mem. Am. Coll. Personnel Assn. (mem. commn. coll. student and his community 1968-71, chmn. position paper on pres.'s comms. on campus unrest 1970-71), Am. Assn. Higher Edn., Am. Personnel and Guidance Assn., Am. Ednl. Research Assn., Phi Delta Kappa, Delta Epsilon. Editor: Calif. Community Coll. Instnl. Research Report, 1973-77. Contbr. to profl. publs. Home: 13720 Ridge Rd Whittier CA 90601 Office: Sch Edn Univ So Calif Los Angeles CA 90089

GRAHAM, CARROLL ADRIAN, state senator, rancher; b. Hardin, Mont., Dec. 14, 1913; s. Joseph Allen and Minnie Frances (Robinson) G.; student Poly. Inst., Billings, Mont., 1935; m. Nelle Yvette Pickard, June 28, 1939; children—Gary Joe, Carroll Allen. Rancher, Lodge Grass, Mont., 1936—; mem. Mont. Senate, 1961—, mem. Legis. Council, Agrl. and Livestock Com., Hwys. and Transp. Com., Adminstrn. Com., Rules Com.; mem. Nat. Indian Task Force. Mem. Mont. Stockgrowers Assn., Farmers Union, Farm Bur., Reservation Ranchers. Democrat. Clubs: Masons; Shriners; Elks; Kart Patrol.

GRAHAM, CHARLOTTE BRANT, dietary service director; b. Belle Fourche, S.D., Jan. 21; d. Charles Clyde and Inga Evelyn (Marby) B.; B.A., Walla Walla Coll., 1945; B.S., Loma Linda U., 1949; postgrad. U. Wash., Seattle, 1950-51; m. William Graham, July 6, 1947; 1 son, William. Dir. food service Lancaster (Mass.) Sch. Girls, 1949-50, Riverside (Calif.) Gen. Hosp., 1952-54; nutritionist Los Angeles City Dept. Health, 1955-56; dir. dietary service Whittier (Calif.) Hosp., 1962-81; dir. food and nutrition mgmt. services Am. Med. Internat., Circle City Hosp., Corona, Calif.; instr. Calif. Community Colls. Mem. Am. Soc. Hosp. Food Service Adminstrs. (sec. So. Calif. chpt. 1973-75), Am. Dietetic Assn., Calif. Dietetic Assn., Am. Heart Assn. Republican. Club: Soroptimists.

GRAHAM, CHRISTINE ROGERS, management consultant to the financial industry; b. Winner, S.D., July 31, 1944; d. Harry Bernard and Mildred V. (Tideman) Rogers; B.A., Calif. State U., San Diego, 1967, M.A., 1975; divorced. Adminstrv. asst. to pres. Percy H. Goodwin Real Estate Co., San Diego, 1967-69; research asst. econ. research and site and mktg. research Security Pacific Nat. Bank, Los Angeles, 1970-73; research analyst Am. Savs. & Loan Assn., Beverly Hills, Calif., 1973-74; v.p., dir. br. devel. and mktg. research Calif. Fed. Savs. & Loan Assn., Los Angeles, 1974-82; v.p., dir. corp. planning Western Fed. Savs. & Loan Assn., 1982-83; v.p. Newport Group, Irvine, Calif., 1983—. Recipient cert. achievement YMCA Leaders Club, 1978. Mem. Nat. Assn. Bus. Economists (exec. com. 1977-79), Savs. Instn. Mktg. Soc. Am. (vice chmn. research com. 1980, speaker convs. 1977-81). Calif. Savs. and Loan League (chmn. industry devel. com. 1977-78), Los Angeles C. of C. Office: 18009-L Sky Park Circle Irvine CA 9274

GRAHAM, CLIVE, JR., real estate broker; b. Long Beach, Calif., Dec. 11, 1948; s. Clive Graham and Josephine (Bernhardt) G.; B.S., U.S. Naval Acad., 1971. Commd. ensign U.S. Navy, 1971, advanced through grades to lt., 1975; naval gunfire officer 3d Marine Div., 1975-76; adminstrv./legal officer Naval Mobile Constrn. Bn., 1976-79; counselor Naval Drug Rehab. Center, San Diego, 1979-82; ret., 1981; mem. Res.; chief fin. officer Graham Mgmt. Corp., Long Beach, Calif., 1979-82, pres., 1982 . Mem. bd. outreach 1st Congl. Ch., Long Beach. Mem. Nat. Assn. Realtors, Calif. Assn. Realtors, Inst. Real Estate Mgmt., Assn. HUD Mgmt. Agts. (2d v.p.), Long Beach Bd. Realtors (chmn. legis./taxation com.), U.S. Naval Inst., U.S. Naval Acad. Alumni Assn., Naval Acad. Athletic Assn. Clubs: Army-Navy Country/(Arlington, Va.); Army and Navy (Washington); Marines Meml. (San Francisco); Kiwanis (ch. liaison com.) (Long Beach). Home and office: 800 E Ocean Blvd Long Beach CA 90802

GRAHAM, DOUGLAS JOHN, museum administrator, banker; b. Dunfermline, Scotland, July 6, 1934; s. Hugh Merton and Ellen Charlotte (Podmaniczky) G.; B.A., N.Y. Inst. Fin., 1961; came to U.S., 1959, naturalized, 1965; children—Robert, Christopher, Anabel. Ptnr. Mitchell, Hutchins & Co., N.Y.C., William D. Witter Inc., N.Y.C., 1959-72; founder., dir. The Turner Mus., Denver, 1973—; pres. Internat. Bank Holdings Ltd., Denver, 1979—. Past council mem. St. Andrew's Soc. Colo. Served with M.I., Brit. Army, 1952-59. Mem. Unity Ch.

GRAHAM, FRANCIS WILLIAM, II, company executive; b. Urbana, Ill., Aug. 2, 1937; s. Francis William and Mary G. (Gleason) G.; m. Helen T. Grady, Dec. 31, 1960; children—Francis William III, James Brian, Mary Helen, Katherin Grady, David Michael. B.S., U. Notre Dame, 1959; M.B.A., Harvard U., 1964. With Gen. Mills, Inc., Mpls., 1964—, div. gen. mgr., 1969-71, v.p. gen. mgr., 1971-73, group v.p., 1973-77; corp. v.p. Pres. Home and Comml. Products Group, Dart & Kraft, Inc., Los Angeles, 1977-82; sr. exec. v.p. and chief operating officer Cambridge Plan Internat., Monterey, Calif., 1982—. Served to lt. (j.g.) USN, 1959-62. Roman Catholic. Contbr. articles to jours. in field. Office: Cambridge Plan Internat 2711 Garden Road Monterey CA 93940

GRAHAM, JOHN EDGAR, orchestra manager; b. Jacksonville, Fla., June 18, 1941; s. John Edgar and Nadine M. (McCullough) G.; B.A. in History, U. Va., 1963; M.P.A., U. Wash., Seattle, 1971. Dir. devel. Seattle Symphony Orch., 1971-78; gen. mgr. Oreg. Symphony Orch., Portland, 1978—. Served with USN, 1963-69. Mem. Am. Symphony Orch. League, Oreg. Advocates for Arts. Club: Rotary.

GRAHAM, JUDITH, physician; b. Des Moines, July 23, 1932; d. W. Walter and Elizabeth (Haw) Graham; B.A. cum laude, U. Colo., 1953; M.D., State U. Iowa, 1957. Intern, resident State U. Iowa, 1957-61, NIH diabetes trainee, 1961-62; practice medicine specializing in internal medicine, Alhambra, Calif., 1962-67, Gt. Falls, Mont., 1967-76, Seattle, 1980—; med. officer Seattle-King County Jails, 1977-78; instr. internal medicine State U. Iowa, 1961-62; clin. instr. internal medicine Loma Linda U., 1962-67, U. So. Calif., 1964-67; clin. asst. prof. U. Wash., 1978—; staff Gt. Falls (Mont.) Clinic, 1967-76; cons. VA Hosp., Ft. Harrison, Mont., 1967-75; attending staff Harborview Med. Center, Seattle, 1978—. Mem. Mont. Commn. for Nursing and Nursing Edn., 1974-76; exec. com. Cascade County Emergency Med. Services Council, 1974-75. Mem. council Trail Riders Canadian Rockies, 1970-78, v.p., 1974, sr. v.p., 1975; mem. planning com. Mont. Gov.'s Conf. on Nursing and Nursing Edn., 1971-72; adv. com. Mont. State U. Coll. Nursing Postgrad. Continuing Edn. Project, 1972-73. Diplomate Am. Bd. Internal Medicine. Mem. Wash. State Med. Assn., King County Med. Soc., Am. Diabetes Assn., Mont. (dir. 1969-76, v.p. 1970-71, pres. 1973-74), Wash. State (dir. 1978—), Am. (dir. 1974-76) heart assns., Mont. Diabetes Assn. (v.p. 1971-74, dir. 1971-76), ACP, Seattle Acad. Internal Medicine, Phi Beta Kappa, Alpha Omega Alpha, Pi Beta Phi. Congregationalist. Home: 2502 Canterbury Ln E Seattle WA 98112 Office: 508 Medical-Dental Bldg Seattle WA 98101

GRAHAM, LEO RICHARD, clinical psychologist, author, publisher; b. Taft, Calif., Aug. 14, 1918; s. John Ellis and Nellie Elvira (Greeson) G.; B.A., Calif. State U.-Fresno, 1949, M.A., 1952; Ph.D., UCLA, 1955; m. Sarah Nell Vanzant, Jan. 4, 1970; children—Marianne Elizabeth, Terril Lee. Tchr., Reef-Sunset Elem. Sch. Dist., Avenal, Calif., 1949-51; instr. UCLA, 1955-58; practice clin. psychology, 1955-80; sr. v.p. Sanford Mgmt. Services, Inc., Los Angeles, 1965-68; exec. dir. Tarzana (Calif.) Ctr., children's treatment ctr., 1970-71; prof. Sch. Bus. and Adminstrn., Pepperdine Coll., 1969-70, 77-80; lectr. U. So. Calif., 1978-79; talk show host KCSN, 1980. Served with USN, 1936-40, USNR, 1941-45. Lic. clin. psychologist, Calif. Mem. Am. Psychol. Assn., AAAS, Sigma Xi, Kappa Delta Pi. Democrat. Clubs: Elks; Royal Aloha Vacation. Home: 22707 Enadia Way Canoga Park CA 91307 Office: 17277 Ventura Blvd Suite 201 Encino CA 91316

GRAHAM, PAMELA SMITH, distributing company executive, artist; b. Winona, Miss., Jan. 18, 1944; d. Douglas LaRue and Dorothy Jean (Hefty) Smith; m. Robert William Graham, Mar. 6, 1965 (div.); children—Jennifer, Eric; m. 2d, Thomas Paul Harley, Dec. 4, 1976; stepchildren—Tom, Janice. Student U. Colo., 1962-65, U. Cin., 1974-76. Cert. notary pub., Colo. Profl. artist, craft tchr., art exhibitor Colo., N.J., Ohio, 1968-73; property mgmt. and investor Cin., 1972-77; acct., word processor Borden Chem. Co. div. Borden, Inc., Cin., 1974-78; owner, pres. Hargram Enterprises, Cin., 1977-81; owner, pres. Graham & Harley Enterprises, Morrison, Colo., 1981—; tchr.; cons. County committeewoman Bergen County, N.J., 1972, clk. of session, 1975-79, conv. chmn., 1981; campaign chmn. United Appeal, 1977. Recipient numerous awards for art exhibits, bus. achievements, 1962—. Mem. Nat. Assn. Female Execs., United Sales Leaders Assn., Alpha Gamma Chi, Kappa Kappa Gamma. Republican. Mormon. Club: Queen City Racquet. Office: Graham & Harley Enterprises 4303 S Taft St Morrison CO 80465

GRAHAM, ROBERT MAURICE, accountant; b. Mt. Pleasant, Utah, Oct. 22, 1930; s. Tilman R. and Edda (Sumsion) G.; m. Joyce Sorensen, Apr. 17, 1953; children—Teri Lynn, Diane, Carolyn. A.S., Snow Coll., 1950; B.S., Brigham Young U., 1956; J.D., U. Utah, 1960. Bar: Utah 1960; C.P.A., Utah. With Deloitte Haskins & Sells, San Francisco and San Jose, Calif., 1960-70, Salt Lake City, 1970—, ptnr., 1972—. Pres., Salt Lake Estate Planning Council; pres. deferred gifts com. Primary Children's Med. Ctr., Salt Lake City. Served with U.S. Army, 1953-55. Mem. Am. Inst. C.P.A.s, Utah Assn. C.P.A.s, Utah State Bar Assn. Club: Rotary. Home: 3735 Viewcrest Circle Salt Lake City UT 84117 Office: 50 S Main St Suite 1800 Salt Lake City UT 84144

GRAHAM, ROGER JOHN, journalist; b. Phila.; s. William K. and Peggy E. (Owens) G.; A.A., Los Angeles Valley Coll., 1961; B.A. (Stanley Stemmer Beaubaire Meml. Journalism scholar), Fresno State Coll., 1962; M.A., Calif. State U., Fresno, 1967; postgrad. UCLA, 1976; children—John Roger, Robb Curt. Display advt. Turlock (Calif.) Daily Jour., 1962, Fresno (Calif.) Guide, 1963; tchr. Riverdale (Calif.) Elem. Sch., 1964, Raisin City (Calif.) Sch., 1965; tchr., counselor Calif. Prison, Sierra Conservation Center, Jamestown, 1966; tchr.-trainer and coordinator Western Center for Community Edn. and Devel., U. Calif.-Fresno, 1967; prof. journalism Los Angeles Valley Coll., 1968—; editorial bd. The Journalist, 1972—; vis. prof. Pepperdine U., 1976; reader, reviewer Ednl. Resources Info. Ctr. (ERIC), Clearinghouse on Reading and Communication Skills, 1976-78; photography judge Los Angeles County Fair, 1973-79. Served in USN, 1957. Recipient Los Angeles Mayor Tom Bradley's Outstanding Citizen award, 1974; Nat. Dedication awards to upgrade Journalism, 1972, 73, 74, 75, 76; Extraordinary Services award UCLA Ctr. for Research and Edn., 1971. Mem. Assn. Edn. in Journalism, Adult Edn. Assn. USA, So. Calif. Journalism Assn. of Jr. Colls. (pres. 1972), Community Coll. Journalism Assn. (articulation com. 1972—), Calif. Journalism Assn. Community Colls. (pres. 1973), Nat. Community Coll. Journalism Assn. (pres. 1978), Phi Delta Kappa, Sigma Delta Chi, Beta Phi Gamma, Pi Lambda Theta. Author: (with Wm. Payden) Observations on the Mass Media, 1976, 78; contbr. articles to various mags.; photog. illus. The San Fernando Valley Past and Present, 1980; contbg. photographer PhotoJournalism, 1980. Home: 438 E Rustic Rd Santa Monica CA 90402 Office: Los Angeles Valley Coll 5800 Fulton Ave Van Nuys CA 91401

GRAHAM, SHIRLEY ANN, law firm data processing official; b. Hattiesburg, Miss., May 21, 1953; d. Delbert Wayne and Aileen Tesola (Loper) Stephens; student public schs., Houston; m. Charles F. Graham, Aug 19, 1972; children—Megan Elise, Stephen Donald. Mem. tech. staff Sam Houston State U. Library, 1972-73; word processing specialist firm Baker & Botts, Houston, 1973-76; word processing specialist firm Miller, Nash, Wiener, Hager & Carlsen, Portland, Oreg., 1976-77, word processing systems analyst, 1977-79, tech. systems coordinator, 1979—; instr. Portland Community Coll., spring 1981; mem. adv. bd. for word processing curriculum Portland State U., 1983—; speaker for coll., high sch. groups. Mem. Assn. Info. Systems Profls. (v.p. membership Willamette Valley chpt. 1980-81, Portland chpt. 1981-82, co-dir. 1981 and 1983 Equipment Show and Symposium, pres. 1983), Oreg. Pioneer Word Processing Assn. (charter; coordinator public relations 1977-78, v.p. 1978-79), Associated Wang Users (charter; coordinator membership 1979-80, chair 1983). Author co. manuals. Home: 4921 SE 85th St Portland OR 97266 Office: 111 SW 5th Ave Portland OR 97204

GRAHAM, THOMAS KENT, banker; b. Lynn, Mass., Aug. 13, 1940; s. John F. and Barbara (Thomas) G.; B.A., Dartmouth Coll., 1962; M.B.A., Drexel U., 1971; m. Beverly Young, Apr. 27, 1963; children—T. Douglas, T. Mark, Tameson Lynn. Trainee to sr. v.p. 1st Pa. Bank, 1965-77; sr. v.p., dist. mgr. Crocker Nat. Bank, San Diego, Calif., 1977-80; pres., chief exec. officer Calif. Commerce Bank, Los Angeles, 1980—. Bd. dirs. San Diego County YMCA, United Way of San Diego, Combined Arts and Edn. Council San Diego. Served to lt. (j.g.) USNR, 1962-65. Mem. Corp. Fin. Council San Diego (pres. roundtable), San Diego C. of C. (dir.). Clubs: California, La Jolla Country. Office: 811 Wilshire Blvd Los Angeles CA 90017

GRAHAM, WALTER, painter, sculptor; Toledo, Ill., Nov. 17, 1903; s. Elijah and Florence (Cramer) G.; m. Alma L. Raber, May 5, 1952; 1 son, David. Student Chgo. Art Inst., Chgo. Acad. Art, also pvt. instrn., 1924-30. Owner, operator, Nugent Graham Studios, 1939-49; fine arts painter murals, sculptor; pres. Central Wash. Mus., 1960; mem. Wash. State Arts Commn., 1960; former illustrator Street and Smith Pubs., Western Story, Western Life. Recipient 1st prizes Chgo. Galleries, 1937, 38, 42, Bronze medal Nat. Advt. Assn., 1954, 55, 56. Mem. Palette Chisel Acad. (Gold medal 1940), Soc. Animal Artists N.Y., North Central Wash. Mus. (past pres.), Seattle Art Dirs. Soc. (hon. mention). Prin. works include murals Rocky Reach Dam, Wenatche, Wash.; fountain sculpture for Lincoln Savs. Bank, Spokane; Paintings on Alaskan steamships; commd. paintings for Northwest banks; paintings in TV and films, including Exploration Northwest, Chief Joseph's War Trail. Home and Studio: 201 S Elliott Apt 9 Wenatchee WA 98801

GRAHAM, WILLIAM BAGLEY, retired electronics engineer; b. Eugene, Oreg., Aug. 14, 1920; s. David M. and Mildred E. (Bagley) G.; m. Dorothy M. Reilly, Feb. 1946 (dec.); m. 2d, Helen Sturgis Gelinas, Mar. 25, 1967; children—David, Kathleen, Richard Gelinas, Suzanne Gelinas, George Gelinas. Lab. asst. MIT, 1940-42, mem. Walker Meml. staff, 1940-42; engr. Lockheed Aircraft Co., Burbank, Calif., 1942; radio engr. Fed. Tel. & Tel. Labs., Nutley, N.J., 1942-43; with Sperry Gyroscope Co., Lake Success, N.Y., 1946-50; mem. research staff Rand Corp., Santa Monica, Calif., 1950-58, assoc. head engring. div., 1958-60, head electronics dept., 1960-68, head engring. and applied scis. dept., 1968-77, mem. corp. research staff, 1977-82, ret., 1982. Cons., mem. Pres.'s Sci. Adv. Com.; mem. USAF Sci. Adv. Bd., Dept. Def. Sci. Adv. Bd.; vice chmn. Naval Research Adv. Com. Served with USN, 1943-46. Mem. AAAS, Am. Radio Relay League, Calif. Acad. Sci. Home: 781 Ranch Ln Pacific Palisades CA 90272 Office: Rand Corporation 1700 Main St Santa Monica CA 90406

GRAINGER, GORDON EDWARD, avionics instrument technician, union official; b. Regina, Sask., Can., Mar. 22, 1938; s. Edward and Freda Kuene (Bubnick) G.; m. Linda Faye Grainger, July 4, 1975; children—Deborah, Kimberly, Michael, Gordon. Student pub. schs., Stockton, Calif. Solid propellant operator Aerojet Gen. Corp., 1960-63; credit sales mgr. Goodyear Tire and Rubber Co., Fresno, Calif., 1964-67; avionics technician McDonnel Douglas Corp., Long Beach, Calif., 1967-70; avionics instrument technician U.S. Civil Service, George AFB, Calif., 1971—; pres. local 977, Nat. Federation Fed. Employees, 1979—. Served to sgt. USAF, 1956-60. Presbyterian. Clubs: Masons, Scottish Rite, Shriners. Home: 22682 Sitting Bull Rd Apple Valley CA 92307 Office: PO Box 523 George AFB CA 92392

GRALEY, GARY JAMES, photographer; b. Buffalo, June 27, 1951. B.A., SUNY-Buffalo, 1973; M.F.A., Rochester Inst. Tech., 1975. Shows include: George Eastman House, Rochester, N.Y., 1976, Los Angeles Inst. Art, 1979, San Francisco Art Inst., 1980, Ctr. Creative Photography, Tucson, 1981; represented in permanent collections: George Eastman House, Albright-Knox Gallery, Buffalo, Mus. Modern Art, N.Y.C., Commns. include Ariz. Dept. Tourism, Phoenix, 1979, Sierra Club, Flagstaff, Ariz., 1980. Mem. S.W. Assn. Photog. Art, Upstate N.Y. Soc. Photographers, Am. Soc. Photog. Expressionism. Office: care M M Cargill 8108 E Buena Terra Scottsdale AZ 85258

GRAMBIHLER, JAMES WILLIAM, trade association executive, consultant; b. Chgo., Jan. 9, 1950; s. William and Mary (Turturillo) G.; B.S. in Journalism, Mass Communications and Psychology, U. Utah, 1978. With communications dept. Utah Copper div. Kennecott Copper Corp., Salt Lake City, 1977-78; pvt. practice cons., Salt Lake City, 1978—; assoc. dir. Utah Petroleum Assn., Salt Lake City, 1980—. Mem. Pub. Relations Soc. Am. (chmn. Intermountain chpt.). Roman Catholic. Home: 1057 Topaz Dr Salt Lake City UT 84116 Office: Utah Petroleum Assn 10 W Broadway St Suite 611 Salt Lake City UT 84101

GRAMLICH, JOHN BRISTOL, surgeon; b. Omaha, Apr. 10, 1915; s. Ralph Clifford and Justine (Bristol) G.; A.B., Morningside Coll., 1934; M.D., Columbia U., 1939. Surg. intern St. Lukes Hosp., N.Y.C., 1939-40, resident in surgery, 1941-42, 45-47; resident in surgery Babies Hosp., N.Y.C., 1940-41; practice medicine, specializing in surgery, Cheyenne, Wyo., 1946—; instr. surgery Columbia U., N.Y.C., 1946-47; instr. anatomy U. Colo. Sch. Medicine, Denver, 1948-52, asst. clin. prof. surgery, 1952-61, assoc. clin. prof. surgery, 1961-69, clin. prof. surgery, 1969—; mem. staff Meml. Hosp., Cheyenne, DePaul Hosp., Cheyenne, Colo. Gen. Hosp., Denver; vis. prof. surgery and surg. anatomy Guy's Hosp. and Med. Sch., London, 1971. Chmn. Civic Center Devel. Com., Cheyenne, 1977-81; mem. Gov.'s Steering Com. on Med. Edn. in Wyo., 1974-79; mem. adv. bd. United Way of Cheyenne, 1976—; bd. dirs. Wyo. Info. and Referral Service, 1973—, Cheyenne Symphony and Choral Soc., 1972—, Laramie County (Wyo.) Council on the Arts, 1967-73. Served to lt. col. M.C., U.S. Army, 1942-45; ETO. Recipient Gold medal U. Colo., 1977. Diplomate Am. Bd. Surgery. Fellow ACS (bd. govs. 1978—); mem. Am. Surg. Assn., Western Surg. Assn., Internat. Soc. Surgery, Southwestern Surg. Congress, Rocky Mountain Traumatological Soc., Denver Acad. Surgery, Am. Cancer Soc. (Bronze Medal award 1953, hon. dir. 1966—), Nat. Rehab. Assn. (hon.), Halsted Soc., Wyo. Med. Soc., Laramie County Med. Soc., Academie Internationale Medicin, Am. Guild of Organists, Am. Orchid Soc., Newcomen Soc. Episcopalian. Clubs: Young Mens Literary, Rotary. Author books in field; contbr. articles on surgery to profl. jours. Home: 435 Cherokee St Cheyenne WY 82001 Office: 1616 E 19th St Cheyenne WY 82001

GRAMS, THEODORE CARL WILLIAM, librarian, educator; b. Portland, Ore., Sept. 29, 1918; s. Theodore Albert and Emma Elise (Boehne) G. B.A., U. Wash., 1947; postgrad. Harvard Law Sch., 1947-48; M.S. in L.S., U. So. Calif., 1951. Land title asst. U.S. Bonneville Power Adminstrn., Portland, 1939-45, accountant, 1948-50, librarian, 1951-52; head cataloger, lectr. Portland State U. Library, 1952-59, dir. processing services, 1960—, prof., 1969—. Panelist on community action N.W. Luth. Welfare Assn. Conf., 1969; mem. adv. council Area Agy. on Aging, 1974-75; commr. City-County Commn. Aging, Portland-Multnomah County, 1975-80. Bd. dirs. Hub-Community Action Program, Portland, 1967-70, Project ABLE, 1972-74. HEW Inst. fellow, 1968-69. Mem. Am., Med., Oreg., Pacific N.W. library assns., AAUP, Am. Soc. for Info. Sci. (panelist on impact new technologies on info. sci. 1974, Library of Congress services 1976), Portland Area Spl. Librarians (pres. 1954-55), Spl. Libraries Assn., Beta Phi Mu. Lutheran. Clubs: Multnomah Athletic, University, Portland. Author: Allocation of Joint Costs of Multiple-Purpose Projects, 1952; Textbook Classification, 1968. Editor: Procs. 4th Am. Soc. Info. Sci. Midyear Meeting, 1975; Special Collections in Libraries of the Pacific Northwest, 1979. Home: 1000 SW Vista Ave Portland OR 97205

GRAND, JEREMY HERBERT, computer applications consultant; b. Vancouver, B.C., Can., Feb. 26, 1944; s. William H. and Ann H. (Jeremy) G.; m. Carmen T. Bernier, May 10, 1975; children—William Jeremy, Juliana Teresa. B.S. in Math., Portland State U., 1972, M.S. in Math., 1974. Mem. tech. staff Clapp and Mayne Inc., San Juan, P.R., 1976-78; methods analyst Pacific Power & Light Inc., Portland, Oreg., 1978-81; systems analyst Esco Corp., Portland, 1981-82; customer support rep. William Shaw and Assocs. Ltd., Portland, 1982—. Served with U.S. Army, 1967-68. Mem. Assn. Computing Machinery (chmn. Willamette Valley chpt. 1982-83), Assn. Systems Mgmt. (pres. Portland chpt. 1983-84). Clubs: City, Toastmasters (Portland). Office: William Shaw and Assocs 2075 SW 1st St Portland OR 97201

GRANDEY, GERALD WAYNE, lawyer, energy fuels company executive; b. Long Beach, Calif., June 25, 1946; s. Loren F. and Elizabeth M. Grandey; P.E., Colo. Sch. Mines, 1968; J.D., Northwestern U.; m. Bettina Brown, Sept. 7, 1973; children—Krista, Peter. Bar: Colo. 1973. Assoc. firm Holland & Hart, Denver, 1973-77; v.p. legal and regulatory affairs Energy Fuels Corp., Denver, 1977—. Active Rocky Mountain Mincral Law Found. Served to 1st lt. C.E., U.S. Army, 1968-70. Mem. ABA, Colo. Bar Assn. Contbr. articles to profl. jours. Office: 1515 Arapahoe St Suite 900 Denver CO 80202

GRANDY, WALTER THOMAS, JR., physicist; b. Phila., June 1, 1933; s. Walter Thomas and Margaret Mary (Hayes) G.; B.S., U. Colo., 1960, Ph.D., 1964; m. Patricia Josephine Langan, Dec. 27, 1955; children—Christopher, Neal, Mary, Jeanne. Physicist, Nat. Bur. Standards, Boulder, Colo., 1958-63; mem. faculty U. Wyo., Laramie, 1963—, prof. physics, 1969—, head dept., 1971-78; Fulbright lectr. U. Sao Paulo, Brazil, 1966-67, vis. prof., 1982; vis. prof. U. Tübingen (W. Ger.), 1978-79. Served with USNR, 1953-57. Fellow AAAS; mem. Am. Phys. Soc., Brasilian Phys. Soc., Am. Assn. Physics Tchrs., Sigma Xi, Sigma Pi Sigma. Author: Introduction to Electrodynamics and Radiation, 1970; research on statis. mechanics, quantum theory. Home: 604 S 18th St Laramie WY 82070

GRANGER, CLIVE WILLIAM JOHN, economics educator; b. Swanasea, Wales, Sept. 4, 1934; came to U.S., 1974; s. Edward John and Evelyn Agnes (Hessey) G.; m. Patricia Anne Loveland, May 14, 1960; children—Mark, Claire. B.A. with first class honors in Math., U. Nottingham (Eng.), 1955, Ph.D. in Stats., 1959. Lectr., reader, prof. math. and econs. U. Nottingham, 1953-74; chmn., prof. econs. U. Calif.,

San Diego, 1982—; vis. prof. Stanford U., Princeton U., Inst. for Advanced Studies, Vienna, Australian Nat. U.; dir. Quantitative Econ. Research, Inc. Harkness fellow, 1959-60, Princeton U. fellow Econometric Soc., 1973. Mem. Royal Stats. Soc., Econometric Soc. Author: (with M. Hatanaka) Spectral Analysis and Economic Time Series, 1964; (with P. Newbold) Forecasting Economic Time Series, 1977; Forecasting in Business and Economics, 1980. Office: Dept Economics D-008 U Calif San Diego La Jolla CA 92093

GRANGER, PHILIP CLARK, marriage and family therapist; b. Ada, Okla., Jan. 13, 1946; s. Donald Clark and Elna Lucille (Webster) G.; m. Viviane Nell Tholl, Mar. 20, 1969; 1 dau., Heather Disa. B.A., U. Colo.-Denver, 1972, M.A., 1975, Ph.D., 1976—. Substitute tchr. Denver pub. schs., 1974-82; research asst. Communication Research Labs., Denver, 1974-76; instr., tchr., counselor in educ. U. Colo.-Boulder and Denver, 1974-80; counselor U. Colo.-Boulder, 1977-80; therapist Arvada Psychol. & Family Services, (Colo.), 1979-80; owner, dir. Wheat Ridge Counseling, (Colo.), 1981—; bd. dirs. several community child care ctrs.; lobbyist at state legislature on behalf mental health and counseling profession. Democratic Party candidate for state legislature, 1982; house dist. vice chmn., dist. captain, precinct committeeperson Dem. Party. Mem. Am. Personnel and Guidance Assn. Methodist. Home: 3002 Benton St Wheat Ridge CO 80033 Office: Wheat Ridge Counseling 3895 Upham St Suite 20 Wheat Ridge CO 80033

GRANNIS, CHARLES OTIS, III, sales exec.; b. Colombia, S.C., Feb. 6, 1942; s. C. Otis and Alberta Lee (McCullagh) G.; A.S., Marion Mil. Inst., 1962; B.C.E., Tri-State U., 1966; m. Diana Cresci Grannis, Aug. 25, 1949; children—Bradley O., Shanon Lee. Engr., Fla. Power & Light Co., Miami, Fla., 1966-69; engr. A.B. Chance Co., Centralia, Mo., 1969-71, product mktg. mgr., 1971-76, account rep., San Bruno, Calif., 1976-78, regional mgr., Amman, Jordan, 1978-80, regional account mgr., Birmingham, Ala., 1981—. Registered Profl. Engr., Mo. Mem. Pacific Coast Elec. Assn., Nat. Soc. Profl. Engrs., Am. Mgmt. Assn. Republican. Patentee foundation systems, 1973, 74. Office: 2909 Coat Bridge Ln Birmingham AL 35243

GRANNIS, SCOTT FREDERICK, economist, consultant; b. Altadena, Calif., June 13, 1949; s. Donald Frederick and Peggy (Harriman) G.; m. Norma Garcia, July 30, 1971; children—Gabriela, Nicole, Ryan. B.A., Pomona Coll., 1971; M.B.A., Claremont Grad. Sch., 1980. Cons. to local govt. and industry, Argentina, 1975-79; Latin Am. economist Claremont (Calif.) Econs. Inst., 1980-82, internat. economist, dir. adminstrn., 1982—; cons. fin. strategies for multinat. corps. Served to lt. (j.g.), USCG, 1971-75. Contbr. numerous articles on polit. and econ. devels. in Latin Am. to profl. jours. Office: 415 W Foothill Blvd Claremont CA 91711

GRANT, ANTHONY WAYNE, interior designer; b. Watsonville, Calif. Sept. 27, 1948; s. Douglas Harold and Bernice Leora (Leppink) G.; m. Nanette Rodriguez July 6, 1974; children—Brooke Leora, Alexis, Keill Anthony. B.F.A. in Industrial Design, Brigham Young U., 1976. Mgr. comml. interior design div. Anita Brooks Design Assocs., Las Vegas, 1976-81; prin. Tony Grant, Nev. Design Corp., 1981—; cons. in field. Del. Clark County Democratic Conv. 1981; scout leader Boy Scouts Am. Served with USAF, 1968-72. Mem. Am. Soc. Interior Designers, (2d prize Flexalum Design Competition 1980, merit award 1983), Nat. Council Interior Design Qualification. Democrat. Mormon. Design work pub. in Designer, Feb. 1981, Las Vegan, Oct. 1980. Office: Tony Grant Nev Design Corp 3333 W Desert Inn Rd E Las Vegas NV 89102

GRANT, DONALD WEBSTER, insurance executive; b. Essex, Eng., Sept. 24, 1924; s. John Webster and May Sarah (Perkins) G.; m. Jean Margaret Brooke, Sept. 10, 1949; children—Gary, John, Donna; m. 2d Gigi Boschy, Oct. 4, 1974. Student London U., 1940-41; Keyman, dir. Fairfield, Ellis & Grant Ltd., Montreal, 1947-60; mgr. indsl. risk ins., dir. Grant & Russell Ltd., Montreal, 1960-64; exec. v.p. M.B. Buettner & Co., Inc., Los Angeles, 1964-79; pres. Western reins. mgrs. Western Reins. Brokers Inc., Los Angeles, 1971—. Bd. dirs. Pres. Reagan's Task Force. Served with Brit. Mcht. Marine, 1941-46. Decorated campaign medals. Mem. Am. Assn. Mng. Gen. Agts., Calif. Surplus Line Assn., Calif. Fair Plan (alt. del.) Los Angeles World Affairs Council (bd dirs.). Republican. Clubs: Los Angeles (bd. dirs.), Riviera Tennis. Home: 10501 Wilshire Blvd Apt 1010 Los Angeles CA 90024 Office: 3325 Wilshire Blvd Suite 301 Los Angeles CA 90010

GRANT, EUGENE LODEWICK, educator; b. Chgo., Feb. 15, 1897; s. Bertrand Eugene and Eva (Lodewick) G.; B.S., U. Wis., 1917, C.E., 1928; M.A., Columbia, 1928; D.Engring. (hon.), Mont. State U., 1973; m. Mildred Brooks Livingston, Sept. 4, 1923 (dec.); 1 dau., Nancy Livingston (Mrs. Edward North Chamberlain) (dec.). Instr. civil engring. to prof. indsl. engring. Mont. State Coll., 1920-30; faculty Stanford U., 1930-62, prof. econs. of engring., 1940-62, exec. head dept. civil engring., 1947-56; cons. C.E., U.S. Army, U.S. Bur. Reclamation, Calif. Dept. Water Resources, others. Mem. Palo Alto Bd. Public Works, 1931-37; chmn. com. on hwy. engring. economy Hwy. Research Bd., 1960-64. Served with USN, 1918-19. Recipient Disting. Service citation Coll. Engring. U. Wis., 1964; Founders award Am. Inst. Indsl. Engrs., 1965, Wellington award, 1979. Fellow ASCE (Rowland prize 1944), Am. Statis. Assn.; mem. Am. Soc. Quality Control (hon., Shewhart medal 1952), Am. Soc. Engring. Edn., Soc. Math. Stats. and Probability, Internat. Acad. Quality (hon.), Sigma Xi, Tau Beta Pi. Author: Principles of Engineering Economy, 1930, (with W.G. Ireson and R.S. Leavenworth) 7th edit., 1982; Statistical Quality Control, 1946, (with R.S. Leavenworth) 4th edit., 1972, 5th edit., 1980; (with P.T. Norton, Jr.) Depreciation, 1949; Basic Accounting and Cost Accounting, 1956, (with L.F. Bell) 2d edit., 1964. Editor: (with W.G. Ireson) Handbook of Industrial Engineering and Management, 1955. Home: 850 Webster St Palo Alto CA 94301

GRANT, GERALDINE HUGHES, govt. ofcl.; b. Warren, Ark., June 27, 1923; d. Willie and Daisy (Hunter) Hughes; student Ark. Bapt. Coll., 1940-41, 44-46, Los Angeles Jr. Coll. Bus., 1957, Los Angeles City Coll., 1958-60; M.Sci. of Adminstrn., Calif. State U., 1979; m. Joseph Grant, Jan. 12, 1962; 1 son, William Thomas. Tchr. elem. pub. schs., Ark., 1944-47; posting machine operator, Kansas City, Mo., 1952-53; file clk. Immigration and Naturalization Service, Dept. Justice, Los Angeles, 1954-56, info. clk., 1956-62, supervisory contact rep., 1962-70, immigration insp., 1970-75, immigration examiner, 1975-78, acting immigration examiner supr., 1978-78, supervisory immigration examiner, 1978—. Minister of music children's dept. Sunday sch. Victory Bapt. Ch., 1955-61, adult Sunday sch. tchr., 1962—, mem. Voices of Victory Choir, 1953—. Recipient Cert. of Appreciation, Shelley Sch. Child Devel. Center, Raleigh, N.C., 1979. Mem. Nat. Council Negro Women (life), Am. Inst. Parliamentarians (pres. local chpt. 1977-78, 80-81), Alpha Kappa Alpha, Eta Phi Beta (pres. local chpt. 1973-74, 80—, rec. sec. 1965-66, western regional dir. 1969-73, grand dir. edn. 1974-78, nat. 2d v.p. 1982—), Black Women's Forum. Democrat. Club: Toastmistress (council del. 1979-80). Home: 3010 S Bronson Ave Los Angeles CA 90018 Office: 300 N Los Angeles St Los Angeles CA 90012

GRANT, JOHN CARRINGTON, advertising agency executive; b. St. Louis, Feb. 2, 1937; s. George Nelson Whitfield and Mary Frances (Tissier) G.; m. Judith Ann Thompson, Oct. 20, 1962; children—Christopher, Susan. Student Westminister Coll., 1960; B.S., Washington U., St. Louis, 1969. Account mgr. Darcy, McManus & Masius, St. Louis, N.Y.C. and San Francisco, 1960-68; with Gardner Advt., St. Louis, 1963-66, McCann-Erickson, Seattle, 1974-75; stockbroker Dean Witter, San Francisco, 1968-74; pres. Tracy-Locke/BBDO, 1975-80; pres. Grant Pollack Advt., Denver, 1980—; mem. faculty Met. State Coll., Denver, 1981-82. Mem. Denver Advt. Fedn. Home: 8506 E Mineral Circle Englewood CO 80112 Office: Grant & Pollack Advt 1660 17th St Denver CO 80202

GRANT, JON BARTON, dentist; b. Elmhurst, Ill., July 17, 1943; s. Russell Sutherland and Louise Winona (Brown) G.; student Colo. State U., 1961-63; D.D.S., U. Nebr., 1968. Group practice dentistry, Colorado Springs, Colo., 1968-74; pvt. practice dentistry, Foster City, Calif., 1974—. Paul Harris fellow, 1980. Fellow Acad. Gen. Dentistry (state pres. 1972-75, regional v.p. 1973-74, nat dir. 1974-75, dir. Calif. 1980—), Acad. Internat. Dental Studies, Acad. Dentistry Internat.; mem. ADA, Calif. Dental Assn., San Mateo County Dental Assn., Am. Assn. Endodontists, Am. Soc. Preventive Dentistry, Am. Acad. Dental Group Practice (charter mem., charter nat. treas.), Nat. Analgesial Soc. (nat. v.p. 1974), Foster City C. of C. (pres. 1980-81), Am. Water Ski Assn., U.S. Parachute Assn. Rotary (charter mem. Foster City, pres. 1978-79). World record holder in parachuting, 1977. Home: 2990 Summit Hillsborough CA 94010 Office: 1289 E Hillsdale Blvd Foster City CA 94404

GRANT, LINDA KAY, alcoholism programs administrator, counselor, educator; b. Seattle, May 13, 1945; d. James M. and Inez M. (Randall) Long; m. Paul A. Reynolds, July 4, 1980; 1 dau., Shelley. B.S. in Psychology, Central Wash. U., 1973; M.S. in Counseling Psychology, 1979. Cert. alcoholism counselor. Instr. alcoholism and psychology Yakima (Wash.) Valley Coll., 1975-81; instr. psychology dept. Central Wash. U., Ellensburg, 1973-82; dir. Kittitas County Community Alcohol Ctr., Ellensburg, 1974-82; exec. dir. Assn. of Alcoholism Programs in Wash. State, Ellensburg, 1981—. Mem. Wash. Women United, Nat. Assn. for Female Execs., Wash. State Council on Alcoholism, Nat. Assn. Alcoholism and Drug Abuse Counselors (regional v.p. 1980-83), Alcoholism Profl. Staff Soc. of Wash. (pres. 1980-82). Author surveys relating to alcohol use and alcoholism. Office: PO Box 1172 Ellensburg WA 98926

GRANT, MERRILL ALAN, superintendent of schools; b. Milw., Apr. 3, 1936; s. Harry and Fay Grant; B.S., U. Wis., 1959; M.S., U. Toledo, 1963, Ph.D., 1973; m. Donna Lipman, Sept. 8, 1957; children—Ronald, Richard, James, Susan. Tchr., prin., exec. dir. Toledo pub. schs., 1969-71; asst. supt. schs., Sylvania, Ohio, 1971-74; supt. schs., Green Bay, Wis., 1974-79, Tucson, 1979—. Mem. exec. bd. Green Bay United Way, 1976-79, Tucson United Way, 1980—. Mem. Am. Assn. Sch. Adminstrs. Office: Tucson USD 1 Box 40400 Tucson AZ 85717

GRANT, PATRICIA JOHNS, advertising agency executive; b. La-Crosse Wis., Apr. 28, 1949; d. Robert David and Patricia (Holmes) Johns; m. Frederick A. Grant, Dec. 28, 1974 (div.); 1 son, Frederick Peter. B.A. Northwestern U., 1971, M.S.J., 1972. Account exec. J. Walter Thompson, Chgo., 1972-78; Chgo. instr. The Exec. Technique, 1979-81; account dir. Foote Cone and Belding, Los Angeles, 1981—; instr., Barrat Coll., Lake Forest, Ill., 1979. Active Jr. League, Chgo., Pasadena. Mem. Advt. Club Los Angeles. Republican. Office: Foote Cone and Belding 2727 W 6th St Los Angeles CA 90060

GRANT, STANLEY, marketing executive; b. Los Angeles, Feb. 22, 1940; s. Frank Paul and Betty Jane (Evans) G.; m. Cheryl Lynne Miller, 1969; m. Mary Susan McElveen, Oct. 9, 1972; 1 child, Jamie. B.S. in Bus., U. So. Calif., 1964; M.B.A., Pepperdine U., 1977. Stockbroker, Mitchum, Jones & Templeton, Los Angeles, 1965-70; health care adminstr. Los Angeles County, 1970-77; health care cons. Cooper & Lybrand, Los Angeles, 1977-79; v.p. mktg. Creative Age Publs., North Hollywood, Calif., 1979-81; mktg. dir. Cedars Sinai Med. Ctr., Los Angeles, 1979-81; exec. v.p. mktg., sales and planning Vascular Diagnostic Services, Inc., Woodland Hills, Calif., 1981—; cons. Mem. Glendale Housing Adv. Commn. Served with U.S. Army, 1958-60. Mem. Glendale C. of C. (chmn. housing zoning com.), Am. Mktg. Assn., Med. Mktg. Assn., Am. Coll. Hosp. Adminstrs. Office: 20300 Ventura Blvd Woodland Hills CA 91364

GRANT, THOM, advertising executive; b. Englewood, N.J., July 29, 1936; s. Thomas and Lucia (Sacchi) Gramaglia; m. Susan Middleton, July 29, 1978; children—John Christopher, Nicholas Middleton. A.B. in English, Wagner Coll., 1957; postgrad., NYU, 1958. Account exec., account supr. Ellington & Co., N.Y.C., 1961-63; v.p., account supr. West, Weir & Bartel, Inc., N.Y.C., 1963-65; v.p., gen. mgr. Cadwell, Davis Co., N.Y.C., 1965-67; v.p., then sr. v.p. account mgmt. McCann-Erickson Worldwide, N.Y.C., 1967-79; exec. v.p., gen. mgr. McCann-Erickson, Inc., Los Angeles, 1979—; dir. McCann-Erickson U.S.A.; dir. Western Tourism Commn. Mem. Western States Advt. Agys. Assn. (bd. dirs.), Pacific Area Travel Assn., Bank Mktg. Assn. Club: Bel-Air Country (Los Angeles). Home: 3658 Mandeville Canyon Rd Los Angeles CA 90049 Office: 6420 Wilshire Blvd Los Angeles CA 90048

GRANTHAM, DONALD JAMES, engineering educator, author; b. Grantham, N.C., Aug. 1, 1916; s. James Clarence and Nannie (Rose) G.; widowed; children—David S., Philip L. B.A. in Chemistry, U. N.C., 1939. Radio announcer Sta. WJLS, Beckley, W.Va., 1940-42, Sta. WCPO, Cin., 1942, Sta. WOLS, Florence, S.C., Sta. WCHS, Charleston, W.Va., 1946, Sta. WGAD, Gadsden, Ala. and Sta. WSMB, New Orleans, 1947; radio programmer Sta. WLPO, La Salle, Ill., 1947; gen. mgr. Sta. WCRA, Effingham, Ill., 1948-50; founder, pres. Grantham Radio Lic. Sch. (name later changed to Grantham Coll. of Engring.), Los Angeles, 1951—. Mem. Calif. Statewide Adv. Com. for Pvt. Schs., Colls. and Univs., 1968-70. Served with U.S. Army, 1942-46. Mem. IEEE, ASEE, Articulation Council of Calif. (engring. liaison com. 1981—). Home: 9628 Oakmount St Cypress CA 90630 Office: 2500 S La Cienega Blvd Los Angeles CA 90034

GRANTON, JAMES, software engr.; b. Chgo., Nov. 3, 1922; s. James and Julia (Harris) G.; student U. Ill., Chgo., 1947-49; B.S. in Math., Ill. Inst. Tech., 1954, M.S. in Math., 1957; m. Eddie Mae Witchard, Feb. 15, 1958; stepchildren—Lawrence Johnson, Richard Johnson, Frederick Johnson. Tchr. math. Lindbloom Tech. High Sch., Chgo., 1957-58; analyst U.S. Naval Ordnance Lab., Corona, Calif., 1958-65; staff engr. Hughes Aircraft Co., Fullerton, Calif., 1965-80; cons., quality engr. ballistic missiles div. Def. and Systems Group, TRW Systems, San Bernardino, Calif., 1980-83, software engr., 1983—; tchr., tutor in field. Served with U.S. Army, 1942-46. Mem. Electronic Industries Assn. (Computer Resources Task Group com., author papers on software configuration mgmt.). Adventist. Office: PO Box 1310 Norton AFB San Bernardino CA 92402

GRANZOW, OTTO JOACHIM, psychiatrist; b. Burg Stargard, Germany, Aug. 16, 1923; s. Wilhelm and Margarete (Peters) G.; student U. Berlin, 1941-42, 43-44, U. Wuerzburg, 1942-43, 44-45; M.D., U. Hamburg, 1946; m. Inge Johanna Stephan, 1970; children—Joachim Wilhelm, Christian Lars. Came to U.S., 1950, naturalized, 1955. Intern internal medicine U. Hamburg, 1947-48; resident ob-gyn, surgery St. Georg Hosp., Hamburg, 1948-50; course in tropical medicine Inst. Tropical Diseases, Hamburg, 1948; psychiat. tng. Mass. Dept. Mental Health, 1950-52; rotating intern St. John's Hosp., Santa Monica, Calif., 1952-53; child psychiatry fellow Pasadena (Calif.) Child Guidance Clinic, 1953-54; fellow child psychiatry Harvard U., 1954-55; surgeon Grace Line, 1955-56; practice medicine specializing in psychiatry, child psychiatry, Los Angeles, 1956—; mem. staff St. John's, Santa Monica, Marina Mercy, Serra Meml. hosps.; clin. instr. psychiatry UCLA, 1956-64; cons. Los Angeles Sch. Guidance Clinic, 1956-65, Calif. Dept. Rehab., 1970—; med. examiner Workmen's Compensation Appeals Bd., 1972—; med. cons. German Consulates Gen., Los Angeles and San Francisco. Served with M.C., German Air Force, 1940-45. Mem Calif., Los Angeles County med. assns. Republican. Lutheran. Office: 2021 Santa Monica Blvd Santa Monica CA 90404 also 4701 W Imperial Hwy Inglewood CA 90304

GRAPER, EDWARD BOWEN, research mechanical engineer; b. Los Angeles, June 1, 1941; s. Robert Edward and Clare (Bowen) G.; m. Barbara Lea Heyl, June 22, 1968. B.S. in Mech. Engring., U. Calif.-Berkeley, 1965, postgrad., 1967. Engr. Unified Sci. Assn., Pasadena, Calif., 1965-68; project engr. Sloan Tech., Santa Barbara, Calif., 1967-73; pres. Lebow Co., Goleta, Calif., 1973—; cons. on thin films; tchr. thin film tech. Recipient IR100 award for beryllium metal, 1977, ultrathin metal, 1979. Mem. Am. Vacuum Soc., Am. Optical Soc. Contbr. articles in profl. jours. Home: RR 1 Box 230A Goleta CA 93117 Office: Lebow Co 38 Gerald Cass Pl Goleta CA 93117

GRASSL, THEODORE PETER, newspaper exec.; b. Stratford, Wis., Nov. 12, 1931; s. Ferdinand V. and Rebecca M. (Fandre) G.; B.B.A., U. Wis., Madison, 1959; m. Marlene Joan Palmer, Aug. 25, 1962; 1 dau., Melody Karen. Advt. and sales promotion acctg. supr. Pillsbury Co., Mpls., 1959-62, sr. computer analyst, 1962-63, acctg. and control mgr. comml. devel. div., 1963-67; systems supr. Control Data Corp., Mpls., 1967-69; bus. systems mgr. Mpls. Star & Tribune Co., 1969-71, EDP mgr., 1971-75; bus. mgr. Trenton (N.J.) Times Corp., 1975-76, v.p., gen. mgr., 1976-78; gen. mgr. Los Angeles Herald Examiner, 1978—. Bd. dirs. New Trenton Corp., 1977; bd. dirs. George Washington council Boy Scouts Am., 1976-77; Minn. state pres. Nat. Campers and Hikers Assn., 1973-75. Served with USN, 1951-55. Mem. Inst. Newspaper Controllers and Fin. Officers, Town Hall Calif., Beta Alpha Psi. Republican. Roman Catholic. Clubs: Los Angeles Athletic; Malibu Riding and Tennis. Contbr. articles to profl. jours. Home: 12401 Littler Pl Granada Hills CA 91344 Office: 1111 S Broadway Los Angeles CA 90015

GRATT, LAWRENCE BARRY, engineer, educator; b. Chgo., Sept. 20, 1940; s. Jack J. and Bette V. (Goldbloom) G.; m. Dona Jean Janecek, Aug. 21, 1963; children—Robyn, Gambyl, Alexis, Natalee. B.S. in Engring. with honors, UCLA, 1962, M.S. (Hughes Fellow), 1964, Ph.D. (AEC fellow), 1969. Mem. tech. staff Hughes Aircraft Co., 1962-65; sect. head TRW, Inc., 1965-73; asst. v.p. Sci. Applications Inc., La Jolla, Calif., 1973-79; pres. IWG Corp., San Diego, 1979—; instr. West Coast U., UCLA. Mem. Am. Nuclear Soc., AIAA, AAAS, Am. Chem. Soc., Geothermal Resource Council, Soc. for Risk Analysis, Tau Beta Pi. Contbr. articles to profl. jours. Office: 975 Hornblend St Suite C San Diego CA 92109

GRATTAN, JAMES GARDINER, physician; b. San Rafael, Calif., Dec. 27, 1948; s. Joseph George and Katherine (Gardiner) G.; A.B. with honors, Stanford U., 1972; M.D., N.Y. Med. Coll., 1975; m. Leslie Gail Best, June 18, 1969; children—Laura, Anna. Intern, resident in medicine Mayo Grad. Sch. Medicine, Rochester, Minn., 1975-78, fellow in cardiovascular disease Mayo Clinic, from 1976; now cardiologist Sansum Med. Clinic, Santa Barbara, Calif. Diplomate Am. Bd. Internal Medicine, Am. Coll. Cardiology. Fellow Am. Coll. Cardiology. AMA, Zumbro Valley Med. Soc., Minn. Med. Soc., Zumbro Valley Med. Soc. (mem. exec. com. 1978-80). Home: 2064 Las Tunas Rd Santa Barbara CA 93103 Office: Sansum Med Clinic Santa Barbara CA 93103

GRAVES, GLEN EDWARD, advertising executive; b. Burns, Oreg., June 15, 1934; s. Herbert Watson and Roselle Graves; m. Marlene June Freel, Jan. 2, 1954; children—Michael Edward, Carrie Lin, Jennifer Ann. B.S., U. Oreg., 1958. Display advt. rep. Eugene (Oreg.) Register & Guard, 1958-60; prodn. mgr. Pacific Nat. Advt. Agy., Portland, Oreg., 1960-61; account exec. Richard Montgomery Advt., Portland, 1961-63; asst. v.p., advt. and publicity mgr. PSNB, Tacoma, Wash., 1963-69; pres. Graves & Assocs., Tacoma, 1970—. Trustee Friends of Lakes Dist. Library, 1966-69, Lakewood Gen. Hosp.; sec., publicity chmn., bd. dirs. Tacoma World Affairs Council, 1969-72; exec. bd. Pierce County chpt. March of Dimes, 1967-70; co-chmn. Wash. State Nat. Library Week Com., 1969; bd. dirs. Tacoma Goodwill Industries, 1971-74; bd. dirs. United Way of Pierce County, also exec. com., past pres.; bd. dirs. Tacoma-Pierce County chpt. NCCJ. Recipient Lakewood Jaycees disting. service award, 1968, Mcpl. League disting. citizen's award, 1972. Mem. Seattle Advt. Club, Pub. Relations Soc. Am., Tacoma Advt. Club (chmn. bd. dirs., past pres.), Am. Advt. Fedn. (past gov. Dist. 11, past sec. Western Region), Bank Pub. Relations and Mktg. Assn. (past state chmn.), Tacoma C. of C. (past bd. dirs., exec. com.), Puget Sound Advt. Fedn. (past bd. dirs., 1st v.p.). Republican. Presbyterian. Club: Tacoma Rotary (pres. 1982-83). Home: 6016 119th St SW Tacoma WA 98499 Office: 107 Tacoma Ave N Tacoma WA 98403

GRAVES, JOHN GARLAND, advertising agency executive; b. San Francisco, Jan. 19, 1949; s. Garland Drewry and Florence (Johnson) G.; m. Sharon Spencer, Jan. 9, 1953. Student Seattle U., 1968-71, U. Wash., 1973; B.A., Humboldt State U., 1975. Program, news and prodn. dir. Sta. KFMI-FM, Eureka, Calif., 1976-77; v.p. MTC Advt. div. The Minor Theatre Corp., 1977-80; pres. MTC Assocs., Inc., Arcata, Calif., 1980—. Mem. Retail Advt. Conf. (best TV comml. award in U.S. award 1982, 83, for western states 1981, 2d place for U.S. TV campaign 1982), No. Calif. Assn. Advt. Agys. Democrat.

GRAVES, LARRY RICHARD, chemist; b. Tacoma, May 5, 1942; s. Rodney Wilbur and Ruth Etta (Rayton) G.; B.S. in Chemistry, U. Puget Sound, 1965; m. Sondra Lee Somers, June 6, 1964; 1 dau., Kelly Ann. Chemist, Hooker Chem. Corp., Tacoma, 1962-66; chemist Hercules Inc., Tacoma, 1966-69, chief lab. chemist, 1969-73; sr. chemist/group leader Pacific Resins Chems./Ga. Pacific Corp., 1973—; asst. treas. Pacific Resins Fed. Credit Union, 1976, 78, pres., 1977, treas./mgr., 1979-80. Vice pres. Hercules Men's Club, 1971-72, trustee, 1973; v.p. Summit Youth Ctr., Tacoma, 1980; v.p. Summit Youth Ctr. Athletic Assn. Tacoma, 1980. Served with USAF, 1966. Recipient award of recognition Summit Youth Center Athletic Assn., 1980; Disting. Scientist award Ga. Pacific Corp., 1982. Mem. TAPPI, Am. Chem. Soc. Republican. Clubs: Brookdale Golf and Country; Elks (Tacoma). Home: 9914 58th Ave Ct E Puyallup WA 98373 Office: PO Box 2277 Tacoma WA 98401

GRAVES, PHILIP EARL, economics educator; b. Hammond, Ind., Dec. 20, 1945; s. Earl Edwin and Ruth Marie (Carmichael) G.; m. Patricia J. Neal, June 10, 1967 (div.); children—Wendy Marie, Jessica Joanne. A.B., Ind. U., 1968; M.A., Northwestern U., 1971, Ph.D. 1973. Asst. prof. econs. Ariz. State U., 1971-74; research fellow dept. econs. U. Chgo., 1974-78, vis. asst. prof., 1977-78; vis. assoc. prof. UCLA, 1982; now assoc. prof. U. Colo. Mem. Am. Econs. Assn., Air Pollution Control Assn., Western Econ. Assn., Assn. Environ. and Resource Economists, Internat. Assn. Energy Economists, Phi Beta Kappa. Contbr. articles to profl. jours. Home: 889 14th St Boulder CO 80302 Office: University of Colorado Department Economics Boulder CO 80309

GRAVES, ROY DANNER, public relations executive, consultant; b. Indpls., Mar. 2, 1943; s. Robert Harrison and Ardis Louise (Danner) G.; m. Rebecca Jane Cole, Oct. 30, 1971; children—Gavin Matthew, Aaron

Todd. B.A., Butler U., 1964; M. Communication, U. Wash.-Seattle, 1972. Pub. relations specialist Cummins Engine Co., Columbus, Ind., 1969-71; marine systems pub. relations specialist Boeing Aerospace Co., Seattle, 1972-75; account exec. Communication N.W., Seattle, 1975-77, pres./owner, 1978—. Active Seattle Chamber Pres.' Club, Intiman Theatre (pub. relations com.). Served to comdr. USNR, 1961—. Mem. Pub. Relations Soc. Am., Counselors Acad. (exec. com., publ. chmn.), Assn. Wash. Bus. Club: Seattle Athletic. Contbr. article to profl. jour. Home: 3476 W Blaine Seattle WA 98199 Office: 514 2d Ave W Seattle WA 98119

GRAVES, THEODORE DUMAINE, psychological anthropologist, social science consultant; b. Concord, Mass., June 2, 1932; s. Theodore Eliot and Cordelia (Dumaine) G.; m. Nancy Beatrice Russell, Mar. 3, 1967; children—Christopher, David, Lisa, Lauren, Kit, Ricky. B.A., Earlham Coll., 1954; M.A., U. Colo., 1957; Ph.D., U. Pa., 1962. Asst. prof. U. Colo., Boulder, 1963-67, assoc. prof., 1967-69; prof. UCLA, 1969-73; Capt. James Cook fellow Royal Soc. N.Z., 1973-75; co-dir. So. Pacific Research Inst., N.Z., 1975—; research assoc. U. Calif.-Santa Cruz, 1976—; cons. in field. Mem. Am. Psychol. Assn., Am. Anthrop. Assn. (Ctr. Advanced Study Behavioral Scis. fellow, 1977-78). Contbr. articles to profl. jours. Home: 136 Liberty St Santa Cruz CA 95060 Office: Oakes Coll U Calif Santa Cruz CA 95064

GRAVES, WILLIAM HENRY BASCOM, geologist, geological consulting company executive; b. Wheatland, Wyo., May 12, 1928; s. William C. and Edythe Janet (Curtis) G.; m. Jeannine A. O'Bryan, July 17, 1948; 1 son, Douglas L. B.S. in Geology, U. Wyo., 1962. Chief mine engr. Fed.-Am. Ptnrs., 1962-66; chief geologist, div. mgr. Northwest U.S., AMAX, 1966-70; chief geologist, advisor to bd. NEDCO, Lander, Wyo., 1970-72; owner, geologic cons. Graves & Assocs., Ltd., Riverton, Wyo., 1972—; dir. Universal Fuels, Advanced Monitoring Systems, Inc., Bishop Cable Communications Corp.; mem. adv. bd. Wyo. Geol. Survey, 1982—. Served with U.S. Army, 1952-54. Mem. Wyo. Geol. Assn., Soc. Mining Engrs., Soc. Econ. Geologists, Colo. Mining Assn., Am. Mining Congress. Democrat. Clubs: Riverton Country, Elks, VFW. Contbr. articles to profl. jours. Home: 130 Fairway Dr PO Box 2129-C Riverview Riverton WY 82501 Office: 922 Federal Blvd PO Box 1686 Riverton WY 82501

GRAVES, (WILLIAM) KENT, school counselor; b. Glendive, Mont., May 24, 1947; s. Marvin Albert and Frances (Andrews) G.; m. Randi Lee Ferch, Aug. 26, 1972; 1 son, Trevor Gary. A.A. in English, Dawson Coll., 1967; B.A. in English, U. Mont, 1969, M.A. in Guidance Counseling, 1972. Elem. sch. counselor, Great Falls (Mont.) Pub. Schs., 1972-74, head counselor, Title I, 1974—. Bd. dirs. Mental Health Assn.; on-site chmn. Mont. Edn. Fair, 1983; vol. tutor Children's Receiving Home; mem. screening com. Miss Great Falls Pageant, 1973; leader People-to-People Russian Tour, 1976; v.p. Teen Coffeehouse, 1975-77; United Way vol., 1975—. Served with Peace Corps, Babol, Iran, 1970. Mem. Am. Personnel and Guidance Assn., Mont. Personnel and Guidance Assn. (Disting. Service award 1982), Great Falls Area Counselors Assn. (past pres., Counselor of Yr. 1982), Am. School Counselor Assn., Mont School Counselor Assn. (founding chmn. 1981), NEA, Mont. Edn. Assn., Great Falls Edn. Assn., Phi Delta Kappa. Methodist. Club: Glacier Racquet (Great Falls). Developed 9 counseling programs, contbr. articles to profl. jours. Home: 3013 Carmel Dr Great Falls MT 57404 Office: Great Falls Public Schools PO Box 2428 Great Falls MT 59401

GRAVITZ, SIDNEY I., aerospace industry engineering executive; b. Balt., June 28, 1932; s. Philip and Sophie (Korim) G.; m. Phyllis Bilgrad, June 14, 1964; children—Deborah, Elizabeth. B.S., MIT, 1953, M.S. in Aero. Engring., 1954, Aero. Engr., 1957. Research engr. dept. aero. engring. MIT, part-time 1952-57, edn. cons., 1974-77; dynamics group engr. N.Am. Aviation, Columbus, Ohio, 1957-60; dynamics group engr., structures research and devel. chief, systems engring. mgr., flight ops. mgr., software devel. mgr., system requirements mgr. Saturn/Apollo, space shuttle, inertial upper stage, 747, 757/767, energy mgmt. programs Boeing Co., Seattle, 1960—. Loaned exec. King County United Good Neighbor Fund, 1968; regional chmn. MIT Alumni Fund Puget Sound, 1970; mem. NASA-Industry Space Shuttle Design Criteria Working Group, 1970; mem. Tech. NW Organizing Com., 1981-82. Served to 1st lt. USAF, 1954-56. Mem. AAAS, ASME, AIAA, Sigma Xi, Sigma Gamma Tau. Contbr. articles to profl. jours. Home: 8428 SE 62d St Mercer Island WA 98040 Office: PO Box 3707 Seattle WA 98124

GRAVLEE, GRADY JACKSON, SR., educator; b. Birmingham, Ala., May 31, 1930; s. Gaines Grady (dec.) and Olathe (Parsley) (dec.) G.; student William Jewell Coll., 1952-53; B.A., Samford U., 1955; M.A., La. State U., 1958, Ph.D., 1963; m. Rhonda Lynn Cooley, Oct. 10, 1953; 1 son, Grady Jackson, Jr. (dec.). Instr., U. Houston, 1959-61; asst. prof. U. N.Mex., Albuquerque, 1962-64; asso. prof. Auburn (Ala.) U., 1964-65; mem. faculty Colo. State U., Fort Collins, 1965—, prof. rhetorical history, 1974—, chmn. dept. speech communication, 1975—. Served with USAF, 1948-52. Recipient Lory Disting. Service award Colo. State U., 1975, Faculty Research grantee, 1972, 76, 78. Mem. Speech Communication Assn., So. Speech Communication Assn., Western Speech Communication Assn., Conf. Brit. Studies, Rhetoric Soc. Am., Colo. Broadcasters Assn., Hist. Soc. Episcopal Ch. Democrat. Episcopalian. Editor: (with James R. Irvine) Pamphlets and the American Revolution, 1976, Speech Coursebook, 1977; contbr. articles to various publs. Home: 1409 Country Club Rd Fort Collins CO 80524 Office: Dept Speech Communication Colorado State U Fort Collins CO 80523

GRAY, BURL BRADLEY, research psychologist; b. Mattoon, Ill., June 1, 1938; s. Lawrence Albert and Virginia (Bradley) G.; m. Sheila Gay Tedrick, Sept. 8, 1962; children—Bradley Kent, Kara Dawne; m. 2d, Pamela Gleason, Oct. 19, 1982. B.S., So. Ill. U., 1960, M.S., 1961, Ph.D., 1963. Research fellow U. Ill., 1962; asst. prof., dir. speech sis. lab. U. Ariz., Tucson, 1963; research psychologist, dir. research Behavioral Scis. Inst., Carmel, Calif., 1964-76; Distinguished scholar in residence Wichita (Kans.) State U., 1976—; sr. staff scientist Human Resources Research Orgn., 1976-78; v.p. McFann Gray & Assos., 1978-81, pres., 1981—. HEW grantee, 1964, 66, 68, 73; Def. Dept. grantee, 1976. Fellow Behavior Therapy and Research Soc., Am. Speech and Hearing Assn.; mem. Am. Psychol. Assn., AAAS. Patentee in field. Author: (with Gene England) Stuttering and the Conditioning Therapies, 1966; (with Bruce P. Ryan) A Program for Non Language Children, 1973. Author ednl. programs in lang., reading and arithmetic; contbr. articles to profl. pubs. Home: 28225 Robinson Canyon Carmel CA 93923 Office: 2100 Garden Rd Suite J Monterey CA 93940

GRAY, ELVA MAE, mfg. co. ofcl.; b. Wichita Falls, Tex., Aug. 15, 1926; d. Joseph and Ella Maude (Drinkard) Matthews; student Delta Jr. Coll., Stockton, Calif., 1962, 70, 75, Humphrey Bus. Coll., 1973-74, Calif. State U., Hayward, 1978; m. Odies Gray, Aug. 15, 1948; children—Donna Sue Gray Jackson, Randolph. Clk.-typist Sharpe Depot, U.S. Army, 1944, Stockton, traffic clk., 1956-62; beautician Cameo Beauty Salon and Elva's Beauty Salon, 1945-54; owner-operated G.I. Cleaners, Stockton, 1962-68; payroll clk. Johns-Manville Co., Stockton, 1968-73, purchasing agt., 1973—, asst. regional purchasing agt., San Mateo, 1979—. Pres. Young Women's Christian Council; pres., dir. choir, youth leader New Hope Ch. of God in Christ, Stockton, 1965-76; supr. women's depts. Glad Tidings Ch. of God in Christ, Hayward, Calif., 1980—. Recipient Superior Performance award Sharpe Depot, U.S. Army, 1961. Mem. Nat. Assn. Purchasing Mgrs. Home: 2155 Eric Ct Apt 3 Union City CA 94587 Office: 2600 Campus Dr San Mateo CA 94403

GRAY, GARY DAVID, communications engineer; b. Orange, Calif., Nov. 7, 1942; s. Albert Eldred and Wilda Minerva (Fender) G.; A.A., Fullerton Jr. Coll., 1963; B.S. Eng. cum laude, Calif. State U., Long Beach, 1969, M.S.E.E., 1974; m. Mary Irene Reilly; children—David Christian, Holly Anne. Communications engring. asst. Gen. Services Agy. Communications div. County of Orange, Calif., 1969-71, communications project engr., 1971-76, communications engr., 1976-82, chief communications engr., 1982—. Electronics adv. com. Santa Ana Coll., 1973-75; Registered profl. elec. engr. Calif., D.C., chartered electronic and radio engr. Eng. Fellow Radio Club of Am., Inst. Advancement Engring.; mem. Instn. Electronic and Radio Engrs. Eng., IEEE (sr.; chmn. Orange County sect. 1974-75), Calif. Soc. Profl. Engrs., Nat. Soc. Profl. Engrs., Associated Pub.-Safety Communications Officers (pres. So. Calif. chpt. 1980), Internat. Mcpl. Signal Assn., Calif. Fire Chiefs Assn., Eta Kappa Nu, Tau Beta Pi. Mem. Christian Ch. Republican. Clubs: Orange County Communicators, Masons. Office: Orange County Communications Center 481 The City Dr S Orange CA 92668

GRAY, GEORGE WALTER, city official; b. Oakland, Calif., Aug. 23, 1927; s. Walter Joseph and Elsie M. (Gefkin) G.; m. Dorothy Florence Damon, Aug. 16, 1953; children—Gordon W., Linda J. A.A. in Fire Service, Merritt Coll., 1967; B.A. in Pub. Mgmt., St. Mary's Coll., Moraga, Calif., 1976; postgrad. Exec. Devel. III, Nat. Fire Acad., 1982. Firefighter, Oakland Fire Dept., 1949-56, fire engr., 1956-58, fire lt., 1958-68, fire capt., 1968-78, bn. chief, 1978-82; asst. chief, 1982, dep. fire chief, 1982—; instr. municipal fire adminstrn. Merritt Coll., Chabot Coll., Hayward, Calif.; mem. adv. com. fire curriculum; Participant rail rapid transit safety workshop, Washington, 1982. Dist. commr. San Francisco Bay Area Council, 1968-70, dist. chmn. bd. dirs., 1975-77; scoutmaster San Francisco Bay Area council Boy Scouts Am., 1970-79, leader 7th & 10th Nat. Scout Jamborees, 13th World Jamboree, Shizuoka, Japan, 1971. Served with U.S. Army, 1946-47. Recipient Silver Beaver award Boy Scouts Am., 1972; Steven R. O'Day award Oakland Fire Dept., 1980. Mem. Nat. Fire Protection Assn. (charter Fire Service Sect.), Bay Area Fire Protection Forum (v.p. 1966). Club: Rotary (pres. East Oakland 1981-82, Paul Harris award 1978). Home: 3518 Rubin Dr Oakland CA 94602 Office: Oakland Fire Dept 1605 Grove St Oakland CA 94612

GRAY, JAMES H., banker, auto dealer; b. Long Beach, Calif., Sept. 27, 1937; s. Brewster and Hester Clay (Niswonger), B.; m. Joann Elaine Gray, Dec. 18, 1956; children—Debra Jo McKay, Diane Elaine Nesland; m. 2d Gail Jean Amundson, Apr. 23, 1982. B.S. in Mktg., Calif. State U.-Long Beach, 1958. Founding dir. Harbor Bank, Long Beach, 1974, pres. chief exec. officer, 1976—; owner, pres. Jim Gray Volvo-Isuzu, 1963—; owner, pres. Long Beach Leasing Inc., 1980—. Elected mem. Long Beach Bd. Edn., 1971-75; mem. Bd. Harbor Commrs., 1977—. Named Long Beach Citizen of Yr., 1978, Outstanding Sales and Mktg. Exec. of Long Beach, Long Beach Exchange Club, 1979, Citizen of Yr., Long Beach Elks. Mem. Calif. Bankers Assn. (dir.), Am. Bankers Assn., Ind. Bankers Assn. So. Calif., Nat. Automobile Dealers Assn., Motor Car Dealers So. Calif., Long Beach Car Dealers (past pres.), Long Beach C. of C. (past pres.). Republican. Clubs: Kiwanis, Virginia Country (Long Beach); Indian Wells Country. Office: 11 Golden Shore Long Beach CA 90802

GRAY, JOHN DELTON, manufacturing executive; b. Ontario, Oreg., July 29, 1919; s. Elmer Roe and Mabel (Ridgley) G.; m. Elizabeth Neuner, Jan. 4, 1946; children—Anne, Joan, Janet, John, Laurie. B.Secretarial Sci., Oreg. State Coll., 1940; M.B.A., Harvard U., 1947; LL.D., Lewis and Clark Coll., 1967. Asst. to pres. Pointer-Willamette Co., Portland, Oreg., 1947; asst. gen. mgr. Oreg. Saw Chain Corp. (now Omark Industries, Inc., Portland, 1948-50, gen. mgr., 1950-53, pres., gen. mgr., 1953-67, chmn. bd., 1961-83; dir. Castle & Cooke, Inc., Precision Castparts Corp., First Interstate Bank Oreg., Tektronix, Inc., Standard Ins. Co. Trustee Reed Coll., Portland, chmn. steering com. capital campaign, chmn. trustees, 1968-82; mem. Com. Econ. Devel., 1967-81; mem. Chief Execs. Orgn.; trustee Oreg. Grad. Ctr.; pres. Portland area council Boy Scouts Am., 1959-61; past pres., mem. exec. bd. Columbia-Pacific Council. Served to lt. col. U.S. Army, 1941-46. Decorated Bronze Star; recipient Silver Beaver award Portland area council Boy Scouts Am. Republican. Episcopalian. Clubs: Multnomah Athletic, Waverley, Arlington, University, Rotary (Portland). Office: 5500 SW Macadam Ave Portland OR 97201

GRAY, MICHAEL HALL, lawyer; b. N.Y.C., Feb. 17, 1946; s. Arthur and Adele (Hall) G.; B.A. in Philosophy, Calif. State U., Northridge, 1969, M.A. in Philosophy, 1971; J.D., Southwestern U., Los Angeles, 1975; m. Leslie Joy Sonners, Aug. 13, 1972; children—Kaili Joy, Jeremiah Schiff. Admitted to Calif. bar, 1975; prof. law Calif. Law Inst., Santa Barbara, 1976-77; individual practice law, Santa Barbara, 1975—; judge pro tem Santa Barbara-Goleta Small Claims Ct., 1976—; bd. dirs. Atty. Referral Service Santa Barbara, 1976-80. Mem. Environ. Def. Center, 1977—, Community Environ. Council, 1978—; mem. steering com. Network, 1979-80; bd. dirs. Advocates for Alternative Child Birth, 1979-80, Family Therapy Inst., 1981—; vice chmn. Santa Barbara City Planning Commn., 1979-81, chmn., 1981-82. Real estate broker, Calif.; community coll. instr. life credential, Calif. Mem. Am. Arbitration Assn., Am. Bar Assn., ACLU (pres. Santa Barbara chpt. 1980, 81), Assn. Trial Lawyers, Calif. State Bar, Nat. Lawyers Guild, Barristers Club (dir., v.p. Santa Barbara), Santa Barbara Tennis Assn. (dir. 1977), Sierra Club. Office: 829 De La Vina St Suite 220 Santa Barbara CA 93101

GRAY, NORMAN EUGENE, fire chief; b. Helena, Mont., Nov. 3, 1937; s. Eugene F. and Gladys I. (Lippert) G.; student public schs., Helena, Mont.; m. Sharon A. Weed, Nov. 21, 1959; children—Debra A., Norman Dean. Clk., IRS, Helena, Mont., 1959; firefighter, Helena, 1960—, fire chief, 1979—, train officer, 1973-79. Served with USN, 1955-58. Mem. Internat. Assn. Fire Chiefs, Western Fire Chiefs Assn., Mont. State Fire Chiefs Assn. Republican. Club: Elks. Office: City of Helena Office of Fire Chief Helena Fire Dept Helena MT 59601

GRAY, PHILIP HOWARD, psychologist, educator; b. Cape Rosier, Maine, July 4, 1926; s. Asa and Bernice (Lawrence) G.; M.A., U. Chgo., 1958; Ph.D., U. Wash., 1960; m. Iris McKinney, Dec. 31, 1954; children—Cindelyn, Howard. Asst. prof. dept. psychology Mont. State U., Bozeman, 1960-65, asso. prof., 1965-75, prof., 1975—; vis. prof. U. Man., Winnipeg, Can., 1968-70; pres. Mont. Psychol. Assn., 1968-70; chmn. State of Mont. Bd. Psychologist Examiners, 1972-74; speaker sci. and geneal. meetings on ancestry of U.S. presidents. Organized exhbns. folk art in Mont. and Maine, 1972-79. Served with U.S. Army, 1944-46. Fellow Am. Psychol. Assn., AAAS; mem. History of Sci. Soc., Nat. Geneal. Soc., New Eng. Historic Geneal. Soc., Deer Isle-Stonington Hist. Soc., Psychonomic Soc., Descendants of the Illegitimate Sons and Daughters of the Kings of Britain, Piscataqua Pioneers, Animal Behavior Soc., Sigma Xi. Author: The Comparative Analysis of Behavior, 1966; (with F.L. Ruch and N. Warren) Working with Psychology, 1963; A Directory of Eskimo Artists in Sculpture and Prints, 1974; contbr. numerous articles on behavior to psychol. jours.; contbr. poetry to lit. jours. Home: 1207 S Black Ave Bozeman MT 59715 Office: Dept Psychology Montana State U Bozeman MT 59717

GRAY, RANDALL JOSHUA, information services administrator; b. Santa Monica, Calif., Sept. 30, 1949; s. Joshua and Eunice M. (Serr) G.; B.A. in English, San Fernando Valley State Coll., 1972; M.L.S., UCLA, 1974, cert. law librarianship, 1974; m. Roberta Christine Johnson, June 15, 1973. Intern, Los Angeles County Law Library, 1973-74; asst. librarian O'Melveny & Myers, Los Angeles, 1974-76; law librarian Adams, Duque & Hazeltine, Los Angeles, 1976-82, dir. info. services, 1982—; instr. Inst. Pvt. Law Librarians, Biltmore Hotel, Los Angeles, 1980, UCLA Extension, 1980, Practising Law Inst., 1981; participant Calif. State Colls. Internat. Studies Program, Uppsala, Sweden, 1971; chmn. 10th Ann. Inst. on Calif. Law, 1982. Cert. law librarian, 1980—. Mem. Am. Assn. Law Libraries, Am. Mgmt. Assn., Am. Soc. Info. Sci., Asso. Info. Mgrs., Def. Research Inst., Info. Industry Assn., So. Calif. Assn. Law Libraries (chmn. cons. com. 1980, v.p. 1981-82, pres. 1982-83), Spl. Libraries Assn., UCLA Grad. Sch. Library and Info. Sci. Students Assn. (pres. 1973-74). Author: Effective Administration: Better Decisions through Information, 1981. information services administrator; b. Santa Monica, Calif., Sept. 30, 1949; s. Joshua and Eunice M. (Serr) G.; B.A. in English, San Fernando Valley State Coll., 1972; M.L.S., UCLA, 1974, cert. law librarianship, 1974; m. Roberta Christine Johnson, June 15, 1973. Intern, Los Angeles County Law Library, 1973-74; asst. librarian O'Melveny & Myers, Los Angeles, 1974-76; law librarian Adams, Duque & Hazeltine, Los Angeles, 1976-82, dir. info. services, 1982—; instr. Inst. Pvt. Law Librarians, Biltmore Hotel, Los Angeles, 1980, UCLA Extension, 1980, Practising Law Inst., 1981; participant Calif. State Colls. Internat. Studies Program, Uppsala, Sweden, 1971; chmn. 10th Ann. Inst. on Calif. Law, 1982. Cert. law librarian, 1980—. Mem. Am. Assn. Law Libraries, Am. Mgmt. Assn., Am. Soc. Info. Sci., Asso. Info. Mgrs., Def. Research Inst., Info. Industry Assn., So. Calif. Assn. Law Libraries (chmn. cons. com. 1980, v.p. 1981-82, pres. 1982-83), Spl. Libraries Assn., UCLA Grad. Sch. Library and Info. Sci. Students Assn. (pres. 1973-74). Author: Effective Administration: Better Decisions through Information, 1981. Home: 521 Ramona Ave Sierra Madre CA 91024 Office: 523 W 6th St Los Angeles CA 90014

GRAY, RICHARD MOSS, coll. pres.; b. Washington, Jan. 25, 1924; s. Wilbur Leslie and Betty Marie Grey; B.A., Bucknell U., 1942; M.Div. summa cum laude, San Francisco Theol. Sem., 1961, Ph.D., U. Calif., Berkeley, 1972; m. Catherine Claire Hammond, Oct. 17, 1943; children—Janice Lynn, Nancy Hammond. Writer, creative dir. N.W. Ayer & Son, Inc., advt., Phila., 1942-58; commd. to campus ministry United Presbyn. Ch., 1961; campus pastor Portland State U., 1961-68; pres. World Coll. of West, San Rafael, Calif., 1972—; trustee San Francisco Theol. Sem., 1968—, Lewis and Clark Coll., Portland, 1972-76. Ruling elder 1st Presbyn. Ch., San Rafael. Served as officer USNR, 1943-46. Mem. Am. Assn. Higher Edn., Assn. World Edn., UN Assn. U.S. (dir. 1980—), Phi Beta Kappa. Republican. Office: Box 3060 San Rafael CA 94912

GRAY, ROBERT HUGH, univ. dean; b. Dallas, Sept. 22, 1931; B.F.A., Yale U., 1959, M.F.A., 1961. Instr. design and visual communication Cooper Union, N.Y.C., 1960-66 instr. drawing, painting and design Silvermine Coll. Art, Conn., 1966-71; also dean; prof. painting, head dept. art Pa. State U., State College, 1972-75; dean visual arts div. SUNY, Purchase, 1975-79; dean Coll. Fine Arts, UCLA, 1979—. Bd. trustees AC-BAW, Westchester County. Mem. Nat. Council Art Adminstrs., Coll. Art Assn., Am. Assn. Higher Edn. Office: Coll Fine Arts Murphy Hall UCLA Los Angeles CA 90024*

GRAY, ROLAND FRANCIS, educator; b. Dover, N.H., June 21, 1923; s. Clarence Sidney and Dorothy Frances (Hussey) G.; B.A. magna cum laude, U. N.H., 1948; M.Ed., 1952; Ph.D., U. Calif. at Berkeley, 1964; m. Barbara Green, 1945; 1 son, Gordon Lester; m. 2d, Doris Claire Bane, Mar. 20, 1951; children—Suzanne Leslie, Edward Roland. Tchr., N.H., 1949-50, Mich., 1951-52, Mont., 1953-55, Calif., 1955-56, 58-59, 61-62, Alaska, 1952-53, 56-58; prin. elementary sch., Dexter, Mich., 1951-52; supt. schs. Fort Yukon, Alaska, 1959-61; mem. faculty edn. U. B.C., Vancouver, 1964—, assoc. prof. edn., 1966-73, prof., 1973—, assoc. dir. elem. div., 1969-73, coordinator C&I, Div. 5, 1979, head dept. C&I studies, 1980—; cons. pub. schs., Palo Alto, Calif., San Francisco, N.W.T. Can., others. Co-chmn. McGovern for Pres. Com., San Juan County, Wash., 1972. Served with USNR, 1942-46. Fellow Royal Geog. Soc.; mem. Am. Ednl. Research Assn., Canadian Soc. for Study of Edn., Nat. Council Tchrs. Math., Canadian Assn. Univ. Tchrs., Phi Kappa Phi, Kappa Delta Pi, Pi Gamma Mu, Phi Delta Kappa. Contbr. articles to profl. jours. Home: 14749 Goggs Ave Whiterock BC V4B 2N3 Canada Office: Faculty Education Univ BC Vancouver BC V6T 1W5 Canada

GRAY, RUSSELL, sch. adminstr.; b. Ft. Ord, Calif., Sept. 26, 1950; s. Donald Courtland and Mary Alice (Rogers) Kessler; A.A., Yuba Coll., 1971; B.A., Calif. State U., 1976, M.A. with honors, 1982; m. Paula Lucille Nance, Aug. 24, 1968; children—Rachelle Kristen, Christina Donn. Dir. children's ministries First So. Bapt. Ch., Fountain Valley, Calif., 1971-72; early childhood edn. dir. First Bapt. Christian Schs., Olivehurst, Calif., 1972-79; adminstr. Hall St. Ministry in Christian Edn., Marysville, Calif., 1979-81; instr. St. James Coll., San Bruno, Calif., 1981—; early childhood edn. cons. Mem. Ch. of the Highlands, San Bruno; chmn. Yuba-Sutter Child Evangelism Com. Mem. Assn. Christian Schs. Internat. (seminar leader 1975—), Full Gospel Businessmen Internat.

GRAY, TOM ROBERT, motion picture executive; b. Jasper, Ala., Mar. 19, 1939; s. Thomas Robert and Elia Margaret (Terry) G.; B.J., U. Mo., 1962; M.A., So. Ill. U., 1964. Entertainment editor Atlanta Constn., 1965-66; with MGM, Chgo. and Washington, 1966-68, Paramount Pictures, Los Angeles, 1968-70, Universal Pictures, 1970-72; dir. corp. pub. relations Lion Country Safari, 1972-74; with Irwin Allen Prodns., 1974-76, Universal Studios, 1976-78, Dino de Laurentis Prodns., 1978-79, 20th Century Fox Films, 1979-80; v.p. world-wide studio publicity United Artists, 1980-81; v.p. publicity and promotion PolyGram Pictures, Culver City, Calif., 1981—; publicist Ladd Co., 1982—. Served with AUS. Mem. Acad. Motion Picture Arts and Scis. Office: Ladd Co Burbank Studios 4000 Warner Blvd Burbank CA 91522

GRAY, WILLIAM PERCIVAL, judge; b. Los Angeles, Mar. 26, 1912; s. Jacob L. and Catherine (Percival) G.; A.B., UCLA, 1934; LL.B., cum laude, Harvard U., 1939;; m. Elizabeth Polin, Nov. 8, 1941; children—Robin Marie, James Polin. Admitted to Calif. bar, 1941; legal sec. to judge U.S. Ct. Appeals, Washington, 1939-40; with firm O'Melveny & Myers, lawyers, Los Angeles, 1940-41; pvt. practice, Los Angeles, 1945-49, partner firm Gray, Pfaelzer & Robertson, Los Angeles, 1950-66; judge U.S. Dist. Ct. Central Dist. Calif., 1966—. Spl. asst. to atty. gen. U.S., 1958-64; chmn. Calif. Conf. State Bar Dels., 1952. Served from 1st lt. to lt. col. AUS, 1941-45. Fellow Am. Bar Found.; mem. Am. Law Inst., Los Angeles County Bar Assn. (pres. 1956), State Bar Calif. (bd. govs. 1960-63, pres. 1962-63). Office: US Courthouse Los Angeles CA 90012

GRAYSON, EDWIN MILTON, realtor; b. Pocatello, Idaho, Dec. 20, 1931; s. William Thomas and Marjorie Jane (Wilcox) G.; student Idaho State Coll., 1955-56, Grimms Sch. Bus., 1956-57; m. Elaine Diane Mooney, Oct. 20, 1957; children—Christine (Mrs. Keith Harding), Michelle (Mrs. Kent Morris), Branda (Mrs. Dave Silva), Cindy (Mrs. Alan Rowbury), Marjorie (Mrs. Mike Carpenter), Jolene (Mrs. John Stokka). Salesman, Shattuck Agy., Idaho Falls, Idaho, 1957-65; owner

Grayson Real Estate & Builders, 1965-73; owner, dir. Grayson Builders, Inc., Idaho Falls, 1973—. Mem. Idaho Real Estate Commn., 1957—, Idaho Falls Realty Bd., 1957—; pres. Idaho Falls Multiple Listing Bur., 1960. Republican precinct committeeman, 1968-70. Bd. dirs. Key Club-Skyline High Sch. Served with USN, 1950-54; PTO. Mem. Nat. Assn. Realtors. Presbyterian. Mason (Shriner), Elk, Kiwanian (Distinguished Service awards 1969, 73, 74). Office: 665 N Holmes St Idaho Falls ID 83401

GRAYSON, JOHN WESLEY, business consultant, computer science educator; b. N.Y.C., Sept. 7, 1941; s. Roger Henry and Dorothy Mae (Kenny) G.; m. Audrey Elize Black, Dec. 22, 1962; children—John Wesley Jr., Carleton Avery. M.A., SUNY-Stony Brook, 1974; postgrad. U. West Los Angeles Sch. Law, 1979. Programmer, Data Stats., Inc., N.Y.C., 1961-62; sr. programmer Computech, Inc., N.Y.C., 1962-65; systems analyst Nat. Shoes, Inc., Bronx, N.Y., 1965-68; sr. systems analyst Acad. Press, Inc., N.Y.C., 1968-69; sr. systems cons. Grumman Aerospace Corp., 1969-71; sr. mgmt. cons. FRB, N.Y.C., 1971-72; coll. lectr., mgr. mgmt. info. systems SUNY-Stony Brook, 1972-76; communications cons. Gen. Telephone Calif., Los Angeles, 1976-79; v.p. Security Pacific Nat. Bank, Los Angeles, 1980; owner, pres. Bus. Cons. Firm, Glendale, Calif., 1981—; assoc. prof. computer sci. Compton (Calif.) Coll.; lectr. SUNY-Stony Brook. Treas., Sunset Baseball Little League, Redondo Beach, Calif.; pres. 147th Bd. Election Dist. Insps., N.Y.; trustee Middle Island (N.Y.) Pub. Library; SBA pres. U. West Los Angeles Sch. Law, 1979; com. examiner Glendale (Calif.) Unified Sch. Dist.; mem. usher bd. St. Francis Episcopal Ch., also mem. choir; scoutmaster Cub Scouts Am., St. James, N.Y.; mem. West High Sch. Band Assn., Torrance, Calif., West High Sch. PTA. Mem. Data Processing Mgmt. Assn., Assn. Systems Mgmt., ACM (treas.). Republican. Clubs: Suffolk County Republican (Brook Haven, N.Y.); Pioneer Track (N.Y.); Los Verdes Men's Golf; Masons, Shriners. Home: 1533 S Pearl Ave Compton CA 90221 Office: 611 N Brand Blvd Glendale CA 91203

GRAYSON, LINCOLN BLAISDELL, constrn. cons.; b. W. Sebois, Maine, June 24, 1907; s. John Watson and Annie Catherine (Blaisdell) G.; student U. Cin., 1925-28; B.C.E., U. Nev., 1930; LL.B., Suffolk U., 1938; m. Grace Riethmuller, Nov. 10, 1946; children—David Arthur, Guy. Shipyard supt. Bethlehem Steel Corp., Boston, 1930-41; project engr. Hydro-Electric Commn., Tasmania, Australia, 1949-52; regional engr. Snowy Mountains Authority, N.S.W., Australia, 1952-55; scheduling engr. Kaiser Engrs., N.S.W., 1955-57, dams estimator, 1957-62; dam engr., 1962-68; dam contract adminstr., London, 1968-72; heavy constrn. cons., Martinez, Calif., 1972—. Vol. crime prevention specialist Martinez Police Dept., 1975—, chmn. Crime Prevention Com. of Contra Costa County (Calif.), 1975—, chmn. citizens tng. subcom., 1976—. Served to maj. C.E., U.S. Army, 1941-49; PTO. Decorated Silver Star. Mem. ASCE, Soc. Am. Mil. Engrs., Instn. Engrs. (Australia), Res. Officers Assn., Ret. Officers Assn. Club: Masons (master lodge Oakland, Calif. 1975; pres. East Bay Masonic Service Bur., Oakland 1976). Address: 1950 Redwood Dr Martinez CA 94553

GREAVES, JAMES LOUIS, art conservator; b. Middletown, Conn., Jan. 25, 1943; s. Wellington North and Mabel (Frazer) G.; divorced; 1 son, Stephen Frazer. B.S. in Biology, Coll. William and Mary, 1965; M.A. in Art History, Diploma in Art Conservation, Inst. Fine Arts, NYU, 1970. Conservation intern Los Angeles County Mus., 1968-70, conservator, 1970, asst. head conservator, 1977-79, acting head conservator, 1979-81, sr. paintings conservator, 1981—; chief conservator Detroit Inst. Arts, 1970-77; cons. conservator Art Gallery of Huntington Library, San Marino, Calif., 1979—; cons. in field; instr. Calif. State U.-Fullerton. Fellow Internat. Inst. Conservation, Am. Inst. Conservation; mem. Western Assn. Art Conservators. Republican. Office: 5905 Wilshire Blvd Los Angeles CA 90036

GREBLER, ARTHUR ROBIN, management, finance, real estate and construction consultant, educator; b. Bklyn., May 21, 1918; s. William and Tonia G.; m. Rene Berger; children—Gillian, Robert, Elizabeth, Harriet. Ph.B., U. Wis., 1940, Ph.M., 1941. Chief project auditor Maumelle Ordinance Works, Marche, Ark., 1942-43; v.p. Grebler & Sons, Inc., Springfield, Ill., 1945-52, chmn. bd., Los Angeles, 1953—; chmn. bd. Universal Cities Real Estate, Inc., Los Angeles, 1953—; lectr. in engring. Calif. State U.-Northridge, 1976—. Served with U.S. Army, 1943-44. Mem. Internat. Inst. Valuers, Nat. Assn. Rev. Appraisers, San Fernando Bd. Realtors, Urban Land Inst. Office: 4386 Lankershim Blvd Toluca Lake CA 91602

GREELEY, CHARLES MATTHEW, painter, ceramcist, educator; b. Teaneck, N.J., Sept. 11, 1941; s. Charles Xavier and Aurelia Lilian (Kvieg) G.; m. Bunny Tobias, Oct. 17, 1964; B.F.A., N.Y. Sch. Visual Arts, 1963. Painter, ceramicist; instr. Glorieta Pass Inst. (N.Mex.), 1973-82; represented in permanent collections: Mus. Modern Art, San Francisco, N.Mex. Mus. Fine Arts, Sante Fe, Longview Mus. (Tex.), Contemporary Arts Mus., Houston, Albuquerque Mus., Home Savs. & Loan Collection, Los Angeles. Recipient 1st prize Southwest Biennial of Weatherhead Found., Santa Fe, N. Mex., 1974, 76, 1st prize Longview Mus. (Tex.), 1977. Home and Office: Box 42 Glorieta NM 87535

GREELY, MICHAEL TRUMAN, atty. gen. Mont.; b. Great Falls, Mont., Feb. 28, 1940; s. Myril Jay and Laura Harriet (Haugh) G.; B.A., Yale U., 1962; J.D., U. Mont., 1967; m. Marilyn Jean Myhre, Dec. 1, 1972; children—Winston Truman, Morgen Myhre. Tchr. pub. schs., Oklahoma City, 1962-63; admitted to Mont. bar, 1967; asst. atty. gen. Mont., 1968-70, atty. gen., 1977—; chmn. Mont. Justice Project, 1975; dep. county atty. Cascade County (Mont.), 1970-74; mem. Mont. Ho. of Reps., 1971-74, Mont. Senate, 1975-77. Pres. 8th Dist. Youth Guidance Home, Great Falls, 1971-72. Mem. Nat. Assn. Attys. Gen. (pres. elect 1982-83), Mont., Cascade County bar assns. Democrat. Office: Dept Justice 208 Capitol Bldg Helena MT 59601*

GREEN, ADELINE ULANOVE MANDEL (MRS. MAURICE L. GREEN), psychiat. social worker, marriage and family counselor; b. St. Paul; d. Meyer and Eva (Green) Ulanove; B.S., U. Minn., 1933, M.S.W., 1955; m. Nathan G. Mandel, July 13, 1938 (div. July 1962); children—Meta Susan (Mrs. Richard Katzoff), Myra (Mrs. Jeffrey Halpern); m. 2d, Maurice L. Green, Aug. 31, 1969. Lic. clin. social worker, Calif. Investigator, Ramsey County Mothers Aid and Aid to Dependent Children, Ramsey County Welfare Bd., St. Paul, 1933-37; psychiat. social worker Wilder Child Guidance Clinic, St. Paul, 1938; psychiat. social worker, supr. outpatient psychiatry clinic U. Minn. Hosps., Mpls., 1955-68; supr., clin. instr. psychiatry social service, outpatient psychiatry clinic, 1968-69; with South Bay Psychiat. Med. Clinic, Campbell, Calif., 1969—; pvt. practice family and marriage counseling. Pres. St. Paul sect. Council Jewish Women, 1950-54; chmn. Diagnostic Clinic for Rheumatic Fever-Wilder Clinic, St. Paul, 1952-54. Lic. clin. psychiat. social worker. Mem. Nat. Assn. Social Workers, Acad. Cert. Social Workers, Minn. Welfare Conf., Am. Assn. Marriage Counselors, Brandeis U. Women. Home: 1696 Miller Ave Los Altos CA 94022 Office: 286 E Hamilton Ave Campbell CA 95008

GREEN, ALAN REESE, data processor; b. LaHabra, Calif., Jan. 27, 1937; s. Dorphus Lee and Joy Evelyn (Griffen) G.; B.S. In Math. and Physics, U. Wichita, 1963; children—Corey Alan, Kevin Troy. Programmer nuclear space physics Boeing Co., 1964-67; systems supr. Wash. Natural Gas Co., 1967-77; systems and programming mgr. Bon Marche, Seattle, 1977-83; systems and devel. mgr. Atherton Industries, Menlo Park, Calif., 1983—. Served with USAF, 1954-57. Cert. Am. Registry of Radiol. Technologists. Mem. Assn. Systems Mgmt., Redmond C. of C. Methodist. Office: Atherton Industries 260 Constitution Dr Menlo Park CA 94025

GREEN, ALICE, rehabilitation counselor; b. Bklyn., Apr. 2, 1928; d. Alexander and Clara (Bernard) Denenholz; m. Stanley J. Green, Apr. 8, 1951; children—David, Douglas, Ronald. B.A., NYU, 1949; M.Ed., U. Pitts., 1973. Cert. rehab. counselor. CETA mental health coordinator Goodwill Industries, Pitts., 1974-77; rehab. counselor Goodwill Industries of Santa Clara County, San Jose, Calif., 1978-82; rehab. counselor Associated Vocat. Services, Campbell, Calif., 1982-83; rehab. counselor Stephenson and Green, San Jose, 1983—. Mem. Nat. Rehab. Assn., Nat. Rehab. Counseling Assn., Am. Personnel and Guidance Assn. Home: 3348 Middlefield Rd Palo Alto CA 94306 Office: Stephenson and Green 1530 Alameda Suite 200 San Jose CA 95126

GREEN, CAROL B., company executive; b. N.Y.C., Nov. 13, 1938; d. Paul and Ruth (Schiffer) Forst; m. Jules Green, Dec. 21, 1957; children—Deborah, David, Daniel. B.A. in Econs., Loretto Heights Coll., 1977. Pres. Weight Watchers Rocky Mountain Region Inc., Littleton, Colo., 1968—; ptnr. Truffles Investment Co.; v.p. Three Dee Investment Co. Mem. Denver C. of C. (bd. dirs.), Centennial C. of C. (bd. dirs., exec. bd.), Com. 200, Women's Forum Colo., Nat. Platform Assn. Office: 1449 W Littleton Blvd Littleton CO 80120

GREEN, CHRISTOPHER JOHN, interior designer; b. Denver, May 4, 1954; s. John Elliot and Mildred (Witt) G. B.Environ. Design, U. Colo., 1976; postgrad. Ill. Inst. Tech. Coll. Architecture, from 1979. Designer graphics and interiors Design Collective, Inc., Columbus, Ohio, 1976-78; head designer facilities planning Ohio Bur. Workers Compensation, Columbus, 1978-79; interior designer Skidmore Owings & Merrill, Chgo., 1979-80; tcaching asst. Ill. Inst. Tech., Chgo., 1980-83; graphics coordinator Environ. Concern, Inc., P.S., Spokane, Wash., 1983—. Mem. ASHRAE, Columbus Soc. Communication arts (student membership coordinator). Office: Environmental Concern Inc PS Spokane WA

GREEN, CORDELL, computer scientist, educator; b. Ft. Worth, Dec. 26, 1941; s. William and Rebecca (Glickman) G.; m. Christine Louise Ochs, June 21, 1979; 1 son, Jeffrey Adam. B.A., B.S., Rice U., 1964, M.S., 1965; Ph.D., Stanford U., 1969. Research mathematician Artificial Intelligence Group, Stanford Research Inst., 1966-69; research and devel. program mgr. Info. Processing Techniques Office, ARPA, 1970-71; asst. prof. computer sci. Stanford U., 1971-78, cons. prof. computer sci., 1979—; chief scientist computer sci. dept. Systems Control Inc., Palo Alto, Calif., 1979-81; dir., chief scientist Kestrel Inst., Palo Alto, 1981—; cons. in field. Served to capt. U.S. Army, 1969-71. Air Force Office Sci. Research grantee, 1978-83; NSF grantee, 1980-83; Rome Air Devel. Ctr. grantee, 1982-83. Mem. Assn. for Computing Machinery (artificial intelligence area editor jour. 1972-79), Advanced Research Projects Agy. (grantee 1973-83). Contbr. articles to profl. jours.; mem. editorial bd. Jour. Cognitive Sci., 1977-80; researcher in field of computer sci. Office: 1801 Page Mill Rd Palo Alto CA 94304

GREEN, DONALD EUGENE, biochem. pharmacologist; b. Napa, Calif., Nov. 25, 1926; s. Joseph and Helen (Rubin) G.; student Mont. Sch. Mines, 1944-45; B.S., U. Calif. at Berkeley, 1948; postgrad. Stanford, 1948; M.S., U. Calif. at San Francisco, 1952, B.S. in Pharmacy, 1955; Ph.D., Wash. State U., 1962; m. Margaret Ann Maurer, July 29, 1951; children—Dennis, Gretchen, Mark, Gary, Sheryl. Instr. pharm. chemistry Idaho State U., Pocatello, 1955-57, 58-60, Wash. State U., Pullman, 1957-58; research biochemist VA Hosp., Palo Alto, Calif., 1962-64; 76-79; sr. engr. Varian Assos., Palo Alto, 1962-70; research asso. Stanford Med. Sch., Palo Alto, 1970-74, 81—; sr. research scientist U. San Francisco Inst. Molecular Biology, 1974-81. Cons. Universal Monitor Corp., Pasadena, 1971-75. Vice pres. Eagle Scout Assn., Santa Clara County, 1970, pres., 1979. Served with USNR, 1944-46, 51-53. Mem. Am. Chem. Soc. (chmn. Santa Clara Valley sect. 1972, councilor 1976-81, 82—), Am. Pharm. Assn., Internat. Assn. Forensic Toxicologists, Calif. Assn. Toxicologists, Am. Soc. Pharmacology and Exptl. Therapeutics, Western Pharmacology Soc., Am. Philatelic Soc., Sigma Xi, Rho Chi, Alpha Chi Sigma (Northwestern dist. councelor 1978—), Phi Delta Chi, Kappa Psi. Patentee in field. Home: 765 Harvard Ave Sunnyvale CA 94087 Office: GRECC 182-B VA Hosp Palo Alto CA 94304

GREEN, DOROTHY MARIE, home economics educator; b. Oneonta, N.Y., Apr. 18, 1946; d. Carl Grant and Elizabeth Mae (Bergh) G. B.S. in Edn., State U. Coll., Oneonta, 1969; M.Ed., U. Ariz., 1977. Cert. home econs. tchr., Ariz., N.Y. Tchr. home econs. Kayenta (Ariz.) Pub. Schs., 1969-71, dir. food service, 1974; staff counselor Koinonia Ch., Potsdam, N.Y., 1971-73; tchr. home econs. Red Mesa High Sch., Chinle, Ariz., 1974-76, Nogales (Ariz.) Pub. Sch., 1976-77; mem. faculty U. Ariz.-Tucson, 1977—, extension agt. in home econs., Chinle, 1977-79, Tuba City, 1979-80, Willcox, Ariz., 1980—. Mem. Am. Home Econs. Assn., Ariz. Home Econs. Assn., Nat. 4-H Agts. Assn., Ariz. 4-H Agts. Assn., Nat. Assn. Extension Home Economists, Ariz. Assn. Extension Home Economists (historian 1980, treas. 1983), Cholla Bowling League. Mem. Assemblies of God Ch. Writer monthly home econs. newsletter. Office: Home Econs Dept U Ariz 450 S Haskell St Willcox AZ 85643

GREEN, EDWARD JOHN, architect; b. Cornwall on Hudson, N.Y., July 14, 1903; s. John Edward and Christine Magdaline (Miller) G.; grad. Benson Poly. Sch., Portland, 1925; B.S., U. Oreg., 1932; m. Helen Angela Curran, Apr. 18, 1936. Pvt. practice architecture, 1932—, Portland, Oreg., 1975—; asso. naval architect U.S. Navy Bur. Ships, 1942-43; asso. Geoge L. Dahl, Dallas, 1953-65, Herrman Blum Co. mech. engrs., Dallas, 1965-67; bridge and civil architect Wash. State Dept. Hwys., Olympia, 1967-73; legis. asst. Wash. State Senate, 1977-83. Dist. commodore USCG Aux., 1959, instr. boating safety, 1946-50, safety patrol comdr., 1956-60. Mem. AIA, Order Blue Gavel. Clubs: Portland Yacht, Royal Victoria Yacht. Recipient 1st prize bridge award Am. Inst. Steel Constrn., 1973, Merit award, 1972. Home: 5250 SW Landing Dr at John's Landing Portland OR 97201

GREEN, FRANCIS WILLIAM, investment consultant; b. Locust Grove, Okla., Mar. 17, 1920; s. Noel Francis and Mary (Lincoln) G.; B.S., Phoenix U., 1955; M.S. in Elec. Engring., Minerva U., Milan, Italy, 1959; M.S. in Engring., West Coast U., Los Angeles, 1965; m. Alma J. Ellison, Aug. 26, 1950 (dec. Sept. 1970); children—Sharmon, Rhonda; m. Susan G. Mathis, July 14, 1973 (div. July 1979). With USN Guided Missile Program, 1945-49; design and electronic project engr. Falcon missile program Hughes Aircraft Co., Culver City, Calif., 1949-55; sr. electronic engr. Atlas missile program Convair Astronautics, San Diego, 1955-59; sr. engr. Polaris missile program Nortronics div. Northrop, Anaheim, Calif., 1959-60; chief, supr. electronic engr. data systems br. Tech. Support div. Rocket Propulsion Lab., USAF, Edwards AFB, Calif., 1960-67, dep. chief tech. support div., 1967-69; tech. adviser Air Force Missile Devel. Center, Holloman AFB, N.Mex., 1969-70, 6585 Test Group, Air Force Spl. Weapons Center, Holloman AFB, from 1970; pvt. investment cons., 1978—. Bd. examiners U.S. CSC; mem. Pres.'s Missile Site Labor Relations Com.; cons. advanced computer and data processing tech. and systems engring.; mem. USAF Civilian Policy Bd. and Range Comdrs. Council. Served as pilot USAAF, 1941-45. Mem. IEEE, Am. Inst. Aeros. and Astronautics; Nat. Assn. Flight Instrs. Contbr. articles to profl. jours. Home and Office: 2345 Apache Ln Alamogordo NM 88310

GREEN, GERALD GALEN, engr.; b. Torrington, Wyo., Jan. 18, 1942; s. Galen Clarence and Lena Alice (Jewett) G.; B.S. in Mech. Engring., U. Idaho, 1965; postgrad. U. So. Calif., 1972; m. Sherry Lynn Witte, Aug. 28, 1965. Product mgr. Wemco div. Envirotech Corp., Sacramento, 1965-69; sales engr. RA Trabert Co., Inglewood, Calif., 1969-74; pres. TEC-ERA Engring. Corp., Torrance, Calif., 1974—; partner AFTEC Co., Redondo Beach, Calif. Registered profl. engr., Calif. Mem. Nat. Soc. Profl. Engrs., Calif. Soc. Profl. Engrs., Soc. Enologists, Oil Mill Supts. Soc., Water Pollution Control Fedn. Patentee in field. Home: 1860 Altmont Dr Felton CA 95018 Office: PO Box 66707 Scotts Valley CA 95066

GREEN, GERTRUDE DORSEY, psychologist; b. Balt., Aug. 18, 1949; d. John S. and Gertrude (Dorsey) G.; 1 son, Ethan Cole Sorrel. A.B., Dickinson Coll., 1971; M.A., Bowling Green State U., 1972; Ph.D., U. Wash., 1981. Lic. psychologist, Wash. Asst. dir. residence life Albion (Mich.) Coll., 1972-74; social worker Big Bros./Big Sisters, Lansing, Mich., 1975-77; pvt. practice psychology, Seattle, 1979—. Bd. dirs. Seattle Counseling Service, 1981—. Active Univ. Friends Meeting, 1977—; regional com. vol. Am. Friends Service Com. Mem. Am. Psychol. Assn., Am. Personnel and Guidance Assn., Assn. Women in Psychology.

GREEN, H. NICHOLAS, optometrist; b. Rochester, Minn., Jan. 15, 1945; s. Harold Garland and Martha Vivian (Berger) G.; m. Kerry Kern, 1974 (div. 1978); 1 son, Nicholas Rand. B.S., San Diego State U., 1968; O.D., So. Calif. Coll. Optometry, 1972. Optometrist, Standard Optical Co., Salt Lake City, 1972-75; pvt. practice optometry, Riverside, Calif., 1975-77; dir. optometry Del Mar (Calif.) Optometric Clinic, 1977—; dir. ops. Calif. Eyecare Plan, San Diego, 1981—; dir. Calif. Med. Plans, Kingsbridge Fin./Mortgage Co. Chmn. Del Parks/Recreation Com., 1980-82. Recipient Merit award Save The Children, 1980, 81, 82. Mem. Am. Optometric Assn., Nat. Eye Research Found. Republican. Mem. Christian Ch. (Disciples of Christ). Club: Kiwanis. Home: 230 11th St Del Mar CA 92014 Office: 1349 Camino Del Mar Del Mar CA 92014

GREEN, HARLAND NORTON, lawyer, accountant; b. Los Angeles, Feb. 14, 1930; s. William and Lena (Schwimer) G.; B.S. in Bus. Adminstrn. with honors, UCLA, 1951, J.D., 1954; LL.M., U. So. Calif., 1962; m. Melva Nudelman, Dec. 20, 1953. Admitted to Calif. bar 1955; acct. J. Arthur Greenfield & Co., Los Angeles, 1956-58; atty. Jerome B. Rosenthal, Beverly Hills, Calif. 1958-61; mem. firm Rosenthal, Cook & Green, Beverly Hills, 1961-65, Rosenthal & Green, 1965-68; practice law, Beverly Hills, 1969-72; pres. Harland N. Green Profl. Law Corp., 1972—. Vice chmn. bd. trustees So. Calif. chpt. Nat. Multiple Sclerosis Soc., named Outstanding Trustee. Served to lst lt. USAF 1954-56. C.P.A.; cert. tax specialist. Mem. Am. (taxation sect.), Calif., Beverly Hills bar assns., Assn. Atty. C.P.A.s (dir.), Los Angeles Copyright Soc., Order of Coif, Phi Beta Kappa, Beta Gamma Sigma. Contbr. numerous articles to profl. jours. Office: 8383 Wilshire Blvd Suite 1056 Beverly Hills CA 90211

GREEN, HAROLD FRANCIS, oil and gas company executive; b. Utica, N.Y., Jan. 4, 1916; s. F. Percy and Mary (Coakley) G.; m. Corena Crase, Dec. 16, 1950; children—Liz Duncan, James C., Richard H. B.A., U. Santa Clara, 1937, J.D., 1940. Vice chmn. Hilliard Oil & Gas, Inc., New Orleans, 1983—. Served as lt. M.I., USN, 1941-46. Decorated Bronze Star. Mem. Calif. Bar Assn., ABA. Clubs: Palo Alto University, Los Altos Golf and Country. Home: 10410 Albertsworth Ln Los Altos Hills CA 94022 Office: 1440 Canal St New Orleans LA 70112

GREEN, HARRY LEE, physician; b. Sewickley, Pa., Aug. 24, 1929; s. William and Tillie (Greenberg) G.; B.S. summa cum laude, U. Pitts., 1951; M.D., Case Western Res. U., 1955; m. Carol Rebecca Gutentag, Aug. 16, 1953; children—Cynthia Lynn, Deborah Ann. Intern, then resident in internal medicine Mt. Sinai Hosp., Cleve., 1955-57; resident in medicine VA Hosp., Los Angeles, 1959-60, sr. resident in gastroenterology, 1960-61; chief resident in internal medicine Mt. Sinai Hosp., Los Angeles, 1961-62; practice medicine specializing in internal medicine and gastroenterology, Los Angeles, 1962—; chief medicine Westwood Hosp.; mem. sr. staff Santa Monica, St. John's, Cedars-Sinai hosps.; asso. clin. prof. medicine U. Calif. at Los Angeles Sch. Medicine, 1963—; cons. in gastroenterology VA Hosp. Served to capt. M.C., USAF, 1957-59. Diplomate Am. Bd. Internal Medicine. Fellow Am. Coll. Gastroenterology; mem. Calif., Los Angeles County med. assns., Am. Gastroenterol. Assn., A.C.P., Am. Soc. Internal Medicine, So. Calif. Soc. Gastroenterology, Guardians of Courage (v.p.), Amity Circle. Jewish. Contbr. to med. jours. Office: 10921 Wilshire Blvd Los Angeles CA 90024

GREEN, JACK, geological educator; b. Poughkeepsie, N.Y., June 19, 1925; s. Louis and Marie (Harris) G.; m. Renee Jean, Sept. 21, 1952; children—Kathy, Jeffrey, Terrence, Nathan, Theresa, Ronald. B.S. in Geology, Va. Poly. Inst., 1950; Ph.D., in Geology, Columbia U., 1953. Registered geologist, Calif. Research geologist Rockwell Internat., Downey, Calif., 1960-65, McDonnell Douglas, Huntington Beach, Calif., 1965-70, cons., 1983; cons. Sci. Applications, Irvine, Calif., 1977-79; prof. geology, Calif. State U., 1970—; geothermal specialist to Tibet and China for Research Soc. for Energy Resources of People's Republic of China, fall 1983; cons. in field. Served with U.S. Army, 1943-46. Recipient NYU Prose Writers award, 1943; N.Y. State Vets. scholar, 1946, NASA grantee, 1972, NASA fellow, 1980. Mem. Geol. Soc. Am., Internat. Assn. Planetology (past pres.), Internat. Lunar Soc. (pres.). Patentee liquid level device. Home: 941 Via Nogales Palos Verdes Estates CA 90274 Office: Geology Dept Calif State U Long Beach CA 90840

GREEN, JAMES CRAIG, computer co. exec.; b. Gladstone, Mich., Apr. 19, 1933; s. Albert Keene and Margaret Josephine (Craig) G.; student Coll. of Gt. Falls, 1951-53, UCLA, 1962; m. Catherine Maxwell, Nov. 1, 1957; children—Cindi, Shelley, Nancy, James W., Robert. Clk., carrier U.S. Post Office, Gt. Falls, Mont., 1951-57; clk. office and sales Mont. Liquor Control Bd., Gt. Falls, 1957-59; payroll clk. Herald Examiner, Hearst Publs., Los Angeles, 1959-67, data processing mgr., 1967-75, data processing ops. mgr. corp. hdqrs. Hearst Publs., N.Y.C., 1975-78; gen. mgr., v.p. Computer/Data Inc., Billings, Mont., 1978—; tax cons., Los Angeles, 1962-75. Cub Scout leader, com. chmn., Los Angeles council Boy Scouts Am., 1973-75; pres. Bus. Office Employees Assn. Los Angeles, 1963-66. Area commr., com. chmn. Black Otter Council Boy Scouts Am., 1982—. Served with USNR, 1951-59. Recipient degree of Chevalier, Order De Molay, 1951; cert. data processing mgr. Mem. Data Processing Mgrs. Assn., Los Angeles Masonic Press Club. Clubs: Masons, Blue Lodge, York Rite, Shrine (charter mem. grotto Gt. Falls). Writer, negotiator contract Bus. Office Employees Assn., Los Angeles, 1965. Office: 2020 Grand Ave Billings MT 59102

GREEN, JAMES LEROY, accountant; b. Chester, Pa., July 20, 1944; s. William and Helen (Bedwell) G.; m. Diane Marie Lois; children—Mark, Georgette, Diana. B.S. in Bus. Adminstrn. cum laude, Widener U., 1969. C.P.A., Pa., Ariz. Sr. acct. Peat, Marwick, Mitchell & Co., Phila., 1969-73; ptnr. Masden and Green, Lake Havasu City, Ariz., 1973-76, officer, dir., 1976—; tchr. Mohave Community Coll. Treas., chmn. fin. com., chmn. bldg. com., chmn. council bd., chmn. bd. trustees St. Michael's United Methodist Ch., 1973-78; treas., bd. dirs. Lake Havasu City Service Unit Salvation Army, 1977-82; treas. bd. dirs. Indsl. Devel. Authority of Lake Havasu City, 1979-82; bd. dirs. Lake Havasu

City Fed. Credit Union, 1982. Mem. Am. Inst. C.P.A.s, Lake Havasu Area C. of C. (dir., chmn. econ. devel. com.), Lake Havasu City Jaycees (Disting. Service award 1975). Republican. Clubs: Lake Havasu City Kiwanis (past pres., Kiwanian of Yr. 1975, 78, Disting. Service award 1979). Home: 2811 Caravelle Dr Lake Havasu City AZ 86403 Office: Masden and Green 2240 McCulloch Blvd Lake Havasu City AZ 86403

GREEN, JAMES WILEY, hospital administrator; b. Eden, Tex., Jan. 1, 1934; s. Gustavas Brooks and Cecil (Lee) G.; m. Marlene Daisey Stoecken, Nov. 27, 1958; children—Jayson Dee, Jamie Lee. B.A., Baylor U., 1958. Hosp. acct., controller Hillcrest Baptist Hosp., Waco, Tex., 1958-62; sr. acct. Daniel M. Smith Jr., C.P.A., Albuquerque, 1962-66; chief acct. Presbyn. Hosp. Ctr. (now Southwest Community Health Services), Albuquerque, 1966-70, dir. fiscal services, 1970-74, controller, 1974-78, v.p. fin., 1978—. Democratic precinct sec., 1982-84, chmn., 1970-74, 1976-80. Served with U.S. Army, 1955-57. Mem. Healthcare Fin. Mgmt. Assn. (advanced mem.), Assoc. Hosp. Systems (sec. fin. council 1978-80). Democrat. Baptist. Office: 1100 Central SE Albuquerque NM 87102

GREEN, JERRY FRANKLIN, physiologist; b. Balt., June 25, 1941; s. Fred H. and Helen (Radesky) G.; B.S. in Biology, Rollins Coll., 1963, B.A. in Psychology, 1963; Ph.D., Johns Hopkins U., 1971. Asst. prof. dept. human physiology U. Calif. Sch. Medicine, Davis, 1971-79, asso. prof., 1979—; vis. asso. prof. dept. environ. health scis. Johns Hopkins Sch. Hygiene and Public Health, Balt., 1980; cons. to USAF, 1972-81. NIH fellow, 1966-71. Fellow Council on Circulation, Am. Heart Assn. (peer rev. com. 1979-83); mem. Am. Heart Assn. Cardiopulmonary Council, Aerospace Med. Assn., Biomed. Engring. Soc., Am. Physiol. Soc., Sigma Xi. Author: Mechanical Concepts in Cardiovascular and Pulmonary Physiology, 1977; Fundamental Cardiovascular and Pulmonary Physiology; An Integrated Approach for Medicine, 1982; contbr. articles on cardiovascular and pulmonary physiology to sci. jours. Office: Dept Human Physiology U Calif Sch Medicine Davis CA 95616

GREEN, KELLE JEAN, interior designer, gift shop buyer and retailer; b. Santa Paula, Calif., April 5, 1954; d. Robert Eugene and Mary Elizabeth (Templeton) Nunn; m. James Allen Green, Dec. 27, 1980; children—Erin Michelle. A.A. in Merchandising, Fashion Inst. of Design and Merchandising, Los Angeles, 1975. Dept. mgr. Camarillo Plumbing & Paint, 1972-75; interior designer, Nettle Creek, Woodland Hills, Calif., 1975-76; head interior designer, Sherwin William's Corp., Glendale, Calif., 1976-78; interior designer, Nettle Creek, Pasadena, Calif., 1978-79; owner, buyer, mgr., designer, Kelle & Co. Designed Interiors and Kelle's Little House of Gifts, Camarillo, Calif., 1979—. Recipient award for retail business beautification by Camarillo Beautiful Community, 1980; first place Best Use of Color award for trade booth, Camarillo Chamber of Commerce, 1981; 1st pl. best seasonal theme award Camarillo C. of C., 1982. Mem. Am. Soc. Interior Designers, Connejo Assn. Profl. Interior Designers. Democrat. Catholic. Room designs pub. House Beautiful and Designers West, 1979-81. Home: 2336 Grandview Dr Camarillo CA 93010 Office: 58 N Glenn Dr Camarillo CA 93010

GREEN, MELVIN M., tax cons.; b. Los Angeles, June 6, 1935; s. Hyman M. and June (Drexler) G.; student UCLA, 1953-60, Kans. State Coll., 1955-56, Coll. William and Mary, 1956-57, U. So. Calif., 1960-61; A.A., Los Angeles City Coll., 1962; B.S. in Accounting, U. Eastern Fla., 1964; M.B.A., Jackson State U., 1966, J.D., 1968; m. Anita Molly Rice, Jan. 1, 1981; children—Michael David, Cary Charles, Scott Howard. Tax cons., North Hollywood, Calif., 1963-64; controller Hood Chem. Corp., Burbank, Calif., 1964-65; mgr. Allen Rael & Assos., 1963-65; pres., gen. mgr., chmn. bd. Melvin Green, Inc., North Hollywood, 1970—; chmn. bd. ACW Med. Products, Inc.; chmn. bd., treas. His Son Audio Corp. of Am., John Wright Plumbing & Heating, Inc.; chmn. bd., v.p. Roden Plumbing & Heating, Inc.; chmn. bd., controller John Yerton Plumbing & Heating, Inc., Robert G. Herring D.D.S., Inc.; sec., dir. South Bay Ednl. Services, Inc., dir., controller Jet, Inc., Job, Inc.; lectr. Assn. Bus. and Tax Cons., 1973-75, Nat. Soc. Pub. Accountants Las Vegas Seminar, 1968. Past dir. Van Nuys Jr. C. of C. Served with U.S. Army, 1954-57. Mem. Assn. Bus. and Tax Cons. (past pres.), Nat. Soc. Pub. Accountants (past sgt. at arms New Orleans Conv. 1971), Mensa, Chi Gamma Iota (past pres.). Clubs: Masons, B'nai B'rith (pres. San Fernando Valley lodge 1981-82). Office: 12431 Oxnard St North Hollywood CA 91606

GREEN, MI MI, theatrical ensemble executive; b. Waco, Tex., Oct. 3, 1947; d. Jeffery Davis and Ruthie Lee (Hubert) G. Student Prairie View A&M Coll., 1967-69. Drama instr. Al Fann Theatrical Ensemble, Hollywood, Calif., 1973—, v.p., 1981—; chmn. charter memberships Fann Inst. for Higher Mind, 1982—, pub. relations dir., 1973—; lectr., writer, actress. Mem. Media Forum, Screen Actors Guild, Am. Fedn. TV and Radio Arts, Nat. Assn. Female Execs., Living Ministries Internat. Office: 6043 Hollywood Blvd Suite 207 Hollywood CA 90028

GREEN, MICHAEL JOSEPH, aerospace research scientist; b. Berkeley, Calif., Aug. 17, 1945; s. Cyril Joseph and Anne Selma Johnson; m. Madeline Raphael Hinojosa, Jan. 19, 1951; 1 dau., Michelle Ann. B.S., Calif. State U., 1970; M.S., U. Santa Clara, 1974. Computer programmer NASA-Ames Research Ctr., Moffett Field, Calif., 1965-69, mathematician, 1969-78, research scientist, 1978—. Mem. sch. council Birchwood Sch., San Jose, Calif.; exec. bd. Ames Recreation Assn., 1982-84. Contbr. articles to profl. jours. Office: Mail Stop 229-4 Moffett Field CA 94035

GREEN, RICHARD MORRIS, constrn. cons.; b. Haxtun, Colo., Dec. 30, 1933; s. William Clarence and Patresa Nell (Hicks) G.; B.S. in Elec. Engring. and Bus. Mgmt., U. Colo., 1961; m. Dawne Marlene Reasbeck, Nov. 25, 1956; children—Joy, Christopher, Jennifer. Quality control engr. Denver div. Martin Marietta Aerospace, 1961-63; cost engr./asst. mgr. cost estimating dept. Denver Equipment Co., 1963-65; constrn. engr. Espro, Denver, 1965-66; pres. Asso. Constrn. Cons., Inc., Aurora, Colo., 1966—. Served with USN, 1953-57. Cert. constrn. estimator. Mem. Am. Soc. Profl. Estimators (Nat. Constrn. Estimator of Year 1975, nat. pres. 1974-75, pres. Denver chpt. 1969, 70, 71, 76), Am. Assn. Cost Engrs., Constrn. Specifications Inst. Office: 1451 Florence St Suite 2 Aurora CO 80010

GREEN, STEPHEN KENNETH, advertising executive; b. Eugene, Oreg., Dec. 30, 1947; s. Kenneth J. and Bernice M. (Armyon) G.; m. Loreen D. Daniel, Sept. 7, 1969; m. 2d, Kathy L. Dix, Jan. 29, 1976; children—Jason, Karissa, Angela, Amanda. B.A., Brigham Young U., 1970. Advt. asst. Eugene (Oreg.) Register-Guard, 1973-76; acct. exec. Statesman-Jour., Salem, Oreg., 1976-78; advt. dir. Van Dahl Publs., Albany, Oreg., 1978—. Mem. Am. Stamp Dealers Assn., Oreg. Newspapers Pubs. Assn. Republican. Mormon. Home: 1465 Kathy St S Salem OR 97306 Office: 520 E 1st St Albany OR 97321

GREEN, WILLIAM FERGUSON, equipment company executive; b. Hilo, Hawaii, May 5, 1934; s. James Simpson and Josephine (Stevens) G.; m. Patricia Allen, June 24, 1961; children—William, Kathleen K.; m. 2d, Barbra Ripson, Nov. 25, 1970; 1 son, Bryan Stevens. B.S. in Agr., Calif. State Poly., 1961; postgrad. Coll. San Luis Obispo, 1957-61. Mgr. Hawaiian Equipment, Lihue, Kauai, Hawaii, 1962-68; shop and contract packing supr. Dole Co., Honolulu, 1968-70; br. mgr. ESCO Corp., Hilo, Hawaii, 1970-78; v.p., gen. mgr. Allied Machinery, Hilo, 1978—. Mem. Kauai Charter Commn., 1968—; mem. Hawaii Bd. Water Supply, 1980—, chmn., 1982-83. Served with USN, 1955-57. Mem. Soc. Agrl. Engrs., Am. Water Works Assn. Club: Rotary (Lihue, Hilo). Home: 100 Kaulani St Hilo HI 96720 Office: Allied Machinery 202 Makaala St Hilo HI 96720

GREEN, WILLIAM PORTER, lawyer; b. Jacksonville, Ill., Mar. 19, 1920; s. Hugh Parker and Clara Belle (Hopper) G.; B.A., Ill. Coll., 1941; J.D., Northwestern U., 1947; m. Rose Marie Hall, Oct. 1, 1944; children—Hugh Michael, Robert Alan, Richard William. Bar: Ill. 1947, Calif. 1948, U.S. Dist. Ct. (cen. dist.) Calif., U.S. Ct. Appeals 5th, 9th and fed cirs.), U.S. Supreme Ct. Practice patents, trademarks and copyright law, Los Angeles, 1947—; mem. firm Wills, Green & Mueth, 1974—. Deacon, San Marino (Calif.) Community Presbyn. Ch. Served to lt. (s.g.), USNR, 1942-46. Mem. ABA, Calif. State Bar (del. conv. 1982-83), Los Angeles County Bar Assn., Am. Patent Law Assn., Los Angeles Patent Law Assn. (past sec.-treas., past bd. govs.), Lawyer's Club Los Angeles County (bd. govs., sec., past treas.), Los Angeles World Affairs Council, Town Hall Calif., Phi Beta Kappa Alumni So. Calif., Phi Beta Kappa, Phi Delta Phi, Phi Alpha, Am. Legion (past post comdr.). Republican. Clubs: Big Ten So. Calif., Northwestern U. Alumni of So. Calif. Bd. editors Ill. Law Rev., 1946. Home: 3570 Lombardy Rd Pasadena CA 91107 Office: 700 S Flower St Suite 1120 Los Angeles CA 90017

GREENAWALT, DAVID F., dairy and agricultural company executive; b. 1933. B.S. in Econs., U. Pa., 1955. Dist. operating mgr. Sealtest Foods div. Dart-Kraft Co., 1959-67; v.p. ops. Farmbest Inc., 1967-73; exec. v.p. Dairylea Coop. Inc., 1973-77; v.p. prodn. and engring. William Underwood Co., 1977-79; sr. v.p. mfg. Knudsen Corp., 1979, exec. v.p. ops., 1980, pres., chief operating officer, dir., 1982—. Served to capt. USMC, 1956-59. Office: Knudsen Corp 231 E 23d St PO Box 2335 Terminal Annex Los Angeles CA 90051*

GREENBERG, CARL, newspaperman; b. Boston, Aug. 19, 1908; s. Harry and Fannie (Herman) G.; student U. Calif. Extension Div., 1927; m. Gladys Bilansky, July 12, 1930; 1 son, Howard Allan. Reporter, Los Angeles Evening Express, 1926-28, City News Service of Los Angeles, 1928-33; reporter Los Angeles Examiner, 1933-43, polit. editor, 1943-62; polit. writer Los Angeles Times, 1962-66, polit. editor, 1966-68, polit. writer, 1968-73. Hon. life mem. Eureka (Ill.) Community Assn.; bd. dirs. 8-Ball Welfare Found.; founder Carl Greenberg scholarship for investigative and polit. reporting. Served with USCGR, World War II. Recipient 1st prize for best news story So. Calif. newspaper writers Los Angeles chpt. Theta Sigma Phi, 1944; Silver award Calif.-Nev. A.P., 1957, Meritorious Pub. Service citation Calif. Newspaper Pubs. Assn., 1961; mem. staff awarded Pulitzer prize gen. local reporting, 1966. Mem. Coast Guard League, Order of Hound's Tooth (charter), Soc. Profl. Journalists-Sigma Delta Chi, Kappa Tau Alpha. Mem. B'nai Brith. Club: Greater Los Angeles Press (hon. life). Home: 6001 Canterbury Dr Culver City CA 90230

GREENBERG, IRA ARTHUR, clinical psychologist, mgmt. cons.; b. Bklyn., June 26, 1924; s. Philip and Minnie (Seligman) G.; B.A. in Journalism, U. Okla., 1949; M.A. in English, U. So. Calif., 1962; M.S. in Counseling, Calif. State U.-Los Angeles, 1963; Ph.D. in Psychology, Claremont (Calif.) Grad Sch., 1967. Editor, Ft. Riley (Kans.) Guidon, 1950-51; reporter, copy editor Columbus (Ga.) Enquirer, 1951-55; reporter Louisville Courier-Jour., 1955-56, Los Angeles Times, 1956-62; free-lance writer, Los Angeles, Montclair, Camarillo, Calif., 1960-69, 76—; counselor Claremont Coll. Psychol. Clinic and Counseling Center, 1964-65; lectr. psychology Chapman Coll., Orange, Calif., 1965-66; psychologist Camarillo State Hosp., 1967-69, supervising psychologist, 1969-73, part time psychologist, 1973—; part time asst. prof. edn. San Fernando Valley State Coll., Northridge, Calif., 1967-69, lectr. psychodrama, social welfare U. Calif. Extension Div., Santa Barbara, 1968-69; vol. psychologist Free Clinic, Los Angeles, 1968-70; staff dir. Calif. Inst. Psychodrama, 1969-71; tng. cons. Topanga Ctr. for Human Devel., 1970-75, bd. dirs., 1971-74, faculty Calif. Sch. Profl. Psychology, 1970—; founder, exec. dir. Behavioral Studies Inst., mgmt. cons., Los Angeles, 1970—; pvt. practice cons. in psychology, psychodrama hypnosis, 1970—; founder, exec. dir. Psychodrama Center for Los Angeles, Inc., 1971—, Group Hypnosis Ctr., Los Angeles, 1976—; producer, host TV talk show Crime and Pub. Safety, Group W Cable, Channel 3, 1983—. Vol. humane officer State of Calif.; res. officer Los Angeles Police Dept. Served with AUS, 1943-46; ETO; USAR, 1950-51. Fellow Am. Soc. Clin. Hypnosis; mem. Am. Soc. Group Psychotherapy and Psychodrama, Am., Calif. personnel and guidance assns., Assn. Research and Enlightenment, Los Angeles Soc. Clin. Psychologists (dir. 1975), Am., Western, Calif., Los Angeles psychol. assns., Am. Soc. for Psychical Research, Group Psychotherapy Assn. So. Calif. (dir. 1974-76, 82—), Soc. for Clin. and Exptl. Hypnosis, Am. Mgmt. Assn., Am. Soc. Bus. and Mgmt. Cons. (nat. adv. council 1977—), So. Calif. Soc. Clin. Hypnosis (dir., exec. v.p. 1973-76, pres. 1977-78), So. Calif. Psychotherapy Affiliation (dir. 1976—), Assn. for Humanistic Psychology, Mensa, Am. Zionist Fedn., Nat. Rifle Assn., Calif. Rifle and Pistol Assn., S.W. Pistol League, Animal Protection Inst. Am., Humane Educators Council (bd. dirs. 1982—), Soc. Sci. Study Sex, Sigma Delta Chi. Clubs: Sierra, Greater Los Angeles Press; B'nai B'rith; Beverly Hills Gun. Author: Psychodrama and Audience Attitude Change, 1968. Editor: Psychodrama: Theory and Therapy, 1974; Group Hypnotherapy and Hypnodrama, 1977. Address: Box A-369 Camarillo State Hosp Camarillo CA 93010 also BSI 11692 Chenault St Suite 206 Los Angeles CA 90049

GREENBERG, JOSEPH SIDNEY, educational administrator; b. N.Y.C., Apr. 10, 1951; s. Oscar and Anita (Hochberg) G.; m. Melody Lynn Johns, Aug. 4, 1974. B.S., SUNY-Oswego, 1973; M.A., Ball State U., 1974; D.Ed., Pa. State U., 1981. Tchr. indsl. arts, graphic arts, photography Wilton (Conn.) High Sch., 1974-79; continuing edn. coordinator Williamsport (Pa.) Area Community Coll., 1979-80; dir. ctr. profl. devel. Coll. Engring and Applied Scis., Ariz. State U., Tempe, 1980—. Mem. Am. Soc. Engring. Edn., Am. Soc. Tng. Devel., Nat. Univ. Continuing Edn. Assn. Office: ECG 148 Ariz State U Tempe AZ 85287

GREENBERG, MARVIN, educator; b. N.Y.C.. June 24, 1936; s. Samuel and Rae (Sherry) G.; B.S. cum laude, N.Y. U., 1957; M.A., Columbia U., 1958, Ed.D., 1962. Tchr. elem. schs., N.Y.C., 1957-63; prof. music edn. U. Hawaii, Honolulu, 1963—, research cons. Center for Early Childhood Research, 1969-71; edn. adminstr. Model Cities project for disadvantaged children Family Services Center, Honolulu, 1971-72. Cons. western region Volt Tech. Services, Head Start program, 1969-71; Head Start worker, 1972-75; Child Devel. Assoc. Consortium rep., 1975—. Recipient several fed. and state grants for ednl. research and curriculum projects. Mem. Hawaii Music Educators Assn., Music Educators Nat. Conf., Soc. for Research in Music Edn., Council for Research in Music Edn., Nat. Assn. for Edn. Young Children. Author: Teaching Music in the Elementary School: Guide for ETV Programs, 1966; Preschool Music Curriculum, 1970; Music Handbook for the Elementary School, 1972; Staff Training in Child Care in Hawaii, 1975; Your Child Needs Music, 1979; also articles. Home: 2575 Kuhio Ave 19-2 Honolulu HI 96815 Office: 2411 Dole St MB203 Honolulu HI 96822

GREENBERG, PAUL ROBERT, lawyer; b. N.Y.C., Sept. 2, 1942; s. Leon and Florence (Litz) G.; A.B. magna cum laude, U. Calif.-Berkeley, 1964; LL.B. magna cum laude, Columbia U., 1968. Bar: Calif. 1968. Assoc., Irell & Manella, Los Angeles, 1968-72; assoc., then ptnr. Nelson, Liker and Merrifield, Los Angeles, 1972-74; pres. Paul R. Greenberg, P.C., 1974-77; ptnr. Cox, Castle & Nicholson, Los Angeles, 1978—; v.p., gen. counsel Shaklee Corp., San Francisco, 1977—. Mem. adv. council Calif. World Trade Commn., Calif. Econ. Devel. Commn. Clubs: Town Hall, Regency (Los Angeles); Commonwealth (San Francisco). Bd. editors Columbia Law Rev., 1967-68. Office: 2049 Century Park E Suite 2800 Los Angeles CA 90067 and Shaklee Corp 444 Market St San Francisco CA 94111

GREENBERG, PAUL STANLEY, physician; b. Los Angeles, Jan. 26, 1949; s. George D. and Margaret (Kanyuk) G.; m. Diana Farley, Sept. 24, 1972; children—George, Jamie. Student U. So. Calif., 1967-69; M.D., U. Ark., 1973. Intern in medicine U. Ala. Hosps. and Clinics, Birmingham, 1973-74; resident in internal medicine U. Calif. Irvine Med. Center, Orange, 1974-76; cardiology fellow Meml. Hosp. Med. Center of Long Beach (Calif.), 1976-78; practice medicine specializing in internal medicine and cardiology, Long Beach, 1978—; coordinator cardiovascular research, div. cardiology Meml. Hosp. Med. Center, Long Beach, 1978—; mem. staff Long Meml. Med. Center and Hosp.; clin. instr. medicine U. Calif., Irvine. Diplomate Am. Bd. Internal Medicine. Fellow ACP, Am. Coll. Cardiology, Am. Coll. Chest Physicians, Am. Coll. Angiology, Council on Clin. Cardiology of Am. Heart Assn.; mem. Am. Soc. Internal Medicine, Long Beach Heart Assn. (dir.), Phi Eta Sigma, Alpha Epsilon Delta. Democrat. Jewish. Contbr. numerous articles on cardiovascular disease to profl. jours. Home: 6531 Mantova Long Beach CA 90815 Office: 2840 Long Beach Blvd Long Beach CA 90806

GREENBERG, RICHARD ALLEN, economist; b. Atlanta, Mar. 18, 1944; s. Sol Harry and Doris Jane (Kleinman) G.; m. Martha Ann Wood, Jan. 27, 1967; children—Jennifer, David; m. 2d, Lynnette Kay Cobb, Sept. 13, 1980. B.A. in Econs., Tulane U., 1965; M.A. in Econs., UCLA, 1967. Market research economist Lockheed-Calif. Co., Burbank, 1966-68; econ. devel. specialist N.D. State U., Fargo, 1971; econ. devel. cons. Office Econ. Opportunity, Ga., Pa., 1972-73; exec. dir. N. Central Pa. Regional Planning and Devel. Commn., Ridgway, 1973-77, Toledo Econ. Planning Council, 1977-81; pres. Pueblo (Colo.) Econ. Devel. Corp., 1982—; asst. prof. dept. geography Mansfield State Coll. (Pa.), 1975-76. Bd. dirs. Colo. Housing Fin. Authority, 1982. Mem. Internat. City Mgmt. Assn., Am. Planning Assn., Council Urban Econ. Devel., Am. Econ. Devel. Assn. Club: Pueblo Rotary. Office: 302 N Santa Fe Ave Pueblo CO 81002

GREENBERG, RUBIN, travel center exec.; b. Los Angeles, Aug. 5, 1926; s. Isaac M. and Minnie (Falick) G.; B.S., U. So. Calif., 1949; M.B.A., Hamilton Coll., 1961; Ph.D., London Inst., 1963; m. Takako Taquchi, Nov. 4, 1966. Vice pres. finance Jacobi Systems Corp., Los Angeles, 1968-71; v.p. fin., dir. Land Dynamics, Fresno, Calif., 1971-73; treas., chief fin. officer, dir. H.S. Watson Co., Emeryville, Calif., 1973-79; pres. Travel Center Inc., Berkeley, Calif., 1979—. Served with USAAF, 1944-46; ETO. Mem. Nat. Assn. Accts. Democrat. Jewish. Clubs: Lions, Masons. Office: 2252 Union St San Francisco CA 94123

GREENBERG, SHARON HELENE, counselor, educator; b. Chgo., Jan. 19, 1945; d. Morris N. and Rose (Siegel) G. B.A., Carleton Coll., 1966; M.A., U. Pa., 1968; Ph.D. in Ednl. Psychology/Counseling, U. Wash., 1982. English instr. Widener Coll., Chester, Pa., 1968-70, 71-72; psychology instr. Bellevue Community Coll. (Wash.), 1981; counseling intern North Seattle Community Coll., Seattle, 1982—; counselor Olympic Mental Health Assocs., Bremerton, Wash., 1981—. Mem. ACLU, Am. Personnel and Guidance Assn., Wash. State Psychol. Assn., Western Assn. Counselor Educators and Suprs., Am. Psychol. Assn., Pi Lambda Theta. Author profl. paper in field. Home: 4015 Woodland Park Ave N Seattle WA 98103 Office: Olympic Mental Health Assocs 237 Sixth St Bremerton WA 98310

GREENBERG, STANLEY ARTHUR, aerospace scientist; b. N.Y.C., Aug. 22, 1935; s. Benjamin and Sara Frieda (Rothstein) G.; m. Dale Lois Van Pelt, Aug. 23, 1958; children—Lisa Leslie, Suzanne Francesca, David Phillip. A.B., Cornell U., 1956; M.S., U. Ariz., 1958, Ph.D., 1960. Mem. sci. staff Lockheed Research Lab., Palo Alto, Calif., 1960-81; mgr. mech. engring. Aerojet Electrosystems, Azusa, Calif., 1981—, cons. to NASA and U.S. Dept. Def. Cubmaster Boy Scouts Am.; track and field ofcl. AAU. Petroleum Research Fund fellow, 1958-60; U. Ariz. dept. chemistry research fellow, 1956-58; NDEA fellow, 1958-60; Cornell State scholar; recipient Lockheed Publs. awards. Mem. AIAA, Am. Chem. Soc., Sigma Xi, Phi Lambda Upsilon. Contbr. articles to profl. jours. Home: 1713 Shenandoah Dr Claremont CA 91711 Office: 1100 W Hollyvale St PO Box 296 Azusa CA 91702

GREENBERG, SUSAN ANNE, university official; b. San Francisco, Oct. 24, 1950; d. Edward and Irene (Arnopole) G. B.A., Calif. State Coll.-Hayward, 1971. Asst. dir. ednl. relations Golden Gate U., 1980-81, dir. corp. mktg., 1981—; cons. mktg. and profl. relations. Mem. Bay Area Exec. Women's Forum (dir.), Am. Soc. Tng. and Devel. Office: 536 Mission St San Francisco CA 94105

GREENBERGER, ELLEN, psychologist, educator, researcher; b. N.Y.C., Nov. 19, 1935; d. Edward Michael and Vera (Brisk) Silver; m. Michael Ladd Burton, Aug. 26, 1979; children by previous marriage—Kari Greenberger, David Greenberger. A.B., Vassar Coll., 1956; M.A., Harvard U., 1959, Ph.D., 1961. Instr., Wellesley Coll., 1962-63, asst. prof., 1963-67; prin. research scientist Ctr. for Social Orgn. of Schs., research assoc. dept. social relations Johns Hopkins U., 1967-75; prof. social ecology U. Calif.-Irving, 1975—, dir. program in social ecology, 1976-80; cons. in field. Nat. Inst. Edn. grantee, 1969-72, 78-79; Spencer Found. grantee, 1979—; Ford Found. grantee, 1979—. Mem. Am. Psychol. Assn., Am. Anthropol. Assn. Contbr. articles to profl. jours. Office: Program in Social Ecology U Calif Irvine CA 92717

GREENBLATT, BERNARD, psychologist, educator; b. Atlantic City, May 5, 1921; s. Isidore and Aliza (Waitsman) G.; m. Margaret Stephenson, Mar. 24, 1943; children—Richard David, Sally Ruth; m. 2d, Adele Kostoff, Mar. 10, 1955; 1 son, Robert David; m. 3rd, Ronnie Drescher, Apr. 10, 1964. B.A., U. Mo., 1942; D.M.D., U. Oreg., 1946, M.A., 1962, Ph.D., 1963; student Postgrad. Ctr. Mental Health, 1962-65. Lic. psychologist, Nev. Gen. practice dentistry, Phila., 1947-54; assoc. prof. social work and psychology, chmn. dept. social services U. Nev., Las Vegas, 1967-70; pvt. practice clin. psychologist, Las Vegas, 1967—. Served with AUS, 1942-44. NIMH fellow, 1963; Danforth fellow, 1968, 69. Mem. Am. Psychol. Assn., Soc. Clin. and Exptl. Hypnosis, Pi Mu Epsilon. Home: 1607 Golden Arrow Dr Las Vegas NV 89109 Office: 4055 S Spencer St Suite 216 Las Vegas NV 89109

GREENE, ALVIN, service co. exec.; b. Pitts., Aug. 26, 1932; s. Samuel David and Yetta (Kroff) G.; B.A., Stanford U., 1954, M.B.A., 1959; m. M. Louise Sokol, Nov. 11, 1977; children—Sharon, Ami, Ann, Daniel. Asst. to pres. Narmco Industries, Inc., San Diego, 1959-62; adminstrv. mgr., mgr. mktg. Whittaker Corp., Los Angeles, 1962-67, sr. v.p. Cordura Corp., Los Angeles, 1967-75; chmn. bd. Sharon-Sage, Inc., Los Angeles, 1975-79; exec. v.p., chief operating officer Republic Distbrs., Inc., Carson, Calif., 1979-81, also dir.; chief operating officer Memel, Jacobs, Pierno & Gersh, 1981—; dir. Sharon-Sage, Inc., True Data Corp.; vis. prof. Am. Grad. Sch. Bus., Phoenix, 1977-81. Served to 1st lt., U.S. Army, 1955-57. Mem. Direct Mail Assn., Safety Helmet Mfrs. Assn., Bradley Group, Alpha Epsilon Pi. Office: 1801 Century Park East Suite 2500 Los Angeles CA 90067

GREENE, BILL, state senator; b. Kansas City, Mo., Nov. 15, 1931; m. Yvonne LaFargue; children—Alisa Rochelle, Jan Andrea. Ed. Lincoln Jr. Coll., U. Mich. Mem. Calif. State Assembly, 1967-75, chmn. indsl. relations com., mem. govt. orgn. and fin. coms., elections and reapportionment, chmn. fin. subcom. on health and welfare; now mem. Calif. State Senate; del. Democratic Nat. Conv., 1980. Clk. Calif. State Assembly; labor cons., legis. adv., legis. asst. to Assemblyman Mervyn Dymally; field rep. Los Angeles County Dem. Central Com.; former regional dir. Calif. Fedn. Young Dems.; mem. YMCA, NAACP, CORE, Urban League. Served with U.S. Air Force. Home: 8514 Broadway Los Angeles CA 90003 Office: California State Senate Sacramento CA 95814*

GREENE, BILL, author, lectr., lawyer, bus. exec., pvt. detective; b. Chgo., 1938; s. William B. Greene; B.A. in Econs., U. Pa., 1958; postgrad. in History, U. Nev., 1968; J.D., John Marshall Law Sch., 1963. Admitted to Ill. bar, 1963, Nev. bar, 1969, U.S. Supreme Ct. bar, 1971; founder, owner Am. Equities Group, 1963—; real estate developer, London, San Francisco, 1970—; lectr. Bill Greene's Tycoon Class, San Francisco, 1975—; hon. consul gen. Senegal, 1970—; partner Lloyd's of London, 1977. Libertarian candidate for Vice-Pres. U.S., 1980; charter mem. Libertarian Party. Served with U.S. Army, 1959-60. Author: Think Like a Tycoon; Tax Revolt; How to Buy Distress Property; How to Trace Missing Heirs; 101 New (Tax) Loopholes. Address: PO Box 850 Mill Valley CA 94942

GREENE, CLYDE CORNELIUS, physician, corporate med. dir.; b. Charlotte, N.C., June 14, 1917; s. Clyde Cornelius and Ellen (White) G.; B.S., Wake Forest Coll., 1937; M.D., Jefferson Med. Coll., 1941; m. Jean H. Eisenhower, Dec. 30, 1972; children—Nancy Ellen Greene Thomas, Ralph Chapman Greene, Clyde Cornelius Greene, Anne Eisenhower, Lyn Eisenhower. Intern, Jefferson Hosp., Phila., 1942; asst. resident in medicine Stanford U. Hosp., San Francisco, 1946-47; practice medicine specializing in internal medicine, San Francisco, 1947-75; examining physician Pacific Telephone Co., San Francisco, 1947-48, asst. med. officer, 1948-57, gen. med. dir., personnel, 1957-75, corporate med. dir., personnel, 1975—; mem. staff Pacific Med. Center; former cons. pharmacy related programs Spl. Research and Devel. Projects Div., HEW. Trustee, former v.p. bd. dirs. San Francisco Hearing and Speech Center; elder Calvary Presbyn. Ch., San Francisco, 1975—. Served to maj M.C., U.S. Army, 1942-46. Recipient Distinguished Alumni award Wake Forest U., 1971. Fellow A.C.P., Am. Occupational Med Assn.; mem. Am. Soc. Internal Medicine (historian, former pres.), AMA, Calif. Med. Assn., San Francisco Med. Soc., Calif. (former officer), San Francisco (former trustee) socs. internal medicine, Am. Acad. Occupational Medicine, Calif. Acad. Medicine, Jefferson Med. Coll. Alumni Assn. (v.p. Calif.), Alpha Omega Alpha, Phi Chi, Kappa Alpha. Republican. Presbyterian. Home: 2757 Green St San Francisco CA 94123 Office: 140 New Montgomery St Room 816 San Francisco CA 94105

GREENE, FRANK S., JR., bus. exec.; b. Washington, Oct. 19, 1938; s. Frank S. and Irma O. (Swygert) G.; B.S., Washington U., St. Louis, 1961; M.S., Purdue U., 1962; Ph.D., U. Santa Clara (Calif.), 1970; m. Phyllis Davison, Jan. 1958; children—Angela, Frank. Part-time lectr. Washington U., Howard U., Am. U., 1959-65; pres. Tech. Devel. of Calif., Santa Clara, 1971—; asst. chmn., lectr. Stanford U., 1972-74. Bd. dirs. NCCJ, Santa Clara, 1980—; regents U. Santa Clara, 1983—. Served to capt. USAF, 1961-65. Mem. Assn. Black Mfrs. (dir., 1974-80), Am. Electric Assn. (indsl. adv. bd., 1975-76), Fairchild Research and Devel. (tech. staff, 1965-71), IEEE, IEEE Computer Soc. (governing bd., 1973-75), Bay Area Purchasing Council (dir. 1978—), Security Affairs Support Assn. (dir. 1980-83), Sigma Xi, Eta Kappa Nu. Author two indsl. textbooks, tech. articles in field; patentee. Office: 3990 Freedom Circle Santa Clara CA 95054

GREENE, JEFFERY DATE, sales engr.; b. Evanston, Ill., Sept. 26, 1953; s. Gordon Date and Jolene Harvey (Nelson) G.; B.A., U. Wyo., 1975. Purchasing agt. Butler Paper Co., Denver, 1975-77, sales rep., 1978-79; with Johns-Manville Corp., 1979—, sr. sales rep., Seattle, 1981—. Mem. ASHRAE, Sigma Chi. Republican. Home: 10770 NE 29th St Apt 191 Bellevue WA 98004 Office: Johns-Manville Corp 2600 Campus Dr San Mateo CA 94403

GREENE, JOHN THOMAS, JR., lawyer; b. Salt Lake City, Nov. 28, 1929; s. John Thomas and Mary Agnes (Hindley) G.; B.A., U. Utah, 1952, J.D., 1955; m. Kay Buchanan, Mar. 31, 1955; children—Thomas B., John B., Mary Kay. Admitted to Utah bar, 1955; law clk. Supreme Ct. Utah. Salt Lake City, 1954-55; asst. U.S. atty. Dist. Utah, Salt Lake City, 1957-59; partner firm Marr, Wilkins & Cannon, Salt Lake City, 1959-69, Cannon, Greene & Nebeker, Salt Lake City, 1969-74; chmn. bd. Greene, Callister & Nebeker, Salt Lake City, 1974—; spl. asst. atty. gen. Utah, 1965-69; spl. grand jury counsel Salt Lake County, 1970; faculty Am. Law Inst.-ABA, 1979—. Pres. Community Services Council, Salt Lake area, 1971-73; Republican chmn. Voting Dist. 47 Salt Lake County, 1969-73; pres. Utah Bar Found., 1971-74; chmn. Utah State Bldg. Authority, 1980—; bd. regents Utah Colls., 1983—. Mem. Utah State Bar (pres. 1970-71, chmn. judiciary com. 1971-77), Am. Bar Assn. (ho. of dels. 1975—, mem. spl. com. delivery legal service 1975-81, council gen. practice sect. 1974-82, chmn. spl. com. on environ. law 1971-75, mem. adv. panel Nat. Legal Service Corp. 1975-82), U. Utah Alumni Assn. (dir. 1968-69), Order of Coif, Phi Beta Kappa, Phi Kappa Phi. Mormon. Clubs: Fort Douglas Country; Salt Lake Tennis. Editor: Utah Law Rev., 1954. Author sect. on mining rights Am. Law of Mining, 1965. Contbr. articles to profl. jours. Home: 1923 Browning Ave Salt Lake City UT 84108 Office: 800 Kennecott Bldg Salt Lake City UT 84133

GREENE, LORRIE LEVIN, interior designer; b. San Francisco, Mar. 4, 1942; d. Harold Theodore and Frances (Friedman) Levin; B.A., U. Calif., Berkeley, 1963; M.A., San Francisco State U., 1969; m. Richard Greene, Jan. 27, 1963; children—Dana, Julie, Elisa. Tchr., Sanchez Sch., San Francisco, 1963-66, Alamo Sch., San Francisco, 1967-69, in-service innovative program adminstr. selected elementary schs., San Francisco, 1968-70, program evaluator, cons. proposals for program funding San Francisco Public Sch. System, 1969-70; interior designer, prin. Lor Elle Interiors, San Francisco, 1966—. Docent, Council San Francisco Fine Arts Museums, 1973—; treas. Belvedere-Tiburon aux. of Fine Arts Museums of San Francisco, 1975-78, pres., 1979-81; Reed Union Sch. dist. adv. council, 1978-79, ad hoc fin., art, transp., sch. site coms., 1972-78; county chmn. county public relations dir. for ann. fund-raising auction public broadcasting sta. KQED, 1971-74; docent info. service Mt. Zion Hosp. and Med. Center, San Francisco, 1977-81; pres. local Parent-Tchr. Club, 1977-78, Dist. Parent-Tchr. Club, 1981—. Republican. Jewish. Club: Tiburon Peninsula (chmn. aims and objectives com., 1977-80). Researcher use of programmed reading materials at elementary level, 1967-68. Office: PO Box 2252 San Francisco CA 94126

GREENE, RICHARD STUART, educator; b. N.Y.C., May 13, 1938; s. Jack and Rose G. B.S., Fla. So. Coll., 1960; student Calif. State U., Fresno, 1964-66; diploma Inst. Children's Lit., 1980. Extension instr. edn. dept. U. Calif., Davis, 1970, U. Calif., Santa Cruz, 1971—; instr. continuing edn. Calif. Lutheran Coll., 1977-79; guest lectr. Calif. State U., Fresno, 1977; spl. educator Thomas Jefferson Sch., Madera, Calif., 1966—; lit. critic Nat. Writers Club, 1979-81; cons. on spl. edn. Am. Correctional Assn. Recipient award of Merit, Madera Police Dept., 1974. Mem. Am. Psychol. Assn., NEA (ednl. critic), Internat. Platform Assn., Am. Assn. Mental Retardation, Am. Parole Assn. Mem. Christian Ch. Author 3 textbooks; editor and founder Exceptional People's Quar., 1980—; contbr. articles on edn. to profl. publs. Home: 5288 N Colonial Ave Apt B Fresno CA 93704 Office: Thomas Jefferson School 1407 Sunset St Madera CA

GREENE, WARREN WICKERSHAM, physician; b. Santa Monica, Calif., Sept. 28, 1912; s. Jesse Benjamin and Ruth (Wickersham) G.; A.B., U. So. Calif., 1935; M.B., Chgo. Med. Sch., 1940, M.D., 1941; m. Josephine Henrietta McLin, Sept. 20, 1938; children—Patricia Josephine (Mrs. Harry Workman), Warren Wickersham, Kathleen Karen (Mrs. Dennis Hynes). Intern, Meml. Hosp., Elmhurst, Ill., 1940-41; resident VA Hosp., Wadsworth, Calif., 1948-50, chief anesthesiology, 1946; chief anesthesiology VA Hosp., Birmingham Hosp., Los Angeles, 1946-50; practice medicine specializing in anesthesiology, Los Angeles, 1950, Santa Monica, 1951—; anesthesiologist Spring Anesthesia Group, Lo chief anesthesiology sect. St. John's Hosp., 1952-59, 64-65, 67-70. Served to capt. M.C., AUS, 1943-45, ETO. Diplomate Am. Bd. Anesthesiology. Fellow Am. Coll. Anesthesiology; mem. Am. Soc. Anesthesists, AMA, Calif. Anesthetists Soc., Calif., Los Angeles County med. socs. Home: 800 Greentree Rd Pacific Palisades CA 90272 Office: PO Box 924 Santa Monica CA 90406 also Box 22222 Los Angeles CA 90022

GREENE, WILLIAM BENNY, guidance counselor; b. Kendrick, Idaho, Dec. 10, 1949; s. Benjamin Richard and Arlene Mae (Riley) G.; m. Sharon Marlene Dryver, May 27, 1972; children—Bethany JoLaine, Bryan Jason. Student U. Idaho, 1970-71, 73; B.A. in Edn., Pacific Luth. U., 1972; M.A. in Edn., Guidance and Counseling, Eastern Wash. U., 1975; cert. in continuing level counseling, vocat. counseling Western Wash. U., 1978. Tchr., St. Maries Sch., Dist. 41 (Idaho), 1972-74; lay asst. Central Luth. Ch., Spokane, Wash., 1973; counselor Dist. 402, Quillayute Valley Sch., Forks, Wash., 1976—. Mem. Am. Personnel and Guidance Assn., Wash. Vocat. Assn., NEA, Wash. Ednl. Assn., Forks Ednl. Assn. Lutheran. Home: Route 3 PO Box 3357 Forks WA 98331 Office: Quillayute Valley Sch Dist 402 Forks WA 98331

GREENFIELD, PATRICIA ANN, hospital administrator, educator, consultant; b. Birmingham, Ala., Jan. 8, 1942; d. E.G. and Ruby Jo (Brazier) Jones; m. Vincent Procopio, Apr. 12, 1961; children—Anthony, Teresa; m. 2d, Jack Edwin Greenfield, Oct. 5, 1968; 1 son, Timothy. Registered nurse diploma Los Angeles County U So. Calif. Med. Ctr. Sch. Nursing, 1975; A.A., East Los Angeles Coll., 1976; student Chapman Coll., 1980—. Registered nurse, Calif.; cert. tchr., Calif. Indsl. nurse Weiser Locks, Inc., South Gate, Fullerton, Calif., 1972-76; nurse Corona (Calif.) Community Hosp., 1976-80, dir. profl. edn., 1980—; adult edn. tchr. nursing Corona-Norco Unified Sch. Dist., 1978-80; cons., gen. mgr., owner Vantage Mgmt. Systems, Corona, 1981—. Mem. mgmt. adv. com. Chaffey Coll., 1982; mem. community edn. adv. com., profl. staff com., curriculum com., support services com. Corona-Norco Unified Sch. Dist. Recipient cert. of Appreciation, Corona Jaycees, 1980. Mem. Bd. Registered Nurses, Edn. Inservice Council Los Angeles, Inland Empire Inservice and Edn. Council, Am. Soc. Tng. and Devel., Am. Mgmt. Assn. Lutheran. Club: Ladies Aux. Fleet Res. Assn. Home: 210 Pinto Pl Norco CA 91760 Office: 469 E Harrison St Suite A Corona CA 91720

GREENGARD, RUSSELL LEON, space and defense company executive; b. Mpls., Dec. 14, 1928; s. Harry H. and Stella (Edelman) G.; B.S., UCLA, 1950; Postgrad. Calif. Inst. Tech., 1950-52, U. So. Calif., 1955; m. Neva Beatrice Kessler, Aug. 30, 1959; children—Gerald Lyle, Kenneth Dale, Alan Randall. Hydrodynamicast, Calif. Inst. Tech., Pasadena, 1950-52; cons. turbo machinery Grovar, Inc., Monterey, Calif., 1952-53; engr., program mgr. Propulsion Research Corp., Santa Monica, Calif., 1953-58; program mgr. Minuteman Missile, systems engr. TRW Corp., San Bernardino, Calif., 1958-69; sr. v.p., spl. asst. to pres. Ultrasystems, Inc., Irvine, Calif., 1969—, also corp. sec., dir. Pres., Broadmoor Hills Home Owners' Assn., 1974. Office: 16845 Von Karman Ave Irvine CA 92714

GREENLAW, ROGER LEE, interior designer; b. New London, Conn., Oct. 12, 1936; s. Kenneth Nelson and Lyndell Lee (Stinson) G.; B.F.A., Syracuse U., 1958; children—Carol Jennifer, Roger Lee. Interior designer Cannel & Chaffin, 1958-59, William C. Wagner, Architect, Los Angeles, 1959-60, Gen. Fireproofing Co., Los Angeles, 1960-62, K-S Wilshire, Inc., Los Angeles, 1963-64; dir. interior design Calif. Desk Co., Los Angeles, 1964-67; sr. interior designer Bechtel Corp., Los Angeles, 1967-70; sr. interior designer, project mgr. Daniel, Mann, Johnson, & Mendehall, Los Angeles, 1970-72, Morganelli-Heumann & Assos., Los Angeles, 1972-73; owner, prin. Greenlaw Design Assos., Glendale, Calif., 1973—; lectr. UCLA, Fashion Inst. Design, Mt. San Antonio Coll., Walnut, Calif. Scoutmaster Verdugo council Boy Scouts Am.; past pres. bd. dirs. Unity Ch., La Crescenta, Calif. Mem. Am. Soc. Interior Designers (treas. Pasadena chpt.), Adm. Farragut Acad. Alumni Assn., Delta Upsilon. Republican. Home: 2100f Valderas Dr Glendale CA 91208 Office: 3460 Oceanview Blvd Glendale CA 91208

GREENLEE, HOWARD NOBLE, JR., book publisher; b. Vincennes, Ind., Nov. 29, 1935; s. Howard Noble and America (Brown) G.; B.A., DePauw U., Greencastle, Ind., 1958; children—Amy, Charles. With Wall St. Jour., Chgo., 1958, Indpls. Star-News, 1959-60; v.p. Franklin Orgn., Chgo., 1960-62; account exec. E.H. Weiss Advt., Chgo., 1962-65; v.p. Sta. WAOV, Vincennes, Ind., 1965-70; pres. Fun Pub. Co., Scottsdale, Ariz., 1970—. Dir. pub. relations, mem. adv. council Mesa Community Coll. Mem. Screen Actors Guild, Phi Kappa Psi. Democrat. Congregationalist. Inventor ednl. toy Learning Talking Machine, 1965. Home: 3520 Creighton Ct Scottsdale AZ 85251

GREENLEE, NORMAN ARLIE, coal research co. ofcl.; b. Corydon, Iowa, May 3, 1932; s. Roy Lester and Eva Rebecca (Green) G.; B.S. in Chem. Engring., Iowa State U., 1954; m. Audrey Johnson, Dec. 22, 1956; children—Arthur Dale, Robert David, John Arlie. Research engr. Spencer Chem. Co., Kansas City, Mo., 1956-63; sr. project engr. Gulf Research and Devel. Co., Merriam, Kans., 1963-72, Harmarville, Pa., 1973; adminstrv. supt. Pittsburg & Midway Coal Mining Co., Dupont, Wash., 1974-75, prodn. supt., 1976-78, dep. plant mgr., 1979, plant mgr., 1980—. Treas. Timberlake Community Assn., 1980. Served with U.S. Army, 1954-56. Mem. Am. Inst. Chem. Engrs. Republican. Methodist. Club: Elks. Co-patentee inventions in area of polymer processing. Home: 8427 E Mineral Circle Englewood CO 80112 Office: PO Box 199 Dupont WA 98327

GREENOUGH, JOSEPH WARREN, marine biologist; b. Spokane, Wash., June 5, 1936; s. Joseph Warren and Agnes (Anderson) G.; B.A., U. Mich., 1959; M.S., U. Wash., 1967; m. Kathrin Woodard, Mar. 25, 1959 (div. 1974); children—Lisa Bale, Phoebe Kathrin. Chief biometrics investigations Auke Bay (Alaska) Lab., 1965-74; sr. scientist Inter-Am. Tropical Tuna Commn., La Jolla, Calif., 1975—. Recipient Silver medal Dept. Commerce. Mem. Sigma Xi. Co-author: International Management of Tuna, Porpoise, and Billfish: Biological, Legal, and Political Aspects, 1979. Office: Inter-American Tropical Tuna Commission care Scripps Institution of Oceanography La Jolla CA 92037

GREENSPAN, SYLVIA HELEN, advertising agency executive; b. Montebello, Calif.; d. Jacob and Lillian (Pollack) G. A.B., UCLA, 1975, M.B.A., 1977. Cert. in litigation atty. asst. tng. program UCLA. Media planner Wells, Rich, Greene, Los Angeles, 1978-80, Della Femina, Travisano & Ptnrs., Los Angeles, 1980-81; media supr. Abert, Newhoff & Burr, Los Angeles, 1981-82; dir. media planning and research Diener/Hauser/Bates, Los Angeles, 1982—. Bd. dirs. Los Angeles Hillel Council.

GREENSPUN, HERMAN MILTON, newspaper pub.; b. Bklyn., Aug. 27, 1909; s. Samuel J. and Anna (Fleischman) G.; student St. John's Coll., 1930-32; LL.B., St. John's Sch. Law, 1934; L.H.D. (hon.), U. Nev., Las Vegas, 1977; m. Barbara Joan Ritchie, May 21, 1944; children—Susan Gail, Brian Lee, Jane Toni, Daniel Alan. Admitted to N.Y. bar, 1936; practice law, N.Y.C., 1936-46; pub. mag. Las Vegas Life, 1946-47; owner, pub. Las Vegas Sun, North Las Vegas News, 1950—; owner Colorado Springs Sun, 1970-75; editorial writer, columnist Las Vegas Sun, 1950—; pres. Las Vegas Sun, Inc., 1950—, KLAS-TV, Las Vegas TV, Inc., 1954-68; owner, pres. CATV-Las Vegas; former owner Sun Outdoor Advt. Co. Bd. dirs. Sun Youth Found. Served from pvt. to maj., AUS, 1941-46; ETO. Decorated Croix de Guerre with silver star; Conspicuous Service cross State N.Y.; recipient Outstanding Journalist award Jewish War Vets, 1957. Mem. Am. Newspaper Pubs. Assn., Am. Soc. Newspaper Editors, Fed. Bar Assn., Nev. Press Assn. (pres. 1957), Internat. Platform Assn., Calif. Newspaper Pubs. Assn., Am. Legion, VFW, DAV. Clubs: Nat. Press; Overseas Press; Variety; Friars; Las Vegas Country (dir.). Author: Where I Stand (autobiography); co-editor; The Day the MGM Burned. Office: Las Vegas Sun 121 S Highland St Las Vegas NV 89106

GREENSTEIN, JAY SCOTT, optometrist; b. Boston, May 19, 1948; s. Morris Abraham and Helen Diane (Lipman) G. B.S. in Psychology, U. Mass., 1970; O.D., Mass. Coll. Optometry, 1976. Lic. optometrist, Colo., Calif. Intern, Hadassah Hosp., Jerusalem, 1975; dir. contact lens services Iranian Med. Inst., Teheran, 1976; assoc. Dr. Stephan Gorden, Denver, 1977; pvt. practice optometry, Denver, 1977—. Mem. Colo. Optometric Assn. (cert. of merit 1974), Am. Optometric Assn., Vol. Optometric Service to Humanity. Home: 222 S Dale Ct Denver CO 80219 Office: 555 A S Broadway St Denver CO 80209

GREENWELL, JAMES OLIVER, JR., health care cons.; b. San Francisco, Feb. 5, 1911; s. James O. and Edith (Snell) G.; A.B., Stanford, 1932, M.D., 1936; m. Lily C. Wilde, Sept. 20, 1953. Intern, San Francisco Hosp., 1935-36; resident physician Santa Clara County Sanatorium, 1936-37; sr. house officer tb San Francisco Hosp., 1937-38; tb physician San Joaquin Gen. Hosp. and Bret Harte Sanatorium, 1938-40; med. dir. San Mateo County Canyon Hosp., Redwood City, Calif., 1941-72; cons. chronic disease care and adminstrn., 1972—; hon. staff Sequoia Hosp., Redwood City, Calif. Choirmaster, St. Peters Episcopal Ch., 1944-51; mem. Evergreen (Colo.) Sch. Ch. Music, 1950-52. Mem. at large Bay Area Social Planning Council, 1958-68; mem. San Mateo County Grand Jury, 1979-80; bd. dirs. San Mateo County Assn. Grand Jurors, pres., 1981-82. Recipient 50th Ann. medal Nat. Tb Assn. 1954. Fellow Am. Coll. Chest Physicians, Royal Soc. Health (Eng.), AMA, Am. Geriatrics Soc.; mem. Am., Calif. (pres. 1956) thoracic socs., Laennec Soc. San Francisco (pres. 1946), Am. Acad. Tb Physicians, Am. Pub. Health Assn., AAAS, Calif. Sanatorium Assn. (pres. 1952), Am. Soc. for Clin. Radiology, Internat. Union Against Tb, San Mateo County Tb and Health Assn. (pres. 1957), Am. Assn. Sr. Physicians, Calif. Hist. Soc. Republican. Episcopalian. Rotarian (charter Redwood City). Clubs: Commonwealth (Calif.); Rotary (Paul Harris fellow 1980). Home: 2107 Edgewood Rd Redwood City CA 94062

GREENWELL, ROGER ALLEN, scientist; b. Santa Maria, Calif., Dec. 4, 1941; s. George C. and Bessie Florence (Sutton) G.; m. Jeannine Pendleton, July 25, 1969; 1 son, George Eli. A.A., Hancock Jr. Coll., 1961; B.S., Calif. Poly. Coll., 1968; M.S., U.S. Internat. U., 1974, D.B.A., 1981. Mathematician Naval Weapons Ctr., China Lake, Calif., 1968, ops. research analyst, Corona, Calif., 1969-70; ops. research analyst Comdr. Naval Forces, Vietnam, 1968-69; mathematician Naval Electronics Lab. Ctr., San Diego, 1970-77; scientist Naval Ocean Systems Ctr., San Diego, 1977—; cons. fiber optics and econ. analysis. Served with U.S. Army, 1964-67. Decorated Bronze Star. Mem. Ops. Research Soc. Am., Inst. Mgmt. Sci., AIAA, Soc. Allied Weight Engrs., Soc. Photo Optical and Instrumentation Engrs. Contbr. chpts. to books, govt. publs., and movies in field. Home: 3778 Eagle St San Diego CA 92103 Office: 271 Catalina Blvd San Diego CA 92152

GREENWOOD, CARL JAMES, real estate exec.; b. Orange, Calif., Jan. 15, 1943; s. Charles Francis and Katharine (Shubunka) G.; B.A., Stanford, 1964; m. Katherine Susanne Root, June 18, 1972; children—Jennifer Susanne, Daniel James. Asso. Greenwood & Son, real estate investments, Tustin, Calif., 1967-72, partner, 1973-76, owner, 1977—. Served to lt. (j.g.) USNR, 1964-67: Vietnam. Mem. Calif. Assn. Realtors (dir. 1969-71), Nat. Assn. Realtors, Tustin C. of C. (dir. 1970-73). Republican. Presbyterian. Rotarian. Home: 12575 Redhill Ave Tustin CA 92680 Office: 17581 Irvine Blvd Suite 200 Tustin CA 92680

GREENWOOD, JERI R., foundry co. exec.; b. Minot, N.D., Mar. 26, 1942; d. George Gerald and Helen Maxine (Holmes) Lillenas; completion certs. Life Office Mgmt. Assn., 1972-73. Various office positions, N.D., Calif., Mont., 1960-65; asst. actuary Sunset Life Ins. Co., Olympia, Wash., 1965-67; exec. sec. to pres. Calif. Handprints, Inc., Los Angeles, 1967-71; brokerage co-ordinator, in-house actuary Conn. Mut. Life Ins. Co., Los Angeles, 1971-73; systems mgr. Fick Foundry Co., Tacoma, 1974—. Mem. Am. Mgmt. Assn., NOW, Cousteau Soc. Democrat. Theosophist. Club: WIBC 600. Office: Fick Foundry Co 1005 East E St Tacoma WA 98421

GREENWOOD, ROBERT WALTER, actor, dir., educator, performing arts adminstr.; b. Hanover, N.H., Mar. 1, 1941; s. Clayton H. and Lillian F. (Bliss) G.; B.A. cum laude (Rufus Choate scholar) with honors, Dartmouth, 1963; M.F.A. with honors, Yale Sch. of Drama, 1964-67. Actor, Columbia Repertory Theatre, N.Y.C., 1967-69; actor-tchr. Dartmouth Repertory Theatre, Hanover, 1969-70; asst. prof. acting, stage movement U. Okla., Norman, 1970-72; dir. Southwest Repertory Theatre, Norman, 1971; actor-dir. Contemporary Arts Found., Oklahoma City, 1971-73; asst. prof. U. Calgary, Alta., 1973-77, chmn. acting-directing, 1973-75; reviewer theatre, dance, films for CBCR and The Albertan, 1977-78; adminstrv. mgr. Arete Contemporary Mime Troupe, 1977-78; actor, dir. Ensemble Players, 1976-77; actor Alta. Show Case on Stage, CBC-TV, 1977, Theatre Calgary, 1978—, Access TV, 1975, 77-79; artistic and mng. dir. Sun-Ergos; communications officer Dance and the Child Internat.; commentator CBC radio and TV. Mem. Southwest Theatre Conf., 1970, Alta. Theatre Conf., 1974; poet, poetry-in-the schs. program, Okla. Arts and Humanities Council, Oklahoma City, 1972-73; mem. World Vision of Can., 1973—; adjudicator Calgary High Sch. Drama Festival, 1974, 75, 76, Alta. Provincial Drama Festival, 1976, Red Deer Provincial Drama Workshop, 1976, 77; bd. dirs. Theatre Can., 1974-78, Festival Calgary, 1975-77; participant Cultural Resources Mgmt. Programme, Banff, 1975, Canadian Council-Touring Office Conf., Red Deer, 1976, Laban Inst. Movement Studies, 1979, Edinburgh Fringe Festival, 1980-82, Swansea (Wales) Festival, 1981-82. Recipient Marcus Heiman award, 1962, Adelbert Ames award, 1963, Citizen of the Age of Enlightenment award, 1976, du Maurier Search for Stars award, 1980, Alta. Cultural Assistance award, 1980; named Actor of Yr., Albertan, 1976. Okla. Arts and Humanities Council grantee, 1973. Mem. Okla. Community Theatre Assn., Canadian Child and Youth Drama Assn., Dance in Can. Assn. (exec. sec. 1976-78, 1st vice chmn. 1978-79), Dance and Theatre Arts Calgary Soc. (pres. 1975-77), Internat. Meditation Soc., Internat. Platform Assn., Humanities Assn. Can., Univ. and Coll. Theatre Assn., Am. Theatre Assn.,

ACTRA, Can. Actors Equity. Home: 2205-700 9th St SW Calgary AB T2P 2B5 Canada

GREER, BARBARA KERR, statistician; b. Pueblo, Colo., Sept. 14, 1955; d. Charles Clithero and Opha Georgia (Thomas) Kerr; m. Richard Lee Greer, Jan. 14, 1983. B.S. in Math. (Pres. Achievement scholar, Mary Lutin scholar), U. So. Colo., 1978; M.S. in Stats., Kans. State U., 1980. Cert. secondary tchr., Colo. Tchr. asst. Pueblo Community Ctr. Sch., 1976-77; tchr. math. Abe Hubert Jr. High Sch., Garden City, Kans., 1977-78; grad. teaching asst. Kans. State U., 1978-80; statistician Rockwell Internat., Rocky Flats Plant, Golden, Colo., 1980—; presenter papers at profl. meetings; lectr. in field. Mem. Rocky Flats Equal Opportunity Adv. Com., 1982-84. Mem. Am. Statis. Assn., Colo.-Wyo. Chpt. Am. Statis. Assn. (newsletter editor 1982-83). Republican. Baptist. Club: Order of Eastern Star. Office: Rockwell Internat PO Box 464 Golden CO 80401

GREER, LARRY EUGENE, transp. engr.; b. Wabash, Ind., Oct. 15, 1942; s. Everett Raymond and Lucille Lenora (Michel) G.; B.S., Manchester Coll., N. Manchester, Ind., 1965; B.S. in Civil Engring., Purdue U., 1966; M.S., Ohio State U., 1968; children—Eric Douglas, Amy Leigh. Civil engring. asst. City Engr's Office, Los Angeles, 1966-69, civil engring. assoc., 1970-73; asso. Barton-Aschman Assocs., Chgo., 1969-70, sr. asso., office mgr., Los Angeles, 1975-78; sr. engr. Crommelin-Pringle Assocs., Los Angeles, 1973-74; v.p. Mohle, Perry & Assos., Fullerton, Calif., 1978-80; owner, prin. Greer & Co., Engrs. & Planners, Anaheim, Calif., 1980—; cons. in field. Mem. Arcadia (Calif.) Auditorium Com., 1977. USPHS fellow, 1967-68; grad. fellow Ohio State U., 1967-68. Registered profl. engr., Calif., Colo. Fellow Inst. Advancement Engring.; mem. Inst. Transp. Engrs. (officer So. Calif. sect. 1975-80; Young Transp. Engr. of Year award So. Calif. sect. 1976), ASCE, Am. Public Works Assn., Met. Assn. Urban Designers and Environmental Planners, Purdue U., Ohio State U. alumni assns. Author papers in field. Home: 1907 Deerpark Pl Apt 491 Fullerton CA 92631 Office: 4095 E La Palma Ave Anaheim CA 92807

GREER, RUTH LINNEA, steel co. exec.; b. Lindsborg, Kans., July 24, 1924; d. George and Ellen (Karlsson) Paulson; student U. Alaska, 1966-67; m. Glenn E. Greer, Apr. 9, 1945; children—David, Linda Helms, Gary, Mark. Co-founder Greer Tank & Welding Inc., Fairbanks, Alaska, 1952, sec.-treas., 1952-68, v.p., 1968-71, pres., chmn. bd., 1971—; pres., Greer Tank Inc. subs., Anchorage, 1972—. Mem. Associated Gen. Contractors, Fairbanks Indsl. Devel. Corp., U.S., Fairbanks chambers commerce, Am. Fedn. Bus. Republican. Episcopalian. Clubs: Rebekah, Order Eastern Star. Home: 1507 4th Ave Fairbanks AK 99701 Office: PO Box 1193 Fairbanks AK 99707

GREFRATH, RICHARD WARREN, librarian; b. Greenwich, Conn., Aug. 7, 1946; s. Warren Paul and Dorothy Lee (Von Bieberstein) G., m. Valentina Mary Lyntkowski, Dec. 23, 1971; children—Jason Richard, David Jonathan. Student Carnegie Inst. Tech., 1964-66; B.A. in English cum laude, NYU, 1968; M.A. in English, Temple U., 1971; M.L.S., U. Md., 1972. Research librarian Coll. Library and Info. Services, U. Md., 1973; reference librarian Pacific Luth. U. Library, Tacoma, Wash., 1973-78; instructional services librarian U. Nev., Reno, 1978—, instr. library sci., 1978—. Served with U.S. Army, 1968-70. Decorated Bronze Star, Army Commendation medal, Vietnamese Commendation medal, Nat. Def. Service medal, Vietnam Service medal. Recipient NYU Founder's Day scholar award, 1968. Mem. Am. Library Assn., Nev. Library Assn., AAUP, 101st Airborne Div. Assn., Vietnam Vets. Am., Phi Beta Kappa. Democrat. Clubs. Faculty of U. Nev., Author: Use of the Library: A Self-Paced Workbook in Library Skills, 1981; book reviewer Library Jour., Am. Reference Books Annual; contbr. articles to profl. jours. Office: U Nev Library Reno NV 89557

GREGERSEN, JACK BRADLEY, safety engineer; b. Richfield, Utah, Mar. 16, 1925; s. Ralph Clifford and Florence (Christensen) G.; student Utah State U., 1945-46; B.S., Brigham Young U., 1951; m. Verla Marie Derricott, Dec. 11, 1952; children—William Randall, Tracy Lynne, Stellan Leo. Prodn. supr. Central Farmers Fertilizer Co., Georgetown, Idaho, 1956-63; resident engr. Ref-Chem Constrn. Co., Conda, Idaho, 1964-65; cost analyst El Paso Products Co., Conda, 1966-68; adminstrv. asst. Mountain Fuel Co., Conda, 1968-69; safety and tng. supr. Stauffer Chem. Co., Leefe, Wyo., 1969—; instr. first aid, CPR, job skills; mem. nat. speakers bur. STAC Program. Served with USAAF, 1944-45; ETO, MTO. Decorated Air medal with 3 oak leaf clusters, others; recipient Am. Indsl. Hygiene Assn. cert. Travelers Ins. Safety Leadership cert. Mem. Mine Safety and Health Adminstrn. (cert., coop. instr. surface mining, underground mining). Mormon. Home: 241 S 8th St Montpelier ID 83254 Office: Stauffer Chem Co PO Box 160 Montpelier ID 83254

GREGG, NANCY VAN SANT, wholesale executive; b. Fostoria, Ohio, Oct. 19; d. Lester A. and Nella C. (Mellott) Van Sant; m. R. Calvin Gregg, Apr. 24, 1960; children—Roger C., Christian V. Student North Central Coll., Naperville, Ill., 1957-58, Ripon Coll., 1958-59, U. Calif.-Santa Barbara, 1962-64; Otis Art Inst., 1968-69. Med. sec. to gen. physician, Fostoria, 1959-60; med. transcriber Oxnard (Calif.) Community Hosp., 1969-72; sales, mktg. rep. Tiny's, Inc., Oxnard, 1972—, v.p. mktg. and advt., 1974—; lctr. in field. Mem. Nat. Assn. Female Execs., Ventura County Bus. Profl. Women's Network, Oxnard C. of C., Better Bus. Bur. Republican. Office: 1237 Saviers Rd Oxnard CA 93033

GREGGS, ELIZABETH MAY BUSHELL (MRS. RAYMOND JOHN GREGGS), librarian; b. Delta, Colo., Nov. 7, 1925; d. Joseph Perkins and Ruby May (Stanford) Bushell; student Colo. Coll., 1943-44; B.A., U. Denver, 1948; m. Raymond John Greggs, Aug. 16, 1952; children—David M., Geoffrey B., Timothy C., Daniel R. Children's librarian Grand Junction (Colo.) Pub. Library, 1944-46, Chelan County Library, 1948, Wenatchee Pub. Library, 1948-52, Seattle Pub. Library, 1952-53; children's librarian Renton Pub. Library, 1957-61, dir., 1962, br. supr. and children's services, 1963-67; area children's supr. King County Library, Seattle, 1968-78, asst. coordinator children's services, 1978—; cons., organizer Tutor Center Library, Seattle South Community Coll., 1969-72; mem. Puget Sound Council for Reviewing Children's Media, chmn., 1974—; cons. to Children's TV Programs. Chmn. dist. advancement com. Kloshee dist. Boy Scouts Am., 1975-78, mem. Bond Issue Citizens Group to build a new Renton Library, 1958, 59. Recipient Hon. Service to Youth award Cedar River dist. Boy Scouts Am., 1971, award of merit Kloshee dist., 1977. Mem. ALA (Newbery-Caldecott com. 1978-79, chmn. com. 1983-84; membership com. 1978-80, Boy Scouts com. children's services div. 1973-78, chmn. 1976-78, exec. bd. for Library Service to Children 1979-81, Top of the News adv. com.), Wash. Library Assn. (exec. bd. children's and young adult services div. 1970-78, chmn. membership com. 1983—), King County Right to Read Council (co-chmn. 1973-77), Pierce-King County Reading Council, Assn. Library Services to Children, Wash. State Literacy Council (exec. bd. 1971-77), Wash. Library Media Assn. (jr. high levels com. 1980—), Pacific N.W. Library Assn. (young readers' choice com. 1981-83, vice-chmn. children's and young adult div. 1981-83, chmn. div. 1983-85, exec. bd. 1983-85), Puget Sound Orton Soc. Methodist. Editor: Cayas Newsletter, 1971-74; cons. to Children's Catalog, Children's Index to Poetry. Home: 800 Lynnwood Ave NE Renton WA 98055 Office: 300 8th Ave N Seattle WA 98109

GREGOR, EDUARD, laser physicist; b. Dnepropetrovsk, USSR, Jan. 9, 1936; s. Waldemar and Concordia (Teschke) G.; came to U.S., 1955, naturalized, 1960; A.A., Pasadena City Coll., 1958; B.S., Calif. State U. at Los Angeles, 1964, M.S., 1966; m. Marie Carlin, June 28, 1968; 1 son, Eduard Joseph. Instr., Calif. State U. at Los Angeles, 1963-66; optical devel. physicist TRW Instruments, El Segundo, Calif., 1966-68; laser physicist, product line mgr. holography Union Carbide Corp., Korad Dept., Santa Monica, 1968-72; operation mgr. Quantrad Corp., Torrance, Calif., 1972-79; sect. head Hughes Aircraft Co., Culver City, Calif., 1979—. Served with AUS, 1959-61. Mem. Optical Soc. Am., Soc. Photog. and Instrumentation Engrs., Sigma Pi Sigma. Republican. Presbyn. Patentee in field. Contbr. to profl. pubs. Home: 820 Las Lomas Ave Pacific Palisades CA 90272 Office: 19900 S Normandie Ave Torrance CA 90502

GREGORIAN, ROUBIK, elec. engr.; b. Iran, Feb. 19, 1950; came to U.S., 1973, naturalized, 1978; s. Djirair and Arshaluise (Balushian) G.; M.S. in Elec. Engring., Tehran U., 1973; M.S. in Elec. Engring., UCLA, 1975, Ph.D. in Engring., 1977. Research asst., elec. engring. dept. UCLA, 1974-76, teaching asst., elec. engring. dept., 1976, research assoc., elec. engring. dept., 1976-77; mem. tech. staff Am. Micro Systems Inc., Santa Clara, Calif., 1977—, sect. mgr., filter design group, 1980—, dept. mgr. design engring., 1982—. Mem. IEEE. Contbr. articles to tech. jours.; patentee in field. Home: 2382 Shoreside Ct Santa Clara CA 95050 Office: Am Micro Systems Inc 3800 Homestead Rd Santa Clara CA 95051

GREGORIOFF, VALERIE JEAN, utility official, bookkeeper; b. Ketchikan, Alaska, July 28, 1952; d. Alec and Lucille (Guthrie) G.; m. Robert E. Ridley, May 27, 1970 (div.); children—Wendy, Gordon, Julie. Student U. Alaska-Fairbanks, 1972-73. Teller, bookkeeper Metlakatla br. Nat. Bank of Alaska, 1974-78; office mgr., payroll clk. Annette Hemlock Mills, La.-Pacific Corp., Metlakatla, 1978-81; office mgr., bookkeeper Metlakatla Power & Light, 1982—. Home: PO Box 562 Metlakatla AK 99926 Office: PO Box 346 Metlakatla AK 99926

GREGORY, CALVIN LUTHER, insurance agent, real estate agent, clergyman; b. Bronx, N.Y., Jan. 11, 1942; s. Jacob and Ruth (Cherchian) G.; m. Rachel Anna Carver, Feb. 14, 1970 (div. Apr. 1977); children—Debby Lynn, Trixy Sue; m. Carla Deane Deaver, June 30, 1979. A.A., Los Angeles City Coll., 1962; B.A., Calif. State U.-Los Angeles, 1964; M.Div., Fuller Theol. Seminary, Pasadena, Calif., 1968; M.R.E., Southwestern Sem., Ft. Worth, 1969; Ph.D. in Religion, Universal Life Ch., 1982; D.D., Otay Mesa Coll., 1982. Notary pub., Calif.; lic. real estate agt., life and disability, casualty agt., Calif.; ordained to ministry Am. Bapt. Conv., 1970. Tchr. polit. sci. Maranatha High Sch., Rosemead, Calif., 1969-70; aux. chaplain Edwards AFB, Calif., 1970-72; pastor 1st Bapt. Ch., Boron, Calif., 1971-72; head youth minister Emanuel Presbyn. Ch., Los Angeles, 1973-74; ins. agt. Prudential Ins. Co., Ventura, Calif., 1972-73, sales mgr., 1973-74; casualty ins. agt. Allstate Ins. Co., Thousand Oaks, Calif., 1974-75; pres. Ins. Agy. Placement Service, Thousand Oaks, 1975—. Counselor, YMCA, Hollywood, Calif., 1964, Soul Clinic, Universal Life Ch., Inc., Modesto, Calif., 1982. Recipient Whole Life Round Table award Prudential Ins. Co., 1972, Man of Month (5 months), 1972, president's citation, 1972, Millionaire award, 1972. Mem. Apt. Assn. Los Angeles, Life Underwriter Tng. Council Ventura. Republican. Clubs: Forensic (Los Angeles); X32 (Ventura); Kiwanis (speaker 1971). Office: Ins Agy Placement Service PO Box 4407 Thousand Oaks CA 91359

GREGORY, JOHN MUNFORD, lawyer; b. Suisun, Calif., May 12, 1904; s. Thomas Tingey Craven and Gertrude Alice (Martin) G.; m. Virginia Christine Denton, Sept. 10, 1926 (div. 1933), children—Joan Gregory Geisen, Virginia Noelle Ellis. A.B., Stanford U., 1927; J.D., U. Calif.-San Francisco, 1931. Bar: Calif., U.S. Dist. Ct. (no. dist.), U.S. Ct. Appeals (9th cir.). Asst. U.S. atty., San Francisco, 1932-33; sole practice, San Francisco, 1934-37; asst. counsel Calif. Pub. Utilities Commn., 1938-46, legal examiner, 1947-72; sole practice, San Francisco, 1972—. Mem. Bar Assn. San Francisco, ABA, Am. Judicature Soc., Conf. Calif. Pub. Utility Counsel. Republican. Episcopalian. Clubs: Pres. Commonwealth of Calif. (San Francisco). Address: 613 32d Ave San Francisco CA 94121

GREGORY, MICHAEL STRIETMANN, educator; b. Oakland, Calif., Oct. 6, 1929; s. Walter and Alexine (Mitchell) G.; A.B., U. Calif., Berkeley, 1952, Ph.D., 1969; m. Ora Thorson, Feb. 2, 1952 (div.); children—Alexa, Tanya; m. 2d, Jan Louise Rosenthal, June 27, 1962; 1 dau., Erika. Instr. English, San Jose (Calif.) State U., 1956-57; mem. Faculty dept. English, San Francisco State U., 1959—, prof., 1971—, dir. NEXA program, 1975—; founding mem. Nat. Bd. Cons., Nat. Endowment for Humanities, 1974—; cons. NSF. Served with USNR, 1951-53. NIMH grantee. Fellow Am. Anthrop. Assn., mem. MLA, AAAS, Am. Assn. Advancement Humanities, Amnesty Internat., Hastings Inst., Joseph Conrad Soc. Am., AAUP. Author books including: Sociobiology and Human Nature, 1978; The Recombinant DNA Controversy: Public Policy at the Frontier of Knowledge, 1978. Home: 351 Melrose Ave Mill Valley CA 94941 Office: Sch Humanities San Francisco State U San Francisco CA 94132

GREGORY, NOBLE K., lawyer; b. Los Angeles, Apr. 19, 1918; s. James Noble and Hazel (Veach) G.; B.A., U. Calif. at Los Angeles, 1939; J.D., U. Calif. at Berkeley, 1946; m. Sara Dunlap, Feb. 21, 1947; children—James, Carol. Admitted to Calif. bar, 1946; law clk. Justice Traynor Calif. Supreme Ct., 1946-48; asso. Pillsbury, Madison & Sutro, San Francisco, 1948-56, partner, 1956—; instr. San Francisco Law Sch., 1947; mem. Calif. Law Rev. Commn., 1970-75. Served to lt. USAAF, 1942-45. Decorated D.F.C., Air medal with 3 clusters, Purple Heart. Mem. State Bar Calif. (chmn. com. on appellate cts. 1974-75), Am., San Francisco (chmn. adminstrn. of justice com. 1966) bar assns., Am. Judicature Soc. Clubs: Commonwealth, San Francisco Commercial. Home: 225 Maywood Dr San Francisco CA 94127 Office: 225 Bush St San Francisco CA 94104

GREGORY, RICHARD BERNARD, lawyer, accountant; b. Ludlow, Mass., Dec. 12, 1944; s. Marion Bernard and Lilian Marguerita (King) G.; m. Nancy Kay Praul, June 30, 1972; children—Jaime Lyn, Christopher William. B.A., Tex. Tech U., 1967; M.B.A., Eastern N.Mex. U., 1972; J.D., U. N.Mex., 1975. Bar: N.Mex. 1975; C.P.A., N.Mex. Tax specialist Peat Marwick Mitchell Co., Albuquerque, 1975-76; assoc. firm Knight and Sullivan, P.A., Albuquerque, 1976-79; pres. Security Trust Co., Albuquerque, 1979-80; sole practice, Albuquerque, 1980-82; mng. ptnr. Reiner and Gregory, Albuquerque, 1982—; chmn. N.Mex. Tax Inst, 1983; dir. Henry Hillson & Co., Inc., Albuquerque, N.Mex. Tax Conf., 1981; adj. prof. Robert O. Anderson Sch. Mgmt., U. N.Mex.; instr. Am. Coll., Bryn Mawr, Pa.; lectr. profl. meetings. Trustee, chmn. devel. com. Menaul Sch., Albuquerque; v.p., ruling elder 1st United Presbyn. Ch., Albuquerque; bd. dirs. N.Mex. State U. Found.; trustees 4-H Youth Devel. Found. of N.Mex.; bd. advisors N.Mex. Boys Ranch; mem. estate planning adv. com. Heights Gen. Hosp., Albuquerque. Served to capt. USAF, 1967-71; Decorated Bronze Star. Mem. ABA, N.Mex. Bar Assn., N.Mex. Estate Planning Council; N.Mex. Cattle Growers Assn., Albuquerque Bar Assn., Am. Inst. C.P.A.s, N.Mex. Soc. C.P.A.s, Western Pension Conf., S.W. Pension Conf., Internat. Assn. Fin. Planners, Eastern N.Mex. U. Alumni Assn. (dir.), Sigma Chi, Sigma Chi Alumni. Contbr. articles to profl. jours.; author of monthly series N.Mex. Stockman Mag. Home: 3713 Valerie NE Albuquerque NM 87111 Office: Reiner and Gregory Attys at Law 200 Lomas Blvd NW Albuquerque NM 87125

GREGORY, ROSE MARIE, nurse; b. Prince Rupert, B.C., Can., Sept. 2, 1930; came to U.S., 1953, naturalized, 1960; d. Elmer Louis and Sarah (Benzies) Hartwig; R.N. diploma, Royal Jubilee Hosp., Victoria, B.C., 1951; B.S. magna cum laude in Nursing, U.Wash. 1962; M.A., U. Calif., Berkeley, 1965; m. Carl Maurice Gregory, Oct. 18, 1968; 1 son, Carl Douglas. Staff, head nurse, supervisory positions in various hosps., Can., Cleve., Seattle, 1952-62; trainee USPHS, Div. Nursing Resources, Washington, 1960; USPHS research fellow, 1962-65; asso. dir. nursing Children's Hosp. and Med. Center, San Francisco, 1965-68; dir. nursing Alta Bates Hosp., Berkeley, Calif., 1968-70; nursing supr. Peninsula Hosp. & Med. Center, Burlingame, Calif., 1970-72, dir. div. patient care services, 1977—; dir. adminstrv. services Community Health Center at Peninsula Hosp. and Med. Center, Burlingame, 1973-77; mem. adv. com. Coll. of San Mateo Sch. Nursing. Mem. Am. Soc. Nursing Service Adminstrs., Calif. Soc. Nursing Service Adminstrs., Nat. League Nursing. Home: 3829 Fairfax Way South San Francisco CA 94080 Office: 1783 El Camino Real Burlingame CA 94010

GREGORY, WILLIAM A., college dean, theatre educator and director; b. Williamston, Mich., Aug. 20, 1924; s. William Alfred and Erna Mae (Roeser) G.; m. JoAnn Alvestrom, June 11; children—Kay, Erna. B.S., Central Mich. U., 1946; M.A., Mich. State U., 1950; Ph.D., U. Minn., 1957. Founder, dir. Lake Michigan Playhouse, Grand Haven, Mich., Vanguard Equity Theatre, Detroit; tchr. high schs., Mich., 1946-50; mem. faculty Alma (Mich.) Coll., 1951-53; prof. theatre Western Wash. U., Bellingham, 1957-60, 69—, dean Coll. Fine and Performing Arts, also theatre dir. Fulbright scholar, Taipei, Taiwan, 1983-84; named Outstanding Alumnus, Central Mich. U., 1981. Mem. Internat. Council Fine Arts Deans, Am. Theatre Assn. Democrat. Author: The Director. Office: Coll Fine and Performing Arts Western Wash U Bellingham WA 98225

GREGORY-GLUCHOWSKI, MATTHIAS GREGORY (ALSO KNOWN AS GREGORY, MATT G.), producer, dir.; b. Araucaria, Parana, Brazil, Nov. 21, 1921; s. Casimer John Gluchowski and Hedwig Mary Gregory; came to U.S., 1946, naturalized, 1955; M. Humanities, Marian Fathers Liceum, Warsaw, poland, 1939; m. Ailsa Marie Winton, Dec. 5, 1964; 1 son, Adam Casimer Gregory-Gluchowski. Script writer for radio, TV., 1947-53; asst. in charge spl. projects Milton Blackstone Agency, N.Y.C., 1946-49; writer radio/TV material, also dir. and personal mgmt. co., San Francisco, 1949-53; in various mgmt., direction and prodn. positions, Las Vegas, 1953-56; pres. Merlin, Inc., doing bus. as Matt Gregory Internat. Cons., Las Vegas, 1956—; mgr. numerous entertainment figures; pres. Merlin Music Pub. Co.; exec. v.p., producer Wonderful World of Youth Corp., 1976—, Wonderful World of Youth Found., 1975—; v.p. Mermaid Inc.; v.p. Dormat, Inc., exec. producer Gambit TV show; asso. Voltaire Cons., London, Brittania Ind. Distbrs., London; cons. Entertainment Internat., Stockholm; lectr. on entertainment industry; producer, dir. variety shows worldwide, nationally and for numerous Nev. hotels and casinos; producer, dir. recordings, syndicated, cable, cassette TV shows, also commls. Served with Polish Air Force (with RAF), 1940-46; lt. col./chief protocol Nev. Air Guard. Decorated Virtuti Militari, Cross of Valor with 2 bars, Air Force Cross, D.F.C.; recipient Jimmy Durante Trendsetter award, 1979. Mem. Ind. Producers Assn., Air Force Assn., Acad. Variety and Cabaret Artists, Entertainment Industry Cons. Assn., Armenian Catholic. Clubs: Paradise Country; Nevern (South Wales) Country. Instrumental in establishing large prodn. shows for hotels, and casinos; creator midi- and mini-revues worldwide; formed, developed and managed Sandler and Young act; past and present clients have been Marlena Dietrich, Joe E. Lewis, Jerry Colona, Jerry Fielding, Leo Damiani, Paul Steffen, Bill Reddie; designer, planner entertainment facilities worldwide, also developer budget and concept policies; developer, producer spl. projects for tourist industry; developer, producer, dir. TV and film projects for cable/cassette industries worldwide. Office: 5 Kensington Park Gardens London W11 3HB England also 2447 Paradise Village Way Las Vegas NV 89120

GREHALVA, RICHARD ANTHONY, facilities management company executive; b. Alhambra, Calif., Dec. 14, 1950; s. Anthony and Patricia Louise (Holmes) G.; children—Michelle, Richard Anthony II. Student in bus. adminstrn. East Los Angeles Coll., 1970-73; B.A. in Bus. Adminstrn., Assoc. Bus. Coll., 1978. Microfilm supr. County of El Paso (Tex.), 1973-75; data ctr. supr. Microfilm Data Systems, Los Angeles, 1975-79; mgr. input preparation/micrographics/control Computer Scis. Corp., Sacramento, 1979—, now dir. publs. and prodn. services Govt. Health Services div.; instr. in mgmt. prins. Nat. Mgmt. Assn. Edn. Program, 1981. Mem. Am. Mgmt. Assn., Nat. Micrographics Assn., Nat. Mgmt. Assn. Home: 2230 P St Sacramento CA 95816 Office: 2000 Evergreen St Sacramento CA 95815

GREINER, MARLENE TRAINOTTI, family, consumer studies educator; b. Beach, N.D., June 14, 1946; d. Mario Victor and Velma May (Babcock) Trainotti; m. Robert Fred Greiner, June 20, 1970 (div.). B.A., Calif. State U.-Long Beach, 1970, M.A., 1972; Ph.D., U. So. Calif., 1975. Elem. sch. tchr., Anaheim, Calif., 1972-75; family and consumer studies prof. South West Coll., 1977-78, West Los Angeles Coll., Culver City, Calif., 1978—. Mem. Phi Delta Kappa. Democrat. Lutheran. Home: 22831 Corralejo Mission Viejo CA 92692 Office: West Los Angeles College 4800 Freshman Dr Culver City CA 90230

GREINER, MAURICE LUTHER, chem. co. exec.; b. Assiniboia, Sask., Can., Jan. 4, 1931; came to U.S., 1971, naturalized, 1979; s. William Morris and Daisy (Weightman) G.; diploma Briercrest Bible Coll., 1952; adminstrn. diploma U. Toronto Extension Program, 1966; grad. Inst. of Fire Engrs., 1968; m. Zelma Alma Ross, June 30, 1951; children—Blayne Maurice, Brenda Gail. Firefighter, instr. City of Regina (Sask., Can.), 1952-66; dir. Regina Emergency Measures Orgn., 1966-68; safety tng. supr. Simplot Chem. Co., Brandon, Man., Can., 1968-71, corp. dir. tng. and safety, Pocatello, Idaho, 1971—; founder; dir. ann. Intermountain Fertilizer Safety Sch., 1974—; mem. safety health task force Fertilizer Inst., Washington, 1975—, vice chmn., 1980—. Recipient Queen's Commendation for brave conduct in fire service, 1966; Disting. service to safety award Nat. Safety Council, 1981; cert. hazard control mgr. Mem. Inst. Fire Engrs., Am. Soc. Tng. and Devel., Am. Soc. Safety Engrs., Vets. of Safety Internat., SAR, Delta Epsilon Chi. Republican. Mem. Ch. of Nazarene. Clubs: Idaho State Symphony (dir. 1977-81), Order St. John. Author: The Greiners of Amityville, Pa., 1700-1900, 1982; editor fertilizer sect. Newsletter for Nat. Safety Council, 1972; contbr. articles to profl. jours.; co-author: Self-Evaluation Manual for Fertilizer Industry, U.S. Dept. Health and Human Services, NIOSH, 1980. Home: 21 Stanford St Pocatello ID 83201

GREINER, RICHARD PETER, JR., automotive exec.; b. Atlanta, Jan. 4, 1950; s. Richard P. and Carmen E. (Frank) G.; m. Rebecca Lee Sedar, Nov. 21, 1975; children—Whitney Lee, Richard P. III. B.S.B.A., U. Ark., 1972. Service dir. Greiner Motor Co., Casper, Wyo., 1972-73, pres., gen. mgr., 1973—; bd. dirs., sec. Security Bank Glenrock; bd. dirs. Bank Casper, Resource Equipment Capital Corp.; pres. Greiner Leasing, Am. Internat. Rent-a-Car. Wyo. Hwy. commr.; former mem. bd. dirs. Casper Boys Club; mem. Dealer Election Action Com. Mem. Nat. Automobile Dealers Assn. (bd. dirs.), Wyo. Automobile Dirs., Rocky Mountain Ford Dealer Advt. Assn. (bd. dirs.), Casper C. of C. (bd. dirs.). Democrat. Roman Catholic. Club: Elks (Casper). Office: PO Box 2460 Casper WY 82602

GRENKO, SUELLEN MARY, educator; b. Dunsmuir, Calif., Apr. 12, 1946; d. Joseph J. and Maureen B. (Roney) G. B.A. in English, Calif. State U.-Chico, 1968; M.A. in Ednl. Adminstrn., Calif. State U.-Rohnert Park, 1982. Cert. secondary tchr., cert. in adminstrv. services, Calif. Tchr. secondary English lit. Livermore (Calif.) Unified Sch. Dist., 1969-71; tchr. english, history and journalism Santa Rosa (Calif.) City Secondary Schs., 1971-73, project coordinator/designer CARMS Vocat. Edn. Project, 1980—, journalism tchr. for newspaper and yearbook, 1972-78; student/family counselor. Active youth work activities. Mem. Profl. Educators Group, Journalism Edn. Assn., Assn. Supervision and Curriculum Devel., Nat. Right to Work Com. Democrat. Office: 217 Ridgway Ave Santa Rosa CA 95402

GRENLEY, PHILIP, physician; b. N.Y.C., Dec. 21, 1912; s. Robert and Sara (Schrader) G.; B.S., N.Y.U., 1932, M.D., 1936; m. Dorothy Sarney, Dec. 11, 1938; children—Laurie (Mrs. John Hallen), Neal, Jane (Mrs. Eldridge C. Hanes), Robert. Intern, Kings County Hosp., Bklyn., 1936-38, resident, 1939; resident in urology L.I. Coll. Hosp., Bklyn., 1939-41; practice medicine specializing in urology, Tacoma, Wash., 1946—; urologist Tacoma Gen. Hosp., St. Joseph Hosp., Drs. Hosp., Mary Bridge Children's Hosp. (all Tacoma), Good Samaritan Hosp., Puyallup, Wash.; pres. med. staff St. Joseph Hosp., Tacoma, 1968-69, mem. exec. bd., 1950-54, 67-68; cons. urologist to Surgeon Gen., Madigan Army Med. Center, Tacoma, 1955—, USPHS McNeil Island Penitentiary, 1955—, Good Samaritan Rehab. Center, Puyallup, 1960—; lectr. in sociology U. Puget Sound, Tacoma, 1960—. Trustee Wash. Children's Home Soc., 1951-60, Charles Wright Acad., 1961-69; trustee Pierce County Med. Bur., 1949-51, 59-61, 71-73, pres., 1973-74, mem. exec. bd., 1975-77. Served with AUS, 1941-46. Diplomate Am. Bd. Urology. Fellow ACS; mem. Am. Urol. Assn., AMA, Wash., Pan Am. med. assns., Pierce County Med. Soc. Clubs: Masons, Shrine (med. dir. 1965-79, divan 1975, 78-82, potentate 1983), Royal Order Jesters, Lions, Elks. Home: 40 Loch Ln SW Tacoma WA 98499 Office: 721 S Fawcett Ave Tacoma WA 98402

GRESSAK, ANTHONY RAYMOND, JR., hotel and food service executive; b. Honolulu, Jan. 22, 1947; s. Anthony Raymond and Anne Tavares (Ferreira) G.; A.A., Utah State U., 1967; postgrad. U.S. Army Inf. Officers Candidate Sch., 1968; m. Catherine Streb, Apr. 11, 1981; 1 son, Anthony Raymond III, 1 stepdau., Danielle. Restaurant mgr. Ala Moana Hotel, Honolulu, 1970-72; gen. mgr. Fred Harvey, Inc., Ontario, Calif., 1972-73, regional mgr. So. Calif., 1972-73, regional mgr. tollway ops., 1973, divisional mgr. Normandy Lanes, 1973, food and beverage dir. Nat. Parks, Grand Canyon, Ariz., 1976-77, gen. mgr. Grand Canyon Nat. Park Lodges, 1977—; resident mgr. Royal Inns of Am., San Diego, 1974; food and beverage dir. Assn. Inns & Restaurant Co. Am., Big Sky, Mont., 1974-75, condomium mgr., Big Sky, 1975, asst. gen. mgr. Naples (Fla.) Bath and Tennis Club, 1975-76; divisional v.p. Food Services Center, Hawley Hale-the Broadway, Los Angeles, 1979—; maitre de table Chaine des Rotisseurs-Napa Valley. Served with U.S. Army, 1967-70. Decorated Silver Star medal, Bronze Star medal, Purple Heart. Mem. Nat. Restaurant Assn., Chefs de Cuisine Los Angeles, Smithsonian Assn., Humane Soc. U.S. Clubs: Town Hall, Industry Hills Country. Roman Catholic.

GRETHER, DAVID MACLAY, economist; b. Phila., Oct. 21, 1938; s. Ewald T. and Carrie Virginia (Maclay) G.; m. Susan Clayton, Mar. 24, 1961; children—Megan Elizabeth, John Clayton. B.S., U. Calif.-Berkeley, 1960; Ph.D., Stanford U., 1969. Research staff economist Cowles Found., Yale U., 1966-70; lectr. econs. Yale U., 1966-68, asst. prof., 1968-70; assoc. prof. econs. Calif. Inst. Tech., 1970-75, exec. officer social scis., 1978-82, prof. econs., 1975—, chmn. div. humanities and social scis., 1982—. Served with USAR, 1960-61. Mem. Econometric Soc., Am. Statis. Assn., Am. Econ. Assn. Author: (with M. Nerlove and J.L. Carvalho) Analysis of Economic Time Series: A Synthesis, 1979. Home: 2116 N Craig Ave Altadena CA 91001 Office: California Institute of Technology Pasadena CA 91125

GREVER, JOHN HENRY, historian, educator; b. 's-Hertogenbosch, Netherlands, Sept. 13, 1942; s. Jacobus B.A. and Petronella (van den Thillart) G.; came to U.S., 1963, naturalized, 1969; B.A., Loyola U. of Los Angeles, 1965, M.A., 1967; Ph.D., UCLA, 1973. Lectr. history Loyola Marymount U., Los Angeles, 1971-73, asst. prof., 1973-80, assoc. prof., 1980—, mem. internat. com. on history of parliamentary instns., 1973—. Mem. Town Hall, Los Angeles, 1978-81. Recipient outstanding tchr. award Coll. Liberal Arts, Loyola Marymount U., 1977, 80, entire univ., 1979. Mem. Am. Hist. Assn., AAUP, Phi Alpha Theta (Pi Beta chpt.). Democrat. Contbr. articles to profl. jours. Home: 7140 Ramsgate Ave Los Angeles CA 90045 Office: History Dept Loyola Marymount U Loyola Blvd at W 80th St Los Angeles CA 90045

GREW, PRISCILLA CROSWELL PERKINS, state official; b. Glens Falls, N.Y., Oct. 26, 1940; d. James Croswell and Evangeline Pearl (Beougher) Perkins; B.A. magna cum laude, Bryn Mawr Coll., 1962; Ph.D., U. Calif.-Berkeley, 1967; m. Edward Sturgis Grew, June 14, 1975. Instr. dept. geology Boston Coll., 1967-68, asst. prof., 1968-72; asst. research geologist Inst. Geophysics, UCLA, 1972-77, adj. asst. prof. environ. sci. and engring., 1975-76; vis. asst. prof. dept. geology U. Calif.-Davis, 1973-74; chmn. Calif. State Mining and Geology Bd., Sacramento, 1976-77; exec. sec., editor Lake Powell Research Project, 1971-77; cons., vis. staff mem. Los Alamos Sci. Lab., 1972-77; dir. Calif. Dept. Conservation, Sacramento, 1977-81; mem. Calif. Public Utilities Commn., 1981—; mem. com. on minority participation in earth sci. and mineral engring. U.S. Dept. Interior, 1972-75; chmn. Calif. Geothermal Resources Task Force, 1977, Calif. Geothermal Resources Bd., 1977-81; mem. earthquake studies adv. panel U.S. Geol. Survey, 1979-83, mem. NRC adv. com., 1982—; mem. mineral and energy resources bd. NRC, 1982—; mem. adv. council Gas Research Inst., 1982—. NSF fellow, 1962-66. Fellow Geol. Soc. Am. (com. on geology and pub. policy 1981—); mem. Am. Geophys. Union, AAAS (electorate nominating com. sect. E 1980—), Soc. Mayflower Descs., Nat. Parks and Conservation Assn. (trustee), Nat. Assn. Regulatory Utility Commrs. (com. on gas 1982—), Appalachian Mountain Club. Editor: Lake Powell Research Project Bull., 1973-77. Contbr. articles to profl. jours. Office: Calif Public Utilities Commn 350 McAllister St San Francisco CA 94102

GRIDER, RONALD MYRON, civil engineer; b. Oakland, Calif., Mar. 31, 1928; s. Ernest E. and Alice (Rodney) G.; B.A., Yale U., 1950; M.A., Columbia U., 1951; law student Harvard U., 1951, Stanford U., 1952-54; m. Martha Helen Riggin, Dec. 8, 1964; children—Ronald Ernest, Sherri, Shauna. Right-of-way agt. State of Calif., San Luis Obispo, 1954-62; real estate broker, appraiser, 1963-64; hwy. engr. Colo. Div. of Hwys., Greeley and Alamosa, 1965-69; pres. A-A-A Engring. and Surveying Assos., Alamosa, 1969-71; br. mgr. Garing, Taylor & Assos., Arroyo Grande, Calif., 1971-74; pres. Unltd. Enterprises, Inc., Arroyo Grande, 1974—, Laser Computer Corp., 1982—. Surveyor, Alamosa County, 1970. Mem. ASCE, Nat., Calif. socs. profl. engrs., Calif. Land Surveyors Assn., Am. Congress Surveying and Mapping. Presbyn. Mason. Club: Toastmasters (treas. 1964). Home: PO Box 149 Arroyo Grande CA 93420 Office: 1367 Newport Ave Arroyo Grande CA 93420

GRIEBE, ROGER WILLIAM, mechanical engineer; b. Chgo., June 26, 1943; s. Henry Gregory and Stella Kathrine Griebe; B.S.M.E., Purdue U., 1964, M.S.M.E., 1966, Ph.D., 1968, S.E.P., 1983; m. Shirley Ruth Babcock, Jan. 23, 1965; children—Karen, Diana, Brian. Project engr. atomic energy div. Phillips Petroleum Co., Idaho Falls, Idaho, 1968-70, Idaho Nuclear Corp., Idaho Falls, 1970-71, Aerojet Nuclear Co., Idaho Falls, 1971-72; div. mgr. Energy Inc., Idaho Falls, 1972-79, v.p., 1975-79, sr. v.p., tech. dir., 1979-83; chmn. bd. JBJ Controls, Idaho Falls, 1982-83; pres. Aisling Inc., Idaho Falls, 1983—; affiliate prof. U. Idaho, Idaho Falls Extension. Mem. ASME, Am. Nuclear Soc., Sigma Xi. Home and office: 2151 Craig Ave Idaho Falls ID 83401

GRIERSON, JOHN ROBERT, physician; b. Miles City, Mont., June 29, 1944; s. John and Marjorie Josephine (Neil) G.; B.S., U. Utah, 1966; M.D., U. Oreg., 1970; children—James Bryan, Krista Neil, Dana Lynn. Intern, Hennepin County Gen. Hosp., Mpls., 1970-71; resident in surgery Phoenix Integrated Surg. Residency Program, 1973-77; practice medicine specializing in surgery; cons. VA Hosp., Miles City; med. dir. units 3 and 4, Bechtel Power Co., Colstrip, Mont.; chmn. Custer County Emergency Med. Services Council; mem. staff Rosebud Community Hosp., Forsyth, Mont.; pres. med. staff Holy Rosary Hosp. Med. dir. Custer County chpt. Am. Cancer Soc. Served with M.C., USPHS, 1971-73. Decorated Commendation medal. Diplomate Am. Bd. Surgery. Fellow A.C.S. (exec. com. Mont.-Wyo. chpt.), Southwestern Surg. Congress (Mont. councillor); mem. Mont. Med. Assn., Southeastern Mont. Med. Assn. (v.p.). Republican. Presbyterian. Home: 26 Sunset Dr Box 3146 Miles City MT 59301 Office: 2200 Box Elder St Miles City MT 59301

GRIESINGER, DONALD WILLIAM, educator; b. Los Angeles, Aug. 8, 1932; s. William Fred and Mildred Mae (Strohm) G.; m. Judith Annette Miller, Dec. 27, 1960; children—Kathryn, John. B.S. in Physics, U. So. Calif., 1954; M.S. in Applied Physics, UCLA, 1960; Ph.D. in Psychology, U. Calif., Santa Barbara, 1970. Assoc. scientist Westinghouse Bettis Atomic Power Labs., Pitts., 1958-59; project mgr. Gen. Electric Co. TEMPO, Santa Barbara, Calif., 1962-71; prof. mgmt. Union Coll., Schenectady, N.Y., 1971-79; v.p. ops. Ray Wilson Co., Los Angeles, 1979-82; prof. mgmt. Claremont (Calif.) Grad. Sch., 1982—, chmn. faculty of mgmt. Grad. Mgmt. Ctr., 1983—; cons. in field. Served to lt. USN, 1954-58. Mem. Acad. Mgmt., Phi Beta Kappa, Sigma Xi. Republican. Episcopalian. Contbr. articles to tech. jours. Home: 2230 Edinboro Ave Claremont CA 91711 Office: Claremont Grad School Claremont CA 91711

GRIESON, RONALD EDWARD, economist, consultant, author, lecturer; b. N.Y.C., Mar. 8, 1943; s. Hans Wilhelm and Stella (Brosse) G.; m. Barbara Ann Uchal, Aug. 29, 1970. B.A., Queens U., 1964; M.A., U. Rochester, 1966, Ph.D., 1972. Prof. econs. MIT, 1969-72, CUNY, 1972-74, Columbia U., 1974-79; vis. prof. econs. Princeton U., 1979-80; prof. econs. U. Calif.-Santa Cruz, 1980—; cons. various govt. agys. NSF fellow, 1964; N.Y. State Regents fellow, 1964; Herbert H. Lehman fellow, 1966. Mem. Am. Econs. Assn., Econometric Soc., Western Econs. Assn. Author: Urban Economics; Readings and Analysis, 1972; Public and Urban Economics, 1970; Urban Economics and Housing, 1982. Contbr. articles to profl. jours. Office: Dept Econs U Calif Santa Cruz CA 95064

GRIEVE, HAROLD WALTER, retired interior designer; b. Los Angeles, Feb. 1, 1901; s. Alexander and Maria (Chapman) G.; m. Jetta Goudal, Oct. 11, 1930. Student Los Angeles art schs., 1920-21, Chouinard Sch. Art, 1920-21, Camillo Innocentie, Rome, 1923-24. Art dir. M.P. Studios, 1920-28; interior designer, Los Angeles, now ret. Interior design work includes homes of George Burns, Jack Benny, Bing Crosby, others. Fellow Am. Inst. Interior Designers (life mem., past nat. pres., past local pres.), Acad. of Motion Pictures (founder mem., life mem.), Hist. Soc. So. Calif. Republican. Clubs: Los Angeles Athletic; Beach (Santa Monica, Calif.).

GRIFFEE, NOREEN JOANNE KILEY, home economist; b. Newhall, Calif., Nov. 14, 1938; d. Clifford James and Mary Elizabeth (Kanaly) Kiley; children—Glenn, Daniel. Student U. So. Calif., 1955-57; B.S. in Home Econs., U. Mont., 1961. Food research asst. Schilling div. McCormick & Co., San Francisco, 1961-62, ednl. rep., 1962-63; assoc. home economist McCall Pattern Co., N.Y.C., 1969-70; dir. home econs. and consumer services Calif. Raisin Adv. Bd., Fresno, 1974-81; dir. consumer services Sun-Diamond Growers Calif., San Ramon, 1981—; community resource guest lectr. Calif. State U., Fresno; mem. consumer edn. com. Fresno City Coll.; mem. oral bd. Fresno County CSC. Mem. Am. Home Econs. Assn., Home Economists in Bus., Soc. Nutrition Edn., Inst. Food Technologists, Soc. Consumer Affairs Profls., Kappa Kappa Gamma. Office: 1320 El Capitan Dr San Ramon CA 94583

GRIFFIN, CHARLES ROBERT, accountant; b. Anchorage, Mar. 5, 1943; s. Edwin Stanley and Wanda Mildred (Gelles) G.; B.S. in Acctg. with distinction, San Jose (Calif.) State Coll., 1970; m. Charlotte Ann Godin, Aug. 5, 1967. Sr. accountant Arthur Young & Co., C.P.A.'s, San Jose, 1970-73; propr. Charles R. Griffin, C.P.A., Palmer, Alaska, 1973—; lectr. income tax acctg. Matanuska-Susitna Community Coll., Palmer, fall 1973, spring 1976; treas., life mem. Mat-Su (Miners) Baseball, Inc., 1978—; treas. Alaska Ind. Baseball League, 1980-82. Bd. dirs. Matanuska Valley Little League, 1974; bd. dirs. Alaska State Fair, 1980—, sec., 1981—. Served with AUS, 1961. C.P.A., Alaska, Calif. Mem. Am. Inst. C.P.A.s (sec. 1983—), Alaska Soc. C.P.A.s (continuing profl. edn. com. 1979—), Am. Acctg. Assn., Greater Palmer C. of C. (dir., treas. 1974-77, 80-82), Classic Thunderbird Assn., Classic Thunderbird Club Internat., Alaska State Fair, Valley Hosp. Assn., Alaska Visitors Assn., U.S. Baseball Fedn., Am. Baseball Coaches Assn., Beta Alpha Psi, Beta Gamma Sigma. Clubs: Matanuska Valley Rotary (treas., dir. 1978-79), Elks, Moose. Home: Star Route B Box 7486 Palmer AK 99645 Office: PO Box 670 Palmer AK 99645

GRIFFIN, JAMES EDWARD, JR., land devel. exec.; b. Fall River, Mass., Jan. 27, 1941; s. James Edward and Marion Beatrice (Johnson) G.; A.A. with honors, Napa Coll., 1965; B.S. with honors, Calif. State U., 1967; m. Audie Leigh Kilwy, July 21, 1963. Auditor, Arthur Young & Co., San Francisco, 1967-69, Providence, 1969-71; v.p. fin. R.I. Land Co., Providence, 1971-79; v.p., treas. Moss Land Co., Sacramento, 1979-82; chief fin. officer David Butler Co., Sacramento, 1982—. Served with U.S. Army, 1959-62. Mem. Am. Inst. C.P.A.s, Calif., Soc. C.P.A.s, Beta Alpha Psi, Beta Gamma Sigma. Home: 8468 Menke Way Citrus Heights CA 95610 Office: 1234 H St Sacramento CA 95814

GRIFFIN, JAMES RAY, research and devel. technician; b. Vancouver, Wash., Mar. 30, 1943; s. William Farrel and Esther Eileen (Joy) G.; A.A., Riverside City Coll., 1976; student Calif. State U., Long Beach, 1978; grad. Cleve. Inst. Electricity, 1971; m. Deanna Rae Turek, Nov. 23, 1962; children—Scott, JoAnn, Paul, Ellen. Research and devel. technician Rockwell Internat., Anaheim, Calif., 1962-69; asso. test engr. Calif. Computer Products, Anaheim, 1969-77; research and devel. technician McDonnell Douglas Corp., Long Beach, Calif., 1977—. Mem. So. Calif. Profl. Engring. Assn. Democrat. Home: 1142 Azalea Circle Corona CA 91720 Office: 3855 Lakewood Blvd Long Beach CA 90846

GRIFFIN, JOHN LAWRENCE, martial arts and Oriental exercise instr., writer, lectr.; b. Butler, Pa., Mar. 16, 1942; s. William and Rose G.; student Wakayama U., Japan, 1964-65; B.A., Calif. State U., Fresno, 1971; postgrad. World U., Ojai, Calif.; pvt. studies psychology and parapsychology Dr. L.J. Bendit, in anthropology Dr. M. d'Obrenovic, FRAI; m. Ann Avery (div.); 1 dau., Erin Marie. Ednl. cons. Laucks Found., 1970-73; instr. Oriental exercise and martial arts, public and pvt. instns., 1965—; mem. faculty phys. edn. U. Calif., Santa Barbara, 1974-78, head coach karate team, 1974-79; lectr. in psychology and parapsychology U. Calif. Extension, 1971-73; lectr. Oriental culture. People-to-People cultural exchange student to Japan, 1964-65; vice chair Tobu City (Japan)-Santa Barbara Sister City Com. Mem. Screenwriters Assn. Santa Barbara, Goju Karate Soc. Am. Contbr. articles on Asian cultural arts and parapsychology to periodicals.

GRIFFIN, JOHN RANDALL, optometrist, educator; b. Decatur, Ala., Jan. 28, 1934; s. Horace Auburn and Jane Ruth (Powers) G.; m. Carol Ann Schmidgall, Oct. 25, 1974; children—Lisa, Angela, Scott. B.S., U. Calif., 1951, M.Opt., 1958, O.D., 1958; M.S.Ed., U. So. Calif., 1976. Field epidemiologist USPHS, Washington, 1962-63; optometrist So. Calif. Permanente Med. Group, Los Angeles, 1963-69; mem. faculty So. Calif. Coll. Optometry, 1969—, asst. prof., 1969-73, assoc. prof., 1973—; mem. optometric adv. bd. Calif. Dept. Motor Vehicles, 1981—. Served to 1st lt. U.S. Army, 1958-62. Mem. Am. Acad. Optometry (diplomate in binocular vision and perception, chmn. sect. binocular vision and perception 1981—), Am. Optometric Assn. (aux. award for research in optokinetic nystagmus 1978), Optometric Extension Program (research award on Van Orcen Star 1978). Republican. Author: Binocular Anomalies, 1976, 2d edit., 1982; (with Howard Walton) Dyslexia Determination Test, 1981; (with Helene Fatt) Genetics of Primary Eye Care Practitioners, 1983; contbg. author Optometric Monthly, 1975—; editor: (Cline and Hofstetter) Dictionary of Visual Science, 3d edit., 1980; contbr. numerous articles to profl. jours. Office: 2001 Associated Rd Fullerton CA 92631

GRIFFIN, ROBERT EUGENE, orthodontist; b. Paris, Tex., Aug. 17, 1938; s. Percy E. and Louise Edwina (Thornal) G.; student U. Colo., 1956-59; D.D.S., Northwestern U., 1963; certificate orthodontics Columbia, 1968; m. Mary Christine Klose, Jan. 13, 1968 (div.); children—John Robert, Christine Louise; m. 2d, Joan Cochran, May 10, 1980. Intern, dept. oral surgery Georgetown U., Washington, 1963-64; practice dentistry specializing in orthodontics, San Rafael, Calif., 1968—; asst. clin. instr. U. Pacific, 1969-71, asso. prof. dept. orthodontics, 1979—. Served to lt. USN, 1966-68. Diplomate Am. Bd. Orthodontics. Presbyterian. Home: 280 Bayview Ave Belvedere CA 94920

GRIFFITH, ARNOLD KOONS, mathematician; b. Providence, July 1, 1942; s. John Ramsbottom and Barbara (Koons) G.; B.A. in Math., Swarthmore Coll., 1964; Ph.D. in Math., MIT, 1970; m. Patricia Ann Martino, July 10, 1971. Research asst. Brown U., 1961; IBM research asst. MIT, 1964-70, research asso., 1970-71; sr. mem. tech. staff Info. Internat., Inc., Culver City, Calif., 1971-76, mgr. advanced applications GRAFIX I systems, 1976-78, dir. O.C.R. devel., 1978-81; cons., 1981—. Mem. ACM, IEEE, Pattern Recognition Soc., Phi Beta Kappa, Sigma Xi. Club: M.I.T. of So. Calif. Contbr. articles to profl. jours. and confs.

GRIFFITH, CARL DAVID, civil engineer; b. Hill City, Kans., Mar. 1, 1937; s. Wilfred Eugene and Veda May (Jackson) G.; m. Tillie Sargoza Luna, Aug. 12, 1967 (div.). B.S. in Civil Engring. summa cum laude, West Coast U., 1978; M.S. in Civil Engring. and Water Resources, U. So. Calif., 1980, M.S. in Engring. Mgmt., 1983. Profl. engr., Calif. Chief draftsman Bear Creek Mining Co., Spokane, Wash., 1959-64; right-of-way technician So. Calif. Edison Co., Los Angeles, 1964-65; engr. treatment plant design and spl. projects sect. Metropolitan Water Dist. So. Calif., Los Angeles, 1965—, com. chmn. employees assn. Sustaining mem. Calif. Republican party. Served with USAF, 1957-58. Mem. ASCE, Am. Water Works Assn., Nat. Mgmt. Assn., Metropolitan Water Dist. Mgmt. Club. Club: Masons. Home: PO Box 4324 Sylmar CA 91342 Office: PO Box 54153 Los Angeles CA 90054

GRIFFITH, DANIEL BOYD, bus. exec.; b. Albuquerque, Aug. 30, 1934; s. Reese Humphrey and Faye (Boyd) G.; B.S., Oreg. State U., 1956; m. Patricia Dawn Mosley, July 26, 1956; 1 dau., Leann Dawn. Pres., Burns Bros., Inc., Portland, Oreg., 1959-61, 69—; mgr. Ga. Pacific Corp., 1961-69; dir. Nat. Tire Corp. Bd. dirs. Oreg. Contemporary Theater, Portland Rotary Found., Tax Payers for a Better Economy. Served with USAF, 1956-59. Mem. Aircraft Owners and Pilots Assn., Portland C. of C. (dir. 1981—), Phi Gamma Delta. Republican. Presbyterian. Clubs: Lake Oswego Country, Mountain Park Racquet, Rotary. Office: 621 SE Union Ave Portland OR 97214

GRIFFITH, DARLENE INEZ, investment and real estate fin. planner; b. South Gate, Calif., June 14, 1938; d. John Joseph and Sarah Inez (Ritchey) G.; student Compton Jr. Coll., 1958-59, Cerritos Jr. Coll., 1960-61, Rio Hondo Jr. Coll., 1966-67, U. Calif.-Berkeley, 1972-74, also investment courses; m. John Baca Lopez, Oct. 15, 1966; children—David Richard Haberbush, John Robert Haberbush. Profl. dancer, choreographer, Hollywood, Calif., 1954-62; mgr., trainer Weaver Airline Personnel Sch., Kansas City, Mo., 1962-67; owner, mgr. co., Whittier, Calif., 1967—; pvt. practice real estate fin. planner, bus. computer counselor, Whittier, 1976—; sec. Los Angeles Bus. Mktg. Group; tchr. Downey (Calif.) High Sch., 1972-76. Grad. Realtors Inst., cert. bus. counselor. Mem. Whittier Dist. Bd. Realtors, Los Angeles Bus. Mktg. Assn. (pres. 1982-83), Calif. Assn. Realtors, Nat. Assn. Realtors, Realtors Nat. Mktg. Inst., Real Estate Securities and Syndication Inst., Nat. Council Exchangors, Internat. Exchangors Assn. Home: 14130 Caswood St Whittier CA 90602 Office: 13217 E Whittier Blvd Whittier CA 90602

GRIFFITH, JOHN ALFRED, psychologist; b. Redlands, Calif., Sept. 29, 1939; s. John E. and Emily B. G.; student Hanover Coll., 1958-60; A.B., San Diego State Coll., 1966; M.Ed., U. Hawaii, 1969, Ph.D., 1973. Field assessment officer U. Hawaii Peace Corps Tng. Center, Hilo, 1967-69, counseling psychologist Counseling and Testing Center, Honolulu, 1970-72; psychologist U.S. Army Support Command Hawaii, Honolulu, 1972-74, alcohol and drug abuse program specialist, 1974-76; pvt. practice psychology, Honolulu, 1976—; instr. U. Hawaii, Pepperdine U.; cons. Hawaii Dept. Edn. Mem. State of Hawaii Commn. on Drug Abuse and Controlled Substances, 1973—; mem. City and County of Honolulu Oahu Substance Abuse Adv. Bd., 1975-76. Lic. psychologist, Hawaii; certified mental health care provider Nat. Register of Health Service Providers in Psychology; lic. instr. Effectiveness Tng. Assos. Mem. Am., Western, Hawaii (pres. 1979) psychol. assns., Am., Hawaii personnel and guidance assns., Nat. Council on Family Relations, Assn. Labor-Mgmt. Adminstrs. and Cons., Am. Soc. Tng. and Devel., Honolulu Marathon Assn. Clubs: Hawaii Masters Track, Honolulu, Kailua Racquet. Home: 210 N Kalaheo Ave Kailua HI 96734 Office: 45 Aulike St Kailua HI 96734

GRIFFITH, MARY CORNWALL, lawyer; b. Denver, Nov. 29, 1915; d. Noah Hayden and Ida (Lindsey) G.; B.A., U. Colo., 1938, J.D., 1941. Bar: Colo. 1941; partner with John L. Griffith, Denver, 1941—. Mem. Colo. Com. on Vet. Affairs, 1947-52; mem. Judicial Council State of Colo., 1957-58; mem. Colo. Commn. Status Women, 1965-75; trustee 1st Bapt. Ch. Denver, 1947-50; exec. bd. Legal Aid Denver, 1951-70; women's advisory com. def. manpower U.S. Dept. Labor, 1951-53; mem. bd. ethics city employees City of Denver, 1971—. Served to comdr., USNR, 1943-46. Mem. Colo., Denver (trustee 1955-57) bar assns.; Am. Legion (vice-comdr. 1956-57), Delta Delta Delta, Delta Sigma Rho. Democrat. Baptist. Clubs: Altrusa (2d v.p. 1970-73), Women's of Denver, Daus. of Nile, P.E.O. Home: 1471 High St Denver CO 80218 Office: 1465 High St Denver CO 80218

GRIFFITH, WANDA ILENE, sociology educator; b. Chelan, Wash., Nov. 17, 1950; d. Evan E. and Ada B. (Moreland) G. B.A., Wash. State U., 1973, M.A., 1974, Ph.D., 1977. Asst. prof. sociology Wash. State U., 1977-78, U. Colo.-Denver, 1978—. NSF grantee, 1978. Mem. Am.

Sociol. Assn., Southwest Social Sci. Assn., Pacific Sociol. Assn., Western Social Sci. Assn. Contbr. articles to profl. jours. Home: 2440 Olive Denver CO 80207 Office: Dept of Sociology U CO 1100 14th St Denver CO 80202

GRIFFITH, WILLIAM ALEXANDER, mining co. exec.; b. Sioux Falls, S.D., Mar. 28, 1922; s. James William and Adeline Mae (Reid) G.; B.S. in Metall. Engring., S.D. Sch. Mines and Tech., 1947; M.S. in Metallurgy, M.I.T., 1950; Mineral Dressing Engr. (hon.), Mont. Coll. Mineral Sci. and Tech., 1971; m. Gratia Frances Hannan, Jan. 27, 1949; children—Georgeanne Reid, James William, Wade Andrew. With N.J. Zinc Co., 1949-57, chief milling and maintenance, 1956-57; metallurgist Rare Metals Corp. Am., Tuba City, Ariz., 1957-58; dir. research and devel. Phelps Dodge Corp., Morrenci, Ariz., 1958-68; with Hecla Mining Co., Wallace, Idaho, 1968—, exec. v.p., 1978, pres., 1979—; pres., dir. Chester Mining Co.; dir. Granduc Mines Ltd., Consol. Silver Corp. Trustee Western Regional Council. Served with USNR, 1943-46. Mem. AIME (Gaudin award 1977, Richards award 1981), Am. Mining Congress (dir.), Idaho Mining Assn. (2d v.p.), Silver Inst. (chmn.), Sigma Tau, Theta Tau. Republican. Clubs: Elks, Gyro. Office: PO Box 320 Wallace ID 83873

GRIFFITHS, BARBARA LORRAINE, psychologist; b. Glendale, Calif., July 15, 1927; d. David William and Mabel Augusta (Gaarder) G.; B.A., U. Calif.-Riverside, 1972; M.S., Calif. State U.-Los Angeles, 1976; Ph.D., Calif. Grad. Inst., Los Angeles; m. Dale Elmo Rumbaugh, Mar. 13, 1948; 1 son, David Wynn; m. Knute Flint, Oct. 13, 1963. Researcher, alcoholism counselor Kaiser Permanente, Los Angeles, 1976-82; editor newsletter Region IX Child Abuse Resource Project, Calif. State U., Los Angeles, 1976-82; pvt. practice psychotherapy, Los Angeles, 1979—; therapist psychiat. unit Coldwater Canyon Hosp., North Hollywood, Calif., 1981—. Mem. Am. Psychol. Assn., Western Psychol. Assn., Calif. State Psychol. Assn. Editor, Directions newsletter Region IX Resource Ctr. for Children and Youth Services, 1982—. Home: 3002 Hyperion Ave Los Angeles CA 90027 Office: 5300 Hollywood Blvd Los Angeles CA 90027

GRIFFITHS, DONALD JAMES, logistics engr.; b. S.I., Nov. 16, 1929; s. Joseph and Teresa Ann (Horenberg) G.; m. Emily Margaret Chrzczonowski, Apr. 25, 1947; children—Eve, Monica, Mark, Donna, Jennifer, Rodger. B.S., NYU, 1952; postgrad. Columbia U., 1955; M.B.A. N.Mex. Highlands U., 1979. Commd. U.S. Navy, 1950, advanced through grades to comdr., 1969, ret., 1980; dir. material mgmt. U. N.Mex. Hosp., Albuquerque, 1980-81; sr. logistics analyst Tracor Internat., Albuquerque, 1981—. Decorated Legion of Merit, Joint Service Commendation medal with oak leaf cluster. Mem. Soc. Logistics Engrs., Alpha Kappa Psi. Republican. Roman Catholic. Clubs: Kiwanis, Kirtland AFB.

GRIFFITHS, DONALD MORGAN, artist; b. N.Y.C., Jan. 16, 1935; s. Harry Donald and Viola Louise (Kostyal) G.; student Coll. of William and Mary, 1957-58, Art Center Sch., 1958-60; B.A., Sacramento State Coll., 1967, M.A., 1970; m. Alynne Cassetty; children—Robin, Jeffrey, Donald. Ednl. TV art dir. WVEC-TV, Hampton, VA. 1957; freelance illustrator, 1958-67; tchr., art dir. Rio Linda Union Sch. Dist., Sacramento, 1967-74; tchr. of workshops for tchrs. Calif. State U., Sacramento, 1970-74; one-man shows: Hollywood (Calif.) Art Gallery, 1962; Kinzels Gallery, Sacramento, 1968, Am. Artists Gallery, Santa Cruz, Calif., 1973; Collectors Cove Galleries, Atlanta, 1975; Phipps Plaza, Atlanta, 1975; Tyrone Sq., St. Petersburg, Fla., 1976, Galerie La Mouffe, Paris, 1978; numerous group shows; represented in public and pvt. permanent collections; owner artist Griffiths Gallery, Fair Oaks, Calif., 1976—; police artist. Served with USMC, 1952-55. Recipient Gold Medal award, World Art Show, 1975, others. Mem. Phi Delta Kappa. Democrat. Episcopalian. Contbr. articles in field to profl. jours.; illustrator various mags. including Field and Stream, Gun Digest, Quarter Horse Jour., Quarter Horse of the Pacific Coast, others; mng. editor Quarter Horse of the Pacific Coast, 1967-68; illustrator: Handbook of Hand Gunning (Paul B. Weston), 1968; Administration of Criminal Justice (Paul B. Weston), 1967. Home: 6016 Sunrise Vista Dr Apt 160 Citrus Heights CA 95610 Office: 6720 Madison Ave Fair Oaks CA 95628

GRIFFITHS, LYN ALLEN, physical disability specialist, counselor; b. Wichita, Kans., May 11, 1943; d. Robert A. and Marjorie (Combs) Allen; m. Lynn Christopher Griffiths, June 18, 1965. Student Wellesley Coll., 1961-62; B.A., Colo. Coll., 1965; postgrad. U. Colo.-Colorado Springs, 1978—. Tchr. French, Colorado Springs Sch., 1963-64; dir. neonate auditory screening program Penrose Hosp., Colorado Springs, 1970-72; juvenile probation counselor City of Colorado Springs, 1972-76; mng. ptnr. Allen, Griffiths & Assocs., Colorado Springs, 1977—; mgr. Diet Ctr. N.W., Colorado Springs, 1982—. Vol. Transcribers for Visually Impaired of Pike's Peak Region. Named vol. of yr., Colorado Springs Sertoma Club, 1975. Mem. Am. Personnel and Guidance Assn., Nat. Rehab. Assn., Colo. Rehab. Assn., AAUW, NOW, Phi Beta Kappa, Pi Gamma Mu, Pi Alpha Alpha. Composer 21 popular songs. Office: Allen Griffiths and Assocs 1705 Culebra Pl Colorado Springs CO 80907

GRIFFITHS, LYNN CHRISTOPHER, economics educator; b. Fremont, Ohio, Feb. 27, 1940; s. Harry George and Betty (Miller) G.; m. Lyn Allen, June 18, 1965; children—Molly, Sarah. B.A., Colo. Coll., 1962; postgrad. U. Chgo., 1962-63; Ph.D., U. Colo., 1970. Instr. econs. U. No. Colo., Greeley, 1966-67; from instr. to assoc. prof. econs. Colo. Coll., Colorado Springs, 1967—, chmn. dept. econs. and bus., 1981—; ptnr. Allen-Griffiths & Assocs., Colorado Springs, 1976—. Bd. dirs., exec. com. Pikes Peak United Way, 1972-76, Pikes Peak Legal Services, 1972-76; treas. Community Vol. Ctr., 1974-76. Recipient Sidney G. Winter prize, 1974, 82. Mem. Am. Econ. Assn., Western Econ. Assn. Staff writer, Jour. Mktg., 1969—; bi-weekly columnist Gazette-Telegraph, Colorado Springs, 1982—; contbr. articles to profl. jours. Office: Colo Coll Colorado Springs CO 80903

GRIGG, JAMES WELLINGTON, insurance company executive; b. Portland, Oreg., Mar. 30, 1951; s. Ronald Arvin and Audrey Marie (Kirby) G.; student Mt. Hood Community Coll., 1969-73, Portland State U., 1977-79; m. Cheryl Lynette Johnson, Feb. 27, 1971. From stockboy to asst. mgr. R.A. Grocery Inc., Portland, 1965-71; head clk. Kienows Grocery, Portland, 1971; supply adminstr. Oreg. Mil. Dept., Portland, 1971-73; mem. ins. sales and mgmt. staff Standard Ins. Co., Portland, 1973-81, Oreg. Group of Conn. Mut. Cos., Portland, 1981—. Bd. dirs. Multnomah County chpt. Am. Cancer Soc., 1978-80, vice chmn. public edn., 1978-79; bd. dirs. Found. of Hope, 1979—. Served with Army N.G., 1969-75. Recipient various ins. awards. Mem. Nat. Assn. Life Underwriters, Oreg. Life Underwriters, Portland Life Underwriters, Rose Festival Assn. Portland. Republican. Club: Lions. Home: 3915 SE Oak St Portland OR 97214 Office: 800 Orbanco Tower 1001 SW 5th Ave Portland OR 97204

GRIGGS, APRIL ROSINA, speech pathologist; b. Ventura, Calif., Apr. 20, 1946; d. Robert Dean and Margarite Terrill (Lyon) Smeltz; student Ventura Coll., 1964-66; B.A., Calif. State U., Fresno, 1968, M.A., 1971; postgrad. The Citadel, 1972-73, San Diego State U., 1977-78; 1 son, Jason. Grad. asst. Calif. State U., 1969-70; speech and lang. pathologist Fresno (Calif.) City Schs., 1969-70, Charleston (S.C.) Speech and Hearing Clinic, 1970-72; speech and lang. pathologist, supr. Charleston County Pub. Schs., 1972-76; speech and lang. pathologist, instr. Southwestern Coll., Chula Vista, Calif., 1976—; pvt. practice speech and lang. pathology, Chula Vista, 1978—. Lic. speech pathologist, Calif., S.C. Mem. Am., Calif. speech and hearing assns. Democrat. Office: 900 Otay Lakes Rd Chula Vista CA 92010 also 3d Ave Suite 103 Chula Vista CA 92011

GRIGGS, BILLY D., building trades educator, real estate agent, contractor; b. Clovis, N.Mex., Nov. 12, 1930; s. Dan and Ida Bell G.; m. LaVerne Bridges, Oct. 14, 1955; children—Alva Dan, Billye Dee. B.A. in Bus., Eastern N.Mex. U., 1953, M.Vocat. Edn., 1977. Cert. vocat. edn.; lic. contractor, real estate agt., N.Mex. Gen. contractor, oil co., 1955-71; real estate agt., Hobbs, N.Mex., 1981—; building trades instr. Eastern N.Mex. U., Clovis, 1971-79; building trades instr. N.Mex. Jr. Coll., Hobbs, 1981—. Sponsor Vocat.-Indsl. Clubs Am. Clubs. Served with U.S. Army, 1953-55. Mem. Am. Vocat. Assn., Home Builders Assn., N.Mex. Vocat. Assn. (Tchr. of Yr. 1973, 82), N.Mex. Trades and Indsl. Assn. Democrat. Baptist. Home: 2027 Adobe Hobbs NM 88240 Office: New Mex Jr Coll Lovington Hwy Hobbs NM 88240

GRIGSBY, CARL EDWARD, aerospace engr.; b. Newport News, Va., July 28, 1926; s. Roy Carlos and Nellie Virginia (Hynson) G.; B.S.M.E., N.C. State U., 1947; m. Audrey Jean Moore, Nov. 18, 1950; children—David Carl, Carolyn Elizabeth, James Edward, Cynthia Lynne. Research scientist Langley Research Center, NASA, 1947-54; aero. engr. Lockheed Corp., Van Nuys, Calif., 1954-56; dept. mgr. Aeronutronic Div., Ford Aerospace & Communication Corp., Newport Beach, Calif., 1956-80; cons. CG Research Assos., Tustin, Calif., 1980—. Mem. AIAA, Am. Def. Preparedness Assn. Baptist. Address: 17531 Chatham Dr Tustin CA 92680

GRIGSBY, JEFFERSON EUGENE, JR., educator, artist; b. Greensboro, N.C., Oct. 17, 1918; s. Jefferson Eugene and Purry (Dixon) G.; B.A., Morehouse Coll., 1938; student J.C. Smith U., 1934-35, Am. Artists Sch., 1938-39; M.A., Ohio State U., 1940; Ph.D., N.Y. U., 1963; D.F.A. (hon.), Phila. Coll. Art, 1965; postgrad. summers Ariz. State U., 1947, 49, Columbia U., 1950, 51; m. Rosalyn Thomasena Marshall, June 12, 1943; children—Jefferson Eugene, Marshall Cephas. Artist-in-residence Johnson C. Smith U., Charlotte, N.C., 1940-41, Bethune-Cookman Coll., Daytona Beach, Fla., 1941-42; head art dept. Carver High Sch., Phoenix, 1946-54; tchr. Phoenix Union High, 1954-58, head art dept., 1958-66; prof. Ariz. State U., Tempe, 1966—; tchr. Children's Creative Center, Brussels World Fair, 1958; co-dir. S.W. region 2d World Festival of Black and African Arts and Culture, Lagos, Nigeria, 1977; chmn. Four Corners Art Edn. Conf., Scottsdale, Ariz., 1982; one-man shows: Wirshem Gallery, Luxembourg City, 1944, Morehouse Coll., Atlanta, 1967, J.C. Smith U., 1967, Central State Coll., Wilberforce, Ohio, 1967; group shows include: Balt. Mus., 1940, Atlanta U., 1938, Ariz. State Fair, 1952, Am. Negro Expn., Chgo., 1940, Black Artists/South, Huntsville Mus., 1979; represented in permanent collections: Mint Mus., Charlotte, N.C., Nat. U. Ghana, Cape Castle, Tex. So. U. Bd. dirs. Phoenix Art Mus., Phoenix Arts Coming Together, Phoenix Opportunities Industrialization Center; judge Young Talent in Okla., 1973; mem. visual arts adjudication panel Art Recognition and Talent Search, Nat. Found. Advancement Arts. Served with AUS, 1942-45. Recipient 75th anniversary Merit medallion U. Ariz., 1960, also disting. research award, 1982-83; 25th Anniverary medallion Nat. Gallery Art, 1966; E.C. Morra award of excellence Nat. Conf. Artists, 1977; Disting. Research award Ariz. State U. Grad. Coll., 1983; elected Danforth Asso., 1974. Fellow African Studies Assn.; mem. Nat. Art Edn. Assn. (v.p. Pacific region 1972-74, co-chmn. minority concerns com. 1978, mem. Grigsby award com. 1980, recipient 1st Grigsby award for contbn. to art edn. 1980, editor com. on minority Concerns newsletter), Ariz. Art Edn. Assn., Ariz. Artists Guild, Am. Assn. Aesthetics, Internat. Soc. Edn. through Art, NEA, Coll. Art Assn., African Heritage Assn., Alpha Phi Alpha. Author: Art and Ethics, 1977. Cons. editor African Arts Mag., 1967-82; contbg. editor. School Arts mag. Home: 1117 N 9th St Phoenix AZ 85006 Office: Art Dept Ariz State U Tempe AZ 85281

GRIJALVA, CARLOS VINCENT, JR., physiol. psychologist; b. Nogales, Ariz., Nov. 3, 1950; s. Carlos Vincente and Lillian (Acuna) G.; student U. Ariz., 1968-69, B.A., 1972; student Santa Barbara City Coll., 1969, Rio Hondo Coll., 1970; M.A., Ariz. State U., 1974, Ph.D., 1977; m. Lynne Cecile Knowles, June 9, 1972. Postdoctoral fellow Center for Ulcer Research and Edn., UCLA, postdoctoral fellow dept. psychology, 1977-80, staff research psychologist, 1980-82, asst. prof. psychology, mem. Brain Research Inst., assoc. Ctr. for Ulcer Research and Edn., 1982—; cons. various profl. jours., research supervision U. Ariz. gen. resident scholar, 1969; Baird scholar, 1969-70; Ford Found. grad. fellow, 1973-77; recipient individual nat. research service award, 1978. Mem. AAAS, Am. Psychol. Assn., Soc. for Neurosci., Am. Assn. Study Obesity, Western Psychol. Assn. Editorial asst. spl. supplement jour. issue, 1980; contbr. articles to med. and physiol. jours. Home: 17151-9 Roscoe Blvd Northridge CA 91325 Office: Dept Psychology UCLA Los Angeles CA 90024

GRIKSCHEIT, GARY MICHAEL, marketing consultant, educator; b. Detroit, Mar. 4, 1940; s. Henry William and Phyllis Marjorie (Rotnour) G.; m. Penelope Ann Steele, June 26, 1965; children—Alyssa Ann, Tracy Cannon. A.B. cum laude, Harvard U., 1963; M.B.A., U. Mich., 1966; Ph.D., Mich. State U., 1971. Spl. agt. Prudential Ins. Co. Am., Detroit, 1963-70; assoc. McKinsey & Co., Cleve, 1970-71; asst. prof. mktg. U. Utah, Salt Lake City, 1971-74, assoc. prof., 1974-80, prof., chmn. dept. mktg., adj. prof. mgmt. Coll. Bus., 1980—; chmn. bd. trustees Utah Mgmt. Inst., 1974-76; cons. in field. Trustee, Utah Am. Revolution Bicentennial Found., 1974-76. NCR Co. research grantee, Dayton, Ohio, 1971. Mem. Am. Mktg. Assn., So. Mktg. Assn., Southwestern Mktg. Assn., Assn. Consumer Research, Beta Gamma Sigma, Phi Eta Sigma. Club: Ft. Douglas (Salt Lake City). Author: Handbook of Selling, 1981; contbr. numerous articles to profl. jours. Home: 2865 Sherwood Dr Salt Lake City UT 84108 Office: Dept Marketing U Utah Salt Lake City UT 84112

GRILLY, EDWARD ROGERS, physicist; b. Cleve., Dec. 30, 1917; s. Charles B. and Julia (Varady) G.; B.A., Ohio State U., 1940, Ph.D., 1944; postgrad. U. Wis., 1940-41; m. Mary Witholter, Dec. 14, 1942 (dec. Sept. 1971); children—David, Janice; m. 2d, Juliamarie Andreen Langham, Feb. 1, 1973. Research scientist Carbide and Carbon Chems. Corp., Oak Ridge, 1944-45; asst. prof. chemistry U. N.H., Durham, 1946-47; mem. staff U. Calif. Los Alamos Sci. Lab., 1947-80; mem. N.Mex. Ho. of Reps., 1967-70. Mem. Los Alamos County Republican Central Com., 1957—, N.Mex. State Central Com., 1961—; mem. Los Alamos County Council, 1976-78. Mem. Am. Phys. Soc. Kiwanian. Club: Los Alamos Golf and Ski. Research in transport properties of gases at low temperatures; thermodynamic properties of liquid and solid helium, hydrogen, neon, nitrogen, oxygen; development of targets for laser fusion. Home: 705 43d St Los Alamos NM 87544

GRIMBLE, MAXINE E. BLANSON, home economics educator; b. Shreveport, La., Dec. 14, 1929; d. Ernest Turner and Zetha (Jefferson) Blanson; m. Willie Lee Grimble. B.S. in Home Econs., So. U., 1951; M.Ed., Va. State U., 1972; Ed.S., N.E. La. U., 1977. Home econs. tchr. Waverly High Sch., Winnsboro, La., 1951-70, Central High Sch., Delhi, La., 1970-74, Winnsboro (La.) High Sch., 1974-78; tchr. Von Tobel Jr. High Sch., Las Vegas, Nev., 1979—, also dept. head. Office: Von Tobel Jr High School 2436 N Pecos St Las Vegas NV 89030

GRIMES, DAVID LEE, retail consultant; b. Dayton, Ohio, Apr. 30, 1917; s. Clarence Leon and Kathleen (Fudge) G.; B.M.E., U. Dayton, 1939; m. Esther Louise Samp, Apr. 17, 1943; children—David Lee, Ronald Alan, Steven Michael. Pres., Narmco Industries, Inc., San Diego, 1953-60; corporate v.p. Whittaker Corp., Los Angeles 1960-70; pres. MLI, Inc., San Diego, 1970-75; v.p. mfg. Bubble Machine, San Diego, 1975-77; dir., cons. Ektelon, San Diego, 1978-80, cons., 1981—; lectr. bus. adminstrn. San Diego State U., Nat. U., San Diego; lectr. NATO, Rome, Nancy, France, London; mem. USAF Sci. Adv. Bd. Served with USAF, 1941-53. Registered profl. engr., Ohio. Mem. Inst. Aero. Scis., Air Force Assn. Presbyterian. Author reports and papers in field. Home and office: 916 El Mac Pl San Diego CA 92106

GRIMES, DONALD WILBURN, water scientist; b. Maysville, Okla., July 28, 1932; s. Thomas Oliver and Georgia Ester (DeGraffenreid) G.; m. Julia Annette, Nov. 23, 1957; children—Janette Ann, Sandra Lynn, Debra Gail. B.S. in Soil Sci., Okla. State U., 1954, M.S. in Soil Sci., 1956; Ph.D. in Soil Sci., Iowa State U., 1966. Soil Scientist Soil Conservation Service, Kans., 1956; irrigation agronomist Kans. State U., 1957-61; agronomist research assoc. Iowa State U., 1962-66; asst. water scientist U. Calif.-Parlier, 1966-71, assoc. scientist, 1971-77, water scientist, 1977—; cons. energy mgmt. firm. Numerous grants on water soil plant relations. Mem. Am. Soc. Agronomy, Soil Sci. Soc. Am., Crop Sci. Soc. Am., Internat. Soc. Soil Sci. Democrat. Roman Catholic. Club: Kiwanis Internat. Contbr. numerous articles to profl. jours.

GRIMES, JOSEPH EDWARD, computer science educator; b. Bloomington, Ill., Sept. 28, 1941; s. Edward A. and Mary Clara (Kleeman) G.; m. Mary Rae Tures, Aug. 8, 1964; children—Joseph, Therese, Christine, Michael, Matthew, Mark. B.A. in Physics, St. Ambrose Coll., 1963; M.S. in Math., Ill. State U., 1968; Ph.D. in Stats., Iowa State U., 1973. Tchr., coach Central Cath. High Sch., Bloomington, Ill., 1963-66; civil engr. McLean County Highway Dept., Bloomington, 1966-68; instr. math. Iowa State U., Ames, 1968-73; prof. computer sci. Calif. Poly. State U., San Luis Obispo, 1973—; researcher NASA-Ames Research Ctr., Moffett Field, Calif., 1974—; cons. County of San Luis Obispo, 1974-75. Office: Dept Computer Sci and Stats Calif Poly State U San Luis Obispo CA 93401

GRIMES, NANCY ANNE, pharmacist; b. Roseburg, Oreg., July 13, 1942, d. Caryl Gerald and Anne Isabell (Gorrie) Van Valzah; B.S. in Gen. Sci., Oreg. State U., 1964, B.A.-B.S. in Pharmacy, 1966; m. Jessee Robert Grimes, July 3, 1967; children—Ryan Colin, Laurie Anne. Pharmacist, Moore & Ripley Drug, Hermiston, Oreg., 1966-69, Payless Drug, Corvallis, Oreg., 1969-70, Albany Gen. Hosp., 1970, Bi Mart, Corvallis, 1970-72, Albany, 1972-73; relief pharmacist, 1976—, Albright & Raw, Corvallis, 1978—. Mem. Am., Oreg. pharm. assns., Acad. Pharmacy Practice. Democrat. Presbyterian. Home: 2219 SW Quinney Dr Pendleton OR 97801

GRIMM, LARRY LEON, school psychologist; b. Goshen, Ind., Aug. 16, 1950; s. Warren Arden and Elizabeth Ann (Rassi) G.; m. Ann Mae Nelson, July 16, 1977. B.S. in Elem. Edn., No. Ariz. U., 1975, M.A., 1977, Ed.D. in Ednl. Psychology, 1983. Cert. sch. psychologist, cert. elem. tchr. Ariz. Tchr. elem. sch. Page (Ariz.) Unified Dist., 1975-76; grad. asst. Coll. Edn., No. Ariz. U., Flagstaff, 1976; tchr. elem. sch. Litchfield Sch. Dist., Litchfield Park, Ariz., 1976-80; grad. assoc. dept. ednl. psychology No. Ariz. U., Flagstaff, 1980-81; sch. psychologist intern Peoria (Ariz.) Unified Dist., 1981-82; adj. faculty Grand Canyon Coll., Phoenix, 1982; sch. psychologist Child Study Services, Prescott (Ariz.) Unified Sch. Dist., 1982—, cons. in field. Mem. Am. Psychol. Assn., Ariz. Assn. Sch. Psychologists, Nat. Assn. Sch. Psychologists, Phi Delta Kappa. Republican. Contbr. articles to profl. jours. Home: 660 Dragonfly Dr Prescott AZ 86301 Office: PO Box 1231 Prescott AZ 86302

GRIMMICK, HENRY WILLIAM, engineering executive; b. Troy, N.Y., July 1, 1945; s. Henry and Margaret Jane (Guerineau) G.; m. Dolores Irene (Mashuta), June 11, 1966; 1 son, Henry Todd. B.S.E.E., San Diego State U. Engring. aide Naval Underseas Research and Devel. Ctr., San Diego, 1971-72; design engr. Teledyne Ryan Aero., 1972-73, product engring. mgr. Burroughs Corp., 1973-80; dir. product engring., dir. assembly, test and finish Silicon Systems, Inc., Tustin, Calif., 1980—. Active Constituency Council for Sen. S.I. Hayakawa. Served with USN, 1964-68. Decorated Nat. Def. Service Ribbon, Vietnam Service medal with two bronze stars; Republic of Vietnam Campaign Medal. Mem. Tau Beta Pi, Phi Kappa Phi. Home: 22736 Barlovento Mission Viejo CA 92692 Office: 14351 Myford Rd Tustin CA 92680

GRIMSHAW, DONALD HARVEY, logistics engineer; b. Turtlecreek Twp., Ohio, June 22, 1923; s. Percy and Louella Rose (Harvey) G.; m. Jean Dolores Mrazek, Nov. 18, 1950; children—Randall, Kimberley, Stuart, Paul, Heather, Matthew. A.B. in Govt., Calif. State U.-Los Angeles, 1959; postgrad. in pub. adminstrn. U. So. Calif., 1960-62. Research asst. Hughes Aircraft, Culver City, Calif., 1951-54, Douglas Aircraft, Santa Monica, Calif., 1954-57; research engr. Northrop Corp., Hawthorne, Calif., 1957-62; research writer Calif. Dept. Water Resources, Los Angeles, 1962-65; tech. staff specialist TRW Def. Systems Group, Redondo Beach, Calif., 1965—. Mem. exec. com. Calif., Los Angeles County and (assembly dist. name?) 53d Assembly dist. Republican Party, 1978—; Rep. nominee for U.S. Rep. from Calif.'s 31st Dist., 1978, 80. Served with USN, World War II; Korea. Mem. Soc. Logistics Engrs. (mng. editor SPECTRUM 1966-68), AIAA, Soc. Tech. Communications, U.S. Naval Inst., VFW. Office: TRW 1 Space Park Redondo Beach CA 90278

GRINBLATT, MARK STEVEN, business educator, researcher; Detroit, Nov. 14, 1956; s. Joseph Eli and Edith (Lodzitch) G. A.B. in Math. and Econs. with high distinction, U. Mich., 1977; M.A. in Econs., Yale U., 1978, M. Phil., 1979, Ph.D. in Econs., 1982. Acting asst. prof. fin. UCLA Grad. Sch. Mgmt., Los Angeles, 1981-82, asst. prof. fin. 1982—. Office: UCLA Grad Sch Mgmt Los Angeles CA 90024

GRINELS, SAMUEL CHAPMAN, advertising agency executive; b. Richmond, Va., Sept. 26, 1944; m. Frances Jean Boggiano, Apr. 20, 1975; children—Jennifer, Cara. Student Old Dominion Tech. Inst., 1962-65; B.S. in Fin., San Jose State U., 1972; M.B.A., U. So. Calif., 1973. Mktg. officer Bank of Am., San Francisco, 1973-75; nat. sales mgr. Sentry Tech., Santa Cruz, Calif., 1975-76; dir. mktg. Community Bank of San Jose (Calif.), 1976-78; account exec. Rauh Good & Darlo, Los Gatos, Calif., 1978-79; pres. Grinels & Assos., San Jose, 1979—; instr. DeAnza Coll., Cupertino, Calif. Served with USMCR, 1965-71. Mem. Am. Advt. Fedn., San Jose Advt. Club (pres.), Beta Gamma Sigma. Republican. Presbyterian. Office: 97 E Brokaw Rd Suite 120 San Jose CA 95112

GRINNELL, WILLIAM JOSEPH, packaging sales engr.; b. Duluth, Minn., Aug. 18, 1920; s. Raymond W. and Margaret Mary (Lyman) G.; student Seattle U., 1955-57; m. Jane Anne Oos, May 27, 1950; 1 dau., Laura Grinnell Zoroya. Group engr. packaging Boeing Co., Seattle, 1939-62; engring. supr. packaging and material handling Northrop Corp., Hawthorne, Calif., 1962-70; gen. mgr. purchasing Dub Harris Corp., 1970-73; packaging sales engr. Geo. B. Woodcock & Co., Inglewood, Calif., 1973—; pres. Coast Systems Corp. Bd. dirs. Packaging Handling Distbn. Edn. Found. Named So. Calif. Man of Year, Soc. Packaging and Handling Engrs., 1964. Mem. Soc. Packaging and Handling Engrs. (nat. v.p. 1970-73, nat. exec. v.p. 1974-75), Western

Packaging Assn., Am. Def. Preparedness Assn., Los Angeles Council Egnrs. and Scientists (dir. 1972, v.p. 1973-74, treas. 1975-76), Inst. for Advancement Engring. (treas. 1977-78), Packaging Inst. U.S.A. Home: 2601 E Victoria #201 Compton CA 90220 Office: 9021 Aviation Blvd Inglewood CA 90301

GRISHAM, JAMES DAVID, civil engineer; b. Glendale, Calif., Nov. 9, 1954; s. James William and Dorothy Cathrine (Barish) G; m. Pamela Jean Walter, Sept. 5, 1980; children—Jessica Ann. B.S. in Engring., Calif. State U.-Fullerton, 1977. Registered profl. engr., Calif. Design engr. Baine Engring Inc., Santa Ana, Calif., 1977-80; design, cons. engr. David A. Boyle Engring, Santa Ana, 1980-83; assoc. civil engr. United Water Conservation Dist., Santa Paula, Calif., 1982—. Mem. Am. Water Works Assn., ASCE. Democrat. Office: 333 W Harvard Blvd PO Box 432 Santa Paula CA 93060

GRISMORE, ROGER, physicist; b. Ann Arbor, Mich., July 12, 1924; s. Grover Cleveland and May Aileen (White) G.; B.S., U. Mich., 1947, M.S., 1948, Ph.D., 1957; B.S. in Computer Sci., Coleman Coll., 1979; m. Marilynn Ann McNinch, Sept. 15, 1950; 1 dau., Carol Ann. Asst. physicist Argonne (Ill.) Nat. Lab., 1956-61, asso. physicist, 1961-62; asso. prof. physics Lehigh U., Bethlehem, Pa., 1962-67; specialist in physics Scripps Instn. Oceanography, La Jolla, Calif., 1967-71, 75-78; prof. physics Ind. State U., Terre Haute, 1971-74; systems analyst Potomac Research, Inc., San Diego, 1978-79; sr. scientist Jaycor, San Diego, 1979—. Served with USN, 1944-46. Mem. Am. Phys. Soc., Am. Geophys. Union, N.Y. Acad. Scis., Sigma Xi. Republican. Contbr. articles in field to profl. jours. Home: 442 Woodland Hills Dr Escondido CA 92025 Office: 11011 Torreyana Rd San Diego CA 92138

GRISWOLD, DANIEL HALSEY, engineering geologist; b. Colorado Springs, Colo., Jan. 10, 1909; s. Clyde Tyler and Grace (Halsey) G.; Geol. Engr., Colo. Sch. Mines, 1930; m. Maud Walton Mays, June 2, 1931; children—Miriam Griswold Miller, Julia Douglas (Mrs. Jude W. Barry). Geophysicist, asst. geologist U.S. Smelting Refining & Mining Co., 1930-31; asst. engr. C.T. Griswold, Mining Engr., 1931-32; lessee Magnolia Petroleum Co., 1932-33; instrumentman Mid Rio Grande Conservancy Dist., 1933; jr. topog. engr. Conservation br. U.S. Geol. Survey, 1933-35; jr. agrl. engr. Soil Conservation Service, U.S. Dept. Agr. (N.Mex.), 1935-38, asst. agrl. engr. (Utah), 1938-40, asso. geologist (N.Mex.), 1941-46, soil conservationist, 1946-49, geologist (N.Mex.), 1949-56, Portland, Oreg., 1956-69; geologist ground water div. Oreg. Engr.'s Office, 1969; sr. geologist Found. Scis., Inc., Portland, 1969-72, assoc. 1972—. Served to lt. col. C.E., AUS, 1941-45. Recipient 20 year service award Soil Conservation Service, Dept. Agr., 1956; 35 years service as fed. employee, 1969. Registered profl. engr., land surveyor, N.Mex.; registered profl. engr., Oreg., Ga.; registered engring. geologist, Oreg., Calif. Fellow Geol. Soc. Am.; mem. Soil Conservation Soc. Am., Geol. Soc. Oregon County, Res. Officers Assn., Assn. Engring. Geologists, AIME, Am. Inst. Profl. Geologists, Soc. Am. Mil. Engrs., Alpha Tau Omega, Theta Tau. Mem. Evangelical Covenant Ch. Mason. Home: 6656 SW Miles Ct Portland OR 97223 Office: 1630 SW Morrison St Portland OR 97205

GRISWOLD-SHUTE, MARY TABOR, data processing systems analyst; b. Greenfield, Mass., July 13, 1950; d. Lyman William and Patricia Marie (Henry) G.; m. Alan Shute, May 20, 1978; 1 son, Ian Lycolm. With Nev. Blue Shield, Reno, 1971—, sr. programmer, 1978-79, data processing mgr., 1979-82, systems analyst, 1982—; RPGII programming instr. Truckee Meadows Community Coll. Mem. Assn. Systems Mgmt. (profl.), Mensa. Republican. Episcopalian. Home: 3130 Comstock Dr Reno NV 89512 Office: 4600 Kietzke Ln Suite 250 Reno NV 89503

GRIVAS, THEODORE, historian, educator; b. Cambridge, Mass., July 11, 1922; s. John T. and Angelina (Jahalidis) G.; A.B. magna cum laude, U. So. Calif., 1952, A.M., 1953, Ph.D., 1958; children—Deborah L., Melanie C., T. Gregory. Instr. history U. So. Calif., 1956-57; asst. prof. history Calif. State U., Fresno, 1957-62; prof., 1962-72, chmn. dept. history and div. social scis., 1962-72; prof. history Calif. State U. at Sonoma, 1972—; cons. HEW, 1965-69, Calif. Dept. Edn., 1970-75, Western Assn. Schs. and Colls., 1975—. Served with USNR, 1942-45; PTO. John Randolph Haynes fellow, 1957; Am. Philos. Soc. fellow, 1963. Mem. Am. Hist. Assn., Western History Assn., Western Writers Assn., Phi Beta Kappa, Phi Alpha Theta, Phi Kappa Phi, Pi Gamma Mu, Phi Delta Kappa. Author: History of the Los Angeles YMCA, 1957; History of Western Civilization Handbook, 1958; California's Military Government 1846-50, 1963. Contbr. articles to profl. publs. Home: 3854 Montecito Ave Santa Rosa CA 95404 Office: History Dept Calif State U 1801 E Cotati Ave Rohnert Park CA 94928

GRIVETTI, LOUIS EVAN, nutrition and geography educator; b. Billings, Mont., Sept. 13, 1938; s. Rex. M. and Blanche I. (Carpenter) G.; m. Georgette Mayerakis; 1 dau., Joanna Elene. A.B., U. Calif.-Berkeley, 1960, M.A., 1962; Ph.D., U. Calif.-Davis, 1976. Research asst. Vanderbilt U., Cairo, 1964-70; adminstrv. asst. Meharry Med. Coll. Gaborone, Botswana, 1973-75; asst. prof. nutrition and geography, U. Calif.-Davis, 1976—; chmn. grad. group in nutrition, 1983—. Served with USPHS, 1962-64. Mem. Botswana Soc., Assn. Am. Geographers, Soc. Nutrition Edn., Asian Geographers, West Coast Nutritional Anthropologists (past pres., v.p., dir.), Am. Inst. Nutrition. Author: Food: The Gift of Osiris, 1977 (Nutrition Founds. Europe, N.Am. award); contbr. articles to profl. jours. Office: Dept Nutrition Univ Calif Davis CA 95616

GRIZZELL, L(LOYD) EARL, JR., radio and television music writer and producer, vocalist; b. McMinnville, Tenn., Aug. 17, 1951; s. Lloyd E. and Joyce E. G.; m. Janet Susan Dill, July 30, 1977; 1 dau., Kara Michelle. A.A., Bakersfield Coll., 1971; B.A. in Music Edn., Calif. State U.-Fresno, 1975. Secondary teaching credential in music. Nat. sales mgr. L & L Broadcast Prodns., 1975-77; western regional sales mgr. O. C. Prodns., 1978-81; pres. producer Grizzell Prodns., Los Angeles, 1981—, also writer; comml. advt. cons. Recipient Best in the West advt. award radio category, 1978; Addy award, radio, 1978; Gold award Sacramento Ad Club, 1980; award Ad Club Ventura County, 1982. Mem. Soc. for Preservation and Encouragement of Barbar Shop Quartet Singing Am., Phi Mu Alpha Sinfonia. Mem. Church of Christ. Office: 6033 W Century Blvd Suite 400 Los Angeles CA 90045

GRIZZLE, CLAUDE OLIVER, physician; b. Campbell, Calif., Aug. 2, 1926; s. Claude and Jeannette (Oliver) G.; student San Jose State Coll., 1946-48; A.B., Stanford, 1949, M.D., 1954; M.S. Neurosurgery, U. Minn., 1959; m. M. Katherine Loden, Mar. 15, 1952; children—Geoffrey Allen, Stephen McRae, Gregory James. Intern, So. Pacific Gen. Hosp., San Francisco, 1953-54; fellow Mayo Found., 1954-58; practice medicine specializing in neurol. surgery, Cheyenne, Wyo., 1958—; chief neurosurg. dept. DePaul Hosp., Cheyenne, 1962-64. Meml. Hosp., 1961-65. Lectr., U. Wyo., 1961—; asso. clin. prof. surgery U. Colo. Med. Center, Denver, 1973—; neurosurg. cons. VA Center, Cheyenne, 1961—; F.E. Warren AFB, Wyo., 1961—; dir. Wyo. Regional Med. Program for Heart Disease, Cancer and Stroke, 1966-73; profl. staff Western Interstate Commn. Higher Edn.; dir. Mountain States Regional Med. Program. Mem. adjudication com. Wyo. Blue Shield, 1959—; mem. Gov.'s Adv. Com. for Comprehensive Health Wyo.; mem. Gov.'s Adv. Com. for Drug Abuse and Control, 1969-70. Bd. dirs. Wyo. Heart Assn.; mem. com. of 50, profl. adv. bd. Epilepsy Found. Am. Served with USNR, 1944-45. Recipient Borden Found. award Stanford, 1953. Diplomate Am. Bd. Neurol. Surgery. Fellow A.C.S., Royal Soc. Health (London); mem. Am. Assn. Neurol. Surgeons, Harvey Cushing Soc., Congress Neurol. Surgeons, AMA, Wyo. Med. Soc., Laramie County Med. Soc., World Fedn. Neurosurg. Socs., Cheyenne C. of C. (med. center com.). Nu Sigma Nu, Tau Delta Phi, Beta Beta Beta. Contbr. articles to profl. jours. Home: 3303 Forest Dr Cheyenne WY 82001 Office: 3100 Henderson Dr Cheyenne WY 82001

GROAH, LINDA KAY, nursing adminstr.; b. Cedar Rapids, Iowa, Oct. 5, 1942; d. Joseph David and Irma Josephine (Zitek) Rozek; B.A., St. Mary's Coll., 1978; student St. Luke's Sch. Nursing, 1960-63; m. Patrick Andrew Groah, Mar. 20, 1975; 1 dau., Kimberly; stepchildren—Nadine, Maureen, Patrick, Marcus. Staff nurse, head nurse U. Iowa, Iowa City, 1963-67; asst. dir. nursing service Michael Reese Hosp., Chgo., 1967-73; dir. operating room Med. Center Central Ga., Macon, 1973-74; nursing dir. operating room U. Calif. Med. Center, San Francisco, 1974—, also asst. dir. hosps. and clins.; clin. instr. U. Calif., San Francisco, 1975—, dir. postgrad. course, 1976—; supr. nurse adv. bd. Dart Industries, 1969-71; mem. nurse panel Am. Cynamid Co., 1969—; mem. Ednl. Material Project Appraisal Panel, Nat. Library of Medicine, 1977—; bd. dirs. Operating Rm. Research Inst., Farnwood, N.J., 1978—; lect. and cons. operating rm. mgmt. and staff devel. Active Center for Democratic Study. Mem. Assn. Operating Rm. Nurses (nominating com. 1980-84), 1980-82), Am. Nurses Assn., Profl. Resources Orgn. of Calif. (dir.), Nat. League Nursing. Author: Operating Room Nursing: the Perioperative Role; contbr. articles in field to profl. jours. Home: 5 Mateo Dr Tiburon CA 94920 Office: Room M 423 B 505 Parnassus St San Francisco CA 94143

GROBE, WILLIAM HOWARD, ret. state ofcl.; b. Winnett, Mont., Feb. 10, 1916; s. Wesley H. and Leota H. (Smith) G.; student Simpson Coll., Indianola, Iowa, 1934-37, Mo. State U., 1937-39, Mont. State Tchrs. Coll., 1940-41; B.S., Mont. State. U., 1947-48; B.S. in Health and Phys. Edn., Miss. Coll., 1951; postgrad. U. Nev., summers 1958-62; m. Jane Singleton, May 7, 1967; stepchildren—John C. Singleton (dec.), Linda G. Moore; children from previous marriage—William H., Robert. Clk. N.P. Ry., Livingston, Mont., 1946-47; student and line coach Mont. State U., Bozeman, 1947-48; coach, phys. edn. tchr. Edgar (Mont.) High sch., 1948-51; athletic dir., coach, phys. edn. tchr., guidance counselor Bridger (Mont.) High Sch., 1951-57, Lassen Union High Sch. Dist., Herlong, Calif., 1957-62; supt. recreation and phys. edn. Calif. Conservation Center, State Dept. Corrections, Susanville, 1962-75, ret. Served with USAAF, 1941-45. Mem. Calif. Employees Assn., Nat. Recreation Assn., Calif. Correctional Assn. Mason. Home: 3485 Lakeside Dr Apt 300 Reno NV 89509

GROBSTEIN, MICHAEL JAY, accountant; b. Chgo., Dec. 24, 1941; s. Henry M. and Mildred (Maniloff) G.; B.S., Calif. State U., 1968; m. Barrie Rona Selman, Aug. 10, 1963; children—Marla, Marc. Jr. acct. Lampert, Rosenthal & Co., Los Angeles, 1964-65; staff acct. Singer, Lewak & Co., Beverly Hills, Calif., 1965-67; proprietor Michael J. Grobstein & Co., Sherman Oaks, Calif., 1967-69; pres. West Coast Home Loan, Sherman Oaks, 1981—; ptnr. Grobstein, Blankstein, Goldman & Co., Sherman Oaks, 1969—; organizer, dir., chmn. audit com. West Coast Bank, 1978—. Bd. dirs. Internat. Coll., 1974-77, Ryokan Coll., 1978—, Inst. for Arteriosclerosis Research, 1977-81, Temple Valley Beth Shalom, 1973-75. Mem. Am. Inst. C.P.A.s, Calif. Soc. C.P.A.s. Office: 15233 Ventura Blvd Sherman Oaks CA 91403

GRODINS, SYLVIA VIOLA, interior designer; b. DeKalb, Ill., May 7, 1916; d. Andrew and Henrika (Anderson) Johnson; m. Fred S. Grodins March 28, 1942. Student No. Ill. U., DeKalb, 1934-35; grad. Augustana Sch. Nursing, 1939; student N.Y. Sch. Interior Design, 1954. Registered nurse Chgo. hosps., 1939-41; interior designer Ponds, Evanston, Ill., 1948-56, Interior Design Inc., Chgo. 1956-58; owner Creative Studios, Chgo., 1958—, Palos Verdes Estates, Calif., 1968—. Mem. Am. Inst. Designers. Contbr. articles to newspapers, profl. publs. Home: 26 Chuckwagon Rd Rolling Hills CA 90274 Office: 2325 Palos Verdes Dr W Palos Verdes Estates CA 90274 also 200 E Walton St Chicago IL 60611

GRODY, MARK STEPHEN, public relations executive; b. Milw., Jan. 1, 1938; s. Ray and Betty (Rothstein) G.; m. Susan Tellem, Mar. 25, 1978; children—Laura, Tori, John, Daniel. B.S. in Journalism, U. Wis., 1960. Mem. pub. relations staff Gen. Motors Corp., Detroit, Buffalo, Los Angeles, Atlanta, 1961-74; v.p. Nat. Alliance Businessmen, Washington, 1973-74; v.p. Carl Terzian Assocs., Los Angeles, 1974-75; chmn. Grody/Tellem Communications, Inc., Los Angeles, 1975—; lectr. pub. relations. Recipient Lulu award, Los Angeles Advt. Women, 1980. Mem. Pub. Relations Soc. Am. (Prism award 1980), Publicity Club. Los Angeles (Pro awards 1979-82). Club: Nat. Press. Office: Grody/Tellem Communications Inc 9100 S Sepulveda Blvd Los Angeles CA 90045

GROENEKAMP, WILLIAM ADOLF, mgmt. cons.; b. Bklyn., Oct. 14, 1933; s. William and Christine (Meyer) G.; B.A. in Econs., Principia Coll., Elsah, Ill., 1955; M.B.A., U. So. Calif., 1963; m. Helen Elizabeth Haines, July 13, 1957; children—William Gregory, Heidi Lynn, Christine Gail. Compensation adminstr. Rand Corp., Santa Monica, Calif., 1960-68; employment mgr. Christian Sci. Ch. and Christian Sci. Monitor, Boston, 1968-69; corp. personnel dir. Informatics, Canoga Park, Calif., 1969-70; cons. mgmt., Los Angeles, 1970-72, 73—; dir. personnel and adminstrv. services Quotron Systems, Inc., Los Angeles, 1972-73; mem. adv. com. and vol. cons. Second Careers Program. Mem. Assn. Personnel Adminstrn., Personnel and Indsl. Relations Assn., Am. Compensation Assn., Los Angeles C. of C. Home: 2922 Oakhurst Ave Los Angeles CA 90034 Office: 8929 Wilshire Blvd Suite 412 Beverly Hills CA 90211

GROFER, EDWARD (TED) JOSEPH, publisher, marketing communications corporation executive, newspaper consultant; b. Cin., Sept. 20, 1934; s. Edward Joseph and Margaret Mary (McGinley) G.; m. Mary Procissi, Aug. 18, 1962; children—Catherine Mary, Laura Marie, Daniel McGinley. B.A., U. Cin., 1957; M.A., U. Iowa, 1959. Asst. dir. pub. relations Champion Paper, Hamilton, Ohio, 1959-61; mktg. dir. The Jam Handy Orgn., Detroit, 1961-69; dir. promotion and research Detroit News, 1969-74; v.p., pub. Desert Sun, Palm Springs, Calif., 1974-80; pres. Ted Grofer Assocs., Inc., Palm Springs, 1980—; pub. Desert Community Newspapers, Inc., Palm Desert, Calif., 1981—; v.p. Desert Mailing Services, Inc., Cathedral City, Calif., 1982—; cons. to several major newspapers; compiler of Newspaper Market Analysis Report, 1980—. Bd. dirs. Palm Springs chpt. Am. Cancer Soc. Mem. Calif. Newspaper Pubs. Assn. (bd. dirs. 1978-80), Internat. Newspaper Promotion Assn. (bd. dirs. 1972-74), Palm Springs C. of C. (pres. 1979-80), Pi Kappa Alpha (nat. v.p. alumni affairs), Pub. Relations Soc. Am. (accredited). Republican. Roman Catholic. Clubs: The Springs (Rancho Mirage); Palm Springs. Home: 584 Fern Canyon Dr Palm Springs CA 92262 Office: Ted Grofer Assocs Inc PO Drawer 1863 Palm Springs CA 92263

GROFF, REGIS F., state senator, educational administrator; b. Monmouth, Ill., Apr. 8, 1935; B.S., Western Ill. U.; M.A., U. Denver, 1972; postgrad. J.F. Kennedy Sch. Govt., Harvard U., 1980; m. Ada Brooks; children—Peter, Traci. Tchr. history East High Sch., Denver; public sch. adminstr. since 1977; former owner Custodial Services Co.; mem. Colo. Senate, 1974—, asst. minority floor leader 51st Assembly, minority floor leader 52d and 53d Assemblies, mem. edn. and judiciary coms. 54th Gen. Assembly. Bd. dirs. NE Denver Mental Health Clinic; mem. Colo. Jud. Adv. Commn. Served with USAF, 1953-57. Mem. Denver Classroom Tchrs. Assn., NEA, Nat. Conf. State Legislatures (bd. dirs.), Nat. State Legislators Leaders Found. (bd. dirs.), ACLU (bd. dirs.) Democrat. Methodist. Office: 2079 Albion St Denver CO 80207

GROGAN, STANLEY JOSEPH, JR., educator, cons.; b. N.Y.C., Jan. 14, 1925; s. Stanley Joseph and Marie (Di Giorgio) G.; A.A., Am. U., 1949, B.S., 1950, M.A., 1955; M.S., Calif. State Coll., Hayward, 1973; Ed.D., Nat. Christian U., 1974; m. Mary Margaret Skroch, Sept. 20, 1954; 1 dau., Mary Maureen. Personnel asst., recruitment asst. CIA, Washington, 1954-56; asst. prof. air sci. U. Calif. at Berkeley, 1963-64, Oakland Tech. Adult Sch., Chabot Coll., 1964-70, Oakland Unified Sch. Dist., 1964—, Hayward Unified Sch. Dist., 1965-68; prof. Nat. Christian U., 1975—, Nat. U. Grad. Studies, Belize, 1975—; pres. SJG Enterprises, Inc., cons., 1967—. Asst. dir. Nat. Ednl. Film Festival, 1971. Pub. relations cons., 1963—. Bd. dirs. We T.I.P., Inc., 1974, Calif. Vets. Coalition, 1978. Served with AUS, 1945, to lt. col. USAFR, 1948-76; col. Calif. State Mil. Res. Decorated Air medal with oak leaf cluster; recipient citation Korea, 1963. Named Ky. col., 1970. Mem. Aviation Space Writers Assn., Nat. Rifle Assn. (life), Am. Def. Preparedness Assn. (life), Assn. Profl. Emergency Planners, Night Fighter Assn. (nat. publicity chmn. 1967), Internat. Platform Assn. (lectr.), Air Force Assn., Res. Officers Assn., Phi Delta Kappa. Clubs: Marines Meml., Presidio officers, Toastmasters. Contbr. articles to profl. jours. and newspapers. Home: 2585 Moraga Dr Pinole CA 94564

GROHMAN, ROBERT T., business executive; b. 1924; student S.D. State Coll., U. Nebr., U. Calif., Davis; married. Gen. mgr. weaving ops. Duplex, 1946-57; gen. mgr. ops. Internat. Playtex Corp., 1957-69; pres. BVD Co., 1969-74; v.p. parent co., pres. internat group Levi Strauss & Co., 1974—, exec. v.p., chief operating officer, from 1976, now pres., chief exec. officer, also dir. Address: Levi Strauss & Co 1155 Battery St San Francisco CA 94106

GROLL, MARY FRANCES GRABNER, state ofcl.; b. Boise, Idaho, Dec. 18, 1935; d. Kenneth McCoy and Frances Marian (Gallet) Grabner; A.A., Boise State U., 1956; B.A., U. Idaho, 1958; M.A., St. Joseph Coll., 1968; M.A. in Communications, U. Denver, 1971; 1 dau., Stacie Susan. With CIA, Washington, 1958-59, Boeing Co., Seattle, 1960-63; affirmative action officer Idaho Personnel Commn., Boise, 1972-82, also sr. personnel analyst State of Idaho; cons. and tng. on affirmative action; personnel mgr. Idaho Dept. Law Enforcement, 1982—. Legis. attache Idaho State Legislature, 1972; bd. dirs., sec. Unitarian Fellowship, 1972-75; chmn. personnel bd. Silver Sage council Girl Scout U.S.A., 1980-83; mem. personnel bd. Idaho Planned Parenthood Assn., 1980-83; mem. Idaho Gov.'s Task Force on Volunteerism, 1980-82. Mem. Internat. Personnel Mgmt. Assn. (assessment council), Am. Soc. Personnel Adminstrn., Am. Assn. for Affirmative Action, Am. Humanist Assn., Internat. Humanist and Ethical Union, Phi Beta Kappa, Pi Beta Phi, Mensa. Democrat. Home: 1409 W Fort St Boise ID 83702 Office: Idaho Dept Law Enforcement PO Box 55 Boise ID 83707

GROLL, RICHARD PENN, accountant; b. Los Angeles, May 1, 1935; s. Oscar and Anne (Penn) G.; m. Judy Ann Weintraub, Sept. 7, 1958; children—Scott, Cindy, Stephanie. B.S. in Acctg., UCLA, 1959; M.B.T., U. So. Calif., 1975. C.P.A., Calif. Staff acct. Finkel & Finkel, Beverly Hills, Calif., 1957-60; Sain & Snyder, Beverly Hills, 1960-62; prin. Richard P. Groll, C.P.A., Los Angeles, 1962-66; ptnr. Wachbrit & Groll, C.P.A.s, Huntington Park, Calif., 1966-79; prin. Wachbrit, Groll & Freedman Accountancy Corp., Beverly Hills, 1979—. Served with USNR, 1954-62. Mem. Am. Inst. C.P.A.s, Calif. Soc. C.P.A.s. Democrat. Club: West Valley Amateur Radio (San Fernando Valley).

GROLLMAN, THOMAS BIRD, orthopedic surgeon; b. Los Angeles, Nov. 8, 1939; s. Julius Harry and Alice Carol (Greenlee) G.; B.A. magna cum laude, Occidental Coll., 1961; M.D., UCLA, 1965; m. Sachiko Kobayashi, July 1, 1972; children—Kiyoshi Mac Cowan, Jay Satoshi. Intern, U. Md. Hosp., Balt., 1965-66; resident in surgery Queens Med. Center, Honolulu, 1969-70; resident in orthopedic surgery U. Calif., San Francisco, U. Hawaii, 1970-73; practice medicine specializing in orthopedic surgery Kauai Med. Group, Lihue, Hawaii, 1973—, also dir.; physician Kauai High Sch., 1974-76; chief of surgery G.K. Wilcox Hosp., 1979-81, chief of staff, 1981-83. Served with Peace Corps, 1966-69: Africa, Ceylon. Diplomate Am. Bd. Orthopedic Surgery. Mem. Am. Acad. Orthopedic Surgeons, Hawaii Orthopedic Assn. (pres. 1978-79), Western Orthopedic Assn. (sec. Hawaii chpt. 1982-83), Kauai County Med. Assn. (v.p. 1983). Home: PO Box 432 Lawai HI 96765 Office: 3420 Kuhio Hwy Lihua HI 96766

GRONER, PAUL STEPHEN, elec. engr.; b. Binghamton, N.Y., May 23, 1937; s. David and Ruth (Sugarman) G.; m. Mildred Jean Ayscue, Sept. 30, 1967; children—Carl Louis, Daniel Jonathan. student M.I.T., 1954-56; B.E.E., Poly. Inst. Bklyn., 1962; postgrad. N.C. State U., 1963-64. Engr., Amperex, L.I., N.Y., 1958-59, technician Sylvania Research Lab., Bayside, N.Y., 1959-61; engr. Bulova Watch Co., 1961; engring. supr. Corning Glass Works, N.Y.C., Raleigh, N.C., 1962-67; engr. Raytheon Computer, Santa Ana, Calif., 1967-69; circuit design group head Hughes Aircraft, Fullerton, 1969-73; mgr. circuit design and advance tech. Varian Data Machines, Sperry-Univac, Irvine, Calif., 1973-82; pres. Creative Silicon, Inc., 1982—; sect. mgr. Computer Consoles Inc., Irvine, 1982—; sci. tchr., N.Y.C., 1962. Served with U.S. Army, 1956-58. Mem. IEEE. Contbr. articles to profl. jours. Patentee in field. Home: 2139 N Ross St Santa Ana CA 92706 Office: 15 Marconi St Irvine CA 92714

GROSE, THOMAS LUCIUS TROWBRIDGE, geologist, educator; b. Evanston, Ill., Dec. 5, 1924; s. Clyde LeClare and Carolyn (Trowbridge) G.; m. Barbara Ann Clark, June 10, 1947; children—Clark Trowbridge, Kathryn. Student, U. Ariz., 1942-44, 46-47; B.S., U. Wash., 1948, M.S., 1949; Ph.D., Stanford U., 1955. Cert. geologist, Calif. Ranger, naturalist Yosemite and Crater Lake Nat. Parks, 1944, 47; petroleum exploration geologist Texaco, Inc., Denver, 1949-52; asst. to assoc. prof. Colo. Coll., Colorado Springs, 1955-64; prof. geology Colo. Sch. Mines, Golden, 1964—; cons. geologist; researcher U.S. Geol. Survey, Nev. Bur. Mines and Geology. Served with USNR, 1944-46; PTO. NSF grantee, 1961-62, 74-77; Office Naval Research grantee, 1974-76; NASA grantee, 1969-70; U.S. Geol. Survey grantee, 1979-82. Fellow Geol. Soc. Am.; mem. Am. Geophys. Union, Am. Assn. Petroleum Geologists, Soc. Econ. Geologists, Colo. Sci. Soc., Soc. Mining Engrs., Rocky Mountain Assn. Geologists. Republican. Club: Explorers. Contbr. articles to prof. jours. Home: 2001 Washington Circle Golden CO 80401 Office: Dept Geology Colo Sch Mines Golden CO 80401

GROSECLOSE, JAY C., civil engineer, consultant; b. Roswell, N.Mex., Aug. 10, 1951; s. J.C. and V. Faye (Owen) G.; m. Earlene Sue Clay, May 28, 1977. B.S.C.E., N.Mex. State U., 1974; student Kans. U., 1978-80. Registered profl. engr., Mo., N.Mex. Project engr. Black & Veatch Cons. Engrs., Kansas City, Mo., 1974-80; project engr., mgr. Scanlon & Assocs. Inc., Santa Fe, 1980-82; staff profl. engr. N.Mex. Interstate Stream Commn., Santa Fe, 1982—. Ofcl. Kansas City Baptist Assn. Youth Basketball League, 1976-80; deacon First Bapt. Ch. Santa Fe, sec.-treas., 1982; pres. Santa Fe chpt. Gideons Internat. Mem. ASCE, Am. Water Works Assn., Engrs. Club Kansas City. Democrat. Home: 120 Calle Don Jose Santa Fe NM 87501 Office: NMex Interstate Stream Commn State Capitol Bataan Bldg Santa Fe NM 87501

GROSFIELD, EVELYNN YBARRA, educator; b. Santa Paula, Calif., Nov. 13, 1955; d. Marcelino Sanchez and Minnie Genevieve (Rodriguez)

Ybarra; A.A. in Liberal Arts, Ventura Coll., 1970; B.A., U. Calif., Santa Barbara, 1973; postgrad. Calif. State U., 1974-75; m. Robert Grosfield, Aug. 24, 1974; 1 dau., Elizabeth. Tchr., Fillmore Unified Sch. Dist., Ventura, Calif., 1973—; owner, pub. Lollipop Publs., Ventura, 1980—; newspaper columnist Lollipop Corner-Just for Kids. Mem. AAUW, Calif. Tchrs. Assn., Soc. Children's Book Writers, Ventura C. of C., Bus. and Profl. Women's Club. Democrat. Roman Catholic. Author booklets: How To Write A Book Report, 1980; Cookbook for Kids, 1982. Office: Lollipop Publs PO Box 6726 Ventura CA 93006

GROSFIELD, ROBERT GERALD, gas co. exec.; b. Ecorse, Mich., Oct. 14, 1943; s. Bert F. and Geraldine (Scott) G.; student Ventura Coll., 1968-70; B.A. in History and Geography, Calif. State U., Northridge, 1972; m. Evelynn Joyce Ybarra, Aug. 24, 1974; 1 dau., Elizabeth. Crew mgr. So. Calif. Gas Co., Santa Barbara, 1974—; free lance cartographer and historian, 1972—; substitute tchr. Ventura Unified Sch. Dist., 1970-72. Served with USAF, 1965-71. Mem. Ventura County Hist. Soc., Santa Barbara Friends of Library, Am. Def. Preparedness Assn., Nat. Rifle Assn. Republican. Roman Catholic. Editor: How to Write a Book Report. Office: PO Box 6726 Ventura CA 93006

GROSKOPF, DORIS MARIE, trucking co. exec.; b. Thief River Falls, Minn., Jan. 8, 1924; d. Ernest Norman and Minnie (Tommerdahl) Rude; student public schs., Crookston, Minn.; m. Charles Joseph Groskopf, Feb. 20, 1944; children—Ronald Stewart, Charlene Ann, Barbara Ann. Sec., U.S. Air Force Washington, 1942-43; teller Bank of Am., Sonoma, Calif., 1943-44; with Groskopf-Weider Trucking Co., Inc. and G-W Tank Lines, Inc., Sonoma, 1944—, sec.-treas., dir., 1956—, chief exec. officer, 1960—; partner Groskopf-Weider Leasing Co., 1946—; expert witness for public utilities comm. State of Calif. rate hearings, 1979-80. Mem. Am. Field Service. Republican. Lutheran. Clubs: Sonoma Valley Bus. and Profl. Women's (pres. 1953-54), Soroptimist, Sonoma Nat. Women's Golf. Address: 1761 Denmark St Sonoma CA 95476

GROSS, BERTRAM MYRON, educator, writer; b. Phila., Dec. 25, 1912; s. Samuel and Regina Fisher (Glass) G.; m. Nora Faine, Aug. 11, 1938; m. Kusum J. Singh, Mar. 10, 1979; children—David, Larry, Samuel, Theodore. B.A., U. Pa., 1933, M.A., 1935. Reporter We the People, 1937; researcher U.S. Housing Authority, 1938-41; staff dir. Senate Small Bus. Com., War Contracts Subcom., Mil. Affairs Com., 1941-46; exec. sec. Pres.'s Council Econ. Advisors, 1946-51; research dir. Nat. Democratic Com., 1952; advisor Prime Minister's Office, Ministry Fin. Govt. Israel, 1953-56; vis. prof. Hebrew U., 1956-60; prof. polit. sci. Maxwell Sch., 1960-68; fellow Ctr. Advanced Study Behavorial Scis., 1961-62; Leatherbee lctr. Harvard Bus. Sch., Cambridge, Mass., 1962-63; dir. Ctr. Urban Studies, Wayne State U., Detroit, 1968-70; cons. UN Pub. Adminstrn., Fin. Div., 1966-76; disting. prof. Hunter Coll., CUNY, 1970-82, emeritus, 1982—; vis. prof.-at-large St. Mary's Coll. Calif., Moraga, 1982—; cons. U.S. Ho. of Reps. Chmn. Nat. Capitol Planning Council; vice-chmn. Arlington County (Va.) Planning Commn., No. Va. Regional Planning Commn. Fulbright grantee, India, 1978; recipient William Mosher award Am. Soc. Pub. Adminstrn., 1972. Fellow AAAS; mem. Am. Polit. Sci. Assn., Soc. Gen. Systems Research (past pres.). Jewish. Author: Friendly Fascism: The New Pace of Power in America, 1980, paperback edit., 1982; Organizations and Their Managing, 1968; The State of the Nation, 1966; The Managing of Organization, 1964; The Hard Money Crusade (with Will Lumer), 1954; The Legislative Struggle: A Study in Social Combat (Woodrow Wilson award), 1953, 2d edit., 1978; editor/co-editor: Toward a More Responsible Two-Party System, 1951; Action Under Planning, 1967; Social Intelligence for America's Future, 1969; Political Intelligence for America's Future, 1969; New Styles of Planning in Post-Industrial America, 1971. Office: St Marys College Moraga CA 94575

GROSS, DEAN CHARLES, engineer, consultant; b. Chgo., Aug. 28, 1953; s. B.G. and Doris L. Johnson; m. Joan O'Malley, Nov. 6, 1981. B.S. in Mech. Engring., Iowa State U., 1975; M.S. in Civil Engring., Northwestern U., 1981. Registered profl. engr., Ill. Engr., Commonwealth Edison Co., Chgo., 1975-78; project engr. Roy F. Weston, Inc., Chgo., 1979-81, project mgr. and mgr. mech. engring. dept. C. E. Maguire, Inc., Honolulu, 1981—, also proposal mgr. Recipient cert. of award Buettner Hydraulics Inst., 1981, value engring. cert. Soc. Am. Value Engrs., 1982. Mem. ASHRAE, Am. Water Works Assn. (cert. of recognition 1978), Water Pollution Control Fedn. Roman Catholic. Home: 419 Atkinson Dr Box 1306 Honolulu HI 96814 Office: 1600 Kapioliani Blvd Honolulu HI 96814

GROSS, EDWARD, sociologist, educator; b. Nagy Genez, Romania; s. Samuel and Dora (Levi) G. m. Florence Rebecca Goldman, Feb. 18, 1943; children—David P., Deborah. B.A., U. B.C. (Can.), 1942, M.A., U. Toronto, 1945; Ph.D., U. Chgo., 1949. Prof. Wash. State U., 1947-51, 53-60, U. Wash., Seattle, 1951-53, 65—, U. Minn., 1960-65. Author: Work and Society, 1958; University Goals and Academic Power, 1968; Changes in University Organization, 1964-71, 1974; The End of a Golden Age: Higher Education in a Steady State, 1981; contbr. numerous articles to profl. jours. Fulbright scholar Australia, 1977. Mem. Am. Sociol. Assn., Pacific Sociol. Assn. (pres. 1971), Internat. Sociol. Assn. Office: U Wash Dept Sociology Seattle WA 98195

GROSS, GORDON EDWARD, physicist; b. Plattner, Colo., July 29, 1925; s. Ben and Edna Pearl (Nelson) G.; B.S. in Math., Central Mo. U., 1947; M.A. in Physics, U. Mo., 1949; postgrad. U. Kans., U. Mo.; m. Shirley Savage, Mar. 7, 1947; children—Gordon Edward, Allen W., Gilbert Lee. Mem. faculty NW Mo. State U., 1949-50; with Libbey Owens Ford Co., Ottawa, Ill., 1952-53; mem. staff Midwest Research Inst., 1953—, prin. scientist, Kansas City, Mo., 1972-77, prin. scientist Solar Energy Research Inst., Golden Colo., 1977-80, chief materials br., 1980—; lectr. U. Mo., Kansas City, 1970-76; energy conservation cons. Mitchell-Webb Assos., San Diego, 1976—. Served with USNR, 1944-46. Registered profl. engr., Mo., Kans., Colo. Mem. Am. Phys. Soc., Nat. Soc. Profl. Engrs., ASHRAE, Assn. Energy Engrs., AAAS, ASTM, N.Y. Acad. Scis., Sigma Xi, Sigma Pi Sigma. Presbyterian. Co-author: Smoke and Flash in Small Arms Ammunition, 1954; contbr. articles to profl. jours. Office: SERI 1617 Cole Blvd Golden CO 80401

GROSS, HOWARD STEVEN, manufacturing executive; b. N.Y.C., Oct. 25, 1948; s. Abner Joseph and Audrey Vera (Janover) G.; m. Joan Pavarini, July 20, 1975. B.A. in Econs. and Math., Cornell U., 1970; M.B.A. in Fin. and Gen. Mgmt., Stanford U., 1972. Sr. assoc. McKinsey and Co., Los Angeles, 1972-77; exec. v.p. Plastiglide Mfg. Corp., Hawthorne, Calif., 1977—. Bd. dirs., v.p. exec. com. Big Bros. Greater Los Angeles, 1975—. Mem. Phi Beta Kappa. Republican. Unitarian. Home: 1058 Villa Grove Dr Pacific Palisades CA 90272 Office: 2701 W El Segundo Blvd Hawthorne CA 90250

GROSS, LEONARD, aircraft company executive; b. N.Y.C., Feb. 10, 1922; s. Maurice and Fay (Schwartz) G.; m. Ruth, Dec. 19, 1943; 1 son, Stephen J. Ph.D. in Physics, Princeton U., 1949. Instr., Princeton (N.J.) U., 1943-49; with Hughes Aircraft Co., El Segundo, Calif., 1949—, v.p., 1967-72, v.p., asst. group exec., engring. for aerospace groups, 1972-78, v.p. NATO affairs, 1978-81, v.p. electro-optical and data systems group, 1981—, mem. policy bd., 1967—; mem. Def. Sci. Bd. Panel on Avionics. Served to 1st lt. U.S. Army, 1944-46. Charles A. Coffin Nat. fellow, 1947-48; AEC fellow, 1948-49. Mem. Am. Phys. Soc., Indsl. and Applied Math., U.S. Naval Inst., Am. Def. Preparedness Assn. (dir. Los Angeles chpt.), AIAA, Assn. U.S. Army, Air Force Assn., Am. Inst. Elec. Engrs., Sigma Xi. Home: 10820 Portofino Pl Los Angeles CA 90077 Office: Hughes Aircraft Company PO Box 902 (M/S E1/A-105) El Segundo CA 90245

GROSS, SIDNEY, engineer; b. Derry, N.H., June 4, 1927; s. Hyman and Ruth (Wexler) G.; B.S. in Chem. Engring., U. N.H., 1950; postgrad., Oreg. State Coll., 1950-51; m. Marguerite Bolton; children—Kathy Lynn, Eric Bolton. Engineer, Boeing Co., Seattle, 1951—, now tech. leader in charge of battery research; cons. in field; advisor in battery research to NASA, 1979-80. Served with USN, 1945-46. Recipient award for tech. paper Conversion Engring. Conf., 1969; registered profl. engr., Wash. Mem. Am. Inst. Chem. Engrs., AAAS. Club: Mountaineers. Author: Battery Design and Optimization, 1979; The Nickel Electrode; inventor various developments on batteries (NASA citation, 1971); organizer, chmn. various symposia in field; contbr. tech. articles to profl. publs. Home: 7201 26 Ave NE Seattle WA 98115 Office: MS 8W-08 Boeing Aerospace Co PO Box 3999 Seattle WA 98124

GROSSBARD-SHECHTMAN, AMYRA, economist, educator; b. Antwerp, Belgium, Oct. 23, 1948; d. Haim and Anna (Propper) Grossbard; m. Amos Shechtman, June 15, 1978; children—Mikhal Hana, Zev Mordehai. B.A., Hebrew U., 1971; Ph.D. in Econs., U. Chgo., 1978. Research assoc. U. So. Calif., 1978-80; fellow Ctr. for Advanced Study in Behavioral Scis., Stanford U., 1980-81; assoc. prof. econs. San Diego State U., 1981—. Mem. Am. Econ. Assn., Population Assn. Am. Contbr. articles to profl. jours. Office: Department economics San Diego State Univ San Diego CA 92182

GROSSMAN, ALVIN, data processing exec.; b. Chgo., Sept. 18, 1924; s. Samuel A. and Rose (Brickman) G.; B.S., U. Ill., 1947; M.Ed., U. Ga., 1950; Ed.D., U. Washington, 1961; m. Marjorie L. Epstein, Oct. 31, 1948 (dec.); m. 2d Doris Pollak, Aug. 5, 1973; 1 son, Gary; stepchildren—Kenneth, Robert. Asst. prof. U. Ga., 1950-51; guidance coordinator Seattle Public Schs., 1953-57; dir. research and guidance Napa (Calif.) County Office of Edn., 1957-59; cons. in guidance Calif. State Dept. of Edn., 1959-63, chief Bur. of Systems and Data Processing, 1963-70; exec. v.p. Anathon Inc., 1971-77; adminstr. Info. Systems, San Mateo County (Calif.) Office of Edn., Redwood City, 1977—; vis. faculty summer sessions U. So. Calif., Stanford U., U. of Pacific, Sacramento State U. Served with USAAF, 1943-46, with U.S. Army, 1951-52. Decorated Air Medal with six oak leaf clusters. NIMH grantee, 1950. Mem. Assn. Ednl. Data Processing, Calif. Ednl. Data Processing Assn. (pres.). Clubs: Am. Spaniel, Mission Valley Cocker Spaniel, Golden Gate English Setter. Co-author: Data Processing for Educators, 1965; author: Breeding Better Cocker Spaniels, 1977, The Standard Book of Dog Breeding, 1980, 83; The Great American Dog Show Game, 1983; editor Jour. of Ednl. Data Processing, 1963-71. Home: 7023 Wooded Lake Dr San Jose CA 95120 Office: 333 Main St Redwood City CA 94063

GROSSMAN, GARY MICHAEL, broadcasting exec.; b. Santa Barbara, Calif., Dec. 5, 1950; s. Emil and Yvonne Anne (Prophet) G.; B.S. in Speech Communications and Theatre Arts cum laude, S. Oreg. State Coll., 1973; m. Barbara Ann Kalin, Sept. 12, 1971; children—Joshua Michael, Bettany Dawn. Program dir. KBOY Broadcasters, Medford, Oreg., 1973-74; salesman, mgr. KRKT-Radio, Albany, Oreg., 1974-76, gen. mgr., 1976—; v.p. broadcasting M3X Corp., Albany. Bd. dirs. YMCA, 1982—. Mem. Nat. Radio Broadcasters Assn. (state dir. 1978-82), Mid-Willamette Valley Broadcasters Assn. (pres. 1977-82), Nat. (regional dir. 1980—), Oreg. (dir. 1979-81, v.p., 1982-83) assns. broadcasters. Republican. Methodist. Clubs: Rotary, Optimist, Jaycees, Gideons. Home: 2477 SE 25th St Albany OR 97321 Office: M3X Corp 1207 E 9th St Albany OR 97321

GROSSMAN, HOWARD BARRY, electrical engineer; b. Bklyn., Oct. 15, 1935; s. Benjamin and Sophie Moses; m. Karen E. Sherman, Mar. 11, 1961 (div. 1969); children—Deborah Sue, Paul Arthur, Michael Eli; m. Kathleen Mueller, Jan. 17, 1970. B.E.E., U. Fla., 1956; M.S.E.E., U. So. Calif., 1959. Sect. head TRW Inc., Redondo Beach, Calif., 1963-67, dept. mgr., 1967-70, asst. lab. mgr., 1970-73, asst. program mgr., 1973—. bd. dirs. Urban League, 1977-79, Joint Powers Authority, 1982—, trustee San Bernardino City Unified Sch. Dist., 1979—. Recipient TRW good neighbor award, 1973, PTA continuing service award, 1973.

GROSSMAN, IRA, psychologist; b. Phila., June 18, 1948; s. Emmanuel and Evelyn (Love) G.; B.S., St. Joseph's Coll., Phila., 1970; M.S., Hahnemann Med. Coll., 1972; Ph.D., Calif. Sch. Profl. Psychology, San Diego, 1975; divorced; 1 son, Matthew. Pvt. practice psychology, San Diego, 1978—; mem. faculty Calif. Sch. Profl. Psychology, 1980—, Chapman Coll., 1982—; cons. mental health. Served with USN, 1975-80. Mem. Am. Psychol. Assn. Jewish. Office: 2830 4th Ave San Diego CA 92103

GROSSMAN, MAURICE, psychiatrist; b. Phila., Dec. 5, 1907; s. Abraham and Sarah (Bernstein) G.; student U. N.C., 1924-27; M.D., Jefferson Med. Coll., 1931; s. Mollie Froman, Nov. 10, 1934 (div. 1953); children—Paul, Kaye, Carl, Roy; m. Marion L. Lewis, July 29, 1956 (div. 1974). Resident Jefferson Med. Coll. Hosp., 1931-34; gen. practice medicine including surg. pathology, Phila., 1934-38; psychiat. tng. VA, Palo Alto, Calif., 1938-39; asst. clin. dir., chief phys. medicine and rehab. San Francisco Psychoanalytic Inst., 1950-55; asst. clin. prof. U. Calif., San Francisco, 1949-58; asst. clin. prof. phys. therapy Stanford U., 1950-69, emeritus clin. prof. psychiatry, 1958—; practice medicine specializing in psychiatry, Palo Alto, Calif., 1953—; cons. to Congl. coms., Calif. legislators, state and fed. agys., pvt. orgns. Served to maj., M.C., U.S. Army, 1944-46. Diplomate Am. Bd. Neurology and Psychiatry. Life fellow Am. Psychiat. Assn. (chmn. task force confidentialtiy 1971-75, past pres. No. Calif. br., Outstanding Achievement award No. Calif. br. 1983); fellow AAAS; mem. Calif. Psychiat. Assn. (a founder, 1st moderator 1961-62), Mid Peninsula Psychiat. Soc. (past pres.), Calif. Med. Assn. (past del.), Santa Clara County Med. Soc., N.Y. Acad. Sci., Soc. Med. Friends of Wine, Phi Beta Kappa. Club: Stanford U. Faculty. Contbg. author: 1977 Annual Review of Medicine, 1978 Law and the Mental Health Professions. Contbr. articles to med. jours. Office: 659 Channing Ave Palo Alto CA 94301 also PO Box 745 Palo Alto CA 94302

GROSSMAN, MAURICE KENNETH, educator, ceramicist; b. Detroit, Sept. 16, 1927. B.S., Wayne State U., 1950, Alfred U., 1951; M.F.A., Ohio State U., 1953. Group shows include: Smithsonian Instn., Washington, 1953, 59, De Young Mus., San Francisco, 1957, Denver Art Mus., 1957, St. Paul Art Gallery, 1959, Scripps Coll. Lang Gallery, Claremont, Calif., 1964, Ark. Art Ctr., Little Rock, 1966, Mus. Contemporary Crafts, N.Y.C., 1968; represented in permanent collections at Detroit Mus. Art, Phoenix Mus. Art, El Paso Mus., Utah State Mus., Salt Lake City, Mills Coll. Art. Mus., Mill Valley, Calif.; instr. ceramics Western Wash. Coll., Bellingham, 1953-54; prof. ceramics U. Ariz., Tucson, 1955—. Recipient Disting. Alumni award Wayne State Univ., 1968, Creative Teaching award U. Ariz. Found., 1978, others. Mem. Am. Crafts Council (southwest area rep. 1963-66), Ariz. Designer-Craftsmen (pres. 1960), Nat. Council Edn. Ceramic Arts (regional rep. 1972), Tucson Art Ctr. (dir. 1968), World Crafts Council. Office: Dept Art University of Arizona Tucson AZ 85721

GROSSMAN, MICHAEL BARRY, govt. ofcl.; b. Pitts., June 18, 1924; s. Samuel Aaron and Della (Stern) G.; B.S. in Metall. Engring., U. Pitts., 1949; postgrad. U. Pitts., 1956, Sacramento State U., 1979-80; grad. program Air War Coll., 1981; m. Faye Evelyn Shatkoff, Dec. 25, 1946; children—Wayne M., Sandra Dee. Welding engr. Towmotor Corp., Cleve., 1949-51; materials engr., supr. heat treatment and plating shop Cadillac Motor Car div. Gen. Motors Corp., Cleve., 1951-56; sr. materials engr. Westinghouse Electric Corp., Pitts., 1956-61; asst. div. mgr., quality program mgr. Aerojet Gen. Corp., Sacramento, 1961-65; sr. value engr. McClellan AFB, Calif., 1965-77, quality assurance div. chief, 1977—. Bd. dirs. cemetery, 1969—; mem. Resettlement Com. for Boat People, 1980. Served with USN, 1943-46. Registered profl. engr., Calif., Pa. Republican. Jewish. Club: B'nai B'rith (3 Man of Yr. awards). Author: (with Lou Haramc) NAV Ships 250-1500-1, MIL-S-18170, MIL-S-18171, MIL-S-22200, 1956; Impact Strength of Ferrous Materials, 1958. Office: McClellan AFB CA 95652

GROSSMAN, MICHAEL S., periodontist; b. Bklyn., Feb. 18, 1940; s. Morris and Rita (Richman) G.; student, Bklyn. Coll., 1956-59; D.D.S., Temple U., 1963; m. Carol Lynne Sugarman, Aug. 30, 1964; children—Mark Steven, Mindi Lynne. Resident in periodontics U. Wash., Seattle, 1965-67; individual practice dentistry, specializing in periodontics, San Diego and La Mesa, Calif., 1967—. Served with USNR, 1963-65. Diplomate Am. Bd. Periodontology. Mem. Am. Acad. Periodontology, Western Soc. Periodontology, San Diego County Dental Soc. Home: 6100 LaJolla Scenic Dr S La Jolla CA 92037 Office: 770 E Washington St Suite 102 San Diego CA 92103

GROSSMAN, ROBERT JOSEPH, lawyer; b. Providence, Nov. 26, 1927; s. Max B. and Anne A. (Feinselber) G.; B.A., U. Calif. at Los Angeles, 1950, J.D., 1953; m. Margery A. Steinberg, Aug. 24, 1958; children—Laurie, Stephanie, Michele. Admitted to Calif. bar, 1954, since practiced in Los Angeles; partner Sax & Grossman, Los Angeles, 1962-66, Grossman, Horwitz & Stein and predecessor firm, Los Angeles, 1971-76, Grossman & Weissman, 1977—; Mem. Calif. State Bar Com. Unauthorized Practice of Law, 1962-67. Vice pres. Med. Center Aides City Hope, Calif., 1967-69; pres. parents council The Herzl Schs., 1979, bd. dirs., 1979-80. Served with AUS, 1945-47. Mem. Calif., Los Angeles County (mem. family law sect. 1970—), Conejo Valley bar assns., Calif. Trial Lawyers Assn., Am. Judicature Soc., Am. Arbitration Assn. (panel of arbitrators), Acad. Legal Arts and Scis. (pres. 1981—), Western Los Angeles Regional C. of C. (dir. 1976-79), Pi Sigma Alpha, Nu Beta Epsilon. Office: 1100 Glendon Ave Los Angeles CA 90024

GROSSMAN, SEYMOUR, gastroenterologist; b. Newark, July 5, 1933; s. Abraham and Sally G. (Pilchman) G.; student MIT, 1950-53; M.D., N.Y. U., 1957; m. Roberta Jane Simon, June 26, 1955; children—Michael Joseph, Deborah Joan. Intern, Cleve. Met. Gen. Hosp., 1957-58, med. resident, 1958-61; NIH clin. research fellow in gastroenterology N.Y. Hosp.-Cornell Med. Center, N.Y.C., 1961-63; pvt. practice medicine, White Plains, N.Y., 1963-65; practice medicine specializing in gastroenterology Permanente Med. Group, Oakland, Calif., 1965-67; chief gastroenterology Kaiser-Permanente Med. Center, Oakland, 1969—; asso. clin. prof. medicine U. Calif. at San Francisco, 1975—; pres. staff assn. Kaiser Found. Hosp., Oakland, 1971-72. Mem. exec. com. Oakland Symphony Chorus, 1970-77. Served to lt. col., U.S. Army, 1967-69. Kaiser Found. Research Inst. grantee, 1973-78, 80—; Liver Center grantee, 1976-77. Diplomate Am. Bd. Internal Medicine and subsplty. in gastroenterology. Mem. ACLU (life), Common Cause, Am. Gastroenterological Assn., AAAS, No. Calif. Soc. for Clin. Gastroenterology (bd. govs., pres. 1984), Nat. Found. for Ileitis and Colitis (chpt. dir., physicians adv. bd.), Am. Soc. Gastrointestinal Endoscopy, Phi Lambda Kappa, Pi Lambda Phi, Phi Lambda Upsilon. Jewish. Home: 2661 Cedar St Berkeley CA 94708 Office: 280 W MacArthur Blvd Oakland CA 94611

GROSSMAN, STEPHEN EUGENE, advertising agency executive; b. N.Y.C., Apr. 24, 1932; s. E. Eugene and Louise (Steefel) G.; B.A., NYU, 1956; B.Engring., CCNY, 1968; m. Karen Lynn Rothstein, May 1973; 1 dau., Emily. Project engr. Radio Engring. Labs., L.I., N.Y., 1968-71; project engr. Litton Industries, South Plainfield, N.J., 1971-72; editor Electronics mag., N.Y.C., 1972-74; sr. staff engr. Fairchild Test Systems, Latham, N.Y., 1974-76; dir. mktg. research Gnostic Concepts, Menlo Park, Calif., 1976-78; pres. Stephen E. Grossman, Inc. Tech. Communications/Advt., Los Altos, Calif., 1978—. Mem. IEEE. Contbr. articles to tech. jours. Home: 977 Spencer Way Los Altos CA 94022 Office: 146 Main St Los Altos CA 94022

GROTEY, GARY DAVID, artist; b. Manhattan, Kans., Apr. 15, 1944; s. Gerald Henry and Beatrice Elizabeth G.; B.A., San Diego State U., 1969. One person shows Biloxi, Miss., 1973, Austin Galleries, Chgo. and Detroit, 1979, Collector's Choice Gallery, Laguna Beach, Calif., 1978, Matise Gallery, Lake Geneva, Wis., 1979; exhibited in group shows Marina del Rey (Calif.) Gallery, 1975, Quail Hollow Gallery, Oklahoma City, 1977, others; represented in permanent collection Chgo. Rehab. Center, DePaul U., Mercantile Bank, Chgo. Recipient 1st place prize Pikes Peat Nat. Art Show, 1973. Baptist. Office: Artco Route 2 Box 109 Long Grove IL 60047

GROTH, BRUNO, sculptor; b. Stolp, Germany, Dec. 14, 1905; came to U.S., 1923, naturalized, 1931; s. Paul and Marie (Jagdman) G.; m. Nita Emsley, 1958; children—David, Nina. Student Otis Art Inst., Los Angeles, 1930. One-man shows: De Young Mus., San Francisco, 1959, Assoc. Am. Artists Galleries, N.Y., 1954, Feingarten Galleries, N.Y.C., San Francisco, Chgo., 1961, Gump Gallery, San Francisco, 1965, Ankeum Gallery, Los Angeles, 1964, 68, 73, 78; groups shows: Brussels World's Fair, Santa Barbara (Calif.) Mus. Art, 1959, Portland (Oreg.) Art Mus., 1959, Mus. Contemporary Crafts, N.Y.C., 1958, works include bronze fountain pieces, cities of Fresno and Crescent City, Calif., wood sculpture Humboldt State Coll.; represented in numerous pvt. collections. Address: PO Box 46 Cornville AZ 86325

GROTHE, PETER (JOHN), political scientist, educator; b. San Francisco, May 28, 1931; s. Walter and Dorothy Swaey (Bromberg) G.; B.A., Stanford U., 1953, M.A. in Communications, 1954; Ph.D. with distrinction, George Washington U., 1970. Fgn. relations advisor to Se. Hubert Humphrey of Minn., Washington, 1960; dep. dir. UN br. Peace Corps, Washington, 1961; research asso. George Washington U., 1968; asst. prof. polit. sci. San Jose State U., 1969-74; vis. prof. Odense U., Denmark, 1976-78; asst. prof. internat. studies Monterey (Calif.) Inst. Internat. Studies, 1979-81, asso. prof., 1981—; lectr. U.S. Internat. Communications Agy. 16 countries in Europe, Africa and Latin Am.; cons. to Peace Corps and USIA, 1969; vis. prof. N.Y. U., Stony Brook, 1973, 74; vis. research scholar Norwegian Inst. Internat. Affairs, Oslo, and Stockholm U., 1970-71. Pres. Hillsborough Democratic Club, 1959; campaign aide to Sen. Claire Engle of Calif., and State Atty. Gen. Stanley Mosk, 1958; del. Dem. Nat. Conf., 1972; active NAACP, Amnesty Internat., Am. Field Service. Served with AUS, 1955-56. Am.-Scandinavian Found. fellow, 1971—; Office of Edn. and Epworth Fund grantee, 1968. Mem. Am. Polit. Sci. Assn., Internat. Studies Assn., Soc. Intercultural Edn., Tng. and Research, No. Calif. Polit. Sci. Assn. (bd. councillors, pres. 1983-84), No. Calif. World Affairs Council. Episcopalian. Club: Sierra. Author: Great Moments in Stanford Sports, 1953; To Win the Minds of Men, 1958; Attitude Change of American Tourists in the Soviet Union, 1969; contbr. numerous articles and book revs. to profl. jours., Washington Post. Home: 966 Fremont St Menlo Park CA 94025 Office: Monterey Institute of International Studies Monterey CA 93940

GROTJAHN, MARTIN, psychiatrist; b. Berlin, July 8, 1904; s. Alfred and Charlotte (Hartz) G.; M.D., Kaiser Friedrich U., Berlin, 1929; came to U.S., 1936, naturalized, 1942; m. Etelka Gross, Aug. 18, 1927; 1 son, Michael. Intern, Hosp. Reinikendaf, Berlin; resident Charité Hosp., Berlin, 1933-36, Menninger Clinic, Topeka, 1936-38, Chgo. Psychoanalytic Inst.; head physician Berlin U. dept. psychiatry and neurology, 1933-36; mem. staff Chgo. Inst. Psychoanalysis, 1938-46; mem. faculty U. So. Calif., 1946—, now prof., tng. analyst emeritus; practice psychiatry, Topeka, Chgo., Beverly Hills, Calif.; ret. Served with M.C., AUS, 1942-46. Recipient Sigmund Freud award Psychoanalytic Physicians, 1976. Mem. Am. Psychoanalytic Assn. (life), Am. Psychiat. Assn. (life), So. Calif. Psychiat. Assn. (life), So. Calif. Psychoanalytic Soc. (life). Author: Beyond Laughter, 1957; Psychoanalysis and the Family Neurosis, 1960; A Celebration of Laughter, 1970; The Voice of the Symbol, 1972; The Art and the Technique of Analytic Group Therapy, 1977; author, co-editor Psychoanalytic Pioneers, 1966, Handbook of Group Therapy, 1982. Contbr. 400 articles to profl. jours. Home: 2169 Century Hill Los Angeles CA 90067

GROVE, ANDREW S., computer component manufacturing company executive; b. 1936; married. With Fairchild Camera & Instrument Co., 1963-67; with Intel Corp., Santa Clara, Calif., 1968—, now pres., chief operating officer, also dir. Office: Intel Corp 3065 Bowers Ave Santa Clara CA 95051*

GROVE, DEAN ALLEN, physician; b. Bryan, Ohio, Mar. 10, 1945; s. Kedric Durward and N. Florence (Stombaugh) G.; B.A., Manchester (Ind.) Coll., 1967; M.D., Ohio State U., 1971; m. Mary Louise Klotz, June 27, 1967; children—Derek Scott, Jason Todd. Intern, Akron (Ohio) City Hosp., 1971-72; univ. physician student-employee health service Ind. U. Med. Sch., Indpls., 1972-76, asst. prof. family medicine, 1974-79; med. dir. Public Inebriate Program Detoxification Center, Indpls., 1974-79; practice medicine specializing in family and geriatric medicine, Indpls., 1972-76; cons. Ind. Blue Cross-Blue Shield, 1976-77, dir. med. affairs, 1977-79; chief physician, occupational health The Boeing Co., Seattle, 1979—; clin. faculty family medicine U. Wash. Coll. Medicine, 1979—. Mem. Greater Indpls. Barbershop Chorus, 1975-77; bd. dirs. Meals on Wheels, Indpls., 1977-79; bass Indpls. Symphonic Choir, 1978-79. Diplomate Am. Bd. Family Practice. Fellow Am. Coll. Preventive Medicine, Am. Acad. Family Physicians; mem. AMA (Physician's Recognition award 1974, 78, 81), Soc. Prospective Medicine (dir. 1980—), Wash. Acad. Family Physicians, Wash. Med. Assn. Methodist. Club: Bellevue Athletic. Office: Boeing Co PO Box 3707 61-40 Seattle WA 98124

GROVER, L. RIDD, business educator; b. Arco, Idaho, Dec. 12, 1926; s. Lowell A. and Merle Rosina (Ridd) G.; m. Geraldine Keller, Mar. 20, 1948; m. Patricia Ann Huggins, Apr. 10, 1976; children—Bruce K., Dennis R., Michael L.; stepchildren—Tereasa Woodyatt, Shelley Woodyatt, Tamara Woodyatt, Susan Woodyatt, Harvey Woodyatt, Dan Woodyatt. A.S. in Bus., Weber State Coll., 1949; B.S. in Secondary Edn., Bus. Adminstrn. and Secretarial Sci., Utah State U., 1951; Cert. tchr., Utah. Acct., office mgr. Packer Motor Co., Brigham City, Utah, 1951-54; bus. tchr., dept. head, treas., Bear River High Sch., Tremonton, Utah, 1954-59; acct., office mgr., auditor Jay Dee Harris Co., Tremonton, 1959-69; tchr. bus., dept. head Box Elder High Sch., Brigham City, 1969—; past chmn. Brigham Office Occupations Tng.; Utah bd. dirs. Future Bus. Leaders Am., 1982-83. Treas. No. Utah Symphony Orch., sect. leader 2d violins; exec. sec. Brigham City 1st Ward Mormon Ch. Served with USN, 1945-47; PTO. Mem. Box Elder Edn. Assn. (sec.), Utah Edn. Assn., Utah Bus. Edn. Assn. (pres.-elect 1981-82, pres. 1982-83), Utah Vocat. Assn. (dir.), Am. Vocat. Assn., NEA, Nat. Bus. Edn. Assn., Western Bus. Assn. (exec. bd. 1981-83). Republican. Home: 235 S 750 E Brigham City UT 84302 Office: 380 S 6th W Brigham City UT 84302

GROVER, MARTELL R., watchmaker, jeweler; b. Sugar City, Idaho, Sept. 29, 1916; s. Daniel Wells and Martha May (Ricks) G.; B.A. B.S., Ricks Coll., 1937; diploma as master watchmaker Am. Acad. Horology, 1948; m. Zell Stevenson, Mar. 21, 1942; children—Fred M., Gail S. Owner, mgr. Grover Jewelry, Rexburg, Idaho, 1948—. Mem. Latter Day Saints Mission to Germany, 1937-39. Served with U.S. Army, 1940-45. Recipient Silver Beaver award Boy Scouts Am., 1977; Outstanding Businessman of Yr. award Rexburg C. of C., 1982. Mem. Intermountain Retail Jewelers (bd. dirs. 1967-73), Rexburg C. of C. (past bd. dirs., past v.p., named Outstanding Businessman of Yr. 1983), Am. Watchmakers Inst., Ret. Jewelers Am., Am. Numismatic Assn. (life), Nat. Assn. Watch and Clock Collectors, Gem State Watchmakers Assn. (dir. 1978-79, pres. 1980-81), Am. Def. Preparedness Assn. (life), Am. Legion, VFW. Clubs: Lions, Rotary. Home: 500 E 350th S Rexburg ID 83440 Office: 58 E Main St Rexburg ID 83400

GROW, DONALD LELAND, ins. co. exec.; b. Los Angeles, June 20, 1938; s. Leonard W. and Dorothy G. (Engberg) G.; student El Camino Coll., 1958-63, U. Calif. at Los Angeles Extension, 1962-67; A.A., Cypress Coll., 1979; m. Shirley Ann Voyda, Aug. 22, 1970; children—Charles Leonard, Kevin Matthew, Kristi Lynn. Collection mgr. Casualty Ins. Co. Calif., Los Angeles, 1957-65, Transit Casualty Co., Los Angeles, 1967-69, Swett and Crawford Co., Los Angeles, 1972-74; collection supr. Mission Equities Ins. Co., Los Angeles, 1965-67; office mgr. Gen. Accident Group, Los Angeles, 1969-72; regional credit mgr. Employers Ins. Wausau, Los Angeles, 1974—; co-editor, tchr. company premium accounting and collections course Ins. Ednl. Assn. and Ins. Credit Mgrs. Assn. Los Angeles. Pres. La Palma (Calif.) Homeowners Assn., 1974; mem. La Palma Traffic Safety Com., 1975—. Mem. Ins. Credit Mgrs. Assn. Los Angeles (pres. 1971, 81), Gardena Jaycees (Jaycee of Month 1969, Jaycee of Quarter 1970, state dir. 1969) La Palma C. of C. (dir. 1976). Republican. Presbyterian. Home: 5954 Thelma St La Palma CA 90623 Office: 3130 Wilshire Blvd Los Angeles CA 90010

GRUBB, SAMUEL PETER, contracting company executive; b. Ashland, Oregon, May 3, 1940; s. Samuel Flynn and Doris Margaret (Lichte) G.; m. Walli Dale Dupuis, Dec. 7, 1960; children—Samuel, Chandra, Julie; m. 2d, Wilma Kelly Aug. 20, 1975. B.S., Portland State Coll., 1968. With Eagle Metals, Portland, 1963-65; salesman automotive parts Federal Mogul, Portland, 1965-67; salesman plastic conduit Western Plastics Corp., Tacoma, Wash., 1967-70; v.p. mech. Pease and Sons, Inc., 1970—. Chmn. Lakewood Summer Festival, 1970; chmn. Pierce County Alcoholism Adminstrn. Bd., 1978-80. Served with USN, 1960-62. Named Kiwanian of Yr., 1978. Mem. Plumbing Heating Cooling Contractors Assn. (pres.) Joint Apprenticeship Tng. Council (bd. dirs.), Assoc. Gen. Contractors, Bldg. Owners and Mgrs. Assn. (treas.), Am. Arbitration Assn. (panel of arbitrators). Clubs: Totem Ski; Marine Indsl. Kiwanis (bd. dirs. 1972—), Tacoma Engrs. (past pres.). Home: 3030 44th St E Tacoma WA 98443 Office: PO Box 44100 Tacoma WA 98444

GRUBER, ALIN, winery exec.; b. Lynn, Mass., June 10, 1932; s. George and Ruth Ann (Hochman) G.; m. Elsa Iris Bloom, Jan. 31, 1956; children—Karin Ann, Michael Barnet. B.A., Dartmouth Coll., 1953; M.S., Purdue U., 1957, Ph.D., 1959. Sr. scientist Dunlap & Assocs., Inc., Darien, Conn., 1959-64; research v.p., group co-mgr. McCann-Erickson, Inc., N.Y.C., 1964-71; v.p. research and new products Norton Simon Communications, Inc., N.Y.C., 1971-75; with Sonoma Vineyards, Inc., Windsor, Calif., 1975—, sr. v.p., 1976-80, exec. v.p., 1980—. Office: Sonoma Vineyards Inc PO Box 368 Windsor CA 95492

GRUBER, IRA LEE, lawyer; b. N.Y.C., Apr. 30, 1940; s. Alexander Philip and Jean (Margoles) G.; B.A., Calif. State U., Los Angeles, 1965; J.D., U. San Fernando Valley, 1976; 1 dau., Lisa Michelle. Admitted to Calif. bar, 1977; individual practice law, Los Angeles, 1977—; cons. atty. Gemi Inc., Grujoh Enterprises, Exo Electronic Co. Served with U.S. Army, 1962-63. Mem. Calif. State Bar, Los Angeles County Bar Assn. Office: 4591 Inglewood Blvd Apt 6 Culver City CA 90230

GRUBIN, DIANA CHERYL, editor, writer; b. Los Angeles, Oct. 22, 1956; d. Carl Milton and Annette Faye Grubin. B.A. in Journalism, Calif. State U.-Long Beach, 1979. Editorial apprentice Los Angeles Mag., 1978; copywriter Denker Creative Services, Los Angeles, 1979-81; methods and procedures writer Pierce Nat. Life, Los Angeles, 1981-82; proofreader, editor Swett & Crawford, Los Angeles, 1982—; cons. to advt. agys.; freelance writer and researcher to various publs. Home: 5309 B Knowlton St Los Angeles CA 90045 Office: 4201 Wilshire Blvd Los Angeles CA 90010

GRUEBER, WILLIAM H., psychotherapist; b. Chgo., Aug. 16, 1933; s. Bernard Shulman and Pepi Rosenthal (Korsower) G.; m. Ronnye J. Morris, June 7, 1959; children—Jill Melanie, Dana Beth. B.S. in Bus. Adminstrn., UCLA, 1959; M.A. in Ednl. Psychology, Calif. State U.-Northridge, 1976. Lic. marriage, family and child counselor Calif. With Lamson Bros., Chgo., 1951-53; sr. account exec. Merrill Lynch Pierce Fenner & Smith, Hollywood, Calif., 1955-69; v.p., mgr. Bateman Eichler, Hill Richards, Beverly Hills, Calif., 1969-75; intern Inst. Human Studies, Sherman Oaks, Calif., 1975-76; founder, dir., psychotherapist Creative Living Ctr., Sherman Oaks, 1977-82; pvt. practice psychotherapy, 1983—; cons., pub. speaker in field. Co-chmn. investment div. United Jewish Welfare Fund, Wilshire Blvd. Temple Brotherhood; active Hollywood YMCA, mem. exec. com. counseling ctr. Mem. Psychotherapy Ctrs. Dirs. Assn. (founding), Beverly Hills N.Y. Stock Exchange Mem. Firms (pres. 1973), Am. Psychol. Assn., Calif. State Psychol. Assn., Western Psychol. Assn., Assn. Humanistic Psychology, Am. Assn. Marriage and Family Therapists, Calif. Assn. Marriage and Family Therapists. Jewish. Home: 12522 Rye St Studio City CA 91604 Office: 4525 Sherman Oaks Ave Sherman Oaks CA 91403

GRUEN, CLAUDE, economist; b. Bonn, Germany, Aug. 17, 1931; s. Walter and Elsbet Gruen; children—Leslie W., Dale J., Adam S., Joshua G., Aaron C. B.B.A., U. Cin., 1954, M.A., 1961, Ph.D., 1964. Instr., Xavier U., Cin., 1963-64; economist Arthur D. Little, Inc., San Francisco, 1964-70; sr. economist Gruen, Gruen & Assocs., San Francisco, 1970—; lectr., sr. economist U. Calif.-Berkeley, 1964-70. Served to capt. USAFR, 1954-57. NSF postdoctoral fellow, 1964. Mem. Am. Real Estate and Urban Econs. Assn., Am. Econ. Assn., Regional Sci. Assn., Western Regional Scis. Assn., Urban Land Inst. Author: Low and Moderate Housing in the Suburbs, 1971; contbr. articles to profl. jours. Home: 8649 Don Carol Dr El Cerrito CA 94530 Office: 564 Howard St San Francisco CA 94105

GRUEN, THOMAS ALEXANDER WANG, bioengr.; b. Sucre, Bolivia, July 14, 1943; came to U.S., 1946, naturalized, 1964; B.S., N.Y. U., 1965; M.S., Columbia U., 1970. Lab. asst. Hosp. for Spl. Surgery, 1969-70; research asst. UCLA, 1970-79; instr. orthopedic research U. So. Calif., Los Angeles, 1979—. Mem. Hip Soc., Orthopedic Research Soc., Soc. Biomaterials, Biomaterials Soc. (Can.), SIROT, ASTM. Office: 2400 S Flower St Los Angeles CA 90007

GRUENDEMANN, BARBARA JEAN, registered nurse; b. LaCrosse, Wis., Mar. 22, 1936; s. Jens and Inga Theresa (Melby) Moilien; B.S., U. Wis., 1959, M.S. in Ednl. Psychology, 1965; M.S. in Nursing, UCLA, 1968; m. Paul A. Gruendemann, Oct. 17, 1959; 1 son, Eric Paul. Instr. operating room nursing Madison (Wis.) Gen. Hosp. Sch. Nursing, 1960-64; instr. nursing Santa Monica (Calif.) Coll., 1968-71; asst. prof. nursing Mount St. Mary's Coll., Los Angeles, 1972-76; operating room nurse clinician Centinela Hosp, Inglewood, Calif., 1976—. Recipient grant USPHS, 1967-68. Mem. Am. Nurses Assn. (western regional accrediting com. 1975-77), Calif. Nurses Assn. (mem. dist. nominating com. 1972-73, mem. continuing edn. com. 1972-73), Assn. Operating Room Nurses (chmn. nat. editorial com. jour. 1971-73, dir. 1974-76, v.p. 1976-78, pres. 1979-80). Lutheran. Club: Valleyrama Toastmistress (rec. sec. 1972-73) (Van Nuys, Calif.). Sr. author: (textbook) The Surgical Patient: Behavioral Concepts for the Operating Room Nurse, 2d edit., 1977; Nursing Audit: Challenge to the Operating Room Nurse, 1974; co-author: Alexander's Care of the Patient in Surgery, 7th edit., 1983. Home: 5613 Ostrom Ave Encino CA 91316 Office: 555 E Hardy St Inglewood CA 90307

GRUENWALD, CHARLES ANDREW, manufacturers representative, consultant; b. Waukegan, Ill., Jan. 11, 1938; s. Charles Andrew and Helen L. (Petitclaire) G.; m. Starr Light, Nov. 14, 1959; children—Peter, Kelly, Kim, Patrick, John. Student Purdue U., 1959-61; B.B.A., Northwestern U., 1966; M.B.A., Marquette U., 1971. With mktg. staff Rex Chainbelt, Chgo. and Milw., 1962-71; dist. sales mgr., mgr. POW-R-Jac div. Phila. Gear Corp., Denver and Phila., 1971-77; pres. Gruenwald & Assocs. Inc., Littleton, Colo., 1977—. Vol., Tech. Assistance Ctr., Denver. Mem. Am. Water Works Assn., Water Pollution Control Fedn., Waters Inc. (treas.). Office: Gruenwald Assocs Inc 5860 Curtice St Littleton CO 80120

GRUENWALD, OSKAR, polit. scientist; b. Yugoslavia, Oct. 5, 1941; s. Oskar and Vera (Wolf) G.; came to U.S., 1961, naturalized, 1967; A.A., Pasadena City Coll., 1964; B.A., U. Calif. at Berkeley, 1966; M.A., Claremont Grad. Sch., 1967, Ph.D., 1972. Internat. economist Office of Asst. Sec. for Internat. Affairs, U.S. Treasury Dept., Washington, 1967-68; vis. research asso. Social Scis. Research Center, U. Erlangen-Nürnberg, W. Ger., 1971-72; lectr. div. social scis. Pepperdine U., Malibu, Calif., 1972-73, Santa Monica (Calif.) Coll., 1973-76; ind. research and writing, 1976—; guest lectr.; cons. to Inst. Advanced Philosophic Research, Colo., 1977—; participant nat. and internat. confs. Served with USAR, 1967-73. Pasadena Edn. Assn. scholar, 1964, Calif. State Grad. fellow, 1969-71; Ludwig Vogelstein Found. grantee, 1976-77. Mem. Am. Polit. Sci. Assn., Am. Philos. Assn., Internat. Polit. Sci. Assn., Internat. Sociol. Assn., Popular Culture Assn., So. Soc. Philosophy and Psychology, Western Social Sci. Assn., Internat. Soc. Polit. Psychology, Internat. Solar Energy Soc., Am. Assn. Advancement of Slavic Studies, Delta Phi Epsilon, Omicron Mu Delta, Delta Tau Kappa. Roman Catholic. Author: The Yugoslav Search for Man: Marxist Humanism in Contemporary Yugoslavia, 1981; contbr. articles on polit. philosophy and comparative communist studies to scholarly jours. Home: 2925 4th St Apt 21 Santa Monica CA 90405

GRUGER, EDWARD HART, JR., research chemist, educator; b. Murfreesboro, Tenn., Jan. 21, 1928; s. Edward Hart and Edith (Sundin) G.; B.S., U. Wash., 1953, M.S., 1956; Ph.D., U. Calif., Davis, 1968; m. Audrey Ruth Lindgren, June 27, 1952; children—Sherri Jeanette, Lawrence Hart, Linda Gay. Chemist, fishery technol. lab. U.S. Bur. Comml. Fisheries, Seattle, 1953-54, 1955-59, project leader, supervisory organic chemist, Seattle, 1955-62; research chemist Pioneer Research Lab., N.W. & Alaska Fisheries Center, Nat. Marine Fisheries Service, Seattle, 1962-65, supervisory research chemist, 1968-83; research assoc. Agrl. Expt. Sta., U. Calif., Davis, 1965-68; research prof. dept. chemistry Seattle U., 1977—. Served with USN, 1946-48. Decorated Victory medal; recipient Spl. Achievement award U.S. Dept. Commerce, 1976. Mem. AAAS, Am. Chem. Soc. (local sect. chmn. 1974, council 1980—), Am. Oil Chemists Soc. (Honor Student award 1967); N.Y. Acad. Scis., Soc. Environ. Toxicology and Chemistry, Sigma Xi. Conglist. Club: Elk. Contbr. numerous articles to profl. publs. Home: 3727 NE 193rd St Seattle WA 98155

GRUHN, CARL VAHLSING, retired educator; b. Jeannette, Pa., Feb. 20, 1903; s. Carl Adolph and Louisa Anna (Vahlsing) G.; B.S., No. State Coll., 1927; postgrad. U. Minn., 1931-33; M.S., U. So. Calif., 1941; postgrad. Claremont Coll., summer 1941; m. Hannah Elizabeth Dyste, Aug. 21, 1941; children—Hannah Gruhn Towle, Diana Gruhn Guthery, Carl. Tchr. sci., math. Ipswich, S.D., 1927-28, Aberdeen, S.D., 1928-31, 33-39, Riverside, Calif., 1939-42, South Pasadena, Calif., 1942-68; tchr. chemistry Flintridge Prep. Sch., La Canada, Calif., 1968-81. Discussion leader various jr. colls. on chemistry; head lab. work various tchr. insts., 1961-67; mem. chem. materials study program NSF, 1960-62. Recipient Cert. of Merit, Industry Edn. Council, 1963. Stanford U. Shell Cos. Found. fellow, 1958. Mem. Smithsonian Assocs., Nat. Acad. Scis., Ret. Tchrs. Assn., Phi Delta Kappa, Phi Kappa Phi. Baptist (Sunday Sch. tchr., supt., choir pres., deacon). Mason. Contbr. articles to profl. jours. Home: 211 S 6th St Apt 210 Alhambra CA 91801

GRUMETTE, STEVE, computer system consultant, film producer; b. N.Y.C., Apr. 22, 1937; s. Murray and Lina (Futterman) G.; m. Elizabeth Kiner, Dec. 28, 1967. B.S., UCLA, 1958, M.S., 1964. Engr. Rand Corp. Santa Monica, Calif., 1958-60; film project supr. Kettering Found., Washington, 1966-67; ind. film maker, Los Angeles, 1968—; computer system cons., Los Angeles, 1975—; cons. to M.G.M.; instr. U. Calif. Recipient Cannes Film Festival Spl. award, 1970. Mem. Internat. Brotherhood Magicians, Tau Beta Pi, Sigma Pi Sigma. Producer films: The Magic Machines (Academy award 1969), 1969; Bright Tempest (14 internat. film awards), 1974. Home and Office: 921 N La Jolla Ave Los Angeles CA 90046

GRUNANDER, CARL L., retailing educator; b. Logan, Utah, June 29, 1947; s. Edward Ray and Ila Jane (Smith) G.; m. Christine Van Orden, Dec. 19, 1969; children—Carl Jason, Todd Ryan, Jennifer Christine. Mgmt. trainee Sears, Roebuck and Co., Ogden, Utah, 1971, dept. mgr., 1971-76; coop. edn. coordinator Weber State Coll., Ogden, Utah, 1976-79, asst. prof. distributive tech., 1979—; pres. Assn. Coop. Educators and Employers Utah, 1981; Utah adviser Delta Epsilon Chi div. Distributive Edn. Clubs Am., 1981—, chmn. exec. com. Western region bd., 1982-83. Fund-raiser United Way, Ogden, 1972-74. Recipient Outstanding Tchrs. award Dept. Distributive Tech., Weber State Coll., 1981. Mem. Am. Vocat. Assn., Distributive Edn. Clubs Am., Utah Vocat. Assn., Utah Mktg. and Distributive Edn. Assn. Republican. Mormon. Home: 943 E 2850 N Ogden UT 84404 Office: 3750 Harrison Blvd Ogden UT 84408

GRUNDMAN, JAMES EDWARD, mfg. co. exec.; b. N.Y.C., Feb. 22, 1944; s. Joseph Vincent and Ellen Joy Grundman; A. Bus. diploma Control Data Inst., 1970; A.Bus. Sci., McIntosh Coll., 1974; diploma in transp. Golden Gate U., 1980. Traffic clk. The Emporium, San Francisco, 1974-76; traffic asst. Koret of Calif., San Francisco, 1976-78, sr. traffic asst., 1978-79, traffic mgr., 1979—. Served with U.S. Army, 1961-63. Mem. Assn. ICC Practitioners, Delta Nu Alpha. Republican. Roman Catholic. Home: 698 Bush St San Francisco CA 94108 Office: 611 Mission St San Francisco CA 94105

GRUNDSTROM, EDWIN VICTOR, lawyer; b. Petaluma, Calif., Nov. 29, 1926; s. Edwin Valentine and Jennie Audry (Vail) G.; A.A., Santa Rosa Jr. Coll., 1948; A.B., U. So. Calif., 1950; J.D., Stanford, 1956; m. Genevieve Lenington, Nov. 5, 1951; children—Jan, Jill, Deidre. Admitted to Calif. bar, 1956, since practiced in Novato; mem. firm Palmer, Grundstrom & Duckworth, Novato, 1956—; partner Soiland & Assos., Novato, 1969. Mem. Republican Central Com., 1958-64; vice chmn. Sonoma State Adv. Bd., 1964-76. Pres., founder Novato Civic Found., 1968-69; bd. dirs. Novato Gen. Hosp., 1960—, pres., 1972-77. Served to 1st lt. USAF, 1945, 50-53. Recipient citation Cal. Parks and Recreation Soc., 1969. Mem. Marin Bar Assn. (dir. 1970—), Sigma Nu, Delta Theta Phi. Baptist. Kiwanian (pres. 1958-59). Home: 100 Old Ranch Rd Novato CA 94947 Office: PO Box 26 7665 Redwood Blvd Novato CA 94947

GRUNDY, GEORGE HENRY (BEN), association executive; b. Estelline, Tex., Jan. 8, 1912; s. Jesse Lee and Cora Anne (Findley) G.; m. Lena Christine Holwick, June 29, 1945; children—Betty Louise Brown, Sharon Ruth Biloff, Sandra Bartlett. City councilman City of Shafter (Calif.), 1950-74, mayor, 1958-62; mgr., sec.-treas. Shafter C. of C., 1980—. Mem. exec. bd. South San Joaquin League Cities, 1958-60; trustee, chmn. bd. Pub. Cemetery Dist. 1 Kern County (Calif.); dir. Calif. Assn. Spl. Dist.; gen. chmn. Shafter Potato and Cotton Festival. Served with U.S. Army, 1942-45. Recipient Kern County Bd. Trade award of merit, 1960; Community Service award Shafter C. of C., 1973; named Shafter Citizen of Yr., 1976. Mem. Calif. Assn. Pub. Cemeteries (past pres.). Clubs: Kiwanis (pres. 1965, lt. gov. Div. 33, 1978-79), VFW, Am. Legion, DAV (Shafter). Office: PO Box 1088 Shafter CA 93263

GRUNFELD, DENIS MAHIR, financial executive; b. Istanbul, Turkey Feb. 19, 1954; came to U.S., 1959; s. Michael and Sonia Arlette (Caraco) G. B.A. in Graphic Design, UCLA, 1976. Pres. DeGrun Designs, Santa Monica, Calif., 1973-80; chief fin. officer, Grunfeld and Brandt, Inc. Los Angeles, 1981—. Mem. Santa Monica C. of C. Democrat. Club: Rotary (Santa Monica). Office: Grundfeld and Brandt Inc 1460 4th St Suite 306 Santa Monica CA 90401

GRUNWALD, ROBERT EDWARD, planning cons., landscape architect; b. Milw., Apr. 16, 1930; s. John Leonard and Olive Althea (Kubiaczyk) G.; B.S., U. Wis., 1952; M.S. in City Planning, U. Calif.-Berkeley, 1956; m. Norma Lee Margaret Ramsey, July 17, 1954; children—Treva Olivia, Theresa Ann, Robert Edward, Stephanie Marie. Asst. planner Tulare County, Calif., 1952-54, Alameda County, Calif., 1954-55; campus planner U. Calif. at Berkeley, 1955, teaching asst., 1955-56; asst. dir. planning Tulare County, 1956-57; dir. planning, Kings County, Calif., 1957-60; pres. Grunwald & Assocs., Hanford, Calif., 1960—; vis. lectr. U. Calif., Calif. State U.-Fresno, Calif. State U.-San Luis Obispo, Bowdoin Coll., Maine, U. Pitts., U. So. Calif. Mem. Gov.'s Adv. Constrn. and Housing Task Force, Calif., 1965-66; mem. Calif. Scenic Hwy. Commn., 1961-70, chmn., 1969-70. Bd dirs. Calif. Roadside Council, Sacred Heart Hosp., Hanford, Kings County Community Action Orgn.; bd. dirs., pres. Taoist Temple Preservation Soc. Served with USNR, 1950. Recipient citation Office Pres. U.S. for contbn. to devel. Plan for Emergency Mgmt. of Resources, 1968. Mem. Am. Inst. Cert. Planners (pres. Calif. chpt. 1964-65, gov. 1969-72), Am. Soc. Landscape Architects, Am. Soc. Planning Consultants (dir. 1975—, v.p. 1976-77, pres. 1978-80), Am. Planning Assn., Calif. Assn. Cons. Planners (pres. 1974-78), Soil Conservation Soc. Am., Urban Land Inst. Club: Elks. Office: 804-C N Irwin St Hanford CA 93230

GRUNWALDT, JOEL JOHN, city agency administrator; b. Green Bay, Wis., Feb. 18, 1944; s. Carl A. and Viola Grunwaldt; m. Noel Ann Furstenberg, Dec. 27, 1966; children—Peter, Paul, Sarah; B.S., U. Wis.-Oshkosh, 1968. Faculty asst. U. Wis.-Oshkosh, 1968-70; geologist, solid waste planner Northeastern Wis. Regional Planning Commn., 1970-72; solid waste coordinator Greater Anchorage Area Borough, 1972-75; dir. solid waste services Municipality of Anchorage, 1975—. Mem. Am. Pub. Works Assn. (sec.-treas. Alaska chpt. 1975, pres. 1976). Home: 8541 Jupiter Dr Anchorage AK 99507 Office: Pouch 6-650 Anchorage AK 99502

GRUTMAN, DAVID STANLEY, corporate executive; b. Oakland, Calif., Dec. 14, 1908; s. Joseph and Anna Gertrude (Brodke) G.; m. Charlotte Donner, Apr. 10, 1912; children—Ann Gail Berland, Jon Anthony. B.A., U. Calif.-Berkeley, 1934. Tchr., Oakland, Calif., 1935-38; various positions to exec. v.p., pres., vice chmn., Barco of Calif., Gardena, 1938—. Democrat. Jewish. Club: Brentwood Country. Home: 9922 Stellbar Pl Los Angeles CA 90664 Office: 350 W Rosecrans Ave Gradena CA 90248

GRUVER, BERNARD FRANCIS, animated film designer, educator; b. Long Beach, Calif., June 25, 1923; s. Joseph and Ethel (Warshafsky) G.; student Long Beach City Coll., 1941-42; grad. Art Center Sch., 1950; m. Adah Coropoff, Aug. 18, 1946 (div. Aug. 1978); children—Nancy, Allison; m. 2d, Jan Green, Sept. 1978. Mem. tech. staff, Graphic Films Co., Los Angeles, 1950-56; designer of TV commercials Kling Studios, Los Angeles, 1954; designer Academy Pictures, N.Y.C., 1954; film dir. story and design John Sutherland Productions, Los Angeles, 1955-56; films include: The Spray's The Thing, 1955, The Golden River, 1956; designer, dir. TV commercials Ray Patin Productions, Los Angeles, 1957-58, Quartet Films Inc., Los Angeles, 1958-59; dir., designer TV commercials and entertainment films Playhouse Pictures Inc., Los Angeles, 1959-65; dir., designer TV commercials and TV entertainment films Bill Melendez Productions, Los Angeles, 1965—; films include: A Charlie Brown Christmas (George Foster Peabody award), 1965, It's The Great Pumpkin, Charlie Brown, 1966; instr. of animation design U. So. Calif., Los Angeles, 1963, 65, 68, 69-76. Recipient numerous awards including: Internat. Broadcasting award, 1963, Golden Eagle award, 1964, Venice Film Festival award, 1954, others. Mem. Acad. of Motion Pictures Arts and Scis., Internat. Animation Soc. (dir. 1963-76), Screen Cartoonist Guild (pres. 1955-57), TV Acad., U. So. Calif. and Art Center Alumni Assns. Home: 5010 Sunnyslope Ave Sherman Oaks CA 91423 Office: 439 N Larchmont Blvd Los Angeles CA 90004

GRUVER, GENE GARY, clinical psychologist, sex therapist; b. Redfield, S.D., Apr. 20, 1935; s. Howard Ezra and Dorothy Elizabeth (Price) G.; m. Dorothy Jane Dykstra, July 24, 1959; B.A. in Psychology, Grand Canyon Coll., 1966; M.A. in Psychology, U. Ariz., 1969, Ph.D. in Clin. Psychology and Physiol. Psychology, 1971. Cert. psychologist, Ariz.; diplomate in clin. psychology Am. Bd. Profl. Psychology; cert. sex therapist, Am. Assn. Sex. Educators, Counselors and Therapists, Nat. Register Health Service Providers in Psychology. Psychol. intern Long Beach VA Hosp., 1969-70; clin psychologist in ind. practice, 1971—; psychologist student counseling service U. Ariz., 1971—, instr., 1973-76. Served with Seabees, USN, 1954-56. Recipient disting. alumnus award, Grand Canyon Coll., 1974; named Handicapped Employee of Yr., Tucson, 1980, distinguished Huronian, Centennial Com., Huron C. of C., 1980; Mem. Paralyzed Vets. of Am. (Ariz. chpt. founding pres. 1965), Ariz. Holistic Health Assn. (bd. dirs.), Am. Psychol. Assn., Western Psychol. Assn., So. Ariz. Psychol. Assn. (pres., 1981-82), Psychologists in Pvt. Practice, Am. Assn. Sex Educators, Counselors and Therapists. Republican. Contbr. papers to ann. meetings, convs.; contbg. author College Student Devel. Revisted (1979); also articles, brochures. Office: Student Counseling Service Old Main U Ariz Tucson AZ 85721

GRUZEN, BENJAMIN MACSON, archtl. cons.; b. Chelsea, Mass., Aug. 21, 1910; s. Max Solomon and Ida Ella (Friedmann) G.; student Coll. Bus. Adminstrn. Boston U., 1929-30, M.I.T., 1930-32, Fairleigh Dickinson U., 1976-78; cert. in architecture Cooper Union, 1943. B.Arch., 1979; B.A. in History, Seton Hall U., 1978; m. Harriet Dorothy Weslock, Oct. 27, 1934; children—John Elliot, Marjorie Gruzen Green. With Housing Study Guild, N.Y.C., 1933-35; asso. econ. analyst Suburban Resettlement Adminstrn., Resettlement Adminstrn., Washington, 1935-36; partner Gruzen Partnership Architects (formerly Kelly & Gruzen), N.Y.C., Newark, San Francisco, 1936-73, cons., 1973-82; fall-out shelter analyst, 1964—; fellow Constrn. Specifications Inst., 1967, pres. Met. N.Y. chpt., 1961-63; mem. N.J. State Bd. Architects, dept. law and public safety, 1969-74, bd. pres., 1973-74; bd. dirs., treas. N.J. Soc. Architects, 1968. Mayor's com. revisions to bldg. code, Newark, Gov. archtl. com. for N.J. Art Commn.; mem. Mus. Soc. and Opera Guild, San Francisco. Served with Seabees USN, 1943-45. Recipient citations Cooper Union, 1978, Constrn. Specification Inst., 1964; Eagle Scout, Boy Scouts Am., 1926. Mem. Nat. Soc. Profl. Engrs. (life), AIA (nat. com. on document review, 1967-68, emeritus, 1978—, Santa Clara Valley chpt.), Phi Alpha Theta. Author: Housing Study Guild Library Manual, 1935; contbr. articles to profl. jours. Home: 5032 Pinetree Terr Campbell CA 95008

GRYCNER, EDWARD, moped mfg. co. exec.; b. Wilno, Poland, May 1, 1924; came to U.S., 1951, naturalized, 1956; s. Robert and Victoria Von Grutzner; M.B.A., Sch. Econs., London U., 1949, B.S. in Fgn. Trade, Sch. Fgn. Trade, 1949; m. Iris Lila Kehr, May 1, 1956; children—Henry, Richard, Gregory, Pamela, Nancy, April, Michelle. Export traffic mgr. George Wehry Co., N.Y.C., 1951-55; export controller U.S. Borax Corp., 1956-66; mgr. internat. ops. Ingersoll Rand, N.Y.C., 1966-67; dir. internat. ops. Revell, Inc., 1967-70; pres. Grycner Toys Internat., Grycner Leisure Group, and Grycner Moped Corp., Palm Springs, Calif., 1970—, chmn. bd., pres. Grycner Moped Corp., 1977—; lectr. fgn. trade state univs. Calif., 1978—. Recipient cert. Am. Soc. Internat. Execs., 1967. Mem. Fgn. Trade Assn. So. Calif., Los Angeles C. of C., Palm Springs C. of C., Am. Sporting Goods Assn., Am. Hobby Assn. Club: Los Angeles Internat. Contbr. numerous articles on internat. trade to mags. Home: 796 N Via Miraleste Palm Springs CA 92262 Office: PO Box 1987 Palm Springs CA 92263

GRYCZ, ANNE ELIZABETH, mental health executive; b. San Francisco, Apr. 7, 1944; d. Albert Winters and Elizabeth Gertrude (Bogle) Cummingham; children—Michal Jozef, Anastasia Christina. B.A., U. San Francisco, 1965, postgrad., 1966; postgrad. San Francisco Theol. Sem. Tchr. Spanish, Peterson High Sch., Santa Clara County (Calif.), 1966; tchr. theology adult edn. dept. Archdiocese of San Francisco, 1967-72; asst. to pres., sec. Behaviordyne, Inc., Palo Alto, Calif., 1976-81, v.p. consumer services, 1981—; cons. workshops on handicapped children. Bd. dirs. Palo Alto Adolescent Services Corp. Mem. Women's Exec. Group (dir.), Corp. Planners Assn., AAUW. Democrat. Roman Catholic. Co-author: The GuidePak, career counselling service; participant film prodn. Sauce for the Goose.

GRYGUTIS, BARBARA, artist; b. Hartford, Conn., Nov. 7, 1946; d. Robert William and Sylvia (Plakson) Zion; B.F.A., U. Ariz., 1968, M.F.A., 1971. Exhibited in group shows including Pima Community Coll., Tucson, 1977, Ariz. Western Coll., 1978, Kay Bonfoey Gallery, Tucson, 1979, Kornbluth Gallery, Fairlawn, N.J., 1979, Dinnerware Artists Coop., Tucson, 1981, Bronx Mus., 1978, Herbert Johnson Mus. Art, Cornell U., Ithaca, N.Y., 1978, Mus. Contemporary Crafts, N.Y.C., 19—, Mus. of Folk Art and Craft, Los Angeles, John Michael Kohler Arts Cntr., Sheboygan, Wis., Renwick Gallery, Smithsonian Instn., Washington, 1977, Vice President's House, Washington, 1978, others; works represented in pub. and pvt. collections; artist in residence Haystack Mountain Sch. Crafts, Maine, 1978; commns. include wall relief Valley Nat. Bank, Payson, Ariz., 1981-82, Tucson, 1981; mural and sculpture Dept. Law, State Capitol, Phoenix, 12 place table setting White House, 1977, mural Navajo County Govtl. Complex, Holbrook, Ariz., 1975-76, Kino Community Hosp., Tucson, 1977; Nat. Endowment for Arts grantee, 1975, 77; Ariz. Commn. on Arts grantee, 1973-74. Address: 273 N Main St Tucson AZ 85705

GRZESIK, JAN ALEXANDER, nuclear engineer; b. Rybnik, Poland, Aug. 7, 1939; s. Alexander Franciszek and Anna (Zurek) G.; came to U.S., 1952, naturalized, 1958; B.A. in Physics with highest honors, UCLA, 1960, Ph.D. in Nuclear Engring., 1977; M.A. in Physics, Harvard U., 1961; m. Renata Ewa Wisniewska, Jan. 4, 1971; children—Renata Lucyna, John Michael. Engr. Aeroneutronic-Philco-Ford Co., Newport Beach, Calif., 1964-65; mem. tech. staff Nat. Engring. Sci. Co., Pasadena, Calif., 1965-67; mem. tech. staff antenna lab. TRW Systems Group, Redondo Beach, Calif., 1968-73; cons. phys. scis. dept. RAND Corp., Santa Monica, Calif., 1973-77; research engr. energy and kinetics dept. Sch. Engring. and Applied Sci., UCLA, 1976-77; mem. tech. staff TRW Energy Devel. Group, Redondo Beach, Calif., 1977—. Woodrow Wilson fellow, 1960-61; NSF fellow, 1961-63. Mem. Am. Phys. Soc., Phi Beta Kappa. Author articles. Home: 5517 Babcock Ave North Hollywood CA 91607 Office: One Space Park Bldg R1 Room 2020L Redondo Beach CA 90278

GUALTIERI, VINCENT, urologist; b. Reggio Calabria, Italy, Jan. 5, 1934; s. Joseph Anthony and Victoria (Cartizano) G.; A.B., UCLA, 1955; M.D., U. Calif., Irvine, 1962; m. Gina Mirella Coggi, May 19, 1963; children—Lisa, Joseph, Stephen. Resident in urology, Los Angeles County Gen. Hosp., 1962-66; urologist Ross-Loos Med. Group, Los Angeles, 1966-68; practice medicine specializing in urology, Sherman Oaks, Calif., 1968—; clin. instr. urology Calif. Coll. Medicine, 1966-68. Diplomate Am. Bd. Urology. Fellow A.C.S.; mem. AMA, Calif. Med. Assn., Los Angeles County Med. Assn., Los Angeles Urol. Soc., Am. Urol. Assn. Republican. Office: 4955 Van Nuys Blvd Sherman Oaks CA 91403

GUARD, DONALD EUGENE, meat company executive; b. Plymouth, Ind., Nov. 18, 1928; s. Orville L. and Lois Erdene (Cramer) G.; student Purdue U., 1949-50, Alexander Hamilton Inst. Bus., 1953-56; m. Dolores Eileen Garber, Sept. 5, 1948; children—Pamela, David, Janet, Richard. Indsl. products mgr. Kraft Foods, Chgo., 1953-60; div. mgr. Leo's Quality Foods, Los Angeles, 1960-68; pres. GRD Food Brokers, Portland, Oreg., 1968-73; regional mgr. R.B. Rice Sausage Co., Lee's Summit, Mo., 1973-77, Jimmy Dean Meat Co., Dallas, 1977—; dir. Casco Devel. Co., Portland, 1972—. Mem. Deshler (Ohio) City Council, 1954-58. Served with AUS, 1946-48. Mem. Nat. Food Distbrs. Assn., So. Calif. Deli Council. Republican. Methodist. Clubs: Elks, Masons. Home: 1539 Worthington St Lake Oswego OR 97034 Office: Jimmy Dean Meat Co 1539 Worthington St Lake Oswego OR 97034

GUARINO, JOHN RALPH, physician; b. N.Y.C., Aug. 17, 1915; s. Joseph John and Marie (Ferrara) G.; B.S., LIU, 1937; M.D., Coll. Phys. and Surg., Boston, 1943; m. Kathleen Paff, Aug. 2, 1947; children—Christopher John, Joseph Charles, Edward James. Intern, Wyckoff Hosp., Bklyn., 1943-44; resident internal medicine VA Hosp., Buffalo, 1955-57; inaugurated, chief artificial kidney service Harlem Hosp., N.Y.C., also L.I. Coll. Medicine Hosp., 1952-53; asst. chief medicine VA Hosp., Livermore, Calif., 1959-69, chief of medicine VA Hosp., Poplar Bluff, Mo., 1969-72, VA Hosp., Topeka, 1972-74; internist VA Hosp., Boise, Idaho, 1974-80, cons., 1980—; clin. asst. prof. medicine U. Wash., 1977-79, clin. assoc. prof., 1979—; pioneer in devel. artificial lung; developed simplified artificial kidney, 1952; cons. dialysis and treatment uremia, 1952—; guest speaker in field. Served as capt. M.C., USAF, 1953-55. Honored by Am. Soc. Artificial Internal Organs, 1979. Diplomate Am. Bd. Internal Medicine. Fellow ACP; charter mem. Am. Soc. Artifical Internal Organs; mem. AMA (Physicians Recognition award 1976, 79), Mass. Med. Soc. Roman Catholic. Developed auscultatory percussion, auscultatory percussion of chest and head; developed a new diagnostic procedure to detect urinary retention. Address: 2404 Ormond St Boise ID 83705

GUBANICH, ALAN ANDREW, biology educator; b. Phoenixville, Pa., Sept. 19, 1942; s. Andrew Joseph and Marie Theresa (Ulishny) G.; m. Rita Carolyn Osborne, Jan. 31, 1970; 1 dau., Kimberly Ann. B.S. in Biology, Wilkes Coll., 1964; M.S. in Zoology, U. Ariz., 1966, Ph.D. in Biol. Scis., 1970. Teaching asst. dept. biology U. Ariz., Tucson, 1964-70; asst. prof. U. Nev.-Reno, 1970-78, assoc. prof., 1978—, dir. gen. biology, 1970—. Recipient Outstanding Tchr. of Yr. award U. Nev. Alumni Assn., 1977, U. Nev. grantee, 1973. Mem. Lahontan Audubon Soc. (editor Pelican newsletter, dir. 1975-78), AAAS, Am. Inst. Biol. Scis., Nat. Wildlife Fedn., Nat. Assn. Biology Tchrs., Assn. Biology Lab. Edn., Flips Gymnastics Club (meets chmn.), U. Nev.-Reno Biology Club (faculty advisor), Phi Kappa Phi. Democrat. Roman Catholic. Author: General Biology in the Laboratory, 1977; contbr. articles to profl. jours. Home: 565 Peter Circle Reno NV 89503 Office: Dept Biology FLS 137 U Nev Reno NV 89557

GUDMUNDSON, BONNIE VIRGINIA STUCKI, speech/lang. pathologist; b. Salt Lake City, Feb. 18, 1930; d. William Theophil and Lucy Marie (Sorensen) Stucki; B.S., U. Utah, 1951, M.A., 1974; m. Ariel George Gudmundson, Aug. 31, 1950; children—Diane Lucy Gudmundson Gardner, Connie Ann Gudmundson Hadden, Denise Allaine Gudmundson Jones, Lois Jan Gudmundson Crawley, Carol Lyn Gudmundson Lemon. Byron James. Instr., Salt Lake City Dept. Recreation, 1947, 48; elem. sch. tchr. Salt Lake Sch. Dist., 1951; communication disorders specialist Davis County (Utah) Sch. Dist., 1975—; pvt. practice speech-lang. pathology, 1981—; clin. instr. U. Utah, Salt Lake City, 1977—. Sec., Bountiful (Utah) Community Concert Assn., 1966-67, publicity chmn. 1967-68. Cert. in elem. teaching, communication disorders-speech pathology, Utah Bd. Edn.; lic. speech/lang. pathologist, State of Utah. Mem. Am. Speech-Lang.-Hearing Assn. (cert. of clin. competence in speech pathology), Utah Speech and Hearing Assn., Davis Edn. Assn., Council for Exceptional Children (legis. info. officer Utah div. Children with Communication Disorders 1980-82), Internat. Assn. Logopedics and Phoniatrics, Utah State Poetry Soc., League of Utah Writers (sec.-treas. chpt. 1981-82). Republican. Mem. Ch. Jesus Christ of Latter-day Saints. Contbr. poetry to Deseret News, Relief Soc. Mag. Office: 425 Medical Dr Bountiful UT 84010

GUE, LESLIE ROBB, educator; b. Medicine Hat, Alta., Can., Aug. 5, 1918; s. Dell Irvin and Annie Matilda (Robb) G.; B.Ed., U. Alta., 1947, postgrad., 1948-49, Ph.D. (Univ. fellow), 1967; B.S.W., U. B.C. (Can.), 1960; m. Lillian Maud Dutton, Sept. 15, 1943 (div.); children—David, Linda, Alison. Clk. Imperial Bank Can., Sangudo, Alta., 1936-40; tchr. Lethbridge (Alta.) Sch. Div., 1947-48, Edmonton (Alta.) Public Sch. Bd., 1949-51; editor Dept. Edn. Alta., Edmonton, 1951-52, supr. sch. broadcasts, 1952-54, supt. schs., 1961-64; coordinator rehab. services Alta. Dept. Welfare, Edmonton, 1954-61; prof. dept. ednl. adminstrn. U. Alta., Edmonton, 1966—; cons. native edn. Can. Edn. Assn., Council Ministers of Edn. Can.; dir. Thailand-Can. Comprehensive Sch. Projects, 1966-80; project mgmt. cons. Thailand Ministry of Edn., 1980-82. Bd. dirs. Goodwill Rehab. Services Alta., 1963-79, pres., 1967-69; mem. leadership com. Internat. Intervisitation Program, 1978-Canada, 1974-78. Served with RCAF, 1940-45. Can. Council travel grantee, 1974. Mem. Amnesty Internat. (nat. exec. com. 1974-77), Can. Soc. Study of Edn., Can. Assn. Study of Ednl. Adminstrn., Can. Assn. Social Workers, Commonwealth Council Edn. Adminstrn., Phi Delta Kappa. Unitarian Universalist. Author: An Introduction to Educational Administration in Canada, 1977. Home: PO Box 4453 Edmonton AB T6E 4T5 Canada Office: Dept Ednl Adminstrn U Alta Edmonton AB T6G 2G5 Canada

GUERRERO, CELINA SISON, pediatrician, child psychiatrist; b. Manila, Philippines, May 18, 1938; d. Guillermo Vinluan and Lucia De La Rosa (Visaya) S.; A.B., U. Philippines, 1957, M.D., 1962; m. Reuben C. Guerrero, June 18, 1962; children—Maria Chiarina, Maria Leonora, Anthony Paul. Intern Philippine Gen. Hosp., Manila, 1961-62, Church Home & Hosp., Balt., 1962-63; resident in pediatrics U. Md. Hosp., Balt., 1963-65, fellow in child psychiatry, 1965-66, asst. dir. Central Evaluation Clinic for Children, 1966-68; practice medicine specializing in child psychiatry, Manila, 1968-73, Honolulu, 1973—. Diplomate Am. Acad. Pediatrics. Fellow Am. Acad. Pediatrics; mem. U. Philippines Alumni Med. Assn., Philippine Med. Assn. Hawaii. Democrat. Roman Catholic. Home: 1424 Ohialoke St Honolulu HI 96821

GUERRERO, REUBEN CASTRO, med. oncologist, internist; b. Manila, Philippines, Aug. 22, 1935; came to U.S., 1962, naturalized, 1978; s. Jacobo Tolentino and Francisca Claravall (Castro) G.; A.A., U. Philippines, Manila, 1952, M.D. (Univ. scholar, 1955-56; United Drug Co. scholar, 1956-57), 1957; m. Celina V. Sison, June 18, 1962; children—Chiarina, Leonora, Anthony Paul. Intern, Philippine Gen. Hosp., Manila, 1956-57; mem. faculty Coll. of Medicine, U. Philippines, 1957-62; resident in medicine, Ch. Home and Hosp., Balt., 1962-64, chief resident, 1965-66; postdoctoral fellow in medicine Johns Hopkins Hosp., Balt., 1964-65, postdoctoral fellow in med. oncology, 1966-68; asst. prof. medicine, chief chemotherapy div. U. Philippines and Cancer Inst., 1968-73; med. oncologist, chmn. cancer com. Straub Clinic and Hosp., Honolulu, 1973—; clin. assoc. prof. John A. Burns Sch. Medicine, U. Hawaii; chmn. research Philippine Cancer Soc., 1969-73; chmn. service and rehab. com., bd. dirs. Hawaii div. Am. Cancer Soc., 1973—. Served with Philippine Army Res., 1957-58. Fellow ACP; mem. Am. Soc. Internal Medicine, Am. Soc. Clin. Oncology, Philippine Soc. Med. Oncology,Honolulu County Med. Soc., Hawaii Med. Assn. (cancer commn.), AMA, Am. Geriatric Soc., Aerospace Med. Assn., Honolulu Marathon Assn. Republican. Roman Catholic. Club: Honolulu. Contbr. articles to profl. jours. Home: 1424 Ohialoke St Honolulu HI 96821 Office: Straub Clinic and Hosp 888 S King St Honolulu HI 96813

GUEST, BERNETTE PARKER, oil company executive; b. Salt Lake City, May 18, 1952; d. Robert Farnsworth and Ilona Leiola (Wiebke) Parker; m. Russel Paul Guest, Sept. 15, 1973; children—Forrest Farnsworth, Robert Russel. B.S. in Fin., Colo. State U., 1973. Transfer agt., sec.-treas. Am. Stock Transfer, Inc., Denver, 1969-70; v.p., dir. 1971-74; corp. sec., controller Golden Oil Co., Denver, 1974-78, treas., 1977—, dir., 1976—, v.p., 1978—; sec.-treas., dir., cons. G & S Service Co., Inc., Tulsa, 1977-79. Mem. Nat. Fedn. Ind. Bus., Ind. Petroleum Assn. Mountain States, Ind. Petroleum Assn. Am., Petroleum Accts. Soc. Colo., Am. Soc. Profl. and Exec. Women, Nat. Assn. Female Execs., Inst. Energy Devel., Am. Mgmt. Assn. Office: 3650 S Yosemite St Suite 430 Denver CO 80237

GUGAS, CHRIS, criminologist; b. Omaha, Aug. 12, 1921; s. Nicholas and Vera (Henas) G.; student U. So. Calif., 1946-49, U. Calif. at Northridge, 1955-56; B.A., M.A. in Pub. Adminstrn., U. Beverly Hills, 1977; D.Div., Ch. Living Sci., 1968; Ph.D., U. Beverly Hills, 1983; m. Anne Claudia Setaro, June 27, 1942; children—Chris, Steven Edward, Carol Ann Gugas Hawker. Asst. dir. security Los Angeles Bd. Edn., 1948-49; spl. agt. CIA, Washington, 1950-54; criminol. cons., Los Angeles, 1955-61; pub. safety dir., Omaha, 1962-65; dir. polygraph services Profl. Security Cons., Los Angeles, 1966—; exec. dir. Calif. Acad. Polygraph Scis., Los Angeles, 1974-76, The Truthseekers, 1975—; instr. Los Angeles Inst. Polygraph, 1979-82, Gormac Polygraph Sch., Los Angeles, 1972-73; chief instr. Las Vegas Acad. Polygraph Sci., 1982-83; columnist Los Angeles Daily Jour., Security World mag., The Truthseekers. Mem. advisory bd., sec. Calif. Dept. Consumer Affairs, 1971-76. Served with USMCR, 1940-45, 47-49. Mem. Marine Corps League (comdr. 1946), Marine Corps Combat Corr.'s Assn. (pres. Los Angeles chpt. 1975-77), Nat. Bd. Polygraph Examiners (pres. 1958), Security Officers Assn. (pres. 1968), Am. Polygraph Assn. (pres. 1971, exec. dir. 1972-73), Am. Soc. Indsl. Security. Club: Los Angeles Press. Author: The Silent Witness; co-author: The National Corruptors; Pre-Employment Polygraph; The Polygraphist in Court; Our National Rebellion, 1982; contbr. numerous articles to various jours. Home: 4018 Dixie Canyon Sherman Oaks CA 91403 Office: 1680 Vine St Hollywood CA 90028

GUGGENHEIM, ALLEN, computer services co. exec.; b. Pitts., Sept. 10, 1939; s. Harold and Minnie (Scott) G.; B.S., U. Pitts., 1961; postgrad. U. Md., 1961-62, George Washington U., 1962, UCLA, 1962-64; m. Karen Merle Copperman, June 18, 1961; children—Stephen Glenn, Scott Evan, Lori Anne. Aerospace technologist NASA, Greenbelt, Md., 1961-62; sect. head Hughes Aircraft, 1962-65; ops. mgr. Data Dynamics Inc., 1965-67; dept. mgr. Computer Scis. Corp., El Segundo, Calif., 1967-68; v.p. ops. CTC Computer Corp., Palo Alto, Calif., 1968-71; pres., chmn. bd. Info. Mgmt. Internat., San Jose, Calif., 1971—; dir. Interscience Systems Inc. Pres. Congregation Beth David, Saratoga, Calif., 1978-80, officer, mem. bd., 1975—; v.p. bd. dirs. No. Calif. region United Synagogues Am., 1978—; mem. exec. com. mem. March of Dimes, San Jose, Calif., 1978—; bd. dirs., v.p., pres., sec., campaign chmn. Jewish Fedn. Greater San Jose, 1978—; pres. Golden State Boychoir Assn., 1976-77; officer N.W. YMCA, Cupertino, Calif., 1971-74. Recipient Community Service award U. Judaism, 1981. Mem. Presidents Assn. of Am. Mgmt. Assn. Contbr. articles to profl. jours. Office: 1101 S Winchester Blvd San Jose CA 95128

GUGGENHIME, RICHARD JOHNSON, lawyer; b. San Francisco, Mar. 6, 1940; s. Richard E. and Charlotte Mary (Johnson) G.; A.B. with distinction in polit. sci. Stanford, 1961; LL.B., Harvard U., 1964; m. Emlen Frances Hall, June 5, 1965; children—Andrew Laurence, Lisa Johnson, Mia Emlen. Bar: Calif. 1966; spl. asst. U.S. Senator Hugh Scott, Pa., 1964; assoc. Heller, Ehrman, White & McAuliffe, attys., San Francisco, 1965-71, ptnr., 1972—. Commr., San Francisco Parking Authority, 1976-78; commr. San Francisco Bd. Permit Appeals, 1978—, pres., 1980-81. Bd. dirs. San Francisco Boys' Club, 1970-73, Univ. Calif. Art Mus., 1966-72, The Guardsmen, 1970-74, San Francisco Univ. High Sch., 1973-77, 83—, Marine World Africa U.S.A., Inc., 1980—; mem. Stanford Assocs., 1969—. Mem. Calif., San Francisco bar assns., Phi Kappa Sigma. Clubs: San Francisco Olympic, University, Bohemian (San Francisco); Silverado (Napa, Calif.); Wine and Food Soc.; Chevalier de Tastavin. Home: 2375 Vallejo St San Francisco CA 94123 Office: 44 Montgomery St San Francisco CA 94104

GUHL, ELDON LOWELL, author, investor, educator, electrical engineer; b. Denton, Tex., Nov. 17, 1908; s. Columbus Ranthemanthus and Roxie Ella (Johnson) G.; B.S. in E.E., U. N.Mex., 1965, B.B.A., 1973; m. Bertha Catherine Verda, Sept. 27, 1936. Enlisted USN, 1928, advanced through grades to comdr., 1954; served on U.S.S. Melville, U.S.S. Pruitt, U.S.S. McCormick, Pacific, 1929-37; U.S.S. Philadelphia, Atlantic, 1937-38; U.S.S. Cincinnati, Pacific, 1938-39; U.S.S. Portland, Pacific, 1939-45; Stationed Pearl Harbor Naval Shipyard, 1945-48; mem. Mil. Mission to Turkey, 1948-50; assigned Electronics Maintenance Sch., Gt. Lakes, Ill., 1950-51, Armed Forces Spl. Weapons Program, Albuquerque, 1951-58, ret., 1958; investor, 1958—; author: A Guide for Advancement in Electrical Ratings, 1943; How to Make an A or at Least A D in a Subject, 1963; How to have $100,000 in 15 Years, 1969; (essay) The Past, Present and the Future, 1976. Mem. Ret. Officers Assn., Nat. Assn. Uniformed Services, Am. Assn. Ret. Persons, Am. Legion. Home: 1602 Aliso Dr NE Albuquerque NM 87110

GUIANG, EVELYN VITAN, educator; b. Cavite City, Philippines, May 16, 1935; came to U.S., 1967, naturalized, 1974; d. Lope M. and

Rosalia P. (Vitan) G.; elem. tchr.'s cert. with honors, Philippine Normal Coll., 1952; B.S. cum laude, U. of the East, Philippines, 1956; ESL cert. UCLA, 1962, M.A. in Edn., 1963; Ed.D., U. of Pacific, 1980. Tchr. elem. schs. Cavite City, Philippines, 1954-61; instr. English, Philippine Sci. High Sch., 1964-67; tchr. primary grades El Portal Sch., Tracy, Calif., 1967-75; reading specialist Tracy pub. schs., 1975—; lang. and culture instr. Philippines tng. programs Peace Corps, summers, 1963, 66, 67, 68. Fulbright-Smith/Mundt fellow UCLA, 1961; recipient E.C. Moore award UCLA, 1962; Outstanding Elem. Tchr. award, 1974; HEW fellow, 1977-80. Mem. Internat. Reading Assn., Assn. Supervision and Curriculum Devel., Calif. Assn. Bilingual Edn., Assn. Filipino-Am. Educators (v.p. 1980-82), Reading Specialists of Calif., Delta Kappa Gamma, Phi Delta Kappa. Republican. Roman Catholic. Home: 3591 Quail Lakes Dr 28 Stockton CA 95207 Office: 315 E 11th St Tracy CA 95376

GUIDO, LOUIE, mfg. co. exec.; b. Oakland, Calif., Apr. 15, 1931; s. Frank and Vintz (Prinzo) G.; A.S. in Bus., San Diego City Coll., 1956; B.S. in Bus. Mgmt., San Diego State U., 1960; m. Joan McGregor, Sept. 2, 1954; children—Donald E., Linda D., David A., Lorraine D. Br. mgr. Brown Engring. Co., 1956-58; standards analyst Ryan Aero. Co., 1958-60; gen. mgr. Hamilton Electro Sales Co., San Diego, 1960-69; co-founder, 1969, v.p., sec., dir. Celtec Co., Irvine, Calif., 1969-81; co-founder, 1977, sec.-treas., dir. Bishop Electronics Corp., Pico Rivera, Calif., 1977-81; co-founder, 1979, partner Lectro Lease, Mission Viejo, Calif., 1979-81, owner, 1981—. Served with USN, 1950-54; Korea. Republican. Mormon.

GUILD, DAVID WILLIAM, data processing executive, consultant; b. Blue Island, Ill., Oct. 1, 1944; s. William Miller and Dolores Jean (Kay) G.; m. Janice Lee Munson, Sept. 3, 1966; children—Wendy L., Jeffrey A. B.A., Knox Coll., 1966. Systems engr. Electronic Data Systems, Dallas, 1971-74, account mgr., 1974-78; fin. systems mgr. Foremost, McKesson Inc., San Francisco, 1978-80, dir. corp. systems, 1980-81, v.p. info. services div., 1981—; cons. Treas. Cowell Homeowners Assn., Concord, Calif., 1980—, pres., 1981—; bd. dirs. Foremost-McKesson Employees Polit. Fund; mem. San Quentin Trade Adv. Council. Served to lt. USN, 1966-71. Clubs: Tennis, Engineers (San Francisco). Home: 4495 Clear Creek Ct Concord CA 94521

GUILD, MONTAGUE, JR., fin. exec.; b. Los Angeles, June 6, 1942; s. Montague and Dorothy (Duncan) G.; B.A., U. Calif. at Santa Barbara, 1964; M.B.A. in Fin., Calif. State U., 1968; m. Andrea Taylor Cole, Dec. 19, 1973. Fin. analyst Security Pacific Nat. Bank, Los Angeles, 1968-69; securities analyst, portfolio mgr. Taurus Partners, Los Angeles, 1969; gen. partner The Himalaya Fund, Santa Monica, Calif., 1969-82; founder, pres. Guild Investment Mgmt., Inc., Malibu, Calif., 1969—; pres. Calif. Ranch Properties, 1978—. Tchr., Transcendental Meditation Program, 1969—; trustee World Plan Exec. Council, 1974—; bd. dirs. Am. Found. for Sci. of Creative Intelligence, 1973—. Served with Calif. Air N.G., 1966-67. Mem. Internat. Platform Assn., Phi Kappa Phi, Delta Tau Delta. Club: Bel Air Bay. Home: 29863 Cuthbert Rd Malibu CA 90265 Office: 23410 Civic Center Way Suite E10 Malibu CA 90265

GUILD, PATRICIA BURKE, educational consultant; b. N.Y.C., June 28, 1943; d. James Francis and Marjorie (Murray) O'Rourke; m. Stephen Eves Guild, Nov. 25, 1972; children—Darren, Michael. B.A., Queens Coll., 1965; M.Ed., U. Mass., 1971, E.Ed., 1980. Mem. program staff M.A.T. program U. Mass., 1970-72, resource tchr., staff devel. coop., 1972-73; workshop dir. Intercultural Assocs., 1974-75; prin., spl. edn. dir. Shutesbury (Mass.) Elem. Sch., 196-80; lectr. Western Wash. U., Bellingham, 1981-82; facilitator prin.'s inservice program Seattle Pub. Schs., 1981-83; assoc. The Teaching Advisory, Seattle; adj. instr. Seattle Pub. U., U. Wash., Seattle U. Recipient Human Relations award B'nai B'rith. Mem. Assn. Supervision and Curriculum Devel., Phi Delta Kappa. Contbr. articles to profl. jours.; author: Cultural Initiative Series: Africa, Latin America, Our Heritage, South and South East Asia, 1974; Latin American and Our Heritage, 1976; (with Susan Carpenter) South and South East Asia, 1978. Office: PO Box 99131 Seattle WA 98199

GUILES, ROBERT EMERSON, artist; b. Addison, N.Y., Oct. 14, 1917; s. Lester E. and Amelia (Kreja) G.; student U. Rochester, 1939, Acad. Art, San Francisco, 1945-46, Indian Valley Colls., Novato, Calif., 1981—; m. Hazel Mae Anderson, June 7, 1947; children—William Alan, Frank Emerson. Asst. art dir. Ruthrauf & Ryan, Advt., 1948; staff artist San Francisco News, 1948-60, News-Call Bull., 1960-65, San Francisco Newspaper Agy., 1965-80; advt. cons., freelance graphic designer, 1980—; polit. cartoonist various labor publs., artist, 1958—. Mem. Black Raven Pipe Band San Francisco, 1966-67. Publicity chmn. Marin Citizens for Responsible Firearms Control. Served to capt. AUS, 1940-45. Mem. Newspaper Guild (pres. local 52 1964, 75-76, treas. 1978-79). Clubs: Sierra. Democrat. Contbr. articles to profl. jours. Home and Office: 1265 Parkwood Dr Novato CA 94947

GUILL, SUSAN ARLOINE, safety/loss control engineer; b. Dubuque, Iowa, Mar. 26, 1952; d. Glenn Eugene Orr and Dorothy Maryland (Coppinger) O.; m. Richard Vernile Guill, Jan. 27, 1971; 1 dau., Jessica. Student Bakersfield Coll., 1970-74; B.A., Calif. State U.-Bakersfield, 1975; postgrad., U. So. Calif., 1982—. Safety rep. State Fund, Bakersfield, 1978-81; loss control engr. Indsl. Indemnity, Bakersfield, 1981—. Instr. ARC. Recipient Recognition award for outstanding safety servicing State Compensation Bd., 1980. Mem. Am. Soc. Safety Engrs., Golden Empire Safety Soc., AAUW, Assn. Oilwell Servicing Contractors. Democrat. Home: 9113 Butternut Ave Bakersfield CA 93306 Office: 2200 19th St Bakersfield CA 93301

GUILLEMIN, ROGER, physiologist, educator; b. Dijon, France, Jan. 11, 1924; s. Raymond and Blanche (Rigollot) G.; B.A., U. Dijon, 1941, B.Sc., 1942; M.D., Faculty of Medicine, Lyons, France, 1949; Ph.D., U. Montreal, 1953; hon. degrees: U. Rochester, 1976, U. Chgo., 1977, Baylor Coll. Medicine, 1978, U. Ulm (Ger.), 1978, U. Dijon (France), 1978, U. Libre de Bruxelles (Belgium), 1979, U. Montreal, 1979; m. Lucienne Jeanne Billard, Mar. 22, 1951; children—Chantal, Francois, Claire, Helene, Elizabeth, Cecile. Came to U.S., 1953, naturalized, 1963. Intern, resident univs. hosps., Dijon, 1949-51; assoc. dir., asst. prof. Inst. Exptl. Medicine and Surgery, U. Montreal, 1951-53; assoc. dir. dept. exptl. endocrinology Coll. de France, Paris, 1960-63; prof. physiology Baylor Coll. Medicine, 1953—; adj. prof. medicine U. Calif. at San Diego, 1970—; resident fellow Salk Inst., 1970—. Decorated Legion of Honor (France), 1974; recipient Gairdner Internat. award, 1974; Lasker Found. award, 1975; Dickson prize in medicine, 1976; Passano award in med. sci., 1976; Schmitt medal in neurosci., 1977; U.S. Nat. Medal of Sci., 1977; Barren gold medal, 1979; Dale medal Soc. Endocrinology (U.K.), 1980; co-recipient Nobel prize for medicine, 1977. Fellow AAAS; mem. Am. Physiol. Soc., Endocrine Soc. (council), Soc. Exptl. Biology and Medicine, Internat. Brain Research Orgn., Internat. Soc. Research Biology Reprodn., Soc. Neuro-sci., Nat. Acad. Sci., Club of Rome. Office: Salk Inst Box 85800 San Diego CA 92138

GUILLIAMS, DONALD LEE, college dean; b. Coshocton, Ohio, Aug. 9, 1934; s. Carlos Albert and Ernestine Katherine (Middy) G.; m. Ann Lester, Sept. 22, 1957 (div.); children—Tim, Steve, Kathy; m. 2d Carole Anderson, Aug. 31, 1980. B.Commerce, Bliss Coll., 1954; B.S., Kent State U., 1960; M.S. Fla. State U., 1962; Ed.D., U. Mo., 1974. Dir. guidance Heath City (Ohio) Schs., 1964-67; Counselor Kellogg (Mich.) Community Coll., 1967-70; assoc. dean Columbia (Mo.) Coll., 1972-74; dean of students and community services Western Wyo. Community Coll., Rock Springs, 1974—. Chmn. Right to Read Task Force, 1977-79; bd. dirs. Mountain Plains Adult Edn. Assn., 1978-80. Served with U.S. Army, 1955-57. Fellow Ednl. Profl. Devel. Act, U. Mo., 1970-71. Mem. Am. Personnel and Guidance Assn., Nat. Council Student Devel., Nat. Council Community Services Continuing Edn. Democrat. Office: Western Wyoming Coll PO Box 428 Rock Springs WY 82901

GUIMARY, RAMON CURTIS, distbn. exec.; b. Portland, Oreg., Aug. 31, 1929; s. Adrian Alturas and Ellen Jean (Lund) G.; student U. Wash., 1948-49; B.S., U. Oreg., 1960; m. Mary Ellen Hull, July 18, 1959; children—Jeannine, Jennifer. Traffic mgr. Albers Milling div. Carnation Co., Portland, Los Angeles, 1954-62; traffic mgr. Omark Industries, Portland, 1964-70, distbn. mgr., 1970—. Sec., gen. mgr. Worjaws Shippers Assn., Portland, 1965-69, pres., 1970-71. Served with AUS, 1950-52. Named Oreg. Transp. Man of Year, 1972. Mem. Am. Soc. Traffic and Transp. (certified), ICC Practitioners Assn., Nat. Council Phys. Distbn. Mgmt., World Trade Com., Portland Air Cargo Assn., Western Internat. Trade Group, Portland C. of C., Dist. Export Council, Delta Nu Alpha. Home: 6707 SE 34th Av Portland OR 97202 Office: 4909 SE International Way Portland OR 97222

GUINN, AL F., music co. exec., band dir.; b. Parkersburg, W.Va., Mar. 25, 1928; s. Alva Foster and Garnett (Creel) G.; B.Sc. in Music Edn., U. Cin., 1952, postgrad., 1960-63; M.Mus. Edn., Miami U., Oxford, Ohio, 1956; Ed.D., East Coast U., 1969; 1 dau., Caryl Joscelyn. Band dir. Mt. Healthy (Ohio) City Schs., 1950-57; band dir., chmn. dept. music Princeton City Schs., Cin., 1957-63; acting dir. U. Cin. Bands, 1963; band dir., chmn. dept. mus. Fine Arts div., assoc. prof. Rocky Mountain Coll., Billings, Mont., 1963-69, 76-78; band dir., assoc. prof. music edn. Wright State U., Dayton, Ohio, 1969-73; owner Al Guinn's Music, Billings, 1973-78; Western Sales rep. L.D. Heater Music Co., Portland, Oreg., 1978-79; band and orch. dir. Butte (Mont.) High Sch., 1979—; flutist Billings Symphony Orch., 1963-69, 73-78; flutist Billings Chamber Orch.; dir. S.-Central Mont. Tri-County Honor Band, 1974-76; instr. flute Rocky Mountain Coll., 1974-78; assoc. prof. Eastern Mont. Coll., 1976; dir., founder Billings Concert Band, 1975-78; assoc. condr. Butte Symphony Orch., 1980—; adjudicator Dist., Region and State Music Festival, Mont., Wyo., N.D., Ohio, Ill.; marching band adjudicator, Mont., Wyo., Ohio. Served as flutist USMC Band, 1946-48. Mem. Music Educators Nat. Conf. (past dist. pres., chpt. sponsor), Mont. Bandmasters Assn., Coll. Band Dirs. Nat. Assn., Ohio Music Educators Assn., Nat. Band Assn., Am. Sch. Band Dirs. Assn., Antique Automobile Club Am., Phi Beta Mu. Club: Rolls-Royce Owners; Rolls-Royce Enthusiasts, Bently Drivers (Eng.). Office: 2000 Dewey Blvd Butte MT 59701

GUINN, GENE, plant physiologist, researcher; b. Prairie Grove, Ark., Mar. 19, 1928; s. John Sherman and Ethel Frances (Grose) G.; m. Mary Sue Crowder, Sept. 17, 1955; children—David Alan, Nancy Elaine. B.S. with honors in Gen. Agr., U. Ark., 1952, M.S. in Agronomy, 1957; Ph.D. in Plant Physiology, Tex. A&M U., 1961. Agt. agronomist Agrl. Research Service, U.S. Dept. Agr., Fayetteville, Ark., 1953-57, research agronomist, College Station, Tex., 1957-61, plant physiologist, Stillwater, Okla., 1961-70, supervisory plant physiologist, Phoenix, 1970—; mem. faculty Okla. State U., 1961-70. Served with U.S. Army, 1946-47. Mem. Am. Soc. Plant Physiologists (editorial bd.), Crop Sci. Soc. Am., Am. Soc. Agronomy. Mem. Ch. of Christ. Contbr. numerous articles to tech. jours. Home: 1138 E Balboa Dr Tempe AZ 85282 Office: 4135 E Broadway Rd Phoenix AZ 85040

GUINN, HENRY ALAN, consultant; b. Bristol, Va., Mar. 22, 1952; s. Henry Virgil and Alsace Lorraine (Jones) G.; B.S., Tenn. Tech. U., 1975, postgrad., 1976; m. Carla Denise Austin Highfill, Sept. 5, 1980; children—Daniel Joseph, Elizabeth Lorraine. Unit mgr. Pizza Hut, Inc., Cookeville, Tenn., 1974-76, Lebanon, Tenn., 1976, area gen. mgr., Waycross, Ga., 1976-77; field service rep. Franchise Services, Inc., Atlanta, 1977-78; nat. mgr. Equipment Sales, Wichita, Kans., 1978-79; franchise ops. rep. Pepsico Food Service Internat., Wichita, 1980-81; dir. francise devel. Can., 1981; gen. mgr. PM Foods Ltd., Calgary, Alta., Can., 1981-82; franchise area dir. Wendy's Internat., Inc., Lake Oswego, Oreg., 1982-83; pres. AVM Mgmt. Cons., Ltd., Calgary, Alta., 1982—. Recipient Pub. Service awards Am. Radio Relay League, 1969-74. Mem. Am. Radio Relay League, Can. Radio Relay League, Woodrow Wilson Ctr. for Scholars, Calgary Amateur Radio Assn., Omicron Delta Kappa. Home: 9824 SW Quail Post Rd Portland OR 97219

GUINTHER, PAULINE, physical education educator; b. Milw., Nov. 3, 1931; s. Walter and Dorothy G.; B.S., U. Wis., LaCrosse, 1953; M.S., Ariz. State U., 1961, Ed.D., 1966. Tchr. public schs., Winneconne, Wis., 1953-54, Whitefish Bay, Wis., 1955-56, Burlington, Wis., 1957-60; tchr. Arcadia High Sch., Scottsdale, Ariz., 1960-70; prof. phys. edn. Calif. State U., 1970—; cons. in field. Mem. Assn. Supervision and Curriculum Devel., AAHPERD (v.p. Ariz. chpt. 1968-69, v.p. S.W. dist. 1975-79, pres. 1979-80, S.W. dist. Honor award 1983), Calif. Assn. Health, Phys. Edn., Recreation and Dance, Western Soc. Phys. Edn. of Coll. Women, Nat. Assn. Phys. Edn. for Higher Edn., Pi Lambda Theta, Kappa Delta Pi. Contbr. articles in field to profl. jours. Home: 1945 Wingfield Way Carmichael CA 95608 Office: 6000 J St Sacramento CA 95619

GULARTE, RICHARD ALVIN, real estate broker; b. San Jose, Calif., Jan. 10, 1933; s. Manuel Souza and Rose Edith (Passadori) G.; A.A., Hartnell Coll., 1953; student Calif. Poly. U.; m. Sara Georgana Grossi, Feb. 28, 1958; children—Richard, Christopher. Owner, Richard Gularte & His Orch., 1953-55; ranch mgr. Gularte Farms, San Juan Bautista, Calif., 1958-63; pres. Richard A. Gularte & Assos., Real Estate, San Juan Bautista, 1964—; sec.-treas. San Juan Assos., Inc., 1967-75. Com. chmn. San Benito County Citizens Advisory Com., 1972-75. Vice-chmn., San Benito County Democratic Central Com., 1974. Served with USN, 1956-57. Mem. San Benito County (pres. 1974), San Juan Bautista (dir. 1970-75) chambers commerce, San Juan Bautista Hist. Soc. (pres. 1973-77), San Benito County Bd. Realtors (pres. 1978-79), Nat. Inst-Farm and Land Brokers, Calif. Real Estate Assn., Nat. Assn. Realtors. Home: 2345 San Juan Canyon Rd San Juan Bautista CA 95045 Office: 308 3d St PO Box 1 San Juan Bautista CA 95045

GULCHER, ROBERT HARRY, aerospace executive; b. Columbus, Ohio, Aug. 26, 1925; s. Alban Henry and Beatrice Margaret (Plohr) G.; m. Anne Winchester, Dec. 14, 1958; m. 2d Suzanne Kone, Apr. 12, 1969; children—Robert G., Jeffery R., Donald A., Andrew N., Kristin M. B.S., U.S. Mcht. Marine Acad., 1945; B.E.E., Ohio State U., 1950. With N. Am. Aviation Co. (merged with Rockwell Internat. Corp. 1968), Columbus, Ohio, 1951—, chief engr., 1966-79, div. dir. research and engring., El Segundo, Calif., 1979-81, v.p. research and engring., 1981—. Served to midshipman USN, 1943-45. Mem. AIAA, IEEE, Nat. Mgmt. Assn. Republican. Lutheran. Clubs: Varsity —O— Ohio State U., Assn. Old Crows. Home: 30034 Via Borica Rancho Palos Verdes CA 90274 Office: 201 Douglas St El Segundo CA

GULLANG-CAPERS, DEBORAH JEAN, psychological therapist, educational administrator; b. Chgo., Sept. 11, 1949; d. Marvin Olaf and Jean Theresa (Conte) Gullang; m. Hedges Capers, Mar. 7, 1982. B.S. with highest honors, U. Ill., 1971; M.S. in Neurosci., U. Calif.-San Diego, 1978; Ph.D. in Psychology, Internat. Coll., 1982. Cert. marriage, family and child counselor intern, Calif. Tchr., adminstr. World Plan Exec. Council, U.S. and Europe, 1971-75; research asst. U. Calif.-San Diego and Salk Inst., La Jolla, Calif., 1975-79; counselor, therapist, tchr., adminstr. San Diego Inst., La Jolla, 1979-83, dir. eating disorders program, 1983—; lectr., tchr. community outreach and edn., pub. relations. Mem. San Diego Arts Found., La Jolla Art Mus., Atheneum Arts. Sloan-Kettering Research grantee, 1975. Mem. Dysorexia Assn., Assn. for Eating Disorders, Phi Beta Kappa, Phi Lambda Delta. Clubs: Women's, Athletic (San Diego). Research, publs. in bulimia. Home: PO Box 1483 La Jolla CA 92038 Office: San Diego Inst 6639 La Jolla Blvd La Jolla CA 92037

GULLEKSON, ELLSWORTH E., management, engineering and energy consultant; b. Beltrami, Minn., Feb. 17, 1912; s. Charles E. and Amelia (Johnson) G.; B.S. in Chem. Engring., U. N.D., 1937; M.S. in Chem. Engring., Calif. Inst. Tech., 1939; m. Beulah Rom, June 14, 1942; 1 dau., Demaris. Research and design engr. Standard Oil Co. Calif., El Segundo, 1939-41, Richmond, 1941-45, asst. mgr. analytical div. comptrollers dept., San Francisco, 1959-60, sec. mgmt. com., mgr. analytical div., 1960-67, asst. mgr. fgn. operations dept., 1967-77; pres. Gullekson Assos., mgmt., engring. and energy cons., 1977—; asst. mgr. rubber research RFC, Washington, 1945-47; supr. tech. service Calif. Research Corp., El Segundo, 1947-49; mgr. process devel. Calif. Oil Co., Perth Amboy, N.J., 1949-58. Recipient Sioux award for outstanding alumni, U. N.D., 1979. Registered profl. engr., Calif. Mem. Sons of Norway, World Affairs Council, U. N.D. Alumni Assn., Calif. Inst. Tech. Alumni Assn., Soc. Profl. Mgmt. Cons. (nat. dir., past pres., treas.), Iron Mask, Blue Key, Phi Beta Kappa, Sigma Xi, Sigma Tau. Republican. Clubs: Commonwealth of California, San Francisco Commercial. Home and Office: PO Box 8088 Foster City CA 94404

GULNAC, HOWARD DEAN, elec. engr.; b. Ridgway, Pa., Jan. 8, 1918; s. Howard Pierce and Ethel Aurora (Frost) G.; B.S.E.E., Bucknell U., 1940; postgrad. Harvard U. and M.I.T., 1942-43, U. Pa., 1947-49, Ariz. State U., 1962-64, U. Calif., 1969-70; m. Fay Bragorgos, June 17, 1967; 1 dau., Donna Lee. Engring. trainee Bell Telephone, Phila., 1940-46; task leader RCA, Camden, N.J., 1946-49; engring. sect. leader Los Alamos Sci. Lab., 1949-57; sect. head Motorola Mil. Electronics Div., Phoenix, 1957-64; design specialist Gen. Dynamics, Pomona, Calif., 1964-65; sr. engr., scientist, McDonnell Douglas Astronautics Co., Huntington Beach, Calif., 1965—. Served with USAF, 1941-46. Patentee, counting rate meter and time delay device. Home: 56 Acacia Tree Ln Irvine CA 92715 Office: 5301 Bolsa Ave Huntington Beach CA 92647

GULSETH, DANA DIANE, accountant; b. Oakland, Calif., Sept. 19, 1951; d. Nye R. and Leah Diane (Heslop) Butler; m. James H. Gulseth, Feb. 29, 1980; 1 dau., Lisa Louise. B.S. with honors in Bus. Adminstrn. and Acctg. (scholar), Calif. State U., 1979. C.P.A., Calif. Staff acct. Deloitte Haskins & Sells, San Francisco, 1979-82; prin. Dana D. Gulseth, C.P.A., Piedmont, Calif., 1983—. Mem. Am. Inst. C.P.A.s, Calif. C.P.A.s Soc., Nat. Assn. Accts., Am. Soc. Women C.P.A.s, Am. Soc. Women Accts., Beta Alpha Psi. Mem. Piedmont Community Ch. Office: PO Box 11315 Piedmont CA 94611

GUMBINER, BURKE FRANKLIN, insurance company executive; b. Long Beach, Calif., Oct. 25, 1950; s. Robert Louis and Josephine (Schlenck) G. B.A., U. Calif.-Santa Barbara, 1972; M.B.A., Calif. State U.-Long Beach, 1977. Mktg. mgr. Family Health Program, Fountain Valley, Calif., 1972-76, mktg. dir., v.p. mktg., 1981—; exec. v.p. Health Maintenance Life Ins., Fountain Valley, 1978-80. Democrat. Club: Kiwanis. Home: 306 21st St Apt B Huntington Beach CA 92648

GUNDERSEN, LEONARD FOND, airline pilot; b. Wis., Apr. 4, 1924; s. Carl Henry and Signe (Fond) G.; student Wis. State U., 1942-43, U. Wis., 1943-44; m. Arlyn Elizabeth Bredahl, Nov. 4, 1945; children—Lynda Jean, Jane Marie. Pilot United Air Lines, 1946—, capt., Los Angeles, 1958—, check airman, 1979—. Exec. sec. Met. Conf., South Pacific Dist., TALC, 1960-71; pres. Westchester Lutheran Ch., Los Angeles, 1969-71; mem. univ. religious council UCLA, 1967-71. Served as aviator USNR, 1943-45. Recipient Programa de Intercambio Matrimonial award, La Plata, Argentina, 1980. Republican. Club: Los Angeles. Lodge: Westchester Rotary. Home: 616 The Strand Manhattan Beach CA 90266

GUNDERSON, CHARLES MARCUS, mechanical consulting engineer; b. Kodiak, Alaska, Aug. 22, 1953; s. Maurice D. and Mary Marjorie (Leiber) G. B.S. in mech. engring., Oreg. State U., 1975. Project engr. Tektronix Inc., Beaverton, Oreg., 1975-78; project engr., then project mgr. Van Gulik and Assocs., Cons. Engrs., Lake Oswego, Oreg., 1978—. Mem. ASME (exec. com. Oreg. sect.), Assn Energy Engrs. Home: PO Box 198 Lake Oswego OR 97034 Office: 543 3d St Lake Oswego OR 97034

GUNDERSON, ELMER MILLARD, state supreme court justice; b. Mpls., Aug. 9, 1929; s. Elmer Peter and Carmaleta (Oliver) G.; student U. Minn., U. Omaha, 1948-53; LL.B., Creighton U., 1956; LL.M., U. Va., 1982; student appellate judges seminar, NYU, 1971; LL.D., U. Pacific; m. Lupe Gomez, Dec. 29, 1967; 1 son, John Randolph. Admitted to Nebr. bar, 1956, Nev. bar, 1958; atty-advisor FTC, 1956-57; pvt. practice, Las Vegas, 1958-71; justice Nev. Supreme Ct., 1971—, chief justice, 1975-76, 81-82; instr. bus. law So. regional div. U. Nev.; adj. prof. McGeorge Sch. Law U. Pacific; lectr., author bills. felony crimes for Clark County Sheriff's Dept.; counsel Sheriff's Protective Assn.; mem. legal staff Clark County Council Civil Def. Agy.; legal counsel Nev. Jaycees. Chmn. Clark County Child Welfare Bd., Nev. central chpt. Nat. Multiple Sclerosis Soc.; bd. visitors Southwestern U. Sch. Law, Los Angeles; hon. dir. Spring Mountain Youth Camp. Served with U.S. Army. Mem. ABA, Nebr. Bar Assn., Nev. Bar Assn., Inst. Jud. Adminstrn., Am. Law Inst., Am. Trial Lawyers Assn., Am. Judicature Soc. (Herbert Harley award), Phi Alpha Delta, Alpha Sigma Nu. Compiler, annotalor Omaha Home Rule Charter; project coordinator Jud. Orientation Manual, 1974. Office: Supreme Ct Bldg Carson City NV 89710

GUNDERSON, JOHN ARNOLD, environ. co. exec.; b. Missoula, Mont., Feb. 2, 1935; s. Cris A. and Louise Annette (Lind) G.; B.S.E.E., Mont. State U., 1960; M.S.E.E., U. So. Calif., 1966; m. Janet Marie Miscoski, Oct. 5, 1973; children—Robert J., Jerry H., Erik M. Tech. staff mem. Hughes Aircraft Corp., Fullerton, Calif., 1960-61; mgr. Northrop Aircraft Corp., Fullerton, 1961-71; mgr., v.p. Olson Labs, Inc., Anaheim, Calif., 1971-78, corporate officer, 1977-78; dir. Systems Control Inc., Anaheim, 1978—. Pres. Diamond Point (Calif.) Bowling League, 1977-78; dir. publicity Jr. All Am. Football League, 1971-72. Served with U.S. Army, 1954-56. Recipient certificate of appreciation U. Wis., Dept. Engring., 1973. Mem. Soc. Automotive Engrs., ASTM (task force on fuel-efficient engine oils, 1978—). Lutheran. Clubs: El Prado Country, Men's. Contbr. research papers in field. Home: 23957 Decorah Rd Diamond Bar CA 91765 Office: Systems Control Inc 421 E Cerritos Ave Anaheim CA 92805

GUNDERSON, TERENCE STARK, music educator, union official; b. Chgo., Sept. 13, 1953; s. Arnie Lee and Kathryn Eileen (Stark) G.; m. Patricia Kaye Anderson, Feb. 17, 1961; Mus.B. in Performance, Colo. State U., 1976; Mus.M. in Performance, U. Miami, Coral Gables, Fla., 1978. Instr. Casper Coll. (Wyo.), 1978—; sec. treas. local 381, Am. Fedn. Musicians, Casper, 1981—; freelance musician. Mem. Percussive Arts Soc. (pres. Wyo. chpt.), Nat. Assn. Jazz Educators, Music Educators Nat. Conf., Coll. Music Soc., Audio Engring. Soc., Nat. Assn. Coll. Wind and Percussion Instrs., Mensa. Roman Catholic. Office: 125 College Dr Casper WY 82601

GUNN, ROBERT DEWEY, educator, chemical engineer; b. Leninakhan, Armenia, May 29, 1928; s. Everett D. and Winifred E. (Dewhirst) G.; m. Francisca Amengual, May 20, 1954; children—Cedric, Alicia. B.S., Kans. State U., 1950; M.S., U. Calif.-Berkeley, 1958, Ph.D., 1968. Geophys. engr. Robert H. Ray Co., Saudi Arabia, 1951-53; petroleum engr. Mobil de Venezuela, 1958-62; asst. prof. chem. engring. U. Tenn., 1967-71; assoc. prof. chem. engring. U. Wyo., Laramie, 1971-75, prof., 1975—, dir. Mining and Mineral Resources Research Inst., 1980—; Disting. guest prof. Tech. U. Aachen (West Germany), 1982-83. Mem. Am. Inst. Chem. Engrs., AAAS, Sigma Xi. Author tech. papers on thermodynamics, freeze drying, underground coal gasification, patterned ground. Office: Dept Chem Engring Univ Wyoming Laramie WY 82071

GUNN, ROCKY WONG, photographer; b. San Francisco, July 31, 1947; s. Fred Wong and Ann (Chang) G.; B.A., Menlo Coll.; m. Kazuko Sakura, July 12, 1970. Freelance photographer, illustrator weddings, Los Angeles; pres. photog. Inovations Internat. Inc.; owner Rocky Gunn Products, Redondo Beach, Calif.; lectr., tchr. photographer various locations; instr. Winona Sch. Profl. Photography. Served with Armed Forces. Fellow Brit. Inst. Inc. Photographers; mem. Profl. Photographers Am. (Master Photography, Photographic Craftsman), Profl. Photographers Calif., Profl. Photographers West. Author: Basic Guide to Wedding Photography; The Wedding Encyclopedia; Your Bridal and Wedding Companion. Contbr. articles to profl. jours. Home: 14826 Archwood St Van Nuys CA 91405

GUNN, WILLIAM JOSEPH, ret. naval officer, engr.; b. N.Y.C., Apr. 16, 1931; s. William Francis and Marie Catherine (Wagner) G.; B.S. in Marine Sci., Maine Maritime Acad., 1952; grad. Armed Forces Staff Coll., 1968, Indsl. Coll. Armed Forces, 1969; m. Geraldine Loo Weeks, July 18, 1953; children—Glenn R., Lynn S., Bonnie J., Laurie B. Commd. ensign, 1952, advanced through grades to capt., 1973; comdr. submarine Grayback, 1964, Clamagore, 1965-67; tech. officer Naval Undersea Ctr., San Diego, 1971-75; sr. submarine mem. Sub-Board Inspection and Survey Pacific, 1975-79; ret., 1979; chief engr. Diving Unltd., Internat., San Diego, 1979-81. Mem. Naval Inst., Nat. Rifle Assn., Am. Radio Relay League (life), DAV (life), Ret. Officers Assn. (life). Author manuals and tech. articles.

GUNNERSEN, UWE, mental health cons.; b. Denmark, Feb. 10, 1935; s. H. Thomas and H. Agneta (Strufe) G.; came to U.S., 1958, naturalized, 1964; B.S., U. Copenhagen, 1956; M.S., U. Hamburg (W. Ger.), 1958; m. Veronica Peper, June 2, 1962; children—Kirsten, Thomas. Psychiat. social worker Div. Psychiatry, Cook County Hosp., Chgo., 1962-68; assoc. adminstr. Martha Washington Hosp., Chgo., 1968-69; program policy adv. Ill. Dept. Mental Health, 1969-71; mental health cons. region V, NIMH, 1971-73; div. dir. Joint Commn. Accrediation of Hosps., 1973-76; pres. Human Services Horizons Inc., San Francisco, 1976-79; exec. dir. Azure Acres Addiction Treatment Ctr., 1979—; mem. task force Pres.'s Commn. Mental Health, 1978, Contra Costa County (Calif.) Council Aging, 1978-79. Cert. mental health adminstr., social worker. Fellow Royal Soc. Health; mem. Nat. Assn. Social Workers, Assn. Mental Health Adminstrs., Assn. Labor Mgmt. Cons. in Alcoholism (bd. dirs. 1980-83), Am. Pub. Health Assn., Am. Health Planning Assn. Lutheran. Author manuals. Home: 3153 Lippizaner Ln Walnut Creek CA 94598 Office: Azure Acres Addiction Treatment Ctr 2264 Green Hill Rd Sebastopol CA 95472

GUNNING, LAURIE FRÖYDIS, vocational counselor; b. Hollywood, Calif., March 11, 1950; d. Everard Frederick Marsek and Fröydis Lenore (Flint) Marsek; m. William Charles Gunning, Jr., Aug. 11, 1973; children—William C., Bryn Taira; B.A. in Sociology, Calif. State U.-Northridge, 1972; M.Ed. in Adult Counseling, U. Mo.-St. Louis, 1980. Vocat. counselor U. Mo.-St. Louis, 1977-80; mgr. edn. div. Mincomp Corp., Denver, 1980-82; pvt. vocat. counselor, cons. Active Jefferson County Pub. Sch. PTA, Columbine West Homeowners Assn. Recipient recognition award U. Denver, Mem. Am. Personnel and Guidance Assn., Colo. Personnel and Guidance Assn., Nat. Vocat. Guidance Assn., Colo Vocat Guidance Assn (treas.) Co-author slide tape presentation and manual in profl. field. Home: 6891 S Yukon Way Littleton CO 80123

GUNTER, MARSIA ADEL, marketing executive, educator; b. Pocatello, Idaho, Mar. 27, 1952; d. Boyd Henry and Edna (Lightfoot) Gunter. B.A. in Journalism, Idaho State U., 1975. Reporter, Pocatello, 1973-74; info. specialist Idaho Dept. Health and Welfare, 1974-75; dir. pub. relations Community Hosp. Idaho Falls, 1975-77; journalism instr. Idaho State U., Pocatello, 1977-80; dir. pub. relations Idaho Falls Consol. Hosps., 1978-80; mktg. instr. Marylhurst Coll., Oreg., 1981—; dir. mktg. and community services Eastmoreland Gen. Hosp., Portland, Oreg., 1980—; speaker. Pres., Bonneville County Heart Assn., 1974; bd. dirs. Idaho Falls YMCA, 1972. Mem. Oreg. Hosp. Pub. Relations Orgn. (pres. 1981-82), Women in Communications (v.p. 1982, pres.-elect 1983), Pub. Relations Soc. Am., Am. Mktg. Assn. Club: City (Portland). Photographs displayed in Portland and Pocatello. Office: Eastmoreland General Hospital 2900 SE Steele St Portland OR 97202

GUPTA, AJAY, civil engineer; b. Amritsar, India, Mar. 4, 1946; came to U.S., 1970, naturalized, 1982; s. Prem Nath and Sheela (Agrawal) A.; m. Rajul Gupta, Jan. 18, 1974; children—Arvin, Ankur. B.S. in Civil Engring., Indian Inst. Tech., 1969; M.S. in Environ. Engring., U. Ill., 1972. Registered profl. engr., Ill., N.Mex. Research assoc. U. Ill., Urbana, 1970-74; project coordinator Greeley & Hansen, Chgo., 1974-80; chief sanitary engr. William Matotan & Assocs., Albuquerque, 1980-83; San. engr. City of Albuquerque, 1983—; cons. in field. Recipient Best Project award Indian Inst. Tech., 1969. Mem. ASCE, Am. Water Work Assn., Water Pollution Control Fedn., Indo Am. Assn. Democrat. Home: 14204 Encantado NE Albuquerque NM 87123

GUPTA, BARBARA MACKAY, educator; b. Berkeley, Calif., Nov. 6, 1948; d. William Robert and Joanne Coby (Willams) MacKay; m. Yogendra Mohan Gupta, June 21, 1975; 1 dau., Anjuli Monica. B.A., Wash. State U., 1970. Cert. tchr., Wash., 1972. Tchr. Edison Elem. Sch., Walla Walla, Wash., 1970-75; tchr. Pinewood Pvt. Sch., Los Altos, Calif., 1975-79, math. dept. supr., tchr. trainer, 1977-81, prin. Grant Campus, 1980-81; curriculum cons., Pullman, Wash., 1981—; workshop dir. Mem. Nat. Council Tchrs. of Math., Assn. for Supervision and Curriculum Devel., AAUW. Address: SW 845 Mies Pullman WA 99163

GUPTA, OM PRAKASH, computer peripherals co. ofcl.; b. Rasra, India, Oct. 1, 1948; came to U.S., 1977; s. Jagannath and Ramrati (Devi) P.; M.Sc., Agra U., 1967; m. Ratna Bhagat, Dec. 10, 1973; children—Manisha (Anshu), Namita (Nitu). Design engr. Philips (India) Ltd., Bombay; reliability engr. Electro-home Ltd., Kichener, Ont., Can., 1971-77; project engr. Can. Aviation Electronics, St. Laurent, Que., Can., 1977-78; group mgr. Tektronix, Inc., Beaverton, Oreg., 1978—. Mem. Am. Soc. Quality Control, Soc. Reliability Engrs., IEEE. Home: 32360 Estates Post Rd Wilsonville OR 97070 Office: Tektronix Inc PO Box 500 Beaverton OR 97077

GUPTILL, WILLIAM KEITH, accountant, business executive; b. Fertilla, Calif., Aug. 20, 1930; s. Sidney Earl and Dorothy Marie (DeRose) G.; A.A., Citrus Jr. Coll., Azusa, Calif., 1957; B.S., Los Angeles State Coll., 1959; m. Olga Bulat, Mar. 25, 1961; 1 dau., Tanya A. Jr. acct. Pacific Fin. Co., Los Angeles, 1958, J. Case, C.P.A., Pomona, Calif., 1959; controller Win Ward Co., Montclair, Calif., 1959-60; internal auditor R.O. Schultz, Covina, Calif., 1960-64; pvt. practice acctg., Covina, 1964—; partner Allen, Allen & Guptill, Investments, West Covina, 1964—, Stegall, Parke & Guptill, Investments, West Covina, 1976—; mng. partner Parke Guptill & Co., C.P.A.s, West Covina, 1970—; chief fin. officer Firebird Internat. Raceway Park, Chandler, Ariz.; dir. North Bend Industries, Pacific Auto Supply, Allen Homes, Inc., Orange County Internat. Raceway, Commodity Import Corp. Mem. spl. coms. U. La Verne. Served with USAF, 1951-55. C.P.A., Calif. Mem. Calif. Soc. C.P.A.s, Am. Inst. C.P.A.s, So. Calif. Motor Car Dealers Assn., Encore Soc. of Claremont Coll. Center for Performing Arts. Republican. Methodist. Club: Masons. Office: 2626 E Garvey Ave Suite 205 West Covina CA 91791

GUREVITCH, ARNOLD WILLIAM, dermatologist; b. Los Angeles, Apr. 3, 1936; s. Leon and Freda S. (Goldman) G.; A.B., Harvard, 1958; M.D., U. Calif. at Los Angeles, 1962; m. S. Camille Abbott, June 12, 1960; children—Douglas Neal, Lara Judith. Intern, Los Angeles County Gen. Hosp., 1962-63; resident in dermatology Los Angeles County Harbor Gen. Hosp., 1963-66, U. Calif. Med. Sch., Los Angeles, 1963-66; practice medicine specializing in dermatology, Los Angeles, 1966-67, Torrance, Calif., 1969—; asst. prof. dermatology UCLA, 1969-76, asso. prof., 1976-82; prof., 1982—; staff physician Harbor-UCLA Med. Center, Torrance, 1969-73, acting chief dermatology, 1973-77, chief dermatology, 1977—; head task force on teaching techniques Nat. Program Dermatology, 1971-75. Chmn. Community Sch., Los Angeles, 1975-76; pres. community advisory council Bancroft Jr. High Sch., Los Angeles, 1978-80, Fairfax High Sch., 1981-83. Served to maj. AUS, 1967-69. Diplomate Am. Bd. Dermatology. Mem. Los Angeles Dermatol. Soc. (pres. 1978-79), Pacific Dermatologic Assn., Am. Acad. Dermatology, Soc. for Investigative Dermatology, Pan Am. Med. Assn., Am. Fedn. Clin. Research, Assn. Am. Med. Colls., Asso. Profs. Dermatology. Home: 2586 Greenvalley Rd Los Angeles CA 90046 Office: 1000 W Carson St Torrance CA 90509

GURY, DONALD DANIEL, accounting services exec.; b. Peoria, Ill., Apr. 19, 1949; s. Joseph F. and Mary Ann (Major) G.; B.A. in Acctg., Bus. Adminstrn., Regis Coll., 1971; M.B.A. with honors, U. Colo., 1973; m. Ellen Eagle Caldwell, June 8, 1974. Pub. acct. integrated services dept. Touche Ross & Co., Denver, 1973-74; v.p. fin. and adminstrn. Neodata Services div. A.C. Nielsen Co., Boulder, Colo., 1974—. Bd. dirs. Jr. Achievement of Greater Boulder County, 1972—, exec. dir., 1973, sec., 1975, chmn. fund raising, 1976-77; team capt. fund raising campaign YMCA, Boulder, 1977; hon. mem. U. Colo. Bus. Adv. Council; bd. dirs. Olde Stage Water Dist. Recipient Outstanding Service to Jr. Achievement of Greater Boulder County award, 1973. Mem. Am. Mgmt. Assn., Nat. Assn. Accts., Boulder C. of C. (chmn. free enterprise council 1978), YMCA, Free Enterprise Council, U. Colo. Alumni Assn. (dir. 1978—), U. Colo. Dean's Assn. Democrat. Roman Catholic. Clubs: Boulder Country, Boulder Rotary, Elks. accounting services exec.; b. Peoria, Ill., Apr. 19, 1949; s. Joseph F. and Mary Ann (Major) G.; B.A. in Acctg., Bus. Adminstrn., Regis Coll., 1971; M.B.A. with honors, U. Colo., 1973; m. Ellen Eagle Caldwell, June 8, 1974. Pub. acct. integrated services dept. Touche Ross & Co., Denver, 1973-74; v.p. fin. and adminstrn. Neodata Services div. A.C. Nielsen Co., Boulder, Colo., 1974—. Bd. dirs. Jr. Achievement of Greater Boulder County, 1972—, exec. dir., 1973, sec., 1975, chmn. fund raising, 1976-77; team capt. fund raising campaign YMCA, Boulder, 1977; hon. mem. U. Colo. Bus. Adv. Council; bd. dirs. Olde Stage Water Dist. Recipient Outstanding Service to Jr. Achievement of Greater Boulder County award, 1973. Mem. Am. Mgmt. Assn., Nat. Assn. Accts., Boulder C. of C. (chmn. free enterprise council 1978), YMCA, Free Enterprise Council, U. Colo. Alumni Assn. (dir. 1978—), U. Colo. Dean's Assn. Democrat. Roman Catholic. Clubs: Boulder Country, Boulder Rotary, Elks. Home: 6423 Red Hill Rd Boulder CO 80302 Office: 1255 Portland Pl Boulder CO 80302

GUSTAFSON, CARL ROHN, management consultant; b. Bklyn., June 6, 1939; s. Richard Melker and Alette (Inger) G.; m. Joanne C. Rinse. Artium degree, Kingsyard Coll., Stavanger, Norway, 1960; B.Sc. in Bus. Adminstrn., U. Calif.-Berkeley, 1963; cert. in internat. bus., Strathclyde U., Glasgow, Scotland, 1961. Prodn. planner Crown Zellerbach, 1963-65; with Carl Gustafson Advt., pub. Civil Service Newsletter and Australia Newsletter, 1965-76; pres. Gustafson Cons., Inc., Walnut Creek, Calif., Newport Beach, Calif. and Dallas, 1976—. Bd. regents John F. Kennedy U., Orinda, Calif., 1978—. Served with Army NG, 1963-69. Address: 3940 N Peardale Dr Lafayette CA 94549

GUSTAFSON, CHARLES IVAN, hosp. adminstr.; b. Chadron, Nebr., June 29, 1931; s. Archie and Adelia (Bawnes) G.; B.S., U. Wash., 1953; M.H.A., U. Mich., 1957; m. Donna Rae Gustafson; children—Laura Kay, Brian Charles. Asst. adminstr. Good Samaritan Hosp., Portland, Oreg., 1957-58; adminstr. Rogue Valley Meml. Hosp., Medford, 1958-80, bd. dirs., 1979; chief exec. officer G.N. Wilcox Meml. Hosp. and Health Center, Kauai, Hawaii, 1980-83; adminstr. Deaconess Hosp., Spokane, Wash., 1983—. dir. So. Oreg. Ednl. Co. Mem. Gov.'s Com. on Comprehensive Health Planning, 1968-72; mem. Oreg. Health Commn. Bd. dirs. Shakespearean Festival, Ashland, Oreg., Rogue Valley Health Found., 1979—, Western Hosp. Found., 1979—. Served with AUS, 1953-55. Fellow Am. Coll. Hosp. Adminstrs.; mem. Am. Hosp. Assn. (Oreg. del. 1968-70), Oreg. Assn. Hosps. (pres. 1968-69), Nat. Assn. Hosp. Devel., Am. Assn. Hosp. Planning. Republican. Episcopalian. Home: 12007 Anna —J— Dr Spokane WA 99218 Office: W 800 5th Ave Spokane WA 99210

GUSTAFSON, CONRAD LEE, ins. co. exec.; b. Portland, Oreg., Dec. 12, 1944; s. Richard Franklin and Lula Elizabeth (Herold) G.; B.S., Oreg. State U., 1968; m. Melody Rae Diegel, Sept. 28, 1968. Premium auditor Argonaut Ins. Co., Portland, 1971-73, premium audit, credit/collection mgr., 1973-77, spl. rep., 1977-78, asst. div. mgr., San Francisco, 1978-79, br. mgr., San Jose, Calif., 1979—. Served with U.S. Army, 1968-71. Mem. Soc. Chartered Property and Casualty Underwriters. Republican. Lutheran. Office: 675 N 1st St San Jose CA 95112

GUSTAFSON, LEIF VALENTINE, consulting engineer; b. Gothenburg, Sweden, Dec. 31, 1911; s. Oscar Gustaf and Olga Alida (Anderson) G.; B.S. in Civil and Structural Engring., Inst. Tech. (Sweden), 1932; postgrad. in bus. adminstrn. Alexander Hamilton Inst., 1969; m. Joan Miller, Nov. 15, 1969; children—Glenn Nordhal, Linda Margaret. Chief structural engr. Elec. Bond & Share Co., N.Y.C., 1947-52; supervising engr. Bechtel Corp., Los Angeles, 1952-61; pres., owner Leif Engring. & Constrn. Corp., Studio City, Calif., 1961-67; mgr. engring. Western Precipitation, Los Angeles, 1967-69; pres., gen. mgr. Esco Internat., Guam, Saipan, 1969-74; dep. dir. pub. works Govt. Am. Samoa, Pago Pago, 1974-76; cons. ballistics and space systems div. U.S. Army, 1962-65; bd. Project 75 Dept. Def. Served with U.S. Army, 1943-45. Mem. Nat. Soc. Profl. Engrs. Republican. Clubs: Swedish (past pres. Los Angeles); Showboat Country. Maj. designer minute man and Atlas launching systems; inventor hydrolaunch system, sonic electrostatic precipitator, acid applications electrostatic precipitator, knob conveyor; contbr. articles on missile launching designs. Home: 319 Banuelo Dr Henderson NV 89015

GUSTAVSON, DEAN LEONARD, architect; b. Salt Lake City, June 27, 1924; s. Ernest L. and Leona (Hansen) G.; B.Arch., U. Calif.-Berkeley, 1951; m. Barbara Knight, Apr. 28, 1944; children—Mark S., Lisa Ann, Clinton K. Pvt. practice architecture, Salt Lake City, 1953-57; pres. Dean L. Gustavson Assocs., Salt Lake City, 1957—, Gustavson Nelson & Panushka, Inc., Salt Lake City, 1976-82; architect, project mgr. U. Utah Med. Ctr. additions, 1975-82; project mgr. Gio-scis. additions complex U. Calif., Berkeley, 1982—; instr. archtl. design U. Utah, 1951-52; chmn. design, coordinating com. Redevel. and Master Plan Study for Salt Lake City joint project of Utah chpt. AIA-Salt Lake Businessmen, 1961-63; co-chmn. Internat. Joint Com. Archtl. Registration and Reciprocity; mem. Architects Exam. Com., 1960-69, chmn., 1963, 66, 69; chmn. World Conf. on Edn. and Reciprocity of Architects, Amsterdam, Netherlands, 1971. Mem. Gov.'s Indsl. Devel. Adv. Council, 1969, Gov.'s Com. Children and Youth, 1970. Recipient Merit award Producers Council Utah, 1969; honored by establishment Dean L. Gustavson award Nat. Council Archtl. Registration Bds., also 1st recipient, 1971. Fellow AIA (nat. urban design com. 1965-69, v.p., sec., treas. Utah chpt. 1957-59, sec. Western Mountain Region 1956-57, chmn. Utah chpt. task force on objectives and means 1974); mem. Nat. Council Archtl. Registration Bds. (pres. 1969-70), U.S. C. of C., Salt Lake City C. of C. (chmn. urban devel. planning and bldg. com., chmn. econ. devel. steering com.), Salt Lake Art Center. Clubs: Fort Douglas Hidden Valley Country, Bloomington (Utah) Country. Contbr. papers to profl. jours. Home: 5775 Highland Dr Salt Lake City UT 84121 Office: 630 E South Temple Salt Lake City UT 84102

GUSTIN, NELSON SAGE, manufacturing co. exec.; b. Detroit, July 7, 1919; s. Nelson Sage and Florence (Sharp) G.; B.A., Pomona Coll., 1943; m. Yvonne Sheridan, July 14, 1943; children—Sheridan, Christopher, David. Pres., N.S. Gustin Co., 1947—, Design Craft Corp., Los Angeles, 1947—. Mem. Young Pres.'s Orgn. Republican. Episcopalian. Office: 1933 S Broadway Los Angeles CA 90007

GUTH, GAIL WILSON, educator; b. Alta., Can., June 24, 1934; came to U.S., 1936; m. 1957; 4 children. Student (PEO scholar), San Diego State Coll., 1952-55, M. Curriculum Devel., 1978; B.A. in Edn., San Jose State Coll., 1959. Dental asst., 1951-52, 57-58; recreation dir. San Diego Parks and Recreation, 1953-54; dir. youth and Christian edn. Kensington Community Ch., 1955-56; tchr. Mountain View (Calif.) Sch. Dist., 1959; tchr. Hearst Elem. Sch., San Diego, 1960-63; pvt. practice tutoring, 1963-67; tchr. San Diego City Schs., 1967—, reading specialist, 1969-70, reading specialist, dir. lang. lab. and visual literacy project, 1971-75, aux. tchr., 1975-79, lang. resource tchr., 1979-80, project resource tchr., 1980—; chmn. reading task force Tchr. Corp, San Diego State Coll., 1971. San Diego Area Writing Project fellow, 1978; Visual Literacy Project grantee, 1969-73; recipient Woman of Distinction award Mexican-Am. Found., 1976. Mem. Internat. Visual Literay Assn. (dir. 1978-82), Internat. Reading Assn., Greater San Diego Reading Assn. (dir. 1976-80), Nat. Council Tchrs. English, Calif. Assn. Tchrs. English, Calif. Assn. Tchrs. English as a Second Lang., Assn. Supervision and Curriculum Devel. Office: 4100 Normal St Annex 4 San Diego CA 92103

GUTHREY, EVELYN MAY, nurse, legal consultant; b. Powell River, B.C., Can., Mar. 26, 1926; came to U.S., 1947, naturalized, 1954; d. Ingvald and Katherine (Voelker) Dahl; m. Edgar Gordon Guthrey Jr., Sept. 7, 1947; children—Edgar III (dec.), Aleta Ann (dec.), Edgar IV, Areta Kay. R.N., San Joaquin Gen. Hosp. Sch. Nursing, 1947; A.A., Diablo Valley Coll., 1968; B.S. in Nursing, Sacramento State U., 1976; J.D., Armstrong Sch. Law, 1982. Nurse in various Calif. communities, 1948-56; nursing office supr. Eden Hosp., Castro Valley, Calif., 1956-61, Peninsula (Calif.) Hosp., 1961-62; nurse Martinez (Calif.) Community Hosp., 1962-65; with John Muir Meml. Hosp., Walnut Creek, Calif., 1965—; head nurse, 1965-66, asst. dept. edn., 1966-69, assoc. dir. nursing, 1969-71, staffing coordinator, 1971-73, asst. edn. coordinator, 1973—; adj. faculty Los Medanos Coll., 1975-80, Contra Costa Coll., 1975-81; cons. and lectr. in field. Bd. dirs. Greater Contra Costa County Cancer Program; mem. Concord Community Adv. Devel. Bd.; mem. Concord Com. Aging, chmn., 1975-76; treas. Shadelands Children's Ctr., Walnut Creek. Mem. Am. Heart Assn. (edn. com. Contra Costa County chpt.), Am. Assn. Critical Care Nurses, Am. Soc. Law and Medicine, Am. Soc. Pharmacy Law. Democrat. Baptist. Home: 1201 Sheridan Rd Concord CA 94518 Office: 1910 Olympic Blvd Suite 220 Walnut Creek CA 94596

GUTHRIE, ANN C., health administrator, physical therapist, consultant; b. Boulder, Colo., Aug. 4, 1943; d. John T. and Ruth I. Guthrie. B.S. in Phys. Therapy, 1966; M.S., U. Notre Dame, 1977. Lic. phys. therapist, Colo. Phys. therapist Mass. Gen. Hosp., Boston, 1965-67, Univ. Hosp., Denver, 1967-70; dir. phys. therapy Mercy Med. Ctr., Denver, 1970-72, dir. allied services and patient rep., 1972-79, adminstrv. dir., 1979—; part-time instr. U. Colo., 1967-70; cons. HEW, 1973-79, grant reviewer Rockville, Md., 1979; acting dir., adminstr. McNamara Hosp. and Nursing Home, Fairplay, Colo., 1975; mem. Colo. Bd. Phys. Therapy, 1973-76. Mem. Nat. Soc. Patient Reps., Colo. Soc. Patient Reps. Democrat. Baptist. Contbr. articles on phys. therapy to profl. jours. Office: 1619 Milwaukee Denver CO 80206

GUTHRIE, DAVID WILLIAM, lawyer; b. Colorado Springs, Colo., Sept. 18, 1947; s. James William and Ruth Virginia (Murchison) G.; B.A., Claremont Men's Coll., 1969; J.D., Bklyn. Law Sch., 1979; 1 son, William Jon. Systems analyst, N.Y.C., 1972-76; instr. N.Y. U., 1976-77; pvt. practice data processing cons. to utilities, mfg. corps. and airlines, N.Y.C., 1978-80; admitted to Calif. bar, 1979, U.S. Dist. Ct. bar, 1979; owner, asso. firm Traveling Atty., San Diego, 1980-82; owner Computer Cons. Services, San Diego, 1982—; instr. Western Sierra Law Sch., 1979—; instr. data processing U. Calif., San Diego, extension div., 1980—. Mem. State Bar Calif., ACLU. Democrat. Contbr. articles to profl. jours. Office: PO Box 84704 San Diego CA 92138

GUTHRIE, JAMES WILLIAMS, educator; b. Chgo., Aug. 28, 1936; s. James Williams and Florence (Harvey) G.; B.A., Stanford U., 1958, M.A., 1960, Ph.D., 1968; m. Paula Humphreys Skene, Feb. 26, 1976; children by previous marriage—Sarah Virginia, James Williams, Shanon Louise, James Kyle. High sch. tchr., Arcata, Calif., 1960-61, Palo Alto, Calif., 1961-64; asst. to dean Sch. Edn., Stanford U., 1965-66; spl. asst. to sec. Dept. HEW, Washington, 1966-67; prof. U. Calif., Berkeley, 1967-70; Alfred North Whitehead postdoctoral fellow Harvard U., 1970; dep. dir. N.Y. State Edn. Commn., 1971-72; edn. specialist U.S. Senate, Washington, 1972-73; prof. edn. U. Calif. at Berkeley, 1973—; dir. Western Community Savs. and Loan Corp.; mem. Calif. Commn. on Tchr. Credentialing, 1982—; cons. HEW, also N.Y., Fla., Calif., Alaska, Oreg. and Wash. state legislatures. Mem. City of Berkeley Bd. Edn., 1975-82, pres., 1976-77. Recipient Cert. of Merit, Am. Public Adminstrn. Assn., 1976; U.S. Office of Edn. grantee, 1968-69; Ford Found. grantee, 1970-73. Mem. Am. Assn. Sch. Adminstrs., Nat. Calif. sch. bd. assns., Calif. Tchrs. Assn., Phi Delta Kappa. Episcopalian. Club: Rotary. Author: Schools and Inequality, 1970; New Models for American Education, 1971, State School Finance Alternatives, 1975; School Finance: Economics and Politics of Public Education, 1978; Educational Administration, 1983. Home: 52 Oakvale St Berkeley CA 94705 Office: Room 3533 Tolman Hall U Calif Berkeley CA 94720

GUTIERREZ, FERNANDO JOSE, counseling psychologist; b. Matanzas, Cuba, Mar. 1, 1951; s. Alberto Rodolfo and Mariana Elena (Cartaya) G.; came to U.S., 1961, naturalized, 1968. B.A. in Psychology, Mich. State U., 1973; M.S. in Edn., Purdue U., 1974; Ed.D., Boston U., 1981. Staff counselor U. Wis., Stevens Point, 1975-77; psychology intern Tri-City Mental Health Ctr., Malden, Mass., 1977-78, Solomon Carter Fuller Mental Health Ctr., Boston, 1978-79; counseling psychologist San Francisco State U., 1980-81, U. Santa Clara (Calif.), 1981—; western region coordinator profl. devel. workshops Nat. Assn. Minority Students, Educators in Higher Edn., 1981-84. Assn. Hispanic Orientation Recreation and Arts, Everett, Mass., 1978-79; mem. children's com. adv.

council to commr. mental health Commonwealth of Mass., 1979-80. Mem. Am. Psychol. Assn., Am. Personnel and Guidance Assn., Am. Coll. Personnel Assn., Assn. Counselor Educators and Suprs., Pi Lamda Theta, Kappa Delta Pi. Democrat. Roman Catholic. Home: 500 King Dr Apt 1008 Daly City CA 94015

GUTKIN, PETER ALAN, sculptor, designer; b. Bklyn., Apr. 23; s. Samuel Sholom and Leonore Ruth (Alpine) G.; m. Vicky Doubleday; 1 son, Miles Alpine. B.F.A., Temple U., 1966; M.F.A., San Francisco Art Inst., 1968. Exhibited in group shows in major mus. and galleries throughout U.S.; furniture designer; mem. faculty U. Calif.-Berkeley, 1972-74, San Francisco Art Inst., 1978, Calif. Coll. Arts and Crafts, 1982. Trustee San Francisco Art Inst., 1972-76. Nat. Endowment for Arts artist fellow, 1980.

GUY, CHARLES WILLIAM, exec. search cons. co. exec.; b. Fairfield, Ohio, Mar. 23, 1945; s. Charles William and Helen S. Guy; student Harvey Mudd Coll., 1963-64, Foothill Coll., 1964-65; B.A. in Economics, Calif. State U.-Northridge, 1967; m. Katherine Elba Hambright, June 16, 1967; children—Robert William, Cynthia Eva. Asst. to v.p. Viking Inds., Inc., Chatsworth, Calif., 1964-67; adminstrv. asst. to chief of police Burbank (Calif.), 1967-69; pres. Environ. Mktg., Los Angeles and St. Louis, 1969-74; dir. hospitality and real estate recruiting Wells Mgmt. Corp., N.Y.C., 1974-75; sr. asso. Korn/Ferry & Assos., Los Angeles, 1975-77; v.p., partner Paul R. Ray & Co., Inc., Fort Worth, 1977-79; v.p./mng. partner Barton Sans, Inc., N.Y./Toronto, Los Angeles, 1979-81; partner Ward Howell Internat., Inc., N.Y.C., Greenwich, Los Angeles, Dallas, Mpls., San Francisco, London, Brussels, Amsterdam, Paris, Mexico City, Sydney, Australia, Melbourne, Dusseldorf, Zurich, 1981—; past chmn. Bank Adv. Bd.; lectr. various univs. and profl. orgns. Active Sister City Program, Symphony Assn., World Affairs Council; bd. dirs., past dist. chmn. Boy Scouts Am. Adv. bd. Adventure/Unltd. Named life mem. Calif. Scholarship Fedn., 1963. Mem. Travel and Tourism Research Assn. (past dir. So. Calif. chpt.), Outreach Love (past pres.), Am. Environ. Assn. (past pres.), Travel Industry Assn., Greater Los Angeles Visitors and Conv. Bur. (past dir.), Alpha Gamma Sigma. Clubs: Kiwanis (past dir. local chpt.), Masons affiliate (chpt. charter officer). Office: 10100 Santa Monica Blvd Suite 900 Century City CA 90067

GUY, JERRY WAYNE, university official; b. San Diego, Oct. 22, 1942; s. Howard Casagrande and Jacqueline Mildred (Hydle) G.; m. Susan Kathleen Straith, July 7, 1979; children—Wendy Kirstin, Jeremy Morgan. A.B., UCLA, 1969; M.S., San Diego State U., 1980. Asst. coach San Diego State U., 1979-80; counselor spl. services Saddleback Community Coll., Mission Viejo, Calif., 1980-82, coordinator spl. services and spl. edn., 1982-83, asst. dean spl. programs, 1983—. Mem. Com. for Quality Edn. Served with USMC, 1960-61. San Diego State U. scholar, 1973. Mem. Assn. Supervision and Curriculum Devel., Nat. Council Student Devel., Audubon Soc., Cousteau Soc., Calif. Assn. Post-Secondary Educators of Disabled, Calif. Tchrs. Assn., Theta Delta Chi, Kappa Iota. Democrat. Clubs: Sierra; Dana Point (Calif.) Canoe.

GUYDISH, JOSEPH RAYMOND, clinical psychology researcher, mental health worker; b. Hazelton, Pa., Nov. 23, 1955; s. Jacob and Mary (Bayzik) G. A.A., U. Md., Heidelberg, W. Ger. Extension, 1976; B.S. in Psychology, Wash. State U., 1977; M.A. in Counseling, Marywood Coll., 1980; M.S. in Clin. Psychology, Ft. Hays State U., 1982; postgrad. in clin. psychology Wash. State U., 1982—. Cert. Addictions Counselor, Pa., Counselor Ft. Knox Confinement Facility, U.S. Army, Ky., 1974-75, Community Drug and Alcohol Ctr., Heilbron, W. Ger., 1975-76, Alcohol and Drug Services, Hazelton, Pa., 1977-78, treatment dir., 1979, exec. dir., 1979-80; statis. cons. Computing Ctr., Ft. Hays State U., Hays, Kans., 1982, research and teaching asst. psychology dept., 1980-82; research asst. student services research Wash. State U., Pullman, 1982—; mental health profl. Whitman Co. Mental Health Ctr., Pullman, Wash., 1983—. Active Greater Hazelton Council Alcoholism, 1979-80. Served with U.S. Army, 1973-76. Decorated Nat. Def. medal; NIMH grantee, 1980-81, 81. Mem. Am. Psychol. Assn., Am. Personnel and Guidance Assn., Am. Mental Health Counselor's Assn., Phi Beta Kappa. Contbr. articles to profl. jours. Home: NE 1540 Merman St Apt 146B Pullman WA 99163 Office: Dept Psychology Wash State U Pullman WA 99164

GUYER, JOHN PAUL, mechanical engineer; b. Sacramento, Feb. 12, 1941; s. Paul M. and Vivian (Mosher) G.; B.S., Stanford U., 1962; postgrad. McGeorge Law Sch., 1962-66; m. Judith M. Overholser, June 28, 1968; children—John Paul, Christopher Meador. Mech. engr., State of Calif., Sacramento, 1962-66; partner Guyer & Santin, Sacramento, 1967-75; pres. Guyer Santin, Inc., Sacramento, 1975—. Recipient Unit commendation Calif. Dept. Water Resources, 1972; Outstanding Service award, Calif. Soc. Profl. Engrs., 1969; Outstanding Jr. C. of C. award, Sacramento Jr. C. of C., 1967, others. Mem. Calif. Soc. Profl. Engrs. (v.p. 1969), Crocker Art Mus. Assn., Sacramento Symphony Assn., Stanford Alumni Assn., ASME, ASCE. Republican. Clubs: The Tennis, Univ., Stanford, El Macero Country, Engrs. (pres. 1968). Home: 3478 Club House Dr El Macero CA 95618 Office: 455 Capitol Mall Suite 302 Sacramento CA 95814

GUYON, ROBERT EDWIN, SR., educator, administrator; b. Pocatello, Idaho, Dec. 14, 1939; s. Edwin F. and Norma M. (Cluff) G.; m. Linda L. Stiles, Aug. 24, 1963; children—Robert E., Stephanie. B.A., Idaho State U., 1963; LL.B., LaSalle U., 1978; M.Ed., Coll. Idaho, 1979. Cert. elem. and secondary adminstr., Idaho. Placement dir. Idaho State U., Pocatello, 1964-66; tchr., Buhl, Idaho, 1966-68; tchr. history and psychology Pocatello Sch. Dist., 1968-69, elem. tchr., 1969-70; elem. tchr. Sch. Dist. 91, Idaho Falls, Idaho, 1970—, prin., 1974—. Chmn. Pocatello Kennedy for Pres. campaign, 1960; precinct committeeman Pocatello-Idaho Falls, 1960-62, 76-78; pres. Young Democrats, 1961-62; chmn. Boneville County (Idaho) Jimmy Carter for Pres. campaign, 1976; vice chmn. Boneville County Dems., 1977. Served to lt. U.S. Army, 1963. Mem. NEA, Idaho Edn. Assn., Idaho Falls Edn. Assn., Am. Personnel and Guidance Assn. (cert.), Am. Sch. Counselor Assn. Mem. Christian Ch. (Disciples of Christ). Home: 960 Jefferson St Idaho Falls ID 83402 Office: Sch Dist 91 Idaho Falls ID 83402

GUYTON, SUZANNE, chiropractor; b. Santa Rosa, Calif., June 7, 1947; d. Robert Eugene and Eleanor May Nixon; m. John Robert Guyton, Oct. 3, 1971 (div.). Dr. Chiropractic summa cum laude, Palmer Coll. Chiropractic. Diplomate Nat. Bd. Chiropractic Examiner; chiropractic lic., Calif. Office mgr., Kenneth E. Bernd, D.C., Santa Rosa, Calif., 1972-74, intern in chiropractic, 1978-79; gen. practice chiropractic, San Jose; cons. to perspective chiropractic students. Mem. Am. Chiropractic Assn., Nat. Assn. Female Execs., Parker Sch. Profl. Successful Woman's Doctors Club, Pi Tau Delta. Republican. Presbyterian. Office: 1361 S Winchester Blvd Suite 105 San Jose CA 95128

GUZY, PETER MICHAEL, medical educator, cardiologist; b. Monongahela, Pa., Oct. 30, 1940; s. Peter and Mary (Yacko) G.; m. Judith Diane Moss, Oct. 9, 1982. B.S., U. Notre Dame, 1962; Ph.D., U. Ky., 1970; postdoctoral fellow in biochemistry U. Cin., 1970; M.D., Med. Coll. Ohio-Toledo, 1973. Intern, McMaster U. Med. Ctr., 1973-74, resident, 1974-75; resident in internal medicine U. Toronto, 1975-76; fellow in cardiology UCLA Med. Ctr., 1976-79, asst. prof. medicine, 1979—, dir. Pacemaker Clinic, 1980—. NIH fellow, 1962-67 Haggin scholar, 1969-70; Med. Coll. Ohio-Toledo scholar, 1970-73; Robert Wood Johnson Clin. scholar, 1976-79; named Tchr. of Yr., UCLA Dept. Medicine, 1982. Fellow Am. Coll. Cardiology, Royal Coll. Physicians and Surgeons of Can.; mem. ACP, Alpha Omega Alpha. Democrat. Roman Catholic. Office: UCLA Div Cardiology CHS 47-123 Los Angeles CA 90024

GWALTNEY, LAMAR EDWARD, state senator; b. Osceola, Ark., Apr. 21, 1933; s. Louie Edward and Lillian (Ward) G.; ed. N.Mex. State U.; m. Mary Gail Anderson, Apr. 1, 1956; children—Cindy, Tracy, Rebecca, Lamar. Pres. Lamar Liquors, Inc., 1958-81, Gail, Inc., 1966—, Andy, Inc., 1970—; mem. N.Mex. Senate, Las Cruces, 1975—. Served with U.S. Army, 1951-59. Democrat. Episcopalian. Office: PO Box 2078 Las Cruces NM 88004

GYEMANT, INA LEVIN (MRS. ROBERT ERNEST GYEMANT), judge; b. San Francisco, Aug. 2, 1943; d. Manuel and Mildred Lita (Woloski) Levin; A.B., U. Calif. at Berkeley, 1965; J.D., Hastings Coll. of Law, 1968; m. Robert Ernest Gyemant, June 7, 1970; children—Robert Ernest, Anne Elizabeth. Admitted to Calif. bar, 1969; clk. chief justice Calif. Supreme Ct., 1969; dep. pub. defender City and County of San Francisco, 1970; individual practice law, San Francisco, 1971; dep. atty. gen. State of Calif., San Francisco, 1972-81; mcpl. ct. judge, San Francisco, 1980—. Mem. Am., San Francisco bar assns.; Calif. Judges Assn., Queen's Bench (dir. 1976-80, pres. 1979), Calif. Women Lawyers, Foster Parents Assn., Alpha Epsilon Phi. Republican. Clubs: Commonwealth Club of Calif. (chmn. law enforcement sect. 1976-79); Barrister's; Criminal Trial Lawyers; Met.; Variety Club of N. Calif. (San Francisco); San Francisco Lawyer's Wives. Office: City Hall San Francisco CA 94102

GYEMANT, ROBERT ERNEST, lawyer, accountant; b. Managua, Nicaragua, Jan. 17, 1944; s. Emery and Magda (Von Rechnitz) G.; came to U.S., 1949, naturalized, 1954; A.B. magna cum laude, U. Calif. at Los Angeles, 1965; J.D., U. Calif. at Berkeley, 1968; m. Ina Stephannie Levin, Feb. 28, 1970; children—Robert Ernest II, Anne Elizabeth. Tax accountant Ernst & Ernst, C.P.A.'s, Oakland, Calif., 1966-68; admitted to Calif. bar, 1969; asso. atty. Orrick, Herrington, Rowley & Sutcliffe, San Francisco, 1968-69; partner law firm Skornia, Rosenblum & Gyemant, San Francisco, 1969-74; law offices Robert Ernest Gyemant profl. corp., San Francisco, 1975; exec. v.p. finance Topps & Trowsers, San Francisco, 1977-79; cons., pvt. investor, 1979—; instr. U. Calif. at Berkeley, 1968. Mem. Calif. Council Criminal Justice Jud. Process Task Force, 1971-73. Mem. Calif. Republican Central Com., 1971—; trustee French-Am. Bilingual Sch., San Francisco, 1978—. Mem. Am., San Francisco (co-chmn. sect. on juvenile justice 1971) bar assns., Am. Judicature Soc., State Bar Calif. (com. on unauthorized practice law 1974-76, spl. com. on juvenile justice 1974—, commr. juvenile justice comm. 1976—), Am. Inst. C.P.A.'s, San Francisco C.P.A. Soc. (mem. accounting prins. com. 1969), San Francisco Barristers Club (chmn. juvenile ct. panel 1969-71), St. Thomas More Soc. Club: N.Y. Athletic. Author publs. in field; editor: Calif. Law Rev., 1967-68. Office: 2891 Vallejo St San Francisco CA 94123

GYOR, HARRIET SUE, therapist, author; b. Holbrook, Nebr., Dec. 25, 1942; d. William A. and Helen Joyce (Davis) Gardner; student Compton Jr. Coll., 1960-61, U. Calif., Berkeley, 1961-62; m. Jon Wesley Gyor, July 6, 1962 (div. 1979); children—Julie Ann, William Jon. Teaching asst. sign lang. elem. sch., Santa Fe Springs, Calif., 1971-74; dir. TERRAP, Orange County, Calif., 1976—; owner PGI Pub. Co., Westminster, Calif., 1980—; dir. Phobia Clinic; hypnotist, 1983—; hypnotherapist, 1983—. Vol., Norwalk State Hosp., 1965-67; asst. coordinator seminars for nurses, on phobias Golden West Coll., 1979, 81. Cert. leader TERRAP programs. Mem. Phobia Soc. Am., Am. Booksellers Assn., Pubs. Assn. So. Calif. Mem. Ch. of Religious Sci. Author: Living in Hell: An Agoraphobic Experience, 1980; (booklet) Anxiety Control Techniques, 1983. Office: 14140 Beach Blvd Suite 204 Westminster CA 92683

HAAG, CAROL ANN GUNDERSON, food co. exec.; b. Mpls.; d. Glenn Alvin and Genevieve Esther (Knudson) Gunderson; B.J., U. Mo., 1969; postgrad. Roosevelt U., Chgo., 1975—; m. Lawrence S. Haag, Aug. 30, 1969. Reporter, Waukegan (Ill.) News Sun, summers 1966-69; pub. relations writer, advt. copywriter Am. Hosp. Supply Corp., Evanston, 1969-70, also free-lance editor Lake County (Ill.) Circle weekly newspaper; asst. dir. pub. relations Rush-Presbyn.-St. Luke's Med. Center, Chgo., 1970-71; asst. mgr. pub. and employee communications Quaker Oats Co., Chgo., 1971-72, mgr. editorial communications, 1972-74, mgr. employee communications programs, 1974-77, mem. corp. office planning com., 1972-77; mgr. public relations Shaklee Corp., San Francisco, 1977-79, dir. public relations, 1979-83; dir. mktg. and communications Discovery Toys, Inc., Pleasant Hill, Calif., 1983—. Adv. bd. dirs. San Francisco Spl. Olympics; bd. dirs. Calif. League for Handicapped; mem. pub. relations com. San Francisco Recreation and Parks Dept.; mem. San Francisco Vol. Bur. Recipient 1st Place cert. award Printing Industry Am., 1972, 74, 1st Place Spl. Communication award Internat. Assn. Bus. Communicators, 1974, First Place Citation for Outstanding Editorial Achievement award Chg. Assn. Bus. Communicators, 1974. Mem. Nat. Acad. TV Arts and Scis., Indsl. Communication Council, Public Relations Soc. Am. Presbyterian. Club: San Francisco Press. Home: 133 Fernwood Dr Moraga CA 94556 Office: 400 Ellinwood Way Pleasant Hill CA

HAAG, JOSEPH ROY, biochemist; b. Clearfield County, Pa., Jan. 25, 1896; s. Carl August and Louisa (Weis) H.; B.S., Pa. State U., 1918, M.S., 1923; Ph.D., U. Minn., 1926; m. Ruth Watts, June 5, 1919; children—Louisa Hope Haag Prescott, Shirley Nelle Haag Byland, Roger Watts. Chemist Aetna Chem. Co., Mount Union, Pa., 1917, Atlas Powder Co., Tamaqua, Pa., 1918-19, R.I. Agrl. Experiment Sta., Kingston, 1919-20, Md. Agrl. Experiment Sta., College Park, 1920-21; instr. agrl. chemistry Pa. State U., State College, 1921-23; instr. agrl. biochemistry U. Minn., St. Paul, 1923-26; prof. agrl. chemistry Oreg. State U., Corvallis, 1927-67, prof. emeritus, 1967—; cons. in animal nutrition, Israel, 1955-56. Williams-Waterman Fund grantee, 1947. Mem. Am. Chem. Soc., Am. Soc. Biol. Chemists, Am. Inst. Nutrition, Nutrition Soc. (Brit.). Contbr. articles on calcium and phosphorus requirements, copper deficiency and molybdenum toxicity, nutritive value of proteins and antithiamine activity of bracken fern to profl. jours. Home: 330 NW 32d St Corvallis OR 97330

HAAG, KENNETH L., city agency executive; b. Columbus, Mont., Dec. 20, 1939; s. Edward P. and Virginia Haag; m. Marie E. Carlson, Oct. 24, 1959; children—Pamela, Vincent, Richard; B.S.C.E., Mont. State U., 1962. Registered profl. engr., Mont. Dist. engr., office engr. Bur. Land Mgmt., U.S. Dept. Interior, Billings, Mont., 1962-63, dist. engr., Miles City, Mont., 1963-65; with Armco Steel Sales, Billings, 1965-69; with N.L. Garrett Constrn. Co., Missoula, Mont., 1969-71; dir. pub. works City of Billings, 1971—. Mem. Traffic Control Bd. Billings; mem. Billings Pub. Works Commn. Mem. Nat. Soc. Profl. Engrs., Mont. Soc. Profl. Engrs., ASCE (pres. eastern br.), Am. Pub. Works Assn. (dir. Rocky Mountain chpt. 1975-80, sec.-treas. 1980-83). Congregationalist. Home: 2634 Louise Ln Billings MT 59102 Office: 4th Floor Parmly Library 501 N Broadway Billings MT 59101

HAAK, HAROLD HOWARD, univ. pres.; b. Madison, Wis., June 1, 1935; s. Harold J. and Laura (Kittleson) H.; B.A., U. Wis., 1957, M.A., 1958; Ph.D., Princeton U., 1963; m. Betty L. Steiner, June 25, 1955; children—Alison Marie, Janet Christine. Asst. prof., assoc. prof. polit. sci., pub. adminstrn. and urban studies San Diego State Coll., 1962-69, dean Coll. Profl. Studies, prof. pub. adminstrn. and urban studies, 1969-71; acad. v.p. Calif. State U. at Fresno, 1971-73, pres., 1980—; v.p. U. Colo. at Denver, 1973, chancellor, 1974-80. Mem. County of San Diego Employee Relations Panel, 1969-71; chmn. Denver Met. Study Panel, 1976-77; bd. dirs. Fresno Econ. Devel. Corp., 1981—, Fresno Philharm., 1981—, Fresno C. of C., 1981—. Mem. Phi Beta Kappa, Phi Kappa Phi. Office: Office of President Calif State U Fresno CA 93740

HAAKE, EUGENE VINCENT, nuclear engr.; b. Cleve., Sept. 25, 1921; s. Eugene Louis and Vincenta Mildred (Hettinger) H.; B.S. in Physics, Western Res. U., 1943; M.A., U. Calif. at Los Angeles, 1948; m. Elsie Warren Burton, Jan. 20, 1951; children—Barbara, Janet, Ronald. Physicist, Oak Ridge Nat. Lab., 1948-52; sr. nuclear engr., nuclear group supr. Convair, Ft. Worth, 1952-62; sr. staff mem., mgr., project engr. Gen. Atomic Co., San Diego, 1962—. Served to 1st lt. AUS, 1943-46. Mem. Am. Phys. Soc., Am. Nuclear Soc. (treas. San Diego sect. 1971-72, exec. com. 1975-78), Phi Beta Kappa. Republican. Lutheran. Patentee nuclear reactor improvements. Home: 3703 Brandywine St San Diego CA 92117 Office: PO Box 81608 San Diego CA 92138

HAAPALA, DAVID ANDREW, psychologist, consultant; b. Tacoma, June 13, 1949; s. Andy Arne and Shirley Theresa (Shannon) H.; m. Jill Claire Kinney, July 26, 1976; 1 son, Scott McCleave. B.S. in Psychology, Wash. State U., 1971, M.A. in Child Devel., 1975; Ph.D. in Psychology, Saybrook Inst., 1983. Pvt. practice psychology, Tacoma, 1974—; cons. dir. tng. Homebuilder Program Catholic Community Services, Tacoma, 1974-77, co-dir., 1977-82; co-dir. Behavioral Scis. Inst., Tacoma, 1981—. HHS grantee, 1980-83. Contbr. articles to profl. jours. Home: 1901 Markham Ave NE Tacoma WA 98422 Office: 1717 341st Pl South Suite C Federal Way WA 98003

HAAS, CHARLES STEVEN, screenwriter, journalist; b. Bklyn., Oct. 22, 1952; s. Philip and Eunice (Dillon) H.; m. Janet Lee Dodson, Sept. 9, 1976 (div.); 2d Barbara Kay Moron, Dec. 23, 1981. B.A. in Creative Writing, U. Calif.-Santa Cruz, 1974. Contbr. to numerous local and nat. mags.; author: (novels) (with Tim Hunter) The Soul Hit, 1977, Over the Edge, 1979; writer screenplays Over the Edge (Warner Bros.), 1979, Tex (Disney), 1982. Recipient CEBA award for excellence, 1981; award of excellence for Screenplay Tex, Film Adv. Bd., 1982. Mem. Writer's Guild Am. West.

HAAS, DEBORAH LYNN, bank officer; b. Chgo., June 11, 1952; d. William Hermann and Elizabeth Dorothy (Badali) H.; B.A., U. Dayton, 1973; M.A., U. Ariz., 1976; M.I.M., Am. Grad. Sch. Internat. Mgmt., 1979. Advt. mgr. Flyer News, U. Dayton (Ohio), 1970-73; instr. U. Ariz., Tucson, 1974-79; consumer lending officer Valley Nat. Bank, Phoenix, 1980-82, comml. lending officer, 1982-83, br. credit officer, 1983— tchr. ESL, 1975-79; tchr. German, U. Ariz., 1974-76. Bd. dirs. Desert Dance Co., 1983—, corp. sec., 1983—; sec. Friends of Refugees, 1982—; instr. Vols. for Refugee Self-Sufficiency, 1982—. Mem. Am. Assn. Tchrs. German, Phoenix T-Birds Alumni Assn. (sec. steering com.), Delta Phi Alpha, Phi Beta Alpha. Address: Sasabe Star Route Box 492 Tucson AZ 85736

HAAS, FRANK ARMEN, advertising agency executive; b. Darby Pa., June 24, 1948; s. Jack Bricker and Lida (Galanderian) H.; m. Susan Ellen Zeman, Sept. 24, 1972. B.S. in Journalism, Northwestern U., 1970, M.Mgmt., 1976. Acct. exec. Leo Burnett Co., Chgo., 1976-80; v.p., acct. supr. Milici Valenti Advt. Co., Honolulu, 1980—. Bd. dirs. Chamber Mus. Hawaii; mem. Transit Coalition for Honolulu. Served to lt. USN, 1970-74. Mem. Pacific Area Travel Assn., Am. Mktg. Assn. (dir. communications Hawaii chpt.). Lutheran. Office: Milici Valenti Advertising Co 700 Bishop St 12th Floor Honolulu HI 96813

HAAS, HELMUT, physician; b. Novi-Sad, Yugoslavia, Dec. 3, 1929; came to U.S., 1952, naturalized, 1957; s. Karl and Elizabeth (Roth) H.; student U. Heidelberg (Germany), 1950-52; B.S., U. Minn., 1956, M.D., 1958; m. Edith E. Raupp, Oct. 16, 1951; children—Peter, Christine, Frederick. Intern, Youngstown (Ohio) Hosp., 1958-59; resident U. Utah Affiliated Hosps., Salt Lake City, 1959-60; resident VA Hosp., Portland, Oreg., 1960-62, asst. chief pulmonary diseases sect., 1966—, med. dir. respiratory care unit, 1976—; assoc. prof. medicine U. Oreg. Health Scis. Center, 1971—. Served to capt. M.C., USAF, 1962-64. Diplomate Am. Bd. Internal Medicine. Fellow Am. Coll. Chest Physicians; mem. Oreg., Am. thoracic socs., Oreg. Critical Care Soc. Author: (with others) Chronic Obstructive Pulmonary Disease, a Manual for Physicians, 1972, 5th edit., 1977. Home: 625 87th Terr NW Portland OR 97229 Office: Sam Jackson Park Rd VA Hosp Portland OR 97207

HAAS, PETER EDGAR, clothing company executive; b. San Francisco, Dec. 20, 1918; s. Walter A. and Elise (Stern) H.; student Deerfield Acad., 1935-36; A.B., U. Calif., 1940; postgrad. Harvard, 1943; m. Josephine Baum, Feb. 1, 1945; children—Peter E., Michael Stern, Margaret Elizabeth. Asst. prodn. mgr. Levi Strauss & Co., San Francisco, 1946-51, v.p., dir., 1951-58, exec. v.p., 1958-70, pres., 1970-82, chief exec. officer, 1976-82, chmn., 1982—; dir. Crocker Nat. Corp., Crocker Nat. Bank, Am. Tel. & Tel. Co. Mem. Golden Gate Nat. Recreation Area Adv. Com.; bd. dirs. Jewish Welfare Fedn.; trustee Stanford U., San Francisco Bay Area Council. Named Leader of Tomorrow, Time mag., 1953. Mem. Calif. Acad. Scis. (vice chmn., trustee), Calif. Alumni Fedn. (trustee). Republican. Jewish. Office: Levi Strauss & Co 1155 Battery St San Francisco CA 94106*

HAAS, RICHARD, biologist, zoologist, educator; b. N.Y.C., July 6, 1929; s. Ignatius and Elizabeth (Varga) H.; m. Vivian Joan Sternlight, June 22, 1952; children—Danielle, Tracy. A.B., UCLA, 1950, M.A., 1958, Ph.D., 1969. Secondary tchr. biology, gen. sci. and German, Los Angeles City Schs., 1955-64; asst. prof. Calif. State U., Fresno, 1969-71, assoc. prof., 1972-75, prof., 1975—; cons. WHO. Served with U.S. Army, 1952-54. Mem. AAAS, Am. Inst. Biol. Sci., Am. Behavior Soc., Am. Soc. Ichthyologists and Herpetologists. Contbr. articles to profl. jours. Home: 5491 N Fruit Fresno CA 93711 Office: Biol Dept Calif State U Fresno CA 93740

HAAS, WILLIAM KARL, aerospace engr.; b. Whitewood, S.D., May 24, 1915; s. Charles and Jane Mae (Pickering) H.; student mech. engring. Internat. Coll. Schs., 1946-50, U. Calif., Los Angeles, San Diego State Coll.; m. Laura Louise Elmore, Dec. 2, 1938; children—Sharon, William, Cynthia. Engring. test technician Solar Aircraft Co., San Diego, 1942-50; test engr., group leader McDonnel Aircraft, St. Louis, 1951-52; research and devel. engr. Marquardt Corp., Van Nuys, Calif., 1953-68; research and devel. engring. sr. Lear Motor Corp., Reno, 1968-69; sr. project engr. Hurst Airheart Corp., Chatsworth, Calif., 1969-71; sr. staff engr. Brake Control Technology, Inc., Glendale, Calif., 1971-73; sr. tst engr. Hydraulic Research/Textron Corp., Valencia, Calif., 1973—. Fellow Am. Inst. Aeros. and Astronautics (asso.); mem. Soc. Automotive Engrs., Soc. Black Hill Pioneers. Democrat. Presbyn. Clubs: Good Sam, Hydraulic Research Mgmt. Inventor load weigh transducer for rapid transit cars. Home: 10118 Oak Park Ave Northridge CA 91325 Office: 25200 W Rye Cyn Rd Valencia CA 91355

HAASE, EDWARD FRANCIS, mined land reclamationist, ecologist; b. Milw., Apr. 29, 1937; s. William M. and Eleanore A. (Treml) H.; m. Joann Meister, Aug. 21, 1965; children—Mark, Timothy, Julie. B.S. in Botany, Marquette U., 1959; M.S., U. Wis.-Milw., 1965; Ph.D., U. Ariz., 1969. Ecologist, S.W. Watershed Research Ctr., Dept. of Agr., Tucson, 1969-70; research assoc., asst. prof. arid land resources U. Ariz., Tucson,

1970-76; head dept. smoke investigation Phelps Dodge Corp., Douglas, Ariz., 1976-79, land use and reclamation coordinator, Phoenix, 1979—; ecol. cons. Oak Ridge Nat. Lab., 1973. Bd. dirs. Douglas Assn. Retarded Citizens, 1978-82, v.p., 1980, pres., 1981; bd. dirs. Pima Assn. Retarded Citizens, also Cochise County Assn. Handicapped, 1976-78. Served to lt. USNR, 1959-62. NSF fellow, 1968; NASA grantee, 1972-73; C.E. grantee, 1971-72. Mem. AAAS, Ecol. Soc. Am., Soc. Mining Engrs., AIME, Air Pollution Control Assn., Sigma Xi, Phi Sigma, Beta Beta Beta. Roman Catholic. Club: Rotary. Contbr. articles on ecology, desert plant utilization, air pollution effects and environ. impacts to profl. jours. Home: 13420 N 82d St Scottsdale AZ 85260 Office: 2600 N Central Ave Phoenix AZ 85004

HAASE, SUSAN MARY, radio station executive; b. Chgo., Dec. 22, 1943; d. Gustav Hermann and Joan (Minarik) Carlson; B.A. (Ill. State scholar), Northwestern U., 1965; M.A., U. Ill., Urbana, 1969; 1 son, Christopher Scott. With public relations dept. Field Enterprises Ednl. Corp., Chgo., 1965-66; program coordinator, trainer Head Start programs, Ga., Miss., 1966-67; instr. English, Parkland Coll., Champaign, Ill., 1969-71; instr. English, teaching fellow U. Nev., Reno, 1972-74; exec. dir. Nev. Assn. Retarded Citizens, Reno, 1976-80; devel. dir. Sta. KUNR-FM, Reno, 1981—. Chmn., Gov.'s Adv. Bd. Mental Hygiene and Mental Retardation, Nev., 1976—; cons. Nev. PTA; bd. dirs. Nev. Spl. Olympics; lobbyist Nev. Legislature, 1977-81. Mem. AAUW. Office: 106 Edn Bldg Sta KUNR Reno NV 89557

HAASER, LUCYNTHIA, interior designer; b. Anderson, Ind., Aug. 29, 1926; d. Charles E. and Miriam I. (Haas) Mattox; student Ind. U., 1944-47, Cornell U., 1945; B.S., U. Cin., 1949; m. Walter L. Haaser, June 14, 1947; children—Deborah K. Haaser Jones, Barbara Susan Haaser Shaner. Tchr., Dept. Def. Schs., Tokyo, 1968-70; designer Denver Dry Goods, Inc., 1972-73; pres. Cindy Haaser Interiors, Inc., Colorado Springs, Colo., 1974—; lectr., cons. on design. Alt. county del. Republican Party; bd. dirs. Assistance League; exec. bd. ch. and arts com. Broadmoor Community Ch.; vol. assn. Fine Arts Center of Colorado Springs. Mem. Internat. Soc. Interior Designers, Colorado Springs Design Guild (pres.), Exec. Women Internat., DAR (dir.), AAUW, Friends of Pioneer Mus., Marine Meml. Assn., Ikebana Internat. (exec. bd.), Hi Fi Investors Assn., Sigma Kappa. Clubs: Eisenhower Golf, Country of Colo., Ports of Call. Home and Office: 3 Loma Linda Dr Broadmoor Colorado Springs CO 80906

HABECKER, EUGENE BRUBAKER, college president; b. Hershey, Pa., June 17, 1946; s. Walter E. and Frances M. Habecker; m. Marylou Napolitano, July 27, 1968; children—David, Matthew, Marybeth. B.A., Taylor U., 1968; M.A., Ball State U., 1969; J.D., Temple U., 1974; Ph.D., U. Mich., 1981. Dir. fin. aid, asst. dean Eastern Coll., St. Davids, Pa., 1970-74; dean students, asst. prof. polit. sci. George Fox coll., Newberg, Oreg., 1974-78; exec. v.p. Huntington (Ind.) Coll., 1979-81, pres., 1981—. Bd. dirs. Christian Coll. Coalition; bd. dirs., sec. Assoc. Colls. Ind.; mem. exec. com. Ind. Conf. on Higher Edn.; mem. steering com. Christians for Polit. Alternatives, Fort Wayne, Ind., 1979. Mem. Am. Assn. Higher Edn., ABA, Christian Legal Soc., Huntington C. of C. (mem. econ. devel. com. 1981), Phi Delta Kappa. Mem. United Brethren Ch. Author: Affirmative Action in the Independent College: A Practical Planning Model, 1977; contbr. articles to profl. jours. Home: 901 Ray St Route 1 Huntington IN 46750 Office: 2303 College St Huntington IN 46750

HABER, JEFFREY S., psychologist; b. N.Y.C., Oct. 10, 1943; s. Morris H. and Elsie J. (Werthelmer) H.; B.S., CCNY, 1967; M.S.Ed., Queens Coll., 1972; Ed.D., U. Denver, 1974; m. Sharon Haber, Aug. 8, 1969; 1 son, Gabriel David. Dir. counseling services Strasburg (Colo.) Public Sch. Dist., 1974-75; asso. prof. dept. human services Met. State Coll., Denver, 1975—; clin. psychologist in pvt. practice Behavior Therapy Inst. and Clinic Colo., Denver, 1976—; clin. supr. York St. Center for Victims Crime and Family Violence, Denver, 1980—. Recipient Disting. Teaching award Met. State Coll., 1977, 78. Mem. Am. Psychol. Assn., Assn. Advancement Behavior Therapy, Nat. Orgn. Human Services Educators, Colo. Psychol. Assn. Jewish. Home: 751 Detroit St Denver CO 80206 Office: 1006 11th St Box 12 Denver CO 80204

HABER, MELVYN, inn owner; b. Bklyn., Oct. 24, 1936; s. Louis and Mary (Tandet) H.; student Fashion Inst. Tech., 1953; children—Gary, Shani. Pres. Auto-Aid Mfg., Inc., White Tone, N.Y., 1955-70, Wallfrin Industries, Bklyn., 1955-75; owner London Trading Ltd., N.Y.C., 1965-75; owner EHS Assocs., Bklyn., 1960-75; owner Ingleside Inn, Palm Springs, Calif., 1975—, Melvyn's and Cecils, Palm Springs, 1976—; dir. Palm Springs Thrift & Loan. Bd. dirs. Angel View Crippled Childrens Hosp., 1981—, Riverside County Vol. Assn., 1980—. Recipient Gold award United Way, 1982; Man of Year award Roundtable Palm Springs, 1981; named Mr. Palm Springs, Man's Best Friend Assn., 1981. Mem. Palm Springs C. of C. Office: 200 W Ramon St Palm Springs CA 92262

HABERMAN, CHARLES MORRIS, mechanical engineering educator; b. Bakersfield, Calif., Dec. 10, 1927; s. Carl Morris and Rose Marie (Braun) H. B.S., UCLA, 1951; M.S.M.E., U. So. Calif., 1954, M.E., 1957. Lead, sr. and group engr. Northrop Aircraft, Hawthorne, Calif., 1951-59; asst. prof. to prof. mech. engring. Calif. State U.-Los Angeles, 1959—; cons. Northrop Aircraft, 1959-61, Royal McBee Corp., 1959-61. Served with AUS, 1946-47. Mem. Am. Acad. Mechanics, Am. Soc. Engring. Edn., AIAA, AAUP. Democrat. Roman Catholic. Author: Engineering Systems Analysis, 1965; Use of Computers for Engineering Applications, 1966; Vibration Analysis, 1968; Basic Aerodynamics, 1971.

HABERMAN, EUGENE GORDON, aerospace engineer; b. N.Y.C., Aug. 18, 1933; s. Nathan and Gussie (Goldstein) H.; m. Barbara Nereustone, June 20, 1954; children—David A., Karen L. B.S. in Chem Engring., CCNY, 1954; M.S. in Mgmt., George Wash. U., 1975; grad. Indsl. Coll. Armed Forces, 1975. With Air Force Rocket Propulsion Lab., Edwards AFB, Calif., 1954—, dir. plans and ops., 1977-79, chief propulsion analysis div., 1979-81, chief liquid rocket div., 1981-83, dir. solid rocket div., 1983—; lectr. Inst. on Missile and Space Tech., U. Conn., 1961-64. Former pres. Congregation Beth Knesset Bamidbar. Assoc. fellow AIAA. Contbr. articles to profl. jours.

HACHTEN, RICHARD ARTHUR, II, hospital administrator; b. Los Angeles, Mar. 24, 1945; s. Richard A. and Dorothy Margaret (Shipley) H.; m. Jeanine Hachten, Dec. 12, 1970; children—Kristianne, Karin. B.S. in Econs., U. Calif.-Santa Barbara, 1967; M.B.A., UCLA, 1969. Mgmt. intern TRW Systems Group, Redondo Beach, Calif., 1969-72; adminstrv. asst. Methodist Hosp., Arcadia, Calif., 1972-73, asst. adminstr., 1973-74, assoc. adminstr., 1974-76, v.p. adminstrn., 1976-80, exec. v.p., adminstr., 1980-81, pres., adminstr., 1981—; instr. health care mgmt. Pasadena City Coll. Bd. dirs., pres. Hospice of Pasadena, Inc. Bd. dirs. ARC, Arcadia. Mem. Am. Coll. Hosp. Adminstrs., Health Care Execs. So. Calif., Hosp. Council So. Calif., Beta Gamma Sigma. Republican. Methodist. Club: Rotary. Home: 1709 Wilson Ave Arcadia CA 91006 Office: 300 W Huntington Dr Arcadia CA 91006

HACK, MAURICE CHARLES, JR., dentist; b. Indpls., Jan. 7, 1935; s. Maurice Charles and Cornelia Gurtrude (Hirsch) H.; D.D.S. (Mosby scholar), Loyola U., Chgo., 1959; m. Barbara Ann Moore, Nov. 25, 1970; children—Patricia, Paul. With Pub. Health Service, Oslo, Norway, 1963-64; gen. practice dentistry, Las Vegas, Nev., 1964—; adviser Vita Plus Corp. Served to lt. comdr. USNR, 1959-62. Named hon. Ky. Col. Mem. Am., Nev., Clark County dental assns., Acad. Gen. Dentistry, Pierre Fachard Acad., Internat. Analgesia Soc., U.S. Naval Inst. Blue Key, Sigma Chi, Xi Psi Phi. Democrat. Roman Catholic. Clubs: Jockey (bd. govs.), Desert Inn Country. Home: 3105 Cabachon Ave Las Vegas NV 89121 Office: 1500 E Desert Inn Rd Las Vegas NV 89109

HACKBARTH, RAYMOND WILLIAM, JR., lawyer; b. Syracuse, N.Y., Sept. 24, 1947; s. Raymond William and Jane Elizabeth (Mason) H.; m. Barbara Louise Windsor, Aug. 31, 1973. B.A., Allegheny Coll., 1968; J.D., Syracuse U., 1974. Bar: N.Y. 1975. Pvt. practice law, Syracuse, 1975-76; account officer The UMET Trust, Beverly Hills, Calif., 1977-78; dir. ins. services Ticor Mortgage Ins., Los Angeles, 1978; v.p., gen. counsel Monarch Properties, Newport Beach, Calif., 1978-79; pres. Monarch Securities, Newport Beach, 1979-80, Ray Hackbarth & Assocs., Inc., Newport Beach, 1979—. Vice pres. Syracuse Univ. Alumni Club So. Calif., 1980-81. Served with AUS, 1969-70. Mem. Am., N.Y. State bar assns., Roosters of Chanteclair, Newport Beach C. of C. Office: PO Box 4466 San Clemente CA 92672

HACKER, ALLEN DAVID, pulmonary toxicologist; b. San Diego, May 30, 1948; s. Charles Arthur and Rose Ida H.; B.A., UCLA, 1971, M.S., 1973; Dr.P.H., 1975; m. Anne Marie Jones, Aug. 20, 1972; children—Jonathan Anthony, Christopher Allen. Postgrad. research biochemist dept. medicine, pulmonary disease div. UCLA, 1975-77, NIH postdoctoral fellow, 1977-78, 80-81, asst. research physiologist, 1978—. Mem. Am. Coll. Toxicology, Am. Thoracic Soc., AAAS, Am. Conf. Govtl. Indsl. Hygienists, Calif. Thoracic Soc., Sigma Xi. Author papers, abstracts in field. Office: Dept Medicine Pulmonary Disease Div C-Lot Research Labs Univ Calif Los Angeles CA 90024

HACKER, KERRY VARINA, lawyer; b. Abilene, Tex., Feb. 27, 1944; d. Leslie Earl and Katherine Emily (Senior) Foreman; m. Wesley D. Hacker, Dec. 29, 1966; children—Dean, Stephanie, Valerie, Douglas. B.A., UCLA, 1967; J.D., Western States Coll. Law, 1978; Bar: Calif. 1978. Controller, Sea Foamed Lightweight Concrete, Inc., Whittier, Calif., 1967-70, treas., 1970-76; sole practice law, Whittier, Calif., 1978—; dir. Sea Foamed Light weight Concrete, Inc., Western Gypsum Floors, Inc. Second v.p. Whittier Com., Spastic Children's League. Mem. ABA, Los Angeles County Bar Assn., Orange County Bar Assn., Whittier Bar Assn. Episcopalian. Club: Los Angeles Athletic. Office: 7915 S Painter Whittier CA 90602

HACKER, ROBERT NORRIS, geologist; b. Macksville, Kans., Aug. 11, 1917; s. John Dole and Laura (Hilts) H.; student U. Houston, 1936-39, U. Okla., 1939-42; A.B., U. Calif. at Berkeley, 1948, M.A., 1950; m. Julienne Marie Hall, July 1, 1950; children—Paul Durland, Marcus Charles (dec.), Adrienne Leigh. Geologist Union Oil Co. Calif., Santa Paula, 1950-56; chief geologist Lloyd Corp. Ltd., Beverly Hills, Calif., 1956-65; cons. petroleum geologist, in pvt. practice, Los Angeles, 1965—. Served with USNR, 1942-45. Mem. Am. Assn. Petroleum Geologists (chmn. Ho. of Dels. 1974-75), Assn. Profl. Geol. Scientists (charter), U. Calif. Alumni Assn., Theta Tau, Pi Kappa Phi. Democrat. Methodist. Mason (Shriner). Club: Woodland Hills (Calif.) Country. Home: 7130 Atheling Way Canoga Park CA 91304 Office: 4907 Topanga Canyon Blvd Woodland Hills CA 91364

HACKETT, CAROL ANN HEDDEN, physician; b. Valdese, N.C., Dec. 18, 1939; d. Thomas Barnett and Zada Loray (Pope) Hedden; B.A., Duke, 1961; M.D., U. N.C., 1966; m. John Peter Hackett, July 27, 1968; children—John Hedden, Elizabeth Bentley, Suzanne Rochet. Intern, Georgetown U. Hosp., Washington, 1966-67, resident, 1967-69; clinic physician DePaul Hosp., Norfolk, Va., 1969-71; chief spl. health services Arlington County Dept. Human Resources, Arlington, Va., 1971-72; gen. med. officer USPHS Hosp., Balt., 1974-75; pvt. practice family medicine, Seattle, 1975—; mem. staff; strategic long range planning com. Overlake Meml. Hosp. Mem. bd. Mercer Island (Wash.) Preschool Assn., 1977-78; coordinator 13th Ann. Inter-profl. Women's Dinner, 1978. Mem. Nat. Assn. Residents and Interns, Wash., King County (chmn. com. TV violence) med. socs., NW Women Physicians (v.p. 1978), Seattle Symphony League, Bellevue C. of C., Sigma Kappa. Episcopalian. Club: Wash. Athletic. Home: 4304 E Mercer Way Mercer Island WA 98040 Office: 1128 112th Ave NE Bellevue WA 98004

HACKETT, JOHN PETER, dermatologist; b. N.Y.C., Feb. 10, 1942; s. John Thomas and Helen(Donohue) H.; A.B., Holy Cross Coll., 1963; M.D., Georgetown U., 1967; m. Carol A. Hedden, July 27, 1968; children—John, Elizabeth, Susanne. Intern, Georgetown U. Hosp., 1967-68, resident, 1968-69; fellow Johns Hopkins Hosp., 1972-75, chief resident, 1975; practice medicine specializing in dermatology, Seattle, 1975—; asst. prof. dermatology U. Wash., 1975; active staff Swedish Hosp.; active staff Providence Hosp.; pres. Psoriasis Treatment Center, Inc.; cons. physician Children's Orthopedic Hosp. Bd. dirs. Mercer Island Boys and Girls Club, 1976-81, Seattle Center for the Blind, 1979-80. Served to lt. comdr. USNR, 1969-71. Diplomate Am. Bd. Internal Medicine, Am. Bd. Dermatology. Mem. Am. Acad. Dermatology, Seattle Dermatol. Soc. (pres. 1981-82), Soc. Investigative Dermatology, Wash. State Med. Soc., King County Med. Soc. (chmn. media relations com. 1977-80), Wash. Physicians Ins. Assn. (adv. bd., chmn. actuarial com.). Clubs: Wash. Athletic, Rotary (Seattle). Contbr. articles to profl. publs. Home: 4304 Mercer Way Mercer Island WA 98040 Office: 716 Cobb Med Center Seattle WA 98101

HACKETT, LE ROY HUNTINGTON, JR., electronics engr.; b. Long Beach, Calif., Dec. 1, 1944; s. LeRoy Huntington and Wilhelmina (Yard) H.; A.A., Cerritos Jr. Coll., 1965; B.S., Calif. State U., Northridge, 1974. Metall. technician McDonnell Douglas Aircraft Co., Long Beach, 1965-67; scanning electron microscopist Rockwell Internat. Co., Thousand Oaks, Calif., 1967-73; semicondr. processing engr. Hughes Aircraft Co., Malibu, Calif., 1973-81, Torrance Research Center (Calif.), 1981—. Pres., Wilshire-Barrington Owners Assn. Recipient 2d prize Am. Soc. Metals, Los Angeles, 1965. Mem. Electron Microscope Soc. So. Calif., Am. Vacuum Soc. Patentee in electronics field. Home: 1418 Bentley 202 West Los Angeles CA 90025 Office: Hughes Aircraft Co 3100 W Lomita St Torrance CA 90509

HACKETT, RANDAL SCOTT, elec. engr.; b. Grand Rapids, Mich., Oct. 1, 1943; s. Hugh Jerry and Phyllis (Weekes) H.; A.A., West Valley Jr. Coll., 1970; B.S., Calif. State U. at San Jose, 1972; m. Lyn Susan Swanson, Jan. 11, 1964; children—Katherine Eileen and Elizabeth Evelyn (twins), Kimberly Michele. Technician, Allen Electronics, 1963-64, Fairchild Semicondr., 1964-65; technician IBM, San Jose, Calif., 1966-68, asso. engr., 1968-71, sr. asso. engr., 1971-81, staff engr., 1981—; owner R.H. Labs., 1975-76, Computer Works, 1982—. Republican. Lutheran. Inventor slave processor measurement control unit, also powering tree checker. Home: 17655 Laurel Rd Morgan Hill CA 95037 Office: Monterey and Cottle Rds San Jose CA 95114

HACKNEY, GARY EDWARD, civil engineer; b. Houston, Oct. 10, 1949; s. Kenneth Ward and Doris Mable (Hastings) H.; B.S.C.E., Calif. State Poly. U., 1974; M.S. in Engring., U. Calif.-Davis, 1981. Registered profl. engr., Calif. Assoc. engr. Stetson Engrs., West Covina, Calif., 1974-77; project engr. L.D. King Engrs., Ontario, Calif., 1977-79, George Tchobanoglous Cons. Engr., Davis, 1980-81; san. engr. John Carollo Engrs., Fountain Valley, Calif., 1982—. Recipient 1st place award small systems design competition Calif. Water Resources Control Bd., 1980. Mem. Am. Water Works Assn. (1st place award 1974), Water Pollution Control Fedn., ASCE. Home: 859 N Mountain Ave Upland CA 91786 Office: John Carollo Engrs 10840 Warner Ave Suite 100 Fountain Valley CA 92708

HACKNEY, ROBERT WARD, plant pathologist; b. Louisville, Dec. 11, 1942; s. Paul Arnold and Ovine (Whallen) H.; B.A., Northwestern U., 1965; M.S., Murray State U., 1969; Ph.D., Kans. State U., 1973; m. Cheryl Lynn Hill, June 28, 1969; 1 dau., Candice Colleen. Postgrad. research nematologist U. Calif., Riverside, 1973-75; plant nematologist Calif. Dept. Food and Agr., Sacramento, 1975—; chmn. Calif. Nematode Diagnosis Adv. Commn., Sacramento, 1981—. Honorable discharge USMC, 1966. NSF grantee, 1974. Mem. Soc. Nematologists, Internat. Council Study of Viruses and Virus Diseases of the Grape, Am. Arbitration Assn. (comml. arbitrator), Delta Tau Delta. Democrat. Methodist. Contbr. articles to profl. jours. Home: 2024 Flowers St Sacramento CA 95825 Office: 1220 N St Room 340 Sacramento CA 95814

HACKWORTH, THEODORE JAMES, JR., city official; b. Denver, Nov. 7, 1926; s. Theodore James and Thelma B. (Hill) H.; m. Doris Evelyn Larson, Dec. 31, 1947; children—James Robert, Joan Evelyn Grady, Linda Jean Hoffman. B.A., U. Denver, 1955. Sales mgr. Continental Baking Co., Denver, 1950-64; mktg. exec. Sigman Meat Co., Denver, 1964-76; v.p. sales Pierce Packing Co., Billings, Mont., 1976-79; city councilman City of Denver, 1979—; cons. EPA. Mem. Denver pub. schs. bd. edn., 1971-77; dir. Urban Drainage and Flood Control Dist., 1981-84; dir. Met. Sewer dist., 1982—; mem. Denver Regional Council Govts., 1979-83, vice chmn., 1981-83; neighborhood commr. Boy Scouts Am., 1968-69, Western Dist. commr., 1970-71; pres. Harvey Park Improvement Assn., 1969; chmn. Denver Met. Library Task Force, 1982. Served with USAF, 1945-47. Republican. Club: Mt. Vernon Country. Contbr. articles to EPA jours. Home: 3955 W Linvale Pl Denver CO 80236 Office: 1601 S Federal Blvd Denver CO 80219

HADDIX, CHARLES E., legis. and regulatory cons.; b. Astoria, Oreg., Nov. 23, 1915; s. Charles H. and Mattie Lee (Wilson) H.; grad. U.S. Maritime Officers Sch., 1943; grad. in traffic mgmt. Golden Gate U., 1951; m. Betty Lee Wylie, Aug. 22, 1948; children—Bruce W., Anne C., C. Brian. Nat. sales mgr. Radio Sta. KLX, Oakland, Calif., 1953-55; West Coast mgr. Forjoe & Co., 1955-60; v.p. Calif. Spot Sales, 1958-60, Radio Calif., KLIP, Fowler, Calif., 1961-63; med. sales rep. Ives Labs., Inc., Sanger, Calif., 1964-73; state govt. relations cons. Marion Labs., Inc., 1973—. Calif. legis. advocate, 1968, 71—; Ariz., Nev., N.Mex., Oreg., Wash., Idaho, Utah and Mont. legis. advocate, 1975—. Served with Marina Mercante Nat., Republic of Panama, 1945, U.S. Mcht. Marine, 1939-50. Mem. U.S. Naval Inst., Internat. Oceanographic Found., Am. Mus. Natural History, Oreg. Hist. Soc., Manuscript Soc., Columbia River Maritime Mus. Club: Commonwealth of Calif. (San Francisco). Address: 3218 N McCall Sanger CA 93657

HADDOCK, JERRY LEON, educational administrator; b. Tahlequah, Okla., Mar. 18, 1950; s. Levi Franklin and Mildred Irene (Garr) H.; m. Lynette Gay Cobb, Aug. 8, 1975; children—Brittany Lynn, Brookelyn Jade. B.S., Northeastern State U., 1972; M.Ed., U. Okla., 1974; Ed.D., U. Ark., 1980. Tchr. Gallup-McKinley County Schs., Zuni, N.Mex., 1973; tchr. Jenks (Okla.) Schs., 1973-77, asst. prin., 1977-79; prin. Justus Pub. Sch., Claremore, Okla., 1980-81, also dir. personnel, budgeting, curriculum and student affairs; cons. Princeton Industries, Okla., 1981-82; prin. Foothill Christian Sch., Glendora, Calif., 1982—. Mem. Assn. for Supervision and Curriculum Devel., Collegiate Assn. for Devel. and Renewal of Educators, Okla. Curriculum Commn., Nat. Assn. Elem. Sch. Prins., Assn. Elem. Sch. Prins. Okla., Coop. Council Okla. Sch. Adminstrs., Phi Delta Kappa. Mem. Assembly of God Ch. Home: 18881 Alford St Azusa CA 91702 Office: 901 S Grand Ave Glendora CA 91740

HADLEY, JANIS TERRY, lawyer; b. Buffalo, Dec. 26, 1946; d. Richard N. and Kirsten Yde (Andersen) Terry; m. John Jay Dystel, June 20, 1969; m. 2d James E. Hadley, Feb. 14, 1981; 1 son, Bryson Oliver. A.B., Brown U., 1968; J.D., U. Wash., 1975. Bar: Wash. 1975. Assoc. firm Schroeter, Goldmark & Bender, 1975-76; asst. sec. Rainier Bancorp., 1980-81; staff counsel Rainier Nat. Bank, Seattle, 1977-80, 81—. Mem. Western Pension Conf., Pension Roundtable, Order of Coif. Club: Brown U. of Wash. (chmn.). Office: Rainier National Bank PO Box 3966 Seattle WA 98124

HADLEY, RAY G., publisher, auditor; b. Salem, Oreg., June 16, 1936; s. Howard E. and Mabel (Thompson) H.; m. Penny Rey Hall, May 16, 1980; children—Heather Renee, Kyle Ray, Jonathan William. B.S. in Humanities, B.S. in English, Western Oreg. State Coll.; A.A. in Bus., U. Oreg. Auditor Oreg. Pub. Utility Commn., 1968-73; chief auditor Oreg. Dept. Agr., 1974-78; pres. R.G. Hadley Co. publ., Salem, Oreg., 1974—; officer R.G. Hadley Mortgage Co., Salem, 1969—; news reporter Salem (Oreg.) Statesman Jour., 1980—. Served with USCG, 1959-63. Mem. Inst. Internal Auditors. Republican. Author, publisher: Simplified Job-Resume Preparation Kit, 1974; Musicians Job Resume and Financial Guide, 1979; publisher, creator: Financial and Property Records for Your Successors, 1978. Office: PO Box 5306 Salem OR 97304

HADLEY, RUTH BANDY POWELL, educator; b. Honolulu, Mar. 28, 1925; d. Edwin R. and Ruth Bandy (Powell) Millikan; B.A., U. Ariz., 1958; M.A., Calif. Poly. State U., 1967; m. John Calvin Hadley, Oct. 9, 1948; children—John Craige, Ruth Bandy Hadley Mallison. With Lompoc (Calif.) Unified Sch. Dist., 1959—, tchr. math. Vandenberg Middle Sch., Vandenberg AFB, Calif. 1979—. Mem. Nat. Council Tchrs. Math., Calif. Math. Council, Assn. Supervision and Curriculum Devel., Curriculum Devel. and Supplemental Materials Commn., Nat. Council Suprs. Math., Calif. Assessment Program Adv. Com. (Assembly Bill 757 Adv. Com.), Calif. Tchrs. Assn., Delta Delta Delta, Delta Kappa Gamma. Episcopalian. Home: 1414 S Wallis St Santa Maria CA 93454 Office: Vandenberg Middle School Cabrillo Campus Consellation Blvd Lompoc CA 93436

HADREAS, JAMES DEMETRIOS, motel exec.; b. LaCrosse, Wis., Aug. 29, 1910; s. John Demetrios and Anna (Rozakis) H.; student U. Calif., Berkeley, 1947-49; m. Catherine Mountanos, Dec. 6, 1942; children—John J., Peter J. Pres., Md. Hotel Bldg. Corp., San Diego, 1946-51, Los Gables Apt. Hotel, Salt Lake City, 1951-57, Sundial Motor Lodge of Redwood City (Calif.), 1960-67, Sundial Motor Lodge, Inc., Hillsborough, Calif., 1967—, Republican candidate for Congress from 13th Dist. Calif., 1974. Mem. Redwood City C. of C. Club: Commonwealth. Home: 903 Tournament Dr Hillsborough CA 94010 Office: 316 El Camino Real Redwood City CA 94062

HADSELL, DOUGLAS LEROY, educator; b. Los Angeles, Sept. 27, 1940; s. Myron LeRoy and Lily Mimosa (Howe) H.; A.A., Pasadena City Coll., 1960; B.A., Calif. State U., Los Angeles, 1963, M.A., 1967; Ph.D., Wash. State U., 1971. Teaching asst. dept. history Wash. State U., 1968-70, instr., 1970-72; asst. prof. history Pasadena City Coll., 1972-74; asst. prof. Rio Hondo Coll., Whittier, Calif., 1974-81; tchr. Los Angeles Unified Sch. Dist., 1982—. OAS fellow, 1973-74. Mem. Am. Hist. Assn., Pacific Coast Council Latin Am. Studies, Calif. State U. Los Angeles Alumni Assn., Los Angeles World Affairs Council, Phi Alpha Theta. Contbr. revs. to profl. jours. Home: 2691 E Del Mar Blvd Pasadena CA 91107

HAECKER, ERNEST EBERHARDT, audiologist; b. Stuttgart, Germany, Apr. 19, 1948; s. Eugene and Luise Johanna (Grassauer) H.; came to U.S., 1954, naturalized, 1965; B.A. cum laude, Messiah Coll., Temple U., 1969; M.S., Central Inst. Deaf, Washington U., St. Louis, 1971. Lang. pathologist Eastern State Sch. and Hosp., Trevose, Pa., 1970; clin. audiologist St. Christopher's Hosp., Phila., 1971-72; adj. instr. U. N.Mex., 1976—; dir. audiology and psychology dept. N.Mex. Sch. for Deaf, Santa Fe, 1972—; clin. instr. Adams State Coll., Alamosa, Colo., 1980-81; cons. sch. dists. N.Mex.; mem. Nat. Adv. Com. on Psychol. Services for Deaf, 1975-77, N.Mex. Task Force on Diagnostic Regulations for Spl. Edn., N.Mex. Task Force on Standards for Edn. of Hearing Impaired. Coordinator spl. human rights project N.Mex. chpt. ACLU, 1980—; bd. dirs. New Vistas Sch., Santa Fe, 1979—. U. N.Mex. fellow, 1974. Mem. Am. Speech, Lang. and Hearing Assn. (cert. clin. competence in audiology, mem. com. on polit. and social responsibility), N.Mex. Speech and Hearing Assn. (pres. 1977-79), Council of State Assn. Pres.'s, Acad. Rehab. Audiology, N.Mex. Assn. Ednl. Diagnosticians, Am. Auditory Soc. Democrat. Lutheran. Home: 626 Kathryn Ave Santa Fe NM 87501 Office: 1060 Cerrillos Rd Santa Fe NM 87501

HAERR, ROBERT KNAUS, instrumentation co. exec.; b. Great Falls, Mont., May 14, 1929; s. George Lester and Eula (Knaus) H.; B.S. in Bus. Adminstrn., U. Utah, 1951; postgrad. U. Calif., Los Angeles Extension, 1954-65; m. Helen Louise Schultz, May 10, 1957; children—Robert Kenneth, Kenneth Paul. Mgr. pricing and planning, asst. to exec. v.p. Hycon Mfg. Co., Pasadena, Calif., 1954-58; mgr. contracts adminstrn. Consol. Systems Corp., Monrovia-Pomona, Calif., 1958-64, SDS Data Systems, Pomona, Calif., 1964-67; dir. adminstrn., program mgr. aerospace div. Perkin-Elmer Corp., Pomona, Calif., 1967—. Cons. in govt. procurement. Served from sgt. to lt. AUS, 1951-54. Certified profl. contracts mgr. Mem. Nat. Contract Mgmt. Assn. (nat. dir. 1963-65), Pomona C. of C., Sigma Nu. Club: Masons. Office: 2771 N Garey Ave Pomona CA 91767

HAFEY, EDWARD EARL JOSEPH, air conditioning company executive; b. Hartford, Conn., June 7, 1917; s. Joseph Michael and Josephine (Pyne) H.; B.S. in Mech. Engring., Worcester Poly. Inst., 1940; postgrad. Johns Hopkins U., 1943, 44; m. Loyette Lindsey, Oct. 21, 1971; children—Joseph M., Barbara Hafey Beard, Edward F. Instr. dept. mech. enging. Worcester Tech. Inst., 1940-41; mgr. Comfort Air Inc., San Francisco, 1946-47; owner, mgr. Havey Air Conditioning Co., San Pablo, Calif., 1947—; cons. air conditioning U.S. Navy, C.E., Japan, Korea, Okinawa. Served to comdr. USNR, 1941-46. Registered profl. engr., Calif.; named Man of Year, San Pablo, 1962. Mem. ASHRAE, Assn. Energy Engrs., Calif. Air Conditioning Service Engring. Soc., World Trade Center Orange County, Internat. Mktg. Assn., San Pablo C. of C. (v.p. 1950), Am. Legion, Ret. Officers Assn., Sigma Alpha Epsilon. Republican. Roman Catholic. Clubs: Exchange of San Juan Capistrano (v.p. 1981-82), Marine's Meml. Office: Havey Air Conditioning Co PO Box 143 San Pablo CA 94806

HAFFEY, JOHN DANIEL, state senator, utility company executive; b. Anaconda, Mont., Sept. 19, 1945; s. John Daniel and Clara (Kloker) H.; m. Susan Marie McGinley, 1968; children—Kelly Ann, John Francis, Daniel Joseph Patricl. B.Math., Carroll Coll., Helena, Mont., 1967; M.B.A., U. Notre Dame, 1972. Mgr. rates Mont. Power Co., Butte, 1978—; mem. Mont. State Senate, Dist. 45, 1981—. Democrat. Roman Catholic. Lodge: K.C. Home: 709 W 4th St Anaconda MT 59711 Office: Montana State Senate Helena MT 59620*

HAFFNER, JAMES WILSON, physicist; b. Ft. Wayne, Ind., Mar. 30, 1929; s. Jesse W. and Ethel (Fowler) H.; student Youngstown Coll., 1947-48; A.B., Miami U., 1950; M.S., Mass. Inst. Tech., 1952, Ph.D., 1955; m. Ann Azadian, Oct. 16, 1955. Prin. engr. Gen. Electric Co., Cin., 1955-59; co. physicist, mgr. indsl. applications RCL, Skokie, Ill., 1959-61; research physicist, group leader Armour Research Found., Chgo., 1961-63; sr. research physicist N.Am. Aviation, 1963—; part time tchr. Grad. Sch., U. Cin., 1956-59, Ill. Inst. Tech., 1961-63, U. Calif. at Los Angeles, 1968-69, Calif. State U., Long Beach, 1978-79. Registered nuclear engr., Calif. Fellow Am. Inst. Aeros. and Astronautics (asso.); mem. Am. Geophys. Union, Am. Phys. Soc., Am. Nuclear Soc., IEEE (sr. mem.), N.Y. Acad. Scis., Sigma Xi. Author: A Study of Space Radiation Shielding; Radiation and Shielding in Space, 1967. Patentee nuclear radiation detector. Home: 3500 Marna Ave Long Beach CA 90808 Office: 12214 Lakewood Blvd Downey CA 90242

HAFFNER, WILLIAM HENRY JOSEPH, physician; b. Jersey City, Mar. 31, 1939; s. William S. and Jean W. (Krueger) H.; M.D., George Washington U., 1965; m. Marlene E. Brings, Aug. 17, 1963; children—Stephanie, Andrea. Intern, George Washington U. Hosp., Washington, 1965-66; resident in ob.-gyn. Sloane Hosp. for Women, Columbia-Presbyn. Med. Center, N.Y.C., 1966-71; med. dir., capt. USPHS, 1971—; chief ob.-gyn. service Gallup Indian Med. Center (N.Mex.), 1973-80, dep. dir. center, 1975-76; chief ob.-gyn. services Navajo area Indian Health Service, 1979-81, sr. clin. cons. ob.-gyn., 1980—; dir. ambulatory care div. ob gyn service Naval Hosp., Bethesda, Md., 1981—, asst. prof. ob.-gyn Uniformed Services Sch. Med., 1981-83, assoc. clin. prob. ob.-gyn., 1983—. Recipient Commendation medal USPHS, 1978. Diplomate Am. Bd. Obstetrics and Gynecology. Fellow Am. Coll. Ob.-Gyn., Am. Fertility Soc.; mem. N.Mex. Obstetrics Soc., D.C. Gynecol. Soc., Commd. Officers Assn. (pres. Navajo br. 1974-76). Home: 11616 Danville Dr Rockville MD 20852 Office: Naval Hosp Bethesda MD 20814

HAFKENSCHIEL, JOSEPH HENRY, JR., physician, educator; b. Youngstown, Ohio, Apr. 2, 1916; s. Joseph Henry and Anna M. (Conroy) H.; A.B., Swarthmore Coll., 1937; M.D., Johns Hopkins U., 1941; postgrad. dept. biology Mass. Inst. Tech., 1947-48; m. Lucinda Buchanan Thomas, July 18, 1942; children—Joseph Henry III, B.A. Thomas, Mark Conroy, John Proctor. Intern, Hosp. U. Pa., 1941-42, resident in medicine, 1948, fellow in medicine-cardiology, 1948-49, staff mem. Robinette Found. Study Cardiovascular Disease at hosp., 1949-66, ward physician, 1946-65; Rockefeller Found. fellow in pharmacology U. Pa., 1946-47; instr. medicine, 1949-51, assoc. medicine, 1951-66, med. dir. Sandoz Pharms. div. Sandoz Inc., 1966-67; clin. instr. medicine Sch. Medicine Stanford, 1966-69, clin. asst. prof., 1969-74, clin. assoc. prof., 1974—; staff Stanford U. Med. Ctr., 1966—. Diplomate Am. Bd. Internal Medicine. Fellow ACP, Royal Soc. Medicine, Council Clin. Cardiology of Am. Heart Assn., Am. Coll. Clin. Pharmacology and Chemotherapy; mem. Am. Inst. Aeros. and Astronautics, Am. Physiol. Soc., Am. Fedn. Clin. Research, Phila. Coll. Physicians, Am. Soc. Pharmacology and Exptl. Therapeutics, Am. Legion (post comdr. 1960-62), Sigma Xi. Clubs: Stanford Faculty, Stanford Golf, Merion Golf (Phila.); San Francisco Golf. Home: 380 Golden Oak Dr Portola Valley CA 94025

HAFLING, C(LARENCE) R(AYMOND) (STEVE), former banker; b. Durango, Colo., Nov. 12, 1920; s. Charles and P. May (Reece) H.; student Columbia U., 1956, m. Jane W. Sprague, June 6, 1942; children Steven R., Constance Joan Chambers, Janet Marie Krogh. Bus. mgr. Anchorage Times, 1947-58; pres. Color Art Printing Co., Anchorage, 1958; chmn. Haf & Haf, Inc., & 1958; chmn. Alaska State Personnel Bd., 1960, Alaska Public Employees Retirement Bd., 1960, Alaska Labor Relations Agy., 1972; mem. Nat. Jud. Coll., 1981-82, Alaska Disability Rev. Bd., 1982—; corporator Alaska Mut. Savs. Bank, 1976. Mem. exec. bd. Western Alaska council Boy Scouts Am., 1955-65. Served to cpl. Signal Corps, U.S. Army, 1941-45. Recipient Silver Beaver award Boy Scouts Am., 1958. Mem. Printing Industry Am., Anchorage C. of C., Internat. Platform Assn. Clubs: Rotary (pres. Anchorage 1973), Nat. Jud. Coll., Elks, pioneers of Alaska. Home: 1147 G St Anchorage AK 99501 Office: 430 W 7th Ave Anchorage AK 99501

HAFNER, CONRAD TAYLOR, educator; b. Fulton, Mo., Apr. 30, 1931; s. Conrad Werner and Jessie Mae (Taylor) H.; B.S., N.E. Mo. State Tchrs. Coll., 1953, M.A., 1958; D.Arts, Western Colo. U., 1972; postgrad. No. Colo. U., 1959-60, Calif. State U. at Los Angeles, 1963-64, No. Ariz. U., 1965-66, U. N.D., 1971, Centro de Artes y Lenguas, Cuernavaca, Mexico, 1974, Instituto Fenix, Cuernavaca, 1975; m. Glenda Jewell Buck, Apr. 14, 1962. Tchr. Liberty dist. 96, Callaway County, Mo., 1949; chmn. bus. dept. Wentzville (Mo.) High Sch., 1955-57, Virginia (Ill.) High Sch., 1957-58; chmn. bus. dept. Reedley (Calif.) Coll., 1958-64; prof. bus. adminstrn. Citrus Coll., Azusa, Calif., 1964—. Sec., Mental Health Soc., Reedley, 1960. Served with AUS, 1953-55. Mem. Delta Pi Epsilon, Pi Omega Pi, Phi Sigma Epsilon. Mason. Home: 1342 Tam O'Shanter Dr Azusa CA 91702

HAFNER, HAROLD JAMISON, steel co. exec.; b. San Francisco, July 6, 1913; s. Steven and Birla (Jamison) H.; B.S., U. Calif. at Berkeley, 1933; m. Elaine Mifflin Bellerue, July 2, 1942; children—Lansing Mifflin, Julie Bryhn. Sales estimator Calif. Steel Products Co., San Francisco, 1933-42; salesman, jr. exec. Gilmore Steel Corp., San Francisco, 1942-49; v.p., gen. mgr. Monarch Steel Products Co., Oakland, Calif., 1949-78; ret., 1978; dir. Gilmore Supply Co., Palo Alto, Calif. Trustee Boilermaker Welfare Trust. Mem. Calif. Metal Trades Assn. (trustee, dir.). Club: Castlewood Country (dir. Pleasanton, Calif.). Home: 29 Camino Don Miguel Orinda CA 94563

HAGA, ENOCH JOHN, educator, author; b. Los Angeles, Apr. 25, 1931; s. Enoch and Esther Bouncer (Higginson) H.; student Sacramento Jr. Coll., 1948-49; A.A., Grant Tech. Coll., 1950; student U. Colo., Denver, 1950, U. Calif., Berkeley, 1954, Midwestern U., 1950-54; A.B., Sacramento State Coll., 1955, M.A., 1958; Ph.D., Calif. Inst. Integral Studies, 1972, diploma tchr. Asian Culture, 1972; m. Elna Jo Wright, Aug. 22, 1957. Tchr. bus. Calif. Med. Facility, Vacaville, 1956-60; asst. prof. bus. Stanislaus State Coll., Turlock, Calif., 1960-61; engring. writer, publs. engr. Hughes Aircraft Co., Fullerton, Calif., 1961-62, Lockheed Missiles & Space Co., Sunnyvale, Calif., 1962, Gen. Precision, Inc., Glendale, Calif., 1962-63; sr. adminstrv. analyst Holmes & Narver, Inc., Los Angeles, 1963-64; tchr., chmn. dept. bus. and math. Amador Valley Dist., Pleasanton, Calif., 1964—; vis. asst. prof. bus. Sacramento State Coll., 1967-69; instr. bus. Chabot Coll., Hayward, Calif., 1970-72; instr. bus. and philosophy Ohlone Coll., Fremont, Calif., 1972; prof., v.p., mem. bd. govs. Calif. Inst. Asian Studies, 1972-75; pres., prof. Pacific Inst. East-West Studies, San Francisco, 1975-76, also mem. bd. govs.; dir. Certification Councils, Livermore, Calif., 1975-80; mem., chmn. negotiating team Amador Valley Secondary Educators Assn., Pleasanton, Calif., 1976-77. Served with USAF, 1949-52, with USNR, 1947-49, 53-57. Mem. Soc. Data Educators (exec. dir. 1970-74). Coordinating editor: Total Systems, 1962; editor: Automation Educator, 1965-67; Automated Educational Systems, 1967; Data Processing for Education, 1970-71; Computer Techniques in Biomedicine and Medicine, 1973; contbg. editor Jour. Bus. Edn., 1961-69, Data Processing mag., 1967-70. Author and compiler: Understanding Automation, 1965. Author: Simplified Computer Arithmetic, Simplified Computer Logic, Simplified Computer Input, Simplified Computer Flowcharting, 1971-72. Editor: Data Processor, 1960-62, Automedica, 1970-76, FBE Bull., 1967-68. Home: 983 Venus Way PO Box 2909 Livermore CA 94550 Office: 4375 Foothill Rd Pleasanton CA 94566

HAGA, THOMAS HARUO, urban planner; b. Waialua, Hawaii, July 22, 1923; s. Chotaro and Akino Haga; m. Mineko K. Kamimura, Aug. 8, 1949; children—Kelly, Sherie, Ken. B.S., Coll. Engring., U. Wis., 1957, J.D., 1956. Research planner Macomb County Planning Commn., 1957-62; dir. zoning and subdiv. adminstrn. Dept. City Planning, City of Syracuse (N.Y.), 1962-64; instr. Wayne State U., Detroit, 1965-67; adj. instr. U. Mich., 1969-74; program coordinator Genessee County Bd. Commrs., Flint, Mich., 1971-73; dir., coordinator Genesee County Met. Planning Commn., Flint, 1964-75, exec. dir., 1974-78; planning cons. Lapeer County, Mich., 1978-80; dir. planning Pueblo (Colo.) Regional Planning Commn., 1980—. Served with U.S. Army, 1943-46. Registered land surveyor, Wis.; profl. community planner, Mich. Mem. Am. Inst. Cert. Planners, Am. Planning Assn. Club: Rotary. Home: 4010 Ridge Dr Pueblo CO 81008 Office: 1 City Hall Pl Pueblo CO 81003

HAGAN, PATRICIA KITTREDGE, health services consultant; b. Milo, Maine, May 12, 1935; d. Milton Donald and Beatrice Alma (Ingalls) Kittredge; B.S., U. Maine, 1971; M.P.A., Calif. State U., 1982. Food service mgr. U. Maine, Orono, 1961-62, Ind. U., 1962-64, U. Tex., Austin, 1965; adminstr. dietary services Cabrillo Med. Center, San Diego, 1965-69, adminstr. gen. services, 1969-70, adminstr. for ops., 1970-73, assoc. adminstr., 1973-76, adminstr., 1976-82, cons., 1982—. Served with USAF, 1954-58. Mem. Am. Coll. Hosp. Adminstrs., Am. Acad. Med. Adminstrs., Am. Hosp. Assn., Am. Dietetic Assn., Asso. Western Hosps. Episcopalian. Club: Altrusa Internat. Home: 1275 Alexandria Dr San Diego CA 92107 Office: 2812 Canon St San Diego CA 92106

HAGELMAN, RONALD RUDOLPH, insurance company executive; b. Houston, June 23, 1926; s. Charles W. and Anna Marie (Griffin) H.; B.A., M.A., U. Tex., 1948; m. Rebecca O'Bannon, Nov. 25, 1953; children—Ronald Rudolph, Carl Frederick, Curt Rudolph, Christa Marie, Claus Edward. Agt. New Eng. Mut. Life Ins. Co., Houston, 1952-54; asst. to v.p. Am. Gen. Life Ins. Co., Houston, 1954-56; asst. dir. agys. Union Nat. Life Ins. Co., Lincoln, Nebr., 1956-57; pres. So. Heritage Life Ins. Co., Charlotte, N.C., 1957-59; chief exec. officer, v.p. Zurich Life Ins. Co., Chgo., 1959-60; pres., dir. Inland Life Ins. Co., Chgo., 1960; pres., dir. Guardsman Life Ins. Co., 1962-80, exec. cons., 1980—; pres., dir. Guardsman Equity Corp., West Des Moines; pres. Delphi Cons.'s; chmn. Delphi Realty, Delphi Brokerage, Tucson, 1980—; dir. Engring. Enterprises, Houston, NORED Corp., Adair, Iowa; non-resident fellow Inst. Higher Studies, Santa Barbara, Calif. Served with USNR, 1944-45, to 1st lt. AUS, 1950-52. C.L.U. Episcopalian. Clubs: Univ., Mid-Am. (Chgo.); Mirador (Switzerland). Home: 6225 Calle Alta Vista Tucson AZ 85715 Office: 6835 Camino Principal Tucson AZ 85715

HAGEN, DONA LOUISE, trainer, consultant; b. Cheyenne, Wyo., Sept. 11, 1943; d. Robert Martin and Virginia Alma (Bell) McManis; m. Paul Thomas Hagen, Aug. 9, 1969; 1 dau., Sydney Anne. Student, U. Wyo., 1961-62, B.S., Eastern Mont. Coll., 1965. Tchr., Sch. Dist. 2, Billings, Mont., 1965-73; owner, ptnr. Hagen/Dunham, Billings, 1981—. Past pres. YWCA; organizer Tng. Core, Jr. League Billings; bd. dirs. Figure Skating Club Billings; past bd. dirs. Community Concert; mem. Mont. Inst. Arts. Mem. Am. Soc. Tng. and Devel. Republican. Roman Catholic. Home: 3014 Forsythia St Billings MT 59102 Office: PO Box 21437 Billings MT 59104

HAGEN, HAROLD KOLSTOE, fishery science educator, consultant, fish farmer; b. Plummer, Minn. Nov. 18, 1924; s. Gudor John and Severine (Kolstoe) H.; m. Mary Hirsig, May 30, 1948; 1 son, Harold Albert. B.S. in Wildlife Conservation, U. Wyo., 1949; Ph.D. in Fisheries Sci., U. Wash., 1956. Formerly aquatic biologist Wyo. Game and Fish Dept., trout water biologist S.D. Game, Fish and Parks Dept., asst. prof. to prof. fish and wildlife biology Colo. State U.; currently owner, operator Hagen, Western Fisheries Inc.; spl. cons. to govts., internat. orgns. Served to sgt. mountain inf. U.S. Army, 1943-45. Decorated Purple Heart; Edmund Niles Nuyck fellow, 1963. Mem. Am. Fish Soc. (cert. fisheries adminstr. and educator), Am. Inst. Fishery Research Biologists, U.S. Trout Farmers Assn. (bd. dirs.), Sigma Xi, Phi Kappa Phi, Phi Sigma. Republican. Contbr. chpts., articles to profl. publs. Office: 237 Wagar Colo State U Fort Collins CO 80523

HAGEN, JOYCE CHLOE, educator; b. Walla Walla, Wash., Jan. 5, 1931; d. Arthur Walter and Evelyn Gladys (Tebelius) H.; B.A., Stanford U., 1952; M.A., UCLA, 1970, Ph.D., 1979; m. Richard N. Sonntag, 1952 (div. 1970); m. Richard W. Young, 1980; children—Richard A., Carol W. and Lynn E. Sonntag. Tchr., Sunnyvale (Calif.) Unified Sch. Dist., 1952-53, Monterey (Calif.) Unified Sch. Dist., 1953-54, Redondo Beach (Calif.) Unified Sch. Dist., 1954-55; faculty Calif. State U., Northridge, 1967—, prof. spl. edn., 1980—; cons. in field. Recipient Disting. Teaching award Calif. State U., Northridge, 1976. Fellow Inst. Advancement Teaching and Learning; mem. Assn. Humanistic Psychology, Calif. Assn. for Gifted, Calif. Assn. Profs. Spl. Edn., Council Exceptional Children, Nat. Assn. Gifted Children, Nat. Soc. Study Edn., Calif. Women Higher Edn., Pi Lambda Theta. Office: Calif State U 18111 Nordhof St Northridge CA 91330

HAGEN, RONALD HENRY, pub. co. exec.; b. Gettysburg, S.D., Aug. 11, 1941; s. Henry W. and Otilla M. (Trefz) H.; B.S., Drake U., 1963; degree in Bus. Mgmt., U. San Francisco, 1965. Mem. sales staff Sunset Mag., 1964-68; v.p., gen. mgr. Korecorp Industries, San Francisco, 1968-70; pres. The Hagen Group, San Francisco, 1970—; pub. U.S. Football League Kickoff. Bd. dirs. Performing Arts Services, San Francisco, 1978, Heartwood Corp., Monterey, Calif., 1978—. Served with USAF, 1964-68. Mem. San Francisco Advt. Club, San Francisco C. of C. (Ideas com.). Republican. Home: 1843 Pine St San Francisco CA 94109

HAGEN, SHELDON GOSTING, realtor; b. LeMars, Iowa, Dec. 9, 1904; s. Henry William and Jessica Maude (Gosting) H.; student U. Wash., 1922, 33, 34, 59; m. Jessica Doak Tannhauser, Feb. 15, 1964. Fed. and state qualified real estate appraiser. Credit, office mgr. Teagarden Products Co., Seattle, 1928-30; mgr. Constrn. Industries Bur., sec. wholesale credit groups Seattle Assn. Credit Men, Seattle, 1931-42; supervising rent examiner OPA, Seattle, 1942-43; dist. dir. War Relocation Authority, U.S. Dept. Interior, Seattle, 1943-45; owner Sheldon G. Hagen Co. Realtors, Guardian 1st Escrow Co., Inc., Guardian Mortgage Co., Seattle, 1945—; v.p. North Shore Properties, Inc., Tacoma, 1958-64. Mem. Nat., Wash. State assns. realtors, Seattle King County Bd. Realtors. Episcopalian. Clubs: Masons, Shriners. Home: 922 NE 150th St Seattle WA 98155 Office: 4000 Aurora Ave N Seattle WA 98103

HAGENSTEIN, WILLIAM DAVID, consulting forester; b. Seattle, Mar. 8, 1915; s. Charles William and Janet (Finigan) H.; B.S.F., U. Wash., 1938; M.F., Duke 1941; m. Ruth Helen Johnson, Sept. 2, 1940; (dec. 1979); m. 2d, Jean Kraemer Edson, June 16, 1980. Field aid entomology U.S. Dept. Agr., Hat Creek, Calif., 1938; logging supt., engr. Eagle Logging Co., Sedro-Woolley, Wash., 1939; tech. foreman U.S. Forest Service, North Bend, Wash., 1940; forester West Coast Lumbermen's Assn., Seattle and Portland, Oreg., 1941-43, 45-49; sr. forester Fgn. Econ. Adminstrn., South and Central Pacific, Costa Rica, 1943-45; mgr., exec. v.p. Indsl. Forestry Assn., Portland, 1949-80, hon. dir., 1980—; pres. W.D. Hagenstein & Assos., Inc., Portland, 1980—; cons. forest engr. U.S. Navy, Philippines, 1952; H. R. MacMillan lectr. in Forestry U. B.C., 1952, 77; Benson Meml. lectr. U. Mo., 1966; S.J. Hall lectr. indsl. forestry U. Calif. at Berkeley, 1973. Trustee Wash. State Forestry Conf., 1948—; trustee Keep Oreg. Green Assn., 1957—, v.p., 1970-71, pres., 1972-73; adv. trustee Keep Wash. Green Assn., 1957—; bd. dirs. Western Forestry Center, 1965—, v.p., 1965-79; trustee Oreg. Mus. Sci. and Industry, 1967-73; mem. U. S. forest products trade mission to Japan, 1968; mem. U.S. delegation World Forestry Congress, Argentina, 1972, Indonesia, 1978; mem. U.S. Forestry Study Team, W. Germany, 1974; mem. Sec. Interior's Oreg. and Calif. Multiple Use Advisory Bd., 1975-76. Recipient Forest Mgmt. award Nat. Forest Products Assn., 1968, Western Forestry award Western Forestry and Conservation Assn., 1972, 79. Registered profl. engr. Wash., Oreg.; registered profl. forester, Calif. Fellow Soc. Am. Foresters (mem. council 1958-63, pres. 1966-69); mem. Am. Forestry Assn. (life, hon. v.p. 1966-69, 74—), Portland C. of C. (mem. forestry com. 1949-79, chmn. 1960-62), Nat. Forest Products Assn. (mem. forestry adv. com. 1949-80, chmn. 1972-73, 78-79), Internat. Assn. Tropical Foresters, Commonwealth Forestry Assn. (life), West Coast Lumbermen's Assn. (v.p. 1969-79), Xi Sigma Pi (named Outstanding Alumnus Alpha chpt. 1973). Republican. Club: Hoo-Hoo. Editor: (asso.) Jour. of Forestry, 1946-53. Author (with Wackerman and Michell) Harvesting Timber Crops, 1966. Contbr. numerous articles pub. in profl. jours. Home: 3062 SW Fairmount Blvd Portland OR 97201 Office: 225 SW Broadway Portland OR 97205

HAGER, THOMAS OTIS, state senator; b. Mpls., Feb. 2, 1938; s. Otis A. and Hazel I. (Hruska) H.; B.S., Mont. State U., 1960; m. Connye L. Idstrom, Oct. 5, 1963; children—Gretchen, Van. Sec.-treas. Hager Leghorn Farms, Billings, Mont., 1967-73; co-owner, sec.-treas., mgr., Hager Bros. Eggs, Billings, Mont., 1973—; mem. Mont. Ho. of Reps., 1972-76, Mont. Senate, 1976—. Republican. Lutheran. Clubs: Kiwanis, Masons. Home: 150 Norris Ct Billings MT 59105

HAGGARD, BETTY ANN, nurse, educator, author; b. Cin., Nov. 8, 1945; s. Roy and Katherine (Detweiler) Haggard. R.N., Michael Reese Hosp., Chgo., 1966; B.S. in Nursing, Pittsburg State U. (Kans.), 1976; M.S. in Health Care Mgmt., Calif. State U.-Los Angeles, 1980; Ph.D., Columbia Pacific U., 1983. Staff nurse, Chgo., 1966-68; head nurse Weiss Meml. Hosp., Chgo., 1968-71; instr. nursing program Franklin Tech. Sch., Joplin, Mo., 1971-74, Valley Coll. Med. Careers, North Hollywood, Calif., 1976-77; coordinator nursing edn. Hosp. of Good Samaritan, Los Angeles, 1977-79; mgmt. devel. coordinator Huntington Meml. Hosp., Pasadena, Calif., 1979—. Recipient Writing award Scholastic Mags., 1962. Mem. Am. Soc. Healthcare Edn. and Tng. (sec. So. Calif. chpt.), Am. Soc. Tng. and Devel., Phi Kappa Phi. Contbr. articles to profl. jours. Office: Edn Dept Huntington Meml Hosp 100 Congress St Pasadena CA 91105

HAGGARD, CLAUDE COLLINS, electrical engineering consultant; b. Ranfurly, Alta., Can., Feb. 6, 1908; s. Joshiah Collins and Adella Elizabeth (Prescott) H.; m. Yvonne May Pickell, Oct. 11, 1933; children—Gloria, Merrill. Student Oreg. schs. With Mountain States Power Co., Tillamook, Oreg., 1926-29; elec. plant operator Calif. Oreg. Power Co., North Bend, Oreg., 1929-39; safety specialist Pacific Power and Light Co., 1963-73; elec. cons. and lectr. Claude Haggard's Seminars, Medford, Oreg., 1973—; instr. War Manpower Commn. Mem. Medford Safety Council; mem. adv. com. Oreg. Inst. Tech.; area dir. health and safety Boy Scouts Am.; dir. Jackson County Red Cross first aid program. Recipient Oreg. Accident Commn. award, 1965; Oreg. Workmen's Compensation award, 1967. Mem. Edison Electric Inst. (cardiopulmonary resuscitation com.), IEEE (sr. mem.; Contbn. award 1972, Hall of Fame 1974), Am. Soc. Safety Engrs., NW Electric Light and Power Assn., Nat. Fire Protection Assn., Vets. of Safety. Republican. Mem. Christian Ch. Producer TV safety programs; developer safety devices.

HAGINO, GERALD TAKAO, state senator, refinery operator; b. Puunene, Maui, Hawaii, July 31, 1949; s. Masao and Lunette (Higashida) H.; m. Cynthia H. Haraguchi, June 30, 1973; children—Steven, Danielle, Sharyse. B.S. in Biology, U. Hawaii, 1971. Operator Hawaiian Ind. Refinery, 1972—; mem. Hawaii Senate, 1982—. Active Wahiawa Community and Businessmen's Assn. Mem. Oahu Met. Planning Orgn. Democrat. Clubs: Lions, Jaycees (Wahiawa). Office: State Capitol Bldg Room 205 Honolulu HI 96813

HAGLEY, THOMAS RAYMOND, public relations executive; b. Cleve., Nov. 2, 1942; s. Raymond Henry and Eugenia (Gorka) H.; m. Margaret Joanne Claflin, Mar. 3, 1944; children—Thomas Raymond, Heather Margaret, Laurel Anne Moreland. B.S. in Journalism, 1968. Reporter Cleve. Plain Dealer, 1964; publs. chief Newport News Shipbuilding & Dry Dock Co., Va., 1967-69; staff asst. internal communications, coordinator mktg. communications, div. mgr. advtg. and pub. relations, supr. corp. communications, Pitts., the Northwest pub. relations mgr., Aluminum Co. of Am. (Alcoa), Vancouver, Wash., 1969-82; v.p., gen. mgr. Columbia Pacific office of Hill and Knowlton, Inc., Portland, Oreg., 1982—; trustee Clark Coll., 1980—; dir. Assn. Wash. Bus., 1980-81. Mem. Citizens' Adv. Com., Vancouver, Wash., 1977-78; asst. coach Battle Ground Youth Soccer Club, Wash., 1977-78; vice chmn., dir. Columbia Arts Ctr.; founder, bd. chmn. Columbia Bus. Community for Arts; adv. bd. Young Audiences SW Wash.; dir. High Valley Homeowners' Assn.; mgmt. task force Vancouver Pub. Schs.; Scoutmaster Columbia Pacific council Boy Scouts Am. Served to 1st lt., U.S. Army, 1964-66; Vietnam. Decorated Bronze Star; cited for Outstanding Contbn. to Arts, Coop. Arts Council, 1982; recipient spl. recognition award Wash. Chpt. Pub. Relations Soc. Am., 1978, Pitts. Advt. Club, 1974, Pitts. Radio Television Club, 1974, Am. Bus. Press, Inc., 1973, Assn. Advancement Journalism Edn., 1968. Mem. Pub. Relations Soc. Am. (Columbia River chpt.), Portland C. of C., Greater Vancouver C. of C. (dir.), Pacific NW Internat. Trade Assn., Western Environ. Trade Assn. (dir.), Oreg. Energy Council, Presbyterian. Office: Suite 300 111 SW Columbia St Portland OR 97201

HAGMANN, LARRY AUGUST, vocational educator; b. Chewelah, Wash., July 1, 1935; s. Merle and Rachel Louella (Greer) H.; m. Shirley Ann Vasconcelles, May 19, 1959; children—Nohea, Keala, Kaai, Lono, Liloa. Student U. Puget Sound, 1957-59; B.Ed., Central Wash. State U., 1961; postgrad. U. Hawaii, summers 1964-66; M.Ed., Wayne State U., 1969; Ed.D., UCLA, 1973. Profl. tchrs. cert., Hawaii; community coll. chief adminstrv. officer credential, Calif. Tchr., Aiea High Sch., 1963-64, Kailua High Sch., 1964-68, 69-70; vocat. edn. researcher Hawaii Adv. Council on Vocat. Edn., 1973-74; vis. asst. prof. U. Hawaii-Manoa, 1974-75, asst. dean Coll. of Continuing Edn. and Community Srevice, 1977-80; curriculum coordinator Ctr. for Continuing Edn. and Community Service, U. Hawaii-Hilo, 1975-76; vocat. edn. evaluator Office of State Dir. for Vocat. Edn., 1976-77; vocat. tchr. Olomana Youth Center, Kailua, Hawaii, 1980-82. Mem. Waimanalo Community Planning Assn., 1973-75, Hawaii County Manpower Planning Council, 1975-76. Served with USN, 1954-56. NDEA fellow, 1968-69; Edn. Professions Devel. Act fellow, 1970-73. Mem. Am. Vocat. Assn. (life), Am. Indsl. Arts Assn. (life), Hawaii Practical Arts and Vocat. Assn., Phi Delta Kappa. Roman Catholic. Club: Olomana Kung Fu (Kailua). Author: (pamphlet) Role of Advisory Committees in Occupational Education, 1971.

HAGOOD, MELVIN ARDENE, cons. irrigation engr.; b. Norman, Okla., Apr. 15, 1922; s. Alvus A. and Edith (Kessler) H.; m. Helen Patricia Glenn, Dec. 18, 1944; children—Diane, Nancy, Cathy, Michael. B.S., Oreg. State U., 1948; M.S., U. Calif.-Davis, 1960. Extension agt. Oreg. State U., Madras, 1948-50, irrigation specialist, 1950-51; irrigation specialist Wash. State U., Prosser, 1951-77; cons., 1977—; cons. FAO, Rome, 1966-67, Bangladesh, 1975, 81, Sultanate of Oman, 1977, Sri Lanka, 1978, 80; lectr., India, 1978, Yemen, 1982; mem. Internat. Commn. Irrigation and Drainage. Served with AUS, 1943-46. Mem. Am. Soc. Agrl. Engrs., Alpha Zeta, Alpha Gamma Rho, Epsilon Sigma Phi. Democrat. Presbyterian. Clubs: Rotary, Elks. Contbr. articles to profl. jours. Home: 1007 Stassen Way Grandview WA 98930

HAGSTROM, ROBERT CHARLES, business executive; b. Oak Park, Ill., Apr. 10, 1930; s. Arvid Gustaf and Emma A. (Ford) H.; m. Lola Anna Gnatz, Aug. 9, 1952; children—Scott, Bonnie-Kathleen. B.S., UCLA, 1957. Asst. treas. Selznick Internat. Pictures, Culver City, Calif., 1957-64; asst. to pres. David O. Selznick, Beverly Hills, Calif., 1964-66; asst. Technicolor Corp., Hollywood, 1966-68; asst. gen. mgr. Pathé Labs., N.Y.C. and Hollywood, 1968-70; controller Berkey Film Processing, Long Beach, 1970-73; treas., chief fin. officer, dir. Ancra Corp., El Segundo, Calif., 1974—; dir. Optical Print Services, Holywood, Selznick Internat. Corp., Culver City. Served with USN, 1948-52. Home: 2165 Fresno St Los Osos CA 93402

HAGSTROM, STIG BERNT, laboratory manager; b. Nassjo, Sweden, Sept. 21, 1932; came to U.S., 1976; s. Johan August and Nanny Victoria (Svanberg) H.; m. Brita Stina Felldin, June 23, 1957; children—Anders, Mats, Karin, Elizabeth. B.S., U. Uppsala (Sweden), 1957, M.S., 1959, Ph.D., 1961, D. in Sci., 1964. Asst. prof. U. Uppsala, 1961-64; resident scientist Lawrence Lab., Berkeley, Calif., 1965-66; assoc. prof. Chalmers (Sweden) U., 1966-69; prof. Linkoping (Sweden) U., 1969-76; lab. mgr. Xerox, Palo Alto, Calif., 1976—; cons. prof. Stanford U., 1976—. Mem. Am. Physicists Soc., AAAS, European Physicists Soc., IEEE. Contbr. articles to profl. jours. Home: 1365 Bay Laurel Dr Menlo Park CA 94025 Office: 3333 Coyote Hill Rd Palo Alto CA 94304

HAHESY, WILLIAM CARRICK, lawyer; b. Tulare, Calif., Oct. 31, 1932; s. William Martin and Roberta Carrick (Clarke) H.; children—William Carrick, Cynthia Ellen. B.A., Fresno State Coll., 1954; J.D., U. Calif.-Berkeley, 1957. Bar: Calif. 1957. Dep. dist. atty. Tulare County, 1958-59; individual practice, 1959—; jud. dist. judge, 1969-76. Pres. Kings Canyon Savs. & Loan Assn., 1968-69; sec., dir. Kaweah Savs. and Loan Assn., 1973-82; mem. adv. com. Gt. Am. Fed. Savings & Loan Assn., 1982—; chmn. bd. dirs. Visalia Community Bank, 1976—. Mem. Tulare Plaza Project, 1964-66; mem. Tulare City Planning Commn., 1960-69; chmn. Task Force Com., Tulare, 1967; chmn. Tulare Redevel. Agy., 1967-81. Chmn., Stanley Mosk for Atty.-Gen., Tulare County, Calif., 1958, 62, Edmund G. Brown for Gov., 1966. Bd. dirs. Tulare County Legal Services, 1964-67, Tulare County Tng. Center for Handicapped, 1962-72, Tulare County Alcoholism Council, 1971-72; bd. dirs., v.p. Tulare Local Devel. Co. Mem. Tulare County Bar Assn. (treas. 1965-68), State Bar Assn. Calif., Lambda Chi Alpha, Pi Gamma Mu, Phi Delta Phi. Democrat. Congregationalist. Clubs: Elks, Kiwanis. Home: 3738 Millcreek Dr Visalia CA 93277 Office: 225 N M St Tulare CA 93274

HAHN, HAROLD THOMAS, phys. chemist; b. N.Y.C., May 31, 1924; s. Gustave Aloysius and Lillie Martha (Thomas) H.; student Hofstra U., 1941-43; B.S. in Chem. Engring., Columbia, 1944; Ph.D. in Chemistry (Naval Bur. Ordnance fellow, Humble Oil fellow), U. Tex., 1953; m. Bennie Joyce Turney, Sept. 5, 1948; children—Anita Karen, Beverly Sharon, Carol Linda, Harold Thomas. Chem. engr. U. Calif. Los Alamos (N.Mex.) Sci. Lab., 1945-50; sr. scientist Gen. Electric Co., Richland, Wash., 1953-58; sect. chief atomic energy div. Phillips Petroleum Co., Idaho Falls, Idaho, 1958-64; staff scientist Lockheed Missiles & Space Co., Palo Alto, Calif., 1964—. Pres., Edgemont Gardens PTA, Idaho Falls, 1963-64; active Boy Scouts Am., 1963-64, 72-81, div. commr. Stanford Area Council, 1974-76, chmn. troop com. Boy Scouts Am., 1975-77. Served with C.E., AUS, 1944-46; col. Res., 1946—. Recipient Meritorious Service award, 1980. Mem. Calif. Acad. Scis., Internat. Platform Assn., Am. Chem. Soc. Am. Inst. Aeros. and Astronautics, Sigma Xi, Phi Lambda Upsilon. Methodist. Patentee method of making uranium oxide-bismuth slurries, nuclear fuel dissol procedure. Home: 661 Teresi Ln Los Altos CA 94022 Office: 3251 Hanover St Palo Alto CA 94304

HAHN, K. ROBERT, corp. exec.; b. 1921; A.B., Oberlin Coll., 1942; LL.B., Cornell U., 1948; m. Practice law, 1948-50; sec., gen. counsel Lake Central Airlines, 1950-51; with Lear Siegler, Inc., 1951—, mgr. mil. sales, 1954-58, v.p., dir. mil. sales, 1958-59, exec. v.p., dir., 1959-62, pres. Power Equipment div., then corp. v.p., 1962-66, sr. v.p., 1966-71, exec. v.p., sec., 1971-72, exec. v.p., dir., 1972—; dir. Rohr Industries, Inc. Office: Lear Siegler Inc 2850 Ocean Park Blvd Santa Monica CA 90406*

HAHN, KURT INSCOE, city official; b. Vallejo, Calif., Aug. 5, 1938; s. Walter Henry and Marian H.; m. Joandell Kelley, Nov. 5, 1967; children—Daniel, David, Walter, Charles. Student U. So. Calif., 1959-61. City adminstr., Riverton, Wyo., 1974-75, Torrington, Wyo., 1976-77; fin. dir. City of Healdsburg (Calif.), 1977—; instr. Golden Gate U., 1979—. Mem. Mcpl. Fin. Officers Assn., Calif. Soc. Mcpl. Fiscal Officers, Calif. Assn. Local Econ. Devel., Am. Planning Assn., Calif. Assn. Pub. Purchasing Ofcls., Calif. Redevel. Assn. Clubs: Kiwanis, Elks, Eagles. Home: 222 Alexandria St Healdsburg CA 95448 Office: 126 Matheson St Healdsburg CA 95448

HAHN, LORENA GRACE, nurse; b. Kalvesta, Kans., Apr. 16, 1914; d. Albert H. and Myrtle (Bingham) Barnes; student Los Angeles County, U. So. Calif. Sch. Nursing, 1944-47, also numerous profl. courses; m. Robert Elwyn Hahn, May 2, 1935. Tchr. tng. Kans. State Normal Sch., 1934-35; Wesleyan ministerial tng. course, including counseling youth career tng., pub. speaking, 1935-44; staff nurse Los Angeles County Sch. Nursing, 1947-50; head nurse Los Angeles County-U. So. Calif Med. Center, 1950—; staff nurse White Meml. Med. Center, 1967—. Recipient 35 Year Perfect attendance certificate Los Angeles County-U. So. Calif. Nurses Alumni Assn., County of Los Angeles Health Dept., 35 Year Service award Los Angeles County-U. So. Calif. Med. Center, 1974, Outstanding Employee Recognition award, 1978, 10 Year Service award White Med. Center, 1977, Nurse of Year award, 1981, Facility Achievement award, 1982. Mem. Am., Calif., Region 6 nurses assns., Nat. Critical Care Inst. Edn., Am. Assn. Critical Care Nurses, Los Angeles County U.-So. Calif. Nurses Alumni Assn., Nat. Honor Soc. (hon. life). Republican. Home: 2431 Sichel St Apt 207 Los Angeles CA 90031

HAIFLEY, TIMOTHY OGDEN, statistician, reliability engineer; b. Long Beach, Calif., Dec. 17, 1948; s. Chester Jo and Marilyn Nadine (Foltz) H.; m. Diann Frearson, Mar. 15, 1973; 1 dau., Paula Anne; m. 2d, Mary Teresa Carmack, Sept. 16, 1977. B.S. in Math., Calif. State Poly. Coll., 1971; M.S. in Biostats., UCLA, 1972. Statistician Veda, Inc., Oxnard, Calif., 1972-73, Lockheed Corp., Sunnyvale, Calif., 1973-77; mgr. reliability Sperry Univac, Santa Clara, Calif., 1977-81; statistician Trilogy Systems Corp., Cupertino, Calif., 1981—; instr. Evergreen Valley Coll., part-time 1974-79. Bd. dirs. Univac Credit Union, 1979-83. USPHS grantee, 1971. Mem. Am. Statis. Assn., Biometric Soc., IEEE, Am. Soc. Quality Control, Kappa Mu Epsilon. Democrat.

HAIG, PIERRE VAHE, radiation oncologist; b. Beirut, Lebanon, Sept. 24, 1917; s. Bahadrian B. and Helen (Kaloustian) H.; came to U.S., 1922; A.B., Occidental Coll., 1938; M.D., U. So. Calif., 1943; m. Alice Jernazian, Jan. 1, 1948; children—Helen, Mari, Theodore. Intern Los Angeles County Hosp., 1942-43; resident in radiology, 1946-49; chief radiation oncology and nuclear medicine Los Angeles County-U. So. Calif. Med. Center, 1950-67; radiation oncologist Kaiser Permanente Med. Group, 1967-70; dr. radiation oncology St. Jude Hosp., Fullerton, Calif., 1970—; assoc. clin. prof. radiology U. So. Calif.; cons. in radiology Long Beach VA Hosp., 1952-79; assoc. clin. prof. radiology Loma Linda U., 1952-68. Served with M.C., AUS, 1943-46; ETO. Diplomate Am. Bd. Radiology. Fellow Am. Coll. Radiology, Los Angeles Acad. Medicine, mem. Radiol. Soc. N.Am., Soc. Nuclear Medicine, AMA, Calif. Radiol. Soc., Calif. Med. Assn., Calif. Radiation Therapy Soc., So. Calif. Radiation Therapy Soc., So. Calif. Soc. Nuclear Medicine, Orange County Radiol. Soc., Los Angeles Radiol. Soc. Orange County Med. Assn., Los Angeles County Hosp. Soc. Grad. Radiologists. Congregationalist. Club: Monarch Bay. Office: 101 E Valencia Mesa Dr Fullerton CA 92635

HAIGHT, WARREN G., land development and management company executive; b. Seattle, Sept. 7, 1929; s. Gilbert Pierce and Ruth (Gazzam) H.; A.B., Stanford U., 1951; m. Suzanne Harr, Sept. 1, 1951; children—Paula Lea, Ian Pierce. Asst. treas. Hawaiian Pineapple Co., Honolulu, 1955-64; v.p., treas. Oceanic Properties, Inc., Honolulu, 1964-67, pres., 1967—; dir. Oceanic Calif., Mililani Town, Inc.; trustee TransAm. Realty. Bd. dirs. Downtown Improvement Assn., Oahu Devel. Conf., Aloha United Way; mem. Transit Coalition. Served with USNR, 1951-55. Mem. Hawaii C. of C., Land Use Research Found., Calif. Coastal Council. Clubs: Outrigger Canoe, Round Hill Country. Office: 130 Merchant St Honolulu HI 96813

HAIL, JAMES ARTHUR, II, newspaper executive; b. St. Louis, July 10, 1949; s. James Arthur and Frances Elizabeth (Koziatek) H.; m. Cynthia Joy Henthorn, May 27, 1972; children—James Arthur III, Laura Elizabeth. Reporter Ft. Scott (Kans.) Tribune and Pittsburg (Kans.) Sun, 1970-73; copy editor Bradenton (Fla.) Herald, 1973-74, sports editor, 1974-75, met. editor, 1975-77; mng. editor Junction City (Kans.) Daily Union, 1977-79; editor, gen. mgr. Golden (Colo.) Daily Transcript, 1979-80; v.p. North Idaho Pub. Co., editor pub. North Idaho Press, Wallace Miner newspapers, Wallace, Idaho, 1980—. Mem. Geary County (Kans.) Tourism and Conv. Com., 1978-80; bd. dirs. George Smith Library, Junction City, Kans., 1978-79; bd. dirs. Colo. Jr. Miss program, 1978—. Mem. Wallace C. of C., Am. Newspaper Pubs. Assn., Idaho Press Club, Idaho Newspaper Assn., Sigma Delta Chi. Republican. Roman Catholic. Home: 146 King St PO Box 1347 Wallace ID 83873 Office: 506 6th St Wallace ID 83873

HAILE, DONALD RALPH, lawyer; b. Santa Cruz, Calif., Dec. 2, 1929; s. Ralph Robert and Wanda Louise (Bunn) H.; B.A., U. San Francisco, 1952; J.D., Hastings Coll. Law, 1958; m. Kathleen Jane Smith, July 11, 1964; children—Colleen Diane, Susan Eileen. Bar: Calif. 1959; assoc. Lucas, Wyckoff & Miller, Santa Cruz, 1959-64; sole practice, Santa Cruz, 1964-66, 77—; ptnr. Atchison & Haile, Santa Cruz, 1966-77, assoc. city atty. City of Santa Cruz; city atty. City of Watsonville, 1971—. Mem. Santa Cruz Water Commn., 1978—. Served with AUS, 1952-55. Mem. ABA, Calif. Bar Assn., Santa Cruz Bar Assn., Nat. Inst. Mcpl. Law Officers. Republican. Episcopalian. Clubs: Rotary, Santa Cruz Yacht (commodore), Elks. Office: 515 Cedar St Santa Cruz CA 95060

HAILE, LAWRENCE BARCLAY, lawyer; b. Atlanta, Feb. 19, 1938; B.A. in Econs., U. Tex., 1958, LL.B., 1961; m. Susan Greene Benson, Sept. 1, 1957 (div. 1967); children—Gretchen Vanderhoof, Eric McKenzie, Scott McAllister. Bar: Calif. 1962, U.S. Supreme Ct. Law clk. to U.S. Judge Joseph M. Ingraham, Houston, 1961-62; practice law, San Francisco, 1962-67, Los Angeles, 1967—; mem. firm Hartman, Haile & Hughes, 1977—; instr. UCLA, Civil Trial Clinics, 1974-76; lectr. law Calif. Continuing Edn. of Bar, 1973-74, 80-83; mem. nat. panel arbitrators Am. Arbitration Assn., 1965—. Mem. adv. bd. Inglewood Gen. Hosp. Mem. State Bar Calif., Tex. bar assns., Internat. Assn. Property Ins. Counsel (past pres.), ASTM, London World Trade Centre Assn. Democrat. Club: Marine (London). Contbr. articles to profl. jours. Home: 9925 Lancer Ct Beverly Hills CA 90210 Office: 50 California St Suite 2221 San Francisco CA 94111

HAIMM, PHILIP M., symphony manager, producer, consultant; b. Bklyn; s. Samuel Morriss and Rae H. B.A. in Econs., Bklyn. Coll.; M.S. in Guidance and Counseling, L.I. U. Tchr. N.Y.C. pub. schs., 1966-70; counselor Beth Israel Med. Ctr., 1971-73; cons. non-profit orgns., 1975-80; gen. mgr. Colo. Music Festival Orch., Boulder, 1980—. Mem. Grants Adv. Council, Colo. Council on Arts and Humanities. Mem. Western Alliance of Arts Adminstrs., Assn. Univ., Coll. and Community Arts Adminstrs., Nat. Choral Soc. Office: 1245 Pearl Suite 210 Boulder CO 80302

HAIMS, ARNOLD BRODY, lawyer; b. N.Y.C., June 19, 1931; s. David Richard and Helen Anna (Brody) H.; A.B., Stanford, 1953; LL.B. J.D., Stanford, 1959; m. Antonia Robb, June 1, 1963; children—Charles Brody, Sally Robb, Katherine Tefft. Admitted to Calif. bar, 1960; clk. to Judge Shoemaker, Calif. Ct. Appeals, San Francisco, 1960; trial atty. So. Pacific Transport Co., San Francisco, 1960-63; assoc. firm Berry, Davis, Lewis & McInerney. Oakland 1963-67; partner firm Berry, Davis & McInerney, Oakland, 1967-76, Haims, MacGowan & McInerney, Oakland, 1976—; lectr. in field. Served to capt., USMCR, 1953-56. Undergrad. tuition scholar Stanford, 1949-50; Royal Charles Victor scholar, 1949-50; Law Sch. scholar, 1957-59. Mem. Calif. State Bar, Alameda County Bar Assn. (chmn. ins. com. 1977—), Assn. Def. Counsel, Nat. Assn. RR Trial Counsel. Republican. Clubs: Olympic (San Francisco); Commonwealth, Ballena Isle Tennis (Alameda, Calif.). Home: 1234 Caroline St Alameda CA 94501 Office: Suite 1402 1330 Broadway Oakland CA 94612

HAINES, DAVID H., marketing executive; b. Kane, Pa., Nov. 23, 1949; s. Joseph Harry and Loma Ruth (Housely) H.; B.A., U. Fla., Gainesville, 1971; M.A., Am. U., Washington, 1974; grad. Exec. Sales Mgmt. Program, Columbia U., 1978. Duty officer Dept. State, Washington Internat. Center, 1972-73; internat. economist Kimberly Case & Co., Washington, 1974-75; mktg. rep. N.Y. Times Info. Service Inc., Washington, 1975-76, Western regional mgr., San Francisco, 1976-81; nat. account mgr. Source Telecomputing Corp., 1981—; guest lectr. info. industry U. Calif., Pub. Relations Soc. Am., lectr. in data retrieval and office of future. Recipient scholarship award, Kiwanis Internat.; data communication award, Interface '78; service fellow Dominican Republic, Ch. World Service, 1972. Mem. Soc. for Internat. Devel., World Future Soc., Commonwealth Club of Calif., Internat. Assn. Bus. Communicatiors, Info. Industry Assn., Asso. Info. Mgrs., Am. U., U. Fla. alumni assns., Friends of Malaysia Soc., San Francisco C. of C. Club. World Trade. Contbr. articles to profl. jours.

HAINES, FRANCIS STEHR, architect, lecturer; b. Bethlehem, Pa., Apr. 7, 1921; s. William Howard and Harriet (Hobbs) H.; m. Margaret Hutchinson, Sept. 8, 1950; children Jane Elise Gordon, Mallory Armstrong, Frederick Stehr. A.B., Princeton U., 1941; M.Arch., MIT, 1948. Registered architect, Hawaii, Guam. Vice pres. Lemmon, Freeth, Haines & Jones, Honolulu, 1951-69; pres. Haines, Jones, Farrell, White & Gima Co., Honolulu, 1969-75; pres. Architects Hawaii, Ltd., Honolulu, 1975—; grad. affiliate faculty Sch. Architecture, U. Hawaii, 1968—; dir. First Fed. Savs. Loan. Vice pres. Habitat, 1981—; mem. adv. bd. Cancer Ctr., 1978—; bd. dirs. Oahu Devel. Conf., 1970—, Hawaii Joint Council on Econ. Edn., 1979 . Served to lt. USNR, 1943-46. Fellow AIA (design award 1962, 63, 65, 70, 75, 81). Republican. Clubs: Pacific (Honolulu); Waialae Country, Rotary. Home: 1016 Koloa St Honolulu HI 96816 Office: 190 S King St Suite 300 Honolulu HI 96813

HAINES, FREDERICK SIDNEY, III, banker; b. San Francisco, Dec. 21, 1929; s. Frederick Sidney Jr. and Eloise (Huggins) H.; m. Dorothy Dennett, Dec. 20, 1954; children—Frederick IV, Sydney Eloise. B.A., U. Wash., 1954. With Rainier Nat. Bank, Seattle, 1957—, sr. v.p. 1976—. Served to capt. USMC, 1954-56. Mem. Assn. Washington Bus., Soc. Info. Mgmt. (nat. pres.). Psi Upsilon. Republican. Episcopalian. Contbr. articles to profl. jours.

HAINES, LAWRENCE ARCHIBALD, manufacturing company executive; b. Boston, May 8, 1928; s. William Lawrence and Doris Alma (Snyder) H.; m. Priscilla June Blake, Mar. 6, 1950; children—William, Robert, Susan, Sandra, Linda, Bradford, Brent, Christopher, Darelyn. A.M.E., Northwestern U., 1953. Gen. sales mgr. Masoneilan Internat., Norwood, Mass., 1951-65; owner, exec. v.p., sec., dir. Valtek Inc., Springville, Utah, 1965—, officer several subsidiaries; lectr. in field. Served with USN, 1945-47. Mem. Instrument Soc. Am. (sr.). Republican. Mormon. Patentee automatic control valves. Office: Box 2200 Springville UT 84663

HAINES, PAUL EDWARD, county official, association executive; b. Sandusky, Ohio, Nov. 27, 1906; s. Edward Jerome and Cary Ellen (Haidet) H.; student Akron U., 1924-25; m. Clair Ann Ross, Mar. 26, 1938; children—Wanda, Cheri Ellen. With B.F. Goodrich Co., Los Angeles, 1929-70, mgr. aerospace div., 1956-70; exec. dir. Calif.-Hawaii Elks Assn. and Maj. Project Inc., 1970-75; mem., chmn. criminal complaints com. Los Angeles County Grand Jury, Los Angeles, 1975-76, chmn., v.p. Los Angeles County Grand Jury Assn., 1978-82. Recipient B.F. Goodrich Co. Winners Circle awards, 1962, 65, 67, 69; Elks Maj. Project hon. awards, 1968, 81. Republican. Roman Catholic. Club: Elks (exalted ruler Pasadena 1956-57, state pres. 1969-70, dist. dep. 1964, leader San Gabriel dist. 1978—). Home: 400 S Los Robles St Pasadena CA 91101 Office: C-21 Sunny Cal Realty 2515 Huntington Dr San Marino CA 91108

HAINES, RICHARD FOSTER, psychologist; b. Seattle, May 19, 1937; s. Donald Hutchinson and Claudia May (Bennett) H.; student U. Wash., 1955-57; B.A., Pacific Luth. Coll., Tacoma, 1960; M.A., Mich. State U., 1962, Ph.D. (NIH predoctoral research fellow), 1964; m. Carol Taylor, June 17, 1961; children—Cynthia Lynn, Laura Anne. Nat. Acad. Sci. postdoctoral resident research asso. Ames Research Center, NASA, Moffett Field, Calif., 1964-67, research scientist, 1967—; cons. Stanford Sch. Medicine, 1966-67, TRW-Systems Group, 1969-70, others; mem. com. on vision NRC; founding mem. advanced tech. applications com. Calif. council AIA and NASA, 1975-80; adv. bd. Space Scis. Center, Foothill Coll., 1976-78; bd. advs. Fund for UFO Research, Washington. Mem. Palo Alto (Calif.) Mayor's Com. on Youth Activities, 1967; chmn. adv. council Christian Community Progress Corp., Menlo Park, Calif. Vice pres. bd. dirs. Center Counselling for Drug Abuse, Menlo Park. Named Alumnus of Year, Pacific Luth. U., 1972. Asso. fellow Aerospace Med. Assn.; mem. Optical Soc. Am., Midwestern Psychol. Assn., Assn. Aviation Psychologists, Sigma Xi. Author: Observing UFOs, 1980; UFO Phenomena and the Behavioral Scientist, 1979; asso. editor Kronos-Jour. Interdisciplinary Synthesis; contbr. publs. to profl. jours.; patentee device for advanced detection glaucoma, optical projector of vision performance data for design engrs. Home: 325 Langton Ave Los Altos CA 94022 Office: Ames Research Center NASA Moffett Field CA 94035

HAINES, ROBERT FREDRICK, electronics engr.; b. Bakersfield, Calif., Feb. 14, 1935; s. Paul Walter and Isabelle Dorothy (Hadel) H.; student Portland State U., 1958-61; B.S. in Elec. Engring., Oreg. State U., 1963; postgrad. Calif. Poly. Inst., 1971-72; M.B.A., West Coast U., 1975; m. Linda K. Hibbard, June 8, 1963; children—Kimberly Dennise,

Terri Lynn. With Western Electric/Bell Telephone Labs., N.C., 1963-64, Calif., 1964-66; sr. engr. Avco Missile Systems Div., Wilmington, Mass., 1966-69; sr. staff engr. electronic design and factory coordination Gen. Dynamics Corp., Pomona, Calif., 1969-77, mktg. mgr. navy shipboard systems, 1977-80; mgr. Lyntone Engring., Inc., Glendora, Calif., 1980—. Mem. IEEE (Best Tech. Paper award 1963), Am. Mgmt. Assn., Tech. Mktg. Soc. Am., Tau Kappa Epsilon (pres. 1959-60). Republican. Home: 126 W Buffington St Upland CA 91786 Office: 215 N Grand Ave Glendora CA 91740

HAINSWORTH, DAVID JAMES, food mktg. and supply co. exec.; b. St. Louis, Nov. 29, 1941; s. Joseph C. and Anna M. Hainsworth; student Coll. of Sch. Ozarks, 1960-63, Forest Park Community Coll., 1967-68, U. Mo., 1968-69; m. Beverly Ann Berner, Oct. 25, 1969; children—Lorry Ann, Jessica Nicole. Purchasing agt. Anheuser-Busch, Inc., St. Louis, 1967-70; asst. to v.p. mktg. D & D Bean Co., Greeley, Colo., 1970-77; asst. mgr. Outwest Bean, Inc., regional mktg. coop., Littleton, Colo., 1977-78, gen. mgr. and treas., 1978-81, pres., 1981—; dir. Nat. Council Farmers Coops., Washington, 1981-82; sec. adv. bd. Wichita (Kans.) Bank for Coops., 1980-82; participant Mktg. and Internat. Trade Conf., 1980; mem. nat. adv. bd. Farm Credit Adminstrn., Washington, 1983—. Active choirs and youth orgns. Oak Hill Presbyn. Ch., St. Louis, 1958-69, First United Meth. Ch., Greeley, 1969-78; supply pastor Hollister (Mo.) Presbyn. Ch., 1961-63; mem. citizen's budget rev. com. Arapahoe County Dist. 6 Sch. Dist., 1980-81; area leader Republican Com. Arapahoe County. Served with USAF, 1963-67; Vietnam. Mem. Rocky Mountain Bean Dealers Assn. (dir. 1979-83, v.p. 1981-83), Englewood C. of C., Traffic Club of Denver. Methodist. Club: Rotary. Home: 6540 S Washington St Littleton CO 80121 Office: 5231 Santa Fe Dr Littleton CO 80160

HAIR, GILBERT MARTIN, airline executive; b. Manila, Philippines, Mar. 16, 1941; s. John Martin and Mary Jane (McMahon) H. (parents Am. citizens); student Internat. Sch. Bangkok, 1958-60; B.A., Am. U., 1966; M.A., Pacific Western U., 1982; m. Susan Jane Christian, Mar. 15, 1969 (div. Nov. 1978); 1 dau., Nicole. With U.S. Govt., Washington, 1963-65; various mgmt. positions Pan Am. World Airways, N.Y.C., 1966-67, Chgo., 1967-71; sr. cons. Welt Internat. Co., Chgo., 1971-72; dir. mktg. Micronesia and Far East, Continental Airlines, Los Angeles, 1972-77; pres., chief exec. officer Westlake Mgmt. Services Inc. (Calif.), 1975-80; asso. Westlake Group, 1980-81; v.p. Corp. planning Air N.Am., Inc., Pasadena, 1982—. Mem. Conejo Republican Action Com., U.S. Olympic Com., So. Calif. Vols., Rep. Nat. Com., Am. Security Council Heritage Found. Served with USMC, 1960-62. Mem. Westlake C. of C., Internat. Sch. Bangkok Alumni Assn. (founder), DAV, Am. U. Alumni Assn., Mercersburg Acad. Alumni Assn., Pacific Area Travel Assn., Accuracy in Media, Citizens for the Republic, Alpha Tau Omega, Republican. Roman Catholic. Clubs: Field House; Shadow Mountain Tennis; Kiwanis, Silver Dollar, Westlake Tennis and Swim, Royal Bangkok Sports. Home: 109 Padua Circle Newbury Park CA 91320 Office: Air North America Inc PO Box 2865 Pasadena CA 91105

HAISKEY, CRIS HUGH, business ofcl.; b. Denver, Jan. 11, 1952; s. Russell and Evelyn H. B.S., U. Colo., 1974. Asst. mgr. Time Tele-Mktg., Denver, 1970-72; dist. mgr. Skil Corp., Chgo., 1974, Des Moines, 1975, Denver, 1976-78; Denver dist. sales mgr. Kemlite Corp., Joliet, Ill., 1978-80; salesman Santec Corp., Denver, 1980-82, Shop-Vac Corp., Aurora, Colo., 1982-83; owner, v.p. Rocky Mountain Power Equipment Inc., 1983—; pres., owner Universal Spltys. Inc., 1983—; owner Profl. Sales Assos., Denver. Mem. Aircraft Owners and Pilots Assn. Home and Office: 15918 E Milan Dr Aurora CO 80013

HAITH, MARSHALL MYRON, psychologist, educator, researcher; b. Chilicothe, Mo., Apr. 23, 1937; s. Nathan and Frances (Rabicoff) H.; m. Sue Ann Schneider, June 11, 1962; children—Michael, Brian Gary. B.A., U. Mo., 1959; M.A., UCLA, 1962, Ph.D., 1964. Postdoctoral fellow Yale U., 1964-66; asst. prof. psychology Harvard U., 1966-70, lectr., 1970-72; prof. U. Denver, 1972—; cons. in field; Guggenheim fellow and vis. prof. psychology U. Rene Descartes, Paris, 1978-79, U. Geneva, 1979; prin. investigator Bilingual Children's TV contract, 1972-73; mem. rev. com. Nat. Found. March of Dimes, 1978—. Recipient Research Scientist award NIMH, 1981-85; Nat. Inst. Child Health and Human Devel. grantee, 1967-71, 69-73, 74-79; NIMH grantee, 1972-82; Grant Found. grantee, 1972-80; Nat. Found. March of Dimes grantee, 1977-80. Fellow Am. Psychol. Assn., AAAS; mem. Soc. for Research in Child Devel., Colo. Psychol. Assn., Internat. Soc. Behavioral Devel. Author books, including: Rules That Babies Look By, 1980; contbr. numerous chpts., articles to profl. publs.; mem. editorial bd. Behavior Research Methods and Instrumentation, 1969—, Child Devel., 1972-78, Jour. Infant Behavior, 1977-78, Harvard U. Press, 1978—, Internat. Jour. Behavior Devel., 1980—; assoc. editor Monographs of the Society for Child Development, 1981; guest reveiwer various jours.

HAITHCOX, JOHN PATRICK, international education director, educator; b. Gafney, S.C., Feb. 6, 1933; s. James Franklin and Margaret Angele (Lowe) H.; m. Marilyn Mattina, July 7, 1957; children—Kevin, Steffan, Kiran. B.A., Oberlin Coll., 1955; M.A., U. Calif.-Berkeley, 1959, Ph.D., 1965. Asst. prof. polit. sci. U. Mich.-Dearborn, 1964-67; asst. prof. govt., then assoc. prof. govt. Carleton Coll., Northfield, Minn., 1967-72; v.p. Associated Colls. of the Midwest, Chgo., 1972-81; dir. internat. edn., assoc. prof. govt. Pomona Coll., Claremont, Calif., 1981—; adv. bd. Beaver Coll. Ctr. for Edn. Abroad; vis. scholar Inter-Univ. Consortium for Polit. Research, Inst. of Social Research, U. Mich., summer 1972; voting mem. Council for Internat. Ednl. Exchange, and Nat. Com. of China Coop. Lang. Program; liaison rep. Council for Intercultural Studies and Programs; steering com. Midwest Faculty Seminars, U. Chgo.; panelist, chmn., contbr. papers to profl. confs. in field; trustee Am. Inst. Indian Studies, 1970-71; dir. Assn. Colls. of the Midwest Program-in-India, 1969. Served with U.S. Army, 1955-57. Am. Baptist scholar, 1951-52; hon. scholar Oberlin Coll., 1951-55; recipient Davella Mills Found. award, 1951-52; grant-in-aid in South Asian studies, U. Calif.-Berkeley, 1958-69; Ford Found. fgn. area tng. fellow for research, India, London, Berkeley, 1961-63; Carnegie teaching fellow, Com. on South Asian Studies, U. Chgo., 1963-64; faculty research grantee Rackham Sch. Grad. Studies, U. Mich., 1965-66; sr. fellow Columbia U., 1967, summer 1968; NSF grantee, 1970, 71; Inst. for Ednl. Mgmt., Harvard Schs. Bus. and Edn. grantee, 1980. Mem. Nat. Assn. for Fgn. Student Advisors, Nat. Com. Internat. Studies and Program Adminstrs., Articulation Council, Assn. Ind. Calif. Calif. and Univs., Internat. Soc. for Ednl. Cultural and Sci. Exchanges, Am. Polit. Sci. Assn., Assn. Asian Studies, UN Assn. (governing bd. Pomona Valley Chpt.). Author: Nationalism and Communism in India; M. N. Roy and Comintern Policy, 1920, 1939, 1971 (also pub. India, Japanese, 2d prize Watumull Found. Biennial Book Prize Competition 1972); contbr. articles in field.

HALAMANDARIS, HARRY, electronics co. exec.; b. Sunnyside, Utah, Sept. 26, 1938; s. Gust and Olga (Konakis) H.; Asso. Sci., Carbon Coll., Price, Utah, 1956; B.S., Math., Utah State U., 1960, B.S. in Engring., 1961, M.S., 1962; m. Sandra Susan Hansen, Aug. 4, 1961; children—Chris Harry, Gina Lee. Tech. staff Hughes Aircraft Co., Culver City, Calif., 1962-65; sr. tech. staff Litton Guidance & Control Systems div., Woodland Hills, Calif., 1965-69; exec. v.p. Satellite Positioning Corp., Encino, Calif., 1969-72; pres. Teledyne Systems Co., Northridge, Calif., 1972—; v.p. Seiscom Delta Co., Houston, 1971-72; lectr. in field; dir. Stinger Antenna Co. Active YMCA. NSF fellow, 1961-62. Mem. Utah State U. Alumni Assn., Wild Goose Assn., Am. Helicopter Soc., Inst. Nav., Sigma Xi, Phi Kappa Phi, Sigma Tau. Democrat. Greek Orthodox. Club: Masons. Contbr. articles to profl. publs. Home: 8055 Clemens St Canoga Park CA 91304 Office: 19601 Nordhoff St Northridge CA 91324

HALBERT, SHERRILL, judge; b. Terra Bella, Calif., Oct. 17, 1901; s. Edward Duffield and Ellen (Rhodes) H.; A.B., U. Calif. at Berkeley, 1924, J.D., 1927; LL.D., McGeorge Coll. Law, 1962; m. Verna Irene Dyer, June 7, 1927; children—Shirley Ellen (Mrs. Stanley J. Eager), Douglas James. Admitted to Calif. bar, 1927; dist. atty. Stanislaus County, 1949; judge Superior Ct. of Calif., 1949-54; U.S. dist. judge Eastern Dist. Calif., 1954—. Chmn. bd. advisers McGeorge Sch. Law, Sacramento. Mem. Selden Soc., Calif. Hist. Soc., Native Sons of Golden West, Am. Camellia Soc. (pres. emeritus), Nat. Pony Express Centennial Assn. (pres.), Alpha Chi Rho, Phi Delta Phi. Lion. Clubs: Ambassador's (Sacramento); Book of Cal., Commonwealth (San Francisco). Contbg. author: Lincoln for the Ages, 1960; Lincoln: A Comtemporary Portrait, 1962. Home: 4120 Los Coches Way Sacramento CA 95825 Office: US Courthouse 650 Capitol Mall Sacramento CA 95814

HALCROMB, VERNON CORTEZ, coll. dean; b. Kansas City, Kans., May 18, 1929; s. Ray Reed and Almeta Frances (Adkins) H.; B.Vocat.Edn., Calif. State U., Long Beach, 1971; M.A., UCLA, 1972, Ed.D., 1975; m. Odessa Marlene Pettis, Sept. 10, 1949; children—Gail, Kent, Brian, Craig, Mark. Instr., counselor Los Angeles Unified Sch. Dist., 1966-69; dir. SE Area Manpower Inst. Devel. Staff, 1969-72; dir. inservice edn. UCLA, 1972-76; dean occupational edn. Pasadena (Calif.) Area Community Coll. Dist., 1976—; adv. com. Pasadena Unified Sch. Dist.; staff Turner Sch. Learning, Pasadena. Mem. Calif. Gov.'s Com. on Employment of Handicapped; mem. planning council Pasadena United Way, 1980-81; mem. Pasadena Pvt. Industry Council, 1980. Served with USNR, 1948-53. Grantee Calif. Dept. Edn., 1972-73, Edn. Professions Devel. Act, 1974; Mem. Am. Vocat. Assn., NEA, Calif. Tchrs. Assn., NAACP. Democrat. Home: 5532 Bedford Ave Los Angeles CA 90056 Office: 1570 E Colorado Blvd Pasadena CA 91106

HALDEMAN, ELOISE ANN, music educator; b. Glendale, Calif., June 11, 1933; d. Glenn M. and Clara (Shain) Haldeman. B.A. magna cum laude, U. Pacific, 1955; B.Mus., U. So. Calif., 1960, M.Mus., 1968; postgrad. Vienna Acad. Music, 1968-69, U. Salzburg, summer 1968. Cert. life teaching, adminstrn., Calif. Ednl. asst. Grace Methodist Ch., Stockton, Calif., 1955-57; recreation leader spl. services Long Beach (Calif.) VA Hosp., 1957-58; gen. and choral music specialist El Rodeo Sch., Beverly Hills, Calif., 1960-77; supr. elem. music Beverly Hills Unified Sch. Dist., 1977—; dir. children's choirs; cons., arranger Macmillan-Collier Pub. Co.; cons. Calif. State Dept. Edn., Calif. State U.-Northridge, U. So. Calif.; active local, state, nat. music confs. Mem. Beverly Hills Community Arts Council, Music Ctr. Performing Arts Council, Los Angeles, Los Angeles County Mus. Art; life mem. Beverly Hills PTA. Mem. NEA, Calif. Tchrs. Assn., Music Educators Nat. Conf., Calif. Music Educators Assn., Los Angeles County Music Educators Assn., So. Calif. Vocal Assn., Am. Choral Dirs. Assn., Orgn. Am. Kodaly Educators, Internat. Soc. Music Edn., Council Basic Edn., Assn. Supervision and Curriculum Devel., Phi Kappa Phi, Pi Kappa Lamda, Friends of Music UCLA. Contbr. articles to profl. publs. Office: Beverly Hills Unified Sch Dist 255 S Lasky Dr Beverly Hills CA 90212

HALE, DEAN EDWARD, social services adminstr.; b. Balt., Aug. 4, 1950; s. James Russell and Marjorie Elinor (Hoerman) H.; B.A.S.W., U. Pa., 1975; postgrad. U. Oreg., 1976, U. London, 1974, U. Mont., 1968-71; m. Lucinda Hoyt Muniz, 1979. Dir. recreation Hoffman Homes for Children, Gettysburg, Pa., 1970; social worker Holt Adoption Program, Inc., Eugene, Oreg., 1975-78; supr. social services Holt Internat. Children's Services, Eugene, 1978—; lectr. U. Oreg.; cons. internat. child welfare, 1982—; co-founder Family Opportunities Unltd. Inc., 1981—. Pres. Woodtique Heights Homeowners Assn., 1980—, Our Saviour's Lutheran Ch., 1981—; bd. dirs. Greenpeace of Oreg., 1979—. Named Outstanding New Jaycee, Gettysburg Jaycees, 1971. Mem. Nat. Assn. Social Workers (bd. dirs. 1978-80, sec. 1979-80), Nat. Assn. Christian Social Workers. Home: 2101 Hawkins Ln Eugene OR 97405 Office: PO Box 2880 1195 City View St Eugene OR 97402

HALE, GEORGE ERWIN, surgeon; b. St. Louis, Oct. 12, 1916; s. Lewis Milton and Hattie (Boff) H.; m. Mary Helen Parker, June 12, 1942; children—John Parker, James Milton, Nancy Ann. B.A. in Chemistry, William Jewell Coll., 1938; M.D., Harvard U., 1943. Diplomate Am. Bd. Surgery. Intern Pa. Hosp., Phila., 1943, med. resident, 1944; instr. Jefferson Med. Ctr., 1944; resident in orthopedic surgery Albany (N.Y.) Med. Ctr., instr. oprthopedica Albany Med. Coll., 1946-47; asst. resident in surgery Washington Hosp. Ctr., 1947-49; surgeon Dr.'s Clinic, Anchorage, 1949-55; practice medicine specializing in surgery, Anchorage, 1955—; surgeon Providence Hosp., Anchorage, 1949—, chief surgery, 1960, 62; mem. founding roup Humana Hosp. Med. Ctr., Anchorage; cons. in surgery Valley Hosp., Palmer, Alaska; asst. chief surgeon Alaska R.R., 1949-51, chief surgeon, 1951-55; chief surgeon Nat. Championship Alpine Ski Races, Mt. Alyeska, Alaska, 1963; founder, trustee Alaska Mut. Savs. Bank; pres. Hale Bldg. Inc., George E. Hale Inc. Bd. dirs. Alaska div. Am. Cancer Soc., pres. Anchorage unit, 1965. Recipient Disting. Service award Am. Cancer Soc., 1979, Alaska div. Nat. Honors awards, 1968, 69, 76. Fellow ACS, Internat. Coll. Surgeons; mem. Anchorage C. of C., Anchorage Med. Soc. (founding group), Alaska Med. Soc. (founding group, 1st pres.), AMA. Club: Anchorage Lions (life mem., dir.). Contbr. articles to sci. and regional mags. Office: 501 L St Anchorage AK 99501

HALE, GUY ALAN, management development and training consultant; b. Pocatello, Idaho, June 28, 1943; s. Ronald Aerot and Beth (Reynolds) H.; B.S., Brigham Young U., 1965, M.B.A., 1967; postgrad. NYU, 1969; m. Nikki Sue Hammontree, July 1, 1965; children—Lance, Leslie, Lane, Lori. Vice-pres. mktg. Campus Mktg. Corp., N.Y.C., 1968-70; regional mgr. Xerox Corp., San Francisco, 1970-74; mng. dir. Kepner Tregoe, Inc., San Francisco, 1974-76; pres. Alamo Cons. Group, Walnut Creek, Calif., 1976—. Mem. Sales and Mktg. Execs. Internat., Am. Soc. Tng. Dirs. Clubs: Olympic, Roundhill Country. Co-author: The Proactive Manager: The Complete Book of Problem Solving and Decision Making, 1982. Office: 47 Quail Ct Suite 300 Walnut Creek CA 94596

HALE, IRVING, investment exec., writer; b. Denver, Mar. 22, 1932; s. Irving, Jr. and Lucile (Beggs) H.; B.A., U. Colo., 1964; m. Joan E. Domenico, Dec. 29, 1954; children—Pamela Joan, Beth Ellen. Security analyst Colo. Nat. Bank, Denver, 1955-58; asst. sec. Centennial Fund, Inc., Second Centennial Fund, Inc., Gryphon Fund, Inc., Meridian Fund, Inc., 1959-68; portfolio mgr. Twenty Five Fund, Inc. (formerly Trend Fund, Inc.), Denver, 1969-72; v.p. Alpine Corp., Denver, 1971-72, Forum Investment Counsel, Inc., 1971-72; dir. research Hanifen, Imhoff & Samford, Inc., Denver, 1973-77; v.p. research First Fin. Securities, Inc., 1977-82; contbg. editor Nat. OTC Stock Jour., 1982—. lectr., Denver Public Schs. Community Talent, 1975—; bd. dirs. Community Resources, Inc., 1981—. Mem. Denver Soc. Security Analysts, Radio Hist. Assn. Colo. (pres. 1977-78), Greater Park Hill Assn., Beta Sigma Tau. Republican. Episcopalian. Columnist, Denver Post; contbr. articles to profl. jours. Home: 1642 Ivanhoe St Denver CO 80220 Office: One Park Central Suite 1585 Denver CO 80202

HALE, JILL JANETTE, legal assistant; b. Wakefield, Neb., Feb. 13, 1950; d. Robert Yates and Gail Harrielle (Warner) Goodell; m. Richard Seth Hale, June 1, 1974. Student Ariz. State U., 1968, Phoenix Coll., 1969-70, Yavapai Coll., 1970, Lamson Bus. Coll., 1971; diploma, Paralegal Inst., 1979. Legal sec. Law Offices Richard Walraven, Prescott, Ariz., 1971-80; legal sec. Walraven, Lange & Mabery, Prescott, 1980-82, legal asst., 1982—; speaker at local schs.; mem. computer adv. com. Yavapai Coll., Prescott. Mem. prodn. com., and chamber singers Prescott Fine Arts Assn. Mem. Yavapai County Legal Secs. Assn. (past pres., Legal Sec. of Yr. 1981-82), Ariz. Assn. Legal Secs. (pres., Legal Sec. of Yr. 1981-82), Nat. Assn. Legal Secs., Nat. Assn. Legal Assts., Prescott Shakespeare Soc. Contbr. articles to profl. jours. Home: 705 Maricopa Dr Prescott AZ 86301 Office: 239 S Cortez St Prescott AZ 86301

HALE, MARY MCBRAYER, geriatric consultant, psychotherapist; b. Iraan, Tex., Nov. 26, 1949; d. Glenvil Maxwell and Mary Elizabeth Hale; B.A., Tex. Tech. U., 1972; M. Counseling, Ariz. State U., 1974. Clin. dir. Terros, Inc., Tucson, 1974; acting dir. Graham-Greenlee Counseling Ctr., Safford, Ariz., 1975-77; therapist Diversified Counseling, Phoenix, 1977-78; clin. supr. Tri-City Mental Health Ctr., Desert Samaritan Hosp., Mesa, 1978-81; geriatric services facilitator 1981—. Vice chmn. Tempe Community Council Com. on Aging, 1983—; bd. dirs. Assn. Retarded Citizens Tempe, 1979; vice chmn. Ariz. Behavioral Health Services Adv. Council, 1981—; founder Practical Alternatives to Violence, 1981. Mem. Am. Assn. Sex Educators, Counselors and Therapists, Am. Geriatrics Soc., Gerontol. Soc. Am., Western Gerontol. Soc., Am. Assn. Marriage and Family Counselors, LWV. Club: Soroptomist. Office: 1454 S Dobson St Mesa AZ 85202

HALE, RON LEE, organic chemist; b. Maud, Okla., Dec. 6, 1942; s. Clayton M. and Hazel May (Arnold) H.; A.S., Murray State Jr. Coll., 1962; B.S., Okla. State U., 1964, M.S., 1965; Ph.D., Ga. Inst. Tech., 1968; postgrad. Stanford U., 1968-71; m. Glenda Beth Gritz, Feb. 28, 1971; children—David, Robert, Sami. Sr. research chemist Hoffman-LaRoche, Inc., Nutley, N.J., 1971-73; sr. research chemist Dynapol, Palo Alto, Calif., 1973-75, mgr. radiochemistry, 1975-80, assoc. dir. chem. synthesis, 1980-82; mgr. pulsed fluorescence chemistry Clin. Assays, Mountain View, Calif., 1982—. NSF fellow, 1965-68; NIH postdoctor fellow, 1969-71. Mem. Am. Chem. Soc., AAAS. Contbr. articles in field to profl. jours. Home: 2477 Louis Rd Palo Alto CA 94303 Office: 110C Pioneer Way Mountain View CA 94041

HALES, BARBARA BAILEY, state official, home economist, consultant; b. Salt Lake City, Apr. 18, 1924; d. Waldamer Francis and Cassandra (Debenham) Bailey; m. Delbert Ray Hales, June 11, 1947 (dec.); children—Karen Hales Meeham, JoAnne Hales Anderson, David Ray, Mark Bailey, Laura Hales Robinson, Carolyn. B.S. Bacteriology, Foods and Nutrition, Brigham Young U., 1947, M.S. in Home Econs. Edn., 1973; postgrad. Utah State U., 1976. Basic profl. cert. Utah Bd. Edn. Grad. asst. in home econs. edn. Brigham Young U., Provo, Utah, 1969-70, instr., 1972-75; edn. specialist for consumer homemaking edn. Utah Bd. Vocat. Edn., Salt Lake City 1975-77, sex equity coordinator, 1977-82, coordinator sex equity and civil rights, 1982—; cons. in field. Auditor Utah Med. Aux., 1960; bd. dirs. utah County Mental Health, 1965-69; mem. adv. council Utah Tech. Coll., Provo, 1972; mem. City-County Bd. Health, Utah County, 1974-81. Mem. Am. Vocat. Assn., Vocat. Equity Edn. Council, Am. Home Econs. Assn., Omicron Nu. Mormon. Author: Families as Consumers, Family Perspective, 1974; (with R.T. Osguthorpe) Equity Education, Readings in Cross Cultured Education for Parents and Teachers, 1983, Equity Idea, Looking Out for Life, Opening Doors to Non-Traditional Employment. Home: 719 E 2730 N Provo UT 84604 Office: Utah Bd Div Vocat Edn 250 E 500 S Salt Lake City UT 84111

HALES, EDWARD SCOTT, interior designer; b. Detroit, Dec. 22, 1945; s. Doyle Charles and Margaret (Scott) H.; m. Michelle Wassom, Apr. 8, 1969; children—Eric Scott and Brian Michael. Degree in color and design, Schaeffer Sch. Design, San Francisco, 1970. Staff designer Shaw-Walker Co., San Francisco, 1970-72; prin. designer John de Vries Interiors, Kentfield, Calif., 1972-77; associated with Ed Smalle, San Francisco, 1977-79; prin. Edward Scott Hales Assocs., San Francisco, 1979-80, Larkspur, Calif., 1980-82; assoc. Quality Interiors, Park City, Utah, 1982—. Recipient Ann McDonald award for Design, 1974. Mem. Am. Soc. Interior Designers. Mormon. Contbr. work to profl. jours. Home: 39 E Pinehurst Ave Tooele UT Office: Quality Interiors Hwy 248 750 E Park City UT 84060

HALEY, FRANK PAUL, design engineer; b. Budapest, Hungary, June 23, 1925; s. Leslie and Magdalena (Reothy) Szerdahelyi; came to U.S., 1963, naturalized, 1969; B.S., Budapest U., 1948; M.S., U. Innsbruck (Austria), 1948; Ph.D., U. Western Calif., 1976; m. Andrea Von Juhasz, June 25, 1978; children—Lisbeth, Ella, Alexandra. Mgr., Automation Marconetti, Buenos Aires, 1952-58; project engr. Danfoss-Kyl Mjolby, Sweden, 1958-60; quality control mgr. Aviation Electric, Montreal, Que., Can., 1960-62; mgr. Upland Engring. Co. (Calif.), 1965, now dir.; sr. systems design engr. FMC Corp., Brea, Calif., 1965-78; chief engr. Marmon Corp., Los Angeles, 1978-80, Titech Internat., Pomona, Calif. and Charleroi, Belgium, 1980—; cons. ind. engr. G.S. May Co. grantee, 1958. Mem. Soc. Quality Control Engrs., Soc. Am. Quality Control Engrs., Soc. Refrigeration Engrs. (Buenos Aires), Nat. Ski Patrol System. Democrat. Roman Catholic. Clubs: Ski Andino, Ski Seefeld, Claremont Tennis, Lions. Patentee in field. Home: 409 W 9th St Upland CA 91786 Office: 4000 W Valley Blvd Pomona CA 91768

HALEY, MARILYN WILSON, educator; b. Durango, Colo., July 23, 1933; d. Henry Elbert and Idonna Elizabeth (Wigglesworth) Wilson; m. Charles Ancil Haley, July 3, 1955; children—Steven Charles, David Scott, Donald Ross. B.S. in Bus. Edn., U. Colo., 1955; M.Ed. in Vocat. Edn., Colo. State U., 1978. Tchr., counselor, sec. to prin. jr. high sch. Cortz (Colo.) Pub. Schs., 1955-59, tchr., dept. head bus. high sch., 1966—; bookkeeper, Wilson and Wilson Investments, 1966-69; sec. treas. Wildihal, Inc., 1969—. Mem. Nat. Bus. Edn. Assn., Mountain-Plains Bus. Edn. Assn., Colo. Educators For/About Bus., Am. Vocat. Assn., Colo. Vocat. Assn., P.E.O., Phi Delta Kappa, Delta Kappa Gamma, Phi Kappa Phi, Beta Sigma Phi. Republican. Methodist. Contbr. articles to ednl. jours. Home: 716 Canyon Dr Cortez CO 81321

HALFERTY, DIANE HARRIET, land devel. co. exec.; b. Tacoma, Feb. 22, 1937; d. Benjamin and Lavina Eleanor (Simmons) Rosen; student U. Miami (Fla.), 1954-56; B.S., Willamette U., Salem, Oreg., 1958; Tech. Asso. of Law, A.A.S., Edmonds Community Coll. and U. Wash., 1976; m. Guy P. Halferty, III, Apr. 5, 1959; children—Geoffrey David, Denise Diane, Keary Douglas, Courney Caryn. Pres., Creativity Unltd., Inc., Edmonds, Wash., 1966-73; pres. Great Pacific Devel. Co., Inc., Federal Way, Wash., 1975—. Mem. King County Housing Task Force, 1978—, King County Ordinance Adv. Com., 1979—; mem. Land Use Research Council; mem. council Shoreline Sch. Dist. Parent-Tchrs.-Student Assn., 1973, exec. bds. Lake Forest Park Sch., Kellogg Jr. High Sch., 1966-78; co-chmn. Little Sch. of Seattle Toy Fair, 1966; participant guardian program King County Juvenile Ct., 1981; chmn. Lake Forest Park Safety Com., 1972; judge AAU, 1978—; mem. long range planning com., auction com. Univ. Prep. Acad., 1982-83; co-chmn. Consumers Against Gen. Motors, 1982-83. Mem. LWV, NOW, Assn. Mobile Home Park Owners (v.p. 1980, pres. 1981, chmn. polit. action com.), Wash. State Horse Show Assn., Wash. State Hunter-Jumper Assn., Sports Car Club Am. (race chairperson N.W. region 1958-59). Unitarian. Club: Wash. Athletic (community affairs com. 1981—). Home: 18036 49th Pl NE Seattle WA 98155

HALFERTY, ROBERT EVANS, college administrator; b. Lancaster, Wis., Nov. 21, 1937; s. Clay Evans and Leone (Burkhardt) H.; B.B.A., U. Wis., 1959. Asst. cashier Union State Bank, Lancaster, 1962-67; adminstrv. analyst U. Calif. at Davis, 1967-73, sr. ednl. facility planner, 1973—, advisor Circle K Club, 1973—. Chmn. Zoning Bd. of Appeals, Lancaster, 1964-67; bd. dirs. Yolo County (Calif.) YMCA, 1977-80, Yolo County Family Services Agy., 1977-83, Yolo County chpt. Am. Cancer Soc., 1977—. Served with U.S. Army, 1959-62, to lt. Res., 1963-69. Recipient Outstanding Faculty Adviser award for Calif., Nev. and Hawaii, Circle K Internat., 1982; Spl. Performance award U. Calif., 1982. Mem. Grant County Bankers Assn. (v.p. 1966), U. Wis. Alumni Assn., Grant County Hist. Soc. (treas. 1964-67), Sierra Club, Sigma Phi Epsilon (chpt. counselor 1976-80). Congregationalist. Clubs: Kiwanis (pres. 1972-73), Commonwealth of Calif. (San Francisco). Home: 307 Antioch Dr Davis CA 95616

HALIGAS, WILLIAM JAMES, bus. exec.; b. Elgin, Ill., May 2, 1926; m. Betty Ann Roberson, Sept. 21, 1951; children—Terrie, Lorie, Larry. Founder, pres. Dry Wall Supply Co., Denver, 1959—. Served with USN, 1943-46. Mem. Colo. Home Builders, Colo. Lumber Dealers. Clubs: Masons, Shriners. Office: 60 Tejon Denver CO 80223

HALL, ADRIENNE A., advertising executive; b. Los Angeles; d. Arthur E. and Adelina P. Kosches; m. Maurice A. Hall; children—Adam, Todd, Stefanie, Victoria. B.A., UCLA. Founding ptnr. Hall & Levine Advt., Inc., 1960-80; vice-chmn. bd. Eisaman, Johns & Laws Advt., Inc., Los Angeles, 1980—. Trustee UCLA; bd. dirs., regent Loyola/Marymount U.; mem. Pres. Circle Los Angeles County Mus. Art, Blue Ribbon Music Ctr.; founding mem. Advt. Industry Emergency Fund. Recipient Woman of Yr. award Am. Advt. Fedn., 1973; Leadership in West award Western States Advt. Agys. Assn., 1975; Silver medal Am. Advt. Fedn., 1978; UCLA Alumni Profl. Achievement award, 1979; Women of Achievement award, 1981; Mktg. and Media Decisions Adperson of West award, 1982; Women in Communications Nat. Headliner award, 1982; Woman of Yr., Boy Scouts, 1983. Founding mem., bd. dirs. Nat. Women's Forum; mem. Com. of 200, western chmn.; mem. Overseas Edn. Fund. Mem. Women in Communications, Fashion Group, Am. Assn. Advertising Agencies (chmn. bd. govs. So. Calif.), Hollywood Radio and TV Soc. (dir.), Los Angeles Advt. Club (pres.), Western States Advt. Agys. Assn. (pres.). Clubs: Calif. Yacht, Stock Exchange (Los Angeles). Office: Eisaman Johns & Laws Advertising Inc 6255 Sunset Blvd Suite 1400 Los Angeles CA 90078

HALL, BRUCE CHARLES, sporting goods sales co. exec.; b. Muskegon, Mich., Aug. 5, 1951; s. Charles Eugene and Alice Lorraine (Nelson) H.; B.S., Calif. State Poly. U., 1974, M.S., 1975; m. Wanda Marie Brown, Aug. 10, 1974; children—Kimberly Marie, Ryan Todd. Sales rep. Sports West Sales, La Habra, Calif., 1974-78; pres., chmn. Bruce Hall Sport Sales, Ontario, Calif., 1978—; pro sales MacGregor Athletic Products, Santa Ana, Calif., 1981—. Mem. Nat. Assn. Profl. Baseball Leagues, Nat. Baseball Congress, U.S. Baseball Fedn., U.S. Golf Assn., Sports Found., Sporting Goods Agts. Assn., Far West Ski Assn., Nat. League Profl. Baseball Clubs, Am. Athletic Trainers Assn., Nat. Sporting Goods Assn. Democrat. Roman Catholic. Clubs: Mountain Meadows Country, Shooters Ski. Home: 1450 S Cypress Ave Ontario CA 91761 Office: 1301 E Warner Ave Santa Ana CA 92705

HALL, BRUCE E., accountant, financial consultant; b. Denver, May 30, 1952; s. Wilbur E. and Dorothy M. (Gawn) H.; m. Kathryn O'Neil, June 8, 1974; B.S.B.A., U. Denver, 1974. C.P.A. Staff acct. Lester Witte & Co., Denver, 1973-76, treas., controller, Jeremiah Corp., Denver, 1976-80, Walton Oil Co., Denver, 1976-80, October Oil Co., 1976-80; part-owner, treas., controller Am. Stock Transfer, Inc., Denver, 1980—; pvt. practice C.P.A., cons., Denver, 1981—, Pres. St. Vrain Valley chpt. Am. Field Service, Longmont, Colo., 1982-83. Mem. Am. Inst. C.P.A.s, Colo. Soc. C.P.A.s. Methodist. Clubs: Kiwanis (Longmont), Fox Hill Country. Office: Suite 477 1825 Lawrence Denver CO 80202

HALL, CARL ALVIN, artist, educator; b. Washington, Sept. 17, 1921; s. Walter Robert and Ella Loretta (Stant) H.; m. Phyllis Naomi Blake, July 12, 1944; children—Merrilee, Carol, Lisa, Eric. Grad., Meinzinger Art Sch., Detroit, 1942. Prof. art Williamette U., Salem, Oreg., 1948—; one-man shows: Am. Realist Painters 1930-1948 Wichita Art Mus., 1981; Willamette U., 1982; Lakewood Ctr. Gallery, 1982; U. Victoria (B.C., Can.), 1981; works represented in permanent collections Boston Mus. Fine Arts, Springfield (Mass.) Art Inst., Detroit Ins. Art, Portland (Oreg.) Art Mus., Whitney Mus. Art, N.Y.C., Wichita Art Mus. Served with inf. AUS, 1942-46; PTO. Nat. Inst. Arts and Letters grantee, 1949.

HALL, DAVID ALVIN, psychiatrist; b. Los Angeles, Nov. 16, 1937; s. Robert D. and Helen Gertrude (McIlwain) H.; B.A., Occidental Coll., 1959; M.D., U. So. Calif., 1968, postgrad., 1969-72; m. Kay Frances Winder, Aug. 6, 1966; children—Bryan Kent, Gregory Scott. Intern, Huntington (Calif.) Meml. Hosp., 1968-69; resident Los Angeles County-U. So. Calif. Med. Center, 1969-72; practice medicine specializing in gen. medicine, South Pasadena, Calif., 1969-72, specializing in psychiatry, 1972-80, specializing in sleep, mood, and fatigue disorders, 1980—; mem. active staff Glendale Adventist Med. Center, Ingleside Mental Health Center; mem. courtesy staff Pasadena Community Hosp., Huntington Meml. Hosp., Meth. Hosp. of So. Calif., Las Encinas Hosp. Recipient Physicians Recognition award AMA/Calif. Med. Assn., 1974. Diplomate Nat. Bd. Med. Examiners, Am. Bd. Psychiatry and Neurology. Mem. AMA (Physicians Recognition award 1971, 73), Calif., Los Angeles County med. assns., Am. Psychiat. Assn., So. Calif. Psychiat. Soc., Pasadena Med. Soc. Patentee with Beckman Instruments on artificial pancreas for diabetics. Office: 1499 Huntington Dr Suite 508 South Pasadena CA 91030

HALL, DAVID HOWARD, industrial engineer; b. Binghamton, N.Y., Oct. 13, 1942; s. Howard Jewell and Patricia Reed (Hounslea) H.; B.S. in Indsl. Engring., Le Tourneau Coll., 1965; M.Tech., M.B.A. (Pres.'s award), Nat. U., 1976; Ph.D. in Mgmt. and Human Behavior, Calif. Pacific U., 1979; m. Pamela K. Parks, Oct. 14, 1979. Tech. illustrator R.G. LeTourneau Inc., Longview, Tex., 1963-64; drafting engr. Aerosonic Corp., Clearwater, Fla., 1965; tech. illustrator Electronics Communications Inc., St. Petersburg, Fla., 1965-67; ops. supr. indsl. engring. for aerospace, energy systems, research and devel. programs Convair div. Gen. Dynamics Corp., San Diego, 1972-80; dep. dir. satellite x-ray test facility program office Maxwell Labs., San Diego, 1980-81; staff asst. Hydro Products/Honeywell, 1981-82; program mgr. Teledyne Ryan Aero., San Diego, 1982—; adj. faculty mem. Nat. U. Served as pilot USNR, 1967-72; Vietnam; comdr. USNR. Registered profl. engr., Calif., Can. Mem. Soc. Mfg. Engrs. (sr., past chpt. chmn.), Am. Inst. Indsl. Engrs. (sr., past chpt. dir.), Nat. U. Alumni Assn. (past dir.), Nat. Mgmt. Assn., Pres.'s Assocs. Nat. U., U.S. Navy League, U.S. Naval Inst., Naval Res. Assn. (life), The Tailhook Assn., San Diego-Edinburgh Sister City Soc. Mem. Christian Ch. Home: 5438 Jamestown Rd San Diego CA 92117 Office: 2701 Harbor Dr San Diego CA 92138

HALL, EDWARD JOHN, safety engineer; b. Chgo., Mar. 9, 1925; s. James Harold and Marie Rose (Lanz) H.; m. Louise V. Goins; children—Daniel E., Vicki Ann, Kathleen M., Patricia G. Student Ill. Inst. Tech., Chgo. 1949, Wright Jr. Coll., Chgo., 1950-52; cert. safety profl., registered profl. engr. Insp., Liberty Mut. Ins. Co., Chgo., 1948-50, service engr. 1950-52; safety engr. Reliance Ins. Co., Indpls., 1955-65; safety engr. CNA Ins. Co., Charlotte, N.C., 1965-68, Orlando, Fla., 1968-79, Denver, 1979; loss control sr. rep. CNA Ins. Co., Denver, 1979—. Served with U.S. Army, 1946-47. Mem. Am. Soc. Safety Engrs. Home: 16771 E Nassau Dr Aurora CO 80013 Office: 720 S Colorado Blvd Suite 700 Denver CO 80217

HALL, GEORGE ELLSWORTH, JR., real estate co. exec.; b. Sterling, Ill., Nov. 20, 1946; s. George E. and Irene (Buckalew) H.; student Brigham Young U., 1972; m. Karla Shepherd, June 15, 1979; children—Kristel, Amanda Lea. Stock broker Wedbush, Noble & Cooke, Las Vegas, Nev., 1972-75; pres. Am. Food Products, Las Vegas, 1975-76; real estate investor, 1976—; pres., chief exec. officer Security Fin. Service; chmn. bd. Sierco, Inc., Salt Lake City, 1980—. Pres., Republican Men's Club, Las Vegas. Served with U.S. Army, 1965-69. Decorated Bronze Star, Army Commendation medal. Mormon. Home: 203 East 600 North Alpine UT 84003 Office: 57 West 200 South Salt Lake City UT 84101

HALL, GORDON CHARLES NAGAYAMA, clinical psychologist; b. Seattle, Dec. 21, 1954; s. Charles W. and Olive T. (Ogawa) H.; m. Jeanne M. Nagayama, Sept. 2, 1979. B.S. in Psychology cum laude, U. Wash., 1977; M.A. Fuller Theol. Sem., 1979, Ph.D. in Psychology, 1982. Research asst. U. So. Calif. Med. Ctr., Los Angeles, 1979-80; postdoctorial fellow dept. psychiatry and behavioral scis. U. Wash. Med. Sch., Seattle, 1982-83; anger mgmt. cons. Mentally Ill Offender Program Western State Hosp., Steilacoom, Wash., 1982—, clin. psychologist Sex Offender Program, 1983—. Elder Japanese Presbyterian Ch., Seattle, 1975—. Mem. Am. Psychol. Assn., Asian-Am. Psychol. Assn., Phi Beta Kappa. Democrat. Contbr. articles to profl. jours. Office: Sex Offender Program Western State Hosp B27-19 Fort Steilacoom WA 98494

HALL, GORDON R., state supreme ct. chief justice; b. Vernal, Utah, Dec. 14, 1926; s. Roscoe J. and Clara (Freestone) H.; B.S., U. Utah, 1949, LL.B., 1951; m. Doris Gillespie, Sept. 6, 1947; children—Rick J., Craig E. Admitted to Utah bar, 1952; individual practice law, Tooele City, Utah, 1952-69; county atty. Tooele County, 1958-69; judge 3d Dist. Utah, 1969-77; justice Supreme Ct. Utah, 1977—, now chief justice. Mem. ABA. Office: 332 Utah State Capitol Salt Lake City UT 84114

HALL, HAROLD ROBERT, computer engr.; b. Bakersfield, Calif., Feb. 7, 1935; s. Edward Earl and Ethel Mae (Butner) H.; B.S., U. Calif. at Berkeley, 1956, M.S. (NSF fellow), 1957, Ph.D., 1966; m. Tenniebee May Hall, Feb. 20, 1965. Chief engr. wave filter div. Transonic, Inc., Bakersfield, 1957-60; chief design engr. Circuit Dyne Corp., Pasadena, Calif., Laguna Beach, Calif., 1960-61; sr. devel. engr. Robertshaw Controls Co., Anaheim, Calif., 1961-63; research engr. Naval Ocean Systems Center, Navy Research Lab., San Diego, 1966—; dir. Circuit Dyne Corp., Pacific Coil Co. Recipient Thomas Clair McFarland award U. Calif. at Berkeley, 1956. Mem. IEEE, Acoustical Soc. Am., Phi Beta Kappa. Home: 5284 Dawes St San Diego CA 92109 Office: Naval Ocean Systems Center San Diego CA 92152

HALL, HARRIET LOUISE, mental health center adminstr.; b. Los Angeles, Oct. 9, 1947; d. Donald Moore and Ethyl Louise (Hartsough) Hall; B.A., Coll. of Wooster, 1969; M.A., U. Wis., Madison, 1971, Ph.D., 1973; m. Randy C. Stith, Nov. 26, 1977; children—Carolyn Annaliese Hall-Stith, Daniel Dag Hall-Stith, Timothy Vernon Hall-Stith. Psychologist, dir. inservice tng. Weld Mental Health Center, Greeley, Colo., 1974-78; child advocacy team mgr. Adams County Mental Health Center, Commerce City, Colo., 1978-80; dep. dir. clin. programs, 1980-81; assoc. dir. programs Jefferson County Mental Health Center, Wheat Ridge, Colo., 1981—. Mem., Adams County Placement Alternative Commn., 1980-81, Adams County Child Protection Team, 1979-80; mem. handicapped child subcom. Colo. Gov.'s Commn. for Children and Families, 1979-80; bd. dirs. Centennial Area Health Edn. Center, 1978, Partners Inc., Greeley, Colo., 1978. Cert. psychologist, Colo. Mem. Colo. Psychol. Assn., Colo. Women Psychologists, NOW, Colo. Com. for Status of Women in Mental (treas. 1981—, Outstanding Woman in Mental Health award 1982). Democrat. Home: 11205 E Vassar Dr Aurora CO 80014 Office: 6195 W 38th Ave Wheat Ridge CO 80033

HALL, IRVING JAMES, statistician; b. Garner, Iowa, May 24, 1933; s. Clarence P. and Clara (Hanna) H.; m. Lois J. Erickson, Aug. 25, 1962; children—Sheila, Lori. Student Pacific Lutheran U., 1952-54; B.A., U. Minn., 1962; M.S., Iowa State U., 1964, Ph.D., 1966. Research scientist Mech. div. Gen. Mills, 1959-62; instr. math. Wis. State U.-River Falls, 1962-64; instr. stats. dept. Iowa State U., Ames, 1964-67; staff mem. stats. and computing div. Sandia Labs., Albuquerque, 1967—. Served with U.S. Army, 1956-58. Mem. Am. Statis. Assn. Lutheran. Club: Scandinavian (Albuquerque). Contbr. articles to profl. publs. Home: 9805 Aztec Rd NE Albuquerque NM 87111 Office: Sandia National Labs Div 7223 Box 5800 Albuquerque NM 87185

HALL, JACK HENRY, TV exec.; b. South Gate, Calif., Sept. 29, 1926; s. Lamont Dupere and Mildred Elizabeth (Hooker) H.; B.A., Calif. State U., Fresno, 1949; m. Peggy Jean Walterscheid, Dec. 27, 1974; children—Julie Anne, Jeffrey Adams; stepchildren—Robert, Jeffrey, April, Steven. Radio singer Sta. KECA, Los Angeles, summer 1938; announcer Sta. KARM, Fresno, 1943-44; asst. theatre mgr. Fox West Coast Ltd., 1944, 46-48; announcer Sta. KSGN, Sanger, Calif., 1949-50, Sta. KMJ, Fresno, 1950-53; dir., announcer Sta. KMJ-TV, Fresno, 1953-81, sta. KSEE, 1981—, community affairs mgr., 1979—; performer, stage dir. Fresno Community Theater, 1960—, pres., 1963-64, 73-74; mem. Fresno Community Chorus, 1955-60, pres., 1959-60. Mem. Easter Seal Soc. Central Calif., 1980—, pres., 1982—. Served with AUS, 1944-45. Recipient Best Actor award Fresno Community Theater, 1965, Pres.'s award, 1971, 72, 77. Mem. AFTRA, Am. Community Theatre Assn. Producer TV documentary Opus 20, 1974; producer, narrator film documentary Lost, 1976. Home: 1435 Park St Sanger CA 93657 Office: 1544 Van Ness Ave Fresno CA 93779

HALL, JOSEPH SARGENT, educator, author; b. Butte, Mont., Aug. 23, 1906; s. Horace Mark and Helen (Kirkendall) H.; A.B., Stanford, 1928; postgrad. Ecole des Hautes Etudes, U. Paris (France), 1933-34; M.A., Columbia, 1936, Ph.D. (Univ. fellow), 1941. Tchr. Latin, Anaheim (Calif.) High Sch., 1930-33; historian student technician U.S. Nat. Park Service, 1937, collaborator, 1939-40; lectr. phonetics and linguistics Hartford Sem. Found., 1940-42; English tutor Bklyn. Coll., 1939-41; asst. prof. English, Mont. State U., 1946-48; instr. English Pasadena (Calif.), City Coll., 1948-63, asso. prof., 1963-70, prof. English, 1970-72. Served with USAAF, 1942-45. Mem. Am., So. Calif. (pres. 1959-60), folklore socs., Am. Dialect Soc. (new words com. 1956-61). Democrat. Episcopalian. Mason, Kiwanian (hon. mem. Pasadena). Club: Sierra. Author: The Phonetics of Great Smoky Mountain Speech, 1942; Smoky Mountain Folks and Their Lore, 1960; Sayings from Old Smoky, 1972; Yarns and Tales from the Great Smokies, 1978; Hall Collection of Great Smokies Speech, Music, and Folklore (170 discs, 50 tapes); research on So. mountain, Gt. Smoky mountains speech, folklore, music. Home: 1455 Lemoyne St Los Angeles CA 90026

HALL, KATHLEEN ANN SHADE, legal asst.; b. Guys Mills, Pa.; d. Glenn C. and Agnes R. (Maxwell) Shade; student Edinboro State Coll., 1958-59, U. West Los Angeles, 1976; m. Robert E. Hall, Aug. 3, 1968 (div.). Exec. sec. Talon, Inc., Meadville, Pa., 1959-62, McDonnell Douglas, Santa Monica, Calif., 1962-64; legal sec. Leon Leonian, atty., Beverly Hills, Calif., 1965-77; prin. Kathleen A. Hall, legal asst., Van Nuys, Calif., 1977—. Mem. Nat. Notary Assn., State Bar Calif. (probate law sect.), Los Angeles Paralegal Assn. Club: Braemar Country. Home: 3915 Benedict Canyon Sherman Oaks CA 91423

HALL, LEONARD EUGENE, building materials executive; b. Portland, Oreg., Nov. 10, 1912; s. Ernest Eugene and Luella (Osgood) H.; div.; children—Peter J., Lenore Kester. Student U. Oreg., 1930-31. Vice pres., gen. mgr. Lumber Products Inc., 1944—; dir. Assoc. Bldg. Materials Inc. Served with USAF, 1942-44. Mem. Pacific Coast Wholesale Hardwood Distbrs., Nat. Plywood Distbrs. Assn. (pres. 1955-56). Republican. Club: Columbia Aviation Country (past pres.). Home: 1425 NW 27th St Portland OR 97210 Office: 2116 NW 20th St Portland OR 97209

HALL, LOIS RIGGS, symphony orch. adminstr., state senator; b. Beeville, Tex., May 22, 1930; d. Ira Franklin and Pearl Ophelia (McCoy) Riggs; student Tex. Women's U., 1947-49, U. Tex., Austin, 1949-50; m. Walter William Hall, Dec. 28, 1950 (dec.); children—Robert Macfarlane, Elaine Denise, Judith Lea. Exec. sec. N.Mex. Symphony Orch., Albuquerque, 1975—; mem. N.Mex. Senate, 1980—. Active Boy Scouts Am., Girl Scouts U.S.A., Officers Wives Clubs; 2d v.p. Albuquerque Symphony Women's Assn.; treas., publicity dir. N.Mex. Aviation Assn. Republican. Home: 620 Ortiz NE Albuquerque NM 87108 Office: PO Box 769 Albuquerque NM 87103

HALL, MARY ANN, principal; b. Los Angeles, Mar. 23, 1942; d. George and Temishia Ellen (Leonard) Newbins; m. Lehman Frederick Smith, Jr., May 1, 1962; 1 son, Lehman Frederick Smith; m. Milton Hall, Aug. 30, 1970. A.A., Los Angeles City Coll., 1972; B.A., Calif. State U.-Los Angeles, 1974, M.A., 1975. Telephone operator, circuit designer, service rep. Pacific Telephone Co., Los Angeles, 1960-68; account specialist IBM, Santa Monica, Calif., 1968-70; tchr. Euclid Elem. Sch., Los Angeles, 1974-77; bilingual coordinator Middleton Elem. Sch., Huntington Park, Calif., 1977-79; compensatory edn. coordinator Edison Jr. High Sch., Los Angeles, 1979-81; asst. prin. Northrup Sch., Alhambra, Calif., 1981; prin. Repetto Sch., Monterey Park, Calif., 1982—. Lectr. edn. adminstrn. Calif. State U.-Los Angeles. Active LWV. Mem. Assn. Calif. Sch. Adminstrs. Educare, Phi Delta Kappa, Delta Kappa Gamma.

HALL, MARY-JO, management consultant, educator; b. Durham, N.C., Jan. 5, 1947; d. Paul Thomas and Miriam Josephine (Burroughs) H.; m. Emmett Eugene Stobbs, July 19, 1975. A.B.T., High Point Coll., 1969; M.Ed. in Human Devel., U. Md., 1972; M.B.A. in Bus., L.I. U., 1980. Cert. tchr., N.Y. Team tchr. Congl. Sch., Rockville, Md., 1969-71; tchr. pub. schs., Durham County, N.C., 1971-72; tchr. Dept. Def. Overseas Schs., Karlsrule, Germany, 1972-74, Seoul, 1974-75; in various adminstrv. and clerical positions, 1975-78; trainer/counselor U.S. Mil. Acad., 1978-81; contract negotiator Naval Surface Weapons Ctr., Duhlgren, Va., 1981-82; contract adminstr. U.S. Air Force, McChord AFB, Wash., 1982; ops./tng. master trainer leadership assessment program 4th ROTC Region Hdqrs., Tacoma, 1983—; instr. Ft. Steila-coom Community Coll.; resident mgr. Personal Dynamics Inc.; pres. M.J. Hall Assocs. Organizer Expanding Horizons Network, Tacoma. Mem. Nat. Contract Mgmt. Assn., Nat. Assn. Female Execs., South Sound Women's Network, Friends of Chambers Creek. Lutheran. Club: Ft. Lewis Officers. Pub., author M.J. Hall Notes, quar. newsletter, 1982—. Office: PO Box 98298 Tacoma WA 98498

HALL, MICHELE MARIE, early childhood educator, consultant; b. Teaneck, N.J., Apr. 13, 1955; d. Daniel James and Carmen Margarita (Munoz) Henriott; m. John Robert Hall, July 20, 1977; children—John Robert. B.A. in Human Devel., U. Kans., 1977; M.A. in Curriculum and Supervision, Nat. Coll. Edn., 1981. Head tchr. Moody Early Childhood Ctr., Chgo., 1978-80; sr. kindergarten tchr. Latin Sch. Chgo., 1980-81; instr. N.W. YMCA Pre-Sch., Arvada, Colo., 1982—; coordinator mothers of pre-schoolers group Calvary Evangelical Free Ch., Broomfield, Colo. Mem. Assn. Supervision and Curriculum Devel., Nat. Assn. Edn. Young. Children. Home: 8327 Yarrow Ct Arvada CO 80005 Office: Northwest YMCA 7160 W 68th Ave Arvada CO 80003

HALL, RADFORD SKIDMORE, II, civil engineer, planner; b. Denver, Sept. 10, 1941; s. Radford Skidmore and Florence (Fulton) H., m. Geraldine M. Bissell, Sept. 3, 1966; children—Romany S., Radford Skidmore III. B.S.C.E., Denver U., 1965; M.S. in Natural Resources Policy, Colo. State U., 1977, postgrad., 1980—. Civil engr. trainee FAA, 1959-65; jr. civil engr. Corps Engrs., San Francisco, 1965-71, sr. civil engr./planner navigation, beach erosion, and water resources, San Francisco, 1971-76, supervisory civil engr., chief permits sect. San Francisco Dist., 1977—; lectr./instr. Colo. State U. Coll. Forestry and Natural Resources, 1980-81; mem. Tech. Com. Susiun Marsh, Calif. Mem. Hillside Preservation Bd., City of Pacifica (Calif.), 1975-78, mem. planning commn., 1978-80, 83—, chmn. planning commn., 1979. Recipient Outstanding Performance award Corps Engrs., 1981; Office of Chief of Engrs. civil works fellow, 1976-77. Mem. Am. Planning Assn., Sierra Club, Phi Kappa Phi, Sigma Chi. Author: Water Use and Management in an Arid Region, 1977.

HALL, RALPH CORBIN, cons. forest entomologist; b. Ellenville, N.Y., May 7, 1899; s. James Harvey and Anna (Newkirk) H.; B.S., Syracuse U., 1925, M.F., Harvard, 1927; Ph.D., U. Mich., 1931; m. Dorothy Dane Colby, Sept. 7, 1930 (dec. Aug. 1981); children—James Dane, Judith Gilmore (Mrs. Pate D. Thomson), John Colby, Joanne Newkirk (Mrs. John F. Parrish) (dec.). Research forest entomologist Bur. Entomology and Plant Quarantine, Columbus, Ohio, 1931-38, Berkeley, Calif., 1938-53; with U.S. Forest Service, 1953-64, entomologist, San Francisco, 1961-64; v.p., dir. Natural Resources Mgmt. Corp., Orinda, Calif., 1970-74; cons. forest entomologist, 1974—. Cons. research grants NSF, 1951—. Mem. nat. council Boy Scouts Am., 1955-66, mem. exec. council Mt. Diablo council, 1947-71. Bd. dirs. Wilderness Found., Calif. Forestry Found., Forest Landowners Calif. Named Man of Yr. by City of Orinda, 1949; recipient Silver Beaver award Boy Scouts Am., 1957; Award of Merit, SUNY, Calif. Acad. Scis., N.Y. Acad. Scis.; registered profl. entomologist, U.S.; registered profl. forester, Calif. Fellow Soc. Am. Foresters (Golden Membership award 1978), AAAS, Internat. Platform Assn., Fedn. Am. Scientists, Explorers Club; mem. Assn. Cons. Foresters, Wildlife Soc., Wilderness Soc., Am. Forestry Assn., Entomol. Soc. Am., Sierra Club, Sigma Xi, Gamma Sigma Delta, Phi Sigma. Address: 72 Davis Rd Orinda CA 94563

HALL, ROBERT EMMETT, JR., investment banker, realtor; b. Sioux City, Iowa, Apr. 28, 1936; s. Robert Emmett and Alvina (Faden) H.; B.A., State U. S.D., 1958, M.A., 1959; M.B.A., U. Santa Clara, 1976; grad. Am. Inst. Banking, Realtors Inst.; m. Marna Thiel, 1969. Grad. asst. State U. S.D., Vermillion, 1958-59; mgr. ins. dept., asst. mgr. installment loan dept. Northwestern Nat. Bank of Sioux Falls, S.D., 1959-61, asst. cashier, 1961-65; asst. mgr. Crocker Nat. Bank, San Francisco, 1965-67, loan officer, 1967-69, asst. v.p., asst. mgr. San Mateo br., 1969-72; v.p., Western regional mgr. Internat. Investments & Realty, Inc., Washington, 1972—; owner Hall Investment Co., 1976—; pres. Almaden Oaks Realtors, Inc., 1976—; instr. West Valley Coll., Saratoga, Calif., 1972—, Grad. Sch. Bus., U. Santa Clara (Calif.), 1981—. Treas., Minnehaha Leukemia Soc., 1963, Lake County Heart Fund Assn., 1962. Treas., Minnehaha Young Republican Club, 1963. Mem. Am. Inst. Banking, San Mateo C. of C., Calif. Assn. Realtors (vice chmn.), Beta Theta Pi. Republican. Roman Catholic. Clubs: Elks, Rotary (past pres.), K.C., Kiwanis, Almaden Country. Home: 6951 Castlerock Dr San Jose CA 95102 Office: 6501 Crown Blvd 100 San Jose CA 95120

HALL, ROBERT JOHN, banker; b. Mitchell, S.D., July 31, 1920; s. James John and Jennie Elizabeth (Bellamy) H.; m. Dorothy Jean Jensen,

Jan. 20, 1945; children—Timothy J., Susan J. Scarpa, Robert T. B.A., U. Puget Sound, 1948; student Pacific Coast Banking Sch., 1965. With Puget Sound Nat. Bank, Tacoma, 1948—, sr. v.p., 1979—; treas. Puget Sound Bancorp, 1982—. Served to 2d lt. U.S. Army, 1940-45. Decorated Purple Heart. Mem. Nat. Assn. Credit Mgmt. (nat. pres. 1977-78, pres. Puget Sound chpt.), Robert Morris Assocs. Republican. Methodist. Clubs: Tacoma Downtown Lions; Fircrest Golf. Home: 3015 N 33d St Tacoma WA 98467 Office: 1119 Pacific Ave Tacoma WA 98402

HALL, ROBERT W., professional photographer; b. Buffalo, Aug. 9, 1928; s. R. V. and Mary A. (Morse) H.; m. Carol Bly, June 24, 1950; children—Deborah, Steven, Craig, Terri, Roberta. Staff photographer, Sandia Corp., Albuquerque, 1957-62; owner, Hall's Studio, Albuquerque, 1962—; supt. photography N.Mex. State Fair. Served in N.Y. N.G., 1947-50. Mem. Profl. Photographers Am. (cert. nat. council), Profl. Photographers N.Mex. (past pres.), Albuquerque Guild Profl. Photographers (past pres.), Photographic Soc. Am. Republican. Presbyterian. Clubs: Exchange (pres.). (Albuquerque). Office: 2414 Juan Tabo Blvd NE Albuquerque NM 87112

HALL, ROBERT WHITNEY, airline executive; b. Upper Derby, Pa., Feb. 9, 1934; s. Arthur Franklin and Ruth Whitney (Flewelling) H.; m. Bertha S. Hall, May 14, 1961; 1 son, Keith T. Student Towson State Coll., U Md., 1951-54. Pilot, Mohawk Airlines, 1959-60, Hawaiian Airlines, 1960, Internat. Air Service Co. (Japan Airlines), 1962-63; asst. to pres. E.L. Forde Ltd. Honolulu, 1960-61; mgr. Hawaii Transp. Co., Hilo, Hawaii, 1961-62; pres. Royal Hawaiian Trading Co. Inc., Honolulu, 1963-67; pres., dir. Robert W. Hall Assocs. Inc. (Hawaii Air Cargo Inc.), 1962-82, Island Airlines Hawaii Inc., 1977-82; chmn., chief exec. officer, dir. Airlines Capital Corp., Inc., 1982—; exec. dir. Hawaii Inst. Biosocial Research, 1981—. Served to capt. USAFR, 1954-59. Mem. Regional Airlines Assn. Am. Republican. Methodist. Clubs: Plaza, Honolulu Press, Honolulu Internat. Country, Shriners (Honolulu). Contbr. articles to profl. jours. Office: 1188 Bishop St Suite 3411 Honolulu HI 96813

HALL, ROBERT WILSON, mfg. co. exec.; b. Kisumu, Kenya, Dec. 17, 1941; s. Robert and Christina Laurie (Jack) H.; B.S. In M.E., Kings Coll. U. Durham (Eng.), 1964; m. Anne Charlotte Watkins, Sept. 26, 1964; children—LeonRobert, Nathan David. Mfg. supr. Lockheed Electronics Co., Los Angeles, 1968-70; prodn. services mgr. Exacta Circuits Ltd., Selkirk, Scotland, 1970-74; mgmt. cons. Currie Coopers & Lybrand, Toronto, Ont., Can., 1974-75; tech. supr. Ont. Hydro, Toronto, 1975-77; v.p. mfg. Tulon Inc., Esterline Corp., Los Angeles, 1977-81; v.p. ops. Megatool Inc., Buena Park, Calif., 1981—. Mem. Inst. Mech. Engrs. Home: 6332 Freeborn Dr Huntington Beach CA 92647 Office: 6880 Orangethorpe Ave Buena Park CA 90620

HALL, RONALD PORTER, savings and loan company executive, security consultant; b. Pitts., Apr. 16, 1947; s. Clarence E. and Betty Lou H.; m. Barbara Shiflet, Feb. 5, 1979; children—Kelli Rae, Brandon C. B.S. in Bus. Adminstrn., Robert Morris Coll., 1967. Cert. protection profl. Spl. agt. FBI, Washington, 1972-77; asst. v.p. Security Pacific Mortgage Co., Denver, 1977-79; fraud analyst investigator Citicorp Person to Person, Denver, 1979-81; mgr. corp. security and investigations Midland Fed. Savs. and Loan Assn., Denver, 1981—; security cons. Mem. Am. Soc. for Indsl. Security, Internat. Assn. Credit Card Investigators (asst. v.p.), Soc. Former Spl. Agts. of FBI, Met. Law Enforcement Assn., Nat. Assn. Chiefs of Police. Contbr. articles on security to profl. jours. Office: 444 17th St Denver CO 80202

HALL, STUART CAMPEN, public affairs consultant; b. San Jose, Calif., June 18, 1935; s. Marshall Spencer and Helen Bernice (Campen) H. B.A., U. Calif. at Berkeley, 1957; M.A., Stanford U., 1961; J.D., Harvard U., 1964. Legis. asst. Calif. Legislature Assembly, 1958-59, asst. clk. 1960, 1st asst. clk., 1961; adminstrv. analyst Office of Pres., U. Calif. at Berkeley, 1960, grad. research analyst, 1960; investigator Office of Dist. Atty., County of Santa Clara, San Jose, 1962-63; cons. Calif. Constn. Revision Commn., Calif. Legislature, San Francisco, 1964-65; lectr. polit. sci., dept. polit. sci. San Jose State Coll., 1965-69; cons. com. on elections and constl. amendments Calif. Assembly, 1969-70; adminstrv. asst. to Calif. State Senator John A. Nejedly, 1970-71; legis. counsel, legis. affairs, agy. Alaska Legislature, 1971-75, sr. legis. counsel, 1975-76; mem. Alaska Pub. Utilities Commn., 1976-83; adj. lectr. pub. adminstrn. U. Alaska, Juneau, 1973-76. Mem. Republican Central Com. Santa Clara County, 1967-70. Trustee Jr. Statesmen Found., 1970-80. Served with USAF Res., 1959—, now maj. Woodrow Wilson fellow, 1957-58. Mem. Calif. Hist. Soc., Nat. Mcpl. League, Am. Soc. for Pub. Adminstrn., Western Govtl. Research Assn., Am. Philatelic Soc., Harvard Law Sch. Assn., Stanford, Cal. alumni assns., Ripon Soc. (nat. governing bd. 1979-81), Sigma Delta Chi. Episcopalian. Clubs: Masons, Rotary, Lions, Commonwealth (San Francisco). Home and Office: 815 Colwell St PO Box 300 Anchorage AK 99510

HALLADAY, ROBERT EUGENE, assn. exec.; b. Provo, Utah, Apr. 19, 1917; s. Thomas Eugene and Fern Elizabeth (Peters) H.; B.S., Brigham Young U., 1942; m. Geraldine Steedman, Dec. 17, 1943; children—Kathie H. (Mrs. Antonio Cano), Robert Greg, Anne H. (Mrs. Virgil Latimer), Thomas Eugene, Paul Andrew, Michael. Missionary to Brazil, Ch. of Jesus Christ of Latter-day Saints, 1937-40; with Utah Welfare Dept., 1942-45; parole agy. Utah Dept. Corrections, 1945-51; mem. staff Provo C. of C., 1951-58, mgr., 1954-58; mgr. Utah Mfrs. Assn., 1958-64, exec. v.p., 1964-82, pres., 1982—. Chmn. Utah Adv. Council on Tech. Edn., 1964-70; mem. exec. com. Utah Com. on Indsl. and Employment Planning, 1958-68; mem. State Adv. Council Unemployment Compensation, 1958—; mem. exec. com. Conf. State Mfrs. Assns.; pres. Utah C. of C. Execs., 1956; mem. N.A.M. Task Force, 1972; vice chmn. NIC, 1974, chmn., 1975—. Mem. alumni bd. Brigham Young U., 1964-67, mem. nat. adv. council Coll. Bus., 1960-78; mem. instnl. council Utah Tech. Coll. at Provo, 1978—. Recipient Outstanding Citizens award City of Provo, 1958. Republican. Mem. Ch. of Jesus Christ of Latter-day Saints (bishop 1955-59, mem. high council 1953-55, 61-67). Kiwanian. Home: 5947 Lakeside Dr Salt Lake City UT 84121 Office: 136 S Main St Salt Lake City UT 84101

HALLAS, CLARK HOWARD, newspaper reporter; b. Washington, May 14, 1935; s. Howard Ensley and Carol May (Harsen) H.; student Mich. State U., 1953-55, Wayne State U., 1956-58, 60; m. Barbara Joy Griffin, Sept. 17, 1977; children—Michael Edward, Kelly Elizabeth. Reporter, UPI, Detroit, 1960-63; asst. night city editor Delaware County Daily Times, Chester, Pa., 1963-64; copy editor Flint (Mich.) Jour., 1964-68; city/county bur. chief, politics writer The Detroit News, 1968-78; investigative reporter Ariz. Daily Star, Tucson, 1978—. Served with U.S. Army, 1958-60. Recipient Detroit Press Club Medallion, 1973; 1st prize for reporting UPI Mich. Newspaper Awards, 1975; 1st place feature writing Mich. AP Editorial Assn.; Don Bolles award for investigative reporting, 1980; Gold Medal, Investigative Reporters and Editors Nat. Awards Competition, 1980; Ariz. Press Club Newsman of Yr. award, 1980; Pulitzer Prize for investigative reporting, 1981. Mem. Investigative Reports and Editors. Clubs: Detroit Press, Ariz. Press, Sigma Delta Chi. Office: 4850 S Park Ave Tucson AZ 85726

HALLBERG, CLAUDIA SKYE, advertising agency executive, consultant; b. Huntington Park, Calif., May 6, 1951; d. Ted Ulf and Lynn (Hansen) H. Student U. London, 1971-72; B.A., Scripps Coll., 1973. Brand mgr. Procter & Gamble Co., Cin., 1973-76; account exec., account supr. Needham, Harper & Steers Advt., Chgo., 1976-78; account supr., mgmt. supr. Tracy Locke Advt., Dallas, 1978-80; mgmt. supr. Young & Rubicam, San Francisco, 1980-82, v.p., gen. mgr., 1982—. Mem. Older Women's League, San Francisco Advt. Club, Phi Beta Kappa. Office: 753 Davis St San Francisco CA 94111

HALLBERG, DALE MERTON, sculptor; b. Spokane, Wash., Aug. 30, 1927; s. Gustaf Philip and Thelma (Bauman) H.; student U. Idaho, 1947-49, Wash. State U., 1949-50, U. Oreg., 1952-54; B.S. in Landscape Architecture, U. Calif., Berkeley, 1955; B.A. in Art, B.Ed., Eastern Wash. State Coll., 1956; postgrad. Claremont Grad. Sch., 1960-62, 62-67; M.A., Calif. State Coll. at Long Beach, 1967; m. Mildred May Lemmon, May 1, 1955. Tchr. art LaHabra (Calif.) High Sch., 1956-62; instr. landscape architecture Calif. State Poly. Coll., 1962-64; art instr. Troy High Sch., Fullerton, Calif., 1964—; pvt. practice landscape architecture, Orange, Calif., 1955-78, Fullerton, 1978—; exhibited sculpture Muckenthaler Cultural Center, Fullerton, 1966, Calif. State Coll. at Long Beach, 1967, Galleria Numero, Venice, 1971, Galleria Fiamma Vigo, Rome, 1971, Art Alliance Safari for Calif. State U. at Fullerton, 1975, Common Ground Artists' Coop., Fullerton, 1978, 79, 80, Bowers Mus., Santa Ana, Calif., others. Served with USMC, 1945-47, 50-52. Recipient certificate of merit Am. Soc. Landscape Architects, 1968; 2d prize Designer-Craftsman Show, Bower's Mus., Santa Ana, 1967; 3d prize sculpture Hillcrest Festival Arts, Whittier, Calif., 1968. Mem. Am. Soc. Landscape Architects, Art. Alliance of Fullerton State U., Laguna Beach Art Assn., Allied Art Assn. Cambria, Orange County Orchid Soc. (trustee). Republican. Presbyterian. Address: 1630 Skyline Dr Fullerton CA 92631

HALLER, HOWARD EDWARD, equipment leasing co. exec.; b. Balt., Mar. 30, 1947; s. Howard Earl and Clemence Anne (Young) H.; B.A. with honors in Polit. Sci., Calif. State U., Northridge, 1970; grad. Am. Inst. Banking, 1970; postgrad. U. So. Calif., 1968-75; M.S. in Mgmt., U. Redlands, 1981; m. Terri Lynne Koster, June 20, 1969; children—Jennifer Louise, Justin Douglas, Jason Davis. Corp. officer Bank of Am., Los Angeles, 1969-71; mgr. Mgmt. Advisory Services, sr. cons. Matthew Wolfson & Co., C.P.A.s, Los Angeles, 1971-73; dist. mgr. U.S. Leasing Corp., Los Angeles, 1973-75; dist. mgr. Chem. Bank of N.Y., Santa Monica, Calif., 1976-77; v.p. Patagonia Leasing Co., Phoenix, 1977; regional leasing mgr. Prime Computer Inc., Woodland Hills, Calif., 1977-81; pres. Haller Co., Woodland Hills, Calif., 1974—; pres., dir. Leasing Dept. Inc., 1981—; chmn. bd. IFC Capital Corp., 1981—; prof. fin. Calif. State U., Northridge, 1981—, trustee univ. trust fund. Served with USAFR, 1968-70. Lic. comml. pilot. Mem. Am. Mktg. Assn., Am. Mgmt. Assn., Nat. Assn. Corp. Dirs., Practising Law Inst., Am. Assn. Equipment Lessors, Inst. Mgmt. Cons., Nat. Assn. Accts., Nat. Assn. Realtors. Republican. Episcopalian. Club: Am. Legion. Office: 23271 Ventura Blvd Woodland Hills CA 91364

HALLER, THEODORE HOWES, developer, contractor, computer company executive, surgeon; b. Blair, Nebr., Mar. 19, 1917; s. William M. and Helen L. (Howes) H.; m. Ann Frost Murray, May 26, 1946; children—Stephen, Theodore, William; m. 2d, Gail Louise Juve, Dec. 31, 1971. B.S., U. Nebr., 1939; M.D., U. So. Calif., 1944. Diplomate Am. Bd. Surgery. Practice medicine, specializing in gen. surgery, Marina Del Rey, Calif., 1953—; founder, pres. Centinela Med. Group, Inglewood, Calif., 1956-73; founder, chmn. bd. U. Beverly Hills, 1975-78, T & H Products, 1975-80; owner, pres. Culver Constrn. Co., 1968—; pres., chmn. bd. Computer Econs., Inc., Marina Del Rey, 1981—; gen. ptnr. Del Rey Profl. Assn., 1967—, Manchester Bus. Park, 1979—; chief exec. officer Rafael Montealegre Designs, 1983—; attending surgeon UCLA, 1953-74; co-sponsor, prodn. officer film Whitewater Sam. Served to capt., M.C., U.S. Army, 1944-46. Fellow Internat. Coll. Surgeons. Clubs: Marina City, Marina City Racquet. Home: 4314 Marina City Dr Apt 630 Marina Del Rey CA 90292 Office: 4560 Admiralty Way Suite 109 Marina Del Rey CA 90292

HALLER, THOMAS FRANCIS, investment company executive; b. Chgo., Dec. 6, 1948; s. Frank Joseph and Margaret Caroline (Kovalcik) H.; B.S. in Econs., U. Ill., Chgo., 1970; M.S. in Bus. Adminstrn., U. Calif. at Los Angeles, 1971; m. Kathy Louise Labovsky, Apr. 8, 1978; children—Melissa Katherine, Julia Caroline. Mgmt. cons., Laventhol & Horwath Co., Los Angeles, 1972-74; controller Eldon Industries/Elpower Corp., Hawthorne, Calif., 1974, nat. sales mgr., 1975; v.p., gen. mgr. U.S. Sales Corp., Pacoima, Calif., 1975-80; portfolio mgr. T.F. Haller Trust, 1980—; pres. Pacific Homes Real Estate Ind. Property Div., 1980-82; v.p. Haney Group, Woodland Hills, Calif., 1982—; pres. T.F. Haller Co., Inc., 1983—; guest lectr. U. Calif. Berkeley, 1976, 77. Mem. Assn. M.B.A. Execs., Am. Mgmt. Assn., Am. Mktg. Assn., U. Ill. Alumni Assn., U. Calif. at Los Angeles Alumni Assn., Sierra Club, Omicron Delta Epsilon. Republican. Roman Catholic. Contbr. article to profl. jour. Home: 16800 Knollwood Dr Granada Hills CA 91344 Office: TF Haller Co Inc 11852 Balboa Blvd Granada Hills CA 91344

HALLFORD, DENNIS MURRAY, educator; b. Abilene, Tex., Feb. 11, 1948; s. Tommy Lamoine and Tiny Elizabeth (Stockton) H.; B.S., Tarleton State U., 1970; M.S., Okla. State U., 1973, Ph.D., 1975; m. Marilyn Williams, Sept. 13, 1971; 1 dau., Amy Denise. Instr., Tarleton State U., Stephenville, Tex., 1970-71; grad. asst. Okla. State U., Stillwater, 1971-75; asst. prof. N.Mex. State U., Las Cruces, 1975-80, asso. prof. animal sci., 1980—. Named Outstanding Tchr. of Yr., N.Mex. State U., 1977; Tchr. of Yr., Coll. of Agr. and Home Econs., 1979-80. Mem. Am. Soc. Animal Sci. (1st place paper award 1974), Sigma Xi, Gamma Sigma Delta, Alpha Zeta, Alpha Chi. Methodist. Contbr. articles to profl. jours. Home: 1135 Calle del Encanto Las Cruces NM 88005 Office: Box 3I NMex State U Dept Animal and Range Sci Las Cruces NM 88003

HALLIBURTON, GENE DENNIS, auto club executive; b. Kennett, Mo., Sept. 17, 1919; s. William Elija and Minnie Ola (Fowler) H.; student U. Kansas City, 1939, U. Ind., 1942-43, Golden Gate Coll., San Francisco, 1950, U. Calif., San Francisco, Berkeley, 1951-52; m. May Gardner, Apr. 3, 1955; children—Randal Brian, Susan Marguerite, Kathryn Elizabeth, Gardner William. Passenger agt. Trans World Airways, Kansas City, Mo., 1940-44; gen. mgr. Ariz. Airways, Phoenix, 1947-49; pres., chief exec. officer, dir. Nat. Automobile Club, San Francisco, 1949—. Served with USAAF, 1944-47. Recipient Man of Year awards East Bay Ins. Men's Assn., 1961, 62. Mem. San Francisco Ins. Forum, Ins. Co. Mgrs. Assn. No. Calif. (past pres.), Am. Automobile Touring Alliance (pres.), Alliance Internationale de Tourisme (mgmt. com.), San Francisco Pub. Relations Round Table (past chmn. bd. govs.), San Francisco Ins. Forum, Pres.'s Assn. Am., San Francisco Bay Area Council. Club: San Francisco Commercial. Office: Nat Automobile Club One Market Plaza San Francisco CA 94105

HALLIDAY, JOHN MEECH, investment company executive; b. St. Louis, Oct. 16, 1936; s. William Norman and Vivian Viola (Meech) H.; B.S., U.S. Naval Acad., 1958; M.B.A., Harvard, 1964; m. Martha Layne Griggs, June 30, 1962; children—Richard M., Elizabeth. Dir. budgeting and planning Automatic Tape Control, Bloomington, Ill., 1964-66; dir. planning Ralston-Purina, St. Louis, 1966-67, v.p. subsidiary, 1967-68, dir. internat. banking, 1967-68; v.p. Servicetime Corp., St. Louis, 1968-70; asso. R. W. Halliday Assos., Boise, Idaho, 1970—; v.p. Sawtooth Communications Corp., Boise, 1970-73; pres., chief exec. officer Sonoma Internat., San Francisco, 1971-77; pres. ML Ltd., San Francisco, 1974—; pres., dir. Halliday Labs., Inc., Reno, 1980—; v.p. Commander Corp., 1979-81; exec. v.p., dir. Franchise Fin. Corp. Am., Phoenix, 1980—. bldg. com. YMCA, 1965; pres. Big Bros. of San Francisco, 1978-81. Served to lt. comdr. USNR, 1958-66. Mem. Nat. Restaurant Assn., Soc. Advancement Food Research, Heart Ill. Restaurant Assn. (v.p. 1969-70), Nat. Assn. Accountants. Republican. Episcopalian. Clubs: Family, New Rotary (San Francisco); Scott Valley Tennis (Mill Valley, Calif.); Harvard Bus. Sch. No. Calif. (v.p.). Home: 351 Corte Madera Ave Mill Valley CA 94941 Office: 625 Market St San Francisco CA 94105

HALLIDAY, L(INDA) SUSAN, employment consultant, dancer, choreographer; b. Long Beach, Calif., Nov. 17, 1950; d. Bernard W. and Frieda (Lander) Baskin; m. Larry Richard Halliday, July 18, 1971. B.A., UCLA, 1971. Programmer/analyst Logicon, San Pedro, Calif., 1971-72; sr. programmer/analyst, cons. NARE Life Service Co., Palo Alto, Calif., 1972-75; data processing cons., mgr. systems and programming Comml. Bankers Life, Newport Beach, Calif., 1975-77; tech. cons., sales rep. Tymshare, Inc., Los Angeles, 1977-79; data processing employment cons. Omicron, Newport Beach, Calif., 1980; pres., ptnr. Intercomp Agy., Los Alamitos, Calif., 1981—; cons. Women's Career Ctr., U. Calif., Irvine, 1983—; asst. dir., choreographer, dancer Dance Kaleidoscope of Orange County modern/jazz performing company, 1975—; gen. ptnr. Food Scheduling and Systems Technology, Los Alamitos, 1982—. Mem. Nat. Assn. Female Execs., The Bus. Forum. Choreographer: Sacramento 55, Videodisk, Objets d'Arts. Office: 10900 Los Alamitos Suite 217 Los Alamitos CA 90720

HALLIDAY, WILLIAM ROSS, med. adminstr., thoracic surgeon, author; b. Emory University, Ga., May 9, 1926; s. William Ross and Jane (Wakefield) H.; B.A., Swarthmore Coll., 1946; M.D., George Washington U., 1948; m. Eleanore Hartvedt, July 2, 1951; children—Marcia Lynn, Patricia Anne, William Ross III. Intern, Huntington Meml. Hosp., Pasadena, 1948-49; resident King County Hosp., Seattle, Denver Children's Hosp., L.D.S. Hosp., Salt Lake City, 1950-57; pvt. practice, Seattle, 1957-65; with Wash. State Dept. Labor and Industries, 1965-76; med. dir. Wash. State Div. Vocat. Rehab., 1976-82; dep. coroner King County, Wash., 1964-66. Mem. Gov's. North Cascades Study Com., 1967-76; mem. N. Cascades Conservation Council, v.p., 1962-63. Dir. Western Speleological Survey, Seattle, 1955-81; pres. Western Speleological Found., Seattle, 1981—; asst. dir. Internat. Glaciospeleological Survey, 1972—. Served to lt. comdr. USNR, 1949-50, 55-57. Fellow Am. Coll. Chest Physicians, Am. Acad. Compensation Medicine, Nat. Speleol. Soc., Explorers Club; mem. Soc. Thoracic Surgeons, Am. Congress Rehab. Medicine, Am. Coll. Legal Medicine, Wash. State Med. Assn., King County Med. Soc., Am. Fedn. Clin. Research, Am. Spelean History Assn. (pres. 1968), Brit. Cave Research Assn., Nat. Trust (Scotland). Clubs: Explorers (fellow); Mountaineers (past trustee); Seattle Tennis. Author: Adventure Is Underground, 1959; Depths of The Earth, 1966, 76; American Caves and Caving, 1974-82. Editor Jour. Spelean History, 1968-73. Contbr. articles in field to tech. jours. Home: 1117 36th Ave E Seattle WA 98112 Office: 1700 E Cherry Seattle WA 98122

HALLIGAN, MICHAEL LEWIS, state senator; b. Jamestown, N.D., July 9, 1949; s. Dwight Mervin and Helen Louise (Kasper) H. B.A., U. Mont., 1975, M. Pub. Adminstrn., 1977, postgrad. Sch. Law, 1982—; postgrad. Gonzaga Sch. Law, 1981-82. Research analyst Mont. State Commn. on Local Govt., Helena, 1975-76; teaching asst. polit. sci. dept. U. Mont., Missoula, 1976-77; asst. dir. Five Valleys Council of Govts., Missoula, 1977-80; owner Halligan & Assocs., 1980-81; mem. Mont. Senate, 1980—; legal intern Missoula County Attys. Office, 1982—. Served to 1st lt. Inf., U.S. Army, 1968-71.

HALLION, RICHARD PAUL, aerospace historian, museum consultant; b. Washington, May 17, 1948; s. Richard Paul and Marie Elizabeth (Flynn). B.A. with high honors in History, U. Md., 1970, Ph.D., 1975. Curator sci. and tech., curator space sci. and exploration Nat. Air and Space Mus., Smithsonian Instn., 1974-80; prof. history, instr. aerospace engring., U. Md., College Park, 1980-81, assoc. prof. gen. adminstrn., Univ. Coll., 1980-81; center historian Air Force Flight Test Ctr., Edwards AFB, Calif., 1982—; museum cons. Recipient Dr. Robert H. Goddard Hist. Essay award Nat. Space Club, 1980; Daniel and Florence Guggenheim fellow, 1974-75. Mem. AIAA (history manuscript award 1976, Young Engr./Scientist award Nat. Capitol sect. 1979), Aviation/Space Writers Assn. (writing citation 1977, 78, Space Lit. award 1979), Am. Astron. Soc., U.S. Naval Inst., Soc. History of Tech., Air Force Hist. Found. (mem. editorial adv. bd.), Air Force Assn. (life), U. Md. Alumni Assn. (life). Roman Catholic. Clubs: Wings (N.Y.C.); Read Room (Washington). Author: Supersonic Flight, 1972; Legacy of Flight: The Guggenheim Contribution to American Aviation, 1977; The Wright Brothers: Heirs of Prometheus, 1978; (with Tom D. Crouch) Apollo: Ten Years Since Tranquillity Base, 1979; Test Pilots: The Frontiersmen of Flight, 1981; Designers and Test Pilots, 1982; contbr. articles to profl. jours. Office: Air Force Flight Test Center 6510 ABG/HO Stop 203 Edwards AFB CA 93523

HALLOCK, BRENT GREGG, soil science educator, consultant; b. South Gate, Calif., July 9, 1947; s. Robert Duane and Cherry (Llewellyn) H.; m. Cathy Renaye Compenell, Mar. 12, 1972; children—Chaudra Lea, Hali Renaye. B.S. in Range Mgmt., U. Calif.-Davis, 1970, M.S., 1972, Ph.D., in Soils and Plant Nutrition, 1976. Research asst. U. Calif.-Davis, 1972-74, assoc. instr., 1974-76; forest soil specialist Wash. State U., Puyallup, 1976-79; prof. Calif. Polytechnic State U., San Luis Obispo, 1979—, head dept. soil sci., 1983—; cons. U.S. Forest Service; workshop coordinator. Active Community for the Year 2000, San Luis Obispo. Dept. Interior grantee, 1982-84; Scotts Fertilizer Co. grantee, 1982; U.S. Forest Service grantee, 1982; recipient Appreciation cert. U.S. Forest Service, 1982. Mem. Soil Sci. Soc. Am., Soil Conservation Soc. (appreciation award, 1981), Profl. Soil Sci. Assn. Calif., South Coast Soil Conservation Soc. (pres. Calif. chpt.), State Soil Survey Com. Author numerous soil sci. manuals. Home: 1671 Pereira Dr San Luis Obispo CA 93401 Office: Dept Soil Sci Calif Polytechnic State U San Luis Obispo CA 93407

HALLOWELL, ROBERT ELLSWORTH, financial executive; b. Seattle, May 28, 1934; s. Lionel Ellsworth and Jeanette Elizabeth (Johnson) H.; m. Claire Isabelle Wernentin, June 13, 1958; children—Jill, Jean. B.A. in Bus. Adminstrn. cum laude, U. Wash., 1958. C.P.A., Wash. Acct., Price Waterhouse & Co., Seattle, 1958-62; asst. to treas. Wash. Title Ins. Co., Seattle, 1962-63; asst. controller Seattle Times, 1963-66, controller, 1966-71, treas., 1970-71, v.p. fin., 1971-75, v.p. adminstrn., 1975-79, v.p. sales and mktg., 1979-81, v.p. fin., 1981—; v.p., dir. Times Communications Co.; treas., dir. Walla Walla Union Bull. Mem. adv. bd. Coll. Bus. and Econs., Wash. State U., 1978-81; bd. dirs. Jr. Achievement Puget Sound Region, 1978-83, v.p., 1981-82; bd. dirs. Edmonds (Wash.) Methodist Ch., mem. fin. com., 1970-72, pres. men's club, 1972; trustee U. Wash. Acctg. Devel. Fund, 1972-83, Pacific Sci. Ctr., Ind. Colls. Wash., Inc., 1970-73. Served with U.S. Army, 1955-57. Recipient C.P.A. Silver medal, 1958. Mem. Fin. Execs. Inst. (nat. dir. 1978-79, pres. Seattle chpt. 1972-73), Inst. Newspaper Controllers and Fin. Officers (nat. dir. 1973-76, mem. exec. com.), Seattle C. of C. (trustee 1970-73, v.p. Pres. Club 1969, Pres. Club award 1969), Alpha Tau Omega, Beta Gamma Sigma, Beta Alpha Psi. Clubs: Sahalie Ski (pres. 1981), Rainier Sea, Wash. Athletic (Seattle). Office: Seattle Times 1120 John St Seattle WA 98109

HALLSTROM, GERALD LINCOLN, newspaper exec.; b. Worcester, Mass., Dec. 29, 1947; s. Lincoln A. and Mary A. H.; student San Francisco City Coll., 1965; m. Colleen Margaret Farrell, Sept. 1, 1967;

1 dau., Heather Aileen. Advt. rep. Tahoe Daily Tribune, South Lake Tahoe, Calif., 1969, mgr. classified advt., 1969-73; mgr. classified advt. Antioch (Calif.) Daily Ledger, 1974-75; dir. classified advt. Contra Costa Times, Walnut Creek, Calif., 1975-79; gen. mgr. Valley Times, Pleasanton, Calif., 1979—. Served with USMC, 1965-69; Vietnam. Mem. Calif. Newspaper Pubs. Assn., Am. Newspaper Pubs. Assn., No. Calif. Classified Advt. Mgrs. Assn. (dir. 1977—), Assn. Newspaper Classified Advt. Mgrs., Western Classified Advt. Mgrs. Assn. Office: 122 Spring St Pleasanton CA 94566

HALLUM, ROSEMARY NORA, educator; b. Oakland, Calif., d. Fred Fain and Edna Henrietta (Becker) Hallum. A.B. with highest honors, U. Calif.-Berkeley, 1954; gen. elementary teaching credential U. of Pacific, 1955; M.A. with honors, Calif. State U., 1960; Ph.D. Walden U., 1975. Accompanist, asst. tchr. in dance studios; pvt. piano tchr.; teaching asst. U. Calif. at Berkeley, 1954-55; high sch. English tchr., elementary sch. tchr., social dance tchr., workshop clinician edn1. writer, West coast cons. Ednl. Activities, Inc., Oakland, Calif., 1960—. Mem. ASCAP, Musicians Union, Music Educators Nat. Conf., Am. Fedn. Tchrs., Phi Beta Kappa, Pi Lambda Theta, Delta Kappa Gamma, Phi Delta Kappa. Roman Catholic. Club: Calif. Writers (Oakland). Early childhood cons., contbg. author New Dimensions in music textbook series, 1970-80. Author: Boxing, 1973; Safe Motorcycle Riding, 1973; Kookie The Motorcycle Racing Dog, 1973; Motocross Racing, 1973; Dr. Marcus A. Foster, 1974; Kookie Rides Again, 1974; Want to Climb a Mountain, 1975; Jet Car Champion, 1977; Oral Language Expansion, 1977; Multicultural Folktales, 1977; I Like to Read, 1981; Kindergarten text Am. Book Social Studies Series, 1982; staff writer Teacher Mag. Producer filmstrips and records. Address: 1021 Otis Dr Alameda CA 94501

HALPER, JANICE ROBIN, organizational consultant; b. Bklyn.; d. Lewis and Fay (Sugarman) H.; B.S. in Human Devel., SUNY, 1977; postgrad. in psychology Columbia Pacific U. Asst. to v.p. ops. Data Recall Corp., El Segundo, Calif., 1970-73; account exec. SSC&B Advt., N.Y.C., 1973-74; founder, organizational cons. Jan Halper Assos., San Francisco and N.Y.C., 1976—. Mem. Am. Soc. Tng. and Devel., Am. Mktg. Assn., Sales and Mktg. Execs., Organizational Devel. Network. Office: 533 Sutter St 419 San Francisco CA 94109 also 7 W 95th St New York NY 10025

HALPERIN, IVAN WARREN, lawyer; b. Los Angeles, Nov. 21, 1946; s. Eugene and Sadella (Weiner) H.; B.S., U. So. Calif., 1968; J.D., U. Calif. Hastings Coll., 1971. Admitted to Calif. bar, 1972; atty., asst. counsel Bank of Am., Los Angeles also San Francisco, 1971-73; asst. counsel Cascars World Inc., Los Angeles, 1973-75; individual practice law, Los Angeles, 1975-76; sr. partner Halperin & Halperin, Los Angeles, 1976—; instr. Hastings Coll. Law, 1974. Mem. U. Calif. Hastings Coll. Law 1066 Found., 1972—, trustee, 1974—. Mem. State Bar Calif., Los Angeles County, Beverly Hills bar assns. Democrat. Jewish. Office: 2049 Century Park E Suite 4000 Los Angeles CA 90067

HALPERIN, KENNETH DEAN, lawyer; b. Los Angeles, Oct. 6, 1950; s. Eugene and Sadella H.; B.A., U. So. Calif., 1972; J.D., U. Calif., San Francisco, 1975; m. Alana Freedman, June 20, 1971 (div.); children—Maximilian Chase, Chloé Lisbeth. Bar: Calif., 1976; mng. partner firm Halperin & Halperin, Los Angeles, 1977-. Pres. Friends of Internat. Inst. for Kidney Disease, UCLA. Mem. Calif. State, Beverly Hills, Century City bar assns., Alumni Assn. U. Calif. Hastings Coll. Law, 1066 Found. Hastings Coll. Law, Assocs. U. So. Calif. Office: 2049 Century Park E Suite 4000 Los Angeles CA 90067

HALPERT, ALBERT L., project engr.; b. Buffalo, Dec. 19, 1922; s. Emanuel G. and Dinath (Grossman) H.; m. Charlotte Batcher, Dec. 24, 1949; children—Leslie Dean, Elena Beth. Student, Rensselaer Poly. Inst., 1941-42; B.S.M.E., NYU, 1944; postgrad. UCLA, 1966-71, U. So. Calif., 1971-72. Gen. mgr. chem. processing Tobin-Halpert, N.Y.C., 1946-53; quality control engr. Republic Aviation Corp., Farmingdale, N.Y., 1953-55, research engr., Fairchild Airplane and Engine Co., Bayshore, N.Y., 1955-59; devel. engr. Brookhan Nat. Lab., Upton, N.Y., 1959-60; chief structural testing Gyrodyne Co. Am., Inc., St. James, N.Y., 1960-64; sr. research engr. Lockheed Aircraft Co., Burbank, Calif. 1965-71; project engr. N.Am. Aircraft, Rockwell Internat., El Segundo, Calif., 1972—; cons. test programs, safety and forensics. Tech. coordinator Calif.-Israel Com. for Trade and Tech. Served with U.S. Army, 1942-46. Mem. AIAA. Home: 8828 Pershing Dr Suite 318 Playa Del Rey CA 90291 Office: NAAO Rockwell Internat Dept 117 GB-10 201 N Douglas St El Segundo CA 90245

HALPIN, EUGENE PIERCE, retired engineering manager; b. Albany, Ind., May 30, 1913; s. Albert Clifton and Ruby Gertrude (Wingate) H.; B.S. in E.E., Purdue U., 1934; spl. courses Harvard and M.I.T.; m. Virginia Lee Beuoy, Aug. 22, 1933; children—Jack Douglas, Sara Diane Halpin DeBellis, Thomas Allon. With Zenith Radio Corp., Chgo., 1934-35; distbn. engr. Indiana Gen. Service Co., Marion, 1935-40; chief engr. Talos Missile Engring., Bendix Corp., Mishawaka, Ind., 1946-57; engring. mgr. Minuteman engring. devel. proposal Bendix Corp., South Bend, 1957-59; mem. new bus. com., sales forecast and contractors, ind. tech. effort Hughes Aircraft, Culver City, Calif., 1959-70; marketing forecaster Missile Systems Group, Hughes Aircraft Co., Canoga Park, Calif., 1971-78; lectr. radar design and engring., Harvard U. Served to lt. col. F.A., also S.C., AUS, 1940-46. Decorated Bronze Star. Mem. Am. Ordnance Assn., Navy League, IEEE, Res. Officers Assn., Am. Def. Preparedness Assn. Republican. Presbyterian. Patentee radar beacon. Home: 3525 Coast View Dr Malibu CA 90265

HALSEY, NORMAN DOUGLAS, aerodynamicist; b. St. Petersburg, Fla., May 17, 1947; s. Norman Cockrem and Virginia (Knighton) H. B.S., U. Fla., 1969; M.S., Calif. State U., 1978. Sr. engr.-scientist Douglas Aircraft Co., Long Beach, 1970—; lectr. Calif. State U., Long Beach, 1980-81. Recipient NASA Cert. of Recognition, 1980. Mem. AIAA, Soc. for Indl. and Applied Math. Democrat. Clubs: Long Beach Windsurfer Fleet, Western Observatorium Astronomy. Contbr. articles to profl. jours. Home: 916 Stevely Ave Long Beach CA 90815 Office: 3855 Lakewood Blvd Long Beach CA 90845

HALSTED, ANNE WATSON, leasing company executive; b. Charleston, W. Va., Nov. 21, 1942; d. Robert Leach and Janet (Watson) H. B.A. in Polit. Sci., Duke U., 1964. Vice pres. personnel U.S. Leasing Internat. Inc., San Francisco, 1969—. Bd. dirs. Internat. Inst., Legal Aid Soc., Telegraph Hill Neighborhood Ctr., Friends of Urban Forest, Telegraph Hill Dwellers; mem. exec. com. San Francisco Planning and Urban Research Assn., Com. Removal Embarcadero Freeway; mem. adv. com. Yerba Buena Ctr., Citizens Com. Open Space Acquisition; mem., chmn. adv. com. Citizens Commn. South Beach/Rincon Point Redevel. Area; mem. Mayor's Com. Econ. Devel.; mem. San Francisco Found. com. Developing Goals for San Francisco. Mem. San Francisco C. of C. (exec. com. women's council). Office: 633 Battery San Francisco CA 94111

HALTON, HARRY JOHN, JR., mfg. engr.; b. Salt Lake City, Sept. 21, 1926; s. Harry John and Fern Julia (France) H.; student Santa Monica City Coll., 1950-51, LaSalle Extension U., 1954-56, Sch. Law, Western State U., 1970-72; m. Ruth Lucile Hemmann, Feb. 25, 1946. Mgr. mfg. Benson Lehner Corp., Van Nuys, Calif., 1963-67, Raytheon Corp., Santa Ana, Calif., 1968-72; mfg. mgmt. cons., Santa Ana, 1972—; plant engr. Leggett & Platt, Los Angeles, 1977; mfg. engr. Weiser Lock Co., South Gate, Calif., 1977—; dir. Benson Lehner Corp. Vice comdr. Mil. Order of Purple Heart, 1947-48. Served with U.S. Army, 1944-46. Decorated Purple Heart, Bronze Star. Mem. ASME. Republican. Lutheran. Club: Elks. Home: 4211 W First St #127 Santa Ana CA 92703 Office: 4100 Ardmore Ave South Gate CA 90280

HALVARSSON-DEWITT, MISHA, architectural and glass designer; b. Oakland, Calif., May 25, 1951; d. Carl Maurice and Ruth Beckner (Ayres) Halvarsson; m. Dennis Craig DeWitt, Dec. 31, 1979. Student World Campus Afloat, Chapman Coll.; student in design and journalism, Union U., Jackson, Tenn., 1971. Sr. designer Halvarsson Design, Oreg., 1975-79, pres., 1978-79; v.p. Icefire Glassworks, Inc., Oreg., 1976-78, corp. gen. mgr., 1977-78; design cons. Van Workshop, Inc., Oreg., 1978-79; pres., archtl. and glass designer, gen. contractor Halvarsson, DeWitt & Assos., Inc., Duvall, Wash., 1979-82; acting dir. Images & Reflections, Inc., Duvall, 1979-82; promotional cons. Marawood Devel. Corp., 1981; sr. designer Chrysalis Studios Inc., Redmond, Wash., 1982—; cons. archtl. glass and Victorian renovation, mktg. cons.; glass designs exhibited: Russell Mus. Fine Arts, Great Falls, Mont., 1981, Lawrence Gallery, Oreg., 1977, 79, 80. Mem. Oreg. Land Conservation and Devel. Com., 1976-79; chmn. Duvall Revitalization Com., 1981—. Mem. Nat. Trust Hist. Prevervation. Editor: Scratchbook Cookery Series, 1980-81. Office: PO Box 2536 Kirkland WA 98033

HALVERSON, CORDELL KENNETH, obstetrician and gynecologist; b. Langdon, N.D., Dec. 26, 1939; s. Kenneth Benford and Annabelle Lee (Yeager) H.; B.A., Jamestown (N.D.) Coll., 1961; B.S. in Medicine, U. N.D., 1966; M.D., Southwestern Med. Sch., Dallas, 1968; m. Patricia Louise Koch, Aug. 20, 1961; children—Jennifer Ann, Leasa Marie, Phillip Andrew. Intern, Meth. Hosp. of Dallas, 1969; practice medicine specializing in family medicine, Ft. Worth, 1969-71; resident in ob-gyn Med. Coll. Ohio Hosp., Toledo, 1971-74; practice medicine specializing in ob-gyn, Las Vegas, N.Mex., 1974—; mem. staff Las Vegas Hosp., chief staff, 1977-78. Vice pres. San Miguel County Fair Bd., 1978-79. Served with M.C., USAF Res., 1971-76. Diplomate Am. Bd. Ob-Gyn. Fellow Am. Coll. Ob-Gyn; mem. AMA, N.Mex. Med. Soc., N.Mex. Obstet. and Gynecol. Soc., San Miguel County Med. Soc. Lutheran. Home: 1623 8th St Las Vegas NM 87701 Office: 720 University St Las Vegas NM 87701

HALVERSON, GEORGE CLARENCE, university dean; b. Greece, N.Y., Apr. 22, 1914; s. Nils and Bertha (Flodquist) H.; A.B. in Govt. and Econs., Antioch Coll., Yellow Springs, Ohio, 1938; M.A. in Internat. Adminstrn., Columbia U., 1944; Ph.D. in Labor Econs., London Sch. Econs., 1952; m. Thelma Lee Cunningham, Sept. 9, 1949; children—Kristine, John. Field examiner NLRB, 1938-41, 48-49; head bus. adminstrn. extension U. Calif., Berkeley, 1952-57, asst. dean Sch. Bus., 1955-56; coordinator mgmt. devel. Ampex Corp., Redwood City, Calif., 1957-61; v.p. Hergenrather Assos., San Francisco, 1961-62; mem. faculty San Jose (Calif.) State U., 1962—, prof. Sch. Bus., 1965—, dean, 1974-81, chmn. manpower adminstrn. dept., 1963-68, asst. to pres., 1970-74. Hon. bd. dirs. Better Bus. Bur., San Jose, 1975—; bd. dirs. Industry Edn. Council Calif., 1977—, Center Creative Arts and Scis., 1978—; bd. dirs. Community Assn. for Retarded, Applied Human Devel. Inc. Served with USCGR, 1942-46. Fulbright fellow, 1949-51. Mem. Acad. Mgmt. Democrat. Unitarian. Co-author: Causes of Industrial Peace: Lockheed Aircraft Corp. and the Machinists, 1955. Contbr. to profl. jours. Home: 149 N Gordon Way Los Altos CA 94022 Office: San Jose State Univ San Jose CA 95192

HALVORSON, GERALD WALTER, microbiologist, army officer, laboratory administrator; b. Bottineau, N.D., June 28, 1935; s. Orville Thurman and Barbara Beverly (Himmelsbach) H.; m. Sally Evelyn Gustafson, June 4, 1960; children—Daniel, Donald. A.S. in Sci., N.D. Sch. Forestry, Bottineau, 1955; B.S. in Edn., Minot State Tchrs. Coll., 1958; M.S. in Microbiology U. Ill., 1969; attended Command and Gen. Staff Coll., 1975-78. Commd. 2d lt. U.S. Army, 1959, advanced through grades to col., 1983; chief virology service 4th U.S. Army Med. Lab., Ft. Sam Houston, Tex., 1968-71; chief microbiology Madigan Army Med. Ctr., Tacoma, 1971-77; chief virology service 10th Med. Lab., Landstuhl, Germany, 1977-79; microbiologist Madigan Army Med. Ctr., Tacoma, 1979-80, lab. mgr. dept. pathology and area lab. service 1980—. Decorated Bronze Star, Meritorious Service medal with 2 oak leaf clusters (U.S.); Cross of Gallantry with palm (Vietnam). Mem. Am. Soc. Microbiology (specialist microbiologist), Soc. Armed Forces Med. Lab. Scientists. Republican. Roman Catholic. Home: 4719 61st Ave W Tacoma WA 98466 Office: Madigan Army Med Ctr Tacoma WA 98431

HALVORSON, RUDELLA (MICKEY), travel agent; b. Coulee, N.D., July 14, 1922; d. Martin J. and Selma C. (Olson) Mikelson; m. Halvor M. Halvorson, Feb. 22, 1941; children—Heidi Halvorson Stejer, Judi Halvorson Rowand, Gail Halvorson DeSmet, Mikel, Ronald Paul Owner, gen. mgr. Red Carpet Travel, Spokane, Wash., 1970—; owner, sec. H. Halvorson, Inc., Spokane, 1945—. Trustee Wampum. Mem. Eastern Wash. Hist. Soc., Spokane C. of C., Assn. Wash. Bus., Am. Soc. Travel Agts., Assn. Retail Travel Agts., N. Am. Travel Assn., Pacific Cruise Conf. Republican. Clubs: Spokane Country, Spokane, Hayden Lake (Idaho) Country. Home: E 1809 Rockwood Pl Spokane WA 99203 Office: Red Carpet Travel S 3009 Grand Blvd Spokane WA 99203

HALZEL, MICHAEL HARRIS, ednl. adminstr.; b. Boston, Apr. 29, 1941; s. George Charles and Ruth C.W. (Baker) H.; B.A., B.Hebrew Lit., Yeshiva U., 1962; M.Jewish Edn., Hebrew Coll., 1974; M.Ed., N.Y. U., 1976; Ed.D., Nova U., 1981; m. Cecelia Heinish, Sept. 2, 1962; 1 son, Avi Samuel. Tchr., prin. Shaar Shalom Congregation, Halifax, N.S., Can., 1962-72; lectr. Dalhousie U., Halifax, 1970-72; prin. North Shore Hebrew Sch., Marblehead, Mass., 1972-76, Hillel Acad. North Shore, Swampscott, Mass., 1974-79; founding headmaster San Diego Jewish Acad., 1979—. Harry H. Fine Meml. grad. fellow, Boston, 1972-74; Am. Assn. for Jewish Edn. grad. fellow, 1974-76. Mem. Jewish Educators Assembly, Nat. Conf. Hebrew Day Sch. Prins., Nat. Assn. Elem. Sch. Prins., Am. Soc. for Curriculum Devel. Democrat. Contbr. articles to Jewish edn. jours. Home: 6260 Camino del Rincon San Diego CA 92120 Office: 6660 Cowles Mountain Blvd San Diego CA 92119

HAM, ANITA SUE, systems engineer, nurse administrator; b. Kewanee, Ill., May 31, 1949; d. Virgil and Mary Lou (Ogle) Ham. B.S. in Nursing, U. Md.-Balt., 1971; M.B.A. with honors, City Coll., Seattle, 1979. Registered nurse, Md., Wash., Calif. Commd. 1st lt. U.S. Army, 1971, advanced through grades to maj., 1983; stationed Madigan Army Med. Ctr., Tacoma, Wash., 1972-73; head nurse drug and alcohol rehab. and psychiat. unit U.S. Army Hosp., Wurzburg, Germany, 1974-76; chief adult day care service, dept. psychiatry Fitzsimmons Army Med. Ctr., Denver, 1976-77, ret., 1977; asst. dir. Seattle City Coll., Tacoma, 1978-80; mgmt. analyst Wash. Dept. Transp., Olympia, 1980; mgr. med. support services Western State Hosp., Ft. Stelacoom, Wash., 1980-81; sr. engr. ops, data base mgmt. Martin Marietta Corp., Vandenburg Air Force Base, Calif., 1981—; cons. U. S. Army Dept. Nursing; Mem. Nat. Assn. Female Execs., Assn. M.B.A. s. Wrote material on systems approach for city colls. Office: Martin Marietta Corp VAFB Ops Mail Stop MI711 Vandenberg Air Force Base CA

HAMAI, JAMES YUTAKA, business exec.; b. Los Angeles, Oct. 14, 1926; s. Seizo and May (Sata) H.; B.S., U. So. Calif., 1952, M.S., 1955; postgrad. bus. mgmt. program industry exec. U. Calif. at Los Angeles, 1963-64; m. Dorothy K. Fukuda, Sept. 10, 1954; 1 dau., Wendy A. Lectr. chem. engring. dept. U. So. Calif., Los Angeles, 1963-64; process engr., sr. process engr. Fluor Corp., Los Angeles, 1954-64; sr. project mgr. central research dept. Monsanto Co., St. Louis, 1964-67, mgr. research, devel. and engring. graphic systems dept., 1967-68, mgr. comml. devel. New Enterprise div., 1968-69; exec. v.p., dir. Concrete Cutting Industries, Inc., Los Angeles, 1969-72; pres. and dir. Concrete Cutting Internat. Inc., Long Beach, Calif., 1973-78, chmn. bd., 1978—. Served with AUS, 1946-48. Mem. Am. Inst. Chem. Engrs., Am. Mgmt. Assn., N.Y. Acad. Scis., Tau Beta Pi, Phi Lambda Upsilon. Lodge: Rotary (gov. dist. 528, 1982-83). Home: 6600 Via La Paloma Rancho Palos Verdes CA 90274 Office: 20963 Lamberton Ave Long Beach CA 90810

HAMAKER, JOHN WARREN, phys. chemist; b. Montreal, Que., Can., Oct. 25, 1917 (parents Am. citizens); s. Roy Ashton and Alice Rosalia (Warren) H.; B.A., UCLA, 1940; Ph.D., U. Calif., Berkeley, 1944; m. Edith Louise Netland, June 24, 1944; children—David Warren, Alice Elizabeth, William Henry, Robert Maurice. With U.S. Manhattan Project, U. Calif., Berkeley, 1944, Napa (Calif.) Jr. Coll., 1944-47, Whittier (Calif.) Coll., 1954; asso. prof. Dow Chem. Co., Seal Beach, Calif., 1954-64, research chemist Agrl. Products div., Walnut Creek, Calif., 1964—. Mem. Am. Chem. Soc., AAAS, Theosophical Soc., Sigma Xi. Editor: (with Goring) Organic Chemicals in the Soil Environment, 1972. Home: 125 Conifer Ln Walnut Creek CA 94598 Office: 2800 Mitchell Dr Walnut Creek CA 94598

HAMAMURA, DENNIS TSUYOSHI, optometrist; b. Honolulu, Jan. 31, 1947; s. Ronald A. and Doris T. (Yamamura) H.; m. Dixie B. Hardy, Aug. 20, 1972 (separated). B.A. in Biology, U. Calif.-Riverside, 1970; O.D., So. Calif. Coll. Optometry, 1975; postgrad. Calif. State U.-Fullerton, 1982—. Lic. optometrist, Calif. Lab. technician U. Calif.-Riverside, 1967-70, lab. asst. dept. entomology, 1967-70; lab. technician Salinity Lab., Dept. Agr., Riverside, 1968-70; assoc. R.A. Wilmer O.D., Santa Monica, Calif., 1975-77, R.J. Anelle, O.D., Colton, Calif., 1977—; asst. prof. optometry So. Calif. Coll. Optometry, 1982—; dir. optometry Sherman Indian High Sch., 1979-81; cons. Toiyabe Indian Health Project, 1981; faculty adv. Gamma chpt. Omega Delta. Japanese Am. Optometric Soc. scholar, 1975; Evening Kiwanis Club scholar, 1965. Mem. Am. Pub. Health Assn., Am. Optometric Assn., Calif. Optometric Assn., Orange Belt Optometric Soc., Japanese Am. Optometric Soc., Nat. Rifle Assn., Calif. Rifle and Pistol Assn., Calif. Golden State Trapshooting Assn. (life; So. Circle 5 Champion 1978, So. Zone Class A Champion 1981, Calif. State Zone Champion 1982). Clubs: Upland (Calif.) Gun; Inland Fish and Game (Redlands, Calif.). Office: 190 W H St Suite 105 Colton CA 92324

HAMANN, CARL L., JR., engineer; b. Hemple, Mo., Nov. 26, 1937; s. Carl L. and Evelyn E. (Pickett) H.; B.S. in Civil Engring., U. Kans., 1963, M.S. in Environ. Health Engring., 1969; m. Sharon K. Cowing, June 22, 1957; children—Mark Allen, Michael Evan. Project mgr. Black & Veatch Cons. Engrs., Kansas City, Mo., 1964-72; dir. water wastewater treatment eastern region, Cornell, Howland, Hayes & Merryfield/Hill, Reston, Va., 1972-76, chief process engr., Corvallis, Oreg., 1976—. Chmn. com. to revise text on Water Treatment Plant Design for Am. Soc. Civil Engrs., Am. Water Works Assn., Conf. State Sanitary Engrs., 1976—. N.T. Veatch scholar, 1961-63; Harry A. Jordan scholar, 1963; recipient Am. Water Works Publications award, 1966; Diplomate Am. Acad. Environ. Engrs; mem. Am. Soc. Civil Engrs., Am. Water Works Assn., Am. Inst. Chem. Engrs., Am. Chem. Soc., Water Pollution Control Fedn. Home: 4365 NW Queens Ave Corvallis OR 97330 Office: 1600 SW Western Blvd Corvallis OR 97330

HAMANN, MARCIA JOANNE, reclamation engineer; b. Seattle, July 25, 1945; d. Donald W. and Jane G. (Lind) H.; B.S. with honors in Biology, U. Puget Sound., 1968; M.S. in Botany (teaching asst.), Wash. State U., 1972; postgrad. Colo. State U., 1977. Teaching asst., research asso. Colo. State U., Ft. Collins, 1977-78; reclamation engr. Kaiser Steel Corp., Raton, N.Mex., 1978—; research project evaluator NSF, 1980—. Recipient Grad. Travel award NSF, 1970; cert. ecologist. Mem. Ecol. Soc. Am., Soc. Range Mgmt., Soil Conservation Soc. Am., Can. Land Reclamation Assn., Soc. Mining Engrs. of AIME, Wildlife Soc., Am. Soc. Surface Mining and Reclamation, N.W. Sci. Assn., Gamma Phi Beta, Phi Sigma, Xi Sigma Pi. Republican. Methodist. Home: 210 Turf Dr Raton NM 87740 Office: PO Box 1107 Raton NM 87740

HAMASSIAN, HARUTUNE, accountant; b. Beirut, Apr. 8, 1955; s. Antranik Manuel and Angel (Ounjian) H.; m. Sona Manjikian, Jan. 20, 1981. A.A., Los Angeles Valley Coll., 1977; B.S. in Bus. Adminstrn., Calif. State U.-Northridge, 1979. Acct. Security 1st Group, Inc., Century City, Calif., 1979-81; sr. acct. Anderson, Satuloff, Machado & Mendelsoh, C.P.A.s, Woodland Hills, Calif., 1981—. Former treas. Armenian Intercollegiate Students Assn.; mem. U.S. Senatorial Club, Republican Presdl. Task Force, Rep. Nat. Com. Mem. Armenian Gregorian Ch.

HAMBLETON, RITA JOAN, educator; b. Harrisburg, Ill., Jan. 6, 1932; d. Edwin Robert and Eva Maude (Cole) Evans; B.S., U. Ill., 1953; student Univ. Nev., 1963-79; m. Harley Ira Hambleton, May 19, 1955; 1 dau., Deborah Renee. Tchr. music Freeport (Ill.) Sch. Dist., 1953-54, Gallup (N.Mex.) Sch. Dist., 1954-55; with Washoe County Sch. Dist., 1956-57, 1962—, tchr. English, Procter R. Hug High Sch., Reno, 1968—. Del., Republican County and State Convs., 1976, 78, 82; mem. Washoe County Rep. Central Com., 1976-80, 82-84; mem. Anne Martin Women's Polit. Caucus, 1978-83; mem. Nev. State Edn. Assn. Polit. Action Com. of Educators, 1978-83; mem. Reno City Council Commn. on Status of Women, 1979-80. Mem. NEA, Nev. State Edn. Assn. (dir.), Washoe County Tchrs. Assn. (pres.; Profl. Leadership award 1978, Pres.'s award 1980), Nat. Council Tchrs. English, No. Nev. Council Tchrs. English, Assn. for Supervision and Curriculum Devel., AAUW, Phi Delta Kappa, Alpha Delta Kappa. Republican. Editor: Washoe Zephyr, 1976-77. Contbr. articles to Washoe Zephyr. Home: 965 Cavanaugh Dr Reno NV 89509 Office: 2880 Sutro St Reno NV 89512

HAMBURGER, WAYNE SCOTT, computer science executive; b. Bklyn., Aug. 13, 1954; s. Marvin Jerry and Rhoda (Farber) H.; S.B. in Math., MIT, 1976. Sci. programmer Nat. Magnet Lab., MIT, Cambridge, 1975-77, systems programmer, mgr., 1977-78; systems performance analyst, programmer Gen. Dynamics, San Diego, 1978-79; sr. systems support rep. Internat. Graphics, San Diego, 1979-80; pres., sr. cons. Computer Software Consultants, San Diego, 1980—; dir. computation INESCO Inc., 1981—; pvt. practice cons., 1978—. Social dir. Westgate Community Assn.; mem. Eastern Mass. Soccer Ofcls. Assn. Mem. Assn. Computing Machinery, IEEE, Digital Equipment Computer Users Soc. Home: 3675 Paul Jones Ave San Diego CA 92117 Office: 11077 N Torrey Pines Rd La Jolla CA 92037

HAMBY, JEANNETTE K., state senator; b. Virginia, Minn., Mar. 15, 1933; d. John W. and Lydia M. (Soderholm) Johnson; m. Eugene Hamby, 1957; children—Taryn Rene, Tenya Ramine. B.S., U. Minn., 1956; M.S., U. Oreg., 1968; Ph.D., Oreg. State U., 1976. Mem. Oreg. Ho. of Reps., 1981-83, Oreg. State Senate, 1983—, mem. trade and econ. devel., aging and minority affairs, intergovt. affairs coms., 1981—. Vice chmn. Hillsboro High Sch. Dist. Bd., 1973-81; mem. Washington County Juvenile Services Comm., from 1980; mem. Suggested Legis. Commn. Council of State Govts., from 1981. Mem. Oreg. Mental Health Assn. (past v.p.), Am. Nurses Assn., Oreg. Nurses Assn., Am. Vocat. Assn., Oreg. Vocat. Assn., Oreg. Vocat./Career Adminstrs., Phi Kappa Phi, Phi Delta Kappa. Republican. Lutheran. Home: PO Box 519 Hillsboro OR 97123 Office: Oregon State Senate Salem OR 97310*

HAME, TREVOR GORDON, elec. engr.; b. London, Aug. 22, 1927; s. Gordon William and Charlotte Elizabeth (Abley) H.; came to U.S., 1957, naturalized, 1964; diploma mech. engring. Regent St. Poly., London, 1949, diploma elec. engring., 1951; postgrad. Ohio State U., 1954-55; m. Billie Jean Lutz, Feb. 23, 1973; children by previous marriage—Penny Ann, Jenice Elizabeth, Sharon Lee, Kerri Jeanette. Sr. engr. EMI Electronics Ltd., Middlesex, Eng., 1951-57; asst. prof., assoc. supr. antenna lab. Ohio State U., 1957-61; dir. advanced devel. electronics div. Gen. Dynamics Corp., Rochester, N.Y., 1961-66, chief engr., San Diego, 1966-75, mgr. Pomona (Calif.) div., 1975-80, dir. tech. programs, 1980-83, dir. planning and research, 1983—; lectr. UCLA extension, 1979-83. Served with Brit. Navy, 1946-48. King George VI Meml. fellow, 1954-55; recipient Best Paper award Poly. Engring. Soc., 1951. Sr. mem. IEEE; mem. Sci. Research Soc. Am., Sigma Xi, Eta Kappa Nu. Republican. Episcopalian. Clubs: Claremont Tennis, Mission Bay Yacht (San Diego). Author papers in field. Home: 1838 Coolcrest Way Upland CA 91786 Office: PO Box 2507 Pomona CA 91766

HAMILL, PATRICK JAMES, physicist; b. Salt Lake City, Apr. 29, 1938; s. Frank Anthony and Ann Jane (McCollom) H.; B.S. in Physics, St. Edward's U., 1959; M.S. in Physics, U. Ariz., 1968, Ph.D., 1972; NCAR postdoctoral fellow U. Chgo., 1971-72; m. Elsa Li Ché, Jan. 14, 1966; children—Carla Alexandra, Candace Joy. Peace Corps vol., Peru, 1963-65; prof. physics, U. Trujillo (Perú), 1964-66; asst. prof. Clark Coll., Atlanta, 1972-74; research scientist NASA-Ames Research Center, Moffett Field, Calif., 1974-78; research scientist Systems and Applied Scis. Corp., Palo Alto, Calif., 1978-81; prof. physics San Jose (Calif.) State U., 1981—; adj. prof. U. Santa Clara, Calif.; vis. prof. U. Católica Andrés Bello, Caracas, Venezuela, 1977; cons. environ. problems. NASA-ASEE summer fellow, 1974-75. Mem. Am. Phys. Soc., Am. Meteorol. Soc., Sigma Xi. Contbr. sci. articles to jours. including Nature, Jour. Atmospheric Scis., Health Physics; contbg. author books in field. Home: 580 Vista Ave Palo Alto CA 94306

HAMILTON, CAROLYN VAGTS, artist, advertising agency executive; corporation executive; b. Seattle; d. Arthur Herman and Mary Elizabeth (Swift) Vagts; m. Gordon F. Hamilton, Jr., May 18, 1963 (div.). A.A. in Comml. Art, Los Angeles Trade Tech. Coll., 1968. Asst. fashion dir. Broadway-Hale Dept. Stores, Los Angeles, 1965-67; free lance comml. artist Carolyn Hamilton Graphic Design, Los Angeles, 1968-70; comml. artist Keye/Donna/Pearlstein Advt., Los Angeles, 1970-72; comml. artist Kelly & Reber Advt., Las Vegas, 1977-78; pres., creative dir. Newman 'n Hamilton Advt., Las Vegas, 1980—; pres. C.M. Products, 1981—; pub. speaker; hostess TV talk show. Charter mem., pres. bd. trustees Greater Las Vegas Found., Inc., 1982-83. Mem. Greater Las Vegas Advt. Fedn. (v.p. 1982—, program chmn. 1982—, Addy awards 1981-82). Democrat. Copyright Original Snowbunny Ski Hat. Office: 2001 E Flamingo Rd Suite 103 Las Vegas NV 89109

HAMILTON, CHARLES HOWARD, metallurgist; b. Pueblo, Colo., Mar. 17, 1935; s. George Edwin and Eva Eleanor (Watson) H.; B.S., Colo. Sch. Mines, 1959; M.S., U. So. Calif., 1965; Ph.D., Case Western Res. U., 1968; m. Joy Edith Richmond, Sept. 7, 1968; children—Krista Kathleen, Brady Glenn. Research engr. Space Div., Rockwell Internat., Downey, Calif., 1959-65, mem. tech. staff Los Angeles div., 1968-75, tech. staff, phys. metallurgy, Sci. Center, Thousand Oaks, 1975-77, group mgr. metals processing Sci. Center, 1977-79, prin. scientist Sci. Center, 1979-81, dir. materials synthesis and processing dept., 1982—, chmn. corp. tech. panel, materials research and engring.; co-organizer 1st Internat. Symposium Superplastic Forming, 1982. Named Rockwell Engr. of Year, 1979; recipient IR100 award Industrial Research mag., 1976, 80. Fellow Am. Soc. for Metals; mem. AIME (shaping and forming com.), Sigma Xi. Contbr. tech. articles to profl. publs. in field; patentee advanced metalworking and tech. Office: 1049 Camino dos Rios Thousand Oaks CA 91360

HAMILTON, CRAIG RALPH WILSON, optometrist; b. San Francisco, June 27, 1947; s. Ralph Wilson and Isobel Mary Baird (Craig) H.; m. Tina Marilyn Brewster, June 19, 1971; children—Ryan Craig and Tara Allison (twins). B.S., U. Nev., 1969; postgrad. U. N.Mex., 1970; O.D. cum laude, So. Calif. Coll. Optometry, 1974. Optometrist, Roos Coos Med. Group, Los Angeles, 1974; pvt. practice optometry, Las Vegas, 1974—; vision cons. to athletic program U. Nev. Las Vegas. Clubs: Rotary, Lions. Office: 4850 S Eastern St Suite 2 Las Vegas NV 89109

HAMILTON, FREDERIC CRAWFORD, oil company executive; b. Columbus, Ohio, Sept. 25, 1927; s. Ferris F. and Jean (Crawford) H.; grad. Lawrenceville Sch., 1945, Babson Coll., 1947; m. Jane C. Murchison, Feb. 14, 1953; children—Christy, Frederic C., Crawford M., Thomas M. Pres., Hamilton Bros. Oil Co., Denver, 1957—; chmn. bd. Hamilton Bros. Canadian Gas Co., Ltd., Calgary, Alta., 1960—; chmn. bd. Hamilton Bros. Oil Co. (Gt. Britain) Ltd., London, Eng., 1964—, Hamilton Bros. Petroleum Corp., Denver, Hamilton Oil Gt. Britain (PLC), London; dir. Celanese Corp., Gates Learjet Corp., Intrawest Fin. Corp., U.S. Trust Co., Skandinaviska Enskilda Banken Internat. Corp., First Matagorda Corp. Served with USAAF, 1944-46. Office: 1600 Broadway Denver CO 80202

HAMILTON, IRVIN CARL, JR., public relations and marketing executive; b. Chgo., Aug. 4, 1935; s. Irvin Carl and Louise Georgia (Rytina) H.; B.S., Northwestern U., 1957; M.A., Calif. State U., San Francisco, 1972; m. Norah Kathleen Davis, May 25, 1976; children—Carl Jeffrey, Laura Emily. Copywriter, 3M Co., Chgo., 1959-60; promotion mgr. Wall St. Jour., Chgo., 1960-63, Nat. Observer, N.Y.C., 1963-64; asst. advt. and public relations mgr. Paul Masson Vineyards, San Francisco, 1964-65; mem. advt. staff Kaiser Aluminum Co., Oakland, Calif., 1965-66, Eastern public relations mgr., N.Y.C., 1966-69; dir. advt. and public relations Kaiser Aetna, Oakland, 1969-73; gen. mgr. SWA Communications, Sausalito, Calif., 1973-74; v.p. Hoefer/Amidei Public Relations, San Francisco, 1974-77; founder, 1977, since pres. Aviso Public Relations, Alameda, Calif.; v.p. Needham Skyles Oil Co., San Francisco, to 1980; v.p. public relations Pinne, Garvin and Hock, San Francisco, 1980-82; speaker, lectr. in field. Served with AUS, 1957-59. Mem. Pub. Relations Soc. Am. (chpt. dir., nat. del.), Alameda C. of C., Oakland C. of C. Author articles in field. Home: 6706 Heartwood Dr Oakland CA 94611 Office: AVISO Inc PO Box 29372 Oakland CA 94604

HAMILTON, JAMES ALEXANDER, psychiatrist; b. Pecatonica, Ill., June 9, 1907; s. Dwight Stoney and Pearl (Blake) H.; A.B., U. Calif., Berkeley, 1928, Ph.D., 1935; M.D., Stanford U., 1941; m. Marjorie Hilder Angell, June 14, 1936. Asst. prof. psychology, asst. dean students U. Calif., Berkeley, 1941-42; clin. instr. psychiatry Stanford (Calif.) U., 1949-55, asso. clin. prof. psychiatry, 1956-75; pvt. practice medicine specializing in psychiatry, San Francisco, Calif., 1948-78; dir., vice chmn. Chemetrics Corp., Burlingame, Calif., 1975-79; researcher in postpartum psychosis, substandard reading, 1955—. Served to maj. U.S. Army 1942-48. Mem. Am. Psychiat. Assn., Marcé Soc. Club: Family, Press. Author: Toward Proficient Reading, 1938; Postpartum Psychiatric Problems, 1962; The Computer Tutor, Language Systems, 1979. Office: 490 Post St Suite 1515 San Francisco CA 94102

HAMILTON, JEFFREY NILS, school principal; b. Marfa, Tex., Oct. 7, 1945; s. Thomas Albert and Nell (Courtney) H.; m. Barbara Lee Ricks, Mar. 23, 1970; children—Ben-Thomas, Michael Matthew. A.B., San Diego State U., 1971; M.A., Point Loma Coll, 1976; Ed.D. (assistantship) No. Ariz. U., 1983. Tchr. pub. schs. Cajon Valley Union Sch. Dist., El Cajon, Calif., 1972-79; program coordinator No. Ariz. U., Flagstaff, 1980-81; prin. Washington Elem. Sch., Mendota Union, Calif., 1981—; inservice speaker Acad. Learning Time. Vice-chmn. Sequoia council Tachi dist. Boy Scouts Am. Served with U.S. Army, 1966-68. Mem. Assn. Calif. Sch. Adminstrs., Assn. Supervision and Curriculum Devel. Democrat.

HAMILTON, JERRY E., business consultant; b. Grinnell, Iowa, Nov. 22, 1937; s. John Herman and Letha Mae (Bosteder) H.; student Los Angeles City Coll., 1970-73; B.B.A., Olympic Coll., 1975; m. Genny Waialae, Sept. 19, 1963; children—John, Dawn, Gerald, Deborah, Geoffrey, Guy. Tchr., adminstr. Harbor City (Calif.) Christian Sch., 1970-72; dir. edn. Calvary Light Ch., Long Beach, Calif., 1972-74; advt. cons., free-lance writer, Los Angeles, 1974-77; tng. rep. Northrop Corp., Hawthorne, Calif., 1977-83; pres. Assistance UnLtd., 1983—. Vice chmn. Fries Elem. Sch. Adv. Council, Wilmington, Calif., 1980-82; sustaining mem. Republican Nat. Com., 1983; mem. Pres. Reagan's Task Force, 1982-83. Served with U.S. Army, 1956-65. Decorated Army Commendation medal. Mem. Am. Mgmt. Assn., Am. Soc. for Tng. and Devel. (dir. of membership 1981-82), Assn. of Dirs. Christian Edn. Club: Toastmasters. Office: 1251 W Sepulveda Blvd Suite 233 Torrance CA 90502

HAMILTON, MADRID BOYD TURNER (MRS. NORMAN WOODROW HAMILTON), social work cons., educator; b. Greensboro, Ga.; d. Paul and Mary (Hubert) Turner; A.B., Spelman Coll.; M.S.W., Atlanta U.; student Syracuse U., Fordham U., U. Mass.; Ph.D., Union Grad. Sch.-West; m. Norman Woodrow Hamilton, June 9, 1948 (dec. 1964); 1 son, Alexander Turner. Asst. prof. sociology Morehouse Coll., Atlanta, 1946-48; organizing program dir. Columbia area YWCA, Phila., 1949-52; sch. social worker Bur. Child Guidance N.Y.C. Bd. Edn.; activities dir. Harlem br., N.Y.C., 1956-57; cons. pub. health social work N.Y.C. Dept. Pub. Health, 1958-64; dir. Western region, mobile unit coordinator Planned Parenthood World Population, N.Y. and San Francisco, 1964-69; rep. Western region Family Service Assn. Am., San Francisco, 1969-72; pres. Hamilton Enterprises, Inc., 1972—; asso. prof. social welfare Grad. Sch. Social Work, San Francisco State U., 1966—; mem. Calif. Gov.'s Population Study Com., 1966—; asso. prof. sociology U. Redlands (Calif.), 1974-77. Nat. bd. dirs. YWCA, 1970-82, v.p., 1979—; v.p., treas., bd. dirs. YWCA, San Francisco, 1969-79, treas., 1982, treas. Redlands YWCA; chmn. community services com. Greater Urban League, N.Y.C., 1960-63; co-founder Calif. Interagy. Council Family Planning, 1967; bd. dirs. United Way Redlands, East Valley Health Commn. Mem. Am. Pub. Health Assn., Social Work Vocat. Bur., Acad. Cert. Social Workers, Acad. Polit. and Social Scis., Nat. Assn. Social Workers, No. Calif. Spelman Coll. Alumnae (pres. and region coordinator 1967-72), Alpha Kappa Delta. Club: Altrusa. Author: Demonstration in Rural Professional Education, 1968; Family Planning: Prejudice and Politics, 1970; Manual on Health Fairs, 1976; Erosive Health, 1979; columnist Metro Reporter. Home: 136 Geneva Ave San Francisco CA 94112

HAMILTON, MARGARET LAWRENCE, psychotherapist; b. Pottstown, Pa., Oct. 12, 1948; d. Mansfield Wiggins and Margaret Lawrence (Van Vechten) Williams; m. Jackson Douglas Hamilton, Dec. 19, 1971; children—Jake, Will. B.A., Skidmore Coll., 1970; M.A., Bryn Mawr Coll., 1974; Ph.D., Internat. Coll., 1983; lic. marriage, family, child cons., Calif. Pvt. practice psychotherapy, Santa Monica, Calif., 1976—; supr. Bel Aire Presbyn. Ch. Counseling Ctr., Calif., 1980—. Mem. Am. Psychol. Assn., Internat. Tranactional Analysis Assn., AAUW. Address: 1760 Sunset Ave Santa Monica CA 90405

HAMILTON, MICHAEL SEYMOUR, political scientist, educator; b. Ithaca, N.Y., June 1, 1946; s. Harry Seymour and Ellen Louise (Moore) H. B.A. in Social Sci. with highest distinction, Colo. State U., 1975, M.A. in Polit. Sci., 1977, Ph.D., 1983. Grad. research asst. Western Regional Power Plant Siting Study, Western Interstate Nuclear Bd., Colo. State U., 1976, research assoc. Los Alamos Sci. Lab., 1977-78, research fellow Colo. Energy Research Inst., 1978-79, 79-80; adminstrv. asst. research Sts. and Traffic Unit, Ft. Collins, Colo., 1980-81; vis. lectr. Grad. Program Energy/Environ. Mgmt., Div. Pub. Adminstrn., U. N.Mex., Albuquerque, 1981—; mem. Impacting Factors Work Group, N.Mex. Energy and Minerals Dept. Contbr. articles to profl. publs. Mem. U. N.Mex. faculty for Anaya for Gov., 1982. Mem. Am. Soc. Pub. Adminstrn., Western Polit. Sci. Assn., Policy Studies Orgn., Am. Polit. Sci. Assn. Democrat. Unitarian. Office: U NMex Div Pub Adminstrn Albuquerque NM 87131

HAMILTON, ROBERT LELAND, mech. engr.; b. Denver, Jan. 8, 1945; s. Robert Boyd and Anna Josephine (Mrachek) H.; B.S. in Mech. Engring., B.S. in Manpower Mgmt., U. Colo., 1970; m. Linda Ruth Wyczawski, June 15, 1968; children—Andrea, Jeff. With Stearns-Roger Engring. Corp., Denver, 1969—, design supr. water tech. group, 1971—, sr. process engr. Registered profl. engr., Colo., N.D., N.J. Mem. ASME, Pi Tau Sigma. Home: 2543 S Oneida St Denver CO 80224 Office: 4500 Cherry Creek Dr Denver CO 80217

HAMILTON, URIAH GEORGE, computer company executive; b. Spanish Town, Jamaica, W.I., Aug. 6, 1943; s. Egerton Constantine and Virginia (Dunkley) H.; m. Elizabeth Doris Williams, July, 1966; m. 2d, Louise Euphemia Henry, Dec. 31, 1977; children—Lydia Hariett. Student Mitchell Coll., 1970-72, U. New Haven, 1973-77, Mission Coll., Santa Clara, Calif., 1979-82. Sr. programmer, analyst Travelers Ins. Co., Hartford, Conn., 1972-73; project mgr. So. New Eng. Telephone Co., New Haven, 1973-78; systems officer Bankers Trust Co., N.Y.C., 1978-79; programming supr. Hewlett Packard Co., Palo Alto, Calif., 1979-80; info. systems mgr. Data Terminals Div. Hewlett Packard, 1980—; cons., lectr. Mem. Jamaica Assn. No. Calif., 1981—; adviser Belleville Widows and Orphans Home, Suffolk, Va., 1978—; mem. Conn. Black Caucus, 1974-77; pres. Black Assn. Registered Republicans, N.E. Conn., 1973-76. Served with USN, 1972-78. Mem. Am. Mgmt. Assn. (v.p. Peninsula chpt. 1982), Data Processing Mgmt. Assn. (pres. Peninsula chpt. 1983). Democrat. Jewish. Club: Family Fitness Ctr. (Foster City, Calif.). Office: 947 E Arques MS 430 Sunnyvale CA 94086

HAMILTON, WENDELL LEE, C.P.A.; b. Upland, Calif., Mar. 23, 1929; s. Perry C. and Nellie (Hampton) H.; m. Marilyn Jean Burge, May 11, 1929; children—Jeannine Hamilton Keevert, Janet. B.S., U. Oreg., 1953. C.P.A., Oreg. Assoc., Winn & Co., Eugene, Oreg., 1954-69, ptnr., 1959-69; ptnr. Coopers & Lybrand, Eugene, Oreg., 1969—. Served with USMCR, 1950-52. Mem. Eugene Area C. of C. (pres. 1982), Am. Inst. C.P.A.s, Oreg. Soc. C.P.A.s. Republican. Ch. Christ. Clubs: Eugene Country, Town, Lions, Civitan (past pres.), Elks. Office: 1600 Oak St Eugene OR 97401

HAMISTER, DONALD BRUCE, electronics co. exec.; b. Cleve., Nov. 29, 1920; s. Victor Carl and Bess Irene (Sutherland) H.; A.B. cum laude, Kenyon Coll., 1947; postgrad. Stanford U. 1948-49, U. Chgo., 1957; m. Margaret Irene Singiser, Dec. 22, 1946; children—Don Bruce, Tracy. Application engr. S.E. Joslyn Co., Cin., 1947-48; regional sales mgr. Joslyn Mfg. & Supply Co., St. Louis, 1950-52, marketing mgr., Chgo., 1953-55, asst. to pres., 1956-57, mgr. aircraft arrester dept., 1958-62, gen. mgr. electronic systems div., 1962-71, v.p., gen. mgr., dir., Goleta, Calif., 1973—, group v.p. indsl. products, 1974—, pres., chief exec. officer, 1978—, chmn. bd., 1979—, also mem. exec. com., pres. Joslyn Stainless Steels div., 1977-78; dir. Joslyn Industries (Can.) Ltd., Porcelanas Pinco S.A., Mex. Served to lt. USNR, 1942-46. Mem. IEEE, Airline Avionics Inst. (pres., chmn. 1972-74). Clubs: Univ. (Chgo.). Office: PO Box 817 Goleta CA 93017

HAMLETT, DALE EDWARD, artist, educator; b. Memphis, Mo., Aug. 15, 1921; s. John Emerson and Gladys Katherine (Reese) H.; B.S. cum laude in Edn., N.E. Mo. State U., 1944; M.A., U. N.Mex., 1963; postgrad. Am. Acad. Art, 1941, Chgo. Art Inst., 1947, Acad. Applied Art, 1946; m. Mozelle Lowe, Aug. 11, 1946; children—Sharon Lynn Hamlett Mullen, Brenda Joy Hamlett Kilmer, Gena Renee Hamlett Camp. Designer, Montgomery Ward and Co., Chgo., 1947-51; comml. artist Ward Hick Advt. Agy., Albuquerque, 1951-64; artist-in-residence N.Mex. Inst. Mining and Tech., Socorro, 1964-69; asso. prof. art Eastern N.Mex. U., Portales, 1969—; one-man shows: N.Mex. Tech. Inst., Pines Gallery, Ruidoso, N.Mex., Albuquerque Pub. Libraries, Eastern N.Mex. U., Territorial Gallery, Roswell, N.Mex., Garrett Studio-Gallery, Boise, Geronimo Mus.-Gallery, Truth or Consequences, N.Mex., Springville (Utah) Art Mus.; represented in various invitational traveling exhbns. with Mus. of N.Mex., Santa Fe, Fedn. of Rocky Mountain States. Denver; judge art shows; condr. workshops; lectr.-demonstrator. Elder First Presbyterian Ch., Portales. Recipient awards for water colors and gouache. Mem. N.Mex. Art League, Artists Equity, N.Mex. Watercolor Soc., Clovis-Portales Arts Council, AAUP, NEA, Llano Estacado Art Assn., Midwest Watercolor Soc. Home: 2104 S Ave H Portales NM 88130 Office: Eastern N Mex U Portales NM 88130

HAMM, E(LEANOR) JEANNE, manufacturing company executive; b. Vandergrift, Pa., Apr. 22, 1921; d. John Isadore and Bessie Gertrude (Hill) Walheim; m. Robert David Hamm, Nov. 2, 1941; children—David R., Patricia J. Hamm Hanson, Betsy A. Hamm Geery. A.A., Thompson Bus. Coll., 1940; student Pa. State U., 1945-46, McHenry County Coll., 1969-70, 1973-74. Sec., York (Pa.) Corp., 1950-59; sec. Packaging Corp. Am., Evanston, Ill., 1960-66; sec. Oak Industries Inc., San Diego, 1966-73, adminstrv. asst. to chief operating officer, 1974-76, asst. corp. sec., 1977-80, corp. sec., 1980—; tchr. office practices McHenry County Coll., 1976-78; lectr. in field. Recipient award as an outstanding woman in bus. San Diego YWCA, 1982. Mem. YWCA, Am. Soc. Corp. Secs. Republican. Club: VFW Aux. Office: Oak Industries Inc 16935 W Bernardo Dr San Diego CA 92127

HAMM, GEORGE ARDEIL, career guidance educator, consultant; b. San Diego, Aug. 13, 1934; s. Charles Ardeil and Vada Lillian (Sharrah) H.; m. Marilyn Kay Nichols, July 1, 1972; children—Robert Barry, Charles Ardeil II, Patricia Ann. B.S. in Music, No. Ariz. U., 1958, M.A. in Music Edn., 1961; M.A. in Ednl. Adminstrn., Calif. Lutheran Coll., 1978, M.S. in Guidance and Counseling, 1981. Cert. secondary sch. tchr., adminstr. pupil personnel services, Calif. Tchr. music Needles (Calif.) High Sch., 1958-61; tchr. career guidance, counselor Hueneme High Sch., Oxnard, Calif., 1961—; cons. applied sport psychology. Served with USMC, 1953-55; Korea. Mem. Am. Personnel and Guidance Assn., N. Am. Soc. Psychology of Sport and Phys. Activity, NEA, U.S. Judo Assn. Inc. (recipient 5th Degree Black Belt award, named sr. level coach of Judo, 1980). Republican. Mormon. Contbr. numerous articles to nat. and internat. Judo jours. Home: 1864 S Bearden Ct Oxnard CA 93033 Office: Hueneme High Sch 500 Bard Rd Oxnard CA 93033

HAMM, PATRICIA MALIZIA, medical technologist; b. Dearborn, Mich., June 15, 1945; d. Vincent Adam and Jeana (Bruno) Malizia; m. Vance Edgar Hamm, Nov. 28, 1971 (div.); 1 dau., Christy Jean. B.A. in Biology, Calif. State U.-Northridge, 1967. Lic. med. technologist, Calif. Tchr. St. Genevieve High Sch., Panorama City, Calif., 1967-69; intern in med. tech. Valley Presbyn. Hosp., Van Nuys, Calif., 1969-71; evening lab. supr. Palm Harbor Gen. Hosp., Garden Grove, Calif., 1971-72; med. technologist La Habra (Calif.) Community Hosp., 1972-75, microbiologist, epidemiologist, 1975—; adult edn. tchr.; cons. Mem. Am. Soc. Microbiologists, Assn. Practitioners Infection Control (sec. chpt. 1983). Contbr. articles to profl. publs. Home: 2549 Branch Ln Brea CA 92621 Office: 1251 W Lambert Rd La Habra CA 90631

HAMM, ROBERT MACGOWAN, research psychologist; b. Phila., Apr. 30, 1950; s. James Robert and Marian Todd (Miller) H. A.B., Princeton U., 1972; Ph.D., Harvard U., 1979. Sr. research assoc. Harvard Bus. Sch., Allston, Mass., 1979-80; tech. specialist Higher Order Software, Cambridge, Mass., 1980-81; research assoc. Ctr. for Research on Judgement and Policy, U. Colo., Boulder, 1981—; operator Sixth Day Consultants, Boulder, 1981—. Active Mass. Citizens Against Apartheid, 1979-80; Com. in Support of People in El Salvador, 1981-83. Recipient dissertation assistance award, NSF, 1978; winner Solomon Competition, Mass. Mental Health Ctr., Boston, 1981, 83. Mem. Am. Psychol. Assn., Judgment and Decision Making Group, Soc. Med. Decision Making, Sigma Xi. Author: (with others): Medical Choices, Medical Chances, 1981.

HAMMAD, DIAH MUHAMMED, electronics engineer; b. Palestine, Aug. 6, 1936; s. Muhamed M. and Mariam Y. Hammad; m. Sonia Lilard, Apr. 1971; children—Mohammed, Besma, Jamila, Tanya; m. Christel Charlotte Huebner, Dec. 3, 1979. Student Cairo Sch. Telecommunications, 1955-57; electronic engring. tech. assoc. degree N.H. Tech. Inst., 1970; B.S. in Engring., Calif. Western U., 1977, M.S. in Electronics Engring., 1982. Second class lic. Internat. Radio Telephony and Radio Telegraph. Engring. aide Applied Microwave, Andover, Mass., 1967-68; group leader Raytheon Mfg. Co., Manchester, N.H., 1970-73; tutor San Diego State U., 1974-75; field engr. Spectral Dynamics Corp., San Diego, 1973-79, Hickok Teaching Systems, Inc., Woburn, Mass., 1979-82; tng. supt. Saudi Consol. Electric Co., Dammam, Saudi Arabia, 1982—; writer tng. programs. Mem. Am. Soc. for Tng. and Devel., Am. Soc. for Engring. Edn. Republican. Moslen. Author elec. textbooks in Arabic.

HAMMAN, HUGH GENE, chiropractor; b. Ashurst, Ariz., Feb. 22, 1927; s. Wayne Michael and Flo (Curtis) H.; student N.Mex. State U., 1944; D.Chiropractics, Tex. Chiropractic Coll., 1948; div.; 1 dau., Nancy Hamman Naylor. Pvt. practice chiropractics, Safford, Ariz., 1950—. Exec. bd. Southeastern Ariz. Govts. Orgn., 1969—, chmn., 1972-73, 82—; chmn. Graham County Bd. Suprs.; Democratic precinct committeeman, Safford, Ariz., 1965-67; mem. conf. com. Nat. Dem. County Ofcls.; mem. governing bd. Health Systems Agy. Southeastern Ariz.; chmn. Graham County Bd. Health. Served with USNR, 1945-46. Named Chiropractor of the Year, Ariz. Chiropractic Assn., 1964. Mem. Am. Chiropractic Assn., Nat. Assn. Counties (public lands steering com., intergovernmental and local determination com., Indian affairs com.), Ariz. Suprs. Assn., Am. Legion. Democrat. Mem. Ch. of Jesus Christ of Latter-day Saints. Elk. Office: 520 11th Ave Safford AZ 85546

HAMMARSTEN, JAMES FRANCIS, internist; b. Grey Eagle, Minn., Mar. 25, 1920; s. Francis Ragnar and Julia Linnea (Hammargren) H.; B.S., U. Minn., 1943, M.B., 1944, M.D., 1945; m. Dorothea Marie Jung, Apr. 15, 1944; children—Linnea L., James E., Richard A. Intern, U. Okla. Hosps., 1944-45; resident in medicine U. Minn. Hosps. and VA Hosp., Mpls., 1947-49; asst. prof. medicine U. Minn., 1949-53; asst. prof. medicine U. Okla., 1953-54, assoc. prof., 1955-61, prof. medicine, 1961-62, Carl Puckett prof. pulmonary diseases and vice chmn. dept. medicine, 1966-67, prof., head dept. medicine, 1967-77, prof., medicine, 1977-78; prof. medicine U. Minn., 1962-66, U. Wash., 1978—; clin. prof. med. scis. U. Idaho, 1978—; adj. prof. health scis. Boise State U., 1978-82, Disting. prof., 1982—; asst. chief med. service VA Hosp.,

Mpls., 1949-53; chief med. services VA Hosp., Oklahoma City, 1953-62; chief medicine St. Paul-Ramsey Hosp., 1962-66; chief med. service Boise VA Med. Ctr., 1978-81; cons. Internat. Union Against Tb, 1977-78; vis. prof. Leannec Hosp., Paris, 1977, 78; mem. adv. council Nat. Heart and Lung Inst., 1970-72; lectr. U. Uppsala (Sweden), 1977. Mem. Crutcho (Okla.) Sch. Bd., 1956-62. Served to capt. AUS, 1945-47, USAF, 1953. Hammasten Conf. Room at VA Hosp., Oklahoma City, Hammersten lectureship at Okla. U. Coll. Medicine named in his honor. Fellow A.C.P., Am. Coll. Chest Physicians; mem. Internat. Union Against Tb, Okla. Heart Assn., Okla. Thoracic Soc. (pres. 1961), Am. Heart Assn., Am.-Israel Med. Found. (trustee), AMA, Assn. Profs. Medicine, Idaho Lung Assn. (dir. 1981), Am. Fedn. Clin. Research (chmn. Midwest sect. 1960), Am. Lung Assn. (dir. 1968-80), Am. Thoracic Soc. (pres. 1969-70), Central Soc. Clin. Research (sec.-treas. 1960-65, pres., 1967-68), Am. Clin. and Climatolgical Assn., Am. Assn. Physicians, AAAS, Am. Geriatric Soc., Sigma Xi, Alpha Omega Alpha. Democrat. Lutheran. Club: Boise Rotary. Editor, Jour. Lab. and Clin. Medicine, 1976; chmn. editorial bd. Med. Sch. sect. Jour. Okla. Med. Assn. 1959-62; contbr. articles to profl. jours., chpts. to books. Home: 2754 Argentina Ln Boise ID 83704 Office: Sch Health Scis Boise State U Boise ID 83725

HAMMER, ARMAND, petroleum co. exec.; b. N.Y.C., May 21, 1898; s. Julius and Rose (Robinson) H.; m. Baroness Olga von Root, Mar. 14, 1927; 1 son, Julian A.; m. 2d. Angela Zevely, Dec. 19, 1943; m. 3d, Frances Barrett, Jan. 26, 1956. B.S., Columbia U., 1919, M.D., 1921; LL.D. (hon.), Pepperdine U., 1978, South Eastern U., Washington, 1978; Columbia U., New York, 1978; University of Colorado, Boulder, 1979; Aix-en-Provence U., France, 1981. Pres., Allied Am. Corp., N.Y.C., 1923-25, A. Hammer Pencil Co., N.Y.C., London and Moscow, 1925-30, Hammer Galleries, N.Y.C., 1930—, United Distillers Am. Inc., N.Y.C., J.W. Dant Distilling Co., N.Y.C. and Dant, Ky., 1943-54; chmn. bd., pres., chief exec. officer Occidental Petroleum Corp., Los Angeles, 1957—; pres., chmn. bd. MBS, 1957-58; chmn. M. Knoedler and Co., Inc., New York, 1972—. dir. First Bank & Trust Co., Perth Amboy, N.J., City Nat. Bank, Beverly Hills, Calif., Can. Occidental Petroleum Ltd., Calgary, Alta., Can., Belgische Petroleum Raffinaderij N.V. (RBP), Antwerp, Belgium; hon. dir. Fla. Nat. Bank of Jacksonville. Mem. Citizens' Food Com., 1945-47; chmn. Am. Aid to France, 1947; mem. adv. bd. Inst. Peace, 1950-54; mem. Com. of Laity for Cath. Charities, 1946-48; active establishment Franklin Delano Roosevelt's residence Campobello as U.S.-Can. Peace Park; mem. Pub. Adv. Com. on U.S. Trade Policy, 1968—, Nat. Petroleum Council, 1968—; mem. econ. devel. bd., exec. com. City of Los Angeles, 1968—; mem. adv. com. Com. for Greater Calif., 1969—; mem. Los Angeles Bd. Mcpl. Art Commrs.; mem. adv. bd. Los Angeles Beautiful, Inc., 1969—; mem. pub. adv. com. on U.S. Trade Policy, 1968-69; mem. vis. com. UCLA, 1947—; bd. govs. MCOSS-Family Health and Nursing, 1949-61; trustee, chmn. exec. com. Salk Inst. Biol. Studies, 1969, sponsor Armand Hammer Center for Cancer Biology; trustee, exec. com. acquisitions com. Los Angeles County Mus. Art; bd. govs. Monmouth Meml. Hosp.; trustee U. N. Africa Assn., Eleanor Roosevelt. Meml. Found., United for Calif.; bd. govs. Eleanor Roosevelt Cancer Found.; bd. dirs. Los Angeles World Affairs Council; bd. govs. UN Assn. of United States, 1976—; Nat. trustee, National Symphony, 1977—; Pres., Found. Internat. Inst. of Human Rights, Geneva, 1977—; mem. Adv. Comm. for the Fogg Art Museum, 1977—; bd. dirs., Corcoran Gallery of Art, Washington, D.C., 1978—; hon. mem., trustees Denver Art Museum, 1980—; bd. dirs., Business Comm. for the Arts, New York, 1980—; mem. Nat. Support Council, U.S. Comm. for UNICEF, New York, 1980—; Hon. mem., Royal Scottish Academy, Edinburgh, 1981—; mem. adv. bd., Center for Strategic and Internat. Studies, Washington, D.C., 1981—; mem. Fine Arts Comm., U.S. Dept. of State, 1981—; chmn., President's Cancer Panel, 1981—; bd. dirs. Nat. Com. U.S.-China Relations, 1982—, Am. Com. East-West Accord, 1982—; internat. bd. govs. Bob Hope Internat. Heart Research Inst.; bd. dirs. Am. Liver Found.; mem. exec. com. Pres.'s Council Internat. Youth Exchange, numerous other civic and polit. activities. Decorated comdr. Order of Crown (Belgium); comdr. Order Andres Bello (Venezuela); Order of Friendship among Peoples (USSR); Mexican Order of the Aztec Eagle; Order of the Legion of Honor, (France); Royal Order of the Polar Star, (Sweden); Grand Officer to the Merit of the Republic, (Italy); recipient Humanitarian award Eleanor Roosevelt Cancer Found., 1962; City commendation Mayor Los Angeles, 1968; Spl. award Los Angeles Econ. Devel. Bd., 1969; Disting. Honoree of Yr., Nat. Art Assn., 1978, numerous other awards and decorations. Mem. Am. Petroleum Inst. (exec. com., dir.), Nat. Petroleum Council, Internat. Inst. Human Rights, AMA, N.Y. County Med. Assn., Alpha Omega Alpha, Mu Sigma, Phi Sigma Delta. Clubs: Los Angeles Petroleum; Lotos. Author: Quest of the Romanoff Treasure; subject of biographies: The Remarkable Life of Dr. Armand Hammer, 1975, Larger than Life (both by Bob Considine). Office: 10889 Wilshire Blvd Los Angeles CA 90024*

HAMMER, FRANK JORGEN, consulting psychologist; b. Appleton, Wis., Jan. 19, 1918; s. Frank Joseph and Marie (Rasmussen) H.; m. Joyce Frances Waldhaus, Apr. 7, 1968; children—Mark, Laurel, Dan, Frank, Aaron, Michelle, Matthew; m. 2d., Emily Sue Speed, Apr. 9, 1983. B.A., Lawrence U., 1942; Ph.D., U. Chgo., 1952. Lic. psychologist, Wash. Chief psychologist Madigan Army Hosp., 1952-55, Community Psychiat. Clinic, Seattle, 1955-64; pvt. practice cons. psychology, Seattle, Mountlake Terrace, Wash., 1964—; cons. Everett Ctr. Youth Services, Seattle Police Dept., King County Juvenile Ct., Valley Gen. Hosp., Snohomish County Family and Juvenile Cts., Seattle Sch. Dist.; clin. instr. U. Wash. Med. Sch. Mayor Mountlake Terrace, 1960-64; chmn., bd. dirs. Source Found. Mentally Retarded Children; bd. dirs. Snohomish County Alcoholism, Mental Health Services; mem. Snohomish County Bd. Freeholders, 1968-69. Served to lt. col. U.S. Army, 1942-55. Recipient football scholarship Lawrence U., 1938-42. Mem. Wash. State Psychol. Assn., Am. Psychol. Assn., Western Psychol. Assn., Am. Group Psychotherapy Assn., Assn. Labor-Mgmt. Adminstrs. and Cons. Alcoholism, Mace, Sigma Xi, Beta Theta Pi. Home and Office: 22506 66th Ave West Mountlake Terrace WA 98043

HAMMER, JULIUS MARX, accountant; b. N.Y.C., May 10, 1921; s. David and Frieda (Komornick) H.; B.S. in Accounting, U. Calif., Los Angeles, 1944; m. Georgine Dombroff, Nov. 24, 1946; children—Linda J. Hammer Krayton, Robert J. Founding partner Cohen Hammer & Co., C.P.A.'s, Beverly Hills, Calif., 1953-72; v.p. Inter Polymer Industries, Inc., Los Angeles, 1967—; partner Alexander Grant & Co., C.P.A.'s, 1972—; chief fin. officer, gen. mgr. Royal Wholesale Cigar Co., Ltd., Los Angeles, 1976—. Served with USAAF, 1942-43. Mem. Am. Inst. C.P.A.'s, Calif. Soc. C.P.A.'s. Republican. Jewish. Clubs: Del Rey Yacht, Masons. Home: 13243 Vanowen St Apt 8 North Hollywood CA 91605 Office: 2939 Bandini Blvd Los Angeles CA 90023

HAMMER, LOUIS EUGENE, educator; b. Lusk, Wyo., Oct. 17, 1955; s. Malcolm I. and Viola L. (Payne) H.; B.A. in Math. and Stats., U. Wyo., 1978, M.S. in Stats., 1980. Head math. dept. Glendo (Wyo.) Pub. Sch., 1980—; community edn. tchr. computer literacy. Vol. Emergency med. tech. Glendo Ambulance Service. Mem. Am. Statis. Assn., Nat. Council Tchrs. Math., Wyo. Edn. Assn., NEA. Home: PO Box 365 Glendo WY 82213 Office: Glendo Pub Sch PO Box 68 Glendo WY 82213

HAMMERS, OLIVER BERTRAND, mechanical contracting company executive; b. St. Joseph, Mo., Nov. 23, 1924; s. Earl E. and Lola M. (Hetherington) H.; B.S. in Elec. Engring., U. Kans., 1950; m. Patricia Ruth Dillman, Nov. 27, 1954; children—Patrick James, David Earl. With Natkin & Co., 1950—, v.p. spl. assignments, Omaha, 1966-68, exec. v.p., mgr. S. Central div., Dallas, 1968-80, res., chief exec. officer, Denver, 1980—, chmn. bd., 1980—, also pres.; dir. Natkin Service Co., Johansen Co.; officer, dir. Charter Page, Inc. Served with AUS, 1942-46. Mem. Mech. Contractors Assn. (Man of Year award Tex. chpt. 1979), Denver C. of C. Clubs: Dallas; Denver Athletic; Columbine Country. Office: Nutkin & Co 2700 S Zuni St Englewood CO 80110

HAMMERSLEY, FREDERICK HAROLD, artist; b. Salt Lake City, Jan. 5, 1919; s. Harold Frederick and Anna Maria (Westberg) H.; student U. Idaho, 1936-38, Chouinard Art Sch., Los Angeles, 1940-42, 46-47, Ecole des Beaux Arts, Paris, 1945, Jepson Art Sch., Los Angeles, 1947-50. One-man shows: Pasadena (Calif.) Art Mus., 1961, Heritage Gallery, Los Angeles, 1961, 63, Occidental Coll., Los Angeles, 1962, Calif. Palace Legion of Honor, San Francisco, La Jolla (Calif.) Art Mus., 1963, Santa Barbara Mus. Art, 1965, Hollis Galleries, San Francisco, 1966, U. N.Mex., Albuquerque, 1969, 75, Middendorf/Lane Gallery, Washington, 1977, L.A. Louver Gallery, Venice, Calif., 1978, 81, others; group shows: Whitney Mus., N.Y.C., 1962, Mus. Modern Art, N.Y.C., 1965, U. Ill., 1968, Los Angeles County Mus. Art, 1977, Albuquerque Mus., 1980-81, M. Knoedler Gallery, Smithsonian Instn., Corcoran Gallery Art, Albright-Knox Art Mus., Walker Art Ctr., J.B. Speed Mus., Houston Mus. Art, Butler Inst. Am. Art, San Francisco Mus. Modern Art, Los Angeles County Mus. Art, Dallas Mus. Fine Arts; rep. in permanent collections; Corcoran Gallery Art, Washington, Butler Inst. Am. art, Univ. Art Mus., Berkeley, Calif., Oakland (Calif.) Mus., Santa Barbara Mus. Art, Los Angeles County Mus. Art, LaJolla Mus. Art, Foote, Cone & Belding, Los Angeles, U. N.Mex., Washington Post, Petersburg Press, London, Eng., also pvt. collections; tchr. painting, drawing and design Jepson Art Sch., Los Angeles, 1948-51, Pasadena Art Mus., 1956-61, Pomona Coll., Claremont, Calif., 1953-62, Chouinard Art Sch., Los Angeles, 1964-68, U. N.Mex., Albuquerque, 1968-71. Served with AUS, 1942-46. John Simon Guggenheim fellow, 1973; Nat. Endowment for Arts grantee, 1975, 77. Address: 608 Carlisle SE Albuquerque NM 87106

HAMMOND, DONNA JEAN, correctional cons.; b. Denver, May 2, 1947; d. Clarence Howard and Rose Marie (Richardson) McCabe; B.A., UCLA, 1969; M.S.W., San Diego State U., 1974. Dep. probation officer Los Angeles County, 1969-72; sch. social worker Lemon Grove Sch. Dist., San Diego, 1973; psychiat. social worker Calif. Dept. Health, Ventura, 1974-75; parole agt. Calif. Youth Authority, Camarillo, 1975-78, treatment team supr., 1979; asst. supt. Fenner Canyon Youth Conservation Camp, Valyermo, Calif., 1979-80; correctional cons. Calif. Youth Authority, Los Angeles, 1981-82. Coordinator, United Way. Recipient Superior Accomplishment award Assn. Cert. Social Workers, 1977-78. Mem. Am. Correctional Assn., Am. Mgmt. Assn., Nat. Assn. Social Workers, Calif. Probation, Parole and Corrections Assn., ACLU, Nat. Polit. Women's Caucus, Women, U.S.A., LWV, Littlerock C. of C. Democrat. Methodist. Office: 143 S Glendale Ave Suite 305 Glendale CA 91205

HAMMOND, ED R., labor relations administrator, educator; b. Winnipeg, Can., Dec. 19, 1941; s. Harry A. and Mary Ethel (Sharpe) H.; m. M. Lise, May 3, 1969. B.S. in Personnel and Indsl. Relations, Utah State U., 1967; M.B.A., U. Nev., 1971; postgrad. U. Ariz., U. Houston. Instr. Rio Salado Community Coll. and Phoenix Community Coll., Ariz., 1978—, U. Phoenix, 1981—; sr. labor relations adminstr. and mgmt. trainer Salt River Project, Phoenix, 1977—. Mem. Employee and Labor Relations com. Am. Soc. Personnel Adminstrn., Phoenix Personnel Mgmt. Assn. (bd. dirs.), Am. Soc. Tng. dirs. Office: The Salt River Project Labor Relations Dept PO Box 1980 Phoenix AZ 85001

HAMMOND, FREDERICK FISHER, musician, educator; b. Binghamton, N.Y., Aug. 7, 1937; s. Clarence Albert and Sarah Reva (Fisher) H.; B.A., Yale U., 1958, Ph.D., 1965. Instr. music U. Chgo., 1962-65; asst. prof. music Queens Coll., CUNY, 1966-68; asst. prof. music UCLA, 1968-73, assoc. prof., 1973-80, prof., 1980—; asst. music dir. Clarion Music Soc., N.Y.C., 1977—, Castel-franco Veneto Festival, 1975—. Am. Acad. Rome fellow, 1965-66, Harvard Centre for Renaissance Studies fellow, 1973. Mem. Am. Musicological Soc., Conn. Acad. Arts and Scis., Elizabethan Club Yale U., Phi Beta Kappa. Democrat. Episcopalian. Contbr. articles on 17th. century music to scholarly jours., edits. medieval music theory. Recs. for Nonesuch, Decca, CRI, Orion, ABC rec. cos. Office: Dept Music U Calif 405 Hilgard Ave Los Angeles CA 90024

HAMMOND, MARK STEVEN, medical services company executive; b. San Diego, Sept. 10, 1956; s. Clyde Newewll and Gloria Genevieve (McKinstry) H. A.A. in Bus. and Psychology, Mesa Coll., 1976; B.A. in Indsl. Psychology, San Diego State U., 1980; M. Bus. Mgmt., U. Redlands, 1983; lic. hosp. adminstr., Calif. Acct., Delta Automotive, San Diego, 1976-78; service asst. dept. personnel Price Co., San Diego, 1978-80; adminstr. Longer Life Found. Ocean View Hosp., Encinitas, Calif., 1980-82; v.p. ops. Indsl. Med. Services, Inc., San Diego, 1982—. Mem. Nat. Soc. Med./Dental Mgmt. Cons., Am. Mgmt. Assn., Med. Group Mgmt., Assn. Republican. Methodist. Club: North Country Personnel. Home: 2640 Angell Ave San Diego CA 92122

HAMMOND, MAUDIE THOMAS, artist, film producer, dancer, Realtor, writer; b. Rexburg, Idaho, d. Ward J. and Loretta (Eckersell) Thomas; student Mills Coll., 1957, U. Calif., Berkeley, 1963-65; children—Dianne Simone, Matthew Henry. Profl. dancer in films and TV, N.Y.C., 1942-46; owner Maudie Hammond Sch. Dance, 1959-64; owner The Hammond Real Estate Co., Orinda, Calif., 1964—. Mem. Contra Costa Bd. Realtors, NOW, League Women Voters, KQED Endl. TV, Calif. Alumni Assn., Media Alliance. Club: Toastmasters. Office: 2 Vashell Way Orinda CA 94563

HAMMOND, ROBERT DEAN, accountant; b. Denver, Sept. 10, 1935; s. James Delbert and Erna (Fillenberg) H.; m. Margaret Murphy Gorrie; children—Lind Ruth Toldness, James Dean, Steven Leroy. C.P.A., Colo. Ptnr. Charles A. Taylor & Assocs. (merged into Clifton, Gunderson & Co.), Denver, 1971—, regional dir. ops., govt. services dir., 1981—. Pres. Northglenn Recreation Dist., 1970. Served as sgt. USAF, 1952-57. Named Boss of Yr., Northglenn Jaycees, 1978. Mem. Am. Inst. C.P.A.s, Colo. Soc. C.P.A.s (contining edn. award, pres. elect), Mcpl. Fin. Officers Assn., Adams County C. of C. (pres.). Republican. Club: Northglenn Rotary. Office: Clifton Gunderson & Co 10190 Bannock St Suite 140 Denver CO 80221

HAMMOND, RONALD ALBERT, elec. engr.; b. Belleville, Ill., Feb. 11, 1938; s. Albert A. and Herma Vera (Dewoody) H.; B.S. in E.E., Purdue U., 1959, M.S. in E.E., 1961; postgrad. U. Washington, 1961-63, U. Ala., 1964-65; m. Barbara Jane Dorward, June 14, 1959; children—Bruce, Katherine, Margaret, Matthew. Controls engr. Caterpillar Tractor Co., Peoria, Ill., 1959-61; controls engr. Boeing Airplane Co., Seattle, 1961-63, Huntsville, Ala., 1963-64; simulation designer IBM Corp., Fed. Systems Div., Huntsville, Ala., 1964-65; control/software engr. Boeing Aerospace, Seattle, 1965-69; simulation engr. Cornell Aero. Lab., Buffalo, 1969-74; software engr., project mgr. Boeing Aerospace/Boeing Computer Services, Seattle, Wash., 1974—; instr. software/computer sci. Boeing, 1979-81; guest lectr. dept. transp. engring. Seattle Univ., 1980—. Recipient Instr. Research fellowship Purdue Univ., 1959-61. Mem. IEEE, Soc. Computer Simulation, Profl. Group Tech. Writing, Sigma Xi. Unitarian. Contbr. articles to various publs. Home: 17164 NE 5th Pl Bellevue WA 98008 Office: 565 Andover Park W Tukwila WA 98188

HAMMOND, RUSSELL IRVING, ret. educator, coll. dean; b. Yorkton, Sask., Can., Aug. 29, 1908; s. Walter Irving and Dora (Claussen) H. came to U.S., 1919; B.A., Morningside Coll., 1929; M.A., U. Colo., 1934; Ed.D., Columbia, 1942; m. Ola Arline Leonard, June 7, 1933; 1 dau., DiAnn Arline. High sch. coach, tchr., Auburn, Iowa, 1929-31; supt. schs., Lanesboro, Iowa, 1931-34, Castana, Iowa, 1934-40, Mt. Vernon, Iowa, 1942-42; instr. Cornell Coll., 1942-44; prof. edn. Willamette U., 1946-47; prof. ednl. adminstrn. U. Wyo., Laramie, 1947-74, prof. emeritus, 1974—, head curriculum and research center, 1947-55, head div. grad. study Coll. Edn., 1956-66, asso. dean Coll. Edn., 1966-74. Dir. Bankers Res Life Ins. Co., Denver. Bd. dirs. Rocky Mountain Ednl. Lab. Served as lt. USNR, 1944-46. Mem. Council Ednl. Facility Planners, NEA, Am. Assn. Sch. Adminstrs., Assn. for Supervision and Curriculum Devel., Nat. Assn. Secondary Sch. Prins., Wyo. Edn. Assn., Nat. Ret. Tchrs. Assn. (Wyo. dir.), Wyo. Ret. Tchrs. Assn., Am. Assn. Ret. Persons, Ret. Officers Assn., Phi Delta Kappa. Methodist. Mason, Lion. Author: Retirement Systems in Selected States of the U.S.; Teacher Supply and Demand; Success of Small-School Superintendents, Teacher Aides, and School Surveys. Home: 816 S 17th St Laramie WY 82070

HAMNER, J. ROBERT, mfg. engr.; b. Nettleton, Ark., Mar. 21, 1938; s. Craig Nettles and Lovena Dudley H.; student Wichita State U., 1957, U. Colo., 1962; B.A. in Bus. Adminstrn., Columbia (Mo.) Coll., 1978; m. Mar. 21, 1959; children—Brent Alan, Kindra Lee. Tool engr. Boeing Aerospace, Wichita, Kans., 1956-59; mfg. engr. Martin-Marietta, Littleton, Colo., 1960-64; tool engr. Dow Chem. Co., Boulder, Colo., 1964-65; cost estimator C.A.W. Norgren Co., Littleton, 1965—. Registered profl. engr., Calif. Mem. Soc. Mfg. Engrs. (certified mfg. engr.). Republican. Clubs: Timberline Toastmasters (treas. 1972-76), Asgard Investment (pres. 1969-71). Home: 4482 E Lake Circle N Littleton CO 80121 Office: 5400 S Delaware St Littleton CO 80120

HAMNER, KARL CLEMENS, ret. educator; b. Salina, Kans., Oct. 15, 1908; s. William Marion and Millie (Swenson) H.; A.B., U. Calif. at Berkeley, 1931; M.S., U. Chgo., 1934, Ph.D., 1935; m. Gladys Gerner, July 24, 1941; children—Lois Karen (Mrs. Phillip A. McLaughlin, dec.), Melinda Lee (Mrs. Itzhak Emanuel Friedman). Asso. plant physiologist U.S. Dept. Agr., Beltsville, Md., 1936-37; instr. botany U. Chgo., 1937-40; plant physiologist U.S. Plant, Soil and Nutrition Lab., Ithaca, N.Y., 1940-48, dir. lab., 1946-48; chmn. dept. botany U. Calif. at Los Angeles, 1948-58, prof. botany, 1958-76. Cons. Atomic Energy project, 1949-54; mem. Gov's. Radiol. Safety Adv. Com. for Calif., 1953-55. Carnegie Inst. fellow, 1949. Fellow AAAS; mem. Am. Inst. for Biol. Scis., Am. Soc. Naturalists, Am. Soc. Plant Physiologists, Bot. Soc. Am., Sigma Xi. Contbr. articles to profl. jours. Home: 11917 Ayres Ave Los Angeles CA 90064

HAMPTON, CLYDE ROBERT, lawyer; b. Worland, Wyo., May 10, 1926; s. Clyde E. and Mabel (Lasley) H.; B.A., Columbia, 1949; LL.B., U. Colo., 1952; m. Dorothy Laura Gaebelein, June 3, 1949; 1 dau., Dorothy Norma. Admitted to Colo. bar, 1952; gen. atty. legal dept. Continental Oil Co., Denver, 1952—. Chmn. adv. com. on rules and regulations Com. on Air and Water Conservation Am. Petroleum Inst.; chmn. Colo. Air and Water Conservation Com., Colo. Petroleum Council. Past pres. Denver Assn. for Retarded Citizens, also mem. bd. dirs.; sec. Denver Bd. for Mentally Retarded and Seriously Handicapped; bd. dirs. Conservative Bapt. Theol. Sem., Denver, 1977—. Served as capt. USNR. Recipient Disting. Service award Colo. Petroleum Council, 1966, 70, Leadership award, 1969. Mem. Am. Petroleum Council, ABA (mem. council natural resources sect., mem. pub. lands com., chmn. water quality subcom. environ. quality com. natural resources sect., chmn. governing council sect., chmn. nominating com. governing council sect.), Denver, Colo. bar assns., Rocky Mountain Oil and Gas Assn. (chmn. environ. affairs com.), Am. Petroleum Inst. (chmn. environ. law com.), Am. Mining Congress (council), Sigma Chi, Phi Alpha Delta. Republican. Clubs: Columbia Alumni of Colo.; Denver Petroleum, Law (Denver), Co-author legal handbook; author articles on pollution and oil industry. Home: 14830 E Jefferson Ave Aurora CO 80014 Office: Anaconda Tower Bldg 555 17th St Denver CO 80202

HAMPTON, LUCILE PAQUIN SMITH (MRS. LAWRENCE CHARLES HAMPTON), artist, educator; b. Dubuque, Iowa, Jan. 7, 1904; d. Albert Hugo and Lola (Lichtenberger) Smith; student Dubuque Acad. Music (Iowa), 1911-21; diploma Chgo. Acad. Fine Arts, 1923; postgrad. Pasadena City Coll., 1947-48, 64, 67-68; UCLA, 1965-66; B.A. in Art, Calif. State U.-Los Angeles, 1973; m. Lawrence Charles Hampton, Dec. 16, 1930 (dec. Apr. 4, 1960); children—Lawrence Charles, Nancy Jeanne (Mrs. Merle Willis Asper, Jr.), Elizabeth Mary (Mrs. John Erskine). Artist advt. dept. Union Lithographing Co., Little Rock, 1923-24; art dir. advt. dept. M. Rich & Bros. Co., Atlanta, 1924-25; head fashion layout artist advt. dept. May Co., Los Angeles, 1925-29; sr. artist advt. dept. David Jones Ltd., Sydney, Australia, 1929-30; fashion illustrator Home mag., Sydney, 1930; cover designer Woman's Budget Mag., Sydney, 1929-30; freelance artist Broadway-Hale Dept. Stores, J.W. Robinson and Co. Dept. Stores, Los Angeles, 1930-35; fashion illustrator Robinson Accents Mag., Los Angeles, 1935; head dept. art, tchr. art essentials and history of art Anoakia Sch. Girls, Arcadia, Calif., 1963-66; substitute tchr. San Marino (Calif.) Unified Sch. Dist., 1973—; freelance artist Lucile Hampton Greeting Cards, San Marino, 1960—. Mem. Girl Scout Leader's Club, San Marino, 1948-56, pres., 1950-51, leader troop 73, 1948-56; mem. PTA, G.S. Stoneman Sch. (exec. bd. 1944-46), H.E. Huntington Sch., San Marino High Sch., 1941-61, South Pasadena-San Marino High Sch. 1950-55. Mem. P.E.O. (pres. chpt. MK 1955-56), DAR (chpt. regent San Marino 1960-61), Children Am. Revolution (sr. adviser, sr. pres. chpt. El Molino Viejo 1958-64, social dir. cotillion ball 1958-59), San Marino Rep. Women's Club Federated, AAUW (bd. dirs. Costa Mesa-Newport Beach br. 1982-83), Kappa Pi (Gamma Tau chpt.), San Marino Community Ch. Women (guild leader), Friday Morning Club Jrs. (dir. fashion show 1934). Republican. Presbyterian. Clubs: Euterpe Opera Reading (bd. dirs. 1956-59), Opera Guild of Los Angeles, Women's Athletic (Los Angeles); Pacific Coast; San Marino Women's. Address: 2775 Mesa Verde Dr East G-106 Costa Mesa CA 92626

HAMRIN, CARL ERIC, govt. ofcl.; b. Falun, Sweden, June 5, 1921; s. Carl Gustav and Hanna Matilda (Nye) H.; came to U.S., 1923, naturalized, 1943; student Wash. State U., 1941, Santa Rosa (Calif.) Jr. Coll., 1942, Reedley (Calif.) Coll., 1956; m. Wanda Marie Nelson, Oct. 14, 1950; children—Karen Marie Hamrin Cox, Mark Eric. Engaged in agribus., Selma, Calif., 1945-50; foreman Consol. Mosquito Abatement Dist., Selma, 1950-65; owner pest control bus., Fresno County, Calif., 1963-65; mgr. Klamath Vector Control Dist., Klamath Falls, Oreg., 1965-70; dist. mgr. Jackson County Vector Control Dist., White City, Oreg., 1970—. Served with AUS, 1942-45. Decorated Bronze Star with oak leaf cluster, Purple Heart with oak leaf cluster. Mem. Am., Utah mosquito control assns., N.W., Calif. mosquito and vector control assns. Republican. Lutheran. Club: Lions. Author papers on mosquito control. Inventor cassette tape eraser. Home: 845 S 5th St Central Point OR 97502 Office: 180 Antelope Rd White City OR 97501

HAN, ITTAH, financial strategy planner, systems designer; b. Java, Indonesia, Jan. 29, 1939; came to U.S., 1956, naturalized, 1972; s. Hongtjioe and Tsuiying (Chow) H.; B.S.E. in Mech. Engring. and Elec.

Engring., Walla Walla Coll., 1960; M.A. in Math., U. Calif., Berkeley, 1962; B.A. in French, U. Colo., 1965, M.S. in Elec. Engring., 1961; M.S.E. in Computer Engring., U. Mich., 1970; M.S. in Computer Sci., U. Wis., 1971; M.B.A. in Mgmt., U. Miami (Fla.), 1973; B.A. in Econs., U. Nev., 1977; M.B.A. in Tax, Golden Gate U., 1979, M.B.A. in Real Estate, 1979, M.B.A. in Fin., 1980, M.B.A. in Banking, 1980. Salesman, Watkins Products, Walla Walla, Wash., 1956-60; instr. Sch. Engring. U. Colo., Denver, 1964-66; systems engr. IBM Corp., Oakland, Calif., 1967-69, Scidata Inc., Miami, Fla., 1971-72; chief of data processing Golden Gate Bridge, Hwy. and Transp. Dist., San Francisco, 1973-74; mgr. info. systems tech. and advanced systems devel. Summa Corp., Las Vegas, Nev., 1975-78; mgr. systems devel. Fred Harvey Inc., Brisbane, Calif., 1978-81; chmn. corp. systems steering com., mgr. systems planning Amfac Hotel & Resorts, Inc., 1978-81 tax planner, chief exec. Ittahhan Corp., 1981—; exec. v.p. Developers Unltd. Group, Las Vegas, 1982—; instr. U. Nev. Sch. Elec. Engring., Reno, 1981—; systems designer, cons. in field. Mem. IEEE, Assn. Computing Machinery, Am. Math. Assn., Inst. Cert. Fin. Planners, Am. Contract Bridge League. Republican. Home and Office: PO Box 27025 Garside Sta Las Vegas NV 89126

HANAN, JOE JOHN, horticulture educator, investigator; b. Buffalo, Jan. 22, 1931; s. Ernest Byron and Leslie Marion (Elliott) H.; m. Julia Watkins, Aug. 24, 1956; children—John Watkins, Ernest Lawrence, Sarah Lois. B.S., U. Mo., 1952; M.S., Colo. State U., 1959; Ph.D., Cornell U., 1963. Greenhouse grower, Mo., 1948-53; greenhouse foreman U. Mo., Columbia, 1950-51; grad. research asst. Colo. State U., Ft. Collins, 1957-59, Cornell U., Ithaca, 1959-63, research assoc., 1963; asst. prof. Colo. State U., Ft. Collins, 1963-67, assoc. prof., 1967-72, prof., 1972-74, prof. and leader, 1974—; cons. Danish Culture Corp, Sardinia, 1969, Julicher's, Johannesburg, S.A., 1969, Israeli Flower Growers, 1970, Cypriot Govt., Paphos Water Project, 1977-78, Carnation producers, Ziticauna, Mex., 1980. Pres. Ft. Collins Poudre Valley Lions Club, 1972, sec., 1977—. Served with USMC, 1953-57. Recipient Best Friend of Industry award Colo. Flower Grower's Assn. 1979. Mem. Am. Soc. Hort. Sci. (Alex Laurie award 1963, 1982, Kenneth Post award 1966, 1976), Internat. Hort. Soc., Am. Soc. Plant Physiologists, Am. Agronomy Soc., AAAS, Sigma Xi, Pi Alpha Xi, Phi Kappa Phi, Gamma Sigma Delta. Republican. Mem. Christian Ch. (Disciples of Christ.). Clubs: Ft. Collins Poudre Valley Lions, Poudre Investment Enterprises. Author: (with W.D. Holley, K.L. Goldsberry) Greenhouse Management, 1978; Plant Environmental Measurement, 1983; contbr. numerous articles to tech. jours. Office: 113A Shepardson Colo State U Ft Collins CO 80523

HANAVAN, GWENDOLYN MAE, accountant; b. Washington, Jan. 21, 1943; d. Arthur N. and Esther J. (Spady) Shane; m. Louis Wayne Hanavan Jr., May 28, 1965; 1 dau., Lisa Dawn. B.S. magna cum laude in Bus. Adminstrn., U. No. Colo., 1978. C.P.A., Oreg. Mem. staff C.P.A. firms in Colo. and Oreg., 1978-80; ptnr. Erickson & Hanavan, C.P.A.s, Eugene, Oreg., 1981—. Bd. dirs. Maude Kern's Art Ctr., v.p., 1981-82; treas. Lane County chpt. ARC, 1982—; bd. dirs. Oreg. Repertory Theatre, 1983—. Recipient Gold Key award Colo. Soc. C.P.A.s, 1978. Mem. Oreg. Soc. C.P.A.s (career activities com.), Am. Inst. C.P.A.s, Profl. Women's Network of Oreg., AAUW. Office: 135 W 10th Eugene OR 97401

HANBERG, MELVIN, Realtor; b. Detroit, May 28, 1923; s. Julius and Betty (Brown) H.; B.S., U. Calif. at Los Angeles, 1948; m. Alice Conn, Dec. 31, 1950; children—Francine B., M. Julian II. Active as engr., 1948-60; owner Active Realty, Hawthorne, Calif., 1960—; communications cons. Served to lt. col. Signal Corps, AUS. Mem. Nat. Assn. Realtors, Am. Family Records Assn. (nat. dir.), Res. Officers Assn. Office: 4444 W El Segundo Blvd Hawthorne CA 90250

HANCE, MARGARET T., mayor Phoenix; b. Spirit Lake, Iowa, July 2, 1923; widow; children—Richard, Galen. Student U. Ariz., 1942-44; B.A., Scripps Coll., 1945. Producer pub. affairs documentaries for TV, 1967-69; writer, producer Holiday World Travel Show for radio, 1971-75; mem. Phoenix Parks and Recreation Bd., 1965-71; mem. Phoenix City Council, 1971-75, mayor, 1975—; dir. valley Nat. Bank; conf. del. OCED, 1979. Mem. Adv. Commn. on Intergovtl. Relations, Presdl. Federalism Adv. Com.; mem. Ariz. Justice Planning Supervisory Bd.; mem. community adv. bd. Salt-Gila Flood Control Study; bd. visitors St. Luke's Hosp.; mem. Jr. League Phoenix; advisor women's aux. Ariz. Kidney Found. Named Woman of Yr., Phoenix Advt. Club, 1978; recipient Don Bolles Meml award Ariz. K.C., 1978, Centennial award Salvation Army, 1978, Alumni Achievement award U. Ariz., 1979. Mem. U.S. Conf. Mayors (trustee), Nat. League Cities (dir.), Nat. Conf. Republican Mayors and Elected Ofcls. (pres.), League Ariz. Cities and Towns (treas.). Office: Office of Mayor 251 W Washington St Phoenix AZ 85003*

HANCHETT, RICHARD BLAKE, radiologist; b. Evanston, Ill., Apr. 19, 1915; s. James Louden and Mabel Ellsworth (Blake) H.; B.S., Am. Internat. Coll., 1937; M.D., Tufts U., 1941; m. Marion Christine Hubach, Oct. 26, 1940; children—Karen Blake Hanchett Miloe, Paul Hubach. Intern, U.S. Naval Hosp., Chelsea, Mass., 1941-42; resident in radiology, Johns Hopkins, Balt., 1949-51; commd. lt. (j.g.) U.S. Navy, 1941, advanced through grades to lt. comdr., 1945, served flight surgeon, ret., 1949; instr. in radiology Johns Hopkins Hosp., Balt., 1951-55; practice medicine specializing in radiology, Balt., San Pedro, Calif., 1950—; asst. clin. prof. radiology UCLA; chmn. dept. of radiology San Pedro Peninsula Hosp., bd. dirs., 1964-70; cons. radiologist U.S. Army Hosp., Ft. MacArthur, 1957-68. Pres. Navy League, Palos Verdes, Calif., 1964. Mem. AMA, Calif. Med. Assn., Am. Coll. Radiology, Med. and Chiruricai Soc. Md., Calif. Radiol. Soc., Md. Radiol. Soc. (hon.), Rocky Mountain Radiol. Soc. (hon.). Republican. Episcopalian. Club: Rotary (San Pedro). Home: 32700 Coastsite Dr Rancho Palos Verdes CA 90274 Office: 1360 6th St San Pedro CA 90732

HANCHEY, SUSAN GALE, ednl. cons.; b. Phila., June 1, 1948; d. Newton and Lorraine (Goldstein) Orovitz; B.S., Temple U., 1969, M.Ed., 1972; M.Ed. in human services and counseling, DePaul U., 1976; postgrad. in psychology Calif. Sch. Profl. Psychology, 1979-80, 83—; m. James D. Hanchey, Aug. 21, 1980. Tchr., Bristol Twp. Sch. Dist., Levittown, Pa., 1969-70, Springfield, (Mass.) pub. schs., 1970-71; tchr. kindergarten Chgo. Bd. Edn., 1971-75, tchr., chmn. primary dept., 1975-76; early childhood edn. coordinator Caruthers Union Elementary Sch. Dist., Caruthers, Calif., 1976-78; psychol. trainee Bridge Counseling Agy., 1978-79; psychol. intern Fresno County Dept. Health-West Outreach, Fresno, Calif., 1979-80; coop. project cons. Fresno County Dept. Edn., Fresno, 1980-82, learning theory/teaching methodology cons., 1982—; part-time instr. women's studies, early childhood edn. Calif. State U.-Fresno, 1981—; instr. West Hills Community Coll., Coalinga, Calif., 78-81, U. LaVerne, Fresno, 1981—. Elem. tchr., community coll. instr., adminstrv. services, pupil personnel services credentials; lic. marriage, family and child counselor, Calif. Home: 2026 N Vagedes Fresno CA 93705 Office: Fresno County Dept Edn 2314 Mariposa St Fresno CA 93721

HANCK, NANCY GOLDEN, psychologist, educator; b. Chgo., Feb. 10, 1944; d. Milton E. and Carlotte A. (Abramson) Golden; m. John J. Hanck, June 16, 1968. B.S., U. Ill.-Urbana, 1965, M.S., 1967; Ph.D., Colo. State U., 1982. Tchr. of hearing impaired Michael Reese Hosp., Chgo., 1965-66; psychoednl. diagnostician, resource tchr. of learning disabled Sch. Dist. 54, Hoffman Estates, Ill., 1967-71; instr. U. No. Colo., Greeley, 1972-77; asst. prof. Colo. State U., Ft. Collins, 1982—; pvt. practice, affiliate Ft. Collins Psychotherapy Group. Mem. Am. Psychol. Assn., Am. Personnel and Guidance Assn., Council for Exceptional Children. Contbr. articles to profl. publs. Office: 1049 Robertson St Fort Collins CO 80524

HANCOCK, DON R., newspaper publisher; b. Centerville, Iowa, June 24, 1928; s. Carl C. and Mayme Ruth (Cooper) H.; m. Bernice Elliott, Apr. 17, 1949; children—Kirklyn, Paige. B.J., U. Okla., 1949. Mgr. Ft. Smith (Ark.) Times Record, 1949; pub., gen. mgr. Effingham (Ill.) Daily News, 1950-59; pub., pres. Bogalusa (La.) Daily News, Coughton (La.) Star, 1959-61; pub. Daily Republic, pres. Fairfield (Calif.) Pub. Co., 1962—; pres. Mother Lode Pub. Co.; pres. Davis Enterprise. Pres. Fairfield C. of C. 1965. Mem. Am. Newspaper Pubs. Assn., Nat. Newspaper Assn., Calif. Newspaper Pubs. Assn. (pres. Gold Unit 1980), Calif. Newspaper Youth Found. (dir.), Calif. Press Assn., Delta Sigma Chi. Clubs: Press (San Francisco); Green Valley Country; Elks, Masons. Office: PO Box 47 1250 Texas St Fairfield CA 94533

HANCOCKS, DAVID MORGAN, zool. gardens adminstr.; b. Kinver, Eng., May 5, 1941; s. Cecil and Eva Alice (Morgan) H.; came to U.S., 1975; B.S. with honors, U. Bath (Eng.), 1966, B.Arch. with honors, 1968. Asst. architect Zool. Soc. London, 1968-69; architect West of Eng. Zool. Soc., Bristol, 1970-71; pvt. practice architecture, Seattle, 1972-74; dir. Brit. Wildlife Park, Salisbury, Eng., 1974-75; dir. Woodland Park Zool. Gardens, Seattle, 1976—; cons. in field. Recipient State of Wash. Gov.'s award for writing, 1975, Disting. Service award Am. Soc. Landscape Architects, 1979; Outstanding Pub. Employee award Seattle Mcpl. League, 1983. Fellow Am. Assn. Zool. Parks and Aquariums; Registered architect, U.K. mem. Royal Soc. Protection of Birds, Audubon Soc., Humane Soc. of U.S. Author: Animals and Architecture, 1971; Master Builders of the Animal World, 1973. Contbr. articles to profl. jours. Office: 5500 Phinney Ave N Seattle WA 98103

HAND, HORACE DE LOS, metals lab. exec.; b. Dillon, Mont., Dec. 18, 1934; s. John William and Ida Barbara (Hartwig) H.; student Mont. Sch. Mines, 1952-57; m. Virginia Lee Stefonic, June 17, 1956; children—Kevin, Danial, Pamela, Randall, Ronald, Tamarilla. Mining engr. Hand Mine, Dillon, 1956-59; lab. technician, chemist Minerals Engring. Co., Dillon, 1960-61; owner, exec. Western Labs., Helena, Mont., 1961—; mem. Small Miners Adv. Com., State of Mont., 1971-73. Mem. architecture and rev. com. Helena Urban Renewal Project, 1970-71; mem. South Area Neighborhood Council, Helena, 1970-71; active Boy Scouts Am. Mem. AIME, Southwestern Mont. Mining Assn. (pres. 1971), Western Mining Assn. (pres. 1972), Mont. Mining Assn. (pres. 1973, exec. sec. 1975), Northwestern Mining Assn., Helena Area C. of C. (chmn. environ. com.). Clubs: Mont., Rotary (pres. 1977-78, sec. 1979-82, dist. gov. 1982-83). Office: PO Box 5359 Western Labs Helena MT 59601

HAND, MICHAEL LAWRENCE, statistics and computer educator, researcher, consultant; b. Pitts., Sept. 10, 1953; s. Donald Eugene and Barbara Ann (Leonard) H.; m. Katherine Chiyeko Takeuchi, Aug. 28, 1976. B.S. in Math., Oreg. State U., 1975, B.S. in Computer Sci., 1975; M.S. in Stats., Iowa State U., 1977, Ph.D. in Stats., 1978. Computer programmer chemistry dept. Oreg. State U.-Corvallis, 1971-72, instr. computer sci. dept., 1972-74, programmer adminstv. Systems Computer Ctr., 1974-75; grad. research asst. Statis. Lab., Iowa State U.-Ames, 1975-77, 77-78; statistician stats. and computer sect. Weyerhaeuser Tech. Ctr., Longview, Wash., summer, 1977; asst. prof. stats. Coll. Bus., U. Denver, 1978-79; asst. prof. appled stats. and info. systems Atkinson Grad. Sch. Mgmt., Willamette U., Salem, Oreg., 1979-82, assoc. prof., 1982—; cons. U.S. Dept. Labor, Cascade Comml. Helicopter, Oreg. Exec. Dept. Oreg. Workers' Compensation Dept., Hewlett-Packard Co.; pub. speaker in field; researcher. U.S. Air Force grantee, summer, 1980; Atkinson Fund research grantee, summer, 1981. Mem. Am. Statis. Assn., Am. Inst. Decision Scis., Soc. Indsl. and Applied Math., Assn. Computing Machinery, Phi Kappa Phi, Mu Sigma Rho, Phi Eta Sigma. Contbr. articles to prof. jours. Office: Atkinson Grad Sch Mgmt Willamette U Salem OR 97301

HANDEL, WILLIAM KEATING, advt. and public relations exec.; b. N.Y.C., Mar. 23, 1935; s. Irving Nathaniel and Marguerite Mary (Keating) H.; B.A. in Journalism, U. S.C., 1959, postgrad., 1959-60; m. Margaret Inez Sitton; children—William Keating II, David Roger. With Packaging div. The Mead Corp., Atlanta, 1960-64, Ketchum, MacLeod & Grove, Pitts., 1964-67, Rexall Drug & Chem. Corp., Los Angeles, 1967-68; owner Creative Enterprises/Mktg. Communications, Los Angeles, 1968-71; creative dir., sales promotion mgr. Beneficial Standard Life Ins., Los Angeles, 1971-72; mgr. advt. and public relations ITT Gen. Controls, Glendale, Calif., 1972-80; mgr. corp. recruitment advt. Hughes Aircraft Co., Los Angeles, 1980-81; mgr. corp. communications Fairchild Camera and Instrument Corp., 1981-82; public relations counsel Calif. Pvt. Edn. Schs., 1978—; chmn. exhibits Mini/Micro Computer Conf., 1977-78. Bd. dirs. West Valley Athletic League; mem. USMC Scholarship Found.; public relations cons. Ensenada, Mexico Tourist Commn., 1978; chmn., master of ceremonies U.S. Marine Corps Birthday Ball, Los Angeles, 1979, 80, 81, 82. Served with USMC, 1950-53. Decorated Silver Star, Bronze Star, Purple Heart (4), Navy Commendation medal with combat V. Recipient Public Service award Los Angeles Heart Assn., 1971, 72, 73. Mem. Bus. and Profl. Advt. Assn. (cert. bus. communicator, past pres.), 1st Marine Div. Assn., Navy League (dir.), Sigma Chi (chpt. adv.). Republican. Roman Catholic. Clubs: Nueva España Boat, Ensenada Fish and Game (Baja, Mexico). Home: 4420 Sarah St #1 Burbank CA 91505

HANDLEY, JAMES HARLAND, JR., marketing executive; b. Lansing, Mich., Oct. 8, 1931; s. James Harland and Lola Gertrude (Madison) H.; B.A., Yale U., 1953; B.Arch., 1957, M.Arch. cert., 1972. Draftsman, Stone, Smith & Parent, Kalamazoo, 1958-60, Warren S. Holmes Co., Lansing, 1960-62; draftsman-designer Manson, Jackson & Kane, Lansing, 1962-64; archtl. designer Del E. Webb Corp., Phoenix, 1966-68; asst. mgr. to mgr. advt. Del E. Webb Devel. Co., Sun City, Ariz., 1968-74, v.p. advt., 1974-82; gen. mgr. Saguaro Advt. Agy., 1974-82; now cons. design and mktg. planned communities. Program annotator. Sun City Symphony Orch. Assn., Inc. Ky. col. Republican. Episcopalian (vestryman). Clubs: Mory's Assn (New Haven); Lakes, Bell Lions (Sun City); Yale (Phoenix). Home: 9921 Hope Circle S Sun City AZ 85351

HANDSCHUMACHER, ALBERT G(USTAVE), mfg. exec.; b. Phila., Oct. 20, 1918; s. Gustave H. and Emma (Streck) H.; B.S., Drexel Inst. Tech., 1940; diploma U. Pitts., 1941, Alexander Hamilton Inst., 1948; m. Inger Stratton, Apr. 1970; children by previous marriage—Albert, David W., Megan, Karin, Melissa. Prodn. mgr. Jr. Motors Corp., Phila., 1938-40; sales engr. Westinghouse Electric, Pitts., 1941; with Lear, Inc., 1945-57, sales mgr. Central dist., asst. to pres., asst. gen. mgr., v.p. and gen. mgr., sr. v.p., dir. sales, 1952-59, pres., dir., 1959-62; pres., dir. Lear Siegler, Inc., 1962-64; chmn. bd. emeritus Aeronca, Inc., Los Angeles, 1965—; v.p., gen. mgr. Rheem Mfg. Co., 1957-59; dir. Accounts Network Inc., Flight Dynamics, Inc., Elliot Group, Inc., Golden West Fin. Corp., 1st Exec. Corp., World Savs. and Loan, Exec. Life Ins. Co., Cramer Investment Co., Lear Siegler, Actair Internat., Informatics Inc.; underwriting mem. Lloyd's of London. Chmn. Am. Heart Assn., Los Angeles; asso. chmn. Los Angeles United Way; trustee City of Hope, Drexel U., Nat. Asthma; mem. exec. com. of adv. council UCLA Internat. Recipient 60th Anniversary Alumni award for outstanding achievements and services field indsl. mgmt. Drexel Inst., 1951; Man of Our Times award City of Hope, 1969; Man of Yr. award Nat. Asthma Found., 1978. Served to maj. USAF, 1942-45. Mem. ASHRAE, Mil. Order World Wars. Clubs: Astro (Phila.); Jonathan; Bel Air Country; Calif. Yacht; Metropolitan, Wings (N.Y.C.); Le Mirador (Switzerland). Home: 1100 Stone Canyon Rd Bel Air Los Angeles CA 90024 Office: 10100 Santa Monica Blvd Century City North Los Angeles CA 90067

HANEY, HAROLD LEVON, state ofcl.; b. Clearfield, Pa., May 23, 1928; s. Ferdnand Nevling and Esther Ulu (Watson) H.; B.A., Brownell U., 1956. Asst. to pres. Louis E. Shecter Advt. Agy., Balt., 1946-47; set designer Alexander Film Co., 1947; prodn. mgr. Glenn L. Brill Advt. Agy., 1948; copy dir. Harold Walter Clark Advt. Agy., 1948-50; pres. H. L. Haney Advt. Co., Denver, 1950-52; asst. dir. travel mktg. State of Colo., Denver, 1952-72, dir., 1972—; dir. Discover Am. Travel Orgn., Inc.; founder Historic Denver Inc., 1969, pres., 1971, chmn. bd., 1973-75; founder Four Corners Regional Tourism Orgn., Inc., 1973, pres., 1973—. Chmn. steering com. Denver Pub. Schs. Recreational and Travel. Recipient Gold Brahm awards, 1966, 67, 69, 70; Internat. Film Festival award, 1961, 62, 64; Am. Film Festival awards, 1961, 62, 65; certificates of Honor by Govts. of Turkey, 1967, Finland, 1970, Germany, 1967, Austria, 1968, Tunisia, 1972; presented Key to City of Berlin by Willy Brandt, 1968. Mem. Western Am. Conv. and Travel Inst., Fedn. of Rocky Mountain States, Soc. Am. Travel Writers, Internat. Harpsichord Soc., Mountain W. Assn. Club: Masons. Collaborating author: The West Nobody Knows, 1973, pub. and editor The Harpsichord, 1969—. Home: 1440 Ash St Denver CO 80220 Office: 500 Centennial Bldg Denver CO 80203

HANEY, PERRY LYNN, chiropractor; b. La Junta Colo., Mar. 4, 1951; s. Chester Dale and Nina Maxine (Dye) H. B.S. U. Colo., 1973; D.C., Palmer Coll. Chiropractic, 1980. Bus. mgmt. advisor Deer and Co., Moline, Ill., 1973-76; pres. Biodynamics Tech., Ltd., Aurora, Colo., 1980-82; pres. Low Back Pain Clinic, Aurora, 1980—. Mem. Ill. Prairie State Chiropractic Assn. (outstanding service award 1979), Internat. Chiropractic Assn., Colo. Chiropractic Assn., Nat. Back Found.; Am. Coll. Sports Medicine. Democrat. Office: Low Back Pain Clinic 11275 East Mississippi Ave Suite 1W5 Aurora CO 80012

HANEY, WILLIAM SAMUEL, JR., aerospace company executive; Vanceburg, Ky., June 28, 1934; s. William Samuel and Mary Louise (Moore) H.; m. Sandra Capone, Aug. 14, 1954; 1 son, William Charles. Flight mechanics and systems engring. positions McDonnell Douglas Astronautics Co., 1957-78, dir., program engr. advanced Systems analysis BMD, 1978—. Assoc. fellow AIAA; mem. Tau Beta Pi. Republican. Office: 5301 Bolsa Ave Huntington Beach CA 92647

HANF, JAMES ALPHONSO, poet, govt. ofcl.; b. Chehalis, Wash., Feb. 3, 1923; s. William G. and Willa DeForest (Davis) H.; grad. Centralia Jr. Coll., 1943; m. Ruth G. Eyler, Aug. 16, 1947; children—Maureen Ruth. Naval architect technician P.F. Spaulding, naval architects, Seattle, 1955-56, Puget Sound Bridge & Dredge Co. (Wash.), 1953-55, Puget Sound Naval Shipyard, 1951-53, 56—; cons. Anderson & Assos., shipbldg.; guest lectr. on poetry and geneal. research methods to various lit. socs., 1969—; contbr. hundreds of poems to lit. jours., anthologies and popular mags.; poetry editor Coffee Break, 1977-82. Recipient Poet Laureate award, 1978, numerous other awards. Mem. Internat. Poetry Soc., World Poetry Soc., Kitsap County Writers Club (pres. 1977-78), Internat. Fedn. Tech. Engrs., Nat. Hist. Locomotive Soc., Kitsap County Hist. Soc., Puget Sound Geneal. Soc., Western World Haiku Soc., Olympic Geneal. Soc. (pres. 1974-75), N.Y. Poetry Forum, World Poets Resource Center, Literarische Union, Internat. Platform Assn., Calif. Fedn. Chaparral Poets, Internat. Biog. Assn., Am. Biog. Inst. Baptist. Home: PO Box 374 Bremerton WA 98310

HANG, AN NGOC, agronomist; b. Cholon, Vietnam, Dec. 10, 1942; came to U.S., 1973, naturalized, 1981; s. Hy Nguon and Dong Thi (Nguyen) H.; Agrl. Engr., Nat. Agrl. Inst., Saigon, 1968; M.S., U. Fla., 1976, Ph.D., 1978; m. Hoa Dat Tran, July 4, 1979; 1 dau., Ann. H. With Wash. State U., Prosser, 1978—, asst. agronomist, 1978—. Mem. Agronomy Soc. Am., Crop Sci. Soc. Am., Soil Sci. Soc. Am., Council for Agrl. Sci. and Tech., Gamma Sigma Delta. Contbr articles to sci. jours. Office: Washington State U PO Box 30 Prosser WA 99350

HANKINS, WALTER GARLAND, psychologist, adminstr.; b. Quincy, Fla., Aug. 20, 1938; s. James Garland and Kathryn Field (Moseley) H.; m. Dawn Nagy, Dec. 28, 1967; children—Kathryn, Sydney, Richard, Mia; m. 2d, Martha Marie Slosson, July 11, 1982. B.A., San Jose State U., 1968; Ph.D., SUNY, Stony Brook, 1972. Research teaching asst., San Jose State U., 1967-69, SUNY Stony Brook, 1969-72; research asst. prof. psychology U. Utah, 1972-73; asst. research psychologist UCLA, 1973-79; dir. acad. affairs Kensington U., Glendale, Calif., 1979—. Bd. dirs. Internat. Acad. Ctr., Tokyo, 1982—. Recipient exec. service award Internat. Police Assn., 1982. Mem. Am. Psychol. Assn., AAAS, Western Psychol. Assn. Democrat. Contbr. articles to profl. jours. Home: 9673 Via Torino Burbank CA 91507 Office: 330 N Glendale Ave Suite 302 Glendale CA 91209

HANKS, EUGENE RALPH, land developer, ret. naval officer; b. Corning, Calif., Dec. 11, 1918; s. Eugene and Lorena B. Hanks; student Calif. Poly. Coll., 1939-41, U. So. Calif., 1949-50, Am. U., 1958-59; grad. Command and Staff Coll., Norfolk, Va., 1960; m. Frances Elliot Herrick, Mar. 4, 1945; children—Herrick, Russell, Stephen, Nina. Served as enlisted man U.S. Navy, 1941-42, commd. ensign, 1942, advanced through grades to capt., 1963; carrier fighter pilot, test pilot Naval Air Test Center, 1946-48; mem. Navy Flight Exhbn. Team, Blue Angels, 1950; comdg. officer fighter squadrons, San Diego, 1957-58, 61; ops. officer U.S.S. Constellation, 1961-62; dir. ops. Naval Missile Center, 1963-66; test dir. Joint Task Force Two, Albuquerque, 1966-69, ret., 1969. Owner, developer Christmas Tree Canyon, Cebolla Springs and Mountain River, subdivs., Mora, N.Mex., 1969—. Decorated Legion of Merit, Navy Cross, D.F.C. with star (2), Air medal (7). Mem. Ret. Officers Assn., Am. Fighter Aces Assn., Combat Pilots Assn., Assn. Naval Aviation, Am. Forestry Assn., Nat. Rifle Assn. Democrat. Home and Office: Christmas Tree Canyon Box 239 Mora NM 87732

HANKS, LARRY BERKLEY, life insurance company executive; b. Idaho Falls, Idaho, Sept. 25, 1940; s. Victor Franklin and Marjorie (Burke) H.; A.B., Brigham Young U., 1964; M.Fin. Sci., Am. Coll., 1982; C.L.U.; chartered fin. cons.; m. Georgia Lee Gammett, Dec. 29, 1965; children—Tiffany, Berkley, Colli, Andrea, Rachel, Jared, Cyrus. Owner, mgr. Larry B. Hanks, C.L.U., ins. and employee benefits, Boise, Idaho, 1969—; pres. Am. Pension Adminstrs. Inc., Boise, 1978—, Integrated Fin. Designs, Inc., 1982—; gen. agt. Mass. Mut. Life Ins. Co., Boise, 1980—; instr. C.L.U. classes Am. Coll., Bryn Mawr, Pa., 1975—. Served with C.E., U.S. Army, 1968-69. Mem. Am. Soc. C.L.U. (dir. Magic Valley chpt.), Nat. Assn. Life Underwriters, Am. Soc. Pension Actuaries, N.E. Idaho Assn. Life Underwriters (dir., officer), Million Dollar Roundtable, Estate Planning Council Boise, Gen. Agts. and Mgrs. Assn. Republican. Mormon. Home: 5669 Fieldcrest Dr Boise ID 83704 Office: 1471 Shoreline Dr Boise ID 83707

HANLEY, MARY BRIDGET, small business owner; b. Seattle, Mar. 23, 1951; d. George Walter and Helen Frances H. Student Foodhill Jr. Coll., 1976-79, De Anza Coll., 1978-79, Coll. San Mateo, 1970-72, Ariz. State U., 1969-70. Exec. sec. Western regional hdqrs. Household Finance Corp., San Mateo, Calif., 1970-71; successively ward sec., sec. to chief otolaryngology, sec. to chief psychology VA Med. Ctr., Palo Alto, Calif.,

1971-79; founder, owner Hanley Secretarial Services, Palo Alto, 1979—. Mem. Peninsula Bus. Services Assn. (founder, treas., membership chmn.). Office: Hanley Secretarial Services 2502 Ash St Palo Alto CA 94306

HANLIN, R. L., agricultural products company executive; b. Sioux Falls, S.D., 1932. Student U. Wash., Los Angeles City Coll. Pres., Sunkist Growers, Inc., Van Nuys, Calif. Office: Sunkist Growers Inc PO Box 7888 Van Nuys CA 91409*

HANLON, CHARLES JOSEPH, state senator; b. Pa., Sept. 15, 1918; s. Charles Hugh and Anna (Darby) H.; student public schs., Greensburg, Pa.; m. Neila Margaret Gaines, Mar. 11, 1943; children—Kathy, Jeffrey. With rock, sand and gravel industry, 1946-58; rancher, Cornelius, Oreg., 1958—; mem. Oreg. Senate, 1974—. Served with Aviation Engrs., AUS, 1941-46; PTO. Democrat. Polit. writer for state newspapers. Office: S-218 Capitol Bldg Salem OR 97310

HANN, DON ROBERT, elec. engr.; b. Ancon, C.Z., Apr. 28, 1946; s. Lyle Ray and Olive Louise (McNicholl) H.; A.S., Barstow Coll., 1970; B.S. in E.E., Calif. Poly. Coll., Pomona, 1973; M.S.E.E., San Diego State U., 1977; m. Bettye Darlene Wilcox, June 15, 1968; children—Valerie Michelle, Robert Douglas. Electronic mechanic U.S. Govt., Barstow, Calif., 1965-70; design engr. Bourns Inc., Riverside, Calif., 1972-73; meters and test engr. San Diego Gas & Electric Co., San Diego, 1973-77, meters and tests supr., 1977-82, distbn. equipment engring. supr., 1982—; mem. steering com, dept. metrology Mesa Coll., San Diego. Registered profl. engr., Calif. Mem. IEEE, Pacific Coast Elec. Assn., Edison Elec. Inst., Tau Beta Pi, Eta Kappa Nu, Kappa Mu Epsilon. Republican. Mem. Assemblies of God Ch. Home: 5511 Mt Aconia Dr San Diego CA 92111 Office: PO Box 1831 San Diego CA 92112

HANNA, BOYD EVERETT, artist, engraver; b. Irwin, Pa., Jan. 15, 1907; s. Roscoe Elton and Grace Belle (Boyd) H.; m. Hazel Mae Bauman, Mar. 20, 1930; children—Sylvia Parr, Philip, Kristina Clark. Student, U. Pitts., 1925-28, Carnegie-Mellon U., 1928-30. Graphic artist Pullman, Inc., Pitts., 1950-70; architect City of Pitts. Water Plant, 1960-65; dir. Hanna Studios, Tucson, 1971—; one man shows: Color Print U.S.A., 1972, Print Club of Albany, 1975, Murphy Gallery, Tucson, 1975; group shows: Audubon Artists, 1974, Arena 76 Art Open, Print Club of Albany, 1972-82, Sander Gallery, Chgo., 1982; works represented in permanent collections: Met. Mus. N.Y., Library of Congress Pennell Collection, Carnegie Inst., Pitts., N.Y. Pub. Library, Boston Pub. Library, Life Mag., Readers Digest, Print Club of Albany, Hunt Inst., Pitts. Illustrator: Longfellow's Poems, 1943-44; Leaves of Grass, Story of Nativity, Compleat Angler, Dreamthorp, 1947-58, Bell Telephone Almanac, 1948; Wild and Wily, 1980. Home: 1475 S Jones St Apt G-16 Tucson AZ 85713

HANNA, JOHN EDWARD, urologist; b. Sarasota, Fla., Oct. 26, 1943; s. James H. and Jane K. (Kaswasten) H.; m. Vicki J. Moore, Oct. 11, 1975; children—Summer, Jimmy. B.A. in Zoology and English, Duke U., 1965; postgrad. in thoracic surgery Aarhus Kummenehospital, Denmark, 1968; M.D., U. N.C., 1970. Diplomate Am. Bd. Urology. Intern, Emory U. and Grady Meml. Hosp., Atlanta, 1970-71, resident in gen. surgery, 1974-75, resident in urology, 1975-78; practice medicine specializing in urology, Mission Viejo, Costa Mesa, Newport Beach and San Clemente, Calif., 1979—. Served with USN, 1971-73. Mem. Orange County Med. Assn., Orange County Urologic Assn., Calif. Med. Assn. Republican. Roman Catholic. Office: 637 Camino de los Mares Suite 138 San Clemente CA 92672 also 275 Victoria St Suite 2B Costa Mesa CA 92626

HANNA, ROBERT CECIL, lawyer, constrn. co. exec.; b. Albuquerque, July 28, 1937; s. Samuel Gray and Orvetta (Cecil) H.; B.A., U. N.Mex., 1959, J.D., 1962. Admitted to N.Mex. bar, 1962; practiced in Albuquerque, 1962-70; organizer, dep. dir. Micronesian Legal Services Corp., Trust Ter. Pacific Islands, 1970-71; practiced in Hilo; Hawaii, 1974; partner Cotter, Atkinson, Kelsey & Hanna, Ortega, Snead, Dixon & Hanna, Albuquerque, 1971-77; owner, pres., prin. Robert C. Hanna & Assos., Albuquerque, 1978-80; pres. Sedco Internat. USA, Inc., Albuquerque, 1977-79, Suncastle Builders, Inc., Albuquerque, 1978—, v.p. Bart Prince & Assos., Inc., Albuquerque, 1982—; mem. Bd. Bar Commrs., Trust Ter. Pacific Islands, 1971-72. Recipient award Rocky Mountain Mineral Law Found., 1962; Public Service award Micronesian Legal Services Corp. Bd. Dirs., 1972. Mem. Hawaii Bar Assn., N.Mex. Bar Assn., Albuquerque Bar Assn. Home: 310 Rio Grande Blvd SW Albuquerque NM 87104 Office: 310 Rio Grande Blvd SW Albuquerque NM 87104

HANNAFORD, PETER DOR, advertising executive; b. Glendale, Calif., Sept. 21, 1932; s. Donald R. and Elinor (Nielsen) H.; A.B., U. Calif., 1954; m. Irene Dorothy Harville, Aug. 14, 1954; children—Richard Harville, Donald R. II. Account exec. Helen A. Kennedy Advt., 1956; v.p. Kennedy-Hannaford, Inc. (name changed to Kennedy, Hannaford & Dolman. Inc. 1965), San Francisco and Oakland, Calif., 1957-62, pres., 1962-67; pres. Pettler & Hannaford, Inc., Oakland, 1967-69; v.p. Wilton, Coombs & Colnett, Inc., 1969-72; pres. Hannaford & Assos., Oakland, 1973; asst. to Calif. Gov., dir. pub. affairs Govs.' Office, 1974; chmn. bd. Hannaford Co. Inc. (formerly Deaver & Hannaford, Inc.), 1975—. Nat. pres. Mut. Advt. Agy. Network, 1968-69; instr. advt. Merritt Coll., Oakland, 1964-67; vice chmn. Calif. Gov.'s Consumer Fraud Task Force, 1972-73. Author: The Reagans: A Political Portrait, 1983. Pres., East Bay div. Republican Alliance, 1968-69; mem. Alameda County Rep. Central Com., Rep. State Central Com. Calif., 1968-74; Rep. nominee for U.S. Ho. of Reps., 1972; mem. Piedmont Park Commn., 1964-67. Dir., mem. exec. com. Oakland Symphony Orch. Assn., 1963-69; bd. dirs. Children's Hosp. Med. Center No. Calif., 1967-70; mem. governing bd. Tahoe Regional Planning Agy., 1973-74. Served as 1st lt. Signal Corps, AUS, 1954-56. Mem. Guardsmen San Francisco, Theta Xi. Presbyterian. Clubs: Univ. (San Francisco); Univ. (Washington). Office: 444 S Flower St Los Angeles CA 90017

HANNAWAY, DAVID BYRON, agronomist; b. Phila., Sept. 14, 1951; s. W. Gordon and Elizabeth (Hunsberger) H.; m. Kimberly Jones, June 22, 1975. M.S., U. Tenn., 1975; Ph.D., U. Ky., 1979. Forage crop specialist crop sci. dept. Oreg. State U., Corvallis, 1980—. Author numerous articles in sci. jours. Mem. Am. Soc. Agronomy, Crop Sci. Soc. Am., Am. Forage and Grassland Council, Am. Soc. Plant Physiologists, Sigma Xi, Gamma Sigma Delta. Home: 2903 NW Hayes Ave Corvallis OR 97330 Office: Crop Science Dept Oreg State U Corvallis OR 97331

HANNON, LENN LAMAR, state senator; b. Roseburg, Oreg., July 4, 1943; s. Leonard Thomas and Irene (Massey) H.; m. Dixie Lynn Gibbs, 1966; children—Michelle R., Patrick L., Rebecca A., Rachel L. Student So. Oreg. State Coll., 1963-64. Mem. Oreg. State Senate, 1975—. Served with U.S. Army, 1961-67. Mem. Jackson County Farm Bur., Fellowship Christian Athletes. Nazarene. Democrat. Lodge: Masons. Home: 240 Scenic Dr Ashland OR 97520 Office: Oregon State Senate Salem OR 97310*

HANOVER, PAUL NORDEN, electronic engineer; b. Hartford, Conn., Sept. 13, 1927; s. Adrian Norden and Ruth (Seide) H.; B.E.E., Rensselaer Poly. Inst., 1952; postgrad. U. So. Calif., 1963, U. Ariz., 1968; m. Margaret Manning, Jan. 17, 1931; children—Nancy, Diane. Electronic engr. Sparrow Missile, Douglas Aircraft Co., Santa Monica, Calif., 1952-54; project engr. radar and spacecraft Hughes Aircraft Co., Culver City, Calif., 1954-63; sr. project engr. missiles Hughes Aircraft Co., Tucson, 1964—; profl. speaker on space programs. Served with USN, 1946-48, to capt. USAF, 1950-57. Recipient Sax Impromptu Speaking prize Rensselaer Poly. Inst., 1952; Impromptu Speaking award Nat. Speakers Assn., 1976. Fellow AIAA (assoc.; Tucson chmn. 1982-83); mem. IEEE (sr.; past chmn. Tucson sect.), Nat. Space Inst., Planetary Soc., Fedn. Aerospace Socs. Tucson (chmn. 1981-83). Republican. Christian Scientist. Club. Masons. Author: Semiconductors, Handle with Care, 1958; (with others) Star Spangled Speakers, 1983; pub., author cassette: Space Shuttle—Your Ticket to Space, 1982. Home: 3551 Winslow Dr Tucson AZ 85715 Office: Hughes Aircraft Co Tucson AZ 85734

HANOWELL, ERNEST GODDIN, physician; b. Newport News, Va., Jan. 31, 1920; s. George Frederick and Ruby Augustine (Goddin) H.; A.B., George Washington U., 1945, M.D., 1948; postgrad. Nat. Heart Inst., 1959-61, Tufts U., 1960-61, Johns Hopkins, 1961-62; m. Para Jean Hall, June 10, 1945; children—Ernest D., Deborah J. Hanowell Orick, Leland H., Dee P. Hanowell Martinmaas, Robert G. Intern, USPHS Hosp., Norfolk, Va., 1948-49; resident in internal medicine USPHS Hosp., Seattle, 1952-55; chief medicine USPHS Hosp., Ft. Worth, 1955-57; dep. chief medicine USPHS Hosp., Boston, 1957-59; chief medicine USPHS Hosp., Memphis, 1964-65, Monterey County Gen. Hosp., 1969-70; mem. staff Kaiser Permanente Med. Group, Sacramento, 1971—; clin. asst. Tufts Med. Sch., 1960-61; cons. chest disease Phila. Gen. Hosp., 1960-61; lectr. medicine Hahnemann Med. Coll., 1960-61; asst. prof. U. Md. Med. Sch., 1961-64; instr. U. Tenn. Med. Sch., 1964-65; asst. clin. prof. Sch. Medicine, U. Calif.-Davis, 1973-81; mem. attending staff Cardiac Clinic, Stanford U. Med. Sch., 1967-69. Mem. sch. bd., Salinas, Calif., 1968-69. Bd. dirs. Am. Heart Assn., Tb and Health Assn. Served with AUS, 1943-46. Diplomate Am. Bd. Internal Medicine. Fellow ACP, Am. Coll. Chest Diseases; mem. AMA, Crocker Art Mus. Assn., Phi Chi. Clubs: Commonwealth (San Francisco); Comstock (Sacramento). Home: 1158 Racquet Club Dr Auburn CA 95603 Office: Kaiser Permanente Found Hosp 2025 Morse Ave Sacramento CA 95825 also Kaiser Permanente Roseville Clinic Riverside Dr Roseville CA 95678

HANSCH, THEODOR WOLFGANG, physicist, educator; b. Heidelberg, W. Ger., Oct. 30, 1941; s. Karl E. and Martha (Kiefer) H.; came to U.S., 1970, Abitur, Helmholtz Gymnasium, Heidelberg, 1961; M.S., U. Heidelberg, 1966, Ph.D., 1969. Asst. prof. physics U. Heidelberg, 1969-70; NATO fellow Stanford, 1970-72, assoc. prof. physics, 1972-75, prof., 1975—. Named Calif. Scientist of Yr., 1973; recipient Alexander von Humboldt Sr. U.S. Scientist award, 1978-79; Otto Klung prize, Ger., 1980; Alfred P. Sloan fellow, 1973-75. Fellow Am. Phys. Soc. (Broida prize 1982), Optical Soc. Am.; mem. Optical Soc. No. Calif. (dir. 1975-78), Deutsche Physikalische Gesellschaft, Sigma Xi. Roman Catholic. Co-editor Metrologia, 1975—; adv. editor Optics Communications, 1975—. Researcher spectroscopy and quantum electronics, devel. powerful monochromatic pulsed dye lasers, high resolution nonlinear spectroscopy of atoms and molecules, contbr. articles to profl. publs. Home: 1510 Oak Creek Dr Apt 405 Palo Alto CA 94304 Office: Dept Physics Stanford U Stanford CA 94305

HANSEN, DARREL CHANCY, educator; b. Lewisville, Idaho, July 13, 1933; s. Chancy Hans and Edith Viola (Forsgren) H.; B.S., Brigham Young U., 1955, M.S., 1971; m. Margaret Doxey, Dec. 20, 1954; children—Julie, Steven, Eric, Wayne. Commd. 2d lt. USAF, 1955, advanced through grades to lt. col.; pilot Robins AFB, Ga., 1957-60; chief maintenance, Spain, 1961-64; maintenance control officer, France, 1964-65; chief pilot Hill AFB, Utah, 1965-66; resigned, 1966; civilian chief publs. mgmt. sect. Hill AFB, 1966-70; tchr. earth sci. and geography Shelley (Idaho) Jr. High Sch., 1973—. Chmn. troop com. Boy Scouts Am., 1970 71; bd. dirs. S.E. Idaho UNISERV. Decorated Air Force Commendation medal. Mem. Assn. Am. Geographers, Idaho Edn. Assn. (dir.), Shelley Edn. Assn. (pres. 1976-77), S.E. Idaho Res. Officers Assn. (pres.), Idaho State Res. Officers Assn. (pres. 1980), Sigma Gamma Upsilon, Gamma Theta Upsilon. Mormon. Contbr. articles to profl. jours. Home: 736 S Park Ave Shelley ID 83274 Office: 330 E Pine St Shelley ID 83274

HANSEN, ELMER HARRIS, ret. customer relations exec.; b. Spokane, Wash., Apr. 28, 1913; s. Emil and Elsie Anna (Johanson) H.; student U. Calif., 1943-44; m. Dorthy Betty Jane Ritt, Mar. 29, 1958; children—Mary Sue, Jane Margaret, James Robert. Vice pres., chief pilot Wash. Aircraft & Transport Co., Seattle, 1934-43, 45-55; sect. chief, flight and ground crew tng. Consol. Vultee Aircraft Corp., San Diego, 1943-45; v.p. Hansen Buick Co., Kirkland, Bellevue, Wash., 1955-61; dir. customer relations Boeing Aerospace Corp., Seattle, 1961-79; instr. flight engring. U. Calif., 1944-45. Mem. AIAA, Ox-5 Aviation Pioneers (pres. Wash. wing), Quiet Birdmen. Lutheran. Home: 12220 NE 39th St Bellevue WA 98005

HANSEN, FLORENCE MARIE CONGIOLOSI (MRS. JAMES S. HANSEN), social worker; b. Middletown, N.Y., Jan. 7, 1934; d. Joseph James and Florence (Harrigan) Congiolosi; B.A., Coll. New Rochelle, 1955; M.S.W., Fla. State U., 1960; m. James S. Hansen, June 16, 1959; 1 dau., Florence M. Caseworker, Orange County Dept. Pub. Welfare, N.Y., 1955-57, Cath. Welfare Bur., Miami, Fla., 1957-58; supr. Cath. Family Service, Spokane, Wash., 1960, Cuban Children's Program, Spokane, 1962-66; founder, dir. social service dept., adminstr. supr. Spokane and Inland Empire artificial kidney center Sacred Heart Med. Center, Spokane, 1967—. Asst. in program devel. St. Margaret's Hall, Spokane, 1961-62; mem. budget allocation panel United Way, 1964-76, mem. planning com., 1968-77, mem. admissions com., 1969-70, chmn. projects com. 1972-73, active work with Cuban refugees; mem. kidney disease adv. com. Wash.-Alaska Regional Med. Program, 1970-73. Mem. Spokane Quality of Life Commn., 1974-75. Mem. Nat. Assn. Social Workers (chpt. pres. 1972-74), Acad. Cert. Social Workers (charter), Am. Soc. Hosp. Social Work Dirs. Roman Catholic. Home: 5609 Northwest Blvd Spokane WA 99205 Office: Sacred Heart Med Center W 101 8th St Spokane WA 99204

HANSEN, FRANCES FRAKES, artist, educator; b. Harrisburg, Mo.; d. Eugene Nelson and Cyrene Bell (Graham) Frakes; m. Claude Bendt Hansen. B.F.A., U. Denver, 1937; postgrad. Sch. Art. Inst. Chgo., 1938; M.A., U. No. Colo., 1941; postgrad. U. So. Calif., 1952-55. Prof. art, dir. dept. art Colo. Women's Coll., Denver, 1942-73; instr., art U. Denver, 1942-45, 52-57; vol. research and display design, dept. anthropology Denver Mus. Natural History, 1973-78; artist, mem. editorial bd., Denver Bot. Gardens, 1976—. Active Denver Symphony Guild, Denver Lyric Opera Guild. Mem. Denver Mus. Natural History, AAUP, Denver Art Mus., P.E.O. Mem. Disciples of Christ Ch. Cover designer Green Thumb—Denver Botanic Gardens, 1976—; illustrator: Song of the Ghost Trains, 1981; designer relief sculpture panel Christian Ch., Harrisburg, Mo., 1982. Home: 700 Pontiac St Denver CO 80220

HANSEN, FRANCES GERALDINE, accountant; b. Swift Current, Sask., Can., Dec. 26, 1921; came to U.S., 1944, naturalized, 1960; d. David Lorne and Frances Esther (Haskell) Acorn; m. Earl M. Hansen, July 15, 1950; 1 son, Joel W. Student pub. schs., Edmonton, Alta., Can. C.P.A., Wash. Employed with various firms, 1944-55; pvt. practice acctg., Walla Walla, Wash., 1955-69; corp. controller Rockcor, Redmond, Wash., 1972-78; owner, prin. F. Geraldine Hansen, C.P.A., Bellevue, Wash., 1980—; dir. Joel Hansen, Inc., Voyages of Discovery, Inc. Mem. Am. Inst. C.P.A.s, Wash. Soc. C.P.A.s, Mensa, Intertel. Republican. Home: 15214 NE 8th St Apt G-29 Bellevue WA 98007 Office: 225 108th Ave NE Suite 100 Bellevue WA 98004

HANSEN, GEORGE VERNON, congressman; b. Tetonia, Idaho, Sept. 14, 1930; s. Dean Erlease and Elmoyne Bendicta (Brewer) H.; A.B. in History and Russian with honors, Ricks Coll., Rexburg, Idaho, 1956; grad. Grimms Bus. Coll., 1958; postgrad. edn. Idaho State U., 1962-63; m. Constance Sue Camp, Dec. 19, 1952; children—Steven, James, Patricia, William, Joanne. Tchr. math. secondary pub. sch., 1956-58; guest lectr. ins. and estate planning colls. and high schs.; spl. agt. N.Y. Life Ins. Co., 1958—; mayor, Alameda, Idaho, 1961-62, city merged with Pocatello, Idaho, 1962, mem. city commn., 1962-65; mem. 89th-90th, 94th-97th Congresses from 2d Idaho dist.; dep. under-sec. agr. for congl. relations and dep. adminstr. Agrl. Stblzn. and Conservation Service, for state and county ops., 1969-71. Chmn., Bannock County Heart Assn., 1962 64. Served with USAF, 1951-54, USNR, 1964-70. Recipient Distinguished Service award Pocatello Jaycees, 1961. Mem. Idaho Municipal League (bd. dirs. 1961-63), Pocatello C. of C., Am. Legion, Idaho Farm Bur., Life Ins. Underwriter Assn. Republican. Mormon. Kiwanian (bd. dirs.). Club: Pocatello 20-30 (past pres.). Office: 1125 Longworth House Office Bldg Washington DC 20515 also PO Box 1330 Pocatello ID 83201

HANSEN, JAMES STUART, state agy. adminstr.; b. Davenport, Wash., June 16, 1931; s. John Peter and Rachel (Echardt) H.; B.A., U. Wash., Seattle, 1953; M.S.W. (State Wash. grantee), Fla. State U., 1960; m. Florence Congiolosi, June 16, 1959; 1 dau., Florence Marie. Child welfare worker, then child welfare supr. State of Wash., Spokane, 1957-63; field instr. U. Wash. at Eastern State Hosp., Medical Lake, 1963-67; social worker in delinquency prevention State of Wash., 1968, 69, regional adminstr. div. devel. disabilities, Spokane, 1969-79, Seattle, 1979-81, chief Office Program Support for Div. Developmental Disabilities, Olympia, Wash., 1982—; field instr. Grad. Sch. Social Work, Eastern Wash. U., 1977-79; mem. Mayor Spokane Adv. Council Employment Handicapped, 1976-79; bd. dirs. Child Guidance Center, Spokane, 1962-63. Served to 1st lt. USAF, 1953-55. Mem. Acad. Cert. Social Workers, Nat. Assn. Social Workers (chpt. chmn. 1964; Inland Empire Social Worker of Year 1975), Am. Assn. Mental Deficiency (regional vice chmn. adminstrn. 1976-78), Wash. Assn. Retarded Citizens. Roman Catholic. Club: Flying Fourteen (pres. 1974). Home: 150 Melrose E Apt 508 Seattle WA 98102 Office: State Office Bldg 2 Olympia WA

HANSEN, JAMES V., congressman; b. Salt Lake City, Aug. 14, 1932; s. Joseph Vear and Sena Utah Ruth (Clawson) H.; m. Ann Burgoyne, June 11, 1958; children—Susan, Joseph, David, Paul, Jennifer. Mem. Utah Ho. of Reps., also speaker; mem. 97th-98th Congresses from 1st Utah Dist. Served with USN. Republican. Mormon. Office: 1113 Longworth House Office Bldg Washington DC 20515

HANSEN, JEFFREY DOUGLAS, writer; b. Glendale, Calif., Jan. 20, 1945; s. Douglas Preston and Marian Dorothy (Modes) H.; m. Lynda Ann Jay, Feb. 5, 1966 (div. June 1970). B.A. in English magna cum laude, Calif. State U.-Northridge, 1970. Reporter, Burbank (Calif.) Daily Rev., 1964-67; night editor Los Angeles City News Service, 1967-68; reporter, asst. city editor Torrance (Calif.) Daily Breeze, 1970-72; met. reporter Los Angeles Times, 1972—; assoc. contract editor Adweek, Los Angeles. Recipient Editorial Excellence award Los Angeles Times, 1980. Mem. Sigma Delta Chi. Democrat. Author: Sports Vision Training, 1982.

HANSEN, JO ANN BROWN, fin. adminstr.; bus. exec.; b. Gallup, N.Mex., July 7, 1929; d. William and Stefi Marie (Schuster) Brown; B.S., U. Ariz., 1950, M.S., 1954, Ph.D., 1966; m. Gordon Eddy Hansen, Mar. 2, 1951; 1 son, Erling Wilhelm II. Clin. microbiologist, histologist pvt. labs., Tucson, 1950-54; teaching fellow, research asst. U. Ariz., Tucson, 1953-54 instr. microbiology, 1954-55, research assoc. in pharmacology Coll. Medicine, 1973-78, project dir. Sci. Career Workshops, 1976-79, research assoc. Cancer Center, 1977-82, program dir. for cancer edn. and grant adminstrn., 1979-82; dir. budget and fin. La Frontera Ctr., Inc., Tucson, 1982—; mem. pres.'s com. on aflatoxin, 1978-79; v.p. Hansen's Auto & Tool Supply Co., 1958-78, pres., 1978—; cons. Research Triangle Inst., 1978—, Nat. Cancer Inst., 1979—, UCLA Jonsson Cancer Ctr., 1981-82, NSF, 1982—, FDA, 1979—; adv. bd. Women in Sci. and Engring., S.W. Inst. Research on Women, 1979-82, chmn., 1980-81; chmn., moderator Forum on Breast Cancer, Community Health Edn., 1974, 78; moderator Forum on Right to Die, 1976, mem. Women's Commn. Health Task Force; cons. Cadre of Ariz. Dept. Edn.; del. People's Republic China, 1976; People-to-People del., S. Am., 1979; del. White House Conf. on Small Bus., 1980. Mem. com. of 100, St. Joseph's Hosp., mem. community adv. bd., 1979-82; active allocations div. United Way, 1979-82; founder, pres. Republican Women's Caucus, 1975-76, v.p., 1976-77, mem. exec. com., 1978—; mem. Rep. Task Force Nat. Women's Polit. Caucus, 1977—. USPHS grantee, 1962-63; Am. Cancer Soc. Inst. Research grantee, 1964-66; AAUW Founder's fellow, 1975-76; NSF grantee, participant Women in Sci. program, 1976-77; Ariz. Found. grantee, 1977, 78; Dept. Labor grantee, 1978-81. Mem. Ariz. Acad. Sci., AAAS, U.S.-Mexican Border, Am., Ariz. pub. health assns., Assn. for Women in Sci., Am. Cancer Soc. (pub. edn. com. 1978-82, profl. edn. com. 1978-81, crusade com. 1982—, dir. Pima County unit 1979—), Am. Soc. Microbiology, N.Y. Acad. Scis., AAUW, Mensa, Ninety Nines, Good Govt. League, Chi Omega, Iota Sigma Pi (nat. del. 1981), Sigma Delta Epsilon. Episcopalian. Research, condr. workshops, participant confs. in field. Home: 4926 E Bermuda St Tucson AZ 85712 Office: 5193 E 22d St Tucson AZ 85711 also La Frontera Ctr Inc 502 W 29th St Tucson AZ 85713

HANSEN, JOHN WILLIAM, hosp. adminstr.; b. Cin., Dec. 7, 1928; s. Hans Christian and Laura Marie (Oeppe) H.; m. Wilma Alice Squires, Dec. 9, 1979; children—John William, Carol, Diane, Steven, Richard, Pamela, Laura, David. Cert. in acctg., U. Cin., 1952. Cost acct. Stearns & Foster Co., Lockland, Ohio, 1949-62; v.p. Tucson Med. Center, 1962—. Bd. dirs. ARC, Tucson, 1977-82, also treas. Mem. Nat. Assn. Accts., Hosp. Fin. Mgmt. Assn., Ariz. Hosp. Assn. (dir. 1976-82, treas. 1980-82). Episcopalian. Home: 8260 E Rockgate Rd Tucson AZ 85715 Office: PO Box 42195 Tucson AZ 85733

HANSEN, KATE PEGGY, editor; b. Washington, Sept. 11, 1948; d. Lester and Louise (Blanton) Leopold; M.A., Bob Jones U., 1970; M.A., San Diego State U., 1979. Instr., Christian Heritage Coll., San Diego, 1970-76; asso. prof. speech San Diego City Coll., 1976-80; editor Where Mag., San Diego, 1980—; communications cons. Pacific Telephone, U.S. Marine Corps, 1979-82. Mem. Western Speech Communications Assn., Communication Arts Group. Republican. Home: 5046 Ducos Pl San Diego CA 92124 Office: 2165 San Diego Ave San Diego CA 92110

HANSEN, KATHRYN GIBBON, retired social service administrator and educator; b. Chgo., Nov. 5, 1908; d. Edmond and Margaret Josephine (O'Donnell) Gibbon; B.S. in Edn., DePaul U., 1942; M.Ed., Loyola U., Chgo., 1944; numerous hon. degrees; m. Ralph E. Hansen, Aug. 15, 1951. Tchr. English to adults Chgo. Bd. Edn., 1947-58, tchr. elementary schs., 1959-75; social adjustment tchr. of 5 high schs. Chgo. Bd. Edn., also art coordinator, 1965-69; dir. Project Family Life, Chgo., 1956-69; founder Chgo. Edn. News, 1962; lectr. TV program, Laguna Hills, Calif., 1972-73. Ecumenical rep. Archdiocese of Los Angeles, Roman Cath. Ch., 1973-75; sec. Laguna Hills Religious Council,

1973-75; ecumenical devel. chmn. Saddleback area Ch. Women United, 1975-77; publicity dir. St. Nicholas Ct. of Cath. Ecumenical Daus. 1977—; pres. Ch. Women United of Laguna Hills, 1973-75; co-chmn. for closed circuit TV program Laguna Hills Religious Council. Recipient engraved gold locket Ch. Women United, 1975. Mem. NEA (life), Ill. Edn. Assn. (v.p., pres.), Chgo. Art Edn. Assn., Exceptional Children's Assn., Adult Edn. Assn., AAUW (sec. Calif. sect. 1970-71), Laguna Hills Art Assn., Laguna Hills Hist. Soc. (adv. com.), Nat. Council Sr. Citizens (rec. sec. chpt. 1982-83), Internat. Platform Assn., Delta Kappa Gamma (pres. Alpha Omega chpt. 1961-63; life). Roman Catholic. Contbr. numerous articles and poems to various jours. and newspapers. Address: 2240-0-Via Puerta PO Box 2323 Laguna Hills CA 92653

HANSEN, LEONARD JOSEPH, editor, publisher, marketing consultant; b. San Francisco, Aug. 4, 1932; s. Einar L. and Margie A. (Wilder) H.; A.B. in Radio-TV Prodn. and Mgmt., San Francisco State Coll., 1956, postgrad. 1956-57; cert. IBM Mgmt. Sch., 1967; m. Marcia Ann Rasmussen, Mar. 18, 1966; children—Barron Richard, Trevor Wilder. Jr. writer (part-time) Sta. KCBS, San Francisco, 1952-54; assoc. producer and dir. Ford Found. TV Research Project, San Francisco State Coll., 1955-57; air promotion dir. and writer Sta. KPIX-TV, San Francisco, 1959-60, crew chief on live and remote broadcasts, 1957-59; pub. relations mgr. Sta. KNTV-TV, San Jose, Calif., 1961; radio and TV promotion mgr. Seattle World's Fair, 1962; pub. relations and promotion mgr. Century 21 Center, Inc., Seattle, 1963-64; pub. relations dir. Dan Evans for Gov. Com., Seattle, 1964; propr., mgr. Leonard J. Hansen Pub. Relations, Seattle, 1965-67; campaign mgr. Walter J. Hickel for Gov. Com., Anchorage, 1966; exec. cons. to Gov. of Alaska, Juneau, 1967; gen. mgr. No. TV, Inc., Anchorage, 1967-69; v.p. mktg. Sea World, Inc., San Diego, 1969-71; editor and publisher Senior World Publs., Inc., San Diego, 1973—; panelist, public affairs radio programs, 1971—; lectr. journalism San Diego State U., 1975-76. Founding mem. Housing for Elderly and Low Income Persons, San Diego, 1977-78; mem. Mayor's Ad Hoc Adv. Com. on Aging, San Diego, 1976-79; vice chmn. Housing Task Force, San Diego, 1977-78; bd. dirs. Crime Control Commn., San Diego, 1980, San Diego Coalition, 1980-83; del. White House Conf. on Aging, 1981. Served with U.S. Army, 1953-55. Recipient numerous service and citizenship awards from clubs and community orgns. Mem. Public Relations Soc. Am. (accredited), Soc. Profl. Journalists (Best Investigative Reporting award 1979), Internat. Platform Assn., San Diego Press Club (Best Newswriting award 1976-77, Headliner of Yr. award 1980), Sigma Delta Chi. Home: 2696 Bayside Ln San Diego CA 92109 Office: 500 Fesler St El Cajon CA 92020

HANSEN, LOWELL HOWARD, physician; b. Clay Center, Kans., Dec. 26, 1929; s. Howard E. and Emma E. (Nachtigal) H.; m. Jesse Jane Hansen, Sept. 1, 1951; children—Susan, Rebecca, Sheree, Kathryn, Peter. B.S. summa cum laude, Wheaton Coll., 1951; M.D., U. Colo., 1955. Diplomate Am. Bd. Radiology, 1967. Practice gen. medicine, Denver, 1958-64, practice radiology, 1966—; chief dept. radiology Mercy Med. Ctr., Denver, 1976—; assoc. clin. prof. radiology U. Colo. Health Services Ctr. Served with USPHS, 1955-58. Fellow Am. Coll. Radiology; mem. Radiology Soc. N.Am., Rocky Mountain Radiology Soc. (pres. 1979), Colo. Med. Soc. Presbyterian. Office: 1633 Fillmore St Suite 2 Denver CO 80206

HANSEN, LUSIA FERNANDEZ, physicist; b. Santiago, Chile, May 23, 1927; d. Alberto Fernández and Esther Morales; B.S., U. Chile, 1949; M.S. in Physics, U. Calif.-Berkeley, 1957, Ph.D., 1959; m. W. L. Hansen, Mar. 1, 1954; 1 son, George Albert. Came to U.S., 1955, naturalized, 1959. Laboratorist in cosmic ray U. Chile, Santiago, 1950-55, asst. prof., 1953-55; research asst. U. Calif.-Berkeley, 1955-59; sr. research physicist Lawrence Livermore Nat. Lab., U. Calif.-Livermore, 1959—, also coordinator and recruiting mem. affirmative action program. Mem. exec. com. Mt. Diablo Ednl. Project, 1972-75; chmn. com. Chileno, 1973-79. Mem. Am. Phys. Soc. (com. on internat. freedom of scientists, com. on status of women in physics), Am. Nuclear Soc., Bay Area Women in Sci. Network, U. Calif. Alumni Assn., AAUW, Sigma Xi. Contbr. articles to profl. jours. Home: 15 Avalon Ct Walnut Creek CA 94595 Office: PO Box 808 Livermore CA 94550

HANSEN, MERLIN, denominational executive, writer; b. Salt Lake City, Feb. 28, 1950; s. Merlin Albert and Helena Kaye (Dakis) H.; m. V. Nannette Pederson, Apr. 9, 1974; children—Matthew David, Benjamin Dale, Joshua Snow. B.S. in Sociology, U. Utah, 1972, M.S. in Sociology, 1976, Ph.Ed. in Ednl. Adminstrn., 1980. Coordinator tng. in gerontology, U. Utah, 1976-78, dir. internat. health care program, 1978-79; mgr. tng. and devel. Ch. of Jesus Christ of Latter-day Saints, Salt Lake City, 1979-81, mgr. adminstrv. services, 1981-82, dir. adminstrv. services, 1982—; mgmt. cons. to numerous orgns. Bd. dirs. Children's Ctr., Salt Lake City, 1971-73, Salt Lake Red Cross, Salt Lake City, 1976-78. Recipient Martin award, 1965; Adminstrn. on Aging tng. grantee, 1972-74. Mem. Am. Soc. Tng. and Devel., Phi Beta Kappa, Phi Kappa. Mormon. Author: Short Term Training, 1975; Grandpa Toby, 1976; Financing Gerontological Programs, 1977; Symbolic Interaction in Short Term Training, 1977; Effects of Finances on University Programs, 1982.

HANSEN, MICHAEL WAYNE, geologist; b. Pocatello, Idaho, Sept. 7, 1942; s. Bill Wayne and Mary (Hansen) H.; B.S. (Idaho Bank and Trust scholar, S.E. Idaho Gem and Mineral Soc. scholar), Idaho State U., 1965; M.S., U. N.C., 1970; Ph.D., U. Ill., 1975; m. Judith Ann Gochenour, July 26, 1963; children—Joni Lyn, Taggart. Sr. teaching asst. Idaho State U., Pocatello, 1964-65; research Ill. State Geol. Survey, 1966, 67-68, 75; educator U. Ill., Urbana, 1968-71; faculty Calif. State U., Fullerton, 1971-72; geologist Triangle Mining Co., Soda Springs, Idaho, 1972; staff geologist J.R. Simplot Co., Pocatello, Idaho, 1974-75; asst. prof. U. Ark., Little Rock, 1975-77; petroleum geologist Amoco Prodn. Co., Denver, 1977-79; sr. exploration geologist Anadarko Prodn. Co., Denver, 1979-81; sr. exploration geologist Williams Exploration Co., Denver, 1981-83; adj. prof. Idaho State U., 1979—; ind. geologist, 1983—. Coordinator, Hist. Geol. Labs., U. Ill., 1971; guest lectr. U. Puget Sound, 1973, geology dept. Idaho State U., 1973. NDEA fellow, 1965-67; honoraria Earth Sci. Curriculum Project, Boulder, Colo., 1970, NSF Earth Sci. Tchr. Preparation Project, Monterey, Calif., 1972; Sigma Xi grantee, 1970; Donaghey Found. research grantee, 1975-76. Mem. Geol. Soc. Am., Rocky Mountain Assn. Geologists, Assn. Women Geoscientists, Am. Assn. Petroleum Geologists, Tobacco Root Geol. Soc. (pres.), Soc. Econ. Paleontologists and Mineralogists, Sigma Xi. Author: Carbonate Microfacies of the Monte Cristo Group (Mississippian), 1974; Crinoid Shoals, Nevada, 1979. Home: 1149 Josephine Denver CO 80206

HANSEN, ROBERT DENNIS, ednl. adminstr.; b. San Francisco, July 17, 1945; s. Eiler Cunnard and Muriel Lenore (Morrison) H.; B.A., U. San Francisco, 1967, M.A. in Counseling and Guidance, 1971, M.A. in Supervision and Adminstrn., 1973; m. Diane Armstrong Messinger, Aug. 14, 1971; children—April Michelle, Allson Nicole. Tchr., dept. chmn., counselor, dir. student affairs, attendance officer South San Francisco Unified Sch. Dist., 1968-74, coordinator, asst. prin. Jurupa Unified Sch. Dist., Riverside, Calif., 1974-78; prin. San Gabriel (Calif.) Sch. Dist., 1978—. Exec. bd. South San Francisco PTA, 1968-74. Named hon. chpt. farmer Future Farmers Am. Mem. U. San Francisco Edn. Alumni Soc. (pres. 1972-73), U. San Francisco Alumni Assn., Assn. Calif. Sch. Adminstrs., Assn. for Supervision and Curriculum Devel., Nat. Assn. Secondary Sch. Prins., Phi Delta Kappa. Democrat. Episcopalian. Mason (32 deg.). Home: 415 Campus View Dr Riverside CA 92507 Office: 1440 Lafayette St San Gabriel CA 91776

HANSEN, ROBERT GUNNARD, scientist, philatelist, numismatist; b. Chgo., Aug. 16, 1939; s. Earl F. and Mildred E. (Hargrave) H.; A.A., Lincoln Coll., 1960; B.A., Culver Stockton Coll., 1962; M.B.A., U. So. Calif., 1966; postgrad. UCLA Extension, 1962-67; m. Bertha Golds, Aug. 10, 1960; children—Karin Lee, Lisa Marie. With Litton Industries, 1962-63, Sterer Engring., 1963-69; mktg. and contracts ofcl. Santa Barbara Research Ctr., 1969-73; pres., chief exec. officer, R.G. Hansen & Assocs., Santa Barbara, 1964—; pres., owner The Silver Penny and Santa Barbara Stamp & Coin, 1969—; guest lectr. Santa Barbara City Coll. Mem. Am. Vacuum Soc., Am. Philatelic Soc. (life), Am. Numismatic Assn., Hawaii Numismatic Assn., Token and Medal Soc. Republican. Presbyterian. Clubs: Masons, York Rite, Scottish Rite, Shriners, Royal Order of Scotland, Channel City, Royal Arch Masons, Toastmasters. Research and publs. on cryogenics, electro-optics, infrared radiation; patentee in field. Office: 1324 State St Santa Barbara CA 93101

HANSEN, RONALD GREGORY, civil engineer; b. Waipahu, Hawaii, Aug. 22, 1929; s. Erling M. and Geraldine J. (Nettleton) H.; m. Theresa J. Cunningham, Feb. 5, 1955; children—Eric L., Karen A., Maureen A., Timothy E. B.C.E., U. Santa Clara, 1952; M.S.C.E., U. So. Calif., 1958, postgrad., 1958-66; M.P.A., U. Alaska, 1981. Registered civil engr., Alaska, Wash., Oreg., Calif. Engr., Calif. Dept. Water Resources, Los Angeles, 1957-67; sr. engr., Water Quality Control Bd., Los Angeles, 1967-71; chief water pollution control State of Alaska, Juneau, 1971-79; sr. engr., EMPS Engring. Juneau, 1981—. Former scoutmaster, now mem. bldg. com. S.E. Alaska, Boy Scouts Am. Served to lt. col., C.E., U.S. Army, 28 yrs. Mem. Am. Water Works Assn., ASCE, Water Pollution Control Fedn., Am. Acad. Environ. Engrs., Am. Water Resources Assn., Internat. Water Resources Assn., Nat. Soc. Profl. Engrs., Republican. Roman Catholic. Home: 4117 Birch Ln Juneau AK 98801 Office: EMPS Engineering Inc Box 2317 Juneau AK 99803

HANSEN, SIGVARD THEODORE, JR., orthopaedic surgeon, medical educator; b. Spokane, Wash., Nov. 30, 1935; s. Sigvard Theodore and Beverly Esther (Means) H.; m. Mary Jane Weinmann, Aug. 20, 1960; children—Christopher Michael, Eric Theodore. B.A. cum laude, Whitman Coll., 1957; M.D., U. Wash., 1961. Diplomate Am. Bd. Orthopaedic Surgery. Intern, King County Hosp., Seattle, 1961-62; resident in surgery U. Wash., Seattle, 1965-69, asst. prof. orthopaedic surgery 1971-75, assoc. prof., 1975-79, prof., 1979—, chmn. dept., 1981—; cons. Madigan Army Hosp., 1975—. Served with USN, 1962-65. NIH summer research fellow, 1957, 58. Mem. Am. Acad. Orthopaedic Surgery, Am. Orthopaedic Assn., Assn. Bone and Joint Surgeons, Western Orthopaedic Assn., Phi Beta Kappa. Club: Sand Point Golf and Country. Contbr. articles to med. jours., chpts. to books. Home: 3512 43d St NE Seattle WA 98105 Office: 325 9th Ave Suite 6S Seattle WA 98104

HANSEN, STANLEY WAYNE, computer systems design engr.; b. Long Beach, Calif., Mar. 16, 1940; s. Royal John and Emma Lois (Mackay) H.; B.S., U. Utah, 1964; m. Lorraine Mitchell, Sept. 3, 1965; children—Jeffrey Kent, Gregory Kirk, Michael Wayne. With Ford Aerospace and Communications Corp., Colorado Springs, Colo., 1965—, project engr. JCS Real Time Computer Complex for Apollo lunar landings, now prin. engr. in charge research/devel. and new computer systems design; co-founder Hyper-Tech. Devel. Corp.; cons. in field. Active Boy Scouts Am., 1951-81. Served with USNG, 1957-65. Recipient Eagle with Palms award, Boy Scouts Am., 1953, Silver Explorer award, 1956. Mormon. Contbr. articles to profl. jours.; patentee several mini/microcomputer designs. Office: 10440 State Hwy 83 Colorado Springs CO 80908

HANSEN, TIMOTHY KARL, fin. exec., city ofcl.; b. Oakland, Calif., Feb. 18, 1941; s. Therman August and Margaret June (Christensen) H.; student, Modesto Jr. Coll., 1958-62; A.A., San Jose City Coll., 1966; B.S. in Accounting, San Jose State Coll., 1970; m. Virginia Cruz Cervantes, Sept. 1, 1963; children—Kirsten Suzette, Lance Erik. Asst. ops. officer Wells Fargo Bank, Foster City, Calif., 1968-72; asst. auditor-controller Kings County, Hanford, Calif., 1972-77; fin. officer and tax collector Clatsop County, Astoria, Oreg., 1977-80; asst. fin. dir. City of Visalia (Calif.), 1980-82, dir. fin. ops., 1982—; instr. acctg. Coll. of Sequoias, Visalia, 1976-77. Candidate for Kings County Treas.-Tax Collector, 1974. Mem. Am. Mgmt. Assn., Mcpl. Fin. Officers Assn., United Ostomy Assn. (past pres. Astoria chpt.), Central Valley Public Mgmt. Assts., Nat. Inst. Govtl. Purchasing, Calif. Assn. Public Purchasing Ofcls., Calif. Mcpl. Treas. Assn., Mcpl. Treas.'s Assn. U.S. and Can., Calif. State Mcpl. Fin. Officers, Nat. Council Self-Insurers, Council Self-Insured Public Agys., Risk and Ins. Mgmt. Soc., Am. Soc. Pub. Adminstrs., Pub. Agy. Risk Mgmt. Assn., Pub. Risk and Ins. Mgmt. Assn. Democrat. Soc. Democrat. Lutheran. Club: Elks. Home: 2738 Dayton St Visalia CA 93277 Office: Visalia City Hall 707 W Acequia St Visalia CA 93291

HANSEN-NEALEY, LEONA IRENE, hospital administrator; b. Odense, Denmark, Mar. 3, 1932; d. Johannes David and Ellan Helene (Madsen) Hansen; m. Horace D. Nealey, Aug. 24, 1953; children—David, Donnell, Michael. Student U. Idaho, 1951-53, Portland State U., 1968-71. Asst. dir. purchasing, assoc. dir. pub. relations and devel. St. Vincent Med. Ctr., 1963-68; adminstrv. asst. Portland State U., 1969-70; dir. vol. services Providence Med. Ctr., Seattle, 1972-79; dir. admitting and client service Pacific Med. Ctr., San Francisco, 1980-81; dir. vol. service O'Connor Hosp., San Jose, Calif., 1981—. Docent Portland Art Mus.; bd. dirs. Seattle Repertory Orgn., Seattle Repertory Theater, 1972-77; bd. dirs. A Contemporary Theater, Seattle, 1977-80; chmn. bd. dirs. Friends of Nursing Stanford U. Hosp., 1981—. Mem. Am. Soc. Dir. Vol. Services, Am. Hosp. Assn., No. Calif. Hosp. Dir. Vol. Services, Calif. Hosp. Assn. (region II advisor), Nat. League Nursing, Calif. League Nursing. Club: Seattle Yacht. Author: Vaer SAA God! A Collection of Danish Country Inn Recipies 1978. Home: 1885 Oak Ave Menlo Park CA 94025 Office: 2105 Forrest Ave San Jose CA 95128

HANSON, CARL DWAYNE, oil co. exec.; b. Fredericktown, Pa., May 31, 1927; s. John Lawrence and Mildred (Cook) H.; B.S. in Petroleum Engring., Pa. State U., 1950; m. Nellda L. Bynum, June 1, 1953; children—Carl Dwayne, Lisa Ann, Jon Bynum. With Forest Oil Corp., 1950—, gen. prodn. mgr., Denver, 1966-73, v.p. prodn., 1973—. Served with USNR, 1945-46. Registered profl. engr., Colo. Mem. AIME, Am. Petroleum Inst., Rocky Mountain Oil and Gas Assn., Ind. Petroleum Assn. Am. Methodist. Clubs: Cherry Hills Country, Columbine Country, Petroleum. Home: 4580 Sumac Ln Littleton CO 80123 Office: 1500 Colorado Nat Bldg Denver CO 80202

HANSON, DONNA MCKINNEY, social service executive; b. Arlington, Ky., Sept. 18, 1940; d. George R. and Louise H. McKinney; m. Robert Gordon Hanson, July 17, 1965; children—David, Steven. B.A. cum laude, Ursuline Coll., Louisville, 1962; M.S.W., St. Louis U., 1964. Social worker Catholic Family Service, Spokane, Wash., 1964-66, Spokane Sch. Dist. 81, 1966-68; instr. sociology Ft. Wright Coll. Holy Names, Spokane, 1968; instr. human services Spokane Falls Community Coll., 1968-69, project dir., 1969, program planner Spokane County Parent Coop. pre-sch. program, 1971; part-time assoc. dir. Cath. Charities, Spokane, 1974-78, exec. dir., 1978—. Founder, Spokane Day Care Ctr., 1966-70; chmn. day-care com. Family Counseling Service Spokane County, 1966-68, bd. dirs., 1966-71; bd. dirs. Spokane YWCA, 1969-71; mem. tutor-aid adv. com. ARC, 1971-72; mem. Spokane County Community Coordinated Child Care Council, 1971-72; founder Suspected Child Abuse and Neglect Ctr., 1972-75; chmn. program adv. com. Spokane Pub. Library Toy Lending, 1973-75; mem. children's and adult services adv. com. Wash. State Dept. Social and Health Services, 1973-76, mem. Gov.'s Select Panel on Dept. Social and Health Services, 1976-77; mem. Spokane Quality Life Council, 1974-76; chmn. sch. and social service task force, mem. coordinating com. Spokane County Comprehensive Planning Com., 1974-76; mem. adv. com. Wash. State Office Community Devel., 1974-77; mem. coordinating com. Wash. State Conf. Women, 1976-77; mem. bd. regents Gonzaga U., 1977-80; chmn. social concerns com. Wash. State Cath. Conf., 1979-83. AAUW fellow, 1972; named Spokane Woman of Distinction, 1978. Mem. Assn. Jr. Leagues (bd. dirs. 1978-80, child advocacy com. 1978-79, pub. issues chmn. 1979-80, Area VI dir.), Jr. League Spokane (chmn. state pub. affairs 1977-78, pres. 1976-77, bd. dirs. 1973-77, chmn. urban affairs interest 1974-75, asst. chmn. community research com. 1971-73, community bd. inst. com. 1971-72), Nat. Assn. Social Workers, AAUS (bd. dirs. Wash. State 1971-72). Home: 620 W 19th Ave Spokane WA 99203 Office: 1023 W Riverside Spokane WA 99210

HANSON, DOUGLAS EUGENE, accountant; b. Glenwood, Minn., June 7, 1945; s. Ferdinand Julius and Hazel Josephine (Skarsten) H.; m. Judith Kay Thompson, Jan. 1, 1978; children—Thomas, Timothy, Erika, Denise, Krista (twins). A.A., Contra Costa Coll., San Pablo, Calif., 1963-66; B.S., Calif. Poly. State U., 1972. C.P.A., Alaska. Various positions to supr. Peat, Marwick, Mitchell & Co., C.P.A.s, 1972-78; sole practice of acctg., Anchorage, 1978—. Served with USAF, 1966-70. Mem. Am. Inst. C.P.A.s, Alaska Soc. C.P.A.s. Mem. Ch. of God. Office: 2805 Dawson St Suite 105 Anchorage AK 99503

HANSON, EVA GIFFORD, educator, consultant; b. Lovell, Wyo., Dec. 23, 1946; d. Andy W. and Lillian M. (Jolley) Gifford; m. Earl Phillip, Hanson, Dec. 20, 1969; children—C. Matthew, Douglas A., Melissa, Stephanie. B.S. in Home Econs. Edn., U. Wyo., 1969; B.S., Eastern Mont. Coll., 1973. Cert. tchr., Wyo. Tchr. home econs. Byron (Wyo.) Jr. and Sr. High Sch., 1969-73; kindergarten tchr. pub. schs., Lovell, 1974-78; tchr. home econs. Lovell High Sch., 1978—; advisor Future Homemakers Am.; cons. Neo-Life. Mem. Wyo. Vocat. Assn., Wyo. Assn. Home Econs. Tchrs., Delta Kappa Gamma. Mormon. Club: Wyo. Extension Group (Lowell). Office: 502 Hampshire Lovell WY 82431

HANSON, FRANK LEWIS, aerospace company executive; b. Vinton, Iowa, Mar. 2, 1925; s. Sven Olaf and Belle Fae (McElhaney) H.; student Central Coll., Fayette, Mo., 1944-45, U. Notre Dame, 1945-46; B.B.A., U. Hawaii, 1963; postgrad. UCLA, 1965-68; m. Bette Ellen Logue, Apr. 6, 1947 (div.); children—Krista Lou, John Christian; m. 2d, Joan Finn. Commd. ensign Supply Corps, U.S. Navy, 1946, advanced through grades to lt. comdr., 1958; ret., 1965; mgr. subcontracts McDonnell Douglas Corp., 1965-76; mgr. subcontracts Rockwell Internat., Newport Beach, Calif., 1976-81, mgr. material, Santa Ana, Calif., 1981—. Fellow Nat. Contract Mgmt. Assn. Democrat. Episcopalian. Office: 3731 W Warner PO Box 11963 Santa Ana CA 92711

HANSON, GEORGE PETER, research botanist; b. Conde, S.D., July 20, 1933; s. George Henry and Rosa Wilhelmina (Peterson) H.; m. Barbara Jean Graves, Aug. 20, 1958; children—David, Carole, Heather, Peter; m. 2d, Gloria Ann Gauntt, June 1, 1969. B.S. in Agronomy, S.D. State U., 1956, M.S. in Plant Breeding, 1958; Ph.D. in Genetics, Ind. U., 1965. Asst. prof. biology Thiel Coll. Greenville, Pa., 1962-65; asst. prof. botany Butler U., Indpls., 1965-67; sr. biologist Los Angeles State and County Arboretum, Arcadia, Calif., 1968—. Mem. Genetics Soc. of Am., Botanical Soc. of Am., AAAS, Am. Inst. Biol. Scis., Guayule Rubber Soc. (pres.), Sigma Xi, Phi Kappa Phi. Republican. Methodist. Contbr. numerous articles in field to profl. jours. Home: 1345 W Haven Rd San Marino CA 91108 Office: 301 N Baldwin Ave Arcadia CA 91006

HANSON, JAMES LEVI, chem. engr., farmer; b. Havre, Mont., Dec. 27, 1946; s. Murvin James and Rae Edith (Bailey) H.; B.S.E., Ariz. State U., 1969; m. Dian Louise Chesser, Apr. 13, 1968; children—Kjelsty, Tansy. Devel. engr. Celanese Fibers Co., Rock Hill, S.C., 1969-73; process engr. Catalytic Inc., Charlotte, N.C., 1974-75; sr. engr. J.E. Sirrine Co., Greenville, S.C., 1976; owner, operator Sunshine Engring., cons., Gildford, Mont., 1976—; mgr. organic dry land wheat farm, Gildford, 1976—; pres. Zarathustra's Garden, Organic Grain Growers Cooperative, 1980. Bd. dirs. Alt. Energy Resources Orgn., Billings, Mont., 1977-79. Served with USAR, 1970-76. Registered profl. engr., Mont., N.C., S.C., Va. Mem. Am. Underground Space Orgn., Internat. Solar Energy Soc., Union Concerned Scientists, Pi Kappa Alpha. Home and Office: PO Box 1776 Gildford MT 59525

HANSON, JAMES PALMER, accountant; b. Waukegan, Ill., Dec. 11, 1945; s. Palmer Benny and Janette Eleanor (Tronnes) H.; B.S., Fresno State Coll., 1968; A.A., Allan Hancock Coll., 1966; m. Kristy Leigh Smith, Dec. 6, 1969; children—Terri Lynn, Sherry Lynn, Bradford James. Tax mgr. Arthur Andersen & Co. C.P.A.s, San Francisco, 1968-75; partner Rogers, Hanson & Co., C.P.A.s, Hayward, Calif., 1975—. Vice pres., treas. Eden Community Found.; bd. dirs., treas. Greater Canyon Assn. Served with USAR, 1968-74. C.P.A., Calif. Mem. Am. Inst. C.P.A.s, Calif. Soc. C.P.A.s. Clubs: Lions (treas. Hayward 1978-81), Hayward Leaders (pres. 1979-81), Hayward Trade (head trader, dir.). Home: 5824 Cold Water Dr Castro Valley CA 94546 Office: 24301 Southland Dr Suite 604 Hayward CA 94545

HANSON, JEROME DOYLE, public relations executive; b. Mpls., Aug. 25, 1942; s. Rolf Rue and Ann Marie (Cashman) H.; m. Sally Ann Sullivan, Aug. 6, 1960; children—Jeffrey, Julliette. B.A., St. Cloud State U., 1964. Dist. mgr. U.S. C. of C., Billings, Mont., 1965-69; v.p. Kampgrounds of Am., Billings, 1969-75; pres. Jerry Hanson & Assocs., Billings, 1975—; pub. speaker Bd. dirs. Eastern Mont. Coll. Found.; v.p. Miss Mont. Pageant. Mont. amateur golf champion, open, single and doubles tennis champion. Mem. Nat. Speakers Assn., Nat. Assn. Expn. Mgrs., Am. C. of C. Execs., Mont. C. of C., Billings C. of C., Nat. Soc. Tng. Dirs. Republican. Club: Hilands Country (Billings). Office: 208 N 29th St Suite 215 Billings MT 59101

HANSON, KENNETH LYLE, marketing and advertising executive; b. Fargo, N.D., Dec. 21, 1942; s. Howard K. and Doris M. (Turner) H.; m. Marcia Packard, June 21, 1979; children—Lori, Scott, Christina. B.A., Colo. Coll. Sales and mktg. mgr. Advance Industries, Mpls., New Orleans and Cleve.; ptnr. Hanson, Pelz & Miller Advt., Colorado Springs, Colo., to 1976; pres., owner Hanson Mktg. & Advt. Inc., Colorado Springs, 1977—. Coach amateur hockey team, Pikes Peak, Colo.; bd. dirs. Jr. Achievement Project Bus., Colo. Coll. Hockey Club. Served with U.S. Army, 1965-67; Vietnam. Mem. Prospectors Assn. (former pres., chmn.), C. of C. (small bus. adv. bd.). Republican. Lutheran.

HANSON, LAWRENCE, art educator, sculptor; b. Winona, Minn., July 28, 1936; s. Glenn Frederick and Zula Angeline (Smith) H.; div.; children—Shawn, Marie, Teresa, David, Paul. B.A., U. Minn., 1959, M.F.A., 1962. Teaching asst. U. Minn., 1959-62, instr., 1961-63; prof. dept. art Western Wash. U., 1963—, dir. Western Gallery, 1966-77, art curator, 1968—; vis. artist Calif. State U.-Los Angeles, 1981-83; numerous one man and group shows; work commd. U. Wash. and Wash.

State Arts Commn. Chmn. Continuing Symposium on Contemporary Art, 1974-75. Nat. Endowment for Arts fellow, 1980; Wash. State Arts Commn. grantee, 1969. Mem. Wash. Art Consortium (chmn. 1975-77, vice chmn. 1979-81). Office: Western Wash U Dept Art Bellingham WA 98225

HANSON, MARY LOUISE, banker; b. Bremerton, Wash., Apr. 24, 1944; d. Lawrence Grant and Ruth Louise (Johnson) Dix; m. Donald Glenn Hanson, Dec. 19, 1964 (div.). Student U. Wash.-Seattle, 1962-64, Am. Inst. Banking, 1972-73, U. Colo., 1973-78. Adminstrv. asst. U. Pa., Phila., 1965-70, Provident Mgmt. Corp., Providence, 1970-72; with 1st Nat. Bank Denver, 1972-80; credit officer, asst. mgr. loan analysis dept., asst. v.p. United Bank of Denver, 1980—; lectr., chmn. adv. council Aton Found. State bd. positions Colo. Libertarian Party, 1976—, nat. vice chmn., 1977-81, regional rep. on nat. com., 1977, nat. fin. chmn., 1980-81, Libertarian candidate for treas. Colo., 1978; trustee Am. Cancer Research Ctr. Mem. Nat. Fedn. Bus. and Porfl. Women, Colo. Fedn. Bus. and Profl. Women (pres.-elect), Downtown Denver Bus. and Profl. Women (pres. 1978-80, state legis. chmn. 1980-81). Home: 812 Harrison Denver CO 80206 Office: 1740 Broadway Denver CO 80217

HANSON, MAUREEN PATER, public relations consultant, educator; b. Cin., Oct. 29, 1954; d. Gordon Mark and Mary Elizabeth (Donahue) Peter; m. Brent Arthur Hanson, Jan. 8, 1983. B.A. with honors, U. Dayton, 1977; M.Pub. Relations with honors, U. So. Calif., 1979. Advt. asst. Dayton (Ohio) Daily News, 1975; community relations coordinator Mayor's Office, City of Dayton, 1976, Stouffer's Hotel, Dayton, 1977; instr. internat. communications U. So. Calif.-Europe campuses, 1978-79; acct. exec. Burson-Marsteller, Los Angeles, 1979-80; v.p. The Hannaford Co., Inc., Los Angeles, 1981—; evening instr. U. So. Calif. Active CORO, 1981—. Mem. Pub. Relations Soc. Am. (pres. citation 1977), Publicity Club of Los Angeles. Republican. Roman Catholic. Editor: China Update, monthly newsletter, 1981—. Home: 3216 Oak Ave Manhattan Beach CA 90266 Office: The Hannaford Co 444 S Flower St Suite 2620 Los Angeles CA

HANSON, NOEL RODGER, mgmt. cons.; b. Los Angeles, Jan. 19, 1942; s. Albert and Madelyne Gladys (Pobanz) H.; B.S. in Indsl. Mgmt., U. So. Calif., 1963, M.B.A. in Fin., 1966; m. Carol Lynn Travis, June 17, 1967; 1 son, Eric Rodger. Asst. dir. alumni fund, then dir. ann. funds U. So. Calif., 1964-66; asst. to Walt Disney for Cal-Arts, Retlaw Enterprises, Glendale, Calif., 1966-68; asst. dir. joint devel. Claremont U. Center, 1968-69; v.p. adminstrn. Robert Johnston Co., Los Angeles, 1969-70; partner Hale, Hanson & Co., Pasadena, Calif., 1970-82, Hanson, Olson & Co., 1982—; pres. Pasadena Services, Inc., 1977—; dir. Pasadena Fin. Cons., Inc., Freeway Motors Ford, Pacific BanCorp, Pacific Island Bank. Trustee Oakhurst Sch., Pasadena, 1973-75; bd. advisers Girls Club Pasadena, 1977 ; mem. U. So. Calif. Assos., 1979—, U. So. Calif. Commerce Assos., 1965—. Republican. Presbyterian. Club: Jonathan (Los Angeles). Address: 1051 LaLoma Rd Pasadena CA 91105

HANSON, PALMER BENNIE, utility executive; b. Ruso, N.D., Oct. 1, 1919; s. Ole and Lisa Frederickson (Rangaard) H.; m. Janette Elinor Tronnes, Mar. 20, 1943; children—James P., Gerald R., Karen L., Robert D. Student Iowa Wesleyan Coll., 1943-44. Communications specialist Ill. Bell Telephone Co., 1942-58; sr. engr. Eckerts Electric Inc., Lompoc, Calif., 1959-60; communications engr. ITT Fed. Electric Co., Vandenberg, AFB, Calif., 1958-59, 60-70; procurement mgr. Quintron Systems Inc., Vanderberg AFB, 1970-78; procurement mgr. telephone div. Citizens Utilities Co., Kingman, Ariz., 1978—. Served with USAAF, 1942-45. Mem. Calif. Real Estate Assn. Methodist. Home: 985 Crestwood Dr Kingman AZ 86401 Office: 3405 Northern Ave PO Box 3609 Kingman AZ 86401

HANSON, PAUL BERNHARDT, banker; b. Bellingham, Wash., July 29, 1935; s. Max Bernhardt and Mae Bernice (Olson) M.; B.A. in Econs., Stanford U., 1957; postgrad. U. Wash. Pacific Coast Savs. and Loan Sch., 1961-62; m. Ann Houston Cilley, Aug. 6, 1965; children—Max Lawrence, Thor Rezeau. Asst. v.p. Bellingham First Fed. Savs. & Loan, 1958-66; trustee, chief exec. officer Mt. Baker Mut. Savs. Bank, Bellingham, 1966—, pres., 1971—; dir., sec. Mt. Baker Recreation Co., Bellingham, 1962—; dir. Builders Concrete, Inc., Savs. Bank Trust Co. NW. Republican precinct committeeman; mem. Whatcom County Rep. Central Com., 1965-67; trustee Western Wash. U., 1971-79, chmn., 1977-79; bd. dirs. Whatcom Devel. Council, 1974-78. Served with AUS, 1957-58. Mem. Am. Inst. Banking, Wash. Bankers Assn., Mut. Savs. Bank Assn. Wash. (pres. 1972-73), Nat. Assn. Mut. Savs. Banks (dir. 1972-73, 79-82), Wash. Savs. League (dir. 1980-82), Bellingham Jr. (past officer), Bellingham (dir. 1966-72) chambers commerce, Alpha Kappa Lambda. Lutheran. Clubs: Rotary (dir. Bellingham 1967-71, v.p. 1973-74, pres. 1975-76), Bellingham Yacht; Hobby, Univ. (Bellingham). Home: 505 17th St Bellingham WA 98225 Office: Mt Baker Mut Savs Bank 1621 Cornwall Ave Bellingham WA 98225

HANSON, PHILIP J., hospital adminstr.; b. Phoenix, Oct. 3, 1932; s. Philip and Freddie Katheryn (Phelps) H.; B.S., Ariz. State U., 1955; m. Barbara Lynn Bloker, Feb. 11, 1978; children—Philip, Leslie Lynne. Personnel analyst Maricopa County Personnel Dept., 1961-64; dir. personnel U. Utah Hosp., 1964-78; dir. personnel services Boswell Meml. Hosp., Sun City, Ariz., 1978—. Vice tng. chmn. Great Salt Lake council Boy Scouts Am., 1965-75. Served with Med. Service Corps, USAR. Recipient Silver Beaver award. Mem. Am. Soc. Personnel Adminstrn., Am. Soc. Hosp. Personnel Adminstrn., Utah Soc. Hosp. Personnel Adminstrn. (past pres.), Utah Personnel Assn. (past pres.), Phoenix Personnel Mgmt. Assn. (pres.), Ariz. Hosp. Assn., Ariz. Hosp. Personnel Assn., Res. Officers Assn. (past chpt. pres.). Republican. Presbyterian. Lodges: Kiwanis, Masons. Home: 4328 W Dahlia Dr Glendale AZ 85304 Office: 10401 Thunderbird Blvd Sun City AZ 85351

HANSON, ROBERT CARL, educator; b. Wichita, Kans., Nov. 5, 1926; s. Otto Albert and Alma Charlotta (Larson) H.; student U. Wyo., 1944, Tex. A. and M. U., 1945; B.A., U. Calif. at Berkeley, 1949, M.A., 1951, Ph.D., 1955; postgrad. Harvard, 1951-52; m. Margaret B. Bremner, Jan. 1, 1950; children—Steven, Holly, Juliana. Instr., Mich. State U., 1955-57, asst. prof., 1957-60; asst. prof. U. Colo., Boulder, 1960-62, asso. prof., 1962-65, dir. Bur. Sociol. Research, 1962-64, acting dir. Inst. Behavioral Sci., 1964-65, prof. sociology, 1965—, research program dir. Inst. Behavioral Sci., 1965-75. Cons. USPHS, Migrant Health Br., 1963-65; mem. Com. on Acad. Disciplines for Study Commn. on Undergrad. Edn., U.S. Office Edn., 1972-75. Served with AUS, 1944-46. Russell Sage Found. Residency grantee, 1960-62, USPHS Research grantee, 1960-63; NIMH Research grantee, 1960-63, 64-70; Council on Research and Creative Work fellow, 1964-65. Mem. AAAS (mem. com. on desert and arid zones research 1961-62), Peace Research Soc., AAUP, Am. Fedn. Tchrs., ACLU, Am. (com. on social statistics 1964-66), Pacific sociol. assns. Author: (with Richard Jessor, Theodore D. Graves and Shirley L. Jessor) Society, Personality and Deviant Behavior, 1968. Contbr. articles to profl. jours. Address: Dept Sociology University of Colo Boulder CO 80309

HANSON, ROBERT JOHN, educator; b. Dubuque, Iowa, Oct. 30, 1919; s. Peter John and Esther Anna (Flynn) H.; m. Josephine Corpstein, June 30, 1943; children—Robert John, David J., Peter T., Christina A. B.S.E.E., U.S. Naval Acad., 1941; M.B.A., U. So. Calif., 1967; postgrad. George Washington U., 1959, U. Va., 1962, UCLA, 1963-64. Commd. ensign, U.S. Navy, 1941, advanced through grades to capt., 1963, ret., 1968; with McDonnell Douglas, Huntington Beach, Calif., 1968-70; faculty Los Angeles Harbor Coll., 1970—, prof. acctg., 1974—; prof. naval sci. U. So. Calif., Los Angeles, 1964-67. Mem. Assn. Naval Aviation, Ret. Officers Assn., Naval Acad. Alumni Assn., Skull and Dagger Soc. Roman Catholic. Clubs: So. Calif. Golf Assn., K.C. Home: 30803 Rue Valois Rancho Palos Verdes CA 90274 Office: 111 Figueroa Pl Wilmington CA 90744

HANSON, ROGER ALL, public policy analyst; b. Alexandria, Minn., Aug. 4, 1942; s. Byron O. and Ruby E. (Swenson) H.; m. Karen A Feste, Jan. 4, 1944; 1 dau., Kristina Feste. B.A., Concordia Coll., 1964; Ph.D., U. Minn., 1972. Vis. assoc. prof. Reed Coll., Portland, Oreg., 1976-77; adminstrv. analyst Math. Policy Research Co., Denver, 1977-79; dir. research ABA, Washington, 1979-80; sr. researcher Inst. Ct. Mgmt., Denver, 1980—. Democrat. Editor Justice System Jour., 1983—; contbr. articles to profl. jours.

HANSON, RONDELL BLAIR, lawyer; b. Rexburg, Idaho, Sept. 1, 1937; s. Edward Blair and Alice (Barnett) H.; B.A., Stanford U., 1959; J.D., U. Calif., Berkeley, 1962; m. Joyce Pugmire, June 20, 1960; children—Jennifer, Elizabeth, Matthew, Andrew. Admitted to Calif. bar, 1962; ptnr. Kindel & Anderson, Los Angeles and Santa Ana, Calif., 1962-70, Layman, Hanson, Jones & Voss, Newport Beach, Calif., 1974-81; prin., gen. counsel Diversified Communities, Newport Beach, 1970-74; organizer, dir. Westlands Bank, 1969-75; lectr. Calif. Continuing Edn. of Bar, U. So. Calif. Tax Inst., U. Calif., Irvine. Bishop, Laguna Beach ward Ch. of Jesus Christ of Latter Day Saints, 1975-80; mgr. Laguna Beach Little League Baseball, 1978-80. Recipient Block S award Stanford U., 1980. Mem. Calif. Bar Assn., Orange County Bar Assn., Calif. Law Rev., Order of Coif. Republican. Clubs: Lincoln, Santa Ana Country. Contbr. legal articles to profl. jours. Home: 529 Emerald Bay Laguna Beach CA 92651 Office: 359 San Miguel Suite 300B Newport Beach CA 92660

HANSON, STANLEY DEAN, optometrist, educator; b. Boulder, Colo., Apr. 23, 1950; s. Russell Howard and Lois Helene H.; student Union Coll., 1968-71, U. Tenn., 1974; B.S., O.D., So. Coll. Optometry, 1975; m. Janenne Marie Wall, Jan. 6, 1979; 1 dau., Christina Janenne. Asst. optometrist C. Vance Bergvall, Optometrists, Littleton, Colo., 1975-77; staff optometrist City and County of Denver Dept. Health and Hosps., 1976-81; pvt. practice optometry, Denver, 1977—; instr. Community Coll. Denver, 1977-79; staff optometrist Kaiser-Permanente Med. Found., Denver, 1981—; asso. optometrist Thomas P. Larkin, M.D., Denver, 1981—. Cert. optometrist Nat. Bd. Optometric Examiners, Colo. Bd. Optometric Examiners, Minn. Bd. Optometric Examiners, Tenn. Bd. Optometric Examiners. Mem. Am. Optometric Assn., Colo. Optometric Assn. (trustee 1979-82, award of merit 1979, 80). Seventh-day Adventist. Contbr. articles to med. jours. Home: 13674 E Evans Aurora CO 80014 Office: 2465 S Downing St No 209 Denver CO 80210

HANZER, PHILIP, econometrician; b. Ft. Lauderdale, Fla., Jan. 8, 1951; s. Edward and Nettie (Ornstein) H.; m. Suzanne Bonnie Blottner, Aug. 8, 1971; children—Leora B., Samuel B. B.A., Fla. State U., Tallahassee, 1972; M.Phil., Columbia U., 1975. Research asst. in econometrics Bur. Applied Social Research, Columbia U., 1972-74, cons. Center for Computing Activities, 1974-75; lectr. dept. math. U. Pacific, 1975-77; asst. prof. dept. econs., 1977-80; econometrician resource planning dept. Sacramento Mcpl. Utility Dist., 1980—; vis. lectr. dept. econs. U. Calif.-Davis, 1982-83; industry cons. Electric Power Research Inst. NSF fellow, 1972-74; recipient Teaching Incentive award U. Pacific, 1979; Outstanding Young Men of Am. award Jr. C. of C. Am., 1980. Mem. Econometric Soc., Am. Statis. Assn., Internat. Assn., Energy Economists, Inst. Math. Stats., Internat. Soc. Forecasters. Author: (with D. Christianson and D. Hughes) Statistics Through Laboratory Experiences, 1977; contbr. articles to profl. jours. Home: 681 Lexington Ave Stockton CA 95204 Office: PO Box 15830 Sacramento CA 95813

HARA, JIMMY HIDEO, physician, adminstr.; b. Rivers, Ariz., Apr. 28, 1945; s. Hanzo and Tatsuye (Hirano) Takesako; B.A., UCLA, 1966; M.D., U. Calif., 1970; m. Diane Harris, May 10, 1975; 1 son, Jeremy Harrison. Intern, VA Hosp., Los Angeles, 1970-71, resident in internal medicine, 1971-72; staff physician So. Calif. Permanente Med. Group, 1974—, physician-in-charge Kaiser-Permanente La Cienega Clinic, 1975-78, Kaiser-Permanente Inglewood Clinic, 1978-82, Kaiser West Los Angeles Acute Care Clinic, 1982—; dir. Physician Asst. Continuing Edn., Kaiser Found. West Los Angeles Hosp., 1975—, chmn. papaprofl. protocol com.; asst. clin. prof. family practice and medicine UCLA; chmn. So. Calif. Permanente Med. Group family practice symposium, 1979-80. Community program dir. Nat. High Blood Pressure Edn. Program, 1975—. Served to lt. comdr. USN, 1972-74. Recipient Physicians Recognition award AMA, 1975, 78; Tchr. of Yr. award Dept. Medicine and Div. Family Practice, UCLA, 1978-79, 79-80, 81-82; diplomate Am. Bd. Family Practice. Fellow N.Y. Acad. Scis., Am. Coll. Angiology (asso.); mem. Soc. Tchrs. of Family Medicine, Am. Acad. Family Physicians, N.Am. Acad. Manipulative Medicine, Center for Integral Medicine, Am. Acad. Med. Dirs., Am. Venereal Disease Assn., Am. Pub. Health Assn., Am. Assn. Health Care Adminstrs., Phi Beta Kappa. Office: 3425 W Manchester Blvd Inglewood CA 90305

HARADON, PENNI PAUL, interior designer; b. Washington, Oct. 10, 1943; d. Philip Franklin and Dorothy (Hite) Paul; m. Fritz Howard Haradon, Sept. 12, 1964; children—Hollie Elizabeth, David Howard. Student U. So. Calif., 1961-62, Chouinard Art Inst., 1961; B.Profl. Arts, Woodbury Coll., 1964. With Country Cousin Interiors, Los Angeles, 1962—, partner, after 1970—, pres., owner, 1979—; tchr. interior design Western Home Furnishing Assn., 1965-81. Mem. Decorative Arts Council, Los Angeles County Mus. Assn. Recipient Certificates of Merit, Scholastic Mag., 1959, 60, 61, Am. Inst. Interior Design, 1964, Los Angeles County Fair, 1969, Am. Soc. Interior Designers, 1975. Mem. Am. Soc. Interior Designers (bd. mem.). Office: 8687 Melrose Ave Suite M48 Los Angeles CA 90069

HARANDA, RONALD PAUL, hospital administrator; b. Detroit, Aug. 5, 1950; s. Clarence Clyde and Patricia Donna (Ragona) H.; m. Cynthia Jean Jarvis, Sept. 23, 1978; children—Kelly, Lawrence. A.S., B.S., U. Mich., 1972; M.B.A., Eastern Mich. U., 1974. Lab. technician Consumers Power Co., Bay City, Mich., 1970, 71; mgmt. engr. Hosp. Systems Improvement Program, Ann Arbor, Mich., 1972-75; sr. cons. Health Mgmt. Advisors, Ann Arbor, 1975-77; sr. staff asst. planning Queen's Med. Ctr., Honolulu, 1977-79, dir. program planning dept., 1979—. Den leader Aloha Council Boy Scouts Am. Mem. Hosp. Assn. Hawaii, Hosp. Mgmt. Services Soc., Soc. Hosp. Planning. Roman Catholic. Clubs: Honolulu, Hosp. Assn. of Hawaii Golf. Office: 1301 Punchbowl St Honolulu HI 96813

HARANO, RICHARD MASAKI, social scientist; b. Sacramento, June 20, 1941; s. Ben T. and Misayo (Hirose) H.; B.A., Sacramento State U., 1963, M.A., 1967; 1 dau., Deborah Leigh. Mem. staff social research analysis, research and statistics sect., mgr. mgmt. and ops. analysis Calif. Dept. Motor Vehicles, Sacramento, 1967-78, mgr. program and policy analysis, 1978—. Instr. psychology San Joaquin Delta Coll., Stockton, Calif., 1969-71; instr. law U. So. Calif., 1979. Recipient Certificate of Commendation, Nat. Safety Council Met. Life, 1972. Mem. Am. Statis. Assn., Am. (accident research com. 1971—), Sacramento Valley psychol. assns. Home: 7406 Alma Vista Sacramento CA 95831

HARARI, OREN, psychology educator; b. Tel Aviv, Israel, July 30, 1949; s. Herbert and Rut (Klein) H.; B.A. in Psychology, San Diego State U., 1970; M.A., 1974, Ph.D., 1978, both in Indsl-Organizational and Social Psychology, U. Calif.-Berkeley. Instr., survey researcher in psychology, indsl. engring. U. Calif., Berkeley, 1975-76; program evaluator St. Mary's Coll., Moraga, Calif., 1976; personel research psychologist U.S. Navy; asst. prof. organizational psychology McLaren Coll. Bus., U. San Francisco, 1977-82, assoc. prof., 1982—. Bd. dirs. Conservatree Paper Co., San Francisco, 1980—. Recipient Disting. Teaching award U. San Francisco, 1981. Mem. Acad. Mgt., Am. Psychol. Assn., Western Psychol. Assn. Author: Resources and Issues in Adjustment (1977); contbr. to Organizational Behavior and Industrial Psychology: Readings with Commentary (1975), Procs. 13th Ann. Meeting of SRA, 1980); contbr. articles to profl. jours. Office: McLaren Coll Bus U San Francisco San Francisco CA 94117

HARASZTI, JOSEPH SANDOR, psychiatrist; b. Ocsa, Hungary, Apr. 23, 1944; came to U.S., 1956, naturalized, 1962; m. Csilla M. Stanzel, Oct. 20, 1979. B.S., Emory U., 1966; M.D., Johns Hopkins U., 1971. Diplomate Am. Bd. Psychiatry and Neurology. Intern in medicine N.Y. Hosp.-Cornell Med. Ctr., N.Y.C., 1971-72; resident in psychiatry U. Chgo. Hosps. and Clinics, 1972-75; chief psychopharmacology research unit Ill. State Psychiat. Inst., 1975-76; practice medicine specializing in psychiatry, Chgo., 1976-81, Norwalk, Calif., 1981—; asst. prof. psychiatry U. Chgo., 1975-78, cons., 1978-81; clin. assoc. dept. psychiatry Northwestern U. Sch. Medicine, Chgo., 1978-80; chmn. therapeutics com. Forest Hosp., Des Plaines, Ill., 1976-81; examiner Am. Bd. Psychiatry and Neurology, 1979. Mem. AMA, Am. Psychiat. Assn., Ill. Med. Soc., Ill. Psychiat. Soc., Chgo. Med. Soc. Club: Quadrangle (U. Chgo.). Editorial reviewer Archives Gen. Psychiatry, 1974—; contbr. articles to med. jours. Office: 12000 E Firestone Blvd Norfolk CA 90650

HARBAUGH, DELBERT LLOYD, JR., educational administrator; b. Rapid City, S.D., May 23, 1932; s. Delbert Lloyd and Julia Antoinette (Wagner) H.; m. Barbara Ruth Bennett, May 11, 1955; children—Sharen, Steven, Staci. B.S. in Edn., Black Hills State U., 1957; M.A. in Math., Boston Coll., 1965. Certified supt., prin., Wyo. Tchr. indsl. arts and math., Ft. Pierre, S.D., 1959-62; tchr. math. pub. schs., Edgemont, S.D., 1959-62, Spearfish, S.D., 1963-64; sch. adminstr., Sundance, Wyo., 1969—, prin. Sundance Elem. Sch., 1972—. Former mem. bd. dirs. Sundance Recreation. Served with U.S. Army, 1953-55. NSF grantee, 1962-63. Mem. Nat. Assn. Elem. Sch. Prins., Wyo. Assn. Elem. Sch. Prins., Assn. Supervision and Curriculum Devel. Republican. Clubs: Lions (Spearfish); Commercial, Lions (Sundance). Home: 714 S 6th St Sundance WY 82729 Office: Sundance Elem Sch 700 Park St Sundance WY 82729

HARBER, DARRELL M., real estate broker; b. St. Louis, July 2, 1952; s. Darrell L. and Georgia J. Harber; m. Betty Bosch, Apr. 28, 1973; children—Angela Jean, Matthew Michael. Student SE Mo. State U., 1972. Real estate agt., Wash., 1975-78; owner Ponderosa Land Co., 1978—; pres. Harber Land & Cattle Co. Chmn. United Way campaign, 1979; dir. transp. Jesus Fair 1979, 80; outpost comdr. Royal Rangers Christian Boys Camping. Served with U.S. Army, 1972-75. Office: Ponderosa Land Co 9703 Meridian S Puyallup WA 98373

HARBOUR, DAVID FRANKLIN, III, b. Coleman, Tex., Sept. 4, 1942; David Franklin and Selma (Koehler) H.; B.A. in English, Colo. State U., 1965; grad. Def. Info. Sch., 1968; M.S., Murray State U., 1971; m. Nikkie Rae Dabling; children Todd Douglas, Benjamin Conrad. Dir. Alaskan affairs Alaskan Meth. U., Anchorage, 1971-72; dir. public relations Murray, Kraft, and Rockey, Inc., Anchorage, 1972-73; dir. public affairs Alaskan Arctic Gas Pipeline Co., Anchorage, 1973, Washington, 1977; regional dir. govt. relations Atlantic Richfield Co., Anchorage, 1978; instr. fin. public relations and mktg. U. Alaska, 1975. Bd. dirs., pres. Common Sense for Alaska; trustee, vice chmn. Alaska Council on Econ. Edn., Commonwealth North; bd. dirs. Coalition Alaska Vets., Resource Devel. Council Alaska. Served to capt. U.S. Army, 1966-70. Mem. Pub. Relations Soc. of Am. (accredited), Alaska C. of C. (dir.), Alaska Press Club (pres.), Alaska Visitors Assn. Contbr. articles to profl. jours. Office: Box 360 Anchorage AK 99510

HARCOURT, ROBERT NEFF, educational administrator; b. East Orange, N.J., Oct. 19, 1932; s. Stanton Hinde and Mary Elizabeth (Neff) H. B.A., Gettysburg Coll., 1958; M.A., Columbia U., 1961. Cert. guidance, secondary edn., career and vocat. guidance, N.Mex. Social case worker N.J. State Bd. Child Welfare, Newark and Morristown, 1958-61; asst. registrar Hofstra U. and asst. to evening dean of student CCNY, 1961-62; housing staff U. Denver, 1962-64; fin. aid and placement dir. Inst. Am. Indian Arts, Santa Fe, 1965—. Donor Am. Indian Library collection Gettysburg (Pa.) Coll. Served with U.S. Army, 1954-56; Ger. Named hon. Okie, Gov. Okla., 1970; col. a.d.c., N.Mex. Mem. Am. Contract Bridge League (exec. bd. unit; advance sr. master) SAR, Santa Fe Council Internat. Relations, Am. Personnel and Guidance Assn., Assn. Specialists in Group Work (charter), Adult Student Personnel Assn., Phi Delta Kappa (exec. bd.), Alpha Tau Omega, Alpha Phi Omega. Home: 720 Acequia Madre #7 Santa Fe NM 87501 Office: Inst Am Indian Arts CSF Campus Santa Fe NM 87501

HARDEN, MARVIN, artist, educator; b. Austin, Tex.; s. Theodore R. and Ethel (Sneed) H.; B.A. in Fine Arts, UCLA, also M.A. in Creative Painting. Tchr. art Calif. State U., Northridge, 1968—, Santa Monica (Calif.) City Coll., 1968; mem. art faculty UCLA Extension, 1964-68; one-man shows include: Ceeje Galleries, Los Angeles, 1964, 66, 67, Occidental Coll., Los Angeles, 1969, Whitney Mus. Am. Art, N.Y.C., 1971, Eugenia Butler Gallery, Los Angeles, 1971, Irving Blum Gallery, Los Angeles, 1972, Los Angeles Harbor Coll., 1972, David Stuart Galleries, Los Angeles, 1975, Coll. Creative Studies, U. Calif., Santa Barbara, 1976, James Corcoran Gallery, Los Angeles, 1978, Newport Harbor Art Mus., 1979, retrospective Los Angeles Mcpl. Art Gallery, 1982; group shows including: U.S. State Dept. Touring Exhbn. in USSR, 1966, Oakland (Calif.) Mus. Art, 1966, UCLA, 1966, Mpls. Inst. Art, 1968, San Francisco Mus. Art, 1969, Phila. Civic Center Mus., 1969, Mus. of Art, R.I. Sch. Design, 1969, N.J. State Mus., 1969, Everson Mus. Art, Syracuse, 1969, La Jolla (Calif.) Mus., 1969, 70, High Mus. Art, Atlanta, 1969, Flint (Mich.) Inst. Arts, 1969, Ft. Worth Art Center Mus., 1969, Contemporary Arts Assn., Houston, 1970, U. N.Mex., 1974, U. So. Calif., 1975, Bklyn. Mus., 1976. Los Angeles County Mus. Art, 1977, Newport Harbor Art Mus., 1977, Frederick S. Wight Gallery, UCLA, 1978, Cirrus Edits., Los Angeles, 1979, Franklin Furnace, N.Y.C., 1980, Art Center, Los Angeles, 1981, Locher Gallery, Calif. Mus. Sci. and Industry, Los Angeles, 1981, Downtown Gallery, Los Angeles, 1981, Alternative Mus., N.Y.C., 1981, Real Art Ways, Hartford, Conn., 1981, Laguna Beach (Calif.) Mus., 1982, Los Angeles Mcpl. Art Gallery, 1982, Nagoya (Japan) City Mus., 1982, Los Angeles Inst. Contemporary Art, 1982, Mus. Contemporary Art. Chgo., Mint Mus., Charlotte, N.C., 1983, De Cordova and Dana Mus. and Park, Lincoln, Mass., 1983, Equitable Gallery, N.Y.C., 1984; represented in permanent collections at: Whitney Mus. Am. Art, N.Y.C., Mus. Modern Art, N.Y.C., Metromedia, Inc., Los Angeles, San Diego Jewish Community Center, Berkeley (Calif.) U. Mus., Home Savs. & Loan Assn., Los Angeles, also pvt. collections; dir. Images & Issues mag. Recipient UCLA Art Council award 1963, awards in visual arts, 1983; Nat. Endowment Arts fellow, 1972; Guggenheim fellow, 1983. Mem. Los Angeles Inst. Contemporary Art (co-founder 1972), Los Angeles Mcpl. Art Gallery Assn. (artists adv. bd. 1983—). Home: PO Box 353

Chatsworth CA 91311 Office: Calif State Univ Northridge 18111 Nordhoff St Northridge CA 91330

HARDER, HILDA LYBOLT, retired educator; b. Wurtsboro, N.Y., Oct. 17, 1915; d. Daniel Everett and Nell Evelyn (Bradley) Lybolt; B.S., State U. N.Y. at New Paltz, 1961; M.A., Calif. State U., Northridge, 1968; M.S., Calif. Luth. Coll., 1977; m. Edmund A. Harder, Dec. 25, 1941; children—Linda Anne, Stefanie, Gerald, Daniel, Kristen. Elem. tchr., N.Y. State, 1936-58; reading tchr., 1959-61; asst. dir. Ventura (Calif.) Reading Improvement Center, 1961-63; dir. Calif. Reading Clinics, Thousand Oaks, 1963-68; instr. U. Calif., Santa Barbara, 1966-68; asst. prof. edn. Calif. Luth. Coll., Thousand Oaks, 1968-77, assoc. prof., 1977-81, prof. emeritus, 1982—; edn. cons. public and pvt. schs. Mem. edn. task force Conejo Future Found. Recipient Woman of Achievement award Bus. and Profl. Women, 1966. Mem. AAUP, Calif. Coll. and Univ. Profs., Calif. Profs. Reading, AAUW, Internat. Reading Assn. (speaker convs. Honolulu 1980, Chgo. 1982, Anaheim, Calif. 1983), NEA, Calif. Assn. for Neurologically Handicapped, Bus. and Profl. Women's Assn., Sigma Pi Sigma, Delta Kappa Gamma, Theta Phi Gamma (pres. 1934-36). Contbr. articles to profl. jours.

HARDER, VIRGIL EUGENE, educator; b. Ness City, Kans., July 19, 1923; s. Walter J. and Fern B. (Pausch) H.; B.S., U. Iowa, 1950, M.A., 1950; Ph.D., U. Ill., 1958; m. Dona Maurine Dobson, Feb. 4, 1951; children—Christine Elaine, Donald Walter. Instr. bus. adminstrn., U. Ill., Urbana, 1950-55, U. Wash., Seattle, 1955—, asst. prof., 1955-59, asso. prof., 1959-67, prof., 1967—, asso. dean sch. bus. adminstrn., 1966-74; dir. Inst. Fin. Edn. Sch. for Exec. Devel., Seattle, 1974—; communications cons. bus. orgns. Served with AUS, 1943-45. Fellow Am. Bus. Communications Assn. (pres. 1965). Club: Trail Blazers. Author: (with Herta Murphy and Charles Peck) Building Favorable Impressions by Mail, 1961; Using PERT in Marketing Research (with Frank Lindell), Marketing Management and Decision Sciences, 1971. Contbr. articles, monographs to profl. publs. Home: 6025 50th Ave NE Seattle WA 98115 Office: Sch Bus Adminstrn U Wash Seattle WA 98195

HARDESTY, JOHN FRANCIS, broadcast cons.; b. Washington, June 18, 1922; s. Charles Phillip and Olive (Padgett) H.; student Am. U., 1940; m. Jeanine Thompson, 1969. Prodn. mgr., promotion mgr. CBS, Washington, 1939-46; promotion mgr. WOL, Washington, 1947-49; sta. relations dir. Nat. Assn. Broadcasters, Washington, 1949-51; promotion mgr. Radio Advt. Bur., N.Y.C., 1951-53, exec. v.p., 1956-59; sales mgr. Westinghouse Broadcasting Co., N.Y.C., 1954-56; pres., dir. Hamilton-Landis & Assos., Inc., San Francisco, 1959-67; pres., dir. Radio Kern, Inc.; broadcast cons., 1967—. Served with USNR, 1942-45. Mem. White House Corrs. Assn., Neptune Soc., U.S. Senate and House Gallery. Clubs: Commonwealth, Brit. American. Home: 115 Retiro Way San Francisco CA 94123

HARDING, JAMES WIRT, adminstrv. analytical chemist, clergyman; b. Houston, Feb. 28, 1927; s. James Wirt and Orlean Clive (Murray) H.; student U. Tex., 1944-45, U. Houston, 1946-47; B.A. in Chemistry, Baylor U., 1948; m. Helen Elizabeth Crump, Oct. 31, 1962; children—Elizabeth Irease, Marla Jaye, Evangeline, Shelley Anne, James Wesley. Advt. chemist Shell Chem. Corp., N.Y.C., 1948-51; research chemist Am. Cyanamid, Fort Worth, 1954-57; chief chemist Big Three Indsl. Gas, Houston, 1961-67; owner, operator Air Lab Inc., Houston, 1967-69; splty. gas mgr. S.W. Cryogenics, Houston, 1969-71; mgr. Rocky Mountain div. Sci. Gas Products Inc., Longmont, Colo., 1971-81; mgr. lab. services Sanco Services, Inc., Denver, 1981—; apptd. to ministry United Methodist Ch., 1975; pastor Mead (Colo.) United Meth. Ch., 1975—; speaker at tech. meetings. Served with USN, 1944-45. Mem. Am. Chem. Soc., Poetry Soc. Tex., Foothills Poets. Republican. Contbr. poems, short story to various publs., 1980-81; poetry editor Riverstone; developed ednl. gas chromatograph kit (IR-100 award Indsl. Research Mag. 1976), 1975. Office: 4950 E 39th Ave Denver CO 80207

HARDING, TERESA JANE, interior designer, consultant; b. Los Angeles, Jan. 14, 1949; d. Edward Joseph and Jane Elisabeth (Gunter) H. B.S. U. Okla., 1971. Interior designer Lawdsaws Co. of Norman (Okla.), 1970-71; buyer W & J Sloane Co., San Francisco, 1971-74, interior designer, Beverly Hills office, 1976-82; interior designer Macy's of Calif., San Francisco, 1974-76; owner, interior designer Harding Interiors Co., Los Angeles, 1978—. Bd. dirs. Jr. Charity League; active Colleague Helpers In Philanthropic Service. Mem. Am. Soc. Interior Designers (cert.) Republican. Roman Catholic. Home and Office: 1361 B S Beverly Glen Blvd Los Angeles CA 90024

HARDING, WAYNE EDWARD, III, accountant; b. Topeka, Sept. 29, 1954; s. Wayne Edward and Nancy M. (Gean) H.; B.S. with honors in Bus. Adminstrn., U. Denver, 1976, M.B.A., 1983; m. Janet Mary O'Shaughnessy, Sept. 5, 1979. Partner, HKG Assos., Denver, 1976-77; staff auditor Peat, Marwick, Mitchell & Co., Denver, 1976-78; auditor Marshall Hornstein, P.C., Wheat Ridge, Colo., 1978-79; sr. auditor Touche Ross & Co., Denver, 1979-80; controller Mortgage Plus Inc., 1980-81; sec.-treas. Sunlight Systems Energy Corp., 1980-81; partner Harding, Newman, Sobule & Thrush, Ltd., Denver, 1981-82; pvt. practice acctg. specializing in multi-family real estate and acctg. systems, 1982—; dir. Harding Transp., Crown Parking Products. Class agt., mem. alumni council Phillips Exeter Acad., Exeter, N.H., 1973—; bd. dirs., treas. Legal Center for Handicapped Citizens, Denver, 1979-80. Mem. Am. Inst. C.P.A.s, Colo. Soc. C.P.A.s, Beta Alpha Psi, Pi Gamma Mu, Beta Gamma Sigma. Republican. Contbr. articles in field of real estate to profl. jours. Home: 6029 S Kenton Way Englewood CO 80111 Office: 6875 E Evans Ave Suite 203 Denver CO 80222

HARDING, WAYNE EDWARD, JR., business executive; b. Fort Smith, Ark., Oct. 13, 1921; s. Wayne Edward and Laura Blanch (Lambiotte) H.; m. Nancy M. Gean, June 22, 1948; children—Lan C., Darra G., Wayne E., Wesley R., Phillip L. B.S., Princeton U., 1944. Cert. comml. investment mem. Realtors Nat. Mktg. Inst. Test pilot, aero. engr. United Aircraft Corp., 1946-48; co-founder, former pres., chmn. bd. dirs. Harding Glass Industries, Inc., Kansas City, Mo., from 1948 (merged into Sun Co.); co-founder, pres. Harding Transp., Inc., 1962—, Parking Systems Engring., Inc., Denver, 1968-73, Harding Tech. Leasing, Inc., 1980—; co-founder, mng. dir. Crown Parking Products Co., Denver, N.Y.C., 1971—; founder, owner, Harding Assocs., Denver, N.Y.C., 1973—. Vice-chmn. Urban Renewal Agency, Topeka, Kans., 1955-59; pres. Flood Control and Water Conservation Bd., Topeka, 1952-54; chmn. Mayor's Aviation Commn., Topeka, 1950-55. Served with USNR, 1944-46. Mem. AIAA, Nat. Flat Glass Mktg. Assn. (pres. 1960-62, chmn. bd. 1962-64, Thompson Merit award 1962), Nat. Parking Assn., Internat. Platform Assn. Republican. Baptist. Club: Rotary (Denver). Home: 3060 S Leyden Denver CO 80222 Office: 6875 E Evans Ave Denver CO 80224

HARDISTY, BETTIE CHRISTENE, educator; b. Dora, N.Mex., May 1, 1934; d. Benjamin Temple and Zella Maye (White) Long; B.S., Eastern N.Mex. U., 1974, M.Ed., 1976; m. Dan Preuit Hardisty, Aug. 17, 1952; children—Kathryn Christene, Dennis Dan. Bookkeeper, Hinkle's Dept. Store, Clovis, N.Mex., 1952-53, Clovis Cattle Commn. Co., 1954-56; cashier Southwestern Investment Co., Clovis, 1956; telephone operator Mt. Bell Tel. & Tel. Co., Clovis, 1956-58; home economist Coop. Extension Service, N.Mex. State U., Clovis, 1975—. Pres., James Bickley Parent Tchr. Orgn., Clovis, 1969-70; sec.-treas. Curry County Affiliate of Am. Diabetic Assn., 1975-79; bd. dirs. Meals on Wheels, Clovis, 1975-77. Named Curry County Cowbelle of the Yr., 1969; N.Mex. Assn. Extension Home Economist Communications award for weekly newspaper column, 1978. Mem. Am. Home Econ. Assn., N.Mex. Extension Home Econ. Assn., Nat. Extension Home Econ. Assn., Phi Kappa Phi. Democrat. Baptist. Club: Pilot Internat.

HARDISTY, DONALD MERTZ, musician, educator; b. Butte, Mont., Feb. 24, 1932; s. George D. and Lauretta (Mertz) Hardisty-Walkup; B.M.E., U. Mont., 1955, M. Music Edn., 1956; D. of Musical Arts, U. Rochester, Eastman Sch. of Music, 1969; m. Barbara Bridges; children—Donald W. and Douglas L. (twins). Bassoonist, U. Mont., 1955, Eastman Wind Ensemble, Rochester, N.Y., 1967-69, Tucson (Ariz.) Symphony, 1958-61, Houston (Tex.) Symphony, 1963, El Paso (Tex.) Symphony, 1973; prin. bassoonist Las Cruces Symphony at N.Mex. State U., 1969—; also featured soloist, 1977; instr. music, asso. choral dir. U. Ariz., Tucson, 1958-61; instr. instrumental music Tucson Pub. Schs., 1962-63; asso. prof. music Houston Bapt. U., 1963-64; asst. prof. music Calif. State U., Chico, 1964-67, also dir. of bands, 1964-67; grad. asst. ensemble and conducting dept. Eastman Sch. Music, Rochester, 1967-69; asso. prof. music N.Mex. State U., Las Cruces, 1969-78, prof., 1979—, acting head music dept., 1979—, grad. adv. music edn., chmn., coordinator theory programs, 1969—, chmn. new music bldg. com., 1980—; bd. dirs. Las Cruces Symphony Assn., 1979—; bd. dirs. Las Cruces Community Concert Assn., 1979—, featured soloist, 1981, 83. Served with U.S. Army, 1956-58; dir. 2nd army choral group, Ft. Meade, Md. Mem. Assn. Composers and Pubs. Am. (ASCAP), Nat. Alliance for Arts in Edn., Nat. Assn. Coll. Wind and Percussion Instrs., Music Tchrs. Nat. Assn. (nat. cert. in theory and bassoon), Internat. Double Reed Soc., Coll. Music Soc., N.Mex. Music Tchrs. Assn. (S.W. v.p. 1980-82, State v.p., pres.-elect 1982-84, composer of yr. 1982), Am. Orff-Schulwerk Assn., (dir. 1979—), N.Mex. Music Educators Assn. (v.p. coll.-univ. music 1977-79, pres. 1979-82), Soc. for Music Theory, Music Educators Nat. Conf. (nat. assembly 1979-83), N.Mex. Alliance Arts in Edn. (chmn. fin. com. 1979-82, pres. 1982—), Assn. Concert Bands Internat. (life, bd. dirs. 1979—). Republican. Author: Six Graded Collections of Original and Transcribed Rounds Arranged for Bassoon Ensembles, 1976; (video instrn. film) Secrets of the Triple Crowing Bassoon Reed, 1981; composer: Pisces of the Zodiac for Woodwind Quintet, 1979; Seven Stages in the Life of Man and His Music; A Cycle of Seven Songs for Choir, 1977; Bassoon Episodes Fantastique with Piano, 1980; contbr. articles to profl. jours. Home: 3020 E Majestic Ridge Las Cruces NM 88001 Office: Dept Music Box 3F New Mexico

HARDS, KATHRYN ELISA, indsl. psychologist; b. Chgo.; b. Arthur O. and D. Caroline (Redcliffe) Olsen; B.A., San Jose State U., 1972, M.S., 1976; m. William Clarence Hards; 1 son, Eric. Indsl. psychologist Four-Phase Systems, Cupertino, Calif., 1976-78; pvt. practice as cons. indsl. psychologist, Cupertino, 1979—; cons. C&H Sugar Co., San Francisco, Real Estate World, Campbell, Calif., Stanford U. Med. Center, Tech. Adv. Service for Attys., Pa., Leasametric, Foster City, Calif., TransUnion Fin. Group, Foster City, Saratoga (Calif.) Inst., Final Approach Mgmt. Systems, San Jose, Calif., SRA, Chgo., Nat. Med. Enterprises, Los Angeles, SRI, Palo Alto, Calif., Two P. Corp., Santa Clara, Calif., Four-Phase Systems, Cupertino; adj. prof. psychology San Jose State U., 1978—; pvt. practice career counseling and vocat. testing, 1979—; dir. K and H Assocs., Cupertino, Calif. Mem. Am. Psychol. Assn., Nat. Assn. Indsl. and Orgnl. Psychologists, Western Psychol. Assn., Profl. and Tech. Cons. Assn., Societe Canadienne de Psychologie, Psi Chi (life). Contbr. articles to profl. jours. Office: K and H Assocs PO Box 1078 Cupertino CA 95015

HARDY, ALICE JOAN, postal service official; b. Corvallis Oreg., Mar. 20, 1949; d. John Pickett and Mary Lorine (Barnes) Williams; m. Michael Hardy, Oct. 11, 1967; children—Taraleen Annette, Shawn Michael. Clk. substitute U.S Postal Service, Chgo., 1970; part time clk, postmaster replacement, Tangent, Oreg., 1973-75, rural letter carrier, Tangent, 1975—. Leader Girl Scouts U.S.A. Troop 209, Corvallis, Oreg., 1981-83; mem. adv. bd. gifted student program Corvallis Sch. Bd., 1981-83. Mem. Oreg. Rural Letter Carrier Assn. Dist. 7, (pres. 1982-84). Republican. Baptist. Clubs: Elks. Home: 1825 NE Noble Ave Corvallis OR 97330 Office: Main Post Office Tangent OR 97389

HARDY, BEN (BENSON B.), orchid nursery exec.; b. Oakland, Calif., Nov. 22, 1920; s. Lester William and Irene Isabell (Bliss) H.; student pub. schs., Oakland, Calif., Concord, Calif.; grad. photo Intelligence Sch., Denver, 1949. Served as enlisted man U.S. Navy, 1942-48; joined USAF, 1948, advanced through grades to capt., 1957; with 67th Reconnaissance Squadron, Korea, 1951-52, Hdqrs. Squadron, Thule AFB, 1956, resigned, 1957; material requirements analyst-coordinator Teledyne Ryan Aero. Co., San Diego, 1958-73; dispatcher-coordinator Cubic Western Data Co., San Diego, 1977-80; owner-partner orchid nursery. Pres. San Diego County Orchid Soc., 1972-73, 75-76, Exotic Plant Soc., 1976-78, 81—, San Diego Gesneriad Soc., 1978; dir. 23d Western Orchid Congress, 1979. Decorated Bronze Star, Letter of Commendation, others. Mem. Am. Orchid Soc., N.Z. Orchid Soc., Orchid Soc. SE Asia, Pacific Orchid Soc. Hawaii, Assn. Hoya Soc. Internat. (pres. 1981-83), Mexicana de Orquideologia, Sociedad Colombiana de Orquideologia, Cymbidium Soc. Am., Orchid Digest Corp. Contbr. articles to orchid jours.; pub. Western Gesneriad Gazette, 1978-79. Home: 9443 E Heaney Circle Santee CA 92071

HARDY, D. ELMO, entomology educator; b. Lehi, Utah, Sept. 3, 1914; s. Horace P. and Ivy (Allred) H.; A.B., Brigham Young U., 1937; M.A., Utah State U., 1938; Ph.D., U. Kans., 1941; m. Agnes Thomas, Sept. 6, 1935; children—Patricia Jane Swiger, Joan Marie Layton, Cheryl Kay Maloy, Dee E. Research Asst. Utah State U., Logan, 1937-38; instr. entomology U. Kans., Lawrence, 1937-41; field supr. Entomol. Surveys, U.S. Dept. Agr., Spokane, 1941; asst. state entomologist, Kans., 1941-42; asst. prof., asst. state entomologist Iowa State U., Ames, 1945-48; asso. prof. U. Hawaii, Honolulu, 1948-58, sr. prof. entomology, 1958-80, prof. emeritus, 1981—; vis. scientist Dept. Primary Industries, Brisbane, Australia, 1979, 82; cons. in field. Mem. State of Hawaii Natural Area Reserves Commn., 1971-75, State of Hawaii Animal Species Adv. Commn., 1978—. Served to maj., U.S. Army, 1942-45. Decorated Bronze Star Medal; recipient NSF Orgn. for European Economic Devel. award, U. Vienna, 1960-61; NSF Scientists and Engrs. in Economic Devel. award, Indonesia, 1975, 79; U. Hawaii award for excellance in research, 1968; Entomol. Soc. Am. Woodward award for outstanding research, 1976; NSF grantee, NIH grantee. Fellow Entomol. Soc. Am.; mem. AAAS, Soc. for Systematic Zoology, Kans. Entomol. Soc., Hawaiian Entomol. Soc., Hawaiian Acad. Sci., Sigma Xi, Gamma Sigma Delta. Mem. Ch. of Jesus Christ of Latter Day Saints. Author several books, chpts. in others, including (with M.D. Delfinado) A Catalog of the Diptera of the Oriental Region; Nematocera, Vol. I, 1973; Brachycera, Vol. II, 1975; Cyclorrhapha, Vol. III, 1977. Contbr. articles in field to profl. jours. Home: 2238 Seaview Ave Honolulu HI 96822 Office: Dept Entomology Univ of Hawaii Honolulu HI 96822

HARDY, JOEL ALLEN, microbiologist, educator; b. Los Angeles, Dec. 1, 1952; s. Allen Williams and Ina Carolyn (Cobia) H.; B.S., Weber State Coll., 1977; M.S., Idaho State U., 1979; m. Vicki Lynn Nickens, Dec. 20, 1974; children—Thomas Joel, Lucas Allen, Janna Marie. Chemist, Firestone Tire & Rubber Co., Salinas, Calif., 1980; instr. microbiology and chemistry Hartnell Coll., Salinas, 1980-82; microbiologist Internat. Shellfish Enterprises, Moss Landing, Calif., 1980-82; research specialist U. Utah Sch. Medicine, Salt Lake City, 1982—. Idaho State U. research grantee, 1979. Mem. AAAS, Am. Soc. for Microbiology, Sigma Xi. Republican. Mormon. Home: 78 W 2550 S Bountiful UT 84010 Office: U Utah Sch Medicine Dept Pathology 50 Medical Dr Salt Lake City UT 84132

HARDY, MARGARETE N., olympic committee exec.; b. Worcester, Mass., June 29, 1948; d. Erving Douglas and Janette (McCreery) Hardy; B.A., Whittier Coll., 1970; M.A., Occidental Coll., 1979; children—Douglas, Sarah. Adminstrv. asst. state senator and then lt. gov. Mervyn Dymally, Los Angeles, 1971-75; sr. asso. Cerrell Asso., Los Angeles, 1975-77; asst. dir. public affairs Calif. State Mus., Los Angeles, 1977-79; public affairs rep. Gen. Telephone Co., Santa Monica, Calif., 1979-83; dir. info. programs Los Angeles Olympic Organizing Com., 1983—. Bd. dirs. Nat. Council Social Services, 1969—, Calif. Spl. Olympics, 1969—; mem. Calif. State Bd. Cosmetology, 1976—, pres., 1980-81; mem. Calif. State Congress of Bds. and Burs., 1978—; mem. Dem. Women's Task Force, 1975—. Recipient Am. Friends of Public Service award, 1978; named Outstanding Woman in Politics, Los Angeles Mag., 1975; Urban Affairs fellow, 1973-74. Mem. NOW, Los Angeles Women's Polit. Caucus, LWV, Los Angeles Social Service Soc., Los Angeles Women's Coalition, Public Relations Soc. Am., Women in Communications, Public Interest in Radio and TV Soc., Radio and TV News Assn., Pi Sigma Alpha. Democrat. Clubs: Chmn.'s Circle, Greater Los Angeles Press. Home: 1843 Midvale Ave Los Angeles CA 90025 Office: Los Angeles Olympic Organizing Com Los Angeles CA 90084

HARDY, NANCY GREAVES, counselor; b. Preston, Idaho, Sept. 29, 1939; d. Donald Kidd and Idana (Swainston) Greaves; m. J. Malin Hardy, Jan. 7, 1932; 1 dau., Susan. B.S., Utah State U., 1961, M.S., 1970. Profl. counselor, Utah. Program editor TV Guide, Salt Lake City, 1960-61; English tchr. Granger High Sch., Salt Lake City, 1962, Granite High Sch., Salt Lake City, 1966-70; counselor Olympus Jr. High Sch., Salt Lake City, 1970—. Contbr. articles to profl. publs. Mem. Women's Legis. Council, 1982-85. Mem. Utah Edn. Assn. (trustee), Utah Sch. Counselor Assn. (Counselor of Year 1977), Utah Personnel and Guidance Assn. (pres. 1978-79), Am. Personnel and Guidance Assn. (pub. chmn. Western Region br., licensure com.), Am. Sch. Counselor Assn. (governing bd. 1983—). Home: 2894 Oakridge Dr Salt Lake City UT 84109 Office: 2217 E 4800 S Salt Lake City UT 84117

HARDY, NEAL, Canadian provinical government official; b. Hudson Bay, Sask., Can., Sept. 21, 1934; s. George and Clara Evelyn (Robinson) H.; m. Darlene Lundy, Dec. 19, 1953; children—Mervin Neal, Lynda Dianne, Donald Wayne, Donna Gail. Student pub. schs., Hudson Bay. Ry. employee, 1953-70; self-employed businessman, 1962—; farmer, 1972—; Reeve of R.M. Hudson Bay 394, 1974-82; elected mem. Legis. Assembly Sask. for Kelsey-Tisdale, 1980; now minister of environment, minister-in-charge Sask. Housing Corp., Govt. Sask., Regina; mem. Sask. Forest Products Corp. and Sask. Water Supply Bd., 1982—. Past pres. Hudson Bay Minor Baseball Assn., Hudson Bay Minor Hockey Assn. Progressive Conservative. Mem. United Ch. Canada. Office: 204 Legis Bldg Regina SK S4S 0B3 Canada*

HARDY, THOMAS R., city manager; b. Salt Lake City, Feb. 13, 1948; s. Kenneth R. and Mary (Thunell) H.; m. Connie Hall, May 29, 1970; children—Janie, Matthew, Jonathan, Marc. B.A., Brigham Young U., 1971, M.P.A., 1973. Mgmt. analyst City of Tallahassee (Fla.), 1972-73; adminstrv. asst. City of Scottsdale (Ariz.), 1973-76; asst. city mgr. City of Buena Park (Calif.), 1976-77; city mgr. City of Ontario (Oreg.), 1977-80; city mgr. City of Bountiful (Utah), 1981—. NSF fellow, 1970. Mem. Internat. City Mgmt. Assn. Mormon. Office: 790 S 100 E Bountiful UT 84010

HARDY, VERNON ERNEST, electronic engineer; b. Oklahoma City, Apr. 5, 1937; s. Ernest Alexander and Sadie Mildred (Patterson) H.; m. Fleta Kate Garrison, June 30, 1966; children—Stephani L., Laura M. B.S.E.E., U. Okla., 1960; M.S.E.E., 1962. Staff engr., engring. mgr. Tex. Instruments, Dallas, 1962-69; engring. mgr. Electronic Memories & Magnetics, Hawthorn, Calif., 1969-71; engring. mgr., dir. engring. Trendata Corp., Santa Ana, Calif., 1971-83; dir. engring. MSI Data Corp., Costa Mesa, Calif., 1983—. Served as officer USAR, 1960-75. Mem. IEEE, Eta Kapa Nu, Tau Beta Pi. Republican. Baptist. Home: 18912 Santa Mariana St Fountain Valley CA 92708 Office: 300 Fischer Ave Costa Mesa CA 92626

HARE, CASPER PATRICK, insurance broker, financial planner; b. San Francisco, Sept. 4, 1921; s. Casper Patrick and Josephine Glydas (O'Manski) H.; LL.B., LaSalle Extension U., Chgo., 1955; teaching cert. U. Calif.-Irvine, 1971; m. Ann C Ninemires, Feb. 6, 1943; children—Garry, Lynda, Mary-Kay, Kristine. Enlisted in USMC, 1939, commd., 1957-59, advanced through grades to capt.; Served in Pearl Harbor, Saipan, Tinian, Korea; ret., 1959; engaged in sales mgmt. Allstate Ins. Co., 1960-69; ind. ins. agt., owner Cass Hare Ins., Tustil, Calif., 1969—; adult edn. tchr., 1971—. Mem. Tustin Planning Commn., 1973; mem. Orange County (Calif.) Democratic Central Com., 1976—; past chmn. Tustin March of Dimes; bd. dirs. Orange County Charities, 1983-84. Mem. Profl. Ins. Agts. Assn., Ret. Officers Assn., Tustin C. of C. (past v.p.), Pearl Harbor Survivors Assn., Order of Alhambra, VFW. Roman Catholic. Clubs: Lions, Elks, K.C. (state advocate 1978-79, treas. 1979-80, sec. 1980-81, state dep. 1981-82). Address: 14322 Pinewood Rd Tustin CA 92680

HARE, JEAN MADISON, data processing manager; b. Viola, Kans., Mar. 13, 1926; s. Lawrence William and Mary Edna (Braden) H.; m. Barbara Ann Pantier, Nov. 14, 1948; children—David Allen, Jean Michael, Catherine Ann. Student Kans. State Coll., 1946-48; A.A., W. Valley Jr. Coll., 1973; B.A., San Jose State U., 1976. Commd. 2d lt. U.S. Army, 1949, advanced through grades to maj., 1969; ret., 1967; with Lebeck's Bus. Equipment, Sacramento, 1967-68; electronics maintenance supr., quality control supr., quality assurance engr. Memorex, Santa Clara, Calif., 1968-77; data processing mgr. ops. Fairchild Corp., San Jose, Calif., 1977—. Served with AC, U.S. Army, 1944-45. Decorated Army Commendation medal with oak leaf cluster. Mem. Assn. Small Systems Users, IBM Users Group. Democrat. Mem. Christian Ch. Club: Toastmasters. Home: 1755 Conrad Ave San Jose CA 95124 Office: 1725 Technology Dr San Jose CA 95115

HARE, JOHN DANIEL, II, data processor; b. Fresno, Calif., Nov. 28, 1921; s. Max William and Laura Minta (Magatagan) H.; A.A., Reedley (Calif.) Coll., 1940; B.A., cum laude, Stanford, 1942; m. Norma Lea Quarles, June 27, 1944; children—John Daniel III, Thomas Christopher. Mng. partner Central Rock & Sand Co., Sanger, Calif., 1946-65; programmer, analyst So. Pacific Transp. Co., San Francisco, 1966-68, asst. mgr. data processing, 1968—. Scoutmaster Sequoia council Boy Scouts Am., 1961-64, dist. leadership tng. chmn., 1965. City planning commr., Sanger, 1961-66. Served to lt. USNR, 1942-46. Mem. Computer Operations Mgmt. Assn. (v.p. San Francisco 1971-72, 75-76), Am. Legion, Stanford Alumni Assn., Phi Beta Kappa, Theta Chi. Republican. Episcopalian. Mason. Home: PO Box 161 Millbrae CA 94030 Office: 1 Market St San Francisco CA 94105

HARELSON, JUANITA LAW, state senator; b. Stratford, Okla., July 4, 1923; d. Ivan and Callie B. (Phillips) Law; B.A., Ariz. State U., 1945; m. James E. Harelson, Aug. 8, 1947; children—Ted, Barry, Patrick, Rex. Public sch. tchr., 1945-49, 67-72; mem. Ariz. Ho. of Reps. from 27th Dist., 1972-82, Ariz. State Senate, 1982—. Republican. Address: 1756 El Camino Tempe AZ 85281

HARGETT, LOUIE THOMAS, agricultural chemistry corporation executive, entomologist; b. Wilmington, N.C., Oct. 19, 1932; s. Louie Fulton and Catherine Cordelia (Thomas) H.; m. Anna Catherine Hazel, June 26, 1954; children—Cheryl Ann, Robert Thomas, Catherine Lynn. B.A., Bridgewater (Va.) Coll., 1953; M.S., Va. Poly. Inst., 1958; Ph.D., Oreg. State U., 1962; A.M.P., Harvard Bus. Sch., 1976. Cert. profl. entomologist. Mem. faculty dept. entomology Va. Poly. Inst., Blacksburg, 1955-58, Oreg. State U., Corvallis, 1958-60; dir. field devel., asst. to v.p. mktg. Geigy, Inc., N.Y.C., 1961-70; dir. devel., gen. mgr. Rhodia, Inc., Monmouth Junction, N.J., 1970-77; asst. to pres. Environ. Research and Tech., Concord, Mass., 1977-78; dir. research, devel. crop protection Sandoz, Inc., San Diego, 1979—. Served with AUS, 1953-55. NIH fellow, 1960-61. Mem. Am. Inst. Biologists, Entomology Soc. Am., Weed Sci. Soc. Am., Sigma Xi. Republican. Protestant. Home: 6827 Corintia St Carlsbad CA 92008 Office: 480 Camino Del Rio S Suite 204 Sandoz Inc San Diego CA 92108

HARGIS, BOB LLOYD, union official; b. Joplin, Mo., Aug. 22, 1935; s. Lloyd E. and Opal (Patrick) H.; m. Mary Ann Hargis, May 17, 1957; m. 2d, Patricia Ann Hargis, Jan. 18, 1979; children—Kathleen (dec.), Barbara, Mike. Student pub. schs., Duenweg, Mo. Collection mgr. Universal CIT Credit Corp., Joplin, 1959-60; warehouseman, shipping clk. Fisher Flour Mills, Seattle, 1961-73; sec., treas., bus. agt. Internat. Longshoremen and Warehousemens Union, Local 9, Seattle, 1973—, also trustee pension fund and trust fund, mem. health and welfare com.; chmn. credit com., dir. Fisher Blend Credit Union. Mem. Puget Sound Labor Council, Seattle. Served with USN, 1954-58. Democrat. Home: 6001 So W Charlestown Seattle WA 98116 Office: 2800 1st Ave Room 76 Seattle WA 98121

HARGROVE, BARBARA JUNE WATTS, sociology educator; b. Ft. Collins, Colo., Apr. 10, 1924; d. Robert Harold Watts and Vera Sophia (Sherred) W.; m. Howard C. Hargrove, Dec. 27, 1942 (dec.); children—Stanley Howard, Kathleen Jo Hargrove Wade, Kenneth Leslie, Dorothy Ellen. B.S. in Social Sci., Colo. State U., 1961, M.S. in Sociology, 1963, Ph.D. in Sociology, 1968. Instr. Hollins Coll., Roanoke, Va., 1967-68, asst. prof., 1968-72, chmn. sociology dept., 1971-72; research assoc. U. Calif.-Berkeley, 1972-73; assoc. prof., chmn. dept. sociology and social welfare U. North Fla., Jacksonville, 1973-75; assoc. prof. sociology of religion Yale Divinity Sch., 1975-79; prof. sociology of religion Iliff Sch. Theology, Denver, 1979—. Chmn. Roanoke Valley Human Relations Council, 1973; bd. dirs. Christian Community Action, New Haven, 1976-79, Operation Nightwatch, Denver, 1982-83, Citizens for Justice, Va., 1971-72. NSF grantee 1968; recipient Nat. Endowment Humanities Younger Humanist award 1972-73. Mem. Am. Sociol. Assn., Soc. Sci. Study Religion, Religious Research Assn., Assn. Sociology Religion, Sociologists for Women in Soc. Presbyterian. Author: Reformation of the Holy, 1971; Sociology of Religion: Classical and Contemporary Approaches, 1979; Religion for a Dislocated Generation, 1981; Women of the Cloth (with Jackson Carroll and Adair Lummis), 1983; (with Stephen Jones) Reaching Youth: Heirs to the Whirlwind, 1983. Home: 2685 S Vine St Denver CO 80210 Office: Iliff Sch Theology 2201 S University Blvd Denver CO 80210

HARGROVE, JOHN JAMES, lawyer; b. Bay Shore, N.Y., May 4, 1942; s. John A. and Cecilia L. (Schultz) H.; m. Jane Ann Nagle, Oct. 21, 1967; children—David, Kristin, Kelly. B.A., U. Notre Dame, 1964, J.D., 1967. Bar: N.Y. 1968, Calif. 1971. Assoc. firm, Gant & Asaro, San Diego, 1972-74; ptnr. firm Weeks, Willis, Hoffman & Hargrove, San Diego, 1974-80, Strauss, Kissane, Davis & Hargrove, San Diego, 1980—. Served with USMC, 1968-72, Vietnam; lt. col. USMCR, 1983—. Decorated Navy Commendation medal with combat V. Mem. ABA, Republican. Roman Catholic. Club: Notre Dame of San Diego (dir.). Office: Suite 305 3838 Camino Del Rio N San Diego CA 92108

HARIVANDI, MOHAMMAD ALI, educator; b. Birjand, Iran, July 9, 1950; came to U.S., 1974; s. Mohammad Hadi and Effat (Jamaalzahi) H.; B.S., Pahlavi U., Iran, 1974; M.S., Colo. State U., 1976, Ph.D., 1980; m. Sue Bobzien Silver, May 27, 1980. Asst. hall dir. Colo. State U., Ft. Collins, 1977-78, teaching asst, 1975-78, research asst., 1974-80; extension advisor U. Calif. Coop. Extension, Hayward, 1980—; cons., lectr. Mem. Soil Sci. Soc. Am., Crop Sci. Soc. Am., Am. Soc. Agronomy, Gamma Sigma Delta, Pi Alpha Xi. Contbr. articles to profl. jours. Home: 5318 Briar Ridge Dr Castro Valley CA 94546 Office: 224 W Winton Ave Rm 162 Hayward CA 94544

HARKINS, PAMELA JEAN, dairy products company executive; b. Seattle, Mar. 30, 1948; d. Lawrence J. and Dorothy L. (Mydland) Sousa; m. Daniel J. Harkins, Apr. 7, 1973; children—Thomas L., John D., Shannan D. Student pub. schs., Seattle. Claims clk. N.Y. Life Ins. Co., Bellevue, Wash., 1969-71; office mgr. Telephone Computing Service, Seattle, 1971-73; personnel asst. Assoc. Grocers Co., Seattle, 1973-77; personnel mgr. Ederer Corp., Seattle, 1977-79, Consol. Dairy Products Co., Seattle, 1979—.

HARLAN, KATHLEEN T. (KAY), business consultant accountant, professional speaker and seminar leader; b. Bremerton, Wash., June 9, 1934; d. Floyd K. and Rosemary (Parkhurst) Troy; student Sanford-Brown Bus. Coll., 1955; m. John L. Harlan, Feb. 16, 1952 (div. 1975); m. 2d, Merlin Habig, June 30, 1979; children—Pamela Kay, Kenneth Lynwood, Lianna Sue. Owner, operator Safeguard N.W. Systems, Tacoma, 1969-79; developer, mgr. Poulsbo (Wash.) Profl. Bldg., 1969-75; pres. Greenapple Graphics, Inc., Tacoma, 1976-79; owner, mgr. Iskrem Hus Restaurant, Pulsbo, 1972-75; pres. Bus. Seminars, Tacoma, 1977—; mem. Organizational Renewal, Inc., Tacoma, 1978-81; asso. mem. Effectiveness Resource Group, Inc., Tacoma, 1979-80; pres. New Image Confs., Tacoma, 1979-82; owner, mgr. Safeguard Acctg. & Data Systems, Bremerton, Wash., 1982—, Safeguard By Harlan, Port Angeles, 1982—, Bellevue Safeguard Computer Ctr., Tacoma, 1982—; owner Total Systems Ctr., Tacoma, 1983—; speaker on mgmt. and survival in small bus. Mem. Wash. State Bd. Boundary Rev. for Kitsap County, 1970-76; mem. Selective Service Bd. #19, 1971-76. Mem. Nat. Speakers Assn., Nat. Assn. Female Execs., Nat. Assn. Accts. Author small bus. manuals; contbg. author: Here is Genius!, 1980. Office: 1702 6th St Bremerton WA 98310

HARLAN, NANCY MARGARET, lawyer, real estate broker; b. Santa Monica, Calif., Sept. 10, 1946; s. William Galland and Betty M. (Miles) Plett; m. Roy Dennis Rebello, May 1, 1967; 1 dau., Laryssa Maria; m. John Hammack Harlan, Dec. 1, 1979; 1 dau., Leea Elyce. B.S. magna cum laude, Calif. State U.-Hayward, 1972; J.D., U. Calif.-Berkeley, 1975. Bar: Calif. 1975, U.S. Ct. Appeals (9th cir.) 1976. Assoc. firm Poindexter & Doutre, Los Angeles, 1975-80; residential counsel Coldwell Banker Residential Brokerage Co., Fountain Valley, Calif., 1980-81; counsel for real estate sub. law dept. Pacific Lighting Corp., Santa Ana, Calif., 1981—; designer, tchr. courses in real estate, professionalism and law. Mem. Community Assns. Inst., 1981—, Town Hall, 1982—, mem. Childrens Aux. Support Assn., La Casa, 1982—; v.p., bd. dirs. Autumnwood Homeowners Assn., 1982 . Mem. ABA, Orange County Bar Assn. (del. to Calif. State Bar Conf. 1983), Los Angeles County Bar Assn., Calif. Women Lawyers Assn., Los Angeles Women Lawyers Assn., Orange County Women Lawyers Assn., Am. Corp. Counsel Assn., Nat. Assn. Female Execs., Bus. and Profl. Women's Club. Office: Pacific Lighting Corp 18 Brookhollow Dr Santa Ana CA 92705

HARLAN, THOMAS CREIGHTON, utility co. exec.; b. Bossier City, La., Oct. 26, 1931; s. Thomas Woodard and Mary Muriel (Harper) H.; A.A., Compton Coll., 1957; B.S. in Petroleum Engring., U. So. Calif., 1959, M.S., 1962; m. Marjorie Harlan; children—Kimberly, Kristen. Gen. supt. Valley Transmission div. So. Calif. Gas Co., Los Angeles, 1969-73, mgr. project analysis, 1973-78, mgr. transmission divs., 1978-80, mgr. engring. services, 1980—. Served with USAF, 1950-53. Mem. Pacific Energy Assn., Am. Gas Assn., Pacific Coast Gas Assn., Soc. Petroleum Engrs. Republican. Home: 28529 Vista Madera Rancho Palos Verdes CA 90732 Office: 810 S Flower St Los Angeles CA 90017

HARLESS, JOHN BEECHER, JR., banker; b. Des Moines, Oct. 6, 1945; s. John Beecher and Helen Elizabeth (Bergman) H.; m. Cheryl Georgia Valko, July 1, 1967. B.S. magna cum laude, U. No. Colo., 1972; grad. Sch. Banking, So. Meth. U., 1980. Mgmt. trainee Central Bank of Denver, 1972, loan and discount and credit analyst, 1972, comml. loan officer, 1973-75, asst. v.p., 1975-78, v.p., 1978, v.p. comml. loan dept. head, 1979-82; pres. Central Bank of Inverness, Englewood, Colo., 1982—. Served with USCG, 1967-70. Mem. Am. Inst. Banking, Robert Morris Assocs., Colo. Bankers Assn., Bank Adminstrn. Inst., Centennial C. of C. Republican. Roman Catholic. Clubs: Columbine Country (Littleton, Colo.); Metropolitan (Englewood). Home: 4664 W Oberlin Pl Denver CO 80236 Office: 11 Inverness Way Englewood CO 80112

HARLEY, ANN, nurse, educator; b. San Juan, P.R.; d. Allen Gotwals and May Miller (Naile) H.; diploma in Nursing, Abington (Pa.) Meml. Hosp., 1954; B.S. in Nursing, U. Pa., 1960, M.S. in Nursing, 1962; Ed.D., Tchrs. Coll. Columbia U., 1978. Curriculum coordinator Presbyn. U. of Pa. Med. Center, Phila., 1968-74; asst. prof. CCNY, 1975-76; asso. prof. Coll. Nursing, U. Nebr. Med. Center, 1976-80; prof. nursing Western Wash. U., Bellingham, 1980—, chmn. dept. nursing, 1980—; cons. in field. Performing mem. Voices of Omaha, 1979. Mem. Am. Nurses Assn., Nat. League Nursing, Internat. Soc. Chronobiology, AAUW, Assn. Supervision and Curriculum Devel., Sigma Theta Tau, Pi Lambda Theta, Phi Delta Kappa, Kappa Delta Pi. Office: Western Washington University Bellingham WA 98225

HARLOW, ARTHUR ALLEN, electric utility exec.; b. Thompson Falls, Mont., Feb. 20, 1935; s. Paul Kidder and Margaret (Barto) H.; B.A. with distinction, Stanford U., 1957, M.A., 1959; m. Michele Lynn Leitch, June 4, 1966; children—Margaret Erin, Melinda Catherine. Agrl. statistician U.S. Dept. Agr., Washington, 1959-62; economist Bonneville Power Adminstrn., Spokane, Wash., 1962-72, area power mgr., 1973—. Bd. dirs. Youth Employment Service, Spokane, 1976—, pres., 1978-81; bd. dirs. United Way of Spokane County, 1974-76, chmn. planning and allocation div., 1975; bd. dirs. Spokane Fed. Credit Union, 1974—, pres., 1975-78. Earheart fellow, Stanford U., 1958; recipient Am. Farm Econ. Assn. award for best pub. research, 1962. Mem. Hist. Auto Soc. Spokane and Inland Empire (dir. 1974-77, pres. 1976). Contbr. articles to profl. jours. Home: S 1130 Wall St Spokane WA 99204 Office: W 920 Riverside Ave Spokane WA 99201

HARLOW, BARBARA ANN, management consultant; b. Kansas City, Kans.; d. James Vernon and Jennie Alice (Flint) Bigler; children—Ronald Eric, Gregory Brent. B.A., U. Nebr., 1970. Exec. dir. March of Dimes, Omaha, 1970-71, regional cons., Kansas City, Mo., 1971-73, nat. cons., 1973-74; pub. relations dir. Crown Ctr. Hotel, Kansas City, 1974-78; corp. dir. tng. and devel. Woolf Bros., Kansas City, 1978-80; pres. Mgmt. Assocs., Inc., cons. in human resource devel., 1980—. Active pub. relations Clark Welfare Council, Clark AFB, Philippines; counselor Neighborhood Youth Corps, Kansas City; mem. women's div. Kansas City Philharm. Orch. Mem. Pub. Relations Soc. Am., Am. Soc. for Tng. and Devel., Kansas City C. of C. Club: Kansas City Ski. Home: 930-B Fontmore Rd Colorado Springs CO 80904

HARMAN, DANNY RAY, oil company executive, accountant; b. Blackfoot, Idaho, July 18, 1947; s. Tom C. and Ruby G. (Ward) H.; m. Janis Lynette Bates, Sept. 30, 1970; children—Priscilla K., Lori L., Daniel W., Angela M., Julie E. B.S., Brigham Young U., 1972. C.P.A., Calif., Wyo., N.Mex., Colo. In-charge auditor Arthur Andersen & Co., Los Angeles, 1972-76; mng. ptnr. Cheyenne (Wyo.) office Townsend Phillips & Co., 1976-81; chief fin. officer Trinity Telecommunications Corp., Ft. Collins, Colo., 1981-82; chief fin. officer Dakota Minerals, Inc., Casper, Wyo., 1982—, also chief fin. officer, sec.-treas. subs. including Extractive Fuels, Inc., Viable Resources, Inc., CTD, Inc., Alkali Butte Coal Co.; pres., chmn. bd. Pleasant Valley Farms, Inc., 1983—. Bd. fin. advisor Cheyenne YWCA, 1981, Cheyenne YMCA, 1979-81, Cheyenne Parents Anonymous, 1981; full time missionary Mormon Ch., 1967-69, sem. instr., 1973-77, ward mission leader, 1979-80, 82—, pres. Seventies, 1978—. Mem. Am. Inst. C.P.A.s, Wyo. Soc. C.P.A.s (report rev. com.), Cheyenne C. of C. (profl. services com. 1979-80). Clubs: Cheyenne Exchange (pres. 1980-81), Cheyenne Social.

HARMAN, ROBERT LEROY, civil engr.; b. Santa Ana, Calif., Mar. 26, 1944; s. Oliver LeRoy and Ruth Jane (Kraft) H.; A.A., Cerritos Jr. Coll., 1965; B.S. in Civil Engring., Calif. State U., Long Beach, 1968; m. Barbara Ellen Phipps, Aug. 27, 1966; children—Rebecca Michelle, Heather Janenne. Exec. v.p., partner Octagon Assos. archtl. engring. Visalia, Calif., 1972—, also sec. bd.; pres. Octagon Enterprises, Visalia, Calif., 1983—; vice chmn. bd. dirs. Mt. Whitney Savs. and Loan, Exeter, Calif. Trustee, 1st Presbyterian Ch. Visalia, 1977, follow up leader Christian Marriage Encounter, 1978; bd. dirs. Gemco Charitable Found., 1976—; pres. Visalia YMCA, 1979. Served to lt., C.E., USN, 1968-72; Vietnam. Lic. comml. pilot. Mem. Visalia C. of C. (pres. 1980-81), Soc. Mktg. Profl. Services, Profl. Services Mgmt. Assn. Republican. Club: Kiwanis (pres. 1978). Home: 3529 Howard St W Visalia CA 93277 Office: 119 Locust St S Visalia CA 93291

HARMON, CHARLES JEROME, educator; b. Adams, N.Y., Apr. 10, 1915; s. William J. and Frances M. (Lawton) H.; m. Mary Phillips, Nov. 4, 1938; children—William, Sarah, Robert. B.S., Cornell U., 1938; M.Ed., Alfred U., 1945; postgrad. various colls. and univs. Cert. tchr./adminstr., N.Mex., Calif.; lic. real estate broker, Calif. Tchr. vocat. agr., pub. schs., York, Alfred, Cato, N.Y., 1938-48, Coolidge and Marana, Ariz., 1948-55; agrl. engring. adviser U.S. Fgn. AID Program to Pakistan, 1955-60; gen. services officer U.S. Fgn. AID Program, Vietnam, Sudan, Belgium, Thailand, Korea, 1960-71; real estate broker, Granada Hills, Calif., 1971-78; tchr. vocat. agr., chmn. vocat. dept. Crownpoint (N.Mex.) High Sch., 1978—. Recipient Service in Vietnam medal AID, 1971. Mem. Am. Vocat. Assn., N.Mex. Vocat. Assn., N.Mex. Assn. Tchrs. of Vocat. Agr. Democrat. Baptist. Home: Drawer M Crownpoint NM 87313 Office: Crownpoint High Sch Drawer D Crownpoint NM 87313

HARMON, GARY RAY, air force officer; b. Ravenna, Ohio, Jan. 7, 1950; s. Raymond A. and Betty (Hassler) H.; m. Jacquelyn Mitchell, Sept. 6, 1981. B.S. in Physics, Ohio State U., 1972, M.S. in Physics, 1974. Commd. 2d lt. U.S. Air Force, 1974, advanced through grades to capt., 1977; space surveillance officer Mt. Hebo Air Force Sta., Oreg., 1974-76, Shemya AFB, Alaska, 1976-77; space program Hdqrs. Aerospace Def. Command, Colorado Springs, Colo., 1977-79; policy analyst office of Sec. of Air Force, Washington, 1979-81, devel. engr. office Spl. Projects, Los Angeles, 1981—. Active Officers Christian Fellowship, 1981—. Decorated Def. Meritorious Service Medal, Meritorious Service medal, Air Force Commendation medal with oak leaf cluster. Mem. AIAA, IEEE, Nat. Space Club, Air Force Assn., Scabbard and Blade. Republican. Baptist. Club: Colo. Mountain (Colorado Springs). Home: 1711 E Pine Ave #4 El Segundo CA 90245

HARMON, GEORGE OLEN, management consultant; b. Hunter, Mo., Mar. 18, 1923; s. George Olen and Mary Mae (Taylor) H.; student George Washington U., 1941-42, Bakersfield (Calif.) Coll., 1946-48; m. Nina Lorene Curtman, Mar. 24, 1945; children—Sharyn Suzanne Harmon Moore, Timothy Olen. Dir. mgmt. systems IBM, White Plains, N.Y., 1952-68; pres. Comma Corp., N.Y.C., 1968-71; v.p. NCR Corp., Dayton, Ohio, 1971-75; pres. Sorbus, Inc., King of Prussia, Pa., 1975-76; v.p., gen. mgr. service Pertec Computer Corp., Los Angeles, 1976-80; pres., chief exec. officer Harmon Assos. Internat. Inc., Los Angeles, 1980—; dir. Indesero Corp., Terminal Service Inc., Service Mgmt. Systems Inc., Taylor Industries. Adv. bd. Abilene Christian U., 1974—, pres. Circle, 1975-77. Served with USNR, 1942-46. Mem. Assn. Field Service Mgrs. (nat. pres. 1977-78; Man of Yr. 1979). Republican. Mem. Ch. of Christ. Home: 2923 Shadow Brook Ln Westlake Village CA 91361 Office: 5655 Lindero Canyon Rd Westlake Village CA 91362

HARMON, JOHN ALAN, engineering executive; b. Everett, Wash., Sept. 2, 1953; s. Ray Alexander and Lena Mae (Bowman) H. Student in Elect. Engring., Wash. State U., 1972-76; student in Indsl. Engring., Eastern Wash. U., 1976-78. Plant engr. Clark Equipment Co., Inc., Spokane, Wash., 1977-80; engring. mgr. E-Z Loader Boat Trailers, Spokane, 1980—. Mem. Soc. Mfg. Engrs. Republican. Methodist. Club: Elks. Office: PO Box 3263 TA Spokane WA 99220

HARMON, SAUNDRA BRYN, educator; b. Oakland, Calif., Dec. 10, 1944; d. Odin Alfred and Lorna Homme Bryn; m. Darrell Arlen Harmon, Jan. 11, 1942; children—Cassaundra Ann, Eric Bryn. B.S., Minot State Coll., 1965; M.A., No. Ariz. U., 1980, Ed.D., 1982. Tchr. English and reading Ironwood Sch., Phoenix, 1972-81; curriculum devel. specialist in reading, 1981—. Mem. Assn. Supervision and Curriculum Devel., Ariz. Sch. Adminstrs., Nat. Council Tchrs. English, Internat. Reading Assn., Alpha Delta Kappa. Democrat. Lutheran. Contbr. articles to profl. jours. Home: 4107 W Hearn Rd Phoenix AZ 85023 Office: 8610 N 19th Ave Phoenix AZ 85021

HARMS, TED E., accountant; b. Chgo., July 29, 1950; s. Theodore P. and Lois J. (McDonald) H.; m. Janet M. Bielfeldt, Aug. 5, 1972; children—Jennifer L., Jeffrey T. B.S. in Accountancy, U. Ill., 1972. C.P.A., Colo. Various positions Peat, Marwick, Mitchell & Co., Denver, 1972-81, ptnr., Denver, 1981—. Recipient Bronze tablet U. Ill., 1972. Mem. Am. Inst. C.P.A.s, Colo. Soc. C.P.A.s, Petroleum Accts. Soc. Colo. (dir.), Club: Denver Petroleum. Home: 5222 E Maplewood Pl Littleton CO 80121 Office: 707 17th St Suite 2300 Denver CO 80201

HARNSBERGER, THERESE COSCARELLI, librarian; b. Muskegon, Mich.; d. Charles and Julia (Borrell) Coscarelli; B.A. cum laude, Marymount Coll., 1952; M.L.S., U. So. Calif., 1953; postgrad. Rosary Coll., River Forest, Ill., 1955-56, U. Calif., Los Angeles Extension, 1960-61; m. Frederick Owen Harnsberger, Dec. 24, 1962; 1 son, Lindsey Carleton. Free-lance writer, 1950—; librarian San Marino (Calif.) High Sch., 1953-56; cataloger, cons. San Marino Hall, South Pasadena, Calif., 1956-61; librarian Los Angeles State Coll., 1956-59; librarian dist. library Covina-Valley Unified Sch. Dist., Covina, Calif., 1959-67; librarian Los Angeles Trade Tech. Coll., 1972—; med. librarian, tumor registrar Alhambra (Calif.) Community Hosp., 1975-79; tumor registrar Huntington Meml. Hosp., 1979—; pres., dir. Research Unltd., 1980—; free lance reporter Los Angeles' Best Bargains, 1981—; med. library cons., 1979—. Chmn. spiritual values com. Covina Coordinating Council, 1964-66. Mem. Calif. Assn. Sch. Librarians (chmn. legis. com.), Covina Tchrs. Assn., AAUW (historian 1972-73), U. So. Calif. Grad. Sch. Library Sci. (life), Am. Nutrition Soc. (chpt. Newsletter chmn.), Nat. Tumor Registrars Assn., So. Calif. Tumor Registrars Assn., Med. Library Assn., So. Calif. Librarians Assn., So. Calif. Assn. Law Libraries, Book Publicists So. Calif., Pi Lambda Theta. contbr. articles to profl. jours. Office: 2809 W Hellman Ave Alhambra CA 91803

HARP, JOHN RUDD, construction company executive; b. Chgo., Dec. 29, 1928; s. Leonard N. and Mae Alta (Rudd) H.; m. Donna Dae Parkison, Apr. 11, 1952; children—Marsha Harp King, Michael, John G. Student, Missoula Bus. Coll., 1956. Engaged in power line constrn., Mont., 1954-57; supt. power line constrn. Darnell Constrn. Co., Lewiston, Idaho, 1957-58; pres. Harp Line Constructors Co., Kalispell, Mont., 1959—; pres. Mont. Evergreen, Inc., Kalispell, 1977—. Life mem. Republican Nat. Com. Served with U.S. Army, 1945-53. Mem. Heritage Found., VFW, C. of C., Nat. Elec. Contractors Assn., Mont. Line Contractors Assn. (pres.), N.W. Elec. Light & Power Assn., N.W. Pub. Power Assn. Baptist. Clubs: Elks, Shriners, Masons. Home: 2233 Whitefish Stage Kalispell MT 59901 Office: Harp Line Constructors Co PO Box 61 Kalispell MT 59901

HARPEL, THOMAS RALPH, naval officer; b. Sandusky, Ohio, Sept. 28; s. Richard Pearl and Mary Katherine (Gross) H.; student City Coll., Sandusky. Joined U.S. Navy, 1965, advanced through grades to chief petty officer, 1973; assigned Vietnam, 1966-73; alcohol and drug abuse counselor, career counselor, leadership/mgmt. instr. USS Ranger, 1976—. Decorated Air medal with oak leaf cluster, others. Mem. U.S., Milpitas (state dir.) jr. chambers commerce, Fleet Res. Assn., Am. Legion. Republican. Address: Grey Eagle Airlines USS Ranger CIA FPO San Francisco CA 96633

HARPER, CAROLYN, telecommunications company sales executive; b. N.Y.C., June 27, 1949; d. Herbert and Rosalie (Leggett) Brown; m. William Henry Harper, III, May 15, 1980; 1 son, Charles Barrett. B.S., Cornell U., 1974. Supr. telephone sales/service Trans World Airlines, Los Angeles, Calif., 1976-81; account exec. Wells, Rich, Greene, Inc., Los Angeles, 1982—; mgr. sales/customer service MCI Telecommunications, Los Angeles. Adv. bd. Inglewood Unified Sch. Dist. Gifted and Talented Edn. program; active La Tijera Parents Assn., Mt. Carmel Bapt. Ch. Mem. Nat. Assn. Female Execs., Mademoiselle Career Mktg. Bd. Democrat.

HARPER, DONALD JACQUES, holding company executive; b. Knoxville, Tenn., June 30, 1928; s. Raymond James and Pauline Jean (Huffstuttler) H.; m. Jayne C. Combs; children—Nancy Lynn (Mrs. Norman Mehl), Danial Ray, Larry F., Lenny G., Lindsay J. Student Wichita (Kans.) State U., 1946-47, Kansas City Coll. Engring., 1948; Indsl. Engr., U. Okla., 1950. Indsl. engr. Coleman Co., Inc., Wichita, 1953-56; agt. Penn Mut. Life Ins. Co., Wichita, 1956-60; gen. agt. Crown Life Ins. Co., Wichita, 1960-62; pres. Fin. Unification Corp., Mark V group of cos., holding co.'s, Scottsdale, Ariz., 1963—. Bd. dirs. Scottsdale Symphony. Served with USNR, 1942-45. Mem. Ariz. Law Soc., Am. Mgmt. Soc., Profl. Consultants, Nat. Soc. Bus. Consultants, Scottsdale C. of C. Home: 5320 E Camelback Rd Phoenix AZ 85018 Office: 6060 E Thomas Scottsdale AZ 85251

HARPER, DONNA T., real estate executive; b. Chgo., Nov. 2, 1943; d. Vito Joseph and Eileen Lillian (Kennelly) Tassone; children—Jeanne Marie, Melissa Leigh. Asst. supt. pub. instn. State of Ill., 1964-66; pres. Venture Property Services, Inc., Phoenix, 1980-83; pres. Valley Income Properties, Phoenix, 1979—.

HARPER, GRACE SONYA, city ofcl.; b. Denver, Apr. 9, 1952; d. Fred Leon and Grace Katherine (Taylor) H.; cert. So. Calif. Pipe Trade Tng. Center, 1977, Los Angeles Trade Tech. Coll., 1980; student vocat. edn. Calif. State U., Long Beach, 1980-83. With Community Design Center, Denver, 1972; apprentice Plumbers and Pipefitters Local Union 575, Boulder, Colo., 1972-76, apprentice-journey level, Local Union 545,

Santa Monica, Calif., 1976-78; plumbing insp., investigator City of Los Angeles, 1978-83, sr. plumbing insp., 1983; career speaker Bur. Apprenticeship Standards, Dept. Labor, 1976—. Cert. journey level plumber, Calif., recipient award Los Angeles City Commn. on Status of Women, 1980; award U.S. Dept. Labor Div. Apprenticeship Standards. Mem. Unified Plumbing and Piping Assn., Internat. Assn. Plumbing and Mech. Ofcls. Office: 200 N Spring St Room 470 Los Angeles CA 90012

HARPER, KENNETH EDWIN, bank executive, consulting company executive; b. Chgo., Mar. 11, 1941; s. Ernest Edwin and Helen Louise (Radoll) H.; m. Sharon Brian, Dec. 8, 1981; children—Michael, Phillip. B.A. in Graphic Design and Art, Western Wash. State U., 1966; M.A. in Edn., San Francisco State U., 1982. Illustration and art dir. Electromec Design Co., Santa Clara, Calif., 1966-70; graphic designer Media Ctr., Sunnyvale (Calif.) Sch. Dist., 1970-74; media design and prodn. technician Los Medanos Coll., Pittsburgh, Calif., 1974-79; tng. dir. Clemco Industries, San Francisco, 1979-80; tng. mgr. auditing div. Wells Fargo Bank, San Francisco, 1980—; pres. Ken Harper and Assocs., Berkeley, Calif., 1981—; hon. mem. tng. dirs. com. Bank Adminstrn. Inst., Chgo. Active environ. concerns Sierra Club, Berkeley. Recipient Corp. Brochure Design award Indsl. Art Methods mag., 1970; Outstanding Multi-Media Presentation award Los Medanos Coll., 1979. Mem. Am. Soc. Tng. and Devel., Nat. Speakers Assn., Sales and Mktg. Execs. Assn. Democrat. Mem. Unity Center Ch. Author: Media Menu; A Guide to the Production of Media, 1974; (booklet) Primer on Educational Copyright, 1979; presented The Nature of Reality, a multimedia award winning show. Home: 1739 Tacoma Ave Berkeley CA 94707 Office: 425 Market St 30th Floor San Francisco CA 94105

HARPER, OWEN HOWE, banker; b. Lunchburg, Va., Sept. 27, 1937; s. Edwin A. and Margaretta S. (Howe) H.; m. Kathleen McEnerney, Oct. 29, 1977; children—Hillary Taylor, Eloise McEnerney, Charles Plimpton. B.A. in Econs., Washington and Lee U., 1959; Program Mgmt. Devel., Harvard U., 1969. Vice pres. Citibank, N.Y.C., 1960-72; 1st v.p. Blyth Eastman Dillon & Co., Inc., N.Y.C., 1972-74; exec. v.p. Crocker Nat. Corp. and Crocker Nat. Bank, Los Angeles, 1974—. Bd. dirs. Am. Heart Assn., Los Angeles YMCA, Hollywood Presbyn. Med. Ctr. Found.; bd. dirs., mem. exec. com. Central City Assn.; trustee Orthopaedic Hosp. Mem. Assn. Res. City Bankers. Republican. Unitarian. Clubs: Los Angeles Country, Calif. (Los Angeles); Pacific Union (San Francisco); Burlingame Country (Hillsborough, Calif.); Links (N.Y.C.). Home: 790 Pinehurst Dr Pasadena CA 91106 Office: 333 S Grand Ave Los Angeles CA 90071

HARR, JOHN MILTON, occupational health and safety administrator, hazardous waste management consultant; b. Reading, Pa., Aug. 28, 1947; s. Bruce Donald Kieffer and Anna Margaret (Everhart) K.; m. Linda Marie Tyrholm, June 26, 1970. B.A., Fla. State U., 1969; M.H.S., San Diego State U., 1978. Cert. radiation safety officer, Calif. Safety engr. cruise missle program Gen. Dynamics Convair, San Diego, 1978-80, radiation safety officer, 1979-80, explosives and pyrotechnics officer, 1979-80, warhead recovery trainer, 1979-80; health and safety adminstr. Litton Guidance and Control, Woodland Hills, Calif., 1980, beryllium specialist, 1980, laser safety coordinator, 1980, hazardous waste mgr., 1981; health and safety mgr. TA Pertec, Chatsworth, Calif., 1981—. Mem. Calif. Earthquake Preparedness Com., 1981. Served with USN, 1970-74. Recipient George Washington Honor medal Freedoms Found., 1965. Mem. Am. Soc. Safety Engrs. (chpt. program chmn.), Alpha Tau Omega. Democrat. Lutheran.

HARRELL, GARY PAUL, educator; b. Texas City, Tex., July 8, s. James E. and Alice (Worley) H.; m. Leigh Evans. B.S., M.A., U. Tex. R.N., Tex., Calif. Charge nurse Seton Med Ctr., Austin, Tex., 1976-78; instr. health edn. U. Tex., Austin, 1978-79; gen. mgr. Nursing Support Services, Austin, 1979-80; dir. edn. Downey (Calif.) Community Hosps., 1980—; adj. prof. nursing Calif. State U.-Long Beach. Served with USNR, 1970-74. Mem. Soc. Pub. Health Educators, Am. Soc. Tng. and Devel., Am. Soc. Health Edn. Tng., Am. Cancer Soc., Am. Heart Assn. (dir. 1983—), Inservice and Health Edn. Council Los Angeles (1982—), Am. Nurses Assn. (cert. adminstr.). Office: Downey Community Hosp 11500 Brookshire Ave Downey CA 90241

HARRELL, JERRY D., public relations executive; b. Santa Ana, Calif., June 20, 1933; s. John Gilbert and Florence Mae (Schnoke) H.; m. Wilhelmina Philippo, Sept. 10, 1960; children—Scott Philip, Wendy Suzanne. B.S. in Journalism, U. Oreg., 1955; postgrad. U. Calif.-Berkeley, 1957. Newsman, AP, Portland, Oreg., 1955, Sacramento, 1957-66, corr. in charge Sacramento Bur., 1964-66; pub. info. officer State of Calif. Dept. Fish & Game, Sacramento, 1966-70; chief pub. affairs staff Calif. Office, U.S. Bur. Land Mgmt., Sacramento, 1970-81; pub. affairs mgr. Eastern Oreg. Region Weyerhaeuser Co., Klamath Falls, Oreg., 1981—. Served with U.S. Army, 1955-57. Recipient award of merit Calif. State Bar, 1960; Spl. Achievement award U.S. Dept. Interior, 1976. Mem. Pub. Relations Soc. Am., Soc. Klamath Basin chpt. ARC, Crater Lake Council Campfire, Klamath County C. of C., Sigma Delta Chi. Republican. Home: 121 Eulalona Ct Klamath Falls OR 97601 Office: PO Box 9 Klamath Falls OR 97601

HARRELL, LEROY FRANKLIN, JR., psychologist, educator; b. N.Y.C., Feb. 12, 1949; s. Leroy Franklin and Ella Blanche (Roberts) H.; m. Carmen Boria, Nov. 16, 1972; children—Liana, Naja. B.S., NYU, 1972; M.S., U. Mass., 1977, Ph.D., 1980. Safety and health specialist, Washington, 1973; ednl. therapist Forest Haven Sch., Washington, 1973-74; research asst., teaching asst. in psychology U. Mass., 1974-75; family therapist Ctr. for Human Devel., Springfield, Mass., 1977-79; predoctoral intern Worcester (Mass.) Guidance Ctr., 1979-80; asst. prof. dept. psychology Colo. State U., Ft. Collins, 1980—, sr. psychologist Counseling Ctr., 1980—; cons. in field. Faculty advisor Afro-Am Students. Mem. Assn. Black Psychologists (Scholarship award Boston chpt. 1977), Am. Psychol. Assn., Am. Personnel and Guidance Assn. Democrat. Contbr. chpt. to book. Office: Univ Counseling Center Colo State U Fort Collins CO 80523

HARRIGAN, DAVID SUMNER, aerospace company engineer, retired air force officer; b. Springfield, Mass., May 1, 1937; s. John Joseph and Marjorie (Harris) H.; m. Jean C. La Pré, Jan. 25, 1958; children—David Jr., Donna, Danny. B.S. in Indsl. Engring., Ariz. State U., 1965; M.S., U. Mass., 1969. Joined U.S. Air Force, 1955, commd. 2d lt., 1965, advanced through grades to lt. col.; maintenance control officer, Vietnam, 1969-70, maintenance analysis officer C-5 Aircraft Test Program, 1970-73, logistics div. chief, 1973-76, squadron comdr. Armed Forces Staff Coll., 1976-77, chief of maintenance Lowry AFB, Colo., 1977-81; ret., 1981; system safety engr. Martin Marietta Aerospace Denver Co., 1981—. Coach youth athletics, 1966-83; bd. dirs., coach Pony League and Little League baseball. area coordinator Neighborhood Watch Program, Englewood, Colo., 1982-83. Decorated Bronze Star medal, Air Force Commendation medal (3). Mem. Air Force Assn., System Safety Soc., Am. Inst. Indsl. Engrs. Roman Catholic. Club: Arapahoe Youth League. Contbr. articles to profl. jours. Home: 7149 E Peakview Pl Englewood CO 80111 Office: 6150 S Ulster St Denver CO

HARRIGAN, JOHN FREDERICK, banker; b. Eau Claire, Wis., June 22, 1925; s. Frederick H. and Marion F. (Farr) H.; student U. Wis., 1946-49; grad. Rutgers U. Stonier Grad. Sch. Banking, 1965; m. Barbara Heald, July 1, 1950; childen—Sarah H. Gruber, Peter Christopher. With First Nat. Bank Oreg., Portland, 1949-71, exec. v.p., 1971; chmn. bd., chief exec. officer Pacific Nat. Bank Wash., Seattle, 1971-74, dir., 1971-80; vice chmn. bd. dirs. United Calif. Bank, Los Angeles, 1974-75; pres., dir. Western Bancorp., Los Angeles, 1975-80; chmn. bd., chief exec. officer, dir. Union Bank, Los Angeles, 1980—; dir. Nordstrom, Inc. Bd. dirs. Los Angeles Civic Light Opera Assn.; bd. visitors Grad. Sch. Mgmt., U. Calif., Los Angeles. Served with USMCR, 1943-45. Mem. Assn. Res. City Bankers, Smithsonian Assos. (dir.), Episcopalian. Clubs: California, Los Angeles Country, El Dorado Country. Address: 445 S Figueroa Los Angeles CA 90071

HARRIMAN, JOHN HOWLAND, banker, lawyer; b. Buffalo, Apr. 14, 1920; s. Lewis Gildersleeve and Grace (Bastine) H.; m. Barbara Ann Brunmark, June 12, 1943; children—Walter Brunmark, Constance Bastine, John Howland. A.B. summa cum laude, Dartmouth Coll., 1942; J.D., Stanford U., 1949. Bar: Calif. 1949. Assoc. firm Lawler, Felix & Hall, Los Angeles, 1949-55; asst. v.p. Security Pacific Nat. Bank, Los Angeles, 1955-61, v.p., 1961-72, sr. v.p., 1972—; sec. Security Pacific Corp., 1971—. Mem. Town Hall, Los Angeles, 1951—; mem. Republican Assocs., 1951—, trustee, 1962-72; mem. Calif. Rep. Central Com., 1956-69, 81—, mem. exec. com. 1960-62, 81—; mem. Los Angeles County Rep. Central Com., 1958-70, exec. com., 1960-62, vice chmn., 1962; chmn. Calif. 15th Congl. Dist. Rep. Central Com., 1960-62, Calif. 30th Congl. Dist. Rep. Central Com., 1962; treas. United Rep. Fin. Com., Los Angeles County, 1969-70; chmn. Commitment '80, Los Angeles County, Reagan-Bush campaign; mem. Los Angeles adv. council Episcopal Ch. Found., 1977-79. Mem. ABA, Am. Soc. Corp. Secs. (pres. Los Angeles region 1970-71), State Bar Calif., Los Angeles Bar Assn., Phi Beta Kappa, Theta Delta Chi, Phi Alpha Delta. Clubs: Beach (Santa Monica, Calif.); California (Los Angeles); Lincoln; Breakfast Panel (pres. 1970-71). Home: 245 S Plymouth Blvd Los Angeles CA 90004 Office: Security Pacific Nat Bank 333 S Hope St Los Angeles CA 90071

HARRIMAN, WANDA JUNE, business educator; b. Clovis, N.Mex., Nov. 16, 1945; d. William Carl and Lola Mae (Pelfry) H. B.S. in Bus. Edn., Eastern N.Mex. U., 1972; M.S., 1975. Tchr., Gallup-McKinley County Schs., Gallup, N.Mex., 1972-75; state supr. bus. office edn. N.Mex. Dept. Edn., Santa Fe, 1979-81; tchr. bus. and office edn. Fort Sumner (N.Mex.) Mcpl. Schs., 1975-79, 81—. Tchr. Sunday Sch., Ch. of Christ, also group youth counselor. Recipient Tchr. of Yr. award Fort Sumner Schs., 1979. Mem. NEA, N.Mex. Edn. Assn., Fort Sumner Edn. Assn., Am. Vocat. Assn., N.Mex. Vocat. Assn., Nat. Bus. Edn. Assn., N.Mex. Bus. Edn. Assn., Beta Sigma Phi, Phi Gamma Nu. Democrat. Home: 601 Lake Ave Fort Sumner NM 88119 Office: PO Box 387 Fort Sumner NM 88119

HARRINGTON, JANE LINZEE SUREN, gemological appraiser, jewelry designer; b. Middlesex, Eng., Feb. 28, 1950; d. Frederick Lewis John and Jean Francis Hood (Linzee) Suren; came to U.S., 1980; m. William C. Harrington, Oct. 3, 1980. Student (Gemological Assn. fellow) Sir John Cass Coll., 1978; B.A. with honors (Inner London Council grantee), Middlesex Poly., 1980. Jewelry designer, appraiser Schaffer & Sons, Northridge, Calif., 1981-82; gemological researcher, appraiser Am. Inst. Gemological Research, Westlake Village, Calif., 1982—. Fellow Gemological Assn. Gt. Britain (cert. diamond appraiser), Assn. Woman Gemologists, Colonial Dames Am. (chpt. XI). Office: Am Inst Gemological Research 30941 W Agoura Rd Suite 230 Westlake Village CA 91361

HARRINGTON, KAREN KETTLEWELL, dietitian; b. Berlis, Wis., Jan. 25, 1953; d. Keith K. and Ruth M. Kettlewell; m. John D. Harrington, May 22, 1976; 1 son, Dana William. B.S., U. Wis.-Stevens Point, 1975; M.S., U. Wis.-Stout, 1978. Registered dietitian. Asst. project dir. Minn. Valley Action Council, Markato, 1978-79; extension food and nutrition specialist U. Wyo.-Laramie, 1979—. Mem. Am. Dietetic Assn., Wyo. Dietetic Assn. (Young Dietitian Yr. 1981), Am. Home Econs. Assn., Wyo. Home Econs. Assn., Soc. Nutrition Edn. Office: Home Econs Dept U Wyo PO Box 3354 Laramie WY 82071

HARRINGTON, MAX GUY, gen. contractor; b. St. Helena, Calif., June 15, 1937; s. Max Cleavland and Della May (Kennedy) H.; student Napa Coll., 1956-57; m. Evelyn June Taxler, July 19, 1959; children—Brent Dean, Brenda June, Bridget May; m. 2d, Enida Figueroa, Sept. 20, 1980. Furniture salesman, interior decorator Town & Valley Furniture, Napa, Calif., 1955-58; precast concrete draftsman Basalt Rock Co., Napa, 1958-59; electronic and mech. draftsman Palomar Sci. Corp., 1961-62; head draftsman Nat. Seal Corp., Redwood City, Calif., 1962; designer, estimator Bleibler Iron Works, Palo Alto, Calif., 1962-65; designer E. Teicheira & Sons, Gen. Contractors, Vallejo, Calif., 1965-71; pres. Tech. Services, Drafting & Design, Napa, 1970-80; pres., chmn. bd. Terrestrial Devel. Corp., San Bruno, Calif., 1980—; engring. technician Mare Island Shipyard, Vallejo, Calif., 1975-77; engring. technician Western div. Naval Facilities Engring. Command, San Bruno, 1977-78, housing mgmt. officer, 1978-80, roof moisture survey program coordinator, 1980—; v.p. engring. Cididel Tech. Corp., San Raphael, Calif., 1978—; chmn. bd. New West Engring. Ltd., San Bruno, Calif. Mem. Assn. Energy Engrs., Elec. Auto Assn. Office: Terrestrial Devel Corp 2560 Valleywood Dr San Bruno CA 94066

HARRINGTON, WALTER HOWARD, JR., lawyer; b. San Francisco, Aug. 14, 1926; s. Walter Howard and Doris Ellen (Daniels) H.; B.S., Stanford, 1947; J.D., Hastings Coll., U. Calif., 1952; m. Barbara Bryant, June 1952 (div. 1973); children—Stacey Doreen, Sara Duval; m. 2d, Hertha Bahrs, Sept. 1974. Admitted to Calif. bar, 1953; dep. legislative counsel State of Calif., Sacramento, 1953-54, 55; mem. firm Walner & Harrington, Sacramento, 1954; dep. dist. atty. San Mateo County, Redwood City, Calif., 1955-62; asso. firm Wagstaffe, Daba & Hulse, Redwood City, 1962-67; practiced in Redwood City, 1967—. Chmn., San Mateo County Criminal Justice Council, 1971-76, San Mateo County Adult Correctional Facilities Com., 1969-71; pro tem referee San Mateo County Juvenile Ct., 1967-72. Served as ensign USNR, 1944-46. Mem. San Mateo County Bar Assn. (pres. 1969, editor publs. 1964-74), State Bar Calif. (editorial bd. 1968-81, vice chmn. 1969, 74-75, chmn., editor 1975-76), San Mateo County Legal Aid Soc. (pres. 1971-72), San Mateo Trial Lawyers Assn., Order of Coif, Delta Theta Phi. Republican. Episcopalian. Club: Sequoia (Redwood City). Office: 333 Bradford PO Box 1064 Redwood City CA 94064

HARRIOTT, BARBARA ANN, sportswear company sales executive; b. N.Y.C., Jan. 5, 1938; d. Anthony and Alice Veronica (Cullen) Militello; m. William James Harriott, June 8, 1963 (div.); children—Joan Marie Harriott, Stephen Byron Harriott. Student Fordham U., 1956-58. Spl. events dir. Nordstom, Inc., Seattle, 1973-80; sales promotion dir. Union Bay Sportswear, Inc., Seattle, 1980—. Bd. dirs. Women's Profl./Managerial Network of YWCA. Mem. Pub. Relations Soc. Am., Fashion Group.

HARRIS, BARBARA HULL (MRS. F. CHANDLER HARRIS), civic worker; b. Los Angeles, Nov. 1, 1921; d. Hamilton and Marion (Eimers) Baird; student UCLA, 1939-41, 45-47; m. F. Chandler Harris, Aug. 10, 1946; children—Victoria, Randolph Boyd. Pres., Victoria Originals, 1955-62; partner J.B. Assos., cons., 1971-73; state-wide dir. vols. Children's Home Soc. Calif., 1971-75. Pres., Silver Spoons vol. group Calif. Pediatric Center, 1958; Los Angeles County Heart Sunday chmn. Los Angeles County Heart Assn., 1965, bd. dirs., 1966-69; mem. exec. com. Hollywood Bowl Vols., 1966—, chmn. vols., 1971, 75; chmn. Coll. Alumni of Assistance League, 1962; bd. dirs. Assistance League So. Calif., 1964-71, 72—, pres., 1976-80; bd. dirs. Nat. Charity League, Los Angeles, 1965-69, 75-76, sec., 1967, 3d v.p., 1968, ways and means chmn., dir. Los Angeles Am. Horse Show, 1969; dir. Coronet Debutante Ball, 1968, Ball bd. chmn., 1969-71, 75, bd. dirs., 1969—; pres. So. Calif. alumni council Alpha Phi, 1961, fin. adviser to chpts. U. So. Calif., 1961-72, UCLA, 1965-72; mem. exec. com., founder chpt. Achievement Rewards for Coll. Scientists, 1983—; benefit chmn. Gold Shield, 1969, 1st v.p., 1970-72; chmn. Golden Thimble III Needlework Exhbn., Hosp. of Good Samaritan, 1975; pres. Hollywood Bowl Patroness Com., 1976; v.p. Irving Walker aux. Travellers Aid, 1976; bd. dirs. Jr. Philharmonic Com., 1976-83, pres., 1981; bd. dirs. Hollywood C. of C., 1980-81, KCET Women's Council, 1979-83, United Way, Region V, 1980-83. Recipient Outstanding Service award Los Angeles County Heart Assn., 1965; Ivy award as outstanding Alpha Phi alumna So. Calif., 1969; Outstanding Achievement award UCLA Alumni Assn., 1978; Eve award Mannequins, 1980. Home: 7774 Skyhill Dr Hollywood CA 90068

HARRIS, CASSIE ANN, advertising manager; b. Medford, Oreg., June 28, 1947; d. William Monte and Evelyn Pauline (Johnson) McIntosh; m. Ronald Lee Harris, Aug. 20, 1966; 1 son, Todd Kimball; m. Stephen Douglas Oien, Feb. 14, 1983. Student Fullerton Coll., 1965-66. Pub. relations dir. McDonald's Restaurants, Lexington, Ky., 1976-77; assoc. dir. Imagebuilders Pub. Relations, Lexington, 1977-78; account exec. Abbott Advt., Lexington, 1978-79; account supr. Caldwell-Van Riper, Inc., Indpls., 1979-80; account exec. Murray/Bradley, Anchorage, 1980-81; advt. mgr., pub. relations dir. Alaska Sales & Services, Inc., Anchorage, 1981—. Bd. dirs. Family Connection; mem. steering com. Better Bus. Bur. Alaska. Mem. Advt. Fedn. Alaska, Nat. Assn. Female Execs., Pub. Relations Soc. Am. Anchorage C. of C. (retail dir.). Home: 202 Mammoth Circle Eagle River AK 99577 Office: Alaska Sales & Service Inc 1300 E 5th Ave Anchorage AK 99501

HARRIS, CHERYL MONTGOMERY, air force officer; b. Phoenixville, Pa., Oct. 8, 1949; d. William Howard and Carol (Hecht) Montgomery; student Philipps U., Marburg, W.Ger., 1970-71; B.A., Muhlenberg Coll., 1972; M.S. in Organizational Behavior, SUNY, Binghamton, 1980; M.S. in Systems Mgmt., U. So. Calif., 1981; m. William T. Harris, Dec. 21, 1974. Commd. 2d lt. U.S. Air Force, 1972, advanced through grades to maj., 1984; chief processing, Hancock Field, N.Y., 1973-74, chief quality force, 1974-76, chief personnel No. Communications Area, Griffiss AFB, N.Y., 1976-78, chief pub. affairs, 1978-79, chief, officer selection br. Directorate of Attaché Affairs, Ft. Belvior, Va., 1979-82; internat. polit.-mil. affairs officer, dep. chief of staff/plans Pacific Air Forces hdqrs., Hickam AFB, Hawaii, 1982—. Decorated Air Force Commendation medal, Meritorious Service medal with oak leaf cluster. Mem. Air Force Assn., Met. Opera Guild, Wolf Trap Assos., Smithsonian Assos., Mensa, Friends of Kennedy Center. Home: 1080 Kaumoku St Honolulu HI 96825 Office: HQ PACAF/XPND Hickam AFB HI 96853

HARRIS, CYNTHIA VIOLA, educational administrator; management consultant; b. San Francisco, Aug. 18, 1948; d. Gilbert and Mary Lee (Barnes) H. B.A. in Speech, Nova U., M.A. in Counseling, now postgrad. Cert. tchr., adminstr., Calif. Tchr. Martin L. King Elem. Sch., Oakland, Calif., 1971-74; teaching v.p. Peralta Year Round Sch., Oakland, 1974-80, prin., 1980—; part-time mgmt. cons. year-round educ., leadership; guest lectr. Mills Coll., LaVerne U. Bd. dirs. Charles Harrison Mason Scholarships. Nominated Outstanding Woman of Am., Alpha Kappa Alpha, 1981; named Outstanding Youth Leader, Nat. Bus. and Profl. Bd., 1981. Mem. Nat. Assn. Female Execs., Nat. Assn. Prins., United Adminstrs. Oakland, Alliance Black Educators, Glamor Working Women's Panel. Democrat. Mem. Pentecostal Ch. Club: Coalition of 100 Black Women. Author: (teaching manual) All about Us, 1980.

HARRIS, DALE RAY, lawyer; b. Crab Orchard, Ill., May 11, 1937; s. Ray Beasley and Aurelia Mae (Davis) H.; B.A., U. Colo., 1959; LL.B., Harvard, 1962; m. Toni Kay Shapkoff, June 26, 1960; children—Kristen, Julie. Admitted to Colo. bar, 1962, U.S. Supreme Ct. bar, 1981; asso. firm Davis, Graham & Stubbs, Denver, 1962-67, ptnr., 1967—, chmn. mgmt. com., 1982—. Mem. Harvard Law Sch. Fund of Colo., Colo. area chmn., 1978-81. Served with AUS, 1962. Mem. Am., Colo. (chmn. antitrust com. 1980—, council corp., banking and bus. sect. 1978—), Denver bar assns., Colo. Assn. Corporate Counsel (pres. 1973-74), U. Colo. Alumni Assos., Colo. Corp. Code Revision Com., Harvard Law Sch. Assn. Colo., Phi Beta Kappa. Clubs: Denver Law (pres. 1976-77); Univ. Home: 2032 Bellaire St Denver CO 80207 Office: 2600 Colorado National Bldg Denver CO 80202

HARRIS, DARRYL WAYNE, publishing co. exec.; b. Emmett, Idaho, July 29, 1941; s. Reed Ingval and Evelyn Faye (Wengreen) H.; B.A., Brigham Young U., 1966; m. Christine Sorenson, Sept. 10, 1965; children—Charles Reed, Michael Wayne, Jason Darryl, Stephanie, Ryan Joseph. Staff writer Deseret News, Salt Lake City, 1965, Post-Register, Idaho Falls, Idaho, 1966-67; tech. editor Idaho Nuclear Corp., Idaho Falls, 1967-68; account exec. David W. Evans & Assos. Advt., Salt Lake City, 1968-71; pres. Harris Publishing, Inc., Idaho Falls, 1971—, pub. Potato Grower of Idaho, 1971—, Snowmobile West, 1974—, The Sugar Producer, 1974—. Counselor to pres. Korean Mission Ch. of Jesus Christ of Latter-day Saints, 1963-64; campaign mgr. George Hansen for Congress Com., 1974, 76. Mem. Agr. Editors Assn., Internat. Snowmobile Industry Assn. (Best Overall Reporting award 1979, 80). Republican. Club: Kiwanis. Office: 520 Park Ave Idaho Falls ID 83401

HARRIS, DAVID TILGHAM, realtor; b. Reading, Pa., May 19, 1920; s. John E. and Pauline (Moore) H.; m. Betty E., Oct. 16, 1981; 1 son from previous marriage. A.B. in Am. History, Yale U. Reporter and sports editor Marysville (Calif.) Appeal Democrat, 1945-46; announcer and sales agt. Sta. KUBA-AM, Yuba City, Calif., 1946-47; sales rep. McClatchy Broadcasting, Sta. KFBK-AM, Sacramento, 1947-50, sta. mgr. Sta. KWG-AM, Stockton, Calif., 1950-53, Sta. KMJ-AM, Fresno, Calif., 1953-57; co-owner Sta. KBIF-AM, Fresno, 1957-59; realtor, Fresno, 1959—; instr. Bd. dirs. Better Bus. Bur., 1976. Served with USAF, 1942-45. Decorated Bronze Star; Paul Harris fellow. Mem. Fresno Bd. Realtors, Farm and Land Inst., C. of C. Fresno. Episcopalian. Clubs: Rotary (pres. 1965), L'Amico (pres. 1982-83), Elks (Fresno). Office: 5064 N Angus Fresno CA 93710

HARRIS, DONNA ELAINE MEAKINS, ednl. adminstr.; b. Austin, Minn., Nov. 15, 1937; d. Lloyd George and Doris DeSales (Duclos) Meakins; A.A., Austin Community Coll., 1970; B.S., Winona State U., 1972, M.S., 1975; Ed.Specialist, 1978; m. Robert Edward Harris, Feb. 13, 1956 (div.); children—Jean, David, Joan, Mark, Richard, Robert, Paul. With Mower County Christian Edn. Center, Austin, Minn., 1965-70, coordinator, dir. preschool program, 1968-70; tchr., Washington-Kosciusko Sch., Winona, Minn., 1972-75; tchr. Goodview Sch.,

Winona, Minn., 1975-77, asst. prin., 1976-77; tchr. Stockton Sch., Winona, 1977-78; elem. sch. prin., Hot Springs County, Wyo., 1978-81, Pine Bluffs, Wyo., 1981—. Mem. bd. N.W. Child Devel. Center. Mem. Council Exceptional Children, Assn. Retarded Citizens, Assn. Supervision and Curriculum Devel., Am. Assn. Public Health. Republican. Roman Catholic. Home: 204 Main St PO Box 314 Pine Bluffs WY 82082 Office: 5th and Elm Sts PO Box 98 Pine Bluffs WY 82082

HARRIS, EDMUND BURKE, management consultant; b. N.Y.C., June 29, 1915; s. Samuel and Rachel (Radin) H.; student St. John's U. N.Y., 1933-36; B.A., U. of Philippines, 1960; M.A., Bklyn. Coll., CUNY, 1966; postgrad. Columbia U., 1963; m. Tarciana M. Mercado y Liad, July 28, 1961; children—Rachel Francis, Edmund Samuel. Enlisted in U.S. Army, 1941, advanced through grades to master sgt., 1949, ret., 1966; with U.S. Dept. Treasury, N.Y.C., 1966; mgmt. cons. Ft. Dix, N.J., 1967, U.S. Marine Corps Supply Center Barstow, Calif., 1968, Marine Corps Air Sta. Iwakuni, Japan, 1970-74; def. attache office Am. Embassy Saigon, Vietnam, 1974-75; head mgmt. engring. br. U.S. Marine Corps Supply Center, Albany, Ga., 1975-79; instr., lectr. mgmt.; adj. prof. mktg. U. Ariz., 1980; instr. bus. adminstrn. and small bus. ops. U. Phoenix, 1980—; instr. Cochise Community Coll., 1982; instr. English lang. Served with U.S. Army, 1941-45, 50-66. Recipient Meritorious Civilian Service award Dept. Navy, 1972. Mem. Small Bus. Adv. Council, C. of C. Albany, Am. Mgmt. Assn. (N.Y.C.), Ind. Consultants Am. (Indpls.). Office: PO Box 1312 Sierra Vista AZ 85635

HARRIS, EDWARD A., producer, writer, dir.; b. Elizabeth, N.J., Dec. 14, 1946; s. Howard E. and Bernice W. H.; student in music composition and theory U. Okla., 1964-67, Los Angeles Community Coll., 1977, UCLA, 1978. Singer, songwriter, 1962—; pres., exec. producer Myriad Prodns., a multi-media entertainment prodn. co., Los Angeles, 1965—; creative dir. Myriad Graphics, Los Angeles, 1976—; producer, assoc. dir. Columbia Music Hall, Hartford, Conn., 1972-75; film and TV producer, 1971—; multi-media entertainment cons., Los Angeles, 1977—; field producer Good Morning Am., also Good Night Am., ABC-TV, 1975-77; exec. producer, dir. The Act Factory, a performing arts services and indsl. show prodn. co., Los Angeles, 1977—; co-exec. producer TV program Buena Vista Hotel; sr. partner Myriad-Fritz Prodns., Los Angeles, 1977—; exec. producer Gateway Group, San Francisco, 1974-75; composer over 30 songs; dir. Performance Evaluation Workshop, Los Angeles Songwriter's Expo, 1978— co-dir. SPVA Performing Arts Workshop, Los Angeles, 1980. Pres. Wintonbury Mall Mchts. Assn., Bloomfield, Conn., 1971-72. Mem. Am. Fedn. Musicians, Am. Guild Variety Artists, Soc. for Preservation of Variety Arts, Alpha Epsilon Pi, Kappa Kappa Psi.

HARRIS, EILEEN LEEPER, artist, art cons.; b. Akron, Ohio, Aug. 4, 1941; d. Morton Samuel and Helen C. L.; student Ohio State U., 1959-61; B.F.A. cum laude, Ariz. State U., 1977; children—Deborah Anne, Tamara Lynn. Free lance designer, Scottsdale, Ariz., 1973-78; interior designer Roche Bobois, Scottsdale, 1978-79; propr. Eileen Harris Art & Design Consultants, Scottsdale, 1979-81; gen. mgr. Roche Bobois, Dallas, 1982-83; motion picture and TV film prodn. and set design John White Prodns., 1978; set decorator TV commls. E.A.T.S., Inc. for Madison, Coleman Muyskins, N.Y.C., 1978; prodn. coordinator, set designer TV commls., asst. dir. Madison, Muyskins, Jones, NY.C., 1980-81; exhibited art at Scottsdale Center for Arts, 1974-77, Ariz. State U., 1974-77; tchr. art in high schs. and jr. colls. Chmn., Phoenix Council for Soviet Jews, 1972; task force photo chmn. City of Phoenix Motion Picture Promotion Office, 1979—. Recipient 2d place award in drawing Ariz. State U. Juried Art Exhbn., 1976. Mem. Am. Soc. Interior Designers (asso., mem. local 1975), Am. Mgmt. Assn., Dallas C. of C., Scottsdale Asso. Mchts. (dir. 1980-81). Republican. Monthly columnist on interior design Phoenix Living mag. Home: 4757 Valley Vista Ln Paradise Valley AZ 85253

HARRIS, ELISABETH ALTSCHUL, advertising executive; b. Dayton, Ohio; d. Malcolm Joseph and Mildred Gladys (Kusworm) Altschul; m. Samuel J. Harris, Jr. (div. 1976); children—Scott M., Kent S., Megan M. Student (Scholar), Northwestern U. Copy chief Willis/Case/Harwood Advt., Dayton, 1966-74; acct. supr. Bart Willis & Assocs. Advt., Dayton, 1974-76; creative dir. The Pattow Agy., Phoenix, 1976-77; owner, mgr. Liz Harris Group Advt. & Pub. Relations, Las Vegas, 1977—; mem. faculty Advt. Age Creative Workshop; mem. various nat. advt. coms. Recipient advt. awards. Mem. Las Vegas Advt. Fedn. (founder). Jewish.

HARRIS, ELLEN GANDY (MRS. J. RAMSAY HARRIS), civic worker; b. Spokane, Wash., Jan. 9, 1910; d. Lloyd Edward and Helen (George) Gandy; student U. Wash.; grad. Smith Coll., 1930; m. J. Ramsay Harris, Jan. 20, 1936; children—Sue Ellen, Hayden Henry. Mem. U.S. com. UNICEF, 1948-66; mem. Def. Adv. Com. Women in Service, 1951-54; nat. co-chmn. Citizens for Eisenhower, 1953-54; Republican candidate U.S. Congress from Denver, 1954; mem. Internat. Devel. Adv. Bd., 1955- 57; nat. co. chmn. Com. Internat. Econ. Growth, 1958-60; regional chmn. Met. Opera Council, 1958-66; mem. Gov. Colo.'s Local Affairs Commn., 1963-66; pres. Colo. Consumers Council, 1965-67; dir. Nat. Safety Council, 1958-60; mem. Nat. Adv. Council on Nurse Tng., HEW, 1969-73; pres. The Park People, 1971-79. Mem. Gov.'s Commn. on Status Women, 1970-75. Vice-pres. 4 Mile Historic Park. Mem. Assn. Jr. Leagues Am. (bd. dirs. 1947-50). Episcopalian. Home: 1077 Race St Denver CO 80206

HARRIS, F. CHANDLER, emeritus univ. adminstr.; b. Neligh, Nebr., Nov. 5, 1914; s. James Carlton and Helen Ayres (Boyd) H.; A.B., U. Calif. at Los Angeles, 1936; m. Barbara Ann Hull, Aug. 10, 1946; children—Victoria, Randolph Boyd. Assoc. editor Telegraph Delivery Spirit, Los Angeles, 1937-39; writer, pub. service network radio programs University Explorer, Sci. Editor, U. Calif., 1939-61; pub. information mgr. UCLA, 1961-75, dir., 1975-82, dir. emeritus, 1982—. Mem. pub. relations com., western region United Way, 1972-75; bd. dirs. Am. Youth Symphony, Los Angeles, 1978—, v.p., 1983—; bd. dirs. Hathaway Home for Children, 1982—. Recipient 1st prize NBC Radio Inst., 1944; Harvey Hebert medal Delta Sigma Phi, 1947, Mr. Delta Sig award, 1972; Adam award Assistance League Mannequins, 1980. Mem. Western Los Angeles Regional C. of C. (dir. 1976-80), U. Calif. Retirees Assn. Los Angeles (pres.-elect 1983—), Sigma Delta Chi, Delta Sigma Phi (nat. pres. 1959-63). Club: UCLA Faculty (sec. bd. govs. 1968-72). Editor Interfraternity Research Adv. Council Bull., 1949-50, Carnation, 1969-80. Home: 7774 Skyhill Dr Hollywood CA 90068 Office: U Calif at Los Angeles Los Angeles CA 90024

HARRIS, FREDERICK EARL, II, investment adviser; b. Los Angeles, Aug. 9, 1940; s. Frederick F. and Maxine (Solomon) H.; U. Calif. at Los Angeles, 1960. Real estate salesman Santa Monica Investment Co. (Calif.), 1964-66; underwater archaeologist Council Underwater Archaeology, Mediterrean Sea, 1966-69; land developer Mustique Island and St. Vincent West Indies, 1969-71; investment adviser for various trusts and pvt. sector, 1972—. Bd. dirs. Am. Cancer Soc.; trustee Santa Monica Heritage Sq. Mus. Served with USCGR, 1958-66. Recipient award of Honor, Compagne Gen. Transalantic, 1971. Mem. Palisades Beach Property Owners Assn. (pres.), Coast Guard Aux. (flotilla and div. staff officer), U.S. Yacht Racing Union, Screen Actors Guild, West Indian Yachting Assn., Screen Actors Guild. Clubs: Calif. Yacht, Ocean Cruising, Los Angeles Yacht; Grenada Yacht; Transpacific Yacht; Royal Ocean Racing. Patentee color adaptable bandages. Office: PO Box 1859 Santa Monica CA 90406

HARRIS, GEORGE ANDERSON, lawyer, real estate broker; b. Los Angeles, Aug. 24, 1946; s. Henry Le Rew and Mary Wallace (Austin) H.; B.S. in Fin., U. So. Calif., 1968, J.D., 1971, M.B.A. in Fin., 1973; married. Bar: Calif.; asst. resident atty. Prudential Ins. Co., Calif., 1973; asst. v.p. Alison Mortgage Investment Trust, 1973-75; v.p., gen. mgr. Ban-Cal Tri State Mortgage Co., 1975-76; v.p. UMET Trust, 1976-78; real estate atty., real estate broker, Los Angeles, 1978—. Mem. ABA, Calif. State Bar, Los Angeles County Bar Assn. Republican. Office: 10960 Wilshire Blvd Suite 422 Los Angeles CA 90024

HARRIS, GEORGE B., federal judge; b. San Francisco, Aug. 16, 1901; s. Bernard Dugan and Gertrude Howard Harris; m. Aileen D. Harris, July 22, 1930; 1 dau., Gail. LL.D., cum laude, U. San Francisco, 1926. Bar: Calif. 1926. Individual practice law, San Francisco, beginning 1926; past assemblyman 27th Dist., San Francisco; judge San Francisco Mcpl. Ct., 1941-46; sr. judge U.S. Dist. Ct. Calif., (No. Dist.) (life appointment by Pres. Harry S. Truman), 1946—. Regent U. San Francisco, 1971. Decorated Knight of Malta, 1962, Knight of St. Gregory, 1966; recipient St. Thomas Moore award, 1966. Mem. Grand Order Knights of Malta. Democrat. Roman Catholic. Office: US Courthouse Dist 83 CA

HARRIS, GODFREY, public policy consultant; b. London, June 11, 1937; s. Alfred and Victoria H.; came to U.S., 1939, naturalized, 1945; B.A. with gt. distinction, Stanford U., 1958; M.A. (disting. mil. grad.), UCLA, 1960; m. Linda Berkowitz, Dec. 21, 1958 (div. 1982); children—Gregrey, Kennith, Mark. Fgn. service officer U.S. State Dept., Washington, Bonn, Germany and London, 1962-65; mgmt. analyst Office Mgmt. and Budget, Washington, 1965-67; spl. asst. to pres. IOS Devel. Co., Geneva, 1967-68; pres. Harris/Ragan Mgmt. Corp., Los Angeles, 1968—; pres. Meter Messages, Inc.; lectr. Rutgers U., 1960-61. Mem. adv. com. on gifted Santa Monica Unified Sch. Dist. (chmn. 1978-79); mem. Los Angeles World Affairs Council, Town Hall Los Angeles; former W. Coast rep. Panamanian Export Promotion and Investment Devel. Center. Served to 1st lt. U.S. Army, 1958-60. Decorated Commendation medal. Fellow Am. Acad. Cons.'s; mem. Assn. Mgmt. Cons.'s, Stanford U. Alumni Assn. (membership sec. N.Am. chpt.), London C. of C. and Industry. Democrat. Jewish. Author: Panama's Position, 1973; History of Sandy Hook, N.J., 1972; (with F. Fielder) The Quest for Foreign Affairs Officers, 1966; founder, editor Almanac of World Leaders, 1957-62, Consultants Directory, 1975—. Office: 9200 Sunset Blvd Los Angeles CA 90069

HARRIS, HOWARD JEFFREY, marketing and printing company executive; b. Denver, June 9, 1949; s. Gerald Victor and Leona Lee (Tepper) H.; B.F.A. with honors, Kansas City Art Inst., 1973, M. of Indsl. Design with honors, Pratt Inst., 1975; postgrad. Graphic Arts Research Center, Rochester Inst. Tech., 1977; m. Michele Whealen, Feb. 6, 1975; children—Kimberly, Valerie. Indsl. designer Kivett & Myers, Architects, 1970-71; indsl. designer United Research Corp., Denver, 1971-72; indsl. designer, asst. to v.p., pres. JFN Assos., N.Y.C., 1972-73; dir. facility planning Abt & Assos., Cambridge, Mass., 1973-74; v.p. design, prodn., and research Eagle Lithographics, Denver, 1974—; pres. HSR Corp., Denver. Bd. dirs. Friends of C. Henry Kemp Ctr., Denver. Mem. Indsl. Designers Soc. Am., Graphic Arts Tech. Found., Design Methods Group, The Color Group, Nat. Assn. Counsel for Children, Am. Advt. Fedn. Democrat. Jewish. Home: 929 Washington St Denver CO 80203 Office: 5105 E 41st Ave Denver CO 80216

HARRIS, JILL SANDRA, advertising agency executive; b. Burbank, Calif., Nov. 5, 1955; d. Norman Richard and Gloria (Singer) H. Student Calif. State U.-Northridge, 1973-76. Media buyer, asst. acct. exec. Hall, Butler, Blatherwick, Co., Los Angeles, 1976-78; media dir., prodn. mgr. Nathanson Advt., Encino, Calif., 1978—. Mem. Los Angeles Advt. Club, Los Angeles Prodn. Mgrs. Club.

HARRIS, JIM HOWARD, educator; b. Minneapolis, Nov. 13, 1940; s. Mac M. and Goldie (Papermaster) H.; 1 dau. Diana. B.S. in Engring., San Francisco State U., 1963; M.S. in Elec. Engring., Columbia U., 1965. Founder, owner Tech. Tng. Ctr., Campbell, Calif., 1980—, dean of faculty, 1981—. Active Community Alert Patrol, pub. Watchdog. Home: 86 Rincon St Campbell CA 95008 Office: One Campbell Ave Campbell CA 95008

HARRIS, JOSEPH DONALD, economics educator, consultant; b. Oklahoma City, Apr. 28, 1927; s. Noah Elmer Dudley and Sarah Louise (Dixon) H.; m. La Vona Sue Davis, Apr. 2, 1961; children—James Daniel, Julia Deborah. Student U. Tulsa, 1947-48, 61-64; B.A. in Bus., Baylor U., 1950; 1950-51; M.B.A., Tex. Christian U., 1965; Southwestern Theol. Sem., 1965; postgrad. U. Okla., 1950-51, Mars Hill Coll., 1969, U. Chgo., 1970, Ariz State U., 1971-74, Grand Canyon Coll., 1971-74. Field office mgr. Sunrayo Corp., Midland, Tex., 1951-52; personnel mgr., dir. Comml. Bus. Coll., Tulsa, 1952-53; acct., engring. clk. Texaco, Tulsa, 1953-55; acct., asst. personnel clk. J. A. Chapman Tulsa, 1955-64; chmn. dept. bus. Mo. Bapt. Coll., St. Louis, 1965-68; personnel profl., acct. Mars Hill (N.C.) Coll., 1968-69; chmn. dept. bus., coll. adminstr. Grand Canyon Coll., Phoenix, 1969—, also asst. dir. fin. aid and scholarship; fin. aid cons., income tax cons. Dist. vice chmn. Boy Scouts Am. Served USAF, 1945- 46. Recipient Good Shepherd award Boy Scouts Am., also Order of Merit, Thunderbird dist., 1981, Silver Beaver, 1982, Order of Arrow, 1981. Mem. Western Econ. Assn., Am. Econ. Assn., Am. Mgt. Assn., Soc. for Advancement Mgt., Nat. Assn. Intercoll. Athletic Coaches, Am. Taxation Assn., Am. Acctg. Assn., Am. Inst. for Decision Scis. (charter), Am. Bus. Law Assn., Phi Delta Kappa, Alpha Iota Delta. Democrat. Baptist. Home: 5035 N 38th Dr Phoenix AZ 85019 Office: 3300 W Camelback Phoenix AZ 85017

HARRIS, LYLE EVERETT, journalism educator; b. Kalispell Mont., July 20, 1939; s. John C. and Barbara M. Star, H.; m. Elizabeth Ann Cargile, Aug. 28, 1964; children—Lyle Everett, John Murry, Nicholas Cargile. B.A. U. Mont., 1962, M.A. 1967; Ph.D., U. Mo., 1979. Reporter, editor UPI, Salt Lake City, 1962-66; reporter Nat. Observer, 1967, Washington Evening Star, 1968-70; assoc. prof. U. Alaska, Fairbanks, 1970-71; dir. bus. journalism program U. Mo., 1971-76; assoc. prof., Western Wash. U., Bellingham, 1976—. Fellow Wash. Journalism Ctr., 1967. Mem. Assn. for Edn. in Journalism, Wash. Journalism Edn. Assn., Am. Fedn. Tchrs., Soc. Profl. Journalists-Sigma Delta Chi. Creator and 1st adminstr. Herbert J. Davenport Fellowships, U. Mo., 1976. Home: 1115 13th St Bellingham WA 98225 Office: Dept Journalism Western Wash U Bellingham WA 98225

HARRIS, LYNN NEWMAN, accountant; b. Logan, Utah, May 3, 1947; s. Newman and Mourine Christine (Andersen) H.; m. Karen Pingree, Aug. 14, 1970; children—Angela, Steven. B.S., Utah State U., 1970; M. in Public Adminstrn., Brigham Young U., 1982. C.P.A., Utah. Office mgr. Brown Equipment, Logan, Utah, 1972-74; mem. acctg. staff Atwood, Johnson & Costley, Ogden, Utah, 1974-76; internal auditor McKay-Dee Hosp., Ogden, 1976-77, budget officer, 1977-82. Chm. Republican voting dist., 1976-80; del. Utah Rep. Conv., 1980. Served with U.S. Army, 1970-72. Mem. Utah Assn. C.P.A.s, Phi Kappa Phi. Mormon. Home: 1178 North 1390 West Layton UT 84041 Office: 3939 Harrison Blvd Ogden UT 84409

HARRIS, MABLE LLOYD, county government administrator, educator; b. Meridian, Miss., Dec. 13, 1928; d. Willie Douglas and Corene (Henderson) Lloyd; children—Sharon Anne, William C., Joyce Faye. B.A., Calif. State U.-San Bernardino, 1972; M.A., U. Redlands, 1973; Ph.D. in Edn., Beverly Hills U., 1980. Tchr. Dependency Prevention Commn., San Bernardino, 1967-71, counselor, supr., 1971-73, dir. 1974-76; dir. San Bernardino County (Calif.) Dept. of Manpower Services, 1976-77, adminstrv. div. chief Family Services Agy., 1977—; cons. in field. Recipient A. Philip Randolph award Operation Second Chance, 1979; City of Rialto (Calif.) award, 1980; City of San Bernardino award, 1981. Mem. NAACP, Urban League, Bus. Profl. Women, Delta Sigma Theta. Democrat. Home: 920 E Home St Rialto CA 92376 Office: 468 W 5th St Suite 110 San Bernardino CA 92376

HARRIS, MARION KIRK, ret. civil engr.; b. Sacramento, June 12, 1914; s. Marion Alva and Nettie (Ireland) H.; B.S. cum laude, U. Calif. at Berkeley, 1951. Engr., Ruth & Going, San Jose, Calif., 1955-58, project engr., 1966-75, ret., 1975; engr. Mark Thomas & Co., 1958-62; project engr. Calif. Pacific Engrs., San Jose, 1962-66. Served with USNR, 1944-46. Mem. AAAS, Am. Congress on Surveying and Mapping, Sigma Xi, Tau Beta Pi, Chi Epsilon. Republican. Contbr. articles to profl. jours. Patentee steam engine details. Home: PO Box 2017 Atascadero CA 93423

HARRIS, MARY BIERMAN, educational foundations educator; b. St. Louis, Feb. 9, 1943; d. Norman and Margaret Bertha (Loeb) Bierman; m. Richard Jerome Harris, June 14, 1965; children—Jennifer, Christopher. B.A., Radcliffe Coll., 1964; M.A., Stanford U., 1965, Ph.D., 1968. Instr. Talladega Coll. (Ala.), 1965-66; mem. faculty U. N.Mex., Albuquerque, 1968—, prof. ednl. founds., 1976—; vis. assoc. prof. psychology Ohio State U., Columbus, 1974-75; vis. prof. psychology U. New South Wales (Australia), 1981-82. Mem. Am. Psychol. Assn. Contbr. numerous psychol. and ednl. articles to profl. publs.

HARRIS, MEL, video company executive; b. Kans. Oct. 9, 1942; s. Arlyss and Melva (Blackmer) H.; m. Ruth, Nov. 25, 1966; 1 son, Chad. B.A., Kans. State U., 1964; M.A., Ohio U., 1965, Ph.D., 1971. Instr. Ohio U., 1970-71; v.p., gen. mgr. Kaiser Broadcasting, Sta. WKBF, Cleve., 1971-74, Sta. WKBS-TV, Phila., 1974-75; with TV sales Metromedia, 1975-77; with Paramount Pictures Corp., Los Angeles, 1977—, pres. Paramount Video, 1981—. Served with U.S. Army, 1968-70. Decorated Bronze Star. Office: Paramount Pictures Corp 555 Melrose Ave Los Angeles CA 90038

HARRIS, MICHAEL DAVID, SR., lawyer; b. Henderson, N.C., Feb. 22, 1936; s. John David and Elsie (Grey) H.; m. Eula J. Harris, Mar. 22, 1959; children—Michael David, Rima M., Jodi C. A.S., Louisburg Jr. Coll., 1966; B.S., N.C. State U., 1968; J.D., U. N.C., 1973. Bar: Calif. 1973. Land surveyor U.S. Dept. Agr., Henderson, 1960-64; loan officer Security Pacific Nat. Bank, Palm Springs, Calif., 1968-70; assoc. Best, Best & Krieger, Palm Springs, 1973-79, ptnr., 1979—, mem. mgmt. com., 1982—; vis. lectr. U. Calif.-Riverside, 1973-74. Chmn. Palm Springs Planning Commn., 1979-82; chmn. Palm Springs dist. Boy Scouts Am.; profl. chmn. United Way of Desert. Served with USN, 1954-57, USAF, 1959-60; Korea. Recipient award of merit Boy Scouts Am., 1976, Silver Beaver, 1980. Mem. ABA, Calif. Bar Assn., Pi Alpha Delta. Republican. Methodist. Clubs: Palm Springs, Lions (dir.). Author: Cable Television Franchising in North Carolina, 1973. Home: 232 NE Cerritos Palm Springs CA 92262 Office: 600 E Tahqitz-McCallum Palm Springs CA 92262

HARRIS, MICHAEL GENE, optometrist, educator; b. San Francisco, Sept. 20, 1942; s. Morry and Gertrude Alice (Epstein) H.; B.S., U. Calif., 1964, M. Optometry, 1965, D. Optometry, 1966, M.S., 1968; m. Andrea Elaine Berman, Nov. 29, 1969; children—Matthew Benjamin, Daniel Evan. Asso. practice optometry, Oakland, Calif., 1965-66, San Francisco, 1966-68; instr., coordinator contact lens clinic Ohio State U., 1968-69; asst. clin. prof. optometry U. Calif. at Berkeley, 1969-73, also dir. contact lens extended care clinic, 1969—, asso. clin. prof., 1973-76, asst. chief contact lens service, 1970-76, asso. chief contact lens service, 1976—, lectr., 1978-80, sr. lectr., 1980—; pvt. practice optometry, Oakland, Calif., 1973-76; lectr., cons. in field. Cons. hypnosis Calif. Optometric Assn., Am. Optometric Assn.; cons. Nat. Bd. Examiners in Optometry, Soflens div. Bausch & Lomb, 1973—, Barnes-Hind Hydrocurve Soft Lenses, Inc., 1974—, Contact Lens Research Lab., 1976—, Wesley-Jessen Contact Lens Co., 1977—, Palo Alto VA, 1980—, Primarius Corp., Aguaflex Contact Lens Co., 1980—. Founding mem. Young Adults div. Jewish Welfare Fedn., 1965—, chmn. 1967-68; commr. Sunday Football League, Contra Costa County, Calif., 1974-78. Bd. dirs. Jewish Community Relations Council of Greater East Bay, 1979—, Campolindo Homeowners Assn., 1981—. Fellow U. Calif., 1971; Calif. Optometric Assn. Scholar 1965, George Schneider Meml. scholar, 1964. Fellow Am. Acad. Optometry (diplomate contact lens sect.; chmn. contact lens papers; mem. contact lens com. 1974—, vice chmn. contact lens sect. 1980-82, chmn. 1982—), Assn. Schs. and Colls. Optometry (council on acad. affairs), AAAS; mem. Am. (proctor 1969—), Calif. optometric assns., Assn. Optometric Contact Lens Educators, Am. Optometric Found., Mexican Soc. Contactology (hon.), Internat. Soc. Contact Lens Referral, Calif. State Bd. Optometry (regulation rev. com.), Mensa. Democrat. Mem. B'nai B'rith. Editor current comments sect. Am. Jour. Optometry, 1974-77; contbr. chpts. to books; author various syllabuses; contbr. articles to profl. pubs. Home: 43 Corte Royal Moraga CA 94556 Office: Univ Calif Sch Optometry Berkeley CA 94720 also 43 Corte Royal Moraga CA 94556

HARRIS, MICHAEL RAYMOND, editor; b. Pensacola, Fla., Jan. 27, 1943; s. Donald George and Alice Ruth H. B.S., So. Ill. U., 1969. Employee communications editor Unicom Systems, Rockwell Internat., Cupertino, Calif., 1966—; service rep. Pan Am Flight Service, San Francisco, 1969-71; pub. relations writer Falstaff Brewing Corp., St. Louis, 1975-78; founder, editor, pub. Peninsula Mag., Palo Alto, Calif., 1979—; co. publs. editor ROLM Corp., Santa Clara, Calif., 1976—. Named First Citizen of San Mateo County, 1976. Mem. Internat. Assn. Bus. Communicators, Pub. Relations Soc. Am., Peninsula Mktg. Assn. Office: 4900 Old Ironsides Dr Mail Stop 626 Santa Clara CA 95050

HARRIS, MIKE ERVIN, optometrist; b. Mohall, N. D., Mar. 6, 1955; s. Leonard O. and Eleanor I. (Larson) H.; m. Cecilia A., Demple, Aug. 30, 1975; children—J.D., Jennifer. Student U. Wyo., 1973-75; B.S., So. Calif. Coll. Optometry, 1979, O.D., 1979. Pvt. practice optometry, Casper, Wyo., 1979—. Named Outstanding committeeman C. of C., 1982, Outstanding First Yr. Mem. Kiwanis Club Casper, 1980, Outstanding Contact Lens Student Bausch & Lomb Co., 1979, Outstanding Visual Therapy Student Bernell Corp., 1979. Mem. Am. Optometric Assn., Wyo. Optometric Assn. Republican. Episcopalian. Clubs: Kiwanis of Casper, Masons. Home: 1932 E 23d St Casper WY 82601 Office: 2510 E 15th St Suite 1 Casper WY 82609

HARRIS, NAOMI, retailer; b. Lufkin, Tex., Aug. 28, 1927; d. Robert Lewis and Ruby Jane Collins; m. John Reagan Harris, Dec. 25, 1945; children—John Robert, Bruce Reagan. Grad. Satterwhite Comml. Coll., Lufkin, 1944. Sec., 1944-47; sec. to asst. adminstrv. officer U.S. Dept. Army, Ft. Huachuca, Ariz., 1952-54; legal sec., 1954-59; office mgr. First Nat. Bank Ariz., Bisbee, 1961-80; propr. retail store, Bisbee, 1976—. Bd. dirs. Bisbee Indsl. Devel. Authority. Mem. Bisbee C. of C. (dirs.). Democrat. Clubs: Bisbee Country.

HARRIS, NORMAN ALLAN, research and devel. co. exec.; b. Los Angeles, Sept. 27, 1933; s. David Jack and Bella (Flack) H.; student

(Univ. scholar) U. So. Calif., 1951; B.A. (Coll. scholar), Occidental Coll., 1955; postgrad. Vanderbilt U., 1955-56; grad. Oak Ridge Sch. Radiol. Physics, 1956; m. Sandra Gail Hill, Feb. 22, 1958; children—Todd, Tracy, Wendy. Project engr. Marquardt, Van Nuys, Calif., 1956-60; project mgr. Atomics Internat., Canoga Park, Calif., 1960-62; sr. asso. Planning Research Corp., Los Angeles, 1962-68; prin. scientist advanced sensor systems McDonnell-Douglas, Santa Monica, Calif., 1968-69; mgr. dept. environ. safety EG&G, Goleta, Calif., 1969-74; exec. v.p. Henningson, Durham & Richardson, Santa Barbara, Calif., 1974—, dir. spl. space shuttle studies, 1974—, dir. M-X EIS prodn. and spl. systems studies, 1976—; pres. Motoracing News, 1978—, Manbourne Inc.; chmn. bd. MI Systems Applications Co., Santa Barbara. Mem. com. to establish tchr. qualifications and evaluation standards, Santa Ynez, Calif. AEC fellow, 1955-56. Mem. Health Physics Soc. (charter), Kappa Mu Epsilon, Sigma Pi Sigma. Author tech. monographs in field. Office: 804 Anacapa St Santa Barbara CA 93101

HARRIS, PATRICIA ANNE, govt. ofcl.; b. Cleve., July 27, 1950; d. George Byron and Lillian Anne (Kippert) Srofe; A.A. cum laude, Anchorage Community Coll., 1979; children—Robert Alan, Mark Andrew, Gregory James. File clk. typist Alcan Aluminum, Warren, Ohio, 1968-69; sec. Manpower, Inc., St. Louis, 1969-70; sec. USAF, Anchorage, 1970-73, adminstrv. systems mgr., 1977-79, chief systems mgmt. div., 1979-83, chief publs. and systems mgmt. div., 1983—; sec. IRS, Anchorage, 1973-75; supervisory clerical asst. Alaska Outer Continental Shelf Office, Anchorage, 1975-77. Recipient USAF Outstanding Adminstrv. officer award, 1979; named Anchorage Fed. Employee of Yr., 1977. Mem. Nat. Assn. Female Execs. Home: PO Box 822 Anchorage AK 99506 Office: HQ AAC/DAY Elmendorf AFB AK 99506

HARRIS, PHILLIP G., utility executive; b. Aberdeen, Miss., Mar. 26, 1948; s. H.W. and Edna L. (Stapp) H.; m. Patricia C. Redwine, Dec. 6, 1970; children—Tracy, Justin. B.S., U.S. Mil. Acad., 1970; B.A., U. No. Colo., 1974. Cert. mgmt. acctg. Inst. Mgmt. Acctg. Mgr. fin., controller Lea County Electric Coop., Inc., Lovington, N.Mex., 1977—; tchr. bus. communications Coll. of S.W. Active 3d and Central Ch. of Christ, Lovington. Served to capt. U.S. Army, 1970-75. Decorated Silver Star, Bronze Star, Army Commendation medal. Mem. Nat. Assn. Accts., Inst. Internal Auditors, Assn. Systems Mgmt., Am. Legion. Contbr. articles to profl. jours. Home: 1911 W Jefferson St Lovington NM 88260 Office: PO Drawer 1447 Lovington NM 88260

HARRIS, ROBERT GEORGE, portrait painter; b. Kansas City, Mo., Sept. 9, 1911; s. Harry George and Lena Mary (Stevens) H.; m. Marjorie Elnora King, Dec. 26, 1935; children—Craig King, Marcia H. Attended Kansas City Art Inst., 1928-30, Art Students League and Grand Central Art Sch., 1931-32. Illustrator, Ladies Home Jour., Saturday Evening Post, McCalls, Good Housekeeping, Cosmopolitan; Cannon Sheet, Schaefer's Beer, Coca Cola, etc., 1937-61; portrait painter (oil medium), 1961—; one-man show, portraits, Phoenix Art Mus., 1962; represented in permanent collections: U.S. Dept. Justice (Washington), Union Pacific Railroad Bd. Room (N.Y.C.), Wabash Coll. (Ind.), Seabury Sem. (Chgo.), various bus. schs., orgns., also personal portraits throughout U.S. and Canada. Mem. Soc. of Illustrators (life mem. N.Y.C. chpt.). Home and Office: 8301 E Serene St Carefree AZ 85377

HARRIS, ROBERT GERALD, business administration educator; b. Bryan, Ohio, Mar. 30, 1943; s. Gerald E. and Mary M. (Merillat) H.; m. Linda Baxter, Mar. 29, 1969; children—Kirsten, Brandon. B.A., Mich. State U., 1965, M.A., 1973; M.A., U. Calif.-Berkeley, 1975, Ph.D., 1977. Pub. relations rep. Gen. Motors, Warren, Mich., 1965-66; v.p. Nat. Student Mktg., Washington, 1966-67; campaign cons. Nelson Rockefeller, Hubert Humphrey, 1968; pres. Young Am. Corp., 1969-71; dep. dir. ICC, Washington, 1980-81; faculty bus. adminstrn., U. Calif., Berkeley, 1977—, assoc. prof., 1983—, chmn. bus. and pub. policy group; faculty dir. exec. program; cons. in antitrust econs. and govt. regulation. Mem. Acad. Mgmt., Am. Econ. Assn., Blue Key, Phi Beta Kappa. Democrat. Club: Claremont Resort and Tennis. Contbr. articles to profl. jours. Home: 2841 Forest Ave Berkeley CA 94705 Office: Sch Bus Adminstrn Univ of Calif Berkeley CA 94720

HARRIS, ROBERT NORMAN, advertising agency executive, consultant; b. St. Paul, Feb. 11, 1920; s. Nathanial and Esther (Roberts) H.; m. Mildred Burton, June 6, 1941; children—Claudia Harris Brown, Robert Norman, Randolph B. B.A., U. Minn., 1941. Exec. v.p. Toni Co. div. Gillette Co., Chgo., 1941-55, Lee King & Ptnrs., Chgo., 1955-60, Wrisley Co. div. Purex Corp. Ltd., Chgo., 1960-62, North Advt. Co., Chgo., 1962-73; pres. Harris Creative Group, Inc., Chgo., 1973-81, San Jose, Calif., 1981—; exec. v.p., gen. mgr. Creamer Inc. Advt., Chgo., 1977-82; dir. Harriscope Broadcasting, Los Angeles, 1975—; instr. advt., mktg. San Jose State U., 1983—. Mem. Republican Presdl. Task Force, 1980—; chmn. activities com. Villages Assn., San Jose, 1982-83. Served with USNR, 1942-44. Mem. Am. Assn. Advt. Agys. (contbg. author A Handbook for Advertising Executives 1978), Am. Mktg. Assn., Nat. Cable TV Assn., Nat. Assn. Broadcasters, Nat. Acad. TV Arts and Scis. Clubs: U.S. Senatorial, Villages Golf and Country, Villages Sons in Retirement. Home: 7220 Via Sendero San Jose CA 95135

HARRIS, THOMAS HALE, manufacturing company official; b. Buffalo, Feb. 25, 1926; s. Alan Hale and Helena Electa (Parker) H.; B.S. in Chem. Engring., U. Minn., 1948; m. Barbara Anne Curtiss, June 17, 1950; children—Susan Day, Peter Graham, Stephen Hale. Plant engr. Conn. Coke Co., New Haven, 1948-55; compressor application engr. Carrier Corp., Syracuse, N.Y., 1955-59; regional engr. Elliott Co., N.Y.C., 1959-62, Eastern marine mgr., 1962-64, compressor mktg. mgr., Jeannette, Pa., 1964-67, Los Angeles dist. mgr., 1967-71, Western regional mgr., 1971-80, mgr. Western ops., 1980-83, mgr. U.S. govt. sales West coast, 1983—. Com. chmn. Troop 720, Boy Scouts Am., 1970-81; advisor/leader Sierra Trek, 1975—; ch. sch. supt. St. Thomas Episcopal Mission, Hacienda Heights, Calif., 1968-70, mem. bishops com., 1974-76. Served with USNR, 1944-46. Mem. Pacific Coast Gas Assn. (bd. dirs. 1979-81; Silver medal 1978, Basford trophy 1980), Pacific Energy Assn. (dir. 1979—, exec. com. 1982-83, Service award of merit 1981, Presdl. citation 1983), Am. Inst. Chem. Engrs., Geothermal Resources Council, Industry Mfrs. Council. Republican. Episcopalian. Clubs: Petroleum of Los Angeles, Candlewood Country, Industry Hills Men's. Home: 15549 LaMoine St Hacienda Heights CA 91745 Office: PO Box 4900 Diamond Bar CA 91765

HARRIS, VELVA JOY, nursing adminstr.; b. Naylor, Mo., Jan. 16, 1936; d. Jack Seamans and Melba Priscilla (Lassiter) Cunningham; R.N., Mo. Bapt. Hosp. Sch. Nursing, 1956; B.S., Washington U., 1962; postgrad. in psychology U. Tex., 1969; m. Fred L. Harris, Apr. 20, 1956 (div.); 1 dau., Kimberly Jo. Psychiat. nurse Mo. Bapt. Hosp., St. Louis, Mo., 1956-61, clin. instr. psychiat. nursing, 1961-63; asst. dir. nurses Northwest Tex. Hosp., Amarillo, Tex., 1967-69; asst. dir. nurses W.I. Cook Meml. Children's Hosp., Ft. Worth, 1970-73; adminstrv. head nurse II, Santa Barbara (Calif.) Gen. Hosp., 1973-78; dir. nurses Santa Barbara County Health Care Services, 1978—; instr. med. aidman course Tex. Army Nat. Guard, Amarillo, Tex., 1968. Mem., Ventura-Santa Barbara Health Systems Agency, 1976—; pres. Western Addiction Services Program, Inc., 1979-80; mem. adv. com. Health Techs. div. Santa Barbara Community Coll., 1979—. Served as capt. Nurses Corps, USAF, 1963-67. USPHS ednl. trainee, 1961-62. Mem. Calif. Soc. Nursing Service Adminstrs., Advocates for Public Health, Nat. Assn. Public Health, Santa Barbara County Employees Assn. (dir. 1975-78), Washington U. Alumni Assn. Episcopalian. Club: Zonta Internat. Home: 257 Brandon Dr Goleta CA 93117 Office: 300 N San Antonio Rd Santa Barbara CA 93110

HARRIS, WILLIAM MERL, chemist; b. Los Angeles, Feb. 23, 1931; s. Merl William Evans and Beatrice Theresa (Hawkins) H.; B.S., UCLA, 1956, Ph.D., 1965; m. Ilse Anneliese Doebrich, Jan. 2, 1957. Mem. tech. staff Hughes Aircraft Co., Culver City, Calif., 1956-59; chemist U.S. FDA, Los Angeles, 1964-65; postdoctoral research fellow in chemistry UCLA, 1965-66, instr., 1966-70; asst. prof. Los Angeles Valley Coll., Van Nuys, Calif., 1970-73, asso. prof., 1973-77, coordinator instrn., 1976-77, prof. chemistry, 1977—, chmn. dept., 1970—; lectr. chemistry U. Calif., Santa Barbara, 1968; vis. prof. chemistry UCLA, 1979. Served with U.S. Army, 1952-54. Named Outstanding Teaching Asst., UCLA, 1962; Hughes fellow, 1957-59; registered patent agt. Mem. Am. Chem. Soc., Royal Soc. Chemistry (Eng.), Patent, Trademark and Copyright Sect. State Bar Calif., Los Angeles Patent Law Assn., Sigma Xi, Phi Lambda Upsilon. Club: Masons (32 deg.). Contbr. articles to profl. jours. Office: 5800 Fulton Ave Van Nuys CA 91401

HARRISON, CAROLE ALBERTA, museum curator, civic worker; b. Dayton, Ohio, Jan. 16, 1942; d. Chester Arthur and Mildred Irene (Focke) Shaw; student U. Dayton, 1959-60, U. Colo., 1960-61; m. Darrell Harrison, Apr. 24, 1962; children—Amelia Holmes, Ann Elizabeth, Abigail. With Council for Pub. TV, Channel 6, Inc., Denver, 1972-78, Hist. Denver, Inc., 1973—; dir. devel. Sewall Rehab. Center, Denver, 1979-80; exec. v.p. Marilyn Van Derbur Motivational Inst., Inc., 1980-82. Bd. dirs. Center for Public Issues, Denver, 1979-82, Passages, 1982—, Hall of Life, 1981— Historic Denver, 1982—, Denver Firefighters Mus., 1979—; bd. dirs. KRMA-TV Vols., 1970—, pres., 1973-74; founder Com. for Support of Arts, Denver, 1978-79; chmn. Graland Country Day Sch. Auction, 1979, 80, Channel 6 Auction, 1971, 72, Colo. Acad. Auction, 1980. Mem. Colo. Assn. Fund Raisers, Denver Advt. Fedn., Leadership Denver Alumni Assn. (dir. 1980-82), Denver C. of C. (govt. relations com. 1983—). Club: Pinehurst Country. Home: 5303 W Oberlin Dr Denver CO 80235 Office: 1326 Tremont Pl Denver CO 80204

HARRISON, CHARLES WAGNER, JR., applied physicist; b. Farmville, Va., Sept. 15, 1913; s. Charles Wagner and Etta Earl (Smith) H.; student U.S. Coast Guard Acad., 1934-36; B.S. in Engring., U. Va., 1939, E.E., 1940; S.M., Harvard U., 1942, M.E., 1952, Ph.D. in Applied Physics, 1954; m. Fern F. Perry, Dec. 28, 1940; children—Martha R., Charlotte J. Commd. ensign USN, 1939, advanced through grades to comdr., 1948; research staff Bur. Ships, 1939-41, asst. dir. electronics design and devel. div., 1948-50; research staff U.S. Naval Research Lab., 1944-45, dir's. staff, 1950-51; liason officer Evans Signal Lab., 1945-46; electronics officer Phila. Naval Shipyard, 1946-48; USN Operational Devel. Force Staff, 1953-55; staff Comdg. Gen., Armed Forces Spl. Weapons project, 1955-57; ret. 1957; cons. electromagnetics Sandia Labs., Albuquerque, 1957-73; instr. U. Va., 1939-40; lectr. Harvard U., 1942-43, Princeton U., 1943-44; vis. prof. Christian Heritage Coll., El Cajon, Calif., 1976. Registered profl. engr., Va., Mass., N.Mex. Fellow IEEE (Electronics Achievement award 1966, best paper award electromagnetic compatibility group 1972); mem. Creation Research Soc., Soc. Harvard Engrs. and Scientists, Internat. Union Radio Sci. (commns. B and H), Sigma Xi. Mem. Fellowship Bible Ch. (founder; chmn. steering com. 1976-77, deacon 1978-81). Author: (with R.W.P. King) Antennas and Waves: A Modern Approach, 1969. Contbr. numerous articles to profl. jours. Home: 2808 Alcazar St NE Albuquerque NM 87110

HARRISON, EARLE, department store executive; b. Rainsville, Ala., May 20, 1905; s. Robert Lee and Sarepta Ophelia (Hansard) H.; A.B., Northwestern U., 1929, grad. student bus. adminstrn., 1942, LL.B., Chgo.-Kent Coll. Law, 1935; m. Joan Mary Jackson, 1942. With Marshall Field & Co., Chgo., 1929—, div. operating mgr., 1958-60, v.p. ops., 1960-64, v.p., treas., 1964-69. Pres., dir. Family Financial Counseling Service of Greater Chgo., 1966-69; cons., adminstr. Lake County Nursing Home, 1973—; adminstr. Condell Meml. Hosp., Libertyville, 1973—, pres., bd. dirs., 1975-77, chmn. bd., 1977—. Mem. bd. dirs. Credit Bur. Cook County, 1949-69, pres., 1958—; mem. Lake County Bd. Suprs.; chmn. Lake County Planning and Zoning Com.; pres. Northeastern Ill. Planning Commn., 1973, mem. exec. com., 1975-78; bus. cons., 1978—. Mem. Phi Delta Phi. Episcopalian. Home: 2712 Chrysler Dr Roswell NM 88201

HARRISON, ETHEL MARGARET, state supreme court clerk; b. Alliance, Ohio, Feb. 5, 1920; d. John William and Edna Lena (Bierry) Streit; m. DeWitt Edward Harrison, June 22, 1941; children—DeWitt Edward, William Douglas. B.F.A. in Silversmithing, Cleve. Inst. Art, 1973. Dep. clk. and recorder Lake County, Mont., 1976-78, clk. Dist. Ct., 1978-81; exec. sec. to sec. of state, State of Mont., 1981-83; clk. Mont. Supreme Ct., 1983—. Participant Leadership Helena, 1982, 83; bd. dirs. Mont. Fedn. Republican Women. Mem. Nat. Conf. Appellate Ct. Clks., Mont. Dist. Ct. Clks. Assn., AAUW. Presbyterian. Clubs: Helena Arts Council, Community Concert Assn. Exhibited silver works: 40th Ann. Nat. Art Exhbn., Cooperstown, N.Y., 1975, Seventh Biennial Beaux Arts Exhbn., Columbus, Ohio, 1973. Office: 215 N Sanders Helena MT 59602

HARRISON, GALE EVANS, city ofcl.; b. Stockton, Calif., Feb. 12, 1947; d. Henry Andrew and Mollie (Wilson) Evans; BS., U. Calif., San Francisco, 1977; divorced; children—Samuel R.F., III, Koranella G. Salary adminstr. Tillie Lewis Foods, Inc., Stockton, 1970-74; personnel analyst City of Stockton, 1974-78; personnel dir. City of Visalia (Calif.), 1978—; lectr. community colls., leader seminars, cons. in field. Chmn., Commn. Status Women, Tulare County, Calif., 1981; adv. bd. selection com. Visalia Unified Sch. Dist. Supt.; bd. dirs. Visalia Unified Sch. Dist. Adult Edn., Tulare County Associated In-Group Donors. Mem. Am. Soc. Public Adminstrn., Calif. Women in Govt., Calif. Public Employees Labor Relations Assn., Nat. Public Employees Labor Relations Assn., Internat. Personnel Mgmt. Assn., Acad. Polit. Sci., Nat. League Cities, NAACP (br. pres. 1980-81), NOW, Delta Sigma Theta. Office: 315 S Johnson St Visalia CA 93277

HARRISON, HELEN MAYER, artist, educator; b. N.Y.C.; d. Henry and Natalia (Perla) Mayer; m. Newton A. Harrison, Aug. 26, 1953; children—Steven, Joshua, Gabriel, Joy. B.A., Queens Coll.; M.A., NYU, 1953. Prof., chmn. dept. visual arts U. Calif.-San Diego; one man shows: Ronald Feldman Fine Arts, 1974, 75, 78, 80, 82, Calif. State Coll.-Fullerton, 1972, Detroit Inst. Arts, 1976, San Francisco Mus. Modern Art, 1977, Portland Ctr. for Visual Arts, 1978, Williams Coll., 1979, Brown U., 1979, Chgo. Mus. Contemporary Art, 1980, Md. Inst. Coll. Art, 1981, Washington Project for the Arts, 1982, Emory U., 1983, San Jose Mus. Art, 1983, San Jose State U., 1983; group shows include: Boston Mus. Fine Art, 1971, Mus. Contemporary Art, Houston, 1972, Propositions Pour Les Halles, Paris, 1974, 75, Santa Barbara Mus. Art, 1979, Contemporary Art of So. Calif., High Mus. Atlanta, 1980, La Jolla Contemporary Mus., 1978, Powers Gallery, Australia, 1974, Scripps Coll., Calif., 1983, Nexus Gallery, Atlanta, 1983, Long Beach (Calif.) Mus. Art, 1983; represented by Ronald Feldman Fine Arts, N.Y.C. Contbr. numerous articles to arts mags. Office: Dept Visual Arts U Calif San Diego La Jolla CA 92014 also PO Box 446 Del Mar CA 92014

HARRISON, J(AMES) RICHARD, business educator; b. Stillwater, Okla., Apr. 20, 1947; s. Charles Arthur and Mary Beatrice (Huggins) H. B.S. with high honors, U. Okla., 1969; Ph.D. in Bus., Stanford U., 1983. Exec. dir. Grad. Student Govt., U. Calif.-Berkeley, 1976-78; mgmt. lectr. Calif. State U.-Hayward, 1979-81; bus. lectr. U. Calif.-Berkeley, 1981, Pepperdine U., 1982; asst. prof. mgmt. U. Ariz., 1983—; v.p., co-founder Siren Records, San Francisco, 1976-78; cons. in bus. strategy, mgmt. Univ. fellow U. Tex., 1969-70; Flood fellow, U. Calif.-Berkeley, 1978-79; Beckendorf fellow Stanford U., 1980-81. Mem. Acad. Mgmt., Am. Sociol. Assn., Am. Math. Soc. (hon.), Phi Beta Kappa. Democrat. Author: The Committee Structure of Corporate Boards of Directors, 1983; founder, pub. The Berkeley Graduate Newspaper, 1976. Home: PO Box 43755 Tucson AZ 85733 Office: Dept Mgmt U Ariz Tucson AZ 85721

HARRISON, JOHN CONWAY, justice; b. Grand Rapids, Minn., Apr. 28, 1913; s. Francis Randall and Ethelyn (Conway) H.; student Mont. State Coll., 1931-34, U. Mont., 1935-37; LL.B., George Washington U., 1940; m. Virginia Flanagan, Aug. 28, 1941; children—Nina Lyn, Robert Charles, Molly M., John C., Frank Randall, Virginia Lee. Admitted to Mont. bar, 1947; practiced in Helena, Mont., 1947-54; pub. prosecutor, 1954-60; atty. Lewis and Clark County, Mont., 1954-60; justice Mont. Supreme Ct., Helena, 1961—. Active Boy Scouts Am. Bd. dirs. Nat. Tb Assn., 1954-61, Mont. Tb Assn., 1947-61; pres. elect Nat. Tb and Respiratory Disease Assn., 1971-72. Served to lt. col. AUS, 1940-45; ETO. Decorated Bronze Star (U.S.); Croix de Guerre (France). Mem. Am., Mont. bar assns., Am. Legion. V.F.W., Sigma Chi. Democrat. Kiwanian (pres. Helena 1951). Home: 516 N Park Helena MT 59106

HARRISON, NEWTON A., artist, educator; b. Bklyn., Oct. 20, 1932; s. Harvey M. and Estelle (Farber) H.; m. Helen Mayer, Aug. 26, 1953; children—Steven, Joshua, Gabriel, Joy. Student Pa. Acad. Fine Arts, 1952-53, 55-57; B.F.A., Yale U., 1964, M.F.A., 1965. Mem. faculty U. N.Mex., 1965-67; prof. visual arts U. Calif.-San Diego, 1967—; one man shows: Ronald Feldman Fine Arts, 1974, 75, 78, 80, 82, Calif. State Coll.-Fullerton, 1972, Detroit Inst. Arts, 1976, San Francisco Mus. Modern Art, 1977, Portland Ctr. for Visual Arts, 1978, Williams Coll., 1979, Brown U., 1979, Chgo. Mus. Contemporary Art, 1980, Md. Inst. Coll. Art, 1981, Washington Project for the Arts, 1982, Emory U., 1983, San Jose Mus. Art, 1983, San Jose State U., 1983; group shows include: Boston Mus. Fine Art, 1971, Mus. Contemporary Art, Houston, 1972, Propositions Pour Les Halles, Paris, 1974, 75, Santa Barbara Mus. Art, 1979, Contemporary Art of So. Calif., High Mus. Atlanta, 1980, LaJolla Contemporary Mus., 1978, Powers Gallery, Australia, 1974, Scripps Coll., 1983, Nexus Gallery, Atlanta, 1983, Long Beach (Calif.) Mus. Art, 1983; represented by Ronald Feldman Fine Arts, N.Y.C. Contbr. numerous articles to arts mags. Office: Dept Visual Arts U Calif San Diego La Jolla CA 92014 also PO Box 446 Del Mar CA 92014

HARRISON, THOMAS SAMUEL, IV, electronic design co. exec.; b. Portland, Oreg., Sept. 24, 1952; s. Thomas Samuel and Margaret (Lindsay) H.; A.B. cum laude, Dartmouth Coll., 1975; m. Karen Anne Hammelman, Oct. 25, 1975; children—Thomas Samuel V., Michael Andrew, Elizabeth Anne. Systems programmer Kiewit Computation Ctr., Dartmouth Coll., Hanover, N.H., 1971-73; system support specialist Grumman Data Systems, Grumman Aerospace Corp., Bethpage, N.Y., 1974; systems analyst/designer Dealer Services div. ADP, Portland, Oreg., 1976-79; owner TS4, Milwaukie, Oreg., 1979—; vol. instr. high sch. programming, 1973. Mem. Assn. for Computing Machinery. Office: TS4 15285 S E Bevington Ave Milwaukie OR 97222-2306

HARRISON, WILLIAM COY, devel. specialist; b. San Antonio, Jan. 26, 1928; s. William Guy and Mary Ellen (Day) H.; children—William G., Carol St. Onge, Mary E. Reinhardt, Betty J., John P. student So. Meth. U., 1948-51. With N.Am. Aviation, 1952-57; supr. ground test equipment Houston Fearless Corp., 1957-60; vacuum technologist Gen. Tech. Corp., Torrance, Calif., 1960-63; devel. specialist Garrett Corp., Torrance, 1963—. Served with U.S. Navy, 1945-46, 51-52. Mem. AAAS, Zeta Epsilon. Democrat. Office: 2525 W 190th Torrance CA

HARRISON, WILLIAM JOSEPH, computer programmer; b. Louisville, Oct. 31, 1933; s. Sterling Stewart and Pearl (Wooley) H.; A.A. in Math., U. Louisville, 1959, B.S. in Physics, 1961; postgrad. UCLA, 1962-63, CCNY, 1964-65, U. Calif., Berkeley, 1969; m. Anna Rose Riley, Mar. 22, 1958; 1 dau., Janet Rose. Cost acctg. clk. Internat. Steel Co., Evansville, Ind., 1951; free-lance portrait photographer, Louisville, 1952; machine acct. IBM, Louisville, 1956-58, computer programmer, Beverly Hills, Calif., 1963-64, N.Y.C., 1964-67; machine acct. Colgate-Palmolive Co., Louisville, 1958-61; mathematician Librascope Inc., Glendale, Calif., 1961-63; staff cons. Info. Mgmt. Inc., San Francisco, 1967-70; systems cons. Fireman's Fund Ins. Co., San Francisco and San Rafael, Calif., 1970—; owner, operator Harrison Enterprises, pub., editor CWP Newsletter for Crossword Puzzle Constructors, 1976-82; editor Challenger Crossword Puzzle Series, Simon & Schuster, 1982—. Mem. nat. research com. Republicans and Independents for Johnson, N.Y.C., 1964. Served with USAF, 1952-56; Korea, Japan. Mem. Assn. Computing Machinery (reviewer Computing Revs.), Optical Soc. Am., Guide and Share (rep.), Nat. Puzzlers League. Democrat. Clubs: Toastmasters, Camera. Author books, most recent being: A Programmer's Guide to Cobol, 1980; patentee automatic focussing range-finding system. Home: PO Box 6366 San Rafael CA 94903 Office: Fireman's Fund Ins Co 1600 Los Gamos Rd CPSD/TSD San Rafael CA 94911

HARRISON-FAULKNER, CYNTHIA ROSS, educational staff development trainer, training consultant; b. Bronxville, N.Y., June 23, 1950; d. George Ross and Shirley Bosworth (Silleck) Harrison; m. Lawrence George Faulkner, July 12, 1975; 1 dau., Elizabeth. B.A. in Sociology, Hollins Coll., 1972; M.A. in Secondary Sch. Adminstrn., U. Colo., 1976. Cert. tchr. and Adminstr., Colo. Substitute tchr. Boulder Valley Sch. Dist. and Adams County, #12, Colo., 1973; organizer September Sch., Boulder, Colo., 1973, dir. Jr.-Sr. High Sch., 1973-78; primary sch. evaluator Rural Primary Project, Ministry Edn., Peace Corps, Jamaica, 1978-79; staff devel. trainer Sch. Dist. 12, Northglenn, Colo., 1980—; psychology instr. Community Coll. Denver, Red Rocks Campus, 1976; ednl. cons. Instructional Improvement Group, Broomfield, Colo., 1981—. Bd. dirs. September Sch., 1980-83. Mem. Assn. for Curriculum and Devel., Nat. Staff Devel. Council. Office: 11285 Highline Dr Northglenn CO 80233

HARRISS, THOMAS T., zoology educator; b. Memphis, Feb. 14, 1918; s. Thomas T. and F. Marie (Bishop) H.; B.S., U. Ariz., 1942; Ph.M., U. Wis., 1943, Ph.D., 1949; m. Lesley R. Matthys; children—Paul R., David G. Asst. prof. biology Whittier (Calif.) Coll., 1949-51, 55-62, assoc. prof. biology, 1962-69; assoc. prof. biology Western State Coll., Gunnison, Colo., 1969-71, prof. zoology, 1971—. Served with AUS, 1945-46, 51-55, USAR, 1947-51, 55-78; lt. col. Res. ret. Mem. Am. Inst. Biol. Scis., Am. Soc. Zoologists, Am. Soc. Parasitologists, Beta Beta Beta, Sigma Xi, Omicron Delta Kappa. Republican. Clubs: Gunnison Valley Naturalists, Gunnison Sportsmens. Home: 119 Floresta Gunnison CO 81230 Office: 208 Hurst Hall Western State Coll Gunnison CO 81230

HARSHA, PHILIP THOMAS, engring. research co. exec.; b. N.Y.C., Feb. 22, 1942; s. Palmer and Catherine (Redinger) H.; B.S. (N.Y. Regents scholar 1958-62), SUNY, Stony Brook, 1962, M.S., 1964; Ph.D., U. Tenn., 1970; m. Jean Ann Quinn, Oct. 23, 1965; children—Peter Charles, Evan Michael. Combustion research engr. Gen. Electric Co., Cin., 1964-67; engr. ARO, Inc., Arnold Air Force Sta., Tenn., 1969-74; research scientist R&D Assos., Marina Del Rey, Calif., 1974-76; sr. staff scientist Sci. Applications, Inc., Chatsworth, Calif.,

1976—. Mem. AIAA, ASME, Combustion Inst., Sigma Xi. Contbr. articles to profl. jours. Home: 24221 St Edens Circle Canoga Park CA 91307 Office: Science Applications Inc 9760 Owensmouth Ave Chatsworth CA 91311

HART, ARTHUR ALVIN, museum director; b. Tacoma, Feb. 13, 1921; s. Arthur Albert and Erma Lola (Maltby) H.; B.A., U. Wash., 1948; M.F.A., 1948; postgrad. Biarritz Am. U., France, 1945, Hans Hofmann Sch. Fine Arts, 1951, U. Calif.-Berkeley, 1952; m. Novella D. Cochran, Feb. 26, 1944; children—Susanna, Robin, Catherine, Allison. Head art dept., chmn. div. fine arts Coll. Idaho, Caldwell, 1948-53; instr. design and art history Colby Jr. Coll., New London, N.H., 1953-54; chmn. art dept., dir. adult evening program Bay Path Jr. Coll., Longmeadow, Mass., 1955-69; dir. Idaho Hist. Mus., Boise, 1969—, Idaho Hist. Soc., Boise, 1975—; lectr. Boise State U., 1970—. Chmn., Longmeadow (Mass.) Conservation Commn., 1968-69; mem. Boise Allied Arts Council, 1971-77; mem. Snake River Regional Studies Adv. Council, 1971—; mem. Boise Am. Revolution Bicentennial Commn., 1974-76. Served with USAAF, 1942-46; ETO. Recipient award for hist. writing Allied Arts Council, 1970; Disting. Citizen award Idaho Statesman Newspaper, 1973; Phoenix award for hist. preservation Soc. Am. Travel Writers, 1982. Mem. Soc. Archtl. Historians (pres. No. Pacific Coast chpt. 1974-76), Am. Inst. Decorators, AIA (hon.), Am. Assn. State and Local History, Popular Culture Assn., Western Museums Conf. (pres. 1979-81), Am. Assn. Museums (regional councillor 1980-83). Author: Steam Trains of Idaho, 1972; contbg. author Space, Style, and Structure: Building in Northwest America, 1974; Fighting Fire on the Frontier, 1976; Historic Boise, 1980; contbr. numerous articles to profl. jours. Home: 8035 Crestwood Dr Boise ID 83704 Office: 610 N Julia Davis Dr Boise ID 83702

HART, BROOK, lawyer; b. N.Y.C., Aug. 24, 1941; s. Walter and Julie Hart; m. Barbara Ingersoll, Nov. 1980; children by previous marriage—Morgan M., Loren L. B.A., Johns Hopkins U., 1963; LL.B., Columbia U., 1966. Bar: N.Y. 1966, Hawaii 1968, U.S. Supreme Ct. 1972, Calif. 1973. Law clk. to chief judge U.S. Dist. Ct. Hawaii, 1966-67; atty. Legal Aid Soc. Hawaii, 1968; assoc. Hyman Greenstein, 1968-69; chief pub. defender State of Hawaii, Honolulu, 1970-72; ptnr. Hart, Levitt, Sherwood, Blanchfield & Hall, Honolulu, 1972-74, Hart, Leavitt, Hall & Hunt, 1974-77, Hart, Leavitt & Hunt, 1977-80, Hart, Leavitt & Hunt, 1980—. Founder, Sons of Poverty, 1968; bd. dirs. ACLU, Hawaii, 1968-76, nat. bd. dirs., 1968-74. Mem. ABA, Hawaii Bar Assn., State Bar Calif., Am. Judicature Soc., Nat. Legal Aid and Defender Assn. (Reginald Heber Smith award 1971), Nat. Assn. Criminal Def. Lawyers; fellow Am. Bd. Criminal Lawyers. Office: Hart & Wolff Suite 610 333 Queen St Honolulu HI 96813

HART, CAROLYN ANNE, marketing executive; b. Ft. Worth, Jan. 13, 1947; d. Edward George and Thelma Estelle (Hibbs) Spahn; m. Charles Gregory Thompson, Sept. 10, 1965 (div.); 1 dau., Deborah Lynn; m. Gerald Randolph Hart, Oct. 27, 1979. B.S. in Bus. Adminstrn. and Mktg., Western Ky. U., 1970. Realtor, Calif., Fla. Asst. mktg. dir. Calif. div. Met. Devel. Corp., Beverly Hills, 1976-81, dir. sales and mktg., Las Vegas div., 1982—; owner, builder, developer Hart to Hart Corp., Belleair Bluffs, Fla., 1981-82; asst. mktg. dir. Mills Devel. Corp., Largo, Fla., 1981-82. Office: 2501 N Green Valley Pkwy Suite 108 Henderson NV 89015

HART, DONALD RAY, publisher; b. Kansas City, Kans., Aug. 13, 1943; s. Isaac Newton and Lulu Irene (Rollins) H.; B.A., Colo. State U., 1966; m. Jane Marie Vondy, Mar. 13, 1971; children—Bradley Ray, Michael Allan. Founder, operator Photo-By Hart Studio, Ft. Collins, Colo., 1962-65; founder, editor, pub. The Campus Tayle, Ft. Collins, 1965-66; salesman Petroleum Pubs., Inc. subs. Bell Publs. Co. (acquired by Data Services Inc. 1970), Denver, 1967-70, pub., 1970-73, editor, 1972-73; founder, pres., editor, pub. Western Oil Reporter and Rocky Mountain Petroleum Directory, Hart Publs., Inc., Denver, 1973—, editor, pub. Drill Bit mag., 1976—; mng. ptnr. Investor Pub. Co., 1981—; pub. Oil and Gas Investor, 1981—, founder Northeast Oil Reporter, 1981, Gulf Coast Oil Reporter, Hart's Rocky Mountain Mining Directory. Mem. Colo. Elephant Club; pres. Russellville Homeowners and Property Owners Assn., 1980. Mem. Rocky Mountain Oil and Gas Assn., Ind. Petroleum Assn. Mountain States, Assn. Petroleum Writers. Baptist. Clubs: Denver Petroleum, Pinery Country. Office: PO Box 1917 Denver CO 80201

HART, GARY, senator; b. Ottawa, Kans., Nov. 28, 1937; grad. Bethany (Okla.) Coll.; LL.B., Yale U., 1964; m. Lee Ludwig, 1958; children—Andrea, John. Admitted to bar, 1964; began career as atty. U.S. Dept. Justice, Washington, then spl. asst. to sec. U.S. Interior Dept.; practiced in Denver, 1967-70, 72-74; nat. campaign dir. Senator George McGovern Democratic Presdl. Campaign, 1970-72; U.S. senator from Colo., 1974—; founder Congressional Mil. Reform Caucus, 1981; founder, 1st chmn. Environ. Study Conf., 1975; Congressional adviser SALT II Talks, 1977; chmn. Nat. Commn. on Air Quality, 1978-81. Bd. visitors U.S. Air Force Acad., 1975—, chmn., 1978-80. Named One of 50 Leaders for Am.'s Future, Time mag. Author: Right From the Start, 1973; A New Democracy, 1983. Office: 1748 High St Denver CO 80218 also SR-237 Russell Senate Office Bldg Washington DC 20510

HART, GARY KERSEY, state senator; b. San Diego, Aug. 13, 1943; s. Newman Lane and Ruth (Kersey) H.; B.A., Stanford U., 1965; M.A.T., Harvard U., 1966; m. Cary Smith, June 21, 1969; children—Elissa, Katherine. Tchr. high sch., Santa Barbara, Calif., 1966-72; extension program adminstr. U. Calif., 1973-74; state assemblyman State of Calif., Sacramento, 1974-82, state senator from 18th dist., 1982—, chmn. Senate edn. com. Calif. Coastal commr., 1973-74; mem. Calif. Commn. on Status of Women, 1976-81. Served to lt. col. Calif. N.G. Democrat. Office: State Capitol Sacramento CA 95814

HART, HERBERT DORLAN, educator; b. Eckert, Colo., Feb. 21, 1910; s. Alpheus Edwin and Jessie (Dorlan) H.; B.S. in Chemistry, U. Denver, 1940, M.S., 1952; m. Constance Joy Spence, Dec. 26, 1940. Sr. resident officer U.S. Fgn. Service, Augsburg, Germany, 1948-50; instr. chemistry Fort Lewis Coll., Durango, Colo., 1954-56, asst. prof., 1956-68, chmn. div. phys. sci., engring and math., 1960-68, acting pres., 1962; asso. prof. chemistry Coll. Notre Dame, Belmont, Calif., 1968-82, chmn. dept., 1968-76; instr. chemistry Canada Coll., Redwood City, Calif., 1982—; cons. on water contamination problems, ranches, fisheries; analyst vanadium and uranium ore Vanadium Corp. Am., 1956. Served to maj. AUS, 1940-48; ETO. Decorated Bronze Star. Fellow Am. Inst. Chemists (cert. profl. chemist, nat. com. for profl. tng. and edn. 1975—); mem. Am. Chem. Soc., Mil. Order World Wars (jr. vice comdr. Peninsula chpt. 1976-77, comdr. 1978-79, 83—), Am. Watchmakers Inst., Sigma Xi, Phi Delta Epsilon, Phi Delta Phi, Phi Delta Kappa, Phi Kappa Alpha. Episcopalian. Home: 1000 Continentals Way #217 Belmont CA 94002 Office: Canada Coll 4200 Farm Hill Blvd Redwood City CA

HART, JOSEPH H., bishop; b. Kansas City, Mo., Sept. 26, 1931. Ed. St. John Sem., Kansas City, St. Meinrad Sem., Indpls. Ordained priest Roman Cath. Ch., 1956, titular bishop of Thimida Regia and aux. bishop, Cheyenne, Wyo., 1976; apptd. bishop of Cheyenne, 1978—. Office: Diocese of Cheyenne Chancery Office Box 426 Cheyenne WY 82001*

HART, JULIA ANN, controller; b. Washington, Aug. 12, 1946; d. Jerry T. and Susan (Finnell) Hart. Student George Wash. U., 1965-69. With Ctr. Policy Studies, George Wash. U., Washington, 1965-69, Social Research Group U. Calif., Berkeley, 1969-72; acct. Rolling Stone mag., San Francisco, 1972-77; tax specialist Peter D. Smith, C.P.A., San Anselmo, Calif., 1977-79; controller Marin Community Workshop, Inc., Mill Valley, Calif., 1979—. Office: Marin Community Workshop 70 Lomita Dr Mill Valley CA 94941

HART, LOIS BORLAND, leadership skills consultant; b. Syracuse, N.Y., May 15, 1941; d. Leslie R. and Laura S. (Styn) Borland; m. Gordan Ide, Nov. 12, 1960; m. 2d, Arnold L. Hart, July 4, 1969; children—Christopher, Richard. B.S., U. Rochester, 1966; M.S., Syracuse U., 1972; Ed.D., U. Mass, 1974. Field services coordinator Program Ednl. Opportunity, U. Mich., Ann Arbor, 1975-78; pres. Organizational Leadership, Inc., East Lansing, Mich., 1978-80; trainer Mgmt. Devel. Ctr., Mountain States Employers Council, Denver, 1980-81; pres. Leadership Dynamics, Lyons, Colo., 1980—. Mem. Am. Soc. Tng. and Devel., Americans for a New Way, AAUW, Zonta Internat., NOW, Colo. Hist. Soc., Lyons Hist. Soc., Toastmasters Internat. Author: The Sexes at Work, 1983; Moving Up! Women and Leadership, 1980, Learning from Conflict, 1981; Saying Hello: How to get Your Group Started, 1983; Conference & Workshop Planners' Manual, 1979; contbr. articles to profl. jours. Home and Office: PO Box 320 Lyons CO 80540

HART, MARGIE RUTH, publisher; b. Chesterfield, S.C., Oct. 28, 1943; d. Lonnie Carson and Carrie Jane (Hancock) Sellers; m. Ben Tucker, Mar. 9, 1963 (div. 1980); children—Chipman D., Sandra L.; m. 2d, Len Hart, Dec. 21, 1980; children—Richard W., Leonard P., Carl S., Karen J. H. Student, Greenville Tech. Sch., 1964-65. Br. mgr. Caroline Emmons Jewelry Co., western S.C., 1978-79; microwave sales specialist western N.C. and S.C., Whirlpool Corp., 19—; sales rep. Cleaves Office Products, 1979; asst. mgr. D & L Assocs., 1977-78; substitute tchr. Picken Jr. High Sch., Pickens, S.C., 1975-79; asst. mgr., co-pub. The Am. Patriot Mag., Barstow, Calif., 1982—. Chmn. 1st supervisorial dist., mem. central com. Am. Independent party, San Bernardino County, Calif.; congl. dist. coordinator Freedom Counsel, San Bernardino County. Recipient Good Establishment cert., Pickens, S.C., 1977, certs. of appreciation Picken PTA, 1978, Second Amendment Found., 1982. Mem. Concerned Women for Am., Moral Majority. Independent. Baptist. Home: 36832 Colby Ave Barstow CA 92311 Office: PO Box 370 Barstow CA 92311

HART, RICHARD HAROLD, agronomist; b. Villisca, Iowa, July 23, 1933; s. Harold J. and Vivian V. (Kelley) H.; m. Helen J. Wetter, Mar. 19, 1960; children—James, Kelley. B.S., Iowa State U., 1954, M.S., 1958; Ph.D., Oreg. State U., 1961. Research agronomist U. Ga., Tifton, 1961-62; research agronomist U.S. Dept. Agr., Tifton, 1962-66, Beltsville, Md., 1966-74, Cheyenne, Wyo., 1974—, research leader, 1974-81; mem. grad. faculty U. Wyo., Colo. State U. Assoc. editor Agronomy Jour.; author numerous articles for sci. publs. Vol., Wyo. State Mus. Served with AUS, 1954-56. Mem. Soc. Range Mgmt. (pres. Wyo. sect. 1979-80), Am. Soc. Agronomy (Crop and Soils Journalism award 1977), Am. Forage and Grassland Council (Merit cert. 1982), Council Agrl. Sci. and Tech. Methodist. Office: 8408 Hildreth Rd Cheyenne WY 82009

HART, RICHARD HENRY, educational administrator; b. Salt Lake City, June 24, 1927; s. Heber L. and Rose Marie (Glissmeyer) H.; m. Arlene Selma Peterson, Sept. 14, 1949; children—Grant, Linnea, Steven, Julie, Laurel, Marie, Vern, Annette, Richard. B.S., U. Utah, 1952; M.Ed., U. Oreg., 1957; postgrad. Ariz. State U., 1967-68. Tchr., Davis County (Utah) Pub. Schs., 1952-54; tchr. pub. schs., Hillsboro, Oreg., 1954-57, prin., 1957-67; prof. edn. Pacific U., 1967-74; dir. curriculum and instrn. Scappoose (Oreg.) Sch. Dist., 1974—; cons. Oreg. sch. dists. Served with USNR, 1945-46. Mem. Confedn. Oreg. Sch. Adminstrs., Assn. Supervision and Curriculum Devel., Assn. Retarded Citizens. Republican. Mormon. Home: 2247 Laurel St Forest Grove OR 97116 Office: PO Box V Scappoose OR 97056

HART, RICHARD LAVERNE, college dean; b. Cozad, Nebr., Dec. 10, 1929; s. David Lane and Carrie Belle (Queale) H.; A.B., Nebr. Wesleyan U., 1950; M.Ed., U. Nebr., Lincoln, 1955, Ed.D., 1960; m. Ramona Jean Fecht, July 28, 1956; children—Jay Huston, David Lane. Tchr. social studies, English, Wakefield (Nebr.) High Sch., 1950-51; tchr. social studies Cozad (Nebr.) High Sch., 1954-57; supr. social studies Univ. High Sch., U. Nebr., 1957-60; asst. prof. edn. U. Maine, 1960-62; asst. prof., asso. prof., chmn. dept. curriculum and instrn. U. Wis., Milw., 1962-69; asso. dean Coll. Edn. Kent (Ohio) State U., 1969-78; dean Coll. Edn., Boise (Idaho) State U., 1978—. Served with U.S. Army, 1951-53; Korea. Coe fellow U. Wyo., summers 1956, 57. Mem. Nat. Council Social Studies, Assn. Supervision and Curriculum Devel. (dir. 1979-81), Idaho Assn. Supervision and Curriculum Devel. (pres. 1979-81), Idaho Assn. Tchr. Edn. (v.p. 1980-81, pres. 1981-83), Phi Delta Kappa, Kappa Delta Pi. Lutheran. Office: Boise State U Boise ID 83725

HART, RONALD EDWARD, aerospace engineer; b. N.Y.C., Nov. 3, 1932; s. Armond E. and Viola H.; m. Sally Jane Sicks, Feb. 3, 1963; children—Karen, Sarah; B.S., U. Wash., 1962; M.A., U. Redlands, 1982; student U. So. Calif., Fresno State Coll., Ga. Inst. Tech. Registered profl. engr., Ga., Calif. Flight test engr. The Boeing Co., Seattle, 1960-64; flight test engr. Lockheed Corp., Marietta, Ga. and Burbank, Calif., 1964-73; aerospace engr. U.S. Air Force, Air Force Flight Test Ctr., Flight Dynamics Div., Edwards AFB, Calif., 1973—, lead engr. flight test, 1974—; guest lectr. USAF Test Pilot Sch., u. Tenn. Space Inst. Mem. Soc. Flight Test Engrs. (dir.). Served with USNR, 1950-53. Republican. Home: 758 E Calmae Dr Lancaster CA 93535 Office: Air Force Flight Test Ctr Flight Dynamics Div Edwards AFB CA 95354

HARTELL, CHARLENE BRADLEY, counselor; b. Santo, Tex., Feb. 3, 1920; d. William H. and Emma F. (Carver) Bradley; m. Harold K. Hartell, July 29, 1944; children—Vickie Isaacs, Edith Archuleta, Deborah, Bradley. B.A., U. N.Mex., 1976, postgrad., 1983—; M.A., N.Mex. Highlands U., 1980; M.A., Webster Coll., 1982. Tchr. schs. no. N.Mex., 1939-42; group leader N.Am. Aviation Corp., Kansas City, Kans., 1942-43; owner-mgr. Hart Dress Shop, Espanola, N.Mex., 1944-50; mgr. ladies' ready-to-wear Hubbards, Los Alamos, 1955-57; in ins. sales and service Prudential Ins. Co., Albuquerque, 1963-77, office mgr., Pojoaque, N.Mex., 1970-73; counselor Counseling Service No. N.Mex., Espanola, 1979-80, dir., 1980-81; dir., counselor Counseling Service del Norte, Espanola, 1981—. Active in fundraising Espanola Hosp.; pres. Espanola Valley Opera Guild, 1978; bd. dirs. McCurdy Sch.; mem. N.Mex. Opera Guild; chmn. N.Mex. Cancer Soc., 1970; mem. Rio Arriba County Democratic Central Com. Mem. Am. Personnel and Guidance Assn., N.Mex. Mental Health Assn., McCurdy Sch. Alumni Assn. (pres. 1977), Espanola Valley Rodeo Assn. Home: Route 2 1400 Montana Vista Espanola NM 87532

HARTER, ROBERT JACKSON, JR., transportation executive, lawyer; b. New Orleans, Nov. 6, 1944; s. Robert and Ann Marie (Carangelo) Jackson; m. Ann Eudean Peebles, Mar. 25, 1972; children—Ryan Scott, Ashley Ann. A.B., Stanford U., 1966; J.D., U. So. Calif., 1969. Bar: Calif. 1970. Law clk. to judge U.S. Ct. Appeals (9th cir.), Los Angeles, 1969-70; assoc. Gibson, Dunn & Crutcher, Los Angeles, 1970-76, Shutan & Trost, Los Angeles, 1976-78; assoc. gen. counsel Tiger Internat., Inc., Los Angeles, 1978-79, v.p. law, 1979-82, v.p. adminstrn., gen. counsel, sec., 1982—. Mem. Democratic Nat. Fin. Council, 1981—, Dem. Bus. Council, 1981—. Served with Air N.G., 1970-76. Mem. ABA, State Bar Assn. Calif., Los Angeles County Bar Assn., Am. Soc. Corp. Secs., Order of Coif. Episcopalian. Lead articles editor U. So. Calif. Law Rev. Office: Tiger Internat Inc 1888 Century Park E Los Angeles CA 90067

HARTINGER, JAMES V., air force officer; b. Middleport, Ohio, Apr. 17, 1925; s. Lawrence C. and Violet H. (Rickard) H.; m. Mickey Christian, Oct. 7, 1979; children—Jimmer, Kris, Mike. B.S., U.S. Mil. Acad., 1949; postgrad. Basic and Advanced Flying Schs., Randolph AFB, Tex. and Williams AFB, Ariz., 1950, Squadron Officer Sch., 1955, Indsl. Coll. Armed Forces, 1966; M.B.A., George Washington U., 1963; Ph.D. (hon.), Norwich U., 1982. Commd. 2d lt. U.S. Air Force, 1949, advanced through grades to gen.; fighter pilot, W.Ger. and Korea, 1950-52; gunnery instr. Williams AFB, Ariz., 1953; fighter pilot, air ops. officer Stewart AFB, N.Y., 1954-58; dir. requirements, Hdqrs. U.S. Air Force, 1958-63; dir. plans Hdqrs. Pacific Air Force, Hickam AFB, Hawaii, 1963-66; F4C replacement tng. officer MacDill AFB, Fla., 1966; comdg. center dir. Hdqrs. 7th Air Force, Ton Son Nhut AB, Vietnam, 1966-68; F-111 test dir., Nellis AFB, Nev., 1968; comdr. 23d Tactical Fighter Wing (Flying Tigers), McConnell AFB, Kans., 1968-70; dir. plans NORAD, Ent AFB, Colo., 1970-73; comdt. Air War Coll., Maxwell AFB, Ala., 1973; comdr. 12th Air Force, Bergstrom AFB, Tex., 1973, 9th Air Force, Shaw AFB, S.C., 1975-80; comdr.-in-chief N.Am. Aerospace Def. Command, Peterson AFB, Colo., 1980—; comdr. U.S. Air Force Space Command, 1982—. Bd. dirs. Air Force Acad. Found., Pikes Peak United Way/USO, Boy Scouts Am., Goodwill Industries. Served as sgt. U.S. Army, 1943-44. Decorated Air Force D.S.M. with cluster, Legion of Merit with cluster, D.F.C., Air medal with 8 clusters, Air Force Commendation medal; Tongil medal (Korea). Mem. Am. Astron. Soc., Air Force Assn., Order Daedalians, Colorado Springs C. of C., Nat. Space Club. Clubs: Rotary, Ohio Commodores. Home: 214 Otis Circle Colorado Springs CO 80916 Office: CINCNORAD/Comdr Space Command Peterson AFB CO 80914

HARTLEY, EARL E., state official, lawyer, real estate broker; b. Curry County, N.Mex., May 29, 1913; s. Plumus B. and Martha P. (Potts) H.; m. Vora V. Lowe, June 9; m. 2d, Mary E. Lawrence, Aug. 19; children—Teddy L., R. Thomas. B.A., U. N.Mex., 1940; LL.B., U. Colo., 1943. Bar: N.Mex. Tchr. schs. Eunice, N.Mex., 1937-39; sec. to U.S. senator, Washington, 1943-44; practice law, Clovis, N.Mex., 1947-60; atty. gen. State of N.Mex., 1961-64; sole practice law, Albuquerque, 1965-82; treas. State of N.Mex.; former city atty., Clovis; former mem. N.Mex. Senate. Mem. Mcpl. Sch. Bd. Served with U.S. Army, 1934-37, 45-46. Mem. N.Mex. Bar Assn., Order of Coif. Democrat. Clubs: Masons, Elks. Office: Box 608 Santa Fe NM 87504

HARTLEY, FRED LLOYD, petroleum and chemical company executive; b. Vancouver, B.C., Can., Jan. 16, 1917; s. John William and Hannah (Mitchell) H.; B.Sc. in Applied Sci., U. B.C., 1939; m. Margaret Alice Murphy, Nov. 2; children—Margaret Ann, Fred Lloyd, Jr. Came to U.S., 1939, naturalized, 1950. Engring. supr. Union Oil Co. of Calif., 1939-53, mgr. comml. devel. 1953-55, gen. mgr. research dept., 1955-56, v.p. in charge research, 1956-60, sr. v.p., dir., 1960-63, exec. v.p., 1963-64, pres., chief exec. officer, 1964-73, chmn., pres., 1974—, also dir.; dir. Rockwell Internat. Corp., Daytona Internat. Speedway Corp., Union Bank. Bd. dirs. Los Angeles Philharmonic Assn., U.S.-Korea Econ. Council; trustee Calif. Inst. Tech., Pepperdine U., Tax Found., Council on Fgn. Relations, Inc., Com. for Econ. Devel.; dir., mem. exec. com. Calif. C. of C. Mem. Nat. Petroleum Council, Am. Petroleum Inst. (chmn.). Office: Union Oil Calif Union Oil Center Los Angeles CA 90017

HARTMAN, A. SCOTT, printing co. exec.; b. Boston, Feb. 28, 1942; s. Ben M. and Barbara H.; B.S., Calif. State U., Northridge, 1963; M.A., U. Calif., Los Angeles, 1964; m. Estelle Lyon, 1966; children—Dale Scott, Holly. Mgr., Far West Communications, Los Angeles, 1963-64; mgr. Stark Printing Co., Los Angeles, 1964-67; pres. Tax Forms Printing Co., Los Angeles, 1967—; pres. United Nat. Industries, Inc. Mem. Nat. Bus. Forms Assn., Nat. Office Products Assn., Data Processing Mgmt. Assn. Office: 9700 Topanga Canyon Pl Chatsworth CA 91311

HARTMAN, ASHLEY POWELL, publishing executive; b. St. Paul, Feb. 26, 1922; s. Thomas and Mollie (Powell) H.; m. Tracy Ellen Robertson, Nov. 19, 1971; children—Timothy, Sabrina Walker Scott, William. B.J., U. Minn., 1948. Advt. sales Cresmer/Woodward, Los Angeles, 1949-52; v.p. Ridder Newspaper Group, Los Angeles, 1952-63; area mgr. McGraw-Hill, Los Angeles, 1963-65; pub. Sea Mag., Long Beach, Calif., 1968-78; western mgr. Yachting Mag., Newport Beach, Calif., 1979-81; pres. Creative Tng. Systems, El Toro, Calif., 1981—; cons. lectr. Served in U.S. Air Force, 1942-46. Mem. So. Calif. Marine Assn. (dir., v.p.), Am. Assn. Newspaper Reps. (past pres.). Republican. Author: Lend Me Your Fears; Set Your Thermostat for Success; numerous articles. Home: 24921 Muirlands Blvd #22 El Toro CA 92530

HARTMAN, CLARENCE HENRY, psychologist; b. Seward County, Nebr., Sept. 22, 1926; s. Henry George and Alma Wilhelmina (Reinhardt) H.; student U. Dubuque, 1944-45; B.A., Iowa State Tchrs. Coll., 1948; M.A., U. Iowa, 1953, Ph.D., 1955; m. Mary Louise Reeve (div.); m. 2d, Joyce McCain, Nov. 24, 1969; children—Kenneth R., Douglas C., Carolyn Sue, Eric P., Kathryn Anne, John K., Kristie L. With VA, 1955-82, chief psychology service VA Med. Ctr., Sioux Falls, S.D., 1959-65, Lincoln Nebr., 1965-69, Salt Lake City, 1969-82; pvt. practice clin. psychology, Rapid City, S.D., 1982—; assoc. prof. psychology U. Utah. Served with USN, 1944-46. Mem. Am. Psychol. Assn., Rocky Mountain Psychol. Assn., Assn. Advancement Behavior Therapy, Biofeedback Soc. Am., Utah Psychol. Assn. (chmn. ethics com.), Am. Pain Soc., Full Gospel Businessmen. Lutheran. Contbr. articles to profl. jours.; pub. audiotape on relaxation tng. Home: 4014 Brookside Dr Rapid City SD 57701

HARTMAN, MAURICE GEORGE, systems engineer; b. Ft. Wayne, Ind., Dec. 15, 1940; s. George Charles and Violet M. (Wilson) H.; m. Theona Catherine Popp, June 12, 1965; children—Joy Charlene, Douglas Alan. B.S. in Engring. Math., Purdue U., 1964; M.S., U. Tulsa, 1966; postgrad. Joint Ctr. Grad. Studies. Instr. math., U. Tulsa, 1966; engring. analyst Universal Oil Products Co., Des Plaines, Ill., 1966-73; sr. engr. Westinghouse, Jacksonville, Fla., 1973-75, Exxon Nuclear Co., Richland, Wash., 1975-78; mem. tech. staff Aerospace Corp., El Segundo, Calif., 1978-82; systems engr. Hughes Aircraft Co., Fullerton, Calif., 1982—; cons. in field. Mem. AIAA, Inst. Nuclear Materials Mgmt., Am. Nuclear Soc., Am. Math. Soc., Soc. Indsl. and Applied Math., Math. Assn. Am., Kappa Kappa Psi, Kappa Mu Epsilon. Contbr. articles to profl. jours. Address: 2709 Bayberry Way Fullerton CA 92633

HARTMAN, MOSHE, sociology educator; b. Kluj, Hungary, Jan. 1, 1936; came to U.S., 1966, naturalized, 1983; s. Yehuda and Lola (Izsak) H.; m. Harriet Stillman, Mar. 17, 1970; children—Niv, Raz, Liat, Maya. B.A. in Sociology and Stats., Hebrew U. Jerusalem, 1964; M.A. in Sociology, U. Mich., Ph.D. in Math. Sociology and Population Studies, 1971. Mem. faculty demography dept. Hebrew U. Jerusalem, 1969-71; mem. faculty sociology dept. Tel Aviv U., 1969-71, asst. prof. sociology, 1971-75, assoc. prof., 1976-78; asst. prof. U. Calif.-Berkeley, 1976; vis. prof. Calif. State U.-Los Angeles, 1978-79; asst. prof. Utah State U., 1979-81, assoc. prof., 1981—, research assoc. Population Research Lab., 1979—; in charge subject matter for 1972 Population and Housing Census, Central Bur. Stats. Israel, 1969-71; researcher Shiloah Inst.,

1978. Ford Found. grantee, 1972-73; Tel Aviv U. Faculty Social Scis. Research Com. grantee, 1974; Inst. Social and Labor Research and Tel Aviv U. grantee, 1973-75; Rockefeller-Ford Found. spl. grantee, 1975-79; Utah State U. grantee, 1980, 81. Mem. Internat. Union for Sci. Study Population, Internat. Sociol. Assn., Population Assn. Am., Am. Sociol. Assn. Contbr. articles to profl. jours.; author papers. Office: Dept Sociology UMC 07 Utah State U Logan UT 84322

HARTMAN, PATRICIA ANNE, social scientist, software consultant; b. Los Angeles, Sept. 8, 1935; d. Earl Hiram and Mary Elizabeth (Wallace) Mathis; children—Mark W. Plank, Craig G. Plank, Kent P. Plank, Karina P. Henry. B.S., Calif. State Poly U., 1967; M.A., Ph.D., U. Minn. Asst. prof. St. Cloud (Minn.) State U., 1969-74; lectr. San Diego State U., 1974-76; research chief County of San Diego, 1976—; microcomputer applications cons. Mem. San Diego Apt. Owners Assn., Apple Corps of San Diego. Minn. State Research grantee, 1971. Mem. Am. Sociol. Assn., Internat. SPSS Software Users Exchange. Contbr. articles to profl. jours. Home: 588 W Chase Ave El Cajon CA 92020 Office: County of San Diego 6255 Mission Gorge Rd San Diego CA 92120

HARTMAN, ROBERT LEROY, artist, educator; b. Sharon, Pa., Dec. 17, 1926; s. George Otto and Grace Arvada (Radabaugh) H.; B.F.A., U. Ariz., 1951, M.A., 1952; postgrad. Colo. Springs Fine Arts Center, 1947, 51, Bklyn. Mus. Art Sch., 1953-54; m. Charlotte Ann Johnson, Dec. 30, 1951; children—Mark Allen, James Robert. Instr. architecture, allied arts Tex. Tech. Coll., 1955-58; asst. prof. art U. Nev., Reno, 1958-61; mem. faculty dept. art U. Calif.-Berkeley, 1961—, prof., 1972—, chmn. dept., 1974-76; one man exhbns. include: Bertha Schafer Gallery, N.Y.C., 1966, 69, 74, Santa Barbara Mus. Art, 1973, Cin. Art Acad., 1975, Hank Baum Gallery, San Francisco, 1973, 75, 78, San Jose Mus. Art, 1983; group exhbns. inlcude: Richmond Mus., 1966, Whitney Mus. Biennial, 1973, Oakland Mus., 1976; represented in permanent collections: Nat. Collections Fine Arts, Colorado Springs Fine Arts Center, San Francisco Art Inst., Roswell Mus., Corcoran Gallery, Washington; mem. Inst. for Creative Arts, U. Calif., 1967-68. U. Calif. humanities research fellow, 1980. Office: Dept Art Univ of Calif Berkeley CA 94720

HARTMAN, ROGER BARTON, engineer, city official; b. Wadsworth, Ohio, June 20, 1948; s. Neil Wade and Thelma Mae (Crouch) H.; m. Susan Postelnek, Aug. 30, 1970; B.S., Ohio U., 1970, M.S., 1972; Ph.D., U. Colo., 1977. Registered profl. engr., Colo. Chief indsl. waste sect. Ohio EPA, 1972-73; asst. prof U. Va., 1977-78; dir. utilities Boulder (Colo.), 1979—; instr. Rocky Mountain Water and Wastewater Sch. Mem. water resources mgmt. adv. com. Denver Regional Council Govs, 1978—, chmn. funding subcom., 1982—. Mem. Am. Water Works Assn., Water Pollution Control Fedn., Am. Pub. Works Assn. Office: PO Box 791 Boulder CO 80306

HARTMAN, SHERON WILSON, medical research center marketing and public relations executive; b. Lodi, Ohio, July 9, 1946; d. Neil G. and Dorothy M. Wilson. B.A. in Journalism, Kent State U., 1969. Feature writer Cleve. Plain Dealer, 1969-70; editor Press-Squire Newspapers, Douglas County, Colo., 1973-76; sr. writer Nat. Asthma Center, Denver, 1976-77; pub. relations dir. Colo. Hosp. Assn., Denver, 1977-81; dir. mktg. and pub. affairs AMC Cancer Research Center, Denver, 1981—. Active various polit. campaigns, including pub. relations adv. to Congl. campaign, Denver, 1983. Recipient 1st place Arthur A. Parkhurst Community Service award Colo. Press Assn., 1974; MacEacher award and cert. of merit for 2d place hosp. cost exhibit Acad. Hosp. Pub. Relations, 1978, for assn. pub. 1980; Gamma Gamma Phi scholar, 1965. Mem. Colo. Soc. Hosp. Pub. Relations (pres. 1982), Am. Soc. Hosp. Pub. Relations (cert.), Pub. Relations Soc. Am., Nat. Fedn. Press Women (2d place award for editorial writing 1975, 2d place award for direct mail promotion 1979), Colo. Press Women. Democrat. Office: 6401 W Colfax Ave Lakewood CO 80214

HARTMAN, WILLIAM ALBERT, naval officer; b. Meriden, Conn., Oct. 7, 1939; s. Casimere William and Elenore Victoria (Lirot) H.; B.S., U.S. Naval Acad., 1961; M.S., U.S. Naval Postgrad. Sch., 1968; M.S., George Washington U., 1977; m. Ismalia Judith Jorge, May 21, 1965; children—Elizabeth, Christopher. Commd. ensign U.S. Navy, 1961, advanced through grades to capt., 1981; exec. officer USS W.S. Sims, 1973-75; asso. chmn. naval systems engring. U.S. Naval Acad., Annapolis, 1975-77; comdg. officer USS Knox, 1977-79; gen. war planner, comdr. 7th fleet staff, San Francisco, 1979-81, exec. asst., dir. research, devel., testing and evaluation, 1982—. Mem. ASME, U.S. Naval Inst., Sigma Xi, (asso.). Roman Catholic. Home: DMS Box 1052 FPO Seattle WA 98762 Office: Staff COMSEVENTHFLT FPO San Francisco CA 96601

HARTWELL, JAY ALAN, optometrist; b. Twin Falls, Idaho, June 2, 1950; s. Albert James and Donna Mae (Thompson) H.; m. Deborah Yvonne Johnson, May 5, 1979; 1 dau., Michelle Marie. A.A., Coll. So. Idaho, 1969; student Idaho State U., 1969-70; B.S., So. Calif. Coll. Optometry, 1972, O.D., 1974. Lic. optometrist, Idaho. Pvt. practice of optometry, Twin Falls, 1974—. Active Boy Scouts Am., 1974-83; v.p. Christian Radio of Magic Valley, 1981-83; precinct com. chmn. Republican Com., 1979—. Recipient Order of Arrow, Boy Scouts Am. Mem. Idaho Optometric Assn., Optometric Assn., Coll. So. Idaho Alumni (pres. 1981), Omega Delta. Clubs: Optimists (bd. dirs. 1980-82, pres. 1982-83, lt. gov. 1983-84), Kiwanis (bd. dirs.), Elks. Home: Route 3 Jerome ID 83338 Office: 628 Main Ave N Twin Falls ID 83301

HARTWIG, MYRON ARTHUR, public relations executive; b. Cleve., Apr. 8, 1944; s. Lawrence Elmer and Helen Cora (Schrauf) H. B.A., U. Mich., 1967. Lectr. Previews of Progress, Gen. Motors Corp., 1968-70, staff asst. pub. affairs, 1970-71, supr., 1971-72, mgr. youth activities, 1972-73, asst. regional mgr., Chgo., 1973-75, regional mgr., Dayton, Ohio, 1975-78, Los Angeles, 1978-79; mgr. European pub. affairs, 1981; counselor to sec. and dir. pub. affairs U.S. Dept. Commerce, Washington, 1980-81; sr. v.p. Hill and Knowlton, Inc., Los Angeles, 1981—. Vice-pres. pub. relations United Way, Dayton, 1976-78, Los Angeles Region IV, 1978-79. Mem. Pub. Relations Soc. Am. Office: Suite 3140 5900 Wilshire Blvd Los Angeles CA 90036

HARTWIG, PAUL DOUGLAS, water superintendant; b. Walla Walla, Wash., Nov. 16, 1954; s. Kenneth Robert and Norma Jean (Anderson) H; m. Tracy L. Stephenson, Feb. 5, 1983; student Northwest Nazarene Coll., 1973-74; A.A., Walla Walla Community Coll., 1975; B.A., Eastern Wash. U., 1977. Water supt. City of College Place (Wash.), 1977—; instr. water/sewer related fields. Mem. Am. Waterworks Assn, Nat. Athletic Trainers Assn. Mem. First Ch. Nazarene. Home: 1028 S College College Place WA 99324 Office: 317 S College College Place WA 99324

HARTWIG, RICHARD PALMER, advertising executive; b. Coalinga, Calif., July 7, 1947; s. Charles Palmer and Katherine Marie (Schamus) H.; m. Rose Marie Dolores Robles, Sept. 13, 1980. A.A. in Advt., Foothill Coll., 1968; B.A. in Advt., Mktg. and Bus., San Jose U., 1970. Prodn. and promotion mgr. The Gap Stores, San Francisco, 1975; asst. advt. mgr. Blue Cross of No. Calif., Oakland, 1975-77; advt. mgr. Ross/Atkins, San Francisco, 1977-78; account exec. retail services KTVU-TV, San Francisco, Oakland, 1978-80, dir. retail services, 1980—; lectr. in field. Mem. San Francisco Film/Tape Council, San Francisco Advt. Club. Club: San Francisco Milline. Contbr. articles to trade publs. Home: 2394 Mariner Sq Dr Alameda CA 94501 Office: 2 Jack London Sq Oakland CA 94607

HARVAT, DENNIS JOSEPH, systems specialist; b. Akron, Ohio, Oct. 28, 1940; s. Joseph Paul and Anne Marie (Pribonic) H.; m. Cynthia Rose Romias, Nov. 25, 1970; children—Nicole, Keegan. B.S. in Bus. Adminstrn., Calif. State U., 1968. With Pacific Telephone, 1964-65, Universal Studios, Los Angeles, 1965-66, MGM Studios, 1966-67; programmer Concept Devel., Los Angeles, 1967-68; with Arco Petroleum Products Co., Los Angeles, 1968—, mgr. systems devel., 1976—. Mgr. supervisory com. Arco Wilshire Fed. Credit Union, 1980-81. Served with USMC, 1958-62. Mem. Am. Mgmt. Assn., Nat. Petroleum Refiners Assn. Republican. Roman Catholic. Home: 13615 Hart St Van Nuys CA 91405 Office: 221 S Figueroa St Los Angeles CA 90012

HARVEY, CLARENCE ALAN, physician; b. Santa Ana, Calif., Mar. 31, 1924; s. Willis Roy and Rachel (Wilmot) H.; student Stanford U., 1941-43, UCLA, 1943-44; M.D., U. So. Calif., 1948; m. Phyllis Kay Boman, Dec. 20, 1947; children—Steven, Diana, Julie, Richard, Scott. Intern, Oakland (Calif.) Naval Hosp., 1948-49, resident, 1953-54; resident St. Mary's Hosp., Duluth, Minn., 1949-50, Ventura (Calif.) practice medicine specializing in family practice/preventive medicine, Oceanside, Calif., 1951—; team physician, med. dir. Mira Costa Community Coll., 1954-81; Edison Co. med. coordinator, 1965—; staff Tri-City Hosp., Oceanside, 1960—; dir. GLH Corp. Trustee, Country Day Sch., La Jolla, Calif. Served with USNR, 1943-46, 47-48, 52-54. Mem. AMA, Calif. Med. Assn., San Diego County Med. Assn., Am. Bd. Family Practice, Am. Acad. Family Practice, Acad. Sports Medicine, Sigma Chi, Nu Sigma Nu. Republican. Office: 2201 Mission St Oceanside CA 92054

HARVEY, JAMES GERALD, educational consultant, counselor, researcher; b. California, Mo., July 15, 1934; s. William Walter and Exie Marie (Lindley) H. B.A. Amherst Coll., 1956; M.A.T. (fellow), Harvard U., 1958, M. Ed., 1962. Asst. to dean grad. sch. edn. Harvard U., Cambridge, Mass., 1962-66, dir. admissions, fin. aid, 1966-69; dir. counseling service U. Calif.-Irvine, 1970-72; ednl. cons., Los Angeles, 1972—. Active ACLU. Served to 1st lt. USAF, 1958-61. Mayo-Smith grantee, 1956-57; Amherst UCLA Adminstrv. fellow, 1969-70. Mem. Am. Ednl. Research Assn., Nat. Council Measurement in Edn., Am. Personnel Guidance Assn. Roman Catholic. Address: 1845 Glendon Ave Los Angeles CA 90025

HARVEY, JAMES ROSS, diversified service co. exec.; b. Los Angeles, Aug. 20, 1934; s. James Ernest and Loretta Berniece (Ross) H.; B.S. in Engring., Princeton U., 1956; M.B.A., U. Calif. at Berkeley, 1963; m. Charlene Coakley, July 22, 1971; children—Kjersten Ann, Kristina Ross. Engr. Standard Oil Co. (Calif.), San Francisco, 1956-61; accountant Touche, Ross, San Francisco, 1963-64; pres., chief exec. officer, dir. Transamerica Corp., San Francisco, 1965—, also chmn. bd.; dir. Transam. Delaval Inc., Transam. Film Service Corp., Transam. Occidental Life Ins. Co., Transam. Fin. Corp., Transam. Airlines, Transam. Ins. Co., Transam. Interway Inc., Transam. Title Ins. Co., Safeway Stores, Inc., Pacific Telephone. Trustee, West Coast Cancer Found.; bd. regents St. Mary's Coll.; bd. dirs. U. Calif. Bus. Sch., Nat. Park Found., Calif. State Parks Found., Fine Arts Museums of San Francisco, Bay Area Council. Served with AUS, 1958-59. Mem. San Francisco C. of C. (dir.). Clubs: Bohemian (San Francisco); Union League (N.Y.C.). Office: 600 Montgomery St San Francisco CA 94111

HARVEY, RICHARD DUDLEY, mktg. cons.; b. Atlanta, Sept. 24, 1923; s. Robert Emmett and June (Dudley) H.; B.A., U. Denver, 1947; postgrad. various bus. seminars Harvard U., Stanford U.; m. Donna Helen Smith, Oct. 12, 1944; 1 dau., Louise Dudley. Various positions in sales, sales promotion and mktg. The Coca-Cola Co., St. Louis, Denver and Atlanta, 1948-60, v.p., brand mgr., mktg. mgr., mktg. dir., Atlanta, 1965-70, v.p. orgn. and mktg. devel., 1970-75; sr. v.p. mktg. Olympia Brewing Co., Olympia, Wash., 1975-78; with Sound Mktg. Services Inc., Seattle; dir. Lone Star Brewing Co., San Antonio. Mem. mayor's housing resources com., Atlanta, 1968-70; program chmn. United Way, Atlanta, 1969; vice chmn. Episcopal Radio-TV Found., Atlanta, 1975—; dir. Oreg. Shakespearean Festival Assn., 1982—. Served with USAAF, 1942-45. Mem. Am. Mktg. Assn. (pres. 1983-84), Mktg. Communications Execs. Internat., Inst. Mgmt. Cons., Seattle C. of C., Phi Beta Kappa, Omicron Delta Kappa. Democrat. Episcopalian. Clubs: Piedmont Driving (Atlanta); The Rainier, Seattle Tennis (Seattle). Home: 3837 E Crockett St Seattle WA 98112 Office: Sound Mktg Services Inc Suite 402 Grosvenor House 500 Wall St Seattle WA 98121

HARWICK, MAURICE, lawyer; b. Los Angeles, Feb. 6, 1933; s. Lester and Fannie (Eisenberg) H.; A.A., Los Angeles City Coll., 1954; J.D., Southwestern U., 1957; m. Saowapa Butranon, July 4, 1970; children—Manasnati, Manasnapa. Admitted to Calif. bar, 1958; U.S. Supreme Ct. bar, 1962; dep. dist. atty. County of Los Angeles, 1958-60; individual practice law, Marina del Rey, and Santa Monica, Calif., 1960—; judge pro tem Municipal Ct., 1966-67, 80, 81. Chmn. bd. rev. Los Angeles Community Colls. and City Schs.; mem. Project Safer Calif. gov.'s com., 1974-75. Mem. Beverly Hills, Los Angeles County, Am. bar assns., State Bar Calif., Criminal Cts. Bar Assn. (pres. 1972, bd. govs.), Los Angeles, Calif. trial lawyers assns., Calif. Attys for Criminal Justice, Nat. Criminal Def. Lawyers Assn., Los Angeles County Dist. Attys. Assn., Vikings. Address: 2001 Wilshire Blvd Suite 600 Santa Monica CA 90403 also 4814 Marina City Dr Suite 916 Center Tower S Marina del Rey CA 90241

HARZ, KARL JOSEPH, financial company executive; b. Paterson, N.J., July 10, 1950; s. Karl Oscar and Vera Marie (Gennaro) H.; B.S., Fairleigh Dickinson U., 1972, M.B.A., 1974; m. Marilyn Lee Kindred, Mar. 3, 1974; children—Alexa Marie, Tiffany Ann. Regional dir., life and disability agt. Lincoln Nat. Life Ins. co., Los Angeles, 1974-76; registered rep. Nat. Plan Coordinators, Inc., Long Beach, Calif., 1976-77; pension cons., fin. planner Mut. Benefit Life Ins. Co., 1977-78; pres., founder Pension Home Loan Corp., 1978-82, Alternative Funding Sources, 1982—; incorporator, pres. Loanlink Corp., 1983—; dir. Province Service Corp. Realtor. Recipient cert. of achievement AAU, 1972. Real estate broker, Tex., Calif. Mem. Nat. Assn. Realtors, Nat. Notary Assn., Rolling Hills Bd. Realtors, others. Clubs: N.Y. Athletic (life); Los Angeles Athletic (profl.). Home: 701 Via Horcada Palos Verdes Estates CA 90274 Office: 2401 Pacific Coast Hwy Suite 101 Hermosa Beach CA 90254

HASAN, SYED MOHAMMAD, chemical engineering consultant; b. Fatehpur, India, Jan. 1, 1931; came to U.S., 1960; s. Siddiq and Summa (Khatoon) H.; B.Sc., U. Karachi (Pakistan); postgrad. in chemistry and chem. engring. U. So. Calif., UCLA, 1964-66; postgrad. in mgmt. sci. West Coast U., Los Angeles, 1974; m. Rashida Khatoon Azim, June 6, 1956; children—Farhat, Khalid, Rafat, Nusrat, Saeeda, Tariq. Tchr. chemistry and physics Marie Colaco English Secondary Sch., Karachi, 1957-60; chemist, chief chemist Globe Elec. Co., Gardena, Calif., 1962-68; sr. mfg. engr. Burroughs Corp., Pasadena, Calif., 1968-69, now cons.; sr. chem. process engr. Lockheed Electronics Co., Los Angeles, 1969-75, cons., 1975—; tech. dir., owner Super Chem Enterprises, Los Angeles, 1975-80; pres. H & R Chems. Inc. (doing bus. as Super Chem Enterprises), Huntington Beach, Calif., 1980—. Mem. Calif. Circuit Assn., Cons. Chemists Assn., Am. Mgmt. Assn., Islamic Soc. Orange County (dir.). Developer metallizing chems. used in mfg. printed circuits and semicondrs. Home: 9852 Vicksburg St Huntington Beach CA 92646 Office: 7573 Slater St Huntington Beach CA 92647

HASBROOK, ALBERT HOWARD, aviation safety consultant; b. Trenton, N.J., July 15, 1913; s. Albert Howard and Mabel Benita (Naar) H.; m. Virginia Randolph Whiting, Nov. 23, 1955; children—Howard Richard Jay (dec.), Barbara Elaine; 1 stepson, Dan C. Grad. Hemphill Engring. Sch. Registered profl. engr. Photog. design engr., freelance tech. writer, 1935-38; equipment design engr., 1939-42; flight instr. U.S. Army Air Force, 1942-44; sales engr., test pilot, 1944-45; flight instr., charter, flight test and agrl. pilot, 1946-49; assoc. dir., chief aircraft accident investigator aviation crash injury research dept. Cornell U. Med. Sch., 1950-55, dir., 1955-60; chief crash safety and accident investigation Civil Aeromed. Research Inst., FAA, Oklahoma City, 1960-68, sr. research scientist, 1960-75, aviation safety specialist, 1968-70, chief flight research and performance, 1970-75; aviation safety cons., accident reconstructionist, Prescott, Ariz., 1975—; prof. Embry-Riddle Aero. U., Prescott, 1982—. Recipient Flight Safety Found. award, 1958, Gen. Spruance award, 1970, Harry G. Moseley award, 1972. Mem. Aerospace Med. Assn., Internat. Soc. Air Safety Investigators, Aircraft Owners and Pilots Assn., Prescott Aviation Adv. Com., Soc. Automotive Engrs. Pioneer in crash injury investigation and crash safety design; contbr. articles to profl. jours.; holder patent on blind flying display. Address: Campwood Route Prescott AZ 86301

HASENOEHRL, DANIEL NORBERT FRANCIS, clergyman; b. Portland, Oreg., July 12, 1929; s. Norbert Frank and Anna (Feucht) H. B.A., Mt. Angel Sem., 1951; M. Ed., U. Portland, 1958. Joined Order of St. Benedict, 1956, Ordained priest Roman Catholic Ch., 1960; counselor Mt. Angel (Oreg.) Prep. Sch., 1960-64, counselor, registrar, academic dean, 1961-71, acting pres. Mt. Angel Sem., 1968-69; chaplain Marylhurst (Oreg.) Coll., 1975-80; chaplain Dammasch State Hosp., Wilsonville, Oreg., 1975—; parish asst. Our Lady of Sorrows Ch., Portland, 1960-72, asst. pastor, 1972-75; prof. psychology Mt. Angel Sem., 1961-72. Served with U.S. Army, 1952-54. Mem. Am. Assn. Higher Edn., Nat. Assn. Cath. Chaplains, Am. Mental Health Counselors Assn., Am. Coll. Personnel Assn., Nat. Vocat. Guidance Assn., Nat. Cath. Guidance Conf. Democrat. Home: PO Box 19113 Portland OR 97219 Office: Pastoral Services Dammasch State Hospital Wilsonville OR 97070

HASHIMOTO, MASANORI, economics educator; b. Tokyo, July 12, 1941; s. Tadaichi and Aki H.; m. Barbara L. Brugman, Nov. 17, 1981; 1 son, Jeffrey Masayuki. B.A., Columbia U., N.Y.C., 1965, Ph.D., 1971. Assoc. prof. econs. U. Wash., Seattle, 1980—. Office: Dept Econs U Wash Seattle WA 98195

HASIN, SIDNEY L., electronic co. exec.; b. N.Y.C., Aug. 5, 1923; s. Charles C. and Florence (Grushen) H.; B.E.E., N.Y. U., 1944; M.S. in E.E., U. So. Calif., 1961; m. Bernice Rothman, Feb. 2, 1947; children—Deborah, Melissa, Tabitha. Asst. project engr. Bendix Radio, Towson, Md., 1951-53; group leader Hughes Aircraft, Culver City, Calif., 1953-57; sr. research engr. Litton Industries, Beverly Hills, Calif., 1957-59; dept. head Ramo Wooldridge, Canoga Park, Calif., 1959-63; div. dir. autonetics information systems N.Am. Rockwell, Anaheim, Calif., 1963-69, v.p., 1969-71, mem. mgmt. council, 1966-71, mem. program devel. council, 1968-71, pres. N.Am. Rockwell Information Systems Co., 1969-71, v.p. electronics group N.Am. Rockwell, 1971, corp. dir. computer requirements and advanced planning, 1971-74, corp. dir. computer tech., 1974-76, corp. dir. computing planning and controls, 1976-81, ret., 1981, cons., 1981—; pres. SLH Assos., 1981; data processing cons. Los Angeles Unified Sch. Dist., 1979-82, So. Calif. Edison, 1979—; v.p. MDR 1 Leasing Ops. Served with Signal Corps, AUS, 1944-45. Mem. IEEE (sr.), Ops. Research Soc. Am., Eta Kappa Nu. Home: 1101 Estelle Ln Newport Beach CA 92660 Office: 2201 Seal Beach Blvd Seal Beach CA 90740

HASKELL, JOHN SINBERG, marketing executive consultant; b. Pitts., Dec. 1, 1942; s. S.K. and Ann (Sinberg) H.; m. Elisabeth Schaye, July 28, 1968; 1 son, David. A.B. in English Lit., Brown U., 1964; M.B.A. in Mktg., Northwestern U., 1966. Consumer mktg. div. trainee Eastman Kodak Co., Rochester, N.Y., 1966-67; sales mgr. instnl. div. Haskell of Pitts., Inc., 1967-69; v.p. mktg. Bentson Office Furniture, 1968-70; v.p. mktg. Haskell of Pitts., Inc., 1970-71; v.p. mktg., gen. mgr. Abbey Rents Furniture, Los Angeles, 1971-73; v.p., chief operating officer Gamble Rents, Mpls., 1973-74; pres. Profl. Mktg. Group, Inc., Los Angeles, 1974—. Recipient soccer award Brown U., 1963. Republican. Jewish. Club: Riviera Tennis. Publisher. Calif. Wine List, 1979—; editor Sports Retailer, 1981—; contbr. articles to profl. jours. Office: 3625 W 6th St 204 Los Angeles CA 90020

HASLAM, GERALD WILLIAM, educator, author; b. Bakersfield, Calif., Mar. 18, 1937; s. Frederick Martin and Lorraine Hope (Johnson) H.; A.B., San Francisco State Coll., 1963, M.A., 1965; Ph.D., Union Grad. Sch., 1980; m. Janice Eileen Pettichord, July 1, 1961; children—Frederick William, Alexandra Ramona, Garth Clark, Simone Britt, Carlos Vicente. Instr. English, San Francisco State Coll., 1966-67; prodn. editor ETC: A Rev. of Gen. Semantics, 1967-69; mem. faculty Sonoma State U., Rohnert Park, Calif., 1967—, prof. English, 1974—; editor Western Writers Series, 1974—, Literary History of the American West, 1978—; mem. nat. acad. adv. bd. Multi-Cultural Inst., 1968-76. Bd. dirs. Petaluma Youth Soccer Program, 1972-75. Served with AUS, 1958-60. Research grantee Gen. Semantics Found., 1965; 1st runner up Joseph Henry Jackson award for fiction San Francisco Found., 1971. Mem. Coll. Lang. Assn., Western Lit. Assn. (dir., v.p.), Calif. Tchrs. Assn., Sierra Club, Calif. Trout, Calif. Native Plants Soc. Roman Catholic. Author: William Eastlake, 1970; The Language of the Oilfields, 1972; Okies: Selected Stories, 1973, 3d edit., 1975; Jack Schaefer, 1976; Masks: A Novel, 1976; The Wages of Sin: Collected Stories, 1980; Hawk Flights: Visions of the West, 1983; editor: Forgotten Pages of American Literature, 1969; Western Writing, 1974; Afro-American Oral Literature, 1974; California Heartland, 1978; author numerous articles, short stories. Office: English Dept Sonoma State Univ Rohnert Park CA 94928

HASS, WILLIAM HARLOW, agrl. co. exec.; b. Outlook, Mont., June 30, 1928; s. William Reinhart and Margaret Isabella (Helander) H.; student U. Chgo., 1950; m. Dorothy M. Irwin, Sept. 28, 1955; children—Michael, Donald, Kimberly, Stephen. Mgr., Hass Farms Inc., Outlook, 1954—, pres., 1956—; pres. Hass Land Co., Outlook, 1967-75, dir., 1956—. Served with USAF, 1951-53. Mem. Mont. Grain Growers Assn., Aircraft Owners and Pilots Assn., Nat. Pilots Assn., Sherwood Pilot Assn., Can. Legion, Am. Legion. Club: Elks. Home and Office: Box 315 Outlook MT 59252

HASSAN, MARK DAVID, psychologist; b. Los Angeles, Jan. 16, 1949; s. Abraham Herman and Joyce Bernice (Ginsberg) H.; m. Elizabeth Worsley Toole, Sept. 19, 1976. B.A. in Criminology, U. Calif.-Berkeley, 1971; M.A. in Clin. Psychology, Calif. Sch. Profl. Psychology, 1974, Ph.D. in Clin. Psychology, 1976. With Los Angeles Suicide Prevention Center, 1971-79, program supr. narcotics and drug abuse rehab. program, 1975-77, assoc. project dir., 1977-79; pvt. practice cons. and clin. psychology, Pasadena, Calif., 1978—; psychol. cons. La Vina Hosp. for Respiratory Diseases, 1978—, Los Angeles Police Dept., 1980; adj. asst. prof. psychology Fuller Sem. Grad. Sch. Psychology. Recipient award for outstanding service and leadership Los Angeles Suicide Prevention Center, 1974. Mem. Am. Psychol. Assn., Calif. State Psychol. Assn., Los Angeles County Psychol. Assn., Pasadena Mental Health Assn., So. Calif. Soc. for Clin. Hypnosis. Club: Pasadena Athletic.

Contbr. articles on milieu treatment of narcotics addicts to profl. jours. Office: 696 E Colorado Blvd Suite 207 Pasadena CA 91101

HASSRICK, PETER HEYL, museum director; b. Phila., Apr. 27, 1941; s. Royal Brown and E. Barbara (Morgan) H.; B.A., U. Colo., 1963; M.A., U. Denver, 1969; m. Elizabeth Drake, June 14, 1963; children—Philip Heyl, Charles Royal. Tchr. Whiteman Sch., Steamboat Springs, Colo., 1963-67; curator collections Amon Carter Mus., Ft. Worth, 1969-75; dir. Buffalo Bill Hist. Ctr., Cody, Wyo., 1976—; mem. nat. adv. bd. Remington Art Mus., 1982—; bd. dirs. Yellowstone Library and Mus. Assn., 1980—. Mem. City of Cody Downtown Devel. Com., 1977—. Mem. Am. Assn. Mus., Wyo. Council Arts, Phi Alpha Theta. Episcopalian. Author: Birger Sandzen, 1970; Frederic Remington, 1973; (with Ron Tyler) The American West, 1974; The Way West, 1977; The Remington Studio, 1981; (with P. Trenton) The Rocky Mountains: A Vision for Artists in the 19th Century, 1983; contbr. articles in field to profl. jours.

HASTIE, BILL, education specialist; b. Salem, Oreg., Nov. 6, 1943; s. William O. and Margaret L. (Jackson) H.; m. Carol L. Paschall, Sept. 22, 1968. B.S., Western Oreg. State Coll., 1969, M.S., 1980. Secondary teaching cert., Oreg. Tchr. sci. Cascade Union Sch. Dist., Turner, Oreg., 1972-76, 77-79; grad. asst. in biology Western Oreg. State Coll., 1976-77; marine edn. cons. Oreg. Dept. Edn., Portland, 1979-82; edn. specialist Oreg. Dept. Fish and Wildlife, Portland, 1982—; mem. Ocean Project Pacific Circle Consortium, U. Hawaii, Honolulu; mem. editorial policy bd. Clearing Publs., Portland State U. Mem. Oreg. Shores Conservation Coalition, Sierra Club, Nature Conservancy. Served to lt. USN, 1969-72. Mem. N.W. Assn. Marine Educators (pres. 1980-81), Nat. Marine Edn. Assn. (dir. 1981-83), Oreg. Sci. Tchrs. Assn., Environ. Edn. Assn. Oreg. (sec. 1982-84). Democrat. Author: Water, Water Everywhere ... (award of excellence Nat. Assn. State Edn. Dept. Info. Officers 1981), 1981 contbr. articles on wildlife to jour. Oreg. Wildlife. Home: 210 18th St NE Salem OR 97301 Office: PO Box 3503 Portland OR 97208

HASTINGS, JOY LABELLE, librarian; b. Long Beach, Calif., Dec. 7, 1946; d. Archie S. and Marian L. Hastings. B.A. in Geography, Calif. State U.-Fullerton, 1969; M.S.L.S., U. So. Calif., 1971. Librarian, Santa Ana (Calif.) Pub. Library, 1971-74; ref. network supr. Santiago Library System-Libraries of Orange County Network, 1974-78; mgr. info. center Hunt-Wesson Foods, Inc., Fullerton, 1978—. Mem. Spl. Libraries Assn., Orange County Library Assn. Office: 1645 W Valencia Dr Fullerton CA 92634

HASTINGS, NORRY MARK, plastic manufacturing company executive; b. Van, Armenia, May 31, 1915; s. Nishan Hagopian and Hranoosh (Jonigian) H.; B.S., Northeastern U., 1940; m. Armine Vartanian, Jan. 23, 1943; children—Michael, Norene. Came to U.S., 1923, naturalized, 1942. Chemist, Makalot Plastics Co., Waltham, Mass., 1942; gen. mgr. Nobell Resin Co., Azusa, Calif., 1945-48; lab. group leader Plastics Lab., N.Am. Aviation, Los Angeles, 1948-52; tech. dir. Rezolin, Inc., Santa Monica, 1952-56; pres. Hastings Plastics Co., 1956—; v.p. Hastings Plastics Stores Inc., 1973—; pres. Western Plastics News Inc., 1974—; organizer, producer Ann. Western Plastics Expn., 1978; organizer, chmn. bd. trustees Western Plastics Mus. and Pioneers Inc., 1978—. Cons., lectr., tech. speaker. Served to lt. USCGR, 1942-45. Recipient editorial award Nat. Soc. Plastics Engrs., 1972; Plastics Engr. 1972 award So. Calif. Soc. Plastics Engrs., 1972; named to Western Plastics Hall of Fame, 1982. Mem. Soc. Plastics Industry (chmn., organizer tooling div. 1952, publicity chmn. Western conf. 1975), Soc. Aerospace Engrs. (founding mem), Soc. Plastics Engrs. (founding mem. 1947, 1st v.p. 1972—, editorial award 1972, 73, 74, gen. chmn. Pacific Coast tech. conf. 1975). Episcopalian (sec., chmn. bishop's com. on laymen's work 1948-56. Club: Armenian Allied Arts Assn. (dir. 1967-71) (Los Angeles). Editor Pacific Coast Plastics and Rubber mag., 1974; editor, pub. Plastics Mag., 1974—. Introduced liquid plastics to tooling use, 1945, liquid plastics to home craft use, 1956, introduced plastics resin to art field, 1960. Home: 539 Via Dela Paz Pacific Palisades CA 90212 Office: 1704 Colorado Ave Santa Monica CA 90404

HASTINGS, RALPH LESLIE, architect; b. Los Angeles, June 2, 1950; s. Ralph Leo and Christine Mae (Shepherd) H.; A.A., Cerritos Coll., 1970; B.S., Calif. State Poly. Coll., 1975; m. Nancy J. Murrill, Sept. 9, 1972; 1 dau., Melissa Cameron. Draftsman, Lott-Collins Architects, Los Angeles, 1971-72, Lott, Collins, DeRevere & Assos., 1973-74; project coordinator Richard Dodd, Architect, Newport Beach, Calif., 1975-76; v.p., project designer Dell H. DeRevere & Assos., Newport Beach, 1976-81; prin. Hastings-Lundstrom Architects, Costa Mesa, Calif., 1981—; instr. Sch. Architecture, Santa Ana Coll. and Cerritos Coll., Norwalk, Calif., 1979—. Served with USNG, 1971-76. Recipient merit award Gold Nuggets Awards for Security Express Hdqrs. Bldg., Santa Ana, Calif., 1981, Riggins Constrn. Mgmt. Corp. hdqrs., 1982. Mem. AIA.

HASTINGS, WILLIAM JEFFREY, brewery official; b. Cleve., July 21, 1951; s. Nelson William and Margaret Elizabeth, (Evans) H.; m. Jessie Vaughn Davidson, May 15, 1982. B.B.A., Cleve. State U., 1973, M.B.A., 1976. Asst. brand mgr. Clorox Co., San Francisco, 1974-77; product mgr. Baxter-Travenol Labs., Chgo., 1978; dir. new products Adolph Coors Co., Golden, Colo., 1979—. Mem. Am. Mktg. Assn. (exec. mem.). Home: PO Box 1297 Golden CO 80401 Office: Adolph Coors Co Mail Number 317 Golden CO 80401

HASTRICH, JEROME JOSEPH, clergyman; b. Milw., Nov. 13, 1914; s. George Peter and Clara (Dettlaff) H.; student Marquette U., 1933-35; B.A., St. Francis Sem., Milw., 1940, M.A., 1941; student Cath. U. Am., 1947. Ordained priest Roman Cath. Ch., 1941; assigned, Milw., then Madison, Wis.; chancellor Diocese Madison, 1952-53, apptd. vicar gen., 1953, aux. bishop, 1963-67; pastor St. Raphael Cathedral, Madison, 1967-69; bishop, Gallup, N.Mex., 1969—. Diocesan dir. Confrat. Christian Doctrine, St. Martin Guild, 1946-69; pres. Latin Am. Mission Program; sec. Am. Bd. Cath. Missions; vice chmn. Bishop's Com. for Spanish Speaking; bd. advisers Religious Life Inst., 1975; founder, epis. moderator Queen of Ams. Guild; pres. Nat. Blue Army. Mem. Gov. Wis. Commn. Migratory Labor, after 1969. Address: 711 S Puerco Dr Gallup NM 87301

HASWELL, FRANK IRVIN, state supreme court justice; b. Great Falls, Mont., Apr. 6, 1918; B.A. in Econs., U. Wash., 1941; J.D., U. Mont., 1947; m. June Elizabeth Arnold, May 5, 1951; children—Frank Warren, Bruce Douglas, John Richard. Admitted to Mont. bar, 1947; practiced in Great Falls, 1947-48; asso. firm Jardine, Chase & Stephenson, 1947-48; city atty. Whitefish (Mont.), 1948-58; pvt. practice law, Whitefish, 1948-51; mem. firm Haswell & Ryan, 1951-54, Haswell & Heckathorn, 1954-58; dist. judge 11th Jud. Dist. Mont., Kalispell, 1958-67; justice Mont. Supreme Ct., Helena, 1967-78, chief justice, 1978—; chmn. Fair Trial-Free Press Com.; chmn. task force on cts./community relations Mont. Bd. Crime Control. Served with USMCR, 1943-46. Mem. Mont. Judges Assn. (pres. 1969-70), Conf. Chief Justices, Six-State Jud. Conf. Clubs: Elks, Eagles, Rotary. Office: Justice Bldg 215 N Sanders Helena MT 59620

HATAMI, MARVIN, architect, urban designer; b. Tehran, Iran, Feb. 14, 1925; came to U.S., 1954, naturalized, 1961; s. Fazlolah and Fahimeh (Sagafi) H.; B.S. in Civil Engring., U. Tehran, 1948; B.Arch. (Engring. Alumni scholar 1957), U. Colo., 1958; M.Arch. (grantee 1961), Yale U., 1961; m. Bernice VanHecke, May 1958 (div. Apr. 1972); children—Todd A., Darium M., Brenna C. Architect, designer archtl. firms in Denver, New Haven and N.Y.C., 1956-65; partner Baume, Polivnick and Hatami, Denver, 1965-67; prin. Marvin Hatami and Assos., Denver, 1967-74, 76—; v.p. URS Corp., Denver, 1974-76; vis. asso. prof. Coll. Environ. Design, U. Colo., 1965-78, Sch. Art, U. Denver, 1972-74; prin. works include: Skyline Urban Renewal project, Denver, 1970; Fisk Planetarium U. Colo., Boulder, 1973; St. Francis Interfaith Center, Auraria Higher Edn. Center, Denver, 1978 (honor award Western Mountain region AIA 1981), Pacific Pl., Denver Housing Authority, 1978. Recipient citation for Skyline Urban Renweal project, Denver, Progressive Architecture mag., 1970, for Communitas, residential and office park devel., Jefferson County, Colo., 1975; honor award for design excellence of renewal project, Denver, HUD, 1970; Inner Elegance 1st award for restoration and renovation of older properties Denver Bd. Realtors, 1979; winner design competition for Boulder (Colo.) Civic Center, 1969, for low-income housing Denver Housing Authority, 1976, 78. Mem. AIA (chmn. commn. on environment Colo. central chpt. 1970, chmn. nat. com. regional devel. and resources 1971), Profl. Ski Instrs. Am., Tau Beta Pi, Sigma Tau. Democrat. Address: 1537 Washington St Denver CO 80203

HATCH, CALVIN SHIPLEY, consumer product company executive; b. Heber City, Utah, Feb. 23, 1921; s. Edwin D. and Veronica (Burton) H.; m. JeNeal Nebeker, Dec. 23, 1945; children—Marcia Hatch Thomas, Julie Hatch Skrdla. B.S., U. Utah, 1942. With Clorox Co. 1971—, v.p. sales, 1972-73, group v.p. mktg. services, 1973-77, exec. v.p., 1977-81, pres., chief exec. officer, 1981-82, chmn., chief exec. officer, 1982—; dir. First Interstate Bank of Calif. Mem. Bus. Sch. Advisory Bd., U. Calif., Bay Area Council, Calif. Round Table, Grocery Mfrs. Am., C. of C. Served to capt. F.A., U.S. Army, 1942-45. Clubs: Orinda Country, Athenian Nile, World Trade, 100. Home: 3853 Palo Alto Dr Lafayette CA 94549 Office: 1221 Broadway Oakland CA 94612

HATCH, DALE, electronics engineer; b. Vernal, Utah, Oct. 14, 1944; s. David Milburn and Grace (Burke) H.; m. Cleone Wilson, Mar. 31, 1972; children—Jeffrey, Brian, Diana, Kimberly. Grad. with honors, Weltech Electronics Coll., 1963; A.A., Brigham Young U., 1968, A.S., 1971, B.S., 1973, M.S., 1974. Systems check-out rep. Kenway Engring. Inc., Salt Lake City, 1973-74; field elec. engr. Rohr Indsl. Systems, San Diego, 1974-75; indsl. engr. NCR Corp., San Diego, 1975-77; sr. electronics/software engr. Gen. Dynamics, San Diego, 1977—; instr. and cons. in field; staff U.S. project. Asst. scoutmaster Boy Scouts Am., 1974; rep. Calif. Constl. Conv., 1972. Served with U.S. Army, 1968-70, Vietnam. Recipient Bronze Star. Mem. Soc. Packaging and Handling Engrs. (profl. cert.), Am. Inst. Indsl. Engrs., Am. Mgmt. Assn. Mormon. Author: APT Systems and Numerical Control Programming, 1981. Office: 5001 Kearny Villa Rd San Diego CA 92138

HATCH, DANIEL JAMES, podiatrist; b. Dixon, Ill., Sept. 13, 1952; s. John Frank (dec.) and Esther Emily (Clover) H.; B.S. in Biology, U. Ill., 1974; Dr. Podiatric Medicine, Ill. Coll. Podiatric Medicine, 1978. Resident surg. podiatry Highlands Center Hosp., Denver, 1978-79; asso. group practice Denver, Boulder, Colo., 1979-80; pvt. practice podiatry, Greeley, Colo., 1980—; chmn. utilization com. Highlands Hosp., 1981—; active resident tng., 1979—. Bd. dirs. Weld County Area Agy. on Aging, 1980—. Recipient Research award Highlands Hosp., 1979. Mem. Colo. Podiatry Assn. (dir.), Am. Podiatry Assn. (pres.-elect), C. of C. Republican. Clubs: Northern Colorado Track; Greeley Jazz; Kiwanis. Office: 2000 16th St Suite 3 Greeley CO 80631

HATCH, EASTMAN NIBLEY, educator, physicist; b. Salt Lake City, June 14, 1927; s. Joseph Eastman and Florence (Nibley) H.; student U. Utah, 1946-48, 51-52; B.S., Stanford, 1950; Ph.D., Calif. Inst. Tech., 1956; m. Anne Clawson, June 21, 1952; children—Joseph Eastman II, Richard Clawson, Anne Florence. Postdoctoral fellow in physics Calif. Inst. Tech., 1956-57; research assoc. physics Brookhaven Nat. Lab., Upton, N.Y., 1957-58, sci. liaison with USN in Frankfurt/Main, Germany, 1958-60; guest physicist Heidelberg U., Germany, 1960-61; assoc. prof. physics Iowa State U., 1961-66, prof. physics, 1966-69, asst dean Grad. Coll., 1967-69, physicist Ames Lab., 1961-66, sr. physicist, 1966-69; prof. physics Utah State U., Logan, 1969—, head dept. physics, 1972-74, dean sch. grad. studies, 1974-79; vis. prof. physics Freiburg U. (W. Ger.), 1979-80; vis. research asso. Los Alamos Sci. Lab., 1971-83. Served with USNR, 1945-46. Fellow Am. Phys. Soc., Phi Beta Kappa, Sigma Xi. Home: 1795 Country Club Dr Logan UT 84321

HATCH, GREG JON, advertising agency executive; b. Sandpoint, Idaho, Nov. 12, 1951; s. John W. and Lois J. H.; m. Julie Ann Osman, Apr. 28, 1974; 1 son, Casey Allan. B.A. in Bus., Whitworth Coll., 1974. Sales rep. Pfizer Inc., Walnut Creek, Calif., 1974-77; media rep. Sta. KXLY-TV, Spokane, Wash., 1977-78; ptnr. Gross-Hatch Assocs., Advt., Spokane, 1978—. Bds. dirs. Big Bros. and Sisters of Spokane, 1981—, Union Gospel Mission of Spokane, 1982—, Greater Spokane Sports Assn., 1982—; mem. Mayor's Prayer Breakfast Com., 1981—, chmn., 1982; exec. com. Inland Empire Billy Graham Crusade, 1982. Mem. Whitworth Alumni Assn. (steering com. 1978-82). Presbyterian. Club: Spokane Valley Rotary. Office: E 5325 Sprague Spokane WA 99206

HATCH, KENNETH L., company executive; b. Vernal, Utah, Aug. 4, 1934; s. Lois and Alva Le Roy Hatch; m. Marsha Kay Rich, Dec. 7, 1974; children—Sean, Ryan, James, Michael, Elizabeth-Ann. B.S. in Banking and Fin., U. Utah, 1957; postgrad. Stanford U., Harvard Grad. Sch. Bus. Gen. sales mgr. KSL, Salt Lake City, 1963-64; gen. sales mgr. KIRO-TV, Seattle, 1964-66, asst. gen. mgr., 1965-67, gen. mgr., 1967-71, sr. v.p., 1971-80, pres., chief exec. officer, 1980—; dir., mem. exec. com., KIRO, Inc.; sr. v.p. Bonneville Internat. Corp.; dir. Bear Creek, Inc., Wash., Olympic Savs. and Loan Assn. Bd. dirs. Seattle Conv. and Bus. Bur. Mem. Ch. of Christ. Club: Rainier of Seattle, Bellevue Athletic, Wash. Athletic, Overlake Golf and Country. Office: 3d Ave & Broad St Seattle WA 98121

HATCH, LYNDA SYLVIA, educator, curriculum consultant; b. Portland, Oreg., Feb. 19, 1950; d. Marley Elmo and Undine Sylvia (Corckard) Sims. Student U. Oreg., 1968-70; B.S., Wash. State U., 1972; M.S., Portland State U., 1975, postgrad. comparative edn. seminar, Eng., 1977. Cert. tchr., supr., Oreg. Elem., outdoor edn. tchr. schs. in Tacoma, Wash., Hillsboro and Bend, Oreg., 1971-72, 78-82; tchr. individualized reading program Hillsboro Elem. Dist. 7, 1972-78; grad. teaching asst. elem. edn. dept. Oreg. State U., Corvallis, 1981—; condr. workshops for tchrs. Active Girl Scouts U.S.A., 1957—; elder, chmn. social concerns, service com. 1st Presbyterian Ch.; mem. Oreg. High Desert Mus., Oreg. Mus. Sci. & Industry. Named Oreg. Tchr. of Year, Oreg. State Dept. Edn., 1982; mem. U.S. Cultural Olympic Team, 1968. Mem. Nat. State Tchrs. of Year Orgn., Oreg. Reading Assn., Oreg. Council Tchrs. of Math., Nat. Council Tchrs. of Math., Oreg. Council Tchrs. of English, Nat. Council Tchrs. of English, Oreg. Assn. Talented and Gifted, Oreg. Edn. Assn., NEA, Bend Edn. Assn., Assn. Supervision and Curriculum Devel., Audubon Soc., Native Plant Soc., Sierra Club, Phi Kappa Phi, Pi Lambda Theta. Home: 20723 Alan-A-Dale Ct Bend OR 97702 Office: 520 NW Wall St Bend OR 97701

HATCH, ORRIN GRANT, U.S. Senator; b. Homestead Park, Pa., Mar. 22, 1934; s. Jesse and Helen (Kamm) H.; B.S., Brigham Young U., 1959; J.D., U. Pitts., 1962; m. Elaine Hansen, Aug. 28, 1957; children—Brent, Marcia, Scott, Kimberly, Alysa, Jess. Journeyman metal lather, 1951-60; admitted to Pa. bar, 1963, Utah bar, 1970; partner firm Thomson, Rhodes & Grigsby, Pitts., 1962-69; sr. v.p., gen. counsel Am. Minerals Mgmt. and Am. Mineral Fund, Inc., Salt Lake City, 1969-71; partner firm Hatch & Plumb, 1976; mem. U.S. Senate from Utah, 1976—. Mem. Am., Utah, Pa. bar assns., Am. Judicature Soc. Mormon. Author: Good Faith Under the Uniform Commercial Code, 1962. Office: Dirksen Senate Office Bldg Room 411 Washington DC 20510*

HATELEY, ENID ELLEN, real estate broker; b. Guayaquil, Ecuador, Mar. 22, 1925; came to U.S., 1944, naturalized, 1948; d. Harry Hawkes and Silia (Blanco) Shephard; B.S., Colegio Guayaquil, 1942; B.A., U. So. Calif., 1946; m. James Charles Hateley, II, Aug. 24, 1946; children—James Charles, Robert, Donald. Asst. credit mgr. Bank of Calif., 1946-49; with IBEC, 1950-51, E.H. Imports, 1952-60; trust adminstr. Bank of Am., 1973-75; broker Coldwell Banker, Los Altos, Calif., 1976—. Named Miss Dominican Republic, 1946; named to Coldwell Banker Million Dollar Club, 1976, 77, 78; recipient Silver Circle award Coldwell Banker, 1979-81. Mem. Nat. Assn. Realtors, Calif. Assn. Realtors, Los Altos Bd. Realtors (life mem. Million Dollar Club). Republican. Roman Catholic. Club: Los Angeles Athletic. Home: 2175 Chuleta Ct Los Altos CA 94022 Office: 301 S San Antonio Rd Los Altos CA 94022

HATFIELD, ELAINE CATHERINE, clinical psychologist, educator; b. Detroit, Oct. 22, 1937; d. Charles Ewald and Eileen Catherine (Kalahar) H. B.A., U. Mich., 1959; Ph.D., Stanford U., 1963. Lic. clin. psychologist, Hawaii. Asst. prof. U. Minn., Mpls., 1963-64, assoc. prof., 1964-66; assoc. prof. U. Rochester (Minn.), 1966-67; assoc. prof. U. Wis., Madison, 1967-68, prof., 1968—; mem. faculty exptl. psychology Oxford U., 1981-82; chmn. dept. psychology U. Hawaii, Honolulu, 1982—; guest research prof., W.Ger., 1972. NIMH grantee, 1965-68, 69-72; NSF grantee, 1966-72. Fellow Am. Sociol. Assn., Am. Psychol. Assn. (council of reps. 1969-74), Soc. for Psychol. Study of Social Issues; mem. Assn. Women Psychologists, Soc. Exptl. Social Psychology (exec. com. 1970-73), Am. Assn. Sex Educators and Counselors, NIMH (grants com. 1977-80), NSF (social scis. com. 1971-74), Nat. Acad. Scis. (aging com. 1978-80), Soc. for Personality and Social Psychology (pub. policy com. 1980—), Wis. Family Studies Inst. (research assoc. 1980-81). Co-author: (with G.W. Walster) A New Look at Love, 1978 (Am. Psychol. Found. award); (with Houston, Bee, Rimm) Introduction to Psychology, 1979; (with W. Griffitt) Psychology & Sexual Behavior, 1981; (with Fogel, Kiesler, Shanas) Aging: Stability and Change in the Family, 1981; contbr. chpts. to books, articles in field to profl. jours. Office: 2430 Campus Rd Honolulu HI 96822

HATFIELD, MARK ODOM, U.S. senator; b. Dallas, Oreg., July 12, 1922; s. Charles Dolan and Dovie (Odom) H.; B.A., Willamette U., 1943, postgrad. Law Sch., 1946-47; M.A., Stanford U., 1948; numerous hon. degrees; m. Antoinette Kuzmanich, July 8, 1958; children—Elizabeth, Mark Odom, Theresa, Charles Vincent. Instr., asst. prof., asso. prof. polit. sci. Willamette U., 1949-56, dean of students, 1950-56; sec. state Oreg., 1957-59, gov. 1959-67; U.S. senator from Oreg., 1967—, chmn. appropriations com., mem. rules and adminstrn. com., mem. energy com. Author: Not Quite So Simple; Conflict and Conscience; Between a Rock and a Hard Place. Office: 463 Russell Senate Office Bldg Washington DC 20510

HATH, DAVID COLLINS, coll. adminstr.; b. San Diego, Mar. 13, 1944; s. Collins Maxwell and Dorothy (Laird) H.; A.A., Porterville Coll., 1964; B.S., Calif. State U., 1966; M.A. in Counseling, Chapman Coll., 1972; postgrad. Pepperdine U., U. Calif., Irvine; m. Deborah Lynn Shively, Apr. 9, 1976; children—Derek Collins, Douglas Alan. Indsl. relations rep. Ford Motor Co., Pico Rivera, Calif., 1966-68; tchr. Tustin Union High Sch., Mission Viejo, Calif., 1968-69; counselor, counseling psychologist Orange (Calif.) Unified Sch. Dist., 1969-75; dean, continuing edn. div. Rancho Santiago Community Coll. Dist., Orange, Calif., 1975—. Mem. community adv. bd. Rehab. Inst. Orange County, 1979—; mem. regional continuing edn. accreditation com. Calif. Dept. Food and Agr., 1980—. Recipient various awards. Mem. Calif. Assn. Marriage and Family Therapists, Calif. Community Coll. Continuing Edn. Assn., Calif. Personnel and Guidance Assn., Assn. Calif. Community Coll. Adminstrs., Phi Delta Kappa, Orange C. of C. Republican. Home: 10744 Rancho Santiago Blvd Orange CA 92669 Office: 541 N Lemon St Orange CA 92667

HATHAWAY, JOHN DAVID, franchise corporation marketing executive; b. Los Angeles, June 26, 1946; s. John Lewis and Jean (Irvine) H.; m. Paula Jean Houle, Apr. 15, 1973; children—David Anthony, Katherine Jean, Elizabeth Ann. B.A., Calif. State U., Long Beach, 1970. Scout exec. Boy Scouts Am., Pasadena, Calif., 1973-74; mktg. mgr. Wienerschnitzel Internat., Inc., Newport Beach, Calif., 1974-80; field mktg. dir. Pioneer Take Out, Inc., Los Angeles, 1980; dir. mktg. Jim Dandy Fast Foods, Santa Monica, Calif., 1980-83; dir. mktg. Numero Uno Franchise Corp., 1983—; cons. mktg., 1981—. Mem. Chino C. of C. Republican. Roman Catholic. Clubs: Praed Street Irregulars (Los Angeles), Baker Street Irregulars (Los Angeles, San Francisco). Home: 12361 Maxon Ln Chino CA 91710 Office: 20335 Ventura Blvd Woodland Hills CA 91364

HATHAWAY, MADELYN KREMER, management consultant; b. Des Moines, Feb. 12, 1915; d. Homer and Bertha Louise (Speth) Kremer; B.A. in Music, Calif. State U., Long Beach, 1976, B.A. in Psychology, 1981; M.A. in Psychology, Newport U., 1979; m. Gordon M. Hathaway, Mar. 21, 1943; children—Spencer Kremer, Scott Craighead. Pres. Hathaway Assocs., Hawthorne, Calif., 1976—; dir. tng. Calif. Inst. Socioanalysis, 1975—; lectr., cons. to bus. and industry in communication and role tng. techniques. Vice pres. Pasadena chpt. World Federalists; docent Los Angeles Philharm. Mem. Am. Soc. for Tng. and Devel., Organizational Developmental Soc. Los Angeles, Am. Soc. Psychodrama, Sociometry and Group Psychotherapy, Sigma Alpha Iota. Democrat. Research on utilization of psychodrama techniques for rehabilitating prisoners. Address: 3209 W 139th St Hawthorne CA 90250

HATLEN, ROE HAROLD, financial executive; b. Kalispell, Mont., Nov. 6, 1943; s. Knute H. and Hilda E. (Lee) H.; m. Beverly J. Thompson, June 18, 1966; children—Kari, Erik, Lars. B.B.A. Pacific Luth. U., 1965; M.B.A. U. Oreg., 1967. Auditor Kohener and Larson, pub. accts., 1967; acct. Herzinger, Porter, Addison and Blind, pub. accts., 1973-76; controller Internat. King's Table, Inc., 1974-76; v.p. fin., treas., 1976-82; founding pres. Central Luth. Found., 1979—. Served with USAR, 1967-73. Mem. Am. Inst. C.P.A.s, Oreg. Soc. C.P.A.s, Nat. Restaurant Assn. Fin. Officers; Oreg. Cash Mgrs. Rep. Lutheran. Home: 782 Kristen Ct Eugene OR 97401 Office: 1500 Valley River Dr Eugene OR 97401

HATTEN, CHARLES WILLIS, oil company executive; b. Fayetteville, Ark., May 21, 1923; s. Joseph Francis and Irene (Moeder) H.; m. Cornelia Ann Eggleston, Oct. 20, 1956; children—Carol Ann, Karen Marie, William E., Charles Willis. B.A., U. Calif.-Berkeley, 1949. Sr. geologist Calif. Exploration Co., Havana, Cuba, 1953-58; chief geologist Pan Am. Hispano Oil Co., Madrid, 1958-62; Pan Am. Indonesia Oil Co., Pakanbaru, Sumatra, 1962-65; exec. v.p., dir. Gt. Basins Petroleum Co., Los Angeles, 1965-67, pres. and dir., 1967-82; pres., dir. Century Prodn. Co. Inc., Pasadena, Calif., 1982—. Trustee, Dunn Sch., Los Olivos, Calif. Served with USN, 1942-46. Mem. Am. Assn. Petroleum Geologists. Republican. Club: Annandale Golf (Pasadena). Contbr. geol. papers to profl. publs.

HAUBERG, JOHN HENRY, forestry mgmt. co. exec.; b. Rock Island, Ill., June 24, 1916; s. John Henry and Suzanne Christian (Denkmann) H.; m. Ann Homer Brinkley, Dec. 1, 1979; children—Fay Page, Sue B. Student Princeton U., 1934; B.S. in Forestry, U. Wash., 1949. Founder Pacific Denkmann Co., Seattle, 1948, pres., 1952—; mem. vis. com. U. Wash. Coll. Forest Resources, 1960—. Vice chmn. Republican Nat. Fin. Com., 1962-64; trustee Seattle Art Mus., 1956—, pres., 1973-78, chmn. bd. trustees, 1978-81; mem. adv. com. for child devel. and mental retardation ctr. U. Wash.; trustee, founder, pres. Pilchuck Glass Sch., Stanwood, Wash.; trustee Bush Sch., Seattle, 1950—, pres., 1954-57; mem. vestry Epiphany Parish Episcopalian Ch., Seattle. Served to 2d lt. F.A. and inf. U.S. Army, 1943-46. Mem. Soc. Am. Foresters, Northwest Hardwoods Assn. (founder, trustee), Phi Beta Kappa, Phi Sigma, Xi Sigma Pi. Clubs: Seattle Tennis, Seattle Golf, Univ., Rainier, City, Bainbridge Racquet Ball. Pub. Pilchuck Tree Farm Notes, 1981—. Office: 216 1st Ave Suite 230 Seattle WA 98104

HAUER, ANDREAS, insurance marketing executive; b. Oslo, June 25, 1946; came to U.S., 1948, naturalized, 1958; s. Karl Andreas and Ellen Bertha (Neilsen) H.; B.S., Linfield Coll., 1967; M.B.A., Golden Gate U., 1974. Asst. brokerage mgr. Pacific Mut. Ins. Co., San Francisco, 1970-72; employee benefit cons. Johnson & Higgins, San Francisco, 1972-80; v.p. employee benefits Bayly, Martin & Fay, Oakland, Calif., 1980-81, Fireman's Fund Ins. Co., San Rafael, Calif., 1981—. Chmn., World Championship Domino Tournament, San Francisco; fund raiser Hunter's Point Boy's Club, San Francisco; bd. dirs. The Guardsmen. Served with USNR, 1968-69; Vietnam. Mem. C.L.U. Soc. (dir. San Francisco chpt. 1975-76). Republican. Lutheran. Clubs: Olympic, Commonwealth. Home: 2101 Sacramento #604 San Francisco CA 94109 Office: PO Box 3330 San Radford CA 94912

HAUFT, NEIL EDWARD, exec. search cons.; b. Hempstead, N.Y., Apr. 19, 1931; s. Laurance Albert and Lena Hauft; B.S. in Mech. Engring., Va. Poly. Inst., 1953; M.B.A., Xavier U., Cin., 1961; m. Dorothy Ann Saba, 1981; children—Amy Gilbert, Robert Florenz. With Gen. Electric Co., 1953-67, mgr. application engring., 1964-67; mgr. space programs Northrop Corp., Los Angeles, 1968-69; partner Peat Marwick Mitchell & Co., C.P.A.'s, Los Angeles, 1970-75;v.p. Korn/Ferry Internat., Los Angeles, 1975-76; pres. N.E. Hauft Assos., Inc., El Segundo, Calif., 1977—; dir. Nat. Needlecraft Corp., Inc. Bd. dirs. Big Bros. Greater Los Angeles; mem. president's adv. council Calif. State U., Long Beach. Served with USAF, 1953-56. Office: 999 N Sepulveda Blvd El Segundo CA 90245

HAUGE, LAWRENCE JESSEN, school administrator; b. Tacoma, Feb. 10, 1928; s. Philip E. and Margrethe (Jessen) H.; m. Beverly J. Milligan, Oct. 17, 1975; children—Jan, Steven, David. B.A. in Speech, Pacific Luth. U., 1950, B.Ed., 1951, postgrad., 1959-62; Ed.D. in Adminstrn., Wash. State U., 1980. Cert. supt., secondary prin., secondary tchr., Wash. Tchr., Hudtloff Jr. High Sch., Tacoma, 1953-57, vice prin., 1957-63; dir. alumni relations Pacific Luth. U., 1963-67; adminstrv. asst. to supt. Clover Park Sch. Dist., Tacoma, 1967-75; coordinator curriculum and instrn. Ednl. Service Dist. 167, Wenatchee, Wash., 1975-77; adminstrv. asst. for curriculum Wenatchee Sch. Dist., 1977—; mem. selection com. Central Wash. U. Program Unit for Preparation of Sch. Adminstrs., 1979-82. Adv. com. Chelan-Douglas Health Dist.; mem. Gov.'s Rural Devel. Confs., 1981-82; mem. regional coordinating com. Partnership for Rural Improvement, 1976-78; mem. planning com. Ft. Steilacoom Community Coll., 1967-69; bd. dirs. North Central Wash. councils Camp Fire Girls; mem. Community Action Council, 1977-82; dist. chmn. Mt. Rainier council Boy Scouts Am., 1972; bd. regents Pacific Luth. U., 1972-78, sec. bd.; pres. Friends of the Lakes Dist. Library, 1969-70; mem. ch. council Grace Luth. Ch., 1977-80. Served with U.S. Army, 1951-53. Mem. Wash. Assn. Sch. Adminstrs., Assn. Supervision and Curriculum Devel., Nat. Sch. Pub. Relations Assn., Appalarians, Phi Delta Kappa, Phi Kappa Phi, Pi Kappa Delta. Club: Kiwanis (local pres. 1966, lt. gov. internat. 1970-71, dist. chmn. 1971-72). Contbr. articles profl. jours. Home: 1608 Washington St Wenatchee WA 98801 Office: Wenatchee School District 246 PO Box 1767 Wenatchee WA 98801

HAUGEN, AGNES GARLAND, hospital administrator; b. Portland, Oreg., June 12, 1935; d. Ray and Anna Grace (Buell) Garland; grad. Good Samaritan Hosp. Sch. Nursing, 1956; m. Harold L. Haugen, Feb. 26, 1956; children—Jan, Marc, Scott, Kim. Staff nurse Good Samaritan Hosp., 1956-57, Emanuel Hosp., 1957-59, U. Oreg. Health Scis. Center, 1961-66; with Newberg (Oreg.) Community Hosp., 1966—, dir. nurses, 1978-79, asst. adminstr. med. services, 1979-81, asst. adminstr., 1981—. Mem. Marion, Polk, Yamhill County Health Systems Agy. Sub-area Council, 1976-80, pres., 1978-79; mem. plan devel. com. Western Oreg. Health Systems Agy., 1978-79; mem. Marion, Polk and Yamhill County Emergency Med. Services Com., 1976-78; pres. bd. advs. Coop. Work Experience Program, Newberg High Sch.; del. Yamhill County Citizens Conv. Mem. Oreg. Emergency Dept. Nurses Assn. (pres.-elect 1978-79), Oreg. Vocat. Assn., Am. Soc. Nursing Adminstrs., Oreg. Soc. Nursing Adminstrs. (mem. legis. com.), Willamette Council Nursing Adminstrs. (pres. 1980-81), Good Samaritan Hosp. Alumni Assn. (pres. 1961-62). Republican. hospital administrator; b. Portland, Oreg., June 12, 1935; d. Ray and Anna Grace (Buell) Garland; grad. Good Samaritan Hosp. Sch. Nursing, 1956; m. Harold L. Haugen, Feb. 26, 1956; children—Jan, Marc, Scott, Kim. Staff nurse Good Samaritan Hosp., 1956-57, Emanuel Hosp., 1957-59, U. Oreg. Health Scis. Center, 1961-66; with Newberg (Oreg.) Community Hosp., 1966—, dir. nurses, 1978-79, asst. adminstr. med. services, 1979-81, asst. adminstr., 1981—. Mem. Marion, Polk, Yamhill County Health Systems Agy. Sub-area Council, 1976-80, pres., 1978-79; mem. plan devel. com. Western Oreg. Health Systems Agy., 1978-79; mem. Marion, Polk and Yamhill County Emergency Med. Services Com., 1976-78; pres. bd. advs. Coop. Work Experience Program, Newberg High Sch.; del. Yamhill County Citizens Conv. Mem. Oreg. Emergency Dept. Nurses Assn. (pres.-elect 1978-79), Oreg. Vocat. Assn., Am. Soc. Nursing Adminstrs., Oreg. Soc. Nursing Adminstrs. (mem. legis. com.), Willamette Council Nursing Adminstrs. (pres. 1980-81), Good Samaritan Hosp. Alumni Assn. (pres. 1961-62). Republican. Home: Rt 4 Box 283 Newberg OR 97132 Office: 501 Villa Rd Newberg OR 97132

HAUGEN, CAROLYN RUTH, elementary school principal; b. Sacramento, Apr. 6, 1939; d. Alfred Franklin and Ruthella (Verran) Schance; m. David Clayton Haugen, July 6, 1973; 1 dau., Kristen Ruthella. A.B., Stanford U., 1961; M.A. in Elem. Edn., 1962; adminstrv. service credential Calif. State U.-Fullerton, 1970; postgrad. Fielding Inst., Santa Barbara, Calif., 1980—. Tchr. elem. schs., Sacramento Unified Dist., 1962-66; tchr. Walnut Valley (Calif.) Unified Dist., 1972-77, coordinator staff devel., 1977-81, prin. elem. sch., 1981—; cons. guest lectr. tchr. prep. program Calif. Poly. U., U. So. Calif., Los Angeles; summer staff mem. bilingual edn., Calif. Poly. U., 1981; mem. adv. bd. sch. adminstrn. Calif. State U.-Fullerton, Chmn., Walnut Valley Mgmt. Council, 1982-83; chmn. bd. dirs. Covina Presbyterian Ch. Day Care Center, 1983-84. Nat. Assn. Elem. Sch. Prins. summer fellow, 1983; recipient Los Angeles County Environ. award, 1974; Evergreen Community Club Recognition award, 1975; Walnut Elem. Community Club Recognition award, 1982. Mem. Walnut Valley Adminstrs. Assn., Assn. Calif. Sch. Adminstrs., Assn. Supervision and Curriculum Devel. (state dir. 1982-84), Nat. Assn. Elem. Sch. Prins., Pi Lambda Theta, Delta Kappa Gamma (rec. sec. 1982-84). Clubs: Stanford (Los Angeles); P.E.O. Contbr. articles in field to profl. jours. Office: 841 S Glenwick Ave Walnut CA 91789

HAUGLAND, NANCY JAEGER, public utility executive; b. Oak Park, Ill., May 5, 1924; d. August Henry and Margaret Reid (Weir) Jaeger; m. Melvin Haugland, Nov. 16, 1951; divorced; 1 son, Gary Paul. B.S. in Home Econ., Iowa State U., 1946. Home economist Pub. Service of Ill., Oak Park, 1946-47, Harper-Maggee, Spokane and Seattle, 1948-50, Coolerator Co., Duluth, Minn., 1950-51; Pacific Nat. Advt., 1964-66; home economist Pacific Power and Light Co., Yakima, Wash., 1966-68, Portland, Oreg., 1968-74, energy and conservation mgr., Walla Walla, Wash., 1974-77, mgr. Coquille (Oreg.) Office, 1977—. Past pres. Myrtle Point C. of C.; mem. bd. Coos County Econ. Devel. Bd. Mem. Am. Home Econ. Assn., Oreg. Home Econ. Assn., Home Econ. in Bus., Elec. Women's Round Table, Coquille C. of C. (dir.). Republican. Clubs: Soroptimist (v.p.), Sawdust Theatre (Coquille). Office: B25 N Adams Coquille OR 97423

HAUK, A. ANDREW, fed. judge; b. Denver, Dec. 29, 1912; s. A.A. and Pearl (Woods) H.; A.B. magna cum laude, Regis Coll., 1935; LL.B., Cath. U. Am., 1938; J.S.D. Yale U., 1942; m. Jean Nicolay, Aug. 30, 1941; 1 dau., Susan. Admitted to D.C. bar, 1938, Colo. bar, 1939, Calif. bar, 1942, U.S. Supreme Ct. bar, 1953; asst. to law librarian Library of Congress, summers 1935-38; spl. asst. to atty. gen., counsel for govt. antitrust div. U.S. Dept Justice, Los Angeles, Pacific Coast, Denver, 1939-41; instr. law Southwestern U., 1939-41; asst. U.S. atty., Los Angeles, 1941-42; asso. firm Adams, Duque & Hazeltine, Los Angeles, 1946-52; individual practice law, Los Angeles, also asst. counsel Union Oil Co., Los Angeles, 1952-64; judge Calif. Superior Ct. Los Angeles County, 1964-66; judge U.S. Dist. Ct. Central Dist. Calif., 1966-80, chief judge, 1980-82, sr. judge, 1982—; lectr. U. So. Calif. Sch. Law, 1947-56, South-Western U. Sch. Law, 1939-41. Vice chmn. Calif. Olympic Com., 1954-61; ofcl. VIII Olympic Winter Games, Squaw Valley, 1960; del. IX Olympic Winter Games, Innsbruck, Austria, 1964; mem., dir. So. Calif. Olympic Com., 1973—. Served from lt. to lt. comdr., Intelligence, USNR, 1942-46. Recipient scrolls for civic and jud. achievements Los Angeles County Bd. Suprs., 1965, 66, 76, 82; award ILGWU, 1938. Alumnus of Yr. award Regis Coll., 1967; named to Nat. Ski Hall of Fame, 1975; Sterling fellow, 1938-39. Mem. Los Angeles County Bar Assn. (chmn. pleading and practice com. 1963-64, membership com., chmn. law day com. 1965-66), State Bar Calif. (corps. com.), Am. Bar Assn. (antitrust sect., criminal law sect., com. on criminal law), Fed. Bar Assn., Nat. Conf. Fed. Trial Judges, Lawyers Club Los Angeles, Am. Judicature Soc., Am. Legion, Navy League, U.S. Lawn Tennis Assn., So. Calif. Tennis Assn. (dir. 1972—), So. Calif. Tennis Patrons Assn. (bd. govs.), Far West Ski Assn. (past dir., v.p. 1947-49), Yale Law Sch. Assn. So. Calif. dir., pres. 1951-56), Town Hall Calif., World Affairs Council, People-to-People Sports Com., Navy League, Am. Legion. Clubs: Yale of So. Calif. (dir. 1964-67); Newman; Valley Hunt (Pasadena); Jonathan (Los Angeles). Numerous pub. decisions and opinions. Office: US Court House 312 N Spring St Los Angeles CA 90012

HAULENBEEK, ROBERT BOGLE, JR., government official; b. Cleve., Feb. 24, 1941; s. Robert Bogle and Priscilla Valerie (Burch) H.; B.S., Okla. State U., 1970; m. Rebecca Marie Talley, Mar. 1, 1965; children—Kimberly Kaye, Robert Bogle, III. Micro paleon. photographer Pan Am. Research Co., Tulsa, 1966-67; flight instr. Okla. State U., 1970; air traffic control specialist FAA, Albuquerque, 1970-73, Farmington, N.Mex., 1973-78, flight service specialist, Dalhart, Tex., 1978-80, Albuquerque, 1980—; staff officer CAP, Albuquerque, 1970-73, Farmington, 1974-78, advanced through grades to lt. col., 1981, now dir. ops. for hdqrs. N.Mex. Wing; mem. faculty Nat. Staff Coll., Gunter Air Force Sta., Montgomery, Ala., 1981-82. Served with U.S. Army, 1964-65. Recipient Meritorious Service award CAP, 1978, 81, 82, Lifesaving award, 1982. Mem. Exptl. Aircraft Assn., Nat. Assn. Air Traffic Specialists (facility rep.). Republican. Presbyterian. Home: 5229 Carlsbad Ct NW Albuquerque NM 87120 Office: FAA Flight Service Sta Albuquerque NM

HAULT, JOHN A., planetarium dir.; b. Halifax, N.S., Can., Aug. 9, 1947; s. George Christie and Lillian Veronica (Steele) H.; student Dalhousie U., 1964-67; m. Esther M. Bruver, May 28, 1977. Planetarium lectr., sci. services asst. N.S. Mus., 1961-66; ednl. coordinator Queen Elizabeth Planetarium, Edmonton, Alta., Can., 1968-69, dir., 1973-80, dir. Queen Elizabeth Planetarium, project coordinator Edmonton Space Scis. Centre, 1980—, Robert J. Lockhart Planetarium, dept. maths. and astronomy U. Man., 1970-72. Mem. Planetarium Assn. Can. (pres. 1979-81), Internat. Planetarium Soc. (exec. councillor 1980-82), Can. Mus. Assn., Royal Astron. Soc. Can. Liberal. Roman Catholic. Club: Royal N.S. Yacht Squadron. Office: Coronation Park Edmonton AB Canada

HAUN, DONALD ARTHUR, construction executive; b. Struthers, Ohio, Feb. 10, 1936; s. Arthur Warren and Margaret Rosella (Eisenbraun) H.; student Thiel Coll., Greenville, Pa., 1954-55, Youngstown (Ohio) U., 1955-57; m. Audrey Ann Slifka, Aug. 6, 1960; 1 dau., Alyssa Ann. Asst. br. mgr. Mahoning Nat. Bank, Youngstown, 1957-61; ins. adjuster Gen. Adjustment Bur. Inc., Painesville, Ohio, 1961-63; claims supr. St. Paul Ins. Cos., Denver, 1963-73; pres. COICO Gen. Constrn. Co. Inc., Denver, 1973—, COICO Devel. Co.; chmn. bd. Colo. Structural Cons. Ltd.; cons. in field. Served with USAF, 1959. Mem. Home Builders Am., Colo. Claims Men's Assn. Republican. Inventor hydraulic drill, truss panel found. system. Home: 9275 Meade St Westminster CO 80030 Office: 7581 N Broadway Denver CO 80221

HAUPTMAN, DAVID SIMON, television station marketing executive; b. Jersey City, Oct. 11, 1951; s. Harry and Gladys E. (Rosenman) H.; m. Ronnie Sue Schindler, June 25, 1978; 1 dau., Rachel. B.S.B.A. in Acctg., U. Denver, 1973; M.B.A. in Mktg., Bernard M. Baruch Coll., CUNY, 1978. Media dir. Exchange Media, N.Y.C., 1973-78; media dir. Karsh & Hagan Advt., Denver, 1978-80; account exec. Sta. KCNC, Denver, 1980-83, mktg. mgr., 1983—; guest lectr. in advt., mktg. U. Denver. Mem. Denver Advt. Fedn., Elcfun Soc.-Gen. Electric, Zeta Beta Tau. Jewish. Office: 1044 Lincoln St Denver CO 80203

HAUSBURG, DAVID EUGENE, research engineeer; b. Chgo., June 13, 1925; s. William Albert and Mary Louise (Watson) H.; A.A.S., Portland Community Coll., 1966; m. Marjorie Ann Wallenstrom, June 16, 1979; 1 dau., Melissa Ann. Field service engr. Honeywell, Inc., Chgo., 1951-56; instrument technician Philips Petroleum Co. Idaho Nat. Engring. Labs., Arco, 1956-63; radio technician Portland (Oreg.) Community Coll., 1964-66; research specialist I, Rockwell Internat., Rocky Flats Plant, Golden, Colo., 1966—. Instr. hunter edn. and wilderness survival Colo. State Div. Wildlife, 1968-82. Served with U.S. Army, 1943-46. Mem. Am. Soc. Cert. Engring. Technicians (pres. Rocky Mountain chpt. 1979, nat. dir. 1980, edn. chmn. 1981—), Instrument Soc. Am. (pres. Boulder sect. 1967, 71), Colo. Minority Engring. Assn. (chmn. tech. adv. task force), Sigma Xi. Clubs: Rocky Flats Photo (treas. 1974-79), Colo. Mountaineering, Rocky Flats Toastmasters (pres. 1978). Home: 1420-D Crete Ct Lafayette CO 80026 Office: PO Box 464 Golden CO 80401

HAUSDORFER, GARY LEE, mortgage bank exec.; b. Indpls., Mar. 26, 1946; s. Walter Edward and Virginia Lee (Bender) H.; A.A., Glendale Coll., 1966; B.S., Calif. State U.-Los Angeles, 1968; m. Debora Ann French, Dec. 17, 1966; children—Lisa Ann, Janet Lee. Research officer Security Pacific Bank, Los Angeles, 1968-73; v.p., mgr. W. Ross Campbell Co., Irvine, Calif., 1973-81; regional v.p. Weyerhaeuser Mortgage Co., Irvine, 1982—. Councilman, City of San Juan Capistrano, 1978—, mayor, 1980-81; vice chmn. Coast Bible Ch., 1979-81; chmn. Orange County Water Dist. 4, 1980-81; chmn. San Juan Capistrano Redevel. Agy., 1983-84. Recipient cert. of commendation Orange County Bd. Suprs., 1981. Mem. Mortgage Bankers Assn. Am., Calif. Mortgage Bankers Assn., Orange County Mortgage Bankers Assn. (dir. 1979-80), Calif. League of Cities. Republican.

HAUSER, HILLARY RIKA, reporter, writer; b. Palo Alto, Calif., Sept. 4, 1944; d. Carl Richard and Mabel (Hensel) H.; B.A., U. Wash., Seattle, 1966. Local editor TV Guide, Los Angeles, 1966-67, nat. programmer, 1967-68; asst. editor Skin Diver mag., Los Angeles, 1968-71; West Coast corr. Ocean Sci. News, Washington, 1971—; spl. features editor Skin Diver Mag., 1971—; freelance writer, Santa Barbara, Calif., 1971—; reporter Santa Barbara News-Press, 1981—; tech. cons. underwater TV films; publicity dir. Diving Equipment Mfrs. Assn., 1978-80. Author: Women in Sports: Scuba Diving, 1976; The Skin Diver's Book of Fishes, 1983; The Living World of the Reef, 1978; contbr. articles to diving and gen. interest mags. Mem. Undersea Med. Soc. (asso.). Home and office: 1655 Fernald Point Ln Santa Barbara CA 93108

HAUSMAN, ARTHUR HERBERT, electronics co. exec.; b. Chgo., Nov. 24, 1923; s. Samuel Louis and Sarah (Elin) H.; B.S. in Elec. Engring., U. Tex., 1944; S.M., Harvard U., 1948; m. Helen Mandelowitz, May 19, 1946; children—Susan Lois, Kenneth Louis, Catherine Ellen. Electronics engr. Engring. Research Assos., St. Paul, 1946-47; supervisory electronics scientist U.S. Dept. Def., Washington, 1948-60, now cons.; v.p., dir. research Ampex Corp., Redwood City, Calif., 1960-63, v.p. operations, 1963-65, group v.p., 1965-67, exec. v.p., 1967-71, exec. v.p., pres., chief exec. officer, 1971-83, now chmn. bd., also dir.; dir. Drexler Tech., Inc.; mem. vis. com. dept. math MIT; invited speaker NATO, 1976. Chmn. tech. adv. com. computer peripherals Dept. Commerce, 1973-75; mem. subcom. on export adminstrn. President's Export Council. Trustee United Bay Area Crusade; bd. dirs. Bay Area Council. Served with USNR, 1944-54. Recipient Meritorious Civilian Service award Dept. Def. Mem. IEEE, Army Ordnance Assn. (dir. chpt. 1969-71). Club: Commonwealth of Calif. Patentee and author publs. in field of radio communications. Home: 55 Flood Circle Atherton CA 94025 Office: 401 Broadway Redwood City CA 94063

HAUSMANN, ROBERT LOUIS, educator; b. Refugio, Tex., Aug. 23, 1933; s. Emil Frederick and Margarite (Ryals) H.; B.S., Tex. A&I U., Kingsville, 1959, M.S., 1964; m. Dorothy Agnes Norris, July 8, 1953; children—Cynthia Anne Hausmann Moore, Linda Kay Hausmann Mayhugh. Public sch. tchr., then jr. high sch. prin., sr. high sch. prin., Tex., 1959-66; program dir. Office of Planning, Tex. Edn. Agy., Austin, 1966-68; regional asso. dir. Adminstrv. Tng. Program, San Angelo, Tex., 1968-70; asst. prof. Lubbock (Tex.) Christian Coll., 1970-75; acad. dean Coll. of the Southwest, Hobbs, N.Mex., 1975-79, faculty ednl. psychology dept., 1979—; ednl. cons. long-range planning, group dynamics. Elder, Jefferson St. Ch. of Christ, Hobbs, 1976—. Served with USAF, 1953-57. Republican. Clubs: Kiwanis, Ambucs (sec., v.p. 1977-79). Office: Coll of Southwest Lovington Hwy Hobbs NM 88240

HAUT, CLAIRE JOAN, painter, sculptor; b. Moline, Ill., Sept. 26, 1918; d. John Louis and Florence Norton (Cameron) Overholt; m. Edward Joseph Haut, Jr., Jan. 21, 1950; 1 dau., Susan Claire Hedley. Student Augustana Coll., 1936-37, Am. Acad. Art, 1937-38, Ill Inst. Tech., 1940-44, Bauhaus-based Sch. Design, studies with Lazlo Moholy-Nagy, Gyorgy Kepes. Designer Ill. Art Project, Chgo., 1939-42; art editor Fairbanks-Morse, Chgo., 1942-44, Cudahy Packing Co., Chgo., 1944-45; freelance advt. artist, Chgo., 1945-52; illustrator, designer Sandia Labs., Albuquerque, 1958-74; freelance painter, sculptor, Albuquerque, 1974—; one-man shows: Jonson Gallery, U. N.Mex., 1979, Artichoke Gallery, Albuquerque, 1980, Go-Shoppe, 1980, 81; group shows: Nat. Watercolor Show, Albuquerque, 1982, Abilene (Tex.) Fine Arts Mus., 1982, Simms Fine Art Gallery, Albuquerque, 1982, Woodworks: 83 United Albuquerque Artists, 1983; work represented in Library of Congress. Recipient numerous awards. Mem. N. Mex. Watercolor Soc., Albuquerque Equity, Nat. League Am. Penwomen. Address: 9836 McKnight NE Albuquerque NM 87112

HAUWILLER, JAMES GEORGE, elementary education educator; b. St. Paul, Nov. 16, 1938; s. Joseph John and Heneritta Marie (Tubirdy) H.; m. Yvonne Carol Sieg, June 5, 1965; children—Tanya Marie, Jay Rahman. B.A., Coll. St. Thomas, 1961; A.M., No. Colo. U., 1968; Ph.D., U. Ill.-Champaign, 1976. Tchr. pub. schs., Isle, Minn., 1962-65; vol. Peace Corps, Freetown, Sierra Leone, West Africa, 1965-67; supervising tchr. Milw. Pub. Schs., 1969-72; assoc. prof. dept. elem. edn. Mont. State U., Bozeman, 1976—. Served with USAF, 1961-62. Mem. Assn. Supervision and Curriculum Devel., Am. Ednl. Research Assn., Nat. Council for Social Studies, Phi Delta Kappa. Contbr. articles to profl. jours. Office: Dept Elementary Edn Mont State U Bozeman MT 59717

HAVEN, SHARON OWEN, interior designer, editor consultant; b. Bell, Calif., Feb. 9, 1943; d. Guilford Achilles Owen and Virginia Hope (Molholm) O; m. Robert Matthew Dorn, Dec. 20, 1966; m. 2d, Clayton Haven, March 4, 1973; children—Matthew, Amy. B.A. magda cum laude, Pomona Coll., 1965; M.A., Columbia U., 1966. Cert. community coll. instr., Calif. Staff writer, researcher, Ctr. for Study Dem. Instns., Santa Barbara, Calif., 1966-67; instr. polit. scis., Westmont Coll., Santa Barbara, 1967-69; co-editor Zero Population Growth Monthly Jour., Palo Alto, Calif., 1972; freelance designer, cons., writer, 1973—; field editor publs., 1979—. Chmn. Mid-Town Property Owner's Assn., 1981; active San Diego Symphony Assn., Mus. of Man, San Diego Zoöl. Soc. Cordell Hull Internat. Relations awardee, 1965; Woodrow Wilson fellow, 1966. Mem. AIA, Am. Soc. Interior Designers. Author: Room to Grow; Making Your Child's Bedroom an Exciting World, 1979. Home: 3136 Falcon St San Diego CA 92103

HAWE, DAVID LEE, consultant; b. Columbus, Ohio, Feb. 19, 1938; s. William Doyle and Carolyn Mary (Hassig) H.; m. Margret J. Hoover, Apr. 15, 1962; children—Darrin Lee, Kelly Lynn. Project mgr. ground antenna systems W.D.L. Labs., Philco Corp., 1960-65; credit mgr. for Western U.S., Am. Hosp. Supply Corp., Burbank, Calif., 1965-74; owner, mgr. Hoover Profl. Equipment Co., contract health equipment co., Guasti, Calif., 1974-75; pres. Baslor Care Services, owners convalescent homes, Santa Ana, Calif., 1975-80; pres. Application Assocs., 1980—; dir. Medisco Co., Casa Pacifica, Broadway Assocs. Bd. dirs. Santa Ana Community Convalescent Hosp., 1974-79, pres., 1975-79. Served with USN, 1954-56. Lic. real estate broker, Calif. Mem. Am. Vacuum Soc. Republican. Roman Catholic. Home: 18082 Hallsworth Circle Villa Park CA 92667

HAWES, GRACE MAXCY, adminstr., writer; b. Cumberland, Wis., Feb. 4, 1926; d. Clarence David and Mabel Hannah (Erickson) Maxcy; student U. Wis., 1944-46; B.A., San Jose State U., 1963, M.A., 1971; m. John G. Hawes, Aug. 28, 1948 (dec.); children—Elizabeth, John D., Mark, Amy. Library asst. NASA, Langley, Va., 1948-49; librarian Hoover Archives, Stanford U., 1976-80, adminstrv. asst. Office of Devel., 1980—. Mem. Soc. Am. Archivists, Women in Hist. Research, Calif. Archivists Assn., Inst. Hist. Study. Author: The Marshall Plan for China: Economic Cooperation Administration, 1948-1949, 1977. Home: 410 Sheridan #220 Palo Alto CA 94306 Office: Office of Development 301 Encina Stanford University Stanford CA 94304

HAWKE, BERNARD RAY, planetary scientist; b. Louisville, Oct. 22, 1946; s. Arvil Abner and Elizabeth Ellen (Brown) H. B.S. in Geology,

U. Ky., 1970, M.S., 1974; M.S., Brown U., 1977, Ph.D. in Planetary Geology, 1978. Geologist, U.S. Geol. Survey, 1967-68; researcher U. Ky., 1972-74, Brown U., 1974-78; planetary scientist Hawaiian Inst. Geophysics, U. Hawaii, 1978—; dir. NASA Pacific Regional Planetary Data Ctr., Honolulu; prin. investigator NASA grants. Served with USAR, 1970-72; Vietnam. Decorated Bronze Star. Mem. Geochem. Soc., Meteoritical Soc., Am. Geophys. Union, Sigma Xi, Sigma Gamma Epsilon, Alpha Tau Omega. Republican. Author papers in field. Address: HIG Univ Hawaii Honolulu HI 96822

HAWKES, GEORGE ROGERS, soil scientist, researcher; b. Preston, Idaho, Oct. 3, 1921; s. William and Anna Rebecca (Rogers) H.; m. Rosa Mae Swainston, Sept. 17, 1947; children—Kathleen, Mark, Douglas, Steven, Michelle. Student U. Utah., 1939-41; A.B., Brigham Young U., 1949; Ph.D., Ohio State U., 1952. Cert. profl. agronomist, profl. soil scientist. Soil scientist U.S. Dept. Agr., Pa. State U. and Beltsville, Md., 1952-57; research agronomist Chevron Chem. Co., Fresno, Calif., 1957-61, regional agronomist, Richmond, Calif., 1961-63, asst. nat. mgr., San Francisco, 1963-70, mgr. soil sci., Richmond, 1970-77, tech. coordinator research and devel., 1977-79, advisor product environ. affairs, San Francisco, 1979—. Mem. agrl. com. Calif. State C. of C., 1979—; mem. agrl. adv. com. Air Resources Bd. State of Calif., 1982—. Served with USN, 1944-46. Recipient Outstanding Service award Calif. Fertilizer Assn., 1975, Man. of Yr. award, 1979; Outstanding mem. award Western Agrl. Chem. Assn., 1982. Mem. AAAS, Am. Soc. Agronomy, Soil Sci. Soc. Am., Western Soil Sci. Soc. Republican. Editor: Western Fertilizer Handbook, 1980; co-editor: Advances in Sugarbeet Production, Principles and Practices, 1971. Office: 575 Market St San Francisco CA 94105

HAWKES, GLENN ROGERS, psychologist, educator; b. Preston, Idaho, Apr. 29, 1919; s. William and Rae (Rogers) H.; m. Yvonne Merrill, Dec. 18, 1941; children—Kristen, William Ray, Gregory Merrill, Laura. B.S. in Psychology, Utah State U., 1946, M.S. in Psychology, 1947; Ph.D. in Psychology, Cornell U., 1950. Asst. prof. to prof. child devel. and psychology Iowa State U., Ames, 1950-66, chmn. dept. child devel., 1954-66; prof. human devel., research psychologist, assoc. dean applied econs. and behavioral scis. U. Calif., Davis, 1966—, chmn. dept. applied behavioral scis., 1982—, chmn. teaching div., 1970-72, prof. behavioral sico. dept. family practice Sch. Medicine; vis. scholar U. Hawaii, 1972-73, U. London, 1973, 80; dir. Creative Playthings Inc., 1962-66. Served with AUS, 1941-45. Recipient numerous research grants from pvt. founds. and govtl. bodies; recipient Iowa State U. faculty citation, 1965, Iowa Soc. Crippled Children and Adults Outstanding Service citation, 1965, Dept. Child Devel. citation, 1980, Coll. Agrl. and Environ. Sics. citation, 1983; named hon. lt. gov. Okla., 1966. Author: (with Pease) Behavior and Development from 5 to 12, 1962; (with Frost) The Disadvantaged Child: Issues and Innovations, 1966, 2d edit., 1970; (with Schutz and Baird) Lifestyles and Consumer Behavior of Older Americans, 1979; (with Nicola and Fish): Young Marrieds: The Dual Career Approach, 1984; contbr. numerous articles to profl. and sci. jours. Home: 1114 Purdue Dr Davis CA 95616 Office: U Calif Dept Applied Behavioral Scis Davis CA 95616

HAWKINS, AUGUSTUS FREEMAN, congressman; b. Shreveport, La., Aug. 31, 1907; s. Nyanza and Hattie H. (Freeman) H.; A.B. in Econs., U. Calif. at Los Angeles, 1931; m. Pegga A. Smith, Aug. 28, 1945 (dec.); m. 2d, Elsie Taylor, June 1977. Engaged in real estate and retail bus., Los Angeles, 1945—; mem. Calif. Ho. of Reps. from Los Angeles County, 1935-62, chmn. rules com., 1961-62; mem. 88th-97th Congresses from 29th Calif. Dist., chmn. Adminstrn. Com., Joint Com. on Printing, vice chmn. Joint Com. on the Library. Democrat. Methodist. Club: Masons. Office: 2371 Rayburn House Office Bldg Washington DC 20515

HAWKINS, CALVIN LEON, locomotive engineer; b. Elko, Nev., Nov. 12, 1930; s. Charles Leroy and Mary Margaret (Origer) H.; m. Nancy Millett Hawkins, Apr. 25, 1961; children—Charles, Edward, Mark, Steven, Tawnya, Donna. Student pub. schs., Winnemucca, N.Y., 1935-1948. Locomotive engr. Western Pacific R.R., Portola, Calif., 1950—; sec., treas., Brotherhood Locomotive Engrs., 1971—. Mem. Am. affiliate Japan Karate Assn. Democrat. Club: Nev. Karate (Sparks). Home: 11760 Pepper Way Reno NV 89506 Office: Western Pacific RR Co Cortola CA 96122

HAWKINS, CHARLES SIMON, historic site manager; b. Lawrence, Kan., Mar. 23, 1917; s. William Simon and Lulu Elizabeth (McQueen) H.; m. Jeanette Ruth Meadows, Oct. 13, 1937; children—Carol Ann Hawkins Wood, Robert Charles. Site mgr. Fort Point Nat. Hist. Site, Presidio of San Francisco, 1968—. Served to master sgt. U.S. Army, 1944-68. Decorated Combat Inf. Badge, Bronze Star, Purple Heart, Army Commendation medal (3). Home: 1631 24th Ave San Francisco CA 94122 Office: Fort Point Nat Instoric Site PO Box 29333 Bldg 989 Presidio of San Francisco CA 94129

HAWKINS, EDWARD FREDERICK, endocrinologist, educator; b. Woodford, Eng., Feb. 12, 1946; came to U.S., 1977; s. Edward Charles and Eileen May (Cotton) H.; B.Sc., Sheffield U., 1967, Ph.D., 1970; m. Ghislaine M. Hawkins, July 14, 1976; 1 son, Edward Gregory. Postdoctoral fellow U. Calif., Berkeley, 1971-73; research endocrinologist Inst. Jules Bordet, Brussels, Belgium, 1973-77; research asso. Johns Hopkins Hosp., Balt., 1977-78; sr. research asso. U. So. Calif., 1978-79, asst. prof. research physiology and biophysics Comprehensive Cancer Ctr., Los Angeles, 1980—. NATO fellow, 1970; Harkness fellow Commonwealth Fund N.Y., 1971-73; Thomas Eckstrom Trust grantee, 1982. Mem. Brit. Soc. Endocrinology, Am. Endocrine Soc., Sigma Xi. Contbr. articles to profl. jours. Office: Univ So Calif Neuromuscular Ctr Good Samaritan Hosp 637 S Lucas Ave Los Angeles CA 90033

HAWKINS, EDWARD W., management consulting company executive; b. Rockville Centre, N.Y., Aug. 29, 1950; s. Anthony and Lavinia B. (Borliss) H.; m. Lucretia Ann Lange, Sept. 5, 1978; 1 son, Gary Edward. B.S. in Bus. Adminstrn., NYU, 1972; M.B.A., U. Conn., 1976. With comml. loan dept. 1st Nat. Bank of N.Y., 1972-74; bus. mgr. Thompson Home Products, Inc., Phila., 1974-78; v.p. fin. dept. Lafayette Engring. Co., St. Louis, 1978-82; sr. v.p. Werik Cons. Corp., San Francisco, 1982—; lectr., cons. in field. Participant telethons Muscular Dystrophy Assn. Mem. Assn. Bus. Cons., Mgmt. Cons. Execs. Assn., Assn. M.B.A. Execs., Sigma Nu. Republican. Baptist. Club: Yacht Harbor. Lodge, Elk. Office: Werik Consultations Corp 24 California St Room 312 San Francisco CA 94111

HAWKINS, JARED WALDO, JR., lawyer; b. Oakland, Calif., July 16, 1912; s. Jared Waldo and Bettie (Stephens) H.; student Modesto Jr. Coll., 1930-32; A.B., U. Calif., Berkeley, 1934; J.D., San Francisco Law Sch., 1945; m. Jacqueline Schwerin, June 30, 1946; children—Jay, Tim. With Calif. Packing Corp., San Francisco, 1934-45; admitted to Calif. bar, 1945; since practiced in Modesto; mem. firm Hawkins and Hawkins, 1945—. Past bd. 55, SSS; past chpt. chmn. Stanislaus County chpt. ARC; bd. dirs. Meml. Hosp. Assn., 1953-75. Recipient Presdl. award for service as mem. SSS, 1973. Mem. Calif. State Bar, Stanislaus County Bar Assn. (past pres.), Calif. Trial Lawyers Assn., Stanislaus County Estate Planning Council (dir.), Modesto C. of C. (legis. com.), U.S. C. of C., Am. Judicature Soc., E. Clampus Vitus (dir., past grand noble), Pi Kappa Phi (Golden Legion award 1983), Sigma Delta Kappa, Native Sons of Golden West. Methodist. Clubs: Optimist (past pres.), Elks, Old Fishermans, Trade, Quarterback. Home: 2913 Parkview Dr Modesto CA 95355 Office: 1119 12th St Modesto CA 95354

HAWKINS, JASPER STILLWELL, JR., architect; b. Orange, N.J., Nov. 10, 1932; s. Jasper Stillwell and Bernice (Ake) H.; B.Arch., U. So. Calif., 1955; children—William Raymond, John Stillwell, Karen Ann, Jasper Stillwell III; m. 2d, Patricia Ann Mordigan, Mar. 1980. Founder, prin. Hawkins & Lindsey & Assos., Los Angeles, 1958-78, Hawkins Lindsey Wilson Assos., Los Angeles and Phoenix, 1978-81; v.p. Hawkins and Lindsey Architects, 1981—; pres. Fletcher Thompson & Assos., Phoenix, Los Angeles, Bridgeport, Conn., 1981. Bd. visitors Nat. Fire Acad., 1978—; mem. Pres.'s Commn. on Housing, 1981; bd. dirs. Nat. Inst. Bldg. Scis., 1976—, chmn. bd. dirs., 1981—, consultative council, 1978—; mem. com. protection of archives and records centers GSA, 1975-77; mem. Nev. Gov.'s Commn. on Fire Codes, 1980-81; mem. archtl. adv. panel Calif. State Bldg. Standards Commn., 1964-70; mem. com. standards and evaluation Nat. Conf. States on Bldg. Codes and Standards, 1971—; chmn. bd. Nat. Inst. Bldg. Scis., 1981-82; maj. works include: Valley Music Theatre, Los Angeles, Houston Music Theatre, Sundome Theatre, Sun City West, Ariz., U. Calif. at Irvine Student Housing, Oxnard (Calif.) Fin. Center, condominium devels. Recipient design awards from Ariz. Rock Products Assn., Theatre Assn. Am., Nat. Food Facilities, House and Home Mag., Practical Builders Mag., Am. Builders Mag., others. Fellow AIA (nat. codes and standards com. 1970—, chmn. 1970-73, nat. liaison commn. with Asso. Gen. Contractors 1969-70, chmn. nat. fire safety task force 1972-74; chmn. Calif. council of AIA state code com. 1964-68, chmn. nat. conf. industrialized constrn. 1969-70, nat. com. bldg. industry coordination 1969-70; nat. rep. to Internat. Conf. Bldg. Ofcls. 1969); mem. Nat. Fire Protection Assn. (com. bldg. heights and areas 1965—, chmn. 1968-72, fire prevention code com. 1974—), ASCE (task force bldg. codes 1971-74). Contbr. articles to profl. jours. Office: 4621 N 16th St Phoenix AZ 85016

HAWKINS, JOSEPH KEY, communications co. exec.; b. Pomona, Calif., Aug. 13, 1926; s. Joseph Key and Helen Ethel (Hourigan) H.; student Lingnan U., Canton, China, 1948-49; B.Sc., Stanford, 1951, M.S., 1952; J.D., Western State U., 1979; m. Kathryn Annette McColl, June 21, 1953 (div. July 1977); children—Ann Patrick, Torrey Sue, Gale Britta. Dir. engring. Alwac Corp., Hawthorne, Calif., 1954-58; dept. mgr. Philco-Ford Co., Newport Beach, Calif., 1959-68; pres. Robot Research Inc., San Diego, 1968—. Lectr. digital computer design U. Calif. at Los Angeles, 1961-66. Served with AUS, 1946-48. Mem. Am. Bar Assn., State Bar Calif., IEEE, Mensa, Phi Beta Kappa. Author: Circuit Design of Digital Computers, 1968; (with Kovalevsky, Muroga, Pankhurst, Watanabe) Advances in Information Systems Science III, 1970. Editor: Pattern Recognition, 1970. Asso. editor Pattern Recognition Soc. Journal, 1968-74. Contbr. numerous articles to profl. jours. Home: 7329 Caminito Cruzada La Jolla CA 92037 Office: 7591 Convoy Ct San Diego CA 92111

HAWKINS, ROBERT EDWARD, savings and loan association public relations executive; writer; b. Chgo., Dec. 27, 1931; s. Robert Gaither and Ina Mae (Lamb) H.; m. Mary Frances Wingo, 1954; m. Leslie Jeanne Foelkner, Nov. 22, 1967; children—Robert A., Lisa Anne, Elizabeth E., Kenneth B., Thomas D. Student Los Angeles City Coll., 1950-51; engring. lic. Radio Operational Engring. Sch., Burbank, Calif., 1951. Announcer/engr. Sta. KWJB, Globe, Ariz., 1952; rec. asst. Les Paul, Los Angeles, 1953; announcer/engr. Sta. KYMA, Yuma, Ariz., 1953; news dir. Sta. KAVL, Lancaster, Calif., 1954; chief announcer Sta. KFBK, Sacramento, 1954; writer, producer, prodn. coordinator Sta. KERO-TV, Bakersfield, Calif., 1955-62; asst. program dir. Sta. KSFO, Golden West Broadcasters Stas., San Francisco, 1962-64, program dir. Sta. KEX, Portland, Oreg., 1964-65, program dir. Sta. KVI, Seattle, 1965-70; sr. account exec. Jay Rockey Pub. Relations, Seattle, 1970-80; v.p. mktg. and communications Wash. Fed. Savs. & Loan Assn., Seattle, 1980—; cons. pub. and media relations; instr. TV tng. seminars; pres. Pub. Relations Round Table, Seattle, 1975. Mem. Pub. Relations Soc. Am. (dir. Seattle chpt. 1979-81), Internat. Assn. Bus. Communicators (award of merit). Republican. Roman Catholic. Author: The Christmas Tree Farm, 1980; Behind the Scenes in Radio, 1983; contbr. numerous articles on history, environ., travel, humor to various mags.; writer TV program: Boomerang Christmas Spl. (Nat. Acad. TV Arts and Scis. Emmy award 1977); author/designer Telephone Manners (named by Ragan Report one of 10 Best Publs. of 1982), 1982. Home: 6255 52d Ave NE Seattle WA 98115 Office: 1423 4th Ave Seattle WA 98101

HAWKINS, ROBERT LEE, social work adminstr.; b. Denver, Feb. 18, 1938; s. Isom and Bessie M. (Hugley) H.; A.A., Pueblo Jr. Coll., 1958; B.S., So. Colo. State Coll., 1965; M.S.W., U. Denver, 1967; m. Ann Sharon Hoy, Apr. 28, 1973; children—Robert, Jeanne, Julia, Rose. Psychiat. technician Colo. State Hosp., Pueblo, 1956-58, 1962-63, occupational therapist asst., 1964-65, clin. adminstr. psychiat. team, 1969-75, dir. community services, 1975—, supr. vol. services, 1975—, mem. budget com., 1975—; counselor (part-time) Family Service Agy., Pueblo, 1968-69, exec. dir., 1969-70; mem. faculty U. So. Colo., 1968-75; partner Human Resource Devel., Inc., 1970-75; mem. nursing adv. com. U. So. Calif., 1982—. Mem. Pueblo Positive Action Com., 1970; chmn. adv. bd. Pueblo Sangre de Cristo Day Care Center, 1969-72; chmn. Gov.'s So. Area Adv. Council of Employment Service, 1975-76; chmn. Pueblo's City CSC, 1976-77; mem. Colo. Juvenile Parole Bd., 1977; bd. dirs. Pueblo United Fund, 1969-74, pres., 1973; bd. dirs. Pueblo Community Orgn., 1974-76, Spanish Peaks Mental Health Center, 1976—, Neighborhood Health Center, 1977-79; mem. local bd. SSS, 1982—. Served with U.S. Army, 1958-62. Mem. Nat. Assn. Social Workers (nominating com. 1973-76), ACLU (dir. Pueblo chpt. 1980—), NAACP, Broadway Theatre Guild. Democrat. Methodist. Club: Kiwanis. Home: 520 Gaylord St Pueblo CO 81004 Office: 1600 W 24 St Pueblo CO 81003

HAWKINS, STEPHEN THOMAS, marketing executive; b. Milw., Oct. 21, 1949; s. Thomas Kenneth and Ursula Linnebelle (Hansen) H.; A.A., Pasadena City Coll., 1970; B.S., San Diego State U., 1972. TV/film producer The Prodn. Co., Sacramento, 1974-75; advt. agt. E.P. McGraw & Co., Santa Clara, Calif., 1975-77; sales mgr. Sunnyvale (Calif.) Cable TV, 1977-79; program mgr. Broadcast Div., Gillcable, San Jose, Calif., 1979-80; comml. mktg. exec. Falcon Cable TV, Alhambra, Calif., 1981—. Mem. Calif. Jr. C. of C. (asst. dir. mktg. and public relations 1980—), Pasadena Jr. C. of C. (v.p. community affairs), Cable TV Adminstrn. and Mktg. Republican. Episcoplian. Clubs: San Jose Advt., So. Calif. Cable. Editor handbook: Your Success Guide to Marketing and Public Relations, 1980. Office: 800 S Date Ave Alhambra CA 91803

HAWKINSON, DOROTHY ANN, social worker, human services program administrator; b. Renton, Wash., Aug. 20, 1951; d. Eric Virgil and Dorothy June H. Student U. Uppsala (Sweden), 1971; B.A. magna cum laude, U. Wash., 1973, M.S.W., 1975. Program coordinator nat. staff Nat. Assn. Social Workers, Washington, 1974-77; social work cons., Atlanta, 1977-78; lineman So. Bell Telephone Co., Douglasville, Ga., 1978-79; yard switchman Seabd. Coast Line R.R., Atlanta, 1979-80; referral agt. program coordinator/vol. tng. coordinator United Way Sacramento Area, 1981—; tech. adv. RENEWS (R.R. Employers New Employment Work Services) Assn. Recipient Citizen Scholar award Rotary Club, Kent, Wash., 1969. Mem. Nat. Assn. Social Workers (chairwoman Calif. chpt. block grant project), Am. Soc. Tng. and Devel., Phi Beta Kappa. Office: 331 J St Suite 204 PO Box 2036 Sacramento CA 95809

HAWLEY, CHARLES CALDWELL, geologist; b. Evansville, Ind., Oct. 23, 1929; s. William McKinley and Evelyn Barnes (Caldwell) H.; A.B., Hanover Coll., 1951; postgrad. U. Wis., 1951-52; Ph.D., U. Colo., 1963; m. Jenny Pearl Lind, July 28, 1951; children—David Lind, William Theodore, Andrew Bruce. Geologist, U.S. Geol. Survey, Denver, 1952-67, Menlo Park, Calif., 1967-69; cons. Anchorage, 1969; pres. C.C. Hawley & Assocs., Inc., Anchorage, from 1974, chmn. bd., 1981—; pres. Coronado Mining Corp., Anchorage, 1980—. Mem. adv. com. Fed.-State (Alaska) Land Use Planning Commn., 1975-79; dir. Citizens Mgmt. Alaska Lands, 1977-80; mem. State of Alaska d-2 Steering Council, 1977-78. NSF fellow, 1962-63; recipient U. Alaska mining award, 1979. Mem. Alaska Miners Assn. (exec. dir. 1976-79), Am. Mining Congress (Western bd. govs. 1979-83), AIME, Geol. Soc. Am. (fellow), Mineral. Soc. Am., Soc. Econ. Geologists, Canadian Inst. Mining and Metallurgists. Unitarian. Club: Petroleum. Contbr. articles to profl. jours. Home: PO Box 2048E Star Route A Anchorage AK 99507 Office: 8740 Hartzell Rd Anchorage AK 99507

HAWLEY, JENNY PEARL, resource company executive; b. Columbus, Ind., July 28, 1930; d. Asa B. and Ella B. (Line) Lind; m. Charles C. Hawley, July 28, 1951; children—David Lind, William Theodore, Andrew Bruce. A.B., Hanover Coll., 1951; postgrad. U. Colo., 1960; teaching cert. U. Denver, 1963. Vice pres. C.C. Hawley & Assocs., Inc., Anchorage, 1974—; exec. dir. Visual Arts Center of Alaska, Anchorage, 1975; exec. v.p. Citizen for Mgmt. of Alaska Lands, Anchorage, 1976; v.p. Coronado Mining Corp., Anchorage, 1980—, Hawley Resource Group, Inc., Anchorage, 1981—. Bd. dirs. State of Alaska Mining and Petroleum Extension Program, 1983—; bd. dirs. Anchorage Republican Women's Club, 1978-82; coordinator traveling exhibits Arctic Winter Games, 1972. Recipient Juror's Choice award All Alaska Juried Art Exhbn., Anchorage, 1977; State Art Council Purchase award, 1976, 77; Print-making award All Alaska Juried Art Exhbn., 1974, others. Mem. N.W. Miners Assn., Alaska Miners Assn., Anchorage C. of C., Anchorage Fine Arts Mus. Assn., Alaska Artists Guild (past pres.). Republican. Unitarian. Works in collection of State of Alaska Artbank, Anchorage Fine Arts Mus.; exhibited in Smithsonian Alaska Exhibition, 1978. Home: SRA Box 2048E Anchorage AK 99507 Office: 8740 Hartzell Rd Anchorage AK 99507

HAWLEY, JEROME CHADBOURN, agricultural business executive; b. Mpls., June 7, 1923; s. Robert and Marguerite (Chadbourn) H.; m. Bonnie Jean Jones, Sept. 13, 1947; children—Mitzi, Suzanne, Marguerite. B.S. in Metall. Engring., U. Minn., 1949. Exec. v.p. Berger Plate Co., San Francisco, 1950-58, exec. v.p. 1958-71, 76—; dir. mgr. Pacific Molasses Co., San Francisco, 1971-76. Served with U.S. Army, 1942-45. Decorated Bronze Star. Republican. Episcopalian. Clubs: Merchants Exchange (San Francisco), Univ. (Palo Alto). Home: 1073 Eden Bower Ln Redwood City CA 94061 Office: 350 Sansome St Suite 900 San Francisco 94104

HAWLEY, NOREEN ANDERSON, educational administrator, curriculum consultant; b. Burley, Idaho, May 6, 1937; d. Harold William and Thora (Whitaker) Anderson; m. Ronald Dale Hawley, Aug. 20, 1959; 1 dau., Natasha. Student Lewis and Clark Normal Sch., 1955-56, Idaho State U., 1956-57; B.S., U. Utah, 1963; M.S., No. Ariz. U., 1968; postgrad. U. Reno, 1979. Cert. tchr., Idaho, Utah, Nev.; cert. adminstr., Nev. Elem. tchr., Eden, Idaho, 1956-59, Idaho Falls, Idaho, 1959-61, Salt Lake City, 1961-62, Bountiful, Utah, 1962-64, Las Vegas, Nev., 1964-80; tchr. cons., 1980-81; elem. prin. Sunrise Acres Elem. Sch., Las Vegas, 1981—; curriculum writer Nev. State Dept. Edn.; curriculum writer, cons. Clark County Sch. Dist., Las Vegas. Pres. Pan Hellenic, Las Vegas, 1979-80. C. of C. scholar, 1955-56. Mem. Assn. Supervision and Curriculum Devel., Nev. Assn. Sch. Adminstrs., Phi Delta Kappa. Democrat. Mormon. Home: 3875 Hoopa Ln Las Vegas NV 89109 Office: 2501 Sunrise Ave Las Vegas NV 89101

HAWLEY, PHILIP METSCHAN, retail exec.; b. Portland, Oreg., July 29, 1925; s. Willard P. and Dorothy (Metschan) H.; B.S., U. Calif., Berkeley, 1946; postgrad. Advanced Mgmt. Sch. Bus., Harvard U., 1967; m. Mary Catherine Follen, May 31, 1947; children—Diane (Mrs. Robert Bruce Johnson), Willard, Philip Metschan, Jr., John, Victor, Edward, Erin, George. Pres., chief exec. officer, dir. Carter Hawley Hale Stores, Inc., Los Angeles; dir. AT&T, Atlantic Richfield Co., BankAmerica Corp., Walt Disney Prodns., The Economist. Mem. vis. com. Harvard U. Grad. Sch. Bus. Adminstrn., UCLA Grad. Sch. Mgmt.; trustee Aspen Inst., Brookings Instn., Com. Econ. Devel., Conf. Bd., Urban Inst., Huntington Library and Art Gallery, Calif. Inst. Tech., U. Notre Dame; vice-chmn. Bus. Council; mem. Bus. Roundtable, chmn. Los Angeles Energy Conservation Com., 1973-74. Served to ensign USNR, 1944-46. Named Calif. Industrialist of Yr., Calif. Mus. Sci. and Industry, 1975; recipient award of Merit, Los Angeles Jaycees, 1974; Coro Pub. Affairs award, 1978; decorated hon. comdr. Order of Brit. Empire; knight comdr. Star of Solidarity (Italy). Mem. Phi Beta Kappa, Beta Gamma Sigma, Beta Alpha Psi. Clubs: California, Los Angeles Country (Los Angeles); Bohemian, Pacific Union (San Francisco); Newport Harbor Yacht (Newport Beach, Calif.); Multnomah (Portland, Oreg.); Links (N.Y.C.). Office: 550 S Flower St Los Angeles CA 90071

HAWLEY, ROBERT CROSS, lawyer; b. Douglas, Wyo., Aug. 7, 1920; s. Robert Daniel and Elsie Corienne (Cross) H.; m. Mary Elizabeth Hawley McClellan, Mar. 3, 1944; children—Robert Cross, Mary Virginia, Laurie McClellan. B.A. with honors, U. Colo., 1943; LL.B., Harvard U., 1949. Assoc. barrister Weller & Friedrich, Denver, 1949-50; sr. atty. Continental Oil Co., Denver, 1952-58, counsel, Houston, 1959-62; ptnr., v.p. Ireland, Stapleton & Pryor, Denver, 1962-81; ptnr. Dechert Price and Rhoads, Denver, 1981—; pres. Highland Minerals, Denver; dir. Yorker Mfg., Denver, Bank of Denver, Calvin Exploration, Denver. Contbr. articles to Oil & Gas Bd. dirs. Am. Cancer Soc., Denver. Recipient Alumni Recognition award U. Colo., Boulder, 1958, Meritorious Service award Monticello Coll., Godfrey, Ill., 1967; Sigma Alpha Epsilon scholar, 1941-43. Mem. Denver Assn. Oil and Gas Title Lawyers (pres. 1983—), Denver Petroleum Club (pres. 1978-79), Harvard Law Sch. Assn. Colo. (pres. 1980-81), Associated Alumni U. Colo. (pres. and bd. dirs. 1956-57) ABA, Colo. Bar Assn., Denver Bar Assn., Tex. Bar Assn., Wyo. Bar Assn., Fed. Energy Bar Assn., Chevaliers du Tastevin. Republican. Episcopalian. Clubs: Denver Country, Univ. (Denver); Colo. Arlberg (Winter Park). Office: Dechert Price & Rhoads 999 18th St Suite 1601 Denver CO 80202

HAWLEY, RONALD DALE, principal; b. Twin Falls, Idaho, Feb. 5, 1934; married, 1 child. B.S. in Psychology, U. Utah, 1963, M.S. in Ednl. Adminstrn., 1964; Ed.D. in Ednl. Adminstrn., U. So. Calif., 1974. Coordinator profl. growth Clark County (Nev.) Sch. Dist., Las Vegas, 1967-68, asst. dir. instructional services, 1968, asst. dir. ednl. TV services, 1968-69, dir. TV services, gen. mgr. channel 10, 1969-81, exec. adminstrv. asst., 1981-82, prin. Madison 6th Grade Center, 1982—; advisor Friends of Channel 10, 1971—; dir. Pacific Mountain Network. Bd. dirs. St. Jude's Ranch Children, 1972-75; mem. adv. bd. Meadows Playhouse. Mem. Nev., Clark County, Am. assns. sch. adminstrs., Nat. Broadcasters Assn., Phi Delta Kappa. Office: 1030 N J St Las Vegas NV 89106

HAWORTH, DENNIS ALLEN, interior designer; b. Sacramento, Feb. 2, 1944; s. Gilbert and Frances Louise Haworth. Student Sacramento City Coll. 1962-63; grad. Rudolph Schaeffer Sch. Interior Design and Color, 1967. Interior designer Wendel Norris & Assocs., Reno, 1973-74; prin. Dennis Haworth & Assocs., Sacramento, 1974—. Mem. Crocker

Art Mus. Recipient Outstanding and Devoted Service Cert. No. Calif. chpt. Am. Soc. Interior Designers, 1975, Presdl. Citation, 1981. Mem. Am. Soc. Interior Designers, (dir. No. Calif. chpt. 1973—, edn. chmn., nat. chmn. student affairs 1980-82). Clubs: El Rancho Racket & Resort (Sacramento). Contbr. design work to publs. in interior design. Home: 944 44th St Sacramento CA 95819 Office: Dennis Haworth Assocs Box 19195 944 44th St Sacramento CA 95819

HAWS, HALE L., physician, ins. co. exec.; b. Anaheim, Calif., June 15, 1923; s. Lloyd A. and Nancy J. (Hale) H.; B.A., Pepperdine U., 1947; M.D., UCLA, 1958; m. Joan Penn, Sept. 5, 1946; children—Kathleen, Jay B., Jerald L. Intern, Gorgas Hosp., C.Z., mem. house staff, 1958-59; physician Pepperdine U. Student Health, also pvt. practice medicine specializing in gen. medicine, Los Angeles, 1959-60; med. dir. Chrysler Corp., Los Angeles, 1960-71; physician and surgeon Calif. Dept. Corrections, Los Angeles, 1961-75; v.p. med. services Pacific Mut. Life Ins. Co., Newport Beach, Calif., 1962-81; dir. Best Life Assurance Co., Newport Beach, Calif., 1981—, also dir.; cons. med. dir., 1982—; med. adviser to state dir. Calif. Selective Service, 1970-75; mem. med. adv. bd. Equifax Services, Inc., Atlanta, 1977—. Served with USN, 1942-46; PTO. Recipient U.S. Presdl. cert. of appreciation, 1975; diplomate Am. Bd. Preventive Medicine, Bd. Life Ins. Medicine. Fellow Am. Coll. Preventive Medicine, Am. Geriatrics Soc., Am. Coll. Angiology, Am. Occupational Med. Assn.; mem. AMA, Assn. Life Ins. Med. Dirs. Am., Am. Council Life Ins., Pepperdine U. Alumni Assn. (dir. 1968-70). Mem. Ch. of Christ. Office: 4201 Birch St Newport Beach CA 92660

HAWS, JULIE, accountant; b. Provo, Utah, May 1, 1952; d. Grant H. and Nelda (Cowan) H. B.S. in Acctg., Brigham Young U., 1976. C.P.A., Idaho. Staff acct. Rudd, DaBell & Hill, C.P.A.s, Rexburg, Idaho, 1976-79; staff acct. Draney & Wells C.P.A.s, Idaho Falls, Idaho, 1979-81, ptnr., 1981—. Mem. Idaho Soc. C.P.A.s, Am. Inst. C.P.A.s, Women's Soc. C.P.A.s. Mormon. Home: PO Box 142 Rexburg ID 83440 Office: Draney Wells & Haws CPAs PO Box 499 185 S Capital St Idaho Falls ID 83402

HAWS, ROBERT DUNN, airline exec.; b. Stamford, Conn., Oct. 30, 1932; s. Henry Ernst and Gabriella Spooner (Dunn) H.; B.A., Yale U., 1954; m. Frances Bailey Pryor, Mar. 12, 1955; children—Robin Frazier, George Allderdice, Cynthia Spooner. Account exec. Hill & Knowlton, Inc., N.Y.C., 1958-62; v.p., treas. Sea Life, Inc., Honolulu, 1962-69; pres., chief exec. officer Royal Hawaiian Airways, Inc., Honolulu, 1969—; dir. Hana Ranch, Inc., 1972—. Served with USN, 1954-58. Mem. Commuter Airline Assn. Am. (vice-chmn. 1977-80). Clubs: Kaneohe Yacht (commodore 1983); Storm Trysail (N.Y.C.). Office: Royal Hawaiian Air Service 3000 Honolulu Internat Airport Honolulu HI 96819

HAWTHORNE, HOWARD ALLISON, health physicist, environmental scientist; b. Stettler, Alta., Can., Nov. 19, 1922; s. Wilmer Glenn and Perle Annie (Spicer) H.; m. Mary Lois Crow, Jan. 7, 1947; children—Sarah, David; m. Nancy Lee Willcox, Aug. 17, 1973; stepchildren—Glen, Alan, Leanna. B.S., U. Calif.-Berkeley, 1949; Ph.D., U. Calif.-Davis, 1956. Cert. profl. soil scientist, 1979. Jr. research soil scientist UCLA, 1956-57, asst. research soil scientist, 1958-72; sr. environ. scientist GE-TEMPO, Sanata Barbara, Calif., 1973-79; sr. health physicist Reynolds Elec. Engring. Co., Las Vegas, 1980-82; research prof. pharmacology U. Utah, Salt Lake City, 1983—. Served to lt. USAAF, 1943-46. Decorated D.F.C. Office: Bldg 351 U Utah Salt Lake City UT 89112

HAWTHORNE, ROWLAND OLIVER, III, furniture executive; b. Anderson, S.C., Sept. 21, 1938; s. Rowland Oliver and Mildred Eastler (McCurdy) H.; m. Nancy Suber, July 8, 1961; children—Miles Brewton, Anna Elizabeth. A.B., Erskine Coll., Due West, S.C., 1960. Asst. to pres. Tomlinson Furniture, High Point, N.C., 1964-65, rep., Dallas, 1965-68; pres. Rowland Hawthorne & Co. Inc., Denver, 1969—. Warden, St. John's Cathedral, Denver, 1980—. Served to lt. j.g. USN, 1960-63. Mem. Internat. Home Furnishings Reps. Assn. Clubs: University (Denver and Salt Lake City); Met. Denver Exec. (pres. 1982-83), Rotary. Home: 380 Marion St Denver CO 80218 Office: 727 E 16th Ave Denver CO 80203

HAY, JOHN LEONARD, lawyer; b. Lawrence, Mass., Oct. 6, 1940; s. Charles Cable and Henrietta Dudley (Wise) H.; A.B. with distinction, Stanford, 1961; J.D., U. Colo., 1964; m. Millicent Victoria Gunnells, Dec. 16, 1967; 1 son, Ian Daniel. Bar: Colo. 1964, Ariz. 1965, D.C. 1971. Practice, Phoenix, 1965—; assoc. Lewis & Roca, Phoenix, 1964-69, ptnr., 1969-82; ptnr. Fannin, Terry & Hay, 1982—. Regional chmn. Stanford U. Ann. Fund, 71-74; bd. dirs. Community Legal Services, 1983; legis. dist. chmn. Democratic party Ariz., 1971-74, precinct and state committeeman, 1966-78. Mem. Am. (dir. 1972-78), Ariz. (dir., pres. 1973-77, Disting. Citizen award 1979), civil liberties unions, Maricopa County Bar Assn. (dir.). Home: 201 E Hayward Ave Phoenix AZ 85020 Office: 100 W Washington St Suite 1465 Phoenix AZ 85003

HAY, JOHN WOODS, JR., banker; b. Rock Springs, Wyo., Apr. 23, 1905; s. John Woods and Mary Ann (Blair) H.; A.B., U. Mich., 1927; m. Frances B. Smith, Dec. 28, 1948; children—Helen Mary, John Woods III, Keith Norbert, Joseph Garrett. Pres., dir. Rock Springs Nat. Bank, 1947—, Rock Springs Grazing Assn., 1939—, Blair & Hay Land & Livestock Co., Rock Springs, 1949—. Trustee, v.p. William H. and Carrie Gottsche Found. Mem. Sigma Alpha Epsilon. Republican. Episcopalian. Clubs: Masons, Shriners, Jesters, Rotary. Home: 502 B St Rock Springs WY 82901 Office: 333 Broadway Rock Springs WY 82901

HAYDEN, KATHY ANN, counseling psychologist, educator; b. Chgo., June 13, 1955; d. Gaylord Jack and Mabel Thomina (Backstrom) H. B.A. cum laude, North Park Coll., 1978; M.S., George Williams Coll., 1981. Resident advisor North Park Coll., Chgo., 1976-78; counselor Wholistic Health Ctr., Woodridge, Ill., 1980-81; psychiat. asst., interpreter hearing impaired team Forest Hosp., Des Plaines, Ill., 1979-81; aftercare coordinator, counselor Comprehensive Alcohol Program, Nome, Alaska, 1981; clinician Norton Sound Family Services, Nome, 1981—; part time faculty N.W. Community Coll.; condr. workshops in field; supr., trainer paraprofl. staff; chmn. Bering Straits Human Service Council. Bd. dirs. Bering Straits Treatment Ctr. Mem. Am. Personnel and Guidance Assn., Nat. Forensic League, Nat. Honor Soc. Home: Box 820 Nome AK 99762 Office: Box 966 Nome AK 99762

HAYDEN, NEIL STEVEN, newspaper publisher; b. Bronx, N.Y., May 23, 1937; s. Aaron Alvin and Selma (Turtletaub) H.; m. Elaine Charlotte Lawson, July 3, 1960 (div. 1975); children—Stephanie, Jennifer, Aaron Alexander II; m. 2d Carolyn Sue Smith, May 8, 1975; 1 stepson, Michael Sean. Student U. Fla., 1955-58, U. Miami, 1958. Mem. copy staff Miami (Fla.) Herald, 1958; reporter Albany (Ga.) Herald, 1959, Hickory (N.C.) Daily Record, 1959-60; editor Jackson Herald, Jefferson, Ga., 1960-62; editor, pub. Hartwell (Ga.) Sun, also pres. Sun, Inc., 1962-67; pub. Athens (Ga.) Banner-Herald, also Daily News, 1967-72; pres., pub. Huntington (W.Va.) Herald-Dispatch and Huntington Advertiser, 1972-76; pres., pub. Salem (Oreg.) Statesman and Capital Jour., 1976-79; pres., pub. Courier-Post, Cherry Hill, N.J., 1979-80, The Bull., Phila., 1980-82; pres., chief operating officer Los Angeles Herald Examiner, 1982—; mem. bus. adv. com. Nat. Alliance Businessmen, 1972—. Bd. dirs. Huntington-Cabell County chpt. ARC, 1972-74, Huntington Galleries, 1973-76, Cammack Children's Ctr., 1973-76, Stella Fuller Settlement, 1973-76, Marion-Polk (Salem) United Way, 1976—, Mission Hill Mus., 1976—, Salem Boys Club, 1976—, Salem Symphony Soc., 1976—, Salem YMCA, 1978—, Oreg. Symphony, 1978—, World Affairs Council, Phila., 1970—, Police Athletic League, 1980—, Phila. Orch. Council, 1979—, United Way Camden County, 1979—; exec. bd. Tri-State area council Boy Scouts Am., 1972-76, pres., 1975-76, exec. bd. Camden County council, 1979; mem. adv. com. Huntington YWCA, 1975-76; adv. bd. Haddonfield Symphony Soc., 1979—. Recipient numerous nat. and state journalism awards, 1961—; Outstanding Young Man of Yr. award Huntington Jaycees, 1972. Mem. Am. Newspapers Pubs. Assn. (prodn. mgmt. com. 1975—), Oreg. Newspaper Pubs. Assn., Pa. Newspaper Pubs. Assn., N.J. Press Assn. (prodn. com. 1980), Nat. Newspaper Assn. (rep. to Am. Council Edn. for Journalism, edn. com. 1977-78), Am. Soc. Newspaper Editors (bull. com. 1976-77, freedom of info. com. 1977-78), South Jersey C. of C. (bd. dirs. 1979—), Women in Communications, Inc., Cherry Hill C. of C. (bd. dirs. 1980—), N.J. State C. of C., N.J. Press Assn., Sigma Delta Chi (mem. undergrad. liaison com. Atlanta chpt. 1968-69, pres. N.E. Ga. chpt. 1969-70, regional dep. dir. 1970). Office: Herald Examiner 1111 S Broadway Los Angeles CA 90015*

HAYES, EDWARD CARY, II, political science educator, consultant; b. Chgo., Dec. 28, 1937; s. Edward Bean and Helen Hammersley (Walker) H. B.A. magna cum laude in Politics and Econ., Swarthmore, 1960; M.A. in Polit. Sci., U. Calif., 1962, Ph.D. with distinction, 1968. Post-doctoral Fellow in Urban Studies and Sociology U. Chgo, 1968-69; asst. prof. polit. sci. U. Wis.-Milw., 1969-72; asst. prof. govt. Ohio U., Athens, 1972-76; dir. small bus. devel. Columbus (Ohio) Catholic Archdiocese, 1976-78; mgr., grants writer fed. job tng. programs ACCESS Corp. San Diego, 1979-82; pres. Metro Assocs., San Diego, 1982—; asst. prof. urban adminstrn. San Diego State U., 1980. Scott Found. fellow, 1958; Ford Found. research fellow, 1959; NSF grantee, 1970-72; Fulbright-Hays sr. scholars fellow (alt.), 1974; Ohio Program in Humanities grantee, 1978. Mem. Am. Polit. Sci. Assn., Internat. Polit. Sci. Assn., Mcpl. Mgmt. Assts. So. Calif., Navy League, Mensa, Republican. Author: Power Politics and Urban Policy, 1972. Home and office: 11112 Polaris Dr San Diego CA 92126

HAYES, ERNEST M., podiatrist; b. New Orleans, Jan. 21, 1946; s. Ernest M. and Emma Hayes; B.A., Calif. State U., Sacramento, 1969; B.S., Calif. Coll. Podiatric Medicine, San Francisco, 1971, D.P.M., 1973; m. Bonnie Ruth Beigle, Oct. 16, 1970. Resident in surg. podiatry Beach Community Hosp., Buena Park, Calif., 1973-74, dir. residency program, 1974-75; practice podiatry, Anaheim, Calif., 1974, Yreka, Calif., 1980—; sr. clin. instr. So. Calif. Podiatric Med. Center, Los Angeles, 1975-78; vice chmn. podiatry dept. Good Samaritain Hosp., Anaheim, Calif., 1978-79. Bd. dirs. Little Bogus Ranches Home Owners Assn., 1981-83, pres., 1983—. Baptist. Club: Kiwanis. Home: PO Box 958 Yreka CA 96097 Office: 519 4th St Yreka CA 96097

HAYES, FORREST L., counselor, consultant, lecturer; b. Tuscaloosa, Ala., Nov. 4, 1930; s. Luther L. and Aimee E. (Collins) H.; m. Moniree V. Heron, Jan. 13, 1951; children—Chris, Pamela, Marla. Student U. Alaska, 1965-69; B.A. in Sociology, U. Tampa, 1971; M.A. in Ednl. Counseling, U. Alaska, 1975; Ph.D. in Human Behavior, U.S. Internat. U., 1979. Diplomate Internat. Acad. Profl. Counselors and Psychologists. Tchr., counselor Dept. Edn., U.S. Air Force, State of Alaska, 1950-72; counselor, test control officer, Anchorage and Fairbanks, Alaska, 1973-78; counselor, student services coordinator U. Alaska, Matanuska-Susitna Community Coll., Palmer, 1978—. Sec. supervisory com. Alaska U.S.A. Fed. Credit Union; deacon Anchorage Evangelical Free Ch. Recipient Outstanding Unit award, combat ready badge. Mem. Am. Psychol. Assn., Internat. Acad. Profl. Counselors and Psychotherapists, Inc., Am. Personnel and Guidance Assn. Club: Masons. Editor Mat-Su Monitor; contbr. articles to profl. jours. Home: 4711 Pavalof St Anchorage AK 99507 Office: U Alaska PO Box 899 Palmer AK 99645

HAYES, JAMES EDWARD, engineer, environment specialist; b. Pitts., Oct. 15, 1946; s. Edward Porter and Marie Antoinette H.; B.S., Old Dominion U., 1976. Design engr. electric boat div. Gen. Dynamics Corp., Groton, Conn., 1976-78, Newport News Shipbldg. Co. (Va.), 1978-79; nuclear engr. Omaha Public Power Dist., 1979-80; mech. engr. TVA, Chattanooga, 1981—, environment specialist Nev. Power Co., Las Vegas, 1981—. Vol. ARC, Omaha. Served with USN, 1968-74. Mem. Am. Meteorol. Soc., Am. Nuclear Soc., Air Pollution Control Assn., Western Energy Supply and Transmission Assn. (mem. air and water quality task force), Edison Electric Inst. (energy and environment com.), Mensa, VFW. Roman Catholic. Club: Nat. Mgmt. Developer acoustic valve leak detector, 1977; designer installing advanced radwaste solidification system, 1980. Home: 1900 E Tropicana Apt 103 Las Vegas NV 89109 Office: Nev Power Co PO Box 230 Las Vegas NV 89151

HAYES, JANAN MARY, chemist; b. Los Angeles, Dec. 10, 1942; d. Paul Louis and Doris (Albright) Hayes; B.S., Oreg. State U., 1964, M.S., 1965; Ph.D., Brigham Young U., 1971. High sch. chemistry and gen. sci. tchr. Fortuna (Calif.) Union High Sch., 1965-67; mem. chemistry faculty Am. River Coll., Sacramento, 1971-79, 80-81; asst. dean sci. and agr. Cosumnes River Coll., Sacramento, 1981—; asso. prof. Calif. State U., Sacramento, 1978-79; cons. Sumar Corp., Foster City, Calif., 1975—; chemist, 1979-80; bd. dirs. Calif. Engring. Found. Bd. dirs. Sacramento Sci. Center and Jr. Mus., 1982—. NSF sci. faculty devel. grantee, 1979-80; NSF Local Assessment of Sci. Edn. grantee, 1978-79. Mem. Am. Chem. Soc. (councilor), Calif. Assn. Chemistry Tchrs. (past pres., dir.), Sigma Xi, Phi Kappa Phi. Delta Sigma Rho, Kappa Delta Pi. Mormon. Contbr. articles profl. jours. Office: Cosumnes River College 8401 Center Pkwy Sacramento CA 95823

HAYES, JANET GRAY, former mayor; b. Rushville, Ind., July 12, 1926; d. John Paul and Lucile (Gray) Frazee; A.B., Ind. U., 1948; M.A., U. Chgo., 1950; m. Kenneth Hayes, Mar. 20, 1950; children—Lindy, John, Katherine, Megan. Mem. San Jose City Council, 1971-82, chmn. Redevel. Agy., 1970-71, chairperson legis. com., vice-mayor San Jose, 1973-74, mayor, 1975-82. Chairperson Santa Clara County (Calif.) Sanitation Dist. 2, Urban Devel. Adv. Com., Gov.'s Task Force on Environ. Goals and Planning, San Jose Redevel. Agy.; mem. Inter-City Council; mem. Santa Clara County Sanitation Dist. 3, Fed. EPA Aircraft/Airport Noise Task Group, Santa Clara Valley Employment and Tng. Bd.; mem. adv. bd. San Jose/Santa Clara Treatment Plant; mem. mayors adv. com. Nat. Council for Econ. Devel.; mem. Calif. Joint Commn. on Fair Judicial Practices, Legis. Action Subcom. on Revenue Sharing and Related Econ. Matters; bd. dirs. Calif. Center Research and Edn. in Govt.; mem. Nat. Democratic Campaign Com., Calif. Dem. Commn. Nat. Platform and Policy. Recipient Woman of Achievement award San Jose Mercury and News, 1975, Community Service award NCCJ, 1980. Mem. Assn. Bay Area Govts. (mem. exec. com., mem. environ. mgmt. task force), League Calif. Cities (dir., chairperson resolutions com.), U.S. Conf. Mayors (mem. resolutions com., mayor's task force on income security, vice chairperson com. urban econs.), AAUW (edn. found. grantee). Democrat. Club: Century. Home: 1155 Emory St San Jose CA 95126

HAYES, JOE LYNN, civil engr., state legislator; b. Bakersfield, Mo., Feb. 18, 1930; s. Norman and Dicy (Cotter) H.; B.S. in Civil Engring., U. Wash., 1955; M.S. in Engring. Mgmt., U. Alaska, 1966; m. Diane Marie Kroesing, Dec. 31, 1977; children by previous marriage—Debra Colleen, Karin Lynn, Laura Beth. Office engr. Cheney Constrn. Co., Anchorage, 1953-57, project engr., 1957-58; engr., dir. pub. works Spenard Pub. Utility Dist., Anchorage, 1959; asso. Tryck, Nyman & Assos. (now Tryck, Nyman & Hayes), Cons. Engrs., 1959-61, partner, 1961-75; pres., dir. Tryck, Nyman & Hayes, Inc., Honolulu, 1971-75; v.p. Borough-City Devel., Inc. v.p., dir. Air Photo Tech., Inc., Anchorage; certified fallout shelter analyst; instr. Anchorage Community Coll., 1961-63. Vice-chmn., mem. Greater Anchorage Platting Bd., 1959-65; judge Greater Anchorage Sci. Fair, 1967-68; mem. Alaska Ho. of Reps., 1977—, minority leader, 1979—, speaker house, 1981—. Registered profl. engr., Alaska, Hawaii, Ariz.; registered profl. land surveyor, Alaska, Ariz. Mem. Greater Anchorage C. of C., Am. Soc. C.E. (pres., dir., 1966—), Am. Congress on Surveying and Mapping, Nat. Soc. Profl. Engrs., Am. Soc. Photogrammetry, Aircraft Owners and Pilots Assn., Alaska Soc. Profl. Engrs. Republican. Lutheran. Home: 9710 Arlene Dr Anchorage AK 99502 Office: 515 D St Suite 201 Anchorage AK 99501

HAYES, LAURA MORGAN, art gallery owner; b. Birmingham, Ala., Nov. 28, 1927; d. Edward Walter Morgan and Ruth Elizabeth Dollar; m. Thomas Grafton Hayes, July 30, 1947; 1 son, Dwight Winston. Head photographic sect. Wyoming state archives, hist. dept., 1965-74; art registrar, 1969-71; curator, art, 1971-79; owner, Wild Goose Gallery, and part-owner, Two Bar H Gallery. Bd. dirs. Cheyenne Frontier Days, Old West Mus. (sec.). Mem. Wyoming Press Women, Nat. Federal Press Women, Wyoming Artists Assn., Quota Club Internat. Republican. Methodist. Home: 2608 E Riding Club Rd Cheyenne WY 82009 Office: 1604 Capitol Ave Suite 521 Cheyenne Wyoming 82001

HAYES, MARY ESHBAUGH, newspaper editor; b. Rochester, N.Y., Sept. 27, 1928; d. William Paul and Eleanor Maude (Seivert) Eshbaugh; B.A. in English and Journalism, Syracuse (N.Y.) U., 1950; m. James Leon Hayes, Apr. 18, 1953; children—Pauli, Eli, Lauri Le June, Clayton, Merri Jess. With Livingston County Republican, Geneseo, N.Y., summers, 1947-50, mng. editor, 1949-50; reporter Aurora (Colo.) Advocate, 1950-52; reporter-photographer Aspen (Colo.) Times, 1952-53, columnist, 1956—, reporter, 1972-77, assoc. editor, 1977—; tchr. Colo. Mountain Coll., 1979. Mem. Nat. Fedn. Press Women (1st prizes in writing and editing 1976-80), Colo. Press Women's Assn. (writing award 1974, 75, 78-80, sweepstakes award for writing 1976, 77, 78). Mem. Aspen Community Ch. Photographer, editor: Aspen Potpourri, 1968. Home: PO Box 497 Aspen CO 81611 Office: Box E Aspen CO 81611

HAYES, PHILIP LOUIS, financial consulting firm executive; b. Watertown, N.Y., Sept. 30, 1934; s. Louis Neville and Lorene (Kerr) H.; B.S. cum laude, Syracuse U., 1960, M.B.A., 1962; m. Catherine M. Sears, June 5, 1955. Dist. credit supr. Eastman Kodak Co., Rochester, N.Y., 1962-64; sr. fin. analyst Indsl. Indemnity Co., San Francisco, 1964-66, asst. mgr. fin. analysis, 1967, mgr. fin. analysis, 1968-71, asst. treas., 1971-74, asst. v.p., asst. treas., 1974-76, v.p., asst. treas., 1976-82; pres. Hayes and Assocs. Fin. Cons., 1982—. Chmn. grad. alumni ann. giving campaign Syracuse U. Sch. Mgmt., 1978; bd. dirs., treas. Marin County Republican party, 1973-76. Served with USCGR, 1952-56. Mem. Ins. Acctg. and Statis. Assn., Syracuse U. Alumni Assn. (nat. bd. dirs.), Belvedere Sailing Soc., San Francisco Mus. Modern Art, M.H. de Young Meml. Mus., San Francisco Symphony Assn., Marin Symphony Assn., Beta Gamma Sigma (chpt. v.p. 1961), Phi Kappa Phi (chpt. v.p. 1960), Alpha Kappa Psi (chpt. social chmn. 1960). Clubs: Syracuse U. San Francisco Bay Area Alumni (pres. 1967-77); Tiburon Penninsula Tennis and Swim; San Francisco Engrs., Commonwealth of Calif. (San Francisco); Scott Valley Tennis and Swim; San Francisco Rotary. Home and office: 104 Sugarloaf Dr Tiburon CA 94920

HAYES, SHIRLEY J., business educator-coordinator; b. Hamburg, Iowa, Nov. 19, 1947; d. Roy Lee and Helen Irene (Tharp) Savage; m. William S. Hayes, Dec. 12, 1969. A.A. in Bus., Mo. Western State U., 1967; B.S. in Bus., Northwest Mo. State U., 1969; postgrad. U. Colo., 1969-71, U. No. Colo., 1972-74, Colo. State U., 1975—. Cert. tchr., vocat. tchr., Colo. Tchr. bus., Denver West, 1969-78, Street Acad., Denver, 1978-79, Manual High Sch., Denver, 1979-80; bus. and office tchr.-coordinator, sponsor Future Bus. Leaders Am., Denver and Montbello, Colo., 1980—. Pres. steering com. Colo. Women's Retriever Club, charter mem., 1980, pres., 1980-82, field trial judge, 1982, field trial chmn., 1983, cons. judge's selection com., ex-officio bd. dirs., 1983; active Rocky Mountain Retriever Club, field trial judge, 1978, 81, field trial sec., 1983, nom. pres. 1983-84; active Ft. Collins Retriever Club, sanctioned trial judge, 1977. Bus./Profl. Women grantee 1965-69; Northwest Mo. State U. grantee 1969. Mem. Am. Vocat. Assn., Nat. Bus. Edn. Assn., Colo. Vocat. Assn., Educators for/about Bus. Home: 4589 Freeport Way Denver CO 80239 Office: 900 Grant St Denver CO 80231

HAYES, WILLIAM FREDERICK, former library adminstrator; b. Brazil, Ind., Dec. 25, 1931; s. Robert William and Viola Elizabeth (Cress) H.; B.A., Ft. Hays (Kans.) State Coll., 1962; M.A., U. Denver, 1963; m. Christine Johnson, June 23, 1955; children—Sheri Lyn, Mark Alvin. Head of tech. processes Kokomo (Ind.) Pub. Library, 1963-65, asst. dir., 1965-66; dir. Boise (Idaho) Pub. Library, 1966-83. Exec. dir. Miss Idaho Pageant, 1973; pres. Collegiate Young Democrats, 1961. Served with AUS, 1949-52, 55-59. Mem. ALA, Pacific N.W. Library Assn. (pres. 1980-81), Idaho Library Assn. Contbr. articles to profl. publs. Home: 7271 Cascade Dr Boise ID 83704

HAYES, WILLIAM RUPERT, JR., distbg. co. exec.; b. Los Angeles, Sept. 19, 1943; s. William Rupert and Gertrude W. Hayes; student public schs.; Verdugo Hills, Calif.; m. Irene Yoshiko Fujimoto Fukui, June 25, 1983; children from previous marriage—William Rupert, Robin Lynn. Pres., Hayes Bolt & Supply, Inc., San Diego, also Hawaii Nut & Bolt, Inc., Honolulu; v.p., sec. We Supply Hawaii, Inc., Honolulu. Mem. S.W. Fastener Assn., Western Assn. Fastener Distributors, Hawaii C. of C., San Diego C. of C. Club: Propeller of U.S. Office: 2298-C Alahao Pl Honolulu HI 96819

HAYNER, JEANNETTE CLARE, state senator; b. Portland, Oreg., Jan. 22, 1919; d. Samuel and Bertha (Gugisberg) H.; B.A., U. Oreg., 1940, J.D., 1942; m. H. H. Hayner, Oct. 24, 1942; children—Stephen J., James K., Judith A. Admitted to Oreg. bar, 1942; legal staff Bonneville Power, Portland, 1943-46; dir. Standard Ins. Co., Portland, 1974—; mem. Wash. State Ho. of Reps., 1972-76, mem. judiciary, edn. and transp. and utilities coms.; mem. Wash. State Senate, 1977—, majority leader, 1981—. Mem. Sch. Bd. Walla Walla (Wash.), 1956-63, chmn., 1960-62; Walla Walla County Republican state committeewoman, 1969-72; bd. dirs. YWCA, 1968-72; dist. chmn. White House Conf. on Children and Youth, 1970; chmn. Mental Health Bd. Walla Walla County, 1970-72; mem. Walla Walla Youth and Family Services Adv. Bd., 1968-72; mem. Wash. Council on Crime and Delinquency, 1970-73; bd. dirs. Walla Walla Meals on Wheels, 1970-74; mem. Bonneville Power regional adv. council, 1970-76; mem. Organized Crime Intelligence Adv. Bd. State of Wash., 1972-80. Recipient award of Merit, Walla Walla C. of C., 1970. Mem. Oreg. Bar Assn., Delta Kappa Gamma. Address: PO Box 454 Walla Walla WA 99362

HAYNES, HAROLD WALTER, aircraft manufacturing company executive; b. Snoqualmie, Wash., Jan. 23, 1923; s. Ralph and Bertha (Sewell) H.; B.A., U. Wash., 1948; m. Barbara J. Tatham, Oct. 11, 1943; children—Christine, Steven, Kevin. With Touche, Ross, Bailey & Smart, C.P.A.'s, Seattle, 1948-54, Boeing Co., Seattle, 1954—, v.p. finance, 1960-70, sr. v.p. finance, 1970-75, exec. v.p., chief finance officer, 1975—, also dir.; dir. First Interstate Bank of Wash., Itel Corp., Safeco. Served as pilot USMCR, 1942-45. C.P.A., Wash. Mem. Financial Execs. Inst.

Home: Highlands Seattle WA 98177 Office: PO Box 3707 10-14 Seattle WA 98124

HAYNES, WILLIAM ERNEST, lawyer, financial consultant, educator; b. Peoria, Ill., Aug. 22, 1936; s. Clarence Ernest and Lucille Ann Haynes; m. Willette Lancia Rothschild, Dec. 2, 1972; children—Lancia Ann, Sharon Elizabeth. B.A. in Fin., Loras Coll., DuBuque, Iowa, 1959; J.D., Marquette U., Milw., 1964; M.B.A. in Bus. Econs., Loyola U., Chgo., 1969. Bar: Wis. 1964, Ill. 1965, Calif. 1970. Corp. counsel Gen. Fin. Co., Evanston, Ill., 1964-69; asst. controller Internat. tax Wells Fargo Bank, San Francisco, 1969-76; tax counsel Kaiser Aluminum and Chem. Corp., Oakland, Calif., 1976-79; prin. Law Offices of William E. Haynes and Assocs., San Francisco, 1979—, prin. The Gryphon Group, San Francisco; prof. taxation, adj. faculty, McLaren Coll. of Bus., U. San Francisco; lectr. on law, taxation and fin. Served with U.S. Army, 1959-61. Mem. ABA, Calif. Bar Assn., Am. Econs. Assn., San Francisco Internat. Tax Group, Internat. Assn. Fin. Planners, Calif. Hist. Soc., San Francisco Mus. Soc., World Affairs Council. Republican. Roman Catholic. Club: Rotary. Office: Suite 1430 Alcoa Bldg One Maritime Plaza San Francisco CA 94111

HAYS, DONALD GRANT, educator; b. San Bernardino, Calif., Aug. 29, 1928; s. John Lorenz and Vera Electra (Folts) H.; m. Eleanor Louise Martin, Mar. 5, 1951; children—John Kenneth, Victoria Lyn, Scott Douglas, Amy Elizabeth. B.A. in Edn., Ariz. State U., 1956, M.A., 1956; Ph.D., U. Wis., 1960. Counselor, Mesa (Ariz.) Pub. Schs., 1956-58; research asst. U. Wis.-Madison, 1958-60; dir. pupil services Fullerton (Calif.) Union High Sch., Jr. Coll. Dist., 1960-65, adminstr. pupil services, 1965—. Served with USN, 1946-48; as 1st lt. USAF, 1949-53. Recipient H.B. McDaniel Found. award, 1982. Mem. Am. Personnel and Guidance Assn., Am. Sch. Counselor Assn., Calif. Personnel and Guidance Assn., Assn. Calif. Sch. Adminstrs., World Future Soc. Republican. Contbr. articles to profl. jours. Office: Fullerton Sch Dist 780 Beechwood Ave Fullerton CA 92635

HAYS, HOWARD H. (TIM), editor, publisher; b. Chgo., June 2, 1917; s. Howard H. and Margaret (Mauger) H.; B.A., Stanford U., 1939; LL.B., Harvard, 1942; m. Helen Cunningham, May 27, 1947; children—William, Thomas. Admitted to Calif. bar, 1946; spl. agt. FBI, 1942-45; reporter San Bernardino (Calif.) Sun, 1945-46; asst. editor Riverside (Calif.) Daily Press, 1946-49, editor, 1949-65, editor, co-pub., 1965-82, editor, pub., 1983—; mem. Pulitzer Prize Bd., 1976—; dir. AP. Bd. dirs. Calif. Tomorrow. Recipient Dist. award Calif. Jaycees, 1951; named Pub. of Yr., Calif. Press Assn., 1968. Mem. Calif. Bar. Assn., Am. Soc. Newspaper Editors (pres. 1974-75), Stanford Alumni Assn. (dir. 1971-74), Internat. Press Inst. (chmn. Am. com. 1971-72, vice-chmn. internat. bd. 1980-82), Am. Press Inst. (chmn. 1978—). Home: 2750 Rumsey Dr Riverside CA 92506 Office: 3512 14th St Riverside CA 92501

HAYS, JACK D. H., state supreme ct. justice; b. Lund, Nev., Feb. 17, 1917; s. Charles Harold and Thelma (Savage) H.; grad. So. Meth. U., 1941; m. Dorothy M. McIntire, Sept. 4, 1971; children by previous marriage—Eugene Harrington, Rory Cochrane, Bruce Harvey, Victoria Wakeling. Admitted to Ariz. bar, 1946; practice law, Phoenix, 1946-49; asst. city atty., Phoenix, 1949-52; U.S. atty., Dist. Ariz., 1952-60; superior ct. judge, Maricopa County, 1960-69; justice Ariz. Supreme Ct., 1969—. Mem. State Justice Planning Bd., 1970-75; awards juror Freedoms Found., Valley Forge, Pa., 1973. Adv. bd. Roosevelt council Boy Scouts Am., Salvation Army. Mem. Ariz. Legislature, 1952; mem. Young Republican Exec. Com., 1948-50, Rep. State Central Com., 1948-53; vice chmn. Maricopa Rep. Com., 1949-53; state chmn. Eisenhower for Pres., 1952. Bd. dirs., past pres. Maricopa Jr. Coll. Found. Served as maj., F.A., AUS, 1941-46. Recipient Big Brother Year award, 1966. Mem. Am. Judicature Soc. (Herbert Lincoln Harley award 1974), Fed., Am., Ariz. bar assns., Am. Law Inst., Ariz. Judges (past pres.), Ariz. Acad., Lambda Chi Alpha, Phi Alpha Delta. Episcopalian. Rotarian. Home: 207 W Clarendon St Suite 2-D Phoenix AZ 85013 Office: Capitol Bldg Phoenix AZ 85007

HAYS, PATRICK GREGORY, hospital executive; b. Kansas City, Kans., Sept. 9, 1942; s. Vance Samuel and Mary Ellen (Crabbe) H.; m. Norma A. Pierce; 1 dau., Julia L.; m. 2d, Penelope Hall Meyer, July 3, 1976; children—Jennifer M. Meyer, Emily J. Meyer, Drew D. Meyer. B.S. in Bus. Adminstrn., U. Tulsa, 1964; M.H.A., U. Minn., 1971. Mfg. analyst N.Am. Rockwell Corp., Tulsa, 1964-66; adminstr. for ops. Henry Ford Hosp., Detroit, 1971-75; exec. v.p. Meth. Med. Ctr. of Ill., Peoria, 1975-77; adminstr. Kaiser Found. Hosps., Los Angeles, 1977-80; pres. Sutter Community Hosps., Sacramento, 1980—; chmn. bd. Sutter Ambulatory Care Corp., Sacramento, 1981—; teaching preceptor Ariz. State U., U. Minn., Tulane U., Xavier U.; bd. dirs. Calif. Hosps. Polit. Action Com.; speaker profl. meetings. Trustee, Sutter Davis Hosp., Davis, Calif.; bd. dirs. Arthritis Found. Northeastern Calif., United Way of Sacramento Area; mem. hon. dinner com. Sacramento Urban League, 1982. Served to capt. Med. Service Corps, U.S. Army, 1966-69. Decorated Army Commendation medal; recipient achievement award U. Tulsa, 1964, cert. of appreciation Dept. Army, 1969, resolution of commendation for EEO efforts Calif. Senate, 1979; USPHS grantee, 1969. Mem. Am. Coll. Hosp. Adminstrs., Nat. League for Nursing, Am. Mgmt. Assns., Hosp. Mgmt. Systems Soc., Am. Hosp. Assn., Royal Soc. for Health, Sacramento-Sierra Hosp. Assn. (pres.), Hosp. Council No. Calif. (various coms.), Sacramento Met. C. of C. (dir.), Kappa Sigma. Democrat. Presbyterian. Club: Sutter (Sacramento). Contbr. articles to profl. jours. Home: 4837 Tiffany Way Fair Oaks CA 95628 Office: 2020 I St Suite D Sacramento CA 95814

HAYTHE, JOHN HUGH MCCOLLUM, marketing executive; b. Oakland, Calif., Feb. 26, 1944; s. Robert O. Sprague (stepfather) and Kristi C. (McCollum) S.; m. Linda M. Klann, Feb. 14, 1981. Student Chaffey Coll, 1967, Calif. Polytech. Coll., 1968-70. Asst. buyer menswear Harris Co., San Bernardino, Calif., 1970-71, menswear buyer, 1971-73, furniture buyer, 1973-75, womenswear buyer, 1975-77; merchandising analyst Retail Merchandising Service Automation Inc., Riverside, Calif., 1978-79, regional dir., 1979-82, nat. dir., v.p. tng. and devel., 1982. Bd. dirs. San Bernardino Symphony, 1975. Served to staff sgt. U.S. Army, 1962-66. Mem. Am. Soc. Tng. and Devel. Club: VFW (Chino); Elks. Office: 6600 Jurupa Ave Riverside CA 92504

HAYWARD, CHARLES SUMNER, II, warehousing and distribution service exec.; b. N.Y.C., July 26, 1915; s. Vincent Sumner and Gertrude Anna (Herbermann) H.; B.A., CCNY, 1936; m. Clara Rachel Steinhardt, July 37 (div. 1953); children—Virginia Louise Malm, Priscilla Anne Schickele, Charles Sumner; m. 2d, Thelma Ida Jones, June 17, 1954 (dec. 1976); m. 3d, Frances E. Hardin, Oct. 4, 1978. Asst. buyer, glass, R.H. Macy & Co., N.Y.C., 1936-45, buyer, china, glassware, silver, Macy's Calif., San Francisco, 1947-50; buyer The Bon Marche, Seattle, 1950-53; buyer Scruggs Vandervoort & Barney, St. Louis, 1953-55; asst. to pres., import mgr., European buyer Vogue Ceramics Industries, Pelham Manor, N.Y., 1955-57; regional sales mgr., West Coast, Cristalleries Du Val St., Lambert, Concord, Calif., 1958-69, Hayward & Askay, Long Beach, Calif., 1960-80, Villeroy & Boch, SasakiGlass, Yamazaki Tableware, Riekes Crisa Corp., Haleiwa, Hawaii, 1980—. Served with AUS, 1945-46. Decorated chevalier Order of Crown, Belgian Govt., 1965. Democrat. Mem. Delta Kappa Epsilon. warehousing and distribution service exec.; b. N.Y.C., July 26, 1915; s. Vincent Sumner and Gertrude Anna (Herbermann) H.; B.A., CCNY, 1936; m. Clara Rachel Steinhardt, July 37 (div. 1953); children—Virginia Louise Malm, Priscilla Anne Schickele, Charles Sumner; m. 2d, Thelma Ida Jones, June 17, 1954 (dec. 1976); m. 3d, Frances E. Hardin, Oct. 4, 1978. Asst. buyer, glass, R.H. Macy & Co., N.Y.C., 1936-45, buyer, china, glassware, silver, Macy's Calif., San Francisco, 1947-50; buyer The Bon Marche, Seattle, 1950-53; buyer Scruggs Vandervoort & Barney, St. Louis, 1953-55; asst. to pres., import mgr., European buyer Vogue Ceramics Industries, Pelham Manor, N.Y., 1955-57; regional sales mgr., West Coast, Cristalleries Du Val St., Lambert, Concord, Calif., 1958-69, Hayward & Askay, Long Beach, Calif., 1960-80, Villeroy & Boch, SasakiGlass, Yamazaki Tableware, Riekes Crisa Corp., Haleiwa, Hawaii, 1980—. Served with AUS, 1945-46. Decorated chevalier Order of Crown, Belgian Govt., 1965. Democrat. Mem. Delta Kappa Epsilon. Office: 61-718 Papailoa Rd Haleiwa HI 96712

HAYWARD, RICHARD LEE, loss prevention engineer; b. Terre Haute, Ind., Sept. 3, 1933; s. Charles Scott and Bessie May (Young) H.; m. Mary Elizabeth Thomas, June 17, 1956; children—Donna, Thomas, Carol. Student U.S. Naval Sch., 1954-55, U. Colo., 1956-57. With Western Electric, Denver, 1957-58; loss prevention engr. Syntex Chemicals, Inc., Boulder, Colo., 1958—; designer solar energy system. Active CAP, Boy Scouts of America; foster parent for trouble youth. Served with USN, 1954-56. Mem. Nat. Rifleman's Assn. Methodist. Created numbering system for identifying, locating vessels in variable plant sites. Office: 2075 N 55th Boulder CO 80302

HAZANI, EMANUEL, electronics engineer; b. Tel-Aviv, Israel, May 25, 1952. Electronics Practical Engr., Israel Inst. Tech., 1976; B.S.E.E., U. Utah, 1980. Chief telecommunication technician Israeli Army, 1971-75; devel. electronics practical engr. Israeli Def. Ministry, Tel-Aviv, 1976-78; integrated circuits design engr. Intel. Corp., Santa Clara, Calif., 1980-82; sr. design engr. Xicor Inc., Milpitas, Calif., 1982—. Mem. IEEE (Internat. Solid-State Circuits Conf. Beatrice Winner award 1982). Contbr. articles to profl. jours. Office: 851 Buckeye Ct Milpitas CA 95035

HAZELHOFER, MICHAEL GREGORY, educational administrator, consultant; b. Oakland, Calif., Feb. 22, 1948; s. Jack and Veronica Yvonne (Ponti) H.; m. Claudia Eileen Burt, Apr. 3, 1982; 1 son, Michael Jason. B.A. San Jose State U., 1970, M.A., 1979; postgrad. in law Golden Gate Coll., 1971; teaching credential Holy Names Coll., 1972. Cert. elem. tchr., kindergarten-12th grades adminstrv. services, Calif. Tchr. grade 6 Livermore Valley Unified Sch. dist., Livermore, Calif., 1972-76, vice prin., 1976-78, prin. elem. sch., 1978—; cons., presenter in field. Round-up chmn. Bay Area council Boy Scouts Am., 1982-83; vol. Zone 2 Spl. Olympics, Newark, Calif., 1982-83. Mem. Nat. Assn. Elem. Sch. Prins., Assn. Supervision and Curriculum Devel., Assn. Calif. Sch. Adminstrs. (pres. Livermore chpt.), I.D.E.A. Prins. Democrat. Roman Catholic. Club: Knights Soccer. Home: 4141 Guilford Ave Livermore CA 94550 Office: 800 Marylin Livermore CA 94550

HAZELTINE, HERBERT SAMUEL, JR., lawyer; b. Huntington Beach, Calif., Dec. 12, 1908; s. Herbert S. and Emma (Phelps) H.; A.B., Stanford U., 1931; LL.D., Harvard U., 1934; m. Frances Sue Coffin, July 5, 1936; children—Susan, Ann, Lynn. Bar: Calif. 1935. Partner Adams, Duque & Hazeltine, Los Angeles, 1945—. Trustee Boys Clubs Found. So. Calif.; bd. dirs. Los Angeles chpt. ARC; trustee U. So. Calif. Served as lt. comdr. USNR, 1942-45. Mem. ABA, Am. Soc. Corp. Secs. Clubs: California; Annandale Golf (Pasadena); Valley (Montecito, Calif.); Cypress Point. Home: 495 Orange Grove Circle Pasadena CA 91105 Office: 523 W 6th St Los Angeles CA 90014

HAZEWINKEL, VAN, corp. exec.; b. Los Angeles, Oct. 2, 1943; s. Ben J. and Betty J. (Bishop) H.; B.S., Calif. State U., Long Beach, 1967; m. Linda Bennett, Sept. 11, 1965; children—Van, Karey. With Daily Indsl. Tools Inc., Costa Mesa, Calif., 1959—, v.p., 1966-78, pres., 1978—. Founding mem. bd. dirs. Greater Irvine (Calif.) Indsl. League, 1970-73. Mem. Soc. Mfg. Engrs. Office: 3197-D Airport Loop Dr Costa Mesa CA 92626

HAZLETT, ROBERT WILKENS, aero. engr.; b. Gaskill Twp., Pa., Apr. 11, 1922; s. Robert Wilkens and Eleanora (Kessler) H.; B.S. in Aero. Engring., Parks Coll., St. Louis U., 1949; M.S. in Aero.-Mech. Engring., Air Force Inst. Tech., 1955, M.S. in Aerospace Engring., 1966; m. Imogene Roberta Elbell, Aug. 16, 1941; 1 son, Robert Wilkens. Liaison engr. Curtis Wright Aircraft, Buffalo, 1941-43, McDonnell Aircraft, St. Louis, 1948-49; B-1 test engr. Rockwell Internat., Los Angeles, 1972-78; space shuttle main engine test engr. Rocketdyne, Los Angeles, 1978-79; air-launched cruise missile fuel test engr. Boeing Co., Seattle, 1979—. Served with U.S. Army, 1943-46, USAF, 1949-70. Decorated Legion of Merit, D.F.C., Silver Star, Air medal. Republican. Clubs: Sertoma, Masons, Shriners. Home: 604 S 298 St Federal Way WA 98003 Office: 20403 68th Ave S Kent WA 98031

HAZZARD, SALLY BOYLES, county government administrator; b. Huntington, Ind., Dec. 4, 1946; d. Frank Blair Boyles and Josephine V. (Jonas) Boyles Zanganas; m. Harold Wayne Donahoo, Oct. 31, 1982. A.B. in Pub. Adminstrn., San Diego State U., 1970, postgrad. in pub. adminstrn. Vocat. counselor, asst. dir. mgmt. service South Bay Trade Schs., San Diego, 1970-72; eligibility worker I and II Dept. Pub. Welfare, San Diego, 1972-73 adminstrv. asst. Dept. Gen. Services, County of San Diego, 1973-76, adminstrv. services mgr., 1976-77, acting asst. dir., 1976-77, exec. asst. 2d Dist. Bd. Suprs., 1977-78, dep. dir. adminstrv. mgmt., 1978-80, dep. dir. Office Mgmt. and Budget, 1980-82, dir. Dept. Animal Control, 1982—. Mem. Calif. Women in Govt. (chmn. 1982-83, bd. dirs. 1981-82), Am. Soc. Pub. Adminstrn. (pres. 1977-78, regional pres. 1977-78), Western Govt. Research Assn., Calif. Assn. Pub. Adminstrn. and Educators, Calif. Elected Women's Assn., Am. Soc. Profl. and Exec. Women, Nat. Assn. Women Execs., Women Officials Nat. Assn. Counties, Am. Polit. Sci. Soc., Pi Alpha Alpha. Democrat. Presbyterian. Office: 1104 Azusa St San Diego CA 92110

HEACOCK, JEANNIE BROCK, teacher educator; b. Santa Fe, May 10, 1942; d. Paul Henry and Lila Winifred (Kleefus) Brock; m. Larry Lee Heacock, Feb. 19, 1962; children—Ryan Mark, Ronda Kay. B.S. Ed., Eastern N.Mex. U., 1976, M.Spl. Ed., 1977. Instr. spl. edn. Eastern N.Mex. U., Portales, 1977—. Mem. Council Exceptional Children (pres. chpt. 1976), Assn. for Gifted, Assn. Supervision and Curriculum Devel., Nat. Assn. Gifted Children, Phi Kappa Phi. Methodist. Home: 209 Floyd Golden Circle Portales NM 88130 Office: Station 25 Education Bldg Eastern NMex Univ Portales NM 88130

HEAD, LAURA DEAN, psychologist, educator; b. Los Angeles, Nov. 3, 1948; d. Marvin Laurence and Helaine Dean (Springer) H.; B.A., San Francisco State Coll., 1971; M.A., U. Mich., 1974, Ph.D., 1978. Teaching asst., asst. project dir. U. Mich., Ann Arbor, 1970-73; instr. U. Calif.-Riverside, 1973-76; project dir., research scientist Urban Inst. Human Services, San Francisco, 1978-80; sr. research scientist, project dir. Far West Lab. Ednl. Research and Devel., San Francisco, 1980-81; assoc. prof. psychology San Francisco State U., 1982—; mem. Com. on Sch. Crime and Violence, Calif. State Dept. Edn., 1981—. Mem. Selective Service Bd.; chmn. Bay Area Black Child Devel. Inst., 1978-81; commn. mem. Marin City Multi-Service Ctr. Calif. State scholar, 1966, Nat. Cath. scholar for Negroes, 1966. Mem. Am. Psychol. Assn. (minority fellow), Assn. Black Psychologists, Children's Def. League, Nat. Black Child Devel. Inst., Soc. Research in Child Devel., Black Women's Forum, Alpha Kappa Alpha. Club: Commonwealth (San Francisco). Home: 3614 Randolph Ave Oakland CA 94602 Office: Black Studies Dept San Francisco State U 1600 Holloway Ave San Francisco CA 94132

HEADLAND, EDWIN HARVEY, naval officer, educator; b. Litchville, N.D., Nov. 15, 1911; s. Edwin Henry and Olga (Strand) H.; m. Margaret McGinnis, Feb. 12, 1942; Student U. Chgo., 1929-31; B.S., U.S. Naval Acad., 1935; postgrad. Nat. War Coll., 1945; M.B.A., U. Puget Sound, 1963, U. Wash., 1968. Commd. ensign U.S. Navy, 1935, advanced through grades to capt., 1954; comdr. ships during World War II; ret., 1961; lectr. econs. and bus. U. Puget Sound, 1963-67, U. Md. Overseas, 1968-79, Fort Steilacoom Community Coll., Tacoma, 1982—. Mem. council Anglican Ch., Munich, Ger., 1976-79. Decorated for combat. Republican. Episcopalian. Mem. AAUP, Psi Upsilon. Clubs: Tacoma Country, Mil. Officers, Lions, Gyro.

HEADLEE, ROLLAND DOCKERAY, assn. exec.; b. Los Angeles, Aug. 27, 1916; s. Jesse W. and Cleora (Dockeray) H.; student UCLA, 1939; m. Alzora D. Burgett, May 13, 1939; 1 dau., Linda Ann (Mrs. Walter Pohl). Asst. mgr. Par Assos., Los Angeles, 1935-43, Finance Assos., Los Angeles, 1946-58; financial cons., lectr., 1958-63; account exec. Walter E. Heller & Co., Los Angeles, 1963-66; exec. dir. Town Hall Calif., Los Angeles, 1966—; dir. Mfrs. Assos., Energy Mgmt. Corp., R.H. Investment Corp., Am. Internat. Bank. Served to 1st lt. AUS, 1943-46. Mem. Los Angeles World Affairs Council, Newcomen Soc. N.Am., Los Angeles Stock Exchange Club, Mensa. Methodist. Clubs: Commonwealth of Calif., Town Hall of Calif. (life), Economic of Detroit. Home: 8064 El Manor Ave Los Angeles CA 90045 Office: 525 W 6th St Los Angeles CA 90014

HEALEY, E. SHEVY, psychologist, consultant; b. Lemberg, Poland, Jan. 29, 1922; came to U.S., 1924, naturalized, 1924; m. Rose F. Spiegel (dec.); 1 dau., Donna E. A.A., Los Angeles City Coll., 1967; B.A., Calif. State U.-Los Angeles, 1969; M.A., Ohio State U., 1971, Ph.D., 1976. Lic. marriage, family, and child counselor, Calif. Intern in psychology Neuropsychiat. Inst., UCLA, 1971-72; pvt. practice clin. psychology and marriage counseling, Los Angeles, 1973—; cons. Reed Neurol. Clinic, UCLA, Nat. Multiple Sclerosis Soc., Los Angeles. Mabel Wilson Richards scholar, 1967-69; State of Calif. fellow, 1969-70; USPHS fellow, 1969-71; Ohio State U. grantee, 1970-71; NIMH fellow, 1971-72. Mem. Am. Psychol. Assn., Calif. Psychol. Assn., Assn. Psychophysiol. Study of Sleep, Western Assn. Women in Psychology, Assn. Humanistic Psychology, Phi Kappa Phi. Contbr. psychol. articles to profl. jours. Home: PO Box 295 Idyllwild CA 92349 Office: 11941 Wilshire Blvd Suite 3 Los Angeles CA 90025

HEALY, LAWRENCE MARTIN, school principal, consultant; b. Valhalla, N.Y., Dec. 13, 1934; s. Hubert Francis (dec.) and Thelma Mae (Dalton) H.; m. Kristen Elaine Fagre, July 31, 1982; children by previous marriage—Lawrence Patrick, Debra Joyce Powell, Megan Deidre. B.S., SUNY, 1961; M.A.T., Mich. State U., 1965; Ed.S., Albany State U., 1975. Tchr. various schs., N.Y., 1961-72; coordinator, Herkimer, N.Y., 1972-75; supt. schs., Telluride, Colo., 1976-77; prin. Bayfield (Colo.) High Sch., 1977-79, Kiana (Alaska) Schs., Naparyarmiut Elicarviat, Hooper Bay, Ak., 1979—. Served with USN, 1952-55. Mem. Lower Yukon Adminstrn. Assn., Nat. Assn. Secondary Sch. Prins., Nat. Assn. Elem. Sch. Prins., Alaska Assn. Secondary Sch. Prins., Assn. Supervision and Curriculum Devel., Nat. Sci. Tchrs. Assn., Alaska Assn. Supervision and Devel. Roman Catholic. Presented sch. program on native arts and crafts, 1982-83. Home: Tundra View N Hooper Bay AK 99604 Office: Naparyarmiut Elicarviat Hooper Bay AK 99604

HEALY, WINSTON, JR., educational adminstrator; b. Evanston, Ill., Oct. 20, 1937; s. Winston and Margaret (Lee) H.; m. Judith Becker, June 24, 1976; children—Nathaniel, Sarah, Jason, Elisabeth. B.A., Williams Coll., 1960; M.A., U. Hawaii, 1968; Ed.D., U. Mass., 1982. Tchr. English, Punahou Sch., Honolulu, 1960-67, chmn. dept. English, 1966-67, dean adminstrn., 1967-69, secondary sch. prin., 1969—. Chmn. bd. Early Sch.; treas. Hilltown Coop. Nursery Sch.; v.p., mem. exec. bd. Hawaii Pub. Radio, 1978-81; mem. Joint Econ. Council; mem. exec. bd. Honolulu Community Scholarship Program. Served with Hawaii Air N.G., 1960-71. Coe fellow, Nat. Assn. Ind. Schs. fellow, 1972-73. Mem. Nat. Assn. Secondary Sch. Prins., Assn. Supervision and Curriculum Devel., Nat. Council Tchrs. English (nat. adv. bd. achievement awards), Hawaii Council Tchrs. English (past pres.). Congregationalist. Home: 45 Piper's Pali Honolulu HI 96822 Office: 1601 Punahou St Honolulu HI 96822

HEAPS, RICHARD ALLYN, psychologist, educator; b. Huntington Park, Calif., Dec. 4, 1942; s. David Richard and Phyllis (Anderson) H.; m. Joyce Ann Claud, June 25, 1964; children—Cassilyn Ann, Christine Joyce, David Allyn, Brian Richard. B.S. cum laude in Psychology, Brigham Young U., 1966; M.A. in Psychology, U. Utah, 1968, Ph.D. in Psychology, 1970. Counseling psychology intern Counseling Ctr., U. Utah, 1968-70; counseling psychologist Brigham Young U., Provo, Utah, 1970—, asst. to assoc. prof. ednl. psychology, 1970—, assoc. dir. Personal Devel. Ctr., 1972-73, dir. career edn. program, 1973-76, dir. personal and career services, 1976—; communications cons. to sch. dist. adminstrs. Mem. troop com. Boy Scouts Am., 1972-74. Brigham Young U. faculty research grantee, 1971-73. Mem. Am. Psychol. Assn., Am. Personnel and Guidance Assn., Assn. Mormon Counselors and Psychotherapists (sec.-treas. 1976-78), Utah Personnel and Guidance Assn. (pres. 1972-74), Am. Assn. Counselor Edn. and Supervision. Mormon. Author: (with Norma Rohde) Interpersonal Communication: A Skill Development Workbook, 1974; producer audio tape series and videotape films in field; contbr. articles to profl. jours. Home: 688 South 630 East Orem UT 84057 Office: B-268 ASB Brigham Young U Provo UT 84602

HEARD, JOANNE O'BRIEN, county official; b. Summit, N.J., Aug. 30, 1936; d. Patrick Earl and Persis (Avery) O'Brien; m. Nathan Eugene Heard. N.Y. State Coll. for Tchrs., 1954-55; A.A., Mira Costa Coll., 1983. Quality control analyst Orange County, Santa Ana, Calif., 1970-72; supr. dept. social services, Santa Ana, 1972-73; eligibility worker San Diego County (Calif.), 1973-74, supr., 1974-76, staff-income maintenance Indochinese Refugee Assistance Program, 1976-77, program instr., 1977-79, data coordinator nat. workfare demonstration, 1979-81, exec. asst. Chief Adminstrv. Office, 1981—. Bd. dirs. Navy Relief Soc.; mem. contract rev. panel United Way. Mem. Nat. Assn. Female Execs., Calif. Women in Govt. (dir. 1981—), Women in Mgmt., County Employees Charitable Orgn. Home: 3223 Mt Whitney Rd Escondido CA 92025

HEARD, ROSE MARIE, bank executive; b. Chgo., Nov. 30, 1930; d. William and Mary Alice Elizabeth (Helm) Horton. Student Wilson Jr. Coll., Chgo., 1947-48, Trinity U., San Antonio, 1950-51; grad. Am. Inst. Banking, 1963; B.A., U. Beverly Hills, 1981, M.B.A., 1981, postgrad., 1982—. With Union Bank, Los Angeles, 1957-76, trust officer, 1970-71, asst. v.p., 1972-76; asst. dir. pension trust dept. Beverly Hills Savs. & Loan Assn., Los Angeles, 1976-78, asst. tng. officer IRA/KEOGH/SEP plans, 1976—, asst. prof., 1978—; instr. retirement plans Inst. Fin. Edn. Served with WAF, USAF, 1948-52. Mem. NAACP, Beverly Hills Bar Assn. Clubs: Topaz, Eastern Star, Heroines of Jericho. Office: 1801 Ave of the Stars Los Angeles CA 90067

HEARIN, JOE KEMP, lumber exec.; b. Tacoma, Wash., Jan. 16, 1912; s. Edward E. and Emma M. (Menson) H.; widower; 1 dau., Joan. Pres. Hearin Forest Industries, Portland, Oreg., 1935—. Home and Office: PO Box 25387 Portland OR 97225

HEARN, CHARLES VIRGIL, clergyman, behavioral scientist; b. Westport, Ind., Sept. 4, 1930; s. Forrest V. and Emma Florence (Marsh) H.; Ph.D., Thomas A. Edison U., 1972; D.D., Trinity Hall Coll. and Sem., 1977; diploma Palm Beach Psychotherapy Tng. Center, 1976; children by previous marriage—Debra Lynn, Charles Gregory, Martin Curtis. Ordained to ministry Methodist Ch., 1958; pastor various Meth. chs., Ind., Tex., Wyo., Calif., 1958-70; interpersonal minister St. Alban's Ch. of the Way, San Francisco, 1974—; clergyman and counselor Green Oak Ranch Boys Camp, Calif., 1969-70; dir. rehab. Mary-Lind Found., Los Angeles, 1970-71; med. asst. Fireside Hosp., Santa Monica, Calif., 1971-72; dir. alcoholism program Patrician Hosp., Santa Monica, 1972-74; propr., exec. dir. Consultation & Referral, Santa Monica, 1974—. Vice chmn. Western Los Angeles Alcoholism Coalition, 1974-78; pres. bd. dirs. Trinity Hall Coll. and Sem. Served with U.S. Army, 1951-53; Korea. Decorated Bronze Star; diplomate Am. Bd. Examiners in Psychotherapy, Bd. Examiners in Pastoral Counseling. Fellow Am. Acad. Behavioral Sci.; mem. Am. Ministerial Assn. (pres. 1981—), Nat. Assn. Alcoholism Counselors, Calif. Assn. Alcoholism Counselors, Cons. on Alcoholism for Communities, Nat. Council Family Relations, Am. Coll. Clinic Adminstrs., Assn. Labor-Mgmt. Adminstrs. Democrat. Contbr. numerous articles on psychotherapy to profl. publs. Address: 1248 11th St Suite B Santa Monica CA 90401

HEARN, KEITH FREDERICK, labor union ofcl.; b. San Francisco, Aug. 30, 1943; s. Charles Sargent and Mildred Virginia (Caldwell) H.; student Stanford U., 1961-65; m. Kathleen Ann Chastain Zerr, Sept. 23, 1978; 1 stepson, Matthew Paul Zerr. Reporter, Palo Alto (Calif.) Times, 1964-67; reporter, editor Asso. Press, Sacramento and Los Angeles, 1967-72; communications mgr. Calif. State Employees Assn., Sacramento, 1973—. Mem. Internat. Assn. Bus. Communicators, Sierra Club. Democrat. Home: 104 Alezane Dr Folsom CA 95630 Office: California State Employees Association 1108 O St Sacramento CA 95814

HEARN, RICHARD JOHN, psychologist, zen master; b. Berkshire, Eng., Oct. 7, 1927; s. George Richard Mant and Louise May (Cormack) H.; m. Kyoko Nozoe, May 9, 1964. B.A. in Clin. Psychology, Antioch Coll. West, 1976; Ph.D. in Social and Clin Psychology, Wright Inst., Los Angeles, 1981. Cert. master in Zen. Various positions as psychiat. nurse, B.C., Can. and Calif., 1958-71; nursing coordinator Westwood Psychiat. Hosp., Los Angeles, 1970-71; abbot, zen master Hui-Neng Zen Tng. Temple, Easton, Pa., 1971-72; v.p. U. Oriental Studies, Los Angeles, 1972-77; postdoctoral fellow Didi Hirsch Calif. Mental Health Ctr., Los Angeles, 1981—; pvt. practice, Los Angeles, 1983—; adminstr. Benjamin Rush Inst., Los Angeles, 1983—; lectr. in field. Vice pres. Psychiat. Nurses Assn. B.C., Can., 1953-54. Mem. Am. Psychol. Assn., Calif. State Psychol. Assn., Am. Assn. Suicidology, Am. Orthopsychology Assn., Western Psychol. Assn. Buddhist. Contbr. articles to profl. jours. Office: 4760 S Sepulveda Blvd Culver City CA 90230

HEARNE, JAMES WILLIAM, accountant; b. Hanna, Wyo., July 25, 1950; s. Frank J. and Annie E. (Tate) H.; m. Margaret L. Tobin, children—Michelle, Kenneth. B.S., U. Wyo., 1972. C.P.A., Wyo. Profl. staff McGladrey Hansen Dunn & Co., Cheyenne, Wyo., 1972-76, supr., 1976, ptnr. McGladrey Hendrickson & Co., 1979—. Bd. dirs. Cheyenne Child Care Ctrs.; mem. contestants com. Cheyenne Frontier Days, The Heels Cheyenne Frontier Days. Mem. Am. Inst. C.P.A.s, Wyo. Soc. C.P.A.s, Am. Acctg. Assn., Beta Alpha Psi. Democrat. Roman Catholic. Club: Lions (Cheyenne) (treas.). Contbr. article to profl. jour. Home: 1702 Newton Dr Cheyenne WY 82001 Office: McGladrey Hendrickson & Co PO Box 1088 Cheyenne WY 82003

HEARST, RANDOLPH APPERSON, publishing co. exec.; b. N.Y.C., Dec. 2, 1915; s. William Randolph and Millicent (Willson) H.; student Harvard, 1933-34; m. Catherine Campbell, Jan. 12, 1938 (div. 1982); children—Catherine, Virginia, Patricia, Anne, Victoria; m. 2d, Maria C. Scruggs, May 2, 1982. Asst. to editor Atlanta Georgian, 1939-40; asst. to pub. San Francisco Call-Bull., 1940-44, exec. editor, 1947-49, pub., 1950-53; pres., dir., chief exec. officer Hearst Consol. Publs., Inc., and Hearst Pub. Co., Inc., 1961-64; chmn. exec. com. The Hearst Corp., 1965-73, chmn. bd., 1973—, dir., 1965—; pres. San Francisco Examiner, 1972—. Trustee Hearst Found. Served as capt., Air Transport Command, USAAF, 1943-45. Roman Catholic. Clubs: Piedmont Driving (Atlanta); Burlingame Country; Pacific Union; Press (San Francisco). Office: 110 5th St San Francisco CA 94103

HEARTFIELD, RANDOLPH, corporation executive; b. Houston, Tex., Nov. 5, 1939; s. Edgar Matthews and Martha Arelia (Tigner) H.; m. Mary Cathryn Sauer, Aug. 8, 1962; children—Alison, Wesley, Laura. B.S. in Chemical Engring., U. Tex., 1962; M.S. in Chem. Engring., 1963; M.B.A. in Fin., Stanford U., 1967. Process engr. Standard Oil of Calif., 1963-65; cons. McKinsey and Co., Los Angeles, 1967-71; v.p. mfg. Superior Fireplace, 1971-73, v.p. and gen. mgr., 1973-75; exec. v.p. Mobex Corp., 1975—. Clubs: Stanford Business School, Los Angeles. Office: 4100 W Commonwealth Ave Fullerton CA 92633

HEATH, BRENT EDWARD, educator; b. Redlands, Calif., Aug. 24, 1953; s. Victor Edward and Dawn Ion (Youngsma) H.; m. Carol Mae Moshier, Aug. 3, 1974; 1 son, Justin Bryant. A.A. in Social Studies, Highline Community Coll., Midway, Wash., 1973; B.A. in History and Edn., Seattle Pacific U., 1975; postgrad. San Jose State U., 1977; M.A. in Secondary Edn., Calif. State U.-Northridge, 1981. Tchr. social studies and English, Christian Center Schs., Dublin, Calif., 1975-77, Los Primeros Sch., Camarillo, Calif., 1977-79; tchr. social studies and TV prodn. Cabrillo Jr. High Sch., Ventura, Calif., 1979-80; tchr. social studies, journalism and English De Anza Jr. High, Ontario, Calif., 1980—, also chmn. dept. social studies. Taft Inst. Govt. fellow, 1977. Mem. Nat. Council for Social Studies, Calif. Council for Social Studies, So. Calif. Social Sci. Assn., Baldy-Vista Social Studies Council, Assn. for Supervision and Curriculum Devel., Calif. Journalism Edn. Assn., So. Calif. Journalism Edn. Assn., Inland Journalism Edn. Assn. Republican. Contbr. articles to profl. jours. Home: 123 W 15th St Upland CA 91786 Office: 1450 S Sultana CA 91761

HEATH, HAROLD HERBERT, computer manufacturing company executive, rancher; b. Sioux Falls, S.D., Dec. 3, 1922; s. Charles Webster and Gladys (Tillery) H.; m. Dorothy Cohee; m. Ernestine M. McCasland, Jan. 14, 1966; children—Bradley, Carleton, Jeffrey, Judy Ann, Bretton, Stuart, Wendy, Holly. Student pub. schs. Sioux City, Iowa. Machinist apprentice, then journeyman Boeing Co., Seattle, 1941-48; pres., chmn. bd., chief exec. officer Heath Tecna Corp., Kent, Wash., 1950-71, chmn. emeritus, 1971-82; mgr. plant ops. then sales CorTec Inc., Cin., 1972-78; v.p. sales and mktg. Access Corp., Cin., 1978-80; dir. several mfg. cos. Past pres. Seattle Opera Assn., Pioneer Coop. Affiliates, half-way house programs, Little Sch., Bellevue, Wash. Served with USAAF, 1943-46. Mem. Am. Mgmt. Assn., Young Pres.'s Orgn. Republican. Club: Rainier (Seattle).

HEATH, MAE BERTHANN, educator; b. Dallas; d. James Lafayette and Allie Mae (Hudson) Jones; m. John Willie Heath, Jr., July 14, 1963 (div.); 1 son, John William. B.S. cum laude, Pepperdine U., 1959; M.S., UCLA, 1960; postgrad. UCLA, Pepperdine U., Chapman Coll. Credentials in elem. edn., secondary edn., gen. adminstrn., pupil personnel services, supervision, homemaking edn., Calif. Tchr. home econs. Bret Harte Jr. High Sch., Los Angeles, 1960-66; counselor Los Angeles High Sch., 1968-72; cons. in consumer home econs. Los Angeles Unified Sch. Dist., 1972-75; regional supr. home econs. edn. Office of Vocat. Edn., Calif. State Dept. of Edn., Los Angeles, 1975—; tchr. Adult Community Schs.; mem. adv. com. J.C. Penny Co. Coordinator, City of Los Angeles Human Relations Bur. Workshops; scholarship fund raiser Wives of Bench and Bar; sustaining mem. YMCA; asst. Sunday Sch. supt. St. Peters Meth. Ch., Crenshaw Meth. Ch.; active Easter Seals 500 Club, NAACP, Urban League. Mem. Am. Vocat. Assn., Calif. Assn. Vocat. Educators, Am. Home Econs. Assn., Assn. Suprs. Vocat. Home Econs., UCLA Alumni Assn., Polit. Study Club, Delta Sigma Theta, Kappa Omicron Phi, Omicron Nu, Alpha Rho Tau. Democrat.

HEATON, KENNETH GORDON, clergyman; b. Zephyr, Ont., Can., Jan. 31, 1935; s. James and Rose Hearty (Rye) H.; came to U.S., 1960; B.A., Olivet Coll., Kankakee, Ill., 1961; B.D., Nazarene Theol. Sem., Kansas City, Mo., 1967; Th.M., So. Bapt. Theol. Sem., Louisville, 1970; D.Min., Sch. Theology, Claremont, Calif., 1976; m. Sylvia Caroline Matheson, June 27, 1959; children—Kenneth Gordon, Caroline Rose. Ordained to ministry United Methodist Ch., 1967; pastor United Meth. Ch., Valencia, Calif., 1972-80; sr. minister First United Meth. Ch., Redondo Beach, Calif., 1980—. Pres. bd. dirs. Santa Clarita Valley Mental Health, Valencia Hills Homeowners Assn.; bd. dirs. Toberman Settlement House, San Pedro; mem. clergy adv. council Torrance YMCA. Mem. Santa Clarita Valley Ministerial Assn. (pres.), C. of C., mem. Redondo Beach Roundtable, South Bay Interfaith Council. Club: Redondo Beach Riviera Rotary. Home: 513 Faye Ln Redondo Beach CA 90277 Office: 243 S Broadway Redondo Beach CA 90277

HEATON, PATTIE JEAN HAYNES, interior designer, educator; b. Ely, Nev., Nov. 28, 1950; d. Reginald Scott and Christie LaVerne (Hermansen) Haynes; B.F.A., Brigham Young U., 1973; m. Russell J. Heaton, Aug. 21, 1970; children—Tisha Brooks, Amber Nettie, Hayley Berle. Head designer House of Lords, Provo, Utah, 1973-74; pvt. practice interior designing, Provo, 1974—; faculty dept. design Brigham Young U., 1974—, Am. Soc. Interior Design club advisor, 1979—. Mem. pres.'s orgn. elem. sch. level PTA, edn. commr., 1979-80, historian, 1980-81. Mormon. Office: 268 Brimhall Bldg Brigham Young U Provo UT 84601

HEATON, TIM B., sociology educator; b. Panguitch, Utah, Dec. 1, 1949; s. W. R. and Berle J. (Jaynes) H.; m. Tamlyn K. Bodine, Aug. 9, 1974; children—Tamara, Michael, Anna, Jonathan. B.S., Brigham Young U., 1974, M.S., 1975; Ph.D., U. Wis.-Madison, 1979; postgrad. U. N.C.-Chapel Hill, 1979-80. Asst. prof. sociology Brigham Young U., Provo, Utah, 1980—; demographic cons. Mormon Ch. Mem. Rural Sociol. Soc., Population Assn. Am., Am. Sociol. Assn. Mormon. Contbr. articles to profl. jours. Home: 305 E 1230 N Springville UT 84663 Office: Brigham Young U 236 KMB Provo UT 84602

HEBERT, BUDD HANSEL, ind. oil and gas operator, state senator; b. Detroit, Aug. 19, 1941; s. L. Hansel and Trudy Hebert; B.Sc. with distinction, Ariz. State U., 1963, M.A., 1964; Ph.D., Ohio State U., 1972; m. Doris Ann Brackeen, Oct. 5, 1963; children—Shirley, Julia. Asst. prof. U. Cin., 1968-71; asst. prof. urban econs. Va. Commonwealth U., 1971-74; economist, project mgr. Dames & Moore, Cin., 1974-77; landman Yates Petroleum Corp., Artesia, N.Mex., 1977-80; land mgr. Marbob Energy Corp., Artesia, 1980-81; v.p. Security Nat. Bank, Roswell, N.Mex., 1981-83; ind. oil and gas operator, 1983—; state senator Dist. 33, N.Mex., 1980—. Vice chmn. United Way, Artesia, 1979; active Conquistador council Boy Scouts Am., Artesia. NSF grantee, 1968-69. Mem. Am. Assn. Petroleum Landmen. Republican. Mem. Ch. of Christ. Club: Kiwanis.

HEBERT, RAYMOND EARL, JR., corporation executive; b. Los Angeles; s. Raymond E. and Marcella (Bente) H.; m. Pamela Ann Kevan, Sept. 23, 1961 (div. 1977); children—Shelly Lin, Stac Allen. B.S., UCLA, 1959; M.B.A., U. Calif., 1963. With sales and mktg. mgmt. Armour & Co., Los Angeles and Chgo., 1961-64; mktg. dir. Hunt Wesson div. Norton Simon, 1964-67; co-founder, pres. AMR Internat., N.Y.C., 1967-78; pres. Wilshire Mktg. Corp. div. Knopp Communications Corp. (Architectural Digest, Bon Apetit, GEO and Home mags), Los Angeles, 1978-82; pres. Hebert & Assocs. Inc., Beverly Hills, Calif., 1982—. Active Republican Nat. Com. Served to lt. USN, 1959-61. Mem. Young Presidents Assn., Jr. C. of C., Sigma Alpha Epsilon. Clubs: Union League (N.Y.C.); Jonathan (Los Angeles). Home: 1296 San Ysidro Dr Beverly Hills CA 90210 Office: 9701 Wilshire Blvd Beverly Hills CA 90212

HEBERT, ROBERT JOHN, construction contractor; b. Oakland, Calif., July 27, 1944; s. Robert Harris and Ramona Josephine (Stevens) H.; B.A., San Francisco State U., 1972. Indsl. videotape producer Bechtel Corp., San Francisco, 1973; profl. photographer, 1974; ednl. film producer Am. Analysis Corp., San Francisco, 1975-77; owner, contractor Robert John Herbert, Hot Tub and Spa Contractor, 1977—. Served with U.S. Army, 1965-68; Vietnam. Home: 53 La Espiral Orinda CA 94563 Office: Box 1778 Orinda CA 94563

HEBERT, YVONNE CECILIA, psychotherapist; b. Detroit, Apr. 20, 1936; d. Philip J. and Ruth V. (Ingalls) H. B.A., Calif. State U.-Los Angeles, 1971; M.A., 1975. Lic. marriage and family therapist, Calif. 1977. Office mgr. print prodn. staff, various public relations and advt. firms, 1954-69; acctg. staff Met. Hosp., Detroit, 1960-61; cost acct. Comprehensive Designers, Sherman Oaks, Calif., 1964-79; freelance writer, artist, Los Angeles, 1962-77; counselor West Los Angeles Coll., 1978-79; pvt. practice marriage, family, child and rehab. counseling, Long Beach, Calif., 1976—. Mem. Calif. Assn. Marriage and Family Therapists, Assn. Christian Therapists, Calif. Assn. Mental Health Counselors (dir. 1981-83), Nat. Rehab. Assn. Roman Catholic. Author: Finding Peace in Pain, 1983; contbr. numerous articles to profl. jours. Office: 4182 Viking Way Suite 108 Long Beach CA 90808

HEBERTSON, WAYNE M., neurologist; b. Provo, Utah, Feb. 19, 1926; s. Thorit Charles and Susan Elmina (Madsen) H.; student Mont. State U., 1944; B.S., Brigham Young U., 1949; M.D., U. Utah, 1952; m. Joan Kearl, Dec. 21, 1956; children—Jonathan Wayne, Elizabeth Germaine, Andrea Bettina, Peter Christian. Intern, med. resident Salt Lake County Hosp., 1952-55; resident in neurology Mass. Gen. Hosp., Boston, 1955-57; clin. clk. Inst. of Neurology, London, 1957-58; fellow in neuropathology Mass. Gen. Hosp., Boston, 1958-59; practice medicine, specializing in neurology, Salt Lake City, 1959—; neurologist, electro-encephalographer St. Mark's Hosp., Salt Lake City, 1959—, staff pres., 1979-80. Mem. Utah Gov.'s Council on Developmentally Disabled, 1968-78; trustee Salt Lake Art Center, 1968-80. Served to 1st lt., U.S. Army, 1944-46; PTO. Fellow Inst. Neurol. Diseases and Blindness; mem. Salt Lake County Med. Soc., Utah Med. Assn., AMA, Am. Acad. Neurology, N.Y. Acad. Sci. Office: 1220 E 3900 S Salt Lake City UT 84117

HEBNER, PAUL CHESTER, oil co. exec.; b. Warren, Pa., Dec. 29, 1919; s. Henry G. and Mabel (Gross) H.; m. Dorothy Farrell, Feb. 16, 1943; children—Richard P., Kathleen D., Susan M., Christine L., Elizabeth A., Jeannie M. Accountant, adminstrv. asst. Altman-Coady Co., Columbus, Ohio, 1940-41; mgr. accounting, exec. adminstr. T & T Oil Co. and asso. cos., Los Angeles, 1954-57; with Occidental Petroleum Corp., Los Angeles, 1957—, sec.-treas., 1958-68, v.p., sec., 1968-80, exec. v.p., sec., 1980—, dir., 1960—; officer, dir. subs. cos. Mem. Los Angeles Beautiful. Served to maj. USAAF, 1942-45. L.S.B. Leakey Found. fellow. Mem. Am. Soc. Corp. Secs. Home: 12 Amber Sky Dr Rancho Palos Verdes CA 90274 Office: 10889 Wilshire Blvd Los Angeles CA 90024

HECHT, ADOLPH, botany educator, genetics educator; b. Chgo., July 25, 1914; s. Mannassa and Bertha (Friedmann) H.; m. Edith Goldstein, July 19, 1942; children—Anton Louis (dec.), Julia Ann. S.B., U. Chgo., 1936, M.S., 1937; Ph.D., Ind. U., 1942. Field asst U.S. Forest and Range Exptl. Sta., Missoula, Mont., 1937-38; instr. botany U. Chgo., 1946-47; asst. prof., prof. botany and genetics Wash. State U., Pullman, 1947-79, prof. emeritus, 1979—, chmn. dept. botany, 1955-70, mem. com. undergrad. edn. in biol. scis., 1966-69. Chmn., Whitman County (Wash.) Democratic Central Com., 1979-82. Served to capt. USAAF, 1942-46; lt. col. Res. ret. Fellow AAAS (pres. Pacific div. 1966-67); mem. Bot. Soc. Am. (chmn. Pacific sect. 1955-56), N.W. Sci. Assn. (pres. 1965-66, hon. life; hon. trustee), Am. Inst. Biol. Scis., Phi Beta Kappa, Sigma Xi. Editor Plant Sci. Bull., 1965-71, Northwest Sci., 1976-79; author: Guide to Graduate Study in Botany for the United States, 1966. Office: Dept Botany Wash State Univ Pullman WA 99164

HECHT, CHIC, congressman; b. Cape Girardeau, Mo., Nov. 30, 1928; m. Gail Kahn; children—Lori, Leslie. B.S., Washington U., St. Louis, 1949. Mcht., banker; mem. Nev. State Senate, 1967-76, minority leader; mem. U.S. Senate, 1983—. Served with U.S. Army, 1951-53. Mem. Las Vegas C. of C., Nat. Mil. Intelligence Assn., Retail Mchts. Bur., Nat. Counter Intelligence Corps. Republican. Office: 297 Russell Bldg Washington DC 20510*

HECHT, KATHRYN A., educator; b. Newark, June 30, 1944; d. Arthur S. and Claire K. (Koehler) H. A.B. with distinction in History, U. Mich., 1965; M.Ed., U. Mass., 1969, Ed.D. (Univ. fellow), 1972. Program asst., program devel. br. Div. Compensatory Edn., Office Edn, HEW, Washington, 1965-67, research assoc. in analysis Survey of Compensatory Edn., Amherst, Mass., 1969-70; dir. social services Head Star, Champlain Valley OEO, Burlington, Vt., summer 1967; evaluation coordinator Brattleboro (Vt.) Follow-Through, Windham S.E. Supervisory Union, 1967-68; assoc. dir. Compensatory Edn. Evaluation and Modification Study, U. Mass., 1968-69; research assoc. Evaluation Service Ctr. for Occupational Edn., Amherst, Mass., 1970; asst. to dir. Community Learning Ctr., Brookdale Community Coll., Lincroft, N.J., 1971; ednl. cons. program evaluation, policy research, problem analysis, Oceanport, N.J., 1972-73, San Francisco, 1979—; asst. prof. edn. Ctr. for No. Ednl. Research (name changed to Ctr. for Cross-cultural Studies 1977), U. Alaska, Fairbanks, 1973-77, assoc. prof., 1977-79, spl. asst. Office of Pres., 1978-79; distbr. personal computers. Ford Found. grantee, 1978. Mem. Am. Ednl. Research Assn., Am. Psychol. Assn., Am. Soc. Tng. and Devel., Evaluation Network, Evaluation Research Soc., Soc. Intercultural Edn. and Research. Contbr. articles to profl. publs.; author profl. papers, reports. Home and Office: 3079 Turk Blvd San Francisco CA 94118

HECHTER, MICHAEL, sociology educator; b. Los Angeles, Nov. 15, 1943; s. Oscar Milton and Gertude (Horowitz) H.; children—Joshua, Rachel. A.B, Columbia U., 1965, Ph.D., 1972. Asst. prof. sociology U. Wash., Seattle, 1970-72, assoc. prof, 1972-81, prof., 1981—. Woodrow Wilson fellow, 1965. Mem. Am. Sociol. Assn., Internat. Sociol. Assn. Author: Internal Colonialism: Pre Celtic Fringe in British National Development, 1936-1966, 1975; editor: The Microfoundations of Macrosociology, 1983. Office: Dept Sociology U Wash Seattle WA 98195

HECKEL, JACK L., aerospace products manufacturing company executive; b. 1931; married. B.S., U. Ill., 1954. With Aerojet-Gen. Corp., 1956—, pres. Space Gen. Corp., from 1970, pres. Aeroject Liquid Rocket Co., from 1972, corp. group v.p., from 1977, corp. pres., La Jolla, Calif., 1981—, also dir. Served with USAF, 1954. Office: Aerojet Gen Corp 10300 N Torrey Pines Rd La Jolla CA 92037*

HECKEL, JOHN LOUIS (JACK), aerospace company executive; b. Columbus, Ohio, July 12, 1931; s. Russel Criblez and Ruth Selma (Heid) H.; m. Jacqueline Ann Alexander, Nov. 21, 1959; children—Heidi, Holly, John. B.S. in Aero. Engring., U. Ill., 1954. With Aerojet-Gen. Corp., La Jolla, Calif., 1956—, mgr. various divs., Azusa, Calif., 1956-59, Seattle, 1959-61, Washington, 1961-70, pres. Aerojet/Space Gen., El Monte, Calif., 1970-72, pres. Aerojet Liquid Rocket Cop., Sacramento, Calif., 1972-77, group v.p. Sacramento Cos., 1977-81, pres. Aerojet-Gen. Corp., 1981—. Mem. chancellor's assocs. U. Calif., San Diego, 1982—. Served to 1st lt. USAF, 1954-56. Recipient Disting. Alumni award U. Ill., 1979. Mem. Aerospace Industries Assn. Am. (gov.), AIAA, Air Force Assn., Am. Def. Preparedness Assn., Nat. Security Indsl. Assn., Navy League U.S. Club: Lomas Santa Fe Country (Solana Beach, Calif.). Home: 14845 Circo Diegueno Del Mar CA 92014 Office: 10300 N Torrey Pines Rd La Jolla CA 92037

HECKENDORF, ROBERT WILLIAM, aviation investment exec., rancher; b. Denver, Jan. 9, 1945; s. Richard Hendrie and June Virginia Heckendorf; B.A., U. Denver, 1969; M.B.A., Calif. Western U., 1981; m. Robyn Lee Florence, Mar. 27, 1969; children—Summer, Fielding, Bronwyn, Dieter. Pres., Harp Ltd., Denver, 1975-77; Summerfield Group, Denver, 1977—; line capt. Johns-Manville Sales Corp., Denver, 1977—. Mem. Nat. Assn. Flight Instrs., Internat. Aerobatic Club, Nat. Bus. Aircraft Assn., Am. Mgmt. Assn., Am. Nat. Cattlemen's Assn., Aircraft Owners and Pilots Assn., Stearman Restorers Assn., Exptl. Aircraft Assn., Warbirds of Am., Colo. Cattlemen's Assn. Home: 21000 E 152nd Ave Brighton CO 80601 Office: Hangar 5 Stapleton Internat Airport Denver CO 80207

HECKER, RICHARD JACOB, research geneticist; b. Miles City, Mont., Mar. 26, 1928; s. John T. and Elizabeth R. H.; m. Diane M., Aug. 12, 1958; children—Carol, John, Ann, Douglas. B.S., Mont. State U., 1958; Ph.D., Colo. State U., 1964. Geneticist, U.S. Dept. Agr., Ft. Collins, Colo., 1959-64, research geneticist, Salinas, Calif., 1964-65, Ft. Collins, 1965-73, research leader, 1973—; affiliate prof. Colo. State U., 1965—. Served with U.S. Army, 1952-54. Recipient Meritorious Service award Am. Soc. Sugar Beet Technologists 1981. Mem. Am. Soc. Agronomy, Crop Sci. Soc. Am., Western Soc. Crop Sci., Am. Soc. Sugar Beet Technologists. Roman Catholic. Club: KC. Contbr. numerous articles to profl. jours. Home: 1100 Morgan St Fort Collins CO 80524 Office: Crops Research Lab Colo State U Fort Collins CO 80523

HECKES, ALBERT ALLEN, chem. engr.; b. Ordway, Colo., June 3, 1930; s. Edward Gerhard and Ethel Mae (Duncan) H.; B.S. in Chem. Engring., U. Kans., 1952, M.S. (Phillips Petroleum Co. fellow 1955-56), 1956; m. Marian Louise Miner, Dec. 23, 1950; children—Frederick A., John A., Helen J., Susan P. Engr., Naval Ordnance Test Sta., China Lake, Calif., 1952, Dow Corning Corp., Midland, Mich., 1956-59; staff mem. Sandia Nat. Lab., Albuquerque, 1959—. Served with U.S. Army, 1952-54. Mem. Internat. Pyrotechnics Soc. (charter), Alumni Assn. U. Kans., Ducks Unlimited, Alpha Chi Sigma. Republican. Presbyterian. Author papers in field. Home: 3616 Mary Ellen St NE Albuquerque NM 87111 Office: Div 9752 Sandia Nat Labs Box 5800 Albuquerque NM 87185

HECKMAN, PAUL EUGENE, educational administrator, researcher; b. Pleasantville, N.J., July 16, 1943; s. Paul Eugene and Theresa (Howell) H., Sr.; m. Sigrid Elizabeth Andresen, July 2, 1966; children—Geoffrey, Erica, Jonathan, Joshua. B.A. in History, Kings Coll., 1966; M.Ed. in English, Boston, U., 1970; Ph.D. in Curriculum and Study of Schooling, UCLA, 1982. Profl. cert., N.H. Asst. prin. Mascenic Regional Sch., New Ipswich, N.H., 1968-70; tchr., team leader Corinne A. Seeds Univ. Elem. Sch., UCLA, 1970-74; research asst. research div. I/D/E/A, Los Angeles, 1974-76, research specialist, 1976-80; asst. dir. lab. in sch. and community edn. Grad. Sch. Edn., UCLA, 1980—; cons. Beaverton, Oreg., Live Oak Sch. Dist., Santa Cruz, Calif., San Diego County Sch. Dist., Fillmore (Calif.) Sch. Dist. Mem. Assn. Supervision and Curriculum Devel., Am. Ednl. Research Assn., Nat. Soc. for Study Edn. Baptist. Contbr. articles to ednl. jours., tech. reports. Office: 405 Hilgard Ave Los Angeles CA 90024

HECKMAN, RICHARD AINSWORTH, chemical engineer; b. Phoenix, July 15, 1929; s. Hiram and Anne (Sells) A.; B.S., U. Calif. at Berkeley, 1950; m. Olive Ann Biddle, Dec. 17, 1950; children—Mark, Bruce. With radiation lab. U. Calif. at Berkeley, 1950-51; chem. engr. Calif. Research & Devel. Co., Livermore, 1951-53; assoc. div. leader Lawrence Livermore Nat. Lab., Livermore, 1953-77, project leader, 1977-78, program leader, 1978-79, energy policy analyst, 1979—. Bd. dirs. Calif. Industries for Blind, 1977-80, Here and Now Disabled Services for Tri-Valley, Inc., 1980. Registered profl. engr., Calif. Mem. AAAS, Nat. Hist. Soc., N.Y. Acad. Scis., Am. Nuclear Soc., Internat. Oceanographic Soc. Club: Island Yacht (commodore 1971) (Alameda, Calif.), Midget Ocean Racing Club (sta. 3 commodore 1982-83), U.S. Yacht Racing Union, Midget Ocean Racing Assn. No. Calif. (commodore 1972). Patentee in field. Home: 5683 Greenridge Rd Castro Valley CA 94546 Office: PO Box 808 Livermore CA 94550

HEDBERG, SALLY BODINE, special education educator; b. Fort Collins, Colo., Oct. 11, 1936; d. Eddie Walter and Ermina (Fallas) Bodine; m. Leonard Nesbit Hedberg, June 27, 1959; children—Julie, Jenny, Linda. B.A., U. Ariz., 1958; M.A., San Francisco State U., 1976. Cert. tchr. physically handicapped, visually impaired and learning disabled, Calif. Resource specialist spl. edn., Miramonte High Sch., Orinda, Calif., 1976-81; project dir. secondary schs. disabled awareness curriculum, Orinda, 1982—; mem. adv. com. Calif. Dept. Rehab., Calif. Adv. Council Vocat. Edn. Calif. Dept. Edn. Title IV-C grantee, 1982-83. Mem. Calif. Tchrs. Assn., NEA, Calif. Assn. Neurologically Handicapped Children and Adults (Waldie award 1980), Kappa Alpha Theta. Home: 52 Overhill Rd Orinda CA 94563 Office: 1212 Pleasant Hill Rd Lafayette CA 94549

HEDEMANN, NANCY OAKLEY, clinical psychologist; b. Honolulu, July 4, 1921; d. George Daniel Oakley and Dorothy Dean (Spry) O.; divorced; 1 son, George Christian. B.A., U. Hawaii, 1948, M.A. in Psychology, 1954, Ph.D., 1969. Clin. psychologist Bur. Mental Hygiene, Hawaii, 1954-66; chief State of Hawaii Children's Day Treatment Ctr., 1966-68, Lanahila Mental Health Clinic, 1968-69, Learning Disability Clinic, 1969-72; pvt. practice clin. psychology, Honolulu, 1982—. Mem. Hawaiian Psychol. Assn., Am. Psychol. Assn. Home: 2120 Kakela Pl Honolulu HI 96822 Office: 4614 Kilauea Ave Suite 567 Honolulu HI 96816

HEDGES, CARL DEVON, inventor, mfr.; b. Rochester, Ind., Sept. 2, 1924; s. Samuel Pope and Cora Myrtle (Wood) H.; student Rochester public schs., spl. courses; m. Margery Eileen Corliss, Aug. 15, 1953; children—Karl Eugene, Karen Eileen. Research dir. KARLEEN Enterprises, 1964-67; research and devel. plastic mktg. mgmt., 1967-70; new product developer, corp. and patent and invention cons., 1970-74; pres., gen. mgr. World-Wide Meml., Inc., Pueblo, Colo., 1974—, maj. stockholder, new product devel. mgr. successor firm World Wide Industries, Inc., 1980—. First aid instr. ARC, 1961-73; merit badge counselor Boy Scouts Am. Served with AUS, 1943-46, PTO. Recipient Internat. Gold Medal award for inventions Internat. Patent and Lic. Expn., 1967, 73. Mem. Ind. Inventors Am., Internat. Ind. Inventors, Am. Plastics and Fiberglass Research and Tech. Assn., DAV (past comdr., life mem., past Ind. state treas.), VFW (life, past comdr.). Republican. Methodist. Inventor, holder 30 patents. Home: 1806 E 3d St Pueblo CO 81001 Office: PO Box 322 Pueblo CO 81002

HEDGES, JONATHAN MARK, restaurateur, musician; b. Beatrice, Nebr., July 24, 1957; s. Dell Gilbert and Marcella Bernice (Clough) H. B.A. in Journalism, U. Nebr., 1981. Advt. dir. Waterbed World, Lincoln, Nebr., 1979; prodn. mgr., art dir. Nebraska Voice Mag., Lincoln, 1980; mgr., art. dir., co-owner Accent Printing, Lincoln, 1981-83; owner, mgr. Dinsdale's Lunch & Lounge, Lincoln, 1983—; mem. country band Shootin' from the Hip, 1980-83; dir. Duplitech, Inc., Lincoln. Mem. Lancaster County Young Republicans. Mem. Advt. Fedn. Lincoln, U. Nebr. Alumni Assn., Phi Kappa Psi Alumni Assn. (bd. dirs.). Methodist. Contbr. printing projects Am. Printer mag., 1982; co-composer numerous songs pub. and rec., 1981-82. Office: Dinsdale's Lunch & Lounge 1228 P St Lincoln NE 68508

HEDIN, EDNA JENKS, musician, educator; b. Ft. Worth, Nov. 15, 1924; d. Edward Lee and Tressie (Jackson) Jenks; A.A., Central Coll. Women, Conway, Ark., 1945; B.Music, Okla. Baptist U., 1948; M.Ed., Tex. Tech. U., 1972; m. Alvin Morris Hedin, Apr. 1, 1947; children—John Alvin, Edward Morris, James Lee. Grad. asst. Central Coll. Women, Conway, 1946-47; pvt. tchr. piano, mus. dir. kindergarten Shawnee, Okla., 1948-49; dir. jr. high choir Crooked Oak Sch., Oklahoma City, 1950-51; tchr. music Norfolk Consol. Sch., Cushing, Okla., 1951-55; Artesia (N.Mex.) pub. schs., 1955—; adj. tchr. N.Mex. State U., Carlsbad; organist First Bapt. Ch., 1955—; tchr. piano and organ; piano soloist and accompanist; judge pianists and ch. choirs. Mem. Nat. Guild Piano Tchrs., Nat., N.Mex., Artesia edn. assns., Internat. Reading Assn., Phi Kappa Phi, Sigma Alpha Iota, Kappa Delta Pi, Delta Kappa Gamma. Democrat. Baptist. Home: 1605 Sears St Artesia NM 88210 Office: Artesia Pub Schs 1105 W Quay St Artesia NM 88210

HEDLUND, EMMA, fabric warehouse co. exec.; b. St. George, Utah, May 14, 1923; d. Gordon and Blanche (Beckstrom) Sullivan; student Phoenix Coll., 1970-72; m. Carl B. Hedlund, June 25, 1960; children—Melinda Marlene Hedlund Millsap, Terry Gordon, Carlene Laurie. With, Hedlund Fabric Supply Co., Phoenix, 1968—, v.p., dir., 1970—. Mem. citizens adv. council Phoenix Union High Sch. Dist., 1977—. Mem. Nat. Assn. Decorative Fabric Distbrs., Automotive Service Industry Assn., Phoenix Met. C. of C. Republican. Mormon. Office: Hedlund Fabrics Supply Co 1710 E Washington St Phoenix AZ 85034

HEDRICK, BASIL CALVIN, museum administrator, educator, consultant, writer; b. Lewistown, Mo., Mar. 17, 1932; s. Truman B. and M. La Veta (Stice) H.; m. Anne Kehoe, Jan. 19, 1957 (div.); 1 dau., Anne Lanier Hedrick Caraker; m. 2d, Susan Elizabeth Pickel, Oct. 2, 1980. A.B. in History and Fgn. Langs., Augustana Coll., 1956; M.A. in Interam. Studies, U. Fla., 1957; Ph.D., Inter-Am. U., Mex., 1965. Tchr., Ill. and N.Mex., 1952-57; asst. dir. Sch. Inter-Am. Studies, U. Fla., 1958-59; asst. to pres., prof. langs. Fullerton Coll., 1963-67; asst. dir. Latin Am. Inst., So. Ill. U., 1959-63, asst. dir. Univ. Mus. and Art Galleries, 1967-70, dir., 1970-72, dean internat. edn., 1972-74, dir. Univ. Mus. and Art Galleries, 1974-77; asst. dir. Ill. Div. of Museums, 1977-80; dir. U. Alaska Mus. and prof. history U. Alaska, Fairbanks, 1980—; cons. in field mem., team leader Am. Assn. Mus. Accreditation Commn.; mem. Alaska State Council on Arts; chmn. Fairbanks Hist. Preservation Commn. Active Fairbanks Symphony Assn. Decorated Cross of Eloy Alfaro (Panama). Mem. Am. Assn. Mus., Museums Alaska, Western Mus. Conf., Soc. Am. Archaeology, Fairbanks Art Assn., Phi Alpha Theta, Sigma Delta Pi. Author, editor 15 books primarily in fields of ethnohistory, archaeology, anthropology; contbr. articles, reviews, monographs to publs. Office: Univ Museum 907 Yukon Dr Univ Alaska Fairbanks AK 99701

HEDRICK, WALLACE EDWARD, planning and mgmt. cons. co. exec.; b. Malad, Idaho, Nov. 11, 1947; s. Clarence Franklin and Beth S. Hedrick; B.S., U. Nev., Reno, 1970; M.A., U. No. Colo., Greeley, 1974; m. Jerrie S. Deffenbaugh, Nov. 20, 1980; children—Ann Elizabeth, Ryan Wallace, Hallie Sue. Regional dir. No. Idaho, Idaho Planning and Community Affairs Agy., Moscow, 1970-73, asso. chief, Boise, 1973-75; project dir. Pacific N.W. Regional Commn., Boise, 1975-76; pres. Resources Northwest, Inc., Boise, 1976—, also chmn. bd. Sec.-treas. Idaho Citizens for Responsible Govt., 1978—. Served with USAR, 1971. Mem. Am. Planning Assn. Democrat. Home: 9413 Knottingham St Boise ID 83704 Office: 775 N 8th St Boise ID 83702

HEDY, CHARLES DUANE, educational administrator; b. Kansas City, Kans., Oct. 6, 1940; s. William T. and Alberta Jane (Acock) H.; m. Ardys I. Yutzie, Dec. 8, 1976; children—John, Laura, D'Lynn, Darin. B.A., Occidental Coll., 1962; B.S., Oreg. State U., 1964, M.S., 1965. Cert. tchr., adminstr. Tchr., Albany (Oreg.) Pub. Schs., 1965-72, vice prin., 1972-75, asst. prin., 1975-79, prin., 1979-82, asst. supt., 1982—. Mem. budget com. Albany Redevel. Agy., 1983—. Mem. Confedn. Oreg. Sch. Adminstrs., Oreg. Assn. Secondary Sch. Adminstrs., Nat. Assn. Secondary Sch. Prins., Oreg. Assn. for Supervision and Curriculum Devel., Nat. Assn. Supervision and Curriculum Devel. Rotarian. Home: 535 SW 11th St Albany OR 97321 Office: 718 SW 7th St Albany OR 97321

HEE, LYLA BONNIE, secondary school administrator, consultant; b. N.Y.C., Mar. 15, 1951; d. Ernest Helge Christian and Carmen (Yap) Berg; m. Clayton Howe Wah Hee, June 11, 1982. Student U. Wash., 1969-71, U. Salzburg, 1971-72; B.A. in English and German, Georgetown U., 1974; M.Ed. in Ednl. Adminstrn. and Supervision, Am. U., 1975; M.Ed. in Curriculum and Instrn., U. Hawaii-Manoa, 1979. Receptionist, sec. Office of U.S. Sen. Daniel K. Inouye, Washington, 1973-74; instr. Paul Jr. High Sch., Washington, 1974-75; vice prin. trainee, adminstr. internship program Wakefield High Sch., Arlington, Va., 1975; instr. Kailua (Oahu) High Sch., 1976-77, Title I reading and lang. arts coordinator, 1977-80; student activities coordinator Molokai High and Intermediate Sch., 1980-81, title I reading and lang. arts program coordinator, 1981-82, vice prin., 1982—; instr. Project Ho'ona-'auao Program Alulike, Inc., 1981—; dance and exercise instr. Molokai Dept. Parks and Recreation, 1981—; aerobics dance instr. Jackie Sorenson Program, Honolulu, 1980; instr. adult edn. Windward Sch. for Adults, Oahu, 1979-80. Sec. Title I Parent Adv. Council; dir. Molokai High Sch. PTSA, Molokai Community Services Council, 1981—; mem. Com. on Status of Women; mem. Kailua High Sch. PTSA, 1976, Waimanalo Ednl. Task Force, 1976-80; mem. Title I Parent Adv. Council; Brownie Troop leader, 1976; mem. Punahou Sch. Alumni Assn. Mem. Internat. Reading Assn., Ka Hui Heluhelu, Assn. Supervision and Curriculum Devel., AAUW, Am. Assn. Tchrs. of German, Alpha Chi Omega. Democrat. Club: Molokai Saddle. Home: PO Box 314 Ho'olehua Molokai HI 96729 Office: PO Box 158 Ho'olehua Molokai HI 96729

HEEGER, JACK JAY, public relations counselor; b. Sioux City, Iowa, Oct. 18, 1930; s. Lester and Etta (Grossman) H.; m. Fern Rubenstein, Feb. 14, 1954; children—Lloyd, Marshall, Laurie. Student U. Iowa, 1949-50. Reporter, writer Sioux City Jour., 1947-49, 50-51, 54; radio news editor UPI, Los Angeles, 1955-57; asst. pub. relations dir. Revell, Inc., Venice, Calif., 1957-59; staff rep. Carl Byoir & Assocs., Inc., Los Angeles, 1959-64, mgr. west coast, 1964-69; owner, pres. Jack J. Heeger Pub. Relations/Communications, Los Angeles, 1969-71; mem. exec. staff Braun & Co., Los Angeles, 1971-74; pub. relations mgr. Sunkist Growers, Inc., Sherman Oaks, Calif., 1974-75, pub. affairs mgr., 1975-76, v.p. pub. affairs, 1976—; instr. pub. relations U. So. Calif., Calif. State U.-Los Angeles; lectr. various univs. Mem. pub. relations adv. bd. John Tracy Clinic, Los Angeles, 1967—; profl. adviser UCLA chpt. Pub. Relations Students Soc., 1969-70; active Boy Scouts Am., 1967-74; bd. dirs. Interracial Council for Bus. Opportunity, 1965-72; trustee Stephen S. Wise Temple, 1975-76. Served with USMCR, 1951-53. Mem. Pub. Relations Soc. Am. (chpt. pres. 1972-73, dir. 1970—, Disting. Profl. award 1976), Nat. Assn. Better Broadcasting (dir.), Phi Epsilon Pi. Lodges: Masons, Shriners. Contbr. articles to profl. jours. Home: 11373 Charnock Rd Los Angeles CA 90066 Office: 14130 Riverside Dr Sherman Oaks CA 91403

HEER, DAVID MACALPINE, sociology educator; b. Chapel Hill, N.C., Apr. 15, 1930; s. Clarence and Jean Douglas (MacAlpine) H.; m. Nancy Whittier, June 29, 1957; m. Kaye Schwarz Heymann, Dec. 11, 1980; children—Douglas (dec.), Laura, Catherine. A.B. magna cum laude, Harvard U., 1960, A.M. in Sociology, 1954, Ph.D. in Sociology, 1958. Statistician population div. U.S. Bur. of Census, Washington, 1957-61; lectr., asst. research sociologist U. Calif.-Berkeley, 1961-64; asst. prof. demography Harvard U. Sch. Pub. Health, Boston, 1964-68; assoc. prof., 1968-72; prof. sociology U. So. Calif., 1972—; mem. population research study sect. NIH, 1971-73. Mem. Population Assn. Am. Nat. Council Family Relations, Am. Sociol. Assn., Internat. Union for Sci. Study Population. Unitarian. Author: After Nuclear Attack: A Demographic Inquiry, 1965; Society and Population, 1968; editor: Social Statistics and the City, 1968; Readings of Population, 1968.

HEFFELFINGER, STEVEN JOHN, aerospace engr.; b. Ely, Eng., Sept. 1, 1954; s. Eugene T. and Valerie Frances (Blyth) H.; student U.S. Mil. Acad., 1972-74; A.S., Mt. Wachusett Community Coll., Gardner, Mass., 1977; B.A., San Jose State U., 1983; m. Gisela M. Wenner, Mar. 11, 1980; children— Michelle, David. Sr. field rep. Sylvania Tech. Systems, Inc., 1978; specialist, curriculum dept. No. Telecom, Inc., 1978-79; satellite ops. engr. Lockheed Missiles & Space Co., Sunnyvale, Calif., 1979-81; mem. tech. staff Applied Research, Inc., Santa Clara, Calif., 1981—. Served with Security Agy., U.S. Army, 1975-78. Mem. Assn. Old Crows. Home: 2406 Alvin St Mountain View CA 94043 Office: 3930 Freedom Circle Santa Clara CA 95054

HEFFERNAN, THOMAS JOSEPH, holding co. exec.; b. Youngstown, Ohio, Sept. 4, 1944; s. Francis Matthew and Muriel Ann (Ryan) H.; B.A., Chgo. City Coll., 1973; postgrad. U. Wash., Seattle; m. Marie T. Arzer, May 1, 1965; children—Mark C., John P., Michael T. Fiduciary tax cons. First Nat. Bank Chgo., 1963-68; controller Microseal Corp., Zion, Ill., 1968-78; v.p. fin., dir. Dietrich-Post Co. Wash., Inc., Seattle, 1978—, Dieterich-Post Co. Can., Ltd., Vancouver, B.C., 1978—, B.C. Industries, Ltd., Vanvouver and Seattle, 1978; controller, dir. Dollco-Industries U.S. and Can., 1978. Mem. Northbook (Ill.) Civic Council, 1969-75; treas., activities chmn. Northbrook troop Boy Scouts Am., 1972-75; mem. fin. com. St. Jude's Roman Catholic Ch. Recipient various certs. of appreciation. Mem. Am. Inst. Corp. Controllers, Nat. Fedn. Ind. Bus. Clubs: Coll. (Seattle); Red-Wood Athletic (Woodinville). Office: Suite 205 2661 Bellevue-Redmond Rd Bellevue WA 98008

HEFFLEFINGER, CLARICE MAE, real estate broker; b. Oregon, Ill., Oct. 5, 1937; d. Ralph Wayne and Wyota Anita (Nashold) Hefflefinger) Thorpe; A.A., Coll. Sequoias, Visalia, Calif.. 1967; m. Jack Kenneth Hefflefinger. Jan. 24, 1970; children—Kenneth, Jack, Deborah, Kevin. Various positions in banking and ins., 1956-76; real estate asso. Lewis Real Estate, Tulare, Calif.. 1977—; substitute tchr. Tulare City Schs., 1979—. Chmn. Tulare County Draft Bd.; Tulare County rep. to state assemblyman. Mem. Nat. Assn. Realtors, Calif. Assn. Realtors (dir.), Tulare C. of C., Tulare Bd. Realtors (dir., pres. 1982), Tulare Amvets Aux. (pres. 1983). Republican. Club: Quota. Home: 1351 Williams St PO Box 1213 Tulare CA 93275

HEFLEY, JOEL M., state senator; b. Ardmore, Okla.; s. J. Maurice and Etta A. (Anderson) H.; B.A., Okla. Baptist U., 1957; M.S., Okla. State U., 1963; m. Lynn Christian, Aug. 25, 1962; children—Janna, Lori, Juli. Exec. dir. Community Planning and Research, Colorado Springs, Colo., 1966—; mem. Colo. Ho. of Reps., 1977-78; mem. Colo. Senate, 1979—. Republican. Presbyterian. Clubs: Rotary, Colorado Springs Country. Office: 25 E San Rafael Colorado Springs CO 80903

HEFTEL, CECIL, congressman; b. Cook County, Ill., Sept. 30, 1924; B.S., Ariz. State U., 1951; postgrad. U. Utah, NYU; m. Joyce Glasmann; children—Cathi, Lani, Peggy, Susan, Christopher, Terry, Richard. Pres., Heftel Broadcasting Co.; mem. 95th-97th Congresses from 1st Hawaii Dist., mem. Ways and Means com. Active March of Dimes. Mem. Am. Legion. Democrat. Clubs: Elks, Eagles, Shriners. Office: 1030 Longworth House Office Bldg Washington DC 20515

HEFTMANN, ERICH, biochemist; b. Vienna, Mar. 9, 1918; s. Salomon and Rosa (Seifert) H.; came to U.S., 1939, naturalized, 1945; m. Brigitte Sander, Mar. 14, 1968; children—Rex, Lisa, Erica. Student U. Vienna, 1936-38; B.S. in Chemistry, NYU, 1942; Ph.D., U. Rochester, 1947. Biochemist, USPHS, Boston, 1947-48, Nat. Cancer Inst., Bethesda, Md., 1948-50, Nat. Inst. Arthritis and Metabolic Diseases, 1950-63, Western Regional Research Ctr., U.S. Dept. Agr., Berkeley, Calif., 1963-83; instr. U. Md., 1942-43, U.S. Dept. Agr. Grad. Sch., 1954-61; lectr. Georgetown U., 1958-59, U. Calif.-Berkeley, 1970; research fellow Calif. Inst. Tech., 1959-64, research assoc., 1964-69; grad. asst. U. Rochester, 1943-47; vis. assoc. prof. U. So. Calif., 1966-69. Recipient A.V. Humboldt award, 1975. Fellow AAAS; mem. Am. Chem. Soc., Am. Soc. Biol. Chemists, Phytochem. Soc. N.Am., Soc. Exptl. Biol. Medicine, Sigma Xi. Author: Chromatography, 1961, 67, 75, 83; Biochemistry of Steroids, 1960; Steroid Biochemistry, 1970; Modern Methods of Steroid Analysis, 1973; Chromatography of Steroids, 1976; contbr. articles to profl. jours.; editor: Jour. Chromatography Symposium Vols., 1983—; patentee in field. Home: 108 Canon Dr PO Box 928 Orinda CA 94563 Office: 800 Buchanan St Berkeley CA 94710

HEGRENES, JACK RICHARD, educator; b. Fargo, N.D., Feb. 27, 1929; s. John and Ivy Anna (Jacobson) H.; B.S., U. Oreg., 1952, M.S., 1955; M.A., U. Chgo., 1960, Ph.D., 1970. Caseworker, Clackamas County Public Welfare Commn., Oregon City, Oreg., 1956-59, casework supr., 1960-62; instr. dept. psychiatry U. Oreg. Med. Sch., Portland, 1962-64, instr. Crippled Children's div., 1966-68, asst. prof., 1969-73, asso. prof. dept. public health and preventive medicine, and Crippled Children's div., 1973—; adj. asso. prof. social work Sch. Social Work, Portland State U., 1973—. La Verne Noyes scholar, U. Chgo., 1958-60; NIMH fellow, U. Chgo., 1964-66. Fellow Am. Orthopsychiat. Assn.; mem. Nat. Assn. Social Workers, Am. Public Health Assn., Soc. for Gen. Systems Research, Am. Assn. for Advancement of Behavior Therapy, Am. Assn. Marriage and Family Therapists. Lutheran. Contbr. articles to profl. jours. Home: 3101 McNary Pkwy 12 Lake Oswego OR 97034 Office: Oreg Health Scis U PO Box 574 Portland OR 97207

HEHN, QUINTON RICHARD, psychotherapist; b. Menno, S.D., Oct. 31, 1948; s. Elver Andreas and Bonnie Lou (King) H. B.A. in Social Welfare, Boston U., 1975, M.Ed. in Counselling and human services, 1975. Clin. supr. intensive care Yellowstone Boys and Girls Ranch, Billings, Mont., 1979, psychotherapist, 1980—. Served to capt. U.S. Army, 1970-78; Vietnam. Decorated Bronze Star, Army Commendation medal. Mem. Am. Personnel and Guidance Assn. Home: 941 Lewis Ave Apt 4 Billings MT 59101

HEIBY, ELAINE MARIE, clinical psychology educator, psychotherapist, consultant; b. Bucyrus, Ohio, Jan. 22, 1952; d. Raymond Woodrow and Geraldine Marie (Schwab) H.; m. James Dubei Becker, June 14, 1980. B.A., Case Western Res. U., 1974; M.A., U. Ill., 1976, Ph.D., 1980. Cert. clin. psychologist, Hawaii. Cons., Human Resources Developers, Chgo., 1975-80; instr. St. Xavier Coll., Chgo., 1979-80; cons. Psychol. Services Inst., Harrisonburg, Va., 1980-81; asst. prof. psychology James Madison U., Harrisonburg, 1980-81; asst. prof. psychology James Madison U., Harrisonburg, 1980-81; asst. prof. clin. psychology U. Hawaii, Honolulu, 1981—; pvt. practice psychotherapy; cons. bus., industry and pub. service instns. Contract rep. U. Hawaii Profl. Assembly. Recipient Revolving Fund award U. Hawaii, 1981-82; James Madison U. grantee, 1980-81. Mem. Am. Psychol. Assn., Western Psychol. Assn., Assn. Advancement Behavior Therapy, Hawaii Psychol. Assn., Biofeedback and Behavioral Medicine Soc. Hawaii. Contbr. psychol. articles to profl. jours. Home: 2542 Date St Apt 702 Honolulu HI 96826 Office: U Hawaii Dept Psychology 2430 Campus Rd Gartley 105 Honolulu HI 96822

HEIDENTHAL, FREDERICK PAUL, JR., computer co. exec.; b. Johnstown, Pa., July 17, 1946; s. Frederick Paul and Sadie Rae (Taylor) H.; B.S. in Acctg., Pa. State U., 1970; divorced; children—Todd, Sharon, Mariah. Controller, gen. mgr., dir. fin., v.p. fin., Splty. Chem., Ltd., Hong Kong and Geneva, 1973-79; auditor, tax acct. Arthur Andersen & Co., San Jose, Calif., 1970-73; v.p. fin., exec. v.p. Televideo Systems, Inc., Sunnyvale, Calif., 1980-82; exec. v.p. Axlon Inc., San Jose, 1982—. Served to 1st lt. AUS, 1965-69. Decorated Bronze Star; C.P.A., Calif. Office: Axlon Inc 70 Daggett Dr San Jose CA 95134

HEIDER, RICHARD JOSEPH, oil company executive; b. Carroll, Iowa, July 7, 1924; s. Joseph A. and Agnes D. (Delaney) H.; m. Marguerite Wallace, July 10, 1950; children—Susan, Beth. B.B.A., Creighton U., 1946, J.D., 1948. Bar: Nebr. 1948, Colo. 1949, Mont. 1950, Wyo. 1952. Landman, Sinclair Oil Corp., Rocky Mountains, 1948-52; div. landman Hancock Oil Co., Casper, Wyo., 1952-56; div. mgr. Petroleum, Inc, Denver, 1956-67; exec. v.p., dir. Inexco Oil Co., Denver, 1968-69; pres., dir. Petromer Trend Corp., Denver, 1970-72; ind. oil ops., Denver, 1973-77; pres., dir. Juniper Petroleum Corp., Denver, 1977—. Served with U.S. Army, 1943-44. Clubs: Denver Petroleum, Arapahoe Tennis. Home: 1880 Cherryville Rd Littleton CO 80121 Office: 1660 Lincoln St Suite 2410 Denver CO 80264

HEIDT, JOHN MURRAY, banker; b. Oceanside, N.Y., Dec. 25, 1931; s. Adaline (Sohns) H.; A.B., Stanford U., 1954; grad. Pacific Coast Banking Sch., 1965; M.B.A., U. So. Calif., 1969; m. Mary Ann Kerans, June 18, 1953; children—John, Ann. With Union Bank, Los Angeles, 1959—, exec. v.p., 1971-75, pres., dir., 1975—; dir. Union Bank, Union Venture Corp. Trustee St. John's Hosp., Marlborough Sch. Served as spl. agt. USAF, 1954-57. Recipient Man of Hope award City of Hope, 1978. Mem. Calif., Am. bankers assns., Assn. Res. City Bankers, Phi Gamma Delta. Clubs: Los Angeles Country, Calif. (Los Angeles); Vintage (Palm Springs). Office: Union Bank 445 S Figueroa St Los Angeles CA 90071

HEIDT, RAYMOND JOSEPH, ins. co. exec.; b. Bismarck, N.D., Feb. 28, 1933; s. Stephen Ralph and Elizabeth Ann (Hirschkorn) H.; B.A., Calif. State U., San Jose, 1963, M.A., 1968; Ph.D., U. Utah, 1977; m. Joyce Ann Aston, Jan. 14, 1956; children—Ruth Marie, Elizabeth Ann, Stephen Christian, Joseph Aston. Claims supr. Allstate Ins. Co., San Jose, Calif., 1963-65; claims mgr. Gen. Accident Group, San Francisco, 1965-69; owner, mgr. Ray Heidt & Assos., Logan, Utah, 1969-76; v.p. claims Utah Home Fire Ins. Co., Salt Lake City, 1976—; with Utah State U., 1970-76; dir. Inst. for Study of Pacifism and Militarism. Active, Republican Party. Served with U.S. Army, 1952-57. Decorated Bronze Star. Mem. Utah Claims Assn. (pres. 1977-78). Mormon. Clubs: Lions, Am. Legion. Home: 3494 Meadowbrook Dr West Valley UT 84119 Office: 3775 Market St Salt Lake City UT 84119

HEIECK, PAUL JAY, wholesale distbg. co. exec.; b. San Francisco, Aug. 6, 1937; s. Erwin N. and Ann C. (Retchless) H.; student Golden Gate Coll., 1958; m. Kathleen Pawela, Oct. 14, 1967; children—Valerie, Yvonne, Elizabeth, Krista, Justin. Sales rep. Heieck & Moran, San Francisco, 1958-63, sec.-treas., 1963-69, Heieck Supply, San Francisco, 1969-76, pres. 1976—; pres., dir. Eureka Supply, Inc., Eureka, Calif.; 1st v.p., dir. San Francisco Bd. Trade, 1978-82. Dir., San Francisco Boys Club, 1972—. Served with U.S. Army, 1955-57. Mem. Nat. Assn. Wholesalers, Am. Supply Assn. (dir. 1984—), No. Calif. Supplier's Assn. (pres. 81-83, dir. 1981—). Republican. Episcopalian. Clubs: Rotary, San Mateo County Mounted Posse, Sharon Heights Country, Ingomar. Office: 1111 Connecticut St San Francisco CA 94107

HEIERTZ, GREGORY PAUL, civil engineer; b. Lynwood, Calif., June 3, 1955; s. John Albert and Margaret Elizabeth (McWatters) H.; m. Carollyn Beth Lobell, May 16, 1981. B.S. in Civil Engring. and Biol. Scis., U. Calif.-Irvine, 1978. Registered profl. engr., Calif. Assoc. engr. James M. Montgomery Cons. Engrs., Irvine, 1978-79; assoc. engr. Irvine Ranch Water Dist., 1979-81, asst. supt. field ops., 1981—. Pres. Woodbridge Park Vista Home Owners Assn. Mem. ASCE, Am. Water Works Assn., Orange County Water Assn.

HEILBRUN, LANCE KNARR, biostatistician; b. Detroit, Mar. 17, 1947; s. Gann W. and Rose M. (Anthony) H.; m. Deborah E. Hutto, July 12, 1970; children—Aaron, Micah, Shana, Noah. B.S. in Math., Wayne State U., Detroit, 1969, M.A. in Math. Stats., 1971; M.P.H. in Biostats., U. Mich., 1974, Ph.D. in Biostats., 1976. Research asst. oncology div. Wayne State U., 1970-72; asst. prof. biometrics M.D. Anderson Hosp., Houston, 1976-79; biostatistician Japan-Hawaii Cancer Study, Honolulu, 1979—; biostatis. cons., 1982—. Bd. dirs. Pohakupu Community Assn., 1983—. USPHS grantee, 1972-74; U. Mich. Cancer Research Inst. fellow, 1975-76. Mem. Am. Statis. Assn., Biometrics Soc., Soc. Epidemiologic Research, Am. Assn. Cancer Research. Contbr. articles to profl. jours. Office: Kuakini Medical Ctr 347 N Kuakini St Honolulu HI 96817

HEILEMAN, JOHN PHILLIP, endocrinologist; b. Phoenix, Feb. 2, 1930; s. Leo M. and Rose M. (Murphy) H.; m. Ann F. O'Hara, Nov. 4, 1961; children—Jeanne Marie, James Andrew, Denise Ann, Matthew J. B.S., Ariz. State U., 1951; M.D., Stritch Sch. Medicine, Loyola U., Chgo., 1955; Intern, U.S. Naval Hosp., Great Lakes Tng. Ctr., Ill.; resident Cook County Hosp., 1959-60 VA Research Hosp, 1960-62 both Chgo.; pvt. practice medicine, Phoenix, 1962-71, practice medicine, pres. Endocrinology Assocs., P.A., Phoenix, 1971—; mem. staff St. Joseph's Hosp., Good Samaritan Hosp., Humana Hosp., St. Luke's Hosp., J.C. Lincoln Hosp., all Phoenix. Served with M.C., USN, 1955-58. Fellow ACP; mem. Am. Soc. Internal Medicine. Republican. Roman Catholic. Office: 3522 N 3d Ave Phoenix AZ 85013

HEIM, WERNER G(EORGE), biology educator; b. Muhlheim Ruhr, Germany, Apr. 7, 1929; came to U.S., 1940, naturalized, 1946; s. Fred and Recha (Hirsch) H.; m. Julie I. Blumenthal, June 25, 1961; children—Susan L., David L.; m. 2d, Suzanne M. Levine, June 24, 1973; children—Elise B. Ginsburg, Lynn A. Ginsburg. B.A. in Zoology, UCLA, 1950, M.A. in Zoology, 1952, Ph.D. in Zoology, 1954. Instr. Brown U., Providence, 1956-57; asst. prof. biology Wayne State U., Detroit, 1957-63, assoc. prof. biology, 1963-67, vice chmn. biology dept., 1961-62, planning coordinator biology bldg. program, 1964-67; mem. faculty Colo. Coll., Colorado Springs, 1967—, prof. biology, 1967—, chmn. biology dept., 1971-76, prof. biophysics and genetics dept. Sch. Medicine, 1978; cooperating geneticist regional genetic counseling program U. Colo. Health Scis. Ctr., Denver, 1978—, Del., Republican State Conv., Denver, 1982. USPHS-Nat. Cancer Inst. fellow, 1952-54; NIH grantee, 1958-67, NSF grantee, 1963-70, Am. Cancer Soc. grantee, 1963-65, Colo. Coll. grantee, 1979-83, Fellow AAAS; mem. Am. Soc. Zoologists, Soc. Developmental Biology, Internat. Soc. Developmental Biologists, Colo.-Wyo. Acad. Sci. (v.p. 1968-69), Nat. Soc. Genetic Counselors (assoc. mem.), Sigma Xi. Contbr. book revs., sci. articles to profl. publs. Office: Colo Coll Biology Dept Colorado Springs CO 80903

HEIMAN, GERALD RICHARD, pesticide co. exec.; b. Beloit, Kans., Sept. 6, 1940; s. Lawrence F. and Josephine J. (Heidrick) H.; B.S., Kans. State U., 1964; m. Sharon L. Potts, June 27, 1964. Sales rep. Thompson-Hayward Chem. Co., Kansas City, Kans., 1964-66; product mgr., 1966-70; mgr. marketing Pestcon Systems Inc. (formerly Phostoxin Sales Inc.), Alhambra, Calif., 1970-77, v.p., dir. mktg., 1977-78, pres., 1978—, also dir.; dir. Agrichem. Ins. Group, Ltd., Grand Caymon, W.I. Mem. Pres. Ford's Com. Food and Agr., 1976. Mem. Assn. Operative Millers, Master Brewers Assn., Am. Assn. Cereal Chemists, Nat. Pest Control Assn., Nat. Agrl. Chems. Assn., Am. Chem. Soc., Sigma Alpha Epsilon. Republican. Roman Catholic. Home: 1210 Wynn Rd Pasadena CA 91107 Office: 2221 Poplar Blvd Alhambra CA 91802

HEIMAN, MICHAEL FRANKLIN, psychiatrist; b. Chgo., May 5, 1945; s. Jerome Marvin and Sylvia May H.; m. Barbara Zukin, June 18, 1967; children—Tamara Beth, Joshua Ben-Israel. A.B. in Computer Sci., U. Calif.-Berkeley, 1968; M.D., U. Calif.-San Francisco, 1972. Intern, Sacramento Med. Ctr., 1972-73; resident in psychiatry Stockton (Calif.) State Hosp., 1973-75; mem. Dept. Mental Health State of Calif., Stockton, 1972-78; assoc. Behavioral Med. Group, Cerritos, Calif., 1978-82; ptnr. Associated Med. Psychiatrists, Paramount, Calif., 1982— . Recipient Young Contbr.'s award Am. Assn. Suicidology, 1976. Mem. Am. Psychiat. Assn., So. Calif Psychiat. Soc., Orange County Psychiat. Soc. (co-editor publ.). Democrat. Jewish. Club: B'nai B'rith. Contbr. articles to profl. jours. Office: Associated Med Psychiatrists 16660 Paramount Blvd Suite 309 Paramount CA 90723

HEIN, MARGARET ALLYCE, banker, lawyer; b. Beloit, Wis., Sept. 22, 1952; d. Allyn J. and Jane M. (McKenna) H.; m. Richard A. Froehlich, July 30, 1976 (div.); 1 son, Aaron B.H. B.A. in Adminstrn. of Criminal Justice, U. Ill.-Chgo., 1974; J.D., U. Puget Sound, Tacoma, 1977. Bar: Wash. 1977. Legal research intern Wash. State Senate, 1976; real estate loan and compliance officer Bank of Arlington (Wash.), 1977-79; v.p. loan rev. and trust Alaska Statebank, Anchorage, 1980—; v.p., asst. sec. Alaska Bancorporation, Alaska Bancshares, Inc. Mem. Wash. State Bar Assn., Bank Adminstrn. Inst., Nat. Assn. Bank Women. Office: PO Bx 240 Anchorage AK 99510

HEINDL, CLIFFORD JOSEPH, physicist; b. Chgo., Feb. 4, 1926; s. Anton Thomas and Louise (Fiala) H.; B.S., Northwestern U., 1947, M.S., 1948; A.M., Columbia, 1950, Ph.D., 1959 Sr. physicist Bendix Aviation Corp., Detroit, 1953-54; orsort student Oak Ridge Nat. Lab., 1954-55; asst. sect. chief Babcock & Wilcox Co., Lynchburg, Va., 1956-58; research group supr. Jet Propulsion Lab., Pasadena, Calif., 1959-65, now mgr. research and space sci. Served with AUS, 1944-46. Mem. Am. Phys. Soc., Am. Nuclear Soc., Am. Inst. Aeros. and Astronautics, Health Physics Soc., Planetary Soc. Research in reactor physics. Home: 179 Mockingbird Ln South Pasadena CA 91030 Office: 4800 Oak Grove Dr Pasadena CA 91103

HEINDSMANN, THEODORE EDWARD, aerospace co. exec.; b. N.Y.C., Aug. 2, 1925; s. Theodore Edward and Alma (Ferrier) H.; student Coll. William and Mary, 1941-43; B.E.E., Rensselaer Poly. Inst., 1944; postgrad. U.S. Naval Acad., 1945; M.S., U. Calif. at Berkeley, 1949; m. Virginia Lee Green, Apr. 17, 1949; children—Sandra Christine, Kenneth Theodore, Emily Lynn. Electronic scientist Navy Underwater Sound Lab., New London, Conn., 1945-47, 49-55; research engr. U. Calif. at Berkeley, 1947-49; research scientist, mgr. Boeing Co., Seattle, 1955—; cons. RIS Assocs., Vashon, Wash. Founding bd. dirs. Vashon Presch.; corp. treas., dir. VM Health Services Center, Vashon Presch. Served as officer, with USNR, 1943-46. Registered profl. engr., Wash. Mem. Vashon-Maury Island C. of C. (pres. 1972-73, bd. dirs. 1966-74), AAAS, Acoustical Soc. Am., IEEE, Marine Tech. Soc. (gen. chmn. Ocean Engring. Conf., 1980, adv. bd. 1984). Presbyterian. (clk. of session, trustee, elder). Club: Vashon Golf and Country. Contbr. articles to profl. jours. Home: Box 433 Route 5 Vashon Island WA 98070 Office: Boeing Co PO Box 3999 Seattle WA 98124

HEINIG, NORMAN THOMAS, cons. co. exec.; b. Chgo., Feb. 20, 1928; s. Oscar William and Agnes Kerchville (Lamar) H.; B.S., Northwestern U., 1955; children—Norman, William, Mary, Barbara, Tanya, Randy. Apprentice, Sanger Plumbing, 1945-50; engr., project mgr. Commonwealth Plumbing Co., Chgo., 1957-65; cons. engr. Architects Mech. Design Service Corp., Chgo., 1965-73; owner Heinig Cons. Plumbing Engring. Co., Mission Viejo, Calif., 1974—. Bd. dirs. Chgo. Boys Club, 1961; pres. PTA, 1967; leader Boy Scouts Am., 1955-65. Mem. Am. Soc. Plumbing Engrs. Republican. Roman Catholic. Clubs: Chgo. Athletic, Royal League, Elks. Home and office: PO Box 2777 Mission Viejo CA 92690

HEINLEIN, OSCAR ALLEN, former air force officer; b. Butler, Mo., Nov. 17, 1911; s. Oscar A. and Katherine (Canterbury) H.; B.S., U.S. Naval Acad., 1932; M.S., Calif. Inst. Tech., 1942; M.S. in Mech. Engring., Stanford, 1949; certificate in mining U. Alaska, 1953; grad. Air War Coll., 1953; student spl. studies U. Ariz., 1956-57; D.D., Universal Sem., 1970; m. Catharine Anna Bangert, May 1, 1933 (div. Apr. 1937); 1 dau., Catharine Anna; m. 2d, Mary Josephine Fisher, Aug. 25, 1939 (dec. Dec. 1977); 1 son, Oscar Allen III; m. 3d, Suzanne Birke, Feb. 23, 1980; 1 son, Michael Andre Bertin. Marine engr. Atlantic Refining Co., Phila., 1934; civil engr. Annapolis Mineral Devel. Co., Calif., 1935-37; enlisted as pvt. U.S. Army, 1937, advanced through grades to col., 1944; comdr. Ladd AFB, Alaska, 1953-54, 11th Air Div., Fairbanks, Alaska, 1954, Air Force Logistics Command Support Group, Vandenberg AFB, Calif., 1960-65, prof. air sci. U. Ariz., Tucson, 1955-58; insp. Gen. Mobile Air Materiel Area, Ala., 1958-60; ret. 1965; now cons.; pres. O.A. Heinlein Merc. Co., Butler, Mo., 1934—; vis. prof. U. Nev., Reno; dep. dir. civil def. Boulder City, Nev., 1967; dir., sec. Boulder Dam Fed. Credit Union, 1973-79; mem. Boulder City Police Adv. Com., 1976; ordained minister Bapt. Ch., 1976. Active Boy Scouts Am. Mem. Clark County (Nev.) Republican Central Com., 1966, Exec. com., 1970; mem. Rep. Central Com., 1966; Rep. candidate Nev. Assembly, 1972; mem. Boulder City Charter Commn. Mem. community coll. adv. bd. U. Nev., 1970. Served with USN, 1928-32; to 2d lt. USMC, 1932-34. Decorated Legion of Merit, Air medal, Army, Navy and Air Force commendation medals. Mem. Inst. Aero. Scis., Am. Meteorol. Soc., Nat. Research Assn., Am. Radio Relay League, SAR, Am. Polar Soc., VFW, Daedalians, Mensa, So. Nev. Amateur Radio Club, Inst. Amateur Radio, Quarter Century Wireless Assn., Ret. Officers Assn., Air Force Assn., Nat. Rifle Assn. (life), Armed Forces Communications and Electronics Assn., CAP, Am. Legion, Am. Assn. Ret. Persons, West Coast Amateur Radio Service, Soc. Wireless Pioneers. Mason. Clubs: MM (San Diego); Intertel (Ft. Wayne, Indiana); Missile Amateur Radio (pres. 1961-65 Vandenberg AFB); Explorers (N.Y.C.); Arctic Circle Prospectors', High Jumpers (Fairbanks, Alaska); Boulder City Gem and Mineral; Stearman Alumnus; Marines Memorial (San Francisco). Author: Big Bend County, 1953. Inventor. Home: 107 Wyoming St Boulder City NV 89005

HEINRICH, BRUCE LEE, financial executive; b. Seattle, Aug. 30, 1946; s. Ernest William and Dorothy Victoria (Stevens) H.; m. Ardeth Dean Lazz, Nov. 12, 1966; 1 dau., Andrea. B.A. in Econs., Wash. State U., 1968, M.B.A. in Fin., 1972. C.P.A., Wash. Fin. analyst Shell Oil Co., Denver and Los Angeles, 1968-70; internat. banking officer, Seattle First Nat. Bank, 1972-74; assoc., dir. acctg. R.W. Beck and Assocs., Seattle, 1974—. Mem. Am. Inst. C.P.A.s, Wash. State Soc. C.P.A.s. Home: 2611 29th St W Seattle WA 98199 Office: 7th Ave at Olive Way Seattle WA 98101

HEINRICH, JOHN HERBERT, Canadian provincial government official; b. Mission City, B.C., Can., Dec. 20, 1936; m. Linda Strachan, July 7, 1962; children—Paul, Kim. B.A., LL.B., U. B.C. Elected mem. Legis. Assembly B.C. for Prince George North, 1979, minister of mcpl. affairs B.C., Victoria, 1970—. Mem. Social Credit Party. Office: Legis Bldg Victoria BC V8V 1X4 Canada*

HEINRICHS, CHARLES LEONARD, aircraft company engineering manager; b. Reedley, Calif., Aug. 6, 1933; s. Abraham Benjamin and Sarah Doris (Koop) H.; B.A., N.W. Mo. State U., 1958; M.B.A., Pepperdine U., 1980. m. Nancy Kathryn Germann, Feb. 24, 1957; children—Debra, Patrice, Gregory, David. Analyst, N.Am. Aviation, Neosho, Mo., 1959-61; jr. statistician Bendix Corp., Kansas City, Mo., 1961-65; sr. scientist Booz-Allen Applied Research, Inc., Ft. Leavenworth, Kans., 1965-66; engring. sect. head Gen. Dynamics Corp., Montreal, Que., Can., and Rochester, N.Y., 1966-70; engring. mgr. Hughes Aircraft Co., Los Angeles, 1970—; indsl. communications cons., 1969-82; communications cons. Speak for Yourself, Inc., 1982—. Served with USAF, 1951-55. Mem. Soc. Logistics Engrs., Reliability, Maintainability, Logistics Symposium (bd. dirs. 1977), Nat. Speakers Assn. Club: Toastmasters Internat. (gov. Area 7 1977-78, Outstanding Toastmaster of Year area 7 dist. 33 1978). Contbr. papers to profl. confs. Home: 755 N Verna Ave Newbury Park CA 91320 Office: 8433 Fallbrook Ave Canoga Park CA 91304

HEINS, MARILYN, pediatrician, medical educator; b. Boston, Sept. 7, 1930; d. Harold and Esther (Berow) H.; m. Milton P. Lipson, Sept. 8, 1958; children—Rachel, Jonathan. A.B., Radcliffe Coll., 1951; M.D., Columbia U., 1955. Intern, N.Y. Hosp., 1955-56; resident in pediatrics Babies Hosp., 1956-58; asst. and assoc. physician dept. pediatrics, asst. to chief Detroit Receiving Hosp., 1960-64; dir. dept. pediatrics Detroit Gen. Hosp., 1965-71; dir. Project PRESCAD, Detroit Gen. Hosp., 1966-71; asst. prof. pediatrics Wayne State U., 1966-70, assoc. prof., 1970-79, asst. dean student affairs, 1971-73, assoc. dean student affairs, 1973-79; assoc. dean acad. affairs, assoc. prof. pediatrics, U. Ariz., 1979—, vice dean Coll. Medicine, 1983—. Chmn. Child Abuse Com. of Detroit Youth Bd., 1971-74; mem. adv. com. Foster Grandparent Program, Detroit, 1968-71; mem. Detroit Council Pub. Services for Children, 1969; bd. dirs. Mich. chpt. Nat. Found. Sudden Infant Death, 1970-79; mem. Joint Commn. Devel. Preventive and Protective Services for Children, Detroit, 1969; mem. adv. council Radcliffe Inst. Program in Health Care, 1973-76; bd. dirs. Planned Parenthood So. Ariz., 1983—; mem. Task Force on Child Abuse and Neglect, City of Detroit, 1976-79. Recipient Alumni Faculty Service award Wayne State U., 1972, Recognition award, 1977. Diplomate Am. Bd. Pediatrics. Fellow Am. Acad. Pediatrics, Am. Orthopsychiat. Assn.; mem. AMA, Am. Pub. Health Assn., Ambulatory Pediatric Assn., Assn. Am. Med. Colls. (nat. chmn. Group on Student Affairs 1977-79), Am. Hosp. Assn., Nat. Bd. Med. Examiners, Western Soc. Pediatric Research. Contbr. articles profl. jours., chpts. in books.

HEINSHEIMER, THOMAS FREDERICK, aerospace company executive; b. N.Y.C., July 28, 1939; s. Hans Walter and Elsbeth Heinsheimer; m. Julianne Weber, June 20, 1963; children—Eric, Eden. S.B.E.E., MIT, 1960; D. Atmospheric Physics, U. Paris, 1966. With Aerospace Corp. El Segundo, Calif., 1968-82, sr. staff scientist, unitl 1982; pres. Atmospherics Co., 1972—; asst. v.p., dir. space programs Titan Systems, Inc.; cons. in space sciences and atmospheric research. Organizer and pres. Gordon Bennett Balloon Race Inc., 1979—; city councilman and mayor, City of Rolling Hills, 1972—. Recipient awards lighter-than-air socs. in U.S., 1975-80; winner records for ballooning Nat. Aero. Assn., 1977. Republican. Contbr. articles to profl. jours. Home: 7 Johns Canyon Rd Rolling Hills CA 90274 Office: 1617 S Pacific Coast Hwy Suite D Redondo Beach CA 90277

HEINTZ, CARL MARTEN, management consultant, accountant, author; b. Pasadena, Calif., May 26, 1949; s. Carl Marten and Gloria Girten (Noblitt) H.; m. Jo Ann Fister, Dec. 20, 1975; children—Matthew, Hilary. B.S. magna cum laude, U. So. Calif., 1971, M.B.A. cum laude, 1976. C.P.A., Calif. Audit supr. Ernst & Whinney, Los Angeles, 1970-75; pres., controller Internat. Mortgage Co., Los Angeles, 1976; pvt. practice acctg., Arcadia, Calif., 1977-80; pres. Am. Mgmt. Techs., Inc., Pasadena, 1980-81; ptnr. Heintz & Assocs., Glendale, Calif., 1981—; instr. acctg. U. So. Calif.; instr. C.P.A. preparation program UCLA. Trustee San Marino Community Ch. Arthur Anderson fellow, 1971. Mem. Am. Inst. C.P.A.s, Calif. Soc. C.P.A.s, Beta Gamma Sigma, Beta Alpha Psi. Republican. Presbyterian. Club: Vergudo (Glendale). Author: Operational Auditing Guidebook, 1975; Building A Successful Accounting Practice, 1980, also articles. Home: 1033 Paloma Arcadia CA 91006 Office: Heintz & Assocs 431 N Brand Blvd Suite 306 Glendale CA 91203

HEINY, BERNARD ARLEN, physician; b. Sterling, Colo., Oct. 15, 1938; s. T. Virgil and Helen G. Heiny; B.S. cum laude, U. Utah, 1961, M.D., 1965; m. Cindy G. Gandy, Sept. 1, 1977; children—Ann, Laura, John. Intern, Letterman Gen. Hosp., San Francisco, 1965-66; resident in gen. surgery U.S. Army Hosp., Ky., 1968-69; resident in otolaryngology U. Colo., Fitzsimon Affiliated Hosps., 1969-72, U. Utah Med. Center, 1972-73, chief resident, 1972-73; practice medicine specializing in otolaryngology Bountiful, Utah, 1973—; asst. clin. prof. otolaryngology U. Utah, 1973—; pres. Bountiful Ear, Nose and Throat Assocs., 1973—; chmn. infectious disease control Lakeview Hosp., 1978-81, vice chmn. dept. surgery, 1977-80, chmn. infectious diseases, vice chmn. dept. surgery, 1977-81. Served from capt. to maj. M.C., U.S. Army, 1965-72. Diplomate Am. Bd. Otolaryngology. Fellow Am. Acad. Facial Plastic and Reconstructive Surgery, Acad. of Opthalmology and Otolaryngology, Soc. Mil. Otolaryngologists; mem. Utah State Med. Assn. (chmn. media relations and pub. edn. com. 1981—, claims rev. panel 1980—), Am. Med. Polit. Action Com., 1981—, Salt Lake Surg. Soc., Davis County Med. Assn., Am. Council of Otolaryngology, Nat. Assn. Residents and Internists, AMA, Utah Soc. of Otolaryngology and Maxiollofacial Surgery, Los Angeles Research Study Club, Nat. C. of C., Bountiful C. of C., Sigma Xi, Rho Chi, Phi Beta Pi. Home: 1489 W Stayner Dr Farmington UT 84025 Office: 425 Medical Dr Suite 205 Bountiful UT 84010

HEINZ, LINDA SINGER, interior designer, educator; b. Chicago, Mar. 8, 1947; d. Joseph and Johanna (Ritzenberger) S.; m. Richard Jacob Heinz, Feb. 28, 1976. B.S. in Home Econs. and Interior Design, So. Ill. U.-Carbondale, 1969. Interior designer Marshall Field and Co., Chicago, 1969-78; interior designer Mehagians Interior Design Studio, Scottsdale, Ariz., 1978—; instr. interior design Scottsdale Community Coll., 1982. Active Phoenix Art Museum Guild, Phoenix Symphony Guild; docent Heard Mus. of Anthropology and Primitive Art. Mem. Am. Soc. Interior Designers. Contr. work to Home and Gardens Christmas Edition, 1978. Home: 7074 E Sweetwater St Scottsdale AZ 85254 Office: Mehagians Interior Design Studio 7175 E Lincoln Dr Scottsdale AZ 85253

HEINZE, DAVID CHARLES, business administration educator; b. Paterson, N.J., June 3, 1941; m. Sandra Lynn Scott, July 9, 1966. B.S. in Math., Ariz. State U., 1963; M.B.A. in Statis. Analysis, 1969; M.S., in Actuarial Sci., U. Wis., 1964. Prof. mgmt. sci. Rochester (N.Y.) Inst. Tech., 1969-74, Va. Commonwealth U., Richmond, 1974-78, No. Ariz. U., Flagstaff, 1978-81, Calif. State U.-Chico, 1981—; cons. mfg. co. and bank. Recipient Profl. Achievement award Calif. State U., 1983; Knapp fellow, 1964; NDEA fellow, 1967-69. Mem. Am. Inst. Decision Scis., Phi Kappa Phi, Beta Gamma Sigma. Republican. Baptist. Author textbooks: Statistical Decision Analysis for Management, 1972; Management Sci., 1978, 2d edit., 1982; Fundamentals of Managerial Statistics, 1980; contbr. articles to profl. jours. Home: 655 La Bonita St Chico CA 95926 Office: Dept Acctg Calif State U Chico CA 95926

HEISE, ARDYS MARY, communications dir.; b. Upland, Calif., May 15, 1927; d. Ralph and Emma (Lenhert) Byer: A.B. in Social Sci., Upland Coll., 1949; postgrad. San Diego State U., 1962; m. Clarence Elmer Heise, II, Aug. 22, 1948; children—Sherilin, Clarence Elmer, Steven. Instr. speech, Upland (Calif.) Coll. and Acad., 1949-53; office mgr., San Diego County Fair, 1962; with Barnes Chase Advt. Agency, 1962-65; owner Ardys Heise and Assocs., 1965; TV and radio coordinator U. Calif., San Diego, 1967; community cons. smoking research, San Diego, 1967; statewide TV coordinator U. Calif., 1969-71; pub. affairs officer Sch. Medicine, U. Calif., San Diego, 1969-74; dir. communications San Diego Community Coll. Dist., 1974—. Vice pres. Health Systems Agency, 1976; apptd. spl. transit review com.; mem. ad hoc com. Status of Women in San Diego; pub. relations advisory com. for Children's Health Center; charter bd. mem. Freedoms Found. Am.; elder La Jolla Presbyterian Church, 1974-76. Recipient Grand award for communications program improvement Council Advancement Edn., 1980; YWCA Twin award, 1980. Mem. Pub. Relations Soc. Am. (Silver Anvil award, 1972). Pub. Relations Club San Diego (named Profl. of Yr. 1974), San Diego Council Adminstrv. Women in Edn. (dir.), Council Advancement and Support of Edn., Calif. Soc. Prevention of Blindness. Contbr. studies, articles to publs. on ednl. TV. Home: 6014 Dirac St San Diego CA 92122 Office: 3375 Camino del Rio S San Diego CA 92108

HEISERMAN, MARY SUSAN, psychologist; b. Anamosa, Iowa, July 12, 1942; d. John Edward and Ruth Louise (Burnstedt) Heiserman. A.A., Cottey Coll., Nevada, Mo., 1962; B.A., U. Ky., 1965; M.S., Iowa State U., Ames, 1967; Ph.D., Mich. State U., 1971. Lic. psychologist, Colo.; cert. psychodramatist. Psychologist, Ingham County Probate Ct., Lansing, Mich., 1969-71; coordinator adolescent program Lincoln Center, Lansing, 1971-72; psychologist Fort Logan Mental Health Center, Denver, 1972-73; cons., 1980; psychologist youth services psychiat. team Colo. Div. Youth Services, Denver, 1973-81; med. cons. disability program Social Security Adminstrn., Denver, 1982—; cons. AMC Cancer Research Center, Denver. Mem. Colo. Psychol. Assn. (dir. 1980-81), Am. Soc. for Group Psychotherapy and Psychodrama, Colo. Women Psychologists (pres. 1983), Phi Kappa Phi, Psi Chi, Phi Sigma Iota. Episcopalian. Club: P.E.O. Office: 570 Detroit St Denver CO 80206

HEISLER, VERDA THIMAS, clinical psychologist; b. Lorenzo, Idaho, Jan. 24, 1919; d. Michael Anton and Myrtle Irene (Fisher) Thimas; m. William Wilbert, June 13, 1941; B.A., U. Utah, 1942; Ph.D. (USPHS fellow), Stanford U., 1951. Diplomate Am. Bd. Examiners Profl. Psychology. Caseworker, USO, Travelers Aid Service, Ogden, Utah, 1944-46; research aide dept. psychology Stanford U., 1946, research asst., 1947; intern Stanford-Lane Hosp., 1949-50, Agnews State Hosp., 1950-51; pvt. practice clin. psychology, San Diego, 1951—; instr. psychol. extension San Diego State Coll., 1955-56; instr. psychology U. Calif. Extension, San Diego, 1958; mem. faculty Calif. Sch. Profl. Psychology, 1972-75; assoc. clin. prof. psychiatry U. Calif., San Diego, 1974-79; cons. United Cerebral Palsy, San Diego, 1963-64, bd. govs.,

1966-76; mem. evaluation com. Bur. Sch. Approvals, Calif. Dept. Edn., 1974; cons. Soc. Crippled Children and Adults Man. (Can.), 1976. Mem. governing bd., newsletter editor Friends of Jung, 1976-77. Recipient Humanitarian Service award United Cerebral Palsy San Diego, 1968, 72, Pres.'s award, 1972, Profl. Services award, 1973; United Cerebral Palsy and Ednl. Found. research grantee, 1964-65, 66-67. Fellow Am. Psychol. Assn.; mem. Am. Acad. Psychotherapist (sec.-treas. Western regional chpt. 1960-62), Soc. Personality/Assessment, Inc., Inst. Religion and Health, Am. Assn. Marriage and Family Counselors, Calif. State Psychology Assn. (mem. com. on standars for continuing edn. 1973-80), San Diego County Psychol. Assn. (pres. 1963), San Diego Soc. Clin. Psychologists (pres. 1966), Acad. San Diego Psychologists, Group Psychotherapy Assn. So. Calif., Phi Beta Kappa, Sigma Xi, Phi Kappa Phi, Alpha Lambda Delta, Psi Chi. Author: A Handicapped Child in the Family - A Guide for Parents, 1972; contbr. articles in field to profl. jours. Home: 3304 Brant St San Diego CA 92103 Office: 3636 1st Ave San Diego CA 92103

HEIST, DAVID WESLEY, manufacturing company executive; b. Lakewood, Ohio, May 17, 1942; s. Carl A. and Ruth E. Heist; m. Linda Elizabeth Brayton, July 11, 1970; children—Jill Christine, Timothy Ryan; m. Helen Elaine Dorsey, Oct. 23, 1982; 1 dau., Sonja Naomi Gulledge. Personnel supr., mgr. Fibreboard Corp., Los Angeles, 1973-77; personnel mgr. Pacific Coast Packaging Corp., Los Angeles, 1977-78, Boise Cascade Corp., Torrance, Calif., 1978-80; personnel/adminstrv. mgr. Manville Forest Products Corp., Bakersfield, Calif., 1980—. Vol. counselor Diogenes Youth Half-Way House. Served to lt. USN, 1964-73; Vietnam. Decorated Air medal with three oak leaf clusters. Mem. Nat. Safety Council. Republican. Mem. Fruitvale Community Ch. Home: 3308 Bisbee Ct Bakersfield CA 93309 Office: 5801 District Blvd Bakersfield CA 93309

HEIST, PAUL A., psychologist, educator; b. Waverly, Iowa, Aug. 2, 1917; s. Ernst G. and Emma K. (Goppelt) H.; children—Martin, Lauren, Jerome. B.A., Luther Coll., Decorah, Iowa, 1939; M.A., U. Ill., 1948; Ph.D., U. Minn., 1956; D.Hum. (hon.), Wartburg Coll., 1972; lic. psychologist, Calif. Counselor, U. Minn., 1948-50; assoc. prof. psychology Oreg. State U., 1950-56; research dir. Ctr. for Study Higher Edn., U. Calif.-Berkeley, 1956-68, dir. Ctr. for Study Undergrad. Edn., 1968-73, prof. higher edn. Grad. Sch. Edn., 1968—; cons. to numerous instns. of higher edn.; staff clinician Holistic Health Assocs. Served with U.S. Army, 1942-46. Fellow Am. Psychol. Assn., AAAS; mem. Am. Ednl. Research Assn., Am. Assn. Higher Edn., AAUP, Western Psychol. Assn. Contbr. articles to profl. jours. Office: 4607 Tolman Hall U Calif Berkeley CA 94720

HEISTAND, JOSEPH THOMAS, bishop; b. Danville, Pa., Mar. 3, 1924; s. John Thomas and Alta (Hertzler) H.; B.A. in Econs., Trinity Coll., Hartford, Conn., 1948, D.D. (hon.), 1978; M.Div., Va. Theol. Sem., 1952, D.D. (hon.), 1977; m. Roberta Crieger Lush, June 1, 1951; children—Hillary Heistand Long, Andrea Deferrier, Virginia Redmon. With Internat. Harvester Co., 1948-49; ordained to ministry Episcopal Ch., 1952; rector Trinity Ch., Tyrone, Pa., 1952-55; chaplain Grier Sch., Birmingham, Pa., 1952-55; asso. rector St. Paul's Ch., Richmond, Va., 1955, rector, 1955-69; rector St. Philip's in the Hill Ch., Tucson, 1969-76; bishop coadjutor Episcopal Diocese Ariz., Phoenix, 1976-79; bishop of Ariz., 1979—. Served with AUS, 1943-45. Decorated Bronze Star with oak leaf cluster, Purple Heart; Croix de Guerre (France). Office: 110 W Roosevelt St Phoenix AZ 85003*

HEITLER, BRUCE F., real estate developer, lawyer; b. Denver, June 12, 1945; s. Emmett H. and Dorothy (Shwayder) H.; m. Susan McCrensky, June 6, 1971; children—Abigail, Sara, Jesse, Jacob. B.A., Yale U., 1967, J.D., 1972; M. City Planning, U.Calif.-Berkeley, 1969. Bar: Colo., 1973. Assoc., Holme Roberts and Owen, Denver, 1972-74; project mgr. Central Devel. Group, Denver, 1975-76; pres. Heitler Devel., Inc., Denver, 1976—; dir. Nexus Corp., Clover Glass Co. Mem. Denver Met. Govt. Study Panel. Mem. Denver Bar Assn., Urban Land Inst., Denver C. of C., Colo. Yale Assn. (treas.). Republican. Jewish. Club: Cactus. Office: 1410 Grant St Suite A-101 Denver CO 80203

HELD, SYLVIA CAROL, guidance counselor for handicapped; b. Camp Lejeune, N.C., Oct. 6, 1944; d. Stanton Leroy and Helen Pearl (Hudson) Williams; m. Donald Bain Coe, II, Jan. 23, 1965; children—Donald Stanton, Mark Shannon; m. 2d Harold Alvin Held, Aug. 14, 1981. B.A., U. N.C., 1973; postgrad. Calif. State U.-Long Beach, 1983—. Vol. tchr., N.C. Assn. for Specific Learning Disabilities, 1972-73; mental health technician, Orange County (Calif.) Mental Health Assn., 1976-77; facilitator of handicapped services, North Orange Regional Occupational Program, Anaheim, Calif., 1981-83; asst. to disabled, vocat. edn. tchr. Coastline Regional Occupational Program, Costa Mesa, Calif., 1983—; mem. core team for chem. dependency intervention. Mem. Orton Dyslexia Soc., Placement Counselors of Orange County. Republican. Mem. Assembly of God. Office: Coastline Regional Occupational Program 1001 Presidio Sq Costa Mesa CA 92626

HELDFOND, SCOTT R., insurance broker; b. Chgo., Oct. 18, 1945; s. Harold S. and Dorothy Fine (Davidson) H.; B.A., U. Calif., Berkeley, 1967; student Menlo Jr. Coll., 1963-64, U. San Francisco Law Sch., 1969; m. Patricia Swig Dinner, June 30, 1968; children—Nicholas, Benjamin, Lucas, Elizabeth. Partner, chief operating officer Dinner Levison Co., Ins. Brokers, San Francisco, 1969—. Mem. exec. com., past pres. Hearing Soc. for Bay Area, Inc.; pres. Presidio Terr. Homeowners Assn., 1981-83; trustee Town Sch. for Boys; vice-chmn., trustee, mem. strategic planning com. St. Francis Meml. Hosp. Served with AUS, 1969. Mem. Am. Cancer Soc., Am. Heart Soc., Am. Jewish Com., Jewish Welfare Fedn., Mechanics Inst., NAACP, Nat. Geog. Found., Nat. Wildlife Fedn., Risk and Ins. Mgmt. Soc., Salvation Army, San Francisco Ballet Assn., San Francisco Hearing and Speech Ctr., San Francisco Symphony Found., San Francisco Zool. Soc., Smithsonian Instn., U. Calif. Alumni Assn., Stock Exchange Club San Francisco, Mchts. Exchange Club of San Francisco. Republican. Jewish. Office: 220 Bush St San Francisco CA 94104

HELDT, JOHN JOURDAN, quality engineer; b. Evansville, Ind., Dec. 19, 1919; s. Carl Anton and Marcella Clara (Bosse) H.; m. Marguerite Virginia Walton, May 11, 1946; children—John Jay, Nicholas W., Rebecca F., Marguerite L., Angela H., Janet M., Marcella B. B.S.E.E., U. Evansville, 1949; M.S.E.E., So. Meth. U., 1961; Ph.D., Sussex Coll. Tech. (Eng.), 1975. Registered profl engr. Calif., Tex., Ind. Engr. various cos., 1952-57; process analyst Gen. Dynamics, Ft. Worth, 1957-62, sr. quality engr., 1970-71; sr. research engr. Lockheed Co., Sunnyvale, Calif., 1962-70 sr. product assurance engr. GTE Lenkurt, San Carlos, Calif., 1971-75, Ampex, Sunnyvale, 1975-76; mgr. audit and receiving inspection Memorex, Santa Clara, Calif., 1977-79; mgr. product assurance design support Watkins Johnson Co., San Jose, Calif., 1979-83; prin. engr. quality assurance Fortune Systems Corp., Belmont, Calif., 1983—; instr. De Anza Coll., Cupertino; faculty U. Phoenix, No. Calif. Learning Ctr., Columbia Pacific U., Mill Valley, Calif.; expert examiner for quality engring. State Bd. Registration, Calif. Mem. quality assurance adv. bd. De Anza Coll., U. Phoenix. Served to 2d lt. inf. AUS, World War II, ETO; to 1st lt. C.E., 1951-52, Korea. Decorated Bronze Star; Research and Innovation grantee De Anza Coll., 1978. Fellow Am. Soc. Quality Control (speaker, E.L. Grant award 1982-83). Democrat. Lutheran. Club: Westgate Cabana (San Jose, Calif.). Patentee in field; contbr. articles to profl. jours.; developer text modules and teaching aids. Home: 2205 Riordan Dr San Jose CA 95130 Office: 300 Harbor Blvd Belmont CA 94002

HELFERT, ERICH ANTON, forest products co. exec.; b. Aussig/Elbe, Sudetenland, May 29, 1931; came to U.S., 1950; s. Julius and Anna Maria (Wilde) H.; B.S., U. Nev., 1954; M.B.A. with high distinction, Harvard U., 1956, D.B.A. (Ford fellow 1956), 1958; m. Anne Langley, Jan. 1, 1983; children—Claire L., Amanda L. Newspaper reporter, corr., Neuburg, W. Ger., 1948-52; research asst. Harvard U., 1956-57; asst. prof. bus. policy San Francisco State U., 1958-59; asst. prof. fin. and control Grad. Sch. Bus. Adminstrn., Harvard U., 1959-65; internal cons., then asst. to pres., dir. corp. planning Crown Zellerbach Corp., San Francisco, 1965-78, asst. to chmn., dir. corp. planning, 1978-82, v.p. corp. planning, 1982—; cons., lectr. in field. Exchange student fellow U.S. Inst. Internat. Edn., 1950. Mem. Am. Acctg. Assn., Am. Econs. Assn., Am. Fin. Assn., Assn. Corp. Growth (pres., dir. San Francisco chpt. 1980-81, Corp. Planners Assn. (past pres., dir.), Phi Kappa Phi. Roman Catholic. Clubs: Commonwealth, Commercial, Harvard Bus. Sch. No. Calif. (past pres., dir.). Author: Techniques of Financial Analysis, 1963, 5th edit., 1982; Valuation, 1966; co-author: Case Book, 1963; Controllership, 1965; contbr. articles to profl. jours. Office: 1 Bush St San Francisco CA 94104

HELFERT, STEPHEN CLARK, wildlife biologist; b. Ft. Brooke, San Juan, P.R., Feb. 23, 1950; s. Peter Allard and Barbara (Blair) H.; m. Rosine Marie Mills, Aug. 19, 1976; m. 2d, Jocinda Lanferman, Aug. 7, 1979; 1 dau., Erin Blair. B.S. in Fish and Wildlife Sci., Tex. A&M U., 1976; M.S. in Biology, U. Tex.-El Paso, 1978. Field asst. Chihuahuan Desert Research Inst., Alpine, Tex., 1976; grad. research asst. Lab. Environ. Biology, U. Tex., El Paso, 1977-78; environ. specialist U.S. Dept. Interior, Bur. Reclamation, Yuma Projects Office, Ariz., 1979-80; environmentalist U.S. Army, Ft. Sam Houston, Tex., 1981-82; wildlife biologist U.S. Air Force, Environ. Planning Div., Norton AFB, Calif., 1982—; Western rep. U.S. Dept. Defense com. for nat. profl. orgn. wildlife mgrs., biologists. Author script, narrator Poisonous Plants of Ft. Sam Houston, Tex., 1981. Served with U.S. Army, 1971-74. U. Tex.-El Paso grad. scholar, 1977. Mem. Wildlife Soc., Desert Tortoise Council, Chihuahuan Desert Research Inst., Beta Beta Beta, AAUP, Wildlife Biology Club. Home: Star Route Box 59 Forest Falls CA 92339 Office: AFRCE-BMS/DEVE Norton AFB CA 92409

HELFORD, PAUL QUINN, broadcasting co. exec.; b. Chgo., June 27, 1947; s. Norman and Eleanor (Kwin) H.; m. Leslie Gale Weinstein, July 11, 1971; children—Ross Michael, Benjamin Keith. B.A., U. Ill., 1969; M.A., Northeastern Ill. U., 1975. Tchr., John Hersey High Sch., Arlington Heights, Ill., 1969-73; self-employed writer Mill Valley, Calif., 1973-75; sales mgr. Sta. KOZY-TV, Eugene, Oreg., 1976-79, sta. mgr., program dir., 1979—. Bd. dirs. Oreg. Repertory Theater, 1982—, Arts Mgmt. Services, 1982—. Jewish. Contbr. articles in broadcasting field to profl. jours. Office: Station KOZY-TV 990 Garfield Eugene OR 97402

HELFRICH, WILLIAM PETER, management consultant; b. Rochester, N.Y., May 7, 1932; s. Lewis James and Alice Elizabeth (Hillen) H.; m. Mary Jane Sullivan, May 6, 1961; children—Katherine Alice, Jennifer Jane, William Peter, Ellen Martha, Gretchen Elizabeth, Samuel Paul, Stephanie Jessica. B.S. in Chemistry, Holy Cross Coll., Worcester, Mass., 1954; grad. Sch. of Psychology, U. Maine, 1968. Commd. ensign U.S. Navy, 1954, advanced through grades to lt. comdr., 1964, resigned, 1964; asst. dir. student aid U. Maine, Orono, 1964-65; coordinator, dir. Penobscott County Community Action Program, Bangor, Maine, 1965-66; pres. Helfrich Enterprises, Ltd., mgmt. cons., 1969—; public speaker; condr. seminars and workshops. Mem. Baron's Assocs., 1977—, chmn., 1983-84; mem. goals and objectives commn. Huntington Beach (Calif.) Unitied Sch. Dist., 1979-81. Mem. Am. Soc. for Tng. and Devel., Assn. Profl. Cons., World Congress Profl. Hypnotists, U.S. Power Squadron. Republican. Roman Catholic. Office: 18471 Mount Langley St Suite P Fountain Valley CA 92708

HELGELIEN, ANNETTE RAE, home economics educator; b. Wessington, S.D., Feb. 14, 1940; d. Robert George and Ethel Beatrice (Hanson) Fisher; m. Duane Elliot Helgelien, June 3, 1962; children—Brent Allen, Brenda Kay. B.S., S.D. State U., 1961; postgrad. Mont. State U., 1966, U. Wyo. Cert. secondary tchr., Wyo. Summer home extension agt. Hyde County, Highmore, S.D., 1959-60; tchr. home econs. Faulkton (S.D.) High Sch., 1961-63, Custer (S.D.) High Sch., 1966-67, Hot Springs (S.D.) High Sch., 1970-71, Wheatland (Wyo.) High Sch., 1976—; mem. adv. bd. Wyo. Future Homemakers Am., 1979-82. Youth group adviser Luther League, Am. Luth. Ch.; moderator meet the candidates panel Edn. Assn. Polit. Action Com., 1982. Mem. NEA, AAUW (v.p. membership), Wyo. Edn. Assn., Platte County Edn. Assn., Am. Vocat. Assn., Wyo. Vocat. Assn., Nat. Assn. Vocat. Home Econs. Tchrs., Wyo. Assn. Vocat. Home Econs. Tchrs. Republican.

HELGESON, DUANE MARCELLUS, librarian; b. Rothsay, Minn., July 2, 1930; s. Oscar Herbert and Selma Olivia (Sateren) H.; B.S., U. Minn., 1952. Librarian, Chance-Vought Co., Dallas, 1956-59, System Devel. Corp., Santa Monica, Calif., 1959-62, Lockheed Aircraft, Burbank, Calif., 1962-63, C.F. Braun Co., Alhambra, Calif., 1963-74; chief librarian Ralph M. Parsons Co., Pasadena, Calif., 1974-79; pres. Mark-Allen/Brokers-in-Info., Los Angeles, 1976-80; phys. scis. librarian Calif. Inst. Tech., Pasadena, 1980—; mem. adv. bd. Los Angeles Trade Tech. Coll., 1974-79, U. So. Calif. Library Sch., 1974-79. Served with USAF, 1952-54. Mem. Spl. Libraries Assn. (chmn. nominating com. 1974). Co-editor: (with Joe Ann Clifton) Computers in Library and Information Centers, 1973. Home: 2706 Ivan Hill Terr Los Angeles CA 90039 Office: Calif Inst Tech Millikan Meml Library Pasadena CA 91125

HELICK, EILEEN JUDGE, public relations executive; b. N.Y.C., June 28, 1930; d. William Joseph and Mary A. (Kelly) Judge; m. R. Martin Helick, Feb. 14, 1954 (div.); children—Reuben Stephen, Deborah Judge. B.A. in Journalism, Calif. State U.-Fullerton, 1977. Ptnr. Regent Graphics Services, Swissvale, Pa., 1954-70; asst. to pub. relations dir. Orange County (Calif.) Unified Sch. Dist., 1971-77; pub. relations dir. Am. Cancer Soc., Newport Beach, Calif., 1977-78; pub. relations cons., Santa Ana, Calif., 1978-79; pub. relations coordinator ATV Systems, Inc., Santa Ana, 1979—. Vol. pub. relations counsel Orange County Commn. on Status of Women. Mem. Women in Communications, Pub. Relations Soc. Am., Sigma Delta Chi. Republican. Club: Toastmasters. Office: ATV Systems Inc 2921 S Daimler St Santa Ana CA 92705

HELIN, JAMES DENNIS, advertising company executive; b. Carmel, Calif., Aug. 30, 1942; s. Richard James and Helen Margaret (Noonan) H.; m. Sally Katharine Pope, July 2, 1966; children—Laurie Ann, Jennifer Katharine, Holly Margaret, Christopher James, Kathleen Patricia. B.S., San Jose State U., 1964. Mktg. asst. Diamond Internat. Co., San Francisco, 1965; product mgr. Purex Corp., Lakewood, Calif., 1966-69; sr. v.p., mgmt. supr. Doyle Dane Bernbach Co., Los Angeles, 1969-81, Dailey & Assocs., Los Angeles, 1981—; instr. 4A's Inst. Advanced Advt. Studies U. So. Calif. Served with USAF, 1964-70. Recipient Alumni of Yr. award, bus. div. San Jose State U., 1979. Mem. Beta Gamma Sigma. Republican. Roman Catholic. Office: Dailey & Assocs 3055 Wilshire Blvd Los Angeles CA 90010

HELLEN, MARIE EVOLINE, occupational health and safety specialist; b. Burbank, Calif., July 31, 1950; d. Robert Owen and Ruth Naomi (Clark) Griffin; m. Jeffrey Hearn Hellen, July 11, 1971; 1 son, Scott Alexander. B.S. in Occupational Safety and Health, San Diego State U., 1979. Cert. healthcare safety profl., 1980. Lab. asst. supr. Paradise Valley Hosp., National City, Calif., 1974-79; safety dir. Sharp Meml. Community Hosp., San. Diego, 1979—. Mem. com. occupational environ. health Am. Lung Assn., 1982-83. Mem. Am. Soc. Safety Engrs., Soc. Fire Protection Engrs., Nat. Fire Protection Assn. Office: 7901 Frost St San Diego CA 92123

HELLER, ROBERT CHESTER, research educator; b. Jersey City, May 16, 1918; s. Chester Eugene and Daisy Katherine (Mahaffey) H.; B.S., Duke U., 1940, M.Forestry, 1941; m. Lois Jean Donehoo, June 27, 1942; children—Sally Katherine, Mary Judith, Martha Jean. Forestry asst. Duke U., Durham, N.C., 1945-46; forester Duke Power Co., Charlotte, N.C., 1946-47; research forester, project leader Forest Service, U.S. Dept. Agr., Md. and Calif., 1947-74; research prof. remote sensing, Coll. Forestry and Wildlife and Range Sci., U. Idaho, Moscow, 1974-81; vis. prof. dept. geography U. Calif.-Santa Barbara, 1983—; cons., 1981—; cons. FAO. Served with USN, 1941-45. Recipient Superior Service award Sec. Agr., 1971; commendation Chief of Forest Service U.S. Dept. Agr., 1970. Mem. Soc. Am. Foresters, Am. Soc. Photogrammetry, Internat. Union Forest Research Orgn. (chmn. remote sensing working group), AAUP (treas. chpt.). Republican. Contbr. chpts. to books. Office: 21 Eastwood Dr Orinda CA 94563

HELLER, ROGER KENNETH, social scientist; b. Beach, N.D., Feb. 17, 1922; s. Oscar Albert and Alma Lenora (Atletved) H.; A.B., U. Calif., Berkeley, 1950, M.A., 1952. Asso., U. Calif., Davis, 1957; tchr. social studies, chmn. dept. San Carlos (Calif.) High Sch., 1961-64; mem. faculty Coll. San Mateo (Calif.), 1963-67; mem. faculty San Jose (Calif.) State U., 1965—, asso. prof. social sci., 1974—. Served with U.S. Army, 1942-45. Decorated Bronze Star with oak leaf cluster, Meritorious Service medal, Combat Inf. badge. Mem. Am. Hist. Assn., Orgn. Am. Historians, Soc. Historians Am. Fgn. Relations, Am. Mil. Inst., Soc. History Tech., Mont. Hist. Soc. Republican. Lutheran. Club: U. Calif. Bears Backers. Author: The 361st Infantry Regiment, 1917-1955, 1955; also articles. Home: 5567 Thomas Ave Oakland CA 94618 Office: Social Sci DMH 221 San Jose State Univ Washington Sq San Jose CA 95192

HELLER, SHEILA RAE, advertising executive; b. Denver, Sept. 16, 1943; d. Joe and Reta (Kleiner) H. B.A. in English Lit., Douglass Coll., 1965. Copywriter, J. Walter Thompson, N.Y.C., N.W. Ayers, London, Sta. KBTV-9, Denver, Sam Lucky Assn., Denver; pres., owner Heller Co., Denver; tchr. Sheila Heller's Creative Copywriting Workshop. Named Advt. Woman of Year, Colo. Women in Communications, 1980. Mem. Denver Advt. Fedn.

HELLICKSON, KATHALEEN PAIGE, home economics educator, counselor; b. Virginia City, Mont., Sept. 8, 1938; d. Orrin Elmer and Ella Mae (Cornforth) Paige; m. Neil Clarence Hellickson, Aug. 15, 1961 (div.); children—Deborah, Rory, Renny. B.S. in Home Econs. Edn., Montana State Coll., 1960; M.S. in Guidance and Counseling, Eastern Montana Coll., 1974. Tchr. Scobey (Mont.) High Sch., 1961-62, C.R. Anderson Sch., Helena, Mont., 1962-63, Harlem (Mont.) High Sch., 1963-67, Bridger (Mont.) High Sch., 1968-70; guidance counselor Grass Range (Mont.) High Sch., 1973-75; guidance counselor, home econs. tchr., community edn. dir. Plains (Mont.) High Sch., 1976—; participant NDEA Disadvantaged Indian Youth Inst., 1965; mem. coordinating com. Improved Career Decision Making Inst., 1982. 4-H leader, judge Sanders County (Mont.); cub scout leader Big Sky council Boy Scouts Am. Named hon. admissions counselor U.S. Naval Acad., 1978. Mem. Montana Personnel and Guidance Assn., Montana Home Econs. Assn., Plains Tchrs. Orgn., Clark Fork Valley Women's Bowling League. Lutheran. Club: Order of Eastern Star (Grass Range). Home: Box 928 Plains MT 59859 Office: Plains High Sch Box 549 Plains MT 59859

HELLMAN, SAUNDRA ANN, foundation executive; b. Mpls., Oct. 17, 1937; d. Wallace McKinley and Alice Mae (Lee) Wadtke; B.A., U. Minn., 1959; M.P.H., U. Calif.-Berkeley, 1962, Dr.P.H., 1971; M.B.A., St. Mary's Coll., 1982; m. Stanley Hellman, July 23, 1964; children—Dara, Carrie. Dir. edn. and services Am. Cancer Soc., Hennepin, Minn., 1959-60, cancer control and accident prevention cons. Dept. Pub. Health, State of Minn., 1960-61; project coordinator Action Research Project, Dept. Pub. Health, San Francisco, 1962-64; ednl. cons., field staff supr. Calif. Nurses Assn., San Francisco, 1964-68; asst. adminstr. Pacific Med. Ctr., San Francisco, 1972-79; pres. Merritt Hosp. Found., Oakland, Calif., 1979-83, Merritt Peralta Found., Oakland, 1983—. Bd. dirs. San Francisco Symphony Assn., Neighborhood Home Owners Assn. Albert Malsin scholar, 1955-56; USPHS trainee, 1960, 68-71; Am. Cancer Soc. awardee, 60, 61. Mem. Am. Coll. Hosp. Adminstrs. Nat. Assn. Hosp. Devel. Calif. Pub. Health Assn., Soc. Pub. Health Educators, Am. Hosp. Educators. Republican. Contbr. articles to profl. jours. Home: 16 Tweed Ter San Rafael CA 94901 Office: Hawthorne Ave and Webster St Oakland CA 94609

HELLON, MICHAEL THOMAS, polit. cons., mgmt. co. exec.; b. Camden, N.J., June 24, 1942; s. James Bernard and Dena Louise (Blackburn) H.; B.S., Ariz. State U., 1972; m. Toni L. Carson; 3 children. Ins. investigator Equifax, Phoenix, 1968-69; exec. v.p. Phoenix Met. C. of C., 1969-76; ins. co. exec. Londen Ins. Group, 1976-78; pres. Hellon Mgmt. Co., 1978—. Mem. Ariz. Occupational Safety and Health Adv. Council, 1972—, Phoenix Urban League, 1972-73, Area Manpower Planning Council, 1971-72, Phoenix Civic Plaza Dedication Com., 1972; pres. Vis. Nurse Service, 1978-79; precinct capt. Republican party, 1973-82; state campaign dir. Arizonans for Reagan Com., 1980; alt. del. Rep. Nat. Conv., 1980; campaign mgr. for various candidates, 1972-82. Bd. dirs. ATMA Tng. Found., 1981—. Served with USAF, 1964-68. Decorated Bronze Star medal, Purple Heart. Recipient George Washington Honor medal Freedom's Found., 1964; commendation Fed. Bar Assn., 1973. Mem. U.S. C. of C. (pub. affairs com. western div. 1974—), Am. C. of C. Execs., Ariz. C. of C. Mgrs. Assn. (bd. mem. 1974—), Phoenix C. of C., Conf. Ariz. Employer Assns. (sec. 1972). Club: Trunk 'N Tusk. Home: 4711E Calle Elegante Tucson AZ 85718 Office: PO Box 32335 Phoenix AZ 85064

HELM, JOHN J., lumber company executive; b. Mexico City, Oct. 12, 1910; s. Jose Maria and Antoinette (Winther) Helm y Correa; m. Ann E. Helm, Sept. 16, 1937 (dec.); 1 son, James A. Student U. Calif.-Berkeley, 1927-31. Salesman, Charles Nelson Co., San Francisco, 1933-34; sales mgr. Sante Fe Lumber Co., to 1946; mgr., pres., chmn. bd. Cascade Pacific Lumber Co., Portland, Oreg., 1946—; dir. Helix Wholesale Co., San Diego. Served to lt. AC, U.S. Army, 1931-41. Mem. N.Am. Wholesale Lumber Assn. Republican. Roman Catholic. Clubs: Arlington, Racquet, University, Waverley Country (Portland).

HELMER, RICHARD GUY, nuclear physicist; b. Homer, Mich., Feb. 19, 1934; s. Hurshul Guy and Edith Maude (Putnam) H.; B.S., U. Mich., 1956, M.S., 1957, Ph.D., 1961; m. Mary Joan Scrivens, June 10, 1956; children—Gary Allen, Carl William. Research assoc. Argonne Nat. Lab., 1958-61; nuclear physicist Phillips Petroleum Co., Idaho Nat. Engring. Lab., Idaho Falls, 1961-65, Idaho Nuclear Co., 1965-70, Aerojet Nuclear Co., 1970-76; sr. scientist EG&G Idaho, Idaho Falls, 1976—. Bd. dirs. Child Devel. Ctr., Idaho Falls, 1968-74, chmn., 1970; bd. dirs. Regional Council, Day Care Center, 1973-82; mem. Sub-Area Council of Idaho Health System Agy., 1976-79; trustee Sch. Dist. #91, 1979—. Fellow Am. Phys. Soc.; mem. AAAS, Am. Nuclear Soc., N.Y. Acad. Sci. Contbr. articles to profl. jours. Home: 792 Sonja Ave Idaho Falls ID 83402 Office: EG&G Idaho PO Box 1625 Idaho Falls ID 83415

HELMER, VIRGINIA E., management and marketing research company executive; b. Portland, Oreg., July 22, 1932; d. Stanley A. and Irene M. (Van Tress) Landers; m. James A. Helmer, May 12, 1951; children—James Lee, Teri Lee. Student Portland Community Coll., 1970-81, Portland State U., 1975-80. Sec., claim clk., manifest clk., billing clk. ONC, Ind., Portland, 1949-52; acct. gen. office J.R. Woodmansee, D.O., Beaverton, Oreg., 1961-66; exec. sec., research asst. Lund, McCutcheon, Jacobson, Inc., Portland, 1969-74; office mgr., sr. analyst, v.p. adminstrn. Mgmt. Mktg. Assocs., Inc., Portland, 1974—. Mem. Inst. Manegerial Profl. Women, Oreg. Pioneer Word-processing Assn., Nat. Inst. Exec. Females. Office: Mgmt Mktg Assocs Bank of Calif Tower Suite 1010 Portland OR 97205

HELMLINGER, TRUDY BENITA, social worker; b. Seattle, Jan. 2, 1942; d. Benjamin V. and Birdie L. (Pettigrove) H. B.A. in Psychology, Calif. State U., Sacramento, 1967, M.S.W. (Nat. Assn. Social Workers scholar), 1969. Psychiat. social worker Children's Protective Services, Sacramento, 1969-70, Placerville, Calif., 1970-71; pvt. practice clin. social work, Sacramento, 1971—; co-owner Linden Advt. Agy.; tchr. American River Coll., Sacramento, U. Calif., Davis, U. Calif., Irvine. Lic. clin. social worker, Calif.; lic. marriage, family and child counselor, Calif. Mem. Nat. Assn. Social Workers, World Fedn. Mental Health, Am. Soc. Journalists and Authors, Sacramento Mental Health Assn. Democrat. Methodist. Author: After You've Said Goodbye, 1977, 2d edit., 1982; contbr. to nat. mags. Home: 7127 Murdock Way Carmichael CA 95608 Office: 2740 Fulton Ave Suite 113 Sacramento CA 95821

HELMS, JAY FREDERICK, cons. engr.; b. San Francisco, June 13, 1931; s. John F. and Zelda L. (Butterfield) H.; B.S., U. Calif., Berkeley, 1952; m. Lucille F. Pearson, Jan. 14, 1956; children—Eric J., Gretchen A. Sr. engr. Jet Propulsion Lab., Calif. Inst. Tech., Pasadena, 1961-65; engring. mgr. Pacific Telephone, San Francisco, 1966-76; chief engr. Ford Aerospace, Palo Alto, Calif., 1977; pres. Helms & Assocs., cons. engrs., Novato, Calif., 1977—; adj. lectr. telecommunications Golden Gate U., San Francisco, 1979. Served with Signal Corps, U.S. Army, 1952-61. Registered profl. engr., Calif. Mem. IEEE, System Safety Soc., Associated Public Safety Communication Officers, Am. Soc. Safety Engrs., Am. Cons. Engrs. Council, Cons. Engrs. Assn. Calif. Republican. Club: Masons. Contbr. articles to profl. jours. Office: 27 Commercial Blvd Suite Q Novato CA 94947

HELMY, ABDELKADER MOHAMED, propulsion scientist; b. Cairo, Feb. 10, 1948; s. Mohamed and Hemiat Helmy; m. Abia M. Eltayeb, May 9, 1952; children—Marwah, Sameh. B.S. in Chem. Propulsion, Cairo U., 1970, M.S., 1975, Ph.D., 1977. Rockets and electronics engr. Research Ctr., Cairo, 1970-77; research engr. Jet Propulsion Lab., Pasadena, Calif., 1978-82; sr. research scientist Teledyne McCormick, Hollister, Calif., 1982—. U. Calgary postdoctoral fellow, 1978; NASA/NRC research fellow, 1979. Mem. AIAA. Moslem. Contbr. articles to profl. jours. Home: 971 Pear St Hollister CA 95023 Office: 3601 Union Rd Hollister CA 95023

HELSELL, ROBERT M., construction executive; b. Seattle, Mar. 29, 1937; s. Frank P. and Ellen (Bringloe) H.; m. Linda M. Clark, Dec. 19, 1961; children—Kristina, Ingrid, Spencer, Alexa. B.A., Dartmouth Coll., 1959, M.B.E., 1960. C.P.A., Wash. With Haskins & Sells, 1961-64; treas. Cascade Natural Gas Co., 1964-68; successively sec.-treas., exec. v.p., pres. and chief exec. officer Howard S. Wright Constrn. Co., Seattle, 1974—. Pres. Seattle Children's Home; treas. Seattle Art Mus. Served to lt. comdr., USCG, 1961-68. Mem. Am. Inst. C.P.A.s, Assoc. Gen. Contractors. Republican. Episcopalian. Clubs: Univ., Rainier, Seattle Tennis, Seattle Yacht, Wash. Athletic (Seattle).

HELVEY, JULIUS LOUIS, II, financial corporate executive; b. Boise, Idaho, May 21, 1931; s. Julius Louis and Adeline (Jonasson) H.; m. Barbara June Ellis, Aug. 29, 1959; children—Janet, Julius Louis, Jennifer, Mary, Rebecca. B.S., USN Acad., 1953; M.B.A., Stanford U., 1959. C.P.A., Calif. Audit supr. Touche Ross & Co., San Francisco, 1959-65, audit mgr., 1967-73; fin. v.p. Golden West Fin. Corp., Oakland, Calif., 1965-67, sr. v.p., 1973—. Scoutmaster, Boy Scouts Am., Lafayette, Calif., 1974-76. Served to lt. j.g. USN, 1949-57. Mem. Calif. C.P.A. Soc., Am. Inst. C.P.A.s, USN Alumni Assn. Rupublican. Mormon. Club: Stanford Bus. Sch. Office: 1970 Broadway Oakland CA 94612

HELZER, JAMES ALBERT, mail order marketing company executive; b. Cheyenne, Wyo., Sept. 11, 1946; s. H. Albert and Bernadette J. (Stalker) H.; B.A. with honors, Yale U., 1968; postgrad. Harvard U. Bus. Sch., 1981—; m. Mary Elizabeth Clark, Mar. 15, 1969; children—Katherine, John. An organizer, 1968, since chmn. bd., chief exec. officer, pres. Unicover Corp., mfr. and mail order marketer collectibles, Cheyenne; chmn. Unicover World Trade Corp., Wilmington, 1981—, Unicover Internat. Sales Corp., Wilmington, 1981—; dir. First Nat. Bank and Trust Co. Wyo. Wyo. co-chmn. Campaign for Yale, 1975-77; mem. Yale Coll. Alumni Admissions Com., 1980—; pres. Wyo. Congl. Award Council, 1983—; bd. dirs. Longs Peak Council, Boy Scouts Am., 1982—; mem. Bus. Com. on Arts, 1978—, bd. dirs., 1980-81; chmn. Wyo. Bus. Conf. on Arts, 1979, Cheyenne Civic Center Dedication Com., 1980-81; bd. dirs., chmn. fin. com. DePaul Hosp., 1979—; commr. Cheyenne-Laramie County Regional Plan Commn., 1980-81; mem. Laramie County Health Planning Com., 1980-81; adv. council Coll. Arts and Scis., U. Wyo., 1980—, Roy Chamberlain disting. speaker, 1980; trustee Seton Cath. High Sch., Cheyenne, 1981—. Recipient Silliman cup Yale U., 1968, citation Am. Stamp Dealers Assn., 1976; Disting. Service in Bus. award Coll. Commerce and Industry, U. Wyo., 1983; Disting. Service award St. Joseph's Children's Home, 1982; asso. fellow Silliman Coll., Yale U., 1976-84. Mem. Direct Mail Mktg. Assn., Indsl. Devel. Assn. Cheyenne (dir. 1973-76, v.p. 1974-75), Newcomen Soc. N. Am., Soc. Illustrators N.Y. (asso.), Assn. Yale U. Alumni (Wyo. del. 1973-75). Clubs: Young Men's Literary (Cheyenne); Rotary. Co-author: A Philatelic Portfolio of America's National Parks, 1972; editor: The Standard First Day Cover Catalog, 1968, 76, 78, 81; co-editor: Catalog of Postage Stamps of the People's Republic of China, 1949-1982, 1983. Home: 4021 Carey Ave Cheyenne WY 82001 Office: 1 Unicover Center Cheyenne WY 82008

HEMANN, RAYMOND GLENN, aerospace co. exec.; b. Cleve., Jan 24, 1933; s. Walter Harold Marsha Mae (Colbert) H.; B.S., Fla. State U., 1957; postgrad. U.S. Naval Postgrad. Sch., 1963-64, U. Calif. at Los Angeles, 1960-62; M.S. in Systems Engring., Calif. State U., Fullerton, 1970, M.A. in Econs., 1972; m. Lucile Tinnin Turnage, Feb. 1, 1958; children—James Edward, Carolyn Frances; m. Leslie K. Lewis, May 23, 1980. Aero. engring. aide U.S. Navy, David Taylor Model Basin, Carderock, Md., 1956; analyst Fairchild Aerial Surveys, Tallahassee, 1957; research analyst Fla. Rd. Dept., Tallahassee, 1957-59; chief Autonetics div. N.Am. Rockwell Corp., Anaheim, Calif., 1959-69; v.p., dir. R. E. Manns Co., Wilmington, Calif., 1969-70; mgr. avionics design and analysis dept. Lockheed-Calif. Co., Burbank, 1970-72, mgr. advanced concepts div., 1976-82; gen. mgr. Western div. Arinc Research Corp., Santa Ana, 1972-76; dir. future requirements Rockwell Internat., 1982—; pres., dir. Avionics Test and Evaluation Corp., 1975-77; asst. prof. ops. analysis dept. U.S. Naval Postgrad. Sch., Monterey, Calif., 1963-64, Monterey Peninsula Coll., 1963; instr. ops. analysis Calif. State Coll., Fullerton, 1963, instr. quantitative methods, 1969-72; pres. Asso. Aviation, Inc., Fullerton, 1965-74; lectr. Brazilian Navy, 1980, U. Calif., Santa Barbara, 1980; cons. to various corps. Troop chmn. Boy Scouts Am. Bd. dirs. Placentia-Yorba Jr. Athletic Assn. Served with AUS, 1950-53. Syde P. Deeb scholar, 1956; recipient certificate appreciation U.S. Naval Postgrad. Sch., 1963; Honor awards Nat. Assn. Remotely Piloted Vehicles, 1975, 76. Comml., glider and pvt. pilot. Fellow AAAS; mem. Ops. Research Soc. Am., IEEE, AIAA, Air Force Assn., N.Y. Acad. Scis., Soaring Soc. Am., Assn. Old Crows, Phi Kappa Tau (past pres.). Episcopalian. Contbr. articles to profl. jours. Home: 2333 Midlothian Dr Altadena CA 91001 Office: PO Box 92098 Los Angeles CA 90009

HEMBROFF, JOHN DAVIS, museum development officer; b. Tacoma, Wash., June 13, 1947; s. Roscoe John and Marian Estelle (Davis) H. B.A., U. Wash., 1969. With Haney Assocs., Inc., Concord, Mass., 1974-78; pub. relations mgr. Seattle Art Mus., 1978-79, assoc. devel. officer, 1979-81, devel. officer, 1981—. Bd. dirs. Wash. State Arts Advocates, 1980—, treas., 1980-82. Served to capt. USAF, 1969-73. Mem. Art Mus. Devel. Officers Assn., N.W. Devel. Officers Assn. Office: 1661 E Olive Way Seattle WA 98102

HEMINGWAY, GEORGE THOMSON, marine biologist, educator, researcher; b. Corvallis, Oreg., Aug. 23, 1940; s. George Danforth and Margaret Roberta Purcell Chadwick (Hardman) H.; B.S., San Diego State U., 1966, M.S., 1973; m. Jean Ann Potym, May 25, 1968; 1 dau., Gillian Christian Allison. With Scripps Instn. Oceanography, U. Calif., San Diego, 1967—, coordinator internat. program, 1977—; prof., chmn. biology Sch. Marine Scis., Autonomous U. Baja Calif., 1973-74. Mem. Tecolote Canyon Citizens Adv. Com. Served with F.A., U.S. Army, 1963-65. Elected prof. honoris causa of marine scis Sch. Marine Scis., Autonomous U. Baja Calif., 1974; NCAA grantee; Tinker Found. grantee. Mem. AAAS, Am. Soc. Zoologists, Western Soc. Naturalists, Am. Inst. Biol. Scis., Hastings Inst. of Soc., Ethics and Life Scis., San Diego Zool. Soc. Republican. Episcopalian. Research on hydrography, chemistry and biology of Calif. current; contbr. articles to profl. jours. Home: 5025 Georgetown Ave San Diego CA 92110 Office: Scripps Instn Oceanography Code A-027 La Jolla CA 92093

HEMMERDINGER, WILLIAM JOHN, artist, art educator; b. Burbank, Calif., July 7, 1951; s. William John Jr. and Eileen Patricia (Fitzmaurice) H.; m. Catherine Lee Cooper, Aug. 8, 1981. Student Art Ctr. Coll. Design, 1967-69, Nat. Palace Mus., Taiwan, 1973; A.A., Coll. of Desert, 1971; B.A., U. Calif.-Riverside, 1973; M.F.A., Claremont Grad. Sch., 1975, Ph.D., 1979; postgrad. Harvard U., 1977. Curator Calif. Mus. Photography, 1973-74; instr. Coll. of Desert, 1974-79, 80—, Calif. State U., Long Beach, 1979-80, Otis Art Inst. Parsons Sch. Design, 1979-80, U. Calif., Riverside, 1981—; group shows include: NAD, Whitney Mus. Am. Art, N.Y.C., UNESCO Mus., Paris, Am. Watercolor Soc., N.Y.C., U. N.Mex. Art Mus., 1979, Los Angeles VA, 1982, Santa Monica City Coll., 1982; works in permanent collections: The Tate Gallery, London, U. Calif. Art Mus., Los Angeles, Smithsonian Instn., D.C. Recipient Calif. Nat. Watercolor Soc. award, 1974, 1979; Ford Found. grantee, 1979; NEA grantee, 1979, NEH grantee, 1980. Mem. Nat. Watercolor Soc. (v.p. 1981-82), Coll. Art Assn., So. Calif. Art Writers Assn. Contbr. articles to profl. jours. Home: 43-409A Martini Court Palm Desert CA 92260 Office: Cirrus Editions Ltd 540 S Alameda St Los Angeles CA 90013

HEMPEL, GARDINER, business exec.; b. Chgo., Dec. 18, 1929; s. John Christopher and Ruth Churchill (Peterson) H.; B.A., U. Chgo., 1949, M.B.A., 1952; m. Darby Grayson, Aug. 23, 1979; children—Amy, Gardiner, Peter. Dist. mgr. sales Rogers Pub. Co., Detroit, 1953-57; pub. Purchasing News, Rogers Pub. Co., Chgo., 1958, asst. to v.p. mktg., 1958-59, gen. sales mgr., tech. services div., Denver, 1960-61; v.p. Info. Handling Services, Inc., Denver, 1961-68; v.p. Arcata Nat. Corp., Menlo Park, Calif., 1968-73; pres. Speedcall Corp., Hayward, Calif., 1973-79; ptnr. Exploration Assocs. and O.F.T. Exploration, San Francisco, 1979—. Bd. dirs. Chamber Soloists of San Francisco; trustee, chmn. bd. San Francisco Art Inst., 1979-82; mem. cabinet U. Chgo. Mem. U. Chgo. Alumni Assn. (exec. v.p., dir. Bay area chpt.), Info. Industry Assn. (dir., v.p. 1970-73), Nat. Microfilm Assn. (dir., treas. 1970-74), Psi Upsilon. Congregationalist. Clubs: Arts (Chgo.); Commonwealth (San Francisco). Home: 3346 Clay St San Francisco CA 94118

HEMPHILL, DUDLEY ROBERT, civil engineer.; b. West Palm Beach, Fla., Aug. 7, 1944; s. Clyde Herbert and Betty Jane (Keebler) H.; m. Nikki Ann Jordan, Aug. 12, 1978; B.S., U. Oreg., 1979. Registered civil engr., Calif. Hwy. designer, traffic engr., Lane County, Oreg., 1964-76; traffic engr., Palm Springs, Calif., 1979-83, dir. pub. works, Coachella, Calif., 1983—. Served with AUS, 1968-70. Decorated Purple Heart. Mem. Inst. Transp. Engrs., Soc. Pub. Adminstrn. Republican Club: Palm Springs Toastmasters (pres.). Home: Route 1 Box 457 Whitewater CA 92282 Office: PO Box 1786 Palm Springs CA 92263

HEMSTREET, JENNIFER JESS, home economics educator; b. Cuero, Tex., Dec. 31, 1943; d. Henry Edwin and Helen (Bredesen) Howe; children—April, Chelsey. Student U. Calif.-Davis, 1962-64, Humboldt State U., 1964-66; B.S., Calif. Poly. State U., 1967, M.A., 1983. Cert. tchr., adminstr., Calif. Tchr., dept. chmn. home econs. Santa Maria (Calif.) High Sch., 1969—, sch. improvement coordinator, 1979—; sch. improvement coordinator Righetti High Sch., Santa Maria, 1980-81; mem. Calif. Dept. Edn. Curriculum Task Force. Named Calif. Home Econs. Tchr. of Yr., 1982; Tchr. of Yr., Nat. Merit winner Am. Home Econs. Assn.-Chesebrough-Ponds, Inc., 1982. Mem. Am. Home Econs. Assn, NEA, Calif. Tchrs. Assn., Home Econs. Tchrs. Assn. Calif., Cal Aggie Alumni Assn. (Davis), Cal Poly Alumni Assn. (San Luis Obispo), Future Homemakers Am., AAUW (br. v.p. 1979, pres. 1980, interbranch chmn. 1981, state membership com. 1982), Santa Maria Mental Health Assn., Phi Upsilon Omicron. Republican. Presbyterian. Implementer of community resource ctr. in home econs. Office: 901 S Broadway Santa Maria CA 93454

HENDERSCHEDT, ROBERT RANDALL, med. center adminstr.; b. Hazleton, Pa., Dec. 24, 1951; s. Herbert Paul and Beatrice Mae (Keck) H.; B.S. in Bus. Adminstrn., Columbia Union Coll., 1972; postgrad. Loma Linda U., 1980—; m. Helen Louise Palmatory, Apr. 16, 1972; children: Stephanie Louise, Stephen Robert. Asst. controller Clasco, Inc., Rockville, Md., 1972-74; controller Tidewater Meml. Hosp., Tappahannock, Va., 1974-77, asst. adminstr., 1977-79; v.p. Loma Linda (Calif.) U. Med. Ctr., 1979—; mem. sub-area council Eastern Va. Health Systems Agy., 1978-79. Bd. dirs. Wythville (Va.) Hosp. Mem. Hosp. Fin. Mgmt. Assn., Am. Mgmt. Assn., Am. Coll. Hosp. Adminstrs. Seventh-day Adventist. Office: Loma Linda U Med Center Room 1160 PO Box 2000 Loma Linda CA 92354

HENDERSON, FREDERICK BRADLEY, III, geologist; b. Oakland, Calif., Dec. 5, 1935; s. Frederick Bradley and Leslie Alice (Phelps) H.; m. Elinor A. Goldbrecker, Feb. 3, 1962; children—Frederick Bradley IV, Ahroon Phelps. B.S. in Geology, Stanford U., 1957, M.S. in Geology, 1960; Ph.D. in Geology, Harvard U., 1966. Mining/research geologist St. Joe Minerals, St. Joseph Mo., 1965-69; project geologist, sr. geologist Kaiser Aluminum, Oakland, Calif., 1969-71; cons. Hend Co., Orinda, Calif., 1971-74; geoscientist Lawrence Berkeley Lab./U. Calif.-Berkeley, 1974-76; pres. Geosat Com. Inc., San Francisco, 1976—; vis. prof. Golden Gate U., 1971-75. Served with USNR, 1957-59. Mem. AIME, Geochem. Soc., AIAA, Prospectors and Developers Assn., Am. Assn. Petroleum Geologists. Republican. Presbyterian. Club: Bohemian (San Francisco). Editor: Geological Remote Sensing From Space, 1976. Home: 37 Camino Don Miguel Orinda CA 94563 Office: 153 Kearny St Suite 209 San Francisco CA 94108

HENDERSON, GLENN VALE, JR., finance educator; b. Akron, Ohio, Dec. 6, 1940; s. Glenn Vale and Linous Eudora (Andrews) H.; m. Kay Marie Gruss, Nov. 7, 1964; children—Tanya Leigh, Tosha Lynn, Terra Lane. B.S. in Bus. Adminstrn., Western Mich. U., 1963; postgrad. U. Cin., 1964; M.S. in Bus. Adminstr., Fla. State U., 1970, Ph.D. in Bus. Adminstrn., 1974. Vice pres. So. Ohio Truck Lines, Inc., Hamilton, 1963-65; comptroller, McKibben Motor Service, Inc., Cin., 1965-66; asst. prof. fin. Ariz. State U., 1972-77, assoc. prof. fin. Ariz. State U., 1980-82, prof. fin., 1982—; assoc. prof. fin., Burton R. Risinger faculty chair La. Tech. U., Ruston, 1977-80; vis. assoc. prof. fin. U. Hawaii, Hilo, 1979-80. Served to 1st lt. U.S. Army, 1966-69. Univ. fellow Fla. State U., 1970-71; fellow Am. Assembly Collegiate Schs. Bus., 1971-72. Mem. Am. Econs. Assn. Am. Fin. Assn., Western Fin. Assn., So. Fin. Assn., Southwestern Fin. Assn., Fin. Mgt. Assn. Republican. Assoc. editor Jour. Fin. Research, 1979-82; co-author: Financing Business Firms (6th edit., 1979); contbr. to profl. jours. Home: 1947 E Manhatton Dr Tempe AZ 85282 Office: Fin Dept Coll Bus Adminstrn Ariz State U Tempe AZ 85287

HENDERSON, HAYDEN MARTIN, trade co. exec.; b. Reno, Nov. 1940; s. Hayden Dewar and Rosalys (Martinez) H.; B.A. in Polit. Sci., U. Nev., 1963; M.B.A., Golden Gate U., 1975; m. Catherine Brine, Oct. 23, 1970. Telecommunications mgmt. staff Qantas Airways, San Francisco, 1970-73, Bechtel Corp., San Francisco, 1973-74, Levi Strauss & Co., San Francisco, 1976-79; telecommunications sales staff RCA Global Communications, San Francisco, 1974-76; pres. Phone Depot, Inc., San Francisco, 1980—; owner Mike Henderson Enterprises, San Francisco, 1979—; dir., sec. Hilltop Corp., 1982-83. Mem. campaign staff Republican candidate U.S. Senate S.I. Hayakawa, 1976; mem. Rep. County Central Com., San Francisco, 1978-83; treas. San Francisco Ednl. Services, 1978-79; bd. dirs. San Franciscans for Neighborhood Enterprise, 1980-81. Served with USAF, 1964-68. Mem. Telecommunications Assn., Internat. Telecommunications Assn., Communications Mgrs. Council (co-chmn. 1973), San Francisco C. of C. Home: 3550 Cabrillo St San Francisco CA 94121 Office: 555 Mission St San Francisco CA 94105

HENDERSON, KENNETH REED, optometrist; b. Mpls., Feb. 1, 1949; s. Warren Duane and Allegra (Friesen) H.; m. Janet Diane Stoupa, Aug. 16, 1975; children—Jennifer Anna, Nathan Silas. A.A., Skagit Valley Coll., 1975; B.S. in Health Sci., Western Wash. U., 1977; B.S. in Visual Sci., Pacific U., 1978, O.D., 1982. Practice optometry, Bellingham, Wash., 1982—; vol. optometrist Optometric Center Seattle, 1982—, bd. dirs., 1982—. Bd. dirs. Citizens Health Care Coop of Whatcom County (Wash.) Inc., 1976-78; mem. Fed. Health Systems Agy. Com. on Healthcare for Low Income and Minorities in N.W. Wash., 1976-77. Served with USN, 1967-71. Vietnam. Mem. Am. Optometric Student Assn., Am. Optometric Assn., Wash. Optometric Assn. Office: 2300 James St Bellingham WA 98226

HENDERSON, KENNETH REED, physician; b. Wheatland, Wyo., Jan. 19, 1935; s. Ralph Elliott and Mansella (Davis) H.; B.S. in Pharmacy, U. Wyo., 1957; postgrad. U. Tulsa, 1959-61; D.O., U. Health Sci., Kansas City, Mo., 1965; m. Nancy Alene Davis, July 31, 1962; children—Trenton Reed, Kira Leigh. Intern, Phoenix Gen. Hosp., 1965-66; gen. practice medicine, Denver, 1966—; mem. staff Valley View Hosp. and Med. Center, Gen. Rose Meml., St. Anthony's North and Mercy hosps.; chief staff Valley View Hosp. and Med. Center, 1975-77, vice chief, 1979; pres. Columbine Med. Group, 1980; bd. dirs. Comprecare, 1978—; mem. Sloans Lake Med. Group, 1980—; founder, dir., chmn. bd. Community First Nat. Bank, Thornton, Colo. Chmn., N. Denver physicians com. United Way, 1980; pres. N. Denver chpt. Colo. Assn. Children with Learning Disabilities, 1977; elder Broomfield Presbyn. Ch. Diplomate Am. Bd. Family Practice, Am. Osteo. Bd. Gen. Practice. Fellow Am. Acad. Family Physicians; mem. AMA (Physicians Recognition award 1977, 80), Colo. Acad. Family Physicians (chpt. pres. 1980-81, dir. 1981-82), Colo. Med. Soc. (ho. dels.), Colo. Osteo. Med. Soc. (trustee), Clear Creek Valley Med. Soc. (chmn. continuing med. edn. com. 1978, chmn. bd. censors and bd. trustees 1980-81, sec.-treas. 1981-82), Tri-County Osteo. Soc. Clubs: Northglenn-Thorton Rotary, Shriners. Office: 8989 Huron St Denver CO 80221

HENDERSON, LESTER KIERSTEAD, photographer, publisher, art agent, photographic illustrator; b. Abington, Mass., May 9, 1906; s. Ernest Lester and Minnie Louise (Kierstead) H.; m. Sydney Danser, Feb. 14, 1982; children—Eleanor, Lester K., Jr., David P., Gale, Toni. B.E.E., Northeastern U., 1927. Freelance portrait photographer, 1927—; art agt., 1932—; pub., 1980—; ann. tours. art mus. on wings. Named to Photography Hall of Fame, Santa Barbara, Calif., 1981. Clubs: Kiwanis, Masons, Elks, Boston Yacht, Scituate Yacht, Stage Harbor Yacht, Monterey Yacht. Author, pub., photographer The Sublime Heritage of Martha Mood, Vol. 1, 1980, Vol. II, 1983. Office: 712 Hawthorne PO Box 3195 Monterey CA 93940

HENDERSON, NEAL SHELLEY, quality engr., govt. adminstr.; b. San Pedro, Calif., July 27, 1925; s. Frederick Oren and Irene Estelle (Neal) H.; student Chabot Jr. Coll., 1968-72, Northwestern U., 1970; m. Charlotte Helen McMahon, Nov. 30, 1946; 1 son, Robert Fortune. Transp. ops. supr. U.S. Navy, Hunters Point, Calif., 1967, test, instrns. and inspn. supr., 1967-73; transp. expert Naval Facilities Engring. Command, San Bruno, Calif., 1973-79; gen. partner Del Loma Resort, Trinity County, Calif., 1980—; dir. transp. ops. Navy Public Works Center, Oakland, Calif., 1979—; cons. Bay Area Marine Inst., San Francisco. Sea scout leader Alameda council Boy Scouts Am., 1965. Served with USCG, 1943-46; ETO, PTO. Decorated Bronze Star with 2 gold stars; recipient cert. of merit Traffic Inst., Northwestern U.; registered profl. engr., Calif. lMem. Fed. Mgrs. Assn. (chmn. transp. safety com. 1979—). Republican. Roman Catholic. Office: Navy Public Works Center PO Box 24003 Oakland CA 94623

HENDERSON, PAUL, III, journalist; b. Washington, Jan. 13, 1939; s. Paul and Doris Olive (Gale) H.; m. JoAnn Burnham, Sept. 10, 1964; children—Leslee, Jill, Polly Ann; m. 2d Janet Marie Horne, Jan. 22, 1982; 1 son, Peter Paul. Student Wentworth Mil. Acad. Jr. Coll., Lexington, Mo., 1957-59, Creighton U., 1963, U. Nebr.-Omaha, 1964-67. Reporter Council Bluffs (Iowa) Nonpareil, 1962-66, Omaha World-Herald, 1966-67; investigative reporter Seattle Times, 1967—; cons. Warner Bros. Co-founder Seattle Forgotten Children's Fund, 1976. Served with U.S. Army, 1959-62. Recipient 1st Place C.B. Blethen award, 1977, 82, Pulitzer prize for spl. local reporting, 1982, 1st Place Roy W. Howard Pub. Service award Scripps-Howard Found., 1982; named one of 50 Outstanding Achievers Am., Am. Acad. Achievement, 1982. Mem. Pacific N.W. Newspaper Guild. Methodist. Office: PO Box 70 Seattle WA 98111

HENDERSON, PHILLIP THEODORE, ready-mix concrete company executive; b. Las Vegas, Nev., June 21, 1945; s. James Robinson and Miriam Lucille (Reynolds) H.; m. Nancy Lee Benner, Aug. 26, 1967; 1 dau., Alyson Elisabeth. B.A. in Bus. Adminstrn., U. Redlands, 1967; student U. Nev., Las Vegas, 1973. Ops. trainee Bank of Am., Claremont, Calif., 1967; v.p., credit mgr. Las Vegas Bldg. Materials, Inc., Calif., 1970-81; pres. LVBM Inc., Las Vegas, 1981—. Bd. dirs. Boys Clubs of Clark County, 1980—, So. Nev. Exec. Council, 1979-82, 1981-82. Served with U.S. Army, 1967-70. Mem. Bus. Council Inst. (adv. bd., chmn. crime com. 1980—), Greater Las Vegas C. of C. (v.p. bus. council, 1979-82), Las Vegas Materialmen's Credit Group (chmn. 1973-74), Employers Assn. So. Nev. (pres. 1982), Credit Mgrs. Assn. So. Calif.

Clubs: Las Vegas Rotary (fellowship chmn. 1977-79), 25 (pres. 1977-79). Home: 3841 Syracuse Dr Las Vegas NV 89121 Office: Las Vegas Bldg Material PO Box 530 Las Vegas NV 89125

HENDERSON, RICHARD, businessman, state senator; b. Hilo, Hawaii, Dec. 20, 1928; B.S. in Econs., U. Pa.; married; 4 children. C.P.A., Henderson, Henderson & Dobbins, 1951-58; pres., dir. Realty Investment Co., Ltd.; dir. Hawaiian Elect. Industries, Inc., Hawaiian Electric, Inc., Hawaii Electric Light Co., Inc.; mem. Hawaii Senate, 1970-78, 80—, asst. minority leader, 1974-78, minority leader, 1980—. Past pres. Hawaii Island United Fund, Big Island Housing Found.; chmn. sustaining membership campaign YMCA, 1979; bd. dirs. Awareness House, Inc., 1979-80. Mem. Hawaii Island C. of C., Kona C. of C., Japanese C. of C. and Industry. Office: PO Box 655 Hilo HI 96720

HENDERSON, ROBERT ALFRED, advertising agency executive; b. Phila., Jan. 25, 1947; s. Joseph Eugene and Mary Elizabeth (Harris) H.; m. Karen Sue Gautereaux, Mar. 27, 1970; children—Christian Michael, Chad Joseph. B.A. in Advt. Design, Calif. State U.-Long Beach, 1969. Retail mgr. B.F. Goodrich Co., 1972-75, mktg. mgr., 1972-75; pres., creative dir. Robert Henderson Design, 1975—; ednl. cons. advt. design. Active Republican Nat. Com. Served to 1st lt., Q.M. Corps, U.S. Army. Recipient advt. award Waterbed Mfrs. Assn. Founder, ClubScene mag., Cuttings monthly; inventor instant picture frame for instant pictures.

HENDERSON, WALTER JAMES, III, ednl. adminstr.; b. Alhambra, Calif., July 31, 1945; s. Walter James and Louise (Whitener) H.; m. Carolyn Janet Epperson, Dec. 24, 1972. A.A., Monterey Peninsula Coll., 1969; B.A., U. N.Mex., 1971; M.Ed., U. Ariz., 1975, Ed.D., 1981. Tchr, Albuquerque Pub. Schs., 1971-74; tchr. Colegio Jorge Washington, Cartagena, Colombia, 1974-75; prin. Santa Cruz Valley Schs., Tumacacori, Ariz., 1977-78; asst. prin. North Pole High Sch., Fairbanks, Alaska, 1978-80; dir. tchr. edn. Sheldon Jackson Coll., Sitka, Alaska, 1981-82; prin. Wasilla (Alaska) High Sch., 1982—; adj. prof. U. Alaska, 1981—; cons. Alaska State Dept. Edn., 1981—. Served with USN, 1966-68. Mem. Nat. Assn. Secondary Sch. Prins., Assn. Supervision and Curriculum Devel., Sigma Alpha Epsilon, Pi Lambda Theta, Kappa Delta Pi, Phi Delta Kappa. Republican. Presbyterian. Club: Rotary. Home: PO Box 3414 Palmer AK 99645 Office: PO Box 1580 Wasilla AK 99687

HENDREN, ED WALTER, lawyer; b. Ft. Sill, Okla., May 13, 1938; s. Ed. V. and Dorthy M. (Schoggen) H.; m. Madeline G. McDonald, May 3, 1979; children—Matthew F., David M., John E., Benjamin C., Ed Walter, Elizabeth Ann, William B. B.S., U.S. Mil. Acad., 1962; M.A., Am. U., 1968; J.D., Stanford U., 1976. Bar: Calif. 1976. Commd. 2d lt., U.S. Army, 1962, advanced through grades to maj., 1968, resigned, 1973; Olmsted scholar U. Freiburg, W.Ger., 1964-67; assoc. prof. sociology U.S. Mil. Acad., West Point, 1969-73; assoc. Wilson, Mosher & Sonsini, Palo Alto, Calif., 1967-78; ptnr. Mosher, Pooley, Sullivan & Hendren, Palo Alto, 1978 ; arbitrator/mediator small claims project Santa Clara County Bar Assn., 1980-82. Decorated Bronze Star medal, Purple Heart, Air Medal, Army Commendation medal. Named Outstanding Educator, U.S. Mil. Acad., 1972-73. Mem. ABA, San Mateo and Santa Clara County Bar Assn. Office: 525 University Ave Suite 1410 Palo Alto CA 94301

HENDREN, ROBERT LEE, JR., furniture co. exec.; b. Reno, Oct. 10, 1925; s. Robert Lee and Aleen (Hill) H.; student U. Idaho, 1943-44, 46-47; m. Merlyn Churchill, June 14, 1947; children—Robert Lee IV, Anne Aleen. Pres., Hendren's Furniture Co., Boise, Idaho; dir. Shore Club Lodge, Inc., 1st Interstate Bank Idaho. Mem. bd. Marriage Counseling Service; exec. com. Mountainview council Boy Scouts Am.; trustee Boise Independent Sch. Dist.; mem. council Ada County Dept. Pub. Assistance; mem. Boise City Planning Commn.; Boise Art Bd.; exec. bd. Boise Philharmonic Orch.; charter dir. Boise Valley Indsl. Found.; chmn. bd. trustees Coll. of Idaho; trustee Boise Ind. Sch. Dist. Served with AUS, 1944-46; PTO. Mem. Idaho Council of Retailers (v.p.), Boise Valley Carpet and Furniture Retailers (pres.), Boise Retail Mchts. (chmn.), C. of C. (pres., dir.), Am. Inst. Interior Designers, Idaho Sch. Trustees Assn., Sigma Chi. Clubs: Arid, Hillcrest, Masons, K.T., Shriner, Rotary. Home: 3504 Hillcrest Dr Boise ID 83705 Office: 516 S 9th St Boise ID 83706

HENDRICK, HAL WILMANS, psychologist, educator; b. Dallas, Mar. 11, 1933; s. Hearold Eugene and Audrey S. (Wilmans) H.; m. Jytte Louridson, Sept. 9, 1972; children—Hal, David, John, Jennifer; stepchildren—Sharon, Debbie, Jackie. M.S. in Human Factors Psychology, Purdue U., 1961, Ph.D. in Indsl. Psychology, 1966. Lic. psychologist, Tex. Commd. 2d lt. U.S. Air Force, 1956; advanced through grades to lt. col., 1972; ret. 1976; with Air Def. Command, 1956-60; human factors psychologist and project engr. C141 aircraft and Dynasoar research and devel. programs Wright-Patterson AFB, Ohio, 1961-64; assoc. prof. U.S. Air Force Acad., 1966-72; chief behavioral scis. Def. Race Relations Inst., Patrick AFB, Fla., 1972-76; assoc. prof. human factors inst. safety and systems mgmt. U. So. Calif., Los Angeles, 1976—; cons. in field. Decorated Meritorious Service medal with one oak leaf cluster, Commendation medal. Mem. Am. Psychol. Assn., Human Factors Soc. (chmn. tech. group), Internat. Ergonomics Assn. (council mem.), Acad. Mgmt., Hawaii, Psychol. Assn., Western Psychol. Assn., Assn. Aviation Psychologists, Assn. Advancement Psychology. Democrat. Unitarian. Contbr. articles to profl. jours. Home: 849 Hahaione St Honolulu HI 96825 Office: Human Factors Dept Inst Safety and Systems Mgmt U So Calif Los Angeles CA 90089

HENDRICKS, CHARLES DURRELL, physicist, researcher in laser fusion, administrator, educator; b. Lewiston, Utah, Dec. 5, 1926; s. Charles Durrell and Louise (McAlister) H.; m. Leah Funk, Mar. 4, 1948; children—Katherine, Martha Jane. B.S. in Physics, Utah State U., 1949; M.S. in Physics, U. Wis., 1951; Ph.D. in Physics, U. Utah, 1955. Mem. tech. staff Lincoln Lab., MIT 1955, vis. prof. dept. elec. engring., 1967-68; asst. prof. U. Ill., Urbana, 1956-63; prof., 1963-66, prof. dept. elec. engring. and nuclear engring., dir. charged particle research lab., 1966; sr. research fellow dept. elec. engring. Southampton U. (Eng.), 1971; leader for target fabrication group in laser fusion program U. Calif. Lawrence Livermore Lab., 1974-80, assoc. program leader, 1980-82, sr. staff scientist, 1982—; vis. lectr. Calcutta U., Saha Inst. for Nuclear Physics, 1961, 65; mem. U.S. del. Internat. Conf. on Controlled Thermonuclear Fusion Research, 1961, 63, 67, 69. Served with USN, 1944-46, 51-52. Dept. of Elec. engring. sr. research fellow Southampton U., 1971; Electrostatics Soc. fgn. fellow, 1977. Fellow Am. Phys. Soc., IEEE, AAAS, AIAA (assoc.); mem. Phi Beta Kappa, Sigma Xi, Tau Beta Pi, Phi Kappa Phi. Mem. Ch. of Christ. Contbr. numerous articles to sci. jours. Home: 2817 Pardee Pl Livermore CA 94550 Office: Lawrence Livermore Nat Lab PO Box 5508 L-482 Livermore CA 94550

HENDRICKS, ED JERALD, pathologist; b. Temple, Tex., Aug. 26, 1935; s. John Gorden and Lucille (Withers) H.; B.A., Rice U., 1957; M.D., Columbia U., 1961; m. Susan Meredith Brown, Sept. 2, 1959; children—David Wesley, Deborah Kay, John Michael, James Gregory. Intern, Parkland Meml. Hosp., Dallas, 1961-62; resident U. Minn., 1962-66; asso. pathologist St. Joseph Hosp., Houston, 1969-72; dir. clin. labs./pathology dept. Fresno Community Hosp. (Calif.), 1972—; dir. clin. labs. Clovis Community Hosp., 1981—; cons. VA Hosp., Fresno, 1981—. Served to capt. USAF, 1966-69. Diplomate Am. Bd. Pathology, Nat. Bd. Med. Examiners. Fellow Am. Soc. Clin. Pathology, Coll. Am. Pathologists; mem. Fresno County, Calif, Am. med. assns., Calif. Soc. Pathologists (dir.), Fresno Pathology Soc. (pres. 1978-79), Phi Beta Kappa, Sigma Xi. Contbr. articles to profl. jours. Clubs: Pres. (Fresno), Fresno Yacht. Home: 5680 E Alluvial Clovis CA 93612 Office: PO Box 1232 Fresno and R Sts Fresno CA 93715

HENDRICKS, PAUL LAUMANN, employee benefit/compensation consulting company executive; b. Tokyo, Mar. 1, 1924; s. Kenneth C. and Grace (Paul) H.; m. Yvonne B. Felton, Dec. 31, 1956; children—Leslie S., Julie A. A.A., Occidental Coll., Los Angeles, 1944; B.A., UCLA, 1946. Cert. employee benefit specialist. Employee benefits specialist Aetna Life & Casualty, various locations, 1947-67; mng. dir. William M. Mercer, Inc., Seattle, 1967—. Bd. dirs. Cardiopulmonary Research Inst. of Seattle/King County; regent Seattle Art Mus. Served to lt. USNR, 1941-47. Mem. Western Pension Conf. (past pres.), Internat. Found. Employee Benefit Plans, Greater Seattle C. of C., Internat. Soc. Cert. Employee Benefit Specialists. Clubs: Arlington (Portland); Wash. Athletic, Harbor (Seattle). Home: 1831 W Mercer Way Mercer Island WA 98040 Office: One Union Sq Suite 3200 Seattle WA 98101

HENDRICKS, ROBERT MICHAEL, insurance company executive; b. St. Louis, Aug. 23, 1943; s. Chester Eugene and Reba Eileen (Leake) H.; B.A., U. Calif., Berkeley, 1965; m. Yvonne Sharon McAnally, Sept. 18, 1971; 1 son, Robert Christian. Dist. mgr. Am. Gen. Life Ins. Co., Los Angeles, 1965-70; gen. ptnr. Hendricks & Assos., Los Angeles, 1970-75; v.p. mktg. U.S. Life Corp., Los Angeles, 1975-76; dir. agys. Bankers United Life Assurance Co., Los Angeles, 1976-77; gen. ptnr. Assurance Distbg. Co., Inc., Los Angeles, 1977-80; pres., chief exec. officer ADCO Re Life Assurance Co., Santa Ana, Calif., 1980—; dir. ADCO Re Life Assurance Co., First Commerce Trust Co., Assurance Distbg. Co., Inc.; instr. C.L.U. and Life Underwriter Tng. Council programs. Recipient various awards in field. Mem. Nat. Assn. Life Underwriters, C. of C., Internat. Platform Assn. Republican. Clubs: Santa Ana Country, Lincoln, Silver Circle, Balboa Bay, Rotary, Masons, Shriners. Home: 1611 La Loma Dr Santa Ana CA 92705 Office: ADCO Re Life Assurance Co 1010 N Main St Suite 525 Santa Ana CA 92701

HENDRICKSON, MICHAEL DALE, accountant; b. Devils Lake, N.D., June 13, 1943; s. Hjalmer Clayton and Mary Elizabeth (Young) H.; m. Karen Louise Skarperud, Dec. 31, 1965 (div.); children—Christine Ann, Craig Michael. B.S. in Bus. Adminstrn., U. N.D., 1965, M.S. in Bus. Adminstrn., 1967. C.P.A., Colo. Wyo. Staff acct. Price Waterhouse, Denver, 1968-71, sr. acct., 1971-74, audit mgr., 1974-78, sr. mgr., 1978-80, ptnr., chmn. acctg., auditing and SEC com. Petroleum Industry Services Group, 1980—; instr. Becker C.P.A. Rev. Course, 1974-76. Bd. dirs. Beaver Ranch Found.; mem. fin. com. Cenikor Found., 1980. Served to lt. U.S. Army, 1966-68. Mem. Am Inst. C.P.A.s, Colo. Soc. C.P.A.s, Ind. Petroleum Assn. Mountain States (dir., exec. com.). Republican. Lutheran. Clubs: Denver Petroleum, Pinery Country, Plum Creek Country, Kiwanis (dir., past pres., Toastmasters (pres. 1974). Office: 950 17th St Suite 2300 Denver CO 80202

HENDRIX, JOHN EDWIN, botany educator; b. Van Nuys, Calif., Aug. 30, 1930; s. John Edwin and Leona (Paul) H.; m. Joan B. Haas, Apr. 10, 1954; children—Janet L. and James A. A.S., Pierce Jr. Coll., 1951; B.S., Fresno State Coll., 1956, A.B. (NSF Fellow), 1961; M.S., Ohio State U., 1963, Ph.D., 1967. Orchard foreman Fresno State Coll., 1958-60; tchr., research asst. Ohio State U., 1960-65, instr. 1965-67; asst. prof. Colo. State U., 1967-72, assoc. prof. 1972—; mem. editorial staff Plant Physiology. Served to 1st lt. U.S. Army, 1951-53. Decorated Air medal. NSF, NASA grantee. Mem. Am. Soc. Plant Physiology, AAAS, Am. Inst. Biol. Scis., Bot. Soc. Am., Colo.-Wyo. Acad. of Sci., Sigma Xi, Phi Lambda Upsilon, Phi Kappa Phi. Republican. Contbr. articles to profl. jours. Office: Dept Botany and Plant Pathology Colo State U Fort Collins CO 80523

HENDRIX, WILLIAM EDWIN, geologist; b. Austin, Tex., Oct. 29, 1916; s. William Samuel and Bertha (Bourdette) H.; B.A., Ohio State U., 1938, M.Sc., 1939; m. Marie Glenn Thrall, Aug. 9, 1940; children—William Steven, Kenneth Alan, Donald Linn. Jr. geologist Magnolia Petroleum Co., Youngstown, Ohio, 1939-40; with Standard Oil Co. Calif., various locations, 1946-72, dist. paleontologist, La Habra, Calif., 1965-68, sr. paleontologist, La Habra, 1968-72; geol. cons., partner Edack Assos., specializing in paleoechology, biostratigraphy, paleovulcanology and mining geology W. coast N.Am., North Sea, Temple City, 1972—. Committeeman, San Gabriel Valley council Boy Scouts Am., 1948; mem. Los Angeles County council 4-H Club, 1960-61; mem. Temple City (Calif.) Citizens Adv. Council on Edn., 1961-62. Bd. dirs. Self Aid Workshops for Mentally Retarded and Physically Handicapped, El Monte, Calif. Served to capt. AUS, 1940-46. Fellow AAAS; mem. Am. Assn. Petroleum Geologists, Soc. Econ. Paleontologists and Mineralogists, Archaeol. Inst. Am., Res. Officers Assn., Am. Def. Preparedness Assn., Ret. Officers Assn., 2d Armored Div. Assn., Retarded Children's Assn. of San Gabriel Valley, Sigma Xi, Pi Kappa Alpha. Developed and adapted for IBM computer, method of foraminiferal correlation of rock strata using complex inter-relationships formed by the cyclical overlapping of occurences of individual species. Address: 6261 N Sultana Ave Temple City CA 91780

HENDRY, JOHN FRANCIS, lawyer; b. N.Y.C., Apr. 22, 1943; B.S., U. Okla., 1968, J.D. with honors, 1978; M.A., Chapman Coll., 1975. Served with U.S. Marine Corps, 1960-81; admitted to Okla. bar, 1978, Calif. bar, 1979; pvt. practice law, Orange, Calif., 1979—. Served to maj. USMC. Mem. Okla. Bar Assn., Calif. Bar Assn., Order of Coif, Phi Delta Phi. Office: 13030 Euclid Ave Suite 205 Garden Grove CA 92643

HENICK, STEVEN EVAN, educator; b. Cleve., Sept. 28, 1956; s. Charles and Florence Shirley (Kronenberg) H. B.A., San Jose State U., 1978; M.Ed., U. Nev.-Las Vegas, 1981; postgrad. in edn. Cert. tchr., Nev., Calif. Tchr. Clark County (Nev.) Sch. Dist., 1979—. Mem. Assn. Supervision and Curriculum Devel., Clark County Classroom Tchr.'s Assn., Phi Delta Kappa, Sigma Pi. Democrat. Jewish. Home: 1555 E Rochelle Ave Apt 123 Las Vegas NV 89109 Office: 4551 Diamond Head Dr Las Vegas NV 89110

HENLEY, JAMES EDWARD, museum director; b. Sacramento, June 14, 1944; s. Rufus F. and Emmiline Helen (Greistner) H.; m. Paula L. Welch, 1978. B.A., Sacramento State Coll., 1966, postgrad., 1966-67. Research asst. Sacramento Historic Landmarks Commn., 1967-69, exec. dir., 1969-73; exec. dir. Sacramento Mus. and History Commn., 1973—. Hist. cons., Old Sacramento Historic area reconstruction; lectr. U. Calif. at Davis, 1975—. Mem. Ry. and Locomotive Hist. Soc. (dir. 1971-74), Sacramento Pioneer Assn. (dir. 1973-75), Am. Assn. State and Local History (merit award 1970). Author: City of the Plain-Sacramento in the Nineteenth Century, 1969; 1849 Scene, 1973; Eagle Theatre, 1973, and others. Home: 2501 N St Sacramento CA 95816 Office: 1930 J St Sacramento CA 95814

HENLEY, PRESTON VANFLEET, former banker, financial consultant; b. Fort Madison, Iowa, July 7, 1913; s. Jesse vanFleet and Ruth (Roberts) H.; m. Elizabeth Artis Watts, Mar. 31, 1940 (div. June 1956); children—Preston Edward VanFleet, Stephen Watts, John vanFleet; m. 2d, Helena Margaret Greenslade, Nov. 29, 1964; 1 adopted son, Lawrence D. Student Tulane U., 1931-34, Loyola U., New Orleans, 1935-36; A.B., Calif. State Coll. at Santa Barbara, 1939; postgrad. U. Wash., 1939-40, N.Y. U., 1943, 46. Teaching fellow U. Wash., 1939-40; sr. credit analyst, head credit dept. Chase Nat. Bank, 45th St. br. N.Y.C., 1942-49; Western sales rep. Devoe & Raynolds, Inc., N.Y.C., 1949-51; v.p., comml. loan officer, mgr. credit dept. U.S. Nat. Bank, Portland, Oreg., 1951-72; loan adminstr. Voyageur Bank Group, Eau Claire, Wis.; v.p. Kanabec State Bank, Mora, Minn., Montgomery State Bank (Minn.), Park Falls State Bank (Wis.), Montello State Bank (Wis.), 1972; v.p., mgr. main office, sr. credit officer So. Nev. region Nev. Nat. Bank, Las Vegas, 1973-75; bus. and fin. cons., 1975—; instr. Am. Inst. Banking, Portland, 1952-65, Multomah Coll., Portland, 1956-62, Portland State U., 1961-72, Mt. Hood Community Coll., 1971-72, Clark County Community Coll., 1979—; adv. dir. Vita Plus, Inc., 1983—; exec. dir. Nev. Minority Purchasing Council, 1979-80; dir., treas. Consumer Credit Counselling Service of Oreg. 1965-72. Treas., Ore. chpt. Leukemia Soc., 1965-66; mem. Menninger Found. 1965-67; mem. St. Rose delima Hosp. Found., 1982—. Served with USNR, 1943-45. Mem. Oreg. Bankers Assn., Robert Morris Assos. (pres. Oreg. chpt. 1959-60, nat. dir. 1961-64), Nat., Oreg. assns. credit mgmt., Credit Research Found., Inst. Internal Auditors, S.A.R., Am. Legion, Navy League, Beta Mu, Leaf and Scarab, Alpha Phi Omega, Portland C. of C., Oreg. Retail Council. Republican. Episcopalian. Mason (32 deg., Shriner), Elk. Club: International. Contbr. articles to profl. jours. Home and Office: 4235 Gibraltar St Las Vegas NV 89121

HENLEY, WILLIAM BALLENTINE, rancher, cattle breeder; b. Cin., Sept. 19, 1905; s. William Herbert and May G. (Richards) Ballentine (later assumed name of stepfather, Charles E. Henley); A.B., U. So. Calif., 1928, student Sch. Religion, M.A., 1930, J.D., 1933, M.S. in P.A., 1935; student Yale U., 1929-30; LL.D., Willamette U., 1937; Sc.D., Kansas City Coll. Osteopathy and Surgery, 1949; L.H.D., Los Angeles Coll., Optometry, 1958; Sc.D. (hon.), Pepperdine Coll., 1966; m. Helen McTaggart, 1942. Engaged as lectr. pub. adminstrn. and asst. to co-ordination officer U. So. Calif., 1928-29; dir. religious edn. First Methodist Ch., New Haven, Conn., 1929-30; lectr. pub. adminstrn. U. So. Calif., 1930-33, exec. sec. Women's Civic Conf., same, 1930-40; pub. speaking instr. and debate coach Am. Inst. Banking, 1928-40; acting dean Sch. of Govt., U. So. Calif., 1937-38, dir. 8th and 9th Inst. of Govt., 1937-38, asst. to dean Sch. of Govt., in charge of in-service tng. Civic Center, 1934-36, asst. prof. pub. adminstrn., 1935-39, asso. prof., 1939-40, dir. co-ordination, 1938-40; pres. Calif. Coll. Medicine, Los Angeles, 1940-66; provost U. Calif. Irvine-Calif. College of Medicine, 1966-70; pres. United Ch. Religious Sci., 1970-78; owner, operator Creston Circle Ranch; exec., speakers' panel Gen. Motors Corp., 1956-74. Mem. Western Interstate Commn. on Higher Edn., 1961-72; v.p. Los Angeles Safety Council, 1972—. Vice pres. bd. dirs. Glendale Community Hosp.; bd. dirs. So. Cal. Cancer Center, Los Angeles County Health Assn.; bd. dirs. Burbank Community Hosp. Found.; mem. Los Angeles Bd. Water and Power Commrs., 1944-62, pres. 1946, v.p. 57-58; mem. Employees' Pension and Retirement Bd. Mgmt. 1946; mem. adv. bd. Los Angeles County General Hospital Unit II; mem. Los Angeles Defense Council, 1941-44, War Council, 1944-45, Calif. Civil Def. Com. Guest observer U.N. Conf., San Francisco, 1945. A.T. Still Meml. lectr., Washington, 1958. Mem. Am., Calif. and Los Angeles bar assns., A.I.M., Def. Orientation Conf. Assn., Am. Saddle Horse Breeding Futurity Assn. (dir.), Am. Aberdeen Angus Breeders Assn., Calif. Cattlemen's Assn., Am. Angus Assn., Sigma Alpha Epsilon, Phi Delta Phi, Phi Kappa Phi, Phi Sigma Gamma, Sigma Sigma Phi, Delta Sigma Rho, Phi Delta Kappa, Pi Sigma Alpha, Alpha Delta Sigma, Phi Eta Sigma, Sigma Sigma, Skull and Dagger. Republican. Mason (32 deg.). Club: Los Angeles Rotary (pres. 1955-56; chmn. Conf. dist. 160-A, gov. dist. 528, 1959-60; mem. internat. community service consultative group; chmn. host club exec. com. for 1962 internat. conv.; mem. world community service com.). Author: The the University of Southern California, 1940; Man's Great Awakening or Beautiful Mud, 1974; also mag. articles. Home: 1224 Geneva St Glendale CA 91207 Office: Creston Circle Ranch Creston Star Route Paso Robles CA 93446

HENNESSEY, JOSEPH PAUL, JR., wind energy specialist; b. Missoula, Mont., May 9, 1944; s. Joseph Paul and Geraldine I. H. B.S. in Math., Marquette U., 1967; B.S. in Meteorology, U. Utah, 1969; M.S. in Atmospheric Scis., Oreg. State U., 1974. Air pollution trainee EPA, 1972-73; energy trainee NSF, 1974-77; research meteorologist Oreg. State U., Corvallis, 1977-79; cons. agrl. meteorologist, 1979-80; head wind resources, wind energy program Calif. Energy Commn., Sacramento, 1980-82; wind energy cons., 1982—. Served to capt. USAF, 1967-72. Decorated Air Force Commendation medal. Mem. Am. Meteorol. Soc., Nat. Weather Assn. (v.p. Willamette chpt. 1976), Air Pollution Control Assn., Crown and Anchor, Sigma Xi, Chi Epsilon Pi. Democrat. Roman Catholic. Contbr. articles and revs. to sci. jours.

HENNESSY, JUDY GAIL, personal computer company official; b. Detroit, Aug. 18, 1947; d. John Harold and Doris Helene (Voigt) H. B.S. in Math. with honors, Mich. State U., 1971, M.S. in Math., 1974. Instr. minicomputers Tex. Instruments, Houston, 1975-77, mgr. S.W. course devel. and sales tng., Austin, Tex., 1977-80; instr. inter-active corp. services dept. Bank of Am., San Francisco, 1981-82; dir. edn. EKOS, Inc., San Rafael, Calif., 1982—; chmn. Bank Am.'s Bankwide Trainer's Forum, 1982. Home: 335 Cascade Dr Fairfax CA 94930 Office: 2165A Francisco Blvd San Rafael CA 94901

HENNING, CHARLES NATHANIEL, educator; b. Pitts., June 20, 1915; s. William P. and Eleanor (Hill) H.; A.B., U. Calif. at Los Angeles, 1938, A.M., 1940, Ph.D., 1953; m. Virginia Marie Doerr, June 30, 1945. Teaching asst., lectr. econs. U. Calif., Los Angeles, 1939-42; economist Far Eastern div. U.S. Dept. Commerce, 1942-48; asst. prof. finance U. Wash., 1948-53, asso. prof., 1953-55, prof. finance, 1955—, dir. bus. adminstrn. faculty publs., 1961-72, coordinator bus. adminstrn. faculty research, 1971-72, acting chmn. dept. finance, bus. econs. and quantitative methods, 1974; mem. extension faculty Pacific Coast Banking Sch., 1954—, ednl. adviser, 1960—; ednl. adviser Pacific Rim Bankers Program, 1977—; dir. Korean Bankers Program, 1980—; cons. various investment firms, banks. Fgn. Transp. Inst., Am. U., 1946, 1948; cons. Operations Research Office, Johns Hopkins, 1952-61, Research Analysis Corporation, 1962-67. Mem. Central Banking Seminar, Fed. Res. Bank of San Francisco, 1951. Mem. U.S. delegation Internat. Conf. on World Trade and Employment, Geneva, Switzerland, 1947. Mem. Am. Econ. Assn., Am. Finance Assn., Seattle C. of C., World Trade Club Seattle, World Affairs Council Seattle, Am. Acad. Polit. and Social Sci., Artus, Pan Xenia, Phi Beta Kappa, Pi Gamma Mu, Alpha Kappa Psi, Beta Gamma Sigma. Author: International Finance, 1958; (with William Pigott and R.H. Scott) Financial Markets and the Economy, 3d edit., 1981; International Financial Management, 1978; contbr. Ency. Brit. Editor: (with James A. Crutchfield and William Pigott) Money, Financial Institutions, and the Economy, 1965; U. Wash. Bus. Review, 1954-71. Address: 12714 42d Ave NE Seattle WA 98125

HENNING, JAMES SCOTT, psychologist, hospital mental health services administrator; b. Duluth, Minn., Dec. 6, 1942; s. Roland John and Margaret Louise (Lynch) H. A.B., Gonzaga U., 1966; M.Div., Jesuit Sch. Theology, Berkeley, Calif., 1973; M.S., U. Wis., 1970, Ph.D., 1974; postgrad. cert. series for mental health profls. U. So. Calif., 1981—. Lic. clin. psychologist, Calif. Teaching asst. U. Wis.-Milw., 1968-70, 73-74; psychol. cons. Suicide Prevention Ctr. Alameda County, Berkeley, 1970-73; research fellow Death and Dying Research Ctr., U. Calif.-Berkeley, 1972-73; clin. intern in psychology Children's Hosp. Med. Ctr., Harvard Med. Sch., Boston and clin. fellow in med. psychology, dept. psychiatry Harvard U. Med. Sch., 1974-75; staff psychologist William Greenleaf Eliot Research Ctr., postdoctoral trainee in clin. psychology, instr. in med. psychology Washington U. Sch. Medicine, St.

Louis, 1975-76; clin. psychologist, pediatric liaison service Div. Child Psychiatry, Harbor-UCLA Med. Ctr., Torrance, Calif., 1976-80; liaison clin. psychologist dept. psychiatry Kaiser Hosp., Bellflower, Calif., 1980—; asst. clin. prof. med. psychology dept. psychiatry and biobehavioral scis. UCLA, 1976-82; cons. Task Force on Psychosocial Impact of Nuclear Advances of Am. Psychiat. Assn., 1979—; mem. Child Abuse Task Force, So. Calif. Permanente Med. Group, 1980—. Trustee, Rossi Fund, Los Angeles. Fellow Am. Orthopsychiat. Assn. (Task Force on Nuclear Issues 1980—); mem. Am. Psychol. Assn. (nat. program reviewer Div. Child and Youth Services, 1978—), Soc. Pediatric Psychology. Democrat. Roman Catholic. Contbr. chpts., articles to profl. jours.; author profl. papers. Office: So Calif Permanente Med Group Downey CA 90242

HENNING, JOHN F., labor union ofcl.; b. San Francisco, Nov. 22, 1915; s. William Henry and Lulu Frances (McLane) H.; A.B., St. Mary's Coll., 1938, LL.D., 1976; LL.D., St. Anselm's Coll., 1965; D.C.S., St. Bonaventure U., 1966; m. Marguerite M. Morand, Nov. 25, 1939; children—John F., Brian H., Patrick W., Nancy R., Daniel M., Thomas R., Mary T. Research dir., adminstrv. asst. to exec. officer Calif. State Fedn. Labor, San Francisco, 1949-58; dir. Calif. Dept. Indsl. Relations, San Francisco, 1959-62; U.S. under sec. of labor, Washington, 1962-67; U.S. Ambassador to N.Z., 1967-69; exec. sec.-treas. Calif. Labor Fedn. AFL-CIO, San Francisco, 1970—. Mem. Bd. Permit Appeals, 1953-56, pres., 1955-56; mem. Pub. Welfare Commn., 1950-53; mem. Equal Employment Opportunities Commn, 1956-59 (all San Francisco); mem. bd. regents U. Calif., 1977—. Office: 995 Market St San Francisco CA 94103

HENNINGS, LONELL HOWARD, counselor; b. Grand Island, Nebr., Oct. 23, 1953; s. Harold Howard and Louise Irene (Luebbe) H.; m. Kelly Maureen Bembry, Apr. 14, 1979. B. S. in Phys. Sci., Kearney State Coll., 1977; M.A. in Counseling, U. Wyo., 1981. Cert. counselor, Wyo. Instr. Gothenburg (Nebr.) High Sch., 1977-79; dormitory dir. U. Wyo., 1979-80; grad. asst., instr., 1980-81; housing mgr. Wyo. Tech. Inst., Laramie, 1980-81; counselor grades kindergarten-12 Guernsey-Wyo.)-Sunrise High Sch., 1981—; cons. spl. services Guernsey-Sunrise Schs., summer 1982. Wyo. Dept. Edn. grantee, 1981-82, 82-83. Mem. Am. Personnel and Guidance Assn., Wyo. Personnel and Guidance Assn., NEA, Wyo. Edn. Assn., Guernsey-Sunrise Edn. Assn. Republican. Lutheran. Home: PO Box 736 Guernsey WY 82214 Office: PO Box 189 Guernsey WY 82214

HENRICH, DANIEL JOSEPH, communication researcher, management/marketing consultant; b. Orange, Calif., Aug. 25, 1951; s. Maurice Riddick and Lois Lorraine (Depp) H.; m. Christine Lynn Klyver, Dec. 29, 1973; children—Caren Anne, Samuel Joseph. B.A., Calif. State U.-Fullerton, 1975, postgrad., 1975-76; postgrad. William Carey Internat. U., 1983—. Registered mgmt. cons., Nigeria. Prin., v.p. Impact Communicators, Anaheim, Calif., 1974—; v.p. devel. M/E Internat., Anaheim, 1974—; tech. dir. Literacy Internat., Lagos, Nigeria, 1980—; mgmt. cons. Olatunbosun Ige Olumide & Assocs., Lagos, 1979—; mem. faculty Immaculate Evangel. Sem., Lagos, 1983—. Elder Plaza Bible Foursquare Ch., 1980—. Named Man of Yr., Santa Ana Coll., 1972. Mem. Am. Vocat. Assn., Am. Multi-Image Soc. Republican. co-developer high speed film projector. Office: 1061 N Shepard St Unit D Anaheim CA 92806

HENRICKS, EDWARD PHILLIP, JR., aerospace sales and distribution corporation executive; b. Evanston, Ill., Mar. 29, 1938; s. Edward P. and Edith Theresa (Schnepp) H.; m. Mary Nardizzi, Nov. 4, 1978; children by previous marriage—Edward P. III, Timothy, Suzanne; 1 step-dau., Victoria. A.A., Alan Hancock Coll., 1962; student Calif. State U., Northridge, 1965-68. With Kahr Bearing Div., Burbank, Calif., 1967-77; sales mgr. Western div. Barry Controls, Burbank, 1977-79, Magnetic Tech. Co., Canoga Park, Calif., 1979; v.p. sales, sec.-treas. Arger Enterprises, Inc., Newbury Park, Calif., 1979—. Served with USAR, 1960-66. Office: Arger Enterprises Inc Suite 113 3533 Old Conejo Rd Newbury Park CA 91320

HENRY, CHARLES LAVON, advertising company executive, marketing consultant, educator; b. Augusta, Ga., June 17, 1947; s. William Clark and Katie Catherine (Quinn) H.; m. Beverly Gonzalez, Aug. 2, 1972 (div.); children—Alisa, Matthew, Adam. B.A. in Communications, Brigham Young U., 1972; bus. mgmt. cert. U. Utah, 1977. Pub. relations supr. Mountain Bell, Salt Lake City, Denver, 1976-78; advt. staff mgr., Denver, 1978-79; dir. mktg. Internat. Communications Assocs., Denver, 1979; instr./lectr. pub. relations Brigham Young U., Provo, Utah, 1980-82; pub. info. officer Fed. Emergency Mgmt. Agy., Denver and Washington, 1981; v.p. mktg. Andres Mines Internat., Denver, Santiago, 1983—; dir. Quinlott Corp., Andes Mines Internat. Bus. Co., Inc.; instr. pub. relations, advt. Brigham Young U. Del., Colo. Assembly, 1980-82; capt. Jefferson County Republican party. Named Communicator of Yr., Internat. Bus. Communicators Assn., 1977; Businessman of Yr., Colo./Okla., 1983; numerous awards for journalism and photography. Mem. Pub. Relations Soc. Am., Am. Mgmt. Assn., Internat. Assn. Bus. Communicators, Sigma Delta Chi. Mormon Author: A Guide to Fire Alarm Systems, 1973; Batteries Not Included, 1982; H.T. (the home teacher), 1982; The Missionary Companion, 1983. Home: PO Box 8555 Denver CO 80201 Office: Andes Mines Internat 12395 W 53d Ave Suite 208 Denver CO 80002

HENRY, CHARLES LEWIS, accountant, educator; b. Raton, N.Mex., Dec. 10, 1946; s. Virgil Oscar and Eloise (Eldridge) H.; m. Carol Ruth Gerken, Nov. 16, 1950; children—Kevin, Eric, Sarah. B.B.A. in Acctg., U. N.Mex., 1970. C.P.A. Surety bond underwriter USF & G, Albuquerque, 1970-71; staff acct. Lewallen & Co., Albuquerque, 1971-74; controller N.Mex. Beverage Co., Albuquerque, 1974; sr. staff acct. Neff & Co. C.P.A.s, Albuquerque, 1974-75; ptnr. Henry & Kardas C.P.A.s, Albuquerque, 1975—; tchr. acctg. U. N.Mex.; pub. speaker. Mem. Am. Inst. C.P.A.s, N.Mex. Soc. C.P.A.s. Democrat. Roman Catholic. Home: 6708 Loftus NE Albuquerque NM 87109 Office: Henry & Kardas 4001 Indian School Rd NE Suite 300 Albuquerque NM 87110

HENRY, CHARLES PATRICK, political scientist, educator; b. Newark, Ohio, Aug. 17, 1947; s. Charles Patrick and Ruth (Holbert) H.; m. Loretta Jean Crenshaw, Aug. 23, 1968; children—Adia, Wesley, Laura. B.A., Denison U., 1969; M.A., U. Chgo., 1971, Ph.D., 1974. Asst. prof. Howard U., Washington, 1973-76; asst. prof., asst. dean Denison U., Granville, Ohio, 1976-81; asst. prof. U. Calif.-Berkeley, 1981—. Cons., mem. Amnesty Internat. Ford Found. grantee, 1969-70, NIMH grantee, 1971-72; NEH fellow, 1980-81. Mem. Nat. Council Black Studies (sec.), Nat. Conf. Black Polit. Scientists, Am. Polit. Sci. Assn. (Congl. fellow 1972-73). Contbr. articles to profl. jours. Office: Dept Afro-American Studies U Calif Berkeley CA 94720

HENRY, EMMA JEAN, educator; b. Taylor, Ariz., June 29, 1939; d. Winston Bernard and Georgianna (Kartchner) Barner; m. G. Tom Henry, Sept. 8, 1956; children—Gene Terry, Vicki Ann, Guy Todd. B.S. in Edn., No. Ariz. U., 1972, M.A. in Phys. Edn., 1975, postgrad.; postgrad. Yavapai Coll., U. Santa Clara, U. Hawaii. Tchr. phys. edn., coach girls sports Camp Verde Sch. Dist., 1969-74; tchr., coach Verde Sch. Dist. #3, Clarkdale, Ariz., 1974—. Mem. NEA, Ariz. Edn. Assn. Republican. Mormon.

HENRY, FAUN DE, small business consultant; b. Cherrypoint, N.C., Nov. 27, 1952; d. James Frazar Henry and Jan Elizabeth (Campbell) R.; m. Dan Martin Shannon, Apr. 3, 1983. Student, Bakersfield Community Coll., 1970-72, U. Houston, 1972-73, U. Md., 1974, Columbia Coll., Denver, 1978. Typist, Seidman & Seidman, C.P.A.s, Houston, 1972-73; pvt. practice cons., Washington, 1973-75, 1976; asst. to pres. Averroes, Inc., McLean, Va., 1975-76; pvt. practice cons., Boston, 1976-77, Denver, 1977; dir. New Directions, Denver, 1977—. Bd. Dirs. Colo. Dance Alliance, 1982-83, pres., 1983—. Mem. Rocky Mountain Career Planning Assn. (treas. 1980-83), Old Girls' Network (co-founder 1979), Women's Exchange (co-founder 1980). Contbr. numerous articles in field to mags.; developer Lifework map, career planning process, 1982. Office: New Directions PO Box 18590 Denver CO 80218

HENRY, JERRY EDWARD, lawyer; b. Kimball, Nebr., Feb. 28, 1941; s. Merle Edward and Natalie Ann (Ebel) H.; m. Nancy Irene Perry, Sept. 25, 1962; children—Karen Ann, Lois Marie, David Charles. A.A., Otero Jr. Coll., Colo., 1961; B.A., San Jose State U., 1965; J.D., San Joaquin Coll. Law, Fresno, Calif., 1974. Bar: Calif. 1974, U.S. Dist. Ct. (ea. dist.) Calif. 1974, U.S. Ct. Appeals (9th cir.) 1981. Journalist, UPI, 1965-74, bur. mgr., 1968-74; dep. dist. atty. Fresno County (Calif.), 1974-75; ptnr. Smurr & Henry, Inc., Kerman, Calif., 1975—. Dir. Kerman State Bank. Mem. ABA, Fresno County Bar Assn. Club: Kiwanis. Office: 441 S Madera Ave Suite C Kerman CA 93630 also 900 Helen Bldg Fresno CA 93721

HENRY, JOHN BRYSON, industrial educator; b. Anadarko, Okla., June 12, 1953; s. Charlene (Saunders) Henry; m. Jerri Ann Landrum, Aug. 17, 1974. B.S., Eastern N.Mex. U., 1978, M.Ed., 1980. Instr., Del Norte High Sch., Albuquerque, 1978-79; grad. asst. Eastern N.Mex. U., Portales, 1979-80; instr. Los Alamos (N.Mex.) High Sch., 1980-81; coordinator graphic arts N.Mex. Jr. Coll., Hobbs, 1981-82; coordinator Area Vocat. High Sch., N.Mex. Jr. Coll., Hobbs, 1982—; cons. Title I TV Prodn., Disadvantaged Vocat. Project, 1982-83. Advisor, Jr. Achievement, 1981-82, 82-83. Named Outstanding Sr. in Indsl. Edn., Eastern N.Mex. U., 1978. Mem. Am. Vocat. Assn., N.Mex. Vocat. Assn., Phi Delta Kappa, Phi Kappa Phi. Baptist.

HENRY, KAREN HAWLEY, lawyer; b. Whittier, Calif., Nov. 5, 1943; d. Ralph Henry and Dorothy Ellen (Carr) Hawley; m. John Dunlap, 1968; m. 2d, Charles Gibbons Henry, Mar. 15, 1975; children—Scott, Alexander, Joshua. B.S. in Social Scis., So. Oreg. Coll., 1965; M.S. in Labor Econs., Iowa State U., 1967; J.D., Hastings Coll. of Law, 1976. Instr., Medford (Oreg.) Sch. Dist., 1965-66; research asst. dept. econs. Iowa State U., Ames, 1966-67; dir. research program Calif. Nurses Assn., San Francisco, 1967-72; labor coordinator Affiliated Hosps. of San Francisco, 1972-79; ptnr. Littler, Mendelson, Fastiff & Tichy, San Francisco, 1979—. Mem. ABA (subcom. on publ. labor arbitration awards labor law sect.), State Bar of Calif., San Francisco Bar Assn., Contra Costa Bar Assn., Soc. Hosp. Attys., Thurston Soc., Order of Coif. Office: 650 California St San Francisco CA 94108

HENRY, KENNETH WESLEY, elec. engr.; b. Brookfield, Mo., Apr. 19, 1939; s. William Howard and Eloisa Grace (Adams) H.; B.S., N.E. Mo. State U., 1961; B.S. in Elec. Engring., U. Mo., Rolla, 1961; M.S., U. N.Mex., 1963; Ph.D., U. Calif., Davis, 1971; m. Elsie McCandlish Taylor, June 20, 1964; children—Kenneth Wesley, Joseph William. With Sandia Labs., Albuquerque, 1961-65, Livermore, Calif., 1965—, materials research engr., 1968-73, sr. engr. non destructive evaluation, 1973—. Mgr., coach Little League, coach soccer; treas. Asbury United Meth. Ch., Livermore, 1974-75; v.p. Am. Little League, Livermore, 1980-81. Mem. IEEE, Eta Kappa Nu, Tau Beta Pi. Republican. Home: 2360 Buena Vista Ave Livermore CA 94550 Office: Sandia Labs Box 969 Livermore CA 94550

HENRY, NANCY M., space planner, interior designer; b. Amarillo, Tex., Mar. 12, 1938; d. Morris Y. and Etta Lee (Poole) Salahi; m. Donald W. Renfro; 1 son, Jay. Student U. Houston, 1958, Tex. A&I Coll., 1963; diploma Inchbald Sch. Design, London, 1976. Freelance designer, Bakersfield, Calif., 1976-79; prin. Nancy Henry Interior Design, 1979—; dir. interior design Design Research Assocs., 1982—; cons., lectr. in field. Chmn. design rev. bd. Bakersfield Redevel. Agy., 1981—; mem. Bakersfield 2000 Commn., 1977-79. Mem. Am. Soc. Interior Designers. Republican. Unitarian. Club: Network (Bakersfield). Project pub. in Designers West mag., Nov. 1982. Office: Nancy Henry Interior Design 4800 Stockdale Hwy Suite 304 Bakersfield CA 93309

HENRY, WALTER L., cardiologist, educator; b. Cumberland, Md., Feb. 20, 1941; s. Walter and Virginia Mae (Keller) H.; B.S. cum laude in Elec. Engring., U. Pitts., 1963; M.D., Stanford U., 1969. Intern, Bronx Mcpl. Hosp., N.Y.C. and Albert Einstein Coll. Medicine, 1969-70, resident in internal medicine, 1970-71; clin. asso. Nat. Heart, Lung and Blood Inst., Bethesda, Md., 1971-73, sr. investigator, 1973-78; prof. medicine, chief div. cardiology U. Calif., Irvine, 1978—. Served with USPHS, 1971-78. Diplomate Am. Bd. Internal Medicine. Mem. Am. Soc. Echocardiography (pres.), N. Am. Soc. Cardiac Radiology, Am. Heart Assn., Am. Fedn. Clin. Research, Eta Kappa Nu, Alpha Omega Alpha, Omicron Delta Kappa. Editorial bd. Am. Heart Jour. Contbr. articles to profl. jours. Office: Cardiology Div U Calif Irvine Med Center 101 City Dr S Orange CA 92717

HENSHAW, WILLIAM CHARLES, optometrist; b. Boston, Nov. 27, 1944; s. Alfred Hugh and Elsie May (Harwin) H.; m. Charlene Lois Gerton, Aug. 27, 1966; children—Theodore William, Marion May, Vernon Charles. B.S., Pacific U., 1966, O.D., 1967. Lic. optometrist, Calif. 1967. Pvt. practice optometry, Seattle, 1968, Lodi, Calif., 1973—; U.S. Army optometrist, Walter Reed Hosp., Washington, Ft. Dedrick, Frederick, Md.; Amway distbr., Lodi, 1977—. Served to capt. U.S. Army, 1968-72. Mem. Am. Optometric Assn., Calif. Optometric Assn., San Joaquin Optometric Assn. (past pres.), Optometric Extension Program, Amway Distbrs. Assn., Lodi C. of C. (polit. activities com.). Republican. Author numerous papers in field. Home: 758 S Crescent Lodi CA 95240 Office: Dr William C Henshaw 801 S Fairmont Lodi CA 95240

HENSLEY, JAMES WILLIS, wholesale co. exec.; b. San Antonio, Tex., Apr. 12, 1920; s. James Louis and Jessie (Mounger) H.; student pub. schs. Phoenix; m. Marguerite Johnson, Mar. 29, 1945; children—Dixie Lea, Kathleen, Cindy Lou. Vice pres., gen. mgr. United Liquor Co., Phoenix, 1945-52; partner Ruidoso Racing Assn. Ariz./N.Mex., Ruidoso, N.Mex., 1952-55; pres., chief exec. officer Hensley & Co., Phoenix, 1955—. Bd. dirs. Doctors Hosp., Phoenix. Served with USAAF, 1941-45. Decorated DFC, Air medal with oak leaf cluster, Purple Heart. Mem. Gov.'s Adv. Commn. on Ariz. Environment, 1973—. Mem. Ariz. Beer and Liquor Wholesale Assn. (pres.), Phoenix C. of C., Phoenix Execs. Club, Exec. Assn. Greater Phoenix, Ariz. Retail Grocers Assn., Ariz. Hotel Assn., Am. Legion. Republican. Clubs: Arizona, Wigwam Country, Plaza, Masons. Home: 7110 Central Ave N Phoenix AZ 85020 Office: 5061 N 51st Ave Glendale AZ 85311

HENZL, ELIZABETH MARY, educator; b. Spokane, Wash., Mar. 22, 1917; d. John Anthony and Freda Elizabeth (Mengert) H.; A.B., Holy Names Coll., 1943; A.M., Portland State U. and U. Oreg., 1954; Ed.D. (fellow), Ind. U., 1969; M.A. in Religious Studies, 1983. Joined Sisters of Holy Names, 1935; instr. Archdiocesan Parochial Elem. and Secondary Schs., Portland, Oreg., also Seattle, 1938-67; mem. faculty geography dept. Ontario Coll. Edn., 1969-70; lectr. geography and edn. Western Wash. State U., 1970-71; assoc. prof. tchr. edn. and geography Tex. Coll., Tyler, 1971-72; asst. prof. tchr. edn. curriculum and instrn. Seattle U., 1973-75, U. Nev., Reno, 1976-78; instr. TESL, Gonzaga U., Spokane, 1980-82. Adult and youth ministry St. Pascal's Parish, Spokane, 1983-84. ERIC research grantee, 1967-69. Mem. Assn. Am. Geographers, Nat. Council Social Studies, AAUP, Nat. Council Geog. Edn., Am. Assn. Curriculum and Supervision Devel., Pi Lambda Theta. Author: Geography Gateways: The United States and Canada, 1967; Visual-Aural Discriminations Series, 1973. Home: W 2911 Fort Wright Dr Spokane WA 99204

HEPLER, MERLIN JUDSON, JR., real estate broker; b. Hot Springs, Va., May 13, 1929; s. Merlin Judson and Margaret Belle (Vines) H.; m. Lanova Helen Roberts; children—Nancy Hepler Mullens, Douglas Stanley. B.S. in Bus., U. Idaho, 1978; grad. Realtors Inst. Enlisted in USAF, 1947; ret., 1967; service mgr. Lanier Bus. Products, Gulfport, Miss., 1967-74; sales assoc. Realty World-Apex Realty, Troy, Idaho, 1978-80, sales mgr., 1980-81, assoc. broker, 1981, broker, prin., 1981—, also dir.; dir. AFPAM, Inc. Mem. Nat. Assn. Realtors, Realtors Nat. Mktg. Inst., Sgts. Assn. Baptist. Clubs: Lions, Am. Legion. Office: 519 S Main St Troy ID 83871

HEPPNER, CLAUS ERICH, designer; b. Wuppertal, Germany, June 13, 1930; s. Erich and Margarete (Romuender) H.; m. Margarete Elizabeth Leber; children—Diana Wiens, Deborah. B.A., Sch. Environ. Design, U. Colo., 1979. Jr. designer Am. Fixture Co., Denver; designer contract dept. Comml. Interiors, Denver, 1956-58, mgr. 1958; pres., owner Claus Heppner & Assocs., Denver, 1967—; theatrical designer. Mem. Am. Soc. Interior Designers. Republican. Clubs: Garden of the Gods (Colorado Springs); Balboa (Mazatlan, Mex.). Home: 1000 S Monaco Apt 104 Denver CO 80224 Office: 1600 Logan Denver CO 80203

HEPWORTH, CAROLYNE, soils engineering company executive; b. Augusta, Ga., Jan. 3, 1942; d. Samuel and Patricia A. (Timm) Steffen; Assoc. Acctg., Columbia Coll., 1981; m. Richard C. Hepworth, Apr. 25, 1981; children—Michelle Denise, Michael John, Diana Lynnette. Sec., U.S. Army Records Ctr., St. Louis, 1960-61, Goodyear Tire & Rubber Co., St. Louis, 1963-67; bookkeeper, office mgr. Hayes C.T.S., Inc., Ironton, Mo., 1971-73; controller Chen & Assocs., Inc., Denver, 1974—. Mem. Women in Constrn., Am. Soc. Women Accts., Nat. Assn. Accts., Profl. Services Mgmt. Assn. Republican. Roman Catholic. Office: 96 S Zuni St Denver CO 80223

HERAMCHUK, LEONARD JOHN, security executive; b. Montreal, Que., Can., Aug. 31, 1943; s. Leonard and Catherine (Lozinski) H.; m. Jocelyne Marie Cyr, Aug. 8, 1975; 1 dau., France Stella. With Royal Can. Mounted Police, eastern Can., 1962-76, spl. investigator Noranda Group, 1976; security mgr. ITT Rayonier Inc., Port Cartier, Que., Can., 1977-80; regional security mgr. ITT Rayonier, Inc., Northwest region, Hoquiam, Wash., 1980—. Mem. Am. Soc. Indsl. Security, Nat. Assn. Chiefs Police, Wash. Timberlands Security Council (chmn.), Twin Harbors Law Enforcement Council. Club: Kiwanis (Aberdeen, Wash.); Masons. Home: 416 Evergreen Ln Aberdeen WA 98520 Office: PO Box 299 Hoquiam WA 98550

HERB, EDMUND MICHAEL, optometrist; b. Zanesville, Ohio, Oct. 9, 1942; s. Edmund G. and Barbara R. (Michael) H.; divorced; children—Sara, Andrew. O.D., Ohio State U., 1966. Pvt. practice optometry, Buena Vista, Colo., 1966—; mem. faculty Ohio State U. Mem. Am. Optometric Assn., Colo. Optometric Assn. Home: Lost Creek Ranch Buena Vista CO 81211 Office: 507 N Highway 24 Buena Vista CO 81211

HERBEL, CARLTON HOMER, range scientist; b. San Antonio, Tex., June 2, 1927; s. Carl Anton and Selma Hermina (Levin) H.; m. Carolene Cae Callahan, Oct. 4, 1952; children—Belinda Ann Fiedler, Kurt Carlton. B.S. in Agr., Tex. A&I U., 1949; M.S., Kans. State U., 1954, Ph.D., 1956. Asst. agronomist Southwest Research Inst., San Antonio, 1949-50; grad. research asst. Kans. State U., 1953-56; agronomist Southwest Found. Research & Edn., San Antonio, 1956; range scientist Agrl. Research Services U.S. Dept. Agr., Las Cruces, N.Mex., 1956—; mem. grad. faculty N.Mex. State U., 1959—. Served with U.S. Army, 1950-52. Fellow AAAS; mem. Am. Soc. Agronomy, Crop Sci. Soc. Am., Soil Sci. Soc. Am., Ecol. Soc. Am., Soc. Range Mgmt., Am. Forage and Grassland Council (Merit cert. 1974), Orgn. Profl. Employees U.S. Dept. Agr. Club: Masons. Contbr. articles to profl. jours. Home: 1804 Half Moon Dr Las Cruces NM 88001 Office: Jornada Exptl Range PO Box 3JER Las Cruces NM 88003

HERBERGER, GEORGE ROBERT, corporate executive; b. Osakis, Minn., Sept. 12, 1904; s. George and Emily (Curry) H.; m. Katherine Kierland, Aug. 25, 1934; children—Gail Roberta, Gary Kierland, Judd Robert. Student Hibbing Jr. Coll., U. Minn. Founder, pres. Herberger-Hart Co., St. Cloud, Minn., 1927; pres., gen. mgr. G.R. Herberger's Inc., 1942-47, chmn. bd., 1950-72, hon. chmn. bd., 1972—; pres. So. Land and Cattle Co., 1937-47, dir., 1937-52; v.p., dir. Keller Drug Co., Mpls., 1946-47; pres. Butler Bros., Chgo., 1947-49, dir., 1948-57, chmn. bd., 1949-50; chmn. bd. Tigrette Enterprises, Inc., 1950-51; pres., dir. Desert Springs Water Co., Scottsdale, Ariz., 1955-71, chmn. bd., 1971-73; pres., dir. Paradise Valley Devel., Inc., 1956-71, chmn. bd., 1971—; pres., dir. Bohmer-Herberger, 1967—; sec., dir. Herberger-Cruse Co., Osakis; v.p., dir. Gainey Water Co., Scottsdale, 1956—; pres. Herberger Enterprises, Phoenix, 1952-71, chmn. bd., 1971—; pres. Chandler Heights Land Co., 1960-74. Chmn. ARC, Stearns County, Minn.; mem. Minn. State Vets. Service Bldg. Commn., 1946-47; mem. UN Bd. State Minn., 1946-47; trustee Phoenix Fine Arts Assn., 1951-70; v.p. dir. Paradise Valley Improvement Assn., 1952-55; bd. dirs. Am. Grad. Sch. Internat. Mgmt., 1952-81, exec. com., 1967-77; mem. pres.'s adv. com. for John F. Kennedy Ctr. for Performing Arts, 1970-77; mem. adv. council SBA, 1970—; chmn. adv. com., mem. adv. council Fiesta Bowl, 1971-81; bd. dirs. Phoenix Symphony Assn., v.p., exec. com., 1962-79; founding mem. Phoenix Chamber Music Soc., 1953-78, bd. dirs., 1960-77; del. Nat. Republican Conv., 1956, alt. del., 1968; mem. Rep. Nat. Fin. Com., 1959-70; trustee Ariz. Sunset Cradle Soc., Evanston, Ill., 1947-53; bd. dirs. U. Minn. Found., 1977-80; mem. dean's adv. council Ariz. State U., 1977—; trustee, dir. numerous civic orgns. Mem. Newcomen Soc. Clubs: Elks; Chgo., Phoenix Execs. (pres. 1967, dir. 1961-68); Alexandria (Minn.) Country. Home: 6439 E Luke Valley AZ 85253 Office: 7045 E Camelback Rd Scottsdale AZ 85251

HERBERT, GAVIN SHEARER, pharmaceutical manufacturing company executive; b. Los Angeles, Mar. 26, 1932; s. Gavin Shearer and Josephine (D'Vitha) H.; m. Dorraine Winter, Oct. 16, 1954; children—Cynthia, Lauri Gavin, Pamela. B.S., U. So. Calif., 1954. Vice pres. Allergan Pharms., 1956-61, exec. v.p., 1961-77; pres., 1977—, chmn. of the bd., chief exec. officer, 1980—; pres. Eye and Skin Care Group, SmithKline Beckman, 1981—. Mem. Pharm. Mfrs. Assn., Beta Theta Pi. Republican. Clubs: Lincoln, Big Canyon Country, The Balboa Bay, Newport Harbor Yacht. Home: 65 Emerald Bay Laguna Beach CA 92651 Office: 2525 Dupont Dr Irvine CA 92713

HERBST, JERRY EDWARD, service station executive, real estate developer; b. Chgo., Jan. 8, 1938; s. E. R. and Loraine G. (Lang) H.; m. Maryanna Anderson, Dec. 26, 1959; children—Ed, Tim, Troy. B.B.A., U. So. Calif., 1960. Owner, pres. Terrible Herbst Oil Co., Las Vegas, 1959—; dir. Valley Bank Nev., Frontier Savs. & Loan Assn. Mem. U. Nev.-Las Vegas Founders Club, President's Assocs., Rebels Booster Club, Las Vegas Founders Club, Gorman High Sch. Booster Club.

Episcopalian. Clubs: Las Vegas Country, Hualapai. Home: 950 Rancho Circle Las Vegas NV 89107 Office: Terrible Herbst Oil Co 5195 Las Vegas Blvd S Las Vegas NV 89119

HERBST, LAWRENCE ROBERT, veterinarian, investment adviser, tax cons., rancher, economist, promoter; b. Haverhill, Mass., Aug. 8, 1946; s. Morton and Ruth I. (Cooper) H.; student UCLA, Alexander Hamilton Bus. Inst., D.V.M., N.Am. Sch. Animal Scis.; D.D., Missionaries of New Truth, Chgo. Owner Total Sound Records, Lawrence Herbst Records, Beverly Hills Music Pubs., 1975—; founder Future World Stores, Larry's Family Restaurant, Heavenly Waterbed Showrooms, 1978; pres., adminstr. Investment Trust Fund, Inc.: Larr Computers, Larr Robots, Larry's Merchandising Data Base, Beverly Hills Music, Total Sound Records, et al. Mem. Broadcast Music, Inc.; pres. Lawrence Herbst Farms; producer Spacee the Lion Cartoon. Pres., adminstr. Lawrence Herbst Found. Mem. Nat. Acad. TV Arts and Scis., Los Angeles Press Club, Internat. Platform Assn., Epsilon Delta Chi. Author: (book and movie) Legend of Tobby Kingdom, 1975; The Good, The Bad, The True Story of Lawrence Herbst; news columnist World of Investments, 1976. Designer 1st mus. electronic amplifier with plug in I.C.s; inventor one-man air car. Office: PO Box 1659 Beverly Hills CA 90213 also PO Box 1003 Milford PA 18337

HERCZEG, FERENC PAL, electro-mech. cons.; b. Kecel, Hungary, May 1, 1932; s. Istvan Janos and Maria Roza (Fajsz) H.; came to U.S., 1956, naturalized, 1962; dip. engr. U. Hungary, 1956; m. Maria Magdolna Lakatos, Dec. 29, 1959; children—Emoke E., Orsi G., Ara G., Dalma K., Hunor F., Tunde, Magor Pal. Staff engr. Fairchild Semiconductor, Palo Alto, Calif., 1966-70; mgr. mech. engring. Gould Inc., Palo Alto, 1970-72; dir. mfg. Continental Telephone Corp., Mountain View, Calif., 1972-74; v.p. mfg. Memories and Magnetics, Inc., Pleasanton, Calif., 1974-76; pres. The Hun Co. Engring./Mgmt. Cons., San Mateo, Calif., 1976—; mem. exec. bd. dirs. Memories and Magnetics, Inc., Pleasanton, 1976-77; faculty Hungarian and ancient history Hungarian Sch., Woodside/Portola Valley, Calif., 1975—. Sec., Hungarian Folk Dance Ensemble, San Francisco, 1974-76. Recipient First Prize Design award IEEE, 1972; Cert. of Merit, SBA, 1977, 78. Mem. Am. Mgmt. Assn. Mem. Ch. of Hungary. Inventor in field. Address: 19 Seville Way San Mateo CA 94402

HERD, SHIRLEY DEAL, writer; b. Wichita, Kans., Sept. 13, 1935; d. James Russell and Dorothy Mae (Powell) Herd; B.S. in Edn., U. of Kans., 1957; children—Michael James DeGood, Mark William DeGood. Freelance writer, author, book reviewer 1957—; books include: The Cruising Cook; Easy Spanish; Blimey, Limey! Wha'd He Say?; author numerous articles on boating, cruising, food preparation; lectr. Mem. Nat. Fedn. of Press Women, Pubs. Group of So. Calif., Outdoor Writers Assn. Am. Republican. Presbyterian.

HERDA, PHYLLIS ANN, clin. social worker; b. Park River, N.D., Nov. 29, 1944; d. Palmer Gustav and Rose Francis (Snaza) Setness; A.A., Bismarck Jr. Coll., 1973; B.S., Mary Coll., Bismarck, 1978; M.S.W., Calif. State U., Sacramento, 1980; m. Peter V. Herda, June 23, 1962 (div. Feb. 1977); children—Alex, Stephen, Dominic, Anthony, Susan, Duncan. Psychiat. social worker Tehama County Mental Health, Red Bluff, Calif., 1980—; jail cons.; liaison county and state residential care homes; outreach social worker Corning Clinic; alcohol and drug counselor 940th Mather Air Force Res., 1979—. Served with USNG, 1974-76. Named Outstanding Airman, 1982. Mem. AAUW. Roman Catholic. Club: Toastmasters (pres.). Home: 635 David Ave Apt A Red Bluff CA 96080 Office: 1860 Walnut St Red Bluff CA 96080

HERDEG, HOWARD BRIAN, physician; b. Buffalo, Oct. 14, 1929; s. Howard Bryan and Martha Jean (Williams) H.; student Paul Smith's Coll., 1947-48, U. Buffalo, 1948-50, Canisius Coll., 1949; D.O., Phila. Coll. Osteopathic Medicine, 1954; M.D., Calif. Coll. Medicine, 1962; m. Beryl Ann Fredricks, July 21, 1955; children—Howard Brian III, Erin Ann. Intern, Burbank (Calif.) Hosp., 1954-55; practice medicine specializing in family practice, Woodland Hills, Calif., 1956—; chief med. staff West Park Hosp., Canoga Park, Calif., 1971-72, trustee, 1971-73; chief family practice dept. West Hills Med. Ctr., Canoga Park, 1982-83, also mem. exec. com. Mem. Hidden Hills (Calif.) Pub. Safety Commn., 1978-82, chmn., 1982; bd. dirs. Hidden Hills Community Assn., 1971-73, pres., 1972; bd. dirs. Hidden Hills Homeowners Assn., 1973-75, pres., 1976-77; bd. dirs. Woodland Hills Freedom Season, 1961-67, pres., 1962. Recipient disting. service award Woodland Hills Jr C. of C., 1966. Mem. Woodland Hills C. of C. (dir. 1959-68, pres. 1967), San Fernando Valley Bus. and Profl. Assn., Theta Chi, Gamma Pi. Libertarian. Home: 24530 Deep Well Rd Hidden Hills CA 91302 Office: 22600 Ventura Blvd Woodland Hills CA 91364

HERDRICH, NORMAN WESLEY, editor; b. Spokane, Wash., July 17, 1942; s. Fred N. and Florice J. (Birchill) H.; B.S. in Agr., Wash. State U., 1969; m. Mary Susan Webb, Aug. 16, 1975; children—Megan Marie, Heidi Susan. Field editor Wash. Farmer-Stockman, Spokane, 1969-78; prodn. editor N.W. unit Farm Mags., Spokane, 1978—. Served with USNR, 1963-65. Mem. Wash. State Grange, Wash. Wool Growers Assn., Spokane Editorial Soc., Nat. Rifle Assn., Sigma Delta Chi. Methodist. Club: Spokane Press. Home: E 12711 Saltese Rd Spokane WA 99216 Office: Review Tower 999 W Riverside Spokane WA 99210

HEREFORD, DANNY JOE, counselor, consultant, researcher, educator; b. Tekoa, Wash., Mar. 22, 1939; s. Joseph Herron and Betty Jane (Shove) H.; m. Juanita Louise Valdez, Oct. 20, 1962; children—Loretta Marie, Joseph John, Cheryl Ann, Daniel John. B.A. cum laude in Behavioral Sci., Nat. U., San Diego, 1980, M.A. in Counseling Psychology, 19—; cert. in alcohol studies U. Calif.-San Diego, 1978. Served as noncommd. officer U.S. Navy, 1957-77; various adminstrv. positions; instr. Service Schs. Command, San Diego, 1968-71; ret., 1977; screener/interviewer USN Alcohol Safety Action Program, San Diego, 1977-80; adj. instr./facilitator U. West Fla., San Diego, 1980-81, U. Arizona, San Diego, 1981-83; instr./facilitator U. Calif.-San Diego, 1982-83, Met. Area Adv. Com., San Diego, 1982-83; clin. research coordinator, program dir. alcohol detoxification and preliminary treatment program Centre City Hosp., San Diego, 1980. Decorated letter of commendation, Navy unit commendation with 3 gold stars; Gallantry Cross (Vietnam). Mem. Nat. Assn. Alcoholism Counselors, Calif. Assn. Alcoholism Counselors, San Diego Area Coalition on Alcohol Problems, Am. Personnel and Guidance Assn., Am. Rehab. Counseling Assn., Calif. Assn. Marriage and Family Counselors, Nat. U. Alumni Assn. (life), Nat. Geog. Soc., Fleet Res. Assn. Roman Catholic. Clubs: North Shores Alano (Pacific Beach, Calif.); Lemon Grove (Calif.) Alano.

HEREM, MAYNARD ALVIN, consulting company executive; b. Rake, Iowa, Aug. 6, 1933; s. Carl O. and Helen (Christenson) H.; m. Helen Carolyn Palmes, Dec. 1, 1956; 1 dau., Karen Kay. B.S., Iowa State U., 1955; M.S., U. Wis.-Milw., 1970; Ph.D., U. Minn., 1979. Instr. Martin Co., Denver, 1959-61; sr. instr. Gen. Motors Corp., Milw., 1961-71; assoc. prof. U. Wis. Extension-Eau Claire, 1971-80; pres. Techtrain Inc., Santa Fe N.Mex., 1980—. Served with USAF, 1955-59. U. Wis. Extension Ednl. fellow, 1976-78. Mem. Santa Fe C. of C., Am. Soc. Tng. and Devel. (exec. com. tech. and skills tng. div. 1976-81), Nat. Soc. Performance and Instrn., Am. Assn. Adult and Continuing Edn. Contbr. articles to profl. jours. Office: 535 Cordova Rd Suite 223 Santa Fe NM 87501

HERENDEEN, LEONARD KING, police chief; b. Long Beach, Calif., July 10, 1929; s. Leonard King and Evelyn Glendora (Hanewinckel) H.; children—Mary Buckley, Terry Massie. B.S., Calif. State U., Long Beach, 1958; M.P.A., U. So. Calif., 1969; grad., cert. FBI Nat. Acad., 1977. With Los Angeles County Sheriffs Dept., 1954-79; police chief City of Antioch (Calif.), 1979—; tchr. adminstrn. of justice Coll. of the Canyons, Valencia, Calif.; Peace Office rep. to Calif. Law Enforcement Telecommunications Adv. Com. Bd. dirs. Delta Hosp. Found. Served with USMC, 1946-48. Mem. Calif. Police Chiefs Assn. (2d v.p.), Sheriffs Relief Assn. (past 1st v.p.), Calif. Peace Officers Assn., Antioch C. of C. Clubs: Antioch Rotary (treas.), Masons (past master, dist. insp.). Office: 301 W 10th St Antioch CA 94509

HERING, WILLIAM MARSHALL, educational research administrator; b. Indpls., Dec. 26, 1940; s. William Marshall and Mary Agnes (Clark) H.; m. Suzanne Wolfe, Aug. 10, 1963. B.S., Ind. U., 1961, M.S., 1962; Ph.D., U. Ill.-Urbana, 1973. Tchr. Indpls. pub. schs., 1962-66; asst. dir. sociol. resources project Am. Sociol. Assn., 1966-70; dir. social sci. curriculum Biomed. Interdisciplinary Project, Berkeley, Calif., 1973-76; staff assoc. Tchrs. Ctrs. Exchange, San Francisco, 1976-82; dir. research Far West Lab. Ednl. Research and Devel., San Francisco, 1979-82, sr. research assoc., 1982—; mem. Nat. Adv. Bd. Educ. Resource Info. Ctr.; cons. U.S. Dept. Edn.; pres. Social Sci. Educ. Consortium, 1981-82, bd. dirs., 1979-81. Nat. Inst. Educ. grantee, 1979-82, 82—. Mem. Am. Ednl. Research Assn., Am. Sociol. Assn., Assn. Tchr. Educators, Social Sci. Educ. Consortium, Nat. Council Social Studies, Nat. Staff Devel. Council, Golden Gate Soc., Nat. Audubon Soc., Phi Delta Kappa. Republican. Episcopalian. Contbr. over 100 articles on social studies edn., staff devel., ednl. research and evaluation to profl. jours. Home: 731 Duboce Ave San Francisco CA 94117 Office: 1855 Folsom St San Francisco CA 94103

HERLOCKER, BARBARA, educator, nutritional/health consultant; b. Los Angeles, May 27, 1936; d. Edwin Heath and Kathryn Mae (Parker) H.; m. Steven F. Holser, Aug. 15, 1956 (div.); children—Carol Holly, Susan Shelly. A.B., U. So. Calif., 1964, M.S., 1966. Cert. secondary tchr., Calif. Sec./asst. to dir. Bay Shore Sanitarium, Hermosa Beach, Calif., 1955-56; med. sec. Doctor's Hosp., Los Angeles, 1956-59; sci. tchr. Los Angeles Unified Sch. Dist., 1966-83; pres. Bardon & Assocs., Torrance, Calif., 1979—; Fulbright scholar, Eng., 1975-76; cons. to health, food, cosmetic, beauty, nutritional and weight loss cos., 1981—. NSF grantee, 1973. Mem. Fulbright Alumni Assn., Calif. Tchrs. Assn. Producer, co-hostess daily television series on health and fitness. Office: Bardon & Assocs PO Box 7000-639 Redondo Beach CA 90277

HERMAN, CAROLYN JEAN, home economist; b. North Platte, Nebr., Sept. 1, 1952; d. Donald E. and Esther M. (Furmanski) Nielsen; m. Kevin D. Herman, July 6, 1975. B.S. in Family and Consumer Edn., U. Wyo., 1975. Cert. extension home economist. Dietary aid Ivinson Meml. Hosp., Laramie, Wyo., 1975-76, transcriptionist med. records, 1976-77; extension home economist Albany County, U. Wyo., Laramie, 1978—; cons. family. Recipient cert. of Appreciation, Laramie Sr. High Sch., 1979; cert. of Merit, Wyo. Future Homemakers Am., 1981; cert. of Appreciation, Albany County K2 Health Fair, 1981, 82. Mem. Wyo. Assn. Extension Home Economists, Laramie Grad. Home Economists. Club: Plant and Pray Garden. Office: Albany County Courthouse Laramie WY 82070

HERMAN, IRVING LEONARD, business educator; b. Seattle, June 6, 1920; s. Joseph and Elizabeth Mitzie (Silverstone) H.; B.A. magna cum laude, U. Wash., 1942; M.A., Stanford, 1949, Ph.D., 1952; m. Jeanne Shirley Hasson, Aug. 31, 1946; children—Michelle (Mrs. Richard Dennis Ferkel), Deborah (Mrs. Tad Steven Shapiro). Research psychologist Air Force Personnel and Tng. Research Center, Lackland AFB and Mather AFB., Calif., 1950-58; engring. psychologist Lockheed Aircraft Corp., Sunnyvale, Calif., 1958, mgr. personnel devel. Aerojet-Gen. Corp., Sacramento, 1958-68; mgr. mgmt. devel. So. Calif. Gas Co., Los Angeles, 1968-69; asso. prof. bus. and pub. adminstrn. Calif. State U., Sacramento, 1969-72, prof., 1972—, chmn. dept., 1978-80; mgmt. cons. to U.S.C.E., Aerojet Gen. Corp., Sacramento Mcpl. Utility Dist. Served to 1st lt. AUS, 1942-45. Certified ASPA Accreditation Inst. as personnel diplomate, tng. and devel. Recipient Presdl. award Sacramento City-County C. of C., 1965. Mem. Am. Soc. for Personnel Adminstrn., Acad. of Mgmt., Sacramento City-County C. of C. (chmn. edn. com. 1964-65), Sacramento Personnel Assn. (pres. 1979-81), Phi Beta Kappa, Sigma Xi, Beta Gamma Sigma, Delta Sigma Pi. Home: 889 Commons Dr Sacramento CA 95825 Office: 6000 Jay St Sacramento CA 95819

HERMAN, JAMES JEROME, electrical engineer, lawyer; b. Sheboygan, Wis., July 23, 1929; s. Jacob and Amalia (Biel) H.; m. Lynn Ruth Willis, Sept. 8, 1951; children—Mark James, Julie Lynn Cross, Matthew James. B.S.E.E., MIT, 1952; B.A., Ripon Coll., 1952; M.S.E.E., U. Wis., 1956; J.D., U. Santa Clara, 1979. Bar: Calif. 1979; registered profl. engr., Calif. Sr. electronics engr. Convair Astronautics, Gen. Dynamics Corp., San Diego, 1956-59; prin. engr. Link div. Gen. Precision, Palo Alto, Calif., 1959-60; research specialist Lockheed Missile and Space Co., Sunnyvale, Calif., 1960—, engring. group supr., 1966-74, sr. staff engr., 1974—; gen. ptnr. Hi-Tech Audio; sole practice law. Bd. dirs. Homemaker Service Santa Clara County, 1982. Served to lt. USAF, 1953-55. Recipient NASA Pub. Service Group Achievement award, 1981. Mem. IEEE, AIAA (tech. com. legal aspects of aeros. and astronautics 1983—), ABA. Republican. Lutheran. Home: 1443 Lewiston Dr Sunnyvale CA 94087 Office: PO Box 504 Sunnyvale CA 94086

HERMAN, JAMES RICHARD, union executive; b. Newark, Aug. 21, 1924; s. Milton Matthew and Larraine Catherine (Kelly) H.; student public schs., N.J. Pres. Internat. Longshoremen's and Warehousemen's Union, San Francisco, 1977—. Bd. dirs. Delancey St. Found., St. Anthony's Dining Rm., Columbia Pk. Boys Club; mem. Dem. State Central Com., Calif. Named Labor Man of Yr., Alameda County Central Labor Council, 1973. Mem. Maritime Inst. for Research and Indusl. Devel. (dir.). Democrat. Roman Catholic. Club: Concordia. Office: 1188 Franklin St San Francisco CA 94109

HERMANN, WILLIAM DARRELL, oil company executive; b. Staplehurst, Nebr., Sept. 18, 1924; s. William Henry and Dora (Graham) H.; m. Janet Sharp, Aug. 17, 1944; children—Kristina Leigh Stevens, William D. B.A. in Econs., Washington U., St. Louis, 1948, M.A., 1962, Ph.D., 1967. Mem. staff mktg. div. Shell Oil Co., St. Louis, 1948-60; program economist AID, Monrovia, Liberia, 1964-67; assoc. prof. S.D. State U., 1967-69; vis. prof. Concordia Coll., Moorhead, Minn., 1969-70; economist Bechtel Corp., San Francisco, 1970-75; chief economist Standard Oil Co. of Calif., San Francisco, 1976—. Served to 1st lt. USAF, 1943-45. Decorated air medal, D.F.C. with three oak leaf clusters. Mem. Am. Econ. Assn., Western Econ. Assn., Nat. Assn. Bus. Economists, Soc. Internat. Devel. Club: Univ. (San Francisco). Contbr. publs. to profl. jours. Home: 1047 Miller Ave Berkeley CA 94708 Office: 225 Bush St San Francisco CA 94104

HERNANDEZ, ERNEST, JR., behavioral science researcher; b. San Antonio, Nov. 18, 1943; s. Ernest and Cielo (Lecea) H.; m. Carol Ann Weiser, May 23, 1965; children—James Je, Robert Re, Summer Ann. A.A., El Camino Coll., 1966; B.A., Calif. State U., 1968, M.A., 1970; Ph.D., U. Calif.-Riverside, 1979. Concert promoter Sta. KMET-FM, Sta. K-LOVE, 1975, Sta. KBCA-FM, 1975-76, also nat. promotion mgr. specialty records and account exec.; dep. probation officer, Los Angeles County, 1974-77; mem. faculty Calif. State U., 1974—; ind. record promoter for mus. groups including STYX, Jose Feleciano, Shango, Richie Lecea, 1974-76; coordinator Chino Community Deliquency Prevention Project, 1972-74; behavioral scis. research analyst III, Los Angeles County, 1977—; pres. E.H.J. & Assocs., El Toro, Calif., 1979—. Bd. dirs. West End Family Counseling Service San Bernardino County, 1972-73; co-chmn. Los Angeles County Research Coordinating Com., 1981-82; chmn. Los Angeles County Research Devel. and Planning Task Force com., 1980-81. Mem. Assn. Police Planning and Research Officers (1st v.p. 1983), Am. Soc. Criminology, Acad. Criminal Justice Sci., Assn. Criminal Justice Researchers Calif., Western Soc. Criminologists, Evaluation Network, Am. Acad. Polit. and Social Sci., Assn. Computing Machinery, Issues Inc., Internat. Assn. Social Sci. and Info. Service Tech. Author: Police Handbook for Applying the Systems Approach and Computer Technology, 1982; Police Chief's Guide to Using Microcomputers, 1983; contbr. articles to profl. jours. Home: 22386 Sunlight Creek St El Toro CA 92630 Office: 211 W Temple St Los Angeles CA 90012

HERNANDEZ, JOANNE FARB, museum administrator; b. Chgo., Nov. 20, 1952; d. Leonard and Leanora (Kohn) Farb; m. Sam Hernandez, Sept. 5, 1976. B.A., U. Wis., 1974; M.A., UCLA, 1975. Accessioner, cataloguer Mus. Cultural History, UCLA, 1974-75; Rockefeller fellow Dallas Mus. Fine Arts, 1976-77; asst. dir. Triton Mus. of Art, Santa Clara, Calif., 1977, dir., 1978—; adj. prof. weaving E. Tex. State U., 1977, mus. studies John F. Kennedy U., 1978; grad. adv. arts adminstrn. San Jose U., 1979-81; dir. Bobbie Wynn and Co. Recipient Ralph C. Altman award Mus. of Cultural History, UCLA, 1975; Trewartha award U. Wis., 1974. Mem. Am. Assn. of Mus., Am. Folklore Soc., Non-Profit Gallery Assn. (dir.), Phi Beta Kappa. Contbr. articles on fine arts to profl. jours.; co-author books and catalogs in field. Office: 1505 Warburton Ave Santa Clara CA 95050

HERNDON, LEW ALLEN, business executive; b. Bremerton, Wash., July 19, 1937; s. Glen Allen and Bernice (Bassett) H.; m. Marie Evelyn Alleger, Apr. 4, 1954; m. 2d, Susan Lynne Dobbins, Jan. 19, 1969; children—Jeryl Taylor, Cheryl M., Kelli L. Gile, Mark T., Karen S. Parker, Craig P. Student San Diego City Coll., 1957-58. Mktg. mgr. Trainex Corp., Garden Grove, Calif., 1967-71; chief exec. The Ungame Corp., Placentia, Calif., 1971—; chmn. bd., dir. Au-Vid, Inc., 1971—; mng. ptnr. Doug Wilson Presents, 1982—. Republican. Methodist. Office: 761 Monroe Way Placentia CA 92670

HERNSTADT, WILLIAM H., broadcasting co. exec., state senator; b. N.Y.C., Nov. 21, 1935; s. William L. and Alma (Cunningham) H.; B.S. in Physics, Rensselaer Poly. Inst., 1957; m. Judith Filenbaum, Oct. 12, 1973; children by previous marriages—Ruth Ellen, Edward William, Liane Winifred, Stephanie Elizabeth. With Globus, Inc., 1960, M.A. Lomasney & Co., 1961; staff security analyst Alleghany Corp., N.Y.C., 1962-67, asst. treas., 1965-67; registered rep. Bruns, Nordeman, Rea & Co., N.Y.C., 1967-78; owner Alvernie Apts., Las Vegas, Nev., 1970-71; pres., gen. mgr., operator Sta. KVVU-TV, Nev. Ind. Broadcasting Corp., Henderson and Las Vegas, 1971-79; treas. Hernstadt Broadcasting Corp., Miami, Fla., operating Sta. WKAT, 1979-80, pres., 1981—; mem. Nev. Senate, 1977—. Bd. dirs. Clark County (Nev.) chpt. Am. Cancer Soc., 1970-72; bd. dirs. Jewish Fedn. Las Vegas, 1974—, 2d v.p., 1979-80, 1st v.p., 1980, pres., 1981-82; bd. dirs. Nev. Kidney Found., 1979—, now 2d v.p. Clubs: Las Vegas Country; Sleepy Hollow Country (Tarrytown, N.Y.); Harmonie of N.Y.C. Home and Office: 3111 Bel Air Dr Las Vegas NV 89109

HERON, WALDO GORDON, agribusiness company consultant; b. East St. Louis, Ill., Sept. 7, 1919; s. Eugene Foster and Edith (Drake) H.; B.S., U. Ill., 1942; m. Barbara Foley, Dec. 3, 1947; children—Patricia Lynn Heron Noll, Martha Ann, Hilary Sue. Latin Am. regional sales rep. Yale & Towne Mfg. Co., Phila., 1946-54; export sales mgr. Am. Can Co., N.Y.C., 1954-64; pres. Food Processing Cons., Fillmore, Calif., 1964—. Served to lt. USNR, 1942-46. Mem. Am. Soc. Agrl. Cons., Assn. Mgmt. Cons., Inst. Food Technologists, Assn. Operative Millers, Nat. Food Processors Assn., Calif. Avocado Soc., Sunkist Growers, Calavo Growers, Calif., Delta Upsilon. Republican. Episcopalian. Club: Rotary. Home: 1950 S Sespe St Fillmore CA 93015 Office: Food Processing Consultants PO Box 85 429 Central Ave Fillmore CA 93015

HERREMA, DONALD JAMES, banker; b. Redlands, Calif., June 8, 1952; s. Russell James and Frances Wilhelmina (vander Kaay) H.; B.A., Whittier Coll., 1974; M.A., U. So. Calif., 1976; m. Maryl Lyn Browne, Sept. 25, 1976; children: Douglas James, Markus Donald. Mgmt. trainee Carnation Co., Los Angeles, 1976-77, group sales mgr., San Francisco, 1977; area sales mgr. Amstar Corp., San Francisco, 1977-78; gen. sales mgr. Instl. Brokerage Co., Inc., San Francisco, 1978, v.p. sales, 1978-81; v.p., officer comml. banking group Wells Fargo Bank, N.A., San Francisco, 1981—; cons. Inst. Econ. Research, 1975; econs. instr. Golden West Coll., Huntington Beach, Calif., 1976-77; mem. founding staff Coastline Community Coll., 1977. Mem. No. Calif. Foodservice Mktg. Assn., Nat. Food Brokers Assn., U. So. Calif. Alumni Assn., Omicron Delta Epsilon. Democrat. Presbyterian. Cons. economist Common Sense Press, 1975-77. Home: 1435 Plaza de Oro Benicia CA 94510 Office: 415 20th St Oakland CA 94612

HERREMAN, GLENN ORRIN, metrology engineer, tool engineer; b. San Francisco, Feb. 16, 1918; s. Orrin Ezra and Eva Myrtle (Harrison) H.; m. Clara V. Nystrom, Dec. 16, 1939; children—Carolyn, Linda, William. Student De Anza Coll., Cupertino, Calif., Foothill Coll., Los Altos, Calif., San Jose State U., U. Calif.-San Francisco. Tool engr. Joshua Hendy Iron Works, Sunnyvale, Calif., 1942; tool engr. Westinghouse Electric Corp., Sunnyvale, 1947-48; tool designer Schlage Lock Co., South Francisco, Calif., 1948-51; tool designer, tool engr., supr., quality engr. Gage Lab., 1951-68; mgr. corp. metrology Hewlett-Packard Co., Palo Alto, Calif., 1968—. Mem. Am. Soc. Quality Control, Soc. Mfg. Engrs., Nat. Conf. Standards Labs. Clubs: Camera (Palo Alto), Masons. Co-inventor, probe assembly, 1959; contbr. articles to profl. jours. Office: 1501 Page Mill Rd Palo Alto CA 94304

HERRERA, CHRISTIAN YANEZ, pediatrician, flight surgeon; b. Santiago, Chile, Mar. 9, 1938; came to U.S., 1968, naturalized, 1973; s. Arturo Segundo and Ernestina Carmen (Yanez) H.; M.D. with scholastic honors, Univ. Chile, 1962; m. Shirley Mae Lagasse, Apr. 29, 1975; children—Karen Anne, Gary John, Ivan Edward, Iwonne Ester. Intern, U. Chile Med. Sch., Santiago, 1960-62; resident in pediatrics Children's Hosp., Boston, 1968-69; fellow in pediatrics Harvard Univ. Med. Sch., Boston, 1962-64, 69-70, instr. in pediatrics, 1971-73; asst. clin. prof. pediatrics Wright State U., Fairborn, Ohio, 1975-77, assoc. clin. prof., 1977-79; chief pediatric services USAF Hosp., Hill AFB, Utah, 1979-82; chief clin. services Andersen AFB, Guam, 1982-83; practice medicine specializing in pediatrics, Boston and Stoneham, Mass., 1971-74, Dayton, 1975-79, Provo, Utah, 1979-82; practice medicine specializing in pediatrics, flight medicine and emergency medicine, Guam, 1982-83; chief med. services USAF Hosp., Hill AFB, Utah, 1983—; regional mil. cons. pediatrics, 1974-79. Served to col., USAF, 1974-82. Recipient Pioneer award Ohio Occupational Therapy Assn., 1978; Physician's Recognition award in Continuing Med. Edn. AMA, 1973—. Diplomate Am. Bd. Pediatrics. Fellow Am. Acad. Pediatrics, A.C.P.; mem. Aerospace Med. Assn., Soc. Air Force Physicians, Soc. USAF Flight Surgeons. Republican. Contbr. articles to med. jours. Home: 3824 N Little Rock Dr West Provo UT 84604 Office: USAF Hosp Hill AFB UT 84056

HERRERA, ROBERT BENNETT, ret. educator; b. Los Angeles, July 24, 1913; s. Royal Robert and Rachel (Mix) H.; A.A., Los Angeles City Coll., 1934; A.B., U. Calif., Los Angeles, 1937, M.A., 1939; m. Agnes Mary MacDougall, May 18, 1941; children—Leonard B., Mary Margaret, William R. Tchr. high sch., Long Beach, Calif., 1939-41; statistician U.S. Forest Survey, Berkeley, Calif., 1941-45; faculty Los Angeles City Coll., 1946-79, prof. math., 1966-79, chmn. math. dept., 1975-79, ret., 1979; lectr. math. U. Calif., Los Angeles, 1952-75; cons. Ednl. Testing Service, Princeton, 1965-68, Addison Wesley Pub. Co., 1966-68, Goodyear Pub. Co., 1970-76. Mem. Math. Assn. Am. (past sec. So. Calif. sect., past gov.), Am. Math. Soc., AAAS, Internat. Oceanic Soc., Phi Beta Kappa, Pi Mu Epsilon. Democrat. Author: (with C. Bell, C. Hammond) Fundamentals of Arithmetic for Teachers, 1962. Home: 6011 Fair Ave North Hollywood CA 91606 Office: 855 N Vermont Ave Los Angeles CA 90029

HERRICK, JOHN JEROME, naval officer; b. Warren, Minn., June 23, 1920; s. James Orval and Lillian Madelaine (Conely) H.; m. Geraldine May Kane, May 1, 1948; children—John Jerome, Patrick, Dennis, Maureen. Student, Superior State Coll., 1938-40; B.S., U.S. Naval Acad., 1943. Commd. midshipman U.S. Navy, 1940, advanced through grades to capt., 1964, chief staff officer 9th Naval Dist., 1970-73, ret., 1973; naval sci. instr. Santa Fe (N.Mex.) High Sch. NJROTC, 1973—. Decorated Navy Commendation medal, Combat Action ribbon. Mem. U.S. Naval Inst., U.S. Naval Acad. Alumni Assn., Ret. Officers Assn. Democrat. Roman Catholic. Clubs: Rotary, Elks. Address: 2100 Yucca Rd Santa Fe NM 87501

HERRICK, TRACY GRANT, fin. cons.; b. Cleve., Dec. 30, 1933; s. Stanford Avery and Elizabeth Grant (Smith) H.; B.A., Columbia U., 1956, M.A., 1958; postgrad. Yale U., 1956-57; M.A., Oxford U. (Eng.), 1960; m. Maie Kaarsoo, Oct. 12, 1963; children—Sylvi Anne, Alan Kalev. Economist, Fed. Res. Bank, Cleve., 1960-70; sr. economist Stanford Research Inst., Menlo Park, Calif., 1970-73; v.p., sr. analyst Shuman, Agnew & Co., Inc., San Francisco, 1973-75; v.p. Bank of Am., San Francisco, 1975-81; lectr. Stonier Grad. Sch. Banking, Am. Bankers Assn., 1967-76; commencement speaker Memphis Banking Sch., 1974; dir. C.D. Anderson & Co., Inc., Jefferies & Co., Inc., T.E.A. Energy Group, Inc., B & H Communications; editor Money Analyst. Bd. dirs. Planned Parenthood Assn., Cleve., 1967-70. Mem. Columbia Coll. Alumni Assn. (dir. 1973—), Nat. Assn. Bus. Economists, San Francisco Bus. Economists Assn., San Francisco Soc. Security Analysts. Republican. Congregationalist. Author: Bank Analysts Handbook, 1978; Timing, 1981; contbr. articles to profl. jours. Home: 1150 University Ave Palo Alto CA 94301

HERRIGEL, HOWARD RALPH, chemical engineer, process engineering company executive; b. Seattle, Sept. 27, 1924; s. Walter Arthur and Violet Cleo (Keirnan) H.; B.S. in Chem. Engring., U. Wash., 1952; postgrad. U. Wash. Grad. Sch., 1953-58, U. Pitts. Grad. Sch. Bus., 1979; m. Judith Esther Robbins, Oct. 23, 1964; children—David Robbins, Nancy Ruth. Jr. engr. Boeing Airplane Co., Seattle, 1943-45; chemist Seattle Gas Co., 1948-49; asst. mgr. Pittsburgh Testing Lab., Seattle, 1950-52; research engr. Boeing Co., Seattle, 1958-71; research engr. Resources Conservation Co., Seattle, 1971-73, chief chemist, 1973-74, process engring. mgr., 1974-80, v.p., chief scientist and dir. tech. devel., 1980—; instr. chem. engring. Seattle U., Seattle, 1956. Recipient Outstanding Contbn. award AIAA. Mem. Am. Chem. Soc., Am. Inst. Chem. Engrs., Sigma Xi, Phi Lambda Upsilon. Club: Seattle Yacht. Patentee in field. Home: 426 36th Ave Seattle WA 98122 Office: 3101 NE Northup Way Bellevue WA 98004

HERRIN, LEXIE ELBERT, engineering firm executive; b. Donna, Tex., May 17, 1925; s. Lexie E. and Mary Frances (Scates) H.; B.S.M.E., U. Mich., 1951, postgrad. 1951; M.B.A., U. So. Calif., 1964; m. Charlotte Frances Campbell, Mar. 9, 1946; children—Christopher Patrick, Timothy Michael, Bradley Terrence. Commd. 1st lt. U.S. Air Force, 1951, advanced through grades to lt. col., 1967, ret., 1969; pres. KOHM Mining and Devel., 1966-69; exec. v.p. Oil Producers & Refiners, Glendale, Calif., 1969-70; gen. mgr. Broadmore Homes of Tex., Waco, 1970-72; pres. Exec. Mobile Home Service, Lighthouse Point, Fla., 1972-74; pres. L.E. Herrin Engr. Cons., Redlands, Calif., 1974-76; v.p., gen. mgr., dir. von Haenel-Herrin & Asso., Glendale, Calif., 1977—; dir. Seagull Industries, 1966-75; chmn. sub-com. on traffic accident reporting Nat. Hwy. Safety Adv. Com.; lectr. U. Calif.-Northridge; arbitrator Am. Arbitration Assn., 1978—; del. com. on transp. Calif. Commn. on the Califs. Active, Boy Scouts Am., 1951-64; co-chmn. Reagan for Pres., San Bernardino County, 1976, asst. to chmn., 1980; del. Calif. Republican Party Conv., 1981. Decorated Air Force Commendation medal with oak leaf clusters. Mem. Am. Inst. Indsl. Engrs., Soc. Automotive Engrs., Am. Assn. Automotive Medicine, Triangle, Sphinx, Michigama, Phi Sigma Kappa. Republican. Clubs: Officers, March AFB Flying, Wheeler Flying, Masons. Editor-in-chief U. Mich. Technic, 1949-51. Office: 102 N Brand Blvd Suite 520 Glendale CA 91203

HERRING, THEODORE MELVIN, JR., obstetrician, gynecologist; b. Battle Creek, Mich., Apr. 15, 1941; s. Theodore Melvin and Myra Elizabeth Herring; B.A., Andrews U., 1963; M.D., Loma Linda U., 1968; m. Rosa Patricia Brown, Nov. 29, 1970; children—Theodore Melvyn III, Jason Lamar, Lisa Monique. Intern, Riverside (Calif.) Gen. Hosp., 1968-69; resident in Ob-Gyn, White Meml. Hosp., Los Angeles, 1969-72; owner, founder Mile-High Women's Clinic, Denver, 1974—, chief of staff, 1975—; clin. instr. dept. Ob-Gyn, U. Colo. Sch. Medicine; pres. Venture Investment Capital, Inc. Served with M.C., U.S. Army, 1972-74. Diplomate Am. Bd. Ob-Gyn. Fellow ACS, Internat. Coll. Surgeons, Am. Coll. Ob-Gyn (speaker ann. meeting, 1973); mem. Am. Assn. Gynecologic Laparoscopists, Am. Fertility Soc., Colo. Gynecol. and Obstetrical Soc., Assn. Profs. of Ob-Gyn. Club: MECTO. Office: 800 Clermont St Suite 130 Denver CO 80220

HERRINGER, FRANK CASPER, business executive; b. Bklyn., Nov. 12, 1942; s. Casper Frank and Alice Virginia (McMullen) H.; m. Nancy Lynn Blair, Dec. 21, 1968; 1 son, William Laurence. A.B., Dartmouth Coll., 1964, M.B.A., Amos Tuck Sch., 1965. Prin. Cresap, McCormick & Paget, Inc., N.Y.C., 1965-71; staff asst. to pres. The White House, Washington, 1971-73; adminstr. U.S. Urban Transp. Adminstrn., Washington, 1973-75; gen. mgr. and chief exec. officer San Francisco Bay Area Rapid Transit Dist., 1975-79; group v.p. Transamerica Corp., San Francisco, 1979—, dir. all major Transamerica subs. Trustee Pacific Med. Ctr., San Francisco Zool. Trust. Republican. Clubs: Bankers, Olympic, Commonwealth, Contra Costa Country. Office: 600 Montgomery San Francisco CA 94111

HERRINGTON, LARRY DAVID, school counselor; b. San Angelo, Tex., June 6, 1943; s. Dwayne Berney and Mary Fawn (Little) Bettis; m. Dixie LaDonna Butler, Aug. 6, 1960; 1 son, Larry David. A.A., San Angelo Coll., 1963; B.S. in Edn., Tex. Tech. U., 1965; M.S. in School Counseling, U. LaVerne, 1978. Cert. tchr., Tex., Hawaii, Alaska. Tchr. phys. edn. McGill Elem. Sch., San Angelo, 1965-68; tchr. A.S. Johnston Elem. Sch., Irving, Tex., 1968-69, Pahala (Hawaii) Elem. Sch., 1969-72; alternative edn. tchr., outreach counselor Kau High Sch., Pahala, Hawaii, 1972-80; counselor Nome (Alaska) Elem. Sch., 1980—; instr. career guidance Northwest Community Coll., Nome. Bd. dirs. Hawaii County Econ. Opportunity Council, 1975-78; pres. Parent Tchr. Student Assn., Kau High Sch., 1978-80. Mem. Alaska Sch. Counselors Assn. (exec. bd.), NEA, Am. Sch. Counselor Assn. Home: PO Box 776 Nome AK 99762 Office: PO Box 131 Suite 202 Nome AK 99762

HERRMANN, STANLEY WILLIAM, former educator, real estate exec.; b. Detroit, Kans., May 11, 1904; s. William Edward and Wilhelmina (Holtz) H.; B.S., Kans. Wesleyan U., 1928; postgrad. Kans. State Tchrs. Coll., 1939-40; M.S., U. Mo., Columbia, 1942; m. Dorothy E. Heinrichs, Aug. 18, 1929; children—Stanley Dwane, Elaine Herrmann Attenborough, Linda Herrman Fuller. Tchr., athletic coach, athletic dir., high sch. prin., Assaria, Lincoln, Salina and Kans., 1942-48; real estate exec., Santa Barbara, Calif., 1953—. Internat. competitor World Masters Championship Track and Field, gold medal winner in discus, Toronto, Ont., Can., 1975, world age records holder all throwing events, winner 17 nat. track championships; Named most valuable over-70 athlete Corona Del Mar Track Club, 1980, winner most outstanding field event competitor award, 1980. Mem. Nat. Ret. Tchrs. Assn. Republican. Methodist. Address: 260 W Alamar #16 Santa Barbara CA 93105

HERRON, ELLEN PATRICIA, judge; b. Auburn, N.Y., July 30, 1927; d. David Martin and Grace Josephine (Berner) Herron; A.B. Trinity Coll., 1949; M.A., Cath. U. Am., 1954; J.D., U. Calif. at Berkeley, 1964. Asst. dean Cath. U. Am., 1952-54; instr. East High Sch., Auburn, 1955-57; asst. dean Wells Coll., Aurora, N.Y., 1957-58; instr. psychology and history Contra Costa Coll., 1958-60; dir. row Stanford, 1960-61; assoc. Knox & Kretzmer, Richmond, Calif., 1964-65; admitted to Calif. bar, 1965; ptnr. Knox & Herron, 1965-74, Knox, Herron and Masterson, 1974-77 (both Richmond, Calif.); judge Superior Ct. State of Calif., 1977— mem. assembly Calif. Judiciary Com. for Ct. Improvement, 1979-80; gen. ptnr. Real Estate Syndicates, Calif., 1967-77. Active numerous civic orgns.; bd. dirs. Rhonoh Sch., Richmond, YWCA, Econ. Devel. Council Richmond; alumnae bd. dirs. Boalt Hall, U. Calif.-Berkeley, 1980—. Mem. ABA, Contra Costa Bar Assn. (exec. com. 1969-74), State Bar Calif., Calif. Trial Lawyers, Nat. Assn. Women Lawyers, Nat. Assn. Women Judges, Calif. Women Lawyers, Applicants Attys. Assn., Calif. Judges Assn. (ethics com. 1977-79, criminal law procedure com. 1979-80), Queen's Bench, Juvenile Ct. Judges Assn. Democrat. Home: 51 Western Dr Point Richmond CA 94801

HERSCHLER, EDGAR J., gov. of Wyo.; b. Kemmerer, Wyo., Oct. 27, 1918; s. Edgar F. and Charlotte (Jenkins) H.; student U. Colo., 1936-41; LL.B., U. Wyo., 1949; m. Kathleen Sue Colter, 1944; children—Kathleen Sue (Mrs. Jerry Hunt), James C. Bar: Wyo. 1949. County and pros. atty. Lincoln County (Wyo.), 1951-59; mem. Wyo. Ho. of Reps., 1961-71; mem. Parole Bd., State of Wyo., 1971-73; now gov. Wyo. Served with USMCR. Decorated Silver Star, Purple Heart. Mem. Wyo. State Bar (pres. 1968-69). Office: Office of Governor State Capitol Bldg Cheyenne WY 82001*

HERSHBERGER, LINDA ANN, communications executive, educator, filmmaker; b. Inglewood, Calif., July 28, 1959; d. Richard Ben and Jane Olive (Taylor) Hershberger. B.A. in Communication Studies magna cum laude, UCLA, 1981, postgrad. (fellow), 1981-83. Newswriter, KABC-TV, Los Angeles, 1978-79; account exec. Communication Develop. Assocs., Inc., Los Angeles, 1979, media cons. and pub. relations dir., 1979—; TV writer Alan Thicke Prodns., Los Angeles, 1980-81; grad. teaching assoc. dept. communication studies UCLA, 1980—; exec. tng. pub. speaking and media relations, career counseling high school and college levels. Mem. Internat. Assn. Bus. Communicators, Soc. Cinema Studies, Pi Beta Phi (del. Nat. Leadership Conv. 1979). Contbr. articles to profl. jours. Home: 140 S Sepulveda Blvd Suite 12 Los Angeles CA 90049 Office: Communication Development Associates Inc 10100 Santa Monica Blvd Suite 470 Los Angeles CA 90067

HERSHEY, GERALD LEE, psychologist; b. Detroit, Mar. 7, 1931; s. Von Waitz and Clementine Hershey; student UCLA, 1949-54; B.A. with honors, Mich. State U., 1957, M.A., 1958, Ph.D., 1961; m. Shirley Gauld, Oct. 2, 1954; children—Bruce, Dale, James. Asst. instr., research asso. Mich. State U., 1958-61; mem. faculty dept. psychology Fullerton (Calif.) Coll., 1961—, prof., 1965—, chmn. dept., 1980—; vis. prof. Chapman Coll., 1962-69. Served to 1st lt. U.S. Army, 1954-56. Mem. Am. Psychol. Assn., Assn. Humanistic Psychology, NEA. Club: Lions. Co-author: Human Development, 2d edit., 1978; Living Psychology, 3d edit., 1981. Office: Fullerton Coll 321 E Chapman Ave Fullerton CA 92634

HERSHEY, R(UTH) CHRISTINE, graphic designer; b. Exeter, Calif., July 27, 1952; d. Richard Ivan and Dorothy Louise (James) H. Student Art Center Coll. of Design, Los Angeles, 1972-74. Graphic artist Los Angeles Times, 1972-74; graphic designer Golden State Graphics, 1974-75; graphic designer, account exec. Ford Graphics, 1975-77; owner, creative dir. Hershey Dalé & Assocs., Los Angeles, 1977—. Active ACLU, People for the Am. Way, Common Cause. Recipient awards Communications Arts Soc., 1977, Western Art Dirs., 1981, DESI, 1982. Mem. Internat. Assn. Bus. Communicators (awards 1977, 82, 83), Printing Industries Am. (awards 1980, 81), Am. Inst. Graphic Arts, Art Dirs. Los Angeles (dir.). Democrat. Unitarian. Office: 3429 Glendale Blvd Los Angeles CA 90039

HERSHFIELD, BEVERLY, psychotherapist; b. Warsaw, Poland; d. Sam and Lilly (Saltzberg) Feldman; children—Lawrence, Pamela, Diane. B.A., Trenton State Coll., 1970, M.A., 1978. Psychotherapist, hypnotherapist, assoc. dir. Ctr. for Change, San Diego, 1981—; pvt. practice psychotherapy, San Diego, 1981—; adj. faculty Nat. U., 1980—; dir. guidance Universal High Sch., Piscataway, N.J., 1977-79; dep. dir. Universal High Sch., 1976-77; spl. edn. tchr. Old Bridge (N.J.) Pub. Schs., 1970-76; cons. in field. Mem. Am. Psychol. Assn., Am. Personnel and Guidance Assn., Calif. Assn. Marriage and Family Therapists. Office: 9820 Willow Creek Suite D San Diego CA 92103

HERTWECK, E. ROMAYNE, educator; b. Springfield, Mo., July 24, 1928; s. Garnett Perry and Nova Gladys (Chowning) H.; m. Alma Louise Street, Dec. 16, 1955; 1 son, William Scott. B.A., Augustana Coll., 1962; M.A., Pepperdine U., 1963; Ed.D., Ariz. State U., 1966; Ph.D., U.S. Internat. U., 1978. Cert. sch. psychologist, Calif. Night editor Rock Island (Ill.) Argus Newspaper, 1961; grad. asst. psychology dept. Pepperdine Coll., Los Angeles, 1962; counselor VA, Ariz. State U., Tempe, 1963; assoc. dir. Conciliation Ct., Phoenix, 1964; instr. Phoenix Coll., Phoenix, 1965; prof. Mira Costa Coll., Oceanside, Calif., 1966—, mem. senate council, 1968-70, chmn. psychology-counseling dept., 1973-75, chmn. dept. behavioral sci., 1976-82; part-time lectr. dept. bus. adminstrn. San Diego State U., 1980—; prof. psychology Chapman Coll. World Campus Afloat, 1970. Bd. dirs. Lifeline, 1969, Christian Counseling Center, Oceanside. Mem. Am., Western, North San Diego County (v.p. 1974-75) psychol. assns., Am. Personnel and Guidance Assn., Nat. Educators Fellowship (v.p. El Camino chpt. 1976-77), Am. Coll. Personnel Assn., Phi Delta Kappa, Kappa Delta Pi, Psi Chi. Club: Kiwanis (charter mem. Carlsbad club, dir. 1975-77). Home: 2024 Oceanview Rd Oceanside CA 92056 Office: Mira Costa Coll 1 Barnard Dr Oceanside CA 92056

HERTZOG, EUGENE EDWARD, visual information specialist; b. Oak Park, Ill., Jan. 30, 1932; s. Charles Demetrius and Julia (McKelvey) H.; grad. high sch.; m. Magdalene D. Tafoya, Nov. 16, 1957; 1 son, Wayne Alan. Project photographer Columbia Basin project U.S. Bur. Reclamation, Ephrata, Wash., 1958-63, regional photographer Lower Colo. region, 1963-80; visual info. officer Bur. Reclamation, 1980—. Served with Signal Corps, AUS, 1949-58. Mem. Profl. Photographers Am. Home: 2520 Golfers St Las Vegas NV 89122 Office: Lower Colo Region Boulder City NV 89005

HERZBERG, DOROTHY CREWS, investment co. administrator; b. N.Y.C., July 8, 1935; d. Floyd Houston and Julia (Lesser) Crews; A.B., Brown U., 1957; M.A., Stanford U., 1964; J.D., San Francisco Law Sch., 1976; m. Hershel Zelig Herzberg, May 22, 1962; children—Samuel Floyd, Laura Jill, Daniel Crews. Legal sec. various law firms, San Francisco, 1976-78; tchr. Mission Adult Sch., San Francisco, 1965-66; tchr. secondary and univ. levels Peace Corps, Nigeria, 1961-63; investigator Office of Dist. Atty., San Francisco, 1978-80; sr. adminstr. Dean Witter Reynolds Co., San Francisco, 1980—; alt. for supr. San Francisco Mayor's Commn. on Criminal Justice, 1978. Bd. dirs. LWV, San Francisco, 1967-69; bd. dirs. Miraloma (Calif.) Improvement Club, 1977—, pres., 1980-81; pres. Council of Co-op Nursery Schs., San Francisco, 1969-71; active with LWV Speakers Bur., 1967-69, 1977-79. Democrat. Unitarian. Lodge: West Portal Toastmistress. Editor Co-op Nursery Sch. Council newsletter, 1969-71, Miraloma Life newsletter, 1976-82, Democratic Women's Forum newsletter, 1980-81. Home: 238 Bella Vista Way San Francisco CA 94127 Office: Dean Witter Reynolds 101 California St San Francisco CA 94111

HERZOG, SUSAN ROCK, librarian; b. Phila., Mar. 31, 1946; d. Milton L. Rock and Shirley Ruth (Cylinder) R.; m. Richard Joseph Herzog, Aug. 5, 1967 (div.); 1 dau., Liza Devon. B.A., U. Mich., 1967, M.A. in Chinese Studies, 1969; M.L.S., U. Calif.-Berkeley, 1976. Reference librarian Fresno County Free Library, 1976—; librarian Thomas, Snell et al Law Firm, Fresno, 1977—, Baker, Manock, Jensen law firm, Fresno, 1978—, U.S. Dept. Agr., 1978—. Home: 1129 E Yale Fresno CA 93704 Office: 2420 Mariposa Fresno CA 93721

HESKETH, KATHLEEN ANN, horticulturist; b. Angola, Ind.; d. James G. and Mary (Williams) H.; B.S., U. Calif.-Davis, 1972, M.S., 1983. Agrl. biologist Office Alameda County Agrl. Commr., Haywood, Calif., 1973-78; urban hort. farm adviser U. Calif. Coop. Extension, Alameda County, Hayward, 1978—. Mem. Am. Soc. Hort. Sci., Weed Sci. Soc. Am. Home: 1010 Sahara Ct Hayward CA 94541 Office: U Calif Coop Extension 224 W Winton Ave Hayward CA 94544

HESKETT, SANDRA LOUISE, nurse, hospital administrator; b. Harrisburg, Pa., Feb. 27, 1947; d. William John and Ruth Mae (McCord) Saltzer; m. William Harry Packer, June 13, 1973; m. 2d William Mark Heskett, Nov. 29, 1982. R.N., Harrisburg Hosp., 1969, student Harrisburg Area Community Coll., 1973-75, No. Va. Community Coll., 1975-77, Phoenix Community Coll., 1977-78, Chapman Coll., 1980-83. Charge nurse surg. ward Harrisburg Hosp., 1969-71, staff nurse operating room, 1971-75; orthopedic team leader operating room Fairfax Hosp., Annandale, Va., 1975-77; head nurse operating room Phoenix Meml. Hosp., 1977-79; head nurse Mesa Lutheran Hosp., Mesa, Ariz., 1979-80, operating room supr., 1980; asst. dir. nurses, dir. operating room-recovery room Pomona (Calif.) Valley Community Hosp., 1980—. Mem. Assn. Operating Room Nurses (del. nat conv. 1979, book rev. panel), Bus. and Profl. Women's Club. Home: 848 Desert Canyon Rd Brea CA 92621 Office: 1798 N Garey Ave Pomona CA 91767

HESS, DAVID FREDRIC, charitable found. exec.; b. Long Beach, Calif., Oct. 11, 1946; s. William Nelson and Maryellen H.; B.S. in Fin., Calif. State U., Long Beach, 1969; m. Donna Darleen Kaspereit, Jan. 31, 1968; children—Jennifer Darleen, Joshua David. Fiduciary tax specialist Security Pacific Nat. Bank, Los Angeles, 1969-75; analyst Computax, El Segundo, Calif., 1975-76; asst. v.p. Security Pacific Nat. Bank, 1976-80; asso. dir. Calif. Community Found., Los Angeles, 1977—, sec./treas., chief fin. officer CCF, Inc., 1980—; lectr. Calif. State U., Northridge, Pepperdine U., Malibu; cons. Japan Assn. Charitable Trusts; condr. workshops Calif. Bankers Assn. Bd. dirs. Los Angeles Council on Careers for Older Americans; mem. Nat. Council on Careers for Older Americans; bd. dirs. SCAPA Praetors-U. So. Calif. Sch. Public Adminstrn. Mem. Council Founds., So. Calif. Assn. Philanthropy (dir.). Republican. Office: 1151 W 6th St Los Angeles CA 90017

HESS, HARRIE FOX, psychologist, educator; b. Hammond, Ind., Mar. 1, 1929; s. Louis Charles and Adelaide Estelle (Fox) H.; m. Beverley Jones, Aug. 20, 1950; m. 2d, Michele Dalton, May 20, 1966; children—Bryant Clark, Krista Lynn, Danielle Adelaide. B.A., U. Nev., 1952; M.A., U. Colo., 1957, Ph.D., 1959. Cert. psychologist, Nev. Instr., U. Oreg. Med. Sch., 1959-60; clin. psychologist Nev. Dept. Mental Health, Las Vegas, 1960-64; chief psychologist Community Child Guidance Ctr., Portland, Oreg., 1964-65; assoc. prof. psychology U. Nev., Las Vegas, 1965-68, prof., 1968—; cons. to state govt., industry; mem., sec.-treas. Nev. Bd. Psychol. Examiners. Served to 2d lt. U.S. Army, 1952-55. Mem. Rocky Mountain Psychol. Assn. (pres. 1978-79), Am. Assn. State Psychology Bds. (pres. 1979-80). Office: 4505 S Maryland Pkwy Las Vegas NV 89154

HESS, PATRICK HENRY, chemist; b. Albia, Iowa, Aug. 6, 1931; s. John Henry and Mary Ellen (Judge) H.; B.S. in Chemistry, U. Iowa, 1953; M.S. in Organic Chemistry, U. Nebr., 1958, Ph.D. in Organic Chemistry, 1960; m. Ann Marie Malone, June 6, 1959; children—Michelle, Maria, Margaret, Catherine, John. Chemist, Iowa State Hygienic Labs., 1953-54; teaching asst. U. Nebr., 1956-57, research asst., 1957-58, research fellow, 1958-60; research chemist Chevron Research Co., Richmond, Calif., 1960-64; research chemist Chevron Oil Field Research Co., La Habra, Calif., 1964-65, sr. research chemist, 1965-69, sr. research asso., 1969—; research group supr., cons. Standard Oil Co. Calif. Active youth sports, PTA. Served with USAF, 1954-55. 3-M research fellow, 1958-59; Monsanto research fellow, 1959-60. Mem. Am. Chem. Soc., Soc. Petroleum Engrs., Sigma Xi, Alpha Chi Sigma, Alpha Tau Omega. Republican. Roman Catholic. Contbr. articles to profl. jours.; U.S., fgn. patentee in field, mainly crude oil recovery. Home: 23615 Sunset Crossing Diamond Bar CA 91765 Office: PO Box 446 La Habra CA 90631

HESS, RONALD EARL, soil chemist; b. Ogden, Utah, Jan. 15, 1945; s. Rex J. and Thora Ann (Roderick) H.; B.S., Brigham Young U., 1969; M.S., No. Ariz. U., 1973; Ph.D., U. Mo., Columbia, 1975; children—Rebekah Ann, Sara Elizabeth. Grad. asst. No. Ariz. U., Flagstaff, 1969-71, U. Mo., Columbia, 1971-75; postgrad. research soil scientist U. Calif., Riverside, 1975-78; pvt. practice as soil chemist, Riverside, 1978—. U.S. Dept. Agr.-Agrl. Research Service fellow, 1975-78. Mem. Am. Chem. Soc., Am. Soc. Agronomy, Soil Sci. Soc. Am., AAAS, Ancient Mystical Order Rosae Crucis, Sigma Xi. Home and Office: 811 Kentwood Dr Riverside CA 92507

HESSE, CHRISTIAN AUGUST, mining co. exec.; b. Chemnitz, Germany, June 20, 1925; s. William Albert and Anna Gunhilda (Baumann) H.; B.Applied Sci. with honors, U. Toronto (Ont., Can.), 1948; m. Brenda Nora Rigby, Nov. 4, 1964; children—Robin Christian, Bruce William. In various mining and constrn. positions, Can., 1944-61; jr. shift boss N.J. Zinc Co., Gilman, Colo., 1949; asst. layout engr. Internat. Nickel Co., Sudbury, Ont., 1949-52; shaft engr. Perini-Walsh Joint Venture, Niagara Falls, Ont., 1952-54; project engr. B. Perini & Sons (Can.) Ltd., Toronto, Ottawa, and New Brunswick, 1954-55; field engr. Aries Copper Mines Ltd., No. Ont., 1955-56; instr. in mining engring. U. Toronto, 1956-57; planning engr. Stanleigh Uranium Mining Corp. Ltd., Elliot Lake, Ont., 1957-58, chief engr., 1959-60; field engr. Johnson-Perini-Kiewit Joint Venture, Toronto, 1960-61; del. Commonwealth Mining Congress, Africa, 1961; with U.S. Borax & Chem. Corp., 1961—, gen. mgr. Allan Potash Mines Ltd., Allan, Sask., Can., 1974, chief engr. U.S. Borax & Chem. Corp., Los Angeles, 1974-77, v.p. engring., 1977-81, v.p. and project mgr. Quartz Hill project, 1981—.

Sault Daily Star scholar, 1944. Mem. AIME, Can. Inst. Mining and Metallurgy, Assn. Profl. Engrs. Ont. Episcopalian. Clubs: Los Angeles, Ambassador Tennis and Health. Office: 3075 Wilshire Blvd Los Angeles CA 90010

HESSELGRAVE, PAUL ARMOUR, JR., research chemist; b. Sparta, Wis., June 19, 1939; s. Paul Armour and Lillian Martha (Staerz) H.; B.S., San Jose State U., 1962; m. Patricia Ann Davison, July 9, 1966. With Lockheed Missiles and Space Co., Sunnyvale, Calif., 1962—, sr. mfg. research engr., 1973-79, research specialist, 1979—. Mem. Am. Chem. Soc., Am. Def. Preparedness Assn. (life), Soc. Mfg. Engrs., Am. Electroplaters Soc. Republican. Roman Catholic. Home: 2462 Gallup Dr Santa Clara CA 95051 Office: PO Box 504 Sunnyvale CA 94086

HESTAND, RONALD EDWARD, psychologist, marriage and family therapist; b. St. Joseph, Mo., Jan. 16, 1944; s. Edward Carlyle and Margaret Wilma (Pugh) H.; m. Carolyn Louise Simmon, Aug. 23, 1963; m. 2d, Andree Yvonne Cuthbertson, Dec. 27, 1982. B.S., Mo. Western State Coll., 1971; M.B.A., Nat. U., 1976; Ph.D., Brantridge Forrest Sch., Sussex, Eng., 1974, D. Psychology, U.S. Internat. U., 1983. Lic. psychologist, marriage, family, child counselor, Calif. Pvt. practice psychology, marriage and family therapy, San Diego, 1983—. Served with USN, 1963-66. Mem. Am. Psychol. Assn., Am. Personnel and Guidance Assn., Acad. Psychologists in Marital, Sex and Family Therapy, Calif. Psychol. Assn., San Diego Acad. Psychologists, Am. Assn. Marriage and Family Therapists, Am. Assn. Mental Health Counselors. Republican. Lutheran. Contbr. numerous articles to profl. jours. Address: 4546 1/2 40th St San Diego CA 92116

HESTER, EDITH GEORGE, educational administrator; b. Evanston, Wyo., Apr. 8, 1940; d. Harold Glen and Phyllis Marie (Smith) George; m. Herschel G. Hester, III, Dec. 26, 1969 (div.); 1 son, Dennis Lee Forsgren, Jr. B.S., Weber State Coll., Ogden, Utah, 1969; postgrad. U. Utah, 1979-82. Office and broadcast prodn. dept. Sta. KLO Radio, Ogden, 1958-61; printing prodn. supr. Boise Cascade Corp., 1962-65; news writer Weber State Coll., 1965-68, publs. coordinator, 1968-72, publs. dir., 1972-77, pub. relations dir., 1977-80, exec. dir. alumni relations and spl. services, 1980—; cons. publs., pub. relations, meeting planning and prodn. Dir. Ogden Ballet Symphony Assn., 1981-82; adv. com. Weber County Schs., 1981-83; budget adv. com. Ogden City, 1982-83. Mem. Am. Bus. Women's Assn. (Woman of Yr. Golden Spike chpt. 1982, pres. 1981-82), Internat. Assn. Bus. Communications (dir. Intermountain chpt. 1977-78, award of excellence total communications 1977-78). Office: 3750 Harrison Blvd Ogden UT 84408

HETHERINGTON, CHERYL KEIKO, lawyer; b. Honolulu, July 24, 1952; d. Sidney Ichiro and Shizuko (Murakami) Hashimoto; m. J. George Hetherington, Nov. 25, 1978. Student Whitman Coll., 1970-72; B.A. U. Wash.-Seattle, 1974; J.D., Hastings Coll. Law, San Francisco. Bar: Hawaii 1979, U.S. Dist. Ct. Hawaii 1979. Counselor Planned Parenthood of Seattle-King County, 1974-76; atty. Law Offices Sidney I Hashimoto, Honolulu, 1979-82; sole practice, Honolulu, 1982—. Area chmn. ann. drive Am. Cancer Soc. Mem. Hawaii State Bar Assn., Hawaii Women Lawyers, ABA (Young Lawyers div., Family Law div.), Nat. Assn. Women Lawyers, U. Wash. Alumni Advisers, Smithsonian Assocs., Nat. Geog. Soc., Hawaii Com. Alcoholism, Hastings Alumni Assn., U. Wash. Alumni Assn., Mortar Board, Alpha Chi Omega Found., Alpha Kappa Delta. Democrat. Club: Kailua Racquet. Contbg. author articles in field. Office: 820 Mililani St Suite 401 Honolulu HI 96813

HETLAND, JOHN ROBERT, educator, lawyer; b. Mpls., Mar. 12, 1930; s. James L. and Evelyn (Lundgren) H.; B.S.L., U. Minn., 1952, J.D., 1956; m. Mildred Woodruff, Dec. 1951 (div.); children—Lynda Lee, Robert John, Debra Ann; m. Anne Kneeland, Dec. 1972; children—Robin T. Kneeland, Elizabeth J. Kneeland. Admitted to Minn. bar, 1956, Calif. bar, 1962; practice law, Mpls., 1956-59; asso. prof. law U. Calif., Berkeley, 1959-60, prof. law, 1960—; practice law cons. to attys., Berkeley, 1959—; vis. prof. law Stanford U., 1971, 80, U. Singapore, 1972. Served to lt. comdr. USN, 1953-55. Mem. State Bar Calif., Am. Bar Assn., Minn. Bar Assn., Order of Coif, Phi Delta Phi. Republican. Author: Hetland, California Real Property Secured Transactions, 1970; Hetland, Commercial Real Estate Transactions, 1972; Hetland, Secured Real Estate Transactions, 1974; California Cases on Secured Transactions in Land, 1975; Hetland, Secured Real Estate Transactions, 1977. Contbr. articles to legal, real estate and fin. jours. Home: 20 Redcoach Ln Orinda CA 94563 Office: 2600 Warring St Berkeley CA 94704

HETRICK, ETHEL WIEST, psychologist, educator; b. Canon City, Colo., Nov. 11, 1943; d. Joseph Emory and Ethel May (Hyatt) Means; m. R. Hugh Hetrick, Feb. 14, 1970; children—John Emory, Samuel Logan. B.S., U. Tex., Austin, 1966; M.A., U. Houston, 1971; Ph.D., Tex. Woman's U., 1976. Cert. psychologist, Ariz.; lic. psychologist, La.; sch. psychologist, La., Ariz. Tchr. Friendswood (Tex.) Sch., 1966-67, Clear Creek Sch. Dist., League City, Tex., 1967-71; spl. edn. counselor Irving (Tex.) Schs., 1971-73; teaching asst. Tex. Woman's U., Denton, 1974-75; psychology intern Fairhill Sch., Dallas, 1975-76; psychologist spl. edn. ctr., adj. instr. Northwestern State U. La., Natchitoches, 1976-78, assoc. prof., head dept. spl. edn. 1978-81; sch. psychologist Tanque Verde Sch. Dist., Tucson, 1982—; pvt. practice child and adolescent psychology. Bd. dirs. Natchitoches (La.) Mental Health Assn., 1979-80, Assn. Children Learning Disabilities, 1978-79. Bur. Edn. Handicapped Personnel Preparation grantee, 1979-82. Mem. Am. Psychol. Assn., Southeastern Ariz. Psychol. Assn., Nat. Assn. Sch. Psychologists, Council Exceptional Children. Contbr. articles to profl. jours. Home: 11261 Hash Knife Circle Tucson AZ 85749 Office: 4202 N Melpommene Tucson AZ 85749

HETT, JOAN MARGARET, ecological consultant; b. Trail, B.C., Can., Sept. 8, 1936; s. Gordon Stanley and Violet Thora (Thors) Hett; B.Sc., U. Victoria (B.C., Can.), 1964; M.S., U. Wis., Madison, 1967, Ph.D., 1969. Ecologist, Eastern Deciduous Forest Biome, Oak Ridge Nat. Lab., 1969-72; coor. sites dir. Coniferous Forest Biome, Oreg. State U., Corvallis and U. Wash., Seattle, 1972-77; ecol. cons., Seattle, 1978—. Mem. Ecol. Soc. Am., Brit. Ecol. Soc., Am. Inst. Biol. Scis., AAAS, Am. Forestry Assn., Sierra Club, Sigma Xi. Contbr. articles to profl. jours.; research in plant population dynamics, land use planning, forest sucession.

HETU, ANNE BRADFORD, counselor; b. Los Angeles, Apr. 15, 1946; d. Bernard Raymond and Cecilia Marguerite (LaRocque) H.; B.A., U. Calif., Santa Barbara, 1967; M.A., Calif. State U., Long Beach, 1969; M.S., Calif. Lutheran Coll., 1977. Tchr., Conejo Valley Unified Sch. Dist., Thousand Oaks, Calif., 1969-78, counselor, 1979—. Mem. Am. Personnel and Guidance Assn., Calif. Personnel and Guidance Assn., Conejo Valley Pupil Personnel Assn., NEA, Calif. Tchrs. Assn., United Assn. Conejo Tchrs., Nat. Council Tchrs. English, Calif. Assn. Tchrs. English, Assn. Supervision and Curriculum Devel., AAUW, Kappa Delta Pi, Delta Kappa Gamma, Alpha Chi Omega. Clubs: North Ranch Country, Foxfield Riding. Office: 2100 E Ave de Las Flores Thousand Oaks CA 91362

HETZ, JOHN NICHOLAS, mfg. co. exec.; b. Newark, Feb. 2, 1943; s. John Nicholas and Marian Hetz; B.A., Rutgers U., 1965; postgrad. in bus. adminstrn. U. Santa Clara, 1971-72; m. Noelle Allen, May 5, 1979; children by previous marriage—Jeff Allen, Mark Allen, Nick. Indsl. relations specialist Western Electric Co., Kearny, N.J., 1966-67; indsl. relations adminstr. Electronic Assos., Inc., West Long Branch, N.J., also Palo Alto, Calif., 1967-70; personnel supr. GRT Corp., Sunnyvale, Calif., 1970-71; personnel cons. Reidburn-Moore Assos., Cupertino, Calif., 1971-74; v.p. human resources Versatec, Inc., Santa Clara, Calif., 1974—. Bd. dirs. Strawberry Square Homeowners Assn., San Jose, Calif., 1975-76; v.p., pres. Dollar Hill I Homeowners Assn., Tahoe City, Calif., 1976-77. Served with N.J. N.G. and U.S. Army Res., 1965-71. Mem. Am. Soc. Personnel Adminstrs., Santa Clara Valley Personnel Assn. (dir. 1978-79). Home: 10842 Wilkinson Ave Cupertino CA 95014 Office: 2710 Walsh Ave Santa Clara CA 95051

HETZEL, JACK HOWARD, II, accountant; b. Dayton, Ohio, Oct. 17, 1947; s. Jack Howard and Beulah Grace (Downing) H.; m. Jacquelyn Williams, Feb. 19, 1970; children—Jennifer, Rachel. B.S., Miami U., Oxford, Ohio, 1970; postgrad. U. Ill.-Chgo., 1971-72. C.P.A., Calif. Gen. acct. J.S. Hoffman Co., Chgo., 1970-71; with Arthur Andersen & Co., Chgo. and San Diego, 1972-80, sr. acct., 1974-78, mgr. in charge small bus. practice, 1978-80; co-owner Hetzel, Stokes & McMains, San Diego, 1980—; dir. Systech Computer Corp. Mem. Dist. IX adv. council SBA; mem. small bus. adv. council San Diego C. of C.; speaker on understanding and use of fin. statements, effective cash mgmt.; trustee Simpson Coll. Mem. Calif. Soc. C.P.A.s, Am. Inst. C.P.A.s. Mem. Christian Missionary Alliance. Office: 9636 Tierra Grande St Suite 103 San Diego CA 92126

HEUSER, KENNETH H., writer, real estate developer; b. Milw., Mar. 11, 1922; s. Hugo and Mabel (Green) H.; m. Margot M. Bretschneider, July 14, 1942; children—Karen, Marie, Lynn, Ann. B.A. U. Wis. Founder, mgr. H & H Constrn. Co., Milw., 1945-60; freelance writer, 1960-69; writer, Vail, then Rifle Colo., 1969—; real estate developer Vail, 1970-75; pres. Lynmar, Inc., Rifle, 1977; instr. creative writing, Colo. Mountain Coll. Served with U.S. Army, 1942-45. Office: Lynmar Inc 3402 226th Rd Rifle CO 81650

HEUSSER, HENRY EARL, JR., assn. exec.; b. Salt Lake City, Feb. 15, 1930; s. Henry Earl and Leona (Erickson) H.; B.S., U. Utah, 1951; M.A., San Jose State Coll., 1962; postgrad. U. Calif., Berkeley, 1963; Ed.D., U. Oreg., 1967; m. Dolly Irene Lloyd, Jan. 9, 1952; children—Karl Gregory, Michael Dexter, Karen Lee, Eric Jay, Kurt Valery, Dawn Sheree. Wildlife biologist Utah Fish and Game Commn., 1954; tchr. Roosevelt Jr. High Sch., Salt Lake City, 1954-58, Blach Jr. High Sch., Los Altos, Calif., 1958-61, Awalt High Sch., Los Altos, 1961-65; asst. prof. edn. U. Alaska, 1967-68; asso. prof. Calif. State U., San Diego, 1968-72; prin. Floyd Dryden Jr. High Sch., Juneau, Alaska, 1972-73; prof. edn., chmn. dept. Western Colo. U., Grand Junction, 1973-82; exec. dir. Nat. Assn. Pvt., Nontraditional Schs. and Colls., Grand Junction, 1982—. Served with USMC, 1951-53. Mem. Nat. Assn. Pvt., Nontraditional Schs. and Colls. (exec. dir. 1975—), Assn. Supervision and Curriculum Devel., Am. Ednl. Research Assn., Nat. Audubon Soc. (pres. Western Colo. 1975-77), Phi Delta Kappa. Democrat. Mormon. Author: Evaluation-Accreditation of Secondary Schools; Accreditation Fact Sheet; Handbook on Accreditation: Guidelines for Accreditation by Contract. Home: 181 1/2 Thompson Rd Grand Junction CO 81503 Office: 182 Thompson Rd Grand Junction CO 81503

HEWETT, JOE JEFFERSON, JR., state ofcl.; b. Clovis, N.Mex., Aug. 8, 1921; s. Joe Jefferson and Nora Lily (Wallis) H.; B.S. in C.E., Tex. Tech U., 1951; postgrad. U.S. Air Force Inst. Tech., 1953; m. Una Elizabeth Scott, Apr. 7, 1950; children—Susan, Christine, Margaret, Joe Jefferson. Project engr. N.Mex. State Hwy. Dept., Roswell, 1964-66, asst. dist. engr., 1966-69, tech. services engr., Santa Fe, 1972-75, traffic services engr., 1975-77, dist. engr., Roswell, 1977-80, chief hwy. adminstr., 1980—; pvt. practice civil engring., Lovington, N.Mex., 1969-72. Served with USAAF, World War II; ETO Decorated D.F.C. with oak leaf clusters (5), Air medal; registered profl. engr., N.Mex.; registered land surveyor, N.Mex. Recipient spl. award Fed. Hwy. Adminstrn., 1982. Mem. N.Mex. Soc. Prof. Engrs. (ex-officio mem. gov.'s cabinet), Am. Assn. State Hwy. and Transp. Ofcls., Western Assn. State Hwy. and Transp. Ofcls. Baptist. Home: 1210 S Sunset St Roswell NM 88201 Office: 1120 Cerrillos Rd Santa Fe NM 87503

HEWETT, ROBERT BURCH, international education administrator; b. Detroit, Dec. 6, 1913; s. Joseph Lancaster and Lulu Marie (Burch) H.; m. Mary Joyce Morgan, Dec. 1, 1952 (dec.); children—Judith, Martha. Student U. Mich., 1931-33. Reporter, Ann Arbor (Mich.) Daily News, 1933-35, Decatur (Ill.) Herald-Rev., 1935-38; capitol corr. AP, Springfield, Ill., 1939-42; AP editor, bur. chief, corr., London, Tehran, Iran, Singapore, Cairo and Beirut, Lebanon, 1946-57; corr. Cowles Publs., Beirut, Hong Kong, London, 1957-67; corp. sec., spl. asst. to pres., curator Jefferson fellowships, East-West Ctr. Honolulu, 1967—. Served to lt. col. USMCR, 1942-45. Decorated Bronze Star., Purple Heart. Recipient Nat. Headliners Club award, 1958; Overseas Press Club award, 1959. Mem. Pub. Relations Soc. Am. (accredited). Club: Army and Navy (Washington). Home: Iolani Ave 504 Honolulu HI 96813 Office: East West Center 1777 East-West Rd Honolulu HI 96848

HEWITT, ARTHUR ELBERT, lawyer; b. Yuba City, Calif., Dec. 9, 1915; s. Charles Oscar and Eva Marie (Smith) H.; A.A., Yuba Coll., 1935; LL.B., U. Calif. at San Francisco, 1938; m. Kathryn Vera Lane, May 12, 1933 (div. 1939); 1 son, Allan A.; m. 2d Irene Flossie Heater, Jan. 15, 1943; children—Arthur Elbert, Ronald C. Admitted to Calif. bar; individual practice law, Marysville, Calif., 1938-42; dist. atty., Yuba County, 1946-47; partner firm Gray, Hewitt, Lenhard & Sanders, Marysville, 1947-75; pres. Hewitt, Lenhard, Sanders and Anderson, P.C., Marysville, Calif., 1975—. State inheritance tax appraiser State of Calif., 1947-59, state inheritance tax referee, 1968—; mem. Yuba County Parole Bd., 1959—; mem. arbitration panel Sutter County Superior Ct., 1978—. Trustee Sutter County Law Library. Served as lt. USNR, 1942-45. Mem. Am., Yuba-Sutter bar assns., State Bar Calif., Am., Calif. trial lawyers assns., Am. Arbitration Assn. (arbitrator 1962—), Yuba Sutter Bar Assn. (pres. 1956-57, mem. disciplinary com. 1965-67). Baptist (chmn. bd. trustees). Home: 1920 Sampson St Marysville CA 95901 Office: 716 D St Marysville CA 95901

HEWITT, FRANK FLOYD, naval officer; b. LaJolla, Calif., July 15, 1945; s. Floyd and Charlotte Marie (Lobel) H.; B.S., U.S. Naval Acad., 1967; grad. Naval Command and Staff Coll., Naval War Coll., 1974; M.S., Naval Postgrad. Sch., Monterey, Calif., 1979; m. Jeanne Madeleine Gallagher, June 22, 1968; children—Jean-Marie Elizabeth, Corinne Alexandra. Commd. ensign U.S. Navy, 1967, advanced through grades to comdr., 1980; engr. officer U.S.S. Sagacity, ocean minesweeper, 1967-69; weapons officer U.S.S. Walke, destroyer, 1969-70, U.S.S. Marvin Shields, destroyer escort, 1970-72; co. officer U.S. Naval Acad., Annapolis, Md., 1972-73; comdg. officer U.S.S. Adroit, ocean minesweeper, 1974-77; exec. officer U.S.S. Goldsborough, guided missile destroyer, 1979-81; chief staff officer Destroyer Squadron 33, 1981-82; now mem. tech. tng. group, San Diego. Mem. U.S. Naval Acad. Alumni Assn., U.S. Naval Inst., Sigma Xi (asso.). Home: 2315 Geranium St San Diego CA 92109 Office: COMNAVSURFPAC Staff San Diego CA 92155

HEWITT, JAMES FRANCIS, lawyer; b. Portsmouth, Va., July 4, 1929; s. Everett Elmer and Margaret (Mulvey) H.; m. Nadine Garrett, Jan. 12, 1957; children—Margaret, Edward, Helen, Nancy. Student Catholic U. Am., 1949-50, 51-52; J.D., U. Richmond, 1955. Bar: Va. 1955, Calif. 1960. Atty. Alameda County (Calif.), 1956-57, Immigration and Naturalization Service, San Francisco, 1957-60; asst. U.S. atty. Dept. Justice, San Francisco, 1960-65; atty. in charge Fed. criminal Def. Office, San Francisco, 1965-71; fed. pub. defender No. Dist. Calif., San Francisco, 1971—; dir. Advanced Criminal Practitioner's Seminars Inc. Served to sgt. U.S. Army, 1946-49, 50-51. Mem. Calif. State Bar, Bar Assn. San Francisco, Nat. Assn. Criminal Def. Lawyers (Ouststanding Contbn. award 1978). Democrat. Roman Catholic. Office: 450 Golden Gate Ave San Francisco CA 94102

HEWITT, JAMES J., provincial government official; b. Toronto, Ont., Can., Jan. 28, 1933; s. James Henry and Mary (Harrison) H.; m. Sheila M. Fox, June 12, 1954 (div.); children—James Russell, Catherine Lee, Robert Allen, Ronald William; m. 2d, Dorothy M. Pickrell, Dec. 27, 1980. With Fruehauf Trailers of Can. Ltd., 1956-62; dir. field services B.C. Credit Union League, 1962-67; gen. mgr. Penticton and Dist. Credit Union, 1967-75; mem. B.C. Legislature, 1975—, now minister of consumer and corp. affairs. Alderman, City of Penticton, 1971-76; bd. dirs. Regional Dist. Okanagan-Similkameen, 1972-74, Union B.C. Muncipalities, 1974-76. Mem. Soc. Mgmt. Accts. Can. Mem. Social Credit Party. Mem. United Ch. Home: 496 Lakeshore Dr Penticton BC V2A 1B9 Canada Office: Parliament Bldgs Victoria BC V8V 1X4 Canada

HEWITT, WILLIAM NELSON, safety and transportation consultant; b. Oklahoma City, Aug. 15, 1932; s. John Nelson and Elizabeth Ann (Adams) H.; grad. Am. Bus. Coll., 1948; B.S. in Social Psychology, U. Okla., 1955; postgrad. Pa. State U., 1966, 67; student Nikon Sch. of Advanced Photography, 1973-75; children—William Nelson, Luanne, Kelly. Vice pres. Am. City Claims Service, Inc., Dallas, 1956-59; safety and transp. cons., 1966—; pres. World Research Co., Phoenix, 1966—; pres., chmn. bd. WNH & Assos., Phoenix, 1972—; pres., chmn. bd. Fleet Photo and Lab., Phoenix, 1973—; chmn. bd. TSI, Inc., Phoenix, 1975-76; guest lectr. on transp. safety, corp. mgmt. and accident reconstrn. and investigation, various univs.; cons. to various mfg. and comml. firms. Served with USN, 1949-53. Mem. World Trade Assn., Am. Trucking Assn. (sr. mem. nat. accident rev. bd. 1972-83), Nat. Freight Claims Congress, Ariz. Motor Fleet Safety Council (pres. 1969-72), Nat. Geog. Soc. Republican. Contbr. articles on accident investigation, indsl. safety, and fed. compliance to profl. jours.; producer multimedia films on safety and transp. Home: 3011 W Ocotillo Phoenix AZ 85017 Office: PO Box 11608 Phoenix AZ 85061

HEYDORN, WILLIAM HOWARD, physician; b. Schenectady, Feb. 10, 1934; s. William August and Lucille (Furbeck) H.; m. Joan Gloria Kilian, Sept. 9, 1956; children—Barbara, Kathryn, William. B.A., Hope Coll., 1955; M.D., Yale U., 1959. Diplomate Am. Bd. Surgery, Am. Bd. Thoracic Surgery. Rotating intern Mary Imogene Bassett Hosp., Cooperstown, N.Y., 1959-60; commd. capt., U.S. Army, 1960, advanced through grades to col., 1974; resident in gen. surgery Letterman Gen. Hosp., 1962-66, resident in thoracic surgery, 1970-72, thoracic surgery staff, 1975-78, chief dept. surgery 1978—; assoc. clin. prof. surgery Uniformed Service U. Health Scis., 1979—; asst. clin. prof. surgery U. Calif.-San Francisco. Decorated Army Commendation medal. Mem. San Francisco Surg. Soc., Assn. Army Cardiology, Soc. Thoracic Surgery, ACS. Republican. Home: 40 Geldert Dr Tiburon CA 94920 Office: PO Box 497 Letterman Army Med Center San Francisco CA 94129

HEYL, ALLEN VAN, JR., geologist; b. Allentown, Pa., Apr. 10, 1918; s. Allen Van and Emma (Kleppinger) H.; student Muhlenberg Coll., 1936-37; B.S. in Geology, Pa. State U., 1941; Ph.D. in Geology, Princeton U., 1950; m. Maxine LaVon Hawke, July 12, 1945; children—Nancy Caroline, Allen David Van. Field asst., govt. geologist Nfld. Geol. Survey, summers 1937-40, 42; jr. geologist U.S. Geol. Survey, Wis., 1943-45, asst. geologist, 1945-47, asso. geologist, 1947-50, geologist, Washington and Beltsville, Md., 1950-67; staff geologist, Denver, 1968—; chmn. Internat. Commn. Tectonics of Ore Deposits. Fellow Instn. Mining and Metallurgy (Gt. Brit.), Geol. Soc. Am., Am. Mineral. Soc.; mem. Inst. Genesis of Ore Deposits, Soc. Econ. Geologists, Geol. Soc. Wash., Colo. Sci. Soc., Rocky Mountain Geol. Soc., Friends of Mineralogy (hon. life), Evergreen Naturalist Audubon Soc. (dir.), Sigma Xi, Alpha Chi Sigma. Lutheran. Contbr. numerous articles to profl. jours., chpts. to books. Home: PO Box 1052 Evergreen CO 80439 Office: Central Mineral Resources Branch MS 905 US Geol Survey Denver Fed Center Denver CO 80225

HEYLER, DAVID BALDWIN, JR., lawyer; b. Los Angeles, May 23, 1926; s. David Baldwin and Andree (Buchwalter) H.; B.A., Stanford, 1948, J.D., 1951; m. Joan Elizabeth Dekker, Aug. 31, 1949; children—Mary Andree, Elizabeth Baldwin, Katherine Dekker. Admitted to Calif. bar, 1952, since practiced in Los Angeles; partner Ward and Heyler. Bd. dirs. Beverly Hills YMCA, v.p., 1961; bd. dirs Beverly Hills Republican Club, 1954-58; trustee Westlake Sch. for Girls, Menlo Sch. and Coll. Served with USNR, 1944-45. Fellow Am. Coll. Trial Lawyers; mem. Am., Los Angeles (trustee 1964), Beverly Hills (pres. 1962, gov. 1954-63) bar assns., State Bar Calif. (chmn. journal com. 1962-63, mem. com. bar examiners 1965-70, chmn. 1968-70, mem. legislation com. 1963—, mem. disciplinary com. 18, 1963-66, chmn. 1965-66, mem. com. on legal edn. 1965-70, 72-74, vice chmn. 1973-74), Beverly Hills Jr. C. of C. (dir. 1953-57, Young Man of Year 1962), Bel Air Assn. (pres. 1972-74, dir.), Stanford Assos., Stanford Alumni Assn. (dir., pres. 1974-75). Episcopalian. Clubs: Beverly Hills Rotary; Los Angeles Country; California; Bohemian of San Francisco. Office: Suite 1475 1901 Ave of the Stars Los Angeles CA 90067

HEYMAN, IRA MICHAEL, educator, univ. chancellor; b. N.Y.C., May 30, 1930; s. Harold Albert and Judith (Sobel) H.; A.B., Dartmouth, 1951; J.D., Yale, 1956; m. Therese Helene Thau, Dec. 17, 1950; children—Stephen Thomas, James Nathaniel. Legislative asst. to U.S. Senator Ives, 1950-51; admitted to N.Y. bar, 1956, Calif. bar, 1961; with firm Carter, Ledyard & Milburn, N.Y.C., 1956-57; law clk. to U.S. Circuit Judge Charles Clark, 1957-58, to Supreme Ct. Justice Earl Warren, 1958-59; prof. law U. Calif. at Berkeley, 1959—, prof. city and regional planning, 1966—, vice chancellor, 1974-80, chancellor, 1980—; Vis. prof. Yale Law Sch., 1963-64, Stanford Law Sch., 1971-72. Mem. adv. bd. to bd. dirs. Pacific Gas & Electric Co. Mem. City of Berkeley Charter Rev. Commn., 1972-74, Calif. adv. com. U.S. Commn. Civil Rights, 1962-67; trustee Dartmouth Coll., 1982—. Served to 1st lt. USMCR, 1951-53. Mem. Am. Law Inst. (asst. reporter). Democrat. Contbr. articles to profl. jours. Home: Univ House U Calif Berkeley CA 94720

HEYNE, PAUL THEODORE, economist, educator; b. St. Louis, Nov. 2, 1931; s. Walter M. and Ruth (Beiderwieden) H.; m. Marjorie Fairchild, Nov. 25, 1955; children—Eric, Margot, Brian; m. 2d, Juliana Becker, Jan. 29, 1966; children—Michelle, Sarah. M.Div., Concordia Sem., St. Louis, 1956; M.A. in Econs. Washington U., St. Louis, 1957; Ph.D., U. Chgo., 1963. Instr., then asst. prof., assoc. prof. econs. Valparaiso (Ind.) U., 1957-65; vis. prof. U. Ill., Urbana, 1965, 66; assoc. prof., econs. So. Meth. U., Dallas, 1966-72, prof. 1972-76; lectr. econs. U. Wash., Seattle, 1976—. Author: Private Keepers of the Public Interest, 1968; The Economic Way of Thinking, 4th edit., 1983. Home: 103 17th Ave E Seattle WA 98112 Office: Econs Dept DK-30 U Wash Seattle WA 98195

HEYWOOD, SANDRA SCHNOOR, volunteer services administrator; b. Mt. Kisco, N.Y., June 26, 1939; d. Richard H. and Lois G. (Brundage) Schnoor; m. John S. Heywood, July 13, 1963; children—Leslie Lynne,

Heidi Lynne. B.A. Middlebury Coll. 1961, M.A. U. Phoenix 1982. Cert. tchr. N.Y.; registered social worker Colo.; cert. sex counselor Am. Assn. Sex Educators, Counselors and Therapists. Tchr. French Scarsdale (N.Y.) Pub. Sch. 1961-63, instr. adult edn. 1963-73; supr. family planning team dept. patient and family counseling Albany (N.Y.) Med. Center 1973-77; program dir. community health edn. Dept. Health and Hosps. City of Denver 1977-79; mgmt. cons. Boone, Young & Assoc., N.Y.C. 1979; dir. vol. services Tucson Med. Center 1979—; v.p. Instn. Devel. Services. Bd. dirs. Arapahoe County Mental Health Assn.; vol. Planned Parenthood. Mem. Am. Soc. Dirs. Vol. Services, Ariz. Hosp. Assn. Contbr. articles to profl. jours.

HIATT, DIANA BUELL, educator; b. Milw., Apr. 3, 1938; d. Paul F. and Mildred R. (Hansen) Buell; m. Charles E. Hiatt, July 6, 1957; children—Charles John, Marianne, Douglas. B.S. in Edn., U. Wis.-Milw., 1960; M.S. in Edn., U. Conn., 1963; Ed.D., UCLA, 1976. Tchr. elem. schs. West Hartford, Conn., 1960-67, Pasadena, Calif., 1968-69; instr. child growth and devel. Santa Monica (Calif.) Coll., 1972-75; cons., specialist early childhood edn. Pales Verdes (Calif.) Unified Sch. Dist., 1973-74; instr. Pepperdine Sch. Edn., Los Angeles, 1973-74, adj. prof. early childhood edn. Sch. Edn., 1974-77, asst. prof. Grad. Sch. Edn., 1977-80, assoc. prof., 1980—; mem. adv. com. Los Angeles County Ednl. Resource Ctr., 1978-79; mem. evaluation com. Los Angeles County Mus. Art, Mar Vista Family Day Care Ctr. Program; lectr. in field, workshop leader. Mem. Am. Assn. Mental Imagery, Assn. Supervision and Curriculum Devel., Am. Ednl. Research Assn., Calif. Assn. Edn. Young Child, Calif. Assn. Program Evaluators (founding), Calif. Council Edn. Tchrs., Calif. Profs. Early Childhood Edn. (dir.), Doctoral Alumni Assn. UCLA (Disting. awards, Alumni chmn., 1982), Edn. Assn. Pepperdine U., Nat. Assn. Ednl. Computing (founding), Soc. Research Child Devel., Nat. Soc. Study Edn., Kappa Delta Pi, Phi Delta Kappa (chmn. planning ann. curriculum conf. 1981), Pi Lambda Theta (So. Calif. Council bd. 1974-77). Mem. Chs. of Christ. Author publs. in fields; contbr. articles to profl. jours; mem. editors adv. council UCLA Educators, 1974-77; editorial reviewer Child Care Quar., 1976—, Merrill-Palmer Quar., 1981—. Office: Pepperdine Grad Sch Edn 3415 Sepulveda St Los Angeles CA 90034

HIATT, DUANE EVAN, educator, writer; b. Payson, Utah, June 16, 1937; s. Ferron E. and Gladys (Wride) H.; m. Diane Robertson, Dec. 15, 1960; children—Daniel, Robert, Joseph, David, John, Matthew, Angela, Callie, Samuel, Benjamin, Katheryn, Thomas, Joshua, Lucy. B.S., Brigham Young U., 1961, M.A., 1982. Singer, comedian, lectr., 1961-75; reporter AP, Provo, Utah, 1960-61; sales mgr. Sta. KFTN, Provo, 1975, news dir., announcer, 1976—; chmn. communications dept., div. continuing edn. Brigham Young, U., Provo, 1979—. Pres. bd. Am.'s Freedom Festival, 1982—, chmn., 1981—; advisor Varsity Scouts; motivational speaker ARC, United Way; fundraiser Am. Cancer Soc. Recipient George Washington medal Freedoms Found. at Valley Forge, 1982; Outstanding Teaching award Div. Continuing Edn., Brigham Young U., 1975; Andy award of Merit, Advt. Club. N.Y., 1975; Best in West First award Am. Advt. Fedn., 1981. Republican. Mormon. Recorded six albums for Capitol Records; writer radio and TV scripts. Home: 4320 N 650 E St Provo UT 84604 Office: 293 HCEB Brigham Young U Provo UT 84602

HIATT, PETER, ednl. adminstr.; b. N.Y.C., Oct. 19, 1930; s. Amos and Elizabeth Hope (Derry) H.; B.A., Colgate U., 1952; M.L.S., Rutgers U., 1957, Ph.D., 1963; m. Linda Rae Smith, Aug. 16, 1968; 1 dau., Holly Virginia. Head, Elmora Br. Library, Elizabeth, N.J., 1957-59; instr. Grad. Sch. Library Service, Rutgers U., 1960-62; library cons. Ind. State Library, Indpls., 1963-70; asst. prof. Grad. Library Sch., Ind. U., 1963-66, asso. prof., 1966-70; dir. Ind. Library Studies, Bloomington, 1967-70; dir. continuing edn. program for library personnel Western Interstate Commn. for Higher Edn., Boulder, Colo., 1970-74; prof., dir. Sch. Librarianship, U. Wash., Seattle, 1974-81, dir. Career Devel. and Assessment Center for Librarians, 1977—; dir. library insts. at various colls. and univs.; adv. project U.S. Office Edn.-ALA, 1977-80. Mem. ALA, Mountain Plains, Pacific N.W. library assns., Spl. Libraries Assn., Am. Soc. Info. Sci., Adult Edn. Assn., ACLU. Author: (with Donald Thompson) Monroe County Public Library: Planning for the Future, 1966, The Public Library Needs of Delaware County, 1967; (with Henry Drennan) Public Library Services for the Functionally Illiterate, 1967; (with Robert E. Lee and Lawrence A. Allen) A Plan for Developing a Regional Program of Continuing Education for Library Personnel, 1969; Public Library Branch Services for Adults of Low Education, 1964; dir., gen. editor The Indiana Library Studies, 1970; mem. editorial bd. Coll. and Research Libraries, 1969-73; co-editor Leads: A Continuing Newsletter for Library Trustees, 1973-75; author chpts., articles on library continuing edn., also monographs in field. Home: 19324 8th Ave NW Seattle WA 98177 Office: Sch of Librarianship U Wash Seattle WA 98195

HIBBARD, JUDITH HOFFMAN, researcher, health educator; b. Los Angeles, Nov. 30, 1948; d. Arnold Mandel and Marian (Corob) Hoffman; m. Michael John Hibbard, Aug. 1, 1968; 1 dau., Johanna L. B.S., Calif. State U.-Northridge, 1974; M.P.H., UCLA, 1975; D.P.H., U. Calif.-Berkeley, 1982. Adj. investigator Kaiser Permanent Med. Care Program, Health Services Research Ctr., Portland, Oreg., 1980—; asst. prof. U. Oreg.; cons. to health agys. Recipient Dissertation Research award Nat. Ctr. Health Services Research, 1981; New Investigator Research award Nat. Inst. Aging, 1983-86; USPHS trainee, 1978-81; Chancellor's fellow in Pub. Health, U. Calif.-Berkeley, 1979-80. Mem. Am. Sociol. Assn., Am. Pub. Health Assn., Soc. Pub. Health Educators, Sociologists for Women in Soc. Office: U Oreg Dept Sch and Community Health Eugene OR 97403

HIBBARD, RICHARD PAUL, industrial ventilation consultant, lecturer; lectr.; b. Defiance, Ohio, Nov. 1, 1923; s. Richard T. and Doris E. (Walkup) H.; B.S. in Mech. Indsl. Engring., U. Toledo, 1949; m. Phyllis Ann Kirchoffer, Sept. 7, 1948; children—Barbara Rae, Marcia Kae, Rebecca Ann, Patricia Jan, John Ross. Mech. engr. Oldsmobile div. Gen. Motors Corp., Lansing, Mich., 1950-56; design and sales engr. McConnell Sheet Metal, Inc., Lansing, 1956-60; chief heat and ventilation engr. Fansteel Metall. Corp., North Chicago, Ill., 1960-62; sr. facilities and ventilation engr. The Boeing Co., Seattle, 1962-63; ventilation engr. environ. health div. dept. preventive medicine U. Wash., 1964-70, lectr. dept. environ. health, 1970-82, lectr. emeritus, 1983—; chmn. Western Indsl. Ventilation Conf., 1962; mem. com. indsl. ventilation Am. Conf. Govtl. Indsl. Hygienists, 1966—; mem. staff Indsl. Ventilation Conf., Mich. State U., 1955—. Served with USAAF, 1943-45, USAR, 1946-72. Recipient Disting. Service award Indsl. Ventilation Conf., Mich. State U., 1975. Mem. Am. Soc. Safety Engrs., ASHRAE, Am. Inst. Plant Engrs., Am. Indsl. Hygiene Assn. (J.M. Dallevalle award 1977), Am. Foundryman's Soc. Clubs: Elks, Masons. Contbr. articles on indsl. hygiene and ventilation to profl. jours. Home: 41 165th Ave SE Bellevue WA 98008

HIBER, JHAN WILLIAM, broadcast consultant, writer; b. Joliet, Ill., Dec. 29, 1946; s. William M. and Marcia Jane (Slappey) H.; m. Lynn E. Palmer, Dec. 27, 1979. Student U. Md., 1964-68; B.A. cum laude, Central Fla. U., 1973; M.A., Am. U., 1977. Cert. radio mktg. cons. Newsman various TV stas., 1969-73; account exec., gen. mgr. radio and TV properties, 1973-76; mgr. radio ratings div. Arbitron Ratings, 1977-78; editor/weekly columnis Radio & Records, Los Angeles, 1979—; pres. Hiber Hart & Patrick Ltd., Pebble Beach, Calif., 1979—, Calif. Lit. Enterprises, Inc., 1982—. Recipient 3 Addy awards, 1972-73; Abraham Lincoln award, 1975. Mem. Internat. Radio and TV Soc., Am. Mktg. Assn., Nat. Assn. Broadcasters, Nat. Radio Broadcasters Assn., Alpha Epsilon Rho. Republican/Libertarian. Presbyterian. Clubs: Sports Car Am., Brit. Sch. Motor Racing. Home: 3102 Bird Rock Rd Pebble Beach CA 93953 Office: PO Box 1220 Pebble Beach CA 93953

HICK, KENNETH WILLIAM, business executive; b. New Westminster, B.C., Can., Oct. 17, 1946; s. Les Walter and Mary Isabelle (Warner) H.; came to U.S., 1950, naturalized, 1956; B.A. in Bus., Eastern Wash. State Coll., 1971; M.B.A. (fellow), U. Wash., 1973. Area sales mgr. Hilti, Inc., Portland, Oreg., 1975-77, regional sales mgr., San Leandro, Calif., 1978-79; gen. sales mgr. Moore Internat., Inc., Portland, 1979-80; v.p. sales and mktg. Phillips Corp., Anaheim, Calif., 1980-81; gen. mgr. K.C. Metals, San Jose, Calif., 1981, pres., chief exec. officer, 1981—; communications cons. Asso. Public Safety Communication Officers, Inc., State of Oreg., 1975-77; numerous cons. assignments, also seminars, 1976-81. Mem. Oreg. Gov.'s Tax Bd., 1975-76; pres. Portland chpt. Oreg. Jaycees, 1976; bd. fellows U. Santa Clara. Served with USAF, 1966-69. Decorated Commendation medal. Mem. Am. Mgmt. Assn., Am. Mktg. Assn., Assn. M.B.A. Execs., Asso. Gen. Contractors, Soc. Advancement Mgmt. Roman Catholic. Contbr. to numerous publs., 1976-81. Home: 566 Cambrian Way Danville CA 94549 Office: 1960 Hartog Dr San Jose CA 95131

HICKETHIER, KARL JAMES, medical center housekeeping administrator; b. San Francisco, Jan. 9, 1944; s. Heinz Waldmeir and Millie (Hollingsworth) H.; m. Lilliam Alejandrina Sanchez, June 4, 1946; children—Jeffrey, Michelle. Student Mich. State U., 1968. Housekeeping asst. Stanford U. Hosp. and Med. Ctr., Palo Alto, Calif., 1964-67, housekeeping supr., 1967-68, head supr., 1969-72, asst. exec. housekeeper, 1973-75, exec. housekeeper, 1975—; cons. Hickethier Assocs., 1978—. Served with USN, 1961-64. Mem. Nat. Exec. Housekeepers Assn. Episcopalian. Home: 4816 Gina Way Union City CA 94587 Office: 300 Pasteur Dr Palo Alto CA 94303

HICKEY, JOHN RAY, university administrator; b. Ontario, Oreg., Aug. 11, 1942; s. William Oscar and Ruth Maxine (Ury) H.; 1 son, Johnny Ray. B.S., Eastern Oreg. State U., 1964; postgrad. Oreg. State U., 1965. Regional mgr. Kappa Systems Inc., Seattle, 1971-76; tng. and mgmt. cons. Palmer Alaska, Arlington, Va., 1976-80; dept. head U. Alaska, Fairbanks, 1980-81, dir. dept. confs. and insts., 1981—. Mem. Fairbanks Festival '84; mem. adv. bd. Community Ctr. Mem. Am. Soc. Tng. and Devel., Adult Edn. Assn., Meeting Planners Internat., Am. Assn. Adult and Continuing Edn. Author tech. publs., research reports. Home: Gen Delivery Ester AK 99725 Office: Dept Confs & Insts U Alaska 117 Erelson Bldg 403 Salcha St Fairbanks AK 99701

HICKEY, SCOTT Y., marketing executive; b. Seattle, May 19, 1951; s. Yates and Marion (McKenzie) H.; m. Priscilla Kathryn Taylor, Mar. 25, 1973; 1 son, Nathaniel Taylor. B.S. in Journalism, U. Oreg., 1972; M.B.A., U. Wash., 1975. Media supr. Kraft Smith Advt., Seattle, 1975-77; brand mgr. Olympia Brewing Co. (Wash.), 1977-80; dir. advt. and pub. relations Alpac Corp., Seattle, 1980—; guest lectr. U. Wash., Seattle. Bd. dirs, v.p. Seafair; mem. exec. com. Muscular Dystrophy Assn. Mem. Seattle Advt. Club. Presbyterian. Club: Washington Athletic (Seattle). Home: 3257 Evergreen Point Rd Bellevue WA 98004 Office: 2300 26th Ave S Seattle WA 98144

HICKEY, SUSAN FOSS, utilities executive, environmental engineer; b. Richmond, Va., Feb. 2, 1948; d. James Benton and Patricia Anne (Foss) H.; m. Sheldon Mark Klapper, July 3, 1982. B.A. in Math. and Russian, magna cum laude, Vanderbilt U., 1970; M.S. in Environ. Engr., U. Fla., 1972. Air pollution analyst EPA, Washington, 1972-74; cons. Energy and Environ. Analysis Inc., Washington, 1974-75; environ. analyst Energy Research and Devel. Adminstrn., Washington, 1975-77; environ. adviser White House Energy Policy/Planning Staff, Washington, 1977; div. dir. environ. planning Dept. Energy, Washington, 1978-79; div. dir. analysis, evaluation Western Sun, Portland, Oreg., 1980-82; div. dir. planning, evaluation Office Conservation, Bonneville Power Adminstrn., Portland, 1982—. Mem. Nat. Assn. Female Execs., Phi Beta Kappa, Phi Kappa Phi. Democrat. Office: Bonneville Power Adminstrn 1002 NE Holladay St Portland OR 97208

HICKEY, WINIFRED E(SPY), state senator, social worker; b. Rawlins, Wyo.; d. David P. and Eugenia (Blake) Espy; children—John David, Paul Joseph. B.A., Loretto Heights Coll., 1933; postgrad. U. Utah, 1934, Sch. Social Service, U. Chgo., 1936. Dir. Carbon County Welfare Dept., 1935-36; field rep. Wyo. Dept. Welfare, 1937-38; dir. Red Cross Club, Europe, 1942-45; commr. Laramie County, Wyo., 1973-80; mem. Wyo. Senate, 1980—; dir. United Savs. & Loan, Cheyenne. Bd. dirs. U. Wyo. Found.; chmn. adv. council div. community programs Wyo. Dept. Health and Social Services; pres. county and state mental health assn., 1959-63; trustee, U. Wyo., 1967-71; active Nat. Council Cath. Women. Named Outstanding Alumna, Loretto Heights Coll., 1959. Democrat. Club: Altrusa (Cheyenne). Pub. Where the Deer and the Antelope Play, 1967.

HICKEY MILL, CHRISTINE, architect; b. Albany, Oreg., Oct. 21, 1947; d. James William and Marie Terese (Dalberti) Hickey; student Oreg. State U., 1965-66; B.Arch., U. Oreg., 1971; m. Richard Allen Mill, Oct. 12, 1975; 1 son, James Richard. Apprentice architect Blanchard-Lamen Architects, Salem, Oreg., 1971-72, 75-76; architect Daniel, Mann, Johnson & Mendelhall, Architects, Portland, Oreg., 1972-73, Robert Hicks Architect, Portland, 1973, Hugh Mitchell Landscape Architect, Portland, 1974-75; prin., owner, architect Christine Hickey Mill, Salem, 1976—; sec. Lebanon Bag Co., Inc. Mem. AIA, Women Entrepreneurs Oreg., Union Internationale Des Femmes Architects. Roman Catholic. Home: 945 Crestview Ct Salem OR 97302 Office: 3385 Liberty Rd S Salem OR 97302

HICKIE, MELVIN RUSSELL, association advertising manager; b. Centerville, Iowa, Nov. 30, 1949; s. John Russell and Mae Leona (Bennett) H.; m. Ruth Anne Jackson, Sept. 1, 1972; 1 son, Brandon Jackson. B.A. in History, N.E. Mo. State U., 1972. Communications cons. Executone, Kansas City, Kans., 1972-73; western div. mgr. The Packer Newspaper, Los Angeles, 1973-77; pres. El Libro Verde, Inc., La Canada, Calif., 1977-80; advt. mgr. Western Growers Assn., Newport Beach, Calif., 1980—. Mem. exec. bd. 1st Methodist Ch. Huntington Beach. Mem. Nat. Agri-Mktg. Assn., West Agrl. Mktg. Assn. (Merit award 1983), Soc. Preservation Vaudevillian Arts. Republican. Author: El Libro Verde Directory to Agriculture in Mexico; contbr. articles to profl. jours.

HICKIS, CHARLES FRANCIS, psychologist, consultant; b. Bronx, N.Y., Aug. 13, 1947; s. Charles J. and Marion S. H.; m. Judy C., Sept. 8, 1979; children—Gregory, Rabecca, Matthew. B.A., Hofstra U., 1970, M.A., 1974; Ph.D. (NIMH fellow), U. Colo., 1978; cert. postdoctoral studies UCLA, 1980. Research asst. dept. psychology U. Colo., 1972-77; asst. prof. psychology Weber State Coll., 1977-79; NIMH postdoctoral trainee physiol. psychology UCLA, 1979-80; clin. dir. Chem. Dependency Ctr., West Park Hosp., Cody, Wyo., 1980—; organizational and motivational cons.; chmn., Wyo. Prevention Planning Com., 1980—. Mem. Am. Psychol. Assn. Democrat. Mormon. Club: Absaroka Flycasters (Cody), N.Am. Hunting Club. Author profl. papers. Home: 2001 24th St Cody WY 82414 Office: Chem Dependency Center West Park Hosp Cody WY 82414

HICKMAN, CECIL RAY, safety engineer, consultant; b. Bug, Ky., Aug. 28, 1936; s. Balos Lewis and Daisy Pearl (Huddleston) H.; m. Hazel Eugena Lee, Feb. 1, 1958; children—Vickie Hickman Pankhurst, Pamela Hickman Southerland, Lisa Hickman Shyface, Eric. B.S. in Indsl. Tech., Tenn. Tech. U., 1960. Cert. safety profl., profl. safety engr. Calif. Safety supr. E.I. DuPont DeNemours, Inc., various locations in U.S., 1962-69; safety supt. Reynolds Elec. and Engring. Co., Inc., Las Vegas, Nev., 1969-73; safety engr. Stone and Webster Engring Corp., Wading River, N.Y., 1973; sr. safety rep. EBASCO, N.Y.C., 1973; chief safety programs Holmes and Narver, Inc., Las Vegas, 1974—; instr. gen. safety tech. Clark County Community Coll. Active Nev. Safety Council, 1978—. Served with USN, 1954-57. Named Safety Profl. of Yr., 1981-82; recipient past pres. award Am. Soc. Safety Engrs. (So. Nev. chpt.). Mem. Am. Soc. Safety Engrs. (nat. admission com. 1978-84). Republican. Baptist. Club: Masons. Home: 5185 Dapple Grey Las Vegas NV 89108 Office: PO Box 1 Mercury NV 89023

HICKMAN, SHARON ROSE, design consultant; b. Kansas City, Kans., May 24, 1951; d. Wilmont and Rose Marie (Cyhel) Lohoefener; m. Billy Ray Lee, July 14, 1969; m. 2d Dan Patrick Hickman, Aug. 7, 1976; children—Jonathan Bryan, Nicole Kristen. Student pub. schs. Overland Park, Kans. Gen. mgr. Bull & Boar Restaurant, Lawrence, Kans., 1971-75, Internat. Restaurant, Lawrence, 1975-76, Sirloin Stockade, Lawrence, 1976-78, Chandler, Ariz., 1978-80; mgr. T.G.I.Friday's, Phoenix, 1980-81; pres., founder Nature's Elves, Inc., Tempe, Ariz., 1981—; design cons. Mem. Exec. Bus. Profl. Women's Club (v.p. Tempe chpt. 1981-82), NOW, Interior Plantscape Assn. Democrat. Roman Catholic. Home and office: 13722 E Williamsfield Rd Gilbert AZ 85234

HICKOK, ERIC HOLOCOMBE, lawyer, accountant; b. Portland, Oreg., Oct. 4, 1948; s. Richard Holcombe Madison and Margaret (Scheffler) H.; m. Stephanie Shooter, Feb. 14, 1979; children—Jaime, Heather, Eric. B.S., Calif. State U.-Los Angeles, 1971; J.D., U. Santa Clara, 1977. Bar: Calif. 1977; C.P.A., Calif. Audit mgr. Ernst & Whinney, Los Angeles and San Francisco, 1971-77; mem. faculty dept. acctg. Menlo (Calif.) Coll., 1975-79; pres. Medi Fund Corp., San Francisco, 1979-80; individual practice law, acctg., Burlingame, Calif., 1980—; dir. Valley Bus. Forms, Inc., Calistoga, Calif., Garrett Press, San Francisco. Mem. Am. Inst. C.P.A.s, ABA, Calif. Soc. C.P.A.s, Calif. State Bar. Republican. Episcopalian. Office: Suite 1 1133 Chula Vista Burlingame CA 94010

HICKS, ADRIENNE SPUUR, telephone communications executive; b. San Francisco, Mar. 27, 1938; d. Henry William and Isabel Katherine (Fagan) Spuur; m. Louis Holland Hicks, Aug. 7, 1965; children—Jeffery, Cynthia, Bernice. A.A., Am. River Coll., 1958; postgrad. Calif. State U.-Sacramento, 1959. Toll operator Pacific Telephone Co., Sacramento, 1956-58, service rep., 1958-61, personnel clk., 1961-63, pub. relations staff asst., 1963-65, instr., 1965-70, bus. office supr., 1970-78, ops. reviewer, 1978-81, phone ctr. zone mgr., 1981-82, zone mgr. Northwestern Calif., 1982—; pub. speaker, mistress of ceremonies. Non-partisan campaign worker, Sacramento, 1982. Recipient Sales award Pacific Telephone Co., 1981. Mem. Nat. Assn. Female Execs., Telephone Pioneers. Club: Sacramento Jeepers, Inc. Office: Pacific Telephone Co 2211 Park Towne Circle Suite 170-A Sacramento CA 95821

HICKS, ROBERT ALVIN, psychologist, educator, research administrator, researcher; b. San Francisco, July 25, 1932; s. James B. and Vera L. (Brand) H.; m. Maralee J., June 15, 1957; 1 son, Gregory James. B.A., U. Calif.-Santa Barbara, 1955; M.A., San Jose State U., 1960; Ph.D. (Univ. fellow), U. Denver, 1964. Psychometrist, San Jose State U., 1956-61, asst. prof. psychology, 1966-68, assoc. prof., 1968-70, prof., 1970—, dir. NIH/Minority Biomed. Support Program, 1980—; instr. U. Denver, 1961-64, asst. prof., 1964-66; cons. to cos. Bd. dirs. San Jose State U. Found. NIH grantee, 1980—; NIMH grantee, 1982—. Mem. Am. Psychol. Assn., Western Psychol. Assn. (dir.), Soc. for Research in Child Devel., Psychonomic Soc., Assn. for Psycho Physiol. Study Sleep, AAAS, Rocky Mountain Psychol. Assn., Sigma Xi. Democrat. Unitarian. Contbr. numerous articles, mainly on research on relationships between sleep and behavior, to profl. jours. Home: 1118 Littleoak Circle San Jose CA 95129 Office: Dept Psychology San Jose State U San Jose CA 95192

HICKS, VERONICA, publicist, advertising executive; b. San Diego, Apr. 19, 1944; d. Ben and Frances Veronica (Patrick) Bagnas; m. Lawrence Raymond Hicks, Aug. 1, 1964 (div.). Student San Diego City Coll., 1963, Mesa Coll., 1976. Pvt. practice real estate agent/broker, San Diego, 1974-76; v.p., regional mgr. Hubbert Advt. & Public Relations, San Diego, 1976-79; prin. Roni Hicks & Assocs., 1979—. Recipient Sales and Mktg. Excellence awards Sales and Mktg. Council of San Diego Bldg. Industry, Assn., 1980, 1982. Mem. Nat. Assn. Real Estate Editors, Bldg. Industry Assn. San Diego County, Home Builders Council, Rep. Bus. and Profl. Club, San Diego Press Club, Ad Club San Diego, San Diego C. of C. Republican. Roman Catholic. Office: 2251 San Diego Ave Suite B-251 San Diego CA 92110

HICKSON, ARNOLD HOWARD, JR., museum director; b. Huntsville, Ala., Sept. 6, 1932; s. Arnold Howard and Lillian Grace (Vann) H.; student U. Nev., 1963-65; B.A., Carson Coll., 1966; m. Betty Alauzet, June 25, 1971; children—Kendall Marc, Andrew Scott, Patrick Lynn; 1 stepson, Ian Parmiter. Profl. artist, designer, photographer, writer, Reno, Nev., 1956-64; one man shows Nev. Art Gallery, Reno, 1961, Tahoe Art Gallery, Lake Tahoe, Calif., 1963; exhibited group shows: St. Mary's of Mountain, Virginia City, Nev., 1960-69, Nev. Artists Assn. exhibits No. Nev., 1959-69; represented in pvt. collections; curator exhibits Nev. State Mus., Carson City, 1964-69; dir. Northeastern Nev. Mus., Elko, Nev., 1969—. Exec. sec. Nev. State Council on the Arts, 1967-76, chmn., 1977; mem. Gov.'s Adv. Bd. on Historic Records, 1975-78; nat. advisor Nat. Trust for Historic Preservation, 1970-76; trustee Elko County Library System, 1970-77; bd. dirs. Western States Art Found., Santa Fe, 1976-77; mem. accreditation, on-site com. Am. Assn. Mus., 1972—. Served with USAF, 1952-56. Recipient Nat. award of Merit, Am. Assn. State and Local History, 1970, 82; Greatest Contbn. to the Arts in Nev., 1980 Critics award Reno Newspapers; named Dean of Museologists, State of Nev., 1979. Mem. Am. Assn. Museums, Am. Assn. State and Local History, Nat. Lawmen and Outlaw Assn., Conf. Internat. Archivists. Republican. Episcopalian. Club: Rotary (pres. 1976-77). Author: Mint Mark: CC; also numerous hist. articles for quars., jours., newspapers. Home: 1965 View Dr PO Box 1046 Elko NV 89801 Office: 1515 Idaho St PO Box 2550 Elko NV 89801

HIDAKA, KENJIRO, elec. engr., inventor, trading co. exec.; b. Tokyo, Japan, Mar. 15, 1934; s. Rishiro and Masako (Nakata) H.; came to U.S., 1964; B.S., Waseda U., Tokyo, 1958; m. Kuniko Michii, Aug. 15, 1959; children—Misa Hidaka, Miki, Lawrence Kitaro. Import mgr. C. Itoh &

Co., Ltd., Tokyo, 1958-64, mktg. mgr. C. Itoh & Co. (Am.) Inc., San Francisco, 1964-70, Los Angeles, 1970-75, v.p. C. Itoh Electronics Inc., Los Angeles, 1975—. Mem. IEEE. Home: 2040 Pelham Ave Los Angeles CA 90025 Office: 5301 Beethoven St Los Angeles CA 90066

HIDDLESTON, RONAL EUGENE, drilling and pump co. exec.; b. Bristow, Okla., Mar. 21, 1939; s. C.L. and Iona D. (Martin) H.; student Idaho State U., 1957-58; m. Marvelene L. Hammond, Apr. 26, 1959; children—Michael Scott, Mark Shawn, Matthew Shane. With Roper's Clothing and Bishop Redi-Mix, Rupert, Idaho, 1960-61; pres., chmn. bd., gen. mgr. Hiddleston Drilling, Rupert, 1961-66, Mountain Home, Idaho, 1966—. Mem. Mountain Home Airport Adv. Bd., 1968—; hon. mem. Idaho Search and Rescue. Cert. driller, Idaho, Utah. Mem. Nat. Water Well Assn. (cert.), Idaho Water Well Assn. (dir., past pres.), Pacific N.W. Water Well Assn. (dir.), N.W. Mining Assn., Nat. Fedn. Ind. Businessmen, Aircraft Owners and Pilots Assn. Clubs: Masons, Shriners, Nat. 210 Owners, Optimist, Ducks Unltd. Designer 3000-foot drilling rig, 1977. Home: 645 E 17th St N Mountain Home ID 83647 Office: Rt 1 Box 610D Mountain Home ID 83647

HIDY, CHRISTINE MARIE, elementary educator; b. Camp Polk, La., Jan. 5, 1954; d. James William and Lavonne Jean (Pooschke) Hidy. B.S., Bethany Coll., 1976; M.A., U. No. Colo., 1981. Cert. tchr., Colo. First grade tchr. Fremont Sch. Dist. Re-2, Cotopaxi, Colo., 1976-79; fourth grade tchr. Lamar Sch. Dist. Re-2, Colo., 1979-81, fifth grade tchr., 1981—; mem. dist. research and devel. com., planning com. Southeastern Ednl. Conf., Colo. Mem. RAMROD Vol. Ambulance, Cotopaxi, 1979, Republican party caucus, 1972; Christian edn. and youth dir. Grace Luth. Ch., Lamar, 1983—. Named Outstanding Young Educator, Lamar Jaycees, 1982. Mem. Assn. Supervision and Curriculum Devel., Lamar Edn. Assn., Colo. Edn. Assn., NEA, Phi Delta Kappa. Home: 406 W Cedar St Lama CO 81052 Office: Lamar Sch Dist Re-2 1105 S 2d St Lamar CO 81052

HIGASHIONNA, RYOKICHI, state ofcl.; b. Gushikawa City, Okinawa Prefecture, Japan, Sept. 8, 1935; s. Ihan and Nae (Hanashiro) H.; B.S. in Civil Engring., U. Hawaii, 1959; M.S. in Civil Engring., U. Ill., 1964, Ph.D., 1970; m. Hiroko Tamashiro, June 11, 1969; children—Carl, Conrad, Eric, Kendall. Structural engr. Park Assos., Inc., Honolulu, 1962-63; research asst. dept. civil engring. U. Ill., Urbana, 1963-65, 1968-70; partner, project engr. Shimazu, Shimabukuro, and Fukuda, Inc., Honolulu, 1970-73; asst. prof. dept. civil engring. U. Hawaii, Honolulu, 1972-74; structural and research engr. Alfred A. Yee & Assocs., Inc., Honolulu, 1974-75; dep. dir Dept. Transp., State of Hawaii, Honolulu, 1975-77, dir., 1978—. Served with C.E., U.S. Army, 1959-62. Decorated Army Commendation medal; registered profl. engr., Hawaii. Mem. ASCE, Structural Engrs. Assn. Hawaii. Democrat. Office: 869 Punchbowl St Honolulu HI 96813

HIGBEE, JILL ANN, home economist; b. Omaha, Apr. 11, 1954; d. Byron Ellsworth and Dorothy Maude (Kidder) Higbee; B.S. in Home Econs. and Bus., N.Mex. State U., 1976. Extension home agt. S.D. Extension Service, Cheyenne River Reservation, Eagle Butte, 1977-79; asst. mgr. McDonalds Restaurant, Craig, Colo., 1979; free-lance home economist, Rock Springs, Wyo., 1979-83; tchr., cons. Cheyenne River Community Coll., Eagle Butte, 1978-79; asst. mgr. Thrifty Drugstores Inc., Rock Springs, 1980-81; letter carrier U.S. Postal Service, Rock Springs, 1981-83, Tempe, Ariz., 1983—. Named outstanding 4-H agt. Yankton (S.D.) Daily Press, 1979. Mem. Nat. Assn. 4-H Agts., Am. Home Econs. Assn., Nat. Assn. Extension Home Economists, Minne Coujou Sioux Cultural Soc., Jaycees. Republican. Baptist. Club: Order of Eastern Star. Home and Office: PO Box 23874 Tempe AZ 85282

HIGBY, WILLIAM FRANK, rancher; b. Sheridan Wyo., July 26, 1940, s. William David and Edith (Drescher) H.; m. Judith Ann Taska, June 17, 1967; children—Michael James, Heather Lynn. Student Colo. State U., 1958-60. Ranch mgr., owner, Monument, Colo., 1970—. Mayor, Monument, Colo., 1968; mem. dist. 38 Sch. Bd., 1973-79; mem. El Paso County 4-H Found. Served with USN, 1963-69. Clubs: Kiwanis (pres., 1971), Masons.

HIGGINS, CHARLES RUSSELL, JR., agronomist; b. Denver, Apr. 20, 1947; s. Charles Russell and Monte Elizabeth (Hall) H.; m. Judy Vern Karten, June 1, 1969; children—Gennette, Russell. B.S., U. So. Colo., 1969; M.S., Colo. State U., 1973, Ph.D., 1981. Vol. tchr. Peace Corps, Ethiopia, 1969-71; extension agt. agronomy, Grand Junction, Colo., 1973-77; extension state agronomist, seed prodn., Colo. State U., Ft. Collins, 1977-81; agronomist Navajo Agr. Products Industry, Farmington, N.Mex., 1981—. Precinct chmn. Democratic Party, 1975-77. Mem. Am. Soc. Agronomy, Crop Sci. Soc., Epsilon Sigma Phi, Sigma Xi. Club: Ram Flying. Home: 4500 South Side River Rd Farmington NM 87401 Office: PO Drawer 1318 Farmington NM 87499

HIGGINS, CLARK WARREN, video/film systems designer; b. Seattle, Aug. 3, 1950; s. Kenneth W. and Charlotte C. (Quash) H. Student U. Wash., 1968-72. Tech. dir. Sta. KEMO-TV, San Francisco, 1972-74; chief engr. Retina Circus Prodns., San Francisco, 1972-76; video instr. Coll. of Marin, Kentfield, Calif., 1976-77; chief engr. Video Prodn. Services, Berkeley, Calif., 1977-79; electronic cinema designer Zoetrope Studios, Hollywood, Calif., 1979-80; video systems designer Lucasfilm Ltd., San Rafael, Calif., 1980-83; video dir. various events, programs, San Francisco, 1972—. Mem. Audio Engring. Soc., Assn. Computing Machinery, Soc. Motion Picture and TV Engrs. Inventor, co-creator Time Code Video Editing of film and electronic cinema prodn. system, 1978. Home and Office: PO Box 2727 San Anselmo CA 94960

HIGGINS, JOSEPH MICHAEL, telecommunications executive; b. Buffalo, N.Y., Jan. 4, 1947; s. Lenord Carl and Elizabeth Mary (Conroy) H.; m. Jill Cecilia Zirnheld, June 21, 1980; 1 son, Todd F.R. B.A. in Sociology, Notre Dame U., 1974; M.S. in Advt., U. Ill.-Urbana, 1975. Mem. faculty Bryant & Stratton Inst., Buffalo, 1975-76; dir. ops. Buffalo Braves (Nat. Basketball Assn.), 1976-78; acct. exec. Arthur Jaffee Advt., Buffalo, 1978-80; acct. exec. Mountain Bell, Billings, Mont., 1980-83, Am. Bell Inc., Billings, 1983—. Mem. Tumbleweed Foster Parent program. Served with USN Intelligence Corps, 1966-70. Mem. Direct Mail Mktg. Assn., Billings C. of C. Libitarian. Roman Catholic. Home: 533 Yellowstone Ave Billings MT 59101 Office: 550 N 31st St Suite 100 Billings MT 59101

HIGGS, DEWITT A., lawyer; b. Soldier, Idaho, Dec. 13, 1907; s. DeWitt P. and Vina (Reedy) H.; LL.B., Calif. Western U., 1934; m. Florence J. Fuller, Dec. 25, 1929; children—Barbara Lee (Mrs. Whelan), Craig DeWitt. Admitted to Calif. bar, 1934, U.S. Supreme Ct., 1939; partner Robbins & Higgs, 1934-36; asso. Weinberger & Miller, 1936-39; partner Higgs & Fletcher, 1939-40, Miller, Higgs, Fletcher & Glen, 1941-47, Miller, Higgs, & Fletcher, 1947-51, Higgs, Fletcher & Mack, 1951-66, Higgs, Jennings, Fletcher & Mack, San Diego, 1966-71, Higgs, Fletcher & Mack, San Diego, 1971—; city attorney, Chula Vista, Calif., 1940-42, 46-47. Bd. regents U. Calif., 1966-82, chmn., 1968-70, vice chmn., 1970-71. Served as lt. comdr. USNR, 1942-45. Decorated Bronze Star medal. Fellow Am. Coll. Trial Lawyers, Am. Bar Found.; mem. Am. (ho. of dels., 1956-62, chmn. standing com. on aeronautical law 1964-66), San Diego County (dir. 1938-40, pres. 1940) bar assns., State Bar Calif. (bd. govs. 1952-55, pres. 1955, judicial council 1960-63), Am. Judicature Soc., Am. Legion (post comdr. 1947). Clubs: San Diego Country (dir.) (Chula Vista). Home: 12 Toyon Ln Chula Vista CA 92010 Office: 1800 Tower 707 Broadway San Diego CA 92101

HIGGS, LLOYD ALBERT, astronomer; b. Moncton, N.B., Can., June 21, 1937; s. Maxwell Lemert and Reta Mae (Jollimore) H.; m. Kathleen Mary Fletcher, Jan. 15, 1966; children—Kevin, Scott, Michelle. B.Sc., U. N.B., Fredericton, 1958; D.Phil., Oxford U., 1961. Research officer Nat. Research Council Can., 1961—, dir. Dominion Radio Astrophys. Obs., Penticton, B.C., 1981—; research officer Leiden U. (Netherlands), 1964-65. Beaverbrook scholar, 1954-58; Rhodes scholar, 1958-61. Mem. Am. Astron. Soc., Royal Astron. Soc., Can. Astron. Soc., Royal Astron. Soc. Can., Internat. Astron. Union. Contbr. articles to profl. jours. Office: Dominion Radio Astrophys Obs Box 248 Penticton BC V2A 6K3 Canada

HIGHAM, THOMAS ROBERTS, JR., assn. exec.; b. Salt Lake City, Feb. 15, 1940; s. Thomas Roberts and Mildred (Vincent) H.; B.A., U. Utah, 1967; m. Janet Housley, Dec. 3, 1965; children—Jody, Mark. Cross connection specialist Salt Lake City Water Dept., 1965-72; plumbing specialist Utah Div. Health, 1972-77; exec. dir. Internat. Assn. Plumbing and Mech. Ofcls., Los Angeles, 1977—. Mem. Am. Soc. Assn. Execs., So. Calif. Soc. Assn. Execs., U.S. C. of C. Republican. Mormon. Office: 5032 Alhambra Ave Los Angeles CA 90032

HIGHMAN, ARTHUR, management consultant, statistician; b. Bklyn., Aug. 5, 1915; s. Max and Mary (Landis) H.; m. Edith Louise Arkoff, Jan. 2, 1944; children—Mark, Louis, Bruce. B.S. in Chem. Engring., Ill. Inst. Tech., 1935; M.B.A., U. Chgo., 1939, Ph.D., 1954. With Royal Mfg. Co., Army & Navy Munitions Bd., Armour & Co., Standard Oil Calif., 1935-51; sr. statistician Stanford Research Inst. (Calif.), 1951-53; prof. stats. Sch. Bus., U. So. Calif., Los Angeles, 1953-58; mgmt. cons., statistician Arthur Highman & Assocs., Encino, Calif., 1953-65, San Rafael, Calif., 1965-70, Los Altos, Calif., 1970—; 1970; prof. mgmt. Sch. Bus., U. Santa Clara (Calif.), 1968-75. Mem. Am. Statis. Assn., Fin. Execs. Inst. Author: (with Charles de Limur) The Highman-de Limur Hypotheses, 1980, contbr. articles to profl. jours. Office: 27100 Byrne Park Ln Los Altos CA 94022

HIGHSMITH, ROBERT JAMES, economics educator; b. Balt., Mar. 19, 1942; s. Raymond Carl and Anna Loretta (Flavin) H.; m. Sarah Lucille Fogg, Oct. 27, 1979. B.A. Towson State U., 1964; M.A., Purdue U., 1967; Ph.D., Ind. U., 1978. Tchr., Baltimore County Pub. Schs., 1963-67; instr. Price Lab. Sch., U. No. Iowa, 1968-69; dir. Ctr. Econ. Edn., St. Cloud State U., 1969-71; exec. dir. Council Econ. Edn. Md., Towson, 1974-79; exec. dir. Econ. Literacy Council Calif., Long Beach, 1979—; instr. econs. Calif. State U., 1979—. Recipient Award for Excellence in Free Enterprise Edn., Freedom Found. of Valley Forge, 1980. Mem. Nat. Assn. Econ. Educators, Am. Econ. Assn., Western Econ. Assn., Nat. Council Social Studies, Phi Delta Kappa. Contbr. articles to profl. jours. Office: 400 Golden Shore Long Beach CA 90802

HIGHT, JOHN DALE, executive search company executive; b. Dallas, Aug. 20, 1940; s. John Calvin and Mozell Ann Hight; B.S. in Bus. Adminstrn. magna cum laude, Calif. State U.-Northridge, 1975; m. Pamela Marie Ward, Oct. 6, 1961; children—Melody Ann, John Edward. From foreman to gen. mgr. Bendix Corp., Slymar, Calif., 1959-71; material control mgr./mgr. mfg. systems James B. Lansing Sound Inc., Northridge, 1975-78; mfg. mgr./dir. materials Info. Internat., Inc., Culver City, Calif., 1978-79; pres. Search Group, Redondo Beach, Calif., 1979—; dir. McAlliffe & Assocs., Inc. Pres. Sky Blue Homeowners Assn., 1966-67; v.p. Citizens Com. to Complete Coll. of Canyons, 1974-75. Mem. Am. Prodn. and Inventory Control Soc., Canyon Country C. of C. Author papers in field. Office: PO Box 7000-378 Redondo Beach CA 90277

HIGHTOWER, JAMES KAY, computer exec.; b. Kalamazoo, Mar. 22, 1937; s. Raymond L. and Jeanne Doris (Matthews) H.; A.B., Kalamazoo Coll., 1958; M.A., Claremont Grad. Sch., 1967, Ph.D., 1970; m. Sharon Joan Wiley, Sept. 7, 1957; children—Matthew Wiley, Elizabeth Joan. Tchr. math. Pomona (Calif.) Unified Sch. Dist., 1959-61; asst. prof. math. and econs. U. Richmond (Va.), 1964-67; asst. prof. Calif. Poly. State Coll., Pomona, 1967-68; asso. prof. Calif. State U., Fullerton, 1969-76, asso. dean Sch. Bus., 1970-73; asso. dir. div. info. systems Calif. State U.-Los Angeles, 1976—; lectr. Claremont Grad. Sch., 1968—. NDEA fellow, 1960-63. Mem. Assn. for Computing Machinery, Am. Assn. for Artificial Intelligence, Ops. Research Assn. Am. IEEE. Home: 4947 Browndeer Ln Rancho Palos Verdes CA 90274 Office: 5670 Wilshire Blvd Suite 2595 Los Angeles CA 90036

HILBERT, GARY MICHAEL, art director; b. San Francisco, May 14, 1953; s. Albert Joseph and Patricia Ann (Son) H. B.A., Calif. State U.-Chico, 1975. Supr. prodn. Ketchum Communications, San Francisco, 1978-79; art dir. Scroggin & Fischer, San Francisco, 1979-83; ind. advt. art dir. Larkspur, Calif. and San Francisco, 1983—. Artist, City of Larkspur's Ofcl. Poster for its Golden Anniversary, 1980-83. Gary Pierce Meml. Journalism scholar, 1973. Mem. San Francisco Ad Club (Cable Car award 1981, past creative chmn.), Sigma Nu Alumni Assn. Democrat. Presbyterian. Home: 14 Skylark Dr Apt 309 Larkspur CA 94939

HILBERT, RICHARD ANDREW, sociologist, educator; b. Glendale, Calif., Oct. 31, 1947; s. Louis William and Beth Cordelia H. B.A., San Diego State U., 1969; M.S., U. Calif.-Santa Barbara, 1974, Ph.D., 1978. Cert. tchr., Calif. Asst. prof. sociology Gustavus Adolphus Coll., St. Peter, Minn., 1978—; on leave as postdoctoral researcher in psychiat. epidemiology UCLA, 1981—. Contbr. articles to profl. publs. Mem. Am. Sociol. Assn. Home: 1411 Moncado Glendale CA 91207 Office: Sch Pub Health U Calif Los Angeles CA 90024

HILBRECHT, NORMAN TY, lawyer, state legislator; b. San Diego, Feb. 11, 1933; s. Norman Titus and Elizabeth (Lair) H.; B.A., Northwestern U., 1956; J.D., Yale, 1959; m. Mercedes L. Mihopulos, Oct. 24, 1980. Admitted to Nev. bar, 1959, U.S. Supreme Ct. bar, 1963; atty.-asso. firm Jones, Wiener & Jones, Las Vegas, 1959-62; asso. counsel Union Pacific R.R., Las Vegas, 1962; partner firm Hilbrecht & Jones, Las Vegas, 1962-69; pres. Hilbrecht, Jones, Schreck & Bernhard, 1969-83; pres. Norman Ty Hilbrecht & Assocs., Chartered, 1983—; assemblyman Nev. Legislature, 1966-72, minority leader, 1971-72; mem. Nev. Senate, 1974-78; asst. lectr. bus. law Nev. So. U. Mem. labor mgmt. com. NCCJ, 1963; mem. Clark County (Nev.) Democratic Central Com., 1959—, 1st vice chmn.; del. Western Regional Assembly on Ombudsman; chmn. Clark County Dem. Conv., 1966, Nev. Dem. Conv., 1966; pres. Clark County Legal Aid Soc., 1964, Nev. Legal Aid and Defender Assn., 1965—. Served to capt. AUS, 1958-67. Named Outstanding State Legislator, Eagleton Inst. Politics, Rutgers U., 1969. Mem. Am. Judicature Soc., Am., Clark County bar assns., Am. Acad. Polit. and Social Sci., Am. Trial Lawyers' Assn., State Bar Nev., Nev. Trial Lawyers (pres. So. chpt., state v.p.), Fraternal Order Police Assos. (v.p.), Phi Beta Kappa, Delta Phi Epsilon, Theta Chi, Phi Delta Phi. Lutheran. Home: 8601 S Mohawk Las Vegas NV 89118 Office: 723 S Casino Center Blvd Las Vegas NV 89101

HILCOSKE, MARY HELEN, law office manager, legal assistant; b. Wadena, Minn., Apr. 20, 1953; d. Alan J. and Marjorie A. (Gleason) H.; m. Neal D. Fried, Aug. 14, 1982. B.A. in Polit. Sci., U. Alaska, Fairbanks, 1976. With Schaible, Staley, DeLisio & Cook, Inc. and predecessor firm Merdes, Schaible, Staley & DeLisio, Inc., Fairbanks, Alaska, 1970-79, legal sec., office mgr., legal asst., Anchorage, 1980—. Mem. Alaska Assn. Legal Assts. (v.p. 1981-82, pres. 1982—). Office: 943 W 6th Ave Anchorage AK 99501

HILDEBRANDT, DARLENE MYERS, university administrator; b. Somerset, Pa., Dec. 18, 1944; d. Kenneth Geary and Julia (Klim) M.; 1 dau., Robin Adaire. A.B., U. Calif.-Riverside, 1970; M.Librarianship, U. Wash., 1971. Info. specialist I, Acad. Computer Center, U. Wash., Seattle, 1970-71, info. II, 1972-73, library assoc., 1974-75, mgr. computing info. center, 1976—. Mem. Assn. for Ednl. Data Systems, IEEE, Soc. Info. Display, AAUW, Spl. Libraries Assn. Republican. Home: 509 S 323d Pl 15H Federal Way WA 98003 Office: U Wash Acad Computer Center 3737 Brooklyn Ave NE Seattle WA 98105

HILDEBRANDT, DAVID EARL, clin. psychologist; b. Watertown, Wis., May 14, 1943; s. Earl Walter and Lucille Gertrude (Wolff) H.; B.S., U. Wis., 1966; M.A., No. Ill. U., 1969, Ph.D., 1975; m. Karen L. Miller, Aug. 13, 1966. Psychologist, Elgin (Ill.) State Hosp., 1972-74; asst. prof. psychology Idaho State U., 1974-76; dir. S.E. Idaho Family Med. and Ednl. Services, Inc., Pocatello, 1976-77; pvt. practice psychology Family Med. Center, Pocatello, 1977-81, Family Practice Group, Pocatello, 1981—; aux. faculty WAMI Program, U. Wash., 1978—. sponsor Multiple Sclerosis Club. Mem. Am. Psychol. Assn., Idaho Psychol. Assn., Pocatello C. of C. Methodist. Home: 4444 Johnny Creek Rd Pocatello ID 83201 Office: Family Practice Group 1070 Hiline Rd Pocatello ID 83201

HILDING, RONALD FREDERICK, psychiatrist; b. Toledo, Aug. 7, 1938; s. John Frederick and Viola Bessie (Pugh) H. B.S., U. Utah, 1961, M.D., 1965. Intern, Maricopa Gen. Hosp., Phoenix, 1965-66; resident in psychiatry Met. State Hosp., U. Calif.-Irvine, Norwalk, Calif., 1968-71, staff psychiatrist 1971-72; chief psychiat. inpatient service Maricopa Gen. Hosp., Phoenix, 1972-75; practice medicine specializing in psychiatry, Phoenix, 1972—; group mem., sec.-treas. Inst. Human Services, Inc.; mem. staff St. Luke's Behavioral Health Services, 1975—, pres. med. staff, 1982—. Served with M.C., U.S. Army, 1966-68. Decorated Bronze Star. Mem. AMA, Am. Psychiat. Assn., Am. Soc. Adolescent Psychiatry, Maricopa County Med. Soc., Phoenix Psychiat. Council, Ariz. Soc. Adolescent Psychiatry. Office: 525 N 18th St Suite 401 Phoenix AZ 85006

HILDRETH, J. JOANNE, word processing co. exec.; b. Toledo, Apr. 10, 1932; d. M.F. and Nedra Kuppe Maloney; ed. Kellogg Coll., Western Mich. U.; m. James R. Hildreth, July 31, 1952; children—Susan, James, Charles, Diana. Pres., owner Word Processing Specialists, Inc., Novato, Calif., 1973-82, owner, pres. Insight Cons., San Francisco, JJ Cons., Petaluma, Calif.; condr. seminars on office automation-employee motivation. Chmn. planning com. Calif. Pvt. Industry Council; mem. Marin County Employers' Adv. Com. Mem. Internat. Word Processing Assn., East Bay Word Processing Soc., Golden Gate Word Processing Exchange, Marin Bus. Owners Assn., Novato C. of C. (dir.), Profl. Assn. Secretarial Services (adv. bd.). Home: 1612 Bodega St Petaluma CA 94952 Office: Word Processing Specialists Inc 14 Pamaron Way Novato CA 94947

HILKER, WALTER ROBERT, JR., lawyer; b. Los Angeles, Apr. 18, 1921; s. Walter Robert and Alice (Cox) H.; B.S., U. So. Calif., 1942, LL.B., 1948; m. Ruth Margaret Hibbard, Sept. 7, 1943; children—Anne Katherine, Walter Robert III. Admitted to Calif. bar, 1949; partner firm Parker, Milliken, Kohlmeier, Clark & O'Hara, Los Angeles, 1955-75; of counsel firm Pacht, Ross, Warne, Bernhard & Sears, Century City, Calif., 1980—; dir. H. & J. Mabury Co. Bd. dirs. Houchin Found., Virginia Steele Scott Found. Served to lt. USNR, 1942-45. Decorated Bronze Star. Mem. Am., Calif., Orange County, Los Angeles bar assns. Republican. Clubs: Spring Valley Lake Country (Apple Valley, Calif.); Balboa Bay (Newport Beach, Calif.). Home: 21 Rustling Wind Irvine CA 92715 Office: 500 Newport Center Dr Suite 800 Newport Beach CA 92660

HILL, A. FERN PARRISH, home economics teacher; b. Carey, Tex., Dec. 4, 1935; d. John Carl Parrish and Eva May (Farmer) Parrish; m. Clarence Morgan Hill, July 16, 1966. B.S. in Home Econs. Edn., U. Colo., 1960; M.S. in Home Econs. Edn., N.Mex. State U., 1973. Teaching certs., N.Mex., Colo. Sch. lunch cons. N.Mex. Dept. Edn., Santa Fe, 1965-67; tchr. home econs. Santa Fe High Sch., 1965-67, Broomfield (Colo.) High Sch., 1972-82; program mgr. vocat. home econs. State of Colo., 1982—; content area resource tchr. Boulder Valley Schs., 1976-82. Named Outstanding Vocat. Home Econs. Educator of Colo., 1980. Mem. Colo. Vocat. Assn., Phi Kappa Phi, Phi Delta Kappa. Republican. Congregationalist. Author: Fern's Favorites, 1977. Home: 1114 East 7th Ave Circle Broomfield CO 80020 Office: 1313 Sherman St Denver CO 80203

HILL, BARBARA JUNE, owner sheet metal firm, educator, consultant; b. Whittier, Calif., June 23, 1929; d. Percy C. and Vera Lydia (Currier) Fauskin; B.Ed., Whittier Coll., 1950, M.Ed., 1963; Ed.D., U. So. Calif., 1973; 1 son, Scott Lance. Tchr. Calif. schs., 1950-67; asst. prin. La Canada (Calif.) Unified Sch. Dist., 1967, dir. personnel, 1968-71; dir. certificated personnel and labor negotiator Bd. Edn., Valley Oaks Union Sch. Dist., Thousand Oaks, Calif., 1971-73; asst. supt. personnel and bd. negotiator Grossmont Union High Sch. Dist., La Mesa, Calif., 1973-77; partner, v.p., treas. Electronic Metal Fabrication, Inc., San Diego, 1976—; pres. BJ Hill Cons., San Diego, 1976—; pres., partner BarTon Aire, San Diego, 1977—. Recipient Edna Boyd award as Outstanding Woman Educator Calif., 1973; Edith M. Bates award as Outstanding Woman Adminstr. Internat., 1974. Mem. Nat. Speakers Assn., Assn. Calif. Sch. Adminstrs., Calif. Tchrs. Assn., DAR, Delta Kappa Gamma. Club: Internat. Toastmistress (pres. 1980-81). Author: Positive Power People, 1981; author articles. Home: 17661 Boca Raton Ln Poway CA 92128 Office: 7034 Clairemont Mesa Blvd San Diego CA 92121

HILL, CAROL AUDREY, pet care center executive; b. South Gate, Calif., Apr. 19, 1934; d. Verne Thomas and Beatrice Audrey (White) Holman; m. Denton Elmer Hill, Nov. 16, 1957 (div.); m. 2d, James Arthur Pennington, Feb. 21, 1981 (div. 1983). Student Butte Coll., Calif., 1974-77. Cert. adult edn. tchr., Calif. Display advt. mgr. J.C. Penney, Chico, Calif., 1954-60; owner, operator Chico Pet Shop (now Carol's Dog-Cat Care Ctr.), 1961—; owner, instr. Dog Obedience Sch., Chico, 1963—; owner operator Designs by Carol, Chico, 1979—. Recipient numerous awards in field. Mem. Greater Chico C. of C., Nat. Assn. Female Execs., Nat. Dog Groomers Assn. Am. Democrat. Author: Dog Obedience Instructors Training Manual, 1983; host TV show Care of Cats, 1964-65. Home: 282 Camino Norte Chico CA 95926 Office: 973-Q East Ave Chico CA 95926

HILL, DIANE SELDON, psychologist, educator; b. Mpls., Sept. 17, 1943; d. Earl William and Geraldine (LeVeille) Seldon; m. David Reuben Hill, May 14, 1966; children—Anna Marion, Jason David. B.A., Mt. Holyoke Coll., 1965; M.A., U. Minn., 1969, Ph.D., 1974. Registered psychologist, Colo.; clin. diplomate Am. Bd. Profl. Psychology. Instr., counselor Student Counseling Bur., U. Minn., Mpls., 1968-70, advisor women's programs, 1970-71; instr. psychology Augsburg Coll., Mpls.,

1970-71; counselor, instr. humanities Emma Willard Sch., Troy, N.Y., 1972-75; dir. counseling Colo. Women's Coll., Denver, 1976-77; pvt. practice psychology, Denver, 1979—; asst. clin. prof. psychology Health Scis. Ctr., U. Colo., Denver, 1979—; vice chmn. Colo. Bd. Psychol. Examiners, 1981. Bd. dirs. Park Hill Elem. Sch. Assn., 1976-78. NDEA fellow, 1967; Rockfeller Family Fund grantee, 1973. Mem. Am. Psychol. Assn., Rocky Mountain Psychol. Assn., Colo. Psychol. Assn. (dir. 1979-81), Mt. Holyoke Club Colo. (pres. 1978-80), Women's Forum Colo. Democrat. Episcopalian. Club: Vail (Colo.). Racquet. Contbr. articles to profl. jours. Home: 2052 Bellaire St Denver CO 80207 Office: 2250 S Albion St Denver CO 80222

HILL, DONALD DAVID, agronomist; b. Fountain City, Wis., June 9, 1904; s. John Edward and Elizabeth (Faulds) H.; 1 dau., Donna Marsh. B.S. in Agr., Ocean State U., 1925; M.S., Kans. State U., 1927; Ph.D., Cornell U., 1936. Mem. agronomy staff Oreg. State U., Corvallis, 1927-59, dept. head, 1943-59; market devel. mgr. Western Wheat Assoc., India, 1960-62; exchange prof. Rutgers U., 1951; seed cons. U.S. Dept. Agr., 1957, 59. Served with AUS, 1917-19. Fellow Am. Soc. Agronomy. Republican. Presbyterian. Author: Grassland Seeds, 1956. Home: 640 NW 35th St Corvallis OR 97330

HILL, DONALD GARDNER, geophysicist; b. Lansing, Mich., May 17, 1941; s. Donald and Florence Beatrice (Waldron) H.; B.S., Mich. State U., 1963, Ph.D., 1969; m. Susan Williams Mitroff, Aug. 6, 1983; 1 son, Jonathan Alan. With Chevron Oil Field Research Co., La Habra, Calif., 1969-78; research geophysicist Chevron Resources Co., San Francisco, 1978-82; sr. devel. geologist Chevron Overseas Petroleum Inc., 1982—; lectr. in field. Bd. dirs. Orange County chpt. Nat. Hemophilia Found., 1975-78, pres., 1976-78. NASA trainee, ship, 1963-66. Mem. Soc. Exploration Geophysicists (reviewer), Soc. Petroleum Engrs. (reviewer), Soc. Profl. Well Log Analysts (reviewer), Am. Geophys. Union, Am. Geol. Inst., European Assn. Exploration Geophysicists, Sigma Xi. Contbr. articles to profl. jours.

HILL, ESTHER JANE, ceramicist; b. Defiance, Ohio, Feb. 7, 1934; d. Richard Maywood and Angela Mable (Burkmeyer) Zedaker; m. John Darrel Hill, Dec. 14, 1948; children—Colleen Kay, John Darrel. Mgr. ceramic craft shop Spl. Services, U.S. Army, Kagnew Sta., Asmara, Ethiopia, 1969-71; owner, mgr. Hill Haven Ceramic Ctr., Huachuca City., Ariz., 1976—. Mem. Huachuca Art Assn., Nev. Ceramic Assn., Internat. Ceramic Tchrs. Assn. (cert. 1980), Nat. Ceramic Mfrs. Assn. (cert. 1978), Nat. Ceramic Assn. (apprentice judge 1981, cert. 1980). Democrat. Ceramics presented to the emperor of Ethiopia by U.S. Army. Home: 719 Mountain View St Huachuca City AZ 85616 Office: Hill Haven Ceramic Ctr 209 Huachuca Blvd Huachuca City AZ 85616

HILL, FREDRIC WILLIAM, educator, nutritionist; b. Erie, Pa., Sept. 2, 1918; s. Vaino Alexander and Mary Elvira (Holmstrom) H.; B.S., Pa. State U., 1939, M.S., 1940; Ph.D., Cornell U., 1944; m. Charlotte Henrietta Gummoe, Apr. 1, 1944; children—Linda Charlotte, James Fredric, Dana Edwin. Research asst. Pa. State U., 1939-40, Cornell U., 1940-44; head nutrition div. research labs. Western Condensing Co., Appleton, Wis., 1944-48; asso. prof., then prof. animal nutrition Cornell U., 1948-59; prof. poultry husbandry, chmn. dept. U. Calif. at Davis, 1959-65, prof. nutrition, 1965—, chmn. dept. nutrition, 1965-73, asso. dean Coll. Agr., 1965-66, asso. dean research, 1976-80, coordinator internat. programs, 1976-80. Mem. subcom. hormonal relationships and applications com. on Animal Nutrition, NRC, 1953, subcom. poultry nutrition, 1953-74, mem. Food and Nutrition Bd., 1975-78; commr. Calif. Poultry Improvement Commn., 1959-65; participant 8th Easter Sch. Agrl. Scis., U. Nottingham (Eng.), 1961, World Conf. Animal Prodn., Rome, Italy, 1963, U.S. AID-Nat. Acad. Sci. Seminar on Protein Foods, Bangkok, 1970, USIA Asia Seminars on Food, Population and Energy, 1974-75; Japan Soc. Promotion Sci. vis. prof. Nagoya U., 1974-75; vis. scientist FDA, 1975, Nutrition Inst., USDA, 1975; cons. French Ministry Agr., 1982. Fellow Danforth Found., 1938; recipient Nutrition Research award Am. Feed Mfrs. Assn., 1958, Newman Internat. Research award British Poultry Assn., 1959; Guggenheim Found. fellow, 1966-67; Pa. State U. Alumni fellow, 1983. Fellow AAAS, Poultry Sci. Assn. (Research prize 1957, Borden award 1961); mem. Soc. Exptl. Biology and Medicine, Nutrition Soc. (Gt. Britain), Council Biology Editors, World Poultry Sci. Assn., Am. Inst. Nutrition (councillor 1982—), Am. Inst. Biol. Scis., Am. Soc. Animal Sci., Am. Chem. Soc., Sigma Xi, Phi Eta Sigma, Gamma Sigma Delta, Phi Kappa Phi, Delta Theta Sigma, Gamma Alpha. Clubs: Cosmos (Washington); El Macero (Davis, Calif.). Contbr. articles profl. jours. Editorial bd. Poultry Sci. Jour., 1960-64; editorial bd. Jour. Nutrition, 1964-68, editor, 1969-79. Home: 643 Miller Dr Davis CA 95616

HILL, GEOFFREY MICHAEL, pschotherapist; b. Barstow, Calif., Oct. 24, 1950; s. William A. and Harriett (Anthony) H. A.A., Orange Coast Coll., 1973, B.A. magna cum laude, So. Calif. Coll., 1975; M.A., Pepperdine U., 1980. Pastor Calvary Chapel, Costa Mesa, Calif., 1978-80, instr. Calvary Bible Coll., Twin Peaks, Calif., 1978; pvt. practice in counseling and psychotherapy, Santa Ana, Calif., 1980—; curator Bob Siemon Art Gallery; instr., lectr. in field. Founder, div. La Résistance, art orgn. Republican. Editor Last Times mag., 1979-80; contbr. articles to gen. interest mags. Home and Office: 2513 S Deegan Dr Santa Ana CA 92704

HILL, GERALD WILLIAM, JR., hosp. adminstr.; b. Akron, Ohio, Oct. 15, 1945; s. Gerald William and Olive Louise (Gaylord) H.; B.A., Miami U., Oxford, Ohio, 1966; M.B.A., Columbia U., 1968. Mktg. analyst Crown Zellerbach, San Francisco, 1972-74; mktg. dir. Children's Hosp., San Francisco, 1975-80; mktg. dir. French Hosp., San Francisco, 1980—. Chmn. bd. mgr. Richmond YMCA, San Francisco, 1980—; bd. dirs. San Francisco Met. YMCA, 1980—. Office: 4131 Geary Blvd San Francisco CA 94118

HILL, HELEN LOUISE, county official; b. Marceline, Mo., May 22, 1938; d. Gordon and Kathleen Mae (Olinger) Courtney; children—Jacob, Jeffrey, John J., Jesse V., Joseph J., Jennifer N. Grad., Parks Bus. Coll., 1958. Field worker Schlumberger Well Survey, Inc., Cortez, Colo., 1958-59; title clk. Adams County Clk. and Recorder, Commerce City, Colo., 1966-69; mgr. Hill Hauling Service, East Lake, Colo., 1965-74; pub. trustee Adams County, Brighton, Colo., 1975-79, treas., 1979—. Mem. Commn. on Women, State of Colo., 1973-79; mem. Colo. State Democratic Central Com., 1972-74; mem. Adams County Democratic Central Com., 1970-79; mem. Colo. Dem. 2d Congl. Dist. Central Com., 1983—; chmn. Colo. Dem. State Senate Dist., 1983—. Recipient Appreciation awards Gov. State Colo., 1978, 77; Outstanding Women's award Adams County Democratic Women's Caucus, 1978-79. Mem. Met. Treas. Assn., Bus. and Profl. Women's Assn., Colo. Treas. Assn., Colo. Pub. Trustee's Assn., Adams County Mental Health Assn., NOW, RSVP Adv. Council. Democrat. Lutheran. Clubs: Adams County Jane Jefferson; Adams County Democratic Women's Caucus. Home: 3225 E 124th Ave Denver CO 80241 Office: 450 S 4th Ave Brighton CO 80601

HILL, IRVING, fed. judge; b. Lincoln, Nebr., Feb. 6, 1915; s. Nathan and Ida (Ferder) H.; A.B., U. Nebr., 1936; LL.B., J.D., Harvard, 1939; D.H.L., Hebrew Union Coll., 1976; m. Maydee Taylor, June 23, 1939; children—Lawrence N., Steven C., Richard F. Admitted to Nebr. bar, 1939, D.C. bar, 1942, Calif. bar, 1946; practiced in Beverly Hills, Calif., 1946-61; spl. asst. to U.S. atty. gens. Biddle and Clark, Dept. Justice, Washington, 1942-46; legal adviser U.S. del. to UNESCO, 1946; judge Calif. Superior Ct., 1961-65; U.S. dist. judge, Los Angeles, 1965—, chief judge U.S. Dist. Ct. for Central Dist. of Calif., 1979-80. Pres. Jewish Fedn.-Council Greater Los Angeles, 1960-63; v.p. Council wish Fedns. and Welfare Fund, 1962-65; dir. gen. bd. United Way Los Angeles County, 1963-72. Served to lt. (j.g.) USNR, 1944-46. Mem. Phi Beta Kappa. Office: US Courthouse 312 N Spring St Los Angeles CA 90012

HILL, JAMES NOAH, physician; b. Fulton, Mo., Aug. 19, 1908; s. Noah F. and Alice (Gingrich) H.; B.S., Warrensburg State Tchrs. Coll., 1933; M.S., U. Kans., 1934; M.D., Creighton U., 1938; postgrad. Johns Hopkins, 1943; m. Mabel Timken, Feb. 28, 1958. Intern, St. Mary's Hosp., Kansas City, Mo., 1938-39; pvt. practice, Hutchinson, Kans., 1940-42; staff mem. Meml. Hosp., St. Francis Hosp., Colorado Springs, Colo.; med. examiner FAA. Served as lt. col., AUS, 1942-46, 5028 Medical Unit, lt. col. Res. (Ft. Carson, Colo.), 1958—. ETO. Mem. AMA, Colo. Med. Soc., El Paso County Med. Soc., Assn. Am. Physicians and Surgeons, Aerospace Med. Assn. Home: 1212 Hermosa Way Colorado Springs CO 80906 Office: 13 S Tejon St Colorado Springs CO 80906

HILL, JAMES ROWLAND, real estate developer, architect; b. Oneida, Tenn., July 12, 1935; s. Ransom Powell and Isabella O. Hill B.A., Columbia U., 1954; M.A., U. Colo., 1980; M.A. in Architecture, Columbia Pacific U., 1982. Lic. gen. contractor, real estate developer, Colo. Gen. mgr. Am. Savs. and Loan, 1964-65; sales mgr. Witkin Homes Inc., Denver, 1966-67; exec. v.p. Golden Key Bldg. Corp., Denver, 1968-71; pres. Regency Homes Inc., Englewood, Colo., 1971—. Served with USAR, 1958-67. Mem. Nat. Assn. Home Builders, SAR. Republican. Presbyterian. Clubs: Heather Ridge Country, Aspen Flying, Sports Car Am., Vail Athletic.

HILL, JEFFREY JOHN, accountant, state senator; b. Pasadena, Calif., May 16, 1948; s. Norman B. and Frances C. (Gies) H.; B.S. in Bus. Adminstrn., U. Ariz., 1972; m. Nancye Jeanne Corbett, June 27, 1970. Sr. acct. ASARCO, Inc., Sahuarita, Ariz., 1972—; ptnr. Hill & Mears, accts., Tucson, 1974—; mem. Ariz. Senate from Dist. 9, 1979—. Chmn., Dist. 10 Republican Com., 1973-75, Dist. 9, 1976. Recipient Scholarship award Alpha Kappa Psi, 1971. Mem. Am. Soc. Tax Cons.'s, Nat. Assn. Tax Consultors. Roman Catholic. Office: 4633 E Broadway Suite 126 Tucson AZ 85711*

HILL, JOHN CONNER, art dealer, publisher; b. Phila., Feb. 17, 1945; s. George H. and Anne (Lux) H.; m. Linda Bowers Sheppard, Feb. 16, 1980; children—May Elizabeth, Matthew Leo, James Leo Conner. B. Indsl. Design, Pratt Inst., Bklyn., 1968. Asst., Cosanti Found., Paradise Valley, Ariz.; with Paolo Soleri, 1972-77; exhibited fabric assemblage applique, Southwest Biennial, Internat Folk Art Mus., 1970, N.Mex. Biennial, 1971, Ariz. Photography Biennial, 1969; art instr. Rough Rock Demonstration Sch., Navajo Nation, Ariz., 1968-69, Ariz. Crafts Ann., Tuscon Art Mus., 1977; art dealer Am. Indian and Am. folk art, pub., Kokopelli Press, art reprodns., posters, notecards, 1972—. Mem. Indsl. Designers Soc. of Am. Office: PO Box 33666 Phoenix AZ 85067

HILL, JOHN GILMORE, geologist; b. El Paso, Tex., Oct. 25, 1937; s. John Elbert and Boone (Gilmore) H.; B.S., Eastern N.Mex. U., 1960; M.S., U. Wis., 1962, Ph.D., 1967; m. Patricia Griffiths Thiel, Aug. 15, 1964; children—Wendy Lee, Kirsten Lynn. Geologist, Amoco Prodn. Co., Denver 1964-72; geologist, tech. supr., div. geologist, geologic specialist Tenneco Oil Co., Denver, 1972-75; geologist Peppard Souders & Assos., Denver, 1975-76; exploration mgr. Patrick Petroleum Co., Denver, 1976-80; cons. petroleum geologist, Denver, 1980—. NSF fellow, 1963-64. Mem. Rocky Mountain Assn. Geologists, Am. Assn. Petroleum Geologists, Wyo. Geol. Assn., Mont. Geol. Soc., N.Mex. Geol. Soc., AAAS, Colo. Hist. Soc. Sigma Xi. Clubs: Southwest Denver Optimist (pres. 1979-80), Denver Petroleum. Office: 1228 15th St Suite 211 Denver CO 80202

HILL, JOHN LEE, optometrist, educator; b. Willcox, Ariz., Apr. 25, 1953; s. Austin William and Gladys Edwina Hill; A.A., Cochise Coll., 1973; student U. Ariz., 1973-74; B.S. in Visual Sci., Pacific U., 1980, O.D., 1980. Lic. optometrist, Ariz. Practice optometry, Tucson, 1980—; instr. contact lenses Pima Coll. Cochise Coll. athletic scholar, 1971. Mem. Am. Optometric Assn., Ariz. Optometric Assn., So. Ariz. Optometric Assn., Omega Epsilon Phi. Republican. Mormon. Office: 1718 W Ajo Way Tucson AZ 85713

HILL, JOHN WORTH, lawyer; b. Portland, Oreg., May 22, 1925; s. Jacob Frederick and Virginia (Thomas) H.; m. Mary Joan Bueermann, Feb. 27, 1981; children—Lawrence L., Steven F. B.S., U. Oreg., 1947, J.D., 1949. Bar: Oreg. 1949. Practiced, Portland; ptnr. Miller, Nash, Yerke, Wiener & Hager, 1954—. Bd. dirs. Western Pension Conf., St. Vincent Hosp. Found., Portland, 1978—; committeeman Columbia Pacific council Boy Scouts Am., 1968-72. Served with USNR, 1943-46. Mem. ABA, Oreg. Bar Assn., Multnomah County Bar Assn. Republican. Clubs: Arlington, Waverley Country, Multnomah Athletic. Office: 111 SW 5th Ave Portland OR 97204

HILL, KENNETH STANLEY, nut company manager; b. Woodland, Calif., Jan. 8, 1939; s. Evart Grant and Florence Marie (Orser) H.; m. Imogene Blue, Feb. 4, 1962; children—Julie, Kenneth; m. Jeanne Keiko Uyetake, Sept. 23, 1973. Ed. pub. schs., Richmond, Calif. Salesman, United Grocers Ltd., Richmond, 1963-67; sales coffee div. Procter & Gamble Distbn. Co., San Francisco, 1967-70, unit mgr., Honolulu, 1970-80; sales mgr. Mauna Loa Macadamia Nut Corp., Honolulu, 1980—. Served with U.S. Army, 1959-63. Mem. Sales and Mktg. Execs. Honolulu. Club: Rotary (Honolulu).

HILL, KRIS ALFRED, optometrist; b. Corvallis, Oreg., Jan. 29, 1955; s. Donald Ramon and Mary Dorothy (Ingram) H.; m. Merry Dawn Milczarek, Mar. 20, 1974; children—Matthew L., Angela D., Kristal L., Nicole M. Student U. Utah, 1972-74; B.S., Pacific U., 1976, O.D., 1978. Pvt. practice of optometry, Tooele, Utah, 1980—. Served to lt. USN, 1978-80. Mem. Utah Optometric Assn. (trustee, 1981—), Am. Optometric Assn., Beta Sigma Kappa. Democrat. Mormon. Home: 724 Kingston St Tooele UT 84074 Office: 300 S Main St Tooele UT 84074

HILL, RALPH H., diversified company executive; b. Miller, Mo., 1914. Chmn., Alfred M. Lewis Inc., Riverside, Calif.; pres., dir. Alfred M. Lewis Properties; dir. M & M; chmn., chief exec. officer Orange Empire Fin. Inc. Bd. dirs. Riverside Community Hosp. Office: Alfred M Lewis Inc 3021 Franklin Ave Riverside CA 92520*

HILL, RAYMOND JOSEPH, agribus. exec.; b. Chanute, Kans., May 4, 1935; s. Raymond Joseph and Emma Leona (Arthurs) H.; Asso. in Engring., Coffeyville (Kans.) Coll., 1955; M.B.A., U. Denver, 1977; m. Bettie Anne Handshumaker, Mar. 2, 1957; children—David, Dianne, Todd, Scott, Jennifer. Field engr. Phillips Petroleum Co., Bartlesville, Okla., 1957-59; design engr. Thiokol Chem. Corp., Brigham City, Utah, 1959-60; tech. supr. Hercules Chem. Corp., Salt Lake City, 1960-68; project mgr. aerospace div. Ball Corp., Boulder, Colo., 1968-70, plant mgr. and v.p. mfg. metal container div., Findlay, Ohio and Denver, Colo., 1970-78, pres. agrl. systems div., Westminster, Colo., 1978—; dir. Navaho Agrl. Products Industries, United Energy Devel.; mem. policy adv. com. to Office of U.S. Trade Rep., 1980—. Mem. Am. Ordnance Assn., Soc. Tool Engrs., Irrigation Assn. Republican. Episcopalian. Club: Rotary. Home: 2575 Briarwood Boulder CO 80303 Office: 9300 W 108th Circle Westminster CO 80020

HILL, SUSAN FORBES, civic worker, rancher; b. Oakland, Calif.; d. Robert Parsons and Dorothy (Adams) Forbes; m. James M. Wells, Sept. 9, 1967; children—Jesse, Lilla, Elizabeth, Jason; m. Anthony Russell Hill, July 8, 1978. B.A., U. Calif.-Berkeley, 1967, postgrad. in bus. adminstrn. Mem., officer bd. dirs., trustee Easter Seal Soc., Oakland, 1968-75, World Coll. West, 1977-82, Head-Royce Sch., 1977-82, Jr. League of Oakland-East Bay, Inc., 1972—, Children's Hosp. Med. Ctr., 1971—, Jr. Ctr. Arts and Sci., 1978-82; internat. host Com. of Calif., 1981—; v.p. Children's Hosp. Found., Oakland, 1983—; pres. Alameda County Children's Interest Commn., 1978—; mem. Piedmont Gen. Plan Com. Recipient Rosalie Stern award U. Calif., 1981—; service recognition award Nat. Ski Patrol System, 1981; Woman of Yr., Children's Hosp. Med. Ctr., 1973. Clubs: Claremont Country, Women's Athletic. Office: PO Box 13176 Oakland CA 94661

HILLER, SUSAN LEE, electronic office equipment company executive; b. Long Beach, Calif., Oct. 23, 1947; d. Robert L. and Mary Louise (Ackerson) Hill. B.A., U. Wyo., 1969. Sec., Div. Plastic Surgery, Stanford (Calif.) Med. Ctr., 1971-77; office mgr. Plastic Surgery Assocs., Eureka, Calif., 1977-79, Electronic Office Equipment Co., Eureka, 1979—. Mem. Bus. and Profl. Women. Contbr. articles to profl. jours. Office: 1480 Myrtle Ave Eureka CA 95501

HILL, THOMAS CLARKE, VIII, bus. exec.; b. Broken Bow, Okla., Mar. 16, 1920; s. James Clifford and Lessie K. H.; student in mech. engring. U. Okla., 1938-39, Purdue U., 1956-57; student So. Meth. U., 1959-60, La. State U., 1963-67; D.D. (hon.), Inst. Life Ins. Mktg.; m. Arlene Mae Wertz, Jan. 7, 1967; 1 son, Thomas Clarke. Owner, operator Hill Oil Co., Long Beach, Calif., 1946-49; sales mgr. Custom Chem. Co., Redondo, Calif., 1948-52; v.p. Am. Ins. Digest, Chgo., 1952-55, owner, pub., Lincolnshire, Ill., 1955—; fin. dir., treas. Village of Lincolnshire, 1975-76; chmn., chief exec. officer Hilson Fin. Corp., Rocklin, Calif., 1976—, Hilson Mgmt. Corp., Rocklin, 1978—; dir. ops. United Nat. Life, Nat. Capital Life; dir. 10 corps.; lectr. univs.; cons. to industry. Served with USNR, World War II. Named hon. ins. commr. State of Okla.; Man of Yr., Home State Corp.; other awards. Republican. Clubs: Millionaires', Century, Gaslight, Execs.; Masons (Long Beach, Calif.); Shriners (Sacramento); Order Eastern Star (Evanston, Ill.). Author: The Profit Sharing Contract, 1968; The Case of New Life Insurance Companies, 1969; Life Insurance as an Investment, 1970; Recruit or Die, 1971; contbr. numerous articles to industry jours., univ. and corps. publs.

HILL, THOMAS LANSDALE (DANNY), advertising and public relations executive; b. Balt., Nov. 3, 1916; s. Howard Clarence and Cornelia Houston (Lansdale) H.; m. Mary Margaret Bumb, June 29, 1952; children—Thomas Lansdale, Elizabeth Allen Aschenbrener, Mary Gunning, Nancy Lansdale. B.A., St. John's Coll., 1941. Reporter Santa Barbara (Calif.) News-Press, 1946-48; assoc. prof., athletic news dir. San Jose (Calif.) State U., 1948-57; liaison officer TV com. Nat. Collegiate Athletic Assn., N.Y.C., 1954, assoc. dir. service bur., 1957-63; ptnr. Darien, Russell & Hill, San Jose, 1963—. Exec. dir. Pacific div. Continental Football League, 1967-69; commr., 1968; commr. Calif. Football League, 1978; mem. San Jose City Sports Commn., 1965, San Francisco Bay Area Olympic Com., 1968. Pres. Santa Clara Valley Music and Arts Found.; v.p. San Jose Civic Light Opera; exec. com. Goodwill Santa Clara County, Santa Clara County Heart Assn. Served with USNR, 1942-46. Mem. Santa Clara Valley Assn Advt. Agys. (dir.), Nat. Sports Library (dir.), Greater San Jose Advt. Golf Assn. (dir.). Clubs: San Jose Country (dir. srs. assn.), Rotary (dir.). Episcopalian. Author: (with others) Complete Handbook of Sports Scoring & Record Keeping, 1974. Home: 826 Cherrystone Dr Los Gatos CA 95030 Office: 3003 Moorpark Ave Suite 200 San Jose CA 95128

HILLENDAHL, WESLEY HARRINGTON, cons. economist; b. Palo Alto, Calif., May 27, 1921; s. John A. and Laura D. Hillendahl; A.B. in Engring., Stanford U., 1942, M.B.A., 1949; m. Marilyn Godshall, Oct. 11, 1965; children—Gregory, Robin, Sandra, William, Nancy, Eric. Aero. engr. NASA, Moffett Field, Calif., 1942-44; sales engr., then dist. engr. Linde Air Products div. Union Carbide Corp., San Francisco, 1949-54; indsl. economist Stanford Research Inst., 1954-57; market research dir. aerophysics devel. div. Curtiss Wright Corp., Santa Barbara, Calif., 1957-58; cons. economist, 1959-66; with Bank of Hawaii, Honolulu, 1966-81, v.p., dir. econs. div., 1967-81; cons. economist, fin. adviser, 1981—. Chmn. Hawaii Council on Revenues, 1980—; chmn. research com. Hawaii Visitors Bur., 1967-72, 77-78; trustee Am. Future, Inc., 1974—, Found. Econ. Edn., 1968—; adv. bd. Salvation Army, 1982—. Served as officer USNR, 1944-47. Decorated Air medal. Mem. Am. Statis. Assn., Com. Monetary Research and Edn., Nat. Assn. Bus. Economists, Urban Land Inst., Small Bus. Council Am., Hawaii Econ. Assn. (pres. 1969-70), Hawaii C. of C. (exec. com. 1975-77, dir. 1975-78), Mfrs. Assn. Hawaii (pres. 1976-77), Waikiki Improvement Assn. (pres. 1974-75). Republican. Club: Honolulu Rotary (dir. 1980—). Office: PO Box 25665 Honolulu HI 96825

HILLER, JANET HUTCHINSON, cooperative extension youth specialist; b. Estherville, Iowa, Nov. 9, 1940; d. Frank Edward and Gladys Mae (Mauss) Hutchinson; m. Larry Keith Hiller, June 9, 1963; children—MarshalKay, David Brian. B.S. in Home Econs. Edn., Iowa State U., 1962; postgrad. SUNY-Cortland, 1971; M.A. in Home Econs., Wash. State U., 1977. Extension home economist Iowa Coop. Extension Service, Madison County, 1962-63, Boone County, 1963-64; grad. teaching asst. dept. child and family studies Wash. State U., Pullman, 1974-77, asst. prof., 1978-79, coop. extension 4-H/youth specialist, 1979—. E.O. Holland travel grantee, Wash. State U., 1976; subcontractor HEW grant, Am. Home Econs. Assn., 1978. Mem. Nat. Assn. 4-H Extension Agts., Am. Home Econs. Assn., Wash. Home Econs. Assn., Pullman Home Econs. Assn., Assn. Faculty Women Wash. State U., Phi Upsilon Omicron, Omicron Nu, Delta Delta Delta. Republican. Methodist. Contbr. articles in field to publs. Office: 313 Agrl Scis Wash State U Pullman WA 99164

HILLER, STANLEY, JR., tool co. exec.; b. San Francisco, Nov. 15, 1924; s. Stanley and Opal (Perkins) H.; ed. Atuzed Prep. Sch.; U. Calif., 1943; m. Carolyn Balsdon, May 25, 1946; children—Jeffrey, Stephen. Dir. Helicopter div. Kaiser Cargo, Inc., Berkeley, Cal., 1944-45; organized Hiller Aircraft Corp. (formerly United Helicopters, Inc.), Palo Alto, Calif., 1945, became pres. and gen. mgr., pres., 1950-64 (co. bought by Fairchild Stratos 1964), became pres. of five operating divs.; resigned as exec. v.p., dir., mem. exec. com. Fairchild Hiller Corp., 1965; chmn. bd., chief exec. officer Reed Tool Co., Houston; chmn. bd. Baker Internat. Corp., 1975, now chmn. exec. com.; partner Hiller Investment Co.; dir. Benicia Industries, Boeing Co., Crocker Nat. Corp., ELTRA Corp. Recipient Fawcett award, 1944; Distinguished Service award Nat. Def. Transp. Soc., 1958; named 1 of 10 Outstanding Young Men U.S., 1952. Hon. fellow Am. Helicopter Soc.; mem. Am. Inst. Aeros. and Astronautics, Am. Soc. of Pioneers, Phi Kappa Sigma. Office: Bldg 2 Suite 260 3000 Sand Hill Rd Menlo Park CA 94025*

HILLES, CAROLE MARIE, moving co. exec.; b. Medford, Oreg., Mar. 13, 1948; d. John Wallace and Phyllis Adele (Allen) Freeland; B.A., U. Redlands, 1970. Market support rep. IBM, Cleve., 1970-72, sales rep. office products, mgr. copier program, 1973-75; sales rep. Xerox Corp., Detroit, 1975-76, regional cons., Chgo., 1976-77, sales tng. mgr. Office Products Hdqrs., Dallas, 1977-79, office products sales mgr., Orange, Calif., 1979-80, dist. sales mgr., 1981-82; regional sales mgr. Bekins Moving and Storage, Glendale, Calif., 1982, dir. nat. account sales,

1982—. Sponsor, Christian Children's Fund, India. Mem. Internat. Wildlife Assn. Home: 2155 Pami Circle Orange CA 92667 Office: 910 Grand Central Ave Glendale CA 91201

HILLIARD, CATHRYN ANN, county ofcl., public affairs mgmt. cons.; b. Los Angeles, July 14, 1942; d. Curtis H. and Eva M. (Jessner) Sampson; A.A., Los Angeles Pierce Coll., 1963; B.A. in Polit. Sci., Calif. State U., Hayward, 1976; cert. U. Calif., Berkeley, 1975; m. Harold James Hilliard, July 6, 1963; children—Frederick Roy, Matthew David. Sec. to congressman from Ind., 1966; legis. aide to senator from Ind., 1966-69; public affairs officer Assn. of Bay Area Govts., Berkeley, Calif., 1970-76; public participation coordinator San Francisco Bay Region Wastewater Solids Study, Oakland, Calif., 1976-79; public participation coordinator Orange and Los Angeles counties Water Reuse Study, Los Angeles, 1979—; guest lectr. career devel. U. Calif., Berkeley, 1977; guest lectr. environ. mgmt. Solano Community Coll., Calif., 1979; public affairs mgmt. cons., 1979—. Mem. public info. com. Am. Cancer Soc., 1976-78. Mem. Am. Soc. Public Adminstrn. (dir. San Francisco sect. 1978), Calif. Water Pollution Control Assn., Nat. Assn. Govt. Communicators, Nat. Assn. County Info. Officers. Clubs: Commonwealth, Town Hall. Home: 3569 Bendigo Dr Rancho Palos Verdes CA 90274 Office: care Met Water Dist of So Calif 1111 Sunset Blvd PO Box 54153 Los Angeles CA 90054

HILLIARD, SARAH (SALLY), insurance company official, educator; b. Whittier, Calif., May 14, 1940. d. Albert Ralston and Elisabeth Kelly (Selix) Said; m. Frank Pappalardo, Feb. 12, 1964; 2 children; m. Robert E. Hilliard, Dec. 14, 1975. Student Golden Gate U., 1971-74, Orange Coast Coll., 1975-78, Santa Ana Coll., 1978-82, Saddleback Community Coll., 1980—. Cert. profl. ins. woman; accredited adviser of ins. With various ins. agys., Berkeley and East Bay Area, Calif., 1967-75; with various agys., So. Calif., 1975; account exec., analyst Infantino & Co., of Irvine, Santa Ana, Calif., 1982—; instr. ins. classes local community colls.; seminar speaker, moderator, panelist. Active Com. of 4000, Newport Beach, Calif. Mem. Ind. Ins. Agts. and Brokers Calif. (dir.), Ind. Ins. Agts. and Brokers Orange County, Newport Irvine Profl. Assn., Nat. Assn. Ins. Women, Irvine C. of C. (charter). Republican. Mem. United Ch. of Christ. Home: 17852 Gillman St Irvine CA 92715 Office: Infantino & Co of Irvine 1750 E Deere St Santa Ana CA 92705

HILLMAN, AARON WADDELL, educational and psychological consultant, poet; b. Chaffee, Mo., 29, 1926; s. Basil Emory and Erthel Dora (Pearman) H.; B.A. in Social Sci., Calif. State U., San Francisco, 1965; M.A. in Edn., U. Calif., Santa Barbara, 1973, Ph.D. in Edn., 1973; m. Rosemary Theresa Witherow, Aug. 6, 1953; 1 son, David Emory. Tchr., Santa Maria (Calif.) High Sch., 1965-68, Dos Pueblos High Sch., Santa Barbara, Calif., 1969-81; pres. Confluent Edn. and Devel. and Research Center, Santa Barbara, 1974-81, dir. ednl. adminstrs. program in confluent edn. 1976-77; pvt. practice bibliotherapy; now pres. Bibliotherapy, Inc.; cons. univs. and schs. U.S., Can., Mex., Spain; therapist. Mem. Assn. Supervision and Curriculum Devel., Nat. Council Social Studies, Am. Ednl. Research Assn., Assn. Humanistic Psychology. Writer, poet; contbr. chpts. to books in field; editor Confluent Edn. Jour., Santa Barbara Book Rev.; contbr. articles to publs. Home: 833 Via Granada Santa Barbara CA 93103 Office: 3887 State St Suite 7 Santa Barbara CA 93105

HILLMAN, CHARLES EDWARD, mfg. co. exec.; b. Erie, Pa., Dec. 24, 1951; s. Lawrence Warren and Helen Violet (Anderson) H.; B.S., M.I.T., 1974; M.E., U. Wis., 1980; m. Gaytha Traynor, Dec. 26, 1971; children—Jessica, Kathryn, Laura. Planner, Southeastern Wis. Regional Planning Commn., Waukesha, 1974-75, asso. planner, 1975-76, sr. planner, 1976-77; engr. A.O. Smith, Milw., 1977-78, sr. engr., 1978-79, mgr. graphic systems, 1979-80; training mgr. G.E. Calma, Sunnyvale, Calif., 1980-81, dir. customer support, 1981—. Registered profl. engr., Wis. Mem. Am. Inst. Planners, Nat. Computer Graphics Assn. Republican. Presbyterian. Home: 3615 Olympic Ct N Pleasanton CA 94566 Office: 352 E Java St Sunnyvale CA 94086

HILLMAN, GARY LEE, educator; b. Fairmont, Minn., Feb. 18, 1939; s. Lawrence Carl and Mabel G. (Kern) H.; B.A., Gustavus Adolphus Coll., 1961; M.S., Mankato State U., 1967; M.A., U. Denver, 1969; Ph.D., U. Colo., 1977; m. Judith K. Gallman, June 27, 1964; children—Gary Lee, Stephani Lane. Tchr., Denver Public Schs., 1962—; part time instr. U. Colo., Denver, 1980—. Experienced tchr. fellow U. Denver, 1968-69; recipient Denver Disting. Tchr. award, 1978. Mem. NEA, Nat. Staff Devel. Council, Nat. Middle Sch. Assn., Colo. Edn. Assn., Colo. Schoolmasters Club, Assn. for Supervision and Curriculum Devel., Phi Delta Kappa. Republican. Lutheran. Contbr. articles to popular mags. Home: 6710 S Washington St Littleton CO 80122 Office: 3800 York St Denver CO 80205

HILLS, FRANK STANLEY, lawyer; b. San Francisco, May 12, 1935. J.D., Stanford U., 1963. Admitted to Calif. bar, 1964, U.S. Dist. Ct. for No. Dist. Calif., 1964, Eastern Dist., 1973, Central Dist., 1973, So. Dist., 1974, U.S. Ct. Appeals bar, 1964, U.S. Supreme Ct. bar, 1969; def. atty. So. Pacific Transp. Co., San Francisco, 1963-67; partner firm Connally & Hills, San Francisco, 1967-69; pres. Frank S. Hills, P.C., San Francisco, 1969—; instr. Hastings Coll. Law, 1972-73. Served with U.S. Army, 1958-60. Mem. Am., Calif., San Francisco (dir.), Los Angeles trial lawyers assns. Author: Experts and Resources Available to Consumers and Their Lawyers, 3d edit., 1981; Handling the Strict Liability Products Case, 1980; (with others) Anatomy of a Personal Injury Trial, 1981, Negotiating the Personal Injury Case, 1981; Personal Injury Preparation and Personal Injury Trial, 1983; contbr. articles to law jours. Won landmark case Barker vs Lull, 1978. Office: Hills Bldg 2506 Clay St San Francisco CA 94115

HILTON, BARRON, hotel exec.; b. 1927; s. Conrad Hilton. Founder, pres. San Diego Chargers, Am. Football League, until 1966; v.p. Hilton Hotels Corp., 1954, pres., chief exec. officer, 1966—, chmn., 1979—, also dir.; mem. gen. adminstrv. bd. Mfrs. Hanover Trust Co., N.Y.C. Address: care Hilton Hotels Corp 9880 Wilshire Blvd Beverly Hills CA 90210*

HILTON, GILBERT WALTER, mfg. co. exec.; b. San Jose, Calif., Sept. 27, 1920; s. Starr Gilbert and Anita Pauline (Zolezzi) H.; student indsl. mgmt. LaSalle Extension U., 1941-43; student mech. engring. San Jose State Coll., 1950-59; m. Melba L. Frasher, Oct. 31, 1941; 1 dau., Judy Diane. With Joshua A. Hendy Iron Works, Sunnyvale, Calif., 1941-46; company acquired by Westinghouse Electric Co., 1946, area mgr. missile launching and handling equipment, 1975—. Served with USNR, 1937-41. Mem. Soc. Mfg. Engrs. Republican. Club: Masons. Home: 729 Millstream Dr San Jose CA 95125 Office: Box 37 Hendy Ave Sunnyvale CA 94088

HILTON, HART DALE, commercial interiors company executive; b. Los Angeles, May 24, 1913; s. Lewis Dale and Nora Elizabeth (Hart) H.; m. Doris King, May 20, 1939; 1 dau., Margaret Pamela. B.S. in Engring., U. So. Calif., 1936; diploma Naval War Coll., 1955; M.A., Nat. Def. U., 1963. Commd. officer U.S. Navy, 1937, advanced through grades to capt., 1956, commd. officer USS Mauna Kea, 1959-60, Aircraft Carrier USS Lexington, 1960-62, asst. to chief naval ops. for Joint Chiefs of Staff matters, 1963-65, ret., 1965; v.p. alumni affairs U. So. Calif., Los Angeles, 1967-81; v.p., div. mgr. Cannell & Chaffin Comml. Interiors, Inc., Los Angeles, 1981—; guest lectr. World Geography, U. So. Calif., 1975-81. Adv. bd. Los Angeles Philanthropic Soc. Recipient Alumni Merit award U. So. Calif., 1966, Alumni Service award, 1982. Mem. Am. Arbitration Assn., Aircraft Owners and Pilots Assn., Navy League, Assn. Naval Aviation, World Affairs Council, Newcomen Soc., U. So. Calif. Assocs. (life). Republican. Clubs: Rotary, Wilshire Country. Home: 1240 Clubhouse Dr Pasadena CA 91105

HILTS, JOHN WARREN, financial corporation executive; b. Los Angeles, May 14, 1923; s. Joseph Earle and Lillian Mary (Gibson) H.; student Glendale Coll., 1941-42, U. Calif. at Los Angeles, 1942-43; B.S., U. So. Calif., 1949; M.S., Calif. State U., Los Angeles, 1972; m. Phyllis Ruth Overton, June 27, 1945; children—Jill Robyn, Judith, Nancy Suzanne Hilts Dunsire. Dist. mgr. Pacific Finance Corp., Los Angeles, 1949-60; partner Overton Labs., Hollywood, Calif., 1960-62; dist. mgr. Pacific Finance Loans, Los Angeles, 1962-70; v.p. Transam. Financial Corp., Los Angeles, 1970—. Active Jr. Achievement Program, United Fund. Bd. dirs. Glendale chpt. Am. Field Service, 1965—. Served with USNR, 1943-47. Mem. Calif. (dir. pub. relations 1970—), Ariz. (dir. 1970—) loan and finance assns., N.Mex. Consumer Loan and Finance Assn. (dir. 1970—, chmn. pub. affairs 1970—), Wash. Consumer Finance Assn. (dir. 1970—), Am. Legion. Club: Oakmont Country (Glendale, Cal.). Contbr. articles to profl. jours. Single and multi-engine comml. pilot. Office: 1150 S Olive St Los Angeles CA 90015

HILTY, ROBERT EDWARD, software systems specialist; b. Lexington, Nebr., Sept. 21, 1941; s. Robert Raymond and Ruby Viola (Jewett) H.; student U. So. Colo., 1965-68; m. Susan Gail George, Dec. 28, 1963; children—Jennifer Suzanne, Julie Ann. Computer operator, programmer, analyst Wolf Research & Devel. Corp., Boston, 1961-68; computer programmer, analyst Fed. Civil Service, Colorado Springs, Colo., 1968-70, chief USAF nat. space hist. data system, 1970-74, chief computer systems requirements div., asst. to dir. NORAD computer systems, Cheyenne Mountain Complex, Colo., 1974-77; dep. dir. ADP resources N.Am. Air Def. Command, Peterson AFB, Colo., 1977-82, chief software systems requirements and testing, 1982—. Recipient Meritorious Civilian Service award Dept. Air Force; Spl. Achievement award Aerospace Def. Command (7); Merit award Dept. Air Force (8). Mem. Assn. Computing Machinery, Armed Forces Communications and Electronics Assn. Methodist. Office: 1520 E Willamette Colorado Springs CO 80909

HIMBER, ROBERT, mag. editor; b. N.Y.C., Oct. 9, 1944; s. Richard and Nina Enamar (MacDougald) H.; B.A., Friends World Coll., 1971; M.A., Calif. State U., 1973. Bd. dirs. Family Resource Center, Boulder, Colo., 1974; instr. psychology Calif. State U., Humboldt, Arcata, Calif., 1972-73; instr. communication U. Colo., Boulder, 1976-77; sr. field editor Omega Group, Ltd., Boulder, 1975-81; mng. editor Survive, Boulder, 1981-82; editor Self Reliance Digest, Santa Fe, 1983—. Served with U.S. Army, 1965-67. Decorated Cross of Gallantry (Vietnam), recipient N.Y. State Scholar Incentive award, 1967, 68. Mem. Nat. Rifle Assn., Assn. Former Intelligence Officers. Contbr. article to various publs. Office: 1406 Luisa St Suite 2 Santa Fe NM 87501

HIMENO, EDWARD TORAO, child psychiatrist; b. Honolulu, May 15, 1926; s. Bunzo and Irene Yoshiko (Kudo) H.; B.A., LaSierra Coll., 1950; M.D., Loma Linda U., 1958; m. Miyoko Kusuhara, June 5, 1952; children—Cheryl Aimee, Guy Randall. Intern, Los Angeles County U. So. Calif. Med. Center, 1958-59, resident gen. psychiatry, 1959-62, child psychiatry, 1963-65; practice medicine specializing in child psychiatry, Monterey Park, Calif., 1965—, Cerritos, Calif., 1983—; assoc. prof. psychiatry Loma Linda U. Sch. Medicine, 1967-77, assoc. clin. prof. psychiatry, 1977-80, dir. child psychiatry services, 1967-77; dir. child psychiatry unit Riverside (Calif.) Gen. Hosp., 1972-81; med./clin. dir. Children's Residential Care and Intensive Day Treatment Ctr., Riverside County, Calif., 1981-83; mem. child psychiatry staff Los Angeles County, U. So. Calif. Med. Center, 1962 63, 65 67; dir. Inst. Family and Group Therapy, Riverside, 1977-80; cons. Inland Adolescent Clinic, San Bernardino, Calif., 1973-83, Desert Community Mental Health Services, Indio, Calif., 1977-80; cons. child and adolescent unit mental health services San Bernardino County Gen. Hosp., 1973-75; cons. adolescent and young adult program Patton (Calif.) State Hosp., 1968-73, Boy's Republico, Chino, 1970-74, adolescent and adult unit Ingleside Mental Health Center, Rosemead, 1962-81; bd. dirs. Ingleside Mental Health Center, Rosemead, 1974-81, 2d v.p., 1975-81; chmn. med. adv. profl. symposiums, Riverside, Calif., 1979—. Mem. City of Monterey Park Human Relations Commn., 1970. Dist. chmn. Alhambra Monterey Park council Boy Scouts Am., 1969-70. Served with AUS, 1944-45. Recipient several hons. by various profl. and civic groups. Mem. Japanese Am. Med. Assn. (v.p. 1969, 81-82, sec. 1979-80, pres.-elect 1983—). Home: 1142 Ridgeside Dr Monterey Park CA 91754 Office: 823 S Atlantic Blvd Monterey Park CA 91754 12506 South St Cerritos CA 90701

HIMSL, MATHIAS ALFRED, state senator Mont.; b. Bethune, Sask., Can., Sept. 17, 1912; s. Victor S. and Clara C. (Engels) H.; came to U.S., 1913; B.A., St. John's U., Collegeville, Minn., 1934; M.A., U. Mont., 1940; m. Lois Louise Wohlwend, July 18, 1940; children—Allen, Marilyn Himsl Olson, Louise Himsl Robinson, Kathleen, Judith Himsl Choury. Tchr., supt. schs., Broadus, Mont., 1934-45; sec. Himsl Wohlwend Motors, Inc., Kalispell, Mont., 1945-68; pres. Skyline Broadcasters, Inc., radio sta. KGEZ, Kalispell, 1958—; part-time instr. Flathead Valley Community Coll., 1969-72; mem. Mont. Ho. of Reps. from Flathead County, 1966-72, Mont. Senate from 9th dist., 1972—. Chmn. Flathead County Republican Com., 1952-64; del. Rep. Nat. Conv., 1964; bd. govs. ARC, 1956-59. Roman Catholic. Club: Elks. Office: 4th Ave E and Center St Kalispell MT 59901

HINCHCLIFF, RICHARD WILBER, engring. cons.; b. Dayton, Wash., Apr. 7, 1939; s. Wilber Louis and Helen Louise (Jackson) H.; student Wash. State U., 1958-59; B.S. in Agrl. Engring., Calif. State Poly. Coll., 1963; m. Denise Kay Price, Sept. 3, 1960; children—Jerry Dennis, Brian Keith. Field mechanic Green Giant Co., summers 1955-60; mechanic McConnel Motors, summers 1961-63; with Merritt Equipment Co., Henderson, Colo., 1961—, welder, engr. trainee, 1963-64, engr., 1964-65, chief engr., 1965-69, co-mgr., chief engr., 1969-71, engring. mgr., 1971-74, Portland plant mgr., 1974-80, v.p. engring., sec. bd. advisors, 1980—; dir. Merritt Profit Sharing Plan. Founder, pres. Blue Berry Hill Homeowners Assn., 1977-79; mem. PTSA, 1977-80; com. chmn. Boy Scouts Am., 1978-79; pres. Bowling League, 1972-73. Recipient James F. Lincoln Welding/Design award, 1964; named Man of Yr., Merritt Equipment Co., 1972; cert. expert witness, trailer engr. Mem. Soc. Automotive Engrs. (dir. Oreg. chpt. 1978-70), Truck Trailer Mfg. Assn. Republican. Methodist. Clubs: Ft. Vancouver Coin (life, pres. 1971-73), Elks. Patentee in field. Home and Office: Route 1 15225 N Lipan St Broomfield CO 80020

HINCHLIFFE, BRUCE GRUETTNER, university development officer, consultant; b. Los Angeles, Dec. 24, 1935; s. Stephen Freeman and Katherine Morris (Gruettner) H.; m. Sandra Lynn Swan Lund, May 15, 1976; children—Gregory, Robert, David, Benjamin, Briana. B.A. in Econs., Stanford U., 1957, M.B.A., 1959. Lectr. in mktg. Butler U., Indpls., 1960-61; asst. to mgr. Hawley Smith Co., Palo Alto, Calif., 1962-63; staff assoc. pace campaign Stanford (Calif.) U., 1963-64, program dir. ann. fund, 1964-67, asst. to v.p. for fin., 1967-68, dir. ann. fund, 1968-72, assoc. campaign dir., Campaign for Stanford, 1972-77, assoc. v.p. for devel., 1977-79, dir. corp. relations, 1979-82, acting v.p. for devel., 1982-83, assoc. v.p. for devel., dir. devel., 1983—; cons. fundraising to non-profit orgns. Served to lt. Fin. Corps, U.S. Army. Democrat. Presbyterian.

HINCKLEY, LAURA L., risk management executive, author; b. Chgo., Mar. 15, 1951; d. Donald B. Donkersloot and Abigail L. Bayer. B.A. (scholar), North Central Coll., 1972; M.B.A., No. Ill. U., 1975. C.P.C.U., Pa. Successively plant acct., prodn. estimator, prodn. planner, prodn. planning supr., staff asst. corp. ins., acting risk mgr. Container Corp. Am., Chgo., 1971-78; account exec., asst. v.p. Fred S. James & Co. of Ill., Chgo., 1978-81; corp. risk mgr. Avery Internat., Pasadena, Calif., 1981—; risk mgmt. instr. Ins. Sch. Chgo., 1978-80, edn. com., 1979-81. Risk mgmt. adviser Los Angeles Olympic Organizing Com., mem. citizen's adv. commn., 1982—. Inst. Soc. C.P.C.U.s (IIA Inst. award, 1977), Risk and Ins. Mgmt. Soc. (industry services liaison com.). Club: Los Angeles Athletic. Author: Risk Control, Student Study Guide for Risk Management Program, 1978; (with Robert E. Kuntz) Risk Financing, Student Study Guide for Risk Management Program, 1978. Office: Avery Internat 150 Orange Grove Blvd Pasadena CA 90291

HINDS, JAMES ROLAND, historian; b. Okmulgee, Okla., Dec. 8, 1937; s. Roland D. and Ina Alice (Richardson) H.; student Am. U., 1956-58; A.B., Washington U. St. Louis, 1960; M.A., So. Ill. U., 1964; m. Yolanda Cruz C., Aug. 2, 1980. Historian, Frederick Douglass Home, Nat. Capital Parks East, Washington, 1966-69; staff historian U.S. Army Aviation Systems Command, St. Louis, 1969-70, USAF Tactical Fighter Weapons Center, Nellis AFB, Nev., 1970—. Sec., Assn. for Preservation of Las Vegas Fort, 1976-78; treas. Preservation Assn. Clark County, 1978, v.p., 1979-80, 81-82, exec. bd., 1980-82, pres., 1982—; acting treas. So. Nev. Hist. Soc., 1976-77, v.p., 1977-80, sec., 1981—. Served with U.S. Army, 1964-66. Mem. Am. Mil. Inst., Council on Abandoned Mil. Posts, Nat. Trust for Historic Preservation. Author ofcl. histories, reports, articles in various jours.; Bulwark and Bastion. Home: 4062 Calimesa St North Las Vegas NV 89110 Office: USAF Tactical Fighter Weapons Center Nellis AFB NV

HINDS, VAN SULLIVAN, moccasin mfg. co. exec.; b. Cleburne, Tex., Dec. 3, 1913; s. John Lee and Myrtle (Izora) S.; B.B.A., Tex. Tech. U., 1935; m. Gladys Moore, Feb. 19, 1938; children—Mary Elizabeth Hinds Powell, Lawrence Lee. Credit mgr. CIT Corp., Amarillo and Lubbock, Tex., 1937-41; partner, owner No. N.Mex Wholesale Co., Taos, 1946-54; pres. Taos Leather Crafts, Inc., 1954-75; chmn. bd., 1975—; chmn. bd. Roca del Mar Inc., Roca del Mar, S.A.; pres. Los Tres Amigos Inc.; dir. 1st State Bank, Taos, La Paleta, S.A., Honduras. Served to lt. USNR, 1941-45. Mem. Taos C. of C. (past dir.). Republican. Clubs: Taos Lions (past pres.), Masons. Address: Box 708 Taos NM 87571

HINDS, WARREN TED, ecologist; b. Ukiah, Calif., Nov. 16, 1936; s. Edward Heaton and Ethel Lourena (Ingram) H.; m. Judy Alice Twitchell, Nov. 18, 1961; children—Randall, Gary, Tara; m. 2d, Nancy René Legato, Feb. 1, 1980. B.S., Northwestern U., 1959; M.S., U. Wash., 1967, Ph.D., 1974; postgrad. Fuller Theol. Sem., 1979. Micrometeorologist Gen. Electric, Hanford Site, Richland, Wash., 1961-67; ecologist Battelle Meml. Inst., Pacific N.W. Labs, 1965-75; land reclamation specialist U.S. Dept. Energy, Washington, 1976-77; sr. ecologist Battelle Meml. Inst., Pacific N.W. Labs., 1978—. Walter P. Murphy Found. scholar, 1954-59; recipient Indsl. Press Award Engring., 1959; Bausch & Lomb Sci. Prize, 1954; Battelle Meml. Inst. fellow, 1973. Mem. AAAS, Am. Inst. Biol. Scis., Am. Sci. Affiliation, Ecol. Soc. Am., N.W. Sci. Assn. Evangelical. Contbr. numerous articles to profl. jours. Home: 2404 Olympia St Richland WA 99352 Office: PO Box 999 Richland WA 99352

HINES, DONALD DOUGLAS, municipal official, program planner; b. Tacoma, May 25, 1946; s. Forrest B., Jr., and Glenna Rowena (Ray) H.; m. Myrna-Lou Eleanor Ostrom, Oct. 4, 1948; children—Paul Douglas, Philip Daniel. B.A., Seattle Pacific U., 1968; M.A. in Journalism, Marshall U., 1972; M.B.A., U. Puget Sound, 1981. Tchr., Tacoma Pub. Schs., 1972; info. specialist Model Cities Program, City of Tacoma, 1972-75; instr. Seattle Pacific U., 1973-74; community services specialist community devel. dept. City of Tacoma, 1975-82, sr. program devel. specialist, 1982—. Mem. Kans. Del. Tribe of Indians, Inc., 1974—; precinct del. Pierce County Republican Com., 1980, mem. Neighborhoods U.S.A., 1983—. Served with U.S. Army, 1968-71. Decorated Army Commendation medal; acad. scholar, 1964-68, 80. Methodist. Contbr. to Grassroots; A Manual for Neighborhood Organizations, 1981. Home: 4214 N Mullen St Tacoma WA 98407 Office: 740 St Helens Ave Suite 1036 Tacoma WA 98402

HINES, JAMES MONROE, mechanical engineer; b. Long Beach, Calif., Oct. 23, 1939; s. Charles Clifford and Helena Mae (Lilla) H.; m. Geraldine Janette Rucker, May 17, 1963; children—Dessa Ann, David James. B.S., Calif. State U.-Long Beach, 1971; M.Engring., UCLA, 1977. Design engr. stamping div. Norris Industries, Los Angeles, 1960-61; project engr. Apollo program Rockwell Internat. Co., Downey, Calif., 1962-70; partner auto repair bus., Bell, Calif., 1970-73; sr. project engr. space shuttle program Rockwell Internat., Downey, 1973-74; sr. mech. engr. nuclear fuel cycle Fluor Engrs. and Constructors Inc., So. Calif. div., Irvine, 1974—; partner UIT Cons.'s, 1970-73. Webelos leader Boy Scouts Am. Mem. Internat. Material Mgmt. Soc. (dir. Los Angeles chpt. 1974-76), Am. Nuclear Soc., Fluor Polit. Action Com. Republican. Baptist. Club: Fluor Suprs., Toastmasters, Masons, Scottish Rite, Shriners (pres.). Home: 9412 Dewey Dr Garden Grove CA 92641 Office: 3333 Michelson Dr Irvine CA 92715

HINES, MARY EMMA, educator; b. Bolton, Miss., July 5, 1934; d. Walter and Emma Mae (Johnson) Harvey; B.S., Jackson State Coll., 1958; B.S., UCLA, 1966; postgrad. Lavern U., Los Angeles; m. Theodore Hines, Dec. 3, 1960; children—Emma Corenia, Herbert Lee, Harold Louis, Joel Lynn, Janee Latricia. Tchr., Hinds County, Miss., 1958-64, Los Angeles City Schs., 1966—; partner H & H Tire Service, South Gate, Calif., 1972—. Pres. Mission True Love Dist. Assn., Los Angeles, 1981—; Sunday Sch. tchr., Bible tchr., youth pres. New Covenant Bapt. Ch. Mem. United Tchrs. Los Angeles, Nat. Edn. Assn., Nat. Council Tchrs. Assn., Gompers Faculty Assn., English Council Los Angeles. Home: 16032 Indian Creek Rd Cerritos CA 90701 Office: 9019 Long Beach St South Gate CA 90280

HINKINS, JOHN-ROGER, educator, consultant, clergyman; b. Rains, Utah, Sept. 24, 1934; s. Parley and Erma Alice (Davis) H. B.S. in Psychology, U. Utah, 1958; teaching cert., UCLA, 1961; D.D., Neotarian Coll. Theology and Philosophy, 1968; Ph.D., Koh-E-Nor U., Los Angeles, 1981. Cert. secondary life tchr., Calif. Ordained to ministry The Ch. of the Movement of Spiritual Inner Awareness. Tchr. English, lit., pub. schs., Calif., 1960-71; tchr., lectr., counselor Movement Spiritual Inner Awareness, Inc., Los Angeles, with extensive travel throughout U.S., Europe, Australia, Mexico, S.Am., Can., N.Z. and Asia, 1967—; lectr., tchr., founder, Ministerial Services in Action, Calif., 1971; lectr. tchr., founder, chmn. bd., chief exec. officer, pres. Prana Theol. Sem. and Coll. of Philosophy, Calif.; mem. faculty, guest lectr. and tchr.-trainer, founder Koh-E-Nor U., Los Angeles; chmn. bd., chief exec. officer, founder, pres. Golden Age Edn., Inc., Calif.; tchr., developer and condr. seminars, workshops and trainings; trainer faciliators for INSIGHT Transformational Seminars, div. Golden Age Edn.; pastor; condr. numerous seminars on personal growth and devel., U.S., Mexico, Australia, Eng., France, Chile, Venezuela, Colombia; chmn. bd., chief exec. officer, founder Baraka, A Holistic Ctr. for Therapy and Research; Heart Felt Found., John-Roger Found., Joint Venture Workshops and Seminars; founder, cons., internat. services dir. Atman Travel Agy.; pres. Ever-Sol Dome, Inc.; dir. Canyon Studios; exec. producer NOW Prodns.; exec. producer That Which Is, weekly series for cable TV;

spiritual dir. Gota de Miel, Ch. of Movement of Spiritual Inner Awareness, Inc.; mem. world adv. bd. Unity-in-Diversity Council; cons. VIVA-TV; radio and TV apperances, including seminar series on Cable TV program That Which Is. Recipient Outstanding Tchr. of Yr. award State Calif., Outstanding Service award Ch. of the Movement of Spiritual Inner Awareness. Mem. Assn. Humanistic Psychology, Inst. for Devel. Human Studies (Colombia, founding), Author numerous books, the most recent being: The Way Out Book, 1980; author monthly series of 92 discourses; condr. semianrson audio and video tapes; contbr. numerous articles to various publs., including The Movement Newspaper, INSIDE INSIGHT, Sci. 66 Mind. Office: 2101 Wilshire Blvd Santa Monica CA 90403

HINKLE, BETTY RUTH, educational administrator; b. Atchison Kans., Mar. 18, 1930; d. Arch W. and Ruth (Baker) Hunt; m. Charles L. Hinkle, Dec. 25, 1950 (div.); children—Karl, Eric. B.A., U. Corpus Christi, 1950; M.S., Baylor U., 1956; M.A., U. North Colo., 1972, Ed.D., 1979. Cert. tchr. Tex., 1950, Mass., 1961, Colo., 1966; cert. adminstr., Colo., 1976. Mem. faculty Alice (Tex.) Independent Sch. Dist., 1950, Waco (Tex.) Ind. Sch. Dist., 1951-52, 1953-58; Hawaii Pub. Schs., Oahu, 1952-53, Newton Pub. Schs., Newtonville, Mass., 1962-63; Colorado Springs (Colo.) Pub. Schs., 1966-75; cons., exec. dir. spl. projects unit Colo. State Dept. Edn., Denver, 1975—; mem. technology com. Colorado Dept. Edn.; alt. foreman Denver Grand Jury, 1983. Recipient Dept. of Edn. Specialists award Colo. Assn. Sch. Execs., 1979. Mem. Am. Assn. School Adminstrs, Colo. Assn. Sch. Execs (coordinating council, 1976-79, v.p. dept. of edn. specialists 1974-75, pres. 1975-76), Assn. for Supervision and Curriculum Devel., Colo. Personnel and Guidance Assn., Nat. Assn. Adminstrs. State and Fed. Programs, Phi Delta Kappa. Republican. Home: 550 E 12th Ave Apt 903 Denver CO 80203 Office: 201 E Colfax Denver CO 80203

HINNERICHS, TERRY DEAN, air force officer, research structural engineer; b. Norfolk, Nebr. Nov. 30, 1946; s. Gilbert Herbert and Nina S. (Peterson) H.; m. Cheryle Anne Newton, Nov. 15, 1969; children—Todd Newton, Christopher Michael. B.S., U. Nebr., Lincoln, 1969; M.S., Colo. State U., 1973; Ph.D. Air Force Inst. Tech., Dayton, 1980. Registered profl. engr., Colo., 1974. Mech. engr. Aircraft Engine div. Gen. Electric, Evendale, Ohio, 1969-70; commd. U.S. Air Force, 1973, advanced through grades to capt., 1977; sect. chief structural response sect. Air Force Weapons Lab., Kirtland AFB, Albuquerque, 1980—. Coach, Am. Youth Soccer Orgn., 1981-82, YMCA basketball, 1981-82; sec. YMCA Indian Guides, 1981-82. Decorated Air Force Commendation medal with oak leaf cluster. Mem. AIAA, ASCE, Acad. of Mechanics, Pi Tau Sigma, Tau Beta Pi, Phi Kappa Phi. Contbr. articles to profl. jours. Home: 3420 Tahoe St NE Albuquerque NM 87111 Office: AFWL/NTES Kirtland AFB Albuquerque NM 87117

HINRICHS, KIT, graphic designer; b. Torrance, Calif., Nov. 15, 1941; s. Gordon Keith and Virginia Louise Hinrichs; student Art Center Coll. Design, 1958-63; m. Linda Evelyn Davis, Dec. 18, 1965; 1 son, Christopher Sejong. Design asst. Designers 3, N.Y.C., 1964; designer Reba Sochis, Inc., N.Y.C., 1965; designer, prin. Russell & Hinrichs, N.Y.C., 1965-72, Hinrichs Design Assocs., N.Y.C., 1972-76; prin. Jonson Pedersen Hinrichs & Shakery, San Francisco, Conn. and N.Y.C., 1976—; instr. Sch. Visual Arts N.Y.C., Acad. Art Coll. San Francisco; guest lectr. Stanford Design Conf., U. Calif., Davis, Calif. Coll. Arts and Crafts, San Francisco U.; designer spl. issue McCall's mag., 1976; designer, illustrator Time mag. covers, 1970-71; design dir. Assets mag., 1979; designer Warner Communications Ann. Report, 1975-79, Crocker Nat. Corp. Ann. Report, 1977-81; represented in permanent collection Mus. Modern Art. Served with USMCR, 1963-69. Recipient awards N.Y. Art Dirs. Club, Am. Inst. Graphic Arts, Soc. Communicating Arts, Soc. Publ. Designers, Ad Club N.Y., Art Dirs. Club Phila., C.A. Ann., Fin. World; named one of most important graphic designers of past 25 years Idea Mag., 1978. Mem. Am. Inst. Graphic Arts (chmn. Calif. 1980-82), Inst. Graphic Design San Francisco. Office: 620 Davis St San Francisco CA 94111

HINSHAW, ERNEST THEODORE, JR., former financial executive, sports executive; b. San Rafael, Calif., Aug. 26, 1928; s. Ernest Theodore and Ina (Johnson) H.; A.B., Stanford U., 1951, M.B.A., 1957; m. Nell Marie Schildmeyer, June 24, 1952; children—Marc Christopher, Lisa Anne, Jennifer, Amy Lynn. Staff asst. to pres. Capital Research and Mgmt. Co., Los Angeles, 1957-58, dir. planning, 1967-68; fin. analyst Capital Research Co., Los Angeles, N.Y.C., 1958-68, v.p., 1962-71, mgr. N.Y. office, 1962-66; dir., exec. v.p. Am. Funds Service Co., Los Angeles, 1968-69, pres., 1969-72, chmn., 1972-82; dir., pres. Capital Data Systems, Inc., Los Angeles, 1971-73, chmn., 1973-79; v.p. Capital Group, Inc., Los Angeles, 1973-83; sr. v.p. Growth Fund of Am., 1973-74, pres., 1974-76, dir., 1974—, chmn. bd., 1976-82; sr. v.p. Income Fund Am., 1973-74, pres., 1974-76, dir., 1974—, chmn. bd., 1976-82; dir. Capital Research & Mgmt. Co.; mem. guest faculty Northwestern U. Transp. Center, 1965-66; mem. ops. com. Investment Co. Inst., 1970-74. Mem. Los Angeles Olympic Organizing Com., commr. yachting 1984 Olympic Games, 1980—. Served to 1st lt. USMCR, 1951-53. Mem. Soc. Airline Analysts (sec. 1965-66), Fin. Analysts Fedn. (chmn. air transport sub-com. 1966-67), Los Angeles Soc. Fin. Analysts, N.Y. Soc. Security Analysts, Am. Statis. Assn., Town Hall Calif., Nat. Kite Class (pres. 1968-69), Lido 14 Internat. Class Assn. (pres. 1978-79), Assn. Orange Coast Yacht Clubs (commodore 1976), U.S. Yacht Racing Union (dir. 1980-81), So. Calif. Yachting Assn. (commodore 1979), B.O.A.T., Inc. (dir. 1977-81), Pacific Coast Yachting Assn. (dir. 1979-80). Democrat. Clubs: Wall St. (N.Y.C.); Univ. (Los Angeles); Lido Isle Yacht (commodore 1973) (Newport Beach, Calif.); St. Francis Yacht (San Francisco); Ft. Worth Boat. Office: 3822 Campus Dr Newport Beach CA 92660

HINSVARK, DON GEORGE, guidance counselor; b. Helena, Mont., Mar. 27, 1934; s. Almer Burton and Carmen Christene (Houston) H.; m. Jacqueline Rica Sarfati, July 10, 1958; children—Jon, Timothy, Michael, Symone. B.A. in Geology, U. So. Calif., 1956; M.A. in Ednl. Counseling, San Diego State U., 1967. Tchr. elem. schs., San Diego, 1962-65, dist. counselor, 1965—. Coach N.Y.C. Mil. League champion basketball team, 1957, San Diego Jr. Olympic champion age group swim team, 1962; mgr. Coronado Sr. Little League champion team, 1977. Served with USN, 1956-61, to capt USNR, 1966-77. Mem. San Diego City Schs. Student Services Assn. (pres.), NEA, Calif. Personnel and Guidance Assn., San Diego Personnel and Guidance Assn., Naval Res. Assn., Res. Officers Assn., Navy League. Office: Guidance Dept 4100 Normal St San Diego CA 92103

HINTZ, KENNETH ALAN, graphic designer; b. Mt. Clemens Mich., Feb. 1, 1950; s. Elmer William and Theresa Ann Mary (Youness) H. B.A. in Advt., Mich. State U., 1976. Asst. graphics tchr., Federal Way (Wash) Sch. Dist., 1976-78; designer advt. graphics, Seattle, 1978-79; designer, Ken Hintz and Friends, Seattle, 1979—; freelance cons., art dir. Served with U.S. Army, 1969-71. Recipient Gold award Broadcaster Promotion Assn., 1981, 82, silver awards, 1982, Hammer and Paper graphics award, 1982.

HINTZ, NORMAN CLARE, army officer; b. Freeport, Ill., Nov. 16, 1937; s. Albert Fred and Rose Lucille (Shadle) H.; B.Arch., U. Ill., 1962, M.Arch., 1963; grad. U.S. Army Engrs. Sch., U.S. Command and Gen. Staff Coll., Armed Forces staff coll., Indsl. Coll. Armed Forces; m. Chong-Sook Yim, Mar. 17, 1979; children—Patrick Jarvis, Alisa Kay. Commd. 2d lt. C.E., U.S. Army, 1962, advanced through grades to col., 1981; personnel mgmt. officer Office of Personnel Ops., Dept. Army, Washington, 1966-68; co. comdr., ops. officer 1st Cav. Div., Vietnam, 1968-69; asst. exec. Office of Chief of Engrs., Washington, 1969-70; dist. sr. adviser, Vietnam, 1971-72; research architect C.E. Constrn. Engring. Research Lab., Champaign, Ill., 1972-74; dep. dist. engr. St. Paul Dist. C.E., 1974-77; dep. engr. I Corps Group, Korea, 1977; comdr. 802d Engrs. Bn., Korea, 1977-78; exec. officer 2d Combat Engr. Group, Korea, 1978-79; staff officer Office of Dep. Chief of Staff for Ops. and Plans, Dept. Army, Washington, 1980-81; asst. dir. mil. programs Office of Chief of Engrs., Washington, 1981; dist. engr., comdr. C.E. dist., Seattle, 1981—. Decorated Legion of Merit, Bronze Star, Air medal (3), and others. Registered architect, Wis., Wash.; registered profl. engr., Wis. Mem. AIA, Soc. Am. Mil. Engrs., Am. Pub. Works Assn., Nat. Soc. Profl. Engrs. Lutheran. Home: 3015 NW 54th St Seattle WA 98107 Office: 4735 E Marginal Way S Seattle WA 98134

HINTZE, JERRY LUND, statistical consultant; b. Richland, Wash., June 11, 1947; s. Royal Sears and Virginia May (Lund) H.; m. Janet Poole, Dec. 19, 1951; children—Eric, Christopher, Holly Ann, Charlotte, Julie Kay. B.A., Brigham Young U., 1971, M.S., 1973; Ph.D., Tex. A&M U., 1976. Instr., U. Denver, 1977; mgr. mgmt. info. ctr. Latter-day Saints Ch., Salt Lake City, 1978-82, computer capacity planner, 1982—. Mem. Am. Statis. Assn. Republican. Mormon. Developed Number Cruncher Statis. Package for Microcomputers. Home: 865 E 400 N Kaysville UT 84037

HINZE, BRENT MAYO, psychologist, therapist; b. Ogden, Utah, Sept. 23, 1941; s. Phillip Mayo and Adele (Carson) H.; m. Sarah Elaine Street, June 3, 1970; children—Krista, Laura, Rodney, Tadd, Sarah Rebekah, Matthew. B.S., U. Wash., 1963; M.S., Central Wash. U., 1965; Ph.D., Utah State U., 1972. Lic. pyschologist Utah. Research asst. U. Wash., Seattle, 1963, Central Wash. U., Ellensburg, 1964; sch. psychologist, Las Vegas, 1964-65, 70-71; psychology instr. Wash. State U., Pullman, 1965-66; research asst., counselor Utah State U., Logan, 1969-70; assoc. prof. psychology, dir. social scis., counseling and testing Sheridan (Wyo.) Coll., 1971-72; dir., instr. Glendale (Calif.) Inst. Religion, 1972-75; counselor, sch. psychologist La Canada, Calif., 1975-76; pvt. practice in psychology Layton, Utah, 1976-81; founder, dir. Hinze Inst. Psychol. and Family Services, Layton, 1981—; instr. psychology and religion Brigham Young U.; missionary Ch. of Jesus Christ of Latter Day Saints, Mex., 1966-68; instr. music and religion Logan Inst. Religion, 1969-70. Chmn. Dist. 3 Citizen's Planning Com., Layton, 1980-82; mem. Mayor's adv. com., 1981-82; youth coach Am. Youth Soccer Orgn., 1981-82; Mormon bishop, 1974-76. Mem. Am. Psychol. Assn., Assn. Mormon Counselors and Psychotherapists, Utah Soc. Clin. Hypnosis, Utah Psychol. Assn. Republican. Home: 1303 N Gillman Dr Layton UT 84041 Office: 1141 W Antelope Dr Layton UT 94041

HIPES, DARRELL DEVON, livestock marketing and credit corporation executive; b. Logansport, Ind., Jan. 26, 1928; s. Roy Lester and Josephine Marie Hipes; m. Sarah Barbara Overman, May 16, 1954 (div.); children—Cindy, Carrie, John, Jill, Jennifer. Student, Wabash Coll., Crawfordsville, Ind., 1946-47, Ind. U., Bloomington, 1947-49. Exec. v.p., gen. mgr. Nat. Live Stock Producers Assn., Denver; dir. Livestock Conservation Inst.; gov. Livestock Merchandising Inst. Served with U.S. Army, 1950-52. Democrat. Clubs: Kiwanis, Masons. Office: 307 Livestock Exchange Bldg Denver CO 80216

HIPPLE, KARL WALTER, soil scientist; b. Meadville, Pa., July 10, 1945; s. Floyd Lewis and Marjorie Lenore (Kreitz) H.; m. Helen Marie Tobin, Nov. 18, 1967; m. 2d, Margaret Mary Flaherty, Dec. 2, 1978; children—Aaron Jacob Smith, Adam Karl. B.S., Old Dominion U., 1972; M.S. in Soil Sci., U. Idaho, 1976, Ph.D. in Soil Sci., 1981. Cert. profl. soil scientist, Idaho. Biology, phys. sci. tchr. Maury High Sch., Norfolk, Va., 1972-73; soil survey scientist Idaho Soil Conservation Commn., Orofino, 1978-79, U.S. Dept. Agrl. Soil Conservation Service, Orofino, 1978-80; soil scientist, soil survey party leader Custer-Lemhi Soil Survey, Salmon, Idaho, 1980—; instr. land judging activities Challis (Idaho) High Sch., 1980-82. Soil instr. Boy Scouts Am., Stanley, Idaho, 1981. Served with USN, 1967-71. Recipient U.S. Dept. Agr. Soil Conservation Service Cert. Merit, cash award, 1980, 83. Mem. Soil Sci. Soc. Am., Soil Conservation Soc. Am., Idaho Soil Scis. Assn. (pres. 1983). Republican. Contbr. articles to sci. jours. Home: 406 Copper St Salmon ID 83467 Office: 201 Church St Salmon ID 83467

HIRAI, CRAIG KAZUO, lawyer, accountant; b. Honolulu, Jan. 3, 1949; s. Ralph Juichi and Tamie (Matsuo) H.; m. Linda K. Goto, Oct. 12, 1980. B.S., U. So. Calif., 1970; M.S., U. Pa., 1971, M.B.A., 1972; J.D., U. Calif.-Hastings, 1978; LL.M. in Taxation, NYU, 1979. C.P.A., Hawaii; bar: Hawaii 1978. Acct., Arthur Young & Co., Honolulu, 1972-73; tax acct. Coopers & Lybrand, Honolulu, 1974-80; assoc. Fong & Miho, Honolulu, 1980-82, Torkildson, Katz, Jossem & Loden, Honolulu, 1982—. Bd. dirs. Po Ailani Inc. Mem. ABA, Hawaii State Bar Assn. (treas. tax sect.), Am. Inst. C.P.A.s, Hawaii Soc. C.P.A.s. Home: 1650 Ala Moana Blvd Apt 613 Honolulu HI 96815 Office: 700 Bishop St Suite 1512 Honolulu HI 96813

HIRAI, WALLACE AZUSA, mechanical engineer; b. Makawao, Maui, Hawaii, Jan. 1, 1929; s. Katsutoshi and Miyuki (Honda) H.; student U. Hawaii, 1946-47; B.S. in Mech. Engring., Iowa State U., 1951; M.B.A., U. Hawaii, 1979; m. Mae Michiyo Iga, Dec. 27, 1951; children—Allen Kazuo, Michael Katsumi. Designer, Douglas Aircraft Co., Long Beach, Calif., 1952; sugar technology trainee Hawaiian Sugar Planters Assn., Honolulu and Wailuku, Maui, 1954-56; project engr. Wailuku Sugar Co., 1956-58; process engr. Hilo Sugar Co., (Hawaii), 1958; project engr. Terminal Steel Co., Honolulu, 1959-62; mech. engr. City and County Honolu Sewer Dept., 1962; chief design engr. C. Brewer & Co., Hilo, 1963-71; pres., mgr. W.A. Hirai & Assos. Inc., Hilo, 1972—. Chmn., Hawaii County Energy Self Sufficiency Com., Hawaii County Plumbing Code Rev. Com., Hawaii County 208 Plan Adv. Com., Hawaii County Underground Injection Control Adv. Com. Served to 1st lt. C.E., AUS, 1952-54; Korea. Registered profl. engr., Hawaii. Mem. Hawaii Island C. of C., Japanese C. of C. and Industry Hawaii, ASME, Nat. Soc. Profl. Engrs., Hawaiian Sugar Technologists, Hawaii Soc. Profl. Engrs. (pres. 1982-83). Home: 1172 Kumukoa St Hilo HI 96720 Office: 109 Holomua St Hilo HI 96720

HIRAOKA, NANETTE EIKO, educational administrator; b. Papaikou, Hawaii, Dec. 3, 1940; d. Richard Minoru and Ethel Chiyoko (Higa) Jitchaku; m. Setsuo Hiraoka, June 25, 1966; children—Susan, Sherri Lynn. Ed.B., U. Hawaii, 1962, 5th year diploma, 1963, M.S. in Secondary Edn., 1980; lic. secondary tchr., sch. adminstr., Hawaii. Sci. tchr. Kalanianaole Intermediate Sch., Papaikou, 1963-68, tchr., 1972-73; beginning tchr. supr. Hawaii Dist., Hilo, 1968-72; tchr. Hilo High Sch., 1973-81, counselor, 1981-82; vice prin. Honokaa High and Elem. Sch., 1982—. Leader 4-H club, 1980—; chmn. State Pres.'s Council, 1980-82. Recipient Nat. Sci. Tchrs. Assn./Ford Motor Co. Ford Future Scientists Am. Tchr. Award, 1967; Nat. Sci. Tchrs. Assn., NASA Space Shuttle Student Involvement Symposium attendee, 1981. Mem. Hawaii Govt. Employees Assn., Assn. Supervision and Curriculum Devel., Alpha Delta Kappa (Delta chpt. pres. 1978-80, chmn. state pres.'s council, 1980-82. Democrat. Buddhist. Club: Hilo Y's Menettes. Office: PO Box 237 Honokaa HI 96727

HIRATA, RHONDA GAY, advertising executive; b. Oxnard, Calif., Aug. 21, 1953; d. Willis Masato and Marlene Matsuye (Kozuki) H.; m. Donnell Wong Choy, Aug. 25, 1979. B.A., U. Calif.-Berkeley, 1975. Account exec. McCann-Erickson, Inc., San Francisco, 1976-79, D'Arcy, MacManus & Masius, Inc., San Francisco, 1979-81; account supr. Dancer Fitzgerald Sample, Inc., Corporate Advt. Group, San Francisco, 1981—. Bd. dirs. Chinatown YWCA, San Francisco, 1980; exec. com. Nihonmachi Polit. Assn., San Francisco, 1981; exec. com. Asian-Am. Dance Collective, San Francisco, 1981; mem. Bay Area Vol. Mktg. Council, Girl Scouts U.S.A., 1983. Democrat. Office: 1010 Battery St San Francisco CA 94111

HIRAYAMA, TETSU, librarian, educator; b. Visalia, Calif., Mar. 1, 1923; s. George Takuzo and Taka (Kido) H.; B.A., Andrew U., 1947; M.A., San Jose State Coll., 1964; M.L.S., U. Hawaii, 1968; m. Betsy Toshiko Terukina, June 2, 1947; children—Lynn Aiko, Shirley Sumiko. Tchr., prin. Wahiawa Mission Sch., Wahiawa, Hawaii, 1948-50; instr., dean boys Hawaiian Mission Acad., Honolulu, 1950-52; tchr. Hawaiian Mission Elementary Sch., Honolulu, 1952-66; instr., librarian Hawaiian Mission Acad., 1966-70; instr. Hawaiian Mission Acad., 1970—. Mem. ALA, Nat. Council Social Studies, Internat. Platform Assn. Home: 1553 Thurston Ave Honolulu HI 96822 Office: 1438 Pensacola St Honolulu HI 96822

HIROTA, SAM OSAMU, cons. civil engr.; b. Ewa, Oahu, Hawaii, May 23, 1912; s. Hiroyoshi and Ko H.; B.S., U. Hawaii, 1935; m. Yukino Yamane, Mar. 12, 1938; children—Dennis I., Jed, Wendy M. State dep. dir. transp., Honolulu, 1960-63; interim state dir. transp., 1962-63; spl. cons. to State Dept. Transp., 1963—; pres. Sam O. Hirota, Inc., cons. civil engrs. and surveyors; v.p. Aquatic Scis., Inc., Investors Finance, Inc. Past commr. Bd. Registration Profl. Engrs., Architects and Surveyors. Served to capt. USAAF, 1951-57. Named Disting. Alumnus U. Hawaii. Fellow ASCE (life, past pres. Hawaii sect.); mem. Hawaii Soc. Profl. Engrs. (charter; Engr. of Yr. award 1980), Highway Research Bd. (asso.), Engring. Assn. Hawaii (past dir., Disting. Community Service award), Cons. Engrs. Council Hawaii (charter), Am. Congress on Surveying and Mapping (past chmn. Hawaii sect., nat. dir.), Cons. Engrs. Council U.S.A. (past nat. chmn. ethical practice com.), Calif. Council Civil Engrs. and Land Surveyors (Disting. Service award, hon. mem.), Hawaii Bowling Proprietors' Assn. (pres. 1960-62). Congregationalist. Clubs: Ala Moana Rotary, Kiwanis (past pres. Internat. Airport club). Home: 4925 Poola St Honolulu HI 96821 Office: 345 Queen St Honolulu HI 96813

HIRSCH, CHERYL RAINESS, marketing executive; b. N.Y.C., Apr. 8, 1952; d. Maurice and Phyllis Barbara (Fox) Rainess; m. Stephen Morris Affron, June 19, 1976 (div.). B.A., U. Colo., 1974. Mgmt. trainee J.C. Penney Co., Inc., N.Y.C., 1974-75; mktg. rep. Allied Stores Mktg. Corp., N.Y.C., 1976-78; buyer Stewart and Co., Balt., 1978-79; account exec. Saber Air Freight, San Bruno, Calif., 1980—. Recipient Winner's Circle award Saber Air Freight, 1981-82. Mem. Nat. Assn. Profl. Saleswomen (bd. dirs., Keynote speaker coordinator), Internat. Trade Council. Club: Oakland Traffic. Office: Saber Air Freight 1061 Sneath Ln San Bruno CA 94066

HIRSCH, JANE ELIZABETH, nurse administrator, educator; b. Bonne Terre, Mo., Dec. 26, 1948; d. John George and Rita Bernice (Gaffney) Hirsch; m. Jeffrey L. Splitgerber, Feb. 16, 1979. B.S., U. Mo.-Columbia, 1971; M.S., U. Calif.-San Francisco, 1975. R.N., Calif. Staff nurse U. Mo.-Columbia, 1971; staff nurse U. Calif.-San Francisco, 1971-72, sr. staff nurse, 1972-75, head nurse, 1975-77, staff devel. instr., 1977-79, clin. nurse V, 1979-81, asst. dir. nursing, 1981—; asst. clin. prof. U. Calif.-San Francisco Sch. Nursing; instr. CPR. Mem. Am. Soc. Nursing Service Adminstrs., Calif. Soc. Nursing Service Adminstrs., Sigma Theta Tau. Editor: (with Leslie Hannock) Mosby's Manual of Clinical Nursing Procedures, 1981; contbr. articles to profl. jours.; mem. editorial bd. C.V. Mosby Co. Nursing Dictionary.

HIRSCH, PHILIP GOODHART, accountant; b. Chgo., Dec. 19, 1952; s. Richard Irwin and Nancy (Lesser) H.; A.B., U. Pa., 1975, B.S. in Fin., 1975; M.B.A., Northwestern U., 1976; m. Gail Lee Gibbons, May 10, 1980. Acct., Price Waterhouse & Co., Phoenix, 1976-78; v.p. fin. and adminstrn., corp. sec. Noble Multimedia Communications, Inc., Noble Broadcast Cons.'s, Inc., San Diego, 1978-80; pres. Philip G. Hirsch & Co., mgmt. and fin. cons. specializing in broadcasting, San Diego, 1980-81; v.p. fin. planning Channel Assos., Inc., Santa Barbara, Calif., 1981-82; acct. Price Waterhouse, Newport Beach, Calif., 1983—. Active Jr. Achievement, United Way, Big Bros. Ariz. Recipient cert. of achievement United Way, 1979, Headstart, 1971; C.P.A., Calif. Mem. Am. Mgmt. Assn., Broadcast Fin. Mgmt. Assn., Nat. Assn. Accts., Am. Inst. C.P.A.s. Clubs: Univ., San Diego Racquet and Tennis (San Diego); Santa Barbara Tennis. Home: 719 Heliotrope Ave Corona del Mar CA 92625 Office: 660 Newport Center Dr Newport Beach CA 92660

HIRSCH, STEVEN M., psychologist; b. Winthrop, Mass., Sept. 10, 1945; s. Kurt M. and Antoinette M. (Giglio) H.; m. Susanne Hirsch, Sept. 25, 1965; children—Christopher, Christina. B.A., U. Mass., Boston, 1969; Ph.D., Tex. Technol. U., 1975. Lic. psychologist, Calif., Ariz., Tex. Dir., Tex. Inst. Alcohol Studies, Austin, 1975-76; exec. dir. Behavioral Health Agy. Central Ariz., Casa Grande, 1976-79; dir. alcohol and drug dependency unit Kaiser Med. Program, San Diego, 1980-81; pvt. practice psychology, El Cajon, Calif., 1982—; dir. psychol. services Raleigh Hills Hosp., El Cajon, 1982—. Mem. Am. Psychol. Assn., Assn. Advancement Behavior Therapy, Calif. Psychol. Assn. Home: 5764 Tortuga Rd San Diego CA 92124 Office: 109 E Chase Ave El Cajon CA 92020

HIRSCH, URBAN S., III, printing ink manufacturing company executive; b. Los Angeles, July 30, 1941; s. Urban S. and Dicky (Pfaelzer) H.; m. Sherri Talbert, Sept. 4, 1981; children—Paul, Carl. With Bowers Printing Ink Co., Hawthorne, Calif., 1960—, v.p., gen. mgr., 1980—. Mem. Am. Motorcycle Assn. Office: Bowers Printing Ink Co 12727 S Van Ness Ave Hawthorne CA 90250

HIRSCH, WERNER ZVI, economist, educator; b. Linz, Germany, June 10, 1920, came to U.S., 1946, naturalized, 1955; s. Waldemar and Toni (Morgenstern) H.; m. Hilde E. Zwirn, Oct. 30, 1945; children—Daniel, Joel, Ilona. B.S. with highest honors, U. Calif.-Berkeley, 1947, Ph.D., 1949. Instr. econs. U. Calif.-Berkeley, 1949-51; econ. affairs officer UN, 1951-52; economist Brookings Instn., Washington, 1952-53; asst. research dir. St. Louis Met. Survey, 1956-57; prof. econs. Washington U., St. Louis, 1953-63; also economist Resources for Future, Inc., Washington, 1958-59; prof. econs., dir. Inst. Govt. and Pub. Affairs, UCLA, 1963—; scholar in residence Rockefeller Study Ctr., 1978; cons. Rand Corp., 1958—, U.S. Senate Com. Pub. Works, 1972, Calif. Senate Select Com. on Structure and Adminstrn. Pub. Edn., 1973, Joint Econ. Com. of Congress, 1975-76, OECD, 1977-80; mem. com. to improve productivity of govt. Com. Econ. Devel., 1975-76. Bd. dirs. Calif. Council Environ. and Econ. Balance, 1973—; Edmund G. Brown Inst. Govt., 1980—, Calif. Found. on Economy, 1979—; pres. Town Hall West of Calif., 1978-79; pres. Friends of Graphic Arts. Mem. Am. Econs. Assn., Western Econ. Assn., Am. Farm Econ. Assn., Western Region Sci. Assn. (dir., pres. 1978-80), Town Hall (chmn. econ. sect.), Los Angeles World Affairs Council, Phi Beta Kappa, Sigma Xi. Author 17 books including: Fiscal Crisis of America's Central Cities, 1971; Program Budgeting for Primary and Secondary Public Education, 1972; Governing Urban America in the 1970s, 1973; Urban Economic Analysis, 1973; Local Government Program Budgeting: Theory and Practice, 1974; Recent Experiences with National Planning in the United

Kingdom, 1977; Law and Economics: An Economic Analysis, 1979; Higher Education of Women: Essays in Honor of Rosemary Park, 1978; Social Experimentation and Economic Policy, 1981; assoc. editor Jour. Am. Statis. Assn., 1980—. Home: 11601 Bellagio Rd Los Angeles CA 90049 Office: Dept Econs UCLA Los Angeles CA 90024

HIRSCHBOECK, JOHN KARL, advertising executive; b. Milw., Nov. 8, 1946; s. John S. and Rosemary C. (Bach) H.; m. Mary C. Prendergast, Mar. 4, 1978. Student St. Mary's Coll., 1965-67; B.A., U. Wis.-Madison, 1969. Account exec. Dancer, Fitzgerald, Sample, N.Y.C., 1969-72, account supr., 1973-78; mgmt. supr. Toyota Motor Sales, Torrance, Calif., 1978—; sr. v.p., mgmt. supr. Dancer, Fitzgerald, Sample, 1980—. Office: Dancer Fitzgerald Sample 3878 Carson St Torrance CA 90503

HIRSCHFELD, TOMAS BENO, chemical engineer; b. Montevideo, Uruguay, Dec. 20, 1939; s. Rudolf Georg Herman and Ruth (Nordon) H., came to U.S., 1966, naturalized, 1974; B.Sc., Vasquez Acevedo Coll., 1956; Ph.D., Nat. U. Uruguay, 1965; m. Judith Berggrun, Nov. 3, 1963; children—Noemi Brenda, Dinorah Jael, Susan Deborah. Asst. prof. spectrochemistry Nat. U. Uruguay, 1965-68; vis. scientist N.Am. Aviation Co., Thousand Oaks, Calif., 1966-67; staff scientist Block Engring. Co., Cambridge, Mass., 1969-71, chief scientist, 1971-79; scientist Lawrence Livermore (Calif.) Lab., 1979—; prof. Ind. U., Bloomington, 1977—. Trustee Temple Beth Sholom, Framingham, Mass., 1974—, chmn. sch. com., 1975-76. Recipient IR-100 award Indsl. Research mag., 1975, 77, 81, 83. Fellow Optical Soc. Am. (editorial adv. jour., editorial bd. Optics Letters); sr. mem. IEEE; mem. Am. Chem. Soc., Coblentz Soc. (governing bd.), Soc. Applied Spectroscopy (Meggers award 1978), Canadian Spectroscopic Assn., Soc. Photo-Instrumentations Engrs., Soc. Automated Cytology. Club: B'nai B'rith. Author, patentee in field. Assoc. editor Jour. Applied Spectroscopy. chemical engineer; b. Montevideo, Uruguay, Dec. 20, 1939; s. Rudolf Georg Herman and Ruth (Nordon) H.; came to U.S., 1966, naturalized, 1974; B.Sc., Vasquez Acevedo Coll., 1956; Ph.D., Nat. U. Uruguay, 1965; m. Judith Berggrun, Nov. 3, 1963; children—Noemi Brenda, Dinorah Jael, Susan Deborah. Asst. prof. spectrochemistry Nat. U. Uruguay, 1965-68; vis. scientist N.Am. Aviation Co., Thousand Oaks, Calif., 1966-67; staff scientist Block Engring. Co., Cambridge, Mass., 1969-71, chief scientist, 1971-79; scientist Lawrence Livermore (Calif.) Lab., 1979—; prof. Ind. U., Bloomington, 1977—. Trustee Temple Beth Sholom, Framingham, Mass., 1974—, chmn. sch. com., 1975-76. Recipient IR-100 award Indsl. Research mag., 1975, 77, 81, 83. Fellow Optical Soc. Am. (editorial adv. jour., editorial bd. Optics Letters); sr. mem. IEEE; mem. Am. Chem. Soc., Coblentz Soc. (governing bd.), Soc. Applied Spectroscopy (Meggers award 1978), Canadian Spectroscopic Assn., Soc. Photo-Instrumentations Engrs., Soc. Automated Cytology. Club: B'nai B'rith. Author, patentee in field. Assoc. editor Jour. Applied Spectroscopy. Home: 1262 Vancouver Way Livermore CA 94550 Office: PO Box 808 Mail Stop L-325 Livermore CA 94550

HIRSCHFIELD, ALAN J., motion picture company executive; B.S., U. Okla.; M.B.A., Harvard U. Vice-pres., Allen & Co., Inc., 1959-67; v.p.-fin., dir. Warner Bros. Seven Arts, Inc., 1967-68; with Am. Diversified Enterprises, Inc., 1968-73; pres., chief exec. officer Columbia Pictures Industries, N.Y.C., 1973-78; vice chmn., chief operating officer 20th Century-Fox Film Corp., Los Angeles, 1979-81, chmn. bd. chief exec. officer, 1981—, also dir.; dir. Straight Arrow Publs. Inc., John D. Coleman Co. Bd. dirs. Film Soc. of Lincoln Center, Cancer Research Inst., Will Rogers Meml. Fund. Mem. Motion Picture Assn. Am. (bd. dirs.). Office: 20th Century-Fox Film Corp Box 900 Beverly Hills CA 90213

HIRSCHI, TRAVIS WARNER, criminologist; b. Rockville, Utah, Apr. 15, 1935; s. Warren G. and Orra (Terry) H; m. Anna Yergensen, Sept. 3, 1955; children—Kendall, Nathan, Justine. B.S., U. Utah, 1957, M.S. 1958; Ph.D. in Sociology, U. Calif.-Berkeley, 1968. Asst. prof., then assoc. prof. U. Wash., Seattle, 1967-71; prof. sociology U. Calif.-Davis, 1971-77; prof. criminal justice SUNY-Albany, 1977-81; prof. pub. policy and sociology U. Ariz., Tucson, 1981—. Served in U.S. Army, 1958-60. Recipient C. Wright Mills award Soc. Study of Social Problems, 1968. Mem. Am. Soc. Criminology (pres. 1982-83), Am. Sociol. Assn. (chair criminology 1982-83). Author: Delinquency Research, 1967; Causes of Delinquency, 1969; Measuring Delinquency, 1981. Home: 1680 W Caspian Dr Tucson AZ 85704 Office: Dept Sociology Social Sci Bldg U Ariz Tucson AZ 85721

HIRSH, NORMAN BARRY, helicopter co. exec.; b. N.Y.C., Apr. 20, 1935; s. Samuel Albert and Lillian Rose (Minkow) H.; B.S.M.E., Purdue U., 1956; postgrad. UCLA, 1979-80; m. Sharon Kay Girot, Dec. 29, 1973; children—Richard Scott, Lisa Robin. Automobile engr. Ford Motor Co., 1956-58; aircraft design engr. Gen. Dynamics-Convair, 1958-62; with aircraft div. Hughes Tool Co. (now Hughes Helicopters Inc.), Culver City, Calif., 1962—, v.p. advanced attack helicopter, 1980—. Served with U.S. Army, 1957. Mem. Am. Helicopter Soc., Assn. U.S. Army, Army Aviation Assn. Office: Hughes Helicopters Inc Centinela and Teale Sts Culver City CA 90230

HIRSON, ESTELLE, ret. educator; b. Bayonne, N.J.; d. Morris and Bertha (Rubinstein) Hirson; student UCLA, U. So. Calif., summers 1949-59, San Francisco, summer 1955, U. Hawaii, 1955; B.E., San Francisco State U., 1965. Tchr. High St. Homes Sch., Oakland, Calif., 1949-54, Prescott Sch., 1955-60, Ralph Bunche Sch., 1960-72; owner Puzzle-Gram Co., Los Angeles, 1946-49; pres. Major Automobile Co., 1948-60. Chpt. v.p. City of Hope, San Francisco, 1962-63; bd. dirs. Sinai-Duarte Nat. Med. Center, 1946-50, also parliamentarian, life mem. Mem. NEA, Calif., Oakland, Los Angeles tchrs. assns., Sigma Delta Tau. Democrat. Mem. Order Eastern Star; Scottish Rite Women's Assn. (v.p. Los Angeles 1982). Rights to ednl. arithmetic game Find the Answer 1948, 51. Home: 8670 Burton Way Apt 328 Los Angeles CA 90048

HIRST, WILMA ELIZABETH, educational psychologist; b. Shenandoah, Iowa; d. James H. and Lena (Donahue) Ellis; m. Clyde Henry Hirst (dec. Nov. 1969); 1 dau., Donna Jean (Mrs. Alan Robert Goss). A.B. in Elementary Edn., Colo. State Coll., 1948, Ed.D. in Ednl. Psychology, 1954; M.A. in Psychology, U. Wyo., 1951. Elem. tchr., Cheyenne, Wyo., 1945-49, remedial reading instr., 1949-54; assoc. prof. edn., dir. campus sch. Nebr. State Tchrs. Coll., Kearney, 1954-56; sch. psychologist, head dept. spl. edn. Cheyenne (Wyo.) pub. schs., 1956-57, sch. psychologist, guidance coordinator, 1957-66, dir. research and spl. projects, 1966—, also pupil personnel, 1973—; vis. asst. prof. U. So. Calif., summer 1957, Omaha U., summer 1958, U. Okla., summers 1959, 60; vis. assoc. prof. U. Nebr., 1961, U. Wyo., summer 1962, 64, extension div., Kabul, Afghanistan, 1970, Catholic U., Goias, Brazil, 1974; investigator HEW, 1965-69; prin. investigator effectiveness of spl. edn., 1983—; participant seminar Russian Press Women and Am. Fedn. Press Women, Moscow and Leningrad, 1973. Sec.-treas. Laramie County Council Community Services, 1962. Speakers bur., mental health orgn.; active Little Theatre, 1936-60, Girl Scout Leaders Assn., 1943-50. Mem. Adv. Council on Retardation to Gov.'s Commn.; mem., past sec. Wyo. Bd. Psychologist Examiners, vice chmn., 1965-74; chmn. Mayor's v.p. Model Cities Program, 1969; mem. Gov.'s Com. Jud. Reform, 1972; adv. council Div. Exceptional Children, Wyo. Dept. Edn., 1974; mem. transit adv. group City of Cheyenne, 1974; bd. dirs. Wyo. Children's Home Soc., treas., 1978—; bd. dirs. Goodwill Industries Wyo., chmn., 1981—; mem. Wyo. exec. com. Partners of Americas, 1970—, ambassador to Honduras, summer 1979; chmn. bd. SE Wyo. Mental Health Center; ruling elder 1st Presbyn. Ch., Cheyenne, 1978—; chmn. adv. assessment com. Wyo. State Office Handicapped Children, 1980, 81. Named Woman of Year, Cheyenne Bus. and Profl. Women, 1974. Diplomate Am. Bd. Profl. Psychology. Fellow Internat. Council Psychologists (chmn. Wyo. div. 1980—); mem. AAUP, Am. Assn. State Psychology Bds. (sec.-treas. 1970-73), Am., Wyo. (pres. 1962-63) psychol. assns., Laramie County (bd. mem., corr. sec. 1963—, pres.), Wyo. mental health assns. (bd. mem.), Internat. Platform Assn., Am. Ednl. Research Assn., Assn. Supervision and Curriculum Devel., Assn. for Gifted (Wyo. pres. 1964-65), Am. Personnel and Guidance Assn., Am. Assn. Sch. Adminstrs., NEA (life, participant seminar to China 1978), AAUW, Cheyenne Assn. Spl. Personnel and Prins. (pres. 1964-65, mem. exec. bd. 1972—), Nat. Fedn. Press Women (dir. 1979), DAR (vice regent Cheyenne chpt. 1975—), Psi Chi, Kappa Delta Pi, Pi Lambda Theta, Alpha Delta Kappa (pres. Wyo. Alpha 1965-66). Presbyn. Mem. Order Eastern Star, Daus. of Nile. Clubs: Wyo. Press Women, Zonta (pres. Cheyenne 1965-66, treas. dist. 12 1974). Author: Know Your School Psychologist, 1963; Effective School Psychology for School Administrators, 1980. Home: 3458 Green Valley Rd Cheyenne WY 82001 Office: Adminstrn Bldg Cheyenne Pub Schs Cheyenne WY 82001

HIRT, JOAN BERNARD, educational administrator; b. Huntington, N.Y., Feb. 20, 1951; d. Warren G. and Ruth Davis (Thomas) H. B.A. in Russian Studies, Bucknell U., 1972; M.A. in Edn., U. Md., 1979. Personnel cons., mgr. br. offices, Schaumburg, Ill. and Rockville, Md., 1973-77; Resident bldg. dir., asst. dir. residential life Humboldt State U., Arcata, Calif., 1979—, instr. peer counseling class, counseling/communication courses. Contbr. articles to profl. jours. Mem. Humboldt County Alcohol Awareness Task Force. Mem. Calif. Assn. Coll. and Univ. Housing Officers (treas., v.p.), Nat. Assn. Student Personnel Adminstrs., Am. Personnel and Guidance Assn., Assn. Coll. Personnel Adminstrs. Democrat. Office: Dept Housing and Food Services Humbolt State U Arcata CA 95521

HITCH, THOMAS KEMPER, economist, banker; b. Boonville, Mo., Sept. 16, 1912; s. Arthur Martin and Bertha (Johnston) H.; A.B., Stanford U., 1934; A.M., Columbia U., 1946; Ph.D. (Econs.), U. London (London Sch. Econ.), 1937; student Nat. U. of Mexico, 1932; m. Margaret Barnhart, June 27, 1940 (dec. 1974); children—Hilary, Leslie, Caroline, Thomas; m. 2d, Mae Okudaira. Mem. faculty Stephens Coll., Columbia, Mo., 1937-42; spl. study of commodity markets Commodity Exchange Adminstrn., U.S. Dept. Agr., 1940; acting head current bus. research sect. Dept. of Commerce, 1942-43; head labor dept. Naval Sch. of Mil. Govt., Princeton, N.J., 1944-45; labor officer for asst. chief of Naval Ops. for Island Govt., 1945-46; labor adviser Vets. Emergency Housing Program, 1946-47; economist with spl. reference to labor econs. Pres.'s Council of Econ. Advisers, 1947-50; dir. research Hawaii Employers Council, Honolulu, 1950-59; sr. v.p. research div. First Hawaiian Bank, 1959—. Chmn. research com. Hawaii Visitors Bur., 1957-60, 62-69; chmn. Gov.'s Adv. Com. on Financing, 1959-62; chmn. Mayor's Fin. Adv. Com., 1960-69; chmn. com. on taxation and finance Constl. Conv. of Hawaii, 1968. Trustee Tax Found. of Hawaii, 1955-71, 74-80, pres., 1969; trustee McInerny Found. Served as lt. O.R.C., 1933-38; lt., USNR, 1943-50; active duty, 1943-46. Mem. Hawaii Joint Council on Econ. Edn. (chmn. 1964-68), C. of C. of Hawaii (dir. 1956-59, 65-67, chmn. 1971), Social Sci. Assn., Phi Beta Kappa, Pi Sigma Alpha. Clubs: Pacific (bd. govs. 1957-60, 63-65); Waialae Country (dir. 1977—, pres. 1979). Author: The Employers Guide to Unemployment Insurance, 1958; The Impact of Exports on Income in Hawaii, 1962; Hawaii the Most Vulnerable State in the Nation, 1973; also bulls. Contbr. articles to profl. jours. Compiler: Economics for the 1960's, 1961. Home: 257 Portlock Rd Honolulu HI 96825 Office: 1st Hawaiian Bank Honolulu HI 96847

HITCHCOCK, DOLORES JEAN, educational administrator; b. Spokane, Aug. 24, 1946; d. Leo Thomas and Lucille Margarite (LaCasse) Gibbons; m. Paul Henry Hitchcock, Sept. 18, 1966. B.A., U. Wash., 1968, M.A., 1976; postgrad Wash. State U., 1982—. Tchr. pub. schs., Imperial Beach, Calif., 1968-69; tchr., reading specialist pub. schs. Federal Way, Wash., 1970-78, prin. elem. sch., 1978-81; asst. prin. Federal Way High Sch., 1981-82, 83—. Recipient Golden Acorn award Parent Tchr. Students Assn., 1981. Mem. Assn. Federal Way Sch. Prins., Nat. Assn. Elem. Sch. Prins., Elem. Sch. Prins. Assn. of Wash., Northwest Women in Ednl. Adminstrn., Assn. Supervision and Curriculum Devel., Phi Delta Kappa.

HITCHCOCK, ROBERT BRIAN, agricultural products company executive; b. Washington, Apr. 9, 1944; s. Charles Roosevelt and Betty Aline (Mahrt) H.; m. Karen Eleen Nicholas; children—Stacy, Carrie; m. 2d, Beverly Hagin; stepchildren—Elisea, Todd, Shonda. B.A. in History, U. Calif.-Davis, 1965; M.B.A., Armstrong Coll., 1967. Office mgr. Nicholas Turkey Breeding Farms, Inc., Sonoma, Calif., 1969-70, controller, 1971-74, dir. fin., 1974-78, v.p., 1978-82, pres., 1982—. Active Sonoma County and Republican Central Com.; v.p. United Way North Bay; chmn. Sonoma Valley United Way. Served to lt. U.S. Army, 1967-69. Decorated Army Commendation Medal. Mem. Poultry and Egg Inst. Am. (dir. 1978—), Sigma Alpha Epsilon. Presbyterian. Club: Commonwealth. Home: 17355 Norrbom Rd PO Box 486 Sonoma CA 95476 Office: 19455 Riverside Dr PO Box Y Sonoma CA 95476

HITCHENS, LINDA SUE, lawyer, educator; b. Milford, Del., Dec. 20, 1949; d. Norris Tilghman and Grace Whaley (Jones) Hitchens. B.S. U. Del., 1972; J.D. cum laude, Loyola U., Los Angeles, 1982. Bar: Calif. 1982. Flight attendant Delta Air Lines, Atlanta, 1972-78; pres. Hitch Oriental Imports, Los Angeles, 1976-81, Foxcroft Fin. Services, Los Angeles, 1978-81; ptnr. Hitchens and Yuen, Los Angeles, 1983—; faculty mem. advanced bus. law Woodbury U., Los Angeles, 1983—. Named Miss Del. Miss-America Pageant, 1970. Mem. ABA. Republican. Office: Suite 3700 Union Bank Square 445 S Figueroa St Los Angeles CA 90071

HITCHINS, DIDDY R. M., political science educator; b. Glasgow, Scotland, May 3, 1945; d. Charles Patrick and Margaret Mary (Thomas) Seyd; m. Cliff L. Hitchins, Mar. 21, 1970; 1 dau., Dzagbe Mary. B.S. in Social Sci., U. Southampton (U.K.), 1967; M.A. in Govt., U. Essex (U.K.), 1968, Ph.D. in Govt., 1975. Research asst. U. Essex, 1968-70; asst. prof. U. Ghana (W. Africa), 1970-74, U. Alaska, Anchorage, 1976-78, assoc. prof., 1978-83, prof., 1983—. Mem. Am. Polit. Sci. Assn., Internat. Poli. Sci. Assn., Polit. Studies Assn. of U.K., Western Polit. Sci. Assn., Alaska World Affairs Council (past pres., v.p.). Contbr. articles on polit. sci. to profl. jours. Office: UAA 3221 Providence Dr Anchorage AK 99508

HITE, ROBERT WESLEY, restaurant co. exec.; b. Ft. Scott, Kans., Mar. 18, 1936; s. Woodard Vannoy and Corinne Winifred (Wright) H.; student Netherlands Coll., Breukelen, Holland, 1956-57; B.A., Colo. Coll., 1958; J.D., N.Y. U., 1961; m. Sarah Catherine Hoper, Aug. 20, 1960; children—Katherine, John, Laura, Martha, Amy. Admitted to Colo. bar, 1961, U.S. Supreme Ct. bar, 1965; mem. firm T. Raber Taylor, Denver, 1965-69; with Mr. Steak, Inc., Denver, 1969—, v.p., gen. counsel, sec., 1970—. Dist. capt. Denver County Republican Com., 1971-74. Bd. dirs. Met. Denver Sewage Disposal Dist., 1970—, sec., 1978, chmn. pro tem, 1979, chmn., 1980—; bd. dirs. Denver Boys, Inc., Montview Bldg. Corp., Alpha Ctr., Inc. Served to lt. USNR, 1965-69. Mem. Am., Colo., Denver bar assns., Colo. Assn. Corp. Counsel (pres. 1972-73). Presbyn. (ruling elder 1970-73). Clubs: Denver Law, Denver Rotary, Denver City (treas., dir. 1970-73). Office: 5100 Race Court Denver CO 80216

HITTLE, LEROY MICHAEL, journalist, state ofcl.; b. Onawa, Iowa, June 10, 1912; s. Thomas Jefferson and Mina Abigail (Covert) H.; student Morningside Coll., Sioux City, Iowa, 1934; B.A., Drake U., 1938; m. Helen L.M. Beroen, June 29, 1941 (dec. 1954); 1 son, Leroy Bradley; m. 2d, Joan Byles David, Apr. 2, 1971. With AP, Des Moines, 1934-39, San Francisco, 1939-41, Reno, 1941-43, Olympia, Wash., 1946-67; mem. Wash. Liquor Control Bd., Olympia, 1967-82, chmn., 1981-82; pres. South Sound Pub. Co., pub. Lacey (Wash.) Leader, 1967-68. Promotion chmn., bd. dirs. Southwestern Wash. Evergreen State Coll. Com., 1965-67; chmn. Regional Civic Auditorium Com., 1968-72. Served with AUS, 1943-46. Recipient 25 Year Service award AP, 1960; Sigma Delta Chi award for outstanding coverage Wash. Legislature, 1960; Gov.'s certificate of merit for 20 years reporting activities Wash. Govt., 1966; Disting. Service award Thurston County Citizen of Yr. Program, 1968, 73. Mem. SAR, Nat. Alcoholic Beverage Control Assn. (pres. 1979-80), Capital City Press Club (past pres.), Sigma Delta Chi, Tau Kappa Epsilon. Lutheran. Clubs: Masons, Shriners, Rotary, Elks; Wash. Athletic (Seattle); Olympia (Wash.) Country and Golf. Home: 5912 Athens Beach Dr NW Olympia WA 98502

HIX, PHYLLIS MARIE, lawyer; b. Bloomfield, Iowa, Mar. 28, 1936; d. Hyle and Myrtle Houston; m. William A. Kurlander (div.); 1 son, Jeff David. Student U. Iowa, 1954-56; B.S. in Occupational Therapy, U. So. Calif., 1959, LL.B., 1962, J.D., 1970. Bar: Calif. 1963, U.S. Dist. Ct. (so. dist.) Calif. 1963. Assoc. Lawler, Felix & Hall, Los Angeles, 1963, Overton, Lyman & Prince, Los Angeles, 1963-67, Dryden, Harrington & Swartz, Los Angeles, 1967-74; sole practice, 1974-76; ptnr. Kurlander & Hix, San Marino, Calif., 1976—; arbitrator Los Angeles Superior Ct. Active U. So. Calif. Town and Gown Scholarship Fund, Tournament of Roses. Mem. State Bar Calif. (bd. govs. 1981—), Los Angeles Adv. Counsel (past nat. dir.), Am. Bd. Trial Advocates. Republican. Congregationalist. Club: Balboa Bay (Newport Beach, Calif.). Office: 1455 San Marino Ave San Marino CA 91108

HIXSON, EARL E., city purchasing officer; b. Paris, Ark., Nov. 10, 1920; s. Henry Earl and Nelly Kelly (Crossno) H.; m. Norma Lee English. B.A., San Diego State U., 1949; student U. Calif.-San Diego, 1959-65. Procurement research adminstr. Gen. Dynamics, San Diego, 1952-72; mgr. ops. research Northrop Corp., Hawthorne, Calif., 1973-77; materials mgr. Geo. A. Fuller Co., Saudi Arabia, 1976-77; mgr. procurement Fortress ICAS, Continental, Iran, 1978-79; purchasing officer City of Oceanside (Calif.), 1979—. Mem. Calif. Assn. Pub. Purchasing Officers, Nat. Assn. Purchasing Mgrs. (cert.), Sigma Pi Sigma. Republican. Office: 704 3d St Oceanside CA 92054

HIZA, MICHAEL DAVID, chem. engr.; b. Quantico, Va., Apr. 11, 1954; s. Michael John, Jr., and Beverly Diane (Masters) H.; B.S. in Chem. and Petroleum-Refining Engring., Colo. Sch. Mines, 1976; m. Mary Charlotte Davis, Dec. 18, 1976; 1 son, Nicholas Alexander. Assoc. mem. tech. staff Ball Aerospace Systems Div., Boulder, Colo., 1977-79; tech. staff scientist Sci. Applications, Inc., Fossil Resource Tech. Devel. Div., Golden, Colo., 1979-81; staff engr. alt. energy and resources dept. Texaco Inc., Englewood, Colo., 1981—. Episcopalian. Condr. research and devel. alternative fuels tech. and low temperature refrigeration systems for space applications. Home: 2332 McKinley Ave Louisville CO 80027 Office: Texaco Inc Englewood CO

HJORTH, GEORGE EARLING, mgmt. cons., former army officer; b. Chgo., Dec. 7, 1922; s. George Louis and Dagmar Sofie (Aarsrud) H.; B.S. in Indsl. Engring., U. Ala., 1949; m. Barbara Marie Wagle, June 3, 1950; children—Debra Marie Hjorth Cluff, Janice Barbara Hjorth Swardson. Commd. 2d lt. U.S. Army, 1949, advanced through grades to col., 1970; mem. C.E., 1949-56; platoon leader, co. exec. officer 3d Engr. Combat Bn., Korea, 1950-51; engr. co. comdr., 1951-52; mem. Ordnance Corps, 1956-75; advanced weapons supply and maintenance officer, 1958-61; project officer Ordnance Bd. and Army Materiel Command Bd. staffs, 1961-64; nuclear weapons officer Hdqrs. U.S. 7th Army, Europe, 1964-66; comdg. officer Navajo Army Depot, Flagstaff, Ariz., 1967-69; project officer U.S. Army Concept Team in Vietnam, 1969-70; comdg. officer Materiel Command Surety Field Office, 1970-73; asst. chief of staff for materiel 2d Support Command VII Corps, Europe, 1973-75; ret., 1975; mgmt. cons., Scottsdale, Ariz., 1975—; mem. Interagy. Bd., U.S. Civil Service Examiners, 1967. Neighborhood commr. Boy Scouts Am., 1968, award, 1938; vol. Phoenix Paradise Valley Village Planning Commn., 1983. Served with Signal Corps, AUS, 1942-46; ETO. Decorated Legion of Merit, Bronze Star with oak leaf cluster, Meritorious Service medal, Army Commendation medal with oak leaf cluster (U.S.); Cross of Gallantry with palm (Vietnam); recipient Disting. Service and Commemorative badges German and Polish Labor Service, 1975. Mem. Mil. Order World Wars, Assn. U.S. Army, Am. Def. Preparedness Assn., Ret. Officers Assn. Republican. Club: Rotary. Home: 5902 E Larkspur Dr Scottsdale AZ 85254

HO, FIRMIN CHUN-SING, physician; b. Hong Kong, May 25, 1953; came to U.S., 1972; s. Hing-Cheung and Yun-Tai (Lee) H.; B.A. summa cum laude with honors in chemistry, Wesleyan U., 1976; M.D., U. Rochester, 1980. Teaching asst. in chemistry Wesleyan U., Middletown, Conn., 1975-76; intern in internal medicine Los Angeles County/U. So. Calif. Med. Center, 1980-81, resident in internal medicine, 1981—. Recipient Ayres prize for highest acad. standing, Wesleyan U., 1973, Silverman prize for excellence in chemistry, 1975; diplomate Nat. Bd. Med. Examiners. Mem. A.C.P., Phi Beta Kappa, Sigma Xi. Home: 400 S Garfield Ave Apt 5 Monterey Park CA 91754 Office: Los Angeles County/Univ of Southern Calif Med Center 1200 N State St Los Angeles CA 90033

HO, PANG T., electrical engineer, communications executive, educator; b. Fukien, China, Nov. 21, 1945; s. Irwine W. and Shiow J. (Wong) H.; m. Nancy N. Leigh, July 4, 1970; children—Katherine, Eric; B.S.E.E., Nat. Taiwan U., Taipei, 1967; M.S.E.E., Princeton U., 1969; Ph.D., Rutgers U., New Brunswick, N.J., 1975. Mem. tech. staff solid state div. RCA Corp., Somerville, N.J., research scientist David Sarnoff Research Ctr., Princeton, 1972-76; dept. mgr. Ford Aerospace & Communications Corp., Palo Alto, Calif., 1976—; asst. prof. San Jose State U., 1977-80; prin. Palo Alto Chinese Lang. Sch. Mem. IEEE, (sr.) AIAA. Republican. Club: Stanford Area Chinese (Palo Alto). Patentee in electronic field; author numerous studies, reports. Home: Office: 3939 Fabian Way Palo Alto CA 94303

HO, WEILYN (LYNN), travel agency executive; b. Honolulu, Feb. 25, 1937; d. Tai-Chun and Bernice Kwai-Jung Lum; m. Ronald Soon-Kong Ho, July 23, 1961; children—Edward (dec.), Edwyna, Ellyna, Gaylynn. Student Honolulu Bus. Coll., 1954-58. Sec. Aloha Airlines Co., 1958; asst. reservation mgr. Trans-Ocean Airlines, 1958; office mgr. Island Holidays San Francisco, 1959-60, office and sales mgr., salesman Chgo. office, 1960; island holidays groups and conv. mgr. City of Honolulu, 1961-66; with Trade-Wind Tours FIT office, Honolulu, 1966-69; owner, mgr. various gourmet shops and restaurant, Maui, Hawaii, 1969-73; mgr. Valley Island Travel, Wailuku, Maui, 1974-75, Travel Bookings, Lahaina, Hawaii, 1975-76, Maui Travel, Lahaina, 1976-78; pres., mgr., owner Travel Masters Ltd., Lahaina, 1978—; tchr. travel agys. courses. Active Roosevelt High Sch.; vestrywoman Holy Innocents Episcopal Ch.; past dist. chmn. Youth Citizen Award, now by-laws chmn. Mem.

Assn. Retail Travel Agts. (dir., past v.p., Hawaii rep. at Western Regional Conf., USSR). Club: Soroptimist (West Maui). Home: 1353 Hoapili St Lahaina Maui HI 96761 Office: Travel Masters Ltd Lahaina Shopping Ctr Office Bldg Suite 210 Lahaina Maui HI 96761

HOADLEY, WALTER EVANS, financial executive, economist; b. San Francisco, Aug. 16, 1916; s. Walter Evans and Marie Howland (Preece) H.; m. Virginia Alm, May 20, 1939; children—Richard Alm, Jean Hoadley Price. A.B., U. Calif.-Berkeley, 1938, M.A., 1940, Ph.D., 1946; D.C.S. (hon.), Franklin and Marshall Coll., 1963; LL.D. (hon.), Golden Gate U., 1968; diploma (hon.), El Inst. Tecnologico Autonomo de Mex., 1974; LL.D. (hon.), U. Pacific, 1979. Economist Fed. Res. Bank, Chgo., 1942-49, chmn., Phila., 1962-66, chmn. 12 Fed. Res. Banks, 1966; exec. v.p., chief economist Bank Am. NT&SA, San Francisco, 1966-81; economist, treas., v.p.-treas., Armstrong Cork Co. (name changed to Armstrong World Industries), Lancaster, Pa., 1949-66, dir. 1962—; sr. research fellow Hoover Inst., Stanford, Calif., 1981—; econ. commentator KRON-TV, San Francisco; dir. Lucky Stores, Inc., Armstrong World Industries, Selected Funds, Soule Steel, Robert A. McNeil Corp., PLM Inc. Chmn. Calif. Gov.'s Council Econ. Bus. Devel., 1980; co-chmn. San Francisco Mayor's Fiscal Adv. Com., 1978-81; mem. adv. council Calif. State Com. Econ. Devel., 1981—. Stanford U. Northeast Asia-U.S. Forum Internat. Fellow Am. Statis. Assn. (pres. 1958), Internat. Acad. Mgmt. Policy fellow, 1982. Nat. Assn. Bus. Economists; mem. Am. Fin. Assn. (pres. 1969), Com. Devel. Am. Capitalism (vice chmn.), Hudson Inst. (trustee), Internat. C. of C. (chmn. com. Internat. Monetary Affairs, U.S.; vice-chmn. Com., Paris), Internat. Conf. Comml. Bank Economists (chmn. 1978-81), Internat. Mgmt. Devel. Inst. Republican. Methodist. Clubs: Commonwealth, St. Francis Yacht, Pacific Union, Bankers, (San Francisco), Silverado Country (Napa), Stanford Faculty. Contbr. numerous articles and books on forecasting and economics; columnist for Dun's Business Month. Office: Bank of Am Center Room 4970 555 California St San Francisco CA 94104

HOAG, ARTHUR ALLEN, astronomer; b. Ann Arbor, Mich., Jan. 28, 1921; s. Lynne Arthur and Wilma S. (Wood) H.; A.B., Brown U., 1942; Ph.D., Harvard U., 1952; m. Marjorie Paulison Beers, Dec. 17, 1949; children—Stefanie (Mrs. William J. Hoel), Thomas. Physicist, U.S. Naval Ordnance Lab., Washington, 1942-45; astronomer U.S. Naval Obs., Washington, 1950-55; dir. U.S. Naval Obs., Flagstaff, Ariz., 1955-65; dir. Stellar Program, Kitt Peak Nat. Obs., Tucson, 1965-75, astronomer, 1975-77; dir. Lowell Obs., Flagstaff, Ariz., 1977—. Served with USNR, 1943-45. Fellow AAAS (councillor sect. D, 1970-71), Ariz. Acad. Sci. (councillor 1961-64, pres. 1965-66); mem. Am. Astron. Soc. (council 1966-69, v.p. 1974-76), Royal Astron. Soc., Astron. Soc. Pacific, Internat. Astron. Union. Home and office: Lowell Observatory PO Box 1269 Flagstaff AZ 86002

HOAG, FRANK STEPHEN, JR., newspaper exec.; b. Pueblo, Colo., June 11, 1908; s. Frank S. and Louise (Allebrand) H.; B.A., Princeton, 1931; Litt.D (hon.), So. Colo. State Coll., 1965, m. LeVert Wiess, June 15, 1935. Pres., Pueblo Star-Jour. and Chieftain, 1943—. Formerly mem. audit com. Asso. Press. Dir. Minnequa Bank, Pub. Service Co. Colo. Dir., v.p. Colo. Public Expenditures Council; formerly mem. Colo. Commn. Higher Edn. Trustee Colo. Coll., Colorado Springs; bd. dirs. USAF Acad. Found., Colorado Springs; trustee Parkview Episcopal Hosp., Pueblo Devel. Found.; trustee, past pres. U. So. Colo. Found. DeMolay Legion of Honor. Named Citizen of Year, Colo. Assn. Real Estate Bds., 1971. Mem. Pueblo C. of C. (past pres.), Am. Soc. Newspaper Editors, Colo. Press Assn. (past pres.), Am. Newspaper Pubs. Assn., Sigma Delta Chi. Presbyn. Mason (32 deg.), Rotarian (past pres.), Elk. Office: 825 W 6th St Pueblo CO 81002

HOAGLAND, PAMELA REDINGTON, educational consultant, administrator; b. Phoenix, June 2, 1937; d. George Appleton and Margaret Tweed (Rae) H. B.A., U. Ariz., 1959; M. Ed. in Reading Edn., 1965, Ed.D. in Reading and Psychology, 1973. Tchr. Tucson Unified Sch. Dist., 1959-73, asst. dir. instruction, reading, lang. arts, library services, 1980—; co-founder, co-dir. Learning Devel. Ctr., Tucson, 1970-74; curriculum specialist and supr. Pima County Spl. Edn. Coop., Tucson, 1973-76; ednl. cons. Redington Cons. Corp., Tucson, 1970—; lectr. in field; bd. dirs. Behavior Assocs. Chmn. Ariz. Right to Read Council, 1978-80; bd. dirs. Tucson Westside Coalition, 1979-80; edn. supr. Grace Episcopal Ch., 1965-67. Mem. Nat. Council Tchrs. English, Internat. Reading Assn. (field cons.), Ariz. State Reading Council (pres. 1969), Assn. Supervision and Curriculum Devel., Alpha Delta Kappa, Pi Delta Kappa (Disting. lecture series award 1978), Pi Beta Phi Alumni Assn. Democrat. Contbr. articles to profl. publs. Office: 2025 E Winsett St Tucson AZ 85719

HOANG, DUC VAN, physiopathologist, educator; b. Hanoi, Vietnam, Feb. 17, 1926; s. Duoc Van and Nguyen Thi (Tham) H.; came to U.S., 1975, naturalized, 1981; m. Mau-Ngo Thi Vu, Dec. 1, 1952; 1 son, Duc-An Hoang-Vu. M.D., Hanoi U. Sch. Medicine, Vietnam, 1953. Dean Sch. Medicine Army of the Republic of Vietnam, Saigon, 1959-63; dean Minh-Duc U. Sch. Medicine, Saigon, 1970-71; clin. prof. pathology, U. So. Calif. Sch. Medicine, Los Angeles, 1978—. Founder, past pres. Movement for Fedn. Countries S.E. Asia; co-founder, past v.p. Movement for Restoration Cultures and Religions of Orient; active Vo-Vi Meditation Assn. Am. Served to lt. col. M.C., Army of the Republic of Vietnam, 1952-63. Mem. AAUP, Am. Com. on Integrating Eastern and Western Medicine (founder), Vo-Vi Meditation Assn. Am. Republican. Roman Catholic. Clubs: U. So. Calif. Staff, U. So. Calif. Faculty Members (Los Angeles) Author: Towards an Integrated Humanization of Medicine, 1957; The Man Who Weighs the Soul, 1959; Eastern Medicine, A New Direction?, 1970; also short stories; translator: Pestis, introduction to the work of Albert Camus, Vietnamese translation of La Peste; editor: The East (co-founder); jour. Les Cahiers de l'Asie du Sud-Est. Home: 3630 Barry Ave Los Angeles CA 90066 Office: Los Angeles County-U So Calif Med Center 1200 N State St Room 12-700 Los Angeles CA 90033

HOARD, DONA, management consultant; b. Bklyn., Jan. 4, 1943; d. Simon and Marcelle (Feiner) Felser; m. David Hoard, Aug. 27, 1966 (div.); children—Daniel, Eliza. A.B., Vassar Coll., 1964; M.P.A., U. Pitts., 1965. Planner Parkins, Roger & Assoc., Detroit, 1965-66; dir. planning Community Action Agy., Lancaster, Pa., 1966-68; asst. to dir. Redevel. Agy., Richmond, Calif., 1969-71; treas. MKGK Incorp., San Francisco, 1971-82; ind. cons., 1982—; pres. Calif. State Bd. for Registration Profl. Engrs. Mem. Oakland Mus. Assn., Oakland Pub. Library Assn., East Bay Zool. Soc., Friends of Central Pl. Recipient awards Nat. Soc. Profl. Engrs., Calif. Soc. Profl. Engrs., Golden Gate sect. Soc. Women Engrs. Bay Area Engrs. Council, San Fernando Valley Engrs. Council, Nat. Soc. Mfg. Engrs. Mem. Nat. Assn. Female Execs. Democratic. Jewish. Co-author: Small Cities Community Development Block Grant Management Handbook, 1981. Office: 580 Market St San Francisco CA 94104

HOBAUGH, BEVERLY GAYLE, brokerage company executive; b. Long Beach, Calif., Apr. 10, 1941; d. Frank Edward and Thelma Dolorus (Knuppe) Hobaugh. B.A. in Sociology, Calif. State U.-Fullerton, 1971; M.B.A., Pepperdine U., 1982. Probation and group counselor Orange County Juvenile Hall, 1968; credit reporter Dun & Bradstreet, Los Angeles, 1971, agy. sales rep., 1971-82; v.p., sec., dir. S & W Engineered Products, Anaheim, Calif., 1982—; account exec. Merrill Lynch, Pierce, Fenner & Smith, Los Angeles, 1982—. Mem. Exec. Women, NOW. Democrat. Office: Merrill Lynch Pierce Fenner & Smith 523 W 6th St Los Angeles CA 90017

HOBBS, CHARLES ALBERT, V, air force officer; b. Balt., Nov. 5, 1948; s. Charles Albert and Shirley Anne (Hager) H.; m. Anne Barrie MacWhinney, Nov. 9, 1973; children—Charles Albert, Thomas Taylor, Ross Hager. B.A., U. Va., 1971; M.B.A, U. Wyo., 1975. Commd. 2d lt. U.S. Air Force, 1972, advanced through grades to capt., 1976; staff auditor, Vandenberg AFB, Calif., 1979-80, audit team leader, Kunsan, Republic of Korea, 1981-82, chief of internal audit Little Rock AFB and Blytheville AFB, 1982—; adj. prof. bus. U. Md., 1982—. Chmn., Little Rock Fed. Credit Union Supervising Com., 1982-83. Decorated Air Force Commendation medal. Mem. Am. Soc. Mil. Comptrollers, Air Force Assn. Republican. Roman Catholic. Clubs: Mensa, Mensa Edn. and Research Found., U. Va. Alumni Assn., U. Wyo. Alumni Assn., Am. Bowling Congress. Home: 133 Alabama Dr Jacksonville AR 72076 Office: AFAA Area Audit Office LRAFB AR 72076

HOBBS, DONALD GORDON, telephone co. exec.; b. Ferndale, Mich., July 9, 1972; s. Reginald Francis and Gladys Hetty (Trusscott) H.; m. Dorothy D. Trembath; children—Jim, Russ, Rick. B.S., Wayne State U., 1950. Acct., Mich. Bell Telephone Co., Detroit, 1950-58; dist. mgr. AT&T, N.Y.C., 1958-61; acct. Pacific Northwest Bell Telephone Co., Seattle, 1961-66; data processing mgr. Bell Labs., N.J., 1966-69; v.p. Wash./Idaho area consumer affairs dept. Pacific Northwest Bell Telephone Co., Seattle, 1978-83, v.p., comptroller, 1983—. Mem. exec. bd. council Boy Scouts Am., 1978; pres. bd. trustees Seattle Central Community Coll. Found., 1978, Downtown Seattle Assn., 1979; mem. exec. bd. Wash. State China Relations Council, 1980; bd. dirs. Citizens Council Against Crime, Econ. Devel. Council, Assn. Wash. Bus., 1982. Mem. Seattle C. of C. Clubs: Wash. Athletic, Rainier, Broadmoor Golf, Rotary (Seattle). Office: 1600 Bell Plaza Room 3108 Seattle WA 98191

HOBBS, GERALD HENRY DANBY, investor; b. Vanouver, B.C., Can., Mar. 11, 1921; s. Charles D. and Victoria M. (Danby) H.; m. Phyllis Rae Nicolson, May 1, 1947; children—David, Leslie, Janet, Phillip. Student Vancouver Coll., 1935-38. Sales mgr. Pacific Bolt Mfg. Co., 1946-55; gen. mgr. Western Can. Steel, Ltd., 1955-64, pres., 1964-68, chmn., chief exec. officer, 1968-72; v.p. Cominco, Ltd., Vancouver, 1968, v.p. Pacific region, 1969-72, exec. v.p., 1972-73, pres., 1973-78, chmn. bd., 1978-80; pvt. investor, Vancouver, 1980—; dir. Bank of N.S., B.C. Telephone Co., Discovery Parks, Inc., MacMillan Bloedel Ltd., N.Am. Life Ins. Co., Suncor, Inc., Glenayre Electronics Ltd. Bd. govs. U. B.C.; chmn. mgmt. com. Health Scis. Ctr. Hosp.; adv. bd. Salvation Army; exec. com. St. John's Ambulance Assn.; mem. adv. bd. Sta. KCTS, Seattle; bd. dirs. Vancouver Bd. Trade. Served with Royal Can. Army, 1940-46. Decorated Comdr. Order of St. John; recipient aux. service award Salvation Army, 1977. Conservative. Anglican. Club: Vancouver. Home: 3803 Marguerite St Vancouver BC V6J 4E8 Canada Office: 1112 W Pender St Vancouver BC V6E 2S1 Canada

HOBBS, NILA ALENE, mfg. co. exec.; b. Colorado Springs, Colo., Mar. 11, 1949; d. Harold Carl and Wilma Ella (French) H.; B.S. with high distinction, Colo. State U., 1971, M.B.A., 1973. Systems analyst Colo. div. Eastman Kodak Co., Windsor, 1974-80, sect. supr. systems devel., 1980—. Mem. Am. Prodn. and Inventory Control Soc, Colo. State U. Alumni Assn., Phi Kappa Phi. Republican. Home: 1037 Parkview Dr Fort Collins CO 80525 Office: DP&SD Bldg C 42 Floor 3 Windsor CO 80551

HOBERT, LEE GORDON, educator, consultant; b. Seattle, Jan. 6, 1927; s. Harold Wesley and Emily Ingaborg (Bumert) H.; m. Laura Sherman, June 16, 1948; children—Loralie, Loren; m. 2d, Jimmie Sue Ragsdale, Feb. 18, 1977. B.Th., Northwest Christian Coll., 1950; M.Div., Phillips U., 1955; L.H.D. (hon.), U. Albuquerque, 1973. Ordained to ministry Christian Ch. (Disciples of Christ), 1950; minister, Trent, Oreg., 1948-50, Wichita, Kans., 1950-52, Jefferson, Okla., 1952-55, Okmulgee, Okla., 1958-60, Mesilla Valley Christian Ch., Las Cruces, N.Mex., 1960-74; dir. The Centering Place, Las Cruces, 1975—; cons. El Paso Housing Authority, El Paso Electric, El Paso Community Coll., Tex. Nursing Home Assn., Mescallero Apache Tribe, Bent-Mescallero Elem. Sch., N.Mex. State Coll. Community and Human Services, U. N.Mex. Dept. Continuing Educ. Mem. Gov.'s Councils on Older Am., 1965, Migrant work, 1966-67; mem. Taos Pueblo Advocate-Bluehake, 1967; chmn. Citizens Adv. Com., Las Cruces; pres. Community Services Council, 1968-72; pres. State Council Chs., 1964-68; chmn. First Ecumenical bd. dirs. Holy Cross Retreat, 1968-73. Served with USN, 1944-46. Recipient Community Services award Community Services Council, 1972; N.Mex. Found. for Humanities grantee, 1974. Mem. Assn. Humanistic Psychology, Am. Personnel and Guidance Assn., Am. Assn. Marriage and Family Therapists, Internat. Transactional Analysis Assn., Las Cruces Jaycees (Disting. Service award 1963), N.Mex. Jaycees (Young Man of Yr. 1963). Republican. Established Hospitality House, East Las Cruces Community Center. Home and Office: 745 Baca Rd Las Cruces NM 88001

HOBLIT, FREDERIC MALTBY, mechanical engineer; b. Los Angeles, July 4, 1916; s. Frederic Maltby and Louise (Barber) H.; m. Iris Munson, Nov. 4, 1950; children—Sidney Louise, Frederic Maltby, Tracy Diane Cook. A.B. in Engring., Stanford U., 1938; M.S. in Marine Engring. and Naval Architecture, U. Mich., Ann Arbor, 1941. Registered mech. engr., Calif. Tech. draftsman Newport News Shipbldg. and Dry Dock Co. (Va.), 1940-42; test engr. Marinship Corp., Sausalito, Calif., 1942-45; with Lockheed-Calif. Co., Burbank, 1945-83, stress engr., 1945-50, structures engr., 1950-56, design specialist, 1956-57, group engr., 1957-71, research and devel. engr., 1971-80, sr. research and devel. engr., project loads dept., 1980-83, cons., 1983—. Bd. mgrs. East San Fernando Valley YMCA, 1967—, chmn. 1976-78. Recipient Robert E. Gross award for tech. excellence and Lockheed's engr.-scientist of yr., 1980. Mem. AIAA. Contbr. publs. to profl. jours. Home: 11555 Amanda Dr Studio City CA 91604

HOBSON, ERIC MILES, educator, school counselor; b. Langley Field AFB, Va., Sept. 26, 1943; s. Oliver Lincoln and Lillian (Miles) H.; m. Ilene Olga Winnick; children—Andrei, Joshua. B.A. in Chemistry, U. Pacific, 1967; M.Ed., U. Nev., 1972. Cert. tchr., Nev. Chemist, Intag Inks, Chgo., 1965-66; instr. chemistry, phys. scis. Fernley (Nev.) High Sch., 1970—, counselor, 1974—. Active Boy Scouts Am., 1980—; bd. dirs. Temple Sinai Religious Sch. Served with U.S. Army, 1967-69; Vietnam. Robert Taft Inst. fellow, 1982. Mem. Am. Personnel and Guidance Assn., Nev. Personnel and Guidance Assn., No. Nev. Personnel and Guidance Assn., NEA. Democrat. Editor Vaquero, 1976—.

HOBSON, GARY JOE, engineer; b. Bedford, Ind., Dec. 29, 1952; s. Warren T. and Mildred L. (Fish) H.; m. Kathleen Corso, Aug. 16, 1980; 1 dau., Kristin Ann. B.S., Ind. U.-Purdue U.-Indpls., 1976. Cert. Nat. Inst. Cert. Engring. Techs. Design engr. Warren T. Hobson & Assocs., Inc., Indpls., 1976-80; project engr. Lowry & Assocs., Irvine, Calif., 1980—. Served in USAFR, 1971-77. Mem. Am. Water Works Assn., Ind. Soc. Profl. Land Surveyors, ASTM, Ind. Univ. Alumni Assn. (life). Republican. Methodist. Home: 8761 Lanark Circle Huntington Beach CA 92646 Office: Lowry & Assocs 17748 Sky Park Blvd Suite 100 Irvine CA 92714

HOBSON, ROBERT LARRIE, manufacturing company executive; b. Longview, Wash., Jan. 11, 1938; s. Howard M. and Mildred F. (Mathisen) H.; m. Delois Jean Cash, Feb. 1, 1958; children—L. Scott, Shelly, Karla, Donna. B.S., Va. Mil. Inst., 1959; M.S., Rensselaer Poly. Inst., 1962, Ph.D., 1965. Registered profl. engr., Calif. Asst. prof. physics U.S. Mil. Acad., West Point, N.Y., 1965-68; sr. engr. Gen. Electric Co., San Jose, Calif., 1968-71, areas sales mgr., 1971-75; mgr. nuclear applications Gen. Electric Tech. Services Co., Tokyo, 1975-78; v.p., rep., dir. Japan Nuclear Fuel Co., Kurihama, 1978-79; mgr. internat. mktg. Gen. Electric Co., San Jose, 1979-83, mgr. domestic projects, 1983—. Mem. high council Ch. of Jesus Christ of Latter Day Saints, Morgan Hill, Calif., 1981—, dist. pres., Tokyo, 1976-79; scoutmaster Boy Scouts Am., San Jose, 1969-70. Served to capt. U.S. Army, 1964-68. Mem. Am. Nuclear Soc. (internat. com.), Soc. Cincinnatus. Republican. Home: 4061 Cienega Rd Hollister CA 95023 Office: Gen Electric Co MC 391 175 Curtner Ave San Jose CA 95125

HOCH, ORION LINDEL, business executive; b. Canonsburg, Pa., Dec. 21, 1928; s. Orion L.F. and Ann Marie (McNulty) H.; B.S., Carnegie Mellon U., 1952; M.S., UCLA, 1954; Ph.D., Stanford U., 1957; m. Jane Lee Ogan, June 12, 1952; children—Andrea, Brenda, John. With Hughes Aircraft Co., Culver City, Calif., 1952-54, Stanford Electronics Labs., 1954-57; sr. engr., dept. mgr., div. v.p., div. pres. Litton Electron Tube div., San Carlos, Calif., 1957-68; group exec. Litton Components Group, 1968-70; v.p. Litton Industries, Inc., Beverly Hills, Calif., 1970, sr. v.p., 1971-74, pres., chief operating officer, 1982—, also dir.; pres. Intersil, Inc., Cupertino, Calif., 1974-82. Served with AUS, 1946-48. Mem. IEEE, Sigma Xi, Tau Beta Pi, Phi Kappa Phi. Office: Litton Industries Inc 360 N Crescent Dr Beverly Hills CA 90210

HOCHADEL, JACK BIRCH, manufacturing company executive; b. Youngstown, Ohio, June 28, 1933; s. John P. and Dorothy E. (Birch) H.; m. Karen K. Kerns, June 26, 1965; children—Julie, John, Jill. M.E., U. Cin., 1956; M.B.A., U. So. Calif., 1961. Systems engr. Hughes Aircraft Co., Culver City, Calif., 1956-61; v.p. Mega Marine Corp., Costa Mesa, Calif., 1961-63; pres. The Willard Co., Fountain Valley, Calif., 1964—, also dir.; chmn. bd. Tankinetics, Inc., Westminster, Calif. and Harrison, Ark. Mem. steering com. for Congressman Robert Badham; dir. Orange County (Calif.) Lincoln Club; county adv. com. mem. Am. Cancer Soc.; past moderator, chmn. bd. trustees Congl. Ch. Newport Harbor; congressional apptd. del. White House Small Bus. Conf., 1980. U. Cin. scholar, 1951. Mem. soc. Naval Architects and Marine Engrs., Am. Def. Preparedness Assn., Navy League of U.S., So. Calif. Marine Assn. (past pres., dir. 1977-83). Republican. Clubs: Capital Hill (Washington); Balboa Bay, Bahia Corinthian Yacht (Newport Beach, Calif.). Contbr. articles in marine field to profl. jours. Home: 1523 Sandcastle Dr Corona Del Mar CA 92625 Office: The Willard Co 11200 Condor Ave Fountain Valley CA 92708

HOCHBERG, FREDERICK GEORGE, accountant; b. Los Angeles, July 4, 1913; s. Frederick Joseph and Lottie (LeGendre) H.; B.A., UCLA, 1937; children—Frederick George, Ann C. Hochberg May. Chief acct., auditor Swinerton, McClure & Vinnell, Managua, Nicaragua, 1942-44; pvt. acctg. practice, Avalon, Calif., 1946-66; designer, operator Descanso Beach Club, Avalon, 1966; v.p. Air Catalina, 1967; treas. Catalina Airlines, 1967; pres. Aero Commuter, 1967; v.p., treas., dir. bus. affairs William L. Pereira & Assos., Planners, Architects, Engrs., Los Angeles, 1967-72; v.p., gen. mgr. Mo. Hickory Corp., 1972-74; prin. Fred G. Hochberg Assos., Mgmt. Cons., 1974—; v.p. Vicalton S.A. Mexico, 1976—; v.p., gen. mgr. Solar Engring. Co., Inc., 1977-79; pres. Solar Assos. Internat., 1979-83. Chmn. Avalon Transp. Com., 1952; sec. Santa Catalina Festival of Arts, 1960; pres. Avalon Music Bowl Assn., 1961; chmn. Avalon Harbor Commn., 1960; pres. Catalina Mariachi Assn., 1961-66; treas. City of Avalon, 1954-62, councilman, 1962-66, mayor, 1964-66; sec. Avalon City Planning Commn., 1956-58; chmn. Avalon Airport Com., 1964-66, Harbor Devel. Commn., 1965-66; bd. dirs. Los Angeles Child Guidance Clinic, 1975—, treas., 1978-79, pres., 1979-81. Served as ensign USNR, 1944-45. Named Catalina Island Man of Yr., 1956. Mem. Avalon Catalina Island C. of C. (past pres.), Soc. Calif. Accountants, Mensa, Am. Arbitration Assn. (panel), Catalina Island Mus. Soc. (treas. 1964), Los Angeles, El Monte chambers commerce, Town Hall-West (vice chmn). Club: Rotary (pres.). Home: 6760 Hill Park Dr 505 Los Angeles CA 90068 Office: 52 E Magnolia Blvd Burbank CA 91502

HOCHSTEIN, PAUL, biochemist; b. N.Y.C., Feb. 7, 1926; s. Samuel and Ida (Leshan) H.; m. Gianna Smith, Mar. 9, 1956; children—Miles, Evon. B.S., Rutgers U., 1950; M.S., U. Md., 1952, Ph.D., 1954. Postdoctoral fellow Nat. Cancer Inst., 1954-57; research assoc. Columbia U., 1957-63; assoc. prof. Duke U., Durham, N.C., 1963-69; prof. biochemistry U. So. Calif., Los Angeles, 1969—, dir. Inst. for Toxicology, 1980—, assoc. dean, 1981—. Served with AUS, 1943-46. Recipient Research Career award NIH, 1965-69. Mem. Am. Soc. Biol. Chemists, Soc. for Toxicology, Am. Soc. Pharmacology and Exptl. Therapeutics, Soc. Gen. Physiologists. Contbr. numerous articles to sci. jours. Office: 1985 Zonal Ave Los Angeles CA 90033

HOCK, OWEN WALTER, advertising and public relations executive; b. Smithfield, Nebr., Aug. 30, 1927; s. Walter Conrad and Magdalena Emma (Bunsen) H.; m. Mina Jane Lorensen, Dec. 27, 1951; children—Greg, Lori. B.S. in Bus. Adm. and Mktg., U. Nebr.-Lincoln, 1952. Mgmt. trainee and advt. mgr. Caterpillar, Peoria, Ill., 1952-59; mktg. supr. Needham, Louis & Brorby, Chgo., 1959-60; v.p and account supr. Marstellar, Chgo., 1960-63; account supr. Young & Rubicam, San Francisco, 1964-68; v.p. and account supr. Lennen & Newell, San Francisco, 1965-69; dir. corp. communications Memorex, Santa Clara, Calif., 1969-74; pres. Pinne, Garvin & Hock, Inc., San Francisco, 1975—. Served with USMC, 1946-48. Mem. Internat. Fedn. Advt. Agys., Nat. Advt./Mktg. Assn., Beta Gamma Sigma. Office: 200 Vallejo St San Francisco CA 94111

HOCKER, RICHARD KELLY, lawyer; b. Buckeye, Ariz., June 14, 1933; s. Conway Holmes and Virginia Estella (Jackson) H.; m. Anna Sue Self, Sept. 10, 1957 (div.); children—Anna Margaret, Charles Conway, Richard Adam. B.A. in Polit. Sci., U. Ariz., 1955; J.D., George Washington U., 1958; postgrad. Hague Acad. Internat. Law, 1970. Bar: Ariz. 1958, U.S. Ct. Mil. Appeals 1959, U.S. Dist. Ct. Ariz. 1962, U.S. Ct. Appeals (9th cir.) 1971, U.S. Supreme Ct. 1971. Assoc., Struckmeyer & Whitney, Phoenix, 1962-63, Caine, Brigham & Hocker, Tempe, Ariz., 1963-67; sole practice, Tempe, 1967-72; ptnr. Hocker & Gilcrease, Tempe, 1972-76; sole practice, R. Kelly Hocker, Ltd., Tempe, 1976-79; ptnr. Hocker, Yarbrough & Gilcrease, Tempe, 1979-82, Hocker & Axford, P.C., Tempe, 1982—; arbitrator Am. Arbitration Assn.; lectr. in field. Served to capt. JAGC, U.S. Army, 1958-62. Mem. State Bar Ariz., Assn. Trial Lawyers Am. (dir. Ariz. chpt. 1973-76), Assn. Trial Lawyers Ariz., Tri-City Bar Assn. (dir. 1971-73), Tempe C. of C. Democrat. Episcopalian. Office: Hocker & Axford PC 6601 S Rural Rd Tempe AZ 85283

HOCKETT, ROBERT GEORGE, college dean, farmer; b. Havre, Mont., Sept. 12, 1925; s. George A. and Sophia (Hegland) H. B.S., Mont. State Coll., 1951; M.S., Oreg. State U., 1968. Farm operator, Havre, Mont., 1950—; soil conservation technician Soil Conservation Service, Havre, 1951-54; instr. No. Mont. Coll., Havre, 1957-79; dean Sch. Tech., 1980—; dir. Farmers Grain Exchange, Havre, 1972—; Bd. dirs. Mont. Council Coops., 1978—; supr. Hill County Conservation Dist., 1960—.

Served with U.S. Army, 1945-46. Mem. Am. Vocat. Assn., Mont. Vocat. Assn. Democrat. Lutheran. Club: Eagles.

HOCKING, THOMAS MESSENGER, accountant; b. Chico, Calif., June 22, 1932; s. Elmer John and Marion Anne (Messenger) H.; m. Diane Knight, Dec. 6, 1959; children—Cynthia J., Thomas, David K. A.A., Yuba Jr. Coll., 1953; A.B., Sacramento State U., 1955. C.P.A., Calif. Mem. staff Barlow, Davis & Wood, San Francisco, 1957-58; ptnr. Hocking, Denton, Palmquist & Co., C.P.A.s, 1959—. Served in USN, 1955-57. Mem. Calif. Soc. C.P.A.s, Delano C. of C. (dir. 1980-82). Republican. Roman Catholic. Clubs: Lions (past pres.). Elks. Home: 1301 Round St Delano CA 93215 Office: 912 High St Delano CA 93215

HOCKMAN, KARL KALEVI, transp. and mgmt. services exec.; b. N.Y.C., Jan. 17, 1924; s. John Laakso and Fanny Maria (Wirtanen) H.; B.A., Shelton Coll., 1956; cert. in indsl. relations U. Calif.-Berkeley, 1968; m. Betty Lou Heyle, June 24, 1970; children—William, James, Karol, Thomas, David, Kathleen. Vice pres. Scroeder Distbg. Co. No. Calif., Oakland, 1960-66; controller Inland Cities Express, Inc., Riverside, Calif., 1967-70; data processing mgr. Moss Motors, Ltd., Goleta, Calif., 1970-73; controller LKL Industries, Fontana, Calif., 1973-82; mng. ptnr. Hockman & Hockman Assocs., Perris, Calif., 1982—; dir. Raemont & Co., Inc., MI Sueno Ranch Nursery, Inc., Quest Electronics Corp., W.R. Eyserbeck Constrn., Inc. Served with AUS, 1942-45; ETO. Mem. Nat. Def. Transp. Assn. Republican. Adventist. Clubs: Valley Transp., Tuxedo Park Masons. Home: 17731 Indian St Perris CA 92370 Office: 17731 Indian St Perris CA 92370

HODDER, JOHN WALTER, industrial engineer; b. Cambridge, Mass.; Nov. 12, 1950; s. Edwin John and Mary Sue (Brown) H.; m. Sheila Laraine Aug. 28, 1971; children—Tracy, Jason, Wendy. B.S., Idaho State U., 1975. Sr. indsl. engr. vegetable div. Ore-Ida Foods, Inc., Boise, Idaho, to 1983; ops. mgr. Cut and Ready Foods, Inc., San Lorenzo, Calif., 1983—. Instr., Jr. Achievement, Boise; active Boise community edn. Mem. Am. Inst. Indsl. Engrs., Am. Contract Bridge League. Democrat. Episcopalian. Contbr. articles in field to profl. jours. Office: 16505 Worthley Dr San Lorenzo CA 94580

HODGE, ALICE MACNAUGHTON, retail advertising executive; b. Honolulu, Feb. 11, 1953; d. Malcolm and Winifred (Sperry) MacNaughton; m. 2d James Blythe Hodge, Jan. 3, 1981; stepchildren—Eric James, Terra Aynsley. A.B., Stanford U., 1975. With Emporium Capwell Co., San Francisco, 1975—, with spl. events dept., 1975-79, spl. events/pub. relations dir., 1979-81, dir. broadcast advt., 1981—; mem. spl. events adv. com. Assoc. Merchandising Corp., 1978-81. Com. mem. Pub. Relations Bd., Vol. Bur. San Francisco, 1980—; pub. relations com. San Francisco Fine Arts Mus., 1981; fundraising vol. Stanford U., 1975—, ann. fund co-chmn. San Francisco, 1980—, mem. Irvine Found. grant com., 1982—; pres. Sacred Heart Schs. Alumnae Assn., 1978-80, mem. Capital Campaign Fund Adv. Com., 1981—; mem. council San Francisco Art Inst., 1981-83; mem. jr. women's com. San Francisco Symphony, 1982-; mem. San Francisco Ballet Aux., 1983—. Recipient five yr. vol. service award Stanford U., 1981. Mem. Bay Area Exec. Women's Forum, Jr. League. Republican. Episcopalian. Club: Commonwealth. Contbr. writings to publs. in field. Office: Emporium Capwell Co 835 Market St San Francisco CA 94103

HODGE, BRADY JOHNSON, marketing executive; b. Los Angeles, July 8, 1951; s. Fred Johnson and Eileen Louise (Holland) H. B.S., U. Calif.-Berkeley, 1974; M.B.A., UCLA, 1976. Dir. mktg. Heavenly Valley Ski Resort, South Lake Tahoe, Calif., 1976—; pres. bd. dirs. Ski Lake Tahoe; bd. dirs., chmn. mktg. com. South Lake Tahoe Visitors Bur.; part time instr. Lake Tahoe Community Coll. Mem. South Lake Tahoe C. of C. (dir.), Assn. M.B.A. Execs. Republican. Club: Lake Tahoe Rotary. Home: PO Box 13081 South Lake Tahoe CA 95702 Office: PO Box AT South Lake Tahoe CA 95705

HODGE, JAMES BLYTHE, lawyer; b. Pasadena, Calif., June 4, 1946; s. Roy Burrows and Virginia Irene (Blythe) H.; m. Alice MacNaughton, Jan. 3, 1981; children—Eric James, Terra A. B.A., U. Wash., 1968; J.D., Columbia U., 1971. Bar: Calif. 1972. Assoc. Morrison & Forester, San Francisco, 1971-74, Cotten, Seligman & Ray, San Francisco, 1974-75; partner Hodge, Buchannan, Falik & DuPree, San Francisco, 1976—. Mem. ABA, Calif. Bar Assn., San Francisco Bar Assn. Episcopalian. Home: 3101 Clay St San Francisco CA 94115 Office: 300 Montgomery St San Francisco CA 94104

HODGE, KENNETH ERNEST, aeronautical engineer; b. Claremont, N.H., Jan. 25, 1928; s. Verden W. and Elizabeth E. (Brownell) H.; m. Kathleen Patricia Henderson, May 30, 1955; children—Kenneth, Marlowe, Andrew. B. Aero. Engring., Rensselaer Poly. Inst., 1951; M. Mech. Engring., Poly. Inst. N.Y., 1956. Registered profl. engr., Calif. Engr., Grumman Aerospace Corp., Bethpage, N.Y., 1951-56; flight test supr. Lockheed-Calif., Burbank, Calif., 1956-72; dir. aero. staff Nat. Aeros. and Space Council, Washington, 1972-73; mgr. transport aircraft office NASA Hdqrs., Washington, 1973-80; dir. engring. Dryden Flight Research Ctr., NASA, Edwards, Calif., 1980-81, chief aero. projects office Dryden Flight Research Facilty, Edwards, 1981—. Recipient design award Aero Digest, 1954; Key award Rensselaer Poly. Inst. Alumni Assn., 1966; Sr. Exec. Service award NASA, 1980. Assoc. fellow AIAA; mem. Aircraft Owners and Pilots Assn. Clubs: Nat. Aviation (Washington); Antelope Valley Amateur Radio (pres. 1981); Aero (Los Angeles, Washington). Contbr. articles to profl. jours. Home: 42846 Cinema Ave Lancaster CA 93534 Office: PO Box 273 Code OP Edwards CA 93523

HODGE, LYNNE GARVEY, training and development specialist; b. Cleve., July 15, 1953; d. Jack Egler and Marion Catherine (Fohl) Garvey; divorced; 1 dau., Hilary Lynne. B.F.A., U. Colo., 1975, M.P.A., 1980. Legal sec. Merkel, Campbell, Dill & Zetzer, Cleve., 1971; customer info. rep. East Ohio Gas Co., Cleve., 1971-72; mgr. central records office Boulder Valley Sch. Dist. (Colo.), 1976-77; sec. corp. reports, energy conservation technician Pub. Service Co. Colo., Denver, 1977-81, tng. and devel. specialist, instr., 1981—. Mem. Am. Soc. Tng. and Devel., Nat. Mgmt. Assn., Exec. and Profl. Women's Council (v.p.). Republican. Presbyterian. Club: Internat. Athletic (Aurora, Colo.). Home: 3500A Telluride Circle Aurora CO 80013 Office: Pub Service Co of Colo 938 Bannock St Suite 320 Denver CO

HODGE, WINSTON WILLIAM, computer cons.; b. Drummondville, Que., Can., Mar. 24, 1940; came to U.S., 1956, naturalized, 1962; s. Russell Alexander and Amelia Eleanor (Lowe) H.; B.A., Chapman Coll., 1962; postgrad. UCLA, 1962-63, Calif. State Coll., Fullerton, 1965; m. Lenda Sue Harvey, June 4, 1961; children—Rusty Hodge, Karen, Nancy. Project engr. Autonetics div. Rockwell, Anaheim, Calif., 1962-69; program mgr. Marshall Data Systems Co., Torrance, Calif., 1969-71; dir. systems div. Trivex/Datapac Co., Irvine, Calif., 1971-73; v.p. engring. Internat. Peripheral & Computer Corp., Santa Ana, Calif., 1973—; founder, pres. Hodge Computer Research Corp., Orange, Calif., 1970—; dir. Great Western Am. Mem. IEEE. Corp. Contbr. articles to profl. jours. Patentee airborne computer architecture. Home: 2603 Hillcrest St Orange CA 92667 Office: 1161 Tustin Ave Orange CA 92667

HODGES, DEWEY HARPER, research scientist; b. Clarksville, Tenn., May 18, 1948; s. Plummer M. and Etha M. (Harper) H.; m. Margaret Elin Jones, Aug. 14, 1971; children—Timothy, Jonathan, David, Philip. M.S., Stanford U., 1970, Ph.D., 1972. Research scientist U.S. Army aeromechanics lab. NASA Ames Research Ctr., Moffett Field, Calif., 1970—, theoretical group leader, rotorcraft dynamics div., 1980—; lectr. dept. aero. and astronautics Stanford U. Elder Christian Community Ch., San Jose, Calif.; prof. theology No. Calif. Bible Coll., San Jose. Served to capt. U.S. Army, 1973-77. Recipient NASA tech. utilization award, 1975; Tech. Brief award, 1976; Dept. Army commendation medal, 1977, ofcl. commendation, 1978; U.S. Army research and devel. achievement award, 1979. Assoc. fellow AIAA; mem. Creation Research Soc., Am. Helicopter Soc., Tau Beta Pi, Pi Tau Sigma. Club: Acacia. Contbr. numerous articles to tech. jours.; assoc. editor AIAA Jour., 1981-83. Home: 3255 Trebol Ln San Jose CA 95148 Office: MS 215-1 Aeromechanics Lab Ames Research Center Moffett Field CA 94035

HODGES, VERNON WRAY, mechanical engineer; b. Roanoke, Va., Dec. 26, 1929; s. Charlie Wayne and Kathleen Mae (Williams) H.; m. Linda Lou Wall, Feb. 3, 1967; children—Kenneth Wray, Kelly Dianne. B.S.M.E., Va. Poly. Inst. and State U., 1951; M.S. in Systems Mgmt., U. So. Calif., 1979. Flight test engr. Boeing Co., Wichita, Kans., 1966-71, systems engr., Seattle, 1971-76; systems test engr. B-1 Bomber, Rockwell Corp., Edwards AFB, Calif., 1976-77, systems design engr. B-1 Bomber, El Segundo, Calif., 1981—; lead systems engr. crew sta. requirements YAH-64, Hughes Helicopters, Culver City, Calif., 1977-81. Deacon, elder Presbyterian Ch., 1973—. Served with USAF, 1951-65. Registered profl. engr., Kans., Wash., Calif. Mem. Air Force Assn., AIAA, ASME, Nat. Soc. Profl. Engrs., Wash. Soc. Profl. Engrs. (sec. South King chpt. 1972-73). Republican. Presbyterian. Clubs: Masons, Shriners. Home: 2731 West Ave J-8 Lancaster CA 93534

HODGES, V(IVIAN) PAULINE, educator; b. Liberal, Kans., Sept. 20, 1929; d. Paul W. and Dora D. (Wilson) Arnett; m. Albert E. Hodges, Sept. 5, 1947 (div.); children—Brent, Mark. B.A. in English summa cum laude, Panhandle State U., 1958; M.A. summa cum laude in Secondary Reading and English, U. Colo., 1973, Ph.D. summa cum laude in Reading, 1973. Tchr. English and speech Forgan (Okla.) Pub. Sch., 1950-66; tchr. remedial English, Liberal Unified Dist. 480, 1966-67; researcher, editor Beaver County Hist. Soc., Okla., 1967-70; tchr. reading Douglas County High Sch., Castle Rock, Colo., 1970-76; assoc. prof. edn. Colo. State U., 1976—; dir. research and devel. Ednl. Cons. Assocs., Englewood, Colo., 1980-81; tchr. adult edn. Accelerated Edn. Dallas, 1969, Contemporary Schs. of Colo., 1970-75; tchr. in-service classes U. No. Colo., 1974-76; tchr. off-campus program U. Albuquerque, 1981; curriculum cons. Colo. pub. schs.; conf. speaker. Mem. Internat. Reading Assn. (dir. Colo. council 1974-77), Nat. Council Tchrs. of English, Colo. Lang. Arts Soc. (pres. 1980-81, dir. 1981—), Western Writers Am., Am. Fedn. Tchrs. (state v.p. 1974-76, treas. Colo. State U. chpt. 1979-80), Phi Delta Kappa. Author: Teaching Speed Reading Grades 7-12, 1977; Teaching Reading in the Content Areas, 1978; Improving Reading/Study Skills, 1979; A Resource Guide for Teaching Reading in the Content Areas, 1980; A Study Guide for Competency in the Basic Skills, 1983; contbr. articles to profl. jours. Office: Dept of Education Colorado State University Fort Collins CO 80523

HODGSON, DAVID LOWELL, energy resources geologist; b. Flushing, N.Y., May 20, 1930; s. Claude Lowell and Sylvia Ann (Riffilmacher) H.; B.S., Fla. State U., 1956; m. Patricia Ruth Patsch Kaiser, May 23, 1982; children—David, Deborah, Michael, Rick, Diana. With Ala. Power Co., 1957-60, TVA, 1960-65; energy resources geologist S. Calif. Edison, Rosemead, 1965—. Served with U.S. Army, 1951-53. Certified mine foreman, Ala.; registered geologist, Calif. Mem. Geol. Soc. Am., Am. Assn. Mining Engrs., U.S. Naval Inst. Club: Seal Beach Yacht. Author, co-author tech. writings and reports in field. Home: 2221 Ocean Ave Apt 207 Santa Monica CA 90405 Office: Southern California Edison Fuel Supply Dept PO Box 800 2244 Walnut Grove Ave Rosemead CA 91770

HODGSON, KENNETH P., mining executive, real estate investor; b. Canon City, Colo., Sept. 20, 1945; s. Cecil L. and Jaunita J. Hodgson Murris; m. Rebecca K. Thompson, Feb. 15, 1967; 1 dau., Amber K.; m. 2d, Rita J. Lewis, Apr. 22, 1979. Student Metro Coll., 1966-68. With Golden Mining Corp., Utah, 1973-79, Windfall Group Inc., Utah, 1976-77; pres. Houston Mining, Ariz., 1979-82; v.p. Silver Ridge Mining, Inc., Gold Ridge Mining Inc., Ariz., 1979-82; pres. Ken Hodgson & Co., Inc., Canon City, 1983—. Recipient numerous safety awards. Mem. AIME. Republican. Baptist. Lodge: Moose. Home: 426 Del Rey Canon City CO 81212

HOEBER, CHRISTOPHER FRANCIS, engineering company executive; b. Berlin, Germany, Mar. 31, 1947; s. Francis Packard and Ethel Thelma (Halverson) H.; m. Mary Lynn Gould, June 7, 1969; 1 son, Brian Richard. B.S.E.E., Cornell U., 1969, M.S.E.E., 1970. Mem. tech. staff Hughes Aircraft Co., El Segundo, Calif., 1970-73, project engr., 1973-75; sr. staff engr. Ford Aerospace and Communications Corp., Palo Alto, Calif., 1975-76, prin. engr., 1976-80, program engring. specialist, 1980-83, program engring. mgr., 1983—. Mem. AIAA, IEEE, Tau Beta Pi, Eta Kappa Nu. Democrat. Unitarian. Club: San Jose Bicycle (Los Altos, Calif.). Contbr. articles to profl. jours. Home: 24421 Summerhill Ave Los Altos CA 94022 Office: 3939 Fabian Way Palo Alto CA 94303

HOEDEMAKER, DAVID CONRAD, architect; b. Phila., July 1, 1933; s. Edward David and Ruth Elisabeth (Shepherd) H.; m. Ivaly Jones, Jan. 3, 1958; children—John Frederick, Linda Anne, Stephen David. B.A., Stanford U., 1955; B.Arch., U. Wash., 1960; M.Arch., Yale U., 1962. Designer Eero Saarinen & Assocs., Bloomfield Hills, Mich., 1960-62; archtl. designer NBBJ Group, Seattle, 1962-68, ptnr., 1968—, mng. ptnr., 1976—; lectr., vis. com. U. Wash. Coll. Architects and Urban Planning, 1978-80. Trustee, Seattle Art Mus., 1977—, Overlake Sch., Redmond, Wash., 1980—; bd. dirs. Seattle Central Community Coll. Found., 1981—. Served to 1st lt. USAF, 1956-58. Recipient numerous local and nat. archtl. design awards; U. Wash. Coll. Architecture and Urban Planning traveling scholar, 1959. Fellow AIA (mem. nat. design com. 1970-72, pres. Seattle chpt. 1973, pres. Sr. Council Architects 1978); mem. Nat. Council Archtl. Registration Bds., Tau Sigma Delta. Clubs: Rotary, Rainier, Seattle Tennis, Univ., Monday. Office: 111 S Jackson St Seattle WA 98104

HOEFER, JOHN HENRY, advertising agency executive; b. St. Cloud, Minn., Nov. 12, 1915; s. John James and Marie Emily (De Long Champs) H.; m. Katherine A. Foster, Sept. 9, 1939; children—Carolyn Pelkam, Susan Witter, John F., William E. B.A., U. Calif.-Berkeley, 1938; M.B.A., Stanford U., 1940. Commd. ensign U.S. Navy Res., 1938, advanced through grades to rear adm., 1965; served in Underwater Defs., Pearl Harbor, 1940-42, as navigator U.S.S. Abner Read, 1942-45, as exec. officer U.S.S. Norris, 1945-46; ret., 1975; pres. Hoefer Dieterich, Brown, Inc., 1946-79; chmn. Chiat/Day/Hoefer Inc., San Francisco, 1979-80, Chiat/Day, San Francisco, 1982—; dir. Lucky Stores, Inc.; chmn. Hoefer/Amidei, Inc., Pub. Relations; mem. No. Calif. Adv. Bd. to Advt. Council. Trustee Pacific Real Estate Trust, Golden State U., Nat. Rowing Found.; cons. Found. Teaching Econs.; counselor U. Calif.-Berkeley Alumni Assn. Decorated Am. Area Naval Res. medal, Commendation ribbon (1 star, 2 permanent citations), Philippine Liberation medal, N.Am. ribbon, World War II medal, Vietnam Service medal, Legion of Merit. Mem. Am. Assn. West (pres.), Am. Assn. Advt. Agys. (sec.-treas. nat bd., chmn. Western Region bd. govs.). Republican. Episcopalian. Clubs: Meadow Golf & Country (Fairfax, Calif.); Belvedere (Calif.) Tennis, San Francisco Advt. (pres.). Home: 32 Peninsula Rd Belvedere CA 94920 Office: 414 Jackson Sq San Francisco CA 94111

HOEFT, ARTHUR PETER, analytical laboratory official, coal sampling consultant; b. Sheboygan, Wis., May 25, 1945; s. Arthur A. and Marjorie A. (Trimberger) H.; m. Patricia A. Slesar, July 10, 1970; children—Alexis, Erika. B.S. in Chemistry, St. Norbert Coll., West DePere, Wis., 1967; M.S. in Chemistry, Colo. State U., Ft. Collins, 1971, M.S. in Bus. (scholar), 1973. Research and devel. chemist Am. Can Co., Neenah, Wis., 1967-68; analytical chemist Core Lab., Inc., Casper, Wyo., 1973-74, lab. supr., 1974-76, coal services coordinator, Denver, 1976-79, coal ops. mgr., Denver, 1980—; cons. coal sampling and testing, analyses, lab. design; condr. coal analysis seminar. Served to 1st lt. U.S. Army, 1967-69. Decorated Army Commendation Medal. Mem. Am. Chem. Soc., ASTM, Colo. Mining Assn., Rocky Mountain Coal Mining Inst., Soc. Mining Engrs., AIME. Contbr. articles to profl. jours.; patentee in field. Home: 8754 E Eastman Ave Denver CO 80231 Office: 1330 S Potomac St Suite 104 Aurora CO 80012

HOELZLE, EUGENE CHRIS, minicomputer maintenance and sales company executive; b. Dayton, Ohio, June 25, 1950; s. Eugene C. and Evelyn K. (Knox) H. Mgmt. Cert., Orange Coast Coll., Costa Mesa, Calif., 1980. Sr. tech. support engr. MSI Data Corp., Costa Mesa, 1973-79; field service mgr. Gen. Terminal Corp., Tustin, Calif., 1979-82; pres. C. Hoelzle Assocs., Inc., Costa Mesa, 1978—. Mem. Costa Mesa Civic Transp. Com. Recipient Achievement award Bank Am., 1968. Mem. Assn. Field Service Mgrs., Nat. Rifle Assn. Office: 1304A Logan Ave Costa Mesa CA 92626

HOFER, DONALD JOSEPH, union executive; b. Petersburg, Nebr., Apr. 15, 1927; s. Arthur W. and Leona (Julich) H.; m. Barbara L. Kelly, June 15, 1948; children—Cynthia Marie, Gregory Stephen, Jerome Vincent. Student Chaunute Jr. Coll., 1946-47, Ranger Jr. Coll., 1954-55. With Sinclair Pipeline Co., Kans., Tex., Mo., 1947-55; plant operator Petro-Tex Chem. Co., Houston, 1958-60; chief exec. officer Retail Clks. Internat. Assn. Local #455, Houston, 1960-68, collective bargaining rep. So. div., Atlanta, 1968-70, internat. dir. research, edn. and collective bargaining, Washington, 1970-71, exec. asst. to internat. dir. orgn., 1971-73, adminstrv. asst. to internat. pres., 1973-75; internat. v.p., dir. United Food and Comml. Workers Internat. Union, Seattle, 1975—; trustee Pension and Health and Welfare Trust; bd. dirs. Pacific N.W. Labor Coll. Served with USN, 1945-46; PTO. Democrat. Roman Catholic. Home: 8534 SE 79th Pl Mercer Island WA 98040 Office: 2819 1st Ave Suite 320 Seattle WA 98121

HOFF, BERNADINE L. RYAN, consultant referral firm executive; b. Creighton, Nebr., Aug. 29, 1926; d. Ralph Russel and Ella Helma (Boysen) Ryan; B.A. summa cum laude, Northeastern Ill. U., Chgo., 1970; M.A., U.S. Internat. U., 1974, Ph.D., 1979; 1 dau. Tchr., English in secondary public schs., Chgo., 1970-73; ednl. adminstr. continuing edn., adminstr. off-campus programs U.S. Internat. U., 1973-74; prof. Pepperdine U., 1974-75; edn. specialist U.S. Navy, 1975-76; asst. prof., dir. continuing bus. edn. U. Minn., 1977-80; dir. continuing edn. San Diego State U. Coll. Extended Studies, 1980-81; pres. Nat. Cons. Referrals, Del Mar, Calif., 1981—. Mem. AAUP, Am. Soc. Tng. and Devel. Home: 1231 Basswood Ave Carlsbad CA 92008 Office: 2120 Jimmy Durante Blvd Suite M Del Mar CA 92014

HOFF, JOHN CONRAD, agronomist, plant breeder; b. Ft. Collins, Colo., May 15, 1931; s. Henry L. and Elizabeth H.; m. Carol Palmer, Aug. 20, 1955; children—Katrina L., Julie E. B.S., Colo. State U., 1953, M.S., 1957; Ph.D., U. Wyo., 1971. Research agriculturist Holly Sugar Corp., Tracy, Calif., 1957-60; agronomist Adolph Coors Co., Golden Colo., 1960-62; farm mgr. The Garden City Co. (Kans.), 1962-64; asst. agronomist Colo. State U., Grand Junction, 1964-68; supply instr. U. Wyo., Laramie, 1968-72; plant breeder Amalgamated Sugar Co., Nyssa, Oreg., 1972—. Councilman, City of Nyssa, 1979—. Served to 1st lt. U.S. Army, 1953-55. Recipient Scholarship award Union Pacific, 1949. Mem. Am. Soc. Agronomy, Corp Sci. Soc. Republican. Presbyterian. Clubs: Elks (Ontario, Oreg.); Eagles (Nyssa). Home: 717 Thompson Ave Nyssa OR 97913 Office: Amalgamated Sugar Co PO Box 1766 Nyssa OR 97913

HOFFENBERG, MARVIN, political science educator, consultant; b. Buffalo, July 7, 1914; s. Harry and Jennie Pearl (Weiss) H.; m. Betty Eising Stern, July 20, 1947; children—David A., Peter H. Student St. Bonaventure Coll., 1934-35; B.Sc. (C.C. Stillman scholar, Univ. scholar) Ohio State U., 1939, M.A. (Univ. fellow), 1940, postgrad., 1941. Asst. chief div. interindustry econs. Bur. Labor Statistics, Dept. of Labor, 1941-52; cons. U.S. Mut. Security Agy., Europe, 1952; cons. Statistik Sentralbyra, Govt. of Norway, Oslo, 1955; dir. research, econ. cons. dept. deVegh & Co., 1956-58; economist RAND Corp., 1952-56; staff economist Com. Econ. Devel., 1958-60; project chmn. Johns Hopkins U., 1960-63; dir. cost analysis dept. Aerospace Corp., 1963-65; research economist Inst. Govt. and Pub. Affairs, UCLA, 1965-67, prof.-in-residence polit. sci., 1967—, dir. M.P.A. program, co-chmn. Interdepartmental Program in Comprehensive Health Planning, 1974-76. Bd. advisors Sidney Stern Meml. Trust; bd. dirs. Vista del Mar Child Center, Los Angeles chpt. Am. Jewish Com., Reiss-Davis Child Study Center. Littauer fellow Harvard U., 1946; recipient Disting. Service award Coll. Adminstrv. Scis., Ohio State U., 1971. Fellow AAAS; mem. Am. Econ. Assn., Policies Studies Orgn., Assn. Pub. Policy Analysis and Mgmt., Acad. Polit. Sci., Interuniv. Seminar on Armed Forces. Jewish. Author: (with Kenneth J. Arrow) A Time Series Analysis of Inter-Industry Demand, 1959; editor: (with Levine, Hardt and Kaplan) Mathematics and Computers in Soviet Economics, 1967; contbr. articles to profl. jours., chpts. to books. Office: Dept of Political Science University of California Los Angeles CA 90024

HOFFLAND, DAVID LAUREN, banker; b. Wheatland, Wyo., June 4, 1933; s. Fred Lauren and Ruth Hazel (Pickerell) H.; m. Marie-Claire Cecile Blouet, May 20, 1960; children—Dorinda Ruth, Timothy David. A.B in Bus., San Diego State U., 1955, M.A. in Econs., 1962. Vice pres., mgr. bank investment portfolio So. Calif. 1st Nat. Bank, San Diego, 1961-73; head securities and investments, v.p., bank portfolio mgr. Fifth Third Bank, Cin., 1973-81; v.p., cashier San Diego Nat. Bank, 1981—. Treas., Community Concert Assn., San Diego, 1967-73; treas., trustee Community Chest and Council, Cin., 1974-79. Mem. Inst. Chartered Fin. Analysts, San Diego Soc. Fin. Analysts (pres. 1970-71), San Diego Mus. Art, San Diego Zool. Soc. Contbr. articles to profl. jours. Home: 7308 Caminito Carlotta San Diego 92120 Office: 535 West A St San Diego CA 92101

HOFFMAN, ANTHONY EARL, vocational educator; b. Detroit, Mar. 31, 1945; s. Earl Joseph and Helen Ruth (Hofland) H.; m. Kathleen Marie Styer, Feb. 14, 1976; children—Timothy, Travis. B.A. in Secondary Edn., Ariz. State U., 1970; M.A. in Indsl. Edn., No. Ariz. U., 1980. Tchr. Coolidge (Ariz.) High Sch., 1970-79; prof. automotive tech. Ariz. Western Coll., Yuma, 1979—; mechanic Garrett Motors, Coolidge, summers 1971, 72. Served with Air Force ROTC, 1965-66. Mem. Coolidge Edn. Assn. (pres. 1976-77). Roman Catholic. Club: Kiwanis (sec.-treas. 1974-76). Office: PO Box 929 Yuma AZ 85364

HOFFMAN, CLIVE, public relations counsel, corporation executive, community education consultant; b. Cape Town, South Africa, July 20, 1937; s. Sydney and Hilda (Bernstein) H.; m. Carol Eunice Rischall, Dec. 18, 1962; children—Jill Lesli, Lisa Kim. B.A. in Communications, UCLA, 1959, postgrad. in polit. studies, 1960-62. Prodn. asst. BBC, 1956; assoc. producer Ziv/UA Television, 1959-61; dir. So. Calif. Com. NCCJ, 1961-63; pub. relations account exec. ICPR, 1963-66; pres. Clive

Hoffman Assocs. Inc., Los Angeles, 1966—; guest lectr. Calif. State U.-Northridge, U. Judiasm. Trustee, Temple Isaiah, 1980-83; mem. Youth Adv. Bd. NCCJ, 1978-83, Urban Affairs Commn. Jewish Fed. Council, 1982-83; chmn. community affairs advt. com. Los Angeles City Schs., 1971-73; press sec. Cranston for Senate, 1964. Mem. Nat. Assn. Real Estate Editors, Nat. Investor Relations Inst. Democrat. Contbg. editorial writer on edn., integration and So. Africa, Los Angeles Times, Post Newspapers, West Los Angeles. Office: 3348 Overland Ave Los Angeles CA 90034

HOFFMAN, CYNTHIA CAROLYN, sociology educator, research consultant; b. Golden, Colo., Feb. 21, 1942; d. William G. and Ann Helene (Nolte) Dwinelle; m. Geoffrey Lee Hoffman, June 28, 1963; children—Michelle, Greg. B.A., U. Colo., 1977, M.A. in Applied Urban Sociology, 1978. Registered radiol. technologist, 1963-71. Sales rep. Morrison & Morrison Realty Co., Broomfield, Colo., 1974-83; v.p. North Washington Dental Group, Thornton, Colo., 1975-83; research asst. dept. sociology, U. Colo., Denver, 1977-78, instr., 1981—, research assoc. Applied Sociol. Research Team, 1978—; cons. computer skills. Mem. Am. Sociol. Assn., Western Social Sci. Assn., Nat. Assn. Female Execs.

HOFFMAN, ELAINE JANET, painter; b. Oak Park, Ill.; d. Dewitt Alexander and Magda Catherine (Christensen) Patterson; m. Carl Rudolph Hoffman, Sept. 11, 1951; Lake Lynda Hoffman Snodgrass, Clayton Carl, Byron Bruce. B.A., Marylhurst Coll., 1978. Works commissioned include: book cover for A Brief History of the Lake Grove Presbyterian Church, 1974, a Christmas card for Waverly Children's Home, 1977. Deacon Lake Grove Presbyterian Church. Recipient Grand Award Soc. Wash. Artists, 1968; Special Merit award Watercolor Soc. Am., 1969, 70; 1st award Lake Oswego Art Festival, 1978, 82; Honor award Clackamas County Fair, 1981. Fellow Am. Artist Profl. League; mem. Lake Area Artists Assn. (pres. 1967-68, 71-72, 76-77), Lake Oswego Art Guild (bd. dirs. 1965-68), Portland Profl. Critique Group, Oreg. Watercolor Soc. Republican. Club: Lake Oswego Mcpl. Golf. Address: 16695 Glenwood Ct Lake Oswego OR 97034

HOFFMAN, FREDERICK, sociologist; b. Long Beach, Calif., May 12, 1934; s. Melvin H. and Isabel P. (Deal) H. B.A., U. of Americas, 1960; M.A., UCLA, 1975, Ph.D., 1979. Reporter, Los Angeles Free Press, 1967-69; editor, pub. Tuesday's Child, Los Angeles, 1970; research analyst Sci. Analysis Corp., Los Angeles, 1975-80; cons. Navajo, Calif. Mission Indians, Los Angeles, 1979-80; acculturation specialist Cuban Refugee Resettlement Program, Los Angeles, 1981—. Mem. Summer Community Orgn. Project, SCLC, 1965; mem. Vietnam Day Com., 1965-69, Friends of Ronald Burleholder, 1977-82. Served in USAF, 1952-56. Mem. Am. Sociol. Assn., Soc. Study of Social Problems, Clin. Sociology Assn. Editor: The Indian Family, 1980; author: Secret Roles and Provocations, 1979; Habilitating the Escoria, 1982. Home: Box 26642 Los Angeles CA 90026

HOFFMAN, HOWARD RICHARD, radio show host; b. Suffern, N.Y., Oct. 6, 1954; s. Charles and Nettie (Kanter) H. Student SUNY-Rockland, 1974. Program dir. Sta. WTBQ, Warwick, N.Y., 1971-73; radio personality Sta. WALL, Middletown, N.Y., 1973-74; prodn. mgr. Sta. WDRQ, Detroit, 1974-75; personality Sta. WPIX-FM, N.Y.C., 1975-77, Sta. WPRO-FM, Providence, 1977-79, Sta. KAUM (ABC), Houston, 1979-80; personality, talk show host Sta. WABC, N.Y.C., 1980-82; radio show host Sta. KOPA-AM-FM, Phoenix, 1981—. Bd. dirs. Ariz. Bapt. Children's Services, 1982—; mem. found. com. Scottsdale Meml. Hosp.-North. Named Radio Personality of Yr., Billboard Mag., 1979; recipient citations Easter Seal Soc., 1979, 1980, 1981, Sta. KUHT-TV (Houston), 1979. Mem. Nat. Assn. Broadcasters, Nat. Assn. Progressive Radio Announcers. Jewish. Illustrator: Cracking The Radio Egg, 1982. Office: Sta KOPA-AM-FM 4601 N Scottsdale Rd Scottsdale AZ 85251

HOFFMAN, HOWARD TORRENS, multi-industry executive, management consultant; b. East St. Louis, Ill., Dec. 30, 1923; s. Edmund Howard and Beulah Esther (Hood) H.; m. Ruth Ann Gisela Koch, June 19, 1947; children—Howard Torrens, Jean Gisele, Glenn Kevin. Student Iowa State U., 1950; M.S. in Elec. Engring., Thomas U., 1972, Ph.D. in Mgmt. Sci., 1977. Registered profl. engr., Mo. Head engring. sect. Joy Mfg. Co., St. Louis, 1950-55; missile systems engr. McDonnell Aircraft Corp., St. Louis, 1955-57; exec. engr. IT&T Labs., Ft. Wayne, Ind., 1957-59; mgr. missile systems Litton Industries, College Park, Md., 1959-60; program mgr., chief engr., div. mgr. Teledyne Ryan Co., San Diego, 1960-69; pres., chief exec. officer Hoffman Assocs., San Diego, 1969—; chmn. bd., exec. dir. H & R Assocs., asset mgrs., mgmt. cons., San Diego, 1970—. Served with U.S. Army, 1943-46. Decorated Bronze Star; recipient community service award United Crusade. Mem. AIAA, IEEE, Nat. Soc. Profl. Engrs., Am. Mgmt. Assn., Nat. Mgmt. Assn., Assn. U.S. Army, Internat. Platform Assn., Armed Forces Communications and Electronics Assn., Iowa State Alumni Assn. Patentee oscillator stabilized inertial navigation system. Home: 5545 Stresemann St San Diego CA 92122 Office: PO Box 22010 San Diego CA 92122

HOFFMAN, NEIL JAMES, art educator, dean; b. Buffalo, Sept. 2, 1938; s. Frederick Charles and Isabel (Murchie) H.; m. Sue Jeffery, Dec. 30, 1960; children—Kim, Amy, Lisa. B.S., SUNY-Buffalo, 1960, M.S., 1967. Art tchr. Grand Island (N.Y.) Jr.-Sr. High Sch., 1965-69; chmn. Unified Arts dept. Grand Island Pub. Schs., 1968-69; assoc. dean, asso. prof. Coll. Fine and Applied Art, Rochester (N.Y.) Inst. Tech., 1969-74; dir. Program in Artisanry, Boston U., 1974-79; dean, chief exec. officer Otis Art Inst. of Parsons Sch. Design, Los Angeles, 1979—; conductor seminars in field; art tchr. Huth Rd. Elem. Sch., 1961-64; draftsman Home Constn. Co., 1957-61; photographer of craft work for profl. pubs. and exhibitions; exhibited photography in Western N.Y. Art Exhibit and Albright Knox Art Gallery, Buffalo, 1968; free lance photographer; mem. evaluation team Western Assn. Schs. and Colls. Accreditation Commn., 1982—; juror Calif. Fine Arts Exhbn., Sacramento, 1982, The Western Edge, 1980; cons. in field. Bd. dirs., v.p. Kidspace, children's mus., 1980-82; bd. dirs. Geisen Trust, 1980—. Mem. Los Angeles Inst. Contemporary Art, Calif. Confedn. Arts, Calif. Council Fine Arts Deans., Phi Delta Kappa. Club: Los Angeles Downtowners. Home: 315 S Plymouth Blvd Los Angeles CA 90020 Office: 2401 Wilshire Blvd Los Angeles CA 90057

HOFFMAN, NORMAN JOHN, lawyer; b. Rochester, N.Y., Dec. 26, 1940; s. Norman John and Marion E. (Bauchman) H.; m. Jacqueline Drozdz, July 15, 1967; children—Eric, Kimberly. B.B.A., St. John Fisher Coll., 1962; LL.B., Syracuse U., 1966; LL.M. in Taxation, Georgetown U., 1970. Bar: N.Y. 1966, Calif. 1973; cert. tax specialist. With Haskins & Sells, 1962-63; trial atty. Dept. Justice, 1966-70; assoc. Martin, Dutcher, Cooke, Mousaw & Vigdor, 1970-73; sr. assoc. Wyman, Bautzer, Rothman, Kuchel & Silbert, 1973-77; ptnr. Jonas, Donahue, Kinigstein & Hoffman, 1978-81; sole practice, Encino, Calif., 1981—; lectr. tax-related matters. Served in USMCR, 1961-67. Mem. ABA, Calif. Bar Assn., Am. Soc. Profl. Cons. Republican. Roman Catholic.

HOFFMAN, PAUL JEROME, research psychologist, testing consultant; b. San Francisco, June 25, 1932; s. Louis and Bessie (Brodofsky) H.; m. Elaine Stroll, Mar. 18, 1944; children—Jonathan, Valerie, Lisa Hoffman Shanley. B.A. in Engring., U. Calif.-Berkeley, 1942; B.A., Stanford U., 1949, Ph.D. in Exptl. Psychology and Statistics, 1953. Lic. indsl. psychologist, Calif. Cons. to research labs. Lowry AFB, Denver, 1953-54; cons. Systems Devel. Corp., Santa Monica, Calif., 1960; asst. prof. dept. psychology U. Oreg., 1957-60, prof., 1967-76; pres. Oreg. Research Inst., Eugene, 1960-77; pres. Paul J. Hoffman Psychometrics, Inc., Palo Alto, Calif., 1977—, Cogitan, Palo Alto, 1978—; adj. prof. U. Calif. Sch. Medicine, 1979—; adj. prof. mgmt. sci. U.S. Naval Postgrad. Sch., Monterey, Calif., 1982—; cons. Nat. Bd. Med. Examiners, Phila., 1974, 75, Am. Bd. Internal Medicine, 1975, 77, IBM, Austin, Tex., 1980-81, Hewlett-Packard, Palo Alto, Calif., 1983—. Served with USAF, 1943-46, USAFR, 1946-51. NSF grantee, 1961, 62; NIH grantee, 1959-77. Fellow AAAS, Am. Psychol. Assn.; mem. Psychometric Soc., Psychonomic Soc., Classification Soc., Human Factors Soc., Oreg. Inventors Council (past pres.), Sigma Xi. Jewish. Contbr. over 50 articles to sci. and profl. jours. Home: 376 Monterey Pl Los Altos CA 94022 Office: 151 University Suite 307 Palo Alto CA 94301

HOFFMAN, ROLLAND EDWARD, association exec.; b. South Bend, Ind., Jan. 20, 1931; s. Edward William and Elsie Martha (Schultz) H.; B.S. in Speech, Northwestern U., 1954; spl. courses Ind. U., U. Notre Dame, U. Chgo., Harvard U.; m. Marilyn Jo McClure, June 20, 1960; children—Chriss, Pamela. Announcer, writer Sta. WKZO, 1954; dir. employee and public relations U.S. Rubber Co., 1956-58; asso. exec. dir. United Fund, South Bend, 1958-62, United Fund and Community Services, Ft. Worth, 1962-65; exec. dir. Tarrant County (Tex.) United Fund and Community Services, 1965-70; pres. Mile High United Way, Denver, 1970—; pub. speaker. Served with U.S. Army, 1954-56. Recipient awards for service to state Govs. of Colo. and Tex. Mem. Denver C. of C. Republican. Mem. United Ch. of Christ. Club: Rotary. Office: 2 Inverness Dr E Englewood CO 80112

HOFFMAN, SUSAN CAMERON, community relations specialist; b. Chgo., Dec. 2, 1947; d. Gordon and Vernon Lucille (Blackwell) Cameron; m. Francis Xavier Hoffman, Jan. 6, 1979. B.S. in Home Econs. Edn., U. Ariz., 1969, M.S. in Consumer Econs./Personel Fin., 1972. Instr., asst. prof. Oreg. State U., U. B.C., Humboldt State U., San Francisco State U., 1972-77; community relations dept., pub. relations div. San Diego Gas & Electric, 1978—; instr. personal income mgmt. course, evening coll. Mesa Coll., 1982—; consumer and homemaking con. San Diego Community Coll., 1978—; atty. gen. San Diego Consumer Task Force Com., 1978-80; active San Diego Republican Businesswomen, 1983—; mem. San Diego City Schs. Adv. Com., 1982—; bd. dirs. San Diego Community Campership Council, 1981-82, chmn. adv. bd., 1982. Mem. Am. Council Consumer Interests, Energy Products and Services Assn. (dir. 1980-82, chmn., co-chmn. coms. 1980-82, membership dir. 1981-82), Central City Assn., Nat. Alliance Bus. (loaned exec. San Diego 1980), San Diego C. of C. Exec. Club (loaned exec. 1978—; one of nat. top 20 vols. U.S. C. of C. 1979, 80), Women in Mgmt. (charter), San Diego Alumni of Kappa Kappa Gamma (dir. 1981-83). Presbyterian. Office: 101 Ash St San Diego CA 92101

HOFFMAN, WAYNE MELVIN, airline executive; b. Chgo., Mar. 9, 1923; s. Carl A. and Martha (Tamillo) H.; B.A. with high honours, U. Ill., 1946, J.D. with high honors, 1947; m. Laura Majewski, Jan. 26, 1946; children—Philip, Karen, Kristin. Admitted to Ill. bar, 1947, N.Y. bar, 1958; atty. I.C. R.R., 1948-52; with N.Y.C. R.R. Co., 1952-67, exec. asst. to pres. 1958-60, v.p. freight sales, 1960-61, v.p. sales, 1961-62, exec. v.p., 1962-67; chmn. N.Y. Central Trans. Co., 1960-67, Flying Tiger Line, Inc., 1967—, N.Am. Car Corp., 1971—; chmn., chief exec. officer Tiger Internat., Inc.; trustee Aerospace Corp., 1975—; dir. Kaufman & Broad, Inc. Mem. Pres. Nixon's Adv. Council on Mgmt. Improvement, 1970-73; mem. vis. com. Grad. Sch. Mgmt., U. Calif. at Los Angeles, 1972—; mem. adv. council Duquesne U. Sch. Bus., 1972—; mem. bus. adv. com. Northwestern U. Transp. Center, 1972—; bd. dirs. So. Calif. Visitors' Council, 1976—; vice chmn. bd. govs. Tyler Ecology of Pepperdine U., 1973—. Served to capt. inf., AUS, World War II. Decorated Silver Star, Purple Heart with oak leaf cluster. Mem. Am. Bar Assn., Internat. Air Transport Assn. (exec. com.), Phi Beta Kappa. Clubs: Calif.; Bel Air Country (Los Angeles); Eldorado Country (Indian Wells, Calif.). Office: Tiger Internat Inc 1888 Century Park E Los Angeles CA 90067

HOFFMAN, WILLIAM GEORGE, physician; b. Allentown, Pa., July 17, 1945; s. Donald B. and Margaret (Gruber) H.; m. Susan Emily Evans, Aug. 10, 1968; children—Andrea, Laura. B.S., Muhlenberg Coll., 1967; M.D., Temple U., 1971. Intern, Hunterdon Med. Center, Flemington, N.J., 1971-72, resident in family practice, 1972-74; family practice physician, adminstr. Yuba Feather Health Center, Brownsville, Calif., 1974—, health planner, 1974-80; health planning cons. Yuba Feather Rural Health Services, 1980—; mem. Yuba-Sutter sub-area health council Golden Empire Health Systems Agy., 1976-81. Pres., Yuba Feather Recreation Com., 1978—; co-chmn. Friends of Yuba Feather Sch., 1981—; bd. dirs. Yuba Feather Communities Services, 1981; founder Brownsville Mountain Fair, 1975, chmn., 1975, 77. Served with USPHS, 1974-76. Recipient Community Recognition award USPHS, 1976, Seventh-day Adventist Public Service award, 1980; Yuba Feather Rural Health Systems grantee, 1977-80, Calif. Proposition II Park grantee, 1978, 81, Roberti-Z'Berg Park Fund grantee, 1979, Adolescent Stop Smoking grantee, 1979. Mem. Am. Assn. Family Practitioners, Calif. Med. Soc., Yuba-Sutter-Colusa Med. Soc., Alpha Omega Alpha, Phi Alpha Theta. Republican. Office: Yuba Feather Health Center PO Box 86 Brownsville CA 95919

HOFFMANN, EVA GOTTSCHALCK, psychologist; b. Hamburg, Germany, July 6, 1913; d. Louis Martin and Anne (Peiser) Gottschalck; B.A. in Psychology, Conn. Coll., 1942; M.A., Columbia U., 1946, postgrad., 1967-69; m. Paul E. Hoffmann, Oct. 23, 1943; children—Beth Anne, Andrew Walter. Personnel clk. Calvert Distilling Co., Relay, Md., 1942-43; sec. to dir. Vocat. Adv. Service, N.Y.C., 1943-44, psychometrist, 1944-47; practice vocat. counseling, 1957-62; psychologist Vocat. Adv. Service, N.Y.C., 1948-62, supr. psychol. services, 1962-66, asst. dir., 1966-70; instr. dept. edn. Herbert H. Lehman Coll., CUNY, Bronx, 1970-73; program coordinator State Project to Implement Career Edn., N.Y.C., 1973-75; mem. faculty Center for N.Y.C. Affairs, New Sch. Social Research, 1975-80; career edn. coordinator dept. spl. edn. Tchrs. Coll., Columbia U., N.Y.C., 1976-80; sec. Petaluma Braille Transcribers, Inc. Treas. Petaluma Symphony Assn. Cert. psychologist, N.Y. Mem. Am., N.Y. State, N.Y.C. (pres. 1976-77) personnel and guidance assns., Nat. Vocat. Guidance Assn., Am., N.Y. State psychol. assns., Assn. Measurement and Evaluation in Guidance (chmn. ethics com. 1970-72). Author of career edn. manuals, 1975-78; contbr. book revs. on personnel guidance to profl. jours. Home: 515 Greenbriar Circle Petaluma CA 94952

HOFFMANN, HANS-WERNER OTTO, industrial engineer; b. Toronto, Ont., Can., July 8, 1954; came to U.S., 1963, naturalized, 1969; s. Walter Otto and Marie Kaete (Klein) H.; B.S. in Indsl. Engring., Calif. Poly. State U., 1978; m. Ruth J. Visco, July 19, 1980. Facilities specialist Gen. Dynamics Corp., Pomona, Calif., 1978-79; facilities planner I, Santa Barbara (Calif.) Research Center, Goleta, 1979—. Recipient Kiwanis Club award, 1973. Mem. Am. Inst. Indsl. Engrs. (sec. 1976-77), Calif. Scholarship Fedn., Nat. Mgmt. Assn., Women in Indsl. Engring., Alpha Pi Mu (pres. 1977-78). Jehovah's Witness. Club: Santa Barbara Mgmt. Home: 2660 Puesta del Sol Apt B Santa Barbara CA 93105 Office: 75 Coromar Dr Goleta CA 93117

HOFSTADTER, ROBERT, physicist, educator; b. N.Y.C., Feb. 5, 1915; s. Louis and Henrietta (Koenigsberg) H.; B.S. magna cum laude (Kenyon prize), Coll. City N.Y., 1935; M.A. (Procter fellow), Princeton, 1938, Ph.D., 1938; LL.D., City U. N.Y., 1961; D.Sc., Gustavus Adolphus Coll.; Laurea Honoris Causa, U. Padua, 1965; D.Sc. (hon.), Carleton U., Ottawa, Can., 1967, U. Clermont-Ferrand, 1967, Seoul Nat. U., 1967, Doctor Rerum Naturalium h.c., Julians-Maximilians U. Wüizburg, 1982; m. Nancy Givan, May 9, 1942; children—Douglas Richard, Laura James, Mary Hinda. Coffin fellow Gen. Electric Co., 1935-36; Harrison fellow U. Pa., 1939; instr. physics Coll. City N.Y., 1941; physicist Norden Lab. Corp., 1943-46; asst. prof. physics Princeton U., 1946-50; asso. prof. physics Stanford U., 1950-54, prof., 1954—, dir. high energy physics labs., 1967-74; dir. KMS Industries, 1973—. Guggenheim fellow. Ford Found., Geneva, Switzerland, 1958-59; Calif. Scientist of Year, 1959; co-recipient of Nobel prize in physics, 1961; Townsend Harris medal Coll. City N.Y. 1961. Fellow Am. Phys. Soc., Phys. Soc. London; mem. Italian Phys. Soc., Nat. Acad. Scis., Am. Assn. Arts and Scis., AAUP, Phi Beta Kappa, Sigma Xi. Author: (with Robert Herman) High-Energy Electron Scattering Tables, 1960. Editor: Investigations in Physics, 1952; Electron Scattering and Nucleon Structure, 1963. Co-editor: Nucleon Structure, 1964. Asso. editor Phys. Review, 1951-53; mem. editorial bd. Review Sci. Instruments, 1953-55; Reviews of Modern Physics, 1958-61. Home: 639 Mirada Ave Stanford CA 94305 Office: Stanford U Dept Physics Stanford CA 94305

HOGAN, F. FAYE HOLLAND, educator, business exec.; b. Baton Rouge, Jan. 15, 1932; d. Oauther Benjamen and Frances (Holland) Hogan; B.S., Tex. Woman's U., 1953; M.A., 1961; Ed.D., U. So. Calif., 1983. Tchr., Marshall (Tex.) High Sch., 1954; field dir. Denison (Tex.) Camp Fire Girls, Inc., 1954-55; tchr. Wichita public schs., 1955-56; instr. Friends U., Wichita, 1956-57; caseworker Tucson Public Social Services and Police Dept., 1957-61; tchr., sch. adminstr. Los Angeles Unified Sch. Dist., 1961-69; asst. prin., prin. Glendale (Calif.) Unified Sch. Dist., 1969-81; owner, diet counselor Diet Center, Inc., 1981—; mem. adv. bd. Diet Center Internat.; cons. personnel selection, ednl. policy evaluation. Mem. vestry St. Mary's Ch. of Palms Anglican Catholic Ch., 1978—, lay reader, chalice bearer, 1980—. Mem. Sociology of Edn. Assn., Women in Ednl. Leadership, Greater Los Angeles Zoo Assn., NOW, ACLU. Democrat.

HOGAN, GREGORY DENHAM, advertising executive; b. Atlanta, Apr. 23, 1950; s. Augustus and Rubye I. (Moffett) H.; m. Jocelyn B. Walker, Dec. 25, 1980; children—Kelli, Marcus. B.S., U. Ill., 1972; M.B.A., Northwestern U., 1974. Account exec. Foote, Cone and Belding, Chgo., 1977-80, account supr. Young and Rubican, 1980-82; regional advt. mgr. McDonald's Corp., Los Angeles, 1982—. Office: McDonald's Corp 10960 Wilshire Blvd Suite 600 Los Angeles CA 90024

HOGG, FREDERICK GLENN, mfg., designer line constrn. equipment; b. Fernald, Iowa, July 31, 1913; s. William Jacob and Lillie (Bell) H.; grad. Fernald High Sch., 1932; m. Margaret Emogene Miskell, Dec., 7, 1936; 1 son, Frederick Neil. With So. Calif. Edison Co., 1940-64; established Hogg and Davis, Inc., Long Beach, 1947—, H & D Sales & Leasing, Inc., 1974, FMN, Inc., 1978. Recipient Edison Electric Inst. medal for sav. life, 1947. Mem. Pacific Coast Elec. Assn. Clubs: Masons, Shriners, Elks. Home: Fullerton CA Office: 2579 E 67th St Long Beach CA 90805

HOGLE, DIANE GOURLEY, guidance counselor; b. Seattle, Feb. 14, 1955; d. Robert M. and Elaine (Stewart) Gourley; m. Andrew Jay Hogle, July 22, 1978. B.A. in Polit. Sci., Wash. State U., 1977; M.Ed. in Guidance and Counseling, Seattle U., 1982. Cert. tchr. Calif., Wash., guidance counselor Wash. Tchr., Mercer Island, Wash., 1978-80, Renton, Wash., 1980-82; guidance counselor Auburn High Sch., Auburn, Wash., 1982—. Recipient U.S. Senate Youth Conf. award State of Wash., 1973; U. Calif.-Davis Grad. Counselor Scholarship award, 1977. Mem. Am. Personnel and Guidance Assn., Am. Sch. Counselor Assn., Mortar Board, Kappa Kappa Gamma. Methodist. Office: Auburn High Sch 800 4th St NE Auburn WA 98002

HOGSETT, VICTOR HOWARD, public relations specialist, consultant; b. Reserve, N.Mex., May 22, 1952; s. John Howard and Maria Elena (Jiron) H.; m. Mary Hilliard, Apr. 11, 1981. B.A. in Journalism, U. N.Mex., 1974. Stringer, reporter Albuquerque Jour., 1972-73; in house publicist Mountain Bell Telephone Co., Albuquerque, 1973; reporter, photographer Los Alamos (N.Mex.) Monitor, 1977-78, Ruidoso (N.Mex.) News, 1978; pub. info. specialist Los Alamos Sci. Lab., 1978-81; liaison officer Office of Atty. Gen., State of N.Mex., Santa Fe, 1981—; cons. in publs. preparation and polit. press relations. Press liaison vol. for Democratic senate campaign, 1981-82. Mem. Pub. Relations Soc. Am. Home: PO Box 8342 Santa Fe NM 87501 Office: Atty General's Office State of NMex PO Drawer 1508 Santa Fe NM 87501

HOGUE, JANET LYN, educator; b. Mpls., Feb. 16, 1953; d. Ervin G. and Annabelle (McClelland) Gross; B.A. cum laude, U. Minn., Duluth, 1975; cert. teaching Weber State Coll., 1976; m. Richard C. Hogue, Dec. 29, 1972. Tchr. biology South Ogden (Utah) Jr. High Sch., 1975-76, North Ogden Jr. High Sch., 1976-77, Sunset High Sch., Beaverton, Oreg., 1979—; researcher Weber State Coll., Ogden, Utah, part time 1975-77. Chmn. energy study LWV, Ogden, 1975-78; chmn. publicity Sierra Club, Ogden, 1976-77. Mem. Cooper Ornithol. Soc., NEA, Audubon Soc., Sierra Club, Sigma Xi, Phi Kappa Phi. Home: 16602 NW Somerset Dr Beaverton OR 97006 Office: PO Box 200 Beaverton OR 97075

HOHU, MARGARET KUULEI, gerontologist, nurse; b. Hilo, Hawaii, Feb. 21, 1924; d. Edmund Kawaianuenue and Fannie Paneohua (Werner) Hohu. A.A. in Nursing, U. Houston, 1947; R.N., Jefferson Davis Hosp. Sch. Nursing, 1947; Cert. R.N. Anesthetist, Baylor U. Med. Ctr. Sch. Nurse Anesthetists, 1953; B.S. in Allied Health, Colo. Women's Coll., 1975; M.A. in Gerontology, U. No. Colo., 1977, Ed.D. in Gerontology, 1979. Staff nurse anesthetist, instr. various hosps. Colo., Hawaii, Utah, 1953-68; chief nurse anesthetist, instr. Denver Gen. Hosp., 1968-69; pvt. practice anesthesia, Denver, 1967-69; dir. anesthesia services and inservice edn. Twin Cities Community Hosp., Deadwood, S.D., 1969-70; nurse anesthetist, instr. Fitzsimons Army Med. Ctr., Denver, 1970-75; nurse anesthetist, Anesthesia Assocs. of Greeley, Colo., 1975-78; adj. prof. gerontology, U. No. Colo., Greeley, 1979—; moderator, panelist Gov.'s White House Conf. on Aging, 1980; adv. bd., steering com. Mt. Evans Hospice, 1980—; field test counselor Am. Personnel and Guidance Assn. aging project, 1981; steering com. Denver Free U. Evergreen br., 1982. Bd. dirs. Greeley Meals on Wheels, 1978-82, pres. 1981. Mem. Colo. Assn. Nurse Anesthetists (trustee 1967), S.D. Assn. Nurse Anesthetists (trustee 1969), Doctoral Vocat. Edn. Assn., Nat. Assn. Female Execs., Nat. Council on Aging, Western Gerontol. Soc. (employment com. 1980), Colo. Gerontol. Soc., AAUP, Kappa Delta Pi. Baptist. Author: Pre-retirement and Retirement Education Program: A Leadership Training Manual, 1979; Tomorrow Is Mine, 1979; contbr. articles to profl. jours. Office: PO Box 159 Evergreen CO 80439

HOITT, LINDA ANN, sales manager; b. Manchester, N.H., Dec. 11, 1947; d. Proctor Hoitt and Elizabeth Ann (Tarasuk) H. Romot; grad. Sch. of Fashion Design, Boston, 1966-69; student Santa Ana Coll., 1979—. Asst. designer Berkshire Apparel, Malden, Mass., 1969-70; sales corr. AMP Inc., Waltham, Mass., 1970-75; sales engr. trainee ITT Cannon Electric, Wakefield, Mass., 1975-76, product specialist, Santa Ana, Calif., 1976-78, product mgr. mktg., 1978-82, also mem. bd. controls Mgmt. Assn. of Cannon Electric; mktg. dir. mil. connectors Stanford Applied Engring., Santa Ana, 1982-83; gen. sales mgr. Tekform

Products, Anaheim, Calif., 1983—. Mem. Electronic Connector Study Group So. Calif., Nat. Assn. Female Execs., Internat. Soc. Hybrid Mfrs. Home: 1104 N Olive St Santa Ana CA 92703 Office: 2770 Coronado St Anaheim CA 92806

HOKE, KAY HUBERT, computer systems official, educator; b. Camp Point, Ill., July 3, 1934; s. Jewell Juett and Margaret Lucille (Gibson) H. B.S. in Chemistry, Ariz. State U., 1957; M.S. in Info. and Computer Sci., U. Hawaii, 1973. Programmer/analyst Computing & Software Inc., Los Angeles, 1960-67; dir. computing ctr. Chathan County (Ga.) Animal Hosp. Savannah, 1967-69; v.p. data processing Rothrock, Reynolds & Reynolds, Miami, Fla., 1969-70; programmer/analyst U. Hawaii, Honolulu, 1970-73, East-West Ctr., 1973-81; dir. computer lab. coll. bus. adminstrn. U. Hawaii, 1981—. Served to 1st lt. U.S. Army, 1957-60. Mem. Assn. Systems Mgmt., Assn. Computing Machinery, Am. Philatelic Soc. Republican. Office: U Hawaii 2404 Maile Way D-310 Honolulu HI 96822

HOLBROOK, ALICE MAE, nursing adminstr.; b. Park City, Utah, Feb. 10, 1938; d. James Llewellyn and Alice (Lefler) Gwilliam; diploma Los Angeles County (Calif. Gen. Hosp. Sch. Nursing, 1959; B.A., U. Redlands, 1975, M.A., 1978; m. Harry Loren Holbrook, Aug. 19, 1960; children—Jimmy Edward, William Loren, Mary Alice, Daniel Raymond. Nurse, VA Hosp., Long Beach, Calif., 1959-61; supervising nurse U. Calif., Irvine Med. Center, 1964-74; patient care coordinator Fountain Valley (Calif.) Community Hosp., 1975-78; supervising nurse Hoag Meml. Hosp., Newport Beach, Calif., 1978-79; dir. nursing service Los Banos (Calif.) Community Hosp., 1979-81; dir. nurses Sonoma Valley Dist. Hosp., 1982—; instr. North Orange County Community Coll. Dist., Merced Community Coll. Mem. Dirs. Nursing Council, AAUW. Mormon. Office: 347 Andrieux St Sonoma CA 95476

HOLBROOK, BOYD LYNN, computer systems engineer; b. Ogden, Utah, Dec. 24, 1947; s. Walter Herbert and Connie (Jorgenson) H.; m. Carlene Weese, July 16, 1965; m. 2d, Margaret Vandenberg, Feb. 3, 1979; children—Sherry Lynn, Christie Sue. B.S. in Computer Sci., Weber State Coll., 1975. Computer programmer White Motor Corp., Ogden, 1975-78; computer analyst Envirotech Corp., Salt Lake City, 1978-79; computer system engr. TRW Corp., Ogden, 1979-81; data processing mgr. R.C. Willey Home Furnishings, Syracuse, Utah, 1981—; cons. Served to sgt. U.S. Army, 1968-69. Decorated Silver Star, Air Medal, Purple Heart, Vietnamese gallantry cross (2). Mem. Assn. Automated Prodn. Inventory Control Specialists, Data Processing Mgmt. Assn., Beta Theta Pi Alumni Assn. Republican. Mormon. Author: (with Arthur Anderson) MX Field Mgmt. Center Study Report, 1980; (with Allen Graves) Implementation Analysis of the Distributed Warehousing and Shipping System, 1981. Home: 1470 Cahoon St Ogden UT 84401 Office: 1693 W 2700 S Syracuse UT 84041

HOLCOMB, LILLIAN PECKHAM, psychologist, special educator; b. Newport, R.I., July 15, 1944; d. Roger Herbert and Ruth Maria (Albro) Peckham; 1 dau., Vivian Lois. B.A., Elmira Coll., 1969; M.A.T., Cornell U., 1971; Ph.D., Syracuse U., 1974. Lic. psychologist, Hawaii. Corrections counselor, N.Y. and Hawaii, 1975-77; lectr. psychology Hawaii colls., 1977-81; pvt. practice psychology, Honolulu, 1977, 80-83; team practice Kahumana Counseling Ctr., Waianae, Hawaii, 1983—; asst. prof. women's studies U. Hawaii, Honolulu, 1980-83. Mem. Honolulu Mayor's Commn. on the Handicapped, 1977. Mem. NOW, Associated Women Entreprenurs, Am. Psychol. Assn., Hawaii Psychol. Assn., Internat. Council Psychologists, Nat. Rehab. Assn., Assn. Advancement Psychology. Mem. Assemblies of God. Contbr. articles to profl. jours. Address: PO Box 1797 Honolulu HI 96806

HOLDCROFT, LESLIE THOMAS, clergyman, educator; b. Man., Can., Sept. 28, 1922; s. Oswald Thomas and Florence (Waterfield) H.; student Western Bible Coll., 1941-44; B.A., San Francisco State Coll., 1950, M.A., San Jose State Coll., 1955, postgrad. Stanford, 1960, 63, U. Cal., 1965-67; D.D., Bethany Bible Coll., 1968; m. Ruth Sorensen, July 2, 1948; children—Cynthia Ruth, Althea Lois, Sylvia Bernice. Instr. Western Bible Coll., 1944-47; instr. Bethany Bible Coll., 1947-55, dean edn., 1955-68, v.p., 1967-68; pres. Western Pentecostal Bible Coll., 1968—; pastor Craig Chapel, 1959-68. Pres., Assn. Canadian Bible Colls., 1972-76. Author: The Historical Books, 1960; The Synoptic Gospels, 1962; The Holy Spirit, 1962; The Pentateuch, 1951; Divine Healing, 1967; The Doctrine of God, 1978. Home: 34623 Ascott Ave Abbotsford BC V2S 4N3 Canada Office: Box 1000 Clayburn BC V0X 1E0 Canada

HOLDEN, RONALD MICHAEL, public relations executive, author; b. Portland, Oreg., July 27, 1942; s. Max Michael and Gertrude Julie (Isaac) H.; m. Glenda Mary McPherson, Dec. 18, 1965; children—Michael, David, Dominic. B.A. in English, Yale U., 1963. TV anchorman, producer news King Broadcasting Co., Portland, Oreg. and Seattle, 1967-74, Westinghouse Broadcasting Co., Balt., 1974-76; pub. affairs mgr. Weyerhaeuser Co., Tacoma, Wash., 1979-81; pres. Holden Pacific, Inc., Seattle, 1981—. Served with U.S. Army, 1964-66. Mem. Pub. Relations Soc. Am., Wash. Wine Writers, Seattle C. of C., Seattle Advt. Fedn. Author: Touring the Wine Country of Oregon, 1982; Touring the Wine Country of Washington, 1983; contbr. numerous articles to local and regional publs. Home: 814 35th Ave Seattle WA 98122 Office: Holden Pacific Inc 207 1/2 First Ave S Seattle WA 98104

HOLDEN, TERRY LEE, educator; b. Dayton, Ohio, July 15, 1946; m. Carol S. Huddleston, Mar. 15, 1974. B.S. in Indsl. Edn., Eastern N.Mex. U., 1974, M.Ed., 1976, Ednl. Specialist, 1981. Vocat. tchr. Portales High Sch. (N.Mex.) 1974—. Served with U.S. Army, 1966-70. Mem. Am. Vocat. Assn., N.Mex. Vocat. Assn., Vocat. Indsl. Clubs Am.

HOLDER, A. W., JR., educator; b. Banning, Ga., Dec. 20, 1937; s. A.W. and Ruth M. (Story) H., Sr.; m. Christine Helene Pilz, Mar. 6, 1958; children—Richard, Eric, Thor. A.A., U. Md., 1976; B.S., So. Ill. U.-Carbondale, 1977; M.Ed., U. Alaska, 1983. Electronic technician U.S. Air Force, 1956-59; electronic materials officer U.S. Navy, 1960-78; tng. engr. Goddard Space Flight Ctr., NASA, 1978-80; prof. electronic tech., dept. chmn. U. Alaska, Fairbanks, 1980—; electronic cons.; mental health counselor. Scoutmaster, Iberian council Boy Scouts Am., 1970-76. Served as petty officer E.T., USN, 1962-76. Mem. Am. Personnel and Guidance Assn., Am. Coll. Personnel Assn. Clubs: Kiwanis (Fairbanks); Key. Office: 327 Duckering Bldg UAF Fairbanks AK 99701

HOLEMAN, DENNIS LEIGH, systems engineer; b. Portland, Oreg., May 10, 1946; s. Donald Sidney and Shirley Barbara (Lash) H.; m. Jeanette Marie Sill, Sept. 12, 1981. B.S. in Engring., Harvey Mudd Coll., Claremont, Calif., 1968; M.E.M.E. (Westinghouse fellow) U. Calif.-Berkeley, 1970. Registered profl. engr., Calif. Project mgr. oceanic div. Westinghouse Electric Corp., Vallejo, Calif., 1968-75; mgr. ops. IMSAI Mfg. Corp., San Leandro, Calif., 1975-78; sr. research engr., SRI Internat., Menlo Park, Calif., 1978—. Mem. AAAS, AIAA, IEEE, Am. Assn. Artificial Intelligence, Soc. Gen. Systems Research, Soaring Soc. Am., Sierra Club. Home: 66 Laurie Meadows Dr Apt 4 San Mateo CA 94403 Office: 333 Ravenswood Ave Suite 30158 Menlo Park CA 94025

HOLFORD, LILLIAN RITA, job referral executive; b. Oakland Calif., July 7, 1936; d. Raymond and Marian (Lewis) Holford; m. Earl J. Robinson, Oct. 19, 1959 (div.); children—Michele, Monica, Mia. B.A. in Social Welfare, U. Calif.-Berkeley, 1958; M.A. in Edn., San Francisco State U., 1973. Adoption agy. recruiter, Children's Home Soc., Oakland, 1965-69; dir. staff tng. Far West Lab. for Endl. Research and Devel., 1970-73; sr. placement interviewer U. Calif. Berkeley, 1973; self-employed seamstress, Oakland, 1973-76; exec. dir. Bay Area Broadcast Skills Bank, San Francisco, 1976—; instr. Peralta Coll. Dist. Active Bay Area Black United Fund. Mem. Progressive Black Bus. and Profl. Women's Assn. (bd. dir.), U. Calif. Black Alumni Club. Office: Bay Area Broadcast Skills Bank 2655 Van Ness Ave San Francisco CA 94109

HOLGATE, GEORGE JACKSON, university president; b. Lakewood, Ohio, Feb. 19, 1933; s. George Curtis and Melba Marguerite (Klein) H.; Mus.B., Baldwin-Wallace Coll., 1953; Mus.M., U. So. Calif., 1954, Ed.D., 1962; Ph.D., Riverside U., 1970, LL.D., 1971; m. Sharon Joy, Dec. 20, 1954 (div. Feb. 1961); 1 dau., Leigh Meredith. Tchr. Oxnard (Calif.) High Sch., 1954-56, Ventura (Calif.) Coll., 1956-60; exec. v.p. Sierra Found., Santa Barbara, Calif., 1960-62; campus coordinator Congo Poly. Inst., Leopoldville, 1962-64; exec. dir. Automation Inst., Sacramento, 1964; pres. Riverside (Calif.) Bus. Coll., 1965-67, Riverside U., 1967—. Minister music St. Paul's Meth. Ch., Oxnard, Calif., 1954-55; condr. So. Calif. Council Protestant Chs. Messiah Chorus, 1954; dir. Ventura Coll. Concert Chorale, 1956-60; condr. Ojai (Calif.) Festivals, 1958; Ventura Bach Festival, 1960; pres. Oxnard Community Concert Assn., 1958; pres. Vineyard Estates Property Owners Assn., 1958. Mem. Calif. State Dem. Central Com., 1962-63; chmn. 13th Congl. Dist. Dem. Council, 1963; bd. dirs. Riverside U., 1967—, Riverside Opera Assn., 1966-71, Riverside Symphony Orch. Soc., 1966—, So. Calif. Vocal Assn., 1955-56. Flotilla comdr. USCG Aux., 1983—. Recipient Disting. Service award U.S. Jaycees, 1962. Mem. NEA, Calif. Council Bus. Schs. (pres. 1970), Calif. Assn. Pvt. Edn. (treas. 1969), Music Educators Nat. Conf., Calif. Choral Condrs. Guild, Internat. Platform Assn., Phi Delta Kappa, Phi Mu Alpha Sinfonia, Sigma Phi Epsilon, Delta Epsilon. Office: 890 N Indian Hill Blvd Pomona CA 91767

HOLLAAR, LEE ALLEN, computer science educator; b. Litchfield, Minn., Mar. 9, 1947; s. Garritt A. and Lyma Marie (Geiger) H.; m. Audrey Mack, Nov. 26, 1968. B.S.E.E., Ill. Inst. Tech., 1969; M.S. in Computer Sci., U. Ill., 1974, Ph.D. in Computer Sci., 1975. Registered profl. engr., Calif. Systems engr., coordinator engring. Datalogics Inc., Chgo., 1969-71, 72-74; design engr. Automation Tech. Inc., Champaign, Ill., 1971-72, grad. research asst. U. Ill., Champaign, 1970-75, asst. prof. aviation and computer sci., 1975-77, asst. prof. computer sci., sr. research engr., 1977-80; assoc. prof. computer sci. U. Utah, Salt Lake City, 1980—, assoc. chmn. dept., 1983—; cons. in field. NASA grantee, 1978; NSF grantee, 1979, 80, 82; IBM Corp. grantee, 1979, 83. Sr. mem. IEEE; mem. Assn. Computing Machinery, AIAA, Inst. Nav., Aircraft Owners and Pilots Assn., Balloon Fedn. Am., Sigma Xi, Phi Kappa Phi, Eta Kappa Nu. Contbr. numerous articles to profl. jours. Patentee in field. Home: 1367 E 100 S Salt Lake City UT 84102 Office: Dept Computer Science 3160 Merrill Engring Bldg U Utah Salt Lake City UT 84112

HOLLADAY, DALE JAY, commercial and portrait photographer; b. Safford, Ariz., Dec. 18, 1945; s. Stanley Charles and Lytha Olive (Cluff) H.; m. Janice Green, Apr. 12, 1968, children—Trevor, Trisha, Stacey, Kristen, Mandy. Student Eastern Ariz. Coll., 1964-65; B.A. in Secondary Edn., Ariz. State U., 1970. Served Mormon Church in Peru, Bolivia, 1965-67; teacher 8th grade sci. Apache Junction Jr. High, 1970-72; teacher biology Safford (Ariz.) High Sch., 1972-75; owner Holladay's Photo Emporium, Safford, 1975—. Recipient various awards for prints in Ariz. exhibits. Mem. Profl. Photographers Assn. Am., Ariz Profl. Photographers Assn. Republican. Mormon. Clubs: Rotary (Safford), Mt. Graham Golf Assn. Office: 429 Main St Safford AZ 85546

HOLLAND, GEORGE HARVISON, film producer, educator, writer; b. Fresno, Calif., Mar. 5, 1937; s. Harvison Catlin and Virginia Rowe H.; m. Jeannie Ann Grubbs, Sept. 14, 1980; children—Kira Lisanne, Krista Michelle. B.S., UCLA, 1958; M.A., U. Calif.-Santa Barbara, 1964, Ph.D., 1968. Assoc. prof. U. Ariz., Tucson, 1967-72; dir. mktg. and sales Am. Ednl. Films, Los Angeles, 1972; v.p. product devel. Phoenix-BFA Films, Pasadena, Calif. and N.Y.C., 1973—; instr. UCLA; free-lance theater and travel writer. Served to lt. (j.g.) USN, 1960-62. Mem. Nat. Council Social Studies, Am. Film Inst., Nat. Council Tchrs. of English. Democrat. Episcopalian. Club: Sierra. Home: 629 S College Ave Claremont CA 91711 Office: 35 S Raymond St Suite 202 Pasadena CA 91105

HOLLAND, GEORGE O., insurance company executive, financial planning consultant; b. Everett, Wash., Nov. 19, 1926; s. Ole J. and Gunhild (Breum) H.; m. Diana Southgate Thorp, July 18, 1953; children—George Donald, Christopher Jon, Peter Thorp. B.A., U. Wash., 1950; M.S. in Fin. Services, Am. Coll., Bryn Mawr, Pa., 1981. C.L.U.; registered health underwriter; chartered fin. cons. Asst. rep. Wash. state Nat. Found. for Infantile Paralysis, Seattle, 1951-52; rep. Western N.Y., Rochester, 1952-54; brokerage mgr. Aetna Life Ins. Co., Seattle, 1954-58; gen. agt. Union Mut. Life Ins. Co., Seattle, 1958—. Pres. Northwest Hosp., Seattle, 1972-73, chmn. bd., 1974-75; bd. dirs. Wash. State Golf Assn., 1974—. Served with U.S. Army, 1945-46. Mem. Nat. Assn. Estate Planning Councils (pres. Seattle council 1983-84), Am. Soc. C.L.U.s (pres. Seattle chpt. 1974-75, western regional bd. dirs. 1983—), Wash. Assn. Health Underwriters (pres. 1961-62), Seattle Gen. Agts. and Mgrs. Assn. (pres. 1981-82) Western Pension Conf., Nat. Assn. Health Underwriters, Sigma Alpha Epsilon. Republican. Congregationalist. Clubs: Seattle Golf, Rainier, Wash. Athletic (Seattle). Contbr. articles to profl. jours. Home: 4208 55th St NE Seattle WA 98105 Office: 600 Stewart St Suite 217 Seattle WA 98101

HOLLAND, JACK HENRY, educator, lectr., clergyman; b. San Diego, Oct 31, 1922; s. Henry Joseph and Hazel M. (Mitchell) H.; student U. So. Cal., 1940-41; A.B., San Diego State U., 1943; grad. student Harvard, 1943; M.B.A., Stanford, 1948; Ph.D. in Theology, Fla. State U.; D.D., Divine Sci. Ednl. Center; hon. degree Faith Sem. Prof., San Jose (Calif.) State U., 1948-79, emeritus, 1979—, head mgmt. dept., 1956-68; sometimes prof. Stanford, summers; sr. asso. Saratoga Inst.; lectr. on human motivation. Ordained minister Ch. Divine Sci.; founder, pres. Inst. Human Growth and Awareness, now lectr., cons., minister; v.p. Internat. New Thought Alliance, Divine Sci. Fedn. Internat.; co-founder, dir. Sci. of Mind Inst. Sch. Ministry, San Jose; minister Divine Sci. Ch. Served from ens. to lt. USNR, 1943-46; PTO. Decorated Purple Heart, Presdl. Unit Citation. Mem. Am. Mktg. Assn., Acad. of Mgmt., Nat. Assn. Purchasing Mgmt., Purchasing Mgmt. Assn. No. Calif., Soc. Advancement Mgmt. (nat. exec. v.p. univ. chpts. 1963-69), Bay Area Bus. Edn. Forum (pres. 1956), Am. Inst. Banking, Beta Gamma Sigma, Phi Kappa Phi., Alpha Tau Omega Alumni Assn. (dir. 1952). Club: Commonwealth of Calif. Author: Outline of Materials Management; An Annotated Biblography for Parapsychology; Man's Victorious Spirit; The Healing Image, 1976; Love: The Scientific Evidence, 1976; Your Freedom To Be, 1977. Office: PO Box 6695 San Jose CA 95150

HOLLAND, JEFFREY R., university president; b. St. George, Utah, Dec. 3, 1940; s. Frank Dennis and Alice (Bentley) H.; A.S., Dixie Coll., 1963; B.S., Brigham Young U., 1965, M.A., 1966; M.Phil., Yale U., 1972, Ph.D., 1973; m. Patricia Terry, June 7, 1963; children—Matthew Scott, Mary Alice, David Frank. Tchr., Latter-day Saints Ch. Ednl. System, 1965-74; dean religious instrn. Brigham Young U., 1974-76, pres., 1980—; commr. edn. Ch. of Jesus Christ of Latter-day Saints, 1976-80; bd. govs. Latter-day Saints Hosp., Salt Lake City. Bd. dirs. Polynesian Cultural Center, Laie, Hawaii; mem. adv. bd. Nat. Multiple Sclerosis Read-a-Thon Com. Contbr. numerous articles to profl. publs. Office: D-346 ASB Brigham Young U Provo UT 84602

HOLLAND, JUDITH RAWIE, television producer, writer; b. Long Beach, Calif., Jan. 25, 1942; d. Wilmer Ernest and Margaret Jane (Towle) Rawie; m. John Allen Holland, July 11, 1964 (div.); children—Daryn Kirsten, Dawn Malia. B.A. in Bus. Adminstrn., Marymount Coll., 1964; B.A. in Visual Arts and Communication, U. Calif.-San Diego, 1978. Producer/writer ednl. series Achieving Basic Skills (Emmy award 1982), distributed through Great Plains Nat. TV Library, also adult edn. series Focus on Parenting combined with PBS Footsteps series, Sta. KPBS, 1979-81; asst. dir. research and video/producer LABC, San Francisco, 1982; dir. programming Group W Cable, Los Angeles area, South Gate, Calif., 1983—. Chmn. publicity 20th Ann. Young People's Summer Show, Palos Verdes Estates (Calif.); leader Explorer Scouts, South Bay Chpt., 1983—. Recipient You Can Make the Difference award S.W. Region Group W, 1983. Mem. Nat. Women in Cable, Women in Communications, Internat. TV Assn. Acad. TV Arts and Scis., Democrat. Episcopalian. Club: Soroptomists (scholarship, publicity com.). Home: 2400 Palos Verdes Dr W 16 Palos Verdes Estates CA 90274 Office: Group W Cable 3125 Firestone Blvd South Gate CA 90280

HOLLAND, KENNETH MILTON, mfg. co. exec.; b. Richmond, Calif., Apr. 12, 1923; s. Charles Arthur and Eleanor Catherine (Morse) H.; B.S. in Chemistry, U. Calif., 1943; m. Dorothy Anne Davis, Sept. 24, 1949; 1 son, David Kenneth. Chemist Chevron Research Corp., Richmond, 1945-46, Reinforced Plastics Devel., Richmond, 1946-48; co-founder, v.p., dir., cons. Hexcel Corp., Dublin, Calif., 1948—. Served to lt. AUS, 1943-45; ETO. Mem. Soc. of Plastics Engrs. (founding bd. mem. Golden Gate sect. 1947), Soc. of Plastics Industry (Outstanding Service award, pres. North Calif. chpt. 1955-56). Clubs: Pacheco, Pebble Beach and Tennis, Monterey Peninsula Country Club. Patentee in field. Home: PO Box 1357 Pebble Beach CA 93953 Office: 650 California St Suite 1400 San Francisco CA 94108

HOLLAND, PHILO KNOWLES, JR., merchandising and public relations executive; b. Altadena, Calif., Mar. 14, 1935; s. Philo Knowles and Florence Holland (Lucas) H.; m. Marilyn Buckley, Jan. 31, 1959; children—Philo Knowles, Dana Elizabeth. B.S., UCLA, 1959, M.B.A., 1960. With Sears Roebuck & Co., 1960 , dir. pub. affairs, 1971 80, mdse. mgr., Santa Monica, Calif., 1964, Bugna Park, Calif., 1965, Hollywood, Calif., 1967, personnel mgr., Long Beach, 1966, spl. assignment Sears Found., Chgo., 1968, exec. dir., 1970, regional pub. relations dir., N.Y.C., 1969, dir. pub. affairs Western Territory, 1980—; v.p. Sears Found., 1980—; vis. prof. Westminster Coll. Mem. founds. com. Los Angeles council Boy Scouts Am.; past bd. dirs. Coro Found.; trustee United Way of Bay Area, Served with U.S. Army, 1955-57. Recipient Disting. Service award Boy Scouts Am., 1976, Disting. Service award Utah Gen. Fed. Women's Clubs, 1977. Mem. Pub. Relations Soc. Am., Los Angeles Pub. Affairs Officers Assn., San Francisco Contbns. Roundtable, Los Angeles C. of C., N.Y. Distributive Edn. Club Am. (hon life), Nat. Alliance Bus. (Disting. Service award 1977). Episcopalian. Club: Jonathan (Los Angeles).

HOLLAND, STEVEN CRAIG, publicist; b. Bakersfield, Calif., Nov. 30, 1948; s. Eugene Ervin and Frances Lorraine (Ruttan) H.; m. Carole Ann Passadori, July 4, 1970, children—Chris, Jeremy. A.A., Bakersfield Coll., 1967; B.A., Calif. State U.-Fresno, 1969; M.A., Calif. State Coll.-Bakersfield, 1977. Secondary tchr. credential, Calif. Sports info. dir. Calif. State U., Bakersfield, 1974-77; tchr. Kern High Sch. Dist., Bakersfield, 1977-78; pub. affairs rep. Getty Oil Co., Bakersfield, 1978—. Trustee Fruitvale Sch. Dist., Bakersfield, pres. bd., 1979—. Served to 1st lt. USAF, 1972-74. Mem. Sigma Delta Chi, Pub. Relations Soc. Am., Internat. Assn. Bus. Communicators, Kern Press Club (past pres.). Republican. United Methodist. Club: Rotary (Bakersfield). Home: 6505 Quailwood Dr Bakersfield CA 93309 Office: Getty Oil Co PO Box 1148 Bakersfield CA 93389

HOLLAND, WILLIAM DAVID, electronics engineer; b. York, Pa., Sept. 3, 1955; s. Allan Lamar and Jane Frieda (Anderson) H. B.S., Calif. Inst. Tech., 1977; postgrad. Stanford U., 1978-82. Cons., Robert Abel Films, Hollywood, Calif., 1972-77; mem. tech. staff Hewlett-Packard, Palo Alto, Calif., 1977—. Ebell scholar, 1976. Mem. Audio Engring. Soc. Clubs: Sierra, Western Wheelers Bicycle, U.S. Parachute Assn. Home: 13331 Wildcrest Dr Los Altos Hills CA 94022 Office: Hewlett-Packard 1501 Page Mill Rd Palo Alto CA 94304

HOLLE, JUDITH ROGERS, dietitian; b. Rochester, N.Y., May 7, 1943; s. Warren A. and Norma B. (Biddle) Rogers; B.S. in Food Adminstrn., Rochester Inst. Tech., 1965. Dietetic intern Peter Bent Brigham Hosp., Boston, 1965-66; chief nutritional service out-patient dept. U. Pa. Hosp., 1966-67; therapeutic dietitian U. Rochester Med. Center, 1967-68, Mass. Gen. Hosp., Boston, 1968-70; research dietitian George Human Clin. Research Found., Washington Hosp. Center, 1970-71; nutrition educator, chmn. consumer nutrition edn. N.Mex. Nutrition Improvement Program, Albuquerque, 1971-73; nutritionist, instr. Checkerboard Area Health System, Cuba, N.Mex., 1973-74; nutritionist Navajo Tribe, Ft. Definace, Ariz., 1974-75; dietetic services cons. mgmt. cons. services Southwest Community Health Services (formerly Presbyn. Hosp. Center), Albuquerque, 1975—. Mem. Am. Dietetic Assn., Soc. Nutrition Edn., Am. Hosp. Assn., Am. Soc. Hosp. Food Service Adminstrs., N.Mex. Dietetic Assn. (chmn. dial-a-dietitian 1971-73), N.Mex. Public Health Assn., N.Mex. Hosp. Assn., Albuquerque Dietetic Assn. Home: PO Box 1611 Corrales NM 87048 Office: Southwest Community Health Services Albuquerque NM 87102

HOLLEMAN, WILBUR JENNINGS, JR., engineering company executive, lawyer; b. Tulsa, Dec. 6, 1931; s. Wilbur Jennings and Maxine (Maxey) H.; m. Jeanne Washburn, Aug. 21, 1954 (div.); children—John Maxey, Eric de Bruch; m. Carol Borden, Mar. 30, 1978. B.A., Princeton U., 1953; LL.B., U. Okla., 1956; LL.M., NYU, 1967. Bar: Okla. 1956, N.Y. 1975, Calif. 1977. Law clk. to presiding judge U.S. Dist. Ct. No. Dist. Okla., Tulsa, 1956-57; atty. law firm, Tulsa, 1957-67; v.p. New Eng. Petroleum Corp., N.Y.C., 1967-75, also dir.; v.p. Flour Corp., Irvine, Calif., 1975—. Episcopalian. Contbr. articles to law jours.

HOLLEN, SALLY GENE, gemology shop owner; b. San Jose, Calif., July 24, 1927; d. George Edward and Arlyne Florence (O'Malia) Hallett; m. Merritt (Mike) Leroy Hollen, Apr. 26, 1950; children—Theresa Mills, Suzanne, Sharon. Student U. Calif., Coll. San Mateo, Gemological Inst. Am. Newspaper reporter Los Angeles Times, 1946-47, Santa Ana (Calif.) Register, 1948; reporter Mineral County News, Hawthorne, Nev., 1949; legal sec. Moyle & Moyle Attys., Salt Lake City, 1950-57; sec. Steinhart, Goldberg, Feigenbaum & Ladar, attys., San Francisco, 1957-59, Chester A. Lebsack, atty., Redwood City, Calif., 1961-63, John Lyons, Conciliation Counsellor, Redwood City, Calif., 1964-66, U.S. Rubber Co., Salt Lake City, 1953-57; part-time sec. Vacu-Blast, Belmont, Calif., 1967-69; owner, pres. Hollen's Broc Shop, Lapidary, San Carlos, Calif., 1982—. Mem. San Carlos Fine Arts Assn., 1982-83; sec. exec. bd. Bayside Intermediate Sch. PTA, San Mateo, Calif., 1959-61; leader Girl Scouts U.S., San Mateo, 1958-60; mgr. Bobby Sox Softball, San Mateo, 1973-75. Mem. Sequoia Gem and Mineral Soc., Gem and Mineral Soc. San Mateo County, Ye Old Times Mineral Club, Nat. Assn. Female Execs., San Carlos C. of C. Republican. Episcopalian. Clubs: Eastern Star (past matron San Mateo), Daus. of Nile (San Francisco). Office: 1585 Laurel St San Carlos CA 94070

HOLLENBECK, CLIFFORD ERNEST, photographer, writer, columnist, pub. cons.; b. Temple, Tex., July 26, 1943; s. Clayton (Holly) Earl and Florence May (Cariveau); H.; A.A. in Journalism, Yakima Valley Coll., 1963; B.A. in Journalism, U.S. Navy, Coronado, Calif., 1967; M.S. in Physiology, U. Australia, 1969; D.D., First Ch. of Research (Va.), 1970; postgrad. in social psychology, Tenn. Christian U., 1977; m. Nancy Eilene Davis, Sept. 23, 1971; 1 son, Craig Eric. Journalist, photographer, editor Fairbanks News Miner, Fairbanks, Alaska, 1968-69; writer, photographer bus., politics Anchorage Daily Times, Anchorage, 1970; asst. v.p. advt., pub. relations Wein Air Alaska, Anchorage, 1971; cons. pub. affairs, aviation Govt. of Can., Ottawa, Ont., 1972-73; dir. pub. affairs, advt. promotion Alaska Airlines, Seattle, 1973-74; v.p. Faces Publs., Inc., Honolulu, Seattle, 1975-76, dir., 1980—; pres. pro tem Indsl. Promotional Toys, Seattle, 1976; prin. Cliff Hollenbeck Agy., Seattle, 1976—; dir. Pacific Advt., Inc., 1979-82. Mem. 7th dist. Congressional Ind. Bus. Adv. Bd., 1978-79. Served with USN, 1963-68. Decorated D.F.C. (2), Air medal (4), numerous others; named Mag. Photographer of Yr., Alaska, 1978, Travel Photographer of Yr., 1982-83. Mem. Am. Soc. Mag. Photographers, Soc. Am. Travel Writers (named One of Top Ten Travel Photographers 1979, 80, 81), Aviation-Space Writers Assn., Nat. Press Photographers Assn., Pub. Relations Soc. Am., Overseas Press Club, Internat. Divers Assn., Nat. Geog. Soc., Alaska Geog. Soc., Profl. Assn. Diving Instrs., Underwater Master Divers Internat., Plonjeurs Internat., Kappa Alpha Mu, Alpha Psi Omega. Club: Siberia-Russia Explorers. Author: Adverse Incident Policy, 1972; A Look into Skyjacking, 1972; (screenplay) High Rockies, 1978; columnist Seattle Post Intelligencer, World Traveling Mag., Welcome to U.S.A., Alaskafest; contbg. editor Pacific Bus. Mag., N.W. World Travel, AlaskaFest, Faces Mag.; contbr. photographs and articles to profl. jours. Office: PO Box 4247 Pioneer Sq Seattle WA 98104 also 6855 Santa Monica Blvd Suite 402 Los Angeles CA 90038

HOLLEY, DANIEL CHARLES, physiologist, educator; b. San Jose, Calif., Aug. 1, 1949; s. Charles E. and Rose Marie (DeLuca) H.; Asso. Sci., Cabrillo Coll., 1969; B.S., U. Calif., Davis, 1971, M.S. in Physiology, 1973, Ph.D. in Physiology (fellow), 1976; m. Darcy Kristine Johnson, Mar. 16, 1968; children—Douglas Charles, David Daniel. Staff research asso. dept. surgery U. Calif. Sch. Medicine, Davis, 1969-73, teaching asst. dept. animal physiology, 1973-74, research asst. dept. animal sci., 1971-76; instr. physiology La. State U. Med. Sch., New Orleans, 1976-78; asst. prof. dept. biol. scis. San Jose (Calif.) State U., 1978-81, asso. prof., 1981—. Mem. Am. Physiol. Soc., Shock Soc., AAAS, Sigma Xi, Alpha Gamma Sigma, Phi Kappa Phi. Contbr. articles on physiology to profl. jours. Office: Dept Biol Scis San Jose State Univ San Jose CA 95192

HOLLEY, GLEN VICTOR, logistics planner; b. Ogden Utah, May 16, 1927; s. George Victor and Myrla May (Wilkinson) H.; m. Lucille Thompson, Mar. 21, 1951; children—Carol Ann Lindquist, Richard, Linda Williams, David. A.A., Weber State Coll., 1948; student Utah State U., 1948, Indsl. Coll. Armed Forces correspondence course, 1956. Lic. real estate, ins. broker, Utah. Mgr. Holley Real Estate and Ins. Co., 1951; logistics planner Hill AFB, Ogden Utah, 1951-79, 1982—. Mormon Ch. mission pres., Mexico, 1979-82. Mem. Ogden Sch. Bd., 1970-79, pres. 1979; mem. exec. council Boy Scouts Am., 1975-79; mem. Airport Planning Adv. Com., 1976, Weber Council Govt., 1978-79, CETA Adv. Council 1978-79. Named USAF Planner of Yr., 1977; recipient USAF outstanding performance and superior performance awards, 1965-78. Republican. Mormon. Club: Desert Gym (adv. bd., 1972-79). Office: Hill AFB Clearfield UT 84056

HOLLEY, ROBERT WILLIAM, biochemist; b. Urbana, Ill., Jan. 28, 1922; s. Charles E. and Viola E. (Wolfe) H.; A.B., U. Ill., 1942; Ph.D., Cornell U., 1947; postdoctoral Wash. State U., 1947-48; m. Ann Dworkin, Mar. 3, 1945. Asst. prof. N.Y. State Agrl. Expt. Sta., Geneva, 1948-50, assoc. prof. organic chemistry, 1950-57; research chemist U.S. Plant, Soil and Nutrition Lab., Agrl. Research Service, U.S. Dept. Agr., Ithaca, N.Y., 1957-64; prof. biochemistry and molecular biology Cornell U., Ithaca, N.Y., 1964-69, chmn. dept. biochemistry, 1965-66; resident fellow Salk Inst. for Biol. Studies, San Diego, 1968—. Recipient Albert Lasker award for basic med. research, 1965; U.S. Dept. Agr. Disting. Service award, 1965; U.S. Steel Found. award in molecular biology, Nat. Acad. Scis., 1967; Nobel Prize for Physiology or Medicine (with M. Nirenberg and H.G. Khorana), 1968. Address: The Salk Inst for Biol Studies PO Box 85800 San Diego CA 92138

HOLLIDAY, GAY, assn. exec.; b. St. Louis, May 30, 1944; d. Stephen Allen and Imogene Holliday; B.S. in Recreation, Ind. U., 1966, M.S. in Edn., 1967. Dir. student activities Endicott Coll., 1967-69; program adv. Ariz. State U. Meml. Union, 1969-71, program dir., 1971-74, asst. dir., 1974-79; coordinator ednl. programs and services Assn. Coll. Unions Internat., Stanford, Calif., 1979—, mem. conf. program planning com., 1976, conf. presenter. Vol. probation officer. Mem. Am. Soc. Tng. and Devel., Ind. U. Alumni Assn. Club: Zonta. Contbr. articles to ann. conf. procs. Assn. Coll. Unions Internat. Home: 584 Lassen St Apt 4 Los Altos CA 94022 Office: 201 480 California St Suite 201 Palo Alto CA 94306

HOLLIE, ANDRÉA RENEE, public transp. exec.; b. Washington, July 11, 1945; d. Percy Eugene, Jr. and Celestine Marie (Wilson) Ricks; B.S., Portland (Oreg.) State U., 1975; m. Adell Nobu Hollie, III, Aug. 10, 1951. Indsl. coordinator/counselor communications and tech. services div. Philco-Ford Corp., Phila., 1968-70; info. systems supr. Model Cities Program, Portland, 1971-74; coordinator, head research and evaluation dept. Portland Human Resources Bur., 1974-77; dir. conv. activities NAACP, 1977-78; exec. dir. corp. devel. Spiral Works, Inc., Portland, 1978-79; minority bus. enterprise officer Tri-County Met. Transp. Dist., Portland, 1980—. Bd. dirs. Albina Art Center, Portland, 1972-74; mem. Portland Bicentennial Commn., 1976; mem. Portland Art Mus., 1974—. Mem. NAACP, Urban League (dir. Portland 1980—), Nat. Black Women's Network (charter 1981—), Schs. for the City (dir. 1980—), Nat. Assn. Female Execs., Delta Sigma Theta (corr. sec. chpt. 1979—). Democrat. Roman Catholic.

HOLLIST, W. LADD, political science educator, author, researcher, consultant; b. Denver, May 30, 1947; s. William D. and Shirley (Penton) H.; m. Marleen Galvez, April 15, 1970; children—Heidi, Nathan Ladd, Amy. B.S. with highest honors, Utah State U., 1971; M.A. in Internat. Politics and Econs., U. Denver, 1973, Ph.D. in Internat. Relations, 1974. Research assoc. dept. polit. sci. Northwestern U., Evanston, Ill., 1974-76; asst. prof. Sch. Internat. Relations, U. So. Calif., Los Angeles, 1976-81, research assoc., dir. program internat. polit. economy research, 1978-81; vis. assoc. prof. Brigham Young U., Provo, Utah, 1981-82, assoc. prof., 1982—; cons. NSF grantee, 1976-80. Mem. Am. Polit. Sci. Assn. (conv. program com. 1983), Internat. Polit. Sci. Assn., Internat. Studies Assn. (chmn. internat. polit. economy sect.). Mormon. Author: Exploring Competive Arms Processes: Applications of Mathematical Modeling and Computer Simulation, 1978; World System Structure: Continuity and Change, 1981; World Systems Debates, 1981; The Political Economy of Global Agriculture, 1984. Home: 371 E 1140 N Orem UT 84057 Office: 760 SWKT Brigham Young U Provo UT 84602

HOLLISTER, CLYDE CARROLL, health care administrator, consultant; b. Sacramento, Oct. 21, 1931; s. Richard Davis and Roxie Arizona (Oliver) H.; m. Patricia Jean Cummins, Sept. 29, 1961; 1 dau., Dana Karlene. A.A., Phoenix Coll., 1957; B.S., Ariz. State U., 1965, M.Ed., 1971. Cert. radiol. technologist, Ariz. Dir. schs. radiol. tech. St. Joseph's Hosp., Phoenix, 1962-67, Good Samaritan Hosp., Phoenix, 1967-73; adminstrv. dir. Prentice Eye Inst. St. Luke's Hosp., Phoenix, 1973-77; dir. Scottsdale (Ariz.) East Homes, Inc., 1980; cons. health care edn. and adminstrn. Scottsdale, 1977-80; coordinator radiol. tech. Ariz. State U., cons. in biomed. electronics. Served with U.S. Army N.G., 1949-57. Mem. Am. Soc. Radiol. Technologists (cert. 1953), Am. Hosp. Assn., Am. Mgmt. Assn., Am. Soc. for Tng. and Devel. Developer radiol. tech. coll. degree programs. Address: 8220 E Garfield St M2 Scottsdale AZ 85257

HOLLORAN, DENNIS MICHAEL, soil scientist; b. Dayton, Ohio, Dec. 16, 1948; s. Thomas Patrick and Shirley Ann Holloran; m. Sharon Grimes, Dec. 15, 1979. B.S. in Agronomy, Ohio State U., 1974. Cert. profl. soil scientist. Soil scientist Ohio Dept. Natural Resources, 1974-77; soil scientist, surveyor Douglas County (Oreg.) Planning Dept. and Soil Conservation Service, 1977-81; soil scientist South Douglas Soil and Water Conservation Dist. and Soil Conservation Service, Roseburg, Oreg., 1981—. Mem. Roseburg Jaycees; chmn. nat. sanctioning com. U.S. Orienteering Fedn.; mem. U.S. team, 1978 World Orienteering Championships, Norway. Served with U.S. Army, 1969-71; Vietnam. Decorated Silver Star (2), DFC (5), Air medal (45). Mem. Am. Soc. Agronomy, Oreg. Soc. Soil Scientists. Home: PO Box 699 Roseburg OR 97470 Office: 2621 NE Stephens St Roseburg OR 97470

HOLLORAN, ROBERT WILLIAM, JR., nuclear engineer, entrepreneur, consultant; b. Logan, Utah, Sept. 14, 1943; s. Robert William and Genevieve (Jordan) H.; m. Nancy Marian Hull, June 19, 1965; children—Peter, John. B.S. in Physics, U. Wash., Seattle, 1965, M.S. in Nuclear Engring., 1975. Registered professional engr. Wash., Calif. Supervisory engr. U.S. AEC, Naval Reactors rep. Portsmouth Naval Shipyard, 1970-73; cons. engr. MPR Assocs., Washington, 1973-74; prin. Holloran Assocs, cons. engrs., 1975—; lectr. dept. nuclear engring. U. Wash., 1976. Chmn., Creston Citizen's Adv. Comm., Seattle; chmn. energy and ecology task force Ch. Council of Greater Seattle. Mem. Am. Nuclear Soc. Mem. United Ch. of Christ. Clubs: Bellevue Athletic, Rotary (Bellevue); Engineers (Seattle). Author profl. papers. Home: 9127 NE 36th St Bellevue WA 98004 Office: 205 108th Ave NE Suite 102 Bellevue WA 98004

HOLLOWAY, J(AMES) HUNTER, information specialist; b. N.Y.C., Sept. 4, 1933; s. Barry James and Jane (Hunter) H.; 1 son, James Hunter. Student Syracuse U., 1951-53, Columbia U., 1956, U. Vt., 1957-59. City editor Vt. Pub. Co., Burlington, 1957-60; with AP, 1960-72, newsman, Troy and Albany, N.Y., news editor, Charleston, W.Va., 1968-69, gen. desk editor, N.Y.C., 1969-70, natural resources editor, Denver, 1970-72; writer U.S. Bur. Reclamation, Dept. Interior, Denver, 1972-75, info. specialist, 1975-77, media relations officer, 1977—. Mission coordinator Colo. Search and Rescue Bd., 1975—, exec. sec., 1977—; field dir. Alpine Rescue Team, Evergreen, Colo., 1981—. Mem. Sigma Delta Chi, Pub. Relations Soc. Am., Denver Press Club. Home: 6170 S Cody Ct Littleton CO 80123 Office: Bur Reclamation Dept Interior Code D 140 Box 25007 Denver Fed Ctr Denver CO 80225

HOLLOWAY, WILLIAM HAROLD, physician; b. Webster City, Iowa, Feb. 27, 1924; s. Harold Earnest and Angie (Allinson) H.; student Purdue U., 1942, Akron U., 1943-44, Pa. State U., 1943; M.D., U. Pitts., 1949; postgrad. Postgrad. Center for Mental Health, 1966-68, Western Inst. Group and Family Therapy, 1971; m. June Dessie Gibson, Dec. 5, 1944 (div. Nov. 1970); children—Gayle Lynn, Joan Lorraine, Shelley Ann; m. 2d, Martha Jeffery, Jan. 1971; children—Jeff, Stephen, Timothy, Patricia. Intern, Riverside Hosp., Toledo, 1949-50; resident Ypsilanti (Mich.) State Hosp., 1954-57; dir. Summit County Mental Hygiene Clinic, Akron, Ohio, 1957-61; practice medicine specializing in psychiatry, Akron, 1958-73, Medina, Ohio, 1973-77, Aptos, Calif., 1977-78, Garden Grove, Calif., 1978-80, Hemet, Calif., 1980—; psychiat. cons. Springhill Sch., Akron, 1958-61, Boys' Village, Smithville, Ohio, 1961-67; cons. group psychotherapy Summit County Receiving Hosp., 1966-69; emeritus sr. med. staff Akron City Hosp., Akron Gen. Hosp.; clin. asst. prof. Ohio State U., 1968-69; clin. asst. prof. psychiatry Case Western Res. U. Sch. Medicine, 1970-76; pres. Nat. Group Psychotherapy Seminars, 1969-70; tng. cons. Family and Children's Service Soc. Summit County; founder, dir. Midwest Inst. Human Understanding Inc., Akron; cons. Medina County Family Guidance Clinic, 1974-76, Brazilian Inst. Transactional Analysis, Sao Paulo, 1976-. Served with U.S. Army, 1943-46; to maj. USAF, 1949-54. Postgrad. Center for Mental Health fellow, 1966-68. Fellow Am. Psychiat. Assn., Am. Group Psychotherapy Assn. (dir. 1970-72, treas. 1974-76); mem. Ohio State Med. Assn. (del. 1969-71), Tri-State Group Psychotherapy Assn. (pres. 1968-70), Internat. Assn. Group Psychotherapy, AMA, Internat. Transactional Analysis Assn. (teaching mem., pres. 1976-78, trustee), Summit County Med. Soc. (sec. 1964-65, mem. council 1969-72), Ohio Psychiat. Assn. (pres. 1969-70, trustee edn. and research found. 1969-73), Phi Beta Pi, Alpha Omega Alpha. Author: (with Martha M. Holloway) Change Now, 1973, Collected Monographs of the Midwest Institute, 1975; Clinical Transactional Analysis, 1974; Transactional Analysis-An Integrative View in Transactional Analysis After Eric Berue, 1977. Address: 41734 Crest Dr Hemet CA 92343

HOLLYWOOD, MICHAEL LEN, ceramic title contractor; b. Hollywood, Calif., Sept. 28, 1946; s. Jack M. and Virginia F. Hollywood; m. Regina E. Carnrite, Nov. 9, 1972; children—Mathew Michael, Jennifer Amy-Marie. Student Santa Barbara City Coll., 1965-66. Profl. golfer, 1969-74; fin. officer Selectile, Santa Barbara, Calif., 1975—; pres. The Tile Collection, Santa Barbara, 1980—; gen. mgr. Santa Barbara Spikers Profl. Volleyball Club, 1979-80. Served with USAR, 1968-69. Democrat. Office: 427 E Montecito St Santa Barbara CA 93102

HOLM, JAMES BRYANT, human services manager; b. Long Beach, Calif., Feb. 6, 1940; s. John Wesley and Elizabeth Mildred (Hoering) H.; m. Starlene Pope, May 29, 1970; children—Angela Marie, James Bryant, John Daniel, Stephen Wesley, Peter Arden. B.S., Brigham Young U., 1971; M.B.A., U. Chgo., 1973. Accredited dir. Goodwill Industries Am. Dir. Newark (Ohio) Goodwill Industries, 1974-76; sr. v.p. Goodwill Industries San Joaquin Valley, Stockton, Calif., 1976-77, pres., 1977-81; mgr. human resources Deseret Industries, Salt Lake City, 1981-82, gen. mgr., 1982—. Bishop Mormon Ch., 1982-83, missionary to Japan, 1966-69; scoutmaster Boy Scouts Am. Served with USAF, 1960-63. Club: Rotary. Home: 9182 S Creponette Dr Sandy UT 84092 Office: 50 E North Temple 7th Floor Salt Lake City UT 84150

HOLM, VICTOR MARTIN, neuropsychiatrist, administrator; b. Tigerton, Wis., Apr. 21, 1929; s. Martin and Gladys Seborg (Loken) Holm; m. Violet Ann Jensen, Aug. 5, 1950; children—Victoria, Lawrence, Steven, Valerie, Jeffrey. Student Augustana Coll., 1952; B.S. in Medicine., U. S.D., 1954; M.D., State U. Iowa, 1956. Diplomate Am. Bd. Psychiatry and Neurology. Rotating intern Emanuel Hosp., Portland, Oreg., 1956-57, resident in internal medicine, 1957; resident in neuropsychiatry Naval Hosp., Oakland, Calif., 1957-60; commd. lt. M.C., U.S. Navy, 1957, advanced through grades to capt., 1970; dir. psychiat. clinic U.S. Naval Sta., Treasure Island, Calif., 1960-64; chief psychiat. service Naval Hosp. Great Lakes (Ill.), 1964-66; chief psychiat. service Naval Hosp., Oakland, 1966-72; asst. chief psychiat. div. Bur. Medicine and Surgery, Washington, 1972-73; dir. intern tng., chmn. dept. psychiatry Nat. Naval Med. Ctr., Bethesda, Md., 1973-76; dir. clin. services, dep. comdg. officer Naval Regional Med. Center, Oakland, 1976-78; ret., 1978; pvt. practice in psychiatry, Portland, 1978-80; clin. dir. Oreg. State Hosp.; assoc. supt. Damasch State Hosp., Wilsonville, Oreg., 1980, supt. 1981—; assoc. prof. clin. psychiatry Oreg. Health Sci. U.; asst. prof. psychiatry Georgetown U. Med. Sch., 1973, assoc. prof., 1976; cons. com. govt. agys., Group Advancement Psychiatry, 1972-75; U.S. Navy del. 2d Nat. Congress on Mental Illness, 1965. Bd. dirs. Lake County (Ill.) Mental Health Soc. and Clinic, 1964-66; v.p. St. James Luth. Ch., San Leandro, Calif., 1970-72; mem. Portland Symphonic Choir. Decorated Meritorious Service Medal with Gold Star, Meritorious Unit Citation. Mem. Nat. Adv. Mental Health Council, 1974, Interagy. Inst. Fed. Health Care Execs., 1975. Fellow Am. Psychiat. Assn. (cert. mental health adminstr. 1980); mem. Golden Gate Group Psychotherapy Assn., (sect. chmn., ann. meeting), Washington (D.C.) Psychiat. Soc., Washington County (Oreg.) Med. Soc., Oreg. Psychiat. Assn., AMA (mil.), Assn. Mil. Surgeons of U.S. Republican. Contbr. articles to profl. jours., govt. publs.; writer, tech. dir. (video tape, film) Combat Psychiatry: Vietnam, 1968. Office: Dammasch State Hosp Wilsonville OR 77070

HOLMAN, PAUL DAVID, plastic surgeon; b. Waynesboro, Va., Mar. 13, 1943; s. Wallace D. and Rosalie S. Holman. B.A., U. Va., 1965; M.D., Jefferson Med. Coll., 1968. Intern, George Washington U. Hosp., 1968-69, resident in gen. surgery, 1969-70, 72-74; resident in plastic surgery Phoenix Plastic Surgery Residency, 1974-76; practice medicine specializing in plastic surgery, Phoenix, 1977—; mem. staff Good Samaritan Hosp., Phoenix, St. Joseph's Hosp., Phoenix, Ariz. Children's Hosp., Tempe. Served to lt. comdr. USNR, 1970-72. Diplomate Am. Bd. Surgery, Am. Bd. Plastic Surgery. Mem. AMA, ACS, Am. Soc. Plastic and Reconstructive Surgeons, Phi Beta Kappa. Office: 1010 E McDowell Rd 303 Phoenix AZ 85006

HOLMAN, STERLING WILLIAM, human services adminstrator; b. Baker, Oreg., Apr. 30, 1936; s. Sterling Arthur and Ruth Hyde (Yancey) Case; m. Leila Helena Sait, July 8, 1967; children—Omar, Edward, Marie, Michelle, Mark. Ph.D. in Psychology, U. Calif.-Berkeley, 1977. Cons. Roche Labs., 1960-66; program dir. dept research Mendocino State Hosp., 1967-72; pvt. practice cons. psychologist, San Francisco, 1972-75; dir. Turk St. Ctr., San Francisco, 1975-78; dir. human services Ft. Hall (Idaho) Indian Reservation (Shoshone-Bannock tribes), 1978—. Regional v.p. Mental Health Assn. Idaho. Served with USN, 1956-60. Recipient U.S. Community Services Adminstrn. Disting. Service award, 1978, Shoshone-Bannock tribes Sho-Ban Cup, 1981. Mem. Am. Orthopsychiat. Assn., Am. Personnel and Guidance Assn., N.Am. Soc. Adlerian Psychology, Assn. Humanistic Psychology, Idaho Psychol. Assn., Idaho Soc. Individual Psychology (pres. elect 1984-85), Idaho Personnel and Guidance Assn. (pres. 1982-83). Democrat. Contbr. articles to profl. jours. Office: PO Box 306 Ft Hall ID 83203

HOLME, BARBARA LYNN SHAW, state senator; b. Long Beach, Calif., May 24, 1946; d. Harry and Lillian (Walton) Shaw; B.A., Stanford U., 1967; Coro Found. intern in pub. affairs, 1967-68; m. Howard Kelley Holme, June 16, 1968; children—Timothy, Lisa. Intern for Rep. Edward Roybal, summer 1966; intern to AID, Washington, D.C., summer 1967; jr. asso. Cogen, Holt and Assocs., New Haven, 1968-69, 71-72; asst. dir. for edn., housing and youth Met. Denver Urban Coalition, 1969-71; housing asst. Denver Housing Adminstrn., 1972-74; mem. Colo. Senate, 1974—; chmn. senate Dem. caucus, 1977-78; asst. Dem. senate leader, 1979-82. Active Mayors Adv. Com. on Youth, Denver, 1969-70; steering com. mem. Colo. Coalition for Social Legislation, 1969-71; co-pres. Colo. Young Dems., 1973-74; bd. dirs. Capitol Hill United Neighborhood, 1974-75. Nominated as Outstanding Young Woman Am., Nat. Bus. and Profl. Women's Clubs, 1976. Mem. Colo. Open Space Council. Jewish. Home: 1243 Fillmore St Denver CO 80206

HOLMES, CHARLES EVERETT, lawyer, banker; b. Wellington, Kans., Dec. 21, 1931; s. Charles Everett and Elizabeth (Bergin) H.; B.A., Wichita U., 1953; LL.B., Okla. U., 1961; m. Lynn Lacy, Jan. 2, 1954; children—Anne Lacy, Charles Everett III, Rebecca. Trainee Halliburton Oil Well Cementing Co., Great Bend, Kans., 1956-58; admitted to Okla. bar, 1961; practiced in Tulsa, 1961—; mem. firm Rogers, Bell & Robinson, 1969-71; v.p. Nat. Bank of Tulsa, 1971—; lawyer Petro-Lewis Corp.; sec. Sinclair Oil & Gas Co., Sinclair Can. Oil Co., Mesa Pipeline Co., Border Pipe Line Co., Sinclair Transp. Co., Ltd. Del. Okla. Council Cath. Diocese, 1966—; chmn. Cath. Parish Governing Body, 1968—; bd. dirs. Youth Services, Travelers Aid, Com. Fgn. Relations. Served with USAF, 1954-56, 61-62. Mem. Am., Okla., Tulsa County bar assns. Home: 4505 S Yosemite #103 Denver CO 80237

HOLMES, DOUGLAS WARREN, computer systems analyst; b. Albany, Calif., Sept. 29, 1941; s. Warren Hawley and Alma Elinor (Schneider) H.; m. Michelle Marcia Heydon, Mar. 18, 1978; 1 dau, Marcia Elizabeth. B.A. in Mathematics, U. Calif.-Berkeley, 1963. Computer applications programmer Crocker Nat. Bank, San Francisco, 1963-66, analyst 1966-67; computer systems analyst Pacific Gas and Electric Co., San Francisco, 1967—. Bd. dirs. (Valley Forge (Pa.), Am. Baptist Churches of U.S., 1974-81, election dist. rep. for North Coastal area Am. Bapt. Ch. of the West, 1974-81, chmn. North Coastal area program bd, 1981-84, mem. exec. com. gen. bd., 1976-79, chmn. com. planning and evaluation, 1974-81. Republican. Home: 322 Blackstone Dr San Rafael CA 94903 Office: 245 Market St Suite 1125 San Francisco CA 94106

HOLMES, HARRY EDWARD, real estate co. exec.; b. Abilene, Tex., Dec. 5, 1925; s. Harry and Rita (Simmons) H.; A.B., U. Calif., Berkeley, 1950; m. Gayle Walter, Sept. 1, 1957; children—Marshall, Hilary, Gay. Mgr., San Ysidro Ranch, Santa Barbara, Calif., 1953-57, Santa Barbara Biltmore, 1957-59, Clift Hotel, San Francisco, 1959-60; v.p. Allied Properties, San Francisco, 1960-62; pres. Am. Convalescent Hosps., San Francisco, 1963-65; v.p., dir. Janss Corp., Thousand Oaks, Calif., 1965-67; pres. Sun Valley (Idaho) Co., 1967-73; pres., chief exec. officer Pebble Beach (Calif.) Corp., 1973—, also dir.; pres. Aspen (Colo.) Ski Co., 1982—. Served with USAAF, 1944-45. Decorated Air medal with 4 oak leaf clusters, Purple Heart. Mem. Am. Hotel/Motel Assn. Clubs: Burlingame (Calif.) Country: Old Capital (Monterey, Calif.); Beach, Cypress Point (Pebble Beach). Home: PO Box 714 Pebble Beach CA 93953 Office: Pebble Beach Corp Box 1098 Pebble Beach CA 93553

HOLMES, PAUL LUTHER, political scientist, educational consultant; b. Rock Island, Ill., Mar. 7, 1919; s. Bernt Gunnar and Amanda Sophia (Swenson) H.; m. Ardis Ann Grunditz, Nov. 1, 1946; children—Mary Ann, David Stephen. B.A., U. Minn., 1940; M.A., Stanford U., 1949, Ed.D., 1968; M.A., George Washington U., 19—. Career officer U.S. Navy, 1941-64, ret. as capt.; adminstr. Laney Coll., Oakland, Calif., 1965-70; dean Contra Costa Coll., San Pablo, Calif., 1970-71; pres. Coll. of Alameda (Calif.), 1971-75, prof. polit. sci., 1975-80; dir. doctoral studies program No. Calif., Nova U., 1975-80; cons. in higher edn., Gig Harbor, Wash., 1981—; regent Calif. Luth. Coll., 1973-76. Decorated Navy Air, Joint Service medals. Mem. AAUP, Am. Polit. Sci. Assn., Navy League, Stanford Univ. Alumni Assn., Phi Delta Kappa. Lutheran. Club: Rotary (Gig Harbor).

HOLMES, PEARL MALOTT, educator; b. Oklahoma City, Dec. 1, 1921; m. Douglas I. Holmes, May 30, 1942; children—Douglas I., Anita J. Holmes Wasinger, Terry J., Merry C. Holmes Logan. Instr. English, Kenjo Girls Coll., Nagoya, Japan, 1954; tchr. Sooner (Okla.) Elem. Sch., 1959-60, Westover (Mo.) Elem. Sch., 1960-62, Belton (Mo.) Jr. High Sch., 1962-63, Misawa (Japan) Dependents' Sch., 1964-66; counselor in practicum Ariz. State U., 1966-67; counselor Sprou1 (Colo.) Jr. High Sch., 1967-68, Widefield Elem. Sch., Colorado Springs, Colo., 1968-75; guidance cons. Colo. Dept. Edn., 1975-77; dir. sch. climate improvement project, coordinator guidance, dir. Title IV, Widefield Sch. Dist., 1977-78; counselor Webster Elem. Sch., Colo., 1978-80; mem. faculty U. Colo. Grad. Sch., Colorado Springs, 1981—. Mem. Gov.'s Council for Children, 1976-77, Colo. ESEA Title IV Adv. Council, 1977-80. First aid and swimming tchr., mem. adv. bd. ARC; officer PTA; pres., chair Air Force Officers' Wives Orgn.; mem. adv. bd. Air Force Family Services; mem. Colorado Springs Opera Aux., Fine Arts Aux.; Sunday sch. tchr.; coordinator parents' and childrens' drug edn. programs; cons. PAYO. Recipient Clifford Houston award Colo. Personnel and Guidance Assn., 1978; named Counselor of Yr., Colo. Sch. Counselors Assn., 18 1982. Mem. NEA (chair human relations com.; Colo. guidance liaison com. 1973-78), Colo. Edn. Assn., Classroom Tchrs. Assn., Collegiate Assn. Devel. and Renewal of Educators, Am. Personnel and Guidance Assn., Colo. Personnel and Guidance Assn., Widefield Counselors Assn., Colo. Assn. Children with Learning Disabilities. Home: 1219 N Tejon Colorado Springs CO 80903

HOLMES, RICHARD HUGH MORRIS, investment management executive; b. Olean N.Y., Dec. 11, 1925; s. Gerald Hugh and Caroline Elizabeth (Morris) H.; m. Dorothy Theone Minnich, Sept. 7, 1944; children—Richard Edward Griffin, James Stuart. Student Brown U., 1942-43. Office Mgr. Red Star Transit Co., Detroit, 1947-55; data processor Nat. Dairy Products Co., Detroit, 1955-58; asst. to controller Am. Sugar Co., San Francisco, 1958-66; with Am. Express Investment Mgmt. Co., San Francisco, 1966-75, pres., 1974-75; v.p. Capital Research & Mgmt. Co., San Francisco, 1975—; pres., dir. Am. Balanced Fund, Inc.; pres., chmn. bd. Endowments, Inc., Bond Portfolio for Endowments, Inc.; pres. Growth Fund Am., Inc., Income Fund Am., Inc. Served to capt. RAF, 1943-46. Mem. Investment Co. Inst., Mensa. Republican. Club: Los Angeles Athletic. Home: 580 Laurent Rd Hillsborough CA 94010 Office: 2 Embarcadero Center Suite 2320 San Francisco CA 94111

HOLMGREN, KENNETH D., aerospace co. exec.; b. Tremonton, Utah, Feb. 23, 1930; s. Delbert K. and Elaine I. (Hokanson) H.; m. Norine Rasmussen, May 12, 1949; children—Debbera, Patricia, Mary Helen. Supr., Holmgren Land & Livestock Co., Bear River City, Utah, 1948-55, sec. and dir., 1965—; owner, mgr. Holmgren Transp. Co., Bear River City, 1955-57; with Thiokol Corp., 1957 , mgr. market research and long-range planning, Brigham City, Utah, 1964-67, mgr. ordnance programs, Brigham City, 1967-72, mgr. Utah div., Ogden, 1972-82, v.p. Utah div., 1982—. Mem. Assn. U.S. Army, Air Force Assn., Am. Def. Preparedness Assn. (founding pres. Utah chpt. 1979-80). Mormon. Home: Bear River City UT 84301 Office: 3350 Airport Rd Ogden UT 84403

HOLMQUIST, WALTER RICHARD, research chemist, molecular evolutionist; b. Kansas City, Mo., Dec. 23, 1934; s. Walter Theodore and Elsie Wilburnia (Seitz) H.; B.S., Washington and Lee U., 1957; B.S., Calif. Inst. Tech., 1961, Ph.D. in Chemistry, 1966; m. Ann Marie Hofer, Sept. 8, 1968; children—Laura Marie, Jon Aron. Lectr. organic chemistry and biochemistry U. Ife, Ibadan, Nigeria, 1966-68; research fellow in biology Harvard U., 1968-70; asst. research chemist Space Scis. Lab., U. Calif., Berkeley, 1970-74, asso. research chemist, 1974-80, research chemist, 1980—, sr. research fellow, 1980-82. Nat. Heart and Lung Inst. grantee, 1971-73; NSF grantee, 1977-81. Mem. AAAS, Am. Chem. Soc., Am. Soc. Biol. Chemists, N.Y. Acad. Scis., Calif. Acad. Scis., Soc. for Study of Evolution, Phi Beta Kappa, Sigma Xi. Editor: Life Sciences and Space Research, 1976-82, mem. editorial bd. Adv. Space Research, 1980—, Jour. Molecular Evolution, 1974—, BioSystems, 1977—. Home: 760 Mesa Way Richmond CA 94805 Office: Space Scis Lab U Calif-Berkeley Berkeley CA 94720

HOLOHAN, WILLIAM ANDREW, state justice; b. Tucson, June 1, 1928; s. Andrew S. and Dorothy L. (Bonnott) H.; LL.B., U. Ariz., 1950; m. Kathryn Dewey, Dec. 12, 1953, children—Mark, Ellen, Brian, Lori. Admitted to Ariz. bar, 1950; asst. U.S. atty., 1953-60; judge Superior Ct., 1963-72; justice Ariz. Supreme Ct., Phoenix, 1972—. Served with U.S. Army, 1950-53. Decorated Bronze Star medal. Office: Ariz Supreme Ct 217 South-West Wing Phoenix AZ 85007

HOLPP, JAMES R., ret. indsl. engr.; b. Tell City, Ind., Mar. 22, 1918; s. John D. and May B. (Patterson) H.; student Ind. U., 1938-39; B.S., Western Ky. U., 1940, M.A., 1948; m. Maryan L. Weber, Aug. 7, 1971; children—Judith, Joseph. Sci. tchr., athletic coach Rineyville (Ky.) High Sch., 1940-41, Elkton (Ky.) High Sch., 1941-42, 46-52, Howevalley (Ky.) High Sch., 1945-46; staff mem. Sandia Nat. Labs., Albuquerque, 1952-53, nuclear research sect. supr., 1953-54, project engr., 1954-58, supr. joint task group div., 1958-60, product acceptance div. supr., 1960-64, data planning div. supr., 1964-81, ret., 1981; conf. speaker; chmn. Project 60 Conf., U. N.Mex., 1962. Del., Democratic State Conv., 1966; scoutmaster Boy Scouts Am., 1940, cubmaster, 1952. Served with USNR, 1943-45. Registered profl. engr., Ky., N.Mex. Mem. Am. Soc. Quality Control (cert., sr.), Peter Tare Motor Torpedo Boat Servicemen's Assn. Roman Catholic. Clubs: Sertoma, Coronado, Elks. Author: (with others) Data System Planning, 1966. Home: 2913 Alcazar St NE Albuquerque NM 87110

HOLSER, MARY ANN, social worker, social services council administrator; b. Detroit, 1928; d. Ray Ward and Ruth Belle (Ferguson) Harris; m. William Thomas Holser, Dec. 23, 1954; children—Thomas Dana, Alec Stuart, Margaret Ann. B.A., U. Mich., 1950; M.S.W., Ohio State U., 1954. Social worker League United Latin Am. Citizens, Anaheim, Calif., 1965-67; psychiat. social worker Crisis Clinic, Orange County U. Calif.-Irvine Med. Sch., 1967-70; psychiat. social worker cons. Los Angeles County Health Dept., 1970; dir. Alcohol Traffic Safety Clinic, Eugene, Oreg., 1971-76; co-dir., founder Drinking Decisions, Inc., Eugene, 1977-78; dir. Behanna House women's residential treatment program, Lane County Council on Alcoholism, Eugene, 1977-78, exec. dir. council, 1979—; mem. Lane County Mental Health Center Bd., 1972-76; sec.-treas. Lane County Substance Abuse Coordinating Com. 1980-81; chmn. Lane County Affirmative Action Com.; mem. Oreg. Community Alcoholism Task Force; mental health examiner State of Oreg., 1973—; vis. asst. prof. U. Oreg., 1973-76; research grantee Max Planck Inst. for Psychiatry, Munich, W.Ger. 1976. Recipient Citizenship award Am. Legion, 1946; winner Eugene Friends of Library Poetry Contest, 1982. Mem. Nat. Assn. Social Workers (dir. 1982-83), Oreg. Assn. Community Alcohol Program Dirs. (sec.-treas.), Oreg. Substance Abuse Profl. Assn., Sierra Club, Obsidians, Smithsonian Assocs., Nat. Geog. Soc., Eugene Family YMCA. Democrat. Congregationalist. Contbr. articles to profl. jours. Home: 2620 Cresta de Ruta Eugene OR 97403 Office: 474 Willamette Suite 308 Eugene OR 97401

HOLST, WILLIAM JAMES, data processor; b. Frederick, Md., Aug. 22, 1945; s. William Walker and Catherine M. (Loggie) H.; m. Patricia Russell, Jan. 27, 1973; children—Jennifer R., Gretchen M., William R. B.S. in Bus. Adminstrn., No. Ariz. U., 1972. Computer ops. mgr. Samaritan Health Service, Phoenix, 1972-75; material requirements mgr. Pepsi-Cola, Flagstaff, Ariz., 1975-78; dir. fiscal/info. services Flagstaff (Ariz.) Med. Center, 1978—. Medic Alert local rep., 1983—; mem., solicitor high tech. equipment, donations No. Ariz. Health Care Found. Served with U.S. Army, 1965-69. Mem. Data Processing Mgmt. Assn. (cert., dir.), Assn. Systems Mgmt., Health Care Fin. Mgmt. Assn., Electronic Computing Health Oriented. Republican. Roman Catholic. Home: 922 N Leroux St Flagstaff AZ 86001 Office: PO Box 1268 Flagstaff AZ 86002

HOLSTE, THOMAS JAMES, artist, educator; b. Evanston, Ill., Jan. 12, 1943; s. Richard Frederick and Ethelyn P. (Bestor) H.; B.A., Calif. State U.-Fullerton, 1964-67, M.A., 1968; M.F.A., Clarmont Grad. Sch., 1970. Prof. art, Calif. State U., Fullerton, 1971—. Nat. Endowment for the Arts Individual Artists Fellowship grantee, 1980-81. One man show: Irving Blum Gallery, Los Angeles, 1972; group shows include: Solomon R. Guggenheim Mus., 1981, Long Beach Mus. of Art, 1982, Ft. Worth Art Mus., 1981, John Weber Gallery, N.Y.C., 1979, Otis Art Inst., Los Angeles, 1979, Mus. Modern Art, N.Y.C., 1976, Newport Harber (Calif.) Art Mus., 1976, Los Angeles County Mus. of Art, 1972, La Jolla (Calif.) Mus. of Contemporary Art, 1970, Newspace Gallery, Los Angeles, 1973-77, 1979, 1981. Works in following collections: Solomon R. Guggenheim Mus., Chase Manhattan Bank, N.Y.C., ITT, N.Y.C., Patrick Lannan Found., N.Y.C., Security Pacific Nat. Bank, Los Angeles, Newport Harbor Art Mus. Newport Beach, Calif., La Jolla Mus. Contemporary Art, Long Bech Mus. of Art. Home: Star Route Box 796 Orange CA 92667 Office: Dept of Art California State U Fullerton Fullerton CA 92634

HOLSTEAD, BOBBY NEAL, psychologist; b. Alexandria, La., May 26, 1952; s. Charles Edward and Leatrice Joy (Davis) H.; B.A. summa cum laude (La. Bd. Edn. scholar 1970-73), N.E. La. U., 1973; M.A., U. Miss., 1975, Ph.D., 1978; m. Deborah Williams Warner, May 22, 1976. Commd. 1st lt. U.S. Air Force, 1977, advanced through grades to capt., 1978; psychologist USAF Hosp., Kirtland AFB, N.Mex., 1978-81; partner Behavior Therapy Assos., 1980—; psychol. dir. Obesity and Risk Factor Program, 1981—. Mem. Am. Psychol. Assn., Assn. Advancement Psychology, Assn. Advancement Behavior Therapy, N.Mex. Psychol. Assn., Soc. Air Force Clin. Psychologists. Democrat. Unitarian. Home: 1706 Ridgecrest Dr SE Albuquerque NM 87108 Office: La Mesa Med Center Suite E22 7000 Cutler NE Albuquerque NM 87110 also St Joseph's Med Towers Suite 308 500 Walter NE Albuquerque NM 87106

HOLSTEIN, TRULA ELAINE, educator; b. Emporia, Kans., Nov. 7, 1945; d. Jack L. and Frances (Shull) Rogers; m. Ben A. Holstein, Dec. 27, 1968; children—Ross Alan, Jenny Louise. Student N.Mex. State U., summers 1963, 64, 65, postgrad., 1970—; B.A., Bethel Coll. and Sem., 1967. Tchr., Scottsdale Elem. Sch., El Paso, 1968-70; tchr. Zia Jr. High Sch., Las Cruces, N.Mex., 1970-71, 72—, head social studies dept., 1974—. Mem. Las Cruces Assn. Classroom Tchrs. (pres. 1980-81), N.Mex. Assn. Classroom Tchrs. (sec. 1983-84), N.Mex. Council Social Studies, Nat. Council Social Studies, Assn. Supervision and Curriculum Devel., Las Cruces Assn. Homebuilder Aux., Delta Kappa Gamma. Republican. Home: 1219 Edgewood St Las Cruces NM 88005 Office: Zia Jr High Sch 1300 W University St Las Cruces NM 88001

HOLT, CHARLES FRANK, economics educator; b. Centralia, Wash., Dec. 30, 1937; s. Jesse James and Frances Louise (Small) H. B.B.A., So. Meth. U., Dallas, 1960; M.S. in Econs., Purdue U., 1967, Ph.D. in Econ. History, 1970. Instr. econs. Purdue U., 1965-68; asst. prof. econs., U. Minn., Duluth, 1969-73; assoc. prof. econs. U. San Diego, 1973—. Served to lt. USN, 1961-65. Krannert Doctoral Research fellow, 1968-69. Mem. Am. Econ. Assn., Econ. History Assn., Western Econ. Assn. Author: The Role of State Government in the Nineteenth-Century American Economy, 1977; contbr. articles to econ. jours. Office: School of Business Administration U San Diego San Diego CA 92110

HOLT, DEAN ANDERSON, physician; b. Salt Lake City, Feb. 8, 1927; s. Harry and Onedia May (Anderson) H.; student Brigham Young U., 1945; B.S., U. Utah, 1950, M.D., 1957; m. Ruth Brown, June 16, 1952; children—Alan, Michael, David, Cathie Ann, Mark, Robert. Intern, Thomas Dee Hosp., Ogden, Utah; 1957-58; resident in neonatal pediatrics U. Utah, Salt Lake City, 1977; county health officer, civil def. med. officer, Evanston, Wyo., 1959-65; partner gen. practice Evanston (Wyo.) Med. Group, 1958-75; chief staff Uinta County Meml. Hosp., Evanston, several times; family practice medicine, Evanston, 1976—; preceptor Medex and nurse practitioners U. Utah Coll. Medicine, Coll. Nursing, 1976-79; preceptor med. students U. Wyo. Coll. Human Medicine, 1979—, clin. assoc. prof. family practice, 1983—; research assoc. Inst. Biomed. Engring., U. Utah, 1968. Bishop, high councilman Ch. of Jesus Christ of Latter day Saints; active Boy Scouts Am. Served with U.S. Army, 1946-47. Recipient Silver Beaver award, Key awards Boy Scouts Am., 1977. Diplomate Am. Bd. Family Practice. Mem. Am. Acad. Family Practice, Wyo. State Med. Soc. (past councilman., del.), Uinta County Med. Soc. Republican. Patentee in field. Office: Suite 302 1237 Uinta St Evanston WY 82930

HOLT, DOUGLAS EUGENE, utility executive; b. Johnson City, Tenn., Jan. 5, 1925; s. John Henry and Alcyone Carolyn (Tate) H.; m. Elizabeth Ann Henderson, Sept. 21, 1948; children—Douglas Eugene, Lisa Gail, John Timothy, Jeffrey Daniel. B.S., U. Tenn., 1948. With Jellico (Tenn.) Electric and Water System, 1948-54, Johnson City Water and Sewer Dept., 1955-56; office mgr. Elizabethton (Tenn.) Electric System, 1956-80, asst. mgr., 1974-80, also sec. bd. dirs.; gen. mgr. Truckee (Calif.)-Donner Pub. Utility Dist., 1980—; instr. Elizabethton Vocat. Tech. Sch., evenings, 1967-80. Bd. dirs. East Tenn. Christian Home, United Fund. Served with USAAF, 1943-44. Recipient Outstanding Citizenship award Carter County C. of C., United Fund. Mem. East Tenn. Pub. Power Accts. Assn., Tennessee Valley Pub. Power Assn., Am. Pub. Power Assn., Carter County C. of C. (past pres.). Republican. Mem. Ch. of Christ. Club: Rotary. Home: PO Box 8351 Truckee CA

HOLT, KRIS EUGENE, marketing executive; b. San Jose, Calif., Jan. 3, 1956; s. Jess Floyd and Joyce Suzanne (Velander) H. A.A., McHenry County Coll., 1976; B.S., So. Ill. U., 1978; student Grad. Bank Mktg. Sch., 1983. Account exec. Smith Advt., Capitola, Calif., 1978-80, KZOZ Radio, San Luis Obispo, Calif., 1980-81; mktg. dir. Mid-State Bank, Arroyo Grande, Calif., 1981—; advt. cons. Recipient Ribbons of Blue Awards, Central Coast Ad Club, 1983. Mem. Bank Mktg. Assn., Am. Bankers Assn. Democrat. Lutheran. Clubs: Exchange of Central Coast, Cal-Poly Mustang Booster, San Luis Obispo Jaycees.

HOLT, RAYMOND MILTON, library cons.; b. San Bernardino, Calif., June 3, 1921; s. Thurman Jess and Mandia Mariah (Groom) H.; A.B., U. Redlands (Calif.), 1942; B.S. in L.S., U. So. Calif., 1947; m. Sarah Vincent Campi, June 25, 1941; children—Harvey Milton, Christine Eileen. Reference librarian Fullerton (Calif.) Public Library, 1947-50; city librarian Pomona (Calif.) Public Library, 1950-70; propr. Raymond M. Holt, library cons., Del Mar, Calif., 1970—; partner Holt-Eggers Partnership, San Diego, 1976—; lectr., cons. Mem. ALA, Library Adminstrn. and Mgmt. Assn., Library Info. and Tech. Assns., Assn. Specialized and Coop. Library Agys., Pacific N.W. Library Assn., Calif. Library Assn. Congregationalist. Author handbooks, proposals, articles, reports in field; editorial bd. Public Library Quar., Library & Archival Security. Office: PO Box 745 Del Mar CA 92014

HOLT, ROBERT GLENN, safety engineer, freelance writer; b. Dallas, Oreg., May 30, 1946; s. Elmer Glenn and Lucille Helen (Paterson) H.; m. Paula Lee Stevens, Oct. 29, 1977; 1 stepdaughter, Angela Sue Crouch. B.S., Portland State U., 1968; student Drury Coll., 1970-71; A.A. in Occupational Safety and Health, Costa Mesa Community Coll., 1975. Cert. safety profl. Geologist Western Geophys. Co., Houston, 1971-72; loss control rep. Continental Ins. Co., Los Angeles, 1972-73; loss control rep. Highlands Ins. Co., Irvine, Calif., 1973-77; loss control surveyor Chubb & Son, Seattle, 1977-79; v.p. loss control Scott Wetzel Services, Bremerton, Wash., 1979—; freelance writer loss control. Served with U.S. Army, 1969-71. Decorated Army Commendation Medal with Oak Leaf Cluster. Mem. Am. Soc. Safety Engrs. (recognition award 1979, sec. Puget Sound chpt., past newletter chmn). Republican. Contbr. articles to profl. jours. Office: 500 Pacific Ave Bremerton WA 98310

HOLTZ, TOBENETTE, aerospace engineer; b. Rochester, N.Y., June 20, 1930; d. Marcus and Leah (Cohen) H.; m. Joseph Laurinovics, Dec. 25, 1964. B.S.A.E., Wayne State U., 1958; M.S.A.E., Ohio State U., 1964; Ph.D., U. So. Calif., 1974. Sr. engr. N. Am. Aviation, Columbus, Ohio, 1954-59; research asso., Ohio State U., Columbus, 1959-60; sr. engr. U. So. Calif. Research Found., Point Mugu, 1960-62; sr. engr. Northrop Corp., Hawthorne, Calif., 1962-67; engring. specialist McDonnell Douglas Corp., Huntington Beach, Calif., 1967-75; staff engr. Acurex Corp., Mountain View, Calif., 1975-76; mgr. reentry systems tech planning Aerospace Corp., El Segundo, Calif., 1976-79, mgr. def. support satellite sensors, 1979-82; dept. mgr. advanced missle systems ops. TRW Def. Systems Group, San Bernardino, Calif., 1982—. Mem. AIAA. Contbr. articles to profl. jours. Office: PO Box 1310 San Bernardino CA 92402

HOLTZCLAW, KENNETH MERTON, analytical chemist; b. La Habra, Calif., Sept. 2, 1929; s. Alvin Raymond and Esther Josephine (Mehrkens) H.; B.S. in Chemistry, Loma Linda U., 1963; m. Margaret Bess Gould, June 13, 1958; children—Kenneth Kelly, Brenda Bea, Brian Lee. Research asst. B. F. Goodrich Aerospace, Rialto, Calif., 1960-61; research asst. Lockheed Propulsion, Mentone, Calif., 1962-63; research asso. U. Calif., Riverside, 1964—, supr. trace mental lab. and basic chem. research, 1970—. Served with U.S. Navy, 1950-54. Recipient Spl. Performance award U. Calif., Riverside, 1980, 83. Mem. Soil Sci. Soc. Am., Am. Soc. Agronomy. Democrat. Home: 13812 Day St Riverside CA 92508 Office: Dept Soil and Environ Scis U Calif Riverside CA 92521

HOLTZMANN, OLIVER VINCENT, plant pathologist, educator; b. Highmore, S.D., June 26, 1922; s. Alphonse Joseph and Mary Lona Gertrude (St. Pierre) H.; m. Cecelia Lucas, June 8, 1957; children—Fredrick John, Kathryn Marie, Nicholas Edward, Joseph Albert, Eleanor Ann. B.S., Colo. State U., 1950, M.S., 1952; Ph.D., Wash. State U., 1955. Grad. asst. Colo. State U., 1950-52, Wash. State U., 1952-55; research asst. prof. N.C. State U., 1955-56; asst. prof. U. Hawaii, 1956-66, assoc. prof., 1966-71, prof., 1971—, chmn. dept. plant pathology, 1970-82. Served with AUS, 1942-45. Mem. Am. Phytopath. Soc., Soc. Nematology, Sigma Xi, Gamma Sigma Delta, Sigma Chi. Roman Catholic. Club: K.C. Contbr. articles to profl. jours. Office: Dept Plant Pathology Univ Hawaii 3190 Maile Way Honolulu HI 96822

HOLUB, ROSHARA JANE, trade association and service company executive; b. Antigo, Wis., Dec. 14, 1945; d. Arthur Carl and Ethelmae (Houghton) Stamm; children—Kathe A., Sandy J. B.B.A. in Mgmt., So. Meth. U., 1971. With Stamm Boat Co., Delafield, Wis., 1964-71; office mgr. North Central Tech. Inst., Wausau, Wis., 1975, 76; coordinator off-campus programs bus. div. Arapahoe Community Coll., Littleton, Colo., 1976-79; dir. edn. and tng. Wyo. Credit Union League, Inc., Casper, 1979-80, pres., 1980—, also pres. Wyo. Credit Union League Services, Inc. Mem. Assn. Credit Union League Execs. (nat. credit union roundtable adv. com.), Credit Union Nat. Assn., Internat. Consumer Credit Assn. (dir.), Credit Women Internat. (treas. 1980, 2d v.p. 1981, chmn. edn. com. 1981, chmn. consumer credit week 1982). Club: Toastmasters (adminstrv. v.p. 1980). Home: 1815 S McKinley St Casper WY 82601

HOLYER, ERNA MARIA, author, educator, artist; b. Weilheim, Bavaria, Germany, Mar. 15, 1925; d. Mathias and Anna Maria (Goldhofer) Schretter; A.A., San Jose Evening Coll., 1964; student San Mateo Coll., 1965-67, San Jose State U., 1968-69, San Jose City Coll., 1980-81; m. Gene Wallace Holyer, Aug. 24, 1957. Free lance writer under pseudonym Ernie Holyer, 1960—; tchr. creative writing San Jose (Calif.) Met. Adult Edn., 1968—; exhibited in group shows Crown Zellerbach Gallery, San Francisco, 1973, 74, 76, 77; I.B.C. Gallery, San Francisco, 1970, Los Angeles 1981. Recipient Woman of Achievement Honor cert. San Jose Mercury-News, 1973, 74, 75; Lefoli award for excellence in adult edn. instrn. Adult Edn. Senate, 1972. Mem. Calif. Writers Club. Author: Rescue at Sunrise, 1965; Steve's Night of Silence, 1966; A Cow for Hansel, 1967; At the Forest's Edge, 1969; Song of Courage, 1970; Lone Brown Gull, 1971; Shoes for Daniel, 1974; The Southern Sea Otter, 1975; Sigi's Fire Helmut, 1975; Reservoir Road Adventure, 1982. Contbr. articles to various mags. and newspapers. Home and Office: 1314 Rimrock Dr San Jose CA 95210

HOLZBOG, THOMAS JERALD, architect, planner; b. Milw., Oct. 25, 1933; s. Walter Charles and Dorothy (Van Holten) H.; B.A. (Hopper fellow), Yale U., 1960; M.Arch., Harvard U., 1968; children—Jessica, Arabella. Asso. architect successively Paul Rudolph, New Haven, Candilis Woods, Paris, Sir Leslie Martin, Cambridge, Eng., Sir Denys Lasdun London, I. M. Pei, N.Y.C., 1960-67; pres. Holzbog & Matloob Assos., Architects and Planners, Los Angeles and Boston, 1967—; mem. faculty Pratt Inst., Columbia U., R.I. Sch. Design, Harvard U., Tufts U., Calif. Poly. U., UCLA; past mem. Mayor's Task Force for Urban Design, N.Y.C.; chmn. Lexington (Mass.) Design Adv. Com.; mem. Hist. Dists. Commn., Lexington. Bd. dirs. Interfaith Housing, Boston. Served to capt. U.S. Army. Recipient numerous archtl. design awards; Agnus T. Hopper fellow, Yale; Fulbright fellow. Mem. AIA (mem. archtl. edn. com. Los Angeles chpt.), Am. Soc. Landscape Architects, Am. Inst. Cert. Planners, Nat. Inst. Archtl. Edn., Archtl. Assn. (London). Contbr. articles to profl. jours.; exhibited work in numerous exhbns. Home: 1301 Warnall Ave Los Angeles CA 90024 Office: 10952 Santa Monica Blvd Los Angeles CA 90025

HOLZMAN, IRVING MURRAY, anesthetist; b. Knoxville, Tenn., Oct. 21, 1936; s. Jacob Leroy and Tessie (Levine) H.; B.A., Vanderbilt U., 1958; grad. Pensacola Jr. Coll. Sch. Nursing, 1960, Mayo Clinic Sch. Anesthesia, 1962. Staff anesthetist U. Fla. Med. Center, Gainesville, 1962-65; asst. chief anesthesia dept. Meml. Hosp., Panama City, Fla., 1965-73, organizer, dir. Sch. Anesthesia, 1968-73; practice anesthesia, Yakima, Wash., 1973—; mem. med. staff New Valley Osteo. Hosp., 1973—, asst. chief of staff, 1979-80, sec.-treas., 1980-81. Acting rabbi Yakima Valley Synagogue, 1974—; mem. Temple de Hirsch Sinai, Seattle, 1978—. United chmn. United Fund, 1971; chmn. Panama City Jaycees Christmas Shopping Tour for Underpriviledged, 1972; patron Allied Arts Council, Yakima, 1977—; commencement speaker Sch. Nursing, Gulf Coast Community Coll., Panama City, Fla., 1973. Recipient Outstanding Young Man of Year award Panama City Jaycees, 1970, Leadership in Action award, 1972. Mem. Am. (mem. nat. conv. steering com. 1972-73, nat. scholarship and loan com. 1973-74; continued profl. excellence certificate 1970, 75), Fla. (trustee 1965-66, pres. 1968-70), Wash. (state conv. chmn. 1974, state edn. chmn. 1974-75, trustee 1975-76, pres. 1977-78, cons. and parliamentarian 1978-82) assns. nurse anesthetists, Am. Soc. Regional Anesthesia, U.S. Power Squadron, YMCA, Am. Contract Bridge League, Ecol. Soc. Washington. Clubs: Rotary, Masons (32 deg.), Elks. Home: PO Box 2314 Yakima WA 98907 Office: 3003 Tieton Dr Yakima WA 98902

HOLZMAN, NEIL JOHN, distribution company executive; b. Oceanside, N.Y., Jan. 4, 1953; s. Ralph Earnest and Florence Marie (Tokach) H.; B.A., U. Colo., 1974; postgrad. Regis Coll., Denver, 1980—; m. Candace Elizabeth Barkey, Aug. 17, 1974; 1 dau., Kelsey Elizabeth.

Research asst. Nat. Center for Atmospheric Research, Boulder, Colo., 1972-74, support scientist, 1975-77; sales exec. Xerox Corp., Aspen, Colo., 1977-79; tng. exec. Kroy Inc., Boulder, 1980-81; mktg. exec. Prolink Corp., Boulder, 1981-82; Western regional mgr. Info Serv div. Nat. Teldata Corp., Boulder, 1982—. Mem. Phi Kappa Tau. Republican. Episcopalian. Home: 3637 Hazelwood Ct Boulder CO 80302 Office: 1495 Canyon Blvd Suite 205 E Boulder CO 80302

HOM, RICHARD YEE, tool engr.; b. Phoenix, July 26, 1950; s. Tommy Look and Betty (Mah) H.; B.S. in Engring. Sci. and Aero. and Aerospace Tech., Ariz. State U., 1973; m. Kathleen Chien. Asst. engr. Sperry Flight System, Phoenix, 1973; sr. engr., composite tool engring. Boeing Comml. Airplane Co., Seattle, 1972—. Mem. Air Force Assn., Soc. Mfg. Engrs., AIAA. Home: 32209 11th Pl S Apt 58 Federal Way WA 98003 Office: M/S 5H-27 PO Box 3707 Seattle WA 98124

HOMBS, KAREN KAY, stockbroker; b. Denver, Aug. 3, 1942; d. Arthur Clark Eugene and Norma May (Urquhart) Ryman; student U. Denver/Colo. Women's Coll., 1980—; m. Thomas Gibson Hombs, Apr. 12, 1978; 1 son, Timothy John. With Samsonite Corp., Denver, 1960-75, employee relations rep., supr., 1965-71, labor relations rep., 1971-75; labor relations rep. Climax Molybdenum Co. (Colo.) div. AMAX, 1975-78, prin. labor relations adminstr., 1978-83; registered rep. Investors Diversified Services, Denver, 1983—. Mem. council Lord of the Mountains Lutheran Ch., Summit County, Colo., 1979-80, founded women's chpt. Luth. Ch. Women, 1976, chpt. chmn., 1976-77, Sunday Sch. supt., 1976-81. Mem. Indsl. Relations Research Assn., Am. Mgmt. Assn. Home: 7640 W 24th Ave Lakewood CO 80215 Office: 10020 E Girard Ave Suite 250 Denver CO 80231

HONEY, CAROL THOMPSON, publishing executive; b. Mauston, Wis., Dec. 3, 1947; d. Lee Bryan Jr. and Mary Eileen (Riley) Thompson; m. David Charles Honey, Nov. 18, 1977. Student Antelope Valley Coll., 1965-66, UCLA Extension, Los Angeles City Coll., 1974. Registered investment adviser, Calif. Project coordinator ITT Cannon Electric, Los Angeles, 1966-68; dir. adminstrn. Rex Land & Assocs., Los Angeles, 1968-77; owner, v.p., mng. editor, sec.-treas. Walker's Manual Inc., Garden Grove, Calif., 1977—. Republican. Office: 14032 Lake St Suite 101 Garden Grove CA 92643

HONEYSETT, WILLIAM LEE, newspaper publisher; b. Wenatchee, Wash., Aug. 13, 1937; s. Harlan H. and Thelma O. (Vaughn) H.; student U. Puget Sound, Tacoma, Wash., 1956-58, Wash. State U., 1962; m. Norma Wilson, June 23, 1962; children—Michelle, Richard. With Bellingham (Wash.) Herald, 1958-77, various positions to gen. mgr., then publisher, 1971-77; pres., pub. San Bernardino (Calif.) Sun, 1977—; v.p. Gannett SW and Pacific Newspaper Group, 1981—; mem. faculty Western Wash. U., 1977. Mem. bd. councillors Calif. State U., San Bernardino, 1977—, chmn., 1980—, adv. bd., 1978—; bd. dirs. San Bernardino YMCA, 1978-79, Arrowhead United Way, 1978-80, Nat. Orange Show, 1978—, St. Bernardino's Hosp. Found., 1977—; trustee Tournament of Roses Parade, 1977-80; chmn. long range planning task force San Bernardino County United Way, 1978-81; pres. Inland Empire Cultural Found., 1980-81; chmn. trustees Redlands (Calif.) United Ch. Christ, 1979-80. Named Citizen of Achievement, San Bernardino LWV, 1979, Urban League of Year, Inland Area Urban League, 1980. Mem. Am. Newspaper Pubs. Assn., Calif. Newspaper Pubs. Assn., Allied Daily Newspapers. Clubs: Bellingham Yacht, Bellingham Golf and Country; Arrowhead Country (San Bernardino). Office: The Sun Co 399 D St San Bernardino CA 92401*

HONG, STEVE, mfg. co. exec.; b. Stockton, Calif., Dec. 26, 1947; s. James and Ng She Hong; B.S., San Jose (Calif.) State U., 1970; m. Gladys Huey, Aug. 8, 1971; children—Roger, Russell, Aimee. Asst. mgr. W.T. Grant Co., San Jose, 1970-71; field underwriter N.Y. Life Ins. Co., 1971-72, asst. sales mgr. Palo Alto, Calif., 1972; with Paul Masson Vineyards, 1972-77, chief acct., 1975-77; asst. controller NPI Corp., 1977-79; controller Forman Industries, Hayward, Calif., 1979, controller, gen. mgr., 1979—. Mem. USNG, 1970-76. Republican. Methodist. Home: 1210 Shriver Ct San Jose CA 95132 Office: 103 Orchard Ave Hayward CA 94544

HOOD, FRED H., mgmt. cons.; b. Granite, Okla., Feb. 23, 1926; s. Fred H. and Gertrude E. (Abel) H.; B.S. in Bus. Mgmt., M.Public Adminstrn., U. No. Colo.; m. Shirley Rose Brenk, July 2, 1964. Served with USN, 1944-47, U.S. Army, 1949-52, U.S. Air Force, 1956-72, ret., 1972; indsl. engr. City of Denver, 1972-74; v.p. Community Devel. Co., 1972-80; mgmt. analyst USAF, Denver, 1974-79; mayor City of Aurora (Colo.), 1975-79; guest lectr. U.S. Conf. Mayors, 1978, Colo. Municipal League, 1978. Mem. Denver Regional Council Govt., 1975-79, Adams County Council Govt., 1975-79, Arapahoe County Council Mayors, 1975-79; mem. transp. com. U.S. Conf. Mayors, 1976-79; mem. policy bd. Colo. Municipal League, 1976-78; pres. Wren Assn., 1980-82. Mem. Am. Inst. Indsl. Engrs., Am. Soc. Mil. Comptrollers, Western Govtl. Research Assn., Am. Mgmt. Assn., Air Force Assn., 45th Inf. Div. Assn., Aurora Hist. Soc., Internat. Platform Assn. Democrat. Clubs: Lions (state sec.-treas. 1980—), Am. Legion (pub. service citation 1976-79), VFW, DAV, Masons, Shriners. Home: 12255 E Louisiana Ave Aurora CO 80012 Office: 1591 Fulton St Aurora CO 80010

HOOD, GREGORY WILLIAM, air force officer; b. Englewood, N.J., Jan. 11, 1950; s. Walter Jacques and Grace Elise (Krieg) H.; m. Leslie Jay Denecke, July 17, 1970; children—Gregory William, Geoffrey A., Amanda B. B.A., Coe Coll., 1972; M.A., U. No. Colo., 1981. Joined U.S. Air Force, 1973, advanced through grades to capt.; missile launch officer FE Warren AFB, Wyo., 1973-80, missile staff officer, 1980-82; space systems dir., chief ops. tng., asst. dir. ops. Shemya AFB, Alaska, 1982-83; missile warning staff officer Peterson AFB, Colo., 1983—; instr. Chapman Coll., 1982-83. Decorated Air Force Commendation medal. Republican. Congregationalist. Home: 4990 Wood Brook Ct Colorado Springs CO 80917 Office: Hdqrs Space Command/DOFW Peterson AFB CO 80914

HOOD, JOHN ROBINSON, JR., Realtor, ret. air force officer; b. Goldsboro, N.C., Dec. 7, 1918; s. John Robinson and Louise (Kivett) H., Sr.; B.S. in Chem. Engring. cum laude, N.C. State Coll., 1941; M.S. in Nuclear Physics, Ohio State U., 1949; grad. Indsl. Coll. of Armed Forces, 1961; m. Wilma Cornelia Faze, Jan. 11, 1943; 1 dau., Dianne McNeil. Chem. engr. E. I. du Pont Co., Gibbstown, N.J., 1941; entered USAAF, 1941, promoted through grades to col., 1951; served as command pilot; research and devel. in nuclear powered aircraft program, nuclear engring. test reactor, Dayton, Ohio, 1950-57, chief prodn. br., div. mil. application AEC, 1957-59, dep. dir. div. mil. applications, 1959-60; dir. advanced systems planning Air Force Systems Command, Dayton, 1961-63, asst. dep. comdr. research and engring., 1963-64, dir. propulsion and power subsystems engring., 1964-65, asst. dep. for Tech. Space Systems Div., 1965-66; ret., 1966; Realtor, real estate broker, Calif., 1966—. Pres., Dayton PTA, 1957; speaker, mem. Civil War Round Table So. Calif. Mem. N.C. State Coll. Alumni Assn. (dir. 1959, nat. chmn. fund dr. 1958, 59), Am. Legion, Mil. Order World Wars, Internat. Platform Assn., Sigma Xi, Tau Beta Pi, Theta Tau, Phi Kappa Phi. Clubs: Masons, Order of Daedalians. Contbr. papers to profl. jours. Address: 27867 Hawthorne Blvd Palos Verdes Peninsula CA 90274

HOOG, THOMAS WILLIAM, airline pilot, cons. firm exec.; b. Ste. Genevieve, Mo., Sept. 21, 1939; s. Leo and Edna (Basler) H.; student in Aero. Engring., U. Ill., 1960; m. Sandra Gary Garrett, Apr. 14, 1962; children—Michael, Mark, Michele. With Continental Airlines, Denver, 1967—, capt., 1978—; pres. Hoog & Assos., Boulder, Colo., 1978—; lectr. Am. U., 1975-78, Metro State U., 1976-79, U. Colo., 1976-79. With John Kennedy for Pres. Campaign, 1960, Bobby Kennedy for Pres. Campaign, 1968, George McGovern for Pres., 1962; state polit. dir. Gary Hart for Senate, 1974; adminstrv. asst. to U.S. Senator Gary Hart, 1975-78; state campaign mgr. Carter/Mondale Presdl. Campaign, 1980. Served with U.S. Navy, 1960-66. Decorated Vietnam Air medal; named U.S. Navy Jr. Officer of Year, 1964. Mem. Assn. Aero. Scientists, Denver C. of C. Roman Catholic. Clubs: Rotary of Denver; Denver City. Contbr. articles to various publs. Home: 6651 Paiute Ave Longmont CO 80501 Office: 1877 Broadway Suite 405 Boulder CO 80302

HOOPENGARNER, ALICE MAE, cattle rancher; b. Milw., Feb. 27, 1925; d. Arthur William and Beryl Caroline (Cook) Kleist; m. Robert C. Hoopengarner, June 22, 1957; 1 dau., Patricia Anne. B.A. with high distinction, Valparaiso U., 1951; M.A., U. Wis., 1954; cert. tchr. Wis., Wyo. History tchr. Elcho (Wis.) High Sch., 1953-54; history, English, German tchr. Morton (Wyo.) High Sch., 1954-56; tchr. Morton Elem. Sch., 1965-69; rancher, dir., sec.-treas. Hoopengarner Cattle Co. Inc., Morton, Wyo. Mem. Episcopal Diocese of Wyo. Commn. on Human Sexuality, 1978-79; lic. lay reader, sr. warden, mem. Bishop's com. Holy Nativity Episcopal Ch., Morton; bd. trustees Wind River Sch. Dist. 6, 1972-80; election judge Precinct 1, Dist. 16, 1979—; troop leader Morton council Girl Scouts U.S.A., 1965-69, troop leader, Gary, Ind., 1950-52, camp counselor, 1950-53, asst. camp dir., 1955-56, camp dir., 1957. Served with U.S. WAC, 1945-47. Recipient Little Red Schoolhouse award Wyo. Sch. Bds. Assn., 1980. Mem. Am. Hereford Assn., Future Farmers Am. Alumni Assn., Pi Gamma Mu. Democrat. Clubs: Lander Racquet, Riverton Tennis, Mensa. Contbr. article to history jour.

HOOPER, FREDERICK RICHARD, ret. educator; b. San Francisco, July 31, 1908; s. John F. and May (Frisbee) H.; A.B., Pomona Coll., 1933; student Claremont Grad. Sch., 1933-34; m. Grace Fletcher Read, June 24, 1937; 1 son, Robert Moore. Master Webb Sch. of Calif., Claremont, 1933-62, head math. dept., 1939-62, dir. studies. 1955-62, mem. exec. com., 1957-62, headmaster, 1962-73, emeritus, 1973—. Troop committeeman Old Baldy council Boy Scouts Am., 1953-56. Mem. Math. Assn. Am., Calif. Assn. Independent Schs. (head mathematics sect 1958-62). Nat. Council of Tchrs. Maths., Headmasters Assn., Cum Laude Soc., Am. Philatelic Soc., S.A.R., John More Assn., Phi Delta Kappa. Conglist. Clubs: Rotary (past pres. Claremont); Commonwealth (San Francisco); Town Hall (Los Angeles); California; Newport Beach Tennis. Address: PO Box 155 Corona Del Mar CA 92625

HOOPER, JAMES ANDREW, III, elec. utility exec.; b. Dallas, Sept. 24, 1937; s. James Andrew, Jr., and Lucille (Hicks) H.; student U. Ark., 1955-57; student UCLA, 1958-60; student public utility exec. program U. Mich., 1977; m. Dorothy Ann Blackford, Feb. 1, 1958; children—LuClare, Cheryl, Deanna, James Andrew IV. Acct., So. Calif. Edison Co., 1957-64, auditor, Los Angeles, 1965-68, supervising auditor, Long Beach, Calif., 1969-70, mgr. audits, Rosemead, Calif., 1971—. Pres. Hacienda Heights Youth Football Program, 1979-80; dir. Hacienda Heights Little League, 1978-79; treas. So. Calif. Baton Assn., 1976-78; pres. Hacienda Heights Bobby Sox Program, 1975, nat. commr., 1975-76; mem. So. Calif. Acctg. Careers Council, 1974-76; loaned exec. United Way, 1963. Cert. internal auditor, info. systems auditor. Mem. Pacific Coast Elec. Assn., Inst. Internal Auditors (internat. treas., dir., chmn. bd. 1983-84, pres. Los Angeles chpt.), Edison Electric Inst. Republican. Roman Catholic. Clubs: K.C. (grand knight 1974-75, faithful navigator 1976-77). Contbr. articles to The Internal Auditor. Home: 1817 S Blazing Star Dr Hacienda Heights CA 91745 Office: 2244 Walnut Grove Ave Rosemead CA 91770

HOOPER, JERE MANN, hotel exec.; b. Brownsville, Tenn., July 6, 1933; s. Carmon Thomas and Annie (Mann) H.; B.A., Vanderbilt U., 1955; m. Alice Anne Caldwell, Feb. 5, 1966; 1 dau., Emily. Exec. trainee Irving Trust Co., N.Y.C., 1958-61; asst. v.p. franchise Holiday Inns, Inc., Memphis, 1961-66; v.p. Chatmar, Inc., San Francisco, 1967-72; v.p. franchise TraveLodge Internat., Inc., El Cajon, Calif., 1972—, also mem. sr. mgmt. group and coordinating council. Served with AUS, 1955-57. Mem. Am. Hotel and Motel Assn., Calif. Hotel-Motel Assn. (dir.), Internat. Franchise Assn., Sigma Alpha Epsilon. Republican. Episcopalian. Club: Cuyamaca. Home: 5141 Marlborough Dr San Diego CA 92116 Office: 600 B St Suite 2015 San Diego CA 92101

HOOPES, MARGARET HOWARD, educator, psychologist; b. Idaho Falls, Idaho, May 12, 1927; d. James Parley and Elizabeth Joyce (Humphrey) Howard; m. Ned Edward Hoopes, June 20, 1958 (div.). B.S., Ricks Coll., Idaho, 1953. M.S., Brigham Young U., 1962; Ph.D., U. Minn., 1969. Tchr. elem. and jr. high sch., Jerome, Idaho, 1948-52; tchr. jr. high sch., Ephrata, Wash., 1955-58; tchr. New Trier High Sch., Winnetka, Ill., 1958-66; instr. U. Minn., 1966-69, asst. prof., 1969-70; assoc. prof. Brigham Young U., Provo, Utah, 1973-81, prof., 1981—. Mem. Am. Assn. Marriage and Family Therapists, Am. Psychol. Assn., Nat. Council Family Relations. Republican. Mormon. Author: (with others) Readings in Ethical and Professional Issues for Marital and Family Therapists, 1980; Family Facilitation: Education, Enrichment and Treatment, 1983. Contbr. articles to profl. jours. Home: 3532 N Piute Dr Provo UT 84604 Office: 257 TLRB Brigham Young Univ Provo UT 84602

HOOTMAN, MARCIA JOAN, author, public speaker, bus. cons.; b. Chgo., May 16, 1939; d. Edward M. and Julie (Chaput) Pearl; 1 son, Marc. B.A. (Univ. scholar), Calif. Western U., 1967; M.A. cum laude, U.S. Internat. U., 1971; Ph.D., Pacific U., 1983. Tchr. Spanish, La Jolla (Calif.) Country Day Sch., 1969-71; real estate mgr. and saleswoman, trainer Realty World, San Diego, 1970-77; corp. pres., broker Hootman-Elliott Resources, Inc., San Diego, 1977-81; corp. v.p. Trans-Pacific Realty, Scottsdale, Ariz., 1980; pub. speaker, 1980—; co-dir. New Wave Cons., La Jolla, 1981—; author: Making The Break, 1982, How To Forgive Your Ex-Husband, 1982; guest speaker real estate broker's courses U. So. Calif. Sch. Continuing Edn.; composer, pianist, including vol. fund-raising performances for non-profit groups, 1978—. Vol. fundraising Kidney Found., La Jolla, Calif. Mem. Nat. Assn. Realtors, Nat. Assn. Female Execs., GROW-Women's Networking Groups, Career Women's Network, AAUW, Publicists So. Calif. Clubs: Soroptomists, Winners' Circle (chairperson chpt. 1979).

HOOTON, JACQUE WOOLVERTON, educational adminstrator; b. Formosa, Ark., May 19, 1927; d. Freeland E. and Artie F. W.; m. Herbert Hillman, June 7, 1947; children—William Dwight, Linda Jean. B.A., U.N.Mex., 1960, M.A., 1965, Edn. Specialist in Adminstrn., 1975. Tchr., Albuquerque Pub. Schs., 1960-66, counselor, 1966-72, coordinator guidance and counseling, 1972-74, ednl. diagnostician, 1974-77, spl. edn. coordinator, coordinator edn. diagnostician, 1977-81, prin. Alamosa Elementary Sch., 1981—. Mem. Assn. Supervision and Curriculum Devel., N.Mex. Div. Ednl. Diagnosticians. Democrat. Baptist. Home: 2401 Norment Rd SW Albuquerque NM 87105 Office: 6500 Sunset Gardens Rd SW Albuquerque NM 87105

HOOVER, DANIEL WAYNE, advertising executive; b. Van Nuys, Calif., Apr. 10, 1947; s. Perry Franklin and Vera Wanda (Johnson) H.; m. Joan Carol Motta, May 29, 1971; 1 son, Timothy Daniel. B.A., San Fernando Valley (Calif.) State Coll.-Northridge, 1969. Prodn. mailer Los Angeles Times, 1965-70; self-employed profl. entertainer Pacific states, 1968-70; regional sales mgr. N.Am. Services Inc., Orange County, Calif., 1970-71; dir., pres. Innovative Med. Systems Inc., Fullerton, Calif., 1971-72; exec. v.p. Hoover & Assocs./Hoover Communications Group Inc., Fullerton and Phoenix, 1972-74; chmn., pres. Estey-Hoover Inc., Newport Beach, Calif., 1975—; ptnr. Hoover & McKay Enterprises, 1979-80; guest lectr. colls. and civic orgns. Founding pres. Sun Valley (Calif.) Jr. Coordinating Council, 1964-65; bd. dirs. Orange County Family Service Assn., 1976-77, Orange County Arts Alliance, Hoag Hosp. 552 Club, Greentree Homeowners Assn., 1980-84; mem. communications com. Orange County United Way, 1979-81; Named Am. Legion Young Man of Yr., Sun Valley, 1965. Mem. Am. Assn. Advt. Agys. (nat. client services com.), Western States Advt. Agys. Assn., Am. Advt. Fedn., Orange County Advt. Fedn., Orange County Profl. Assn., Bus. Forum, Pi Kappa Alpha (pres.). Republican. Club: Newport Balboa Rotary. Feature columnist various bus. pubns.

HOOVER, EVANGELINA (CONKIE), tribal council executive; b. Yuma, Ariz., Mar. 23, 1944; d. Vincent L. and Margaret G. (Leivas) Chavez; m. Robert Dell Hoover, July 17, 1964; children—Dale Cecil, Jamie Ellen. Student Ariz. Western Coll., 1974-80. Acct. Colo. River Indian Tribes, Parker, Ariz., 1975-78; sec./treas. Chemehuevi Indian Tribe, Chemehuevi Valley, Calif., 1979—; bd. mem. Colorado River service unit Intertribal Health Bd. Commr. All Mission Indian Housing Authority, sec., 1983—; del. Calif. Indian Manpower Consortium, 1980-82; chmn. Havasu Landing (Calif.) Adv. Bd., 1981-83. Recipient service award Town of Parker-Colo. River Indian Tribes Colorado River Joint Sewage Venture, 1981. Republican. Clubs: Soroptimist. Does (Parker). Home: PO Box 1774 Valley Mesa Chemehuevi Valley CA 92363 Office: PO Box 1976 Chemehuevi Valley CA 92363

HOOVER, WILLIAM RAY, computer service company executive; b. Bingham, Utah, Jan. 2, 1930; s. Edwin Daniel and Myrtle Tennessee (McConnell) H.; B.S., M.S. U. Utah; m. Sara Elaine Anderson; children—Scott, Robert, Michael, James, Charles. Sect. chief Jet Propulsion Lab., Pasadena, Calif., 1954-64; v.p. Computer Scis. Corp., El Segundo, Calif., 1964-69, pres., 1969—, chmn. bd., 1972—. Office: 650 N Sepulveda Blvd El Segundo CA 90245

HOPCUS, EUGENE PAUL, mfg. co. exec.; b. Harrah, Okla., July 22, 1941; s. Albert Paul and Carolyn Evelyn Hopcus; B.S. in Bus. Adminstrn., Central State Coll., 1964; grad. Famous Artists Sch., Bridgeport, Conn., 1974; m. Sharron Alameda, June 16, 1962; children—Melody Ann, Shanna Michele. Draftsman, designer Black, Sivalls & Bryson, Oklahoma City, 1966-69; draftsman Star Mfg., Oklahoma City, 1969-70, sr. draftsman, 1970-73, estimator, 1973-76; sr. draftsman The Boardman Co., Oklahoma City, 1976-77, chief draftsman, 1977-78, designer, 1978-79; chief estimator Bldg. div. Soule Steel Co., 1979, supr. order entry engring., 1980, supr. drafting, 1980-81, dir. product devel., 1981-82, mgr. contract services, 1982—; freelance graphic designer. Chief advisor Jr. Achievement, Oklahoma City, 1972-75; adult sponsor Vocat. and Indsl. Clubs Am., Choctaw, Okla., 1972-78; pres. PTA, Midwest City, Okla., 1976-77, v.p., 1978. Mem. Am. Soc. Profl. Draftsmen and Artists, Internat. Soc. Artists, Am. Inst. Drafting and Design, Graphic Artists Guild, Assn. Archtl. Artists. Democrat. Roman Catholic. Clubs: Moose, Woodmen of the World, Craftsmen Lodge. Office: 2160 E Domingez St Carson CA 90749

HOPE, RONNIE CORBETT, radio sta. exec.; b. Boston, 1930; d. John M. and Phyllis B. Corbett; student N.Y. U., 1951-53, small bus. mgmt. program U. Hawaii, 1979-81; children—Clinton, Jamie, Edgar, Andrew. Adminstrv. asst. to pres. Kenyon & Eckhart, 1953-54, Dancer, Fitzgerald & Sample, 1954-55; office mgr. Campbell Mithun, Chgo., 1955-56; copywriter, account exec. Lester Harrison, N.Y.C.; copywriter Sta.-KORL, Honolulu, 1976-77; account exec. Sta.-KCCN, Honolulu, 1977, sales mgr., 1978, gen. mgr., 1978—; guest lectr. U. Hawaii; adult edn. instr. Dept. Edn., 1975—, mem. adv. bd. dept. spl. edn., 1979-80. Bd. dirs. Cystic Fibrosis Found., Honolulu, 1979-80; mem. adv. bd. Humane Soc., Honolulu, 1979-80. Mem. Am. Mktg. Assn., Hawaii Assn. Broadcasters (treas. 1981-83, bd. dirs. 1981-83), Hawaii Music Found., Bishop Mus., Honolulu Acad. Arts, Hawaii Acad. Rec. Arts (chmn. bd. dirs. 1981-82), World Fedn. Press Women (pres. Hawaii chpt.), Honolulu Exec. Assn., Nat. Fedn. Press Women (pres. Hawaii chpt.), Hawaii Acad. Rec. Arts (pres. 1981-82), Hawaii Songwriters Soc. (hon.). Club: Press. Office: KCCN 900 Fort St Mall Honolulu HI 96813

HOPKINS, ANNADAWN EDWARDS, coll. pres.; b. Monroe, La., May 24, 1930; d. Robert Crawford and Annadawn (Watson) Edwards; A.B., Tift Coll., 1949; M.B.A., Loyola U., New Orleans, 1968; Ed.D., Seattle U., 1981; postgrad. New Orleans Baptist Theol. Sem., 1949-51, Va. Poly. Inst. and State U., 1969-70; m. James Wesley Hopkins, June 2, 1951 (div. Dec. 1978); children—Dawn Hopkins Warner, Lyn Hopkins Shearon. Adminstrv. sec. to pres. Reed Unit-Fans Inc., New Orleans, 1955-56; instr. sec. scis. Greenleaf Coll., Atlanta, 1958-61, asst. dir., 1959-61; adminstrv. asst. to regional mgr. petroleum supply and transp. div. Humble Oil & Refining Co., New Orleans, 1961-63; adminstrv. asst. to dean Coll. Bus. Adminstrn., Loyola U., New Orleans, 1963-66, dir. adminstrv. practices degree program, asst. prof. bus. adminstrn., 1966-68; asst. prof. bus. Radford (Va.) Coll., 1968-71; instr. Shoreline Community Coll., Seattle, 1972-74, prof. mgmt. and bus. law, 1974—, chmn. bus. adminstrn. div., 1974-83; dir. Archival Mgmt. Cons., Inc., Seattle, 1979—; pres. Everett (Wash.) Bus. Coll., 1980—. Named Sec. of Year, Nat. Secs. Assn., 1963. Mem. Am. Mgmt. Assn., Pacific N.W. Bus. Law Assn. (pres.), Am. Bus. Law Assn., Am. Vocat. Assn., Nat. Bus. Edn. Assn., DAR, Beta Gamma Sigma, Kappa Delta Pi, Phi Chi Theta, Alpha Gamma Beta, Matrix Table. Home: 3847 NE 155th Pl Seattle WA 98155 Office: 16101 Greenwood Ave N Seattle WA 98133

HOPKINS, CECILIA ANN (MRS. HENRY E. HOPKINS), educator; b. Havre, Mont., Feb. 17, 1922; d. Kost L. and Mary (Manaras) Sofos; B.S., Mont. State Coll., 1944; M.A., San Francisco State Coll., 1958, M.A., 1967; postgrad. Stanford U.; Ph.D., Calif. State U., 1977; m. Henry E. Hopkins, Sept. 7, 1944. Bus. tchr. Havre (Mont.) High Sch., Mateo, Calif., 1942-44; sec. George P. Gorham, Realtor, San Mateo, 1944-45; escrow sec. Fox & Cars 1945-50; escrow officer Calif. Pacific Title Ins. Co., 1950-57; bus. tchr. Westmoor High Sch., Daly City, Calif., 1958-59; bus. tchr. Coll. San Mateo, 1959—, chmn. real estate-ins. dept., 1963-76, dir. div. bus., 1976—; cons. to commr. Calif. Div. Real Estate, 1963—, mem. periodic rev. exam. com.; chmn. Community Coll. Adv. Com., 1971-72, mem. com., 1975—; projector direction Calif. State Chancellor's Career Awareness Consortium, mem. endowment fund adv. com., community coll. real estate edn. com., state community coll. adv. com.; mem. No. Calif. Adv. Bd. to Glendale Fed. Savs. and Loan Assn. Recipient Citizen of Day award KABL, Outstanding Contbns. award Redwood City-San Carlos-Belmont Bd. Realtors; named Woman of Achievement, San Mateo-Burlingame br. Soroptimist Internat., 1979. Mem. AAUW, Calif. Assn. Real Estate Tchrs. (state pres. 1964-65, hon. dir. 1962—, outstanding real estate educator of yr. 1978-79), Real Estate Cert. Inst. (Disting. Merit award 1982), Calif. Bus. Edn. Assn. (certificate of commendation 1979), San Francisco State Coll., Guidance and Counseling Alumni, Theta Alpha Delta, Pi Lambda Theta, Delta Pi Epsilon (nat. dir. interchpt. relations 1962-65, nat. historian 1966-67, nat. sec. 1968-69), Alpha Gamma Delta. Co-author: California Real Estate Principles; contbr. articles to profl. jours. Home: 504 Colgate Way San Mateo CA 94402

HOPKINS, FRANKLIN LEE, SR., advertising executive; b. Cin., Sept. 13, 1940; s. Oscar Vern and Mary Winifred (Hirons) H.; m. Grace A.

Jay, Jan. 17, 1960 (div. 1971); children—Franklin Lee, Gary Jay, Jody Lyn, Kelly Todd; m. 2d, Margaret Edith Schlarman, July 17, 1977; children—Darin Mark, Jeffrey Adam, Lisa Margaret Horgan. Student, Cin. U. Applied Arts, 1965-67, Cin. Art Acad., 1962-64. With USPHS, 1961-64, art dir. Gable Advt., Cin. and Columbus, Ind., 1964-66; art dir., percentage owner Avery Studio Art, Columbus, 1966; art dir., account exec. Bauer Kemble, Spicer Advt., Cin., 1966-69; designer, creative dir. Campbell, Turner & Assocs., Inc. Cin., 1969-73; v.p., creative dir. William E. Wilson Advt., Palos Verdes, Calif. and Los Angeles, 1973-75; designer, owner Franklin L. Hopkins and Assocs., Redondo Beach, Calif., 1975-78; owner, pres. Hopkins & Assocs., Inc., Fountain Valley, Calif., 1978—. Served with USN, 1958-61. Recipient award of merit Chgo. Art Dirs., 1965; 1st Place awards Cin. Art Dirs., 1968, Los Angeles Indsl. Advt. Club, 1973. Mem. Orange County Advt. Fedn., Fountain Valley C. of C. (1st v.p.). Republican. Clubs: Omni, Kiwanis, Masons.

HOPKINS, HENRY TYLER, museum ofcl.; b. Idaho Falls, Idaho, Aug. 14, 1928; s. Talcott Thompson and Zoe O. (Erbe) H.; student Coll. Idaho, 1946-49; B.A., Art Inst. Chgo., 1952, M.A., 1955; postgrad. U. Calif. at Los Angeles, 1958-61; m. JoAnne Bybee, Sept. 1, 1954 (div. Oct. 1969); children—Victoria Anne, John Thomas, Christopher Tyler; m. 2d, Jan Butterfield, July 1, 1972. Asst. curator Los Angeles County Mus. Art, 1961, head edn., 1963-66, curator exhbns. and pubs., 1967-68; dir. Fort Worth Art Center Mus., 1968-73; dir. San Francisco Mus. Art, 1974—. Instr. art history Tex. Christian U., Fort Worth, 1968-73; cons. art program Northwood Inst., Dallas, 1969-73; mem. vis. com. fine arts U. Okla., 1971—, Tex. Christian U., 1971-73; dir. U.S. representation 35th Venice (Italy) Bienalle, 1970; dir. art presentation Festival of Two Worlds, Spoleto, Italy, 1970; dir. São Paulo (Brazil) Biennial, 1981. Served with AUS, 1952-54. Decorated knight Order of Leopold, 1981. Mem. Am. Assn. Art Mus. Dirs., Coll. Art Assn., Internat. Animated Film Soc. Contbr. articles to profl. pubs. Home: 735 21st Ave San Francisco CA 94121 Office: San Francisco Mus Art VanNess Ave at McAllister St San Francisco CA 94102

HOPKINS, JAMES RAY, financial executive; b. Long Beach, Calif., Feb. 25, 1936; s. George Howard and Margaret Rae (Shearer) H. B.A., Stanford U., 1957, M.B.A., 1959; C.P.A., Calif., 1962. Auditor, Arthur Young & Co., Los Angeles, 1959-64; treas. Chem-Therm Mfg. Co., Monrovia, Calif., 1964-66; sr. v.p. finance Audiotronics Corp., North Hollywood, Calif., 1966—; dir. Audiotronics Internat., Inc., North Holywood, 1971—. Served with USAR, 1959-65. Office: 7428 Bellaire St North Hollywood CA 91605

HOPKINS, JEAN HUMMER, nurse; b. Cheyenne, Wyoming, Oct. 21, 1942; d. Robert O. and Elizabeth (Bixler) Hummer; m. Raymond William Hopkins, Mar. 29, 1975. Student U. Wyo., 1961-63, Holy Cross Hosp. Sch. of Nursing, 1963-66; B.S.N. (cum laude), Westminster Coll., 1982. Charge nurse Holy Cross Hosp., Salt Lake City, 1966-67, staff nurse intensive care unit, 1967-68, charge nurse intensive care unit, 1968-69, clin. nursing instr. operating room, 1969-72; office nurse Dr. R.O. Hummer, M.D., 1972-74; operating room staff nurse Holy Cross Hosp., 1973-76, asst. operating room supr., 1976-79, staff nurse, 1979—; operating room, obstetrics supr. Holy Cross Jordan Valley Hosp., 1983—; instr. Med. Self Help for Senior Citizens, Salt Lake City, 1976-77; CPR instr., 1982—. Mem. Nat. Assn. Operating Room Nurses (legis. com.), Assn. Operating Room Nurses (cert., chpt. pres.), Nat. League Nursing, Am. Nurses Assn. Contbr. articles to profl. jours. Office: 1045 E 1st So Operating Room Salt Lake City UT 84084

HOPKINS, PATRICIA MARGARET, marketing educator; b. Ilford, Essex, Eng., June 6, 1939; d. Edward George and Freda Miriam (Farrant) Berg; m. McMillen Hopkins, Mar. 5, 1960 (div.); children—Craig Edward, Keith Bryan. B.A., Calif. State U.-Fullerton, 1971, M.B.A., 1972; Ph.D., Claremont Grad. Sch., 1977. Sec. Getty Oil, Los Angeles, 1958-63; statistician Rockwell Internat., Anaheim, Calif., 1965-69; assoc. prof. Calif. State Polytech. U., Pomona, 1975—. Named Calif. State U.-Fullerton Outstanding Student of Yr., 1971. Mem. NOW, Am. Mktg. Assn., Am. Mgmt. Assn., Acad. Mktg. Sci., Beta Gamma Sigma, Phi Kappa Phi, Phi Sigma Epsilon. Democrat.

HOPKINS, PAUL MORTIMER, mining geologist, engr.; b. Edgerton, Mo., Mar. 6, 1918; s. Walter Ashe and Vera Virginia (Denniston) H.; grad. petroleum engr., Colo. Sch. Mines, 1939, geol. engr., 1951; post grad. U. Colo., 1951-52; m. Joyce Lorraine Mundy, Nov. 16, 1946 (div. Oct. 1947); m. 2d, Marian Francis Hawk, Jan. 1, 1954 (div. Nov. 1960); m. 3d, Mary Evelyn Shurtleff Newell, Feb. 20, 1965 (div. Feb. 1977). Employee of Socony Vacuum Oil Co., East St. Louis, Ill., 1939-41; civil engr. U.S. Air Force, Lowry Field, Denver, 1948-49; geologist Leadville Lead Corp., Park County, Colo., 1952-53; geologist engr. Silver Bell Mines, Ophir, Colo., 1952-53; jr. engr. Kennecott Copper Co., Ruth, Nev., 1953-55; cons. engr., mining geologist and engr. Colo., Utah, Nev., Wyo., S.D., N.Mex., Ariz., Idaho, Mont., Can., Alaska, Central and South Am., Africa. Served to capt. AUS, 1941-47. Registered profl. engr., Colo., B.C.; registered geologist, Calif. Mem. Colo. Mining Assn. (dir.), Am. Inst. Mining, Metall. and Petroleum Engrs., Nat. Soc. Profl. Engrs., Canadian Inst. Mining and Metallurgy. Democrat. Mem. Christian Ch. Mason (Shriner). Home and office: 2222 Arapahoe St PO Box 403 Golden CO 80401

HOPKINS, PHILIP JOSEPH, journalist, editor; b. Orange, Calif., Dec. 10, 1954; s. Philip Joseph and Marie Elizabeth (Calnan) H.; m. Barbara Humbird Peters, May 23, 1981. B.A. in Journalism, San Diego State U., 1977. Cert. tissue therapist Center for Decubitis Ulcer Research, 1981. Reporter, La Jolla Light & Journal (Calif.), 1973; editorial cons. San Diego Union, 1974; asst. producer Southwestern Cable TV, San Diego, 1974; corr. Mission Cable TV, San Diego, 1975; photojournalist United Press Internat., San Diego, 1976; editor The Aztec Engr. mag., San Diego, 1977; editor Rx Home Care mag., Los Angeles, 1981, Hosp. Info. Mgmt. mag., 1981; editor, assoc. pub. Arcade mag., 1982; v.p. Humbird Hopkins Inc., Los Angeles, 1983—; dir. Shield Legal Action Com., Ltd., Washington; cons. Am. Gamemakers Assn., Los Angeles. Campaign cons. Republican Congl. and Assembly candidates, 1979-80. Recipient 1st and 4th place awards Nikon, Inc., Photo Contest, 1974; 3rd prize Minolta Camera Co. Creative Photography awards, 1975; Best Feature Photo award Sigma Delta Chi Mark of Excellence contest, 1977; Advt. of Month award Communicator mag., 1980. Mem. Am. Soc. Mag. Photographers, Am. Soc. Picture Profls., Am. Soc. Mag. Editors, Am. Med. Writers Assn., Comml. and Indsl. Properties Assn. (founder), Sigma Delta Chi. Club: Santa Monica Athletic. Author: The Students' Survival Guide, 1977, 78; photographs have appeared in Time and Omni mags., The Mythology of Middle Earth, Beginners Guide to the SLR, NBC-TV's Saturday Night Live. Office: PO Box 49813 Barrington Station Los Angeles CA 90049

HOPKINS, RUTH STEINER, educator; b. Council, Alaska, Oct. 31, 1918; d. Calvin Otto and Mattie (Caldwell) Steiner; student U. Calif., 1937-38, 41-42, U. Colo., 1939, 47-48; B.A., Stanford U., 1949; 1 dau., Susan Ruth. Tchr. Public Schs. Los Altos (Calif.), 1957-59, 62-68, Morocco and Ger., 1960-62, Los Angeles, 1970, Washington, 1973-74; sec., research analyst Stanford (Calif.) Linear Accelerator Center, 1964-68; research analyst High Energy Physics Lab., Stanford U., 1968-69; legal sec., Washington and San Francisco, 1974-77; math. tchr. Oakland (Calif.) Sch. Dist., 1978-80, Dos Palos (Calif.) Joint Union High Sch., 1980-81; instr. math. Merced (Calif.) Coll., 1981; physics/chemistry tchr. DODDS, Turkey, 1981-82, Philippines, 1982—. Mem. NEA, AAAS, Sierra Club. Democrat. Office: Dewey High School FPO San Francisco CA 96651

HOPKINS, STEPHEN WILLIAM, laboratory director, engineering consultant; b. Brockton, Mass., July 23, 1943; s. Royal Carlton and Bertha Irene (Crowell) H.; m. Sandra Grippen, June 23, 1963; children—Stephen R., Susan M., Scott C., Spencer. A.S. in Mech. Engring., Wentworth Inst., 1963; B.S.M.E., U. New Haven, 1971; M.S. in Applied Mechanics, Rensselaer Poly. Inst., 1974; registered profl. engr., Calif. Exptl. research asst. Pratt & Whitney Aircraft Co., North Haven, Conn., 1963-69, sr. materials engr., Middletown, Conn., 1969-76; mng. engr., dir. exptl. and materials lab. Failure Analysis Assocs., Palo Alto, Calif., 1976—; lectr. in field. Mem. Am. Acad. Mechanics, ASME, Soc. Exptl. Stress Analysis (chmn. No. Calif. sect. 1978-79), ASTM, Alpha Sigma Lambda. Contbr. articles to profl. jours. Office: 2225 E Bayshore Rd Palo Alto CA 94303

HOPKINS, WILLARD GEORGE, hospital administrator; b. Balt., Mar. 30, 1940; s. George Conrad and Laura Elizabeth (Elwell) H.; m. Valerie Jewell Hopkins, June 22, 1963; children—Michelle Marie, Tiffany Lynn. B.S. in Civil Engring., U. Md., 1963; M.H.A., Cornell U., 1969, M.B.A., 1969. Cons., Arthur Young & Co., San Francisco, 1969-74, health cons. practice dir., 1974-76, dir. health care cons. practice dir., Washington, 1976-78; health cons. practice dir. Booz Allen & Hamilton, Washington, 1977-79; exec. v.p. Scottsdale (Ariz.) Meml. Hosp., Scottsdale Meml. Health Service Co., 1979—. Served with USPHS, 1963-69. Fellow Am. Coll. Hosp. Adminstrs., Soc. Advanced Med. Systems; mem. N. Am. Soc. Corp. Planning, Am. Health Planning Assn., NAM (mem. employee benefits and compensation policy com., subcom. on nat. health care 1978-79), Assn. Univ. Programs in Health Adminstrn. (mem. com. on minority group affairs 1977-79), Comprehensive Health Planning Assn. Contra Costa County (bd. dirs. 1973-77). Presbyterian. Club: Rotary (Paradise Valley). Mem. editorial adv. bd. Am. Jour. Health Planning, 1976-79. Home: 4711 E Arroyo Verde Dr Paradise Valley AZ 85253 Office: 7400 E Osborn Rd Scottsdale AZ 85251

HOPKINSON, HAROLD ISADORE, artist; b. Salt Lake City, Aug. 8, 1918; s. Ernest I. and Susan Rosella (Smethurst) H.; B.A., U. Wyo., 1949, M.A., 1952; postgrad. Brigham Young U., 1962, U. Utah, 1960, Art Ctr. Sch. Design, Los Angeles, 1960; m. Vivian Hamblin, Nov. 8, 1939; children—Judith DeVine, H. Richard, Glen S., Cynthia Welch. One-man shows include: Voris Gallery, Salt Lake City, 1980, 81, 82, 83, Thunderhorse Gallery, Cody, Wyo., 1981, 82, 83; group show: C.M. Russell Ann., Great Falls, Mont.; represented in pvt. collections; art dir., Rock Springs, Wyo., 1949-52; supt. schs. Byron (Wyo.), 1952-62. Pres., Byron Sch. Bd., 1963-66; pres. Lovell (Wyo.) state Ch. Jesus Christ of Latter-day Saints, 1973-8, bishop Byron Ward, 1970-73. Served with USN, 1943-46; PTO. Recipient Gold Medal award Western Artists Am. Show, Reno, 1980, 82; Gold Medal award and Best of Show, The Arts in St. George (Utah), 1980, 83; others. Mem. Western Artists Am. Address: Box 175 Byron WY 82412

HOPPE, STEVEN PAUL, chemist, environmental consultant; b. Rolla, Mo., May 22, 1952; s. Harry M. and Alice (Fleming) H.; m. Sonja Johnson, June 1982. B.S., No. Ariz. U., 1976, M.S., 1982. Research technician, chemist No. Ariz. U., Flagstaff, 1976-80, instr., 1980; lab. dir. Smith & Smith Environ. Cons., Flagstaff, 1979-81; research chemist Ralph M. Bilby Research Ctr., No. Ariz. U., 1981-82; chemist Western Technologies, Inc., Phoenix, 1982—. Mem. Soc. Applied Spectroscopy Am. Chem. Soc., Am. Water Works Assn., ASTM, Water Pollution Control Assn., Am. Soc. Microbiology, Soc. Indsl. Microbiology. Office: 3737 E Broadway Rd Phoenix AZ 85040

HOPPE, WILLIAM EDWARD, realtor; b. Milw., Mar. 30, 1928; s. Edward Clarence and Claire Emily (Ruthe) H.; student U. Wis., 1945-46; m. Audrey L. Stephen, Oct. 22, 1949; children—Craig Allen, Douglas Dean. Owner, operator H&R Foods, Racine, Wis., 1951-55; partner Ed Hoppe Realty, Las Vegas, Nev., 1958-63, v.p., 1963-71; pres. Hoppe Realty, Inc., Las Vegas, 1971—. Committeeman citizen's adv. council Las Vegas Gen. Plan Program, 1973-74; bd. dirs. Center Bus. and Econ. Research U. Nev. Served with USMCR, 1946-48. Recipient Outstanding Service award Multiple Listing Service, 1970; named Realtor of Yr., Las Vegas, 1976. Mem. Nat. (publicity chmn. conv. com. 1972-74, legis. com. 1976-77, polit. action com. 1979, home protection com. 1980—, dir. 1980—, chmn. program devel. subcom., polit. affairs com. 1982), Nev. (dir. 1972, 75, treas. 1978, pres.-elect 1979 pres. 1980) assns. realtors, Las Vegas Bd. Realtors (1st v.p. 1974, pres. 1975—). Editor: Nev. Realtor, 1972, 74. Home: 716 Starks Dr Las Vegas NV 89107 Office: 708 S 6th St Las Vegas NV 89101

HOPPER, ROBERT E., JR., cons. engring. corp. exec.; b. Houston, Aug. 26, 1946; s. Robert E. and Ollie Mae H.; B.S. in Mech. Engring., U. N.Mex., 1969; m. Patricia Ann Knight, July 16, 1971; children—Kristen Diane, Ryan James. Vice pres. Bridgers & Paxton, Cons. Engrs., Inc., Albuquerque, 1971—; instr. U. N.Mex. Sch. Architecture, 1978, 82; speaker, lectr. various classes and seminars. Served as lt. j.g. USN, 1969-71. Registered profl. engr., N.Mex., Calif., N.Y. Mem. Nat. Soc. Profl. Engrs., ASHRAE (chmn. energy com. to evaluate computer energy analysis programs, 1978), Automated Procedures for Engring. Consultants (trustee 1975-80, nat. pres., 1979). Mem. U.N.Mex. Engring. Alumni Assn. (sec.), Sigma Chi. Democrat. Presbyterian. Clubs: Four Hills Country, Albuquerque Civitan. Contbr. papers in field to profl. publs. and confs. Office: 213 Truman NE Albuquerque NM 87108

HOPPONEN, JERRY D., engr.; b. Fargo, N.D., Mar. 26, 1946; B.S., N.D. State U., 1966; M.S. in Math., U. Ariz., 1968; Ph.D. in Math., U. Colo., 1979. Mathematician applied electromagnetic sci. div. Inst. for Telecommunication Scis., U.S. Dept. Commerce, Boulder, Colo., 1972-77; instr. math. U. Colo., Boulder, 1971-76; staff engr. electronic systems engring., space systems div. Lockheed Missiles and Space Co., Sunnyvale, Calif., 1977—. Office: Lockheed PO Box 504 Sunnyvale CA 94086

HORAN, JOSEPH PATRICK, interior designer; b. Waterloo, Iowa, Feb. 9, 1942; s. Raymond John and Anna Louise (Byrnes) H. B.S. in Applied Art, Iowa State U., Ames, 1964. Staff interior design studio L.S. Ayres & Co., Indpls., 1964-70, W. & J. Sloane, Inc., San Francisco, 1970-82; freelance interior designer San Francisco, 1982—. Served with USAR, 1965-71; Recipient 1st prize and honorable mention awards Am. Soc. Interior Designers Competitions, 1980. Mem. Am. Soc. Interior Designers (profl.; dir. Calif. North chpt. 1983—). Contbr. articles to newspapers and mags. Address: 3299 Washington St San Francisco CA 94115

HORD, JESSE, chemical engineer, government official, researcher; b. Maysville, Ky., Oct. 11, 1934; s. William Wilson and Emma Dee (Huber) H.; m. Martha Ann Oakes, Aug. 31, 1956; children—Cheryl Ann, Karen Lynne, Kevin Taylor. B.S. in Civil Engring., U. Ky., 1956; M.S. in Civil Engring., U. Colo., 1963. Test engr. Rocketdyne div. N.Am. Aviation Co., Canoga Park, Calif., 1956-61; mech. engr. Nat. Bur. Standards, Boulder, Colo., 1961-79, chief thermophys. properties div., 1979-81, dir. Center for Chem. Engring., 1981—; guest lectr. cryogenic engring. UCLA, 1977—, U. Calif.-Berkeley, 1981; mem. engring. devel. council U. Colo., 1974-83. Recipient Russell B. Scott Meml. award for outstanding paper U.S. Cryogenic Engring. Conf., 1975; tech. brief innovation award NASA, 1973, 76; silver medal U.S. Dept. Commerce, 1981. Mem. AIAA, Internat. Assn. for Hydrogen Energy, AAAS, Am. Inst. Chem. Engrs., N.Y. Acad. Scis., Sigma Xi, Tau Beta Pi. Democrat. Presbyterian. Contbr. articles to profl. jours. and tech. publs. Office: 325 Broadway Boulder CO 80303

HORDESKI, MICHAEL FRANK, computer systems consultant; b. Stamford, Conn., Oct. 16, 1939; s. Michael John and Julia Marion (Jablonski) H.; m. Delores Elaine Buell, Feb. 1, 1969. B.S. in Elec. Engring., U. Bridgeport, 1964; M.S. in Elec. Engring., U. So. Calif., 1968. Registered profl. engr., Calif. Elec. engr. Rocketdyne, Canoga Park, Calif., 1964; research engr. Rockwell Internat., Anaheim, Calif., 1964-66, mem. tech. staff, 1966-74; prin. cons. Siltran Digital, Atascadero, Calif., 1974—; assoc. prof. Calif. Poly. State U., 1979—. Mem. IEEE (Control Instrumentation Group 1976), Instrument Soc. Am. (standards rev. bd. 1976), Am. Soc. Profl. Cons. Author: (with others) Handbook on Process Measurement, 1982; Microcomputer Dictionary, 1979; Microprocessor Cookbook, 1979; patentee in field.

HORI, KIYOAKY, anesthesiologist; b. Idaho Falls, Idaho, Nov. 14, 1926; s. Seitaro and Rin (Shimomura) H.; B.S., U. Idaho, 1952; M.D., U. Oreg., 1956; m. Patricia Palms, Oct. 12, 1982; children by previous marriage—Michael K., Nancy Ada. Intern, St. Vincent's Hosp., Portland, Oreg., 1956-57; resident Sacred Heart Hosp., Spokane, 1957-58; resident anesthesiology Tacoma Gen. Hosp., 1958-60, mem. staff, 1960—; pvt. practice, Tacoma, 1960—; mem. staff Mary Bridye Children's Hosp., Tacoma; vol. staff clin. assoc. U. Wash. Med. Sch. Served with AUS, 1945-48. Diplomate Am. Bd. Anesthesiology. Fellow Am. Coll. Anesthesiologists; mem. Am., Wash. (pres. 1972) socs. anesthesiologists, Am., Wash. med. assns., Pierce County Med. Soc., Japanese-Am. Citizens League, Tacoma Surg. Club, Alpha Epsilon Delta, Phi Beta, Theta Kappa Psi. Clubs: YMCA, Rokka Ski. Home: 4102 N 10th St Tacoma WA 98406 Office: 314 K St Suite 202 Tacoma WA 98405

HORIGAN, JAMES EUGENE, lawyer, author; b. Oklahoma City, Sept. 4, 1924; s. Joseph D. Horigan and Mary (Swirczynski) Horigan McRill; step-son Albert L. McRill; student Okla. U., 1942-44, Northwestern U., 1944; J.D., Okla. U., 1949; postgrad. So. Meth. U., 1958, Colo. U., 1966; m. Joan Murry, Mar. 8, 1945; children—Susan, Daniel James, Nancy Jean Horigan Datz. Bar. Okla. 1949, Tex. 1957, N.Y. 1959, Colo. 1961, Law Soc. Eng. (hon.), 1973. Asst. county atty. Oklahoma County, 1949-51; atty. Mobil Oil Corp. (formerly Magnolia Petroleum Co. and Magnolia Pipe Line Co.), Oklahoma City, 1951-57, Beaumont, Tex., 1957, Dallas, 1958; U.S. and Can. counsel, office gen. counsel, N.Y.C., 1959-61, regional gen. atty. Denver regional office, 1961-63; gen. counsel Hamilton Bros. Oil Co. and affiliates, Denver, 1963-69; ptnr. Foliart, Shepherd, McPherson & Horigan, Oklahoma City, 1963, Horigan Thompson & Miller, Denver, 1965-69, individual practice internat. law, London, 1969-70; ptnr. Horigan & Boss, 1971; sr. resident ptnr. London office law firm Vinson, Elkins, Searls, Connally & Smith, 1971-75; of counsel Burns & Wall, 1978; ptnr. Horigan, Jumonville, Broadhurst, Brook & Miller, 1978, Holland & Hart, 1979-81; individual practice law, 1981—; v.p., gen. counsel Charterhall Am. Inc., 1981—. Trustee Town of Bow Mar (Colo.), 1976-78; mem. U.S. Congl. Adv. Bd., 1982—; mem. adv. bd. Internat. Comparative Law Ctr., Southwestern Legal Found., 1983—. Served to lt. USNR, 1943-46. Mem. ABA, Colo. Bar Assn., Okla. Bar Assn., Denver Bar Assn., Internat. Bar Assn., Am. Soc. Internat. Law, Rocky Mountain Mineral Law Found. (gen. chmn. spl. legal inst. 1975), Internat. Platform Assn., Internat. Trade Assn. Colo. (v.p. 1979-81), Phi Delta Phi, Phi Gamma Delta, Delta Sigma Rho. Roman Catholic. Clubs: American (London); Rotary; Denver Petroleum. Author: Chance or Design?, 1979; The Key to Reconcile Modern Science and Religious Thought, 1983; Petroleum Laws of the North Sea, 1975; contbg. author: The Law of Transnational Business Transactions, 1980; Foreign Participation in Domestic Oil and Gas Ventures, 1982, contbr. articles to legal jours.; charter mem. bd. editors Okla. Law Rev., 1947-49. Home: 5100 Bow Mar Dr Littleton CO 80123 Office: Denver CO

HORLER, VIRGINIA LOUISE, financial consultant to local governments; b. St. Louis, Nov. 21, 1940; d. Kenneth James and Elise Deprez (Weck) Palmer; m. Brian Leslie Horler, Sept. 4, 1965; 1 dau., Jennifer Ann. A.A. with honors, Contra Costa Coll., 1976; B.A. in Mgmt. with honors, St. Mary's Coll. of Calif., 1982, postgrad. in bus. adminstrn. Bus. mgr. Heald Bus. Coll., Oakland, Calif., 1965-67; dep. treas. City of Richmond (Calif.), 1967-81, budget analyst, 1981-83; sr. staff cons. Rauscher Pierce Refsnes, Inc., Pub. Fin.-Calif. Div., San Francisco, 1983—; lectr. on pub. fin. at seminars, workshops; student commencement speaker St. Mary's Coll. of Calif., 1982. Mem. Pinole (Calif.) YMCA Swim Team, 1976—, bd. dirs., 1976—, pres., 1980; mem. Pinole Traffic Flow Com., 1980. Recipient 2d place Fine Arts award Bank of Am., Calif., 1958. Mem. Calif. Mcpl. Treas. Assn. (cert. 1981, bd. dirs. 1979-83), Mcpl. Fin. Officers Assn., Calif. Soc. Mcpl. Fin. Officers, YMCA. Author: Guide to Public Debt Financing in California, 1982. Home: 3270 Colusa St Pinole CA 94564 Office: One California St Suite 2650 San Francisco CA 94111

HORN, CLAIRE HELEN, music educator, administrator; b. Richmond, Hill, N.Y., Aug. 16, 1934; d. Albert E. and Helen (Kriger) Capitanio; m. Denis R. Horn, Sept. 5, 1955; children—Jeffrey D., Erica Jeanne, B.S. in Music Edn., Ithaca Coll., 1956; M.A., Calif. State U., 1982. Tchr. music Saddleback Valley Unified Dist., Mission Viejo, Calif., 1971-76; instrumental music tchr. Mission Viejo High Sch., 1975-80; dist. music coordinator Saddleback Valley Unified Sch. Dist., Mission Viejo, 1980—; prin. oboist Saddleback Symphony Orch.; guest lectr. Calif. State U. Nat. Honor Soc. scholar, 1952; N.Y. Regents scholar, 1952; named Tchr. of the Month, Mission Viejo High Sch., 1978. Mem. Orange County Music Adminstrs. (pres.), So. Calif. Sch. Band and Orch. Assn. (sec.), Music Educators Nat. Conf., Assn. Calif. Sch. Adminstrs., Assn. Supervision and Curriculum Devel., So. Calif. Women Mgrs. in Edn., Orange County Music Educators Assn., Calif. Music Educators Assn., Pi Kappa Lambda. Republican. Lutheran. Contbr. articles to profl. jours. Home: 28212 San Marcos St Mission Viejo CA 92692 Office: 25631 Diseno Dr Mission Viejo CA 92691

HORN, DEBORAH PABLO, public relations official, writer, photographer; b. Honolulu, Aug. 28, 1955; d. Laureto R. and Yvonne K. (Fuller) Pablo; m. Thomas Earl Horn, III, May 15, 1977; 1 dau., Tracy Lyn Kaiulani. B.A. in Journalism and Communications, U. Hawaii, 1978. News dir. Sta. KTUH-FM, Honolulu, 1977-78; writer, photographer Trade Pub. Co., Honolulu, 1979-80; asst. pub. relations dir. Honolulu Bd. of Realtors, 1980; pub. relations dir. Hawaii Assn. of Realtors, Honolulu, 1980-82; pub. relations, recruitment coordinator Big Bros. and Big Sisters of Honolulu, 1982—; cons. in pub. relations; freelance writer, photographer. Mem. Pub. Relations Soc. Am., Internat. Assn. Bus. Communicators. Office: Big Bros-Big Sisters of Honolulu 200 N Vineyard Blvd Suite 301 Honolulu HI 96817

HORN, ELIZABETH CAYE, software company official; b. Hamilton, Ohio, Mar. 29, 1954; d. Ira Levaughn and Vivian Millicent (Moritz) Gould. B.S. cum laude, Miami U., Oxford, Ohio, 1976. Staff writer Gibson Greeting Cards, Cin., 1976-77; internal communications coordinator Cincom Systems, Cin., 1977-79; promotional writer Measurex, Cupertino, Calif., 1980-81; dir. advt. and promotion Boole & Babbage, Sunnyvale, Calif., 1981—. Mem. Women in Film, Internat. Documentary Assn. Club: Decathlon (Sunnyvale). Editorial bd. Capacity Mgmt.

Jour. Home: 1431 Saratoga #223 San Jose CA 95129 Office: Boole & Babbage Inc 510 Oakmead Pkwy Sunnyvale CA 94086

HORN, ERIC LAURENS, homebuilding company executive; b. Huntingdon, Pa., Sept. 23, 1946; s. John Chisolm and Solveig Elizabeth (Wald) H.; B.A., Susquehanna U., 1968; M.B.A., U. So. Calif., 1972; m. Eileen Maria Moninghoff, Aug. 11, 1973; children—Brian Fitzgerald, Dennis Chisolm. Asst. to pres. Watt Industries, Los Angeles, 1972-73, pres. Brookline Co. div., Santa Monica, Calif., 1979-82, Hi Valley Enterprises div., Santa Monica, 1980-82; v.p. Bell Canyon Bldg. Co., Canoga Park, Calif., 1974-76, W & A Builders, Inc., Santa Monica, 1976-79, So. Alleghenies Mgmt. Inc., Huntingdon, Pa., 1982—; pres. Springfield Co., Pacific Palisades, Calif., 1982—. Pres. Palisades Homeowners Assn., 1975-76; mem. Redondo Beach Superstar Classic com., 1977-79. Served to lt., USN, 1968-70. Mem. Bldg. Industry Assn. (air quality adv. panel 1977-78), Sales and Mktg. Council, So. Calif. U. Commerce Asso., Am. Enterprise Inst., Bldg. Industry Assn. Homebuilders Council, Moku Golf Partnership. Republican. Lutheran. Club: Los Angeles Athletic. Office: 1816 Michael Ln Pacific Palisades CA 90272

HORN, JOHN LEONARD, psychology educator; b. St. Joseph, Mo., Sept. 7, 1928; s. John Leonard and Nellie Rae (Weldon) H.; m. Darleen Dimmitt, July 26, 1950 (div.); m. 2d, Bonnie Colleen Hoskins-Horn, July 31, 1955; children—John Leonard, James Bryan, Julia Lynn, Jennifer Lee. B.A., U. Denver, 1956; student U. Melbourne (Australia), 1956-57; M.A., U. Ill., 1961, Ph.D., 1965. Asst. prof. U. Denver, 1961-65, assoc. prof., 1965-69, prof., 1970—; research assoc. U. Wis., 1965; vis. lectr. U. Calif., (Berkeley), 1967; research assoc. London, 1972-73, Univ. Hosp., Lund, Sweden, 1982. Served with U.S. Army, 1950-52. Fulbright fellow, Melbourne, Australia, 1956-57, NIH fellow, 1958-61, U.S. Office Edn. fellow, 1965; recipient NIH Research Career award, 1968-73, Soc. Multivariate Explt. Psychologist Disting. Publs. Award, 1973. Mem. Am. Psychol. Assn., Psychometric Soc., Soc. Multivariate Explt. Psychologists. Club: Elks. Contbr. articles to numerous profl. jours. Home: 196 S Corona Denver CO 80209 Office: U Denver Psychology Dept Denver CO 80210

HORN, (JOHN) STEPHEN, univ. pres.; b. Gilroy, Calif., May 31, 1931; s. John Stephen and Isabelle (McCaffrey) H.; A.B. with great distinction, Stanford U., 1953, Ph.D., 1958; M.P.A. (Adminstrn. fellow), Harvard U., 1955; m. Nini Moore, Sept. 4, 1954; children—Marcia Horn Yavitz, Stephen. Adminstrv. asst. to U.S. Sec. Labor James P. Mitchell, 1959-60; legis. asst. to U.S. Senator Thomas H. Kuchel, 1960-66; sr. fellow Brookings Inst., 1966-69; dean grad. studies and research Am. U., 1969-70; vice chmn. U.S. Commn. on Civil Rights, 1969-80, commr., 1980-82; pres. Calif. State U., Long Beach, 1970—; fellow Inst. Politics, Harvard U., 1966-67. Bd. dirs. Nat. Inst. Corrections, Inst. Internat. Edn.; vice-chmn. Long Beach Promotion Com. mem. Calif. Republican League. Congl. fellow Am. Polit. Sci. Assn., 1958-59. Mem. Stanford Alumni Assn. (pres. 1976-77), Stanford Assos., Calif. Scholarship Fedn. (pres. chpt.), Phi Beta Kappa, Pi Sigma Alpha. Author: The Cabinet and Congress, 1960; Unused Power: The Work of the Senate Committee on Appropriations, 1970; (with Edmund Beard) Congressional Ethics: The View from the House, 1975. Office: 1250 Bellflower Blvd Long Beach CA 90840

HORN, NICHOLAS JOHNSON, state senator, businessman, educator; b. Salt Lake City, July 25, 1945; s. Harold Truman and Madge (Rollins) H.; m. Nancy Lynn Ellis, 1971; children—Stacy Lynn. A.A., Ricks Coll., 1968; B.A., Brigham Young U., 1970, M.P.A., 1971. Chmn. dept. bus. adminstrn. Clark County Community Coll., Las Vegas, 1973—; prof., lectr. bus. mgmt. Golden Gate U., Nellis AFB, 1974—; ptnr. Horn & Pool Bus. Cons., Las Vegas, 1974—; mem. Nev. State Assembly, from 1976, now mem. Nev. State Senate. Recipient Outstanding Freshman Assemblyman award, 1977. Mem. Vol. Action Ctr. (dir.), Girls Club So. Nev. (dir.), Clark County Easter Seals (profl. adv. bd. 1975), Western Assn. Coop. Work Experience Educators (conf. chmn.), Am. Soc. Personnel Adminstrs., Pi Sigma Alpha. Democrat. Mormon. Home: 2543 Boise St Las Vegas NV 89121 Office: Nevada State Senate Carson City NV 89710

HORN, ROBERT GENE, ednl. adminstr.; b. Dallas, Sept. 24, 1940; s. Oscar Henry and Agnes Henrietta (Symank) H.; B.A., Concordia Tchrs. Coll., 1962; M.A., U. Calif., Santa Barbara, 1966; Ph.D., Purdue U., 1978; m. Sandra Kirch, June 3, 1962; children—Christopher B., Elizabeth S. Tchr., St. John's Luth. Sch., Oxnard, Calif., 1962-68, Am. Sch., Tokyo, 1968-72; asst. to v.p. for pub. and alumni affairs Valparaiso (Ind.) U., 1972-74; dir. devel. Am. Sch. in Japan, Tokyo, 1974-78; dir. devel. and public affairs Am. Grad. Sch. Internat. Mgmt., Glendale, Ariz., 1979-81, v.p. external affairs, 1981—. Mem. Nat. Soc. Fund Raisers, Council for Support and Advancement of Edn. Republican. Lutheran. Address: Am Grad Sch Internat Mgmt Glendale AZ 85306

HORNAK, THOMAS, electronics executive; b. Bratislava, Czechoslovakia, Oct. 14, 1924; s. Stefan and Elisabeth (Meer) H.; m. Vera Lautner, Mar. 15, 1958; 1 son, Thomas. M.S.E.E., Tech. U. Bratislava, 1947; Ph.D. in E.E., Tech. U. Prague, Czechoslovakia, 1966. Sect. mgr. Tesla Radio Research Lab., Prague, 1947-61; sci. adv. Computer Research Inst., Prague, 1962-68; mem. tech. staff Hewlett Packard Labs., Palo Alto, Calif., 1968-73, dept. mgr., 1973—; vis. prof. Univs. Prague and Brno, 1952-56. Sr. mem. IEEE (chmn. solid state circuits and tech. com., 1979-81; mem. internat. solid state circuits program com., 1978-82). Guest editor IEEE Jour. Solid State Circuits, 1978; contbr. numerous articles to profl. jours.; holder 44 patents in field. Office: 1501 Page Mill Rd Palo Alto CA 94304

HORNBECK, EILEEN RUTH, mfg. co. exec.; b. Evansville, Ind., July 10, 1930; d. Adam Jacob and Clara (Rode) Rettig; student public schs., Evansville; children by previous marriage—Michael Slevin, Pat Slevin, Polly Ann Hornbeck. Sec., Cal-Farm Ins. Co., 1951-53, Convair, 1955-56, Boeing Aviation, 1957-58, N.Am. Aviation, 1959-61; salesperson Humming Boyd Sales Co., Tupperware distbr., Los Angeles, 1969—; unit mgr. Tupperware Co., Los Angeles, 1971—. Home: 427 W Gardena Blvd Gardena CA 90247 Office: 9020 Bellanca St Los Angeles CA 90045

HORNBRUCH, FREDERICK WILLIAM, III, management consultant; b. Bryn Mawr, Pa., Mar. 31, 1942; s. Frederick William and Helen (Novak) H.; B.S., Yale U., 1964; M.B.A., Stanford U., 1969. With Procter & Gamble, Food Mfg. Div., N.Y.C., 1964-67, Trans World Airlines, N.Y.C., summer, 1968, Creative Publs., Inc., 1969-81; sole owner Sundown Properties, 1979—; management cons., Palo Alto, 1981—. Mem. Stanford Bus. Sch. Alumni Assn. (pres. 1981-82), Stanford U. Alumni Assn., Yale U. Alumni Assn., Yale Engring. and Sci. Assn., Nat. Assn. Realtors, Calif. Assn. Realtors, Palo Alto Assn. Realtors, Underwater Photog. Assn., Oceanic and Cousteau Soc., Internat. Assn. Fin. Planners. Address: 4214 Ponce Dr Palo Alto CA 94306

HORNE, FREDERICK FRANKLIN, engring. co. exec.; b. Carriere, Miss., Mar. 24, 1900; s. Frederick and Ida Belle (Vogh) H.; student Miss. A. & M. U., 1917-21; m. Eleanor Isabelle Call, Apr. 16, 1931; children—Mary Eleanor, Barbara Lee, Diana Jean. Salesman, Nat. Cash Register Co., 1922-30; rep. to govts. Addressograph-Multigraph Corp., 1930-39; owner, mgr. Palace Stationery Stores, Monterey, Santa Cruz, Calif., 1940-50; owner, pres. Airrigation Engring. Co., Carmel Valley, Calif., 1950—, also dir. Mem. Water Pollution Control Fedn., Am. Pub. Works Assn. Democrat. Roman Catholic. Patentee waste water tech. Office: Airrigation Engring Co Inc Chaparral Rd Carmel Valley CA 93924

HORNER, DAVID DEAN, university administrator, consultant; b. Pitts., Nov. 28, 1939; s. Harry Ogle and Helen Marie (Reinerth) H.; m. Iris Ogawa, May 25, 1968; children—Tamiko, Mark. B.A., U. Redlands, 1961, M.A., 1965; Ph.D., Wash. State U., 1979. Cert. secondary tchr., adminstr., Calif. Tchr. jr., sr. high sch., Lake Arrowhead, Calif., 1961-63; ESL tchr. Peace Corps, Thailand, 1963-65; East-West Center grantee, U. Hawaii, 1966-67; fgn. student adviser Wash. State U., Pullman, 1967-75, asst. dir. admissions, 1975—; cons. internat. admissions Nat. Assn. for Fgn. Student Affairs, also bd. dirs. 1981-83, chmn. admissions sect., 1981-82; chmn. Commn. on Profl. Devel., coordinator faculty orientation program; ednl. cons. Dept. State and Coll. Bd. Pres. bd. dirs. Pullman YMCA, 1974-77; treas. bd. dirs. United Way, 1979-82; local bd. dirs. ACLU, 1969-72. German Fulbright grantee, 1980; internat. student research grantee Am. Assn. Collegiate Registrars and Admissions Officers, 1979. Mem. Am. Personnel and Guidance Assn., Am. Assn. Collegiate Registrars and Admissions Officers, Nat. Assn. Fgn. Student Affairs, Soc. for Intercultural Edn. Tgn. and Research. Author: Japan Travel Student Style, 1966.

HORNER, JENNIE LINN, educational administrator, nurse; b. Memphis, Tex., Feb. 27, 1932; d. Lester C. and Cecil T. (Knight) Linn; m. Billy A. Gooch, June 4, 1951 (dec.); children—Brenda Michael, Patricia Lynn, Robert Allen; m. 2d Donald M. Horner, July 26, 1975. R.N., U. Tex., 1955; B.S., No. Ariz. U., 1977, M.A., 1978, now postgrad. Cert. tchr., registered nurse, Ariz., Tex. Indsl. nurse Lipton Tea Co., Galveston, Tex., 1955-56; head nurse U. Tex. Med. Br., Galveston, 1956-58; sch. nurse Wash. Sch. Dist., Phoenix, 1970-77; tchr. middle sch., 1977-80; asst. prin. Murphy Sch. Dist., Phoenix, 1980-82; assoc. prin. middle sch. Madison Sch., Phoenix, 1982—; lang. arts coordinator Madison Sch. Dist., Phoenix; med. cons. Medahab, Phoenix. Mem. Assn. Supervision and Curriculum Devel., Sch. Nurses Orgn. Ariz. (pres.), Am. Vocat. Assn., Nat. Assn. Sch. Nurses, Phi Delta Kappa. Democrat. Home: 16063 N 26th Circle Phoenix AZ 85023 Office: 5525 N 16th St Phoenix AZ 85016

HORNIG, CARL ALFRED, mining engineering geologist, chemist, surveyor; b. Allentown, Pa., Sept. 17, 1941; s. Carl Orion and Josephine Marion (Tokas) H.; m. Lilian Alicia Martinez, Nov. 18, 1969; 1 dau., Opal Celeste. B.S. in Agr., Rutgers U., 1965; M.S. in Geology, U. S.C., 1973. Mining geologist W.S. Frey Co., Clearbrook, Va., 1970-74; staff geologist J.R. Simplot Co., Conda, Idaho, 1974-76; civil insp. Bechtel, Inc., Fairbanks, Alaska, 1976-77; city mapper Montpelier, Idaho, 1978-80; civil insp. Alyeska Pipeline Service Co., Anchorage, Alaska, 1980—; pres. Hornig Enterprises, Inc. Former chpt. leader John Birch Soc. Served with U.S. Army, 1966-68. Mem. Am. Soc. Quality Control, Alaska Pipeline Builders Assn., VFW (life). Home: 2914 Willow St Anchorage AK 99503 Office: 1835 S Bragaw St Anchorage AK 99512

HORNING, DEBORAH, office manager; b. Billings, Mont., Mar. 2, 1949; d. George and Mary (Ponessa) McCormick; m. John R. Horning, July 2, 1969. Student Mont. State U., 1967-69; B.S. in Bus. Adminstrn., Eastern Mont. Coll., 1978. Adminstrv. asst. to chief of police Billings Police Dept., 1971-78; city clk. City of Billings, 1978-79; office mgr. Sanderson/Stewart/Gaston Engring., Inc., Billings, 1979—. Mem. Am. Bus. Women's Assn., Pilot Club Internat. Home: 1147 Yellowstone Ave Billings MT 59102 Office: 1629 Ave D Billings MT 59102

HOROWITZ, BEN, medical center administrator; b. Bklyn., Mar. 19, 1914; s. Saul and Sonia (Meringoff) H.; B.A., Bklyn. Coll., 1940; LL.B., St. Lawrence U., 1935; postgrad. New Sch. Social Research, 1942; m. Beverly Lichtman, Feb. 14, 1952; children—Zachary, Jody. Admitted to N.Y. bar, 1941, dir. N.Y. Fedn. Jewish Philanthropies, 1940-45; Eastern regional dir. City of Hope, 1945-50, nat. exec. sec., City of Hope Los Angeles, 1950-53, exec. dir., 1953—; chmn. coordinating com. City of Hope Nat. Med. Center, City of Hope Research Inst., 1980—. Mem. Gov.'s Task Force on Flood Relief, 1969-74. Bd. dirs., v.p. Hope for Hearing Found., UCLA, 1972—. Recipient Spirit of Life award, 1970, Gallery of Achievement award, 1974, Profl. of Yr. award So. Calif. chpt. Nat. Soc. Fundraisers, 1977; Ben Horowitz chair in research established at City of Hope, 1981. Jewish (dir. temple 1964-67). Home: 221 Conway Ave Los Angeles CA 90024 Office: 208 W 8th St Los Angeles CA 90014

HOROWITZ, STEPHEN PAUL, lawyer; b. Los Angeles, May 23, 1943; s. Julius J. and Maxine (Rubenstein) H.; B.S., UCLA, 1966; J.D., 1970; M. Acctg., U. So. Calif., 1967; m. Nancy J. Shapiro, Apr. 4, 1971; children—Lindsey Nicole, Keri Lyn, Deborah Arielle. Bookkeeper, various law and acctg. firms, 1963-70; staff acct. Touche, Ross & Co., C.P.A.s, Los Angeles, 1968, 69; admitted to Calif. bar, 1971, U.S. Dist. Ct. bar, 1971, U.S. Ct. Appeals bar, 1972; individual practice law, Los Angeles, 1971-77; partner firm Horowitz & Horowitz, Los Angeles, 1978-79, prin. firm, 1979—; judge pro tem Los Angeles Mcpl. Ct.; mem. judge pro tem panel Los Angeles Superior Ct., Family Law Dept., classroom speaker Los Angeles County Bar Assn.; arbitrator Better Bus. Bur., Los Angeles County Bar Assn.; ombudsman VA, 1970. Bd. dirs. Vols. Am. Detoxification and Rehab. Center, Los Angeles, 1975-81, treas., 1979, vice chmn., 1980-81; legal adv. chmn., parliamentarian Temple Ramat Zion, Northridge, Calif. Served with U.S. Army, 1961-62. C.P.A., Calif. Mem. Calif. State Bar, Los Angeles County Bar, Calif. Trial Lawyers Assn., Los Angeles Trial Lawyers. Jewish. Clubs: Masons, B'nai B'rith, North Valley Jewish Community Center. Editorial bd. UCLA-Alaska Law Rev., 1968-70, co-editor-in-chief, 1969-70. Office: 8383 Wilshire Blvd Suite 528 Beverly Hills CA 90211

HORRIGAN, JACK ALLEN, computer cons.; b. Des Moines, Aug. 30, 1930; s. Jack William and Earnestine Geraldine (Smith) H.; B.S., Iowa State Coll., 1955; M.A., Oreg. State Coll., 1957; D.D., Neotarian Fellowship and Coll. of Philosophy, 1967, Ph.D., 1969; m. Patricia Ann Austin, June 8, 1963; children—Marianne MiChael, Aileen Elizabeth, William George. Mathematician, tech. rep. Philco, Phila., White Sands Missile Range, N.Mex., 1959-60; with Vitro Silver Spring Lab., 1961; sr. mathematician Litton Data Systems div., Van Nuys, Calif., 1962-66; asst. dept. mgr. Wolf Western div., Sherman Oaks, Calif., 1967; staff mathematician AAI-Pacific, Northridge, Calif., 1968; staff engr. Hughes Aircraft Co., Culver City, Calif., 1969-70; chief ops. research Mental Health Research and Evaluation Team, U. Denver, 1972-76; cons. Clarett McCoy, Denver; co-owner John Paul Jones Mine, Idaho Springs, Colo., 1970—; cons. Westinghouse F-16 computer systems, Balt., 1976-77, ESI, Tempe, Ariz., 1978, Sperry FS, Phoenix, 1979, Lear Siegler, Grand Rapids, Airship Industries, Ramsey, Isle of Man, 1980, Am. Home Video, Denver, 1981-82; system designer over horizon radar Gen. Electric Co. Founder Denver Libertarian Ch., 1976. Served with USCG, 1948-51. Mem. Pi Mu Epsilon. Author: Coordinate Transformations, Ship and Earth Orientated Coordinate Systems, 1962. Contbr. to Behavior Analysis and Systems Analysis: An Integrative Approach to Mental Health Programs, 1974. Contbr. articles to profl. jours. Home: PO Box 06436 Denver CO 80206

HORROCKS, RODNEY DWAIN, agronomy educator, researcher; b. Maeser, Uintah, Utah, Oct. 4, 1938; s. Rodney B. and Phoebe M. (Hatch) H.; m. Barbara Jean Williams, Sept. 9, 1960; children—Rodney, Sharilyn, Janene, Richard, Russell. B.S., Brigham Young U., 1962; M.S., Pa. State U., 1964, Ph.D., 1967. Cert. profl. agronomist. Asst. prof. agronomy U. Mo.-Columbia, 1967-71, assoc. prof., 1971-75, prof., 1975-78; vis. assoc. prof. U. Ariz., Tucson, 1975-76; prof. Brigham Young U., Provo, Utah, 1978—, chmn. dept. agronomy and horticulture, 1982—; environ. researcher; agrl. cons. AID, 1976. Assoc. editor Agronomy Jour., 1983—; contbr. articles to prof. jours. Campaign worker Republican Com., election ofcl., 1967-78. Mem. Am. Soc. Agronomy, Crop Sci. Soc. Am., AAAS, Sigma Xi, Alpha Zeta. Republican. Mormon.

HORSELL, MARY KAY, assn. exec.; b. Roundup, Mont., Nov. 3, 1917; d. Guy Elmer and Mary Catherine (Raridan) Smith; B.S., Fresno (Calif.) State U., 1939; m. Arthur Howard Horsell, June 26, 1937; children—Barbara Jeanne Horsell Koon, Mary Ann Horsell Boyette, Arthur Howard. Owner, operator Food Merchandising Service, Oakland, Calif., 1954—; chmn. bd. Oakland Diocesan Council Cath. Women, 1962-64, program chmn., 1964-65, v.p., program chmn., 1965-66, pres., 1967-69, parliamentarian, Diocesan rep. Ch. Women United Bd., 1969-71, ways and means chmn., 1971-73; province dir. San Francisco Archdiocesan Council Cath. Women, 1973-75; pres. Nat. Council Cath. Women, Washington, 1975—; U.S. rep. from Nat. Council Cath. Women to World Union Cath. Women's Orgns., 1979—, bd. dirs., 1979—; mem. Commn. for Women in Ch., Oakland Diocese, 1978—. Mem. central com. San Francisco Bay council Girl Scouts U.S.A., 1947-55; diocesan bd. mem., health chmn., program chmn., legis. chmn. Parent Tchrs. Groups, 1949-54, pres. East Bay Pres.'s Council, 1954-56, archdiocesan pres., 1958-60, pres. Oakland Diocese, 1962-64; pres. St. Jarlath's Mothers Club, 1946-48, Bishop O'Dowd High Sch. Mothers Club, 1956-58; co-organizer Children's Vision Center of East Bay, 1957, pres., 1971-74; pres. East Bay Motion Picture and TV Council, 1964-66; organizer Vol. Tchr. Assistance Program for elementary schs. in Oakland Diocese, 1965; bd. dirs. Met. Horseman's Assn., 1963-75, now v.p., Past Pres.'s trophy, 1975; vol. counselor juvenile delinquents awaiting trial, 1967—, sec. Fedn. Motion Picture Councils, Inc., 1975-77, pres., 1979-82. Recipient Pro Ecclesia Et Pontifice, 1964, Life membership East Bay Pres.'s Council Parent Tchrs. Groups, 1964; named Oakland Mother of Year, 1970. Club: Zonta Internat. Editor: Newsreel, Fedn. Motion Picture Councils, 1973-75. Home: 11590 Circle Way Dublin CA 94566 Office: Washington DC 20005

HORSMAN, JAMES DEVERELL, Canadian provincial government official; b. Camrose, Alta., Can., July 29, 1935; s. George Cornwall and Kathleen (Deverell) H.; m. Elizabeth Marian Whitney, July 4, 1964; children—Catherine Anne, Diana Lynn, Susan Marian. B.Com., LL.B., U. B.C. Created queen's counsel, 1980. Mem. Alta. Legis. Assembly for Medicine Hat, 1975—, minister of advanced edn. and manpower, 1979-82, minister of fed. and intergovtl. affairs and dep. govt. house leader, 1982—; mem. Alta. Del. to First Ministers Conf. on Constn., 1982; chmn. Provincial Ministers Responsible for Manpower, 1982. Mem., chmn. bd. govs. Medicine Hat Coll., 1972-74; elder St. John's Ch. Medicine Hat. Mem. Medicine Hat C. of C. (pres. 1971-72). Progressive Conservative. Presbyterian. Clubs: Kinsmen (past pres., past dist. officer), Cypress. Lodge: Shriners. Office: 130 Legis Bldg Edmonton AB T5K 2B7 Canada*

HORSMAN, MARSHALL NELSON, hosp. adminstr.; b. Redwood City, Calif., May 12, 1926; s. Nelson Martin and Helen Amelia (Trumble) H.; m. Rose Margaret Lovelace, Dec. 5, 1976; children—Randolph, Mark. B.S., Calif. State U.-Fullerton, 1979; M.B.A., Pepperdine U., Malibu, Calif., 1980. Adminstr., Beaumont (Calif.) Convalescent Hosp., 1966-72, Alvarado Convalescent and Rehab. Hosp., San Diego, 1972-73, Royale Convalescent Hosp., Santa Ana, Calif., 1974—; instr., lectr. Calif. State U., Long Beach, 1981—; mem. Bd. Exams. Nursing Home Adminstrn., 1971-73; chmn. Beaumont Heart Fund drive, 1969; bd. dirs., Riverside County chmn. Am. Heart Assn., 1969-71. Fellow Am. Coll. Nursing Home Adminstrs. (pres. Calif. chpt. 1976-77, gov. Region X 1977-79); mem. Calif. Assn. Health Facilities (v.p. 1969-71; Thomas E. Spinndle award 1971). Republican. Seventh-day Adventist. Home: 3814 S Teakwood St Santa Ana CA 92707 Office: 1030 W Warner Ave Santa Ana CA 92707

HORSTIN, ABRAHAM HUGO, control systems engineer; b. Java, Indonesia, Oct. 13, 1935; s. Hugo and Dora (Nio) H.; m. Alberta Carolina Dieben, June 1967; children—Doreen, Eugene. B.S. in Mech. Engring., The Netherlands, 1958; M.S. in Systems Engring., West Coast U., Los Angeles, 1970; cert. in bus. mgmt. UCLA, 1979. Registered mech. engr., Calif.; registered control systems operator, Calif. Various positions in design and analysis of aerospace controls and flight control systems, Burg Warner, De Laval Turbine, Crane Co., Bendix Corp., until 1980; specialist control systems and systems analysis Rocketdyne div. Rockwell Internat. Canoga Park, Calif., 1980—. Served with Royal Dutch Navy, 1958-60. Mem. ASME, AIAA, Soc. Automotive Engrs. Contbr. to profl. jours. Home: 3473 Avenida Ladera Thousand Oaks CA 91362 Office: Rocketdyne Div Rockwell Internat Corp 6633 Canoga Ave Canoga Park CA 91304

HORTIN, LARRY LAMAR, city librarian; b. Evanston, Wyo., July 13, 1934; s. Glen Malin and Hannah Lucille (Wilde) H.; B.S., Brigham Young U., 1961; M.S. (NDEA grantee), U. Oreg., 1967; m. Carol Holman, May 24, 1957; children—Lesley, Kristen, Bradley, John, Melinda, Michael. Tchr., Carbon County Sch. Dist., Price, Utah, 1961-62; sch. librarian Clark County Sch. Dist., Boulder City, Nev., 1962-69; librarian Brigham Young U., Provo, Utah, 1969-70; library dir. Provo City Library, 1970—. Chmn., Utah Library Legis. Com., 1978-79. Served with AUS, 1956-58. Mem. ALA, Adult Edn. Assn., Utah Library Assn., Utah Ednl. Assn., Nev. Edn. Assn. Republican. Mormon. Club: Rotary. Home: 3675 N 500 E Provo UT 84604 Office: Provo City Public Library 13 N 100 N Provo UT 84601

HORTON, DEBORAH JAN, college administrator, environmental technology training consultant; b. Oskaloosa, Iowa, Feb. 12, 1951; d. Donald Delaine and Elizabeth Joan (Burk) Riddle; m. Gary Francis Horton, Dec. 18, 1971; children—David Francis, Richard Donald. B.A., U. Wyo., 1972; postgrad. Laramie County Community Coll., U. Utah, U. Wis., Calif. State U., 1976-81. Cert. tchr., Wyo., 1976-78. Reading tchr., aide Wyo. Indsl. Inst., Worland, 1975-76; tng., operator cert. officer dept. environ. quality State of Wyo., Cheyenne, 1977-80; dir. environ. tech. Utah Tech. Coll., Provo, 1980—; pres. EnTrain, Springville Utah, 1982—; sec. joint tng. coordinating com. State of Utah; advisor Ad Hoc Com. on Required Cert. EPA grantee, 1982. Mem. Nat. Environ. Tng. Assn. (v.p.), Wyo. Water Quality and Pollution Control Assn., Water Pollution Control Assn. (edn. chmn.), Am. Water Works Assn. Democrat. Presbyterian. Home: 1120 E 1200 S Springville UT 84663 Office: PO Box 1609 Provo UT 84603

HORTON, ERNEST HORACE, JR., educator; b. Pasadena, Calif., Nov. 7, 1926; s. Ernest Horace and Esther Maretta (Virgo) H.; A.B., Los Angeles Pacific Coll., 1946; M.Div., Asbury Theol. Sem., 1949; Ph.D., U. So. Calif., 1956; m. Patricia Mathews, Mar. 6, 1982; 1 dau., Carol Gail Horton-Mann. Instr., U. Redlands (Calif.), 1956-57; vis. lectr. Occidental Coll., Los Angeles, 1957-58; prof. philosophy Glendale (Calif.) Community Coll., 1958—; vis. prof. Sch. Religion, U. So. Calif., Spring 1982. Mem. Am. Acad. Religion, Soc. Bibl. Lit., Royal Inst. Philosophy, Am. Philos. Assn., Glendale Tchrs. Assn. (pres. 1963-64), Calif. Tchrs. Assn. Urban Chpt. Presidents (chmn. 1964-65). Contbr. articles to profl. jours. Home: 4145 Aralia Rd Altadena CA 91001 Office: Dept Philosophy Glendale Community Coll Glendale CA 91208

HORTON, JACK KING, utilities executive; b. Stanton, Nebr., June 27, 1916; s. Virgil L. and Edna L. (King) H.; A.B., Stanford, 1936; LL.B., Oakland Coll. Law, 1941; m. Betty Lou Magee, July 15, 1937; children—Judy, Sally, Harold. Admitted to Calif. bar, 1941; treasury dept. Shell Oil Co., 1937-42; pvt. law practice, San Francisco 1942-43; atty. Standard Oil Co., 1943-44; sec., legal counsel Coast Counties Gas & Electric Co., 1944-51, pres., 1951-54; v.p. Pacific Gas & Electric Co., San Francisco, 1954-59; pres. So. Calif. Edison Co., 1959-68, chief exec. officer, from 1965, chmn. bd., 1968-80, chmn. exec. com., 1980—; dir. United Calif. Bank, Pacific Mut. Life Ins., Lockheed Aircraft Corp., Western Bancorp. Trustee U. So. Calif., Nat. Indsl. Conf. Bd. Mem. State Bar Calif., Tax Found. (trustee), Bus. Council. Clubs: Pacific Union, Bohemian, California, Los Angeles Country, Cypress Point. Office: So Calif Edison Co 2244 Walnut Grove Ave Rosemont CA 91770

HORTON, JOHN EDWIN, sociology educator, researcher; b. Milw., June 3, 1932; s. Merrill Edwin and Alice Eleanor (Buckett) H. B.A. in History, U. Wis.-Madison, 1954; Fulbright scholar Coll. Europe, Bruges, Belgium, 1955; Ph.D., Cornell U., 1960. From instr. to assoc. prof. sociology UCLA, 1959—; staff mem. Inst. Study of Labor and Econ. Crisis, San Francisco. Woodrow Wilson scholar, 1955; Fulbright research scholar, 1981. Mem. Am. Sociol. Assn., Internat. Sociol. Assn., Pacific Sociol. Assn., Am. Polit. Sci. Assn., Internat. Polit. Sci. Assn. Contbr. numerous articles to profl. jours. Office: Dept Sociology UCLA Los Angeles CA 90024

HORTON, LARRY RAY, systems programmer; b. Spokane, Wash., July 11, 1950; s. Robert E. and Vera R. (Archambeault) H.; m. Jacqueline K. Cockrell, Mar. 22, 1974; children—Patrick, Joshua, Curtis. A.A.S. in Data Processing, Spokane Community Coll., 1976. Computer operator Roundup Co., Spokane, 1976-78, programmer analyst, 1978-80, systems programmer, 1980-81; systems programming mgr. West Coast Grocery, Spokane, 1981—. Served USNR, 1970-76. Mem. Assn. Systems Mgmt. Home: E 12815 29th St Spokane WA 99216 Office: West Coast Grocery E 11016 Jackson St Spokane WA 99220

HORTON, LAWRENCE STANLEY, engr., apt. developer; b. Hanston, Kans., July 25, 1926; s. Gene Leigh and Retta Florence (Abbott) H.; B.S.E.E., Oreg. State U., 1949; m. Margaret Ann Cowles, Nov. 26, 1946 (dec., 1964); children—Craig, Lawrence Stanley, Steven J.; m. 2d, Julia Ann Butler Wirrkila, Aug. 15, 1965; stepchildren—Charles Wirkkila Horton, Jerry Higginbotham Horton. Elec. engr. Mountain States Power Co., Calif. Oreg. Power Co., Pacific Power and Light Co., 1948-66; mgr. Ramic Corp., 1966-69; cons. elec. engr. Marquess and Assos., Medford, Oreg., 1969—, sec., bd. dirs.; owner, mgr. Medford Better Housing Assn., Ashland Better Housing Assn.; partner Eastwood Living Group, Jackson St. Properties, T'Morrow Apts., Lake Empire Apts., Johnson Manor; dir. Medford State Bank; developer various apt. complexes, 1969—. Active Medford Planning Commn., Archtl. Review Commn., Housing Authority; pres. United Fund, 1963-64. Served with USN, 1945-46. Named Rogue Valley Profl. Engr. of Yr., 1969. Mem. IEEE, Internat. Assn. Elec. Inspectors (asso.), Nat. Soc. Profl. Engrs., Profl. Engrs. of Oreg., Elec. Safety Research Assn., So. Oreg. Apt. Owners Assn. (pres.), Rogue Valley Geneol. Soc. (v.p.), Medford C. of C. (dir.). Republican. Methodist. Clubs: Kiwanis (sec. Joe Meuse Kiwanis Found. of White City, dir. White City, life mem.), Rogue Valley Yacht (commodore 1974-55, dir., local fleet capt., champion), San Juan 21 Fleet Assn. (western vice commodore, Top Ten San Juan Sailor West Coast, 1980), Jackson Toastmasters (founder 1957). Grad. instr. Dale Carnegie course, 1955, 56; contbr. elec. articles to profl. assns., 1956-61. Office: 1120 E Jackson St PO Box 490 Medford OR 97501

HORTON, LOWELL EUGENE, ecologist, botanist; b. Murray, Iowa; s. John Samuel and Iva Verona (Brooks) H., m. Barbara Dean Hill, Oct. 13, 1951; children—Merlene Kirby, Deborah Gordon, George. Asst. ranger, U.S. Forest Service, Spanish Fork, Utah, 1950-55, dist. ranger, Clayton, Idaho, 1955-58, range conservationist, Provo, Utah, 1958-60, resource staff officer, Vernal, Utah, 1960-66, range conservationist, Ogden, Utah, 1966-70, ecol. specialist, Ogden, 1970-73, regional ecologist, San Francisco, 1973-77, regional botanist, 1977—. Served with U.S. Army, 1944-46. Mem. Ecol. Soc. Am., Soc. Range Mgmt., Calif. Native Plant Soc., Am. Inst. Biol. Scis., No. Nev. Native Plant Soc., Nature Conservancy, Am. Legion. Home: 2537 Prestwick Ave Concord CA 94519 Office: 630 Sansome St San Francisco CA 94111

HORTON, THOMAS CLIFFORD, SR., farmer, rancher, water cooperative executive; b. Venus, N.Mex., Jan. 23, 1916; s. Claude C. and Ethel M. (Madole) H.; m. Rita Shook, Dec. 27, 1937; children—Rita Loy Horton Thomas, Sharron Horton Geilenfeldt, Thomas Clifford. Grad. Menaul Sch. of United Presbyn. Ch., 1936. Farmer, rancher Santa Fe and Bernalillo Counties (N.Mex.), 1936—; farm instr. Edgewood Dist. (N.Mex.) State Coll., 1947-49; sub-contractor road constrn. Allison-Haney Co., Albuquerque, 1953-54, Northwestern Engrs., Denver, 1953-54, Floyd Hake, Santa Fe, 1953-54; gen. contractor, Albuquerque, 1954—; bldg. supr. Bd. Nat. Missions United Presbyn. Ch. U.S.A., N.Mex., Ariz., Utah, Tex., Alaska, 1954-71, asst. dir. Bd. Properties div., 1961-69; founder Entranosa Water Corp. (name changed to Entranosa Water Cooperative 1981), Santa Fe and Bernalillo Counties, 1974—, comptroller, 1982—. Sec. Edgewood Soil Conservation Dist., 1942-43; mem. adv. com. Santa Fe County Long Range Planning Program, 1948-49; organizer no. half Estancia Valley for REA com., 1949-50; pub. relations officer Central N.Mex. Elec. Coop., 1950-52. Mem. Menual Sch. Alumni Assn. Democrat. Clubs: Mason, Moriarty Rotary. Address: PO Box 150 Edgewood NM 87015

HORWITZ, DENNIS NEAL, instrument manufacturing company executive; b. Los Angeles, Sept. 23, 1954; s. Sherwyn Irving and Edythe (Gubman) H.; m. Arlene Nancy Koster, Aug. 14, 1977. B.S. in Engring., UCLA, 1976, M.S. in Engring., Computer Sci., 1981. Research engr. UCLA, 1972-79; v.p. Photodyne Inc., Newbury Park, Calif., 1978—; cons. DBA Micro-Business Concepts, Sherman Oaks, Calif., 1977—. Mem. IEEE, IEEE Computer Soc., Soc. Photo-Instrumentation Engrs. Democrat. Home: 1623 Buena Vista St Ventura CA 93001 Office: Photodyne Inc 948 Tourmaline Dr Newbury Park CA 91320

HORZBERGER, ARTHUR CONRAD, county commissioner; b. Colorado Springs, Colo., Jan. 29, 1917; s. Karl and Emma Barbara Horzberger; m. Lucky Knowles, Jan. 10, 1942; 1 dau., Barbara. D.V.M., Colo. State U., 1939. Practice veterinary medicine, Colorado Springs, 1939-40, 46-57; veterinarian Cheyenne Mountain Zoo, Colorado Springs, 1946-57; pres. Santa's Workshop, North Pole, Colo., 1957-69; pres. Park State Bank, Woodland Park, Colo., 1965-68; real estate developer, Colorado Springs, 1969-72; mem. Colo. State Legislature, 1972-80; commnr. El Paso County, Colorado Springs, 1980—. Bd. dirs. Coral council Girl Scouts U.S.A., El Paso Rehab. Center, United Way; chmn. Colo. Joint Budget Com. Served with AUS, 1940-46. Mem. Colo. Vet. Med. Assn., AVMA. Republican. Clubs: Rotary, Paterson Field Officers, Broadmoor Golf. Home: 1700 Mesa Ave Colorado Springs CO 80906 Office: 27 E Vermijo St Colorado CO 80903

HOSFORD, SANDRA MARLENE, marketing, advertising and public relations executive; b. Burbank, Calif., Nov. 25, 1947; s. Yewed B. and Margarete Pearl (Walsh) Shipp. B.A., Calif. State U.-Northridge, 1973. Exec. sec., pub. relations officer, asst. v.p. Valley Fed. Savs., Los Angeles, 1973-80, v.p. mktg., advt. and pub. relations, 1980—. Mem. Las Companareos Guild Valley Presbyn. Hosp.; mem. Valley Coordinating Roundtable. Mem. Savs. Inst. Mktg. Soc. Am. (pres. So. Calif. chpt.), San Fernando Valley Pub. Relations Roundtable, (past pres.), Los Angeles Publicity Club, Los Angeles Advt. Club, Van Nuys C. of C. Republican. Presbyterian. Club: Soroptomist (v.p.).

HOSTETTER, GENE HUBER, electrical engineering educator; b. Spokane, Wash., Sept. 14, 1939; s. John Huber and Virginia Lane (Yancey) H.; B.S. in Elec. Engring., U. Wash., 1962, M.S., 1963; Ph.D., U. Calif.-Irvine, 1973; m. Donna Rae Patterson, Nov. 30, 1967; children—Colleen Rae, Kristen Lane. Dir. engring. Sta. KOL, Seattle, 1965-67; asst. prof. elec. engring. Calif. State U.-Long Beach, 1967-70, assoc. prof., 1970-75, prof., 1975-81, chmn. dept. elec. engring., 1975-81; prof. electrical engring. U. Calif., Irvine, 1981—, chmn. dept., 1982—. Recipient Outstanding Faculty award Calif. State U., 1975, 77, Engr. Faculty of Yr. award U. Calif.-Irvine, 1982. Mem. IEEE, AAAS, Am. Soc. Engring. Edn., Internat. Fedn. Automatic Control, Sigma Xi. Episcopalian. Author: Fundamentals of Network Analysis, 1980; Design of Feedback Control Systems, 1982; Engineering Network Analysis, 1984. Home: 8811 Gallant Dr Huntington Beach CA 92646 Office: Elec Engring U Calif Irvine CA 92717

HOSTETTER, PAUL ESBENSHADE, clergyman; b. Lancaster, Pa., Apr. 11, 1927; s. Paul Hess and Ada Kathryn (Esbenshade) H.; m. Dorothy Clark, June 7, 1969; children—Mary Elizabeth, Martha Ruth, Rachel Lois. B.A., Wheaton Coll., 1950; M.Div., Western Theol. Sem., Ref. Ch. of Am., 1954; postgrad. U. N.D., 1953, U. Chgo., 1954, Hartford Sem., 1959, Mich. State U., 1967, Fuller Theol. Sem., 1973. Ordained to ministry Reformed Ch. of Am., 1954; missionary linguist, Sudan, 1954-59; dir. W. Pakistan Christian Council Literacy Center, Lahore, 1960-65; pastor Midland Ref. Ch., 1968-72; missionary educator and writer, Mexico, 1973-80; minister of mission and evangelism Crystal Cathedral, Garden Grove, Calif., 1981—. Pres., Friends of the Chiapas Med. Center, Inc., 1982. Served with U.S. Army, 1945-46. Mem. Am. Soc. Missiologists. Contbr. articles to profl. jours.; developed system for writing African langs. in Sudan with Arabic script. Home: 1138 E Chestnut Ave Orange CA 92667 Office: 12141 Lewis St Garden Grove CA 92640

HOSTLER, CHARLES WARREN, business executive; b. Chgo., Dec. 12, 1919; s. Sydney M. and Catherine (Marshall) H.; 1 son, Charles Warren. B.A., UCLA, 1942; postgrad. U. Bucharest (Rumania) Law Sch., 1945-46; M.A., Georgetown U., 1951, Ph.D., 1957; M.A., Am. U., Beirut, 1955; A.A., San Diego Community Coll., 1978. Commd. 2d lt. U.S. Air Force, 1942, advanced through grades to col., 1951; mem. policy planning staff Office Sec. Def.; asst. to dir. disarmament Dept. Def., sr. dep. U.S. Del. Nuclear Test Ban Conf., Geneva, Switzerland; U.S. air attache Lebanon, Jordan, Cyprus, mem. strategic plans group Joint Chiefs Staff, Washington; mil. affairs officer Am. Embassy, Beirut, Lebanon, chief combat info. br. Am. Mission to Aid Turkey, U.S. mil. rep. Allied Control Mission, Rumania; adj. prof. Am. U. Sch. Internat. Service, Washington, 1955-63; ret. 1963; dir. internat. ops. Middle East and Africa, mgr. internat. ops. Europe and Middle East, mgr. internat. mktg. missiles and space McDonnell Douglas Corp., 1963-69; chmn. bd. dirs. Irvine (Calif.) Nat. Bank, 1969-74; dep. sec. for internat. commerce, dir. Bur. Internat. Commerce, U.S. Dept. Commerce, Washington, 1974-76; regional v.p. Middle East and Africa, E-Systems Inc., Dallas, 1976-77; pres. Hostler Investment Co., San Diego, 1971—; pres. Hostler Leasing Co., Tustin, Calif., Pacific S.W. Capital Corp., San Diego; lectr. in field. Bd. govs. Middle East Inst., Washington, 1962-80; pub. mem. Calif. Contractors State Lic. Bd., San Diego County Local Agy. Formation Commn.; adv. bd. Hubbs/Sea World Research Inst., San Diego; bd. govs. San Diego Coalition for Econ. and Environ. Balance, Mission Thrift and Loan, San Diego; mem. exec. com. Friends Scripps Clinic, La Jolla, Calif.; life mem. Republican Nat. Com. Decorated Legion of Merit, grand comdr. Greek Order of Phoenix, Order Holy Sepulchre, Orders St. Peter and St. Paul, Lebanese Order Cedars, Haitian Order Honor and Merit, Peoples Republic of China Order Cloud and Banner; named hon. citizen Cyclades Island, Greece, hon. dep. sheriff San Diego, Sacramento counties, col. Calif. State Mil. Res. Mem. Am. Polit. Sci. Assn. Clubs: Nat. Press, Balboa Bay, Confrerie des Chevaliers du Tastevin, Chaine des Rotisseurs. Author: Turkism and the Soviets, 1957; The Challenge of Science Educations, 1959; contbr. articles to profl. jours. Home: PO Box 9976 San Diego CA 92109 Office: 9580 Black Mountain Rd Suite H San Diego CA 92126

HOTCHKIS, PRESTON, business exec.; b. Los Angeles, June 19, 1893; s. Finlay Montgomery and Flora Cornelia (Preston) H.; A.B., U. Calif.-Berkeley, 1916; postgrad. U. So. Calif. Law Sch., 1916-17; LL.D., Pepperdine U., 1955, Whittier Coll., 1957; m. Katharine Bixby, Dec. 11, 1923 (dec. 1979); children—Katharine Hotchkis Johnson, Joan Hotchkis, Preston Bixby, John Finlay; m. 2d, Georgina Hicks Mage, 1981. Asst. sec., later sec. Calif. Delta Farms, Inc., Los Angeles, 1919-25; admitted to Calif. bar, 1920; asso. in founding Pacific Fin. Corp., 1920, Pacific Indemnity Co., 1926; organized Founders' Ins. Co., 1946; chmn. bd. Fred H. Bixby Ranch Co. Councilman city of San Marino, 1940-55. U.S. rep. Econ. and Social Council UN, 1954-55; grad. mem. Bus. Council; mem. Hoover Commn. Task Force on Fed. Lending Agys., 1954-55, State Calif. Reconstrn. and Reemployment Commn., 1942-47, Govs. Tax Com., 1942; chmn. Calif. Water Project Campaign, 1960, Southland Water Com.; pres. Colo. River Assn., 1947-52; chmn. Local Agy. Formation Commn. Los Angeles County, 1963-75; chmn. Navy Relief Soc. Campaign for So. Calif. (citation from Sec. Navy), 1942; chmn. War Chest campaign for Greater Los Angeles Area (citation War Chest) 1945; mem. nat. adv. council Girl Scouts U.S.; mem. pres.'s adv. council U. Redlands; mem. pres.'s bd. Pepperdine U.; chmn. So. Calif. Com. for Radio Free Europe, 1969-70. Mem. Tng. within Industry com. War Manpower Bd. So. Calif., 1942-45 (citation War Manpower bd.). Mem. War Fin. Com. of U.S. Treasury Dept. for Calif., 1942-45 (citation from Treasury Dept.); del. Rep. Nat. Conv., Calif. rep. resolutions com., Phila., 1940, Chgo., 1944, San Francisco, 1964, alt. del., 1948-52; v.p., trustee Good Hope Med. Found., S.W. Mus., hon. trustee Harvey Mudd Coll.; regent U. Calif., 1935-36; mem. adv. council Calif. State Parks Found.; co-founder, hon. bd. dirs. Los Angeles World Affairs Council, pres., 1967-69; bd. dirs. Met. Water Dist. So. Calif. Served from seaman to ensign USN, 1917-18. Mem. Calif., Los Angeles bar assns., Calif. Alumni Assn. (pres. 1935-36), Calif. State C. of C. (pres. 1942-43), Sigma Nu, Phi Delta Phi. Presbyn. Clubs: Calif., Univ. (Los Angeles); Valley Hunt (Pasadena); Bohemian, Pacific Union (San Francisco). Home: 1415 Circle Dr San Marino CA 91108 Office: 523 W 6th St Los Angeles CA 90014

HOTCHKISS, HENRY WASHINGTON, banker; b. Meshed, Iran, Oct. 31, 1937; s. Henry and Mary Bell (Clark) H.; B.A., Bowdoin Coll., 1958. French tchr. Choate Sch., Wallingford, Conn., 1959-62; v.p. Chem. Bank, N.Y.C., 1962-80, v.p. Chem. Bank Internat. San Francisco, 1973-80; dir. corp. relations Crédit Suisse, San Francisco, 1980—; dir. Indonesia-U.S. Bus. Seminar, Los Angeles, 1979. Asso. bd. regents L.I. Coll. Hosp., 1969-71, pres., 1971, bd. regents, 1971-73. Served to capt. U.S. Army Res., 1958-59. Mem. Explorers Club, Calif. Council Internat. Trade (dir. 1976—, chmn. membership com. 1977-79, treas. 1978-79), New Eng. Soc. in City Bklyn. (v.p., dir. 1968-73). Clubs: Heights Casino (bd. govs. 1971-73) (Bklyn.); St. Francis Yacht, Golden Gate Anglers (San Francisco), Internat. Folkboat Assn. San Francisco (cruise chmn. 1976-77, pres. 1977-79, membership chmn. 1979—). Home: 1206 Leavenworth St San Francisco CA 94109 Office: 50 California St San Francisco CA 94111

HOTSON, HUGH HOWISON, corp. exec.; b. Seattle, Jan. 26, 1916; s. John William and Jennie (Doak) H.; B.S., U. Wash., 1938, M.S., 1940; Ph.D. in Plant Pathology, U. Minn., 1950; postgrad. Cornell U., 1940-41, Harvard U., 1941, Yale U., 1949-50; m. Josephine Frances Richardson, Dec. 23, 1939; children—Josephine Ann, John Richardson, Hugh Howison. Teaching fellow U. Wash., 1939-40; Herbarium curator, Cornell U., 1941; teaching asst. Yale U., 1949-50; research asso. U. Minn., 1950-51; dep. chief C div. Dugway Proving Ground, 1951-52, asst. chief BW div., 1952-53; mgr. agrl. chem. project Minn. Mining and Mfg. Co., 1953-58, cons. bus. mgmt., 1958—; pres. Maritime Corp., Seattle, 1961—. Pres., Pat Smith Kontum Hosp. Fund, 1965-71; treas. English Speaking Union, 1974—; active Seattle council Boy Scouts Am. Served to lt. col. U.S. Army, 1941-47. Recipient Book of Yr. award, Ency. Britannica, 1950. Mem. Am. Chem. Soc., AAAS, Geothermal Resource Council, N.Y. Acad. Sci., Seattle C. of C., U. Wash. Alumni Assn. (pres. Minn. chpt. 1958), Sigma Xi, Phi Kappa Psi. Clubs: Rainier, Seattle Tennis. Author monographs in field of botany. Office: 911 Western Ave Seattle WA 98104

HOTTENSTEIN, EVELYN KENNY, devel. tng. co. exec.; b. Glasgow, Mont., Mar. 4, 1948; d. Daniel Patrick and Miriam (Phelan) Kenny; B.A., Carroll Coll., 1970. Speech coach, English tchr. Mont. State Sch. for Girls, Helena, 1970-72; exec. dir. Camp Fire council, Helena, 1972-73, mgr. adminstr., exec. orientation program Camp Fire, Inc., Nat. Service Center, Englewood, Colo., 1974-76; owner, mgr. H & G Devel. Co., Cheyenne, Wyo., 1976-78; owner Lifework Assocs., Westminster, Colo., 1978—, Public Speaking for the Profl., 1979—; public speaker; instr. U. Colo., 1979—, U. Denver, 1982—; cons. Assn. for Vol. Adminstrn. Co-chmn. Mont. Gov.'s Commn. on Status of Women, 1973; mem. Nat. Commn. on Mgmt. Standards, Camp Fire, Inc., 1975-76; mem. adv. bd. Vol. Mgmt. Program, U. Colo., Boulder, 1979, 80. Mem. Am. Soc. Tng. and Devel., Career Devel. Group, Mgmt. Tng. Group, Assn. for Vol. Adminstrn. Unitarian-Universalist (bd. dirs. service com.). Office: 4155 E Jewell Suite 405 Denver CO 80222

HOTTOIS, JAMES WILLIAM, political scientist, college administrator; b. Batavia, N.Y., June 16, 1943; s. George Joseph and Ethel Holly Hottois; m. Suanne Jo Hottois, Aug. 14, 1965; children—Jo-Elle, Robert Paul. B.A., SUNY-Albany, 1965; M.A., SUNY-Buffalo, 1968, Ph.D., 1971. Asst. prof. polit. sci. Grinnell (Iowa) Coll., 1969-73; assoc. prof. polit. sci. U. San Diego, 1977, assoc. dean Coll. Arts and Scis., 1980—. Served with USMCR, 1962-67. Mem. Am. Polit. Sci. Assn., Western Polit. Sci. Assn., Western Social Sci. Assn., Policy Studies Orgn., Nat. Counsel Univ Research Adminstrs. Author: The Sex Education Controversy, 1975; contbr. articles to profl. jours. Home: 4882 Mt Ashmun Dr San Diego CA 92111 Office: U San Diego Coll Arts and Scis San Diego CA 92110

HOTZ, HENRY PALMER, physicist; b. Fayetteville, Ark., Oct. 17, 1925; s. Henry Gustav and Stella (Palmer) H.; B.S., U. Ark., 1948; Ph.D., Washington U., St. Louis, 1953; m. Marie Brase, Aug. 22, 1952; children—Henry Brase, Mary Palmer, Martha Marie. Asst. prof. physics Auburn (Ala.) U., 1953-58, Okla. State U., Stillwater, 1958-64; asso. prof. Marietta (Ohio) Coll., 1964-66; physicist, scientist-in-residence U.S. Naval Radiol. Def. Lab., San Francisco, 1966-67; asso. prof. U. Mo., Rolla, 1967-71; physicist Qanta Metrix div. Finnigan Corp., Sunnyvale, Calif., 1971-74; sr. scientist Nuclear Equipment Corp., San Carlos, Calif., 1974-79; sr. scientist Envirotech Measurement Systems, Palo Alto, Calif., 1979-82; sr. scientist Dohrmann div. Xertex, Santa Clara, Calif., 1982—; cons. USAF, 1958-62. Served with USNR, 1944-46. Mem. AAUP (sec. Okla. State U. chpt. 1959-64), Am. Phys. Soc., Am. Assn. Physics Tchrs., AAAS, Phi Beta Kappa, Sigma Xi, Sigma Pi Sigma, Pi Mu Epsilon, Sigma Nu (sec. 1947-48). Methodist. Mason. Home: 290 Stilt Ct Foster City CA 94404 Office: 3240 Scott Blvd Santa Clara CA 95050

HOU, STERLING SHANLIN, electronics company executive; b. Hunan, China, Sept. 3, 1938; came to U.S. 1962, naturalized, 1972; s. Fisher T. and Lotus H.C. (Chu) H.; m. Vivian Wang, July 4, 1965; children—Patricia, Tina. B.S. in E.E., Nat. Taiwan U., 1961; M.S. in E.E., U. Mo., 1964; postgrad. Stanford U., 1966-68. Design engr. Nat. Cash Register Co., Dayton, Ohio, 1964-65; project mgr. IBM, San Jose, Calif., 1965-70; dir. engring. Telex Corp., San Jose, 1970-72; project mgr. Hewlett Packard, Palo Alto, Calif., 1972-73; program mgr. Ampex, Sunnyvale, Calif., 1973-74; engring. mgr. Intel, Santa Clara, Calif., 1974-77; dir. devel. Nat. Semiconductor, Santa Clara, 1977-80; founder, v.p. Envision Tech. Inc., San Jose, 1981—. Pres. Sino America Culture & Economy Assn., 1981. Served to 2d lt. Chinese Mil. Police, 1961-62. Mem. IEEE, Chinese Inst. Engrs. (dir. Bay Area chpt.). Office: 631 River Oaks Pkwy San Jose CA 95134

HOUCHENS, JAMES HENRY, packaging executive; b. Mpls., June 22, 1939; s. John H. and Margaret M. (Sodergren) H.; m. DiAnne M. Randin, July 8, 1961; 1 son, Jeremy B. B.S. in Chemistry, U. Minn. Inst. Tech., 1966; M.A., Webster Coll., St. Louis, 1976; cert. packaging profl. Mem. Product devel. staff 3M Co., St. Paul, 1966-70; supr. package devel. Travenol Labs., Round Lake, Ill., 1971-75; mgr. tech. packaging Sunmark Cos., St. Louis, 1975-78; unit mgr. packaging devel. Clorox Co., Pleasanton, Calif., 1978-80; mgr. packaging tech. Cutter Labs. Inc. div. Miles Labs., Inc., Berkeley Calif., 1980—. Maj. CAP Aux., USAF. Mem. Packaging Inst. No. Calif. (pres., treas.), Soc. Packaging and Handling Engrs., Packaging Inst. U.S.A. Democrat. Lutheran. Office: PO Box 1986 Berkeley CA 94701

HOUCHIN, DAVID EVERETT, corp. exec.; b. Glendale, Calif., Aug. 15, 1949; s. Dick Albert and Dorothy Berniece (Stoughton) H.; B.S. in Bus. Adminstrn., Biola U., 1971; m. Sue Elta, Oct. 3, 1970; children—Dick Eugene, Jason, David, Kerry Sue. Rural missionary Village Missions, No. Calif., 1973-77; chief acct. Neptune Soc. Corp., San Pedro, Calif., 1973-77; chief fin. officer Trio Tech Internat., Burbank, Calif., 1977-81; chief fin. officer, mgmt. info. systems dir. Knudsen & Sons, Chico, Calif., 1981—; dir. Neptune Soc. Corp., San Pedro, Calif.; instr. Los Angeles Bapt. Coll., 1980-81; cons. in field. Mem. Nat. Assn. Accts., Am. Mgmt. Assn., Credit Mgmt. Assn. Republican. Mennonite. Home: Route 6 Box 404B Chico CA 95926 Office: PO Box 369 Chico CA 95927

HOUCK, ALAN PAUL, accountant; b. Portland, Oreg., June 29, 1947; s. Albert Lyle and Pauline Roberta (Jones) H.; m. Kathleen Ruth Elwood, Aug. 15, 1969; children—Eric Alan, Mark Andrew, Brian Christopher; B.A. in Math., Seattle Pacific U., 1969; M.A. in Math., Cleve. State U., 1971, B.B.A. in Acctg., 1973. C.P.A., Oreg. Tchr. math. and computer programming Cleve. Pub. Schs., 1969-72; staff acct. Brubaker, Helfrich & Taylor, C.P.A.s, Cleve., 1972-74; staff acct. Minihan, Kernutt, Stokes & Co., Eugene, Oreg., 1974-79, ptnr. in charge data processing and mgmt. services dept., 1979—; cons. to small bus. Treas. Emerald Exec. Assn., Eugene, 1978—; bd. dirs., treas. Eugene Christian Sch., 1975—; treas. local polit. campaigns. Mem. Am. Inst. C.P.A.s, Oreg. Soc. C.P.A.s, Assn. Time-sharing Small Computer Users. Republican. Club: Kiwanis (Eugene). Office: 1170 Pearl St Eugene OR 97401

HOUCK, C(ARLOS THOMPSON) (CUB), state senator, construction contractor; b. Salem, Oreg., Apr. 17, 1930; s. Roy L. and Grace F. (Thompson) H.; m. Kathleen Moore, Dec. 26, 1951; children—Ronald, Donald, Darah Ann. B.S., Oreg. State U., 1952. Vice pres. Roy L. Houck Sons' Corp., Salem, 1954-69; corp. officer Houck-Carrow Corp., Salem, Oreg., 1983—, Houck-McCall, Salem, 1983—; mem. Oreg. Senate,

1983—; owner, operator cattle ranch, 1983—; corp. officer Beaver State Sand & Gravel & Fabricators Inc.; active mgmt. real estate co., ins. agy., loan instn., state-wide devel. co. Pres. Salem City Council, 1967-69, alderman, 1966-69; chmn., mem. sch. bd., 1975-80. Served to 1st lt. USAF; Korea. Recipient Salem Disting. Service awards, 1971, 76, Council of Govt. Service award, 1965, Oreg. Gov. Ethic Commn. State Senate award, 1983. Republican. Lutheran.

HOUGH, WILLIAM HENRY, contractor; b. Phila., July 2, 1940; s. Samuel Jones and Margaret H. Hough; m. Shelley Boyle, Oct. 1, 1976; children—Alden, Benjamin. B.A. in Econs., U. Calif.-Berkeley, 1964, M.A., 1966. Lectr. econs. Ahmadu Bello U., Zaria, Nigeria, 1966-69; partner Team Constrn., Santa Cruz, Calif., 1970-74; v.p. Get-It Up Constrn., Inc., Santa Cruz, 1974-76, pres., 1976—. Mem. Overall Econ. Devel. Com., Santa Cruz County, 1976—. Address: 1720 Vine Hill Rd Santa Cruz CA 95064

HOUGHTON, RICHARD BURDETTE, bio-med. cons. co. exec.; b. Yakima, Wash., Apr. 26, 1925; s. Floyd Albert and Carolyn (Loveland) H.; B.S., U.S. Naval Acad., 1946; postgrad. U. Calif., Los Angeles, 1956-58; m. Anne Plowden, Jan. 19, 1972; children—Jill, Rebecca, Richard. Vice pres. engring. Acoustica Assos., Los Angeles, 1958-60; pres. Electro-Sonic Systems, Inc., Los Angeles, 1961-65; mgr. research and devel. Genisco Tech., Los Angeles, 1965-66; sr. research engr. Statham Inst., Oxnard, Calif., 1966-68; pres., chief cons. Phoenix Electronix, Inc., Irvine, Calif., 1968—; dir. Electro-Sonic Systems, 1961-65, In Vivo Metric Systems, 1968; cons. Aerojet Gen., Narco Bio-Systems, Bentley Labs., Edwards Labs., Cavitron, Bird Corp. subs. 3M Corp., Vascor subs. Johnson & Johnson. Served with USN, 1943-48. Mem. Am. Rocket Soc., Am. Ordnance Assn., U.S. Naval Acad. Alumni Assn., Sigma Alpha Epsilon. Developer early control systems for Dr. Michael E. DeBakey's left ventricular bypass pumps, 1966-67; patentee in field of ultrasonic power. Office: 19211 Sierra Gerona Rd Irvine CA 92715

HOUGIE, CHRISTOPHER JOHN, gift company executive; b. London, Apr. 10, 1951; s. Cecil and Barbara B. Hougie; came to U.S., 1955. B.A., U. Calif.-Berkeley, 1973; M.B.A., Stanford U., 1976. Co-founder, pres. Am. Gift Corp., San Diego, 1976-78, Santa Cruz, Calif., 1978—. Mem. Santa Cruz C. of C. Office: Am Gift Corp 986 Tower Pl Santa Cruz CA 95062

HOUGLAND, PATRICIA ANN, interior designer; b. Wellington, Kans., May 13, 1945; d. Ramon Pratt and Rachel Elizabeth (Golightley) Braun; m. David Allison Hougland, Aug. 7, 1965; children—Shea Allison, Noel David. B.F.A. in Interior Design, U. Kans., 1968. Qualified Nat. Council Interior Design. Interior designer Emporium Dept. Store, Palo Alto, Calif., 1971-72; art tchr. Los Altos (Calif.) Parks Dept., part-time 1974-75; designer, assoc. Don Stevenson, Ltd., Portland, Oreg., 1976-80; prin., ptnr. Noell Assocs., Inc., Portland, 1980-81; interior design project mgr. Design Through Research, Portland, 1981—. Vol. cons. Easter Seal Soc., Portland, 1979-80; mem. exec. bd. Portland Beautification Assn., 1980-81; bd. dirs., chmn. personnel Irvington Community Day Care, Portland, 1980-81. Mem. Am. Soc. Interior Designers (past dir., Recognition awards 1978, 79, 80), PTA. Democrat. Office: Design Through Research 319 SW Washington St Suite 720 Portland OR 97204

HOUK, JUDITH ANN, librarian, editor, publisher; b. Muncie, Ind., Feb. 2, 1935; d. William Harrison and Allie Maude (Allen) H. B.A. with honors, Ind. U., 1958, M.A. in Library Sci., 1959. Reference asst. and govt. document librarian Dayton (Ohio) and Montgomery County Pub. Library, 1959-63; reference librarian U.S. Air Force Inst. Tech., br. librarian Civil Engring. Center and Sch. of Systems and Logistics Wright-Patterson AFB, Ohio, 1963-64; librarian Westminster (Colo.) Pub. Library, 1964-67; regional librarian Inter-County Regional Planning Commn., Denver, 1967-68; system librarian Central Colo. Public Library System, Denver, 1968-72; exec. dir. Library Reports and Research Service Inc., Westminster, 1972-76; reference and documents librarian Colo. State Library, Denver, 1976-78, supr. State Govt. Info. Services, 1978-81; pres., treas. Library Reports and Research Service, Inc., Westminster, 1972—, exec. dir., 1981—; cons. acad. programs; vis. lectr.; seminar leader: asso. in urban affairs Nat. Inst. Public Affairs, Conf. Program on Met. Affairs, 1968. Mem. ALA (councilor-at-large 1972-76), Spl. Libraries Assn., Colo. Library Assn. (exec. bd. 1966-72, pres. 1967-68, exec. sec. 1970-72), Phi Beta Kappa, Beta Phi Mu. Democrat. Roman Catholic. Author: Classification System for Ohio State Documents, 1962; Public Libraries in the Denver Metropolitan Area: A Plan and Program for Public Library Development to 1985, 1968; contbr. articles on libraries to profl. jours. Home: 4140 W 80th Pl Westminster CO 80030 Office: Writers Tower Suite 400 1660 S Albion Denver CO 80220

HOUSE, JAMES PHILIP, public relations director; b. Kansas City, Mo., June 9, 1944; s. Frank Teays and Martha Ellen (Philp) H.; m. Betty Irene Bond, June 18, 1966; children—Sarah Beth, Jennifer Lynn. B.S. in Journalism, U. Wis., 1966, M.S. in Pub. Relations, 1967. Editor, Continental Ill. Nat. Bank & Trust Co. of Chgo., 1967-69; communications mgr. Am. Nat. Cattlemen's Assn., Denver, 1969-76; pub. relations dir. Broyles, Allebaugh & Davis, Inc., Denver, 1976—. Elder Reformed Ch. Am. Recipient Gold Key, Colo. chpt. Bus./Profl. Advt. Assn., 1980; Author Achievement award Gates Rubber Co., 1979. Mem. Pub. Relations Soc. Am. (Gold Pick award Colo. chpt. (2) 1979), Internat. Assn. Bus. Communicators, Nat. Agri-Mktg. Assn. (past chpt. pres.). Clubs: Rocky Mountain Road Runners, Trout Unlimited. Contbr. articles to profl., sports, religious publs. Office: 31 Denver Technol Ctr Englewood CO 80111

HOUSE, PATRICK LORY, mechanical engineer; b. Boise, Idaho, Sept. 1, 1940; s. Anthony Lee and Josephine Mary (Jullion) H.; m. Bonnie Jean Evans, Dec. 3, 1966; children—Brian, Christopher, Stephen, Phillip. B.S. in Mech. Engring., U. Wyo., Laramie, 1963; lic. profl. engr. Idaho, Wyo., Mont. Cons. Smith and Monroe Engrs., Boise, 1964-69; v.p., ptnr. Felts-House Engring. Inc., Boise, 1969—. Bd. dirs. Boise Youth Baseball, 1980—. Mem. ASHRAE (edn. dir. Idaho sect.), Idaho Soc. Profl. Engrs., ASME. Roman Catholic. Home: 4205 Green Meadow Dr Meridian ID 83642 Office: 8131 Crestwood Dr Boise ID 83704

HOUSE, REESE MILTON, counselor, educator, therapist, consultant; b. Noblesville, Ind., May 18, 1938; s. William Kenneth and Myrtle Audrey (Gustin) H.; children—Martha Kelly, Karen Elizabeth. B.S. in Bus. Edn., Ball State U., 1960; M.A. in Counseling, 1961; Ed.D. in Counseling, Oreg. State U., 1970. Cert. counselor, sch. psychologist Oreg. Counselor Tipton Twp. Schs., Onward, Ind., 1961-62, Monroe-Woodbury Schs., Monroe, N.Y., 1962-68; counselor-educator Western Oreg. State Coll., Monmouth, 1969—; pvt. counselor, cons. Bd. dirs. City Ballet Portland, 1983-85, Phoenix Rising Service Ctr., 1982-85. Recipient Disting. Service award Oreg. Personnel and Guidance Assn., 1976, 80, Leona Tyler award, 1982. Mem. Am. Personnel and Guidance Assn., Oreg. Personnel and Guidance Assn., Assn. Counselor Edn. and Supervision, Assn. Specialists Group Work, Am. Sch. Counselor Assn., Oreg. Sch. Counselor Assn. Democrat. Office: Dept Counseling Western Oreg State Coll Monmouth OR 97361

HOUSEN, JACK HOBART, educational administrator; b. Huntington, W.Va., Dec. 25, 1922; s. James Hobart and Hazel (Shelton) H.; m. Grace La Nelle Coley, Sept. 10, 1955; children—Nicole, Jill, Jack. B.A., W.Va. State Coll., 1948; M.Ed., Springfield (Mass.) Coll., 1950. Tchr., coach State Tchrs. Coll., Elizabeth City, N.C., 1950-52, 2d Ward High Sch., Charlotte, N.C., 1952-57; adminstrv. asst. Dept. Army, Huntington, 1957-58; tchr. Robinson Jr. High Sch., Toledo, Ohio, 1958-62; dir. phys. edn., coach Fontana (Calif.) Jr. High Sch., 1962-65; asst. prin. Aldar Jr. High Sch., Fontana, 1965-66; asst. prin. Marshall Jr. High Sch., Pomona, Calif., 1966-68, prin., 1968-78; prin. Ganesha High Sch., Pomona, 1978-83; prin. Lorbaar Jr. High Sch., Diamond Bar, Calif., 1983—. Served to 1st lt. AUS, 1943-46. Mem. Assn. Supervision and Curriculum Devel., Nat. Assn. Secondary Sch. Prins. Office: Diamond Bar Blvd Diamond Bar CA

HOUSE-SHARP, KATHLEEN TRACEY, tax consultant, accountant; b. Indianola, Okla., Jan. 1, 1928; d. George Rolland and Cordelia Mae (Higgins) House; m. Robert S. Sharp, Jan. 23, 1947 (dec.); children—R. Steven, Rebecca Sue Sharp Stine, Karen Kay Sharp Spurlock. Student, Modesto Jr. Coll., 1959-75, Stanislaus State Coll., Turlock, Calif., 1978. Enrolled agt., U.S. Dept. Treasury, 1981. Office mgr. I.C. Refrigeration, Inc., Modesto, Calif., 1959-62; chief acct. Miller Mfg. Inc., Turlock, 1962-63; acct., office mgr. Winter Motor, Inc. & Winter Volvo, Inc., Sacramento, 1971-73; owner House-Sharp Bus. Service, Hughson, Calif., 1978—; pvt. practice tax preparation, acctg., 1955-83. Served with USAF, 1963-71. Mem. Nat. Soc. Enrolled Agts., Calif. Assn., Enrolled Agts., Inland Soc. Tax Cons., Nat. Assn. Tax Cons., Nat. Soc. Pub. Accts., VFW Aux. Mem. Ch. of Christ. Club: Women of Moose. Office: 7312 E Whitmore St Hughson CA 95326

HOUSEWORTH, RICHARD COURT, banker; b. Harveyville, Kans., Jan. 18, 1928; s. Court Henry and Mabel (Lynch) H.; m. Laura Jennings, Nov. 1, 1952; children—Louise, Lucile, Court II. B.S., U. Kans., 1950; grad. Pacific Coast Banking Sch., 1962. Trainee, Lawrence Nat. Bank (Kans.), 1951-52; pres. and cashier, 1st Nat. Bank, Harveyville, 1952-55; asst. cashier Farmers & Stockmens Bank, Phoenix, 1955-58; asst. v.p. and mgr. Ariz. Bank, Scotsdale, 1958-62, v.p. and mgr. Phoenix home office, 1962-64, v.p., mgr. coml. loan dept., 1964-67, sr. v.p. and area supr. Tucson br., 1967-72, exec. v.p. br. adminstrn. Phoenix, 1972-82, exec. v.p., sr. corp. bus. devel. officer, 1982—. Pres. Barrow Neurol. Found., 1983; bd. dirs., chmn. Phoenix Urban League; treas. Valley of the Sun United Way, 1982, also dir.; bd. dirs. Vol. Bur. Maricopa County Scottsdale C. of C., Tucson Conquistadores. Served with U.S. Army, 1946-48. 1st recipient Scottsdale Jr. C. of C. Disting. Service award. Mem. Arizona Bankers Assn. (dir., chmn. govt. relations com. and resolutions com.), Robert Morris Assocs. Republican. Episcopalian. Clubs: Phoenix Country, Paradise Valley Country (Ariz.). Office: 101 N First Ave Phoenix AZ 85003

HOUSH, PHYLLIS IRENE BAKER, secretary; b. Pueblo, Colo., Aug. 23, 1934; d. Samuel Elvin and Rosella Pearl (Smith) Baker; student pub. schs., Pueblo; m. Sidney William Housh, May 19, 1951; children—Barbara Louise Housh Stewart, Michael William, Rebecca Kay. Typist, High Country News, 1964-65; clk.-typist, then prin. clk. stenographer So. Colo. State Coll., Pueblo, 1966-74; sec. to dean U. So. Colo., Pueblo, 1974-79; adminstrv. asst., sec. to pres. Pueblo Vocat. Community Coll., 1979-82; sec. to gov. Coll. Council, 1979-82; sec. U. So. Colo., 1982-83. Mem. Classified Employees Adv. Council; mem. classified staff, mem. legis. com., del. Statewide Liaison Council Higher Edn.; leader Girl Scouts U.S.A., 1960-67; chmn. March of Dimes; pres. PTA; pres., sec. Job's Mothers Club. Mem. Am. Bus. Women's Assn., Nat. Secs. Assn., Pueblo Vocat. Community Coll. Women's Orgn., VFW Aux. Republican.

HOUSHOLDER, KENNETH ADELBERT, architect; b. Dallas, Jan. 18, 1918; s. T. Franklin and Selma (Nicholson) H.; B.A., So. Meth. U., 1942; B.Arch., Yale, 1947; M.A., U. Calif. at Berkeley, 1965. Pvt practice architecture, Dallas 1947-50; mem. firm Marsh, Smith & Powell, Los Angeles, 1950-53; pvt. practice, San Francisco, 1953-64; exec. v.p. Donald Francis Haines, San Francisco, 1964-73; architect San Francisco Bur. Architecture, 1973—; now prof. history Golden Gate U.; lectr. history architecture, San Francisco, 1962-71. Mem. AIA, Soc. Archtl. Historians, Nat. Trust for Historic Preservation, San Francisco Symphony Soc., San Francisco Opera Guild, San Francisco Ballet Assn., Oakland Museum Soc., Nat. Wildlife Soc., Delta Chi, Alpha Rho Tau, Alpha Rho Chi. Republican. Christian Scientist. Clubs: Press (San Francisco); Oakland Athletic: S.M.U. Alumni, Rolls Royce Owners; Yale of San Francisco. Works include Oakland (Calif.) Post Office, 1965, San Mateo (Calif.) Jr. Coll., 1959. Home: 40 Lincoln Ave Piedmont CA 94611

HOUSKA, ROBERT BARON, college administrator, consultant; b. Chamberlain, S.D., Sept. 14, 1933; s. Raymond L. and Hazel E. (Potter) H.; m. Beverly Florence Ponto, Feb. 13, 1960; children—Derrick, Cerise, Carina. Student S.D. Sch. Mines, 1951-53; B.S., U. S.D., 1959; M.Ed., U. N.D., 1961; Ed.D., N. Mex. State U., 1969. Dir. guidance Juneau-Douglas Schs., Juneau, Alaska, 19—; dormitory mgr. N. Mex. State U., 1965-69; cons. Minn. Higher Edn. Coordinating Commn., St. Paul, 1969-70; asst. acad. dean Nat. Coll. Bus., Rapid City, S.D., 1970-74; v.p. service area devel. Colo. Northwestern Community Coll., 1974—; pub. relations coordinator Am. Sch. Counselor Assn., 1964-65. Bd. dirs. Craig (Colo.) C. of C., 1981-83; mem. Craig Planning and Zoning Commn., 1982—; candidate for county Commr. Moffat County (Colo.), 1982. Recipient Nat. Educator of Yr. award Outstanding Educators Am., 1972; NSF scholar, 1960; NDEA scholar, 1960-61. Mem. Am. Vocat. Assn., Psi Chi, Phi Delta Kappa, Phi Kappa Phi. Republican. Mem. Ch. of Christ. Clubs: Lions, VFW, Shriners, Elks (Craig); Masons. Office: 775 Yampa Craig CO 81625

HOUSKEEPER, BARBARA ANN, artist, art educator; b. Ft. Wayne, Ind., Aug. 25, 1922; d. Clarence Paul and Mary Louise (McCormick) Rossberg; m. Harold Lee Houskeeper, Jan. 5, 1946; children—Lee Paul, Ann Kathryn, Kathryn Louise. Student Knox Coll., 1940-42, R.I. Sch. of Design, 1942-43; Sch. of Art Inst. Chgo., 1944-46. Art instr. various Chgo. area schs. including Columbia Coll., Chgo., Countryside Art Ctr., Arlington Heights, Ill., 1962-78; dir. OxBow Summer Sch. Art, Saugatuck, Mich., 1974-75; artist and art instr., vis. artist San Francisco area, 1978-83; San Francisco State U., 1981, San Francisco State U., 1982; dir. workshops, El Granada, Calif., 1978-83; one woman shows: Michael Wyman, Chgo., 1972, Countryside Art Ctr., Arlington Heights, Ill., 1972, Habitat Gallery, Detroit, 1973, Zaks Gallery, Chgo., 1977, Artimesia Gallery, Chgo., 1979, San Jose State U., 1981, Montalvo Ctr. for Arts, 1982; group shows, include: U. Mo., Kansas City, 1977, Name Gallery, Chgo., 1977, Evanston (Ill.) Art Ctr., 1977, Kohler Art Ctr., Sheboygan Wis., 1979, Klein Gallery, Chgo., 1982. Docent Coyotte Point Museum San Mateo County, Calif.; mem. human resources group for Calif. schs. Recipient first prize New Horizons Exhibit, Chgo., 1969, 70. Mem. Arts Club of Chgo., Woman's Caucus for the Arts, Delta Delta Delta. Episcopalian. Home: 930 Columbus St El Granada CA 94018 Office: PO Box 1148 El Granada CA 94018

HOUSSELS, JOHN KELL, JR., hotel/casino exec., lawyer; b. Denver, Dec. 11, 1922; s. John Kell and Alice Mary Houssels; m. Nancy Claire Wallace, May 23, 1970; children—John Kell III, Leslie Jeanne, James O'Shaughnessy, Kelly Claire, Eric. B.S., U.S. Mil. Acad., 1945; LL.B., Stanford U., 1948. Bar: Nev. 1948. Asst. dist. atty. Clark County, 1948-50; individual practice law, Las Vegas, 1950-57; gen. mgr. El Cortez Hotel, Las Vegas, 1958-62; pres., dir. Hotel Tropicana and Showboat Hotel, Las Vegas, 1962-72, exec. v.p., dir. Union Plaza Hotel/Casino, Las Vegas, 1972—; vice. chmn. bd., v.p. Showboat Hotel/Casino, 1972—. Assemblyman, Nev. Legislature; chmn. United Fund Clark County; active Boulder Dam Area council Boy Scouts Am., So. Nev. Drug Abuse Council, NCCJ; bd. dirs. Taxpayers Assn. Served as 2d lt. Inf., AUS, 1941-42. Mem. ABA, Nev. Bar Assn., Calif. Thoroughbred Breeders Assn., Nev. State Horse Owners and Breeders Assn., Nev. Resort Assn. (pres.), Las Vegas C. of C. (dir.). Clubs: Las Vegas Country, Showboat Country. Office: One Main St Las Vegas NV 89101

HOUSTON, BRUCE, artist; b. Iowa City, Jan. 23, 1937; s. Robert W. and Ruth Harriet (Thamert) H.; (div.); 1 son, Chris. B.A., U. Nebr., 1959; M.F.A. in Painting, U. Iowa, 1974. Vis. artist Calif. Inst. Arts, Valencia, 1976, Otis Art Inst., Los Angeles, 1977, 80, Los Angeles City Coll., 1980, U. Iowa, 1980, Claremont (Calif.) Graduate Sch., 1980, N. Tex. State U., Denton, 1981, U. Ga., Athens, 1982. One-man shows: Orlando Gallery, Encino, Calif., 1977, 78, 80, Shade Gallery, Lenox, Mass., 1979, Molly Barnes Gallery, Los Angeles, 1980, 82, Jehu Galleries, San Francisco, 1981, Framingdun, Omaha, 1981, Allan Stone Galleries, N.Y.C., 1981; group shows: Los Angeles Inst. Contemporary Art, 1975, 78, 80, 81, San Diego Mus. Art, 1980, Dayton (Ohio) Art Inst., 1981, El Paso (Tex.) Mus. Art, 1981, Siegel Contemporary Art, 1982, N.Y.C., Downey (Calif.) Mus. Art, 1976, 82, Fresno (Calif.) Arts Center, 1982. Served with Air N.G. Episcopalian. Work reviewed in numerous profl. jours. Address: 600 Moulton Ave Suite 300 Los Angeles CA 90031

HOUTS, MARSHALL WILSON, lawyer, author, editor; b. Chattanooga, June 28, 1919; s. Thomas Jefferson and Mary (Alexander) H.; A.A., Brevard Jr. Coll., 1937; B.S. in Law, U. Minn., 1941, J.D., 1941; m. Mary O. Dealy, Apr. 27, 1946; children—Virginia, Kathy, Marsha, Patty, Tom, Cindy, Tim. Admitted to Tenn. bar, 1940, Minn. bar, 1946, U.S. Supreme Ct. bar, 1967; spl. agt. FBI, Washington, Brazil, Cuba, Boston, 1941-44; partner Palmer & Houts, Pipestone, Minn., 1946-51; municipal judge, Pipestone, 1947-51; gen. counsel Erle Stanley Gardner's Court of Last Resort, Los Angeles, 1951-60; prof. law UCLA, 1954, Mich. State U., East Lansing, 1955-57; adj. prof. Pepperdine U. Law Sch., 1972—; clin. prof. forensic pathology Calif. Coll. Medicine, U. Calif., Irvine, 1972—; creator, editor TRAUMA, 1959—; cons. police depts. Served with OSS, 1944-46; CBI. Decorated Bronze Arrowhead. Author: Houts: Lawyer's Guide to Medical Proof, 1967; From Gun to Gavel, 1954; From Evidence to Proof, 1956; The Rules of Evidence, 1956; From Arrest to Release, 1958; Courtroom Medicine, 1958; Courtroom Medicine: Death, 3 vols., 1964; Photographic Misrepresentation, 1965; Where Death Delights, 1967; They Asked for Death, 1970; Proving Medical Diagnosis and Prognosis, (13 vols.), vols.), 1970; Cyclopedia of Sudden, Violent And Unexplained Death, 1970; King's X: Common Law and the Death of Sir Harry Oakes, 1972; Courtroom Toxicology, 6 vols., 1980; Art of Advocacy: Appeals, 1981; Art of Advocacy: Medical Cross-Examination, 1981. Address: 313 Emerald Bay Laguna Beach CA 92651

HOUX, MARY ANNE, investment company executive; b. Kansas City, Mo., Aug. 16, 1933; d. Rial Richardson and Geraldine Marie (McHale) Oglevie; B.S. in Edn., U. Kans., 1954; postgrad. U. Mo., Calif. State U., Chico; m. Phillip Clark Houx, May 12, 1962 (dec. 1974); 1 son, Clark Oglevie. Tchr. schs. in Mo., 1954-57; asst. to v.p. Woolf Bros., Inc., Kansas City, Mo., 1957-58; Midwest dir. C.A.R.E., Inc., 1960-63; legal sec., 1962-75; co-owner No Bull Custom Meats, Chico, Calif., 1975-79; owner H&P Investments, Chico, Calif., 1979—. Mem. Calif. Republican Central Com., 1972-74; mem. Butte County Rep. Central Com., 1972-76, sec., 1974-76; pres. Chico Rep. Women, 1973; adv. coms. Chico Unified Sch. Dist. Bd. Trustees, 1977—, pres., 1979-81; v.p. Chico State Assocs., 1981-83; mem. federated council Calif. Interscholastic Fedn., 1981—. Mem. Chico C. of C., Calif. Sch. Bds. Assn. (del. Butte County 1978—), Alpha Phi. Roman Catholic. Clubs: Butte Creek Country, Cosmos, Chico State Assos., Chico State U. Women, Chico State Faculty Wives (pres. 1969-70). Address: 860 Filbert Ave Chico CA 95926

HOVANCSEK, JOHN EUGENE, podiatrist; b. Cleve., July 28, 1934; s. Steven J. and Elizabeth (Moore) H.; student Ohio State U., 1953-56; D.P.M., Ohio Coll. Podiatric Medicine, 1972. Switchman, N.Y. Central R.R., Cleve., 1953-72; pvt. practice podiatry, Aberdeen, Wash., 1972—. Com. chmn. project review com. Health Systems Agy., S.W. Wash. Regional Council; treas. Timberland Opportunities Sheltered Workshop; mem. adv. bd. Twin Harbor Rural Health Consortium; mem. Trouble Shooters Adv. Council, Grays Harbor Assn. Retarded Citizens. Served with U.S. Army, 1957-59. Mem. Nat. Fedn. Ind. Bus., Am. Podiatry Assn., Podiatry Polit. Action Com., Am. Assn. Podiatry Adminstrn. Republican. Roman Catholic. Clubs: Friends of the Library, K.C. (past pres.), Lions (past pres.). Home: 2127 N B St Aberdeen WA 98520 Office: 2218 Simpson Ave Aberdeen WA 98520

HOVING, ROBERT ANDRE, utility exec.; b. Grand Rapids, Mich., Jan. 18, 1919; s. Robert and Jennie Andree H.; m. Mary MacLean Thompson, Aug. 31, 1940; children—Robert H., Maria Hoving Friedman, Schuyler. With Booth Newspapers Inc, 1946-72, mem. staff Jackson (Mich). Citizen Patriot, 1946-65, Washington bur., 1965-72; dir. pub. info. Detroit Edison Co., 1972-76, Colo.-Ute Electric Assn., Montrose, 1976—; chmn. pub. info. com. Western Systems Coordinating Council; cons. pub. relations. Trustee Mich. Heart Assn., 1959-63. Served with USN, 1944-46, USNR, 1946-51. Recipient award best news story of year Mich. AP, 1952, 53, 62, Headliner Medallion award, 1960. Mem. Internat. Assn. Bus. Communicators, Engring. Soc. Detroit (vice-chmn. publs. com. 1974-75, chmn. pub. relations com. 1975-76), Colo. Press Assn. Episcopalian. Club: Nat. Press (membership chmn. 1969-71). Chief judge elections standing com. corrs. in U.S. House and Senate press galleries, 1970. Home: 66110 Juniper Ct Montrose CO 81401 Office: PO Box 1149 Montrose CO 81402

HOWARD, DAVID, artist, collector; b. N.Y.C., Jan. 25, 1952; s. John Charles and Florence (Martino) H. M.F.A., San Francisco Art. Inst., 1974. Vis. artist, art historian San Francisco City Coll., 1973; grad. workshop instr. San Francisco Art Inst., 1973. One man shows: Images Gallery, N.Y.C., John Boles Gallery, San Francisco, Thomas J. Crowe Gallery, Los Angeles, Ohio U., Athens, San Francisco Art Inst.; group shows: Hansen-Fuller-Goldeen Gallery, San Francisco, Oakland Mus. Ultra Films, Palace of Fine Arts, San Francisco, De Saisset Art Gallery and Mus., Santa Clara, Calif., San Francisco Art Festivals, 27th thru 31st, San Francisco Art Inst., De Young Mus., Guggenheim Gallery, Orange, Calif., Neary Gallery, Santa Cruz, Calif.; represented in permanent Collections: Mus. Modern Art, N.Y.C., San Francisco Mus. Modern Art, Oakland Mus., De Saisset Art Gallery and Mus. Author: Photography for Visual Communicators, 1978; Perspectives, Interviews with Ansel Adams, Jerry Uelsman, Ralph Gibson, Robert Heineckin, 1979; contbr. articles to profl. jours. Office: 49 Rivoli San Francisco CA 94117

HOWARD, DONNA MARTA, educational administrator; b. Many, La., Sept. 18, 1942; d. Walter Anthony and Martha Virginia (Tischoff) Pennino; m. Bruce Hayes Howard, July 1, 1967; children—Kimberly Merrill, Matthew Glen. B.A., Pa. State U., 1965; M.Ed., U. Hawaii, 1975. Spl. asst. to press sec. U.S. Senator Harry F. Byrd, Jr., Washington, 1965-67; curriculum specialist U. Hawaii, Manoa, 1971-73; exec. dir. Kailua Satellite City Hall, Honolulu, 1973-78; v.p. instl. devel. Hawaii Loa Coll., Kaneohe, 1978—. Commr. Honolulu Bd. Water Supply; v.p. bd. dirs. Hale Kipa; bd. dirs., v.p. Kailua Community Council; founder Kailua Town Arts Fair, Windward Jazz Festival. Edn.

Professions Devel. Act fellow, 1972. Mem. Pub. Relations Soc. Am., Council Advancement and Support Edn., Pi Lambda. Democrat. Club: Plaza (Honolulu). Office: 45-045 Kamehameha Hwy Kaneohe HI 96744

HOWARD, ERNEST FREDERICK, accountant; b. Key West, Fla., Aug. 22, 1950; s. Franklin Sanford and Florence Isabel (Andersen) H.; A.A., El Camino Coll., 1973; B.S., Calif. State U., Dominguez Hills, 1975; children—Sarah M., Taira M. Accountant, Peat, Marwick, Mitchell & Co., Los Angeles, 1974-76; audit sr. Fox & Co., Century City, Calif., 1976-78; audit sr. Touche Ross & Co., Los Angeles, 1978; pvt. practice acctg., Playa Del Rey, Calif., 1978—; lectr. acctg. Calif. State U., Dominguez Hills, 1979; mem. mgmt. adv. com. Calif. State U. Dominguez Hills Sch. Mgmt., 1977-79. C.P.A., Calif. Mem. Am. Inst. C.P.A.s, Calif. Soc. C.P.A.s, Venice C. of C., Westchester C. of C., South Bay Bus. Round Table, Calif. State U. Dominguez Hills Alumni Assn. (fin. v.p., pres. acctg. chpt. 1977-80. Republican. Office: 323 Pershing Dr Playa Del Rey CA 90293

HOWARD, GEORGE THOMAS, theatre consultant; b. Portland, Oreg., June 8, 1929; s. George Thomas and Jeannette Olga (Eppenstein) H.; m. Karen Miriam Holm, June 16, 1950; children—Dana, Tamara, Christopher. B.A. in Physics, Reed Coll., 1951; B.S. in Elec. Engring., MIT, 1951, M.S. in Elec. Engring., 1952. Registered profl. engr. Calif., Ga., Ill., Iowa, Ky., Mass., Nev., N.J., N.C., Ohio, Oreg., Tenn., Wash., Wis. Supr. scene shop, instr. scenery design and constrn. Reed Coll., Portland, Oreg., 1947-50; instr. MIT, sr. div. elec. engring. and math. course in-plant students, Cleve., 1955-56; engr. large lamp div. Gen. Electric, Cleve., 1950-58; Western regional mgr. Wakefield Lighting div. I.T.T., Portland, 1962-65; exec. v.p., gen. mgr. Kliegl Bros., Western Corp., Los Angeles, 1965-70; vis. lectr. theatre architecture, engring. Calif. State U.-Northridge, 1972; cons. in theatrical and presentation facilities George Thomas Howard Assocs., Hollywood, Calif., 1958—; U.S. del. Theatre Engring. and Safety Orgn. of Internat. Scenography and Theatre Technicians, Hamburg, W. Ger., 1978. Fellow U.S. Inst. Theatre Tech. (exec. com. So. Calif. sect.); mem. Assn. Profl. Cons., IEEE, Illumination Engring. Soc. (western vice chmn., theatre, TV and film lighting com., 1923), Soc. Motion Picture and TV Engrs., Am. Soc. Theatre Cons. (dir. 1982), Nat. Acad. TV Arts and Scis., Nat. Fire Protection Assn., Am. Theatre Assn., Internat. TV Assn., Nat. Soc. Profl Engrs., Assn. Cons. Elec. Engrs., Profl. Engrs. Oreg., Profl. Engrs. Nev., Internat. Alliance Theatrical Stage Employees, Hex-Alpha, Eta Kappa Nu, Tau Beta Pi. Office: 7046 Hollywood Blvd Suite 711 Hollywood CA 90028

HOWARD, JAMES WEBB, investment banker, lawyer; b. Evansville, Ind., Sept. 17, 1925; s. Joseph Randolph and Velma Cobb (Johnson) H.; B.S. in Mech. Engring., Purdue U., 1949; M.B.A. in Finance, Western Res. U., 1962; J.D., Western State U., San Diego; m. Phyllis Jean Brandt, Dec. 27, 1948; children—Sheila Rae, Sharon Kae. Jr. engr. Firestone Tire & Rubber Co., 1949-50; gen. foreman Cadillac Motor Car div. Gen. Motors Corp., 1950-53; mgmt. cons. M.K. Sheppard & Co., 1953-55; plant mgr. Lewis Welding & Engring., 1956-58; investment banker Ohio Co., 1958-59; chmn. dir. Growth Capital, Inc., Cleve., 1960-68, San Diego, 1970—; pres. Meister Brau, Inc., Chgo., 1966-73; pres. Santana Rancho, Inc.; pres., dir. The Home Mart, The Bus. Mart, San Diego; also dir. various cos. Served with 69th Inf. Div., AUS, 1943-46. Registered profl. engr., Ind., Ohio. Mem. ASME, Nat. Assn. Small Bus. Investment Cos. (past pres.), Am. Mgmt. Assn., Nat. Assn. Realtors, Am. Bar Assn., Calif. Bar Assn., San Diego Bd. Realtors, Pi Tau Sigma, Beta Tau Epsilon, Tau Kappa Epsilon. Presbyterian. Mason. Home: PO Box A-80427 San Diego CA 92138 Office: 701 B St Suite 1300 San Diego CA 92101

HOWARD, JANE OSBURN (MRS. ROLLINS STANLEY HOWARD), ednl. cons.; b. Morris, Ill., Aug. 12, 1926; d. Everett Hooker and Bernice Otilda (Olson) Osburn; B.A., U. Ariz., 1948; M.A., U. N.Mex., 1966, Ph.D., 1969; m. Rollins Stanley Howard, June 5, 1948; children—Ellen Elizabeth, Susan (Mrs. John Karl Nuttall). Instr. U. N.Mex. Sch. Medicine, Santa Fe, 1968-70, mem. staff pediatrics, deaf blind children's program, Albuquerque, 1971-72, asst. dir. N.Mex. programs for deaf blind children, 1972—, instr. psychiatry, instr. pediatrics, coordinator deaf-blind children's program, 1972—. Cons. Mountain-Plains Regional Center for Services to Deaf-Blind Children, Denver, 1971-74, Bur. Indian Affairs, 1974. Active Cystic Fibrosis, Mother's March, Heart Fund, Arthritis Found., Easter Seal-Crippled Children. Trustee Harwood Sch. Recipient fellowships U. N.M., 1965, 66, 66-67, 67-68, U. So. Calif. John Tracy Clinic, 1973. Fellow Royal Soc. Health; mem. Council Exceptional Children, Am. Assn. Mental Deficiency, Nat. Assn. Retarded Children, AAUW, Pi Lambda Theta, Zeta Phi Eta, Alpha Epsilon Rho, Republican. Methodist. Home: 615 Valencia Dr SE Albuquerque NM 87108

HOWARD, JOHN VERNON, accountant; b. Monte Vista, Colo., May 30, 1950; s. Harold Stroup and Ellen Nora (Lamke) H.; B.A., Adams State Coll., 1972; m. Susan Marie Williams, Aug. 19, 1978. Office mgr. Ranch Way Inc., Monte Vista, Colo., 1972-75; v.p., staff acct. Dorr Acctg. P.C., Gillette, Wyo., 1975-78; partner Dorr & Assos., 1978—; dir. Abstract & Title Co. of Gillette. Vice-pres. Big Bros. Central Wyo., 1975-77; chmn. Gillette Civic Center Com., 1977-80. C.P.A. Mem. Am. Inst. C.P.A.s, Wyo. Soc. C.P.A.s, Colo. Soc. C.P.A.s, Campbell County C. of C. (treas., dir. 1980-83). Republican. Clubs: Optimists (v.p. 1978), Rotary, Elks. Home: 2500 Maple St Gillette WY 82716 Office: 710 W 8th St Gillette WY 82716

HOWARD, LARRY LADON, health service adminstr., educator; b. Elvins, Mo., Oct. 10, 1936; s. Lawrence Elmer and Clara Mabel (MacFarland) H.; A.A., Hannibal-LaGrange Coll., 1956; B.A., Baylor U., 1958; M.A., U. Mo., 1965, Ed.D., 1971; m. Janel Louise Norris, June 1, 1957; children—Jeffrey Lynn, Leslie Kent. Tchr. English, William Chrisman High Sch., Independence, Mo., 1960-64; instr. English Hannibal-LaGrange Coll., Hannibal, Mo., 1964-66, dir. curriculum, 1966-67, dean faculty, 1967-70; dean, v.p. acad. affairs Mo. Bapt. Coll., St. Louis, 1970-75; asso. prof. edn., chmn. dept. edn. Grand Canyon Coll., Phoenix, 1975-79; dir. organizational devel. Samaritan Health Service, Phoenix, 1979—; team leader accreditation visitation Nat. Assn. Trade and Tech. Schs., 1977-80; editorial cons. secondary English textbooks Alpha Omega Publs., 1979; lectr. in field; seminar facilitator for civil/religious orgns. Adv., Jr. Achievement, 1979-80. Edn. Professions Devel. Act fellow, 1968-70. Mem. Assn. Tchr. Educators, Tchr. Edn. Coordinating Council, Phi Delta Kappa. Baptist. Editor secondary English textbooks, 1977-79. Home: 4237 W Frier Dr Phoenix AZ 85021 Office: 1500 E Thomas Rd Phoenix AZ 85014

HOWARD, LORRAINE HARRIS, university dean; b. LaPine, Oreg., Dec. 17, 1921; d. Sidney Daly and Judith Crawford (Donahue) Harris; m. Nov. 1944 (div.); children—Joseph Sidney, Daniel William, William Weaver. Student Linfield Coll., 1941-42; B.S., Oreg. State U., 1945, Ed.M., 1961, Ph.D., 1964; postgrad. Portland State U., 1959, U. Oreg., 1961-62. Lic. marriage, family and child counselor, Calif.; secondary and vocat. credential in home econs., Oreg. Lab. technician Cutter Lab., Berkeley, Calif., 1943; asst. buyer Meier & Frank Co., Portland, Oreg., 1944-45; quality control chemist Hawley Pulp & Paper Mill, Oregon City, Oreg., 1946-47; dental asst. and technician, Portland, 1948-49; asst. dir. Fruit Flower Day Nursery, Portland, Oreg., 1949-50; counselor Corvallis (Oreg.) Sr. High Sch., 1960-61; juvenile case worker Corvallis Juvenile Dept., 1962-63; lectr. Gen. Extension Evening Div. continuing edn. for women Oreg. State System Higher Edn., Portland, 1962-64; grad. asst. Sch. Edn., Oreg. State U., 1963; assoc. dean women, Calif. Poly. State U., 1964-81, asst. prof. 1964-68, assoc. prof., 1968-74, prof., 1974-81, assoc. dean student affairs, 1981—; prof. human devel. Evening Div., Cuesta Coll., 1967-68; prof. human devel. Evening Div., Calif. Men's Colony, San Luis Obispo, Calif., 1979—; vol. counselor Family Service Counseling, 1970—; cons. in field. Recipient Cardinal Key, Calif. Poly. State U., 1972. Mem. AAUW (Calif. Poly. State U. rep. 1964-83), Calif. Assn. Women Adminstrs. and Counselors (rep. 1964-83), Calif. State Employees Assn. (v.p. 1967-68, chmn. Support Services Council 1968-73, pres. 1969-70, del. 1971-73), San Luis Obispo County Psychol. Assn. (pres. 1981-82, dir. 1982-83), Calif. Assn. Marriage and Family Counselors (rep. 1972-79), Am. Psychol. Assn., Am. Personnel and Guidance Assn., Calif. Women in Higher Edn., Panhellenic Council, Kappa Delta (v.p. 1942-43, pres. 1943-44, dir. 1976-77, treas. House Corp. Bd. 1977-78, mem. bd., 1977-82), Phi Kappa Phi (sec.-treas. 1965-66, pres. 1971-72), Omicron Nu, Phi Kappa Phi pres. 1981-82), Kappa Delta Pi, Delta Kappa Gamma. Home: 1724 Lee Ann Ct San Luis Obispo CA 93401 Office: Student Affairs Calif Poly State U San Luis Obispo CA 93407

HOWARD, MARGUERITE EVANGELINE BARKER (MRS. JOSEPH D. HOWARD), bus. exec., civic worker; b. Victoria, B.C., Can., July 30, 1921; d. Reuel Harold and Frances Penelope (Garnham) Barker; brought to U.S., 1924, naturalized, 1945; B.A., U. Wash., 1943; m. Joseph D. Howard, June 16, 1952; children—Wendy Doreen Frances, Bradford Reuel. Vice pres., dir. Howard Tours, Inc., Oakland, Calif., 1953—; co-owner, gen. mgr. Howard Travel Service, Oakland, 1956—, mng. dir. Howard Hall, Berkeley, Calif., 1964-75; co-owner, asst. mgr. Howard Investments, Oakland, 1960—; sec., treas. Energy Dynamics Inc. Bd. dirs. Piedmont council Campfire Girls, 1969-79, pres., 1974-79, mem. nat. council, 1972-76, zone chmn., 1974-76, 77-83, nat. bd. dirs., 1976-83; bd. dirs. Oakland Symphony Guild, 1969—. pres., 1972-74; mem. exec. bd. Oakland Symphony Orch. Assn., 1972-74, bd. dirs., 1972—; bd. dirs. Piedmont Jr. High Sch. Mothers Club, 1968-69. Mem. Oakland Mus. Assn., U. Wash. Alumni Assn., East Bay Bot. and Zool. Soc., Young Audiences, Am. Symphony Orch. League, Assn. Calif. Symphony Orchs., Chi Omega Alumni Seattle, Chi Omega East Bay Alumni Berkeley. Republican. Clubs: Womens Univ. (Seattle); Womens Athletic (Oakland). Home: 146 Bell Ave Piedmont CA 94611 Office: 526 Grand Ave Oakland CA 94610

HOWARD, MARTHA JAMISON, educator; b. Pasadena, Calif., Apr. 24, 1939; d. Edward Benjamen and Ada (McKeown) Jamison; m. Jerry Neal Howard, Nov. 23, 1974; 1 dau., Terese Ann. B.S., UCLA, 1961; postgrad. Mt. St. Mary's Coll., 1961-69; M.Edn., San Jose State U., 1975, postgrad., 1981-83. Tchr. phys. edn. and English, Bishop Montgomery High Sch., Torrance, Calif., 1961-62; tchr. 6th grade St. Jerome's Sch., Los Angeles, 1966-68; tchr. 5th grade St. Frances Solano-Sonoma (Calif.), 1968-69; tchr. phys. edn. and social studies Ortega Jr. High Sch., Cupertino, Calif., 1969-78; tchr. lang. arts and social studies Cupertino Jr. High Sch., 1981—, also dist. inservice tchr.; mem. staff devel. com. Cupertino Sch. Dist.; tchr. cons., writer South Bay Writing Project. Recipient cert. of appreciation, Cupertino Edn. Assn. Mem. Cupertino Tchrs. Assn. (v.p. 1981), Nat. Council Tchrs. English, Calif. Council Tchrs. of English, Central Council Teaching English (dir.). Roman Catholic. Office: 1650 Bernardo Ave Sunnyvale CA 94087

HOWARD, MARTHA WALLING, educator, writer; b. Shreveport, La., Jan. 28, 1916; d. Joseph Macon and Moss (Turner) Walling; B.A., Randolph-Macon Woman's Coll., 1937; M.A., George Washington U., 1942; Ph.D., U. Md., 1967; m. George Wilberforce Howard, June 5, 1938; children—George Wilberforce III, James Ewing. Instr. Latin, All Saints Coll., Vicksburg, Miss., 1937-39, Gunstan Hall Jr. Coll., Washington, 1940-42, public schs. Stafford and Fairfax Counties, Va., 1950-66; lectr. Greek and Latin, Am. U., Washington, 1965-66; lectr. humanities U. Ariz., Tucson, 1966-74, asso. prof. humanities, 1974-76; freelance writer, 1976—; books include: All Things to Sea (lyric poetry), 1942; Plutarch in the Major European Literatures of the Eighteenth Century, 1970, Comparative Literature Study (Choice List of outstanding acad. books), 1972; The Roland Woman: A Biography, 1983. Named to Hall of Fame, U. Ariz., 1975. Mem. Humane Soc. Tucson, Ariz. Hist. Soc., Phi Beta Kappa (Alpha chpt. Ariz.), Mortar Bd. Republican. Episcopalian. Club: U. Ariz. President's. Home: 177-C S Paseo Sarta Green Valley AZ 85614

HOWARD, THAYA MARGARET, businesswoman; b. Marion, Ind., Mar. 3, 1942; d. Paul Eugene and Margaret Hannah (Wonderly) Williams; m. Stanley E. Howard E. Jr., Sept. 1, 1961, children—Jeffrey Scott, Eileen Linnae. Student U. Oreg., 1960-63, N.W. Christian Coll., 1960-62, Coll. Sequoias, 1976-77, 80; B.A. in Home Econs., Calif. State U.-Fresno, 1978. Asst. librarian Eugene (Oreg.). Pub. Library, 1962-64; library clk. Gen. Dynamics, Ft. Worth, 1966; research asst. San Mateo County Library, 1974; dance instr. YMCA, Visalia, Calif., 1975-79; owner, prin., interior designer Process Design, Visalia, 1978-81; owner, prin., tng. dir. Contemporary Computers. Mem. Eugene C. of C., Am. Soc. Interior Designers (assoc.). Republican. Mem. Christian Ch. Office: Contemporary Computers 1478 Willamette Eugene OR 97401

HOWARD, VICTOR, mgmt. cons.; b. Montreal, Que., Can., Aug. 12, 1923; s. Thomas and Jean (Malkinson) H.; B.A., Sir George Williams U., 1947; B.Sc., 1948; Ph.D., Mich. State U., 1954; m. Dorothy Bode, Dec. 25, 1953. Mech. design engr. Canadian Vickers Ltd., Montreal, 1942-46; with Aluminum Co. Can., 1946-48, E.B. Badger Co., Boston, 1948-50; asst. prof. Mich. State U., 1952-56; social scientist Rand Corp., 1956-58; staff exec., personnel dir. System Devel. Corp., Santa Monica, Calif., 1958-66; staff cons. Rohrer, Hibler & Replogle, San Francisco, 1966-69; mng. dir. Rohrer, Hibler & Replogle Internat., London and Brussels, 1969-74, partner, 1974, mgr. San Francisco, 1974—, dir., 1979—. Mem. Am., Western psychol. assns., U.S. Power Squadron (comdr. Sequoia Squadron 1981, lt. col. Calif. State Mil. Res. 1981), Sigma Xi, British Inst. Dirs. Clubs: Reform, Hurlingham (London); Thames Motor Yacht (Molesey, Eng.); Stockton Yacht; Univ. (San Francisco); Mason, Shrine. Home: 1460 Cherrywood Dr San Mateo CA 94403 Office: 1601 Old Bayshore Hwy Burlingame CA 94010

HOWARD, WALTER EGNER, vertebrate ecologist, educator; b. Woodland, Calif., Apr. 9, 1917; s. Walter Lafayette and May Belle (Cooper) H.; m. Elizabeth Ann Kendall, June 12, 1940; children—Thomas Kendall, Kathryn Spencer, John Casey. A.B., U. Calif., 1939; M.S., U. Mich., 1941; Ph.D. 1947. Fellow U. Mich., 1942, 1946-47; instr. zoology to prof. wildlife biology U. Calif.-Davis, vertebrate ecologist expt. sta., 1947—; frequent overseas UN cons. FAO and WHO. Served with AUS, 1942-46. Fellow AAAS; mem. Animal Behavior Soc., Brit. Ecol. Soc., Am. Soc. Mammalogists, Wildlife Soc., Ecol. Soc. Am., Western Soc. Naturalists, Sigma Xi, Phi Kappa Phi. Clubs: Rotary, Commonwealth. Contbr. over 300 articles to profl. jours. Home: 24 College Park Davis CA 95616

HOWE, DRAYTON FORD, JR., lawyer; b. Seattle, Nov. 17, 1931; s. Drayton Ford and Virginia (Wester) H.; m. Joyce Arnold, June 21, 1952; 1 son, James Drayton. A.B., U. Calif.-Berkeley, 1953; LL.B., U. Calif.-San Francisco, 1957. Bar: Calif. 1958, C.P.A. Calif. Atty. IRS, 1958-61; tax dept. supr. Ernst & Ernst, San Francisco, 1962-67; ptnr. Bishop, Barry, Howe & Reid, San Francisco, 1968—; lectr. on tax matters U. Calif. extension, 1966-76. Mem. Calif. Bar Assn., San Francisco Bar Assn. (chmn. client relations com. 1977), Calif. Soc. C.P.A.s.

HOWE, EDWIN HENRY, grain and cotton farmer; b. Hanford, Calif., June 7, 1926; s. Edwin Henry and Maude (Burr) H.; student public schs., Hanford; m. Larella Loraine Fincher, June 16, 1949; children—John Nelson, Rachel Loraine. With Westlake Farms, Inc., Stratford, Calif., 1946—, v.p., 1965-82, pres., 1983—; del. Nat. Cotton Council. Bd. dirs. Central Union Elem. Sch. Dist., 1960-76; pres. Kings River Conservation Dist., 1969; chmn. Kings County Water Commn., 1972, Kings River Water Assn., Empire Irrigation Dist., 1969, Tulare Lake Basin Water Storage Dist., 1969, Hacienda Water Dist., 1978. Served with USN, 1944-46. Recipient Carnegie medal for act of heroism, 1983. Lic. comml. pilot; amateur radio licensee. Mem. Assn. Calif. Water Agencies (dir. 1972—). Republican. Home and Office: 23311 Newton Ave Stratford CA 93266

HOWE, GARY KENNETH, national park administrator; b. Chgo., July 22, 1938; s. William Arthur and Mary Ellen (Oliver) H.; B.S., Colo. State U., 1962; m. Sondra Jean Bolitho, June 8, 1957; children—Russell B., Ronald D., Christine D. Bldg. mgr. GSA, Denver, Cheyenne, Wyo., Santa Fe, N.Mex., 1963-68; maintenance supt. Nat. Park Service, Grand Canyon Nat. Park, Santa Fe, 1969-71, Tumacalori Nat. Monument, Ariz., 1972-74; bicentennial coordinator Harpers Ferry (W.Va.) Design Ctr., 1975-76; mgmt. asst. Canyonlands Nat. Park, Moag, Utah, 1976-80; supt. Fort Laramie (Wyo.) Nat. Historic Site, 1980—. Office: Fort Laramie Nat Historic Site Fort Laramie WY 82212

HOWE, GEORGE EDWARD, geneticist; b. Indpls., Aug. 18, 1941; s. Edward Sheldon and Lee Atta (Hiatt) H.; student U. Vt., 1965-68; B.S., Purdue U., 1963; M.S. in Forestry, U. Wash., 1965; Ph.D., Mich. State U., 1971; m. Sharon Diane Emery, June 10, 1978; 1 dau., Summer Ann; stepson, David E. Stephenson. Forestry aid Forest Inventory, Bur. Land Mgmt., Baker, Ore., summer 1962; research/teaching asst. Forestry Sch., U. Wash., Seattle, 1964-65; asso. plant geneticist, sugar maple research Forest Service, U.S. Dept. Agr., Burlington, Vt., 1965-68; research asst. dept. forestry Mich. State U., East Lansing, 1968-70; regional geneticist Forest Service No. Region, U.S. Dept. Agr., Missoula, Mont., 1971—; faculty U. Mont. Sch. Forestry, Missoula, 1971—; vis. scientist Internat. Maize & Wheat Improvement Center, Mexico, 1977. Bloedel grad. scholar, U. Wash., 1963. Mem. Soc. Am. Foresters, N. Am. Quantitative Forest Genetics Group, Western Forest Genetics Assn. Unitarian Universalist. Clubs: Rocky Mountaineers of Western Mont. (pres. 1977-78), Missoula Hellgate Ski, Missoula Handball Assn., Toastmasters (pres. 1977). Author: The Forest Genetics Program for the Northern Region, 1973; contbr. articles to profl. jours. Home: 915 Parkview Way Missoula MT 59801 Office: Federal Bldg Missoula MT 59807

HOWE, L. NORMAN, marketing executive; b. Detroit, Oct. 6, 1931; s. Paul LaVerne and Mary (Parks) H.; m. Gloria Michael, Nov. 27, 1981; children—Kevin, Kelly. Mktg. dir. Kal Kan Foods, 1962-70; v.p., gen. mgr. Bill Burrud Prodns., Los Angeles, 1970-71; owner L. Norman Howe & Assocs., Los Angeles, 1972—, House of Mktg., Los Angeles, 1976—. Exec. dir. Coupons of Hope for City of Hope. Served with USMC, 1951-54. Mem. Am. Mgmt. Assn., UCLA Alumni Assn. Pub.: Pictures & Quotes, 1982; creator animal conservation TV series Animal World, 1970.

HOWE, MAYNARD ALFRED, JR., psychotherapist, educator; b. St. Paul, June 1, 1947; s. Maynard Alfred and Dorothy Marie (Schmidt) H.; 1 dau., Kara. B.S. with full honors, Rochester Inst. Tech., 1970; M.S., U. Maine, 1975; Ph.D., U.S. Internat. U., 1980. Lic. clin. sports psychologist Calif. Prof. psychology, asst. dir. grad. program psychology and clin. sport psychology U.S. Internat. U., San Diego, 1978—; psychotherapist, cons. San Diego Sport Psychology Ctr.; sr. exec. cons. indsl. psychology Behavioral Mgmt. Inst., San Diego, dir., commentator Human Agenda Sta. KUSI TV, San Diego; cons. to bus., industry and sports teams. Mem. Am. Psychol. Assn., Assn. Advancement Psychology, Internat. Assn. Sport Psychology, N.Am. Soc. Sport Psychology and Phys. Edn., Am. Assn. Coll. and Univ. Coaches, Western Psychol. Assn., Am. Coll. Sports Medicine. Contbr. articles to profl. jours. Home: 2567 Myrtle San Diego CA 92104 Office: 10455 Pomerado Rd San Diego CA 92121

HOWE, RICHARD C., state supreme ct. justice; b. 1924; B.S., J.D., U. Utah. Admitted to Utah bar, 1949; now justice Utah Supreme Ct., Salt Lake City. Office: State Supreme Ct State Capitol Salt Lake City UT 84114

HOWE, RICHARD ESMOND, JR., educator, musician; b. Murray, Utah, Apr. 30, 1927; s. Richard Esmond and Louise (Hill) H.; student U. Utah, 1946; B.S. in Music, Juilliard Sch. Music, 1951, M.S. in Music, 1952; student U. Florence (Italy), 1952-53; D.Mus. Arts, Eastman Sch. Music, 1956; m. Agnes Jensen, May 31, 1949; 1 dau., Mary Katherine. Mem. faculty Grinnell (Iowa) Coll., 1956-73, prof. music, 1963—, chmn. dept., 1959-62, 65-67, 70-72, chmn. div. humanities, 1971-72; dean San Francisco Conservatory Music, 1973—. Served with USNR, 1945-46. Fulbright grantee, Italy, 1952-53, 53-54. Spl. research keyboard music of Baldassare Gallupi. Contbr. articles to mus. jours. Home: 409 Countyview Dr Mill Valley CA 94941

HOWELL, ALAN PETER, lawyer; b. Honolulu, Aug. 1, 1927; s. Hugh and Mavis Halcyon (Cochran) H.; B.A., Yale, 1950; LL.B., Cornell U., 1953; m. Sara Lynn Grounds, Dec. 26, 1954; children—David Wallace, Brian Cochran. Bar: Hawaii 1954. Law clk. to chief justice Supreme Ct. Hawaii, Honolulu, 1953-54; asst. pub. prosecutor City and County of Honolulu, 1954-58; mem. firm Hogan, Howell & Rother, Honolulu, 1958-71; sole practice, Honolulu, 1971—. Sixth dist. magistrate Dist. Ct. Honolulu, 1963-67. Pres. Kainalu Park Homeowners Assn., 1970. Served with AUS, 1946-47; to 1st lt. USAF Res., 1950-59. Mem. Am. Bar Assn., Am. Arbitration Assn. (nat. panel arbitrators), Bar Assn. Hawaii (chmn. Law Day com. 1964), Am. Judicature Soc., Hawaii Estate Planning Council, Bishop Mus. Assn., Honolulu Acad. Arts, Aircraft Owners and Pilots Assn., Exptl. Aircraft Assn. (chpt. pres.), Musicians Assn. Hawaii. Christian Scientist. Clubs: Pacific, Outrigger Canoe (Honolulu). Home: 76 Kailuana Pl Kailua HI 96734 Office: 733 Bishop St Suite 2515 Honolulu HI 96813

HOWELL, LAWTON WADE, corp. exec.; b. McKensive, Tenn., Aug. 20, 1948; s. Arden Keith and Rachael June (MacFadden) H.; student U. Pacific, 1966-68, agy. mgmt. courses U. Calif., Los Angeles, 1975, 78; m. LaValle Jean Dobretz, Jan. 4, 1969; 1 son, Lawton Wade. Office mgr. Robert J. Meath & Assos., Stockton, Calif., 1969-73; v.p. Buethe/Howell Assos. Ins., Stockton, 1973-75; chmn. bd. Inxuramerica Corp., Irvine, Calif, 1975—; chmn. bd. Dataxurance Corp., chief exec. officer Stratford-Lloyds, Ltd.; chmn. bd. Fabugraphics Corp.; chmn. bd., chief exec. officer CommuniGroup USA, Howell Corp., 1982—; cons. in data processing; internat. lectr. mgmt. and mktg.; Bd. dirs., mem. Advanced Practice Enrichment Team. Named Mr. Chmn., Assn. Mng. Gen. Agts., 1975. Mem. Calif. Ins. Assn. (dir. 1973-76, v.p. Orange County chpt. 1977), Fire Mark Soc. (cert. 1974), Soc. Cert. Ins. Counselors (cert.). Republican. Clubs: 552; Saddleback Court. Author ins. agy. personnel manual; author, editor bimonthly vet. medicine newsletter, bimonthly Practice Planning Manual for Veterinarians; designer computerized risk mgmt. analysis system for ins. brokers, data processing systems for comml. lithography, vet. hosp. mgmt. System. Contbr. articles to nat. trade publs. Office: 34169 Coast Hwy Suite 245 Dana Point CA 92629

HOWELL, NANCY, media specialist, copywriter, painter; b. San Francisco, Oct. 17, 1952; d. Kenneth Warren and Frances Dee

(Crawford) Howell. B.A. in Humanities, San Francisco State U., 1975. Co-pres., Rodell Co., San Francisco, 1977-79; v.p. Criswell Div., advt. and pub. relations, San Francisco, 1979-82; freelance media specialist, writer, San Francisco, 1982—. Mem. San Francisco Advt. Club, San Francisco Women in Advt. Address: San Francisco CA 94117

HOWELL, WARREN RICHARDSON, book dealer, publisher; b. Berkeley, Calif., Nov. 13, 1912; s. John Gilson and Rebecca Ruskin (Richardson) H.; student Stanford, 1930-32; m. Antoinette Oostermayr, Dec. 31, 1953. With John Howell-Books, rare book dealers, pubs., San Francisco, 1932-40, partner firm, 1940-45, mng. partner, 1945-56, owner 1956-71, pres., 1972—. Dir. English Speaking Union, 1956-61; sec., trustee Calif. Hist. Soc., 1956-60; 72-74; dir. Book Club Calif., 1956-71, v.p., 1972, pres., 1973—; dir. Manuscript Soc., 1960-65; founding mem., mem. exec. council Friends of Bancroft Library, 1957— mem. adv. council regions 9 and 10, Nat. Archives, 1972; mem. vis. com. Stanford U. Libraries, 1972-78, 82—. Served to lt. USNR, 1942-45; in U.S.S. Essex; comdr. amphibious forces Pacific fleet, 1943-45. Decorated Bronze Star medal with Combat V.; recipient 1st Warren R. Howell award Stanford U. Libraries, 1982. Life fellow Morgan Library, N.Y.C.; recipient Warren R. Howell award for outstanding service Stanford U. Libraries, 1982. Fellow Calif. Hist. Soc. (Henry R. Wagner Meml. award 1980); mem. Antiquarian Booksellers Assn. Am. (v.p. 1960-62, gov. 1964-67, 1968-72, v.p. 1974-76, pres. 1976-78), Sir Frances Drake Assn. (pres. 1957-59), Lincoln Sesquicentennial Assn. Calif., (v.p. 1959-60), Soc. Calif. Pioneers (hon. life). Clubs: Century, Grolier (N.Y.C.); Bohemian, Roxburghe, Chevaliers Du Tastevin (San Francisco); Pacific Union. Contbr. articles on Californians and Western Americana to hist. jours. Home: 1052 Chestnut St San Francisco CA 94109 Office: 434 Post St San Francisco CA 94102

HOWELLS, DANIEL PATRICK, business executive; b. Salt Lake City, Mar. 17, 1941; s. Daniel E and Quata (Lindsay) H.; m. Linda Peterson, Sept. 30, 1965; children—Brittney, Justyn, Adrianna, Tori, Kindra. B.S. in Journalism, U. Utah, 1966; M.S. in Advt. and Mktg., Northwestern U., 1967. Account exec. Grey Advt., N.Y.C., 1967-68; product mgr. Chesebrough Ponds, N.Y.C., 1968-69; product mgr. Internat. Paper, Oxnard, Calif., 1969-72; dir. mktg. Six Flags Over Tex., Arlington, 1972-75, v.p., gen. mgr., 1975-79; v.p., gen. mgr. Six Flags Magic Mountain, Valencia, Calif., 1979-82; pres., chief exec. officer Six Flags Corp., Los Angeles, 1982—; dir. Tex. Am. Bank. Bd. dirs. Tex. Tourist Council, 1975-79. Named hon. senator Tex., 1975. Mormon. Office: 515 Figueroa St 11th Floor Los Angeles CA 90071

HOWELLS, GARY NEIL, psychologist, educator; b. Eugene, Oreg., June 29, 1942; s. Edward Wyman and Eva Mae (Hart) H.; m. Jane Tsurue Kise, June 10, 1964; m. 2d, Christina Louise Doebele, July 14, 1978; children—Craig Edward, Kaeti Marie, Emily Jean. B.S., Oreg. State U., 1964; M.A., U. Utah, 1970, Ph.D. (NDEA fellow), 1971. Lic. profl. psychologist, Calif., 1978. Asst. prof. Raymond-Callison Coll., U. Pacific, 1971-79, assoc. prof. dept. psychology, U. Pacific, 1979—, dir. behavioral medicine clinic; pvt. practice clin. psychology and behavioral medicine, 1978—. Served with USN, 1964-67; to comdr. USNR, 1967—. Recipient Environ. Improvement award State Calif., 1977; Teaching Incentive award, 1978. Mem. Am. Psychol. Assn., Western Psychol. Assn., Nat. Register Health Service Providers Psychology, Soc. Behavioral Medicine, Sierra Club, Sigma Xi, Phi Kappa Phi. Democrat. Contbr. articles to profl jours. Home: 4533 Rialto Pl Stockton CA 95207 Office: U Pacific Stockton CA 95211

HOWERY, ERLE G., public relations agency executive; b. Montgomery, W.Va., May 5, 1923; s. Claude Erle and Mildred Mona (Conway) H.; student Concord State Coll., 1941-42, 46-47, U.S. Def. Lang. Inst., 1954; m. Margaret Jane Beamer, Dec. 7, 1954; 1 dau., Janis Eryl Howery Welch. Civilian publ. coordinator U.S. Army Far East Theatre, 1957; mem. editorial staff Stockton (Calif.) Record, 1957-58, Oakland (Calif.) Tribune, 1959-65; pub. newspapers, Fremont and Modesto, Calif., 1965-67; dir. public relations Calif. Sch. Employees Assn., San Jose, 1967-83; owner Erle Enterprises, Milipitas, Calif., 1983—. Served with U.S. Army, 1942-46, 52-56. Mem. Ednl. Press Assn. Am. (awards for editorial excellence 1973—). Club: East Bay Press (charter mem., past v.p.). Author: (with others) Two Years of Progress, 1957; Style Book, Media and Public Relations, 1978. Home: 620 Saturn Ave Fremont CA 94539 Office: Erle Enterprises 142 W Calaveras Blvd Milipitas CA 95035

HOWLAND, JAMES CHASE, engineer, consultant; b. Oregon City, June 2, 1916; s. Arthur Cornell and Sade Agusta (Chase) H.; m. Ruth Louise Meisenhelder, June 14, 1941; children—Joyce, Eric, Mark, Peter. B.S. in Civil Engring., Oreg. State U., 1938; M.S. in Civil Engring., MIT, 1939. Engr. Standard Oil Co. Calif., 1939-41; gen. mgr., dir. personnel, cons. CH2M Hill Engrs. Inc., Corvallis, Oreg., 1946—. Mem. City Planning Comn., Corvallis, 1961-74; trustee Linfield Coll., 1978—. Served with U.S. Army, 1941-45. Decorated Bronze Star. Mem. Nat. Soc. Profl. Engrs., Am. Cons. Engrs. Council, Profl. Engrs. Oreg., ASCE; Republican. Episcopalian. Mailing Address: CH2M Hill Inc PO Box 428 Corvallis OR 97339 Home: 2575 S Whiteside Dr Corvallis OR 97333 Office: 2300 NW Walnut Blvd Corvallis OR 97333

HOWLETT, PATRICIA ERSKINE, public relations executive, editor; b. Moscow, Maine, June 12, 1930: d. Charles Samuel and Elvina Mary (Thompson) Erskine; A.B., Colby Coll., 1952; M.A., U. San Francisco, 1979; children—Lorin Ann, Charles Erskine. English tchr. public schs., Orleans, Beverly and Brookline, Mass., 1952-57; tchr. English, Mt. Diablo Schs., Concord, Calif., 1960-67; broadcaster Radio Sta. KWUN, Concord, Calif., 1971-74; info. officer Mt. Diablo Unified Sch. Dist., Concord, 1974-79; dir. bd. devel. Calif. Sch. Bds. Assn., 1980; public relations exec. Assn. Calif. Sch. Adminstrs., 1980—; also pub./editor Thrust Mag., EDCAL edn. weekly newspaper. Bd. dirs. Sch./Community Relations Found., 1979—. Mem. Internat. Assn. Bus. Communicators, San Francisco Pub. Relations Round Table, Nat. Sch. Public Relations Assn. (accredited; Calif. coordinator 1981-83), Public Relations Soc. Am. (accredited), Calif. Sch. Public Relations Assn.(pres. 1979-80), Am. Assn. Sch. Adminstrs., Ednl. Press Assn. Am., Public Relations Round Table, Am. Soc. Assn. Execs., Phi Delta Kappa. Clubs: Commonwealth, San Francisco Press, Ninety Nines. Author: How to Work with the Media, 1979; Single Woman, (poetry), 1983; Independent Woman, 1983. Office: Assn Calif Sch Adminstrs 1575 Old Bayshore Hwy Burlingame CA 94010

HOWLEY, PETER A., telephone co. exec.; b. Phila., Mar. 5, 1940; s. Frank L. and Edith Jenkins (Cadwallader) H.; B. Indsl. Engring., N.Y. U., 1962, M.B.A., 1970; m. M. Mavin Renz, June 25, 1966; children—Tara Noel, Christina Maeve, Sean-Francis Cadwallader. With Long Lines div. AT&T Co., N.Y.C., 1965-73; dir. ops., dir. policy and procedures MCI Telecommunications, Inc., Washington, 1973-76; spl. assignment to Calif., Citizens Utilities Co., Stamford, Conn., 1976-77, gen. mgr. Ariz. Telephone div. Citizens Utilities Co., Kingman, 1977—, Citizens Utilities Rural Co., Kingman, 1977—. Dist. chmn. Boy Scouts Am., 1978—; 1st v.p. The Kingsmen, 1978-80, pres., 1979-80. Served with USAF, 1962-65, 68-69. Decorated Air Force Commendation medal. Mem. Kingman C. of C. (econ. devel. com. 1977-81, now 1st v.p.), Ariz. C. of C. (dir.), U.S. Ind., Rocky Mountain (2d v.p.), Ariz-N.Mex. (dir.) telephone assns., Am. Legion. Roman Catholic. Clubs: Rotary, Kingman Country, Hualapai Racquet (pres. 1977-78), Elks. Home: 3750 Cantle Dr Kingman AZ 86401 Office: 3405 Northern Ave Kingman AZ 86401

HOWSLEY, RICHARD THORNTON, regional govt. adminstr.; b. Medford, Oreg., Jan. 31, 1948; s. Calvin Nevil and Arvilla Constance (Romine) H.; B.A., Willamette U., 1970; M.S., Va. Poly. Inst. and State U., 1974; J.D., Lewis and Clark Law Sch., 1984; m. Susan Erma Johnson, Oct. 23, 1971; children—James Denver, Kelly Ann. Tech. editor U.S. Bur. Mines, Arlington, Va., 1971-72; program mgr., sr. planner KRS Assos., Inc., Reston, Va., 1972-74; exec. dir. Rogue Valley Council Govts., Medford, 1974-78; exec. dir. Regional Planning Council of Clark County, Vancouver, Wash., 1978—; vice chmn. Oreg. Council of Govts. Dirs. Assn., 1976-77, chmn., 1977-78. Mem. regional adv. com. So. Oreg. State Coll., 1975-78; mem. Medford-Ashland Air Quality Adv. Com., 1977-78. Carpenter Found. scholar, 1966-70, Leonard B. Mayfield Meml. scholar, 1966-67, Albina Page Found. scholar, 1966-70. Mem. Am. Planning Assn., Am. Inst. Cert. Planners, Internat. City Mgmt. Assn. Democrat. Methodist. Home: 13011 NE 9th Ave Vancouver WA 98665 Office: 1408 Franklin St Vancouver WA 98668

HOYE, WALTER BRISCO, college administrator; b. Lena, Miss., May 19, 1930; s. William H. and LouBertha (Stewart) H.; m. Vida M. Pickens, Aug. 28, 1954; children—Walter B. II, JoAnn M. B.A., Wayne State U., 1953. Sports/auto editor Detroit Tribune, 1958-65; sports editor Mich. Chronicle, 1965-68; assoc. dir. pub. relations San Diego Chargers Football Co., 1968-76; media liason NFL, 1972-75; community services officer San Diego Coll. Dist., 1976-78; placement officer Ednl. Cultural Complex, San Diego, 1978-80, info. officer, 1980-82, placement officer, adminstrv. asst., 1982—; cons. in field. Bd. dirs. San Diego County ARC; active San Diego Conv. and Tourist Bur., Joint Ctr. Polit. Studies, Am. Cancer Soc., San Diego Urban League, Neighborhood Housing Assn., Public Access TV. Named San Diego County Citizen of Month, May, 1979; recipient United Way Award of Merit, 1974. Mem. Am. Personnel and Guidance Assn., San Diego Career Guidance Assn., Nat. Mgmt. Assn., Assn. Calif. Community Coll. Adminstrs. Home: 6959 Ridge Manor Ave San Diego CA 92120 Office: 4343 Ocean View Blvd Suite 60-A San Diego CA 92113

HOYER, IVAN CEDRIC, investment corporation executive; b. Battle Creek, Iowa, Nov. 28, 1926; s. Verne B. and Ella V. (Warnock) H.; m. June L. Hughes, Aug. 14, 1949; children—Karen Hoyer Winters, Verne B. III, Gary W. B.S., U. Oreg., 1953, postgrad. 1953-55. Acct., writer, 1955-59; pub. relations dir. On-to-Oreg. Cavalcade, 1961-69; operator, mgr. sta. KNND, Cottage Grove, Oreg., 1961-69; pres. Lane Ventures, Inc., Cottage Grove, 1969. Vice chmn. Oreg. State Tax Examiners. Served with USAAF, 1945-46; Mem. Assn. Tax Cons., Oreg. Soc. Tax Cons., Kappa Rho Omicron. Republican. Rotary Internat. Office: Lane Ventures Inc 516 Whitteaker Ave Cottage Grove OR 97424

HOYMAN, JOHN, b. Dubuque, Iowa, July 14, 1924; s. Frank and Salome K. (Kinsella) H.; m. Dorothy P. Cox, Nov. 17, 1950; children—Deborah, Stefan, Timothy, Patrick. Student Loras Coll., 1940-49, Iowa U., 1949-50; B.S., J.D., Denver U., 1950. Bar: Colo. 1950. Chmn., Planning and Zoning Bd. Arvada (Colo.), 1960-67; mcpl. judge, Arvada, 1968-70; sole practice, Greeley, Colo., 1970—; tchr., lectr. Children's Hosp., Denver, 1975-83. Served with USAF Parachute Forces, 1943-46. Mem. VFW. Clubs: Elks, Moose. Office: 1115 11th Ave Greeley CO

HOYT, ANTHONY SAYER, advertising director; b. N.Y.C., Nov. 3, 1938; s. Everett Wilson and Elizabeth Alice (Sayer) H.; div.; children—Heidi France, Elizabeth Dow, Robert Everett. Student U. Va., 1957-60. Account supr. Rumrill-Hoyt Inc., N.Y.C., 1970-73; W. Coast mgr. N.Y. Mag., advt. mgr. New West, Beverly Hills, Calif., 1973-77; pres., chief exec. officer Tony Hoyt & Assocs., Los Angeles, 1977-80; advt. dir. Calif. Mag. (formerly New West), Beverly Hills, 1980—. Served with AUSR, 1968-72. Mem. Advt. Club Los Angeles, Mag. Resps. So. Calif., Western Pub. Assn. (mem. bd.). Democrat. Episcopalian. Club: Bel Air Bay (Pacific Palisades). Office: 9665 Wilshire Beverly Hills CA 90212

HOYT, JACK WALLACE, engring. educator; b. Chgo., Oct. 19, 1922; s. Claire A. and Fleta M. (Wheeler) H.; B.S., Ill. Inst. Tech., 1944; M.S., UCLA, 1952, Ph.D., 1962; m. Helen Rita Erickson, Dec. 27, 1945; children—John A., Katheryn M. (Mrs. Richard Everett), Annette M. (Mrs. Walter Butler), Denise M. Research engr. gas turbines Cleve. Lab., NACA, 1944-47; mem. staff Naval Ocean Systems Center, Navy Dept., DOD, San Diego, 1948-79, asso. for sci. fleet engring. dept., 1967-79, now cons.; vis. prof. mech. engring. Rutgers U., New Brunswick, N.J., 1979-81; prof. mech. engring. San Diego State U., 1981—. Mem. ASME (Freeman scholar 1971), N.Y. Acad. Scis., Soc. Naval Architects and Marine Engrs. Author, patentee in field. Editorial bd. Internat. Shipbldg. Progress, 1965—. Spl. research propulsion and hydrodynamics. Home: 4694 Lisann St San Diego CA 92117

HOYT, JAMES ROBERT, school administrator; b. Stockton, Calif., Aug. 15, 1927; s. Frederick Carrington and Elphie Viola (Stohl) H.; m. Mary Patricia Boyd, May 24, 1952; children—Frederick, Mary, Janette, Thomas. A.A., Coll. San Mateo, 1948; B.S., Calif. Poly. State U., 1951; M.S., Kans. State Tchrs. Coll., 1966; Ed.D., U. Idaho, 1973. Cert. adminstr., tchr., Calif., Idaho, Wyo. Tchr. various schs. Calif., 1954-65; prin. Del Oro High Sch., Loomis, Calif., 1966-69, Colfax (Calif.) High Sch., 1969-71; asst. prof. edn. U. Idaho Moscow, 1973; assoc. prof. edn. Calif. State Coll.-Stanislaus, 1974; prin. Moscow Sch. Dist., 1974-78, asst. sup., 1979-81, supt., 1978-79; asst. supt. Converse County (Wyo.) Sch. Dist. 2, 1981—; ednl. cons. various projects. Served with U.S. Army, 1951-54. Acad. Year fellow NSF, 1965-66. Mem. Am. Assn. Sch. Adminstrs., Assn. Supervision and Curriculum Devel., Phi Delta Kappa. Republican. Roman Catholic. Club: Rotary (Moscow, Idaho). Contbr. articles to profl. jours. Home: PO Box 2042 Glenrock WY 82637 Office: Converse County Sch Dist 2 PO Box 1300 Glenrock WY 82637

HOYT, LEEZA LEE, public relations/advertising firm executive; b. Cairo, Egypt, Nov. 27, 1955; (parents Am. citizens); d. Harry Grant Hoyt and Lucille Hoyt Kasner. B.A. cum laude in Pub. Relations, U. So. Calif., 1977; M.B.A., Loyola U., Los Angeles, 1983. Lic. in real estate sales, Calif. Real estate salesperson Ladera Realty, Los Angeles, 1976-78; account coordinator/jr. account exec. Lewis & Assocs., Los Angeles, 1978-79; jr. account exec. Ayer Jorgensen Macdonald (now N.W. Ayer, ABH Internat.), advt. firm, Los Angeles, 1979; recruitment adminstr. Lawler, Felix & Hall, Los Angeles, 1980-81; account exec. Clive Hoffman Assocs., Los Angeles, 1981—. Fund-raising chmn. for 1980 Spl. Olympics, Los Angeles Jr. C. of C. Named to Outstanding Young Women Am., U.S. Jaycees, 1980. Mem. Pub. Relations Soc. Am., Soc. Mktg. Profl. Services, Los Angeles C. of C. Republican. Clubs: U. So. Calif. South Bay Young Alumni (2d v.p. bd. dirs. 1982), Trojan Jr. Aux. (dir. 1978-80), Alpha Gamma Delta Alumni (exec. council 1983-84), Los Angeles Athletic.

HOYT, RICHARD C., psychologist; b. Corona, L.I., N.Y., Nov. 15, 1929; s. Charles Edward and Julia (Mahoney) H.; A.A., Calif. Sch. Profl. Psychology, 1974, M.A., 1975, Ph.D., 1977; m. Phyllis E. Iritano, Oct. 8, 1966; children—Tania S., Michelle D. Radio announcer, disc jockey Stas. WAVZ, New Haven, Conn., WBRC, Birmingham, Ala., WOR, N.Y.C., 1957-62; actor, N.Y. and Hollywood, 1962-72; pvt. practice psychology, Encino, Calif., 1977—, Simi Valley, Calif., 1980—; faculty Laverne U., 1980—. Served with USN, 1946-48. Diplomate Am. Bd. Profl. Psychotherapy, 1981. Mem. Am. Psychol. Assn., Calif. Psychol. Assn., Los Angeles County Psychol. Assn., AFTRA, Screen Actors Guild, Mensa. Home: 2537 Verda Ct Simi CA 93065 Office: 2345 Erringer Rd Suite 211 Simi Valley CA 93065

HOYT, RICHARD WALTER, real estate appraiser, educator; b. Winchester, Mass., Apr. 16, 1939; s. Wendell Robert and Marian Pearl (Stoddard) H.; m. Robert Inez Buzo, Dec. 19, 1944; children—Jeffrey Richard, Matthew Robert. B.A., Calif. State U.-Long Beach, 1966, M.B.A., 1970; Ph.D., U. Ark., 1976. Right-of-way agt. Calif. Dept. Transp., Los Angeles, 1966-68; research assoc. U. Ark., Fayetteville, 1972-73; assoc. prof. real estate U. Nev., Las Vegas, 1973—; real estate appraiser, cons., Las Vegas, 1973—. Served with U.S. Army, 1959-62. Barrick Faculty Devel. grantee U. Nev., summers 1981, 82, 83. Mem. Soc. Las Vegas Exchangors, Am. Real Estate and Urban Econs. Assn., Real Estate Educators Assn. Republican. Contbr. articles to periodicals. Office: Coll Bus and Econs Univ Nevada Las Vegas NV 89154

HRPCHA, RICHARD JOHN, health care executive; b. Joliet, Ill., May 5, 1936; s. Joseph John and Olga (Balnis) H.; m. Virginia Pasternak, Oct. 27, 1962; children—Bridget, Gina. B.S. in Mgmt. Acctg., Lewis U., 1969; M.P.A., DePaul U., 1975. Mgr. data processing A.L. Mechling Barge Lines, Joliet, Ill., 1960-69; asst. to controller St. Joseph Hosp., Joliet, 1969-70; dir. fin. St. Anthony Hosp., Chgo., 1970-74; corp. fin. officer Rose Med. Ctr., Denver, 1974—; pres. Romed Corp., Denver, 1982—; part-time faculty Webster Coll. Served with U.S. Army, 1958-60. Mem. Hosp. Fin. Mgmt. Assn. (pres. Colo. chpt. 1977-78). Roman Catholic. Club: Edelweiss. Home: 6232 South Adams Dr Littleton CO 80121 Office: 4567 E 9th Ave Denver CO 80220

HSIAO, BRYAN CHIHGHSANG, cable TV and satellite communications products company executive; b. Taiwan, Nov. 16, 1951; came to U.S., 1976, naturalized, 1978; s. Tze-Chang and Tzung H.; B.S. in Mech. Engring., Nat. Cheng Kung U., Taiwan, 1973; M.S. in Mgmt. Engring., L.I. U., 1978; postgrad. Grad. Sch. Mgmt., UCLA, 1980; Materiel system analyst Marine Corps, Taiwan, 1973-74; mech. engr. 1st Nuclear Powerplant, Taiwan Power Co., 1975-76; info. system analyst Northrop Corp., Hawthorne, Calif., 1977-78; founder, pres. Hitek Systems Group, Torrance, Calif., 1979-82; pres., chief exec. officer Expertech Corp., Montebello, Calif., 1982—. Mem. Assn. Computing Machinery, IEEE, Ops. Research Soc. Am. Home: 4346 W 176th St Torrance CA 90504

HSIAO, FRANK S. T., economics educator; b. Taiwan, Sept. 14, 1933; came to U.S., 1961, naturalized, 1972; s. Chi-Lai and Chao-Chi (Pan) H.; m. Mei-Chu Wang, July 20, 1968; children—Edward C., Victoria C. B.A., Nat. Taiwan U., 1956, M.A., 1959; M.A., U. Rochester, 1964, Ph.D., 1967. Research asst. U. Mich., Ann Arbor, 1965-66; from asst. prof. to prof. econs. U. Colo., Boulder, 1966—; mem. internat. editorial bd. Irving Fisher Monograph Award and Frank W. Taussig Award Competition, 1970—. Fulbright-Hays fellow, 1975-76; Summer Research Initiation Faculty fellow, Grad. Sch., U. Colo., 1969, grantee, 1972-78; U. Rochester Fellow, 1961-64. Mem. Am. Econ. Assn., Econometric Soc., Asian Studies Assn., N.Am. Taiwanese Prof. Assn. Contbr. articles to profl. jours.; editorial advisor H.K. Econ. Papers, 1980—. Office: Dept Econs U Colo Boulder CO 80309

HSIEH, MIKE MING-CHENG, design engr.; b. Taipei, Taiwan, Aug. 10, 1951; s. Cheng-Noan and Hui-Inn (Chu) H.; m. Millie I-Jiuann Lee, May 19, 1979; 1 son, Allen Michael. M.S., Nat. Chiao Tung U., Taiwan, 1975; Ph.D., Tex. Tech. U., Lubbock, 1980. Sr. design engr. Intel Corp., Chandler, Ariz., 1980—. Mem. IEEE. Baptist. Home: 1324 W Brooks St Chandler AZ 85224 Office: Intel Corp MS418 5000 W Williamsfield Rd Chandler AZ 85224

HSU, CHIN-SHUNG, elec. engr.; b. Taiwan, Aug. 10, 1948; s. Chin-Chong and Mei-Yu (Chang) H.; Ph.D., Oreg. State U., 1978; m. Ning Wang, Dec. 4, 1976. Vis. asst. prof. Wash. State U., Pullman, 1978-79, Cleve. State U., 1979-80; asst. prof. elec. engring. Wash. State U., 1980—. Mem. IEEE, AAAS, Sigma Xi. Contbr. articles to profl. jours. Office: Dept Elec Engring Wash State U Pullman WA 99164

HSU, ELMER MING, engineering manager, statistical consultant; b. Kiangsu, China, Dec. 8, 1943; s. Ginn I. Hsu and Imei H. Huang; came to U.S., 1967, naturalized, 1978; m. Grace B. Lee, July 10, 1971; children—Edwin, Christina. B.A. in Acctg., Nat. Chung Hsing U., Taipei, Taiwan, 1965; M.S. In Stats., U. Southwestern La., 1971, Ph.D., 1974. Sr. scientist, prin. scientist, supr., then co-project mgr. Lockheed Electronics Co., Houston, 1974-80; statis. cons. Air Products and Chemicals, Allentown, Pa., 1980-81; tech. head Hughes Aircraft Co., Los Angeles, 1981—. Named an Outstanding Young Man Am., U.S. Jaycees, 1978. Mem. Am. Statis. Assn., Nat. Mgmt. Assn., Chinese Am. Profl. Assn. Roman Catholic. Home: 3644 Blair Way Torrance CA 90505 Office: R5/1753 PO Box 92426 Los Angeles CA 90009

HSU, GEORGE CHI, chem. engr.; b. Chung Ching, China, Sept. 10, 1942; came to U.S., 1965, naturalized, 1976; s. Lincoln Lin and Yun Tan (Chang) H.; B.S.Ch.E., Tunghai U., Taiwan, 1964; M.S.Ch.E., Ill. Inst. Tech., Chgo., 1967; Ph.D.Ch.E. (research fellow), Calif. Inst. Tech., Pasadena, 1971; m. Ingrid Ing-Ging Tang, June 15, 1969; children—Oscar K.W., Katherine W.I. Research engr. Nat. Cash Register Co., Dayton, Ohio, 1967; sr. engr., group leader, mem. tech. staff Jet Propulsion Lab., Pasadena, 1972—; cons. Recipient recognition on 10 tech. inventions NASA; Jet Propulsion Lab. in-house grantee in coal research, 1975-78. Mem. Am. Inst. Chem. Engrs., Am. Chem. Soc., Sigma Xi. Democrat. Baptist. Contbr. articles to profl. jours., chpt. in book. Patentee in field; inventor coal desulfurization and liquefaction processes. Home: 2622 Timberlake Dr La Crescenta CA 91214 Office: 4800 Oak Grove Dr Pasadena CA 91103

HSU, HSIANG-LIN, computer scientist; b. Szechuan, China, Mar. 30, 1944; came to U.S., 1967, naturalized, 1977; d. Fan-chi and Pin-hwei (Feng) K.; m. Kang Hsu, Dec. 21, 1968; children—Kang, Hsuan L., Lin. B.S., Tunghai U., Taichung, Taiwan, 1965; Ph.D. U. Nebr., 1971. Postdoctoral research assoc. Ohio State U., 1972-76; chem. info. scientist Chem. Abstracts Research Service, Columbus, Ohio, 1977-79; tech. staff engr. Hughes Aircraft Co., Fullerton, Calif., 1979-80, Rockwell Internat., Anaheim, Calif., 1980—. NSF fellow, Mainz, Germany, 1969; NATO fellow, Netherlands, 1976. Mem. Chinese Am. Profl. Soc., South Coast Chinese Culture Assn., Chinese Engrs. and Scientists Assn. So. Calif. Contbr. articles to profl. jours. Office: 3370 Miraloma MH 6 Anaheim CA 92803

HSU, HSIN-HUNG, agronomist, researcher; b. Taiwan, Republic of China, June 10, 1947; came to U.S., 1975; s. Yun-Hei and Chang-Mei (Lo) H.; m. Ruby Ching-Ying, Jan. 15, 1974; children—Paul, Alice. Ph.D., Miss. State U., 1979. Research asst. Taiwan Plant Protection Ctr., 1972-73; tchr. Taipei Mcpl. A&M Profl. High Sch., Taiwan, 1973-75; research asst. Miss. State U., 1975-79; head dept. agr. Albion Labs., Inc., Clearfield, Utah, 1979—; cons. in field. Mem. Am. Soc. Agronomy, Council of Agrl. Scis. and Technology. Contbr. in field. Home: 2128 N 1300 W Clinton UT 84015 Office: 101 N Main St Clearfield UT 84015

HSU, MING-TEH, nuclear engr.; b. Taiwan, June 10, 1940; came to U.S., 1969, naturalized, 1981; s. Kuai-teng and Chin-ju (Tong) H.; B.S. in Nuclear Engring., Nat. Tsing-Hua U., Taiwan, 1968; M.S. in Nuclear Engring., U. Md., 1974, Ph.D. in Nuclear Engring., 1974; m. Chun-mei, Jan. 27, 1979; 1 son, Johnny Meng. Engr., Singer Co., Silver Spring, Md., 1975; sr. application engr. Control Data Corp., Rockville, Md., 1975-78; sr. engr. Idaho Nat. Engring. Lab., Idaho Falls, 1978-81, Bechtel Power Corp., Norwalk, Calif., 1981—. Mem. Am. Nuclear Soc., Nat. Geog. Soc., Sigma Xi, Phi Kappa Phi. Author papers in field. Home: 513 Lyons

Way Placentia CA 92670 Office: 12400 E Imperial Hwy Norwalk CA 90650

HSU, PEI-CHENG, metallurgist; b. China, Dec. 18, 1947; came to U.S., 1972, naturalized, 1979; s. Simon Shiao-Kung and Tsu-Ven (Wu) H.; B.S. in Metall. Engring., Nat. Cheng Kung U., Taiwan, 1970; M.S. in Metallurgy, N.Mex. Inst. Mining and Tech., 1974; m. Shenn-Song Lee, Aug. 25, 1978; 1 dau., Vivian Ming-Hua. Research asst. N.Mex. Inst. Mining and Tech., 1973-74, 75-78; research asst. John D. Sullivan In-Situ Mining Research Ctr., Socorro, N.Mex. 1975-78; metallurgist solution mining div. UNC Teton Exploration Drilling Co., Casper, Wyo., 1978-80; plant supt. Uranerz, U.S.A. Inc. In-Situ Project, Casper, 1980. Mem. Soc. Mining Engrs. of AIME, Can. Inst. Mining and Metallurgy, Sigma Xi, Alpha Sigma Mu. Author articles in field. Home: 4040 Placid Dr Casper WY 82604 Office: 190 Pronghorn Casper WY 82601

HSU, YUNG-SHING, research and devel. engr.; b. Hangchow, China, Sept. 14, 1921; s. Cheng-Tze and Ba-Yin H.; came to U.S., 1963, naturalized, 1972; B.S. in Mech. Engring., Hunan U., China, 1943; M.S., Ore. State U., 1966; m. Debbie Liang, June 15, 1973; children—Fun-Gee Lien-Gee, May-Gee, Jin-Gee. Ballistics specialist 50th Arsenal, Chung King, China, 1943-46; instr. Kiang-Su Coll., China, 1946-47; engr., supr., dir. tech. tng. Air Asia Co., Taiwan, 1947-63; devel. engr., Omark Industries, Portland, Oreg., 1965-67, project engr., 1967-68; dir. engring. Omark-CCI, Lewiston, Idaho, 1968—. Registered profl. engr., Oreg., Idaho. Mem. Am. Soc. M.E., Am. Soc. for Metals, Soc. Automotive Engrs., Am. Soc. Quality Control, Nat. Soc. Profl. Engrs. Patentee in field. Home: 2414 6th St Lewiston ID 83501 Office: PO Box 856 Lewiston ID 83501

HU, CAN BEVEN, chemist; b. Taipei, Taiwan, Oct. 31, 1949; came to U.S., 1975; s. Der-Chang and Shen-Chi Hu; B.S., Nat. Taiwan U., 1972; M.S., U. Ky., 1976; Ph.D., M.I.T., 1980. Teaching asst. dept. chemistry U. Ky., Lexington, 1975-76; research asst. M.I.T., Cambridge, Mass., 1976-80; polymer scientist Thoratec Labs. Corp., Berkeley, Calif., 1980—. Whitaker Health Scis. fellow, 1978-80. Mem. Am. Chem. Soc., Soc. Plastics Engrs., Sigma Xi. Mem. Christian Ch. Contbr. articles on polymer chemistry to sci. jours. Home: Apt 6A 1741 Grove St Berkeley CA 94709 Office: 2023 8th St Berkeley CA 94710

HU, JACKSON KWO-CHAIN, electronic engr.; b. Taichung, Taiwan, Aug. 26, 1949; s. Lin-yun and Pi-Hsien (Lai) H.; m. Michelle Yee-Kuang, Jan. 20, 1954. Ph.D. in Computer Sci., U. Ill., Urbana, 1978. Staff engr. Zilog Inc., Campbell, Calif., 1978—. Mem. Assn. Computing Machinery, Chinese Inst. Elec. Engrs. Contbr. articles to profl. jours. Office: 1315 Dell Ave Campbell CA 95008

HU, JOHN CHIH-AN, chemist, research engr.; b. Nanchang, Hupeh, China, July 12, 1922; came to U.S., 1954, naturalized, 1965; s. Chi-Ching and Chao-Hsian (Tsen) Hu; B.S. in Chemistry, Nat. Central U., Nanking, China, 1946; M.S. in Organic Chemistry, U. So. Calif., 1957, postgrad., 1957-61; m. Betty Siao-Yung Ho, Oct. 26, 1957; children—Arthur, Benjamin, Carl, David, Eileen, Franklin, George. Dir. research dept. Plant 1, Taiwan Fertilizer Mfg. Co., Chilung, 1947-54; research asso. chemistry dept. U. So. Calif., Los Angeles, 1957-61; research chemist Chem Seal Corp. Am., Los Angeles, 1961-62; research chemist Products Research & Chem. Corp., Glendale, Calif., 1962-66, sr. research engr., materials and tech. unit, Boeing Co., Seattle, 1966-71, specialist engr. Quality Assurance Labs., 1971 ; lectr., China, profl. confs. Mem. Am. Chem. Soc., Phi Lambda Upsilon. Patentee Chromatopyrography; contbr. articles on analytical pyrolysis, gas chromatography, mass spectrometry, polymer characterization, chemistry and tech. of sealants and adhesives profl. publs. in Chinese and English. Home: 16212 122 SE Renton WA 98055 Office: Boeing Co M/S 23-22 PO Box 3999 Seattle WA 98124

HU, JOSEPH S. Y., lawyer; b. Honolulu, Mar. 7, 1953; s. Rene Choy Kee and Mary S.H. Hu. B.A. in Psychology, U. Hawaii, 1974, J.D., 1978. Bar: Hawaii 1978. Ptnr. Douthit, Darrah and Hu, Honolulu, 1978-80; asso. dir. Hawaii State Ethics Commn., 1981; ptnr. Hu and Tsuji, Honolulu, 1982—. Recipient U.S. Law Week award, 1978. Mem. ABA, Immigration and Nationality Assn., Hawaii Bar Assn. (dir.), Honolulu Chinese Jaycees (dir.), Hawaii Wilderness Adventure Travel Soc. (founder). Democrat. Office: 900 Fort St Mall Suite 910 Honolulu HI 96813

HU, STEVE SENG-CHIU, scientific research director, educator; b. Yangchou City, Kianksu Province, China, Mar. 16, 1922; s. Yubin and Shuchang (Lee) H.; m. Lily Li-Wan Liu, Oct. 2, 1977; children—April, Yendo, Victor. M.S., Rensselaer Poly. Inst., N.Y., 1940; Ph.D., MIT, 1942; postgrad. UCLA, 1964-66. Mng. tech. dir. China Aircraft/China Motor Programs, Douglas Aircraft Co., Calif., N.J., 1945-48, Kelly Engring Co., N.Y., Ariz., 1949-54; systems engr., meteorol. sci. dir. R.C.A., Ariz., 1955-58; research specialist Aerojet Gen., Calif., 1958-60; research scientist Jet Propulsion Lab., Calif., 1960-61; dir. research analysis Northrop Corp., Calif., Ala., 1961-72; dir. Century Research, Inc., Am. Tech. Coll., and U. Am. United Research Inst., Gardena, San Bernardino, Calif., 1973—. Dir., exec. v.p. Am. Astronautical Soc., Wash., 1963-70; cons. Hsin-Hwa Nuclear Reactor Program, Taiwan, 1954-58; prof. Auburn U., U. Ala., U. Ariz., U. So. Calif., 1957-73. Fellow Calif. Inst. Tech., 1943-44. Recipient MIT Salisbury prize and Sloane prize, 1941-42, Commission Aeronautical Affairs, Republic of China cert. of merit and cash award, 1945, Northrop Corp. cert. of merit, 1965. Mem. Am. Astronautical Soc., AIAA, Nat. Assn. Tech. Schs. Office: Century Research Bldg 16935 S Vermont Ave Gardena CA 90247

HUANG, FRANCIS FU-TSE, educator; b. Hong Kong, Aug. 27, 1922; s. Kwong Set and Chen-Ho (Yee) H.; B.S., San Jose State Coll., 1951; M.S., Stanford, 1952; profl. mech. engr. Columbia, 1964; m. Fung-Yuen Fung, Apr. 10, 1954; children—Raymond, Stanley. Came to U.S., 1945 naturalized, 1960. Design engr. M.W. Kellogg Co., N.Y.C., 1952-58; faculty San Jose (Calif.) State U., 1958—, asso. prof. mech. engring., 1962-67, prof., 1967—, chmn. dept., 1973-81; hon. prof. heat power engring. Taiyuan Inst. Tech., People's Republic China, 1981—. Served to capt. Chinese Army, 1943-45. NSF faculty fellow, 1962-64. Named Tau Beta Pi Outstanding Engring. Prof. Year, 1967, 76; recipient Calif. State Coll. System Distinguished Teaching award, 1968-69. Mem. ASME, Am. Soc. for Engring. Edn., AIAA, N.Y. Acad. Scis., AAAS, AAUP. Author: Engineering Thermodynamics—Fundamentals and Applications, 1976. Home: 1259 Sierra Mar Dr San Jose CA 95118 Office: Dept Mech Engring San Jose State Univ San Jose CA 95192

HUANG, GEORGE WENHONG, educator; b. Taiwan, China, Apr. 20, 1936; s. A-ch'un and Jun'keng (Jao) H.; came to U.S., 1962, naturalized, 1971; B.A., Taiwan Normal U., 1960; M.A., George Peabody Coll. Tchrs., 1963; M.Ed., N.Mex. Highlands U., 1967; Ph.D., U. Idaho, 1969; m. Linda Hsueh-hong Hsu, Dec. 10, 1961; children—John, Joseph. Librarian, China Nat. Library, Taipei, Taiwan, 1959-60; tchr., librarian Provincial Hsin Chu High Sch., Taiwan, 1961-62; librarian Taipei Am. Sch., Taiwan, 1962; asst. librarian N.Mex. Highlands U., 1963-67; teaching fellow U. Idaho, 1967-69, instr. library sci., 1969; prof. dept. edn. Calif. State U., Chico, 1969—, coordinator Asian studies, 1979—. Mem. ALA, Calif. Media and Library Educators Assn., Assn. Asian Studies, Tri-County Sch. Librarians Assn., Internat. Assn. Sch. Librarianship, Chinese Librarians Assn., Phi Delta Kappa. Club: Toastmaster (Chico pres. 1974, area gov. 1980—). Editorial bd. The University Journal, Calif. State U., Chico, 1979—. Contbr. articles in field to profl. jours. Office: Dept Edn Calif State U Chico CA 95929

HUANG, JOSEPH JUIN-SHYONG, structural engr.; b. Taiwan, China, Nov. 20, 1941; s. Huang Chuan Shou and Huang Juan Hsu; came to U.S., 1966, naturalized, 1977; B.S. in Civil Engring., Nat. Taiwan U., 1965; M.S., Lehigh U., 1968, Ph.D., 1973; m. Vivian Weiwei Wang, June 20, 1970; children—Peter B., Andrew B. Post-doctoral research asso. Lehigh U., Bethlehem, Pa., 1973; sr. structural engr. Skidmore, Owings & Merrill, Chgo., 1973-75; sr. structural engring. specialist Sargent & Lundy, Chgo., 1976-81; supr. Bechtel Power Corp., San Francisco, 1981—. Recipient A.F. Davis Silver medal Am. Welding Soc., 1971; registered profl. and structural engr., Ill., Calif. Mem. ASCE, Am. Concrete Inst., Structural Engrs. Assn. Ill., Sigma Xi, Contbr. engring. articles to profl. jours. Home: 35682 Gleason Ln Fremont CA 94536 Office: Bechtel Power Corp 50 Beale St San Francisco CA 94105

HUANG, ROBERT YU, aerospace company executive; b. Manila, Philippines, Jan. 20, 1932; s. Chen Jung and Chiao Ti (Yu) H.; m. Rita W. Wong. B.S. in Elec. Engring., Purdue U., 1952, M.S. in Elec. Engring., 1954; Ph.D., Syracuse U., 1962. Engr., Curtiss Wright Corp., Carlstadt, N.J., 1954-58; research engr., instr. Syracuse (N.Y.) U., 1958-62; sr. staff engr. TRW Systems, Redondo Beach, Calif., 1962-81, mgr. electronics and tech. ops. TRW Electronics Systems Group, 1981—. Mem. IEEE, Sigma Xi. Contbr. articles to profl. publs. Office: TRW Systems 1 Space Park Redondo Beach CA 90278

HUANG, WOONTSING WALLY, petroleum engr.; b. Pingtung, Taiwan, Nov. 12, 1949; came to U.S., 1974; s. Yun-Chun and Yu-Chun (Chien) H.; B.S., Nat. Central U., Taiwan, 1972; M.S., U. Okla., 1977; Ph.D., U. So. Calif., 1980; m. Grace Y. Lin, Aug. 14, 1977. Research asst. geomagnetism and paleomagnetism lab. U. Okla., Norman, 1975-76, Petroleum Engring. Sch., 1976-77, dept. petroleum engring. U. So. Calif., Los Angeles, 1977-79; research engr. Union Oil Co. of Calif., Brea, Calif., 1979—; physics tchr. Chinese Inf. Training Sch., Fonshan, Taiwan, 1973-74. Served to 2d lt. Chinese Army, 1972-73. Hampin scholar, 1971; Chunpu scholar, 1972. Mem. Soc. Petroleum Engrs. of AIME, Sigma Xi, Sigma Pi Epsilon. Contbr. articles to profl. jours. Home: 2328 Fallen Dr Rowland Heights CA 91748 Office: 376 S Valencia Ave Brea CA 92621

HUBBARD, DONALD, marine artist, writer; b. Bronx, N.Y., Jan. 15, 1926; s. Ernest Fortesque and Lilly Violet (Beck) H.; student Brown U., 1944-45; A.A., George Washington U., 1959, B.A., 1958; student Naval War Coll., 1965-66; m. Darlene Julia Huber, Dec. 13, 1957; children—Leslie Carol, Christopher Eric, Lauren Ivy. Commd. ensign U.S. Navy, 1944, advanced through grades to comdr., 1965; served naval aviator, ret., 1967; founder Ocean Ventures Industries, Inc., Coronado, Calif., 1969, operator, 1969-77; marine artist; author: Ships-in-Bottles, A How to Guide to a Venerable Nautical Craft, 1971; Buddleschiffe: Wie Macht Man Sie, 1972; The Complete Book of Inflatable Boats, 1979; editor: The Bottle Shipwright; contbr. articles in field to publs. SCUBA instr.; lectr. on marine art. Decorated Air Medal. Mem. Ships-in-Bottles Assn. Ipres. N.Am. div. 1982—), Nature Printing Soc., Writers Guild, San Diego Watercolor Soc. (bd. dirs. 1981-82), La Jolla Art Assn., Am. Soc. Marine Artists, Marine Hist. Soc., San Diego Maritime Assn., Nautical Research Guild. Home and Office: 1022 Park Pl Coronado CA 92118

HUBBARD, GREGORY SCOTT, physicist; b. Lexington, Ky., Dec. 27, 1948; s. Robert Nicholas and Nancy Clay (Brown) H.; B.A., Vanderbilt U., 1970; postgrad. U. Calif., Berkeley, 1974-76; m. Susan Artimissa Ruggeri, Aug. 1, 1982. Lab. engr. physics dept. Vanderbilt U., Nashville, 1970-73, staff scientist Lawrence Berkeley Lab. Dept. Instrument Techniques, Berkeley, Calif., 1974-80; dir. research and devel. Canberra Industries, Inc., Detector Products Div., Novato, Calif., 1980-82; v.p., gen. mgr. Canberra Semicondr., Novato, Calif., 1982—; cons. SRI Internat., Menlo Park, Calif., 1979 ; lectr. in field. Recipient Founders Scholarship, Vanderbilt U., 1966. Mem. IEEE, Am. Soc. Psychical Research, Materials Research Soc. Office: 24 Digital Dr No 1 Novato CA 94947

HUBBARD, HOWARD LELAND, banker; b. San Francisco, June 19, 1931; s. Albert Giles and Lorena (Watts) H.; m. Lou Juan M. Anderson, Nov. 3, 1951; children—Steven, Thomas, Richard. Student Sacramento City Coll., 1949-50; B.A., Sacramento State Coll., 1958; postgrad. U. Calif. Extension, 1958-61, Ind. U. Inst. Fin. Edn. Grad. Sch., 1974-76. Real estate salesman Watrous, McClory, Inc., Sacramento, 1957-58; loan officer Buhler Mortgage Co., Sacramento, 1959; asst. mgr. Capital Fed. Savs. & Loan Assn., Sacramento, 1959-63; exec. v.p. Senator Savs. & Loan Assn., Sacramento, 1963-71; pres. Equitable Savs. & Loan Assn., Portland, Oreg., 1971-82, also dir.; pres. Washington Fed. Savs. & Bank, Hillsboro, Oreg., 1982—, also dir.; dir. Cascade Natural Gas Corp., Oreg. Title Ins. Co. Chmn. Oreg. Consumer Adv. Bd., Home Owners Warranty Program Oreg.; bd. dirs., mem. exec. com. United Way Portland, 1977-83; bd. dirs. Oreg. Symphony Assn., 1977—, also past pres.; bd. dirs. Portland State U. Found., 1979—, pres., 1983; mem. exec. bd. N.W. Synod Luth. Ch. Am., 1973-80; regent Pacific Luth. U., 1979—. Served with USN, 1951-54. Mem. Portland C. of C. (dir. 1978-81). Republican. Clubs: Waverly Country, Arlington (Portland); Rotary (Hillsboro); Masons. Home: 4685 NW Malhuer Ave Portland OR 97229 Office: Washington Fed Savs & Bank 314 E Main St PO Box 9 Hillsboro OR 97123

HUBBARD, LYLE TURNER, JR., anthropologist, biologist, educator; b. Long Beach, Calif., Dec. 22, 1935; s. Lyle Turner and Jewel (Green) H. A.B., Linfield Coll., 1958; M.S., Oreg. State U., 1967; M.A., U. Oreg., 1970; Ph.D., Wash. State U., 1983. Research assoc., instr. dept. oceanography Oreg. State U., 1961-65; grad. teaching asst. in anthropology U. Oreg., 1966-69; environ. field officer Dept. Environ. Conservation, Juneau, Alaska, 1972-74; grad. teaching asst. in anthropology Wash. State U., 1979-80; assoc. prof. biology/anthropology U. Alaska, Juneau, 1980—; oceanographic and anthrop. field worker, 1958-79. Served with U.S. Army, 1958-60. Recipient award Alaska Native Health Service, 1981. Mem. Systematics Assn. (U.K.), Soc. Systematic Zoology, Soc. for Study Evolution, Soc. Vertebrate Paleontology, Am. Inst. Biol. Scis., AAAS, Paleontol. Soc., Am. Assn. Phys. Anthropologists, Am. Quaternary Assn., Am. Soc. Zoologists, Human Biology Council, Internat. Soc. Cryptozoology, Western Soc. Naturalists, Alaska Anthrop. Assn., N.Y. Acad. Scis., Pi Gamma Mu. Contbr. articles to profl. jours. Office: Sch Fisheries and Sci U Alaska 11120 Glacier Hwy Juneau AK 99801

HUBBARD, MARYJOANNE CHRISTINE, psychologist; b. Benton Harbor, Mich., Jan. 12, 1939; d. Harvey Howard and Vivian (Wolford) Halsey; children—Kim Rene, Craig Martin, Nicole Elizabeth. B.A., Calif. State U.-Fullerton, 1970, M.S., 1976; Ph.D., U.S. Internat. U., San Diego, 1981. Cert. marriage, family and child counselor, Calif. Counselor Orange County Juvenile System, 1967-69; psychometrist San Diego State U., 1970-71; grad asst. dept. psychology Calif. State U.-Fullerton, 1974-75; intern Olive-Vista Psychiat. Hosp., Pomona, Calif., 1975, Met. State Hosp., Norwalk, Calif., 1975-76; marriage, family and child counselor, Fullerton, 1976—; juvenile diversion psychologist Santa Ana (Calif.) Police Dept., 1976-80, police psychologist, 1980—; psychol. asst. Town and Country Psychol. Services, Orange, Calif., 1981—; instr. Orange County Sheriff's Acad., 1980—. Bd. dirs. Mariposa Women's Ctr., 1981—, COPES, 1979. Mem. Acad. Criminal Justice Scis., Soc. Police and Criminal Psychology, Calif. Assn. Marriage and Family Counselors, Calif. Psychol. Assn., Am. Psychol. Assn., Psi Chi. Contbr. articles to profl. jours. Office: Santa Ana Police Dept 24 Civic Center Plaza Santa Ana CA 92701

HUBBARD, RICHARD LEE, accountant, educator; b. Durango, Colo., Mar. 28, 1949; A.S., Mesa Coll., 1971; B.S., Ariz. State U., 1974; diploma in programming Barnes Sch. Commerce, 1967. Lead programmer Stockmen's Bank, Gillette, Wyo., 1976-78; field auditor Wyo. Dept. Revenue and Taxes, Gillette, 1978—; instr. Sheridan Coll., Gillette campus, 1977—; prin. Hubbard Acctg., Gillette, 1981—. C.M.A., Wyo. Republican. Methodist. Clubs: Masons, Shriners, Elks, Moose. Home: Box 804 Gillette WY 82716 Office: Box 2193 Gillette WY 82716

HUBBARD, ROBERT LANE, research chemist; b. Portland, Oreg., Apr. 12, 1948; s. Lyle Turner and Jewel (Green) H.; B.S. in Chemistry, Oreg. State U., 1970; Ph.D. in Chemistry, Tex. A&M U., 1976; m. Dianna K. Jones, Sept. 22, 1979; 1 dau., Colleen Marie H. Research chemist advanced displays br. Central Research Labs., Tex. Instruments, Inc., Dallas, 1976-78; sr. research chemist Display Research Group, Tektronix, Inc., Beaverton, Oreg., 1978—. Mem. Am. Chem. Soc. Author books, articles in field. Patentee in field. Home: 14370 SW Hart Rd Beaverton OR 97005 Office: Tektronix Inc Box 500 MS 50-426 Beaverton OR 97077

HUBBELL, ROBERT NEWELL, psychologist; b. Neenah, Wis., Oct. 23, 1931; s. Ralph Newell and Ruth Elizabeth (Lindsey) H.; m. Joann Marguerite Jansen, Aug. 14, 1954; children—Scott David, Brian Jansen. B.S. (ROTC scholar) Northwestern U., 1954; M.A., U. Wis., 1961, Ph.D., 1964. Lic. psychologist, Colo. Dean of men, asst. prof. U. Iowa, 1964-67; Am. Council on Edn. intern U. Calif.-Santa Barbara, 1967-68; assoc. prof., staff psychologist Colo. State U., Ft. Collins, 1968-72; coordinator Community Counseling Ctr., Granby, Colo., 1972-76; coordinator mental health services West Central Mental Health Ctr., Canon City, Colo., 1976-77; pvt. practice clin. psychology, Canon City, 1977—; behavioral sci. intern Nat. Tng. Labs., Bethel, Maine, summer 1968; cons. Pomona Coll., summer 1969, Luth. Ch. Am., 1969-70, Higher Edn. Assocs., 1970-72; adj. prof. Walden U., Naples, Fla., 1971—, Colo. State Penitentiary, 1977-79. Served to lt. (j.g.) USNR, 1954-57. Mem. Biofeedback Soc. Am. (cert.), Am. Soc. Clin. Hypnosis, Nat. Register Health Service Providers in Psychology, Am. Council Edn., Colo. Psychol. Assn. Methodist. Contbr. articles to profl. jours. Home: 2317 Greenway Circle Canon City CO 81212 Office: PO Box 687 Canon City CO 81212

HUBBS, JACK ROLLAND, printing co. exec.; b. Modesto, Calif., Jan. 27, 1937; s. Caleb Edmond and Evelyn Gertrude (Dotta) H.; B.S., Calif. Poly. State U., 1958; m. Barbara Louise Welsh, Dec. 4, 1975; children—Cassandra, Geoffrey, Alicia. Product mgr. Am. Type Founders, San Francisco, 1958-61; plant mgr. Del Monte Corp., Oakland, Calif., 1961-74; v.p. mfg. Jeffries Banknote Co., Los Angeles, 1974-78; pres. Graphic Press, Inc., Los Angeles, 1978-80; v.p. ops. Ticor Printing Group, Inc., Los Angeles, 1980—; pres. Jeffries Banknote Co., Los Angeles, 1981—. Mem. adv. bd. Calif. Poly. State U.; bd. dirs. Central City Assn. Los Angeles. Mem. Printing Industries Am., Graphic Arts Tech. Found., Nat. Assn. Printers and Lithographers, Internat. Assn. Printing House Craftsmen Republican. Clubs: La Casa De Vida, Poso Creek; Regency; Jonathan. Home: 28304 Golden Meadow Dr Rancho Palos Verdes CA 90274 Office: 1330 W Pico Blvd Los Angeles CA 90015

HUBER, BEVERLY JEAN, computer systems and human resources specialist; b. Minot, N.D., Mar. 30, 1932; d. Fred William and Bernice Lorrayne (Cooley) Buchwitz; B.S. in Edn. cum laude, Minot State Coll., 1951; B.M. in Piano, Am. Conservatory Music, Chgo., 1953; M.S.W., U. Calif., Berkeley, 1967; cert. Computer Learning Center, Los Angeles, 1981. Pvt. music tchr., pianist, accompanist, N.D. and Chgo., 1947-58; tchr. high sch. music, English and sci., N.D. and Calif., 1951-52, 59-63; med. caseworker Los Angeles County Bur. Med. Social Service, 1963-65, clin. social worker, summer 1966, 67 72; dir. social service St. Vincent Med. Center, Los Angeles, 1973 80; tchr. Computer Learning Center, 1982—; field work supr. UCLA Grad. Sch. Social Work, 1979-80. VA grad. fellow in psychiat. social work, 1966-67, NSF summer fellow in botany and chemistry, 1961; registered social worker, Calif.; licensed clin. social worker Calif. Acad. Cert. Social Workers. Mem. Soc. Clin. Social Workers, Nat. Assn. Social Workers, Roman Catholic. Club: Town Hall Calif. Home: 750 E Carson St Space 25 Carson CA 90745 Office: 3130 Wilshire Blvd Los Angeles CA 90010

HUBER, JOSEPHINE ECKERT, interior designer; b. Santa Fe, Jan. 20, 1915; d. Charles Joseph and Josephine (Perea) Eckert; m. Oscar Joseph Huber, Aug. 3, 1955; children—Josephine Huber Cook, Oscar Joseph. Owner, interior designer Eckerts' Inc., Albuquerque, 1946—. Bd. dirs. Casa Angelica, Boys Club of Am. Friends of Music, Albuquerque Opera Guild, N.Mex. Opera Assn., Santa Fe. Papal Order of Holy Sepulchre of Jersuleum awardee, 1977. Mem. Am. Soc. Interior Designers (founder, past pres. N.Mex. chpt.), Albuquerque C. of C. (past chmn. woman's com.). Roman Catholic. Clubs: Pilot, (past pres.), Albuquerque (past pres.).

HUCK, LARRY RALPH, manufacturers representative; b. Yakima, Wash., Aug. 10, 1942; s. Frank Joseph and Helen Barbara (Swalley) H.; student Wash. Tech. Inst., 1965-66, Seattle Community Coll., 1966-68, Edmonds Community Coll., 1969-70; 1 son, Larry Ralph. Salesman, Kirby Co., Seattle, 1964-68, sales mgr., 1968-69; with Sanico Chem. Co., Seattle, 1968-69; salesman Synkoloid Co., Seattle, 1970-71; tech. sales rep. Vis Queen div. Ethyl Corp., Seattle, 1971-75; Western sales mgr. B & K Films, Inc., Belmont, Calif., 1975-77; pres. N.W. Mfrs. Assos., Inc., Bellevue, Wash., 1977—; nat. sales mgr. Gazelle, Inc., Tomah, Wis., 1979-81; dir. sales Prime Time Travel Co.; owner Mad Platter Record Co.; owner Combined Sales Group, Seattle. Served with USMC, 1959-64. Mem. Nat. Council Salesmen's Orgns., Mfrs. Agts. Nat. Assn., Am. Hardware Mfrs. Assn., Northwest Mfrs. Assn. (pres.). Hardware Affiliated Reps., Inc., Door and Hardware Inst. Roman Catholic. Office: 3805 108th St NE Suite 220 Bellevue WA 98004

HUCK, LEONARD WILLIAM, banker; b. Sioux City, Iowa, Dec. 4, 1922; s. Jay Myles and Eula Lea (Pinkley) H.; m. Suzanne Lesher, July 26, 1947; children—Leonard William, Robert C., Wendy. B.A., Depauw U., 1944; postgrad. Southwestern Grad. Sch. Banking, 1965, Harvard U., 1944. Asst. mgr. Camelback Inn, Phoenix, 1946-50; summer resort mgr. St. Mary's Glacier Lodge, Idaho Springs, Colo., 1950; mgr. Ariz. Country Club, Phoenix, 1950-57; pres. Valley Nat. Bank, Phoenix, 1957—; faculty Assembly for Bank Dirs., 1968—; dir. Southwestern Sch. Banking, 1966—, dean for bankers, 1973-75. Pres. Phoenix and Valley of the Sun Conv. and Visitors Bur., 1975, dir., 1975-77; chmn. Maricopa County Heart Assn., 1967, Desert Found., 1966-71; pres. Scottsdale (Ariz.) Boys Club, 1965, St. Luke's Hosp., 1972-74; trustee, sec. Phoenix Art Mus., 1971. Served with USN, 1942-46. Named Phoenix Man of Yr., 1978. Mem. Bank Mktg. Assn. (dir. 1976—, pres. 1981-82), Phoenix C. of C. (pres. 1977, dir. 1974-79), Am. Inst. Banking, Ariz. Club Mgrs. Assn., Ariz. Hotel and Motel Assn., Ariz. Heart Assn., Ariz. Acad., Ariz. Bus.-Industry-Edn. Council (pres. 1980), Exec. Com. Blood Systems (dir.), Sigma Chi (named Significant Sig 1981). Episcopalian. Clubs: Valley of the Sun Kiwanis (pres. 1961), Scottsdale Dinner (pres. 1967), Paradise Valley Country (dir. 1974-77, sec., 1976), Kiva (pres. 1970-71), Phoenix Thunderbirds (big chief 1964), Valley Field Riding and Polo (v.p. 1978-79). Office: PO Box 71 Phoenix AZ 85001

HUCKABY, DAVID GEORGE, biology educator; b. Ponca City, Okla., Dec. 8, 1942; s. George Portal and Gladys (Roach) H.; m. Geraldine Renee Daigle, Dec. 26, 1967; 1 son, Scott David. B.S., La. State U., 1963, M.S., 1967; Ph.D., U. Mich., 1973. Assoc. prof. dept. biology Calif. State U.-Long Beach, 1973—. Mem. AAAS, Am. Inst. Biol. Scis., Am. Soc. Mammalogists, Soc. for Study of Evolution, Soc. Systematic Zoology, Am. Soc. Zoologists, Sigma Xi. Office: Dept Biology Calif State U Long Beach CA 90840

HUCKEBY, KAREN MARIE, graphic arts exec.; b. San Diego, June 4, 1957; d. Floyd Riley and Georgette Laura (Wegimont) H. Student Coll. of Alameda, 1976; student 3-M dealer tng. program, St. Paul, 1975. Staff Huck's Press Service, Inc., Emeryville, Calif., 1968—, v.p., 1975—. Recipient service award ARC, 1977. Mem. East Bay Club of Printing House Craftsman (treas. 1977-78), San Francisco Mus. Soc., Internat. Platform Assn., Am. Film Inst. Home: 509 Civic Center Richmond CA 94804 Office: 1311A 63d St Emeryville CA 94608

HUCKINS, CHARLES ALBERT, botanist; b. Honolulu, July 4, 1941; s. Thomas Averill and Sue (Edwards) H.; B.A. in Biology, Brown U., 1963; M.S. in Horticulture, Cornell U., 1967, Ph.D. in Botany, 1972; m. Mathilde Germaine Demisay, Sept. 27, 1975. Curator tropical plants Mo. Bot. Garden, St. Louis, 1974-77, asst. chief horticulturist, 1977-78, chmn. indoor horticulture dept., 1978-79; dir. Desert Bot. Garden, Phoenix, 1979—; adj. assoc. prof. dept. botany-microbiology Ariz. State U., 1980—; cons. S.I. Bot. Garden Assn., 1974-79; cons. hort. therapist Clove Lakes Nursing Home, S.I., 1974-79; cons. hort. taxonomist N.Y.C. Dept. Parks, 1973-74. Served with USMC, 1963-69. Oxford (Eng.) U. research grantee; recipient Wm. Frederick Dreer award Cornell U. Mem. Am. Assn. Bot. Gardens and Arboreta (chmn. plant collections com.), Central Ariz. Museums Assn. (v.p.), Ariz. Bot. Garden Assn. (founding), Sigma Xi, Phi Kappa Phi, Pi Alpha Xi. Author: Flower and Fruit Keys to the Ornamental Crabapples Cultivated in the U.S., 1967; A Revision of the Sections of the Genus Malus Miller, 1972; Chromosome Numbers of Phanerogams-Rosaceae, 1977. Office: 1201 N Galvin Pkwy Phoenix AZ 85008

HUCKLEBRIDGE, MARK HAROLD, hospital executive; b. Riverside, Calif., May 27, 1952; s. Ted H. and Ruth Helen (Bischoff) H.; m. Trish Jann, June 9, 1979; 1 dau., Molly Erin. B.A., U. So. Calif., 1974; student Pacific U., 1970-72; M.A., U. Wis., 1976. Research asst. Elvirita Lewis Found. for Geriatric Health and Nutrition, Santa Cruz, Calif., 1976-78; dir. research and info., 1978-80; dir. community relations Watsonville (Calif.) Community Hosp., 1980—. Mem. Hosp. Pub. Relations Assn., Am. Soc. Hosp. Pub. Relations, Pub. Relations Roundtable (founder, pres. 1980-82). Democrat. Presbyterian. Office: Watsonville Community Hosp PO Box 310 Watsonville CA 95077

HUDAK, PAUL ALEXANDER, reliability engr.; b. Youngstown, Ohio, Oct. 8, 1930; s. B.S. in Math., Youngstown U., 1958; m. Ingrid Gertrud Matzke, June 27, 1964; children—Frank, David, Greta. Chem. lab. technician Republic Steel Corp., Youngstown, 1950-51; chem. analyst N.Am. Aviation, Los Angeles, 1958-64; design engr. Douglas Aircraft Corp., Long Beach, Calif.; reliability engr. Chrysler Corp., Sterling Heights, Mich., 1973-77; sr. reliability engr. product assurance support group Boeing Airplane Co., Seattle, 1977—. Served with USMC, 1951-53. Mem. IEEE. Home: 10514 NE 120th Pl Kirkland WA 98033 Office: PO Box 3707 Mls 9W-13 Seattle WA 98124

HUDDLESTON, ROGER FRANCIS, youth-family therapist; b. Alamagordo, N.Mex., Oct. 18, 1941; s. R.F. and Virginia L. (Schwabach) H.; m. Judith Rose Smith, July 3, 1964; children—Garret, Hilary. M.A. in Edn. and Counseling, No. Ariz. U., 1981. Cert. tchr. spl. edn., Ariz. Correctional counselor Ariz. Dept. Corrections, Alpine, 1969-72; prin. Youth Vocat. Tng., Prescott, Ariz., 1972-79; counselor Quixote Community, Prescott, 1979-81; program mgr., asst. dir. Prescott Child Devel. Ctr., 1981—. Mem. Foster Care Orgn., Prescott; founder, instr. Prescott Child-Parent Tng. Group. Served with U.S. Army, 1962-64. Recipient Community Service award Dept. Econ. Security, 1982. Mem. Am. Personnel and Guidance Assn., Am. Orthopsychiat. Assn. Established first therapy foster home in No. Ariz. Home: 2106 Richard St Prescott AZ 86301 Office: Prescott Child Devel Ctr 710 Whipple St Prescott AZ 86301

HUDNUT, DAVID BEECHER, leasing company executive, lawyer; b. Cin., Feb. 21, 1935; s. William Herbert and Elizabeth Allen (Kilborne) H.; m. Robin Fraser, Apr. 12, 1958; children—David Beecher, Marjorie Elizabeth, Joshua Fraser, John Marshall, Benjamin Parker. A.B., Princeton U., 1957; J.D., Cornell U., 1962. Bar: N.Y. 1962, U.S. Supreme Ct. 1967. Assoc., Hughes, Hubbard & Reed, N.Y.C., 1962-67; v.p. U.S. Leasing Internat., Inc., San Francisco, 1969-76, sr. v.p., 1976—; dir. Assn. for Corp. Growth, 1977-79. Bd. dirs. Donaldina Cameron House, 1969-76, 80—, Services for Srs., 1970—; bd. dirs. No. Calif. Presbyn. Homes, 1971-77, chmn., 1973-76, 79—; bd. dirs. The Choate Sch., Wallinford, Conn., 1973-76, Edgewood Children's Ctr., 1979—, Ind. Colls. No. Calif., 1981—. Mem. Calif. Friends of Robert Frost. Republican. Presbyterian. Office: US Leasing Internat Inc 633 Battery St San Francisco CA 94111

HUDNUT, THOMAS CUSHMAN, educational administrator; b. Rochester, N.Y., May 8, 1947; s. William Herbert, Jr., and Elizabeth Allen (Kilborne) H.; B.A. magna cum laude, Princeton U., 1969; M.A., Fletcher Sch. Law and Diplomacy, Tufts U., 1970; m. Deirdre Steele Moran, Mar. 7, 1970; children—Sarah, Spencer, Peter. Tchr., dean of students St. Albans Sch., Washington, 1970-77; headmaster The Norwood Sch., Bethesda, Md., 1977-82, The Katharine Branson/Mt. Tamalpais Sch., Ross, Calif., 1982—; dir., v.p. Assn. Ind. Schs. Greater Washington, 1980-82; dir. Assn. Ind. Md. Schs., 1980-82, chmn. legis. affairs com., 1980-82. Bd. dirs. Wolf Trap Assocs., 1981-82; trustee Maret Sch., Washington, Cathedral and St. Mark's Sch., Calif.; dir. Assembly of Elem. Schs., Middle States Assn. Colls. and Schs., 1978-82; fin. chmn. Morella Congressional campaign, 1980; mem. fin. com. Mathias Senatorial re-election campaign, 1978. Naumberg fellow in voice, 1965; NSF grantee, 1969; Neil A. McConnell Found. grantee, 1968. Mem. Am. Guild Musical Artists, Assn. Ind. Schs., Nat. Assn. Prins. Schs. for Girls, Cum Laude Soc. Republican. Presbyterian. Clubs: Cosmos, Colonial. Author: L'Algerie, de Gaulle et l'Armée, 1975; contbr. articles to ednl. publs. including Independent School. Home: Box 1394 Ross CA 94957 Office: Box 887 Ross CA 94957

HUDSON, BARBARA, author; b. St. James, Minn., Feb. 2, 1921; d. Lloyd Edwin and Lois (Hardin) Hudson; B.A., U. Iowa, 1942; M.A., U. So. Calif., 1951; children—Jean Lois Powers Cross, Cathy Colleen Powers. Youth dir. Hollywood Presbyn. Ch., 1945-47; prin. Isabelle Buckley Schs., Van Nuys, Calif., 1948-50; asso. prof. drama, dir. church drama Calif. Lutheran Coll., Thousand Oaks, Calif., 1961-77; dir. drama Calvary Community Ch., 1977-82; pres. Barbara Hudson Ministries, Inc., 1982—; writer, producer, dir. pageants, for convs., all synods of Lutheran Ch., 1967-75; works include: Going with God, 1953; Henrietta Mears Story, 1957; Where Is God?, 1973; Bridge of Nothing Less, 1975; God's Power in Your Life, 1975; Bathsheba, 1983; also 1000 radio scripts. Served as lt. USMCR, 1943-45. Recipient Outstanding Actress award U. So. Calif., 1947, 48; winner Story contest Guideposts mag., 1977. Mem. Conejo Players, Am. Ednl. Theater Assn., Nat. Collegiate Players, DAR, Town Hall Calif., Internat. Platform Assn., NEA, Zeta Phi Eta, Gamma Phi Beta. Republican. Home: 1851 Village Ct Thousand Oaks CA 91360

HUDSON, DAVID EARL, cons. engr.; b. Clanton, Ala., Sept. 6, 1931; s. William Frank and Cecil E. (Parker) H.; B.A., Bob Jones U., 1954, M.Div., 1956; M.B.A., Western Mich. U., 1970; m. Shirley Hayward, Aug. 21, 1954; children—David, Stephen, Rebecca, Rosalie. Chief engr. Sta. WCMR, Elkhart, Ind., 1956-59; chief engr. Okinawa Network, Far East Broadcasting Co., 1960-67, dir. engring., 1967-79; cons. engr. Hammett & Edison, Inc., San Francisco, 1979-82; staff engr. Lockheed Aircraft Service Co., Ontario, Calif., 1982—. Registered profl. engr., Calif. Mem. IEEE (sr.), Soc. Broadcast Engrs., Internat. Computer Soc., Bioelectromagnetics Soc., Assn. Fed. Communications Cons. Engrs., Am. Nat. Standards Inst. (mem. C95 com.), Internat. Platform Assn. Baptist. Contbr. articles to Religious Broadcasting. Home: 12003 Maybrook Ave Whittier CA 90604 Office: Lockheed Aircraft Service Co PO Box 33 Ontario CA 91761

HUDSON, DEE TRAVIS, anthropologist; b. Denver, July 3, 1941; s. Oscar Melvin and Aileen Mae (Gurley) H.; m. Janice Ellen Mowers, Aug. 18, 1963; children—Lisa Marie and Laura Ann (twins), Michael Scott. A.A., Santa Ana Jr. Coll., 1968; B.A. cum laude, Calif. State U.-Long Beach, 1970; M.A., Ariz. State U., 1973, Ph.D., 1974. Test technician and supr. ITT Gilfillan Inc., Azusa, Calif., 1964-65; product support engr. FMA Inc., Los Angeles, 1965-66; computer test engr. Calif. Computer Products, Anaheim, Calif., 1966-70; curator anthropology Santa Barbara (Calif.) Mus. Natural History, 1973—; research assoc. Marine Sci. Inst. U. Calif., Santa Barbara, 1974-81, asst. research anthropologist dept. anthropology, 1982—; cons. and lectr. in field. Served with USN, 1962-64. NSF trainee, 1970-73; grantee Nat. Endowment Arts, NSF, NEH, Wenner-Gren Found., Smithsonian Instn.; Nat. Acad. Scis. exchange scholar to USSR. Fellow Am. Anthrop. Assn.; mem. Soc. for Am. Archeology, S.W. Anthrop. Assn. Author: The Holocene Prehistory of Old-World Arid-Lands: A Research Appraisal, 1974; editor: The Chumash Indians of Southern California: Selected Readings, 1979; contbr. numerous chpts. to books, articles to profl. jours. Home: 622 Burtis St Santa Barbara CA 93111 Office: Santa Barbara Museum Natural History 2559 Puesta Del Sol Rd Santa Barbara CA 93105

HUDSON, DOROTHY MORGAN, businesswoman; b. Omaha, May 23, 1928; d. Glover and Maria Elizabeth Morgan; student U. Colo., 1967-68, Metropolitan State Coll., 1974-75, Colo. Women's Coll., 1979-80; cert. Equal Employment Opportunity Commn. Acad., 1975; m. Harrison Hudson, Aug. 29, 1964; 1 dau., Ronnette Marie Marshall Davis. Owner, propr. D.M.H. Enterprises; pres. City Park Sundries, 1980-83; investigator, conciliator Equal Opportunity Commn., Denver, 1974-75, pay audit technician Air Force Finance Center, Denver, 1956-74. Committeewoman, Democratic party; neighborhood task force rep. Denver City Council. Recipient cert. of honor City of Denver, 1976, Colo. Centennial-Bicentennial Archivist Pin, 1976; named Colo. Outstanding Woman of Yr., 1979. Mem. NAACP, Nat. Council Negro Women, Colo. Black Women for Polit. Action, Nat. Assn. Ret. Fed. Employees, Nat. Profl. Writers Club, Nat. Fedn. Bus. and Profl. Women's Clubs, Nat. Assn. Female Execs. (rep. Nat. Ind. Bus. Assn.), LWV (bd. mem. 1977-78, editor newsletter), Colo. Press Assn., Adult Edn. Council Met. Denver, Greater Park Hill Community, Inc., Sigma Gamma Chi. Baptist. Clubs: Denver Jane Jefferson, Denver Century.

HUDSON, EDWARD VOYLE, linen supply co. exec.; b. Seymour, Mo., Apr. 3, 1915; s. Marion A. and Alma (Von Gonten) H.; student Bellingham (Wash.) Normal Coll., 1933-36, also U. Wash.; m. Margaret Carolyn Greely, Dec. 24, 1939; children—Edward G., Carolyn K. Asst. to mgr. Natural Hard Metal Co., Bellingham, 1935-37; partner Met. Laundry Co., Tacoma, 1938-39; propr., mgr. Peerless Laundry & Linen Supply Co., Tacoma, 1939—; propr. Independent Laundry & Everett Linen Supply Co., 1946-74, 99 Cleaners and Launderers Co., Tacoma, 1957-79; chmn. Tacoma Public Utilities, 1959-60; trustee United Mut. Savs. Bank; bd. dirs. Tacoma Better Bus. Bur., 1977—. Pres., Wash. Conf. on Unemployment Compensation, 1975-76; pres. Tacoma Boys' Club, 1970; v.p. Puget Sound USO, 1972—; elder Emmanuel Presbyn. Ch., 1974—; past campaign mgr., pres. Tacoma-Pierce County United Good Neighbors. Recipient Disting. Citizen's cert. U.S. Air Force Mil. Airlift Com., 1977; U.S. Dept. Def. medal for outstanding public service, 1978. Mem. Tacoma Sales and Mktg. Execs. (pres. 1957-58), Pacific NW Laundry, Dry Cleaning and Linen Supply Assn. (pres. 1959, treas. 1965—), Internat. Fabricare Inst. (dir. dist. 7 treas. 1979, pres.-elect 1980), Am. Security Council Bd., Tacoma C. of C. (pres. 1965), Air Force Assn. (pres. Tacoma chpt. 1976-77), Navy League, Puget Sound Indsl. Devel. Council (chmn. 1967), Tacoma-Ft. Lewis-Olympia Army Assn. (past pres.) Republican. Clubs: Elks, Shriners (potentate 1979), Masons, Scottish Rite, Tacoma, Tacoma Country and Golf, Jesters, Rotary (pres. Tacoma chpt. 1967-68), Tacoma Knife and Fork (pres. 1964). Home: 3901 N 37th St Tacoma WA 98407 Office: 2902 S 12th St Tacoma WA 98405

HUDSON, FREDERIC MINER, profl. grad. sch. exec. and educator; b. Lyons, N.Y., May 25, 1934; s. Albert Frederic and Clara (McChesney) H.; m. Pamela McLean, June 9, 1979; children—Jeffrey, John, Lisa Sue, Christopher. B.A., Kalamazoo Coll., 1956; M.Div. Colgate Rochester Div. Sch., 1959; Ph.D., Columbia U., 1968. Assoc. dean, instr. in philosophy Stephens Coll., 1961-64; asst. prof. philosophy, religion, and human devel. Colby Coll., 1964-69; acad. dean, grad. dean Lone Mountain Coll., 1969-72; pres., prof. adult devel. Fielding Inst., A Grad. Sch. for Mid-Career Study in Profl. Psychology and Human and Orgn. Devel., Santa Barbara, Calif., 1973—; cons. adult devel. issues, including stress, burnout, mid-life crisis, intimacy issues, career counseling. Rockefeller fellow, 1956; Danforth fellow, 1956-68. Office: 226 E de la Guerra Santa Barbara CA 93101

HUDSON, ROBERT H., artist; b. Salt Lake City, Sept. 8, 1939. B.F.A., San Francisco Art Inst., 1962, M.F.A., 1963. Works exhibited in permanent collections; Los Angeles County Mus., San Francisco Mus. Art, Stedelijk Mus., Netherlands, Oakland Mus. Art, Calif.; exhibits: Whitney Mus. Art Ann, N.Y.C., 1964-72, Los Angeles County Mus. Art., 1967, Phila. Mus. Art, 1967, Art Inst. Chgo., 1967, Walker Art. Ctr., Mpls., 1969, Moore Collection of Art, 1977; solo exhibits; Univ. Art Mus., Berkeley, Calif., 1972, San Francisco Mus. Modern Art, 1973, Hansen Fuller Goldeen Gallery, San Francisco, 1973, 75, 79, 82, Portland Ctr. for Visual Arts, 1977, Moore Coll. Art, Phila., 1978; group exhibits: Corcoran Gallery, Washington, 1975, Hayward Gallery, London, 1975, San Francisco Mus. Modern Art, 1978, 1st Western State Biennial Exhibit, 1979. Instr. San Francisco Art Inst., 1964-65, chmn sculpture and ceramic dept., 1965-66; asst. prof. art, U. Calif.-Berkeley, 1966-73; asst. prof. art San Francisco Art Inst., 1976—. Recipient Purchase prize San Francisco Art Festival, 1961, San Jose State Coll., 1964; Nellie Sullivan award, San Francisco, 1965; Guggenheim fellow, 1976; NEA grantee, 1972. Office: San Francisco Art Inst 800 Chestnut St San Francisco CA 94133*

HUDSON, RONALD JAY, university administrator, psychologist, educator; b. Los Angeles, Sept. 26, 1950; s. L. C. and Earlene (Nichols) H.; m. Arlene Marie Matthews, Dec. 29, 1979; children—Tiffany, Rashida, Ronald Jay II. A.A., East Los Angeles Coll., 1972; B.A. (Sears and Roebuck Found. scholar), U. Calif.-Irvine, 1974, Ph.D. (Regent fellow), 1979. Coordinator spl. services U. Calif.-Irvine, 1976-77, counseling psychologist, 1979-80, post doctoral intern, 1979-80, asst. to dean grad. div., 1980; asst. dean Stanford (Calif.) U., 1981—; lectr. psychology Calif. State Coll.-San Bernadino, 1978, Pepperdine U., Newport Beach, Calif., 1979. Recipient Univ. Services award, U. Calif. Mem. Third World Counselors Assn. (dir. Calif. chpt.), Black Council (chmn., sec. bd. dirs.), Assn. Black Psychologists. Contbr. articles to profl. jours.

HUDSON, SUSAN LYNNE, petroleum company office manager; b. Artesia, N.Mex., Mar. 20, 1959; d. Paul and Roetta Bell (Reves) H. Student N.Mex. State U.-Carlsbad, 1977, Las Cruces, 1977, Midland Coll., Tex., 1978, Met. State Coll., Denver, 1979—, Colo. Women's Coll., 1983—. Dental asst. Dr. R.A. Harden, Artesia, N.Mex., 1976; office mgr. William Siegnathaler, Artesia, 1977; sec. Oscar Rios Credit Collections, Las Cruces, 1977; draftperson J.W. Humbard and Assocs., Midland, Tex., 1978; orthodontic asst. Dr. Glen Rogers, Midland, Tex., 1978; sec., asst. Dr. Sohr, Denver, 1979; sec., Devon Corp., Denver, 1979-80; sec. Lewis Energy Corp., Denver, 1980-82; office mgr. Callon Petroleum Co., Denver, 1982—. Clubs: Deca (sec. 1977), Desk and Derrick of Denver (vice chmn. edn. com. 1982, chmn. edn. com. 1982—) named mem. of yr. 1982).

HUDSON, THOMAS RUSSELL, JR., advertising executive; b. Dalles, Oreg., Nov. 11, 1921; s. Thomas R. and Florence Christina (Koontz) H.; m. Pauline Gordon, Apr. 7, 1947; children—Thomas E., Heidi Hudson Baer. B.S., U. Oreg., 1943. Ins. agt. Thomas R. Hudson Ins., The Dalles, Oreg., 1947-68; newspaper pub. Blue Mountain Eagle, John Day, Oreg., 1968-69; advt. display salesman Medford Mail Tribune (Oreg.), 1969-72, advt. mgr., 1972—. Regent Boys and Girls Aid Soc. of Oreg., 1976—; bd. dirs. Jackson County chpt. ARC, 1982—; bd. dirs. Jacksonville Hwy. Water Dist., 1978—, Jackson County Legal Services, 1979—; mem. Oreg. Ho. of Reps., 1951-53. Served to capt. inf. U.S. Army, 1943-46. Mem. Sigma Delta Chi. Republican. Episcopalian. Clubs: Rotary, Masons, Elks. Home: 3255 Hollywood Ave Medford OR 97501 Office: Medford Mail Tribune 33 N Fir St Medford OR 97501

HUDSON, WILLIAM FREDERICK, aerospace and marine systems co. exec.; b. Seattle, May 26, 1944; s. William Traylor and Edna Margreta (Fredlund) H.; B.S. in Elec. Engring., U. Wash., 1966, M.S. in Indsl. Engring., 1971; exec. program cert. in mgmt. UCLA, 1981. Project engr. Naval Sea Systems Command, Washington, 1971-76; project mgr. Honeywell Co., Seattle, 1976; mgr. systems engring., program mgr. acoustic warfare Librascope div. Singer Co., Glendale, Calif., 1976—. Served to lt. USN, 1966-70. Decorated Navy Commendation medal. Mem. Nat. Security Indsl. Assn. Club: La Canada/Flintridge Country (La Canada, Calif.). Office: Librascope Div Singer Co 833 Sonora Ave Glendale CA 91201

HUESTON, HARRY RAYMOND, II, director public safety, consultant, educator; b. Pitts., Aug. 8, 1949; s. Harry and Nancy (Helm) H.; m. Maryann Malone, Sept. 4, 1971; children—Kristine, Colleen. B,A., Kent State U., 1971; M.A., Ohio State U., 1975. Cert. Ohio Peace Officer's Tng. Council, 1975. Police officer Ohio State U., Columbus, 1971-72, criminal investigative agt., 1972-75, coordinator/investigator, 1976-78, dir. student security aide program, 1977-78; cons. Human Systems Devel. Inc., Los Angeles, 1979—; dir. pub. safety Loyola Marymount U., Los Angeles, 1978—. Served as capt. U.S. Army, 1972-80. Mem. Am. Soc. Criminology, Internat. Assn. Chiefs Police, Am. Soc. Safety Engrs. Presbyterian. Contbr. articles to profl. jours. Home: 647 Jenny Dr Newbury Park CA 91320 Office: 7101 W 80th St Los Angeles CA 90045

HUETER, JAMES WARREN, painter, sculptor, art educator; b. San Francisco, May 15, 1925; m. Alabelle M. Hueter, Mar. 5, 1948. B.A. Pomona Coll., 1948; M.F.A., Claremont Grad. Sch., 1951. Painter, sculptor, draftsman, Claremont, Calif., 1951—; instr. Pomona Coll., Claremont, 1959-60, Claremont Grad. Sch., summer 1963, Pitzer Coll., Claremont, 1971, Mt. San Antonio Coll., 1951-80; group exhbns. include: 38th Corcoran Biennial of Am. painting, Washington, 1983. works represented in numerous collections. Served with U.S. Army, 1943-46. Recipient 1st prize Pasadena Art Mus., 1952, Frye Mus., 1957, Los Angeles County Mus., 1955, Long Beach State U., 1961; Nat. Design award Boulder Ctr. for Visual Arts, 1982. Address: 190 E Radcliffe Claremont CA 91711

HUEY, CRAIG ALAN, advertising executive; b. Los Angeles, June 16, 1950; s. Philip Albert and Anna (Aden) H. A.A., El Camino Coll., 1972; B.A., Long Beach State Coll., 1975. Account exec. Infomat, Inc., Rolling Hills Estates, Calif., 1972-75, pres., 1976—. World Youth Crusade for Freedom scholar, Taiwan, 1969. Mem. Direct Mail Mktg. Assn., European Direct Mktg. Assn., Newsletter Assn. Am. Republican. Club: Libertarian Supper. Office: 708 Silver Spur Rd Rolling Hills Estates CA 90274

HUEY, WILLIAM EDWARD, golf course cons.; b. Lakewood, Ohio, Apr. 14, 1930; s. William Edward and Virginia (Higgins) H.; B.A., Dartmouth, 1952. Sales rep. Mobil Oil Corp., Los Angeles, Tacoma, 1954-56; partner Elmer Langguth Brokearge Co., San Francisco, 1957-75; partner Forrest Randolph Co., San Francisco, 1957-75; cons. Dalgety Ltd., San Francisco 1976-79; internat. sales/mktg. exec. William Sherman Co., San Rafael, Calif., 1980—. Adviser, Black boys clubs, San Francisco, 1959—; mem. Job Therapy Calif., Spl. Com. on Parolee Employment, San Quentin; pres. bd. dirs. Booker T. Washington Community Service Center. Served with USNR, 1952-54 (Korea), 61-62 (Vietnam). Mem. U.S. Navy League, Kappa Sigma. Mason (32 deg., Shriner), Elk. Clubs: Dartmouth of California, Commonwealth of California (San Francisco); W. Atwood Yacht (Los Angeles). Co-editor: San Franciscan, 1960-61. Contbr. articles to Future, house organ U.S. Jr. C. of C.; editor internat. newsletter Greenline. Home: 2586 Las Gallinas Ave San Rafael CA 94903 Office: 880 Las Gallinas San Rafael CA 94903

HUEY, WILLIAM SAMPSON, mem. senatorial staff; b. Wichita Falls, Tex., Mar. 26, 1925; s. Bill and Homer Ella (Morrow) H.; B.S., N.Mex. State U., 1952; postgrad. N.Mex. State U., 1962, Colo. State U., 1972; m. Mary Blue, Jan. 5, 1948. Chief spl. services Dept. Game and Fish, State of N.Mex., Santa Fe, 1963-64, chief game mgmt., 1964-70, asst. dir., 1970-75, dir., 1975-77, sec. dept. natural resources, 1977-82; state coordinator U.S. Senator Jeff Bingaman, 1983—. Bd. dirs. Santa Fe Animal Shelter, also past pres.; mem. U.S. del. to Conv. on Trade in Endangered Species. Served with USAAF, 1943-46. Recipient George W. Allan Meml. award Internat. Wild Waterfowl Assn., 1962; Winchester award Game Conservation Internat., 1971; citation Jicarilla Tribal, 1972; Honors award Ducks Unlimited, 1978; N.Mex. State U. Award of Merit, 1978; Profl. of Yr., Western Assn. Fish and Wildlife Agys., 1980; Spl. Conservation award Nat. Wildlife Fedn., 1982; N.Mex. Disting. Pub. Service award, 1982. Mem. Wildlife Soc., Internat. Assn. Game Fish and Conservation Commrs., Am. Ornithol. Soc., East African Wildlife Soc., South African Wildlife Soc., Whooping Crane Conservation Assn. (pres. 1973—), N.Mex. Ornithol. Soc. (past pres.), N.Mex. Wildlife Fedn. Episcopalian. Club: Masons. Contbr. articles in field to profl. jours. Office: 231 Washington Ave Santa Fe NM 87501

HUFF, ALBERT KEITH, plant physiologist, chemist; b. Burlington, Wash., Apr. 16, 1942; s. Robert F. and Helen J. (Freday) H.; m. Ingrid Margaret Gjertsen; children—Rebecca Anne, Heather Maria. B.S., U. Wash., 1964; Ph.D., Colo. State U., 1974. Chemist radiation biology lab. AEC, U. Wash., 1965-67; lectr. Summer Sci. Inst., 1966, 67; research assoc. Colo. State U., 1972-74, S.D. State U., 1974-77; asst. prof. U. Ariz., Tucson, 1977—; invited lectr., cons. univs. Cairo, Alexandria and Menoufia, Egypt, 1981. NSF fellow, 1968; NDEA fellow, 1969. Mem.

Am. Chem. Soc., AAAS, Am. Soc. Plant Physiologists, Fedn. Am. Scientists, Internat. Citrus Soc., Sigma Xi, Phi Kappa Phi. Club: Seven Pipers Soc. (Tucson). Contbr. articles and papers to profl. jours. Office: Dept Plant Scis U Arizona Tucson AZ 85721

HUFF, HOWARD LEE, artist, educator; b. Kansas City, Mo., July 18, 1941; s. Elbridge Lee and Mildred Irene (Fulton) H.; m. Holly Arleen Black, Oct. 3, 1964. B.A. cum laude, Coll. Idaho, 1963; M.F.A., U. Idaho, 1967. Tchr. art Boise pub. schs., 1964-65; asst. prof., Boise State U., 1968-72, assoc. prof., 1973-76, prof., 1977—; group shows include: Photospiva '81, Joplin, Mo., Photog '78, Colby, Kans.; represented in permanent collections: Boise Cascade Corp., Ore-Ida Corp., State of Oreg., City of Boise, Idaho 1st Nat. Bank, Boise, Boise Gallery of Art, U. Idaho, Coll. Idaho. Served with Idaho N.G., 1963-69. Office: 1910 University Dr Boise ID 83725

HUFF, NORMAN NELSON, systems company executive, educator; b. San Diego, Apr. 22, 1933, s. George Peabody and Norma Rose (Nelson) H.; B.S., San Diego State U., 1957; cert. UCLA, 1972; M.B.A., Golden Gate U., 1972; A.A., bus. cert., Victor Valley Coll., 1972; m. Sharon Kay Lockwood, Sept. 30, 1979. Chemist, Convair, San Diego, 1954-55, astrophysicist, 1955-56; mgmt. trainee, chem. engr. U.S. Gypsum Co., Plaster City, Calif., 1957-58; instr. data processing Victor Valley Coll., Victorville, Calif., 1967-70, chmn. data processing, 1970-81; owner High Desert Data Systems, 1972—; mgmt. info. systems cons. Pfizer Inc., 1970-72, Mojave Water Agy. Calif., 1972-74. Served with USNR, 1950-54, to capt. USAF, 1954-67; Vietnam. Recipient Presdl. Achievement award, 1982. Mem. Calif. Ednl. Computing Consortium (chmn.), Am. Mgmt. Assn., Calif. Bus. Edn. Assn. (treas. 1967-73), Inst. Aero. Sci. (pres. 1956-57), Soaring Soc. Am. (life). Author 4 computer sci. texts. Office: 16746 Sunset Dr Victorville CA 92392

HUFF, ROBERT ALLEN, state education ofcl.; b. Kansas City, Kans., July 25, 1931; s. H. G. and Helen F. H.; B.S., U. Kans., 1953; M.A., U. Mo., Kansas City, 1958; D.Ed., U. Oreg., 1969; m. Mary Ann Strumillo, Aug. 8, 1953; children—Stephen, Susan. Biology tchr. Punahou Acad., Honolulu, 1953-55; lang. arts tchr. Shawnee Mission High Sch. Dist., Prairie Village, Kans., 1955-56; social studies tchr. Medford (Oreg.) Public Schs., 1956-64, guidance dir., scholarship chmn., 1964-67; research asst. Bur. Ednl. Research, Coll. Edn., U. Oreg., Eugene, 1967-68; adminstrv. asst. to supt. Salem (Oreg.) Public Schs., 1968-69; asso. dir. Nat. Center Higher Edn. Mgmt. Systems, dir. applications and implementation unit, Boulder, Colo., 1969-74; prof. higher edn. Va. Poly. Inst. and State U., Blacksburg, 1974-75; exec. sec. Bd. Ednl. Fin. and Commn. Postsecondary Edn. for N.Mex., Santa Fe, 1975-78; exec. dir. Ariz. Bd. Regents, Phoenix, 1979—. Named Hon. Prof., Fed. U. Santa Maria, Brazil, 1974. Mem. Am. Assn. Higher Edn., Assn. Instl. Research, NEA, State Higher Edn. Exec. Officers, Phi Delta Kappa. Club: Kiwanis (Phoenix). Office: State Ariz Ariz Bd Regents 1535 W Jefferson St Phoenix AZ 85007

HUFFINE, CAROL LYNNE, sociologist, educator; b. Elgin, Ill., Jan. 8, 1937; d. Cecil Byron and Carolyn Elizabeth (Kern) H. B.A., Ariz. State U., 1962, M.A., 1967; Ph.D., U. Calif., 1972. Asst. prof. sociology Sacramento State Coll., 1968-69; Sociol. scientist Johns Hopkins U. Sch. Medicine, Balt., 1969-72; research sociologist U. Calif.-Berkeley, 1972—; research specialist Inst. Research Social Behavior, Oakland, Calif., 1975-81; dir. research Calif. Sch. Profl. Psychology, Berkeley, 1981—; adj. assoc. prof. U. Calif.-Berkeley, 1981—. Mem. AAAS, Am. Sociol. Assn., Pacific Sociol. Assn., Gerontol. Soc. Am. Contbr. numerous articles to profl. jours. Office: IHD 1203 Tolman Hall U Calif Berkeley CA 94720

HUFFINE, DENNIS BERNS, rehabilitation counselor, vocational consultant; b. Sewal, Iowa, Dec. 5, 1948; s. Berns E. and Faye L. (Horner) H.; m. Marcia Luann Johnson, June 3, 1971; m. Marcy Lynn Patten, May 15, 1982. B.A., U. Iowa, 1971; M.A., U. No. Colo., 1976. Rehab. coordinator Underwriters Adjusting Co., Santa Ana, Calif., 1975-76; rehab. counselor Rehab. Cons., Inc., Orange, Calif., 1976-77; rehab. counselor, office mgr. Valpar Corp., Long Beach, Calif., 1977-78; services coordinator Specialists Rehab. Center, West Los Angeles, Calif., 1978-79, owner, pres. Huffine & Assocs., Inc., Glendale, Calif., 1979—; cons. to ins. cos.; career counselor. Sec. bd. dirs. Sunland (Calif.) Oaks Homeowner Assn., 1982—. Served to capt. USAF, 1971-75. Decorated Air medal. Mem. Am. Personnel and Guidance Assn., Nat. Rehab. Assn., Rehab. Nurses Soc., Am. Rehab. Counselors Assn., Valley Indsl. People, So. Counties Rehab. Exchange, Calif. Assn. Rehab. Profls. Republican. Methodist. Office: 229 N Central Ave Suite 400 Glendale CA 91203

HUFFMAN, ALVIN DONALD, chemical company executive; b. Windsor, Ont., Can., May 2, 1924; s. Donald Alfonso and Katherine Dora (Bailey) H.; m. Lois Joyce Smale, Aug. 1, 1949; children—Robert, Janet, Catherine. B.Applied Sci., U. Toronto, 1949. Registered profl. engr., Can. From plant engr. to prodn. supr. Sifto Salt div. Domtar Ltd., Goderich, Ont., 1949-53, from supt. to plant mgr., Unity, Sask., 1953-57, from tech. dir. to indsl. sales mgr., Montreal, 1957-63, from mktg. mgr. to asst. gen. mgr., 1967-71, gen. sales mgr. Lime div., Montreal, 1963-67, gen. mgr. Converted Papers div., Toronto, 1971-77; pres., dir. Prairie Malt Ltd., Biggar, Sask., 1978—. Served as flying officer RCAF, 1942-45. Mem. Assn. Profl. Engrs. Sask., Assn. Profl. Engrs. Ont., Chem. Inst. Can., Brewing and Malting Barley Research Inst. (dir.), Engring. Inst. Can., Can. Soc. Chem. Engring., Assn. Chem. Profession Ont. Club: Lions. Patentee salt prodn. Home: 421 5th Ave W Biggar SK S0K 0M0 Canada Office: PO Box 1150 Biggar SK S0K 0M0 Canada

HUFFMAN, DENNIS KEITH, national park manager; b. Rock Falls, Ill., Oct. 24, 1939; s. Carl Victor and Dorothy Ione (Eddy) H.; children—Todd Matthew, James Andrew. B.S., U. Utah, 1967. Test engr. Sperry Utah Corp., Salt Lake City, 1961-63; park ranger, park mgr. Nat. Park Service, 1964—; park mgr. Colo. Nat. Monument, Fruita, 1980—. Served with USN, 1957-61. Home and Office: Colo Nat Monument Fruita CO 81521

HUFFMAN, NONA GAY, financial planner; b. Albuquerque, June 22, 1942; d. William Abraham and Opal Irene (Leaton) Crisp; m. Donald Clyde Williams, Oct. 20, 1961; children—Debra Gaylene, James Donald; m. 2d Earl George Huffman, Sept. 22, 1973. Student pub. schs. Lawndale, Calif. Lic. ins., securities dealer, N.Mex. Sec. City of Los Angeles, 1960, Los Angeles City Schs. 1960-62, Aerospace Corp., El Segundo, Calif., 1962-64, Albuquerque Pub. Schs., 1972-73, Pub. Service Co. N.Mex., Albuquerque, 1973; rep., fin. planner Waddell & Reed, Inc., Albuquerque, 1979—; tchr. money mgmt. seminars for sr. citizens ctr. Mem. Profl. Orgn. Women (dir.), Nat. Assn. Female Execs. Office: 5101 Copper NE Albuquerque NM 87108

HUFFSTETLER, LINDA LOU, counselor; b. Eustis, Fla., Dec. 3, 1950; d. Lewis Earl and Evelyn Louise H. B.A. in Psychology, Rollins Coll., 1979; M.A. in Counseling, U. Ariz., 1981. With Office of Sec. of State, Winter Park, Fla., 1969-76; with Office of Grad. Program in Edn., Rollins Coll., Winter Park, 1976-79; pvt. counselor sexual assault and sexual abuse, Tucson, 1981—; cons. on incest to hosps., Social Service agys. and govtl. agys. Counselor Parents United, sponsored by Child Protective Services, State of Ariz., Tucson. Mem. Am. Personnel and Guidance Assn., Specialists in Group Work. Democrat. Office: 239 N Warren Ave Tucson AZ 85719

HUFNAGEL, WENDY, lawyer; b. Milw., Oct. 6, 1949; d. Roland John and Lilliam Josephine (Kail) H.; m. Joseph E. Tesch, Nov. 10, 1979. B.A. Marquette U., 1971, J.D., 1974. Bar: Wis. 1974, Utah 1977. Asst. dist. atty. Milw. County, 1974-77; asst. county atty. Salt Lake City, 1977-80; ptnr. Tesch and Hufnagel, 1980—; dep. atty. Wasatch County (Utah). Mem. Wis. Bar Assn., Utah Bar Assn., Heber Valley Horse Assn. (pres.). Democrat. Home: 3413 East Center Creek Rd Heber Valley UT 84032 Office: Tesch and Hufnagel 353 East 4th St South Suite 100 Salt Lake City UT 84111 also 30 N Main St Suite 2 Heber City UT 84032

HUG, PROCTER RALPH, JR., judge; b. Reno, Mar. 11, 1931; s. Procter Ralph and Margaret (Beverly) H.; B.S., U. Nev., 1953; LL.B., J.D., Stanford, 1958; m. Barbara Van Meter, Apr. 4, 1954; children—Cheryl Ann, Procter James, Elyse Marie. Admitted to Nev. bar, 1958; with firm Woodburn, Wedge, Blakey, Folsom & Hug, Reno 1963-77; U.S. judge 9th Circuit Ct. Appeals, Reno, 1977—. Chmn. Nev. State Bar Com. on Jury Inst.; dep. atty. gen. State of Nev.; v.p., dir. Nev. dir. Nev. Tel. & Tel. Co., 1958-77, Vice pres. Young Democrats Nev., 1960-61. Chmn. bd. regents U. Nev.; bd. visitors Stanford Law Sch. Served to lt. USNR, 1953-55. Recipient Outstanding Alumnus award U. Nev., 1967. Mem. Am. Bar Assn. (gov. 1976—), Nat. Assn. Coll. and Univ. Attys. (past mem. exec. bd.), U. Nev. Alumni Assn. (past pres.), Stanford Law Soc. Nev. (pres.). Office: Suite 600 50 W Liberty St Reno NV 89501*

HUGGINS, CHARLOTTE SUSAN HARRISON, educator; b. Rockford, Ill., May 13, 1933; d. Lyle Lux and Alta May (Bowers) H.; student Knox Coll., 1951-52; A.B. magna cum laude, Radcliffe Coll., 1958; M.A., Northwestern U., 1960, postgrad., 1971-73; m. Rollin Charles Huggins, Apr. 26, 1952; children—Cynthia Charlotte Peters, Shirley Ann, John Charles. Asst. editor Hollister Publs., Inc., Wilmette, Ill., 1959-65; tchr. advanced placement English New Trier High Sch. East, Winnetka, Ill., 1965—, asst. sponsor Echoes, 1981, Trevia, 1982, 83; pres. Harrison Farm, Inc., Lovington, Ill., 1976—. Mem. women's bd. St. Leonard's House, Chgo., 1965-75; Central Sch. PTA Bd., Wilmette, 1960-64; mem. jr. bd. Northwestern U. Settlement, Chgo., 1965-75. Recipient DAR Citizenship award, 1953, Phi Beta Kappa award, 1957; Am. Legion award, 1959; named Master Tchr., New Trier High Sch., 1979. Mem. NEA, Ill. Edn. Assn., New Trier Edn. Assn., Nat. Council Tchrs. English, Ill. Assn. Tchrs. English, MLA, Northwestern U. Alumni Assn., Jr. Aux. Chgo. Cancer Research Bd., Mary Crane League, Pi Beta Phi. Clubs. Nat. Huguenot Soc., Ill. Huguenot Soc., Womans' of Wilmette, Univ. of Chgo., Mich. Shores, Knox Coll., Radcliffe Coll. of Chgo. Author: A Sequential Course in Composition Grades 9-12, 1979; A History of New Trier High School 1982; Doom of a Dynasty: An Anaheim Tragedy, 1983. Home: 700 Greenwood Ave Wilmette IL 60091 or Ptarmigan Meadows Creede CO 81130 Office: 385 Winnetka Ave Winnetka IL 60093

HUGHES, ALICE MARLENE, retail co. exec., b. Peru, Nebr., Mar. 16, 1935; d. George Dewey and Lela (Gerdes) Jones; m. Archie Benton Hughes, Oct. 11, 1980; children by previous marriage—Kathleen, Louise, Steve, Judith. With Fred Meyer Inc., Portland, Oreg., 1970—, asst. buyer, 1975-80, buyer, 1980—. Lutheran. Home: 2411 SE 105 Portland OR 97216

HUGHES, BRADLEY RICHARD, mktg. exec.; b. Detroit, Oct. 8, 1954; s. John Arthur and Nancy Irene (Middleton) H.; A.A., Oakland Community Coll., 1974, B.S. in Bus., U. Colo., 1978, B.S. in Journalism, 1979, M.B.A., 1981; m. Linda McCants, Feb. 14, 1977; 1 son, Bradley Richard. Buyer, Joslins Co., Denver, 1979; mktg. adminstr. Mountain Bell, Denver, 1980—; tech. cons. Art Info. Systems, 1983—. Bd. dirs. Brandychase Assn. Mem. Assn. MBA Execs., U.S. Chess Fedn., Internat. Platform Assn. Mensa, Intertel. Republican. Home: 14453 E Jewell Ave Aurora CO 80012 Office: 6200 S Syracuse Englewood CO 80111

HUGHES, CHARLES CAMPBELL, behavioral scientist, anthropologist; b. Salmon, Idaho, Jan. 26, 1929; s. Charles Frederick and Grace Jean (Campbell) H.; A.B. magna cum laude, Harvard U., 1951; M.A., Cornell U., 1953, Ph.D., 1957; m. Jane Ellen Murphy, Feb. 5, 1951 (div. 1962); m. 2d, Patricia D. Devereau, Aug. 8, 1964 (div. 1969); m. 3d, Leslie Ann Medert, Mar. 7, 1970; children—John Charles Campbell, Calisse Marie. Acting asst. prof. sociology and anthropology Cornell U., 1957-62, asst. prof. psychiatry Med. Coll., 1959-62, asso. dir. program in social psychiatry, 1959-62; asso. prof. sociology and anthropology Mich. State U., 1962-64, prof. anthropology, 1964-73, prof. psychiatry Coll. Human Medicine, 1970-73, dir. African Studies Center, 1962-70; chmn. div. behavioral sci. dept. family and community medicine U. Utah Coll. Medicine, 1973-78, prof. behavioral sci., 1973—, prof. anthropology, 1975—, dir. grad. studies, 1979—; fellow Center for Advanced Study in Behavioral Scis., 1961-62. Recipient Disting. Faculty award Mich. State U., 1967. Mem. Am. Anthrop. Assn., Am. Sociol. Assn., Soc. Applied Anthropology (pres. 1969-70), Am. Ethnol. Soc., AAAS, African Studies Assn., Arctic Inst. N.Am., Assn. Behavioral Scis. and Med. Edn. (pres. 1979-80), Soc. Med. Anthropology (pres. 1981-82), Phi Beta Kappa, Sigma Xi, Phi Kappa Phi. Author: An Eskimo Village in the Modern World, 1960; (with others) Peoples of Cove and Woodlot, 1960; (with others) Psychiatric Disorder Among the Yoruba, 1963; Eskimo Boyhood: An Autobiography in Psychosocial Perspective, 1974; contbr. numerous articles to profl. jours.; editor: Make Men of Them, 1972; Custom-Made: Introductory Readings for Cultural Anthropology, 1976. Home: 7453 Enchanted Hills Dr Salt Lake City UT 84121 Office: Dept Family and Community Medicine U Utah Med Center Salt Lake City UT 84132

HUGHES, DAVID ROLLAND, air force officer; b. Honolulu, June 14, 1939; s. William R. and Jessie Marion (Twine) H.; m. Lynn P. Birkland, Sept. 13, 1959; 1 son, Steven Rolland. B.S., Mont. State Coll., 1961; M.S., Air Force Inst. Tech., 1969; disting. grad. Air Command and Staff Coll., 1971-72; postgrad. U.S. Army War Coll., 1976-77. Commd. U.S. Air Force, 1961, advanced through grades to col.; squadron comdr., 1977-79, base comdr. Howard AFB, Panama, 1980-82, dep. comdr. for resource mgmt. George AFB, Calif., 1983—; mgmt. cons. Pres., Panama area Boy Scouts, 1982. Decorated Air Medal, Air Force Commendation medal with oak leaf clusters (4), Purple Heart. Mem. Combat Control Assn., Air Force Assn., Red River Valley Fighter Pilots Assn., U.S. Parachute Assn., C. of C. (dir. 1979-80. Congregationalist. Clubs: Rotary, Antelope Valley Soaring, Internat. Cartridge Collectors Assn. Contbr. articles to profl. jours. Home: 207 Sheppard St Victorville CA 92392 Office: 831 Air Division Victorville CA 92392

HUGHES, EDWIN JAMES, librarian; b. Adrian, Wash., Nov. 30, 1922; s. Guy Allen and Lucy (Norman) H.; student Eastern Wash. State Coll., 1948-49; B.A., U. Minn., 1952, M.A., 1961; B.S., Mankato State Coll., 1962; M.Pub. Adminstrn., U. So. Calif., 1973; m. Edith Luverne Carter, June 17, 1951; children—James, Nancy, David. Sr. clk. U.S. P.O., Ephrata, Wash., 1941-43, 46-48; county librarian Martin County Library, Fairmont, Minn., 1954-69; library dir. Oxnard (Calif.) Pub. Library, 1969—; mem. faculty Library Inst. Seminar, U. Minn., 1956; pres. Minn. Library Film Circuit Corp., 1966-68; mem. state adv. council Inter-Library Coop., 1967-68; incorporator So. Minn.-No. Iowa Edn. TV Corp., 1967; v.p. Total Inter-Library Exchange Network, 1978-79, pres., 1979-80. Chmn. Martin County Red Cross, 1957-59; dist. finance chmn. Boy Scouts Am., 1960-66; fund chmn. Fairmont Community Chest, 1965. Bd. dirs. Ventura County Mental Health Assn. Served with AUS, 1943-46; ETO. Named Key Man, Jr. C. of C., 1955. Mem. ALA, Minn. (chmn. sect. 1958), Calif. library assns., Pub. Library Execs. Assn. So. Calif. (sec./treas. 1982-83), Jr. C. of C. (sec. 1957), Alpha Phi Omega. Methodist (chmn. ofcl. bd. 1966). Club: National Exchange (sec. 1958-60 Fairmont). Home: 1021 Ivywood Dr Oxnard CA 93030 Office: 214 S C St Oxnard CA 93030

HUGHES, EUGENE MORGAN, university president; b. Scottsbluff, Nebr., Apr. 3, 1934; s. Ruby Melvin and Hazel Marie (Griffith) H.; diploma Neb. Western Coll., 1954; B.S. in Math. magna cum laude, Chadron State Coll., 1956; M.S. in Math., Kans. State U., 1958; Ph.D. in Math., George Peabody Coll. for Tchrs., Vanderbilt U., 1968; m. Caroline Mae Hartwig, Aug. 1, 1954; children—Deborah Kaye, Greg Eugene, Lisa Ann. Grad. asst. dept. math. Kans. State U. at Manhattan, 1956-57; instr. math. Nebr. State Tchrs. Coll. at Chadron, 1957-58; asst. prof. math., head dept. Chadron State Coll., 1958-66, asso. prof., 1966-69, prof. math., 1969-70, dir. research, 1965-66, asst. to the pres., 1966-68, dean adminstrn., 1968-70; grad. asst. dept. math. George Peabody Coll. for Tchrs., Nashville, 1962-63, 64-65, asst. to undergrad. dean, 1964, asst. to pres., 1964-65, instr. Peabody Demonstration Sch., 1963-64; prof. math. No. Ariz. U., Flagstaff, 1970—, dean Coll. Arts and Scis., 1970-71, provost univ. arts and sci. edn., 1971-72, acad. v.p., 1972-79, pres., 1979—. Cons. Nebr. Dept. Edn., 1966-70; mem. staff bd. trustees Nebr. State Colls., Lincoln, 1969-70; co-dir. workshop tchr. edn. N.Central Assn., U. Minn., 1968-70; officer various fed. ednl. programs Nebr. and Ariz., 1966—; bd. dirs. Am. Assn. State Colls. and Univs., 1979—, mem. com. on accreditation, 1980—; bd. fellows Am. Grad. Sch. Internat. Mgmt., 1980—. Mem. Chadron Housing Authority, 1968-70; bd. dirs. Flagstaff Summer Festival, Ariz. Council on Humanities and Public Policy, Mus. No. Ariz., Grand Canyon council Boy Scouts Am., Ariz. Acad. NSF fellow, 1963, 64. Mem. Math. Assn. Am. (vis. lectr. secondary schs. western Nebr. 1962), Nat., Ariz. edn. assns., N.Central Assn. Colls and Secondary Schs. (co-ordinator 1968-72, cons.-evaluator 1977—), Nat. Council Tchrs. of Math, Flagstaff C. of C. (dir.), Blue Key, Pi Mu Epsilon, Phi Delta Kappa, Kappa Mu Epsilon, Phi Kappa Phi. Clubs: Masons, Elks, Rotary (past pres.). Home: 1407 N Aztec Flagstaff AZ 86001 Office: Northern Ariz Univ Box 4092 Flagstaff AZ 86011

HUGHES, JERRY M., state senator; b. Yonkers, N.Y., Feb. 16, 1944; s. Thomas F. and Anna J. (Mahoney) H.; m. Sally A. Kostecka, 1974; children—Shannon, Erin, Sean. B.A., Gonzaga U., 1966; postgrad. Eastern Wash. State Coll., 1969-71, Whitworth Coll., 1972-74. Mem. Wash. Ho. of Reps., 1976-80, Wash. State Senate, 1980—. Vice pres. Gonzaga U. Young Democrats, 1964-65, pres., 1965-66; mem. Spokane Zool. Soc., Irish-Israeli-Italian Soc.; dir. Good Shephard Home. Served to col., U.S. Army. Mem. Wash. Gen. Assn., NEA. Democrat. Roman Catholic. Clubs: Ski, Calif. Home: N 3504 Milton St Spokane WA 99205 Office: Washington State Senate Olympia WA 98504*

HUGHES, JOHN DANIEL, television executive; b. Madrid, Spain, Jan. 21, 1946, came to U.S., 1951, naturalized 1967; s. Emmet John and Mari Francis (Pfeifer) H. B.A., U. Miami, 1970; postgrad. UCLA, 1976-78. Vice-pres. sales Playboy, Chgo., 1971-76; account exec. KTTV, Los Angeles, 1977-79, nat. sales mgr., 1979-80, v.p., nat. sales mgr., 1980-82, v.p., local sales mgr., 1982—. Mem. Am. Mgmt. Assn., Exceptional Children's Found., Am. Film Assn. Democrat. Roman Catholic. Clubs: Athletic (Los Angeles); Calif. Yacht (Marina Del Rey); Riviera Country. Office: KTTV 5746 Sunset Blvd Hollywood CA 90028

HUGHES, JOHN MEREDITH, dentist; b. Hollywood, Calif., Apr. 7, 1929; s. John M. and Margaret Emma (Abell) H.; m. Inez Mitchel Meier, Oct. 5, 1968; children—Robert A. Meier, Susie Z. Evans, Miki Bottomly, Peggy Ruyle, Matt, Kim. A.A., UCLA, 1952; D.D.S., U. So. Calif., 1956. Pvt. practice dentistry, Ventura, Calif., 1959—; clin. instr. U. So. Calif. Dental Sch., 1959-62; dir. Am. Comml. Bank. Served with USNR, 1955-59. Fellow Acad. Gen. Dentistry, So. Calif. Assn. Endodontists; mem. Ventura-Santa Barbara Dental Soc., Calif. Dental Soc., ADA, U. So. Calif. Alumni Assn., Western Soc. Periodontists. Republican. Club: Lions. Home: 1957 Swift St Ventura CA 93003 Office: 3390 Loma Vista Ventura CA 93003

HUGHES, MADELON GRACE, accountant; b. Seattle, July 21, 1926; d. Lawrence Christopher and Thelma May (McKay) Prentice; student public schs., Seattle; m. James Robert Hughes, Apr. 29, 1967; children—Robert, Kathleen, Teresa, Linda. With Pacific Iron & Metal Co., Seattle, 1965-66; acct. Judson Park Retirement Home, Des Moines, Wash., 1966-69, Budget Rent A Car of Tacoma, Medved Auto Parks, Inc., 1969-72; self employed bookkeeping service and Tax acct., Torrance, Calif., 1972—. Treas., St. James Women's Council, 1974-75. Mem. Nat. Soc. Pub. Accts., Nat. Assn. Enrolled Agts. (sec. 1974-78; pres. Los Angeles chpt. 1977-78, dir. 1978-80), Calif. Soc. Enrolled Agts. (sec. 1977, 80-81, pres. South Bay chpt. 1981-82, dir. 1982-83), Southwood Homeowners Assn. Home and Office: 5227 Lillian St Torrance CA 90503

HUGHES, MALCOLM SAMUEL, real estate developer, constrn. exec.; b. Wednesbury, Staffordshire, Eng., May 26, 1936; came to U.S., 1978; s. Samuel Trevor and Gladys Rosalie (Bayer) H.; B.A., U. Cambridge, 1959, M.A., 1963; m. Ursula Margret Voigt, Mar. 15, 1974; children—David C.S., Mark A., Susanne, Christina. Chmn., Maxim Investments Ltd., 1964—, pres. Maxim Pacific, Inc., San Diego, 1978—. Served with Army of Gt. Brit., 1954-56. Home: 1105 La Jolla Rancho Rd La Jolla CA 92037 Office: 600 B St Suite 2000 San Diego CA 92101

HUGHES, MARTHA HANNAH, educator; b. Pitts., Nov. 25, 1939; d. Jesse and Ethel May (Booker) Foreman; m. John Davis Thompson, Nov. 10, 1963; children—Jewell L. Johnson, Jawanna L. Thompson; m. 2d, Virgil Hughes; Nov. 27, 1971; 1 son, Virgil L. B.A., Chgo. State U., 1975; postgrad. Pepperdine U., 1979; postgrad. U. Calif.-Dominguez Hills, 1979-80. Mail order clk. Montgomery Ward Co., Chgo., 1958-59; file clk. Spiegel, Inc., Chgo., 1959-62; sec. Allied Radio Corp., Chgo., 1965-71; tchr. history pub. schs., Chgo., 1972-78; tchr. history pub. schs., Unified Sch. Dist., Los Angeles, 1978-80; tchr. spl. edn. jr. high sch., Los Angeles, 1980—. Active Los Angeles Philharmonic Assn., 1982-83, Assn. Children and Adults with Learning Disabilities, 1982-83; inmate reception clk. Los Angeles County Jail; mem. St. Philomena Women's Council. Mem. Nat. Congress Parents and Teachers.

HUGHES, MICHAEL RICHARD, radiology administrator; b. Springfield, Mo., Dec. 30, 1947; s. Richard F. and Evelyn E. (Rippee) H.; 1 dau., Holly Michelle Davolt. Student, Calif. State U., 1977-80, Santa Monica Coll., 1976-78, S.W. Mo. State U., 1968, 69; cert. registered technologist, St. Johns Hosp. Sch. X-Ray Tech., Springfield, Mo., 1965-67. Staff radiologic technologist St. Johns Hosp. Springfield, Mo., 1967-69; supr., float radiologic technologist Bapt. Meml. Hosp., Kansas City, Mo., 1969-71; chief radiologic technologist Med. Center, Independence, Mo., 1971; tech. dir. PM shifts St. Joseph Hosp. and Med. Center, Phoenix, 1972-74; staff radiologic technologist Martin Luther Hosp., Anaheim, Calif., 1974-75; staff radiologic technologist St. Johns Hosp., Santa Monica, 1975-76; asst. chief technologist Cedars-Sinai Med. Center, Los Angeles, 1976-81; adminstrv. dir. radiology services St. Joseph Med. Center, Burbank, Calif., 1981—. Mem. Am. Hosp. Radiology Adminstrs. Inc., Calif. Soc. Radiologic Technologists (pres. 1978), Am. Soc. Radiologic Technologists, (legis. com. 1975-77), Ariz. Soc. Radiologic Technologists. Democrat. Methodist. Office: Buena Vista and Alameda Sts Burbank CA 91505

HUGHES, NORMA JEAN, museum director; b. Cin., Dec. 29, 1930; d. Carl Edward and Juanita Grace Moore; m. Louis Ray Sandefur, Jan.,

1953; 1 son, Jeffrey Mark; m. 2d, William Holcomb Hughes, Apr. 18, 1964; 1 dau., Melinda Ann. B.S., Western Ky. U., 1952. Cytotechnologist, cancer control unit, field investigation demonstration br. Nat. Cancer Inst., NIH, Memphis, 1954-57; supr. cytotechnology lab., pathology dept. Bapt. Meml. Hosp., Memphis, 1957-60, Barger and Likos Med. Lab., Phoenix, 1960-63; tchr. Flagstaff, Ariz., Memphis, Twin Falls, Idaho, 1965-71; cytotechnologist Automated Pathology Services, Phoenix, 1973-75, supr., 1975-76; dir. Mohave Mus. of History and Arts, Kingman, Ariz., 1979—. Mem. exec. bd. Kingman Centennial Commn., 1979-83; mem. Kingman Historic Preservation Commn., 1979-83. mem. Kingman Republican Women. Mem. AAUW, Ariz. Hist. Soc., Ariz. Paper and Photograph Conservation Group, LWV, Mohave and Craftsmen's Guild (bd. dirs.). Methodist. Club: Soroptimists Internat. of Kingman (sec. 1981, pres.-elect 1982). Home: 300 Astor Kingman AZ 86401 Office: 400 W Beale Kingman AZ 86401

HUGHES, ROBERT HARRISON, trade association executive; b. Puunene, Mani, Hawaii, Mar. 23, 1917; s. Robert E. and Alice T. (Walker) H.; m. Nadine J. Hegler, Aug. 24, 1940 (div. Jan. 1983); children—Robert L., Linton Alice Hughes Breen, Carole N. Hughes Trefts; m. Judith Dean Gething, Jan. 28, 1983. B.S. in Sugar Tech., U. Hawaii, 1938. with Hawaiian Comml. & Sugar Co., 1939-65, sugar mill supt., 1951-63, prodn. mgr., 1963-65; v.p. tech. services C. Brewer & Co., Ltd., Honolulu, 1965-69, sr. v.p. Hawaiian ops., 1969-77, exec. v.p. 1977-80, dir. subs., 1966-80; pres. Hawaiian Sugar Planters Assn., Aiea, 1981—; dir. C. Brewer & Co., Ltd., Olekele Sugar Co., Ltd., Hawaiian Sugar Transp. Co.; chmn. Hilo Coast Processing Co. Bd. regents U. Hawaii, 1961-66; turstee Hawaii Conf. Found., 1966—, Hawaii Loa Coll., 1980—; trustee U. Hawaii Found., 1963-65, 73-78, pres., 1967-68; bd. dirs. Hawaii Multi-Cultural Ctr., 1979-82; chmn. adv. bd. Cancer Ctr. Hawaii, 1979-81; pres. Hawaii conf. United Ch. of Christ, 1962-63. Mem. Hawaiian Sugar Technologists. Republican. Clubs: Oahu Country, Pacific, Honolulu. Home: 7148 Kukii St Honolulu HI 96825 Office: PO Box 1057 Aiea HI 96701

HUGHES, ROBERT MERRILL, engineer; b. Glendale, Calif., Sept. 11, 1936; s. Fred P. and Gertrude G. (Merrill) H.; A.A., Pasadena City Coll., 1957; 1 dau., Tammie Lynn Cobble. Engr. Aerojet Gen. Corp., Azusa, Calif., 1957-64, 66-74; pres. Automatic Electronics Corp., Sacramento, 1964-66; specialist Perkin Elmer Corp., Pomona, Calif., 1974-75; gen. mgr. Hughes Mining Inc., Covina, Calif., 1975-76; project mgr. L&A Water Treatment, City of Industry, Calif., 1976-79; dir. Hughes Industries Inc., Alta Loma, Calif., 1979—; pres. Hughes Devel. Corp., Carson City, Nev.; chmn. bd. Hughes Mining Inc. Registered profl. engr., Calif. Mem. Nat. Soc. Profl. Engrs., Instrument Soc. Am., Am. Inst. Plant Engrs. Republican. Patentee in field. Home: 10039 Bristol Dr Alta Loma CA 91701 Office: Box 723 Alta Loma CA 91701

HUGHES, W. JAMES, optometrist, public health administrator; b. Shawnee, Okla., Oct. 15, 1944; s. Willis J. and Elizabeth Alice (Nimohoyah) H. B.A. in Anthropology, U. Okla., 1966, M.A. in Anthropology, 1972; O.D., U. Houston, 1976; M.P.H., U. Tex., 1977. Lic. Optometrist, Okla., Tex., W. Va. Physician's asst., Houston, Dallas, 1969-70; teaching asst. in clin. optics U. Houston, 1973-74, contact lens research asst., 1974; Wesley Jessen Contact Lens Rep., 1974-76; extern eye clinic Tuba City Indian Hosp., 1975; teaching fellow pub. health optometry U. Houston, 1975-76; Indian Health Service optometrist, Eagle Butte, S.D., 1976; optometrist vision care project Crockett Ind. Sch. Dist., 1977; vision care program dir. Bemidji Area Indian Health Service, 1977-78; optometrist Navajo Area Indian Health Service, Chinle Health Ctr., 1978-79; adj. prof. So. Calif. Coll., U. Houston, 1978—; optometrist Shiprock USPHS Indian Hosp., 1979—, chief vision care program. Served with U.S. Army, 1966-69. Decorated Bronze Star, Purple Heart. Recipient House of Vision award 1974; Community Health Optometry award 1976; Better Vision scholar, 1973-76. Mem. Am. Pub. Health Assn., Am. Optometric Assn., Tex. Optometric Assn. Commd. Officers Soc., Assn. Am. Indian Physicians, Beta Sigma Kappa. Democrat. Roman Catholic. Contbr. articles to profl. jours.

HUGHES, WILLIAM ALAN, fin. exec.; b. Denver, Jan. 31, 1952; s. William Earl and Lila Maxine (Dinsmoore) H.; B.S., Nat. Coll. Bus., 1974; m. Barbara Jo Hendrix, Feb. 23, 1980. Staff acct. Blue Cross-Blue Shield Wyo., Cheyenne, 1975-77; comptroller Ideal Aerosmith, Inc., Cheyenne, 1977—, also treas. bd. dirs. Mem. U.S. C. of C., Cheyenne Job Service Employers Council, Nat. Rifle Assn., Greater Cheyenne C. of C. (econ. edn. com., mem. state affairs com.), S.E. Wyo. Wildlife Assn. (dir.). Methodist. Club: Kiwanis. Home: 4208 Carla Dr Cheyenne WY 82001 Office: 2505 E Fox Farm Rd Cheyenne WY 82001

HUGHS, MARY GERALDINE, accountant, social service adminstr.; b. Marshalltown, Iowa, Nov. 28, 1929; d. Don Harold, Sr., and Alice Dorothy (Keister) Shaw; A.A., Highline Community Coll., 1970; B.A., U. Wash., 1972; m. Charles G. Hughs, Jan. 31, 1949; children—Mark George, Deborah Kay, Juli Ann, Grant Wesley. Asst. controller Moduline Internat., Inc., Chehalis, Wash., 1972-73; controller Data Recall Corp., El Segundo, Calif., 1973-74; fin. adminstr., acct. Saturn Mfg. Corp., Torrance, Calif., 1974-77; sr. acct., adminstrv. asst. Van Camp Ins., San Pedro, Calif., 1977-78; asst. adminstr. Harbor Regional Center, Torrance, Calif., 1979—; active bookkeeping service, 1978—; instr. math. and acctg. South Bay Bus. Coll., 1976-77. Sec. Pacific N.W. Mycol. Soc., 1966-67; treas., bd. dirs. Harbor Employees Fed. Credit Union. Recipient award Am. Mgmt. Assn., 1979. Mem. Beta Alpha. Republican. Methodist. Club: Holiday Health Spas. Author: Iowa Auto Dealers Assn. Title System, 1955; Harbor Regional Center Affirmative Action Plan, 1980; Harbor Regional Center - Financial Format, 1978—; Provider Audit System, 1979; Handling Client Funds, 1983. Office: 21231 Hawthorne Blvd Torrance CA 90509

HUGLEY, CLARENCE LEE, army officer; b. Opelika, Ala., June 11, 1949; s. David and Leo (Cole) H.; m. Lou Ethel Hall, July 5, 1975. B.S. in Biology, Tuskegee Inst., 1967; M.A. in Hosp. Adminstrn., Webster Coll., 1978. Commd. 2d lt. U.S. Army, 1972; advanced through grades to capt., 1976; adj. med. dept. Redstone Arsenal, Ala., 1972-74; adminstrn. officer Yonson Health Clinic, Seoul, Korea, 1975-76; comdr. B Co., 1st bn., acad. brigade Acad. Health Scis., Ft. Sam Houston, Tex., 1976, comdr. A Co., 3d bn., 1976-77, med. detachment comdr., adj. Inst. Surg. Research, 1977-79; hdqrs. comdr., specialist 4th med. bn., Ft. Carson, Colo., 1980-82, chief ancillary br., clin. support div. U.S. Army Hosp., 1982—. Decorated army commendation medals (2). Mem. Kappa Alpha Psi (keeper records Colo. Springs alumni chpt.). Democrat. Baptist. Home: 2249 Farnsworth Colorado Springs CO 80916 Office: US Army Hosp Fort Carson CO 80913

HUI, PETER H., hotel executive; b. Hong Kong, Dec. 13, 1952; came to U.S., 1974; s. Sui Fai and Lap Kim (Chan) H.; B.A. in Hotel and Restaurant Mgmt., S.W. State U., 1976; married. Mgr. Denny's Restaurant, Houston, 1976-78; innkeeper Holiday Inn-China Town, Los Angeles, 1979-81; gen. mgr. Ramada Inn, Hollywood, Calif., 1981-82, Holiday Inn, Montebello, Calif., 1982—. Recipient Four Diamonds award Automobile Assn. Am., 1981. Mem. Hotel Sales Mgmt. Assn., Pico Rivera (Calif.) C of C. (bd. dirs.). Clubs: Rotary (program chmn.), City of Commerce. Office: 7709 Telegraph Rd Montebello CA 90640

HULBERT, BRUCE WALKER, banker; b. Evanston, Ill., Feb. 5, 1937; s. Bruce Walker and Mary Alice (Utley) H.; m. Linnette Ott, June 19, 1963; children—Christina, Jennifer, William. B.S. in Bus., Northwestern U., 1961. With 1st Interstate Bank of Calif., Los Angeles and San Francisco, 1962-78, sr. v.p. planning and devel., asst. to chief exec. officer, 1975-77, regional adminstr., Los Angeles, 1977-78; pres., chief exec. officer, dir. 1st Interstate Bank of Denver, 1978—; dir. 1st Interstate Services Co., bd. regents Stonier Grad. Sch. Banking. Active nat. bd. trustees, exec. com., regional chmn. Inst. Internat. Edn., 1979—; mem. community adv. bd. Jr. League Denver, 1980—; trustee Denver Found., 1978—; bd. dirs. Lutheran Med. Ctr. Found., Denver, 1979—, Denver Partnership, 1978— Colo. U.S. Olympic Com., 1982—, Nat. Jewish Hosp., 1983—; vice chmn. Denver Civic Ventures, Inc., 1978—; mem. exec. bd. Denver Area Council Boy Scouts Am., 1981—; bd. dirs., treas. Mile High United Way, Denver, 1981—; bd. dirs., mem. exec. com. NCCJ. Mem. Am. Bankers Assn., Colo. Assn. Bank Holding Cos. (exec. com., dir.), Colo. Bankers Assn., Denver Clearing House Assn. (dir.), Denver C. of C. Republican. Clubs: Chevaliers du Tastevin, Cherry Hills Country, Denver, Denver Petroleum. Office: First Interstate Bank 17th and Stout Sts Denver CO 80201

HULCE, JOSH T., building materials company executive; b. Chelsea, Mich., Apr. 2, 1942; s. Elwin Leigh and Thelma Ursel (Bahnmiller) H.; m. Carol Ann Jones, Nov. 27, 1964; 1 dau., Hillary Megan. B.A., Northwestern U., 1964; J.D., U. Mich., 1967. Bar: Pa. 1967, Colo. 1975. Assoc., Pepper, Hamilton & Scheetz, Phila., 1967-72; assoc. corp. counsel Manville Corp., Denver, 1972-75, asst. to chmn. bd., 1976-79, v.p. purchasing, 1979-81, div. gen. mgr., 1981-82, pres., 1983—; pres. Johns-Manville Corp., 1982—. Mem. Phila. Bar Assn., Colo. Bar Assn., ABA, Nat. Assn. Purchasing Mgrs., Ky. Cols., Phi Delta Theta, Phi Delta Phi.

HULEATT, RICHARD SHOVELTON, library exec.; b. Boston, Aug. 13, 1931; s. Joseph Alexander and Miriam Wesley (Shovelton) H.; student Boston U., 1949-51; m. Irene Meymaris, Oct. 2, 1955; children—John Joseph, Richard Shovelton, Paul Henry. Tech. info. mgr. Lab. for Electronics, Inc., Boston, 1960-67; chief librarian Gen. Dynamics Electric Boat Div., Groton, Conn., 1967-68; tech. info. mgr. Stone & Webster Engring. Corp., Boston, 1968-75; ind. library cons., Phoenix, 1975-76; mgr. library services Armour Research Center Library, Scottsdale, Ariz., 1976-80; vice chmn. panel counsellors New Eng. Library Bd., 1973-75; pres. Info. Intelligence, Inc., Phoenix, 1980—. Bd. dirs. Framingham (Mass.) Jr. C. of C., 1965. Served with USAF, 1951-54. Mem. Spl. Libraries Assn. (pres. Boston chpt. 1971-72), Ariz. Library Assn. News editor Online Mag., Database Mag., 1979; editor, pub. Ariz. Handbook. Contbr. articles on library adminstrn. and mgmt. to profl. jours. Home: 3815 E Shangri-La Rd Phoenix AZ 85028 Office: PO Box 31098 Phoenix AZ 85046

HULEN, MARJORIE JANE, med. center exec.; b. Denver, Sept. 23, 1921; d. Perry E. and Garnet W. (Doty) Kellogg; student pub. schs., Redondo Beach, Calif.; m. Ray Romaine Hulen, June 10, 1950; 1 child, Lynn Robert. With A. O. Smith Corp., Los Angeles, 1948-60, exec. sec., 1956-60; exec. sec. Sterling Electric Motors, Los Angeles, 1960-61; research sec. Pasadena (Calif.) Found. for Med. Research, 1961-65; exec. sec. Profl. Staff Assn., Los Angeles County/U. So. Calif. Med. Center, Los Angeles, 1965-70, office mgr., 1970-74, bus. mgr., 1974-79, exec. dir., 1979—. Instl. rep. Los Angeles Regional Family Planning, 1977-79. Nat. Pub. Relations award Nat. Assn. Accts., 1979. Mem. Am. Soc. Assn. Execs., Nat. Secs. Assn., Soc. Research Adminstrs., Nat. Assn. Accts. Democrat. Home: 2311 El Paseo St Alhambra CA 91803 Office: 1739 Griffin Ave Los Angeles CA 90031

HULL, CONSTANCE (CONNIE) MAE, educator, librarian/media specialist; b. Pitts., Nov. 29, 1928; d. Lysle Latourelle and Lillian Henriett (Frahm) Gilman; m. Albert Emil Ahrens Jr., m. Howard Donald Hull, Feb. 19. B.S. in Elem. Edn., Oreg. State U., 1966, also postgrad.; M.L.S., U. Oreg., 1968, M.S. in Ednl. Media, Oreg. Coll. Edn., 1976, also postgrad. Various teaching and office positions, St. Paul, 1940-57, Missoula, Mont., 1957-61; co-founded library/media program, Sweet Home, Oreg.; dist. adminstr., dir. Instnl. Materials Ctr., library supr. Sweet Home Sch. Dist. 55, 1961—; tchr. children's lit., media cons.; presenter at state confs. Mem. Oreg. Ednl. Media Assn., Dist. Oreg. Edn. Media Assn., Confedn. Oreg. Sch. Adminstrs., Oreg. Women Ednl. Adminstrn., N.W. Women Ednl. Adminstrn., Am. Assn. Sch. Adminstrs., Assn. Suprs. and Curriculum Dirs., Oreg. Instnl. Media Assn. (co-founder continuing edn. com.), Assn. Ednl. Communication and Tech., AAUW, Delta Kappa Gamma (state media cons.). Republican. Presbyterian. Contbr. to profl. publs. Home: 42899 Green River Dr Sweet Home OR 97386 Office: 1920 Long St Sweet Home OR 97386

HULL, CORDELL WILLIAM, business executive; b. Dayton, Ohio, Sept. 12, 1933; s. Murel George and Julia (Barto) H.; B.E., U. Dayton, 1956; M.S., M.I.T., 1957; J.D., Harvard U., 1962; m. Susan G. Ruder, May 10, 1958; children—Bradford W., Pamela H., Andrew R. Admitted to Ohio bar, 1962; atty. Taft, Stettinius & Hollister, Cin., 1962-64, C & I Girdler, Cin., 1964-66; gen. counsel, treas., pres. C&I Girdler, Internat., Brussels, 1966-70; v.p. Bechtel Overseas Corp., San Francisco, 1970-73; pres., dir. Am. Express Merchant Banks, London, 1973-75; v.p., chief fin. officer Bechtel Group, Inc., San Francisco, 1975—; dir. Bechtel prin. operating cos.; dir. Sequoia Ventures Inc., Bechtel Investments Inc. Trustee, exec. com. World Affairs Council, San Francisco, 1978-82. Served with C.E., U.S. Army, 1956. Mem. ABA, Ohio Bar Assn., Am. Soc. Maro-Engring. Democrat. Clubs: Pacific Union, Bankers, Commonwealth (San Francisco); Knickerbocker, Harvard (N.Y.C.). Mem. adv. bd. Tech. in Society; contbr. articles to profl. jours. Office: 50 Beale St San Francisco CA 94105

HULL, DENNIS JACQUES, counselor; b. Orange, N.J., June 8, 1945; s. Jacques L. and Ora May (Holdman) H.; m. Elizabeth Ann Martin, Sept. 7, 1969; 1 son, Jonathan. B.A. in Psychology, Calif. State U.-Hayward, 1968, M.S., 1975. Cert. counselor. Drug counselor, asst. dir. base drug and alcohol rehab. and edn. U.S. Air Force, 1971-72; group counselor, Contra Costa County (Calif.) Juvenile Hall, 1973-75; counselor Bay Area Quest Program, San Francisco, 1975-76; youth employment counselor, job search workshop leader Calif. Dept. Employment Devel., Pittsburg, 1977-78; adminstv. asst. Los Angeles Harbor Coll., 1978-79, counselor, 1979—. Served in USAF, 1968-72. Mem. Am. Personnel and Guidance Assn., Calif. Personnel and Guidance Assn., Los Angeles Community Coll. Counselors Assn. (pres.), Calif. Community Coll. Counselors Assn. (chmn. So. Calif. Conf. 1983). Office: Los Angeles Harbor Coll 1111 Figuerua Pl Wilmington CA 90744

HULL, DIANA, psychologist; b. Lawrence, N.Y., Aug. 13, 1924; d. Louis Albert and Rosalyn Diamont) Jaffre; B.A., CUNY, 1946; M.S.W., U. Mich., 1954; Ph.D., Sch. Public Health, U. Tex. Health Scis. Center, 1975; children—Marcy Burton, Allison Langdon Boomer; m. 2d, David P. Hull, Dec. 27, 1969. Mem. clin. faculty Baylor Coll. Medicine, Houston, 1966-80; pvt. practice individual, group and family therapy, Houston, 1964—; cons. Tex. Inst. Family Psychiatry, Children's Psychiat. Clinic of Baylor Coll. Medicine. Fellow Am. Group Psychotherapy Assn. (nat. faculty); mem. Southwestern Group Psychotherapy Soc. (dir., officer, sr. faculty), Am. Psychol. Assn. (health, psychology and population sects), Calif. Psychol. Assn. (chmn. div. VI 1983), Assn. Media Psychology (sec.), AAAS, Am. Public Health Assn., Houston Group Psychotherapy Soc. (pres. 1967), So. Calif. Demographic Forum, N.Y. Acad. Scis., Sierra Club. Unitarian. Contbr. articles to books and profl. jours. Home: 815 Cima Linda Ln Santa Barbara CA 93108

HULL, ELEANOR HORNER, writer, editor, cons.; b. Dallas; d. Lee Meridan and Frances (Connor) Horner; student So. Meth. U.; spl. courses Columbia U.; m. Leon Gay Hull, Aug. 23, 1921 (div. July 1948); 1 dau., Carol Jean (Mrs. Jack Raymond Clark). Free-lance advt. research, 1936-40, 41-42; promoter fashion booklets, copywriter, copyreader Sterling Agy., N.Y.C., 1942-44; supr. editor govt. tng. material War Dept. Q.M. Army Corps, 1944-45; account exec. copywriter Gussow-Kahn Advt. Agy., 1945-46; advt. mgr. Kramer Bros., 1945-46; publicity dir. Henry Glass & Co., 1946-50; pres. Shoulderite, Inc., 1946-51; instr. fashion dept., extension div. CCNY, 1951-63, supr. dept., 1959-63; lectr., instr. Traphagen Sch. Fashion, 1956-67; mem. staff Fashion Digest mag., 1957-67, assoc. editor, 1962-67. Served with motor corps ARC, 1942-45. Mem. Woman's Press Club, Alpha Omicron Pi. Patentee in field. Designer Flag of States. Home: 3131 N 7th Ave Phoenix AZ 85013

HULL, ROBERT EDWIN, mechanical engineer; b. Ames, Iowa, Nov. 30, 1926; s. Fred Harold and Margaret Frances (Lush) H.; m. Barbara Ione Peterson, Oct. 2, 1948; children—Bruce Robert, Lee Allan, Roger Mark, Bryan Scott. B.S.M.E. with distinction, Worcester Poly Inst., 1946; M.S.M.E., Rennssalaer Poly. Inst., 1957. Asst. project engr. Pratt & Whitney Aircraft, East Hartford, Conn., 1948-58; sr. staff engr. Lockheed Missiles & Space Co., Sunnyvale, Calif., 1958—. Asst. Scoutmaster Boy Scouts of Am. Served to lt. USNR, 1944-47. Mem. ASME, AIAA, Conn. soc. Genealogists, Orange Hist. Soc., Santa Clara County Hist. and Geneal. Soc., Stratford Hist. Soc., Sigma Xi. Republican. Presbyterian. Clubs: Apple II, Commonwealth. Patentee gas turbine engine fuel control, gas turbine engine air bleed control.

HULLIHEN, ALICE ALVINA, safety administrator; Mellette, S.D., Aug. 5, 1932; d. Henry and Alvina Magdalena (Heinert) Reister; m. Clair Wayne Rahn, Oct. 29, 1949 (dec.); m. 2d, Robert Gene Hullihen, July 28, 1979; children—Donna Jordan, Diane Hanson, James, Jerry. Student Black Hills (S.D.) State Coll., 1968-69, Glendale (Ariz.) Community Coll., 1978-79, Ariz. State U. Asst. to supt. Hot Springs (S.D.) Pub. Schs., 1963-71, State S.D. Dept. Pub. Instrn., 1971-72; safety and health mgr. Holsum Bakery, Phoenix, 1980—; cons. fleet safety and accident prevention. Mem. Ariz. Workers Compensation Assn., Internat. TV Assn., Am. Soc. Safety Engrs., Nat. Assn. Ednl. Office Personnel, Ariz. Safety Engrs. Assn. (1st v.p., outstanding safety and accident prevention award), Am. Soc. Pub. Adminstrn. (outstanding superior pub. service award), Bus. and Profl. Women's Assn. Recipient Motor Fleet Safety award Continental Ins. Co.; Outstanding Safety award, Argonaut Ins. Cos. Republican. Lutheran. Office: 408 S 23d Ave Phoenix AZ 85005

HULLIN, SUSAN LEE, public relations executive; b. Walla Walla, Wash., May 22, 1944; d. Edward O. and Wilberta M. (Kirkman) Kanz; m. Tod Robert Hullin, May 6, 1967. B.A. in Polit. Sci., U. Wash., 1966. Exec. asst. to chmn. Garfinckel's, Washington, 1977-81; press relations/spl. events coordinator Emporium-Capwell, San Francisco, 1981—. Active San Francisco Symphony 500, Arts Council of Eureka Coll. (Ill.); bd. dirs. Historic Alexandria Found. Mem. Pub. Relations Soc. Am., San Francisco Bay Area Publicity Club, Fashion Group Jr. League of San Francisco. Republican. Presbyterian. Clubs: Commonwealth of Calif., Press of San Francisco, Army-Navy Country (Arlington, Va.). Home: 1702 Vallejo St San Francisco CA 94123 Office: 835 Market St San Francisco CA 94103

HULLIN, TOD ROBERT, real estate executive; b. Seattle, May 28, 1943; s. Jack Elmer and Floretta Elizabeth (Light) H.; m. Susan Lee Kanz, May 6, 1967. B.A. in Bus. Adminstrn., U. Wash., 1966. Staff asst. domestic council White House, Washington, 1973-74, assoc. dir. domestic council for housing and community devel., 1974-76; prin. asst. sec. def. for pub. affairs, Washington, 1976-77; v.p. Interstate Gen. Corp., St. Charles, Md., 1977-81; pres. Interstate Condominiums Inc. affiliate Interstate Gen. Corp., Albany, Calif., 1981—. Served to 1st lt. U.S. Army, 1967-69. Decorated Army Commendation medal; recipient award for outstanding pub. service Sec. of Def., 1977. Mem. Nat. Assn. Home Builders, Greater Washington Bd. Trade, U. Wash. Alumni Assn. (trustee, gov. Mid-Eastern region 1979-81), Sigma Nu. Republican. Presbyterian. Club: Army-Navy Country (Arlington, Va.). Home: 8 Campo Verde Circle San Pablo CA 94806 Office: 555 Pierce St Albany CA 94706

HULME, ROBERT DOUGLAS, film director; b. N.Y.C., Aug. 6, 1943; s. Horace Lincoln and Ann Marie (Marancy) H.; m. Diane Marie Vennerstrom, Dec. 14, 1968; children—Matthew, Aaron. B.S. in Bus., Ariz. State U., 1966. Assoc. creative dir. Foote, Cone & Belding, San Francisco, 1970-73; creative dir. Botsford Ketchum, San Francisco, 1973-77; dir. Robert Hulme Prodns., Hollywood, Calif., 1978—, dir. Paisley Prodns. Served with USAR, 1963-69. Mem. Dirs. Guild, Screen Actors Guild, AFTRA.

HULS, DURWOOD CRAIG, computer cons.; b. Preston, Idaho, July 15, 1940; s. D.F. and Elva Retta (Knudsen) H.; m. Laura Frick, Dec. 8, 1961; children—Scott, Stephen, David, Carrie. B.A., U. Wash., 1971. Mgr. data processing Heathtecna, Seattle, 1966-72; computer sales Benchmark Systems, Seattle, 1972-78; pres. Huls & Assocs., Portland, Oreg., 1974—; ptnr., v.p. Diamond Computer, Beaverton, Oreg., 1980—; lectr. in field. Served with U.S. Army, 1962-65. Developer software for sales mgmt. and motivation, bus. acctg. systems. Home: PO Box 260 Seaside OR 97138 Office: 15555 SW Bangy Rd Lake Oswego OR 97034

HUMBERGER, FRANK EDWARD, career and family counselor; b. Troy, Ohio, July 10, 1914; s. Frank Longfellow and Myrtle May (McDowell) H.; B.S., Case Inst. Tech., 1935; B.D., San Francisco Theol. Sem., 1959; Th.D., Pacific Sch. Religion, 1967; m. Jackeline H. Armstrong, Apr. 14, 1973; children by previous marriage—Sallie Marshall, Edward McDowell, Janet Gayle. Owner, mgr. Tech. Metal Processing, Inc., Cleve., 1945-57, Aerobraze Corp., 1953-57; ordained teaching elder, United Prebyterian Ch. U.S.A., 1959; pastor Presbyn. Ch., Turlock, Calif., 1960-68; pres. Interpersonal Relations, Inc., Bellevue, Wash., 1964-83, Exec. Services Assocs., Bellevue, 1978-83; IPR, Inc., 1983—; prof. mgmt. dept. San Francisco State U., 1967-70; asso. prof. psychology John F. Kennedy U., Moraga, Calif., 1967-70; pres. Calif. Health Group, 1974-78; lectr. Sch. Edn., U. Pacific, Stockton, Calif., 1975-77. Chmn. Grower-Worker Reconciliation Task Force, United Presbyn. Ch. U.S.A., San Joaquin Valley, Calif., 1965-68; dir. coll. community relations San Francisco State U., 1970. Fellow Am. Assn. Pastoral Counselors; mem. Am. Assn. Marriage and Family Therapists (cert. supr.; clin. mem.), Am. Soc. Tng. and Devel., Blue Key, Tau Beta Pi. Republican. Clubs: St. Francis Yacht, Bellevue Athletic, Orcas Island Yacht, Orcas Tennis. Author: Your Personal Career, 1973; Developing Effective Communication Styles, 1979; Outplacement and Inplacement Counseling, 1983; contbr. articles to profl. jours. Home: PO Box 100 Star Route Eastsound WA 98245

HUMBURG, NEIL EDWARD, agronomist, contract researcher, consultant; b. LaCrosse, Kans., May 16, 1933; s. Harold Bernreuter and Alvene Martha (Markwart) H.; m. Renae Bygel, June 17, 1961; children—Karen, James. B.S., Colo. State U., 1955, M.S., 1965; Ph.D., U. Wis., 1970. Rancher-farmer, Ness City, Kans., 1955-62; grad. research asst. Colo. State U., Fort Collins, 1963-65; grad. research asst., research asst. U. Wis., Madison, 1965-70; asst. prof. dept. agronomy Kans. State U., Manhattan, 1970-75; agronomist Humburg Ranch, Inc.,

Ness City, 1975-76; asst. prof. weed sci. U. Wyo., Laramie, 1976—; cons. to Saudi Arabia; external reviewer Dept. Agr. Central Gt. Plains Field Sta. Mem. adminstrv. bd. First United Methodist Ch., Topeka, Kans., 1972-74; mem. troop com. Boy Scouts Am., 1981—. Grantee in field. Mem. Weed Sci. Soc. Am. (chmn. herbicide handbook com.), Am. Soc. Agronomy, Western Soc. Weed Sci. (chmn. resolutions com.), Crop Sci. Soc. Am., Plant Growth Regulator Soc. Am., Soil Sci. Soc. Am., Antique Automobile Club of Am. Sigma Xi, Gamma Sigma Delta. Republican. Club: Lions (Laramie). Contbr. articles to weed sci. to profl. jours.; editor: Herbicide Handbook of Weed Sci. Soc. Am., 1983. Home: 1974 N 17th St Laramie WY 82070 Office: PO Box 3354 University Sta Laramie WY 82071

HUMBURG, RENAE BYGEL, vocational education planner/researcher; b. Sault Ste. Marie, Mich., Sept. 10, 1936; d. Clayton Maxwell and Ruth Viola Maureen (Kullberg) Bygel; m. Neil Humburg, June 17, 1961; children—Karen, Jim. Student North Tex. State U., 1958, U. Colo., 1959; M.A. in Teaching, Colo. State U., 1965; Ed.D., U. No. Colo., 1978. Bus. instr., adult edn. tchr. various schs., 1959-74; career edn. coordinator Central Kans. Area Vocat. Tech. Sch., Newton, 1974-76; vocat. edn. instr. U. Wyo., Laramie, 1976-77, research assoc., 1977-78; state planner/researcher vocat. edn. Wyo. State Dept. Edn., Cheyenne, 1979—; Mem. PEO, AAUW, Nat. Bus. Edn. Assn., Am. Vocat. Assn., Phi Delta Kappa, Delta Pi Epsilon. Democrat. Contbr. articles to profl. jours. Home: 1974 N 17th St Laramie WY 82070 Office: State Dept Education Hathaway Bldg Cheyenne WY 82002

HUME, MERRIL WAYNE, statistician, educator; b. San Francisco, Apr. 30, 1939; s. Wayne Stanford and Esther Alberta (Crow) H.; m. Nancy Johnson, Oct. 16, 1938; children—David, James, Ellen. B.S. in Physics, Coll. William and Mary, 1960; M.S. in Math. Stats., Va. Poly. Inst., 1964, Ph.D., 1966. Asst. prof. math. stats. Case Western Res. U., Cleve., 1966-70; assoc. prof. U. Mo., Rolla, 1970-74; research specialist Rockwell Internat., Rocky Flats, Colo., 1974—; tchr., cons. NIH grantee. Mem. Am. Statis. Assn., Nat. Mgmt. Assn., ASTM (chmn. C26.06), Sigma Xi, Phi Kappa Phi, Pi Mu Epsilon, Sigma Pi Sigma, Beta Gamma Sigma. Contbr. articles to profl. jours. Home: 6564 W 85th Ave Arvada CO 80003 Office: Rockwell Internat Golden CO 80401

HUMMEL, FRED EDWARD, consulting engineer, mining, metallurgical, petroleum and mechanical engineer; b. Los Angeles, May 8, 1906; s. Albert Edward and Minnie Louise (Hardegen) H.; m. Ruth Glenna Horton, May 1, 1926 (dec. Feb. 1955); children—Fred Ernest, Marilyn Jean; m. Marianne Pance, Aug. 10, 1958. B.S., S.D. Sch. Mines and Tech., 1931, Metall. Engr., 1938. Registered profl. engr., Calif. Chemist Holy Sugar Corp., 1926-27; metall. engr. Am. Smelting & Refining Co., 1931-35; petroleum and mech. engr. Shell Oil Co., 1935-47; cons. mining, metall., petroleum and mech. engr. Hummel & Christianson Cons. Engrs., Ojai, Calif., 1947—; dir. Moburg Labs.; dir., pres. El Roblar Corp. Named Engr. of Yr., Ventura and Santa Barbara Counties, 1980. Mem. Am. Petroleum Inst., AIME, Soc. Petroleum Engrs., Nat. Soc. Profl. Engrs., Calif. Soc. Profl. Engrs., Ventura County Engrs. Republican. Club: Play Boy. Patentee in field. Home: 338 Bonita Dr Ojai CA 93023 Office: 102 E Alisa St PO Box 577 Ojai CA 93023

HUMPAL, DONALD STANLEY, agriculturalist; b. Wilmington, N.C., June 25, 1952; s. Stanley Francis and Joyce Gertrude (Green) H.; m. Leah Louise Jordan, Dec. 28, 1974; 1 son, Patrick Jordan. B.S. in Biology, Yale U., 1974; M.S. in Internat. Agrl. Devel., U. Calif.-Davis, 1977. Staff agriculturalist Devel. Alternatives, Inc., Washington, 1978—. Mem. Am. Soc. Agronomy, Soil Sci. Soc. Am., Crop Sci. Soc. Am., Nitrogen Fixing Tree Assn., Yale Alumni Assn., Calif. Aggie Alumni Assn. Office: Devel Alternatives Inc 624 9th St NW 6th Floor Washington DC 20001

HUMPHERYS, ALFRED GLEN, museum director; b. Montpelier, Idaho, May 7, 1939; s. Alfred and Ivie Mae (Wood) H.; m. Marilyn Stanley, June 6, 1963; children—Alan Glen, Kenneth Dean, Grant Warren. B.S., Brigham Young U., 1963, M.A., 1964; Ph.D., U. N.Mex., 1974. Tchr., Can. Cardston Sch. Div. (Alta.), 1964; history instr. Ricks Coll., Rexburg, Idaho, 1965-69, fgn. student advisor, 1966-69; ranger, historian Nat. Park Service, Washington, 1966; grad. teaching asst. U. N.Mex., Albuquerque, 1970-73; sargent at arms Utah Senate, 1974; curator, dir. Wheeler Hist. Farm, Salt Lake City, 1976—. Exec. dir. Wheeler Farm Friends, Inc. Recipient award Standard Oil Calif., 1957; Union Pacific R.R. scholar, 1957. Mem. Utah Mus. Assn., Western History Assn. Republican. Mem. Ch. Jesus-Christ of Latter-day Saints. Contbr. articles to profl. jours. Office: 6351 S 9th St E Salt Lake City UT 84121

HUMPHERY, JOSEPH FRANKLYN, banker; b. Hollywood, Calif., Sept. 25, 1941; s. Franklin Levant and Grace Elizabeth (Jackson) H.; m. Sheila Marie Boylston, June 15, 1968 (div.); children—Elizabeth Grace, Catherine Anne. A.B., Occidental Coll., 1963; M.B.A., Stanford U., 1965; Ph.D., U. So. Calif., 1970. Asst. prof. dept. econs. Occidental Coll., Los Angeles, 1967-78, chmn. dept., 1975-78, dean of men, 1969-73; asst. v.p. Fed. Home Loan Bank San Francisco, 1978-81, v.p., 1981—, dir. research, 1981—. Recipient Lincoln Found. prize, 1970; Haynes Found. grantee, 1976-78; Mellon Found. grantee, 1978. Mem. Am. Econ. Assn., Western Econ. Assn., Phi Beta Kappa. Episcopalian. Contbr. articles to profl. jours.

HUMPHREY, SEBRON ARTHUR, lawyer; b. El Paso, Tex., Sept. 22, 1951; s. Howard and Annie (Williams) H. B.A., Morehouse Coll., 1974; M.A., Tufts U., 1976; J.D., Howard U., 1980. Bar: Tex. 1981. Legal asst. Bergson, Borkland, Margolis and Adler, Washington, 1976-78; law clk. Office of Mayor, City of Washington, 1978; law clk. GSA, Washington, 1978-80; exec. dir. Humphrey and Assocs., Sacramento, Calif., 1979—; columnist Sacramento Observer, 1983—; assoc. No. Calif. Law Ctr., Sacramento, 1983—; cons. bus. devel.; tchr. internat. relations Calif. State U.-Sacramento. Morehouse Coll. scholar, 1970-74; Tufts U.-Fletcher Sch. Law and Diplomacy Pub. Service fellow, 1975. Mem. Nat. Bar Assn., Wiley Manuel Bar Assn., NAACP, Delta Theta Phi. Democrat. Baptist. Author: Legal Relations Among Modern Nations, 1983.

HUMPHREY, THOMAS WARD, librarian; b. Hartford, Ky., Oct. 20, 1948; s. James William and Violet Rene (Ward) H.; m. Billie Powell Staton, May 20, 1973; children—Sybil Rene, Laura Nicole. B.A., Ky. Wesleyan Coll., 1970; M.L.S., Peabody Coll., Nashville, 1972. Librarian, Ky. Wesleyan Coll., Owensboro, 1970-79, faculty Library Sch., 1973-79; head librarian Central Wyo. Coll., Riverton, 1979; library dir. Eastern N.Mex. U., Clovis, 1983—. Mem. Wyo. Library Assn., Mountain-Plains Library Assn., Ky. Hist. Soc., West Central Ky. Family Research Assn., Nat. Grigsby Family Assn., Wyo. Edn. Assn., Fremont County (Wyo.) Geneal. Soc. Democrat. Methodist. Author: Index to the History of Daviess County, Kentucky 1883, 1981. Home: 900 Collins Ave Clovis NM 88101 Office: Eastern NMex U Clovis NM 88101

HUMPHREYS, EVAN TIMOTHY, educator; b. Seattle, Mar. 2, 1948; s. Walter Stanley and Alva Margaret (Moev) H. B.A., Seattle Pacific U., 1971, M.Ed., 1982; postgrad. Central Wash. U., 1973-75. Cert. secondary sch. counselor, tchr., Oreg.; cert. tchr., Wash. Plant mgr., truck driver Pearcy Fruit Co., 1965-66; truck driver Seattle Times, U.S. Post Office, 1967-71, 80; instr. A.C. Davis Sr. High Sch., Yakima, Wash., 1971-78; campus life coordinator Youth for Christ, 1978-80; guidance counselor South Albany High Sch., Albany, Oreg., 1982—; ch. cons.; free lance photographer; speaker at service clubs. Recipient Outstanding Advisor award Key Club, 1973; selected commencement speaker A.C. Davis Sr. High Sch., 1973, sr. class speaker, 1980. Mem. Am. Psychol. Assn., Am. Personnel and Guidance Assn., Oreg. Personnel Guidance Assn., Wash. Edn. Assn., Oreg. Edn. Assn., NEA. Club: Kiwanis. Contbr. articles to profl. jours.

HUMPHRIES, MARTHA JEAN, learning resources director, b. Camden, N.J., July 19, 1950; d. William Harry and Mary Catherine (Aust) Nethery; B.A., Alma (Mich.) Coll., 1972; M.A., Mich. State U., East Lansing, 1977; M.A.M., U. Phoenix, 1981; m. James David Humphries, III, June 8, 1974. Music tchr. Stockbridge (Mich.) Community Schs., 1972-74; media librarian Mich. Law Enforcement Officers Tng. Council, Lansing, 1976; media librarian, dir. learning resources No. Ariz. U., Flagstaff, 1976-78; dir. learning resources Embry-Riddle Aero. U.-West, Prescott, Ariz., 1978—. Vol., A.R.C., 1965-76. Mem. Assn. Ednl. Communications and Tech., Am. Assn. Aerospace Educators, Am. Aviation Hist. Soc., Univ. Aviation Assn., Flight Safety Found., Future Airline Profls. Am., ALA, Soaring Soc. Am. (dir. aerospace edn. resource center), Ariz. Library Assn. Presbyterian. Author bibliographies. Office: 3200 N Willow Creek Rd Prescott AZ 86301

HUNDLEY, JOHN KENNETH, foundation executive; b. Nowata, Okla., Feb. 27, 1942; s. Loris and Annie Laurie (LaBarr) H.; m. Michele Maria Chastang, July 2, 1967; children—James Michael, Colette Elizabeth, John Robert, Kimberly Victorine, JoAnn Ruby. A.A. in Police Sci., Cerritos Coll., 1969. Supr. Los Angeles County Sheriff's Dept., 1963-75; tchr., program supr. ABC Unified Sch. Dist., Cerritos, Calif., 1969-77; pres., chmn. bd. Better Citizens Found., Hawaiian Gardens, Calif., 1977—; cons. traffic safety programs. Mem. Bd. Edn. Huntington Beach High Sch., 1977-79. Mem. Hawaiian Gardens C. of C., Calif. Assn. Traffic Schs. Republican. Club: Magic Island (Newport Beach). Office: 12018 E Centralia Rd Hawaiian Gardens CA 90716

HUNG, CHING-MAO, research scientist; b. Taiwan, May 28, 1941; s. Yi-shiang and Yeh (Huang) H.; m. Pei-jean Lee, Jan. 1, 1970; children—Jeffrey, Emilie, Albert. B.S.M.E., Nat. Taiwan U., 1965; M.S. in Engring., Cornell U., 1968, Ph.D., 1972. Lic. mech. engr., Calif. Research assoc. scientist Lockheed Missiles and Space Co., Huntsville, Ala., 1972-73; NRC felow NASA Ames Research Ctr., Moffett Field, Calif., 1973-75, research scientist, 1978—; cons. DCW Industries, Studio City, Calif., 1975-78. Treas. Taiwanese Alliance Interculture, 1977-80. Served to 2d lt. Taiwan A.F. Nat. Taiwan U. honor student scholar, 1963, 64, 65; Cornell U. John McMullen fellow, 1967; recipient NASA spl. achievement award, 1980. Mem. AIAA, N.Y. Acad. Scis., Sigma Xi. Contbr. articles to tech. jours. Home: 994 Nettle Pl Sunnyvale CA 94086 Office: Computational Fluid Dynamics Branch NASA Ames Center Moffett Field CA 94035

HUNG, FRED CHIA-CHUN, economist, educator; b. Shanghai, China, Apr. 28, 1925; s. Sun Chang and Tsui Tseng)King) H.; m. Hwa Ching Lok, 1955; children—Cynthia Hung Stahl, David, Jeanette. A.B., St. John's U., Shanghai, 1947; Ph.D., U. Wash., 1955. Predoctoral assoc., acting instr., acting asst. prof., research assoc. U. Wash., 1950-56; research fellow Harvard U., 1956-57; asst. prof. U. Calif.-Davis, 1957-60; asst. prof. econs. U. Hawaii, Manoa, 1960-62, assoc. prof., 1962-68, prof., 1968—, chmn. dept., 1981, chmn. East Asian studies, 1968-74, 76-81; dir. Econ. Research Ctr., 1962-65; external examiner econs. and commerce Nanyang U., Singapore, 1971-74. NDEA related Fulbright-Hays fellow, Taiwan, 1965-66. Mem. Am. Econ. Assn., Western Econ. Assn., Hawaiian Econ. Assn., Asian Studies on the Pacific Coast. Author: (with others) Interlocking Relationship in Hawaii and Public Regulation of Ocean Transportation, 1961; Current Economic Status of the Hawaiian Sugar Industry with Special Reference to the General Excise Tax, 1962.

HUNGERFORD, CURTIS RANDALL, education educator, consultant, researcher; b. Fresno, Calif., Aug. 1, 1930; s. Samuel Sylvester and Evelyn Hungerford McKenna; m. Mabel Darleen Burton, Dec. 22, 1956; 1 dau., Mary Hungerford Lund. B.A., in Theatre and Philosophy, Stanford U., 1952; M.A. in Telecommunication, U. So. Calif., 1956, Ph.D. in Higher Edn. Administration and Communication, 1967. Cert. community coll. adminstr., tchr., Calif. Dir. pub. relations, asst. to pres. Los Angeles State Coll., 1957-62, assoc. dean Coll. Continuing Edn. U. So. Calif., 1962-69; dean acad. affairs faculty and grad. sch., Western N.Mex. U., Silver City, 1969-73; asst. to pres., dir. edn. dept. Woodbury U., Los Angeles, 1973-74; v.p. Investors Research Internat., Pace Corp., Beverly Hills, Calif., 1974-75; western regional adminstr. human factors faculty Inst. Safety and Systems Mgmt., U. So. Calif., 1975-77; prof. ednl. adminstrn. Brigham Young U., Provo, 1977—. So. Calif. coordinator state constrn. bonds; pres. Community Concerts Assn.; sec. Los Angeles Town Hall; active Mayor's Los Angeles Sr. Citizen Edn. Com., dir. Everywoman's Village; active Smithsonian Assocs., Govs. Higher Edn. Council Improving Quality of Life N. Mex., Acad. Council Higher Edn. N. Mex., N. Mex. Commn. Humanities; bd. dirs. Festival Faith and Freedom Found., Beverly Hills. Served with U.S. Army, 1952-54. Western N. Mex. U. grantee, 1972-75; recipient Stanford U. Mother's Club award 1952; U. So. Calif. Telecommunication's award 1960; Brigham Young U. award excellence in edn. 1981. Mem. Am. Assn. Higher Edn., Am. Soc. Tng. and Devel., Nat. Soc. Study Communication, Am. Coll. Pub. Relations Assn., AAAS, Am. Acad. Polit. and Social Sci., N. Central Regional Accrediting Assn., Alpha Epsilon Rho, Phi Delta Kappa. Club: Los Angeles Athletic. Contbr. numerous articles to profl. jours. Home: 3000 Iroquois Dr Provo UT 84601 Office: MCKB 310-C Dept Edn Adminstrn Brigham Young U Provo UT 84602

HUNGERFORD, DALE, health care company executive; b. La Grange, Ill., May 16, 1936; s. Jonathan Donald and Helen Blanche (Junker) H.; B.S. in Bus. Administrn., Bowling Green State U., 1958; postgrad. U. Md., 1963-64; m. Beverly Ann Derrick, May 6, 1961; children—Lance Byron, Rex Lee, Kimberly Derrick. Personnel interviewer Allstate Ins. Co., Harrison, N.Y., 1961-62, personnel asst., 1967-69; mgr. salary adminstrn. Dun & Bradstreet, N.Y.C., 1969-71; dir. personnel Cooper Labs., Inc., Palo Alto, Calif., 1971-80, v.p., 1976—, v.p. personnel and adminstrv. services, 1980—. Treas., Cub Scouts, Westchester-Putnam council Boy Scouts Am., 1972-73. Served to capt. U.S. Army, 1959-61, 62-67. Mem. Am. Compenation Assn., Am. Soc. Personnel Adminstrn. (dist. dir. 1974-75, v.p. 1982—), No. Calif. Human Resources Council, Pharm. Mfrs. Assn., Health Industry Mfrs. Assn. (spl. compensation survey com. 1981—), Westchester Personnel Mgmt. Assn. (dir. 1973-75, pres. 1974, Person of Yr. 1975), Santa Cruz Mountain Trail Assn. Republican. Lutheran. Club: Brookside. Home: 19241 Brockton Ln Saratoga CA 95070 Office: Cooper Labs Inc 3145 Porter Dr Palo Alto CA 94304

HUNKIN, GEOFFREY GILBERT, cons. engr.; b. Cornwall, Eng., Aug. 2, 1923; came to U.S., 1968, naturalized, 1975; s. Edwin Gilbert and Florence Adelaide (Bunt) H.; B.S., Sch. of Mines, Cornwall, 1949; m. Margot A.E., Drinkwater, Nov. 30, 1945; children—Philip Bingham, Elinor Patricia, Geoffrey Bingham. With Mysore Gold Mining, India, 1949-52, Macalder Mines, Kenya, Africa, 1952-57, Rio Algom Mines, Can., 1957, Stanrock Mines, Can., 1958, Silvermines, Ireland, 1965-68, Anaconda Co., Utah and N.Mex., 1968-71; mgr. mining and engring. Westinghouse Electric Corp., Denver, 1971-74; cons. engr. in pvt. practice, Can., Australia, U.S., 1974; pres. Hunkin Engrs., Inc. and Ground Water Sampling, Inc., Littleton, Colo., 1976—; lectr. in field. Served to lt. Royal Navy, 1940-45. Recipient Robert Earll McConnell award AIME, 1977; named Disting. mem. Soc. Mining Engrs., 1977. Fellow Inst. of Mining and Metallurgy; mem. Nat. Soc. Profl. Engrs., Cons. Engrs. Council Am., Soc. Mining Engrs. of AIME, Soc. Petroleum Engrs. of AIME, Can. Inst. Mining, Metall. and Petroleum Engrs. Republican. Episcopalian. Clubs: Columbine Country, Petroleum of Denver, Masons, Shriners. Patentee in field. Address: 9 Meadow Lark Ln Littleton CO 80123

HUNKINS, RAYMOND BREEDLOVE, lawyer; b. Culver City, Calif., Mar. 19, 1939; s. Charles Franklin and Louise (Breedlove) H.; student U. Colo., 1957, U. Mont., 1958-61; B.S., U. Wyo., 1967, J.D., 1968; m. Deborah McBride; children—Amanda Louise, Blake McBride, Ashley Marie. Admitted to Wyo. bar, 1968; partner firm Jones, Jones, Vines and Hunkins, Wheatland, 1968—; dir. Am. Bank of Wheatland; bd. dirs. Wyo. Inst., Wyo. Law Enforcement Acad., 1968—. Mem. exec. com., sec., chmn. subcom. edn. and tng. Wyo. Gov.'s Crime Commn., 1968-78; chmn. Platte County Republican Central Com., 1972-74; bd. dirs. Platte County March of Dimes, 1968, chmn., 1968; mem. adv. council Coll. Commerce and Industry, U. Wyo., 1971—, vice chmn., 1977-78, chmn., 1978-79. Served with USMCR, 1956-58. Mem. Am. Bar Assn. (aviation com. litigation sect.), Am. Trial Lawyers Assn., Wyo. Trial Lawyers Assn. (pres. 1981-82), Wyo. Stockgrowers Assn., Am. Polled Hereford Assn., U. Wyo. Alumni Assn. (v.p. 1972, pres. 1973-74), Platte County Bar Assn. (pres. 1972). Mem. Ch. of Christ (trustee 1970-75). Clubs: Elks, Lions; Wheatland Golf (dir. 1969-72). Home: 309 10th St Wheatland WY 82201 Office: PO Drawer 189 Wheatland WY 82201

HUNNER, WALTER CLARK, soil scientist; b. Palo Alto, Calif., Aug. 21, 1951; s. Earl Eugene and Helen Christine (Baxter) H.; m. Sherry Fischer, Jan. 14, 1983. B.S. in Earth Scis., Stanford U., 1974; M.S. in Watershed Mgmt., Humboldt State U., Arcata, Calif., 1983. Geology phys. technician U.S. Geol. Survey, Menlo Park, Calif. and Lakewood, Colo., 1974; geologist Cities Service Minerals Corp., Anchorage, 1975, 76; soil scientist U.S. Forest Service, Upper Lake, Calif., 1978, Soil Conservation Service, Anchorage, 1979, Bur. Land Mgmt., Arcata, 1980; soil scientist hydrology dept. Colville Confederated Tribes, Nespelem, Wash., 1981—; teaching asst. dept. natural resources Humboldt State U., 1980-81. Mem. Soil Sci. Soc. Am., Internat. Soc. Soil Sci., Soil Conservation Soc. Am., Natural Resources Def. Council, Sierra Club. Home: PO Box 242 1007 Camas St Coulee Dam WA 99116 Office: PO Box 647 Hwy 155 Nespelem WA 99155

HUNNICUTT, ANN SPROULE, dental hygienist; b. Norfolk, Va., July 18, 1930; d. Samuel Jackson and Alfreda (Jones) Sproule; m. Glen Charles Luff, Aug. 17, 1955; children—Susan Carol, David Gerrish; m. 2d, William Howard Taake, July 18, 1981. A.A., Harcum Jr. Coll., 1950; cert. Thomas W. Evans Sch. Oral Hygien, U. Pa., 1953; B.S. with honors in Speech Pathology, Eastern N.Mex. U., 1968; postgrad. McGeorge Sch. Law, U. Pacific, 1973-77. Registered dental hygienist, Calif., Pa. Dental hygienist, 1967—; owner, operator ind. dental hygiene practice, Santa Barbara, Calif., 1977—; lectr. in field. Founder, 1st pres. Davis (Calif.) Soc. for Prevention of Cruelty to Animals, 1971. Recipient Humanitarian of Yr. award Sacramento Soc. for Prevention of Cruelty to Animals, 1974. Mem. Santa Barbara Dental Hygiene Assn. (pres. 1977, 78), Santa Barbara C. of C., Alumni U. Pa. Republican. Author: Be Your Own Boss, 1979; contbr. articles to profl. jours. Office: 1514 Anacapa St Santa Barbara CA 93101

HUNNICUTT, RICHARD PEARCE, metall. engr.; b. Asheville, N.C., June 15, 1926; s. James Ballard and Ida (Black) H.; B.S. in Metall. Engring., Stanford, 1951, M.S., 1952; m. Susan Haight, Apr. 9, 1954; children—Barbara, Beverly, Geoffrey, Anne. Research metallurgist Gen. Motors Research Labs., 1952-55; sr. metallurgist Aerojet-Gen. Corp., 1955-57; head materials and processes Firestone Engring. Lab., 1957-58; head phys. scis. group Dalmo Victor Co., Monterey, 1958-61, head materials lab., 1961-62; v.p. Anamet Labs., Inc., 1962—; partner Pyrco Co. Served with AUS, 1943-46. Mem. Electrochem. Soc., AIME, Am. Soc. Metals, ASTM, Am. Welding Soc., Am. Soc. Lubrication Engrs. Research on frictional behavior of materials, devel. armored fighting vehicles; author: Pershing, A History of the Medium Tank T20 Series, 1971; Sherman, A History of the American Medium Tank, 1978. Home: 2805 Benson Way Belmont CA 94002 Office: 2827 7th St Berkeley CA 94702

HUNSAKER, DOUGLAS JAMES, consumer products company executive; b. Salt Lake City, Nov. 22, 1939; s. Milton L. and Mary Rose (Ferrlen) H.; m. Olivia Jane Schwan, Nov. 18, 1961; children—Milton, Amanda. B.S., U. Utah, 1963; M.B.A., St. Marys Coll., Moraga, Calif., 1980. With Albertson's Inc., 1961-66; salesman Bristol Myers Products, Inc., 1966-68, key account mgr., 1969, nat. sales promotion mgr., N.Y.C., 1969-70; dist. mgr. N.Y. and N.J., 1970-75, dist. sales mgr. no. Calif. and no. Nev., 1975—; mem. faculty Diablo Valley Coll., Pleasant Hill, Calif., 1980—. Recipient Merchandiser of Yr. award Bristol Myers and Point of Purchase Advt. Inst., 1968; Salesman of Yr. award Bristol Myers, 1969. Mem. Kappa Nu. Democrat. Roman Catholic.

HUNSAKER, FLOYD B., accountant; b. Collinston, Utah, Sept. 6, 1915; s. Allen G. and Mary Ann (Bowcutt) H.; grad. high sch.; m. Zella D. Hepworth, Mar. 3, 1943; children—Marcia (Mrs. Marvin Bahr), Charlene (Mrs. Abelino Ancira), Sonia (Mrs. Val Fisher), Rhonda (Mrs. Kim Veigel), Tamara. Owner, operator dairy farm, Bedford, Wyo., 1946-70; accountant, Afton, Wyo., 1959—; owner Credit Bur. Star Valley, Afton, 1967—; municipal judge Town of Afton, 1967-77; local office claimstaker Wyo. Unemployment Compensation Dept., 1975—. Pres., Holdaway Sch. PTA, 1960; active Boy Scouts Am., 1946-49, 58-67; bd. dirs. Star Valley Sr. Citizens, 1981-83; pres. Lower Valley 4-H council, 1961-62, leader, 1959-63; chmn. Star Valley chpt. Am. Revolution Bicentennial Adminstrn., 1975-76, Star Valley chpt. ARC, 1976—. Served with Devils Brigade, 1941-45; ETO. Mem. Nat., Wyo. socs. pub. accountants, Farm Bur. (exec. sec. Lincoln County 1961-66), Nat. Platform Assn., Afton C. of C. (dir. 1973-74), VFW (dist. comdr. Wyo. 1974-75, 77-78, state dept. jr. vice comdr. 1978-79, state comdr. 1980-81, dist. comdr. 1982-83). Mem. Ch. of Jesus Christ of Latter-day Saints. Home: 323 Adams St Afton WY 83110 Office: 498 Washington St Afton WY 83110

HUNSAKER, M. LEON, safety educator, consultant; b. Brigham City, Utah, Nov. 27, 1944; s. Allen Collins and Clara (Harmston) H.; m. Barbara Lynn Blanie, July 15, 1974; children—Becky, Jesse. B.S., Utah State U., 1967, M.S., 1969. Safety dir. Ariz. div. ARC, Phoenix, 1970-73, Maricopa County chpt., 1968-73; safety dir. Ariz. Safety Council, Phoenix, 1973-76; safety specialist, instr. and instructional coordinator Extension Safety Edn. Service, Utah State U., Logan, 1978—; coordinator safety instructional programs Utah bus. and industry. Mem. Am. Soc. Safety Engrs., Associated Safety Engrs. Ariz. (pres., 1974-75), Sigma Phi Epsilon. Office: UMC 83 Logan UT 84322

HUNSBERGER, CHARLES WESLEY, county librarian; b. Elkhart, Ind., Sept. 25, 1929; s. Charles August and Emma Edna (Zimmerman) H.; m. Hilda Carol Showalter, July 3, 1949 (div.); children—Jonathan Wesley, Jerald Wayne, Jane Wannette. B.A., Bethel Coll., Mishawaka, Ind., 1952; M.L.S., Ind. U., 1967. Mem. Ft. Wayne (Ind.) Library Staff, 1960-62; dir. Columbia (Ind.) City Library, 1962-64, Monroe County Library, Bloomington, Ind., 1964-71, Clark County Library Dist., Las Vegas, Nev., 1971—; cons. sch. pub. libraries, 1968-70; lectr. library schs. Ind. U., 1970-71, U. Ariz., 1974, U. Nev., Reno, 1976; mem. Nev. Council on Libraries, 1973—, chmn., 1980-81. Mem. Calif. Library

Assn., ALA, Nev. Library Assn. Democrat. Club: Las Vegas-Paradise Rotary (pres. 1979-80). Home: 1544 Hialeah Dr Las Vegas NV 89109 Office: Clark County Library Dist 1401 E Flamingo Rd Las Vegas NV 89109

HUNT, ARLON JASON, physicist; b. Iowa, Oct. 8, 1939; s. Frank and Dorothy H.; B.A. in Physics, U. Minn., 1963; M.S., U. Ariz., 1971, Ph.D., 1974; m. Mary Quinby, July 10, 1971; children—Elena, Robb. Asst. physicist Univac Corp., St. Paul, 1959-63; physicist Stanford Research Inst., Menlo Park, Calif., 1963-65; vol. tchr. Peace Corps, Malaysia, 1965-67; research assoc. U. Ariz., 1968-74, postdoctoral asso. Optical Scis. Center, 1974-76; staff scientist Lawrence Berkeley Lab., U. Calif., Berkeley, 1976—; pres. Particle Tech. Assos.; cons. in field. Precinct committeeman Tucson, 1972-74. Mem. Am. Phys. Soc., Optical Soc. Am., AAAS, Am. Meteorol. Soc., Internat. Solar Energy Soc. Research, numerous publs. on physics and optics of small particle systems, solar energy, electro optics and alt. energy systems; patentee in field. Home: 2025 Manzanita Dr Oakland CA 94611 Office: 90-2024 Lawrence Berkeley Lab Berkeley CA 94720

HUNT, BRIAN LINDSAY, aerospace engr.; b. Cambridge, Eng., May 10, 1937; came to U.S., 1979; s. Frederick William and Ethel Lindsay (Jamieson) H.; M.A., Cambridge U., 1961; Sc.M., Brown U., 1965, Ph.D., 1967; m. Julia Vyse, Aug. 27, 1960; children—Tony Stephen, Andrea Jane. Performance engr. Bristol (Eng.) Siddeley Engrs. Ltd., 1961-63; lectr. U. Bristol, 1967-76, reader, 1976-79; propulsion research mgr. Northrop Corp., Hawthorne, Calif., 1979-82, aeroscis. research mgr., 1982—; cons. Rolls-Royce Ltd., Brit. Aerospace, Unilever Co., 1970-79. Served as pilot officer RAF, 1956-58. State scholar, U.K., 1958-61; Corinna Borden Keen fellow, Brown U., 1964-65; chartered engr. Fellow Royal Aero. Soc., AIAA (asso.). Club: Squash Club Internat. (Torrance, Calif.). Contbr. research writings to publs. in field. Home: 17284 Walnut St Fountain Valley CA 92708 Office: One Northrop Ave Hawthorne CA 90250

HUNT, ELIZABETH HOPE, psychologist; b. Hattiesburg, Miss., Oct. 14, 1943; d. Emory Spear and I. Elizabeth (Burkett) Hunt; m. John Volney Allcott, III, Sept. 9, 1978; 1 son, Hunt. A.B., Sweet Briar Coll., 1965; M.S.W., U. Pa., 1971; Ph.D., U. Oreg., 1980. Lic. psychologist, Oreg. Peace Corps vol., Santiago, Chile, 1967-69; civil rights specialist Region III, HEW, Phila., 1971-74; doctoral fellow Rehab. Research and Tng. Ctr. in Mental Retardation, U. Oreg., Eugene, 1974-77; intern Phila. Child Guidance Ctr., U. Pa., Phila., 1977-78; psychologist in pvt. practice, Oreg. Family Ctr., Eugene, 1980—; lectr., workshops in field. Bd. dirs. Lane County Relief Nursery for Abused and Neglected Children, 1981—. Nat. Inst. Handicapped Research grantee, 1977-79. Mem. Am. Psychol. Assn., Oreg. Psychol. Assn., Lane County Psychologists Assn., Physicians for Social Responsibility (co-chmn. Eugene speakers bur. 1982—), Profl. Women's Network of Oreg. Contbr. articles to profl. jours. Home: 2650 Cresta De Ruta Eugene OR 97403 Office: 3225 Willamette St Suite 3 Eugene OR 97405

HUNT, HAROLD KEITH, marketing specialist, educator; b. Ames, Iowa, Apr. 16, 1938; s. Harold Gilbert and Dorothy Harriet (Petro) H.; B.S., U. Utah, 1961, M.B.A., 1962; Ph.D., Northwestern U., 1972; m. Carolyn Sue Sedgwick, Aug. 21, 1961; children—David, Nathan, Tacy, Cale, Sara, Katie, Adria, Hayley. Instr., Imperial Valley Coll., 1962-64, Northwestern U., 1964-67; asst. prof. bus. adminstrn. and journalism U. Iowa, 1967-73; consumer behavior and mktg. research specialist FTC, Washington, 1973-74; assoc. prof. bus. adminstrn. U. Wyo., 1974-75; prof. bus. mgmt. Brigham Young U., 1975—; co-sponsor ann. conf. Consumer Satisfaction/Dissatisfaction and Complaining Behavior, 1976—; cons. FDA, FTC. Mem. Assn. Consumer Research (exec. sec., past pres.), Am. Acad. Advt. (exec. sec., past pres.), Am. Council Consumer Interests, Am. Psychol. Assn., Am. Mktg. Assn. Mormon. Editor: Jour. Advt., 1978-83. Home: 835 E High Country Dr Orem UT 84057 Office: 632 TNRB Grad Sch Mgmt Brigham Young U Provo UT 84602

HUNT, JOHN MAURICE, found. exec.; b. Mpls., Sept. 23, 1944; s. Maurice Glenn and Mary Alice (James) H.; student St. Michael's Coll., 1962-64; B.A., Mt. Angel Sem. Coll., 1966, postgrad., 1966-68. Coordinator activities therapy Nazareth Hosp., Albuquerque, 1969-74; adminstr. arthritis project, div. regional med. programs U. N.Mex. Sch. Medicine, 1974-76; exec. dir. Arthritis Found., Albuquerque, 1975—, mem. nat. research com., 1978. Chmn. Nat. Health Agencies Coordinating Com., 1976-77; mem. human research com. Presbyn. Hosp. Center, 1976—; profl. adv. bd. Share Your Care/Sr. Daily Living program, 1977—; exec. com. Hosp. Home Health Care/St. Joseph's Presbyn. Hosps., 1978, profl. adv. group mem., 1976—, chmn., 1978; bd. dirs. N.Mex. Assn. Home Health Agencies, 1975-77; instr. U. N.Mex. Community Coll., 1979, 80; cons. to consultation edn. dept. Bernalillo County Mental Health/Mental Retardation Center, 1980, 81. Mem. Profl. Staff Assn. Arthritis Found. Democrat. Home: 1028 Georgia St SE Albuquerque NM 87108 Office: 5112 Grand Ave NE Albuquerque NM 87108

HUNT, MARY LOU, counselor, consultant; b. Bell, Calif., Apr. 23, 1932; d. David Allen and Ruth Irene (Bolton) Smith; m. Earl Busby Hunt, Dec. 20, 1954; children—Robert David, Susan Mary, Alan James, Steven Thomas. B.A. cum laude in Psychology, Stanford U., 1954, M.A., 1954. Counselor, tchr. Women's Guidance Ctr., U. Wash., Seattle, 1972; counselor, sec./treas. Individual Devel. Ctr., Inc., Seattle, 1972-74; co-dir., counselor, cons., v.p., treas., 1974—. Bd. dirs. Together in Employment, 1982-83, Focus Parttime Employment, 1976, Seattle Day Nursery, 1974-76. Mem. Am. Personnel and Guidance Assn., Am. Soc. Tng. and Devel. (dir. membership Puget Sound chpt. 1981, 82, bd. dirs. 1980), Am. Soc. Personnel Adminstrn. Office: Individual Devel Ctr Inc 1020 E John St Seattle WA 98102

HUNT, PATRICIA ANN, educator; b. Memphis, Aug. 21, 1938; d. John William and Virginia Lee (Arnold) H.; children—Erin Leigh Manning and Lauren Elisa Manning. B.A., Upper Iowa Coll., 1967; M.A., U. Iowa, 1972, Ph.D., 1976. Asst. prof. English, coordinator writing program Northland Coll., Ashland, Wis., 1977-79; lectr. writing programs UCLA, 1980—. NEH Summer Seminar fellow, 1979, research fellow, 1979-80. Mem. MLA, Am. Studies Assn., Nat. Council Tchrs. English, Assn. Can. Studies in U.S. Unitarian. Contbr. articles to profl. jours. Home: 118 S Sherbourne Dr Apt 2 Los Angeles CA 90035 Office: 302 Royce UCLA Los Angeles CA 90024

HUNTER, BERTRAM HARRY, JR., interior designer; b. Bakersfield, Calif., May 1, 1917; s. Bertram Harry and Margaret Kathryn (Cartwright) H.; m. Virginia Hawes, Mar. 30, 1941; children—Margaret Susan Hancock, Gail Elizabeth Haynes. Student Central Calif. Comml. Coll., 1934-35, Fresno State Coll., 1935-36, Stanford U., 1937-38. Draftsman Taylor & Wheeler, Fresno, Calif., 1936-37; sales mgr. J.C. Ferger Co., Fresno, 1938-42, B.H. Hunter, Inc., Fresno, 1946-56; owner Harry Hunter Interiors, Fresno, 1946-58, Hunter Shops, Fresno, 1948-77; pres. mgr. Connell & Chaffin, Fresno, 1958-77; ret. 1977; cons. in field. Served to maj. USMC, 1942-46. Mem. Am. Inst. Interior Designers (bd. govs. 1970). Republican. Christian Scientist. Clubs: Kiwanis (Fresno); Commonwealth (San Francisco); Masons. Home and Office: 5336 N Colonial Apt 101 Fresno CA 93704

HUNTER, BETTY KATHERINE, executive search consultant; b. Los Angeles, May 28, 1945; d. Robert Cecil and B. Fay (McLean) H. B.S. in Psychology, U. So. Calif., 1967, postgrad. 1968. Ednl. cons. Los Angeles Unified Sch. Dist., 1968-80; exec. search cons. Korn/Ferry Internat., Los Angeles, 1980-81; prin. Betty K. Hunter, exec. search cons., Los Angeles, 1982—; lectr. U. So. Calif., UCLA; TV-radio personality. Mem. Calif. Republican Assocs.; mem. Jr. League, Los Angeles. Recipient hon. life award for excellence in edn. PTA, 1976; fundraising award and trophy U. So. Calif. Grad. Sch. Bus., 1983. Mem. Las Floristas, Los Angeles World Affairs Council, Town Hall of Calif., U. So. Calif. Commerce Assocs. (dir. 1974—), U. So. Calif. Educare, Internat. Platform Assn., Nat. Speakers Assn., Hollywood Bowl Jrs. Republican. Contbr. articles to profl. jours. Home: 4201 Via Marina Apt 265 Marina Del Rey CA 90292 Office: 2029 Century Park E Suite 2150 Los Angeles CA 90067

HUNTER, DUNCAN LEE, Congressman; b. Riverside, Calif., May 31, 1948; J.D., Western State U., 1976; m. Lynne Layh, 1973; children—Ducan Duane, Robert Samul. Admitted to Calif. bar, 1976; practiced in San Diego; mem. 97th Congress from 42d Dist. of Calif., 98th Congress from 45th Dist. Calif., asst. regional whip. Served to 1st lt. U.S. Army, 1969-71. Mem. Navy League. Baptist. Republican. Office: 117 Cannon House Office Bldg Washington DC 20515

HUNTER, E. ALLAN, electric utility executive; b. Grantsville, Utah, May 27, 1914; s. James Austin and Francis (Fraser) H.; B.S. in Elec. Engring., U. Utah, 1937; postgrad. U. Mich., 1955; m. Helen Spindler, July 12, 1941; children—Edward Allan, James Scott. With Utah Power and Light Co., Salt Lake City, 1937—, various positions including asst. to pres., comml. mgr., 1937-62, v.p., 1963-68, asst. gen. mgr., dir., 1966-68, pres., chief exec. officer, 1969-79, chmn. bd., 1979—; pres., dir. Western Colo. Power Co., 1969-74; pres. WEST Assos., 1970-72; dir. First Security Corp., ZCMI. Mem. Utah Nuclear Energy Commn., 1970-73; mem. industry adv. com. Def. Electric Power Adminstrn., 1975-77; mem. electric utilities com. Fed. Energy Adminstrn., 1975-77; mem. Western Regional Council; mem. Gov.'s Mineral Lease Fund Adv. Com.; bd. dirs. Utah Bus. Devel. Corp., Nat. Assn. Electric Cos., 1974-77. Mem. adv. council Weber State U. Sch. Bus. and Econs., 1967-71 Brigham Young U., 1969-71; mem. nat. bd. advisors U. Utah Coll. Bus., 1976—; campaign chmn., dir. Utah United Funds, 1968-69. Trustee, treas. Utah Blue Cross, 1969-74; trustee Utah Found.; bd. dirs. Ballet West, 1969-74. Utah Symphony. Served from 1st lt. to maj. AUS, 1942-46; ETO. Decorated Bronze Star, Purple Heart; named Utah Outstanding Engr. in Industry, 1968. Registered profl. engr., Utah. Mem. Utah N.G. Hon. Cols. Assn., Salt Lake Area C. of C. (pres. 1971-72, bd. govs.), Edison Electric Inst., (dir. 1974-77), Nat. Soc. Profl. Engrs. (past pres. local chpt.), Utah Mfrs. Assn. (dir. 1963-70; Mfr. of Year award 1971), N.W. Electric Light and Power Assn. (past dir.), N.A.M. (former dir. Utah), Nat. Elec. Contractors Assn. (citation 1974), High Temperature Reactor Devel. Assn. (trustee 1970-73), U. Utah Alumni Assn. Emeritus Club. Mem. Ch. Jesus Christ of Latter-day Saints. Rotarian. Clubs: Alta, Timpanogos, Salt Lake Country. Office: Utah Power & Light Co 1407 W North Temple St PO Box 899 Salt Lake City UT 84116

HUNTER, GEORGE WILLIAM, III, parasitologist, educator; b. N.Y.C., Jan. 27, 1902; s. George William and Emily Isabel (Jobbins) H.; m. 2d, Adelaide Louise White, July 11, 1941 (div.); m. 3d, Fern Emily Wood, May 15, 1972; children—Anita Anderson, Gay Culp, Mina F. Sage. Student Carleton Coll., 1919-20; B.S., Knox Coll., 1923; M.S., U. Ill., 1924, Ph.D., 1927; cert. tropical and mil. medicine, 1944. Commd. 2d lt. U.S. Army Res. 1923, advanced through grades to maj. AUS, 1943, to col. U.S. Army, 1949; asst. chief dept. parasitology Army Med. Sch., 1942-45, chief, 1946-47, staff mem. tropical and mil. medicine course, 1942-47; chief sect. med. zoology 406th Med. Gen. Lab., Tokyo, 1947-51; chief sect. parasitology-entomology 4th Army Med. Lab., 1951-55; exec. officer commn. schistosomiasis Army Epidemiol. Bd., Philippines, 1945; dep. blood adminstr. Far East Command, Korea, 1950-51; ret., 1955; interim prof. biol. sci. U. Fla., Gainesville, 1956-57, lectr. biol. scis. and tropical medicine Coll. Medicine, 1957-67, prof. microbiol. Med. Sch., 1966-67, prof. emeritus, 1967—; res. coordinator, chief sect. parasitology La. State U. Internat. Ctr. Med. Research Tng., research prof. med. parasitology, sch. medicine; mem. faculty U. Costa Rica, 1961-63; clin. prof. parasitology, div. epidemiol., dept. community medicine U. Calif. Sch. Medicine, San Diego, 1974—. Decorated Bronze Star with oak leaf cluster; Harvard U. research fellow, 1940; NIH immunology schistosomiasis grantee, 1956-64; WHO schistosomiasis grantee, 1978-80; recipient Knox Coll. Alumni Achievement award, 1954, Carlos J. Finlay award, Cuba, 1958; named hon. citizen with distinction Kurume, Japan. Fellow Royal Soc. Tropical Medicine and Hygiene, AAAS, Am. Pub. Health Assn.; mem. Entomol. Soc. Am., Japan Soc. Parasitologists, Am. Soc. Zoologists Am. Micros. Soc., Wash. Acad. Scis., Assn. Southeastern Biologists, Southeastern Soc. Parasitologists (co-founder), Royal Inst. Pub. Health and Hygiene, Am. Soc. Parasitologists (charter, emeritus), Am. Soc. Tropical Medicine and Hygiene, Union Am. Biol. Socs. (exec. com. 1941-44), So. Calif. Parasitologists, Helminthological Soc. Wash., Japanese Soc. Parasitology, Assn. Mil. Surgeons U.S., Phi Beta Kappa, Sigma Xi, Delta Sigma Rho, Phi Eta, Beta Theta Phi. Clubs: Mil. Order Boars, Mil. Order World Wars, Mil. Order Carabao; Lions. Author: (with W.W. Frye, J.C. Swartzwelder), A Manual of Tropical Medicine, 4th edit., 1966; (with J.C. Swartzwelder and David Clyde) Tropical Medicine, 5th edit., 1976; Hunter's Tropical Medicine (G.T. Strickland) 1983. Contbr. numerous articles to med. jours. Home: 17760 Camino Murrillo PO Box 28286 Rancho Bernardo San Diego CA 92128

HUNTER, HOWARD WILLIAM, church official, ofcl., lawyer; b. Boise, Idaho, Nov. 14, 1907; s. John William and Nellie Marie (Rasmussen) H.; J.D. cum laude, Southwestern U., 1939; m. Clara May Jeffs, June 10, 1931; children—Howard William (dec.), John Jacob, Richard Allen. Engaged in banking in Calif., 1928-34; admitted to Calif. bar, 1939, practiced in Los Angeles until 1959; mem. council of 12, Ch. of Jesus Christ of Latter-day Saints, 1959—; dir. Beneficial Life Ins. Co., Salt Lake City, Watson Land Co., Los Angeles, Heber J. Grant & Co., First Security Corp., 1st Security Bank of Utah, Deseret Fed. Savs. and Loan Assn., Continental Western Life Ins. Co. Pres., Polynesian Cultural Ctr., Hawaii. Mem. Calif., Utah bar assns., Geneal. Soc. Utah (dir., past pres.). Home: 2833 Sherwood Dr Salt Lake City UT 84108 Office: 47 E South Temple Salt Lake City UT 84150

HUNTER, IRENE WIBERG, credit agency executive; b. Arlington, Wash., Sept. 3, 1922; d. Frank and Anna Marie (Burns) Wiberg; m. Charles Daniel Hunter, July 18, 1942; children—Linda Hunter McCammon, Steven Jeffrey. Student U. Wash., 1940, Seattle Coll., 1940-42, Seattle Bus. Sch., 1943. Cert. credit bur. exec., collection agy. exec. With Peoples Nat. Bank, Seattle, 1943-44; with various banks Calif., Ariz., 1944-45; co owner, mgr. Washington Credit, Inc., Bellevue, 1950—. Mem. fundraising coms. YMCA, 1976-83; leader Girl Scouts Am., 1953-55; den mother Boy Scouts Am., 1955-57; instr. water safety ARC, 1954-60; mem. coms. PTA Lake Washington Sch. Dist., 1951-65; vol. Community Services for the Blind, Seattle, 1975-77, Griffin Boys Home, 1977-78. Mem. Bellevue Credit Women Internat. (founder, past pres.), Seattle Consumer Credit Assn. (speakers bur.), Seattle Better Bus. Bur. (arbitration com. 1972—), Credit Women Internat. (dir. dist. 10 1972-73). Mem. Unity Ch. Office: PO Box 1378 Bellevue WA 98009

HUNTER, JEFFREY CHARLES, chemist, label company manager; b. San Diego, Oct. 19, 1938; s. Theodore Lee and Dorothy (Wilson) H. B.S., San Diego State U., 1962, M.S., 1964; M.A. in Mgmt., U. Redlands, 1979. Sr. chemist Avery Label Co., Azusa, Calif., 1966-76, product devel. specialist consumer div., 1976-79, project mgr. Avery consumer div., Consumer and Office Products div. Avery Internat., 1980—; grad. bus. instr. U. Redlands, 1980—; mem. faculty in bus. and sci. Coll. Profl. Studies, U. San Francisco, 1981—, state chmn. curriculum design com. Coll. Profl. Studies, 1982-84. Vol. account exec. United Way, 1980—. Calif. community coll. teaching credentials in bus. and chemistry. Mem. Council of Reprographics Execs., Assn. M.B.A. Execs., Am. Chem. Soc., TAPPI. Republican. Episcopalian. Clubs: Ontario Pkwy. Kiwanis (sec., 1980, 81, 82, Circle K Club adv. Mt. San Antonio Coll.). Co-author articles in field. Home: 923 N San Antonio St Pomona CA 91767 Office: 777E Foothill Blvd Azusa CA 91702

HUNTER, JESS EVAN, life insurance company executive; b. Des Moines, Aug. 4, 1923; s. Jesse Early and Helen Margaret (Smith) H.; m. Naomi Irene Wade, Dec. 8, 1951; children—Laura K., Sara Amy. B. Comml. Sci., Drake U., 1948. C.L.U. With Bankers Life Ins. Co., Des Moines, 1948-57; life underwriter Producers Life Ins. Co., Phoenix, 1957-64, Independence Life Ins. Co., Pasadena, Calif., 1964-65; chief underwriter Anchor Nat. Life Ins. Co., Phoenix, 1965—, v.p. Anchor Nat. Life Calif., 1968—. Active Anchor Nat. Life Polit. Action Com. Served to USAAF, 1942-45. Decorated Air medal. Fellow Life Mgmt. Inst., Assoc. Acad. Life Underwriting. Club: Phoenix Underwriters.

HUNTER, ROBERT LESLIE, educator; b. Delaware County, Ohio, June 29, 1921; s. Rollin Clarence and Adelia Wave (Adams) H.; B.A., Ohio Wesleyan U., 1943, M.A., 1949; Ph.D., U. Mich., 1954; m. Ilene Iola Donner, Feb. 16, 1944; children—Jean Eileen, Richard Collins, Joanne Irene, Janet Wave. Instr. to asso. prof. Dept. Anatomy, U. Mich., Ann Arbor, 1953-63; asso. prof. Dept. Anatomy, Stanford (Calif.) U. Sch. Medicine, 1963-66; prof. Dept. Human Anatomy, Med. Sch., U. Calif., Davis, 1966-68, dept. chmn., 1968-74, now prof.; hon. prof. Fed. U. of Pernambuco, Recife, Brazil, 1969. Mem. City of Davis Hist. Commn., 1978-79. Served with M.C., U.S. Army, 1943-46; ETO. Edgar Rice summer scholar, Ohio Wesleyan U., 1946. Mem. Histochem. Soc. (pres. 1968-69), Histochem. Soc. Finland (hon.), AAAS, Am. Inst. Biol. Sci., Am. Assn. Anatomists, Exptl. Aircraft Assn., Sigma Xi, Phi Kappa Phi, Phi Mu Alpha. Editorial bd. Jour. Histochemistry & Cytochemistry, 1966-72, Electrophoresis, 1980—. Home: 803 Plum Ln Davis CA 95616 Office: Dept Human Anatomy Sch Medicine Univ of Calif Davis CA 95616

HUNTER, WILMONT LENNINGTON, computer scientist; b. Chgo., July 23, 1927; s. Howard Walter and Eve Lynn (McKinstry) H.; B.S. in Elec. Engring., U. So. Calif., 1959; m. Gloria Catherine Swanson, Feb. 20, 1961; 1 son, Brian John. Elec. engr. Hoffman Labs., Los Angeles, 1953-55, Lockheed MSD, Van Nuys, Calif., 1955-57; engring. specialist Litton Industries, Van Nuys, 1957-67; electronics engr. Interstate Electronics Corp., Anaheim, Calif., 1967-70; mem. tech. staff Rockwell Internat. Co., Los Angeles, 1971-73; sr. devel. engr. Honeywell, Inc., Seattle and West Covina, Calif., 1973-75; mem. tech. staff Tex. Instruments Inc., Dallas, 1975-78; specialist engr. Boeing Co., Seattle, 1978—. Served with USNR, 1944-46. Decorated Commendation medal. Mem. Assn. Computing Machinery, Mensa, Eta Kappa Nu. Mem. Libertarian Ch. Author, patentee in field. Home: 7236 S 128th St Seattle WA 98178 Office: Boeing Co PO Box 3999 Seattle WA 98124

HUNTER-BOWINGTON, DOROTHY DIANA, educator, consultant; b. Chgo., Dec. 21, 1930; d. William Paul and Dorothy (Proud) Hunter; m. James Paul Gingrich, July 31, 1948; children—James, Mark, Chris, Suzanne Gingrich Black, Margaret, Eric, John; m. 2d, Howard F. Bowington, Feb. 14, 1975. A.A., Am. River Coll., Sacramento, 1967; B.A., Calif. State U.-Sacramento, 1969, postgrad., 1969-74; M.A.V.E., Calif. State Consortium, Sacramento, 1975; postgrad. Calif. State U.-Chico, 1969-73. Cert. in adminstrn., secondary home econs. for mentally retarded, as specialist for learning handicapped and resource specialist, Calif. Vocat. specialist for spl. needs students Grand Union High Sch. Dist., North Highlands, Calif., 1969—; asst. prof. vocat. edn. Calif. State Consortium, 1977—; cons. spl. needs workshop State Calif.; mem. ednl. adv. com. for spl. needs students Calif. State U.; chmn. pro tem Calif. Assn. Vocat. Edn.-Nat. Priority Students, 1982-83. Mem. Calif. Gov.'s Com. for Hired the Handicapped; mem. Gold Country Hire the Handicapped Com., Sacramento, 1982-83. Named Vocat. Trainer of Yr., Sacramento C. of C., 1978; Calif. Dept. Edn. grantee, 1980-82. Mem. Am. Vocat. Assn., Calif. Assn. Vocat. Edn. (pres. elect), Am. Vocat. Assn. for Spl. Needs Students, Council Exceptional Children. Author job-seeking curriculum, 1975; author health handbook adopted by Los Angeles Community Colls., 1976.

HUNTHAUSEN, RAYMOND GERHARDT, archbishop; b. Anaconda, Mont., Aug. 21, 1921; s. Anthony G. and Edna Marie (Tuchscherer) H. B.A., Carroll Coll., 1943; M.Div., St. Edward's Sem., Kenmore, Wash., 1946; postgrad. St. Louis U., 1947, Cath. U. Am., 1948-49, Fordham U., 1950; M.S., U. Notre Dame, 1953. Ordained priest Roman Catholic Ch., 1946, consecrated bishop, 1962; mem. faculty Carroll Coll., 1946-57, pres., 1957-62; bishop of Helena, Mont., 1962-75; archbishop of Seattle, 1975—; prof. Carroll Coll., Helena, 1946-57; athletic dir., 1957-62; domestic prelate, 1958-62. Inducted into Nat. Assn. Athletics Hall of Fame. Office: Archdiocese of Seattle Chancery Office 907 Terry St Seattle WA 98104*

HUNTINGTON, BARBARA WEEKS, computer company executive; b. Albuquerque, June 20, 1946; d. Paul R. and Ruth Irene (Looney) Weeks; m. Fred W. Huntington III, June 25, 1978; children—Melody, Dale. Student U. Wash., San Diego State U., 1965-68; B.S. in Zoology with distinction, Los Angeles State U., 1971. Cert. elem. tchr., Calif. Tchr. elem. schs. Los Angeles, 1968-71, Escondido, Calif., 1971-79, Corcoran, Calif., 1980-82; owner, pres. Huntington Computing, Corcoran, 1981—. Life judge Am. Rose Soc. Baha'i. Contbr. articles to profl. jours. Office: PO Box 1297 Corcoran CA 93212

HUNTINGTON, DOROTHY SPATZ, psychologist; b. N.Y.C., Nov. 12, 1927; d. Morris and Rose (Burrows) Spatz. B.A., Barnard Coll., 1948; M.A., Harvard U., 1952, Ph.D., 1954. Lic. psychologist, Calif. Sr. clin and research psychologist Beth Israel Hosp., Boston, 1955-67; chief child devel. sect. Research Found. of the Children's Hosp. of D.C., 1967-71; chief child and family services Peninsula Hosp., 1972-80; dir. research and evaluation Ctr. for the Family in Transition, Corte Madera, Calif., 1980—; assoc. clin. prof. psychiatry U. Calif.-San Francisco, 1981—; clin. asst. prof. dept. psychiatry Stanford U., 1975-81; assoc. research prof. pediatrics, child devel. George Washington U., 1968-71. Active Internat. Hospitality Ctr., San Francisco, World Affairs Council; mem. Task Panel on Orgn. and Structure of Services, Pres.'s Commn. on Mental Health, 1977-78. Mem. Boston Psychoanalytic Soc., San Francisco Psychoanalytic Inst., Am. Psychol. Assn., Soc. for Research in Child Devel. Contbr. articles to profl. jours. Office: 5725 Paradise Dr Suite 100 Corte Madera CA 94925

HUNTINGTON, ROBERT WATKINSON, ret. physician; b. Hartford, July 2, 1907; s. Robert Watkinson and Constance (Willard) H.; A.B., Yale, 1928, M.D., 1933; m. Katherine Bond Upchurch, Mar. 21, 1936; children—Robert Watkinson III, Ann Bowles Huntington Heldman, Edith Willard Huntington Lopez, Deborah Lathrop Huntington Ward. Intern, New Haven Hosp., 1932-33, asst. resident, 1934-35; research fellow Yale, 1933-34; fellow St. Louis Children's Hosp., 1935-38; instr. pathology Cornell U., 1938-41; asso. prof. pathology U. So. Calif., 1946-65, clin. prof. pathology, 1965-75; pathologist Kern County Gen. Hosp., Bakersfield, Calif., 1950-75, also dir. med. services;

mem. exec. bd. Calif. Tumor Tissue Registry, 1955-75. Pres. Kern County unit Am. Cancer Soc., 1959-60; bd. dirs., Kern County Safety Council, 1959-75; exec. bd. Kern County council Boy Scouts Am. Served to comdr. USNR, 1941-46. Recipient Silver Beaver award Boy Scouts Am., 1965; Pub. Interest award Kern County Safety Council, 1966. Recorder of assembly Coll. Am. Pathologists, 1961-63. Episcopalian (standing com. San Joaquin Diocese 1961-65). Author numerous papers in profl. jours. Home: Wellington Dr Cambria San Luis Obispo County CA 93428

HUNTLEY, ALICE MAE, mfg. exec.; b. Atoka, Okla., May 9, 1917, d. Joseph LaHay and Lula May (Stapp) Howe; B.A. U. Okla., 1939; m. Loren Clifford Huntley, Nov. 7, 1942; children—Loren Lee, Marcia Lynn. Reporter, McAlester (Okla.) News Capital, 1939-41; sec., asst. to pres. and chmn. bd. N.Am. Aviation, Los Angeles, 1941-63; v.p., co-owner Tubular Specialties Mfg., Inc., Los Angeles, 1966—. Former sec. 1st Baptist Ch. of Westchester; sec. Westchester-Del Rey Republican Women, 1959-60; asso. mem. Rep. State Central Com., 1973. Cert. profl. sec.; named Outstanding Sec. in So. Calif., So. Calif. chpt., 1954, Internat. Sec. of Year, 1955 (both Nat. Secs. Assn.). Home: 8238 Calabar Ave Playa del Rey CA 90293 Office: 13011 S Spring St Los Angeles CA 90061

HUNTLEY, ROBERT CARSON, JR., justice Idaho Supreme Court; b. Union City, Pa., Aug. 7, 1932; s. Robert C. and Mildred (Kaltenmark) H.; m. Elfreda Garvens, Feb. 11, 1955; children—Chris, Tony. B.S., U. Idaho, 1954, J.D., 1959. Bar: Idaho, 1959; mem. Pocatello, Racine, Huntley, Olson, Nye & Cooper, Boise, Idaho, 1959-82; justice Idaho Supreme Ct., 1982—. Served to capt. USNR, 1954-80. Mem. ABA, Idaho Bar Assn. Democrat. Unitarian. Lodge: Elks.

HUPKA, LAWRENCE GLEN, accountant, consultant; b. Tecumseh, Nebr., Apr. 29, 1945; s. Glen L. and Victoria (Lempka) H.; m. Catherine Anne Davisson, Sept. 27, 1969; children—Jennifer, Steven. B.S., U. Nebr., 1972. C.P.A., Colo., Tex. Programmer, analyst U. Nebr., Lincoln, 1969-72; mgmt. cons. Price Waterhouse Co., Dallas, 1973-77, Denver, 1977-83, ptnr., 1983—. Served with U.S. Army, 1966-69. Decorated Army Commendation medal. Mem. Am. Inst. C.P.A.s, Colo. Soc. C.P.A.s, EDP Auditors Assn. Republican. Roman Catholic. Clubs: Columbine Country, Internat. Athletic. Office: Price Waterhouse Co 950 17th St Suite 2300 Denver CO 80202

HUPKA, RALPH BERND, psychology educator; b. Hamburg, Germany, Feb. 23, 1938; came to U.S., 1951, naturalized, 1956; s. Walter and Yvonne Waltraud (Kimmel) H. B.A., San Francisco State U., 1963, M.A., 1965; Ph.D., U. Mass., 1969. Prof. psychology Calif. State U.-Long Beach, 1969—. Served with U.S. Army, 1956-59. Mem. Am. Psychol. Assn., Western Psychol Assn., Internat. Council Psychologists, Soc. Psychol. Study Social Issues. Contbr. articles to profl. jours. Office: Dept Psychology Calif State U Long Beach CA 90840

HURABIELL, JOHN PHILIP, lawyer, entrepreneur, ins. exec.; b. San Francisco, June 2, 1947; s. Emile John and Anna Beatrice (Blumenauer) H.; student U. San Francisco, 1965-66, 69-71, San Francisco State U., 1968-69; J.D., San Francisco Law Sch., 1976; m. Judith Marie Worner, June 7, 1969; children—Marie Louise, Michele Anne, Heather Ann Epiphany, John Philip, Jr. Agt., Provident Mut. Ins. Co., 1968-70; cons. Riedy & Casey, Inc., San Francisco, 1970-75; agt. Banker Life Ins. Co. Iowa, 1971-81; spl. cons. Acacia Mut. Life, 1981—; chmn., chief fin. officer Direct Mail Marketing Services, Inc., San Francisco, 1979—, Advt. Mail Services, Inc., Reno, Nev.; chmn. Curry Graphics, Inc., Reno; v.p., gen. counsel Ionikon Corp., Partitions by Design, Mag Tech Systems, Diversified Fin. Concepts Service Corp.; owner Hurabiell Ins. Services, San Francisco, 1974—; sec., gen. counsel Eu Mar Corp., Lee-Mil, Inc., Sellers Mfg. Corp., Symposia Prodns. and Publs., 1979—, numerous other corps. and non-profit orgns.; admitted to Calif. bar, 1976, since practiced individually in San Francisco. Served with USNR, 1966-68; Vietnam. Mem. Nat. (vice chmn. field practices com.), Calif. (past chmn. bus. practices com.) assns. life underwriters, San Francisco Life Underwriters Assn. (dir., pres. 1981-82), Am. (mem. small bus. subcom., com. on taxation, real property probate and trust com., internat. law com.), Calif., San Francisco bar assns., Am. Trial Lawyers Assn., Calif. Trial Lawyers Assn., Lawyers Club San Francisco, Barristers Club, San Francisco Estate Planning Council, Trout Unltd., Fedn. Fly Fishermen, Am. Orchid Soc., San Francisco S.A.F.E. (chief fin. officer), Calif. Rifle and Pistol Assn. (life mem.), Nat. Rifle Assn. (benefactor mem.), Internat. Order Alhambra (Neophyte of Year 1979, grand comdr. 1981-82, regional dir. 1983—). Republican. Roman Catholic. Clubs: KC (grand knight 1978-80, dist. dep. 1980-81, state legis. chmn., asst. membership dir. State of Calif. 1981-82, state membership dir. 1982-83, legal advisor 1983—), San Francisco Tennis. Home: 1958 18th Ave San Francisco CA 94116 Office: 45 Polk St 2d Floor San Francisco CA 94102 also 144 Townsend St San Francisco CA 94107

HURKOS, PETER, author; b. Dordrecht, The Netherlands, May 21, 1911; came to U.S., 1956, naturalized, 1959; s. Jakobus and Plonia (Van Ysden) Van der Hurk; Ph.D. in Psychology, U. Wis., 1967; m. Stephany Farb, May 11, 1970; 1 dau., Gloria Ann. Author: Psychic, 1959; Psychic World of Peter Hurkos, 1970; I Have Many Lives, 1975; actor appearing in The Boston Strangler, 1970, Mysterious Monsters, 1976, The Amazing World of Psychic Phenomena, 1978, Now I Lay Me Down to Sleep, 1979, Boxoffice, 1982; TV and radio appearances; psychic detective on cases involving mission persons and murder victims including The Stone of Scone, London, The Boston Strangler, Missing Thi Silk King - Jim Thompson, The Ann Arbor (Mich.) Co-Ed Murders, The Sharon Tape Multiple Murders, Los Angeles, Ronald Hughes - the missing Manson Atty., Los Angeles. Hon. police chief, N.J., Redondo Beach, Calif., Palm Springs, Calif., Phoenix, Chgo., Syracuse, N.Y., Miami. Served with Dutch Underground, 1939-45. Mem. AFTRA, Screen Actors Guild. Republican. Jewish. Home and Office: 12214 Viewcrest Rd Studio City CA 91604

HURLEY, CAROL REYNOLDS, marketing consulting company executive; b. Stamford, Conn., Sept. 21, 1932; d. Walter Buxton and Esther (Nelson) Reynolds; m. Edward Daniel Hurley, Sept. 5, 1964. Grad. Katharine Gibbs Sch., N.Y.C., 1951. Exec. sec., pub. relations dir. Interchurch Ctr., N.Y.C., 1957-63; editor Combined Book Exhibit, N.Y.C., 1963-64; sec.-treas. Hurley Assocs., Los Angeles, 1964—; exec. sec. Associated Rehab. Ctrs., Evanston, Ill., 1967-69; asst. to pres. Intercole Inc., Brentwood, Calif., 1974-78; asst. to chmn. Donegal Internat. Machinery Ltd., Ballyshannon, Ireland, 1977—; v.p. Lodestar Prodns., Los Angeles, 1978—; mgr. adminstrn. Hesburgh Internat., Inc., Pacific Palisades, Calif., 1978—. Founder Pacific Palisades Hunger Walk orgn., 1975, Pacific Palisades Hospice Vols. orgn., 1980. Mem. Nat. Assn. Female Execs., Am. Bonsai Soc., Sunset Succulent Soc. Home: 1330 Monument St Pacific Palisades CA 90272 Office: Hesburgh Internat Inc Suite 200 15135 Sunset Blvd Pacific Palisades CA 90272

HURLEY, FRANCIS T., archbishop; b. San Francisco, Jan. 12, 1927. Ed. St. Patrick's Sem., Menlo Park, Calif., Cath. U., Washington. Ordained priest Roman Catholic Ch., 1951, consecrated bishop, 1970; titular bishop Daimlaig, 1970-71, aux. bishop diocese of Juneau, Alaska, 1971-76, ordinary of See, 1971-76; archbishop of Anchorage, 1976—. Address: PO Box 2239 Anchorage AK 99510*

HURLEY, MARGARET ELLEN, state senator; b. Winnebago, Minn.; d. David Hall and Margaret Matilda (Lafey) Morse; B.A., Ft. Wright Coll., Spokane, Wash., 1959; student Eastern Wash. State Coll., 1956, Whitworth Coll., 1957, Gonzaga U., 1958; m. Joseph E. Hurley, June 27, 1935 (dec. 1968); children—Patrick, John, Stephen, Mary Margaret. Mem. Wash. Legislature, 1953-83, caucus sec., 1972-73, chmn. parks com., 1973-76; mem. Wash. State Senate, 1980-81. chmn. parks and recreation, 1980—. Bd. dirs. Eastern Wash. U. Found. Named Woman of Year, City of Spokane and Wash. State, Bus. and Profl. Women, 1968; recipient Marion Medal award, Ft. Wright Coll., 1968. Mem. Nat. Order Women Legislators. Home: E 730 Boone Spokane WA 99202

HURLEY, MARK JOSEPH, bishop; b. San Francisco, Dec. 13, 1919; s. Mark Joseph and Josephine (Keohane) H.; A.B., St. Joseph's Coll., 1941; postgrad. U. Calif., Berkeley, 1944-45; Ph.D., Cath. U. Am., 1947; J.C.B., Lateran U., Rome, 1963; LL.D., U. Portland, 1971. Ordained priest Roman Cath. Ch., 1944, consecrated bishop, 1968; asst. supt. schs. Archdiocese of San Francisco, 1944-51; prin. Bishop O'Dowd High Sch., Oakland, Calif., 1951-58, Marin Cath. High Sch., Marin County, Calif., 1959-61; supt. schs. Diocese of Stockton (Calif.), 1962-65; adminstr. St. Eugene's Ch., Santa Rosa, Calif., 1959, St. John's Ch., San Francisco, 1961; chancellor Diocese of Stockton, 1962-65; asst. chancellor Archdiocese of San Francisco, 1965-69; aux. bishop of San Francisco, 1967-69; bishop of Santa Rosa, 1969—; mem. U.S.A. Bishops Com. for Cath.-Jewish Relationships, 1965—; chmn. Bishops Com. for Ecumenical and Interreligious Affairs, 1970, Bishop's Com. Human Values, 1975-78. Mem. bd. State of Calif. Com. for Study of Edn., 1955-60; del. State of Calif. White House Conf. on Youth, 1960; trustee N.Am. Coll., Rome, Cath. U. Am. Recipient Saint Francis award City of San Francisco, 1975, Alumni award for Outstanding Achievement in social service Cath. U. Am., 1975. Mem. Vatican Secretariat for Non-Believers, Nat. Conf. Cath. Bishops (mem. adminstrv. com.), Nat. Catechetical Com. Syndicated columnist, 1944-66. Contbr. articles to profl. and religious jours. Office: PO Box 1297 Santa Rosa CA 95403

HURST, DAVID THOMAS, lawyer, educator; b. Mechanicsburg, Pa., Oct. 6, 1949; s. Thomas J. Betty E. (Suplee) H.; m. Linda D. Davidson, July 19, 1980. Student Montclair State Tchrs. Coll., 1971-75; B.S. in Laws, Western State U., 1978, J.D., 1979. Bar: Calif. 1980. Head tchr. westlaw computer Western State U., Fullerton, Calif., 1977-78; dep. pub. defender Solano County, Fairfield, Calif., 1980-81; ptnr. Hearn and Hurst, San Ramon, Calif., 1981-82; assoc. Law Offices William E. Glass, Martinez, Calif., 1982—; tchr. John F. Kennedy U., Law Sch., Walnut Creek, Calif. Served with USAF, 1967-71. Recipient Am. Jurisprudence awards Western State U., 1977. Mem. Calif. Trial Lawyers Assn., Contra Costa County Bar Assn., Calif. Attys. Criminal Justice, ABA, Calif. State Bar Assn., Assn. Trial Lawyers Am., Alameda Contra Costa Trial Lawyers Assn. Democrat. Office: Suite 1 900 Court St Martinez CA 94553

HURST, JAMES C., university official, psychologist; b. Ogden, Utah, June 19, 1935; s. Leo Calvin and Deseret Ione (Salt) H.; m. Joan Rees, May 16, 1958; children—Kathy, Jeff, Brad, Jennifer. A.S., Weber State Coll., 1959; B.S. with high honors, U. Utah, 1961; Ph.D., Brigham Young U., 1966. Lic. psychologist, Colo., Tex. Intern counseling psychology Duke U., Durham, N.C., 1965-66; counselor, asst. prof. dept. psychology Oreg. State U., Corvallis, 1966-67; asst. dir. counseling ctr., asst. prof. psychology Colo. State U., Ft. Collins, 1967-70, dir. counseling ctr., assoc. prof. psychology U. Tex., Austin, 1970-76, dean of students, asst. v.p. student affairs, 1976-81, prof. counseling psychology, 1980-81; assoc. v.p. acad. affairs, prof. clin. psychology, U. Wyo., Laramie, 1981—; vis. prof. Kans. State U., 1981; cons. assoc. Rocky Mountain Behavioral Sci. Inst., 1970—. NDEA fellow, 1962-65; Brigham Young grad. scholar, 1965; recipient Margaret C. Berry award U. Tex., 1977; Tejas Club award, 1979; services for handicapped U. Tex. students award, 1979; U. Tex. Union award, 1980; U. Tex. Ombudsman award, 1982. Fellow Am. Psychol. Assn.; mem. Wyo. Psychol. Assn., Rocky Mountain Psychol. Assn., Am. Personnel and Guidance Assn., Am. Coll. Personnel Assn. (sec. 1979-81, contbn. to knowledge award 1982), Nat. Assn. of Student Personnel Adminstrs., Am. Coll. Personnel Assn. (media bd.), Internat. Assn. of Counseling Services (field visitor), Sigma Xi, Phi Kappa Phi, Omicron Delta Kappa, Phi Eta Sigma (hon.). Co-author: (with Morrill and Oetting) Nine Outreach Programs, 1974; (with K.G. Kitchener) Manual for Education Through Student Interaction, 1975; (with W.H. Morrill) Dimensions of Intervention for Student Development, 1980; contbr. chpts. to books and articles to profl. jours. Home: 1070 Hidalgo Dr Laramie WY 82070 Office: 204 Old Main PO Box 3066 U Wyoming Laramie WY 82071

HURST, MARY KATHLEEN, electronics company executive; b. Beverly, Mass., Apr. 3, 1952; d. Louis N. and Mary J. (McAllister) Donohoe; m. Cody W. Hurst, Jan. 3, 1973 (div.); 1 son, John. B.A. in History, Gonzaga U., 1975. Cert. tchr., Wash. Switchboard operator Password Answering, Spokane, 1973; asst. mgr. Annex Motel, Spokane, 1973-74; receptionist-cashier Moose Lodge, Spokane, 1974-75; prodn. supervisor Keytronics Corp., Spokane, 1975-83; sec.-treas. D.B. Electronics, Spokane, 1983—; lectr. continuing edn. Mem. Nat. Assn. Female Execs. Republican. Roman Catholic. Office: D B Electronics Inc S 169 Stevens Spokane WA 99204

HURST, WILLIAM SUTCLIFFE, telecommunications cons.; b. Salt Lake City, June 23, 1953; s. Floyd H. and Irene E. (Sutcliffe) H.; m. Jeri Lu Gehmlich, Sept. 22, 1975; children—Heidi, Matthew, Julee. B.S.E.E., U. Utah, Salt Lake City, 1978. Registered profl. engr., Utah. Vice pres. test ops. Communication Cert. Labs., Salt Lake City, 1975—; telecommunication cons.; condr. seminars; instr. continuing edn. George Washington U. Nat. Camp Sch. aquatics dir. Boy Scouts Am. Mem. IEEE. Home: 5779 Carranza Dr Salt Lake City UT 84118 Office: 2290 W Custer Rd Salt Lake City UT 84104

HURT, ROBERT GLENN, investment banker; b. Pasadena, Calif., Jan. 31, 1919; s. Leslie Milton and Effie Mae (McKim) H.; A.B., U. So. Calif., 1940; postgrad. Harvard, 1941. With sales dept. Calvin Bullock, Ltd., N.Y.C., Los Angeles, 1946-50, No. Calif. mgr., San Francisco, 1950-65, west coast mgr., San Francisco, 1965-66, v.p., San Francisco, 1967—. Mem. pres.'s circle U. So. Calif. Served from pvt. to lt. col. AUS, 1941-46. Named Ky. Col. Mem. San Francisco, Los Angeles stock exchange clubs, Mil. Order World Wars, Am. Legion. Clubs: Commonwealth (San Francisco); Andreas Canyon (Palm Springs, Calif.). Home: 937 Ashbury St San Francisco CA 94117 summer North Forty Middletown CA 95461 Office: 931 Mills Bldg 220 Montgomery St San Francisco CA 94104

HUSNEY, ELLIOTT RONALD, lawyer, fin. co. exec.; b. Mpls., July 24, 1940; s. Edward and Betty H.; A.A., U. Minn., 1962; B.S. in Bus. Adminstrn., U. Denver, 1965, J.D., 1968; m. Gloria Lynne Rudd, Jan. 10, 1962; children—Ronald Edward, Kenneth Logan, Evan James. Staff examiner Nat. Assn. Securities Dealers, Inc., 1965-67; admitted to Colo. bar, 1966; trial atty. SEC, 1967-68; house counsel Denver Corp., 1968-70; house counsel and v.p. Petro Search, Inc., Denver, 1971-72; pres. Denver Venture Capital, Inc., 1972-75; individual practice law, Denver, 1975-78; of counsel Pansing and Pansing, Denver, 1983—; chmn. Elliott Enterprise Group; chmn. bd. Am. Heliothermal Corp., Denver, 1978-81, U.S. Israel Investments, Ltd., 1977—; dir. Miromit Ashkelon Metal Products, Ltd., 1978-81, Aquaculture Prodn. Tech., Ltd. Tech. Products, Inc., Taraco, Inc.; bd. govs. Oil Investment Inst., 1969-70. Vice chmn. United Way Drive, 1978—; v.p. Rocky Mountain Planned Parenthood, Denver chpt., 1971-72; mem. energy conservation com. Cherry Creek Sch. Dist., Colo., 1977-78; co-chmn. group work youth and edn. com. Allied Jewish Fedn., 1977-78, chmn. energy com., 1978—; mem. Colo. Solar Advisory Com., 1978-82; bd. dirs. Am. Jewish Com., Denver chpt., 1983—. Recipient Distinguished award Allied Jewish Fedn. of Denver, 1976, Distinguished Service award Denver Jaycees, 1977, Adolf Kiesler Young Leadership award, 1978. Mem. Am. Bar Assn., Colo. Bar Assn., Denver Bar Assn., Solar Energy Industries Assn. (govt. relations and ethics com.). Republican. Jewish. Inverness Country. Author articles on venture capital, solar energy, drilling programs and securities laws.

HUSS, CHARLES MAURICE, building company executive; b. Chgo., Nov. 11, 1946; s. Charles Maurice and June Pierce (Bailey) H.; A.A., Kendall Coll., 1979; m. Winifred Louise Traughber, Dec. 24, 1973; children—Amber Elaine, Ra Ja Lorraine, Micah Alexander, Gabriel Joe, Cameron M., Jordan Charles. Traffic mgr. The Harwald Co., Evanston, Ill., 1966-67, asst. v.p., 1968-69; traffic mgr. Northwestern U. Press, Evanston, 1969-71; fire chief City of Kotzebue (Alaska), 1971-76, asst. city mgr., 1973-76; dir. maintenance USPHS Hosp., Kotzebue, 1976-79; pres., gen. mgr. Action Builders, Inc., Kotzebue, 1979-82; gen. mgr. Husky Maintenance Services, 1982—. Chmn., Kotzebue Planning Commn., 1978-82, Kotzebue Sch. Bd., 1974-79; founding vice chmn. Kotzebue chpt. ARC; mem. Alaska Criminal Code Revision Commn., 1976-78; mem. Alaska Fire Fighter Tng. Commn.; vol. Kotzebue Vol. Fire Dept., 1972-76, 82—. Pullman Found. scholar, 1964-65; Blackburn Coll. scholar, 1964-65; Ill. State scholar, 1964-66. Mem. Constrn. Specifications Inst., Soc. Fire Service Instrs., Alaska Firefighters Assn., Internat. Assn. Fire Chiefs, Home Builders Assn. Alaska, Nat. Fire Protection Assn., Kotzebue C. of C. Guest essayist: Seven Days and Sunday (Kirkpatrick), 1973. Home and Office: PO Box 277 Kotzebue AK 99752

HUSTED, JUNE ROSE, psychologist, educator; b. Highland Park, Mich., Dec. 10, 1934; A.B., UCLA, 1962, M.A., 1967, Ph.D., 1972. Staff psychologist Long Beach VA Med. Center, 1971-73, chief Day Treatment Center, 1973—; clin. asso. prof. U. So. Calif., 1973—; clin. asso. prof. Fuller Theol. Sem., 1977—; clin. asst. prof. U. Calif., Irvine, 1979—, UCLA/Harbor Med. Center, 1980—; dir. Who's Who Internat., a Calif. corp. Recipient Superior Performance award Long Beach VA Hosp., 1975, 81. Mem. Am. Psychol. Assn., Western Psychol. Assn., Am. Soc. Clin. Hypnosis, So. Calif., Soc. Clin. Hypnosis, Phi Beta Kappa. Contbr. chpts. to books, articles to profl. jours. Office: 5901 E 7th St Long Beach CA 90822

HUSTED, MARY KATHRYNE, corp. exec.; b. Newton, Kans., Dec. 23, 1935; d. Eldon F. and Alta Mae (Hershberger) Martens; student Wichita State U., 1953-55; grad. Mt. Carmel Acad., 1953; m. Loren Paul Husted, July 8, 1960; children—Bradley Jay, Kevin Michael. Self-employed in fashion industry, Wichita, Kans. and San Jose, Calif., 1957-77; head telecommunications Fireman's Fund Ins. Co., San Jose, 1965-70; account exec. Solari & Sanfilippo Ins. Agy., San Jose, 1970-78; exec. dir. The Executaries/The Execs., Suite One, Campbell, Calif., 1978—; ins. instr. County of Santa Clara Supt. Schs.; cons. Mem. Am. Telephone Answering Service Assn., Campbell C. of C. Republican. Roman Catholic. Office: 274 E Hamilton Ave Suite B Campbell CA 95008

HUSTON, JOHN RICHARD, physician; b. Columbus, Ohio, May 1, 1920; s. Harvey and Harriet Elizabeth (Schubert) H.; B.A., Ohio State U., 1947, M.D., 1947; m. Patricia Wilkinson, Oct. 17, 1940 (dec. Oct. 1970); children—Shirley J., Bonnie L., Valerie E., John Richard; m. 2d., Martha Rankin, Oct. 16, 1971 (div. 1979); m. 3d, Beverly E. Gerrish, Apr. 21, 1982. Intern, U.S. Naval Hosp., Phila., 1947-48; resident in pathology U.S. Naval Hosp., Bethesda, 1948-49, internal medicine Phila. Naval Hosp., 1951-52, internal medicine Ohio State U., 1953-54, cardiology Ohio State U. Hosp., 1954-55; clin. instr. medicine Ohio State U., Columbus, 1953-60, clin. asst. prof., 1960-64, clin. asso. prof., 1964-74; pvt. practice medicine, specializing in internal medicine and cardiology, Columbus, 1955-74; med. dir. United Comml. Travelers, Columbus, 1966-74; staff dept. internal medicine VA Hosp., Phoenix, 1974—, also dir. affiliated med. residency program, asst. chief of medicine; pres. Acad. Medicine Columbus and Franklin County, 1965. Served with USNR, 1944-46, 47-53. Diplomate Am. Bd. Internal Medicine. Mem. Am., Ohio med. assns., Am. Heart Assn., Internat. Platform Assn. Contbr. articles to med. jours. Home: 2828 E Desert Cove Phoenix AZ 85028 Office: VA Hosp 650 E Indian Sch Phoenix AZ 85012

HUTA, HENRY NICHOLAUS, financial executive; b. Traunstein, Germany, Nov. 16, 1947; came to U.S., 1963, naturalized, 1968; s. Mykola and Bertha (Hoffman) H.; m. Kay Crouch, Nov. 14, 1978; children—David, Scott. A.S. with honors, Suffolk County Community Coll., 1974; B.S. magna cum laude in Acctg., C.W. Post Coll., L.I. U., 1976; M.S., West Coast U., 1981. Acctg. supr. Loeb Rhoades & Co., N.Y.C., 1967-71; auditor Albrecht Viggiano Zurich, C.P.A.s, N.Y.C., 1974-76; sr. cons. Arthur Young & Co., N.Y.C., 1976-78; pres. R&B Info. System, West Los Angeles, 1978-80; mgr. Price Waterhouse & Co., Los Angeles, 1980-81; v.p. ops. and adminstrn. Bay Beer Distbrs., Redondo Beach, Calif., 1981—, also treas., asst. corp. sec. Served with USMC, 1964-67. Mem. Nat. Assn. Accts., Am. Inst. C.P.A.s, Calif. Soc. C.P.A.s, Data Processing Mgmt. Assn., Assn. Computer Users. Republican. Home: 4233 Fir Ave Seal Beach CA 90740 Office: 2420 Santa Fe Ave Redondo Beach CA 90278

HUTCHENS, FRED JAMES, public works director; b. LaBelle, Idaho, Aug. 13, 1920; s. William Aaron and Martha Alvina (Anglesey) H.; m. Wanda Mary McCulloch, Nov. 27, 1941 (dec.); children—James, Jack; m. 2d Frances Rushton, May 10, 1957; children—Ellen, Terri, John, David. Grad. high. sch., trade courses sponsored by EPA Health Dept. 1967-80. Cert. water, sewer and cross connection control. Pub. works dir. City of Rigby (Idaho), 1947—. Served to sgt. U.S. Army, 1940-45. Mem. Am. Water Works Assn., Pacific N.W. Pollution Control Assn., VFW, Rigby Hist. Soc. Mormon. Home: 151 W Short Rigby ID 83442 Office: 158 W Fremont Rigby ID 83442

HUTCHESON, ALAN GERARD, communications co. exec.; b. Buffalo, Dec. 4, 1943; m. Gabriell M. Maciola, Dec. 31, 1976; children—Alan, Patrick, Nicole, Alexander. B.S.E.E., Mich. State U., 1965. Staff supr. Automatic Electric Labs., Northlake, Ill., 1970-73; mgr. electronic switching Lynch Communication Systems, Inc., Reno, Nev., 1973-79, v.p., product line mgr., 1979-81, v.p. corp. planning, 1981—. Served to capt. USAF, 1966-70. Decorated Air Force Commendation medal. Patentee in field. Office: 204 Edison Way Reno NV 89520

HUTCHESON, JERRY DEE, manufacturing company executive; b. Hammon, Okla., Oct. 31, 1932; s. Radford Andrew and Ethel Mae (Boulware) H.; B.S. in Physics, Eastern N. Mex. U., 1959; postgrad. Temple U., 1961-62, U. N.Mex., 1964-65; m. Lynda Lou Weber, Mar. 6, 1953; children—Gerald Dan, Lisa Marie, Vicki Lynn. Research engr. RCA, 1959-62; sect. head Motorola, 1962-63; research physicist Dikewood Corp., 1963-66; sr. mem. tech. staff Signetics Corp., 1966-69; engring. mgr. Litton Systems, Sunnyvale, Calif., 1969-70; engring. mgr. Fairchild Semiconductor, Mountain View, Calif., 1971; equipment engr., group mgr. Teledyne Semiconductor, Mountain View, 1971-74; dir. engring. DCA Reliability Labs., Sunnyvale, 1974-75; founder, prin. Tech. Ventures, San Jose, Calif., 1975—; chief exec. officer VLSI

Research, Inc., 1981—. Democratic precinct committeeman, Albuquerque, 1964-66. Served with USAF, 1951-55. Registered profl. engr., Calif. Mem. Nat. Soc. Profl. Engrs., Profl. Engrs. Pvt. Practice, Calif. Soc. Profl. Engrs., Semiconductor Equipment and Materials Inst. Presbyterian. Club: Masons. Contbr. articles to profl. jours. Home: 5950 Vita Coop San Jose CA 95124 Office: 826 N Winchester Blvd Suite 2H San Jose CA 95128

HUTCHESON, MARK ANDREW, lawyer; b. Phila., Mar. 29, 1942; s. Jack Robert and Helen (Willis) H.; m. Julie Olander, June 13, 1964; children—Kirsten, Mark, Megan. B.A., U. Puget Sound, 1964; LL.B., U. Wash., 1967. Staff counsel U.S. Senate Com. on Commerce, Washington, 1967-68; assoc. firm Davis, Wright, Todd, Riese & Jones, Seattle, 1968-72, ptnr., 1973—; lectr. in field; Trustee Epiphany Sch., pres., 1978-81; bd. dirs. Virginia Mason Hosp., 1981—. Mem. ABA, Wash. State Bar Assn., Seattle-King County Bar Assn., Am. Soc. Hosp. Attys., Wash. State Soc. Hosp. Attys. Episcopalian. Clubs: Seattle Tennis, Rainier (Seattle).

HUTCHINGS, FRANCEY JOAN, school principal, consultant; b. Auburn, Calif., Aug. 26, 1946; d. Frank Lawrence Bringman and Jobyna Ralston (Schlarman) B.; m. John A. Hutchings (div.); 1 dau., Laura Marie. B.A. in English and Sociology, U. Nev., 1969, M.A. in Elem./Secondary Edn., 1974, ednl. specialist sch. adminstrn., 1981. Cert. sch. adminstr., reading specialist, elem. educator, secondary educator, Nev. Tchr. reading and English, Sparks (Nev.) Middle Sch., 1969-75; dir. Summer Fun Program, Sparks, 1971-73; coordinator and tchr. O'Brien Middle Sch., Sparks, 1975-81; program asst. reading Washoe County (Nev.) Sch. Dist., 1981-82; prin. Stead Elem. Sch., Reno, 1982—. Vice-pres. O'Brien PTA, Sparks Middle Sch.; council mem. St. Peter Canisius Catholic Ch.; chairperson Washoe County Parks Commn., Sun Valley Pool Com.; coach Sparks Bobbysocks Softball; v.p., coach Miss Softball. Recipient Nev. State Edn. Assn. Outstanding Achievement award 1983; Washoe County Sch. Dist. Incentive grantee 1982, block grantee 1983. Mem. Assn. Supervision and Curriculum Devel., Internat. Reading Assn., NEA, Nev. State Edn. Assn., Washoe County Edn. Adminstrs. Assn., Nat. Assn. Elem. Sch. Prins., Nev. Assn. Sch. Adminstrs. Democrat. Roman Catholic. Home: 528 Aloha Way Sparks NV 89431 Office: 10580 Stead Blvd Reno NV 89506

HUTCHINSON, JOSEPH CANDLER, foreign language educator; b. Hazelhurst, Ga., Jan. 10, 1920; s. George Washington and Lillie Arizona (Rowan) H.; m. June Cruce O'Shields, Aug. 12, 1950; children—Junie O'Shields, Joseph Candler. B.A., Emory U., 1940, M.A., 1941; Ph.D., U. N.C., 1950; postgrad. U. Paris, summers 1951, 53. Tchr., Tech. High Sch., Atlanta, 1941-42; instr. French, German, Italian, Emory U., Atlanta, 1946-47; instr. U. N.C., Chapel Hill, 1947-50, asst. prof., 1954, assoc. prof., to 1957; asst. prof. Sweet Briar (Va.) Coll., 1950-51, 53-54; asso. prof. Tulane U., New Orleans, 1957-59; fgn. lang. specialist U.S. Office Edn., Washington, 1959-64; acad. adv. hdqrs. Def. Lang. Inst., Washington, 1964-74, Monterey, 1974-77, dir. tng. devel. Def. Lang. Inst. Fgn. Lang. Center, Monterey, Calif., 1977-82, asst. acad. dean, 1982—; vis. prof. U. Va., Charlottesville, 1966, Arlington, 1970, Georgetown U., 1968, Am. U., 1971; cons. Council of Chief State Sch. Officers, 1960, U. Del., 1966, U. Colo., 1968, U. Ill., 1968; U.S. del. Bur. Internat. Lang. Coordination, NATO, 1964-79, 81, 82. Served with U.S. Army, 1942-46, 51-53. Decorated Bronze Star. Mem. Am. Council on Edn. (task force on internat. edn. 1973), NEA (sec. dept. fgn. langs. 1961-64), Higher Edn. Assn. Monterey Peninsula, Am. Council on Teaching of Fgn. Lang., MLA, Am. Mgmt. Assn., Monterey Peninsula Choral Soc. Episcopalian. Clubs: Presidio of Monterey Officers and Faculty, Washington Linguistics (v.p. 1970-72). Contbr. articles to profl. jours.; author: Using the Language Laboratory Effectively, School Executives Guide, 1964; The Language Laboratory: Equipment and Utilization in Trends in Language Teaching, 1966, others. Office: Def Lang Inst Fgn Lang Center ATFL-AD Monterey CA 93940

HUTCHINSON, ROBERT NEWMAN, optometrist; b. Salt Lake City, Sept. 21, 1926; s. Oliver and Elizabeth M. (Newman) H.; m. Elizabeth N. McNicol, Feb. 20, 1954 (dec.); children—Laurie Jean, Robert Oliver. B.S., U. Utah, 1956; O.D. cum laude, So. Calif. Coll. Optometry, 1976. Lic. optometrist, Calif., Fla., Wash. Pvt. practice optometry, San Juan Capistrano, Calif., 1976—. Cons. Laguna Hills Lions Vision Aids Clinic. Bd. dirs. Lions Sight and Hearing Found., Inc. Served to lt. col. USMC, 1951-72. Decorated D.F.C., Air medal with eleven clusters, Navy Commendation medal; Bausch and Lomb Soflens, Inc. fellow, 1975. Mem. Low Vision Cons. Calif., Am. Optometric Assn., Calif. Optometric Assn., Orange County Optometric Soc., Mil. Order World Wars, USMC Assn., Ret. Officers Assn., C. of C. Republican. Mormon. Club: Lions. Contbr. article to profl. jour. Home: 25502 Via Inez San Juan Capistrano CA 92675 Office: 31876 Del Obispo Suite 3 San Juan Capistrano CA 92675

HUTCHISON, FANNIE MAE, educator; b. Coschocton, Ohio, Nov. 11, 1929; d. Lewis Leroy and Mary Esther (Wells) H.; B.S., Muskingum Coll., 1952; M.A., Chapman Coll., 1974; M.S., U. So. Calif., 1975; postgrad., 1976—. Tchr. elem. schs. Ventura, Calif., 1953-78, tchr. educationally handicapped, 1979-80, spl. edn. resource specialist, 1980—. Mem. Ventura Unified Edn. Assn. (pres. 1972-73), Sch. Resource Network (dir. 1977-78), Orton Soc., Council Exceptional Children, EDUCARE, Assn. Supervision and Curriculum Devel., Calif. Tchrs. Assn., NEA, Phi Delta Kappa. Home: 956 Sharon Ln Ventura CA 93001 Office: 120 E Santa Clara St Ventura CA 93001

HUTCHISON, WILLIAM HENRY, III, data processing consulting company executive; b. Denver, Sept. 11, 1943; s. Carl Kenneth and Florence Jane (Mayhall) H.; tng. Burroughs Corp., 1966-67. Salesman, Caribou-Wards, Anchorage, 1965-66; field engr. trainee to sr. field engr. Burroughs Corp., Anchorage, 1966-78; owner, mgr. Alaska Systems, Anchorage, 1978-81; pres. Alaska Systems Consultants, Inc., Anchorage, 1981-82; owner, mgr. The Hutchison Co., Anchorage, 1982—; cons. in field. Served with USAF, 1961-65. Mem. Assn. Computing Machinery, Nat. Rifle Assn., U.S. Chess Fedn. Clubs: Commonwealth N., No. Bytes, Ketchikan Rod & Gun (sec.-treas. 1971-72), Anchorage Chess (v.p. 1976-77). Office: 2900 W Northern Lights Blvd Anchorage AK 99503

HUTELMYER, JAMES JOHN, advertising executive; b. Providence, R.I., Feb. 11, 1937; s. Joseph Vincent and Marie Rose (O'Neill) H.; m. Elizabeth Laffey, June 5, 1971; 1 son, James John. Asst. acct. exec. APCL&K, Phila., 1961-63; asst. acct. exec. Compton Advt., N.Y.C., 1964-65; acct. exec. Cunningham & Walsh, N.Y.C., 1966-68; acct. supr. Doyle Dane Bernbach, N.Y.C., 1969-78; sr. v.p. Bozell & Jacobs, Union, N.J., 1978-80, gen. mgr. Phoenix, Ariz., 1980-82; pres. Hutelmyer & Lavidge, Inc., Phoenix, 1982—; guest lectr. Ariz. State U., Scottsdale Community Coll. Bd. dirs. Phoenix Symphony, Compas, Phoenix Better Bus. Bur. Served with USAFR, 1960-64. Mem. Phoenix Advt. Club (bd. dirs., pres.), Phoenix C. of C. Republican. Roman Catholic. Clubs: University, Village Tennis, Notre Dame (Phoenix). Office: 3737 N 7th St Suite 207 Phoenix AZ 85014

HUTH, SYLVIA TERESA, industrial engineer; b. Youngstown, Ohio, Mar. 25, 1945; d. John Patrick and Lois Virginia (Mirth) DeNicola; m. Robert Alexander Huth, Nov. 1, 1975. B.A., San Jose (Calif.) State U., 1967. Assoc. indsl. engr. Rockwell Internat., Downey, Calif., 1968-70; sr. adminstrv. analyst Chief Administrv. Office, County of Los Angeles, 1970-78; sr. mgmt. engr. Kaiser Permanente Med. Care Program, Los Angeles, 1978-81; asst. dir. planning and devel. So. Calif. Permanente Med. Group, Los Angeles, 1981—. Mem. Inst. Indsl. Engrs., Am. Mgmt. Assn., Nat. Assn. Exec. Females. Republican. Contbr. articles to profl. publs. Office: 4747 Sunset Blvd Los Angeles CA 90027

HUTMACHER, JOHN STEVEN, steamship co. exec.; b. Columbus, Ohio, Dec. 14, 1944; s. John Joseph and Margaret M.H.; B.A., Detroit Conservatory of Music, 1964; M.B.A., UCLA, 1967; m. Margo M. Hutmacher, July 21, 1976; 1 son, Johnny. With Manchester Liners, Seattle, 1974—, mgr. West Coast, 1978—; owner, v.p. internat. mktg. Lancaster Group Internat., Seattle, 1976—; owner, internat. dir. Rain Rose Internat., Seattle, 1979—. Mem. Am. Ordnance Assn., AIAA, World Affairs Council. Clubs: Masons, Elks, Propeller, World Trade. Home: 31725 47th Ln SW Div A Federal Way WA 98003 Office: Manchester Liners 821 2d Ave 2001 Exchange Bldg Seattle WA 98104

HUTNER, HERBERT LOEB, financial consultant, lawyer; b. N.Y.C., Dec. 21, 1908; s. Nathan M. and Ethel (Helhor) H.; m. Marjorie Mayer, Oct. 1, 1962 (div.); children—Jeffrey J., Lynn M. Colwell; m. 2d., Zsa Zsa Gabor, Mar. 20, 1967 (div.); m. 3d., Juli Reding, Nov. 28, 1969. B.A., Columbia U., 1928, J.D., 1931. Bar: N.Y. 1928. Ptnr., Osterman & Hutner, mem. N.Y. Stock Exchange, N.Y.C., 1945-57; successively pres. N.E. Life Insurance Co., N.Y.C.; chmn. bd. Sleight & Hellmuth Inc., N.Y.C.; chmn. bd. Pressed Metals of Am., Port Huron, Mich.; chmn. bd. Struthers Wells Corp., Warren, Pa., Plateau Mining Co. Inc., Oak Ridge; investor, cons., Los Angeles, 1963—; dir. United Artists Communications Inc., 1965—. Chmn., Pres.'s Adv. on the Arts for the Kennedy Ctr., 1982—; founder Los Angeles Music Ctr.; chmn. profl. sports com. United Way. Decorated title DATO, Sultan of Johore, Malaysia, Order of the Crown, 1981. Mem. ASCAP, Nat. Republican Senatorial Club. Club: Deepdale Golf (Manhasset, N.Y.). Composer: The Super Bowl Song, Go Rams Go, others.

HUTTENBACK, ROBERT ARTHUR, university chancellor; b. Frankfurt, Germany, Mar. 8, 1928; s. Otto Henry and Dorothy (Marcuse) H.; B.A., U. Calif. at Los Angeles, 1951, Ph.D., 1959; postgrad. Sch. Oriental and African Studies, U. London (Eng.), 1956-57; m. Freda Braginsky, July 12, 1954; 1 dau., Madeleine Alexandra. Mem. faculty Calif. Inst. Tech., Pasadena, 1958-78, asst. prof., 1960-63, asso. prof., 1963-66, prof. history, 1966-78, master student houses, 1958-69, dean students, 1969-72, chmn. div. humanities and social scis., 1971-77; chancellor U. Calif., Santa Barbara, 1978—; cons. Jet Propulsion Lab., Pasadena, 1966-68. Served to 1st lt. U.S. Army, 1951-53. Mem. Assn. Asian Studies, Am. Hist. Assn. Author: British Relations with Sind, 1799-1843, An Anatomy of Imperialism, 1962; (with Leo Rose, Margaret Fisher) Himalayan Battleground-Sino-Indian Rivalry in Ladakh, 1963; The British Imperial Experience, 1966; Gandhi in South Africa, 1971; Racism and Empire, 1976. Home: 543 Channel Islands Rd Santa Barbara CA 93106

HUTTENHOFF, ROBERT L., newspaperr publisher; b. Colton, Calif., Nov. 15, 1920; s. Otto F. and Henrietta (Sherman) H.; m. Patricia A. Pfifer, Dec. 27, 1947; children—Veronica Leonard, Damian, Honora. A.B., U. Kans., 1942; B.S., U.S. Mcht. Marine Acad., 1944. Salesman, Salinas Californian, 1950-51, retail advt. mgr., 1952-61; dir. advt., 1962-72, pres., pub., 1972—. Bd. dirs. Calif. Rodeo Assn. Served to lt. (j.g.) USNR, 1944-46. Mem. Calif. Advt. Execs. Assn. (past pres.), Internat. Advt. Execs. Assn., Calif. Newspaper Pubs. Assn. (dir.), Am. Newspaper Pubs. Assn., Assn. U.S. Army (nat. dir., past pres.), Salinas C. of C. Republican. Roman Catholic. Clubs: Kiwanis (past pres.), Rotary (Salinas); Commonwealth (San Francisco); Elks, KC. Home: 656 San Miguel Ave Salinas CA 93901 Office: PO Box 81091 Salinas CA 93901

HUTTER, JAMES RISQUE, lawyer; b. Spokane, Wash., Mar. 20, 1924; s. James R. and Esther (Nelson) H.; B.S., U. Calif. at Los Angeles, 1947; J.D., Stanford, 1950; m. Patricia Ruth Dunlavy, Aug. 12, 1951; children—Bruce Dunlavy, Gail Anne, Dean James, Karl Nelson. Admitted to Calif. bar, 1951, U.S. Supreme Ct. bar, 1965; assoc. Gibson, Dunn & Crutcher, lawyers, Los Angeles, 1950-58, partner, 1959—; dir. Fifield Manors, Los Angeles, 1955—, v.p., 1964—. Bd. dirs., chmn. finance com. Congl. Found. for Theol. Studies, Nat. Assn. Congl. Christian Chs., 1961-68; mem. San Marino (Calif.) City Planning Commn., 1968—, chmn., 1976—. Served to 1st lt., inf. AUS, 1943-46. Decorated Purple Heart. Mem. State Bar Calif. (com. on corps. 1973-76, exec. com. bus. law sect. 1976-78), Am., Los Angeles County, Beverly Hills (bd. govs. 1968-70) bar assns., Am. Judicature Soc., Town Hall, Phi Delta Phi, Beta Gamma Sigma, Phi Kappa Psi. Republican. Congregationalist. Clubs: Stock Exchange of Los Angeles, Valley Hunt. Home: 1400 Circle Dr San Marino CA 91108 Office: 333 S Grand Ave Los Angeles CA 90071

HUTTON, RONDELL BRUCE, marketing educator, market research executive; b. Arkansas City, Kans., Aug. 6, 1947; s. Morris Wayne and Dorothy Pearl H.; m. Sally Elaine; 1 dau. Abby Calla. B.S. in Bus. Adminstrn., Okla. State U., 1970, M.B.A., 1971; Ph.D., U. Fla., 1977. Instr. bus. adminstrn. S.E. Mo. State U., 1971-73; asst. prof. U. Denver, 1976-77; program mgr., market research cons. U.S. Dept. Energy, 1976-77; chmn. dept. mktg. U. Denver, 1978—; exec. v.p. Market Analysis Profls., Inc., 1980—; dir. Newstrak Info. Tech., Inc.; advisor Colo. State Energy Office, Solar Energy Research Inst., Colo. Assn. Gift Giving. Active Spl. Olympics, 1977. Recipient Ann. Vol. Service award 1978. Mem. Am. Mktg. Assn. (grantee 1976, doctoral consortium rep. 1975), Assn. Consumer Research, Mktg. Sci. Inst., Mu Kappa Tau, Beta Gamma Sigma. Contbr. numerous articles to profl. jours.

HUZURBAZAR, VASANT SHANKAR, statistics educator, researcher; b. Kolhapur City, India, Sept. 15, 1919; came to U.S., 1979; s. Shankar Abaji and Ganga Shankar (Kanetkar) H.; m. Prabha Wasudeo Gadgil, Dec. 26, 1959; children—Snehalata, Aparna. B.A. with honors, Bombay U. (India), 1940; M.A., Barnaras Hindu U. (India), 1942; Ph.D., Cambridge U. (Eng.), 1949. Sampling expert Bur. Econs. and Stats., Govt. Bombay, 1950-52; statis. reader Lucknow (India) U., 1952-53; sr. prof., head dept. math. and stats. U. Poona (India), 1953-76; Fulbright vis. prof. Iowa State U., Ames, 1962-64, U. Man. (Can.), Winnipeg, 1976-79; prof. stats. U. Denver, 1979—; researcher, cons. Recipient Chancellor's Gold medal Banaras Hindu U., 1942; Adams prize Cambridge U., 1959-60; Padma Bhushan award Pres. India, 1974; Nat. Lectr., Univ. Grants Commn. India, 1975-76. Fellow Am. Statis. Assn., Royal Statis. Soc. (London), Indian Nat. Acad. Sci., Cambridge Philos. Soc.; mem. Internat. Statis. Inst. Author: Sufficient Statistics, 1976, contbr. articles to profl. jours. Home: 3755 E Buchtel Blvd #206 Denver CO 80210 Office: Coll Bus Adminstrn U Denver Denver CO 80208

HWANG, CORDELIA JONG, chemist; b. N.Y.C., July 14, 1942; d. Goddard and Lily (Fung) Jong; m. Warren C. Hwang, Mar. 31, 1969; 1 son, Kevin. Student Alfred U., 1960-62; B.A., Barnard Coll., 1964; M.S., SUNY-Stony Brook, 1969. Research asst. Columbia U., N.Y.C., 1964-66; analytical chemist Veritron West Inc., Chatsworth, Calif., 1969-70; asst. lab. dir., chief chemist Pomeroy, Johnston & Bailey Environ. Engrs., Pasadena, Calif., 1970-76; research chemist Met. Water Dist. So. Calif., Los Angeles, 1976—; mem. Joint Task Group on Instrumental Identification of Taste and Odor Compounds; instr. Citrus Coll., 1974-76. Mem. Am. Chem. Soc., Am. Water Works Assn. (cert. water quality analyst level 3, Calif.-Nev.). Office: Met Water Dist So Calif 700 N Moreno St La Verne CA 91750

HYATT, CAROLYN JOYCE, career counselor, educator of deaf, writer, photographer; b. Los Angeles, Jan. 30, 1952; d. John Russell and Edna Mae (Long) H.; A.A. in Journalism with honors, Fullerton Coll., 1975; B.A. in Communications with honors, Calif. State U.-Fullerton, 1978; M.A. in Counseling of Hearing Impaired, Gallaudet Coll., 1981. Cert. in pupil personnel service, Calif. Free-lance writer, photographer, 1974—; practicum counselor adult edn. program Gallaudet Coll., spring 1980, Maritua Elem. sch., Fairfax, Va., fall 1980; counseling intern Fla. Sch. for Deaf and Blind, St. Augustine, spring 1981; career counselor/tchr. Calif. Sch. for Deaf, Fremont, 1981—; cons. teaching and counseling deaf youth. Recipient Woman of Distinction award Alpha Gamma Eta, Fullerton Coll. chpt. 1975, Mem. Am. Personnel and Guidance Assn., Calif. Assn. tchrs. of Hearing Impaired, Nat. Assn. of Deaf, Conv. Am. Instrs. of Deaf, Am. Assn. Owners and Breeders of Peruvian Paso Horses. Roman Catholic. Contbr. photographs, articles, chpt. to various publs. Office: 39380 Gallaudet Dr Fremont CA 94538

HYBL, WILLIAM JOSEPH, investment company executive, foundation executive, lawyer; b. Des Moines, July 16, 1942; s. Joseph A. and Geraldine (Evans) H.; m. Kathleen Horrigan, June 6, 1967; children—William J., Kyle. B.A., Colo. Coll., 1964; J.D., U. Colo., 1967. Bar: Colo. bar, 1967, U.S. Sup. Ct. 1978, U.S. Tax Ct. 1977, U.S. Ct. Apls. 1978, U.S. Dist. Ct. 1969-70. Dep. dist. atty. El Paso County, Colo., 1970-72; asst. dist. atty. El Paso and Teller Counties, Colo., 1972-73; ptnr. Murphy, Morris & Hybl., 1972-73; mem. Colo. Ho. of Reps., 1972-73; pres., dir. El Pomar Investment Co., Colorado Springs, also pres., dir. El Pomar Found., 1983; dir. Broadmoor Hotel, Inc., Broadmoor Mgmt. Co., Garden City Co., Manitou and Pikes Peak Ry., Mt. Manitou Incline Ry., Ft. Carson Nat. Bank; spl. White House csl., 1981. Bd. trustees Colo. Coll.; bd. dirs. Council on Founds., Am. Council Young Polit. Leaders; pres., trustee Air Force Acad. Found.; exec. com. Atlantic Assn. Young Polit. Leaders, Pikes Peak United Way. Served to capt., AUS, 1967-69. Mem. ABA, Colo. Bar Assn., El Paso County Bar Assn. Republican. Roman Catholic. Clubs: Broadmoor Golf, Cheyenne Mountain Country, El Paso (Colorado Springs). Home: 2 Heather Circle Colorado Springs CO 80906 Office: 10 Lake Circle Colorado Springs CO 80906

HYDE, JOHN WALLACE, motion picture company executive; b. Jackson, Mich., Mar. 29, 1941; s. Neil W. and Doris (Brown) H.; B.A., NYU, 1963; 1 son, John W. With ABC, 1963; exec. asst. MCA-Universal, 1963-69, assoc. producer numerous films, 1963-69; v.p., exec. asst. to pres. Filmways, Inc., Los Angeles, 1969-72; founder, pres. Acmelab, Ltd., Hollywood, Calif., 1972-76; v.p. Film Fin. Group, Ltd., Los Angeles, 1976-81; v.p. Guinness Film Group, Los Angeles, 1976-81; vice chmn. Producers Sales Orgn., Los Angeles, 1981—. Mem. Acad. Motion Picture Arts and Scis. Office: 10100 Santa Monica Blvd Suite 1580 Los Angeles CA 90057

HYDE, RONALD GREGORY, educational administrator; b. Pocatello, Idaho, May 2, 1929; s. Milton D. and Mildred Yvonne (Gregory) H.; m. Mary Helen Frampton, Dec. 12, 1956; children—Kerrie Hyde Summerhays, Nathan, Paul, Catherine, Amy. B.S., U. Idaho, 1951; M.S., Brigham Young U., 1963. Field rep. Patterson Sales Clinic, Phoenix, 1957-58; alumni fund dir. Brigham Young Univ., Provo, Utah, 1958-64, exec. dir., 1964-78, spl. asst. to pres., 1981-82, asst. exec. v.p. Univ. Relations, 1982—; pres. Eng. Birmingham Mission, 1978-81. Served with USAF, 1951-53. Recipient Exceptional Achievement award Council for Advancement and Support of Edn., 1982; Time/Life award Am. Alumni Council, 1974; Ernest T. Stewart award 1970; Alumni Adminstrn. award, 1969. Mem. Council for Advancement and Support of Edn. (trustee 1974-75), Pub. Relations Soc. Am., Internat. Pub. Relations Assn., Am. Alumni Council (bd. chmn. 1974), Am. Provo C. of C. (dir. 1983). Republican. Mormon. Home: 540 S Palisade Dr Orem UT 84057 Office: C-366 ASB Brigham Young University Provo UT 84602

HYLAND, FRANCIS PAUL, JR., information management executive, retail management consultant; b. Oil City, Pa., Oct. 17, 1929; s. Francis Paul and Gertrude Elizabeth (Bullock) H.; m. Margaret Ellen Hannon, Oct. 9, 1954; children—Kevin Paul, Timothy Francis; m. 2d Muriel Anderson, Dec. 3, 1983. Student U. Calif.-San Francisco, 1949; B.A., U. Omaha, 1962. Enlisted U.S. Air Force, 1947; advanced through grades to maj., 1966; officer in charge Diplomatic and Mil. Courier Net, S.E. Asia, 1963-65; staff officer SAC, 1965-70; ret., 1970; mgr. data services Manhattan Industries, 1971-77; team chief fin. research and devel. Datapoint Corp., San Antonio, 1977-78; v.p. data processing Am. Indsl. Cons., San Antonio, 1978-80; bus. systems specialist info. service Am. Express, San Rafael, Calif., 1980—; pvt. practice cons. retail bus. systems. Decorated D.F.C. with 2 oakleaf clusters, Air medal with 8 oakleaf clusters, Bronze Star with 2 oakleaf clusters. Mem. Assn. Systems Mgmt., Data Processing Mgmt. Assn., Air Force Assn., Mensa. Republican. Clubs: Treasure Island Yacht (San Francisco); Pt. San Pablo Yacht (Richmond, Calif.). Office: 1600 Los Gamos ASD/CIS San Rafael CA 94901

HYLAND, KATHLEEN NOLAND, company executive; b. Long Beach, Calif., July 3, 1945; d. Richard Lee and Grace Irene Noland; m. Richard N. Gary, Nov. 1982. B.A., U. Wash., 1967. Asso. editor Kaiser News, Kaiser Aluminum & Chem. Corp., Oakland, Calif., 1968-73; dir. communications Kaiser Engrs., Oakland, 1973-74; mgr. internal communications Kaiser Industries Corp., Oakland, 1975-77; dir. pub. relations and advt. Kaiser Steel Corp., Oakland, 1977-80; corp. v.p. pub. affairs and communications Syntex Corp., Palo Alto, Calif. Bd. dirs. Calif. Health Products Info. Council. Mem. Public Relations Soc. Am., World Affairs Council, Calif. Mfrs. Assn. (dir.), Pharm. Mfrs. Assn., Mortar Bd., Gamma Phi Beta. Club: Sea Ranch Assn. Author: (with Don Fabun) Dimensions of Change, 1971, Children of Change, 1970. Office: Syntex Corp 3401 Hillview Ave Palo Alto CA 94304

HYMAN, EDWARD JAY, psychologist, information scientist, educator, consultant; b. Roslyn, N.Y., Oct. 25, 1947; s. Herbert H. and Edith T. Hyman; A.B., Columbia U., 1969; postgrad. Harvard U., 1969; Ph.D. (Regents fellow), U. Calif.-Berkeley, 1975. Editorial asst. Huntley-Brinkley Report, NBC News, 1968; residential therpist New Community Sch., 1969; coordinator Center for Ednl. Change, U. Calif.-Berkeley, 1970-72, research asst., 1973, teaching asst. dept. psychology, 1974; psychology intern Santa Cruz County (Calif.) Health Dept., 1974; fellow Center for Social Research, 1975; lectr. U. Calif.-Berkeley, 1976-77; sci. dir. Center for Social Research, Berkeley, 1977—, dir. social ecology project, 1978-79; asst. prof. U. San Francisco, 1979-82; clin. dir. Inst. Labor and Mental Health, 1983—; cons. Exxon, 1977, Edison Electric Inst., 1978—. Coordinator, Berkeley Legal Def., 1970-71; co-chmn. Democratic Nat. Com. Voter Registration, 1972. Lic. psychologist, Calif. Mem. Am. Psychol. Assn., Calif. State Psychol. Assn., Am. Orthopsychiat. Assn., Am. Child Abuse Prevention Soc. (dir. 1977—), Am. Acad. Polit. and Social Sci., Am. Assn. Marriage and Family Therapists, AAUP, Internat. Soc. Polit. Psychology, Internat. Soc. Applied Psychology, AAAS, Soc. for Psycho. Study of Social Issues, Internat. Congress Psychology. Contbg. author: Life Stress; Marcuse Festschrift; co-author: Random House Instructional Support System; contbr. articles to psychol. jours. Office: Center for Social Research 439 Boynton Ave Berkeley CA 94707

HYMAN, ZACHARIAH HENRY, engineer; b. Bklyn., Mar. 11, 1929; s. Zachariah Henry and Maria Lillie (Plummer) H.; m. Helena Cecelia Hyman, June 12, 1953; children—Monica Louise Hyman Bullock,

Yvette Cecelia. B.S. in Structural Engring., N.C. A&T State U., 1951. Lic. engr. Tchr., N.C. A&T State U., 1951-52; designer Curtiss Wright Aero. Corp., Woodbridge, N.J., 1952-53; engr. Engring. Ctr., Columbia U., 1953-56; with Electric Boat div. Gen. Dynamics Corp., Groton, Corp., 1956—, program mgr., 1973-76, asst. to exec. v.p. aerospace, 1978-80, dir. mfg. engring. Convair div., 1980-81, dir. engring. bus. mgmt. Convair div., 1982—; exec. v.p., chief engr. Seatrain Shipbldg. Corp., 1976-78. Mem. nat. bd. govs. ARC. dir. of mfg. Convair div. Mem. AIAA, Soc. Naval Architects and Marine Engrs. Democrat. Methodist. Home: 18197 Valladares Dr San Diego CA 92127 Office: General Dynamics/Convair Division PO Box 80877 San Diego CA 92138

HYNDMAN, LOUIS DAVIES, Canadian provincial government official; b. Edmonton, Alta., Can., July 1, 1935; s. Louis Davies and Muriel (MacKintosh) H.; m. Mary Evelyn Maclennan, June 2, 1962; children—Mary Jennifer, Bruce Louis Davies, Peter. B.A., LL.B., U. Alta. Hon. aide-de-camp to Lt. Gov. Alta., 1960-62; exec. asst. to Minister of Citizenship and Immigration Ottawa, 1962-63; mem. Legis. assembly Alta. for Edmonton Glenora prov. g.e., 1967—, minister of edn., 1971-75, minister of fed. and intergovtl. affairs and govt. house leader, 1975, treas. Province Alta., 1979—. Served to ltd. R.C.N. Res., ret. 1962. Progressive Conservative. Anglican. Office: 323 Legis Bldg Edmonton AB T5K 2B7 Canada*

HYNDS, FRANCES JANE, public relations and communications consultant; b. Martin, Tenn., Oct. 27, 1929; d. Loyd Orion and Hunter Elizabeth (Goad) H. B.S. in Journalism, McMurry Coll., 1951; M.A. in Telecommunications, U. So. Calif., 1961, Ph.D. candidate in Communications, 1983. Dir. pub. info., instr. journalism McMurry Coll., Abilene, Tex., 1951-53; dir. pub. relations Oklahoma City U., 1953-55; acct. exec., corp. sec. Joe Leighton & Assocs. Inc., Hollywood, Calif., 1956-65; prin. Hynds Co., Los Angeles, 1965—; sr. lectr., adj. faculty, dir. pub. relations program for mgmt. U. So. Calif. Sch. Journalism and Coll. Continuing Edn. Mem. Pub. Relations Soc. Am. (dir. 1975-77, nat. assembly del.), Women in Communications Inc. (dir. 1967-72; Far West region Woman of Achievement 1980, Los Angeles chpt. Freedom of Info. award, Nat. Founders award, 1982). Author (with Norma L. Bowles): Psi Search, The New Investigation of Psychic Phenomena that Separates Fact from Speculation, 1978, transl. French, 1983, contbr. articles to profl. jours.

HYNEK, FREDERICK JAMES, architect; b. Minot, N.D., May 24, 1944; s. Frederick Frank and Esther Irene (Hermanson) H.; B.Arch., N.D. State U., 1968; m. Jane Rebecca Lowitz, June 9, 1966; children—Tyler James, Scott Anthony. Intern archtl. firms in Bismarck, N.D., 1967-72; architect Gerald W. Deines, Architect, Casper and Cody, Wyo., 1972-73; v.p. Gerald Deines and Assos., 1973-77; propr. Fred J. Hynek, AIA/Architect, Cody, 1977-80; pres. Design Group, P.C., Architects/Planners, Cody, 1980—; mem. selection com. for archtl. students for Western Interstate Commn. for Higher Edn. Profl. Student Exchange Program, U. Wyo., 1979—. Mem. Big Horn Basin Resource Conservation and Devel. Council; bd. dirs. Cody Stampede, Inc., 1977-82, Cody Econ. Devel. Council, 1982. Served with USAR, 1967-68. Mem. AIA (dir. Wyo. chpt. 1976—, pres. 1980, 81; conf. chmn. Western Mountain region 1977, mem. awards jury 1981, treas. 1982; chmn. design awards jury N.D. 1981), Constrn. Specifications Inst., Cody County C. of C. (dir., pres. 1982). Republican. Presbyterian. Clubs: Cody Elks, Cody Country Ambassador. Mem. editorial adv. bd. Symposia mag. Home: 708 Southfork Rd Cody WY 82414 Office: 1371 Sheridan Ave Cody WY 82414

HYSTER, ELIZABETH MILLER, contract specialist; b. Boston, June 4, 1951; d. James Fitzgerald and Elizabeth (Meath) Miller; m. David Robert Hyster, May 26, 1977; 1 son, Scott. A.B. with honors, Mt. Holyoke Coll., 1973. Contract specialist Atomic Energy Commn., Schenectady, N.Y., 1973-75; budget analyst AEC-ERDA, Schenectady, 1975-77; auditor ERDA, Montville, Conn., 1977-79; contract specialist Dept. Energy, Idaho Falls, 1979—. Mem. Nat. Contract Mgmt. Assn., Nat. Assn. Femal Execs., Idaho Falls Chorale.

IACHETTI, ROSE MARIA ANNE, educator; b. Watervliet, N.Y., Sept. 22, 1931; d. Augustus and Rose Elizabeth Archer (Orciuolo) I.; B.S., Coll. St. Rose, 1961; M.Ed., U. Ariz., 1969. Joined Sisters of Mercy, Albany, N.Y., 1949-66; tchr. various parochial schs. Albany (N.Y.) Diocese, 1952-66; tchr. Headstart Program, Troy, N.Y., 1966; tchr. fine arts Watervliet Jr. and Sr. High Sch., 1966-67; tchr. W.J. Meyer Sch., Tombstone, Ariz., 1968-71, Colonel Johnston Sch., Ft. Huachuca, Ariz., 1971-78, Myer Sch., Ft. Huachuca, 1978—. Ann. chmn. Ariz. Children's Home Assn., Tombstone, 1973-74; trustee Tombstone Sch. Dist. #1, 1971-80; active Democratic Club; mem. Bicentennial Commn. for Ariz., 1972-76, Tombstone Centennial Commn., 1979-80; chmn. Tombstone Centennial Ball, 1980; pres. Tombstone Community Health Services, 1978-80; mem. Tombstone City Council, 1982—. Mem. Ariz. Edn. Assn. (so. regional dir. 1971-73), Tombstone Dist. 1 Educators Assn. (pres. 1969-71), Ft. Huachuca Edn. Assn., Ariz. Sch. Bd. Assn., NEA (del. 1971-73), Ariz. Classroom Tchrs. Assn., Internat. Platform Assn., Tombstone Bus. and Profl. Women's Club, Am. Legion Aux., Phi Delta Kappa, Pi Lambda Theta, Delta Kappa Gamma (pres. 1982—). Club: Ft. Huachuca Lakeside Officers. Home: Round Up Trailer Ranch Box 725 Tombstone AZ 85638 Office: Myer School Fort Huachuca AZ 85613

IACONO, GEORGE DANTE, optometrist; b. Chgo., Oct. 21, 1922; s. Carl Umberto and Emma (Decrecchio) I.; m. Rosemary Marie Maksym, Nov. 28, 1928; children—Carl Dante, Georgeann Louise. O.D., Chgo. Coll. Optometry, 1948. Sole practice optometry, Tucson, 1948—; dir. Tucson Reading Inst., 1953-62; cons. Fellow Nat. Eye Research Found.; mem. Am. Optometric Assn., Ariz. Optometric Assn., Internat. Orthokeratology Assn., Am. Interprofl. Assn. Office: 2553 E Broadway Tucson AZ 85716

IACULLO, ROBERT LEWIS, obstetrician, gynecologist; b. Chgo.; s. Joseph Petrino and Josephine (Loizzo) I.; M.D., Autonomous U. Guadalajara, 1972. Intern, Calif. Hosp. Med. Center, Los Angeles, 1972-73; practice medicine specializing in ob-gyn; mem. staff Southeastern Gen. Hosp. and Med. Center; pres. Montgomery Surg. & Orthopedic Center, 1979—, Ala. Family Practice Center, Montgomery, 1979-80. Diplomate Am. Bd. Surgery. Fellow Am. Soc. Abdominal Surgeons; mem. AMA, Am. Fertility Soc., Am. Soc. Contemporary Medicine and Surgery, Am. Assn. Gynecologic Laparoscopists, Assn. Profs. Gynecology and Obstetrics, Pan-Pacific Surg. Assn., Soc. Tchrs. Family Medicine. Democrat. Roman Catholic. Home: 4248 Via Marina #86 Marina Del Rey CA 90291 Office: 2007 Wilshire Blvd Los Angeles CA 90057

IAMS, BETTY ANN, advertising executive; b. Allen, Okla., Sept. 24, 1936; d. Isaac Sylvester and Minnie Floy (Miller) Horton; student Lassen Coll., 1953-54; M.S., U. So. Calif., 1958; m. Robert Sherwin Iams, Apr. 25, 1962; children—K. Evonne, Kevin Robert. Adminstrv. asst. Ameron Corp., South Gate, Calif., 1958-63; owner Betty Iams Piano & Organ Studios, Cypress, Calif., 1963-70, Clef House Publs., Temecula, Calif., 1963-79, Allegro Art/Type, Temecula, 1979—. Bd. dirs. Calif. Republican Assembly, 1980—. Mem. Music Tchrs. Assn., Mildred Alexander Tchrs. Assn. Club: Bus. and Profl. Women's. Author: Bread Baking from A to Z, 1978; also music books; editor Calif. Woman. Home: 29848 Villa Alturas Temecula CA 92390 Office: 27780 Front St Temecula CA 92390

IAMS, DONNA RUTH, consumer sciences educator, researcher; b. Wheeling, W. Va., Aug. 18, 1950; d. Charles H. and Gertrude R. (Parson) Gassaway; m. Richard W. Iams, May 27, 1972. A.B., Marshall U., 1972, M.A., 1974; Ph.D., Tex. Woman's U., 1979. Tchr. art Elyria (Ohio) City Sch. Dist., 1972-73; tchr. vocat. home econs. Warren Local Sch. Dist., Vincent, Ohio, 1974-77; asst. prof. consumer studies U. Ariz.-Tucson, 1979—. Named Outstanding Young Alumna, Marshall U., 1981. Mem. Am. Home Econs. Assn., Am. Council on Consumer Interest, Am. Assn. Housing Educators. Office: Sch of Home Econs U Ariz Tucson AZ 85721

IANNOLO, FRANK PLACID, aerospace marketing executive; b. Bklyn., May 24, 1925; s. John and Angela (Bruno) I.; m. Peggy Lois Newton, Mar. 5, 1950; 1 son, Gregory. Student Concord Coll., Athens, W.Va., 1943-44; B.S. in Aerospace Engring., Va. Poly. Inst., Blacksburg, 1949. Design draftsman Republic Co., N.Y.C., 1949-51; sales engr. Curtiss Propeller, Caldwell, N.J., 1951-52; sr. sales engr. Wright Aerospace div. Curtiss-Wright Corp., Woodridge, N.J., 1952-58; support engring. mgr. Gen. Dynamics-Convair, San Diego, 1958-65; mktg. mgr. turbomach div. Solar Turbines, San Diego, 1965—. Served with USAAF, 1943-45. Mem. AIAA, Army Aviation Assn., Helicopter Assn. Am., Assn. U.S. Army. Republican. Episcopalian. Home: 3642 Mt Acadia Blvd San Diego CA 92111 Office: 4400 Ruffin Rd San Diego CA 92123

IANZITI, ADELBERT JOHN, indsl. designer; b. Napa, Calif., Oct. 10, 1927; s. John and Mary Lucy (Lecair) I.; student Napa Jr. Coll., 1947, 48-49; A.A., Fullerton Jr. Coll., 1950; student UCLA, 1950, Santa Monica Community Coll., 1950-51; m. Doris Moore, Aug. 31, 1952; children—Barbara Ann Ianziti Haines, Susan Therese Ianziti Shifflett, Joanne Lynn Ianziti Lely, Jonathan Peter, Janet Carolyn. Design draftsman Basalt Rock Co. Inc. div. Dillingham Heavy Constrn., Napa, 1951-66, chief draftsman plant engring., 1966-68, process designer, 1968-82, pres. employees assn., 1967; now self-employed indsl. design cons. Vice-pres., Justin-Siena Parent-Tchr. Group, 1967. Mem. Aggregates and Concrete Assn. No. Calif. (vice-chmn. environ. subcom. 1976-77), Am. Ordinance Assn., Constrn. Specifications Inst., Italian Catholic Fedn. Republican. Roman Catholic. Clubs: Toastmasters, Napa Valley Runners. Home and Office: 2650 Dorset St Napa CA 94558

IAQUINTO, SHIRLEY LORRAINE, school administrator; b. Chgo., Aug. 5, 1923; d. Roy D. and Frances Ethel (Brown) Rann; student U. Tampa, 1946; B.A., Ariz. State Coll., 1951, M.A., 1961; m. Joseph Iaquinto, Apr. 28, 1945; children—Sharon Lee, Jeri Lynn, Michael Joe, Mark Steven. Sec., Ceco Steel Products Co., Cicero, Ill., 1941-43; substitute tchr. Tempe (Ariz.) Elem. Sch. Dist., 1951-54, tchr., 1954-61; substitute tchr. Kyrene (Ariz.) Elem. Sch. Dist., 1951-54, Tempe (Ariz.) High Sch. Dist., 1964-66; instr. manpower devel. and tng. center Maricopa Community Coll., Phoenix, 1967-69; career edn. project dir. Roosevelt Sch. Dist., Phoenix, 1973-82, asst. to prin., 1982—; cons. U.S. Office Edn., Sch. dists., corps., civic groups; presentor nat. and state confs. Mem. Parks and Recreation Bd., 1970-76, chmn., 1974-76; mem. Tempe Long Range Planning Com., 1980-81. Served with WAVES, 1943-45. Mem. Am. Soc. for Tng. and Devel., Ariz. Dirs. Career Edn., Assn. Supervision and Curriculum Devel., Toastmasters Internat., Roosevelt Sch. Dist. Adminstrs. Assn. (pres. 1979-81), Phi Delta Kappa, Phi Kappa Phi. Contbr. articles to profl. jours. Home: 510 W 19th St Tempe AZ 85281 Office: Roosevelt School District #66 Julian Sch 2149 E Carver Dr Phoenix AZ 85040

IBBETSON, EDWIN THORNTON, bus. developer; b. Los Angeles, Apr. 17, 1923; s. Robert Edwin and Ann (Thornton) I.; student Long Beach Jr. Coll., 1941-42, Calif. Inst. Tech., 1942-43; m. Harriett Alice Hudson, Dec. 28, 1947; children—Elizabeth Ann Ibbetson Hitchock, Douglas Hudson, Gregory Bruce, Timothy Edwin, Julia Katherine Ibbetson Zilinskas, Erika Alice Ibbetson Hertzog. With Union Devel. Co., Cerritos, Calif., 1944—, pres., 1961—; partner Paramount Constrn., Cerritos, 1948—; v.p. Valley Properties, Inc., Imperial Valley, 1962—; chmn. bd. Dutch Village Bowling Center, Inc., Lakewood, 1965—; partner Ibbetson-Marsh Realtors, 1975—; vice chmn. bd. Equitable Savs. and Loan Assn., 1977—. Bd. dirs. Met. Water Dist. So. Calif., 1959—, sec., 1979-82, chmn. bd., 1983—; chmn. Bellflower Water Devel. Com., 1965—; mem. Los Angeles County Citizens Com. Real Estate Mgmt., 1974—, now chmn.; bd. dirs. armed services YMCA, Long Beach, 1962-72. Trustee St. Mary's Hosp., Long Beach. Served with USNR, 1942-46. Named Young Man of Year, Bellflower Jaycees, 1959. Realtor of Year, Bellflower Dist. Bd. Realtors, 1962, 67, 71. Mem. Am. Soc. Real Estate Counselors (gov., pres. 1977), Calif. Assn. Realtors (treas. 1972-77, dir., hon. life pres.), Internat. Real Estate Fedn., Nat. Assn. Realtors (dir.), Nat. Inst. Real Estate Brokers (cert. comml. investment mem.), Inst. Real Estate Mgmt. (cert. property mgr.), Bellflower Dist. Bd. Realtors (pres. 1961), Central Basin Water Assn. (dir.), Calif. Real Estate Polit. Action Com., Internat. Council Shopping Centers, Lambda Alpha. Roman Catholic. Clubs: Elks, Kiwanis (pres. 1958); International Traders, So. Calif. Tuna (Long Beach). Office: 16550 Bloomfield Cerritos CA 90701

ICERMAN, LARRY, research engineering administrator; b. Muncie, Ind., Sept. 22, 1945; s. Charles and Janelyn (Mock) I. B.S., MIT, 1963, M.S. U. Calif.-San Diego, 1971, Ph.D., 1976; M.B.A., San Diego State U., 1976. Research engr. U. Calif.-San Diego, 1976; asst. prof. tech. and human affairs, Washington U., St. Louis, 1976-79, assoc. prof., 1979-80; dir. Energy Inst., N. Mex. State U., Las Cruces, 1980—. Author: (with S.S. Penner) Energy: Demands, Resources, Impact Technology and Policy, 1974, 81, Energy: Non-Nuclear Energy Technologies, 1976; (with R. P. Morgan) Renewable Resource Utilization for Development, 1981. Home: 4212 Colt Rd Las Cruces NM 88001 Office: 3EI N Mex State U Las Cruces NM 88003

IDLEMAN, ELFRIEDA LOUISE, educator; b. Youngs Point, Mont., Mar. 10, 1928; d. Emil and Amalia Kober; B.S., Mont. State U., 1951; postgrad. Eastern Mont. Coll., 1952-53, U. Utah, 1956-57, No. Mont. Coll., 1969-70; m. Wilfred Eldon Idleman, Aug. 22, 1960 (dec. 1978). Tchr. bus., pub. schs., Rosebud, Mont., 1951-56, Belgrade, Mont., 1956-58, Belfry, Mont., 1958-60, Billings (Mont.) West High Sch., 1962, Billings Sr. High Sch., 1964—; tchr. adult edn., 1966-68. Mem. Mont. Edn. Assn., Billings Edn. Assn. (sec. 1970-71), Mont. Bus. Edn. Assn. (pres. 1966-67, 80-81, v.p. 1978-79), Western Bus. Edn. Assn. (treas. 1970-71, conv. chmn. 1975). Lutheran. Compiler history of Park City. Home: 319 W 29th St Billings MT 59102 Office: 425 Grand Ave Billings MT 59101

IGNELZI, MICHAEL GUIDO, college administrator; b. Hollywood, Calif., Nov. 10, 1954; s. Guido Anthony and Frieda Emma I. B.A. in Psychology, U. Calif.-Riverside, 1976; M.A., Ohio State U., 1980. Activities asst. U. Calif.-Riverside, 1977-78; grad. adminstrv. asst. Ohio State U., Columbus, 1978-80; resident dir. U. Calif.-Davis, 1980-82; housing dir. Menlo Coll., Atherton, Calif., 1982—; trainer, cons. cultural awareness. Recipient Chancellor's award U. Calif.-Riverside, 1976. Mem. Am. Coll. Personnel Assn., Nat. Assn. Student Personnel Adminstrs., Am. Assn. Coll. and Univ. Housing Officers. Democrat. Co-author manual: Taking the First Step: A Cultural Awareness Training and Programming Manual, 1981. Office: Menlo Coll 1000 El Camino Real Atherton CA 94025

IHARA, GRACE REIKO, speech pathologist; b. Newell, Calif., Nov. 17, 1943; d. Tamotsu and Betsy Shizue (Ito) I.; B.A., U. Hawaii, 1965; M.S. (Vocat. Rehab. Adminstrn. grantee), U. Oreg., 1966. Staff speech pathologist Syracuse VA Hosp., 1966; dir. adult speech and lang. program Mt. Diablo Therapy Center, Pleasant Hill, Calif., 1967-70; chief speech pathology Pacific Inst. Rehab. Medicine, Honolulu, 1970-72; pvt. practice as speech pathology cons., Honolulu, 1972—; dir. Spl. Edn. Center of Oahu; cons. Dept. Social Services, Hawaii Ear, Nose & Throat Group, Kuakini Med. Center, Castle Hosp., 15 skilled nursing and intermediary care facilities; guest lectr. KMC Gerontology Series; commr. State Bd. Speech Pathology and Audiology; faculty and guest lectr. Hawaii Stroke Seminar. Stroke com. Hawaii Heart Assn., 1976—, recipient Community Service award. Mem. Am. Speech and Hearing Assn. (cert.), Council Exceptional Children, Hawaii Assn. Retarded Children, Phi Beta. Club: Quota (charter pres.). Office: Suite 209 1380 Lusitana St Honolulu HI 96813

IHLE, JOHN LIVINGSTON, artist, educator; b. Chgo., Feb. 1, 1925; s. Chester and Martha Elizabeth (Schneider) I.; B.F.A., Ill. Wesleyan U., 1950; M.A., Bradley U., 1951; postgrad. San Francisco State U., 1954; m. Marguerite Poeschel, July 30, 1955; children—Lars Eric, Jean Elain. Exhibited one-man shows San Francisco Mus. Art, 1960, 66, 77, Palace of Legion of Honor, San Francisco, Hansen Gallery, 1964, 68, Henry Gallery, U. Wash., 1965, U. Alta., Edmonton, 1969, others; group shows Library of Congress, Washington, 1950, 51, 53, 55, 58, 61, Pa. Acad. Fine Arts, Phila. Mus., 1950, 53, 59, 61, 65, Bklyn. Art Mus., 1951, 52, 62, 66, numerous others; represented in permanent collections; faculty San Francisco State U., 1955—, prof. art, 1968—, univ. grantee, 1966, 73, 75. Served with U.S. Army, 1943-46. Decorated Purple Heart. Mem. Calif. Soc. Printmakers (pres. 1959), San Francisco Tapestry Workshop (chmn. bd. 1977—).

II, JACK MORITO, aerospace engr.; b. Tokyo, Japan, Mar. 20, 1926; s. Iwao and Kiku Ii; came to U.S., 1954, naturalized, 1966; B.S., Tohoku U., 1949; M.S., U. Washington, 1956; M. in Aero. Engring., Cornell U., 1959; Ph.D. in Aero. and Astronautics, U. Wash., 1964; Ph.D. in Engring., U. Tokyo, 1980; m. Aiko Nouno, Nov. 14, 1952; children—Keiko, Yoshiko, Mutsuya. Reporter, Asahi Newspaper Press, Tokyo, 1951-54; aircraft designer Fuji Heavy Industries Ltd. Co., Tokyo, Japan, 1956-58; mem. staff structures research The Boeing Co., Seattle, 1962—. Mem. AIAA, Japan Shumy and Culture Soc. (pres. 1976—), Sigma Xi. Mem. Congregational Ch. Contbr. numerous articles on aerodyns. to profl. jours. Office: M/S 41-10 The Boeing Co Seattle WA 98124

IIDA, DAVID TAKASHIGE, toy mfr.; b. Vancouver, Wash., Mar. 20, 1923; s. Kametaro and Koma (Inoue) I.; B.A., U. Yokohama, 1943; M.B.A., U. Chgo., 1956; m. Kazu Suzuki, Apr. 10, 1958; children—Elizabeth and Margaret (twins). With Louis Marx & Co., Inc., 1956-73, gen. mgr. Far East, Tokyo, Hong Kong, Far East coordinator, Stamford, Conn., 1973-76; pres. Tomy Corp., Carson, Calif., 1976—; dir. Tomy Kogyo. Mem. Toy Mfrs. Am. (dir.), Am. Toy Inst. (trustee), Am. Mtmg. Assn., Los Angeles Area C. of C. Clubs: Rolling Hills Country (bd. dirs.), Japan (pres.), Mesa Verde Country. Home: 26742 Nokomis Rd Rancho Palos Verdes CA 90274 Office: 901 E 233d St Carson CA 90745

IKEDA, MOSS MARCUS MASANOBU, ednl. adminstr.; b. Los Angeles, Sept. 11, 1931; s. Masao Eugene and Masako (Yamashina) I.; B.E., U. Hawaii, 1960, M.Ed., 1962; postgrad. Stanford U., 1961-62; M.Mil. Art and Sci., U.S. Army Command and Gen. Staff Coll., 1975; grad. U.S. Army War Coll., 1976; m. Shirley Yaeko Okimoto; children—Cynthia Cecile Ikeda Tamashiro, Mark Eugene, Matthew Albert. Tchr., Farrington High Sch., Honolulu, 1962-64; vice-prin. Kailua Intermediate Sch. 1964-65; adminstrv. intern Central Intermediate Sch., Honolulu, 1965-66; vice-prin. Kaimuki High Sch., Honolulu, 1966-67; prin. Kawananakoa Intermediate Sch., Honolulu, 1967-68, Kailua High Sch., 1969-71, Kalaheo High Sch., Kailua, 1972-77; ednl. specialist Hawaii Dept. Edn., Honolulu, 1977-79; ednl. adminstr. Hawaii Dept. Edn., Honolulu, 1979—. Served with AUS, 1951-57, 68-69, col. Res. Decorated Army Commendation medal. Mem. Nat. Assn. Secondary Sch. Prins., Assn. U.S. Army, Res. Officers Assn., Hawaii Govt. Employees Assn., Phi Delta Kappa, Phi Kappa Phi. Home: 47-494 Apoalewa Pl Kaneohe HI 96744 Office: 3430 Leahi Ave Honolulu HI 96815

ILANIT, TAMAR, psychologist; b. Tel Aviv, Israel, May 5, 1929; s. Aharon and Ada (Berman) Pougatch; came to U.S., 1950, naturalized, 1970; grad. Levinski Tchr. Sem., 1949; Ph.D., U. So. Calif., 1959; m. Apr. 15, 1948; children—Rona, Gill. Research dir. United Cerebral Palsy Assn., Los Angeles, 1959-61; instr. Pepperdine U., Los Angeles, 1962-64; spl. cons. White Meml. Med. Center, Los Angeles; pvt. practice clin. psychology, Los Angeles, 1963—; mem. disability evaluation panel Social Security Adminstrn., 1961—. Mem. Am. Psychol. Assn., Los Angeles County Psychol. Assn., Sigma Xi, Phi Beta Kappa, Phi Kappa Phi. Jewish. Contbr. articles to profl. jours. Office: W Olympic Blvd Los Angeles CA 11665

ILETT, FRANK, JR., trucking co. exec.; b. Ontario, Oreg., June 21, 1940; s. Frank Kent and Lela Alice (Siver) I.; B.A., U. Wash., 1962; M.B.A., U. Chgo., 1969; m. Donna L. Andlovec, Apr. 3, 1971; children—James Frank, Jordan Lee. Accountant, Ernst & Ernst, Boise, Idaho, Cleve., Spokane, Wash., 1962-69, mgr., Boise, 1970-72, regional mgr., San Francisco, 1972-73; treas. Interstate Mack, Inc., Boise, 1973-81, pres., chief exec. officer, 1981-82; pres. Interstate NationaLease, Inc., Boise, 1975-81; pres. Contract Carriers, Inc., Boise, 1983—; adj. lectr. Boise State U., 1964-67; cons. Calif. Hosp. Commn., 1973, Idaho Hosp. Assn., 1974; chmn. Mack Truck Western Region Distbr. Council, 1979—; mem. nat. distbr. adv. com. Mack Trucks, Inc., 1980—; dir. standards enforcement Idaho State Bd. Accountancy, 1983—. C.P.A., Idaho, Ill., Wash. Mem. Am. Inst. C.P.A.'s, SAR. Episcopalian. Clubs: Hillcrest Country (Boise), Masons, Shriners. Contbr. articles in field to profl. jours. Home: 1701 Harrison Blvd Boise ID 83702 Office: 4450 Enterprise St Boise ID 83705

ILFELD, FREDERIC WILLIAM, JR., psychiatrist; b. Los Angeles, Dec. 19, 1940; s. Frederic and Jane Agnes (Mandelbaum) I.; B.A., Yale U., 1962; M.D., Harvard U., 1966; M.A., Stanford U., 1969; m. Holly Cohan, May 6, 1979; children—Brian, Jeffrey, Benjamin. Research assoc. Intramural Research div. NIMH, 1970-72; chief Crisis Clinic, U. Calif.-Davis Sch. Medicine, 1972-74; pvt. practice psychiatry, Sacramento, 1974—; assoc. clin. prof. U. Calif.-Davis Sch. Medicine, 1978—. Served with USPHS, 1967-72. Recipient Pawlowski Peace Prize, 1974. Mem. Calif. Psychiat. Assn., Calif. Med. Assn. Democrat. Jewish. Office: 718 Alhambra Blvd Sacramento CA 95816

ILIFF, WARREN JOLIDON, zoo administrator; b. Madison, Wis., Nov. 5, 1936; s. Warren Jolidon and Wilma Marie (Lowenstein) I.; A.B., Harvard U., 1958; m. Ghislaine DeBergeyck, Feb. 13, 1970. Agrl. spray pilot Allied Helicopters, Honduras and Guatemala, 1962-67; dir. airport facilities Air Transport Assn., Washington, 1967-68; spl. asst. Nat. Zoo, Washington, 1967-71, asst. dir., 1973-76; exec. dir. Friends of Nat. Zoo, 1971-73; dir. Washington Park Zoo, Portland, Oreg., 1976—. Trustee Catlin Gable Sch., Columbia River council Girl Scouts U.S. Served with USMC, 1958-62. Mem. Am. Assn. Zool. Parks and Aquariums (chmn. ethics com. 1979-81, dir. 1982—), Greater Portland Conv. and Visitors Assn. (treas.), Willamette Valley Devel. Officers (pres.), Internat. Union Dirs. Zool. Gardens. Club: Rotary. Contbr. articles in field to profl. jours. Home: 01865 SW Palatine Hill Rd Portland OR 97219 Office: 4001 SW Canyon Rd Portland OR 97221

ILLANGASEKARE, TISSA HARISCHANDRA, hydrologist; b. Sri Lanka, Feb. 19, 1949; came to U.S., 1974; s. James and Anula (Jayasingha) I.; B.S. with honors, U. Ceylon, 1971; M.Engring., Asian Inst. Tech., 1974; Ph.D., Colo. State U., 1978; m. D.V.N.M. Paulis, Aug. 29, 1977; 1 dau., Samantha Lakmali. Mem. faculty U. Ceylon, 1971-72; research faculty Asian Inst. Tech., 1973-74; asst. prof. civil engring. Colo. State U., Ft. Collins, 1978—. Gen. sec. Student Union, Asian Inst. Tech., 1972. Recipient president's honor award Asian Inst. Tech., 1974; named outstanding research faculty mem. dept. civil engring. Colo. State U., 1981-82; various research grants state and fed. agys.; registered profl. engr., Colo. Mem. Nat. Soc. Profl. Engrs., Profl. Engrs. Colo., Am. Geophys. Union, ASCE, Sigma Xi. Condr. research on surface and ground water mgmt.; contbr. writings to research publs. Home: 2201 Suffolk St Fort Collins CO 80526 Office: Colorado State Univ Foothills Campus Fort Collins CO 80523

ILLING, HANS ALFONS, sociologist; b. Berlin, Germany, Aug. 15, 1913; s. Leopold and Alice G. (Beermann) I.; Ph.D., Friedrich Wilhelm U., 1936; B.A., U. Utah, 1944; M.S.W., Tulane U., 1948; m. Lillian E. Ulrich, Apr. 19, 1962; 1 stepson, Theodore Lloyd Baker; came to U.S., 1939, naturalized, 1944. Clin. social worker VA Outpatient Clinic, Los Angeles, 1959-60; adminstrv. asst. Calif. Home for the Aged, Reseda, 1960-62; sr. psychiat. social worker Parole Outpatient Clinic, State of Calif., Los Angeles, 1960—; staff mem. The Hacker-Clinic, Beverly Hills and Lynwood, Calif., 1962-70; charter mem. Social Work Treatment Service, 1963—, Westchester Mental Health Clinic, 1962—; pvt. practice, 1970—; mem. faculty Los Angeles Inst. for Psychoanalytic Studies, 1970—; lectr. in field; cons. M.C. Air Force workshop, 1956; speaker Nat. Conf. Social Work, 1957, Am. Psychiat. Assn., 1964; cons. Airport Marina Counseling Service, Los Angeles, 1962-75. Mem. UCLA Art Council, Goethe House, N.Y.; pres. Westport Heights Democratic Club, 1964-70. Diplomate Conf. Advancement of Pvt. Practice in Social Work. Fellow Am. Group Psychotherapy Assn., (speaker nat. conv. 1956, 58, 67, 68, 79), Am. Orthopsychiat. Assn. (life; speaker nat. conv. 1970, 78), Am. Assn. Suicidology, Soc. Clin. Social Work; mem. Nat. Assn. Social Workers (Gold Card mem.), So. Calif. Psychotherapy Assn., Internat. Soc. Study Prenatal Psychology, Assn. Rec. Sound Collections, Berlin Mus., Salzburg Mozarteum; mem. Group Psychotherapy Assn. So. Calif. (co-founder, charter mem.), Los Angeles Group Psychotherapy Soc., Los Angeles County Mus. Art, Music Library Assn., Beethoven Haus (Bonn), Mendelssohn Gesellschaft, Heinrich von Kleist Gesellschaft, Met. Opera Guild, Chamber Symphony Soc. Calif., Wilhelm Furtwängler Soc. (founder, pres.), Goethe Gesellschaft, Hugo von Hofmannsthal Gesselschaft. Contbr. numerous articles to profl. jours. and books. Cons. editor: Internat. Jour. Psychiatry, 1965—; book rev. editor: Modern Austrian Literature; contbg. editor Dynamische Psychiatrie, Berlin, Germany. Home: 6112 W 77th St Los Angeles CA 90045 Office: 656 Aerick St Inglewood CA 90301

IMAD, AZMI PHILIP, environ. health and safety specialist; b. Shweir, Lebanon, Nov. 12, 1942; came to U.S., 1976; s. Philip Khattar and Zakieh Philip (Hanna Besharah) Emad; B.S., Am. U. Beirut (Lebanon), 1963; M.Sc., U. London, 1966. Chmn., project officer environ. health and hazards program Am. U. Beirut, 1969-72, dir. safety center, univ. health physicist, safety officer, 1972-76; environ. protection specialist U. Md., College Park, 1976-79; dir. environ. health and safety dept., radiation safety officer U. Colo., Boulder, 1979—; safety cons. NIH, Bethesda, Md., 1976-77. IAEA fellow, 1964-66; cert. safety profl.; registered profl. safety engr., Calif. Mem. Am. Soc. Safety Engrs., Health Physics Soc., Campus Safety Assn. Office: Univ Colo Campus Box 375 Boulder CO 80309

IMAMURA, ELAINE JOY, counselor; b. Denver, Dec. 27, 1954; d. Roy S. and Priscilla Miyuki (Hamada) Hiratsuka. B.A. in Psychology, Adams State Coll., 1976, M.A. in Guidance and Counseling, 1978. Counselor, cottage parent Colo. Boys Ranch, LaJunta, 1978-79; program mgr., counselor Billings Childrens' Receiving Home, 1979-80; counselor Advance By Choice, Mont. State U., Bozeman, 1980—. Mem. Am. Personnel and Guidance Assn., Mont. Personnel and Guidance Assn., Wheelchairs, Crutches and People Club. Office: Advance By Choice Mont State U Bozeman MT 59717

IMAN, RONALD L., statistician; b. Phillipsburg, Kans., Oct. 1, 1940; s. I.J. and E. Lucille (Pool) I.; m. V. Rae Forssberg, Apr. 10, 1960; children—Deborah Sue, Susan Rae. B.S., Kans. State U., 1962, M.S., 1970, Ph.D., 1973; M.A., Kans. State Tchrs. Coll., 1965. High sch. tchr. math., Derby and Norton, Kans., 1962-67; grad. teaching asst. Kans. State U., Manhattan, 1967-68, instr., 1970-73; math. statistician White Sands Missile Range (N.Mex.), 1968-70; asst. prof. Western Mich. U., Kalamazoo, 1973-75; biostatistician Upjohn Co., Kalamazoo, 1974-75; statis. cons. Sandia Nat. Lab., Albuquerque, 1975—. Fellow Am. Statis. Assn.; mem. Biometric Soc. Republican. Lutheran. Author: (with W.J. Conover) A Modern Approach to Statistics, 1983, an Introduction to Modern Business Statistics, 1983, Modern Business Statistics, 1983; contbr. articles to profl. jours. Office: Sandia Nat Lab Div 7223 Albuquerque NM 87185

IMAN, STEPHEN CHARLES, aircraft company executive; b. Seattle, Oct. 14, 1940; s. Raymond Stephen and Carla Ester (Cook) I.; m. Sally Ann Baker, June 1, 1967 (div.). B.S., Yale U., 1962; M.S., U. Mich., 1967, Ph.D. in Organizational Psychology, 1972. Asst. prof., chmn. dept. psychology Claremont (Calif.) Men's Coll., 1972-76; from prof. assoc. to prof. mgmt. Sch. Bus., Calif. State Poly. U., Pomona, 1976-82; mem. faculty Claremont Grad. Sch. Exec. Mgmt. Program, 1966-82; mgr. mfg. tng. and devel. Hughes Aircraft, Fullerton, Calif., 1982—; pres. Mgmt. Resource Assocs.; pres. Hillhomes of San Antonio Heights; cons. WHO; mem. faculty regional schs. Credit Union Nat. Assn. Mem. Am. Psychol. Assn., Organizational Devel. Network, Am. Mgmt. Assn., Yale Alumni Assn. Contbr. articles to profl. jours. Office: 617-PP212 Hughes Aircraft Ground Systems Fullerton CA 92633

IMANA, JORGE GARRON, artist; b. Sucre, Bolivia, Sept. 20, 1930; s. Juan S. and Lola (Garron) I.; grad. Fine Arts Acad., U. San Francisco Xavier, 1950; cert. Nat. Sch. for Tchrs., Bolivia, 1952; came to U.S., 1964, naturalized, 1974; m. Cristina Imana; children—George, Ivan. Prof. art Nat. Sch. Tchrs., Sucre, 1954-56; prof. biology Padilla Coll., Sucre, 1956-60; head dept. art Inst. Normal Simon Bolivar, La Paz, Bolivia, 1961-62; propr., mgr. The Artists Showroom, San Diego, 1973—. Numerous one-man shows of paintings in U.S., S. Am. and Europe, 1952—, latest being: Gallery Banet, La Paz, 1965, Artists Showroom, San Diego, 1964, 66, 68, 74, 76, 77, San Diego Art Inst., 1966, 68, 72, 73, Contrast Gallery, Chula Vista, Calif., 1966, Central Public Library, San Diego, 1969, Universidad de Zulia, Maracaibo, Venezuela, 1969, Spanish Village Art Center, San Diego, 1974, 75, 76, La Jolla Art Assn. Gallery, 1969, 72, 73, 74, 75, 78, Internat. Gallery, Washington, 1976, Galeria de Arte L'Atelier, La Paz, 1977; numerous group shows including: Fine Arts Gallery, San Diego, 1964, Mus. of Modern Art, Paris, 1973, exhibits in galleries of Budapest (Hungary), 1973, Moscow (USSR), 1973, Warsaw (Poland), 1976, represented in permanent collections: Museo Nacional, La Paz, Bolivia, Museo de la Universidad de Potosi, Bolivia, Muse Nacional de Bogota, Colombia, S. Am., Ministerio de Edn., Managua, Nicaragua, Bolivian embassy, Moscow, also pvt. collections in U.S., Europe and Latin Am.; executed many murals including: Colegio Padilla, Sucre, Bolivia, 1958, Colegio Junin, Sucre, Bolivia, 1959, Sindicato de Construccion Civil, Lima, Peru, 1960. Hon. consul of Bolivia, So. Calif., 1969-73. Served to lt. Bolivian Army, 1953. Recipient Mcpl. award Sucre, Bolivia, 1958. Mem. San Diego Art Inst., San Diego Watercolor Soc., Internat. Fine Arts Guild, La Jolla Art Assn. Home: 3357 Caminito Gandara La Jolla CA 92037 Office: 2168 Chatsworth Blvd San Diego CA 92107

IMHOFF, CAROL ANN, nursing administrator; b. Los Angeles, June 15, 1934; d. Neal and Frances M. (Roberts) Vogelsang; m. James C. Imhoff, Aug. 10, 1957; children—Jean, Robert, Christopher, Mary Angela. B.S.N., U. Utah, 1973; diploma Holy Cross Hosp. Sch. Nursing, 1955. Staff nurse Holy Cross Hosp., UCLA Med. Ctr., 1955-58, staff nurse, part time supr., 1960-66, unit supr. rehab., 1977-82, rehab. clinician, 1982-83; dir. nursing Bountiful Care Convalescent Ctr., 1983—; vis. staff nurse Community Nursing Service, Salt Lake City, 1966-69; head nurse med. supportive care rehab. McKan Dee Hosp., Ogden, Utah, 1969-77. Mem. edn. com. Am. Heart Assn., 1969-81, chmn., 1972-73; bd. dirs. Utah Heart Assn., 1976—; sec. Home Sch. Assn. Mem. Am. Nurses Assn., Assn. Rehab. Nurses (certs. for service, nat. pres. 1982-83), Rehab. Services Adv. Council, Utah Nurses Assn. (past dist. treas., bd. dirs., 2d place Nurse of Yr.), Beta Sigma Phi, Sigma Theta Tau. Roman Catholic. Club: Does. Home: 4581 Taylor S Ogden UT 84403 Office: 350 S 400 E Bountiful UT 84010

IMMASCHE, SONIA MARGOLIN, university administrator; b. Omaha, Aug. 3, 1946; d. Morton Leonard and Bonnie (Seldin) Margolin; m. Michael Lyle ImMasche, Aug. 11, 1974; 1 son, Elias Kyle. B.A., Colo. Coll., 1968; M.A. with highest honors, U. Denver, 1970; postgrad. Hebrew Union Coll. Bibl. and Archeol. Sch., Jerusalem, summers 1968-71, Western Ill. U., Colo. State U. Cert secondary tchr. history, Colo. Hall dir. U. Denver, 1969-70; head resident advisor Western Ill. U., 1970-74; asst. dir. women's programs Colo. State U., 1974-75, asst. dir. student relations and fraternal programs coordinator, 1975-79, Greek advisor, asst. coordinator Student Orgns. Resource Ctr., 1979—, faculty affiliate dept. history, 1977—; mem. resource faculty Mid Am. Panhellenic/Interfraternity Council Assns. Mem. Ft. Collins Jewish Community; community coordinator United Way for student affairs div. Colo. State U.; mem. Ft. Collins Alumnae Panhellenic. Denver Classroom Tchrs. scholar, 1964; Mem. Assn. Fraternity Advisors (sec.-treas.), Nat. Assn. Women Deans, Adminstrs. and Counselors, Am. Personnel and Guidance Assn., Assn. Coll. Personnel Adminstrs., Alpha Lambda Delta (nat. council), Alpha Phi, Kappa Delta Pi. Democrat. Jewish. Club: Longs Peak Alumnae of Alpha Phi. Home: 730 Cottonwood Dr Fort Collins CO 80524 Office: Student Orgns Resource Ctr 200 A Lory Student Center Colo State U Fort Collins CO 80523

IMMENSCHUH, WILLIAM TABER, aeronautical engineer; b. Monte Vista, Colo., June 12, 1917; s. Aldie Philip and Helen Francis (Taber) I.; Tech. Cert., Ryan Aero. Sch. Aeronautics and Engring., 1940; m. Joan Palmer, Dec. 31, 1969; children—Cheryl McCurdy, William P., Edwin; stepchildren—Pamela Massey, Janet Martin. Designer, Teledyne Ryan Aero. Co., San Diego, 1940-44, project engr., 1944-56, chief test ops., 1956-61, chief engr., 1961-65, dir. aircraft programs, 1965-69, asst. to pres., 1965-69, mgr. systems engring., 1969-72, mgr. test ops., 1972-82; pres., chief exec. officer San Diego Aerospace Mus., Balboa Park, 1980—. Pres., Internat. Aerospace Hall of Fame, San Diego, 1967-69; bd. dirs. San Diego Aerospace Mus., 1968—. Recipient Silver Knight award Am. Mgmt. Assn., 1981. Registered profl. engr., Calif. Asso. fellow AIAA (pub. service award San Diego sect. 1981); mem. Soc. Automotive Engrs. Republican. Club: Teledyne Ryam Mgmt. Home: 4621 Euclid Ave San Diego CA 92115 Office: 2001 Pan Am Plaza Balboa Park San Diego CA 92101

INADOMI, ROBERT JOHN, supermarket co. exec.; b. Los Angeles; s. Yosh and Ruth K. Inadomi; B.S., U. Calif., Berkeley, 1969; S.M., Sloan Sch. Mgmt., M.I.T., 1971; 1 dau., Mary Catherine. Asst. to gen. mgr. Boise Cascade Corp., Honolulu, 1971-74; exec. v.p., gen. mgr. Jonsons Markets, Inc., Los Angeles, 1974—, also dir.; data processing cons. City of Somerville (Mass.), Pacific Telephone Co. Mem. Am. Mgmt. Assn., Calif. Grocers Assn., Food Mktg. Inst., Beta Gamma Sigma. Clubs: M.I.T. of So. Calif., Toastmasters (pres. 1974). Office: 3425 Whittier Blvd Los Angels CA 90023

INBODEN, FREDERICK VINTON, aerospace medical technician; b. Lancaster, Ohio, Nov. 10, 1951; s. Harles Vinton and Phyllis Ann (Abram) I. Student Foothill Coll., 1978, U. Ariz., 1982; West Hills Coll., 1983—. Enlisted U.S. Navy, 1970; technician coronary care unit Portsmouth Naval Hosp., 1972-73; ICU technician emergency rm. Boone Clinic Naval Dispensary, 1973-74; respiratory therapist Portsmouth Naval Hosp., 1974, Oakland Naval Hosp., 1974-75; biomed. technician human test subject Naval Med. Research Inst., 1975-77; med. dept. rep. Patrol Squadron 40, 1977-81, aerospace med. technician, med. dept. rep., 1979-81; leading chief petty officer of aviation medicine Lemoore (Calif.) NAS, 1981—. Mem. Aviation Space and Tech. Assn. Methodist. Clubs: DeMolay, Masons. Home: 265 E Hanford-Armona Rd Apt 8 Lemoore CA 93245 Office: Naval Hosp Annex NAS Lemoore CA 93245

INGALL, BEVERLY HELLER, botanist; b. N.Y.C., Jan. 30, 1926; d. Morris and Rose (Hollander) Heller; B.A., Bklyn. Coll., 1947; M.S., U. So. Calif., 1949; postgrad. Calif State U.-Long Beach, 1951-52; m. William Elfric Ingall, Jan. 18, 1951 (dec.); children—Oliver Elfric, Glynnis Beth Ingall Katz, Alan Eliot, Ellery Duke. Instr., Bklyn. Coll., 1949; research technician Mistaire Lab., Millburn, N.J., 1949-51; tchr. Westridge Sch., Pasadena, Calif., 1978-79; research asst. Guayule research project Los Angeles Arboretum, 1979-82; scientist Phytogen Inc., 1982—. Mem. Guayule Rubber Soc., AAAS, Am. Inst. Biol. Scis., N.Y. Acad. Sci., Sigma Xi. Office: Phytogen Inc 101 Waverly Dr Pasadena CA 91105

INGALLS, HENRY A., accountant; b. Albuquerque, July 8, 1946; s. Henry A. and Lucile I.; m. Donna L. Korbitz, June 5, 1969; children—Matt, Jay. B.B.A., U. N.Mex., 1969. C.P.A., N.Mex. Ptnr. Peat, Marwick, Mitchell & Co., Albuquerque, 1969—. Chmn.-elect. Better Bus. Bur. N.Mex. Mem. Am. Inst. C.P.A.s, N.Mex. Soc. C.P.A.s, C. of C., Sigma Chi. Clubs: Tanoan Country, Albuquerque Petroleum, Elks, Angel Fire Country. Home: 3912 General Bradley St NE Albuquerque NM 87111 Office: 20 First Plaza Suite 500 Albuquerque NM 87102

INGEBRITSON, JACK GORDON, real estate developer, financier; b. Berwyn, Ill., Mar. 22, 1946; s. Gordon L. and Hazel J. (Ulberg) I. B.S. in Bus. Adminstrn., Northwestern U., 1968, postgrad., 1969; postgrad. Ariz. State U., 1971. Mem. advt. dept. Chgo. Tribune, 1970; pres. Wellington Investment & Devel. Co., Inc., Phoenix, 1971-73, Ingebritson Investment Co., Inc., Phoenix, 1973—; gen. partner J.I. Assocs., Ltd., La Espanada, Ltd.; partner Residential Mktg. Systems, Crystal Technologies Ltd.; pres. Stonewood Devel. Corp., Benison Constrn. Co., Inc., Nicholas Gordon Ltd., Mistwood Devel. Co., Inc.; dir. Spear S Land & Cattle Co., Inc.; cons. maj. corps. 1st v.p. Royale Gardens II, 1977—; adv. panel Fiesta Bowl, 1970. Recipient award for Spengler Manor Complex, 1975; lic. real estate broker, Ariz. Mem. Solar Energy Inst., Urban Land Inst., Nat. Assn. Real Estate Bds., Ariz. Assn. Realtors, Nat. Inst. Real Estate Brokers, Home Builders Assn. of Central Ariz., Sales and Mktg. Council, Phoenix C. of C., Scottsdale C. of C., Friends of Channel 8, Phi Delta Theta. Republican. Lutheran. Clubs: Jockey, Metro Athletic. Adv. panel Housing Mag., 1980-81. Home: 1905 E Medlock St Phoenix AZ 85016 Office: Suite 103 5301 N 7th St Phoenix AZ 85014

INGELS, HAROLD CLAYTON, video engineer; b. Annapolis, Md., Sept. 18, 1941; s. Albert Clayton and Elizabeth Francis (Philbrick) I.; m. Clairette Eveline Ingels, Jan. 28, 1967; children—Michelle, David. A.A., San Diego City Coll., 1962; student San Diego State Coll., 1962-63. With various radio stas., San Diego, 1960-65; sr. video engr. NBC Inc., Burbank, Calif., 1965—. Chmn. emergency communications Crescenta Radio Club, 1980-83. Served with U.S. Army, 1962-64. Recipient Emmy award for electronic camera work, 1982. Mem. Nat. Acad. TV Arts and Scis., Nat. Assn. Broadcast Employees and Technicians. (treas. 1977, regional v.p. 1983). Office: NBC Inc 3000 W Alameda Ave Burbank CA 91523

INGELS, MARTY, theatrical agent, TV and motion picture production company executive; b. Bklyn., Mar. 9, 1936; s. Jacob and Minnie (Crown) Ingerman; m. Jean Maire Frassinelli, Aug. 3, 1960 (div. 1969); m. 2d, Shirley Jones. Student Erasmus High Sch., 1951-53, Forest Hills High Sch., 1953-55. Star Dickens and Fenster series ABC-TV, 1964; co-star Pruitts of Southampton, 1968-69; films include Armored Command, 1962, Horizontal Lieutenant, 1965, Busy Body, 1967, Ladies Man, 1966, If It's Tuesday This Must Be Belgium, 1970, Wild and Wonderful, 1965, Guide for a Married Man, 1968; numerous TV appearances; founder Ingels, Inc., 1975—; formed Stoneypoint Prodns., 1981. Active various charity drives. Office: 7560 Hollywood Blvd Hollywood CA 90046

INGERMAN, MICHAEL LEIGH, hospital consultant; b. N.Y.C., Nov. 30, 1937; s. Charles Stryker and Ernestine (Leigh) I.; B.S., George Washington U., 1963; m. Marie Ann Cosner, Apr. 19, 1962; children—Shawn Marie, Jenifer Lyn. Health planner, Marin County, Calif., 1969-70, 70-72; regional cons. Bay Area Comprehensive Health Council, San Francisco, 1972-73; hosp. cons. Booz, Allen & Hamilton, San Francisco, 1974; health planning coordinator Peralta Hosp., Oakland, Calif., 1975-76; pres. Ingerman & Assocs., Inc., hosp. cons., Nicasio, Calif., 1976—; instr. Golden Gate U., 1981—. Asst. chief Nicasio Vol. Fire Dept., 1976—; dep. coroner Marin County, 1980-83; nat. bd. dirs. Am. Friends Service Com., 1980-81; bd. dirs. Hospice of Marin, 1983—. Mem. Marin County Civil Grand Jury, 1977-78; mem. Nicasio Design Rev. Com., 1979-83; mem. fin. com. John Woolman Sch., 1980—; bd. dirs. Hospice of Marin. Mem. Am. Hosp. Assn., Calif. Hosp. Assn., Western Hosp. Assn. Home: 2101 Nicasio Valley Rd Nicasio CA 94946

INGERSOLL, BRUCE KEMPTON, mechanical contractor; b. Miles City, Mont., May 21, 1927; s. Lynn and Bernice (Kempton) I.; married; children—Bruce Kempton, Bernice, Robert, David, Glenn, Tony, Dion, Sevila. Various positions in oil, steel, constrn. industries, 1946-70, owner, operator Ingersoll Heating and Sheet Metal, Anchorage, 1970—; lectr. on energy mgmt. Served with U.S. Army, 1945. Mem. ASHRAE. Mem. Metaphysical Ch. Home: PO Box 4-2189 Anchorage AK 99509 Office: 6723 Arctic Spur Rd Anchorage AK 99509

INGERSOLL, TED MERIAM, marketing executive; b. Cleve., Oct. 3, 1939; s. Edmund Meriam and Helen Winifred (Stephan) I.; m. Jean Carol McCutcheon, June 30, 1962; children—Karen, Kris, Kimberley. Student St. Lawrence U., 1957-61; B.F.A. in Speech, Kent State U., 1962. Pub. relations account exec. The Jayme Orgn., Cleve., 1968-69; v.p. account supr. The Marschalk Co., Cleve., 1969-73; v.p. mgmt. supr. Tracy-Locke Advt., Denver, Dallas, 1973-81; exec. v.p. mktg. and corp. relations 1st Columbia Fin. Corp., Denver, 1981—. Served with USAF, 1962-68. Mem. Denver Advt. Fedn., Soc. Mktg. Execs. Republican. Presbyterian. Club: Hiwan Golf (Evergreen, Colo.). Home: 32329 Inverness Dr Evergreen CO 80439 Office: PO Box 17127 Denver CO 80217

INGHAM, LYNN MARIE, advertising/circulation director; b. Butte, Mont., Sept. 17, 1952; d. Michael Edwin Hollenbeck and June Marie White; m. John Timothy Ingham, June 17, 1972 (div.). B.A. cum laude in Journalism/English, U. Mont., 1976. English and journalism tchr. C.M. Russell High Sch., Great Falls, Mont., 1977-79; staff writer San Francisco mag., 1979-80, advt. sales coordinator, 1979-80, advt. salesperson, 1980-81, dir. advt., 1981-82; advt./circulation dir. Resort Mgmt. mag., San Diego, 1982—. Mem. Writers Workshop, Alpha Phi. Home: 365 Bon Air #11 La Jolla CA 92037 Office: Resort Management Mag 4501 Mission Bay Dr San Diego CA 92109

INGHAM, ROBERT EDWIN, cardiologist; b. Berkeley, Calif., Dec. 30, 1944; s. Theodore Alton and Mary Lou (Bailey) I.; B.A., U. Calif.-Berkeley, 1966; M.D., Cornell U., 1970; m. Linda Bridges, Aug. 17, 1968; children—William Robert, Douglas James. Intern, Cornell-N.Y. Hosp., N.Y.C., 1970-71, resident internal medicine, 1971-72; fellow in cardiology Stanford (Calif.) U., 1973-74; practice medicine specializing in cardiology Naval Regional Med. Center, Oakland, Calif., 1974-76; mem. staff John Muir Meml. Hosp., Walnut Creek, Calif., 1976—, sec.-treas. staff, 1981, vice-chief of staff, 1982-83, chief of staff, 1983, dir. non-invasive cardiology lab., 1979-81, dir. cardiac exercise program, 1978—, also bd. dirs. hosp.; assoc. clin. prof. medicine U. Calif.-Davis, 1976—. Former bd. dirs. Danville (Calif.) Fire Protection Dist.; bd. dirs., past pres. Contra Costa County chpt. Am. Heart Assn. Served with M.C., USNR, 1974-76. Diplomate Am. Bd. Internal Medicine; Leopold Schepp Found. scholar, 1968-69. Fellow Am. Coll. Cardiology, ACP; mem. Am. Heart Assn., Soc. Med. Friends of Wine. Contbr. articles to profl. jours. Office: 1515 Ygnacio Valley Rd Walnut Creek CA 94598

INGLESBY, THOMAS PAUL, editor, writer, media producer; b. Chgo. Apr. 7, 1940; s. Thomas Robert and Grace Florance (Bochenek) I.; m. Karen Harris, Jan. 15, 1958 (dec.); m. Janet Kay Libit, Dec. 31, 1966 (div.); m. Patricia Shallcross, Oct. 31, 1979 (div.). B.S. in Sociology, Ariz. State Coll., 1962; M.S. in Pub. Adminstrn., U. Ariz., 1964; postgrad. U. Ill., 1965-66. News dir. Sta. KEOS, Flagstaff, Ariz., 1959-62, Sta. KHOS, Tucson, 1962-64; instr. English U. Ill.-Chgo., 1965-67; sr. audio producer Ency. Brit. Edn. Corp., Chgo., 1968-74; ind. audio-visual producer Birdhouse Prodns., Downers Grove, Ill., 1971-78; editor PSQ mag. Pratt & Whitney Aircraft Co., 1978-80; assoc. editor Assembly Engring. mag. Hitchcock Pub. Co., 1980-82, sr. editor Infosystems mag. ABC Publs. Group, 1982-83; free-lance writer/editor Photo Media!, Sunnyvale, Calif., 1983—; tchr. audio prodn. Coll. of DuPage, Glen Ellyn, Ill., 1974-76. Founding mem. Johnson for Pres. Com. of Ariz., 1964. Served to lt. Spl. Forces Intelligence, U.S. Army, 1964-65. Decorated Purple Heart, Bronze Star. Recipient numerous film festival awards for best ednl. films, 1969-74. Mem. Am. Soc. Bus. Press Editors, Aviation-Space Writers Assn., AIAA, Soc. Mfg. Engrs., IEEE, Audio Engring. Soc., AFTRA. Pub. numerous films, filmstrips, recs., booklets, 1967-83; author: Diary of a Pitch, 1978; They Call the Wind David, 1980.

INGLISH, SUMTER RUSSELL, III, hosp. exec.; b. St. Louis, July 20, 1950; s. Russell II and Rebecca Frances (Duley) I.; B.A., Westminster Coll., 1969-73; M.H.S.A., Ariz. State U., 1974-76; m. Diane Adler, Sept. 4, 1976. Service coordinator St. Luke's Hosp. and Med. Center, Phoenix, 1973-76; asst. v.p. Phoenix Bapt. Hosp. and Med. Center, 1976-79; asst. adminstr. Placentia-Linda Community Hosp., Placentia, Calif., 1979—, also v.p., dir. Sumter R. Inglish Assocs., Inc., Sun City, Ariz., 1978—; preceptor adminstrv. residency Loma Linda U. Sch. Public Health; mem. Orange County Health Systems Agy.; mem. health adv. council Orange County Health Planning Council; mem. Orange County exec. and planning com., chmn. emergency Services com. Hosp. Council So. Calif. Mem. Am. Hosp. Assn., Am. Coll. Hosp. Adminstrs., Am. Acad. Med. Adminstrs., Placentia C. of C. (dir., v.p., chmn. comml. and indsl. com.). Office: 1301 Rose Dr Placentia CA 92670

INGRAM, ALVIN DEAN, JR., distributive education educator; b. Iowa City, Iowa, Nov. 15, 1948; s. Alvin Dean and Carolyn Ruth (Cox) I.; m. Connie Marie Hersh, Apr. 16, 1970; 1 son, Shawn Dean; m. 2d Rhonda Leigh Cozad, Nov. 21, 1980. A.A.S. in Mgmt., Aims Community Coll., 1982; student U. No. Colo., 1982—. Quality control supr. Monfort Packing Co., Greeley, Colo., 1970-77; bull rider, bareback rider Profl. Rodeo Circuit Am., Denver, 1977-79; instr. distributive edn. Aims Coll., Greeley, Colo. 1983—; advisor bus. profl. tutoring service. Vol. probation counselor, 1976; block capt. Neighborhood Crime Prevention, 1982-83. Served with U.S. Army, 1967-69. Recipient Achievement award in mgmt. decision making State of Colo., 1982; Outstanding Student award Nat. Register Mag. for Jr. Colls., 1982. Mem. Am. Vocat. Assn., Colo. Vocat. Assn., Colo. Assn. Distributive Edn. Tchrs., Delta Epsilon Chi (presdl. honor list 1981, 82, Merchandising award 1983, pub. relations dir. 1983). Republican. Mem. Pentecostal Ch. Office: Bus Div Aims Community Coll PO Box 69 20th St Greeley CO 80632

INGRAM, HELEN MOYER, political science educator; b. Denver, July 12, 1937; d. Oliver Weldon and Hazel Margaret (Wickard) Hill; children—Mrill, Maia, Seth. B.A., Oberlin (Ohio) Coll., 1959; Ph.D., Columbia U., N.Y.C., 1967. Lectr., asst. prof. polit. sci. U. N. Mex., 1962-69; cons. Nat. Water Commn., Washington, 1969-72; assoc. prof. polit. sci. U. Ariz., Tucson, 1972-77, prof. polit. sci., 1979—; sr. fellow Resources for the Future, Washington, 1977-79, cons., 1979—; mem. agr. and renewable resources bd. Nat. acad. Scis., 1977-80. Mem. Ariz. Council on Humanities; mem. council, exec. com. Policy Studies Orgn., 1978—. Mem. Am. Polit. Sci. Assn., Western Polit. Sci. Assn. (past pres., v.p.). Author: (with Dean Mann) Why Policies Succeed or Fail, 1980; (with Nancy Laney and John McCain) A Policy Approach to Representation: Lessons from the Four Corners States, 1980. Home: 3244 E Waverly Tucson AZ 85716 Office: Dept Polit Sci U Ariz Tucson AZ 85721

INGRAM, KEITH TALBERT, agronomist; b. Corona, Calif., Aug. 18, 1953; s. Billy Gean and Suzanne Lois (Giese) I.; A.B., U. Calif.-Riverside, 1974, M.S., 1976; Ph.D., U. Fla., 1980; m. Christine Marie Roser, Nov. 22, 1980. Teaching asst. plant sci. dept. U. Calif.-Riverside, 1975-76; research asst. dept. agronomy U. Fla., Gainesville, 1976-80, vis. asst. research scientist agrl. engring. dept., 1980-81; assoc. agronomist Hawaiian Sugar Planters Assn., Aiea, 1981—. Mem. Am. Soc. Agronomy, Soil and Crop Sci. Soc. Fla., Crop Sci. Soc. Am., AAAS, Hawaiian Sugar Technologists, Phi Beta Kappa, Gamma Sigma Delta, Phi Kappa Phi. Club: Toastmasters Internat. Office: PO Box 1057 Aiea HI 96701

INJERD, WILLIAM GEORGE, chemist; b. Tucson, Aug. 2, 1951; s. Howard Wesley and Dorothy Mae (Welty) I.; B.S., UCLA, 1973; m. Kathryn Diane Edleman, June 2, 1979; 1 dau., Diane Elizabeth. Research asso. Inst. Geophysics, UCLA, 1972-74; tchr. chemistry and physics Yucapia (Calif.) High Sch., 1975-77; mfg. research and devel. engr. Boeing Co., Everett, Wash., 1978—; owner Bi-Chem Supply, 1982—. Mem. Am. Chem. Soc., Nat. Assn. Corrosion Engrs. Mem. Ch. Assembly of God. Club: Sons of Norway. Patentee in countersink sealant nozzle. Home: Lake Stevens WA

INLOW, RUSH OSBORNE, chemist; b. Seattle, July 10, 1944; s. Edgar Burke and Marigale (Osborne) I.; B.S., U. Wash., 1966; Ph.D., Vanderbilt U., 1975; m. Gloria Elisa Duran, June 7, 1980. Chemist, sect. chief U.S. Dept. Energy, New Brunswick Lab., Argonne, Ill., 1975-78, chief nuclear safeguards br. Albuquerque ops., 1978—. Served with USN, 1966-71. Tenn. Eastman fellow, 1974-75. Mem. Am. Chem. Soc., Sigma Xi. Republican. Episcopalian. Contbr. articles to profl. jours. Home: 1900 Butterfly Maiden NE Albuquerque NM 87112

INMAN, STUART K., professional basketball team manager; m. Elinor; children—Nancy, Sandy, Janice, Carol, David. B.S., San Jose State U., 1950. Basketball coach San Jose State U., 1957-66; with Portland Trailblazers, Nat. Basketball Assn., 1970—, now gen. mgr. Office: Portland Trailblazers 700 NE Multnomah Lloyd Bldg Suite 950 Portland OR 97232*

INOUYE, DANIEL KEN, U.S. senator; b. Honolulu, Sept. 7, 1924; s. Hyotaro I. and Kame Imanaga; B.A., U. Hawaii, 1950; J.D., George Washington U., 1952; m. Margaret Shinobu Awamura, June 12, 1949; 1 son, Daniel Ken. Engaged as asst. pub. prosecutor Honolulu, 1953-54; practice law, Honolulu, 1954—; dir. Central Pacific Bank. Majority leader Territorial Ho. of Reps., 1954-58, Senate, 1958-59; mem. 86th-87th U.S. Congresses from Hawaii, mem. com. on agr.; U.S. Senator from Hawaii, 1963—, mem. Commerce com., Appropriations com., D.C. com., 1971-76, mem. Select Intelligence com., 1976—, chmn., 1976-78, mem. select com. on Indian Affairs, 1979—, asst. majority whip, 1965-76; vice chmn. Democratic senatorial campaign com., 1969-71; sec. Senate Dem. Conf., 1977—; mem. Senate Dem. Policy Commn. select com. on Presdl. campaign activities, 1973-74. Temp. chmn., keynoter Dem. Nat. Conv., 1968; chmn. rules com. Dem. Nat. Conv., 1980. Served from pvt. to capt. AUS, 1943-47. Decorated D.S.C., Purple Heart with cluster, Bronze Star medal; named 1 of 10 Outstanding Young Men, U.S. C. of C., 1960, 1 of 100 Most Important People in U.S., Life mag., 1962; recipient Alumnus of Year award George Washington U., 1961, Splendid Am. award from the Thomas A. Dooley Found., 1967, Distinguished Alumnus award George Washington Law Assn., 1973, Am. Legion Nat. Comdr.'s award, 1973. Mem. Am., Hawaii bar assns., John Howard Assn., Honolulu Council Chs., U. Hawaii Alumni Assn., D.A.V. (past comdr. Hawaii), Phi Delta Phi. Methodist. Lion. Author: Journey to Washington. Office: 105 Russell Senate Office Bldg Washington DC 20510

INTISO, FRANK JOSEPH, cable TV company executive, accountant; b. Los Angeles, Feb. 11, 1947; s. Joseph T. and Josephine (Raia) I.; m. Lee Allison Merritt, May 28, 1977. B.S. cum laude in Acctg., Calif. State U.-Northridge, 1969; M.B.A., UCLA, 1970. C.P.A., Calif. Mgr., dir. personnel Seidman & Seidman, C.P.A., Beverly Hills, Calif., 1971-79; exec. v.p. Falcon Communications, Los Angeles, 1979-82, chief operating officer Falcon Cable TV Co. No. Calif., Los Angeles, 1982—. Mem. Am. Mgmt. Assn., Calif. Soc. C.P.A.s, Am. Inst. C.P.A.s, Calif. Cable TV Assn., Nat. Cable TV Assn. Democrat. Roman Catholic. Club: So. Calif. Cable. Home: 22405 Dardenne St Woodland Hills CA 91364 Office: Falcon Cable TV 10889 Wilshire Blvd Suite 1260 Los Angeles CA 90024

INTRIERE, ANTHONY DONALD, physician; b. Greenwich, Conn., May 9, 1920; s. Rocco and Angelina (Belcastro) I.; M.D., U. Mich., 1944; m. Carol A. Yarmey, Aug. 1, 1945; children—Sherry Lynn, Michael, Nancy, Lisa. Intern, New Rochelle (N.Y.) Hosp., 1944-45; pvt. practice medicine, Greenwich, Conn., 1947-53, Olney, Ill., 1956-61, Granite City, Ill., 1961-74, San Diego, 1975—; fellow in internal medicine Cleve. Clinic, 1953-55; fellow in gastroenterology Lahey Clinic, Boston, 1955-56. Served from 1st lt. to capt. M.C., AUS, 1945-47. Fellow Am. Coll. Gastroenterology (asso.); mem. A.C.P. (asso.), Am. Soc. Internal Medicine. Home: 9981 Caminto Chirimolla San Diego CA 92131

IRELAND, JERRY MEADE, marketing director; b. Cody, Wyo., Oct. 19, 1944; s. Earl Strawn and Mary Mildred (Warren) I.; m. Corinda Miriam Barbour, Apr. 14, 1979; 1 son, Fraser Barbour. B.S. in Polit. Sci., Tufts U., 1966; M.B.A., Stanford U., 1971. Brand asst., sales trainee, asst. brand mgr. Clorox Co., Oakland, Calif., 1971-74; product mgr. Holubar Mountaineering Co., Boulder, Colo., 1975; ind. cons., Oakland, 1976; account exec., supr. Hoefer, Dieterich & Brown, San Francisco, 1977-79; advt. mgr. Levi Strauss & Co., San Francisco, 1979-82, dir. olympic projects, 1983—. Served to 1st lt. U.S. Army, 1966-69. Gen. Motors scholar, 1962-66. Home: 41 Robert Rd Orinda CA 94563 Office: Levi Strauss & Co 1155 Battery St San Francisco CA 94106

IRISH, GARY GENE, hosp. exec.; b. Lancaster, Wis., Sept. 17, 1951; s. Clyde Gene and Florence Adele (Haudenshield) I.; B.A., Andrews U., 1973; M.P.H., Loma Linda U., 1975; M.B.A., UCLA, 1980; m. Karen L. Seinhart, Aug. 18, 1974. Asst. health planner Inland Counties Comprehensive Health Planning Council, San Bernardino, Calif., 1975; adminstrv. resident Corona (Calif.) Community Hosp., 1976; health planner Inland Counties Health Systems Agy., Riverside, Calif., 1977-78; dir. resource mgmt. and planning Loma Linda U. Med. Ctr., 1978-82; exec. dir. Loma Linda Gyn-Ob Med. Group, 1982—. Mem. Am. Hosp. Assn., Hosp. Mgmt. Systems Soc., Hosp. Planning Soc., Med. Group Mgmt. Assn., Am. Pub. Health Assn. Home: 23020 Merle Ct Grand Terrace CA 92324 Office: Loma Linda Univ Med Ctr Loma Linda CA 92354

IRITANI, WILLY MASAO, educator; b. Denver, Apr. 28, 1923; s. Frank and Chitose Iritan; m. Eiko Totoki, May 29, 1953. B.S., U. Minn.; M.S., U. Idaho; Ph.D., U. Ill., 1958. Horticulturist, U. Idaho, Moscow, 1958-68; prof. horticulture Wash. State U., Pullman, 1968—. Mem. Potato Assn. Am. (dir. 1979-81), European Potato Assn. Club: Kiwanis. Office: Washington State University Dept Horticulture Pullman WA 99164

IRVIN, FRED MADDOX, artist; b. Chillicothe, Mo., Nov. 19, 1914; s. Clifford Herbert and Maude E. (Jarrell) I.; student Kansas City Art Inst., 1935, Chgo. Acad. Fine Arts, 1935-36, Art Students League, 1940, 46; m. Betty Smith, Sept. 13, 1947; children—John Maddox, Jarrell Lee. Mag. story and cover artist, N.Y.C., 1946-56; artist, art dir. Sta. KEY-TV, Santa Barbara, Calif., 1960-64; animation layout artist artist Hanna Barbera, Hollywood, Calif., 1978—; illustrator more than 50 children's books and textbooks, 1960—, including: Sea Lion Island, 1972, Hit the Bike Trail, 1974, McMillan Dictionary for Children, 1976, Great Moments in Fiction, 1977, My Son Dan, 1978. Served with AUS, 1942-46. Decorated Bronze Star. Mem. Soc. Illustrators of Los Angeles, Santa Barbara Art Assn. (treas. 1972—, dir. 1980-81), Artist Equity Assn., Internat. Platform Assn. Presbyterian. Address: 1702 Hillcrest Rd Santa Barbara CA 93103

IRVIN, MICHAEL JACOBS, accountant; b. Barrington, N.J., Aug. 6, 1938; s. Donald Frederick and Margaret Abigail (Jacobs) I.; m. Diana Jean Gibson, June 16, 1963; children—Susan Dashiell, Kimberly Jean. B.A., Augustana Coll., Rock Island, Ill., 1960; M.B.A., Ind. U., 1962. C.P.A., Calif. Jr. acct. Price Waterhouse & Co., San Francisco, 1962; staff asst. Bruce G. Fielding, Palo Alto, Calif., 1963, George J. Moshofsky, Palo Alto, 1964-65; controller Idylmoor, Inc., Sunnyvale, Calif., 1966-67; pvt. practice acctg., Palo Alto, 1966-80; ptnr. Irvin, Abrahamson & Co., C.P.A.s, Palo Alto, 1981—; teaching assoc. Ind. U., 1961; instr. acctg. Foothill Coll., 1966-67; dir. numerous small corps. Treas., mem. ch. council Grace Lutheran Ch., 1976-78; coach Palo Alto Girls' Softball League, 1977-83; life mem. Wildlife Rescue, Inc.; mem. Bike Centennial. Served with U.S. Army, 1962-68. Mem. Calif. Soc. C.P.A.s, Am. Inst. C.P.A.s. Republican. Clubs: Palo Alto Kiwanis (dir. 1982-83). Home: 630 Scale Ave Palo Alto CA 94301 Office: 438 Cambridge Ave Palo Alto CA 94306

IRVINE, MARION HELEN, nun, educator; b. San Francisco, Oct. 9, 1929; d. Walter A. and Mabel L. (Keane) I. B.A., Dominican Coll., San Rafael, Calif., 1953, M.S., 1971. Standard teaching cert., 1969; gen., secondary cert., Calif., 1961; adminstrv. services cert., 1975. Joined Dominican Order, Roman Catholic Ch., 1947; dean of students St. Mary's High Sch., Stockton, Calif., 1959-64; dean of students Junipero Meml. High Sch., Monterey, Calif., 1964-69, prin., 1969-70; prin. St. Vincent's High Sch., Vallejo, Calif., 1970-76; coordinator of edn. Dominican Sisters of San Rafael, 1976—. NSF grantee U. Calif.-Berkeley, 1957; NDEA grantee SUNY-Geneseo, 1968. Mem. Nat. Cath. Edn. Assn., Assn. Supervision and Curriculum Devel., Conf. Religious Dirs. of Edn., Supervision, Personnel and Curriculum Developers. Clubs: Dolphin South End Runners, Nor Cal Srs. (San Francisco). Set records in Great Sanford Race, 1981, Pacific Sun 10K Meml. Day race, 1982; set records for women over 50 in Great Berkeley 15K, 1982, Capitol City 20K, 1983; completed Boston Marathon, 1981, Pike's Peak run, 1982. Address: Dominican Convent 1520 Grand Ave San Rafael CA 94901

IRVINE, ROBERT GERALD, elec. engr., educator; b. Salt Lake City, July 27, 1931; s. Francis Gerald and Bernice (Henckel) I.; m. Joan Laura Granberg, Aug. 26, 1955; children—Gerald Andrew, John Robert. B.S.E.E., Utah State U., 1956; M.S.E.E., Calif. State U.-Los Angeles, 1975. Elec. engr. Gen. Dynamics, Ponoma, Calif., 1956-61; asst. prof. engring. Calif. State Poly. U., Ponoma, 1959-66, assoc. prof., 1976-82, prof., 1983—; sr. engr. Ling Electronics, Anaheim, Calif., 1966-70; owner, operator Stretch & Sew Fabrics, Claremont, Calif., 1971-72; sr. research and devel. engr. Safetran Systems Corp., 1972-76; mem. faculty Citrus Jr. Coll., U. LaVerne, San Bernardino Valley Coll.; cons. in field. Mem. ch. council Good Shepherd Lutheran Ch., Claremont, Calif., 1979-81; mem. exec. bd. Old Baldy council Boy Scouts Am., 1980—. Served with U.S. Army, 1949-50. Registered profl. engr., Calif. Mem. IEEE (sr.; chmn. sect. 1966-67, award of Merit 1967), Am. Soc. Engring. Edn., Precision Measurements Assn., Measurement Sci. Conf., Nat. Soc. Profl. Engrs., Tau Alpha Pi, Eta Kappa Nu. Republican. Clubs: Optimists; Masons (Salt Lake City). Author: Operational Amplifier Characteristics and Applications, 1981. Office: Dept Elec and Computer Engring Calif State Poly U 3801 W Temple Ave Ponoma CA 91768

IRVINE, VESS EDMUND, computer executive; b. New Rochelle, N.Y., Oct. 7, 1945; s. Vess Edmund and Grace Alma (Langeler) I. B.S., John Hopkins U., 1967; M.Aerospace Engring., Cornell U., 1968; M.S. in Mgmt. Sci., U. So. Calif., 1975. Registered profl. engr., Calif. Aero. engr. Lockheed Aircraft Corp., Burbank, Calif., 1968-74; grad. instr. U. So. Calif., Great Falls, Mont., 1975; branch mgr. STSC Inc., Dallas, 1976-80; pres., chmn. bd. Windfall Systems Inc., Englewood, Colo., 1981—; cons. in field. Mem. APL Users Group (a founder). Republican. Author: Flexibility in Accounting Systems, 1980; contbr. articles to tech. jours. Home: 33589 Robin Ct Elizabeth CO 80107 Office: 5555 DTC Pkwy Suite 1024 Englewood CO 80111

IRVINE, WILLIAM GROVER, architect; b. St. Maries, Idaho, Nov. 8, 1936; s. Grover and Kathryn Bernice (Whalen) I.; m. Donna Marie Nowicka, Aug. 21, 1965; 1 dau., Michelle Lynn. B.Arch., U. Idaho, 1959; Dir. architecture Internat. Environ. Dynamics, Menlo Park, Calif., 1969-71; pres. Irvine Architects, Inc., Saratoga, Calif., 1971—; mem. Cupertino (Calif.) Archtl. Site Control Com., 1975-79; prin. works include I.E.D. Bldg., Mountain View, Calif., 1970, Hayward (Calif.) Air Plaza, 1978; tech. cons. for residence and sch. USSR mission, UN bldg., Riverdale, N.Y., 1974; others. Served with AUS, 1959. Mem. AIA. Patentee suspended bldg. system, bldg. curtain wall system. Home: 10560 Castine Ave Cupertino CA 95014 Office: 1162 Capri Dr Campbell CA 95008

IRVING, DONALD J., university dean; b. Arlington, Mass., May 3, 1933; m. Jewel P. Irving; children—Kevin William, Todd Lawrence. Ed. Mass. Coll. Art, 1955; student Tchrs. Coll., Columbia U., 1956, Ed.D., 1963. Tchr. art White Plains (N.Y.) High Sch., 1958-60; instr. art SUNY-Oneonta, 1960-62; prof. art, dean Moore Coll. Art, Phila., 1963-67; chmn. art. dept., dir. Peabody Mus. Art, George Peabody Coll. Tchrs., Nashville, 1967-69; dir. Sch. Art Inst. Chgo., 1969-82; dean faculty fine arts U. Ariz., Tuscon, 1982—; mem. U.S. del. Conf. Nat. Soc. Edn. through Art, Prague, Czechoslovakia, 1966; cons. ednl. TV series Art Now, Sta. WRCV-TV, Phila. Mem. Nat. Assn. Schs. Art (treas., dir. 1975-77), Union Ind. Colls. Art (chmn. dir.), Nat. Council Art Adminstrs. (dir. 1969-82), Internat. Council Fine Arts Deans, Fedn. Ind. Ill. Colls. and Univs. (dir.), Nat. Art Edn. Assn. (officer Eastern region 1966-68), Eastern Arts Assn. (council 1964-66, mgr. conv. 1959-64), Nat. Council Arts in Edn., Internat. Soc. Edn. through Art, Coll. Art Assn., Phi Delta Kappa. Author: Sculpture Material and Process, 1970; contbr. articles to profl. jours. Home: 5810 E Paseo San Valentine Tuscon AZ 85715 Office: Faculty Fine Arts U Ariz Tuscon AZ 85721

IRVING, ROBERT, aerospace engr.; b. Bradford, Pa., Sept. 6, 1925; s. Ralph Edison and Dorothy Lovina (Hogarth) I.; B.S.N.S., Brown U., 1946; M.S.E.E., U.S. Naval Postgrad. Sch., 1954; M.S.M.S., Calif. State U., Northridge, 1975; children—Conrad Paul, Ronald John, Frank Thomas, George Michael, Diane Elizabeth, James Charles, Dorothy-Jean Rebekah. Served as enlisted man U.S. Marine Corps, 1943-44, U.S. Navy, 1944-46; commd. ensign U.S. Navy, 1946, advanced through grades to lt. comdr., 1957; various assignments including U.S.S. Randolph, U.S.S. Macon, U.S.S. Philippine Sea, also Polaris program; ret., 1964; staff engr. Bunker-Ramo Corp., Canoga Park, Calif., 1964-66; sr. staff engr. Hughes Aircraft Co., Canoga Park, 1966—; adv. First State Bank. Fellow AAAS; mem. Marine Tech. Soc., IEEE, Inst. Navigation, U.S. Naval Inst., Internat. Oceanographic Found., Ret. Officers Assn., Soc. Naval Engrs., Sigma Xi. Contbr. articles to profl. jours.; patentee in field. Home: 8637 Bothwell Rd Northridge CA 91324 Office: Hughes Aircraft Co Mail Sta T-96 Canoga Park CA 91304

IRWIN, DIANNE E., psychology educator; b. Madison, Wis., July 22, 1946; d. Donald J. and Dorothy R. (Shaw) I. B.A., Calif. State Coll., 1972; M.A., Calif. State U., 1974; Ph.D., U.S. Internat. U., 1979. Lectr., instr. Calif. State Coll.-San Bernardino, 1974, psychometrist, 1974-78, dir. learning ctr., 1974—; lectr. Valley Coll., San Bernardino, Calif. State U., Fullerton, 1974. Mem. Calif. Statewide Legal Compliance com. instructionally related material review, 1979-83. Mem. Am. Psychol. Assn., Student Personnel Assn., Western Coll. Reading Assn., Western Psychol. Assn., Am. Personnel and Guidance Assn. Contbr. articles to profl. jours. Home: 918 W Edgemont Dr San Bernardino CA 92405 Office: Calif State College San Bernardino CA 92407

IRWIN, DONALD MOWRY, heavy machinery manufacturing company executive; b. Albuquerque, July 3, 1925; s. Mowry A. and Marian E. (Rider) I.; m. Margaret Julia Strong, June 22, 1951. A.B. in History, U. Calif.-Berkeley, 1945; postgrad. Cornell Law Sch., 1946-47; postgrad. in econs. U. Calif.-Berkeley, 1947-50; postgrad. in bus. econs. Harvard U., 1953-55, 1962-63. Adminstrv. asst. Dept. Labor, Washington, 1956-57; mgr. personnel research and planning Chrysler Corp., Detroit, 1957-68; mem. internat. labor relations staff Deere & Co., Moline, Ill., 1968-70; regional dir. Dept. Labor, Chgo., 1971-73; adminstr. Office Wage Stblzn., Exec. Office of Pres., Cost of Living Council, Washington, 1973-74; v.p. employee relations PACCAR Inc., Bellevue, Wash., 1974—. Pres. Health Care Purchases Assn. Puget Sound. Mem. Indsl. Relations Research Assn., Am. Econ. Assn. Club: Washington Athletic. Office: PACCAR Inc 777 106th St NE Bellevue WA 98004

IRWIN, DOROTHY ANNE, ednl. adminstr.; b. Kelvington, Sask., Can., Mar. 24, 1932; d. John A. and Mary B. (Fallon) I.; B.A., U. Ottawa, 1968; Ed.B., U. Sask., 1971, diploma, 1975; postgrad. in continuing edn.; m. John Darl VanDusen, Nov. 11, 1982; children—Marie, Vincent, Jerome, Francis, Monica, Sheila. Tchr. elem. and secondary public schs. Uranium City, Sask., Can., 1958-62, Esterhazy, Sask., 1963-68; instr. Camosun Coll., Victoria, B.C., Can., 1969-74; edn. cons. Sask. Indian Cultural Coll., Saskatoon, 1975-76; adult upgrading instr. St. Mary's Sch., Dept. Indian Affairs, Cardston, Alta., Can., 1976-78; edn. counselor Dept. Indian Affairs, Blackfoot Res., Gleichen, Alta., 1978; program developer Inst. for Devel. of Indian Govt., Prince Albert, Sask., 1978-79; edn. counselor Dept. Indian Affairs, Ft. McMurray, Alta., 1979-80; coordinator distance edn. Sask. Indian Federated Coll., U. Regina (Sask.), 1980—, also editor Mem. Assn. for Ednl. Data Systems, Sask. Assn. for Computers in Edn., Royal Canadian Legion. Telidon. Home: Apt 4 1415 Mc Kercher Dr Saskatoon SK S7H 5J8 Canada Office: Saskatchewan Indian Federated Coll U Regina Classroom Bldg C-4 Regina SK S4S 0A2 Canada

IRWIN, JAMES BENSON, former astronaut, found. exec.; b. Pitts., Mar. 17, 1930; s. James and Elsie (Strebel) I.; B.S., U.S. Naval Acad., 1951; M.S. in Aero. Engring., U. Mich., 1957, D. Astronautical Sci., 1971; D.Sc., William Jewell Coll., 1971, Samford U., 1972; m. Mary Ellen Monroe, Sept. 4, 1959; children—Joy Carmel, Jill Cherie, James Benson, Jan Caron, Joe Chau. Commd. 2d lt. USAF, 1951, advanced through grades to col., 1971; project officer Wright Patterson AFB, 1957-60; test dir. ASG-18/AIM-47 armament system, Edwards AFB, Calif., 1961-63; test pilot F-12 Test Force, Edwards AFB, 1963-65; br. chief Advanced Systems Hdqrs. Air Def. Command, Colorado Springs, Colo., 1965-66; astronaut NASA, 1966-72; mem. support crew Apollo 10; backup lunar module pilot Apollo 12; lunar module pilot Apollo 15 moon landing crew, July 30, 1971; internat. lectr. Founder, chmn. bd. trustees evang. found. High Flight, Colorado Springs, Colo., 1972. Decorated NASA Distinguished Service medal, D.S.M. (USAF), City N.Y. Gold medal, UN Peace medal, City Chgo. Gold medal; Order of Leopold (Belgium); recipient David C. Schilling trophy, 1971, Kitty Hawk meml. award, 1971, Haley Astronautics award AIAA, 1972, John F. Kennedy trophy Arnold Air Soc., 1972, George Washington medal Freedoms Found., 1973, Citizenship award Nat. Chaplains Assn., 1978, others. Mem. Air Force Assn., Soc. Exptl. Test Pilots. Baptist. Author: To Rule the Night; More Than Earthlings. Address: PO Box 1387 Colorado Springs CO 80901

IRWIN, JOHN (HENRY) BARROWS, astronomer; b. Princeton, N.J., July 7, 1909; s. Frank and Mary Eleanor (Barrows) I.; m. Elizabeth Ruth Catherwood, July 19, 1936; children—Esther Catherwood, Paul Manning, Nancy Barrows, Alan William. B.S.M.E., U. Calif.-Berkeley, 1933, Ph.D. in Astronomy, 1946. Jr. astronomer U.S. Naval Obs., 1937-39; research asst. Calif. Inst. Tech., 1942-43, research assoc., 1943-45; asst. prof. astronomy U. Pa., 1946-48; assoc. prof. Ind. U., 1948-51, prof., 1952-64; research assoc. Carnegie Inst. of Washington, La Serena, Chile, 1964-67; assoc. prof. Kean Coll. N.J., 1971-77, ret., 1977; vis. prof. UCLA, 1961, 68-70, U. Basel, 1962, U. So. Calif., 1964, U. Ariz., 1967-68, La. State U., 1971; vis. prof. Fulbright prof., U. Chile, 1959; Office Naval Research grantee, South Africa, 1950. Recipient 1st prize Hughes Griffith Observer, 1981; Lick fellow 1941; Guggenheim fellow, 1955. Mem. Am. Astron. Soc., Astron. Soc. Pacific, Royal Astron. Soc., AAAS, Am. Radio Relay League. Presbyterian. Research in photoelectric photometry, binary star orbits, cepheid variables, seeing; contbr. articles to popular mags. Home: 2744 N Tyndall Ave Tucson AZ 85719

ISAAC, ROBERT MICHAEL, lawyer, mayor Colorado Springs; b. Colorado Springs, Colo., Jan. 27, 1928; s. Isaac Albert and Sigrid Elvira (Oksa) I.; student U. Colo., 1945-46; B.S., U.S. Mil. Acad., 1951; J.D., U. So. Calif., 1962; m. Betsy Lou McDonald, Sept. 8, 1972; children—Leslie Ann Isaac Williams, Julia Hermine, Melissa Sue, Tiffany Ann,

Chance Robert. Sales engr. Trane Co., Los Angeles, 1957-62; practice law and dep. city atty. City Colorado Springs, 1962-64; asst. dist. atty. 4th Jud. Dist. Colo., 1965-66; judge Colorado Springs Mcpl. Ct., 1966-69; partner firm Trott, Kunstle, Isaac & Hughes, 1969-72, Isaac, Walsh & Johnson, 1972-74, Isaac, Johnson & Alpern, 1974—; councilman City of Colorado Springs, 1975-79, mayor, 1979—. Gen. chmn. YWCA/YMCA/USO fund dr., past pres. Pikes Peak Y/USO; past pres. El Paso County Soc. Crippled Children and Adults; past mem. Nat. USO Council; chmn. Pikes Peak Area Council Govts., 1976-78. Served as officer inf. U.S. Army, 1951-57. Mem. Am. Bar Assn., Colo. Bar Assn. Calif. Bar Assn., El Paso County Bar Assn. Episcopalian. Home: 4150 Brigadoon Ln Colorado Springs CO 80909 Office: 550 United Bank Bldg Colorado Springs CO 80903

ISAACS, ARLINE, author, photojournalist; b. N.Y.C., Mar. 20, 1927; d. Louis and Fay (Durst) Goldberg; student N.Y. U. and Parsons Sch. Design, 1945-48, UCLA, Calif. State U. (Fullerton), 1966-68; m. A. David Isaacs, Jan. 7, 1950; children—Ellen, Dean. Interior designer Henry Roth, N.Y.C., 1947-50; freelance author, photojournalist newspapers, 1950—; publicist, public relations ofcl., photojournalist Bullocks Realty, Santa Ana, Calif., 1966-70; owner, operator SunBox Press, Laguna Beach, Calif., 1979—. Commr., sec.-treas. Laguna Beach Arts Commn., 1978-81, recipient award; bd. dirs. Laguna Beach Mus. Art, 1979—; chmn. 1st Ann. Beaux Arts Ball, Laguna Beach, 1978, recipient placque. Mem. Nat. Fedn. Press Women, Orange County Press Women, Women's Nat. Book Assn., Orange County Arts Alliance, Am. Council for the Arts, Women in Communications, Am. Soc. Mag. Photographers, Nat. League Am. Penwomen (1st pl. photography 1983). Author: Who's Cooking in Laguna Beach, 1980; one woman show of photographs, Laguna Niguel, Calif., 1975. Home and Office: 750 Alta Vista Way Laguna Beach CA 92651

ISAACS, GREGORY SULLIVAN, marketing communications executive; b. Cin., Jan. 18, 1947; s. Robert E. and Imogene S. Isaacs. B.A., U. Miami, 1969; M.A., Ind. U., 1971. Instr. Simpson Coll., Indianola, Iowa, 1971-73; marketer U.S. Postal Service, N.E. region, N.Y.C., 1973-76; mktg. communications mgr. Pacesetter Systems, Sylmar, Calif., 1976-80; mgr. mktg. communications ITT Gen. Controls Div., Glendale, Calif., 1980—. Bd. dirs. West Coast Opera Assn., Los Angeles. Office: 801 Allen Ave Glendale CA 91201

ISAACS, JULIE CORCORAN, health care executive; b. Oak Park, Ill., Apr. 20, 1957; d. F. Joseph and Margaret (Leydon) Corcoran; m. Donald Gompers Isaacs, May 3, 1981. B.S., U. Ariz., 1979. Adminstrv. asst. Intergroup of Ariz., Tuscon, 1979-81; health maintenance orgn. cons., 1981, dir. Intergroup of Ariz. now subs. Tuscon Clinic, P.C., also pub. relations dir. health maintenance orgn. Tucson Clinic, 1981—. Mem. Pub. Relations Soc. Am., AAUW, Med. Group Mgmt. Assn. (editorial bd. mem. Nat. Patient Edn. Council). Office: Tucson Clinic PC 116 N Tucson Blvd PO Box 26926 Tucson AZ 85726

ISAACS, ROBERT WOLFE, structural engr.; b. Clayton, N.Mex., Sept. 22, 1931; s. Robert Phillip and Eva Estella (Freeman) I.; student So. Meth. U., 1949-50, Amarillo Jr. Coll., Tex. Tech U.; B.S. in Civil Engring., UCLA, 1959; m. Ruth Marie Peffley, Jan. 12, 1951; children—Robert Philip, Jeannette Lucille Isaacs Darlington, Charlotte Ruth Isaacs Frye, Rebecca Grace. Structural engr. N.Am. Aviation, Rockwell Internat., Los Angeles, 1959—. Asst. scoutmaster, com. mem., fund raiser, Order of Arrow Gt. Western council Boy Scouts Am., 1964—; active Rep. Party. Served with U.S. Army, 1955. Lic. profl. engr., Tex.; named Pacemaker of Scouting, 1966. Mem. ASCE, Nat. Rifle Assn (life), Calif. Rifle and Pistol Assn. (life), Nat. Muzzleloading Rifle Assn. (So. Calif. rep. 1976—), Western States Muzzleloading Rifle Assn. (charter), Calif. Muzzleloading Rifle Assn., Colo. State Muzzleloading Rifle Assn., Nat. Assn. Primitive Riflemen, High Desert Muzzleloaders. Clubs: Piute Mountain Men, Sante Fe Trail Gun, Rockwell Rod and Gun, Masons. Condr. research design and devel. press diffusion bonding of titanium, aircraft design and structure; underwing and overwing inflatable seals. Home: 1028 H-1 Lancaster CA 93534 Office: Bldg 1623 Edwards AFB CA 93523

ISAACSON, LAURETTA MARIE, accountant; b. Baldwin, Wis., Feb. 5, 1931; m. Eugene I. Isaacson, June 20, 1952; children—Lynne, Nancy, Carol. B.B.A. with honors, Idaho State U., 1979, M.B.A., 1981. Sec., Archer Daniels Midland Co., Mpls., 1954-57, Austin Typog. Union (Tex.), 1967-69, Rocky Mountain Dist. Council of Carpenters, Pocatello, Idaho, 1972-77; acct. Southeastern Dist. Health Dept., Pocatello, 1982—. Mem. fin. com. Lutheran Ch. of Good Shepherd. Mem. Am. Soc. Personnel Adminstrs., Am. Soc. Tng. and Devel., AAUW. Office: Southeastern Dist Health Dept 465 Memorial Dr Pocatello ID 83201

ISAAK, ARNOLD, insurance co. exec.; b. Germany, Apr. 18, 1926; came to U.S., 1939, naturalized, 1944; s. Leopold and Melita (Strauss) I.; student Northwestern U., 1946-48; grad. Air Tech. Intelligence Advanced Lang. Sch., 1946; m. Carole Lois Klein, June 19, 1948; 1 dau., Robin Lee (dec.). TV producer Oscar Levant Show, 1948-63; pres. Mayflower Ins. Agy. Inc., Palm Springs, Calif., 1964—; cons. credit card mktg. Active Guide Dogs for the Blind, Am. Cancer Soc., Los Angeles County Mus. Art. Served with USAAF, 1944-46. Mem. Ind. Ins. Agts. Am., Ind. Ins. Agts. Calif., Am. Bankers Assn. Creator Charge-A-Surance. Office: 1301 N Palm Canyon Dr Palm Springs CA 92262

ISAAK, G. EUGENE, lawyer; b. Bismarck, N.D., Nov. 23, 1937; s. Gotthilf C. and Caroline (Jassman) I.; m. Melva Elizabeth Baguet, Aug. 3, 1968; children—Jason Eugene, Melissa Elizabeth. B.S. in Bus. Adminstrn., U. N.D., 1959, J.D., 1961; LL.M., NYU, 1962. C.P.A., N.D., Ariz.; bar: N.D. 1961, Ariz. 1963. Assoc., Dunseath, Stubbs & Burch, Tucson, 1962-73, Miller & Pitt, P.C., Tucson, 1973—. Legal adv. U. Ariz. Found.; mem. adv. com. Greater Tucson Area Found.; mem. CAP. Mem. ABA, State Bar Ariz., Pima County Bar Assn., So. Ariz. Estate Planning Council, Am. Assn. Atty.-C.P.A.s. Republican. Lutheran. Office: Miller & Pitt P C 111 S Church Ave Tucson AZ 85701

ISALY, SHARON MARTIN, interior designer, construction and land development executive; b. Columbus, Ohio, July 31, 1946; d. John W. and Patricia M. Martin; student in edn. No. Ariz. U., 1964-66; m. Charles W. Isaly, Nov. 5, 1966; children—Jeffrey Scott, Bradley William. Interior designer John Martin Constrn., Phoenix, 1967-72; v.p., interior designer Martin Devel. Co., Missoula, Mont., 1972-79; v.p., partner Security-West Devel. Co., Missoula, 1979-82, also dir.; pres., owner SMI Interiors, Missoula, 1979-82; sec.-treas. Prospect Assocs./Devel. Co., Missoula, 1979-83, also dir.; with John Martin Constrn. Co., Phoenix, 1983—. Vice pres. Missoula Civic Symphony, 1977-78; bd. dirs. Missoula Children's Theatre, 1977-78. Mem. Am. Soc. Interior Designers, Women in Design, LWV, Delta Delta Delta. Republican. Methodist. Home: 4814 E Marston Dr Phoenix AZ Office: 10439 N Cave Creek Rd Suite 110 Phoenix AZ 85020

ISBELL, HAROLD MAX, banker; b. Maquoketa, Iowa, Sept. 20, 1936; s. H. Max and Marcella E. I.; B.A. cum laude (scholar), Loras Coll., 1959; M.A. (fellow), U. Notre Dame, 1962; grad. U. Mich. Grad. Sch. Bank Mgmt., 1982; m. Mary Carolyn Cosgriff, June 15, 1963; children—Walter Harold, Susan Elizabeth, David Harold, Alice Kathleen. Instr., U. Notre Dame, South Bend, Ind., 1963-64; asso. prof. St. Mary's Coll., 1969-72; asst. prof. San Francisco Coll. for Women, 1964-69; with Continental Bank & Trust Co., Salt Lake City, 1972—, v.p., 1977—, comml. credit officer, 1978—, also dir. Trustee, Judge Meml. Cath. High Sch., Salt Lake City; mem. Utah Council for Handicapped and Developmentally Disabled Persons, 1980-81; bd. dirs. Ballet West, 1983—; active ACLU, Common Cause. Mem. MLA, Mediaeval Acad. Am., Robert Morris Assos. Democrat. Roman Catholic. Club: Alta. Editor and translator: The Last Poets of Imperial Rome, 1971; contbr. to publs. in field of classical Latin lit. and contemporary Am. Lit. Office: PO Box 30177 200 S Main St Salt Lake City UT 84130

ISELY, BARBARA JOHNSON, sociologist, educator; b. Winfield, Kans., Dec. 28, 1941; d. Lyman S. and S. Elise (Isely) Johnson; m. Charles C. Langford, June 30, 1968., M.A. in Sociology, U. Oreg., 1975, Ph.D. in Sociology, 1981. Research asst. dept. sociology U. Oreg., 1970, research assoc., 1974-76, NIMH trainee in evaluation research, 1976-77; instr. sociology Oreg. State U., Corvallis, 1979—; spl. lectr. in sociology Annamalai (India) U., 1978, 82, Madras (India) U., 1982; series lectr. Madurai (India) Inst. Social Work, 1982; cons. for curriculum and syllabus creation Indian univs., 1982 Mem. Am. Sociol. Assn., Population Assn. Am. Office: Dept Sociology Oreg State U Corvallis OR 97331

ISENBERG, EDWIN, real estate company executive; b. Max and Mae (Safran) I.; B.S., U. So. Calif., 1952; m. Susan Gay Ehrenberg, June 28, 1959; children—David, Daniel. Pres., Isenberg's Womens Apparel, Pomona, Ontario and Riverside, Calif., 1957-69; v.p. Grubb & Ellis Brokerage Co., Beverly Hills, Calif., 1975-81; chmn. bd. Standard Indsl. Properties, Los Angeles, 1981—; prin. Donaty Group Corp. Real Estate, 1981. Mem. Town Hall of Calif., 1979-81. Served with U.S. Army, 1952-55. Mem. Beverly Hills C. of C., Beverly Hills Bd. Realtors (chmn. land use com.), Internat. Council Shopping Ctrs., Am. Indsl. Real Estate Assn., Real Estate Inst., Blue Key. Republican. Jewish. Clubs: Los Angeles Athletic, Masons. Office: 1636 W 8th St Los Angeles CA 90017

ISENBERG, LIONEL, energy systems cons.; b. Detroit, Feb. 26, 1925; s. William and Ida (Levy) I.; B.S., UCLA, 1950; M.S., U. So. Calif., 1953; M.B.A., Princeton U., 1970; m. Virginia Ann Germain, Dec. 18, 1949; children—Diane, Peter, Jill. Chemist, plant mgr. Prudential Chems., Los Angeles, 1953-57; asst. div. mgr. Aerojet-Gen. Corp., Azusa, Calif., 1957-63; program mgr. tech applications Rockwell Internat. Corp., Downey, Calif., 1963-72; pres. IR Assos., Downey, 1971-80; cons. energy programs Fairchild Industries, 1976-80, mgr. energy programs jet propulsion labs., 1981—; pres. IR Assos., 1980—. Served with U.S. Army, 1943-46. Mem. AIAA (asso. fellow), Am. Inst. Chem. Engring., Am. Chem. Soc., Am. Inst. Chemists, AAAS, Sigma Xi. Author: Solar Energy, 1979; Synthetic Fuels, 1980; contbr. articles to profl. jours.; patentee in field. Home: 1205 Sunbird Ave LaHabra CA 90631 Office: PO Box 1026 Downey CA 90240

ISENBERG, PHILLIP L., state legislator; b. Gary, Ind., Feb. 25, 1939; s. Walter M. and Violet R. (Phillips) I.; B.A., Sacramento State Coll., 1961; J.D., U. Calif., Berkeley, 1967; m. Marilyn Y. Araki, July 13, 1963. Exec. sec. com. legis. representation Calif. senate, 1961; admitted to Calif. bar, 1967, since practiced in Sacramento; adminstrv. asst. to Calif. Assemblyman Willie L. Brown, Jr., 1967-69; chief cons. com. ways and means Calif. Assembly, 1971; mem. Sacramento City Council, 1971-75; mayor City of Sacramento, 1975-82; mem. Calif. Assembly from 10th Dist., 1982—. Mem. Calif., Sacramento County bar assns. Democrat. Office: State Capitol Sacramento CA 95814*

ISHAK, WAGUIH SHAFIK, electronics engineer; b. Cairo, Dec. 4, 1949; came to U.S., 1978; S. Shafik Ishak Kolta and Laila Mehany Tadros; B.Sc. with 1st class honors in Elec. Engring. (univ. scholar 1967-71), Cairo U., 1971; B.Sc. with 1st class honours in Math. (univ. scholar 1971-73), Ain Shams U., Cairo, 1973; M.Engring. (teaching and research scholar 1973-75), McMaster U., Hamilton, Ont., Can., 1975, Ph.D., 1978; m. Ragaa Kamel Takla, Aug. 24, 1974; children— Edward Waguih, Andrew Waguih. Teaching fellow Cairo U., 1971-73; teaching asst. Am. U., Cairo, 1972; teaching fellow, postdoctoral fellow McMaster U., 1973-78; NRC Can. fellow, 1975-79; project leader Hewlett-Packard Research Labs., Palo Alto, Calif., 1978—. Mem. IEEE, Assn. Profl. Engrs. Ont., Syndicate Profl. Engrs. Egypt. Mem. Coptic Orthodox Ch. (treas.) Author papers, revs. in field. Home: 1572 Meadowlark Ln Sunnyvale CA 94087 Office: 1651 Page Mill Rd Palo Alto CA 94304

ISHAM, DELL, state senator; b. San Rafael, Calif., Apr. 30, 1944; s. Quentin D. and Leah (Sabo) I.; student Boise State Coll., 1962-64; B.S., Weber State Coll., 1967; M.A., Colo. State U., 1969; m. Paulette Oblock, Dec. 17, 1966; children—Shane Gordon, Shaun Lane, Shannon Leah. Tchr., Siuslaw High Sch., Florence, Oreg., 1971-76; ins. agt., Danforth, Isham & Sprague Ins., Lincoln City, Oreg., 1977—; mem. Oreg. State Senate, 1977—, majority leader, 1980-83. Mem. West Lane County Planning Commn., 1977-78; mem. Oreg. State Democratic Central Com., 1974, 76-83. Served with U.S. Army, 1969-71. Decorated Bronze Star. Mem. Nat. Conf. State Legislators, C. of C., Farm Bur., Common Cause. Clubs: Lions, Rotary, Elks, Eagles. Author: Rock Springs Massacre, 1885, 1969. Office: PO Box 107 Lincoln City OR 97367

ISKANDER, KAMAL SADEK, mech. engr.; b. Cairo, Egypt, Dec. 11, 1941; came to U.S., 1968, naturalized, 1974; s. Sadek Iskander and Odet Nassif (Mourcous) Abdelmalek; B.S. in M.E., Cairo U., 1964; postgrad. USSR Aero Sch., 1968; M.S., Calif. State U., 1972; m. Rosanna W. Khalil, Sept. 16, 1972; children—Kamal J., Maria E. Prodn. engr. Egyptian Pipe Prodn. Co., Cairo, 1964; aircraft test engr. Egypt Air, Cairo, 1965; application engr. Robertshaw Controls Corp., Anaheim, Calif., 1968; asst. project engr. Caltrans, Calif., Los Angeles, 1969; solar engr. Los Angeles Dept. Water and Power, 1974-79, energy cons., 1977-79; pres. Kamal S. Iskander & Assos., Inc., Los Angeles, 1980—. Registered profl. engr., Calif. Mem. Power Engrs. Club, Instrument Soc. Am., ASHRAE, Am. Soc. Plumbing Engrs. Coptic Orthodox. Club: Internat. Gliders. Home: 350 N Acaso Dr Walnut CA 91789 Office: 2101 S Atlantic Blvd Los Angeles CA 90040

ISRAEL, FRANKLIN DAVID, architect; b. N.Y.C., Dec. 2, 1945; s. Irving Isadore and Zelda (Carr) I. B.A., U. Pa., 1967; postgrad. Yale U., 1967-68; M.Arch., Columbia U., 1971. Urban designer N.Y.C. Planning Commn., 1968-70; designer Giovanni Pasanella Assocs., N.Y.C., 1971-73; sr. architect Shakestan Pahlavi, Teheran, Iran and London, Llewelyn Davies Assocs., London, 1975-77; lectr. archtl. design UCLA, 1977-83, adj. assoc. prof. Sch. Architecture and Urban Planning, 1983—. Sponsor, Oppositions, N.Y., 1975; bd. dirs. Archtl. League N.Y., 1978; mem. Com. for Profl. Responsibility, Los Angeles, 1983. William Kinney fellow, 1970; recipient Lucille Snyder award, 1971; Gold medal AIA, 1970; recipient Rome prize, 1973-75; Progressive Architecture award with Llewelyn Davies, 1977. Corr. Gentlemen's Quar. Mag.; contbr. articles to profl. publs. Address: 1326 N Laurel Ave Los Angeles CA 90024

ISRAEL, RICHARD V., professional sports promoter; b. Palo Alto, Calif., Mar. 12, 1956; s. Robert and Joyce Anne (Beitz) I.; m. Marilou Quinby, May 25, 1980; 1 son, Jason David. B.S. in Bus. Adminstrn., San Diego State U., 1979. Sales mgr., ops. dir. San Diego Friars tennis team, 1977-78; dir. advt. and promotion, San Diego Chargers Football Team, 1978—. Recipient Bank of Am. achievement award, 1974. Mem. Am. Mktg. Assn.; Advt. Club San Diego. Office: 9449 Friars Rd San Diego CA 92108

IUPPA, ALESSANDRO ANTHONY, food service company executive; b. Bristol, Conn., June 3, 1953; s. Vittorio M. and Mary Iuppa; B.A., St. Michael's Coll., 1975; M.P.A., Suffolk U., 1980; m. Donna Tizio, Sept. 24, 1977. With Fairchild Republic Co., Farmingdale, N.Y., 1977-78; pres. Energy Program Mgmt., Marblehead, Mass., 1979-81; v.p. adminstrn., dir. Vidor, Inc., Reno, Nev., 1981—. Club: Boston Yacht. Home: 1181 Wagonwheel Rd Reno NV 89503 Office: 3429 McCarran Blvd Reno NV 89503

IVANCIE, FRANCIS J., mayor, writer; b. Marble, Minn., July 19, 1924; s. John and Mary (Mayerle) I.; m. Eileen Louise O'Toole, May 30, 1950; children—Gwen, Joan, Jim, Dan, John, Celeste, Mary, Paul, Peter, Tommy. B.A. in Sociology, U. Minn., 1948; M.A. in Edn., U. Oreg., 1955. Cert. tchr., sch. adminstr. Tchr., sch. adminstr., pub. schs., 1948-56; exec. asst. to mayor City of Portland (Oreg.), 1957-66, city commr., mem. city council, 1966-80, mayor, 1980—; speaker in field; weekly columnist This Week mag., Portland. Chmn. Columbia Willamette Air Pollution Authority; bd. dirs. Columbia Region Assn. Govts. Served with USAAF, World War II. Mem. League Oreg. cities (past pres.). Democrat. Roman Catholic.

IVE, JAMES ANTHONY, architect; b. Seattle, Oct. 28, 1941; s. Charles Anthony and Nora Cecelia (McGrath) I.; B.Arch., U. Wash., 1964. Owner, J. Anthony Ive, Architect, Seattle and Honolulu, 1972—. Roman Catholic. Home: 6453 NE 130th Pl Kirkland WA 98033 Office: 321 16th S Seattle WA 98144 also Suite 1717 733 Bishop St Honolulu HI 96813

IVERS, JAMES, mining engineer; b. Salt Lake City, Aug. 2, 1949; s. James and Katherine (Meagher) I.; A.B., Colo. Coll., 1970; M.E., U. Utah, 1979; m. Sandra Smith, July 10, 1976; 1 son, James V. Mine supt. Lost Packer Mining Co., Lost Packer Mine, Loon Creek, Idaho, 1972-79; shift boss Consolidated Silver Mine, Hecla Mining Co., Wallace, Idaho, 1980-81, mine engr. Lucky Friday Mine, 1981—. Served with USN, 1970-72. Mineral and Fuel Conservation fellow, 1977-79. Mem. AIME, N.W. Mining Assn. Home: 410 River St Wallace ID 83873 Office: Box 320 Wallace ID 83873

IVERSON, DWAINE JOHN, accountant; b. Poplar, Mont., Dec. 16, 1953; s. Merland N. and Ruth E. (Johnson) I.; m. Barbara J. Ruffatto, Nov. 25, 1955; children—Kristi, Rebecca, John, Elizabeth, Colleen. B.S. in Bus., Mont. State U., 1976. C.P.A., Mont. Staff acct. Misfeldt & Garnett, Great Falls, Mont., 1976-77, br. office mgr., Shelby, Mont., 1977—, ptnr. Hamilton Misfeldt & Co. (merger), Shelby, 1980—; dir. Mont. Oil & Gas Assn. Recipient Wall Street Jour. award Mont. State U., 1975; Spark Plug award Shelby Jaycees, 1978-79, 81-82, named Boss of Yr., 1982. Mem. Am. Inst. C.P.A.s, Mont. Soc. C.P.A.s, Shelby C. of C. (dir. 1980-83), Shelby Jaycees (v.p. 1981). Republican. Lutheran. Clubs: Kiwanis, Elks (Shelby). Home: Box 687 Shelby MT 59474 Office: Hamilton Misfeldt & Co 301 1st St S Suite 2 Shelby MT 59474

IVES, CATHLYN LAURIE KLAIBER, nurse, psychotherapist; b. Milw., Jan. 30, 1945; d. Charles Lawrence and Esther Dorothy (Luhm) Klaiber; B.S., U. Wis.-Milw., 1971; M.S., U. San Diego, 1982; m. Warren Charles Ives, Aug. 7, 1971. Instr. nursing San Diego City Coll., 1980, Hillcrest Coll., 1978-80; med. clk. instr. San Diego City Schs., 1980; staff nurse Sharp Hosp., San Diego, 1973-75; inservice dir. Highsmith-Rainey Meml. Hosp., Fayetteville, N.C., 1972-73; instr. psychiat. nursing Point Loma Coll., 1982—; cons. vocat. nurse program San Diego City Schs., 1980. Bd. dirs. Battered Women's Services; sec. Children's Hosp. Aux., 1976-78; bus. mgr., advt. treas. Mercy Hosp. Ball, 1976-80; mem. citizens adv. com. San Diego City Council, 1976-77. NIMH grantee, 1980-82. Mem. Calif. Nurses Assn., San Diego Soc. Specialists Psychomental Health, Beta Beta Beta, Alpha Phi. Republican. Research in alcoholism and schizophrenia. Home: 6506 Ridge Manor Ave San Diego CA 92120

IVEY, PATRICIA MELGIE, author/photographer; b. Omaha, Mar. 5, 1941; d. Wilbur and Mabel Gertrude (Morton) Ward; student Colo. State U., 1959, U. Alaska, 1976-80; children—Perry Gene Vaughn, Jr., Stephen Michael Vaughn. Various secretarial positions, 1966-69; exec. asst. to v.p. indsl. mktg., sales div. Spartan Mills Inc., Spartanburg, N.C., 1969-74; freelance writer, photographer, 1976—; profl. model, 1977-78; sec., then adminstrv. sec. Alaska Coop. Extension Service, U. Alaska, Fairbanks, 1975—; condr. workshops, speaker, lectr. in field. Public relations chmn. Fairbanks chpt. Am. Heart Assn., 1978. Mem. Nat. Fedn. Press Women, Alaska Press Women (pres. No. region 1977-79), Alaska Heritage Writers Assn. (exec. dir. 1982—). Home: PO Box 60634 Fairbanks AK 99706

IVIE, WARREN CURTIS, JR., advertising executive; b. Ft. Lauderdale, Fla., Aug. 10, 1948; s. Warren Curtis and Mary Ann (Kenyon) I.; m. Sharon Kay Rader, May 23, 1974; children—Sharon Renee, Brandon Warren. B.F.A. in Advt. Design and Theory, North Tex. State U., 1973. Designer Brougham Industries, Sanger, Tex., 1972; artist Skaggs Albertsons, Richardson, Tex., 1973, advt. mgr., 1974-81; v.p. advt. services Skaggs Co., Salt Lake City, 1981—. Served to sgt. AUS, 1970-72. Mem. Dallas/Ft. Worth Soc. Visual Communications. Office: 5201 Amelia Earhart Salt Lake City UT 84130

IVORY, CHRISTIAN W., computer software consultant; b. Payson, Utah, Jan. 1, 1949; s. Fredrick Ross and Inez (Lee) I.; m. Susan Lorie Pryor, Aug. 1, 1978; children—Mathew Ross, Adam Christian. B.S. in Math., Brigham Young U., 1973; M.B.A., U. R.I., 1976. Fin. analyst FIRSTMARK, Providence, 1973-76; analyst/programmer GATY Leasing, San Francisco, 1975-79, QARTEL Corp., San Francisco, 1979-80; cons. computer software, El Sobrante, Calif., 1980—; leveraged lease analyst, 1980—. Scoutmaster, Mt. Diablo council Boy Scouts Am. Republican. Mormon. Home: 5700 Amend Rd El Sobrante CA 94803 Office: 180 Grand Ave Suite 900 Oakland CA 94612

IWAI, RINZO, marketing executive; b. Tokyo, Jan. 3, 1926; s. Toranosuke and Chiyo (Suzuki) I.; came to U.S., 1981; m. Yoko Wakabayashi, Nov. 2, 1952; 1 son, Shigeo. Degree in Mech. Engring., Tokyo Coll. Tech. Dep. group gen. mgr. computer group, then asst. group gen. mgr. internat. mktg. Fujitsu Ltd., Tokyo, 1947—; pres. Fujitsu Am., Inc., Santa Clara, Calif., 1981—. Dir. Amdahl Corp. Mem. Info. Processing Soc. Japan, Electronics and Communication Soc. Japan. Patentee stepping motor, electronic magnetic relay, others. Office: Fujitsu Am Inc 2945 Oakmead Village Ct Santa Clara CA 95051

IZDEBSKI, KRZYSZTOF, speech and hearing educator, voice and laryngology scientist; b. Milanowek, Poland, Mar. 6, 1945; came to U.S., 1970, naturalized, 1976; s. Julian and Halina Heliodara (Szymanska) I. Fil.Kand., U. Lund (Sweden), 1970; M.A., UCLA, 1972; postgrad. U. Calif.-Santa Barbara, 1972-73; Ph.D., U. Calif.-San Francisco, 1976. Asst. prof. otolaryngology U. Calif.-San Francisco, 1978—, dir. Voice Sci. Lab., 1979—. Earl C. Anthony grantee, 1975-76 Nat. Inst. Communicative Disorders and Stroke grantee, 1979-82; VA trainee, 1973-76; recipient cert. of appreciation Am. Speech Lang. and Hearing Assn., 1982. Mem. Internat. Assn. Exptl. Research in Singing (officer), Am. Assn. Phonetic Scis., Polish-Am. Congress, Sigma Xi. Democrat. Roman Catholic. Author: Common Speech Disorders in Otolaryngology Practice, 1980; contbr. articles to profl. jours., chpts. to books; inventor reaction time device for measurement phonation. & Current work: Research in physiology and pathophysiology of phonation and laryngeal mechanics. Home: 2024 14th Ave San Francisco CA 94116 Office: U Calif-San Francisco Med Center 533 Parnassus R-U494 San Francisco CA 94143

IZENSTARK, JOSEPH LOUIS, physician, educator; b. Chgo., Mar. 29, 1919; s. Paul and Flora (Berger) I.; B.A., U. Calif., Berkeley, 1948; M.D., U. Calif., San Francisco, 1951; m. Elizabeth Kaplan, June 25, 1944; children—Susan Rebecca, John Kenneth, Florence Pauline. Intern, USPHS, Chgo., 1951-52; resident Kern Gen. Hosp., Bakersfield, Calif., 1952-53; resident radiology Cedars of Lebanon Hosp., Los Angeles, 1955-56; chief radiology resident Los Angeles County Harbor Gen. Hosp., Torrance, Calif., 1957-58; practice medicine, specializing in radiology, Inglewood, Calif., 1953-55, Bakersfield, 1971—; dir. radiology Imperial Hosp., Inglewood, 1959-60; asst. prof. radiology Tulane U., 1960-62, assoc. prof., 1963; assoc. prof. radiology Emory U., 1963-67, dir. nuclear medicine, 1963-67; prof. radiology U. So. Calif., 1969—; prof. health scis. Bakersfield State Coll., 1973—; chief nuclear medicine Cedars of Lebanon Hosp., 1968-71; spl. cons. radiol. health USPHS, Bur. Radiol. Health State of Calif., U.S. Army; mem. La. Atomic Energy Adv. Council; dir. nuclear medicine Crawford W. Long Meml. Hosp.; mem. USPHS Commn. on Radiation Exposure Evaluation; mem. Calif. Bd. Med. Quality Assurance, 1982—. Diplomate Am. Bd. Radiology, Am. Bd. Nuclear Medicine. Fellow Am. Cancer Soc., Am. Coll. Radiology; mem. Soc. Nuclear Medicine (pres. So. Calif. chpt. 1976), So. Valley Radiol. Soc. (pres. 1975), Kern County Med. Soc. (pres. 1978). Author: Anatomy and Physiology for X-ray Technicians, 1961. Contbr. articles to profl. jours. Home: 4007 Brae Burn Dr Bakersfield CA 93306 Office: 1703 27th St Bakersifeld CA 93301

IZUMO, PATSY MASUDA, multimedia services director, educator; b. Paia, Maui, Hawaii, June 24, 1934; d. Charles Takechiyo and Gladys Kikue (Wada) Masuda; m. Hiromu Izumo; children—Terry Ann Kiku Annon, Darren Isamu, Colin Hiro. B.E., U. Hawaii, 1956, 5th year diploma in Elem. Edn. and Library Studies, 1957, M.Ed. in Ednl. Adminstrn, Counseling and Guidance, 1967, M.Ed. in Ednl. Communications and Tech., 1968. Cert. profl. tchr., librarian, media specialist, adminstr., Hawaii. Tchr. pub. schs., Hawaii, 1957-61, sch. librarian, 1961-65; adminstrv. trainee, vice prin. Kuhio and Puuhale Schs., Hawaii, 1965-66; program specialist Sch. Library Services, Hawaii Dept. Edn., 1966-74, dir. Multimedia Services Br., 1974—. Active Manoa Community Assn., Friends of the Library. Mem. Hawaii Assn. Sch. Librarians, Hawaii Library Assn., ALA (council 1983—), Nat. Assn. State Media Profls., Internat. Assn. Sch. Librarians, Hawaii Assn. Supervision and Curriculum Devel., Assn. Supervision and Curriculum Devel., Hawaii Adult Edn. Assn., Hawaii Assn. Tchrs. of English, Nat. PTA, Delta Kappa Gamma, Pi Lambda Delta. Congregationalist. Club: Zonta. Reviewer School Media Quartlery, ALA. Office: 641 18th Ave Honolulu HI 96816

JAACKS, JOHN WILLIAM, ret. air force officer, aerospace co. exec.; b. Chgo., Sept. 3, 1928; s. Oren Ernst and Mathilda (Dritlein) J.; B.S. in Indsl. Adminstrn., U. Ill., 1949, B.S. in Indsl. Engring., 1962; M.B.A., U. So. Calif., 1970; m. Marilyn Joyce Walker, Sept. 24, 1952; children—John W. II, Jeffrey A., Holly S. Entered USAF, 1950, commd. 2d lt., 1952, advanced through grades to lt. col., 1968; navigator Fighter Interceptor Squadron, Alaska, 1952-55, pilot, fighter squadron ops. officer, Youngstown, Ohio, 1957-60, chief avionics and aircraft maintenance, Soesterberg, Holland, 1962-65, chief program mgmt. Space Systems div., Los Angeles, 1966-67, dir. program control space launch vehicles Missile Systems Orgn., Los Angeles, from 1967; ret., 1973; now with Hughes Aircraft Corp., Culver City, Calif. Chmn. Los Angeles council Boy Scouts Am., Torrance and Palos Verdes Calif. Mem. Am. Inst. Indsl. Engring., Am. Inst. Aeros. and Astronautics, Air Force Assn., U. Ill. Alumni Assn., Phi Kappa Psi. Lutheran. Home: 3310 Seaclaire Dr Rancho Palos Verdes CA 90274 Office: Hughes Aircraft Corp El Segundo CA 90009

JACINTO, GEORGE ANTHONY, counselor, educator, consultant; b. Gilroy, Calif., Dec. 21, 1949; s. George Peter and Isabelle Agnes (Joseph) J. B.S. in Criminology-Corrections, Calif. State U.-Fresno, 1974; postgrad. Wash. Theol. Union, 1975, Boise State U., 1981; M.Ed. in Guidance, Counseling-Gen. Personnel Services, Coll. Idaho, 1982. Intern, counselor drug and alcohol Mt. Carmel Guild, Patterson, N.J., 1974; dir. recreation program Summer Markham, Toronto, Ont., Can., 1973, pastoral asst. Ch. St. Peter, Toronto, 1973, youth minister Ch. St. Michael, Olympia, Wash., 1976-77; dir. youth ministry St. James Congregation, Franklin, Wis., 1977-80; diocesan youth dir. Catholic Diocese, Boise, Idaho, 1980—; intern counselor, grant writer Salvation Army Drug Rehab. Ctr., Boise, 1982; parish dir. youth ministry; cons. youth programming. Active diversion program Union St. Ctr., Olympia, Wash.; campaign leader for children's toys Indo-China Refugee Relief, Milw.; adv. community agys. concerned with youth issues; coordinator community service program for young people, Franklin, Wis. Mem. Am. Personnel and Guidance Assn., Assn. Humanistic Educ. and Devel., Assn. Religious and Value Issues in Counseling, World Future Soc., Region XII Youth Ministry Coalition (assoc. regional dir.), Nat. Fed. Cath. Youth Ministry, Assn. Transpersonal Psychology, Fellowship of Reconciliation. Democrat. Roman Catholic. Home: PO Box 5092 Boise ID 83705 Office: 7003 Franklin Rd Boise ID 83709

JACK, WAYNE ELMO, savings and loan executive; b. Pasadena, Calif., Jan. 26, 1943; s. Elmo C. and Nadine E. (Waite) J.; m. Barbara Gautier, Mar. 18, 1963; children—Doug, Steve, Beckey. Student, Orange Coast College, 1961, Pasadena Coll., 1962. Real estate salesman Parsons-Cambell Realtors, Pasadena, 1962-63; appraiser, loan mgr. Calif. Fed. Savs., Los Angeles, 1964-73; pres., chief exec. officer First Fed. Savings & Loan Assn. Hawaii, Honolulu, 1974—; dir. Nat. Savings and Loan League, 1977—; dir. Fed. Home Loan Bank Seattle, 1980-82; pres. Hawaii Savings & Loan League, 1981-82. Com. chmn. Boy Scouts Am., 1975-77, vice chmn. fin., 1982-83; adv. bd. U. Hawaii Sch. of Architecture, 1981—; dir. Downtown Improvement Assn., 1983; council dir. Oahu Devel., 1983. Mem. Mortgage Bankers Assn., Calif. Saving & Loan League. Club: Oahu Country (Honolulu). Office: 851 Fort St Mall Honolulu HI 96813

JACKS, RICHARD NELSON, educator, psychologist; b. Lewiston, Idaho, Oct. 31, 1938; s. Wilbur D. and Myrtle E. (Gooch) J.; m. Riett Brown, Mar. 23, 1977; children—Christopher Nelson, Eric Wayne. B.A., Eastern Wash. U., 1962, M.Ed., 1963; Ph.D. in Counseling Psychology, Stanford U., 1972. Cert. psychologist, Wash., Calif. Mem. faculty, counselor Olympic Coll., Bremerton, Wash., 1963-69; mem. faculty, staff psychologist Stnford U., 1972-79; assoc. prof. psychology, dir. counseling Whitman Coll., Walla Walla, Wash., 1979—. Mem. Am. Psychol. Assn., Am. Coll. Student Personnel Assn., Wash. State Psychol. Assn. Club: Elks. Home: 516 Catherine St Walla Walla WA 99362 Office: Whitman Coll Walla Walla WA 99362

JACKSON, BEVERLEY JOY JACOBSON, columnist, lectr., photographer; b. Los Angeles, Nov. 20, 1928; d. Phillip and Dorothy Jacobson; student U. So. Calif., U. Calif. at Los Angeles; m. Robert David Jackson (div. Aug. 1964); 1 dau., Tracey Dee. Daily columnist Santa Barbara (Calif.) News Press, 1968—; nat. lectr. Santa Barbara history, hist. China recreated, also China today; free lance writer, fgn. corr. Bd. dirs. Santa Barbara br. Am. Cancer Soc., 1963—; mem. art mus. council Los Angeles Mus. Art, 1959—, mem. costume council, 1983—; chmn. Santa Barbara Fiesta Ball, 1967, 68, 82, mem. com., 1965—; docent Los Angeles Mus. Art, 1962-64; mem. exec. bd. Lobero Theater Found., 1963-69; mem. exec. bd. Channel City Women's Forum, 1969—; mem. Santa Barbara Mission New Library Com., 1967—. Bd. dirs. Heart and Lung Found. Bd., Hospice of Santa Barbara, 1981—; chmn. Santa Barbara Com. for Visit Queen Elizabeth II, 1982—. Mem. Women in Communications. Club: Scorpio (pres.). Author: Dolls and Doll Houses of Spain, 1970; (with others) I'm Just Wild About Harry, 1979. Home: PO Box 5118 Santa Barbara CA 93108

JACKSON, BRUCE GEORGE, lawyer, banking and finance executive; b. Portland, Oreg., July 15, 1942; s. George William and Sally Marie (Dorner) J.; m. Jane Harris, Sept. 8, 1972; children—Yvette, Scott. B.S. cum laude, U. Oreg., 1966; J.D., U. Calif.-Berkeley, 1970. Bar: Hawaii 1971, U.S. Dist. Ct. Hawaii 1971. Assoc., Case, Kay & Lynch, Honolulu, 1970-74; v.p., treas., dir. Curtis W. Carlsmith, A Law Corp., Honolulu, 1974-76; sole practice, Honolulu, 1977-81; pres., chmn. bd. Bruce G. Jackson, Atty. at Law, A Law Corp., Honolulu, 1981—. Trustee Artisan Sch. Interior Design, Honolulu, 1981—. Mem. Hawaii State Bar Assn., ABA (real property and probate sect., banking and comml. law sect.), Sigma Phi Epsilon. Democrat. Clubs: Honolulu, Downtown Honolulu Exchange. Home: 46-224 Yacht Club St Kaneohe HI 96744 Office: 190 S King St Suite #1132 Honolulu HI 96813

JACKSON, DALE EDWARD, program mgr. co. exec.; b. Sacramento, Feb. 21, 1950; s. Leonard Franklin and Georgia Lee (Guild) J.; A.A., Am. River Coll., 1971; B.S., U. Calif., Davis, 1973, M.A., 1979; m. Rose Estelle Sherman, Nov. 21, 1982. Police officer City of Roseville, Calif., 1973-77; spl. agent CIA, Washington, 1977-80; owner, corporate dir. Jackson & Assos., Investigators, San Francisco, 1980—; splty. gas lab. dir. Liquid Carbonic Corps., San Carlos, Calif., 1980-81; quality program mgr. Hysol div. Dexter Corp., Pittsburgh, Calif., 1981—. Asst. commandant cadets Calif. Cadet Corps San Juan Unified Sch. Dist., Carmichael, Calif., 1968—. Mem. Am. Chem. Soc., AAAS, Calif. Peace Officers Assn., Peace Officers Assn. Calif. Republican. Baptist. Clubs: Lions, Rotary. Contbr. articles in field to profl. jours. Office: PO Box 312 Pittsburg CA 94565

JACKSON, DAVID GEORGE, government official; b. Santa Fe, July 31, 1933; s. David E. and Mili (Stakich) J.; m. Peggy H. Hooper, June 5, 1957; children—Laurel, Kim, Melissa. B.A. in Journalism, U. N.Mex., 1958; M.A. in Speech (Radio, TV), 1969. Reporter, Albuquerque Jour., 1957-58, Amarillo (Tex.) Globe-Times, 1958; asst. dir. info. and edn. N.Mex. Game and Fish Dept., Santa Fe, 1958-64; dir. info. services N.Mex. Inst. Mining and Tech., Socorro, 1964-69; dir. office pub. affairs Nev. ops. office U.S. Dept. Energy, Las Vegas, 1969-80, Albuquerque Office 1980—. Served with U.S. Army, 1954-56. Recipient Bicentennial Service award State of Nev., 1976. Mem. Pub. Relations Soc. Am., Sigma Delta Chi. Produced motion pictures and TV documentaries for Dept. Energy nuclear weapons programs. Office: Dir Pub Affairs Office Albuquerque Ops US Dept Energy PO Box 5400 Albuquerque NM 87115

JACKSON, DAVID WAYNE, engring. exec.; b. Dayton, Ohio, Aug. 5, 1941; s. Eugene Arnold and Charlotte LaVanda (Dokken) J.; B.S. in Physics, Iowa State U., 1963; M.S. in Elec. Engring., Stanford U., 1965; m. Palma Karen Paulson, June 22, 1968; children—Christine Diane, Suzanne Annette. Research engr. laser applications Stanford U., 1963-67, program mgr., 1967-69; program mgr. Electro-optics, Stanford Research Inst., Menlo Park, Calif., 1969-76; bus. area mgr. electro-optics Probe Systems, Sunnyvale, Calif., 1976-80, dir. engring., 1980-82; sr. tech. staff ESL, Inc., Sunnyvale, 1982—. Mem. Optical Soc. Am., Soc. Photo-Optical Instrumentation Engrs., Assn. Old Crows, Sigma Xi, Phi Kappa Phi, Pi Mu Epsilon.

JACKSON, DICK STANLEY, entomologist; b. Dayton, Wash., Sept. 15, 1932; s. Walter Scott and Gertrude Ethel (Carder) J.; B.S., Wash. State U., 1960; m. Naley Frances Blaak, Nov. 28, 1952; children—Arthur, Ardis, Anthony, Arlene, Alan. Craftsman, Hanford Atomic Works, Richland, Wash., 1954-57; entomologist U.S. Dept. Agr., Spokane, 1960—, area dir. plant protection and quarantine programs, Animal & Plant Health Inspection Service, 1975—, dep. dir. Medfly Project, Calif., 1981-82, vector control officer Western Regional Emergency Animal Disease Eradication Orgn. Dept. Agr., 1974—, dist. dir., Wash., Oreg. and Alaska; alt. rep. for Civil Defense, Wash., Oreg., Idaho, 1970-74, mem. Wash. State Emergency Bd., 1974—. Served with USNR, 1950-54. Recipient Superior Service award U.S. Dept. Agr., 1979, Disting. Service award, 1983. Profl. regulatory entomologist, Wash., Oreg., Idaho, Wyo., Colo., Utah, Mont., N.D., S.D. Mem. Entomol. Soc. Am., Hawaii Entomology Soc. Clubs: Toastmasters Internat., Patentee Jackson Fruit Fly Trap, 1967. Home: 21634 NE 17th Pl Redmond WA 88052 Office: Room 8004 Fed Bldg Seattle WA 98174

JACKSON, DONALD WILLIAM, JR., educator; b. Cleve., Jan. 7, 1944; s. Donald William and Barbara Ann (Dolsen) J.; m. Sylvia Kay Schroen, July 22, 1972; B.A., Albion Coll., 1966; M.B.A., Mich. State U., 1968, Ph.D., 1973. Mgmt. intern Eastern Airlines, N.Y.C., 1966; personnel mgr. Mich. Bell Telephone Co., Detroit, 1967; asst. prof. mktg. Ariz. State U., Tempe, 1972-75, assoc. prof., 1975-79, prof., dir. research, 1979—; cons. in mktg. to firms and trade assns., Bd. dirs. Ariz. Econ. Roundtable, Maricopa County Housing Study. Mem. Am. Mktg. Assn., Am. Psychol. Assn., Acad. Mktg. Scis., So. Mktg. Assn., Sales and Mktg. Execs. of Phoenix (dir.), Beta Gamma Sigma (past pres.), Pi Sigma Epsilon, Alpha Kappa Psi. Republican. Methodist. Author: Marketing Profitability Analysis: An Annotated Bibliography, 1977; mem. editorial bd. Journal of Mktg.; contbr. articles to prof. jours. Office: Coll of Bus Adminstrn Ariz State U Tempe AZ 85287

JACKSON, EDWARD NATHANIEL, electronic engr., educator; b. Los Angeles, Aug. 7, 1933; s. Edward N. and Aileen (McDaniel) J.; A.A., Los Angeles City Coll., 1960; B.S. in E.E., U. So. Calif., 1962; Ph.D., Calif. Western U., 1974; m. Mary Collier; children—Anastasia, Edward, Lisa Anne. Project research and devel. engr. AC Spark Plug, 1962; circuit designer Litton Systems, Woodland Hills, Calif., 1963-64, equipment designer, 1964-68, advanced systems engr., 1968-72, systems engring. mgr., 1972—; prof. electronic engring. Pacific State U., 1965—. Served with U.S. Army, 1950-52. Mem. IEEE, Inst. Nav., AAAS, Am. Soc. Engring. Edn. Home: 1655 Indiana St South Pasadena CA 91030 Office: 5500 Canoga Ave Woodland Hills CA 93167

JACKSON, FRANK CLINE, JR., management consultant; b. Seattle, Aug. 14, 1920; s. Frank C. and Bertha J. (TeRoller) J.; B.S. in Pre-medics, U. Wash., 1942; B.S. in Animal Sci., Wash. State U., 1947; postgrad. Harvard U., 1954, Columbia U., 1955, Pacific Luth. U., 1966; m. Helen Elaine Bonner, Jan. 12, 1943 (dec. 1978); children—Stanley Allan, Bruce Edward, Paul Bonner, David Brian; m. 2d, Joan Marion Hurd, Dec. 29, 1979. Vets. agrl. instr. Puyallup (Wash.) High Sch., 1947-52; vet. rep. Pfizer Labs. div. Charles Pfizer Co., Inc., 1952-53, nat. sales mgr. vet. dept., N.Y.C., 1953-57, mgr. vet. dept., 1957-61; gen. mgr. Am. Wilbert Vault Co., Inc., Puyallup, 1961-65; chmn. Pierce County Co-op Extension Service, Wash. State U., Tacoma, 1966-78; chmn. Jefferson County Coop. Extension Service div. Wash. State U., Port Townsend, 1978-79; mgmt. cons., 1979—; founder Pacific N.W. Vet. Suppliers Assn., 1955, pres., 1955-56, dir., 1956-59; founder, dir. Wash. Meml. Soc., Seattle, 1962-64. Troop chmn. Tacoma council Boy Scouts Am., 1950-60; bd. dirs. Tacoma Rescue Mission, 1970-78; Bible tchr., lectr., 1965—. Served with U.S. Army, 1942-46; PTO. Decorated Purple Heart (4), Bronze Star; recipient Disting. Citizen award Mcpl. League Tacoma, 1978, Jefferson award Am. Inst. for Public Service, 1977. Mem. Community Devel. Soc., Nat. (Disting. Service award 1979), Wash. assns. county agrl. agts., Nat. Sales Execs. Assn. Republican. Presbyterian. Club: Elks, Tacoma Yacht. Home and Office: 3109 SW 319th Pl Federal Way WA 98003

JACKSON, FRANKLIN D. B., business exec.; s. J.H. and Mary Evelyn (Logan) J.; B.S., U. No. Colo., 1976; M.P.A., U. N.C., 1978; M.H.A., Webster Coll., 1979; A.A., Community Coll. Denver, 1975; div.; 1 son, Franklin. With EEOC and EPA, 1978; housing officer HUD, 1978; pres., owner Jackson's Enterprises, Ltd., Denver, 1966—. Treas., Opportunities Industrialization Center, 1978; chmn. publicity U. Colo., 1971. Served with U.S. Army, 1976. Decorated Army Commendation medal, Bronze Star, Meriotorious Service medal; recipient U.S. Leadership award Am. Conf. on Leadership. Mem. Am. Soc. Public Adminstrs., Am. Soc. Health Adminstrs., Kappa Alpha Psi. Democrat. Baptist. Club: East Denver Democrat; Masons. Home: 9931-East Ohio Ave Denver CO 80231 Office: PO Box 7096 Denver CO 80207

JACKSON, HARRY ANDREW, artist; b. Chgo., Apr. 18, 1924; s. Harry and Ellen Grace J.; m. Valentina Moya Lear, Feb. 22, 1974; children—Matthew, Margot, Jesse, Luke, Chloe. One man exhbns. include: Amon Carter Mus., Fort Worth, 1961, 68, Smithsonian Inst., Washington, 1964, Whitney Gallery Western Art, Cody, Wyo., 1964, Mont. Hist. Soc., 1964; S.W. Mus., Los Angeles, 1979, (retrospective) Buffalo Bill Hist. Center, 1981, Palm Springs Desert Mus., 1981, Pro-Rodeo Hall of Champions, 1981; represented in permanent collections: Am. Mus. to Gt. Britain, U.S. State Dept, Lyndon Baines Johnson Meml. Library, Nat. Cowboy Hall of Fame, Wyo. State Mus., Whitney Mus. Western Art, Buffalo Bill Hist. Center, Plains Indian Mus., Amon Carter Mus., Woolarac Mus., Mont. Hist. Soc., Gilcrease Mus.; founder pvt. foundry, Camaiore, Italy, 1964—; founder Wyo. Foundry Studios, 1965—; founder Western Fine Arts Found., 1974—; commd. works include: mural Fort Pitts Mus., Pitts., monument Plains Indian Mus., Cody, Wyo. Served with USMC, 1942-45. Decorated Purple Heart; recipient gold medal Nat. Acad. Design, 1968; Best Cover Art of 1969 award for sculpture of John Wayne, Am. Inst. Graphic Arts, 1969; Fulbright grantee, 1954. Fellow Am. Artists League, Nat. Acad. Western Art; Mem. Nat. Sculpture Soc. Club: Bohemian (San Francisco). Author: Lost Wax Bronze Casting, 1972, 79; subject of Harry Jackson (Goddard and Pointer), 1981, Harry Jackson, 40 Years of His Work, 1941-1981, 1981. Office: PO Box 2836 Cody WY 82414

JACKSON, HELEN, army nurse; b. Cleve., Dec. 22, 1925; d. James and Idell (Hann) J.; R.N., Cleve. City Hosp., 1948; B.S. in Nursing, Boston U., 1957. From staff nurse to supr. communicable disease sect. Cleve. City Hosp., 1948-55; commd. capt. Nurse Corps, U.S. Army, 1957, advanced through grades to col., 1977; service in Korea, W. Ger. and Vietnam; asst. chief dept. nursing Letterman Army Med. Center, San Francisco, 1977-80, ret., 1980. Decorated Army Commendation medal with oak leaf cluster, Meritorious Service medal; Republic of Vietnam Cross of Gallantry with palm, Bronze Star, Legion of Merit. Mem. Am. Nurses Assn., Nat. League Nursing, Assn. Mil. Surgeons, Am. Legion (comdr. San Francisco nurses' post 452, historian 7th dist. council Calif., commr. Dept. Calif. Children and Youth Commn. 1982—, jr. v.p. honor soc. women Legionnaires echelon 37 1982-83). Address: 100 Font Blvd Apt 11C San Francisco CA 94132

JACKSON, HENRY MARTIN, U.S. senator; b. Everett, Wash., May 31, 1912; s. Peter and Marine (Anderson) J.; ed. pub. schs.; LL.B., U. Wash. Law Sch., 1935; m. Helen Hardin, Dec. 16, 1961; children—Anna Marie, Peter Hardin. Admitted to Wash. bar, 1935; asso. with Black and Rucker; pros. atty. Snohomish County, 1938-40, mem. 77th-82d Congresses, Wash. 2d Dist.; U.S. senator from Wash., 1953—; ranking minority mem. Com. on Energy and Natural Resources, mem. Armed Services Com., mem. Govt. Ops. Com. Chmn. Dem. Nat. Com., 1960-61. Mem. Wash. bar assn., Phi Delta Phi, Delta Chi. Democrat. Presbyterian. Home: 1703 Grand Ave Everett WA 98201 Office: Senate Office Bldg Washington DC 20510

JACKSON, HOWARD WORDELL, electronics executive, consultant; b. Glendale, Calif., Mar. 2, 1931; s. Wordell Carter and Nannie Louise (Murrell) J.; m. Dorothy Marree Taylor, Nov. 7, 1953 (div.); children—Joyce, Janice, Braden, Brent; m. 2d, Constance Lee Jarrett, Sept. 18, 1979. B.S. in Physics, UCLA, 1953; M.B.A., U. Chgo., 1961; postgrad. Am. U., 1967-70. Commd. officer U.S. Air Force, 1953, advanced through grades to lt. col., research physicist, research and devel. mgr./program dir. U.S. Air Force, 1953-74; ret., 1974; cons. research and devel. mgmt., Glendale, Calif., 1974-78; sr. program mgr. Allegheny Internat. Corp., Santa Ana, Calif., 1978-80; mgr. applied sci. dept. EG&G, Santa Barbara, Calif., 1980—; dir. DESA, Inc.; pres. Sci. and Engring. Council Santa Barbara, Inc. Mem. AIAA (assoc. fellow), Am. Nuclear Soc. Republican. Methodist. Club: Monticeto Country. Patentee in field of photography, electronics, instrumentation and nucleonics. Home: 498 Scenic Dr Santa Barbara CA 93103 Office: 130 Robin Hill Rd Goleta CA 93117

JACKSON, JACQUELINE DELORES SKILLERN, psychologist, consultant; b. Oakland, Calif.; d. Elton Earl and Virginia Ruth (Trotty) Skillern; m. Alvin H. Jackson, Jr., Aug. 22, 1970. B.A., San Francisco State U., 1969, M.A., 1972; Ph.D. in Counseling Psychology, Stanford U., 1980. Audiologist, San Francisco, 1971-72; diagnostician, speech therapist, audiologist Ravenswood City Sch. Dist., East Palo Alto, Calif., 1972-74; instr. dept. spl. edn. San Francisco State Coll., 1974; aide to dean for advisement and recruitment of minority student counselors Sch. Edn., Stanford U., 1978-79; cons. Ravenswood City Sch. Dist., 1978-80; counselor DeAnza Community Coll., Cupertino, Calif., 1981; program coordinator Nat. Safety Council-Central Counties, San Jose, 1981-82; psychologist, cons. San Mateo County Mental Health, East Palo Alto, 1981—; cons., trainer, therapist Project Pegasus, Inc., Palo Alto, 1981—; pvt. practice psychology, 1981—. Mem. Am. Psychol. Assn., Assn. Black Psychologists, Nat. Black Alcoholism Council, Am. Personnel and Guidance Assn., Am. Speech and Hearing Assn., Calif. Speech and Hearing Assn. Democrat. Baptist.

JACKSON, J. L., urban planning cons.; b. Los Angeles, Jan. 27, 1940; s. Jack and Rose (Rosenberg) F.; A.A. in Earth Sci., Los Angeles City Coll., 1960; B.A. in Geography, UCLA, 1962; M.A. in Geography, Calif. State U., Northridge, 1971; 1 son, Michael Justin. City planner Los Angeles City Planning Dept., 1964-73; v.p., chief environ. planner Engring. Technology, Inc., Los Angeles, 1973-74; pres. Geomega Planning Services, Inc., Los Angeles, 1974-76; dir. planning Socio-Econ. Systems, Inc., Los Angeles, 1976; pres. Geomega Corp., Los Angeles, 1977—, Wensac Internat., 1981—; dir. Environ. Scis. Div., ZOSCO, 1983—. Participant first West Coast Olympic Fencing Devel. Camp, 1964; jr. varsity fencing coach UCLA, 1980-82. Pres., Sherman Oaks Property Owners Assn., 1969-71; bd. dirs. Sherman Oaks Homeowners Assn., 1975-81; bus. adv. com. Congresswoman Bobbi Fiedler. Served to lt. comdr. USCGR, 1957-80. Recipient J. Stuart Neary meml. award for outstanding contbns. to sport of fencing UCLA, 1962. Mem. Assn. Environ. Profls. (charter), Assn. Pacific Coast Geographers, Sherman Oaks C. of C. (dirs., 1974-81), Sigma Tau Sigma. Republican. Jewish. Clubs: Brit. United Services, So. Calif. Bouvier des Flandres. Contbr. articles in field to profl. publs.

JACKSON, JOHN HERBERT, computer software co. exec.; b. Lima, Peru, Jan. 11, 1944; s. Herbert John and May Edith (Lyon) J.; B.S., Miami U., Oxford, Ohio, 1967; M.B.A., Loyola U., Chgo., 1974; m. Candace Wolf, Aug. 21, 1976; children—Mathew John, Melissa Joan. From sales rep. to product planning mgr. Formica Corp., Cin., 1969-74; salesman Boole & Babbage Inc., San Francisco, 1974-80, dist. mgr., 1980-81, also field rep. product rev. com., chmn. tech. rev. bd.; account mgr. Candle Corp., 1981—. Recipient various sales awards. Republican.

Presbyterian. Club: Toastmasters. Home: 5 Caddy St Novato CA 94947 Office: 359 Belmarin Keys Blvd Suite 10 Novato CA 94947

JACKSON, JOSIE JO ANN LEAVER, health adminstr.; b. Salt Lake City, June 14, 1938; d. Samuel C. and Edna Irene (Connary) Leaver; student U. Utah, 1956-57, Westminster Coll., 1957-58; cert. Patricia Stevens Career Coll., 1963; m. Duane C. Jackson, Aug. 9, 1958; children—Cheryl, Randal, Samuel. Dir. and mgr. Patricia Stevens Career Coll., Salt Lake City, 1963-66; mgr. Makoff Co., Salt Lake City, 1966-67; personnel counselor J.C. Bonner & Assos. St. Louis, 1967-68; leasing mgr. Mansion House Center, St. Louis, 1968-69; asst. to v.p. mktg. Mayer Co., St. Louis, 1969; dir. Browning Bus. div. Southwest Coll., Albuquerque, 1970-72; credit mgr. Midwest Floor Co., St. Louis, 1972-73; sec., Christian Hosp. Northwest, Florissant, Mo., 1973-75; adminstrv. asst. Cottonwood Hosp. Lab., Murray, Utah, 1976-78; placement dir., instr. Bryman Sch., Salt Lake City, 1978-79; exec. asst., dir. ops. Comprehensive Health, Salt Lake City and asst. dir. Salt Lake Clinic, 1980—. Named Utah Woman of Yr., 1967. Mem. Med. Group Mgrs. Assn., Utah Med. Group Mgrs. (sec.), Am. Soc. Personnel Adminstrn., Utah Personnel Assn., Beta Sigma Phi. Baptist. Office: Salt Lake City UT

JACKSON, KARL WENDELL, psychologist; b. Houston, Apr. 7, 1941; s. Norman Walker and Winefred Carver J.; B.A. summa cum laude, Washington U., St. Louis, 1967, Ph.D., 1975; m. Mary Louise Sanders, July 22, 1977. Research asso. Social Sci. Inst., 1968-70; instr. Grad. Inst. Edn., Washington U., 1969-70; instr. psychology U. Nebr., 1970-73, psychol. asst., cons., program dir. Counseling and Therapy Center, 1973-77; psychologist, dir. Riverside (Calif.) Psychol. Cons., 1977—; dir. Center for Personal and Profl. Devel., Jackson, Sanders & Assos.; staff psychologist, adult program dir. Kellogue Psychiat. Hosp., Corona, Calif.; lectr. Calif. State U., Long Beach, Eastern Wash. U., U. Calif., Riverside; cons. in field. NDEA fellow, 1966-70. Mem. Am. Psychol. Assn., Orgn. Devel. Network, World Future Soc., Calif. Psychol. Assn., Inland So. Calif. Psychol. Assn., Sigma Xi. Author: (with others) Enhancing Motivation Change in the Classroom, 1976. Office: 3717 McCray St Riverside CA 92506

JACKSON, LINDA ROSE, personnel exec.; b. Newark, Oct. 18, 1947; d. Emil S. and Priscilla J. (Durocher) Morelli; B.A., Caldwell Coll., 1969; M.A., Fairleigh Dickinson U., 1972; m. Riley Venning Jackson III, Aug. 22, 1981. Mktg. coordinator Airtron Div. Litton Industries, Morris Plains, N.J., 1969-70; research asst. dept. neuropsychology N.J. Neuropsychiat. Inst., Princeton, 1970-72; asst. dir./counselor S.I. (N.Y.) Rehab. Center, United Cerebral Palsy of N.Y.C., 1972-75; asst. v.p. Corroon & Black, San Francisco, 1975—. Mem. Assn. Women in Psychology, Ins. Personnel Mgrs. Assn., Calif. Unemployment Ins. Council, No. Calif. Human Resources Council, San Francisco Employers Adv. Com.

JACKSON, LOIS KATHRYN, educational institution executive; b. Flint, Mich., July 31, 1927; d. Milo N. and Edith (Kelly) Wood; m. Warren G. Jackson, Oct. 27, 1945; children—Connie L., Edith A., Christine K. B.A. cum laude, Asbury Coll., 1956; student U. Coimbra, Lisbon, Portugal, 1957-59, Scarritt Coll., Vanderbilt U., 1956-57. Treas., cost acct. Mobil Home Co., 1948-52; missionary educator Bd. Global Ministries, United Meth. Ch., Angola, Zaire, 1959-77; administrv. asst. to supt. Navajo United Meth. Mission Sch., Farmington, N.Mex., 1978-81; bus. mgr. Navajo Mission Acad., Farmington, 1981—. Past chmn. program Council on Ministries United Meth. Ch. Mem. Nat. Assn. Female Execs. Office: 1200 W Apache St Farmington NM 87401

JACKSON, MARGUERITE MCMILLAN, nurse epidemiologist, educator; b. Statesboro, Ga., Sept. 1, 1943; d. Clifford Heindel and Jessie Stafford (Neville) McMillan; m. Crawford Gardner Jackson, Jr., June 12, 1965; 1 son, Crawford Gardner III. B.A., Vanderbilt U., 1964; M.S., Miss. U. for Women, 1968, A.A., 1973. Registered nurse. Research assoc. Miss. U. for Women, 1967-74; asst. to mng. editor Ecol. Soc. Am., 1974-77; mem. infection control team U. Calif. Med. Ctr., San Diego, 1977-80, team coordinator, 1980—, asst. clin. prof. community and family medicine, 1981—; mem. adj. faculty Nat. U., San Diego, 1981—; tech. cons. Centers for Disease Control, Atlanta; v.p. Certification Bd. Infection Control, 1983. Mem. Assn. Practitioners in Infection Control, Am. Pub. Health Assn., Phi Kappa Phi, Sigma Theta Tau. Episcopalian. Staff editor Am. Jour. Infection Control, 1980—; contbr. articles to profl. jours. Office: U Calif-San Diego Med Center 225 Dickinson St H-951 San Diego CA 92103

JACKSON, ROBERT RAYMOND, advertising executive; b. Indpls., Dec. 13, 1951; s. Robert F. and Jean M. J. B.S., Valparaiso U., 1974; M.B.A., Butler U., 1977. Account exec. Ruben Montgomery & Assoc., Indpls., 1974-77; advt. mgr. ITT Ednl. Services, Indpls., 1977-79, Wickes Bldgs., Indpls., 1980-81; account supr., dir. mktg. Tracy-Locke Advt., Denver, 1981—; cons., profl. speaker. Mem. Direct Mktg. Assn., Rocky Mountain Direct Mktg. Club, Denver Advt. Fedn., Am. Mktg. Assn., Bus. Profl. Advt. Assn. Presbyterian. Office: Tracy-Locke Advt/BBDo Direct Mktg 7503 W Marin Dr 2-B Anglewood CO 80111

JACKSON, RUTHIE FAY, government manager; b. Wynne, Ark., June 2, 1948; d. Tyree and Ruth (Perry) Weaver; m. Charles Mack Jackson, July 6, 1974; children—Vanessa, Casey. A.A., Seattle Community Coll., 1968; postgrad. U. Wash., 1971. Sec., Mobil Oil Corp., 1969-70, U.S. HEW, 1970-74; equal opportunity specialist U.S. Office for Civil Rights, Seattle, 1974-78; program specialist Office of Child Support Enforcement, Dept. Health and Human Services, Seattle, 1978-80, dept. regional rep., 1980-81, regional rep., 1981—. Recipient Letter of Commendation U.S. HEW, 1978; U.S. Dept. Health and Human Services award, 1980. Mem. Nat. Assn. Exec. Females. Mem. Ch. of God in Christ. Office: 2901 3d Ave M/S 415 Seattle WA 98121

JACKSON, VICTOR LOUIS, naturalist; b. Thanh-Hoa, Viet Nam, July 2, 1933; s. Richmond Merrill and Hazel Irene (Peebles) J.; B.S., Wheaton Coll., 1955; m. Lois Annetta Scott, Apr. 4, 1959; children—Nathan Ray, Sharon Ruth. Chief park naturalist Organ Pipe Cactus Nat. Monument, Ajo, Ariz., 1963-66; asst. chief naturalist Grand Teton Nat. Park, Moose, Wyo., 1966-73; chief park naturalist Zion Nat. Park, Springdale, Utah, 1973—. Mem. adv. bd. So. Utah, Folklife Festival. Served with Signal Corps, U.S. Army, 1956-58. Recipient Spl. Achievement award Nat. Park Service, 1972, 79, Freeman Tilden award, 1982. Mem. Zion Natural History Assn. (ex-officio mem. bd. dirs.). Republican. Author, photographer: Discover Zion, 1978.

JACOB, DELIA LEGGETT, high technology recruiter; b. Los Angeles, Sept. 16, 1950; d. Charles William and Delia (Marin) Leggett; m. John Edward Jacob, Feb. 14, 1979; 1 son, Jonathan Michael. Student U. So. Calif., 1968-70; B.A. with honors, Stanford U., 1972; M.A., U. Mich., 1979. Study coordinator Am. Psychol. Assn., Ann Arbor, Mich., 1973; teaching fellow U. Mich., Ann Arbor, 1974-76, acad. advisor Coll. Lit., Sci. and Arts, 1979-80; research assoc. Survey Research Ctr., Ann Arbor, 1977-78; personnel asst. Martec Services, Los Angeles, 1981; asst. personnel dir. Cox, Castle & Nicholson Law Offices, Los Angeles, 1981-82; recruiting specialist TRW, Redondo Beach, Calif., 1982—; instr. Stanford U., 1971; mem. Career Mktg. Bd., Mademoiselle mag. Recipient Calif. Employee's Assn. Book award, 1968; Calif. Gov.'s scholar, 1968; Ford Found. fellow, 1972-77; U. Mich. fellow, 1976-79. Mem. Am. Psychol. Assn., Women in Communication. Democrat. Author: Gender and Sex Roles as Factors in Person Perception, 1978; Chicanos in Higher Education, 1978; Retention of Minority Graduate Students, 1976; Reports in Minorities in the Youth Conservation Corps, 1975. Office: One Space Park Dr MS R1-2194 Redondo Beach CA 90278

JACOB, NANCY LOUISE, university administrator; b. Berkeley, Calif., Jan. 15, 1943; d. Irvin Carl and Ruby (Roberts) Feustel; m. George B. Fotheringham, Dec. 22, 1972. B.A. magna cum laude, U. Wash., 1967; Ph.D. in Econs. magna cum laude, U. Calif.-Irvine, 1970. Chmn. dept. fin., bus. and econs. and quantitative methods, econ. analyst, summer research staff Ctr. for Naval Analysis, Arlington, Va., 1969; with Weyerhaeuser Co., Tacoma, 1963-65; mem. faculty U. Wash., Seattle, 1970—, dean Sch. and Grad. Sch. Bus. Adminstrn., 1981—, prof. fin., 1981—; trustee Coll. Retirement Equities Fund, N.Y., 1980—; dir. Puget Sound Power & Light Co., Bellevue, Wash. Bd. dirs. Jr. Achievement, Seattle, 1982—, Wash. Council on Internat. Trade, Seattle, 1981—. Recipient Wall St. Jour. Achievement award U. Wash., 1967; NDEA Title IV fellow, 1968-70. Mem. Am. Econ. Assn., Am. Fin. Assn., Western Fin. Assn., Seattle Soc. Fin. Analysts. Clubs: Rainier, Nat. League Am. Pen Women. Contbr. articles to profl. jours. Office: Sch Grad Bus Adminstrn DJ 10 Univ Wash Seattle WA 98195

JACOBS, ARTHUR DIETRICH, health services executive, educator; b. Bklyn., Feb. 4, 1933; s. Lambert Dietrich and Paula Sophia (Knissel) J.; m. Viva Jane Sims, Mar. 24, 1952; children—Archie (dec.), David L., Dwayne C., Dianna K. B.S. in Bus. Adminstrn., Ariz. State U., 1962, M.B.A., 1966. Enlisted U.S. Air Force, 1951, commd. 2d lt., 1962, advanced through grades to maj., 1972, ret., 1973; indsl. engr. Motorola, Phoenix, 1973-74; mgmt. cons. state of Ariz., 1974-79; mgmt. cons. Productivity Internat., Tempe, Ariz., 1974-79; faculty assoc. Coll. Bus. Adminstrn., Ariz. State U., Tempe, 1977—; productivity advisor Scottsdale (Ariz.) Meml. Health Services Co., 1979—. Bd. dirs. United Way of Tempe, 1979—. Mem. Ariz. State U. Alumni Assn. (bd. dirs. 1979-82, pres. 1973-79), Inst. Indsl. Engrs., Am. Soc. for Quality Control, Ops. Research Soc. Am., Sigma Iota Epsilon, Beta Gamma Sigma, Delta Sigma Pi. Club: Optimist (Tempe). Contbr. articles to profl. jours. Office: 7400 E Osborn Rd Scottsdale AZ 85251

JACOBS, BARBARA LEEDS, interior designer; b. Chgo., Oct. 5, 1941; d. Albert Joseph and Gertrude (Klein) Leeds; A.A. in Interior Design, West Valley Coll., 1978; m. Melvin Jacobs, June 16, 1933; children—Jonathan, Matthew, Alexander. Pres., Barbara Jacobs Interior Design, Saratoga, Calif., 1978—. Mem. Am. Soc. Interior Designers (chpt. sec.), Jr. League San Jose. Office: 12340 Saratoga-Sunnyvale Rd Suite 2-3 Saratoga CA 95070

JACOBS, CARL DAVID, restaurant chain executive, consultant; b. Phila., Apr. 14, 1944; s. Leonard and Margery (Goldberg) J.; m. Francine Berger, Dec. 24, 1972; children—Bonnie Jean, Scott Andrew. B.S., U. Calif.-Berkeley, 1965; M.A., So. Methodist U., 1967. Project specialist Eastern Airlines, Miami, Fla., 1968-70; adminstrv. trainer RCA, Princeton, N.J., 1970-71; sr. mgmt. devel. specialist Xerox Corp., Rochester, N.Y., 1971-73; sr. prin. Hay Assocs., Los Angeles, 1973-78; dir. staff orgn. devel. Anheuser Busch Co., St. Louis, 1978-79; gen. mgr. Host Internat., Los Angeles, 1979-82; sr. v.p. human resources Sambos Restaurants, Carpinteria, Calif., 1982—; guest lectr. NYU, UCLA, U. Mo.; cons. in human resources. HEW grantee, 1972. Mem. Am. Soc. Tng. and Devel., Am. Soc. Personnel Adminstrs. Club: Kiwanis. Contbg. author: Work in America, 1972; Quality of Working Life, 1975. Office: 6400 Cindy Ln Carpinteria CA 93013

JACOBS, DIANA PIETROCARLI, botanical illustrator; b. Glen Cove, N.Y., Aug. 22, 1950; d. Frank and Elizabeth (Ranaldo) Pietrocarli; m. David Jacobs, Feb. 12, 1977; children—Aaron Michael, Molly Sarah. B.A., U. Pitts., 1971. Cert. bot. and zool. illustrator, Los Angeles County Mus. Comml. artist agt. Mary Louise Flock Assn., N.Y.C., 1971-74; free lance illustrator, painter, Los Angeles, 1976—; bot. illustrator Huntington Bot. Gardens, San Marino, Calif., 1981—.

JACOBS, LAURENCE DAVID, editor; b. Bournemouth, Eng., May 16, 1947; came to U.S., 1964, naturalized, 1973; s. George and Lena (Flank) J.; B.A. in English, SUNY-Albany, 1969. Instr. in English pub. schs., N.Y., 1969-79, Columbia-Greene Community Coll., Hudson, N.Y., 1978-79; mng. editor Craftsman Book Co., Carlsbad, Calif., 1980—. Mem. Personnel Mgmt. Assn., San Diego Writers and Editors Guild. Home: 778 Bracero Rd Encinitas CA 92024 Office: 6058 Corte Del Cedro Carlsbad CA 92008

JACOBS, LAURENCE WILE, marketing educator, consultant, researcher; b. Cin., May 26, 1939; s. Arthur Leonard and Josephine (Yuster) J.; m. Susan Stone, Aug. 1, 1965; children—Andrew Wile, Julie Bridget. B.S., U. Pa., 1961; M.B.A., Ohio State U., 1963, Ph.D., 1966. Mgmt. trainee F&R Lazarus Co., Columbus, Ohio, 1961-62; grad. asst. Ohio State U., Columbus, 1963-65; research assoc. Mktg. Sci. Inst., Phila., 1965-66; asst. prof. mktg. U. Hawaii, Honolulu, 1966-69, assoc. prof., 1969-73, prof., 1973—, dept. chmn. mktg., 1981-83. Mem. Am. Mkgt. Assn., Sales and Mktg. Execs., Hawaii Profl. Sales Assn. Author: Timsim: A Computerized Game for Travel Industry Management, 1967; developer advt. and promotion for retailing, 1972. Office: 2404 Maile Way Honolulu HI 96822

JACOBS, PETER ALAN, artist, educator; b. N.Y.C., Jan. 31, 1939; s. Peter A. and Elsie Kathrine (Hirschi) J.; m. Nanci Ann Gardner, Apr. 1, 1961; children—Christopher, Cathi. B.S., SUNY-New Paltz, 1960, M.A., 1962; Ed.D., Vanderbilt U., 1965. Chmn. dept. art, prof. U. Wis.-Whitewater, 1965-70; chmn. dept. art No. Ariz. U., 1970-74, Central Mich. U., 1974-76; chmn. art dept., dir. spl. arts programs Colo. State U., 1976—; tchr. Native Am. arts, sculpture, drawing; one-man shows include: Horizons Gallery, Ft. Collins, Colo., Saginaw (Mich.) Art Mus., Port Huron (Mich.) Mus. Art, Scottsdale (Ariz.) Fine Art Ctr., DeVry Inst. Tech., Phoenix, Pima (Ariz.) Coll., Central Mich. U., Northwesten Mich. Coll., Lake Superior State Coll., Muskingum (Ohio) Coll., Prescott (Ariz.) Art Ctr., Grand Canyon Nat. Park Visitors Ctr., Ariz. Western Coll., Northwestern U., Luth. Sch. Theology, Chgo., U. Wis., New Paltz Art Gallery, Gallery 1309, Boulder, Colo., Gallery 5, Duluth, Minn., Ripon (Wis.) Coll., Tex. A&I U., Ohio State U., Sneed Gallery, Rockford, Ill., Behind the Brewery Gallery, LaCrosse, Wis., U. Wyo. Art Mus., VI Internat. Biennale of Humor and Satire in Art, Gabrovo, Bulgaria, U. N.Mex., Centro Documentazione Archivio, Castel San Giorgio, Italy. Fulbright scholar to India, 1980. Mem. Nat. Council Art Adminstrs. (founder, 1st pres., now dir.), Coll. Art Assn., Nat. Art Edn. Assn. Lutheran.

JACOBS, RANDOLPH, JR., banker, lawyer; b. Missoula, Mont., Feb. 7, 1944; s. Randolph and Barbara (Harris) R.; m. Stacey Needham, July 10, 1976; 1 son, Eric M. B.A. in Econs., Whitman Coll., 1966; J.D., U. Mont., 1969. Bar: Mont. 1969; comml. loan officer First Interstate Bank, San Francisco, 1969-72; sr. v.p. First Enterprise Bank, Oakland, Calif., 1972-78; pres., chief exec. officer, Mont. Bank of Billings, 1978—; adminstr. Mont. Bancsystems, Inc. Pres. Jr. Achievement, Billings; bd. dirs. United Way, Billings, Downtown Billings Assn. Mem. Mont. Bankers Assn. (pres. group 7B), Mont. Bar Assn. Club: Yellowstone Country, Billings. Home: 203 Clark Billings MT 59101 Office: 201 N Broadway Billings MT 59101

JACOBS, STEPHEN EMANUEL, engineering geologist; b. Los Angeles, Aug. 10, 1949; s. Charles and Florence (Werne) J.; B.S., UCLA, 1971; M.S., U. Nebr., Lincoln, 1974, postgrad., 1973-74; M.S., Calif. State U., Los Angeles, 1982. Grad. asst. U. Nebr., Lincoln, 1971-74, teaching asst., 1971-74; ins. clk. Charles Jacobs Co., Los Angeles, 1974-79; staff geologist Le Roy Crandall & Assocs., Los Angeles, 1979-81; staff geologist Lockwood-Singh & Assocs., Los Angeles, 1981—. NDEA Title IV fellow, 1972; Shell Oil Co. fellow, 1971-73. Mem. Geol. Soc. Am., Assn. Engring. Geologists, Sigma Xi. Contbr. articles to profl. publs. Home: 118 N Beachwood Dr Los Angeles CA 90004 Office: 1944 Cotner Ave Los Angeles CA 90025

JACOBS, WILBUR RIPLEY, historian, educator; b. Chgo.; s. Walter R. and Nona I. (Deutsch) J.; B.A., M.A., UCLA, Ph.D.; postgrad. (John Martin Vincent scholar) Johns Hopkins U.; m. Priscilla Dehmel, 1981. Jr. instr. Johns Hopkins, Balt.; instr. history Stanford U.; faculty Am. history U. Calif., Santa Barbara, asst. prof., 1951-55, asso. prof., 1955-60, prof., 1960—, dean men, 1950-51, research lectr., 1956, chmn. dept. history, 1959-63; acad. asst. to pres. U. Calif. at Berkeley, 1964-65; mem. editorial bd. history panel U. Calif. Press, 1965-68. Vis. prof. Ind. U., U. Colo., U. Calif. at Los Angeles, 1964, Claremont Grad. Sch., 1968; William L. Clements library lectr. U. Mich., 1967; U.S. State Dept. del. Cultural Exchange Program Yugoslavia, 1965, Anglo-Am. History and Reading Conf., York, Eng., 1972; Fulbright vis. prof. Australian Nat. U., 1969; Fulbright designate Kyoto Clinic (Japan), 1983; lectr. U. Papua New Guinea, 1969, Melbourne U., 1969; cons. Nat. Endowment for the Humanities, NSF, 1975—. Served with USAAF. Research grantee Rockefeller Found., 1949, Am. Philos. Soc., 1956, 69, Huntington Library, 1960, 64, 70, 79, Ford Found., 1962. Mem. Am. Hist. Assn. (council mem. Pacific Coast br., Pacific Coast prize 1947, v.p. Pacific Coast br. 1975, pres. 1976-77, mem. Beveridge and Dunning prize com. 1969-72), Orgn. Am. Historians, History Guild So. Calif. (mem. council Conf. for Peace Research in History, 1966-72), Am. Soc. for Ethnohistory (exec. bd. 1966—, pres. elect 1978-79), Am. Soc. Environ. History (pres. 1978-79). Author: Wilderness Politics and Indian Gifts, 1966; The Historical World of Frederick Jackson Turner, 1968; Dispossessing the American Indian, 1972; also articles in Ency. Britannica and other reference works, scholarly jours., mags., newspapers. Co-author: Turner, Bolton and Webb, 1979; American Indian Environments, 1980. Editor: Letters of Francis Parkman, 2 vols., 1960 (selected for J.F. Kennedy White Ho. collection of distinguished books); The Appalachian Indian Frontier, 1967; The Paxton Riots and the Frontier 1967; Benjamin Franklin, Philosopher-Statesman or Materialist?, 1972; Frederick Jackson Turner's Legacy, 1977. Research on early Am. history, Am. frontier, native Am. Indian and environmental history, historiography. Editorial bd. Pacific Hist. Rev., 1966-70, American West mag., 1969—, Western Hist. Quar., 1969-74, Am. History and Life, 1969—, Am. Indian Quar., 1974—, Environ. Rev., 1977—, Public Historian, 1980—. Office: Dept History U Calif Santa Barbara CA 93106

JACOBSEN, KIM, publisher; b. Escanaba, Mich., Nov. 19, 1933; s. Arthur and Charlotte (Smith) J.; grad. Mich. State Normal Coll., 1955. Publisher, Hawaii Bus. Pub. Corp., Honolulu, 1968—. Served with U.S. Army, 1955-57. Mem. Assn. Bus. Publs. (dir. 1980). Office: 825 Keeaumoku St Honolulu HI 96814

JACOBSEN, LAREN, systems analyst; b. Salt Lake City, June 15, 1937; s. Joseph Smith and Marian (Thomas) J.; B.S., U. Utah, 1963; m. Audrey Bartlett, July 29, 1970; children—Andrea, Cecily, Julian. Programmer, IBM Corp., 1963-70; systems programmer Xerox Computer Services, 1970-79; sr. systems analyst Quotron Systems, Los Angeles, 1979—; pres. Prescient Investments Co., 1975-82. Served with USAR, 1961. Mem. Am. Guild Organists (dean San Jose chpt. 1967), Mensa. Home: PO Box 91174 Los Angeles CA 90009 Office: 5454 Beethoven St Los Angeles CA 90066

JACOBSEN, LAWRENCE E., state senator; b. Gardnerville, Nev., July 1, 1921; m. Betty Lundergreen; children—Bruce, Gary, Susan, Tim. Mem. Nev. Assembly, 1963-77, mem. Legis. Commn., 1965-66, 69-78, 79-81, vice chmn., 1966, chmn., 1970-71, 74-75, speaker pro tem, 1969, speaker of Assembly, 1971; mem. Nev. Senate, 1979—, minority floor leader, 1981—. Mem. Douglas County Republican Central Com.; mem. State Rep. Central Com.; chmn. Marlette Lake Adv. Com. Served with USN. Mem. Motor Transport Assn. (dir.), Council State Govts. (chmn. energy com.), Nat. Conf. State Legislatures (mem. energy com., co-chmn. nat. legis. service and security adv. com.), Am. Legion. Lutheran. Clubs: Buckbrush Gun, Douglas County Sportsman, Rotary. Office: Nevada State Senate Carson City NV 89710*

JACOBSEN, PARLEY PARKER, accountant; b. Hou, Denmark, July 21, 1924; s. Anders and Anna (Sorensen) J.; came to U.S., 1929, naturalized, 1938; student U. Wis., 1942-43, Henager's Bus. Coll., 1946-47; student acctg. U. Utah, 1947-51; m. Alice White, Mar. 15, 1946 (div. 1978); children—Karen Ann, Steven Craig, Kelli, Kathleen Alice, Kimberli; m. 2d, Malia J. Luengthada, Feb. 11, 1983. Staff acct. Ernst & Ernst, C.P.A.s, 1952-55; owner, sec.-treas. Abajo Petroleum Co., also Kmoco Oil Co., 1957-59; partner Hansen, Jacobsen & Barnett, C.P.A.s, Salt Lake City, and predecessor firm, 1955-63; partner H&J Investment Co., Real Estate, Salt Lake City, 1963-80; v.p. Harman-Mgmt. Corp., 1978—, v.p. legal and auditing, also dir.; pvt. practice acctg., cons. in field. Served with USNR, 1942-46, USAR, 1959-61. C.P.A.; cert. internal auditor, data processing auditor. Mem. Am. Inst. C.P.A.s, Utah Assn. C.P.A.s (com. auditing procedures 1955-56), Data Processing Mgmt. Assn., Am. Mgmt. Assn., Nat. Mgmt. Assn., EDP Auditors Assn. (bd. dirs. 1981-83), Inst. Internal Auditors, VFW, Salt Lake C. of C., Blanding Finance Clk. Club: Fort Douglas. Home: 1027 Luehu St Pearl City HI 96782 Office: 1270 E 2100 S Salt Lake City UT 84106

JACOBSEN, ROBERT ALLEN, civil engr., cons.; b. Cloquet, Minn., Feb. 4, 1931; s. Magnus and Gunhild Lynn (Johnson) J.; m. Darlene Joan Tansom, July 28, 1956; children—Robert J., Richard A., Ronald B., Julie L. B.C.E., U. Minn., 1964. Registered profl. engr., Minn., Wis., Mich., Calif., Nev., Ariz. Bridge insp. Minn. Hwy. Dept., St. Paul, 1959-63; structural engr. Weyerhaeuser & Co., St. Paul, 1962-63; structural engr. Durox Mgmt. Co., Lake Elmo, Minn., 1963-64; civil and structural engr. Green Giant Co., LeSueur, Minn., 1964-69; project engr. E. & J. Gallo Winery, Modesto, Calif., 1969-71; ptnr. Morgan & Jacobsen, Modesto, 1971-77; pres. Robert Jacobsen & Assocs., Inc., Modesto, 1977—. Mem. Modesto C. of C. Served to cpl. USMCR, 1951-52. Mem. Nat. Soc. Profl. Engrs., Calif. Soc. Profl. Engrs., Costrn. Specifications Inst., Am. Concrete Inst., Structural Engrs. No. Calif., Am. Soc. Mil. Engrs., Am. Inst. Plant Engrs. Republican. Presbyterian. Office: 1101 M St Modesto CA 95350

JACOBSEN, THOMAS HAROLD, genealogist; b. Ballerup, Denmark, Aug. 12, 1918; s. Anders and Anna E. M. (Sorenson) J.; brought to U.S., 1929, naturalized by Act of Congress; student U. Utah; m. Erika Elfriede Seiter, Jan. 31, 1940; children—Carma Erika, Kathryn Irene, Connie Leah, Harold Andrew. Coordinator records div. Geneal. Soc., Salt Lake City, 1936-51, coordinator microfilm div., 1951-61, asst. treas., 1956-61; Utah State archivist, records adminstr., 1963-83. Served with AUS, 1944-48, maj. Res. ret. Fellow Nat. Micrographics Assn.; mem. Nat. Rifle Assn., Nat. Assn. State Archivists and Records Adminstrs., Utah Hist. Soc. Inventor microfilm accessories, archival table. Author: Ancestry of Carma Erika Jacobsen, 1943, 44; Genealogical Lesson Plans, 3 vols., 1954; Manual to Microfilming, 1959; Microfilming in the State of Utah, 1964; Guide to Official Records of Genealogical Value in the State of Utah, 1980. Contbr. articles on archives, geneology, law to publs. Home: 196 W 2900 S Bountiful UT 84010 Office: State Capitol Salt Lake City UT 84114

JACOBSON, ALBERT DALE, pediatrician; b. Portland, Oreg., Mar. 28, 1942; s. Leonard Dale and Alice Cleo (Wiesendanger) J.; B.S. in Acctg., Ariz. State U., 1964; M.D. (Oreg. Heart fellow 1966), U. Oreg., 1969; m. Donna Marie Shaw, Aug. 8, 1964; children—Heidi, Craig, Bryan, Chad. Intern, Good Samaritan Hosp., Phoenix, 1969-70; resident pediatrics Naval Hosp., San Diego, 1970-72; chief pediatrics Pacific Command-Navy, Pearl Harbor, 1972-75; staff pediatrics Health Maintenance Assos., Phoenix, 1975-77; pvt. practice medicine specializing in pediatrics, Phoenix, 1977—; mem. staffs Good Samaritan, J.C. Lincoln, Phoenix Bapt., Ariz. Crippled Children's hosps. Mem. planning com. Health Systems Agy., 1977-78. Served to lt. comdr. U.S. Navy, 1970-75. Mem. AMA, Ariz. Med. Assn., Maricopa County Med. Assn., Maricopa County Pediatric Soc. (pres.-elect), Am. Acad. Pediatrics, Ariz. Pediatric Soc. (sec.). Republican. Roman Catholic. Clubs: Arizona Biltmore Tennis; Plaza; Sports Village Country. Author: Development of Ear, 1966. Home: 11 E Linger Lane Phoenix AZ 85020 Office: 333 E Virginia St Suite 210 Phoenix AZ 85004

JACOBSON, DONALD PAUL WHITFIELD, manufacturing company marketing executive; b. Sringfield, Mass., July 13, 1953; s. William Norman and Shirly May (Kingsbury) J.; m. Pamela Jean Whitfield, Dec. 29, 1976; 1 son, James. B.A. in History, Northwestern U., 1975. Reporter, editor City News Bur., Chgo., 1976; advt. editor Sandy Corp., Southfield, Mich., 1977; advt. coordinator Toyota Indsl. Trucks USA Inc., Carson, Calif., 1977-78, advt. mgr., 1978-81, market planning mgr., 1981; market planning mgr. Komatsu Fork Lift USA Inc., La Mirada, Calif., 1981—. Mem. Bus. Profl. Advt. Assn. Democrat. Contbr. articles to trade jours. Office: 14815 Firestone Blvd La Mirada CA 90638

JACOBSON, DONALD THOMAS, mgmt. cons.; b. Powers Lake, N.D., June 5, 1932; s. Martin I. and Gladys E. (Thronson) J.; B.A., Whitman Coll., 1954; M.B.A., Stanford U., 1956; m. Andrea Marie Moore, Aug. 14, 1954; 1 dau., Kathryn Elaine. Sales and mktg. mgmt. Guy F. Atkinson Co., Portland, Oreg., 1959-63; sales control mgr. Boise Cascade Corp., Portland, 1964-66; v.p. and dir. research Lund, McCutcheon, Jacobson, Inc., Portland, 1966-74; pres. Mgmt./Mktg. Assocs., Inc., Portland, 1974—; chmn. Oreg. Bus. Workshops, 1974-76; exec. com., dir. Full-Circle, Inc., 1971-77. Served to lt. U.S. Army, 1956-59. Decorated commendation ribbon; recipient Oreg. Econ. Devel. award, 1973; cert. mgmt. cons. Mem. Am. Mktg. Assn. (pres. Oreg. chpt. 1972-73), Am. Mgmt. Assn., Inst. Mgmt. Consultants (pres. Pacific N.W. chpt. 1980-81), Am. Econ. Assn., Mktg. Research Assn., Nat. Assn. Bus. Economists, Am. Arbitration Assn., Portland C. of C. (chmn. mktg. task force 1983), U.S. Dept. Commerce Nat. Def. Exec. Res. (chmn. Oreg.-Idaho assn. 1969-70), Oreg. Hist. Soc., Whitman Coll. Alumni Assn. (pres. 1975-77), Stanford U. Bus. Sch. Assn. (pres. Oreg. chpt. 1971-72), Phi Beta Kappa. Republican. Lutheran. Club: University (Portland). Contbr. articles on mgmt. and mktg. to profl. jours. Home: 18844 Red Wing Way Lake Oswego OR 97304 Office: 707 SW Washington Portland OR 97205

JACOBSON, GARY CHARLES, political science educator; b. Orange, Calif., July 7, 1944; s. Charles William and Ruth Hope (Brown) J.; m. Martha Ellen Blake, June 2, 1979. A.B. in Polit. Sci., Stanford U., 1966; M.Phil., Yale U., 1969, Ph.D. in Polit. Sci., 1972. From instr. to assoc. prof. Trinity Coll., Hartford, Conn., 1970-79; from assoc. prof. to prof. polit. sci. U. Calif.-San Diego, 1979—. Woodrow Wilson fellow, 1969; NSF grantee, 1980-82. Mem. Am. Polit. Sci. Assn. (Gladys E. Kammerer award 1981), Western Polit. Sci. Assn., Midwest Polit. Sci. Assn., So. Polit. Sci. Assn. Author: Money in Congressional Elections, 1980; (with Samuel Kernell) Strategy and Choice in Congressional Elections, 1981; The Politics of Congressional Elections, 1983. Office: Dept Polit Sci Q-060 U Calif San Diego La Jolla CA 92093

JACOBSON, JOSEPH WILLIAM, welding engineer; b. San Antonio, Oct. 10, 1932; s. Dave and Ionia Morine (Langston) J.; B.S. in Mech. Engring., U. Tex., 1956; m. Lucy Mildred Miller, Aug. 30, 1956; children—Lucy Annette (dec.), Ionia Elizabeth, Dave Espy. Metall. turn foreman U.S. Steel, Duquesne (Pa.) Works, 1956-58, metall. lab. dir. Consol. Western Steel, Los Angeles, 1958-64, asst. to welding engr. Am. Bridge div., Los Angeles, 1964-66, staff welding engr. Ameron Inc., Los Angeles, 1966-73; mgr. engring. tech. services Fluor Engring. and Constrn. Inc., Irvine, Calif., 1973—; welding and metall. cons., 1960-80. Registered profl. metall. engr., Calif. Mem. ASME (first winner Old Guard prize 1956), Am. Soc. Metals, Am. Welding Soc., Phi Alpha Tau, Beta Phi Gamma. Contbr. article to profl. jour. Home: 6410 Nixon Lakewood CA 90713 Office: 3333 Michelson Dr Irvine CA 92730

JACOBSON, JUDITH HELEN, state senator; b. South Bend, Feb. 26, 1939; d. Robert Marcene and Leah (Alexander) Haxton; m. John Raymond Jacobson, 1963; children—JoDee, Eric, Wendy. Student U. Wis., Milw. and Madison, 1957-60. Mem. Mont. State Senate, 1980—, mem. human resources com., 1981—; del. Nat. Conf. State Legislators. Dir. Easter Seal Soc., 1980—; legis. chmn. Mont. Med. Aux., 1981—. Mem. Alpha Gamma Delta. Democrat. Lutheran. Home: 1400 W Gold St Butte MT 59701 Office: Montana State Senate Helena MT 59620*

JACOBSON, KAY CHRISTENSEN, school psychologist, counselor, educator; b. Spanish Fork, Utah, Aug. 16, 1944; d. Lorimer Simmons and Phyllis (Tanner) C.; m. Sterling Russell Jacobson, June 24, 1965; children—Kristi, Sterling Kim, Kevin Russell. B.S., Utah State U., 1966; M.A., Brigham Young U., 1968. Cert. Tchr., Utah. Counselor-psychologist Provo (Utah) Sch. Dist., 1968—; instr., Brigham Young U., part-time, 1978—; pvt. practice hypnosis, Provo, 1981—. Mem. Nat. Assn. Sch. Psychologists, Am. Personnel and Guidance Assn., Utah Assn. Sch. Psychologists, Utah Edn. Assn., Nat. Edn. Assn., Provo Edn. Assn., Psi Chi, Delta Kappa Gamma. Mormon. Home: 3967 N 450 W Provo UT 84604 Office: 280 W 940 N Provo UT 84601

JACOBSON, RONALD JOEL, lawyer, artist, b. Chgo., May 17, 1948; s. Abraham and Julia E. (Lazarus) J. B.A., U. So. Calif., 1970, J.D., UCLA; postgrad. Otis Art Inst., Los Angeles, 1970-71, 76-78. Bar: Calif. 1973. Assoc. counsel Bank of Am., Los Angeles, 1974-78, Paramount Pictures Corp., Los Angeles, 1979-81; counsel Filmways, Inc., Los Angeles, 1981; sr. assoc. Stein & Kahan, Santa Monica, Calif., 1982; of counsel Katsky, Ker & Hunt, Los Angeles, 1982-83, sr. atty. Paramount Pictures Corp., Los Angeles, 1983—; one man shows: COR Gallery, Los Angeles, 1978, Knights, Ltd., Beverly Hills, Calif., 1979, Ross Lawrence Silver Gallery, Los Angeles, 1981; group shows include: Fisher Gallery, Los Angeles, Gallery Plus, Los Angeles, 1976, Los Angeles County Mus. Sic. and Industry, 1979, Form and Function Gallery, Atlanta, 1983. Bd. dirs. Social and Pub. Arts Resource Ctr, Los Angeles; bd. govs. Mcpl. Elections Com. of Los Angeles. Mem. Calif. State Bar. Democrat. Jewish. Club: Jim Morris (Los Angeles). Contbr. articles to legal jours. Office: 9200 Sunset Blvd Suite 618 Los Angeles CA 90069

JACOBSON, THOMAS JOSEPH, child guidance counselor; b. Chgo., Dec. 2, 1935; s. Melvin George and Lorraine Bell (Fredericks) J.; m. Marilyn Louise Carlson, June 7, 1958; children—Jon Karl, Mark David. B.S., Iowa State U., 1957; M.A. in Ednl. Adminstrn., Roosevelt U., Chgo., 1962; Ph.D. in Counselor, Edn., Fla. State U., 1968. Assoc. prof. guidance, Fla. A&M U., 1967-68; guidance coordinator S.D. County Dept. Edn., 1968-73; dir. pupil personnel services Grossmont Union High Sch. Dist., La Mesa, Calif., 1973-78; dir. grants and contracts, sch. improvement, 1978—; counseling cons., lectr. Sch. Edn., U. San Diego; sr. research scientist Ednl. Indsl. Testing Service, San Diego. Chmn. music com. First United Meth. Church, San Diego. Served to lt. col. USAR. Mem. Nat. Vocat. Guidance Assn. (Merit award 1974), Am. Personnel and Guidance Assn., Calif. Personnel and Guidance Assn. (disting. service award 1974), Am. Psychol. Assn., Res. Officers Assn. Contbr. numerous publs. to profl. jours. and textbooks. Home: 5945 Highgate Court La Mesa CA 92041 Office: PO Box 1043 Grossmont Union Hi Sch Dist La Mesa CA 92041

JACOBUS, LOUISE MARTHA, counselor and therapist, educator, consultant; b. Summit, N.J., Apr. 4, 1950; d. John L. and Nancy R. (Favorite) J. B.A., U. Mich., 1972; M.A. in Counseling Psychology, Lewis & Clark Coll., 1981. With Home Health Care, Vis. Nurses Assn., Portland, Oreg., 1976-77; co-founder, instr., pvt. practice health edn. and stress mgmt. Inst. Preventive Medicine, Portland, 1977-79; co-founder, adminstr., therapist Everett Community Ctr., Portland, 1979-81; counselor Office of Counseling and Cons., U. Portland, 1981—; personal counseling, Portland, 1981—; speaker, active seminars. Active Physicians for Social Responsibility. Mem. Am. Personnel and Guidance Assn., Mensa. Office: 5709 SE Lafayette Portland OR 97206

JACQUES, MARY JO, educator; b. Denver, Jan. 2, 1932; d. Mary E. (Nelson) Swanson; m. Jean Louis Jacques, Aug. 27, 1955; children—Stephen, Paula. A.B., St. Mary Coll., Xavier, Kans., 1959; M.A., U. Colo., 1962; postgrad. U. No. Colo., 1983—. Vocat. edn. cert., secondary tchr. cert., vocat. guidance specialist cert., Colo. Field dir. Camp Fire Girls, 1954-57; tchr. St. Mary Acad., Denver, 1957-58; tchr. pub. schs., Adams County, 1958-59; tchr., counselor pub. schs., Jefferson County, Colo., 1959-62, asst. prin., 1962-64; counselor Met. Youth Edn. Ctr., Denver, 1966—. Mem. Am. Vocat. Assn., NEA, Colo. Vocat. Assn., Colo. Edn. Assn., Colo. Guidance Assn., Denver Classroom Tchrs. Roman Catholic. Home: 12985 W 16th Dr Golden CO 80401 Office: 27 S Garfield St Denver CO 80209

JAECH, DANIEL WINFRED, trust officer; b. Tacoma, Wash., Apr. 24, 1943; s. Karl John and Josephine Frances (Ott) J.; B.A., Pacific Luth. U., 1965; student U. Wash. Law Sch., Seattle, 1965-66; grad. Pacific Coast Banking Sch., Seattle, 1978; grad. Coll. for Fin. Planning, Denver, 1983; m. Betty Jo-Anne Applegate, Feb. 15, 1980; children by previous marriage—Benjamin Andrew, Matthew Aaron. Trust officer Rainier Nat. Bank, Seattle, 1969-78; v.p., trust officer Laird, Norton Trust Co., Seattle, 1978—. Wash. State treas. United Negro Coll. Fund, 1977, 78. Served with AUS, 1966-69. Mem. Estate Planning Council, Inst. Cert. Fin. Planners, Mensa. Republican. Club: Harbor (Seattle). Office: 13th Floor Norton Bldg Seattle WA 98104

JAECH, JOHN LEWIS, statistical consultant, educator; b. Tacoma, Jan. 20, 1929; s. Karl Johannes and Josephine Frances (Ott) J.; m. Lorna Mavis Schmidt, Apr. 10, 1930; m. 2d, Alyce Ann Schaeffer, Feb. 11, 1931; children—James Quigley, Jeffrey, Jeremy, Deborah Quigley, Justin, Jonathan, Jennifer, Joseph. B.A. in Math., U. Wash., 1952, M.S. in Math., Stats., 1953. Statis. cons. Gen. Electric, Richland, Wash., 1953-63, Vallecitos, Calif., 1963-66; mgr. stats., then applied math. depts., Battelle N.W., Richland Wash., 1966-70; statis. cons. Exxon Nuclear Co., Richland, Wash., Bellevue, Wash., 1970—; cons. IAEA; tchr. statis. methods nuclear materials safeguards. Mem. Inst. Nuclear Materials Mgmt. (chmn.; Spl. award 1978), Am. Statis. Assn., Am. Soc. Quality Control, Biometrics Soc. Baptist. Author: Statistical Methods in Nuclear Materials Control, 1973; contbr. articles to profl. jours. Office: Exxon Nuclear Co 600 108th Ave NE Bellevue WA 98009

JAEGER, BRENDA KAY, artist; b. Fairbanks, Alaska, July 20, 1950; d. Paul and Catherine Elias (Simon) J.; M.A. in Teaching, Whitworth Coll., 1975; m. James T. Hanlen, Apr. 26, 1969; children—Bent Omar, Shishaldin Simone Augustina. Instr. art Whitworth Coll., Spokane (Wash.) Art Sch., E.S.D. 101, 1974-75; vis. artist, Washington State Cultural Enrichment Program, 1975-76, 77-78; instr. art Columbia Basin Coll. and Walla Walla (Wash.) Community Coll., 1976-77; U. Alaska, Anchorage, 1978; dir. Cold Mountain Visual Arts, Anchorage, 1978, Longview, Wash.; owner arts and crafts bus., Cold Mountain Visual Arts, Longview; represented in permanent collections Alaska State Council on Arts, Alyeska Pipeline Service Co., Anchorage Hist. and Fine Arts Mus., Gonzaga U. Press, Intertext Press affiliated with Artique, Ltd., Anchorage, Gallery West, Portland, Oreg., also others in Spokane, Wash., Juneau, Alaska, Anchorage. Winner 1st place awards art show, McClelland Art Center, Longview, 1979, All Alaska Juried Watercolor Show, 1979, 81. Mem. Artists Equity Assn., Alaska Artists Guild, Alaska Watercolor Soc., N.W. Watercolor Soc., World Print Council, Anchorage Fine Arts Mus. Assn., Midwest Watercolor Soc., Visual Artists and Galleries Assn., Fairbanks Art Assn., Allied Arts Assn. Tri-Cities, Allied Art Council Walla Walla Valley, Nat. Watercolor Soc., Provincetown Art Assn. and Mus., Oreg. Sch. Arts and Crafts. Handmade papers featured in publs. in field. Office: Box 2152 Longview WA 98632 also Box 100014 DT Station Anchorage AK 99510

JAFFA, LAWRENCE MARVIN, clergyman, educator; b. Palo Alto, Calif., Aug. 19, 1923; s. Milton Jerome Katzky and Aileen Raby Jaffa; B.S. in Bus. Adminstrn., U. Calif., Berkeley, 1944, postgrad. in Edn., summers 1954, 56; M.Div., Harvard U., 1949, postgrad. Grad. Sch. Bus. Adminstrn., 1944-45; m. Jarmila Mikulasova, June 14, 1951 (div. 1972); 1 son, Thomas Emerson. Ordained to ministry Unitarian-Universalist Ch., 1949; minister First Parish Ch., Pembroke, Mass., 1948-52; elem. sch. tchr., Hanford, Calif., 1953-59; minister to Unitarian Fellowship, Hanford, Visalia, Modesto and Bakersfield, Calif., 1953-60; tchr. Lafayette (Calif.) Elementary Schs., 1959-60; minister First Ch. of Christ (Unitarian), Groton, Mass., 1960-63; asso. minister for religious edn., Worcester, Mass., 1963-64; minister Unitarian-Universalist chs., Ashby and Hubbardston, Mass., 1964-70; social sci. tchr. Central Cath. High Sch., Modesto, Calif., 1970-72, Laloma Jr. High Sch., Modesto, 1972-81; instr. parapsychology Merced Community Coll., 1971-81; minister United Community Ch. of San Joaquin Valley, 1980—; hon. assoc. minister No. Congl. Ch., Berkeley, Calif. Chaplain Pendola Scout Reservation, Boy Scouts Am., 1973, 75, 79, Camp Wanocksett, 1962-70; mem. Musicians and Actors Serving the Ch.; regional council on the arts Calif. State Stanislaus; sponsor Modesto Symphony; chmn. sch. bldg. study com. Ashby, Mass., 1965-67; library trustee Ashby, 1967-70; town chmn. United Fund, Ashby, 1968; Rep. town com., Ashby, 1968-70; faculty chmn. United Way, Modesto, 1977-81; active Big Bros. of Stanislaus County, 1976—; mem. San Francisco Mus. Soc.; pres. Y's Men's Club, 1978-79; bd. dirs. Modesto Community Concerts, 1979-83; mem. Modesto Arts Adv. Council, 1980—; trustee Modesto Bd. Edn., 1983—; active Modesto Civic Theatre. Served with USNR, 1943-46. Recipient Silver Beaver award Mt. Whitney council Boy Scouts Am., 1958; mem. Modesto Dist. Mentally Gifted Minors Adv. Com., 1978—, sec., 1979—; hon. life mem. Calif. PTA. Mem. NEA (life), Calif. Tchrs. Assn., Modesto Tchrs. Assn., Calif. Assn. for Gifted, Modesto C. of C., Calif. Council on Geographic Edn., Transpersonal Psychol. Assn., Inst. Noetic Scis., Unitarian-Universalist Ministers Assn., Uniterian-Universalist Psi-Symposium, Unitarian-Universalist Christian Fellowship, Spiritual Frontiers Fellowship (area chmn. 1978—, nat. council 1980—), Assn. for Research and Enlightenment, Parapsychology Assn., U. Calif. Alumni Assn. (life), Harvard Div. Alumni Assn., Harvard Bus. Sch. Alumni No. Calif., Calif. Writers Club, Calif. Fedn. Chaparral Poets (charter), Calif. State Poetry Soc. (treas. 1976-78), Mensa. Clubs: Merced Coll. Boosters, Downey High Sch. Boosters, Modesto Color Camera, Modesto North Rotary (pres., 1976-77, Paul Harris fellow 1981), Masons (Cornerstone Duxbury, Mass.), Scottish Rite, Yosemite Order of Arrow (vigil hon. Boy Scouts Am.), Am. Legion. Editor: Unitarian-Universalist Christian Quarterly, 1969-71; contbr. poetry to anthologies, 1971, 73, 75, 77, 79; winner prizes for color photography Stanislaus County Fair, 1975, Modesto Color Camera Club, 1978. Home and Office: Casa Quixote 1105 Wellesley Way Modesto CA 95350

JAFFE, DENNIS THEODORE, psychologist, educator; b. N.Y.C., Sept. 20, 1946; s. Sidney and Rhoda (Oltarsh) J.; children—Oren, Kai. B.A., Yale U., 1967, M.A. in Mgmt., 1969, Ph.D. in Sociology, 1973; lic. clin. psychologist. Lectr. dept. psychiatry UCLA Sch. of Medicine, 1973—; dir. Learning for Health Clinic, Los Angeles, 1976—; co-dir. Health Studies Saybrook Inst., San Francisco, 1981—; cons. Recipient Med. Self-Care Book Award, 1980; NIMH trainee, 1971-74. Author: Number Nine: Autobiography of an Alternate Counseling Service, 1973; In Search of a Therapy, 1974; Worlds Apart: Young People and Drug Programs, 1974; TM: Discovering Inner Energy and Overcoming Stress, 1975; Adult Psychology: Contemporary Perspectives, 1978; Abnormal Psychology in the Life Cycle, 1978; Healing from Within, 1980; From Burnout to Self-Renewal, 1983; Body, Mind, and Health: Toward an Integral Medicine, 1983; contbr. articles to profl. jours. Home: 254 Throckmorton St Mill Valley CA 94941 Office: Westwood Blvd Suite 107 Los Angeles CA 90024 also 1772 Vallejo St San Francisco CA 94123

JAFFE, IRA S., film educator; b. N.Y.C., Aug. 19, 1943; s. Samuel and Lillian (Kupietz) J.; A.B., Columbia U., 1964, M.F.A., 1967; Ph.D., U. So. Calif., 1975. Lectr. U. So. Calif., 1970-72; lectr. U. N.Mex., 1972-75, asst. prof., 1975-79, assoc. prof., 1979—. Mem. Univ. Film Assn., Soc. Cinema Studies. Contbr. articles to profl. jours. Office: Coll Fine Arts U NMex Albuquerque NM 87107

JAFFE, NISSEN ASHER, engring. co. exec.; b. San Francisco, Mar. 3, 1936; s. Simon Baer and Mona (Brown) J.; B.S., U. Calif.-Berkeley, 1958, M.S., 1960, Ph.D., 1962. Sr. scientist McDonnell Douglas, Long Beach, Calif., 1968-77; gen. mgr. Gas Generation Assos., div. Acurex Corp., Reading, Pa., 1978-79; mgr. bus. devel. Acurex Corp., Mountain View, Calif., 1979—; lectr. UCLA, 1963-68, Ohio State U., 1974, Cranfield (Eng.) Sch. Aeros., 1967, Cambridge (Eng.) U., 1967, M.I.T., 1968, many others; mem. Brit. Adv. Com. Aeros. and Astronautics, 1967. Brit. Ministry of Aviation grantee and lectr. Oxford (Eng.) U., 1966-67; NATO grantee, Belgium, 1969. Fellow AIAA (asso.). Jewish. Contbr. articles to profl. jours., chpts. to books. Office: 485 Clyde Ave Mountain View CA 94042

JAGLA, KEVIN NEIL, data processing company executive; b. Middleboro, Mass., July 19, 1949; s. Andrew and Mary (Duggan) J.; m. Pamela Lee Fallon, July 14, 1973. B.A., Colby Coll., 1972; M.B.A., Boston Coll., 1978. Site rep., cons., computer specialist Optimum Systems, Santa Clara, Calif., 1978-79; programmer, analyst Georgia-Pacific, Portland, Oreg., 1979-80; fin. analyst Electro Sci. Industries, Inc., Portand, 1980—. NSF grantee, 1967. Mem. Assoc. Systems Mgrs. Roman Catholic. Clubs: Wianno Yacht (Osterville, Mass.), Island Yacht (Portland). Office: Electro Scientific Industries Inc 13900 NW Scientific Park Dr Portland OR 97229

JALLOW, RAYMOND, economist; b. Baghdad, Iraq, Oct. 10, 1930; s. Jawad M. and Naima (Hussain) J.; B.A., U. Baghdad, 1951; M.A., U. So. Calif., 1956; Ph.D., U. Calif. at Los Angeles, 1966. Came to U.S., 1953. Supr. revenue dept. Iraqi Rys., Baghdad, 1947-52; auditor Robert Young, C.P.A., Pasadena, Calif., 1956-57; economist, mgr. econ. research and planning dept. United Calif. Bank (now First Interstate Bank), Los Angeles, 1959-66, v.p., chief economist, 1966-70, v.p., chief economist, dir. research and planning div., 1966-70, sr. v.p., chief economist, dir. research and planning div., 1970-81; chief economist Western Bancorp., 1979-81; pres. Jallow Internat. Ltd., Los Angeles, 1981—; faculty mem. U. Calif. Extension, 1964-68; dir. Barrick Investment Ltd., Triad Am. Corp., Midwestern Cos., Inc.; lectr. econs. and monetary fields; advisor govts. and corps. Europe, Middle East and Far East; guest econ. commentator on TV and radio networks. Mem. Real Estate Adv. Council; bd. regents, mem. Calif. Luth. Coll.; mem. fin. com. Seavers Inst.; mem. adv. bd. Calif. Poly. State U.; chmn. bd. of U.S. OMEN, 1972 U.S. Omen. Trust Com., 1972—. Mem. Am. Bankers Assn. (econ. adv. com.), Am., Western, So. Calif. econ. assns., Nat. Assn. Bus. Economists (pres. So. Calif. chpt. 1968-69), Am. Statis. Assn., Am. Mgmt. Assn., U.S.-Arab C. of C. (dir.), Blue Key, Beta Gamma Sigma. Home: 2530 Park Oak Ct Los Angeles CA 90068 Office: 2049 Century Park E Suite 2520 Los Angeles CA 90068

JALLU, OFA, artist; b. Alameda, Calif., May 5, 1907; d. Wilbur Oliver and Minnie Jean (Mead) Hayes; A.B. with honors in Art, U. Calif., Berkeley, 1928, M.A. in Art, 1931; student summer sessions univs., adult classes, workshops, pvt. tchrs.; m. Frank Marcel Jallu, Apr. 8, 1972; children by previous marriage—Gaylan John Hayes, Vivian Stein Hayes, James Hayes Irvine. Artist in oils, watercolors, drawing, etchings, acrylics; works exhibited extensively in Central Calif., 1954-72, in San Diego, La Jolla, Los Angeles, Redlands, and Del Mar, Calif., 1972—; one-person shows: La Jolla Art Assn. Gallery, 1973, 75, 77, Foothills Art Assn., La Mesa, Calif., 1976, H. Hery Gallery, San Diego, 1978, First Unitarian Ch., San Diego, 1976, R.J. Software Systems, La Mesa, 1978, Glendale Fed. Savs., Pacific Beach, Calif., 1978; 2-person show: La Jolla Art Assn. Gallery; tchr. art and home econs. Calif. schs., 1931-71; judge Ramona Art Guild Show, 1976, Nat. Fedn. Women's Club Art Show, 1976; demonstrator collage techniques, figure drawing techniques. Recipient numerous awards including: Sweepstakes award Dist. 25, S.D. Women's Club, 1983. Mem. Nat. League Am. Pen Woman (Woman of Achievement award 1977, pres. San Diego br. 1976-78, award in graphics), San Diego Art Guild, San Diego Art Inst., Assoc. Sr. Artists, San Diego Watercolor Soc., Artists Equity Assn., Foothills Art Assn., La Jolla Art Assn., Central Calif. Art League (past pres.). Home: 5445 Collier Ave San Diego CA 92115

JALONEN, NANCY LEE, arts administrator; b. Hollywood, Calif., Oct. 28, 1927; d. Earle Reynolds and Hazel Lee (Griffin) MacNaught; B.A., Stanford U., 1948, M.A., 1950; m. John William Jalonen, June 26, 1955; children—Wendy Anne, Christopher Lee. Instr. drama Pasadena (Calif.) City Coll., 1950-55; instr. eve. coll. Coll. of San Mateo (Calif.), 1956-78; producer, moderator ednl. TV, Sta. KCSM-TV, San Mateo, 1965-78; communications cons., 1977-79; exec. dir. San Mateo County Arts Council, 1978—. Mem. Bicentennial com. City of San Mateo. Mem. AAUW, Am. Council Arts. Republican. Office: 1219 Ralston Ave Belmont CA 94002

JAMES, BERTHA SANDERS, educator; b. Ft. Wayne, Ind., Mar. 3, 1940; d. Mark and Maggie (Crews) Sanders; m. John W. James, Jr., Aug. 27, 1967; children—Mark, Tiffany, Jon. Student Ft. Wayne Bus. Coll., 1956-58, Calif. Bus. Coll., 1968-69. Coordinating instr. Bryman Sch. Med. Assts., Rosemead, Calif., 1970-73, tchr. remedial reading Calvary Bapt. Elem. Sch., Gardena, Calif., 1978-80; tchr. 1st grade, dir. reading lab. Redeemer Alternate Sch., Los Angeles, 1980-83; founder, prin. Carson (Calif.) Christian Sch., 1983—. Missionary, Apostolic Pentecostal Ch. Mem. Assn. Supervision and Curriculum Devel.

JAMES, CHRISTOPHER MARTIN, finance educator; b. Detroit, Oct. 12, 1951; s. Norman McKinley and Lois Ann (McNierney) J.; B.A., Mich. State U., 1973; M.B.A., U. Mich., 1977, Ph.D., 1978; m. Kay Kiner, Oct. 5, 1950. Asst. prof. fin. U. Oreg., Eugene, 1978-82, assoc. prof., 1982—; sr. econ. advisor Comptroller of the Currency, 1980-81. Mem. Am. Econ. Assn., Am. Fin. Assn. Home: 5040 Nectar Way Eugene OR 97405 Office: Dept Finance Univ Oregon Eugene OR 97403

JAMES, DAVID LESLIE, commercial construction company executive, accountant; b. Garden City, Kans., Sept. 18, 1951; s. John Leslie and Beverly Jean J.; m. Melanie Kay Hulse, May 15, 1971; children—Kira Briana, Brent Nathan. B.S. in Acctg. and Bus. Adminstrn. with distinction, U. Kans. C.P.A., Ariz. Mem. staff Lester White & Co., C.P.A.s, Phoenix, 1974-77; controller/officer D. K. Realtec, Inc., real estate cons., Phoenix, 1977-80; treas. Joe E. Woods, Inc., Mesa, Ariz., 1980—. Mem. Ariz. Soc. C.P.A.s, Am. Inst. C.P.A.s. Methodist. Home: 4707 S McAllister Tempe AZ 85282 Office: 122 N Country Club Mesa AZ 85201

JAMES, ELIZABETH WICK, nutritionist; b. Youngstown, Ohio, Jan. 4, 1950; d. Carl Gilbert Jr. and Adeline (Wick) J. B.S. in Food and Nutrition, U. Ariz., 1972; postgrad. Calif. State U.-Los Angeles, 1976-77. Gourmet chef, caterer Liz's Little Lunches, Los Angeles, 1975-77; food editor Party mag., Los Angeles, 1977; self-employed food stylist, cons. nutritionist Los Angeles area, 1978—. Mem. Womans Referral Service, Alpha Delta Pi. Presbyterian. Club: Jr. League Los Angeles. Contbr. articles to gen. mags. Coordinator, stylist Los Angeles Times Home mag. Home and Office: 4128 Hood Ave Suite A Toluca Lake CA 91505

JAMES, FRANK EDWARD (JIMMY), accountant; b. Seattle, Aug. 2, 1929; s. Frank E. and Edith (O'Brien) J.; m. Mary Watson, Dec. 30, 1952 (div.); children—Chris Frutrich, Elinor Frutrich, Frank E., Mary Minor; m. Susanne Hackett, Dec. 9, 1972. B.B.A., U. Wash., 1951. C.P.A. Wash. With Sears Roebuck & Co., Seattle, 1948-62, Selo Electric, Seattle, 1962-63, Eltek Inc., Seattle, 1963-71, City Electric, Seattle, 1971, Wash. Dept. Revenue, 1971-73, Wash. Dept. Labor and Industry, Seattle, 1973-77; acct. Weber & Bennett, Settle, 1977-80; sole practice James & Assocs., Seattle, 1980—; cons. Bd. dirs. Seafair; treas. Crystal Mountain Ski Patrol. Served with USMCR, 1950-52. Mem. Seattle C. of C. (past pres.), Am. Inst. C.P.A.s, Wash. Soc. C.P.A.s. Clubs: Seattle Yacht, Elks. Office: 1200 Westlake Ave N Suite 809 Seattle WA 98109

JAMES, GEORGE BARKER, II, forest products co. exec.; b. Haverhill, Mass., May 25, 1937; s. Paul Withington and Ruth Arlene (Burns) J.; A.B., Harvard U., 1959; M.B.A., Stanford U., 1962; m. Beverly A. Burch, Sept. 22, 1962; children—Alexander North, Christopher Burch, Geoffrey Abbott, Matthew Bradstreet. Fiscal dir. EG&G, Inc., Bedford, Mass., 1963-67; asst. to treas. Am. Brands, Inc., N.Y.C., 1967-69; v.p. Pepsico Leasing Corp., N.Y.C., 1969-72; sr. v.p. Arcata Corp., Menlo Park, Calif., 1972-82; exec. v.p. Crown Zellerbach, San Francisco, 1982—; dir. Pacific States Industries, Inc. Mem. Andover (Mass.) Town Com., 1965-67. Chmn., Towle Trust; v.p., trustee San Francisco Ballet Assn.; trustee Nat. Corp. Fund for Dance, Cate Sch.; Inc. Served with AUS, 1960-61. Mem. Newcomen Soc. N.Am., Fin. Execs. Inst. Clubs: Commonwealth of Calif.; Harvard (Boston, N.Y.C.); Menlo Circus (Atherton, Calif.); Harvard Varsity (Cambridge, Mass.); Stock Exchange (San Francisco). Author: Industrial Development in the Ohio Valley.

JAMES, GEORGE ROBERT, artist, educator, illustrator, consultant; b. Detroit, Feb. 16, 1932; s. Leonard Phillip and Florence Eleanor (Stickley) J.; m. Isabel Marie Gowen, Dec. 27, 1957; children—Anne Isabel, Joseph George. Student Choinard Art Inst., 1953, Rex Brant Sch. Painting, 1952-54; B.A., Calif. State U.-Long Beach, 1956 M.A., 1957. Chmn. art dept. Savanna High Sch., Anaheim, Calif., 1960-68; prof. Calif. State U.-Fullerton, 1968—, chmn. visual arts dept., 1979-83; one man shows: Orlando Gallery, 1971-75, 78, 80, 82; group shows include: Am. Watercolor Soc., N.Y.C., 1970, Nat. Acad. Design, N.Y.C., 1970, 71, Calif. Nat. Watercolor Soc., 1970, 71-73, Cerritos Open, 1970, The Old Bergen Art Guild Travel Show, Calif. Nat. Watercolor Soc. 51st Ann. Exhbn., 1971, 52d Ann., 1972, Watercolor U.S.A., 1972; represented in permanent collections: Long Beach Mus. Art, North Orange County Jr. Coll. Dist., Home Savs. and Loan, Los Angeles, City of La Mirada (Calif.), Orange County Illustrated Mag.; also numerous pvt. collections. Served with U.S. Army, 1956-58. Recipient Windsor Newton award Watercolor West Exhbn., 1979. Mem. Nat. Watercolor Soc. (1st v.p. 1978-79). Roman Catholic.

JAMES, HERB MARK, found. exec.; b. Trail, B.C., Can., Jan. 30, 1936; s. George William and Violet Ethyl (Corbin) J.; student bus. adminstrn. Simon Fraser U., 1965-69; m. Patricia Helen Boyd, Nov. 1, 1958; 1 son, Brad Mark. Founder, pres. Internat. Sound Found., Nanaimo, B.C., Can., 1967—, Blaine, Wash., 1975—; mem. bus. adv. bd. U.S. Senate, 1981—; mem. Can. Internat. Devel. Agy.; founder Better Hearing Better Life projects, Fiji, Kenya, Cayman Islands, Nepal, Costa Rica, Pakistan. Govt. of Can. grantee, 1973-83. Mem. Blaine C. of C. Clubs: Masons, Shriners, Demolay. Home: J3 Rural Route 2 Nanaimo BC V9R 5K2 Canada Office: 1045 Howie Ave COQ Vancouver BC V3J 1T5 Canada also Am Bldg PO Box 1587 Blaine WA 98230

JAMES, JON DOUGLAS, rehabilitation counselor; b. Slaton, Tex., June 18, 1939; s. Ivory and Estelle (Houston) J.; m. Jo Ann Stanley, Sept. 8, 1973. Cert. rehab. counselor N.Mex.; diplomate Internat. Acad. Profl. Counseling and Psychotherapy, 1982. Tchr. Home Gardens Elem. Sch., Corona, Calif., 1964-65, asst. prof. edn. Prairie View (Tex.) A&M Coll., 1967-68; asst. prof. edn., asst. to adminstrv. dean, asst. to chmn. grad. council Lincoln U., Jefferson City, Mo., 1969-70; vocat. rehab. counselor III, Carlsbad, N.Mex., 1973—; motivational interviewer N.Mex. State Govt. employees, Eddy County. Chmn. Carlsbad Inter-Agy. Council, 1977-78; mem. prin. screening com. Carlsbad Mcpl. Schs., 1979; v.p. Eddy County chpt. NAACP, 1979-81; chmn. Community Housing and Resource Bd. Served with USN, 1958-62. Mem. Nat. Rehab. Counseling Assn., N.Mex. Rehab. Counseling Assn. (Counselor of Yr. 1978, pres.'s cert. for outstanding service 1978, 82), Nat. Job Placement Assn., N.Mex. Job Placement Assn., Am. Personnel and Guidance Assn., N.Mex. Personnel and Guidance Assn., N.Mex. Mental Health Counselors Assn., Am. Assn. Marriage and Family Therapy, Am. Orthopsychiat. Assn., Internat. Acad. Profl. Counseling and Psychotherapy. Democrat. Home: 2021 Manzana Rd Carlsbad NM 88220 Office: 1095 N Canal Unit 1 Carlsbad NM 88220

JAMES, RICK E., data processing specialist; b. Los Angeles, Sept. 20, 1951; s. Julian B. and Barbara Jean (Minyard) J.; A.A. in Bus. Adminstrn., Rio Hondo Coll., 1982; student Whittier Coll., 1982—; m. June Elise Montgomery, Nov. 17, 1979; children— Jeffrey Scott, Christopher Bradley. Electronic technician Western Gear Corp., Industry, Calif., 1974-75, Delco Electronics Goleta, Calif., 1975; computer programmer, analyst Data Systems Support, Inc., Woodland Hills, Calif., 1977-79; dir. software Ice, Inc., Carson, Calif., 1979-80; pres. James Computing Services, Whittier, Calif., 1980—; pres. Inhouse Systems, Inc., 1983—. Served with USAF, 1969-73. Mem. Am. Mgmt. Assn., Computer Cons. Assn., Assn. for Computing Machinery, Data Processing Mgrs. Assn. Address: 6321 Whittier Ave Whittier CA 90601

JAMES-OLSEN, LACRETIA, business consultant; b. Walnut Ridge, Ark., June 30, 1943; d. Wade Hampton and Vera Marie (Henry) James; children—Tamara, Brent, Angela; m. Rex James-Olsen. B.A. in Psychology, Colo. Womens Coll., 1975; M.S.W., U. Denver, 1978. Team leader intensive treatment unit Excelsior Youth Ctr., Denver, 1973-76; psychiat. intern U. Colo. Med. Ctr., Denver, 1976-78; mgr. corp. tng. and devel. Storage Tech. Corp., Louisville, Colo., 1978-82; pres. James-Olsen, Inc., Golden, Colo., 1982—. Nat. Assn. Mental Health scholar, U. Denver. Mem. Orgnl. Devel. Network, Denver Cons. Group., Am. Soc. Tng. and Devel. (Outstanding Tng. Dept. in Colo. award, 1982). Home and office: 24648 Foothills Dr Golden CO 80401

JAMESON, CHARLES SCOTT KENNEDY, marketing educator; b. Bonnieville, Ky., May 25, 1925; s. Charles Scott and Gillie (Addcox) J.; A.A., Ventura Coll., 1948; B.A., U. So. Calif., 1950, M.S., 1951, M.B.A., 1959, Ph.D., 1963. Asst. registrar U. So. Calif., Los Angeles, 1950-55, adminstrv. asst. to dean Sch. Bus., 1955-58, instr. bus. adminstrn., 1958-61, assoc. prof. mktg. and communications, 1963-82, prof. emeritus, 1982—; assoc. prof. Ariz. State U., Tempe, 1962-63; assoc. prof. mktg. and mgmt. Calif. State U.-Dominguez Hills, 1982—. Cons., Auto Club Soc. Calif., Long Beach Community Hosp., Calif. Dairy Council, Blue Cross Ins., others. Served with USNR, 1943-46. Mem. Am. Bus. Communication Assn., AAUP, Am. Mus. Natural History (asso.), Phi Delta Kappa, Delta Pi Epsilon, Alpha Kappa Psi, Beta Gamma Sigma, Omicron Delta Epsilon, Theta Xi. Home: 624 S Irena St Redondo Beach CA 90277 Office: Sch Bus Univ So Calif Los Angeles CA 90007

JAMESON, DARLENE TAYLOR, sch. adminstr.; b. Shelby, Ohio, Jan. 19, 1938; d. Ervin L. and Elaine R. (Schiffer) Smith; B.A., U. Calif., Davis, 1963; student McGeorge Sch. Law, 1977-79; children—Tammi, Thomas, Traci, Kelly. Tchr. English, Vacaville (Calif.) High Sch., 1963-66; Terra Nova High Sch., Pacifica, Calif., 1966-69; Woodland High Sch., 1969-78, chmn. dept., 1976-78, dean of girls, 1978-80, asst. prin., 1980—. Vice-pres. bd. trustees Woodland Meml. Hosp. Found., 1978-81, pres. bd. trustees, 1981—; mem. Woodland City Council, 1980—; mem. Holy Rosary Sch. Bd., 1973-75. Mem. Am. Cancer Soc., Nat. Council Tchrs. English, Assn. Calif. Sch. Adminstrs., Nat. Council Adminstrv. Women, Calif. Elected Women, Assn. for Edn. and Research, Assn. Mgmt. Personnel, Mensa. Democrat. Home: 609 Del Oro Woodland CA 95695 Office: 21 N West St Woodland CA 95695

JAMIESON, DAVID WILSON, mgmt. cons.; b. West Chester, Pa., Mar. 25, 1947; s. Samuel David and Esther Jane (Wilson) J.; B.S., Drexel U., 1970; Ph.D. in Mgmt., UCLA, 1976; m. Josephine Volpe, Oct. 12, 1968; children—Brian David, Christopher Michael. Adminstrv. asst. Office of Student Affairs, Drexel U., Phila., 1968-70; sr. assoc. MGR Assocs., Los Angeles, 1973-78, partner, 1978—; adj. faculty mem. UCLA, U. So. Calif., Calif. State U., Northridge, Union Grad. Sch. Bd. dirs. Los Angeles Voluntary Action Center, Center for Non-Profit Mgmt. Mem. Acad. Mgmt., Orgn. Devel. Network, Am. Soc. Tng. and Devel. (pres. Los Angeles chpt., nat. v.p., 1980—, pres.-elect 1983, dir.), World Future Soc. Office: 10801 National Blvd Los Angeles CA 90064

JAMISON, DAVID W., marine scientist; b. Portland, Oreg., Apr. 23, 1939; s. Edgar W. and Nina (Ray) J.; m. Susan Elizabeth Porter, Dec. 23, 1962 (div. 1974); children—Adam, Elizabeth; m. 2d, Nancy Louise Kasper, Apr. 7, 1979; stepchildren—Kevin, Keith, Kelly. B.S., Whitman Coll., 1961; postgrad. U. Oreg., 1961-62; M.S., U. Wash., 1966, Ph.D., 1970. Remote sensing scientist Wash. Dept. Natural Resources, Olympia, 1969-70, marine scientist, 1970-74, 78-80, mgr. forestry research and devel., 1980-82, dir. marine research and devel., 1982—, supr. baseline studies dept. ecology, 1974-78; gov.'s rep. U.S. Dept. Interior outer continental shelf research adv. com., 1974-78; cons. NOAA Interagy. Com. on Ocean Pollution Research, Devel. and Monitoring, 1981. Bd. dirs. Boston Harbor Assn., 1980-82, chmn. utilities com., 1981—; mem. Thurston County Shorelines adv. com., 1973-74, 82-83. Mem. Am. Soc. Photogrammetry, Marine Tech. Soc., Sigma Xi. Contbr. articles to profl. jours. Office: Dept Natural Resources Olympia WA 98504

JAMISON, JAMES LEROY, airline pilot; b. Mpls., Aug. 16, 1938; s. Edgar LeRoy and Margaret Opel (Ellis) J.; student Colo. Coll., 1956-57; B.A., U. Colo., Boulder, 1961; grad. U.S. Naval Justice Sch., 1964; student law U. Nebr., 1966-67; m. Tara Kane Finlay, July 13, 1963; children—Erin Kathleen, Jennifer Leigh, Amanda Colleen. Pilot, capt. Continental Airlines, Los Angeles, Houston and Denver, 1967—. Pres. Huntington Beach/Fountain Valley YMCA, 1972-73, Layman of Year, 1973; bd. dirs. Met. Denver YMCA, 1977-79; chmn. bd. Littleton (Colo.) YMCA, 1977-79, bd. dirs., 1975—, Layman of Year, 1977, Lowell Linnes Leadership award Nat. Council, 1978; bd. dirs. Chatfield (Colo.) YMCA, 1980—; bd. dirs. Columbine Knolls Met. Recreation Dist., 1974—, pres., 1978—; pres. Littleton Press Council, 1979—, Meadowridge Homeowners Assn., 1975-78; pres. Jeffco Jets Girls Track Club, AAU, 1979, treas., dir., 1981—; active Littleton Center Cultural Arts; bd. dirs. Denver Regional Park and Recreation Council, 1979—Faith Community Ch., 1981—. Served to lt. comdr. USN, 1961-66. Mem. Air Line Pilots Assn., Alumni Assn. U. Colo., Nat. Recreation and Park Assn. (dir. Midwest regional council 1981—), Colo. Park and Recreation Soc. Club: Rotary (Littleton). Home: 12738 Grizzly Dr Littleton CO 80127 Office: Stapleton International Airport Denver CO 80207

JAMTGAARD, DALE EUGENE, psycho-physical therapist; b. Sioux Falls, S.D., Apr. 30, 1930; s. Arnold L. and Ellen Clara J.; m. Patricia Margaret O'Regan, June 15, 1957; children—Arne, Peter, Paul, Laurel. B.A., Augustana Coll., 1954; M.S.W., U. Chgo., 1956; M.Div., Luther Theol. Sem., St. Paul, 1960. Registered clin. social worker, Oreg.; ordained to ministry American Lutheran Ch., 1960. Social worker Luth. Social worker Luth. Social Service of Wis., Milw., 1956-57; pastor Ascension Luth. Ch., Milw., 1960-67; dir. ednl. services, counselor Luth. Family Service of Oreg., Portland, 1967-80; dir., therapist, cons. Life and Health Ctr., Milwaukee, Oreg., 1980—; founder, dir. Quest Fellowship. Served with USN, 1950-52. Mem. Am. Soc. Tng. and Devel., Internat. Transactional Analysis Assn. (clin. mem.), Humanistic Psychol. Assn. Lutheran.

JANES, JOHN MICHAEL, electronics co. exec.; b. Chgo., Nov. 7, 1931; s. Michael and Tacia B. (Chaltis) J.; B.S., U. Ill., 1954; M.S., Ill. Inst. Tech., 1956; LL.B., LaSalle U., 1975; m. Celine Herzing, Apr., 1980; children by previous marriage—Pamela, Lawrence, John M., Lynda, Christopher, Nicole. Mgr. mfg. engring. ITT-Telecommunications, Chgo., N.Y.C., N.J., 1956-62; mfg. mgr. Raytheon Co., Mass., Calif., 1962-69; v.p., div. mgr. Rucker Co., Oakland, Calif., 1969-72; gen. mgr. Marantz div. Superscope Inc., Sun Valley, Calif., 1973-75; dir. mfg. ops. Vivitar Corp., Santa Monica, Calif., 1975-79; v.p., gen. mgr. Marantz Div., Chatsworth, Calif., 1980—; pres. JKW/Ltd., Internat. Trade and Devel., 1981—; dir. ops. Superscope, Inc., 1979-80; cons. Conejo Valley Bd. Realtors, 1977-78, China Trade and Devel. Corp., Taipei, Taiwan, Lucas Industries, Auckland, N.Z., 1981; faculty U. Calif. Extension, Santa Barbara. Served with U.S. Army, 1949-52. Mem. Am. Mgmt. Assn., Am. Inst. Indsl. Engrs., Sigma Iota Epsilon, Tau Beta Pi. Author: Developing Creativity, 1965; Theory and Practice of Improvement Curves, 1963; Production Line Balancing and Model Mix Optimization, 1969; Productivity Improvement, 1970. Home: 5801 Valley Circle Woodland Hills CA 91367 Office: 20525 Nordhoff Chatsworth CA 91311

JANES, PATRICIA ELLEN, accountant; b. San Jose, Calif., Feb. 16, 1944; d. Albert G. and Grace E. (Freeman) McCracken; m. Clair W. Janes, Nov. 12, 1965. B.Sc., San Jose State U., 1965; M.B.A., U. Santa Clara, 1970. C.P.A., Calif. Mem. audit staff Touche, Ross & Co., San Jose, 1965-67, Chgo., 1967-68; lectr. San Jose State U., 1969-72; tax mgr. Peat, Marwick, Mitchell & Co., San Jose, 1972-80; tax ptnr. Armstrong, Bassow & Potter Accountancy Corp., San Jose, 1980—. Mem. Am. Inst. C.P.A.s, Calif. Soc. C.P.A.s (pres. San Jose chpt. 1979-80), Beta Alpha Psi, Beta Gamma Sigma, Phi Kappa Phi. Republican. Episcopalian. Office: 177 Park Center Plaza Suite 300 San Jose CA 95113

JANETOS, GEORGE PETER, radiologist; b. Hamilton, Ohio, Jan. 18, 1932; s. Peter Andrew and Photini Janetos; B.A., Miami U., Oxford, Ohio, 1954; M.D., U. Cin., 1958; m. Jane Kathryn Hannah, Jan. 18, 1958; 1 dau., Andrea Lynn. Intern, Stanford U. Hosp., 1958-59; resident in radiology Ochsner Clinic and Hosp., New Orleans, 1961-64; staff radiologist Palo Alto (Calif.) Med. Clinic, 1964—, chief radiology, 1975—, also mem. exec. com.; bd. dirs. Palo Alto Med. Found., Community Physicians for Patient Care; clin. assoc. prof. Stanford U. Med. Sch.; del. No. Calif. Cancer Program. Served as officer M.C., USNR, 1959-61. Diplomate Am. Bd. Radiology. Mem. Am. Coll. Radiology, Radiol. Soc. N.Am., Am. Roentgen Ray Soc., Am. Soc. Clinic Radiologists, AMA, Am. Group Practice Assn. (trustee 1981—, v.p. 1981, pres. 1982), Calif. Med. Assn., Calif. Radiol. Soc., Santa Clara County Med. Soc., S. Bay Radiol. Soc. Republican. Mem. Greek Orthodox Ch. Club: Sharon Heights Golf and Country. Contbr. articles med. jours. radiologist; b. Hamilton, Ohio, Jan. 18, 1932; s. Peter Andrew and Photini Janetos; B.A., Miami U., Oxford, Ohio, 1954; M.D., U. Cin., 1958; m. Jane Kathryn Hannah, Jan. 18, 1958; 1 dau., Andrea Lynn. Intern, Stanford U. Hosp., 1958-59; resident in radiology Ochsner Clinic and Hosp., New Orleans, 1961-64; staff radiologist Palo Alto (Calif.) Med. Clinic, 1964—, chief radiology, 1975—, also mem. exec. com.; bd. dirs. Palo Alto Med. Found., Community Physicians for Patient Care; clin. assoc. prof. Stanford U. Med. Sch.; del. No. Calif. Cancer Program. Served as officer M.C., USNR, 1959-61. Diplomate Am. Bd. Radiology. Mem. Am. Coll. Radiology, Radiol. Soc. N.Am., Am. Roentgen Ray Soc., Am. Soc. Clinic Radiologists, AMA, Am. Group Practice Assn. (trustee 1981—, v.p. 1981, pres. 1982), Calif. Med. Assn., Calif. Radiol. Soc., Santa Clara County Med. Soc., S. Bay Radiol. Soc. Republican. Mem. Greek Orthodox Ch. Club: Sharon Heights Golf and Country. Contbr. articles med. jours. Office: 300 Homer Ave Palo Alto CA 94301

JANIS, JUEL MENDELSOHN, university administrator; b. Los Angeles, May 17, 1934; d. Leonard T. and Ida (Miller) Mendelsohn; m. Jay Janis, Sept. 7, 1954; children—Laura, Jeffrey. B.A., George Washington U., 1956; M.S., U. Miami, 1961; Ph.D., U. Md., 1971. Head Start coordinator Dade County Community Action Agy., Dade City, Fla., 1971-73; assoc. prof. Fla. Internat. U., Miami, 1973-75; dir. behavioral sci., assoc. prof. pediatrics U. Mass. Med. Sch., Worcester, 1976-77; exec. asst. to U.S. Surgeon Gen., asst. sec. health Dept. Health and Human Services, 1977-81; asst. dean, Sch. Public Health, UCLA, 1981—; participant profl. confs. William T. Grant doctoral fellow Inst. for Child Study, U. Md., 1968-69. Mem. Am. Psychol. Assn., Am. Pub. Health Assn., Am. Orthopsychiat. Assn., AASA, Assn. for Advancement of Psychology, Phi Kappa Phi. Democrat. Jewish. Contbr. articles to profl. jours., chpts. to profl. books. Office: Dean's Office UCLA School of Public Health 16-035 CHS Los Angeles CA 90024

JANOVICI, ROBERT, city planner, zoning adminstr.; b. N.Y.C., Nov. 5, 1942; s. Murray and Celia (Pollack) J.; m. Susan Wexstein, Feb. 23, 1974; children—Michael, Erica. B.A., UCLA, 1965; J.D., U. San Diego, 1968. Bar: Calif. 1970, U.S. Dist. Ct. (cen. dist.) Calif. 1970. Personnel analyst Los Angeles Bd. Edn., 1968-69; city planner Los Angeles Dept. City Planning, 1969-82, assoc. zoning adminstr., 1982—; vol. Legal Aid Soc. Mem. ABA, Am. Planning Assn. Office: Office of Zoning Adminstrn City Los Angeles Room 600 Los Angeles City Hall Los Angeles CA 90012

JANTZEN, J(OHN) MARC, educator; b. Hillsboro, Kans., July 30, 1908; s. John D. and Louise (Janzen) J.; A.B., Bethel Coll., Newton, Kans., 1934; A.M., U. Kans., 1937, Ph.D., 1940; m. Ruth Patton, June 9, 1935; children—John Marc, Myron Patton, Karen Louise. Elem. sch. tchr. Marion County, Kans., 1927-30, Hillsboro, Kan., 1930-31; high sch. tchr., 1934-36; instr. sch. edn. U. Kans., 1936-40; asst. prof. Sch. Edn., U. of Pacific, Stockton, Calif., 1940-42, assoc. prof., 1942-44, prof., 1944-78, prof. emeritus, 1978—, also dean sch. edn., 1944-74, emeritus, 1974—, dir. summer sessions, 1940-72. Past chmn. commn. equal opportunities in edn., Calif. Dept. Edn.; mem. Nat. Council for Accreditation Tchr. Edn., 1969-72. Bd. dirs. Ednl. Travel Inst., 1965—. Recipient Hon. Service award 8th Dist. Calif. Congress of Parents and Tchrs., 1981. Mem. Am. Ednl. Research Assn. (emeritus), Calif. Ednl. Research Assn., Calif. Council for Edn. Tchrs., Calif. Assn. of Colls. for Tchr. Edn. (sec.-treas. 1975—), NEA, Phi Delta Kappa. Methodist. Club: Rotary (Paul Harris fellow 1980). Home: 117 W Euclid Ave Stockton CA 95204

JANUSZ, NORBERT VICTOR, mfg. co. exec.; b. Youngstown, Ohio, July 23, 1927; s. Peter and Helen (Wydro) J.; B.S.I.E., Youngstown U., 1952; M.B.A., Calif. Western U., 1965; m. Maria Carmen Cabrera, Apr. 17, 1951; children—Norma, Maria, Monica, Victor, Karla. Plant mgr. Hexcel Corp., San Francisco, 1965-70, Gen. Dynamics-Electronics, San Diego, 1970-73; mgr. mfg. services Rainbird Sprinkler, Glendora, Calif., 1973-75; mgr. mfg. Criton Corp., Kent, Wash., 1975—; cons. in field. Served with USAAF, 1946-47. Mem. Am. Inst. Indsl. Engrs., Am. Inst. Plant Engrs., Am. Prodn. and Inventory Control Soc. Contbr. articles to profl. jours. Home: 8000 SE 65 St Mercer Island WA 98040 Office: 19819 84 St S Kent WA 98031

JANWAY, DALE WAYNE, mining co. exec.; b. Carlsbad, N.Mex., Oct. 17, 1944; s. Ardell Haskell and Gloria Kathryn Janway; student N.Mex. State U., Carlsbad, 1963-64; student in bus. adminstrn. Internat. Corr. Schs., 1967; m. Cheryle Jean Allen, May 30, 1966; children—Scott, Robin, Stephen. With U.S. Borax Co., Carlsbad, 1963-73, Teledyne Potash Co., 1973-74; safety supr. Mississippi Chem. Corp., Carlsbad, from 1974, now mgr. safety and tng.; condr. safety and emergency care workshops. Pres., Eddy County (N.Mex.) Young Republicans, 1966; organizational vice chmn. Eddy County Central Rep. Com. Interagy. Council, 1979-80, sec., 1980; bd. dirs. Pecos Valley Mental Health, 1975, sec.-treas., 1976, v.p., 1977, pres., 1978-79; pres. Carlsbad Area Counseling and Resources Center, 1979; bd. dirs. N.Mex. Dist. 6 Mental Health Bd.; Eddy County coordinator for Congressman Joe Skeen, 1980-82; bd. dirs. Hacienda de Esperenza; co-chmn. United Way campaign, 1981, campaign gen. chmn., 1982, v.p., mem. exec. com.,1973; chmn. Eddy County Republican Party, 1983; mem. N.Mex. Behavioral Health Adv. Group Com., 1979. Served with USNG. Mem. Am. Soc. Indsl. Security, Nat. Safety Mgmt. Soc. (N.Mex. v.p. ops. 1979-80), N.Mex. Mining Assn. (Operator of Yr. 1976, 77, 78), Am. Soc. Safety Engrs., Nat. Safety Council (Mining Div. winner 1977, 78, 79, award of Merit 1978), N.Mex. Mine Rescue Assn., Carlsbad C. of C. (legis., edn. coms.), Potash Basin Safety Engrs. Assn. (chmn. 1979-80). Baptist. Club: Elks. Office: PO Box 101 Carlsbad NM 88220

JAPENGA, JACK WALLACE, radiologist; b. Chgo., June 22, 1928; s. Jacob Martin and Theresa Alberta (Jaax) J.; Ph.B., U. Chgo., 1949, M.D., 1953; m. Laurena Booker, Nov. 1, 1952; children—William Martin, Ann Theresa, Charles Albert, Diana. Intern, USPHS Hosp., San Francisco, 1953-54; resident in radiology U. Chgo., 1956-59; practice medicine specializing in radiology, Glendora, Calif., 1959—; mem. staffs Magan Med. Clinic, Covina, Calif., San Dimas (Calif.) Community Hosp., Foothill Presbyn. Hosp., Glendora, Glendora Community Hosp.; chmn. pub. health commn. County of Los Angeles, 1975-82; former chief of staff Glendora Community Hosp., San Dimas Community Hosp.; dir. InBank, InBancorp. Served with USPHS, 1953-56. Mem. Am., Calif. (ho. of dels.), Los Angeles County (past pres. Foothill Dist.) med. assns.,

Am. Coll. Radiology, Los Angeles Radiol. Soc., Calif. Radiology Soc. Am. Fedn. Physicians and Dentists (pres. Calif. council), Glendora Radiol. Assn. Inc. (pres., dir.), Am. Thermographic Soc. Republican. Home: 2452 N Cameron St Covina CA 91724 Office: 210 S Grand St Glendora CA 91740

JAPPELLE, JOYCE E., management consultant; b. N.Y.C., Apr. 26, 1945. B.S. in Edn., Bklyn. Coll., 1966, M.S. in Edn., 1969. Tchr., N.Y.C. Pub. Schs., 1966-73; asst. prof. edn. Met. State Coll., Denver, 1974-76; dir. human devel. Nat. Farmers Union Ins., Denver, 1978-83; mgmt. cons.; instr. Regis Coll., Denver, U. Colo., Boulder. Recipient Colo. Service award, 1977. Mem. Exec. Profl. Women's Council, Am. Soc. Tng. and Devel. (pres.-elect), Nat. Soc. Performance and Instrn., Colo. Humane Soc., Longmont Humane Soc., AAUW.

JAQUITH, GEORGE OAKES, ophthalmologist; b. Caldwell, Idaho, July 29, 1916; s. Gail Belmont and Myrtle (Burch) J.; B.A., Coll. Idaho, 1938; M.B., Northwestern U., 1942, M.D., 1943; m. Pearl Elizabeth Taylor, Nov. 30, 1939; children—Patricia Ann Jaquith Mueller, George, Michele Eugenie Jaquith Smith. Intern, Wesley Meml. Hosp., Chgo., 1942-43; resident ophthalmology U.S. Naval Hosp., San Diego, 1946-48; pvt. practice medicine, specializing in ophthamology, Brawley, Calif., 1948—; pres. Pioneers Meml. Hosp. staff, Brawley, 1953; dir., exec. com. Calif. Med. Eye Council, 1960—; v.p. Calif. Med. Eye Found., 1976—. Sponsor Anza council Boy Scouts Am., 1966—. Gold card holder Republican Assos., Imperial County, Calif., 1967-68. Served with M.C., USN, 1943-47; PTO. Mem. Imperial County Med. Soc. (pres. 1961), Calif. Med. Assn. (del. 1961—), Nat., So. Calif. (dir. 1966—, chmn. med. adv. com. 1968-69) socs. prevention blindness, Calif. Assn. Ophthalmology (treas. 1976—), San Diego, Los Angeles ophthal. socs., Los Angeles Research Study Club, Nathan Smith Davis Soc., Coll. Idaho Assos., Am. Legion, VFW, Res. Officers Assn., Basenji Assn., Nat. Geneal. Soc., Phi Beta Pi, Lambda Chi Alpha. Presbyn. (elder). Clubs: Cuyamaca (San Diego); Elks. Home: 665 S Western Ave Brawley CA 92227 Office: 116 N Plaza St Brawley CA 92227

JARAMILLO, MARI-LUCI, university dean; b. Las Vegas, N.Mex., June 19, 1928; d. Maurilio and Elvira (Ruiz) Antuna; m. J. Heriberto Jaramillo, Jan. 3, 1972. B.A., N.Mex. Highlands U., 1955, M.A., 1959; Ph.D., U. N.Mex., 1970. Tchr., Las Vegas Schs., 1955-64; prof. U. N.Mex., Albuquerque, 1964-76, prof., spl. asst. to pres., 1981—, assoc. dean Coll. Edn.; ambassador, Honduras, 1977-80. Recipient N.Mex. Disting. Citizen award Gov. N.Mex., 1977; Medal of Honor, Hispanic U., 1982. Mem. Assn. Supervision and Curriculum Devel., Mexican Am. Women's Assn. Democrat. Roman Catholic. Home: 2301 Artesanos Ct NW Albuquerque NM 87107 Office: Coll Edn U NM Albuquerque NM 87131

JARMAN, BERNARD ALVIN, psychotherapist; b. Harmon AFB, Nfld., Can., May 15, 1948; s. Clarence Bernard and Stella Mary (White) J., B.A. (Achievement Award scholar, A.S. Sullivan Award scholar), Rollins Coll., 1970; M.A. in Counseling Psychology, Chapman Coll., 1975; Ph.D. in Counseling Psychology (tuition scholar), Ariz. State U., 1982; m. Deborah Ann Smith, June 30, 1971; 1 son, Todd Wellington. Biology tchr., tennis coach Bishop Moore High Sch., Orlando, Fla., 1970-71; psychology asst. to chief psychologist Naval Regional Med. Center, San Diego, Calif., 1971-75; psychotherapist Muscles Shoals Mental Health Center, Florence, Ala., 1975-77; counseling psychology intern The Center, Mesa Luth. Hosp., Ariz., 1977-78, staff psychotherapist, 1978—; cons. Lauderdale County Probation Dept., Home Health Agy., HELP, Inc. Vol. staff counselor Newman Center of Rollins Coll., 1970-71; personnel adv. com. Muscles Shoals Mental Health Center, 1977. Served with USN, 1971-75. Recipient George Washington cert. Freedoms Found., 1975. Mem. Am. Psychol. Assn., Ariz. Psychol. Assn. (assoc.), Ariz. Assn. Health Psychology (assoc.), Pi Lambda Theta. Roman Catholic. Contbr. to Power Over Your Pain Without Drugs (Neal H. Olshan), 1980. Home: 1206 W Alamo Dr Chandler AZ 85224 Office: Mesa Lutheran Hospital 525 W Brown Rd Mesa AZ 85201

JARMAN, JAMES PETER, advertising executive; b. N.Y.C., Aug. 11, 1931; s. James Roger and Ruth Elizabeth (McNamara) J. Student U. Colo., 1949-51; A.B., Columbia U., 1958. Advt. mgr. Careers Inc., N.Y.C., 1960-66; copywriter, account exec. Warner, Bicking and Fenwick, N.Y.C., 1966-70; account exec. Mohr and Co., N.Y.C., 1970-73; exec. v.p., ptnr. Jarman, Spitzer and Felix, N.Y.C. and San Diego, 1973—. Served in USAF, 1951-55.

JARMIE, NELSON, physicist; b. Santa Monica, Calif., Mar. 24, 1928; s. Louis and Ruth (Wydman) J.; B.S., Calif. Inst. Tech., 1948; Ph.D., U. Calif.-Berkeley, 1953. Staff mem. Los Alamos Nat. Lab., 1953—. Vis. prof. U. Calif.-Santa Barbara, 1960; adj. prof. U. N.Mex., 1957-71; mem. adv. council Los Alamos Grad. Center, 1958—, participant Vis. Scientist Program, 1965-71. Contbr. numerous articles on nuclear physics, medium-energy particle physics and astrophysics to sci. jours. Mem. Econ. Devel. Council Los Alamos County, 1968. Fellow Am. Phys. Soc., AAAS; mem. Am. Assn. Physics Tchrs., Sigma Xi, Tau Beta Pi. Office: Los Alamos Nat Lab Los Alamos NM 87545

JARRELL, WESLEY MICHAEL, soil science educator, researcher, consultant; b. Forest Grove, Oreg., May 23, 1948; s. Burl Omer and Edith LaVerne (Sahnow) J.; m. Linda Ann Illig, June 24, 1972; children—Benjamin George, Emily Theresa. B.A., Stanford U., 1970; M.S., Oreg. State U., 1974, Ph.D., 1976. Grad. research asst. Oreg. State U., 1971-76; asst. prof. soil sci. U. Calif.-Riverside, 1976—; internat. cons. agr. Mem. Soil Sci. Soc. Am., Am. Soc. Agronomy, AAAS. Democrat. Lutheran. Contbr. articles to profl. jours. Home: 25865 Mountain Park Dr Sun City CA 92380 Office: 2247 Geology U Calif Riverside CA 92521

JARROW, LYLE MITCHELL, mfg. co. exec.; b. Bklyn., July 20, 1923; s. S. Morrell Hirst and Miriam Cee Jarrow; B.S. in Chem. Engring., Mich. Technol. U., 1950. Process engr. Northrop Aircraft, Hawthorne, Calif., 1951-54; mfg. engr. Narmco Mfg., LaMesa, Calif., 1954-57; sr. process engr. Swedlow Plastics, Los Angeles, 1957-60; chief process engr. Deutsch Connector, Banning, Calif., 1960-62; sr. specialist process engring. Douglass Aircraft, Santa Monica and Seal Beach, Calif., 1962-63; chief applied research ITT Cannon Electric, Anaheim, Calif., 1963-65; product mgr. component assemblies Teledyne Semicondr., Hawthorne, 1965-72; chmn. bd. dirs., pres. Advanced Devel. Corp., Oxnard, Calif., 1972-76; chmn. bd. dirs., pres. ADC Resins, Ventura, Calif., 1976—. Mem. mgmt. adv. panel Chem. Week, 1977-79; v.p. bd. dirs. The Villages. Served with USAAF, 1942-45. Mem. Los Angeles Rubber Group, Soc. Aerospace Materials and Process Engrs. Patentee in field; formulator numerous epoxy adhesives, exotic silicone, fluorosilicone, fluorocarbon, neoprene elastomers; originator compounds and processes for ablative applications, metal bonding tech., solid state assembly tech. Home and office: 2410 Peninsula Rd Oxnard CA 93030

JARVIS, DONALD BERTRAM, judge; b. Newark, Dec. 14, 1928; s. Benjamin and Esther (Golden) J.; B.A., Rutgers U., 1949; J.D., Stanford U., 1952; m. Rosalind C. Chodorcove, June 13, 1954; children—Nancy, Brian, Joanne. Admitted to Calif. bar, 1953; law clk. Justice John W. Shenk, Calif. Supreme Ct., 1953-54; asso. Erskine, Erskine & Tulley, 1955; asso. Aaron N. Cohen, 1955-56; law clk. Dist. Ct. Appeal, 1956; asso. Carl Hoppe, 1956-57; adminstrv. law judge Calif. Public Utilities Commn., San Francisco, 1957—; pres. Calif. Adminstrv. Law Judges Council, 1978-83; mem. faculty Nat. Jud. Coll., U. Nev., 1977, 78, 80. Chmn. pack Boy Scouts Am., 1967-69, chmn. troop, 1972; class chmn. Stanford Law Sch. Fund, 1959, mem. nat. com., 1963-65; dir. Forest Hill Assn., 1970-71. Served to col. USAF Res., 1949-79. Decorated Legion of Merit. Mem. Am. Bar Assn., State Bar Calif., Bar Assn. San Francisco, Calif. Conf. Pub. Utility Counsel (pres. 1980-81), Nat. Panel Arbitrators, Am. Arbitration Assn., Air Force Assn., Res. Officers Assn., De Young Museum Soc. and Patrons Art and Music, San Francisco Gem and Mineral Soc., Stanford Alumni Assn., Rutgers Alumni Assn., Phi Beta Kappa (pres. No. Calif. 1973-74), Tau Kappa Alpha, Phi Alpha Theta, Phi Alpha Delta. Home: 530 Dewey Blvd San Francisco CA 94116 Office: State Bldg 350 McAllister St San Francisco CA 94102

JARVIS, NORMA MARIE, interior designer; b. Sanger, Calif., Oct. 24, 1927; d. William Henry and Mary (Bender) Heintz; divorced; m. 2d, Kenton James Jarvis, Nov. 24, 1951 (div. Mar. 1982); children—Cheryl M., Jeffrey Kent. Apprentice interior designer LeRoy's, Fresno, Calif., 1950-56; founder, owner Golden Dawn Interiors, Fresno, 1956-74, San Luis Obispo, Calif., 1974-78; owner Interiors by Norma, San Luis Obispo, 1981—; personnel dir., advisor Grad. Restaurants, Inc. Grad. Restaurants II, Inc., 1972—. Pres. John Washington Sch. PTA, 1968. Assoc. mem. Am. Soc. Interior Designers. Methodist. Club: Fresno Cotton Wives Aux. (past pres.). Home: 2460 Coburn Ln Apt G Shell Beach CA 93449 Office: 990 Industrial Way San Luis Obispo CA 93449

JARVIS, PAUL SAMUEL, hotel chain exec.; b. Schenectady, Jan. 5, 1937; s. Samuel Frank and Mary Jane (Moraski) J.; B.A. in Econs., U. Coll., 1959; M.B.A., U. Pa., 1961; m. Jacquelyn T. Buksa, Feb. 9, 1963; children—Jeffrey, Todd. Mgr. advt. and sales promotion Gen. Electric Co., N.Y.C., 1962-68; dir. mktg. Mohawk Airlines, Utica, N.Y., 1968-70; mgr. leisure mktg. Eastern Air lines, N.Y.C., 1970-71; gen. mgr. Norton Sealants, Granville, N.Y., 1972; v.p. leisure mktg. and sales Hertz Corp., N.Y.C., 1972-75; v.p. mktg. and sales Bekins Co., Los Angeles, 1975-79; v.p. U.S. Photog. Sales div. Vivitar Corp., Santa Monica, Calif., 1979-80; v.p. mktg. and sales Del Webb Hotel Group, Las Vegas, Nev., 1980—. Served with U.S. Army, 1961. Mem. Sales and Mktg. Execs., Union Coll. Alumni Assn. Democrat. Roman Catholic. Home: 3361 S Westwind Rd Las Vegas NV 89102 Office: Del Webb Hotels 300 S 4th St Las Vegas NV 89101

JARVIS, STEPHEN BAYARD, safety manager; b. Anchorage, Feb. 18, 1950; s. Irby B. and Lois Jeanne (Carter) J. Student Tex. A&M U., 1968, U. Md., Tokyo, 1969-70, Universidad De Guanajuato, Mex., 1970-71; B.A. in Polit. Sci., U. Tex., El Paso, 1976. Advt. mgr. Alpha Distbg. Corp., Austin, Tex., 1976; forestry technician U.S. Forest Service, Gila Nat. Forest, 1977-79; safety asst. Sharon Steel Corp., Bayard N.Mex., 1979-80; safety engr. Quintana Minerals Corp., Hillsboro, N.Mex., 1980—. Mem. Am. Soc. Safety Engrs., Am. Trucking Assn. Council Safety Suprs., Nat. Safety Council, N. Mex. E.M.T. Registry. Clubs: Hillsboro Rugby and Rowing. Home: PO Box 502 Hillsboro NM 88042 Office: PO Drawer 472 Truth or Consequences NM 87901

JARVIS, STEVEN LEE, corporate executive, engineer, researcher; b. Herkimer, N.Y., July 1, 1949; s. Alexander Bruce and Lucille Margaret (Rankins) J.; m. Cynthia Sue Turner, June 12, 1961; 1 son, Christopher. B.S. in Elec. Engring., SUNY, 1972; M.B.A. in Fin., U. N.Mex., 1982. Staff research electro-optics TRW, Redondo Beach, Calif., 1973-78, project mgr. laser tech., 1976-78, product line mgr. laser systems, 1981—; dist. office mgr. TRW, Albuquerque, 1978-81. Bd. dirs. N.Mex. Symphony Orch. Music Festival, 1982. Mem. AIAA, Tech. Mktg. Soc. Am., Theta Chi. Republican. Clubs: TRW Recorder, Ski and Golf. Contbr. articles to profl. jours. Home: 23526 Carlow Rd Torrance CA 90505 Office: TRW MS-81/1673 1 Space Pk Redondo Beach CA 90278

JASKIE, JAMES EDWARD, mechanical engineer; b. Chgo., Feb. 18, 1951; s. Zygmunt and Genevieve Louise (Mikosz) J.; B.S.E., Ariz. State U., 1973, Ph.D., 1980; m. Cynthia Ann Black, May 22, 1973; children—Michael, Kristen. Research staff Los Alamos Sci. Lab., 1977; v.p. Black & Ryan Engring., Phoenix, 1982—; mem. engring. staff Motorola (G.E.D.), Scottsdale, Ariz., 1980-82, sr. scientist semicondr. sector, 1982—; sr. scientist Solavolt Internat. (Joint Solar Energy Venture of Motorola and Shell Oil), 1982—; cons. Magma Engring., Queen Creek, Ariz., 1979—; mem. faculty Ariz. State U., Tempe, 1980—. Mem. AIAA, ASME, Sigma Xi, Tau Beta Pi, Eta Kappa Nu. Contbr. articles to profl. jours. Home: 8323 E Monterey Way Scottsdale AZ 85251 Office: PO Box 2934 Phoenix AZ 85062

JASMER, DAVID L., educator; b. South Milwaukee, Wis., Oct. 17, 1942; s. Joseph Henry and Ruth Evelyn (Stevens) J.; 1 dau. by previous marriage, Sharon Kaye. B.S., U. Wis., LaCrosse, 1969; M.A., U. No. Colo., 1972, Ed.D., 1980; grad. Preacher Lewis Sch. Ministry, Albuquerque, 1983. Tchr. English, speech, pub. schs., DeSoto, Wis., 1969-70, Fountain-Ft. Carson High Sch., Fountain, Colo., 1970-71; tchr. English, reading, Apache culture Globe (Ariz.) High Sch., 1974-75; tchr. English, reading Window Rock High Sch., Ft. Defiance, Ariz., 1980—; Served with USAF, 1960-64. Mem. Assn. Supervision and Curriculum Devel., NEA, Ariz. Edn. Assn., Window Rock Edn. Assn., Internat. Reading Assn., Nat. Council Tchrs. English. Democrat. Episcopalian.

JASPER, LETTA WALTERS, consumer economics and marketing educator; b. Phil, Ky., Sept. 26, 1919; d. Carlisle and Flossie (Meeks) Walters; divorced; 1 son, Robert Lawrence Jasper. B.S., Berea Coll., 1944; M.S., U. Ky., 1964; postgrad. Colo. State U., 1968-81. Jr. clk. Fed. Res. Bank, San Francisco, Los Angeles, 1944-45; tchr. home econs. secondary schs., Marion, Ky., 1945-46; receptionist, bookkeeper Berea Coll. Hosp. (Ky.), 1946-47; county extension home economist Madison County, Berea, 1947-54; extension specialist in home furnishing U. Ky., Lexington, 1954-55; extension specialist in mktg. info. for consumers, Louisville, 1957-67; extension specialist for consumer mktg. Colo. State U., Ft. Collins, 1967-69, assoc. prof. consumer econs. and mktg., 1969—. Farm Found. scholar, 1961; Nat. Extension scholar, 1963; NDEA scholar, 1964. Mem. Am. Home Econs. Assn., Colo. Home Econs. Assn., Am. Agrl. Econs. Assn., Am. Assn. Consumer Interests, Am. Women in Radio and TV (dir., sec. program planning com.). Democrat. Unitarian. Club: Zonta (Zontian of Yr. award 1983). Contbr. articles to newsletters and newspapers. Home: 221 E Stuart St Fort Collins CO 80525 Office: 152 Aylesworth Hall SE Colo State U Fort Collins CO 80523

JASPER, MOLLY JANE, environmental scientist; b. Zanesville, Ohio, Mar. 19, 1952; d. James Eugene and Iris L. (Kinsey) Jasper; m. Terrence Dale Guilbault, May 20, 1979; 1 son, Caton Andre. B.S. in Environ. Sci., Bowling Green State U., 1974. Lic. wastewater operator, Ohio. Lab. technician, City of Bowling Green (Ohio), 1973-75; sci. tchr. Peace Corps, Fiji Islands, 1975-77; lab. scientist State of N.Mex., Albuquerque, 1979-81; environ. scientist, Santa Fe, 1981—; mem. Gov.'s Com. to Save Our Water. Mem. Am. Water Works Assn., Water Pollution Control Fedn. Methodist. Club: Parencraft. Contbr. articles to profl. jours. Home: 8501 Edith NE Albuquerque NM 87113 Office: State of New Mexico Water Supply Program PO Box 968-Crown Bldg Santa Fe NM 87504

JASTREM, JOHN FRANK, accountant; b. Plains, Pa., May 28, 1955; s. Frank J. and Bernadine J.; B.S. cum laude in Commerce and Fin., Wilkes Coll., 1977. Jr. acct. Andrew Kovalchek, C.P.A., Wilkes-Barre, Pa., 1976; internal auditor Ingersoll-Rand Co., Woodcliff Lake, N.J., 1976; experienced sr. acct. Arthur Andersen & Co., Los Angeles, 1977—, also audit mgr. Mem. Am. Mgmt. Assn., Nat. Assn. Accts. (pres.), Los Angeles Jaycees. Roman Catholic. Club: K.C. Home: 631 1st St Hermosa Beach CA 90254 Office: Arthur Andersen & Co 911 Wilshire Blvd Los Angeles CA 90017

JAUHAR, PREM PRAKASH, cytogeneticist; b. West Punjab, India, Sept. 15, 1939; s. Ram Lal and Maya Devi (Bhatla) J.; m. Raj Trehan, May 15, 1965; children—Rajiv, Sandeep, Suneeta. M.Sc., Agra U., India, 1959; Ph.D., U. New Delhi, 1965. Prof. U. New Delhi, 1963-72; sr. sci. officer U. Wales, Aberystwyth, 1972-75; research assoc. U. Ky., Lexington, 1976-78; research cytogeneticist U. Calif.-Riverside, 1978-81; research assoc. City of Hope Nat. Med. Ctr., Duarte, Calif., 1981; research dir. U.S. Agr. Labs., Research and Devel. Corp., 1982—. Area capt. Am. Heart Assn., Riverside. Recipient Chancellor's medal, United Provinces, India, 1957, Irwin Gold medal, 1957; Harcourt Butler medal United Provinces Bd. Edn., 1958; Golden Jubilee Gold medal Agra U., 1959; Genetics Soc. Am. travel award, 1978. Fellow Linnean Soc. London Indian Soc. Genetics and Plant Breeding, Tissue Culture Assn., Am.; mem. Genetics Soc. Am., Crop Sci. Soc. Am., Am. Genetic Assn., Am. Soc. Agronomy. Author: Cytogenetics and Breeding of Pearl Millet and Related Species, 1981. Contbr. chpts. in books, numerous articles to internat. jours. Discovered regulatory mechanism controlling chromosome pairing in polyploid species of Festuca. Home: 230 W Campus View Dr Riverside CA 92507 Office: US Agr Labs Research and Devel Corp Bldg 4C 12155 Magnolia Ave Riverside CA 92503

JAUNZEMS, IMANTS, jewelry co. exec.; b. Riga, Latvia, Oct. 18, 1931; came to U.S., 1948, naturalized, 1955; s. Max and Elza (Dembrovsky) J.; grad. UN Lang. Sch., 1948; student Lewis Hotel Sch., Washington, 1960-61, U. Puget Sound, 1960; m. Rita Pezkins, Dec. 5, 1969. Investigator, translator Wash. State Liquor Control Bd., Seattle, 1948-50; mgr. Winthrop Hotel, Tacoma, 1956-58; owner Tiki Club, Tacoma, 1958-60; mgr. Fleur de Les, Honolulu, 1960-62; mfr.'s rep., Honolulu, 1962-70; mgr. Rainbow Products, Zamco Jewelry and Alpha Jewelry, Honolulu, 1962—; mortgage broker United Mortgage Co., Inc. Mem. adv. bd. Am. Security Council; mem. U.S. Congl. Adv. Bd.; mem. Republican Nat. Com. Served with U.S. Army, 1950-56. Decorated Combat Inf. badge. Mem. DAV, VFW. Lutheran. Clubs: Tacoma Sportsmen's, Eagles. Home and Office: 2825 A Waialae Honolulu HI 96826

JAY, DAVID JAKUBOWICZ, management consultant; b. Danzig, Poland, Dec. 7, 1925; s. Mendel and Gladys Gitta (Zalc) Jakubowicz; came to U.S., 1938, naturalized, 1944; B.S., Wayne State U., 1948; M.S., U. Mich., 1949, postgrad., 1956-57; postgrad. U. Cin., 1951-53, Mass. Inst. Tech., 1957; m. Shirley Anne Shapiro, Sept. 7, 1947; children—Melvin Maurice, Evelyn Deborah. Supr. man-made diamonds Gen. Electric Corp., Detroit, 1951-56; instr. U. Detroit, 1948-51; asst. to v.p. engring. Ford Motor Co., Dearborn, Mich., 1956-63; project mgr. Apollo environ. control radiators N.Am. Rockwell, Downey, Calif., 1963-68; staff to v.p. corporate planning Aerospace Corp., El Segundo, Calif., 1968-70; founder, pres. PBM Systems Inc., 1970—; pres. Cal-Best Hydrofarms Coop., Los Alamitos, 1972-77, others. Pres., Community Design Corp., Los Alamitos, 1971-75. Served with USNR, 1944-46. Registered profl. engr., Calif., Mich., Ohio. Mem. Inst. Mgmt. Sci. (chmn. 1961-62), Western Greenhouse Vegetable Growers Assn. (sec.-treas. 1972-75), Tau Beta Pi. Jewish. Patentee in air supported ground vehicle, others. Home: 885 Holly Glen Dr Long Beach CA 90815 Office: 5212 Katella Ave Suite 106 Los Alamitos CA 90720

JAY, JAMES EARL, agronomist; b. Salida, Colo., Aug. 31, 1916; s. Cyril E. and Ruby L. (Ramey) J.; student Western Colo. State Coll., 1935-37; B.S. in Agronomy, Colo. A&M U., 1940; m. Margaret O'Connell, Nov. 30, 1939; children—J. Michael, Patricia Rae Jay Nelson. Clk., Bur. of Census, Washington, 1940-41; trainee soil survey Soil Conservation Service, Ga., 1941-42, soil surveyor, Warren, Ark., 1942-43, party leader soil survey, Hot Springs, Ark., 1943-44, Harrison, Ark., 1944-45, Monte Vista, Colo., 1946-51, Chandler, Ariz., 1951-56, area soil scientist, Casa Grande, Ariz., 1956, Tucson, 1956-58, range soil specialist, Phoenix, 1958-60, correlation specialist, Phoenix, 1960-61, asst. state soil scientist, Phoenix, 1961-77; land classifier Bur. of Reclamation, Monte Vista, Colo., 1945-46; soil cons. Espey, Huston & Assos., Houston, 1979-80. Recipient cert. of merit Soil Conservation Service, 1969, 71, 73. Mem. Soil Sci. Soc. Am., Gamma Sigma Delta, Beta Beta Beta, Lambda Delta Lambda, Alpha Zeta. Contbg. author: Landscaping with Native Arizona Plants, 1973. Address: 6112 W Indianola Ave Phoenix AZ 85033

JAY, RAYMOND RALPH, analytical research chemist; b. Chgo., Mar. 30, 1922; s. Alexander R. and Pauline M. (Bochte) J.; m. Janine M. Kwiatt, Nov. 3, 1945; children—Lawrence A., Charles A., Nancy J. Gamiz, Marianne B. B.S. in Chemistry, Ill. Inst. Tech., 1947, postgrad. in Organic Chemistry, 1947. Analytical chemist Sinclair Research Labs., Inc., Harvey, Ill., 1947-55; research chemist Am. Potash & Chem. Co., Whittier, Calif., 1955-56; research chemist, asst. dept. mgr. Aerojet Gen. Corp., Azusa, Calif., 1956-71; v.p., gen. mgr. Analytical Research Labs., Inc., Monrovia, Calif., 1971—. Served to 2d lt. USAF, 1943-45. Mem. Cons. Chemists Assoc. Los Angeles (pres. 1981—), Am. Chem. Soc. Roman Catholic. Clubs: K.C., Elks. Contbr. articles to profl. jours. Home: 3620 N Shadyglen Dr Covina CA 91724 Office: 160 Taylor St Monrovia CA 91016

JAYARAM, SUSAN ANN, professional secretary; b. Stockton, Calif., Nov. 23, 1930; d. George Leroy and Violet Yvonne (Rushing) Potter; m. M. R. Jayaram, July 2, 1960. Student Pasadena Coll., 1951-52; Woodbury Coll., 1961; A.A., Long Beach City Coll., 1979. Cert. profl. Sec. Sec. to mgr. First Western Bank, Los Angeles, 1953-56; sec. to pres. Studio City Bank (Calif.), 1957-60; sec. to exec. vice-pres. Union Bank, Los Angeles, 1962-81; sec. to vice chmn. Imperial Bank, Los Angeles, 1981-82; personal sec. to Howard B. Keck, chmn. W.M. Keck. Found., 1982—. Sec., bd. advisors Citizens for Law Enforcement Needs, 1972-74; corr. sec., dir. Los Angeles/Bombay Sister City Com. Mem. Nat. Secs. Assn., DAR (Susan B. Anthony chpt.), Windsor Sq./Hancock Park Hist. Soc., Assistance League So. Calif., Freedoms Found. at Valley Forge (Los Angeles women's chpt.), League of the Americas (1st v.p., dir.). Republican. Clubs: Los Angeles (dir., sec. 1967-81), Lancer Yacht. Editor: Los Angeles Club Panorama, 1979-80; California Clarion, 1978-80. Office: HB Keck 555 S Flower St Los Angeles CA 90071

JAYE, ROBERT DONALD, architect, planner; b. Chgo., Sept. 10, 1927; s. John Leopold and Helene (Statkiewicz) Jasinski; student Ill. Inst. Tech., 1952-53; m. Evelyne Marie Campbell, May 20, 1958; children—Robert Donald, Scott M., Kurt W., Eric C.; m. 2d, Teruyo Kaneko, Oct. 10, 1975. Pvt. practice architecture and planning, Chgo., 1957-61, Los Angeles, 1962—; co-author plan for deep water internat. port for Chgo. and Gary, Ind., 1958; author plan for Internat. Center Transp. and Trade with off-shore SST airport in Santa Monica Bay, Calif., 1968. Served with USNR, 1944-46. Lic. comml. pilot. Mem. Japanese Am. Soc., Aircraft Owners and Pilots Assn. Prin. works include Playboy Mag. Office Bldg., Chgo., 1957, Playboy Townhouse, 1962, Hugh M. Hefner's Brownstone Mansion swimming pool, grotto, recreation area, underwater lounge, 1961, Richard Young Residence, Malibu Colony, Calif., 1963, Tree Houses, West Mag., 1969, Curtis Sch., Los Angeles, 1983. Office: 2522 18th St Santa Monica CA 90405

JAYME, WILLIAM NORTH, writer; b. Pitts., Nov. 15, 1925; s. Walter A. and Catherine (Ryley) J.; student Princeton, 1943-44, 47-49. With Young & Rubicam Advt., Inc., 1949, Charles W. Gamble & Assos., 1949-50; asst. circulation promotion mgr. Fortune mag., 1950-51, Life mag., 1951-53, copy dir., sales and advt. promotion CBS Radio Network, N.Y.C., 1953-55; sr. copywriter McCann-Erickson, Inc., 1955-58; established own advt. creative service, 1958-71; pres. Jayme, Ratalahti, Inc., 1971—. Producer U.S. Army radio program Music Motorized, 1945-46; editor, producer Time, Inc. TV programs Background for Judgment, 1951, Citizen's View of '52; script editor CBS Radio-UPA motion picture Tune in Tomorrow, 1954; author script adaptations for Studio One and other TV programs, articles and stories in periodicals. Served as sgt., 2d Armored Div., AUS, 1944-46. Democrat. Episcopalian. Club: Century Assn. Author: (with Roderick Cook) Know Your Toes and Other Things to Know, 1963; (with Helen McCully, Jacques Pepin) The Other Half of the Egg, 1967; (opera libretto, with Douglas Moore) Carry Nation. Address: 2306 Leavenworth St San Francisco CA 94133

JEFFE, SHERRY BEBITCH, political scientist; b. Trenton, N.J., Nov. 27, 1942; d. Herman L. and Pauline (Harrison) Bebitch; m. Douglas Jeffe, Sept. 15, 1968. B.A., Goucher Coll., 1964; M.A., Rutgers U., 1966; Ph.D., Claremont Grad. Sch., 1980. Tchr. pub. schs., Trenton, N.J., 1964-65; staff Calif. State Legislature, Sacramento, 1966-68; staff coordinator Calif. Students for R.F. Kennedy, Los Angeles, 1968; polit. cons., press staff Humbert Humphrey for Pres. Campaign, 1968; adminstrv. asst., v.p. acad. affairs Calif. State U., Los Angeles and asst. dir. Center for Study of Spl. Edn., 1969-70; adminstrv. asst. Hon. Jesse M. Unruh, Los Angeles, 1971; investigator/researcher Legislative Ethics/Campaign Financing Study, Eagleton Inst. Politics, Los Angeles, 1971-75; vis. instr. polit. sci. Loyola Marymount U., Los Angeles, 1974-77; asst. prof. polit. studies Pitzer Coll., Claremont, Calif., 1978-82; project dir. Calif. State Legislative Leadership Study, 1982—; faculty U. So. Calif. Inst. Politics and Govt., 1981—; vis. faculty Claremont McKenna Coll., 1982-83. Bd. dirs. Calif. Center for Edn. Pub. Affairs, 1982—; mem. adv. council U. So. Calif. Inst. Politics and Govt., 1980—; mem. Los Angeles County Dept. Health Services Task Force, 1982—; mem. permanent governing bd. Health Systems Agy. of Los Angeles County, 1977-79; vice chmn. Peninsula County Formation Rev. Commn., State of Calif., 1977-78; mem. adv. com. Rev. of Elections Code, Calif. State Legislature, 1975-77; mem. State Central Com., Calif. Dem. Party, 1975-77. Eagleton Inst. Politics fellow, 1965-66; N.J. State scholar, 1960; Goucher Alumni scholar, 1960-64; Proctor and Gamble scholar, 1960-64; Ahmanson Found. grantee, 1982-83. Mem. Am. Polit. Sci. Assn., Am. Acad. Polit. and Social Sci., Western Polit. Sci. Assn., Center for Study of the Presidency, Women in Pub. Affairs, Calif. Elected Women's Assn. for Edn. and Research. Jewish. Contbr. articles to profl. jours. Home: 5019 W 63d St Los Angeles CA 90056 Office: JEF 110 University Park MC 1292 Los Angeles CA 90089

JEFFERDS, MARY LEE, environmental edn. assn. exec.; b. Seattle, July 16, 1921; d. Amos Osgood and Vera Margaret (Percival) Jefferds; A.B., U. Calif. at Berkeley, 1943, gen. secondary teaching certificate, 1951; M.A., Columbia, 1947; certificate Washington and Lee U., 1945. Sec., Fair Play Com. Am. Citizens Japanese Ancestry, 1943-44; adminstrv. asst. U.C. Alumni Assn. book Students at Berkeley, 1949; dir. Student Union Monterey Jr. Coll., 1949-50; mgr. Nat. Audubon Soc. Conservation Resource Center, Berkeley, 1951-66; dir. Nat. Audubon Soc. Bay Area Ednl. Services, 1966-71; curriculum cons. Project WEY, U. Calif. Demonstration Lab. Sch., Berkeley, 1972—. Cons. Berkeley Sch. Dist., Alameda County Schs. Mem. land use com., environ. edn. com. East Bay Municipal Utility Dist., 1968—; mem. steering com. Nat. Sci. Guild, Oakland Mus., 1970-76; community adviser Jr. League of Oakland, 1972-76. Mem. Berkeley Women's Town Council, 1970—. Bd. dirs. East Bay Regional Park Dist., 1972—, pres., 1978-80; bd. dirs. Save San Francisco Bay Assn., 1969—, People for Open Space, 1977—, Calif. Natural Areas Coordinating Council, 1968—; bd. dirs. Living History Ctr., 1982—, Bay Area Environ. Edn. Alliance, 1982—; v.p. Friends of Bot. Garden, U. Calif., Berkeley, 1976-80. Served with USAAF, 1944-46. Recipient Merit award Calif. Conservation Council, 1953; Woman of Achievement award Camp Fire Girls, 1976; Merit award Am. Soc. Landscape Architects, 1979. Mem. Prytanean Alumnae, Inc. (pres. 1969-71, chmn. adv. council 1971-73), AAUW (Calif. com. 1970-73), Nature Conservancy (chmn. no. Calif. chpt. 1970-71), LWV, Regional Parks Assn., Nat. Women's Polit. Caucus, Golden Gate Audubon Soc., Sierra Club (environ. edn. com. No. Calif. chpt. 1973-77), Urban Care, Stiles Hall, U. Calif. Art Council, U. Calif. Alumni Assn., Inst. Calif. Man in Nature, NAACP, Calif. Assn. Recreation and Park Dists. (v.p. 1978—), Calif. Elected Women for Edn. and Research, Nat. Assn. Environ. Edn., Calif. Native Plant Soc., Planning and Conservation League, Cousteau Soc., Soroptomists, Pi Lambda Theta, Mortar Board, Gavel (pres.). Democrat. Adv. com. natural history guide series U. Calif. Press. Home: 2932 Pine Ave Berkeley CA 94705

JEFFERIES, BOYD LAVON, institutional brokerage company executive; b. Los Angeles, Nov. 10, 1930; s. J.B. and Avrice (Boyd) J.; B.S., UCLA, 1952; m. Sharon Klukas, May 13, 1972; 1 dau., Carol B. Ptnr. Noble, Tulk & Jefferies, Los Angeles, 1956-62; chmn. Jefferies & Co., Inc., Los Angeles, 1962—. Mem. Laguna Beach Mus. Art. Mem. Nat. Council Tchr. Retirement, Los Angeles Stock Brokers Soc., Fin. Analysts Assn., Los Angeles Town Hall, Nat. Assn. State Retirement, Beta Theta Pi. Club: Jonathan, Balboa Bay, Newport Beach, El Dorado Country, Palm Desert, Aspen. Office: 445 S Figueroa St Suite 3300 Los Angeles CA 90071

JEFFERIS, ALLEN LEE, electronics co. exec.; b. Eaton, Ohio, Jan. 26, 1938; s. Raymond H. and Glenna D. (Younce) J.; B.S.E.E., Ohio U., 1961; postgrad. U. Santa Clara, 1965-66; mgmt. devel. program cert. Coll. Notre Dame, Belmont, Calif., 1977. Systems integration engr. Hughes Aircraft Co., Fullerton, Calif., 1961-62; various engring. instrn. positions Lockheed Missile & Space Co., Sunnyvale, Calif., 1962-66, sr. missile systems engr., 1966-68; successively sales devel. and tng. engr., tng. mgr., product support mgr. Hewlett Packard Co., Palo ALto, Calif., 1968-78; microcomputer tng. mgr. Intel Corp., Santa Clara, Calif., 1978—. Mem. IEEE, IEEE Computer Soc., IEEE Edn. Soc., Am. Soc. Tng. and Devel., League to Save Lake Tahoe, Sierra Club, Am. Mgmt. Soc., Calif. Acad. Sci. Author Dept. Def. classified documents. Home: 1025 Wunderlich Dr San Jose CA 95129 Office: 3065 Bowers Ave Santa Clara CA 95051

JEFFREDO, JOHN VICTOR, manufacturing company executive; b. Los Angeles, Nov. 5, 1927; s. John Edward and Pauline Matilda (Whitten) J.; grad. in aero. engring. Cal-Aero Tech. Inst., 1948; A.A., Pasadena City Coll., 1951, Palomar Coll., 1978; postgrad. U. So. Calif., 1955-58; M.B.A., La Jolla U., 1980, postgrad., 1981—; m. Elma Jean Nesmith, July 1953 (div. 1958); children—Joyce Jean Jeffredo Ryder, Michael John; m. 2d, Doris Louise Hinz, Feb. 18, 1958 (div. 1980); children—John Victor, Louise Victoria; m. 3d, Gerda Adelheid Pillich, Nov. 29, 1980. Design engr. Douglas Aircraft Co., Long Beach and Santa Monica, Calif., 1955-58; devel. engr. Honeywell Ordnance Corp., Duarte, Calif., 1958-62; cons. Honeywell devel. labs., Seattle, 1962-65; supr. mech. engr. dept. aerospace div. Control Data Corp., Pasadena, Calif., 1965-68; project engr. Cubic Corp., San Diego, 1968-70; supr. mech. engring. dept. Babcock Electronics Co., Costa Mesa, Calif., 1970-72; owner, operator Jeffredo Gunsight Co., Fallbrook, Calif., 1971-81; chief engr. Western Designs, Inc., Fallbrook, 1972-81, exec. dir., 1981; owner, operator Western Designs, Fallbrook, 1981—; pres. JXJ, Inc., San Marcos, Calif., mgr. Jeffredo Gunsight div. JXJ, Inc., 1981—, exec. dir. JXJ, Inc., 1981—; owner, mgr. Energy Assos., San Diego, 1982—; engring. cons. Action Instruments Co., Inc., Gen. Dynamics, Alcyon Corp., Systems Exploration, Inc. (all San Diego); dir. Indian World Corp. Mem. San Diego County Border Task Force on Undocumented Aliens, 1979-80, 81-82; chmn. Native Californian Coalition, 1982—. Served with U.S. Army, 1951-53. Recipient Superior Service Commendation U.S. Naval Ordnance Test Sta., Pasadena, 1959. Mem. Nat. Hist. Soc., Nat. Rifle Assn. (life), San Diego Zool. Soc., Sierra Club, Nat. Wildlife Fedn. Republican. Patentee: agrl. frost control system, deep sea pressure hull, internal combustion engine emission control, vehicle off-road drive system, recoil absorbing system for firearms, telescope sight mounting system for firearms, breech mech. sporting firearm, elec. switch activating system, others. Home: 1629 Via Monserate Fallbrook CA 92028 Office: 133 N Pacific St Suite D San Marcos CA 92069

JEFFREY, D. BALFOUR, psychologist; b. Washington, May 3, 1943; s. H. Newman and Mildred Jeffrey; B.S., Wayne State U., 1968; M.A., U. Utah, 1971, Ph.D., 1973; m. Rashel Levine, Dec. 20, 1968; children—Erica Rose, Thomas Balfour. Asst. prof. psychology Emory U., Atlanta, 1973-76; asst. prof. U. Mont., Missoula, 1976-79, asso. prof. psychology, 1979. NIMH trainee, 1968-71. Mem. Am. Psychol. Assn., Assn. for Advancement of Behavior Therapy, AAAS, Western Psychol. Assn., NAACP. Democrat. Author: Take it Off and Keep It Off: A Behavioral Program for Weight Loss and Health Living, 1977. Office: Dept Psychology Univ Mont Missoula MT 59812

JEFFREY, DAVID GORDON, advertising agency executive; b. Pawtucket, R.I., July 31, 1946; s. David Gordon and Clara Ellen (Wilson) J.; m. Pamela Kunatz, Jan. 25, 1980; 1 dau., Alexandra Elizabeth. B.A., Furman U., 1968; M.B.A., Wake Forest U., 1971. With mktg. staff Hanes Corp., Winston-Salem, N.C., 1969-71, Wilson Sporting Goods Co., Chgo., 1971-73, Levi Strauss & Co., San Francisco, 1973-74; pres., creative dir. David/MacAlister/Jeffrey Inc. subs. Gt. Western Sporting Goods Co. Inc., Caledonia Group Inc., San Francisco, 1974—. Dir. San Francisco Advt. Softball League, 1978-80, commr., 1981-83. Served to 1st lt. U.S. Army, 1968-69. Republican. Episcopalian. Home: 5009 Diamond Heights Blvd San Francisco CA 94131 Office: David/MacAlister/Jeffrey Inc 1668 Lombard St San Francisco CA 94123

JEFFRIES, ROBERT ALAN, physicist; b. Indpls., Nov. 11, 1933; s. Seth Manes and Mary Elizabeth (Christmas) J.; B.S., U. Okla., 1954, M.S., 1961, Ph.D., 1965; m. Kelly Grisso, June 5, 1954; children—Russell A., D. Craig. Project engr. Pontiac (Mich.) Motor div. Gen. Motors Corp., 1954-55; mem. staff Los Alamos Sci. Lab., 1957-76, group leader, 1976-77, asst. div. leader, 1977-79, program mgr., 1979-83, office leader nat. security programs, 1983—. Chmn. Los Alamos County Econ. Devel. Council, 1967; bd. dirs. Los Alamos Cancer Clinic, 1977-80. Served with USAF, 1955-57. Mem. Am. Phys. Soc., Sigma Xi. Home: 160 La Cueva Los Alamos NM 87544

JEGHERS, SANDERSON JOHN, hosp. adminstr.; b. Boston, May 7, 1945; s. Harold Joseph and Isabel Jean (Wile) J.; m. Kathleen Marie Guiney, Apr. 21, 1982; B.B.A., U. Miami, 1972; M.B.A., George Washington U., 1974. Adminstrv. intern St. Vincent Hosp., Worcester, Mass., 1969-71; adminstrv. resident St. Luke's Hosp. Med. Center, Phoenix, 1973-74, asst. adminstr., 1974-76; sr. mktg. cons. Ernst & Whinney, Los Angeles, 1977-78; asst. dir. Santa Monica (Calif.) Hosp. Med. Center, 1978-80, sr. v.p., 1980-83; pres., chief exec. officer Overlake Meml. Hosp., Bellevue, Wash., 1983—; dir. H.A.S.S., Inc., Los Angeles; guest lectr. UCLA, 1977-78, U. So. Calif., Los Angeles, 1977-78, Golden Gate U., San Francisco, 1980-83. Spl. asst. to exec. dir. Pres. Ford Com., San Diego, 1976. Served with USAF, 1965-69. Mem. Am. Coll. Hosp. Adminstrs., Am. Hosp. Assn., Am. Mktg. Assn., Hosp. Fin. Mgmt. Assn., George Washington U. Alumni Assn., Bellevue C. of C. Republican. Club: Rotary. Contbr. articles to profl. jours. Office: 1035 116th Ave NE Bellevue WA 98004

JELINEK, JOHN JOSEPH, editor; b. San Pedro, Calif., Sept. 3, 1955; s. Joseph Francis and Patricia Valerie (Powers) J.; A.B., Loyola U., Los Angeles, 1977; M.A., Loyola Marymount U., Los Angeles, 1983. Advt. account exec. United Western Newspapers, Santa Monica, Calif., 1975-76; asso. editor E-GO Enterprises Publications, Sherman Oaks, Calif., 1976-77; advt. dir., editorial cons. Select Promotions, Irvine, Calif., 1977-78; editor SCORE Internat. News, Westlake Village, Calif., 1978-79; editor Automotive div. Petersen Pub. Co., Los Angeles, 1979—. Recipient award Calif. Newspaper Pubs. Assn.; lic. competetion driver Sports Car Club Am. Mem. Am. Film Inst., Am. Auto Racing Writer & Broadcasters, Outdoor Writers Assn. Am., Nat. Rifle Assn., Aircraft Owners and Pilots Assn. (life mem.), Nat. Notary Assn., Air Safety Found. Air Safety Found. Roman Catholic. Club: Am. Sportsman's. Office: 8490 Sunset Blvd Los Angeles CA 90069

JELLINEK, L. ROBERT, sales executive; b. Ridley Park, Pa., Nov. 8, 1941; s. Leslie and Gladys Evelyn (Marquette) J.; m. Carol Olga Gonday, Mar. 30, 1962; children—Laura Renee, Sheree Lynne, Derek Anthony, Tiffini Diana. Student Rutgers U., 1969-72, Regis Coll., 1975-77; B.S. in Bus. Adminstrn. and Mktg. Mgmt. magna cum laude, U. Colo., 1977. Cost acct. Johns-Manville Corp. (N.J.), 1960-64, prodn. coordinator, 1964-68, chief scheduler, 1968-70, div. indsl. engr. Finderne, N.J., 1970-72, sr. systems analyst, Denver, 1972-78, pipe div. mcpl. sales, Casper Wyo., 1978-81, territory sales mgr., 1981—. Served with USCG, 1959. Mem. Am. Water Works Assn., Water Pollution Control Fedn., Wyo. Engring Assn., Wyo Water Quality Assn., S. D. Water and Wastewater Assn. Republican. Clubs: Rocky Mtn. Gun (Casper); Falcon Skeet and Trap (Denver). Home: 2024 Kelly Dr Casper WY 82609

JENG, RAYMOND ING-SONG, civil engineering educator, consultant; b. Taipei, Taiwan, Jan. 1, 1940; came to U.S., 1963, naturalized, 1977; s. Juen-hsin and Yuen-lien (Chang) J.; m. Young Y. Tsai, July 18, 1971; children—Lily, Sophia. B.S. in Hydraulics, Nat. Taiwan U., 1962; M.S. in Civil Engring., Colo. State U., 1965, Ph.D., 1968. Registered profl. engr., Calif. Asst. prof. Calif. State U.-Los Angeles, 1968-74, assoc. prof., 1974-79, prof., 1979—, chmn. dept. civil engring., 1980—; cons. ground water, flood control. Mem. ASCE, Am. Water Works Assn., Am. Geophys. Union. Contbr. articles in field to profl. jours. Office: Dept Civil Engring 5151 State U Dr Los Angeles CA 90032

JENKINS, BRUCE STERLING, fed. judge; b. Salt Lake City, May 27, 1927; s. Joseph and Bessie Pearl (Iverson) J.; B.A. with high honors, U. Utah, 1949; J.D. (bd. editors law rev.), 1952; m. Margaret Watkins, Sept. 19, 1952; children—Judith Margaret, David Bruce, Michael Glen, Carol Alice. Admitted to Utah bar, 1952; individual practice, Salt Lake City, 1952-59; asst. atty. gen. State of Utah, 1952; dep. county atty. Salt Lake County, 1954-58; asso. in practice with George McMillan, Salt Lake City, 1959-65; bankruptcy judge U.S. Dist. Ct. Dist. Utah, 1965-78, U.S. dist. judge, 1978—. Mem. Utah Senate, 1959-65, minority leader, 1963, pres., 1965; vice chmn. Commn. Orgn. Exec. Br. Govt., 1965-66; adv. com. Utah Tech. Coll., 1967-72; mem. instl. council Utah State U., 1976. Served with USN, 1945-46. Mem. Am. Bar Assn., Fed. Bar Assn., Utah Bar Assn., Salt Lake County Bar Assn., Phi Beta Kappa. Order of Coif, Phi Kappa Phi, Phi Eta Sigma, Pi Sigma Alpha, Tau Kappa Alpha. Democrat. Mormon. Author articles, essays in field. Office: Room 235 US Courthouse 350 S Main St Salt Lake City UT 84010

JENKINS, B(URTON) CHARLES, plant breeder; b. New Westminster, B.C., Can., June 13, 1920; s. Robert James and Edith Ora (Schofield) J.; B.Sc., U. Alta., 1941, M.Sc., 1944; Ph.D., U. Calif.-Berkeley, 1950; m. Doris Irene Shaw, Sept. 4, 1947; children—Wendie Lou, April Doris, Hilary Charles, Rhett James. Asst. cerealist Can. Agr., Sask., 1944-48, Lethbridge, Alta., 1948-50; assoc. prof. U. Sask., Saskatoon, 1950-54; research prof. U. Man., Winnipeg, 1954-66; dir. research Jenkins Found. for Research, Salinas, Calif., 1968-80; sta. head, sr. plant breeder Dessert Seed Co., Inc. (name changed to ARCO Seed Co. 1983), Salinas, 1980—. Mem. Agrl. Inst. Can., AAAS, Am. Soc. Agronomy, Crop Sci. Soc. Am., Am. Registry Cert. Profls. in Agronomy, Crops and Soils, N.Y. Acad. Scis., Am. Hort. Soc., N.Am. Gladiolus Council, Am. Iris Soc., Sigma Xi. Home: 418A Cayuga St Salinas CA 93901 Office: 1072 Industrial St Salinas CA 93902

JENKINS, CHARLES RILEY, aerospace company executive; b. Coffee Springs, Ala., Apr. 5, 1926; s. Charlie Morrell and Lessi Belle Jenkins; children—Charles Michael, Treasa Louise Friend. M.A., Midwestern U., 1973, Ph.D. (hon.), 1974. Buyer, Bomarc program Boeing Co., Eglin AFB, Fla., 1959-60; buyer-supr. Minuteman missile, Cape Canaveral, Fla., 1961-65, Saturn program, Kennedy Space Ctr., Fla., 1965-71; contracts adminstr. Boeing Services Internat., Inc., Kennedy Space Ctr., 1971-77, contracts mgr., 1977-81, contracts mgr. U.S. Army Nat. Tng. Ctr., Ft. Irwin, Calif., 1981—. Served with U.S. Army, 1944-46; col. Res. Mem. Res. Officers Assn. (pres.), Nat. Contract Mgmt. Assn., N.G. Assn. U.S. Democrat. Baptist. Club: Masons. Home: 1900 Dill St Apt 24 Barstow CA 92311 Office: Bldg 487 Fort Irwin CA 92310

JENKINS, DONALD JOHN, art mus. dir.; b. Longview, Wash., May 3, 1931; s. John Peter and Louise Hazel (Pederson) J.; B.A., U. Chgo., 1951, M.A., 1970; m. Mary Ella Bemis, June 29, 1956; children—Jennifer, Rebecca. Mus. asst. to asst. curator Portland (Oreg.) Art Mus., 1954-69; asso. curator Oriental Art, Art Inst. Chgo., 1969-74; curator Portland Art Mus., 1974; dir. Portland Art Assn., 1975-80; dir. Portland Art Mus., Portland, Oreg., 1980—; mem. gallery adv. com. Asia House Gallery, N.Y.C.; reviewer div. pub. programs Nat. Endowment of Humanities, Washington. Mem. Pittock Mansion Adv. Commn. Bur. Parks, City of Portland, 1975—; mem. Portland Mall art steering com. Met. Arts Commn., City of Portland, 1976-78; co-chmn. Northwest Regional China Council, 1981. Assn. Art Mus. Dirs. grantee, Mus. Mgmt. Inst. grantee, 1979. Mem. Portland C. of C., Am. Assn. Museums, Assn. Art Mus. Dirs., Internat. Hajji Baba Soc., Soc. Japanese Arts and Crafts, Western Assn. Art Mus. art mus. dir.; b. Longview, Wash., May 3, 1931; s. John Peter and Louise Hazel (Pederson) J.; B.A., U. Chgo., 1951, M.A., 1970; m. Mary Ella Bemis, June 29, 1956; children—Jennifer, Rebecca. Mus. asst. to asst curator Portland (Oreg.) Art Mus., 1954-69; asso. curator Oriental Art, Art Inst. Chgo., 1969-74; curator Portland Art Mus., 1974; dir. Portland Art Assn., 1975-80; dir. Portland Art Mus., Portland, Oreg., 1980—; mem. gallery adv. com. Asia House Gallery, N.Y.C.; reviewer div. pub. programs Nat. Endowment of Humanities, Washington. Mem. Pittock Mansion Adv. Commn. Bur. Parks, City of Portland, 1975—; mem. Portland Mall art steering com. Met. Arts Commn., City of Portland, 1976-78; co-chmn. Northwest Regional China Council, 1981. Assn. Art Mus. Dirs. grantee, Mus. Mgmt. Inst. grantee, 1979. Mem. Portland C. of C., Am. Assn. Museums, Assn. Art Mus. Dirs., Internat. Hajji Baba Soc., Soc. Japanese Arts and Crafts, Western Assn. Art Mus. Home: Route 2 Box 331 Portland OR 97231 Office: Portland Art Mus 1219 SW Park Ave Portland OR 97205

JENKINS, JERRY PRESTON, cosmetic co. exec.; b. Roanoke, Va., May 9, 1938; s. Orbrey W. and Mildred R. (Reynolds) J.; B.A. in Econs. and Bus. Adminstrn., Roanoke Coll., 1961; m. Rosetta Albert, May 17, 1969; children—Kimberly, Preston. Dist. sales mgr. No. Calif. and Pacific N.W., Coty div. Pfizer Co., 1977-79; regional sales mgr. No. Calif. and Pacific N.W., Charles of the Ritz, Danville, Calif., 1979-82; v.p. for west coast sales Helena Rubinstein, Inc., 1982—. Bd. dirs. Clifton Forge (Va.) Jaycees, 1967; membership chmn. Charlottes (Va.) Jaycees, 1968. Served with USAR, 1961-64. Democrat. Baptist. Home: 71 St Timothy Ct Danville CA 94526 Office: 319 Diablo Rd Suite 206 Danville CA 94526

JENKINS, LAWRENCE WILLIAM, business executive; b. Portland, Oreg., Dec. 19, 1937; s. Mark Berry and Eleanore (Glass) J.; B.S., Brigham Young U., 1962; M.B.A., Stanford U., 1968; m. Sally Jo Murdock, Feb. 19, 1960; children—David, Julie, Douglas, Janna, Jennifer. With Hyland div. Travenol Labs., Costa Mesa, Calif., 1968-71, dir. product mgmt., 1969-71; regional mgr., v.p. commercialization Devel. & Mktg. Internat., San Diego, 1972; dir. mktg. Advt. Mgmt./Mktg. Mgmt., Salt Lake City, 1973-74; dir. mktg. Vacudent Co., Salt Lake City, 1975-77; dir. mktg. A Dec, Inc., Newberg, Oreg., 1977-80; pres. L.W. Jenkins & Assos., cons., Beaverton, Oreg., 1980-81, Douglas Pacific Corp./Neilsen N.W. Corp., Salem, Oreg., 1981-82, CFG Financial, Inc./EMARC, Oakland, Calif., 1982—. Asso. chmn. Fremont dist. Explorer Scouts Am., 1974, chmn. Fremont dist., 1975-76; fin. chmn. Sunset Trails dist. Boy Scouts Am., 1980-81; del. Utah Republican Conv., 1976. Served to capt. USAF, 1963-67; Vietnam. Decorated Bronze Star; recipient Dist. award of merit Boy Scouts Am., 1976. Mem. Assn. M.B.A. Execs. Republican. Mormon. Club: Sycamore Court. Office: 1 Kaiser Plaza Suite 485 Oakland CA 94612

JENKINS, LLOYD GARY, personnel agency executive; consultant; b. N.Y.C., June 23, 1941; s. Lloyd S. Clyne and Georgia (Keith) Jenkins Burton. B.S. in Polit. Sci., Rutgers U., 1963. Personnel asst. Ford Motor Co., Metuchen, N.J., 1963-65; mgr. employee relations, gen. form div. Tenneco Chems., Inc., N.Y.C., 1965-68; owner, pres. Dunhill Personnel of Harlem, Inc., N.Y.C., 1969-71; corp. personnel adviser Atlantic Richfield Co., N.Y.C. and Los Angeles, 1971-74; dir. employee relations Xerox Data Systems, Xerox Corp., Los Angeles, 1974-76; corp. search cons., ptnr. Robert Turner & Assocs., Inc., San Francisco, 1983—; speaker personnel div. Am. Mgmt. Assn. Bd. dirs. Pride Found., San Francisco, San Francisco Arts and Athletics; co-founder Consortium of Responsible Profls., San Francisco. Mem. Golden Gate Bus. Assn., Bay Area Black Personnel Adminstrs. Democrat. Home: 38 Museum Way San Francisco CA 94114 Office: Robert Turner & Assocs Inc San Francisco CA 94114

JENKINS, MYRA ELLEN, historian, archivist; b. Elizabeth, Colo., Sept. 26, 1916; d. Lewis Harlan and Minnie (Ackroyd) Jenkins; B.A. cum laude, U. Colo., 1937, M.A., 1938; Ph.D., U. N.Mex., 1953. Instr. pub. schs., Climax, Colo., 1939-41, Granada, Colo., 1941-43, Pueblo, Colo., 1943-50; fellow U. N.Mex., 1950-52, asst., 1952-53; free-lance historian and hist. cons., Albuquerque, 1953-59; archivist Hist. Soc. N.Mex., Santa Fe, 1959-60; sr. archivist N.Mex. Records Center and Archives, 1960-69, dep. for archives, 1968-70; N.Mex. state historian, 1967-80; ret., 1980; instr. St. Michael's Coll., 1962-63, Coll. of Santa Fe, 1966-74, 81-82, N.Mex. State U., 1983. Mem. Soc. Am. Archivists, Western History Assn., Hist. Soc. N.Mex., Phi Beta Kappa, Phi Kappa Phi, Phi Alpha Theta, Kappa Delta Pi. Democrat. Episcopalian. Author: (with Albert H. Schroeder) A Brief History of New Mexico, 1974; Guides and Calendars to the Spanish, Mexican and Territorial Archives of New Mexico; contbr. articles to profl. jours. and book revs. Home: 1022 Don Cubero St Santa Fe NM 87501

JENKINS, ROBERT RICHARD, leasing co. exec.; b. Chgo., June 1, 1938; s. Matthew N. and Marion (Shelby) J.; B.S., Loyola U., 1960, M.A., 1962; m. Mary Ellen Thulis, May 31, 1969; children—Tracy Jane,

David Robert. Product mgr. Nat. Steel Corp., Evanston, Ill., 1965-69; sales mgr. Xerox Corp., Chgo., 1969-71; regional mgr. Gelco Corp., N.Y.C., 1971-77, v.p. mktg., Eden Prairie, Minn., 1977-80; v.p. The Van Arnem Co., Bloomfield Hills, Mich., 1980-81; exec. v.p. Republic Fin. Corp., 1981—. Mem. Planning Commn. City of Westport, Conn., 1975-77. Served with USNR, 1963-65. Mem. Sales Exec. Club N.Y., Am. Equipment Leasing Assn., Sales and Mktg. Exec. Mpls., Denver Area Lessors Assn. (bd. dirs.), New Eng. T Register, Colo. MG T Club, Am. Automotive Leasing Assn. Clubs: Decathlon, Mpls. Athletic, Colo. Racquet, Smoky Hill Rotary (bd. dirs.). Editor: Guide, 1978-80. Home: 6212 S Jamaica Ct Englewood CO 80111 Office: 2015 S Dayton St Denver CO 80231

JENKINS, ROGER LESLIE, utilities engineer; b. Staples, Minn., Jan. 17, 1941; s. Leslie Elmer and Mayme Margaret (Hunter) J.; B.S. in History and Geology, U. Minn., 1964; M.S. in Geography, U. N.D., 1971; postgrad. Bemidji State U., Macalester U., U. Alaska, Alaska Pacific U. Instr., Menahga (Minn.) pub. schs., 1964-67; grad. asst. dept. geography U. N.D., Grand Forks, 1967-69; departmental adminstr. pub. works City of Anchorage, 1969-75; cons. geologist Roger Jenkins Geol. Services, Anchorage, part-time 1973—; agreement engr. public works Municipality of Anchorage, 1975; engr. Anchorage Water and Wastewater Utility, 1981—; officer CCCu, Inc., Gravest, Inc., Anchorage, 1973—. Bd. dirs. Alaska Miners, 1977-78; mem. Alaska Republican State Central Com., 1972-76; Rep. chmn. Alaska Dist. 9, 1974-76. Mem. Assn. Am. Geographers, Alaska, N.W. miners assns., Alaska Geol. Soc., Am. Congress Surveyors, Jaycees, CTM Toastmasters, Chugach Gem and Mineral Soc. Republican. Methodist. Club: Moose. Contbr. articles to profl. jours. Home: 3007 Arctic #3 Anchorage AK 99503 Office: 3500 Tudor Rd Anchorage AK 99507

JENKS, KARL THOMAS, computer programmer, researcher; b. Los Angeles, June 29, 1948. S. Lynn Moore and Gisela Vera (Sesse) J.; m. Barbara Jean Kennedy, May 31, 1982. B.A., UCLA, 1970; postgrad. in Math., Calif. State U., Los Angeles, 1970-72. Money mgmt. diplomate Coneducor Corp. Programmer/analyst City of Los Angeles Data Service Bur., 1972—, also project leader Network Communications System. Active 1 gubernatorial, 2 presdl. campaigns Democratic Party. Mem. Engrs. and Architects Assn., UCLA Alumni Assn., Sierra Club. Office: Los Angeles Data Service Bur 200 N Main St Los Angeles CA 90012

JENKS, MARLOWE DRYDEN, hatchery exec.; b. Tangent, Oreg., Mar. 3, 1917; s. Enoch M. and Elizabeth (Moser) J.; B.B.A., U. Oreg., 1941; m. Edna Elizabeth Bowles, Feb. 14, 1939; children—Sharon, Gregory, Gary, Larry. Pres., Jenks Hatchery, Inc., Tangent, 1941—, Shore Pines Inc., mobile home devel., Tangent, 1958—; sec.-treas. Jenks-Smith Corp., 1968—, United Poultry Inc.; dir. Pederson's Poultry, Inc. Bd. dirs. Albany Boys Club, 1964—. Mem. Poultry and Egg Inst. Am. (dir. for Oreg. 1964-73), Oreg. Poultry Hatchery Assn. (dir. 1955—, past pres., Meritorious award 1965), Willamette River Power Squadron (dir. 1973), Nat. Rifle Assn. (life). Methodist (chmn. bd. trustees 1972). Clubs: Masons, Shriners, K.T., Rotary (treas. 1977-81, v.p. 1981-82, pres. 1983-84; Paul Harris fellow); Order Eastern Star. Address: 32521 Hwy 99 E Tangent OR 97389

JENNE, RUTH MARIE, aerospace company financial executive; b. Providence, Apr. 7, 1947; d. Robert Charles and Concetta Therese (Iacovelli) J. B.A., Calif. State Coll., 1970; M.B.A., U. Phoenix, 1983. Paymaster Charlton Co., Compton, Calif., 1974-79; payroll adminstr. Northrop Corp., Hawthorne, Calif., 1979-82, fin. mgr., payroll, 1982—. Recipient Performance Achievement award Northrop Corp., 1983. Mem. Nat. Assn. Female Execs. Democrat. Roman Catholic.

JENNINGS, BRUCE MARTIN, III, service company official; b. Woodward, Okla., Aug. 25, 1947; s. Bruce M. and Ruby Berneice (Locke) J., Jr.; m. Jennifer Littleton, Dec. 23, 1970; children—Beau Ryan, Tate Alan, Erica Lyn. B.S., Tex. A&I U., 1970, M.A., 1974. Div. chemist S.W. Tex. div. Halliburton Services, Alice, 1974-79; mgr. research and devel. Nat. Cementers, Grand Junction, Colo., 1979-80, sta. mgr., 1981—; gen. mgr. U.S. ops. Am. Franmaster, Inc., Chanute, Kans., 1980-81. Served with USNR, 1970-72. Recipient Order of Arrow-Brotherhood, Eagle scout with 2 palms; Rob and Bessie Welder Wildlife Found. research grantee, 1972-74; Caesar Kleberg Fund research grantee, 1972-75. Mem. Soc. Petroleum Engrs. Republican. Presbyterian. Clubs: Country, Eagles. Author: Engineering Handbook, 1980; Products Manual, 1980; Price Manual, 1980; National Cementers Sales Brochure, 1980. Home: 325 Music Ln Grand Junction CO 81501 Office: Box 2370 Grand Junction CO 81502

JENNINGS, FRANK W., III, real estate exec.; b. Eufaula, Ala., May 19, 1949; s. Frank Wilkins and Ruth (Aurin) J.; B.S., U. Ill., 1971; student in Real Estate, U. Calif., Los Angeles, 1975; m. Gloria Fisher, Aug. 11, 1974; 1 son, Jay R. Asso. producer Chuck Barris Prodns., Hollywood, Calif., 1971-73; comml. talent agent William Schuller Agy., 1973-74; comml. investment sales asso. George Elkins Co., Beverly Hills, Calif., 1974-76; owner, pres. Frank Jennings & Assos., Beverly Hills., 1976—; West Coast rep. Jacobs Kahan & Co., Chgo.; Western region real estate mgr. Midas-Internat. Corp., Fullerton, Calif.; cons. to real estate developers, nat. chains; mem. arbitration panel Beverly Hills Bar Assn.; real estate rep. Tuneup Masters, Woodland Hills, Calif. Mem. Beverly Hills C. of C. and Civic Assn., Beverly Hills Bd. Realtors (co-chmn. income-investment div.), Calif. Assn. Realtors, Nat. Assn. Realtors, Realtors Nat. Mktg. Inst., Beverly Hill Bus. and Profl. Men's Assn., Town Hall of Calif., Aircraft Owners and Pilots Assn., Phi Delta Theta. Clubs: Beverly Hills Men's (dir.), Kiwanis (v.p.). Home: 144 N Wetherly Dr Beverly Hills CA 90211 Office: 9701 Wilshire Blvd Beverly Hills CA 90212

JENNINGS, JASON WILLIAM, broadcasting executive, TV interviewer, consultant; b. Ishpeming, Mich., May 31, 1952; s. William Allen and Beverly Mae (Johnson) J. Student No. Mich. U., 1970-72; B.A. in Polit. Sci., U. Detroit, 1974. Gen. mgr. Sta. WUPY-WMOT, Marquette, Mich., 1970-72; exec. asst. to chmn., v.p. radio Patten Corp., Detroit, 1973-76; pres. Jennings-McGlothlin and Co., San Francisco, 1977-81, World Pacific Radio, Inc., Tiburon, Calif., 1981—; cons. and lectr. in field. Active Republican Party. Mem. Nat. Assn. Broadcasters, Nat. Radio Broadcasters Assn. Lutheran. Author numerous books and cassette programs on broadcast mgmt. Office: 106 Redhill Circle Belvedere-Tiburon CA 94920

JENNINGS, TIMOTHY ZEPH, rancher, state senator; b. Roswell, N.Mex., Sept. 4, 1950; s. James Traynor and Frances Mitchell (Schultz) J.; m. Candy W. Jennings. Student N.Mex. State U., 1968-69; B.S. in Bus. Adminstrn., Creighton U., 1972. With Bill Deane Goodyear, San Jose, Calif., 1973; operator Penasco River Ranch, Roswell, 1973—; pres. First Roswell Co.; mem. N.Mex. Senate, 1978—, mem. conservation com., chmn. edn. com. Mem. Chaves County Bd. Commrs., 1974-78; mem. N.Mex. Standards and Goals Com. for Juvenile Justice, 1974-76. Democrat. Roman Catholic. Lodge: Elks. Office: PO Box 1797 Roswell NM 88201*

JENNINGS, WILLIAM PALMER, JR., economist, educator; b. Oakland, Calif., Apr. 9, 1948; s. William Palmer and Florence Ann (Case) J.; m. Kathleen M. Ball, Dec. 19, 1974. B.A. in Econs., Calif. State U.-Hayward, 1970; M.A., UCLA, 1974, Ph.D., 1981. Asst. prof. Calif. State U.-Northridge, 1977—; cons. Klein Assocs., Los Angeles, 1980—. Home: 14302 Summertime Ln Culver City CA 90230 Office: 18111 Nordoff Ave Northridge CA 91330

JENNY, DIETRICH ALFRED, electronics cons.; b. Ennenda, Switzerland, Aug. 15, 1920; came to U.S., 1947, naturalized, 1952; s. Dietrich and Johanna (Tschudi) J.; M.S., Swiss Fed. Inst. Tech., 1946, Ph.D., 1950; m. Selly C. Jenny, Oct. 30, 1954; 1 son, Dietrich IV. Research physicist RCA Labs., Princeton, N.J., 1947-53, head of exploratory research, 1953-58, dir. component research and engring., 1958-60; gen. mgr. Secleta Generale Semicondutori, Milan, Italy, 1960-62; mgr. microelectronics div. Hughes Aircraft Co., Newport Beach, Calif., 1962-65; pres. Iota Ltd., Wilmington, Del., 1965—. Served with Swiss Army, 1939-46. Fellow IEEE; mem. Am. Phys. Soc., Sigma Xi. Republican. Episcopalian. Author: Electronic Semiconductors, 1952; contbr. articles to profl. jours. Patentee in field. Home and office: PO Box 9102 Incline NV 89450

JENSEN, ALAN WILLIAM, bank executive, educator; b. Castle Dale, Utah, Nov. 5, 1941; s. William Charles and Elzora Helen (Jones) J.; m. Mary Joyce Avery, July 29, 1966; children—Suzanne Marie, Mark Alan, Amy Joyce, Julie. A.S. in Journalism, Coll. Eastern Utah, 1962; B.S. in Communications, Brigham Young U., 1966, M.A. in Communications, 1981. Tchr. English and journalism Weber County High Sch., Ogden, Utah, 1967-70; pub. relations account exec. Jennings & Thompson/FCB, Phoenix, 1970-74; store mgr. Vegas Village Shopping Corp., Cedar City, Utah, 1974-76; pub. communications officer Valley Nat. Bank Ariz., Phoenix, 1976—; instr. Glendale (Ariz.) Community Coll., 1977—. Vice chmn. bd. dir. Latter-day Saints Book & Supply, Phoenix, 1980—. Recipient Best in West award Am. Advt. Fedn., 1973, 1st place award nat. specialty advt., 1973; Master's Thesis of Yr. award Found. Pub. Relations Research and Edn., 1981. Mem. Pub. Relations Soc. Am., Phoenix Press Club, Sigma Delta Chi. Republican. Contbr. article to profl. jour. Office: Valley Nat Bank Ariz 241 N Central Ave Phoenix AZ 85073

JENSEN, ALTON DEAN, architect; b. Centerfield, Utah, May 9, 1927; s. Alton H. and Arvilla (Roylance) J.; cert. archtl. drafting Utah Tech. Coll., Salt Lake City, 1950; m. Anita Heaton, Mar. 14, 1953; children—Bradley Dean (dec.), Dale Alton, Ryan Heaton. Chief draftsman, office mgr. Miles E. Miller, Salt Lake City, 1950-54; chief draftsman Robert L. Springmeyer, Salt Lake City, 1954-58; asso. Donald H. Panushka & Asso. Architects, Salt Lake City, 1958-62; practice architecture Alton Dean Jensen Architect, Salt Lake City, 1962—; cons. architect; chmn. adv. com. Graphic Arts dept. Utah Tech. Coll.; mem. master plan com. Salt Lake City Internat. Airport No. 1, 1979-81, No. 2, 1979-81; mem. airport master plan com. Wasatch Front Regional Council, 1979—. Squadron comdr. CAP, 1951-59. Served with USNR, 1945-46. Registered architect, Utah, Nev., Ariz., Colo., Idaho, Wyo., Oreg., Calif., Wash.; cert. Nat. Council Archtl. Registration Bds. Recipient Testimonial Honor award Salt Lake Trade Tech. Inst. Mem. Utah Pilots Assn. (dir. 1978, pres. 1979, chmn. bd. dirs. 1980), Silver Wings. Mormon. Home: 268 U St Salt Lake City UT 84103 Office: 646 S 9th E Salt Lake City UT 84102

JENSEN, ARTHUR ROBERT, educational psychologist, educator: b. San Diego, Aug. 24, 1923; s. Arthur Alfred and Linda Mary (Schachtmayer) J.; m. Barbara Jane DeLarme, May 6, 1960; 1 dau., Roberta Ann. B.A., U. Calif.-Berkeley, 1945; M.A. in Psychology, San Diego State U., 1952; Ph.D., Columbia U., 1956. Asst. psychologist Psychiat. Inst., U. Md., 1955-56; USPHS research fellow Inst. of Psychiatry, U. London, 1956-58; asst. prof. ednl. psychology U. Calif.-Berkeley, 1958-62, assoc. prof., 1962-66, prof., 1966—. Guggenheim fellow, 1964-65; fellow Ctr. Advanced Study Behavioral Scis., 1966-67. Fellow Am. Psychol. Assn., AAAS; mem. Am. Ednl. Research Assn., Behavior Genetics Soc., Am. Soc. Human Genetics, Soc. Social Biology, Psychometric Soc., Psychonomic Soc., Engenics Soc. (London). Author: Genetics and Education, 1972; Educational Differences, 1973; Educability and Group Differences, 1973; Bias in Mental Testing, 1980; Straight Talk About Mental Tests, 1981. Contbr. articles to psychol. and ednl. jours. Office: Institute of Human Learning U Calif Berkeley CA 94720

JENSEN, DONALD CARL, mining consulting company manager; b. St. Joseph, Mich., Sept. 14, 1949; s. Donald S. and Jeanne V. (Erickson) J.; B.S. in Engring. and Math., U. Ariz., 1971; m. Mary Lynn Wood, July 16, 1977; children—Christina, Angela. Co-founder Computing Assocs. Inc., Tucson, 1971-78; mgr. Computing Assocs. Internat., Tucson, 1978—. Served with U.S. Army, 1972-73. Republican. Home: 10660 E Rusty Spur Tucson AZ 85715 Office: 6420 E Broadway Tucson AZ 85710

JENSEN, DONALD EUGENE, mktg. exec.; b. Milaca, Minn., Aug. 25, 1939; s. Elvin Eugene and Cleo Laraine (Hulett) J.; B.S., St. Cloud State U., 1961; M.S., Purdue U., 1963, Ph.D., 1966; m. Janet Ann Folta, June 12, 1961; children—Deborah, Dean, Sean, Julie. Field biologist State of Minn., summers, 1959-60; grad. teaching asst. Purdue U., West Lafayette, Ind., 1961-63; staff researcher Procter & Gamble Co., Cin., 1966-73; asst. prof. Colo. State U., Ft. Collins, 1974-75; pres. Jandon Internat. Enterprises, Ft. Collins, 1976—, Color-Ado, 1982—. NIH fellow, 1964-65. Mem. Nat. Fedn. Ind. Bus., Sigma Xi. Republican. Mem. Christian Ch. Clubs: Order of DeMolay, Optimists (pres. 1976). Mem. editorial bd. Jour. Applied Microbiology, 1974-75. Home: 1801 Pawnee Dr Fort Collins CO 80525

JENSEN, EDMUND PAUL, banker; b. Oakland, Calif., Apr. 13, 1937; s. Edmund and Olive (Kessell) J.; m. Marilyn Norris, Nov. 14, 1959; children—Juliana L., Annika. B.A., U. Wash., 1959; postgrad. Stanford U., 1981. Lic. real estate broker, Oreg., 1972; licensed sales in real estate, Calif., 1968. Mgr. fin. analysis/mktg. and prodn. coordinator Dole/Castle & Cooke, 1960-67; mgr. fin. planning and evaluation Technicolor, Inc., Los Angeles, 1967-69; group v.p. Nat. Industries and Subsidiaries, Louisville, 1969-72; v.p. fin. Wedgewood Homes, Beaverton, Oreg., 1972-74; exec. v.p. U.S. Bancorp, Portland, 1974—. Vice pres. econ. devel. Portland C. of C., 1981-84; bd. dirs. Multnomah County Health Care Commn., 1981-82, mem. blue ribbon com., 1982-83; mem. Gov.'s Econ. Recovery Council, 1982-83; trustee St. Helen's Hall, 1981—; bd. dirs. Sat. Acad., 1983—. Served to capt. USAR, 1959-67. Club: Rotary (dir.). Home: 10210 SW Terwilliger Pl Portland OR 97219 Office: 309 SW 6th St Portland OR 97204

JENSEN, ERNEST M., accountant; b. St. Anthony, Idaho, Oct. 27, 1944; s. Leonard Elmer and Mary Phyllis (Miller) J.; m. Elaine Kearsley, May 26, 1967; children—Lezlie Ann, Kirk E. B.S., Brigham Young U., 1969; M.B.A., U. Puget Sound, 1972. C.P.A., Idaho, Wash. Acct., Crown Zellerbach, San Francisco, 1969; jr., then sr. Wesley A. Bubb, C.P.A., Tacoma, 1973-75; sr., mgr., prin. Burnett, Humpherys & Mason, P.A., Idaho Falls, 1975—. Vice-pres., treas. East Idaho Estate Planning Council. Treas., bd. dirs. United Way Idaho Falls and Bonneville County, Inc. Served with U.S. Army, 1969-71. Mem. Am. Inst. C.P.A.s, Idaho Soc. C.P.A.s (auditing standards com.), Wash. Soc. C.P.A.s. Republican. Mormon. Club: Kiwanis (Idaho Falls) (pres.). Office: 490 Memorial Dr PO Box 700 Idaho Falls ID 83402

JENSEN, ERNST O., general contractor; b. Billum, Denmark, Aug. 26, 1937; came to U.S., 1961, naturalized, 1968; s. Niels Brown Ostergaard and Anna (Hansen) J.; m. Linda Darlene Purcell, Oct. 5, 1968. Gen. contractor, Seattle. Home: 2459 1st Ave W Seattle WA 98119

JENSEN, GORDON REX, mfg. co. exec.; b. Aurora, Utah, Jan. 12, 1935; s. Rex Wilford and Verla (Madsen) J.; B.S. in Journalism, U. Utah, 1956; m. Mary Allred, Jan. 12, 1973; children—Justin W., Jordan David. Sales mgr. Modernfold Industries, New Castle, Ind., 1961-67, gen. mgr. Western div., 1968-69, exec. v.p., St. Lambert, Que., Can., 1970, dir. mktg., 1971-72; owner, pres. Holland Equipment Co. and Interior Space Systems, Salt Lake City, 1973—; prin. partner Jenead Investments. Chmn. bd. trustees Salt Lake City Police Athletic League. Served with USAF, 1957-60. Mem. Salt Lake Area C. of C., Utah Mfrs. Assn., Associated Gen. Contractors Utah, Bldg. Owners and Mgrs. Assn. Mormon. Clubs: Fort Douglas Country, Canyon Racket. Office: 2420 W 2100 S Salt Lake City UT 84119

JENSEN, GWENDOLYN MARIE, petroleum geologist; b. Los Angeles, June 24, 1944; d. Oscar Bernhard and Cora Theresa (Bergh) Jensen; m. Jeffrey Charles Heller, Nov. 25, 1972. B.S., UCLA, 1967. Geologist Cities Service Co., Los Angeles, 1968-72, exploration geologist, Denver, 1979-81, geol. assoc. exploration 1981—; asst. field trip chmn. Rocky Mountain Assn. Petroleum Geologists, 1978; lectr. subsurface stratigraphy Idaho State U., Pocatello, 1981. Mem. Colo. NOW, ERA Taskforce, 1982; publicity com. Colo. Nat. Abortion Rights Action League, 1982; mem. LWV, Denver Women's Polit. Caucus, AAUW, Jung Soc., Women's Equity Action League. Named Woman of Yr., Assn. Women Geoscientists, 1981. Mem. Am. Assn. Petroleum Geologists, Rocky Mountain Assn. Geologists, Wyo. Geol. Assn., Soc. Econ. Paleontologists and Mineralogists, Assn. Women in Sci., Assn. Women Geoscientists (dir., publicity com. 1981). Democrat. Office: 1600 Broadway Suite 900 Denver CO 80202

JENSEN, HAROLD ARTHUR, real estate broker; b. Salt Lake City, June 22, 1924; s. Harold Arthur and Ragnhild Laura (Wedding) J.; student U. Idaho, 1946, George Washington U., 1947; B.A., U. Utah, 1950; M.A., cert. Russian Inst., Columbia U., 1956; m. Helen Jane Larsen, Aug. 27, 1960. Mgmt. cons. Norman Jaspan Assos., N.Y.C., 1956-57, George S. May Co., Chgo., 1957-59; exec. v.p., sec. ICOA Life Ins. Co., Salem, Oreg., 1959-68; cons. Exec. Life Ins. Co., Beverly Hills, Calif., 1968-69; broker A.A. Larsen, Inc., Salem, 1969—. Served with USAF, 1942-45, 50-52. Mem. Am. Hereford Assn. Home: 3635 Bethel Heights Rd NW Salem OR 97304 Office: AA Larsen Inc 3635 Bethel Heights Rd NW Salem OR 97304

JENSEN, HELEN, musical artists mgmt. co. exec.; b. Seattle, June 30, 1919; d. Frank and Sophia (Kantosky) Leponis; student public schs., Seattle; m. Ernest Jensen, Dec. 2, 1939; children—Ernest, Ronald Lee. Co-chmn., Seattle Community Concert Assn., 1957-62; sec. family concerts Seattle Symphony Orch., 1959-61; hostess radio program Timely Topics, 1959-60; gen. mgr. Western Opera Co., Seattle, 1962-64, pres. 1963-64; v.p., dir., mgr. public relations Seattle Opera Assn., 1964—, preview artists Coordinator, 1981-83, bus. mgr. Portland (Oreg.) Opera Co., 1968, cons., 1967-69; owner, mgr. Helen Jensen Artists Mgmt., Seattle, 1970—. First v.p. Music and Art Found., 1981-83. Recipient Cert., Women in Bus in the Field of Art, 1973. Mem. Am. Guild Mus. Artists, Music and Art Found., Seattle Opera Guild (pres., award of distinction 1983), Ballard Symphony League (sec.), Seattle Civic Opera Assn. (pres. 1981-83), Portland Opera Assn., Portland Opera Guild, Seattle Civic Opera Assn., 200 Plus One, Aria Preview, Lyric Preview Group, Past Pres. Assembly (pres. 1977-79) North Shore Performing Arts Assn. (pres. 1981). Clubs: Helen Jensen Hiking, Kenmore Community. Home: 19029 56th Ln NE Seattle WA 98155 Office: 716 Joseph Vance Bldg Seattle WA 98101

JENSEN, MARVIN ELI, agricultural engineer; b. Clay County, Minn., Dec. 23, 1926; s. John M. and Inga C. (Haugness) J.; m. Doris A. Lundberg, Sept. 4, 1947; children—Connie Heidemann, Jeffrey, Eric. B.S., N.D. State U., 1951, M.S., 1952; Ph.D., Colo. State U., 1965. Instr. to asst. prof. N.D. State U., 1952-55; agrl. engr. Agrl. Research Service, Bushland, Tex., 1955-58, Ft. Collins, Colo., 1959-64, Kimberly, Idaho, 1964-69; dir. Snake River Research Ctr., 1969-78; nat. program leader, Beltsville, Md., 1979-81, Ft. Collins, Colo., 1982—. Bd. dirs. Twin Falls (Idaho) United Fund, 1968-74. Served with USNR, 1944-46. Fellow Am. Soc. Agrl. Engring. (Hancock engring. award 1974, John Deere Gold medal); mem. ASCE (Huber research prize 1968, Royce J. Tipton award, 1982), AAAS, Soil Conservation Soc. Am. Lutheran. Club: Rotary (Twin Falls). Contbr. numerous article to profl. publs. Office: 2625 Redwing Rd Executive Plaza Bldg Suite 130 Fort Collins CO 80526

JENSEN, OTTO J., fire chief; b. Coulee City, Wash., Aug. 28, 1929; s. Otto Johannes and Mary (Armbruster) J.; m. Betty June Pierpoint, Apr. 8, 1948; children—Jenifer, Jonathan, James, Jane, Jerry; A.S., Big Bend Community Coll. With Moses Lake (Wash.) Fire Dept., 1956-70, fire chief, 1963-70; chief Olympia (Wash.) Fire Dept., 1970-77; chief Vancouver (Wash.) Fire Dept., 1977—. Mem. Gov.'s Adv. Com., Wash. State Bldg. Code. Mem. Internat. Assn. Fire Chiefs, Wash. State Assn. Fire Chiefs. Clubs: Kiwanis, Elks. Home: 610 Palo Alto Dr Vancouver WA 98661 Office: 900 W Evergreen St Vancouver WA 98660

JENSEN, ROBERT MARTIN, aircraft engr.; b. Denver, Mar. 31, 1926; s. Reuben Maynard and Mary Marguerite (Weston) J.; student Cal-Aero Tech. Inst., 1946-47; m. Ruth Darline Spahr, Dec. 22, 1946. Aircraft electrician Grand Central Aircraft Co., Glendale, Calif., 1947-53; elec. systems engr. Lear, Inc., Santa Monica, Calif., 1953-57; sr. project engr. Pacific Airmotive Corp., Burbank, Calif., 1957-70; chief systems engring. DeVore Aviation Corp., Albuquerque, 1970—; designated engring. rep. FAA. Served with USAAF, 1944-45. Mem. AIAA. Republican. Presbyterian. Home: 14213 Marquette Ave NE Albuquerque NM 87123 Office: 6104 B Kircher Blvd Albuquerque NM 87109

JENSEN, ROBERT TRYGVE, lawyer; b. Chgo., Sept. 16, 1922; s. James and Else (Uhlich) J.; m. Marjorie Rae Montgomery, Oct. 3, 1959; children—Robert Trygve, James Thomas, John Michael; m. Barbara Mae Jensen, Aug. 5, 1974. B.S., LL.B., J.D., Northwestern U., 1949; LL.M., U. So. Calif., 1955. Bar: Calif. 1950. Asst. counsel Douglas Aircraft Co., Inc., Santa Monica, Calif., 1950-52, 58-60; counsel El Segundo div. Douglas Aircraft Co., 1952-58; gen. counsel Aerospace Corp., El Segundo, 1960—, asst. sec., 1961-67, sec., 1967—. Served with U.S. Army, 1942-46; PTO. Mem. ABA, Beverly Hills Bar Assn., Fed. Bar Assn., Am. Arbitration Assn. (nat. panel arbitrators), Alpha Delta Phi, Phi Delta Phi. Home: 10610 Ashton Ave Los Angeles CA 90024 Office: 2350 E El Segundo Blvd El Segundo CA 90245

JENSEN, RONALD ALAN, automobile co. ofcl.; b. San Bernardino, Calif., Dec. 12, 1948; s. Lyle J. and Leila (Wessel) J.; A.B. in History, U. Calif., San Diego, 1971; M.B.A., U. Calif., Riverside, 1976; m. Karen Marie Kirish, Aug. 18, 1978. Vice pres., adminstrv. services mgr. Santa Fe Fed. Savs. and Loan Co., San Bernardino, 1974-78; v.p. mgmt. systems Pacific Fed. Savs. & Loan, 1978-82; corporate office automation and communications mgr. Nissan Motor Corp. U.S.A., 1982—. Instr., Sch. Bus. Adminstrn., Calif. State U. Pres. Inland Adolescent Clinic, 1977-78. Mem. Inst. Fin. Edn. (pres. Tri-County chpt. 1976-77, state dir.). Club: Rotary of San Bernardino (Bus. Exchange award Rotary Found., 1978). Office: 18501 S Figueroa St Gardena CA 92407

JENSEN, VERLYN NADELL, lawyer; b. Reno, Nev., Oct. 31, 1939; s. NaDell and Evelyn (Mitchell) J.; m. Cecilia Diane Hamilton, Oct. 5, 1958; children—Jeffrey, Melinda, Bryan, Jay. B.A., U. Calif.-Berkeley, 1961, LL.B., 1964. Bar: Calif. 1965. Sr. partner firm Jensen, Sanders and

McConnell, Santa Ana, Calif., Washington, 1980—; legis. adv. for Orange County (Calif.), Washington, 1980—; gen. counsel select com. on coms. U.S. Ho. of Reps., 1979-80. Dist. rep. Congressman Jerry M. Patterson, 38th Congressional Dist. of Calif., 1974-79. Mem. Am., Orange County bar assns., The State Bar of Calif., Sierra Club, Boalt Hall Alumni Assn. (pres. 1973), Phi Delta Phi. Office: 902 N Main St Santa Ana CA 92701

JENSEN, WARREN MARTIN, materials and processes engineer; b. Olympia, Wash., Apr. 22, 1941; s. Martin H. and Roberta W. (Vanden Hoek) J.; m. Charlotte A. Anderson, Sept. 14, 1963; children—Matthew A., Jonathan A. B.S. in Chem. Engring., U. Wash., 1964. Registered profl. engr., Calif. Engr., Boeing Comml. Airplane Co., Renton, Wash., 1964-68; sr. engr. Jet Propulsion Lab., Pasadena, Calif., 1968-76; engr. specialist Litton Guidance & Control Systems, Grants Pass, Oreg., 1976-78; group leader, sr. specialist engr. Boeing Aerospace Co., Seattle, 1978—. Mem. Soc. Advancement Material and Process Engring. (1st vice chmn. Seattle chpt., Delmonte award 1982), Inst. Interconnecting and Packaging Electronic Circuits (chmn. working group). Republican. Baptist. Patentee in field. Home: 12017 NE 68th Pl Kirkland WA 98033 Office: PO Box 3999 MS 88 40 Seattle WA 98124

JENSON, DAVID PAUL, accountant; b. Tooele, Utah, Mar. 9, 1945; s. R. Leo and Claris Jenson; m. Lynda S. Homer, Aug. 22, 1964; children—Stacy, Jeffery, Tiffany, Teri. B.S., Brigham Young U., 1967. C.P.A., Calif., Utah. Sr. acct. Solar div. Internat. Harvester, San Diego, 1967-71; with Touche Ross & Co., Salt Lake City, 1971—, mgr., 1977-80, ptnr., 1980—; mem. adv. com. dept. acctg. Utah State U., 1979—. Mem. Am. Inst. C.P.A.s, Calif. Soc. C.P.A.s, Utah Assn. C.P.A.s. Mormon.

JENSON, NORMAN CARLTON, JR., music educator, church organist, choir master, musical theatre director; b. Glendale, Calif., Nov. 3, 1937; s. Norman Carlton and Mildred (Erickson) J.; m. Carolyn Keyser, Aug. 10, 1968; children—Jennifer, Lynn, Lisa Ann. B.A., Occidental Coll., 1959; M.Mus., Ariz. State U., 1970. Music tchr. Wilson Jr. High Sch., Pasadena, Calif., 1963-65, Pasadena High Sch., 1965-69, Coronado High Sch., Scottsdale, Ariz., 1971-72; music faculty Scottsdale Community Coll., 1972—; organist Sepulveda (Calif.) Community Methodist Ch., 1953-55, St. James. Presbyterian Ch., Tarzana, Calif., 1955-56, North Hollywood (Calif.) First Presbyn. Ch., 1956-60, 63-67; organist, choirmaster Camp Smith Protestant Chapel, Pearl Harbor, Hawaii, 1960-63, First Congregational Ch., Pasadena, 1968, First Presbyn. Ch., Phoenix, 1970-72, Scottsdale United Presbyn. Ch., 1972-81, Mountain View Presbyn. Ch., Scottsdale, 1981—; dir. musical theater Calif. and Ariz.; founding dir. Scottsdale Masterworks Chorals; guest choral condr., choral adjudicator, guest organist. Active fin. fund drive Scottsdale YMCA, 1983. Served to lt. USNR, 1960-63. Named one of two American choral condrs. to participate J.S. Bach Acad., Stuttgart, W.Ger., summer 1980. Mem. Am. Choral Dirs. Assn., Am. Guild of Organists, Music Educators Nat. Conf., Ariz. Music Educators Assn., Ariz. Choral Dirs. Assn., Phoenix Fedn. Musicians. Republican. Presbyterian. Home: 8513 E Edward Ln Scottsdale AZ 85253 Office: Scottsdale Community Coll 9000 E Chaparral Rd Scottsdale AZ 85253

JEPPSON, GERALD W., educator; b. Driggs, Idaho, Aug. 7, 1930; s. Gerald Jeppa and Maude Christina (Weekes) J.; m. Joan Cluff, Apr. 2, 1954; children—G. Paul, M. Terry, John D., Marianne, Joseph C. B.S., Ricks Coll., Rexburg, Idaho, 1956; Ed.M., Oreg. State U., Corvallis, 1964; postgrad. U. Utah, 1959, Idaho State U., 1961-70, Boise State U., 1971-75, Eastern Wash. State U., Cheney, 1978. Tchr., Edmunds Sch., Rexburg, Idaho, 1955-57; tchr. Parker (Idaho) Elem. Dist. 215, 1957-62, tchr. Sugar Salem High Sch., Sugar City, Idaho, 1962-63; counsellor Rigby (Idaho) High Sch., 1964—. Mem. Sugar City Bd. Trustees, also chmn. Mem. NEA, Idaho Edn. Assn., Jefferson County Tchrs. Assn. Republican. Mormon. Home: Box 126 Sugar City ID 83448 Office: 125 N 1W Rigby High School Rigby ID 83442

JEPPSON, ROBERT BAIRD, JR., bus. exec.; b. Rexburg, Idaho, Apr. 23, 1920; s. Robert Baird and Elsie (Smith) J.; B.S., U. Calif., 1942; grad. Advanced Mgmt. Program, Harvard U., 1963; m. Edith Abigail French, Jan. 9, 1947; children—Jane Elizabeth, James Robert, Virginia K. Commd. ensign U.S. Navy, 1942, advanced through ranks to capt., 1962; ret., 1969; bus. mgr. Reno Radiol. Assos. (Nev.), 1969-78; broker Alpine Realty Assos., 1971—; mgmt. cons., 1978—; gen. mgr., partner BHLS Investments. Republican. Mormon. Home: 2675 Everett Dr Reno NV 89503 Office: PO Box 7011 Reno NV 89510

JERATH, SUKHVARSH, structural engineering educator; b. Khaur, Pakistan, May 27, 1942; came to U.S., 1971; s. Ram Partap and Raj Rani Jerath; m. Saroj Shahi, Oct. 1, 1968; children—Aradhana, Rahul. B.E., Birla Engring. Coll., Pilani, India, 1962; M.E., Birla Inst. Tech. and Sci., Pilani, 1968; M.S., Brigham Young U., 1972; Ph.D., U. Ill., 1977. Registered profl. engr., Ill., Ind. Asst. prof. civil engring. Birla Inst. Tech. and Sci., 1962-71; teaching asst. U. Ill., Urbana, 1972-74, 75-77; research asst. Constrn. Engring. Research Lab., U.S. Army, Champaign, Ill., 1974-75; sr. engr. Custodis Constrn. Co. div. Research Cottrell, Inc., Terre Haute, Ind., 1977-80; asst. prof. civil and environ. engring. Wash. State U., Pullman, 1980—. Merit scholar Brigham Young U., 1972. Mem. ASCE, ASME, Sigma Xi, Phi Kappa Phi. Contbr. articles to profl. jours. Home: NW 1705 Turner Dr Pullman WA 99163 Office: Dept Civil and Environ Engring Wash State U Pullman WA 99164

JERNIGAN, JEAN ALLEN, adminstrv. asst.; b. Brookline, Mass., May 26, 1923; d. Langdon and Dorothy (Talbot) Allen; A.A., Garland Jr. Coll., 1942; m. Roger R. Jernigan, May 31, 1943; children—Roger, Jeffrey, Bruce, Linda. Fashion and beauty editorial asst. Boston Herald Traveler, 1942-44; news editor Sun Newspapers, Contra Costa County, Calif., 1958-64; aide to county supr. Contra Costa County, 1964-66; dir. public relations Children's Hosp. Med. Center, Oakland, Calif., 1966-68; women's editor, feature writer Berkeley (Calif.) Gazette, 1968-78; dir. public relations, asst. exec. dir. Berkeley-East Bay Humane Soc., 1978-81; reporter Contra Costa Sun, Lafayette, Calif., 1979-80; now adminstrv. asst. to v.p. fin. Cetus Corp. Recipient McQuade award, 1970. Mem. Women in Communication, East Bay Press Club, Contra Costa Press Club. Republican. Office: 1400 53d St Emeryville CA 94608

JERREMS, ALEXANDER STAPLER, aerospace co. exec.; b. Kansas City, Mo., May 9, 1919; s. William G. and Anna (Stapler) J.; B.S. in Elec. Engring., Calif. Inst. Tech., 1942; postgrad. M.I.T., 1946-48; m. Eva Lion, Aug. 22, 1954; 1 son, Brian David. Mem. tech. staff radiation labs. M.I.T., 1942-45, research asso., 1946-48; sr. staff scientist Los Alamos Sci. Lab., 1945-46; tech. dir. aerospace group Hughes Aircraft Co., Culver City, Calif., 1948-70, dir. tech., 1970-82, corp. staff v.p. tech., 1982—; cons. Def. Sci. Bd., Washington, 1974—; mem. engring. dean's council UCLA, 1977—; mem. UCLA Chancellor's Assos., 1979—. Mem. Sci. Research Soc. Am., IEEE, AAAS, Am. Soc. Engring. Edn., Sigma Xi, Tau Beta Phi. Author profl. articles. Home: 141 N Anita Los Angeles CA 90049 Office: 200 N Sepulveda Blvd El Segundo CA 90245

JESSE, BERNARD W., safety and health administrator, metallurgist; b. Alliance, Nebr., Aug. 20, 1931; s. Bert H. and Mary A. (Yeager) J.; m. Cecile M. Shankenburg, Jan. 3, 1952; children—Christine Jesse Brown, Charlotte Jesse Sparks, Justin, Alberta, Philip. Student Ariz. Western, 1976-78; San Jose State U., 1979. Contract miner iron mine, Sunrise, Wyo., 1953-56; tunnel foreman and supt. Gates and Fox Gen. Contractors, Burlingame, Calif., 1956-59; supt. shaft and tunneling Morrison and Knudson Co., Boise, Idaho, 1960-64; specification compliance insp. and engr. U.S. Bur. Reclamation, Denver, 1964—; tunneling and hydroelectric constrn. safety engr., Yuma, Ariz., 1976-79, Gilroy, Calif., 1979-81, Oroville, Wash., 1981-83; safety mgr. Oroville-tonasket Irrigation Project, Wash., 1983—; cons.; welding insp. Republican. committeeman Pima Creek; active Holy Rosary Cath. Council, Knights of Columbus. Served with U.S. Army, 1949-52. Recipient Purple Heart. Mem. Am. Soc. Safety Engrs., Nat. Safety Council (defensive driver instr.), Nat. Rifle Assn. Roman Catholic. Club: Kiwanis. Home: 29 Crumbacher Rd Tonasket WA 98855 Office: PO Box 929 11th and Fir St Oroville WA 98844

JESSEN, DAVID WAYNE, accountant; b. Albuquerque, Jan. 13, 1950; s. Irving Matthew and Lucille Barbara (Huber) J.; B.B.A. in Acctg., U. N.Mex., 1972; m. Melissa Meyer, Oct. 4, 1975; children—Jennifer Leigh, Kimberly Paige. Staff acct. local C.P.A. firm, Albuquerque, 1971-74, jr. partner, 1974-75; mgr. in charge Santa Fe office Alford, Meroney & Co., C.P.A.s, 1975-80, prin. in charge Santa Fe office, 1980-82; dir. taxes N.Mex. offices Arthur Young & Co., Santa Fe, Albuquerque, 1980—. Asst. scoutmaster Boy Scouts Am.; bd. dirs. Kiwanis Found. C.P.A., N.Mex.; Eagle Scout. Mem. Am. Inst. C.P.A.s, N.Mex. Soc. C.P.A.s (taxation com., v.p. Santa Fe chpt. 1980), Santa Fe C. of C., Santa Fe Jaycees, Albuquerque Jaycees, Alpha Kappa Psi. Republican. Lutheran. Clubs: Elks, Downtown Santa Fe Kiwanis. Home: 4908 Calle del Cielo Ct NE Albuquerque NM 87103

JEWELL, DAVID WILLIAM, educator, therapist, administrator, clergyman; b. Cherry Valley, Ill., Oct. 27, 1925; s. Earl Branch and Elsie (Barton) J.; m. Elaine Steffensrud, June 10, 1949; children—Randi Jewell Budwit, Martha Jewell Gomez, Phebe B. A.B., Carleton Coll., 1948; M.Div., Union Theol. Sem., 1951; Ed.D., Tchrs. Coll., Columbia U., 1957. Instr. religious edn. and psychology Union Theol. Sem., N.Y.C., 1955-57; assoc. prof. Christian edn. Bangor (Maine) Theol. Sem., 1957-61; assoc. prof., dir. Schenffler Div. Religious Edn. and Social Work Theology, Oberlin Coll., 1961-66; assoc. prof. Christian edn. Divinity Sch. Vanderbilt U., 1966-69; exec. dir. Met. Campus Ministry Assn., Houston, 1969-76; aftercare coordinator, asst. to clin. dir. Akeela House Inc., Anchorage, 1979—; lectr. Co-pres. Am. Field Service Internat. Scholarships, Clear Lake, Tex., 1971-73; lectr. in-service tng. program Houston Ind. Sch. Dist., 1974-76. Served with USN, 1943-45. Research grantee Vanderbilt U. 1966. Mem. Am. Personnel and Guidance Assn., Am. Mental Health Counselors Assn. Mem. United Ch. of Christ. Contbr. chpts. to books, articles to religious jours.

JEWELL, HELEN STEVENS, educator; b. Elkhart, Iowa, Sept. 10, 1920; d. Ralph William and Ethel Eleanor (Peters) Stevens; m. Louis C. Jewell, Dec. 7, 1942 (div.); children—H. Richard, Janis I.; m. Stanley S. Sims, Jan. 2, 1980. Tchr. primary grades, Iowa, 1943-45; substitute tchr., Monmouth, Ill., 1965-72; tchr. Harding Sch., Monmouth, 1972-77; coordinator curriculum, instr. early childhood edn. Carl Sandburg Community Coll., Galesburg, Ill., 1976-81; lead tchr. lab. sch. Anna Bing Arnold Childrens Ctr., Calif. State U.-Los Angeles, 1981—; presenter profl. workshops So. Calif. Assn. Edn. for Young Children, 1982. Mem. exec. bd. Girl Scouts U.S.A., 1965-75, dir. Brownie day camp, 1965, 66, dist. dir., 1966-67, leader, 1965-77; vol. sch. for handicapped children; mem. bldg. fund com. YMCA. Mem. AAUW, AAUP, Ill. Children's Assn., Nat. Assn. Edn. Young Children, Phi Kappa Phi. Republican. Presbyterian. Clubs: Garden, Country. Home: 13180 St Andrews Dr Seal Beach CA 90740 Office: Lab Sch Anna Bing Arnold Childrens Ctr Calif State U Los Angeles CA

JEWELL, NICHOLAS PATRICK, biostatistics educator, researcher, consultant; b. Paisley, Scotland, Sept. 3, 1952; came to U.S., 1976, naturalized, 1982; s. Brian McCalmont and Phyllis Mary J.; m. Debra Jean Cederborg. B.Sc., U. Edinburgh, 1973, Ph.D., 1976. Research fellow med. computing and stats. unit U. Edinburgh, 1978-79; asst. prof. dept. stats. Princeton (N.J.), 1979-82; asst. prof. biostats. U. Calif.-Berkeley, 1982—. Office: Sch Pub Health U Calif Berkeley CA 94720

JEWELL, PEARL PECK (PEP), school principal; b. Kalispell, Montana; Aug. 19, 1947; d. Raymond L. and Ilse C. (Sonnek Wagner) Peck; m. Wallace Austin Jewell, Aug. 16, 1969; 1 son, Jeremy. B.A. in English and Psychology, Coll. Great Falls, 1969; M.A. in Career Edn., No. Mont. Coll., 1974; postgrad. in Ednl. Adminstrn., Mont. State U., 1980—. Tchr. English, librarian Centerville High Sch., Sand Coulee, Montana, 1969-70; tchr. English, psychology Bozeman (Mont.) Sr. High Sch., 1970-72; tchr. English, counselor Havre (Mont.) High Sch., 1972-79, intern Women in Sch. Adminstrn., Livingston, Mont., 1979-80; asst. prin. Hellgate High Sch., Missoula, Mont., 1979-81; prin. Havre Jr. High Sch., 1981—; cons. Office Pub. Instrn.; lectr. in field. Loaned exec. United Way, 1980; bd. dirs. Havre Encourages Long-Range Prevention Program (HELP), 1981—. Recipient Nat. award Outstanding Service Gamma Sigma Sigma, 1969; named Outstanding Young Educator, Havre Jaycees, 1977; Title IV grantee, 1978. Mem. Nat. Middle Sch. Assn., Assn. Supervision and Curriculum Devel., Mont. Assn. Elem. Sch. Prins. Phi Delta Kappa, Delta Kappa Gamma., Gamma Sigma Sigma (nat. service v.p. 1970-71). Democrat. Roman Catholic. Home: Box 1935 Havre MT 59501 Office: Havre Jr High Sch Box 7791 Havre MT 59501

JEWETT, GEORGE FREDERICK, JR., forest products executive; b. Spokane, Wash., Apr. 10, 1927; s. George Frederick and Mary Pelton (Cooper) J.; m. Lucille Winifred McIntyre, July 11, 1953; children—Mary Elizabeth, George Frederick III. B.A., Dartmouth Coll., 1950; M.B.A., Harvard U., 1952. With Potlach Corp., San Francisco, 1955—, sr. v.p. 1972-77, vice chmn. bd. adminstrn., 1977-78, vice chmn., 1979—. Trustee, Asia Found., Pacific Med. Ctr., Calif. Acad. Sci., Carnegie Instn. of Washington; chmn. Asian Art Found.; mem. Asian Art Commn. of San Francisco. Served with USN, 1945-46. Republican. Presbyterian. Clubs: St. Francis Yacht, N. Y. Yacht, Marin Yacht, Bohemian, Pacific Union. Home: Skyland Way Ross CA 94957 Office: Potlach Corp One Maritime Plaza Suite 1340 San Francisco CA 94111

JEWETT, LUCILLE MCINTYRE (MRS. GEORGE FREDERICK JEWETT, JR.), civic worker; b. St. Louis, Jan. 1, 1929; d. Charles Edwin and Elizabeth (Newbery) McIntyre; student U. Puget Sound, 1950; m. George Frederick Jewett, Jr., July 11, 1953; children—Mary Elizabeth, George Frederick III. Mem. Jr. League, Tacoma. Bd. dirs. Lewiston-Clarkston YWCA, Lewiston, Idaho, 1957-65, v.p. bd. dirs., 1959-65, mem. internat. div. com. nat. bd., 1958-71, mem., world service council. 1967—; trustee emeritus San Francisco Ballet Assn.; bd. dirs. Lewiston-Clarkston United Fund, 1959-65, Internat. Hospitality Center, San Francisco; adv. com. China Inst. Am.; trustee U. Puget Sound, Tacoma, Coro Found., San Francisco; Nez Perce County Rep. State Committeewoman, 1962-65; pres. Nez Perce County Republican Women's Club, 1961; alt. del. Rep. Nat. Conv., 1964; nat. council Nat. Women's Rep. Club, 1964—. Mem. Order St. John of Jerusalem, Pi Beta Phi. Presbyterian. Club: Francisca. Home: PO Box 236 Ross CA 94957

JILLSON, KENNETH RAYMOND, life insurance company executive; b. Los Angeles, Aug. 28, 1932; s. LeRoy Wilcox and Edith (Orr) J.; m. Pauline Elizabeth Lyman, Aug. 1, 1954; 1 son, Paul Christopher; m. Gloria del Carmen Castillo, Dec. 30, 1966; children—Teresa del Carmen, Kenneth Raymond, Deborah Edith del Carmen; 1 stepson, Rene Aristides Picota. B.A. in Econs., UCLA, 1954. C.L.U., Am. Coll.; cert. fin. planner, Coll. Fin. Planning. Served as midshipman U.S. Navy, 1950-54, advanced through grades to lt., 1961; ret., 1969; agt. field mgmt. Pacific Mut. Life Ins. Co., Los Angeles, Corona del Mar, Calif., 1961-66; regional dir. Am. Life Ins. Co., Ltd., Wilmington, Del. and Panama, 1966-69, v.p., Seguros and Caracas, Venezuela, 1971-73; with Hawaiian Life Ins. Co., Ltd., Honolulu, 1974—, pres., chief exec. officer, 1980—, dir., 1979—, chmn. exec. com., 1981—; cert. Model-Netics instr., 1981—. Trustee, Chaminade U. Ednl. Found., 1978—; bd. regents Chaminade U. of Honolulu, 1980—; bd. dirs. Jr. Achievement of Hawaii, 1981-83, Hawaii Joint Council on Econ. Edn., 1981—, Catholic Youth Orgn., 1981-83. Fellow Life Mgmt. Inst.; mem. Nat. Assn. Life Underwriters, Hawaii Assn. Life Underwriters, Honolulu Assn. Life Underwriters, Am. Soc. C.L.U.s (Hawaii chpt. dir. 1976—, pres. 1982-83), Golden Key Soc., Gen. Agts. and Mgrs. Assn., Hawaii Estate Planning Council, Sales and Mktg. Execs. Honolulu (past v.p.). Republican. Roman Catholic. Club: Pacific (Honolulu). Home: 211 Kawaihae St Honolulu HI 96825 Office: Hawaiian Life Ins Co Ltd PO Box 3149 Honolulu HI 96802

JIMENEZ, AGUSTIN JESUS, federal educational program administrator; b. Camaguey, Cuba, July 14, 1950; came to U.S., 1962, naturalized, 1977; s. Agustin J. and Flora Maria (Dominguez) J.; m. Minerva L. Gomez, Aug. 6, 1977; children—Andres, Agustin. B.A., Calif. State U.-Long Beach, 1977; M.A., Claremont Grad. Sch., 1979. Asst. tchr. Head Start Program, South Whittier (Calif.) Sch. Dist., 1971-73; tchr. Rio Hondo Area Action Council, Pico Rivera, Calif., 1973-75, asst. dir., 1975-76; tchr. Los Nietos (Calif.) Sch. Dist., 1976; asst. dir. compensatory edn. program Whittier (Calif.) High Sch., 1977-79; dir. Head Start State Presch., Foothill Area Community Services, Inc., Pasadena, Calif., 1979—; prof. Pacific Oaks Coll., Pasadena, 1981—. Mem. adv. council Pasadena City Coll. Child Care Services; bd. dirs. Child Care Info. Service, Pasadena. Served with USCGR, 1968-70. Mem. Assn. Parents and Dirs. Together, Nat. Head Start Assn. (past treas.), Am. Mgmt. Assn. Democrat. Roman Catholic. Office: 193 E Orange Grove Blvd Pasadena CA 91103

JIMENEZ, ANDRES EUGENIO, social and political science researcher, educator; b. Los Angeles, Oct. 19, 1953; s. Higinio and Irene (Montoya) J.; m. Maria Juana Martinez, Aug. 8, 1981. A.B. in Politics, Latin Am. Studies, U. Calif.-Santa Cruz, 1975; M.A., U. Calif.-Berkeley, 1978. Teaching assoc. coll. natural resources U. Calif.-Berkeley, 1979, asst. coordinator program in Mexican studies, 1981—; pres. Inst. Research and Info. on Mex.-Am., 1983—; lectr. dept. Chicano studies Calif. State U.-Northridge, 1979-80; coordinator No. Calif. Conf. on U.S. Immigration Policy, 1977; mem. Bay Area Com. on Immigration, 1977-79. Active Librería Latinoamericana. Ford Found. grad. fellow, 1975-79. Mem. Am. Polit. Sci. Assn., Chicano Polit. Economy Collective (contbg. editor 1977—), Nat. Assn. Chicano Studies. Democrat. Roman Catholic. Co-editor: Informe—Review of Mexican America, 1984. Office: Mexican Studies 2334 Bowditch U Calif Berkeley CA 94720

JIMIRRO, JAMES P., entertainment and communications executive; b. Donora, Pa., Jan. 23, 1937; s. Paul F. and Lee (Meyers) J. B.A., Pa. State U., 1958, postgrad., 1960-63; M.A., Syracuse U., 1959. Program dir. Sta. WPBS, Phila., 1963-65; account exec. CBS, 1965-67, internat. sales mgr., 1967-70, dir. internat. sales, 1970-71; dir. internat. sales Viacom Internat., N.Y.C., 1971-73; dir. internat. sales Walt Disney Ednl. Media Co., 1973-74, exec. v.p., 1974-80; pres. Walt Disney Telecommunications, Burbank, Calif., 1980—; pres. Disney Channel, 1982—; prof. communications UCLA extension seminar program, 1981. Bd. dirs. Flight Attendant Vol. Corps. Mem. Hollywood Radio and TV Soc., Assn. Ednl. Communications and Tech., Internat. Radio and TV Soc., Speech Communications Assn., Ednl. Film Library Assn., Internat. Tape/Disc Assn. (bd. dirs.), Sigma Delta Chi. Contbr. articles to profl. jours. Home: 10787 Wilshire Blvd Apt 704 Los Angeles CA 90024 Office: 4111 W Alameda St Burbank CA 91505

JINKENS, ROBERT CARL, accountant, educator, real estate broker; b. Montebello, Calif., Nov. 17, 1945; s. Victor Carl and Irene (Tuttle) J. B.S. in Bus., U. So. Calif., 1969, B.A. in Math., 1971; M.B.A., U. Calif.-Irvine, 1982. C.P.A., Calif. Acct., Balboa Island, Calif., 1977—; real estate broker, Balboa Island, 1973—; faculty Saddleback Coll., Mission Viejo, Calif. Mem. Am. Inst. C.P.A.s, Calif. Soc. C.P.A.s, NEA, Calif. Tchrs. Assn., U. So. Calif. Alumni Assn., Alpha Kappa Psi. Republican. Methodist. Clubs: Masons, DeMolay. Home: 326 1/2 Onyx Ave Balboa Island CA 92662 Office: PO Box 331 Balboa Island CA 92662

JIO, STEVEN S., optometrist; b. San Jose, Calif., Nov. 20, 1950; s. Sa and Aiko J. A.B., U. Calif.-Berkeley, 1972, O.D., 1979. Pvt. practice optometry, Los Osos, Calif., 1980—. Mem. San Luis Obispo County Band, Morro Bay White CapS Community Band. Mem. Am. Optometric Assn., Calif. Optometric Assn., Tri-Counties Optometric Soc., Low Vision Cons. So. Calif., Am. Heart Assn. (dir. San Luis Obispo), Los Osos Baywood Park C. of C. (dir.), U. Calif. Optometry Alumni Assn., Natural History Assn. San Luis Obispo Coast. Club: Lions (sec.).

JITTLOV, MIKE JOHN, film producer, director, writer, animator, actor; b. Los Angeles, June 8, 1948; s. Vadim Serge and Marie Anne (Pacolt) J. B.A. in Motion Pictures and TV Prodn./Direction, UCLA, 1971. Ind. film producer, Los Angeles, 1971—; clients include Walt Disney Studios, Alan Landsburg Prodns., Liberty Pictures, numerous others; short subject films include Good Grief, 1972, Swing Shift, 1973, The Interview, 1973, Animato, 1977, Time Tripper, 1978, The Collector, 1979, Wizard of Speed and Time, 1980; co-starred in 2 Disney TV spls., 1978, 79; created Disney channel Mouse Satellite, 1982; animated 1st stop-motion Mickey Mouse film, 1978; producer, dir., cameraman numerous other TV spots and promotional films; lectr. film spl. effects. Recipient Norman McLaren award Chgo. Film Fest, 1980, Gold Cindy and Spl. Achievement Animation award Informational Film Producers Am., 1979; grand prize Aspen Film Fest, 1980, Houston Internat. Film Fest, 1980; 4 times finalist for Acad. Award nomination. Mem. Dirs. Guild Am., Screen Actors Guild, AFTRA, Sci. Fiction Cons. Home and office: 902 N Waltman Ave Los Angeles CA 90026

JOAQUIM, RICHARD RALPH, hotel exec.; b. Cambridge, Mass., July 28, 1936; s. Manuel and Mary (Marrano) J.; B.F.A., Boston U., 1955, Mus. B., 1959; m. Nancy Phyllis Reis, Oct. 22, 1960; 1 dau., Vanessa Reis. Social dir., coordinator summer resort, Wolfeboro, N.H., 1957-59; concert soloist N.H. Symphony Orch., Vt. Choral Soc., Choral Arts Soc., Schenectady Chamber Orch., 1957-60; coordinator performance functions, mgr. theatre Boston U., 1959-60, asst. program dir., 1963-64, dir. univ. programs, 1964-70; gen. mgr. Harrison House of Glen Cove; dir. Conf. Service Corp., Glen Cove, N.Y., 1970-74, sr. v.p., dir. design and devel.; v.p. Arltec, also mng. dir. Sheraton Internat. Conf. Center, 1975-76; v.p., mng. dir. Scottsdale (Ariz.) Conf. Center and Resort Hotel, 1976—; pres. Internat. Conf. Resorts, Inc., 1977, chmn. bd., 1977—; pres. Western Conf. Resorts; concert solist U.S. Army Field Band, Washington, 1960-62. Creative arts cons., editorial cons., concert mgr. Commr. recreation Watertown, Mass., 1967—; mem. Spl. Study Com. Watertown, 1967—; mem. Glen Cove Mayor's Urban Renewal Com. Bd. dirs. Nat. Entertainment Conf. Served with AUS, 1960-62. Mem. Assn. Coll. and Univ. Concert Mgrs., Am. Symphonic League, Am. Fedn. Film Socs., Assn. Am. Artists, Am. Personnel and Guidance Assn., Knights of the Vine, Nat. Alumni Council Boston U. Office: 7700 McCormick Pkwy Scottsdale AZ 85258

JOBE, ALICE, transp. co. exec.; b. Little Rock, Nov. 24, 1935; student Long Beach City Coll., 1960-61; m. K.L. Jobe, Mar. 12, 1957; 1 dau.,

Cathy. With Nat. Equity Life Ins. Co., Little Rock, 1954-55, Cash Wholesale Co., Little Rock, 1956-57; with Bekins Internat., subs. Bekins Co., Wilmington, Calif., 1959-77, v.p., 1971-77; exec. v.p. Imperial Internat., Inc., Torrance, Calif., 1977-80, dir., 1977-81; pres. Imperial Van Lines Internat., Inc., 1980-81; industry cons., 1981-82; founder, pres. Caddo Internat., freight forwarding, Los Alamitos, Calif., 1982—. Mem. Household Goods Forwarders Assn. (exec. com. 1977-78), Nat. Def. Transp. Assn. (life), Am. Soc. Profl. Women. Republican. Office: Caddo Internat PO Box 666 4772 Katella Ave Los Alamitos CA 90720

JOBES, PATRICK CLARK, sociologist, educator; b. Los Angeles, s. Ralph Clark and Dorothy Marie (Johnston) J.; m. Sally Owens, June 19, 1965; children—Genevieve, Peter. A.B., Vanderbilt U., 1962; M.A., U. Colo., 1965; Ph.D., U. Wash., 1970. Asst. prof. U. Colo., Boulder, 1969-71; asst. prof. Mont. State U., Bozeman, 1971-73, assoc. prof., 1973-81, prof., 1981—. Chmn. bd. trustees Malmborg Sch.; mem. bd. Bozeman Environ. Info. Ctr. NSF grantee, 1970, 72, 76, 78, 80, 82. Mem. Am. Sociol. Assn., Pacific Sociol. Assn., Rural Sociol. Soc., Western Social Sci. Assn., World Congress Sociology, No. Plains Resource Council. Democrat. Author numerous research papers and articles in field. Home: 19 W Story Bozeman MT 59715 Office: 217 Wilson Hall Mont State U Bozeman MT 59715

JOBS, STEVEN PAUL, computer company executive; b. 1955; s. Paul and Clara J. Student Reed Coll., Portland, Oreg. Designer video games Atari, Inc., 1974; founder (with Steven Wozniak) Apple Computer, Inc., Cupertino, Calif., 1976, now chmn. Office: Apple Computer Inc 10260 Bandley Dr Cupertino CA 95014*

JOFFRE, STEPHEN PAUL, consulting chemist; b. N.Y.C., Mar. 12, 1913. B.A. in Chemistry, NYU, 1938; postgrad. Columbia U., 1939-40; Ph.D., Poly. Inst. N.Y., 1946. Medicinal research chemist S.L. Ruskin & Assocs., 1938-40; chief chemist Loeser Lab. div. Parenteral Mfg., William S. Merrell & Co., N.Y.C., 1940-44; chief chemist devel. control labs. and mfg. Drug Products Co., Inc., L.I. and Passaic, N.J., 1944-49; dir. organic research Shulton, Inc., Clifton, N.J., 1949-63; research dir. Germaine Monteil Cosmetiques, L.I., 1964-66; mgr. exploratory research and devel. dept. Max Factor & Co., Hollywood, Calif., 1966-71; dir., owner Stephen P. Joffre & Assocs., Magalia, Calif., 1971—. Fellow AAAS, Am. Inst. Chemists; mem. Am. Chem. Soc., Soc. Cosmetic Chemists, Intersci. Research Found. Calif., Phi Lambda Upsilon. Contbr. articles to profl. jours.; patentee in field. Address: 6194 Kilgord Ct Magalia CA 95954

JOHANNESSEN, EDWARD L. H., oil company executive; b. San Luis Obispo, Calif., Dec. 3, 1919; s. H.K. and Ruth M.C. (Anderson) J.; m. Juliet M. Pasquini, June 13, 1943; 1 dau., Judyth R. Johannessen Lewis. A.B. in Econs., Stanford U., 1941; postgrad. Calif. Maritime Acad., 1943; M.A. in Econs., U. Calif.-Berkeley, 1948; postgrad. Columbia U. Sch. Bus., 1964. Personnel analyst Standard Oil of Calif., Inc., San Francisco, 1948-54, Labor relations counselor, 1955-60, sr. labor relations counselor, 1960-63, asst. mgr., 1963-68, mgr. corp. labor relations, 1968—. Served to lt. comdr. U.S. Maritime Service, 1944-46. Mem. Nat. Assn. Mfrs. (indsl. relations com.), Nat. Petroleum Refiners Assn. (indsl. relations com.), Indsl. Relations Research Assn., U.S. Council Internat. Bus. (indsl. relations com.), U. Calif. Bus. Alumni Club, Stanford U. Alumni Club, Columbia U. Bus. Alumni Club, Phi Delta Theta. Clubs: San Francisco Comml., Press of San Francisco. Author: The Hawaiin Labor Movement, 1956. Home: 30 Los Ranchitos Walnut Creek CA 94595 Office: Standard Oil Co of Calif 225 Bush St Suite 1055 San Francisco CA 94104

JOHANNING, CLIFFORD CARLOS, investment consultant; b. Dallas, Mar. 4, 1952; s. Douglass Henry and Phyllis May (Saunders) J. B.S. in Edn., Stephen F. Austin State U., 1976. Promotions dir. Athletes in Action Basketball team, Tustin, Calif., 1978-80; pres., founder Pro-Players West, Inc., Irvine, Calif., 1980-82; investment exec. Univ. Securities, Irvine, Calif., 1980—; Baraban Securities, Fullerton, Calif., 1980—. Bd. dirs. Thessalonika Found., 1980-83, Fieldstead Inst., 1980—. Republican.

JOHANOS, DONALD, condr.; b. Cedar Rapids, Iowa; student Eastman Sch. Music, Rochester, N.Y. Music dir., prin. condr. Dallas Symphony Orch., from 1962; former asso. condr. Pitts. Symphony; music dir. Honolulu Symphony, 1979—, artistic dir. Hawaii Opera Theatre; guest condr. numerous orchs. including: Boston Symphony Orch., Phila. Orch., San Francisco Symphony, Chgo. Symphony, New Orleans Philharm., Hong Kong Philharm., orchs. of St. Louis, Atlanta, Toronto, Indpls., Mexico City; condr. opera prodns., Pitts., Phila., Ambler Festival; head opera dept. So. Meth. U., Dallas; guest condr. Concertgebouw Orch., Amsterdam, Mostly Mozart Festival, N.Y.C. Rockefeller Found. grantee. Office: Honolulu Symphony Honolulu HI

JOHL, JUGRAJ SINGH, biomed. researcher; b. Yuba City, Calif., Aug. 7, 1952; s. Karm Singh and Swarn Klaur (Grewal) J. A.S. in Math., Yuba Coll., 1972, A.S., 1972; student U. Calif.-Davis, 1972-73; B.A. in Biology, Chico State U., 1976, B.A. in Chemistry, 1976, postgrad., 1977-80. Farm mgr. KSV Ranch, Yuba City, Calif., 1969—; biomedical researcher Stanford Research Inst. Internat., 1981—; agrl. cons. Mem. AAAS, Am. Chem. Soc., Am. Inst. Biol. Scis., Calif. Acad. Scis. Democrat.

JOHLER, JOSEPH RALPH, physicist; b. Scranton, Pa., Feb. 23, 1919; s. Joseph Jacob and Lillian (Dietzel) J.; B.A., Am. U., 1941; B.S.E., George Washington U., 1950; m. Nora Stella Callahan, Sept. 16, 1953; children—Dennis Ralph, Mark Stephen, Paul Norman, Annette Diane. Ballistic mathematician Ballistic Research Lab., Aberdeen Proving Grounds, Md., 1942-45; with Nat. Bur. Standards, Washington, 1946-51, electronic engr. Boulder Labs., 1951-65, chief electromagnetic theory sect., 1961-65; program leader, electromagnetic theory program Environmental Sci. Services Adminstrn., Inst. Telecommunication Scis. and Aeronomy, U.S. Dept. Commerce, Boulder, 1965-70, physicist, project scientist Office Telecommunications 1970-72, chief nav. and D-Region Sci. sect., 1972-76; pres. Colo. Research and Prediction Lab., Boulder, 1976—. Served with USNR, 1944-46. Research Nat. Bur. Standards Disting. Authorship award, 1963, 66. Mem. AAAS, Am. Geophys. Union, Am. Math. Soc., Sci. Research Soc. Am., Internat. Union Radio Sci., IEEE (sr. mem.), Internat. Radio Consultative Com., Soc. Indsl. and Applied Math., Wild Goose Assn. (Gold Medal of Merit award 1982). Contbr. articles to profl. jours. Home: 16796 W 74th Pl Golden CO 80403 Office: PO Box 1056 4801 N 63d St Boulder CO 80306

JOHNEN, ELIZABETH THERESA, reading educator; b. Homestead, Pa., July 20, 1953; d. Russell Joseph and Florence Theresa (Stankevich) Mastrota; m. Robert Allan Johnen, Aug. 28, 1976. B.S. in Edn. of Exceptional Children, Pa. State U., 1975; M.S. in Reading, Elmira (N.Y.) Coll., 1981. Spl. edn. tchr. pub. schs., Cresson, Pa., 1975-76, Wellsboro, Pa., 1977-79; resource room tchr. Tooele County (Utah) Sch. Dist., 1980-81; reading instr. Blue Mountain Community Coll., Pendleton, Oreg., 1981-83; adult basic educator Boise (Idaho) State U., 1983—; basic skills cons. EDL/Arista, Concord, Calif., 1983—; test item writer GED, Am. Coll. Testing Program. Active Assn. for Retarded Citizens, 1975—. Mem. Council for Exceptional Children, Internat. Reading Assn., Oreg. Developmental Studies Orgn., Oreg. Reading Assn., NOW, Western Coll. Reading and Learning Assn., Assn. Supervision and Curriculum Devel., Nat. Assn. Remedial/Developmental Studies in Postsecondary Edn., NW Adult Edn. Assn., Pi Lambda Theta, Phi Kappa Phi. Democrat. Roman Catholic. Author: Challenging Adults to Read Effectively: A Guide for Teacher and Tutors, 1982. Home: 970 N 12 East Mountain Home ID 83647

JOHNS, DAVID CLARENCE, electrical engineer, utility company executive; b. Great Falls, Mont., Aug. 2, 1923; s. Francis Hayes and Rose Nell (Bosckis) J.; m. Edith Shirley, Apr. 23, 1945; children—Shirley, Constance, Susan. B.S. in Elec. Engring., Mont. State U., 1948, M.S., 1949. With Mont. Power Co., Butte, 1949—, jr. engr., 1949-50, asst. engr., 1950-53, asst. div. supt., 1953-57, div. supt., 1957-60, gen. office distbn. and transmission engr., 1960-62, gen. office supt. transmission and distbn., 1962-73, mgr. transmission and distbn. budget, 1973—; pres., dir. World Mus. Mining, 1973—. Served with USN, 1944-46. Mem. Mont. Profl. Engrs., N.W. Elec. Light and Power Assn. Rep. Clubs: Rotary, Butte Exchange.

JOHNS, ROBERT MICHAEL, advertising company executive; b. Los Angeles, July 13, 1943; s. Bernard William and Elizabeth Jane (Sorensen) J.; m. Sharon Ruth Andersen, Sept. 9, 1965; children—Jennifer, Susan, Robert, Stephen, Sherry, Kimberly, Julie. A.A., Pasadena City Coll., 1964; B.S., Brigham Young U., 1966. Sales and med. center rep. Hoffman-LaRoche, Inc., Los Angeles, 1966-74; So. Calif. dist. sales mgr. IVAC Corp., Los Angeles, 1974-75; fin. planner Conn. Gen. Life Ins., Los Angeles, 1975-79; pres. Common Carrier Advt., Inc., Los Angeles and Salt Lake City, 1979-81; chmn., pres., chief exec. officer AdMedia Internat., Inc., Salt Lake City, 1981—; dir. Common Carrier Advt., Inc. Instl. rep. Boy Scouts Am., 1969-71, explorer advisor, 1967-69, varsity scout coach, 1979-80; mem. high council of Ch. Jesus Christ Latter-day Saints, 1971-73, 77-79, 81—, ordained bishop, 1979; soccer coach, 1978. Recipient Conn. Gen. Life Ins. Co. awards 1976, 77, 78; named Outstanding Young Man, U.S. Jaycees, 1979. Mem. Assn. Life Underwriters. Republican. Co-innovator and pioneer of supermarket/convenience store advertising medium. Office: 942 E 7145 S Suite 201 Midvale UT 84047

JOHNS, ROY CLINTON (BUD), JR., writer, publisher, apparel manufacturing company executive; b. Detroit, July 9, 1929; s. Roy Clinton and Isabel (Horton) J.; m. Ann Barbour Grieve, June, 1957; m. 2d, Judith Spector Clancy, Mar. 28, 1971. B.A., Albion Coll., 1951. Reporter Flint (Mich.) Jour., 1947-51, 1953-56, San Diego Union, 1956-60; bur. chief Fairchild Publs., San Diego, 1960-61, San Francisco, 1961-69; pres. Synergistic Press Inc., San Francisco, 1968—; dir. pub. relations Levi Strauss & Co., San Francisco, 1969-71, dir. corp. communications, 1971-79, v.p. corp. communications, 1971-81, mgr. continuing spl. projects, 1981—; author: The Ombibulous Mr. Mencken, 1968; contbr. numerous articles to various mags.; author film script; What is This Madness?, 1976; exec. producer The Best You Can Be (CINE award), 1980; co-editor: Bastard in the Ragged Suit, 1977. Bd. dirs. Stern Grove Festival Assn., San Francisco, 1970-83, Documentary Research Inc., Buffalo, 1978—, San Francisco Contemporary Music Players, 1981—, People for Open Space, 1982—; mem. Nat. Council for Mus. Am. Indian, 1980—. Served with USMC, 1951-53. Home: 3985 Sacramento St San Francisco CA 94118 Office: 1155 Battery St San Francisco CA 94106

JOHNS, SIDNEY MARVIN, accountant, educator; b. Carey, Idaho, May 17, 1937; s. Carl Emris and Louise (Wilde) J ; B.A., Idaho State U., 1963, B.B.A., 1964; postgrad., Calif. State U., 1980; M.B.A., Golden Gate U., 1982; m. JoAnne Goodsell, July 12, 1961; children—Cristina, David Stuart, Darrin Keith, Juanita, Maria. Instr. Spanish, Idaho State U., Pocatello, 1963-64, commd. 2d lt. Fin. Corps, U.S. Army, 1964, advanced through grades to maj., 1973, resigned, 1979; supervising acct. So. Calif. Rapid Transit Dist., Los Angeles, 1979—. Bd. dirs., treas. Transit Employees Fed. Credit Union; pres. Chino stake Spanish-speaking mission Latter-Day Saints Ch. Decorated Commendation medals. Mem. Res. Officers Assn. Home: 407 Navajo Springs Rd Diamond Bar CA 91765 Office: Southern California Rapid Transit District 425 S Main St Los Angeles CA 90013

JOHNS, VARNER JAY, JR., med. educator; b. Denver, Jan. 27, 1921; s. Varner Jay and Ruby Charlene (Morrison) J.; B.S., La Sierra Coll., 1944; M.D., Coll. Med. Evangelists, 1945; m. Dorothy Mae Hippach, Dec. 7, 1944; children—Marcia (Mrs. David B. Hinshaw, Jr.), Donna (Mrs. Don Bennett), Varner Jay III. Intern, White Meml. Hosp., Los Angeles, 1944-45, resident, 1945-47; resident pathology Loma Linda (Calif.) U., 1947-48; head physician Los Angeles County Hosp., 1951; assoc. dean. Sch. Medicine Loma Linda U., 1951-54, chmn. dept. medicine, 1956-69, 80—, prof. medicine, 1957—, assoc. dean continuing edn. Sch. Medicine, 1975—; chief medicine service White Meml. Hosp., Los Angeles, 1956-62, co-chmn., 1978-80; chief medicine service Loma Linda U. Hosp., 1964-69, 80—; physician-in-chief Los Angeles County Hosp., 1958-64; cons. Office Surgeon Gen. Dept. Army, 1956-67; vis. colleague Inst. Cardiology, London, Eng., 1962-63; hon. vis. physician Nat. Heart Hosp., London, 1962-63; pres. Alumni Fedn. Bd. Govs., Loma Linda U., 1970-71 dir. Audio/Digest, 1975—. Served to maj. M.C. AUS, 1954-56. Diplomate Nat. Bd. Med. Examiners, Am. Bd. Internal Medicine, Am. Bd. Cardiovascular Disease. Fellow ACP (gov. 1972-76), Am. Coll. Cardiology; mem. Los Angeles Acad. Medicine (mem. governing bd. 1965-68, 74-77, treas. 1977-78, v.p. 1978-79, pres. 1979-80), San Bernardino County Heart Assn. (dir. 1966-72), Am. Heart Assn. (fellow council clin. cardiology), Western Assn. Physicians, Royal Soc. Medicine, Internat. Soc. Internal Medicine, Am. Fedn. Clin. Research, AMA, Calif. Med. Assn. (del. 1974—), Los Angeles Soc. Internal Medicine (pres. 1961-62), Inland Soc. Internal Medicine, Alpha Omega Alpha, San Bernardino County Med. Soc. (v.p. 1972-73, pres. 1974-75). Clubs: Torch (pres. 1971-72) San Bernardino Valley, Calif.); Redlands Country (Calif.). Mem. editorial bd. Calif. Medicine, 1964-74. Contbr. articles to profl. jours. Home: 11565 Hillcrest Ct Loma Linda CA 92354

JOHNS, WILLIAM KENT, wholesale drug co. exec.; b. San Jose, Calif., Aug. 29, 1941; s. Harvey William and Sue J.; B.A., San Jose State U., 1968. Field foreman Mayfair Packing Co., San Jose, 1950-62; exec. office engring. asst. Ruth & Going Assos., San Jose, 1962-64; mgr. camera dept. Payless Drugs, Oakland, Calif., 1964-68; tech. support mgr. McKesson Drug Co. Economost System, San Francisco, 1970—; dir. Best Studios, Inc. Advisor, Jr. Achievement, 1979. Mem. Friends of Photography, Santa Clara Profl. Wine Soc. Office: 1 Post St San Francisco CA 94104

JOHNS, W(ILLIAM) LLOYD, univ. pres.; b. East St. Louis, Ill., May 25, 1930; s. William C. and Beatrice G. (Schoenen) J.; B.S., N.E. Mo. State Coll., 1952, M.A., 1956; Ed.D., U. So. Calif., 1966; postgrad. Inst. Ednl. Mgmt., Harvard U., 1974; m. Dorene Ann Hill, Oct. 11, 1975; children—Victoria Johns Parsons, Michelle Lynn, Terri Lee. Tchr. music schs. in Mo., 1950-54, Calif., 1958-59; prin. schs. in Mo., 1954-58, Calif., 1958-65; prof. ednl. adminstrn. Calif. State U., Northridge, 1965-75, asst. to dean edn., 1968-70, dir. audiovisual services, 1970-72, asso. v.p. bus. and adminstrv. affairs, 1972-75; v.p. adminstrv. affairs and ednl. services, then acting pres. Sonoma State Coll., Rohnert Park, Calif., 1975-77; exec. v.p. Calif. State U., Sacramento, 1977-78, pres., 1978—; chmn. accreditation com. Western Assn. Schs. and Colls., 1965-76; chmn. mgmt. adv. com. Calif. State Univs. and Colls., 1972—, chmn. public safety adv. com., 1978—; tng. inst. dir. Leadership Tng. Area of Deaf, Rehab. Services Adminstrn., 1967-70. Pres. bd. dirs. Helping Hand Fund, Sacramento; adv. bd. Sacramento Salvation Army; bd. dirs. Sacramento United Way; chmn. membership subcom., long-range planning com. Golden Empire council Boy Scouts Am. Recipient various service awards. Mem. Am. Mgmt. Assn., Phi Delta Kappa. Club: Comstock (Sacramento). Co-author: Systematic Instructional Strategy, 1971; co-editor: Readings in Educational Leadership, 1969; contbr. articles to profl. publs. Office: Calif State Univ 6000 J St Sacramento CA 95819

JOHNSON, ABIGAIL RIDLEY, tour and travel consultant; b. Vancouver, B.C., Can., Jan. 28, 1945; d. Frederic Neville and Cara Lee (Smith) Ridley; m. Ralph Maxwell Johnson, Sept. 17, 1971 (div.). B.A. in Music, Colo. Woman's Coll., 1967; postgrad. San Jose State U., summer 1967. Cert. travel counselor. Co. rep. Manhattan Festival Ballet, N.Y.C., 1967-68; asst. booking mgr. Western Opera Theatre, San Francisco, 1968-69; asst. to consul and trade commr. Can. Consulate Gen., San Francisco, 1969-71; office mgr. Whitney Properties, San Francisco, 1971-72; supr. Bel-Air Travel, Los Angeles, 1972-73; dir., owner Sutter Travel Service, San Francisco, 1973—; founder, dir. Tour Arts, San Francisco, 1978—; cons. Arts Internat. and Roman Assocs. Bd. dirs., devel. com. and tour fund raising Marin Ballet Assn., 1980—; exec. com. Friends of Am. Conservatory Theatre; mem. San Francisco Com. for Joffrey Ballet, 1981—; active San Francisco Opera, Symphony, Ballet, Internat. Visitors Ctr., Met. Opera Guild, 1976—, Republican Party, San Francisco, 1981—. Mem. Am. Soc. Travel Agts., Pacific Area Travel Assn., Inst. Cert. Travel Agts. Episcopalian. Clubs: English Speaking Union, Jr. League San Francisco. Office: 231 Franklin St San Francisco CA 94102

JOHNSON, ADOLPH, JR., college administrator; B.A. magna cum laude, U. Calif.-Santa Barbara; M.S. in Edn., U. So. Calif., also M.B.A., Ph.D. Research asst. U. Calif.-Santa Barbara, 1967-70; teaching asst. U. So. Calif., 1971-72; asst. to dean evening div. Compton (Calif.) Community Coll., 1972-73; instr., coordinator coop. edn. program, 1972-76, instr., 1973-79, dean continuing edn. evening div., 1979—; asst. prof. Grad. Sch. Edn. Pepperdine U., Los Angeles, 1977—, dir. community outreach, 1977—. Mem. Am. Assn. Higher Edn., Am. Assn. Community and Jr. Colls., Calif. Community Coll. Continuing Edn. Assn., Calif. Community and Jr. Coll. Assn., Phi Delta Kappa.

JOHNSON, ANDREA JACKQUELINE, mgmt. info. services co. ofcl.; b. Oakland, Calif., Sept. 3, 1948; d. Andrew Johnson and Iris Willien (Ward) J.; student San Jose State U., 1979—. Trainee operator Info. System Design Co., Oakland, 1973-75; with Intel Corp., Santa Clara, Calif., 1975-80; with San Jose, Calif., 1980, Aloha, Oreg., 1980—, ops. supr., 1980—, systems analyst, 1982—. Mem. Nat. Assn. Female Execs. Club: Altrusa. Office: 3585 SW 198th Ave Aloha OR 97006

JOHNSON, ANITA LORRAINE, nurse practitioner; b. San Bernardino, Calif., July 24, 1942; d. Adam and Ursula Lorraine (Evans) Jones; A.A. in Nursing, San Bernardino Valley Coll., 1975; student U. Calif., San Francisco, 1977, Harbor Gen. Hosp. UCLA Sch. Medicine, 1978; B.A. in Bus., U. Redlands, 1983; m. Morsell Johnson, Dec. 26, 1977; children—Ursula Ballard, Dawna Ballard. R.N., San Bernardino County Gen. Hosp., 1975; nurse practitioner San Bernardino County Health Dept., 1977-82, West End Women's Med. Group, 1982—; realtor assoc., co-owner Morsell Johnson Real Estate, 1979—. Nursing trainer Nat. Council Negro Women, 1976-79. Mem. NAACP (chmn. Freedom Fund), Nat. Assn. Nurse Practitioners in Family Planning, Inland Empire Nurse Practitioner Assn., Nat. Assn. Realtors, San Bernardino Valley Bd. Realtors, Calif. Assn. Realtors, San Bernardino Bus. and Profl. Women. Democrat. Baptist (supt. jr. dept. Sunday sch. 1981—). Home: 1558 N Chestnut St Rialto CA 92376 Office: 5050 San Bernardino St Montclair CA 91763

JOHNSON, ARNOLD IVAN, consulting engineer; b. Madison, Nebr., June 3, 1919; s. Casten Henry and Awilda May (Reeves) J.; B.S.C.E., U. Nebr., 1949, A.D., 1950, postgrad., 1950-54; m. Betty Lou Spencer, June 3, 1941; children—Robert Arnold, Bruce Gary, Carmen Sue Johnson Mark. With U.S. Geol. Survey, 1948-79, asst. chief Office Water Data Coordination, Washington, 1971-79; water resources cons. Woodward-Clyde Cons., Denver, 1979—; faculty affiliate Colo. State U., 1969-70; bd. dirs. Renewable Natural Resources Found., 1971-81; pres. Internat. Commn. Ground Water, 1972-75, Internat. Commn. Remote Sensing and Data Transmission, 1980—; v.p. U.S. nat. commn. Internat. Union Geodesy and Geophysics, 1976-79. Served with USNR, 1942-44. Recipient Award of Merit Dept. Interior, 1962, Meritorious Service award, 1977; Engr. of Yr. award Profl. Engrs. in Govt., 1969; registered profl. engr., Colo., D.C. Fellow ASCE, ASTM, Am. Water Resources Assn. (pres. 1972, rep. to Nat. Acad. Sci. 1971—); mem. Am. Geophys. Union (sec., sect. on hydrology 1973-77), Assn. Engring. Geologists, Internat. Assn. Hydrological Scis. (1st v.p. 1975-79), Internat. Soc. Soil Sci., Internat. Soc. Soil Mechanics and Found. Engring., Internat. Assn. Hydrogeology, Assn. Geohydrologists Internat. Devel., Nat. Soc. Profl. Engrs. (chpt. pres. 1970-71), Archaeol. Inst. Am., Bibl. Archaeol. Soc. Author, editor 80 reports and books in field. Office: 7600 E Orchard Rd Harlequin Plaza N Englewood CO 80111

JOHNSON, ARTHUR WILLIAM, JR., planetarium executive; b. Steubenville, Ohio, Jan. 8, 1949; s. Arthur William and Carol (Gilcrest) J.; B.Mus., U. So. Calif., 1973. Lectr., Griffith Obs. and Planetarium, 1969-73; planetarium writer, lectr. Mt. San Antonio Coll. Planetarium, Walnut, Calif., 1970-73; dir. Fleischmann Planetarium, U. Nev., Reno, 1973—. Organist, Trinity Episcopal Ch., Reno, 1980—; bd. dirs. Reno Chamber Orch. Assn., 1981—. Nev. Humanities Com., Inc. grantee, 1979-83. Mem. Am. Guild Organists (mem. exec. council No. Nev. chpt.), Cinema 360 Assn., Pacific Planetarium Assn. Republican. Episcopalian. Writer, producer: (with Donald G. Potter) Beautiful Nevada, 1978. Office: Fleischmann Planetarium U Nev Reno NV 89557

JOHNSON, BARBARA BEE, investments cons., businesswoman; b. Larned, Kans., Dec. 15, 1921; d. Thomas Kilburn and Hattie Leara (Fisher) Balman; student schs. Neosho, Mo.; m. Eddie Jack Johnson, Jan. 28, 1942 (dec.); children—Judith Ann, Jackie Carolee (dec.). Farm mgmt., Brawley, Calif., 1942-83; mgr., owner riding stable, Descanso, Calif., 1960-65; office sec., Imperial Valley, Calif., 1965-75; owner, mgr. rental complex, Brawley, 1965-73; owner, operator real properties, money mgmt., Barbara Bee Johnson Investments Co., Palm Desert, Calif., 1973—; prin. Johnson & Briggs Devel Co., 1980—, Bee Johnson Enterprises, 1981—. Democrat. Office: PO Box 2406 Palm Desert CA 92261 also PO Box 61 Solana Beach CA 92075 also PO Box 205 Ramona CA 92065

JOHNSON, BARBARA LANGNER, educational adminstrator; b. N.Y.C., June 17, 1946; d. Sidney and Geraldine (Brownstein) Langner; m. Sherman Lee Johnson, June 19, 1976; children—Damian Michael, Emily Elizabeth. B.A., NYU, 1968; M.A., U. No. Colo., 1973; Ed.D., No. Ariz. U., 1978. Tchr. spl. edn., Mount Kisco, N.Y., 1973-74, Phoenix, 1974-79; asst. prin. Fruitvale Elem. Sch., Grand Junction, Colo., 1979-80; asst. prin. Lincoln Orchard Mesa Elem. Sch., Grand Junction, Colo., 1980-82; prin. Mesa View Elem. Sch., Grand Junction, 1982—. Active Am. Cancer Soc. Mem. AAUW, Nat. Assn. Elementary Sch. Prins., Council Exceptional Children, Colo. Assn. Sch. Execs., Phi Delta Kappa. Democrat. Jewish. Office: Mesa View Elementary 2967 B Rd Grand Junction CO 81503

JOHNSON, BILL J., safety administrator, consultant; b. Greatbend, Kans., Dec. 21, 1942; s. George W. and Estor Marie J.; children—Jeffery James, Jennifer Marie, Deborah Ann. Student Central State U., 1961-63,

Okla. State U., 1974-75, Tulsa Jr. Coll., 1979-80. Safety insp. and premium auditor Md. Casualty Co., Oklahoma City, 1964-68; owner Midam. Fire Equipment Co. and B.J.J. Safety Cons., 1968-79; sr. loss control engr. Aetna Life and Casualty, Tulsa and Los Angeles, 1979-81; loss control mgr. Unigard Ins. Co., Fountain Valley, Calif., 1981—. Bd. dirs. Okla. Arson Adv. Council; mem. adv. bd. S. Oklahoma City Jr. Coll., Tulsa Jr. Coll.; active Big Bros. Am., Jaycees, 1965-70. Mem. Am. Soc. Safety Engrs., Internat. Assn. Drilling Contractors, Nat. Fire Protection Assn., Nat. Safety Mgmt. Soc., Vets. Safety. Republican. Clubs: Optimist Internat. (pres.), Black Gold. Contbr. articles to profl. jours. Home: PO Box 89 Midway City CA 92655

JOHNSON, BRADLEY ARTHUR, def. systems exec.; b. Tokyo, Nov. 11, 1947 (parents Am. citizens); s. Harold Ernest and Viola (Markarian) J.; m. Kathleen Marie Baumgartner, June 29, 1970; children—Jennifer Leigh, Matthew Philip. B.S., Va. Poly. Inst., 1969. Engr., Indsl. Tech. Assos., Alexandria, Va., 1969-70; v.p. Ionics Internat., Alexandria, 1970-71; self-employed, 1971-73; program mgr. command and control systems Westinghouse/DESC, Balt., 1973-75; v.p. Def. Systems div., dir. OAO Corp., El Segundo, Calif., 1975—; dir. Ionics Internat. Recipient Pres.'s award Fairchild Industries, 1976; ASTP Achievement award NASA, 1975; ATS-6 Achievement award, 1975. Mem. Am. Mgmt. Assn., Data Processing Mgmt. Assn., Assn. Computing Machinery, AF Assn., Armed Forces Communications and Electronics Assn., Assn. Old Crows, Assn. U.S. Army, Naval Inst. Research on advanced def. and NASA system architecture and design. Office: 225 E Imperial Hwy Suite 600 El Segundo CA 90245

JOHNSON, BURLEY RAY, consultant; b. Long Beach, Calif., Feb. 10, 1946; s. Burley and Bessie Beatrice (Babcock) J.; m. Dorothy Elizabeth Hahl, Mar. 11, 1978; children—Christianna Elizabeth, David Alojzy, Frederick William. A.A., Los Angeles Harbor Jr. Coll., 1966; B.S., Calif. State U.-Long Beach, 1971; B.A., Brigham Young U., 1972; M.B.A., U. So. Calif., 1976. Cost analyst Garrett Airesearch, Los Angeles, 1974-78; v.p. Quantum Fin. Corp., Palos Verdes, Calif., 1979-80; pres. Seventy Services, San Pedro, Calif., 1981—; dir. Las Vegas Mgmt. Group, Great Western Hotels Corp. Pres., Informed Voters League, 1981. Mem. Nat. Assn. Accts., Am. Acctg. Assn., San Pedro C. of C. (legis. com.). Republican. Mem. Ch. Jesus Christ of Latter-day Saints. Office: 555 W 9th St #24 San Pedro CA 90732

JOHNSON, CAROL JOY, publishing company executive; b. Rye, N.Y., Jan. 28, 1938; d. Jack and Blanche Isabelle (Akin) Pacanda; 1 son, Jason. Editorial asst. Fairchild Publs., N.Y.C., 1968-69; copywriter, adminstrv. asst. Petersen Pub. Co., Los Angeles, 1969-73, mgr. mail advt., 1973-74, mgr., 1974-79, dir. advt. adminstrn., 1979—. Office: 8490 Sunset Blvd Los Angeles CA 90069

JOHNSON, CAROLYN (HASSLER), librarian, educator; b. Oakland, Calif., May 29, 1921; d. Ferdinand Oren and Clara Wells (Humphrey) Hassler; m. Benjamin Alfred Johnson, Feb. 12, 1943; children—Robin Rebecca, Anne Elizabeth, Delia Mary. Grad. in Journalism, U. Calif.-Berkeley, 1946; M.L.A., Immaculate Heart Coll., Los Angeles, 1968. State sch. library credentials, Calif. Asst. children's librarian, Fullerton (Calif.) Pub. Library, 1951-58, coordinator children's services, 1958-80, city librarian, 1980—; instr. Rio Hondo Jr. Coll., 1970-72, Grad. Sch. Librarianship Calif. State U., Fullerton, 1972-77; pres. So. Calif. Council on Lit. for Children and Young People, 1977-79. Life mem. PTA; mem. LWV, YWCA. Mem. ALA, Calif. Library Assn. (pres. Children's Services Chpt. 1979), Calif. Media Educators Assn., AAUW, Phi Beta Kappa, Theta Sigma Phi. Office: 353 W Commonwealth Ave Fullerton CA 92632

JOHNSON, CHARLES FOREMAN, architect, architectural photographer, consultant; b. Plainfield, N.J., May 28, 1929; s. Charles E. and E. Lucile (Casner) J.; student Union Jr. Coll., 1947; B.Arch., U. So. Calif., 1958; postgrad. UCLA, 1959-60; m. Beverly Jean Hinnendale, Feb. 19, 1961 (div. 1970); children—Kevin, David. Draftsman, Wigton-Abbott, P.C., Plainfield, 1946-48; archtl. cons., graphic designer and interior designer, 1952—; designer, draftsman with H.W. Underhill, Architect, Los Angeles, 1953-55; teaching asst. U. So. Calif., Los Angeles, 1954-55; designer with Carrington H. Lewis, Architect, Palos Verdes, Calif., 1955-56; grad. architect Ramo-Wooldridge Corp., Los Angeles, 1956-58; tech. dir. Atlas weapon system Space Tech. Labs., Los Angeles, 1958-60; advanced planner and systems engr. Minuteman Weapon System, TRW, Los Angeles, 1960-64, div. staff ops. dir., 1964-68; cons. N.Mex. Regional Med. Program and N.Mex. State Dept. Hosps., 1968-70; prin. Charles F. Johnson, architect, Los Angeles, 1953-68, Sante Fe, N.Mex., 1968—; free lance archtl. photographer, Sante Fe, 1971—. Major archtl. works include: residential bldgs. in Calif., 1955-66; Bashein Bldg. at Los Lunas (N.Mex.) Hosp. and Tng. Sch., 1969, various residential bldgs., Santa Fe, 1973—, Kurtz Home, Dillon, Colo., 1981, Whispering Boulders Home, Carefree, Ariz., 1981, Hedrick House, Santa Fe, 1983, Kole House, Green Valley, Ariz., 1984. Casa Largo, Santa Fe (used for film The Man Who Fell to Earth), 1974. Pres., Santa Fe Coalition for the Arts, 1977; set designer Santa Fe Fiesta Melodrama, 1969, 71, 74, 77, 78, 81. Mem. Delta Sigma Phi. Club: El Gancho Tennis. Contbr. articles on facility planning and mgmt. to profl. publs.; contbr. archtl. photographs to mags. in U.S., Eng., France, Japan and Italy. Recognized for work in organic architecture. Address: 14 General Sage Dr Santa Fe NM 87501 also Camino de la Cruz Blanca Santa Fe NM

JOHNSON, CHARLES H., info. systems co. exec.; b. Ogden, Utah, Mar. 6, 1948; s. Charles M. and Gracie Johnson; student U. Calif., Berkeley, 1979—; m. Darelena Allen, Nov. 11, 1968; children—Konia Kofi, Zalika Nayo. With Bank of Am. San Francisco, 1967-75; with Rand Info. Systems, San Francisco, 1975—, mgr. ops., 1980—. Served with AUS, 1968-70. Office: 98 Battery St San Francisco CA 94111

JOHNSON, CLARISSA M. TORRES, school administrator; b. El Paso, May 27, 1947; d. Arturo C. and Clara S. (Kozarek) Torres; m. David C. Johnson, July 20, 1969; children—Lara Eileen, Alexander David. B.S. in Elem. Edn., N.Mex. State U., 1969, M.A. in Reading, 1976. Cert. elem. tchr., prin. N.Mex. Tchr. Alamogordo (N.Mex.) Pub. Schs., 1969-71, 74-76, prescriptive reading tchr., 1976-78, dist. instructional coordinator, 1978-82, prin. Heights Elem. Sch., 1982—; tchr. Roswell (N.Mex.) Ind. Sch., 1971-74. Mem. Assn. Supervision and Curriculum Devel., N.Mex. Assn. Elem. Sch. Prins., Delta Kappa Gamma, Kappa Kappa Iota. Democrat. Methodist. Office: 2410 10th St Alamogordo NM 88310

JOHNSON, CLAYTON ERROLD, poultry company executive; b. DeSota, Wis., Apr. 20, 1921; s. James and Louella (Goodin) J.; student U. Wis., 1940-41, Tex. A. and M. Coll., 1946; m. Betty J. Higenbotham, May 23, 1943; children—Roderick and Ronald (twins), Richard. Pres. Flavor Fresh Brand, Inc., 1949—; Calif. gen. bldg. contractor, 1947—. Served with USAAF, 1942-45. Home: 3111 Bel Air Dr Las Vegas NV 89109

JOHNSON, CLIFFORD LEE, bus. assn. exec.; b. Belleville, Kans., Sept. 15, 1917; s. Russell L. and Lillian Rena (Carlson) J.; student Inst. Orgn. Mgmt., U. Mont., 1949-56, U. Colo., 1957; m. Evelyn J. Hunt, Aug. 6, 1939; 1 dau., Jerry Lee Dunn. Super market mgr. Great Atlantic & Pacific Tea Co., Kansas City, Mo., 1935-43; buyer Herbolsheimer Men's Wear, Belleville, Kans., 1946-49; mgr. Fort Morgan (Colo.) C. of C., 1949-52; membership dir. Colo. C. of C., Colorado Springs, 1952-56; exec. v.p. Estes Park (Colo.) C. of C., 1956-60; mgr. Elkhorn Lodge, Estes Park, 1960-61; owner Range Restaurant, Estes Park, 1963-66; exec. v.p. Longmont (Colo.) C. of C., 1966-71; dir. fin. and adminstrv. affairs Colo. Assn. Commerce and Industry, Denver, 1971—. Served with USN, 1943-46; PTO. Recipient Outstanding Service award Colo. C. of C. Execs., 1959, Outstanding Leadership award Colo. C. of C. Execs., 1971, Service award Longmont Centennial Commn., 1970, Distributive Edn. Appreciation award Longmont High Sch., 1971; cert. chamber exec. Am. C. of C. Execs., 1974. Mem. Am. C. of C. Execs. Colo. C. of C. Execs. (pres. 1958-59), chambers of commerce execs., Mountain States Assn. (dir. 1970-79), Assn. Membership Execs. (pres. 1975-76), Colo. State Firemen's Assn. Republican. Clubs: Order Eastern Star, Shriners, Masons. Editor: Colo. C. of C. Execs. Newletter, 1974-79, Mountain States Assn. Newsletter, 1974-79. Home: 1225 Cornell Dr Longmont CO 80501 Office: 1390 Logan St Denver CO 80203

JOHNSON, CONOR DEANE, mech. engr.; b. Charlottesville, Va., Apr. 20, 1943; s. Randolph Holiday and Louise Anna (Deane) J.; B.S. in Engring. Mechanics, Va. Poly. Inst., 1965; M.S., Clemson U., 1967, Ph.D. in Engring. Mechanics, 1969; m. Laura Teague Rogers, Dec. 20, 1966; children—William Drake, Catherine Teague. With Anamet Labs., Inc., 1973-82, sr. structural analyst, Dayton, Ohio, 1973-75, prin. engr., San Carlos, Calif., 1975-81, v.p., 1981-82; program mgr. Aerospace Structures Info. & Analysis Center, 1975-82; co-founder, pres. CSA Engring., Inc., Palo Alto, Calif., 1982—. Served to capt. USAF, 1969-73. Decorated Commendation medal. NDEA fellow, 1967-68. Registered profl. engr., Calif. Mem. AIAA, ASME (award for structures and materials 1981), Sigma Xi. Methodist. Contbr. articles to profl. jours. Home: 3425 Lodge Dr Belmont CA 94002 Office: 560 San Antonio Rd Suite 101 Palo Alto CA 94306

JOHNSON, CRAIG WALTER, plumbing contractor; b. Spanish Fork, Utah, July 11, 1947; s. Marcus Walter and Catherine Holley J.; B.S. in Mgmt., Weber State U., 1970; postgrad. Brigham Young U., 1975-76. Plumbing contractor Idaho, 1970-71; property mgr. western states Village Properties, 1971-73; foreman, estimator Marcus Johnson Plumbing, Salt Lake City, 1973-75, gen. mgr., 1977—, sec.-treas., 1977—; pvt. practice bldg. contractor, Provo, Utah, 1975-77. Served to 2d lt. Utah N.G., 1966-72. Mem. Mech. Contractors Assn., Utah Plumbing-Heating-Cooling Contractors, Salt Lake Home Builders. Mem. Ch. of Jesus Christ of Latter-day Saints. Club: Sports Mall (Salt Lake City). Home: 5815 Waterbury Way No 4 Salt Lake City UT 84107 Office: 222 E 4050 S Salt Lake City UT 84107

JOHNSON, DAVID EASTERBROOK, optometrist, health care administrator; b. Cleve., May 7, 1932; s. Vernon Frank and Edna Harriet (Easterbrook) J.; m. Lois Jean Repine, Apr. 19, 1954; children—Deborah Lynn, Scott David. B.S. in Optometry, Ohio State U., 1954; M.P.H., U. Mich., 1969. Diplomate Am. Acad. Optometry. Commd. 2d lt. U.S. Army, 1955, advanced through grades to lt. col., 1970; research optometrist, chief optometrist U.S. Army, 1955-70; cons. optometry Surgeon Gen. Army, Washington, 1971-72; chief optometry service 5th Gen. Hosp., Stuttgart, Germany, 1972-75, Letterman Army Med. Ctr. San Francisco, 1975-76; asst. dean Coll. Optometry, Pacific U., Forest Grove, Oreg., 1976-78; chief optometry service Schofield Barracks, Hawaii, 1979-82; staff optometrist Straub Clinic and Hosp., Honolulu, 1983—; TV series host: You and Eye. Pres. Stuttgart Am. High Sch. PTA 1974-75; bd. dirs. Enchanted Lake Assn. 1983. Mem. Am. Optometric Assn., Armed Forces Optometric Soc. (pres. 1973-74), Am. Pub. Health Assn., Am. Acad. Optometry. Home: 940 Akumu St Kailua HI 96734 Office: Eye Dept Straub Clinic and Hospital 888 S King St Honolulu HI 96813

JOHNSON, DEANE HENRY RAE, county extension agent; b. Marcus, Iowa, June 10, 1931; s. Carl Oscar and Dorothy Helen (Fairchild) J.; m. Lorna Roberta Gatherers, Sept. 11, 1954; children—Douglas Leo, Cheryl Marie Johnson Vance. B.S., N.D. State U., 1958; postgrad. U. Minn., 1962—; M.Extension, Wash. State U., 1969; postgrad. 1971. County 4-H agt. Clay County, U. Minn., 1958-64; 4-H and youth agt. Lewis County, Wash. State U., Chehalis, 1964-82, staff chmn., 4-H youth agt., 1982—. Active Mayfield Lake Youth Camp Assn., 1974—, v.p., 1981—. Served to cpl. U.S. Army, 1952-54. Mem. Wash. 4-H Assn., Nat. Assn. Extension 4-H Agts. (Disting. Service award 1975). Club: Sertoma (Twin City, Wash.). Home: 554 N W Penn Ave Chehalis WA 98532 Office: PO Box 708 Court House Annex Chehalis WA 98532

JOHNSON, DENA NANCEAN, real estate company executive; b. Des Moines, May 31, 1944; d. William W. and Genevieve Garland (Myrick) den Hartog; m. Richard K. Johnson, Jan. 9, 1965; children—Scot Richard, Kurt William. Student Central Coll., Pella, Iowa, 1962-65, Coe Coll., summer 1965; B.A., Central Mo. State U., 1968; student Dijon (France) U., summer 1967; postgrad. Fla. State U., 1969; interior design cert. Griffith Opportunity Sch., 1975. Tchr., Gadsen County Sch. System, Quincy, Fla., 1969; with Junction Realty, Evergreen, Colo., 1977-79; salesman Pine Ridge Realty, Evergreen, 1979, 82-83; v.p. Tamarac Ltd., Evergreen, 1978—; salesman, treas. Tamarac Homes, Ltd., Evergreen, 1974—. Pres. Bear Mountain Homeowners' Assn., 1980-82. Lic. real estate salesman, Colo. Mem. Nat. Assn. Realtors, Colo. Assn. Realtors, Jefferson County Bd. Realtors, Evergreen Bd. Realtors, AAUW (charter mem. Lakewood), P.E.O. (chpt. treas.). Mem. Unity Ch. Club: Newcomers (Evergreen). Office: PO Box 1567 Evergreen CO 80439

JOHNSON, DIANE KAY, solid waste collection and landfill services contractor, registered nurse; b. Coeur d'Alene, Idaho, Apr. 24, 1937; d. Raymond Francis and Irene Winifred (Nelson) Lavonture; m. Louis Bryan Granger, Aug. 10, 1958; children—Joseph, Relene; stepchildren—Richard, Kelly; m. 2d, Richard David Johnson, Aug. 16, 1969 (dec. 1979); 1 son, Rex. Diploma, Deaconess Hosp. Sch. Nursing, Spokane, Wash., 1958; B.S. in Nursing, U. Oreg., 1966. R.N., Idaho, Wash.; lic. pub. works contractor, Idaho. Head nurse surg.-psychiat. unit No. State Hosp., Sedro Wooley, Wash., 1958-59; night charge nurse surg. unit St. Mary's Hosp., Port Arthur, Tex., 1959-60; head nurse recovery room Lake City Gen. Hosp., Coeur d'Alene, 1960-62; pub. health nurse Panhandle Dist. Health Unit, Coeur d'Alene, 1962-64; staff nurse U. Oreg. Med. Sch. Out-Patient Clinic, Portland, 1966, head nurse med. unit Kootenai Meml. Hosp., Coeur d'Alene, 1967; instr. practical nursing N. Idaho Coll., Coeur d'Alene, 1967-70; owner Latah Sanitation, Inc., Moscow, Idaho, 1970—. Mem. Statewide Health Coordinating Council, 1979; bd. dirs. Gritman Meml. Hosp., Moscow, 1972—. Mem. N.Central Idaho Comprehensive Health Planning Council (sec. 1973-74), Idaho Nurses Assn. (v.p. 1973-76), Idaho Health Systems Agy., Idaho San. Service Inst., Inc. (pres. 1980-83), Moscow C. of C., Am. Nurses Assn., Nat. Solid Waste Mgmt. Assn. Presbyterian. Founder teen-age vol. program for hosp. and convalescent ctrs., Moscow, 1971. Home: PO Box 8931 Moscow ID 83843 Office: Latah Sanitation Inc 3339 Hwy 8 Moscow ID 83843

JOHNSON, DORIS ELIZABETH, plant geneticist; b. Woodstock, Ont., Can., Dec. 12, 1942; d. John Smith and Doris Evelyn (Goodwin) Hamill; m. Clayton Aaby Johnson, Nov. 21, 1970 (dec.). B.Sc., U. Western Ont., 1965; Ph.D., U. Hawaii, 1970. Research asst. Brookhaven Nat. Lab., N.Y.C., 1967-68; geneticist Molokai (Hawaii) Seed Service, 1969-72; mgr. Molokai Research Sta., Funk Seeds Internat., 1972—. Treas. Molokai 4-H Club. Mem. Am. Soc. Agronomy. Home: Puili Pl Kaunakakai HI 96748 Office: Box 371 Kaunakakai HI 96748

JOHNSON, DOUGLAS ALLAN, plant physiologist, researcher; b. Montevideo, Minn., Dec. 6, 1949; s. Thomas W. and Dorothy I. (Dove) J.; m. Kathryn E. Rosine, Jan. 1, 1972; children—Thomas H., Kira D. B.A. summa cum laude, Augustana Coll., 1971; M.S., Utah State U., 1973, Ph.D., 1975. Research fellow, research asst. Utah State U., Logan, 1971-75, research plant physiologist Forage and Range Improvement Program, Agrl. Research Service, U.S. Dept. Agr., Crops Research Lab., 1976—; postdoctoral research asst. Naval Arctic Research Lab., Barrow, Alaska, 1975; fed. collaborator dept. range sci. U. State U., Logan. Recipient Coop. Research grant, 1981-82. Mem. Soc. for Range Mgmt., Am. Soc. Agronomy, Crop Sci. Soc. Am., Am. Soc. Plant Physiologists, Beta, Beta, Beta. Club: Lions (past pres., sec.-treas.). Office: Crops Research Lab Utah State U 63 Logan UT 84322

JOHNSON, DOUGLAS MCFARLIN, school counselor; b. States, Idaho, Aug. 20, 1945; s. Carl Alfred and Frances (Verlee) J.; m. Marlene Kay Moggenborg, Aug. 9, 1980. B.S., Lewis-Clark State Coll., 1969; M.Ed., Idaho State U., 1974; postgrad. U. Idaho, 1982. Tchr., coach Clearwater Valley Hgh Sch., Kooskia, Idaho, 1969-71; counselor Wendell (Idaho) High Sch., 1974-80, Moscow (Idaho) High Sch., 1980—. Mem. Am. Personnel and Guidance Assn., Idaho Personnel and Guidance Assn., Idaho Soc. Individual Psychology, NEA, Idaho Edn. Assn. Elk. Office: 401 E 3d St Moscow ID 83843

JOHNSON, DUANE CURTIS, sales trainer; b. Vanport, Oreg., Mar. 30, 1945; s. Glen V. and Florence M. (Wang) J.; m. Wendy M. Bradbury, Sept. 6, 1969; m. 2d, Teresa A. Haley, Oct. 28, 1977; children—Curt, Stephanie, Kristofer. B.A., Gustavus Adolphus Coll., 1967; M.A., Lewis and Clark Coll., 1971; M.B.A., U. Portland, 1974. Bus. tchr., coach Colton (Oreg.) High Sch., 1967-68, Centennial High Sch., Gresham, Oreg., 1969-72; sales rep. Purex Corp., Portland, Oreg., 1972-73; market research analyst Freightliner Corp., Portland, 1974-75; sales rep. Employers Ins. of Wausau, Beaverton, Oreg., 1975-76; mgr. sales tng. Freightliner Corp./Mercedes-Benz Truck Co., Portland, 1976—; cons. in field. Asst. coach West Linn Baseball-Softball Assn.; mem. alumni adv. bd., mem. fin. com. U. Portland Grad. Sch. Bus., 1982; advisor Jr. Achievement Portland Area, 1979-80. Woodbury scholar, 1963; Gustavus Adolphus Coll. grantee, 1963. Mem. Am. Soc. Tng. and Devel. Democrat. Lutheran. Clubs: West Linn Soccer, Oregon State Grange. Author numerous slide sound programs, sales aides, brochures and tng. programs. Office: PO Box 3849 Portland OR 97208

JOHNSON, EARL, JR., judge; b. Watertown, S.D., June 10, 1933; s. Earl Jerome and Doris Melissa (Schwartz) J.; B.A. in Econs., Northwestern U., 1955, LL.M., 1961; J.D., U. Chgo., 1960; m. Barbara Claire Yanow, Oct. 11, 1970; children—Kelly Ann, Earl Eric, Agaarn Yanovitch. Admitted to Ill. bar, 1960, 9th Circuit bar, 1964, D.C. bar, 1965, U.S. Supreme Ct. bar, 1966, Calif. bar, 1972, U.S. Dist. Ct. (cen. dist.) Calif., 1982; trial atty., organized crime sect. Dept. Justice, Washington, Las Vegas, Nev., 1961-64; dep. dir. Neighborhood Legal Services Project, Washington, 1964-65; dep. dir. OEO Nat. Legal Services Program, 1965-66, dir., 1966-68; vis. scholar Center for Study of Law and Soc., U. Calif., Berkeley, 1968-69; assoc. prof. U. So. Calif. Law Center, Los Angeles, 1969-75, prof. law, 1976-82, dir. Program for Dispute Systems Research, Social Sci. Research Inst., 1975-82, dir. clin. semester, 1970-73; assoc. justice Ct. Appeal, State of Calif., Los Angeles, 1982—; mem. Los Angeles County Regional Planning Commn., 1980-81; co-dir. Access to Justice Project, vis. scholar Inst. Comparative Law, U. Florence (Italy), 1973, 75, 79; cons. Ct. Assistance Project, Inst. Advanced Studies in Justice, Am. U., 1976-80; cons. Sci. Applications, Inc., 1979-82; adv. panel Legal Services Corp., 1976-80; legis. impact panel Nat. Acad. Scis., 1977-80; faculty Asian Workshop on Legal Services to Poor, 1974; mem. Internat. Center Legal Services in Developing Countries, 1972-75; Robert H. Jackson lectr. Nat. Jud. Coll., 1980. Founder, bd. mem. Action for Legal Rights, 1971-74; pres., trustee Western Center on Law and Poverty, 1972-73, 76-80; v.p., chmn. exec. com. Calif. Rural Legal Assistance Corp., 1973-74; sec. Nat. Resource Center for Consumers of Legal Services, 1974-83; bd. dirs. Beverly Hills Bar Found., 1972-73; trustee Los Angeles Legal Aid Found., 1969-71; mem. exec. com. Nat. Sr. Citizens Law Center, 1980-82. Served with USNR, 1955-58. Recipient Dart award for acad. innovation U. So. Calif., 1971; 1st Loren Miller award for legal services to Calif. poor, 1977; named So. Calif. Citizen of Week, 1978; Ford Found. fellow, 1960; Dept. State lectr., 1975; grantee Ford Found., Russell Sage Found., Law Enforcement Assistance Adminstrn., NSF. Mem. Am. (com. chmn. 1972-75, mem. spl. com. resolution minor disputes 1976-81, mem. com. on non-jud. resolution of disputes 1981—), Calif. (standing com. on legal services to poor 1977-81), Los Angeles bar assns., Law and Soc. Assn., Nat. Legal Aid and Defenders Assn. (dir. 1968-77), Am. Acad. Polit. and Social Sci., Soc. Am. Law Tchrs., Order of Coif. Democrat. Author: Justice and Reform: The Formative Years of the American Legal Services Program, 1978; Toward Equal Justice: A Comparative Study of Legal Aid in Modern Societies, 1975; Outside The Courts: A Survey of Diversion Alternatives in Civil Cases, 1977; Dispute Processing Strategies, 1978; editor U. Chgo. Law Rev., 1960. Contbr. articles to books and periodicals. Home: 1627 Monterey Blvd Hermosa Beach CA 90254 Office: Ct Appeal 2d Appellate Dist 3580 Wilshire Blvd Los Angeles CA 90010

JOHNSON, ELAINE CHARNAK, educator; b. N.Y.C., Aug. 17, 1943; d. Nelson Charnak and Rose (Chesin) C.; m. Robert Malcolm Johnson, Nov. 8, 1970. B.A., U. Calif.-Berkeley, 1965; M.A., Calif. State U.-San Francisco, 1967. Cert. secondary tchr., Calif. Braille transcriber Berkeley Unified Sch. Dist., 1965-66; tchr. of blind, San Francisco, 1968; humanities tchr. Reed Union Sch. Dist., Tiburon, Calif., 1968-69; English tchr. Tamalpais Union High Sch., Marin County, Calif., 1969—; co-chmn. Asilomar Lang. Arts Conf. 32, 1982; cons. Novato Union High Sch. Dist., 1977, Bay Area Writing Project Ednl. Testing Service. Active Sierra Club, ACLU, Coalition Labor Union Women, Simon Weisenthal Ctr., Calif. Abortion Rights Action League; pres. Am. Fedn. Tchrs. Local #1985, 1980-82; trustee Central Labor Council, Calif. Labor Fedn., AFL-CIO. Calif. Parent Tchr. Student Assn. grantee 1967; U.S. Govt. Study grantee 1966-67. Mem. Calif. Assn. Tchrs. English. Democrat. Co-editor: The Tamalpais Teacher, 1979—.

JOHNSON, ELLIOTT WILLARD, lawyer; b. Mt. Vernon, Wash., Feb. 18, 1949; s. A. Elliott and Eileen (Willard) J.; m. Victoria Annette Goodman, Aug. 28, 1970; children—Ann Kay, Meredith Christine. A.A., Skagit Valley Coll., 1969; B.A., U. Wash., 1971; J.D., Willamette U., 1974. Bar: Wash. 1974, U.S. Dist. Ct. (ea. and we. dists.) Wash. 1975, U.S. Ct. Appeals (9th cir.) 1979, U.S. Supreme Ct. 1979. Sole practice, Mt. Vernon, 1974-75; ptnr. Mullen, Angevine & Johnson, Mt. Vernon, 1975-77, Angevine & Johnson, Mt. Vernon, 1977-80, Angevine, Johnson & Barth, Mt. Vernon, 1980—. Adminstr., Pacific N.W. Dist. of Key Clubs, 1980—. Recipient Am. Jurisprudence award, 1971. Mem. Am. Trial Lawyers Assn., Wash. State Trial Lawyers Assn., ABA, Wash. State Bar Assn., Skagit County Bar Assn., Phi Delta Phi. Republican. Methodist. Home: 310 E Washington St Mount Vernon WA 98273 Office: Angevine Johnson & Barth 709-711 S 1st St Mount Vernon WA 98273

JOHNSON, FREDERICK HAROLD, furniture company executive, interior designer; b. Mitchell, S.D., July 26, 1931; s. Harold Jacob and Alice (Nieveen) J.; m. Shirley Ann Dowell, Feb. 22, 1965 (div. 1977); 1 stepson, Scott Marshall Dolph; m. 2d, Athena Callas, Nov. 27, 1978. B.A., U. Ariz., 1952; postgrad. Rudolph Schaeffer Sch. of Design, 1952-53. Sales staff Union Furniture Co., San Francisco, 1952-53, W. R.

Shearman Furniture Co., Tucson, 1953-54; pres., owner Johnson's Furniture, Inc., Tucson, 1954—; bus. mgr. Voorlas-Johnson Group, Mgmt. Cons. Charter pres., co-founder, Downtown 20-30 Club, 1958; charter mem. Tuscon Chpt. Air Force Assn. (council mem., v.p. 1970-76); mem. bd. dirs. Tuscon Symphony Soc. (past v.p., exec. com. mem.), pres. Ariz. Touring Orch., 1982—. Mem. Ariz. Shippers Assn. (cir. 1973-75), Tucson C. of C. (chmn. aviation com.), Nat. Home Furnishings Assn., Alpha Tau Omega, Alpha Kappa Psi, Alpha Delta Sigma. Republican. Episcopalian. Clubs: Tucson Country (dir. 1974-75), Skyline Country, Rotary. Home: 6910 N Mamaronick Dr Tucson AZ 85718 Office: Johnson Furniture Inc 4380 E Broadway St Tucson AZ 85711

JOHNSON, FREDERICK WILLIAM, Canadian provincial chief justice; b. Sedgley, Staffordshire, Eng., Feb. 13, 1917; s. Edwin Priestley and Laura (Caddick) J.; m. Joyce Marilyn Laing, July 30, 1949; children—William Frederick, Royce Laing Caddick, Sheila Frederika. B.A., U. Sask. (Can.), 1947, LL.B., 1949. Bar: Sask. 1950, created queen's counsel, 1963. With Johnson, Bayda, Trudelle & Beke; justice Ct. of Queen's Bench Sask., Regina, 1967-77, chief justice, 1977—; chmn. Royal Commn. on Govt. Adminstrn. (Sask.), 1964-65. Trustee Regina Pub. Sch. Bd., 1956-60. Served with RCA, 1941-46; U.K. and Western Europe. Mem. Law Soc. Sask. (bencher 1960-65). Mem. United Ch. Canada. Clubs: Assiniboia, United Services Inst. Office: Ct of Queen's Bench Courthouse 2425 Victoria Ave Regina SK S4P 3V7 Canada*

JOHNSON, GARDINER, lawyer; b. San Jose, Calif., Aug. 10, 1905; s. George W. and Izora (Carter) J.; A.B., U. Calif., 1926, J.D., 1928; m. Doris Louis Miller, Sept. 28, 1935; children—Jacqueline Ann, Stephen Miller. Bar: Calif. 1928; practice San Francisco, 1928—; ptnr. Johnson & Stanton, 1952—. Mem. nat. drafting com. Council State Govts., 1944-47, chmn. Gov.'s Conf. Edn., 1955; chmn. Calif. delegation White House Conf. Edn., 1955; mem. Calif. Legislature from 18th Assembly Dist., 1935-47, speaker pro tem, 1940; mem. Republican State Central Com., 1934-46, 50—; mem. Alameda County Rep. Central Com., 1934-47, 59—; alternate del. Rep. Nat. Conv., 1940, del., 1956, 60, 64, 68, 76; pres. Calif. Rep. Assembly, 1959; mem. Rep. Nat. Com., 1964-68; mem. Citizens Legis. Adv. Commn., 1957-61; bd. dirs. U. Calif. Hosps. Aux., 1960-70, pres., 1962, 64-65; bd. dirs. Florence Crittenton Home, San Francisco, 1960-69, 76—, pres., 1967-69; bd. dirs. Florence Crittenton Assn. Am., 1969-75, v.p., 1973-75; bd. dirs. Spring Opera of San Francisco, 1963-69, Child Welfare League Am., 1976—; bd. govs. San Francisco Heart Assn., 1963-70, chmn., 1966-69; mem. council Save-the-Redwoods League, 1970—; bd. dirs. San Francisco unit Am. Cancer Soc., 1971-77, pres., 1973-75. Recipient Disting. Service medal U. Calif. Hosps., 1976. Fellow Am. Coll. Trial Lawyers; mem. Assn. Trial Lawyers Am., Internat. Bar Assn. (alternate del. 8th Conf. Salzburg 1960), Inter-Am. Bar Assn., ABA (com. state legislation 1957-59, vice chmn. com. pub. contracts 1959), State Bar Calif. (chmn. exec. com. Conf. State Bar Dels. 1956-57, chmn. legislative com. 1965), Bar Assn. San Francisco (dir. 1951-57, pres. 1958-59), Calif. Hist. Soc. (trustee 1961-71, pres. 1968-70), San Francisco C. of C. (dir. 1964-67, v.p. 1967), Presidio Soc. (dir. 1981—), Phi Beta Kappa, Phi Delta Phi, Kappa Delta Rho. Republican. Episcopalian. Clubs: Pacific-Union, Claremont Country, Lawyers (San Francisco), Commonwealth of Calif. (bd. govs. 1954-64, pres. 1958-59). Home: 329 Hampton Rd Piedmont CA 94611 Office: 221 Sansome St San Francisco CA 94104

JOHNSON, GARY KENT, management education company executive; b. Provo, Utah, Apr. 16, 1936; s. Clyde LeRoy and Ruth Laie (Taylor) J.; m. Mary Joyce Crowther, Aug. 26, 1955; children—Mary Ann Johnson Harvey, Gary Kent, Brent James, Jeremy Clyde. Student Brigham Young U., 1954-55, U. Utah, 1955-58, 60-61, U. Calif.-Berkeley, 1962. Sales rep. Roche Labs., Salt Lake City, 1958-61, sales trainer, Denver, 1962, sales trainer, Oakland, Calif., 1962, div. mgr., Seattle, 1962-69, sec.-treas. Western Mgmt. Inst., Seattle, 1969-71, pres. WMI Corp., Bellevue, Wash., 1971—; dir. Lamson Products; speaker, cons. various nat. orgns. Bd. dirs. Big Bros.; del. King County Republican Com. Served with U.S. N.G., 1953-61. Walgreen scholar, 1955-58; Bristol scholar, 1958. Mem. Am. Soc. Tng. and Devel., Phi Sigma Epsilon. Mormon. Club: Bellevue Athletic. Author: Select the Best, 1976; Antitrust Untangled, 1977; The Utilities Management Series, 1979; Performance Appraisal, A Program for Improving Productivity, 1981. Office: 1309 114th Ave SE Suite 212 Bellevue WA 98004

JOHNSON, GARY MICHAEL, restaurant conglomerate executive; b. Phoenix, Oct. 13, 1946; s. Woodrow Victor and Victoria (Romley) J.; m. Bernadette Ellen Vidrine, Aug. 15, 1969; children—Holly, Troy, Cody. Student U. Ariz., 1963-67. From restaurant mgr. to pres. Macayo Restaurants Corp. (name now Macayo's Inc.), Phoenix, Tucson and Las Vegas, 1968-83, pres., chief exec. officer, 1983—; mem. western adv. council Kemper Ins. Co. Bd. dirs. Arthritis Found., Phoenix, 1982-83; chmn. Metro Pops Orch., Phoenix, 1981, 82-83. Mem. Nat. Restaurant Assn., Scottsdale Jaycees (head honcho), C. of C. Am., Ariz. Desert Bighorn Sheep Soc., Assoc. Hwy. Patrolmen Ariz., Frat. Order of Police. Republican. Episcopalian. Office: Macayo's Inc 4001 N Central St Phoenix AZ 85012

JOHNSON, GEORGE GILBERT, accountant; b. Frankfort, Mich., May 24, 1930; s. Gilbert George and Blanche Louise (Natzel) J.; m. Sharon Elizabeth Thurber, June 11, 1955; children—Cynthia, Angelia, Denise, George. Asso. Commerce, Northwestern Mich. Coll., 1955. Sec./treas. subs. Kysor Heater Co., Cadillac, Mich., 1955-62; fin. dir. N.Mex. Dept. Hosps., 1962-69; fin. dir. St. Joseph Hosp., Albuquerque, 1969-77; v.p. fin. Driscoll Children's Hosp., Corpus Christi, Tex., 1977-78; dir. spl. acctg. S.W. Community Health Services, Albuquerque, 1978—. Bd. chmn. St. Francis Gardens Nursing Home, 1979-81, bd. dirs., 1982. Served with U.S. Army, 1951-53. Mem. Healthcare Fin. Mgmt. Assn., N.Mex. Healthcare Fin. Mgmt. Assn. Republican. Methodist. Lodge: Elks. Home: 8530 Yeager Dr NE Albuquerque NM 87109 Office: 1100 Central SE Albuquerque NM 87102

JOHNSON, GERALD HARLAN, engineer; b. Peoria, Ill., July 26, 1920; s. Frank Llewellyn and Bertha Francis (Doubet) J.; m. Margaret Ileen Boydstun, June 2, 1946; children—Gerald H., Randy L., Neil R., Peggy L. Registered profl. engr., Calif., 1978. Patrolman, Ill. State Police, 1953-56; plant protection officer Hughes Aircraft Co., 1956-64; dir. loss prevention Anamax Mining Co., Sahuarita, Ariz., 1965-83. Served with USAAF, 1941-45. Mem. Nat. Safety Council, Am. Soc. Safety Engrs. Republican. Clubs: Masons, (32 deg.), Shriners. Contbr. articles to profl. jours. Home: Rt 1 Box 19 Sahuarita AZ 85629

JOHNSON, GWENAVERE A., artist; b. Newark, S.D., Oct. 16, 1909; d. Arthur E. and Susie Ellen (King) Nelson; m. John Wendell Johnson, Dec. 17, 1937; 1 son, John Forrest. Student Mpsl. Sch. Art, 1930; B.A., U. Minn., 1937; M.A., San Jose State U., 1957. Cert. gen. elem., secondary, art tchr., Calif. Art tchr., supr. Austin (Minn.) Schs., 1937-38; art tchr. Hillbrook Sch., Los Gatos, Calif., 1947-52; art tchr., supr. Santa Clara (Calif.) Pub. Schs., 1952-55; art tchr., dept. chmn. San Jose (Calif.) Unified Schs., 1955-75; owner Tree Tops studio, San Jose, 1975—. Juried shows: Los Gatos Art Assn., 1976, 77, 78, 79 (1st and 2d awards), Treeside gallery, Los Gatos, 1980, 81 (1st awards); Livermore Art Assn., 1977 (2d award), Los Gatos Art Mus., 1981 (1st award), 82 (2d award), Rosicrucean Mus., 1983; creator Overfelt portrait Alexian Bros. Hosp., San Jose, Calif., 1977. Recipient Golden Centaur award Acad. Italia, 1982, others. Mem. San Jose Art League, Los Gatos Art Assn., Santa Clara Art Assn., Soc. Western Artists, Nat. League Am. Penwomen, Academia Italia. Home and Office: 2054 Booksin Ave San Jose CA 95125

JOHNSON, H. THOMAS, university administrator; b. Chgo., Apr. 18, 1938; s. Harold M. and Ellen J. (Peterson) J.; m. Elaine Bowe, July 17, 1971; 1 son, Thomas. A.B., Harvard U., 1960; M.B.A., Rutgers U., 1961; Ph.D., U. Wis., 1969. C.P.A., Mass., Wash. Auditor, Arthur Andersen & Co., Boston, 1961-64; assoc. prof. econs. U. Western Ont. (Can.), London, 1968-78; prof., chmn. dept. acctg. Wash. State U., Pullman, 1978-80; dir. Sch. Bus., U. Puget Sound, Tacoma, 1982—. NDEA Title IV fellow, U. Wis., 1965-68; recipient Newcomen award Newcomen Soc., 1978. Mem. Acad. Acctg. Historians (pres.; Hourglass award 1981), Am. Acctg. Assn., Am. Inst. C.P.A.s, Am. Econ. Assn. Club: Tacoma. Author: System and Profits, 1981; contbr. articles to profl. jours. Home: 6202 50th St Ct W Tacoma WA 98467 Office: Sch Bus Univ Puget Sound Tacoma WA 98416

JOHNSON, JAMES ARNOLD, business consultant, venture capitalist; b. Detroit, June 15, 1939; s. Waylon Z. and Elsie Jean (Peuser) J.; m. Glenda Lin Chow; 1 dau., Stephanie Louise. B.A., Stanford U., 1961; M.B.A., U. Chgo., 1968. C.P.A., Hawaii, Calif. Asst. cashier internat. banking First Nat. Bank of Chgo., 1965-68; ptnr. in charge mgmt. cons. Peat, Marwick, Mitchell & Co., Honolulu, 1968-79, ptnr. in charge small bus. services, 1977-80; co-mng. ptnr. Asia/Pacific Initiatives Ltd., Honolulu, 1980—; pres. Johnson Internat., Inc., Honolulu, 1980—; gen. ptnr. numerous investment partnerships. Bd. dirs. Honolulu Symphony Soc. Served to lt. USNR, 1962-65. Mem. Am. Inst. C.P.A.s, Hawaii Soc. C.P.A.s (past chmn. mgmt. adv. com.). Clubs: Waikiki Yacht, Honolulu, Sales and Mktg. Execs. of Honolulu. Home: 1221 Victoria St Apt 2705 Honolulu HI 96814 Office: 737 Bishop St Suite 2770 Honolulu HI 96813

JOHNSON, JAMES CALVIN, typewriter company executive; b. Portland, Oreg., Sept. 7, 1941; s. Leif Erickson and Fletta Olive J.; grad. Portland State U., 1964; m. Virginia Van Dyke, Apr. 15, 1971. Sales rep. H & M Bus. Products Co., Portland, 1969-72; sales mgr. Gestetner Corp., Salem, Oreg., 1972-73; co-owner, v.p. sales and service Newport Typewriter Co. (Oreg.), 1973—. Mem. Lincoln County Justice Facility Com., 1982—. Served with AUS, 1967-69. Mem. Nat. Office Machine Dealers Assn., Am. Mgmt. Assn., U.S. Golf Assn., Oreg. Shakespeare Festival Assn. Republican. Clubs: Agate Beach Men's, Elks, Eagles. Office: Newport Typewriter Co 324 SW Coast Hwy Newport OR 97365

JOHNSON, JAMES EDWARD, synthetic fuels mfg. co. exec.; b. Midland, Mich., Oct. 13, 1947; s. James Edward and Eunice Rebecca (Payton) J.; B.A., Calif. State U., Long Beach, 1970, M.B.A., 1978; m. Linda Ann Melohusky, Oct. 26, 1968; children—Brian Edward, Adam Michael, Todd Ryan. Mgmt. trainee Continental Can Co., San Pedro, Calif., 1970; prodn. supr. Pacific Electricord Co., Gardena, Calif., 1971-73; assembly supr. Avon Products, Inc., Monrovia, Calif., 1973-75; mgr. inventory control Hunt-Wesson Foods, Inc., Fullerton, Calif., 1975-79; indsl. relations adminstr. Westen Gear Corp., Lynwood, Calif., 1979-80; mgr. human resources Getty Synthetic Fuels Inc., Signal Hill, Calif., 1981—. Mem. vocat. edn. adv. coms. Lynwood and Compton Sch. Dists., 1979-80; mem. pack com. Cub Scouts Am., 1980-81; coach youth soccer, 1977-80. Served with USMCR, 1966-72. Mem. Am. Soc. for Personnel Adminstrn. (accredited personnel mgr.), Personnel and Indsl. Relations Assn., Kappa Sigma, Epsilon Pi Tau. Republican. Presbyterian. Home: 12408 Destino St Cerritos CA 90701 Office: Getty Synthetic Fuels 2750 Signal Pkwy Signal Hill CA 90806

JOHNSON, JAMES GWYNN, lawyer; b. Santa Monica, Calif., Mar. 22, 1949; s. James Robert and Shirley Laura (James) J.; A.B. in Econs., UCLA, 1971; J.D., Calif. Western U., 1974; LL.M., Georgetown U., 1975. Bar: Calif. 1974; mem. firm McLaughlin & Irvin, Los Angeles and San Francisco, 1974-77; ptnr. Hill, Farrer & Burrill, Los Angeles, 1977—. Mem. ABA, Calif. Bar Assn. (del.), Los Angeles County Bar Assn. (exec. com. labor law sect.). Contbr. articles to profl. jours. Office: 445 S Figueroa St 34th Floor Los Angeles CA 90071

JOHNSON, JAMES HARDING, business executive, b. Perry, Iowa, Sept. 26, 1940; s. Richard Harding and Dorothy Margarite (Nelson) J.; m. Kathy Novak, Dec. 27, 1980; 1 dau., Ann Katherine; children by previous marriage—Jennifer Lynn, James Harding. B.A., U. Wash., 1963; Ph.D., U. Minn., 1972. Lic. psychologist, Utah, Va., Ill. Asst. prof. psychology U. Utah, Salt Lake City, 1975-77, dir. div. psychology Med. Sch., 1976-77; assoc. prof., vice chmn. dept. psychiatry Eastern Va. Med. Sch., Norfolk, 1977-79; chmn. Va. Consortium for Profl. Psychology, Norfolk, 1978-79; prof., dir. clin. psychology Ill. Inst. Tech., Chgo., 1979-83; pres. Human Edge Software, Inc., Palo Alto, Calif., 1983—; dir. Psych Systems, Inc., Balt. Recipient Rush bronze medal Am. Psychiat. Assn., 1975. Mem. Am. Psychol. Assn., Am. Psychopathol. Assn., Soc. for Personality Assessment, Psychonomic Soc. Author: Mental Health in the 21st Century, 1979; Technology in Mental Health Care Delivery Systems, 1980; mem. editorial bd. Behavior Research Methods and Instrumentation, 1977; contbr. articles to profl. jours. Home: 93 Fair Oaks Ln Atherton CA 94025 Office: Human Edge Software Inc 2445 Faber Pl Palo Alto CA

JOHNSON, JANE A., college administrator; b. Great Falls, Mont., May 27, 1936; d. Darold L. and Mildred (Tompkins) Sauer; m. Evertt Philip Johnson, Sept. 3, 1958; children—Milanne Galles, Phyllis Jane. B.A., Ariz. State U., 1957; M.A., UCLA, 1961; postgrad. U. So. Calif., Ariz. State U., Stanford U., U. Calif.-Berkeley, Banff Sch. Fine Arts. Assoc. producer Faith of Our Children, NBC, 1959-61; creative dir. Owens & Assocs., Phoenix, 1961-62; asst. mktg. dir. Flair Sch. Modeling and Charm, Phoenix, 1961-63; instr. speech Spokane Community Coll./Spokane Falls Community Coll., 1963-67, pub. info. coordinator, 1967-70, communications mgr. dist. 17, 1970-82, on loan as communications dir. Expo '74, 1973-74, dir. communications and devel., 1982—; project dir. Wash. Ofcl. Bicentennial Traveling Festival, 1975-76; trustee, chmn. pub. relations Greater Spokane Found.; mem. adv. bd. Salvation Army; mem. radio-TV prodn. adv. council Eastern Wash. U., 1977—; mem. Task Force on Pub. TV for Spokane Sch. Dist. 81. Mem. Council Advancement and Support Edn. (chmn. elect. nat. council 1982, recipient nat. writing awards, 1979, 77), Pub. Relations Soc. Spokane (v.p.), Spokane Advt. Fedn., Women in Communications, Spokane C. of C., Nat. Council Community Relations, Pub. Relations Soc. Am., PEO, Pi Beta Phi (named outstanding young woman in Wash. by alumni chpt. 1970). Author: Marketing Resource Study Book, 1979; editor: New Directions for Institutional Advancement: The Two-year College Advancement Program (Jossey-Bass series), 1982; contbr. articles to profl. jours. Home: W518 Hastings Rd Spokane WA 99218 Office: N2000 Greene St Spokane WA 99207

JOHNSON, JAY M., advertising agency executive, consultant; b. Spokane, Wash., Feb. 8, 1952; s. Melvin O. and Ann Brown (McCulloch) J.; m. Liza M. Belgarde, July 10, 1977; 1 dau., Heather. B.A. in Radio-TV Mgmt., Eastern Wash. U., 1974. Ops. mgr. Sun River Broadcasting Co., Great Falls, Mont., 1975-81; dir. advt. and pub. relations Sun Wise Solar Products, Great Falls, 1981-82; mktg. mgr. Reierson Health Ctr., Pleasant Hill, Calif., 1983—; prin. J & L Communications, Pleasanton, Calif., 1983—. Recipient Polit. Reporting award S.E. Idaho News Assn., 1976; Best New Project award Sun Wise Solar Products, 1981; named Jaycee of Yr. Mont. Jaycees, 1979. Mem. Mont. Solar Industries Assn., Jaycees (pres. Great Falls 1980), Great Falls C. of C. Editor Solar Flare, 1981-82. Home and office: J & L Communications PO Box 1793 Pleasanton CA 94566

JOHNSON, JENNY LEES, public relations director; b. Wahkon, Minn., June 10, 1944; d. Howard Edward and Frances Mildred (Wilson) Hartzie; m. Wayne Charles Johnson, Sept. 16, 1962; children—Clinton, Stacie, Kristie. Student pub. schs., Wahkon, and Oakland, Calif. Mgr. coffee shop Depot Restaurant, Reno, 1975-79; escrow sec. Title Ins. and Trust, Reno, 1980-81; with collection dept. 1st Comml. Title, Reno, 1981-82; dir. pub. relations Universal Helicopters, Reno, 1982—. Democrat. Roman Catholic. Office: Universal Helicopters PO Box 20814 Reno NV 89510

JOHNSON, JOE WILLIAM, engineering educator, consultant; b. Pittsburg, Kans., July 19, 1908; s. Ernest Conrad and Carrie Auroa (Saunders) J.; m Virginia Burke, June 11, 1940; children—Christina Johnson Dean, Cornelia. B.S. in Civil Engring., U. Calif.-Berkeley, 1931, M.S. in Civil Engring., 1934. Registered engr., Calif. Hydraulic researcher, Waterways Exptl. Sta., Vicksburg, Miss., 1934-35; sediment transport researcher, Soil Conservation Service, Washington, 1935-42; asst. prof. to prof. hydraulic engring., U. Calif., Berkeley, 1942-75, prof. emeritus, 1975—; cons. coastal engr. Recipient citation, U. Calif., Berkeley, 1975, Disting. Service Medal, C.E., 1972; Guggenheim fellow, 1955. Mem. ASCE (hon.), Am. Shore and Beach Preservation Assn., Nat. Acad. Engring. Episcopalian. Contbr. writings to tech. publs. Office: 412 O'Brien Hall Univ Calif Berkeley CA 94720

JOHNSON, JOHN HASKELL, JR., mining company executive; b. Longview, Tex., July 21, 1939; s. John Haskell and Dorothy Naomi (Glover) H.; m. Rosalie Spencer, Aug. 29, 1959; children—Cynthia, Jenna. B.A., Tex. A&M U., 1960; postgrad. South Tex. Coll. Law, Houston, 1965-67. Publs. editor Shell Oil Co., Houston, 1961-62; personnel asst. Trunkline Gas Co., Houston, 1962-67; dir. indsl. relations Duval Corp. (Pennzoil Co.), Houston, 1967-73; dir. compensation services Pennzoil Co., 1971-73; v.p. NAM, Washington, 1973-74; v.p. Newmont Services Ltd., Tucson, 1974—; v.p. Newmont Exploration Ltd.; pres. Telluride Valley Corp.; v.p. CG Properties Inc., Tucson, 1974—. Pres. Catalina Foothills Sch. Dist. Bd., Tucson, 1978-82. Mem. Am. Mining Congress, AIME. Republican. Methodist. Clubs: Mining (N.Y.C.); Oro Valley Country (Tucson). Home: 6830 N Montezuma Dr Tucson AZ 85718 Office: 200 W Desert Sky Rd Tucson AZ 85704

JOHNSON, JOHN HERBERG, high school principal; b. Fargo, N.D., Dec. 20, 1922; s. John J. and Olga M. (Herberg) J.; m. Donna M. Harris, Aug. 6, 1950; children—Michael, Steven, Randi, Glynis. B.A., B.S., Moorhead State U., 1949; M.A., U. Wyo., 1955. Cert. adminstr., Mont. Mem. faculty Roseau (Minn.) pub. schs., 1949-53; instrumental music dir. Glendive (Mont.) pub. schs., 1953-60; prin. Dawson County High Sch., Glendive, 1960—. Chmn. Eastern Mont. 75th Statehood Jubilee, Glendive Bicentenniel Commn. Served with U.S. Army, 1943-46. Mem. Mont. Assn. Secondary Sch. Prins. (pres., 1969-70), Nat. Assn. Secondary Sch. Prins. (dir. 1973-77). Lutheran. Clubs: Lions, Elks. Home: 124 Gresham Glendive MT 59330 Office: 900 N Merrill Ave Glendive MT 59330

JOHNSON, JOHN RICHARD, nurse; b. St. Paul, Nov. 25, 1945; s. Arthur M. and Margaret E. (Edison) J.; R.N., Los Angeles Valley Coll., 1972; B.S. in Community Health Edn., Calif. State U., Northridge, 1975; M.S. in Health and Safety, Calif. State U., Los Angeles, 1981; m. Susan Johnson, Aug. 15, 1963; children—John, Steven, James, Scott. Nursing and teaching positions in Los Angeles area, 1970—; asst. prof. health and safety edn. Calif. State U., Los Angeles, 1977; chmn. immunization action com. San Gabriel Valley region Los Angeles Dept. Health Services, 1977-80; chmn. child health task force Pasadena/Foothill Child Care Consortium, 1978-80; dir. nursing edn. Los Angeles/Orange counties blood services Los Angeles chpt. ARC, 1980-82; chmn. patient service com. So. Calif. chpt. Nat. Multiple Sclerosis Soc., 1980—; bd. dirs. San Fernando Valley chpt. ARC, 1972-75. Recipient Clara Barton Humanitarian award ARC, 1976; Cert. of Appreciation Los Angeles County Dept. Health Services; others. Mem. Nat. League Nursing, Inservice and Health Edn. Council Los Angeles, Am. Nurses Assn. Home: 325 Fremont Ave South Pasadena CA 91030

JOHNSON, JOHNNY BURL, architect, planner; b. Bryan, Tex., Mar. 2, 1944; s. Leonard Walter Johnson and Lois (Moon) Barker; B.Arch., Tex. A. and M. U., 1969; m. Stephanie Lynne Bates, Dec. 26, 1964; 1 dau., Jennifer Lea-Bates. Draftsman, designer William E. Nash, Architect, Bryan, Tex., 1968-69; designer R. Keith Hook & Assos., Inc., Colorado Springs, Colo., 1969-71, planning dir., 1969-76; v.p., dir. planning and architecture R. Keith Hook & Assos., Inc., 1976-80; owner Becker-Johnson & Assos. (formerly R.K. Hook & Assos., Inc.), 1980—. Mem. Colorado Springs Park Bd. Recipient Ernest Langford award Tex. A. & M. U., 1969. Mem. AIA (nat. energy com. 1979-80), Homebuilders Assn. (chmn. subdiv. com. 1973-74, vice chmn. urban devel. council 75), Colo. Soc. Architects (dir., pres. chpt. 1978, sec. 1979), Colorado Springs Homebuilders Assn. (mem. com. 1969—), Urban Transp. Inst., Urban Land Inst., Pikes Peak Area Hist. Preservation Com., Colorado Springs C. of C. (mem. indsl. com.), Colorado Springs Fine Art Center. Club: Sertoma. Designer Pikes Peak Olympic Flame. Home: 116 E Columbia St Colorado Springs CO 80907 Office: 2545 E Platte Pl Colorado Springs CO 80909

JOHNSON, JOYCE ALINE, hosp. exec.; b. Los Angeles, Dec. 21, 1946; d. Charles Edmund and Vivian Aline (Doak) J.; B.S. in Nursing, Calif. State U.-Los Angeles, 1968; M.A. in Edn., Calif. State U.-Northridge, 1979; postgrad. Columbia Pacific U. Nurse, Good Samaritan Hosp., Los Angeles, 1968-70, nursing instr., 1970-73, dir. inservice edn., 1973-77, dir. edn., 1977-79; mgr. human resources devel. Huntington Meml. Hosp., Pasadena, Calif., 1979—; mem. adv. council vocat. nursing Los Angeles Trade Tech. Coll., 1976-79; adj. clin. faculty Azusa Pacific U., 1981—. Instr. C.P.R., Am. Heart Assn., 1971—. Mem. Assn. Western Hosps. (Edn. and Tng. chmn. 1981), Am. Soc. Health Manpower Edn. and Tng. (pres. local chpt. 1983), Inservice and Health Edn. Council Los Angeles, Am. Soc. for Tng. and Devel. Presbyterian. Club: Jobs Daughters (past queen). Office: 100 Congress St Pasadena CA 91105

JOHNSON, JOYCE LYNN, vocational consultant; b. Orange, N.J., Mar. 30, 1951; d. William Veader and Doris Squier (Mae) J. B.A. in Sociology, U. R.I., 1973; M.S. in Rehab. Counseling, U. Ariz., 1976. Cert. rehab. counselor Calif. Extended campus Coordinator Devereux Found., Santa Barbara, Calif., 1976-78; supr. Internat. Rehab. Assocs., North Hollywood, Calif., 1978-80; mgr. Emeritus, Santa Barbara, 1980-81; self-employed cons., owner Johnson & Assocs., Santa Barbara, 1982—. Mem. Nat. Rehab. Assn., Rehab. Nurses Soc. Am. Personnel and Guidance Soc., Nat. Assn. Rehab. Profls. Office: 735 State St Suite 612 Santa Barbara CA 93101

JOHNSON, JUDY LEE, contract bookkeeping co. executive; b. Hobbs, N.Mex., Sept. 11, 1953; d. Henry Leroy and Verna Jo (McDougal) Landusky; m. Roger Dale Johnson, Mar. 31, 1983. B.B.A. in Mktg., Tex. Tech. U., 1975. Cert. petroleum sec. Assn. Desk & Derrick Clubs. Owner, mgr. Landusky Enterprise & Assocs., Hobbs, N.Mex., 1976—. Mem. Nat. Assn. Female Execs., Lefthanders Internat., Desk & Derrick Club (recipient 3d pl. award of merit 1981). Democrat. Baptist. Home: 421 W Kiowa St Hobbs NM 88240 Office: 3220 W County Rd Hobbs NM 88240

JOHNSON, LARRY EUGENE, public relations executive, public affairs officer; b. Greenfield, Mo., Nov. 18, 1931; s. Virgil Lee and Leona Lucille J.; m. June Ione Burge, June 26, 1955; children—Laura Louise, Brian David, Victoria Lee. B.Journalism, U. Mo., 1954; M.B.A., Pepperdine U., 1975. Reporter, Kansas City (Mo.) Star, 1958-59; editor Fin. Publs., Inc., Kansas City, 1959-61; pub. relations mgr. Pacific Tel. & Tel., San Francisco and San Jose, Calif., 1962-70, dist. staff mgr. pub. relations, San Francisco, 1973—; pub. relations mgr. AT&T, N.Y.C., 1970-73; reserve chief for western region Office of Pub. Affairs, U.S. Air Force, Los Angeles. Chmn., Opportunities Industrialization Ctr., San Jose, 1969-70; pres. Order of Mil. Wine Tasters, San Francisco, 1980—. Served to Col. USAFR, 1955—. Named Outstanding Mobilization Augmentee Officer of Yr., Air Force Service Info. and News Ctr., Kelly AFB, Tex., 1982. Mem. Pub. Relations Soc. Am., Res. Officers Assn., Air Force Assn., Sigma Delta Chi. Club: Marines' Memorial (San Francisco). Lutheran. Office: Pacific Tel & Tel 140 New Montgomery St San Francisco CA 94105

JOHNSON, LARRY EUGENE, lawyer; b. Hill City, Kans., July 18, 1947; s. Eugene V. and Betty (Lee) J.; m. Linda Jean Rathbun, Jan. 26, 1969. A.B. in History, Ft. Hays Kans. State Coll., 1969; J.D., U. Kans., 1972; LL.M. in Taxation, Georgetown U., 1977. Bar: Kans. 1972, Mont. 1978. Assoc. gen. counsel Kans. Farm Bur. and affiliated cos., 1972-76; research asst. Scribner, Hall, Thornburg & Thompson, Washington, 1976-77; assoc. Boone, Ellison & Smith, Tulsa, 1977-78; tax counsel 1st Nat. Bank & Trust Co., Tulsa, 1978; ptnr. James, Gray & McCafferty, Great Falls, Mont., 1978—. Mem. Mont. Bar Assn., ABA, Community Beautification Assn., Humane Soc. Cascade County, Mont. Farm Bur. Assn. Methodist. Office: 615 2d Ave N Great Falls MT 59401

JOHNSON, LAWRENCE HANFORD, lawyer; b. Cedar Rapids, Iowa, May 30, 1926; s. Harry Stainbrook and Florence (Wagner) J.; m. Joyce Howard, Nov. 21, 1962; 1 dau., Regina Elise Francis. Student Okla. State U., 1945; A.B. in Econs., Coe Coll., 1949; LL.B. U. Mich., 1952. Bar: Iowa 1952, N.Mex. 1953. Assoc. U.M. Rose, Atty., Hobbs, N.Mex., 1953; ptnr. Rose and Johnson, Hobbs, 1954-78, prin. 1978—. Trustee Hobbs Pub. Library, 1957—; treas. Lea County (N.Mex.) Republican Com., 1956-67, chmn. 1967-71; treas. N.Mex. Rep. Com., 1971-75; mem. N.Mex. Rep. Central Com., 1967—, N.Mex. Rep. Exec. Com., 1971-77. Served with USNR, 1944-46. Mem. ABA, State Bar N.Mex., Lea County Bar Assn. (pres. 1970-71), Hobbs C. of C., Am. Legion, VFW, Delta Theta Phi, Tau Kappa Epsilon. Presbyterian. Home: 702 Seco St Hobbs NM 88240 Office: Rose and Johnson 308 W Taylor St PO Box 159 Hobbs NM 88240

JOHNSON, LAYMON, JR., dynamics engr.; b. Jackson, Miss., Sept. 1, 1948; s. Laymon and Bertha (Yarbrough) J.; m. Charlene J. Johnson, Nov. 13, 1982. B.Tech., U. Dayton, 1970; M.S. in Systems Mgmt., U. So. Calif., 1978. Mem. tech. staff Rockwell Internat., Canoga Park, Calif., 1975-77; sr. dynamics engr. Gen. Dynamics, Pomona, Calif., 1978—. Served to lt. USNR, 1970-75. Mem. Assn. Systems Mgmt., Ops. Research Soc. Am., Los Angeles County Mus. Art, Smithsonian Assos., Nat. Hist. Soc., Archimedes Circle, Tau Alpha Pi. Democrat. Roman Catholic. Office: General Dynamics Pomona Div PO Box 2507 Pomona CA 91766

JOHNSON, LEANNE MARY, home economist, emergency medical technician; b. Forest Grove, Oreg., Nov. 2, 1950; d. James W. and Mary V. (Fearn) J. B.S., U. Wyo., 1973, M.S. in Home Econs. Edn., 1976. Cert. emergency med. tech., Wyo. Home econs. tchr. Farson High Sch., Farson, Wyo., 1973-75; extension home economist Agr. Extension Service, U. Wyo.-Afton, 1976—; ambulance attendant Star Valley Ambulance Service, 1982—. Mem. Wyo. Assn. Extension Home Economists, Nat. Assn. Extension Home Economists, Star Valley Emergency Med. Techs., Wyo. Ambulance and Emergency Med. Service Assn. Baptist. Clubs: Daughters of the Nile, Order of Eastern Star. Office: Home Econs Dept PO Box 308 Afton WY 83110

JOHNSON, LEONARD MORRIS, pediatric surgeon; b. Gowanda, N.Y., June 11, 1931; s. Leonard Brynolf and Helen Berdena (Morris) J.; m. Ann Marie Homer, Mar. 30, 1968; children—Hilding Leif Brynolf, Nils Anders Christian. B.A., Haverford Coll., 1954; M.D., U. Pa., 1958; M.S. in Surgery, U. Minn., 1966. Intern, Colo. Gen. Hosp., 1958-59; fellow in surgery Mayo Clinic, Rochester, Minn., 1959-63; surgeon S.S. Hope, Guayaquil, Ecuador, 1964, surgeon, asst. chief of staff, Conakry, Guinea, 1965, pediatric surgeon, dir. med. edn., Corinto, Micaragua, 1965-66, pediatric surgeon, Cartegena, Colombia, 1967, Colombo, Sri Lanka, 1968; fellow in pediatric surgery Mercy Children's Hosp., Kansas City, Mo., 1964-65; vis. pediatric surgeon Univ. Hosp., Uppsala, Sweden, 1967; registrar in pediatric urology Alder Hey Children's Hosp., Liverpool, Eng., 1967-68; practice medicine specializing in pediatric surgery, Oakland, Calif., 1969—; mem. staff Children's Hosp. Med. Ctr., 1969—, chief div. gen. surgery, 1974-80, pres. med. staff, 1977-78. Decorated Orden de Ruben Dario (Nicaragua). Fellow ACS, Am. Acad. Pediatrics; mem. AMA, Calif. Med. Assn., Alameda-Contra Costa Med. Assn., Am. Trauma Soc., Am. Pediatric Surg. Assn., Brit. Assn. Pediatric Surgeons, Pacific Assn. Pediatric Surgeons, East Bay Surg. Soc., San Francisco Surg. Soc., Continental Surg. Club. Republican. Presbyterian. Club: Rotary (Oakland). Home: 7 Charles Hill Ln Orinda CA 94563 Office: Suite 1000 3300 Webster St Oakland CA 94609

JOHNSON, LLOYD ERWIN, public relations consultant, writer; b. Salina, Kans., Dec. 12, 1931; s. Lloyd Erwin and Melda Marie (Mohler) J.; m. Janet Ellen Austad, Aug. 15, 1953; children—Margaret Ellen, Rebecca Ann, Brad Erwin; m. 2d, Ginger Lea Scott, Aug. 9, 1980. B.S. in Bus. Law, U. Idaho, 1953. Pub. relations asst. Aluminum Co. Am., Wenatchee, Wash., 1956-59, Vancouver, Wash., 1959-61, asst. editor The Alcoa News, Pitts., 1961-64; asst. v.p., dir. pub. relations Pitts. Nat. Bank, 1964-67; pres. L.E. Johnson & Assocs., Pub. Relations & Advt. Agy., Boise, Idaho, 1967-76; cons. Erv Johnson, Accredited Pub. Relations, Boise, 1976—; vis. lectr. communications dept. U. Idaho, Moscow. Past chmn. Idaho Commn. on Post-Secondary Edn.; mem. Idaho com. Council on Fgn. Relations; mem. parking commn. City of Boise; past pres. Boise Little Theatre. Served to capt. U.S. Army, 1954-56. Recipient appreciation cert. Radio Free Europe, 1969. Mem. Pub. Relations Soc. Am. (accredited; chmn.-elect North Pacific Dist., past pres., v.p. Idaho chpt., mem. jud. com., membership com.), Idaho Pub. Relations Roundtable (founder), Beta Theta Pi, Gamma Gamma (editor newsletter). Republican. Methodist. Author: Retail Bank Marketing, 1966, The Terteling Story, 1975; Rosey Posey, 1976; author TV scripts.

JOHNSON, LOUIS RAYMOND, publishing company executive; b. Boring, Oreg., Oct. 25, 1936; s. Mathis Steven and Vera Madeline (Salmon) J.; m. Carole Ann Denham, June 11, 1960 (div.); children—Kenneth, Tammy, David, Steven; m. 2d, Patricia Ann Safra. A.A., Long Beach City Coll., 1960; B.A., Long Beach State U., 1962. With Arcata Graphics, Los Angeles, 1960-72, mgr. purchases, traffic, warehouse, 1961-72; mgr. purchasing and traffic Petersen Pub., Los Angeles, 1972-77; dir. prodn. CBS Consumer Pub., Newport Beach, Calif., 1977—. Leader, YMCA. Mem. Western Pub. Assn., Purchasing Mgmt. Assn., Traffic Club of Los Angeles, Los Angeles Litho. Roman Catholic. Home: 22232 Camino Arroya Seco Laguna Hills CA 92653

JOHNSON, LYNN SCOTT, clinical psychologist; b. Portland, Oreg., Dec. 26, 1945; s. Willis Andrew and Leah Annabelle (Cutler) J.; m. Kaye Vandiver, Sept. 6, 1969; children—Brant, Rhett, Cort, Dirk, Trais. B.A. (Univ. scholar), Stanford U., 1969; M.S., Brigham Young U., 1971, Ph.D. (Univ. fellow), 1975; lic. psychologist, Mont. Grad. asst. Brigham Young U., 1969-73, instr., 1973-74; research psychologist Timpanogos Community Mental Health Center, Provo, Utah, 1972-74; intern in psychology Palo Alto (Calif.) Vets. Hosp., 1974-75; asst. prof. psychology U. N.D., Grand Forks, 1975-79; clin. psychologist, program evaluator North Central Mont. Commn. Mental Health Center, Gt. Falls, 1979—; cons. Lake Region Human Services Center, Devils Lake N.D., 1976-79; co-dir. U. N.D. Psychol. Services Center, 1978-79. Bishop, Chief Jesus Christ of Latter-day Saints, Gt. Falls, 1978—; Explorer adv. Mont. council Boy Scouts Am., 1977-81, committeeman, 1981—. U. N.D. grantee, 1976, 80; Brigham Young U. grantee, 1980. Mem. Am. Psychol. Assn. Contbr. articles to profl. jours. Home: 4178 5th Ave S Great Falls MT 59405 Office: PO Box 3048 Great Falls MT 59403

JOHNSON, MARGARET MARIE, special education teacher, consultant; b. Greeley, Colo., Aug. 1, 1948; d. Robert Walter and Rita M. (Wykert) J. Ph.D., U. Ariz., 1984. Cert. tchr., Tex., Colo. Tchr. work coordinator Weld BOCES, La Salle, Colo., 1971-79; tchr./cons. Ysleta Ind. Sch. Dist., El Paso, Tex., 1982—; cons. U. Ariz.; part-time affiliation with U. Texas-El Paso; conf. presentor at nat. and regional convs. Mem. Assn. for Children with Learning Disabilities, Council for Exceptional Children, Nat. Assn. Vocat. Edn. for Spl. Needs Personnel. Office: 2430 McRae St El Paso TX 79925

JOHNSON, MARTIN BRUCE, economist, consultant; b. St. Paul, Sept. 11, 1933; s. Martin Ivar and Evelyn Hazel (Paul) J.; m. Elenore Kershner, Mar. 21, 1964; children—Karla, Paula, Martin. B.A., Carleton Coll., 1955; Ph.D., Northwestern U., 1962. Asst. prof. U. Wash., Seattle, 1962-68; assoc. prof. econs. U. Calif.-Santa Barbara, 1968-72, prof., 1972—; vis. prof. UCLA, 1975-76; assoc. dir. Law and Econs. Ctr., U. Miami, 1976-77; pres. Econs. Group, Inc., 1979—; cons., expert witness. Mem. Am. Econs. Assn., Western Econs. Assn. (pres. 1981-82), Internat. Assn. Bus. Economists, Nat. Assn. Bus. Economists. Author: The Attack on Corporate America, 1978; Resolving the Housing Crisis, 1982; The Efficient Pricing of Electricity, 1981.

JOHNSON, MARY DOROTHY, computer scientist; b. Long Beach, Calif., June 1, 1944; d. James Peter and Mary Delarosa (Francken) Kurthy; m. David Frank Johnson, Oct. 28, 1967; children—Jeremy James, Miranda Michelle. B.S. in Physics, Long Beach State U., 1967; M.S. in Mgmt. Sci., Naval Postgrad. Sch., Monterey, Calif., 1977. Physicist, engr. U.S. Navy Civil Service Pacific Missile Test Ctr., Point Mugu, Calif., 1967-79; sr. mgmt. analyst, asso. ctr. dir. Litton Mellonics, Camarillo, Calif., 1979-81; dept. mgr. computer scientist, sr. engring. analyst Combat Systems Ctr. applied tech. div. Computer Scis. Corp., Oxnard, Calif., 1981—; cons. in field Active Boy Scouts Am., Girl Scouts U.S. NSF grantee, 1961, 62; Naval Aviation Exec. Inst. masters program appointee, 1976-77. Mem. AIAA. Republican. Roman Catholic. Club: Calif. Broadcasters. Contbr. articles to tech. jours. Office: 601 Daily Dr Suite 123 Camarillo CA 93010

JOHNSON, MICHAEL, engineer, statistician; b. Cardiff, Wales, Sept. 29, 1934; s. Frederick and Henrietta Blanche (Cook) J.; came to U.S., 1963, naturalized, 1968; m. Anne Lavington, Mar. 21, 1959 (div.). B.Sc., U. Bristol (Eng.), 1956. Registered profl. engr., Calif. Engring. apprentice Bristol Aircraft Co. (Eng.), 1956-58, non-destructive test technician 1958-60; non-destructive test specialist Rolls Royce Aero Engines, Montreal, Can., 1960-63; quality assurance engr. Garrett Airesearch, Phoenix, 1963-64; physicist, sr. engr. mgr. computer dept. Gen. Electric Co., Phoenix, 1964-70; pres. Plan-Test Assocs., Phoenix, 1970—; statis. methods cons. Mem. Am. Statis. Assn. (pres. Ariz. chpt. 1976), Am. Soc. Quality Control, Ariz. Council Engring. Sci. Assns. (chmn. 1982), Am. Soc. Non-Destructive Testing (vice-chmn. Eastern Can. sect. 1962), Mensa. Home: Unit 22 3012 N 32d St Phoenix AZ 85018 Office: Suite 609 3443 N Central Ave Phoenix AZ 85012

JOHNSON, NICHOLAS LEROY, principal technologist, author; b. Mpls., Jan. 31, 1950; s. Francis LeRoy and Marjory Madelene (Nelson) J.; m. Mary Elizabeth Porter, Apr. 5, 1969; 1 son, Kevin LeRoy. B.S. in Physics magna cum laude, Memphis State U., 1974; postgrad. Rice U., 1974-75. Dir. Heat Transfer and Fluid Flow div. U.S. Naval Nuclear Power Sch., Orlando, Fla., 1976-79; prin. technologist Soviet space systems Teledyne Brown Engring., Costa Mesa, Calif., 1979—. Served with USAF, 1969-72, USN, 1975-79. Decorated Air Force Commendation medal; Cross of Gallantry (Vietnam). Fellow Brit. Interplanetary Soc.; mem. AIAA. Author: Handbook of Soviet Lunar and Planetary Exploration, 1979; Handbook Soviet Manned Space Flight, 1980; Soviet Year in Space: 1981, 1982, Soviet Military Strategy in Space; contbr. articles to profl. jours. Home: 980 War Eagle Dr N Colorado Springs CO 80919 Office: 3595 E Fountain Blvd Suite A-1 Colorado Springs CO 80910

JOHNSON, NOBLE MARSHALL, scientist; b. San Francisco, Feb. 23, 1945; s. Donald Raymond and Frances (Romer) J.; B.S. in E.E. cum laude, U. Calif., Davis, 1967, M.S. in E.E., 1969; Ph.D., Princeton U., 1974; m. Alice Wheeler, June 22, 1968; children—Pamela, Elaine. Research engr. SRI Internat., Menlo Park, Calif., 1974-76; mem. research staff Gen. Scis. Lab. Xerox Palo Alto Research Center, Palo Alto, Calif., 1976—. NDEA fellow, 1969-73. Mem. Am. Phys. Soc., Am. Vacuum Soc., IEEE, Sigma Xi, Eta Kappa Nu. Author numerous articles on electronic materials and devices. Office: 3333 Coyote Hill Rd Palo Alto CA 94304

JOHNSON, NORA ANN TONER, charter company executive, interior designer; b. Juneau, Alaska, Mar. 1, 1952; d. Felix Joseph and Mary Fredericka (Vander Leest) Toner; m. Paul Evert Johnson, Dec. 29, 1981. Student U. Idaho, 1970-73; B.S. in Bus. Adminstrn., U. Portland, 1978. Pvt. practice interior design, Juneau, Alaska, 1973—; sec. Toner & Nordling, Juneau, 1973-74; statis. tech. Alaska Dept. Labor, Juneau, 1974-75; village acct. Sealaska, Juneau, 1978-79; jr. acct. Alaska Div. Legis. Audit, Juneau, 1979-81; ptnr. Chicago of Charters, Elfin Cove, Alaska, 1981—; mgr. grocery store, liquor store, laundromat, inn, fish buying scow. Democrat. Roman Catholic.

JOHNSON, PATRICIA GAYLE, corporate communication executive, writer; b. Conway, Ark., Oct. 23, 1947; d. Rudolph and Frances Modene (Hayes) J. Student U. Calif.-Irvine, 1965-68. Advance rep. Disney on Parade, Los Angeles, 1971-75; mktg. dir./dir. field ops. Am. Freedom Train, 1975-77; publ. relations mgr. Six Flags, Inc., Los Angeles, 1977-81; mgr. corp. communications Playboy Enterprises, Inc., Los Angeles, 1981-82; external relations mgr. Kal Kan Foods, Inc., Los Angeles, 1982—; lectr. U. So. Calif., UCLA, Calif. State Coll.-Northridge. Mem. Pub. Relations Soc. Am. (dir.), Publicity Club Los Angeles (dir.), Pub. Affairs Council. Methodist. Collaborator TV scripts; contbr. articles to mags. in field. Office: Kal Kan Foods Inc 3386 E 44th St Vernon CA 90058

JOHNSON, PHILIP RONALD, educational travel company executive; b. Stockport, Eng., Aug. 1, 1952; s. Ronald Warren and Phyllis (Bewlay) J.; came to U.S., 1975; m. Kristine Rampton, Dec. 30, 1977; children—Kirsten Ashley, Lacey Catherine. B.A., U. Sussex, 1974. Ops. mgr. Fgn. Study League (U.K.) Ltd., London, 1974-75; asst. to internat. v.p. FSL Inc./Readers Digest, Pleasantville, N.Y., Los Angeles, 1975-77; v.p. EF Inst., Los Angeles, also Greenwich, Conn., 1977-79; mng. dir. Lang. Colls. Ltd., Brighton, Eng., also Luzern, Switzerland, 1979-81; v.p. Am. Internat. Edn. and Tng., San Francisco, 1981—. Mem. Travel Industry Assn. Am., Former Sussex Students Assn. Democrat. Home: 13 Cinnamon Teal Ln Novato CA 94947 Office: 5725 Paradise Dr Corte Madera CA 94925

JOHNSON, PRESCOTT KENT, association executive; b. Norwood, Mass., June 4, 1930; s. Albert Kent and Eleanor Farley (Gove) J.; m. Darolyn Louise Mooers, July 18, 1953; children—Kent Linwood, Scott Whitcomb, Blake Farley. B.S., U. Maine, 1952; M.S., Springfield Coll., 1956; Ph.D., Ohio State U., 1962. Asst. phys. edn. dir. YMCA, Westfield, Mass., 1956-57, dir. health, phys. edn., 1957-60; dir. health, phys. edn. Latin Am. Confed. YMCA's and asst. dir. Instituto Tecnico YMCA Coll., Montevideo, Uruguay, 1962-72; asst. v.p. health, phys. edn. YMCA Met. Milw., 1972-80; health, phys. edn. specialist Pacific Region YMCA, Foster City, Calif., 1980—; cons. 300 YMCA's in Pacific Region. Served as 1st lt. U.S. Army, 1952-54. Recipient Roberts-Gulick award YMCA of U.S.A., 1971; Roberts-Gulick fellow, 1960-62. Mem. Assn. Profl. Dirs. YMCA, Am. Coll. Sports Medicine (cert. exercise technician), Council Nat. Cooperation in Aquatics. Republican. Mem. United Ch. of Christ. Home: 1017 Lark Ln Foster City CA 94404 Office: Pacific Region YMCA 1111 Chess Dr Foster City CA 94404

JOHNSON, QULAN ADRIAN, software engr.; b. Gt. Falls, Mont., Sept. 17, 1942; s. Raymond Eugene and Bertha Marie (Nagengast) J.; m. Helen Louise Pocha, July 24, 1965; children—Brenda Marie, Douglas Paul, Scot Paul, Mathew James. B.A. in Psychology, Coll. Gt. Falls, 1964. Lead operator 1st Computer Corp., Helena, Mont., 1966-67; v.p., sec.-treas. Computer Corp. of Mt., Great Falls, 1967-76, dir., 1971-76; sr. systems analyst Mont. Dept. Revenue, Helena, 1976-78; software engr. Mont. Systems Devel. Co., Helena, 1978-80; programmer/analyst III info. systems div. Mont. Dept. Adminstrn., Helena, 1980-82; systems analyst centralized services Dept. Social and Rehab. Services State of Mont., 1982—. Mem. Assn. for Systems Mgmt., Mont. Data Processing Assn., Data Processing Mgmt. Assn., Mensa. Club: K.C. (rec. sec. 1975-76). Home: 2231 8th Ave Helena MT 59601 Office: Centralized Services Div Mont Dept Social and Rehab Services Helena MT 59602

JOHNSON, RANDALL ARTHUR, animal nutritionist, cons.; b. Los Angeles, Sept. 28, 1946; s. Arthur J. and Jean A. (Raith) J.; B.S., Calif. Poly. State U., Pomona, 1968; M.S. (research asst.), U. Mo., 1973, Ph.D., 1977; m. Sally Kay Caruthers, July 30, 1977; children—Scott Thomas, Ryan Arthur. Dir. student services and placement, asst. to dean coll. Agr., U. Mo., 1973-77; mgr. quality control and nutrition Nat. Pet Food Corp., 1977-79; mgr. tech. services S.W. Feed and Seed Co., 1979-80; pres. Agri-Data Systems, Inc., Phoenix, 1980—, Agri-Data Systems Internat., Ltd. Mem. adv. bd. CETA, Maricopa County (Ariz.), 1978. Served with USMC, 1968-71; Vietnam; maj. Res. Decorated Bronze Star. Mem. Am. Soc. Animal Sci., Am. Dairy Sci. Assn., Marine Corps Assn., Marine Corps Res. Officer Assn., Am. Quarter Horse Assn., Alpha Zeta, Gamma Sigma Delta. Author numerous articles in field; asso. editor Outlook mag. Office: 5050 W 19th Ave Suite 204 Phoenix AZ 85015

JOHNSON, (REDA) KAY, banker; b. Downey, Idaho, Sept. 28, 1935; d. Loren Gunter and Elva Ruth (Underwood) Egan; m. Leland Theron Johnson, Feb. 12, 1960; 1 dau., Lori Johnson Manning. Student Idaho State U., 1954-55, Grimms Bus. Coll., 1955-56; diploma in trust ops., U. Wis. Sch. Bank Adminstrn., 1980-83. With proof dept. Crocker Citizens Bank, San Francisco, 1956-58; with proof and bookkeeping dept. IB&T Co., Pocatello, Idaho, 1958-60, proof supr., 1960-64, research and proof supr., 1964-75, supr. ops. adminstrn., 1975-78, asst. ops. officer adminstrn., 1978-79, asst. auditor, 1979-81, auditor, 1981—. Mem. Bank Adminstrn. Inst., Am. Inst. Banking, Nat. Assn. Bank Women (treas.), Am. Bus. Women Assn. (treas., Woman Yr. 1979). Mormon. Club: Elks. Office: IB&T Co PO Box 1788 Pocatello ID 83201

JOHNSON, RICHARD DAMERAU, aero. scientist; b. Zanesville, Ohio, Oct. 28, 1934; s. Earl G. and Merlie D. Johnson; A.B., Oberlin (Ohio) Coll., 1956; M.S., Carnegie-Mellon U., 1960, Ph.D., 1962; S.M., M.I.T., 1982; m. Catherine Collins, Dec. 30, 1969; children—Laurana, Karen, Eric, Gregory. Postdoctoral fellow UCLA, 1961-62; sr. scientist Jet Propulsion Lab., Pasadena, Calif., 1962-63; with NASA, 1963—, chief life scis. flight expts. office, 1973-76, chief biosystems div. Ames Research Center, Moffett Field, Calif., 1976—; vis. lectr. Stanford U. Recipient Exceptional Service medal NASA, 1976; Alfred P. Sloan fellow M.I.T., 1981-82. Mem. Am. Chem. Soc., AAAS, AIAA, N.Y. Acad. Scis., Peninsula Home Enologists Workshop. Club: Stanford (Palo Alto, Calif.). Author, papers in field. Office: Mail Stop 236-5 Code LB NASA/Ames Research Center Moffett Field CA 94035

JOHNSON, RICHARD EARL, architect; b. Bogota, Colombia, July 10, 1944 (parents Am. citizens); s. Mark Waldo and Raquel Olga (Ortiz) J.; student U. Minn., 1964-67, McNeese U., 1973-74; B.Arch., U. N.Mex., 1975, M.Arch. (Fulbright fellow), 1976; m. Danielle Charlotte Fazan, July 6, 1973; 1 dau., Karie Michéle. Tchr. arch. and planning U. N.Mex., 1978; designer interiors Engel Kieding Design Assos., Denver, 1978-79; interior architect Cannell & Chaffin Comml. Interiors, Denver, 1979-80; interior architect, designer Muchow & Partners Architects, Denver, 1980-82; prin. Richard Johnson Architects & Interiors, Denver, 1982—; tchr. vernacular archtl. research in Amazon and S.Am. Andes. Recipient 1st prize La. Architects Assn., 1973. Mem. AIA (Henry Adams medal 1977), Nat. Council Archtl. Registration Bds., Phi Kappa Phi. Home: 1727 Emerson St Denver CO 80210 Office: 1865 S Pearl St Denver CO 80210

JOHNSON, RICHARD EDWIN, employee benefits cons. co. exec.; b. Tacoma, Aug. 29, 1945; s. Edwin Richard and Paula Irene (Gebo) J.; B.A. in History, Pacific Lutheran U., Tacoma, 1970; m. Kendall Dawn Yeagle, Apr. 19, 1974; children—Dawn Elaine, Kathryn June. Owner, Health Au Naturel, health foods, Tacoma, 1972-73; account rep. Pacific N.W. Bell Telephone Co., 1974-75; dir. mktg. Wash. Physicians Service, Seattle, 1976-78; asst. v.p. William M. Mercer, Inc., Seattle, 1978—; lectr. nutrition, 1972-76; chmn. Western Conf. Prepaid Med. Service Plans, 1977; condr. seminars. Mem. Sales and Mktg. Execs. Internat. (membership chmn. Seattle 1977-78), Seattle C. of C. (health care com.), Internat. Found. Employee Benefit Plans, N.W. Health-Welfare-Pension Adminstrs., Employee Benefits Planning Assn., Western Pension Conf., Smithsonian Assos., Anchorage C. of C., U.S. Handball Assn. Republican. Congregationalist. Club: Wash. Athletic (Seattle). Home: 5011 91st Ave SE Mercer Island WA 98040 Office: Norton Bldg Seattle WA 98104

JOHNSON, ROBERT LEWIS, management systems consultant; b. Chgo., Apr. 29, 1937; s. Robert Lewis and Dorthy Swift (Anderson) J.; B.S., Purdue U., 1964; M.B.A., Pepperdine U., 1979; m. Dolores Ann McCain, June 16, 1972; children—Dana K., Kyle P. Field engr. Beckman Instruments, 1964-66; programmer analyst to dir. research and devel. Chgo. N.W. R.R., Systems Engring. Labs. and Hewlett Packard, 1967-79; sec. Flexible Interactive Bus. Systems, 1979; mgmt. cons. process and software engring., 1979—; owner, operator RJ Enterprises, Cupertino, Calif., 1979—. Served with USNR, 1958-62. Mem. Assn. Mgmt. Cons., Profl. and Tech. Cons. Assn. Republican. Club: Decathlon. Home and Office: 7533 Kingsbury Ct Cupertino CA 95014

JOHNSON, ROGER MILES, marketing research and consulting company executive; b. Mpls., Oct. 30, 1921; s. Arthur H. and Ella M. (Mortensen) J.; m. Marian Elizabeth Scott, June 12, 1943; children—

Craig W., Brian L. Student DePauw U., 1939-40; B.S., Northwestern U., 1943. Exec. asst. Ford Sammis, mktg. economist, Los Angeles, 1946-49; mktg. cons. George Fry & Assocs., Chgo., 1950-51; sr. v.p., mktg. dir. Erwin Wasey Co., Los Angeles, 1952-64, N.W. Ayer Co., 1964-68; mgr., mktg. cons. Peat, Marwick, Mitchell & Co., Los Angeles, 1968-69; pres. Roger Johnson & Assocs., Inc., Arcadia, Calif., 1969—; lectr. mktg. research Calif. State U.-Los Angeles, 1979—, chmn. mktg. adv. bd., 1982—. Served to lt. USN, 1943-46. Recipient Guy E. Marion award Los Angeles C. of C., 1974. Mem. Am. Mktg. Assn. (Mktg. Success Yr. award 1979, former pres. So. Calif. sect., v.p., nat. dir. 1969—). Republican. Club: Rotary (Los Angeles). Editor: Dynamics of the Youth Explosion, 1967; What Makes Southern California Different, 1970. Home: 1725 N Santa Anita Ave Arcadia CA 91006 Office: Roger Johnson & Assocs 150 N Santa Anita Ave Suite 645 Arcadia CA 91006

JOHNSON, RONALD KAYE, retail company executive; b. Abilene, Tex., Feb. 26, 1939; s. Vernon Floyd and Mattye Sue (Milburn) J.; m. Sally Ann Fleet, Nov. 22, 1962 (div.); 1 dau., Sheri May. B.A. with honors in Theatre Arts, Eastern Wash. State U., 1971. Div. mgr. Nutrition Centers Fred Meyer, Inc., Portland, Oreg., 1971—, v.p. Nutrition Ctrs. div., 1979—. Actor Lake Oswego (Oreg.) Civic Theatre, 1979—. Recipient Best Supporting Actor award Spokane Civic Theatre, 1967-68; Oreg. Theat. Soc. Best Actor award, 1980-81. Breeder 1965 Nat. Grand Champion Appaloosa mare. Republican. Presbyterian. Office: Fred Meyer Inc PO Box 42121 Portland OR 97242

JOHNSON, RONALD LEROY, material handling engineer; b. Stillwater, Okla., July 5, 1947; s. James Lawrence and Lois Leone (Helgeland) J.; B.S., Mich. State U., 1970; m. Renee Marie Swift, Sept. 29, 1979. Packaging engr. Control Data Corp., Rochester, Mich., 1971-75; sr. material handling engr. Hughes Aircraft Co., Fullerton, Calif., 1975—. Served as capt. Army N.G., 1970—. Mem. Soc. Packaging and Handling Engrs., N.G. Assn. U.S., N.G. Assn. Calif. Republican. Methodist. Home: 1820 Hamer Dr Placentia CA 92670

JOHNSON, ROSS BYRON, geologist; b. Ladd, Ill., June 4, 1919; s. Ray Ryland and Katherine Effie (Wolfe) J.; B.S., U. N.Mex., 1946, M.S., 1948; m. Mary Louise Wallenhorst, June 29, 1942. Geologist, U.S. Geol. Survey, Albuquerque, 1948-58, Denver, 1958-62, research geologist, Denver, 1963-74; pvt. research geologist, cons., Denver, 1974-82. Mem. Denver Audubon Soc., 1968—, Denver Bot. Gardens, 1972—, Denver Mus. Natural History, 1973—. Served to capt. AUS, 1941-45; ETO. Fellow Geol. Soc. Am.; mem. SAR (state pres. 1982-83), Soc. Mayflower Descs. (state gov. 1975-77), Order Crown Charlemagne in U.S.A., Nat. Soc. Sons Am. Colonists, Descs. Colonial Govs., Descs. Colonial Clergy (councillor 1976-78), Huguenot Soc. (state registrar 1975-79, state pres. 1979-81), Magna Charta Barons, Descs. Knights of Garter, Plantagenet Soc., Sons and Daus. Pilgrims (state organizing gov. 1976-78, state gov. 1978-81), Mil. Order World Wars (Denver chpt. comdr. 1978-80, state comdr. 1980-81), St. Andrew Soc., S.R., Ams. of Armorial Ancestry, Flagon and Trencher, Gen. Soc. War of 1812, Gen. Soc. Colonial Wars, Ancient and Honorable Arty. Co. of Mass., Am. Legion, VFW, Nat. Audubon Soc., Denver Field Ornithologists, Colo. Field Ornithologists, English-Speaking Union, Nat. Sojourners, Sigma Xi. Presbyterian (elder). Clubs: Masons, Shriners. Author: The Great Sand Dunes of Southern Colorado, 1967; Geology of the Igneous Rocks of the Spanish Peaks Region, Colorado, 1968; Pecos National Monument, New Mexico: Its Geologic Setting, 1969. Contbr. articles to profl. jours. Home: 240 Quay St Lakewood CO 80226

JOHNSON, ROY ERICK, school counselor; b. Pasadena, Calif., Nov. 23, 1926; s. Erick Konrad and Ida Theresa (Hedman) J.; m. Gloria Hall, Nov. 25, 1954; children—Gregory, Mark. B.A., Whittier Coll., 1954; M.A. in Edn., No. Ariz. U., 1967; postgrad. Walden U., 1982— . Cert. sch. counselor, Ariz. Tchr. schs. Alamitos Sch. Dist., Calif., 1954-61, Westminster, Calif., 1963-67; tchr., guidance counselor U.S. Bur. Indian Affairs, Brimhall, N.Mex., Nazumi, Ariz., 1961-63; counselor schs. Winslow, Ariz., 1967-70, Holbrook, Ariz., 1970—; mem. Master Tchr. Corps., Cadre, Ariz. Active Boy Scouts Am. Served with U.S. Army, 1943-46. Named Tchr. of Yr., Holbrook Schs., 1978. Mem. Am. Personnel and Guidance Assn., Ariz. Personnel and Guidance Assn. Republican. Lutheran. Home: 410 W Hampshire St Holbrook AZ 86025 Office: Holbrook Schs Box 640 Holbrook AZ 86025

JOHNSON, ROY MELVIN, microbiology educator, consultant, researcher; b. Chgo., Sept. 8, 1926; s. Carl Henning and Ebba Dorothy (Helstrom) J.; m. Betty Lou Schutt, Sept. 6, 1952; children—Renee M., Roberta M., Rhonda M., Regan M. A.B., U. Chgo., 1949, M.S., 1951; Ph.D., U. N.Mex., 1955; postgrad. Ind. U., 1963-64. Asst. prof. Ariz. State U., Tempe, from 1955, prof. dept. botany and microbiology, 1967—. Served to 1st lt. U.S. Army, 1944-46. NIH fellow, 1963-64. Mem. Am. Soc. Microbiology, Ariz. Acad. Sci. Contbr. articles to profl. jours. Office: Dept Microbiology Ariz State Univ Tempe AZ 85287

JOHNSON, RUSSELL EDWARD, clergyman; b. Memphis, Mar. 9, 1944; s. Lawrence Russell and Mildred Louise (Schwarz) J.; m. July 30, 1967; children—Lorraine Denise, Douglas Richard. B.A., Loma Linda U., 1967; M.Div., Andrews U., 1969, D.Min., 1975; M.B.A., Calif. State U., 1982. Ordained to ministry Seventh-Day Adventist Chs., 1973. Assoc. pastor White Meml. Ch., Los Angeles, 1969-71; pastor East Los Angeles Ch., 1971-74, Hawthorne (Calif.) Seventh-Day Adventist Ch., 1975—. Mem. Am. Prodn. and Inventory Control Soc. (pres.). Office: 3939 Compton St Hawthorne CA 90250

JOHNSON, S. EDMUND, data communications equipment mfg. co. exec.; b. Los Angeles, Nov. 9, 1945; s. Joseph Edmund and Miney Oleta (Stanley) J.; m. Dorothy B. Lopez, Nov. 12, 1966; 1 son, Carl Edmund. Technician, AT&T, Oakland, Calif., 1963-68; staff engr. Kaiser Broadcasting Co., San Francisco, 1968-69; staff engr. ABC Owned Stas. div., San Francisco, 1969-77, chief engr. Sta. KSFX, 1977-80; pres. Madzar Corp., Fremont, Calif., 1980—, also chmn. bd. Served with USMCR, 1966-71. Mem. Soc. Broadcast Engrs., Bay Area Broadcast Engrs. Soc. Republican. Lutheran. Office: 37490 Glenmoor Dr Fremont CA 94536

JOHNSON, SAMUEL BURKETT, agronomist, soil scientist, consultant; b. Glendale, Calif., Aug. 4, 1941; s. S. Burkett and Mary Louise (Godfrey) J.; m. Norma Rae Thoyre, July 1, 1966. B.S., U. Calif.-Davis, 1962. Cert. profl. agronomist, pest control adviser. Soil scientist Soil Conservation Service, U.S. Dept. Agr., Dixon, Calif., 1963-65; vol. Peace Corps, Honduras, 1965-67; extension/research horticulturist Libby, McNeill & Libby, P.R., 1968-72; chief agronomist Basico, Inc., Costa Rica, 1972-75; agronomist, soil scientist AgWest, Inc., Sacramento, 1979-82; pvt. practice as cons. agronomist, Sacramento, 1982—; agronomist, soil scientist Pacific Agrl. Labs., Inc., Oceanside, Calif., 1983—. Vice pres. Alzheimers Disease and Related Disorders Assn., Sancramento, 1982—. Mem. Soil Sci. Soc. Am., Agronomy Soc. Am., Crop Sci. Soc. Am., Soil Conservation Soc. Am., Am. Soc. Hort. Sci. Home: 4602 Twin Haven Rd Oceanside CA 92054

JOHNSON, SANDRA LYNN, real estate broker; b. Stockton, Calif., July 30, 1948; d. Oscar F. and Carolyn M. Carlson; m. Garen L. Johnson, Aug. 19, 1967; children—Jollyne Marie, Janelle Renee. Sec. to dist. psychologist and high sch. counseling dept. Tracy (Calif.) pub. schs., 1966-71; saleswomen Nimmo Realty, Atascadero, Calif., 1979-81, broker, owner, 1981—. Mem. adv. council Santa Margarita (Calif.) Elem. Sch. Mem. Nat. Assn. Realtors, Calif. Assn. Realtors, Atascadero Bd. Realtors (treas. 1982-83, chmn. fin. and budget com. 1982-83). Republican. Lutheran. Office: 7360 El Camino Real Atascadero CA 93422

JOHNSON, SKIP, advt. sales exec.; b. Omaha, Sept. 5, 1953; s. Charles M. and Constance O. (Anderson) J.; B.S. in B.A., U. Nev., 1976. Gen. mgr. Valley Yamaha, Las Vegas, Nev., 1975-77; sales mgr. Bates & Bertges Real Estate Inc., Las Vegas, Nev., 1977-78; with Cycle News, Inc., Long Beach, Calif., 1978—, nat. sales mgr., 19—. Voter registrar, State of Nev., 1974, 75, 76. Mem. Am. Motorcyclist Assn., Alpha Kappa Psi. Democrat. Baptist. Clubs: Silver City Scramblers, Motorcycle. Home: 2277 Pacific Ave A-103 Costa Mesa CA 92627 Office: 2201 Cherry Ave Long Beach CA 90801

JOHNSON, TERRY ALLYN, federal agency administrator; b. North Tonawanda, N.Y., Oct. 24, 1942; s. Whitney Alfred and Hilda Elizabeth (Robbins) J. B.S. in Edn., Central Mo. State U., Warrensburg, 1971, M.S. in Indsl. Safety. Safety specialist Norfolk Naval Shipyard, Dept. Navy, Portsmouth, Va., 1972-74; safety specialist Naval Weapons Sta., Dept. Navy, Concord, Calif., 1974-78; safety specialist Fish and Wildlife Service, Dept. Interior, Portland, Oreg., 1978-80; safety and health mgr. Pacific N.W. Forest and Range Experiment Sta., Dept. Agr., Portland, 1981—. Served with U.S. Army, 1963-66. Mem. Am. Soc. Safety Engrs. Home: 163 NE 18th Ave Hillsboro OR 97123 Office: US Forest Service-Pacific NW Forest and Range Experiment Station 319 SW Pine St Portland OR 97208

JOHNSON, THERA CHRISTENSEN, public sch. adminstr.; b. Richfield, Utah, Sept. 18, 1921; d. Archie Bert and Sarah (Curtis) Christensen; B.S. in Child Devel., Brigham Young U., 1942; M.S. in Counseling, Utah State U., 1959, Profl. Adminstr., 1963; m. Howard Melvin Johnson, Aug. 12, 1943 (dec.); children—Ralph Howard, Susan Kay Johnson Okroy, Linda Lou Johnson Marriott. Nursery and elementary sch. tchr., Utah, 1943-49, 55-57; jr. and sr. high sch. tchr. and counselor, Utah, 1959-75; mem. adminstrv. staff Weber County Sch. Dist., Ogden, Utah, 1975—, supr. pupil counseling and career services, 1977, supr. student services, career guidance and handicapped programs, 1978—; mem. Nat. Adv. Council Women's Ednl. Programs, 1976-80. Co-chmn. Greater Ogden Area Jr. Achievement; mem. Weber County Human Services Youth Adv. Bd.; mem. com. Ogden Rape Crisis Center. Mem. NEA, Am. Personnel and Guidance Assn., Am. Vocat. Assn., Utah Edn. Assn., Utah Counselors Assn., Utah Farm Bur., Delta Kappa Gamma, Phi Delta Kappa. Mormon. Club: Weber State Coll. Faculty Women's. Home: 3616 Van Buren Ave Ogden UT 84403 Office: 1122 Washington Blvd Ogden UT 84404

JOHNSON, THOMAS STODDARD, speech-language pathologist; b. Tremonton, Utah, Dec. 16, 1941; s. Heber Guy and Emorett (Stoddard) J.; m. Carol Lue Smith, June 24, 1964; children—Jay Robert, Jarey Guy, Jann, Thomas Sterling. B.S., Utah State U., 1964, M.S., 1967; Ph.D., U. Kans., 1969. Asst. prof. dept. communicative disorders Utah State U., Logan, 1969-71, assoc. prof., 1971-82, prof., 1982—, chmn. dept., 1976—. Bd. dirs. Exceptional Child Ctr., Logan. Mem. Am. Speech-Lang. Hearing Assn., Nat. Council Grad. Programs in Speech Pathology (exec. bd.), Assn. Curriculum Devel. and Supervision. Mormon. Author: Voice Therapy for Children, 1983. Office: Dept Communicative Disorders Utah State U Logan UT 84322

JOHNSON, VICKI R., insurance company manager; b. Glens Falls, N.Y., June 19, 1952; d. Leonard H. and Rose (Petrosky) J.; A.B., Franklin and Marshall Coll., 1974; postgrad. U. Portland, 1979—; m. Robin James Johnson, Nov. 24, 1979. Mgr. Prudential Ins. Co. Am., Woodland Hills, Calif., 1974—. Pres., Ridgeview Condominium Assn., 1978-81. Mem. Los Angeles Life and Health Claim Assn. Home: 21931 Burbank #16 Woodland Hills CA 91367 Office: 6000 Canoga Ave Woodland Hills CA 91367

JOHNSON, WALTER EARL, geophysicist; b. Denver, Dec. 16, 1942; s. Earl S. and Helen F. (Llewellyn) J.; Geophys. Engr., Colo. Sch. Mines, 1966; m. Ramcy Kandice Kayes, Aug. 6, 1967; children—Gretchen, Roger, Aniela. Geophysicist, Pan. Am. Petroleum Corp., 1966-73, seismic processing supr. Amoco Prodn. Co., Denver, 1973-74, marine tech. supr., 1974-76, div. processing cons., 1976-79, geophys. supr. No. Thrust Belt, 1979-80; chief geophysicist Husky Oil Co., 1981-82, exploration mgr. Rocky Mountain and Gulf Coast div., 1982—; pres. Sch. Lateral Ditch Co.; cons. engr. Bd. dirs. Rocky Mountain Residence, nursing home. Registered profl. engr., cert. geologist, Colo. Mem. Denver Geophys. Soc., Soc. Exploration Geophysicists. Republican. Baptist. Office: 6060 S Willow Dr Englewood CO 80111

JOHNSON, WALTER WILLIAM, librarian; b. Grand Rapids, Mich., Oct. 21, 1925; s. Carl and Dewey (Vander Mass) J.; B.A., Mich. State U., 1949, M.A. in Art, 1950; M.S. in L.S., U. So. Calif., 1957; m. Marcelon Cadeaux Matteson, Apr. 9, 1948; children—Koe Johnson-Orneles, Brook, Camille, Leigh, Stacy Ferl, Chad. Tchr. art Poly. High Sch., Long Beach, Calif., 1950-51, Artesia (Calif.) High Sch., 1952-53; librarian Calif. State U., Long Beach, 1956-58; dir. Library Info. and Cultural Resource Center, Huntington Beach, Calif., 1958—; sec. to Allied Arts Bd.; liaison to Allied Arts Assn. Former pres. Orange Coast Unitarian-Universalist Ch. Served with inf. AUS, 1944-45. Decorated Bronze Star, Purple Heart. Mem. Public Adminstrs. Orange County (past pres.), Orange County Library Assn. (past pres.), Public Library Execs. So. Calif., Calif. Library Assn., ALA. Club: Rotary. Office: Library Information and Cultural Resource Center 7111 Talbert St Huntington Beach CA 92646

JOHNSON, WARREN COTTLE, ofcl. Navy Dept.; b. Gilroy, Calif., Oct. 3, 1926; s. Edward Martin and Frances Estelle (Cottle) J.; B.S., U. Santa Clara (Calif.), 1951; grad. Advanced Mgmt. Program, Harvard, 1971; m. Ruth Elaine Wendt, Apr. 15, 1954; children—Shannon E., Shelagh L., Lisa R.; m. 2d, Simone Bernede, June 30, 1970. Materials engr. Area Public Works Office, U.S. Navy, Navy Dept., Dept. Def., Marianas Islands, 1956-58; sr. soils engr. Edwards & Kelcey, Baghdad, 1958-59; civil engr., Paris, 1961-62; chief soils engr. Capitol Engring. Corp., Saigon, 1959-61; hwy. br. mgr., dir. design officer charge constrn., Thailand, 1962-69, dir. design div., officer charge constrn., Saigon, Vietnam, 1969-71; dir. design div. Pacific div. Naval Facilities Engring. Command, 1971—; lectr. soil mechanics SEATO Postgrad. Sch., Bangkok, 1967. Mem. Guam Parks, Mus. and Monuments Commn., 1957. Served with AUS, 1944-46. Decorated Army Commendation medal; recipient Outstanding Performance award, 1970-72, Meritorious Civilian Service award, 1975, Superior Civilian Service medal, 1982 (all Navy Dept.), Vietnam Civilian Service medal, 1970, S.E. Asia Civilian Service award, 1967; Civic Enrichment award AIA, 1981. Registered profl. engr., Mass. Fellow ASCE; mem. ASTM, Soc. Am. Mil. Engrs., Nat. Soc. Profl. Engrs. Clubs: Royal Bangkok Sports; Elks; Cirque Sportif Saigon. Contbr. articles to profl. jours. Home: 1230 Mapuana St Kailua HI 96734 Office: Code 04 USN COMPACDIV NAVFACENCOM Pearl Harbor HI 96860

JOHNSON, WAYNE CARRINGTON, political consultant; b. Roanoke, Va., Apr. 8, 1952; s. Gustaf A. Johnson and Lois (Ingersoll) Johnson Bettis; m. Jennifer Crawford, Dec. 19, 1973; children—Rebecca Ann, Nathan Dabney. Student (Edison Fund grantee) Georgetown Inst. for Comparative Polit. and Econ. Systems, summer 1971; B.A., Purdue U., 1973. Nat. sales adminstr. Henri Fayette, Inc., Chgo., 1974-75; adminstrv. asst. to Senator H. L. Richardson, Sacramento, Calif., 1976; sr. v.p. Computer Caging Corp., Citrus Heights, Calif., 1977-82; pres. Wayne C. Johnson & Assocs. Inc., Sacramento, 1983—; dir. Dominion Mining Co.; mgr. numerous state legis. campaigns including mgr. U.S. Senate Campaign in Calif., 1980; mem. 11-mem. statewide steering com. Calif. Reagan for Pres. campaign, 1980. Elder Covenant Reformed Ch. of Sacramento; trustee Chalcedon Found. Mem. Direct Mktg. Assn., Phi Alpha Theta. Republican. Clubs: 20/30, Comstock of Sacramento. Home: 8335 Allene Creek Ct Citrus Heights CA 95610 Office: 8915 Folsom Blvd Suite H Sacramento CA 95826

JOHNSON, WAYNE HAROLD, librarian, state ofcl.; b. El Paso, Tex., May 2, 1942; s. Earl Harold and Cathryn Louise (Greeno) J.; B.S., Utah State U., 1968; M.P.A., U. Colo., 1970; M.L.S., U. Okla., 1972; m. Patricia Ann Froedge, June 15, 1973; 1 dau., Meredith Jessica. Circulation librarian Utah State U., Logan, 1968, adminstrv. asst. librarian, 1969; research Okla. Mgmt. and Engring. Cons., Norman, 1972; chief adminstrv. services Wyo. State Library, Cheyenne, 1973-76, chief bus. officer library archives and hist. dept., 1976-78, Wyo. state librarian, 1978—; trustee Bibliog. Center for Research, Denver, pres., 1982, 83. Fin. chmn. Cheyenne dist. Longs Peak council Boy Scouts Am., 1978-79; mem. Cheyenne Airport Authority, 1981—, pres., 1981, 82. Served with USCG, 1960-64. Mem. ALA, Wyo. Library Assn., Mountain Plains Library Assn., Aircraft Owners and Pilots Assn., Cheyenne C. of C. (chmn. transp. com. 1982, 83). Democrat. Presbyterian. Club: Masons. Office: Wyo State Library Cheyenne WY 82002

JOHNSON, WILLIAM HERBERT, JR., rancher; b. Duncan, Okla., June 10, 1918; s. William Herbert and Mattie May (Jones) J.; m. Edwina Crabtree, July 23, 1941; children—William Herbert III, Nancy Nell Curtis. Student Cameron Coll., Lawton, Okla., 1936-37, Okla. State U., 1938-40. Pres., dir. Johnson Ranches Inc., Wyo., Okla., 1958—. Mem. state coms. Farmers Home Adminstrn., 1961-63, Agrl. Stblzn. and Conservation, 1977-81; mem. Platte County Sch. Bd., 1956-81, pres., 1973-81; dir. Wyo. Sch. Bd. Assn., 1974-78; dir. Platte County Sch. Dist. 1 sch. facilities authority, 1976-81, chmn. project area coordinating council, 1976-81; chmn. Platte County Dem. Central Com., 1952-60. Recipient Golden Bell award Wyo. Sch. Bd. Assn., 1981. Served to capt. U.S. Army, 1942-46. Mem. Laramie Peak Stock Growers Assn. (past pres.). Baptist. Clubs: Glendo Lions (past pres.); Masons. Home and Office: Cassa Ranch Glendo WY 82213

JOHNSON, WILLIAM HUGH, JR., hosp. adminstr.; b. Bklyn., Oct. 29, 1935; s. William Hugh and Florence Patricia (Seinsoth) J.; B.A., Hofstra U., 1957; M.Ed., U. Hawaii, 1969; m. Gloria C. Stube, Jan. 23, 1960; children—Karen Anne, William Hugh III. Asst. adminstr. U.S. Army Hosp., Berlin, 1959-62, West Point, N.Y., 1962-65, Tripler Med. Center, Honolulu, 1966-70; staff officer Hdqrs. Dept. of Army, Washington, 1970-74; dir. personnel Walter Reed Army Hosp., Washington, 1974-77; adminstr. U. N.Mex. Hosp., Albuquerque, 1977—; asst. prof. U.S. Mil. Acad., 1962-65. Vice pres., exec. bd. Albuquerque Vis. Nurse Service, 1978—. Served with M.C., U.S. Army, 1957-77. Decorated Legion of Merit, Army Meritorious Service medal. Mem. Am. Hosp. Assn. (mem. governing council pub. gen. hosp. sect.), Nat. Assn. Pub. Hosps. (bd. dirs.), N.Mex. Hosp. Assn. (dir. at large), Albuquerque Area Hosp. Council (pres.), Am. Coll. Hosp. Adminstrs. Roman Catholic. Club: Tanoan Country (Albuquerque). Home: 7920 Sartan Way NE Albuquerque NM 87109 Office: 2211 Lomas Blvd Albuquerque NM 87106

JOHNSON, WILLIAM LARRY, mathematics educator; b. Tyler, Tex., Jan. 19, 1943; s. Henry William and Martha Marie (McMurray) J.; m. Annabel Marie Bek, June 2, 1974. B.S. in Edn., North Tex. State U., 1967; M.Ed., Tex. Christian U., 1976; Ed.D., Tex. Tech U., 1980. Secondary educator, 1967-76; project dir. Pedamorphosis, Inc., Lubbock, Tex., 1979-80, asst. treas., 1980-81; statistician Tex. Tech U., Lubbock, 1979-81; chmn. dept. math. Ambassador Coll., Big Sandy, Tex., 1981—. Helen DeVitt Jones leadership fellow, 1978-79. Mem. Hawkins Classroom Tchrs. Assn. (pres. 1976-77), Am. Ednl. Research Assn., Nat. Soc. Study Edn., Omicron Delta Kappa, Phi Delta Kappa, Alpha Chi, Phi Delta Kappa. Mem. Ch. of God. Clubs: Summit, Plaza, Haps Hazards Square Dance (v.p. 1979), Lubbock Spokesman (pres. 1980-81). Patentee in field. Home: Route 2 PO Box 517 Big Sandy TX 75755 Office: PO Box 111 Ambassador Coll Big Sandy TX 75755

JOHNSON, WILLIAM POTTER, newspaper pub.; b. Peoria, Ill., May 4, 1935; s. William Zweigle and Helen Marr (Potter) J.; A.B., U. Mich., 1957; m. Pauline Ruth Rowe, May 18, 1968; children—Darragh Elizabeth, William Potter. Gen. mgr. Bureau County Republican, Inc., Princeton, Ill., 1961-72; pres. Johnson Newspapers, Inc., Sebastopol, Calif., 1972-75, Evergreen, Colo., 1974—, dir. First Nat. Bank, Evergreen, Colo. Alt. del. Republican Nat. Conv., 1968. Served to lt. USNR, 1958-61. Mem. Colo. Press Assn., Nat. Newspaper Assn., San Francisco Press Club, Denver Press Club, Beta Theta Pi, Sigma Delta Chi. Republican. Roman Catholic. Clubs: Hiwan Country (Evergreen); Oro Valley Country (Tucson); Grand Lake (Colo.) Tennis. Home: 445 W Rapa Pl Tucson AZ 85701 Office: 4009 S Colorado Hwy 74 Evergreen CO 80439

JOHNSON, WILLIAM R., bishop; b. Tonopah, Nev., Nov. 19, 1918; ed. St. Patrick's Sem., Menlo Park, Calif., St. John's Sem., Camarillo, Calif.; B.S. in Social Work, Cath. U. Am. Ordained priest, 1944; staff Cath. Welfare Bur., Archdiocese of Los Angeles, 1948-76, dir., 1956-76; pastor Holy Name of Jesus Ch., Los Angeles, 1962-68, Am. Martyrs Ch., Manhattan Beach, Calif., 1968-70; parochial vicar St. Vibiana's Cathedral, Los Angeles, 1970-76; consecrated titular bishop of Blear and aux. bishop of Los Angeles, 1971; bishop of Orange (Calif.), 1976—. Registered social worker, Calif.; lic. clin. social worker, Calif. Mem. Nat. Assn. Social Workers, Acad. Cert. Social Workers. Office: 2811 Villa Real Dr Orange CA 92667*

JOHNSTON, BRUCE FOSTER, economics educator; b. Lincoln, Nebr., Sept. 24, 1919; s. Homer K. and Ethel (Hockett) J.; m. Harriet L. Pollins, Mar. 31, 1944; children—Bruce C., Patricia C. B.A., Cornell U., 1941; M.A., Stanford U., 1950, Ph.D., 1953. Agrl. mktg. adminstrn. U.S. Dept. Agr., 1941-42; chief food br. econ. and sci. sect. SCAP, Tokyo, 1952-54; agrl. economist Food and Agr. div. U.S. Mission to NATO and European Regional Orgn., Paris, 1952-54; assoc. prof., assoc. economist Food Research Inst., Stanford (Calif.) U., 1954-59, prof., economist, 1959—; cons. World Bank, FAO, others. Cons., mem. steering com., research and action programme concerning tech. and employment ILO, 1971—. Served to capt. U.S. Army, 1942-46. Guggenheim fellow, 1962; Internat. Inst. Applied Systems Analysis fellow, 1978-79. Mem. Am. Agrl. Econs. Assn., Am. Econ. Assn., African Studies Assn., Phi Beta Kappa, Phi Kappa Phi. Author: (with Clark) Redesigning Rural Development: A Strategic Perspective, 1982; (with Anthony, Jones and Uchendu) Agricultural Change in Tropical Africa, 1979; (with Kilby) Agriculture and Structural Transformation: Economic Strategies in Late-Developing Countries, 1975; co-editor, contbr. (with Ohkawa and Kaneda) Agriculture and Economic Growth: Japan's Experience, 1969. Home: 676 Alvarado Row Stanford CA 94305 Office: Food Research Inst Stanford Univ Stanford CA 94305

JOHNSTON, CYNTHIA COCHRAN, physician, educator; b. Kansas City, Mo., Oct. 2, 1952; d. John A. and Mary L. (Leffler) Cochran; B.S. in Zoology with high honors, Ariz. State U., 1974; M.D., U. Ariz., 1976; m. Bruce G. Johnston, Dec. 29, 1973; children—Lauren Elizabeth, Stephen Shepherd. Resident in family practice U. Ariz., Tucson, 1976-79, chief resident in family practice, 1978-79; med. officer San

Xavier Indian Health Center, Tucson, 1979, dir., 1979-82; assoc. faculty dept. family and community medicine U. Ariz., Tucson, 1979-81, adj. asst. prof., 1981—; staff physician Tucson Clinic, 1982—; Ariz.'s rep. to Nat. Conf. Family Practice Residents, 1978, 79. Served with USPHS, 1979—. Recipient John Grobe award for outstanding family practice resident in Ariz., 1979. Mem. Am. Acad. Family Physicians (Warner-Chilcot award for outstanding tchr. 1979), Ariz. Acad. Family Physicians, (dir. 1981—), Soc. Tchrs. in Family Medicine, Phi Beta Kappa. Contbr. articles to profl. jours. Home: 6307 E Paseo Otono Tucson AZ 85715 Office: PO Box 26926 Tucson AZ 85726

JOHNSTON, DAVID CHARLES, psychiatrist; b. Calgary, Alta., Can., Jan. 30, 1925; came to U.S., 1950, naturalized, 1956; s. Franklin Melvin and Dorothy Alma (Corneille) J.; M.D., U. Toronto, 1950; m. Lily Martha Bell, Dec. 15, 1972; children by previous marriage—Susan Johnston Amselem, David C., Kenneth D. Intern medicine and surgery Buffalo Gen. Hosp., 1950-52; resident ob-gyn Millard Fillmore Hosp., Buffalo, 1952-55; practice medicine, specializing in ob-gyn, Buffalo, 1955-60, Long Beach, Calif., 1960-62; practice medicine, specializing in psychiatry, Beverly Hills, Calif., 1962—, also Long Beach; clin. instr. U. Calif.-Irvine, 1967—; cons. U. Calif.-Long Beach, also VA Hosp., 1966—. NIMH fellow, 1963-66. Mem. Calif. (v.p.), So. Calif., Orange County (past pres.), Harbor socs. clin. hypnosis, Am. Psychiat. Assn., AMA, Am. Bd. Med. Hypnosis (dir., pres., examiner), Phi Delta Theta. Clubs: Balboa Bay (Newport); Royal Canadian Yacht (Toronto); Huntington Harbour Yacht. Pioneered hypnotic childbirth; nat. precedent hypnoanalytic film as evidence Calif. Superior Ct., 1968. Home: 16078 Bonaire Circle Huntington Harbour CA 92649 Office: 4729 E Anaheim Long Beach CA 90804

JOHNSTON, DENNIS L., advertising and marketing executive; b. Peoria, Ill.; s. LaVerne F. and Lucille K. Johnston; m. Teresa E. Daugherty; children—Erica Lynn, Jason Andrew. Ed. pub. schs. Mktg. dir. Melvin Simon & Assocs., Pekin, Ill., 1970-76; art dir. sta. WMBD-TV, Peoria, 1976-80; devel. dir. sta. WTVP-TV, Peoria, 1975-77; county mgr. Times Call, Longmont, Colo., 1977-81; pres. Crimson Blue Advt. Inc., Longmont, 1981—; adv. com. cons. Career Devel. Ctr. Served with USMCR, 1965-71. Recipient nat. devel. award Corp. Pub. Broadcasting, 1976, others. Lutheran. Clubs: Lions, Optimists.

JOHNSTON, HELEN SMITH HEAD, art dealer; b. Atlanta; d. Philip and Helen (Smith) Head; widowed. A.B. in Journalism, U. Ga.; M.F.A. (hon.) San Francisco Acad. Fine Arts Coll., 1982. Dir. pub. relations M.H. DeYoung Memorial Mus., San Francisco, 1953-65; dir. Focus Gallery, San Francisco, 1966—. Recipient award for outstanding contbn. to photography in Calif., Profl. Photographers No. Calif., 1968; Dorothea Lang award Oakland (Calif.) Mus., 1972. Mem. Western Assn. Art Museums, Assn. Internat. Photography Art Dealers, Women in Communications. Established oldest continually operating photography art gallery in the U.S.

JOHNSTON, JACQUELYN JUANITA, banker; b. St. Louis, June 17, 1936; d. Lucious and Louise Elizabeth (Mobley) Carey; student St. Louis U., 1954; student U. Calif., Berkeley; m. Charles Fredrick Rice Johnston, Apr. 17, 1955; children—Charles Fredrick Rice, Marion Louise, Errol Kevin. Credit investigator Sears Roebuck & Co., St. Louis, 1967-69; with Mo. Div. Welfare, St. Louis, 1969-70; credit investigator/verifier Westinghouse Credit Corp., Anaheim, Calif., 1970; credit mgr. Broadway Jewelers, Oakland, Calif., 1971; records/info. analyst Crocker Nat. Bank, San Francisco, 1973—. Sunday ch. sch. youth supt. Bapt. Ch., Oakland, 1977—, youth coordinator, 1977—; bd. dirs. Allen Temple Sr. Citizens Center. Mem. Nat. Micrographics Assn., Assn. Records Mgrs. and Adminstrs. Baptist. Club: Toastmasters (area gov. 1976-77, pres. 1977-78). Home: 8129 Earl St Oakland CA 94605 Office: 111 Sutter St San Francisco CA 94104

JOHNSTON, JOHN, economics educator; b. Belfast, with honors, No. Ireland, Mar. 13, 1923; s. John R. and Elizabeth (Clenaghan) J. B.Com.Sc. with honors, Queen's U., No. Ireland, 1947; Ph.D., U. Wales, 1957; M.A. (hon.), U. Manchester, 1962. Faculty, Harvard U., Cambridge, Mass., 1957-58, CUNY, 1967-68, U. Wales, 1948-53, U. Wis.-Madison, 1958-59; Stanley Jevons prof. econometrics U. Manchester, 1959-78; prof. econs. U. Calif.-Irvine, 1978—; cons. Recipient Gold medal in Econ. Theory, Queen's U., 1947; Houblon-Norman Research grantee Bank of Eng., 1951. Fellow Econometric Soc.; mem. Royal Econ. Sco., Am. Econ. Assn., Royal Statis. Soc., Am. Statis. Assn., others. Author: Statistical Cost Analysis, 1960; Econometric Methods, 1963, 2d edit., 1973; contbr. articles to profl. jours. Office: Sch Social Sci U Calif Irvine CA 92717

JOHNSTON, LINDA OSGOOD, lawyer; b. Pitts., Mar. 24, 1949; d. Steven S. Osgood and Estelle (Richest) Zangwill; B.A. in Journalism, 1970; J.D., Duquesne U., 1980; vis. student U. So. Calif., 1978-79; m. Frederick Dean Johnston, May 21, 1977; children—Frederick Jarrit (Eric), Keith Nicholas. Writer, editor MATCOM Ledger, Zweibruecken, Germany, 1971-72; account exec., media liaison Steve Osgood & Assos., Pitts., 1972-77; summer law clk. Meyer, Unkovic & Scott, Pitts., 1978; admitted to Pa. bar, 1980, Calif. bar, 1980; asso. firm Fenwick, Stone, Davis & West, Los Angeles, 1980—. Mem. Pa. Bar Assn., Calif. Bar Assn., Los Angeles Bar Assn. Contbr. articles to legal publs. Office: 707 Wilshire Blvd Suite 5400 Los Angeles CA 90017

JOHNSTON, MARJORIE DIANE, computer programming consultant; b. Fullerton, Calif., Sept. 19, 1943; d. Earl Lawrence and Ruth Junita (Long) Whipple; m. Roy L. Johnston, Oct. 30, 1971; children—Stephen, Deborah. Grad computer programming LaSalle U., Chgo., 1973. Computer programmer Los Alamos Nat. Lab., 1972-81; analyst Computer Assistance, Inc., programmer and applications cons., Tulsa, 1981-82, Denver, 1982—. Clubs: Rebekah, Order Eastern Star (past matron). Home: 5709 W 71st Circle Arvada CO 80003

JOHNSTON, MARY ANNE CLAIBORNE, educator; b. Atlanta, Apr. 6, 1938; d. Thomas Sterling and Dorothy (Rhorer) Claiborne; m. Richard Boles Johnston, Jr., Aug. 13, 1960; children—Richard Boles III, Sterling Claiborne, Kristin Marie. B.A. cum laude, Vanderbilt U., 1960; M.A., U. Ala., 1975; Ph.D., U. Colo., 1979; Montessori presch. diploma, St. Nicholas Tng. Ctr., London, 1971. Tchr., Emsworth Sch., Nashville, 1960-62, Grace Episcopal Day Sch., Newton, Mass., 1968-69, Montessori Creative Presch., Birmingham, Ala., 1972-73; instr. women's studies program U. Ala., Birmingham, 1974-75, teaching asst. Grad. Sch. Edn., 1975, instr. Summer Grad. Sch. Edn., 1978, 79; asst. prof. dept. edn. Colo. Women's Coll., Denver, 1978-81; asst. prof. dept. tchr. edn. Met. State Coll., Denver, 1981—, dir. edn. project Fed. Emergency Mgmt. Agy., 1981-82; cons. in field. Mem. Am. Ednl. Studies Assn., Assn. Experimental Edn., Assn. for Supervision and Curriculum Devel., Phi Delta Kappa, Kappa Delta Pi. Contbr. articles to profl. jours. Office: Sch Edn Box 21 Metropolitan State Coll 1006 11th St Denver CO 80204

JOHNSTON, NETTA RITCHIE, medical equipment manufacturing company adminstrator; b. Muthill, Perthshire, Scotland, Feb. 24, 1931; d. Duncan McDonald and Mary (Cameron) MacNaughton; came to U.S., 1960, naturalized, 1981; m. George Mathieson Johnston, Apr. 10, 1957 (div.); children—Brian Duncan, Bruce Mathieson. Diploma in Edn. Dundee (Scotland) Tng. Coll., 1952. Tchr. elem. schs. Dundee, Scotland, 1952-56, Coupar Angus, Scotland, 1956-57, Lachine, Que., Can., 1957-60; bookkeeper Wells Fargo Bank, Palo Alto, Calif., 1960-63; office mgr. Channel Disposal Co., Santa Barbara, Calif., 1974-80; adminstr. Endotek Corp., Santa Barbara, 1980—. Home: 729 N Ontare Santa Barbara CA 93105 Office: 824 E Ortega Santa Barbara CA 93103

JOHNSTON, ROBERT WAYNE, manufacturing and organization development company executive, management consultant, educator; b. Dayton, Ohio, Nov. 8, 1929; s. Clinton Silas and Dorothy Pearl (Eicher) J.; m. Isabel Marie Mingiraulli; children—Wayne Robert, Randall Kent, Kara Lee. B.A. in Psychology, Calif. State U.-Los Angeles, 1955; postgrad. Boston U., 1966-67; Ph.D. in Behavioral Sci., Calif. Western U., 1975; post-doctoral work in mgmt., orgn. devel. New Sch. Social Research, 1975, in psychology U.S. Internat. U., 1977, in self-mgmt. Menninger Found., 1980. Mgr. personnel space systems div. Lockheed Missiles and Space Co., 1955-61; corp. staff specialist Itek Corp., 1961-67; mgr. mgmt. and orgn. devel. Honeywell Info. Systems Corp. Group, 1967-70; prin. cons. Personnel Mgmt. Assocs., Huntington Beach, Calif., 1970-74; mgr. orgn. devel. and tng. McCulloch Corp., Los Angeles, 1974-76; mgr. mgmt. devel. Kaiser-Permanente Med. Care Program, Los Angeles, 1977-78; corp. mgr. orgn. devel. Western Gear Corp., Lynnwood, Calif., 1978-83; pres. Robert Wayne Johnston Assocs., Huntington Beach, 1983—; adj. prof. behavioral scis. Pepperdine Grad. Sch. Bus. and Mgmt. cons. in field. Vol. tchr. non-profit Mgmt. Inst., Los Angeles, 1980—. Recipient numerous honorariums, awards Western Gear Corp., 1981, 82, 83. Mem. Am. Soc. Tng. and Devel., Orgn. Devel. Network, Assn. Humanistic Psychology, World Futurist Soc., Acad. Mgmt., Assn. Transpersonal Psychology. Author numerous publs., manuals in field; contbr. articles to profl. jours.

JOHNSTON, STEPHEN CRAIG, advertising agency executive; b. Mpls., Apr. 28, 1943; s. Donald Grover and Evelyn Marcella (Veigel) J.; m. Leslie Ann Miller, Sept. 13, 1964; m. 2d, Suzanne Kirk, Apr. 15, 1978; children—Marisa, Monika, Morgen. B.A., Calif. State Coll.-Long Beach, 1972. Owner, mgr. Leysen & Johnston Advt., Newport Beach, Calif., 1972—; writer, producer cassette digests Man in Black (Johnny Cash), The Late Great Planet Earth; author: Jerry Brown Verbatim, 1976; The Newport Beach Answer Book, 1982, The Republican Answer Book, 1983. Bd. dirs. Natural History Found. Orange County. Served with AUS, 1966-71. Recipient Thomas Jefferson award for narration The End of the War to End All Wars, Freedom's Found., Valley Forge, 1969; Emmy for PBS Narration The Bus. Exchange, 1982; Best Film strip award Xerox Corp., 1978. Democrat. Elder, Presbyterian Ch. Home: 5 Landfall Ct Newport Beach CA 92663 Office: 359 San Miguel Dr #201 Newport Beach CA 92660

JOHNSTON, STODDARD PINTARD, radio and television station executive; b. Elkins, W.Va., Aug. 16, 1924; s. Mrs. John A. Kennedy; B.A., Yale, 1950; m. Patricia Kelly, Feb. 1, 1953 (dec. Mar. 1979); children—Bruce Lee, Azile Kelly, John Stoddard. Chmn. bd. KMST TV, Monterey, Calif., 1965-79; pres. Johnston Broadcasting (Sta. KMBY, Seaside-Monterey, Calif.), 1968—; gen. mgr. KWAV, Monterey, 1966-80; pres. PG-Asilomar Operating Corp.; chmn. Econ. Devel. of Monterey County, 1982—. Pres., Monterey Peninsula Found., 1978-80; bd. dirs. Girl Scouts U.S.A., 1975-78, mem. fin. com., 1980-81; mem. Calif. Health Facilities Commn., 1973-77; chmn. Library and Museums Commn., Oakland, Calif., 1959-61. Served with AUS, 1942-46, to 1st lt., 1951-52. Mem. Calif. Broadcasters Assn. (bd. dirs., chmn. 1980-81). Address: 2640 Ribera Rd Carmel CA 93923

JOHNSTON, SUZANNE MOORE, ballet company artistic director, choreographer; b. Macon, Ga., Dec. 12, 1928; d. Arthur Raymond and Alice Arie (Hollomon) Moore; m. Sidney F. Johnston, III, May 10, 1952; children—Suzanne Cary, Bridget Hollomon, Sidney Fowler, IV. Student Peabody Coll., 1948-49, Nashville Ballet Soc., Edna McRae Sch. Dance, Chgo., Edwin Strawbridge Summer Dance Camps, Am. Sch. Ballet N.Y.C., Ballet Art Carnegie Hall N.Y.C., Edward Caton Sch. Ballet N.Y.C., Chester Hale Sch. Ballet N.Y.C., and others. Appeared as solo dancer in Our Gang movies; ballerina, Nashville Ballet Co., 1941-45; appeared as featured dancer in Broadway plays: High Button Shoes, Miss Liberty, Oklahoma; originator, dir. Knoxville Civic Ballet Co., 1949-51; founder Suzanne Concert Dancers, Albuquerque, 1963—; owner, pres., dir. Suzanne Sch. Classical Ballet, Albuquerque, 1963—; owner, pres. Suzanne Johnston Agy., Albuquerque, 1978—; founder, artistic dir. N.Mex. Ballet Co. Albuquerque, 1972-76; ballet tchr. continuing edn. program U. N.Mex., 1978—; chmn. dance panel N.Mex. Arts Commn., 1976-77. Republican. Presbyterian.

JOHNSTON, THOMAS ALIX, artist, educator; b. Oklahoma City, June 4, 1941. B.A., San Diego State Coll., 1965; M.F.A., U. Calif.-Santa Barbara, 1967; student Atelier 17, Paris, 1980. Group shows include Library Congress, Washington, Seattle Art Mus., 1972, U. Calgary (Alta., Can.), 1975, Rochester Inst. Tech., 1978, Evergreen (Wash.) State Coll., 1980, Traver Gallery, Seattle, 1980, Bklyn. Mus., 1980; one-man show at Whatcom Mus., Bellingham, Wash., 1971; works represented in permanent collections at Henry Art Gallery U. Wash., U. N.D., Grand Forks, Seattle Art Mus., Modern Art Mus., Kobe, Japan, Cheney Cowles Mus., Spokane; asst. prof. printmaking Western Wash. U., 1967-73, assoc. prof., 1974-82, prof., 1982—; vis. artist, prof. various colls. and univs. Recipient 1st Place Graphics award Calif. State U.-Chico, 1970. Office: Western Washington State College Dept Art Bellingham WA 98225

JOHNSTON, VIRGINIA EVELYN, editor; b. Spokane, Wash., Apr. 26, 1933; d. Edwin and Emma Lucile (Munroe) Rowe; student Portland Community Coll., 1964, Portland State U., 1966, 78-79; m. Alan Paul Beckley, Dec. 26, 1974; children—Chris, Denise, Rex. Proofreader, The Oregonian, Portland, 1960-62, teletypesetter operator, 1962-66, operator Photon 200, 1966-68, copy editor, asst. women's editor, 1968-82, editor FOODday/UPDATE, 1982—; pres. Matrix Assocs., Inc., Portland, 1975—, chmn. bd., 1979—; cons. Democratic party Oreg., 1969, Portland Sch. Dist. No. 1, 1978. Mem. Women in Communications, Inc., Inst. Profl. and Managerial Women, Nat. Assn. Female Execs. Democrat. Editor Principles of Computer Systems for Newspaper Mgmt., 1975-76. Home: 4140 NE 137th Ave Portland OR 97230 Office: 1320 SW Broadway Portland OR 97201

JOHNSTON, WARREN E., agricultural economics educator, consultant; b. Woodland, Calif., May 27, 1933; s. Henry H. and Margaret G. Johnston; m. Donna M. Hamblet; children—Kimberly Ann, Douglas Stuart. B.S., U. Calif.-Davis, 1959; M.S., N.C. State U., 1963, Ph.D., 1964. Prof. agrl. econs. U. Calif., Davis, 1963—, acting assoc. dean applied econs. and behavioral scis., Coll. Agrl. and Environ. Scis., 1980-81, chmn. dept. agrl. econs., 1981—. Served with U.S. Army, 1953-57. Alexander von Humboldt research scholar, W.Ger., 1969-70; Fulbright research scholar, N.Z., 1976-77. Mem. Am. Agrl. Econs. Assn., Western Agrl. Econs. Assn., Am. Soc. Farm Mgrs. and Rural Appraisers, Internat. Assn. Agrl. Economists. Office: Dept Agrl Econs Univ Calif Davis CA 95616

JOHNSTON, WILLIAM R., city official; b. Kansas City, Mo., Sept. 7, 1937; s. John F. and Dorothy Dolores (Welch) J.; m. W. Jean Freeman, Feb. 28, 1959; children—William J., Ernest L., Dorothy J.; A.A., El Camino Coll., 1971. Sanitation foreman City of Inglewood (Calif.), 1960-73; sanitation supt. City of Manhattan Beach (Calif.), 1973-77; comml. refuse mgr. City of Beverly Hills (Calif.), 1977-79; sanitation supt. City of Mesa (Ariz.), 1979—; cons. UN, WHO, 1976. Served with USN, 1954-57. Mem. Govtl. Refuse Collection and Disposal Assn. (pres. 1976, treas. Ariz. chpt.). Dem. Office: PO Box 1466 Mesa AZ 85201

JOHNSTONE, LINDA K(AY), educator; b. Billings, Mont., Apr. 1, 1945; d. McKay L. and Ina M. (Sunset) Welling; m. George R. Johnstone, Aug. 2, 1968; children—Jason Nicholas, Shadd Arthur, Jillyn. B.S. in Home Econs., U. Wyo., 1967. Tchr. schs., Riverton, Wyo., 1967-69, Mill Creek Sch., Wind River Reservation, 1970-76, Lander Valley High Sch., Lander, Wyo., 1976—. Recipient local and state Diana award, Epsilon Sigma Alpha, 1982. Mem. Am. Vocat. Assn., Wyo. Vocat. Assn., Nat. Experienced Based Career Edn. Assn. Republican. Mormon.

JOHNTZ, JAMES ANDREW, JR., radio sta. exec.; b. Oakley, Idaho, Nov. 10, 1919; s. James Andrew and Florence Cecil (Datzel) J.; B.A. magna cum laude, Stanford U., 1942; m. Willa M. Maxey, Feb. 14, 1945; children—James Andrew III, Kevin R. Chief engr. KIDO, 1943-47, KDSH radio, Boise, 1947-64; v.p. engring. Boise Valley Broadcasters, 1964-73; pres., gen. mgr. Boise Valley Broadcasters, Inc. KBCI-TV, 1974—; chmn. Idaho adv. com. FCC. Mem. Idaho Citizens Com. on Crime and Delinquency, 1974-75; past pres. Cystic Fibrosis Assn. Idaho, pres. Gem. State chpt. Bd. dirs. Mayors Com. on Employment of Handicapped, 1972-81. Registered profl. engr., Idaho. Mem. Boise C. of C., Phi Beta Kappa. Methodist. Lion (past pres.). Office: KBCI-TV Eugene Television Inc 1007 Jefferson St Boise ID 83707

JOLLEY, DONAL CLARK, painter; b. Zion National Park, Utah, Oct. 20, 1933; s. Donal Jones and Nora (Crawford) J.; m. 2d, Virginia Elizabeth Harrison, Nov. 14, 1971; children—Karen Elizabeth, Donal Dean, Keith Paul. B.S. in Art and Psychology, Brighman Young U., 1959. Illustrator, Space Tech. Labs., Los Angeles, 1960-61, Aerospace Corp., San Bernardino, Calif., 1961-71; freelance illustrator, Rimforest, Calif., 1971—. Served with U.S. Army, 1956-57. Decorated Army Commendation medal; recipient numerous awards. Mem. Nat. Watercolor Soc. (Members award 1981), Watercolor West, Whiskey Painters Am. Address: PO Box 156 Rimforest CA 92378

JOLLEY, JERRY CLYDE, sociologist, educator; b. Murray, Utah, Feb. 9, 1945; s. Merlin Duane and Alice May (Frazier) J.; m. Carol Elaine Free, May 21, 1971; children—Darin, Jennifer. B.A., U. Utah, 1969, M.A., 1970, Ph.D., 1975. Cert. secondary tchr., Utah. Teaching asst. U. Utah, Salt Lake City, 1970, teaching fellow, 1972-75; instr. Kans. State Tchrs. Coll., Emporia, 1970-72; from asst. prof. to prof. Lewis-Clark State Coll., Lewiston, Idaho, 1975—, coordinator Criminal Justice program. Mem. Am. Sociol. Assn., Acad. Criminal Justice Scis., Idaho Sociol. Assn. (pres. 1979-80), Idaho Correctional Assn., Criminal Justice Soc., Sigma Gamma Chi. Mormon. Contbr. articles to profl. jours. Home: 1022 Hemlock Dr Lewiston ID 83501 Office: Lewis-Clark State College Lewiston ID 83501

JOLLY, JAMES A., educator; b. Oceanside, Calif., Nov. 2, 1921; s. Peter Benjamine and Amelia (DeMuth) J.; B.A., U. Pacific, 1951; M.B.A., U. Santa Clara, 1963, Ph.D., 1970; m. Rose Calvina Binkley, Jan. 14, 1945; children—Mayeve O. Jolly Tate, David O., Heidi O. Jolly Wolf. Research physicist Eitel McCullough, San Bruno, Calif., 1951-54, prodn. engr., 1954-59, mgr. prodn. engring. and indsl. engring., 1959-60, mgr. advanced devel., 1960-64; mgr. indsl. microwave activity Varian Assos., Palo Alto, Calif., 1964-69; asso. prof. Naval Postgraduate Sch., Monterey, Calif., 1969-76; prof. Sch. Bus., Calif. State U., Sacramento, 1976—. Mem. IEEE (sr.), Internat. Microwave Power Inst. (past pres.), Acad. Mgmt. Author: (with J.W. Creighton) Technology Transfer Process Model and Annotated Selected Bibliography, 1978. Editor: (with J.W. Creighton) Technology Transfer in Research and Development, 1975; asso. editor Jour. Microwave Power, 1973—; editor Jour. Tech. Transfer, 1976—. Home: 905 Dunbarton Circle Sacramento CA 95825

JOLY, JOHN GERARD, marketing executive; b. Detroit, June 15, 1939; s. Louis George and Gertrude Katherine (Begley) J.; m. Judith Ellen Vielhaber, June 24, 1967; children—Jennifer Anne, James Louis, Janine Elizabeth. B.A. in Journalism, U. Detroit, 1968. Printer Detroit Times, 1957-60; promotion copywriter Detroit Free Press, 1962-68; humor columnist Detroit News, 1963; editor Lowell (Mich.) Ledger, 1970; editor Ada (Mich.) Suburban Life, 1970; promotion mgr. Miami (Fla.) Herald, 1970-77; promotion mgr. El Miami Herald en Espanol; mktg. dir. Seattle Post-Intelligencer, 1977-83; pres. John Joly Inc., Seattle, 1983—; cons. newspaper mktg.; lectr. promotion Knight-Ridder Inst. Tng., Miami, 1972-77; lectr. Internat. Newspaper Promotion Assn., Atlanta, Mexico City, Seville, Spain, San Francisco. Served with U.S. Army, 1961-63. Recipient Found. award Detroit Free Press Club, 1968, awards Editor and Publisher Mag., 1978-82. Mem. Sales and Mktg. Execs. of Seattle (pres. 1982), Mktg. Communications Execs. Internat., Can. Soc. of Northwest (exec. dir. Seattle 1983), Seattle Advt. Fedn. (dir.), Seattle Home Show (dir.). Club: Seattle Athletic. Columnist, Ham on Wry, 1962-65. Office: 521 Wall St Seattle WA 98121

JONAS, ADRIENNE HAZEL, clothing manufacturing company executive; b. London, Feb. 9, 1935; came to U.S., 1957, naturalized, 1968; d. Henry and Sadie (Clapper) J. Gen. cert. edn., Regent St. Poly., London, 1952. Sec. to consulting engrs. and real estate cos., London, 1952-55; sec. purchasing dept. Canadian Govt., Toronto, 1955-56; sec. Lash, Lash & Pringle, Toronto, 1956-57, J.C. Penney Co., San Francisco, 1957-58; with Levi Strauss & Co., San Francisco, 1959—, sundries purchasing mgr. Jeanswear div., 1975—. Active San Francisco Big Sisters, 1972—. Mem. Nat. Purchasing Assn. No. Calif., Nat. Assn. Female Execs. Democrat. Jewish. Office: 1155 Battery St San Francisco CA 94120

JONDAHL, GERALD ROBERT, school administrator; b. Ruthven, Iowa, Sept. 13, 1932; s. Ernest and Hazel Irene (Kummerfeldt) J.; m. Jean Elizabeth Steege, Nov. 20, 1955; children—Jennifer Lynne, Jeffry Alan, Julianne. B.A., Iowa State Tchrs. Coll., 1954; M.Ed., U. Ariz., 1967; postgrad. No. Ariz. U., 1969—. Tchr. instrumental, vocal music Denver (Iowa) Consol. Community Schs., 1954-56, Geneva (Iowa) Community Schs., 1956-59, Allison (Iowa) Community Schs., 1959-61; tchr. instrumental music Yuma (Ariz.) Elem. Schs., 1961-69, dept. coordinator, 1967-69; prin. James D. Price Sch., Yuma, 1969-71, Mary Elizabeth Post Sch., Yuma, 1971-77, 4th Ave. Jr. High Sch., Yuma, 1977-83, assoc. supt. for ednl. services, 1983—; mem. Developing Task Force for Ednl. Mgmt. System based on Zero Base Budgeting Model, 1979-82. Bd. dirs. Yuma Symphony Assn., 1964-69; founding bd. dirs. Yuma Child Abuse/Neglect, 1978, pres., 1978—; Republican precinct committeeman, 1982—. Mem. NEA, Ariz. Edn. Assn. (profl. policies commn. 1969-72, chmn. 1971-72), Yuma Edn. Assn. (pres. 1966-67), Ariz. Sch. Adminstrs. Assn., Nat. Assn. Middle Sch./Jr. High Adminstrs., So. Ariz. Assn. Middle Sch./Jr. High Adminstrs., Am. Assn. Sch. Adminstrs., Assn. Supervision and Curriculum Devel., Phi Delta

Kappa. Nominated Yuma County Citizen of Yr., Yuma Daily Sun, 1978. Methodist. Home: 790 W 7th St Yuma AZ 85364 Office: Yuma Sch Dist 1 450 W 6th St Yuma AZ 85364

JONER, BRUNO, aero. engr.; b. Oskarström, Sweden, Dec. 17, 1921; came to U.S., 1962, naturalized, 1967; s. Algot and Hanna (Erickson) J.; B.S. in Aero. and Mech. Engring., Stockholm Inst. Tech., 1940; m. Ingrid Gustafsson, Oct. 3, 1953; children—Peter, Eva, David. Tech. dir. Ostermans Aero AB, Stockholm, 1946-52; devel. engr. mgr. STAL Finspong, Sweden, 1952-57; mgr. aviation dept. Salen & Wicander, AB, Stockholm, 1957-62; project engr. Boeing Vertol Co., Phila., 1962-77, Boeing Marine Systems Co., Seattle, 1977—. Served with Swedish Air Force, 1942-43. Assoc. fellow AIAA; mem. U.S. Naval Inst., Nat. Assn. Unmanned Vehicle Systems (charter). Club: Swedish (Seattle). Author papers in field; co-author: Feasibility Study of Modern Airships, 1975. Home: 16621 SE 21st Pl Bellevue WA 98008 Office: PO Box 3707 Seattle WA 98124

JONES, ARTHUR LEE, engineer; b. Longview, Tex., Aug. 20, 1939; s. Jack Edwin and Elizabeth Anne (Watson) J.; m. Margaret Lea Simmons Porter, Aug. 1, 1975; m. Frankie Lou Russell, May 26, 1962; children—Gay Lynnette, Brandon A. B.S. in Aerospace Engring., U. Okla., 1962, M.S., 1963. Registered profl. engr., Wash. Engr., Boeing Aerospace Co., Seattle, 1963—. Mem. AIAA. United Ch. of Christ. Office: M/S 8K-91 Boeing Aerospace Co PO Box 3999 Seattle WA 98124

JONES, BART ANTHONY, architect; b. Sacramento, Nov. 6, 1942; s. Robert John and Mary Adelaide (Chipmen) J.; student art and architecture U. Oreg., 1960-61; B.Arch., U. Calif., Berkeley, 1967; m. Diana Mae Crestetto, Feb. 16, 1963; children—Monica Ann, Anthony Clay, Anna Laura. Engr. aide Continental Heller Constrn., Sacramento, 1965-69; archtl. cons. Redevel. Agy., City of Oakland, Calif., 1965-69; staff architect Building Block Modules Inc., Fremont, Calif., 1969-73; owner, prin. architect Bart Jones Architects, Kensington, Calif., 1973—; dir. Coventry Land Corp.; cons. architect Kuwaiti Archtl. Consultants, Al Kuwait, 1976—, San Leandro (Calif.) Unified Sch. Dist., 1976—. Bd. dirs. Kensington Improvement Assn.; vol. architect various civic improvement projects, 1976—. Lic. architect, Calif. Mem. U. Calif. Alumni Assn., Nat. Trust for Hist. Preservation, Nat. Anti-Vivisection Soc. Roman Catholic. Works include reconstrn. Stanford Bros. Bldg., Hist. Sacramento; co-architect United Real Estate Office/Retail Complex, Al Kuwait; co-author design for concrete modular housing system, 1971 (award of merit); contbr. archtl. projects to publs. in U.S., Japan. Office: 264 Arlington Ave Kensington CA 94707

JONES, BERNARD LEE, engring./constrn. co. exec.; b. Spokane, Wash., Aug. 31, 1939; s. Alfred Frederick and Yvonne Elizabeth (Ball) J.; L.P.N., St. Joseph's Sch. Nursing, Lewiston, Idaho, 1959; B.S. in Safety Engring., Northwestern Coll., Tulsa; m. Mary Jessie McKay, Apr. 28, 1961; children—Geraldine, Craig, Margaret, Paul. Heavy constrn. safety-med.-security-fire supr., 1959-65; from safety engr. to chief safety engr. Morrison Knudsen Co., Inc., Saigon, South Vietnam, 1965-72; safety-fire supr. Crystal River (Fla.) nuclear power plant J.A. Jones Inc., 1972-74; from safety rep. to safety dir. Alyeska Pipeline Service Co., Fairbanks, Alaska, 1974-78; safety security-fire supr. Bechtel Inc., San Francisco, Hassi R'Mel, Algeria, 1978-79, safety fire supr., Jubail, Saudi Arabia, 1979-81, mgr. project safety and fire (petrochem. complex), Yanbu, Saudi Arabia, 1981—. Mem. Am. Soc. Safety Engrs., Idaho Lic. Practical Nurse Assn., Nat. Fire Protection Assn., Nat. Safety Mgmt. Soc. Roman Catholic. Home: 121 15th Ave Lewiston ID 83501 Office: Safety Div Bechtel Inc 50 Beale St San Francisco CA 94119

JONES, BETTE-JEAN GABRIEL, management assistant; b. Ruislip, Eng., Apr. 16, 1956; d. James S. and Helga M. (Negel) Gabriel; m. William B. Jones, Jr., Aug. 11, 1979. B.A., Marymount Coll., Arlington, Va., 1977; M.B.A., U. West Fla., 1981. Clk., typist, CAB, Washington, 1977-78, head sec., 1978-79, transp. industry analyst, 1979-80; supply clk, Naval Air Sta., Pensacola, Fla., 1980-81; mgmt. asst. Whidbey Island, Oak Harbor, Wash., 1983—; sales auditor Brumfield's Dept. Store, Pascagoula, Miss., 1981-82; instr. Chapman Coll., Oak Harbor. Recipient spl. achievement award CAB, 1980. Democrat. Club: Officer's Wives (Oak Harbor). Home: 1254 Cascade Dr Oak Harbor WA 98277 Office: SUPP-1 NAS Whidbey Island Bldg 116 Oak Harbor WA 98278

JONES, BEVERLY ANN MILLER, nursing adminstrator; b. Bklyn., July 14, 1927; d. Hayman Edward and Eleanor Virginia (Doyle) Miller; B.S.N., Adelphi U., 1949; m. Kenneth Lonzo Jones, Sept. 5, 1953; children—Steven Kenneth, Lonnie Cord. Chief nurse regional blood program ARC, N.Y.C., 1951-54; asst. dir., acting dir. nursing M.D. Anderson Hosp. and Tumor Inst., Houston, 1954-55; asst. dir. nusing Sibley Meml. Hosp., Washington, 1959-61; assoc. dir. nursing service Anne Arundel Gen. Hosp., Annapolis, Md., 1966-70; asst. adminstr. nursing Alexandria (Va.) Hosp., 1972-73; dir. nursing service Longmont (Colo.) United Hosp., 1977—; instr. ARC, 1953-57; mem. adv. bd. Boulder Valley Vo-Tech Health Occupations Program, 1977-80; chmn. nurse enrollment com. D.C. chpt. ARC, 1959-61; del. nursing adminstrs. good will trip to Poland, Hungary, Sweden and Eng., 1980. Bd. dirs. Meals on Wheels, Longmont, Colo., 1978-80; bd. dirs. Longmont Coalition for Women in Crisis; mem. Colo. Hosp. Assn. Task Force on Nat. Commn. on Nursing, 1982; mem. utilization com. Boulder (Colo.) Hospice, 1979—; mem. council labor relations Colo. Hosp. Assn., 1982; mem.-at-large exec. com. nursing service adminstrs. Sect. Md. Nurses' Assn., 1966-69. Mem. Am. Soc. Nursing Service Adminstrs. (chmn. com. membership services and promotions), Colo. Soc. Health Care Nursing Service Adminstrs. (dir. 1978-80, pres. 1980-81). Home: 8902 Quail Rd Longmont CO 80501

JONES, BOBBIE LEE, air force officer; b. Soper, Okla., Sept. 27, 1933; s. Russell Lee and Juanita (Archer) J.; m. Barbara Jean Hanna, May 1, 1982; children by previous marriage—Kimberly Ann, Wendy Allison. B.S. in Mech. Engring., U. Okla., 1956; M.S., Fla. State U., 1974; postgrad. Air War Coll., 1978-79. Static stress engr. McDonnell Aircraft Co., St. Louis, 1956-57; commd. 2d lt. U.S. Air Force, 1957, advanced through grades to col., 1968; dep. dir. Metallurgy and Cermaics Research Lab., Aerospace Research Labs., Wright-Patterson AFB, Ohio, 1968-70; research plans officer, Plans Office, dir. sci. and tech. Hdqrs. Air Force Systems Command, 1971-72; dir. programs Aerospace Research Labs., Wright-Patterson AFB, 1974-76, chief applications office, Air Force Aero Propulsion Lab., 1976-78; dep. for acquisition logistics U.S. Air Force Space Div., Los Angeles AFS, Calif., 1979—. Decorated Air Force Meritorious Service medal, Commendation medal with 2 oak leaf clusters; recipient Commandants award, Air War Coll., 1979; Disting. Grad., Air Force Inst. Tech., 1974. Mem. Air Force Assn., Beta Gamma Sigma. Democrat. Clubs: Officers, Elks. Contbr. articles to profl. jours. Home: 17782 Crestmoor Ln Huntington Beach CA 92649 Office: USAF Space Div AL LA AFS PO Box 92960 Los Angeles CA

JONES, CARLA PADILLA, state official, real estate broker; b. Albuquerque, Sept. 2, 1940; d. Julian and Suzanna Padilla; m. Ronald A. Jones, Apr. 28, 1960; children—Mary Padilla Davis, Suzanna. Student El Camino Jr. Coll., Inglewood, Calif., Albuquerque Career Inst. Lic. Realtor. Vice pres. Julian Padilla and Assocs., Southwest Bankers Investment Co.; sec. of state State of N.Mex., 1983—. Bd. dirs. Albuquerque Career Inst.; 1st vice chmn. Bernalillo County chpt. Las Amigas de Nuevo Mejico; pres. Bernalillo County Democratic Women; mem. rules com. N.Mex. Dem. Com. Mem. N.Mex. Kindey Found., Hispano C. of C. (bd. dirs.), La Compañia del Teatro (bd. dirs.), Nat. Bus. and Profl. Women's Orgn., N.Mex. Bus. and Profl. Women's Orgn., Albuquerque Career Inst., Southwest Bankers Assn., Nat. Assn. Secs. of State, N.Mex. GI Forum. Roman Catholic. Club: Zonta Internat. Home: 228 Crestview Dr SW Albuquerque NM 87105 Office: Exec Legis Bldg Santa Fe NM 87501

JONES, CARY DENNIS, broadcast executive; b. Los Angeles, July 20, 1950; s. Edward Douglas J. and Alice (Stanton) Serrao; m. Gail Blanchard, Nov. 22, 1980; children—Christina Peyton, Tylor Stanton. B.A., Washington U., St. Louis, 1972. Account exec. TeleRep Inc., Los Angeles, 1973-75; group sales mgr. Harrington, Righter & Parsons, Los Angeles, Chgo., 1975-80; gen. sales mgr. Eastman CableRep, New York, 1980-81; sr. v.p., sta. mgr. Peyton Broadcasting Ltd. and Sta. KTRV-TV, Nampa, Idaho, 1981—; v.p. Mohawk Broadcasting Ltd. Mem. Assn. Ind. TV Stas., Idaho State Broadcasters Assn. Democrat. Episcopalian. Home: 1574 Sendero Ln Boise ID 83702 Office: Peyton Broadcasting Ltd PO Box 1212 Nampa ID 83651

JONES, CHARLES MARTIN (CHUCK), author, producer, director; b. Spokane, Sept. 21, 1912; s. Charles Adams and Mabel (Martin) J.; grad. Chouinard Art Inst., Los Angeles, 1931; m. Dorothy Webster, Jan. 31, 1935 (dec. 1978); 1 dau., Linda Jones Clough. Animator, Warner Bros., 1933-38, dir., 1938-63; creator Road Runner, Coyote, Pepe le Pew, other animated characters; writer, producer, dir. TV spls. for ABC and CBS, including The Cricket in Times Square, How the Grinch Stole Christmas, Rikki-Tikki-Tavi, Bugs Bunny in King Arthur's Court, Raggedy Ann and Andy in the Great Santa Claus Caper, numerous others, 1963—; tchr., lectr. schs. and colls. throughout U.S. Recipient Acad. award for best animated cartoons for For Scenti-Mental Reasons, 1950, The Dot and The Line, 1965, best documentary short subject for So Much for So Little, 1950; Best Ednl. Films for 24th Ann. Columbus Film Festival, 1976; 1st prize Tehran Festival Films for Children, 1977; Brit. Film Inst. tribute, 1979; Cine award for The Dot and The Line, The Cricket in Times Square, Rikki-Tikki-Tavi, The White Seal and Mowgli's Brothers. Mem. Nat. Council Children and TV, Acad. Motion Picture Arts and Scis., Screen Writers Guild, Acad. TV Arts and Scis., Screen Actors Guild. Democrat. Unitarian. Author articles. Office: 789 W 20th St Costa Mesa CA 92627

JONES, CLARA PADILLA, state official; b. Albuquerque, Sept. 2, 1940; d. Julian and Suzanna Padilla; m. Ronald A. Jones, Apr. 28, 1960; children—Mary Jones Davis, Suzanna. Student El Camino Jr. Coll., Albuquerque Career Inst. Vice pres. S.W. Bankers Investment Co., Santa Fe, Julina Padilla & Assocs., sec. State of N.Mex., 1983—. Bd. dirs. Albuquerque Career Inst. Mem. Nat. Assn. Secs. of State, Nat. Bus. and Profl. Womens Club, N.Mex. Bus. and Profl. Womens Club. Democrat. Roman Catholic. Club: Zonta. Office: Office of the Secretary of State Executive Legislative Bldg Santa Fe NM 87501

JONES, CLARIS EUGENE, JR., botanist; b. Columbus, Ohio, Dec. 15, 1942; s. Claris Eugene and Clara Elizabeth (Elliott) J.; B.S., Ohio U., 1964; Ph.D., Ind. U., 1969; m. Teresa Diane Wagner, June 26, 1966; children—Douglas Eugene, Philip Charles, Elizabeth Lynne. Asst. prof. Calif. State U., Fullerton, 1969-73, assoc. prof., 1973-77, prof. botany, 1977—, dir. Fullerton Arboretum, 1970-80, dir. Faye MacFaddan Herbarium, 1969—. Mem. Am. Inst. Biol. Sci., AAAS, Bot. Soc. Am., Internat. Assn. Plant Taxonomy, Am. Soc. Plant Taxonomists, Soc. Study of Evolution, Systematics Assn., Ecol. Soc. Am., Calif. Bot. Soc., Sigma Xi. Methodist. Author: A Dictionary of Botany, 1980. Editor Handbook of Exptl. Pollination Biology, 1983. Contbr. articles to profl. jours. Office: 800 N State College Blvd Fullerton CA 92634

JONES, CLARK DAVID, restaurant executive, accountant; b. Wells, Nev., May 23, 1935; s. Waldo LeRoy and Beatrice (Bollschweiler) J.; m. LaRue Morrison, Nov. 20, 1953; children—Debra, Pam, David, Diane, Christy. B.S. in Acctg., U. Nev., 1957; postgrad. U. Utah, 1964-65. C.P.A., Nev. Mgr., Al Huber, C.P.A., Elko, Nev., 1960-62; ptnr. Main Hurdman C.P.A.s, Salt Lake City, 1962-70; v.p. fin. JB's Restaurants, Inc., Salt Lake City, 1970-81, pres., 1981—. Served to 1st lt. U.S. Army, 1958-60. Mem. Utah Soc. C.P.A.s, Am. Mgmt. Assn., Am. Inst. C.P.A.s. Republican. Mormon. Club: Rotary of Sugarhouse. Home: 4614 Ledgemont Dr Salt Lake City UT 84117 Office: JB's Restaurants 1010 W 2610 S Salt Lake City UT 84119

JONES, CLINTFORD ROSS, engring. co. exec.; b. Schenectady, Nov. 5, 1934; s. Maynard Carlton and Evalina (Witbeck) J.; B.S. in Metall. Engring., Mo. Sch. Mines and Metallurgy, 1958; M.S., Northwestern U., 1976; M.B.A., Loyola Marymount U., 1981; m. Alba Riveros, May 11, 1963. With P.R. Mallory, Lab. Phys. Sci., Burlington, Mass., 1963-67; sr. metallurgist Handy & Harman, Fairfield, Conn., 1969-71; sr. metall. engr. Bechtel Corp., San Francisco, 1971-74; project engr. Holmes & Narver, Orange, Calif., 1974-76; sr. project engr. Jacobs Engring. Group, Pasadena, Calif., 1976-81; prin. chem. engr. C F Braun, Alhambra, Calif., 1981—. Bd. dirs. Escalon Sch. for Atypical Children, Pasadena, 1980—. Registered profl. engr., Ill., Nev., Calif. Mem. Nat. Soc. Profl. Engrs., AIME, Am. Soc. Metals, Calif. Soc. Profl. Engrs., Am. Chem. Soc., Mensa. Club: Toastmasters. Patentee, author in field. Home: 20262 Ravenwood Ln Huntington Beach CA 92646 Office: C F Braun and Co Alhambra CA 91802

JONES, CORINNE MALMIN, writer; b. Mary's Igloo, Alaska, Nov. 14, 1918; d. Cornelius Knutson and Christine (Skillingstad) Malmin; student Pacific Luth. U., 1936-38; children—Jan W. Sande, Christine Jones Chagnon, Rebecca Jones Murphy. Rewriter, Alaska Sportsman mag., Ketchikan, Alaska, 1938-42; office worker, Seattle, 1942-46; saleswoman, 1946-48; office worker, Fairbanks, Alaska, 1948-50, St. Louis, Houston, 1950-52; with direct sales, Valdez, Alaska, 1953-58; editor, writer This Alaska mag. and Our Alaska Bus. & People mag., 1971-78; news and feature writer Anchorage (Alaska) Daily News, 1976; corp. sec. Gallagher-Jones & Assos., Inc., Anchorage, 1973—. Recipient certs. Mine Safety and Health, U.S. Dept. Labor, 1978, Am. Soc. Safety Engrs., 1979, 81. Mem. Nat. Fedn. Press Women (award 1972), Alaska Press Women (17 awards 1971-78), Am. Soc. Safety Engrs., Associated Gen. Contractors Am., Inc. Republican. Lutheran. Club: Pioneers of Alaska.

JONES, DANIEL M., radiologist; b. Samaria, Idaho, Apr. 30, 1928; s. Daniel Williams and Mary Olwen (Matthews) J.; B.S., U. Wash., 1951, M.S., 1952; M.D., Yale U., 1960; m. Carolyn Irene Hahn, Sept. 8, 1951; children—Lauralyn Ann, Daniel Mark, Gareth Allan. Commd. ensign U.S. Navy, 1952, advanced through grades to capt., 1977; intern U.S. Naval Hosp., St. Albans, N.Y.C., 1960-61, resident in radiology, 1961-64; head energy dependence sect. biophysics br. Naval Radiol. Def. Lab., San Francisco, 1953-56; chief of radiology Naval Hosp., Memphis, 1964-66, Naval Hosp., Yokosuka, Japan, 1966-69; ret., 1978; dir. radiology Kaweah Delta Dist. Hosp., Visalia, Calif., 1976—; cons. Naval Hosp., Lemoore, Calif. Diplomate Am. Bd. Radiology. Mem. Central Valley Radiol. Soc. (past pres.), Tulare County Med. Soc. (past pres.), Calif. Med. Assn. (del.), Am. Coll. Radiology (del.), Soc. Nuclear Medicine, Radiol. Soc. N.Am. Republican. Presbyterian. Club: Kiwanis. Contbr. articles to sci. and med. jours. Office: 400 W Mineral King St Visalia CA 93277

JONES, DANIEL YOUNG, pvt. investigation co. exec.; b. Los Angeles, Sept. 21, 1949; s. John Jay and Peggy (Johnson) J.; A.A., Los Angeles Valley Coll., 1976; postgrad. U. So. Calif., 1976-77; hon. degree, Van Nuys Coll. Bus.; m. Cheryl L. Blair, May 21, 1983; 1 dau., Beverly Jane. Mgr. S.S. Kresge Co., 1970-74; br. rep. Transamerica, 1974-75; mgr. P & C Investigation Agy., Encino, Calif., 1975-77; partner Costello, Jones & Assos., Burbank, Calif., from 1977, sr. mng. partner, now owner; chief exec. officer D.Y. Jones & Assocs., Inc. Mem. Calif. Assn. Lic. Investigators (dir. 1979, 81, chmn. bd. dirs. 1983-84, chmn. investigator security polit. action com. 1982-83), Council Internat. Investigators, World Assn. Detectives. Home: 2431 N Lamer Burbank CA 91504 Office: 301 E Olive Ave Suite 200 Burbank CA 91502

JONES, DAVID B., venture capitalist, corporation executive; b. Jamestown, N.Y., Oct. 12, 1943; s. Gustav E. and Jeane Louise (Nord) J.; m. Cornelia Corson Morris, Sept. 3, 1966; children—Caroline Vaughan, David Kristofer. A.B., Dartmouth Coll., 1965; M.B.A., U. So. Calif., 1967, J.D., 1970. Admitted to Calif. bar, 1971; assoc. firm Hufstedler, Miller, Carlson & Beardsley, Los Angeles, 1970-72; v.p. Union Venture Corp., Los Angeles, 1972-78; v.p. fin. Am. Technology, Inc., Northridge, Calif., 1978, The Tannery West Corp., San Francisco, 1978-79; pres. First Interstate Capital, Inc. and First Interstate Equities Corp., Los Angeles, 1979—; dir. Sutter Biomed., Inc., Trilog, Inc., Novatech Corp., Gigabit Logic, Inc., Computer Power Systems, Corp., Animated Playhouses Corp. Mem. Western Assn. Venture Capitalists (former v.p., dir.), So. Pacific Regional Assn. Small Bus. Investment Cos. (former pres.), Nat. Assn. Small Bus. Investment Cos. (bd. govs.) (exec. com.). Club: Los Angeles Athletic, Jonathan. Office: 707 Wilshire Blvd Suite 1850 Los Angeles CA 90017

JONES, DAVID JOHN, aerospace executive; b. Pueblo, Colo., Jan. 21, 1934; s. David John and Clare Elizabeth (Bronish) J.; m. Margaret Alice Hoagland; children—David Robert, Pamela Ruth. A. Engring., Pueblo Jr. Coll., 1954; B.S. in Aero. Engring., U. Colo., 1956; Exec. Program, Stanford U., 1977. Engr., Ryan Aero., 1956-59; program mgr. Convair div. Gen. Dynamics Corp., 1959-71, program mgr. space, 1971-75, dir. conventional applications of Tomahawk Cruise Missile, 1975-79, dir. advanced space systems, 1979-80; dir. space techs. System Devel. Corp., Santa Monica, Calif., 1980-82, dep. gen. mgr. Space and Control Systems div., 1982, v.p., gen. mgr. Space and Control Systems div., 1982—; mem. Joint NASA/Congl. Budget Com., 1964-65; mem. planning com. on space NASA, 1975-76. Cons. Jr. Achievement Project Bus., 1980—; mem. San Diego council Boy Scouts Am., 1967-70, San Diego Multiple Sclerosis Com., 1973. Assoc. fellow AIAA (dir., Nat. Service award San Diego chpt. 1977, 80); mem. Aerospace Industries Assn., Nat. Mgmt. Assn., Assn. U.S. Army, Am. Def. Preparedness Assn., Assn. Unmanned Vehicle Systems, Porsche Club Am., SDC Mgmt. Assn. Contbr. articles to profl. jours. Home: 2372 Bahia Dr LaJolla CA 92037 Office: 2500 Colorado Ave Santa Monica CA 90406

JONES, DEE WALKER, public relations executive; b. Chgo., Dec. 15, 1921; d. Francis John and Dessie (Lawes) Walker; m. Warren Worth Jones, Dec. 8, 1944; children—Christopher, Philip, Stephen. B.A. in Journalism, La. State U., 1943. Mem. editorial staff Courier News, Plainfield, N.J., 1943-44, World Jour., San Juan, P.R., 1944-45, U.P., Washington, 1945-46, News Jour., Pensacola, Fla., 1946-47; editor Young Am., Washington, 1954-55, Jour., Northgate, Wash., 1956-61, Seattle Times, 1961-62; owner Dee Jones Public Relations, Seattle, 1962-73; communications dir. Wash./Alaska Regional Med. Program, 1973-76; dir. public relations Swedish Hosp. Med. Ctr., Seattle, 1976—. Mem. Women in Communications (past regional v.p.), Am. Soc. Hosp. Public Relations (pres. Wash. chpt. 1983—). Office: 747 Summit Ave Seattle WA 98104

JONES, DENNIS WILLIAM, SR., illumination engineer; b. Pomona, Calif., Nov. 7, 1953; s. Roy Leslie and Etta Mae (Williams) J.; student Santa Ana Coll., 1971-73; m. Marian Durst, Nov. 20, 1976; children—Dennis William, Gregory Arthur. Prin., sr. design engr. Elec. Systems Design, Orange, Calif., 1973—; pres. SUNATCO Co. Mem. Illuminating Engring Soc. (recipient 4 awards 1980-82, bd. dirs. Orange chpt.), Elec. Industries Assn., IEEE, AIA, Orange County Electric Club. Republican. Lighting sect. editor The Landscape Architects Reference Manual, 1977-80; innovator interior and exterior lighting systems and landscape lighting. Office: 707 E Chapman St Orange CA 92666

JONES, DONOVAN JAMES, safety management executive; b. Cushing, Okla., June 19, 1933; s. Daniel and Hope Marie Jones; student Ariz. State Coll., 1950-51, Weber State Coll., 1965-67; m. Katie Pearl Short, Nov. 19, 1955; children—Melody Elizabeth, Michael Donovan, Meshell Danise. Ammunition surveilance inspector Navajo Ordnance Depot, Flagstaff, Ariz., 1955-57; safety engr. Hughes Aircraft Co., Tucson and Culver City, Calif., 1957-60, N.Am. Aviation, Los Angeles, 1961; sr. safety engr. Norair/Northrop Corp., Rapid City, S.D., 1961-62; systems safety engr. Thiokol Chem. Corp., Brigham City, Utah, 1962-67; dir. safety and workmen's compensation Talley Industries, Inc., Mesa, Ariz., 1967-82, corp. coordinator safety, 1982—; dir. safety and workmen's compensation Talley Industries Ariz., Inc., 1982—; mem. adv. com. Ariz. Div. Occupational Safety and Health, 1971—; lectr. safety orgn. and mgmt. Ariz. State U., Tempe, 1972, Grand Canyon Coll., 1979; lectr. in field, 1969—. Served with U.S. Army, 1953-55. Cert., Bd. Cert. Safety Profls. Mem. Am. Soc. Safety Engrs. (profl.), Ariz. Safety Assn. (dir. 1978—, sec. 1981), Ariz. Assn. of Industries (chmn. safety com. 1971—), Nat. Council Self-Insurers (mem. bd. mgrs. 1976—, sec. 1981), Ariz. Self-Insurers Assn. (dir. 1972—, pres. 1973, 83), S.W. Safety Congress Assn. (dir. 1974—, gen. chmn. 1978, Al Geiser award 1981), Veterans of Safety, Phoenix C. of C. (mem. state govt. com. 1976-79). Republican. Baptist. Home: 6107 N 87th Pl Scottsdale AZ 85253 Office: 3500 N Greenfield Rd Mesa AZ 85205

JONES, DOROTHY CAMERON, educator; b. Detroit, Feb. 5, 1922; d. Vinton Ernest and Beatrice Olive (Cameron) J.; B.A., Wayne State U., 1943, M.A., 1944; Ph.D., U. Colo., 1965. Attendance officer Detroit Bd. Edn., 1943-44; English tchr. Denby High Sch., Detroit, 1946-56, 57-58; exchange tchr., Honolulu, 1956-57; instr., asst. prof. English, Colo. Women's Coll., Denver, 1962-66; faculty U. No. Colo., Greeley, 1966—, prof. English, 1974—, Faculty research grantee, 1970, 76. Served with WAVES, USNR, 1944-46. Mem. Internat. Shakespeare Assn., Central States Renaissance Soc., Rocky Mountain Medieval and Renaissance Soc., Rocky Mountain MLA, Patrististic, Medieval, and Renaissance Conf., Delta Kappa Gamma, Pi Lambda Theta. Contbr. papers to profl. lit. Home: Apt 312 1009 13th Ave Greeley CO 80631 Office: Dept English 40 Michener Library U No Colo Greeley CO 80639

JONES, EARL, former college president, research specialist; b. Canton, Okla., Aug. 4, 1925; s. Hercel C. and Florence (Hill) J.; B.S., Oreg. State U., 1949; M.S., Inter-Am. Inst. of OAS (Turrialba, Costa Rica), 1958; Ed.D., Mont. State U., 1962; m. Eleanor Harriett Vance, July 15, 1952; children—Beverly Anne, Mark Earl, James Richard, Cindy Kay. Tchr. public schs. Ontario, Oreg., 1949-55; dir. rural programs KSRV, Ontario, 1955-56, KSLM, Salem, Oreg., 1956; vocat. dir. Arcata (Calif.) Public Schs., 1956-57; instr. Inter-Am. Inst., 1957-58, asst. prof.,

1960-62; asso. prof. sociology UCLA, 1963-66; prof. sociology, edn., asso. dean Tex. A&M U., Coll. Edn., College Station, 1967-71; pres. Incarnate Word Coll., San Antonio, 1971-73; sr. research specialist Devel. Assos., San Antonio, 1974—, dir. research office, 1977—; prof. Antioch U./West, San Antonio, 1977—; dir. research Caribbean Inst. Sociology and Anthropology, Caracas, Venezuela, 1963-65; chair prof. U. Chile Sch. Law, Santiago, Valparaiso, 1965-66; vis. prof. Royal Danish Acad., Copenhagen, 1955, U. P.R., Mayaguez, 1960, Cath. U., Caracas, 1963-65, U. Pacific, 1966, Calif. State Coll., Los Angeles, Calif. State Coll., San Francisco, 1968; prof. Antioch Coll., 1973—; cons. Mexican-Am. Cultural Center, San Antonio, 1973-75; mem. Gov.'s Coms. on Confluence of Tex. Cultures, 1969-76, to Reconstruct Tchr. Edn., 1969-72; cons. Cabinet Com. on Spanish Speaking Peoples, 1972-75. Served with USMCR, 1943-46. Recipient Presdl. citation Republic Guatemala, 1969; Standard Oil Disting. Teaching award, 1970. Mem. Am. Sociol. Assn., Rural Sociol. Soc., Soc. Comparative Edn., NRA, Alpha Zeta, Phi Delta Kappa. Democrat. Roman Catholic. Club: Lions. Author: Rural Youth in the Americas, 1960; Lideracao, 1961; A Study of the Costa Rican Extension Service, 1962; The Cooperative Extension Services of Jamaica, 1962; Supervision en Extension Agricola, 1963; Latin American Literature for Youth, 1968; Some Perspectives on the Americas, 1968; Self-Identification and the Americas, 1970; Social Attitudes of South Texas Primary Children, 1976; (with others) Teacher Classroom Behaviors, 1977; Case Studies in Educational Change, 1978; Client Satisfaction with Services to Limited and Non-English-Speaking Students in California, 1980; Study of Food for Peace in Ghana, Evaluation of Food for Peace in Panama, 1981; Handbook for the Evaluation of AID Cooperative Projects, Evaluation of Private Sector Development in Dominican Republic, 1982; Study of Rural Technologies Program in Honduras, 1983. Home: 2695 37th Ave San Francisco CA 94116 Office: 693 Sutter St 3d Floor San Francisco CA 94102

JONES, GERALD JOSEPH, former broadcasting exec.; b. Saginaw, Mich., May 22, 1920; s. LaVern Pierce and Yvonne Maria (Berthaud) J.; student Los Angeles Jr. Coll., 1939; m. Madelyn Fio Rito, Nov. 15, 1970; children by previous marriage—Jennifer Jones Batteau, Steven G. Account exec. Murray Dymock, 1946, West-Holliday, 1947-50, The Katz Agy., Inc., 1950-60, v.p., 1967-78, West Coast mgr., 1977-78, v.p. sta. and industry relations, 1978-80. Served to flight lt. RCAF, 1941-45. Decorated D.F.C.; col. Staff of Gov. John McKeithen, La., 1971. Mem. Pacific Pioneer Broadcasters, So Calif. Advt. Golfers Assn. Republican. Clubs: Bel Air, Woburn Golf and Country (Milton Keynes, Eng.), Milline (sec. 1963-66); Thunderbird Country. Home: 10690 Somma Way Los Angeles CA 90024

JONES, GERALD THOMAS, aerospace engineer; b. East St. Louis, Ill., Dec. 10, 1924; s. Gerald Montague and Loretta (Thomas) J.; m. Noreen Virginia Wells, Jan. 1, 1946; children—Cynthia R. Clark, Dennis R., Ellana R. Hollmuller, Brian R. B.S. in Aerospace Engring., Tri State U., 1947. With McDonnell Aircraft Co., 1947—, mgr. prodn. planning, 1975-79; dir. prodn. planning Douglas Aircraft Co., Long Beach, Calif., 1979—. Former sr. warden, treas. St. Paul's Episcopal Ch., Overland, Mo. Served with USN, 1942-46. Mem. AIAA, VFW. Republican. Home: 8485 Kington Way Cypress CA 90630 Office: 3855 Lakewood Blvd MC 2-43 Long Beach CA 90846

JONES, HARRY MCCOY, cons. engr., investor; b. Stillwater, N.Y., Oct. 19, 1896; s. Louis Benson and Isabelle (Gray McCoy) J.; B.S., U.S. Naval Acad., 1918; M.B.A., N.Y. U., 1928; m. Caroline A. Murray-Browne May 10, 1969. Financial work Wall Street, 1927-28; engring. work Walker Signal Equipment Co., 1928-30; distbn. mgr. Dry-Ice Corp. of Am., 1930-34; pvt. practice cons. engring., 1934-37; partner Weaver Assos., 1937-39; sr. partner Dunn & Jones, cons. engrs., 1940-48, sole partner, 1949-65; pres., dir. H-H Inc., real estate, investments and ranching, 1940—. Founder U.S. Naval Acad. Found., 1946, chmn., 1946-64, trustee, 1946—; trustee Textile Mus., Washington, 1967-72. Served as midshipman USN, 1915-18, ensign to lt., 1918-26, lt. to lt. comdr. USNR, 1926-43. Recipient Meritorious Pub. Service citation Dept. Navy; Scroll of Honor, Navy League U.S., 1963; Ann. Man of Year award U.S. Naval Acad. Assn. N.Y., 1961; named Hon. Adm., Brigade of Midshipmen, U.S. Naval Acad. Mem. Mil. Order World Wars, Soc. Am. Mil. Engrs., Am. Ordnance Assn., Am. Soc. Naval Engrs., Soc. Naval Architects and Marine Engrs., Am. Inst. Iranian Studies, Brit. Inst. Persian Studies, Assn. Interstate Commerce Practitioners, U.S. Naval Acad. Athletic Assn., Friends of Winterthur, U.S. Naval Acad. Alumni Assn., Navy League U.S. (life), Naval Inst. (life), Rug Soc. Washington (pres.), Internat. Hajji Baba Soc. (chmn. bd.). Episcopalian. Clubs: Army and Navy Country, Cosmos, Arts (Washington); Hajji Baba, Army and Navy (N.Y.); Family, Marines' Memorial (San Francisco); Prospectors (Reno); Oriental Rug (Toronto, Can.); Las Cruses (Baja California, Mexico). Lectr., writer and collector antique Oriental rugs and Am. antiques. Donor antique oriental rugs and Americana collection to H.M. deYoung Mus., San Francisco, 1980. Home: 1250 Del Monte Ln Reno NV 89511

JONES, J., consultant; b. San Francisco, June 1, 1922; s. Enoch Roscoe L. and Remedios (Ponce De Leon) J.; student U.S. Mcht. Marine Acad., 1942-44, San Francisco City Coll., 1941-42, 46-47; A.B., U. Calif., Berkeley, 1949, M.A., 1952. Ins. insp. Ins. Cos. Insp. Bur., San Francisco, 1959-62; pub. relations cons., San Francisco, 1962-67; ins. insp. Am. Service Bur., San Francisco, 1967-72; propr., mgr. Dawn Universal Research Services, San Francisco, 1972—. Mem. Calif. Republican Assembly, 1978—. Mem. Am. Hist. Assn., Internat. Acad. Criminology, Calif. Assn. Lic. Investigators, Am. Law Enforcement Officers Assn., SAR (sec., editor San Francisco chpt. 1979—), U. Calif. Alumni Assn. Republican. Episcopalian. Hist. research on causes of crime. Office: PO Box 4239 San Francisco CA 94101

JONES, JACK, chem. co. exec.; b. Oklahoma City, Dec. 9, 1927; s. S.J. and Mildred (Autry) J.; B.A., U. Okla., 1948, LL.B., 1951; m. Betty Lee, Aug. 11, 1947 (dec.); children—Scott, Summer, Skye. News reporter Daily Oklahoman, Oklahoma City, 1948-58, Toledo Blade, 1958-61; mgr. public relations Dow Chem. Co., Sacramento, 1961-70, Western mgr. govt. and public relations, Sacramento, 1970—, mem. Western Mgmt. Bd., 1970—. Chmn. Calif. Chem. Industry Council, 1971-74. Mem. Calif. Mfrs. Assn., Soc. Plastics Industries, San Francisco Press Club, San Francisco Bay Publicity Club (pres. 1969-71). Sigma Delta Chi. Republican. Presbyterian. Club: Sutter. Contbr. short fiction stories, articles to gen. publs. Office: Dow Chem Co 925 L St Suite 1425 Sacramento CA 95814

JONES, JAMES THOMAS, lawyer, state government official; b. Twin Falls, Idaho, May 13, 1942; s. Henry C. and Eunice Irene (Martens) J.; m. Nancy June Babson, Nov. 25, 1972; 1 dau., Katherine A. Student, Idaho State U., Pocatello, 1960-61; B.A., U. Oreg., 1964; J.D., Northwestern U., 1967. Bar: Idaho 1967. Legis. asst. to U.S. Senator Len B. Jordan, Washington, 1972; practice law, Jerome, Idaho, 1973-82; atty. gen. State of Idaho, Boise, 1983—; mem. Idaho State Bd. Land Commrs.; mem. Idaho State Bd. Examiners. Bd. dirs. Vietnam Vets. Leadership Program, 1983—; bd. dirs. Idaho Cancer Soc. Served wi to capt. U.S. Army, 1967-69. Decorated Bronze Star, Army Commendation medal, Air medal with four oak leaf clusters, Vietnamese Cross of Gallantry. Mem. ABA, Idaho State Bar, Idaho Trial Lawyers Assn. Republican. Lutheran. Office: Statehouse Boise ID 83720

JONES, JOE CHESTER, aerospace co. exec.; b. Birmingham, Ala., Sept. 18, 1922; s. James Marion and Cynthia (Byram) J.; B.S. in Aero. Engring., Auburn (Ala.) U., 1943; S.M. in Indsl. Mgmt. (Sloan fellow), M.I.T., 1957; m. Mary Emma Bowdon, Aug. 17, 1940; children—Cynthia Louise Jones Wertz, Cheri Lynn Jones Hall, James Marion, Joe Chester. With Dept. Air Force, 1947-73, dep. asst. sec. research and devel., 1966-73; asst. to chmn. bd. Northrop Corp., Los Angeles, 1974-79, v.p., asst. to chief exec. officer for aero. systems, 1979—; mem. research and tech. adv. com. aeros. NASA, 1968-70. Served to capt. USAF, 1943-46. Recipient Air Force Exceptional Civilian Service award, 1965, 69, 73, Dept. Def. Disting. Service award, 1972. Mem. Air Force Assn., Soc. Sloan Fellows, Sigma Nu. Republican. Office: 1800 Century Park E Los Angeles CA 90067

JONES, JUANITA YVONNE, business executive; b. Bainbridge, Ga., Nov. 14, 1938; d. James and Dorothy (Johnson) Ealey; m. William S. Walden, Nov. 28, 1959; children—Bergandi G.E., William S.; m. 2d, Larry Jones, June 25, 1975. Student Clark Coll., Atlanta, 1955-56; B.A., So. U., 1959; postgrad. UCLA, 1960; A.A. in Computer Lang., El Camino Coll., Torrance, Calif., 1972. Lic. real estate agt., Calif. Tchr., Thomasville (Ga.) Pub. Schs., 1959-60; library asst. UCLA, 1960-63; yellow page rep. So. Bell Telephone Co., Atlanta, 1963-65; computer operator Western A/L, Los Angeles, 1965-75; press inerviewer Lundberg Co., North Hollywood, Calif., 1975-76; owner Bride's Choice Wedding Chapel, Los Angeles, 1976—; exec. dir. L & J Assocs., Los Angeles, 1975—; agt. Lee/Sugita Realty, Beverly Hills, Calif., 1979—. Recipient Calif. Blind Assn. award, 1978. Mem. Nat. Notary Assn., Calif. Bd. Realtors, Nat. Female Exec. Assn., Am. Photographers Internat., NAACP. Democrat. Roman Catholic. Home: 2843 Hillcrest Dr Los Angeles CA 90016 Office: 2800 S Robertson Blvd Los Angeles CA 90034

JONES, KAREN ALICE, statistician; b. San Jose, Calif.; d. Henry and Florence Elizabeth (Johnson) Neergard; m. Randolph Dana Jones, Jan. 23, 1971 (div.); children—Alicia Carey, Scott Alexander. A.B., Occidental Coll., 1965. With Div. Labor Stats., Dept. Indsl. Relations, State of Calif., San Francisco, 1968—, research mgr., work injury and illness stats. sect., 1979—. Mem. Am. Statis. Assn. (pres.-elect San Francisco Bay chpt.). Democrat. Presbyterian. Office: 525 Golden Gate St 4th Floor San Francisco CA 94102

JONES, KENNETH CAREY, scientist; b. Santa Monica, Calif., June 15, 1946; s. Bill Thorlin and Geraldine Marie (Meadows) J.; m. Jean Carol Langerberg, Oct. 14, 1966; children—Glen Edwin, Robert Earl. B.S. in Physics, Calif. State U.-Northridge. Scientist E.H. Plesset Assocs., Santa Monica, 1965-68; scientist EG&G, Santa Monica, 1968-70, Los Alamos, 1970-76, mgr. 1978—; scientist U. Calif.-Los Alamos, 1976-78. Mem. Los Alamos Ski Patrol. Mem. Optical Soc. Am., Soc. Photo-Optical Instrumentation Engrs. Clubs: Los Alamos Sportsmen's (past pres.), Los Alamos Mountaineers. Contbr. articles to profl. jours. Home: 2470 Club Rd Los Alamos NM 87544 Office: EG&G Inc PO Box 809 Los Alamos NM 87544

JONES, KENNETH LAMAR, biol. scientist, educator; b. Ogden, Utah, May 31, 1931; s. Kenneth Parks and Lucille (McEntire) J.; Asso. Sci., Weber Coll., 1955; B.S., Utah State U., 1958, M.S. in Parasitology, 1960, postgrad. U. Calif., Riverside, U. Calif., Irvine, Stanford; children—Allison, Kathryn; m. Frances Jones, Aug. 12, 1982; stepchildren—Bradley Bullock, Gary Trisler, Guy Trisler. Gen. sci. tchr. Los Angeles City Schs., 1960-62; prof. biol. scis. Mt. San Antonio Coll., Walnut, Calif., 1962—. Pres., Pomona Area Health Council, 1967, bd. dirs. Walnut Area Counseling Center, 1975—, San Gabriel Valley Council on Alcoholism, 1969. Served with USN, 1950-54; Korea. Recipient regional certificate of appreciation Am. Cancer Soc., 1968-70. Mem. NEA, AAAS, Am. Coll. Health Assn., Am. Sch. Health Assn., Calif. Tchrs. Assn., Calif. Assn. Health, Phys. Edn. and Recreation, Sigma Nu. Democrat. Mormon. Club: Kiwanis. Author: Health Science, 1968, 71, 74, 78, 6th edit., 1984; Dimensions V, 1982; Principles of Health Science, 1975; Sex, 1969; Age of Aquarius, 1971; Drugs and Alcohol, 1969, 73, 78; Drugs: Substance Abuse, 1970-75; Disease, 1970; Emotional Health: Foods, Diet and Nutrition, 1970-75; Environmental Health, 1971; Consumer Health; The Human Body, 1971; Total Fitness, 1972; V.D., 1974; Sex and People, 1976; Dimensions of Human Sexuality, 1984. Home: 22448 Ridge Line Rd Diamond Bar CA 91765 Office: 1100 N Grand Ave Walnut CA 91789

JONES, KYLE EDWARD, coast guard officer; b. Beckley, W.Va., Dec. 19, 1942; s. Kyle Edward and Mary Rosalie (Scott) J. B. Aeronautics, Embry-Riddle Aero. U., 1979. Commd. lt. U.S. Coast Guard, 1968, advanced through grades to lt. comdr., 1976; stationed U.S. Coast Guard Air Sta., Barbers Point, Hawaii, 1976-81; comdr. C-13 Aircraft, 1976-83, flight safety officer, 1977—. Decorated air medal with oak leaf cluster. Mem. Aircraft Owners and Pilots Assn. Republican. Club: Rotary. Home: PO Box 1289 USCG Air Station Kodiak AK 99619

JONES, LINDA MAY, travel industry executive; b. El Dorado, Kans., Nov. 9, 1937; d. Forrest Edward and Edith May (Heck) Carlson; student U. Kans., 1955-57, Wichita State U., 1958, U. Denver, 1962-64, U. Colo., 1970-71; children—Chris Dale, Carin Dene, Curtis Dean. Wrangler, counselor Skyland Camp, Crested Butte, Colo., 1954-56; tour guide Queen City Tours, Denver, 1976—, tour guide writer, 1979—, coordinator, 1979—, mgr. tour guide services, 1982—; lead coordinator Am. Travel Brokers, 1983—; moving cons. Kamp Moving & Storage, Denver, 1978-83; tour guide Molly Brown House, Hist. Denver, 1975-81, day chmn., 1976-81, vice-chmn. vol. council, 1977-78; vol. chauffeur Christian Fellowship of Blind, 1977-83. Named Outstanding Young Woman of Am., 1970. Mem. Nat. Assn. Profl. Saleswomen (sec. Mile High chpt.), Mensa, U. Kans. Alumni Assn. (life), Phi Alpha Theta, Alpha Phi. Republican. Methodist. Club: D.A.R. (Outstanding Jr. Mem. in Colo. 1970, Outstanding Jr. Mem. Western div. 1970). Author: (with Vickie Schroeder) Mile High Denver: A Guide to the Queen City, 1981; columnist Rocky Mountain Christian, 1964-69. Home: 12857 Hwy 119 Route 4 Golden CO 80403 Office: Queen City Tours 2695 Alcott Suite 213-S Denver CO 80211

JONES, MAX DAVID, insurance agency executive, vocational education consultant; b. Bisbee, Cochise County, Ariz., Sept. 25, 1937; s. David Adam and Gladys Ornett (Barham) J.; m. Ina Lee Wilson, Jan. 30, 1959; children—Melinda Lea Jones Sherman, David Troy, Rachelle Susan. B.A., N. Mex. Western Coll., 1961; M.A., Western N. Mex. U., 1964. Cert. tchr., Ariz., N. Mex., Guam; cert. ins. agent, broker, surplus lines and life, Ariz. Tchr. indsl. arts Patagonia (Ariz.) Union High Sch., 1961-64; prin. Guam Trade and Tech. Sch., Agana, Ter. of Guam, 1964-68; dir. Micronesian Occupational Ctr., Palau, Western Caroline Islands, 1968-70; supt. adult, higher vocat. edn. Trust Ter. of Pacific Islands, 1970-72; owner, mgr. Jones-Wilson Ins. Agy., Benson, Ariz., 1972—; vocat. edn. cons. Benson Vol. Fire Dept., 1972—; leader 4-H Club, Catalina council Boy Scouts Am., 1972-79; mem. Indsl. Devel. Authority (Benson), 1983—. Served with USN, 1956-62. Decorated Ancient Order fo Chammori, Gov. Ter. Guam. Mem. Am. Indsl. Arts Assn., Am. Vocat. Assn., Ariz. Indsl. Edn. Assn., Guam Indsl. Edn. Assn. (founder), Micronesian Indsl. Edn. Assn. (founder), Ariz. Fire Chiefs Assn., Ariz. Fire Fighters Assn., Ariz. Ind. Ins. Agts. Assn., Nat. Ind. Ins. Agts. Assn., Cochise County Ind. Ins. Agts. Assn., Benson C. of C., Iota Lambda Sigma, Kappa Pi, Epsilon Pi Tau. Democrat. Clubs: Masons, Scottish Rite, Eastern Star, Eagles. Office: 700 W 4th St Benson AZ 85602

JONES, MERRIWEATHER, public administrator; b. Eudora, Miss., Apr. 20, 1930; s. Fred Milton and Bessie Mae (Hobbs) J.; m. Bernice Hearn, May 3, 1952; 4 children; m. 2d, Catherine Sue Lewis, May 5, 1973; 2 children. B.S., Western Oreg. State Coll., 1977; postgrad. Williamette U., 1977-78. Enlisted U.S. Army, 1951, ret. sgt., 1971; vocat. instr. Fairview Tng. Ctr., Salem, Oreg., 1972-74, dir. maintenance, 1974-77; asst. dir. housekeeping Oreg. Health Scis. U., Portland, 1978—. Mem. budget com. Chemeketa Community Coll., Marion County (Oreg.) Democratic Com. Served as maj. Army N.G., 1972—. Mem. Nat. Exec. Housekeepers Assn. (cert. exec. housekeeper, ofcl. Pacific Trails chpt.), Nat. Rifle Assn., State Mgmt. Assn., Oreg. Health Scis. Univ. Mgmt. Assn. Club: Four Corners Rifle and Pistol. Office: 3181 SW Sam Jackson Park Rd Portland OR 97201

JONES, MICHAEL BRUCE, psychologist; b. Los Angeles, Mar. 23, 1954; s. Robert Bruce and Carol Louise (Anderson) J. B.S., Brigham Young U., 1977; M.A., Calif. Sch. Profl. Psychology, 1979, Ph.D., 1982. Psychology intern Calif. Community Services Ctr., Los Angeles City Coll. Student Mental Health Clinic, 1977-78, Los Angeles Child Guidance Clinic, 1978-79, Intercommunity Child Guidance Clinic, Whittier, Calif., 1979-80, VA, Wadsworth Hosp. Ctr., Los Angeles, 1980-81; psychology fellow Coordinated Child Psychiatry Clinic div. child psychiatry and child devel. Children's Health Council, Children's Hosp., Stanford U. Med. Ctr. Palo Alto, Calif., 1982—. Mem. Am. Psychol. Assn., Calif. State Psychol. Assn., Tourette Syndrome Assn., Psi Chi, Alpha Epsilon Delta. Mem. Ch. of Jesus Christ of Latter-day Saints. Home: 130 Brookwood Rd Woodside CA 94062

JONES, MILDRED JEAN, mfg. co. ofcl.; b. Algoma, W.Va., Jan. 5, 1946; d. Dan Sanders and Eva Mae (Pilson) Price; B.S. in Tng. and Devel., Grand Canyon Coll., 1979; B.S. in Behavior Sci., 1979; postgrad. Ariz. State U., 1982; children—Jeri Lynn, Alton James, Justin Sanders. Trainer, Motorola, Inc., Phoenix, 1978-79; affirmative action coordinator Unidynamics/Phoenix, Inc., Goodyear, Ariz., 1979—, also tng. mgr.; notary pub.; adj. faculty Embry-Riddle U. Active Phoenix Urban League; adv. bd. Phoenix NAACP, 1979—, 2d v.p., 1983; mem. Operation PUSH, 1978—; del. Nat. Bapt. Conv. Am., Salt River Valley Gen. Missionary Bapt. State Conv. Ariz; mem. Bapt. Joint Com. Public Affairs. Am. Soc. Tng. and Devel. scholar; named Mrs. Black Ariz., 1983-84. Mem. Am. Soc. Tng. and Devel., Ariz. Adult Edn. Assn., Top Ladies of Distinction, Inc., League Bus. and Profl. Women, Ariz. Affirmative Action Assn., Pi Lambda Theta, Phi Beta Lambda. Office: Unidynamics Phoenix Inc PO Box 2990 Phoenix AZ 85062

JONES, PEGGY LAVERNE, health educator, administrator; b. Tampa, Fla., Dec. 25, 1939; d. James Andrew and Hazel Angelina (Wyrick) Menghini; children—Matthew, Erin, Todd. Student U. Tampa, 1959-61, Orange Coast Coll., Costa Mesa, Calif., 1963-64, Cerritos (Calif.) Jr. Coll., 1967-69. Free lance pub. relations specialist, 1964-74; clinic coordinator Planned Parenthood of No. Nev., Reno, 1975-76; exec. dir. Multiple Sclerosis Soc. Nev., Reno, 1976-79; supr. Washoe County Med Soc., Reno, 1979-80; head dept. St. Mary's Hosp., Reno, 1980-82, program dir. Heart Inst. No. Nev., 1982—, mem. cardiac task force 1982—. Bd. dirs. Homemaker Upjohn Home Health Corp., 1979-81; mem. adv. bd. Ret. Sr. Vol. Persons, 1980-82; mem. adv. bd. Com. to Aid Abused Women and Children, 1981-82. Mem. Am. Hosp. Assn., Health Adminstrs. No. Nev., Reno Women in Advt., Am. Bus. Women's Assn., Am. Mgmt. Assn., Am. Soc. Dirs. Vol. Dirs. of Vol. in Agys., Nat. Assn Women Execs., Nat. C. of C. for Women. Democrat. Baptist. Office: 667 N Arlington Ave Reno NV 89503

JONES, ROBERT ALONZO, economist; b. Evanston, Ill., Mar. 15, 1937; s. Robert Vernon and Elsie Pierce (Brown) J.; A.B., Middlebury Coll., 1959; M.B.A., Northwestern U., 1961; m. Kathleen Mary Bush, Aug. 16, 1958; children—Lindsay Rae, Robert Pierce, Gregory Alan, William Kenneth. Sr. research officer Bank of Am., San Francisco, 1969-74; v.p., dir. fin. forecasting Chase Econometrics, San Francisco, 1974-76; chmn. bd. Money Market Services, Inc., Belmont, Calif., 1974—; dir. Money Market Services, Ltd., London, Money Market Services, Ltd., Hong Kong; chmn. bd. dirs. Inst. Econ. and Monetary Affairs, Incline, Nev., 1982—; instr. money and banking, Am. Inst. Banking, San Francisco, 1971, 72. Councilman, City of Belmont (Calif.), 1970-77, mayor, 1971, 72, 75, 76; dir. San Mateo County Transit Dist., 1975-77. Hon. life mem. Calif. PTA; named to Kappa Delta Rho Nat. Hall of Fame. Mem. San Mateo County Council Mayors (chmn. 1975-76), Nat. Assn. Bus. Economists, San Francisco Bond Club. Republican. Methodist. Author: U.S. Financial System and the Federal Reserve, 1974. Office: 490 El Camino Real Belmont CA 94002

JONES, ROBERT KIRK, industrial hygienist; b. Harrodsburg, Ky., Jan. 8, 1931; s. William Hobert and Celestine Goddard (Phillips) J.; m. Wilma Ruth Boughton, Nov. 26, 1960 (div.); children—Krista Marie, Alan Todd, Bradley Kirk. B.A. in Chemistry, Centre Coll. Ky., 1952. Cert. Am. Bd. Indsl. Hygiene, Safety Profls. Chemist, Reynolds Metals Co., Louisville, 1954-56, Ky. Utilities Co., Burgin, 1957-65; indsl. hygienist Ky. Dept. Health, Frankfort, 1966-69; dir. Coal Workers' Pneumoconiosis Program, 1970-71; regional indsl. hygienist Shell Oil Co., Wood River, Ill., 1972-74, Stamford, Conn., 1975-77, staff indsl. hygienist, San Ramon, Calif., 1978—. Served as lt. USNR, 1949-64. Mem. Am. Acad. Indsl. Hygiene (Diplomate), Am. Indsl. Hygiene Assn., Am. Soc. Safety Engrs., ASTM, Calif. Mfrs. Assn. Western Oil and Gas Assn. Democrat. Methodist. Home: 1515 Prairie Grove Dr Houston TX 77077 Office: 1078 One Shell Plaza Houston TX 77002

JONES, ROBERT LEWIS, ednl. adminstr., educator, consultant; b. Omaha, Aug. 12, 1924; s. James Robert and Georgia Evelyn (Clark) J.; student Idaho State U., 1943-44; B.A., U. Ariz., 1949; M.A., Ariz. State U., 1969, Ph.D., 1975; m. Wauneeta Marie Gamelgaard, June 8, 1949; 1 dau., Stacey Kathleen. Announcer/writer, Sta. KYUM, Yuma, Ariz., 1949-52; writer, TV continuity dir. Sta. KTAR, Phoenix, 1952-56; with Ariz. Public Service Co., Phoenix, 1956-75, manpower resources mgr., 1970-72, exec. devel. mgr., 1972-75; dir. Center for Bus. Studies, prof. bus. Grand Canyon Coll., 1975-81; mgmt. cons. Thoren Group, Tempe, Ariz., 1981—; cons. bus.; v.p. Applied Tng. Concepts. Mem. Phoenix Civil Service Bd., 1971-72, hearing officer, 1973-75; mem. various community adv. bds. Served to capt. USNR. Recipient award Ariz. State Dept. Edn., 1968, Phoenix C. of C., 1971, Maricopa Mental Health Assn., 1972, Dept. Labor, 1972, SBA, 1977. Mem. Am. Soc. Tng. and Devel. (pres. chpt. 1978, asst. regional v.p. 1979-81, Torch award 1980, Gordon Bliss award). Author: (with Rudolph Moore) General Business, 1976; contbr. articles to profl. jours. Home: 1114 E Leeward Ln Tempe AZ 85283 Office: 5410 Lakeshore Dr Tempe AZ 85283

JONES, ROBERT STUART, publisher; b. Pasadena, Calif., Apr. 1, 1942; s. Edward Winslow and Jean Eileen (Wolfe) J.; A.A., DeAnza Coll., 1972; B.A., Calif. State U., Fullerton, 1976; m. Nancy Anne Spindle, Jan. 11, 1964; children—Carolyn Jean, Robert Stuart. Mil. acct. exec. Nat. Semi-condr. Corp., Santa Clara, Calif., 1971-73; sr. sales engr. Intel Corp., Santa Clara, 1973-75; pres., editor-in-chief, pub. Interface Age Mag., Cerritos, Calif., 1975—; editor-in-chief Computer User, Cerritos, 1983—, Computer Book base; chief exec. officer I.M.M.; pres., pub., editor-in-chief Interface Age Internat., Inc.; dir. Tech-Ser, Inc., rep. orgn. Served with U.S. Army, 1962-65. Mem. Soc. Bus. Press Editors (charter), Western Pubs. Assn. (Maggie award 1978, 79, 83). Author booklets: A Tutor on Small Business Computing, 1977; Starting Your Own Computer Business: Aspects of Promotion, Sales, and Marketing, 1978. Office: 16704 Marquardt St Cerritos CA 90701

JONES, RODDIS STEWART, construction and land development executive; b. Marshfiled, Wis., Jan. 11, 1930; s. Henry Stewart and Sara Roddis J.; B.A.M.E., Auburn U., 1952; P.M.D., Harvard U., 1960; postgrad. U. Wis.-Madison, 1959; m. Anne Crook Orum, Jan. 7, 1955; children—Patricia, Jeffrey, Jennifer. Project engr. Marathon Corp., Rothschild, Wis., 1955-57; prodn. supt. indsl. engring., mgr. cost acctg. Roddis Plywood Corp., Marshfield, Wis., 1957-60; br. mgr. Weyerhaeuser Co., Hancock, Vt., Oakland, Calif. and Federal Way, Wash., 1960-78; pres., gen. mgr. Roddis Jones Cos., Solarcrete N.W., Investment Bldg. & Devel. Co., Paneling Place, Seattle, 1978—. Served as officer USN, 1952-55. Mem. Seattle Master Builders. Republican. Episcopalian. Clubs: Rotary, Elks, Masons. Home and Office: 104 Cascade Key Bellevue WA 98006

JONES, ROY STEVEN, business forms manufacturing executive; b. Weston, W.Va., Dec. 22, 1944; s. Lloyd Hall and Ethel Marie (Flinn) J.; student W.Va. Wesleyan Coll., 1962-63, Glenville (W.Va.) State Coll., 1963; A.A., Santa Barbara City Coll., 1967; B.A., U. Calif.-Santa Barbara, 1973; m. Rebecca Susan Piercy, Mar. 26, 1964; children—Stephanie Lynne, Allyson Elise. Hwy. insp. W.Va. Rd. Commn., Weston, 1964-66; shipping clk. Automated Bus. Forms Inc., 1966-68, collator, pressman, 1968-72, asst. plant mgr. prodn., 1972-79, co-owner, plant mgr., corp. sec., 1979—; instr. vocal. printing Santa Barbara Community Coll., 1983—. Active Citizens for Good Water, 1978-79; chmn. bd. dirs. Vocat. Instrn. Pub. Schs.; exec. dir. Com. for Goleta Valley, 1978-82; mem. Santa Barbara County Democratic Central Com., 1979—, Calif. Small Bus. Council, 1981—; v.p. bd. dirs. Goleta Valley Community Center, 1981-82; v.p. Combined Health Agys. Drive, campaign chmn., 1981-82; v.p. Goleta Valley Dem. Club, 1979—. Mem. Goleta C. of C. (pres. 1983—), Tri-Counties Graphic Industries Assn., Nat. Bus. Forms Assn. (corporate). Democrat. Baptist. Club: Montecito Country. Home: 6171 Verdura Ave Goleta CA 93017 Office: 137 Aero Camino Goleta CA 93017

JONES, RUSSELL WARD, optometrist; b. La Junta, Colo., Dec. 11, 1946; s. William Russell and Josephine J. (Mahill) J.; m. Daphne Sue Dean, Dec. 29, 1966; children—Ean Trent, Chian Alicia. B.S., U. Colo., 1968; M.S., U. Ariz., 1972; O.D., Pacific U., 1976. Lic. optometrist, Ariz., Oreg. Practice optometry, Flagstaff, Ariz., 1976—; cons. Title 1 Reading Dept., Flagstaff pub. schs. Mem. Am. Optometric Assn. Ariz. Optometric Assn. (v.p. 1983), Metroptic, Am. Pub. Health Assn., Beta Sigma Kappa (Medal award 1977). Democrat. Club: Rotary (pres. club 1982-83) (Flagstaff). Home: 3214 N King St Flagstaff AZ 86001 Office: 410 N San Francisco St Flagstaff AZ 86001

JONES, SALLY NEIGHBOR, counselor; b. Ft. Worth, Nov. 3, 1943; d. Frank and Hazel D. Neighbor; m. James C. Jones, Feb. 10, 1964; children—Donald, Michael. B.A., U. Wyo., 1966, M.A., 1974, Ph.D., 1976. English tchr. Kelly Walsh High Sch., Casper, Wyo., 1966-68; grad. asst. in counseling, U. Wyo., Laramie, 1972-76, acad. counselor for athletics, 1976—; cons. State Dept. Edn., U.S. Office Edn. Exec. bd. U. Wyo. Faculty Senate, 1980-82; bd. dirs. U. Wyo. Employees Credit Union, v.p., 1982-83. Wyo. State Dept. Edn. grantee, 1975. Mem. Nat. Assn. Acad. Advisors for Athletics (pres. 1983), Am. Personnel and Guidance Assn., Wyo. Personnel and Guidance Assn. (Outstanding Grad. Student 1975), Phi Kappa Phi, Phi Delta Kappa. Author: Learning About Me, 1974. Office: PO Box 3414 Univ Sta Laramie WY 82071

JONES, STEVEN RAY, podiatrist; b. Salt Lake City, Aug. 27, 1949, s. Clyde Ray and Cherril (Christiansen) J.; B.S. in Biology, U. Utah, 1973; D.Podiatric Medicine, Calif. Coll. Podiatric Medicine, 1979; m. Vicki Green, Aug. 24, 1973; children—Emily Melissa, Lara Alene, Kami Lynn. Owner The Athlete's Foot, Salt Lake City, 1975-76; pvt. practice podiatry, Salt Lake City, 1979—. Mem. Utah Podiatry Assn., Am. Podiatry Assn. Mormon. Office. 2367 Murray-Holladay Rd Salt Lake City UT 84117

JONES, SUZETTA JEAN, systems company executive; b. Wheeling, W.Va., Jan. 18, 1949; d. Harold Stuart and Eva Jean J.; B.S. in Home Econs. and Edn., W.Va. U., 1970. Sales rep. Wang Labs., San Mateo, Calif., 1974-75, Gen. Bus. Systems, Burlingame, Calif., 1975-77; sales rep. NBI Inc., San Francisco, 1977-78, br. mgr., San Jose, Calif., 1978—; owner Office Systems Experts, 1981—; bd. dirs. Word Processing/Office Equipment Trade Show, 1978—. Mem. Internat. Word Processing Assn., Santa Clara Valley Word Processing Assn. Office: PO Box 1330 Mountain View CA 94042

JONES, TERRY EARL, mental health consultant, writer, educator, lecturer; b. Grand Coulee, Wash., Mar. 5, 1940; s. Earl Harold and Maria Caroline (Hunich) J.; m. Judy Haworth, (div.); 1 son, Jason; m. 2d, Linda Lauretta Buccola; children—Caleb, Nicole, Amy, Joshua, Jeremy. B.A. in History, Sonoma State U., 1968, M.A. in History, 1970; M.Ed. in Counseling, Lewis and Clark Coll., 1976. Asst. dir. Sonoma County Drug Abuse Council, Santa Rosa, Calif., 1970-71; dir. Portland Youth Advocates Runaway, Oreg., 1971-72; community alcohol and drug specialist Oreg. Mental Health Div., 1972-79; founder, pres. Oreg. Substance Abuse Profl. Assn., Prepared Childbirth Assn., 1975-78; owner Employees Assistance Service, Portland, 1979—; bd. dirs. Occupational Program Cons. Assn., 1980—. Served with USAF, 1962-66. Mem. Assn. Labor-Mgmt. Adminstrs. and Consultants in Alcoholism, Occupational Program Cons. Assn., Am. Personnel and Guidance Assn., Am. Soc. Tng. and Devel. Author: Industry, A Caretaker, 1974; the Heroin Lovers, 1977, Employee Assistance Programs in Industry, 1980; (with Paul Kadota) Biography of Kanaye Nagasawa, 1983.

JONES, THELMA LOUISA, chamber of commerce exec.; b. Price, Utah, Feb. 5, 1939; d. Levi and Luella Josephine (Heaps) Tyron; m. Vernon W. Jones, July 5, 1958; children—Brian W., Kurt A., Vicki M. Student Coll. of Eastern Utah, 1957-59. Owner/mgr. Thelma's Fabrics, 1970-76; exec. dir. Carbon County C. of C., Price, Utah, 1974—. Chmn. bd. dirs. Coll. of Eastern Utah Prehistoric Mus. Recipient Outstanding Community Service award Price Rotary Internat., 1979; Woman of Yr. award Bus. and Profl. Women of Price, 1980; Community Service award City of Price, 1981. Mem. U.S. C. of C., Utah C. of C. (dir.), Castle Country Travel Council (chmn. bd. dirs.), Bus. and Profl. Women of Price, LWV (pres. 1982-83). Democrat. Mormon. Clubs: Soroptimist Internat. (pres. 1978-80), Ladies of Elks. Home: 734 North 600 East Price UT 84501 Office: 200 E Main North Entrance Price UT 84501

JONES, THOMAS GREGORY, advertising agency executive; b. Jersey City, Jan. 22, 1949; s. Paul John and Eileen (Harris) J.; A.A., Brookdale Coll., 1974; B.A., Thomas Edison Coll., 1978. Copywriter, Charisma Media Cons., 1972-75; edn. dir. Users, Inc., Valley Forge, Pa., 1975-78; mktg. analyst Communications Design, Sacramento, 1978-80; prin. Thomas G. Jones Assocs., Fair Oaks, Calif., 1981; founder, exec. dir. Summit Mktg. Resources div. Summit Info Systems Corp., Corvallis, Oreg., 1981—; lectr. in field. Served to sgt. U.S. Army, 1967-69. Decorated Bronze Star, Air medal. Mem. Portland Advt. Fedn. Home: 42529 Green Mountain Dr Lebanon OR 97355 Office: Summit Mktg Resources Div 850 SW 35th St Corvallis OR 97330

JONES, THOMAS VICTOR, aerospace company executive; b. Pomona, Calif., July 21, 1920; s. Victor March and Elizabeth (Brettelle) J.; student Pomona Jr. Coll., 1938-40; B.A. with gt. distinction, Stanford, 1942; LL.D., George Washington U., 1967; m. Ruth Nagel, Aug. 10, 1946; children—Ruth Marilyn, Peter Thomas. Engr., El Segundo div. Douglas Aircraft Co., 1941-47; tech. adviser Brazilian Air Ministry, 1947-51; prof., head dept. Brazilian Inst. Tech., 1947-51; staff cons. Air Staff of USAF, Rand Corp., 1951-53; asst. to chief engr. Northrop Corp., 1953, dep. chief engr., 1954-56, dir. devel. planning, 1956-57, corporate v.p., 1957, sr. v.p., 1958-59, pres., 1959-76, chief exec. officer, 1960—, chmn. bd., 1963—. Bd. dirs. Los Angeles World Affairs Council; trustee Inst. for Strategic Studies, London, Eng. Fellow Am. Inst. Aeros. and Astronautics; mem. Los Angeles C. of C., Navy League U.S. (life), Aerospace Industries Assn., So. Calif. Symphony Assn., U. So. Calif. Assos., Town Hall. Clubs: Calif.; The Beach (Santa Monica); Georgetown; Calif. Yacht; Bohemian. Author: Capabilities and Operating Costs of Possible Future Transport Airplanes, 1953. Office: Northrop Corp 1800 Century Park E Century City Los Angeles CA 90067

JONES, THOMAS WILLIAM, painter; b. Lakewood, Ohio, Aug. 13, 1942; s. Robert W. and Roberta (Poske) J.; m. Carrie Pemberton, July 21, 1973. B.F.A., Cleve. Inst. Art, 1964. Group shows: Frye Art Mus., Seattle, 1973, Seattle Art Mus., 1975, 79, Colo. Heritage Ctr. Mus., Denver, 1981-82, Nat. Acad. Art Western Heritage Ctr., Oklahoma City, 1980, 81, 83; series of watercolors commd. by Gen. Telephone Co. of N.W., 1967-68; watercolors represented in numerous public and corp. collections. Served with U.S. Army N.G., 1964-70. Recipient numerous awards. Mem. N.W. Watercolor Soc., Am. Acad. Taos N.Mex., Fedn. Can. Artists. Work published in numerous art jours. Address: 1420 W Lake Sammamish Pkwy NE Bellevue WA 98008

JONES, VERNON QUENTIN, surveyor; b. Sioux City, Iowa, May 6, 1930; s. Vernon Boyd and Winnifred Rhoda (Bremmer) J.; student UCLA, 1948-50; m. Rebeca Buckovecz, Oct. 1981; children—Steven Vernon, Gregory Richard, Stanley Alan. Draftsman III Pasadena (Calif.) city engr., 1950-53; sr. civil engring. asst. Los Angeles County engr., Los Angeles, 1953-55; v.p. Treadwell Engring. Corp., Arcadia, Calif., 1955-61, pres., 1961-64; pres. Hillcrest Engring. Corp., Arcadia, 1961-64; dep. county surveyor, Ventura, Calif., 1964-78; propr. Vernon Jones Land Surveyor, Riviera, Calif., 1978—; city engr. Needles (Calif.), 1980—. Chmn. graphic tech. com. Ventura Unified Sch. Dist., 1972-78, mem. career adv. com., 1972-74; mem. engring. adv. com. Pierce Coll., 1973; pres. Mgmt. Employees of Ventura County, 1974. Vice pres. Young Republicans of Ventura County, 1965. Pres., Marina Pacifica Homeowners Assn., 1973. Mem. League Calif. Surveying Orgns. (pres. 1975), Am. Congress on Surveying and Mapping (chmn. So. Calif. sect. 1976), Am. Soc. Photogrammetry, Am. Pub. Works Assn., County Engr. Assn. Calif. Home: 913E San Juan Ct Riviera AZ 86442

JONES, VICTOR EMORY, chief of police; b. Long Beach, Calif., July 10, 1935; s. Walter Jacob and Lillian Merble (Roberts) J.; A.A., Riverside City Coll., 1971; B.S., Calif. State U.-Los Angeles, 1973; M.P.A., U. So. Calif., 1975; grad. F.B.I. Nat. Acad., Quantico, Va., 1976; m. Sharon Kaye Burns, Dec. 24, 1961; children—Victoria Suzanne, Robert Eugene. With Rohr Corp., Riverside, Calif., 1958-61; with Riverside Police Dept., 1961—, chief of police, 1977—. Cert. peace officer standards and tng. exec., Calif. Mem. Internat. Assn. Chiefs of Police, U. So. Calif. Scapa Practor, F.B.I. Nat. Acad. Assos., Calif. Police Chiefs Assn. Republican. Clubs: U. So. Calif. Lifetime Alumni, Masons, Shriners, Elks, Moose, Riverside Kiwanis (dir.). Office: 4102 Orange St Riverside CA 92501

JONES, WILLIAM PAUL, clinical psychologist, educator; b. Clovis, N.Mex., Aug. 23, 1939; s. Paulie C. and Mary Louise (Homer) J.; m. Dorothy Ravac Wright, Mar. 19, 1983; children from previous marriage —Donna, Cindy, Jann. B.A., Eastern N.Mex. U., 1961, M.A., 1963; Ed.D., N.Mex. State U., 1969. Registered psychologist, N.Mex., Nev. Tchr., adminstr. pub. schs., Roswell, N.Mex., 1961-64; research psychologist Sci. Research Assocs. subs. IBM, Chgo., 1967-70; prof. psychology N.Mex. State U., Alamogordo, 1970-79; pvt. practice psychology, Las Vegas, 1979—; cons. Nev. Service to Blind, N.Mex. Sch. Visually Handicapped. Bd. dirs. Community Mental Health, Alamogordo, 1975-79, pres. 1977-78; bd. dirs. Nat. Accreditation Council Agys. Serving Blind and Visually Handicapped. Mem. Am. Personnel and Guidance Assn., Am. Assn. Sex Educators, Counselors, and Therapists (cert. 1976). Republican. Baptist. Club: Rotary (Las Vegas). Author: Assessing Basic Competencies: Visually Impaired, 1981; cassette tape programs on self control; contbr. numerous articles to profl. jours. Home and Office: Dr W Paul Jones 1020 E Desert Inn Las Vegas NV 89109

JONES, WILLIAM RUSSELL, university administrator; b. Midland, Tex., Sept. 6, 1921; s. William Russell and Cora C. (Castellaw) J.; B.S., N.Mex. State U., 1942; M.B.S., U. Colo., 1958, Ed.D., 1969; m. Donna J. Flanery, Feb. 14, 1977; children—Jo Lynn, Russell Ward, Carolyn Sophia. Instr. vocat. agr. Pueblo (Colo.) Jr. Coll., 1947-50; tchr. Crowley Public Sch., 1954-57; prin. Crowley County Sch. Dist., Ordway, Colo., 1958-61, supr., 1961-64; supt. Arickaree Sch. Dist., Anton, Colo., 1964-69; dir. div. instrn. Dept. Edn., State of Alaska, 1969-71; prof. ednl. adminstrn. and acad. adminstr. U. Alaska, Juneau, 1971-80, dean acad. affairs, 1980-81, vice chancellor acad. affairs, 1981-82, exec. vice chancellor, 1982—; mem. Alaska Profl. Teaching Practices Commn., 1978—. Served with USAF, 1942-46. Decorated Air medal. Mem. Am. Assn. Sch. Adminstrs., Am. Assn. Univ. Adminstrs., Soc. Coll. and Univ. Planning, Phi Delta Kappa. Presbyterian. Clubs: Rotary, Lions (past pres.), VFW (past dist. comdr.). Contbr. in field. Home: 15795 Glacier Hwy Juneau AK 99801 Office: 11120 Glacier Hwy Juneau AK 99801

JONES, WINFORD LIONEL, computer software company executive, seed distributor; b. Sterling, Idaho, Nov. 22, 1926; s. John William and Florence Viola (Hardy) J.; m. Jo Ann Groesbeck, Jan. 30, 1953; children—Stuart Douglas, William Lance, Alan Charles, Carol. Student pub. schs. Aberdeen. Missionary, Ch. of Jesus Christ of Latter-day Saints, western Can., 1950-51; farmer, eastern Idaho, 1952-70; regional sales mgr. Trojan Seed Co., Olivia, Minn., 1970-75; regional sales mgr. Pfizer Genetics, St. Louis, various locations, Utah, Idaho, Colo., 1975-79; wholesale seed distbr. Paymaster Seed Co., Mpls., various locations, Utah, Idaho, Oreg., Wash., 1980—; pres. Jo-Se-Co, Inc., Aberdeen, Idaho, 1980—, pres. Bus. Service Group div., 1981—; sec. Countryside Data, Inc., Idaho Falls, 1981—. Precinct committeeman, 1960-70. Served with U.S. Army, 1945-46. Republican. Copyright holder in field. Office: 718 N Skyline Dr Idaho Falls ID 83401

JONES, WYMAN H., librarian; b. St. Louis, Dec. 17, 1929; s. Jay Hugh and Nina Marie (Dallas) J.; student So. Ill. U., 1945-47; Washington U., St. Louis, 1948-50; B.A., Adams State Coll., Alamosa, Colo., 1956; student U. Iowa, 1956-57; M.S. in L.S., U. Tex., 1958; children—Gregory Foster, Mark Jay, Manson Matthew, Ross Christopher. Head sci. and industry div. Dallas Pub. Library, 1958-60, chief br. services, 1960-64; dir. Ft. Worth Pub. Library, 1964-70, Los Angeles Pub. Library System, 1970—; cons. library bldg. and site selections, 1962—. Bd. dirs. Young Symphony Orch., Ft. Worth, 1967-70. Served with USAF, 1951-55. Mem. ALA (legis. com. 1975—), Calif. Library Assn. Author: (with E. Castagna) The Library Reaches Out, 1964; also articles, monthly column Library Jour. Home: Promenade West 880 W 1st St Los Angeles CA 90012 Office: Los Angeles Pub Library 630 W 5th St Los Angeles CA 90017

JONES-TWIGHT, ANGENETT, organization development company executive; b. Loma Linda, Calif., Feb. 13, 1940; d. Horace Darwin and Alice (Goen) Jones; m. Peter Alan Twight, July 3, 1958; children—Nicholas Peter, Jessica, Cedric Dixon. B.S., U. Calif.-Berkeley, 1971; M.S. in Orgn. Devel. cum laude, Pepperdine U., 1977. Orgn. devel. cons. Central Atlantic Conf., United Ch. of Christ, Silver Spring, Md., 1972-73; mgmt. cons. Corplan, Chico, Calif., 1973-74; owner, ptnr. Process for Planned Change, Richmond, Calif., 1974-77, pres., cons., Aptos, Calif., 1977—; convenor Team Leadership Process Consortium, Aptos, 1980—; mem. adj. faculty Pepperdine U. Sch. Bus. and Mgmt., 1983—. Mem. Orgn. Devel. Network, Bay Area Orgn. Devel. Network (steering com.). Republican. Presbyterian. Club: N.Am. Trail Riding Conf. Author: Proc. of 1976 New Prospectives on Recreation Mgmt. Conf.; (with William R. Daniels) Stress Reduction Strategies: A Training Curriculum For Public Contact Employees, 1975, rev. edit., 1977, Handbook: Effective Supervisory Practices Training, 1974, rev. edit., 1976. Home and office: 5552 Freedom Blvd Aptos CA 95003

JOOST-GAUGIER, CHRISTIANE L., art history educator; b. Ste. Maxime, France; d. Louis Clair and Agnes L. Gaugier. A.B. with honors, Radcliffe Coll., 1955; A.M., Harvard U., 1959, Ph.D., 1973; postgrad. U. Munich, 1956-57. Mem. faculty Mich. State U., 1959-60, U. Mich., 1960-61, Tufts Coll., 1969-73; prof. dept. art N.Mex. State U., Las Cruces, 1975—. Fulbright grantee, 1956-57; AAUW Vassie James Hill fellow, 1979-80; Am. Philos. Soc. grantee, 1981-82; Am. Council Learned Socs. grantee, 1981-82. Mem. Coll. Art Assn. Am. (bd. dirs.), Renaissance Soc., South Cen. Renaissance Conf., Rocky Mountain Medieval and Renaissance Assn., Soc. Archtl. Historians, Women's Caucus Art (adv. bd.), Southeastern Coll. Art Assn., Mid-Am. Coll. Art Assn. Author: Cathedral Tour, 1958; Jacopo Bellini: Selected Drawings, 1980; contbr. articles to profl. jours. and exhbn. catalogues. Office: Dept Art New Mexico State Univ Las Cruces NM 88003

JORDAN, BONITA (BONNIE) ADELE, TV producer; b. Dayton, Ohio, Mar. 9, 1948; d. Theodore and Faye Annette (Fields) Sampson; student Habor Jr. Coll., Wilmington, Calif., 1966-68; divorced; 1 son, Brett Anthony. Asso. producer Dick Clark Prodns., Hollywood, Calif., 1972-73, sta. KNBC-TV, Los Angeles, 1973-75; account exec. Ameron Co., Monterey Park, Calif., 1976; prodn. coordinator Movie of the Week for CBS, Paramount Studios, Hollywood, 1977-78; in film/TV devel. and casting 20th Century Fox, 1978—, now asst. to producer The Fall Guy, Glen Larson Prodns. Co-chmn., asst. to producer telethon United High Blood Pressure Found., 1977, mem. exec. bd., 1975 78, treas., 1977. Recipient cert. achievement City of Los Angeles and UCLA Mardi Gras, 1974. Mem. Nat. Assn. Media Women (corr./rec. sec. 1974-75), Women in Film. Home: 15050 Sherman Way 207 Sherman Oaks CA 91405 Office: PO Box 900 Beverly Hills CA 90213

JORDAN, CARL HARVEY, mechanical engineer; b. Los Angeles, June 29, 1933; s. Carlos Webster and Elizabeth Leile (Sanderson) J.; B.S.M.E., Fresno (Calif.) State Coll., 1955; postgrad. U. Calif. Extension; m. Wilma Fay Dupuy, Aug. 21, 1954, children—Daniel Scott, Kurt Michael. Asst. chief engr. Buonaccorsi & Assos., cons. engrs., San Francisco, 1957-66; v.p. G.L. Gendler & Assos., cons. engrs., Berkeley, Calif., 1966-73; dir. mech. and elec. engring. Skidmore, Owings & Merrill, architects and engrs., San Francisco, 1973—. Mem. Berkeley Energy Commn., 1979-82; leader Boy Scouts Am.; leader YMCA Indian Guides. Served with AUS, 1955-57. Registered profl. engr., Calif., Nev., Wash., Hawaii. Mem. ASHRAE (chpt. pres. 1976-77), ASME, Nat. Soc. Profl. Engrs., Bldg. Owners and Mgrs. Assn., Sigma Alpha Epsilon. Club: Berkeley Yacht (commodore 1980). Contbr. articles on mech. engring. and energy conservation to profl. jours. Home: 646 Colusa Ave Berkeley CA 94707 Office. One Maritime Plaza San Francisco CA 94111

JORDAN, CHARLES CLARK, manufacturing company executive; b. Fullerton, Calif., Feb. 21, 1948; s. Charles Earl and Elizabeth Inez (Hatch) J.; B.S. in E.E., Stanford U., 1970; M.B.A., Columbia U., 1972; m. Linda Louise Street, Dec. 9, 1978; children—JoAnne, Michael, Kathleen, David, Lacey. Fin. analyst Rockwell Internat., Anaheim, Calif., 1972-73; controller George-Good Corp., City of Industry, Calif., 1973-77; gen. mgr. Domestic Products, George-Good Corp., 1977-81; fin./adminstrv. v.p. Pulse Engring. div. Varian Assocs., San Diego, 1981-82, div. gen. mgr. delay lines, 1982—. Mem. Am. Electronics Assn. Democrat. Office: 7250 Convoy Ct San Diego CA 92111

JORDAN, FRANCESCA, banker; b. Boston, May 25, 1953; d. Frank Wysong and Virginia (Leahy) J. A.B., Smith Coll., 1975; postgrad. Ecole Superieure des Sciences Economiques et Commerciales, Cergy-Pontoise, France, 1976; M.B.A., Northwestern U., 1977. With Wells Fargo Bank N.A., San Francisco, 1977-79, asst. v.p., regional mktg. coordinator Oakland region, 1979-80, asst. v.p., mgr. bus. devel. Credit Card div., San Francisco, 1980-83, asst. v.p. bus. div., 1983—. Mem. exec. bd. Christian Sci. Ch., San Francisco. Smith Coll. scholar, 1971-75. Mem. San Francisco Profl. Womens Network. Office: Wells Fargo Bank 394 Pacific St San Francisco CA 94163

JORDAN, GARY BLAKE, electronics engr.; b. Urbana, Ill., Feb. 3, 1939; s. Robert Leslie and Lois Evelyn (Schildhammer) J.; B.S. in Elec. Engring., Ohio U., Athens, 1961; D.Eng., Pacific So. U., 1977; Ph.D. (hon.), Sussex Coll. Tech., 1977; m. Gloria Jean Heppler, Mar. 21, 1969; children—Gareth Kylae, Glynis Jerelle. Sr. engr. Martin-Marietta Corp., 1963-65; mem. profl. staff ITT Aerospace Co., 1965-68, TRW Inc., 1968-71; exec. v.p. EW Orgn., Hermosa Beach, Calif., 1969—; asst. to v.p. Antekna Inc., Mountain View, Calif., 1972-73; tech. dir. spread spectrum mktg. Ford Aerospace & Communications Corp., Palo Alto, 1973-78; with ESL div. TRW Inc., 1979—; dir. Nat. Intelligence Agy., 1979—. Fellow Am. Biog. Inst.; mem. Washington Acad. Scis., AAAS, IEEE (Outstanding Author award Electronic Engr. mag. 1966, 67), Wash. Acad. Sci., Soc. Tech. Communications (charter), Soc. Profl. Communication, Am. Def. Preparedness Assn. (life), Armed Forces Communications and Electronics Assn. (corp.), Radio Soc. Gt. Britain, Ohio Acad. Scis., U.S. Naval Inst., Assn. Old Crows, Lambda Xi Pi (life fellow). Contbr. profl. jours. Home: 1012 Olmo Ct San Jose CA 95129 Office: PO Box 3689 Stanford CA 94305-0047

JORDAN, GLEN GARY, marketing executive; b. Warren, Ohio, Feb. 28, 1940; s. Glen William and Velma Clare (Ball) J.; m. Patricia Delores McLaughlin, May 16, 1964; 1 son, William Gary. Mktg. rep. Black & Decker Power Tools, Harrisburg, Pa., 1964-73, exec. v.p. Novinger Supply Co., Harrisburg, 1973-77; mgr. Spl. Markets div. Homelite Corp., Charlotte, N.C., 1977-81; v.p. mktg. Relton Corp., Arcadia, Calif., 1981—; dir. Trac Internat. Corp. Coach Am. Youth Soccer Assn. Served with USMCR, 1964-69. Mem. Mfrs. Agts. Nat. Assn., Splty. Tool and Fasteners Distbrs. Assn., Am. Rental Assn. Republican. Club: Claremont Tennis. Contbr. articles to trade publs. Home: 3947 Northampton Ave Claremont CA 91711 Office: 317 Rolyn Pl Arcadia CA 91006

JORDAN, JOSEPH HENRY, mechanical engineer; b. Giesen, Germany, Sept. 9, 1933; m. Florence Friedman, Mar. 22, 1956; children—Terrie, Laurence. B.M.E., NYU, 1955, M.M.E., 1959. Engr., Sperry Gyroscope Co., Great Neck, N.Y., 1955-66; engring. mgr. Hamilton Standard Systems Ctr., Farmington, Conn., 1966-70; dir. engring. Guidance and Control Systems div. Litton Systems, Inc., Woodland Hills, Calif., 1970-80, v.p., chief engr. Aero Products div., 1980—. Mem. ASME, AIAA, ION. Office: 6700 Eton Ave Canoga Park CA 91303

JORDAN, PHILLIP LOWELL, retail company financial executive; b. Washington, May 13, 1947; s. William Douglass and Elizabeth May (Merrick) J.; m. Judith Anne Jones, Aug. 5, 1972; 1 son, Andrew Jones.

Student U.S. Air Force Acad., 1964; B.B.A., U. Wash., 1968. C.P.A., Wash. Acct. Main Lafrentz & Co., C.P.A.s, Seattle, 1968-70, Coopers & Lybrand, C.P.A.s, Seattle, N.Y.C., 1970-80; ptnr. Moss, Adams & Co., C.P.A.s, Seattle, 1980-83; exec. v.p., chief operating officer Early Winters, Ltd., Seattle, 1983—; lectr. Sch. Bus., U. Wash.; speaker tech. bus. topics various trade, profl. orgns. Treas. United Cerebral Palsy Assn. Wash., 1979—; mem. Seattle Art Museum, Seattle Opera Assn., Seattle Symphony Assn., Pacific NW Ballet. Mem. Am. Inst. C.P.A.s, Wash. Soc. C.P.A.s, Am. Acctg. Assn., Nat. Assn. Accts. for Coops., Am. Mgmt. Assn. Seattle C. of C. (higher edn. com.), Sigma Chi Alumni Assn. Episcopalian. Clubs: Seattle Yacht, Seattle Tennis, Wash. Athletic. Office: Early Winters Ltd 110 Prefontaine Pl S Seattle WA 98104

JORDAN, PHYLLIS HENRY, law firm administrator; b. Boston, Mar. 6, 1932; d. Andrew Kidder and Phyllis Elizabeth (Brown) Henry; m. Winthrop D. Jordan, Aug. 30, 1952 (div.); children—Joshua Henry, James Mott, Winthrop Eliot. Student Radcliffe Coll., 1950-53; B.A., Barnard Coll., 1954. Tchr. high sch. English, Providence, 1956-59; tchr., writer, editor, community activist, Berkeley, Calif., 1963-78; legal asst., paralegal supr., sec. Golden Gate chpt. Assn. Legal Adminstrs., San Francisco, 1980—; with Lasky, Haas, Cohler & Munter, San Francisco, 1979-82. Mem. adv. com. Berkeley Sch. Bd., Berkeley City Council. Mem. Assn. Legal Adminstrs. Democrat. Episcopalian. Clubs: Ivy, Harvard, Barnard (San Francisco). Contbr. articles to mags., introdns. to books, poems to newspapers, anthologies. Home: 1107 Milvia St Berkeley CA 94707 Office: 505 Sansome St Suite 1200 San Francisco CA 94111

JORDAN, RAYMOND BRUCE, health services cons.; b. Holland, Mich., Mar. 10, 1912; s. Albert Raymond and Aimee (Best) J.; m. Dorothy Caig, June 6, 1942. B.A., Sacramento State Coll., 1952; M.B.A., Stanford U., 1959. Pub. acct., Calif. Acct., auditor State Bd. Equalization, Calif. Dept. Employment, 1947-48, mgmt. analyst, 1948-52, chief analyst, 1952-59; chief mgmt. analyst Hdqrs. Office, Calif. Dept. Mental Hygiene, 1959-63; bus. adminstr. Atascadero State Hosp., 1963-68, Patton State Hosp., San Bernardino, Calif., 1968-70; mgmt. cons. hosps., Victoria, B.C., Can., 1970-72; instr. Sacramento City Coll., 1951-62; cons. Govt. Iran, faculty, U. Tehran, 1956; instr. U. Calif.-Davis, 1963, Cuesta Coll., San Luis Obispo, 1967-68, Monterey Peninsula Coll., 1974-76; professorial lectr. Golden Gate U., Monterey Campus, 1974-78; chmn. grievance rev. bd. Monterey Peninsula Unified Sch. Dist., 1976. Pres., Monterey County Ombudsman Program, 1976-79; founder, adv. bd. mem. Monterey County Sr. Hearing Ctr., 1977-78; treas. Experience, Inc., 1973-78; bd. dirs. Monterey County Sr. Aide Program, 1976-78; mem. adv. bd. Alliance on Aging, 1976-78; founder, pres. Concerned Sr. Citizens, Monterey Peninsula Club, 1974-77; mem. adv. group Monterey Sr. Day Care Ctr., 1977-78. Recipient Bronze Achievement award Mental Hosp. Service, 1963. Served with U.S. Army, 1943-46. Clubs: Rotary, Toastmasters. Author: Management Analysis in Health Services, 1982; Supervision—Effective Management, 1982; contbr. articles to profl. jours. Home: 200 Glenwood Circle Apt G-8 Monterey CA 93940

JORDAN, ROBERT ELDER, banker; b. Galesburg, Ill., Sept. 5, 1926; s. Cecil Asbury and Dorothy (Garrett) J.; m. Nancy Carol Anderson, July 5, 1950; children—Michael, Thomas. B.F.A., U. Nebr., 1950. Advt. mgr. W.A. Jordan Co., Galesburg, 1950-57; mgr. pub. relations Mountain States Bank, Denver, 1957-59, asst. v.p., 1959-64, v.p., 1964—. Bd. dirs. Mile Hi chpt. ARC, Rocky Mountain Better Bus. Bur. Recipient Silver Medal award Am. Advt. Fedn./Denver Advt. Fedn., 1982. Mem. Bank Mktg. Assn., Denver Advt. Fedn. (Advt. Man of Yr. 1973, Fame and Fortune award 1980), Advt. Club Denver (pres. 1970), Colo. Bank Mktg. Assn. (pres. 1975). Club: Advt. Golf Assn. (pres. Denver). Home: 41 Scott Drive S Broomfield CO 80020 Office: Mountain States Bank 1635 E Colfax Ave Denver CO 80218

JORDAN, ROGER LYNN, optometrist; b. Livingston, Mont., Dec. 6, 1953; s. Russell Leroy and Marlys Mae (Seeback) J.; m. Virginia Rae Phillips, Apr. 2, 1976 (div.). B.S. with honors in Zoology, Mont. State U.-Bozeman, 1976; O.D. magna cum laude, So. Calif. Coll. Optometry, 1980. Lic. optometrist, Calif., Mont., Wyo. Optometrist Gillette (Wyo.) Optometric Clinic, 1980—, Wright (Wyo.) Vision Clinic, 1981—. Trustee Prince of Peace Luth. Ch.; mem. Community Theatre. Mem. Wyo. Optometric Assn., Am. Optometric Assn., Am. Acad. Optometry, Gillette C. of C., Beta Sigma Kappa, Omega Epsilon Phi. Republican. Clubs: Gillette Jaycees, Ducks Unlimited (Gillette).

JORGENSEN, GORDON DAVID, engring. co. exec.; b. Chgo., Apr. 29, 1921; s. Jacob and Marie (Jensen) J.; B.S. in Elec. Engring., U. Wash., 1948, postgrad. in bus. and mgmt., 1956-59; m. Nadina Anita Peters, Dec. 17, 1948 (div. Aug. 1971); children—Karen Ann, David William, Susan Marie; m. 2d, Barbara Noel, Feb. 10, 1972 (div. July 1976). With R.W. Beck & Assos., Cons. Engrs., Phoenix, 1948—, partner, 1954—; pres. Beck Internat., Phoenix, 1971—. Served to lt. (j.g.) U.S. Maritime Service, 1942-45. Recipient Outstanding Service award Phoenix Tennis Assn., 1967; Commendation, Govt. Honduras, 1970. Registered profl. engr., Alaska, Ariz., Calif., Colo., Nev., N.Mex., N.D., Utah, Wash., Wyo. Mem. IEEE (chmn. Wash.-Alaska sect. 1959-60), Nat. Soc. Profl. Engrs., Am. Soc. Appraisers (sr. mem.), Ariz. Cons. Engrs. Assn., Ariz. Soc. Profl. Engrs., Internat. Assn. Assessing Officers, Southwestern Tennis Assn. (past pres.), U.S. Lawn Tennis Assn. (2d v.p., chmn. U.S. Davis Cup com.). Presbyterian (elder). Project mgr. for mgmt., operation studies and reorgn. study Honduras power system, 1969-70. Home: 5329 N 25th St Phoenix AZ 85020 Office: 3003 N Central St Phoenix AZ 85012

JORGENSEN, JAMES RICHARD, accountant, financial manager; b. Racine, Wis., July 29, 1948; s. John F. and June M. (Kuhmsted) J.; m. Janet L. Uran, Aug. 9, 1969; children—Scott, Daniel, Kathryn, B.B.A., U. Wis., 1970; M.B.A., Stanford U., 1971-73. C.P.A., Calif. Acct. Peat, Marwick, Mitchell & Co., San Francisco, 1970-72; v.p. Tennis Am., Palo Alto, Calif., 1973; pres. King Enterprises Inc., San Mateo, Calif., 1973-78, Women's Sports Pub. Co., San Mateo, 1973-76, Soviet Union Nat. Tennis Team, Phila., Moscow, 1975-76; sr. ptnr. Jorgensen & Co., Los Angeles, 1978—; dir. Nat. Legal Network, Nottingham Fin. Corp., Am. Yellow Page Network; lectr. U. Redlands. Trustee Women's Sports Found. Recipient Sells award Am. Inst. C.P.A.s 1973; Elwell award U. Wis. 1969; Calif. State fellow, 1972. Mem. Calif. Soc. C.P.A.s, Am. Inst. C.P.A.s. Author: Hallelujah Jamboree, 1981, Tennis Women, 1974. Home: 19700 Komar Dr Tarzana CA 91356 Office: Jorgenson & Co 1801 Ave of the Stars Suite 235 Los Angeles CA 90062

JORGENSEN, JUDITH ANN, psychiatrist; b. Parris, Island, S.C., Aug. 31, 1941; d. George Emil and Margaret Georgia J.; B.A., Stanford U., 1963; M.D., UCLA, 1968; m. Ronald Francis Crown, July 11, 1970. Intern, Meml. Hosp., Long Beach, Calif., 1968-69; resident in psychiatry San Diego County (Calif.) Mental Health Services, 1970-73, gen. med. physician, 1969-70, staff psychiatrist dept. profl. edn., 1973-76, dept. children and adolescent services, 1973-78; practice medicine specializing in psychiatry, La Jolla, Calif., 1973—; mem. clin. faculty U. Calif., San Diego, 1976—; chairperson dist. 14 med. quality rev. com. Calif. Bd. Med. Quality Assurance. Diplomate Am. Bd. Psychiatry and Neurology. Mem. Am. Psychiat. Assn., San Diego Psychiat. Soc. (v.p. 1978-80), Am. Soc. Adolescent Psychiatry, San Diego Soc. Adolescent Psychiatry (pres. 1981-82), Soc. Sci. Study Sex, Am. Assn. Sex Educators, Counselors and Therapists, Masters and Johnson Inst., San Diego Soc. Sex Therapy and Edn., Am. Med. Women's Assn., NOW. Office: 470 Nautilus St Suite 211 La Jolla CA 92037

JORGENSEN, LOU ANN BIRKBECK, social worker; b. Park City, Utah, May 14, 1931; d. Robert John and Lillian Pearl (Langford) Birkbeck; student Westminster Coll., 1949-51; B.S., U. Utah, 1953, M.S.W., 1972, D.S.W., 1979; grad. Harvard Inst. Ednl. Mgmt., 1983; m. Howard Arnold Jorgensen, June 9, 1954; children—Gregory Arnold, Blake John, Paul Clayton. Social work adminstr. nursing home demonstration project, dept. family and community medicine U. Utah Med. Center, Salt Lake City, 1972-74; mental health ednl. specialist Grad. Sch. Social Work, U. Utah, 1974-77, 77-80, asst. prof., 1974-80, asso. prof., 1980—; regional mental health cons. Bd. dirs. Info. and Referral Center, 1975-82, United Way of Utah, 1976-82, Pioneer Trail Parks, 1977-83, Rowland Hall-St. Marks Sch., 1980—; Salt Lake County housing commr.; pres. Human Services Conf. for Utah, 1979-80. Mem. Council on Social Work Edn., Nat. Assn. Social Workers (pres. Utah chpt. 1978-79), Adminstrs. of Public Agys. Assn., Human Services Assn. Utah, Jr. League of Salt Lake City, Phi Kappa Phi. Republican. Episcopalian. Clubs: Ft. Douglas Country, Town, Eastern Star. Author: Explorations in Living, 1978; Social Work in Business and Industry, 1979; Handbook of the Social Services, 1981; contbr. articles to profl. jours. Home: 3442 East Oaks Dr Salt Lake City UT 84117 Office: Grad Sch Social Work U Utah Salt Lake City UT 84112

JORNACION, OSCAR LICTAOA, accountant, publisher, entrepreneur; b. San Juan, La Union, Philippines, Oct. 13, 1951; s. Eleuterio Pimentel and Consuelo Lictaoa J.; B.S. in Bus. Adminstrn. magna cum laude, U. East, Manila, 1973; postgrad. Calif. State U., Los Angeles, 1975-76; M.B.A., Pepperdine U., 1982; m. Gilda Arroyo, June 15, 1980. Auditor, Price Waterhouse & Co., Philippines, 1973-74, acctg. supr., Los Angeles, 1974-76; mgr. acctg. Ticor Mortgage Ins. Co., Los Angeles, 1976-77, dir. acctg., 1977—; pres., pub. Fil-Am Enterprises, Inc., 1981—, Calif. Examiner, 1982—. Recipient Leadership award U. of East, Manila, 1973. C.P.A., Calif., Philippines. Mem. Am. Entrepreneurs Assn., Los Angeles C. of C., Beta Epsilon Sigma (Grand Lord chancellor 1972-73). Roman Catholic. Home: 7511 Laurelgrove Ct North Hollywood CA 91605 Office: 6300 Wilshire Blvd Los Angeles CA 90048

JORSS, EMMA BARBARA, university president; b. Odessa, Russia; foster dau. Jacob and Wilhelmina Bauman; student Dakota Wesleyan Coll., 1930-31, U. Calif., Berkeley, 1931-32, U. So. Calif., 1932-37, U. Omaha, 1964-65; J.D., Lincoln U., 1950; m. Harry Charles Jorss, 1932; 1 dau., Margaret. Mgr., Eversharp Inc., San Francisco, 1939-45; bus. mgr. YWCA, San Francisco, 1945-53, exec. v.p. Lincoln U., San Francisco, 1953-78, pres., 1978-83, pres. emeritus, 1983—, sec.-treas. bd. trustees, 1953-80, founding mem., dir. Lincoln U. Found., founder Lincoln U. Law Sch., Sacramento. Mem. Nat. Assn. Women Deans, Adminstrs. and Counselors, Am. Assn. Higher Edn., AAUP. Republican. Episcopalian. Club: Commonwealth. Exec. producer cable TV series This Is Your Law, 1974. Office: Lincoln U 281 Masonic Ave San Francisco CA 94118

JOSEFOWITZ, NATASHA, educator, author, consultant; b. Paris, France, Oct. 31, 1926; d. Myron and Tamara (Fradkin) Chapro; came to U.S., 1939, naturalized, 1947; children—Nina, Paul. B.A., Scripps Coll., 1948; M.S.W., Columbia U., 1965; Doctorans, U. Lausanne (Switzerland), 1974; Ph.D., Sussex (Eng.) Coll., 1977. Family therapist Child Guidance Clinic, Lausanne, 1965-74; prof. social work, Ecole d'etudes Sociales, Lausanne, 1965-74, prof. psychology Lausanne U., 1972-74; assoc. prof. mgmt. Whittemore Coll. Bus., U. N.H., Durham, 1974-80; prof. mgmt. San Diego State U., 1980—; dir. Nat. Tng. Lab. Inst., 1981—. NIMH grantee, 1976. Mem. Am. Soc. Tng. and Devel., Acad. Mgmt., Orgn. Devel. Network, Cert. Consultants Internat., Nat. Assn. Social Workers. Author: Paths to Power; 1980; Is This Where I Was Going, 1983; In a Nutshell, 1982; contbr. articles to profl. jours. Office: Coll Bus San Diego State U San Diego CA 92115

JOSEPH, RAYMOND GENE, water power company executive; b. Walla Walla, Wash., Sept. 25, 1936; s. Gabe S. and Emily F. (Ferris) J.; B.A. in Bus. Adminstrn., U. Wash., 1960; m. Lilia Farah, June 25, 1961; children—Craig, Cami, Shawn. Owner, mgr. Family Store, Walla Walla, 1953-63; adminstrn. ops. supr. Safeco Ins. Co., Seattle, 1963-68; indsl. engr., systems analyst Boeing Co., Seattle, 1968-71, orgn. planning and manpower coordinator Wash. Water Power Co., Spokane, 1971—. Mem. budget panel United Way, 1973, loaned exec., 1964; bd. dirs. Inland Empire chpt. Nat. Rehab. Assn. Served with USAF, 1961-67. Mem. Am. Soc. Personnel Adminstrn. (nat. v.p.), N.W. Electric Light and Power Assn., Pacific N.W. Personnel Mgmt. Assn. (pres.), Assn. Systems Mgmt., U. Wash. Alumni Assn. Republican. Episcopalian. Club: Elks. Office: PO Box 3727 Spokane WA 99220

JOSHI, AIDA ALCALA, educator; b. Daraga, Albay, Philippines, July 12, 1935; came to U.S., 1961, naturalized, 1978; d. Jose Arboleda Imperial and Eufemia Alcala Alcala; m. Sudhakar Bhalachandra Joshi, Aug. 18, 1971. M.A., U. Calif.-Berkeley, 1962, Ph.D., 1971. Cert. tchr., supr., Calif. Asst. prof. edn. U. Ark.-Montecello, 1971-72; asst. prof. edn. Calif. State U.-Hayward, 1972-73; asst. prof. edn. San Francisco State U., 1973-74; asst. prof. edn. U. San Francisco, 1975-78, assoc. prof. edn., 1978—; cons. schs. dists., Calif. State Dept. Edn., Nat. Inst. Edn. Mem. AAUP, Nat. Council Social Studies, Council Calif. Social Studies, Assn. Supervision and Curriculum Devel., Nat. Assn. Asian and Pacific Islander Am. Edn., Calif. Women in Higher Edn., U. Calif. Alumnae Assn. Home: 6910 Cutting Blvd El Cerrito CA 94530 Office: 2130 Fulton St Sch Edn U San Francisco San Francisco CA 94117

JOSHUA, AARON, investment company executive; b. Los Angeles, Aug. 26, 1957; s. Elmo and Pineniece Penny (Starks) J.; m. Valeri Janien. B.A. in Bus. Adminstrn., Whittier Coll., 1978, M.B.A., 1980. Life ins. agt. ITT Ins. Corp., Marina del Rey, Calif., 1977; pres., chmn. bd. Pleasure Jet Entertainment Centre Inc., Inglewood, Calif., 1980—; gen. ptnr. Joshua Investments, Ltd., Beverly Hills, Calif., 1980—. Mem. Am. Mgmt. Assn., Beverly Hills C. of C. (edn. com.), Inglewood C. of C. Republican. Baptist. Club: Inglewood Rotary. Office: 311 S Robertson Blvd Beverly Hills CA 90211

JOSLEN, ROBERT ANDREW, automobile dealer; b. Altadena, Calif., June 28, 1929; s. Fred L. and Elsie A. (Westlake) J.; B.S. in Bus. Adminstrn., Anderson (Ind.) Coll. and Theol. Sem., 1952; M.B.A., George Washington U., 1966; m. Eldine Frazee, Dec. 18, 1949; children—Robert, Lisa, Nancy. Adminstrv. asst., adminstrv. resident Washington Hosp. Center, Washington, 1965-67; asst. dir. U. Mo. Med. Center, Columbia, 1967-69, also mem. faculty dept. community health and med. practice U. Mo. Med. Sch.; adminstr. St. Bernard Hosp., Chgo., 1969-73; pres. Saginaw (Mich.) Osteo. Hosp., 1973-78; preceptor adminstrv. residents in hosp. adminstrn. Trinity U., San Antonio, 1971—, George Washington U., 1975—; now owner, operator Joslen Chevrolet, Pagosa Springs, Colo. Bd. dirs. Englewood Sr. Citizens Centers, 1969-73, chmn., 1970-71; bd. dirs. Comprehensive Research and Devel., 1971-73, Englewood Manor Apts., 1969-73, Group Health Service Mich., 1975-78, Community Hosp. Services, 1973-78; bd. dirs., treas. Dr. Mary Fisher Med. Center, Pagosa Springs, 1979—; chmn. bd. dirs. Upper San Juan Hosp. Dist. Served with AUS, 1946-48. Fellow Am. Coll. Hosp. Adminstrs., Mich. Hosp. Assn. (trustee 1977-78; chmn. unemployment compensation com. 1975-77); mem. Mich. Osteo. Hosp. Assn. (v.p. 1977-78 dir. 1974-78), Am. Hosp. Assn., Am. Pub. Health Assn., Acad. Health Care Consultants. Clubs: Elks, Rotary. Home: PO Box 961 Pagosa Springs CO 81147 Office: Joslen Chevrolet 5th & San Juan Pagosa Springs CO 81147

JOSPE, MICHAEL, med. psychologist; b. Johannesburg, South Africa, Feb. 12, 1944; s. Leonhard and Gerda J.; B.A., U. Leeds (Eng.), 1965; M.A., U. Minn., Mpls., 1970, Ph.D., 1974. Chief psychologist Newington (Conn.) Children's Hosp., 1975-76; coordinator pediatric consulation and liaison psychiatry Kaiser-Permanente Med. Ctr., Los Angeles, 1979; asst. clin. prof. consultation and liaison psychiatry Neuropsychiat. Inst., UCLA Med. Ctr.; program faculty Calif. Sch. Profl. Psychology. Mem. Am. Psychol. Assn. Author: The Placebo Effect in Healing, 1968; Psychological Factors in Health Care: A Manual for Practitioners, 1980; contbr. articles to profl. jours. Office: 4900 Sunset Blvd Room 2005 Los Angeles CA 90027

JOST, FRANZ ALPHONS, marketing executive; b. Lucerne, Switzerland, Feb. 27, 1950; s. Francois and Heidy B. (Walther) J.; m. P. Ellen Kling, Mar. 19, 1977. B.S. in Internat. Econs. and Fin., U. Ill., 1972, M.B.A., 1974. Internal auditor The Greyhound Corp., Phoenix, 1974-75; dir. mktg. Greyhound Support Services, Inc., Phoenix, 1976-78, v.p. corp. devel., 1979—. Home: 11043 N St Andrews Way Scottsdale AZ 85254 Office: 3120 Greyhound Tower Phoenix AZ 85077

JOVAN, ANDRÉANNA, ednl. adminstr.; b. San Diego, May 16, 1947; d. Richard J. and Emily Jeanette (Barber) Wallingford; Asso. Sci., Grossmont Coll., 1967; B.B.A. summa cum laude, Nat. U., 1979, postgrad., 1979-80; children—Garidean Coartney, Tammie Colleen Coartney. Dep. sheriff San Diego Sheriff's Dept., 1971-74; mgr. Claudia's Waterbed Store, Lemon Grove, Calif., 1976-77; owner, mgr. Eishtar Sunshine Co., San Diego, 1977-81; dean North County Coll., 1981—. Mem. Internat. Soc. Arboriculture. Home: 3225 Citrus St Lemon Grove CA 92045

JOWER, GORDON WAYNE, podiatrist; b. San Mateo, Calif., July 30, 1943; s. Lawrence Harold and Mabel Camile (Fong) J.; B.A., U. Calif.-Berkeley, 1966; B.Med. Scis., Calif. Coll. Podiatric Medicine, 1975, D. Podiatric Medicine, 1976; children—Matthew Wayne, Kristen Michelle. Tchr. biology, Sierra Vista High Sch., Baldwin Park, Calif., 1971-73; clin. instr. biomechanics and foot surgery Calif. Coll. Podiatric Medicine, San Francisco, 1978-79; practice podiatry Foster City, Calif., 1976—; prof. Chinese medicine Ctr. Chinese Medicine, Los Angeles, 1982—. Instr. CPR, Am. Heart Assn., San Mateo County, bd. dirs., 1979-82, pres., 1981-82. Served with AUS, 1968-70. Fellow Am. Acad. Foot Orthopedists, Am. Acad. Podiatric Sports Medicine; mem. Calif. Podiatry Assn. (recipient Presidents award 1980), Am. Podiatry Assn., San Mateo San Francisco Podiatry Soc. (pres. 1982-83), Am. Coll. Foot Surgeons (assoc.), Foster City C. of C. Roman Catholic. Clubs: Rotary, Foster City Joggers, Masons, KC, St. Luke's Burning Bush Folk Group. Contb. author: The Foot Books: Advice for Athletes, 1976. Office: 1289 East Hillsdale Blvd Foster City CA 94404

JOY, CARLA MARIE, educator; b. Denver, Sept. 5, 1945; d. Carl P. and Theresa M. (Lotito) J. A.B. cum laude, Loretto Heights Coll., 1967; M.A. (Ford Found. fellow), U. Denver, 1969. Instr. history Community Coll. Denver, Red Rocks Community Coll., Golden, Colo., 1970—; cons. for innovative ednl. programs. Instr. vocat. edn. Mile High United Way, Jefferson County, 1975. Cert. in vocat. edn. Colo. State Bd. Community Colls. and Occupational Edn. Recipient cert. of appreciation Kiwanis Club, 1981; Master Tchr. award U. Tex. at Austin, 1982. Mem. Am. Hist. Assn., Nat. Council for Social Studies, Nat. Geog. Soc., Inst. Early Am. History and Culture, Phi Alpha Theta. Democrat. Episcopalian. Designer individualized instructional programs for world civilization, 1972—. Home: 1849 S Lee St Apt D Lakewood CO 80226 Office: 12600 W 6th Ave Golden CO 80401

JOYCE, JAMES DONALD, oil company executive; b. Appleton, Wis., July 1, 1936; s. Donald Mathew and Elizabeth Alice (Breitenstein) J.; B.S. in Chem. Engring., U. Wis., 1963; M.S. in Chem. Engring., N.J. Inst. Tech., 1967; J.D., John F. Kennedy U., 1980; m. Joan Elizabeth Matt, Sept. 12, 1959; 1 dau., Kimberly Joan. Research chemist Shell Oil Co., 1963-67, product devel. engr., 1967-70, tech. service rep., 1970-73, regional rep. safety/health, 1973-77, W. Coast rep. environ. affairs, San Ramon, Calif., 1977-81, staff engr.-atty., 1981—; admitted to Calif. bar. Pres., Walnut Walk (Calif.) Homeowners Assn., 1974-81, also bd. dirs. Served with USAF, 1954-57. Mem. Am. Inst. Chem. Engrs., Calif. Mfrs. Assn. (co. rep. 1974—), Western Oil and Gas Assn. (co. rep. 1977—), Bay Area League Indsl. Assns. (tech. cons. to br. 1977-81). Republican. Roman Catholic. Club: Commonwealth of San Francisco. Patentee rapid setting epoxides, 1965.

JOZWIK, FRANCIS XAVIER, agrl. bus. exec.; b. El Paso, Tex., July 4, 1940; s. Andrew and Dagmar Elizabeth (Wettermark) J.; student Casper Coll., 1958-60, U. Idaho, 1960; B.S., U. Wyo., 1962, M.S., 1963, Ph.D., 1966; postgrad. Wash. State U., 1964; m. Phyllis Ann Angevine, Dec. 28, 1974; children—Melissa, John, Monika. Asst. prof. plant physiology Wis. State U., Oshkosh, 1966-67; rangelands scientist Commonwealth Scientific & Indsl. Research Orgn., Canberra, Australia, 1967-69; owner, mgr. Johnny Appleseed, Inc., Casper, Wyo., 1969—; owner Beaver Creek Land & Cattle Co., Custer County, S.D. NSF fellow, 1963. Mem. U.S. C. of C., Sigma Xi. Roman Catholic. Contbr. articles in field to profl. jours. Home: 8364 W Yellowstone St Casper WY 82601 Office: 8340 W Yellowstone St Casper WY 82601

JUCKETT, RUSSELL BERNARD, JR., lawyer; b. Hopkinsville, Ky., Oct. 26, 1943; s. Russell Bernard and Alice Muriel (Barbo) J.; A.A., Skagit Valley Coll., 1963; B.A., U. Wash., 1965; J.D., Vanderbilt U., 1971; m. Marsha Gay Madeiras, Mar. 31, 1973; children—Stacy Malia, Paige Alison. Admitted to Tenn. bar, 1972, Wash. bar, 1973; adjudicator VA, Nashville, 1971-72; mem. firm Mathew D. Griffin, Everett, Wash., 1972-78; prosecuting atty. Snohomish County, Everett, 1979-82; ptnr. firm Hulbert, Hawes & Juckett, Everett, 1983—. Mem. Everett City Council, 1976-77; pres. Snohomish County unit Am. Cancer Soc., 1980-81; bd. dirs. Rape Relief, March of Dimes, Snohomish County Assn. for Retarded Citizens; mem. adv. bd. Wash. State Patrol Explorer Post 700; chmn. bd. Mothers Against Drunk Drivers. Served with U.S. Army, 1965-68. Mem. Am. Trial Lawyers, ABA, Wash. Bar Assn., Wash. Assn. Pros. Attys. (chmn. county powers and revenue legis. com.), Snohomish County Peace Officers Assn., Lambda Chi Alpha, Phi Delta Phi. Republican. Methodist. Clubs: Toastmasters, Mason, Kiwanis (pres. 1979-80), Shriners, Elks. Home: 2801 Panaview Blvd Everett WA 98203

JUDGE, JAMES ROBERT, lawyer; b. Milw., Mar. 19, 1948; s. Robert James and Margaret (Weseli) J.; m. Joan M. Illingworth, Aug. 21, 1971; children—Robert Kanoa, Corrie Malia. B.B.A., U. Hawaii, 1970; J.D., U. Calif.-Hastings Coll. Law, 1973. Bar: Hawaii 1973; real estate broker, Hawaii. Assoc. Okano, Noguchi & Wong, Honolulu, 1973-75; assoc. Mukai, Ichiki, Raffetto & MacMillan, Honolulu, 1976, ptnr., Wailuku, Maui, 1977-82; ptnr. Foley, Maehara, Judge, Choi, Nip & Okamura, Honolulu and Wailuku, Maui, 1983—; lectr. U. Hawaii Coll. Bus. Adminstrn., 1973-76; judge per diem Dist. Ct. (2d cir.), Hawaii, 1981—. Bd. dirs. Friends of Maui Symphony, 1980-81, Maui Community Arts and Cultural Ctr., 1983—. Mem. ABA, Hawaii Inst. Continuing Legal Edn. (dir. 1977-81), Bar Assn. Hawaii (chmn. continuing legal edn. com. 1975), Maui County Bar Assn. (pres. 1979-80). Office: 2233 Vineyard St PO Box 1268 Wailuku HI 96793

JUHASZ, JOSEPH BORIS, psychologist, educator; b. Budapest, Hungary, Jan. 30, 1938; came to U.S., 1951, naturalized, 1956; s. William P. and Mary Antonia (Christianus) J.; A.B., Brown U., 1961; Ph.D., U. Calif., Berkeley, 1969; postgrad. U. Otago, 1971; m. Suzanne Hecht, June 12, 1963 (div. 1981); children—Alexandra Jeanne, Jennifer Anne, Antonia Janis; m. 2d, Lorraine Wood, May 1981. Faculty of social scis. Bennington (Vt.) Coll., 1968-71; asst. prof. Bucknell U., Lewisburg, Pa., 1971-74; asst. prof. Coll. Environ. Design, U. Colo., Boulder, 1974-78, asso. prof., dir. Environ. Design Div., Coll. Environ. Design, 1978—; vis. asst. prof., fellow Oakes Coll., U. Calif., Santa Cruz, 1973-74; vis. asso. prof. U. Toronto, 1981; cons. on grants Carnegie Found., Colo. Humanities Program, NSF, HUD; bd. dirs. Windstar Found., Wright-Ingraham Inst., EDAW Inc., Joint Venture, Inc. Exec. com. AFT local U. Colo., Boulder, 1979-80. Served as officer USN, 1961-65. NSF postdoctoral fellow, 1971-72, predoctoral traineeship, 1967-68; grantee NIH, 1971-72, Jefferson County Commrs., 1975-77. Fellow Am. Psychol. Assn.; mem. Environ. Design Research Assn., Soc. for Psychol. Study of Social Issues. Democrat. Roman Catholic. Club: Brown Club of N.Y.C. Co-author: Environments: Notes and Selections on Objects, Spaces and Behavior, 1974; guest editor Jour. of Architectural Education, 1981; editor Am. Psychol. Assn. newsletter, div. on psychology and the arts, 1979—; contbr. writings to profl. publs. Home: 1081 Lincoln Pl Boulder CO 80302 Office: Coll of Design and Planning U Colo Boulder CO 80309

JUHL, SUSAN ELLEN, writer; b. San Jose, Calif., May 5, 1941; d. Robert C. and Jane M. (Moorehead) Doerr; m. Jerry R. Juhl, June 27, 1965. B.A., San Jose State U., 1963; postgrad. Goethe Inst. (West Berlin, W. Ger.) 1964. Head of continuity, announcer Sta. KRPM-FM, San Jose, Calif., 1959-60; researcher Muppets Inc., N.Y.C., 1965; art dir. Ted Memeth Studios, N.Y.C., 1965-66; Arthurian researcher, London, 1976-80; editorial asst., writer Fraggle Rock, Toronto, Can., 1982—; researcher to head writer Muppets, 1965—; co-dir. Under Milkwood, Cambria, Calif., 1975; co-producer 4 plays Calif. Artists Repertory Theatre, Cambria, 1975. Officer, N. Coast Property Owners Assn., Cambria, 1974-75, Central Coastal Handweavers Guild, San Luis Obispo, Calif., 1974, Environ. Ctr. San Luis Obispo, 1974, Mozart Festival Bd., San Luis Obispo, 1980-83. Mem. Writers Guild Am. Democrat. Home and Office: 775 Ardath Dr Cambria CA 93428

JUHLIN, SHARYL ANN, consumer electronics company advertising executive; b. Pontiac, Mich., June 19, 1943; d. Grant Edmund and Bonnie Jeanne Hoople; student UCLA, 1960-61; m. Jon Charles Juhlin, June 23, 1978; stepchildren—Jon Christian, Eric Sheffield. Dir. mktg. coordinator ednl. prodns. Audio Magnetics Corp., Gardena, Calif., 1969-73; coordinator mktg. services The Data Corp., Los Angeles, 1973-74; pvt. practice mktg. and advt. cons., Los Angeles, 1974-75; advt. mgr. Hitachi Sales Corp., Compton, Calif., 1975-78; advt. promotions mgr. 7-Up Bottling Co. of So. Calif., Los Angeles, 1978-79; advt. mgr. Pioneer Electronics Am., Long Beach, Calif., 1979—. Mem. Sales and Mktg. Execs. of Los Angeles, Los Angeles Advt. Club (dir. 1980, 81). Republican. Home: Santa Monica CA 90402 Office: 1925 E Dominguez Long Beach CA 90810

JUI, WEN, elec. engr.; b. Nanking, China, Aug. 3, 1948; d. Kuang-Hwai and Mar-Ching (Kwang) Jui; came to U.S., 1970; B.S.E.E., Nat. Taiwan U., 1970; Ph.D. (Univ. fellow, Teaching fellow), Vanderbilt U., 1977; m. Rodney Carl Threadgill, Aug. 15, 1977. Mem. research staff Teledyne Brown Engring. Corp., Huntsville, Ala., 1977-78; lead engr. Harris Corp., Melbourne, Fla., 1978-79; project engr. Hughes Aircraft Co., Space and Communications Group, Los Angeles, 1979—. Research asst. fellow Research Inst. Physics, Stockholm, 1973-74. Mem. IEEE (space communications tech. com.), Am. Phys. Soc., Sigma Xi. Home: 218 Pasteur Pl Placentia CA 92670 Office: Hughes Aircraft Co Space and Communications Group PO Box 92919 Bldg 550 MS-X337 Los Angeles CA 90009

JULIAN, CAROL PATRICIA, medical center administrator; b. Portland, Oreg., Apr. 14, 1942; d. John Joseph and Alice Lucille (Riggs) J. B.S. in Nursing, U. Oreg., 1964, M.S. in Edn., 1969. Med./surg. nurse Providence Hosp., Portland, 1964-65, gerontological nurse Hassler Hosp., San Francisco, 1965-67; med. nurse St. Lukes Hosp., Denver, 1968-69, inservice instr., 1969-70, dir. edn., pres., 1970—. Mem. Am. Nurses Assn., Colo. Soc. Nurse Execs., Nat. Accreditation Bd. Continuing Edn. Democrat.

JULIEN, JANE A. PIERCE, librarian; b. Detroit, July 1, 1932; d. Frank Johnson and Margaret Elizabeth (Norgrove) Pierce; B.A., Wayne State U., 1964, M.S.L.S., 1968; Ed.S., No. Ariz. U., 1974; Ph.D., Ariz. State U., 1979; m. Daniel J. Julien, Jan. 24, 1953; children—Paul Daniel, Timothy Frank, Mark James. Tchr., Southfield (Mich.) High Sch., 1963-67; univ. librarian No. Ariz. U., Flagstaff, 1967-77, mem. faculty Coll. Edn., 1972, 74-75, 78, 80; librarian Coconino High Sch., Flagstaff, 1980—. Mem. Flagstaff City-Coconino County Public Library Bd., 1975-83, chairperson, 1978-80. Mem. Assn. Supervision and Curriculum Devel., Ariz. State Library Assn. (sec. 1976-77), Ariz. Assn. Supervision and Curriculum Devel., NEA, Ariz. Edn. Assn., Flagstaff Edn. Assn. (bldg. rep. 1981-83), Phi Kappa Phi, Phi Delta Kappa, Alpha Delta Kappa. Christian Scientist. Home: 507 N James Flagstaff AZ 86001 Office: 2801 N Izabel Flagstaff AZ 86001

JUN, JONG SUP, public administration educator; b. Sunsan, Korea, July 26, 1936; came to U.S., 1961; s. Myung D. and Jum S. (Pai) J.; m. Soon Ye, Sept. 16, 1964; children—Eugene, Amy. LL.B., Taegu Coll., 1960; M.A., U. Oreg., 1964; Ph.D., U. So. Calif., 1969. Research assoc. U. So. Calif., Los Angeles, 1968; prof. pub. adminstrn. Calif. State U., Hayward, 1968—, chmn. dept., 1973-76; cons. to various govt. agys. Nat. Assn. Pub. Affairs and Adminstrn. fellow, 1972-73; Social Sci. Research Council grantee, 1978; Mem. Am. Soc. Pub. Adminstrn. (acad. achievement award San Francisco-Santa Clara chapts., 1982), Am. Soc. Polit. Sci. Democrat. Author: Tomorrow's Organizations: Challenges and Strategies, 1973; Administrative Alternatives in Development Assistance, 1973; Management by Objectives in Government, 1976; contbr. articles to profl. jours.; mem. editorial bd. Pub. Adminstrn. Rev., 1976-78, Jour. of Comparative Adminstrn., 1972-74. Home: 5600 Trail Side Ct Castro Valley CA 94546 Office: Dept Pub Adminstrn Calif State U Hayward CA 94542

JUNCHEN, DAVID LAWRENCE, pipe organ mfg. co. exec.; b. Rock Island, Ill., Feb. 23, 1946; s. Lawrence Ernest and Lucy Mae (Ditto) J.; B.S. in Elec. Engring. with highest honors, U. Ill., 1968. Founder, owner Junchen Pipe Organ Service, Sherrard, Ill., 1968—; co-owner Junchen-Collins Organ Corp., Woodstock, Ill., 1975-80; mng. dir. Baranger Studios, South Pasadena, Calif., 1980-81. Named Outstanding Freshman in Engring. U. Ill., 1963-64. Mem. Am. Inst. Organ Builders, Am. Theatre Organ Soc., Mus. Box Soc., Automatic Mus. Instrument Collectors Assn., Tau Beta Pi, Sigma Tau, Eta Kappa Nu. Author: Encyclopedia of American Theatre Organs; contbr. to Ency. Automatic Mus. Instruments; composer, arranger over 90 music rolls for self-playing mus. instruments. Office: 280 E Del Mar Suite 311 Pasadena CA 91101

JUNE, ROY ETHIEL, lawyer; b. Forsyth, Mont., Aug. 12, 1922; s. Charles E. and Elizabeth F. (Newnes) J.; m. Laura Brautigam, June 20, 1949; children—Patricia June Rossitto, Richard Tyler. B.A., U. Mont., 1948, B.A. in Law, 1951, LL.B., 1952. Bar: Mont. 1952, Calif. 1961. Sole practice, Billings, Mont., 1952-57, Sanders and June, 1953-57; real estate developer, Orange County, Calif., 1957-61; ptnr. Dugan, Tobias, Tornay & June, Costa Mesa, Calif., 1961-62; city prosecutor, Costa Mesa, 1962-63, asst. city atty., 1963-67, city atty., 1967-78; sole practice, Costa Mesa, 1962—. Atty. Costa Mesa Hist. Soc., Costa Mesa Playhouse Patron's Assn., Red Barons Orange County, The Redcoats, Inc., Costa Mesa Meml. Hosp. Aux., Harbor Key, Child Guidance Ctr. Orange County, Fairview State Hosp. Therapeutic Pool Vols., Inc.; active Eagle Scouts Am., Harbor Area Boy Scouts Am., YMCA; atty. United Fund/Community Chest Costa Mesa and Newport Beach; bd. dirs. Boys' Club Harbor Area, bd. dirs. Mardan Ctr. Ednl. Therapy. Served with USAF, World War II. Decorated Air medal with oak leaf cluster, D.F.C. Mem. Mont. Bar Assn., Calif. Bar Assn., Orange County Bar Assn., Harbor Bar Assn., Costa Mesa C. of C. (bd. dirs.). Clubs: Masons, Scottish Rite, Shriners, Santa Ana Country, Amigos Viejos, Los Fiestadores. Office: 695 Town Center Dr 8th Floor Costa Mesa CA 92626

JUNG, GARY BRUCE, financial planner; b. Cin., Nov. 23, 1939; s. Gordon Clifford and Mary Lee (Stoveall) J.; student Colo. State Coll., 1958-59, George Washington U., 1967-68. Personnel supr. Control Data Corp., 1968-70; pres. Kono Kai Enterprises, Honolulu, 1970-79; pres. Diversified Fun. Planning, Honolulu, 19—; pres. E.A. Buck Planning Services, Inc., Honolulu, 1982—; lectr.; Pacific area dir. Audit Guard, Inc., 1981-82. Mem. Mayor's Water Safety Com., 1979. Served with U.S. Army, 1960-62. Recipient Mayor's award Honolulu, 1979. Mem. Internat. Assn. Fin. Planning (pres. Hawaii chpt. 1982-83, Outstanding Mem. of Yr. 1983), Hawaii C. of C., Hawaii Council Dive Clubs (pres. 1978). Club: Honolulu. Fin. planning columnist Hanalike mag. Home: 425 Ena Rd #1001B Honolulu HI 96815 Office: 900 Fort St Mall Suite 1590 Honolulu HI 96813

JUNGE, BARBARA JACKSON, education specialist; b. Los Angeles, Dec. 1, 1931; d. Thomas Edward and Llellwyn Dolores (Smith) Jackson; m. Bjarne Junge, Sept. 7, 1953; children—Maria, Karina. B.A., UCLA, 1953; M.A., San Jose State U., 1961; Ph.D., U. Colo., 1972. Cert. elem. tchr., secondary tchr., sch. adminstr., Calif. Adviser evaluation UNESCO, Thailand, 1976-77, chief tech. adviser primary edn., Nigeria, 1978-82, cons. female edn., Nepal, 1983—; asst. prof. edn. Coll. Notre Dame, Calif., 1972-75. Mem. UNESCO Field Staff Assn., Internat. Reading Assn., Assn. Supervision and Curriculum Devel., Phi Delta Kappa. Author: New Patterns in Educational Leadership, 1981; Family Life Education, 1982.

JUNGHERR, ANTON, mgmt. cons.; b. New Haven, Jan. 5, 1933; s. Erwin L. and Marie H. Jungherr; B.S., U. Conn., 1954; M.P.A., Syracuse U., 1958; Ed.M., Columbia U., 1971; m. Mary Jane Mikuriya; children—Karen, Lisa, Anna, Anton. Asst. city mgr. City of Lake Forest (Ill.), 1958-61; controller Anchorage Ind. Sch. Dist., 1961-63, City of Anchorage, 1963-65; asst. supt. bus. Pearl River (N.Y.) Sch. Dist., 1965-71; dir. fin. City of Newark, 1971-73; dep. supt. schs. City of Yonkers (N.Y.), 1973-75; bus. mgr. San Francisco Unified Sch. Dist., 1975-80; mgmt. cons., 1981—. Served with Adj. Gen. Corps, U.S. Army, 1954-56. Mem. Am. Mgmt. Assn. Unitarian. Author: (with Robert F. Alioto) Operational PPBS for Education: A Practical Approach to Effective Decision Making, 1971. Home and Office: 361 Mississippi St San Francisco CA 94107

JUNIEL, EUNICE KIMBROUGH, clergywoman; b. Magnolia, Ala., Sept. 12, 1931; d. Joseph and Emma Lee (Jenkins) Kimbrough; B.A. in Sociology, Calif. State U., 1969, M.A., 1974; D. Metaphysical Sci., U. Metaphysics, Los Angeles, 1981; children—Josephus, Cheryl, Michael, Kathleen. Psychiat. technician State of Calif., Walnut, 1962-64; tchr. Los Angeles public schs., 1971-81; founder, dir. weekly program Patterns for Living, Sta. KTYM, Los Angeles, 1982—. Founder, pres. Universal Truth Found., 1982—. Mem. Los Angeles Urban League, Phi Delta Kappa, Psi Gamma Mu. Democrat. Office: PO Box 11088 Marina Del Rey CA 90295

JUREK, WALTER, management consultant; b. Cleve., 1937; B.S. in Mech. Engring., Ohio U., 1960, B.S. in Commerce, 1960; M.B.A., Case Western Res. U., 1963; D.B.A., U. Colo., 1966. Pres. Quality Services, Inc., Mgmt. Cons., Santa Barbara, Calif., 1967—; pres. Trans-Western Services, Inc., real estate investments, Goleta, Calif., 1978—; chmn. bd. Vulcan Trailer Mfg. Co., Birmingham, Ala., 1983—; pub. Acquisition/Divesture Weekly Report and Ann. Merger and Acquisition Directory. Office: Quality Services Inc 3887 State St Santa Barbara CA 93105

JUST, RICHARD E., agricultural economist, educator, consultant, commodity analyst; b. Tulsa, Feb. 18, 1948; s. William and Leah (Flaming) J.; m. Jane Ann Hardie, Jan. 3, 1949; children—Angela, David. B.S., Okla. State U.-Stillwater, 1969; M.A., U. Calif.-Berkeley, 1971, Ph.D., 1972. Assoc. prof. agrl. econs. and stats. Okla. State U., 1972-75; prof. agrl. and resource econs. U. Calif.-Berkeley, 1975—; cons. World Bank, GAO, Oak Ridge Nat. Lab. Mem. econs. position com. Dem. Nat. Com., 1981. Recipient Quality of Research Discovery award Am. Agrl. Econs. Assn., 1977, 1980; Best Pub. Research award Western Agrl. Econs. Assn., 1975; Best Jour. Article award Am. Agrl. Econs. Assn., 1982. Mem. Am. Agrl. Econs. Assn., Western Agrl. Econs. Assn., Am. Econs. Assn., Econometric Soc. Democrat. Mormon. Contbr. articles to profl. jours. Office: 207 Giannini Hall U Calif Berkeley CA 94720

JUST, RONALD ANDREW, med. facilities adminstr.; b. Chgo., June 8, 1934; s. Andrew Anthony and Arielle Donna (LaVoy) J.; student La. State U., 1956-58; B.S. in Indsl. Mgmt., Whitworth Coll., 1982; m. Ruth Catherine Brunette, June 7, 1954; children—Andrew John, Pamela Ruth. Painting and decorating contractor, Chgo., 1956-59; painter, glazier Stanford U., 1959-67, maintenance coordinator, insp., 1967-71, maintenance supr., 1972-75, work measurement analyst, 1975-76, asst. ops. mgr., 1976-77, facilities projects mgr., 1977-79, assoc. dir. facilities Stanford U. Hosp./Med. Center, 1979-82, dir. ops. and maintenance, 1982—. Served with USAF, 1952-56. Mem. Am. Mgmt. Assn., Assn. Phys. Plant Adminstrs., Pacific Coast Assn. Phys. Plant Adminstrs. Democrat. Roman Catholic. Club: Elks. Office: Stanford U Hosp Room E012B Stanford CA 94305

JUSTI, CHRISTIAN LEROY, fin. and engring. cons.; b. Kenosha, Wis., Jan. 4, 1928; s. Harald Christian and Gertrude Emma (Schulz) J.; B.S. in Engring., Johns Hopkins U., 1950; M.S. in Fin. and Econs., N.Y. U., 1953, Ph.D., 1955; m. Rose Marie Leon, Feb. 14, 1982; children from previous marriage—Paul, Ann. Engr., Johnson Corp. (acquired by Martin Marietta Corp.), Balt., 1946-50; pro-asst. cashier fgn. dept. Bank Am., Internat., N.Y.C., 1950-55; petroleum and fin. engr. ARCO, Los Angeles, also dir. adminstrn. Vehicle Research Corp., Pasadena, Calif., 1955-60; propr. Fin. Engring. Cons., West Covina, Calif., 1960—. Mem. adv. and youth bds. Los Angeles County Dist. Atty., 1965—; pres. West Covina Beautiful, 1965-67, 81-82, Republican Assembly San Gabriel-Pomona Valley, 1971-73; advisor Nat. Commn.-Youth in Action, 1976—, Nat. Youth Commn., 1981—. Recipient numerous awards for civic contbns. Mem. Am. Inst. Econ. Research, Nat. Assn. Accountants, Nat. Registry Engrs., West Covina C. of C. (dir., Ambassador of Yr. 1980). Roman Catholic. Home: 3133 Sunset Hill Dr West Covina CA 91791 Office: 652 Sunset Suites 208-215 West Covina CA 91790

JUSTICE, LARRY, engineer; b. Borger, Tex., May 11, 1955; s. Dane Carter and Audrey Maxine J.; B.S., Tex. A&M U., 1978; m. Rebecca Jane Dimmitt, Dec. 30, 1977. Product planning and devel. engr. Meiller Research, College Station, Tex., 1976-77; ptnr. Seventy-Seven Cons., College Station, 1977-78; acctg. coordinator Microswitch div. Honeywell, Salt Lake City, 1978-80, product adminstr., 1980, field sales engr., 1980-82, field sales engr. Process Controls div. MS&S Honeywell, 1982-83. Republican. Methodist. Club: Elks. Home: 826 E Scirlein Sandy UT 84070

KABACK, ELAINE, counselor/cons.; b. Phila., Feb. 22, 1939; d. Sol and Evelyn Zitman; student Pa. State U., 1956-58; B.A., Temple U., 1960; M.S., Calif. State U., 1977; children—Douglas, Stephen, Michelle. Tchr. English, Sayre Jr. High Sch., Phila. Public Schs., 1960-62; tchr. English and history Beth Rfiloh Pvt. Day Sch., Balt., 1968-72; mgmt. cons., trainer Sandra Winston Assos., Palos Verdes, Calif., 1975—; counselor Career Planning Center and Mid-Life Center, Long Beach City Coll., 1977-78, instr. in assertion tng. coll. extension; dir. program devel. Univance Career Centers, Inc., Los Angeles, 1978-80; pvt. practice counseling and consulting, 1980—; trainer/presenter, various classes, UCLA Extension, coordinator program devel. Career Planning Program, 1980—. Pres. Palos Verdes chpt. NOW, 1974-76, chairperson, lectr. Speaker's Bur., 1977—; treas. S.W. chpt. Nat. Women's Polit. Caucus, 1973, 78; bd. dirs. STEP Adult Edn. Programs, Palos Verdes, Calif., 1974—, cert. community coll. life counselor, Calif.; cert. tchr., Pa. Mem. Calif. Personnel and Guidance Assn., Calif. Career Guidance Assn., Nat. Assn. Female Execs., Am. Soc. Tng. and Devel., Phi Kappa Phi. Home: 2813 Via Barri Palos Verdes Estates CA 90273 Office: 24222 Hawthorne Blvd Suite B Torrance CA 90505

KACAKAVITCH, PASHA, political scientist; b. Desrovia, Yugoslavia, Dec. 16, 1938; came to U.S., 1956, naturalized, 1965; s. Irving and Euphates (Ragamuff) K.; B.S. in Polit. Sci., Stanford U., 1960, J.D., 1962; M.B.A. in Fin., U. So. Calif., 1965; LL.B., UCLA, 1968; Ph.D. in Fin., Pepperdine U., 1972; m. Samantha Smith, Sept. 19, 1964; children—Acheck, Chip. Chmn. bd. Planning Services, Pasadena, Calif., 1973—. Chmn. emeritus Yugoslavian Am. League, 1975—, Man. of Yr. award, 1980. Mem. Greek Orthodox Ch. Clubs: Balboa Bay, Newport Beach, Bohemian of San Francisco; California (Los Angeles); Variety of So. Calif.; Trojan, Buck. Office: 701 Burleigh Dr Pasadena CA 91105

KACKLEY, EVAN MORGAN, physician; b. Soda Springs, Idaho, Mar. 30, 1906; s. Ellis and Ida (Sarver) K., B.S. with distinction, Stanford, 1927; M.D., Harvard, 1930; m. Lois Louise Lynch, Oct. 2, 1940; children—Ellis N., Alvin E. Intern Los Angeles County Hosp., 1930-31; preceptorship in urology Washington U. Med. Sch., St. Louis, 1933-35; practice medicine specializing in urology, Soda Springs, 1933-41, supt. Caribou County Hosp., Soda Springs, 1935-37. Dir. Phillip-Daucker Mfg. Co., Astoria, Oreg., Caribou Water Devel. Co., Soda Springs. Mem. Idaho Bd. Med. Examiners, 1937-39. Mem. Idaho Senate, Bear River Interstate Compact Commn., 1965-67, Idaho Water Resource Bd., 1967-69. Served to comdr. USNR, 1942-45. Mem. Phi Beta Kappa. Club: Arid (Boise, Idaho). Contbr. articles to profl. jours. Research in carcinoma of the prostate. Co-developer Caulk-Kackley transurethral resectoscope, 1934. Home: 2323 Ellis Ave Boise ID 83702

KADEN, BARBARA ANN, educator; b. Milw., May 2, 1934; d. David Charles and Esther Elizabeth (Schroth) Schilke; m. Harold R. Kaden, July 21, 1956; children—Kristin Sue, Laurie Ann. B.S., Concordia Tchrs. Coll., 1955, M.A., U. San Francisco, 1975; postgrad. Calif. State U.-Sacramento, 1964-70. Tchr., Immanuel Luth. Sch., Albuquerque, 1955-56, St. Paulus Luth. Sch., San Francisco, 1956-57, Town and Country Luth. Sch., Sacramento, 1958-71, Legette Sch., Fair Oaks, Calif., 1972-82, Sch. for Gifted Children, Orangevale, Calif., 1982—. Pres., pub. relations dir. Luth. Women's Missionary League, 1974-80; pres. Theatre Ballet Assn., 1981-82. Mem. Calif. Assn. Gifted, Sacramento Area Gifted Assn. Lutheran. Club: River City Chorale. Author: Opening Wider Doors: An Approach to Gifted Education, 1975. Home: 2740 Tioga Way Sacramento CA 95821 Office: 9010 Pershing Ave Orangevale CA 95662

KADIN, MARSHALL EDWARD, hematopathologist; b. Milw., July 19, 1939; s. George and Mildred (Goldberg) K.; B.A., Northwestern U., 1961, M.D., 1965; m. Martha LuClare Hutchinson, June 15, 1980. Intern, Milw. County Gen. Hosp., 1966; resident in pathology Barnes Hosp., Washington U., St. Louis, 1967-68; NIH fellow in surg. pathology Stanford (Calif.) U., 1969-70; fellow in clin. hematology U. Calif., San Francisco, 1972-73, asst. prof. medicine, clin. pathology and research assoc. Cancer Research Inst., 1974-77; assoc. prof. pathology and lab. medicine U. Wash., Seattle, 1977-82, prof., 1982—, adj. assoc. prof. medicine, 1981—; asso. Fred Hutchinson Cancer Center, Seattle, 1980—. Served to maj. M.C., U.S. Army, 1970-72. Decorated Bronze Star; diplomate Am. Bd. Pathology. Mem. Soc. for Hematopathology, Am. Assn. for Cancer Research, Am. Soc. Hematology, Am. Soc. Cytology, Internat. Acad. Pathology, Acad. Clin. Lab. Physicians and Scientists, Phi Beta Kappa. Republican. Jewish. Contbr. articles to profl. jours.; editor: (with Sam Newcom) Diagnosis and Management of Hematologic Malignancies, 1981. Home: 5711 61st St NE Seattle WA 98105 Office: Dept Lab Medicine SB 10 Univ of Wash Seattle WA 98195

KADZIELSKI, MARK ANTHONY, lawyer; b. Cleve., July 1, 1947; s. Karl Aloysius and Ann Therese (Krol) K.; m. Marilyn Elizabeth Manis, 1977; 1 son, John Joseph. A.B. magna cum laude, John Carroll U., Cleve., 1968; J.D., U. Pa., 1976. Bar: Calif. 1976. Atty. firm Weissburg & Aronson, Los Angeles, 1981—; acad. counselor U. West Los Angeles Law Sch., 1978—, prof. law, 1980—; sec. sect. legislation and adminstrn. of justice Town Hall Calif., 1977-81, v.p., 1981—. Served as officer USAR. Mem. ABA, State Bar Calif. (chmn. history of law com. 1981—), Am. Soc. Legal History, Los Angeles County Bar Assn., Fed. Bar Assn., Alpha Sigma Nu, Phi Alpha Theta. Author Articles in field. Vice chmn. Los Angeles Lawyer, 1981—. Address: 2049 Century Park East Suite 3200 Los Angeles CA 90067

KAESER, LINDA, human services administrator, educator; b. Cape Girardeau, Mo., Dec. 25, 1926; d. Ernest Elden and Hazel (Evans) Arterburn; children—Cyd, Even, Jill, Susan, Deborah, Margot. R.N., B.S., Skidmore Coll., 1950; M.S.W., Portland State U., 1970; Ph.D., Cornell U., 1981. Adminstr. Youth Services Bur., Multnomah County, Portland, Oreg., 1971-73; planner dept human service Multnomah County, 1973-74; researcher Sch. Social Work, Portland State U., 1974-75; lectr. Cornell U., 1975-76; chief exec. officer Oreg. Adult and Family Services, Salem, 1976-78; assoc. prof. Oreg. Health Scis. U., Portland, 1978—, dir. Oregon. teaching nursing home program, 1982—, pres. faculty senate, 1982-83. Commr. Portland Housing Authority, 1979—; mem. Oreg. Gov.'s Mental Health Task Force, 1980-81; mem. Medicaid Reimbursement Task Force, 1982-83. LEA grantee, 1970; HEW grantee, 1971; Robert Wood Johnson Found. grantee, 1982. Mem. Am. Nurses Assn. (rep. to long term care accreditation com. Joint Council Accreditation of Hosps. 1982), Oreg. Nurses Assn., Am. Soc. Nurse Adminstrs., Oreg. Soc. Nurse Adminstrs., Nat. League Nursing, Oreg. League Nursing, Western Gerontol. Assn., Am. Pub. Health Assn., Oreg. Pub. Health Assn., Assn. Oreg. Faculties, Nat. Assn. Social Workers, Acad. Cert. Social Workers, Oreg. Assn. Social Workers, Sigma Theta Tau. Democrat. Unitarian. Office: 3181 SW Sam Jackson Park Rd Portland OR 97201

KAFKA, VINCENT WINFIELD, university administrator, management consultant; b. Bklyn., Feb. 6, 1924; s. Victor and Tunde (Brajjer) K.; m. Elizabeth Murphy, Aug. 19, 1950; children—Anne, John, Rosemary, Patricia, Sue, Thomas. B.I.E., N.C. State U., 1948; M.B.A.,

Drexel U., 1956. With Gen. Electric Co., Phila., Schenectady, N.Y., 1950-66; mgr. indsl. learning systems Gen. Learning Co., Washington, 1963-67; tng. dir. Pacific Gas and Electric Co., San Francisco, 1967-81; assoc. dean sch. mgmt. John F. Kennedy U., Orinda, Calif., 1981—, dir. mgmt. ctr.; pres. Effective Learning Systems, Inc. Served with U.S. Army, 1943-46, 50-52. Mem. Am. Soc. Tng. and Devel. Roman Catholic. Author: (with John H. Schaefer) Open Management, 1975; contbr. numerous articles to profl. jours. Home: 360 Deerfield Dr Moraga CA 94556

KAGAWA, CLIFTON YUKIO, public relations exec.; b. Madison, Wis., Apr. 12, 1950; s. Charles Masayuki and Mari (Toki) K.; m. Lucy Ahn. B.B.A., U. Hawaii, 1972; student Tex. Christian U., 1968-70. Media dir. Fawcett McDermott Cavanagh, Honolulu, 1973-76; account exec. MiliciValenti Advt., Honolulu, 1976-78; pres. Communications-Pacific, Inc., Honolulu, 1978—. Trustee, Hawaii Bound, 1979-81; active Aloha United Way, 1979-81; bd. dirs. Honolulu Symphony Guild, 1980-81; mem. pub. relations com. Honolulu YMCA. Mem. Am. Mktg. Assn. (pres. 1978-79, Award of Merit 1978-79, bd. dirs. 1973-79, council of govs. 1979—), Sales and Mktg. Execs. (bd. dirs.), Better Bus. Bur. (advt. rev. com.), Public Relations Soc. Am. Club: Rotary (Honolulu). Office: 820 Mililani St Suite 400 Honolulu HI 96813

KAGIN, DONALD H., numismatist, investment counselor; b. Des Moines, Sept. 22, 1950; s. Arthur Meyer and Henrietta (Spitz) K.; m. Sara Ellen Gildiner, Oct. 10, 1976; children—Adam, Justin. B.A. in History, Northwestern U., also B.A. in Numismatics; Ph.D. in Numismatics, Union Grad. Sch., Union for Experimenting Univs. Profl. numismatist, 1968—; numismatist, Hollinbeck-Kagin Coin Co., Des Moines, 1968-73; ptnr., exec. v.p. A.M. & Don Kagin, Inc., 1974-80; owner, pres., chief exec. officer Kagin Numismatic Investment Corp., Des Moines, San Francisco, N.Y.C., London, 1980—, Kagin Numismatic Services, Ltd., Kagin Numismatic Auctions, Inc., Mktg. and Media, Inc.; cons. Am. Numismatic Assn. Cert. Service. Recipient Heath Lit. award for best articles, 1972, 73. Mem. Am. Numismatic Assn. (life), Nat. Assn. Numismatic Profls. (v.p.). Jewish. Lodge: Masons (past master Lodge 647). Author: Private Gold Coins and Patterns of the United States, 1982 (best book of year award Numismatic Lit. Guild 1982); columnist: Coin World, Fact Mag., Miami Reb.; contbr. to Financial Planner, Trust and Estates, The Numismatics, Barrons. Office: 4 Embarcadero Suite 2800 San Francisco CA 94111

KAHAN, JAMES PAUL, psychologist; b. N.Y.C., Oct. 15, 1942; s. Robert Helmen and Janet (Rieders) K.; div.; 1 dau., Rebecca. B.A., Reed Coll., 1964; M.A., U. N.C., 1966, Ph.D., 1968. Lic. psychologist, Calif. NATO postdoctoral fellow Université de Provence, Aix-en-Provence, France, 1968-69; asst. prof. dept. psychology, U. So. Calif., Los Angeles, 1970, assoc. prof., 1975-80; fellow-in-residence Netherlands Inst. for Advanced Study in the Humanities and Social Scis., Wassenaar, 1977-78; vis. prof. dept. psychology U. Haifa (Israel), 1980-81; behavioral scientist RAND Corp., Santa Monica, Calif., 1981—; cons. in field. NSF grantee. Mem. Am. Psychol. Assn., Soc. Psychol. Study of Social Issues, Soc. Exptl. Social Psychology. Contbr. articles to profl. jours. Office: RAND Corp 1700 Main St Santa Monica CA 90406

KAHLENBERG, MARY HUNT, consultant and dealer in antique textiles; b. Wallingford, Conn., Oct. 19, 1940; d. Joel Paddock and Emma-Louise (Warner) Barnes; m. Robert T. Coffland, Sept. 23, 1982. B.A., Boston U., 1962; student Austrian Acad. Applied Arts, 1962-63, Berlin Acad. Fine Arts, 1963-64, Master Sch. Crafts, Berlin, 1964-65, Art Inst. Chgo., 1965-66. Instr. textile design U. Tenn., 1965; conservationist Textile Conservation Ctr. London, 1966-67; asst. curator Textile Mus., Washington, 1967-68; vis. lectr. UCLA, 1975, Calif. State U.-Fullerton, 1968-78; curator Los Angeles County Mus. Art, 1968-78; pres. Textile Arts, Inc., Los Angeles, 1978—; cons., dealer in antique and ethnographic textiles. Nat. Endowment for Arts travel grantee, 1975; IBM fellow. Mem. Folk Council, Craft and Folk Art Mus. Author: (with Tony Berlant) Walk in Beauty The Navajo and Their Blankets, 1977; A Book About Grass, Its Beauty and Uses, 1983. Address: 1424 N Ogden Dr Los Angeles CA 90046

KAHN, BLOSSOM, motion picture exec.; b. N.Y.C., Aug. 16, 1936; d. Jules Franklin and Anita Beatrice (Arkin) K.; B.A. in English, Hofstra Coll., Hempstead, N.Y., 1958; postgrad. Columbia U. Sch. Journalism, N.Y.C. Exec., story dept. Universal Pictures Corp., N.Y.C., 1963-64; head motion picture, TV and play depts. Curtis Brown Lit. Agy., N.Y.C., 1964-68; pres. Kahn-Penney Lit. Agy., Los Angeles, 1968-77; dir. creative affairs First Artists Prodns., Los Angeles, 1977-78; exec. in charge creative projects Avco-Embassy Pictures, Los Angeles, 1978-82; v.p. Zupnik-Curtis Enterprises, 1982—; lectr. Sherwood Oaks Coll., Marymount Coll., Los Angeles. Mem. Women in Film, Women in Communication. Office: 9229 Sunset Blvd Los Angeles CA 90069

KAHN, IRWIN WILLIAM, indsl. engr.; b. N.Y.C., Feb. 3, 1923; s. Milton and Clara (Clark) K.; B.S., U. Calif.-Berkeley, 1949; student Cath. U., 1943-44; m. Mildred Cross, May 14, 1946 (dec. May 1966); children—Steven Edward, Michael William, Evelyn Ruth, Joanne Susan; m. 2d, Marajayne Smith, Oct. 9, 1979. Chief indsl. engr. Malsbary Mfg. Co., Oakland, Calif., 1953-57, Yale & Towne Mfg. Co., San Leandro, Calif., 1957-60; sr. indsl. engr. Eitel McCulloch, San Carlos, Calif., 1961-62, Lockheed, Sunnyvale, Calif., 1962-69; v.p. Performance Investors, Inc., Palo Alto, 1969-74; with Kaiser-Permanente Services, Oakland, 1974-76; nat. mgr. material handling Cutter Labs., Berkeley, Calif., 1976-83; sr. mgmt. engr. Children's Hosp. Med. Ctr., Oakland, 1983—; tchr. indsl. engring. Laney Coll., Oakland, 1967—, Chabot Coll., Hayward, Calif. Chmn. Alameda County Library Adv. Commn., 1965—. Served with AUS, 1943-46. Registered profl. engr., Calif. Mem. Am. Inst. Indsl. Engrs. (chpt. pres. 1963-64, chmn. conf. 1967 nat. publ. dir. aerospace div. 1968-69), Calif. Soc. Profl. Engrs. (pres. chpt.). Club: Toastmasters (dist. gov. 1960-61). Home: 4966 Elrod Dr Castro Valley CA 94546 Office: Children's Hosp Med Ctr 51st and Grove Sts Oakland CA 94609

KAHN, LINDA MCCLURE, actuary; b. Jacksonville, Fla.; d. George Calvin and Myrtice Louise (Boggs) McClure; m. Paul Markham Kahn, May 20, 1968. B.S. with high honors, U. Fla.; M.S., U. Mich., 1964. Actuarial trainee N.Y. Life Ins. Co., N.Y.C., 1964-66, actuarial asst., 1966-69, asst. actuary, 1969-71; v.p., actuary US Life Ins., Pasadena, Calif., 1972-74; mgr. Coopers & Lybrand, Los Angeles, 1974-76, sr. cons., San Francisco, 1976-82; dir. program mgmt. Pacific Maritime Assn., San Francisco, 1982—. Sec.-Treas., Pacific Heights Residents Assn., 1981. Fellow Soc. Actuaries, Conf. Actuaries in Pub. Practice; mem. Internat. Actuarial Assn., Internat. Assn. Cons. Actuaries, Actuarial Studies Non-Life Ins., Am. Acad. Actuaries, Western Pension Conf., Actuarial Club Pacific States, San Francisco Actuarial Club (pres. 1981). Clubs: Metropolitan Soroptimist (v.p. 1973-74), Commonwealth. Home: 2430 Pacific Ave San Francisco CA 94115 Office: Pacific Maritime Assn 635 Sacramento St San Francisco CA 94111

KAHN, MARVIN WILLIAM, clinical psychologist; b. Cleve., Feb. 1, 1926; s. Alexander L. and Ida E. (Solowitz) K.; m. Gale Carla Utti, Sept. 18, 1982; children—Karen, David. Ph.D., Pa. State U., 1952. Diplomate Am. Bd. Psychology; lic. psychologist, Ariz. Prof. psychology Yale U., New Haven, 1952-54, U. Colo., Denver, 1954-64, Ohio U., Athens, 1964-69, U. Ariz., Tucson, 1969—. Served with USMC, 1943-46. Fellow Am. Psychol. Assn. Author: Basic Methods for Mental Health Practitioners, 1981. Office: Psychology Dept U Ariz Tucson AZ 85721

KAHN, PAUL MARKHAM, actuary; b. San Francisco, May 8, 1935; s. Sigmund Max and Alexandrina K. (Strauch) K.; B.S., Stanford U., 1956; M.A., U. Mich., 1957, Ph.D., 1961; m. Linda P. McClure, May 20, 1968. Asst. actuary Equitable Life Assurance Soc., N.Y.C., 1961-71; v.p., life actuary Beneficial Standard Life, Los Angeles, 1971-75; v.p., actuary Am. Express Life Ins. Co., San Rafael, Calif., 1975-77, P.M. Kahn & Assos., 1977—. Fellow Soc. Actuaries (Triennial prize 1961-64), Canadian Inst. Actuaries, Conf. Actuaries in Pub. Practice; mem. Am. Acad. Actuaries, Internat. Actuarial Assn., Inst. Actuaries (Eng.), Spanish, Swiss, German, Italian actuarial assns. Clubs: Zamorano (Los Angeles); Roxburghe; Press, Concordia-Argonaut, Commercial (San Francisco). Editor: Credibility: Theory and Practice, 1975; Computational Probability, 1980. Address: 2430 Pacific Ave San Francisco CA 94115

KAHN, ROBERT IRVING, bus. counselor; b. Oakland, Calif., May 17, 1918; s. Irving Herman and Francesca (Lowenthal) K.; A.B. with honors, Stanford U., 1938; M.B.A. (Baker scholar), Harvard U., 1940; LL.D. (hon.), Franklin Pierce Coll., 1977; m. Patricia Elizabeth Glenn, Feb. 14, 1946; children—Christopher Glenn Kahn, Roberta Anne Kahn. Researcher exec. R.H. Macy's, N.Y.C., 1940-41; controller Smiths and Moneyback Smiths, Inc., Oakland, 1946-51, dir., v.p., treas. Sherwood Swan & Co., Oakland, 1953-56; owner Robert Kahn & Assos., Mgmt. Cons., 1956—; pres. Kahn & Harris, Inc., fin. counselors, 1973—; v.p. Hambrecht & Quist, investment bankers, San Francisco, 1977-80; v.p., dir. Marc Paul, Inc. and related cos., Oakland; sec., dir. Coast Med. Corp., Concord, Calif.; dir. Piedmont Grocery Co., Oakland, Menlo Trading Co., Burlingame, Calif., Wal-Mart Stores, Inc., Bentonville, Ark., Lipps, Inc., Santa Monica, Calif., Berkeley Enterprises, Newtonville, Mass., Components Corp. Am., Dallas pub. Retailing Today. Active treas. United Way Bay Area and predecessor orgns., 1946-82, past chmn. ad hoc affiliate agy. com., mem. membership com., past v.p., treas., chmn. fin., personnel, allocations coms.; past mem. Nat. Budget and Consultation Com.; past dir. Bay Area Council for Social Planning, Downtown Property Owners Assn., Oakland; past dir. Oakland chpt. ARC, Oakland council Boy Scouts Am.; past bd. dirs., mem. fin. com. San Francisco Bay council Girl Scouts; past vice chmn. Jewish Community Relations Commn. Alameda-Contra Costa Counties. Mem. adv. council on fed. reports Retail Industry Com. Served from 2d lt. to lt. col. USAF, 1941-46, 51-52; ret. lt. col. Res. Mem. Nat. Retail Mchts. Assn., Stanford Alumni Assn., Harvard Bus. Sch. Alumni Assn., Res. Officers Assn., Air Force Assn., Nat. Rifle Assn., Assn. Mgmt. Cons. (past pres.), Inst. Mgmt. Cons. (a founder), Ret. Officers Assn., Mensa, Phi Beta Kappa. Home: 3684 Happy Valley Rd Lafayette CA 94549 Office: PO Box 249 Lafayette CA 94549

KAIGHAN, HERBERT VINCENT, employee benefit consulting company executive; b. Vancouver, B.C., Can., July 1, 1940; came to U.S., 1951, naturalized, 1958; s. John Newton and Vera (McDonald) K.; B.A., Immaculate Heart Coll., Los Angeles, 1967; m. Mary Catherine Flanagan, Apr. 29, 1966; children—Christina Marie, Kimberly Anne, Michael John. Sales/service rep. Blue Cross Co., Los Angeles, 1965-68; with William M. Mercer (formerly Marsh & McLennan), Los Angeles, 1968—, asst. v.p., 1974-77, v.p., mgr. group cons., 1977-83, prin., mgr. Los Angeles cons. practice, 1983—. Mem. Employee Benefit Planning Assn. (dir. Los Angeles chpt. 1978-79). Club: Los Angeles. Home: 23 Oceanaire Dr Rancho Palos Verdes CA 90274 Office: 3303 Wilshire Los Angeles CA 90010

KAIMOWITZ, BARBARA S., psychotherapist; b. Bklyn., Nov. 9, 1955; d. Carl and Mildred Fishman (Shenkman) K. B.A. in Psychology, Clark U., 1977; M.A. in Counseling Psychology, Humboldt State U., 1980. Psychology intern Humboldt County (Calif.) Outpatient Clinic, 1977-78; crisis intervention counselor Humboldt Crisis Intervention Service, 1978-79; out-patient therapist Family Service Ctr., Eureka, Calif., 1978-79; sexual abuse counselor Child Protective Services, Eureka, 1979; mental health worker Psychiat. Inpatient Unit, Alameda County (Calif.) Services, 1980—; mental health counselor forensic unit Napa County (Calif.) Services, 1982—. Mem. Marriage Family and Child Therapists, Am. Personnel and Guidance Assn. Jewish. Office: Mental Health Services 2344 Old Sonoma Rd Napa CA 94559

KAISER, MICHAEL NORMAN, advertising executive; consultant; b. Bklyn., Feb. 23, 1941; s. Samuel and Hilda (Schwartz) K.; m. Gita Endore, Jan. 3, 1969; 1 son, Guy; m. 2d., Sharon Kay Emanuelli, Aug. 15, 1982. A.B., Hamilton Coll., 1962; postgrad. Ind. U., 1962-64. Sr. publicist Columbia Pictures Corp., 1964-65; ptnr. Kaiser & Father, Los Angeles, 1975-78, Brown Kaiser Advt., Los Angeles, 1980-81; dir. advt. Filmways Pictures, Los Angeles, 1981-82, Orion Pictures Corp., Los Angeles, 1982—. Auctioneer Contemporary Craft Council, Los Angeles, Craft and Folk Art Mus. Mem. Acad. Motion Picture Arts and Scis. Home: 1502 N Ave So Los Angeles CA 90042 Office: Orion Pictures Corp 1875 Century Park E Los Angeles CA 90067

KAISER, WALTER EDWARD, law enforcement official; b. Albany, N.Y., Sept. 29, 1947; s. Rudy and Esther Elizabeth (Bergman) K.; m. Judy Lee Holderegger, Mar. 24, 1952; children—Jason Thomas, William Erich. Student, San Jose City Coll., 1974; B.A., U. San Francisco, 1976. Patrolman, then detective, Mountain View (Calif.) Police Dept., 1971-79, spl. agt. Bur. Narcotic Enforcement, Calif. Dept. Justice, San Jose, 1979—, tchr. Advanced Tng. Ctr., Sacramento, 1980-83. Served with U.S. Army, 1967-70. Mem. Motorcycle Safety Found., Calif. Narcotic Officers Assn. Republican. Club: Blue Knight Law Enforcement Motorcycle (Sunnyvale, Calif.). Office: 2025 Gateway Pl Suite 474 San Jose CA 95110

KAITSCHUK, ROBERT CHARLES, psychologist, travel agency exec.; b. Oak Park, Ill., Sept. 28, 1934; s. Oscar C. and Victoria Marguerite (Schmaus) K.; B.A., Wittenberg U., 1956; M.A., Pepperdine U., 1967. Tchr., Henry Ford II Sch., Chicago Ridge, Ill., 1961-64; counselor, psychologist, div. vocat. edn. West Covina (Calif.) Unified Sch. Dist., 1966-70; prin. Renaissance High Sch., Santa Paula, Calif., 1970-72; personnel mgmt. specialist Ventura County Personnel Dept., Ventura, Calif., 1972-73; vocat. psychologist Calif. Dept. Rehab., Bakersfield dist., 1974-76; psychologist, account exec. Dean Witter & Co., Inc., 1976-77; owner, pres. Elegant Travel, Inc., Mission Viejo, Calif., 1977—; mem. pres. adv. bd. Mission Viejo Nat. Bank, 1982—. Bd. convocators Calif. Luth. Coll., Thousand Oaks, 1969-77; bd. dirs. Santa Paula Boys Club, 1971-74, Kern County Campfire Girls, 1976-77; v.p. Orange County Assn. for Retarded Citizens, 1978-79. HEW grantee, 1970. Mem. Am. Psychol. Assn., Western Psychol. Assn., Calif. Psychol. Assn., Assn. Retail Travel Agts., Am. Soc. Travel Agts., Soc. Advancement Travel Handicapped. Assn. Calif. Sch. Adminstrs., Phi Kappa Psi, Theta Alpha Phi. Republican. Lutheran. Clubs: Rotary (sec. 1978-79, v.p. 1979-80, pres. 1980-81) (Mission Viejo); Mission Viejo Country; Town Hall of Calif. Home: 25751 Knotty Pine Laguna Hills CA 92653 Office: 24000 Alicia Pkwy Suite 16 Gateway Center Mission Viejo CA 92691

KALAHAR, PAT ANN, marketing and communications executive; b. Fort Collins, Colo., Aug. 1, 1951; d. James N. and Florence B. Kalahar; m. James A. Jamison, Apr. 28, 1977 (div.). B.A. in Tech. Journalism, Colo. State U., Fort Collins, 1974. Info. specialist, tech. writer Tri-State Generation and Transmission Assn., Denver, 1978-80; tech. editor, dir. communications Willard Owens Assocs., Inc., Denver, 1980; self-employed, Golden, Colo., 1981; project mgr. U. Colo. Health Scis. Ctr., Denver, 1981-82; dir. mktg., tech. editor Muller Engring. Co., Inc., Lakewood, Colo., 1982-83; dir. bus. devel. BHCD Engrs. Inc., Denver, 1983—; cons. in field. Active Jefferson County Young Republicans. Recipient Best Staffer award Rocky Mountain News, 1969. Mem. Soc. Mktg. Profl. Services (cert. excellence 1983), Profl. Women in the Pub. Sector (award appreciation 1981), Nat. Assn. Female Execs. Lutheran. Contbr. articles to various publs. Home: 3355 S Flower #85 Lakewood CO 80226

KALB, BARBARA, psychologist; b. N.Y.C., Mar. 23, 1935; d. Joseph and Ruth Fliederbaum; B.A. summa cum laude with high honors in Psychology (acad. scholar), Hofstra U., 1973, Ph.D. in Psychology, 1978, postgrad. in public adminstrn., 1980—; children—Austin, Rodney, Todd. Counselor, Tempo Drug Rehab. Center, Woodmere, N.Y., 1969-71; cons. Biofeedback Research Inst., Los Angeles, 1971-76; research analyst Nassau County Dept. Sr. Citizens Affairs, Carle Place, N.Y., 1973-76; research scientist Nassau County Dept. Mental Health, Mineola, N.Y., 1977-80; clin. psychologist Martin Luther King Hosp. day treatment program, Los Angeles, 1980—; clin. psychologist Beverly Hills Community Clinic, Los Angeles; adj. asso. prof. Grad. Sch., C.W. Post Coll., L.I. U., 1978-80; prof. U. Humanistic Studies, Los Angeles, 1980—; research cons., 1976-80; pvt. practice biofeedback, clin. psychology, 1978-80, clin. psychology, 1980—. Sec., Long Beach Republican City Com.; Long Beach del. Nassau County Fedn. Rep. Women; committeewoman Long Beach Election Dist. 16. Cert. biofeedback clinician. Mem. Am. Psychol. Assn., Biofeedback Soc. Am., Am. Assn. Biofeedback Clinicians (charter), New Eng. Biofeedback Soc., Psi Chi. Jewish. Club: Hofstra U. Home and Office: 448 Bellflower Blvd Long Beach CA 90814

KALB, BENJAMIN STUART, television producer; b. Los Angeles, Mar. 17, 1948; s. Marcus and Charlotte K.; B.S. in Journalism, U. Oreg., 1969. Sportswriter, Honolulu Advertiser, 1971-76; traveled with tennis profl. Ilie Nastase, contbr. articles N.Y. Times, Sport Mag. and Tennis U.S.A., 1976; editor Racquetball Illustrated, 1978-82; segment producer PM Mag., 1983—; instr. sports in soc. U. Hawaii, 1974-75. Served with Hawaii Army N.G., 1970-75. Named Outstanding Male Grad. in Journalism, U. Oreg., 1969. Mem. Sigma Delta Chi (chpt. pres. 1968). Democrat. Jewish. Contbr. articles to mags. and newspapers. Home: 605 San Vicente Blvd Apt 104 Santa Monica CA 90402

KALBFLEISCH, KENNETH LEROY, veterinarian; b. Filer, Idaho, June 10, 1940; s. Lawrence Sherman and Golda Mae (Meyers) K.; student N.W. Nazarene Coll., Nampa, Idaho, 1958-61; D.V.M., Colo. State U., 1965; m. Glenda Louise Heppell, Aug. 18, 1961; children—Kurt LeRoy, Cindy Lou. Small animal veterinarian Ingleside Animal Hosp., Phoenix, 1965-66; mixed practice veterinarian Kindness Animal Hosp., Nampa, 1966-67; owner successor Kindness Small Animal Med. Center, Nampa, 1967—; veterinary, cons., founder vol. group Canyon County Pet Haven, humane soc.; speaker in field; mem. Mayor Nampa Com. Animal Control, 1977. Past pres. Camelot Water Assn., Nampa; Sunday sch. supt., chmn. fin. com. Ch. of Nazarene, Nampa; trustee Nampa Christian Schs. Mem. AVMA, Am. Animal Hosp. Assn., S.W. Vet. Assn., Idaho Vet. Assn., Idaho Acad. Vet. Medicine. Home: 1309 Camelot Dr Nampa ID 83651 Office: 1803 12th Ave Rd Nampa ID 83651

KALED, DAVID ALEC, clothing co. exec.; b. Sioux City, Iowa, Feb. 3, 1943; s. Abraham and Bertha (Ferris) K.; B.S., Iowa State U., 1965; M.B.A., U. Pa., 1967; m. Linda Caluya, May 12, 1974; children—Eric, Gregory. With Vertol div. Boeing Co., 1967; with Levi Strauss & Co., San Francisco, 1970—, dir. corp. planning, 1977-80, v.p. corp. planning and policy, 1980—; pres. K-Cal, Inc., San Rafael, Calif., 1979—. Served with U.S. Army, 1968-70. Mem. N.Am. Soc. Corp. Planning. Unitarian. Club: Stock Exchange. Office: 1155 Battery St San Francisco CA 94106

KALEJS, KARLIS, aerospace engineer; b. Tukums, Latvia, June 23, 1926; came to U.S., 1949, naturalized 1955; s. Janis and Olga (Smits) K.; m. Klitija Pilmanis, Apr. 5, 1953; children—Lija, Nora, Valdis. A.A., Los Angeles City Coll., 1952; B.S., U. So. Calif., 1962, M.S., 1965. Registered profl. mech. engr., Calif. Design engr. Weber Aircraft Co., Burbank, Calif., 1955-59; design engr. Marquardt Aircraft Corp., Van Nuys, Calif., 1959, N.Am. Aviation, Canoga Park, Calif., 1959-61; sr. design engr. Rocketdyne div. N.Am. Rockwell, 1961-65; mem. tech. staff Rocketdyne div. Rockwell Internat., 1965—. Pres. Peace Luth. Ch. of Los Angeles, 1969-72; v.p. Latvian Welfare Assn. So. Calif., 1970—; chmn. bd. Latvian Community Ctr. So. Calif., 1978—; bd. dirs. Baltic Am. Freedom League, 1981—. Served with USAF, 1948-49. Recipient Apollo Achievement award NASA, 1969; cert. of appreciation of contbn. to Apollo II, NASA and Rocketdyne, 1969; tech. utilization cert. George Marshall Space Ctr., 1972. Mem. AIAA, Latvian Engrs. Assn., Deutsche Gesellschaft fur Luft- und Raumfahrt. Club: Latvian Community. Home: 3822 Markridge Road La Crescenta CA 91214 Office: 6633 Canoga Ave Apt FA 03 Canoga Park CA 91304

KALENSCHER, ALAN JAY, physician and surgeon; b. Bklyn., July 9, 1926; s. Abraham and Julia (Horwitz) K.; B.S., Union Coll., Schenectady, 1945; M.D., N.Y. U., 1949; m. Hannah Blaufox, June 18, 1949; children—Judith Lynne, Mark Robert. Intern Morrisania City Hosp., N.Y.C., 1949-50; surg. resident Maimonides Med. Center, Bklyn., 1950-51, 54; asst., then chief resident Bronx Mcpl. Hosp. Center, 1954-56; mem. faculty surgery dept. Albert Einstein Coll. Medicine, 1956-59; practice medicine specializing in surgery, Sacramento, 1959—; attending surgeon Sacramento Med. Center and Clin. Faculty, 1970-75; sr. staff Sutter Community Hosps., Sacramento. Served with USNR, 1943-45, 51-53; ETO, Korea. Recipient citation N.Y.C. Cancer Com., 1959. Diplomate Am. Bd. Surgery, Nat. Bd. Med. Examiners (examiner 1957-59). Fellow Am. Soc. Contemporary Medicine and Surgery; mem. AAAS, AMA, Calif. Med. Assn., Sacramento County Med. Soc., Am. Soc. Abdominal Surgeons, Am. Diabetes Assn., Am. Heart Assn., Am. Occupational Med. Assn., Am. Mensa Ltd., Far West Ski Assn., League to Save Lake Tahoe. Office: 2 Scripps Dr Suite 208 Sacramento CA 95825

KALENSHER, BERNARD EARL, physicist, consultant; b. Beaumont, Tex., May 4, 1927; s. Alphonse and Julia (Richker) K. B.S., U. Tex., 1949, Ph.D., 1954. Sr. research engr. Jet Propulsion Lab., Pasadena, Calif., 1954-1960; sr. physicist Xerox Corp., Pasadena, 1961-76; sr. analytical physicist Phrasor Sci. Inc., Duarte, Calif., 1977—. Served with USNR, 1945-46. Mem. AIAA. Republican. Contbr. articles to profl. jours. Home: 551-B Linwood Ave Monrovia CA 91016 Office: 1536 Highland Ave Duarte CA 91010

KALIS, MURRAY, advertising agency executive, writer; s. Bernard and Bernis Kalis. B.S. in Communications, U. Ill., 1961; postgrad. Drake U., 1963-64, U. Iowa, 1964-70. Chmn. art dept. Midwestern Coll., Denison, Iowa, 1965-70; creative dir., v.p. Leo Burnett Advt., Chgo., 1970-81, Marsteller Advt., Los Angeles, 1982—. Served to 1st lt. U.S. Army, 1961-63. Recipient cert. of merit N.Y. Art Dirs. One Show; Bronze Lion, Cannes Festival; gold medal Chgo. Film Festival; intaglio art in permanent collection Phila. Mus. Art. Club: Creative. Author: Candida by Amy Voltaire, 1979; Love in Paris, 1980.

KALLAY, MICHAEL FRANK, II, med. devices co. mgr.; b. Painesville, Ohio, Aug. 24, 1944; s. Michael Frank and Marie Francis (Sage) K.; B.B.A., Ohio U., 1967; m. Irma Yolanda Corona, Aug. 30, 1975; 1 son, William Albert. Salesman, Howmedica, Inc., Rutherford, N.J., 1972-75, Biochem. Procedures/Metpath, North Hollywood, Calif.,

1975-76; surg. specialist USCI div. C. R. Bard, Inc., Billerica, Mass., 1976-78; western and central regional mgr. ARCO Med. Products Co., Phila., 1978-80; Midwest regional mgr. Intermedics, Inc., Freeport, Tex., 1980-82; Western U.S. mgr. Renal Systems, Inc., Mpls., 1982—. Mem. Am. Mgmt. Assn., Phi Kappa Sigma. Home and Office: 6515 Marengo Dr Anaheim Hills CA 92807

KALLENBERG, JOHN KENNETH, librarian; b. Anderson, Ind., June 10, 1942; s. Herbert August and Helen Elizabeth (Suttles) K.; A.B., Ind. U., 1964, M.L.S., 1969; m. Ruth Ann Barrett, Aug. 19, 1965; children—Jennifer Ann, Gregory John. Reader's adv. Fresno County Library, Fresno, Calif., 1965-67, librarian Fig Garden br., 1967-70, county librarian, 1976—; asst. dir. Santa Barbara Pub. Library, 1970-76; chmn. adv. council, bd. dirs. Calif. Authority for Systems and Services, 1978-80. Mem. ALA, Calif. Library Assn. (adminstrv. council 1975-77), Am. Soc. Public Adminstrn., Calif. County Librarians Assn. (pres. 1977). Presbyterian. Club: Kiwanis (treas. 1974-75, v.p. 1975-76 North Santa Barbara, dir. Fresno 1977-78, 79-80, v.p. 1980-81, pres. 1981-82). Office: Fresno County Free Library 2420 Mariposa St Fresno CA 93721

KALLGREN, JOYCE KISLITZIN, political science educator; b. San Francisco, Apr. 17, 1930; d. Alexander and Dorothea (Willett) K.; m. Edward E. Kallgren, Feb. 8, 1953; children—Virginia, Charles. B.A., U. Calif.-Berkeley, 1953, M.A., 1955; Ph.D., Harvard U., 1968. Jr. researcher to asst. researcher Ctr. Chinese Studies, U. Calif.-Berkeley, 1961-65; from lectr. to prof. polit. sci. U. Calif.-Davis, 1965—. Contbg. editor: China after Thirty Years, 1979; contbr. articles to profl. jours., chpts. to books; editor Jour. Asian Studies, 1980-83; research assoc. Ctr. Chinese Studies, U. Calif.-Berkeley, 1965—, chair, 1983—; editorial bd. Polit. Sci. Quar., Asian Survey, World Affairs; cons. Ford Found. awardee, 1978-79. Mem. Am. Polit. Sci. Assn., Assn. Asian Studies, China Council, Nat. Com. U.S./China Relations. Home: 28 Hillcrest Road Berkeley CA 94705 Office: Ctr Chinese Studies U Calif Berkeley CA

KALLMAN, PATRICIA RINCON, city official, planning consultant; b. El Paso, Apr. 29, 1942; d. Jose Ramon and Ruth (Torres) Rincon; m. Maxwell Morrison Kallman, Feb. 4, 1968 (div.); children—Lisa Ruth, Kimberly Jane. B.A. in Biol. Sci., U. Tex. El Paso, 1964; postgrad. U. Tex.-Arlington, 1967-68, M.Urban and Regional Planning (Denver Regional Council Govts. fellow), U. Colo.-Denver, 1978. Cert. pub. sch. tchr., Tex. Intern physician's office, 1962-63; elem. sch. tchr., El Paso, 1964-67; high sch. tchr., Ft. Worth, 1968-70; data input operator Colo. Nat. Bank, Denver, 1971; terminal operator Samsonite Corp., Denver, 1972; planning intern Planners ETC., Denver, 1978; planning intern, planner I, City of Arvada (Colo.), 1978; long range planner II, City of Thornton (Colo.), 1979—, long range planner, 1983—; planning cons. Vol. leadership trainer Family Community Leadership Program, Kellogg Found., Denver; mem. Main St. Redevel. Assn., Village E. Homeowners Assn.; pres. Planners Alumni Assn., U. Colo.-Denver. Mem. Am. Planning Assn., Colo. Council Local Energy Ofcls. (v.p.), Urban Design Forum (dirs.). Democrat. Roman Catholic. Editor Colo. Council Energy Ofcls. Network News. Office: 9500 Civic Center Dr Thornton CO 80229

KALMBACH, JOHN HENRY, oil co. exec.; b. Drexel Pa., Oct. 17, 1952; s. Charles Frederic and Elizabeth (Uhl) K.; B.S.E. with high honors, Princeton U., 1973; A.M. with distinction, Harvard U., 1975; m. Cecilia Elizabeth Rice, June 22, 1974; 1 dau., Hilary Elizabeth. Cons. geologist, Boston, 1976-78; geologist, credit exec. First Nat. Bank Boston, 1978-80; asst. to pres., corp. officer Pauley Petroleum, Inc., Los Angeles, 1980—; dir. Blacktop Materials Co., Sun Valley, Calif. NSF grad. fellow, 1973-76. Mem. Am. Inst. Mining Engrs., ASME, Geol. Soc. Am., Soc. Econ. Geologists, Am. Assn. Petroleum Geologists, Sigma Xi, Tau Beta Pi. Clubs. Jonathan, Petroleum (Los Angeles); Princeton Ivy; Harvard of Boston. Author: Notes on the Upper Crataceous Invertebrate Fauna of Haddonfield, 1969. Home: 20452 Califa St Woodland Hills CA 91367 Office: Pauley Petroleum Inc 10000 Santa Monica Blvd Los Angeles CA 90067

KALPAKIAN, SARKIS ARSHAG, trading company executive; b. Sudan, Dec. 6, 1922; came to U.S., 1968, naturalized, 1973; s. Arshag Sarkis and Nouritsa (Ekmekjian) K.; cert. Comboni Coll., Sudan, 1939; m. Dora Melikian, Dec. 5, 1954. With Shell Internat. Petroleum Co., 1962-68, sales mgr., Sudan and Saudi Arabia, 1965-68; dir. West Coast ops. Borneo Sumatra Trading Co., San Mateo, Calif., 1968—. Mem. West Coast Metal Importers Assn. (dir.). Republican. Armenian Orthodox. Club: Elks. Office: 30 W 39th Ave Suite 106 San Mateo CA 94403

KALT, HOWARD MICHAEL, public relations executive; b. Racine, Wis., June 11, 1943; s. Nat and Fay (Schwartz) K.; m. Barbara Lee Schowalter, Feb. 2, 1963; children—Jennifer, Jeffrey. B.S. in Journalism, U. Wis., 1964. Writer, Wis. State Jour., Madison, 1963-64; v.p. Gardner, Jones & Co., Chgo., 1964-74, v.p. communications Fred S. James & Co., Chgo., 1974-75; dir. communications The Marmon Group, Chgo., 1975-76, v.p. Ruder & Finn, San Francisco, 1976-77, Hoefer Amidei Assocs., San Francisco, 1977-79; v.p. communications ISU Cos., Inc., San Francisco, 1979-82; ptnr., co-owner Kalt & Hamlin Pub. Relations, San Francisco, 1982—. Life mem. Community Renewal Soc. Chgo.; mem. pub. affairs com. Bay Area Urban League. Mem. Pub. Relations Soc. Am. (accredited, best pub. relations program No. Calif. chpt. 1980, dir., v.p., chmn. fin. com. San Francisco chpt.), San Francisco Pub. Relations Round Table. Jewish. Club: The Family. Office: Kalt & Hamlin Pub Relations 100 Bush St Suite 1100 San Francisco CA 94104

KALTENBACH, RICHARD JOSEPH, engr.; b. Mt. Clemens, Mich., Aug. 26, 1930; s. Francis William and Agnes Bea (Frazho) K.; student U. Detroit, 1952-53; B.S., UCLA, 1956, postgrad., 1957-59; m. Elba Rodriguez, Apr. 21, 1961; children—Richard Louis, John Joseph. With Gilfillan Corp., ITT, Van Nuys, Calif., 1956—, now system tech. specialist. Served with USN, 1948-52; Korea. Mem. U.S. Air Force Assn., Tau Beta Pi. Home: 17522 Candia St Granada Hills CA 91344 Office: 7821 Orion Ave Van Nuys CA 91409

KALTSOUNIS, THEODORE, educator, school administrator; b. Albania, Feb. 15, 1930; s. Haralampos and Sophia (Pappas) K.; m. Maria Mesires, Aug. 25, 1963; children—Sophia T., George H., Andreas T. B.A., McPherson Coll., 1956; M.A., Wichita State U., 1959; Ph.D., U. Ill., 1961. Asst. prof. edn. SUNY-Oswego, 1961-65, prof., 1965-67; vis. prof. U. Wash. Coll. Edn., Seattle, 1967-68, assoc. prof., 1968-71, prof., 1971—, chmn. curriculum and instrn., 1979-81, assoc. dean, 1981—. Fulbright grantee, 1972-73. Mem. Am. Ednl. Research Assn., Nat. Council Social Studies (nat. pres. 1981), Phi Delta Kappa. Greek Orthodox. Lodge: Rotary. Author: Elementary School Curriculum, 1972; Teaching Social Studies in the Elementary School, 1979; State and Regions, 1982; also textbooks. Home: 5839 NE 181st St Seattle WA 98155 Office: U Wash 201 Miller Hall Seattle WA 98195

KAM, PAUL HING-KWOK, university administrator; b. Canton, China, Nov. 6, 1947; came to U.S., 1969; s. Scheng and Roly (Lo) K.; m. May Poon, Feb. 1, 1975; 1 dau., Vannessa. B.S. in Mktg. Mgmt., Calif. Poly. U., 1975, B.S. in Hotel and Restaurant Mgmt., 1977. Asst. dir. food service Azusa (Calif.) Pacific U., 1973-75, dir. food service, 1975-76, dir. aux. service, 1976-79, dir. gen. service, 1979—. Mem. Nat. Mgmt. Assn., Nat. Assn. of Coll. Aux. Services, Assn. Phys. Plant Adminstrs. of Univs. and Colls., Nat. Assn. Coll. Univ. Services, Pi Sigma Epsilon. Office: Highway 66 at Citrus Azusa CA 91702

KAMBACK, MARVIN CARL, psychologist; b. Yankton, S.D., July 15, 1939; s. Carl Melvin and Pauline Elizabeth (Albrecht) K.; children—Elizabeth, Christopher. B.A. in English, U. S.D., 1961, M.A. in Psychology, 1962; Ph.D., Vanderbilt U., 1965. Cert. psychologist, Md. Lic. psychologist, Wyo., Calif. Instr. U. S.D., Sioux Falls, 1962, asst. prof. dept. psychology, physiology, 1967-71; fellow neuro-psychology Stanford (Calif.) U. Med. Sch., 1966-67; psychol. intern Balt. City Hosps., 1971-74, family therapy intern, 1974-78; asst. prof. John Hopkins U. Med. Sch., Balt., 1971-74; assoc. prof. U. Md. Med. Sch., College Park, 1974-78; dir. Washakie County Mental Health Services, Worland, Wyo., 1978-79; dir. psychol. services Raleigh Hills (Calif.) Hosps., 1979—; clin. psychologist Behavior Therapy & Research Inst., Newport Beach, Calif., 1979—; dir. psychol. services Alcoholism Program, Advanced Health Services, Newport Beach, 1979—. NIMH fellow, Mem. Am. Psychol. Assn., AAAS, Md. Psychol. Assn., Rocky Mountain Psychol. Assn., Nat. Register Health Service Providers in Psychology, Soc. for Gen. Systems Research. Club: Rotary. Contbr. chpts. to books and articles to profl. jours. Home: 372 Calle Guaumas San Clemente CA 92672 Office: 1300 Bristol St North Newport Beach CA 92663

KAMEL, AHMED ALY, aerospace co. exec.; b. Alexandria, Egypt, Nov. 21, 1940; came to U.S., 1965, naturalized, 1979; s. Aly Ahmed and Habiba Amin (Abdo) K.; B.Sc. with 1st class honors, Alexandria U., 1963; M.S., Stanford U., 1965, Ph.D., 1970; m. Zeimab M. Housni, Feb. 12, 1976; children—Wael, Ayman, Waleed, Sameh. Teaching asst. Alexandria U., 1963-65; research asst. Stanford (Calif.) U., 1967-69, research asso., 1969-71; sr. engring. specialist Ford Aerospace & Communication Corp., Palo Alto, Calif., 1971-78, supr. orbit dynamics sect., system analysis dept., 1978—; cons. dept. aeros. and astronautics Stanford U., 1970-72. Egyptian Govt. fellow, 1965-70. Mem. AIAA, Am. Astron. Soc. Democrat. Moslem. Contbr. articles to profl. jours. Home: 723 Jura Way Sunnyvale CA 94087 Office: 3939 Fabian Way Palo Alto CA 94303

KAMERMAN, KENNETH M., accounting co. exec.; b. N.Y.C., June 21, 1931; B.S. in Textile Engring., U. Lowell, 1953; M.B.A., U. N.Mex., 1970; m. Pati Kleinhein, Dec. 21, 1957; children—Kim Patrice, Brett Padraic, Trent Irving. Mgr. customer relations Lytle Corp., Albuquerque, 1956-61; bus. mgr. Teaching Machines, Inc., Albuquerque, 1961-65; adminstrv. mgr. Westinghouse Learning Corp., Albuquerque, 1965-71; mgr. personnel and adminstrv. services Bellamah Corp., Albuquerque, 1972-78; v.p. Honor Corp., Albuquerque, 1979-81; firm adminstr. Rogoff, Diamond & Walker, Albuquerque, 1981-82; v.p. Battery Power Specialists, Albuquerque, 1982—; dir. Design Products, Inc., Learning Mgmt. Corp. Vice chmn. Republican Party Bernalillo County, (N.Mex.), 1978-81; chmn. Police Adv. Bd., Albuquerque, 1978-80; mem. central com. Republican Party N.Mex., 1976—; sec. bd. trustees Bernalillo County Mental Health/Mental Retardation Center, 1981—. Served with Supply Corps, USN, 1953-56. Republican. Home: 3305 Utah St NE Albuquerque NM 87110 Office: 2522 1st St NW Albuquerque NM 87102

KAMERMAN, MORTON, photo processing company executive; b. N.Y.C., Jan. 28, 1927; s. David and Martha (Chill) K.; B.S., NYU, 1948; J.D., St. John's U., 1952; m. Sheila Brody, Sept. 11, 1947; children—Nathan, Elliot, Laura. Admitted to N.Y. bar, 1953; mem. firm Kamerman and Kamerman, N.Y.C., 1948-60; partner Ira Haupt & Co., stock brokers, N.Y.C., 1960-63; v.p. Germaine Monteil Co., N.Y.C., 1963-69; now chmn. bd., chief exec. officer Technicolor, Inc., Los Angeles. Office: Technicolor Inc 2049 Century Park E Los Angeles CA 90067

KAMERSCHEN, ROBERT K., cosmetic company executive; b. 1936. B.S., Miami U., Ohio, 1957, M.B.A., 1958. Sr. v.p. mktg. Dunkin Donuts, 1973-76; pres., chief operating officer Chanel Inc., 1976-79, also sr. v.p. Norton Simons Inc., parent co.; pres., chief exec. officer Max Factor & Co., Hollywood, Calif., 1979—, also dir. Office: Max Factor & Co 1655 N McCadden Pl Hollywood CA 90028*

KAMHOLTZ, STANLEY, financial planning company executive; b. Bklyn., May 10, 1928; s. John S. and Anna (Schwartz) K.; m. Marilyn Heckler, May 31, 1953; children—Valerie Jean, David Stuart, Mark Lawrence, Terry Lynn, George Harrison. Student Ohio State U., 1948, Bklyn. Coll., 1950, UCLA, 1960, Coll. Financial Planning, 1980-81. Registered investment adviser. Mgr., Universal Advt. Agy., L.I., N.Y., 1952-53; chief insp., engring. liaison Republic Aviation, Farmingdale, N.Y., 1952-57, project adminstr., writer, 1957-59, tech. writer top secret projects, 1959-60; contract adminstr. Support Services Airesearch, Torrance, Calif., 1960-68; agt. John Hancock Ins. Co., Torrance, 1968-70, supr., 1971-74, supr., fin. planner, 1974-79; pres. Fin. Planning Assocs., Inc., Torrance, 1979—. Dist. commr. Boy Scouts Am., 1962-64, commr., 1964—. Served with USAF, 1946-49. Decorated Purple Heart. Mem. Calif. Assn. Underwriters (ethics chmn.), Am. Rocket Soc., Instrument Soc. Am., South Bay Estate Planning Assn., Internat. Assn. Fin. Planners, Inst. Cert. Fin. Planners, Writers' Guild, Nat. Assn. Life Underwriters, Air Force Assn., Aircraft Owners and Pilots Assn., Power Squadron. Republican. Jewish. Club: B'nai B'rith. Office: 2733 Pacific Coast Hwy Suite 305 Torrance CA 90505

KAMIENIECKI, SHELDON, political scientist, educator; b. Bklyn., Jan. 29, 1952; s. Joseph and Rachel (Supraski) K.; m. Eilza Sanasarian, Apr. 20, 1981. B.A., SUNY-Buffalo, 1974, M.A., 1976, Ph.D., 1978. Asst. prof. polit. sci. Calif. State Coll.-San Bernardino, 1978-81; asst. prof. polit. sci. U. So. Calif., Los Angeles, 1981—. Contbr. articles to profl. jours. Mem. Mem. Am. Polit. Sci. Assn., Midwest Polit. Sci. Assn., Policy Studies Orgn., Western Polit. Sci. Assn., So. Calif. Fedn. Scientists, Sierra Club. Author: Public Representation in Environmental Policymaking, 1980. Office: U So Calif Dept Political Science Los Angeles CA 90089

KAMIMOTO, DAVID ROSS, college admissions counselor; b. Gilroy, Calif., Jan. 5, 1956; s. Kay K. and Yoshiko (Tamura) K. B.A. in Psychology and Social Welfare, U. Calif.-Berkeley, 1978; M.S. in Counseling, San Francisco State U., 1980. Program coordinator Cogswell Poly. Coll., 1979-80; admissions counselor, U. Calif.-Santa Cruz, 1980—. Mem. Nat. Assn. Coll. Admissions Counselors, Western Assn. Coll. Admissions Counselors, Am. Personnel and Guidance Assn., Calif. Personnel and Guidance Assn., Calif. Coll. Personnel Assn., Asian-Pacific Am. Caucus, Phi Lambda Theta. Clubs: Calif. Alumni Assn., Calif. Alumni Band, Am. Field Services. Home: 115 Felix St Apt 8 Santa Cruz CA 95060 Office: Office of Admissions Cook House University of California Santa Cruz CA 95064

KAMITA, KATHERINE T., nurse; b. Honolulu, May 9, 1932; d. Takeo and Kimiko (Okamura) Shigeta; R.N., St. Francis Hosp., Honolulu, 1953; m. Kenneth Kamita, Aug. 6, 1955; children—Kevin, Keith, Kent, Kery, Stephanie. Hosp. and pvt. duty nurse, 1953-81; pvt. scrub nurse neurology dept. Straub Clinic, Honolulu, 1960; mem. nursing staff Castle Hosp., Kailua, Hawaii, 1966—, supr. operating room, 1979—. Mem. Assn. Operating Room Nurses. Roman Catholic. Home: 45-1106 Maka Pl Kaneoke HI 96744 Office: Castle Hosp Kailua HI 96734

KAMSKY, EARL CHARLES, human resource development specialist, educator, consultant; b. Chgo., Sept. 3, 1946; s. William and Anne Frieda (Gerstein) K.; B.A., Beloit Coll., 1969; M.S., U. Oreg., 1976; student U. Granada, 1965-66; postgrad. San Francisco Theol. Sem., 1969-70. Faculty mem. Wallace Sch. Community Service, Pub. Affairs, U. Oreg., Eugene, 1976-81; acad. dir. Sch. Internat. Tng., Ahmedabad, India, 1979; tng. devel. officer, City of Portland (Oreg.), 1981-83; human resource devel. specialist Portland Gen. Elec., 1983—; orgn. devel. cons., 1976—. Mem. Head Start adv. bd., 1977 Oreg. State Career Devel. Com., 1973. HEW grantee. Mem. Am. Soc. Tng. and Devel., Am. Pub. Works Assn., U.S.-China People's Friendship Assn. Democrat. Toured China in 1978. Office: 121 SW Salmon St TB 14 Portland OR 97204

KAN, JOSEPH RUCE, physicist, educator; b. Shanghai, China, Feb. 10, 1938; s. John H. S. and Mary A. (Chen) K.; m. Rosalind J. Chen; children—Christina, Deborah, Steven. Ph.D., U. Calif.-San Diego, 1969. Asst. prof. U. Alaska, Fairbanks, 1972-76, assoc. prof., 1976-81, prof. geophysics, 1981—. NSF research grantee, 1974—. Mem. Am. Geophys. Union, Am. Phys. Soc., AAAS. Contbr. papers to profl. publs. including: Jour. Geophysical Research, Jour. Plasma Physics, Solar Physics, Planetary and Space Sci., Geophysical Research Letters, Rev. of Space Physics. Office: Geophysical Inst Univ Alaska Fairbanks AK 99701

KANAGAWA, ROBERT KIYOSHI, citrus co. exec.; b. Sanger, Calif., Sept. 10, 1917; s. Yasoichi T. and Jitsuyo (Sumii) K.; B.B.A., Central Calif. Comml. Coll., 1939; m. Yukiye Nakamura, Feb. 12, 1944; children—Rodney M., Floyd A., Dallas W. Vice pres., treas. Kanagawa Citrus Co., Sanger, 1939-65, pres., 1965—; charter dir. Sequoia Community Bank, 1980—, chmn. bd., 1981—. Chmn. Agrl. Exhibit, Fresno Dist. Fair, 1953-58, Nations Christmas Tree Festival, Sanger, 1959, Sanger Grape Bowl Festival, 1964-74; bd. dirs. Valley Children's Hosp., 1968-72; bd. trustees St. Agnes Hosp., 1972-80, v.p., 1979, 81—; bd. trustees Fairmont Elem. Sch., 1954-58, Sanger Union High Sch., 1958-65, Sanger Unified Sch. Dist., 1965-69, Sanger Parks and Recreation Commn., 1963-73, Sanger Sr. Citizens Commn., 1975-79; mem. Republican. State Central Com., 1972-76; bd. dirs. 21st Dist. Agrl. Assn., 1970-79, pres., 1977; exec. bd. Sequoia council Boy Scouts Am., 1971—, v.p., 1979—; mem. Calif. Council Humanities in Public Policy, 1977-82; campaign chmn. Am. Heart Assn., 1981-82, v.p. Central Valley chpt., 1983—; bd. dirs., treas. Calif. Agrl. Mus., 1980—. Named Man of Yr., Sanger Dist. C. of C., 1968; recipient Golden Apple award Fresno County Sch. Adminstrs., 1976. Mem. Sanger Citrus Assn. (dir. 1961-72, pres. 1972), Orange Cove-Sanger Citrus Assn. (dir., v.p. 1973—), Sanger Japanese Am. Citizens League (charter, charter pres., dist. gov. 1977-78). Republican. Methodist. Club: Rotary of Sanger (pres. 1970-71, dist. gov. internat. 1974-75). Home: 16156 E McKinley Ave Sanger CA 93657 Office: 2720 Jensen Ave Sanger CA 93657

KANDAL, TERRY ROBERT, sociology educator; b. Chgo., Sept. 17, 1940; s. Terry Olaf and Gertrude Linda (Eich) K.; m. Nancy Jean Fried, Mar., 1965; 1 son, Joshua Terry; m. 2d, Anita Aurora Acosta, June 25, 1978. A.A., City Coll. San Francisco, 1963; A.B. in Sociology, U. Calif.-Berkeley, 1965, M.A., 1967, Ph.D., 1974. Lab. technician Reynolds Aluminum, McCook Ill., 1958-60; teaching asst. U. Calif.-Davis, 1965-66, Berkeley, 1966-67; assoc. prof. sociology Calif. State U.-Los Angeles, 1968—; cons. Mexican-Am. edn. commn. Los Angeles Bd. Edn., 1969-70; tchr. sociology U.S. Student Parole Program, Calif. Instn. for Women, Fontana, Calif. Instn. for Men, Chino, 1973-74. Vice pres. Community Adv. Council, Glassell Park Elem. Sch., Los Angeles United Sch. Dist. Comparative studies tng. program grantee U. Calif.-Berkeley, 1967-69; Calif. State U.-Los Angeles Found. grantee. Mem. Am. Sociol. Assn., Internat. Soc. Sociology of Knowledge, Midwest Sociol. Soc., Soc. Applied Spectroscopy. Office: Dept Sociology and Soc Work Calif State U 5157 State U Dr Los Angeles CA 90032

KANDELL, MARSHALL JAY, public relations counselor; b. Bklyn., Dec. 5, 1937; s. Harry and Mollie Rebecca (Remstein) K.; m. Judith Ann Zeve, May 20, 1961; children—Paul Bryon, Robin Pilar. A.A. in Journalism, Los Angeles City Coll., 1958; student Calif. State U.-Los Angeles, 1963-65. Cert. tchr. community colls., Calif. Pub. relations staff City of Hope (Calif.) Nat. Med. Ctr., 1966-68; v.p. Roger Beck Pub. Relations, Sherman Oaks, Calif., 1968-71; account supr. Laurence Laurie & Assoc., Los Angeles, 1971-72; community relations dir. St. Mary Med. Ctr., Long Beach, Calif., 1972-75; dir. pub. relations Cedars-Sinai Med. Ctr., Los Angeles, 1975; founder Marshall Jay Kandell Pub. Relations, Huntington Beach, Calif., 1976—; vis. faculty mem. Calif. State U.-Long Beach, mem. founding faculty Coastline Community Coll. Pres. Encino Jaycees, 1970-71; pres. Community Vol. Office, Long Beach, 1975-76; bd. dirs. Long Beach chpt. ARC, 1974-75; mem. Citizen's Adv. Commn. 1984 Olympic Games; v.p. Irvine Jewish Community, 1973; founding mem., v.p. Congregation B'nai Tzedek, Fountain Valley, Calif., 1976. Served in USAF, 1958-63. Recipient Disting. Service award Encino Jaycees, 1972; MacEachern award Acad. Hosp. Pub. Relations, 1973-74; Best written story award Press Club Greater Los Angeles, 1965. Mem. Pub. Relations Soc. Am., Counselors Acad., So. Calif. Soc. Hosp. Pub. Relations. Democrat. Jewish. Club: Pacific Coast Press. Contbr. numerous articles to profl. jours. Home: 18882 Deodar St Fountain Valley CA 92708 Office: 18700 Beach Blvd Huntington Beach CA 92648

KANDLER, PAUL ALFRED, opthalmologist; b. N.Y.C., Nov. 30, 1939; s. Paul Alfred and Edith Ann (Reichhard) K.; m. Mary Kathryn Gibbons, May 7, 1966; 1 dau., Kirsten Lynn. B.A., Johns Hopkins U., 1961; M.D., U. Md., 1965. Diplomate Am. Bd. Opthalmology. Commd. ensign U.S. Navy, 1962, advanced through grades to comdr., 1973; intern U.S. Naval Hosp., Gt. Lakes, Ill., 1965-66; med. officer in U.S.S. Delta, 1966-68; resident in ophthalmology U.S. Naval Hosp., Oakland, Calif., 1969-72; chief ophthalmology U.S. Naval Regional Med. Ctr., Gt. Lakes, 1972-74; ret., 1974; practice medicine specializing in opthalmology, Monterey, Calif., 1974—; asst. prof. surgery Chgo. Med. Sch., 1974-75. Fellow Am. Acad. Ophthalmology; mem. AMA. Club: Beach and Tennis (Pebble Beach, Calif.). Home: 3580 Edgefield Pl Carmel CA 93923 Office: 757 Pacific St Monterey CA 93940

KANDO, THOMAS MATHEW, sociology educator, author; b. Budapest, Hungary, Apr. 8, 1941; came to U.S., 1965; s. Jules and Ata Edith (Gorog) K.; m. Anita Chris Costa, June 30, 1973; children—Danielle, Leah. Student Union Coll., 1960-61; B.S., U. Amsterdam (Netherlands), 1965; M.A., U. Minn., 1967, Ph.D., 1969. Asst. prof. sociology U. Wis.-Stout, Menomonie, 1968-69; cons. Calif. Dept. Parks and Recreation, Sacramento, 1969-70; asst. prof. Calif. State U.-Sacramento, 1969-72, U. Calif.-Riverside, 1972-73; assoc. prof. Calif. State U.-Sacramento, 1973-77; assoc. prof. recreation and parks Pa. State U., 1978-79; prof. sociology and criminal justice Calif. State U.-Sacramento, 1979—. U. Amsterdam fellow, 1962-65; U. Minn. fellow, 1967; Fulbright fellow, 1960-61. Mem. AAUP (pres. local chpt. 1974—, pres. statewide 1976-78), Am. Sociol Assn., Internat. Sociol. Assn., Internat. Com. Leisure Research, Nat. Recreation and Parks Assn., Pacific Sociol. Assn., Popular Culture Assn., Internat. Com. on Sports Sociology, Athletic Congress, Phi Sigma Kappa. Republican. Author: Sex Change: The Achievement of Gender Identity Among Feminized Transsexuals, 1973; Leisure and Popular Culture in Transition, 1975, 80; Social Interaction, 1977; Sexual Behavior and Family Life in Transition, 1978; assoc. editor Pacific Sociol. Rev., 1973-78; Contemporary Sociology, 1975-79; contbr. numerous articles to profl. jours, popular mags. Home: 8267 Caribbean Way Sacramento CA 95826 Office: Dept Sociology Calif State U 6000 Jay St Sacramento CA 95819

KANE, BATHOLOMEW ALOYSIUS, librarian; b. Pitts., Nov. 2, 1945; s. Bartholomew A. and Ruth Mary (Loerlein) K.; m. Kathleen Anne Osborne; 1 dau., Leah. B.A. in Journalism, Pa. State U., 1967; M.L.S., U. Pitts., 1971. Dir., El Dorado (Kans.) Library, 1972-74; librarian Lanai (Hawaii) Library, 1975-79, Lilha (Hawaii) Library, 1979; librarian research and eval. services sect. State of Hawaii, 1979-82, state librarian, 1982—; instr. U. Hawaii at Manoa, 1983. Founder, pres. Lanai Community Services Council, 1975-79; founder, treas. Hawaii Visual Arts Consortium, 1977-83. Hazel McCoy fellow Friends of Library of Hawaii, 1970; Alumni Meml. scholar Pa. State U., 1963-67; Senatorial scholar Pa. Assembly, 1967. Mem. ALA, Hawaii Library Assn., Librarians Assn. Hawaii. Office: 809 8th Ave Suite G-5 Nonolulu HI 96816

KANE, CHARLES ARTHUR, neurologist; b. Boston, Oct. 2, 1917; s. Meyer Charles and Alice Louise (Richardson) K.; m. Mildred Elizabeth Johnson, Sept. 10, 1944; children—Charles A., Priscilla E., Richard J.; m. Rita Margaret Abbott, Nov. 10, 1966. A.B., Harvard U., 1939, M.D. cum laude, 1943. Diplomate Am. Bd. Psychiatry and Neurology. Intern, Harvard U.-Boston City Hosp., 1943; resident in medicine Western Res. U., 1947; chief resident in neurology VA Hosp., Bronx, N.Y., 1948-51; instr. neurology Cornell U., 1948-51; asst. prof., then assoc. prof. and prof. neurology Boston U., 1951-66; instr. neurology Harvard U., 1951-66; chief of neurology, chmn. med. records research com., mem. instnl. rev. bd. Kaiser-Permanente, Hayward, Calif., 1961—. Exec. com., med. advisor Los Amigos de las Americas, 1968-80. Served to maj. M.C., AUS, 1944-46. Named Citizen Ambassador, Pres. Eisenhower, 1983. Fellow Am. Acad. Neurology (past pres.); mem. Am. Epilepsy Soc., Am. Heart Assn., World Fedn. Neurology, San Francisco Neurol. Soc. (pres.-elect), Sigma Xi, Alpha Omega Alpha. Democrat. Roman Catholic. Club: Las Positas Golf (Livermore, Calif.). Contbr. articles med. jours., chpts. in med. textbooks. Home: 614 Thornhill Rd Danville CA 94526 Office: 27400 Hesperian Blvd Hayward CA 94545

KANE, DAVID HOWARD, educator; b. Honolulu; s. Saburo and Kiyono (Watanabe) Shigekane; A.A., Los Angeles City Coll., 1960; B.B.A., Woodbury U., 1955; B.A., Los Angeles State U., 1962; M.A., Columbia U., 1965. Exec. sec., dir. community services Los Angeles County, 1955-58; tchr. bus. edn. Los Angeles City Schs., 1962-64, 65-68; instr. Los Angeles S.W. Coll., 1968; asso. prof. bus. Foothill Coll., Los Altos Hills, Calif., 1968—. Served with U.S. Army, 1951-53; Japan. Mem. Internat. Soc. Bus. Edn., Nat. Bus. Edn. Assn., Am. Bus. Communications Assn., Calif. Bus. Edn. Assn., Am. Vocat. Assn., Western Bus. Edn. Assn., Phi Gamma Kappa, Kappa Delta Pi, Gamma Rho Tau, Delta Pi Epsilon. Republican. Contbr. articles to profl. jours.; co-author: Proofreading Precision, 1982. Named Bus. Tchr. of Yr., Adminstrv. Mgmt. Soc., 1973; recipient Teaching Excellence award Foothill Community Coll., 1975. Home: 4029 Oella Ct San Jose CA 95124 Office: Foothill College 12345 El Monte Rd Los Altos Hills CA 94022

KANE, ELIZABETH VERONICA, educator; b. Kildare, Ireland, Apr. 5, 1944; came to U.S., 1965, naturalized, 1973; s. Patrick Anthony and Johanna Josephine (Murphy) K.; 1 son, Patrick D. B.A., St. Mary's Coll., New Orleans, 1971; M.R.E., Notre Dame Sem., New Orleans, 1976; postgrad. U. San Francisco, 1978—. Cert. tchr., Calif., Alaska. Tchr. high sch. English and typing, Ireland, 1962-65; tchr. elem. sch., Miss. and La., 1965-72; tchr., parish dir. religious edn. St. John's Elem. Sch., Gulport, Miss., 1972-77; tchr. St. Roberts Sch., San Bruno, Calif., 1977-80; individualized ednl. specialist N.W. Arctic Sch. Dist., Kotzebue, Alaska, 1980-81; tchr. elem. sch. Noorvik (Alaska) schs., 1981—. Mem. IRA, Alaska State Reading Assn., NEA, Assn. Supervision and Curriculum Devel., Smithsonian Inst. Democrat. Roman Catholic. Club: Encore Travel. Developed systems for individualized teaching. Home: PO Box 36 Noorvik AL 99763 Office: Noorvik Elementary School Noorvik AK 99763

KANE, FLORA, investment cons.; b. Lyon, France, Apr. 2, 1948; d. Henry Greenbaum and Rochelle (Selmanowicz) Greenbaum; dental technician degree with honors, UCLA, 1967; degree in paralegal bus. orgns., 1980; m. Alan Steven Kane, Mar. 15, 1969 (div. Apr. 1977); 1 dau., Dawn Elizabeth-Marie. Fin. coordinator for physician, 1968-69; owner, office mgr. Ditto of Calif., Inc., clothing mfrs., 1969-75; cons. in fin. and investments, Woodland Hills, Calif., 1975—; notary public, 1980—; real estate agt., So. Calif., 1980—. Active Orphans Aid Soc., Tel Aviv, 1975-77. Lic. real estate agt. Mem. San Fernando Valley Bd. Realtors, Exec. Female, Internat. Assn. Med. Assistance to Travellers, Save Children Fedn., Am. Entrepreneurs Assn., Acad. Magical Arts, Nat. Notary Assn. Republican. Jewish. Address: 3410 San Martin Circle Palm Springs CA 92262

KANE, FRANCIS XAVIER, aerospace engineer; b. Phila., Dec. 12, 1918; s. John Joseph and Elinor Marie (Houlihan) K.; m. Virginia C. Cegelski, Oct. 3, 1946; 1 dau., Kathleen N. Kane Dove. B.S., U.S. Marine Acad., 1943; M.A., Georgetown U., 1949, Ph.D., 1960. Served to col. U.S. Air Force, 1943-70; mgr. requirements analysis TRW Def. and Space Systems Group, Redondo Beach, Calif., 1970-81; dir. aerospace concepts Rockwell Internat., El Segundo, Calif., 1981—; initiated space programs NAVSTAR; cons. U.S. Air Force; tchr. Cath. U., UCLA, Pepperdine U. Decorated Legion of Merit with oak leaf cluster. Assoc. fellow AIAA; mem. U.S. Strategic Inst., Internat. Inst. Strategic Studies, Los Angeles Council Fgn. Relations, Air Force Assn. (past dir. chpt.). Club: Springs (Rancho Mirage). Author: The Fateful Ends and Shades of SALT, Past .. Present .. and Yet to Come?, 1979; contbr. numerous publs. to profl. jours. Office: 2230 E Imperial Hwy El Segundo CA 90245

KANE, JOHN LAWRENCE, JR., judge; b. Tucumcari, N.Mex., Feb. 14, 1937; s. John Lawrence and Dorothy Helen (Bottler) K.; B.A., U. Colo., 1958; J.D., U. Denver, 1961; m. George Ann Berger, Oct. 17, 1969; children—Molly, Meghan, Sally, John Pattison. Bar: Colo. 1961. Dep. dist. atty. Adams County, Colo., 1961-63, pub. defender, 1964-67; dep. dir. Peace Corps, Calcutta, India, 1967-69; ptnr. firm Holme, Roberts & Owen, Denver, 1970-77; judge U.S. Dist. Ct., Denver, 1977—; instr. Met. State U., Denver, 1972-75; adj. prof. law U. Denver Coll. Law, 1978—; lectr. Colo. Continuing Legal Edn. Fellow Internat. Acad. Trial Lawyers, Internat. Soc. Barristers, Cath. Lawyers Guild (pres. elect 1977), Am. Law Inst., Union Internationale des Avocats. Club: Cactus. Contbr. legal jours. Office: Room C-218 US Courthouse Denver CO 80294

KANEKO, RYOJI LLOYD, training administrator; b. Los Angeles, Apr. 11, 1951; s. Hayao and Yoshiko Kaneko. B.A. in English, Calif. State U.-Long Beach, 1974. Marching instr. Third Generation Drum and Bugle Corps, Los Angeles, 1973-75; trainer, supr. Teledyne-Geotronics, Long Beach, Calif., 1975-79; tng. coordinator, supr. tng. and procedures, tng. adminstr. Hughes Aircraft Co., El Segundo, Calif., 1979—; guest lectr., speaker, cons. in field. Deacon, chmn. stewardship dept., exec. bd. mem.-at-large, mem. chancel choir Bellflower (Calif.) First Christian Ch. Mem. Am. Soc. Tng. and Devel. (cert. outstanding service 1982, editor Los Angeles Interchange newsletter), All-Am. Judges Assn., Pacific Coast Field Bank Assn. Club: Calif. State U.-Long Beach Alumni Assn. Columnist Drum Corps News, contbr. articles to various gen. interest publs. Home: 906 Torrance Blvd Apt 5 Redondo Beach CA 90277 Office: 2000 El Segundo Blvd MS E4/P156 El Segundo CA 90245

KANTOR, ROBERT EDWIN, graduate school president, psychologist; b. N.Y.C., June 6, 1915; s. Samuel and Jenny Kantor; m. Harriet Sayer, Sept. 25, 1940; m. 2d Sharon Dudlettes, May 25, 1980; children—Donald Macfarlane, Judith Kantor Vining, Robin Renée. A.B., Bklyn. Coll., 1935; M.A., U. Calif.-Berkeley, 1953, Ph.D., 1956. Research fellow Coll. Physicians and Surgeons, Columbia U., 1938-39; staff psychologist N.Mex. State Hosp., Las Vegas, 1940-43; chief clin. psychologist, dir. tng. and research for psychology interns VA, Menlo Park, Calif., 1946-51; pvt. practice clin. psychology, Palo Alto, Calif., 1951-74; program dir., chmn. mental hygiene com. Santa Clara County (Calif.), 1959-60; research assoc., cons. Palo Alto (Calif.) Med. Research Found., 1961-63; research fellow, bd. dirs., Mental Research Inst., Palo Alto, 1963-68; sr. staff scientist Office of Edn. grantee Stanford Research Inst. Internat., Menlo Park., 1968-71; pres. Multi-Media Prodns. Inc., Mountain View, Calif., 1972-82; pres. Pacific Grad. Sch., 1975—; mem. clin. faculty Stanford U. Med. Sch., 1960-61, clin. prof. psychology, dept. dermatology, 1979—; vis. faculty dept. art Stanford U., 1966-67. Served with U.S. Army, 1942-46. Mem. Am. Psychol. Assn., Calif. State Psychol. Assn., Am. Sociol. Assn., Soc. Projective Techniques. Clubs: Bohemian (San Francisco); Stanford Faculty. Author: Reactive and Process Schizophrenia, 1966; (with others) Contemporary School Psychology, 1970; contbr. articles to profl. jours.; author numerous audio-visual programs. Home: 340 Stevick Dr Atherton CA 94025 Office: 431 Burgess Dr Menlo Park CA 94025

KAO, RICHARD HSIUNG-FEI, marketing educator; b. Hupei, Taiwan, June 1, 1941; s. Yuh H. and Yin (Wu) K.; m. Nancy Wen-Bih, Sept. 6, 1969; 1 child, Yuh-Ting. B.B.A., Nat. Chengchi U., 1964; M.B.A., Mich. State U., 1971; Ph.D. in Bus. Adminstrn., U. Mich., 1978. Assoc. dir. Metal Indsl. Research Labs., Taipei, Taiwan, 1971-75; assoc. prof. Nat. Chengchi U., Taipei, Taiwan, 1978-80; assoc. prof. mktg. Calif. State U.-Los Angeles, 1981—. Mem. Am. Mktg. Assn., Acad. Internat. Bus., Chinese Inst. Mgmt. Sci., Beta Gamma Sigma (hon.). Office: 5151 State University Dr Los Angeles CA 90032

KAPCSANDY, LOUIS ENDRE, building products executive, engineering consultant; b. Budapest, Hungary, June 5, 1936; s. Lajos Endre and Margit Ilona (Toth) K.; m. Roberta M. Henson, Jan. 25, 1964; 1 son, Louis. B.S. in Chem. Engring., Tech. U. Budapest, 1956; student U. San Francisco Law Sch., 1961-63; M.Petroleum Tech., U. Calif., Berkeley, 1966. Profl. football player San Diego Chargers, 1961-65; western regional mgr. Norton Co., 1965-72; product mgr. Koch Engring., 1972-74; v.p., gen. mgr. Flow Industries, 1974-78; pres., chief exec. officer Fentron Bldg. Products, Inc., Seattle, 1978—; chem. engring. cons. Coach Mercer Island Youth Soccer; mem. United for Wash. Served with AUS, 1959-61. Fellow Am. Inst. Chem. Engrs.; mem. TAPPI, Am. Chem. Soc., Archtl. Aluminum Mfrs. Assn., Single Insulated Glass Mfg. Assn. Republican. Roman Catholic. Clubs: Rotary, Bellevue Athletic, Rainier. Research on high vacuum fractionation of crude oil, high pressure purification of hydrogen, azeotropic distillation of Vitamin E, computer controlled waterjet slitting of corrugated paper, cezium ion exchange with molecular sieves. Office: 2801 NW Market St Seattle WA 98117

KAPLAN, BARRY ROBERT, podiatrist; b. Bklyn., Aug. 29, 1938; s. Louis and Ruth (Sunshine) K.; student L.I. U., 1956-58; Dr. Podiatric Medicine, Ohio Coll. Podiatric Medicine, 1962; m. Nancy Mardick, Jan. 25, 1979; children—Abbie, Stacey, Alyssa. Surg. resident Ohio Coll. Podiatric Medicine, Cleve., 1962-63, clin. instr., 1963-64; pvt. practice podiatric medicine, Cleve., 1963-69, Phoenix, 1970—; chief podiatric surg. dept. Community Hosp. Phoenix, 1975-77. Active, Jewish Community Center, Temple Beth Israel, 1970—. Mem. Ariz. Podiatry Assn. (v.p.), Acad. Ambulatory Foot Surgery (sec.), Am. Podiatry Assn. Club: Mason. Office: 1901 W Glendale Ave Phoenix AZ 85015

KAPLAN, GARY, exec. recruiter; b. Phila., Aug. 14, 1939; s. Morris and Minnie (Leve) K.; B.A. in Polit. Sci., Pa. State U., 1961; m. Linda Ann Wilson, May 30, 1968; children—Michael Warren, Marc Jonathan, Jeffrey Russell. Tchr. biology N.E. High Sch., Phila., 1962-63; coll. employment rep. Bell Telephone Labs., Murray Hill, N.J., 1966-67; supr. recruitment and placement Univac, Blue Bell, Pa., 1967-69; pres. Electronic Systems Personnel, Phila., 1969-70; staff selection rep. Booz, Allen & Hamilton, N.Y.C., 1970-72; mgr. exec. recruitment M&T Chems., Rahway, N.J., 1972-74; dir. exec. recruitment IU Internat. Mgmt. Corp., Phila., 1974-78; v.p. personnel Crocker Bank, Los Angeles, 1978-79; mng. v.p., partner Korn/Ferry Internat., Los Angeles, 1979—. Bd. dirs. Vis. Nurse Assn. Los Angeles. Served to capt. Adj. Gen. Corps, U.S. Army, 1963-66. Mem. Hollywood Radio and TV Soc. Home: 5150 Solliden Ln La Canada CA 91011 Office: Korn/Ferry Internat 1900 Ave of Stars Los Angeles CA

KAPLAN, HERMAN, psychiatrist, educator; b. N.Y.C., Aug. 17, 1928; s. Isaac and Goldie (Rubin) K.; A.B., N.Y. U., 1948, D.D.S. (N.Y. State scholar), 1953; M.D. (Armed Forces scholar), SUNY, 1963, postgrad., 1972; m. Joyce Esther Citron, Oct. 27, 1956; children—Lori Beth, David Elliott, Douglas Steven. Intern, San Francisco Gen. Hosp., 1963-64; resident oral surgery VA Hosp., Buffalo, 1957-59; practice medicine specializing in oral surgery, Oakland, Calif., 1964-71; resident in psychiatry Presbyn. Hosp., Pacific Med. Center, San Francisco, 1972-75; practice medicine specializing in psychiatry, Lafayette, Calif., 1975—; asso. prof. oral surgery U. Pacific Sch. Dentistry, San Francisco, 1964-72, asso. clin. prof. medicine, 1972-80, adj. prof. diagnostic scis., 1980—, dir. student health service, 1970—; cons. oral surgery Fresno Gen. Hosp., 1965-68, Mt. Zion Hosp., San Francisco, 1965—, Cowell Hosp., U. Calif.-Berkeley, 1967—, WHO, 1979-80; cons. psychsomatic problems of dentistry; cons. Facial Pain Research Ctr., 1982—. Bd. dirs. No. Calif. Diabetes Assn., 1973-77. Served to lt. comdr. USNR, 1953-56; capt. Res. Fellow Acad. Dentistry Internat.; mem. AMA, AAUP, Am. Psychiat. Assn., AAAS, Calif. Med. Assn., N.Y. Acad. Scis., Alameda Contra Costa Med. Soc., Am., No. Calif., East Bay psychiat. assns., Alpha Omega Alpha, Omicron Kappa Upsilon. Author: Handbook on Physical Diagnosis in Dentistry, 1967; Handbook on Emergency Medical Conditions in Dentistry, 1968. Home: 38 Arroyo Dr Moraga CA 94556 Office: 3688 Mt Diablo Blvd Lafayette CA 94549

KAPLAN, IRVING EUGENE, data processor; b. N.Y.C., Nov. 29, 1946; s. Maurie C. and Celia M. (Chasin) K.; m. Suzanne Folsom, July 30, 1946; 1 dau., Robyn Ann. B.S. in Math., CCNY, 1967; M.B.A. in Mgmt., Rochester Inst. Tech., 1978. Data processor Xerox Corp., Rochester, N.Y., 1973-78; developer minicomputer strategy Crocker Nat. Bank, San Francisco, 1979; mgr. systems and programming Rolm Corp., Santa Clara, Calif., 1979—. Served to capt. U.S. Army, 1968-73. Decorated Bronze Star, Air medal, Army Commendation medal. Office: Old Ironsides Dr Santa Clara CA 95050

KAPLAN, JOSEPH M., safety council administrator; b. Cleve., May 29, 1914; s. Edward and Mamie Kaplan; m. Henrietta Lurie, Mar. 30, 1941; children—Paul Dana, Drew Alan. B.A., UCLA, 1935; M.A., Harvard U., 1938. Cert. hazard control mgr. Internat. Hazard Control Mgr. Certification Bd. With Greater Los Angeles chpt. Nat. Safety Council, 1939—, pres., 1979—; cons. White House Conf. Traffic Safety. Nat. chmn. Conf. State and Local Safety Orgn.; bd. dirs. March of Dimes, So. Calif. War Manpower Conservation Program. Served U.S. Army, World War II. Recipient award of honor Assn. Safety Councils, 1973; named Assn. Exec. of Yr., So. Calif. Soc. Assn. Execs., 1979. Mem. Am. Soc. Safety Engrs., Inst. Traffic Engrs., Assn. Expn. Mgrs., So. Calif. Indsl. Safety Soc., Calif. Assn. Safety Councils, Vets. Safety Internat. (pres. 1976), Am. Soc. Assn. Execs. (Key award 1974), Inst. Safety and Systems Mgmt. Club: Rotary. Home: 8871 St Ives Dr Los Angeles CA 90069 Office: 616 S Westmoreland Ave Los Angeles CA 90005

KAPLAN, LAWRENCE DAVID, linguistics educator; b. Los Angeles, Jan. 23, 1950; s. Nathan and Barbara Ida (Hade) K. A.B., U. Calif.-Berkeley, 1971; M.A., San Diego U., 1974, Ph.D., 1979. Inupiaq Eskimo linguist Alaska Native Lang. Ctr., U. Alaska, Fairbanks, 1974—, asst. prof. linguistics, 1979—. Mem. Linguistics Soc. Am., Inuit Studies Assn. (editorial bd. jour. 1980—). Home: PO Box 82003 Fairbanks AK 99708 Office: Alaska Native Lang Center U Alaska Fairbanks AK 99701

KAPLAN, MARJORIE ANN, educational adminstrator; b. Bronx, N.Y., Apr. 10, 1940; d. William B. and Laura L. Pashkow; m. Marvin R. Kaplan, Aug. 12, 1962 (dec.); children—Eliot L., Mara E. B.A., Smith Coll., 1962; M.A., Ariz. State U.-Tempe, 1974, Ph.D., 1980. Tchr., coordinator fed. projects, prin. Washington Sch. Dist., Phoenix, 1972-80; asst. supt. Paradise Valley Unified Sch. Dist., Phoenix, 1981—; adj. prof. Ariz. State U., Tempe, 1980—. Mem. Am. Assn. Sch. Adminstrs., Assn. Supervison and Curriculum Devel., Phi Beta Kappa, Phi Delta Kappa. Office: 3012 E Greenway Rd Phoenix AZ 85032

KAPLAN, PETER LOUIS, psychologist; b. Miami, Fla., Jan. 24, 1949; s. Seymour and Marvelle Beatrice Kaplan; B.S., U. Fla., 1970; M.A., Fla. Atlantic U., 1973; Ph.D., Colo. State U., 1977; m. Helen Sobel, Nov. 25, 1970; children—Ben, Joshua. Vis. asst. prof. dept. psychology U. B.C., Vancouver, Can., 1977-78; Nat. Inst. Neurol. Communicative Diseases and Stroke fellow, dept. psychology Colo. State U., 1978-80, instr., 1981-82; psychol. therapist Larimer County Mental Health Center, Ft. Collins, Colo., 1981—; pvt. practice clin. psychology, Ft. Collins, 1981—; cons. Larimer County Sheriff's Dept. Mem. AAAS, Am. Psychol. Assn., Fedn. Am. Scientists, Sigma Xi. Democrat. Jewish. Home: 1417 Beech Ct Fort Collins CO 80521 Office: Dept Psychology Colo State U Fort Collins CO 80521

KAPLAN, PHILIP IRWIN, publishing company graphics executive; b. San Diego, Aug. 2, 1936; s. Joseph Jack and Claire Louise (Klaskin) K.; B.A. in Art, San Diego State U., 1958; student Art Inst. Chgo., 1959, Ill. Inst. Tech., 1960; m. Martha Lynn Ray, Nov. 30, 1969 (div.); 1 son, Neal Bennett. Book designer Harper & Row, Evanston, Ill., 1959-61; art dir. Playboy Mag., books, Chgo., 1961-67; art dir. Atlanta Mag., 1967-70; owner, art dir. Philip Kaplan Graphic Design, San Diego, 1970-75; graphics dir. Archtl. Digest, Bon Appetit mags., Knapp Communications Corp., Los Angeles, 1975-77, v.p. graphics, 1976-83, v.p. internat. editorial 1983—. Served with AUS, 1955-63. Recipient awards Art Dirs. Clubs of N.Y., Los Angeles Chgo., Soc. Typog. Arts (Chgo.), Soc. Publ. Designers, N.Y.C., 1977-78, award for visual excellence Columbia Sch. Journalism, 1978. Mem. Am. Inst. Graphic Arts, Soc. Publ. Designers, Art Dirs. Club Atlanta (Best of Show award 1978), Art Dirs. Club San Diego (award), 8th AF Hist. Soc. Designer: Minamata, book of photog. documenting indsl. pollution affects in Japan, 1974; author: One Last Look, 1983. Office: Knapp Communications 5900 Wilshire Blvd Los Angeles CA 90036

KAPLAN, RALPH JOSEPH, internat. affairs specialist, writer, cons.; b. Riga, Russia, Nov. 22, 1912; came to U.S., 1950; naturalized, 1956; s. Joseph and Doris K.; m. Aug. 30, 1967. M.A. in Philosophy Riga U., 1934; Ph.D. in Edn. and Human Relations, NYU, 1954; postgrad. in lang., psychology and polit. sci. Cambridge (Eng.) U., 1944. Founder, dean Universal Coll., Tel Aviv, 1938-50; prof. edn. NYU Sch. Edn., 1950-54, cons. Ctr. Human Relations Studies and Communication, 1950-54; writer, columnist and radio commentator on internat. fin., indsl. and econ. subjects, 1950—, author syndicated column Ralph Kaplan Reports, 1936—, fgn. news editor Radio KIEV, Los Angeles, 1962—; econ. cons. on multinat. bus. 1950—; economist, head dept. econ. research, devel. cons. to mgmt. Beverly Hills Bancorp. (Calif.), 1971-74; pres. Kaplan Communications, internat. relations cons., Los Angeles, 1970—; internat. affairs analyst Intermountain Network, 1964-68; U.S. corr. Broadcasting Corp. China, Taiwan, 1965-67; lectr. UCLA-Extension Sch. Journalism, 1965-82; mem. faculty Hebrew Union Coll., Los Angeles, 1968—; writer, producer, narrator Focus On Eichman documentary Sta. KCOP TV, Los Angeles, and nat. syndication, 1964; hist. cons. to Let My People Go, TV documentary (George Foster Peabody award 1966), 1965, 66; ann. lecture tours throughout U.S.; communications cons. Davidson Conf. Ctr., U. So. Calif., 1982—; condr. seminars, lectr. on countering appeal of Communism, U.S. Army Inst. Mil. Assistance, Ft. Bragg, N.C., 1968. Mem. Los Angeles County (Calif.) Hosp. Commn., 1970-73, 80-83; mem. Calif. Postsecondary Edn. Commn., 1981-86; mem. Los Angeles Mayor's Council on Internat. Vis. and Sister Cities, 1968—, chmn., 1969-71; mem. community relations com. Jewish Fedn. Council Greater Los Angeles; mem. exec. bd. Pacific S.W. region Anti-Defamation League B'nai B'rith; mem. Am. Jewish Com. Mem. Internat. Inst. Strategic Studies (London), Nat. Acad. TV Arts and Scis., Consular Press Orgn. (formerly Fgn. Govts. Press Assn.) founder; (life mem.), Le Grand Conseil L'Academie du Vin (grand conseiller) (Bordeaux), AFTRA, Radio and TV News Assn. So. Calif., Phi Delta Kappa.

KAPLAN, RICHARD ALAN, defense and strategic affairs specialist; b. San Francisco, Mar. 20, 1951; s. Murray M. and Beatrice (Ray) K. A.A., Canada Coll., 1973; B.A., San Francisco State U., 1975; B.A., 1976, M.A., 1981. Mng. editor Jour. Contemporary Revolutions, 1974-76; New Labor Rev., 1976-78; researcher Dept. War Studies, U. London King's Coll., 1978-80; def. and strategic affairs specialist Com. on Armed Conflict, Am. br. Internat. Law Assn., N.Y.C., 1981-82; mem. nat. adv. bd. Am. Security Council, Washington, 1978-83; spl. advisor U.S. Congl. Adv. Bd., 1982-83. Mem. SSS Appeal Bd. (eastern jud. dist.), State of Calif.; apptd. Nat. Def. Exec. Res. Fed. Emergency Mgmt. Agy., Washington. Served with U.S. Army, 1968. Recipient cert. Appreciation U.S. Congl. Adv. Bd., 1982. Fellow Royal Geog. Soc., Inter-Univ. Seminar Armed Forces and Soc., Internat. Inst. Humanitarian Law; mem. Internat. Inst. Strategic Studies, Royal United Services Instn. Defence Studies, Royal Inst. Internat. Affairs, Brit. Atlantic Com., Brit. Hist. Assn., U.S. Strategic Inst., U.S. Naval Inst., Air Force Assn., Assn. U.S. Army, Internat. Law Assn., Am. Soc. Internat. Law, Am. Security Council, Am. Def. Preparedness Assn. Democrat. Jewish.

KAPLAN, RICHARD EMANUEL, aeronautics and astronautics engineer; b. Phila., July 4, 1938; s. Albert and Eleanor (Savadove) K.; m. Mimi J. Greenfield, Aug. 14, 1960; children—Hilary Jane, David Michael. S.B. in Aeronautics and Astronautics, MIT, 1961, M.S., 1961, Sc.D., 1964. Asst. prof. aerospace engring U. So. Calif., Los Angeles, 1964-68, assoc. prof., 1968-74, prof., 1974—, dir. systems simulation lab., 1969-71, interim dir. engring. computer lab., 1982—. Guggenheim fellow, 1971-72; Fulbright vis. lectr., 1971-72, 75-76. Mem. Am. Phys. Soc., AIAA. Home: 2717 Arizona Ave 1 Santa Monica CA 90404 Office: PHE 202 U So Calif CA 90089

KAPLAN, RICHARD JAY, research psychologist; b. Hartford, Conn., Sept. 12, 1930; s. Leon S. and Minnie (Glass) K.; m. Vera Servi, June 23, 1954; m. 2d., Adrienne Kranz, June 17, 1961; children—Carisa, Seth. B.A., Williams Coll., 1953; M.A., Columbia U., 1954; Ph.D., UCLA, 1957. Lic. psychologist, Calif. With Litton Industries, Beverly Hills, Calif., 1957-59, TRW, Canoga Park, Calif., 1959-61, System Devel. Corp., Santa Monica, Calif., 1961-65; psychologist Rand Corp., Santa

Monica, Calif., 1965-71, ops. research specialist, 1981—; research scientist U. Mich., Ann Arbor, 1971-81. Mem. Am. Psychol. Assn., Am. Acad. Polit. and Social Sci., Assn. Computing Machinery, Human Factors Soc., AAAS, Sigma Xi. Contbg. author articles in field. Home: 11701 Texas Ave Apt 101 Los Angeles CA 90025 Office: Rand Corp 1700 Main St Santa Monica CA 90406

KAPLAN, ROBERT B., linguistics educator, consultant, researcher; b. N.Y.C., Sept. 20, 1929; s. Emanuel B. and Natalie Kaplan; m. Audrey A. Lien, Apr. 21, 1951; children—Robin Ann Kaplan Gibson, Lisa, Robert Allen. Student Champlain Coll., 1947-48, Syracuse U., 1948-49; B.A., Willamette U., 1952; M.A., U. So. Calif., 1957, Ph.D., 1962. Teaching asst. U. So. Calif., 1955-57, instr. coordinator, asst. prof. English communication program for fgn. students, 1965-72, assoc. prof., dir. English communication program for fgn. students, 1972-76, assoc. dean continuing edn., prof. applied linguistics, 1976—; instr. U. Oreg., 1957-60; cons. field service program Nat. Assn. Fgn. Student Affairs, 1964—; Fulbright sr. scholar, Australia, 1978. Served with inf. U.S. Army; Korea. Mem. Am. Anthrop. Assn., AAAS, Am. Assn. Applied Linguists, AAUP, Association Internationale de Lingiustique Applique, Association Interrationale Pour La Researche et al Diffusion Des Methods Audio-Visuelles et Structuro-Globales, Assn. Tchrs. English as Second Lang., Calif. Assn. Tchrs. English to Speakers Other Langs., Can. Council Tchrs. English, Nat. Assn. Fgn. Student Affairs (nat. pres. 1983-84), Linguistics Soc. Am. Author: Reading and Rhetoric: A Reader, 1963; (with V. Tufte, P. Cook and J. Aurbach) Transformational Grammar: A Guide for Teachers, 1968; (with R.D. Schoesler) Learning English Through Typewriting, 1969; The Anatomy of Rhetoric: Prolegomena to a Functional Theory of Rhetoric, 1971; On the Scope of Applied Linguistics, 1980; The Language Needs of Migrant Workers, 1980; contbr. articles to profl. jours., U.S., Australia, Brazil, Can., Germany, Holland, Japan, Mexico, N.Z., Philippines and Singapore; contbr. notes, revs. to various profl. jours., U.S. and abroad; gen. editor: Annual Review of Applied Linguistics, 1980—. Office: Dept Linquistics U So Calif Los Angeles CA 90089

KAPLAN, SANDRA, artist, color consultant, educator; b. Cin., May 23, 1943; d. Howard and Helen (Katz) Kaplan; student Art Acad. Cin., 1960-61; B.F.A. with honors, Pratt Inst., Bklyn., 1965; postgrad. CUNY, 1968-70; m. Stanley Joseph Dragul, June 21, 1964 (div.); 1 dau., Sacha. Color cons. to archtl. firm Anderson Assocs., Denver, 1976—, interior design firm Assocs. III, Denver, 1976—, Standard Textile of Cin., 1976—; guest instr. art Denver U., 1978-79, Met. State Coll., 1977-78, 82-83, others; exhibited in one-man shows and group shows, Denver, Cin., N.Y.C., Santa Fe, San Francisco, also represented in pvt. collections; commns. include art for guest rooms Vail (Colo.) Athletic Club, 1979, water color mural Prince Khalid, Saudi Arabia, 1980, paintings for lobby Hyatt Regency Hotel, Dubaii, 1981, art for Atlantic Richfield Corp. Offices, Denver, Amoco Oil, Denver. Recipient Dean's medal in graphic arts Pratt Inst., 1965; Rocky Mountain Nat. Watermedia award Foothills Art Ctr., Golden, Colo., 1979; Jocelyn Biennial award Jocelyn Art Mus., Omaha, 1980. Mem. Artists Equity Assn. U.S., Denver Art Mus., Colo. Lawyers for the Arts. Home: 828 S Pennsylvania Denver CO 80209 Office: 1537 Platte St Denver CO 80202

KAPLAN, SANFORD SANDY, geologist; b. N.Y.C., Oct. 2, 1950; s. Lawrence J. and Jeanne (Leon) K.; m. Joanne Mandel, June 5, 1975; children—Elicia Anne, Shira Frieda. A.B., Lafayette Coll., 1971; M.S., Lehigh U., 1976; Ph.D., U. Pitts. 1980. Engr., U.S. Steel Corp., Monroeville, Pa., 1976; geologist coal preparation div. U.S. Dept. Energy, Bruceton Research Sta., Pa., 1979-80; exploration geologist Pennzoil Exploration and Production Co., Denver, 1980—; vis. lectr., teaching asst. various colls. and univs. Vol. KCFR Pub. Radio and pub. TV, Denver, 1980—; scout leader Boy Scouts Am., 1968-71, 83—. Served to lt. comdr. USNR, 1969—. Mem. Am. Assn. Petroleum Geologists, Geol. Soc. Am., Soc. Econ. Paleontologists and Mineralogists, Rocky Mountain Assn. Geologists, Am. Econ. Assn., Can. Mineral. Assn., Naval Res. Assn., Res. Officers Assn., Alpha Phi Omega. Jewish. Editor-in-chief Rocky Mountain sect. Soc. Econ. Paleontologists and Mineralogists Newsletter; contbr. articles to profl. jours. Office: Pennzoil 1600 Broadway Denver CO 80202

KAPPAS, JOHN G., hypnotist, institute director; b. Chgo., Sept. 11, 1925; s. George John and Frances (Anton) K. B.A. in Psychology, Antioch Coll., 1976; M.A., Lindenwood Coll., 1978; Ph.D., Internat. Coll., 1979. Lic. marriage counselor; hypnosis cert. Counselor, instr., dir. Hypnosis Soc. Am., Los Angeles, 1963-67, Self-Improvement Soc., Los Angeles, 1967-68; counselor, instr., dir. Hypnosis Motivation Inst., Van Nuys, Calif., 1968—. Served with USN, 1941-45. Mem. Am. Psychol. Assn., Can. Psychol. Assn., Marital Therapists Union (charter), Hypnotists Union (founder Local 472, past pres., now tech. advisor), Hypnotists Exam. Council Calif. (past v.p., tech. advisor), Counselors on Alcholism and Related Dependencies (cert. addictions counselor), Am. Hypnosis Assn. (founder, past pres., now tech. advisor), Am. Assn. Sex Educators, Counselors and Therapists. Author: Your Sexual Personality, 1975; The Professional Hypnotism Manual, 1975; Success Is Not an Accident, The Mental Bank Concept, 1982. Office: Hypnosis Motivation Inst 14640 Victory Blvd Suite 210 Van Nuys CA 91401

KAPPES, BRUNO MAURICE, clinical psychologist; b. Nancy, France, Dec. 14, 1951; came to U.S., 1956, naturalized, 1960; s. Harold A. and Simone F. (Bedigie) K. B.A., U. Mo., 1973, M.A., 1975; Ph.D., Kans. State U., 1978. Cert. biofeedback profl.; lic. clin. psychologist. Research analyst U. Mo., Columbia, 1975, research assoc., 1976, also testing adminstr.; asst. prof. stats., research methods and ednl. psychology Kans. State U., 1978-79; asst. prof. psychology U. Alaska, Anchorage, 1979-82, assoc. prof., 1982—. Recipient Outstanding Teaching award U. Mo., 1975; Research award Mo. Psychol. Assn., 1976; Outstanding Tchr. of Yr. award U. Alaska, 1981; U. Alaska Coll. Arts and Scis. fellow, 1980. Mem. Am. Psychol. Assn., Alaska Psychol. Assn., AAUP, Am. Assn. Biofeedback Clinicians, Biofeedback Soc. Am., Biofeedback Soc. Alaska (founder, past pres.), Phi Kappa Phi. Contbr. psychol. articles to profl. jours. Home: 3431 Boniface Pkwy Anchorage AK 99503 Office: Psychology Dept U Alaska Anchorage AK 99508

KARAKEY, SHERRY JOANNE, aerospace manufacturing company executive; b. Wendall, Idaho, Apr. 16, 1942; d. John Donald and Vera Ella (Frost) Kingery; m. George W. Karakey, Mar. 11, 1961 (div.); children—Artist Roxanne, Buddy W., Kami JoAnne, Launi JoElla; m. 2d, James J. Dalgleish, Oct. 6, 1973 (div.). Student Ariz. State U., 1960. Various secretarial positions D-Velco Mfg. of Ariz., Phoenix, 1959-62, exec. v.p., sec.-treas., dir., 1972—; sec. AiResearch Mfg. Co., Phoenix, 1962-63; corp. sec.-treas. Karbel Metal Co., Phoenix, 1963-67; sec. to pub. Scottsdale (Ariz.) Daily Progress, 1969-72. Mem. Nat. Tool and Die Assn. Republican. Home: 5912 E Larkspur Scottsdale AZ 85254 Office: 401 S 36th St Phoenix AZ 85034

KARALIS, GEORGE DEMETRIUS, psychiatrist; b. Chgo., Nov. 1, 1945; s. Demetrius Nicholas and Pauline Georgia (Gianakopulos) K.; M.D., U. Calif., Irvine, 1970; J.D., Golden Gate U., 1980; LL.M. in Taxation, 1981. Practice medicine specializing in psychiatry, med. hypnosis, legal medicine, Berkeley and San Francisco, 1973—; faculty lectr. Soc. Med. Hypnoanalysts, 1980—. Mem. Soc. Med. Hypnoanalysts, Am. Soc. Clin. Hypnosis, Soc. Clin. and Exptl. Hypnosis, Internat. Soc. Hypnosis, Soc. Legal and Ednl. Hypnosis (dir.), San Francisco Acad. Hypnosis, Am. Coll. Legal Medicine. Greek Orthodox. Club: Commonwealth of California. Office: PO Box 664 San Francisco CA 94101

KARAWINA, ERICA, painter, stained glass designer; b. Ger., 1904; d. Paul wilhelm and Meta (Jaenecke) K.; came to U.S., 1923, naturalized, 1937; studied under Charles J. Connick; m. Sidney C. Hsiao, June 21, 1938. One-woman shows: Grace Horne Gallery, Boston, 1933, U. N.H., 1936, Art Club, Lancaster, Pa., 1937, Wadsworth Atheneum, 1938, Colby (Maine) Coll., 1938, U. Dayton, Ohio, 1939, Okla. Art Center, 1939, Grand Rapids Mich., 1940, Ferargil Galleries, 1947, Fitchburg Art Mus., 1949, Currier Gallery, 1949, Beaux Arts Gallery, Honolulu, 1952, Gima's, 1953, China. Inst., Taipei, 1956, The Gallery, Honolulu, 1957, Contemporary Arts Center, 1977; numerous stained glass commns. Hawaii; represented in permanent collections: Library of Congress, Washington, Boston Mus. Fine Arts, Met. Mus., Worcester (Mass.) Fine Arts Mus., Colorado Springs Art Center, Addison Gallery, Mus. Modern Art, N.Y.C., Honolulu Acad. Arts, Tennent Art Found. Recipient John Poole Meml. Prize, James C. Castle award Narcissus Festival of Arts, 1961. Fellow Internat. Inst. Arts; mem. Hawaii Artists League, Arts Council Hawaii, Stained Glass Assn. Hawaii. Address: 3529 Akaka Pl Honolulu HI 96822

KARDUSH, MARCELLE M(ARIE), psychologist, educator; b. Port-Said, Egypt, July 5, 1937; came to U.S., 1962; d. Issa Michael and Mathilde Kardouche; B.A. (Rockefeller fellow), Am. U. Beirut, 1962; Ph.D., U. Calif., Berkeley, 1967; children—Stefon Kardush-Podell, Andrei Kardush-Podell. Research and teaching asst. U. Calif., Berkeley, 1963-67, research assoc., 1965-67; asst. prof. psychology San Francisco State U., 1967-74, assoc. prof., 1974-81, prof., 1981—; human resource devel. cons. to industry, social service agys., alt. ednl. systems, health care delivery systems, govt. agys.; condr. public workshops in human relations and communication. NIH grantee, 1968-69. Mem. Am. Psychol. Assn., Western Psychol. Assn., United Profs. Calif., Am. Soc. Tng. and Devel., AAAS, Assn. Humanistic Psychology, Personal Dynamics Assn., AAUP, Orgn. Devel. Network. Contbr. articles to profl. publs.; editor Group and Orgn. Studies, 1975-79. Home: 950 Bollinger Canyon Rd Moraga CA 94556 Office: San Francisco State U Psychology Dept 1600 Holloway Ave San Francisco CA 94132

KARGER, MICHAEL JAY, lawyer; b. Bronx, N.Y., Nov. 16, 1948; s. Leo and Sylvia K.; B.A., SUNY, Binghamton, 1969; J.D., SUNY, Buffalo, 1974; m. Lauryne M. Miller, May 6, 1978. VISTA vol., Edwardsville, Ill., 1969-70; asst. project dir. Williamsburg Urban Renewal Project, Bklyn., 1970-71; dep. city atty., Santa Ana, Calif., 1974-77; asst. city atty., Gardena, Calif., 1977-82, city atty., 1982—. Mem. Am. Bar Assn., Los Angeles County Bar Assn. Office: 1700 W 162d St Gardena CA 90247

KARLE, JUDITH NANCY, information systems training coordinator; b. Buffalo, N.Y., May 14, 1951; d. Carl J. and Veronica E. (Stark) K. Student Colo. State U., 1969-70, Arapahoe Community Coll., 1972-73; cert. in mgmt. Denver U. Tax analyst Johns-Manville Corp., Denver, 1971-74, data adminstrn. clk. 1974-76, data processing assoc. systems analyst, 1976-79; divisional systems analyst Petro-Lewis Corp., Denver, 1979-81, systems analyst, 1982—; data processing adviser/speaker at high schs., 1981—, Women and Bus. Conf., 1983. Active in vol. activities for NOW, Safe House (battered women's facility); fund-raiser for Michael Lawrence Multiple Sclerosis Found. and Holiday Project. Mem. Am. Bus. Women's Assn. (Women of Yr. 1983, v.p. 1983), Info. Systems Trainers Group (membership coordinator), Nat. Assn. Female Execs., Women's Resource Council. Clubs: Profl. Singles Group, Ski. Office: PO Box 2250 Denver CO 80201

KARLESKINT, BARRY MICHAEL, retail store exec.; b. Santa Maria, Calif., May 25, 1941; s. John Peter and Mary Alward (Fitzgerald) K.; student Calif. State Poly. U., 1959-62; m. Brenda Signorelli, July 20, 1963; children—Kenneth Brian, Robert Jasen, Ann Marie. Foreman, Landscape Dept., Karleskint's Florist & Nursery, San Luis Obispo, 1962-67; gen. mgr. Landscape Dept., Karleskint-Crum, Inc., San Luis Obispo, Calif., 1969, v.p., 1969, v.p., retail gen. mgr., 1975, pres., 1980—, dir., 1967—; co-owner Comput-A-Swim; instr. San Luis Coastal Sch. Dist. Adult Sch., 1977-78; cons. in field. Mem. organizing com. Obispo Beautiful Assn., 1970; pres. Mission-Nativity Parents Assn., 1974-76, mem. sch. bd., 1974-76; pres. Nativity of Our Lady Cath. Ch. Council, 1977; mem. San Luis Obispo City Parks and Recreation Commn., 1981—, San Luis Obispo City Tree Com., 1981—. Served with U.S. Army, 1962, USAR, 1962-66, USNG, 1966-68. Cert. nurseryman, Calif. Mem. Calif. Assn. Nurserymen (chpt. dir. 1978-80), Calif. Landscape Contractor's Assn. (chpt. dir. 1964-66). Roman Catholic. Clubs: San Luis Obispo Swim (pres. 1977-78); KC, Old Mission Sch. Booster (sec. 1961-63) Home: 623 Jeffrey Dr San Luis Obispo CA 93401 Office: 225 Suburban Rd San Luis Obispo CA 93401

KARLIN, RICHARD JOSEPH, metallurgical engineer; b. Denver, Mar. 16, 1947; s. Laurence William and Gracella Elizabeth (Iven); m. Mary Sue Supanich, Feb. 26, 1947; children—Tyler, Stacey. Met.E., Colo. Sch. Mines, 1969. Registered profl. engr., Colo. Dist. engr. Colo. Dept. Health, Denver, 1972-79, chief drinking water sect., 1979—; cons. in water treatment. Mem. Am. Water Works Assn. (research com., trustee Rocky Mountain sect.), Tau Beta Pi. Contbr. articles to tech. jours. Home: 4652 S Quitman Denver CO 80236 Office: 4210 E 11th Ave Denver CO 80220

KARLOVAC, MARYLIE, psychologist, educator, researcher; b. Madison, Wis., Aug. 29, 1953; d. Jesse N. and Henrietta (Ver Meer) Williams; B.A. with high honors, Coll. William and Mary, 1975; M.A., Princeton U., 1977, Ph.D., 1979. Instr. psychology Drew U., Madison, N.J., 1979, So. Meth. U., Dallas, 1979-81, Calif. Poly. State U., San Luis Obispo, 1981-82; assoc. prof., dir. instl. research and grants Calif. Grad. Inst., Los Angeles, 1982—. Mem. Am. Psychol. Assn., Soc. Psychol. Study Social Issues, Am. Psychology-Law Soc., Group Psychotherapy Assn. So. Calif., Calif. State Psychol. Assn. Contbr. articles to profl. jours. Home: 969 Hilgard Ave 706 Westwood Los Angeles CA 90024 Office: Calif Grad Inst 1100 Glendon Ave West Los Angeles CA 90024

KARLTON, LAWRENCE K., judge; b. Bklyn., May 28, 1935; s. Aaron Katz and Sylvia (Meltzer) K.; student Washington Sq. Coll.; LL.B., Columbia, 1958; m. Mychelle Stiebel, Sept. 7, 1958. Admitted to Fla. bar, 1958, Calif. bar, 1962; acting legal officer Sacramento Army Depot, Dept. Army, 1959-60, civilian legal officer, 1960-62; individual practice, Sacramento, 1962-64; mem. firm Abbott, Karlton & White, 1964, Karlton & Blease, until 1971, Karlton, Blease & Vanderlaan, 1971-76; judge Calif. Superior Ct. for Sacramento County, 1976-79; judge U.S. Dist. Ct. Eastern Dist. Calif., 1979—, chief judge, 1983—. Co-chmn. Central Calif. council B'nai B'rith Anti-Defamation League Commn. 1964-65; treas. Sacramento Jewish Community Relations Council, chmn., 1967-68. Mem. ACLU (chmn. lawyers panel 1966-76). Am. Sacramento County bar assns., Am. Trial Lawyers Assn., Assn. Criminal Def. Attys. Mem. B'nai B'rith (past pres.). Home: 7039 Garden Hwy Sacramento CA 95837 Office: 650 Capitol Mall Sacramento CA 95814

KARNOW, MICHAEL, public relations executive; b. Phila., Jan. 9, 1941; s. Michael and Eleanor (Bachelor) K.; m. Mary Ellen Rhodes, July 3, 1962; children—Michael, Michelle. B.A., Bucknell U., 1964; M.A., Johns Hopkins U., 1969. Editor Garden State Pub. Co., Sea Isle City, N.J., 1964-66; mgr. periodicals and publ. div. Johns Hopkins Press, Balt., 1966-68; lectr. writing and lit., Bucknell U., Lewisburg, Pa., 1969-73; advt. and pub. relations account exec. Tektronix Inc., Beaverton, Oreg., 1976-81, mgr. corp. mktg. pub. relations, tech. pub. relations, 1981—. Johns Hopkins U. teaching fellow, 1968-69. Mem. Pub. Relations Soc. Am. Home: 687 NW Queens Ct E Hillsboro OR 97123 Office: PO Box 500 Y3-408 Beaverton OR 97077

KARP, CHERYL L., psychologist; b. San Francisco, July 19, 1946; d. Vernon Arthur and Kathleen Marian (Taylor) Davison; B.A., U. Ariz., 1968, M.Ed., 1972, Ph.D., 1978; m. Leonard Irwin Karp, June 10, 1967; children—Alan, David (dec.), Scott. With Catalina Psychologists, Tucson, and rural sch. psychologist Pinal County, Ariz., 1976-80; lectr. developmental psychology and psychology of learning U. Ariz., Tucson, 1979-80; pvt. practice psychology, Tucson, 1980—; police psychologist Dept. Pub. Safety, Tucson, 1981—; research cons. U. Ariz., Tucson, 1978-80; trainer behavior cons. Dept. Econ. Security, 1978-80. Mem. Young Jewish Leadership Council, 1970-72; div. co-chmn. Combined Jewish Appeal, 1974; bd. dirs. Brewster Home Aux., 1973-75, Brandeis U. Nat. Women's Com., 1970-74; sec. Pima County Bar Aux., 1971-72. Mem. Am. Psychol. Assn., Am. Soc. Clin. Hypnosis, Internat. Soc. Hypnosis, Assn. Advancement of Behavior Therapy, Ariz. State Psychol. Assn. (sec. 1982-84, membership/pub. info. chmn. 1981-82, Meritorious Achievement award 1981), So. Ariz. Psychol. Assn., Ariz. Council Attys. for Children, Inc. Democrat. Jewish. Office: 5190 E Farness St Bldg 1000 Suite 1006 Tucson AZ 85712

KARP, MICHAEL, psychologist; b. Bklyn., Apr. 6, 1951; s. Bernard and Estelle (Rudman) K.; B.S. Psychology cum laude, Bklyn. Coll., 1973; M.A. in Clin. Psychology, SUNY-Plattsburgh, 1979. Lic. marriage, family and child counselor, Calif. Rural psychologist Cumberland River Comprehensive Care Ctr., Williamsberg, Ky., 1979-80; alcohol and substance abuse counselor Behavioral Health Services, Inglewood, Calif., 1980—; cons. in field. Mem. Am. Psychol. Assn. (assoc.), Sierra Club. Office: 279 W Beach Ave Inglewood CA 90302

KARPENKO, VICTOR NICHOLAS, mech. engr.; b. Harbin, China, Jan. 23, 1922; s. Nicholas Stephan and Sophia Andrea (Kootas) K.; came to U.S., 1941, naturalized, 1943; student San Francisco State Coll., 1941-42, Oreg. State Coll., 1943; B.S. in Mech. Engring., U. Calif., Berkeley, 1948; m. Lydia Kamotsky, June 23, 1950; children—Victor, Mark, Alexandra. Staff engr. Atomic Products Equipment div. Gen. Electric Co., San Jose, Calif., 1956-57; project engr. nuclear explosives engring. Lawrence Livermore (Calif.) Lab., 1957-65, sect. leader nuclear explosives engring., 1965-66, div. leader Nuclear Test Engring. div., 1966-76, project mgr. Mirror Fusion Test Facility, 1976—; mem. fusion reactor safety com. Dept. Energy; mem. Containment Evaluation Panel, ERDA; cons. undergrounding of nuclear reactors. Dist. chmn. U. Calif. Alumni Scholarship Program, 1976—; com. mem. U. Calif. Alumni Scholarship Program, 1972-76; com. mem. San Ramon High Sch. Boosters, 1969; pres. San Ramon AAU Swim Club, 1964. Served with AUS, 1943-46. Registered profl. mech. and nuclear engr., Calif. Mem. Am. Nuclear Soc., Calif. Alumni Assn. Republican. Greek Orthodox. Home: 613 Bradford Pl Danville CA 94526 Office: PO Box 808 East Ave Livermore CA 94550

KARPILOW, CRAIG, physician; b. San Francisco, Oct. 23, 1947; s. David and Babette (David) K.; B.Sc., U. Alta. (Can.), 1967; M.A., U. So. Calif., 1970; M.D., Dalhousie U., 1973. Intern, Dalhousie U., Halifax, N.S., Can., 1974-75; resident in family practice medicine Meml. U. Nfld. Hosp., St. John's, 1975-77; practice medicine specializing in family medicine with subsplty. dermatology and rheumatology, Carson City and Dayton; Nev., 1978-81; practice medicine, Snohomish, Wash., 1981-83; med. health officer Storey County, Nev., 1978-80; med. dir. Med. Center, Carson City, Nev.; pres. Internat. Profl. Assos. Ltd., 1979—. Diplomate Am. Bd. Family Practice; licenciate Med. Coll. Can. Fellow Am. Acad. Family Practice; mem. AMA, Wash. State Med. Assn.; Snohomish County Med. Soc.; Wash. Acad. Family Physicians, Coll. Family Physicians of Can., Can. Med. Assn., Kappa Sigma. Clubs: Rotary, Everett Yacht. Home: 406 Glen St Snohomish WA 98290 Office: PO Box 604 Snohomish WA 98290

KARRELS, KENNETH VERNON, organizational psychologist, adminstr.; b. Chgo., July 31, 1941; s. Vern F. and Irene G. (Sylvester) K.; B.S. in Psychology, Bradley U., 1963, M.A. in Clin. Psychology, 1964; M.A. in Mgmt., U. Phoenix, 1983; m. Mary K. Flory, Nov. 14, 1970; children—Kathryn Rose, Kenneth Karsten. Psychology intern Elgin (Ill.) State Hosp., 1964, dir. transitional care program, 1967-74; devel. disabilities adminstr. Dept. Mental Health and Retardation, Elgin, 1974; asso. exec. dir. Ray Graham Assn., Addison, Ill., 1975-77; mgr. ops. Dist. II State of Ariz., Tucson, 1977—; cons. career counseling, indsl. psychology, human resource mgmt.; lectr. time mgmt., staff tng. and devel. Bd. dirs. Pima County Assn. for Retarded Citizens; Tanque Verde Homeowners' Assn.; mem. Sch. Bd. Planning Com. Tax Reform Com. Recipient Gerty award Gov. of Ill., 1967; registered psychologist, Ill., Ariz. Mem. Am. Psychol. Assn., Internat. Assn. Quality Circles, Am. Soc. Personnel Adminstrn., Am. Soc. Tng. and Devel., Ariz. Psychol. Assn., Internat. Assn. Quality Circles, Am. Assn. on Mental Deficiency, Nat. Registry Health Service Providers in Psychology. Unitarian. Clubs: Civitan, So. Ariz. Soc. Model Engrs. Contbr. articles to profl. confs. Home: 3930 N Smokey Topaz Tucson AZ 85715 Office: PO Box 13178 Tucson AZ 85732

KARSTEN, PETER, zoo director; b. Goettingen, Ger., Nov. 8, 1937; s. Wolfgang and Marie-Luise (Karsten) immigrated to Can., 1962, naturalized, 1966; diploma Agr. Coll., Witzenhausen, Ger., 1961; m. Margrit Marie Helen Thomas, May 6, 1962; children—Werner, Karen. Farmer in Germany, 1955-59; student Aske Gard, research farm, Sweden, 1960; rancher, DeWinton, Alta., Can., 1962-64; mem. staff Calgary (Alta.) Zoo, 1964—, dir., 1975—; cons. zoo masterplan Moose Jaw (Sask.) Wild Animal Park. Achieved wildlife artist. Mem. Canadian (founding pres. 1975), Am. (Achievement award 1975) assns. zool. parks and aquariums. Office: PO Box 3036 Sta B Calgary AB T2M 4R8 Canada*

KARSTENSSON, LEWIS, economics educator; b. McCloud, Calif., Oct. 14, 1939; s. Hans and Iris Alameda (Smith) K.; m. Kathleen Ann Barta, June 17, 1967; children—Kristina, Linne. B.A. in Social Sci., Humboldt State Coll., 1962; M.A. in Econ. Edn., Ohio U., 1970, Ph.D., 1974. Tchr. Marysville (Calif.) High Sch., 1964-69; asst. prof. Ohio U., Athens, 1974-75; asst. prof. North Tex. State U., Denton, 1975-79; assoc. prof. econs. U. Nev., Las Vegas, 1979—, chmn. dept., 1982—. Mem. Am. Econ. Assn. Contbr. articles to profl. jours. Office: Dept Econs Univ Nev Las Vegas NV 89154

KART, STUART LIONEL, accountant; b. Chgo., May 4, 1933; s. Irving L. and Camille (Ehrenberg) K.; m. Sandi L. Olins, Mar. 31, 1957; children—Deborah, Beth. B.S., Calif. State U.-Los Angeles, 1960. C.P.A., Calif. Jr. acct. Price Waterhouse, Los Angeles, 1960-61; sr. acct. Pritkin, Finkel & Co., Beverly Hills, Calif., 1961-63, Roseman & Stern, Beverly Hills, 1963-65; ptnr. Glass, Kart & Co., Beverly Hills, 1965-78; ptnr. Edison-Kart & Co., Sherman Oaks, Calif., 1978—, ptnr.-in-charge, 1979—; part-time faculty acctg. dept. Calif. State U.-Los Angeles, 1979—. Served with USN, 1953-57. Mem. Am. Inst. C.P.A.s, Calif. Soc. C.P.A.s (dir., pres. Los Angeles chpt. 1983-84). Club: Seniors Track. Office: 14011 Ventura Blvd Suite 301 Sherman Oaks CA 91423

KARTER, MARY LOUISE, home economist, educator; b. Granite City, Ill., Mar. 16, 1943; d. Elmer and Elva (Gundlach) Johnson; m. Thomas G. Karter, June 22, 1963; children—Thomas G., Scott. B.S. in Home Econs., Purdue U., 1963; M.S. in Edn., Portland State U., 1973. Cert. home econs., health tchr. Tchr. pub. schs., Portland, Oreg., 1967—, Mt. Tabor Middle Sch., 1968—; home econs. mem. Area III Curriculum Council, chmn. Parenting Curriculum Com., coordinator career edn., chmn. co-op.; mem. Dist. Home Econs. Steering Com. Mem. Oreg. Vocat. Assn., Am. Home Econs. Assn., Portland Fedn. Tchrs. (legis. com., area rep.), Dist. Home Econs. Tchrs. (pres.), Alpha Delta Kappa. Republican. Lutheran. Clubs: Lion Aux. (Portland). Home: 2516 NE 25th St Portland OR 97212 Office: Mt Tabor Middle Sch 5800 SE Ash St Portland OR 97215

KASHI, JOSEPH LEON, lawyer; b. Hazleton, Pa., June 17, 1950; s. Stephen A. and Adeline (Genetti) K. B.S., MIT, 1972, M.S., 1973; M.A. in Polit. Sci., J.D., Georgetown U., 1976. Bar: Pa. 1976, Alaska 1978, U.S. Supreme Ct. 1981, U.S. Ct. Appeals (9th cir.) 1982, U.S. Ct. Appeals (D.C. cir.) 1977, U.S. Dist. Ct. Alaska 1978. Intern, U.S. Senate Joint Econ. Com.; assoc. Jones, Day, Reavis & Pogue, Washington, 1975; researcher Office of Telecommunications, U.S. Dept. Commerce, 1975-76, atty., 1976-77; dep. borough atty. Kenai Peninsula Borough (Alaska), 1977-82; ptnr. Garnett & Kashi, Kenai, Alaska, 1982-83, Kashi & Tempel, 1983—; instr. photography Kenai Peninsula Community Coll.; founder Central Peninsula Conflict Resolution Ctrs. Recipient miscellaneous photography awards. Mem. ABA, Alaska Bar Assn. Democrat. Club: Kenai-Soldotna Rotary. Home: Soldotna AK 99669 Office: PO Box 2073 Soldotna AK 99669

KASKEL, NEAL T., marketing executive, educator; b. Buffalo, Oct. 6, 1943; s. David and Bertha (Perlmuter) K.; m. Geraldine Slutsky, Apr. 3, 1966; children—Amy, Robert. B.S., DePaul U., 1966; M.B.A., Northwestern U., 1972. Project dir. D'Arcy Advt., Chgo., 1966-67; research supr. Foote, Cone & Belding, Chgo., 1967-72; mktg. research mgr. Armour-Dial Co., Phoenix, 1972-74, Hunt-Wesson Foods, Fullerton, Calif., 1974-79; corp. dir. mktg. services Family Health Program, Fountain Valley, Calif., 1979-81; mktg. mgr. TCM div. Smith Internat., Inc., Tustin, Calif., 1981-83; market research dir. Geneva Corp., Santa Ana, Calif., 1983—; instr. mktg. Calif. State U., 1975—; instr. Advt. Ctr., Los Angeles, 1983—. Vice-pres. Jewish Family Service Orange County, 1980—; mem. supt.'s adv. com. Fountain Valley Sch. Dist., 1980—, proficiency com., 1981—; Served to lt., USNR, 1968-74. Mem. Am. Mktg. Assn., World Future Soc., Internat. Inst. Forecasters, Alpha Epsilon Pi. Democrat. Office: 2933 Pullman Ave Santa Ana CA 92705

KASLOFF, STEVE, motion picture studio executive, writer; b. N.Y.C., Nov. 13, 1952; s. Lawrence Alvin and Yvette Shirley (Reiser) K. B.F.A. cum laude, Pratt Inst., 1974. Art dir., writer Young & Rubicam, Inc., N.Y.C., 1974-76; writer Carl Ally Inc., N.Y.C., 1976; writer, supr. Marsteller, Inc., N.Y.C., 1977-79; sr. writer, supr. Scali, McCabe & Sloves, Inc., N.Y.C., 1979-82; v.p., creative dir. Columbia Pictures, Inc., Burbank, Calif., 1982—; tchr. creative thinking Pratt Inst., 1975. Pres., Tree-Lined Apt. Corp., N.Y.C., 1979. Recipient Citizenship award B'Nai B'rith, 1970; Print Casebooks award, 1978; Clio award Dannon Yogurt Soviet Sr. Citizens TV Comms., 1978; Clio award Sierra Club, 1979; One Show Silver and Gold awards, 1976, 77, 81. Democrat. Jewish. Author and editor: The Rainy Day Yearbook, 1974; conceiver, designer The Little Apple T-shirt and trademark for Roosevelt Island, 1977; TV commls., printwork on permanent display The One Show Worldwide Exhibit, 1974-82. Office: Columbia Pictures Columbia Plaza Burbank CA 91505

KASPER, FRANKLIN VANDA, securities company executive; b. Oakland, Calif., Apr. 15, 1937; s. Henry J. and May Kasper; B.S., Calif. State U., 1964; m. Susan Taneen, Apr. 4, 1964; 1 dau., Kristin Sue. Account exec. Merrill Lynch Pierce Fenner & Smith, Pasadena, Calif., 1964-69; 1st v.p. Shearson Hammill & Co., San Francisco, 1969-74; v.p. Loeb Rhoades & Co., San Francisco, 1974-78; pres., chmn. Van Kasper & Co., San Francisco, 1978—; dir. Barringer Resources. Chmn. Exploratorium San Francisco. Served with AUS. Office: 50 California St San Francisco CA 94111

KASSEBAUM, GENE GIRARD, sociology educator, research consultant; b. St. Louis, June 24, 1929; s. John G. and Flora (Girard) K.; m. Gayathuri Rajapur, Aug. 15, 1966; 1 son, Krishna John. A.B., U. Mo., 1951; M.A., Harvard U., 1955, Ph.D., 1958. Mem. faculty Cornell Med. Sch., N.Y.C., 1957-60; Mem. faculty Sch. Pub. Health, UCLA, 1960-65; mem. faculty Am. U. Cairo, Egypt, 1965-68; prof. sociology U. Hawaii, Honolulu, 1968—. Served to cpl. U.S. Army, 1951-53. Fulbright sr. lectr., India, 1973-74; Fulbright research grantee, 1981-82. Mem. AAUP, Am. Sociol. Assn., Phi Beta Kappa. Co-author: Women's Prison, 1965; Prison Treatment, Parole Survival, 1971; author: Delinquency and Social Policy, 1974; co-editor: Narcotics; contbr. numerous articles to profl. jours. Office: Dept Sociology U of Hawaii Honolulu HI 96822

KASSEL, GLORIA LAISELLE, marketing professional; b. Cape Girardeau, Mo., Dec. 14, 1927; d. Otto Fredrick and Myrtle M. (Morrison) K. A.A. in Bus. Adminstrn., Ala. State U., 1955; cert. in radiology St. Francis Hosp., Wichita, Kans., 1961. Registered radiol. tech. Gen. switchboard operator Bell Telephone Co., Salina, Kans., 1944-48; radiol. technician Good Samaritan Hosp., Portland, Oreg., 1961-64; security officer Lawless Detective Agency, Denver, 1965-68; med. office mgr., Montclair, Calif., 1968-76; emergency room mgr. Ontario (Calif.) Community Hosp., 1976-1980, mktg. dir., 1980—; cons., speaker in field. Served to 1st lt. U.S. Women's Army Corps, 1948-58. Mem. Acad. Pub. Relations, Women in Communications, Inc., Pub. Relations Soc. Am., So. Calif. Soc. Hosp. Public Relations, Internat. Assn. Bus. Communicators, Am. Hosp. Assn. Pub. Relations, Ontario C. of C., Rancho Cacamonga C. of C., Am. Legion, Women's Army Corps Vets. Democrat. Roman Catholic. Club: Soroptimists (Ontario). Home: 609 East F St Ontario CA 91764 Office: Ontario Community Hosp 550 N Monterey Ave Ontario CA 91764

KASSEL, MICHAEL PHILLIP, data processing consulting co. exec.; b. Chgo., Feb. 10, 1948; s. Erwin Lawrence and Anita (Goldberg) K.; B.S. in Bus., U. Wis., 1968; m. Susan Rose Bernstein, Aug. 16, 1970; 1 son, Ryan Eric. Recruiter Western Cons., Encino, Calif., 1969-71; recruiting mgr. Dunhill Employment Agy., Los Angeles, 1971-74; recruiter E.D.P. Staff-Cons., Marina del Rey, Calif., 1974-76; regional recruiting mgr. Cutler-Williams, Marina del Rey, 1976-78; v.p. Comml. Programming Systems, Inc. Coach Culver City Lancers Football for Youth, 1969-79, pres., 1973-75, 79; coach Culver City Babe Ruth, 1969-80, equipment dir., 1976. Office: 3400 W 6th St Los Angeles CA 90020

KAST, NANCY LEA, personnel analyst; b. Fresno, Calif., Dec. 2, 1955; d. Lawrence M. and Bertharene Kast; B.S., Calif. State U., Fresno, 1979, postgrad., 1980—. Personnel analyst St. Agnes Med. Center, Fresno, Calif., 1979-80; personnel analyst classified State Center Community Coll. Dist., Fresno, 1980, personnel analyst certificated, 1980—; staffing cons. Fresno Conv. Bur. Mem. Calif. State U. Fresno Alumni Assn., Alpha Kappa Psi. Republican. Baptist. Office: 1525 E Weldon Ave Fresno CA 93705

KASTEN, GERALD ALLEN, mktg. specialist; b. Bklyn., July 24, 1943; s. Alexander and Etta (Karlikow) K.; B.S., N.Y. U., 1965; M.A. in Mktg., CCNY, 1969; m. Hermine Rochell Gottlieb, Jan. 10, 1971; children—Mallary Jill, Ainsley Brooke, Lauren. Analyst, Dun & Bradstreet, N.Y.C., 1966; asst. mgr. advt. Phillips Van Heusen Corp., N.Y.C., 1966-69; mgr. promotions Ideal Toy Corp., N.Y.C., 1969-71; dir. mktg. Perl-Mack Cos., Denver, 1971-76; mgr. mktg. services Info. Handling Services, Denver, 1976—; exec. v.p. The Denver Avalanche, profl. indoor soccer team, 1980; dir. mktg. Precision Visuals Inc., computer graphics software, 1980—. Bd. dirs. Colo. Celebration of the Arts, 1976-78. Served with U.S. Army, 1966-68. Mem. Denver Advt. Fedn. (past chmn. community communications com.), Soc. Photo-Optical Instrumentation Engrs., Bus. Profl. Advt. Assn., N.Y. U. Alumni Assn. Club: Town (Denver). Home: 4620 E Oxford St Cherry Hills Village Englewood CO 80111 Office: 800 E Prentice St Englewood CO 80110

KASTLER, BERNARD ZANE, natural gas company executive; b. Billings, Mont., Oct. 30, 1920; s. B.Z. and Elsie (Grossman) K.; student U. Colo., 1940-41; LL.B. with high honors, U. Utah, 1949; m. Donna Irene Endicott, July 24, 1948; children—Lynn, Kerry Sue. Admitted to Utah bar, 1949, Mont. bar, 1948; pvt. practice law, Salt Lake City, 1949-52; counsel Salt Lake City Civil Service Commn., 1949-50; with Mountain Fuel Supply Co., Salt Lake City, 1952-58, sec., asst. treas., gen. counsel, 1958-68, v.p. fin., treas., 1968-72, pres., 1972-80, chief exec. officer, 1974-82, chmn. bd., 1976—; chmn. bd. Entrada Industries, Inc., Mountain Fuel Resources, Inc., Wexpro Co.; dir. Albertson's, Inc., Bonneville Internat. Corp., Intermountain Health Care, Inc., 1st Security Corp.; mem. Utah Ho. of Reps., 1963-64. Bd. dirs. Mountain States Legal Found. Served with USNR, World War II. Mem. Salt Lake City C. of C. (bd. govs. 1967-78, v.p. govt. and pub. affairs council 1968-69, pres. 1977-78), U. Utah Alumni Assn., Am., Utah, Salt Lake County, Mont. bar assns., Am. Gas Assn., Pacific Coast Gas Assn. (chmn. 1980), Rocky Mountain Oil and Gas Assn., Order of Coif, Phi Kappa Phi, Phi Delta Phi. Conglist. Mason, Kiwanian (pres. 1967-68). Contbr. articles to profl. jours. Office: Mountain Fuel Supply Co 180 E 1st South St Salt Lake City UT 84139 Mailing address: PO Box 11368 Salt Lake City UT 84139

KASZNIAK, ALFRED WAYNE, neuropsychologist; b. Chgo., June 2, 1949; s. Alfred H. and Ann Virginia (Simonsen) K.; B.S. with honors, U. Ill., 1970, M.A., 1973, Ph.D., 1976; m. Mary Ellen Beaurain, Aug. 26, 1973; children—Jesse Beaurain, Elizabeth Beaurain. Instr. dept. psychology Rush Med. Coll., Chgo., 1974-76, asst. prof. dept. psychology, 1976-79; from asst. prof. to assoc. prof. dept. psychiatry U. Ariz. Coll. Medicine, Tucson, 1979-82, assoc. prof., 1982—; staff psychologist Presbyn.-St. Luke's Hosp., Chgo., 1976-79; mem. behavioral scis. rev. group and spl. study sect. div. research grants NIH, 1981—. Trustee So. Ariz. chpt. Nat. Multiple Sclerosis Soc., 1980-82; mem. med. and sci. adv. bd. Nat. Alzheimer's Disease and Related Disorders Assn., 1981—; mem. med. adv. bd. Fan Kane Fund for Brain-Injured Children, Tucson, 1980—. Nat. Inst. Aging grantee, 1978—. Mem. Am. Psychol. Assn. (Disting. Contbr. award div. 20 1978), Internat. Neuropsychol. Soc., Soc. for Neurosci., Gerontol. Soc., Soc. Psychophysiol. Research, Biofeedback Soc. Am., AAAS, N.Y. Acad. Scis., Soc. Behavioral Medicine. Editorial cons. Jour. Gerontology, 1979—. Contbr. articles to profl. jours. Home: 7630 N Chapalla Pl Tucson AZ 85704 Office: Dept Psychiatry Univ Ariz Coll Medicine 1501 Campbell Tucson AZ 85724

KATASHIBA, KEN N., computer and semicondr. co. exec.; b. Tokyo, Feb. 27, 1940; came to U.S., 1963; B.A., Keio U., Tokyo, 1963; postgrad. Tex. Christian U., 1963-64. Project leader Control Data Corp., Mpls., 1967, sr. systems specialist, 1969-72; with Fujitsu Am. Inc., Santa Clara, Calif., 1972—, dir. internat. ops. service, 1972-75, dir. Central ops. office, 1975-77, dir. program mgmt., 1979-80, v.p. ops. mgmt., 1980—. Mem. Am. Mgmt. Assn. Clubs: Decathlon; Fgn. Corr. Japan.

KATHER, GERHARD, air force base administrator; b. Allenstein, Germany, Jan. 30, 1939; came to U.S., 1952, naturalized, 1959; s. Ernst and Maria (Kempa) K.; m. Carol Anne Knutsen, Aug. 18, 1962; children—Scott T., Cynthia M., T. Stephen, Chris A.; m. Mary Elsie Frank, Oct. 25, 1980. B.A. in Govt., U. Ariz., 1964; M.P.A., U. So. Calif., 1971. Tchr. social studies, Covina, Calif., 1965-67; tng. officer Civil Personnel, Ft. MacArthur, Calif., 1967-70; chief employee tng. and devel. Corps Engrs., Los Angeles, 1970-72; chief employee tng. and devel. Frankfurt Area Army Personnel Office, 1972-73; chief employee relations and tng. brs. Corps Engrs., Los Angeles, 1973-74; chief employee devel. and tng. Kirtland AFB, N.Mex., 1974—. Mem. adv. com. Albuquerque Tech.-Vocat. Inst., 1982—. Served with USAF, 1958-64. Mem. Am. Soc. Tng. and Devel., Paralyzed Vets. Am. Democrat. Roman Catholic. Office: 1606 ABW/DPCT Kirtland AFB NM 87117

KATZ, ELINOR LIPIT, educator, ednl. adminstr.; b. Bklyn., June 17, 1942; d. Morris and Hannah (Krales) Lipit; B.A., Bklyn. Coll., 1964; M.A., U. Denver, 1977, M.P.A., 1981, Ph.D., 1981; m. Seymour Katz, June 23, 1963; children—Andrew, Lori. Spl. edn. tchr., 1964-68; coordinator Univ. for Youth, U. Denver, 1979-81; faculty gifted and talented program Denver U., 1979-81, dir. Bur. Ednl. Services, Sch. Edn., 1982-83; cons. gifted edn. Mem. Nat. Assn. for Gifted Children, Colo. Assn. for Gifted and Talented (pres.), Council for Exceptional Children, Assn. for Supervision and Curriculum Devel., Phi Delta Kappa, Kappa Delta Pi. Co-editor Jour. for Education of the Gifted. Office: University of Denver School of Education BC-5 Denver CO 80208

KATZ, GENE IRWIN, electronics engr.; b. Richmond, Calif., Aug. 30, 1951; s. Robert Sidney and Durene Evon (Short) K.; B.E.E., Calif. State Poly. U., 1973; m. Chantal Vogel, Aug. 27, 1971; 1 son, Etienne J. Frameman, Pacific Telephone Co., San Luis Obispo, Calif., 1969-73; research engr. Advanced Linear Products div. Fairchild Semicondr., Mountain View, Calif., 1973-74; electronic systems engr. Nat. Controls, Inc., Santa Rosa, Calif., 1974-80; v.p. engring. Flex-Weigh Corp., 1980—, also dir.; instr. digital systems Santa Rosa Jr. Coll.; guest speaker confs. Recipient Top Honors award Valler Processing Achievements, 1976. Mem. Nat. Scalemen's Assn. (electronic com.), Instrument Soc. Am. Republican. Roman Catholic. Contbr. articles to profl. publs. Office: 3158 Condo Ct Santa Rosa CA 95405

KATZ, JERRY BENJAMIN, ins. co. exec.; b. Louisville, Jan. 8, 1947; s. David Frederick and Carolyn K.; student Bradley U., 1964-65; B.A., U. Louisville, 1968; m. Mary Kathleen Brown, Mar. 29, 1969; children—Kristen Carole, Damon Michael, Danielle Laura. With Indsl. Indemnity Co., San Francisco, 1972-78; asst. v.p. Fremont Indemnity Co., Los Angeles, 1978—, home office auditor and collections mgr., 1978-79, asst. v.p. audit and collections, 1979-81, asst. v.p. workers' compensation underwriting, 1981—. Served with USCG, 1968-72. Mem. Calif. Ins. Audit Mgrs. Assn., Ins. Credit Mgrs. Assn. of Los Angeles, Phi Kappa Tau. Home: 5408 Vista Fortuna Cypress CA 90630 Office: 1709 W 8th St Los Angeles CA 90017

KATZ, LEAH EVANS, nurse anesthetist, educator; b. Columbus, Ohio, Mar. 6, 1941; d. Leslie Malcolm and Elizabeth (Stoughton) Evans; m. Ronald Lewis Katz, Apr. 1, 1976. B.S. in Nursing, Ohio State U., 1962, postgrad. in anesthesia, 1965; M.A., Lindenwood Coll., 1977; Ed.D., Pepperdine U., 1982; law student Loyola U., Los Angeles, 1983. Cert. R.N.; cert. R.N. anesthetist, Ohio. Nursing instr. Ohio State U., 1962-64; nurse anesthetist Cleve. Clinic, 1965-68; nurse anesthetist and instr. Baylor Coll. Med., Houston, 1968-73; dir. anesthesia Martin Luther King Hosp., Los Angeles, 1973-74; program dir. nurse anesthesia UCLA Sch. Med., 1974-82, assoc. prof., 1981—; cons. Mem. Am. Assn. Nurse Anesthetists, Calif. Assn. Nurse Anesthetists, Sigma Theta Tau, Phi Delta Kappa. Republican. Episcopalian. Contbr. numerous articles to profl. jours. Home: 3063 Greentree Ct Los Angeles CA 90077 Office: UCLA Program of Nurse Anesthesia CHS 56-125 Los Angeles CA 90024

KATZ, MICHAEL GORDON, lawyer; b. Chgo., Apr. 5, 1947; s. Jack J. and Sarah L. K.; m. Susan B. (Katz), July 6, 1969; 1 son, Daniel Gordon. B.A. in Polit. Sci., U. Mich., 1969, M.A. in English Lit., 1973; J.D., U. Ill., 1973. Bar: Fla. 1973, Colo. 1976. Asst. pub. defender Broward County (Fla.), 1973-74, asst states atty., 1974-76; staff atty., instr. U. Colo. Law Sch., Boulder, 1976-77, dir. legal aid clinic, 1977-78; asst. fed. pub. defender Dist. Colo., Denver, 1978-79, fed. pub. defender, 1979—. Mem. Colo. Criminal Def. Bar, Nat. Assn. Criminal Def. Lawyers. Office: 1961 Stout Suite 1754 Denver CO 80294

KAU, MELVIN EDWARD, optometrist; b. Shanghai, China, June 10, 1938 (parents Am. citizens); s. Edward Young and Eleanor (Moo) K.; m. Kathleen Tom, Dec. 30, 1973. B.A., Dartmouth Coll., 1960; O.D., So. Calif. Coll. Optometry, 1970. Lic. optometrist, Hawaii, Calif. Gen. practice optometry, Honolulu, 1970—. Served to lt. with USN, 1960-63; to lt. comdr., M.S.C., USNR, 1979—. Recipient So. Calif. Coll. Optometry Bartley Optical award, 1970. Mem. Armed Forces Optometric Assn., Naval Res. Assn. (v.p. health services), Res. Officer Assn. (v.p. Navy), Assn. Mil. Surgeons. Episcopalian. Clubs: Masons (Waikiki), Shriners. Home: 98-099 Uao Pl Apt 1407 Aiea HI 96701 Office: 1507 S King St Room 203 Honolulu HI 96826

KAUFFMAN, DONALD GOODWIN, food broker; b. Hillsboro, Wis., Jan. 13, 1918; s. Jesse and Grace (Goodwin) K.; m. Ethelynn Helen Bays, Feb. 22, 1942; children—Camille Taylor, Donald G., Patrick Taylor, Thomas W.; m. 2d, Marilyn Jean Miller Taylor, Dec. 2, 1960; Ph.B., U. Wis., 1940. Salesman, food brokerage co., Portland, Oreg., 1946-47; owner D.G. Kauffman Co., 1947-48; pres., gen. mgr. Stater-Kauffman Co., Portland, Oreg., 1948-61, Edwards/Kauffman Co., Portland, 1961-79; founder, pres. Erlandson-Kauffman, Seattle, 1965-80; sr. v.p. charge corp. devel. Bromar, Inc., Newport Beach, Calif., 1979—, dir., 1980—. Dir. ops. and tng. Oreg. Air N.G., 1946-50; chmn. food div. Multnomah County ARC, 1953, United Fund Drive, 1955; bd. deacons St. Andrews United Presbyn. Ch., 1959-62; v.p. USO for Oreg., 1977-80, bd. dirs., 1978-80. Served to maj. USAAF, 1941-45. Decorated Air medal with oak leaf cluster. Mem. Portland Food Brokers Assn. (past pres.), Nat. Food Brokers Assn. (regional dir. 1965-66), Portland C. of C.. Republican. Presbyterian. Clubs: Multnomah Athletic, Waverley Country, Bermuda Dunes Country, Eldorado Country, Rotary (pres. 1975-76). Home: 4014 SW 36th Pl Portland OR 97221 Office: Lloyd 500 Bldg 500 NE Multnomah St Suite 1203 Portland OR 97232

KAUFFMAN, WILLIAM MILLER, aerospace engr.; b. Los Angeles, Apr. 19, 1920; s. William Miller and Margaret Mary (Flynn) K.; B.M.E., Santa Clara U., 1942; m. Mary Jane Spear, May 27, 1945; children—Karen Kauffman Schmitt, Celeste Kauffman Weekley, John. Aero. research scientist flight research br. NACA, Ames Aero. Lab., Moffett Field, Calif., 1942-56; tech. asst. to mgr. astrionics div. Aerojet-Gen. Corp., Azusa, Calif., 1956-66; staff scientist systems engring. Aeronutronic Ford Corp., Palo Alto, Calif., 1967-70; tech. specialist systems engring. Aerojet Electrosystems Co., Azusa, 1970-75; cons. Avanti Aviation Co., Chino, Calif., 1975; cons. Aerojet Electrosystems Co., 1976, staff tech. specialist, 1977-79; sr. engr. Intermetrics, Inc., Huntington Beach, Calif., 1979-80; cons. ULA design, 1981-82. Served with USNR, 1946-47. Recipient A.S. Flemming award, 1955, L.T. Barbour award, 1967. Assoc. fellow AIAA; mem. Tau Beta Pi. Democrat. Roman Catholic. Author papers in field. Address: 434 Emerson St Costa Mesa CA 92627

KAUFMAN, ALAN STEPHEN, psychology educator, test developer; b. N.Y.C., Apr. 21, 1944; s. Max and Blanche (Levine) K.; m. Nadeen L. Bengels, Dec. 20, 1964; children—Jennie, David, James. A.B., U. Pa., 1965; M.A., Columbia U., 1967, Ph.D., 1970. Asst. dir. Psychol. Corp., N.Y.C., 1968-74; assoc. prof. U. Ga., Athens, 1974-79, U. Ill.-Chgo., 1979-80; prof. Nat. Coll. Edn., Evanston, Ill., 1980-82; prof. psychology Calif. Sch. Profl. Psychology, San Diego, 1982—; Recipient Outstanding Research award Ariz. Assn. Sch. Psychologists, 1980. Mem. Am. Psychol. Assn., Am. Ednl. Research Assn., Council for Exceptional Children, Nat. Assn. Sch. Psychologists. Developer psychol. tests for children; contbg. author articles in profl. jours., chpts. in profl. books. Editorial bd. numerous profl. jours. Home: 8960 Montrose Way San Diego CA 92122 Office: 3974 Sorrento Valley Blvd San Diego CA 92121

KAUFMAN, DAVID GRAHAM, constrn. co. exec.; b. North Canton, Ohio, Mar. 20, 1937; s. DeVere and Josephine Grace (Graham) K.; student Kent State U., 1955-57; grad. Internat. Corres. Schs., 1965; postgrad. Calif. Coast U.; m. Carol Jean Monzione, Oct. 5, 1957 (div. Aug. 1980); children—Gregory Allan, Christopher Patrick. Machinist apprentice Hoover Co., North Canton, Ohio, 1955-57; draftsman-designer Goodyear Aircraft Co., Akron, Ohio, 1957-60, Boeing Co., Seattle, 1960-61; designer Berger Industries, Seattle, 1961-62, Rubens & Pratt Engrs., Seattle, 1963-65; pres. Kaufman Inc., Juneau, Alaska, 1965—, Kaufman-Alaska Inc., Juneau, 1975—, Kaufman-Alaska Constructors Inc., Juneau, 1976—; constrn. mgr. U. Alaska, 1979—, instr. constrn. tech., 1980. Mem. Constrn. Specifications Inst., Portland (Oreg.) C. of C., N.Y. Inst. Photography. Republican. Roman Catholic. Home: PO Box 648 Juneau AK 99801 Office: PO Box 648 Juneau AK 99801

KAUFMAN, KAREN LYNN, construction company executive; b. Akron, Ohio, Mar. 19, 1948; d. William B. and Edith (Gruber) Rogovy; div.; children—Amanda, Jonathan. Student U. Akron, 1966-68, Tex. Tech U., 1968-69, U. Calif.-Riverside, 1977-80; B.S., U. San Francisco, 1981. Lic. contractor, Calif. Project mgr. Bilsar Corp., Riverside, 1977-79; housing specialist County of Riverside, 1979-80; project mgr. Lewis Homes of Calif., 1980-81; cons. Williams & Burrows, Belmont, Calif., 1982—; owner, mgr. Amajon, Upland, Calif., 1982—. Mem. Bldg. Industry Assn., Nat. Assn. Home Builders, Community Assns. Inst., Comml. Indsl. Council. Democrat. Jewish. Club: Aero Club of So. Calif.

KAUFMAN, NADEEN LAURIE, psychologist, researcher; b. N.Y.C., Jan. 17, 1945; d. Seymour and Hannah Sarah (Chavetz) Bengels; m. Alan Stephen Kaufman, Dec. 20, 1964; children—Jennie, David, James. B.S. in Edn., Columbia U., 1965, M.A. in Psychology, 1972, M.Ed. in Reading and Learning Disabilities, 1975, Ed.D. in Learning Disabilities, 1978. Cert. tchr., N.Y.; cert. sch. psychologist, Ga., Ill. Tchr. Pub. Schs., Norristown, Pa., 1965; research cons. Psychol. Corp., N.Y.C., 1971-74, Coll. Entrance Exam. Bd., N.Y.C., 1972-74; psychologist Rutland Psychoednl. Ctr., Ga., 1975-77; asst. prof. early childhood edn. U. Ga., Athens, 1978-79; asst. prof. learning disabilities DePaul U., Chgo., 1979-80; prof. sch. psychology Nat. Coll. Edn., Evanston, Ill., 1980-82; program developer Calif. Sch. Profl. Psychology, San Diego, 1982—. Recipient Sch. Psychology Research award Ariz. Assn. Sch. Psychologists, 1981. Mem. Am. Psychol. Assn., Council Exceptional Children, Nat. Assn. Sch. Psychology, Am. Ednl. Research Assn., Internat. Reading Assn. Democrat. Author: Clinical Evaluation of Young Children with the McCarthy Scales, 1977; (with Alan S. Kaufman) The Kaufman Assessment Battery for Children, 1983; assoc. editor Sch. Psychology Rev., 1981—; contbr. articles to profl. jours. Home: 8960

Montrose Way San Diego CA 92122 Office: 3974 Sorrento Valley Blvd San Diego CA 92121

KAUFMAN, SUSAN JANE, bank executive; b. Denver, Nov. 13, 1942; d. William Douglas and Catherine Sue (Orrison) Morrison; m. Jerry Allen Kaufman, Mar. 10, 1962; children—Eric Douglas, Carrie Annette. B.A., U. Colo., 1968; M.A., U. Denver, 1972; M.B.A., John F. Kennedy U., Orinda, Calif., 1981. Librarian, Littleton (Colo.) Pub. Library, 1972-74, Kent Denver Country Day Sch., 1974-76; exec. dir. Colo. Library Assn., Denver, 1974-76; customer service rep. bus. office Pacific Telephone Co., Berkeley, Calif., 1977-80; br. mgr., asst. v.p. Citicorp Savs., Orinda, 1981—. Mem. Contra Costa County M-11 Commn. (Calif.), 1983—. Mem. Jr. League Oakland/East Bay, Orinda C. of C., Orinda Hist. Soc., Am. Heart Assn., Les Dames du Coeur, Delta Gamma. Republican. Club: Soroptimists. Home: 6 Lavenida Orinda CA 94563 Office: 77 Moraga Way Orinda CA 94563

KAUFMAN, THOMAS ALLEN, school administrator; b. Wichita, Kans., May 22, 1940; s. Edward Emil and Cecelia Josephine Kaufman; m. Rose Marie G. Valente, June 16, 1962; children—Gregory Thomas, Matthew Edward, Scott Anthony. B.A., Colo., U., 1964; M.A., U. No. Colo., 1968, Ed.D., 1979. Tchr. social studies Baseline Jr. High Sch., Boulder, Colo., 1966-68; asst. prin. Lafayette High Sch., Boulder, 1968-69; prin. Cache La Poudre Jr. High Sch., Ft. Collins, Colo., 1969-81; prin. Lesher Jr. High Sch., Ft. Collins, Colo., 1981—; mem. adv. com. dept. edn. Colo. State U. Precinct chmn. Democratic Party, Ft. Collins; pres. St. Joseph's Parish Council, Ft. Collins. Served with U.S. Navy, 1957-63. NDEA fellow, 1968; named outstanding Educator, Acad. Am. Educators, 1973. Mem. Nat. Assn. Secondary Prins., Colo. Assn. Secondary Prins., Colo. Assn. Sch. Execs., Poudre Assn. Sch. Educators, Assn. Sch. Curriculum Developers, Phi Delta Kappa. Roman Catholic. Club: Ft. Collins Kiwanis (disting. pres. 1978-79). Home: 1112 Pitkin St Fort Collins CO 80524 Office: 1400 Stover St Fort Collins CO 80524

KAUFMAN, WILLIAM I., writer, photographer, designer, consultant; b. N.Y.C., June 8, 1922; children—Iva Anne, Lazare Seeley. With NBC TV Network, 1947-63; writer, editor 141 pub. works in areas of food, wine, travel, music, photography and TV, 1963—; works include numerous UNICEF, gen., TV, art books and cookbooks, most recent being: Mormon Pioneer Songbook, 1980; Watch Your Weight Series, 1980; Diet, Diary, Calories, Carbohydrates, Fiber, Cholesterol, Natural Foods, 6 books, 1980; The Traveler's Guide to the Vineyards of North America, 1980; Pocket Encyclopedia of California Wine (Gold Vine award), 1981, 82, 83; California Wine Drink Book, 1982; Pocket Encyclopedia of American Wines East of the Rockies, 1984; photographer; 21 one-man shows include: Assignment Children—1971, UN, 1972; All God's Children, Tenn. Arts Commn., 1973-74; Internat. Invitational of Photography, 1975; Family of Children, Plaza Hotel, N.Y.C., 1976; California Mus. Sci. and Industry, 1976; The Treasures, GF Industries, 1977; The Artisans, La Fortaleza, San Juan, P.R., 1979; lectr. on subjects of food, wine and photography; cons. new product devel. in areas of food and food appliances; creator spl. interest travel programs for maj. airlines; TV spokesman various corps. Bd. dirs. Ctr. for Improvement of Child Caring. Decorated comdr. de Bordeaux, Master Knight of the Vine; recipient Chrisopher award, 1971. Mem. Authors Guild, Screen Actors Guild, Overseas Press Club, Chevalier du Tastevin, Confrerie des Vignerons de Saint Vincent, Bontemps de Medoc and des Graves, Officiers de l'Ordre des Coteaux.

KAUFMANN, CYNTHIA SICKMANN, educational adminstrator; b. San Francisco, Mar. 23, 1950; d. Hubert A. and Betty Jean (Davis) Sickmann. B.A., Bethany Coll., 1972; M.Ed., U. Va., 1975; M.P.A., U. Denver, 1981, Ph.D., 1983. Tchr. first grade Prince William County Schs., Va., 1972-74, learning disabilities specialist, 1974-76, asst. prin., 1976-79; research asst. U. Denver, 1979-81; prin. Garfield County Sch. Dist. 16, Parachute, Colo., 1981—; instr. No. Va. Community Coll., Woodbridge, 1975-76. Bd. dirs. United Way campaign, Garfield County, Colo., 1982. Research asst. fellow U. Denver, 1979-81. Mem. Colo. Assn. Sch. Execs., Phi Delta Kappa, Alpha Delta Kappa. Presbyterian. Author: A Handbook for Coping with Decelerating Resources, 1981. Home: PO Box 39 Parachute CO 81635 Office: PO Box 68 Parachute CO 81635

KAUFMANN, THOMAS DAVID, educator; b. Rye, N.Y., July 23, 1922; s. Fritz and Irma (Heiden) K.; B.A., Oberlin Coll., 1943; M.P.A., Harvard U., 1947, M.A., 1947, Ph.D., 1949; m. Maureen Liebl, June 4, 1983; children—Peter F., David T. Economist, U.S. del. NATO and OEEC, Paris, 1949-56; dir. new bus. Amax, Inc., N.Y.C., 1956-67; v.p. Alumax, Inc., Greenwich, Conn., 1967-69; dir. bus. planning Hunter-Douglas, London, 1969-75; trader Asoma, N.Y.C., 1975-77; cons. Daniel K. Ludwig, N.Y.C., 1977-82; Philip Bros. prof. mineral econs. Colo. Sch. Mines, Golden, 1982—. Served with U.S. Army, 1943-46. Mem. Am. Econ. Assn., Phi Beta Kappa. Jewish. Club: Queens. Home: 1966 Mount Zion Dr Golden CO 80401 Office: Colo Sch Mines Golden CO 80401

KAUN, STEVEN LYNN, advertising executive; b. Glendale, Calif., Sept. 13, 1955; s. Terry Lynn and Betty Lorraine (Keller) K.; m. Cheryl Ann Riley, Nov. 23, 1974; children—Devin, Aaron. Grad. in Communications, Calif. State. U.-Fullerton, 1977. Asst. to dir. Schnitzer Prodns., Hollywood, Calif., 1976-77; exec. v.p. Trimagination Creative Services, Santa Ana, Calif., 1977-79; exec. v.p. McCreery/Pacific, Newport Beach, Calif., 1979-80; v.p., gen. mgr. Food Fundamentals, Irvine, Calif., 1980—. Club: Toastmasters. Office: 2107 N Broadway Suite 105 Santa Ana CA 92706

KAUNE, JAMES EDWARD, ship repair co. exec., former naval officer; b. Santa Fe, N.Mex., Mar. 4, 1927; s. Henry Eugene and Lucile (Carter) K.; B.S., U.S. Naval Acad., 1950; Naval Engr. degree Mass. Inst. Tech., 1955; B.S. in Metallurgy, Carnegie-Mellon U., 1960; m. Pauline Stamatos, June 24, 1956; children—Bradford Scott, Audrey Lynn, Jason Douglas. Commd. ensign U.S. Navy, 1950, advanced through grades to capt., 1970; asst. gunnery officer U.S.S. Floyd B. Parks, 1950-52; project officer U.S.S. Gyatt, Boston Naval Shipyard, 1955-57; main propulsion officer U.S.S. Tarawa, 1957-58; asst. planning officer Her Majesty's Canadian Dockyard, Halifax, N.S., Can., 1960-62; repair officer U.S.S. Cadmus, 1962-64; fleet maintenance officer Naval Boiler and Turbine Lab., 1964-68; various shipyard assignments, 1968-70, material staff officer U.S. Naval Air Forces Atlantic Fleet, 1971-74; production officer Phila. Naval Shipyard, 1974-79; comdr. Long Beach Naval Shipyard, Calif.; exec. v.p. Am. Metal Bearing Co., Garden Grove, Calif., from 1979; gen. mgr. San Francisco div. Topp Shipyards, Alameda, Calif., v.p. engring. Point Richmond Shipyard (Calif.). Mem. Am. Soc. Naval Engrs., Am. Soc. Quality Control, Soc. Naval Architects and Marine Engrs., U.S. Naval Inst., Am. Soc. Metals. Episcopalian. Club: Masons. Contbr. articles to profl. jours. Home: 403 Camino Sobrante Orinda CA 94563 Office: San Francisco Div Todd Shipyards Alameda CA 94501

KAUR, INDERJIT, marriage, group counselor; b. West Pakistan, Jan. 22, 1935; came to U.S., 1972; d. Kartar Singh Uppal and Rawel Kaur Bedi; m. Harbhajan Singh Khalsa, Jan. 22, 1953; children—Ranbir S. Bahi, Kulbir S. Bhai, Kamaljit K. Kohli. Student, Punjab U., 1951-54; B.A., Coll. of Santa Fe, 1979; M.A. (hon.), U. N.Mex., 1981, postgrad., 1981—; postgrad. U. Humanistic Studies, San Diego, 1981—. Tchr., instr. lang. 3HO Found., Los Angeles, 1972—, counseling specialist, pub. relations officer for eastern hemisphere, 1972—; tchr., trainer, counselor Khalsa Women's Tng. Camp, Albuquerque, 1972—; cons. Khalsa Med. Clinic, Berkeley, Calif., 1980—; internat. guest speaker TV, radio talk shows, 1974—; founder counseling clinics, Espanola and Albuquerque, N.Mex., Los Angeles. Recipient Appreciation cert. N.Mex. Sec. State, Gov., Lt. Gov., 1982. Mem. Am. Personnel Guidance Assn., I-A Women's Assn. (pres. 1977—), Santa Fe Opera Guild. Club: Women's Garden of Espanola. Author: Punjabi Handbook, 1975. Address: 219 Amhurst St SE Albuquerque NM 87106

KAUS, OTTO MICHAEL, judge; b. Vienna, Austria, Jan. 7, 1920; s. Otto F. and Gina (Wiener) K.; came to U.S., 1939, naturalized, 1942; B.A., UCLA, 1942; LL.B., Loyola U., Los Angeles, 1949; m. Peggy A. Huttenback, Jan. 12, 1943; children—Stephen D., Robert M. Admitted to Calif. bar, 1949; pvt. practice, Los Angeles, 1949-61; judge Superior Ct. Calif., 1961-64; asso. justice Calif. Ct. Appeal, 2d appellate dist., div. 3, Los Angeles, 1965-66, presiding justice div. 5, 1966-81; assoc. justice Calif. Supreme Ct., San Francisco, 1981—; mem. faculty Loyola U. Law Sch., 1950-75, U. So. Calif., 1974-77. Served with U.S. Army, 1942-45. Mem. Am. Law Inst., Phi Beta Kappa, Order of Coif. Office: Calif Supreme Ct State Bldg San Francisco CA 94102

KAUT, STANLEY WILLIAM, elec., nuclear and control system engr.; b. Huntington, N.Y., Nov. 28, 1943; s. Stanley William and Marie Patricia (Rhyne) K.; A.A.S., Rochester Inst. Tech., 1963, B.S. in Elec. Engring., 1966; m. Nina Kharchenko, Apr. 16, 1966; children—William Alexander, Kristian Stanley, Corrina Cheri. Field engr., project engr. Gen. Electric Co., N.Y., Pa., Calif., Minn., 1963-70; engr., sr. engr., mgr. Nuclear Services Corp., Campbell, Calif., 1970-75; engring. mgr., engring. dir., chief cons. Nutech, San Jose, Calif., 1975—. Mem. exec. bd. YMCA, 1979-80, mem. br. bd., 1977-80, youth program participant/leader, 1972-81, fund campaigner, dir., 1973-81, youth sports coach, 1974-81. Registered profl. engr., Calif. Mem. Am. Nuclear Soc., IEEE. Home: 6657 Copperwood Circle San Jose CA 95120 Office: 6835 Via Del Oro San Jose CA 95119

KAVANAUGH, BILL MICHAEL, nuclear engineer; b. Seattle, Feb. 22, 1938; s. Joseph Patrick and Mary Bill (Smith) K.; m. Joan Delores Engdahl, Apr. 6, 1963; B.S.M.E., U. Wash., 1961; M.S. in Engring., U. Ala., Huntsville, 1968. Registered profl. engr., Ala. Mech. engring. asst. U.S. Army Missile Command, Redstone Arsenal, Ala., 1961-63; sr. product engr. Chrysler Space Div., Huntsville, 1963-69; sr. engr. thermodynamics McDonnal-Douglas Astronautics Co., St. Louis, 1969-73; nuclear engr. Puget Sound Naval Shipyard, Bremerton, Wash., 1973—. Served with U.S. Army, 1961-63. Mem. Profl. Engrs. in Govt. (Wash. state chmn., nat. chmn., employment relations com. bd. gov.), Nat. Soc. Profl. Engrs., ASME, AIAA, U.S. Power Squadron, Lamda Chi Alpha. Clubs: Toastmasters (Port Orchard, Wash.); College (Seattle). Home: 1891 Sequoia St SE Port Orchard WA 98366 Office: Code 2320.7 Puget Sound Naval Shipyard Bremerton WA 98314

KAVELIN, JOHN HOWARD, scenic designer; b. Jackson, Miss., Jan. 7, 1944; s. Howard Borrah and Martha Louise (Hamilton) K. B.F.A., Carnegie Inst. Tech., 1965; M.F.A., Brandeis U., 1970. Instr. stage design Pa. State U., State College, 1965-66; asst. prof. scenic design N.C. Sch. of Arts, Winston-Salem, 1970-73, Conservatory of Theatre Arts, Webster Coll., St. Louis, 1974-78; show designer WED Enterprises, Walt Disney Prodns., Glendale, Calif., 1978—; theme park Wild Ride of Mr. Toad, Snow White's Scarey Adventures, projects (stage) Close Ties, Los Angeles Pub. Theatre (Drama-logue award), Two By South, Los Angeles Actor's Theatre, Little Foxes, Hay Fever, Tennessee Williams Fine Arts Ctr.; (touring prodns.) Daisy Mayme nat. tour, Tom Jones/A Musical midwest tour; chmn. bd. dirs. Light*Years Internat., Los Angeles; co-host TV series The Spiritual Revolution. Chmn. Spiritual Assembly Baha'is of Los Angeles. Served with U.S. Army, 1966-77. Mem. United Scenic Artists Assn. Local 350. Home: Apt 2 4707 Finley Ave Los Angeles CA 90027 Office: 1401 Flower St Glendale CA 91201

KAWAGUCHI, IKE ICHIRO, agronomist; b. Roy, Utah, Feb. 8, 1936; s. Kanichi and Teruko (Sase) K.; A.S. (tuition scholar 1958-59), Weber State Coll., 1959; B.S. (tuition scholar 1959-60), Utah State U., 1963, M.S., 1964; m. Chizuko Endow, Dec. 5, 1959; children—Jeffrey Brian, Kevin Todd. Truck farmer, Roy and Layton, Utah, 1954-62; welder Gen. Machine Co., Ogden, Utah, 1958; with Layton (Utah) Sugar Co., 1958-59; research agronomist, sta. dir. Waterman Loomis Co., Bakersfield, Calif., 1964-79, sr. research agronomist, sta. dir., 1979-81; dir. alfalfa breeding Plant Genetics Inc., Davis, Calif., 1982—. Mem. Western Alfalfa Improvement Conf. (chmn. 1969-71), Nat. Alfalfa Improvement Conf. (dir. 1969-71, 80-81), Am. Genetic Assn., Am. Soc. Agronomy, Crop Sci. Soc. Am., Soil Sci. Soc. Am., Western Soc. Crop Sci., Council Agrl. Sci. and Tech., Calif. Agrl. Prodn. Cons. Assn. Republican. Counselor, leader Boy Scouts Am. Club: Kiwanis (dir., chmn. agr. and conservation com.). Breeder alfalfa varieties. Home: 208 Jalisco Pl Davis CA 95616 Office: 1930 5th St Davis CA 95616

KAWANA, KOICHI, educator, artist; b. Asahikawa, Hokkaido, Japan, Mar. 16, 1930; s. Kiichi and Toki (Takeda) K.; B.S., Yokohama (Japan) Municipal U., 1951; A.B., UCLA, 1955, M.A., 1959, M.F.A., 1964; Ph.D., Pacific Western U., 1979; Master of Painting honoris causa, Internat. Seminar Modern and Contemporary Art. Lectr. landscape design, Japanese art history UCLA, 1962—, univ. research artist, 1964-66, lectr. art, 1966, asst. prof. art in residence, 1966, sr. artist dept. architects and engrs., 1968-70, design. cons., archtl. asso., 1970-73, prin. archtl. assoc., 1973—. Sumi paintings included collections White House, Washington, Grunwald Graphic Arts Found., garden design for Wattles Park, Los Angeles, Mo. Bot. Garden, St. Louis, Chgo. Hort. Soc. Bot. Garden, Glencoe, Ill., Denver Bot. Gardens, others; chmn. Environ. Design Assocs., 1966—; v.p. Kapa Co., 1969—. Recipient Seikyojo rank award Adachi-shiki Sch. Floral Design, 1961, Design award Progressive Architecture, 1972, Gold medal Accademia Italia delle Arti e del Lavoro; winner Nat. Soc. Interior Designers competition, 1961; recipient Order of Merit, Mil. and Hospitaller Order of St. Lazarus of Jerusalem. Mem. Am. Soc. Interior Designers, So. Calif. Hort. Inst., Japan Am. Soc. So. Calif. (council 1965—, Distinguished Service award 1965, Victor H. Carter Diamond award 1980), Los Angeles County Mus. Art, Far Eastern Art Council, Pi Gamma Mu, Pi Sigma Alpha. Club: UCLA Faculty Center. Contbr. articles to profl. jours. Home: 633 24th St Santa Monica CA 90402 Office: U Calif 601 Westwood Plaza Los Angeles CA 90024

KAWASAKI, DUKE T., businessman, state senator; b. Honolulu, Dec. 9, 1920; student Schillinger Music Sch., Boston; married, 2 children. Real estate broker-developer, Honolulu; mem. Hawaii Senate, 1966—. Past pres. Young Democrats of Oahu; past vice chmn. Dem. Com. Hawaii; mem. Young Dems. Nat. Com.; mem. Nat. Small Bus. Adv. Council. Served with U.S. Army, 1944-46. Office: Room 231 State Senate Honolulu HI 96813*

KAWECKI, LEON STANLEY, artist, art dir.; b. nr. Chojnice, Poland, July 2, 1921; s. Adam and Elizabeth (Link); came to U.S., 1952, naturalized, 1956; grad. State Coll. Graphic Arts Poznan (Poland), 1939; student Pitts. Art Inst., 1952-54, Otis Art Inst., 1964, Calif. Inst. Arts, 1966-67, Art Center Coll. Design, 1968, U. Calif. at Irvine, 1968-71; m. Jacqueline Salamey, Apr. 25, 1953; children—Raymond Mark, Steven James, Daniel Noel, Barbara Rachelle. Comml. artist Fuller Label & Box Co., Pitts., 1952-57; packaging designer Standard Packaging Corp., Pitts., 1957-60; art dir. Mead Packaging, Los Angeles, 1960—; exhibited in shows in Warsaw, Poland, Dusseldorf, Germany, Pasadena, Calif., Los Angeles, Mexico City; designer U.S. Bicentennial Commemorative medal Freedom Founders, Polonus Commemorative medal, 1979 Internat. Philatelic Exhbn., Commemorative medal John Paul II - A Son of Poland, Polish-Am. Numis. Assn., commemorative medal 300th Anniversary Relief of Vienna-King John III, Polish Am. Numis. Assn., commemorative medal King John III Sobieski Savior of Christianity, Polish Am. Congress, 1983. Supporting mem. Pitts. Symphony Orch., 1957-58; exec. officer Ariz.-Calif. Nat. Copernicus Com., 1971-73. Served with Polish Armed Forces, 1939-47. Recipient Silver medal All-Polish Scholastic Exhbn., 1936; Grand award U. Pitts., 1960; Gold and Silver medals Folding Box Internat. competition, 1963; Silver medal U.S. Folding Box competition, 1966; Gold medal 500th anniversary Copernicus celebration Adler Planetarium, Chgo., 1973; Silver medal 500th anniversary Copernicus Celebration, Warsaw, Poland, 1973; Grand Prix, World Folklore Philat. Exhbn., Chgo., 1978, award of excellence for exhibit Orange County Advt. Fedn., 1978, State Order Cultural Merit, Polish Ministry Arts and Culture, 1978, hon. medal and diploma 50th anniversary Regional Mus., Chojnice, Poland, others. Mem. Pasadena Arts League, Fountain Valley Arts Assn. (founding), Am. Philatelic Soc., Nat. Soc. Art Dirs., Art Dirs. Club Los Angeles, Polonus Philatelic Soc., Polonus Philatelic Soc. (hon.). Club: Town Hall of Calif. Research in coins and crowns of Poland from 14th to 18th century. Address: 6400 Valley View St Buena Park CA 90620

KAY, DOUGLAS HAROLD, optometrist, optometry educator; b. Oakland, Calif., Oct. 7, 1949; s. Marvin Jack and Lois Natalie (Bernstein) K. A.B., U. Calif., 1971, B.S. in Optometry, 1973, O.D., 1975. Registered optometrist, Calif. Assoc. Woodland Clin. Med. Group (Calif.), 1975-78; cons. Calif. Vision Service Plan, Sacramento, 1977-82; pvt. practice optometry, Davis, Calif., 1978—; clin. instr. Sch. Optometry, U. Calif., Berkeley, 1983—; mem. supervisory com. Calif. Optometric Credit Union. Dir. Valley Artist Prodns.; dir. Library Assocs., U. Calif.-Davis. Named Young Optometrist of Yr., Sacramento Valley Optometric Soc., 1981. Mem. Am. Optometric Assn., Calif. Optometric Assn., Sacramento Valley Optometric Soc., Vision Conservation Inst., C. of C. (dir. membership Davis Area). Democrat. Jewish. Club: Rotary (Davis). Office: 1111 Kennedy Pl Suite 6 Davis CA 95616

KAY, PETER, state senator; b. N.Y.C., Feb. 18, 1924; s. E.M. and S.V. Kay; m. Miriam Spitalny, 1949; children—Karen, Dianne. A.B., U. N.C., 1944; postgrad. Stanford U., 1943-44, LL.D., Southwestern U., 1949. Casualty claims adjuster Ariz. Adjustment Agy., 1952-69; formerly mem. Ariz. Ho. of Reps., now mem. Ariz. State Senate. Precinct capt. Ariz. Republican State Central Com., 1952-69. Served to sgt., U.S. Army, 1943-46; CBI. Mem. Ariz. Claimsmen's Assn. Home: 5002 E Calle Redonda Phoenix AZ 85018 Office: Arizona State Senate Phoenix AZ 85007

KAYA, MAURIECE HIROMU, environmental engineer; b. Hilo Hawaii, Oct. 29, 1949; s. Hisao and Hagie (Minamoto) K.; m. Shelley Shizuko, July 22, 1971; children—Katherine Noelani, Jennifer Malia Akemi. B.S.C.E. with distinction, U. Hawaii-Honolulu, 1970, M.S.C.E., 1971. Registered profl. engr., Hawaii. Design engr. Sunn, Low, Tom and Hara, Honolulu, 1971-72; project mgr., assoc., Gray, Rhee, and Assocs., Inc., 1972-78; civil engr., environ. engr., mgr., environ. br. Facilities Engring Div., Navy Pub. Works Ctr., Pearl Harbor, Hawaii, 1978-82, div. dir., 1982-83; dep. dir. Dept. Pub. Works, City and County of Honolulu, 1983—. Active Mauhawili Estate Community Assn. NSF Fellow, 1970-71. Mem. ASCE, Am. Water Works Assn., Water Pollution Control Fedn., Hawaii Water Pollution Control Assn. (pres.), Phi Kappa Pi. Democrat. Contbr. articles to profl. jours. Office: Dept Public Works City and County of Honolulu 650 S King St Honolulu HI 96813

KAYA, ROBERT MASAYOSHI, contractor; b. Waialua, Oahu, Hawaii, Feb. 3, 1914; s. Jinhichi and Aki (Tanimoto) K.; student pub. schs.; m. Florence Shinayo Okinaka, Mar. 15, 1939; children—Kathleen Tatsue, Merle Nobue, Virginia Sachie, Winifred Fumie. Carpenter, Hawaiian Contracting Co., 1935, carpenter, foreman D. Orita, contractor, 1936-37; owner contracting bus., Honolulu, 1937—; dir. City Bank Honolulu. Active YMCA; bd. dirs. Kuakini Med. Ctr. Mem. Gen. Contractors Assn. Hawaii, Oahu Contractors Assn. (pres. 1954-55), Building Industry Assn. Hawaii (pres. 1956), Honolulu C. of C., Honolulu Japanese C. of C. (pres. 1974-75), Nat. Assn. Home Builders (life dir. 1976—), Nat. Fedn. Ind. Bus., Japan Am. Soc. Honolulu, Bishop Museum Assn., U.S. Army Museum, U. Hawaii Found. Buddhist (pres. Zen sect. Soto Mission 1973-74). Clubs: Lions (dist. gov. Hawaii 1964-65, pres. 1955-56; life mem.), 200 (Honolulu). Home: 2380 Beckwith St Honolulu HI 96822 Office: 1087 Dillingham Blvd Honolulu HI 96817

KAYE, ALAN STEWART, linguist, educator, researcher; b. Los Angeles, Mar. 2, 1941; s. Sammy and Ray (Finkel) K.; m. Susan Marianne Mazur, Sept. 21, 1972; children—Jennifer D., Jeremy D. B.A. with honors, UCLA, 1965; M.A., U. Calif.-Berkeley, 1968, C.Phil., 1969, Ph.D., 1971. Teaching asst. U. Calif.-Berkeley, 1967-69; asst. prof. linguistics U. Colo., Boulder, 1969-71; asst. prof. linguistics, Arabic and Hebrew Calif. State U.-Fullerton, 1971-74, assoc. prof., 1974-78, prof., 1978—, dir. Lab. for Phoentic Research, 1971—; prof. Hebrew Shalom Bible Inst., Orange, Calif. Trustee North Orange County Community Coll. Dist., Fullerton, 1977—, Yorba Linda Library Dist., 1980-82. Fulbright grantee 1967, 78-79; NSF grantee, 1969-70; NEH grantee, 1973-74; Am Philos. Soc. grantee, 1973-74, 75-76. Mem. Am. Oriental Soc., Linguistic Soc. Am., Philol. Assn. Pacific Coast, Philol. Soc. Republican. Author: Chadian and Sudanese Arabic in the Light of Comparative Arabic Dialectology, 1976; A Dictionary of Nigerian Arabic: English-Arabic, 1982; A Dictionary of Nigerian Arabic: Arabic-English, 1983. Home: PO Box 32 Atwood CA 92601 Office: Department of Linguistics Calif State U Fullerton CA 92634

KAYE, ALEX R. (SANDY), mfg. co. exec.; b. N.Y.C., Dec. 24, 1936; s. Saul and Vilma (Boorstyn) K.; B.B.S., Coll. City N.Y.; m. Farida Karoon, June 27, 1954; 1 dau., Loretta Kaye Mintz. Div. mgr. Sears Roebuck & Co., N.Y.C., 1958—; v.p. mktg. Field Enterprises Corp., Chgo., 1958-77; pres., chmn. bd. Energy Assos., Ltd., Latham, N.Y., 1966-71, Land N' Sea Craft, Inc., San Jose, Calif., 1969-73, Porta-Bote Internat., Menlo Park, Calif., 1973—. Chmn. bd. San Francisco Better Bus. Bur. Dist. Sales Ethics Com., 1968-69; bd. dirs. San Mateo Better Bus. Bur., 1971-75, Am. Boat and Yacht Council, 1969-71. Recipient Fisher Body Craftsman's Guild award Gen. Motors, 1951; award City Coll. Div. Big Bro. Orgn., Mem. Soc. Automotive Engrs. 1955. Club: Commonwealth San Francisco. Office: PO Box 2287 Menlo Park CA 94025

KAYE, ELLEN SUE, university dean; b. Cleve., Sept. 28, 1953; d. Samuel and Aline Betty (Emerman) K. B.S., U. Calif.-Berkeley, 1975; M.B.A., Nat. U., 1980; postgrad. U. So. Calif., 1982. Park aide Yosemite Nat. Park, summers 1972-73, project dir. NSF grantee, 1974; environ. cons. No. Plains Resource Council, Billings, Mont., 1975-77; county land-use planner Stillwater County (Mont.), 1977-78; dean continuing edn. Nat. U., 1978—, tchr. mgmt. workshops, 1979—; organizer Fin. Planning Program for Women, career devel. programs Mgmt. Devel. Inst.; lectr., mgmt. cons. to bus., industry; pub. quar. Continuing Edn. Catalog Named Outstanding Young Woman Am., U.S. Jaycees, 1980, 81, Outstanding Alumna Nat. U. Alumni Assn., 1980, Outstanding Young Citizen San Diego, San Diego Jaycees, 1981; recipient 1st Place award Am. Coll. Testing, Nat. U. Continuing Edn. Assn. Innovative

Award in Continuing Edn., 1981; Outstanding Service award City San Diego, 1979, 80, 81, 82, others. Mem. Nat. Mgmt. Assn. (pres. chpt. 1982), Am. Soc. Tng. and Devel. (pres. chpt. 1982-83), Nat. Univ. Continuing Edn. Assn. (award 1980), Women in Bus., World Trade Assn., Career Guidance Assn., Career Women's Assn. (founder 1979, pres. 1979-80), San Diego Wellness Council, San Diego Navy League, Nat. U. Alumni Assn. (chmn. 1983). Author: Black Bear Population of Yosemite, 1974. Home: 5626 Abalone Pl La Jolla CA 92037 Office: 4141 Camino Del Rio S San Diego CA 92108

KAYE, KENNETH, ins. ofcl.; b. Bklyn., Sept. 16, 1946; s. William and Gladys K.; m. Nancy Friedland, Mar. 24, 1974; children—Lisa Rachel, Deborah Alaina. B.A. cum laude in Classics, Bklyn. Coll., 1968; M.A. in Classics, U. Calif., Santa Barbara, 1970. Tchr., UCLA Extension, 1973-76; lectr. U. So. Calif., 1974-76; underwriter Occidental Life Ins. Co., 1976-77, Gordon Co., 1978-79; regional tng. coordinator Wausau Ins. Cos., Los Angeles, 1979—; instr. Ins. Ednl. Assn., 1980—; adj. asst. prof. Western div. Coll. of Ins., 1982—. Modern and Classical Lang. Assn. So. Calif. scholar, 1971. Mem. Am. Soc. Tng. and Devel., Ins. Co. Edn. Dirs. Soc. Office: 3130 Wilshire Blvd Los Angeles CA 90010

KAYE, LORI, lecturer, author, consultant, educator, actress; b. N.Y.C., June 19; d. Eldin Bert and Katherine Angeline (Varkulas) Onsgard. Student Detroit Inst. Art, 1956-57, U. N.Mex., 1958-60. Cons., v.p. Electron Industries, Torrance, Calif., 1961-70, Freeze-Air Internat., Torrance, 1961-70; actress Warner Bros., Burbank, Calif., 1960-64; speech and drama instr. John Robert Powers, Los Angeles, 1960-73, v.p., owner, dir., regional dir., 1962-73, nat. sales dir., 1964-70; owner, pres. Lori Kaye Cosmetics, Los Angeles, 1965-73; sch. dir. Caroline Leonetti Ltd., Hollywood, Calif., 1975-79; internat. cons. Glendale (Calif.) Coll. Bus. and Paramed., 1980, Acad. Pacific, Hollywood, 1981; internat. cons., dir. Internat. Career Acad., Van Nuys, Calif., 1972—; pres. KLM Advt., Studio City, Calif., 1979-83; internat. cons., nat. dir. admission A&T Inst. Travel and Tourism, North Hollywood, Calif., 1982-83; pres. Molori Publs., Studio City, 1979—; radio and TV commls., Los Angeles, 1960—; world wide travel lectr., instr., cruise ship lectr.; guest speaker various orgns. and firms. Vol. Camarillo (Calif.) State Hosp., 1963-67; N.Mex. Job Corps cons. with Senator F. Chavez, Albuquerque, 1967. Served with CAP, 1956-58. Recipient Mental Health Spl. Achievement award Camarillo State Hosp., 1967; named dir. of year John Robert Powers Schs. of Self Devel., Los Angeles, 1966; recipient participation award U.S.-Australia First Internat. Meet, Masters Swimming Internat., 1974. Mem. Nat. Assn. Female Execs., Screen Actors Guild, AFTRA, Smithsonian Assocs., Internat. Platform Assn., Nat. geog. Soc., Am. Film Inst. Author various tng. manuals and works in field. Home: 5438 1/4 Vesper Van Nuys CA 91411 Office: Malori Publs 11684 Ventura Blvd Suite 134 Studio City CA 91604 also A&T Inst of Travel and Tourism 12123 Magnolia North Hollywood CA 91607

KAYFETZ, VICTOR JOEL, journalist, editor; b. N.Y.C., July 20, 1945; s. Daniel Osler and Selma Harriet (Walowitz) K.; B.A., Columbia U., 1966; postgrad. U. Stockholm (Sweden), 1966-67; M.A. in History, U. Calif.-Berkeley, 1969. Teaching asst. in Swedish, U. Calif., Berkeley, 1969-70; tchr., adminstr. Dalaro Folk Coll., Sweden, 1970-71, Visingso Folk Coll., Sweden, 1972-73; head tchr. English, Studieframjandet Adult Sch., Stockholm, 1973-74, sec. head, 1974-75; corr. Reuters, Stockholm, 1975-78; sub-editor Reuters World Ser., London, 1978; corr. London Fin. Times, Stockholm, 1979-80; copy editor, translator Scandinavian Bus. World, 1981-82; free lance translator Swedish, Danish, Norwegian, 1967—; free lance journalist, editor Swedish and Am. mags., Stockholm, 1979-80, San Francisco, 1980—. Harry Evans traveling fellow, 1966-67; Nat. Def. Fgn. Lang. fellow, 1967-69; Thord Gray fellow Am.-Scandinavian Found., 1970. Mem. Stockholm Fgn. Press Assn., Media Alliance, World Affairs Council No. Calif., Sierra Club, Phi Beta Kappa. Club: Swedish Nat. Press. Author: Sweden in Brief, 1974, 2d edit., 1977; editor, translator numerous books and articles Swedish Inst., 1971—; editor, translator Swedish Industry Faces the 80s, 1981; others. Office: Scan Edit World Trade Center Room 268 San Francisco CA 94111

KAYS, DOUGLAS BRUCE, lawyer; b. Eugene, Oreg., Mar. 14, 1954; s. James W. and Marilyn (Griffith) K.; m. Jean Marie McEvoy, Aug. 14, 1982. B.S., Willamette U., 1976; J.D., Southwestern U., 1979. Bar: Calif. 1980. Gen. counsel McMahan's Furniture Co., Santa Monica, Calif., 1980—; sole practice law, Santa Monica, 1980—; staff counsel Western Home Furnishings, 1982—; lectr. in field. Bd. dirs. Greater Los Angeles Consumer Credit Assn., 1982-83, Santa Monica Y's Men's, 1982-83, Santa Ana Taxpayers Assn., 1982-83. Named Future First Citizen, Eugene, 1972; Am. Legion award, 1969. Mem. ABA, Calif. Bar Assn., Los Angeles County Bar Assn. Republican. Methodist. Home: 859 Harvard St Santa Monica CA 90403 Office: 2121 Wilshire Blvd Santa Monica CA 90403

KAYS, JAMES WILLIAM, investment executive; b. Princeton, Ind., Aug. 19, 1924; s. James Oscar and Mildred June (Hedge) K.; m. Marilyn Griffith, June 13, 1948; children—J. Alan, Nancy Lynn Kays Read, Douglas B., David W., Scott T., Holly J., John P. B.S. in Bus. Adminstrn., U. Oreg., 1948. Gen. mgr. Eugene (Oreg.) Country Club, 1948-53; supr. Standard Ins. Co., 1953-58; with Adams, Hess, Moore & Co., Eugene, and predecessor E.M. Adams & Co., 1958—, chmn. bd., 1982—; dir. R.A. Chambers & Assocs.; pres. Eugene Open, Inc. Mem. Eugene Civic Ctr. Comm.; fin. chmn. Oreg. Bach Festival; chmn. 1st United Methodist Ch. Found.; bd. dirs. Sr. Masters Golf Assn.; trustee Eugene Symphony Endowment Fund. Served with AUS, 1943-45; ETO. Named Eugene Jr. 1st Citizen, 1954; Boss of Yr., Nat. Secs. Assn., 1972. Mem. Roundtable, Nat. Assn. Corp. Dirs. Republican. Clubs: Eugene Country (past pres.), Lions (past pres.), Town (dir.) (Eugene). Home: 2085 Sunrise Blvd Eugene OR 97405 Office: 975 Oak St Suite 560 Eugene OR 97405

KAYS, WILLIAM MORROW, engineering school dean; b. Norfolk, Va., July 29, 1920; s. Herbert Emery and Margaret (Fechteler) K.; A.B., Stanford U., 1942, M.S., 1947, Ph.D. in Mech. Engring., 1951; m. Alma Campbell, Sept. 14, 1947 children—Nancy, Leslie, Margaret, Elizabeth. Asst. prof. mech. engring. Stanford U., 1951-54, asso. prof., 1954-57, prof., 1957—, chmn. dept., 1961-72, dean Sch. Engring., 1972—; dir. Acurex Corp.; cons. Served with AUS, 1942-46. Fulbright fellow, 1959-60; NSF sr. postdoctoral fellow, 1966-67. Fellow ASME (Heat Transfer Div. Meml. award 1965); mem. Am. Soc. Engring. Edn., Nat. Acad. Engring. Author: Compact Heat Exchangers, 1964; Convective Heat and Mass Transfer, 1979; adv. bd. Internat. Jour. Heat and Mass Transfer, 1982—. Office: Sch Engring Stanford U Stanford CA 94305

KAZANJIAN, PHILLIP CARL, lawyer; b. Visalia, Calif., May 15, 1945; s. John Casey and Sat-ten Arlene Kazanjian; B.A. with honors in Speech and Polit. Sci., U. So. Calif., 1967; J.D. with honors, Lincoln U., 1973; m. Wendy Coffelt, Feb. 5, 1972. Admitted to Calif. bar, 1979; comdg. officer Navy Internal Relations Activity, Los Angeles, 1975—; chief exec. officer Trident Communications, Inc., Glendale, Calif., 1978—; ptnr. firm Brakefield & Kazanjian, Los Angeles, 1979—. Mem. Calif. Atty. Gen.'s advv. commn. on community-police relations, 1973; v.p. bd. trustees Glendale Community Coll., 1981; bd. dirs. Los Angeles County Naval Meml. Found., Inc., 1981. Served with U.S. Army, 1968. Recipient tribute U.S. Ho. of Reps. Congl. Record, 1974; Centurion award Chief of Naval Ops., 1978. Mem. ABA (Gold Key award 1972), Calif. State Bar Assn., Los Angeles County Bar Assn., Assn. Am. Trial Lawyers, Scribes, Am. Soc. Writers on Legal Subjects, Los Angeles Trial Lawyers Assn., Res. Officers Assn. U.S. (nat. judge adv.), Naval Res. Assn. (pres. Rose Bowl chpt.), Naval Inst. Republican. Episcopalian. Clubs: Am. Polar Soc., Explorers Club, Polar Regions Soc. (dir.), Town Hall of Calif., Commonwealth of Calif. Author: The Circuit Governor, 1972; editor-in-chief: Lincoln Law Rev., 1973. Office: 417 S Hill St Suite 770 Los Angeles CA 90013

KAZANOWSKI, ALBIN DANIEL, operations research manager, consultant; b. Terryville, Conn., Aug. 22, 1926; s. Matthew H. and Mary M. (Sosinski) K.; m. Mary A. Kotuli, July 24, 1949; children—Carol K., Matthew D. Student, MIT, 1944-45, B.S. in Chem. Engring., Northeastern U., Boston, 1951; M.B.A., Harvard U., 1953; cert. cost analyst Inst. Cost Analysis, 1982. Systems/ops. analyst Kaiser Aluminum & Chem. Corp., Spokane, 1953-60; mgmt. cons. United Research Inc., Beverly Hills, Calif., 1960-62; sr. tech. specialist/supr./sr. mem. tech. staff ops. analysis group advanced systems Space Div., Rockwell Internat., Downey, Calif., 1962-80; mgr. The Aerospace Corp., Los Angeles, 1980—; cons. design and analysis of biomed. expts., 1957-59; lectr. local univs. and colls. Served with USAF, 1946-47. Fellow AAAS, Inst. for Advance of Engring.; mem. AIAA, Ops. Research Soc. Am., Inst. Cost Analysis, World Future Soc., Town Hall Calif. Republican. Roman Catholic. Clubs: Harvard Bus. Sch. (Los Angeles). Home: 21869 Woodland Crest Dr Woodland Hills CA 91364 Office: PO Box 92957 Los Angeles CA 90009

KAZEMI, HOSSEIN, petroleum engineering executive; b. Iran, Mar. 11, 1938; s. Ali Akbar and Bozorg K.; m. Bonnie M. Killian, July 31, 1964; children—Greg H. Steve K., Karen L. B.S. in Petroleum Engring., U. Tex., Austin, 1961, Ph.D., 1963. Registered profl. engr., Colo. Research scientist, sr. research scientist Sinclair Research and Atlantic Richfield Co., 1963-69; advanced research scientist, sr. research scientist, research assoc. Marathon Oil Co. Denver Research Ctr., 1969—, mgr. engring. dept., 1981—; lectr. Tulsa U. 1967-69, Colo. Sch. Mines, 1981—. Recipient Henry Mattson Tech. Service award Denver Petroleum sect. Soc. Petroleum Engrs., 1980; Engring. fellow, U. Tex., 1961. Mem. Soc. Petroleum Engrs. of AIME. Contbr. articles to profl. jours. Office: PO Box 269 Littleton CO 80160

KAZLO, MARTHA PEYTON, psychologist, consultant; b. Cumberland, Md., Nov. 18, 1945; d. Orvel Patrick and Henrietta Maria (Peyton) K.; B.S., U. Md., 1967, M.Ed., 1972, Ph.D., 1975. Registered psychologist, Calif. Field dir. Shawnee council Girl Scouts, U.S., Cumberland, Md., 1967-70; research asst. U. Md., College Park, 1970-72; asst. dir. commuter services, 1973-74, psychol. intern counseling ctr., 1974-75; counseling psychologist Calif. State Coll., San Bernardino, 1975—; tchr. and mgmt. cons. Bd. dirs. YWCA, San Bernardino, Calif., 1977-79; mem. Nat. Women's Polit. Caucus. Mem. Am. Psychol. Assn., Am. Personnel and Guidance Assn., Am. Coll. Personnel Assn., now (pres.). Democrat. Office: Counseling Center Calif State Coll San Bernardino CA 92407

KAZOR, VIRGINIA ERNST, curator, architectural historian; b. Detroit, Sept. 28, 1940; d. Frederic William and Marjorie F. (Fobert) Ernst; m. Eugene L. Kazor, Nov. 27, 1970. B.A. in Art and Archtl. Hist., U. So. Calif., 1963. Asst. curator modern art Los Angeles County Mus. Art, 1965-68; curator Fred and Marcia Weisman Collection, Los Angeles, 1969; curator Mcpl. Art Gallery, Los Angeles, 1970-78, Frank Lloyd Wright's Hollyhock House, Los Angeles, 1978—; bd. dirs. Los Angeles Conservancy, 1982-83; exhibits include Greene & Greene: The Architecture & Related Designs of Charles Sumner Greene and Henry Mather Greene, 1976. Pres. Ridgewood-Wilton Neighborhood Assn., Los Angeles, 1982. Mem. Soc. Archtl. Historians (pres. So. Calif. chpt. 1981—), Los Angeles Conservancy. Office: 4808 Hollywood Blvd Los Angeles CA 90027

KEADY, WILLIAM LEO, JR., elec. equipment co. exec.; b. Newport, R.I., Nov. 8, 1928; s. William Leo and Margaret (Jennings) K.; B.S., Trinity Coll., 1951; m. Shirley Kathryn Davenport, Nov. 5, 1955; children—William McCall, Robert Jennings, Margaret Kathryn. Sales engring. Charles S. James Co., San Francisco, 1956-60; sales engring. exec. v.p. Balloon Tire Mould Corp., Los Angeles, 1960-66; adminstrv. v.p. Advalloy, Inc., Palo Alto, Calif., 1966-67, pres., 1968—; dir. Viking Container Corp., San Jose, Calif. Pres. Alpine Little League, Inc., Portola Valley, Calif., 1972-76; founder Alpine Sr. League, 1969, Alpine Big League, 1972; pres. Woodside Priory Found., Woodside Priory Sch., Portola Valley, 1971-78. Mem. central com. Republican party, San Mateo County, Calif., 1971—. Served to comdr. USAF, 1952-56. Mem. Research Inst. Am., Am. Welding Soc., Am. Irish Hist. Soc. (life), Air Force Assn., Semicondr. Materials Inst., Gun Owners Am., Gun Owners Calif., Navy League, Am. Electronics Assn., Nat. Rifle Assn., Second Amendment Found., Ducks Unltd., Mil. Order World Wars, Law and Order Com., Calif. Rifle and Pistol Assn., Calif. Waterfowl Assn., Calif. Wildlife Fedn., Portola Valley Trails Assn., Am. Metal Stamping Assn., San Mateo County Horseman's Assn., Citizens Com. for Right to Keep and Bear Arms, Lincoln Continental Owner's Club. Clubs: Shack Riders Inc. (dir.), Portola Valley Polo (dir. 1978), Portola Valley Duck (pres. 1975-82), Cementary Riders, Tenn. Squires. Home: 15 Shoshone Pl Portola Valley CA 94025 Office: 844 E Charleston Rd Palo Alto CA 94303

KEAHEY, PETE FRANCIS, mining company administrator; b. Newborn, N.C., Jan. 31, 1936; s. Joe Judson and Cathelene Elizabeth (Turgeon) K.; m. Yvonne Jean Goodwin, Feb. 8, 1958 (dec.); children—Geoffrey, Debra, Mark; Amy. m. 2d, Patricia Mae Bernhardt, June 9, 1979. Student Boise Jr. Coll., 1955-56, Oreg. State Coll., 1956-57. Petroleum engr. Phillips Petroleum Inc., Bartelsville, Okla., 1966-75; drilling and blasting foreman Peabody Coal, St. Louis, 1975-78; dept. head drilling and blasting Kayenta Mine Peabody Coal Inc., Page, Ariz., 1978—. Republican. Club: Elks.

KEALA, FRANCIS AHLOY, security adminstr.; b. Honolulu, June 1, 1930; s. Samuel Louis and Rose (Ahloy) K.; B.A., U. Hawaii, 1953; m. Betty Ann Lyman, Nov. 28, 1952; children—Frances Ann, John Richard, Robert Mark. With Honolulu Police Dept., 1956-83, detective, 1962-65, lt., 1965-68, capt., 1968-69, chief of police, 1969-83; dir. security Hawaiian Telephone Co., Honolulu, 1983—. Bd. dirs. Aloha council Boy Scouts Am., Hawaii chpt. ARC, Boys' Club Honolulu, Palama Settlement, Honolulu Muscular Dystrophy Assn.; mem. civilian adv. group U.S. Army; trustee St. Louis High Sch. Served with U.S. Army, 1953-55. Mem. Internat. Assn. Chiefs of Police, Hawaii State Law Enforcement Ofcls. Assn., FBI Nat. Acad. Assocs., Nat. Ednl. Inst. Assocs. Club: Rotary. Office: 1455 Beretania St Honolulu HI 96815

KEANE, JOHN, architect, graphic designer; b. N.Y.C., Sept. 28, 1940; s. John Joseph and Flavia (Heaney) K.; m. Nadasha Halupke, Mar. 20, 1977. B.Arch., Columbia U., 1968. Asst. project architect William B. Tabler, N.Y.C., 1961-62; project architect Edgar Tafel, N.Y.C., 1963-64, Justin Henshell-Arthur Drexler, N.Y.C., 1968-69; asst. prof. architecture Dutchess County Community Coll., Poughkeepsie, N.Y., 1969-70; prin. archtl.-graphic design firm, San Francisco, 1972—; cons. Community Design Ctr., San Francisco, Community Coop. Berkeley, U. Calif. Served with USNR, 1962-63. Recipient Western Art Dirs. Club award (Gap Stores), 1976; Progressive Architecture citation (Community Design Ctr. project), Yerba Buena Planning Ballot, 1977. Mem. AIA. Roman Catholic. Graphic designs include Cow Palace, Kaiser Hosps. Signing System, Stinson Beach Houses, Stinson Beach, Calif., Poolside House, Sausalito, Calif., Bethsaida Ch., Marin City, Calif. Office: 1603 Howard St San Francisco CA 94103

KEANE, WILLIAM FRANCIS, photographer; b. La Habra, Calif., June 8, 1948; s. William Edward and Joan Francis Keane; m. Beverly Paul, May 5, 1973; children—Cameron Patrick, Chelsea Shannon. B.A., Claremont Men's Coll.; craftsman photographer Profl. Photographers Am., 1980. Owner, Bill Keane Photography, Claremont, Calif., 1968-71; apprentice Charis Studios, Pasadena, Calif., 1971; chief photographer Fotomat Corp., La Jolla, Calif., 1972-75; owner Keane Studios, Santa Ana, Calif., 1982—, San Diego, 1976—; founder The Bridal Bazaar, San Diego, 1975—; lectr. in field. Mem. Profl. Photographers Am., Profl. Photographers Calif., Am. Soc. Photographers. Republican. Columnist, Profl. Photographer, 1978-81, Rangefinder, 1981-82. Office: 7341 Claremont Mesa San Diego CA 92111

KEAR, FRED WINSTON, manufacturing company executive; b. Clayton, N.Mex., Nov. 11, 1930; s. James Clifford and Lillie Mae (Ogle) K.; student Union Coll. (Nebr.), 1950-51; m. Fonda Anita Scott, Jan. 11, 1953; children—Steven Scott, Stephanie Kay, Pamela Mae. Dir. research and devel. lab. Lytle Corp., Albuquerque, 1960-64; chief mfg. engr. Sparton S.W., Inc., Albuquerque, 1964-72, 77—; sr. quality assurance engr. Singer Bus. Machines, Albuquerque, 1972-75; mgr. mfg. MRL S.W., Albuquerque, 1975-76; engr. supr. GTE Lenkurt, Albuquerque, 1977—. Served with USN, 1950-54. Mem. Soc. Mfg. Engrs. Democrat. Seventh-Day Adventist. Author: The Design and Manufacture of Printed Circuits, 1971; Production Engineering, 1973; Manufacture of Electronic Assemblies, 1979; contbr. articles to profl. jours.; chief contbr. to Handbook of Electronic Circuits, 1969, others. Home: 1729 Shirley St Albuquerque NM 87112 Office: 1 Camino De Lenkurt Albuquerque NM 87123

KEAR, MARGARET IRVIL, instrument co. exec.; b. Pottsville, Pa., May 17, 1935; d. Carl Irvin and Alice Mildred (Guensch) K.; A.B., Wilson Coll., 1957; M.S. in Edn., U. Maine, 1976; D.A., Idaho State U., 1978; children—Geoffrey William Snyder, Margaret Elizabeth Pease. Tchr. public schs., Pa., Maine, Idaho, 1962-79; fuel allocationist, program mgr. transp. Idaho Office of Energy, Boise, 1979-80; funding project dir. Idaho Assn. Soil Conservation Dists., Boise, 1980-82; exec. sec. Demaray Sci. Instrument, Ltd., Pullman, Wash., 1982—. Unitarian. Home: NW 725 Ritchie Pullman WA 99163 Office: SE 1122 Latch St Pullman WA 99163

KEARNEY, CHERYAL ANN, set decorator, interior designer; b. Los Angeles; d. Donald Ray and Henrietta (Robinson) K. B.A., Woodbury U., Los Angeles, 1964; degree in interior design Parson Sch. Design-Musee Des Arts Decoratifs, 1979. Set decorator for TV shows including Cannon, 1971, Harry-O, 1973, 74, Spiderman, 1978, Tucker's Witch, 1981; set decorator films including Sounder II, 1975, Bad News Bears, 1975, Mother, Jugs and Speed, 1975, A Hero Ain't Nothin' But a Sandwich, 1976, Semi-Tough, 1977, The Promise, 1978, Lazarus Syndrome, 1979, Under the Rainbow, 1980, Poltergeist, 1981, Two of a Kind, 1982. Active Los Angeles Urban League, NAACP, Los Angeles. Mem. Am. Soc. Interior Designers, Acad. Motion Picture Arts and Scis., Acad. TV Arts and Scis. (Emmy 1980). Clubs: Media Forum, Los Angeles. Home: 8856 Guthrie Ave Los Angeles CA 90034 Office: Unique Design Experience 4506 Valdina Pl Los Angeles CA 90043

KEARNEY, JOHN ALLEN, banker; b. Columbus, Tex., Aug. 8, 1944; s. Charles W. and Mackie (Boswell) K.; m. Betty Arlene Thompson, Feb. 10, 1971; children—John Allen, Alison Lyn. B.S., Tex. A&M U., 1966; M.S., Purdue U., 1968; grad. Stonier Grad. Sch. Banking Rutgers U., 1982. Analyst trainee Bank of Southwest, Houston, 1970-73; investment officer/asst. v.p. Tex. Commerce Bank, Houston, 1973-76; v.p. Valley Nat. Bank Ariz., Phoenix, 1976—. Bd. dirs., treas. City of Phoenix Indsl. Devel. Authority. Served to 1st lt. U.S. Army, 1968-70. Club: Phoenix Stock and Bond. Home: 9037 N 29th St Phoenix AZ 85028 Office: Valley Nat Bank of Ariz PO Box 29514 Phoenix AZ 85038

KEARNS, DONN KENYON, air force officer; b. Topeka, Dec. 3, 1949; s. Gilbert Paul, Jr., and Helen (Hyer) K.; m. Elizabeth Ann Spingler, June 15, 1974. B.S. in Math., U. Ga., 1971, M.S. in Stats., 1974. Commd. 2d lt. U.S. Air Force, 1974, advanced through grades to capt., 1976; served as computer systems analyst, Gunter AFS, Ala., 1974-78, chief computer mgmt. sect., Hickam AFB, Hawaii, 1978-79, chief computer acquisition and devel. office, 1979-81, dep. chief of computer program mgmt. office, 1981-82, dep. chief intelligence and tactical systems div., 1982—. Named Pacific Air Forces Outstanding Data Automation Officer of Year, 1982. Episcopalian. Mem. various sports clubs. Contbr. profl. procs. to publs. Home: 98-814C Kaonohi St Aiea HI 96701 Office: HQ PACAF/ACDI Hickam AFB HI 96853

KEARNS, WILLIAM JOSEPH, computer co. exec.; b. Pitts., Aug. 30, 1922; s. William J. and Ida Louise (Rotter) K.; B.S., Carnegie Mellon U., 1949; m. Joan Brandenberg, Apr. 22, 1950; children—James William, Alan John, David Paul. Vacuum engr. Carnegie Inst. Tech., Pitts., 1949-51; tube devel. engr. Gen. Electric Co., Schenectady, 1951-62, mgr. ion pump devel., 1962-64; mgr. electron devices Electro-Optical System, Pasadena, Calif., 1964-67; mgr. system analysis Xerox Co., Pasadena, 1967-71; co-founder, mgr. materials and process engring. Duplicon Corp., Newport Beach, Calif., 1971-75; cons., Costa Mesa, 1975; co-founder, v.p. New World Computer Corp., Costa Mesa, Calif., 1976-82, patent agt., cons. product devel., 1982—. Mem. Democratic Com., East Glenville, N.Y., 1963-64. Served with USAAF, 1944-45. Decorated Air medal. Mem. Am. Phys. Soc., Am. Vacuum Soc., Instrument Soc. Am. Patentee in field. Home: 3350 California St Costa Mesa CA 92626

KEATING, PATRICK DAVID, educator, administrator; b. Flandreau, S.D., Feb. 25, 1939; s. Leonard Michael and Mildred Ione (Sedelmeier) K.; m. Judith Ann Madson, Aug. 12, 1961; children—Todd James, David Patrick. B.A., Huron Coll., 1961; M.A., Adams State Coll., 1964. Tchr., coach, Gettysburg (S.D.) High Sch., 1961-63; grad. asst., coach Adams State Coll., Alamosa, Colo., 1963-64; tchr., coach, Ceres (Calif.) High Sch., 1967-74; tchr., coach Salinas (Calif.) High Sch., 1967-74; vocat. coordinator, dir. Mission Trails Regional Occupation Program, 1978—. Bd. dirs. Continental Little League, 1973-76; active YMCA; bd. dir. Pop Warner Football, 1977-80. Mem. Am. Vocat. Assn., Calif. Vocat. Assn., Calif. Dirs. Vocat. Edn., Phi Delta Kappa. Democrat. Roman Catholic. Club: Lions. Home: 1360 Cherokee Dr Salinas CA 93906 Office: 867 E Laurel Dr Salinas CA 93905

KEATING, THOMAS FRANCIS, state senator; b. Langdon, N.D., Nov. 26, 1928; s. Thomas Delbert and Olive Mary (Bear) K.; student Eastern Mont. Coll., 1951; B.A. in Bus. Adminstrn., U. Portland, 1953; m. Anna Louise Walsh, Aug. 22, 1953; children—Thomas J., Patrick, Michael, Kathryn, Terence. Landman, Mobil Oil Corp., Billings, Mont., 1954-61, Oklahoma City, 1961-66, Burlington No. R.R., Billings, 1966-67; Mont., landman, Billings, 1967-81; mem. Mont. Senate, 1981—. Served with USAF, 1946-49. Mem. Mont. Assn. Petroleum Landmen (pres. 1969), Am. Assn. Petroleum Landmen (dir. 1971-73), Ind. Petroleum Assn., Billings C. of C. Republican. Roman Catholic. Office: PO Box 20522 Billings MT 59104

KEATING, WALTER JAMES, fin. exec.; b. Atlantic City, May 23, 1947; s. John J. and Alice (Mercer) K.; B.B.A., U. Okla., 1970; m. Aug. 6, 1969; children—Jennifer Lynn, Jared Alan. Loan officer Security Pacific Bank, Westwood Village, Calif., 1970-72; account exec. Merrill Lynch, Long Beach, Calif., 1972-75; with E.F. Hutton, Long Beach, 1975-78; with Paine Webber, City of Industry, Calif., 1978—, nat. trust and devel. officer, 1979-80, br. mgr., Walnut Creek, Calif. 1980-81, City of Industry, 1982, sales mgr./asso. mgr. Los Angeles regional hdqrs., 1982—. Trustee, Mt. Diablo Health Care Found., 1981—; chmn. community adv. com. Torrance Meml. Hosp., 1975-76. Mem. City of Industry C. of C. Republican. Methodist. Club: Rotary. Office: 700 S Flower St Los Angeles CA 90017

KEATINGE, RICHARD HARTE, lawyer; b. San Francisco, Dec. 4, 1919; A.B. with honors, U. Calif.-Berkeley, 1939; M.A., Harvard U., 1941; J.D., Georgetown U., 1944; m. Betty West, Apr. 20, 1944; children—Richard West, Daniel Wilson, Nancy Elizabeth. Bar: D.C. 1944, N.Y. 1945, Calif. 1947, U.S. Supreme Ct. 1964. Economist, sr. indsl. specialist WPB, Washington, 1941-44; practice law, N.Y.C., 1944-45, Washington, 1945-47, Los Angeles, 1947—; sr. ptnr. Keatinge, Pastor & Mintz, and predecessor firms, Los Angeles, 1948-79; ptnr. Reavis & McGrath, 1979—; spl. asst. atty. gen. State of Calif., 1964-68; pub. mem. Adminstrv. Conf. U.S., 1968-74. Mem. Calif. Law Revision Commn., 1961-68, vice chmn., 1963-65, chmn., 1965-67; del. Democratic Nat. Conv., 1952, 64; trustee Dem. Assos., Inc., 1958-70, chmn., 1967-70; trustee Coro Found., 1965-73; trustee, mem. exec. com. U. Calif.-Berkeley Found., 1973—, v.p., 1978-82, chmn. bd. trustees, 1983—. Fellow Am. Bar Found. (life); mem. Am. Law Inst., ABA (chmn. adminstrv. law sect. 1967-68, 74-78, mem. council adminstrv. law sect. 1961-64, 65-69, mem. council econs. of law practice sect. 1974-75, mem. ho. of dels. 1974-81, 82—, mem. standing com. on resolutions 1973-74, vice chmn. adv. commn. housing and urban growth 1974-77, com. on law and economy 1976-78, vice chmn. 1977-78, chmn. coordinating com. immigration 1983—, bd. govs. 1978—), Los Angeles County Bar Assn. (chmn. taxation sect. 1966-67, del. Conf. State Bar Dels. 1966-67, 77—), Internat. bar assns., State Bar Calif. (exec. com. pub. law sect. 1976-78), Am. Judicature Soc., Assn. Bus. Trial Lawyers Los Angeles (bd. govs. 1974-76, v.p. 1977-78, pres. 1978-79), Inter-Am. Assn., Nat. Planning Assn. (nat. council 1956—), Am. Arbitration Assn. (nat. panel arbitrators 1950—), Lawyers Club Los Angeles, Phi Beta Kappa. Episcopalian. Bd. editors Georgetown Law Jour., 1943-44. Home: 1141 S Orange Grove Pasadena CA 91105 Office: 700 S Flower St 6th Floor Los Angeles CA 90017

KECK, GWENDOLYN ODESSA, marketing executive; b. Seattle, May 18, 1950; d. Shelby Rochal and Veroqua Earline (Simpson) Smith; m. Steven Walter Keck, Dec. 19, 1970; 1 son, Ryan Justin. B.S. in Textiles and Clothing, Colo. State U., 1972. Various consumer, tchr. positions in textiles, Indpls., 1973-74; coordinator to pres. JHB Imports, Inc. (name changed to JHB Internat. 1981), Denver, 1975-77; asst. dir. edn. and info. Am. Sheep Producers Council, Inc., Denver, 1977-82, dir. wool info., 1982—. Adv. bd. Colo. State U. Home Econs. Dean's Alumni; mem. program adv. com. Jefferson County Pub. Schs., 1978-79. Mem. Home Economists in Bus. (chmn. 1982-83), Am. Home Econs. Assn., Colo. Home Econs. Assn., Fashion Group, Aux. Colo. Soc. C.P.A.s. Home: 12489 E Amherst Circle Aurora CO 80014 Office: Am Sheep Producers Council 200 Clayton St Denver CO 80206

KECK, ROBERT RYGER, banker; b. Salem, S.D., Feb. 28, 1927; s. Dallas Lester and Margarette (Elizabeth) Ryger) K.; m. Lahoma Moreland, Feb. 24, 1951; children—Dennis Ryger, Janet Denene Keck Davis. B.S., Ariz. State U., 1951; grad. Am. Banking Inst., 1966, Pacific Coast Banking Sch., 1971. Successively loan collector, asst. mgr., br. mgr., asst. v.p., mgr. 1st Interstate Bank of Ariz., N.A., Phoenix, v.p., mgr., 1972-77, v.p., regional mgr., 1977—; mem. polit. action com., good govt. com. 1st Nat. Bank of Ariz. Bd. dirs., pres. N.E. Phoenix YMCA, Tri City YMCA. Served with U.S. Army, 1952. Mem. Am. Banking Inst., Am. Philatelic Assn., Ariz. Philatelic Assn. Lodge: Elks. Office: 1769 Grand Ave Phoenix AZ 85007

KEECH, DOROTHY ANN, environ. chemist; b. Alhambra, Calif., Jan. 27, 1954; d. Jack William and Elizabeth Marie (Dellinger) K.; B.S. with high honors, U. Calif., Riverside, 1976, Ph.D. in Soil Sci., 1979. Research asst. U. Calif., Riverside, 1976-79; research co-worker Universitat Hohenheim, Stuttgart, W.Ger., 1979-80; research chemist Chevron Oil Field Research Co., LaHabra, Calif., 1981—. Mem. Soil Sci. Soc. Am., Internat. Soil Sci. Soc., Agronomy Soc. Am., Sigma Xi. Contbr. articles to profl. jours. Office: PO Box 446 LaHabra CA 90631

KEEDY, CURTIS RUSSELL, radiochemist, educator; b. Selma, Calif., Sept. 14, 1938; s. Ralph Wellington and Virginia Alice (Whitlow) K.; B.A. cum laude, Occidental Coll., 1960; Ph.D., U. Wis., 1965; m. Wendy Hardy, Aug. 28, 1976; children—Camille Rebekka, Alexander Woodard. Research assoc. chem. engring. div. Argonne (Ill.) Nat. Lab., 1964-66; asst. prof. chemistry dept. Reed Coll., Portland, Oreg., 1966-70; asst. prof. chemistry dept. Lewis and Clark Coll., Portland, 1970-75, assoc. prof., 1975—, chmn., 1983—. Mem. Am. Chem. Soc. (chmn. Portland sect. 1977), Am. Nuclear Soc., AAUP, Sigma Xi, Alpha Chi Sigma. Home: 7118 SE Reed College Pl Portland OR 97202 Office: Lewis and Clark Coll Portland OR 97219

KEEFER, ROLAND JESSE, computer science educator, researcher, consultant; b. Billings, Mont., Aug. 29, 1935; s. William Lester and Zylpha Leone (Palmerlee) K. B.S., U. Mont., 1958, M.S., 1961; postgrad. Northwestern U., 1967; student Texas A&M Coll., 1958-59, U. Ariz., 1958-61. Assoc. prof. computer sci. Eastern Wash. U., Cheney, 1961—; vis. prof. U. Wis., 1966, 67; co-founder Forefront, Inc., Spokane, Wash., 1982—. Mem. Assn. for Computing Machinery, Pi Mu Epsilon, Alpha Pi Mu. Patentee Datalyzer. Home: 1717 W 14th St Spokane WA 99204 Office: care Dept Math and Computer Sci Eastern Wash U Cheney WA 99004

KEEHN, NEIL FRANCIS, aerospace executive; b. Massillon, Ohio, Oct. 24, 1948; s. Russell Earl and Mary (Danner) K.; B.S. in Math., Ariz. State U., Tempe, 1970, postgrad. in elec. engring., 1970. Mem. tech. staff Tech. Service Corp., Santa Monica, Calif., 1972-74, Hughes Aircraft, El Segundo, Calif., 1974-77; program mgr. TRW Inc., Redondo Beach, Calif., 1977-79; mgr. advanced concepts Mil. Space Systems div. Sci. Applications Inc., El Segundo, 1979-80; pres. Strategic Systems Scis., Santa Monica, 1980—. Mem. IEEE (vice chmn. aerospace def. systems panel 1972-76, chmn. 1976-79), AIAA, U.S. Strategic Inst. Contbr. articles to profl. jours.; patentee in digital signal processing.

KEELER, REX S(AUNDERS), accountant; b. Evansville, Ind., Jan. 22, 1952; s. Mark V. and Leola (Saunders) K.; m. Christine Pettit, Sept. 18, 1978. B.S.B.A., U. Fla., 1973, postgrad., 1974-75. C.P.A., Utah. Mgr. Exec. Tax Service, Salt Lake City, 1975-77; ptnr. DeWaal and Keeler, Salt Lake City, 1977—. Office: 711 First Security Bank Bldg Salt Lake City UT 84111

KEELEY, MICHAEL CLARK, economist; b. Kearney, Nebr., May 5, 1947; s. Benjamin Joseph and Helen Irene (Moon) K.; m. Maryann Bezich, June 24, 1973. S.B. in Math., MIT, 1969; A.M., U. Chgo., 1971, Ph.D. in Econs., 1974. Economist TEMPO, Ctr. Advanced Studies, Gen. Electric Corp., Washington, 1973-75; sr. economist SRI Internat., Menlo Park, Calif., 1975-81, mgr. antitrust econs. cons. group, 1981-83; economist San Francisco Fed. Res. Bank, 1983—; vis. assoc. prof. econs. U. Santa Clara (Calif.), 1982. Mem. Am. Econ. Assn., Econometric Soc., Population Assn. Am., Western Econ. Assn. Author: Population, Public Policy, and Economic Development, 1976; Labor Supply and Public Policy; A Critical Review, 1981; contbr. articles to profl. jours. Home: 2703 Sequoia Way Belmont CA 94002 Office: 101 Market St San Francisco CA 94105

KEENAN, EDWARD JAMES, pharmacologist; b. Shelton, Wash., Sept. 6, 1948; s. Robert Hart and Mildred Pauline (Stoick) K.; student U. Wash., 1966-68; B.S., Creighton U., 1970, M.S., 1972; Ph.D., W.Va. U., 1975; m. Shelley C. Hall. Research fellow dept. surgery Oreg. Health Sci. U., 1975-76; research asst. prof. surgery, 1976-78, asst. prof. surgery, 1978-82, assoc. prof. surgery, 1982—, asst. prof. pharmacology, 1978—, dir. Clin. Research Ctr. Lab., 1976—, dir. Hormone Receptor Lab., 1976—. Mem. Endocrine Soc., Soc. Study Reprodn., Am. Soc. Pharmacology and Exptl. Therapeutics, Western Pharmacology Soc., AAAS, Am. Soc. Andrology, Sigma Xi. Home: 4110 NE Klickitat Portland OR 97212 Office: Hormone Receptor Lab Oreg Health Scis U Portland OR 97201

KEENAN, EDWARD JOSEPH, hospital management engineer; b. N.Y.C., Oct. 3, 1932; s. Edward Joseph and Leona (Tansey) K.; married; 2 children. B.A., U. Minn., 1967; M.A. in Edn., Chapman Coll., 1977. Enlisted U.S. Air Force, 1951, advanced through grades to master sgt., 1969; ret., 1971; ptnr. Edrian-Keenan & Assocs., San Bernardino, Calif., 1971-73; adminstr. for pvt. law firms, Los Angeles and Beverly Hills, Calif., 1973-78; West Coast mgr. B. W. Hildebrandt & Co., cons. to law firms, Encino, Calif., 1978-79; sr. mgmt. analyst Cedars Sinai Med. Ctr. Los Angeles, 1979—; instr. law office mgmt. U. So. Calif., U. West Los Angeles; cons. in field. Mem. Am. Inst. Indsl. Engrs., Assn. Legal Adminstrs. (charter; pres. Beverly Hills chpt. 1977-78). Republican. Lodges: Elks, Moose, K.C. Office: 8700 Beverly Blvd Los Angeles CA 90048

KEENAN, KATHLEEN DOYLE, public relations specialist; b. San Mateo, Calif., Aug. 29, 1950; d. John Louis and Barbara (Moore) Doyle; m. Thomas A. Keenan, Jr., Apr. 22, 1972; 1 dau., Kerry Doyle. B.A., Beloit Coll., 1972, M.A., 1973, Prodn. editor Am. Life Ins. Assn., Washington, 1973-76; mng. editor Pharmacy West mag., Los Angeles, 1976-78; pub. info. coordinator Accurex Corp., Mountain View, Calif., 1979-80; assoc. pub. relations dir. TFB Pub. Relations div. Tycer, Fultz-Bellack, Palo Alto, Calif., 1980—. Mem. Pub. Relations Soc. Am., Women in Communications. Office: TFB Pub Relations 1731 Embarcadero Rd Palo Alto CA 94303

KEENAN, MARY LOU, hotel executive, consultant; b. Oklahoma City, Jan. 19, 1931; d. Richard Alexander and Lulua Della (Plowman) Stewart; m. Robert Millard, Feb. 27, 1950; children—Deborah Jean, Valerie Lynn, Robert Stuart, Ralph Edward. Student Napa Coll., 1965-69. Pres. Burgundy House Inc., Yountville, Calif., 1973—, Burgundy House Antiques, 1973—; div. Calif. Health Care Delivery Service for Inns; cons. in field. Recipient Upper Napa Valley Assn. award of merit for restoration of 1870 stone bldg., 1977. Mem. Am. Hotel and Motel Assn., Calif. Hotel and Motel Assn., Am. Mgmt. Assn., Smithsonian Assocs., Nat. Trust Historic Preservation, Calif. Hist. Soc., Napa C. of C., Yountville C. of C., Am. Contract Bridge League. Republican. PO Box 2766 Yountville CA 94599 Office: 6600 Washington St Yountville CA 94599

KEENAN, ROBERT LOUIS, biomed. engr.; b. Los Angeles, Aug. 12, 1928; s. Louis Albert and Cleone (Test) K.; B.S., U. Calif., 1955; postgrad. Pacific Union Coll., 1958-59, UCLA, 1966; m. Helen Zinke, Dec. 20, 1970. Electronic engr., physicist U.S. Naval Ordnance Test Sta., China Lake, Calif., 1959-63; electronic engr., attending staff assn. Rancho Los Amigos Hosp., Inc., Downey, Calif., 1964-68, sr. systems analyst, sr. biomed. engr., med. research engr. City of Hope Med. Ctr., Duarte, Calif., 1968-79; systems engr. Glendale (Calif.) Adventist Med. Center, 1979—. Served with Calif. State Guard, 1944-45, AUS, 1946-48. Registered profl. engr., Calif. Mem. IEEE (sr.), ASME, Creation Research Soc., Sierra Club, Chi Epsilon. Contbr. articles to profl. jours. Home: PO Box 9510 Glendale CA 91206 Office: Glendale Adventist Medical Center Glendale CA 91206

KEENE, KENNETH PAUL, lawyer; b. Torrington, Wyo., Oct. 29, 1940; s. Lyndell Franklin and Marion (Morgan) K.; m. Katherine La Heist Keith, Sept. 10, 1966; children—Elizabeth La Heist, Kenneth Paul, Susan Morgan. Student Miami U., Oxford, Ohio, 1958-61; B.S., U. Nebr., 1962, J.D., 1965. Bar: Nebr. 1965, Colo. 1968. Ptnr., treas. Cole, Hecox, Tulley, Keene & Beltz, P.C., Colorado Springs, Colo., 1970—. Bd. dirs. Silver Key Sr. Services, Colorado Springs, 1973-79, pres., 1977-79; active Pikes Peak chpt. ARC. Served to capt. JAGC U.S. Army, 1965-69. Mem. ABA, Nebr. Bar Assn., Colo. Bar Assn. Republican. Home: 2615 Pavo Pl Colorado Springs CO 80906 Office: 316 N Tejon St Colorado Springs CO 80903

KEENE, RUTH FRANCES, army ofcl.; b. South Bend, Ind., Oct. 7, 1948; d. Seymour and Sally (Morris) K.; B.S., Ariz. State U., 1970; M.S., Fairleigh Dickinson U., 1978. Inventory mgmt. specialist U.S. Army Electronics Command, Phila., 1970-74, U.S. Army Communications-Electronics Materiel Readiness Command, Fort Monmouth, N.J., 1974-79; chief inventory mgmt. div. Crane (Ind.) Army Ammunition Activity, 1979-80; supply systems analyst Hdqrs. 60th Ordnance Group, Zweibruecken, W. Ger., 1980—. Mem. Federally Employed Women (chpt. pres. 1979-80), Nat. Assn. Female Execs., Soc. Logistics Engrs., Assn. for Computing Machinery, AAAS, Am. Soc. Pub. Adminstrn., Soc. Profl. and Exec. Women, Internat. Info./Word Processing Assn., NOW. Democrat. Jewish. Home: 4916 W Pinchot Ave Phoenix AZ 85031 Office: Hdqrs 60th Ordnance Group Attn AEROD-MS APO 09052

KEERAN, DANIEL MELVIN, psychotherapist; b. Marion, Ohio, Nov. 29, 1947; s. Melvin Forest and Ruth Huldah (Armintrout) K.; B.A., David Lipscomb Coll., 1968; M.A., U. Ky., 1972; M.S. in Social Work, U. Louisville, 1977; m. Jennie Lynn Gilliam, July 24, 1976; children—Phoebe Reba, Seth Benjamin. Social worker Bur. Social Services, Louisville, 1974-76; dir. El Paso (Tex.) Christian Services, 1977-79; psychotherapist Psychiat. Center, Weyburn, Sask., 1979-81; prof. Bible and psychology Western Christian Coll., Weyburn, 1979-82; psychotherapist Psychiat. Day Hosp., U. Alta. Hosp., Edmonton, 1983— Served with U.S. Army, 1969-70. Mem. Nat. Assn. Social Workers, Australian Assn. Social Workers. Mem. Ch. of Christ.

KEEVER, ROBERT ELLIS, engring. cons. co. exec.; b. Dodge City, Kans., Aug. 6, 1940; s. Earl Edgar and Mary Ellen (Bryant) K.; m. Vickie Stockwell, June 10, 1961; children—Sarah Ellen, Janna Marie. B.A., Kans. Wesleyan U., 1962; B.S. in Civil Engring., Kans. State U., 1963. Registered profl. engr., Calif., Kans., Md., Tex., Wis., Tenn., Iowa, Wash.; lic. pvt. pilot FAA. Engr., Pacific Gas & Electric Co., San Francisco, 1963-65; engr. Gen. Electric Co., San Jose, Calif., 1965-70; gen. mgr. Nuclear Services Corp., Campbell, Calif., 1970-74; exec. v.p. NUTECH, San Jose, Calif., 1974-81, chmn. bd., 1975-81, pres., 1981—. Mem. Am. Concrete Inst., ASCE, ASME, Am. Nuclear Soc. U.S. Congressional Adv. Bd., Young Pres.' Orgn., Korea Engrs.' Club, Kenna Club. Patentee in field. Office: 6835 Via Del Oro San Jose CA 95119

KEGEBEIN, JAMES ALBERT, industrial hygienist; b. LaPorte, Ind., Feb. 17, 1951; s. Robert Royal and Jeanette (Howard) K.; m. Valerie Jeanne Nygra, Feb. 13, 1981; 1 dau. Kimberly Ann. B.S., Ind. State U., 1973; postgrad. Mo. State U., 1977-79. Registered pub. sanitarian, Ind. Sanitarian Elkhart (Ind.) County Health Dept., 1974; sr. environ. health tech. Bethlehem Steel Corp., Burns Harbor, Ind., 1974-79; field indsl. hygienist Bechtel Power Corp., Midland, Mich. and Port Gibson, Miss., 1979-81, indsl. hygienist, San Francisco, 1981—. Adv. com. safety program Cogswell Coll., San Francisco. Mem. Am. Indsl. Hygiene Assn., Am. Soc. Safety Engrs. Home: 1244 S Mary Sunnydale CA 94087 Office: Box 3965 San Francisco CA 94119

KEHLE, ANTHONY GEORGE, III, insurance agency executive; b. Toledo, Jan. 18, 1938; s. Anthony George and Jeanne Esther (Kurts) K.; B.B.A., U. Toledo, 1960; postgrad. U. Stetson Law Sch., 1961-62; children—Kelly McGhee, Kory Sean. State mgr. Alaska Combined Ins. Co. Am., Anchorage, Alaska, 1964-72; owner, pres. Schweitzer Ins. Agy. Inc., Sandpoint, Idaho, 1973—; pres. Idaho Coach Corp., Sandpoint, 1977—, Mountain States Distbg. Co. Inc., Sandpoint, 1977—; owner Ponderay Ranch Inc., 1972—. Mem. fin. com. Republican Nat. Com., 1969-70. Served with USMCR, 1956-60. Named C.I.C.A. Internat. Man of Yr., 1964. Mem. Life Underwriters Assn., Idaho State Draft Horse Assn. (mgr./founder Internat. 1977-79, cert. appreciation 1979), North Idaho Draft Horse Assn. (dir. 1977, 78), U. Toledo Alumni Assn. (life), Pi Kappa Alpha Alumni (life). Clubs: Spokane Polo, Spokane Athletic, Round Table. Author: poetry Girdwood, 1972. Home: Drawer D Sandpoint ID 83864 Office: Schweitzer Ins Agy Inc PO Box D Sandpoint Idaho 83864

KEHLMANN, ROBERT, glass artist, critic; b. Bklyn., Mar. 9, 1942. B.A., Antioch Coll., 1963; M.A., U. Calif.-Berkeley, 1966. Group shows include: San Jose (Calif.) Mus. Art, 1977, Leigh Yawkey Woodson Art Mus., Wausau, Wis., 1978, 81, Mus. Contemporary Crafts, N.Y.C., 1978, Corning (N.Y.) Mus. Glass, 1979, Jacksonville (Fla.) Art Mus., 1980, Triton Mus. Art, Santa Clara, Calif., 1980; represented in permanent collections at Corning Mus. Glass, Leigh Yawkey Woodson Art Mus., Hessisches Landes Mus., W.Ger., Bank of Am. World Hdqrs., San Francisco, Mus. Fur Moderne Kunst, Goslar, W.Ger.; instr. glass design Calif. Coll. Arts and Crafts, Oakland, 1978-80; instr. glass design Pilchuck Glass Ctr., Stanwood, Wash., 1978-80; contbg. editor Glass Art Mag., Oakland, Calif., 1975-76, editor Glass Art Soc. Jour., Berkeley, Calif., 1981—. Nat. Endowment Arts grantee, 1977, 78. Mem. Glass Art Soc. (dir. 1980), Stained Glass Assn. Am. Office: William Sawyer Gallery 3045 Clay St San Francisco CA 94115

KEHOE, LAWRENCE HERBERT, public affairs executive; b. Passaic, N.J., Sept. 20, 1948; s. Robert B. and Sylvia K.; B.A., N.Mex. Highlands U., 1972; m. Linda Mae Duran, Nov. 10, 1968, children—Lawrence G., Brian. Planner, N.Mex. State Planning Office, 1972-73, fuel allocation officer, 1973-75; sales rep. Shell Oil Co., 1975-76; dep. dir. N.Mex. Legis. Energy Commn., 1976-77; liaison officer Energy Research Bd., 1977-78; public affairs rep. Kerr McGee, 1978-79; sec. N.Mex. Energy and Minerals Dept., Santa Fe, 1979-82; mgr. public affairs Kerr McGee Corp., 1982—; mem. Community Assistance Council, 1979-82; bd. dirs. N.Mex. Energy Research and Devel. Inst., 1981-82. Dist. chmn. Cub Scouts, 1979; dist. chmn. Boy Scouts Am., 1980, v.p. council, 1981, dist. award of merit, 1979. Served with USMC, 1968-70; Vietnam. Recipient Disting. Public Service award State of N.Mex., 1981. Mem. VFW, Vietnam Vets. Assn. Democrat. Roman Catholic. Office: 113 Washington St Santa Fe NM 87501

KEIL, DAVID JOHN, educator; b. Elmhurst, Ill., Dec. 13, 1946; s. John Bell and Clara Elizabeth (Thomas) K.; B.Sc., Ariz. State U., 1968, M.Sc., 1970; Ph.D., Ohio State U., 1973. Herbarium asst. Ariz. State U., Tempe, 1967-68, grad. teaching asst., 1968-70, postdoctoral researcher, 1975-76; NDEA Title IV fellow botany Ohio State U., Columbus, 1971-72, grad. teaching assoc., 1972-73, lectr., 1973; vis. asst. prof. biology Grand Valley State Colls., Allendale, Mich., 1973-74; research asst. Ohio State U., Columbus, 1974; asst. prof. biology Franklin (Ind.) Coll., 1975; lectr. biology Calif. Poly. State U., San Luis Obispo, 1976-78, asst. prof., 1978-80, assoc. prof., 1980—, dir. Robert F. Hoover Herbarium, 1978—. Served with U.S. Army, 1970. Recipient Disting. Teaching award Calif. Poly. State U., 1980. Mem. Internat. Assn. Plant Taxonomy, Am. Soc. Plant Taxonomists, Bot. Soc. Am., Soc. Systematic Zoology, Sociedad Botanica de Mexico, Western Soc. Naturalists, Calif. Bot. Soc., Calif. Native Plant Soc., Torrey Bot. Club, Sigma Xi. Contbr. articles to profl. jours. Office: Biol Scis Dept Calif Poly State U San Luis Obispo CA 93407

KEIL, ROBERT ALVIN, operations research analyst; b. Chgo., Sept. 9, 1919; s. Walter Alvin and Della Sophia (Danielson) K.; B.S. in Bus. (fellowship), U. Richmond, 1941; M.A., U. Hawaii, 1963; m. Betsy Tingle Breece, Feb. 21, 1945 (dec.); m. 2d, Louise Victoria Wigchert, Apr. 25, 1981. Exec. trainee C & P Telephone Co. of Va., 1941-42; assoc. Planning research Corp., Honolulu, San Diego, 1964-67; ops. research analyst Naval Ocean Systems Ctr., San Diego, 1967-80, scientist, 1980—. Pres., Coronado Residential Assn., 1968-71; chmn. Coronado Planning Commn., 1975, 77, 78, commr., 1972-78. Served with USN, 1942-64. Mem. Mil. Ops. Research Soc., U.S. Naval Inst., Phi Beta Kappa, Omicron Delta Kappa, Phi Kappa Sigma. Episcopalian. Club: Rotary. Contbr. tech. research papers. Home: 110 Carob Way Coronado CA 92118 Office: 271 Catalina Blvd San Diego CA 92152

KEIM, HARRY EDWARD, ednl. adminstr.; b. Lakewood, Ohio, May 15, 1941; s. Herbert E. and Mary Kathryn (Fairbanks) K.; B.S., Ohio Univ., 1963, M.B.A., 1965; m. Marilyn Sue Sherlock, Aug. 17, 1963; children—Kipp Gregory, Kenneth David. Budget analyst Cummins Engine Co., Columbus, Ind., 1963-65; dir. budget Ohio Univ., Athens, 1965-73; mem. faculty Univ. Alaska, Juneau, 1973—, dir. adminstrv. services, 1973-81, vice chancellor adminstrv. services, 1981—, part-time instr. bus. and finance, 1973—. Pres. Athens Jr. C. of C., 1973; mem. mayor's adv. com. Eaglecrest Ski Area, 1979-82, chmn. bd. dirs., 1982—. Mem. Juneau Jr. C. of C. (pres.), Western Assn. Coll. Univ. Bus. Ofcls., Delta Sigma Pi. Club: Rotary. Home: 17655 Lena Loop Rd Juneau AK 99801 Office: 11120 Glacier Hwy Juneau AK 99801

KEIM, PAUL FERDINAND, civil engr., educator; b. Falls City, Nebr., Apr. 22, 1902; s. Will Seward and Fernande Rose (Godfirnon) K.; B.Sc., U. Calif., Berkeley, 1925; M.Sc., C.E., U. Nebr., 1932; m. Marjorie Little, Dec. 31, 1927 (dec. Dec. 1982); children—Seward Russell (dec.), Charles Bruce. Engr. contracting co., Los Angeles, 1925-26; instr. civil engring. U. Nebr., 1926-32; cons. Platte Valley Public Power and Irrigation Dist., (Nebr.), 1933-36, Calif. Hwy. Div., Marysville, 1936-37; hydraulic engr. Los Angeles County Flood Control Dist., 1937-39; prin. engr. FPC, Washington, 1939-41, 46; served from lt. comdr. to capt. USNR, 1941-46; public works officer, damage control officer, Midway Islands, 1942; public works and constrn. officer Whidbey Island Naval Air Sta., 1943; staff civil engring. officer Naval Air Command, 13th Naval Dist., 1944-46; mem. Res., from 1946; cons. transp. and water supply U.S. Dept. State Econ. Mission to Liberia, 1947-48; asso. Tippetts Abbett, McCarthy, Stratton, Engrs., N.Y.C., 1948-52; ops. Greece, Turkey, Alaska, throughout U.S., 1948-52; prof. civil engring. U. Calif., Berkeley, 1952-69, prof. emeritus, 1970—; on leave cons. ports Taiwan, 1957; adv. to dir. U.S. Ops. Mission Egypt, tchr. Grad. Sch., U. Cairo, 1959-61; cons. Calif. Joint Senate-House Com. Water Resources, various times, 1952-59; chief staff civil engr. Ralph M. Parsons Co., Pasadena, Calif., Peru, Greece, Argentina, Mex., Tunisia, Morocco, 1968-71; cons. Internat. Exec. Service Corps, N.Y.C.; port cons., Taiwan, 1975; OAS cons., Brazil, 1971; FMC cons., Rumania, 1972. Recipient citation for disting. profl. conduct during Battle of Midway, 1942; registered profl. engr., Calif., Oreg., Wash. Fellow ASCE (life; chmn. student activities com. Los Angeles sect. 1977-81); mem. Los Angeles Council Engrs. and Scientists (pres. 1979-81), Inst. Advancement Engring. (pres. elect 1981, emeritus dir. 1983-84, award of merit 1982), Am. Soc. Engring. Edn., Nat. Reclamation Assn., Am. Geophys. Union, Soc. Mil. Engrs., Chi

Epsilon, Tau Beta Pi. Clubs: Commonwealth of Calif., Town Hall of Calif., Los Angeles Breakfast, Lions. Contbr. articles to profl. publs. Address: 4552 Fountain Ave Apt 2 Los Angeles CA 90029

KEIM, ROBERT THOMAS, computer science educator, consultant, researcher; b. St. Marys, Pa., Jan. 12, 1949; s. Robert Charles and Ida Florence (Radin) K.; m. Judy Conti, Sept. 12, 1970. B.S. in Math., U. Pitts., 1970, M.B.A., 1971, Ph.D., 1976. Asst. prof. Fla. State U., 1974-79; asst. prof. computer info. systems Coll. Bus. Adminstrn., research assoc. Bur. Bus. and Econ. Research, Ariz. State U., 1979-82, asst. prof., 1979—; cons. design, programming, implementation and evaluation of computer info. systems. Mem. steering com., leadership, tng. and devel. program Mesa (Ariz.) C. of C. Mem. Acad. Mgmt., Am. Inst. Decision Scis., Assn. Systems Mgmt., Inst. Mgmt. Sci. Club: Optimists (Mesa). Home: 1039 W Natal Ave Mesa AZ 85202 Office: Coll Bus Adminstrn Ariz State U Tempe AZ 85287

KEIM, WILLARD DENNIS, educator; b. Fairbury, Nebr., Dec. 16, 1932; s. S. Irvin and Merle Alice (Eichelberger) K.; m. Chiem Thuc Tran, Sept. 17, 1964. Ph.D., U. Hawaii, 1969. Assoc. prof. polit. sci. U. Hawaii, Hilo, 1976—. Recipient East-West Ctr. scholarship, 1963-65; Fulbright fellow, 1972-73. Mem. Am. Polit. Sci. Assn., Am. Sociol. Assn. Author: The Korean Peasant at the Crossroads, 1979. Office: U Hawaii 1400 Kapiolani St Hilo HI 96720

KEIRNS, JANELLE RAY, education, child development consultant; b. Oklahoma City, July 14, 1949; d. James Robert and Nadine Maureen (Minyard) Ray; m. Jon William Keirns, Sept. 10, 1947; children—Jacquelyn Gail, Jason Randel. B.A. in Edn., Central State U., 1971, M.Ed., 1978; postgrad. Okla. State U., 1978—. Cert. Gesell Devel. Examiner. Secondary tchr. English Okla. City Pub. Schs., 1971-72; presch. tchr., dir., co-owner, Edmond, Okla., 1974-77; field supr. Head Start, Oklahoma City, 1978-79; adj. prof. psychology-child devel. South Oklahoma City Jr. Coll., 1978-79; teaching asst. ednl. psychology Okla. State U., 1979; founder, cons. Learning and Sch. Readiness, Inc., Oklahoma City, 1977-80; now cons./lectr. edn., child devel. Gesell Inst. Human Devel., New Haven; active tchr. tng. workshops, ednl. counselor. Mem. Bd. Edn. Bayfield Pub. Schs. Mem. Assn. Supervision and Curriculum Devel., So. Assn. for Children Under Six, Okla. Assn. Children Under Six, Nat. Assn. Edn. Young Children, Colo. Assn. Edn. Young Children, Kappa Delta Pi. Democrat. Baptist. Co-editor: Gesell Inst. School Readiness Scoring Notes, 1982. Home: 44105 Hwy 160 Bayfield CO 81122

KEIRSEY, RUTH ANN, lab. mgr.; b. Shreveport, La., Dec. 8, 1946; d. James H. and LaVera L. Parrish; A.S. in Plastics Tech., Mt. San Antonio Coll., 1980; A.A. in Liberal Arts, Mt. San Antonio Coll., 1980; B.A. in Bus. Mgmt., U. Redlands, 1981; children—David James and Michelle Lynn Tiemann. Quality control technician Hysol div. Dexter Hysol Corp., Industry, Calif., 1976, technician, 1976-78, tech. specialist, 1978-80, project leader, 1980-81, group mgr. liquid projects, 1981, lab. mgr., 1981—. Mem. Soc. Advancement Materials and Plastics Engrs., Soc. Plastics Engrs., Am. Soc. Profl. and Exec. Women, U. Redlands Alumni. Office: 15051 Don Julian Rd Industry CA 91749

KEISER, JOHN HOWARD, university president; b. Mt. Olive, Ill., Mar. 12, 1936; s. Howard H. and Lorraine G. K.; B.S. in Edn., Eastern Ill. U., 1958; M.A., Northwestern U., 1960, Ph.D. in History, 1964; m. Nancy Peterka, June 27, 1959; children—John, Sam, Joe. Prof. history Westminster Coll., Fulton, Mo., 1963-65, Eastern Ill. U., Charleston, 1965-71; v.p. acad. affairs Sangamon State U., Springfield, Ill., 1971-78; pres. Boise State U., 1978—, also instr. U.S. History. Bd. dirs. Abraham council Boy Scouts Am., Springfield, 1977-78, Ore-Ida council, Boise, 1979-80. Recipient Harry E. Pratt Meml. award, Jour. Ill. History, 1970, 72. Mem. Orgn. Am. Historians, Am. Hist. Assn., Labor History Soc., Boise C. of C. Roman Catholic. Club: Rotary. Author: Building for the Centuries, Illinois, 1865-1898, 1977; Illinois Vignettes, 1977. Office: 1910 University Blvd Boise ID 83725

KEITH, BRUCE EDGAR, political analyst, genealogist; b. Curtis, Nebr., Feb. 17, 1918; s. Edgar L. and Corinne E. (Marsteller) K.; m. Evelyn E. Johnston, Oct. 29, 1944; children—Mona Louise, Kent Marsteller, Melanie Ann. A.B. with high distinction, Nebr. Wesleyan U., 1940; M.A., Stanford U., 1952; grad. Command and Staff, Marine Corps Schs., 1958, Sr. Resident Sch., Naval War Coll., 1962; Ph.D., U. Calif.-Berkeley, 1982. Commd. 2d lt. U.S. Marine Corps, 1942, advanced through grades to col., 1962, ret., 1971, comdg. officer 3d Bn., 11th Marines, 1958-59, ops. officer, Pres. Dwight D. Eisenhower visit to Okinawa, 1960, G-3 ops. officer Fleet Marine Force, Pacific, Cuban Missile Crisis, 1962, mem. U.S. del. SEATO, Planning Conf., Bangkok, Thailand, 1964, G-3, Fleet Marine Force, Pacific, 1964-65, head Strategic Planning Study Dept., Naval War Coll., 1966-68, genealogist, 1967—, exec. officer Hdqrs. Marine Corps programs, Washington, 1968-71; election analyst Inst. Govtl. Studies, U. Calif.-Berkeley, 1974—; teaching asst. U. Calif.-Berkeley, 1973-74. Bd. dirs., Bay Area Funeral Soc., 1980-83, v.p., 1981-83. Decorated Bronze Star, Navy Commendation medal, Presdl. Unit citation with 3 bronze stars. Recipient Phi Kappa Phi Silver medal Nebr. Wesleyan U., 1940, Alumni award, 1964. Mem. Am. Polit. Sci. Assn., Acad. Polit. Sci., Am. Acad. Polit. and Social Sci., Marine Corps Assn., Ret. Officers Assn. Phi Kappa Phi, Pi Gamma Mu. Republican. Unitarian. Club: Masons. Contbg. author: The Descendants of Daniel and Elizabeth (Disbrow) Keith, 1979-81; author: A Comparison of the House Armed Services Coms. in the 91st and 94th Congresses: How They Differed and Why, 1982; The Johnstons of Morning Sun, 1979; The Marstellers of Arrellton, 1978; The Morris Family of Brookville, 1977; Japan-the Key to America's Future in the Far East, 1962; A United States General Staff: A Must or a Monster?, 1950; co-author: California Votes, 1960-72, 1974; The Myth of the Independent Voter, 1977; The Longer You Look, The More They Lean, 1983. Address: PO Box 156 El Cerrito CA 94530

KEITH, GORDON, publisher; b. Kent, Wash., Aug. 27, 1913; s. John Albert and Grace (Calkins) K.; student San Jose State Coll., 1938-39, U. Calif. at Oakland, 1940; m. Barbara Louise Henson, Sept. 4, 1953 (div. Apr. 1979); 1 dau., Michelle Louise. Operator several small chain dance schs. No. Calif., 1933-42; free lance writer, 1945-50; pub., editor Dance Digest, 1951-62; pub., printer Personnel Improvement Booklets, also specialized greeting cards, note paper, San Jose, Calif., 1962—; feature writer Island Sounder newspaper, San Juan, 1971—. Served with AUS, 1942-45. Mem. Dance Masters Am. (past pres. Calif., dir.). Lion (sec. 1972). Author: (booklets) A Special 48-State Survey on Examining and Licensing of Dance Teachers in America, 1958; Why You Should Belong to an Accredited Dance Teachers' Organization, 1958; Private Dance Schools vs. Recreation Departments, 1960; (books) (with Roderic Marble Oizendam) Liberty's Grandson, An Unconventional Autobiography, 1977, It Came to Pass in the San Juan Islands, 1978; Green Gold for America, 1981; Voices from the Islands, 1982. compiler, editor The James Francis Tulloch Diary 1875-1910, 1978; The Ferryboat Islands: A Practical Guide to Washington State's San Juan Islands, 1984. Home and Office: PO Box 280 Eastsound Orcas Island WA 98245

KEITH, IRENE MARIE, interior designer; b. Stamford, Conn., Aug. 16, 1942; d. Peter Steven and Mary Ann (Neforos) Anargirou; m. Michael Martin Keith, May 13, 1966 (div.); 1 son, Steven Martin. B.A. in Interior Design, Calif. State U.-Long Beach, 1974. Interior designer various design firms, Long Beach, Calif., 1969-74; pres. Irene Keith & Assoc., Long Beach, 1975—; chmn. dept. interior design Brooks Coll., Long Beach, 1977—; tchr. various colls. Mem. Los Angeles County Mus. Art; mem. Pub. Corp. for the Arts, Long Beach. Mem. Am. Soc. Interior Designers (bd. dirs., presdl. award 1981, editor newsletter), Interior Design Educators Council, AIA (affiliate), Nat. Council Interior Design Qualifications (chmn. 1981—), Republican. Contbr. articles to profl. jours. Office: 4825 E Pacific Coast Hwy Long Beach CA 90804

KEITH, PHILIP ALLEN, investment broker; b. Springfield, Mass., Aug. 24, 1946; s. Forrest Allen and Edith (Tower) K.; B.A., Harvard U., 1968; m. Trudy Ann Keith; children—Jennifer Annemarie, Lisa-Marie Ashley. Customer service rep. Crown Zellerbach Corp., 1973-74; project mgr. Trident missle program Westinghouse Electric Corp., 1974-76; mgmt. cons., 1976-77; account exec. Kidder Peabody & Co., Newport Beach, Calif., 1977-78; v.p. Sutro & Co., Newport Beach, 1978-80; exec. v.p., partner Beaumont & Co. Inc., Newport Beach, 1980-82; exec. v.p. TBR & Co., Lake Arrowhead Village, Calif., 1982—. Mem. Laguna Niguel (Calif.) Planning Commn., 1979-80, parks and recreation dir., 1980-91. Served as aviator USNR, 1968-73; Vietnam. Decorated D.F.C., Air medal, Purple Heart, Navy Commendation medal. Mem. Nat. Soc. Registered Reps., U.S. Naval Inst. Republican. Lutheran. Author articles in field. Home: 27334 Matterhorn Dr Lake Arrowhead CA 92352 Office: Suite F-240 Lake Arrowhead Village CA 92382

KELLEHER, DIANA LEE, vitamin company marketing executive; b. Phila., July 9, 1947; d. Lee Roy and Margaret Hopkins (Hey) McKean; m. Gregory Kelleher, Feb. 9, 1968 (div.). B.S. in Fin., Drexel U., 1969; M.B.A., U. Chgo., 1975. With McKinsey & Co., Inc., Chgo., 1970-75; mgr. merchandise group forecasts and tech. service Sears Roebuck & Co., Chgo., 1975-77; assoc. dir. mktg. planning, mktg. mgr. Kitchens of Sara Lee, Consolidated Foods Co., Chgo., 1977-80; mktg. mgr. E & T Gallo Winery, Modesto, Calif., 1980-82; dir. mktg. Pharmavite Corp., Arleta, Calif., 1982, v.p. mktg., 1982—. Tchr. Jr. Achievement classroom course, 1983. Mem. AAUW. Office: Pharmavite Corp 12801 Wentworth Ave Arleta CA 91331

KELLEHER, ROBERT JOSEPH, judge; b. N.Y.C., Mar. 5, 1913; s. Frank and Mary (Donovan) K.; A.B., Williams Coll., 1935; LL.B., Harvard, 1938; m. Gracyn W. Wheeler, Aug. 14, 1940; children—R. Jeffrey, Karen Kathleen. Admitted to N.Y. bar, 1939, Calif. bar, 1941, U.S. Supreme Ct. bar, 1954; atty. U.S. War Dept. 1941-43; asst. U.S. atty. So. Dist. Calif., 1948-50; pvt. practice law, Beverly Hills, Calif., 1951-71; judge U.S. Dist. Ct., Central Dist. Calif., 1971—. Mem. So. Calif. Com. for Olympic Games, 1964; capt. U.S. Davis Cup Team, 1962-63; treas. Youth Tennis Found. So. Calif., 1961-64. Served from ensign to lt. USNR, 1942-45. Mem. So. Calif. Tennis Assn. (v.p. 1958-64), U.S. Lawn Tennis Assn. (pres. 1967-68), Am., Los Angeles County, Beverly Hills, Fed. bar assns., Am. Judicature Soc., State Bar Calif., Delta Kappa Epsilon. Club: Williams (N.Y.C.); Harvard of Southern Calif. Office: US Courthouse 312 N Spring St Los Angeles CA 90012

KELLER, BEN ROBERT, JR., obstetrician, gynecologist, educator; b. Big Springs, Tex., July 9, 1936; s. Ben R. and Rowena (Gibson) K.; m. Janice Elizabeth Scott, Mar. 17, 1977; children—Gwenyth Sue, Jennifer Lynn, Amy Jo, Qurisha Leigh, Ben R., Destry Scott Lance. B.A., U. Tex.-Austin, 1957, M.D., 1961. Diplomate Am. Bd. Ob-Gyn. Intern, Hermann Hosp., Houston, 1961-62, resident in ob-gyn., 1962-65; practice medicine specializing in ob-gyn, Arlington, Tex., 1967-79, Glenwood Springs, Colo., 1979—; asst. clin. prof. Colo. U.-Denver; chmn. ob-gyn dept., Valley View Hosp., Glenwood Springs. Chmn. Physicians Speaker Bur., Am. Cancer Soc., 1968-73; mem. Texpac com. for Tarrant County, 1968-75, chmn., 1972-75; mem. Arlington Drug Abuse Com., 1969-72. Served to capt. USAF, 1965-67. Named Outstanding Young Man of Yr., Arlington Jr. C. of C., 1970-71. Mem. Tarrant County Med. Soc. (del. 1972), Tex. Med. Assn. (del. 1972, sec. ob-gyn sect. 1972, chmn. 1973-74, treas. 1974, 79), AMA, Tex. Inst. for Med. Assessment (bd. dirs. 1976), Am. Coll. Ob-gyn, Colo. Med. Soc., Mt. Sopros Med. Soc. Club: Rotary. Home: 0263 119 Rd Glenwood Springs CO 81601 Office: Dr Ben Keller Jr 410 23rd St Suite 300 Glenwood Springs CO 81601

KELLER, DIXON WILLIAM, med. service rep.; b. San Diego, July 19, 1954; s. William Carl and Eleanor Ruth (Dixon) K.; A.A., Chapman Coll., 1980; B.A. in Bus. Adminstrn., Columbia Coll. of Mo. Extension, 1981; m. Christine Marie Sandstrum, Nov. 21, 1981 children—Jameson William-Paul and Lindsay Nicole (twins). Enlisted U.S. Navy, 1974, advanced through grades to petty officer first class, 1980; student aircraft launch and recovery systems sch., Lakehurst, N.J., 1974; assigned to U.S.S. Enterprise, 1974-78; mem. U.S. Navy Career Recruiter Force, Navy Recruiting Sta., Salem, Oreg., 1978-81; assigned U.S.S. Ranger, 1981-82; resigned, 1982; med. service rep. Roerig div. Pfizer Pharm. Crew mem. studios public broadcasting system sta. KVDO-TV, Salem; res. dep. Marion County Sheriff's Res. Orgn., Salem; local media and public relations cons.; high schs. and colls. mil. liaison. Recipient recruiting gold wreath awards, Navy Achievement medal for recruiting. Mem. Am. Film Inst., Navy League. Republican. Club: Rotary. Producer film documentary: Underway, 1976-80. Home: 1285 Woodside Dr Eugene OR 97401

KELLER, DOROTHY JEAN, college dean; b. Bath, N.Y., Feb. 18, 1937; d. Daniel Raidy and Anna Laing (Cooper) K. A.B., Russell Sage Coll., 1959; M.A., Cornell U., 1961; Ed.D., U. Rochester, 1974. Asst. to dir. housing U. Buffalo, 1961-62; supr. women's housing SUNY-Buffalo, 1962-65; assoc. dir. residence halls U. Rochester, 1965-68; asst. dean students in charge of resident program Russell Sage Coll., 1970-72, dean resident living, 1973-74; dean of students Mills Coll., Oakland, Calif., 1974—. NDEA fellow, 1968-70. Mem. Nat. Assn. Student Personnel Adminstrs. (dir. 1982-83). Office: Mills Hall Mills Coll Oakland CA 94613

KELLER, GARY LEE, automotive rental company executive; b. Ong, Nebr., Dec. 15, 1944; s. Ralph Edward and Betty Jean (Coverdale) K.; ed. high sch.; m. Catherine Swett, Aug. 30, 1968; children—Shaunett, Bridget. Sec.-treas. Custom Inc., also gen. mgr. Thrifty Rent-a-Car, Thrifty Rent-a-Truck, and Quality Leasing Co., Salt Lake City, 1967-78, mem. nat. advt. com. Thrifty Rent-a-Car System, 1974-78; pres. Utah Car and Truck Rentals Inc. dba Am. Internat. Rent-a-car, Salt Lake City, 1978—; dir. Mountain Tours, Inc.; Am. Internat. Rent-a-Car licensee, Ogden, Utah, Park City, Utah, Idaho Falls, Idaho, Mem. Salt Lake Valley Visitors and Conv. Bur. Served with USAF, 1963-67. Mem. Car and Truck Renting and Leasing Assn. (sr. v.p. Utah chpt. 1976-78, pres. 1979, v.p. 1981), Am. Car Renting Assn., Utah Ski Assn. Club: Skal (sec.). Home: Office: Utah Car and Truck Rentals Inc 1380 W North Temple St Salt Lake City UT 84116

KELLER, GEORGE MATTHEW, oil co. exec.; b. Kansas City Mo., Dec. 3, 1923; s. George Matthew and Edna Louise (Mathews) K.; B.S. in Chem. Engring., Mass. Inst. Tech., 1948; m. Adelaide McCague, Dec. 27, 1946; children—William G., Robert A., Barry R. Mem. engring. dept. Standard Oil Calif., San Francisco, 1948-63, fgn. ops. staff, 1963-67, asst. v.p., asst. to pres., 1967-69, v.p., 1969-74, dir., 1970—, vice-chmn., 1974-81, chmn., chief exec. officer, 1981—; dir. First Interstate Bancorp., First Interstate Bank Calif., The Boeing Co. Trustee M.I.T., Notre Dame Coll., Belmont, Calif., Am. Enterprise Inst. Served to 1st lt. USAAF, 1943-46. Mem. M.I.T. Club No. Calif. (dir. 1972—), Am. Petroleum Inst. (dir.), Council Fgn. Relations, World Affairs Council No. Calif. (trustee 1972-79). Clubs: Peninsula Golf and Country (San Mateo, Calif.); San Francisco Golf, World Trade, Bankers, Stock Exchange (San Francisco). Home: San Mateo CA Office: 225 Bush St San Francisco CA 94104

KELLER, GORDON WAYNE, elec. engr.; b. Los Angeles, Feb. 14, 1938; s. Earl Francis and Clio Marilla (Sorkness) K.; B.S.E.E. summa cum laude, U. Calif., Berkeley, 1965, M.S.E.E., 1968, Ph.D., 1970; m. Anna Victoria Menges, Dec. 25, 1975. Sr. engr. Systems Control Corp., Palo Alto, Calif., 1970-73, Rolm Corp., Cupertino, Calif., 1973-76; v.p. engring. Pick & Assos., Irvine, Calif., 1976-77; dir. advanced products Basic Four Corp., Tustin, Calif., 1977-79; v.p. engring. Qantel Corp., Hayward, Calif., 1979-82; chief exec. officer DataMac Corp., 1982—; lectr. U. Calif., Irvine, 1977-79. Served with USN, 1957-60. NSF fellow, 1967-70; Western Electronics Mfg. Assn. scholar, 1964. Mem. Assn. for Computing Machinery, IEEE, Tau Beta Pi. Republican. Clubs: Brotherhood Knights of Vine, Clan Campbell Soc. Home: 2345 Holly Oak St Danville CA 94526 Office: 4142 Point Eden Way Hayward CA 94545

KELLER, JEROME A., advertising executive; b. Berkeley, Calif., Aug. 22, 1933; s. Max and Rose (Berkowitz) K.; m. Gloria Cambell, July 11, 1973; children—Scott, Randall, Kimberly. B.A., U. Calif., 1954, M.B.A., 1958. Market research analyst Del Monte, 1958-61; account supr. Ketchum Communications, 1961-64; sr. v.p. internat. Dailey and Assocs., San Francisco, 1964-76, sr. v.p., dir. Travel div., 1976—. Served with USMC, 1954-56. Mem. San Francisco Charter Internat. Advt. Assn., San Francisco Ad Club. Jewish. Clubs: World Trade (San Francisco), Concordia Argonaut. Home: 42 19th Ave San Francisco CA 94121 Office: Dailey & Assocs 574 Pacific Ave San Francisco CA 94133

KELLER, JOHN CHARLES, law enforcement agency researcher; b. Rapid City, S.D., Feb. 9, 1952; s. John Edward and Jessie Jean (Arnold) K.; m. Catherine Lynn Schexnayder, Aug. 18, 1973; children—John Christopher, Julie, Lauren. B.A. with honors in Econs., Harvard U., 1975. Analyst, Calif. Hwy. Patrol, Sacramento, 1975-80, research mgr. long-range planning sect., 1981—; adv. panel Transp. Research Bd. Scholar Harvard U. Roman Catholic. Clubs: Capital Auto Racers (v.p.), Parkway Soccer (Sacramento).

KELLER, LEROY SCOTT, airline co. exec.; b. Logan, Utah, Oct. 8, 1918; s. Leroy Franklin and Sarah Stoddard (Scott) K.; m. Marlene, Jan. 20, 1979; children by previous marriage—Leroy Scott II, Robert Kay. B.B.A., Utah State U., 1940. Commd. capt. U.S. Air Force, 1945; ret., 1967; with Frontier Airlines, Kalispell, Mont., v.p. 1978; v.p., chief pilot Stockhill Aviation, 1978— flight examiner FAA. Decorated Air medal. Mem. Airline Pilots Assn., Aircraft Owners and Pilots Assn., Ret. Pilots Assn. Republican. Clubs: Elks, Kiwanis. Home: 375 Grandview Dr Kalispell MT 59901 Office: Stockhill Aviation 1893 Airport Rd Kalispell MT 59901

KELLER, PATRICK ERLE, property analyst; b. Los Angeles, June 5, 1947; s. Olin Thomas and Helen Elizabeth (Sell) K.; B.S. in Fin., Calif. State U., Long Beach, 1971, M.B.A., Pacific Northwestern U., 1973; m. Maud May Kahalolani Napoleon, May 10, 1975; children—Amy Patricia, Katie Kaholalani, Erle Teminihi, Hilarie Kulamanukaekaeluni, Naomi Kaipoakelani, Leslie Kznai. Engaged in real estate appraising, 1964—; owner, chief appraiser Patrick E. Keller & Assos., Hawthorne, Calif., 1976—; dir., founder First Nat. Bank El Segundo; dir., fin. officer Southbay Credit Union; founder, dir. 1st Nat. Bank of El Segundo. Res. police officer, Hawthorne, 1975—; fin. officer local Mormon Ch., 1977-80; treas. Flag. of the Free Com., 1978-81, Republican Central Com. of Los Angeles County, 1978—; city clk., Hawthorne, 1981—; bd. dirs. Meml. Hosp. of Hawthorne; active local YMCA, Boy Scouts Am. Sr. mem. Nat. Assn. Rev. Appraisers. Am. Assn. Cert. Appraisers, Nat. Assn. Ind. Fee Appraisers; mem. Am. Soc. Appraisers, Soc. Real Estate Appraisers (assoc.), Nat. Register Real Estate Appraisers (pres.), Nat. Soc. Real Estate Appraisers, Internat. Orgn. Real Estate Appraisers (pres. So. Calif. chpt., regional v.p. West Coast), Internat. Inst. Valuers, Inst. Real Property Analysts, Internat. Soc. Real Estate Economists, Hawthorne C. of C. (dir. 1978-80). Republican. Club: We-Tip. Address: 4734 W Broadway Hawthorne CA 90250

KELLER, PHILIP BECKWITH, manufacturing executive; b. Salt Lake City, July 18, 1917; s. George Philip and Winifred Westbrook (Gatrell) K.; student UCLA; m. Margaret Cook, July 3, 1946; children—Timothy, Paul, Marilyn. Engr., N.Am. Aviation, 1938-52; dir. new product devel. Collier Corp., Los Angeles, 1952-55; dir. mfg. Stillman Rubber Co., Culver City, Calif., 1955-62; owner, pres. Fizz-Whiz Co., Los Angeles, 1957—. Mem. ASME, Engrs. Assn. Honolulu, Advt. Splty. Inst. Clubs: Santa Monica Yacht, Honolulu Book, Elks. Patentee in field. Home: 258 Poipu Dr Honolulu HI 96825 Office: 1527 Pontius Ave Los Angeles CA 90025

KELLER, ROBERT WILLIAM, lawyer; b. Chgo., Feb. 8, 1940; s. Joseph H. and Irene C. (Annis) K.; B.S. in Elec. Engring., Ill. Inst. Tech., 1961, M.S. in Elec. Engring., 1963; J.D. with honors, De Paul U., 1968; m. Judith M. Barnes, Mar. 8, 1969; 1 son, Thomas. Teaching asst. Ill. Inst. Tech., Chgo., 1961-63, research engr. Ill. Inst. Tech. Research Inst., 1963-67; admitted to Ill. bar, 1968, Calif. bar, 1970; assoc. firm Hofgren and Wegner, Chgo., 1967-69; patent lawyer IBM, San Jose, Calif., 1969-73, Schatzel and Hamrick, Santa Clara, Calif., 1973-77; sr. patent counsel TRW Electronics and Def. Sector, Redondo Beach, Calif., 1977—. Bd. dirs. Legal Aid Soc. Santa Clara County, 1970-77. Mem. Calif. Bar Assn., Ill. Bar Assn., Am. Patent Law Assn., Calif. Patent Law Assn., Los Angeles Patent Law Assn., Nat. Security Indsl. Assn., Ill. Soc. Profl. Engrs., Tau Beta Pi. Home: 30170 Matisse Dr Rancho Palos Verdes CA 90274 Office: One Space Park Redondo Beach CA 90278

KELLER, TRUDY THAL, sales exec.; b. Fairfield, Calif., Feb. 16, 1944; d. Warren Adolph and Sybil (Wessendorf) Thal; A.A., Stephens Coll., 1963; student U. Mo., 1963-64; B.S., Black Hills State Coll., 1966; M.A., Calif. State U., Los Angeles, 1979; m. Robert J. Keller; children from previous marriage—Pete Heyden, Kristen Cosette. Instr. art Mountain Home (Idaho) Sch. Dist., 1966-69; sales rep. Art et Decor, Mission Viejo, Calif., 1976-77; sales rep. Kraft Food Service, Carson, Calif., 1977-79; account exec. Sta. KWAV-FM, Monterey, Calif., 1979—; sales exec. Keller & Assos.; instr. sales Cabrillo Coll., Aptos, Calif., 1980. Vol., Hotline for Youth Salt Lake City, 1972-74. Hudson Rousher scholar, 1975. Mem. Nat. League Am. Penwomen, Nat. Assn. Profl. Saleswomen, Am. Soc. Tng. and Devel. Home: 1612 Escalona Dr Santa Cruz CA 95060

KELLER, WAYNE DONALD, safety engineer, consultant; b. Decatur, Ill., Sept. 17, 1926; s. Theodore T. and Neda Ruth (Hughes) K.; grad. Sch. Ministerial Studies, Kent, Ohio, 1964; B.S., Northwestern Coll., 1979; Psy.D., Neotarian Coll. Philosophy, 1982; m. Lee Dotson Walker, Nov. 12, 1958; children—Michael, Debra, Susan. Design engr. Lockheed Aircraft Co., Smyrna, Ga., 1966-70, McDonnell Aircraft Co., St. Louis, 1970-73; safety dir. Nev. Machine Engring. Co., Las Vegas, 1973—; Quantum-Data Co., Las Vegas, 1974—; safety and health rep. State of Nev., 1979—. Chmn. first aid com. Las Vegas chpt. ARC, 1974—. Served with USN, 1944-45. Mem. Nat. Fire Protection Assn., Nat. Safety Mgmt. Soc., Am. Soc. Safety Engrs., Epsilon Delta Chi. Club: Toastmasters (Mo. lt. gov. 1970, pres. Sunset club, Las Vegas 1973). Home: 5157 Champions St Las Vegas NV 89122 Office: PO Box 3078 Laguna Hills CA 92653

KELLERMAN, SALLY CLAIRE, actress; b. Long Beach, Calif., June 2, 1937; d. John Helm and Edith Baine (Vaughn) K.; student Los Angeles City Coll., Actor's Studio, N.Y.C.; pupil Jeff Corey, Los Angeles; m. Jonathan D. Krane, May 11, 1980; 1 dau., Clare. Stage appearances include Breakfast at Tiffany's, Singular Man, N.Y.C., Holiday, Los Angeles; films include M*A*S*H*, Brewster McCloud, Last of the Red Hot Lovers, Reflection of Fear, Slither, Lost Horizon, Rafferty and the Gold Dust Twins, The Big Bus, The Boston Strangler, It Rained All Night The Day I Left, Head On, The April Fools, Welcome to L.A., A Little Romance, Foxes, Serial, Loving Couples; also TV roles Mannix, It Takes a Thief, Crysler Theatre; TV films Verna: USO Girl, 1978, The Big Blonde, 1980. Nominee Acad. and Golden Globe awards for M*A*S*H*. Mem. Actor's Equity, AFTRA, Screen Actors Guild. Office: care Robert Colbert Guild Mgmt 9911 Pico Blvd Los Angeles CA 90067

KELLEY, JOHN JAMES, neurosurgeon; b. Stoughton, Mass., June 15, 1930; s. Timothy Francis and Agnes Josephine (O'Halloran) K.; B.S., Stonehill Coll., 1952; M.S., Boston Coll., 1954; M.D., Georgetown U., 1958; m. Patricia Ann Stone, Aug. 13, 1960; children—James Matthew, Michael John. Resident in neurosurgery Mayo Clinic, Rochester, Minn., 1962-66, asso. cons., 1967-68; practice medicine specializing in neurosurgery Phoenix, 1968—; mem. staff St. Josephs Hosp., Good Samaritan Hosp., Phoenix Bapt. Hosp., Ariz. Childrens Hosp. Mem. Maricopa County Commn. on Trial Ct. Appointments, 1976—; trustee Maricopa Found. Med. Care, 1977—; bd. dirs. Hope-A Head Trauma Support Group. Served with AUS, 1957-62. Diplomate Am. Bd. Neurol. Surgery. Fellow A.C.S.; mem. Mayo Alumni Assn., Ariz. Med. Assn., AMA, Rocky Mountain Neurosurg. Soc., Congress Neurol. Surgeons, Am. Assn. Neurol. Surgeons, Am. Judicature Soc., Alpha Omega Alpha. Office: 6036 W 19th Ave Phoenix AZ 85015

KELLEY, NEIL DAVIS, meteorologist; b. Clayton, Mo., Jan. 8, 1942; s. Davis Franklin and Louise Minnie (Zager) K.; divorced; B.S. in Meteorology, St. Louis U., 1963; M.S., Pa. State U., 1968. Mem. staff Meteorology Research Inc. Altadena, Calif., 1963-66; field supr. Exxon Research and Engring., Linden, N.J., 1967; instr. meteorology Pa. State U., 1969-71; chief of capability devel. Research Aviation Facility, Nat. Ctr. for Atmospheric Research, Boulder, Colo., 1972-77; prin. scientist Solar Energy Research Inst., Golden, Colo., 1977—. Recipient spl. award Nat. Ctr. Atmospheric Research, 1974; outstanding award Solar Energy Research Inst., 1982. Mem. Instrument Soc. Am., Am. Meteorol. Soc., AAAS, AIAA, Am. Theater Organ Soc., Sigma Xi. Club: Elks. Contbr. articles to profl. jours. Office: 1617 Cole Blvd Golden CO 80401

KELLEY, PAULA GARRETT, film studio advertising executive; b. Okmulgee, Okla., Aug. 6, 1946; d. Paul and Elva (Harmon) Bryson; m. William Charlton Kelley, Jan. 2, 1976. B.A., U. Wash., 1968. Advt. agy. media dir., Portland, Oreg., 1968-72, David Evans Advt., San Francisco, 1972, Nat. BankAmericard Inc. (now VISA USA), San Francisco, 1973-75; assoc. media dir. J. Walter Thompson, San Francisco, 1976-77, acct. exec., 1978; acct. exec. D'Arcy-MacManus-Masius, San Francisco, 1979; media mgr. Columbia Pictures, Burbank, Calif., 1980, media dir., 1981, v.p. media advt., 1982, sr. v.p. media advt., 1982—. Office: 2083 Columbia Plaza S Burbank CA 91505

KELLEY, RICHARD CHARLES, political science educator; b. Salt Lake City, July 8, 1950; s. Vincent Charles and Dorothy Jean (McArthur) K.; m. Theresa B. Doyle, Aug. 17, 1980. B.A. cum laude, Harvard U., 1970; M.P.A., U. Wash., 1976, Ph.D., 1983. Staff aide to U.S. Rep. Brock Adams, 1970; chief dep. auditor Clark County (Wash.), 1971-72; vice chmn. King County (Wash.) Democratic Com., 1972-76; dep. mayor, Seattle, 1977-79; mem. chmn. Seattle Civil Service Commn., 1981-83; asst. prof. politics and govt. adminstrn. St. Mary's Coll., Moraga, Calif., 1983—. Del., Dem. Nat. Conv., 1974-76; bd. dirs. Central Seattle Community Council Fedn., 1974-76, Assn. for Retarded Citizens, 1976; mem. recombinant DNA research com. U. Wash., 1978-79. Nat. Merit. scholar, 1967; J. Allen Smith fellow U. Wash., 1975. Mem. Am. Polit. Sci. Assn., Western Polit. Sci. Assn., Pacific Northwest Polit. Sci. Assn., Am. Soc. Pub. Adminstrn., Pub. Choice Soc. Roman Catholic. Author: (with Sara J. Weir) Unwrapping the Blanket Primary, 1981, 2d edit., 1983. Office: Dept Govt St Mary's Coll Moraga CA 94575

KELLEY, ROBERT LLOYD, history educator; b. Santa Barbara, Calif., June 2, 1925; s. Loyd Amos and Berta Lee (Winniford) K.; B.A., U. Calif., Santa Barbara, 1948; M.A., Stanford U., 1949, Ph.D., 1953; m. Madge Louise Naumchik, June 10, 1972; children (by previous marriage)—Sandra Lee Kelley Gory, Brian Michael, Alison Gail Kelley Eason, Dorcas Louise; stepchildren—Christopher John Naumchik, Lisa Ann Naumchik. Historian Air Def. Command, Colorado Springs, Colo., 1953-54; instr. history Santa Barbara City Coll., 1954-55; prof. history U. Calif., Santa Barbara, 1955—, asst. to chancellor, 1960-62, chmn. grad. program public hist. studies, 1975-81, chmn. acad. senate, 1973-75; vis. prof. U. Mich., Ann Arbor, 1969-70; mem. U.S. history adv. selection com. Council Internat. Exchange of Scholars, 1979-82; cons. on water history of Sacramento Valley. Served to capt. USAF, 1943-46, 51-53. Mem. Calif. Commn. Tchr. Preparation and Licensing, 1973-74. Recipient Harold J. Plous Meml. award U. Calif., Santa Barbara, 1962; Louis Knott Koontz prize Pacific Coast br. Am. Hist. Assn., 1965; Nat. Endowment Humanities fellow, 1975-76; Fulbright-Hays prof. Moscow U., 1979; Guggenheim fellow, 1982-83; fellow Woodrow Wilson Internat. Center for Scholars, 1982-83. Mem. Am. Hist. Assn., Orgn. Am. Historians (program chmn. ann meeting 1974, exec. bd. 1980—). Democrat. Episcopalian. Author: Gold vs. Grain: The Hydraulic Mining Controversy in California's Sacramento Valley, 1959; The Transatlantic Persuasion: The Liberal-Democratic Mind in the Age of Gladstone, 1969; The Shaping of the American Past, 3d edit., 1982; The Sounds of Controversy: Crucial Arguments in the American Past, 1975; The Cultural Pattern in American Politics: The First Century, 1979; Transformations: UC Santa Barbara 1909-1979, 1981; contbr. articles to profl. publs.

KELLEY, ROBERT PAUL, JR., marketing company executive; b. Mansfield, Ohio, Mar. 27, 1942; s. Robert Paul and Rachel Marie Kelley; B.B.A., Notre Dame U., 1964; M.B.A., Harvard U., 1969; m. Mimi Grant, June 15, 1975; children—Robert, Laura, Elizabeth. Mktg. cons., supr. Laventhol & Horwath, Los Angeles, 1972-73; dir. mktg., entertainment and mdsg. Knott's Berry Farm, Buena Park, Calif., 1974-76; sr. v.p. mktg. Am. Warranty Corp., Los Angeles, 1978-80; chief exec. officer Five Star Mktg. Services, Inc., Santa Ana, Calif., 1976—. Served with USNR, 1964-67. Home: 13992 Malena Dr Tustin CA 92680 Office: 555 Parkcenter Dr Santa Ana CA 92705

KELLEY, SANDRA DEE, educator, researcher, b. Hot Springs, S.D., Aug. 9, 1937; d. Edwin Donald and Lucile Olga (Wickstrom) Kachelhoffer; m. Gregory Michael Kelley, Aug. 16, 1975; children—Jayne Elaine Gerlach, William S. Lundy, Alice Ann Lundy, Michael R. B. Kelley. B.S., S.D. State U.-Brookings, 1959; M.A., N.Mex. Highlands U., 1972; postgrad. N.Mex. State U.-Las Cruces, 1980—. Cert. counselor, tchr., N.Mex. Grad. teaching asst. S.D. State U.-Brookings, 1958-59; pres., bd. dirs. Creative Living Assocs., Los Alamos, 1973-76; grad. teaching asst. N.Mex. State U., Las Cruces, 1979-82; research assoc. dept. curriculum and instrn. 1982—. N.Mex. State U. grad. fellow, 1982-83. Mem. Assn. for Supervision and Curriculum Devel., N.Mex. Assn. for Supervision and Curriculum Devel., N.Mex. Assn. for Supervision and Curriculum Devel., Phi Kappa Phi, Alpha Psi Omega, Phi Delta Kappa. Democrat. Unitarian. Home: 238 1/2 W Madrid St Las Cruces NM 88005 Office: N Mex State U PO Box 3 AC Las Cruces NM 88003

KELLEY, VINCENT CHARLES, pediatrician; b. Tyler, Minn., Jan. 23, 1916; s. Charles Enoch and Stella May (Ross) K.; B.A., U. N.D., 1934, M.A., 1935; B.S. in Edn., U. Minn., 1936, Ph.D. in Biochemistry, 1942, B.S. in Medicine, 1944, M.B., 1945, M.D., 1946; m. Dorothy Jean MacArthur, Sept. 5, 1942; children—Nancy Jean, Thomas Vincent, Richard Charles, William MacArthur, Robert Kenneth, Jean Elizabeth, James Joseph. Prof. chemistry Emory and Henry Coll., 1941; Rockefeller research fellow U. Minn., 1941-42, Swift fellow in pediatrics, 1948-50, intern in pediatrics, 1945-46, instr., 1949-50; asst. prof. organic chemistry Coll. St. Thomas, 1942-43; asso. prof. pediatrics U. Utah, 1950-58; prof., head div. endocrinology, metabolism and renal disease dept. pediatrics U. Wash., 1958—; dir. Utah State Heart Labs., 1953-58. Served with U.S. Army, 1943-45, M.C., USAAF, 1946-48. Recipient E. Mead Johnson award for pediatric research, 1954, Ross Pediatric Edn. award, 1971; diplomate Am. Bd. Pediatrics. Mem. Am. Acad. Pediatrics, AAAS, AAUP, Am. Inst. Biol. Scis., Am. Heart Assn., AMA, Am. Pediatric Soc., Am. Rheumatism Assn., Am. Soc. Nephrology, Internat. Endocrine Soc., N.Y. Acad. Scis., Pan-Am. Med. Assn., Soc. Exptl. Biology and Medicine, Endocrine Soc., Soc. Pediatric Research, Western Soc. Clin. Research, Western Soc. Pediatric Research, Phi Beta Kappa, Sigma Xi, Phi Lambda Upsilon, Phi Eta Sigma, Kappa Kappa Psi. Contbr. numerous articles on biochemistry, pediatrics and endocrinology to profl. jours.; editor: Metabolic, Endocrine and Genetic Disorders of Children, 3 vols., 1974; Infections in Children, 1982; Practice of Pediatrics, 8 vols., 1958—; editorial bd. Audio Digest, 1956-72, Med. Digest, 1956-75, Am. Jour. Diseases Children, 1958-69, Internat. Med. Digest, 1960-71. Home: 8611 45th Ave NE Seattle WA 98115 Office: Dept-Pediatrics RD-20 U Wash Seattle WA 98195

KELLMAN, HAROLD RICHARD, financial consultant; b. Bronx, N.Y., Dec. 15, 1944; s. Jack and Ann (Schneider) K.; B.S., Mich. Tech. U., Houghton, 1966; M.B.A., U. Mich., 1968; m. Mary Elizabeth Sadowski, June 6, 1970; children—Suzanne Elizabeth, David Haven. Elec. engring. asst. Fed. Pacific Electric Co., Newark, 1964-65; treas., v.p. fin. Interactive Systems, Inc., Ann Arbor, Mich., 1968-69; pres. HRK Enterprises, Fremont, Calif., 1969—. Recipient Wall St. Jour. award, 1966; Mich. Coll. scholar, 1967; Chrysler fellow, 1968. Mem. IEEE, Assn. Venture Founders, Phi Eta Sigma, Phi Kappa Phi. Investments editor Detroit Discovery mag., 1973-75. Address: 38164 Miller Pl Fremont CA 94536

KELLNER, RICHARD GEORGE, computer scientist; b. Cleve., July 10, 1943; s. George Ernest and Wanda Julia (Lapinski) K.; B.S., Case Inst. Tech., 1965; M.S., Stanford U., 1968, Ph.D., 1969; m. Charlene Ann Zajc, June 26, 1965; children—Michael Richard, David George. Staff mem. Los Alamos (N.M.) Scientific Lab., 1969-79; co-owner, dir. software devel. KMP Computer Services, Inc., Los Alamos, 1979—; co-owner Computer-Aided Communications, 1982—; cons., 1979—. Mem. IEEE, Assn. Computing Machinery. Home: 4496 Ridgeway Dr Los Alamos NM 87544 Office: KMP Computer Services Inc 703 Central Ave Los Alamos NM 87544

KELLOGG, BERTRAM CECIL, safety consultant; b. Port Angeles, Wash., Sept. 16, 1924; s. Bertram Fredrick and Lorette Louise (Woods) K.; student UCLA, 1961, U. Wash., 1966, U. So. Calif., 1956-57, U. Minn., 1967, Anchorage Community Coll., 1956, Calif. State U., Sacramento, 1968; children—Bertram Scott, Mary Alice, Deborah Jo Ellen Kellog Douglas, Dennis Bertram. Mgr. engring. Fireman's Fund Am., Seattle, 1965-69; dir. indsl. relations Feather River Lumber Co., Loyalton, Calif., 1960-62; v.p., gen. mgr. Kelor Corp., Anchorage, 1969-76; mgr. loss control div. Aetna Cravens Dargar & Co., Sacramento, 1978-81; safety cons. Callosha Cons. Service, Sacramento, 1981—; cons. City of Pasadena. Dir. safety services and disasters ARC, Pasadena, 1957-60. Served with U.S. Mcht. Marine, 1944-47. Mem. Am. Soc. Safety Engrs. (profl.), Nat. Fire Protection Assn., U.S. Power Squadron, Vets. of Safety, Engring. Council Sacramento Valley. Republican. Episcopalian. Clubs: Lions, Toastmasters, Elks. Contbr. articles to profl. jours. Home: 161 Magnolia Ave Sacramento CA 95828 Office: 2424 Arden Way Sacramento CA 95825

KELLOGG, BRUCE MICHAEL, real estate investor and agent; b. Buffalo, Jan. 3, 1947; s. Harlan Wood and Hilma Moore (Yarrington) K.; m. Diane Linda Mancuso, Dec. 25, 1979; children—Jeremy, Catherine, Michael, Elizabeth. B.S.E.E., Rutgers U., 1969; M.B.A., Golden Gate U., 1976, Securities investor, Wilmington, N.C., 1970-73; real estate investor, San Jose, Calif., 1973—; assoc Gt. Am. Realty, San Jose, 1982—. Mem. Tri-County Apt. Assn., Calif. Apt. Assn. Nat. Apt. Assn., San Jose Bd. Realtors, Calif. Assn. Realtors, Nat. Assn. Realtors, Nat. Multihousing Council, Internat. Platform Assn. Republican. Roman Catholic. Contbr. articles to profl. jours. Office: Great American Realty 100 N Winchester Blvd Suite 370 San Jose CA 95128

KELLOGG, FREDERICK, historian; b. Boston, Dec. 9, 1929; s. Frederick Floyd and Stella Harriet (Plummer) K.; A.B., Stanford U., 1952; M.A., U. So. Calif., 1958; Ph.D., Ind. U., 1969; m. Patricia Kay Hanbery, Aug. 21, 1954, (dec., 1975); 1 dau., Kristine Marie Calvert; m. 2d, Rebecca Anne Boone, July 11, 1979. Instr., Boise State U., 1962-64, asst. prof., 1964-65; vis. asst. prof. U. Idaho, 1965; asso. prof. Boise State U., 1966-67; instr. history U. Ariz., 1967-68, asst. prof., 1968-71, asso. prof., 1971—. Founder, chmn. Idaho Hist. Conf., 1964. U.S.-Romania Cultural Exchange Research scholar, 1960-61; Sr. Fulbright-Hays Research scholar, Romania, 1969-70. Recipient Am. Council Learned Socs. Research grant, 1970-71; Internat. Research and Exchanges Bd. Sr. Research grant, 1973-74. Mem. Am. Hist. Assn., Am. Assn. Advancement Slavic Studies, Am. Assn. Southeast European Studies. Mng. editor Southeastern Europe, 1974—; contbr. articles to scholarly publs. Office: Dept History U Ariz Tucson AZ 85721

KELLOGG, GERALD LEE, instructional designer; b. Chgo., May 4, 1953; s. Laurel Wells and Terry Catherine (Bermes) K.; m. Josefina Cuevas, June 25, 1977. B.A. in Telecommunications, U. Calif.-Riverside, 1975, M.A. in Instructional Media and Tech., Calif. State U.-Los Angeles, 1982. Audio visual prodn. specialist Action/Peace Corps, Dominican Republic, 1976-78; media coordinator Burroughs Jr. High Sch., Los Angeles, 1978-80; instructional media specialist Los Angeles Trade Tech. Coll., 1979-81; instructional designer Hughes Aircraft Co., Santa Fe Springs, Calif., 1981-82, Calif. State U. Consortium, Long Beach, 1983—. Recipient Calif. State U.-Los Angeles Hartford Bridges award, 1980. Mem. Am. Soc. Tng. and Devel., Nat. Soc. Performance and Instruction. Home: 25937 Oak St Apt 9 Lomita CA 90717

KELLOGG, LLOYD EDMUND, lawyer, educator; b. Sioux City, Iowa, May 25, 1935; s. Lloyd C. and Catherine Irene (Donohue) K.; m. Colette Mulvey, June 25, 1960; children—Marie C., Carol D., Edmund C. B.A., U. Notre Dame, 1958; M.A., Calif. State U.-Los Angeles, 1972; J.D., Van Norman U., 1962. Bar: Calif. Prof. law Pasadena City Coll., 1972—; sole practice, Glendale, Calif., 1970—. Mem. Los Angeles Bar Assn., Glendale Bar Assn., Phi Alpha Delta. Republican. Roman Catholic. Club: Oakmont Country. Home: 951 E Dryden St Glendale CA 91207 Office: 1570 E Colorado St Pasadena CA 91106

KELLOGG, MEG ANN, medical center administrator; b. Chgo., Oct. 24, 1948; d. Harry E. and Kathleen M. (Cahill) K. B.A. in French, U. Calif.-Berkeley, 1970, M.S. in Community Health and Phys. Therapy, Stanford U., 1972. Pub. health analyst Med. Services Adminstrn. HEW, Washington, 1972-73, br. chief Systems Devel. Bur. of Qualty Assurance, Rockville, Md., 1973-75; coordinator accreditation and regulation Kaiser-Permanente Med. Care Program, Oakland, Calif., 1975-80; dir. corp. planning Pacific Med. Ctr., Inc., San Francisco, 1980—; lectr. in field. Bd. dirs. San Francisco Opera Guild. Recipient HEW Outstanding Service Merit award, 1975. Mem. Health Care Execs. No. Calif., Soc. Hosp. Planning, N.Am. Soc. Corporate Planning, Am. Assn. Colls., Phi Beta Kappa. Roman Catholic. Club: San Francisco Bay. Office: PO Box 7999 San Francisco CA 94120

KELLOGG, REBECCA BOONE, librarian; b. Springfield, Ohio, Mar. 7, 1946; d. Roger S. and Elizabeth Lupton (Walker) Boone; m. Dennis David Ash, June 8, 1967 (div.); m. 2d Frederick Kellogg, July 11, 1979; 1 dau., Kristine Marie Kellogg Calvert. Student Earlham Coll., 1964-67; B.A., Case Western Res. U., 1968; M.L.S., U. N.C., 1970. Asst. reference librarian Princeton (N.J.) U., 1970-76; head central reference dept. U. Ariz. Library, Tucson, 1976—. Mem. ALA, Ariz. Library Assn., Nat. Assn. Female Execs., Execs. Women's Council So. Ariz. Mem. Soc. Friends. Home: 1018 E Greenlee Pl Tucson AZ 95719 Office: U Ariz Library Tucson AZ 95721

KELLY, ARTHUR FRANCIS, aviation exec.; b. Tombstone, Ariz., Feb. 22, 1913; s. J.J. and Grace (Angelus) K.; m. Sally Payne, Jan. 31, 1942; children—James J. III, Arthur Francis II. A.B., U. Utah, 1933. Exec. sec. Salt Lake City Airport Commn., 1933-35; with United Air Lines, 1935-37; with Western Air Lines, Inc., Los Angeles, 1937—, v.p. sales, 1949-68, sr. v.p., 1968-70, sr. v.p. mktg., 1970-73, pres., chief exec. officer, 1973-76, chmn. bd., chief exec. officer, 1976-79, chmn. bd., chmn. exec. com., 1979—, also dir.; dir., audit com. MGM/VA Home Entertainment Corp., Inc.; dir., vice chmn. Hollywood Park, Inc.; dir. Fireman's Fund Ins. Cos. Trustee Alaska Pacific U. Served to col. USAAF, World War II. Decorated Bronze Star. Mem. Air Force Assn. (pres. 1952—), Sigma Chi. Office: Western Air Lines Inc 6060 Avion Dr Los Angeles CA 90009

KELLY, CONNIE DIANE, real estate development company executive; b. Reno, July 22, 1951; d. Angelo Bernard and Florence Irene (Powell) Landa. Student U. Nev., Truckee Meadows Community Coll. Lic. real estate broker, Nev. Loan processing supr. 1st Nat. Bank Nev., Reno, 1973-76; loan officer, asst. v.p. Family Savs. and Loan Assn., Reno, 1976-78; br. mgr. Lomas & Nettleton Co., Reno, 1978-81; ptnr. Homes & Land Mag., Reno, 1980-81; project adminstr. R.J.B. Devel. Co., Reno, 1982—; counselor Am. Inst. Fgn. Studies. Mem. Nat. Assn. Female Execs., Winners Circle. Clubs: Sierra Yacht, Multihull Racing Assn., Prindle Fleet 8. Home: 12405 Westridge Dr Reno NV 89511 Office: 100 N Arlington St Suite 340 Reno NV 89501

KELLY, CORNELIUS BERNARD, III, energy co. exec.; b. Cohoes, N.Y., Sept. 23, 1931; s. Cornelius Bernard, Jr. and Agnes Kathleen (Horan) K.; B.A., Providence Coll., 1953; M.A., Am. U., 1971; m. Arlene Rose Holdforth, May 12, 1956; children—Sharon, Diedre, Debora, Patty, Peggy, Terry, Cornelius. Commd. 2d lt. USAF, 1953, advanced through grades to col., 1972; service in Vietnam; ret., 1977; mgr. prodn. services Atlantic Richfield Co., Los Angeles, 1977—; audi-visual cons. Decorated D.F.M., Air medal with oak leaf cluster, Bronze Star. Mem. Internat. Tape Assn., Internat. Audio Visual Assn., Am. Inst. Graphic Arts, Design Mgmt. Inst. Home: 2730 Ardmore St San Marino CA 91108 Office: 515 S Flower St Los Angeles CA 90071

KELLY, ERIC DAMIAN, lawyer, city planner; b. Pueblo, Colo., Mar. 16, 1947; s. William Bret and Patricia Ruth (Ducy) K.; B.A., Williams Coll., 1969; J.D., U. Pa., 1975, M.City Planning, 1975; m. Viana Eileen Rockel, 1980; children—Damian Charles, Eliza Jane, Valissitie Christina Heeren, Douglas Ray Heeren. Bar: Colo. 1975, U.S. Dist. Ct. 1976, U.S. Tax Ct. 1976. Chief citizens' participation unit EPA, Region III, Phila., 1971-72; project planner Beckett New Town, N.J., 1972-73; v.p., project mgr. Rahenkamp Sachs Wells & Assocs., Inc., Denver and Phila., 1973-76; sole practice law, Pueblo, 1976—; instr. U. Colo. Coll. Environ. Design, 1975—, land use seminars Fed. Publs., Inc., 1976—; spl. counsel City of Westminster, Colo., 1976—; pres. Color Radio, Ltd., 1979—; sec., dir. Lodging Service Corp., 1980—; dir. Steel City Agencies, Inc., Mar Tec Broadcasting Corp., Capital Ideas Fund, Inc., Flower Aviation, Inc.; cons. Colo. Land Use Commn., 1976-77, Wyo. Land Use Adminstrn., 1977-78, City of Santa Fe, 1981—. Bd. dirs. Broadway Theatre League, Pueblo, 1976-77, Pueblo Beautiful Assn., 1978—; trustee Sangre de Cristo Arts and Conf. Ctr., 1981—, Christ Congregational Ch., 1982—. Served with U.S. Army, 1969-71. Named outstanding student Am. Inst. Planners, 1975. Mem. Am. Inst. Cert. Planners (charter), Am. Planning Assn., Urban Land Inst., Am., Colo., Denver, Pueblo County bar assns., Williams Coll. Alumni Assn. (class sec. 1969-74, regional sec. 1980—). Democrat. Clubs: Pueblo Country, Rotary. Author: Land Use Controls, 1976, 77, 78, 79, 80, 82 editor, prin. author: The Roadtripper, 1969; contbr. articles to profl. planning and legal jours. Home: 11 Fireweed Ct Pueblo CO 81001 Office: 200 E Abriendo Ave Pueblo CO 81004

KELLY, JACK EDWARD, newspaper advertising executive; b. Susanville, Calif., Aug. 28, 1946; s. Robert Vern and Jeanne Effie (Bath) K.; m. Suzanne Maxine Smith, June 10, 1972; children—Ryan Chandler, Erin Angelyn. B.B.A., Eastern Wash. U., 1972. Dist. circulation mgr. Tri-City Herald, Pasco, Wash., 1972-74, city circulation mgr., 1974-76, classified advt. mgr., 1976-81, advt. sales mgr., 1981-82, advt. dir., 1982—. Served with USN, 1969-71; Vietnam. Mem. Pacific Northwest Assn. of Classified Advt. Mgrs. (bd. dirs., past pres., Bill Totten Achievement award 1983), Pacific Northwest Newspaper Advt. Execs. Assn., Internat. Newspaper Advt. Mktg. Execs., Am. Advt. Fedn. bd. dirs., v.p. Tri-Cities chpt.) Club: Pasco Kennewick Rotary (bd. dirs.). Home: 1002 Rd 55 Pasco WA 99301 Office: PO Box 2608 Pasco WA 99302

KELLY, JAMES FRANCIS, JR., naval officer; b. New Haven, Nov. 18, 1930; s. James Francis and Ann Evelyn (Smith) K., m. Charlane Agnes Hughes, Jan. 22, 1955; children—Terence, Robina, Carisa. B.S., So. Conn. State U., 1952; M.S., U.S. Naval Postgrad. Sch., 1966; postgrad. Harvard U., 1971. Commd. ensign U.S. Navy, 1953, advanced through grades to capt., 1973; comdr. 3 ships Pacific Fleet, 1969-80; asst. chief of staff Comdr. Naval Surface Force, U.S. Pacific Fleet, 1978-80; comdg. officer Navy Personnel Research & Devel. Ctr., San Diego, 1980—. Decorated Legion of Merit, Bronze Star; recipient Award of Merit for Authorship, U.S. Naval Inst., 1979. Mem. U.S. Naval Inst., Harvard U. Alumni Assn. Roman Catholic. Contbr. articles to profl. jours; regular contbr. commentaries to Navy Times, 1978—. Home: 3403 Kennelworth Ln Bonita CA 92002 Office: Navy Personnel Research and Devel Center San Diego CA 92152

KELLY, JAMES LESTER, electronics executive; b. Granite Falls, Minn., Oct. 15, 1931; s. Lester G. and Barbara (Rand) K.; m. Lora Lamborn, Jan. 31, 1953; children—John Sorrick, Pamela. B.S., U. Calif.-Berkeley, 1954; M.B.A., Harvard U., 1958. With Ampex Corp., Redwood City, Calif., 1958-62; Cons. Booz Allen & Hamilton, Inc., San Francisco, 1962-66; mgr. fin. analysis TRW Electronics, Los Angeles, 1966-69; div. mgr. TRW Holyoke Wire & Cable, South Hadley, Mass., 1969-74; v.p., gen. mgr. TRW Datacom Internat. Inc., Los Angeles, 1974—; adv. bd. Scott Sci. & Tech.; instr. U. Calif. Extension. Bd. dirs. St. Kitts Biomed. Found., Childrens Hosp., Huntington Library. Served to 1st lt. inf. AUS, 1954-56. Calif. Alumni scholar, 1950-54. Mem.

Electronic Industries Assn., World Affairs Council, Town Hall, Calif. Hist. Soc. Republican. Episcopalian. Clubs: Rotary, Vikings of Scandia. Home: 20352 Delita Dr Woodland Hills CA 91364 Office: 10880 Wilshire Blvd Suite 1812 Los Angeles CA 90024

KELLY, PATRICIA DUCY, civic worker; b. Pueblo, Colo., Nov. 11, 1923; d. Damian Patrick and Ruth Russell (Taylor) Ducy; B.A., U. Colo., 1948; m. Bret Kelly, Mar. 25, 1944; children—Eric Damian, Kate Kelly Schweitzer. Dir., Steel City Agys., Inc., 1973—; mem. Fed. Home Loan Bank Bd. Topeka, 1977-83. Mem. Colo. Council on Arts and Humanities, 1967-71; mem. Pueblo City Council, 1970-78, v.p., 1972-73, chmn. exec. com., 1974-75, 77; mem. exec. bd. Colo. Mcpl. League, 1970-74, v.p. exec. bd., 1972-73; mem. So. Colo. Econ. Devel. Dist. Exec. Bd., 1975-77; mem. steering com. Colo. Front Range Project, 1979—; bd. dirs. Pueblo Conservancy Dist., 1977—, chmn., 1977-79; mem. Pueblo Energy Commn., 1975—, chmn., 1975-77; mem. environ. steering com. Nat. League of Cities, 1971-76; mem. consumer affairs/spl. impact adv. com. Fed. Energy Adminstrn., 1976-77; mem. energy extension adv. com. Dept. Energy, 1978—; mem. citizens adv. com. Colo. Office of Energy Conservation, 1978-80; mem. Colo. Bicentennial Commn., 1972-74; trustee Sangre de Cristo Arts and Conf. Center, 1971-77; chmn., founding mem. Pueblo Greenways Found., 1983—. Recipient Disting. Woman award U. So. Colo., 1970; outstanding achievement in arts award Pueblo C. of C., 1970; Disting. Citizen award Pueblo Rotary Club, 1976; Energy Conservation award Denver Fed. Exec. Bd., 1977. Mem. Women's Forum of Colo. (founding mem., dir. 1977-78). Democrat.

KELLY, PATRICIA JEAN, creative director, writer, designer, illustrator, photographer; b. St. Louis, Dec. 27, 1946; d. Edward Eugene and Helen Marie (Montgomery) K. Student U. Mo. and Washington U., 1965-67, Webster Coll., 1967-69; B.A., U. Colo., 1976. Designer curriculum material, Cemrel, St. Louis, 1969-73; photographer, designer, tchr. U.S. Park Service, Gulf Islands Nat. Seashore, Santa Rosa Island, Fla., 1973-74; dir. pubs. Met. State Coll., Denver, 1975—; co-founder Pinon Press, Denver, 1979-82. Campaign worker candidates for lt. gov. and state legislature, 1978; announcement designer for Women in Communications. Recipient spl. creativity award U.S. Park Service 1974; Art Direction Creativity award N.Y. 1976; St. Louis Art Dir. Club Creativity award, 1975. Mem. Women in Communication, Denver Art Dirs. Club, Denver Advertising Fedn., Soc. Children's Book Writers, Univ. and Coll. Designers Assn., Higher Edn. Assn. of the Rockies. Illustrations, photographs, books displayed in Smithsonian traveling exhbn., U.S. and Can.; illustrator numerous books for Viking Press, Wadsworth Pub. and Lincoln Ctr. Home: 3415 Wyandot St Denver CO 80211 Office Met State Coll 1041 9th St Denver CO 80204

KELLY, PATRICK JOSEPH, manufacturing company executive; b. Chillicothe, Ohio, July 14, 1947; s. Roger Edmond and Ruth Elizabeth (Emmett) K.; m. Patricia Ann Santangelo, Jan. 2, 1970; children—Alyssa, John. B.S. in Physics, U. Dayton, 1969; M.B.A., Loyola Coll., 1980. Supr. mfg. cad/cam systems Newport News Shipbldg. div. Tenneco (Va.), 1969-77; mgr. systems and programming Balt. Aircoil div. Merck & Co., 1977-81; mgr. mgmt. info. systems Paco Pumps div. Merck & Co., Oakland, Calif., 1981—. Mem. Assn. Systems Mgmt. Roman Catholic. Office: 9201 San Leandro St Oakland CA 94604

KELLY, PAUL JOSEPH, JR., lawyer; b. Freeport, N.Y., Dec. 6, 1940; s. Paul J. and Jacqueline M. (Nolan) K.; B.B.A., U. Notre Dame, 1963; LL.B., Fordham U., 1967; m. Ruth Ellen Dowling, June 27, 1964; children—Johanna, Paul Edwin, Thomas Martin, Christopher Mark, Heather Marie. Law clk. Cravath, Swaine & Moore, N.Y.C., 1964-67; admitted to N.Mex. bar, 1967; asso. firm Hinkle, Bondurant, Cox & Eaton, Roswell, 1967-71, partner, 1971—; mem. N.Mex. Bd. Bar Examiners; mem. N.Mex. Ho. of Reps., 1976-81, chmn. public affairs com., mem. judiciary com. Mem. N.Mex. Pub. Defender Bd.; pres. Roswell Drug Abuse Com., 1970-71. Pres. Chaves County Young Republicans, 1971-72; vice chmn. N.Mex. Young Republicans, 1969-71, treas., 1968-69. Bd. dirs. Zia council Girl Scouts Am., Roswell Girls Club, Chaves County Mental Health Assn., 1974-77; bd. dirs. Roswell Symphony Orch. Soc., 1969-82, treas., 1970-73, pres., 1973-75; mem. Eastern N.Mex. State Fair Bd., 1978-83. Mem. ABA, State Bar N.Mex. (v.p. young lawyers sect. 1969, co-chmn. ins. sub-com. 1972-73, mem. continuing legal edn. com. 1970-73). Roman Catholic (pres. parish council 1971-76). K.C. Home: Route 9 Box 90V Sunlit Hills Santa Fe NM 87501 Office: PO Box 2068 Santa Fe NM 87501

KELLY, PETER JAMES, financial planner; b. Albany, N.Y., Apr. 18, 1941; s. James Raymond and Ann (Lansing) K.; children—Elaine Anna, Sean Peter. Student Georgetown U., 1959-64; postgrad. in fin. services Am. Coll., 1980-82. CLU. Mgr., 1789 Restaurant, Washington, 1962, Clyde's, Washington, 1963, Marriott Corp., Washington, 1963-65, Stittig's, Albany, N.Y., 1966-67; comml. audit mgr. Calif. Casualty, 1967-68; sales rep. to sales mgr. Acacia Mut. Life Ins., 1968-77; pres., founder PJK Assocs. and successor corp. Fin. Directions, Inc., Oakland, Calif., 1970—; dir. East Bay Underwriters; prin. Computer Aid, Fin. Planners Equity Corp. Bd. dirs. St. George's Home, 1982-83, Sch. of the Madelene, 1979. Mem. Am. Soc. C.L.U.s, Internat. Assn. Fin. Planners, Life Underwriters Assn., Inst. Fin. Planning, Oakland Estate Planning Council, Calif. Life Underwriters Assn., Golden Key Soc. Roman Catholic. Club: Oakland Athletic. Home: 5 Commodore Dr Apt 202 Emeryville CA 94612 Office: 428 13th St Oakland CA 94612

KELLY, RITA MAE, political science educator, researcher, consultant; b. Waseca, Minn., Dec. 10, 1939; d. John Francis and Agnes Mary (Lorentz) Cawley; m. Vincent Peter Kelley, June 2, 1962; children—Patrick Joseph, Kathleen Theresa. B.A. in Russian, U. Minn., 1961; M.A. in Polit. Sci., Ind. U., 1964, Ph.D., 1967. Research scientist Am. Insts. Research, Kensington, Md., 1968-70, sr. research scientist, 1970-72; cons. OEO, Washington, 1972-73; pres. Rita Mae Kelly & Assocs., Elizabeth, N.J., 1973-75; assoc. prof. Camden (N.J.) Coll. Rutgers U., 1975-77, prof., 1979-82; prof. ctr. for pub. affairs Ariz. State U., Tempe, 1982—; mem. editorial bd. Evaluation Rev., 1978-81, Women and Politics, 1980, Jour. Internat. and Comparative Pub. Policy; bd. dirs. Eagleton Inst. Politics, Rutgers U., 1980-82, Inst. Comparative Social and Cultural Studies. Pres. Cabin John Citizens Assn., 1973. Ford Found. fellow, 1962-73; recipient Merit award Rutgers U., 1979; Outstanding Achievement award Camden County YWCA, 1980. Mem. Am. Polit. Sci. Assn., Am. Soc. Pub. Adminstrn. (outstanding achievement award N.J. chpt. 1981), Am. Psychol. Assn., Soc. for Psychol. Study of Social Issues (chmn. nat. task force on Productivity in pub. sector 1975-80), Northwestern Polit. Sci. Assn. (bd. dirs. 1977-79, pres. women's caucus, 1978-79), N.J. Polit. Sci. Assn. (bd. dirs. 1976-81), Evaluation Research Soc., Phi Beta Kappa. Author: Pilot Police Project, 1972; Community Control of Economic Development, 1977; The Making of Political Women, 1978. Contbr. articles in field to profl. jours. Home: 1335 E Ellis Dr Tempe AZ 85282 Office: Ariz State U Ctr for Pub Affairs Tempe AZ 85287

KELLY, ROBERT E., air force officer, educational administrator; b. Albany, N.Y., Nov. 3, 1933; s. Frank Benedict and Helen Marie (Parker) K.; m. Margaret Elizabeth Odell, Apr. 9; children—Patrick (dec.), Michael, Christopher, Karen, Kathleen, Robert E. Jr. (dec.), Diana, Colleen. B.A., Rutgers U.; M.A., George Washington U. Commd. 2d lt. U.S. Air Force, 1956, advanced through grades to lt. gen.; vice comdr. Tech. Air Command Air Weapons Ctr., Eglin AFB, Fla., 1977-78; comdr. 836th Air Div., Davis-Monthan AFB, Ariz., 1978-79; comdr. Tech Air Command Fighter Weapons Ctr., Nellis AFB, Nev., 1979-81; supt. USAF Acad., Colorado Springs, Colo., 1981—. Bd. dirs. Air Force Acad. Found.; mem. Gov's Commn. on Cancer, Las Vegas, 1980-81; mem. Gov.'s Task Force on Drunk Driving, 1981-83. Decorated D.S.M., Legion of Merit, D.F.C., Bronze Star, Air medal with 10 oak leaf clusters, Air Force Commendation medal; Armed Forces Honor medal 1st class (Republic of Vietnam). Mem. Order of Daedalians, Mil. Order of World Wars, Air Force Assn., U.S. Squash Racquets Assn., Chi Psi. Roman Catholic. Club: Las Vegas Country. Office: Office of Supt USAF Academy Colorado Springs CO 80840

KELLY, ROBERT JEROME, public affairs executive; b. Anaconda, Mont., Aug. 27, 1946; s. Robert J. and Mary C. (Cunningham) K.; m. Sandra J. Jensen, Nov. 22, 1974. B.S. in Biology, U. Mont., 1964-69; M.P.H. in Environ. Sci., U. Minn., 1971-72; USPHS grantee, 1971-72. Environ. affairs aide to U.S. congressman, Washington, 1972-74; mgr. Ecol. Cons. Services, Helena, Mont., 1974-75; dir. air, water, land reclamation programs The Anaconda (Mont.) Co., 1975-76; pub. affairs mgr. Champion Internat. Corp., Rocky Mountain Region, Missoula, Mont., 1976—; sec. HEW Nat. Coal Mine Health Research Adv. Council, 1974-76, Agr.'s Continental Divide Nat. Scenic Trail Adv. Council, 1979—; mem. Am. Forest Inst. Western Communications Com., 1976—. Mem. Mont. Council on Econ. Edn., 1980—; bd. dirs. YMCA Youth Government, 1979—, Western Environ. Trade Assn., 1978—, Mont. Internat. Trade Commn., 1982—. Served to lt. A.C., USN, 1969-71. Mem. Internat. Assn. Bus. Communicators, Pub. Relations Soc. Am. Roman Catholic. Club: Rotary Internat. Office: 619 SW Higgins Missoula MT 59803

KELLY, SHARON YVONNE, insurance company executive; b. Martinez, Calif., May 18, 1937; d. John Edgar and Doyle B. (Keeling) Heyne; m. James Lowell Kelly, May 18, 1954 (dec.); children—Lowell Zane, Patrick Shaun. Assoc. in Liberal Arts Sci., North Idaho Coll., 1974; B.S. in Psychology, Western Oreg. Coll., 1979. Lic. real estate broker, Oreg. Sales agt. Bankers Life & Casualty, Spokane, Wash. and Salem, Oreg., 1974-76, Floyd McNall Real Estate, Salem, 1976-80; mktg. cons. Saif Corp., Salem, 1980—. Precinct com. woman Republican Party, Kootena. Recipient numerous awards in field. Mem. Am. Bus. Women, Nat. Assn. Female Execs., Salem Bd. Realtors, Salem C. of C. Baptist. Club: Toastmasters (Salem). Home: 1766 Icabod Ct NE Salem OR 97305 Office: 400 High St Salem OR 97305

KELLY, THOMAS EUGENE, hydrologist; b. Wichita, Kans., May 30, 1935; s. Eugene Edward and Anna Augusta (Vollmer) K.; student Creighton U., 1953-55; B.S., U. Dayton, 1959; M.S., U. Kans., 1961; postgrad. U. N.D., 1964; m. Rose Marie Malone, Aug. 23, 1958; children—Elizabeth Ann, Hugh Thomas, Sean Eugene. Geologist, Kans. Geol. Survey, Lawrence, 1959-61; reservoir engr., devel. geologist Standard Oil of Calif., LaPort, Tex., 1961-62; project, subdist. supr. U.S. Geol. Survey, Grand Forks, N.D., 1962-68, Albuquerque, 1968-75; co-founder, v.p., treas. Geohydrology Assos., Inc., Albuquerque, 1975—, pres., 1978—. Served with U.S. Army, 1955-57. Mem. Am. Assn. Petroleum Geologists (sec.-treas. energy minerals div.), Nat. Water Well Assn., N.Mex. Geol. Soc., Albuquerque Geol. Soc. (v.p. 1978, pres. 1979). Republican. Roman Catholic. Contbr. articles to profl. jours. Home: 148 Whitetail Rd NE Albuquerque NM 87122 Office: 4015 Carlisle Blvd NE Albuquerque NM 87107

KELLY, TIM, state senator; b. Sacramento, Aug. 15, 1944. Formerly legis. aide to Calif. and Nev. Legislatures; self-employed; active youth sports; mem. Alaska Ho. of Reps., 1976-78, Alaska State Senate, 1978—. Served with USMC, Alaska Air NG. Office: Alaska State Senate Juneau AK 98111*

KELLY, WILLIAM BRET, ins. exec.; b. Rocky Ford, Colo., Sept. 28, 1922; s. William Andrew and Florence Gail (Yant) K.; B.A. cum laude, U. Colo., 1947; m. Patricia Ruth Ducy, Mar. 25, 1944; children—Eric Damian, Kathryn Gail Kelly Schweitzer. With Steel City Agencies, Inc., and predecessor, Pueblo, Colo., 1946—, pres., 1961-76, chmn. bd., 1977—; dir. United Bank Pueblo, 1963—, chmn. bd., 1983—; dir. Pub. Expenditure Council, 1967—; v.p. Colo. Ins. Edn. Found., 1981, pres., 1982. Mem. Pueblo Area Council Govts., 1971-73; trustee Pueblo Bd. Water Works, 1966-80, pres., 1970-71; pres. Pueblo Single Fund Plan, 1960-61, Pueblo Heart Council, 1962, Family Service Soc. Pueblo, 1963; mem. 10th Jud. Dist. Nominating Com., 1967-71; trustee U. So. Colo. Found., 1967—, Jackson Found., 1972—, Farley Found., 1979—, Roselawn Cemetery Assn., 1982—. Served with inf. AUS, 1943-45. Decorated Silver Star, Bronze Star with oak leaf cluster, Purple Heart with oak leaf cluster; C.P.C.U. Mem. Soc. C.P.C.U.'s, Pueblo C. of C. (past pres.), Phi Beta Kappa. Democrat. Clubs: Pueblo Kiwanis (past pres.), Pueblo Country (treas. 1964-66). Home: 700 W 17th St Pueblo CO 81003 Office: 1414 W 4th St Pueblo CO 81004

KELMAN, STUART LAURANCE, rabbi, religious educator; b. Bridgeport, Conn., Feb. 13, 1942; s. Wilson and Esther (Levin) K.; m. Victoria Kolton, Dec. 20, 1964; children—Navah, Ari, Etan, Elana. B.S., Columbia U., 1964; B.H.L., Jewish Theol. Sem., 1964, M.R.E., 1967; Ph.D., U. So. Calif., 1978. Rabbi, 1969. Prin., Herzl Schs., Los Angeles, 1973-74; regional dir. United Synagogue Youth, Los Angeles, 1969-73; asst. prof. Jewish edn. Hebrew Union Coll., Los Angeles, 1978—; chmn. Coalition for Alternatives in Jewish Edn., 1982—. Recipient Weinberg Chai award Jewish Fedn. Council Los Angeles, 1978. Mem. Rabbinical Assembly, Jewish Educators Assn., Central Conf. Am. Rabbis, Assn. Jewish Studies, Bd. Rabbis, Phi Delta Kappa. Office: 3077 University Ave Los Angeles CA 90007

KELSEY, JOHN PAUL, naval officer; b. Kewanna, Ind., Nov. 14, 1942; s. Lawrence E. and Catherine L. (Cooney) K.; B.S., U.S. Naval Acad., 1964; Ocean E. in Naval Engring. and S.M. in Elec. Engring., M.I.T., 1972; m. Vera M. Vlcek, July 9, 1966; children—Lara Jo, John L., Ramona L. Commd. ensign U.S. Navy, 1960, advanced through grades to comdr., 1978; service in Europe, Western Pacific, Indian Ocean; dep. for ship material, comdr. Naval Air Force, U.S. Pacific Fleet, San Diego, 1978—. Mem. IEEE, Am. Soc. Naval Engrs., Am. Soc. Quality Control, Am. Radio Relay League, Sons of Norway, Sigma Xi. Home: 5304 Robinwood Rd Bonita CA 92002 Office: Comdr Naval Air Force US Pacific Fleet NAS North Island San Diego CA 92135

KELSEY, JUDY L., city official; b. Los Angeles, May 30, 1944; d. Roy T. and Opal (Parman) K.; B.S., U. So. Calif., 1966, M.P.A., 1969. Adminstrv. asst., European positions, 1966-67; sr. adminstrv. asst. Los Angeles Police Dept., 1967-71; asst. to city mgr. City of Newport Beach (Calif.), 1971-74; asst. city adminstr. City of Westminster (Calif.), 1974-78; city mgr. City of Eureka (Calif.), 1978-80; asst. city mgr., dir. mgmt. services City of Sunnyvale (Calif.), 1980—; instr. Calif. State Long Beach, 1977-78. Bd. dirs. Eureka chpt. Am. Cancer Soc., 1979-80; account exec. United Crusade, 1976; campaign chmn. City Newport Beach United Way, 1972-73. Mem. Internat. City Mgrs. Assn. (mem. com. on fin. 1972-73, v.p. 1976-78), League Calif. Cities (mem. com. govt. and adminstrn. 1973-75), Peninsula Profl. Women's Network, Am. Soc. Pub. Adminstrn., Western Govtl. Research Assn. (pres. 1974-75). Office: PO Box 60607 Sunnyvale CA 94088

KELSON, VIRGINIA PAUL, social services agency director; b. Salt Lake City, Jan. 26, 1929; d. Leslie J. and Viola (Love) Paul; m. A. William Kelson, Aug. 12, 1950; children—Martin Paul, Leslie. B.S., U. Utah, 1950; M.B.A., U. Utah, 1972. Founder, cons. Phoenix Inst., Salt Lake City, 1971-77, exec. dir., 1977—; founder, cons. Phoenix Ctr., 1972-77; founder, ptnr. Network mag., 1978—; organizational devel. and assertiveness cons. NEA and state affiliates, 1981—. Chmn., Salt Lake County Merit Council, 1976-82; bd. dirs. Salt Lake United Way, 1977-84. Recipient Planning to Meet the Changing Needs of Women award Am. Planning Assn., 1980; Susa Young Gates award Utah Women's Polit. Caucus, 1979. Mem. Am. Soc. Training and Devel. Author: Career Education in the Environment, 1972; Personal Money Management Trainers Manual, 1973; Non-Traditional Job Preparation for W.I.N. Registrants, 1981; Manual for Displaced Homemaker Program Operators, 1981; The Assertive Workbook, 1982, others.

KELTY, JAMES OWEN, trade show official; b. Ft. Wayne, Ind., Sept. 15, 1952; s. Edward Richard and Loretta Marie K. Student Ind. U., 1971-76. Advt. supr., trade show mgr. Hardware Wholesalers Inc., Ft. Wayne, Ind., 1970-78; account exec. Sanford Orgn., Rolling Meadows, Ill., 1978-80; ops. mgr. Three Way Corp.-Internat. Shows Div., Sunnyvale, Calif., 1980—. Mem. Nat. Assn. Expn. Mgrs., Nat. Assn. Miniature Enthusiasts, Nat. Trade Show Exhibitors Assn. (exec. com. chpt.), Exhibit Designers and Producers Assn. W. (adv. bd.). Office: 1150 Karlstad Dr Sunnyvale CA 94086

KELVER, ANN ELKINS, librarian; b. Delaware City, Del., Sept. 6, 1915; d. Dennie and Carrie Ridgeway (Cox) Elkins; B.A. with honors, Goshen (Ind.) Coll., 1964; M.A. in Secondary Edn., U. Denver, 1966, M.A. in L.S. (Colo. State Library scholar 1967-69), 1969; m. Gerald O'dell Kelver, Aug. 24, 1938. Cost accountant Miles Labs., Elkhart, Ind., 1944-62; librarian Jimtown (Ind.) High Sch., 1964-65; library dir. Arapahoe Regional Library Dist., Littleton, Colo., 1966—. Pres. Elkhart council Girl Scouts, 1959-61. Recipient Nell I. Scott award Friends of Library, Denver, 1978. Mem. ALA, Colo. Library Assn., Mountain Plains Library Assn., U. Denver Alumni AAUW. Republican. Methodist. Contbr. articles to profl. pubs. Home: 13490 Kennedy Ave Brighton CO 80601 Office: 2305 E Arapahoe Rd Littleton CO 80122

KELVIN, PATRICIA ROSEMARY, public relations director; b. London, Jan. 31, 1945; d. Richard and Pauline (Okun) K.; came to U.S., 1952, naturalized, 1965; student Radcliffe Coll., 1962-63; B.S., U. Calif.-Davis, 1966; postgrad. Pepperdine U. Sch. Bus. Adminstrn., 1974-76; m. Hamilton Todd Messinger, Dec. 29, 1973. Publicity dir. San Francisco State U. Sch. Creative Arts, 1966-67; med. editor, research assoc. Tufts New England Med. Ctr., Boston, 1969-71; pub. relations dir. Children's Hosp. of Orange County (Calif.), 1972-74, Little Co. of Mary Hosp., Torrance, Calif., 1974-75, St. John's Hosp. and Health Ctr. and St. John's Hosp. and Health Ctr. Found., Santa Monica, Calif., 1975-76; pres. Patricia R. Kelvin & Assos., Long Beach, Calif., from 1976; now dir. pub. relations Mercy Med Ctr., Roseburg, Oreg.; also v.p. Mercy Found.; public relations con., lectr. Cerritos Coll. Children's Theatre, Rio Hondo Community Coll.; speaker Hosp. Council So. Calif., Western Hosp. Assn. Conv. and Conf. on Pub. Info. in Public Sector. Mem. Mayor's Task Force, 1979, Fine Arts Affiliates; bd. dirs. Umpqua Symphony Assn. Recipient William V. Cruess award No. Calif. Inst. Food Tech., 1964; award of merit for communications excellence So. Calif. Indsl. Editors Assn., 1972, 73. Mem. Public Relations Soc. Am., Internat. Assn. Bus. Communicators, Long Beach C. of C., Oreg. Hosps. Pub. Relations Orgn. (pres.-elect). Jewish. Writer, producer Campus on the Move TV series, 1965. Home: 857 SE Watson Roseburg OR 97470 Office: 2700 Stewart Pkwy Roseburg OR 97470

KEMBLE, GORDON BENJAMIN, JR., designer, communications director; b. Wakarusa, Ind., May 26, 1939; s. Gordon B. and Ruth Ellen K.; student U. Ill., 1959; B.D., Denver Sem., 1963; B.A., Sch. of Art Inst., Chgo., 1965, M.A., 1967; M.A., U. Toronto, 1969; m. Sharon Kay Van Camp, Dec. 11, 1971; children—Gregory Donald, Daniel Gordon, Lavender Elizabeth, Fawn Victoria, Joshua David. Ordained to ministry Evang. Ch. Alliance; art dir. Christian Service Brigade, Chgo., 1963-66; art dir. dept. graphic services U. So. Calif., Los Angeles, 1978; now designer, dir. communications Avalon Communications, Hawthorne, Calif. Bd. dirs. Camfel Prodns., Fellowship Artists in Cultural Evangelism; chmn. Evangelism Missions com. dir. 1st Baptist Ch., La Crescenda, Calif. Recipient Belding award Advt. Club, Los Angeles, 1975; Maggie, Western Pubs. Assn., 1978. Mem. Montrose/Verdugo City C. of C. (past pres.), Art Dirs. Club Los Angeles. Republican. Club: U. So. Calif. Faculty-Staff. Home: 9805 Cabanas Ave Tujunga CA 91042 Office: Avalon Communications 1290 Crenshaw Blvd Hawthorne CA 90250

KEMMIS, DANIEL ORRA, state legislator, lawyer; b. Fairview, Mont., Dec. 5, 1945; s. Orra Raymond and Lilly Samantha (Shidler) K.; m. Jeanne Marie Koester, June 9, 1978; 1 son, Abraham; children by previous marriage—Deva, John. B.A. magna cum laude in Govt., Harvard U., 1968; J.D. with honors, U. Mont., 1978. Bar: Mont. 1978. Practice law, Missoula, Mont., 1978—; mem. Mont. Ho. of Reps., 1974—, minority leader, 1981-82, Speaker of the House, 1983—; lectr., writer. Nat. Merit scholar, 1964; Harvard scholar, 1964-68; recipient Young Alumnus award U. Mont., 1981. Mem. Mont. Bar Assn. Democrat. Roman Catholic. Contbr. articles to legal publs. Office: PO Box 8687 Missoula MT 59807

KEMNITZ, WILLIAM HERMAN, JR., holding co. exec.; b. Detroit, July 25, 1916; s. William Herman and Amanda Katherine (Neumann) K.; A.B. in Econs. and Polit. Sci., U. Mich., 1939; postgrad. San Francisco State U.; m. Frances Souza, Sept. 1, 1943 (dec. 1982). Enlisted U.S. Army, 1941, advanced through grades to lt. col., 1960; service in Britian, Europe, Far East; ret., 1967; cons. in reorgn. John Rich Enterprises, 1967-72; dir. Energy Absorption Systems, Inc., Sacramento, 1973—, Quixote Corp., Chgo., 1980—; cons. Patton, Inc. Life mem. Am. Ordnance Assn., Am. Def. Preparedness Assn. Republican. Club: Masons. Office: 860 S River Rd West Sacramento CA 95691

KEMP, DONNA RENEE, political science educator, public policy educator, administrator; b. Idaho Falls, Idaho, Apr. 12, 1945; d. Glen E. and Maybel A. (Smith) K.; m. Geoffrey K. Guss, Apr. 11, 1970 (div.); 1 dau., April R. Kemp. Student Chapman Coll., 1963-65; B.A. cum laude in Polit. Sci., Coll. Idaho, 1967, M.Edn., 1978; M.A., U. Oreg., 1970; M.P.A., U. Idaho, 1977, Ph.D., 1978. Lic. social worker, Idaho, 1982. Dir. vol. services, coordinator foster grandparents program Idaho State Sch. and Hosp., Dept. Health and Welfare, Nampa, 1971-75; planner Exec. Office of Gov. Div. Budget and Policy Planning, Boise, Idaho, 1975; program mgr. Idaho Office Energy, Boise, 1978-80; prin. planner Idaho Dept. Health and Welfare, Boise, 1980; assoc. prof. polit. sci., coordinator govt. and pub. service program Winthrop Coll., Rock Hill, S.C., 1980-81; assoc. prof. pub. policy and adminstrn., coordinator healthcare mgmt. program Calif. State Coll., Bakersfield, 1981—; adj. prof. Coll. Idaho, Caldwell, 1970-72, Boise State U., 1972-80; cons. in field, 1976—; marriage and family counselor Haven House, Bakersfield, 1982—. Bd. dirs. Kern County chpt. Am. Lung Assoc., 1982—; mem. adv. bd. Retired Sr. Vol. Program, 1982—. Whittenberger fellow U. Idaho, 1977, recipient Affirmative Action Faculty Devel. program award Calif. State U. System, 1983; Stillinger scholarship U. Idaho, 1976. Mem. Am. Soc. Pub. Adminstrn., Am. Polit. Sci. Assn., Acad. Mgmt., Am. Pub. Health Assn., Calif. Assn. Marriage, Family Therapists, Am. Personnel and Guidance Assn., Am. Mental Health Counselors Assn., NOW, ACLU, LWV, Sierra Club. Contbr. articles to profl. jours. Office: Dept Pub Policy and Adminstrn Sch Bus and Pub Adminstrn Calif State Coll Bakersfield CA 93309

KEMP, GARY FENTON, school administrator, educator; b. Hollywood, Calif., Jan. 24, 1937; s. James Fenton and Gertrude Pauline (Peacock) K.; m. Nancy Marie Jane Elliott, children—Elliott, David Ray, Cynthia Marie, Thomas W. B.A., Occidental Coll., 1959; M.A., Calif. State U.-Los Angeles, 1969; Ed.D., Brigham Young U., 1977. Tchr. phys. edn., physiology, various Calif. schs., 1959-69; vice prin., Corcoran, Calif., 1970-72, prin., 1972-78; supt. schs., Woodrow, Colo., 1978-81; prin. Willows (Calif.) Unified Sch. Dist., 1981-82, supt., 1982—. Mem. Assn. Calif. Sch. Adminstrs., Assn. Am. Sch. Adminstrs., Assn. Supervision and Curriculum Devel., Pacific Soaring Council, Chico (Calif.) Soaring Club. Republican. Mormon. Club: Rotary (Willows). Columnist Westwind; contbr. articles to profl. jours. Home: PO Box 405 Willows CA 95988 Office: Willows Unified Sch Dist 823 W Laurel St Willows CA 95988

KEMP, GREGORY ALEXANDER, accountant; real estate developer; b. Ogden, Utah, July 31, 1947; s. Dale Desmond and Mary Elaine (Alexander) K.; m. Beverly Ruth Racker, Sept. 9, 1969; children—Steven, Brian, Anna, Daniel, Camille, Allison. B.S., Weber State Coll., 1971. C.P.A., Utah. Internal auditor IRS, Ogden, Utah, 1968-71; sr. acct. Fox & Co., Salt Lake City, 1971-73, mgmt. cons., 1973-75; sr. ptnr. Carter, Kemp & Adams, St. George, Utah, 1975—; mayor City of Bloomington (Utah), 1978-80. Mem. Am. Inst. C.P.A.s, Utah Assn. C.P.A.s, St. George C. of C. (v.p. 1976-79, named Outstanding Young Businessman 1979). Republican. Mormon. Clubs: Bloomington Country, Exchange (pres. 1978-79). Developer of First S. Plaza, St. George. Home: 1151 Baneberry St Saint George UT 84770 Office: Carter Kemp & Adams 50 E 100 S St Suite 301 Saint George UT 84770

KEMP, ROGER LARK, city manager, author; b. St. Paul, Minn., Aug. 1, 1946; s. Charles Woodrow and Eva Audrey (Blair) K.; m. Jill Baumbach, Jan. 14, 1951; 1 son, Jonathan David; B.S., San Diego State U., 1972, M.P.A., 1972; Ph.D., Golden Gate U., 1979; Dipl., Harvard U. Program for Sr. Execs. in Local Govt., 1982. Asst. to city mgr., Oakland, Calif., 1977-78; city mgr., Seaside, Calif., 1978-83, Placentia, Calif., 1983—; grad. instr. Golden Gate U., 1978-83; lectr.; author: Coping With Proposition 13, 1980; Managing With Lee, 1980. Served with USCGR, 1966-70. Mem. Am. Soc. Pub. Adminstrn. (past pres. Monterey Bay chpt.), Internat. City Mgrs. Assn., Golden Gate U. Alumni Assn., Harvard U. Alumni Assn. Contbr. numerous articles to profl. jours. Home: 1345 Mescal St Seaside CA 93955 Office: 401 E Chapman Ave Placentia CA 92670

KEMP, WAYNE RUSSELL, educator, geologist; b. Chgo., May 2, 1948; s. Russell Milton and Doris Eileen (Bender) K.; B.S., U. Mo. at Rolla, 1970; M.S., U. Nev. at Reno, 1972, Ph.D., 1982. Uranium exploration Union Carbide Exploration Corp., Corpus Christi, Tex., summers 1968-70; lab. technician Mo. Geol. Survey, Rolla, 1969-70; teaching asst., lectr. geology U. Nev., 1972-77, Calif. State U., Fresno, 1977-78; cons. geologist, Reno, 1971-79; exploration geologist Freeport Exploration Co., Reno, 1979-81, Denver, 1982—. NDEA Title IV fellow, 1970-73; V.H. McNutt scholar, 1968-70; recipient Penrose research grant Geol. Soc. Am., 1972-73. Mem. Geol. Soc. Am., Soc. Econ. Geologists (asso.), Am. Assn. Petroleum Geologists, Sigma Xi, Phi Kappa Phi, Sigma Gamma Epsilon. Home: 26881 Hilltop Rd Evergreen CO 80439 also PO Box 3055 Evergreen CO 80439

KEMPER, DORLA DEAN (EATON), real estate broker; b. Calhoun, Mo., Sept. 10, 1929; d. Paul McVey and Jesse Lee (McCombs) Eaton; student William Woods Coll., 1947-48, B.S. in Edn., Central Mo. State U., 1952; m. Charles K. Kemper, Mar. 1, 1951; children—Kevin Keil, Kara Lee. Tchr. pub. schs., Twin Falls, Idaho, 1950-51, Mission, Kans., 1952-53, Burbank, Calif., 1953-57; real estate saleswoman Minn., 1967-68, Calif., 1971-73; Deanie Kemper, Realtor (name changed to Deanie Kemper, Inc. Real Estate Brokerage 1976), Loomis, Calif., 1974-76, pres., 1976—, also dir. Organizing pres. Battle Creek Park Elementary Sch. PTA, St. Paul, 1966-67; mem. Placer County (Calif.) Bicentennial Commn., 1976; mem. adv. com. Sierra Coll., 1981—. Named to Million Dollar Club (lifetime) Sacramento and Placer County bds. realtors, 1978; designated Grad. Realtors Inst., Cert. Residential Specialist. Mem. Nat., Calif. assns. realtors, Sacramento, Placer County (mem. profl. standards com.) bds. realtors. Republican. Mem. Christian Ch. Clubs: DAR (chpt. regent 1971-73, organizing chpt. regent 1977-78, dist. dir. 1978-80, state registrar Calif. 1980-82, state vice regent 1982—, nat. resolutions com. 1981—), Hidden Valley Women's (pres. Loomis club 1970-71), Auburn Travel Study (pres.). Home: 8165 Morningside Dr Loomis CA 95650

KEMPER, JAMES STUART, consulting safety engineer; b. Marion, Ky., Nov. 7, 1918; s. Robert Henry and Mona Belle (Hunt) K.; student Merritt Coll., 1966-68, Ohlone Coll., 1976-77; m. Maebelle Clark, Oct. 24, 1943; children—Donna, Anita. Chief reactor plant operator engr. Westinghouse Electric Co., Idaho Falls, 1957-62; with Gen. Electric Co., San Jose, Calif., 1962-82, safety engr. nuclear energy bus. group, 1981-82; instr. Chabot Coll. Served in U.S. Navy, 1937-57. Registered profl. safety engr., Calif. Mem. No. Calif. Indsl. Safety Soc. (pres. 1971), Twin Valley Fire Chiefs Assn. (pres. 1972), Am. Soc. Safety Engrs. (profl. mem.), Nat. Fire Protection Assn., Vets. of Safety. Clubs: Masons, Shriners, Mensa, Order Ky. Cols. Home: 1343 Vernal Ave Fremont CA 94539

KEMPER, JOHN DUSTIN, educator, former college dean; b. Portland, Oreg., May 29, 1924; s. Clay Wallace and Leona Bell (Landis) K.; B.S., UCLA, 1949, M.S., 1959; Ph.D., U. Colo., 1969; m. Barbara Jeanne Lane, June 28, 1947; 1 dau., Kathleen Lynne. Chief mech. engr. Telecomputing Corp., North Hollywood, Cal., 1949-55, H.A. Wagner Co., Van Nuys, Calif., 1955-56; v.p. engring. Marchant div. SCM Corp., Oakland, Calif., 1956-62; faculty U. Calif., Davis, 1962—, prof. engring., 1967—, dean Coll. Engring., 1969-83. Served with USAF, 1944-46. Fellow ASME (chmn. San Francisco sect. 1962-63), AAAS; mem. Am. Soc. Engring. Edn., Nat. Soc. Profl. Engrs. Author: Engineers and their Profession, 3d edit., 1981. Office: College of Engineering University of California Davis CA 95616

KEMPF, KARLTON, optical instrument mfg. co. exec.; b. Ill., Mar. 1949; s. Paul S. and Dorothea R. Kempf; B.S. in Biology, San Diego State U., 1972, M.S. in Radiol. Physics, 1975. Gen. mgr. Metron Marker Co., Solana Beach, Calif., 1972-73; v.p. ops. Metron Optics, Inc., Solana Beach, 1977-79, exec. v.p., 1979—; pres. Metron Concepts, Inc., Solana Beach, 1979—, also dir.; lectr. physics San Diego State U. Mem. Health Phycis Soc., Sigma Phi Sigma. Office: 813 Academy Dr PO Box 690 Solana Beach CA 92075

KENCHT, GEORGE NOEL, biology educator, plant physiologist, researcher; b. Taylor, Pa., Dec. 28, 1939; s. George and Mildred Dorothy (Graff) K.; m. Maria Elena Ortiz, Dec. 22, 1976. B.S., Rutgers U., 1962, M.S., 1969; Ph.D., U. Ariz., 1975. Lab. technician Rutgers U., 1962-69; research assoc. Environ. Research lab. U. Ariz., Tucson, 1969-73; lectr. dept. biol. scis. Calif. Poly. State U., San Luis Obispo, 1973-74, asst. prof., 1974-78, assoc. prof., 1978—. Mem. AAAS, Am. Soc. Agronomy, Council for Agr. Sci. and Tech. Crop Sci. Soc. Am., San Luis Obispo County Zool. Soc. Contbr. articles to profl. jours. Office: Biol Sci Dept Calif Poly State U San Luis Obispo CA 93407

KENDALL, KATHERINE MARY, educational consultant; b. Los Angeles, Jan. 1, 1946; d. Cecil Alvernin and Jane Curtis (Fox) K.; m. Robert Oaks, Dec. 16, 1967 (div.). B.A. in Zoology, U. Calif.-Riverside, 1967; M.P.H. in Tropical and Infectious Medicine, UCLA, 1971; Ph.D. in Edn., Claremont Grad. Sch., 1978. Cert. tchr., adminstr., counselor, Calif. Tchr., counselor Venice High Sch., Los Angeles, 1968-75; adminstrv. dean Univ. High Sch., Los Angeles, 1975-78; asst. prin. Mark Twain Jr. High Sch., Los Angeles, 1978-79; asst. prin. Beverly Hills (Calif.) High Sch., 1979-82; owner, dir. Kendall & Assocs., Los Angeles, 1981—. Mem. Assn. Calif. Sch. Adminstrs., Women in Ednl. Leadership, Western Assn. of Coll. Admissions Counselors, Nat. Assn. of Female Execs. Republican. Episcopalian. Office: 10350 Santa Monica Blvd Suite 100 Los Angeles CA 90025

KENDALL, KEITH LEON, electrical engineer; b. Weiser, Idaho, Aug. 2, 1951; s. Karl E. Kendall and Nola (Batty) K.; m. Carol Rae Hennum, Nov. 14, 1974. B.S.E.E., Brigham Young U., Provo, Utah, 1977. Computer operator Bringham Young U. Computer Services, 1973-77; reliability engr. Sperry Univac, 1977-79, test engr., 1979-80; product engr. Nat. Semiconductor, West Jordan, Utah, 1980-82; design engr. Am. Microsystems, Pocatello, Idaho, 1982—. Mem. IEEE Clubs: Personel Program Center, Toastmasters Internat. Home: 435 S 19th Ave Pocatello ID 83201 Office: 2300 Buckskin Rd Pocatello ID 83201

KENDALL, PATRICIA ANN, food science and nutrition extension specialist, columnist; b. Superior, Nebr., Mar. 3, 1947; d. Myron K. and Evonne G. (Switzer) Intermill; m. Lawrence M. Kendall, June 12, 1972; children—Kristin, Matthew. B.S. magna cum laude, Kans. State U., 1969; M.S., 1973. Registered dietitian. Foods research tech. Kans. State U.-Manhattan, 1973-74; research assoc. food sci., nutrition dept. Colo. State U.-Fort Collins, 1974-75, extension specialist, assoc. prof., 1976—. Recipient F.A. Anderson award Colo. State U., 1980; Gen. Food fellow, 1972. Mem. Am. Dietetic Assn., Soc. Nutrition Edn., Am. Home Econs. Assn., Sigma Xi (Univ. Research Excellence award), Phi Kappa Phi, Omicron Nu, Alpha Delta Kappa, Gamma Delta. Contbr. articles to profl. jours.; author of Colo. State U. bulls.

KENDALL, ROGER LANE, newspaper editor; b. Salem, Ind., July 25, 1944; s. Ralph Leonard and Maycel Maude (Durham) K.; m. Susan Elaine Lowe, May 14, 1967; children—Jeffrey Edward, Grace Elizabeth. Sports editor Salem (Ind.) Democrat, 1960-62; reporter Sparks Newspapers, Hayward and Livermore, Calif., 1969-71, bur. chief and mng. editor, 1971-73; copy editor Palo Alto (Calif.) Times, 1973-77; asst. met. editor San Jose (Calif.) Mercury-News, 1977-80; mng. editor The Argus, Fremont, Calif., 1980—. Mem. Sigma Delta Chi. Office: The Argus 37427 Centralmont Place Fremont CA 94537

KENDEL, DORLA DEAN (MRS. ROBERT LEWIS KENDEL), mfrs. rep. co. exec.; b. Los Angeles, Apr. 16, 1930; d. Thomas Weston and Lois May (Oliver) Hall; grad. high sch.; m. Robert Lewis Kendel, Aug. 13, 1949; children—Robert L., Michael L., Richard L. Tchr. oil painting, LaCrescenta, Calif., 1960-62; with Air Conditioning Specialties Co., Inc., mfrs. rep., LaCrescenta, 1962-79, corp. sec.-treas., 1970-79; now involved in constrn. industry. Active Scouting, sch. and sport activities, 1956-70. Mem. Am. Soc. Heating Refrigerating and Air Conditioning Engrs. Address: 46-058 Verba Santa Palm Desert CA 92260

KENDRICK, PAUL JOSEPH, air force officer; b. Charleroi, Pa., Dec. 26, 1947; s. Thomas Bernard Flgar and Agnes Victoria (Turtzer) K.; B.S. in Aero. Engring., U. Cin., 1972; M.S. in Aero. Engring., U. Dayton, 1973; m. Libby Ann Roos, June 10, 1972; children—Paul Thomas, Laura Marsh. Commd. 2d lt. U.S. Air Force, 1974, advanced through grades to capt., 1978; instr. navigator 644 Bomb Squadron, K.I. Sawyer AFB, Mich., 1975-78; student USAF Test Pilot Sch., Edwards AFB, Calif., 1979; test navigator B-52 Offensive Avionics System Test Force, Wichita, Kans., 1980-81, B.-1B Combined Test Force, Edwards AFB, 1981—. Mem. AIAA, Air Force Assn., Aircraft Owners and Pilots Assn. Home: 6774 Rickenbacker Edwards CA 93523 Office: 6510 Test W/TEVI Edwards AFB CA 93523

KENDRICKS, JAMES WILLIAMS, financial services company executive; b. Van Lear, Ky., Feb. 28, 1938; s. Roy Johnson and Clara Eugena (Newland) K.; m. Christine Johnson, Dec. 26, 1962 (div. Mar. 1965); 1 dau., Angel R., m. 2d, Earsey Marie Pryor, Apr. 6, 1968, children—Jacquelyn Rene, Jeanine Marie. Student, Hillsdale Coll., 1961-63, Pepperdine Coll., 1965; B.A., Calif. State U.-Los Angeles, 1967; J.D., UCLA, 1971. Systems analyst Arco, 1967-71; legal fellow Regionald Heber-Smith, 1971-73; hearing officer Los Angeles Police Commn., 1972-73; dep. dir. Los Angeles Urban Coalition, 1973-75; founder, exec. dir. Afro-Am. Cultural Edn. Center, 1974-80; v.p. Social Engring. Tech., Los Angeles, 1978-81; organizer, cons. GHS Enterprises, Los Angeles, 1981—; pres. James W. Kendricks & Assocs., Los Angeles, 1981—. Campaign mgr. David L. Pierson to Calif. Legislature, 1972; spl. cons. Govt. Nigeria, 1978; cons. bus. and govt. activities Govt. Indonesia. Served with USAF, 1957-61. Mem. NAACP, Fellowship Falcons, Tau Kappa Epsilon. Republican. Office: 4966 N Grand Ave Coving CA 91724

KENIGSBERG, EUGENE MICHAEL, allergist; b. N.Y.C., July 16, 1946; s. Benjamin and Mary K.; B.S., CCNY, 1967; M.D., SUNY, Syracuse, 1971. Intern and resident in pediatrics Albert Einstein Coll. Medicine, 1971-74; commd. lt. comdr. USPHS, 1974; resigned, 1976; fellow in allergy and clin. immunology U. Colo., Nat. Jewish Hosp., Denver, 1976-78; allergist Kaiser-Permanente Med. Center, Panorama City, Calif., 1978—; assoc. clin. prof. pediatrics U. So. Calif.-Los Angeles County Med. Center, 1979—. Diplomate Am. Bd. Pediatrics, Am. Bd. Allergy and Immunology. Fellow Am. Acad. Pediatric, Am. Acad. Allergy, Am. Coll. Allergists; mem. Los Angeles Soc. Allergy and Clin. Immunology, Alpha Omega Alpha. Office: 13652 Cantara Panorama City CA 91402

KENISTON, STANLEY FRED, architect; b. San Diego, Aug. 24, 1948; s. Fred Wilson and Mabel Elvira (Humphreys) K. B.Arch., U. Calif., Berkeley, 1971. Designer, draftsman Delawie, Macy & Henderson, Architects, 1972-75; jr. analyst Energy Mgmt. Consultants, Inc., 1975-76; designer, energy analyst Deems/Lewis & Partners, Architects, 1976-77; sr. analyst Energy Mgmt. Consultants, Inc., 1977-78, v.p., 1979—; asso. Michael Weinstein & Assos., energy planning, 1979-80; owner Stanley Keniston, Architect, 1977-80; partner Keniston & Mosher, Architects, AIA, San Diego, 1980—; works include Jordan solar residence (AIA and Pacific Coast Builders Conf. Gold Nugget awards), Adams solar residence (Pacific Coast Builders Conf. award of merit), Froehlich solar residence (spl. award AIA), passive solar test bldg. research project for Calif. Energy Com. and Dept. Energy; lectr. U. So. Calif., UCLA, So. Calif. Inst. Architecture; cons. San Diego Assn. Govts.; mem. San Diego Citizen's Solar Energy Com. Mem. AIA, Internat. Solar Energy Soc., So. Calif. Solar Energy Assn. (dir.). Democrat. architect; b. San Diego, Aug. 24, 1948; s. Fred Wilson and Mabel Elvira (Humphreys) K. B.Arch., U. Calif., Berkeley, 1971. Designer, draftsman Delawie, Macy & Henderson, Architects, 1972-75; jr. analyst Energy Mgmt. Consultants, Inc., 1975-76; designer, energy analyst Deems/Lewis & Partners, Architects, 1976-77; sr. analyst Energy Mgmt. Consultants, Inc., 1977-78, v.p., 1979—; asso. Michael Weinstein & Assos., energy planning, 1979-80; owner Stanley Keniston, Architect, 1977-80; partner Keniston & Mosher, Architects, AIA, San Diego, 1980—; works include Jordan solar residence (AIA and Pacific Coast Builders Conf. Gold Nugget awards), Adams solar residence (Pacific Coast Builders Conf. award of merit), Froehlich solar residence (spl. award AIA), passive solar test bldg. research project for Calif. Energy Com. and Dept. Energy; lectr. U. So. Calif., UCLA, So. Calif. Inst. Architecture; cons. San Diego Assn. Govts.; mem. San Diego Citizen's Solar Energy Com. Mem. AIA, Internat. Solar Energy Soc., So. Calif. Solar Energy Assn. (dir.). Democrat. Office: 666 State St San Diego CA 92101

KENN, CHARLES WILLIAM, travel lectr. and cons.; b. Honolulu, Jan. 2, 1907; s. Solomon Kahaokamoku and Mine Halualani (Haines) K. B.A., U. Hawaii, 1931; student Whittier Coll., 1933-35. Editor, Hawaii's Youth monthly, 35; dir. Hawaiian activities City and County of Honolulu, 1934-35; parole officer Terr. Prison, Terr. of Hawaii, 1935-45, juvenile parole officer, 1945-47; lectr., cons. on travel, Hawaii, 1932—; vis. scientist anthropology and folklore UCLA, 1948-49; cons. Hawaiian studies Kamehameha Sch., Honolulu, 1978-79; hon. cons. and lectr. on Hawaiiana, Ch. Coll., 1963-67; hon. lectr. Brigham Young U., 1980; cons. Hawaiiana; translator Hawaiian. Bd. dirs. YMCA, Honolulu, 1933-47; treas. Republican Precinct Club, Honolulu, 1929-67, sec., 1947, v.p., 1946, pres., 1947-67. Recipient prize for excellence in speaking U. Hawaii Forum, 1930, Alu Like award, 1978; named 1st Living Treasure of Hawaii, 1976; Found. History and Research grantee, 1976. Mem. Am. Anthrop. Assn., Hawaiian Anthrop. Soc. (charter; treas. 1930-47), Am. Probation Assn., AAAS, Hawaiian Acad. Sci., Inter-Am. Soc. Anthropology and Geography, Conf. Calif. Hist. Socs., Huna Research Assn. (hon. life), Honolulu Orchid Club, Am. Orchid Soc. Club: Hawaiian Civic. Author: Moolelo of Ancient Hawaii, 1976; Fire Walking from The Inside, 1949. Home: PO Box 791 Kaneohe HI 96744

KENNEDY, BRUCE R., airline executive; b. Denver, Oct. 11, 1938; s. Roger W. and Jean (Converse) K.; B.B.A., U. Alaska, 1963; m. Karleen Isaacson, Nov. 21, 1965; children—Kevin, Karin. Corp. sec. Alaska Continental Devel. Corp., Fairbanks, 1959-64, v.p., 1964-67, pres., 1967-72, chmn., 1972; dir. Alaska Airlines, Inc., Seattle, 1972, sr. v.p. properties, 1973-78, pres. 1978—, chief operating officer, from 1978, chmn., 1979—, also chief exec. officer; dir. Pelican Cold Storage, Inc. Served to 1st lt. U.S. Army, 1965-67. Mem. Assn. Local Transport Airlines (chmn.). Republican. Presbyterian. Office: Alaska Airlines Inc PO Box 68900 Seattle WA 98168

KENNEDY, CHARLES F., communications executive; b. Springfield, Mass., July 12, 1931; s. Stephen J. and Grace M. (Mahoney) K.; m. Jean M. Molin, Apr. 19, 1952; children John, Patrick, David. Student Northeast U., 1948-52. With Outlet Broadcasting, 1970—, gen. sales mgr. Sta. WJAR-TV, Providence, 1970-75, v.p., gen. mgr. sta. WNYS-TV, Syracuse, N.Y, 1975-78, v.p. corp. planning, Providence, 1978, sr. v.p. corp. TV group, 1979-80, pres., gen. mgr. sta. KOVR-TV, Sacramento, 1980—. Bd. dirs. ARC, Salvation Army, United Way. Mem. Nat. Assn. TV Programmers and Execs., Calif. Broadcasters Assn. (dir.), Nat. Assn. Broadcasters, Sacramento C. of C. Clubs: R.I. Yacht, Turks Head (Providence); Sutter (Sacramento). Office: 1216 Arden Way Sacramento CA 95815

KENNEDY, DAVID KITTLE, educational administrator, clergyman; b. Alamusa, Colo., Oct. 29, 1932; s. Harry Sherbourne and Katharine Jane (Kittle) K.; m. Anna Marie Hemberger, Nov. 1, 1956; children—Chris W., Paul K., Karl S., Eric D. B.A., Trinity Coll., 1954; M.Div., Ch. Div. Sch. of the Pacific, 1963. Ordained priest Episcopalian Ch., 1964; vicar St. Barnabas' Ch., Ewa Beach, Hawaii, 1968-73; rector St. Peter's Ch., Honolulu, Ch. of the Ascension, Kwajalein Atoll, Marshall Islands, 1968-73, St. Timothy's Ch., Aiea, Hawaii, 1973-81; headmaster St. Andrew's Priory Sch., Honolulu, 1981—. Mem. Gov.'s Commn. Jud. Qualifications, 1970-76, Hawaii State Health Coordinating Council, 1977-82, State Health Cert. of Need Com., 1978—. Served with USAF, 1954-60, USAFR, 1969—. Recipient Diocesan Disting. Service Cross, 1969. Mem. Nat. Assn. Ind. Schs., Nat. Assn. Secondary Sch. Prins., Nat. Assn. Prins. Schs. for Girls. Democrat. Clubs: Plaza, Rotary (Honolulu). Home: 98-1138 Malualua St Aiea HI 96701 Office: Saint Andrews Priory Sch 224 Queen Emma Square Honolulu HI 96813

KENNEDY, DEBRA JOYCE, hospital marketing and community relations official; b. Covina, Calif., July 9, 1955; d. John Nathan and Drea Hannah (Lancaster) Ward; m. John William Kennedy, Sept. 3, 1977 (div.). B.S. in Communications, Calif. State Poly. U., 1977. Pub. relations coordinator Whittier (Calif.) Hosp., 1978-79, pub. relations mgr., 1980; pub. relations dir. San Clemente (Calif.) Hosp., 1979-80; dir. pub. relations Garfield Med. Ctr., Monterey Park, Calif., 1980-82; dir. mktg. and community relations Charter Oak Hosp., Covina, 1983—. Mem. Am. Soc. Hosp. Pub. Relations, So. Calif. Soc. Hosp. Pub. Relations, Alhambra C. of C. Republican. Methodist. Club: Soroptimists. Contbr. articles to profl. jours.

KENNEDY, DENNIS LEO, mgmt. cons., educator; b. Youngstown, Ohio, Nov. 26, 1943; s. John P. and Mary I. (Hall) K.; B.G.S., Roosevelt U., 1972; M.M., Northwestern U., 1974; Ph.D., Ill. Inst. Tech., 1979; m. Dianna Marie Ledesma, June 20, 1970. Customer engr. IBM, Chgo., 1963-66; mgr. EDP, Northwestern U., 1966-68; systems analyst/dir. edn. Honeywell Inc., Chgo., 1968-69; sr. system analyst Internat. Timesharing Corp., Chgo., 1969-70; asst. prof. indsl. and organizational psychology North Central Coll., 1976-79; pres. Kennedy, Heller & Drehmer Inc., Chgo., 1979-81; chmn. div. bus. and mgmt. Northeastern Ill. U., Chgo., 1979-81; asso. prof. human resource mgmt. Calif. State U., Sacramento, 1981—. Vol., Thresholds Half-Way House. Served with USAF, 1961-63. Mem. Phi Sigma Phi. Address: 4432 Sierra Springs Dr Pollock Pines CA 95726

KENNEDY, DONALD, university president, educator; b. N.Y.C., Aug. 18, 1931; s. William Dorsey and Barbara (Bean) K.; m. Jeanne Dewey, June 11, 1953; children—Laura Page, Julia Hale. A.B., Harvard U., 1952, A.M., 1954, Ph.D., 1956. Mem. faculty Syracuse U., 1956-60, Stanford (Calif.) U., 1960-77, prof. biol. scis., 1965-77, dept. chmn., 1965-72, v.p., provost, 1979-80, pres., 1980—; commr. FDA, 1977-79; sr. cons. Office of Sci. and Tech. Policy, Exec. Office of Pres., 1976. Mem. bd. overseers Harvard U., 1970-76. Fellow Am. Acad. Arts and Scis., AAAS; mem. Nat. Acad. Scis., Am. Physiol. Soc., Soc. Gen. Physiologists, Am. Soc. Zoologists, Soc. Explt. Biology (U.K.). Author: (with W.H. Telfur) The Biology of Organisms, 1965; also articles. Editor: The Living Cell, 1966; From Cell to Organism, 1967; editorial bd. Jour. Exptl. Zoology, 1965-71, Jour. Comparative Physiology, 1965-76, Jour. Neurophysiology, 1969-75, Science, 1973-77. Office: Office of the President Stanford Univ Stanford CA 94305

KENNEDY, GAY LOUISE, social services administrator; b. Hollister, Calif., May 23, 1931; d. Howard Ross and Harriet Elizabeth (Douglass) K.; m. Andrew Milos Gall, Aug. 30, 1952 (div.); children—Steven H., Kenneth J. (dec.). B.S. in Acctg., Calif. State U.-Fresno, 1981. Ptnr. Sergel Bus. Service, 1956-58; owner, mgr. Cardland, 1965-75, Anytime Bookkeeping, 1965-75; dir. Sr. Aides, Fresno, 1979—. Mem. Human Rights Commn.; mem. Human Services Coalition; mem. citizens adv. com. City of Fresno; v.p. Displaced Homemakers Network; mem. state steering com. Nat. Women's Polit. Caucus. Mem. Western Gerontol. Soc., Nat. Council Sr. Citizens, Older Women's League. Democrat. Roman Catholic. Office: 2048 Kern St Fresno CA 93721

KENNEDY, GERALDINE ANN, urban planner; b. McKeesport, Pa., Sept. 1, 1940; d. Joseph and Mary Markos; B.A., Pa. State U., 1962; M.A., UCLA, 1980; m. James W. Kennedy, 1965; 3 children. Tchr., U.S. Peace Corps, Liberia, 1962-64; archtl. designer Geraldine Kennedy Design, Santa Monica, Calif., 1975-78; analyst Urban Projects Inc., Los

Angeles, 1979; researcher Urban Innovations Group, Los Angeles, 1980; asso. Econs. Research Assos., Los Angeles, 1980-82; cons. Environ. Mgmt. Inst., U. So. Calif., 1977-80; strategic planner Investors Mortgage Service Co., 1982—. Mem. Santa Monica Planning Commn., 1977-81; founder/dir. Community Planning Coalition, Santa Monica, 1976—; bd. dirs., v.p. Santa Monica YWCA, 1971-73; bd. dirs. Santa Monica LWV, 1977-79, Los Angeles Community Design Center, 1982—. Mem. Am. Inst. Cert. Planners, Am. Planning Assn. Author: MGM, A Handbook for Parents of Gifted Children, 1976; editor: Liberia One, 1962-1982, A Peace Corps 20th Anniversary Album, 1982; editorial bd. West Plan, 1983. Home: Santa Monica CA 90405 Office: 1405 N San Fernando Blvd Burbank CA 91504

KENNEDY, JEANNE DEWEY, hospital administrator; b. Worcester, Mass., Jan. 4, 1933; d. Charles Nichols and Barbara Plum (Bruske) Dewey; m. Donald Kennedy, June 11, 1953; children—Laura Page, Julia Hale. B.A., Smith Coll., 1954. Fin. mgr. William Kaufmann Inc., Los Altos, Calif., 1972-74; indexer Stanford U. Press, 1961-76; assoc. dir. med. devel., assoc. gen. sec. Stanford U., 1976-77; dir. resources devel., spl. asst. to pres. Inst. Medicine Nat. Acad. Scis., Washington, 1977-79; dir. community relations Stanford U. Hosp., 1979—. Mem. com. art Stanford U., 1961—, treas., 1966-68, chmn., 1968-70, advisor, 1979—; bd. dirs. Children's Health Council, 1980—. Mem. Soc. Patient Reps., Am. Hosp. Assn., Calif. Soc. Patient Reps. Club: Stanford Faculty. Office: Stanford Univ Hosp P3018 Stanford CA 94305

KENNEDY, LINDA MARY, advertising representative; b. Detroit, Apr. 15, 1952; d. Daniel Peter Kennedy and Gwendolyn Barbara Mann; A.A., Eastern Mich. U., 1973. Receptionist/sec. ABD Federal Credit Union, Warren, Mich., 1970-72; sec. Eastern Mich. U., 1973-74; stenographer, Colo. Interstate Gas Co., Colorado Springs, 1973-74; advertising rep., trade coordinator Sperry Flight Systems, Phoenix., 1974; advt. cons. Office: 21111 N 19th Ave T-14 Phoenix AZ 85027

KENNEDY, PAMELA CHARLENE, public relations executive; b. Chgo., Feb. 15, 1947; d. Kenneth J. and Rubye M. (Green) K.; student Ariz. State U., 1965-66, Phoenix Coll., 1967-73, U. Phoenix, 1983—; diploma LaSalle Extension U., 1978; m. John William Kennedy, June 1, 1974; 1 dau., Christina Larisa. Dir. public relations Maryvale and Glendale Samaritan Hosps., 1966-73; dir. communication services Blood Systems, Inc., Scottsdale, Ariz., 1973-77; propr., public relations exec. The Communicators, Phoenix, 1977-81; v.p., sec. Vantage Devel. and Mgmt. Corp., 1976-82; exec. v.p., chief exec. officer Stonebridge Corp., 1982-83; corp. dir. pub. affairs, chief exec. officer of devel. Sun Health Corp., 1983—. Chmn. State Pub. Info. Com., 1974-80; bd. dirs. Am. Cancer Soc., Ariz. div., 1974—, v.p., 1979-81, pres., 1982-83, chmn. bd., 1983-84; coordinator pub. relations sect. First Joint Conf. of Am. Nat. Red Cross Blood Program and Council Community Blood Center, 1977. Recipient Gold Quill award of Excellence, 1977. Mem. Internat. Assn. Bus. Communicators (award 1974, 77, accredited 1976), dir. 1971-76, pres. Phoenix chpt. 1975), Public Relations Soc. Am., Am. Soc. for Hosp. Public Relations (v.p. Ariz. chpt. 1972, pres. 1973, treas. 1983-84). Club: Soroptimists Internat. (del. to nat. 1976-77). Editor: Blood Program Manager's Reference Guide, 1977. Home: 616 E Manzanita Dr Phoenix AZ 85020 Office: 1 N 103d Dr Sun City AZ 85351

KENNEDY, RAYMOND MCCORMICK, interior designer; b. Glendale, Calif., Sept. 19, 1930; s. Raymond McCormick and June (Sparks) K.; B.A. in Architecture, U. Calif.-Berkeley, 1956. Draftsman, Bechtel Corp., San Francisco, 1956-58; draftsman/designer Maher & Martens, Architects, San Francisco, 1956; free lance designer, San Francisco, 1966-67; designer Bernard J. Block, Architect, San Francisco, 1967-69; v.p. Rodgers Assocs., San Francisco, 1969-77; pres. RMK Design, Inc., San Francisco, 1977-83; pres. Kennedy-Bowen Assocs., Inc., San Francisco, 1983—; mem. faculty Acad. of Art Coll., San Francisco, 1982—. Bd. dirs. San Francisco Easter Seals Soc., 1974-79. Served with U.S. Army, 1952-54. Mem. Golden Gate U. Assocs., Am. Soc. Interior Designers (dir., v.p. N. Calif. chpt. 1983), Nat. Trust for Hist. Preservation, Assocs. for San Francisco's Archtl. Heritage. Presbyterian. Club: Commonwealth. Office: 930 Lombard St San Francisco CA 94133

KENNEDY, REGINALD, stockbroker, b. Eng., Oct. 29, 1919; s. Henry and Hanna (Hall) K.; came to U.S., 1950; m. Mary, Nov. 10, 1940. Mng. ptnr. Davis Skaggs and Co., 16 years; now vice-chmn. Morgan, Olmstead, Kennedy and Gardner, Inc., San Francisco. Served to lt. comdr. Royal Australian Naval Vol. Res., 1945. Clubs: Engineers, Queen's. Home: 57 Amador Ave Atherton CA 94025 Office: 160 Sansome St Suite 1200 San Francisco CA 94104

KENNEL, JOHN MAURICE, physicist, aerospace engineer; b. Sioux City, Iowa, Oct. 7, 1927; s. Elmer M. and Blanche (Augsburger) K.; A.B., Miami U. (Ohio), 1948; Ph.D., U. Tex., 1955; m. Clara Jane Whaley, Dec. 28, 1952; children—Susan, Sandra, John, William. Physicist, Naval Ordnance Lab., 1949-51; engr. Aerophysics Lab., N.Am. Aviation, 1951-52; teaching fellow U. Tex., 1952-55; successively engr., engring. supr., project engr., engring. program mgr. Inertial Navigation Autonetics div. N.Am. Aviation, 1955-67; program mgr. research and devel. Microelectronics div. Rockwell Internat., 1967-71, mgr. liquid crystal devel., 1971-75, engr. ICBM guidance, 1975—. Mem. Am. Phys. Soc., AAAS, AIAA, Soc. Automotive Engrs., Town Hall Calif. Home: 11591 Suburnas Way Santa Ana CA 92705 Office: 3370 Miraloma Ave Anaheim CA 92803

KENNER, R. ROBERTSON, psychiatrist, hospital administrator; b. Williamsport, Ind., Nov. 2, 1937; s. R. Schultz and Juanita Jean (Robertson) Schultz; m. Kathryn Terry, Oct. 9, 1976. M.D., Ind. U., 1964. Resident in psychiatry Vanderbilt U. Hosp., Nashville, 1969-72; clin. dir. Jackson (Tenn.) Community Mental Health Ctr., 1972-74; med. dir. NE Ga. Community Mental Health Ctr. Athens, 1974-76; clin. dir., dist. 4 W. Mental Health and Mental Retardation, LaGrange, Ga., 1976-77; pres. Clinic Psychiat. Treatment and Research, Pine Mountain, Ga., 1976-78; supt. W. Central Ga. Regional Hosp., Columbus, 1977-78; supt. Ariz. State Hosp., Phoenix, 1978—; exec. com. State Mental Health Forensic Dirs.; mgmt. cons. Proctor and Gamble. Served to lt. comdr. USN, MC, 1965-69. Mem. Am. Psychiat. Assn., Ariz. Phychiat. Soc., Phoenix Psychiat. Council, Assn. Advancement Behavior Therapy, Am. Soc. Clin. Hypnosis, Sigma Chi. Contbr. paper to jour. in field. Office: 2500 E Van Buren Phoenix AZ 85008

KENNEY, ALAN ADAMS, lawyer; b. Richfield, Utah, Nov. 2, 1939; s. Don Earl and Armenia (Adams) K.; m. Margaret Compton, Apr. 30, 1976; children—Matthew, Travis. B.S., Brigham Young U., 1964; J.D., U. Colo., 1969. C.P.A., Colo., 1970; bar: Colo. 1969. Mem. tax staff Arthur Andersen & Co., Denver, 1969-70; tax atty. Samsonite Corp., Denver, 1979-72; gen. counsel Storage Tech. Corp., Louisville, Colo., 1972—; dir. STC Communications Corp., Media Tech. Corp. Served in USAF, 1962-66. Mem. Am. Corp. Counsel Assn. (dir. Colo. chpt.), ABA, Colo. Bar Assn., Denver Bar Assn., Computer Law Assn., Am. Soc. Corp. Secs., Beta Alpha Psi. Office: 2270 S 88th St Louisville CO 80028

KENNEY, CAROLYN TERRY, surgical products company sales executive; b. Aberdeen, S.D., Apr. 5, 1950; d. Raymond Joseph and Esther M. (Mullally) Reis; m. Raymond Nelson Kenney, June 17, 1972 (dec.). B.A. in Drama and Sociology, U. Wash., 1973. Profl. sales rep. Bristol Labs., Seattle, 1974-77; sales rep. med. ctr. Roche Labs., Seattle, 1977-80; heart valve specialist Shiley Labs., Seattle, 1980-82; surg. specialist Bard Implants div. C.R. Bard, Seattle, 1982—. Bd. dirs. Benefactor for Issaquah Village Theatre; active Young Widows United Way group. Recipient Rookie of Yr. award Shiley, Inc., 1981; named Young Career Woman of Yr., Seattle Bus. and Profl. Womens Assn., 1978. Mem. Nat. Assn. Female Execs., Bus. Profl. Women's Assn. Democrat. Roman Catholic. Clubs: Pres.'s U. Wash., Bellevue Athletic.

KENNON, ROBERT BRUCE, internat. trade co. exec., mgmt. cons., educator; b. Flatonia, Tex., Jan. 15, 1920; s. Robert Bruce and Jessie Caledonia (Epperson) K.; B.A., U. Calif., Berkeley, 1944, M.A., 1945; Ed.D., Nova U., Ft. Lauderdale, Fla., 1977; m. Cohuita Price, Jan. 14, 1949; 1 dau., Adah Frances. Pres., Am. Inst. of Addis Ababa (Ethiopia), 1946-47; cons. to Ethiopian govt., 1946-47; prof. history and govt. Tex. So. U., Houston, 1948-51; pres. Kennon Co., Sacramento, 1957—; bus. rep. to various African and Middle Eastern firms, 1957—; prof. polit. sci. Sacramento City Coll., 1968—. Julius Rosenwald Travelling fellow, 1946, Fulbright Internat. fellow, 1975. Mem. Am. Polit. Sci. Assn., Am. Mgmt. Assn., Calif. Tchrs. Assn., AAUP, Alpha Phi Alpha. Home: 7018 23d St Sacramento CA 95822 Office: 3915 7th Ave Sacramento CA 95817

KENNY, MICHAEL H., bishop; b. Hollywood, Calif., June 26, 1937; ed. St. Joseph Coll., Mountain View, Calif., St. Patrick's Sem., Menlo Park, Calif., Cath. U. Am. Ordained priest, Roman Cath. Ch., 1963; ordained bishop of Juneau (Alaska), 1979—. Office: 419 6th St Juneau AK 99801*

KENT, JANET, computer consultant, school psychologist; b. Los Angeles, Nov. 8, 1941; d. Samuel and Sylvia (Laskowitz) Schrager; m. Leonard Kent, Nov. 7, 1964. B.A., UCLA, 1964; M.A., Calif. State U.-Los Angeles, 1967. Cert. tchr., sch. psychologist, adminstr., learning handicapped specialist, Calif. Tchr. educationally handicapped Hermosa Beach (Calif.) City Schs., 1967-72, dist. counselor, 1973-79, dist. sch. psychologist, 1979-83; pres. Kent Data Mgmt. Services, Inc., Palos Verdes, Calif., 1983—; instr. Pepperdine U., Whittier Coll. NDEA fellow, 1966. Mem. Council for Exceptional Children, Am. Personnel and Guidance Assn., Pi Lambda Theta. Office: Kent Data Mgmt Services Inc 904 Silver Spur Rd Suite 127 Rolling Hills Estates CA 90274

KENT, PAULA (MRS. STANLEY J. LLOYD), pub. relations, mktg. and mgmt. cons., lectr.; b. Bklyn.; d. John and Estelle (Frye) Smith; B.S., State Tchrs. Coll., Worcester, Mass., 1939; M.S., Grad. Sch. Bus. Adminstrn., Boston U., 1941; m. Stanley J. Lloyd, Jan. 23, 1943; children—Diane Adrienne Noel, Robin Michele Cheri, Kevin Christopher Kent, Gisele Nicolette Jolie. Methods engr. Internat. Bus. Machines, 1941-42; personnel dir. Daily Jour., San Diego, also radio sta. KSDJ, 1946-48; fashion editor The San Diego Union, 1949; promotion dir. The San Diego Union and the Evening Tribune, 1948-70, also U. Calif. at Los Angeles Extension Div. Faculty, 1961-63; pub. relations, marketing and mgmt. cons., 1970—; v.p. La Jolla Clin. Labs., 1970—. Lectr. marketing workshop tour, Brussels, London, Paris, Madrid, 1972. Formerly active ARC, Am. Cancer Soc., Med. Aux. San Diego. Recipient over 158 awards 1950—, including: 39 nat., 18 western states, over 100 Calif. state awards, 1 local award, resulting from ann. competitions sponsored by, Los Angeles Advt. Women's Club, Nat. Newspaper Assn. Mgrs., N.Y. Stock Exchange, Calif. Newspaper Publs. Assn., Calif. Press Women, Nat. Fedn. Press Women, Editor and Pub. Mag.; civic awards City of San Diego, Distinguished Service award Investment Edn. Inst., Detroit, 1969, Golden Spear award Twin Cities Sales Promotion Execs. Assn., Mpls., 1965; named Woman of Achievement, 1958, 59, 64, Woman of Valor, 1958, Woman of Year, San Diego, 1965, Woman of Achievement, Nat. Fedn. Bus. and Profl. Women's Clubs, 1966, Advt. Man of Distinction, San Diego, 1970. Mem. Advt. and Sales Club San Diego (former dir.), Sales Execs. Club San Diego (pres. 1970-71), Personnel Mgmt. Assn. (hon. mem.), Sales and Marketing Execs. Internat. (dir. at large 1970—), Sales Promotion Execs. Assn. Los Angeles (Man of Year 1965), Am. Advt. Fedn. (western region chmn. edn. com., mem. nat. edn. com. 1971-72) Nat. Newspaper Promotion Assn. (pres. Western region 1964, dir. 1968-70), Calif. Assn. Press Women, Nat. Fedn. Press Women, Internat. Newspaper Promotion Assn. (bd. dirs.), Am. Mgmt. Assn. Roman Catholic. Club: San Diego. Editor: Monthly Bull., Personnel Mgmt. Assn., 1955-59, monthly bull., Sales Execs. Club. Chmn. San Diego's Ann. Giant Sales Rally, 1953-55, 70-71, co-chmn., 1964, 65; chmn. Advt. Recognition Week Campaign, Nat. Unltd. Hydroplane Races, San Diego, 1953-54; pub. relations adviser Nat. Mrs. Am. Pageant, San Diego 200th Anniversary celebration, Holiday for Housewives, San Diego, 1955-60; exec. dir., producer San Diego Ann. Golden Gloves Boxing Tournament, San Diego Ann. Metrotennis Championships, Ann. Power Boat Regatta, Ann. Model Yacht Regatta, Ann. Jr. Golf Championships, Ann. Hole-in-One Tournament, Ann. Investment Clinic. Commd. ensign, Women's Reserve, USNR, 1942, transferred USCG, served from ensign to lt. (s.g.), 1943-46. Traveled throughout Europe, Japan, Hong Kong, Hawaii, Macao, West Indies, C.Am., Colombia, Mex., Russia, 1953—. Home: 515 Bon Air St La Jolla CA 92037 Office: PO Box 2243 La Jolla CA 92038

KENT, RICHARD S., data processing cons.; b. Bronx, N.Y., Nov. 6, 1942; s. Martin L. and Shirley (Satinsky) K.; B.S., N.Y. U., 1967, M.S., 1969; children—Paul, Neil. Sr. systems analyst, dir. data processing N.Y. U., 1960-72; dist. mgr. AT&T, N.Y.C., 1972-74; mgr. customer support ISD, Santa Clara, Calif., 1974-76; pres., chmn. bd. DLM Cons., Inc., Sunnyvale, Calif., 1976—; instr. DeAnza Coll., Cupertino, Calif.; lectr. on data processing cons. Mem. Assn. Computing Machinery, Data Processing Mgmt. Assn., Assn. Computer Programmers and Analysts, Ind. Computer Consultants Assn. Co-pub., editor Computer Money: How to Make it in Data Processing Consulting. Address: 566 Croyden Ct Sunnyvale CA 94087

KENYON, DOUGLAS ALAN, safety profl.; b. Binghamton, N.Y., Jan. 8, 1953; s. Douglas Walter and Edith (Noble) K.; A.S., Merritt Coll., Oakland, Calif., 1979; B.S., U. Redlands, 1981; m. Marsha G. Smith, Mar. 17, 1973. Safety coordinator Washington Hosp., Fremont, Calif., 1975-77; safety and health asst. Stanford U. Med. Center, 1977-78; mgr. safety and environ. health Pacific Med. Center, San Francisco, 1978—; instr. safety studies Cogswell Coll., San Francisco, 1981—. Served with USN, 1970-74. Mem. Nat. Safety Council (chmn. region 9 health care sect. 1980—), Profl. Health Care Safety Assn., Am. Soc. Safety Engrs., Nat. Safety Mgmt. Soc., No. Calif. Indsl. Safety Soc., Am. Soc. Hosp. Engring., Nat. Fire Protection Assn., World Safety Orgn. Contbr. in field. Office: Pacific Med Center Clay and Buchanan Sts San Francisco CA 94115

KENYON, JULIA CAROLINE, educator; b. Harvard, Nebr., Jan. 3, 1919; d. Peter J. and Anna Marie (Bartholoma) Pauley; B.S., U. Nebr., 1941; M.Ed., Colo. State U., 1968; postgrad. (Colo. scholar), U. No. Colo., 1970, Utah State U., 1979, Colo. State U., 1980, others; m. Meril T. Kenyon, May 10, 1949. Tchr. home econs., Philips, Nebr., 1941-43, Grand Island, Nebr., 1943-44; home supr. Loup City (Nebr.) Schs., 1945-46; home extension agr. Perkins County, Nebr., 1947—; tchr. home econs. Holyoke (Colo.) High Sch., 1959—. Served with WAVES, 1944-46. Recipient Outstanding Home Econs. Humanitarian award State of Colo., 1977. Mem. NEA, Colo. Edn. Assn., Holyoke Edn. Assn., Am. Vocat. Assn., Colo. Vocat. Assn., Am. Home Econs. Assn., Colo. Home Econs. Assn., Gen. Fedn. Women's Clubs (dist. treas. 1954-55, pres. 1954-55), Sigma Kappa, Alpha Kappa, Delta Kappa Gamma. Methodist. Clubs: Venango Fairy Dell (pres.), Mary Jane Extension, Order Eastern Star (past matron). Home: 205 S Belford St Holyoke CO 80734 Office: PO Box 193 Holyoke CO 80734

KEOWEN, SHERALEE JUNE, electronics company exec., personnel adminstr.; b. Coquille, Oreg., Nov. 14, 1939; d. Ernest Harrell and Willeta P. (Strong) O'Dell; m. Terence Neil Grasteit, June 20, 1958; children—Chris, Michele, Misty; m. 2d, Andrew Peter Keowen, Mar. 14, 1976. Student, El Camino Coll., Torrance, Calif., 1958-59. Personnel adminstr. Control Data Corp., Los Angeles, 1964-66; corp. adminstr. Computer Scis. Corp., Century City, Calif., 1966-69; personnel mgr. Computer Micro-Image Systems, Chatsworth, Calif., 1969-71; personnel and adminstrn. mgr. Vector General, Inc., Woodland Hills, Calif., 1971-78, adminstrn. dir., asst. corp. sec., 1978-81, v.p. adminstrn, asst. corp. sec., 1981—; v.p., dir. Warner Ctr. Credit Union; dir. Lanseair Travel, Inc. Bd. dirs. Woodland Hills C. of C., Pierce Coll. Adv. Com. Mem. Personnel and Indsl. Relations Assn. (bd. dirs., exec. com.), Am. Soc. Personnel Adminstrn., Am. Compensation Assn., Exec. Women Internat., Travel and Transp. Council, Los Angeles. Office: 21300 Oxnard Street Woodland Hills CA 91367

KEPLER, RAYMOND GLEN, physicist; b. Long Beach, Cal., Sept. 10, 1928; s. Glen Raymond and Erma Martina (Larsen) K.; B.S., Stanford, 1950; M.S., U. Cal. at Berkeley, 1955, Ph.D., 1957; m. Carol Flint, Apr. 19, 1953; children—Julianne, Linda, Russell B., David L. Mem. tech. staff central research dept. E.I. duPont de Nemours & Co., 1957-64; div. supr. Sandia Labs., Albuquerque, 1964-69, dept. mgr., 1969—. Active Boy Scouts Am., Girl Scouts U.S.A. Mem. Am. Phys. Soc. (chmn. edn. com.), A.A.A.S., Sierra Club, Sigma Xi. Home: 9004 Bellehaven NE Albuquerque NM 87112 Office: Sandia Labs Albuquerque NM 87115

KEREM, ABRAHAM, aero. engr.; b. Bagdad, Iraq, June 27, 1937; s. Moshe and Flora (Yehuda) Kiflawi; came to U.S., 1977; B.Sc.Ae., Technion (Israel), 1960; m. Dina Schlifer, Mar. 31, 1966; children—Gail, Yael. Head advanced design Israel Aircraft Industries, 1970-74; pres. Matoss Aviation Industry, Lod, Israel, 1974-77; project engr. Devel. Scis., Inc., Industry, Calif., 1977-80; pres. Leading Systems, Inc., Hacienda Heights, Calif., 1980—; tchr. Technion, 1974-75; cons. Israel Mil. Industries, 1976-77, Teledyne Ryan Aero., 1980. Served with Israeli Air Force, 1960-69. Recipient Israel Defense award, 1965. Mem. Exptl. Aircraft Assn., Acad. Model Aeros. Home and Office: 3308 S Olaf Hill Hacienda Heights CA 91745

KERMAN, BARRY MARTIN, ophthalmologist, educator; b. Chgo., Mar. 31, 1945; s. Harvey Nathan and Evelyn (Bialis) K.; B.S., U. Ill., 1967, M.D. with high honors, 1970; m. Pamela Renee Berliant, Aug. 18, 1968; children—Gregory Jason, Jeremy Adam. Intern in medicine Harbor Gen. Hosp., Torrance, Calif., 1970-71; resident in ophthalmology Wadsworth VA Hosp., Los Angeles, 1971-74; fellow in diseases of the retina, vitreous and choroid Jules Stein Eye Inst. UCLA, 1974-75; fellow in ophthalmic ultrasonography Edward S. Harkness Eye Inst., Columbia U., N.Y.C. and U. Iowa Hosps., Iowa City, 1975; asst. prof. ophthalmology UCLA, 1976-78, Harbor Gen. Hosp., 1976-78; asst. clin. prof. ophthalmology UCLA, 1978-83, assoc. clin. prof., 1983—, dir. ophthalmic ultrasonography lab., 1976—; cons. ophthalmologist, Los Angeles, 1976—. Served with USAFR, 1971-77. Diplomate Am. Bd. Ophthalmology. Fellow Am. Acad. Ophthalmology; mem. Calif. Med. Assn., Los Angeles County Med. Assn., Los Angeles Soc. Ophthalmology, Am. Inst. Ultrasound in Medicine, Am. Soc. Ophthalmic Ultrasound, Am. Registry of Diagnostic Med. Sonographers (exec. bd.). Contbr. articles to profl. jours. Office: 2080 Century Park E Suite 800 Los Angeles CA 90067

KERN, CLIFFORD DALTON, meteorologist; b. Oakland, Calif., Jan. 6, 1928; s. Arthur William and Blanche Naomi (Brown) K.; A.B., U. Calif., Berkeley, 1952; certificate in Meterology, UCLA, 1953, M.A., 1958; Ph.D., U. Wash., 1965; m. C. Joyce Durant, Feb. 21, 1951; children—Michael Richard, Janice Rae, Michelle Ann. Commd. 2d lt. USAF, 1952, advanced through grades to lt. col., 1972; staff meteorologist Air Force Systems Command, McClelland AFB, Calif., 1953-55, Hanscom Field, Mass., 1955-56, 58-61, Vietnam, 1964-65, Air Force Satellite Control Facility, Sunnyvale, Calif., 1965-67, Air Force Global Weather Central Offutt AFB, 1969-71, Los Angeles Air Force Sta., 1971-72; ret., 1972; asst. prof. St. Louis U., 1972; vis. scientist Nat. Center Atmospheric Research, Boulder, Colo., 1972-73; with Atomic Energy div. E.I. duPont de Nemours & Co., Savannah River Lab., Aiken, S.C., 1973-78; with Space Systems div. Lockheed Missiles & Space Co., Sunnyvale, Calif., 1978—. Served with AUS, 1946-48. Decorated Bronze Star medal, Air medal with one oak leaf cluster. Mem. Am. Meteorol. Soc., Am. Geophys. Union, Sigma Xi. Mason. Home: 556 Hacienda Dr Scotts Valley CA 95066 Office: PO Box 504 Sunnyvale CA 94086

KERN, EDWARD LANE, chemist; b. Toledo, Ohio, Sept. 15, 1934; s. Edward Allen and Marie (Van Zandt) K.; B.S., Case Inst. Tech., 1956, Ph.D. in Phys. Chemistry, 1960; children—Susan, Edward, Michael. Mgr. solid state research and devel. Dow Corning Corp., Midland, Mich., 1963-70; pres. High Performance Tech., Inc., Midland, Mich., 1970-72; sr. scientist Hughes Aircraft Co., Carlsbad, Calif., 1973-81; pvt. cons. semicondr. materials, 1981—. Vice chmn. Com. for Nuclear Power, Midland, 1970. Served with USAF, 1960-63. Fellow Am. Inst. Chemists; mem. Am. Assn. Crystal Growers (dir. Western sect.), Am. Chem. Soc., Electrochem. Soc. Presbyterian. Contbr. articles to profl. jours. Patentee in field. Home: 13655 Ruette Le Parc Del Mar CA 92014 Office: Edward Kern & Assocs 201 Lomas Santa Fe Dr Suite 500 Solana Beach CA 92075

KERN, ERNST F., JR., marketing executive; b. Detroit, Sept. 18, 1939; s. Ernst F. and Janet (Bragaw) K.; m. Janis Eileen Dodson, May 8, 1976; children—Kathryn, Ernst III, Jan Marie. B.A., Dartmouth Coll., 1961; M.B.A., U. Mich., 1965. Fin. analyst, product planner Ford Motor Co., Dearborn, Mich., 1962-69; nat. mktg. mgr. parts Toyota Motor Sales USA, Torrance-Calif., 1969-72, nat. sales adminstrn. mgr., 1973-74, nat. dealer planning and placement mgr., 1974-75, asst. regional mgr. So. Calif., 1975-76, regional mgr. No. Calif., 1976-77, v.p. sales and mktg. Gulf States, 1977-80; nat. mktg. mgr. Am. Isuzu Motors, Whittier, Calif., 1980—. Mem. Am. Mktg. Assn., Advt. Club Los Angeles. Office: 2300 Pellissier St Whittier CA 90601

KERN, HAL COLEMAN, III, marketing sales executive; b. Long Beach, Calif., Oct. 8, 1949; s. Hal C. and Robyn (Adair) K.; m. Phyllis Grable, Dec. 16, 1967 (div.); children—Keri Mari, Kasey Elizabeth. B.S. in Criminal Justice, Calif. State U., 1967; M.A. in Edn., Pepperdine U., 1971. With U.S. Secret Service, 1976-77; sr. security specialist Fluor Corp., Irvine, Calif., 1977-80; v.p. Shield Security, Orange, Calif., 1980-82; mgr. security and safety Air Cal, Newport Beach, Calif., 1981-82; loss prevention dir. Sav-on Drugs Inc., Anaheim, Calif., 1982-83; mgr. mktg.-sales Taser Industries, Inc., 1983—; instr. criminal justice. Bd. dirs. Irvine Harvest Festival Com. Served as maj. USMC, 1967-76, to lt. col. USMCR. Mem. Am. Soc. Indsl. Security, Am. Soc. Safety Engrs., Am. Mgmt. Assn. Republican. Presbyterian. Office: 22642 Lambert St Suite 406 El Toro CA 92630

KERN, VIRGINIA KNOX, reading specialist; b. Springfield, Mass.; d. Hugh V.B. and Jean R.K. Knox; B.A. in Edn., Methodist Coll., Fayetteville, N.C., 1964; M.A. in Counseling, Chapman Coll., Orange, Calif., 1972; m. Martin C. Kern; children—Daniel, Natalya A., Crystal L. Tchr., Headstart program Cumberland County Community Action,

Fayetteville, 1964-66; tchr. Santa Ana (Calif.) Unified Dist., 1966-67; lang. arts specialist in early childhood program Lompoc (Calif.) Unified Sch. Dist., 1973-74, reading specialist, 1968—, classroom mgmt. coach, 1981-83. Cert. specialist tchr. in reading, Calif.; specialist in auditory and visual perception; trainer of vol. parents. Mem. Internat. Reading Assn. (pres. elect Tri-Valley council 1976-77, pres. 1977-78), Day Care and Child Devel. Council Am., Orton Soc., Reading Specialists of Calif., Lompoc Mental Health Assn. Editor: Tri-Valley News Notes, 1981. Office: Crestview Sch Utah Rd Vandenberg AFB CA 93437

KERNEN, WILLIAM ARNOLD, corporate executive, financial planner; b. Butte, Mont., Apr. 29, 1928; s. Arnold Roy and Eve Eunice (Hull) K. m. Betty Mae Nelson, June 8, 1947; children—William C., Belinda Susan. B.A., LaVerne U., 1972. C.P.A.; cert. fin. planner. Controller, Allied Stores Corp., Yakima, Wash., 1952-57; Rhodes Dept. Stores, Tacoma, Wash. and Portland, Oreg., 1957-62, Robinson's Dept. Stores, Los Angeles, 1962-63; pres. Stockwell & Binney, San Bernardino, Calif., 1963—; pres. Diversified Investors, San Bernardino. Bd. dirs. San Bernardino C. of C.; commr. Parking Pl. Commn. Mem. Internat. Soc. Fin. Planners, Nat. Office Products Assn. Baptist. Club: Kiwanis. Office: PO Box 5429 San Bernardino CA 92412

KERNER, DIANE LOUISE, educator; b. Portland, Oreg., Aug. 3, 1953; d. John Ovila and Dolores Mae (Haebe) Daoust; m. Keith Allen Kerner, Aug. 8, 1981. Cert. tchr. adult edn., Calif. Tutor for autistic adult, San Luis Obispo, Calif., 1977-78; substitute adult edn. tchr., Casade Vida, San Luis Obispo, 1979-80, program coordinator, Life Edn. and Advancement Program, 1980-82, spl. edn. tchr., sign lang. cons., 1982—. Mem. Calif. Tchrs. Assn. Co-planner, co-developer Friendship Sch. LEAP I for severely physically disabled adults; planner, developer Friendship Sch. LEAP II for profoundly retarded adults. Office: CdV 879 Meinecke St San Luis Obispo CA 93401

KERNER, FRANCIS XAVIER, lawyer; s. Louis Philip and Mary Gertrude (Uren) K.; A.B., U. San Francisco, 1929; LL.B., Stanford U., 1932; m. Virginia Cain, Oct. 1, 1934; children—Joan, Peter. Admitted to Calif. bar, 1932; asso. firm Linforth & Cannon, San Francisco, 1932-33; asst. counsel Farm Credit Adminstrn., Berkeley, Calif., 1933-45; individual practice law, San Francisco, 1945-67; partner Kerner, Colangelo & Imlay, San Francisco, 1967—. Mem. Nat. Council Farmer Coops. (legal tax and acctg. com.), Am. Bar Assn., Calif. Bar Assn., San Francisco Bar Assn. Roman Catholic. Club: Serra. Contbr. articles to profl. jours. Home: 90 Biscayne Dr San Rafael CA 94901 Office: Kerner Colangelo & Imlay 114 Sansome St San Francisco CA 94104

KERNER, JEREMIAH WADSWORTH, radiologist; b. N.Y.C., Sept. 8, 1910; s. Sigmund S. and Rose S. (Seligman) K.; student U. Ga., 1934; B.S., Duke U., 1934, M.D., 1937; m. Jeannette Victoria Herman, Jan. 20, 1939; children—Jeffrey S., Jordan R. Intern, Los Angeles County Hosp., 1937-59, resident, 1940-43, attending radiologist, 1946-71; radiologist, chief staff West Covina (Calif.) Hosp., 1960-83; assoc. clin. prof. U. So. Calif. Med. Sch., Los Angeles, 1937-65. Bd. dirs. Am. Cancer Soc., San Gabriel Valley br.; mem. com. admissions Duke U. Med. Sch., 1950-76. Served to lt. col., M.C., AUS, 1943-46. Fellow Am. Coll. Radiology; Mem. AMA, Am. Bd. Radiology, Radiol. Soc. N.Am., Calif. Med. Assn., Los Angeles County Med. Assn., Calif. Radiol. Soc., Phi Delta Epsilon. Clubs: So. Hills Country, Industry Hills Country. Office: 725 S Orange Ave West Covina CA 91790

KERNODLE, UNA MAE, educator; b. Jackson, Tenn., Mar. 4, 1947; d. James G. and Mary E. (McLemore) Sikes. B.S. in Home Econs., U. Tenn., 1969; M.Edn., U. Alaska, 1974. Tchr. Chugiak High Sch., Anchorage; instr. Anchorage Community Coll.; edn. cons. State of Alaska, Anchorage Talent Bank. Active Women's Resource Ctr. Mem. Am. Home Econs. Assn., Anchorage Assn. Edn. Young Children, NEA, Am. Vocat. Assn. Democrat. Baptist. Office: Chugiak High School PO Box 218 Eagle River AK 99577

KERR, BAINE PERKINS, JR., lawyer, writer; b. Houston, June 23, 1946; s. Baine Perkins and Mildred Pickett (Caldwell) K.; m. Cynthia Anne Carlisle, May 1, 1974; children—Dara, Baine. B.A., Stanford U., 1968; M.A., U. Denver, 1976, J.D., 1979. Bar: Colo. 1979, U.S. Dist. Ct. (Colo.) 1979, U.S. Ct. Appeals 1979. Editor-in-chief Place Mag., Palo Alto, Calif. 1971-74; ptnr. Hutchinson, Black, Hill, Buchanan & Cook, Boulder, 1979—; fiction writer; educator. Active Nat. Wildlife Fedn., Colo. Open Space Council, Sierra Club. Nat. Endowment Arts fellow 1983; work appeared in Houghton Mifflin Co. Best American Short Stories of 1977. Mem. ABA, Colo. Bar Assn., Boulder County Bar Assn. (co-chmn. civil litigation com. 1983). Democrat. Author: Jumping Off Place, 1981; contbr. numerous short stories and articles to periodicals and literary jours.; contbr. legal articles to law reviews. Home: 411 Spruce Boulder CO 80302 Office: 1215 Spruce Boulder CO 80302

KERR, DAVID EMMETT, general contracting company executive; b. Albany, Calif., May 13, 1944; s. Ralph Emmett and Evelyn Linnea (Johnson) K.; B.S. in Civil Engring., U. Calif.-Berkeley, 1967; m. Carrie Elizabeth Hansel, Feb. 12, 1972; children—Stephanie Linnea, Michael Erin. Estimator, A.A. Johnson & Sons, Contractors, Berkeley, Calif., 1962-67; project engr. Munro-Burns Jackson Bros., Honolulu, 1967-68; Hawaii div. mgr., 1970-80; pres., owner David E. Kerr, Inc., Gen. Contractor, Honolulu, 1980-82; project mgr. Hawaiian Dredging and Constrn. Co. Served with AUS, 1968-70. Mem. Nat. Assn. Home Builders, Gen. Contractors Assn. Hawaii, Bldg. Industry Assn. Hawaii, Chi Epsilon. Republican. Congregationalist Clubs: Oahu Country, Honolulu. Home: 1176 Koloa St Honolulu HI 96816 Office: P O Box 4088 Honolulu HI 96813

KERR, EUGENE GARNER, educational and technological consultant; b. Orofino, Idaho, Oct. 7, 1935; s. Frank Walter and Fern Eliza (Perry) K.; B.A., U. Wash., 1957, M.Ed., 1966; Ed.D., Wash. State U., 1974; m. Beverly J. Shaw, Aug. 5, 1960; children—Kevin Frank, Shawn Harold. Dir. computing Wash. State U., 1966-69; dir. edn. div. McDonnell Douglas Automation, St. Louis, 1969-73; dir. computing Western Inst., Waco, Tex., 1973-74; exec. cons., Waco, 1974-76; N.W. dist. mgr. edn. Control Data Corp., Seattle, 1976—; cons., dir. Bibl. Instrn. and Tech. Found., Video Tech., Inc.; founder, pres. Spirit 2000, Inc. NSF grantee, 1968; N.W. Regional Edn. Lab. grantee, 1968. Mem. Assn. Ednl. Data Systems, Assn. for Devel. Computer Based Instrn. Systems, Am. Soc. Tng. and Devel., Nat. Assn. Performance and Instrn., Phi Delta Kappa. Presbyterian. Contbr. numerous articles on application of computers to edn. to profl. jours. Home: 9441 NE 16th St Bellevue WA 98004

KERR, FARNUM WOODWARD, planning, engineering and management consultant; b. San Francisco, Nov. 27, 1925; s. William John and Dorothy Campbell (Fish) K.; student Colo. U., 1943-44; B.S.E., U. Mich., 1946; M.C.P., U. Calif., Berkeley, 1956; m. Verna M. Berlin, July 29, 1952; children—John C., Robert T., Andrew E., Meghon E., Gena F. Asst. profl. planning and civil engring. positions, No. Calif., 1946-54; prin. partner Farnum Kerr Assos., planners, architects, engrs., Inc., Napa, Calif., 1954-66, pres., 1967-72; cons., Napa, 1972—; guest lectr. U. Calif., Berkeley, Davis and Irvine, Santa Clara U.; participant Congrès Fédération Internationale des Géomètres, Switzerland, 1981. Served to maj. USMCR, 1943-46, 51-52. Recipient award of merit Calif. Council Civil Engrs. and Land Surveyors, 1964. Mem. Am. Inst. Cert. Planners, ASCE (outstanding service award; chmn. land use planning com. 1969-74), Calif. Council Civil Engrs. and Land Surveyors (dir. 1958—, pres. 1983), 20-30 Club (dist. gov. 1958), Alpha Tau Omega, Chi Epsilon. Clubs: Elks, Rotary. Author: Ecology, Environmental Quality and Public Works, 1971; (with others) Environmental Impact Analysis, 1972. Contbr. articles to jours. Home: 19 Oak Grove Way Napa CA 94559 Office: 1700 2d St Suite 276C Napa CA 94559

KERR, JAMES WILFRID, artist; b. N.Y.C., Aug. 7, 1897; s. James Fairbairn and Leah M. (Galer) K.; grad. Poppenhusen Inst., 1914, N.Y. Sch. Fine and Applied Arts, 1923; m. Rose R. Netzorg, June 24, 1922; children—Andra Gail (dec.), Paul F. (adopted); m. 2d, Mary N. Wenzel, Aug. 27, 1980. Dir., Art Summer Sch., Detroit, 1923-24; artist, lectr., art adminstr., 1923—; painter in oils, tchr.; one-man and group shows include: Galeria Del Sol, Allied Artists Am., NAD, Am. Vets. Soc., N.J. Painters and Sculptors Soc., Carnegie Inst. Pitts., 1949 (by invitation), Conn. Acad. Fine Arts, Davenport (Iowa) Mus., Houston Mus., Irvington (N.J.) Mus., Norfolk Mus. Arts and Scis., Dialists Exhibit, N.J. Artists, Newark Mus., Ridgewood, N.J., Salmagundi Club, N.Y.C., Delgado Mus., New Orleans, Art U.S.A., Madison Sq. Garden, N.Y.C., 1958, Richmond Mus., Artists Equity Assn. show Botts Meml. Hall, Albuquerque, 48th-50th Fiesta shows at Mus. Fine Arts, Santa Fe, Springville, Utah, 1962-63, 1st Air Force Acad. Exhbn., 1962-63, Juried Arts Nat. Exhbn., Tyler, Tex., 1963, Western Mich. U., Kalamazoo, 1983; Western Mich. U., Kalamazoo, 1983; represented in permanent collections: Mus. City N.Y., Joslyn Art Mus., Omaha, Newark Mus., Mus. Albuquerque, Fla. So. Coll., Lakeland, N.Mex. State Fair, Fergusson Library, Albuquerque, Waldwick (N.J.) Elem. Sch. Trustee, Mus. Albuquerque. Recipient awards, prizes N.J. State Exhibit, Montclair, 1943 (hon. award); NAD, 1945 (1st Altman prize); Plainfield (N.J.) Art Assn. (hon. award), 1946; prize Oil, Morristown (N.J.) Art Assn.; Irvington Art and Mus. Assn., 1st prize in Oil, 1948, 49; Ridgewood (N.J.) Art Assn., 1st prize Oil, 1948; Art Council N.J., 2d Oil prize, 1948; Am. Vets. Soc. Artists purchase award, 1951; Ridgewood (N.J.) Art Assn. (hon. award), 1952; citation Fla. So. Coll., Lakeland, 1952; 1st prize 50th Fiesta Show, Mus. N.Mex., 1963; purchase prize N.Mex. State Fair, 1963, grand award, 1964; silver medal Am. Vets. Soc. Artists, 1963; prizes Ouray County Ann. Exhbn., 1964, State Fair, 1966. Served with USN, World War I. Mem. Allied Artists Am. (treas. 1952, mem. jury awards oil painting 1958, dir. 1955, chmn. membership com. 1955), Internat. Assn. Plastic Arts (Joint com. for Am. participation), Asso. Artists N.J. (dir.), Artists Equity Assn. (chmn. nat. mus. com., co-chmn. nat. artists-museums com. 1958, nat. treas. 1959), Dialists (N.J.), Grand Central Galleries (artist-mem.), Irvington (N.J.) Art and Mus. Assn. (artist mem.), N.J. Soc. Painters and Sculptors, New Mexican Art League (dir. 1966), Ridgewood Art Center (past pres.), Salmagundi Club (artist mem.), Art Assn. New Orleans, Artists Equity Assn. (nat. treas. 1952-55), Am. Vets. Soc. Artists (pres. 1958-60), Albuquerque Mus. Assn. (pres. 1967-68, dir.), Pres.'s Club Western Mich. U. Co-artist, author: Historic Design for Modern Use; also articles on art for School Arts mag. and Everyday Art mag. Lectr. women's clubs, high schs., colls., univs., art clubs and assns. on painting, graphic arts, modern movements in arts, and psychology related to art, radio and TV. Address: 7017 Bellrose Ave NE Albuquerque NM 87110

KERR, KLEON HARDING, educator, state senator; b. Plain City, Utah, Apr. 26, 1911; s. William A. and Rosemond (Harding) K.; Asso. Sci., Weber Coll., 1936; B.A., George Washington U., 1939; M.S., Utah State U., Logan, 1946; m. Katherine Abbott, Mar. 15, 1941; children—Kathleen, William A., Rebecca Rae. Tchr., Bear River High Sch., Tremonton, Utah, 1940-56, prin. jr. high sch., 1956-60, prin. Bear River High Sch., 1960-71; city justice Tremonton, 1941-46; sec. to Senator Arthur V. Watkins, 1947. Mayor, Tremonton City, 1948-53; mem. Utah Local Govt. Survey Commn., 1954-55; mem. Utah Ho. of Reps., 1953-56; mem. Utah State Senate, 1957—, chmn. appropriation com., 1959—, majority leader, 1963; mem. Utah Legis. Council. Dist. dir. vocat. edn. Box Elder Sch. Dist. Recipient Alpha Delta Kappa award for outstanding contbn. to edn., 1982, award for outstanding contbrs. to edn. and govt. Theta Chpt. Alpha Beta Kappa, 1982. Mem. NEA, Utah, Box Elder edn. assns., Nat., Utah secondary schs. prins. assns., Bear River Valley. C. of C. (sec., mgr. 1955-58), Phi Delta Kappa. Mem. Ch. of Jesus Christ of Latter-day Saints. Lion, Kiwanian. Author: Open My Eyes (poetry), 1983; We Remember, 1983. educator, state senator; b. Plain City, Utah, Apr. 26, 1911; s. William A. and Rosemond (Harding) K.; Asso. Sci., Weber Coll., 1936; B.A., George Washington U., 1939; M.S., Utah State U., Logan, 1946; m. Katherine Abbott, Mar. 15, 1941; children—Kathleen, William A., Rebecca Rae. Tchr., Bear River High Sch., Tremonton, Utah, 1940-56, prin. jr. high sch., 1956-60, prin. Bear River High Sch., 1960-71; city justice Tremonton, 1941-46; sec. to Senator Arthur V. Watkins, 1947. Mayor, Tremonton City, 1948-53; mem. Utah Local Govt. Survey Commn., 1954-55; mem. Utah Ho. of Reps., 1953-56; mem. Utah State Senate, 1957—, chmn. appropriation com., 1959—, majority leader, 1963; mem. Utah Legis. Council. Dist. dir. vocat. edn. Box Elder Sch. Dist. Recipient Alpha Delta Kappa award for outstanding contbn. to edn., 1982, award for outstanding contbrs. to edn. and govt. Theta Chpt. Alpha Beta Kappa, 1982. Mem. NEA, Utah, Box Elder edn. assns., Nat., Utah secondary schs. prins. assns., Bear River Valley. C. of C. (sec., mgr. 1955-58), Phi Delta Kappa. Mem. Ch. of Jesus Christ of Latter-day Saints. Lion, Kiwanian. Author: Open My Eyes (poetry), 1983; We Remember, 1983. Home: Box 246 Tremonton UT 84337

KERRI, KENNETH DONALD, civil engineering educator; b. Napa, Calif., Apr. 25, 1934; s. Kenneth R. and Eunice E. (Beck) K.; m. Judith Reeves, Aug. 22, 1958; children—Christopher, Kathleen. B.S.C.E., Oreg. State Coll., 1956; M.S. in San. Engring., U. Calif.-Berkeley, 1959; Ph.D., Oreg. State U., 1965. Registered profl. engr., Calif. San. engr. U.S. Pub. Health Service, San Francisco, 1956-58; prof. civil engring. Calif. State U.-Sacramento, 1959—; cons. civil engring., Sacramento, 1960—. Recipient Trainer of Yr. award Nat. Environ. Tng. Assn., 1982; ABC Pres. Service award, 1982; Sacramento State Coll. Faculty Research award, 1969. Mem. ASCE, Am. Water Works Assn., Water Pollution Control Fedn. (Collection System award 1977), Assn. Environ. Engring. Profs., Calif. Water Pollution Control Assn., Sigma Xi, Phi Kappa Phi, Tau Beta Pi, Sigma Tau. Author textbooks: Operation of Wastewater Treatment Plants, 1970, 2d edit., 1980; Operation and Maintenance of Wastewater Collection Systems, 1976, 2d edit., 1983; Water Treatment Plant Operation, 1983; Water Supply System Operation, 1983. Home: 5839 Shepard Ave Sacramento CA 95819 Office: Calif State U 6000 J St Sacramento CA 95819

KERSHAW, VICKI LYNN, controller, accountant; b. Tulsa, Mar. 6, 1949; d. Arnold Leslie and Doris Evelyn (Lotspeich) Ayers; m. Gary L. Kershaw, May 31, 1976; children—Kristine, Meredith, Brandt. B.B.A. in Acctg. with high honors, Idaho State U., 1980. C.P.A., Idaho. Staff acct. Touche Ross & Co., Pocatello, Idaho, 1980-82; controller Bannock Regional Med. Ctr., Pocatello, 1982—. Treas., bd. dirs. Jr. Achievement of Pocatello, 1981—. Mem. Am. Inst. C.P.A.s, Idaho Soc. C.P.A.s, Hosp. Fin. Mgmt. Assn., Zonta Internat. (treas. chpt. 1983—), Alpha Kappa Psi, Beta Gamma Sigma, Phi Kappa Phi, Mortar Board. Home: 2515 Woodhill Way Pocatello ID 83201 Office: Bannock Regional Med Ctr Memorial Dr Pocatello ID 83201

KERSTEN, RICK BOYCE, publishing company executive; b. Shawano, Wis., June 15, 1941; s. Raymond Fred and Alice Elizabeth (Wochinske) K.; m. Ellen Jane Stonehouse, Dec. 17, 1967; 1 son, Matthew. Student, Ariz. State U., 1959-62. Vice-pres. Kersten Bros. Greeting Cards Co., 1968-79, pres., 1979—. Served with USN, 1962-68. Mem. Nat. Assn. Greeting Card Pubs. Republican. Lutheran. Office: Kersten Bros Greeting Card Co 9312 N 94th St Scottsdale AZ 85258

KERSTEN, TIMOTHY WAYNE, economics educator; b. Algona, Iowa, Nov. 18, 1944; s. Harold Arthur and Marcella (Heger) K.; m. Carol Ann Kersten, Dec. 23, 1967; 1 son, Jeffrey. B.A., Calif. State U., 1957; M.A., U. Oreg., 1970, Ph.D., 1973. Asst. prof. econs. Calif. Poly. State U. 1971-75, assoc. prof. 1976-80, prof. 1980—, chmn. acad. senate 1980-82; cons. in field. Mem. citizens adv. com. City Council of San Luis Obispo, Calif. 1976-77. Fed. research fellow 1969-71. Mem. Am. Econ. Assn., Western Econ. Assn., Phi Mu Alpha, Omicron Delta Epsilon. Author: Instructor's Guide to Accompany Contemporary Economics 1975. Office: Dept Econs Calif Poly State Univ San Luis Obispo CA 93407

KERTESZ, LOUIS ROBERT, mfg. co. ofcl.; b. Chgo., June 25, 1947; s. Louis Walter and Katherine Ann (Depile) K.; B.A., Iowa Wesleyan Coll., 1969; M.B.A., U. Nebr., 1980; m. Sylvia Ann Bijjani, Dec. 21, 1970. Admissions counselor Iowa Wesleyan Coll., Mt. Pleasant, 1970-72; asst. sales mgr. Aetna Life & Casualty, Des Moines, 1972-73; asst. indsl. relations mgr. Delavan Mfg. Co., Des Moines, 1973-75; indsl. relations rep. Becton-Dickinson, Columbus, Nebr., 1975-79, mgr. indsl. relations, Los Gatos, Calif., 1980-82; dir. human resources Endevco Corp. div. Becton, Dickinson & Co., San Juan Capistrano, Calif., 1982—. Served with USAR, 1969-70. Mem. Am. Soc. Safety Engrs., San Juan Capistrano C. of C. (dir. 1983—). Home: 27752 Torija Mission Viejo CA 92691 Office: 30700 Rancho Viejo Rd San Juan Capistrano CA 92675

KERVICK, RICHARD JOHN, career planning exec.; b. Worcester, Mass., Jan. 12, 1924; s. John Anthony and Elizabeth Frances (McKeon) K.; B.B.A., Holy Cross Coll., 1945; M.A., Georgetown U., 1949; m. Mary Jane Walpole, Nov. 22, 1951 (dec.); children—Andrea Lisa, Sarah Elizabeth, Daniel Walpole, Mimi Angelique. Dist. sales mgr. Peninsular Grinding Wheel Co., Chgo., 1950-55; regional mgr. Rogers Pub. Co., Phila., 1955-59; mktg. mgr. Chilton Co., Chgo., 1959-64; dir. publs. Soc. Mfg. Engrs., Detroit, 1964-67; dir. mktg. U.S. Industries, Inc., Detroit, 1967-69; v.p., gen. mgr. Consoweld Corp., Wis. Rapids, Wis., 1970-74, pres. Consoweld Distbrs., Inc., 1971-74, also dir.; pres., cons. Richard J. Kervick & Assocs., San Francisco and San Jose, Calif., 1974—. Bd. dirs. Riverside Hosp., Wisconsin Rapids, 1972-74, United Way Fund Drive, San Jose, 1976. Served with USN, 1943-47. Mem. Am. Mgmt. Assn., Soc. Profl. Mgmt. Consultants, Soc. Am. Bus. and Economic Writers, Am. Mktg. Assn. Clubs: Commonwealth, Almaden Country. Author research papers in field. career planning exec.; b. Worcester, Mass., Jan. 12, 1924; s. John Anthony and Elizabeth Frances (McKeon) K.; B.B.A., Holy Cross Coll., 1945; M.A., Georgetown U., 1949; m. Mary Jane Walpole, Nov. 22, 1951 (dec.); children—Andrea Lisa, Sarah Elizabeth, Daniel Walpole, Mimi Angelique. Dist. sales mgr. Peninsular Grinding Wheel Co., Chgo., 1950-55; regional mgr. Rogers Pub. Co., Phila., 1955-59; mktg. mgr. Chilton Co., Chgo., 1959-64; dir. publs. Soc. Mfg. Engrs., Detroit, 1964-67; dir. mktg. U.S. Industries, Inc., Detroit, 1967-69; v.p., gen. mgr. Consoweld Corp., Wis. Rapids, Wis., 1970-74, pres. Consoweld Distbrs., Inc., 1971-74, also dir.; pres., cons. Richard J. Kervick & Assocs., San Francisco and San Jose, Calif., 1974—. Bd. dirs. Riverside Hosp., Wisconsin Rapids, 1972-74, United Way Fund Drive, San Jose, 1976. Served with USN, 1943-47. Mem. Am. Mgmt. Assn., Soc. Profl. Mgmt. Consultants, Soc. Am. Bus. and Economic Writers, Am. Mktg. Assn. Clubs: Commonwealth, Almaden Country. Author research papers in field. Office: 50 Francisco St Suite 485 San Francisco CA 94133

KESSELRING, JOHN PAUL, engineering executive; b. Detroit, Mar. 26, 1940; s. Paul Herbert and Gwendolyn (Currie) K.; m. Jane Edwards, July 23, 1940; children—Joan Paula, Thomas Max. B.S., U. Mich., Ann Arbor, 1961; M.S., Stanford U., 1962, Ph.D., 1968. Registered profl. mech. engr., Calif., Tenn., 1975. Research engr. Rocketdyne Div., N.Am. Aviation, Canoga Park, Calif., 1962-63, mem. tech. staff, 1967-69; asst. prof. engring. U. Tenn., Knoxville, 1969-74; research engr. Acurex Corp., Mountain View, Calif., 1974-79, assoc. mgr., 1980-82; v.p. devel. Alzeta Corp., Mountain View, 1982—; lectr. Stanford U.; cons. U.S. Army Missile Command, Huntsville, Ala. N.Am. Aviation fellow, 1963-67; named Outstanding Young Teacher, Coll. Engring., U. Tenn., 1971; Outstanding AIAA Faculty Adv. U. Tenn., 1972-73. Mem. AIAA, ASME, Combustion Inst., Sigma Xi, Tau Beta Pi. Methodist. Author over 50 tech. publs. on combustion; patentee in catalytic combustion, U.S. and Can. Office: 500 Clyde Ave Mountain View CA 94043

KESSLER, A. D., property development company executive, consultant; b. N.Y.C., May 1, 1923; s. Morris William and Belle Miriam (Pastor) K.; m. Ruth Schwartz, Nov. 20, 1944; children—Brian Lloyd, Judd Stuart, Earl Vaughn. Student U. Newark, 1940-41, Rutgers U., 1941-42, 46, Albright Coll., 1942, Newark Coll. Engring., 1946; M.B.A., Kensington U., 1976, Ph.D. in Mgmt. nd Behavioral Psychology, 1977. Sr. cert. rev. appraise; cert. exchangor. Pvt. practice real estate and ins. sales, N.J. and Pa., 1946; pres. Armor Corp., Newark, 1947-68; pres. Folding Carton Corp., Am., N.Y.C., 1958-68; exec. v.p. Henry Schindau Assocs., N.Y.C., 1966-67; tax rep. Calif. State Bd. Equalization, 1968-69; aviation cons. transp. div. Calif., Dept. Aeros., also pub. info. officer; 1969-71; broker, mgr. La Costa (Calif.) Sales Corp., 1971-75; chmn. bd. Profl. Ednl. Found., 1975—, Timeshare Resorts Internat., 1975—, Interex, Leucadia, Calif., 1975-82, The Kessler Orgn., Leucadia, 1975—; publisher, editor in chief Creative Real Estate Mag., 1975-82, 83— pres. Who's Who Assocs., Inc., Marina del Rey, Calif., 1982-83; chmn. bd. The Brain Trust, Rancho Santa Fe, Calif., 1977—; cons. and lectr. in field. Scoutmaster Orange Mountain council Boy Scouts Am., 1955-62; harbor master N.J. Marine Patrol, 1958-67; dep. sheriff, Essex County, N.J., 1951-65. Served with USAF, 1942-45. Decorated D.F.C., Air medal, Purple Heart. Mem. Am. Soc. Editors and Publishers, Author's Guild, Internat. Platform Assn., Nat. Speakers Assn., Nat. Press Photographers Assn., Guild Assn. Airport Execs., Aviation and Space Writers Assn., Internat. Exchangors Assn. (founder), Nat. Press Club, Overseas Press Club. Clubs: La Costa Country, Cuyamaca, Mason (320), Shriner, Who's Who Internat. Assocs. Author: A Fortune At Your Feet, 1981; editor: The Real Estate News Observer, 1975-82; speaker for radio and TV as The Real Estate Answerman, 1975—. Home: PO Box 1144 Rancho Sante Fe CA 92067 Office Box 2446 Leucadia CA 92024

KESSLER, HELEN JOYCE, architect; b. N.Y.C., July 11, 1952; d. John Otto and Eva Magdalena (Bondy) K. B. Arch., U. Ariz., 1975; student U. Coll. London, 1973-74. Registered architect, Ariz. Grad. architect Vista Vol., Tucson Community Devel./Design Ctr., 1975-76; assoc. editor Harris Sobin & Assoc., Tucson, 1967-77; project. architect Environ. Research Lab., W. Ariz., Tucson, 1977—; lectr., 1979-80; cons. Solar archtl. design. Commr. Ariz. Solar Energy Commn., 1979—, Tucson-Pima Met. Energy Commn., 1981—; vice chmn., bd. dirs. Ariz. Solar Energy Assn., 1978-82; co-founder, coordinator Women's Design Network, 1980-81, 82-83. Am. Solar Energy Commn. grantee 1979, 82-83. Mem. AIA (council dels.), Am. Solar Energy Soc., Ariz. Solar Energy Assn., N.Mex. Solar Energy Assn., Nat. Trust Historic Preservation. Columnist Ariz. Daily Star; designer house Tucson Solar Parade Homes; contbr. articles to archtl. mags. Office: Environ Research Lab Tucson Internat Airport Tucson AZ 85706

KESSLER, HILDA, clinical psychologist; b. N.Y.C., June 6, 1932; d. Joseph and Ida (Golemborsky) Waxman; m. Seymour Kessler, Oct. 17, 1953; children—C. Elliot, Zev A. B.A., Stanford U., 1968; M.S., San Jose

State U., 1973; Ph.D., Wright Inst., Berkeley, Calif., 1978. Lic. clin. psychologist, marriage, family and child counselor, Calif. Counseling internships, Calif., 1967-72; substitute tchr., East Palo Alto, Calif., 1969; counselor Redwood City (Calif.) Youth Corps, 1970; coordinator Mountain View (Calif.) High Sch. Drop-in Ctr., 1971-72; psychol. asst. Victor Lovell, Palo Alto, Calif., 1972-74; mem. psychol. staff Collective Psychotherapy Ctr., Palo Alto, 1972-75; pvt. practice marriage, family and child counseling, Palo Alto, 1976—, clin. psychology, 1981—; mem. faculty San Francisco State U., 1981—. Mem. Assn. Mental Health Affiliation with Israel, Alameda County Psychol. Assn., Am. Psychol. Assn., Calif. Psychol. Assn., Feldenkrais Guild (dir. 1978-81), Santa Clara County Mental Health Assn. Democrat. Jewish. Home: 770 Hilldale Ave Berkeley CA 94708 Office: 1635 Solano Ave Berkeley CA 94707

KESSLER, JERRY LEYLAN, civil engineer; b. Medford, Oreg., Oct. 25, 1935; s. Ernest Walter and Kathryn Jane (Antle) K.; B.S. in Civil Engrng., U. Idaho, 1958; M.S. in Civil Engrng. (Am. Petroleum Inst. grantee), U. Wis., 1961; m. Margaret Arlene Young, Sept. 5, 1959. Civil engr. Bechtel Corp., San Francisco, 1961-63, New Zealand, 1963-65; asst. resident engr. Sverdrup & Parcel, Inc., Bend, Oreg., 1965-66; resident engr. Harza Engrng. Co., Reykjavik, Iceland, 1967-69, Addis Ababa, Ethiopia, 1969-72; resident engr. Durham Advanced Wasterwater Treatment Plant, Stevens, Thompson & Runyan, Portland, Oreg., 1972-76; chief resident engr. Bedok Wastewater Treatment Plant, Camp Dresser & McKee Internat., Singapore, 1976-80; project engr. La Mesa Water Treatment Plant, Manila, Philippines, 1980-82; resident engr. City of Everett (Wash.) Water Treatment Plant, 1982—. Served to lt. USN, 1958-60. Registered profl. engr.; Wash., Oreg., New Zealand, Singapore. Mem. Nat. Soc. Profl. Engrs., ASCE, Oreg. Profl. Engrs., Cons. Engrs. Council, New Zealand Inst. Engrs., Inst. Engrs. Singapore. Republican. Clubs: Mason. Home: 14004 Maple Ln Milwaukie OR 97222 Office: 4055 21st Ave W Seattle WA 98199

KESSLER, LAWRENCE PHIL, psychologist, educator; b. Los Angeles, Aug. 12, 1926; s. Joseph and Sonia (Kanovitz) K.; m. Dawn, June 4, 1978; children—Craig, Carrie. B.A., UCLA, 1957; M.A., Occidental Coll., Los Angeles; Ph.D., Internat. Community Coll., Los Angeles, 1977. Lic. psychologist, Calif. Remedial tchr., counselor, psychometrist Dubnoff Sch. Ednl. Therapy, Los Angeles, 1953; tchr. retarded children Los Angeles Sch., 1954-57; tchr., counselor, psychometrist, Los Angeles Jr. High Sch., 1957-59; sch. psychologist Torrance Sch. Dist., Los Angeles, 1965-69; psychodiagnostician, psychotherapist Psychol. Guidance Ctr., Anaheim, Calif., 1959—; psychotherapist Vt. Gardens Home, Los Angeles, 1976—; prof. Los Angeles Community Coll. Dist., 1970—; pvt. practice psychodiagnostics, psychotherapy, Los Angeles. Mem. State Commn. Crime Control and Violence Prevention, Los Angeles Fedn. Community Coordinating Councils; mem. planning council United Way mental health devel. commn. Served with USN, 1944-46. Mem. Am. Psychol. Assn. (task force dir. criminal justice div.), Nat. Assn. Sch. Psychologists and Psychometrists (charter mem.), NEA, Western Psychol. Assn. Calif. State Psychol. Assn. Calif. Assn. Sch. Psychologist and Psychometrists, Calif. Tchrs. Assn., So. Calif. Group Psychotherapy Assn., Orange County Psychol. Assn., Los Angeles County Psychol. Assn., Los Angeles Humanistic Psychology Assn. Republican. Office: 855 N Vermont Ave Los Angeles CA 90029

KESSLER, MARCIA SUE, service organization executive; b. Cleve., Sept. 30, 1947; d. Max and Guta (Small) K. B.S., U. Cin., 1970; M.S., U. Oreg., 1981. Tchr., Shaker Heights (Ohio) City Schs., 1971-72; with juvenile delinquency prevention project-youth devel. program Case Western-Res. U., Cleve., 1973-75; with Women's Growth Coop., Cleve., 1976-79; guest lectr. Gestalt Inst. Cleve., 1978-79; dir. crisis services Free Med. Clinic, Cleve., 1971-79; co-leader Eugene (Oreg.) Cancer Support Group, 1980-81; dir. scheduling Ross Anthony for Congress, Eugene, 1981; coordinator/trainer vols. Womenspace-Battered Women's Shelter, Eugene, 1982—; therapist Hospice of Lane County, 1980-82; cons. child abuse, Domestic Violence Helpline, 1983—; presenter Oreg. Coalition Against Sexual and Domestic Violence Conf., 1982, numerous workshops. Trustee Community Health and Edn. Clinic, 1979-81; active Students for a Democratic Soc., 1966-73. Mem. Am. Personnel and Guidance Assn., Assn. Humanistic Psychology, Phi Sigma Sigma. Democrat. Home: 991 W 12th St Eugene OR 97402 Office: Womenspace PO Box 5485 Eugene OR 97405

KESSLER, MARY EMELINE, nurse; b. Benton, Ky., Sept. 15, 1932; d. Albert and Christine Marie (Stubblefield) Penney; m. James Patrick Kelly, Oct. 6, 1958; 1 dau., Ann Marie; m. 2d, Paul Armand Chenette, Oct. 6, 1964; children—Marie, Jacqueline, Jean-Paul; m. 3d, Irving Isadore Kessler, Aug. 24, 1974. Diploma St. Anthony Sch. Nursing, Louisville, 1954. Registered nurse, Ky., Calif. Staff nurse St. Anthony Hosp., Louisville, 1954-58, Sherman Oaks (Calif.) Community Hosp., 1960-74; staff nurse, operating room supr., freelance surgery emergency call nurse Hollywood (Calif.) Presbyterian Hosp., 1974-79; staff operating room Parkwood Community Hosp., Canoga Park, Calif., 1979-81, supr. operating room, 1981—. Mem. Assn. Operating Room Nurses. Democrat. Roman Catholic. Home: 6117 Manton Ave Woodland Hills CA Office: Parkwood Community Hosp 7011 Shoup Ave Canoga Park CA 91307

KESSLER, SHEILA, psychologist; b. Seattle; d. Chester Milton and Elouse Martha (Rogers) K.; Ph.D., U. Wash., 1971; m. Barry J. Halsted, June 1, 1973. Assoc. prof. Ga. State U., 1973-80; dir. Nat. Inst. Profl. Tng., Fountain Valley, Calif., 1975-82; dir. U. San Francisco, 1980-81; mgmt. devel. and tng. specialist Fluor Engrs., Irvine, Calif., 1981—; cons. Nat. Inst. Profl. Tng., 1975-82. Mem. exec. bd. Assn. Family Conciliation Cts. Recipient Outstanding Service award Office of Personnel Mgmt., 1975; U.S. Govt. grantee, 1975-79. Mem. Am. Mgmt. Assn., Am. Psychol. Assn. Office: M D and T Fluor Corp 3333 Michelson St Irvine CA 92730

KESTENBAUM, RICHARD, school psychologist, consultant neuropsychology; b. N.Y.C., Nov. 16, 1955; s. Ralph and Evelyn (Rose) K. B.S., SUNY-Buffalo, 1977; M.A., U. Colo., Boulder, 1979, Ph.D., 1983. Cert. sch. psychologist, Colo. Staff psychologist San Luis Valley Bd. Coop. Ednl. Services, Alamosa, Colo., 1980-81; cons. psychologist Porter Meml. Hosp., Denver, 1981; staff psychologist Jefferson County Schs., Lakewood, Colo., 1981—; instr. U. Colo., Boulder, 1982-83; pvt. practice cons. neuropsychol. psychology Boulder, 1981—; workshop lectr. nat., state, local confs. Mem. Rocky Flats Conversion Campaign, 1978-79; bd. dirs. Boulder County Youth Planning Council, 1979-80. Recipient Henry S. Loeb Brotherhood award, 1973; N.Y. State Regents scholar, 1973-77; State of Colo. grad. grantee, 1981-83, fellow, 1981-82. Mem. Am. Psychol. Assn., Nat. Assn. Sch. Psychologists, Colo. Soc. Sch. Psychologists, Psi Chi, Kappa Delta Pi. Home: 4456 Greenbriar Blvd Boulder CO 80303

KETCHAM, HENRY HOLMAN, JR., lumber executive; b. Seattle, Oct. 24, 1922; s. Henry Holman and Gena (Peters) K.; m. Nancy Kerr; children—Mary Frances, Henry H., Kathryn, Sally. B.A. in Internat. Relations, Yale U., 1944. Salesman, Blyth and Co., Portland, Oreg., 1949-53; salesman Ketcham Lumber Co., 1954-72, sec.-treas., 1954—; dir. West Fraser Timber Co., Vancouver, B.C., 1955-77, chmn., 1978—. Served with USAF, 1943-45. Clubs: Seattle Tennis; Vancouver Tennis. Home: 12267 Country Club Rd Bainbridge Island WA 98110 Office: PO Box 9887 Seattle WA 98107

KETCHERSID, WAYNE LESTER, JR., hospital laboratory administration, chemist, educator; b. Seattle, Oct. 16, 1946; s. Wayne Lester and Hazel May (Greene) K.; m. Wilette LaVerne Mautz, Oct. 6, 1972; 1 son, William Les. Staff technologist Tacoma Gen. Hosp., 1978-79, chemistry supr., 1979-81, head chemistry, 1981—. Mem. Nat. Republican Com. Served with U.S. Army, 1966-68. William E. Slaughter Found. scholar, 1975-76. Mem. Am. Assn. Clin. Chemistry, Am. Soc. Med. Tech. (cert.), Wash. State Soc. Med. Tech. (chmn. biochemistry sect. 1983—, cert. merit 1983). Lutheran. Contbr. articles to profl. jours. Home: 2906 S 274th Pl Auburn WA 98002 Office: 315 S K St Tacoma WA 98405

KETCHUM, GEORGE HENRY, petroleum co. exec., cons.; b. Albuquerque, July 31, 1910; s. James Hampton and Irene (Troutman) K.; student Compton Coll., 1929-30, UCLA, 1936-40; m. Beryle Josephine Healy, Sept. 9, 1933. With Mobil Oil Corp., 1936-74, West Coast regional land advisor, Los Angeles, asst. sec., 1966-74; asst. sec. No. Natural Gas Producing Co., N.Y.C., 1966-74; petroleum cons., 1974—; v.p. Minoco So. Corp., 80-82, Cliffwood Energy Co., 1982—; pres. Phoenix Energy Services, Inc., 1980—. Mem. adv. bd. Internat. Oil and Gas Ednl. Center of Southwestern Legal Found. Served with AUS, 1943-45. Mem. Am. (treas. 1966-67), Los Angeles (pres. 1958-59) assns. petroleum landmen, Am. Petroleum Inst., Rocky Mountain, Western (chmn. pub. lands com. Los Angeles 1963-64) oil and gas assns., Los Angeles C. of C., Petroleum Club Los Angeles. Author: Business Beneath the Seas, 1973; also profl. articles. Home: 16742 Octavia Pl Encino CA 91436

KETTEL, EDWARD JOSEPH, oil co. ofcl.; b. N.Y.C., Sept. 13, 1925; s. Harold J. and Evelyn M. (Melbourne) K.; student St. John's U., 1943; B.A., St. Francis Coll., 1949; M.A., Columbia U., 1953; m. Janet M. Johnson, Nov. 27, 1952; children—Dorothy A., David A. Ins. mgr. Arabian Am. Oil Co., 1950-56, Ethyl Corp., 1956-65; asst. treas. Atlantic Richfield Co., Los Angeles, 1965—; chmn. bd. Oil Ins., Ltd.; pres. Greater Pacific, Ltd.; dir. Am. S.S. Owners Mut. Protection and Indemnity Assn., Inc., Internat. Tanker Indemnity Assn., Ltd. Served with inf. AUS, 1943-46. Decorated Bronze Star, Purple Heart with oak leaf cluster. Mem. Am. Petroleum Inst., Mfrs. Chem. Assn., Nat. Fire Protection Assn., Risk and Ins. Mgmt. Soc. Clubs: N.Y. Athletic, Los Angeles Athletic, Palos Verdes Country. Office: 515 S Flower St Los Angeles CA 90071

KETTER, DAVID E., lawyer; b. Ft. Benning, Ga., Jan. 1, 1945; s. Victor Eugene and Ruth Maxine (Ratekin) K.; m. Sally Marian Vance, June 1, 1954. B.A. magna cum laude, Augustana Coll., Rock Island, Ill., 1967; M.A. with honors in English, U. Ill., 1969; J.D., Georgetown U., 1975. Bar: Iowa 1975, Ill. 1975, Wash. 1978, U.S. Tax Ct. 1978. Assoc. Klochau, McCarthy et al, Rock Island, Ill., 1975-77, W.V. Clodfelter, Seattle, 1977-78; owner, prin. Law Offices of David Ketter, P.S.C., 1979—. Pres. bd. trustees Conservatory Theater, Seattle; pres. Sidney Fund, Seattle. Served as 1st lt. Med. Service Corps., U.S. Army, 1969-72. Mem. Am. Bar Assn., Wash. Bar Assn., Seattle-King County Bar Assn., Ill. Bar Assn., Omicron Delta Kappa. Lutheran. Office: 1415 Park Pl Bldg Seattle WA 98101

KETTERMAN, IVAN JAY, accountant, educator; b. Lancaster, Pa., June 11, 1950; s. Warren D. and Dorothy Alberta (Sweigart) K.; m. Patricia Ann Benefiel, Dec. 23, 1972; children—Traci Lauree, Tara Lisette. B.S. in Acctg., Bob Jones U., 1972. C.P.A., Ohio, Hawaii. Auditor, U.S. Gen. Acctg. Office, Cin., 1972-74, U.S. Dept. Interior, Guam/Saipan, 1974-75; semi-sr. acct. Touche Ross & Co., Sacramento, 1975-76; supervisory auditor Red Carpet Corp. Am., Walnut Creek, Calif., 1976-77; staff, sr. acct. Peat, Marwick, Mitchell & Co., Hilo, Hawaii, 1977-81, audit supr., 1981-82; pvt. practice acctg., Kailua-Kona, Hawaii, 1982—; treas., dir. Polynesian Gifts Inc.; dir. Kona Helicopters Inc.; tchr. Kona Community Sch. Recipient Highest C.P.A. in Bus. Sch. award Wall St. Jour. Mem. Am. Inst. C.P.A.s, Hawaii Soc. C.P.A.s, Kona Coast C. of C. (treas. 1983-84). Baptist. Clubs: Kuakini Exchange (pres. 1983), Hawaii Dist. Exchange (treas. 1980-83). Home: PO Box 4689 Kailua-Kona HI 96740 Office: 75-5722 Kuakini Hwy Suite 106 Kailua-Kona HI 96740

KETTLESON, J. BENTON, safety engineer; b. St. Paul, Apr. 26, 1937; s. John B. and Dorothy Susan (Elkins) K.; m. Wanda Lee Minnix, Apr. 12, 1963; children—Sean Benton, Amy Lee. Student Macalester Coll., 1955-58; B.A. in Psychology, U. Minn., 1960. Asst. youth dir. YMCA, St. Paul, 1960; traveling passenger rep. Great No. Ry., St. Paul and Seattle, 1961; with St. Paul Fire and Marine Ins. Co., 1961—, field rep., St. Paul, 1965, prevention rep./auditor, 1966-70, state engr./auditor, Albuquerque, 1970—. Mem. Am. Soc. Safety Engrs., Ins. Auditors Assn. (Road Runners) (treas.). Home: 6221 Cuesta Pl NW Albuquerque NM 87120 Office: 2700 San Pedro NE Suite 102 Albuquerque NM 87110

KEUL, ROBERT PETER, insurance company executive; b. Kenosha, Wis., Feb. 24, 1939; s. Robert Mathew and Marcella Gertrude (Zens) K.; m. Janet Marie Kramer, Jan. 16, 1971; 1 son, Kristoffer Jason. B.S. U. Wis.-Milw., 1962. Sr. account analyst Travelers Ins. Co., San Francisco, 1967-70; asst. mktg. mgr. Frank B. Hall Co., San Francisco, 1970-72; sr. v.p. Swett & Crawford Group, Los Angeles, 1972-80; regional v.p. Montgomery & Collins, Inc., Los Angeles, 1980, pres., 1980—. Pres. Wimbledon Estates Civic Assn., 1976-78. Served to lt. USN, 1962-67. Mem. Nat. Assn. Profl. Surplus Lines Offices (bd. dirs. 1982-84), Calif. Surplus Lines Assn. (exec. com.). Republican. Club: Los Angeles. Home: 25728 Tamarisk Pl Valencia CA 91355 Office: Montgomery & Collins Inc 3807 Wilshire Blvd Suite 1010 Los Angeles CA 90010

KEVANE, RAYMOND A., career consultant, management consultant; b. Rembrandt, Iowa, Dec. 18, 1928; s. Michael and Sarah A. (Distel) K.; m. Lillian A. Schiltz, July 26, 1972; children—Karen, Mark, Mary. B.A., Loras Coll., Dubuque, Iowa, 1950; S.T.L., Gregorian U., Rome, 1954; Doctorate, Lateran U., Rome, 1957. Adminstr. social programs and assistance to disadvantaged projects, 1957-71; chief cons., assoc. dir. J. Frederick Marcy & Assocs., Portland, Oreg., 1972-78; pres., chief cons. R.A. Kevane & Assocs., Inc., Portland, 1978—. Served to capt. Army N.G., 1959-61. Mem. Am. Personnel and Guidance Assn., Portland C. of C., Nat. Vocat. Guidance Assn., Am. Mgmt. Assn. Club: City (Portland). Author: Career Development Manual, 1979; Business Procedure Manual, 1982. Office: 522 SW 5th Ave Suite 1105 Portland OR 97204

KEY, JOHN WALTER, V, soil scientist; b. San Jose, Calif., July 31, 1946; s. John Walter and Carolyn Claire (Kennedy) K.; m. Loretta Anne Bellue, Apr. 17, 1982; children—John Walter, Christopher Brooks. B.S. in Agr., Calif. Poly. State U., 1969, M.S., 1974. Cert. profl. soil scientist. Asst. ranch foreman Superior Farming Co., Bakersfield, Calif., 1974-75, research agronomist, 1975-76; soil scientist U.S. Dept. Agr. Soil Conservation Service, Bakersfield, 1976-78; soil scientist U.S. Dept. Interior Bur. Land Mgmt., Bakersfield, 1978—. Served to maj. USAR. Recipient U.S. Dept. Interior Bur. Land Mgmt. Quality Increase award, 1981. Mem. Am. Soc. Agronomy, Am. Soc. Photogrammetry, Assn. U.S. Army, Calif. Acad. Sci., Calif. Forest Soils Council, Calif. Native Plant Soc., Calif. Soil Survey Com., Ducks Unltd., Internat. Soc. Soil Sci., Res. Officers Assn. (life), Soil Conservation Soc. Am., Soil Sci. Soc. Am., Profl. Soil Sci. Assn. Calif. Contbr. articles to sci. jours. Home: 1001 Dwina Ave Bakersfield CA 93308 Office: 800 Truxtun Ave Room 311 Bakersfield CA 93301

KEY, MARY RITCHIE (MRS. AUDLEY E. PATTON), linguist, author, educator; b. San Diego, Mar. 19, 1924; d. George Lawrence and Iris (Lyons) Ritchie; student U. Chgo., 1954, U. Mich., 1959; M.A., U. Tex., 1960, Ph.D., 1963; postgrad. UCLA, 1966; children—Mary Helen Key Ellis, Harold Hayden Key, Thomas George Key. Asst. prof. linguistics Chapman Coll., Orange, Calif., 1963-66; asst. prof. linguistics U. Calif., Irvine, 1966-71, asso. prof., 1971-78, prof., 1978—, chmn. program linguistics, 1969-71, 75—; cons. Am. Indian langs., Spanish, in Mexico, 1946-55, S. Am., 1955-62, Easter Island, 1975, also English dialects, 1968-74; cons. Calif. State Dept. Edn., 1966, 70, 71, 74-75, Center Applied Linguistics, Washington, 1967, 69; lectr. in Bolivia, Chile, Germany. Recipient Friends of Library Book award, 1976; Fulbright-Hays grantee, 1975; U. Calif. Regent's grantee, 1974. Mem. AAUW, Linguistic Soc. Am., MLA, Am. Dialect Soc. (exec. council, regional sec. 1974—), Internat. Reading Assn. (dir. 1968-72), Delta Kappa Gamma (local pres. 1974-76). Author numerous books, including: Bolivian Indian Tribes, 1967; Comparative Tacanan Phonology, 1968; Male/Female Language, 1975; Paralanguage and Kinesics, 1975; Nonverbal Communication: A Research Guide and Bibliography, 1977; The Grouping of South American Indian Languages, 1979; The Relationship of Verbal and Nonverbal Communication, 1980; Catherine the Great's Linguistic Contribution, 1980; editor: Notas Lingüísticas, 1959-66; founder, editor newsletter Nonverbal Components of Communication: Paralanguage, Kinesics, Proxemics, 1972-76; editorial bd. Forum Linguisticum, 1976—, Lang. Scis., 1978—, La Linguistique, 1980—; editor (with others) Organization of Behavior in Face-to-face Interaction, 1975; contbr. articles to profl. jours. Office: Program in Linguistics U Calif Irvine CA 92717

KEY, WILLIAM GENE, health care adminstr.; b. Phoenix, Jan. 17, 1935; s. William B. and Virginia (Brown) K.; B.A., Stanislaus State U., 1972; M.A., Chapman Coll., 1974; m. Martha J. Little, May 21, 1977. Ordained to ministry, Baptist Ch., 1958; minister chs., Calif., Mex., 1959-66; adminstr. HEW, Bakersfield, Calif., 1970-72, Vis. Nurse Assn., Modesto, Calif., 1972-76; founder, exec. dir. Omnicare, Inc., health agy., Modesto, 1977—. Bd. dirs. Modesto Hospice, 1978-81, Turlock (Calif.) Emanuel Hospice, 1979-81; dir. Advocacy Com. for Disabled, Modesto, 1977-80; arbitrator Better Bus. Bur., 1978—; mem. Calif. State Democratic Party, mem. exec. com., 1981—; chmn. Stanislaus County Dem. Central Com., 1981-83. Recipient Meritorious Service award, Health Systems Agy., 1979. Mem. Calif. State Coll. Stanislaus Alumni Assn., Health Systems Agy. Democrat. Baptist. Club: Lions (chpt. pres. 1976—). Author: Psychology of Aging, 1976. Office: 726 14th St Modesto CA 95353

KEYES, JAMES BONDURANT, business consultant; b. Des Moines, May 22, 1927; s. Arthur Hyde and Dorothy (Bondurant) K.; B.S., Iowa State U., 1950; M.B.A., Northwestern U., 1951; m. Mary Jane McAfee, July 26, 1957; children—Edward, Jason. Asst. cashier Bank of Am., Los Angeles, 1952-57; profl. bus. cons. Dental Bus. Adminstrn., Laguna Beach, Calif., 1957—. Pres. Laguna Beach Community Chest, 1961-62; treas. Orange County (Calif.) United Way, 1972-74. Treas. Orange County Republican Central Com., 1960-62; pres. Young Reps., 1960-61. Served with AUS, 1945-46. Mem. Acad. Prof. Mgmt. Cons.'s (pres. 1973-74), Soc. Profl. Bus. Cons.'s (pres. 1974-75), Inst. Cert. Profl. Bus. Cons.'s, Delta Upsilon. Episcopalian. Editorial cons. Dental Mgmt. Mag., 1972—, Dental Econ. Mag. Address: 1125 Emerald Bay Laguna Beach CA 92651

KEYES, JOHN WILLIAM, air force officer; b. Schenectady, Apr. 25, 1950; s. John Aloysius and Mary Ann (Connell) K.; student Portland State U., 1970-71; B.A., U. Portland, 1973. Civil engring. technician Bur. of Pub. Rds., Portland, Oreg., 1970-73; commd. 2d lt., U.S. Air Force, 1973, advanced through grades to capt., 1977, completed initial navigator training at Mather AFB, Sacramento and Castle AFB, Merced, Calif., 1974, B52G navigator, Wing Standardization/Evaluator, Fairchild AFB, Wash., 1975-77, served with USAFR, 1977—; flight examiner, aerial delivery specialist in C-141, McChord AFB, Wash., 1977—; control tower operator FAA. Decorated Air Force Commendation medal; cert. multi-engine flight instr. for instruments. Roman Catholic. Clubs: Mt. Hood Ski Patrol, Res. Officers Assn., Nat. Ski Patrol. Home: 643 SW Burlingame Ter Portland OR 97201

KEYES, ROBERT WYATT, economist; b. Montreal, Que., May 28, 1921; s. Lorne Royce and Gladys (Wyatt) K.; B.Commerce with honors, U. Man., 1946; M.in Commerce (Kresge fellow), U. Toronto, 1950; postgrad. Toronto U., 1949-51; m. Roberta Jean McQueen, June 11, 1947; children—Robert Douglas, Nancy Joanne, Barbara Jean. Asst. sec. N.Am. Life Assurance Co., Toronto, Ont., 1946-50; economist Imperial Oil Ltd., Toronto, 1950-56; economist asst. to chmn. Man. Hydro, Winnipeg, 1956-60; chief economist Western Can. Steel Ltd., Vancouver, B.C., 1961-81; group economist Cominco Ltd., Vancouver, 1975-81; cons. economist, 1982—; instr. U. Toronto Sch. Bus., 1950-52; mem., sessional instr. dept. econs. Simon Fraser U., 1965-67, sessional lectr., 1973—. Bd. dirs., chmn. budgets United Community Services, Vancouver, 1963-66; trustee, chmn. bd. West Vancouver Sch. Bd., 1968-72; bd. dirs. Pacific NW Econ. Conf., 1971—, Ednl. Research Inst. B.C., 1969-72, chmn., 1971; mem. council, chmn. primary and energy resources com., chmn. bus. and arts com., treas. Vancouver Bd. Trade, 1973—; mem. Sci. Council B.C., 1978, chmn., 1981. Served to capt. Can. Army, 1942-45. Mem. Am., Can. econ. assns., Nat. Assn. Bus. Economists, Western Regional Sci. Assn. (dir.). Club: University (Vancouver). Mem. editorial bd. Can. Public Policy, 1974—. Home and Office: 765 South Borough Dr West Vancouver BC V7S 1N1 Canada

KHAJAVI, ABOL GHASSEM, radiologist; b. Tehran, Feb. 11, 1932; came to U.S. 1978; s. Gholam Ali and Khadijeh (Gharib) K.; m. Shirin Jabali, June 18, 1962; children—Nushin, Sharmin, Ramin. M.D., Tehran U., 1955. Diplomate Am. Bd. Radiology; cert. Calif. Bd. Med. Examiners. Resident in radiology Thomas Jefferson Hosp., Phila., 1957-61; mem. radiology staff Nemazee Hosp., Shiraz, Iran, 1961-78; chief dept. radiology NAPA State Hosp., Imola, Calif., 1978—; assoc. prof. radiology Shiraz U., 1963-78; vis. prof. radiology UCLA, 1974-75. Mem. Am. Coll. Radiology, Calif. Radiol. Soc., Redwood Empire Radiol. Soc. Contbr. articles to profl. jours.

KHAN, M. AZAM, surgeon; b. Hafizabad, Pakistan, Apr. 11, 1948; s. Mahboob Alam and Khursid (Begum) K.; M.D., King Edward Med. Coll., Lahore, Pakistan, 1970; m. Naghma Khan, Feb. 5, 1977; children— Uzma, Aqsa. Intern, Knickerbocker Hosp., N.Y.C., 1971-72; resident in surgery Misericordia Hosp., Bronx, N.Y., 1972-76; attending physician Pelham Bay Gen. Hosp. and Lincoln Hosp., Bronx, 1976-77, Mohave Gen. Hosp., Kingman, Ariz., 1977—; practice medicine specializing in gen. and vascular surgery, Kingman, 1977—; pres. med. staff Mohave Gen. Hosp., Kingman, 1983—; med. dir. Dynamic Health Services, Kingman; pres. M. Azam Khan, M.D., P.C. Diplomate Am. Bd. Surgery. Fellow Internat. Coll. Surgeons, Am. Soc. Abdominal Surgeons; mem. AMA, Ariz. Med. Assn., Mohave County Med. Soc. Republican. Contbr. research pancreatic and biliary diseases. Home: 3703 Castle Dr Kingman AZ 86401 Office: 1330 Sycamore Ave Suite C Kingman AZ 86401

KHAN, WASEEM AHMAD, business educator; b. Karachi, Pakistan, Mar. 3, 1953; s. Ghulah Ahmad and Amat-ul-Hai Khan. B.A., Forman Christian Coll., Lahore, Pakistan, 1973; M.B.A., Claremont Grad. Sch., 1976, Ph.D., 1981. Asst. prof. bus. Calif. State Coll., San Bernardino, 1979-82; assoc. prof. fin. and econs. U. So. Colo., Pueblo, 1982—; vis.

prof. bus. U. Calif., 1979—; cons. Office Tax Analysis, U.S. Dept. Treasury, Ernst and Whinney, C.P.A.s. Lincoln Found. fellow, 1977-79; Texaco Found. grantee, 1980. Mem. Am. Econ. Assn., Am. Acctg. Assn., Inst. Mgmt. Acctg., Western Econ. Assn., Fin. Mgmt. Assn. Republican. Muslim. Contbr. articles to profl. jours. Home: 60 Douglas Ln Apt 226 Pueblo CO 81001 Office: Sch Bus U So Colo Pueblo CO 81001

KHANDELWAL, UMESH CHANDRA, safety engr.; b. Agra, India, Feb. 13, 1936; s. Sukhdev Prasad and Sarla (Gupta) K.; B.Tech. in Mech. Engring., Indian Inst. Tech., Kharagpur, 1957; m. Asha Khandelwal, May 7, 1960; children—Manoj, Anuj. Design engr. Texmaco, Calcutta, India, 1957-58, Ideal Industries, Ahmedabad, India, 1959; chief engr. Khandelwal Mfg. Corp., Bombay, India, 1959-63; engr. trainee Demag A.G., Duisburg, W. Ger., 1963-64; tech. mgr. Khandelwal Mfg. Corp., Bombay, 1964-68; chief engr. Engring. Cottage Industries, Kanpur, India, 1968-70; draftsman Gaffers & Sattler, Los Angeles, 1971-72; safety engr. div. indsl. safety State of Calif., Los Angeles, 1972-73, cons. safety engr., 1973-76; sr. safety engr. UCLA, 1976-81; corp. safety and health engr. Data Products Corp., Woodland Hills, Calif., 1981—. Founder, sec. India Cultural Soc. Conejo and Simi Valley. Registered profl. engr., Calif. Mem. Am. Soc. Safety Engrs., Am. Indsl. Hygienists Assn., Soc. Fire Prevention Engrs., Nat. Fire Protection Assn., So. Calif. Indsl. Safety Soc. Home: 3378 Avenida Simi Simi Valley CA 93063 Office: 6200 Canoga Ave Woodland Hills CA 91365

KHANG, CHULSOON, economics educator; b. Kaesong City, S. Korea, May 10, 1935; s. Woon-sung and Ji-chung (Lim) K.; m. Yee Yu Lau, Sept. 15, 1959; children—Kenneth, Maurice; B.A. in Econs., Mich. State U., 1959; M.A. in Econs., U. Minn.-Mpls., 1962, Ph.D. in Econs., 1965. Asst. prof. econs. San Diego State U., 1963-66; asst. prof. econs. U. Oreg., Eugene, 1966-69, assoc. prof., 1969-73, prof. 1973—; vis. prof., research grantee U. New South Wales (Australia), 1972-73; vis. prof., Fulbright fellow Hanguk U. Fgn. Studies, Seoul, Korea 1979. Mem. Eugene Area Korean Assn. (pres.), Am. Econ. Assn. Republican. Referee, Am. Econ. Rev., Jour. Internat. Econs., Rev. Econ. Studies, Jour. Fin., Jour. Polit. Econs., Jour. Banking and Fin., Jour. Econs. and Bus., Internat. Econ. Rev.; contbr. articles to profl. jours. Home: 30 Coachman Dr Eugene OR 97405 Office: Dept Econs U Oreg Eugene OR 97403

KHASIGIAN, AMOS, economist, educator, farmer; b. Fresno, Calif., Nov. 21, 1918; m. Anna Rose Machoian, June 27, 1930; children—Paul A., Mary E. B.A., UCLA, 1950; M.A., U. So. Calif., 1958, Ph.D., 1971. Farmer, Fowler, Calif., 1961—; prof. econs. Los Angeles Pierce Coll., 1970—. Active Los Angeles council Boy Scouts Am. Served with Signal Corps, AUS, 1941-49; PTO. Mem. Am. Econ. Assn., Am. Hist. Assn., Orgn. Am. Historians, Am. Acad. Polit. and Social Sci., History of Econs. Soc., Econ. History Assn. Mem. Armenian Apostolic Ch. Club: Knights of Vartan. Home: 5647 W 64th St Los Angeles CA 90056 Office: Los Angeles Pierce Coll 6201 Winnetka Ave Room 4F02 Woodland Hills CA 91371

KHAZANIE, RAMAKANT GOVIND, mathematics educator, researcher, author; b. Goa, India, Jan. 21, 1935; s. Govind Krishna and Padmavati (Bhatcar) K.; m. Jeevan Sukerker, Sept. 7, 1975; children—Amita, Uma. M.S., Bombay U., 1957; Ph.D., Purdue U., 1964. Prof. math. Western Ill. U., 1964-65, U. Vt., 1965-69, San Diego State U., 1969-74, Humboldt State U., Arcata, Calif., 1974—. Mem. Am. Statis. Assn., Sigma Xi. Author: Introduction to Mathematics, 1974; Basic Probability Theory and Applications, 1976; Elementary Statistics in a World of Applications, 1979; contbr. research papers to Biometrika, Jour. Applied Probability, various med. jours. Home: 685 California Ave Arcata CA 95521 Office: Math Dept Humboldt State Univ Arcata CA 95521

KHO, BING KUANG, accountant, consultant; b. Indonesia, Sept. 9, 1952; s. Ah Hui and Sang Nio (Lie) K.; m. Ching Ching Wong, Mar. 5, 1978. B.S. in Acctg. (hon.), Woodbury U., 1978; degree in taxation UCLA, 1980. C.P.A., Calif. Acct., Lionel Daley & Co., C.P.A.s, 1979; sr. acct. Brown, Loyd & Stevenson, C.P.A.s, 1980-81; ptnr. Heintz & Assocs., C.P.A., Glendale, Calif., 1982—; bus. and tax cons.; columnist. Mem. Calif. Soc. C.P.A.s. Home: 3866 Torrey St Baldwin Park CA 91706 Office: 431 N Brand Blvd 306 Glendale CA 91203

KHO, JAMES WANG, computer science educator; b. Manila, Philippines, Sept. 6, 1944; came to U.S., 1966; naturalized, 1973; s. Eng-Too Lao and Lour-Chii Lim (Wang) K.; M.S., U. Wis., 1968, Ph.D., 1972; m. Joanne Jane Chan, June 22, 1976. Project and research specialist U. Wis., Madison, 1966-71; prof. computer sci. Wayne State U., Detroit, 1971-73; prof. computer sci. Calif. State U., Sacramento, 1973—, chmn. dept., 1977—; computer sci. cons. State of Calif., 1975—; lectr. in field for univs.; cons.; owner, operator import bus. Mem. Assn. Computing Machinery, Am. Inst. Decision Scis., Soc. Computer Simulation, Soc. Gen. Systems Research, Ops. Research Soc. Am., Data Processing Mgmt. Assn., Beta Gamma Sigma, Phi Kappa Phi, Pi Gamma Mu. Contbr. articles to profl. jours. Office: 6000 Jay St Sacramento CA 95819

KHOSLA, VED MITTER, oral surgeon, educator; ed. U. Cambridge (Eng.), U. Edinburgh; L.D.S., Coll. Dental Surgeons, Sask., Can., 1962; m. Santosh Ved; children—Ashok M., Siddarth M. Intern, oral surgery Selly Oak Hosp., Birmingham, 1950; resident in oral surgery Nottingham Gen. Hosp., 1957-58, Nottingham City Hosp., 1957-58; prof. oral and maxillofacial surgery U. Calif. at San Francisco, 1967—; chief oral surgery and clin. dentistry San Francisco Gen. Hosp., 1968—; dir. postdoctoral studies in oral surgery U. Calif., 1968—; cons. oral surgeon Mwanza Hosp., Govt. Tanzania, 1959-62; cons. oral surgery San Quentin State Prison, 1968—; cons. oral and maxillofacial surgeon VA Hosp., Palo Alto, Calif.; lectr. oral surgery. Fellow Royal Coll. Surgeons Edinburgh, Internat. Assn. Oral Surgeons, AAAS, Royal Soc. Health, Internat. Coll. Applied Nutrition, Internat. Coll. Dentists, Am. Coll. Dentists; mem. Brit. Assn. Oral Surgeons, Am. Dental Soc. Anesthesiology, ADA, Canadian Dental Assn., Internat. Assn. Maxillofacial Radiology, N.Y. Acad. Scis., U. Calif. Sch. Dentistry Alumni Assn., Omicron Kappa Upsilon. Club: Masons. Author, contbr. numerous tech. papers. Office: 1525 Lakeview Dr Hillsborough CA 94010

KHOTIN, LEONID, editor; b. Leningrad, USSR, July 29, 1930; s. Samuel and Alexandra (Korsunskaya) K.; came to U.S., 1975, naturalized, 1981; B.S., U. Kazan, 1950; M.S., U. Ural, 1953; m. Galina Gezintzvey, Jan. 20, 1960; 1 dau., Tanya. Instr. Russian, Def. Lang. Inst., Monterey, Calif., 1976-78; cons. dept. econs. U. Calif., Berkeley, 1979—; chief editor, pub. Soviet Emigre Press Abstracts Mag., Monterey, 1981—. Mem. Soc. Russian Jews (v.p. 1981—), Am. Assn. Advancement Slavic Studies. Home: 235 17 Mile Dr Pacific Grove CA 93950

KIDD, DAVID THOMAS, lawyer, transp. and natural resources legal exec.; b. Laramie, Wyo., Feb. 1, 1934; s. David T. and Lucille (Love) K.; student Dartmouth, 1952-55; B.A., U. Wyo., 1957, J.D., 1960; m. Sally Louise Noble, Sept. 1, 1956; children—Lynden Louise, David Thomas II. Admitted to Wyo. bar, 1960; asso. firm Brown, Healy, Drew, Apostolos & Barton, Casper, Wyo., 1960-62; mem. firm McCrary, Schwartz, Bon & Kidd, Casper, 1962-74; Western natural resources counsel Union Pacific Corp., 1974—; atty. Wyo. Ho. of Reps., 1961-62; mem. Wyo. Ho. of Reps., 1962-67; municipal judge City of Casper, 1963-68; mayor Casper, 1971; pres. Jewett-Kidd Ranches, Big Piney, Wyo., Jewett Land and Livestock Co., Big Piney & Kidd Ranches Casper and Big Piney sec.-treas., dir. Wyo. Indsl. Devel. Corp., Capital Corp. Wyo., Casper; mem. bd. litigation Mountain States Legal Found., Denver; sec.-treas., exec. com. Wyo. Coal Info. Com., Casper; Wyo. bus. leader People to People Mission, China, 1981. Trustee Wyo. Heritage Found., Cody. Mem. Petroleum Assn. Wyo. (v.p. legal), Rocky Mountain Oil and Gas Assn. (chmn. legal com.), Am., Wyo. State, Natrona County (sec.) bar assns., U. Wyo. Alumni Assn. (v.p., dir.), Sigma Chi, Pi Delta Epsilon. Republican. Club: Petroleum of Casper. Home: 2076 Willow Creek Rd Casper WY 82604 Office: 1st Interstate Bldg Casper WY 82601

KIDD, MARINA VON LINSOWE, data processing executive; b. Indpls., July 21, 1952; d. Carl Victor and Dorothy Mae (Quinn) von Linsowe; m. Russell W. Kidd, Mar. 21, 1982; 1 dau., Kira Christina von Linsowe. Student Am. River Coll., Portland State U. Verbal operator Credit Bur. Metro, San Jose, Calif. and Portland, Oreg., 1970-72; computer clk. Security Pacific Bank, San Jose, 1972-73; proof operator Crocker Bank, Seaside, Calif., 1973-74; proof supr. Great Western Bank, Portland, 1974-75; bookkeeper The Clothes Horse, Portland, 1976-78; computer operator Harsh Investment Co., Portland, 1978-79; data processing mgr. Portland Fish Co., 1979-81; data processing mgr. J & W Sci. Inc., Rancho Cordova, Calif., 1981-83; search and recruit specialist, data processing mgr. Re:Search Exec. Recruiters, Sacramento, Calif., 1983—; computer conversion cons. and tng. First violinist Am. River Orch. Recipient Bank of Am. Music award, 1970. Mem. Nat. Assn. Female Execs., Am. Mgrs. Assn., MENSA. Republican. Lutheran. Home: 3405 Jutewood Ct Sacramento CA 95826

KIDD, REUBEN PROCTOR, garage owner; b. Bedford, Va., Feb. 18, 1913; s. Oscar Kibbler and Estelle (Johnson) K.; B.S., Va. Poly. Inst., 1936; m. Margaret Jerome, June 23, 1952. Pres., Frito Corp. of Roanoke (Va.), 1947-49; indsl. engr. USAF, Sacramento, 1956-73; chmn. bd. USDR, Inc., Sacramento, 1961-69, MEN Internat., Inc., Mpls., 1977—; owner, operator Precision Tune-Up, Sacramento, 1974—. Served to capt. U.S. Army, 1942-46, to maj., 1949-51. Decorated Silver Star; registered profl. engr., Calif. Republican. Presbyterian. Home: 5809 Northgrove Way Citrus Heights CA 95610 Office: 6241 Spruce Ave Sacramento CA 95841

KIDD, VERNON GEORGE, aerospace engineer; b. Monrovia, Calif., May 26, 1927; s. Kiddson Lyles and Marquise (Klepper) K.; B.S. in Public Adminstrn., U. So. Calif., 1952, M.S. in Systems Mgmt., 1975; m. Lynn Terry, Apr. 14, 1976; 1 son, Edward George. Served as enlisted man U.S. Navy, 1945-47; commd. ensign U.S. Navy, 1952; advanced through grades to lt., 1955, ret., 1960; various tech., engring. and supervisory positions Lockheed Missiles & Space Co., 1961—, group leader base ops. Strategic Weapons Facility-Pacific, Bremerton, Wash., 1977—. Mem. IEEE, AIAA, Nat. Mgmt. Assn., Nature Conservancy, Cousteau Soc., Sierra Club (hon. life). Republican. Methodist. Club: Masons. Home: 22009 Clear Creek Rd NW Poulsbo WA 98370 Office: Box 6429 Naval Submarine Base Bangor Bremerton WA 98315

KIDDE, THOMAS SLOAN, lawyer; b. Pasadena, Calif., Apr. 26, 1950; s. Gustave Edgar and Mary Sloan (Orear) K.; grad. Phillips Acad., 1968; B.A., Stanford U., 1971; J.D., U. Calif. Hastings Coll. Law, 1974; m. Donnette Elsie Heal, Feb. 7, 1981; 1 dau., Katherine. Bar: Calif. 1974. Assoc. Macdonald, Halsted & Laybourne, Los Angeles, 1974-80, ptnr., 1980—. Mem. State Bar of Calif., Los Angeles County Bar Assn., ABA, Am. Arbitration Assn. (panel mem.), Phi Delta Phi. Republican. Episcopalian. Clubs: California; Valley Hunt; Los Angeles Athletic. Office: 1200 Wilshire Blvd Los Angeles CA 90017

KIEBERT, KERMIT V. V., contractor, educator, state senator; b. Clarkfork, Idaho, July 18, 1942; s. Kermit V. and Ruth G.V. (Coulthard) K.; m. Diane M. Kunz, Aug. 19; children—Travis J.V., Kiley V.V. B.S. in Edn., U. Idaho, 1964. Tchr. pub. schs., 1964-77; contractor, Idaho, 1977—; mem. Idaho State Senate, 1974—, now minority leader. Democrat. Home: Box 187 Spring Creek Rd Hope ID 83836

KIEFER, PATRICIA MERLENE, mfg. co. exec.; b. Dunkirk, N.Y., Sept. 28, 1946; d. Anthony Michael and Clarabelle Merline (Wardlow) Siembieda; m. David Michael Kiefer, June 9, 1973; children—Andrew Patrick, Christopher David. B.S., Calif. State U., Northridge, 1968; M.S. in Library Sci., U. So. Calif., 1969. Librarian, U.S. Army Dept. Spl. Services, Korea, Boston, 1969-73; receptionist Space Vector Corp., Northridge, Calif., 1973-74, asst. contract adminstr., 1974-76, contracts adminstr., 1976-78, dir. contracts, 1979-80, v.p., dir. contracts, 1981—. Mem. Nat. Contract Mgmt. Assn. Democrat. Roman Catholic. Home: 18729 Cohasset St Reseda CA 91335 Office: 19631 Prairie St Northridge CA 91324

KIEFERT, JAMES JOHN, educational administrator; b. Green Bay, Wis., Sept. 21, 1938; s. Michael Henry and Gertrude Mary (Cygan) K.; m. Linda Carol Kuhl, Aug. 21, 1962 (div.); children—Susan, Peter, John, Sandra, Wendy, Kamela. B.S., Wis. State U., 1960; M.Ed., U. N.D., 1965; Ed.D., U. N.D., 1967. Tchr., coach, Merrill, Wis., 1960-64; research asst. U. N.D., Grand Forks, 1965-67; prof. edn. Wash. State U., Pullman, 1967-71; asst. supt. Ednl. Service Dist. No. 121, Seattle, 1971—; adj. prof. U. Wash., Seattle, 1971-79, Seattle Pacific U., 1978-83; cons. Electro-Sci. Industries, Portland, Oreg., 1980—. Mem. Gov.'s Task Force on Edn.; scoutmaster Boy Scouts Am. Recipient Fed. Grants, 1967, 71, 73, 75, 77-83; Golden Key award Wis. Jaycees, 1963; Kettering Found. fellow, 1979, 80, 81, 82; NDEA scholar, 1965; NDEA fellow, 1966. Mem. N.W. Evaluation Assn. (pres. 1975, 82), Wash. Ednl. Research Assn. (pres. 1978), Am. Ednl. Research Assn., Am. Assn. Sch. Adminstrs., Phi Delta Kappa. Democrat. Roman Catholic. Clubs: Corinthian Yacht (Tacoma); Elks. Author: The Teaching Learning Process, 1977; Program Project Evaluation Guide, 1978. Home: 5802 Upland Terrace NE Tacoma WA 98422 Office: 1 S 200th St Seattle WA 98148

KIEHNE, ANNA MARIE, accountant, educator; b. Preston, Minn., Dec. 15, 1947; d. Alvin H. and Anna M. (Goldsmith) K. B.B.A., Winona State U.; postgrad. Calif. State U.-Los Angeles, 1974-78; postgrad. in systems analysis UCLA, 1983—. Acct. Murray Howard Realty, Los Angeles, 1974-78; staff acct. Bowest Corp., La Jolla, Calif., 1978-79; acctg. supr. Majestic Investment, Denver, 1979-81; adminstrv. acct. ECA/Intercomp. Denver, 1981-83; corp. acct. Plaza Mortgage, Los Angeles, 1983—; tchr. adult edn. Election judge, Denver; del. to primary, county, state Democratic convs., 1980, 82. Mem. Nat. Assn. Accts. (cert. in flexible budgeting and performance reporting), Nat. Assn. Female Execs.; Nat. Women's Polit. Caucus. Lutheran. Home: 944 Arroyo Dr South Pasadena CA 91030 Office: Plaza Mortgage 5615 Wilshire Blvd Los Angeles CA 90036

KIEL, PATRICIA HALL, medical equipment sales representative; b. Drexel Hill, Pa., June 14, 1942; d. Robert Coleman and Dorothy (Bidelman) Hall; m. Alan L. Kiel, Feb. 1, 1964; children—Susannah, Jennifer; m. 2d, Kenneth E. Lightle, July 7, 1979. A.A., Centenary Coll., Hackettstown, N.J., 1962; student Delaware Valley Coll., Doylestown, Pa., 1976-77, Calif. State U.-Fullerton, 1978—. Exec. sec. to product safety dir., nat. sales mgr. and v.p. mktg. Air-Shields, Hatboro, Pa., 1974-77, tech. sales rep., So. Calif., 1978, terr. sales mgr., So. Calif., 1979, area sales mgr., So. Calif., 1980—. Recipient numerous awards Air-Shields Co. Mem. Nat. Assn. Profl. Saleswomen, Nat. Assn. Female Execs. Republican. Episcopalian.

KIELMEYER, WILLIAM HENRY, research engineer; b. Columbus, Ohio, Jan. 6, 1943; s. Peter Henry and Dorothy Ruth (Potts) K.; B.S. in Ceramic Engring., Ohio State U., 1966, M.S., 1973; m. Marjorie E. Kaufman, Oct. 5, 1968; children—Cheryl A., Thomas W. Project engr. Owens-Corning Fiberglas Corp., Granville, Ohio, 1968-72; research engr. Johns-Manville Sales Corp., Littleton, Colo., 1973-78, sr. research engr., 1978—. Mem. Am. Ceramic Soc., Mineral Insulation Mfrs. Assn. Republican. Lutheran. Co-patentee process for making high-purity silica fiber for use in space shuttle reusable surface insulation; loose-fill residential insulation, comml. insulation systems. Home: 3374 W Chenango Ave Englewood CO 80110 Office: 10100 W Ute Ave Littleton CO 80123

KIELSMEIER, CATHERINE JANE, sch. adminstr.; b. San Jose, Calif; d. Frank Delos and Catherine Doris (Sellar) MacGowan; M.S., U. So. Calif., 1964, Ph.D., 1971; m. Milton Kielsmeier; children—Catherine Louise, Barry Delos. Tchr. pub. schs. Maricopa, Calif.; sch. psychologist Campbell (Calif.) Union Sch Dist., 1961-66, asst. prof. edn. and psychology Western Oreg. State Coll., Monmouth, 1966-67, 70; asst. research prof. Oreg. System Higher Edn., Monmouth, 1967-70; dir. spl. services Pub. Schs., Santa Rosa, Calif., 1972—. Bd. dirs. Sonoma County Council Community Services, 1976—, Sonoma County Orgn. for Retarded/Becoming Independent, 1978—. Mem. Council for Exceptional Children. Home: 7495 Poplar Dr Forestville CA 95436 Office: 211 Ridgeway Ave Santa Rosa CA 95402

KIENHOLZ, LYN SHEARER, arts projects coordinator, collector; b. Chgo.; d. Mitchell W. and Lucille M. (Hock) Shearer; student Sullins Coll., Md. Coll. Women. Assoc. producer Kurt Simon Prodns., Beverly Hills, Calif., 1963-65; owner, mgr. Vuokko Boutique, Beverly Hills, 1969-75; bd. dirs. Los Angeles Inst. Contemporary Art, 1976-79, Fellows of Contemporary Art, 1977-79, Internat. Network for Arts, 1979—, Los Angeles Contemporary Exhbns., 1980-82; exec. sec., bd. dirs. Beaubourg Found. (now George Pompidou Art and Culture Found.), 1977-81; visual arts adv. Performing Arts Council, Los Angeles Music Center, 1980—; bd. govs. Calif. Inst. Tech. Baxter Art Gallery, 1980—; mem. adv. bd. dirs. Fine Arts Communications, pub. Images & Issues mag., 1981—; founder, pres. bd. dirs. Calif./Internat. Arts Found., 1981—; bd. dirs., western chmn. Art Table 1983—; treas., exec. bd. Sovereign Fund.

KIEREIN, JOHN, aerospace engineer; b. South Bend, Ind., Nov. 29, 1936; s. Leo John and Norma (Shoop) K.; m. Serena Ruth Reighard, Apr. 15, 1963; children—Kathryn, Rebecca, Pamela. B.S. in Physics, U. Notre Dame, 1959; M.B.A., Ind. U., 1961. Sr. engring. planner McDonnell Douglas, St. Louis, 1963-68; supr. Skylab sci. expts. Martin-Marietta, Denver, 1968-75; mgr. spaceshuttle payload integration studies Rockwell space div., Downey, Calif., 1975-77; mgr. shuttle payload programs Ball Aerospace systems div., 1977—; dep. program mgr. Combined Release and Radiation Effects Satellite; antigravity tchr. Martin-Marietta Inst., 1973-75. Served with U.S. Army, 1961-63. Union Carbide scholar, 1955-59; recipient NASA Skylab awards, 1974. Mem. AIAA, Astron. Soc. Pacific, Am. Astronautical Soc., Planetary Soc., Assn. for Pushing Gravity Research (1st place research awards 1966, 80). Author: Kamikaze No Trump, 1977. Contbr. articles to profl. jours. Office: Ball Aerospace Systems Div PO Box 1062 Boulder CO 80306

KIERSCH, GEORGE ALFRED, geological consultant, emeritus educator; b. Lodi, Calif., Apr. 15, 1918; s. Adolph Theodore and Viola Elizabeth (Bahmeier) K.; m. Jane J. Keith, Nov. 29, 1942; children—Dana Elizabeth Kiersch Haycock, Mary Annan, George Keith, Nancy McCandless Kiersch Bohnett. Student Modesto Jr. Coll., 1936-37; B.S. in Geol. Engring., Colo. Sch. Mines, 1942; Ph.D. in Geology, U Ariz., 1947. Geologist, 79 Mining Co., Ariz., 1946-47; geologist underground explosion tests and Folsom Dam/Reservoir Project, U.S. C.E., Calif., 1948-50; supervising geologist Internat. Boundary and Water Commn., U.S.-Mex., 1950-51; asst. prof. geology U. Ariz., 1951-55; dir. Mineral Resources Survey, Navajo-Hopi Indian Reservations, 1952-55; exploration mgr. resources survey So. Pacific Co., San Francisco, 1955-60; assoc. prof. geol. scis. Cornell U., Ithaca, N.Y., 1960-63, prof., 1963-78, prof. emeritus, 1978—, chmn. dept. geol. scis., 1965-71; geol. cons., Ithaca, N.Y., 1960-78, Tucson, 1978—. Adv. council to bd. trustees Colo. Sch. Mines, 1962-71; mem. coms. Nat. Acad. Engring./Nat. Acad. Scis., 1966—. Served to capt. C.E., U.S. Army, 1942-45. Recipient award for best article Indsl. Mktg. Mag., 1964; NSF sr. postdoctoral fellow Tech. U. Vienna, 1963-64. Fellow Geol. Soc. Am. (chmn. div. engring. geology 1960-61, cert. of appreciation 1980, mem. U.S. nat. com. on rock mechanics 1980—), ASCE; mem. Soc. Econ. Geologists, U.S. Com. on Large Dams, Internat. Soc. Rock Mechanics, Internat. Assn. Engring. Geologists (U.S. com. 1980—, chmn. com. 1983—), Assn. Engring. Geologists (1st recipient Claire P. Holdredge award 1965). Republican. Episcopalian. Clubs: Cornell (N.Y.C.); Statler, Tower (Ithaca, N.Y.); Masons. Author: Engineering Geology, 1955; Mineral Resources of Navajo-Hopi Indian Reservations, 3 vols., 1955; Geothermal Steam-A World-Wide Assessment, 1964. Editor: Case Histories in Engineering Geology, 4 vols., 1963-69; editorial bd. Engring. Geology/Amsterdam. Home and Office: 4750 N Camino Luz Tucson AZ 85718

KIERULFF, STEPHEN, psychotherapist, educator; b. Los Angeles, June 17, 1942; s. Charles Taylor and Barbara Phillips (Smith K.; m. Carol Winter, June 14, 1970 (div.); 1 son, Benjamin Ernest. B.A. in Anthropology, U. Calif.-Berkeley, 1963; M.A. in Teaching, Paterson Coll., 1974; Ph.D. in Psychology, U.S. Internat. U., 1980. Clin. psychology intern Wyandotte (Mich.) Gen. Hosp., 1979; research asst. System Devel. Corp., Santa Monica, Calif., 1979; asst. prof. psychology Chapman Coll. San Diego, 1981; therapist Psychology and Psychiatry Ctr., Los Angeles, 1982-83; pvt. practice psychotherapy Beverly Hills, Calif., 1983—; cons. in field. Mem. Am. Psychol. Assn., Calif. Assn. Marriage and Family Therapists, Psi Chi. Presenter papers at profl. meetings. Home: 358 S Bentley Ave Los Angeles CA 90049

KIESCHNICK, WILLIAM FREDERICK, petroleum company executive; b. Dallas, Jan. 5, 1923; s. William Frederick and Effie Elizabeth (Meador) K.; B.S., Rice U., 1947; Certificate Physics/Meterology, U. Calif. at Los Angeles, 1943; postgrad. Scripps Inst., 1943; m. Betty Jane Camp, Sept. 25, 1948 (dec.); children—Michael Frank, Meredith Jane; m. 2d, Keithann Chapman Allen, Apr. 21, 1979. Research engr. Atlantic Richfield Co., Dallas, 1947-59, asst. to gen. mgr. exploration, 1959-61, dist. mgr. prodn. and exploration Eastern Region, Lafayette, La., 1961-63, regional mgr. dists. exploration and prodn. North Am. Producing Div., Dallas, 1963-67, v.p. synthetic fuel and mineral ops., 1967-69, v.p. ARCO Chem. Co., Phila., 1970-72, v.p. corp. planning, Los Angeles, 1972-73, exec. v.p., 1973-75, group exec. v.p. chem., fuels and transp. divs., 1975-78, vice chmn. bd., in charge of ops., 1979-81, pres., chief operating officer, 1981 , chief exec. officer, 1982 , dir., 1973—; dir. 1st Interstate Bancorp. Mem. Leadership Council, Elderhostel, Inc.; trustee Aspen Inst. Humanistic Studies, Calif. Inst. Tech.; bd. govs. Rice U.; bd. dirs. Am. Petroleum Inst.; vice chmn. Corp. Fund for John F. Kennedy Ctr. for Performing Arts; bd. dirs. So. Calif. region NCCJ; mem. exec. com. United Way; pres. bd. trustees Mus. Contemporary Art. Served to capt. USAAF, 1943-46. Decorated Bronze Star; felow Aspen Inst. Humanistic Studies. Contbr. articles to profl. jours. Office: 515 S Flower St Los Angeles CA 90071

KIESLING, HERMAN ERNST, animal nutritionist, educator; b. Miles, Tex., Jan. 23, 1938; s. Willie and Emma (Wolf) K.; student Angelo State U., 1956-58; B.S., Tex. Tech U., 1961; M.S., N.Mex. State U., 1968;

Ph.D., Okla. State U., 1972; m. Sarah L. Sofge, Aug. 24, 1962; children—Sherry Kay, Terry Gay. Mgr., P & B Feed Store, Talpa, Tex., 1962-63; tchr. vocat. agr. Fluvanna (Tex.) High Sch., 1963-66; nutritionist Taylormade Feeds, Las Cruces, N.Mex., 1972-75; asst. and asso. prof. animal sci. N.Mex. State U., Las Cruces, 1975—; nutrition cons. for beef feedlot and dairy ops., N.Mex. Mem. adminstrv. bd. Univ. United Meth. Ch., Las Cruces, 1973-75, 79-81; mem. awards com. Dona Ana County (N.Mex.) 4-H, 1977-79, chmn. com. 1978-79, project leader, 1972-80, council adviser, 1975-77, bd. dirs. fair, 1979—. Served with Army N.G., 1961-66. Named Hon. State Farmer, Future Farmers Am., Tex., 1966, N.Mex., 1978; recipient Okla. Feed Mfrs. Assn. award, 1970, Asso. Mem. award N.Mex. Alpha Zeta, 1979. Mem. Am. Soc. Animal Sci., Council Agrl. Scis. and Tech., Sigma Xi, Phi Kappa Phi. Methodist. Club: Lions (pres. club 1979-80). Contbr. numerous articles to profl. publs. Home: PO Box 1077 Mesilla Park NM 88047

KIESLING, ROY ADOLPH, JR., consumer affairs consultant, land developer; b. Houston, Mar. 11, 1934; s. Roy Adolph and Ninon (Collins) K.; B.A., Yale U., 1955; J.D., U. Tex., 1959; B.A., San Jose State Coll., 1966; m. Nancy Lou Hunt, Dec. 22, 1955 (div. 1975); children—Eugenia Collins, John Brady, Stephen Howard, Roy Adolph; m. 2d, Ann Adrian, Aug. 7, 1980. Research contract adminstr. Lockheed Missiles & Space Co., Sunnyvale, Calif., 1960-62, systems test engr., 1966-69; staff mem. Zero Population Growth, Los Altos, Calif., 1969-70; cons. environ. and consumer affairs, Palo Alto, Calif., 1970—. Past pres. Consumer Fedn. Calif., Consumers Co-op Palo Alto. Lic. real estate broker, Calif. Mem. Tex. Bar Assn. Address: 97 Douglass Way Atherton CA 94025

KIESSLING, GERD, sales rep.; b. Duerrenberg, Germany, May 8, 1942; came to U.S., 1966, naturalized, 1976; s. Alfred Ernst and Helene Paula (Wiese) K.; student Interpreter Sch., Cologne, Germany, 1961-63, Acad. Bus. and Econs., Cologne, 1961-66, U. Evansville, 1966-67; m. Carole Judy Cook, Jan. 25, 1969; m. 2d, Mary K. Schnitker, Dec. 8, 1981. Export sales specialist heavy steel forgings Wuppermann, Ltd., Leverkusen, Germany, 1961-63; prodn. control ofcl. Ford Motor Co. of Germany, Cologne, 1963-66; auditor Fruehauf Corp., Detroit, 1967-68, material controller, 1968-70; material cost analyst Ford Motor Co. of Europe, Cologne, 1971-74; purchasing agt Telemation, Inc., Salt Lake City, 1974-75; realtor asso. Ken Mayne, Inc., Salt Lake City, 1975-78; sales rep. Cline's Mazda, Murray, Utah, 1978—. Mem. Nat. Right to Work Com. Mem. Am. Security Council (nat. adv. bd.). Republican. Mormon. Club: Bonneville Kiwanis (Salt Lake City). Research on ops. cost control. Home: 258 W Benson Way Sandy UT 84070 Office: 4528 S State St Murray UT 84107

KILBOURNE, BECKY ANNE, utility adminstr.; b. Albuquerque, Apr. 5, 1954; d. H. Wells and S.V. K.; B.B.A. in Acctg., U. N.Mex., 1976, M.B.A. in Fin., 1980. Plant and property acct. Public Service Co. of N.Mex., Albuquerque, 1977-78, auditor, 1978-80, acct., 1980-82, sr. rate analyst, supr. regulatory affairs, 1982—. Cert. mgmt. acct. Mem. Inst. Mgmt. Acctg., Nat. Assn. Accts., Alpha Chi Omega. Republican. Home: 10219 Oso Grande NE Albuquerque NM 87111 Office: PO Box 2267 Albuquerque NM 87103

KILBOURNE, THOMAS CHAMBERLAIN, manufacturing executive; b. Shiloh Valley, Ill., Jan. 1, 1947; s. Philip Alward and Phyllis (Chamberlain) K.; m. Joan Kennedy, Apr. 9, 1982; 1 son, Peter Michael. B.S. in Human Relations and Organizational Behavior, U. San Francisco, 1982. Ptnr. Electronic Acoustic Research, San Jose, Calif., 1970-71; engr. Solid Sound, Hollywood, Calif., 1971-72; electronic technician Singer Instrumentation, Palo Alto, Calif., 1973-75; test supr. Wiltron Co., Mountain View, Calif., 1975-76, prodn. control supr., 1976-77, test mgr., 1977-81, mfg. mgr., 1981—. Facilities planner Morgan Hill Bus. Park. Served with Air Def. Arty., U.S. Army, 1966-69. Mem. Am. Prodn. and Inventory Control Soc. Office: 825 E Middlefield Rd Mountain View CA 94042

KILBURN, CANDACE HALLMAN, retail company executive; b. Chgo., Sept. 10, 1953; d. Donald Joseph and Anita Jane (Grubb) Hallman; m. Randall Richard Kilburn, May 31, 1975. B.S. in Bus. summa cum laude, U.S. Internat. U., 1975; M.B.A., Chapman Coll., 1977; cert. in personnel mgmt. U. Calif.-San Diego, 1982. Sales cons. Buffums' of So. Calif., San Diego, 1970-75; audit coordinator Handyman of Calif., Inc., San Diego, 1975-77, mgr. tng. and devel., 1977-79, dir. human resources, 1979—; tng. cons. Edison Bros. Stores, St. Louis. Vol. worker Children's Mus. San Diego. Mem. Am. Soc. for Tng. and Devel., Am. Soc. Personnel Adminstrs., Personnel Mgmt. Assn., Internat. Assn. Bus. Communcators. Republican. Methodist. Club: San Diego Ski.

KILGORE, EUGENE STERLING, JR., surgeon; b. San Francisco, Feb. 3, 1920; s. Eugene Sterling and Mary (Kirkpatrick) K.; m. Marilynn H. Wines, June 23, 1950; children—Eugene Sterling III, Marilynn Ann Bee. B.S., U. Calif.-Berkeley, 1941; M.D., U. Calif.-San Francisco, 1949. Intern medicine Harvard service Boston City Hosp., 1949-50; intern surgery Roosevelt Hosp., N.Y.C., 1950-51, resident gen. surgery, reconstructive hand surgery, 1951-55; practice medicine specializing in surgery and reconstructive hand surgery, San Francisco, 1955—; asso. clin. prof. surgery U. Calif.-San Francisco, 1955-75, clin. prof., 1975—; chief hand surgery, dept. surgery U. Calif. Hosp., also San Francisco Gen. Hosp., 1965—; chief hand service Ft. Miley VA Hosp., San Francisco, 1965—, Martinez (Calif.) Vets. Hosp., 1970—, Livermore (Calif.) VA Hosp. 1965—; chief hand service plastic surgery tng. service St. Francis Meml. Hosp., 1965—, chief surgery, 1979—; cons. hand surgery numerous private hosps., San Francisco, 1955—. Served to lt. col. inf. AUS, 1941-45. Decorated Bronze Star medal. Recipient Gold Headed Cane, AOA medal; Kaiser award for excellence in teaching U. Calif. San Francisco Sch. Medicine, 1976. Mem. AMA, A.C.S., Am. Assn. Surgery of Trauma, Am. Trauma Soc., Am. Soc. Surgery of Hand, Carribean Hand Soc., San Francisco Surg. Soc. (pres. 1979-80), Pacific Coast Surg. Assn. Rotarian. Club: Bohemian (San Francisco). Author numerous publs. in field. Office: 450 Sutter St San Francisco CA 94108

KILGORE, MARGARET ADELAIDE, public relations director, writer; b. Ravenna, Ohio, Mar. 1, 1935; d. Alfred D. and Donna Page (Voorhees) K. A.A., Stephens Coll., 1955; B.A., Syracuse U., 1957; M.B.A., Pepperdine U., 1982. Reporter, editor UPI, 1957-73; reporter Los Angeles Times, 1973-79; asst. v.p. pub. relations Caesars World, Inc., Los Angeles, 1979-82; regional dir. communications Ernst & Whinney, Los Angeles, 1982—; lectr. in field. Bd. dirs. Santa Monica YWCA. Named Outstanding Alumnae, Stephens Coll., 1977; Ford Found. Walter Lippman Fellow, 1976. Mem. Pub. Relations Soc. Am., Washington Press Club (pres. 1968-69), Sigma Delta Chi, Delta Delta Delta. Contbr. numerous articles to popular mags.

KILIAN, AUSTIN F., art educator, artist; b. Lyons, S.D., Sept. 19, 1920; s. Ward Van and Mabel A. Kilian; m. Elizabeth J.; children—Michael, Amy. B.A. in Art, Augustana Coll., Sioux Falls, S.D., 1942; M.F.A. in Drawing, State U. Iowa, Iowa City, 1949; postgrad. Atelier Fernand Leger, Paris, 1951, Mexico City Coll., 1952, Ohio State U., 1953-55. Instr. U. Idaho, Moscow, 1949-50, Dillard U., New Orleans, 1950-53; assoc. prof. Baylor U., Waco, Tex., 1953-59; asst. prof. Calif. Western U., San Diego, 1959-64; prof. Woodbury U., Los Angeles, 1964-66; prof. art Coll. of the Desert, Palm Desert, Calif., 1970—; wardrobe man Ringling Bros., Barnum and Bailey Combined Shows, 1948; dir. Art in All Media Exhbn., So. Calif. Expn., Del Mar, 1963-67; one-man shows: Athenaeum, La Jolla, Calif., 1961; Stephen F. Austin State Coll., Nacogdoches, Tex., 1957; Baylor Theater, Waco, 1955; Terry Nat. Art Exhbn., Miami, 1952; Art Assn. New Orleans, 1953-56; Tex. Fine Art Assn., Austin, 1953-59; Cedar City (Utah) Exhbn., 1957; D.D. Feldman Collection of Contemporary Art, Dallas, 1955-58; Art Ctr. in La Jolla, 1960; Inland Empire Community Coll., San Bernardino, Calif., 1981. Pres., San Diego Art Guild, 1962-63; bd. dirs. Mus. Contemporary Arts, Waco, 1959; citizens coordinator San Diego Planning Comm., 1963. Served with Combat Engrs., AUS, 1942-45. Mem. Palm Springs Mus. Art, Art Historians of So. Calif., 39th Engrs. Combat Regiment Assn. Home: 3720 Wawona Dr San Diego CA 92107 Office: 73286 Juniper St Palm Desert CA 92260

KILKENNY, WILLIAM H., industrial equipment manufacturing company executive; b. 1919. Grad. Willamette U.; postgrad. Harvard U. Grad. Sch. Bus., MIT. With Hyster Co., Portland, Oreg., 1946—, mgr. Los Angeles retail br., 1949, mgr. Danville plant, 1960, corp. v.p., 1962, exec. v.p., 1967, exec. v.p., chief ops. officer, 1970, pres., chief ops. officer, 1971, pres., chief exec. officer, 1975, chmn. bd., chief exec. officer, 1976, also dir.; dir. Omark Industries Inc., Jantzen Inc., Bancal Corp., Bank of Calif., No. Specialty Sales Inc. Trustee Willamette U. Office: Hyster Co 700 NE Multonomah St PO Box 2902 Lloyd Bldg Portland OR 97208*

KILLAM, ROBERT CRAIG, JR., data tech. cons.; b. Honolulu, June 2, 1945; s. Robert Craig and Jane (Winn) K.; A.B., U. Puget Sound, 1969; m. Erin Cook, Aug. 30, 1969; 1 son, Keith Scott. Gen. mgr. Pacific Laundry-Maui div. Island Service Industries (Hawaii), 1969-78; pres. Aeolean Industries Inc., Lahaina, Hawaii, 1978-82; systems analyst C & E Cons., Lahaina, 1982—; cons. computer sales and data processing. Mem. Am. Mgmt. Assn., Textile Rental Assn. Am. Club: Elks. Home: 418 Front St Lahaina HI 96761 Office: 418 Front St Lahaina HI 96761

KILLEBREW, DAVID SCOTT, physician; b. Indpls., Jan. 27, 1939; s. Clarence E. and Ruth V. (Vinson) K.; A.B., Coll. Wooster, 1962; M.S., U. Mich., 1964, M.D., 1973; m. Peggy A. Starr, July 22, 1977; children—Steven, Allen, Brian, Nicole. Resident in surgery Jewish Hosp., St. Louis, 1973-74; resident in otorhinolaryngology Barnes Hosp., St. Louis, 1974-78; practice medicine specializing in otorhinolaryngology, Great Falls, Mont., 1978—. Mem. AMA, Am. Council Otorniolaryngology, Am. Council Facial Plastic and Reconstructive Surgeons, Mont. Med. Assn. Republican. Club: Meadowlark Country. Home: RR Box 5409 Great Falls MT 59401 Office: Suite 8 1300 28th St Great Falls MT 59405

KILLERMANN, ROSEMARY DONOVAN, technology cons. co. exec.; b. Chgo., Apr. 24, 1929; d. Timothy V. and Mabel (Hederman) Donovan; student Fla. So. U., U. Wis., Northwestern U.; children—Adam, Mark, Lisa, Stephen, Kevin, Jeffrey, Susan. With Intercon Research Assos. Ltd., Evanston, Ill., 1965-79, technology cons., Ft. Collins, Colo., 1979—; lectr. in field. Mem. Licensing Exec. Soc. Office: Intercon Research Assos 1304 Hillside St Fort Collins CO 80524

KILLHAM, KENNETH STUART, microbiologist, consultant; b. Liverpool, Eng., Mar. 1, 1957; came to U.S., 1981; s. Bryan and Norma Lilliam (McClure) K. B.S. 1st Class, Sheffield U. (Eng.), 1981; Ph.D. in Microbiology, 1981. Research microbiologist U. Calif.-Berkeley, 1981—; cons. to EPA; instr. biochemistry U. Calif.-Berkeley. Regional leader Brit. Conservation Corps, 1980; chmn. Environ. Sci. Soc., 1977-78. Recipient Brit. Natural Environment Research Council award, 1978-81; Bramley award for Outstanding Research, 1981. Mem. Inst. Biology, Am. Soc. Microbiology, Am. Soc. Agronomy. Mem. Ch. of England. Contbr. articles to profl. jours. Home: 706 The Alameda Berkeley CA 94707 Office: Dept Plant and Soil Biology U Calif Berkeley CA 94720

KILLMASTER, JOHN HENRY, III, artist, educator; b. Allegan, Mich., Dec. 2, 1934; s. John H. and Ora Mae (Backus) K.; m. Linda Aileen Olson, Mar. 27, 1965; m. 2d, Jeanette Esther Hendricks, May 15, 1971; children—Dana, Karen, John Henry IV. B.A. cum laude, Hope Coll., Holland, Mich., 1968; M.F.A., Cranbrook Acad. Art, Bloomfield Hills, Mich., 1969. Artist, designer Ambrose Assocs., 1953-56, LaDriere Inc., Detroit, 1957-62; asst. prof. art Ferris State Coll., Big Rapids, Mich., 1966-67, 69-70; prof. art Boise State U., 1970—; important works include: exterior mural Boise Gallery of Art, 1974; sculpture City of Portland, 1977; lobby mural Morrison Knudsen Corp., Boise, 1982; wall sculpture Idaho First Nat. Bank, 1980. Recipient Gov.'s award for excellence in the arts State of Idaho, 1978; Western States Art Found. grantee, 1975. Mem. Nat. Enamelist Guild, Idaho Art Assn., N.W. Designers and Craftsmen. Home: 220 Cotterell St Boise ID 83709 Office: 1910 University Dr Boise ID 83725

KILLMER, DONALD EDWARD, computer systems company executive; b. Charlotte, N.C., Dec. 19, 1938; s. Donald Franklin and Grace Emily (Elliott) K.; m. Melinda Jane Bock, Oct. 25, 1974; stepchildren—Rodrigue, Christopher, Kevin. B.S. in Math., N.Mex. State U., 1961. Sci. programmer, phys. sci. lab. N.Mex. State U., 1960-62; mgr. flight ops. Astromet div. Thiokol Co., Ogden, Utah, 1964-65; sr. engr. Litton Data Systems, Van Nuys, Calif., 1965-67; pres. Elliott Data Systems Inc., N.Y.C., 1967-72; mgr. systems programming United Computing Corp., Carson, Calif., 1972-78; pres. Creative Software Systems Co., Fountain Valley, Calif., 1978—; cons. Served to 1st lt. U.S. Army, 1962-64. Methodist. Home: 18813 Santa Isadora St Fountain Valley CA 92708

KILLMER, WAYNE EVERETT, television executive; b. Minot, N.D., Oct. 6, 1928; s. Marion Dennis and Agnes Ovidia (Nybakken) K.; m. Shirley Anne Carvo, Aug. 12, 1951; m. 2d, JoAnn Croft, Nov. 21, 1959; children—Rich, Kristi, Bradley, Michael. B.A., U. Wash., 1951; postgrad. Nat. Assn. Broadcasters seminars Harvard U. Grad. Sch. Bus., 1967, 68. With Sta. KELA, Centralia, Wash., 1951-53, Sta. KALE, Richland, Wash., 1953-55; owner Sta. KODI, Cody, Wyo., 1955-59; gen. sales mgr. Sta. KULA, Honolulu, 1959-61; gen. mgr. Sta. KGMB-AM-TV, Honolulu, 1961-65; v.p., gen. mgr. Sta. KIRO AM-FM, Seattle, 1965-72; gen. mgr. Sta. KGVO-TV, Missoula, Mont., 1975-77; Sta. KCFW-TV, Kalispell, Mont., 1975-77; Sta. KTVM-TV, Butte, Mont., 1975-77; gen. sales mgr. Sta. KULR-TV, Billins, Mont., 1977-78; v.p., gen. mgr. Sta. KBAK-TV, Harriscope Broadcasting Corp., Bakersfield, Calif., 1978—. Active Concerned Citizens for Quality Edn., Republican Presdl. Task Force. Served to lt. USAF, 1952-53. Recipient Man of Year award Honolulu Advt. Club, 1962; Golden Mike award So. Calif. Radio and TV News Dirs. Assn., 1982. Mem. Nat. Assn. Broadcasters, Nat. Assn. TV Programming Execs., Broadcast Promotion Assn., Calif. Broadcasters Assn., Bakersfield C. of C. Republican. Mormon. Clubs: Rotary, Elks, Stockdale Country (Bakersfield). Office: 1901 Westwind Dr Bakersfield CA 93301

KILLOUGHEY, DONNA MARIE, lawyer; b. Chgo., Nov. 27, 1949; d. John Joseph and Gertrude A. (Smith) K.; m. Gary Eugene Bird, June 12, 1982. B.A. in Secondary Edn., DePaul U., 1971; J.D., Ariz. State U., 1978. Bar: Ariz. 1979. Jud. clk. to judge Ariz. Ct. Appeals, 1979—; assoc. firm McGowan & Johnson, Phoenix, 1979-81, ptnr., 1982—; speaker in field. Recipient Dean's award for leadership and service, 1978. Mem. ABA (legal econs. com.), State Bar Ariz. (legal econs. com., com. on legal services for elderly), Maricopa County Bar Assn., Nat. Order of Barristers, Assn. Trail Lawyers Am., Ariz. Trial Lawyers Assn., Ariz. State U. Coll. of Law Alumni Assn. (bd. dirs.), Phoenix C. of C. (small bus. com.). Contbr. writings in field to profl. publs.

KILPATRICK, BEVERLY AVIS, advertising/public relations executives; b. Sacramento, Mar. 1, 1936; d. Frank and Irene J. (Avis) Bernardo; m. Joseph W. Kilpatrick, June 7, 1958; 1 son: Joseph Warren. Ed. Sacramento State Coll. Tchr., Lakeland Sch. Dist., Goldwater, Mich., 1960-61; copywriter Sta. WTVB Radio, Angola, Ind., 1961; dep. Unemployment Dept., State of Ind., Ft. Wayne, 1961-63; copywriter/prodn. Sta. KXRQ Radio, Sacramento, 1963-65; media dir. Dannenfelser, Runyan & Craig, Inc., 1965-73; v.p., sec.-treas. Boyle/Kilpatrick & Assocs., Modesto, Calif., 1973—; dir. Stanislaus Media and Advt. Club, 1976-78. Vice chmn. Modesto Selective Service Bd., 1982—; v.p. bd. dirs. Stanislaus County MCA, 1976-79; sec. bd. dirs. Bldg. Industry Assn. Central Calif., 1979-82; bd. dirs. Stanislaus County United Way, 1982—, Scenic Gen. Hosp. Found., 1982—; exec. bd. Valley Video Network for Community TV, 1979-81, others. Recipient YMCA Appreciation for Service to Youth plaque, 1978; Bldg. Industry Assn. of Central Calif. Assoc. of Yr., 1980. Mem. Network, Nat. Assn. Female Execs. Clubs: Cabrillo Civic, Modesto Trade (dir.), Soroptimist (past pres. Modesto). Home: 1708 Plaza De San Joaquin Modesto CA 95350 Office: 1226 11th St Suite C Modesto CA 95354

KILPATRICK, FRANK STANTON, publishing and communications executive; b. San Jose, Calif., Dec. 2, 1950; s. Frank George and Marian (Polk) K.; B.A., U. Calif., Berkeley, 1975, postgrad., 1976; student U. Wis., 1968-71, Stanford U. Grad. Sch. Bus., 1981. Successively writer, advt. sales rep., Midwest regional mgr., Western mktg. mgr. 13-30 Corp., pub. Esquire mag., 1970-74; with Grey Advt., 1977; mktg. mgr. East/West Network, 1978-79; mktg. dir. Calif. Bus. mag., Los Angeles, 1979-81; v.p. mktg. Laufer Co. div. Harlequin Enterprises, 1981; mgr. new venture devel. Knapp Communications Corp. (pub. Archtl. Digest, GEO, Bon Appétit and Home mags.), 1981—; co-gen. ptnr. Pacific Cellular, 1982—; gen. ptnr. Calif. Coast Communications, 1981—. Mem. Los Angeles Advt. Club (Belding award 1980), Direct Mktg. Assn., Town Hall, U. Calif. Alumni Assn., Stanford Bus. Sch. Alumni Assn. Home: 1302 N Harper Ave Los Angeles CA 90046 Office: 5900 Wilshire Blvd Suite 2900 Los Angeles CA 90036

KILPATRICK, MELL WILTON, production engineer; b. Santa Ana, Calif., Oct. 14, 1927; s. Mell Wilton and Katherine Eliza (Woodworth) K.; m. Sarah Ann Beatty, June 15, 1952; 1 son, Kent Alan. Student Santa Ana Jr. Coll., 1949-51. With The Register, Santa Ana, 1949—, prodn. mgr., 1970—; adv. bd. Fullerton (Calif.) Jr. Coll. Served with U.S. Army, 1945-48. Mem. Western Newspaper Prodn. Conf. (charter). Episcopalian. Clubs: Elks, Irvine Coast Country. Office: 625 N Grand Ave Santa Ana CA 92705

KILSBY, MARY ELLEN GREEN, minister, lecturer; s. Los Angeles, June 20, 1934; d. Lester Eugene Green and Mary Anna (Erickson) Green; m. Graham Perry Kilsby, Feb. 11, 1956; children—Mary Kathleen Kilsby Dunstan, Richard Perry, Christi Ann, Robin Lynn. B.A., Pomona Coll., 1956; M. Rel., M. Div., Sch. Theology Claremont, 1975, D. Min., 1978. Ordained to ministry United Methodist Ch., 1975. Asst. pastor Claremont United Meth. Ch., 1975; assoc. pastor Claremont United Ch. of Christ, 1975-82; sr. minister Altadena (Calif.) United Ch. of Christ, 1982—; lectr. Sch. Theology, Claremont, Calif. Trustee Claremont Unified Sch. Dist., 1970-78, pres. 1976-78; del. Calif. Sch. Bds. Assn.; bd. dirs. So. Calif. Conf. United Ch. of Christ, 1980-82. Recipient So. Calif. Sch. Theology at Claremont Wilshire Preaching award, 1978. Home: 470 Blaisdell Dr Claremont CA 91711 Office: 943 E Altadena Dr Altadena CA 91001

KILZER, FRANK JAMES, chemist, educator; b. Milw., Oct. 18, 1933; s. Albert Alphonse and Catherine Mary (Strubert) K.; B.S., U. Calif., Berkeley, 1956; Ph.D., Iowa State U., 1962; children—Sharon A., Paul J. DuPont teaching fellow Iowa State U., 1959-60; chemist, sr. scientist U.S. Forest Service, U.S. Dept. Agr., 1962-68; instr. Cabrillo Coll., 1968-69, Feather River Coll., Quincy, Calif., 1969—, Peralta Community Coll. Dist., sabbatical leave, 1977-78. Mem. Am. Chem. Soc., AAAS, Sigma Xi, Phi Lambda Upsilon. Contbr. sect. to book, articles to profl. jours. Office: Feather River College Box 1110 Highway 70 N Quincy CA 95971

KIM, CHONG CHOL, physicist, educator; b. Seoul, Korea, Nov. 6, 1918; s. Kook Bae and Byong Ok (Kong) K.; came to U.S., 1954, naturalized, 1963; B.S. in Physics, Keijo Imperial U., 1944; Ph.D., U. Iowa, 1960; m. Marguerite Sangju Kim, Nov. 14, 1943; children—William C., Michael E. Asst. physics Keijo Imperial U., 1944-45; lectr. Kyung Sung U., 1945-46; mem. faculty Nat. Seoul U., 1946-57, assoc. prof. physics, 1954-57, head dept., 1953-54, head acad. affairs Coll. Liberal Arts and Scis., 1953-54; research assoc. U. Iowa, 1960; research assoc. U. So. Calif., 1960-69, sr. research physicist, 1969-72, dir. undergrad. physics lab., 1969-76, dir. physics lecture demo. lab., 1976—; cons. Sci. Museum, Seoul, Korea. Grantee Am. Korean Found., 1954. Fellow Korean Phys. Soc.; mem. Am. Phys. Soc., Korean Scientists and Engrs. Assn., Sigma Xi. Home: 3563 Twin Lake Ridge Westlake Village CA 91361 Office: Physics Dept Univ So Calif Los Angeles CA 90007

KIM, DEWEY HONGWOO, public service consultant; b. Washington, July 4, 1928; s. Henry Cu and Edith (Ahn) K.; B.A. with honors, U. Hawaii, 1950; M.P.A. with highest distinction, Maxwell Sch., Syracuse (N.Y.) U., 1961; LL.D. (hon.), Myong Ji U., Seoul, Korea, 1981; m. Lila Lee, Mar. 10, 1951; children—Melissa, Dewey Hongwoo, Michael. Personnel officer 14th Coast Guard Dist., 1953-54; with IRS, 1956-68, dir. mgmt. tng., 1966-68; asso. dean Coll. Continuing Edn., U. Hawaii, 1968-70, asst. v.p. acad. affairs, 1970-78, vice-chancellor for community colls., 1978-80, chancellor community colls., 1980-83, chancellor emeritus, 1983—; dir. Pacific and Asian affairs Pub. Adminstrn. Service, 1983—; mgmt. cons., 1960—; dir. Island Fed. Savs. & Loan Assn., 1st Fed. Savs. & Loan Assn. Exec. asst. Honolulu Fed. Exec. Bd., 1967—; chmn. Hawaii Task Force Police and Public Protection, 1970-74; commr. Accrediting Commn. Jr. and Community Colls. Trustee U. Hawaii Found., 1972-82. Recipient awards IRS, 1958, 59, 67, 68; William E. Mosher fellow, 1960-61. Mem. Am. Soc. Pub. Adminstrn. (pres. Honolulu 1959), Honolulu Fed. Businessmen's Assn., Western Assn. Schs. and Colls. (chmn. and pres. 1981-83), Phi Kappa Phi.

KIM, HARRY HYUNKIL, urban geographer; b. Seoul, Korea, Jan. 17, 1938; came to U.S., 1964, naturalized, 1971; s. Yoon Ha and Saeng Kun (Chong) K.; M.A., U. Wash., Seattle, 1967, Ph.D., 1972; m. Jiyon Kim, May 9, 1970; children—Peter H., Hanna H. Urban planner II, King County Planning Commn., Seattle, 1972-74; prof. U. South Fla., Tampa, 1974-79; housing mgmt. asst. U.S. Dept. HUD, Seattle, 1979—; Fulbright scholar, India, 1978; cons. urban environment, water/solid waste; lectr. urban geography, community devel., housing mgmt. to profl. and civic groups. Bd. dirs. program agy. Presbyn. Ch. U.S.A. Served with Korean Army, 1960-62. Fla. State Energy Office grantee, 1976. Mem. Assn. Am. Geographers, Nat. Geog. Soc., Am. Geog. Soc., Presbyn. Housing Assn. (pres.), Presbyn. Ministry Inc. (bd. dirs.), Seattle-Wash. Korean Assn. (chmn. bd. dirs. 1982), Tampa Korean Assn. in Fla. (pres. 1976). Republican. Presbyterian (staff personnel com. Synod of Alaska-N.W., mem. strategy com. dept. mission and evangelism Presbytery of Seattle). Contbr. articles to profl. jours. Home: 4239 NE 74th St Seattle WA 98115 Office: HUD 1321 2d Ave Seattle WA 98101

KIM, JOYCE YOUNG, optometrist; b. Seoul, Korea, Aug. 18, 1954; came to U.S., 1971, naturalized, 1981; d. Tom H.S. and Rohi (Park) Shin; m. Dennis H.J. Kim, Aug. 8, 1981. B.A., U. Calif.-Berkeley, 1977; O.D.,

Pacific U., 1981. Pvt. practice optometry, San Jose, Calif., 1981—. Mem. Santa Clara County Optometric Assn., Calif. Optometric Assn., Am. Optometric Assn. Democrat. Baptist. Home: 21060 Filora Vista Cupertino CA 95014 Office: 1711-D Hamilton Ave San Jose CA 95125

KIM, KEITH, freight forwarding co. exec.; b. Seoul, Korea, Oct. 11, 1935; s. Rinsuk and S.E. (Chu) K.; came to U.S., 1953, naturalized, 1969; A.A., Los Angeles City Coll., 1955; B.A., Los Angeles State Coll., 1957; m. Theresa Lee, Sept. 5, 1968; children—Dominick, Glenn. Import mgr. Judson Sheldon Internat. Corp., Los Angeles, 1965-69; import mgr. P.I.E. Transport, Inc., Inglewood, Calif., 1969-70; v.p. Shiloh Internat., Inc., Los Angeles, 1970-76, pres., 1976—; corporate v.p., cons. Dunbar Customs Services, Inglewood, 1973-77; pres. Alpha Cargo Service, 1978—. Licensed customshouse broker U.S. Treasury Dept. Home: 28523 Rothrock Dr Rancho Palos Verdes CA 90274 Office: 1222 E Imperial Ave El Segundo CA 90245

KIM, LAUREEN OK SUN, human relations administrator; b. Honolulu, Jan. 22, 1955; d. Alfred Kui Dong and Laura Kam Chin (Luke) K. A.B. in Psychology, Stanford U., 1977. Counselor, mem. admissions com. Grad. Sch. Bus., Stanford U., 1977-81, admissions office supr., 1980-81; mgr. personnel Silvar-Lisco, Palo Alto, Calif., 1981—; instr. seminar Stanford U., 1974. Counselor, advisor Collective Rehab. Clinic, Palo Alto, 1972-73. Office: 1801 Page Mill Rd 220A Palo Alto CA 94304

KIM, PUM KI, exporter; b. Seoul, Korea, Dec. 28, 1938; s. Jin Won and Chon (Park) K.; m. Gill Ah, June 30, 1972; children—Bonny, Grant, Ann. Student Am. U. Pres., Arm-Kor Hide Co., Inc., Los Angeles, 1971—. Mem. U.S. Hide, Skin and Leather Assn. Office: 3600 Wilshire Blvd Suite 1726 Los Angeles CA 90010

KIMBALL, DICK (CHARLES RICHARD ROBATOR), organist, educator; b. Essex, Mass., June 19, 1937; s. Lionel William and Viola May (Kimball) R.; A.A., Seattle Community Coll., 1981; div.; children—Julie Marie, Carson Leonard. Organist, cocktail lounges, Helena, Mont., 1959-61, Everett and Seattle, 1961-69; organ instr. Holiday Music Co., Seattle, 1971-78, Evans Music Co., Seattle, 1980-82, Sherman-Clay Co., San Francisco, 1982—; organist Seattle Totems Hockey Club, 1973-75, Seattle Supersonics basketball, 1974-75, Seattle Sounders Soccer Club, 1976-78, Seattle Mariners Baseball Club, 1977-82. Mem. Am. Fedn. Musicians, Am. Theatre Organ Soc. Record album: A Natural Man. Home: 22 Gardenside Dr #14 San Francisco CA 94131

KIMBALL, JESSIE LOURRAINE, tour director; b. Elko, Nev., Nov. 15, 1930; d. Louis Frederick and Winifred Ruth Kelley (Smith) Simonsen; m. Donald J. Reinertson, Feb. 26, 1953 (div.); m. 2d, David Miller Kimball, Feb. 11, 1965; children—Judith Ricco, John, Jane Novielle. Supr. Bell Telephone Co., Reno, 1948-53; model Sta. KOLO-TV, Reno, 1954-58; buyer Wonder Dress & Millinery Reno, 1954-60; sec. 1st Nat. Bank, Reno, 1960-65; tour. dir. Sr. Citizens Travel Club, Las Vegas, Nev., 1978—. Active Sunrise Hosp. Aux., Las Vegas; dist. chmn. Girl Scouts U.S.A., 1972-73, bd. dirs., 1972-77, field v.p., 1973-77, nat. del., Washington, 1976. Named Mrs. Nevada, 1955; recipient Thanks Badge Girl Scouts Am., 1973, Las Vegas Frontier award, 1974, Susie Scout award, 1977. Mem. Nat. Assn. Female Execs., Bus. and Profl. Women's Club. Democrat. Episcopalian. Clubs: Simi Garden, Busy Doe Homemakers, PEO. Address: 4908 Dunkirk Ave Las Vegas NV 89121

KIMBALL, RANCH SNOW, construction company executive, architecture educator; b. Salt Lake City, May 29, 1934; s. Ranch Shipley and Helen Rogers (Snow) K.; children by previous marriage—Ranch C., Cornell, Rebecca. A.B., Columbia Coll., N.Y.C. 1956; postgrad. in architecture U. Utah, 1960-61. Estimator, field coordinator Cannon Constrn. Co., Salt Lake City, 1960-61; gen. mgr., 1961-70, v.p., 1970-72, pres., part-owner, 1972—; pres. Cannon/Galensburg Constrn., Salt Lake City, 1972-75, Vik/Cannon Constrn., Eugene, Oreg., 1979-82; faculty Grad. Sch. Architecture, U. Utah, 1969—; chmn., dir. Utah Builder's Bargaining Unit. Chmn. bd. dirs. Children's Ctr., Salt Lake City, 1966-70; treas. Salt Lake Art Ctr., 1970-74; bd. dirs. Friends of KUED Pub. T.V., Salt Lake City, 1969-78; trustee Utah Heritage Found., 1981—; bd. dirs. Utah Environment Ctr., 1969-73. Served to 1st lt. USAF, 1956-59. Mem. Associated Gen. Contractors, Constrn. Specifications Inst., Am. Concrete Inst. Democrat. Clubs: Alta, Hidden Valley (Salt Lake City). Author articles on cold weather concrete constrn. Office: PO Box 2186 Salt Lake City UT 84110

KIMBALL, RAYMOND ALONZO, association executive; b. Kanosh, Utah, Apr. 28, 1918; s. Abraham Alonzo and Mary Jane (Gardner) K.; m. Adrus Hansen, Sept. 30, 1943; children—Kristine Kimball Harris, Diane Kimball Wilcox, Treo Kimball Winterrose, Colette Kimball Rolandelli, Melanie Kimball Shaha. B.S., Utah State U., 1941; M.S., U. Denver, 1946; postgrad. Stanford U., 1951-52. Dir. research Colo. Pub. Expenditure Council, Denver, 1947-51, 52-58; asst. tax commr. Colo. Fuel & Iron Corp., Denver, 1958-61; asst. to pres. Denver Dry Goods Co., 1963-65; pres., chief exec. officer Colo. Assn. Commerce and Industry, Denver, 1965—. Patriarch, Church of Jesus Christ of Latter-day Saints, 1981—. Served to lt. USNR, 1942-45. Mem. Colo. Soc. Assn. Execs., Council Western Retail Assns., Colo. C. of C. Clubs: City, Rotary. Office: Colorado Association of Commerce and Industry 1390 Logan St Suite 308 Denver CO 80203

KIMBALL, REID ROBERTS, psychiatrist; b. Draper, Utah, June 29, 1926; s. Crozier and Mary Lenore (Roberts) K.; B.S., Brigham Young U., 1949; M.D., U. Utah, 1951; m. Barbara Joy Radmore, Aug. 3, 1962; children—Valery, Michael, Pauline, Karen, Kay. Intern, Thomas D. Dee Hosp., Ogden, Utah, 1951-52; resident Norristown (Pa.) State Hosp., 1952-53, Oreg. State Hosp., Salem, 1953-55, Palo Alto (Calif.) VA Hosp., 1956; practice medicine specializing in psychiatry, Eugene, Oreg., 1957-60, Salem, Oreg., 1960-72, Portland, Oreg., 1972-77; dir. Outpatient Clinic Oreg. State Hosp., Salem, 1956-57; mem. staff Sacred Heart Hosp., Eugene, consultation/liaison psychiatry, 1977—; asst. prof. psychology U. Oreg., Eugene, 1957-65, prof., 1977—; asst. prof. psychiatry U. Oreg., Portland, 1965, adj. asst. prof., 1982—. Mem. Lane County Community Mental Health Adv. Bd., 1980-81. Served with USN, 1943-45. Mem. Am., Oreg. (chmn. psychiatry sect. 1973-74) med. assns., Lane County Med. Soc., Am. (pres. Oreg. dist. br. 1973-74), Pacific N.W., Lane County (pres. 1979-80) psychiat. assns., Am. Gerontology Soc. Home: 2005 Law Ln Eugene OR 97401 Office: 132 E Broadway Suite 303 Eugene OR 97401

KIMBALL, ROBERT GORDON, lawyer; b. Springfield, Mass., Nov. 27, 1951; s. Irving S. and Pearl S. (Silverman) K.; m. Alicia Stacey Beach, Mar. 31, 1979; children—Samantha, Brett. B.A. cum laude, Harvard U., 1973; J.D. with honors, George Washington U., 1977. Bar: D.C. 1977, Ariz. 1979. Atty., King & King, Washington, 1977-79, Doshoff & Sacks, Phoenix, 1979—; adj. prof. law George Washington U., 1978-79. Home: 5217 N 24th St Phoenix AZ 85016 Office: 3300 N Central Ave 20th Floor Phoenix AZ 85012

KIMBALL, ROGER STANLEY, physician; b. Portland, Oreg., May 18, 1935; s. Stanley M. and Sylvia M. (Seymour) K.; B.A., Stanford U., 1957; M.A., U. Calif., Berkeley, 1958; M.D., Albany Med. Coll., 1962; m. Patricia M. Wadsworth, Apr. 11, 1970; children—Keri Ann, Dyana Jean. Intern, Highland Hosp., Oakland, Calif., 1962-63; resident U. Calif Med. Center, San Francisco, 1963-67; practice medicine specializing in internal medicine, San Francisco, 1969—; mem. staffs U. Calif. Hosps., Ralph K. Davies Med. Center Hosp.; fellow in cardiology, dept. medicine Stanford U., 1965; asso. clin. prof. medicine Sch. Medicine, U. Calif., San Francisco. Mem. AMA, Am. Soc. Internal Medicine, Calif. Med. Soc. Presbyterian. Home: 183 Los Robles Dr Burlingame CA 94010 Office: 350 Parnassus Ave San Francisco CA 94117

KIMBALL, SPENCER WOOLLEY, clergyman; b. Salt Lake City, Mar. 28, 1895; s. Andrew and Olive (Woolley) K.; student Gila Jr. Coll., 1910-14, Brigham Young U., 1917, U. Ariz., 1917; LL.D., Brigham Young U., 1969; m. Camilla Eyring, Nov. 17, 1917; children—Spencer LeVan, Olive Beth (Mrs. Grant M. Mack), Andrew Eyring, Edward Lawrence. Mem. Council of Twelve Apostles of the Ch. of Jesus Christ of Latter-day Saints, 1943—, now pres.; on mission, Mo., 1914-16; pres. Seventies Quorum, stake clk., Thatcher, Ariz., 1918-38; counselor St. Joseph Stake Presidency, 1924-36; pres. Mt. Graham Stake, 1938-43; teller, clk. later asst. cashier Ariz. Trust & Sav. Bank, Safford, 1918-23, Bank of Safford, 1923-26; pres., mgr. Kimball Greenhalgh Ins. & Realty Co., Safford. Ariz., 1927-43; sec. Gila Valley Irrigation Co., 1935-43; organizer, part owner Gila Broadcasting Co., Safford, 1935—. Mem. Ariz. Assn. Tchrs. Retirement Bd., Thatcher and Safford (Ariz.) city councils; bd. dirs. ARC, Safford; chmn. war fund drives; trustee Gila Coll.; active Boy Scouts Am. Clubs: Rotary Internat. (dist. gov.); Rotary (pres.) (Safford). Office: 50 E North Temple St Salt Lake CIty UT 84111*

KIMBALL, WILFORD WAYNE, JR., artist, lithographer, educator; b. Salt Lake City, July 15, 1943; s. Wilford Wayne and Ruth (Burton) K.; m. Pamela Barton, June 29, 1967; children—Erika, Wilford Wayne, Paula, Abraham, Jacob, Samuel, Aaron. B.A., So. Utah State Coll., Cedar City, 1968; M.F.A., U. Ariz., 1970. Artist-in-residence Roswell Mus. and Art Ctr. (N.Mex.), 1972; asst. prof. U. Wis.-Madison, 1972-73; asst. prof. San Diego State U., 1973-74, 77-78; asst. prof. Calif. State U., Long Beach, 1974-75; asst. prof. U. Tex., San Antonio, 1975-77; assoc. prof. Ariz. State U., Tempe, 1978-83, prof., 1983—, co-dir. Print Research Facility, 1979—; represented in permanent collections, Nat. Gallery Fine Arts, Washington, N.Y.U., Library of Congress, Tamarind Lithography Workshop, Prudential Ins. Co. Am., Phila. Mus. Art, Bklyn. Mus., others. Mem. Ch. Jesus Christ of Latter-day Saints. Office: Sch Art Ariz State U Tempe AZ 85287

KIMBELL, MARION JOEL, systems engring. cons.; b. McDonough, Ga., Sept. 7, 1923; s. Charles Marvin and Mary (McMillian) K.; B.S. in Civil Engring., U. Houston, 1949, M.Chem. Engring., 1953; m. Judy Weidner, Dec. 18, 1946; children—Nancy, Susan, Candice. Civil engr. U.S. Dept. Interior, Lemmon, S.D., 1954; chief piping engr. M.W. Kellog Co., Paducah, Ky., 1955; nuclear engr. Westinghouse Atomic Power Div., Pitts., 1956-59; control systems prin. engr. Kaiser Engrs., Oakland, Calif., 1959-80; control systems supervising engr. Bechtel Inc., San Francisco, 1980—; control systems tchr. Laney Coll. cons. engr. NASA, Gen. Atomic Co.; advisory bd. Chabot Collage on radiation tech. Served as sgt. U.S. Army, 1943-46. Registered profl. nuclear engr., Calif.; control systems engr., Calif. Mem. Instrument Soc. of Am. (sr. mem. exec. com.). Clubs: Moose. Contbr. articles to profl. jours. Home: 22324 Ralston Ct Hayward CA 94541 Office: 50 Beal St PO Box 3965 San Francisco CA 94119

KIMBRELL, LEONARD BUELL, art historian; b. Archibald, La., Aug. 3, 1922; s. Lee Baines and Jessie Mae (Wilson) K.; m. B. Evelyn Davis, Dec. 19, 1922; children—Anna Kathryn Ritchie, Rebecca Lynn. B.A., Northwestern State Coll., La., 1942; M.S., U. Oreg., 1950, M.F.A., 1954; Ph.D., U. Iowa, 1965. Tchr. Roseburg (Oreg.) Sr. High Sch., 1946-49, Parkrose Sr. High Sch., Portland, Oreg., 1954-56; instr. Eastern Oreg. State Coll., 1956-62; mem. faculty Portland State U., 1962—, prof. art, 1966—, head dept., 1976—. Served with AUS, 1942-46. Mem. Coll. Art Assn., Pacific N.W. Soc. Archtl. Historians, Pacific N.W. Renaissance Soc., Samuel Johnson Soc. Democrat. Contbr. articles to profl. jours.

KIMME, ERNEST GODFREY, research communications engr.; b. Long Beach, Calif., June 7, 1929; s. Ernest Godfrey and Lure Elizabeth (Dake) K.; B.A. magna cum laude, Pomona Coll., 1952; M.A., U. Minn., 1954, Ph.D., 1955; m. Margaret Jeanne Bolen, Dec. 10, 1978; children by previous marriage—Ernest G., Elizabeth E. Kimme Browning, Karl Frederick. Mem. grad. faculty Oreg. State U., Corvallis, 1955-57; mem. tech. staff Bell Telephone Labs., Murray Hill, N.J., 1957-65, supr. mobile radio research lab., 1962-65; head applied sci. dept. Collins Radio Co., Newport Beach, Calif., 1965-72; research engr. Northrop Electronics, Hawthorne, Calif., 1972-74; sr. staff engr. Interstate Electronics Corp., Anaheim, Calif., 1974-79; dir. advanced systems, dir. advanced communications systems, tech. dir. spl. communications programs Gould Navcomm Systems, El Monte, Calif., 1979-82; pres. Cobit, Inc, 1982—; prin. assoc. Ameta Cons. Technologists; mem. adj. faculty in behavioral scis. Pepperdine U. Mem. AAAS, ACM, Am. Math. Soc., IEEE (sect. chmn.), Soc. Indsl. and Applied Math., Am. Mgmt. Assn., Inst. Math. Stats., Smithsonian Instn., Am. Mus. Natural History, Nat. Geog. Soc., Aircraft Owners and Pilots Assn., Phi Beta Kappa, Sigma Xi. Contbr. articles to profl. jours. Home: 301 Starfire St Anaheim CA 92807 Office: care PMP 224 N Sunset St Industry CA

KIMMONS, KEITH DEWAYNE, rehabilitation counselor; b. Chgo., Sept. 25, 1954; s. Norman Benjamin and Edith Elizabeth (Hundley) K.; A.A., Olive-Harvey Coll., 1974; B.A., Chgo. State U., 1976; M.A., Govs. State U., 1978. Rehab. tng. supr./counselor Vincennes Spl. Industries, Chgo. Assn. Retarded Citizens, Chgo., 1976-78; vocat. counselor Kennedy Sch. and Tng. Ctr., Palos Park, Ill., 1978-79; coordinator asst. Center for Program Devel. and the Handicapped, Chgo. City-Wide Coll., 1980; rehab. counselor, group coordinator Jewish vocat. Services/Vocat. Adjustment Ctr., Chgo., 1979-80; rehab. counselor New Horizons/San Fernando Valley Assn. Retarded, Inc., Sepulveda, Calif., 1980—; behavior technician Jay Nolan Ctr. Residential Program, Newhall, Calif., 1981-83; communication specialist Commn. Cultural and Ethnic Minorities, 1977-78. Mem. Am. Personnel and Guidance Assn., Am. Rehab. Counselor Assn., Ill. Rehab. Counselor Assn., Ill. Guidance and Personnel Assn., Assn. Humanistic Edn. Devel., Commn. Cultural and Ethnic Minorities. Address: 23515 Lyons Ave Apt 220 Valencia CA 91355

KIMURA, DANIEL KEIZO, fisheries biometrician; b. Sidney, Nebr., Aug. 29, 1945; s. Kaz and Masako (Kato) K.; m. Etsuko Hashimoto, Oct. 2, 1982. B.S., U. Wash., 1967, Ph.D., 1972. Fisheries biometrician Wash. Dept. Fisheries, Seattle, 1974—; math. statistician Nat. Marine Fisheries Service, Seattle, 1983—. Mem. Biometric Soc., Am. Statis. Assn. Contbr. numerous articles to profl. jours.

KIMURA, TY HIROSHI, real estate exec.; b. Honolulu, Feb. 27, 1944; s. Takao and Michiko (Higashimura) K.; B.A. in Psychology, U. Hawaii, 1967; diploma in data processing and computer programming Capitol Radio Engring. Inst., Washington, 1973; grad. Realtors Inst., 1976. Ind. fee staff appraiser Alexander & Alexander, Ltd., Honolulu, 1973; fee appraiser, Realtor-asso. Tad Fukumoto, SRPA, Honolulu, 1973-74; self-employed appraiser and cons., Honolulu, 1974-77; Realtor asso. Tooru Hara, Realtors, Honolulu, 1974-75; Realtor, Aaron M. Chaney, Inc., Honolulu, 1975-77; pres. Ty H. Kimura Corp., appraisers and cons., Honolulu, 1977—; chief appraiser, cons. Appraisal Analysts & Cons., Honolulu, 1977—; prin. broker Ty Property Cons., Honolulu, 1977—; guest instr. continuing edn. and community services dept. U. Hawaii, 1979-80. Served to capt. U.S. Army, 1967-73; Vietnam. Decorated Bronze Star with V device, Air medal with 2 oak leaf clusters, Joint Services Commendation medal; Cross of Gallantry with bronze star. Mem. Investment Group Realtors (pres. 1981, Counselor of Year award 1978), Internat. Coll. Real Estate Cons. Profls., Nat. Assn. Rev. Appraisers, Am. Assn. Cert. Appraisers, Soc. Real Estate Appraisers, Internat. Orgn. Real Estate Appraisers (internat. sec. 1981-83), Internat. Right of Way Assn., Inst. Cert. Bus. Counselors, Realtors Nat. Mktg. Inst., Internat. Exchangors Assn., Nat. Assn. Realtors, Hawaii Assn. Realtors, Honolulu Bd. Realtors. Club: Honolulu (a founder). Home: 811 16th Ave Honolulu HI 96816 Office: 1560 Kanunu St Suite 420 Honolulu HI 96814

KIMZEY, LOUIS LEE, publisher; b. South Gate, Calif., Mar. 15, 1928; s. Albert Lee and Elvera L. (Bosque) K.; divorced; children—Louis L., John A., Nancy I. B.S., Woodbury Coll., 1950. Artist Enthusiast Publs., Burbank, Calif., 1950-52; art dir. Quinn Publs., Burbank, 1952-57; managing editor Peterson Publishing, Hollywood, Calif., 1957-58; self-employed pub. Mag. Pub. Service, Los Angeles, 1958-70, Paisano Publs., Malibu, Calif., 1970—. Served with USCG, 1946-48. Office: 28210 Dorothy Dr Agoura CA 91301

KINCAID, DIXIE ONALEE, interior designer; b. Sparta, Wis., Sept. 17, 1942; d. Francis DeWolf and Maxine Onalee (Budde) Mullins; m. James Marvin Kincaid (div.); 1 son, J. Brent. Student San Jose State Coll., 1961-62, 66-67, Chaffey Jr. Coll., 1964-65, Coll. Redwoods, 1965-66, Humboldt State Coll., 1965-66; B.S. in Interior Design, U. Wis., 1979. Artist; exec. sec. nat. radio broadcaster, Washington, 1968-70; slide librarian Freer Gallery Aot Smithsonian Instn., Washington, 1970; numerous secretarial positions in Utah and Wis., 1971-74; sec. dept. ednl. adminstrn. U. Wis., Madison, 1974-81; draftsman Hal-Ken Engring., Madison, 1979, RE Assocs., Space Planners and Designers, Dallas, 1981; with Wallace N. Cooper, Architects and Assocs., Salt Lake City, 1981—. Recipient Exceptional Performance award Dept. Ednl. Adminstrn. U. Wis., 1976. Mem. Am. Soc. Interior Designers, Omicron Nu, Phi Upsilon Omicron. Republican. Mormon. Office: PO Box 125 North Salt Lake City UT 84054

KINCAID, RALPH WILSON, drilling company executive; b. Kansas City, Mo., Apr. 20, 1938; s. Ralph Davis and Helen Lucille (Wilson) K.; B.A., William Jewell Coll., 1960; m. Bobbi Joan Reed, Apr. 13, 1963; children—Ashlie Lynn, Michelle René. With Marion Labs., Kansas City, Mo., 1966-68, Hyland Labs., Denver, also Mobile, Ala., 1968-70; owner Profl. Lab. Supply, Birmingham, Ala., 1970-73; sales mgr. Hycel, Inc., Denver, 1973-74; dir. leasing and fin. Sturgeon Electric, Denver, 1974-75; owner Profl. Investments, Inc., Denver, 1975-76; with Atco Drilling, Inc., Denver, 1976-81, gen. mgr., 1979-81; mgr. Shelby Drilling Inc., Denver, 1981-82; pres., chief exec. officer Kopco Drilling Co., Denver, 1982—. Served to capt. USMC, 1960-65. Mem. Soc. Petroleum Engrs., Internat. Assn. Drilling Contractors (dir. 1980-81). Office: Suite 180 6969 S Spruce Englewood CO

KINDER, PATRICIA JUANICE, nurse administrator, educator; b. Malvern, Ark., Sept. 29, 1933; d. Roy James and Nancy Emily (Stewart) Nichols; divorced; children—Christopher, Kirk, Joseph. R.N., A.S. Long Beach Community Coll., 1968; B.S. in Health Care Adminstrn., U. Redlands, 1981. Cert. acute and intensive care nurse. Nursing supr. emergency dept. St. Mary Med. Ctr., 1958-79, trauma nurse coordinator, 1981—; dir. emergency dept. California Hosp., Los Angeles, 1979-81; instr. Long Beach Community Coll., 1975-79, Med. Mgmt. Acad., Marina del Rey, 1979-80, Long Beach City Coll., Long Beach Heart Assn.; cons. in emergency dept. mgmt. Bd. suprs. Trauma Systems of Los Angeles County, 1980. Mem. Emergency Dept. Nurses Assn.

KINDRED, ANN JOHNSON, accountant, accounting firm executive; b. Helena, Mont., May 5, 1921; d. Frank A. and Dorothy (Dickerson) J.; m. Jack M. Kindred, Dec. 28, 1950 (div.); children—Dea Kindred Maude, Dunn. Student U. Mont., 1939-43; B.A. in Bus. Adminstrn and Econs., U. Wash., 1944; M.B.A., NYU, 1950. C.P.A., Mont. wage rate analyst 12th Regional War Labor Bd., Seattle, 1944-45; analyst indsl. relations div. E. R. Squibb & Sons, N.Y.C., 1946-51; staff acct. Galusha Higgins & Galusha, C.P.A.s, Helena, Mont., 1955-60, Anderson-Zurmuehlen & Co., C.P.A.s, Helena, 1961-65; pvt. practice acctg., Helena, 1966-76; sr. ptnr. Kindred Holland & Co., Helena, 1976—; mem. Small Bus. Adv. Bd., 1964-67; mem. Mont. Gov.'s Com. on Personnel Classification, 1967-68; sec. Mont. bd. Pub. Accountancy, 1969-71, chmn., 1971-73. Mem. Am. Inst. C.P.A.s, Mont. Soc. C.P.A.s (dir. 1965-68, chmn. legis. com. 1961-63, 69-70, C.P.A. of Yr. 1969). Congregationalist. Club: Montana (Helena). Home: 710 Power St Helena MT 59601 Office: 555 Faller Helena MT 59601

KINDRED, LESLIE WITHROW, education educator emeritus; b. Boston, Dec. 27, 1905; s. Leslie Withrow and Veronica (Vatter) K.; student Clark U., 1924-26; A.B., U. Mich., 1928, A.M., 1934, Ph.D., 1938; m. Helen F. Parmenter, Dec. 24, 1932; children—James W., Robert H. Tchr. pub. schs., Ann Arbor, Mich., 1928-34; critic, demonstration tchr. U. High Sch., U. Mich., 1934-38; dir. Marsh Found., Van Wert Ohio, 1938-39; cons. Mich. Dept. Pub. Instrn., 1939-40; asst. prof. edn. Temple U., 1940-43, assoc. prof. edn., 1943-44, prof. edn., from 1945, now prof. emeritus, dir. dept. ednl. adminstrn., 1953-58, prof. ednl. adminstrn., from 1958, now prof. emeritus; instr. comparative edn. course in Europe, summers 1958, 59, S.Am., summers 1961-62, 66, 69. Mng. dir. Pub. Edn. and Child Labor Assn. Pa., 1943-45. Mem. Nat. Sch. Pub. Relations Assn. (editorial adv. bd. 1953), Middle Atlantic States Assn. Colls. and Secondary Schs. (chmn. evaluation com. 1940-50), Pa. Edn. Assn. (sec. div. higher edn. 1949-51), Am. Assn. Sch. Adminstrs., Pa. Schoolmen's Club, Phi Delta Kappa, Phi Kappa Phi, Tau Kappa Alpha, Kappa Phi Kappa. Author: (with Leo M. Chamberlain) The Teacher and School Organization, 4th edit., 1966; compiler, editor: Public Relations in Secondary Schs., 1948; Supervisory Problems in the Secondary School, 1950; contbr.: Citizen Cooperation for Better Public Schools, 1954; School Public Relations, 1957; Study Guide and Case Book for School Public Relations, 1957; How to Tell the School Story, 1960; The Intermediate Schools, 1968; The School and Community Relations, 1975, 3d edit., 1984; Middle School Curriculum, 1976, 2d edit., 1980. Editor: Communications Research and School-Community Relations, 1965. Contbr. to Preparatory Programs for School Administrators, 1963; Critical Incidents in Teaching, 1964. Home: 8 Carrizo Dr Santa Barbara CA 93105

KING, BARNELLE STOKES, educational administrator; b. Tyler, Tex., Apr. 19, 1941; d. Robert and Grace Elizabeth (Hood) S.; m. Russell A. King, Oct. 23, 1970; children—Lisa Gayle, Tanishya Kelley. B.S., Tex. Coll., Tyler, 1963; M.Ed., East Tex. State U., 1972; postgrad U. N.Mex., 1978-79. Tchr., Nenahnezad Boarding Sch., Fruitland, N.Mex., 1964-68; tchr. kindergarten Gallup/McKinley County Schs., Gallup, N.Mex., 1968-78; elem. sch. adminstr. Gallup Pub. Schs., 1979-81, secondary sch. adminstr., 1981—, asst. prin., 1981—; part-time instr. Gallup Branch Coll., 1980—. Bd. dirs. Mental Health Clinic, NAACP, Democratic Assn. Mem. Am. Soc. Curriculum and Devel., Assn. Edn. Young Children, N.Mex. Assn. Edn. Young Children, Internat. Reading Assn., NEA, Phi Delta Kappa, Delta Kappa Gamma, AAUW. Democrat. Methodist. Clubs: Golden Circle, Eastern Star, Black Orgn. for Women. Home: 301 Cora Lee Dr Gallup NM 87301 Office: 600 S Boardman St Gallup NM 87301

KING, BERNICE, history educator; b. Tuscaloosa, Ala., May 27, 1952; d. Eldridge Jonathan and Laura Lee (Merritt) K. B.A., U. Calif.-San Diego, 1974, M.A., 1976; postgrad. U. San Diego, 1974-75. Tchr. Opportunity Sch., Vista, Calif., 1977-78, Vista High Sch., 1978-80; tchr. Washington Middle Sch., Vista, 1980—, also chmn. dept. Active United Negro Coll. Fund, 1981-82. Leshay Grad. fellow, 1975-76. Mem. Nat. Council Social Studies, Assn. Calif. Sch. Adminstrs. Democrat. Baptist. Office: Dist Warehouse Vista Unified Sch Vista CA 92083

KING, CANDACE MCCARTHY, human services/health services administrator, consultant; b. Kansas City, Mo., Feb. 16, 1951; d. Max Eugene and Jeanne Margaret (McRae) McCarthy; m. Philip Warren King, Jan. 5, 1980. B.A., Barat Coll., 1972; M.P.A., U. Ariz., 1977. Chief caseworker Office of Congressman R. P. Hanrahan, Chgo., 1973-75; program dir. Town of Worth (Ill.), 1975-76; program dir. protection and advocacy for developmentally disabled Ariz. Ctr. for Law in Pub. Interest, Phoenix, 1977-81; exec. dir. Ariz. Congress for Action Ind. Living Ctr., Phoenix, 1981-82; pvt. practice advocacy, guardianship, and tng. services, Phoenix, 1982—; mem. Ariz. State Employment and Tng. Council, 1980-82, arbitrator Am. Arbitration Assn., 1982—; field instr. Ariz. State U. Sch. Social Work, 1978-79. Mem. Am. Personnel and Guidance Assn., Ariz. Assn. for Retarded Citizens (dir. guardianship and advocacy, chmn. edn. com. 1983—), Nat. Assn. Protection and Advocacy Systems (regional rep. 1979-80, v.p. 1980-81), Nat. Assn. for Ind. Living (bd. dirs. 1981-82). Republican. Roman Catholic. Co-author: Attendant Training Manual, 1982; Advocacy Manual, 1980; Guardianship Self-Help Kit, 1980; It's a Question of Human Rights for the Developmentally Disabled in Arizona, 1977. Home: 913 W Marshall Ave Phoenix AZ 85013

KING, CARL STANLEY, state corrections administrator; b. Salisbury, N.C., Feb. 9, 1934; s. Clayborne Stanford and Vivian Pearl (Kester) K.; A.B., Lenoir Rhyne Coll., 1955; B.D., Luth. Theol. Sem., 1958, M.Div., 1972; M.A. L.I. U., 1972; postgrad. in edn. Ariz. State U., 1981—; m. Harriette Naoma Collins, May 22, 1955; children—Elizabeth Carol, Patricia Leigh. Ordained to ministry Luth. Ch. in Am., 1958; pastor Richfield (N.C.) Luth. Parish, 1958-59, St. Thomas Luth. Ch., Charlotte, N.C., 1959-63; commd. 1st lt. Chaplain Corps, U.S. Army, 1963, advanced through grades to lt. col., 1980; served various mil. posts, including 7th Missile Bn., 2d Arty., Toksan ni, Korea, 1964-65, 23d Field Arty. Group, Vietnam, 1969-70, 1st Signal Brigade, Yongsan, Korea, 1976-77, Ft. Huachuca, Ariz., 1977-78; inactive res. status, 1978—; supr. pastoral activities Ariz. Dept. Corrections, Phoenix, 1979-83, unit mgr., correctional program supr. Alhambra Reception and Treatment Center, 1983—; mem. affiliate faculty Cochise Coll., 1977-80; mem. vis. faculty South Mountain Coll., 1980—; mem. adj. faculty Ottawa U., Phoenix, 1981—. Decorated Bronze Star with oak leaf cluster, Army Commendation medal with 2 oak leaf clusters, Air medal, Meritorious Service medal. Mem. Am. Correctional Assn., Ariz. Probation, Parole and Corrections Assn., Adult Edn. Assn., Mensa. Home: 1725 N Date #14 Mesa AZ 85201 Office: Ariz Dept Corrections 1924 E University Phoenix AZ 85034

KING, CAROL SOUCEK, editor, journalist, b. Los Angeles, Sept. 8, 1943; d. Romus and Anne (Merrill) Soucek; m. Douglas Manley Sandefur, 1969; m. 2d, Richard Carlton King, Jan. 31, 1976. B.A. in English Lit., U. So. Calif., 1966, Ph.D., 1976; M.F.A., Yale U., 1966. Lectr. contemporary theater U. So. Calif., Los Angeles, 1969; drama critic Santa Monica (Calif.) Evening Outlook, 1972-73; staff writer Los Angeles Herald Examiner, 1973-77, editor Lifestyle sect., 1977; editor in chief, Designers West Mag., Los Angeles, 1978—. Mem. Am. Soc. Interior Designers, Internat. Soc. Interior Designers, Nat. Home Fashions League, Women in Bus. Office: Designers West 8564 Melrose Ave Los Angeles CA 90069

KING, CHARLA ROSEMARY, restaurant executive, consultant; b. Pasadena, Calif., Dec. 22, 1944; d. Charles Valentine and Rosemary Barbara (Lyne) K. Student Gonzaga U., 1962-63; B.A. in English, Occidental Coll., Los Angeles, 1966. Asst. to v.p. Shareholders Mgmt. Co., Los Angeles, 1968-69; sec. to asst. sec. Rand Corp., Santa Monica, Calif., 1971; adminstrv. asst. to v.p. corp. planning Dart Industries, Los Angeles, 1972-73; regional dir. pub. relations and advt. Davre's div. ARA Services, Inc., Los Angeles, 1973—; cons. Mem. Los Angeles the Beautiful, 1980—, The Downtowners, 1982-83. Mem. Publicity Club Los Angeles, Peninsula Press Club. Republican. Roman Catholic. Contbr. articles to newspapers. Office: Davres 505 S Flower St Los Angeles CA 90071

KING, CLARENCE EARL, JR., constrn. co. exec.; b. Charlottesville, Va., Apr. 6, 1917; s. Clarence Earl and Nell (Wingfield) K.; B.S., U. Va., 1937; m. Elizabeth Ann Ryan, Apr. 23, 1949; children—David R., Gary W., Sarah E., Rebecca A., John R. With Morrison Knudsen Co., Inc., various locations, 1951—, dir. adminstrn., Boise, Idaho, 1972-76, v.p. internat., 1976—. Served to capt. AUS, 1941-45. Mem. Phi Beta Kappa. Club: Hillcrest Country. Home: 1602 Brumback St Boise ID 83702 Office: 400 Broadway Boise ID 83729

KING, CLARENCE HILYER, JR., management consultant; b. San Diego, Sept. 24, 1915; s. Clarence H. and Lucille (Brown) K.; m. Betty Lou Pennell, Nov. 11, 1944. B.Sc., U. So. Calif., Shipping supt. Ratner Mfg. Co., San Diego, 1940-42; cost acct. Consol. Vultee Aircraft, San Diego, 1942-44; mgr. data processing Golden State Mut. Life Ins. Co., Los Angeles, 1946-62; project adminstr. Rockwell Internat., Los Angeles, 1962-81; ind. mgmt. cons., Los Angeles, 1981—. Served with U.S. Army, 1944-45. Mem. Assn. for Systems Mgmt. (past internat. pres., disting. service award, 1981), Data Processing Mgmt. Assn., Quarter Century Wireless Assn., Amateur Radio Relay League. Club: Masons. Home and office: 3951 Carmona Ave Los Angeles CA 90008

KING, DAVID QUIMBY, aerospace engr.; b. Summit N.J., Sept. 5, 1953; s. William Henry and Jane (Gurnee) K.; B.S.M.E., Rutgers U., 1976; M.A., Princeton U., 1978, Ph.D., 1982. Sr. engr. NASA Jet Propulsion Lab., Pasadena, Calif., 1981—. Mem. AIAA, Tau Beta Pi, Pi Tau Sigma. Contbr. articles to profl. jours. Home: 3131 Montrose Ave #20 La Crescenta CA 91214 Office: Jet Prop Lab/M/ 277-102 4800 Oak Grove Dr Pasadena CA 91109

KING, DAVID THOMAS, Canadian provincial government official; b. Perth, Ont., Can., June 22, 1946; s. Albert Edward and Ethel (Dickson) K.; m. Clare Elaine Ann Piven, Oct. 19, 1968; children—Troy Oliver Albert, Jason Darren Tod. Attended U. Victoria, 1964-65, U. Alta., 1965-67, 69-70. Mem. Legis. Assembly Alta. (Can.), Edmonton, 1971—, minister of edn. Alta., 1979—. Progressive Conservative. Mem. United Ch. Canada. Office: 319 Legis Bldg Edmonton AB T5K 2B6 Canada*

KING, FRANK WILLIAM, writer; b. Port Huron, Mich., Oct. 1, 1922; s. William Ernest and Catherine Theresa (Smith) K.; student U. Utah, 1963-65, Santa Monica City Coll., 1941, 48-49; B.A., Marylhurst Coll., 1979; M.A., U. Portland, 1982; m. Carma Morrison Sellers, Sept. 16, 1961; children—Rosanne, Jeanine Nell, Melanie, Lisa June; one stepson, Michael Sellers. Air traffic controller FAA, Salt Lake City, Albuquerque and Boise, Idaho; 1949-65, info. officer Western Region, Los Angeles, 1965-68; pub. affairs officer Los Angeles Dist. C.E., U.S. Army, 1968-69, Walla Walla (Wash.), 1969-77, N. Pacific div., Portland, Oreg., 1977-79; dir. pub. relations U. Portland, 1979-80; adj. asst. prof. communications U. Portland, 1982—; freelance writer, 1980—. Exec. asst. Los Angeles Fed. Exec. Bd., 1965-67; chmn. Walla Walla County Alcoholism Adminstrv. Bd., 1974-75; vice-chmn. Walla Walla County Human Services Adminstrv. Bd., 1976-78, chmn., 1977-78. Served with USMCR, 1942-45. Decorated Air medal; William Randolph Hearst scholar, 1965. Mem. Soc. Profl. Journalists, Pub. Relations Soc. Am. (accredited), Soc. Am. Mil. Engrs., Kappa Tau Alpha. Democrat. Roman Catholic. Home: 4106 N Montana Ave Portland OR 97217 Office: 413 Board of Trade Bldg 310 SW 4th Ave Portland OR 97204

KING, FREDERIC, health services company executive, educator; b. N.Y.C., N.Y., May 9, 1937; s. Benjamin and Jeanne (Fritz) K.; m. Linda Ann Udell, Mar. 17, 1976; children by previous marriage—Coby Allen, Allison Beth, Lisa Robyn, Daniel Seth. B.B.A. cum laude, Bernard M. Baruch Sch. Bus. and Public Adminstrn., CUNY, 1958. Dir. adminstrn. Albert Einstein Coll. Medicine, Bronx, N.Y., 1970-72; assoc. v.p. health affairs Tulane Med. Ctr., New Orleans, 1972-77; dir. fin. Mt. Sinai Med. Ctr., N.Y.C., 1977-78; v.p. fin. Cedars-Sinai Med. Ctr., Los Angeles, 1978-82; pres. Vascular Diagnostic Services, Inc., Woodland Hills, Calif., 1982—; assoc. adj. prof. Tulane U. Sch. Pub. Health; asst. prof. Mt. Sinai Med. Ctr.; instr. Pierce Coll., Los Angeles. Served with U.S. Army, 1959-62. Mem. Hosp. Fin. Mgmt. Assn., Am. Pub. Health Assn. Democrat. Jewish. Home: 4530 Willens Ave Woodland Hills CA 91364 Office: 20300 Ventura Blvd Suite 150 Woodland Hills CA 91364

KING, GARY FREDRIC, accountant; b. Detroit, Nov. 30, 1946; s. Roland Elwood and Esther Janet (Hawley) K.; m. Linda Jean Canning, Aug. 17, 1968; children—Christopher, James David. B.A., U. Mich., 1968, M.B.A., 1972. C.P.A., Calif. Staff acct. Deloitte Haskins & Sells, Los Angeles, 1972-81, ptnr., 1981—. Chmn. allocation com. United Way of Los Angeles. Served with inf. U.S. Army, 1968-69; Vietnam. Decorated Bronze Star. Mem. Calif. Soc. C.P.A.s, Am. Inst. C.P.A.s. Republican. Club: Jonathan (Los Angeles). Home: 8417 Bleriot Ave Los Angeles CA 90045 Office: 333 S Grand Suite 2800 Los Angeles CA 90071

KING, GEOFFREY ROBERT, management educator; b. Hull, Eng., Feb. 10, 1918; s. William Ralph and Agnes (Morgan) K.; m. Mary Elsie Wheeler, July 27, 1940; children—Robert William, Gillian. B.S., Calif. State U.-Los Angeles, 1964, M.S., 1966; M.A., U. So. Calif., 1968, Ph.D. in Econs., 1972. Registered profl. engr. Ont., Can. Contracts mgr. Aerojet Gen., Downey, Calif., 1960-66; mgr. contract adminstrn. Interstate Electronics, Anaheim, Calif., 1966-72; prof. mgmt. Calif. State U.-Fullerton, 1973—, chmn. dept. mgmt., 1975-79. mem. Laguna Greenbelt, Laguna Beach Homeowners Assn., LWV. Mem. Assn. Profl. Engrs. Ont., Omicron Delta Epsilon, Beta Gamma Sigma. Contbr. articles to profl. jours. Office: Calif State U Dept Mgmt Fullerton CA 92634

KING, GUNDAR JULIAN, ednl. adminstr.; b. Riga, Latvia, Apr. 19, 1926; s. Attis K. and Austra (Dale) Kenins; student J. W. Goethe U., Frankfurt, Germany, 1946-48; B.B.A., U. Oreg., 1956; M.B.A., Stanford U., 1958, Ph.D., 1964; m. Valda K. Andersons, Sept. 18, 1954; children—John T., Marita A. Came to U.S., 1950, naturalized, 1954. Asst. field supr. Internat. Refugee Orgn., Frankfurt, 1948-50; br. office mgr. Williams Form Engring. Corp., Portland, Oreg., 1952-54; project mgr. Market Research Assos., Palo Alto, Calif., 1958-60; asst. prof., asso. prof. Pacific Luth. U., 1960-66; prof., 1966—, dean Sch. Bus. Adminstrn., 1970—; vis. prof. mgmt. U.S. Naval Postgrad. Sch., 1971-72. Mem. Gov's. Com. on Reorgn. Wash. State Govt., 1965; mem. study group on pricing U.S. Commn. Govt. Procurement, 1971-72; pres. N.W. Univs. Bus. Adminstrn. Conf., 1965-66. Served with AUS, 1950-52. Mem. AAUP (past chpt. pres.), Am. Mktg. Assn. (past chpt. pres.), Assn. Advancement Baltic Studies (pres. 1970), Western Assn. Collegiate Schs. Bus. (pres. 1971-72), Alpha Kappa Psi, Beta Gamma Sigma. Author: Economic Policies in Occupied Latvia, 1965; articles in field. Home: PO Box 44401 Parkland WA 98444 Office: Pacific Luth U Tacoma WA 98447

KING, HARTLEY HUGHES, research engineer; b. Fresno, Calif., Apr. 21, 1936; s. Ralph Edgar and Esther Mae (Hughes) K.; m. Beverly Hartman, Aug. 18, 1962; children—Adriane H., Audrey H. B.S., U. Calif.-Berkeley, 1957, M.S., 1959, Ph.D., 1963. Lic. profl. mech. engr. Calif. Engr. Electro-Optical Systems, Pasadena, Calif., 1962-65, General Motors Delco, Santa Barbara, Calif., 1965-68; engr. General Research Corp., Santa Barbara, 1968-75, sr. research engr., 1983—; sr. research engr. Effects Technology Inc., Santa Barbara, 1975-83; tchr. fluid dynamics courses U. So. Calif., 1965, U. Calif., Berkeley, 1972, 78. Mem. AIAA, IEEE. Home: 212 Canon Dr Santa Barbara CA 93105 Office: 5383 Hollister Ave Santa Barbara CA 93111

KING, JAMES BRUCE, newspaper editor; b. Enterprise, Oreg., Oct. 30, 1922; s. Oscar Lawrence and Julia Etta (Bruce) K.; student Lower Columbia Community Coll., 1941-43, Whitman Coll., 1943-44; B.A. in Journalism U. Wash., 1948; m. Betty Ruth Berkley, June 27, 1944; 1 son, James Bruce. With Seattle Times, 1948—, beginning as reporter, successively copy editor, asst. news editor, news editor, asst. mng. editor, 1948-75, mng. editor, 1975-77, exec. editor, 1977—, v.p. news, 1980-82, editor, v.p. news and editorial, 1982—. Vis. com. U. Wash. Sch. Communications, 1971-77; Pulitzer Prize judge, 1981-83; mem. Community Devel. Round Table Seattle; former cons. self-improvement group McNeil Island Fed. Penitentiary. Served to lt. comdr. USNR, 1943-46; PTO. Mem. AP Mng. Editors (dir. 1977—), Am. Soc. Newspaper Editors (dir. 1982—), U. Wash. Alumni Assn., Soc. Profl. Journalists, Sigma Delta Chi, Beta Theta Pi. Episcopalian. Clubs: Wash. Athletic, Blue Ridge Community Ranier. Office: Seattle Times PO Box 70 Seattle WA 98111

KING, JAMES ROGER, physiologist; b. San Jose, Calif., Mar. 12, 1927; s. James Raymond and Dorothy Lydia (Donnelley) K.; m. Eleanor Porter, June 16, 1950; children—Julia, Robert, Joanna. A.B., San Jose State U., 1950; M.S., Wash. State U., 1953, Ph.D., 1957. Asst. prof. exptl. biology U. Utah, 1957-60, asst. prof., 1960-62, assoc. prof., 1962-67, prof. zoophysiology, 1967—; chmn. dept. zoology Wash. State U., 1972-78; assoc. editor The Auk, 1961-63; editor The Condor, 1965-68; chmn. subcom. standards for birds, Nat. Research Council, 1973-76; panel mem. Program Environ. Biology, NSF, 1973-76; co-dir. NSF Workshop Nat. Plan Ornithology, 1975-78; Investigador Visitante, Instituto Miguel Lillo, Universidad Nacional de Tucuman, Argentina, 1969-70; Maytag vis. prof. zoology Ariz. State U., 1979. Served with AUS, 1945-46. NIH Research Career Devel. awardee, 1963-67; fellow Guggenheim Found., 1969, AAAS, 1978; Brewster medalist, 1974. Mem. AAAS, Am. Physiol. Soc., Am. Ornithol. Union (pres. 1980-82), Cooper Ornithol. Soc. (council pres. 1977-78), Am. Soc. Zoologists, Ecol. Soc. Am., Am. Inst. Biol. Scis. Co-editor Avian Biology/A Multivolume Treatise, 1971; contbr. numerous articles in field to profl. jours. Home: NW 910 Fisk St Pullman WA 99163 Office: Dept Zoology Wash State U Pullman WA 99164

KING, JANET ANN, educator; b. Dayton, Ohio, Nov. 9, 1949; d. William C. and Rosetta V. (Mahle) K.; m. Andrew M. Junken, Apr. 3, 1982 (div.). A.A., Manatee Jr. Coll., 1969; B.S., Fla. State U., 1971. Tchrs. certs. Fla., Ohio, Colo. Home econs. tchr. Dayton, Ohio, 1972-76, Woodland Park (Colo.) High Sch., 1982—; guest speaker health fields; youth activities counselor; advisor Future Homemakers Assn. Active WHO, Better Health Coop. Recipient Outstanding Leadership award Manatee Jr. Coll., 1969, Joe Fant award, 1969. Mem. NEA, Am. Home Econs. Assn. Home: Box 1936 Woodland Park CO 80863 Office: Box 99 Woodland Park CO 80863

KING, JAY FREDRIC, personnel director; b. Joliet, Ill., May 6, 1946; s. William Fred and Shirley Inez (Couch) K.; m. Patricia Louise DeMik, June 15, 1968; children—Daniel Jay, Amy Christine. B.S. in Personnel Mgmt., No. Ill. U., 1972, M.B.A., 1976. Asst. dir. personnel St. Joseph Hosp., Joliet, Ill., 1972-76, dir. personnel, 1976-78; dir. human resources Lovelace Med. Ctr., Albuquerque, 1978-81; dir. personnel San Antonio Hosp. Upland, Calif., 1981—; cons. Served with USN, 1969-70. Mem. N.Mex. Soc. Personnel Adminstrn. (past pres.), Am. Soc. Personnel Adminstrn., Am. Soc. Hosp. Personnel Adminstrn., Hosp. Personnel Assn. Mgmt. Assn. So. Calif., Sigma Iota Epsilon. Lutheran. Contbr. articles to profl. jours.; developer effective position control system. Home: 6233 Opal Alta Loma CA 91701 Office: 999 San Bernardino Rd Upland CA 91786

KING, JERRY ALLEN, manufacturing company executive; b. Balt., Oct. 12, 1941; s. Clarence Eugene and Olive Lucille (Lindley) K.; B.A., U. Calif.-Irvine, 1974, postgrad., 1974-76; M.A., UCLA, 1983—; m. Sharon Jean Pipoly, June 29, 1968; 1 son, John Lindley. Ops. officer First Nat. Bank Orange County, 1962-66; property mgr. Grant Corp., comml. shipping centers, 1968-70; asst. to v.p. Irvine Co., residential devel., 1971-72; assoc. Ashley Econs. Inc., 1973-74; gen. mgr. King Engring. Co., and predecessor Star Screw Products, Inc., Costa Mesa, Calif., 1975-76, pres., owner, 1977—; pres. Universal Metals Corp., 1980-82; owner, chmn., chief exec. officer J.A. King & Assocs. Chmn. Newport Beach (Calif.) Planning Commn., 1981-83, Newport Beach Water Quality Commn., 1980—, Newport Beach Environ. Quality Adv. Commn., 1976-81, Newport Beach Environ. Impact Rev. Commn., 1976; mem. facilities com. Orange County Music Ctr., 1981—; bd. dirs. U. Calif. Indsl. Assocs; bd. dirs. Orange Coast YMCA, 1983—; mem. Santa Ana region Water Quality Control Bd., 1983—; mem. steering com. Rural/urban Design Assistance Team, Newport Beach, 1983—. Served with USMC, 1966-68; Vietnam. Mem. Am. Soc. Metals, Soc. Mfg. Engrs., Robotics Internat., Credit Mgrs. Assn., Am. Planning Assn., U. Calif.-Irvine Alumni Assn. (dir.), World Affairs Council Orange County, Town Hall Calif. Republican. Catholic. Club: Rotary. Home: 979 Sandcastle Dr Corona Del Mar CA 92625 Office: 3585 Cadillac Ave Costa Mesa CA 92626

KING, JOHN DOUGLAS, management analyst; b. Beckenham, Kent, Eng., June 1, 1934; s. Douglas Stanley and Mary (Carpenter) K.; m. Shirley Anne Spencer; children—Linda, Alan, Douglas, Pamela, Lynn Angela, Gary. B.S., Oglethorpe U., 1956; M. Aerospace Ops. Mgmt., U. So. Calif., 1969; Dr.Bus.Adminstrn., U.S. Internat. U., 1980. Commd. officer, U.S. Navy, 1956, advanced through grades to lt. comdr., 1965, ret., 1977; mem. faculty Troy State U., Kolsaas, Norway, 1976; with Davlyn Enterprises, San Diego, 1977, Northrop Services, Inc., San Diego, 1977-78, Intercon Corp., Camp Pendleton, Calif., 1978-79; tech. staff P.E. Systems, Inc., San Diego, 1979—; research asst. U.S. Internat. U., San Diego, 1981—; cons. in field. Bd. dirs. Scripps Ranch Community Theatre, 1979-80, 83—. Decorated Navy Commendation medal. Lowry Meml. scholar, 1956. Mem. Am. Mgmt. Assn., Am. Soc. Tng. and Devel., Assn. Old Crows. Mem. Anglican Ch. Home: 10287 Grayfox Dr San Diego CA 92131 Office: 1663 Rosecrans St San Diego CA 92106

KING, JOHN WALTER, wildlife biologist; b. East Ely, Nev., May 18, 1942; s. Harry Cameron and Lois Nancy (Bally) K.; B.S. with high distinction, U. Nev., Reno, 1977, M.S. in Biology, 1982; m. Mary Ervene Williams, Nov. 23, 1962; 1 son, John Cameron. Mech. supt., asst. Elko (Nev.) Daily Free Press, 1970-73; teaching fellow dept. biology U. Nev., Reno, 1977-78; fisheries biologist Nev. Dept. Wildlife, Verdi, 1978-80, hunter safety coordinator, Reno, 1980—. Chmn., City of Elko Planning Commn., 1971-73; nature related merit badge counselor Boy Scouts Am., 1976—. Mem. N. Am. Assn. Hunter Safety Coordinators, Wildlife Soc., Western Assn. Hunter Edn. Coordinators, Sigma Xi. Presbyterian. Club: Masons. Office: 1100 Valley Rd Reno NV 89520

KING, JOSEPH JERONE, assn. exec.; b. Spokane, Wash., Sept. 27, 1910; s. Joseph Jerone and Alice (Halferty) K.; B.A. with gt. distinction, Stanford U., 1935; M.A., Duke U., 1937; m. Irma Kathleen Martin, Aug. 22, 1937; children—Sally Jo (Mrs. John S. Thompson), Nikki Sue (Mrs. Dennis Ring), Cindy Lou (Mrs. Richard Mullen). Instr. econs. Black Mountain Coll., 1937-38; numerous adminstrv. positions Farm Security Adminstrn., U.S. Dept. Agriculture, Portland, 1939-51; Oreg. state dir. Christian Rural Overseas Program, 1950-51; sr. civilian for indsl. relations Puget Sound Naval Shipyard, 1951-58; public affairs dir. Assn. Wash. Industries, Olympia, 1958-78, exec. cons., 1978—; Western mgr. Inst. Applied Econs., 1981—. Mem. President's Assos., Central Wash. U.; mem. Gov.'s Council for Reorg. Wash. State Govt.; dir. manpower Statewide Public Edn. Mgmt. Survey; mem. Gov.'s Commn. on Employment of Physically Handicapped; mem. adv. council, dept. econs. and bus. adminstrn. Central Wash. U., 1973—; mem. profl. edn. adv. council Wash. State Dept. Public Instrn., 1977—, chmn. community edn. adv. council, 1981—; chmn. adv. com. for Anderson Landing Wildlife Project, Kitsap County (Wash.) Bd. Commrs.; bd. dirs. Wash. State Council Econ. Edn., State-Wide Project Bus. Liaison with Edn. Served with USAAF, 1944. Recipient Outstanding Service awards DAV, Assn. Wash. Bus.; named hon. citizen City of Vancouver (Wash.), hon. Wash. adm., hon. Wash. gen. Mem. Am. Soc. Pub. Adminstrn., Am. Legion (hon. life mem.), Phi Beta Kappa, Pi Gamma Mu. Clubs: Washington Athletic, Kitsap Country, Elks, Masons (Shriner). Author: Winning, 1961. Home: Ioka Beach-Hood Canal 11655 Ioka Way NW Silverdale WA 98383

KING, MARCIA, librarian; b. Lewiston, Maine, Aug. 4, 1940; d. Daniel Alden and Clarice Evelyn (Curtis) Barrell; m. Howard P. Lowell, Feb. 14, 1969 (div.); m. 2d Richard G. King, Aug. 9, 1980. B.S., U. Maine, 1965; M.L.A., Simmons Coll., 1967; postgrad. in Orgn. Devel., Boston U. Cons., reference, Bookmobile librarian Maine State Library, Augusta, 1965-69; dir. Lithgow Pub. Library, Augusta, 1969-72; exec. sec. Maine Library Adv. Com., 1972-73; dir. Wayland (Mass.) Free Pub. Library, 1973-76; state librarian Oreg. State Library, Salem, 1976-82; dir. Tucson Pub. Library, 1982—; library and organizational cons. Active Exec. Women's Council So. Ariz. Mem. ALA, Pub. Library Assn., Ariz. State Library Assn., Oreg. State Library Assn., Pacific NW Library Assn., AAUW, Assn. Specialized and Coop. Library Agys. Unitarian. Office: PO Box 27470 Tucson AZ 85726

KING, MARY ELIZABETH, anthropologist, museum administrator, educator; b. Williamsport, Pa., Sept. 7, 1929; d. Layton Ellsworth and Elizabeth Bird (Champion) K. A.B. in Anthropology, Cornell U., 1951; M.A., Columbia U., 1958; Ph.D., U. Ariz., 1961. Cert. anthropologist. Asst. to state archaeologist Pa. State Mus., Harrisburg, 1951-52; part-time vol. mus. asst. Am. Mus. Natural History, N.Y.C., 1952-53, profl. asst. to Junius Bird, 1953; mus. asst. Textile Mus., Washington, 1953-54, librarian, 1954-59, curator Western Hemisphere Textiles, 1957-67; teaching asst. U. Ariz., Tucson, 1959-60, instr. anthropology, 1961; mus. asst. Ariz. State Mus., Tucson, 1960-61; part-time lectr. anthropology Am. U., Washington, 1963; part-time lectr. anthropology Howard U., Washington, 1963-67, asst. prof. anthropology, 1967-79, assoc. prof., 1969-71; curator of anthropology Mus. Tex. Tech U., assoc. prof. anthropology, assoc. prof. mus. sci. Tex. Tech U., Lubbock, 1971-75, curator of anthropology, Mus., assoc. prof., acting coordinator mus. sci. program, 1975-76, curator of anthropology, Mus., prof. and acting coordinator mus. sci. program, 1976-77, acting chmn. mus. sci. dept., curator of anthropology, Mus., 1977-78; keeper of collections Univ. Mus., U. Pa., adj. prof. anthropology U. Pa., Phila., 1978-81; dir.

Univ. Mus., prof. anthropology N.Mex. State U., Las Cruces, 1982—; cons. on textiles; research assoc. Textile Mus., Washington, Carnegie Mus. Natural History, Pitts.; faculty Am. Law Inst.-ABA course on legal problems of mus. adminstrn., 1979, 81, 82; mem. permanent planning com. for roundtable on mus. textiles, Textile Mus., 1973—. Fellow Am. Anthropol. Assn. (Royal Anthropol. Inst., AAAS; mem. Soc. Am. Archaeology, Current Anthropology (assoc.), Am. Assn. Mus. (council 1978-80), Internat. Com. Mus. of Ethnography (exec. bd. 1980-83), Assn. Sci. Mus. Dirs., Mountain-Plains Mus. Conf., Western Regional Mus. Conf., Sigma Xi, Delta Delta Delta. Episcopalian. Club: Soc. Women Geographers N.Y.C. Assoc. editor Am. Antiquity for Current Research, 1970-75; contbg. editor Quar. Rev. of Archaeology; contbr. articles to profl. publs. Office: Box 3564 New Mexico State Univ Las Cruces NM 88003

KING, MICHAEL STEPHEN, accountant; b. Vero Beach, Fla., July 8, 1949; s. Andrew Alfred and Margaret Elaine (Hines) K.; student Mesa Coll., 1968-69, San Diego State U., 1970-71, U. San Diego, 1971; m. Geraldine Diane Dykstra, Aug. 25, 1972; children—Joel Richard, Micah Andrew. Partner, sr. staff acct. Maranhao & King, San Diego, 1970-73; mng. sr. staff Drummond Bates & Co., San Diego, 1973; treas., dir. ECI Industries, Inc., Beverly Hills and San Diego, 1974-75; owner, mgr. King & Co., San Diego, 1975-78, 82—, Fresno, Calif., 1978—. Mem. adv. com. San Diego Community Colls. Mem. Nat. Assn. Accts., Fresno C. of C. Republican. Co-author: Accounto-metrics/Graphics. Office: 9939 Hilbert St Suite 207 San Diego CA 92131

KING, PETER JOSEPH, JR., utilities exec.; b. Concord, N.H., Aug. 5, 1921; s. Peter Joseph and Helen (Hallinan) K.; m. Louise Lynch, Sept. 11, 1948; children—Anne, Peter J. III. B.S., Georgetown U., 1942; LL.B., Harvard U., 1958, postgrad. Harvard Bus. Sch. advanced mgmt. program, 1966. Bar: N.H. 1949. Sole practice law, Concord, 1948-51; atty. AEC, Portsmouth, Ohio, 1952-53; with Colo. Interstate Gas Co., Colorado Springs, 1953—, pres., 1976—, dir. Colorado Springs Nat. Bank. Bd. dirs. The Stratton Home. Served to lt. U.S. Army, 1942-45, 51-52. Mem. Interstate Nat. Gas Assn., Gas Research Inst. Roman Catholic. Clubs: Denver Petroleum, Broadmoor Golf, Garden of the Gods, El Paso. Home: 7 Chase Ln Colorado Springs CO 80906 Office: PO Box 1087 Colorado Springs CO 80944

KING, RICHARD LOUIS, author, editor, publisher, librarian; b. Portland, Oreg., May 21, 1937; s. Louis and Mary Elizabeth (White) K. B.A. in History, Calif. State U., Sacramento, 1964; postgrad. UCLA, 1964, M.S. in Library Sci., 1970. Head circulation dept., acting curator history, bus. and econs., library of Grad. Sch. Mgmt., UCLA, 1966-70, head bus. and econs. reference dept. library, 1971-77, acting head social scis. reference dept., 1976-77, bus. librarian, 1977-78; lectr. seminars for realty profls. library Calif. State U., Long Beach, 1980; cons. to law firms, businesses, acad. insts., Los Angeles, 1966—. Served with USAF, 1960-64. Mem. Calif. Library Assn., ALA (chmn. bus. reference services com., 1973-75). Author: Airport Noise Pollution: a Bibliography of Its Effects on People and Property, 1973; editor, pub. noise pollution publs. Address: 12614 E Park St Cerritos CA 90701

KING, RICHARD MAURICE, JR., planning executive; b. Wilmington, N.C., Jan. 15, 1935; s. Richard Maurice Sr. and Eleanor Pearl (Watson) K.; m. Edith Page Stevenson, Dec. 26, 1960 (dec.); 1 dau., Eleanor Elizabeth. B.S. in Math., U. N.C., 1956. Statis. engr. E.I. du Pont, Parlin, N.J., 1957-59; research statistician Am. Cyanamid, Stamford, Conn., 1959-65, group leader, 1965-71; prin. mem. tech. staff Xerox Corp., Rockville, Md., 1971-76, cons. mem. tech. staff, El Segundo, Calif., 1976-78, mgr. Advanced Systems, Arlington, Va., 1978-81, mgr. 9700 Planning, El Segundo, 1981—. Mem. Am. Statis. Assn. Home: 28738 Covecrest Dr Rancho Palos Verdes CA 90274 Office: Xerox Printing Systems 880 Apollo St El Segundo CA 90245

KING, ROBERT PAUL, mgmt. cons.; b. Anniston, Ala., Feb. 10, 1938; s. S. S. and Maedel Odessa (Strickland) K.; B.Engring. Physics, Auburn U., 1961; postgrad. UCLA, 1964, U. So. Calif., 1965-66; m. Aug. 10, 1968; children—Kendra Elizabeth, Natasha Christine. Deep space telecommunications devel. engr. Calif. Inst. Tech./Jet Propulsion Lab., Pasadena, 1964-65; dir. project mgmt. and adminstrn. Astrodata, Inc., Anaheim, Calif., 1965-70; area mgr. State of Nev. for Dale Carnegie Courses, 1970-71; pres. Robert King & Assos., Inc., Anaheim, Calif., 1971—; lectr. in field. Co-chmn. election com. Bruce Nestande for Calif. Assembly, 1970; mem. spl. task force City of Anaheim, 1967. Served to 1st lt. U.S. Army, 1962-63. Recipient Disting. Service award City of Anaheim, 1968; Letter of Accommadation, United Way of Orange County, 1975; Cert. of Appreciation, U.S. Army's 6th Recruiting Dist., 1973. Mem. Internat. Soc. for Gen. Semantics, Am. Soc. for Tng. and Devel., Am. Mgmt. Assn., Auburn U. Alumni Assn., World Future Soc. (life), The Humanist. Patentee in field; contbr. articles to profl. jours. Office: 2415 S Manchester St Suite E Anaheim CA 92802

KING, RODNEY LYNN, real estate appraiser, broker; b. Ada, Okla., Sept. 27, 1946; s. Sparkey and Irene Elizabeth (Green) K.; A.A., Modesto Jr. Coll., 1967; B.A., Calif. State U., Fullerton, 1969; m. Phyllis J. Dye, Feb. 10, 1973; children—Matthew Rodney, Eric Michael. Right of way agt. Calif. Div. Hwys., San Bernardino, 1969-72; real estate appraiser Ray R. Hastings, San Bernardino, 1972-75; owner, mgr. King Realty and Investment Co., Redlands, Calif., 1975—, Rodney L. King Inc., 1978—; instr. Crafton Hills Coll., 1973-79. Served to lt. (j.g.) USCG, 1973-77. Mem. Soc. Real Estate Appraisers (asso.), San Bernardino Real Estate Bd., Nat. Assn. Realtors, Tau Kappa Epsilon. Republican. Methodist. Office: 1025 Calle de Acacia Redlands CA 92373

KING, ROSALIE ROSSO, educator; b. Tacoma, May 22, 1938; d. Stanley and Gertrude Emma (Conrad) Rosso; B.S., U. Wash., 1960, Ph.D., 1975; M.Ed., Mass. State Coll., Framingham, 1965; m. Indle Gifford King, Sept. 10, 1960; children—Indle Gifford, Paige Phyllis. Product devel. Lyndens (Wash.) State Coop., 1960; with Seattle Times, 1961; acad. adv. U. Wash., Seattle, 1965-67, asso. and lectr., 1967-75, chmn. div. textile sci. and costume studies, 1975-82; mem. flammable fabrics adv. com. Consumer Product Safety Commn., 1977-79; cons. textile flammability litigation. Pres., Mercer Island Sch. PTA, 1972-73; active Cub Scouts, Girl Scouts. Denney fellow, 1973-74. Mem. Am. Assn. Textile Chemists and Colorists, Am. Chem. Soc., ASTM, Nat. Assn. Coll. Profs. Textiles and Clothing, Fashion Group, Pi Beta Phi, Omicron Nu (nat. v.p. 1978-80, pres. 1981-83). Clubs: Women's Univ., U. Wash. Faculty (dir.). Contbr. articles to profl. jours.; participant fiber art exhbns. Home: 5075 W Mercer Way Mercer Island WA 98040 Office: U Wash Seattle WA 98195

KING, ROY EDWARD, safety engineer; b. San Francisco, Apr. 2, 1921; s. Walter John Hartman and Ella Anna (Kauck) K.; m. Marilyn Audrey Happ, Sept. 22, 1946; 1 son, Brian Edward. Grad. in engring. U.S. Mcht. Marine Acad., 1943; law student Oakland City Coll., 1957, U. Calif., 1959. Lic. safety engr., Calif. Personnel and safety dir. Am. Manganese Steel Co., Oakland, Calif., 1952-58; safety engr. Crum & Forester, Reliance Ins. Co., Pacific Employers Ins. Co., San Francisco, 1958-66; mgr. safety Transam. Ins. Co. Sacramento br., 1976—; safety cons. Sacramento, Lodi and Rio Vista, Calif. Served with USN, 1943-46. Named to World Golf Hall of Fame, 1976. Mem. Am. Soc. Safety Engrs. (exec. com., legis. affairs com.), No. Calif. Indsl. Safety Soc. Republican. Roman Catholic. Clubs: U. Calif. Alumni, Engrs., Toastmakers, Oakland 20-30.

KING, SAMUEL PAILTHORPE, judge; b. Hankow, China, Apr. 13, 1916 (parents Am. citizens); s. Samuel W. and Pauline (Evans) K.; B.S., Yale, 1937, LL.B., 1940; m. Anne Van Patten Grilk, July 8, 1944; children—Samuel Pailthorpe, Louise van Patten, Charlotte Lelepoki. Admitted to D.C. bar, Hawaii bar, 1940; practiced in Honolulu, 1941-42, 46-61, 70-72, Washington, 1942; atty. King & McGregor, 1947-53, King & Myhre, 1957-61; judge 1st Circuit Ct., Hawaii, 1961-70, sr. judge Family Ct., 1969-70; judge U.S. Dist. Ct., Hawaii, 1972—, chief judge, 1974. Faculty, Nat. Coll. State Trial Judges, 1968-73, Nat. Inst. Trial Advocacy, 1976—; mem. com. to implement Criminal Justice Act, U.S. Jud. Conf., 1979—. Chmn., Hawaii Republican Central Com., 1953-55. Served with USNR, 1942-46; capt. Res. Mem. Hawaii Bar Assn. (pres. 1953). Episcopalian. Co-editor: The Theory and Practice of Go. Office: PO Box 50128 Honolulu HI 96850

KING, SHARON DENISE, legal secretary, poet; b. Dallas, Dec. 6, 1949; d. John Charles and Patsy Marie (Carter) K. Student Glendale Community Coll., 1968-72. Legal sec. Filler, Paytas, Shannon, Fleming and Stephenson, Phoenix, 1968-75, Kenneth K. Miller, 1976-79, F. Reid Nathan, Ltd., 1979-81, Gillenwater and Meyers, P.C., 1981, Warner, Angle, Roper and Hallam, 1981—. Democrat. Baptist. Author: (pen name Sharon Walters) Cast a Ray of Light, 1978.

KING, SHELDON SELIG, hosp. adminstr.; b. N.Y.C., Aug. 28, 1931; s. Benjamin and Jeanne (Fritz) K.; A.B., N.Y.U., 1952; M.S., Yale, 1957; m. Ruth Arden Zeller, June 26, 1955; children—Tracy Elizabeth, Meredith Ellen, Adam Bradley. Adminstrv. intern Montefiore Hosp., N.Y.C., 1952-53, 55; adminstrv. asst. Mt. Sinai Hosp., N.Y.C., 1957-60, asst. dir., 1960-66, dir. planning, 1966-68; exec. dir. Albert Einstein Coll. Medicine-Bronx Municipal Hosp. Center, Bronx, N.Y., 1968-72; asst. prof. Albert Einstein Coll. Medicine, N.Y.C., 1968-72; dir. hosps. and clinics Univ. Hosp., asso. clin. prof. U. Calif., San Diego, 1972-81, acting head div. health care scis., dept. community medicine Sch. Medicine, 1978-81; exec. v.p., dir. Stanford U. Hosp., 1981—; clin. assoc. prof. dept. family, community and preventive medicine Stanford U.; Council of Teaching Hosps. rep. to gen. assembly Assn. Am. Med. Colls., 1978—; mem. adminstrv. bd. Council of Teaching Hosps., 1982—; preceptor George Washington U., Ithaca Coll., Yale, U. Mo., City U. N.Y. Chmn. health care com. San Diego County Immigration Council, 1974-77; adv. council Calif. Health Facilities Commn., 1977-83. Bd. dirs. Hosp. Council San Diego and Imperial Counties, 1974-77, treas., 1976—, pres., 1977—; bd. dirs. United Way San Diego, 1975-80, Brith Milah Bd. Served with AUS, 1953-55. Fellow Am. Coll. Hosp. Adminstrs., Am. Pub. Health Assn., Royal Soc. Health; mem. Am. Hosp. Assn., Calif. Hosp. Assn. (trustee 1978-81). Mem. editorial bd. Jour. Med. Edn., 1979—; mem. editorial adv. bd. Who's Who in Health Care. Home: 989 Cottrell Way Stanford CA 94305 Office: C-204 Stanford U Hosp Stanford CA 94305

KING, WILLIAM MICHAEL, elec. systems tech. advisor, investor; b. San Diego, Nov. 13, 1941; s. Billy Woodruff and Maria Seraphina Rosario (Vaca-Calderon) K.; student Capitol Radio Engring. Inst., 1962; m. Jo Ann Franchetto, July 2, 1960 (div. Sept. 1982); children—Shannon (dec.), Stephanie, Christopher; m. Rosamarie Adams, 1983. Retail audio store mgr., 1959; elec. lab. supr. Cornell-Dubilier Electronics, Los Angeles, 1960-63; engring. mgr. West Coast systems Filtron Co., Culver City, Calif., 1963-66; sr. tech. specialist Garrett Airesearch Co., Torrance, Calif., 1966-67; asst. chief engr., lab. mgr. radar relay div. Teledyne Corp., Santa Monica, 1967; mgr. EMI/EMC ops. Cornell-Dubilier Electronics, Venice, Calif., 1967-77; mgr. pvt. investments, 1977—; tech. advisor in electromagnetic compatibility to computer industry and mil. contractors; free-lance sound rec. engr., ind. record producer, 1959-63. Pres., Exceptional Children's Found., 1978-80; bd. dirs. Calif. Assn. for Retarded, 1978-79. Mem. Soc. Automotive Engrs. (group AE-4). Researcher in fields of electrostatic discharge susceptibility data processing equipment, cardiac pacemakers. Patentee enhanced safety method of interference suppression in hand-held elec. devices, others. Home and Office: 2709 Cardinal Dr Costa Mesa CA 92626

KINGDON, KATHLYN LEE, law firm executive; b. Long Beach, Calif., Jan. 4, 1947; d. John Eldon and Thelmalee (Murphey) K. B.A. in Music, Harding U., 1970; M.M.Ed., U. Colo., 1972. Tchr. Pueblo (Colo.) Sch. Dist. 60, 1972-74; co-owner, mgr. Pueblo Printing & Lito Supply Co., The Lens, La Graphiques Excalibre, Pueblo, Colo., 1974-79; coordinator art dept. Waddell Press, Denver, 1979-80; services supr. Davis, Graham & Stubbs, Denver, 1980—; pvt. tutor; speaker in field. Bd. dirs., singing mem. Classic Chorale. Mem. Nat. Assn. Female Execs. Republican. Home: 17193 E 16th Ave Aurora CO 80011 Office: Davis Graham & Stubbs 950 17th St Denver CO 80202

KINGERY, JAMES, real estate developer; b. Union County, Iowa, June 14, 1935; s. James E. and Lela Vesta (Sanders) K. B.S., U. So. Calif., 1957. Asst. controller Western Lithograph Co., Los Angeles, 1960-62, Pasco Steel Corp., Pomona, 1962-63; exec. v.p. Calprop Corp., Los Angeles, 1963-83; real estate developer, 1983—. Served with U.S. Army, 1958-60. Republican. Methodist. Home: 8747 Shoreham Dr Los Angeles CA 90069 Office: 8680 Melrose Ave Los Angeles CA 90069

KINGSBURY, CAROLYN ANN, aerospace systems engr.; b. Newark, Ohio, Aug. 4, 1938; d. Cecil C. Layman and Orpha Edith (Hisey) Layman Dick; m. James Kingsbury, Apr. 25, 1959; children—Donald Lynn, Kenneth James. B.S. in Math., B.S. in Info. and Computer Scis., U. Calif.-Irvine, 1979; postgrad. West Coast U., 1982—. Integrated test engr. Rockwell Internat., Downey, Calif., 1979-82, system engr., analyst, 1982—. Pres., PTA, Manhattan Beach, Calif., 1971-73; Cub Scout den mother Boy Scouts Am., Manhattan Beach, 1972-73. Recipient. Service award Calif. Congress Parents and Tchrs., 1973; named Outstanding Woman in Industry, YWCA, Los Angeles, 1980. Mem. Nat. Assn. Female Execs., Nat. Mgmt. Assn., AAUW. Republican. Club: Newtowners (pres. 1962). Home: 11392 Stonecress Ave Fountain Valley CA 92708 Office: 12214 Lakewood Blvd Downey CA 90241

KINGSBURY, KENNETH EARL, psychotherapist, social sevices bureau administrator; b. Bozeman, Mont., July 6, 1948; s. Kenneth Euell and Phyllis Mae (Johnson) Funk; m. Janice Ruth Lower, Aug. 7, 1971; 1 son, Taylor Phillip. A.A., Cerritos Coll., 1972; B.A. in Psychology, Calif. State U.-Fullerton, 1974, M.S. in Community/Clin. Psychology, 1976. Intern, Met. State Hosp., Norwalk, Calif., 1971; lectr. in psychology Calif. State U., Fullerton, 1975; intern in psychology Orange County (Calif.) Mental Health Agy., 1975-76; clin. coordinator Teen Help-Youth Service Bur., Fountain Valley, Calif., 1976-80, exec. dir., 1980—; pvt. practice marriage and family therapy, Huntington Beach, Calif., 1980—; cons. counseling, non-profit mgmt.; mem. adv. bd. Orange County Coalition in Alcohol and Drug Abuse and Disabled; chmn. Fountain Valley Sch. Attendance Rev. Bd. Mem. United Way Campaign Cabinet, West Orange County, 1982; co-chmn. Orange County Health Care Agy./Social Sci. Agy. Adv. Bd. Served with USAF, 1966-70. Named Orange County Outstanding Citizen, KNOB, 1982; lic. marriage, family and child therapist, cert. hypnotherapist, Calif. Mem. United Youth Agys. (chmn.), Orange County Prevention Network (co-chmn.), Psi Chi, Phi Kappa Phi. Democrat. Club: Omni Business. Home: 4612 Fox Glen La Verne CA 91750 Office: 10200 Slater Ave Fountain Valley CA 92708

KINGSBURY, KENNETH EARL, JR., publisher; b. Black Rock, Ark., Sept. 30, 1945; s. Kenneth Earl and Dora (Bell) K.; A.A. in Bus. Mgmt., El Camino Coll., Torrance, Calif., 1977. Freelance film dir., N.Y.C., 1968-71; ednl. cons. Programmed Systems Co., Los Angeles, 1972-77; credit cons. Computer Credit Co., 1977-78; credit mgr. Windsor Publs. Co., Woodland Hills, Calif., 1978-80; pres. Black Stallion Country, Inc., also sec.-treas. King-Bart Group, Inc., Culver City, Calif., 1980—; editor, pub. Kingsbury's Who's Who In Country and Western Music, 1981. Served with USAR, 1963-68. Mem. Variety Entertainers Guild Am. (sec.-treas. 1975-77), Country Music Assn., Acad. Country Music, Country Music Found. (assoc.). Republican. Mem. Salvation Army. Office: PO Box 2250 Culver City CA 90230

KINGSLEY, SHERWOOD CLARK, accountant; b. Los Angeles, July 5, 1939; s. William Jackson and Eleanor Nevin (Veale) K.; m. Rona Toby Fretter, Nov. 8, 1980; 1 son, Aron Sherwood. Staff acct. Arthur Young & Co., Los Angeles, 1965-66; supr. accounts payable Interpace Co., Los Angeles, 1966-67; controller Illig Constrn. Co., Los Angeles, 1967-73; supr. John F. Forbes Co., Los Angeles, 1974; practice public acctg., Los Angeles, 1975—. Organizer alumni fund raising orgn. Webb Sch. C.P.A., Calif. Mem. Am. Inst. C.P.A.s, Calif. Soc. C.P.A.s, SAR. Republican. Congregationalist. Clubs: Lions (pres. 1981-82), Masons (master 1976). Home: 4159 Keystone Ave Culver City CA 90230

KINION, EDWARD FRANKLIN, law enforcement administrator; b. Casper, Wyo., June 4, 1933; s. Ernest Lemial and Jessie Irene (Phillipsen) K.; m. Doris Marlene Hahn, Aug. 5, 1956; children—Kimberly Irene, Karen Louise. A.A. in Law Enforcement, Casper Coll., 1959, A.S., 1967. Cert. profl. peace officer, Wyo. With Casper (Wyo.) Police Dept., 1959—, sgt. in charge of traffic div., 1969-73, master lt. in charge of traffic div., 1973-76, comdr. patrol div., 1976-80, chief of police, 1980—; instr. driver tng. Casper Coll., 1969-76; cert. assessor Police Assessment Center for Hirings and Promotions. Served with M.P., U.S. Army, 1955. Named Peace Officer of Yr., Casper Exchange Club, 1967; recipient Frank Morgan award Explorer Scouting, 1977. Mem. Internat. Assn. Chiefs of Police, Nat. Assn. Chiefs of Police, Wyo. Assn. Chiefs of Police (pres.), Wyo. Peace Officers Assn. (1st v.p.). Republican. Lodges: Kiwanis, Masons. Founder Community Service Patrol, Casper, 1976, hit and run accident investigative unit, 1980, crime prevention programs, 1980, Crime Watch Program, 1982; co-founder Explorer Post, 1974. Office: 200 N David St Casper WY 82601

KINNEE, SANDY (FLOYD AMOS, III), artist; b. Port Huron, Mich., Mar. 30, 1947; s. Floyd A., Jr., and Annabel V. (O'Hare) K.; m. Gale B. Murray, Jan. 22, 1977; 1 dau., Lauren. Student Port Huron Jr. Coll., 1965-67; B.F.A. in Printmaking, U. Mich., 1969, postgrad., 1970; M.F.A. in Printmaking, Wayne State U., 1976; Atelier 17, Paris, 1979. Printmaker, painter, papermaker; one-man shows include: Hollins Coll., Va., 1974, Peter M. David Gallery, Mpls., 1976, 78, 80, Huber Gallery, Washington, 1978, Allport Gallery, Larkspur, Calif., 1978, Two Plus Gallery, Denver, 1978, St. Clair County Community Coll., Port Huron, Mich., 1979, Webb and Parsons Gallery, New Canaan, Conn., 1980, Dubins Gallery, Los Angeles, 1980, Davidson Galleries, Seattle, 1980, New Provincetown Group Gallery, Provincetown, Mass., 1981, Blue Door Too Gallery, Denver, 1981, Orion Gallery, N.Y.C., 1981, Midwest Mus. Am. Art, Elkhart, Ind., 1981, Creighton U., Omaha, 1981, Phila. Art Alliance, 1981, Marcus/Gordon, Pitts., 1981, Lambert/Miller, Phoenix, 1982, Mather Gallery, Case Western Res. U., Cleve., 1982, Gallery Moos, Calgary, Alta., Can., 1983; works represented exhbns. including Mus. Modern Art, N.Y.C., 1976, Nat. Collection Fine Arts, Washington, 1977, Smithsonian Traveling Exhbn., 1978-80, Phila. Mus. Art, 1979, Western States Arts Found. Traveling Exhbn., 1980-82, Lerner/Heller, N.Y.C., 1981, Madison (Wis.) Art Ctr., 1982; represented in permanent collections: Met. Mus. Art, N.Y.C., State Office Bldg., Columbus, Ohio, Allen Art Mus., Oberlin, Evergreen State Coll., Wash., N.Mex. Mus., Portland (Oreg.) Art Mus. Printmakers fellow Western States Arts Found., 1979, recipient awards including Purchase award Mus. N.Mex., Santa Fe, 1978. Contbr. to profl. publs.

KINNEY, GORDON DICKINSON, educator; b. Portland, Oreg., July 25, 1922; s. Robert Crouch and Althea Edna (Moores) K.; m. Gloria Dandell Eaton, Aug. 31, 1947; children—Janice Lee, Alan Gordon, Pamela Susan, Diana Joyce Bianchini. B.A. in Edn., Central Wash. U., Ellensburg, 1974. Sr. electronics technician, insp. calibration lab., tech. writer and editor Boeing Co., Seattle, 1957-64; instr. electronics and math. Seattle Sch. Dist., part-time 1959-64; instr. electronics Clover Park Vocat. Edn. Ctr., Tacoma, Wash., 1964-66; tech. writer Milmanco, Renton, Wash., 1966-67; vocat. tchr. math. and sci., guidance counselor Wash. State Reformatory, Monroe, 1967-82; tutor, proctor edn. corr. program Seattle Breakers Hockey Club, part-time 1982-83. Discussion-action group leader Puget Sound Coalition. Served with USAAF, 1942-46. Mem. Am. Vocat. Assn., Wash. Vocat. Assn. (pres. guidance sect. 1982-83), Soc. for Tech. Communications. Congregationalist. Home: 7519 S Taft St Seattle WA 98178

KINNEY, HARRY EDWIN, mayor, former bldg. contractor, mech. engr.; b. Trinidad, Colo., June 7, 1924; B.S. in M.E., U. N.Mex., 1945; m. Carol N. Roberts, Aug. 1970; 2 children. Staff mem. Sandia Labs., 1956-73; chmn. Middle Rio Grande Council Govts. of N.Mex., 1970-72; chmn. City-County Joint Alcoholism Bd., 1969-72; pres. Albuquerque-Bernalillo County Econ. Opportunity Bd., 1964-66, N.Mex. Conf. Social Welfare, 1965-67; commr. City of Albuquerque, 1966-73, vice chmn., 1970-71, chmn., 1971-73; commr. Bernalillo County, 1956-58, 61-65; spl. asst. to U.S. senator, 1973-74; mayor Albuquerque, 1974-77, 81—; mem. adv. bd. U.S. Conf. Mayors, 1975-77, 82—, chmn., 1977; mem. mgmt. adv. group constrn. grants EPA, 1982—; mem. Adv. Com. Intergovtl. Relations, 1975-77. Pres. Ams. for Rational Energy Alternatives, 1980—; mem. met. bd. dirs. YMCA, 1978-81; 2d v.p. Chaparral council Girl Scouts U.S.A., 1978-81. Served with USNR, 1943-46, 50-53. Mem. ASME, Naval Res. Assn., Kappa Sigma. Episcopalian. Address: 3006 Vista Grande NW Albuquerque NM 87120

KINNEY, JACK ALANSON, sociologist, scientist; b. Port Allegany, Pa., Sept. 11, 1921; s. Alanson and Hazel Belle (Greer) K.; student Pa. State U., 1946-47, George Williams Coll., 1947-48, Roosevelt U., 1948; M.A., U. Chgo., 1951; postgrad. U. N.C., 1958-60, Boston U., 1964-66; m. Shirley J. Davis, Nov. 10, 1953; children—J. Alleyn, Jothen S. With Inst. for Juvenile Research, Chgo., 1949-51, Ill. Youth Commn., Rock Island, Ill., 1951-52, Rock Island Arsenal, 1952-54, Ordnance Civilian Personnel Agy., Rock Island, 1954-57, U.S. Army Research Office, Durham, N.C., 1957-61, U.S. Navy Personnel Research Activity, Washington, 1961-64; naval research asso. chief of naval ops. Center Naval Analyses, 1964-65; with Inst. Naval Studies, Cambridge, Mass., 1965-66; supervisory staff asso. Arthur D. Little, Inc., Cambridge, 1966-74; sr. scientist Anacapa Scis., Inc., Santa Barbara, Calif., 1974—. Commr. Explorer Scouts, Durham council Boy Scouts Am., 1958-60; active Civitan Internat., 1958-61. Served with USAAF, 1942-46. Decorated Air medal with 2 oak leaf clusters, Purple Heart; recipient Presdl. award Arthur D. Little Inc., 1973; Cert. of Recognition, Australian Dept. Bus. and Consumer Affairs, 1979. Mem. Human Factors Soc., Am. Soc. Criminology, Soc. Gen. Systems Research, Acad. Criminal Justice Scis., Nat. Council on Crime and Delinquency, Am. Judicature Soc., Internat. Assn. Chiefs of Police, Soc. Police and Criminal Psychology, Am. Soc. Indsl. Security, Nat. Criminal Justice Assn., Western Soc. Criminology, Western and Pacific Assn. Criminal Justice Educators, Assn. Criminal Justice Research, Internat. Assn. Law Enforcement Intelligence Analysts, Am. Soc. Indsl. Security, Sigma Chi. Home: 5182 Vista Bahia Santa Barbara CA 93111 Office: 901 Olive St Santa Barbara CA 93102

KINNEY, JEANNE JONES, geologist; b. Spokane, Wash., Mar. 31, 1955; d. Robert Keith and Margaret Dora (Renard) Jones; B.S. in Geology, U. Wyo., 1977; m. Andrew J. Kinney, May 15, 1976; 1 son, Aaron Timothy. Office technician Getty Oil Co., Ventura, Calif., 1974; student geologist Panhandle Eastern Pipeline Co., Liberal, Kans., 1975; 208 specialist Wyo. Conservation Commn., Cheyenne, 1977-78; geologist U.S. Bur. Mines, Albany, Oreg., 1978—, profl. rep. fed. women's program, 1978—. Founding mem. Women's Inst. Fin. Edn., 1979—. Recipient Spl. Achievement award Bur. Mines, 1982. Mem. Geol. Soc. Am., Am. Inst. Profl. Geologists, Soc. Miscellaneous Oreg. Geoscientists, Sigma Xi, Beta Sigma Phi. Author tech. report U.S. Bur. Mines. Home: 1600 SW Takena St Albany OR 97321 Office: PO Box 70 1450 SW Queen St Albany OR 97321

KINNEY, MARJORIE SHARON, mktg. and fin. exec.; b. Gary, Ind., Jan. 11, 1940; d. David Harrison and Florence Clara Dunning; student El Camino Coll., 1957-58; L.H.D., West Coast U., 1982; m. Daniel Dean Kinney, Dec. 31, 1958 (div. 1973); children—Steven Daniel, Michael Alan, Gregory Lincoln, Bradford David. Exec. v.p. Kinney Advt., Inc., Inglewood, Calif., 1958-68 founder, chmn. bd. Person to Person, Inc., Cleve., 1969-72; chief exec. officer, pres. Kinney Mktg. Corp., Encino, Calif., 1972-80; sr. v.p. Beverly Hills Savs. and Loan Assn., 1980—; dir. Safeway Stores, Inc., Chubb/Pacific Indemnity Co.; adv. bd. Marine Nat. Bank; lectr. profl. groups, univs. Bd. dirs. ARC, 1976-81, United Way, 1979-81; trustee West Coast U.; adv. bd. U.S. Human Resources. Mem. Savs. Inst. Mktg., Calif. Savs. and Loan League, Women of Wall Street West (bd. dirs.), Fin. Inst. Mktg. Assn. Republican. Presbyterian. Office: 450 N Roxbury Dr Beverly Hills CA 90210

KINNEY, PAUL HARRIS, production company executive; b. Sacramento, Apr. 26, 1944; s. Melvin Eldon and Dorothy Jean (Williams) K.; m. Viola Loretta Sentman, Sept. 5, 1965; children—Jason Paul, Kristina Marie; m. Patricia Ann Davis, Aug. 25, 1979; 1 son, Taryn Davis. B.S., Calif. State U.-Hayward, 1968; M.A., U. Calif.-Berkeley, 1971. Pub., editor Union City (Calif.) Leader, 1969-72; adminstrv. asst. to Calif. Assemblyman, Ventura, 1972-74; dir. Assembly Majority Cons., Calif. Legislature, 1975-81; owner, mgr. Paul Kinney Prodns., Sacramento, 1981—. Recipient Best Weekly News Story award San Francisco Press Club, 1970, 1971. Democrat. Producer Capitol Restoration Gala, 1982, Harvest Jazz at Paul Maisson Winery, others.

KINNEY, ROBERT BRUCE, mechanical engineering educator; b. Joplin, Mo., July 20, 1937; s. William Marion and Olive Frances (Smith) K.; m. Carol Stewart, Jan. 29, 1961; children—Rodney, David, Linda. B.S., U. Calif.-Berkeley, 1959, M.S., 1961; Ph.D., U. Minn., 1965. Sr. research engineer United Aircraft Research Labs., East Hartford, Conn., 1965-68; assoc. prof. mech. engring. U. Ariz., Tucson, 1968-78, prof., 1978—, assoc. dept. head, 1980—. Alexander von Humboldt grantee, 1976-77. Fellow AAAS, AIAA; mem. ASME. Office: Aerospace/Mech Engring Dept U Ariz Tucson AZ 85721

KINNICUTT, PHILIP HEYWOOD, energy company marketing executive; b. Worcester, Mass., Sept. 3, 1941; s. Roger and Janet (Heywood) K.; m. Annetta Lynn Johns, June 21, 1969; children—Kainoa R. C., Leiana J. B.A., Williams Coll., 1963; M.B.A., U. Hawaii, 1979. Advt. salesman Hawaii Bus. Pub. Corp., Honolulu, 1963-65; spl. projects dir. Hawaii Bus. Pub. Corp., Honolulu, 1969-71; mgr. advt. and sales promotion Gasco, Inc., subs. Pacific Resources, Inc., Honolulu, 1971-77, dir. pub. relations Pacific Resources, Inc., 1977-79, v.p. pub. relations Pacific Resources, Inc., 1979-83, v.p. mktg. Gasco, Inc., 1983—. Chmn. pub. relations steering com. Aloha United Way, 1981. Served to lt. j.g. USNR, 1965-68. Mem. Pub. Relations Soc. Am. (accredited; pres. Hawaii chpt. 1982), Am. Mktg. Assn. (pres. Hawaii chpt. 1975-76). Clubs: Kaneohe (Hawaii) Yacht, Pacific (Honolulu). Home: 341 Iliaina St Kailua HI 96734 Office: PO Box 3379 Honolulu HI 96842

KINNISON, ROBERT RAY, statistician; b. Los Angeles, Sept. 10, 1934; s. Ray Hiram and Helen Louise (Krozek) K.; m. Karen Dale Wingo, July 10, 1959; children—Sharon Dale, Donald Ray. B.A., Pomona Coll., 1956; Ph.D., UCLA, 1971. Pharmacologist, Rexall Drug and Chem. Co., Los Angeles, 1960-68; research statistician U. Calif.-San Francisco, 1971-72; statistician EPA, Las Vegas, 1972-79, Battelle Pacific N.W. Labs., Richland, Wash., 1979—; adj. assoc. prof. math. U. Nev.-Las Vegas, 1974-79. Mem. Am. Statis. Assn., Biometric Soc., AAAS, Simulation Council, Sigma Xi. Democrat. Methodist. Club: Masons. Assoc. editor: Jour. Simulation, 1972—. Home: 700 N Montana Pl Kennewick WA 99336 Office: Battelle Pacific NW Labs Battelle Blvd Richland WA 99352

KINNISON, ROBERT WHEELOCK, certified public accountant; b. Des Moines, Sept. 17, 1914; s. Virgil R. and Sopha J. (Jackson) K.; m. Randi Hjelle, Oct. 28, 1971; children—Paul F., Hazel Jo Huff. B.S. in Acctg., U. Wyo., 1940. C.P.A., Wyo., Colo. Ptnr. 24 hour auto service, Laramie, Wyo., 1945-59; pvt. practice acctg., Laramie, Wyo., 1963-71, Las Vegas, Nev., 1972-74, Westminster, Colo., 1974-76, Ft. Collins, Colo., 1976—. Served with U.S. Army, 1941-45; PTO. Mem. Am. Soc. C.P.A.s, Wyo. Soc. C.P.A.s, Am. Legion (past comdr.), Laramie Soc. C.P.A.s (pres. 1966), VFW. Clubs: Laramie Optimist (pres. 1950), Sertoma. Home: 401 N Summit View Dr Fort Collins CO 80524 Office: 2050 Airway Ave Fort Collins CO 80524

KINRADE, KERRY FRANCIS, ins. exec.; b. Los Angeles, Oct. 1, 1936; s. John T. and Claire (Bovee) K.; B.A., UCLA, 1959; M.P.A., U. So. Calif., 1969; m. Linda C. Wolf, May 31, 1969. With State Compensation Ins. Fund, San Francisco, 1960—, supervising mgmt. analyst, 1979—. Mem. Am. Soc. Public Adminstrn., Nat. Micrographics Assn., Office Automation Research Forum. Lutheran. Office: 1275 Market St San Francisco CA 94103

KINRICH, JEFFREY HAROLD, management consultant; b. Los Angeles, Apr. 2, 1955; s. J. Ken and Sara (Feldman) K.; m. Juli B. Bliss, May 25, 1980. B.A. in Math. summa cum laude, Pomona Coll., 1976; M.S. in Stats., Stanford U., 1977; M.B.A. in Fin., U. Md., 1980. Statistician Lawrence Livermore Lab., Livermore, Calif., 1977-78, BDM Corp., McLean, Va., 1978-80; sr. cons. Price Waterhouse, Los Angeles, 1981-82; mgr., mgmt. adv. services dept. Price Waterhouse, Century City, Calif., 1982—. Recipient Outstanding Grad. award U. Md. Grad. Sch. Mgmt., 1980. Mem. Am. Statis. Assn., Phi Beta Kappa. Democrat. Jewish. Office: 1880 Century Park East Los Angeles CA 90067

KINSELLA, WILLIAM RAPHAEL, accountant; b. Los Angeles, Aug. 11, 1954; s. William Patrick and Mercedes (Taboada) K.; m. Janet Louise Ungaro, July 7, 1979. B.S., Loyola U., 1975; M.B.A., U. So. Calif., 1979. With Arthur Young & Co., Los Angeles, 1975—, tax mgr., 1980—; lectr. tax acctg. Loyola Marymount U., 1978—. Mem. Am. Inst. C.P.A.s, Calif. Soc. C.P.A.s, Delta Sigma Pi. Club: So. Calif. Alumni (pres.). Office: 515 S Flower St Los Angeles CA 90071

KINSER, RICHARD EDWARD, management consultant; b. Los Angeles, May 14, 1936; s. Edward Lee and M. Yvonne (Withes) K.; B.A. in Econs., Stanford U., 1958; m. Suzanne Carol Logan, Mar. 22, 1958. Mgr., U.S. Steel Corp., San Francisco, 1958-65; v.p. Booz-Allen & Hamilton, Inc., San Francisco, 1965-78, Washington, 1971-73; sr. v.p., dir. William H. Clark Assocs., Inc., San Francisco, 1979-82; dep. dir. presdl. personnel The White House, Washington, 1982—; dir. Measurmatic, Inc., San Francisco. Bd. dirs. San Francisco Bicentenial Com., 1976. Mem. World Affairs Council. Republican. Clubs: Bankers; Orinda Country, Commonwealth. Office: 517 Washington St San Francisco CA 94111 also 2533 Waterside Dr NW Washington DC 70008

KINSEY-CALORI, JOANNE, broadcasting co. exec.; b. McKeesport, Pa.; d. George Morris and Pauline Vivian (Anderson) Kinsey; B.A.-M.A., Ohio State U., 1976; Ph.D., Harvard U., 1982; m. Dan John Calori, June 6, 1952 (div.); children—Paula Christine, Kevin Kinsey. Reporter, Sta. WOSU, Ohio State U., Columbus, 1969-70, communications asst. dept. continuing edn., 1970-72, public relations dir. Coll. Adminstrv. Sci., 1974-75, acting asst. prof. communications and psychology, 1971-76; editor Columbus region Internat. Harvester Corp., 1973-77; pres., co-owner Profl. Broadcasting Services, Redondo Beach, Calif., 1976—. Pres., PTA, Marburn, Ridgeview, Whetstone schs., Columbus, 1965-70; campaign mgr. Republican party Franklin County, 1965-68. Recipient spl. award for outstanding community service Columbus Pub. Schs. Mem. Nat. Acad. TV Arts and Scis., Women in Communications, So. Calif. Wine Writers (charter), Archaeology Soc. Columbus, Pacific Pioneer Broadcasters, Mirrors and Chimes, Jr. League, Phi Beta Kappa, Phi Kappa Phi. Presbyterian. Clubs: Worthington Music, Clintonville Women's, Columbus Players. Office: Suite 10 625 Esplanade Redondo Beach CA 90277

KINTZELE, JOHN ALFRED, lawyer; b. Denver, Aug. 16, 1936; s. Louis Richard and Adele (Humphreys) K.; B.S., U. Colo., 1958; m. Shirley Ann Asklof, June 25, 1965; children—John A., Marcia A., Elizabeth A. Admitted to Colo. bar, 1961; pvt. practice law, Denver, 1962—; sr. ptnr. Kintzele & Assos., Denver, 1978—; corp. officer, dir. Kintzele, Inc., Denver, 1979—. Election commr. City of Denver, 1975-79. Served to 1st lt. U.S. Army, 1965-68. Mem. ABA, Colo. Bar Assn. (chmn. statewide lawyer referral service), Denver Bar Assn., Am. Judicature Soc. Democrat. Roman Catholic. Home: 2040 Clermont St Denver CO 80207 Office: 1317 Delaware St Denver CO 80204

KINYON, GILBERT EUGENE, anesthesiologist; b. Tipton, Iowa, June 4, 1921; s. Virgil Fern and Lena (Regennitter) K.; B.A., U. Iowa, 1946, M.D., 1950; m. Jessie Marie Morris, Feb. 16, 1952 (dec.); children—Michelle, Leslie; m. 2d, Mary Johnston, Nov. 29, 1975. Intern, Methodist Hosp., Indpls., 1950-51; resident anesthesia Univ. Hosps., Iowa City, 1951-53; practice medicine specializing in anesthesiology, La Jolla, Calif., 1953-63; chief anesthesiology San Diego County Hosp., 1963-66; dir. anesthesiology Mercy Hosp. and Med. Center, San Diego, 1968—; assoc. clin. prof. anesthesia U. Calif., San Diego; cons. U.S. Naval Hosp., San Diego. Pres., Arthur E. Guedel Anesthesia Meml. Center, San Francisco. Served with AUS, 1942-45. Decorated Bronze Star medal with oak leaf cluster, Purple Heart with oak leaf cluster. Diplomate Am. Bd. Anesthesia. Mem. Am., Calif. (dir., past pres.) socs. anesthesiologists, Am. Coll. Anesthesiologists (gov. 1975—), Am. Acad. Anesthesiology, Internat. Soc. Anesthesia, Calif. Med. Assn. (Aesculapius award). Contbr. articles to profl. jours. Home: 5252 Chelsea St La Jolla CA 92037 Office: 4077 5th St San Diego CA 92103

KIONKA, BERNARD CARL, educator; b. Racine, Wis., May 14, 1942; s. Carl Bernard and Evelyn Marguerite (Pagel) K.; B.S., Dana Coll., 1964; M.S., Creighton U., 1969; Ph.D., U. Colo., 1972; m. Edna Lou Schram, Aug. 11, 1967; children—Michael, Kurt. Sci. tchr. Omaha public schs., 1965-67; environ. engr. Charles T. Main Engring., Denver, 1974-75; tchr. biology and chemistry, Pomona High Sch., Arvada, Colo., 1976—; pvt. practice environ. cons., 1975—; environ. cons. firms including Conoco, CH2M-Hill Engring. Mem. Am. Fisheries Soc., Colo.-Wyo. Acad. Sci., NEA, Colo. Edn. Assn., Jefferson County Edn. Assn., Sigma Xi, Alpha Sigma Nu. Republican. Lutheran. Author three biol. lab. manuals; author articles and curriculum materials. Home: 6731 Field St Arvada CO 80004 Office: 8101 W Pomona Dr Arvada CO 80003

KIPP, HENRY WILLIAM, forester, range conservationist; b. Pitts., Dec. 14, 1930; s. Harold Ambrose and Margarita (Boettger) K.; m. Elaine Jane Maki, June 22, 1962; children—Thomas J., Laurie A. B.A. in History, Trinity Coll., Hartford, Conn., 1954; postgrad. U. Pitts., 1955-56, Duke U., 1956-58; B.S. in Forestry, U. Idaho, 1960; M.R.A., U. Mont., 1972. Forestry technologist Bur. Land Mgmt., 1960; forester Idaho Dept. Lands, 1961; with Bur. Indian Affairs, 1962—, supervisory natural resources specialist Rocky Boy's Reservation, Mont., 1968-83, natural resources mgr. Jicarilla Apache Reservation, Dulce, N.Mex., 1983—; lectr. in natural resources No. Mont. Coll., 1973-83; served on Project '80 Extension, water studies commns.; tchr. Triangle Youth Conservation Camps; participant in preparation forest history Rocky Boy's Reservation with Hist. Research Assocs., Missoula, Mont.; tree farmer. Ruling elder First Presbyterian Ch., Havre, Mont., 1972-80; participant Havre C. of C. and Chippewa-Cree Tribe winter outdoor recreation devel. at Bear Paw Ski Bowl, 1975-80; assoc. supr. Hill County (Mont.) Soil and Water Conservation Dist., 1976-83. Recipient 5-Yr. Safety award Bur. Indian Affairs, 1973; letter of commendation Senator Len B. Jordan, Idaho, 1973, Senator John Melcher, Mont., 1981; Havre C. of C. award, 1974. Mem. Soc. Range Mgmt., Soc. Am. Foresters. Republican. Methodist. Contbr. articles in field to Havre Daily News, Bear Paw Sentinel, Rocky Boy's Native Voice. Home: Gen Delivery Dulce NM 87528 Office: Bur Indian Affairs Jicarilla Agy PO Box 167 Dulce NM 87528

KIRBY, CALVIN JON, aircraft co. exec.; b. Bklyn., Sept. 1, 1940; s. Major Henry and Helen Eleanor (Sorell) K.; B.S. in Physics, Long Beach State U., 1969; M.Engring., UCLA, 1979; m. Ann White, Nov. 28, 1963. Tech. supr., Teledyne Semiconductor Co., Hawthorne, Calif., 1970-71; research and devel. engr. TRW Semiconductor, Hawthorne, 1971-72; mem. tech. staff Hughes Aircraft Co., El Segundo, Calif., 1972—, engring. supr., 1973-75, sr. staff engr., 1975-76, head engring. dept., 1976-78, engring. mgr., 1978—; cons. in metallic attachment techniques with indsl. applications, 1975—. Mem. Soc. Mfg. Engring., Am. Def. Preparedness Assn. Mem. Christian Ch. Home: 16165 Mount Gustin Fountain Valley CA 92708 Office: 2060 E Imperial Hwy El Segundo CA 90245

KIRBY, FRANCIS MARION (FRANK), aerospace company program manager; b. Birmingham, Ala., Sept. 13, 1932; s. Francis Marion and Bessie Mae (Nichols) K.; m. Donna Grace Hosegood, Sept. 1, 1962; children—Keith Allen, Leslie Ann, Kyle Norman. B.A. in Physics, UCLA, 1959; M.S.M.E., U. So. Calif., 1970. Mem. tech. staff Advanced Programs, Rocketdyne Div. Rockwell Internat., Canoga Pk., Calif., 1959-76, project engr., 1976-78, program devel. mgr., 1978-80, program mgr. Div. Propulsion Programs, 1980—; mem. chem. propulsion subcom. of space systems tech. adv. com. NASA; mem. Propulsion Tech. Panel U.S. Air Force Space Systems and Tech. Workshop. Served with USAF, 1951-55. Mem. AIAA (Liquid Propulsion Tech. Com.), Nat. Mgmt. Assn. Democrat. Methodist. Contbr. articles to profl. jours. Office: 6633 Canoga Ave Canoga Park CA 91304

KIRBY, WARREN LLOYD, mortgage banking co. exec.; b. Chgo., Mar. 31, 1919; s. Clarence James and Elizabeth Marie (Houlihan) K.; student YMCA Coll., Chgo., 1939, Northwestern U., 1946-48; m. Patricia Hall, Aug. 22, 1942; children—Patricia Diane (Mrs. George R. Schneider), Gregory H., Valerie A. (Mrs. Jamesharvey Biswell). With Brunswick Balke Collender Co., Chgo., 1936-37, Gamble Hinged Music Co., Chgo., 1937-41, Bur. Fgn. and Domestic Commerce, U.S. Dept. Commerce, Chgo., 1941-42, 46-48; with Securities-Intermountain, Inc., Portland, Oreg., 1948—, v.p., 1956—; pres. Fairview Properties Inc. Pres., Simco Fed. Credit Union, Portland, 1964-69. Served with USAAF, 1942-46. Mem. Nat. Office Mgr.'s Assn., Portland Opera Assn. Club: International (Portland).

KIRCHHOFFER, JAMES HAWLEY, fin. planner, investment adv.; b. Mobile, Ala., Jan. 24, 1933; s. Richard Ainslie and Arline Leister (Wagner) K.; A.B., Wabash Coll., 1955; M.Div. (Wabash Coll. scholar), Va. Theol. Sem., 1958; C.F.P., Coll. Fin. Planning, 1980; m. Elaine Marie Pope Biagini, Sept. 16, 1978; children—Lisa, Stephanie, Ann Margaret; stepchildren—Trese, Leslie. Ordained to ministry Episcopal Ch., 1958; vicar Trinity Ch., Lawrenceburg, Ind., 1958-60; asso. rector St. John's Episcopal Ch., Youngstown, Ohio, 1960-62; vicar St. Giles Ch., Moraga, Calif., 1962-67; field underwriter Mut. New York, Berkeley, Calif., 1967-69; owner, operator Personal & Profl. Planning, San Francisco, 1969-70; agt. Bell Funding, Orinda, Calif., 1970-71; agt. Investment Fund Assocs., Orinda, 1971-77; br. mgr. Pvt. Ledger Fin. Services, San Rafael, Calif., 1977-78; registered prin., investment adv., pub. Value Ventures, R&M Investment Mktg., San Rafael, 1978—; instr. adult div. Acalanes High Sch. Dist., Lafayette, Calif. Mem. bd. examining chaplins Diocese Calif.; pres., Inland Valley Elem. Parents Club, Orinda, Inland Valley Intermediate Parents Club, Orinda; mem. book rev. com. Orinda Sch. Dist.; chmn. adv. com. for selection Dixie Sch. Dist. Supt., 1981; commr. Dixie Soccer; bd. dirs. Planned Parenthood, Youngstown; meet dir. All Orinda Swim Meet, 1975-77; bd. dirs. Moraga Valley Pool, Orinda; bd. dirs. founder Orinda-Moraga Fair Housing Council. Registered investment advisor. Mem. Internat. Assn. Fin. Planners (dir. North Bay), Inst. Cert. Fin. Planners Nat. Assn. Tax Consultors. Lodge: Orinda Lions (pres. 1974-75). Home: 835 Greenberry Ln San Rafael CA 94903 Office: 1368 Lincoln Ave San Rafael CA 94901

KIRCHNER, DON F., educator; b. Detroit, Sept. 28, 1931; s. Ralph T. and Frances I. (Schriener) K.; A.B., Mich. State U., 1953; M.B.A., U. Detroit, 1959; Ph.D., U. Calif., Los Angeles, 1969; m. Cecile Dumas. Research analyst Maxon, Inc., Detroit, 1950-53; mgr. merchandising Security Cos., Detroit, 1956; v.p. Richardson-Shaw, Inc., Detroit, 1956-62; chmn. dept. mktg. Calif. State U., 1962—. Served with USAF, 1954-56. Mem. Am. Mktg. Assn., Advt. Club Los Angeles (dir. 1977-81), So. Mktg. Assn., Acad. Mktg. Sci., Am. Acad. Advt., Assn. Consumer Research, Western Mktg. Educators Assn., Sierra Club, Nature Conservancy, Audubon Soc. Roman Catholic. Office: Dept Mktg Calif State U Northridge CA 91330

KIRK, CASSIUS LAMB, JR., lawyer, real estate exec.; b. Bozeman, Mont., June 8, 1929; s. Cassius Lamb and Gertrude Violet (McCarthy) K.; A.B., Stanford U., 1951; J.D., U. Calif., Berkeley, 1954. Admitted to Calif. bar, 1955; asso. firm Cooley, Godward, Castro, Huddleson & Tatum, San Francisco, 1956-60; staff counsel for bus. affairs Stanford U., 1960-78; chief bus. officer, staff counsel Menlo Sch. and Coll., Menlo Park, Calif., 1978-81; pres. Eberli-Kirk Properties, Inc., Menlo Park, 1981—; mem. faculty Coll. Bus. Adminstrn. U. Calif., Santa Barbara, 1967-73. Served with U.S. Army, 1954-56. Mem. Calif. Bar Assn., Stanford Assos., Order of Coif, Phi Alpha Delta. Republican. Clubs: Stanford Faculty, Menlo Faculty. Home: 1330 University Dr Apt 52 Menlo Park CA 94025 Office: 211 E Hacienda Ave Campbell CA 95008

KIRK, CHRISTY LYNN, metals company consumer affairs manager; b. Covina, Calif., Mar. 15, 1951; d. George Oliver and Lois Marie (Jacobs) Stock; m. Randolph William Kirk, Sept. 6, 1969. B.S. in Home Econs., Calif. State U.-Long Beach, 1979. Sec., Reynolds Metals Co., Los Angeles, 1972-74, regional consumer sales rep., 1975-79, regional consumer affairs mgr., 1980—. Mem. Am. Home Econs. Assn., Home Economists in Bus., Soc. Consumer Affairs Profls., Internat. Microwave Power Inst., Grocery Mfrs. Assn. Home: 5108 Huck Finn Ln Culver City CA 90230 Office: Reynolds Metals Co 5670 Wilshire Blvd Los Angeles CA 90036

KIRK, DALE EARL, agricultural engineeer, educator; b. Payette, Idaho, July 2, 1918; s. Earl E. and Susan Lillian (Kent) K.; B.S., Oreg. State U., 1942; M.S., Mich. State U., 1954; m. Esther Lucille Lathrop, Apr. 6, 1939; children—Janet E., Stanley D., Carolyn J., Joyce L., Marvin E. County supr. Agrl. Adjustment Adminstrn., Payette, Idaho, 1939-41; agrl. engr. Oreg. State U., Corvallis, 1942—, faculty, 1942—, prof., 1962—, acting head agrl. engring. dept., 1969-71, 75-76, 80-81; cons. Oreg. Turf & Chem. Co., 1952-62. Leader Boy Scouts Am., 1946-64, 4-H Youth, 1954-60. Served with USNR, 1944-46. Registered profl. engr., Oreg. Fellow Am. Soc. Agrl. Engrs.; mem. Inst. Food Tech., Agrl. Engring. Research Found., Izaak Walton League Am., Sigma Xi. Congregationalist. Contbr. articles in field to profl. jours. Home: 8150 N W Mitchel Dr Corvallis OR 97330 Office: Dept Agrl Engring Oreg State U Corvallis OR 97331

KIRK, HELEN WHITE (MRS. KENNETH BURSON KIRK), club woman; b. Detroit; d. William John and Grace (Ramsay) White; B.A., U. Mich.; m. Kenneth Burson Kirk; children—Cynthia Grace, Helen Victoria. Sec.-treas., dir. Kirk Dial Corp., Beverly Hills, Calif., Dir. Beverly Hills Women's Club, 1936-37, Palm Springs (Calif.) Women's Club, 1953-54; pres. Lifelighters, 1955-56, 71-72, Palm Springs chpt. W.A.I.F., 1958-59; chmn. Bookworms of Assistance League So. Cal., 1967-68; mem. adv. bd. Los Angeles Women's chpt. Freedom's Found., 1972-74, 81; mem. women's com. Los Angeles Philharmonic Orch., Opera Guild Soc. Calif., Bel-Air Guild Children's Hosp.; gen. chmn. ladies div. Rotary Internat. Conv., 1962; pres. Palm Springs chpt. Nat. Charity League, 1965; v.p. women's aux. Desert Hosp., 1965. Mem. Internat. Platform Assn. Clubs: Beverly Hills Garden (pres. 1978-79, 79-80); Ebell of Los Angeles; Beverly Hills Women's. Home: 702 N Bedford Dr Beverly Hills CA 90210 also 155 S Belardo Rd Palm Springs CA 92262

KIRK, JOHN MELVILLE, lawyer; b. Colo. Springs, Colo., Sept. 25, 1946; s. John Melville and Helen Elvira (Rufer) K.; m. Linda C. Lane, Apr. 21, 1973 (div.); children—Kristen Michelle, Timothy Carter. A.B., Johns Hopkins U., 1968; J.D. cum laude, U. N.Mex., 1975. Bar: N.Mex. 1975. Assoc. Johnson & Lamphere, Albuquerque, 1975-79; ptnr. Kirk & Williams, Albuquerque, 1979—; sr. v.p. ops. St. Joseph Hosp., 1983—. Active Albuquerque C. of C. Served lt., USNR, 1968-71. Mem. ABA, N.Mex. Bar Assn., Nat. Health Lawyers Assn., N. Mex. Health Lawyers Assn. (founder), Am. Soc. Hosp. Attys., Omicron Delta Kappa. Democrat. Lutheran. Office: 400 Water NE Albuquerque NM 87102

KIRK, JOHN RICHARD, safety engineer; b. Dowagiac, Mich., May 20, 1950; s. Norman R. and Bernedean E. (Hicks) K.; m. Kathy Marie Maes, Nov. 11, 1977; 1 dau., Sarah Nicole. B.A., Ariz. State U., 1972. Cert. safety profl., Nev. Account mgr. Gibbens Co., Inc., Reno, 1976-77; safety/health rep. Dept. Occupational Safety and Health, Las Vegas, Nev., 1977-79; safety engr. Reynolds Elec. & Engring. Co., Inc., Las Vegas, 1979-80; instr. Clark County Community Coll., Las Vegas, 1979; sr. loss control cons. State Indsl. Ins. System, Reno, 1981—; cons. Mem. Am. Soc. Safety Engrs. (chmn. Sierra Nev. sect.), Am. Soc. Tng. and Devel., System Safety Soc. Democrat. Home: 26 E J St Sparks NV 89431 Office: PO Box 10950 Reno NV 89510

KIRK, REA HELENE (GLAZER), social services administrator, educator; b. N.Y.C., Nov. 17, 1944; d. Benjamin and Lillian (Kellis) Glazer; 3 stepdaughters. B.A., UCLA, 1966; M.A., Eastern Mont. Coll., 1981. Life cert. spl. edn. tchr., Calif., Mont. Spl. edn. tchr., Los Angeles, 1966-73; clin. sec. speech and lang. clinic, Missoula, Mont., 1973-75; spl. edn. tchr., Missoula and Gt. Falls, Mont., 1975-82; dir. Women's Resource Ctr., Gt. Falls, Mont., 1981-82; dir. Battered Woman's Shelter,

Rock Springs, Wyo., 1982—. Pres. bd. dirs. battered woman's shelter, Gt. Falls, Woman's Resource Ctr., Gt. Falls; founder, advisor Rape Action Line, Gt. Falls; founder Jewish religious services, Missoula; 4-H leader; hostess Friendship Force; mem. YMCA Mont. and Wyo. Recipient honors Missoula 4-H. Mem. Council for Exceptional Children (v.p. Gt. Falls 1981-82), Assn. for Children with Learning Disabilities, Delta Kappa Gamma, Psi Chi. Democrat. Jewish.

KIRK, RICHARD A., banker; b. Morristown, N.U., Oct. 19, 1930; s. William T. and Edith K.; B.A., Haverford (Pa.) Coll., 1952; diploma Stonier Grad. Sch. Banking, 1967; A.M.P., Harvard U., 1973; m. Gladys Nicholson, June 4, 1955; children—Laura Faust, Pamela Goodrich, Elizabeth Ely. Mgmt. trainee 1st Nat. City Bank, N.Y.C., 1955-57, Warner Lambert Pharm. Co., 1957-58; with United Bank of Denver, 1958—, sr. v.p. charge personal banking, 1969-73, exec. v.p., 1973-77, pres., chief operating officer, dir., from 1977, now pres., chief exec. officer, chmn. bd.; dir. United Banks Colo., Inc., ROMCOE, Inc. Pres. Downtown Denver, 1973-74; bd. dirs., pres. Denver Bot. Gardens, 1968-74, v.p. Served with USNR, 1952-54. Mem. Mountain States Bankcard Assn., W. Am. Bankcard Assn., Am. Bankers Assn., Assn. Res. City Bankers, Denver Clearing House Assn., Denver C. of C., Nat. Alliance of Bus. (Western Regional Council), Nat. Western Stockshow, NCCJ. Republican. Episcopalian. Clubs: Denver Country, Mile High, Met. Denver Exec., Univ., Denver Rotary, Confrerie des Chevaliers du Tastevin, Colo. Harvard Bus. Sch. Office: United Bank of Denver 1740 Broadway Denver CO 80217

KIRKBY, GORDON WELLESLEY, lawyer; b. Ft. Qu'appelle, Sask., Can., Mar. 21, 1928; s. Robert Wellesley and Helga Marie (Berg) K.; LL.B., U. Sask., 1955, B.A., 1956; m. Lois Gwendolyn Stevenson, Sept. 4, 1954; children—Gordon Merrill, Janet Marie Lynne, Robert Duncan. Admitted to Sask. bar, 1957; mem. firm Dokken & Kirkby, 1957-60, Gordon W. Kirkby, Prince Albert, Sask., 1960—; solicitor Bank Montreal, Can., 1960—; agt. of atty. gen. Alderman, City of Prince Albert, 1967-68. Apptd. Queen's Counsel, 1982. Mem. Royal Can. Humane Assn. (hon.), Prince Albert, Can. bar assns., Law Soc. Sask. (bencher). Clubs: Masons, Shriners, Rotary. Anglican. Home: 710 Cuelenaere St Prince Albert SK S6V 2S9 Canada Office: Leefs Bldg 196B 9th St E Prince Albert SK X6V 5T3 Canada

KIRK-FAIRCLOUGH, CATHIE SUE, educational psychologist, aerobic exercise instructor; b. Mercer, Pa., Dec. 13, 1945; d. Edgar Merle and Betty Mae (Brown) Burns; m. Theo D. Kirk, Nov. 27, 1968 (dec.); m. 2d, Ronald D. Fairclough, July 5, 1982. B.A. in Polit. Sci., Psychology, U. Wash., 1968; M.A. in Psychology, Central Wash. U., 1975, postgrad., 1978—; Cert. tchr., sch. psychologist, Wash. Tchr. pub. schs., Longview, Wash., 1969-71; grad. asst. Central Wash. U., Ellensburg, 1972-73; sch. psychologist Ednl. Service Dist. 114, Port Townsend, Wash., 1973-80, Sequim (Wash.) Sch. Dist., 1980—; owner, instr. Aerobic Conditioning Techniques, Sequim, 1979—; cons. State of Wash. Social Security disability div.; cons. Quileyute Indian Tribal Sch., La Push, Wash. Mem. Wash. Assn. Sch. Psychologists, NEA, Nat. Found. Cancer Research, NOW, Nat. Abortion Rights Action League. Republican. Presbyterian. Author: Student Modification of Teacher Behavior, 1975.

KIRKHAM, ROGER LESLIE, management consultant, engineering and management educator; b. Salt Lake City, Apr. 23, 1944; s. Ralph N. and Mary (Barkdull) K.; m. Judy Ann Gowans, July 2, 1945; children—Nathan, Heather, Ryan, Darin, Kellie. B.S. in Indsl. Engring., U. Utah, 1969, M.Engring. Adminstrn., 1971. Registered profl. engr., Utah. Project engr. Inst. Biomed. Engring., 1968-73, asst. adminstr., 1973-76; instr. indsl. engring. U. Utah, 1976-78, research instr. surgery, 1971—, adj. asst. prof. indsl. engring., 1974—; pres. Am. Tng. Alliance, Salt Lake City, 1978—; mgmt. trainer and cons. to corps. and govt. agencies. Mem. Salt Lake Area C. of C., Am. Soc. Tng. and Devel., Inst. Indsl. Engrs. (sr.), Sigma Xi. Republican. Mormon. Club: Evergreen Swim and Tennis. Contbr. articles to profl. jours. Office: PO Box 8193 Salt Lake City UT 84108

KIRKLAND, BERTHA THERESA (MRS. THORNTON CROWNS KIRKLAND, JR.), estimator, engineer; b. San Francisco, May 16, 1916; d. Lawrence and Theresa (Kanzler) Schmelzer; m. Thornton Crowns Kirkland, Jr., Dec. 27, 1937 (dec. July 1971); children—Kathryn Elizabeth, Francis Charles. Supr. hosp. ops. Am. Potash & Chem. Corp., Trona, Calif., 1953-54; office mgr., T.C. Kirkland, elec. contractor, 1954-56; sec.-treas., dir. T.C. Kirkland, Inc., San Bernardino, Calif., 1958-74; design-install estimator Add-M Electric, Inc., 1972-82, v.p., 1974-82; estimator/engr. Corona Indsl. Electric, Inc. (Calif.), 1982-83. Episcopalian. Club: Arrowhead Country (San Bernardino). Home: 526 E Sonora St San Bernardino CA 92404

KIRKLAND, JACQUELINE CERCEK, school counselor; b. Langley Field, Va., Aug. 29, 1945; d. John Frank and Helene Susan (Grienciwicz) Cercek; m. Richard C. Kirkland, Apr. 11, 1965; 1 son, Kristian Jon. B.S. in Health Edn., U. Nev.-Reno, 1976, B.A. in Psychology, 1977, M.A. in Counseling and Guidance, 1980. Cert. secondary tchr., counselor, sch. psychologist, Nev. Agt. United Airlines, Reno, 1966-69; supr. Western Airlines, Reno, 1969—; elem. sch. counselor Washoe County Sch. Dist., Reno, 1980—; instr. Meadows Community Coll. Chmn. Washoe County Guidance adv. council. U. Nev.-Reno Davis Mature Women's scholar, 1975-77. Mem. Am. Personnel and Guidance Assn. (newsletter editor Nev. br.), Am. Sch. Counselors Assn., Nat. Vocat. Guidance Assn., NEA, Nat. Assn. Sch. Psychologists, Nev. Personnel and Guidance Assn., Nev. Sch. Counselors Assn., Nev. State Edn. Assn. Republican. Roman Catholic.

KIRKLAND, VIRGIL WAYNE, elec. engr.; b. Carthage, Tex., July 29, 1939; s. J. B. and Evelyn Virginia K.; B.S. in Elec. Engring., Lamar State U., 1962; m. Inci M. Heybeli, Mar. 14, 1973; 1 dau., Olga Lynn. With Hughes Aircraft Co., Fullerton, Calif., 1962—, mgr. tech. staff, 1979—, asst. program mgr., 1980—. Mem. Air Force Assn. Republican. Baptist. Office: PO Box 3310 Fullerton CA 92634

KIRKLEY, JAMES ARTHUR, coll. police adminstr.; b. Union, N.J., Sept. 5, 1927; s. Arthur James and Hilda Elizabeth (Brown) K.; student N.Y. Inst. Criminology, 1955-56, Calif. State U., Los Angeles, 1970-71, Loyola Marymount U., 1972-73; div.; children—Lawrence A., Laura Kirkley Lee, Kevin Vance. Security police officer McDonnell Douglas Aircraft Co., Long Beach, Calif., 1966-70; capt. security dept. Whittier Coll., 1969-70, chief security, 1970-72; chief security police Loyola Marymount U., 1972-76; dir. security police Claremont Colls., 1976—; guest lectr. crime on campus, 1972-74; cons. security to colls. and univs. Served with USAAF, 1946-47. Mem. Internat. Assn. Police Chiefs (rev. com.), Nat. Orgn. Black Law Enforcement Execs., Internat. Assn. Coll. and Univ. Security Dirs., So. Calif. Campus Police and Security Assn. Methodist. Contbr. articles to Police Chief Mag. Office: 1030 Dartmouth Ave Claremont CA 91711

KIRKORIAN, DONALD GEORGE, coll. ofcl., mgmt. cons.; b. San Mateo, Calif., Nov. 30, 1938; s. George and Alice (Sergius) K.; B.A., San Jose State U., 1961, postgrad., 1963, 68, M.A., 1966; postgrad. Stanford U., 1961, (fellow) U. So. Calif., 1966; Ph.D., Northwestern U., 1972. Tchr., Los Angeles City Schs., 1963; instructional TV coordinator Fremont Union High Sch. Dist., Sunnyvale, Calif., 1963-73; assoc. dean instrn. learning resources Solano Community Coll., Suisun City, Calif., 1973—; owner, pres. Kirkorian & Assocs., Suisun City; field cons. Nat. Assn. Edn. Broadcasters, 1966-68; extension faculty San Jose State U., 1968-69, U. Calif. at Santa Cruz, 1970-73, U. Calif. at Davis, 1973-76. Pres., Western Ednl. Soc. Telecommunications, 1976-77; exec. dir. Learning Resources Assn. Calif. Community Colls., 1976—; chmn. Bay Area Community Coll. TV Consortium, 1976-77; adv. panel Speech Communication Assn./Am. Theater Assn. tchr. preparation in speech, communication, theater and media, N.Y.C., 1973-77; chmn. Solano County Media Adv. Com., 1974-76; bd. dirs. Napa-Solano United Way, 1980-82. Mem. Nat. Assn. Ednl. Broadcasters, Assn. for Edn. Communications and Tech., Broadcast Edn. Assn., Calif. Assn. Ednl. Media and Tech. (treas.), Western Ednl. Soc. for Telecommunications (Calif. dir. 1973-75), Learning Resources Assn. Calif. Community Coll. (sec.-treas.), Assn. Cal. Community Coll. Adminstrs., Phi Delta Kappa. Editor: Media Memo, 1973—; Intercom: The Newsletter for Calif. Community Coll. Librarians, 1974-75; Exploring the Benicia State Recreation Area, 1977; California History Resource Materials, 1977; Time Management, 1980. Contbr. articles to profl. publs. Home: 1655 Rockville Rd Suisun CA 94585 Office: PO Box 246 Suisun CA 94585

KIRKPATRICK, MORRIS L., safety engineer, flight instructor; b. Blair, Nebr., Dec. 31, 1949; s. Don J. and Ann P. (Whitehurst) K.; B.S. in Contrn. Mgmt., U. Nebr., 1974; M.S. in Indsl. Engring., U. Utah, 1979. Cert. safety professional. Loss control rep. St. Paul Co., Denver, 1974-77, state loss control cons., Salt Lake City, 1977-79; safety dir. Stearns-Roger Whitney Canyon Project (Amoco Oil), Evanston, Wyo., 1979-81; loss control mgr. Aetna Ins., Denver, 1981-82; corp. loss control mgr. Wendy's Internat., 1982—. Mem. Am. Soc. Safety Engrs. Democrat. Office: 5488 Wilcox Rd Dublin OH 43017

KIRKPATRICK, R. GEORGE, sociology educator; b. Wharton, Tex., Aug. 15, 1943; s. Burke and Loretta (Van Pelt) K.; m. Adreain Ann Ross, June 6, 1966 (div.). B.A., U. Tex., 1965, M.A., 1967, Ph.D. in Social Psychology and Sociology, 1971. Asst. prof. U. Okla., Norman, 1969-71; assoc. prof. sociology San Diego State U., 1971—; dir. Ocean Front Inst. Social Research. NIMH fellow, 1965. Mem. Am. Sociol. Assn., Soc. for Study Social Problems, Am. Humanist Assn. Mem. Zen Ctr. of Los Angeles. Author: (with Louis A Zurcher, Jr.) Citizens for Decency: Anti-Pornography Crusades as Status Defense, 1976.

KIRKPATRICK, RICHARD ALAN, internist; b. Rochester, Minn., Jan. 17, 1947, s. Neal R. and Ethel C. (Hull) K.. B.A. in Chemistry with honors, U. Wash., 1968, B.S. in Psychology, 1968, M.D., 1972; m. Dorelie Ann Berg, Sept. 14, 1968; children—James N., Ronald S., David B., Mary J. Intern, resident in internal medicine Mayo Grad. Sch., Rochester, 1972-76, spl. resident in biomed. communications, 1974-75; practice medicine specializing in internal medicine, Longview, Wash., 1976—, sr. ptnr. Kirkpatrick Richards Thorson Zeilenga Gee Gorton Peterson Internal Medicine Clinic; mem. clin. faculty U. Wash.; dir. cardiac rehab. program St. John's Hosp. Mem. City Council, Longview; bd. dirs. YMCA, Youth Symphony. Diplomate Am. Bd. Internal Medicine. Fellow ACP; mem. Wash. State Soc. Internal Medicine (trustee, pres.-elect), Am. Geriatrics Soc., Am. Soc. Echocardiography, Am. Soc. Internal Medicine, Wash. Med. Assn. (council med. service), Am. Cancer Soc. (local bd. dirs.), Am. Soc. Clin. Oncology, AMA, Am. Med. Writers Assn. Editor: Drug Therapy Abstracts, Wash. Internists; mem. editorial adv. bd. Your Patient and Cancer; contbr. articles to med. jours. Office: PO Box 578 748 14th Ave Longview WA 98632

KIRKSEY, JIMMIE MOORE, petroleum engineer, petroleum company executive; b. Huntingdon, Tenn., May 5, 1950; s. Leon Marshall and Lucy Marguerite (Holladay) K.; m. Cheryl Winn, Oct. 2, 1976; children—Laurel, Marie. B.S. in Petroleum Engring., Miss. State U., 1974. Field engr. Dowell div. Dow Chem., Worland, Wyo., 1975-76; service sales engr., Vernal, Utah, 1976-77, dist. engr., 1977-78, dist. sales supr., Williston, N.D., 1978-80; petroleum engr. Burkhalter Engring., Grand Junction, Colo., 1980-81; pres., sr. petroleum engr. Prodn. Assocs., Grand Junction, 1981—; v.p., dir. West Exploration and Prodn., Grand Junction; pres., dir. Grand Valley Gas Transmission Co. Mem. AIME (Soc. Petroleum Engrs. div.), Am. Petroleum Inst. Club: Petroleum and Mining (Grand Junction). Office: Prodn Assocs 1401 N 1st Grand Junction CO 81501

KIRSCH, LYNN FRANCES, personnel executive; b. Johannesburg, S. Africa, June 10, 1945; came to U.S., 1978; d. Peter and Cecelia (Newman) Kirsch. B.A., U. Witwatersrand, Johannesburg, 1965, postgrad. in librarianship, 1966. Asst., Thorold's Bookstore, Johannesburg, 1967-70; asst. media mgr., accounts exec. PN Barrett Advt., Johannesburg, 1970-72; dir. personnel Westin Hotels, various locations, 1972—, Detroit, 1978-80; dir. personnel Carlton Hotel, Johannesburg, 1972-78, Century Plaza Hotel (Westin Hotels), Los Angeles, 1981—; tchr. So. Calif. Instl. Laundry Mgrs. Assn. Mem. Calif. employment devel. dept. Employer's Adv. Council; assoc. Leakey Found., Los Angeles. Named Employer of the Yr. for Employment of Handicapped, Detroit Jewish Vocat. Rehab., 1979; recipient Dale Carnegie Leadership award Carlton Hotel, 1978. Office: Century Plaza Hotel 2025 Ave of the Stars Los Angeles CA 90067

KIRSCHBAUM, JOEL BRUCE, molecular geneticist; b. Palo Alto, Calif., Aug. 29, 1945; s. Howard William and Wilhelmina (Jensen) K.; m. Felicity Russell, Sept. 14, 1974. B.A. in Chemistry, Pomona Coll., 1967; Ph.D., Harvard U., 1972. Chargé de recherche U. Geneve (Switzerland), 1975-77; research assoc. in neurosci. Children's Hosp. Med. Ctr., Boston, 1977-81; instr. neuropathology Harvard Med Sch., Boston, 1977-81; supr. microbial genetic engring. sect. Stauffer Chem. Co., Richmond, Calif., 1981—; asst. instr. Cold Spring Harbor bacterial genetics course, 1971; course instr. European Molecular Biology Orgn., 1976. Woodrow Wilson fellow, 1967-68; Helen Hay Whitney fellow, 1973-75; fellow Med. Found. of Boston, Inc., 1978-80; prin. investigator Am. Cancer Soc. research grant, 1979-81. Mem. AAAS. Contbr. articles to profl. jours. Office: Stauffer Chem Co Western Research Ctr 1200 S 47th St Richmond CA 94804

KIRSCHBROWN, RICHARD HARRY, computer software company executive; b. Oakland, Calif., Jan. 14, 1947; s. Milton and Cecil Cynthia (Linden) K.; B.S. in Computer Sci., Calif. State U., Chico, 1970, M.S. with distinction in Computer Sci., 1972; m. Suzanne Eileen Griffin, Sept. 18, 1968; children—Kimberly Dawn, Kari Elizabeth. Assoc. cons. Arnovick Assos., Chico, Calif., 1970-72; mgr. data processing Enterprise Sch. Dist., Redding, Calif., 1972-73; systems engr. IBM Corp., Reno, 1973-76; owner, founder Med. Accounts Receivable Service, Reno, 1976-80; pres., founder Computer Shop etc., Reno, 1979-82; pres. Frontrunner Computer Industries, 1982—; tchr. Calif. State U., Chico, Yuba Coll., Western Nev. Community Coll. Mem. Assn. Computing Machinery. Cert. data processor. Home: 595 Hunter Lake Dr Reno NV 89509 Office: 316 California Ave Suite 712 Reno NV 89509

KIRSHEN, EDWARD JEROME, obstetrician and gynecologist; b. Syracuse, N.Y., Oct. 30, 1944; s. Gerald Bernard and Corrine (Markson) K.; B.A., Syracuse U., 1962-65; M.D., SUNY, Syracuse, 1969. Intern, then resident in ob-gyn U. Calif. Med. Center, San Diego, 1969-73; fellow in reproductive endocrinology Boston Hosp. Women, also instr. Harvard U. Med. Sch., 1973-74; practice medicine specializing in ob-gyn, San Diego, 1974—; mem. staff Donald Sharp Hosp., Mission Bay Hosp.; clin. instr. U. Calif. Med. Sch., San Diego. Mem. Am. Coll. Ob-Gyn, Am. Fertility Soc., Am. Assn. Gynecol. Laparoscopy, Pacific Coast Fertility Soc., Calif. Med. Assn., San Diego County Med. Soc. Office: 304 Ivy St San Diego CA 92101

KIRTLAND, RICHARD LEE, lawyer; b. New Bedford, Mass., Apr. 24, 1907; s. Charles L. and Flora (Ellis) K.; B.S. in Bus. Adminstrn., U. So. Calif., 1929, J.D., 1932; m. Antoinette Schamoi, Jan. 29, 1983; children—Richard Lee III, Robert Hackney. Admitted to Calif. bar, 1933; practiced in Los Angeles, 1933—; assoc. Fred O. Reed, 1935-45; ptnr. Reed & Kirtland, 1945-56; sr. ptnr. Kirtland & Packard, 1956-72, Kirtland, Darby & Hager, 1972—; lectr. State Bar Calif., 1949-55; assoc. prof. med. jurisprudence Loma Linda U. Bd. dirs. Huntington Inst. Applied Med. Research. Fellow Am. Coll. Trial Lawyers, Internat. Acad. Trial Lawyers; mem. U. So. Calif. Law Alumni Assn. (past pres.), Gen. Alumni Assn. U. So. Calif. (gov.), ABA, Internat. Bar Assn., Internat. Assn. Ins. Counsel, Legion Lex (past pres.), SAR, USC Assocs., Commerce Assocs., Phi Delta Phi. Republican. Clubs: San Gabriel Country, San Marino City, Overland, Masons, Shriners. Home: 2657 Oak Knoll Ave San Marino CA 91108 Office: 251 S Lake Ave Suite 601 Pasadena CA 91101

KIRVEN, ELIZABETH JOY, chamber of commerce executive; b. Altoona, Pa., Mar. 14, 1949; d. Paul Augustine and Catherine Regina (Kinney) Adams; m. Timothy Joseph Kirven, Oct. 31, 1970; 1 dau., Kristen Barbara. Student inst. orgn. mgmt. U. Colo., 1979-82. Reporter, photographer, Casper (Wyo.) Star Tribune, 1976-79; exec. dir. Buffalo (Wyo.) C. of C., 1979—. Chmn., Buffalo optional 1 per cent sales tax election, 1979, 80, 82; bd. dirs. Buffalo Fine Arts Council, 1981; pres. Johnson County LWV, 1980-81; mem. Buffalo Human Resource Council; bd. dirs. Buffalo SSS; mem. Wyo. Pvt. Industry Council, 1980-82, Wyo. Travel Commn., 1981-85. Mem. Wyo. Assn. C. of C. Execs. (pres. 1981-82), Wyo. Conv. and Visitors Bur., N. Wyo. Travel Assn. Republican. Roman Catholic. Home: 606 Kearney Buffalo WY 82834 Office: 55 N Main St Buffalo WY 82834

KISCH, LOUIS U. C., banker; b. Tucson, Sept. 29, 1935; s. Joseph E. and Elizabeth R. (Hercek) K.; M. Genevieve Louise Placko, June 13, 1959; children—Loretta, Lorraine, Glenn, Leslie, LuAnn. B.S. in Bus. Adminstrn., U. Ariz., 1963. Ind. ins. agt. T. F. Leehan Ins. Agy., Tucson, 1956-63; asst. branch mgr. Valley Nat. Bank Ariz., Phoenix, 1963-68, credit mgr. Master Charge dept., 1969-70, mgr. Compensation Div., 1971-76, v.p., mgr. Trust Employee Benefits Dept., 1976—; guest instr. Ariz. State U. Bus. Coll.; treas. Western Pension Conf., Phoenix chpt.; mem. Central Ariz. Estate Planning Council. Served with U.S. Army, 1954-56. mem. Phoenix Met. C. of C. Office: Valley Nat Bank Ariz 241 N Central Ave Dept A 814 Phoenix AZ 85001

KISER, CAROL ANN, accountant, bookkeeping consultant; b. Denver, Jan. 19, 1949; d. Clark Harry and Iva Lucy (Hill) Skinner; m. Roger Lynn Kiser, Sept. 6, 1970; 1 son, Zachary Aaron. B.S., Met. State Coll., 1976. Acct., Montgomery & Assocs., Arvada, Colo., 1974-76; acctg. supr. Auraria Higher Edn. Ctr., Denver, 1976-78; acct. Met. Denver Sewage Disposal Dist. No. 1, Denver, 1978-80; pvt. practice acctg., bookkeeping, Lakewood, Colo., 1980—; trainer bookkeepers for small bus. Mem. Embroiderer's Guild. Democrat. Methodist.

KISER, ELLIS EUGENE, police chief; b. North Platte, Nebr., Feb. 22, 1936; s. Coy D. and Dorthy M. (Todd) K.; m. LuElla M. Faught, June 7, 1958; 1 son, Tim E. Student Eastern Mont. Coll., 1955-59. With Billings (Mont.) Police Dept., 1961—, chief of police, 1977—. Bd. dirs. Mont. Bd. Crime Control, 1981—. Mem. Internat. Assn. Chiefs of Police, Mont. Police Chiefs Assn. Baptist. Club: Exchange. Office: Billings Police Dept PO Box 1554 Billings MT 59101

KISH, LESLIE PAUL, entomologist, educator; b. Johnstown, Pa., Nov. 28, 1944; s. Joseph August and Evelyn Celeste (Tomasel) K.; student U. Mass., 1963; B.S., U. Fla., 1970, M.S., 1971, Ph.D., 1975; 1 dau., Heather Kathleen. Research assoc. U. Fla., Gainesville, 1973-75, asst. research scientist, 1975-78, assoc. prof. entomology U. Idaho, Moscow, 1978—; cons. Fla. Dept. Nat. Resources, 1973-77; Multi-state research coordinator Chalkbrood Program, Wash., Oreg., Nev., Idaho and Utah, 1978—; cons. Interam. Inst. Agrl. Scis., 1979—. Served with USAF, 1962-66. Idaho Alfalfa Seed Com. grantee, 1978-82, Wash. Alfalfa Seed Com. grantee, 1978-82; Nev. Seed Council grantee, 1978-82; Malheur County (Oreg.) Seed Growers grantee, 1978-82; NSF travel grantee, 1979; Idaho Research Council grantee, 1980; U.S. Dept. Agriculture grantee, 1979—. Mem. Entomol. Soc. Am., Mycol. Soc. Am., Soc. for Invertebrate Pathology, Sigma Xi. Roman Catholic. Club: Lions. Contbr. articles to profl. jours. Home: 723 East F St Moscow ID 83843 Office: Dept Plant Soil and Entomological Sciences Univ Idaho Moscow ID 83843

KISHEL, GREGORY FRANCIS, management consultant; b. Wilkes-Barre, Pa., Aug. 18, 1946; s. Joseph John and Josephine (Krzywicki) K.; m. Patricia Charlotte Gunter, July 1, 1977. B.S., San Jose U., 1973; M.S. in Bus. Adminstrn., Calif. State U.-Long Beach, 1977. Cert. Calif. Community Coll. instr., Calif, real estate broker. Asst. nat. bank examiner Office Comptroller of Currency, Los Angeles, 1973-78; partner K & K Enterprises, Marina del Rey, Calif., 1978—. Served to sgt. USAF, 1964-68. Mem. Authors Guild. Author: The Student Survival Guide, 1979; How to Start, Run and Stay in Business, 1981; Your Business is a Success; Now What?, 1983; contbr. articles to bus. mags. and newspapers. Home and Office: 4572 Via Marina Apt 309 Marina del Rey CA 90292

KISSIL, KAY ELAINE, disaster services administrator; b. Omaha, July 17, 1935; d. Harvey and Gertrude Emma (Mewius) Spancer; m. George Kissil, Sept. 24, 1954; children—Natasha, Andrew. A.A., Skyline Coll., San Bruno, Calif., 1979; B.S. cum laude, U. San Francisco, 1980. Recreation supr. U. Calif., San Francisco, 1965-70; mgr., coach San Francisco Merionettes, 1970-74; program cons. Safety Programs ARC, San Francisco, 1974-77, asst. dir., 1977-78, asst. dir. disaster services, 1978-79, asst. regional mgr., San Mateo, 1980-81, dir. disaster services, Los Angeles, 1981—, instr. and coach synchronized swimming. Vice chmn. San Mateo County Disasters Preparedness Commn. Mem. So. Calif. Emergency Services Assn., Nat. Assn. Female Execs., Inc. Republican. Lutheran. Office: 2700 Wilshire Blvd PO Box 57930 Los Angeles CA 90057

KISSLING, CHARLOTTE ELAINE, real estate broker; b. Jacksonville, Fla.; d. Albert Jacob and Viola Gertrude (Olive) K. B.A. magna cum laude, Carleton Coll.; M.A.T. in History, Harvard/Radcliffe Sch. Edn., 1961. Real estate broker, Calif.; cert. tchr., Calif. Guide, World's Fair, Brussels, Belgium, 1958; tchr. history, French and English, Newton (N.J.) High Sch., 1960-61, Montclair (N.J.) High Sch., 1961-62; adminstrv. officer Inst. Internat. Edn., San Francisco, 1962-69; publications officer, editor adult edn. UNESCO, Paris, 1969-72; broker, agent Hill Co. Real Estate, San Francisco, 1972—. Bd. dirs. YWCA, Bay Area, 1982-83. Mem. Phi Beta Kappa (past pres. No. Calif. 1979-80). Democrat. Presbyterian. Clubs: Harbor Point Tennis, Radcliffe, Commonwealth. Contbr. articles to profl. jours. Home: 1 Harbor Point Dr Apt 204 Mill Valley CA 94941

KISTER, BENJAMIN JOSEPH, optometrist; b. Worland, Wyo., May 11, 1951; s. Victor and Millie (Lehman) K.; m. Dorthy Ellen Baker, Dec. 27, 1972; children—Stephanie Suzanne, Tyson John, Megan Marie. Student U. Wyo., 1969-72; B.S. with honors, Pacific U., Forest Grove, Oreg., 1974, O.D. with distinction, 1976. Pvt. practice optometry, Riverton, Wyo., 1978—; state dir. Optometric Extension Program, Oreg. Served to lt. (s.g.) U.S. Navy, 1976-78. Mem. Am. Optometric Assn., Wyo. Optometric Assn. (treas. 1981—), C. of C., Alpha Omega Epsilon,

Beta Sigma Kappa. Republican. Club: Rotary (chmn. youth exchange 1981—).

KITADA, SHINICHI, biochemist; b. Osaka, Japan, Dec. 9, 1948; came to U.S., 1975; s. Koichi and Asako Kitada; M.D., Kyoto U., 1973; M.S. in Biol. Chemistry (Japan Soc. Promotion Sci. fellow 1975-76), UCLA, 1977, Ph.D., 1979. Intern, Kyoto U. Hosp., 1973-74, resident physician Chest Disease Research Inst., 1974-75; research scholar lab. nuclear medicine and radiation biology UCLA, 1979—. Mem. Am. Oil Chemists Soc., N.Y. Acad. Scis., Sigma Xi. Author papers in field. Home: 478 Landfair Ave Apt 5 Los Angeles CA 90024 Office: 900 Veteran Ave Los Angeles CA 90024

KITAGAWA, CHISATO, educator; b. Tokyo, July 29, 1932; came to U.S., 1958, naturalized, 1967; s. Chiaki and Sumi (Ishii) K.; M.A., U. Mich., 1961, Ph.D., 1972; Th.M., Episcopal Theol. Sch., 1964; m. Mary Joan Messinger, June 17, 1961; children—Kristen Sumi, Jeffrey Chiaki. Ordained priest, Episcopal Ch., 1964; asst. minister Grace Episcopal Ch., Amherst, Mass., 1964-67; Protestant chaplain Eastern Mich. U., 1969-70; vicar Holy Cross Episcopal Ch., Saline, Mich., 1970-72; asst. prof. Asian studies U. Mass., 1972-76; asso. prof. Oriental Studies, U. Ariz., Tucson, 1976—, co-dir. East Asia Center, 1980-82; non-stipendiary priest St. Philip's in the Hills Episcopal Ch., Tucson, 1978—. Mem. Japan-Am. Soc. (v.p. Tucson chpt. 1981—), Linguistic Soc. Am., Assn. Tchrs. Japanese. Democrat. Episcopalian. Home: 3332 N Bentley St Tucson AZ 85716 Office: Oriental Studies Dept Univ Ariz Tucson AZ 85721

KITCHEN, LAWRENCE OSCAR, aerospace company executive; b. Ft. Mill, S.C., June 8, 1923; s. Samuel Sumpter and Ruby Azalee (Grigg) K.; m. Marjorie Dawn Bridges, Feb. 18, 1945; children—Brenda, Alan, Janet; m. 2d Brenda Colleen Lenhart, Nov. 25, 1978. Ed. Foothill Coll., Los Altos, Calif., also various exec. tng. programs. With U.S. Navy Bur. Aeros., Washington, 1946-58, asst. chief of bur., 1958; with Lockheed Missiles & Space Co., Sunnyvale, Calif., 1958-70, mgr. product support logistics, 1964-68, dir.-fin. controls, 1968-70; v.p. fin. Lockheed-Ga. Co., Marietta, 1970-71, pres., 1971-75; pres. Lockheed Corp., Burbank, Calif., 1975—, chief operating officer, 1976—. Mem. bd. visitors Emory Inst.; mem. founding bd. Hollywood Presbyterian Hosp.; mem. nominating com. Aviation Hall of Fame; trustee Calif. Museum Found. Served with USMC, 1942-46. Mem. Nat. Def. Transp. Assn., AIAA, Nat. Assn. Accts., Navy League, Am. Def. Preparedness Assn., Soc. Logistics Engrs., Air Force Assn., Assn. U.S. Army. Clubs: Lakeside Golf (Toluca Lake, Calif.); Wings (N.Y.C.); Cherokee Town and Country, Capital City (Atlanta). Office: PO Box 551 Burbank CA 91520

KITCHEN, RICHARD ELBUR, photographer; b. Altadena, Calif., Oct. 19, 1946; s. Elbur Creston and LaVerne Madilene (Considene) K. Student Long Beach Community Coll., Cerritos Coll. Owner, photographer R & R Photography, Bellflower, Calif.; owner Richard Kitchen Enterprises, Bellflower, 1982—; cons. in field. Served with USN, 1967-69. Mem. Assoc. Photographers Internat., Am. Entrepreneurs Assn., Nat. Forensic League. Office: 9832 Flower St Suite 219 Bellflower CA 90706

KITCHENER, SAUL LAURENCE, zoo adminstr.; b. Passaic, N.J., Mar. 22, 1938; s. Benjamin and Sylvia (Frost) K.; B.A., U. Maine, 1959; M.S., U. Okla., 1963; m. Barbara Aisuss, Apr. 15, 1972; 1 son, Joshua Harry. Curator primates Oklahoma City Zoo, 1963-65; gen. curator Henry Doorly Zoo, Omaha, 1965-67; gen. curator Lincoln Park Zoo, Chgo., 1967-69, asst. dir., 1970-75; dir. San Francisco Zoo, 1975—. Fellow Am. Assn. Zool. Parks and Aquariums (dir.). Office: San Francisco Zoo San Francisco CA 94132

KITSON, JANE, marketing professional; b. Wabash, Ind., Nov. 7, 1952; d. Richard Sherman and Madaline Fern (Goehler) K. B.S. in Russian-Soviet Studies, Am. U., 1975; M. Internat. Mgmt., Am. Grad. Sch. Internat. Mgmt., 1982. Asst. to gen. consul Am. Embassy, Moscow, 1976; asst. to pres. Am. Data Home and Office Computer, Washington, 1979; dir. mktg. Systems Research, Inc., Washington, 1980-82; product mgr., acctg. and fin. mgmt. software Application Software div. Univ. Computing Co., Dallas, 1982—; lectr. Oxford U., 1977. Active St. Vladimir's Theol. Found., Scarsdale, N.Y. Mem. Nat. Assn. Accts. Office: UCC Tower Exchange Park Dallas TX 75235

KITTELL, ARTHUR CALLEN, JR., educational administrator, vocational educator, coach; b. Durango, Colo., Nov. 14, 1929; s. Arthur Callen and Virginia Ann (Harmon) K.; m. Wilda Janet Rogers, Mar. 21, 1954; children—Lee Callen, Sharron Ann, Arthur Callen. A.A., Ft. Lewis, Colo., 1958; B.A., Adams State Coll., 1960; M.A., Colo. State U., 1965; postgrad. U. Wyo., 1966—. Cert. tchr., adminstr., Ariz., Colo., N.Mex., Wyo. Gen. mgr. Aerex Co., 1952-58; owner, mgr. Art Kittell Constrn. Co., 1952-57; tchr., coach, Colo., 1959-66; sch. adminstr., Wyo., 1966-72, Ariz., 1974-79; sch. adminstr. Chinle and Kayenta, Ariz., 1979-82; supt. schs., Lake Arthur, N.Mex., 1982—; guide, Mesa Verde, Colo., 1961; recreation dir. Uinta Nat. Forest, 1968. Boys' State counselor, N.Mex., 1955-57, 80-83, Wyo., 1973-74, Colo., 1978. Served with USAF, 1947-50. NDEA grantee, 1967, 69; named Basketball Coach of Yr., 1964, Football Coach of Yr., 1974; recipient Meritorious Service awards 4-H, 1970. Am., Mem. Am. Assn. Sch. Adminstrs., N.Mex. Assn. Sch. Adminstrs., Am. Vocat. Assn. (life), Am. Indsl. Arts Assn. (life), Am. Legion (post comdr. 1956-58, dist. comdr. 1957-59), Phi Delta Kappa, Iota Lambda Sigma. Republican. Baptist. Clubs: Lions (past pres.), Rotary. Home: PO Box 104 Lake Arthur NM 88253 Office: PO Box 98 Lake Arthur NM 88253

KITTERMAN, NANCY L., educator; b. Monte Vista, Colo., Sept. 4, 1934; d. Darrel and Evelyn Akers; m. Jack Kitterman, July 25, 1964; children—William, James, Jodeen, Dennis. B.A., Adams State Coll., 1964, M.A., 1971; postgrad. U. No. Colo.-Greeley, Colo. State U.-Ft. Collins, 1971-82. Cert. tchr. Tchr. Sargent High Sch., Monte Vista, Colo., 1968-74, San Luis Valley Vocat. Sch., Monte Vista, 1974-76; tchr. bus., office Alamosa High Sch., 1977—; adviser Future Bus. Leaders Am. Recipient Service award Future Bus. Leaders Am., 1982. Mem. Am. Vocat. Assn., Colo. Vocat. Assn., NEA, San Luis Valley Vocat. Assn., Colo. Edn. Assn. (Disting. Service award 1979), Alamosa Community Edn. Assn., Colo. Educators for and about Bus., Phi Delta Kappa. Republican. Presbyterian. Club: PEO. Office: Alamosa High Sch 401 Victoria St Alamosa CO 81101

KITTLESON, CHARLES HOWARD, loss control consultant; b. St. Cloud, Minn., Jan. 12, 1952; s. Howard Benjamin and Adeline Josephine (Ziton) K. B.S. in Engring., St. Cloud State U. 1973. Assoc. safety profl. Mech. engring. aide Minn., N.D., S.D., Wis., Iowa, 1965-73; loss prevention rep. St. Paul Cos., Bloomington, Ill. and Houston, 1974-77, Aetna Ins. Co., Mpls., 1977-79; sr. loss control engr. CNA Ins. Co., Mpls., 1979-81, Argonaut Ins. Co., San Jose, Calif., 1981—. Mem. Am. Soc. Safety Engrs. (v.p.). Republican. Lutheran. Home: 4102 Thain Way Palo Alto CA 94306 Office: 675 N 1st St Suite 306 San Jose CA 98112

KITTO, FRANKLIN CURTIS, university administrator; b. Salt Lake City, Nov. 18, 1954; s. Curtis Eugene and Margaret (Ipson) K.; m. Collette Madsen, 1982. B.A., Brigham Young U., 1978, M.A., 1980. Sta. operator KUED-TV, Salt Lake City, 1972-73; sta. operator KBYU-TV, Provo, Utah, 1973-78, chief operator, 1977-78; student instr. TV prodn. Brigham Young U., Provo, 1978-80; cable TV system operator U. Utah, Salt Lake City, 1980-82, supr. media ctr., mgr. data processing, 1982—; tech. developer media Harrison & Assocs., Provo, 1979-80. Recipient Kiwanis Freedom Leadership award, 1970; Golden Microphone award Brigham Young U., 1978. Mem. Am. Ednl. Research Assn., Assn. Ednl. Communications and Tech., Eastern Communication Assn., Phi Eta Sigma, Kappa Tau Alpha. Mormon. Home: 390 E 4140 S Apt 15 Murray UT 84107 Office: 207 MBH U Utah Salt Lake City UT 84112

KITTO, KETHLEEN LEONE, metallurgical engineer, educator; b. Butte, Mont., Oct. 7, 1956; d. Howard Stanley and Elizabeth Mary (Murphy) Kitto. B.S. with high honors, Mont. Coll. of Mineral Sci. and Tech., 1978, M.S., 1981. Student engr. Hanna Mining Co., Hibbing, Minn., 1978-81; research engr., instr. Mont. Coll. of Mineral Sci. and Tech., Butte, 1981—; cons. Mineral Research Ctr.; pres. Micromet, Inc. Ptnr., Expanding Your Horizons Workshop; judge high sch., city sci. fairs. Mem. Am. Ceramic Soc., Am. Soc. Metals, AIME, Metall. Soc., Alpha Sigma Mu, Mu Beta Pi. Republican. Roman Catholic. Contbr. numerous articles to profl. jours. Home: 643 S Main St Butte MT 59701 Office: Dept Metallurgy Mont Coll of Mineral Sci and Tech W Park St Butte MT 59701

KITTRICK, JAMES ALLEN, soil chemist, mineralogist, educator; b. Milw., Aug. 4, 1929; s. James Allen and Anita C. (Kasper) K.; m. Lucy Jane Neff, June 19, 1953; children—Bruce, Carol. B.S., U. Wis., 1951, M.S., 1953, Ph.D., 1955. Assoc. prof. Wash. State U.-Pullman, 1955-67, prof., 1967—. Chmn. Wenaha-Tucannon Wilderness Council. Fellow Am. Soc. Agronomy, Soil Sci. Soc. Am.; mem. Clay Minerals Soc. (counselor), Mineral. Soc. Am., Sierra Club. Author books; contbr. articles to research jours. Home: NW 465 Orion St Pullman WA 99163 Office: Dept of Agronomy and Soils Wash State U Pullman WA 99164

KITTSON, AUGUSTAN, building materials company executive, land developer; b. St. Louis, Oregon, Aug. 15, 1913; s. Nazaire (Ned) and Virginia Elizabeth (Brouillard) K.; m. Myrna Ann Nickisch, Dec. 3, 1947; children—Janet Grace Kittson Hartman, Cynthia Jane Kittson Peterson, Nicki Jean Kittson Keohohou, Lori Lee Kittson Turping, Constance Kittson Rogers, Augustan Daniel. Student U. Alaska, 1946. Constrn. engr. many Alaskan firms, 1946-48; gen. foreman electricians Atkinson-Jones, Richland, Wash., 1948-53; gen. foreman electrician Foothill Electric, Richland, 1953-55; owner/pres. Kennewick (Wash.) Indsl. and Elec. Supply, Inc., 1955—. Active Republican Nat. Com. Served with C.E. U.S. Army Air Corps, 1943-46. Recipient Internat. Boss of Yr. award Tri-Cities Credit Women, 1981; Cert. of Recognition, Nat. Rep. Congl. Com., 1982; Presdl. Achievement award Pres. Ronald Reagan. Republican. Club: Riverside Investment. Club: Elks. Home: 407 W 29th Ave Kennewick WA 99336 Office: 113 E Columbia Dr Kenniwick WA 99336

KLAAS, PHILIP JOHN, systems co. exec.; b. Dubuque, Iowa, Nov. 16, 1928; s. Paul and Ida Louise (Schroeder) K.; B.A., Loras Coll., 1949; Ph.D., U. Notre Dame, 1953; m. Therese Mary Winters, Apr. 16, 1955; children—Vincent, Virginia, John, Stephen, Kenneth, Mary, Gerald. Research chemist Esso Research and Engring. Co., Linden, N.J., 1952-62; mgr. Product Assurance Lab., Aerojet Tactical Systems Co., Sacramento, Calif., 1962—. Served with USN, 1954-57. Registered profl. engr., Calif. Mem. Am. Chem. Soc., Am. Soc. Quality Control. Roman Catholic. Home: 5109 Melvin Dr Carmichael CA 95608 Office: PO Box 13400 Sacramento CA 95813

KLAISNER, LOWELL ALAN, electrical engineer; b. San Francisco, Dec. 30, 1938; s. William and Clara Elizabeth (Grey) K.; m. Marilyn Regina Wolff, July 11, 1959; children—Mark Alan, Beth Anne; m. 2d, Sharon Louise Burkitt, June 24, 1972; children—Jennifer Lynn, Shawn Lewis, Sheryl Allice. B.S. in Elec. Engring., Stanford U., 1960, M.S., 1961. Registered profl. engr. Wash., 1979. Engr. Argonne (Ill.) Nat. Lab., 1961-68; chief engr. Nat. Accelerator Lab., Batavia, Ill., 1968-72; founder, v.p. mktg. Kinetic Systems Corp., Lockport, Ill., 1972-78; program mgr. Eldec Corp., Lynnwood, Wash., 1978-80; engring. mgr. Intermec Corp., Lynnwood, 1980—; cons. Lowell A. Klaisner & Assocs.; instr. Coll. DuPage (Ill.). Mem. IEEE, Instrument Soc. Am. (sr.). Presbyterian. Contbr. articles to profl. jours. Home: 17427 5th Ave W Bothell WA 98011 Office: Intermec Corp PO Box C-N Lynwood WA 98036

KLAKEG, CLAYTON HAROLD, physician; b. Big Woods, Minn., Mar. 31, 1920; s. Knute O. and Agnes (Folvik) K.; student Concordia Coll., Moorhead, Minn., 1938-40; B.S., N.D. State U., 1942; B.S. in Medicine, N.D. U., 1943; M.D., Temple U., 1945; M.S. in Medicine and Physiology, U. Minn.-Mayo Found., 1954; children—Julie Ann, Robert Clayton, Richard Scott. Intern, Med. Center, Jersey City, 1945-46; mem. staff VA Hosp., Fargo, N.D., 1948-51; fellow in medicine and cardiology Mayo Found., Rochester, Minn., 1951-55; internist, cardiologist Sansum Med. Clinic Inc., Santa Barbara, Calif., 1955—; mem. staff Cottage Hosp., St. Francis Hosp. Bd. dirs. Sansom Med. Research Found. Served to capt. M.C., USAF, 1946-48. Diplomate Am. Bd. Internal Medicine. Fellow ACP, Am. Coll. Cardiology, Am. Coll. Chest Physicians, Am. Heart Assn. (mem. council on clin. cardiology); mem. Calif. Heart Assn. (pres. 1971-72, Meritorious Service award 1968, Disting. Service award 1972, Disting. Achievement award 1975), Santa Barbara County Heart Assn. (pres. 1959-60, Disting. Service award 1958, Disting. Achievement award 1971), Calif. Med. Assn., Los Angeles Acad. Medicine, Santa Barbara County Med. Assn., Mayo Clinic Alumni Assn., Santa Barbara Soc. Internal Medicine (pres. 1963), Sigma Xi, Phi Beta Pi. Republican. Lutheran. Club: Channel City. Contbr. articles to profl. jours. Home: 4772 Calle Cammarada Santa Barbara CA 93110 Office: Sansum Med Clinic Inc 317 W Pueblo St Santa Barbara CA 93102

KLAMMER, JOSEPH FRANCIS, management consultant; b. Omaha, Mar. 25, 1925; s. Aloys Arcadius and Sophie (Nadolny) K.; B.S., Creighton U., 1948; M.B.A., Stanford, 1950; cert. in polit. econs. Grad. Inst. Internat. Studies, U. Geneva, 1951. Adminstrv. analyst Standard Oil Co. Calif., San Francisco, 1952-53; staff asst. No. Natural Gas Co., Omaha, 1953-57; mgmt. cons. Cresap, McCormick and Paget, Inc., San Francisco, 1957-75, v.p., mgr. San Francisco office; mgmt. cons., prin. J.F. Klammer Assocs., Inc., San Francisco, 1975—. Served to 1st lt. USAAF, 1943-46; lt. col. USAFR (ret.). Rotary Found. fellow, 1950-51. Republican. Roman Catholic. Clubs: Univ. Home: 1998 Broadway San Francisco CA 94109 Office: 1970 Broadway St Oakland CA 94612

KLAWITTER, RALPH ALEX, forester; b. Chgo., July 28, 1927; s. Alex John and Veronica Irene (Kowalczyk); B.S. in Forestry, Mich. State U., 1952; M.F., Duke U., 1956, D.F. (Brunswick Pulp & Paper Co. fellow 1960-62), 1962; m. Lillian June McVannel, Apr. 19, 1952; children—Victoria June, Laura Lynn, Michael Ralph, Mark Ralph. With U.S. Forest Service, 1953-80, asst. dir. Northeastern Forest Expt. Sta., Upper Darby, Pa., 1969-72, asst. dir. Intermountain Forest and Range Expt. Sta., Missoula, Mont., 1972-80; faculty affiliate Sch. Forestry, U. Mont., 1973-80, cons., 1980—. Served with USNR, 1945-47. Mem. Soc. Am. Foresters (cert. ser. 1964), Mont. Water Research Inst. (advisory bd. 1974—), Idaho Water Research Inst., Missoula C. of C., Sigma Xi, Alpha Zeta, Xi Sigma Pi, Theta Chi. Roman Catholic. Contbr. articles to profl. publs. Home: 104 39th St Missoula MT 59803 Office: 104 39th St Missoula MT 59803

KLECKNER, JAMES H., clin. psychologist, con.; b. Brooklyn, Jan. 4, 1934; s. Albert and Ann (Handsman) K.; m. Mary S. Tilson, April 8, 1970. B.A., Cornell U., 1955; M.S. Rutgers U., 1964; Ed.D., Tchrs. Co. Coll., Columbia U., 1968. Lic. psychologist, Calif.; lic. marriage, family and child counselor, Calif. Staff psychologist Kings County (N.Y.) Hosp., 1962; staff therapist Queens County (N.Y.) Neuropsychiat. Inst., 1962-66; asst. prof. U.S. Internat. U., San Diego, 1966-71; dir. Fed. Drug Abuse Program, San Diego, 1968-80; pvt. practice San Diego, 1966—; cons. Chaplain's Office, Naval Air Sta., Miramar, Calif. Mem. Republic Nat. Com. Served to capt. USAFR, 1955-59. Mem. Am. Psychol. Assn., Am. Assn. Marriage and Family Therapists, Calif. State Psychol. Assn., Acad. San Diego Psychologists. Clubs: Cornell of San Diego, K.P. Editor, contbg. author: Readings in Marriage and Mental Health, 1968; contbg. editor Bull. Psychologists in Substance Abuse; contbg. author Psychology. Home: 5679 Tortuga Ct San Diego CA 92124 Office: 5402 Ruffin Rd 202 San Diego CA 92123

KLEEMANN, GARY LEWIS, educational consultant; b. Pasadena, Calif., June 8, 1945; s. Ernest Wilhard and Martha May (Lewis) K.; m. Balvina Setelo, Sept. 12, 1970; children—Robert, Michael. B.A., San Jose State U., 1968; M.S., Oreg. State U., 1973; postgrad. Ariz. State U. Dir. student activities, asst. union dir. Boise (Idaho) State U., 1970-72; asst. dean students U. Calif.-Irvine, 1973-74; dir. univ. ctr. U. Pacific, Stockton, Calif., 1974-79; coordinator Associated Students, Ariz. State U., Tempe, 1979—; cons. Garvi Assocs. Served with USN, 1968-70. Mem. Am. Assn. Higher Edn., Am. Ednl. Research Assn., Assn. Coll. Unions Internat. (research com.), Nat. Assn. Student Personnel Adminstrs. Home: 1831 E Cornell St Tempe AZ 85283 Office: M U 208A Arizona State U Tempe AZ 85287

KLEEN, STEVEN ROY, optometrist; b. Des Moines, Nov. 18, 1953; s. Merle Dean and Irene Leone (Mueller) K.; m. Janet Marie Nielsen, June 26, 1976; 1 dau., Kristen Anne. O.D., So. Calif. Coll. Optometry, 1979. Cert. optometrist, Calif. Chief contact lens and low vision depts. Redlands (Calif.) Eye Med. Group, 1979—. Chmn. Annual Retinitis Pigmentosa Golf Benefit, Redlands, 1983. Recipient Apollo Laser award So. Calif. Coll. Optometry, 1979. Mem. Am. Optometric Assn., Calif. Optometric Assn., Orange Belt Optometric Soc. Lutheran. Clubs: Kiwanis, Redlands Noon. Office: 245 Terracina Blvd 102 Redlands CA 92373

KLEHS, HENRY JOHN WILHELM, ret. civil engr.; b. Dornbusch bez Stade, Germany, Dec. 7, 1910; s. Frederick and Anna (Mahler) K.; B.S., U. Calif., 1935; m. Clodell Peters, July 17, 1948; came to U.S., 1920, naturalized through father, 1922. Engr. So. Pacific Transp. Co., 1936-75, supr. hazardous materials control, until 1975; ret., 1975. Mem. Calif. Fire Chiefs Assn., Internat. Assn. Fire Chiefs, Steuben Soc. Am., Am. Ry. Engring Assn., ASCE. Home: 604 Glenwood Isle Alameda CA 94501

KLEIMAN, JOSEPH, life sciences co. exec.; b. Grand Rapids, Mich., Oct. 1, 1919; s. Jacob and Bessie (Targowitch) K.; B.S. in Engring., U. Mich., 1941, M.S., 1942; m. Shirley Ruth Present, Aug. 30, 1942; children—Richard Neil, Robert Alan, William Jay. Engr., Reeves Instrument Corp., N.Y.C., 1946-51; v.p., gen. mgr. Belock Instrument Corp., College Point, N.Y., 1951-58; v.p., gen. mgr. Whittaker Gyro div. Telecomputing Corp., Los Angeles, 1958-59, exec. v.p. corp., 1959-64; v.p. corp. devel. Whittaker Corp., 1964-67, sr. v.p., 1967—; dir. Yardney Electric Corp., Whittaker Corp., Diagnostic Products Corp. Vice chmn. Union Am. Hebrew Congregations, 1975-79, 81—. Mem. Nat. Soc. Profl. Engrs., Calif. Soc. Profl. Engrs., Sigma Xi, Phi Lambda Upsilon, Iota Alpha. Jewish. Home: 11240 Chalon Rd Los Angeles CA 90049 Office: 10880 Wilshire Blvd Los Angeles CA 90024

KLEIN, ARNOLD WILLIAM, physician; b. Mt. Clemens, Mich., Feb. 27, 1945; s. David and Malvina K.; B.A., U. Pa., Phila., 1967, M.D., 1971. Intern, Cedars-Sinai Med. Center, Los Angeles, 1971-72; resident dermatology Hosp. U. Pa., Phila., 1972-73; resident dermatology UCLA Med. Center, 1973-75, chief dermatol. resident, 1975, asst. prof., 1975—; attending physician Cedars-Sinai Med. Center, Century City Hosp., Mid-Way Hosp., Los Angeles New Hosp.; asst. prof. Stanford U.; cons. in field, also lectr.; cons. Am. Cancer Soc. Haney scholar, 1963-67; Measey scholar, 1967-71; Phila. Found. fellow, 1970; USPHS postdoctoral fellow, 1972-73. Mem. Beverly Hills C. of C., Pepper Med. Soc., Los Angeles Med. Soc., Met. Dermatologic Soc., Soc. Investigative Dermatology, Am. Acad. Dermatology, Am. Venereal Disease Assn., Nat. Psoriasis Found., Nat. Scleroderma Found., Pediatric Derm. Soc., Am. Soc. Cosmetic Surgeons, Delphos, Phi Beta Kappa, Sigma Tau Sigma. Author: The Skin Book; Drug-Trip Abroad; editor: The Med. Reader; mem. editorial bd. Shape. Home: 553 S Windsor St Los Angeles CA 90005 Office: 435 N Roxbury Dr Beverly Hills CA 90210

KLEIN, CARL GOTTLIEB, oil well service company executive; b. Billings, Mont., July 13, 1932; s. Carl Gottlieb and Esther Evelyn (Swecker) K.; student Eastern Mont. Coll., 1951-52, 68-71, Rocky Mt. Coll., 1958, U. Mont., 1969, Billings Bus. Coll., 1954-55; m. Eldora Hochhalter, Dec. 2, 1952; children—Jacqueline Ann, Susan Pamela. Owner, officer Western Oil Well Service Co., Billings, 1955-82, also dir.; owner, officer Oilfield Constrn. Service Co., Billings, 1969—, also dir.; dir. Western Bank of Billings; tchr. Eastern Mont. Coll., 1965-66. Served with U.S. Army, 1952-54. Mem. Am. Petroleum Inst., Am. Mgmt. Assn., Assn. Oilwell Servicing Contractors, Billings Petroleum Club, Nat. Rifle Assn., Am. Legion. Clubs: Exchange, Billings Rod & Gun, Ducks Unlimited, Elks. Office: 2812 1st Ave N Room 404 Billings MT 59101

KLEIN, DAVID BALLIN, clinical psychologist, writer; b. N.Y.C., Apr. 15, 1897; s. Phillip and Julie (Hirsch) K.; m. Rosa, Sept. 13, 1923; m. 2d, Anne, Feb. 5, 1959. Ph.D., Columbia, U., 1930. Diplomate in clin. psychology. Prof. psychology, dir. Psychol. Service Ctr., U. So. Calif., Los Angeles, 1948-62, prof. emeritus, 1962—. Author: General Psychology, 1936; Mental Hygiene-Psychology of Personal Adjustment, 1944, 56; Abnormal Psychology, 1951; A History of Scientific Psychology-Origins and Philosophic Backgrounds, 1970; The Unconscious: Invention or Discovery-A Historico-Critical Inquiry, 1977; The Concept of Consciousness, 1983. Address: 3422 E Calle Azul Laguna Hills CA 92653

KLEIN, EUGENE VICTOR, football exec.; b. N.Y.C., Jan. 29, 1921; s. Benjamin and Sadie (Olsen) K.; student N.Y.U., 1939-40; m. Joyce Fay Finberg, Feb. 10, 1976; children by previous marriage—Randee, Michael Gary. Automobile dealer, Calif., 1946-55; automobile distbr., Calif., 1955-60; chmn. bd. Columbia Savs. & Loan Assn., Los Angeles, 1955-65; pres., dir. Nat. Theatres & TV, Inc., 1955-59; chmn. bd., pres. Nat. Gen. Corp., 1961-73; pres., gen. partner San Diego Chargers Football Club, 1966—; dir. City Nat. Bank, Zenith Nat. Ins. Co. Active local civic groups and orgns. Recipient Medallion of Valor State of Israel, 1969. Home: PO Box 2468 Rancho Santa Fe CA 92067

KLEIN, JEFFREY BRUCE, hosp. adminstr.; b. N.Y.C., May 8, 1948; s. Herbert and Rose (Ginsberg) K.; B.A., Alfred U., 1970; M.B.A., Temple U., 1972; m. Barbara Cynthia Greenstein, May 12, 1973. Adminstrv. extern L.I. Jewish Med. Center, New Hyde Park, N.Y., 1968; pub. health asst. Nassau County Dept. Health, Minneola, N.Y., 1970; adminstrv. resident Frankford Hosp., Phila., 1971-72; asso. dir. community medicine Brookhaven Meml. Hosp., Patchogue, N.Y., 1972-73; adminstrv. asst. Moss Rehab. Hosp., Phila., 1973-74, asst. adminstr., 1974-78; assoc. adminstr. Daniel Freeman Hosp., Inglewood, Calif., 1978—. Mem. council on aging Fedn. Jewish Agys., Phila., 1974-. Fellow Am. Acad. Med. Adminstrs.; mem. Am. Hosp. Assn., Am. Coll. Hosp. Adminstrs., Am. Pub. Health Assn., Nat. Fire Protection Assn.,

Royal Soc. Health (London), Beta Gamma Sigma. Home: 10856 Topeka Dr Northridge CA 91324 Office: 333 N Prairie Ave Inglewood CA 90301

KLEIN, JOSEPH DAVID, audio video producer; b. Chgo., July 2, 1953; s. Morey and Florence (DuBow) K. Grad. high sch. Tech. engring. asst. Ryder Sound Service, Hollywood, Calif., 1969-70; disc jockey, prodn. man KAFY Radio, Bakersfield, Calif., 1971; engr., producer, ptnr. Hollywood Spectrum, Inc., Los Angeles, 1972-77; producer, pres. L.A. Trax, Inc., Los Angeles, 1977—; music and comml. cons. Recipient Clio award, 1982, 83, numerous others. Mem. SAG, AFTRA, Nat. Assn. Rec. arts and Scis. Democrat. Jewish. Office: LA Trax Inc 8033 Sunset Blvd Suite 1010 Los Angeles CA 90046

KLEIN, KENNETH, computer co. exec.; b. Bklyn., Apr. 19, 1939; s. Irving and Ruth (Poplinger) K. Student Rutgers U., 1972-76. Computer programmer Block Drug Co., N.Y.C., 1965-67, Diners Club, N.Y.C., 1967; systems analyst Norelco, N.Y.C., 1967-75; project mgr. APL Corp., Damon Creations, N.Y.C., 1976-78; owner Stoneware Computer Products, San Rafael, Calif., 1978—. Served with U.S. Army, 1960-63. Address: 50 Belvedere St San Rafael CA 94901

KLEIN, LAWRENCE ROBERT, investment consultant, educator; b. N.Y.C., May 27, 1938; s. George Samuel and Miriam Gertrude (Billig) K.; m. Joan Deana Kramer, Sept. 17, 1960; children—Lisa Susan, Amy Lynn, Randi Beth. B.A., N.Y.U., 1960; M.B.A., Adelphi U., 1965. Cert. fin. planner, 1969; securities exchange commn.; registered investment advisor; registered options prin.; registered rep., commodity futures prin. sr. account exec. Merril Lynch Pierce, N.Y.C., 1960-70, sr. v.p., mgr., various locations, 1970-80; v.p. investments Shearson/Am. Exprexx, Encino, Calif., 1981—; pres. Lawrence R. Klein and Assocs., Westlake, Calif., 1980—; dir. UCLA Sch. Fin. Planning, 1981—. Contbr. articles on fin. to profl. jours. Vice pres. so. Calif. div., Nat. Leukemia Assn., Los Angeles, 1980—; commr. Pop Warner Jr. Football, Conejo Valley, Calif., 1980—; bd. govs. Adelphi U. Sch. Banking Mgmt. Named Outstanding Educator, UCLA, 1980, 81. Mem. Internat. Assn. Fin. Planners (v.p. 1980—), Nat. Assn. Retired Persons (advisor to group 1980—). Republican. Jewish. Clubs: Mason, Shriners. Home: 715 Arroyo Oaks Dr Westlake Village CA 91362 Office: Shearson/Am Express 15760 Ventura Blvd Encino CA 91346

KLEIN, MINNIE FRANCES, education educator; b. Arcadia, Fla., July 21, 1932; d. David Ferguson and Margaret (Dampier) Jones; m. William A. Klein, Aug. 11, 1963; children—Karen Lisa, Steven Gregory. B.S., Fla. State U., 1954; M.S., UCLA, 1959, Ed.D., 1963. Elem. sch. tchr. Englewood (Fla.) Sch., 1954-61; cons., sr. staff mem. Inst. for Devel. of Ednl. Activities Los Angeles, 1974-80; prof. edn., Pepperdine U., Los Angeles, 1975-80; assoc. prof. edn. U. So. Calif., Los Angeles, 1980—. Mem. Am. Ednl. Research Assn., Assn. Supervision and Curriculum Devel., Profs. of Curriculum, Nat. Soc. for Study Edn. Democrat. Author (with John I. Goodlad) Looking Behind the Classroom Door, 1974; (with Goodlad, Novotney and Tye) Toward a Mankind Curriculum, 1974; About Learning Materials, 1978, How To Study a School, 1983. Home: 928 23d St Santa Monica CA 90403 Office: 702 Waite Phillips Hall USC Los Angeles CA 90004

KLEIN, NIEL K., advertising agency executive; b. Chgo., Sept. 7, 1938; s. Louis Charles and Edith M. (Shrove) K.; m. Kaye Miller Jackson, June 18, 1960; children—Jeffrey, Tracy; m. 2d, Valerie Ann Hays, May 30, 1975; children—Hilerie, Tyler. B.A. in Creative Writing, Stanford U., 1960; M.A. in Music Composition, UCLA, 1964. Product mgr. Procter & Gamble, Cin., 1964-67; account exec. Doyle Dane Bernbach Advt., Los Angeles, 1967-72; account supr. Keye Donna Pearlstein Advt., Los Angeles, 1972-73; dir. devel. Viviane Woodward Cosmetics, Panorama City, Calif., 1973-74; ptnr. Hale Hanson & Co. Consulting, Pasadena, Calif., 1974-75; pres. Klein/Richardson Advt., Beverly Hills, Calif., 1975—; mktg instr. Advt. Ctr., Los Angeles, pres., 1982. Treas. West Los Angeles Montessori Sch., pres., 1982. Served to lt. (j.g.) USNR, 1960-62. Mem. Advt. Club of Los Angeles, Beverly Hills C. of C. Republican. Presbyterian. Club: Stanford (Los Angeles). Office: Klein/Richardson Inc 8665 Wilshire Blvd Suite 409 Beverly Hills CA 90211

KLEIN, SUSAN JEAN, sociologist, consultant; b. Cin., Jan. 3, 1947; d. Harry S. and Imogene A. (Laudeman) Ditchett; m. Kenneth M. Klein, Sept. 13, 1966; 1 son, Kevin B.; m. 2d William M. Marine, Mar. 17, 1979; 1 dau., Alice L. Student U. Pa., 1965-67; B.A. summa cum laude, U. Minn., 1969, Ph.D., 1975. Asst. prof. Health Scis. Ctr., U. Colo., Denver, 1975-78; program dir. health resources Western Interstate Commn. Higher Edn., Boulder, Colo., 1979-82; writer, cons. in field of health, social scis., 1982—; vis. researcher dept. community medicine U. Edinburgh (Scotland), 1982. NIMH trainee U. Minn., 1971-75; WHO travel fellow, 1978. Mem. Am. Pub. Health Assn., Am. Sociol. Assn., Conf. on Social Scis. in Health, Assn. Behavioral Scientists in Med. Edn. Congregationalist. Author: (with Simmons and Simmons) The Gift of Life: Social and Psychological Impact of Organ Transplants, 1977; Vision Manpower Needs in the Western States, 1979; Rural Health in the West: An Inventory of Education and Administration, 1981; Effects of Chronic Kidney Disease and Transplantation on Adolescents in the Disabled and Chronically Ill Adolescent, 1983.

KLEIN, WILLIAM BRUCE, architect; b. Kansas City, Mo., Sept. 22, 1945; s. William Charles and Margaret Anna (Folger) K.; B.A., Colo. Coll., 1967; M.Arch., U. Utah, 1974; m. Gay Larae Keen, Aug. 31, 1974. Architect, Historic Bldgs. Survey, Nat. Park Service, Washington, 1974-75; archtl. apprentice Architects and Planners/Alliance, Salt Lake City, 1976-78, Johnson, Hobson & Partners, Denver, 1978; prin. Bill Klein Architect, Sandpoint, Idaho, 1979—; architect in schs., 1979-82. Served with U.S. Navy, 1967-71. Home: PO Box 1393 Sandpoint ID 83864 Office: 111 Cedar St Suite 3 Sandpoint ID 83864

KLEINMAN, GARY STEVEN, accountant; b. Los Angeles, Mar. 28, 1945; s. Morrie and Anne Rose (Sharp) K. B.S., St. Jose State Coll., 1968; M.B.A., Calif. State Coll.-Long Beach, 1969. C.P.A., Calif. Acct., Arthur Young & Co., Los Angeles, 1969-73, Freedman, Kinzelberg & Broder, Los Angeles, 1974-79; pres., controlling stockholder Gary S. Kleinman Accountancy Corp., Los Angeles, 1979—; mem. adv. bd. First Pacific Bank. Active Beverly Hills (Calif.) Men's Charities. Served with USAF, 1966-67. Mem. Calif. Soc. C.P.A.s, Am. Inst. C.P.A.s, Soc. Calif. Accts. Club: Touch (Los Angeles). Office: 12304 Santa Monica Blvd Suite 119 Los Angeles CA 90025

KLEINSCHUSTER, STEPHEN JOHN, III, biologist; b. Bath, Pa., June 3, 1939; s. Stephen John and Elizabeth (Morrow) K.; student Baylor U., 1963; B.S. in Biology, Colo. State U., 1963, M.S., 1966; Ph.D., Oreg. State U., 1970; m. Karen Kreutzer, June 25, 1965; children—Stephan John IV, Luke. Postdoctoral fellow devel. biology U. Chgo., 1971; lectr. Community Coll. Denver, 1972; asst. prof. Met. State Coll., Denver, 1971-73; affiliate prof. Colo. State U., Fort Collins, 1973, asst. prof., 1973-75, asso. prof., 1975-77; asso. prof., head dept. animal dairy and vet. scis. Utah State U., Logan, 1977—, dir. animal tumor program, 1977—. Recipient Ellis Scholarship award, 1960, Aylesworth Scholarship award, 1961, Achievement award NASA, 1976, Spl. Service award Colo.-Wyo. Jr. Acad. Sci., 1978; NASA fellow, 1961-63, USPHS fellow, 1966-70, NIH fellow, 1970-71. Mem. AAAS, Am. Astronautical Soc., Am. Assn. Anatomists, World Assn. Vet. Anatomists, Am. Assn. Vet. Anatomists, Am. Soc. Zoologists, Am. Soc. Animal Sci., Oreg. Marine Biol. Soc., Colo.-Wyo. Acad. Sci., Utah Acad. Sci., N.Y. Acad. Sci. Roman Catholic. Contbr. articles in field to profl. jours. Home: 1071 Lamplighter Dr River Heights UT 84321 Office: Dept Animal Dairy and Vet Sci Utah State U Logan UT 84322

KLEINSMITH, GENE, artist; b. Madison, Wis., Feb. 22, 1942; B.A., Augustana Coll., Sioux Falls, S.D., 1963; M.A., U. No. Ariz., Flagstaff, 1969; m. Judy; children—Jon Darin, Paul, Christin. Tchr. art high schs. in S.D., Colo., Minn. and Calif., 1963-71; mem. faculty San Bernardino Valley Coll., eves. 1967-71; instr. ceramics Victory Valley Coll., Victorville, Calif., 1971—, chmn. art dept., also coordinator artist-in-residence programs; lectr., condr. workshops in field; one-man shows include U. Minn., Mankato, 1967, U. Calif., Riverside, 1969, U. S.D., 1976, No. Ariz. U., 1980, Olive Tree Gallery, Ft. Collins, Colo., 1966, Yavapai Coll., Prescott, Ariz., 1976, Apple Valley, Calif., 1977, Hi-Desert Symphony, Victor Valley, 1979; group and invitational exhbns., 1963—, including Gallery II, Charlottesville, Va., 1983, Nat. Council on Edn. for Ceramic Arts, Atlanta, 1983; represented in permanent collections Mpls. Art Inst., Valparaiso (Ind.) U., Gustavus Adolphus Coll., St. Peter, Minn., No. Ariz. U., Ariz. Western Coll., Yuma, S.D. State U., Brookings, U. S.D., U. Minn., Mankato, Miami-Dade Community Coll., also pvt. collections; presenter workshops, lectr. in Naples, Florence, Sesto Fiorentino, Vicenza, Bologna, Milan, Venice (all Italy), Vallauris, Cap d'Antibes (both France), 1982. Faculty fellow Victor Valley Coll., 1973. Mem. Nat. Council Art Adminstrs., Nat. Council Edn. for Ceramic Arts (mem. exhbns.), Am. Crafts Council, Calif. Art Assn., Inst. Ceramic History, Los Angeles County Art Mus., Phi Delta Kappa, Kappa Delta Pi. Author: Earth, Fire, Air and Water, 1974; Clay's The Way, 2d edit., 1980; contbg. writer TV series Search. Address: 13925 Kiowa Apple Valley CA 92307

KLEINSMITH, JAMES JOSEPH, data processor; b. Murdo, S.D., Oct. 23, 1934; s. Frederick John and Monica Rose (Herber) K.; student George Washington U., 1953-55; B.S. in Physics, Spring Hill Coll., 1962; M.A. in Philosophy, 1963; M.B.A., St. Mary's Coll., 1981; m. Nicole Michelle Bridelle, Aug. 15, 1966; children—David, Nicole, Niela. Systems designer, analyst Systems Devel. Corp., Santa Monica, Calif., 1965; tchr. various primary, secondary schs., colls., U.S.A. and fgn. countries, 1963, 65-67; research technician U.S. Bur. Standards, 1957-58; communication systems program mgr., European announcement mgr. IBM, Paris, 1972-75; distributed processing systems specialist for comml. banks and savs. and loan assns., San Francisco, 1976—. Active in city planning and devel., Clayton, Calif., 1976—. Served with U.S. Army, 1955-57. Mem. Data Processing Mgmt. Assn., Sigma Pi Sigma. Republican. Roman Catholic. Club: Toastmasters. Home: 8 London Ct Clayton CA 94517 Office: 475 14th St Oakland CA 94612

KLEMETSON, STANLEY LOUIS, civil engineer, educator; b. Bellflower, Calif., May 10, 1941; s. Karl William and Viola Fern (Peterson) K.; B.S.C.E., San Jose State U., 1968; M.S.C.E., U. Mo., Rolla, 1974; Ph.D., Utah State U., 1975; m. Margaret Ellen Benson, Oct. 19, 1961; children—Richard Aaron, Glenn Allen, Camille, Kathryn. Engr., Guy F. Atkinson, San Francisco, 1968-71; asst. prof. N.D. State U., Fargo, 1974-77; assoc. prof. civil engring. Colo. State U., Fort Collins, 1977-81, Brigham Young U., Provo, Utah, 1981—; pres. Klemetson Engring., Ft. Collins, Colo., 1977-81, Orem, Utah, 1981—; owner Klemetson Constrn. Co., Ft. Collins, 1978-81. Precinct committeeman Republican Party, Ft. Collins, 1978-81, dist. capt., 1980-81. Mem. ASCE, Water Pollution Control Fedn., Internat. Assn. Water Pollution Research, Am. Soc. Engring. Edn., Assn. Environ. Engring. Profs., Sigma Xi, Tau Beta Pi, Chi Epsilon. Republican. Mem. Ch. of Jesus Christ of Latter-day Saints. Contbr. articles in field to profl. jours. Home: 20 W 1200 E Orem UT 84057 Office: 371 CB Brigham Young U Provo UT 84602

KLEPPE, JOHN ARTHUR, scientist, engr., educator, corp. exec.; b. Oakland, Calif., Feb. 21, 1939; s. Arthur William and Musa (Anderson) K.; B.S. in Elec. Engring., U. Nev., Reno, 1961, M.S. in Elec. Engring., 1967; Ph.D., U. Calif., Davis, 1970; m. Julianna Marie Galli, Aug. 12, 1961; children—John Frederick, Johanna Beth, Judith Anne. Prof. elec. engring. U. Nev., Reno, 1970—, dir. Engring. Research and Devel. Center, 1976—; pres., research cons. Sci. Engring. Instruments, Inc., Reno, 1968—, pres. Klepco, Inc., 1976—; cons. in tech.; chief engr. NSF weather expdn. to Antarctica, 1977; del. White House Conf. on Small Bus., 1980. Served to lt., C.E., USN, 1961-65. Registered profl. engr., Nev., Calif. Mem. IEEE, Sigma Xi, Tau Beta Pi. Contbr. articles, papers to publs. and confs. in U.S., Switzerland, Eng., Holland, France, Mex., Can. Home: 2425 Greensboro Dr Reno NV 89509 Office: SEI 1275 Kleppe Ln 14 Sparks NV 89431

KLEPPER, ELIZABETH LEE, plant physiologist, researcher; b. Memphis, Mar. 8, 1936; d. George Madden and Margaret Elizabeth (Lee) K.; B.A., Vanderbilt U., 1958; M.A., Duke U., 1963, Ph.D., 1966. Research scientist Commonwealth Sci. and Indsl. Research Orgn. div. Irrigation Research, Griffith, Australia, 1966-68; asst. prof. dept. botany and microbiology Auburn (Ala.) U., 1968-72; research scientist ecosystems dept. Battelle N.W. Labs., Richland, Wash., 1972-75, sr. research scientist, 1975-76; plant physiologist Columbia Plateau Conservation Research Ctr., Agrl. Research Service, U.S. Dept. Agr., Pendleton, Oreg., 1976—. Recipient Founders medal Vanderbilt U., 1958; NSF fellow, 1964-66; Marshall scholar, 1958. Mem. AAAS, Am. Soc. Plant Physiology, Am. Soc. Agronomy, Soil Sci. Soc. Am., AAUW, Crop Sci. Soc. Am., Phi Beta Kappa, Sigma Xi, Gamma Sigma Delta. Editorial bd. Plant Physiology, 1976—, contbr. articles to profl. jours. Home: 1454 SW 45th St Pendleton OR 97801 Office: Columbia Plateau Conservation Research Ctr PO Box 370 USDA-ARS Pendleton OR 97801

KLEPSA, RADMILA VITA, financial executive, business manager; b. Pisek, Czechoslovakia, June 6, 1946; came to U.S., 1970; naturalized, 1978; d. Jaroslav and Marie (Volfova) Vita; m. Eric Mirek Klepsa, July 22, 1967. M.B.A. with honors, Karl's U., Prague, 1968; postgrad. UCLA, 1978. Bus. sec., acct. Mary Pickford Co., Beverly Hills, Calif., 1974-76; controller Wakeford/Orloff, Los Angeles, 1976-77; dir., controller Dreyfus Agy., Los Angeles, 1978-80; v.p. fin., treas. BBDO/West, Inc., Los Angeles, 1980—; dir., treas. Advt. Industries Emergency Fund. Mem. Nat. Assn. Accts., Motion Picture and TV Controllers Assn. Republican. Roman Catholic. Office: BBDO/West Inc 10960 Wilshire Blvd Suite 1630 Los Angeles CA 90024

KLEYN, HANS E., hospital executive; b. Socrabaya, Indonesia, Dec. 27, 1926; s. Isaac and Ann (Hofmeester) K.; m. Ila, Aug. 29, 1952; children—Gertrude Christina, Jacques J. B.A., U. Amsterdam, 1948; B.D., M.A., U. Chgo., 1955; research fellow U. Groningen (Netherlands), 1956. Comptroller bursar Chgo. Coll. Osteo. Medicine, Ill., 1956-72; v.p. fin. Children's Meml. Hosp., Chgo., 1972-75; v.p. fin. St. Joseph Hosp., Denver, 1975—. Episcopalian.

KLIEN, WOLFGANG JOSEF, architect; b. Hollabrunn, Austria, Sept. 29, 1942; s. Josef and Maria (Kainz) K.; Dipl. Ing., Vienna Tech. U., 1967; m. Charlotte Olga Kutscherer, Aug. 14, 1968; children—Christina Olga, Angelika Maria. Designer, E. Donau, Architect, Vienna, 1968; with C. Nitschke & Assos., Architects, Columbus, Ohio, 1968-71; project architect GSAS Architects, Phoenix, 1971-75, 77-78; prodn. architect Harry Glueck, Vienna, 1976-77; v.p. architecture Am. Indian Engring. Inc., Phoenix, 1978-81; pres. S.W. Estate Group, Inc., real estate devel., San Diego, 1980-82; exec. v.p. Ariz. br. office SEG-S.W. Estate Group, Inc., Phoenix, 1982—. Mem. AIA. Roman Catholic. Home: 214 E Griswold Rd Phoenix AZ 85020 Office: 6530 N Scottsdale Rd Scottsdale AZ 85253

KLINE, FRED WALTER, communications corporation executive; b. Oakland, Calif., May 17, 1918; s. Walter E. and Jean M. Kline; m. Verna Marie Taylor, Dec. 27, 1952; children—Kathleen, Nora, Fred Walter. B.A. in Calif. History, U. Calif.-Berkeley, 1940. With Walter E. Kline & Assocs. and successor Fred Kline Agy., Inc., from 1937; chmn. bd., pres. Kline Communications Corp., Los Angeles, 1956 ; pres. Capitol News Service. Commr. Los Angeles County Fire Services Commn., Calif. Motion Picture Devel. Council; former fed. civil def. liaison; developer state-wide paramedic rescue program; Calif. chmn. Office of Asst. Sec. Def.; mem. Calif. Com. for Employer Support of Guard and Res. Served with USAAF, World War II; brig. gen. Calif. Mil. Dept. Recipient Inter-Racial award City of Los Angeles, 1963, named Man of Yr., 1964. Mem. Acad. Motion Picture Arts and Scis., Radio and TV News Assn. So. Calif., Pub. Relations Soc. Am., Calif. Newspaper Pubs. Assn., Cath. Press Council (founding mem.), Pacific Pioneer Broadcasters, Footprinters Internat., Am. Mil. Govt. Assn. (past pres.), Navy League, Calif. State Police Officers Assn., Internat. Assn. Profl. Firefighters (hon. life), Peace Officers Assn. Los Angeles County (life), Internat. Assn. Chiefs of Police, Internat. Assn. Fire Chiefs, Calif. Fire Chiefs Assn., Fire Marshals Assn. N.Am., Nat. Fire Protection Assn., Nat. Fin. Writers Assn., Hollywood C. of C., Nat. Fire Sci. Acad., Calif. State Mil. Forces, Calif. Pubs. Assn., So. Calif. Cable Club. Sigma Delta Chi. Clubs: Greater Los Angeles Press, Media (Los Angeles), Sacramento Press. Columnist Calif. newspapers. Office: 1741 N Ivar Ave Suite 204 Los Angeles CA 90028

KLINE, J(OHN) ANTHONY, judge; b. N.Y.C., Aug. 17, 1938; s. Harry and Bertha (Shapiro) K.; m. Susan Sward, Nov. 25, 1982. B.A. with honors, Johns Hopkins U., 1960; M.A., Cornell U., 1962; LL.B., Yale U., 1965. Bar: N.Y., Calif. Law clk. to Justice Raymond Peters, Calif. Supreme Ct., 1965-66; assoc. Davis Polk & Wardwell, N.Y.C., 1966-69; chief litigating atty. Nat. Housing and Econ. Devel. Law Project, Boalt Hall, U. Calif., Berkeley, 1969-70; co-founder, mng. ptnr. Public Advocates, Inc., San Francisco, 1970-75; apptd. legal affairs sec. to Gov. Calif., 1975-80; apptd. Superior Ct. judge, San Francisco, 1980-82; apptd. presiding justice Calif. Ct. Appeals, Dist. 1, Div. 2, San Francisco, 1982—. Bd. dirs. San Francisco Pvt. Industry Council; bd. dirs. No. Calif. div. Am. Jewish Congress. Alfred P. Sloan fellow Cornell U., 1960-62; recipient various awards from bar assns.; Cherini and Sutherland Cup prizes Yale U. Mem. Calif. Judges Assn. Democrat. Jewish. Contbr. articles to legal publs. Office: Calif Court Appeals State Bldg San Francisco CA 94102

KLIORE, ARVYDAS JOSEPH, radio scientist; b. Kaunas, Lithuania, Aug. 5, 1935; came to U.S., 1949, naturalized, 1955; s. Bronius Joseph and Antonia (Valaitis) K.; B.S., U. Ill., 1956; M.S., U. Mich., 1957; Ph.D., Mich. State U., 1962; m. Birute Anna Ulenas, Sept. 3, 1960; children—Saule Andrea, Rima Birute. Research engr. Armour Research Found., Chgo., 1956-58, sr. scientist, 1962-65; mem. tech. staff, research scientist Jet Propulsion Lab., Calif. Inst. Tech., Pasadena, 1965—; lectr. UCLA, 1963-64. Recipient NASA medal, 1972, also several Group Achievement awards. Mem. Internat. Com. for Space Research (exec.), Am. Astron. Soc. (a founder div. for planetary scis.), Am. Geophys. Union, AAAS, Planetary Soc., Am. Lithuanian Commn. (council), Sigma Xi. Roman Catholic. Club: Backa Athletic. Contbr. radio sci. articles to profl. jours. Office: Jet Propulsion Lab Calif Inst Tech 4800 Oak Grove Dr Pasadena CA 91103

KLIPP, BRIAN RANDOLPH, architect; b. Coalinga, Calif., Jan. 5, 1950; s. James E. and Lois M. K.; m. Deanna L. Corbin, Oct. 4, 1980. B.Arch., U. Colo., 1973. Cert. Nat. Council Archtl. Registration Bds. Designer, Nixon-Brown-Brokaw-Bowen, Architects, Boulder, Colo., 1971-75; asso. architect Warren Flickenger & Assos., Denver, 1975-77; partner Anderson/Klipp, Architects and Engrs., Denver, 1977-78; prin. architect Klipp Assocs., P.C., Denver, 1979—. Mem. AIA, Denver C. of C. Office: 3003 E 3d Ave Denver CO 80206

KLIPSCH, LEONA KATHERINE, former newspaper publisher-editor; b. Vancouver, Wash., Feb. 24, 1914; d. Louis John and Marie Rosetta (Debitt) Hinkel; A.B., Smith Coll., 1935; student Sorbonne, Paris, 1934, Columbia U. Grad. Sch. Library Service, summers 1942-44; m. Robert Darius Klipsch, Nov. 25, 1937; children—Phyllis Marie Klipsch Smith, Katharine Klipsch Abbott, Marjorie Klipsch McCracken. Tchr. French and library sci. Marshall U., Huntington, W.Va., 1949-54, br. librarian Albuquerque Public Library, 1955-56; high sch. librarian, Gallup, N.Mex., 1963-65; co-owner, editor Defensor Chieftain, Socorro, N.Mex., 1965-82, pub., 1980-82. Bd. dirs. Socorro Gen. Hosp. Mem. N.Mex. Press Assn. (dir.), Nat. Investigative Reporters, PEO, Sigma Delta Chi. Republican. Presbyterian. Author: Treasure Your Love (Librarian prize for jr. novel 1958); (as Jean Kirby) A Very Special Girl, 1963. Home: 1304 Kitt Pl Socorro NM 87801

KLOBE, THOMAS MICHAEL, art gallery director; b. Mpls., Nov. 26, 1940; s. Charles Sylvester and Lorna Cecilia (Effertz) K.; B.F.A., U. Hawaii, 1964, M.F.A., 1968; postgrad. UCLA; m. Delmarie Pauline Motta, June 21, 1975. Mem. faculty Calif. State U., Fullerton, 1969-72, Santa Ana Coll., 1972-77, Orange Coast Coll., 1974-77; acting dir. Downey (Calif.) Mus. Art, 1976; gallery dir. U. Hawaii, 1977—. Grantee Nat. Endowment Arts, 1979, 81 (2), 82. Mem. Art Mus. Assn., Hawaii Mus. Assn. (sec. 1979, dir. 1980). Author exhbn. catalogues. Office: Dept Art U Hawaii Honolulu HI 96822

KLOPATEK, JEFFREY MATTHEW, ecologist, educator; b. Milw., Dec. 5, 1944; s. Raymond Matthew and Clare Louise (Seramur) K.; m. Barbara Ann Brooks, Mar. 18, 1967; 1 son, Joshua Matthew. B.S. in Conservation, U. Wis.-Milw., 1971, M.S. in Botany, 1974; Ph.D. in Ecology, U. Okla., 1978. Cert. sr. ecologist. Research asst. Okla. Biol. Survey, U. Okla., Norman, 1973-76; research ecologist Oak Ridge Nat. Lab., 1976-81; prof., research ecologist Ariz. State U., Tempe, 1981—; cons. Electric Power Research Inst., 1981—. Chmn. Met. Planning Commn., Farragut, Tenn., 1980-81. Served to 1st lt. U.S. Army, 1966-69. Grantee Dept. Energy, 1977-81, EPA, 1981, U.S. Forest Service, 1980-83, Ariz. State U., 1982-84. Mem. Ecol. Soc. Am., Internat. Assn. Ecology, AAAS, Am. Inst. Biol. Scis. Clubs: Am. Saddlebred Assn. Contbr. articles to books, profl. jours. Home: 1218 E Knight Ln Tempe AZ 85284 Office: Dept Botany Ariz State U Tempe AZ 85287

KLOPFER, JEAN MCQUARY, design educator; b. Lexington, Ky., Sept. 30, 1922; d. Rodney L. and Helen Maurine (Longman) McQuary; m. Florenz Dudley, June 26, 1945; children—Richard Dean, Linda Maurine. B.A. summa cum laude, U. Minn., 1944; M.A., Wash. State U., 1950. Mem. faculty Wash. State U., Pullman, 1950-62, 67—, assoc. prof. design and interior design, 1975—, acting chmn. dept., 1982—. Mem. Environ. Design Research Assn., Interior Design Educators Council, Am. Home Econs. Assn., Assn. Faculty Women. Home: NW 1420 Orion Dr Pullman WA 99163 Office: Dept Clothing Interior Design and Textiles Wash State U Pullman WA 99164

KLOPP, KENNETH HAROLD, camping equipment executive; b. Spokane, Wash., Feb. 7, 1942; s. Kenneth Henry and Dolores Alma (Rowland) K.; m. Margot Ann Latimer, June 18, 1964; children—Kelly, Matthew. B.A., Stanford U., 1964, M.B.A., 1966. Adminstr., White Pine Sash Co., Spokane, 1964-66; gen. mgr. The Ski Hut, Berkeley, Calif., 1966-68; pres. The North Face, Berkeley, 1968—. Bd. dirs. Mexican

Mus., 1980-82; pres. Buildres, Inc., 1982—. Am. Apparel Mfg. Assn. (dir. 1980—, pres. down apparel div. 1979-82). Democrat.

KLOSTERMAN, DONALD FRANCIS, public health administrator, educator; b. Elkton, S.D., June 1, 1939; s. Myles Francis and Frances Marie K.; m. Veralyn Joyce, June 8, 1939; children—Philip, Kara, Scott. M.P.A., Lewis and Clark Coll., 1982; Ph.D. (Univ. Bd. Regents fellow), U. Nebr., 1973. Project cons. Lincoln (Nebr.) Hosp. and Health Council, 1971; prin. investigator research project Edutek, Inc., Lincoln, 1972; dist. dir. and coordinator community mental health/social sci. services Human Relations Services, Biddeford, Maine, 1972-75; dir. psychology Fairview Tng. Center, Salem, Oreg., 1975-81, asst. supt., 1981-83; asst. pub. health adminstr. Marion County Dept. Health, Salem, 1983—; instr. Linfield Coll., 1981—. Mem. Democratic precinct committeeman, Salem, 1976—; mem. allocations panel United Way, Salem, 1979—. Served with U.S. Army, 1958-60. Mem. Am. Psychol. Assn., Oreg. Soc. Tng. Dirs. Presbyterian.

KLOTZ, DOLORES RAMONA, aircraft mfg. co. tech. staff; b. Los Angeles, Dec. 22, 1931; d. Sigurd Daniel and Aasta (Dybwad) Shervik; B.A., Pacific Luth. Coll., 1953; m. Carol Robert Klotz, Feb. 24, 1973; children—Jean Marie Croonquist, David Frank Croonquist. Scientific computer programmer Lockheed Aircraft, Burbank, Calif., 1968-74, fuel systems flight programmer B-1 bomber, El Segundo, Calif., 1974—. Republican. Lutheran. Clubs: Channel Cruising, Sons of Norway. Office: 201 N Douglas St El Segundo CA 90245

KLUCKMAN, JAMES MICHAEL, army officer, optometrist; b. Oceanside, Calif., July 1, 1950; s. Wilson Anthony and Donna Isabelle (Melville) K.; m. Tamie Sue Dunn, Dec. 9, 1978; children—Sean Michael, Brian James. B.S., SUNY-Albany, 1981; O.D., So. Coll. Optometry, Memphis, 1974. Commd. 2d lt. U.S. Army, 1973, advanced through grades to capt. Med. Service Corps, 1976; div. optometrist 307th Med. Bn., 82d Airborne Div., Ft. Bragg, N.C., 1974-76; chief optometry clinic U.S. Army MEDDAC, Tehran, Iran, 1976-78; clin. optometrist Brooke Army Med. Ctr., Ft. Sam Houston, Tex., 1978; asst. chief optometry service Walter Reed Army Med. Ctr., Washington, 1978-82; chief optical div. and adj. U.S. Army Med. Equipment and Optical Sch., Acad. of Health Scis., Aurora, Colo., 1982—, instr. optical lab. specialist course, 1982—; mem. adj. faculty, optometric externship program New Eng. Coll. Optometry, Boston, 1980-82, Pa. Coll. Optometry, Phila., 1980-82, Coll. Optometry, U. Houston, 1980-82; affiliate prof. Regis Coll., Denver, 1982—. Decorated Army Commendation medal. Mem. Am. Optometric Assn. (membership services adv. com. 1983—), Armed Forces Optometric Soc. (pres. 1982, newsletter editor 1980-82), Beta Sigma Kappa. Roman Catholic. Office: Commander USAMEOS ATTN HSHA-MEO-O Aurora CO 80045

KLUDT, DAROLD LEROY, logger; b. Cottonwood, Idaho, July 31, 1944; s. Virgil Charles and Frances (Landmark) K.; m. Becky Margaret Kirk, June 24; children—Erica Lee, Kirk David. B.Mus.Ed., U. Idaho, 1969. Dir. music Pomeroy (Wash.) Schs., 1970-72; ptnr. Kludt Bros. Logging, Orofino, Idaho, 1972—. Vice chmn. Dist. 171 Sch. Bd., 1975-82; mem. exec. bd. Idaho Sch. Bd. Assn., 1980-82; mem. adv. bd. Idaho Educators Inservice, 1980-82; bd. dirs. Clearwater Community Concert Assn., 1977-82; pres. Grangemont PTA, 1981-82; Clearwater county coordinator Mitchell for Lt. Gov., 1982. Mem. Associated Logging Contractors Idaho, Delta Sigma Phi. Democrat. Home and Office: Star Route 2 Box 160 Orofino ID 83544

KLUGMAN, ROBERT, marketing executive; b. Phila., Sept. 20, 1947; s. Jack and Marian (Eveloff) K.; m. Kathleen Martin, Apr. 28, 1979. B.A., Amherst Coll., 1969; M.B.A., Harvard U., 1973. Vice pres., account supr. Leo Burnett U.S.A., Chgo., 1973-79; v.p. mktg. Adolph Coors Co., Golden, Colo., 1979—. Office: Adolph Coors Co Golden CO 80401

KLUSMANN, EUGENE BELZER, engr., chemist; b. Pasadena, Calif., Apr. 17, 1929; s. Carl Dietrech and Beulah Ree (Belzer) K.; B.S., UCLA, 1957; m. Ellene Mae Wonnenberg, May 11, 1951; children—Eric Eugene (dec.), Evalena Karen, Erlynda Mae. Research chemist Olin Mathieson Chem. Corp., 1957-59, Nat. Engring. Sci. Co., 1959-66, Aerojet-Gen. Corp., 1966-70, Chem. Systems, Inc., Irvine, Calif., 1970-75; engr. So. Calif. Gas Co., Los Angeles, 1975-79; sr. supply analysis engr. 1979—. Served with USAF, 1950-52. Mem. Am. Chem. Soc., Pacific Energy Assn. Republican. Contbr. articles to profl. jours. Patentee in field. Home: 2134 Rocky View Rd Diamond Bar CA 91765 Office: 720 W 8th St Los Angeles CA 90017

KLUTE, ARNOLD, soil scientist, educator; b. Galien, Mich., Sept. 24, 1921; s. Benjamin M. and Hazel Vera (Wright) K.; m. Helen Miller, June 26, 1948; children—Sally, Marjorie, Jeffrey, Karen. B.S., Mich. State U., 1947, M.S., 1948; Ph.D., Cornell U., 1951. Research engr. Schlumberger Well Surveying Corp., Ridgefield, Conn., 1951-53; prof. soils U. Ill. Urbana, 1953-70; soil scientist, prof. Agrl. Research Service, U.S. Dept. Agr. and Colo. State U., Ft. Collins, 1970—. Served to tech (s.g.) U.S. Army, 1942-45. Mem. Soil Sci. Soc. Am., Am. Soc. Agronomy (Soil Scientist award 1965), Western Soc. Soil Sci., Am. Geophys. Union. Office: Dept Agronomy Colo State Univ Fort Collins CO 80523

KNAEBEL, MICHAEL LEE, naval officer, electronics technician; b. New Albany, Ind., July 29, 1946; s. Vincent Joseph, Jr. and Anna Lee (Milligan) K.; children—Nicole Marie, Michael Lee. B.S.E.S.C., Purdue U., 1975, M.S.E. (Sec. Navy scholar), 1976. Cert. electronics technician Internat. Soc. Cert. Electronics Technicians; lic. real estate salesperson, Calif. Commd. ensign U.S. Navy, 1975, advanced through grades to lt., 1980; electronics technician, 1967-75; main propulsion asst USS. Blandy, 1976-79; head missile systems br. engring. div. Naval Plant Rep. Office, Strategic Systems Project Office, Sunnyvale, Calif., 1979—; lectr. design of missile systems. Recipient award of merit Purdue U.-Gen. Dynamics Corp., 1975. Mem. AIAA, Am. Soc. Naval Engrs., U.S. Naval Inst. Planetary Soc., Order of the Engr., Am. Legion, Purdue Alumni Assn. Phi Beta Kappa, Tau Beta Pi, Phi Kappa Phi, Sigma Pi Sigma. Roman Catholic. Home: 1611 New Brunswick Ave Sunnyvale CA 94087 Office: PO Box 504 Sunnyvale CA 94086

KNAGGE, ALICE C., businesswoman; b. Tucson, Sept. 11; d. Carlos M. and Louisa F. (Felix) Escalante; widow; children—Deborah Ann, William Charles Grider, Michael F. Knagge. B.A., U. Ariz., 1951. Owner, operator DBM Entprises, trucking, Sasabe, Ariz., 1962—, Sasabe Store and Adobe, 1962—; owner Jefferson House Apts., Tucson. Clk., Sasabe Sch. Bd., 1977-83; precinct committeewoman, 1977. Roman Catholic. Home and Office: 43000 S Sasabe Rd Sasabe AZ 85633

KNAPP, CLEON T., publisher; b. Los Angeles, Apr. 28, 1937; s. Cleon T. and Sally (Brasfield) K.; student UCLA, 1955-58; m. Elizabeth Ann Wood, Mar. 17, 1979; children—Jeffrey James, Brian Patrick, Aaron Bradley, Laura Ann. With John C. Brasfield Pub. Corp. (purchased co. in 1965, changed name to Knapp Communications Corp. 1977), now pub. Bon Appetit mag., Archtl. Digest, GEO mag., Home mag., Los Angeles, 1958—, pub., chief exec. officer, 1965—, also pres., chmn. bd.; organizer, dir. Wilshire Bancorp. Office: 5900 Wilshire Blvd Los Angeles CA 90036

KNAPP, DENISE LYNETTE, dental plan executive; b. Fresno, Calif.; d. John J. and Melba K. Knapp; m. John R. Robinson, Dec. 29, 1978. Student Fresno State U., San Francisco State Coll. Assoc. dir. profl. relations and adminstrv. asst. to exec. dir. Calif. Dental Service, San Francisco, 1965-76; dir. profl. relations Delta Plan of Mont., Nev. and Utah, Salt Lake City, 1977-78; exec. v.p., chief exec. officer Delta Dental Plan of Alaska, Anchorage, 1978—; mem. Alaska State Med. Care Adv. Com. Chmn. Anchorage Women's Club Free Com. Mem. So. Alaska Life Underwriters Assn., Nat. Life Underwriters Assn., Women Life Underwriters Assn., C. of C. (legis. study com.). Home: PO Box 4-787 Anchorage AK 99509 Office: PO Box 3-726 Anchorage AK 99501

KNAPP, EBER GUY, accountant; b. Seattle, Sept. 18, 1916; s. Eber G. and Ernestine C. (Venter) K.; student Wilson's Bus. Coll., 1938-39, U. So. Calif., 1946-47; m. M. Lorraine Knapp, July 2, 1947; children—Candyce Lorraine, Ardyce Christine, Carol Lynn. Owner, Knapp's Tax & Bus. Service, Westminster, Calif., 1959—; overall coordinator Orange County (Calif.) Am. Assn. Ret. Persons Tax-Aide Program. Served with U.S. Army, 1941-45. Mem. Inland Soc. Tax Cons., Assn. Bus. and Tax Cons. Orange County (v.p.), Am. Legion, VFW. Republican. Mem. Christian Ch. Author: Groom's Survival Handbook, or How to Teach Your Bride to Cook, 1982. Home: 7152 Santee Ave PO Box 1 Westminster CA 92684

KNAPP, JERRY WILSON, economist; b. Idaho, Oct. 9, 1937; s. Lloyd Wilson and Dorothy June (Erickson) K.; m. Kullaya Wongbantao, Mar. 10, 1968; children—Malisa Lynn, Anthony James. B.S. in Agrl. Econs., U. Idaho 1959, M.S. in Econs., 1961. Economist, U.S. Bur. Reclamation, 1961-66; econ. advisor Royal Irrigation Dept., Bangkok, Thailand, 1966-70; staff asst. Sec. of Interior, Washington, 1970-74; sr. economist Harza Engring. Co., Chgo., 1974-78; dir. resource econs. CH2M Hill, Sacramento, 1978-81, v.p., dir. econs., 1981—. Mem. Am. Econ. Assn., Am. water Resources Assn., Internat. Commn. Irrigation Drainage and Flood Control, Alpha Zeta. Contbr. to books and articles to profl. jours. Home: 3103 Shelter Cove Davis CA 95616 Office: 555 Capitol Mall Suite 1290 Sacramento CA 95814

KNAPP, RONALD HARRISON, mech. engr., educator; b. Tuscola, Ill., July 20, 1944; s. Robert Harrison and Bessie Margaret (Teel) K.; B.S.M.E. with honors, U. Hawaii, 1967, Ph.D. in Ocean Engring., 1973; M.S.M.E., Calif. Inst. Tech., 1968. Mech. engr. Naval Ocean Systems Center, Kaneohe, Hawaii, 1968-75; vice-pres. Ocean Engring. Consultants, Inc., Honolulu, 1972-80; asso. prof. dept. mech. engring. U. Hawaii, Honolulu, 1975—; pres. Knapp Engring. Inc., Aiea, Hawaii, 1980—. U.S. Navy Grad. fellow, 1970-72; Alexander von Humboldt Found. (W. Ger.) postdoctoral fellow, 1981-82. Registered profl. engr. Mem. ASME (mem. exec. com. ocean engring. div.), Marine Tech. Soc., Internat. Assn. Spatial and Shell Structures, Nat. Soc. Profl. Engrs., AAUP, Hawaii Edn. Assn. Methodist. Patentee, contbr. articles to profl. jours. Home: 98-1033 Kupukupu Pl Aiea HI 96701 Office: U Hawaii Dept Mech Engring 2540 Dole St Holmes Hall 302 Honolulu HI 96822

KNAPP, TERRY SCOTT, mfg. co. exec.; b. Lemmon, S.D., Jan. 26, 1945; s. Theron Scott and Gladys Jane (Walter) K.; student in Chemistry and Math., Western Wash. State Coll., 1963-66; m. Laura Joanne Gaborit, Sept. 11, 1965; children—Michael John, Jon David. Chief insp., quality control mgr. Kawecki Berylco Industries, Wenatchee, Wash., 1967-72; mgr. mfg. Zirtech div. KBI, Albany, Oreg., 1972-76; mgr. mfg. and materials Nichols Homeshield, Davenport, Iowa, 1976-79; plant supt. Selkirk Metalbestos div. Household Internat., Nampa, Idaho, 1979-80, plant mgr., 1980—. Mem. Soc. Mfg. Engrs., Nampa C. of C. Home: 999 Eagle Hills Way Eagle ID 83616 Office: 1820 E Fargo Ave Nampa ID 83651

KNAPP, THOMAS EDWIN, sculptor, painter; b. Gillette, Wyo., Sept. 28, 1925; s. Chester M. and Georgia Mabel (Blankenship) K.; student Santa Rosa Jr. Coll., 1952-53; A.A., Calif. Coll. Arts and Crafts, Oakland, 1953-54; student Art Center Sch., Los Angeles, 1954-55; m. Dorothy Wellborn; children—Gordon, Kathy, Dan, Kent, Keith. Animation artist Walt Disney Studios, Burbank, Calif., 1954-56, Portrait & Hobby Camera Shops, WyoFoto Studies, Cody, Wyo., 1956-64; owner Rocky Mountain Land Devel. Corp., Cody, 1965-66; comml. artist Mountain States Telephone Co., Albuquerque, 1966-69; one man shows: Cody County Art League, 1968, Jamison Gallery, Santa Fe, 1969, Mesilla Gallery, 1971, Inn of Mountain Gods, Mescalero Apache Reservation, N.Mex., 1978, Mountain Oyster Club, Tucson, 1978, Dos Pajaros Gallery, El Paso, 1978; joint shows (with wife) Rosequist Gallery, Tucson, 1975, 77, Colony House, Roswell, N.Mex., 1974, 75; (with Michael Coleman) Zantman Gallery, Palm Desert, Calif., 1977; group shows: Saddleback Inn, Santa Ana, Calif., 1968-77, Zantman Gallery, Carmel, Calif., 1975, 76, 77; Solon Borglum Meml. Sculpture Exhbn. Nat. Cowboy Hall of Fame, Oklahoma City, 1975-76, Maxwell Gallery, San Francisco, 1975, others; represented in permanent collections: Whitney Gallery of Western Art, Cody, Wyo., Senator Quinn Meml. Auditorium, Spencer, Mass., Heritage Mus., Anchorage, Indpls. Mus. Art, Mescalero (N.Mex.) Tribe; works include: Dance of the Mountain Spirit (Blue Ribbon award 1976), Laguna Eagle dancer (Spl. award 1974, Blue Ribbon Los Angeles Indian Art Show 1975-76), Santa Clara Buffalo dancer (Spl. award San Antonio Indian Nat. show 1974, spl. award Los Angeles Indian show 1976), Mandan chieftan (spl. award San Diego Indian Show 1974, Los Angeles Indian Show 1976); lectr. at art seminars. Active Boy Scouts Am., 1947-68. Served with USN, World War II, Korea. Decorated Air medal; recipient Order of Arrow award Boy Scouts Am., 1968. Mem. Am. Foundrymen's Soc., N.Mex. Amigos. Club: Safari Internat. Home and office: PO Box 510 Ruidoso Downs NM 88346

KNECHTLI, RONALD CHARLES, research scientist; b. Geneva, Aug. 14, 1927; s. Alfred Charles and Edith (Beran) K.; m. Diane Frances Weisul, Nov. 3, 1953; children—Alain, Bernard, Daniel. Diploma, Swiss Fed. Inst. Tech., 1950, Ph.D., 1955. Research engr. Brown Boveri & Co., Switzerland, 1950-51, 52-53, research labs. RCA, 1953-58; asst. MIT, 1951-52; sr. scientist Hughes Reseach Labs., Hughes Aircraft Co., Malibu, Calif., 1958—. Recipient award for outstanding research RCA Labs., 1957, L.A. Hyland Patent award, 1974. Mem. Am. Phys. Soc., IEEE, AIAA, Sigma Xi. Republican. Presbyterian. Contbr. articles profl. jours. Patentee in field. Home: 22929 Ardwick St Woodland Hills CA 91364 Office: 3011 Malibu Canyon Rd Malibu CA 90265

KNEEDLER, JULIA ANNE, nursing educator, cons.; b. Martinez, Calif., Mar. 27, 1938; d. John F. and Marge G. (Curl) Williams. B.S. in Nursing, Walla Walla Coll., 1961; M.S. in Nursing, Loma Linda U., 1967; Ed.D. in Adult Continuing Edn., U. No. Colo., 1976. R.N., Colo. Staff nurse Greater Bakersfield (Calif.) Meml. Hosp., 1961-63, Loma Linda (Calif.) U. Hosp., 1963-67; med.-surg. supr. Iowa Luth. Hosp., Des Moines, 1967-69; operating room supr. Porter Meml. Hosp., Denver, 1969-72, asst. dir. nursing service, staff devel., 1980—; assoc. Operating Room Nurses Inc., Denver, asst. dir. edn./continuing edn., 1972-80; cons. Edn. Design, Inc.; leader seminars. Mem. Am. Nurses Assn., Colo. Nurses Assn. (dir. 1976-77, commn. cert. 1973-74, ad hoc. com. C.E. 1974-78, commn. nursing service and edn. 1976-78, del. Am. Nurses Assn. Conv. 1976, 78, 78), Assn. Operating Room Nurses (regional joint rev. com., chmn. 1973-75), Am. Soc. Tng. and Devel., Adult Edn. Assn. U.S.A., Colo. Soc. Health Care Nursing Service Adminstrn., Sigma Theta Tau. Republican. Seventh-day Adventist. Contbr. numerous articles to profl. jours.; author: (with Diane F. Schoenrock) Operating Room Orientation Program for the New Graduate Nurse, 1974; (with Barbara J. Gruendemann, et al) Nursing Audit: Challenge to the Operating Room Nurse, 1975; Speciality Nursing Courses: Operating Room, 1976; (with Nancy Ertl, et al) Peer Review for Nursing Practice: Operating Room, 1977; (with Bradley J. Manuel, Dorris L. David) Surgical Experience: A Model for Professional Nursing Practice in the Operating Room, 1978; (with Carol A. Lindeman, et al) The Relationship Between Operating Room Nursing Activities and Patient Outcomes: An AORN-WICHE Report, 1978; (with Bradley J. Manuel) Design for Continuing Education Activities, 1979; (with Lowen Dodge) Postoperative Patient Care, 1983; compiler and editor: Guidelines for ORT Refresher Course, 1973, AORN Nat. Seminar Brochure, 1977-78, 78-79, 79-80; developed modular ind. learning systems. Home: PO Box 31975 Aurora CO 80041 Office: PO Box 31975 Aurora CO 80041

KNEISEL, ROBERT PRENTICE, energy economist, educator; b. Louisville, Aug. 14, 1946; s. Paul Robert and Emily Prentice (Bryant) K. B.A. in Geophysics, UCLA, 1968; M.A. in Econs., U. Calif.-Riverside, 1976, Ph.D. in Econs., 1979. Lectr. econs. Calif. State Coll., San Bernardino, 1973-77; asst. prof. econs. Earlham Coll., Richmond, Ind., 1977-78; staff economist Mayor's Energy Office, Los Angeles, 1980-81; conservation planner So. Calif. Edison Co., Rosemead, 1981—; cons. Cost Effectiveness of Energy Ordinances, City of Riverside (Calif.). Mem. Riverside City Interim Energy Commn., 1980. Served with USAF, 1969-71. Regents scholar, 1966-68; UCLA Soc. of Exploration Geophysicists scholar, 1966-68. Mem. Am. Econ. Assn. Soc. Exploration Geophysicists. Author: Economic Impact of Lane Use Control: The California Coastal Zone Conservation Commission, 1979; co-author: Federal and State Mandating in Local Governments: An Exploration of Issues and Impacts, 1979, The Energy/LA Action Plan, 1981. Office: So Calif Edison Co Conservation Div Room 391 2244 Walnut Grove Ave Rosemead CA 91770

KNIERIM, K. PHILLIP, lawyer; b. Tacoma, Nov. 18, 1945; s. Oscar Fitzpatrick and Dorothy Margaret (King) K.; B.S. in Sociology, U. Wash., Seattle, 1968; J.D. (Harlan Fiske Stone scholar 1971-72, James Kent scholar 1972-74), Columbia U., 1974; m. Pamela Gail Waller. Human resources planning dir. N.Y. Telephone Co., 1969-71; atty. firm Pillsbury, Madison & Sutro, San Francisco, 1974-76, Hughes, Hubbard & Reed, Los Angeles, 1976-77, Fulop, Polston, Burns & McKittrick, Beverly Hills, Calif., 1976-81, Gordon, Weinberg & Zipser, Los Angeles, 1982—; judge pro tem Beverly Hills Mcpl. Ct., 1979—; guest lectr. Pepperdine U. Law Sch., Los Angeles, 1981; mem. Los Angeles City Atty.'s Regulatory Reform Task Force, 1982—; mem. U.S. Army War Coll. Nat. Security Seminar, 1984. Chmn. public affairs Planned Parenthood N.Y.C., 1971-74; gen. counsel Los Angeles Ballet, 1979-80; chmn. bd. Bethune Ballet, 1981-82, pres., 1982-83. Served with RNSC, 1957-63; with USNR, 1969. Decorated Nat. Def. Service medal; Order Hosp. St. John Jerusalem. Mem. Am. Bar Assn. (vice chmn. young lawyers div. com. jud. tenure, selection and performance 1980-81), Calif. State Bar (del. 1980-83), Los Angeles County Bar Assn. (arbitrator 1979-83), Beverly Hills Bar Assn. (chmn. environ. law com. 1979-82, vice chmn. resolutions com. 1983—), Beverly Hills Barristers (gov. 1979-81), English Speaking Union. Anglican. Club: Brit. United Services. Exec. editor Columbia Jour. Transnat. Law, 1973-74. Home: 11700 Iowa St Apt 304 Los Angeles CA 90025 Office: 1901 Ave of Stars Suite 800 Los Angeles CA 90067

KNIERIM, ROBERT VALENTINE, elec. engr.; Oakland, Calif., Sept. 27, 1916; s. Otto Valentine and Edith May (Bell) K.; B.S., U. Calif. at Berkeley, 1941; postgrad. U. Pitts., 1942, U. Colo., 1944-45; grad. Westinghouse Grad. Student Course, 1942, Raytheon Field Engring. Sch., 1945; m. Esther Perry Bateman, July 10, 1954; children—Kathleen Dianne, David Lyell, Daniel Goddard. Grad. student engr. Westinghouse Corp., East Pittsburgh, Pa., 1942; marine elec. engr. U.S. Maritime Commn., Oakland, 1943-44; elec. engr. U.S. Bur. Reclamation, Denver, 1944-45, Sacramento, 1945-48; field engr. Raytheon Corp., Walthm, Mass., 1945; electronics engr. Sacramento Signal Depot, 1948-49; asso. elec. engr. Calif. Office Architecture and Constrn., 1949-57, sr. elec. engr., 1957-76; pvt. cons. engr., 1976—. Mem. Century Club of Golden Empire council Boy Scouts Am., 1969—, instnl. rep., 1948-54, dist. chmn. camping and activities com., 1951-54. Registered profl. elec. engr., Calif. Mem. Sacramento Engrs. Club (charter), IEEE (sr.), Sierra Club (life, chpt. treas. 1962-65), Nat. Assn. Corrosion Engrs., Calif. Alumni Assn. (life), Eta Kappa Nu, Alpha Phi Omega. Republican. Congregationalist. Club: Masons. Home and Office: 4441 60th St Sacramento CA 95820

KNIGHT, ALEXA RANDALL, educator; b. Gloster, Miss., Nov. 26; d. Byron H. and Gueretta (McDaniel) Randall; B.S., U. Colo., 1955; M.A., Calif. State U., Long Beach, 1980; divorced; children—Pamela Ann, Janet Alexa, William Edward. Tchr., Cheney (Wash.) High Sch., 1956-59; sec. Hilderbrand Constrn. Co., Edmonds, Wash., 1969-73; tng. coordinator, instr. office occupations Edmonds Community Coll., Lynnwood, Wash., 1972-74, N. Orange County Regional Occupational Program, Anaheim, Calif., 1975—. Vice pres. membership Lynnwood PTA, 1967. Mem. Internat. Info./Word Processing Assn. (chpt. v.p. membership 1978-80), Am. Vocat. Assn., Calif. Bus. Edn. Assn., Calif. Assn. Vocat. Edn., Calif. Assn. Regional Occupational Programs/Centers, Phi Delta Gamma, Kappa Delta Pi, Epsilon Pi Tau. Republican. Episcopalian. Author articles in field. Developer word processing curriculum for blind/deaf. Home: 1876 New Jersey St Costa Mesa CA 92626 Office: 830 S Dale St Anaheim CA 92804

KNIGHT, DIANA SANCHEZ, beverage company executive; b. San Antonio, Tex., Nov. 17, 1945; d. Manuel R. and Mercedes F. (Flores) Sanchez; children—Frederick, Joseph, Charles. B.S., Tex. Women's U., 1967. Dept. mgr. Sears Roebuck & Co., San Antonio, 1972-74; sales person J.C. Penney Co., Colorado Springs, Colo., 1974-76; exec. dir. SER-Jobs for Progress, Colorado Springs, 1976-80; community affairs rep. Adolph Coors Co., Golden, Colo., 1980—. Named Outstanding Mem. Am. G.I. Forum, 1980; recipient Cert. of Recognition, Mexican Am. Assn. W. Tex. State U., 1981. Mem. Bus. Profl. Women, League United Latin Am. Citizens, AAUW, Nat. Women's Polit. Caucus. Home: 11213 E Harvard Dr Aurora CO 80014 Office: Dept 342 Adolph Coors Co Golden CO 80401

KNIGHT, KIRK LAY, venture capital investment mgmt. exec.; b. Winnetka, Ill., Apr. 17, 1939; s. Harry William and Agnes Louise (Berger) K.; B.A., Amherst Coll., 1961; M.B.A., Harvard U., 1963; J.D., Stanford U., 1966; m. Virginia Harrison, Feb. 24, 1973; 1 son, Rodney Harrison. Research asso., mem. teaching staff Grad. Sch. Bus., Stanford U., 1966-69; founder, chmn. bd. dirs. Kirk Knight & Co., Inc., Menlo Park, Calif., 1969-79; pres., chmn. bd. dirs. Menlo Fin. Corp., Menlo Park, 1974—; pres. Menlo Venture Corp., 1976—; gen. partner Menlo Venture Partners, 1980—. Bd. dirs. Project Hear; trustee Menlo Sch. and Coll. Mem. Nat. Assn. Small Bus. Investment Cos. (bd. govs.), Am. Electronics Assn. Clubs: Menlo Country, Univ. Office: 3000 Sand Hill Rd Menlo Park CA 94025

KNIGHT, PAUL FORD, computer company executive; b. Washington, Aug. 8, 1947; s. Herbert Paul and Eleanor Kent (Hall) K.; m. Yvonne M. Adams, Aug. 6, 1977. B.A., U. Minn., 1969, M.S., 1971. Planning analyst Royal Globe Ins. Co., N.Y.C., 1971-72, sr. planning analyst, 1972-74; fin. analyst Pfizer, Inc., N.Y.C., 1974, fin. mgr., 1974, div. controller, 1975, asst. group controller, 1976, group product mgr., 1976-78, dir. mktg., 1978-81; pres. Touch Dialogues Inc., Ft. Collins, Colo., 1981—. Mem. Am. Mktg. Assn., Pharm. Advt. Club. Republican. Methodist. Club: Jaycees. Home: 767 Sandpiper Point Ft Collins CO 80525 Office: 333 W Drake Rd Suite 32 Ft Collins CO 80526

KNIGHT, PHILIP HAMPSON, shoe company executive; b. Portland, Oreg., Feb. 24, 1938; s. William and Lota (Hatfield) K.; m. Penelope Parks, Sept. 13, 1968; children—Matthew, Travis. B.B.A., U. Oreg., 1959; M.B.A., Stanford U., 1962. C.P.A. Acct., Coopers & Lybrand, Portland, Oreg., 1963-64, Price Waterhouse, Portland, 1964-67; asst. prof. bus. adminstrn. Portland State U., 1967-69; pres. NIKE, Inc., Beaverton, Oreg., 1969—, also chmn. Trustee Reed Coll. Served with U.S. Army, 1959-60, USAR, 1960-67. Named Corp. Exec. of Yr., Oreg. Bus. Mag., 1982. Mem. Oreg.-Korea Econ. Cooperation Com., Nat. Council U.S.-China Trade, ASEAN-U.S. Bus. Council, Am. Inst. C.P.A.s. Office: 3900 SW Murray Blvd Beaverton OR 97005

KNIGHT, RICHARD CARL, financial planner; b. Kimball, Nebr., Aug. 28, 1929; s. Lewis Ralph and Gladys Sophia (Falk) K.; m. Phyllis Maxine Whipple, June 4, 1950; children—Robin Hambre, Lori DeMartino. B.A. Pacific U., Forest Grove, Oreg., 1950; cert. fin. planner Coll. Fin. Planning, Denver, 1975. Teacher, Heppner (Oreg.) High Sch., 1950-53; owner OK Tire Store, Hillsboro, Oreg., 1953-57; resident v.p. Waddell & Reed, Inc., Kansas City, Mo., 1957-77; v.p. Foster & Marshall/Am. Express Inc., Seattle, 1977—; adj. faculty mem. Coll. Fin. Planning. Mem. Inst. Cert. Fin. Planners (div.), Eastside Estate Planning Council. Republican. Clubs: Elks (Bellevue, Wash.), Masons.

KNIGHT, SUSAN EFFORD, psychotherapist; b. Los Angeles, Dec. 15, 1950; d. John R.T. and Marth L. (Wait) K. B.S. in Community Edn. and Counseling, U. of Calif.-Davis, 1973; M.S.W., San Francisco State U., 1982. Lic. clinical social worker, Calif. Psychotherapist in pvt. practice, San Francisco, 1982—; prof. John F. Kennedy U., Orinda, Calif., 1982-83, Calif. Grad. Sch. of Marriage and Family Therapy, San Rafael, Calif., 1983—; cons. United Cerebral Palsy Assn., San Francisco, 1981-83; dir. sex and disability unit U. Calif., 1973-82. Mem. Adv. Comm. for the Hearing Impaired; active Big Sisters of San Francisco; mem. adv. comm. Am. Soc. of Allied Health Professions. Mem. No. Calif. Clinical Hypnosis Assn., Nat. Assn. Social Workers. Author (with David Bullard): Sexuality and Physical Disability: Personal Perspectives, 1981. Office: 5709 Geary Blvd San Francisco CA 94121

KNIGHT, TONY CHRISTOPHER DAVID, aerospace corp. exec.; b. London, Feb. 11, 1936; came to U.S., 1966, naturalized, 1978; s. Cyril Bertram and Edith Grace (Stansfield) K.; B.Sc. in Physics with spl. honors, U. Bristol (Eng.), 1957; m. Bernice Elizabeth Rose Lane, 1957; children—David John, Gillian Mary, Jeffrey Richard, Graham Charles, Andrew Michael. Instr. physics, 1957-62; nuclear reactor physicist Nuclear Power Group, Eng., 1962-66; sr. staff engr. Aerospace Systems div. Bendix Corp., Ann Arbor, Mich., 1966-70; program mgr. Martin Marietta Aerospace Corp., Denver, 1970—. Recipient NASA Public Service medal, 1977. Mem. AAAS, Am. Soc. for Mass Spectrometry. Home: 2370 S Brentwood St Lakewood CO 80227 Office: Martin Marietta Aerospace Corp PO Box 179 Denver CO 80201

KNIGHT, VICK, SR., advt. exec., composer; b. Moundsville, W.Va., Aug. 5, 1908; William Eugene and Stella Vernon (Shimp) K.; student Cleve. Prep. Sch., 1923-25; m. Janice Adele Higgins, July 21, 1927; children—Vick, Virginia, Nancy. Asso. editor Cleve. Citizen, 1927-29; program dir. radio sta. WGAR, Cleve., mdse. mgr. radio sta. WHK, 1929-32; dir. radio, writer, producer, 1932-40; v.p. Biow Co., 1941; v.p., dir. Foote, Cone & Belding, 1942-43; staff writer MGM, 1946; pres. Vick Knight, Inc., pres. Key Records, Los Angeles, 1947—, also mng. dir. Adver-Tunes; dir. Playersville, Inc., dir.; exec. producer Big Show, Australia; dir. Eddie Cantor Stage Presentations; producer Hollywood Bowl Appearance Pres. Eisenhower, Ann. New England Rally for God, Family and Country, Boston; writer, dir. Coffee Hours for Eisenhower, MacArthur's Legacy, 1971; pres. Round Table Music Publs.; owner The Pumpkin Press, Tune Text Publs.; producer Ronald Reagan audio unit Rendezvous With Destiny, 1981, also med. tapes on ileostomy and colostomy. Bd. dirs. Matt Cvetic Found.; mem. United States Day Com. radio chmn. March of Dimes; bd. dirs. Americanism Ednl. League, Parents Adv. League; v.p. Ostomy Assn. of Los Angeles. Served to lt. AUS, 1944-45. Decorated D.S.M. with oak leaf cluster; Mil. Order British Empire; Songwriters Hall of Fame; recipient Merit award Congress of Freedom. Mem. Hist. Soc. Wis., ASCAP, Am. Guild Authors and Composers, Am. Legion, VFW, Internat. Platform Assn. Republican (state central com., radio-TV chmn., Rep. Assos.). Club: West Atwood Yacht. Author: (poetry) England's a Lot Like Illinois, 1944; Cartwheel (play); (song) Halls of Ivy; (books) What Happened to the Bees, 1964, Young John Steinbeck, 1975; Audiography of Louis Armstrong, 1976; Contbr. textbooks, mags., tech. publs. Address: PO Box 46128 Los Angeles CA 90046

KNIGHT, VICK (RALPH), JR., hospital official; b. Lakewood, Ohio, Apr. 6, 1928; s. Vick Ralph and Janice (Higgins) K.; B.S., U. So. Calif., 1952; M.A., Los Angeles State Coll., 1956; postgrad. Whittier Coll., 1959-61, Long Beach State Coll., 1960-61, Calif. State Coll.-Fullerton, 1961-64, Claremont Grad. Sch., 1963-65; Ed.D., Calif. Coast U., 1984; m. Beverly Joyce McKeighan, Apr. 14, 1949 (div. 1973); children—Stephen Foster, Mary Ann; m. 2d, Carolyn Schlee, June 6, 1981. Producer-dir. Here Comes Tom Harmon radio series ABC, Hollywood, Calif., 1947-50; tchr., vice-prin. Ranchito Sch. Dist., Pico Rivera, Calif., 1952-59; prin. Kraemer Intermediate Sch., Placentia, Calif., 1959-64; dir. instructional services Placentia Unified Sch. Dist., 1964-65, asst. supt., 1965-71; program dir. World Vista Travel Service, 1970-72; dir. grad. extension La Verne Coll., 1971-73; v.p. Nat. Gen. West Investments, 1971-74; dir. community relations and devel. Childrens Hosp. of Orange County (Calif.), 1974—; pres. Aristan Assocs.; dir. Key Records, Hollywood. Dist. chmn. Valencia council Boy Scouts Am.; chmn. Cancer Soc. Partners of Ams., also chmn. Sister City Com.; chmn. of Community Chest Drives; chmn. adv. com. Esperanza Hosp.; mem. Educare; hon. life mem. Calif. PTA. Bd. dirs. U. Calif.-Irvine Friends of Library, pres., 1975-77; bd. dirs. Muckenthaler Cultural Groups Found.; chmn. bd. William Claude Fields Found. Served with USN, 1946-48. Named One of Five Outstanding Young Men, Calif. Jr. C. of C., 1959; recipient Distinguished Citizen award Whittier Coll., 1960; Educator of Yr. award Orange County Press Club, 1971; Author and Book award U. Calif., 1973; Children's Lit. award Calif. State U.-Fullerton, 1979; Bronze Pelican award Boy Scouts Am. Mem. Nat. Sch. Pub. Relations Assn. (regional v.p.), U.S. (dir.), Calif. (state v.p.), Pico Rivera (pres.) jr. chambers commerce, Audubon Soc., Western Soc. Naturalists, Calif. Tchrs. Assn., NEA, Internat. Platform Assn., ASCAP, Soc. Children's Book Writers, Authors Guild, Authors League Am., Anti-Slubberdegullion Soc., Bank Dicks, Assn. Hosp. Devel., Art Experience, Good Bears of World, Los Compadres con Libros, Blue Key, Skull and Dagger, Les Amis du Vin, Phi Sigma Kappa, Alpha Delta Sigma, E Clampus Vitus, Theta Nu Epsilon. Kiwanian (pres.), Mason. Club: West Atwood Yacht (commodore). Writer weekly Nature Notebook newspaper columns, 1957—; fine arts editor Placentia Courier. Editor curriculum guides: New Math., Lang. Arts, Social Scis., Pub. Relations, Biol. Sci. Substitute Tchrs. Author: (ecology textbooks) It's Our World; It's Our Future; It's Our Choice; Snakes of Hawaii; Earle the Squirrel; Night the Crayons Talked; My Word!; Send for Haym Salomon!; Joby and the Wishing Well; Twilight of the Animal Kingdom; A Tale of Twos; Who's Zoo; A Navel Salute; Friend or Enema?; also math. instrn. units; contbr. articles to various jours. Home: PO Box 4664 Canyon Lake CA 92380 Office: Childrens Hosp 1109 W La Veta St Orange CA 92668

KNIGHT, VIRGINIA LUCINDA, interior designer; b. Cleve., Dec. 10, 1931; d. Vick Ralph and Janice (Higgins) Knight. Student Los Angeles City Coll., 1951, UCLA, 1975—. Designer Albert Van Luit Wallpaper Co., Los Angeles, 1955; interior designer W. & J. Sloane Co., Beverly Hills, Calif., 1955-62, Barnett Bros., Beverly Hills, 1962-69; sr. designer for Cannell & Chaffin, 1969-82; free lance designer, 1982—; instr. UCLA Extension, 1981—. Mem. bldg. and sites com. Los Angeles Epilepsy Soc.; bd. dirs. Los Angeles Community Design Center, 1974—. Mem. Am. Inst. Interior Designers (corp. mem. bd. govs., v.p. 1971-76, chmn. community affairs com.), Am. Soc. Interior Designers (corp. mem. 1975—), Archtl. Guild U. So. Calif. Republican. Club: Altrusa (charter; South West Los Angeles, pres. 1967-69, dir. 1969-72). Home: 1601 Sunset Plaza Dr Los Angeles CA 90069 Office: 1601 Sunset Plaza Dr Los Angeles CA 90069

KNIGHT, WARREN VAN HORN, air force officer; b. Pensacola, Fla., Jan. 23, 1945; s. Robert Clark and Patricia Gould (Roos) K.; B.S. in Engring. Mechanics, Va. Poly. Inst., 1967; M.B.A., Oklahoma City U., 1971. Commd. 2d lt. U.S. Air Force, 1967, advanced through grades to lt. col., 1983; aircraft structural engr., aircraft accident investigator, Tinker AFB, Okla., 1963-71; aircraft damage repair engr., Vietnam, 1972; flight test engr., flight test dir., 1973-75; chief test and evaluation tech. publs., Edwards AFB, Calif., 1975-76; logistics program mgr., fgn. sales mgr. Naval Air Systems Command, Washington, 1976-79; space system analyst, Los Angeles Air Force Sta., 1979-82; system test program mgr., 1983—. Decorated Air Force Commendation medal (2). Mem. Air Force Assn., Tech. Mktg. Soc. Am., U.S. Parachute Assn., Soc. Air Safety Investigators (founding officer, sec.-treas. Oklahoma City chpt. 1969-70). Club: South Bay Ski. Home: 2213 Mathews Ave Apt B Redondo Beach CA 90278 Office: Air Force Space Div El Segundo CA 90009

KNIGHT, WESLEY MELVIN, geophysicist; b. Jasper, Alta., Can., Mar. 24, 1944; came to U.S., 1980; s. George Allen and Edna May (Bowen) K. Student pub. schs., Jasper; 1 dau., Jodi Lynne. Sr. survey crew supr. Govt. Can., Jasper, 1965-70; surveyor high Arctic, Western Geophys. Can., Alta., B.C., 1974-75; chief surveyor Western Geophys. Am., North Africa, 1975-77; party mgr. Western Geophys. Can., high Artic, 1977-80; ops. supr. Seis-Port Explorations, Denver, 1980—. Mem. Denver Geophys. Soc., Soc. Exploration Geophysicists (assoc.). Anglican. Club: Internat. Athletic. Home: 812 Engleman Pl Loveland CO 80537 Office: Suite 2000 1616 Glenarm St Denver CO 80202

KNIGHTS, RONALD MICHAEL, business educator; b. Bronx, N.Y., Mar. 6, 1943; s. Nehemiah and Eramae K.; B.B.A., U. N.Mex., 1968, M.Vocat. Counseling (grantee), 1972, Ph.D. in Counseling Psychology, 1976; m. Mimi Benumann, July 26, 1980. Sr. counselor Office Manpower and Devel., Albuquerque, 1968-72; personnel counselor, then employee adv. City of Albuquerque, 1972-79; mgr. employee relations RMS Co., Englewood, Colo., 1979-80; mgr. tng. and devel. RCSI Co., Englewood, 1980-82; asst. prof. mgmt. Met. State Coll. Sch. Bus., 1982—; mem. affiliate faculty Regis Coll. Bus. Sch., Denver; faculty mem. U. Phoenix, 1982; cons. in field. Served with USAR, 1969. Recipient Watusi award Albuquerque Econ. League, 1976; appreciation award USAF Contract Mgmt. Assn., 1975. Mem. Am. Soc. Tng. and Devel. Democrat. Roman Catholic. Home: 3126 Clayton St Denver CO 80205 Office: 1006 11th St Denver CO 80204

KNIPE, WILLIAM BERNARD, JR., real estate broker, consultant; b. Emmett, Idaho, July 27, 1923; s. William Bernard and Frances Kathryn (Jones) K.; student U. Idaho, 1941-42, 46, Boise State U., 1946-47, U. Ariz., 1947-49; B.S., Calif. Western U., 1978, M.B.A., 1979; Ph.D., Calif. Coast U., 1983; m. Diane Adele Shaw, Nov. 25, 1960; children—Bradford T., Quentin M., John P., William Bernard III, Curtis A., Karen, Kathleen, Kellett. Staff adjuster Motor Ins. Corp., Gen. Motors Corp., Boise, Idaho, 1949-51; gen. mgr. The Sawtooth Co., Boise, 1952-62; cattle rancher, Horseshoe Bend, Idaho, 1963-69; pres. Robison Realty, Inc., Boise, 1974—, Knipe Land & Livestock Co., Boise, 1976—, William Knipe & Assos., Boise, 1970—; cons. to farms and ranches, 1967—. Mem. adv. bd. Am. Security Council, 1968—, Security and Intelligence Fund, 1969—, Nat. Com. for Employer Support of the Guard and Res., 1973—. Served with USAAF, 1943-46; ATO. Cert. residential specialist. Mem. Jerusalem Cattle Assn. (pres. 1966-68), Farm and Land Inst. (accredited), Nat. Assn. Realtors, Nat. Mktg. Inst., Nat. Cattlemen's Assn., Am. Soc. Farm Mgrs. and Rural Appraisers, Nat. Pilots Assn., Nat. Assn. Rev. Appraisers (cert. rev. appraiser), Assn. M.B.A. Execs., Am. Soc. Agrl. Consultants (cert.). Phi Delta Theta. Republican. Roman Catholic. Club: Elks. Contbr. articles to profl. jours. Office: 1120 Lewis St Boise ID 83702

KNISELY, TERRENCE LEE, optometrist; b. Cleve., Sept. 4, 1949; s. Victor Donald and Lydia (Sichau) K. B.S. in Biology, Bowling Green State U., 1971; D. Optometry, Ill. Coll. Optometry, 1975; M.S., Colo. State U., 1983. Cert. optometrist, Colo., Ill. Optometrist Division-Pulaski Med. Ctr., Chgo., 1975; chief optometry clinic 56th Gen. Hosp., Baumholder, W. Ger., 1976-78; practice optometry, Ft. Collins, Colo., 1979—. Vol. Channel 9 TV Health Fair, 1980-81. Served to capt. U.S. Army, 1975-77. Mem. Am. Optometric Assn., Colo. Optometric Assn., Assn. Research in Vision and Ophthalmology. Lutheran. Home: 121 Dartmouth Trail Apt 301 Fort Collins CO 80525 Office: 2601 S Lemay Suite 4 Fort Collins CO 80525

KNODELL, CLAYTON WILLIAM, financial executive; b. Enterprise, Oreg., Mar. 19, 1927; s. Clayton Leroy and Isel Ruby (Hunter) K.; m. Donna Mae Paulson, Sept. 16, 1950; children—Steven William, Brad Clayton, Kathy Diane, Susan Gail. B.S. in Bus. Adminstrn., Oreg. State U., 1951; postgrad. U. Oreg., 1952. C.P.A., Oreg. Sr. acct. Peat Marwick, Mitchell & Co., Portland, Oreg., 1952-56; div. controller Textron, Inc., Coquille, Oreg., 1956-59; fin. v.p. Western Kraft Corp., Portland, 1959-71; fin. v.p. Willamette Industries, Portland, 1971-77, exec. v.p., chief fin. officer, sec., treas., 1977—; sec., dir. Keller Enterprises, Inc.; dir. Pacific Am. Liquid Assets, Inc. Trustee, treas. Good Samaritan Hosp. and Med. Ctr., Portland; exec. com. Columbia Pacific council Boy Scouts Am.; trustee Oreg. State U. Found. Served with U.S. Army, 1945-47. Mem. Fin. Execs. Inst. (nat. dir. 1967, Portland chpt. pres. 1965), Am. Inst. C.P.A.s, Oreg. Soc. C.P.A.s, Nat. Assn. Accts., Tax Execs. Inst., Am. Legion. Lutheran. Clubs: Arlington, University (Portland). Office: 3800 First Interstate Tower Portland OR 97201

KNOEBEL, BETTY LOU MARGARET, food service executive; b. Hobart, Ind., July 12, 1931; d. Frank Orville Burnett and Louise Caroline (Sohn); m. Daniel R. Lynch, Mar. 10, 1954; m. 2d, F. C. Knoebel, Apr. 27, 1974. Student Ind. U., 1950-52, Calif. Coast U., 1976—. Radiology technician Meth. Hosp., Gary, Ind., 1948-51; med.-surg. asst., R. Nilges & M. Bernard, Gary, 1951-63; exec. sec. Anderson Co., Gary, 1963-70; x-ray technician, adminstr. Melissa Meml. Hosp., Holyoke, Colo., 1970-71; adminstrv. asst., dir. Nobel/Sysco Food Services Co., 1971—; corp. sec., dir. Gen. Mgmt. Corp., Capital Warehouse Co., Denver, 1971—. Am. Cancer Soc. grantee, 1950-51. Mem. Am. Businesswomen's Assn., Ind. Soc. Radiologic Technicians, Colo. Republican Women.

KNOEFEL, HUGH KARL, newspaper publisher; b. St. Paul, July 7, 1910; s. George Gustav and Caroline Freda (Schneider) K.; m. Maxine Manning, Jan. 29, 1937; children—Jeanne, Lynn, Patricia; m. Dorothy Mildred Stevenson, Sept. 1, 1962. B.S., Macalester Coll., 1932. Classified advt. mgr. St. Paul Daily News, 1932-37; advt. solicitor St. Paul Dispatch Pioneer Press, 1937; classified advt. mgr. Denver Rocky Mountain News, 1938-39; advt. dir. Wyo. Eagle Tribune, Cheyenne, 1939-46; editor-pub. No. Wyo. Daily News, Worland, 1946—; pres. Big Horn Basin Newspapers, Inc., Worland, 1980—, also dir.; pres. Worland Bldg. Co., 1955—; dir. Laramie Newspapers, Inc. Trustee sec. Washakie County Meml. Hosp., Worland, 1960-80; mem. adv. bd. Wyo. N.G. Armory, 1960—; mem. Wyo. Selective Service Bd., 1948-73, chmn., 1960-73. Served with USN, 1944-45. Mem. Nat. Newspaper Assn., Wyo. Press Assn., Colo. Press Assn., Sigma Delta Chi. Republican. Presbyterian. Clubs: Worland Country, Cloud Peak, Masons, Consistory, Royal Order Jesters, Shriners Elks. Author: Wyoming's Bloodiest Fourth of July, 1969. Office: 723 Robertson Ave Worland WY 82401

KNOERNSCHILD, KURT WESLEY, educational administrator, consultant; b. Waterbury, Conn., July 11, 1950; s. Kenneth George and Maryellen (Earle) K.; m. Sally Claire Nogg, Apr. 11, 1981. B.A., U. Conn., 1973; M.A., U. N.Mex., 1981. Tchr. Rough Rock (Ariz.) Demonstration Sch., 1973-76; dir. Black Mesa Community Sch., Chinle, Ariz., 1976-80; spl. asst. N.Mex. Research and Study Council, Albuquerque, 1980—, sec. grad. students in ednl. adminstrn., 1980—, mem. U. N.Mex. Senate Library Com., 1981-82. Recipient Outstanding Service award N.Mex. Research Study Council, 1981, 82, Academic Excellence award Phi Kappa Phi, 1981. Mem. Am. Assn. Sch. Adminstrs., N.Mex. Council Computer Users in Edn., Phi Beta Kappa. Democrat. Home: 401 Montclaire Dr SE Albuquerque NM 87108 Office: University New Mexico 214 Onate Hall Albuquerque NM 87131

KNOLL, ROBERT EUGENE, sociologist; b. Pasadena, Calif., Feb. 20, 1930; s. Gordon G. and Molly E. (Learn) K.; divorced; 1 dau., Susan Lynn. B.A. in Psychology, UCLA, 1953, M.S., 1958; Ph.D., U. So. Calif., 1965. Lic. tchr., clin. social worker Calif. Teaching asst. in social research UCLA, 1957-58; asst. supr. child welfare Los Angeles City Schs., 1958-63; research asst. U. So. Calif., 1962-63, lectr. in criminology, 1964-65, asst. prof. sociology, 1965-66; assoc. prof. sociology Chapman Coll., Orange, Calif., 1966-69; br. exec. Cath. Youth Orgn., Los Angeles, 1969-70; supr. Social Work II Calif. Youth Authority, Norwalk, 1970-80; exec. dir. Social Research Inst., Glendale, Calif., 1980—. Served with USNR, 1948-58. UCLA Clevenger scholar, 1958. Mem. Am. Sociol. Assn., Nat. Assn. Social Workers, Am. Soc. Criminology, Pacific Sociol. Assn., Am. Statis. Assn. Republican. Episcopalian. Author numerous articles for profl. publs. Address: 1520 Columbia Dr Suite B Glendale CA 91205

KNOLL, SAMSON BENJAMIN, historian, ednl. adminstr.; b. Stanislaus, Poland, Feb. 11, 1912; s. Elias and Regina (Gronich) K.; student U. Berlin, 1930-33, U. Paris, 1933-35, U. Calif., Berkeley, 1938-41; M.A., U. Colo., 1936; Ph.D., Stanford U., 1953; m. Elsa Elizabeth Uppman, Aug. 9, 1940; came to U.S., 1935, naturalized, 1943. Instr. German, U. Colo., 1935-37; instr. fgn. langs. Colo. State Coll. Edn., 1937-38; teaching asst. German, U. Calif., Berkeley, 1938-41; instr. fgn. langs. Menlo Jr. Coll., 1941-42, history Stanford, 1947-52, history and fgn. langs. Menlo Coll., 1952-62; dean div. polit. arts, head dept. history Monterey Inst. Fgn. Studies, 1962-67, chancellor, 1967-69, 74-75, dean of faculty, 1969-73, acad. v.p., 1973-74, v.p., prof. history, 1975-78, prof. history, chancellor emeritus, 1978—; research asso. Center for Advanced Study in Behavioral Scis., 1957-58; vis. prof. Stanford Inst. for Advanced Study in German, 1967. Bd. dirs. Internat. Acad., Santa Barbara, Calif.; trustee Inter Future, 1972-78. Served with U.S. Army, 1943-45. Mem. Am. Hist. Assn., MLA, Am. Soc. Eighteenth Century Studies, Am. Assn. Advancement Humanities, Am. Assn. Tchrs. German (pres. No. Calif. 1961-62), Ernst Barlach Gesellschaft, Fgn. Lang. Assn. No. Calif. (pres. 1963-65), Calif. Council Fgn. Lang. Tchrs. Assns. (pres. 1967-68), World Affairs Council Monterey Peninsula (pres. 1969-72, 77-79), World Affairs Council No. Calif. (trustee 1969-72, 77-79), Carmel Music Soc. (dir. 1969-78, pres. 1975-77), ACLU (dir. Monterey chpt., chmn. 1980—). Co-author: The Development of Historiography, 1954; Kurt Breysig-Stefan George, 1960; UNESCO, History of Mankind, Cultural and Scientific Development, Vol. IV, 1969; co-author/co-editor: Johann Gottfried Herder, Innovator Through the Ages, 1982. Contbr. articles to Ency. Brit., Ency. Americana, profl. jours. Home: Route 1 Box 200 Carmel CA 93923 Office: 425 Van Buren St Monterey CA 93940

KNOLLMILLER, JAMES GEORGE, lawyer, accountant; b. Toledo, May 28, 1938; s. George Albert and Beatrice Ernest (Smith) K.; m. Carol Ann Corwin, July 24, 1965; children—Robyn, Timothy, Dana, Jay. B.B.A., U. Mich., 1960, M.B.A., 1961, LL.B., 1964. Bar: Ariz. 1965; C.P.A., Ariz. Tax mgr. Arthur Andersen & Co., Phoenix, 1964-74; ptnr. Knollmiller, Herrick & Brown, Tempe, Ariz., 1974—. Mem. Am. Inst. C.P.A.s, Ariz. Soc. C.P.A.s, State Bar Ariz., Tri-City Bar Assn., Maricopa County Bar Assn., Tri-City Estate Planners, Lost Chord Soc. (dir.). Republican. Mormon. Home: 8349 E Via de Belleza Scottsdale AZ 85258 Office: Knollmiller Herrick and Brown 1232 E Broadway Suite 120 Tempe AZ 85282

KNORR, DONALD ROBERT, architect; b. Chgo., Dec. 25, 1922; s. Arthur Herman and Esther Gertrude (Sternbeck) K.; B.S., U. Ill., 1947; postgrad. Cranbrook Acad. Art, 1948; m. Anne Hall, May 14, 1949; children—Torin Jon, Kipp D., Guy Douglass. Designer Eero Saarinen & Assos., 1947-49; designer, project mgr. Skidmore, Owings & Merrill, San Francisco, 1949-51; prin. Knorr Assos., San Francisco, 1951-56; partner Knorr-Elliott & Assos., San Francisco, 1956-73, Don Knorr & Assos., San Francisco, 1973—; vis. critic Calif. State Poly. Coll. Sch. Architecture, 1969, 71. Mem. San Francisco Mus. Art. Served to lt. (j.g.) USNR, 1943-46. Recipient Nat. awards Archtl. Record, Progressive Architecture; 1st prize N.Y. Mus. Modern Art, Internat. Furniture Design Competition, 1949. Fellow A.I.A. (numerous regional and nat. awards). Home: 888 Francisco St San Francisco CA 94109 Office: 950 Battery St San Francisco CA 94111 also 600 Barrow St Anchorage AK 99501

KNORR, DONNA DANIEL, advertising executive; b. Topeka, Kans., Aug. 9, 1932; d. Eddie Dean and Lorene (Donnelley) Glosup; m. Theodore H. Knorr, Nov. 7, 1971; children—Shellee Richardson, Deborah Richardson, Karen, Jeff Scales. B.B.S., Woodbury Coll., 1952; cert. in Advanced Advt. Studies, U. So. Calif., 1979. Clk., St. Luke Hosp., Altadena, Calif., 1963-64; sec. Stacoswitch, Costa Mesa, Calif., 1965-70; with Casa Advt., Orange, Calif., 1970—, pres., 1976—; account exec. Hunter Barth Advt., 1983—; guest lectr. various colls. Mem. Orange County Advt. Fedn., Western States Advt. Agys. Execs., Internat. Soc. Gen. Semantics, NOW, Nat. Assn. Female Execs. Clubs: Patrons, Costa Mesa Playhouse. Home: 293 Bowling Green Dr Costa Mesa CA 92626 Office: 1532 Brookhollow Dr Santa Ana CA 92705

KNOTT, WILLIAM ALAN, library director, library management and building consultant; b. Muscatine, Iowa, Oct. 4, 1942; s. Edward Marlan and Dorothy Mae (Holzhauer) K.; m. Mary Farrell, Aug. 23, 1969; children—Andrew Jerome, Sarah Louise. B.A. in English, U. Iowa, 1967, M.A. in L.S., 1968. Asst. dir. Ottumwa (Iowa) Pub. Library, 1968-69; library cons. Iowa State Library, Des Moines, 1968-69; dir. Hutchinson (Kans.) Pub. Library and S. Central Kans. Library System, Hutchinson, 1969-71; dir. Jefferson County Pub. Library, Lakewood, Colo., 1971—. Served with U.S. Army, 1965-67. Mem. Western Conservation Congress (sec.-treas.), Colo. Library Assn. Author: Books by Mail: A Guide, 1973; co-author: A Phased Approach to Library Automation, 1969; editor: Conservations Catalog, 1982. Office: 10200 W 20th Ave Lakewood CO 80215

KNOWLER, WILLIAM C., physician, epidemiologist, statistician; b. Iowa City, June 20, 1946; s. Lloyd A. and Faith M. (Stamler) K.; m. Kathleen D. Albright, July 5, 1970; children—Harrison, Marden, Heidi

Margaret, Robin Faith. B.A. with highest distinction and honors, U. Iowa, 1968; M.D. in Spl. Field cum laude, Harvard U., 1973, M.P.H., 1973, D.P.H., 1980. Statistician, Sheller-Globe Corp., 1963-66; USPHS NIMH trainee dept. psychiatry Harvard U., 1970-71; intern in internal medicine Faulkner and Lemual Shattuck hosps., Boston, 1973-74; mem. staff VA Hosp., Boston, 1974-75; resident in preventive medicine dept. epidemiology Harvard U. Sch. Pub. Health, Boston, 1974-75; staff physician Nat. Inst. Arthritis, Metabolism and Kidney Diseases, Phoenix, 1977-79, chief Southwestern Field Studies sect., 1979—, dep. chief Epidemiology and Field Studies br. 1981—; commd. jr. asst. USPHS, 1972, advanced through grades to sr. surgeon, chief surgeon, 1981—; mem. staff Phoenix Indian Med. Ctr., USPHS Hosp., Sacaton, Ariz.; cons., presenter seminars, lectr. in field, 1976—; mem. com. to plan gallbladder disease research in Health and Nutrition Exam. Survey, Nat. Ctr. Health Stats., 1979—. Fellow Am. Coll. Preventive Medicine; mem. Am. Diabetes Assn., Soc. Clin. Trials, Soc. Epidemiologic Research, Phi Beta Kappa, Sigma Xi, Omicron Delta Kappa. Author: Quality Control Training Manual, 2d edit., 1965; (with others) Quality Control by Statistical Methods, 1969; contbr. chpts., numerous articles and abstracts to profl. publs. Office: 1440 E Indian School Rd Phoenix AZ 85014

KNOWLES, GLORIA BALL, personnel administrator; b. Magna, Utah, Mar. 14, 1937; d. Alfred Thomas and Virginia Booth (Hatton) Ball; m. Sanderson Lewellyn Knowles, Apr. 2, 1955; children—Douglas Llyn, Thomas Ross. Bookkeeper, Wells Fargo Bank, San Francisco, 1954-56; bookkeeper, utility clk. Bank of Am., Richmond, Calif., 1956-60; credit and loan analyst Central Bank, Concord, Calif., 1972-73; sr. acctg. clk., produce div. Safeway Stores, Inc., Oakland, Calif., 1973-75, affirmative action rep., 1975-76, affirmative action rep., supply divs., Walnut Creek, Calif., 1977-81, employee relations supr., 1981—; mem. Contra Costa County Regional Occupational Program Adv. Com., 1978—; mem. secretarial sci. com. Diablo Valley Coll., 1979-81; bd. dirs. Shadelands Children's Ctr. Mem. Federated Employers of Bay Area, Diablo Valley Indsl. Personnel Soc., Am. Mgmt. Assn., Nat. Assn. Female Execs. Republican. Mormon. Office: 2800 Ygnacio Valley Rd Walnut Creek CA 94598

KNOWLES, MARILYN RAE, ballet co. adminstr.; b. Fresno, Calif., Sept. 23, 1937; d. Lawrence Earl and Phyllis Marie (Faus) Evans; B.F.A., U. Utah, 1959, M.F.A., 1960; m. Lawrence Rowland, Oct. 9, 1960; children—Stuart Ashley, Paul Joseph. Soloist, Pacific Ballet, San Francisco, 1961-71; artistic dir. Fresno Civic Ballet, 1973—; tchr. ballet Severance Sch. Dance, Fresno, 1971—. Mem. La Paloma Guild Fresno City and County Hist. Soc., Delta Delta Delta. Office: 1432 Fulton St Fresno CA 93721

KNOWLES, RICHARD THOMAS, retired army officer; b. Chgo., Dec. 20, 1916; s. John T. and Signe (Almcrantz) K.; student U. Ill., 1939-42, Command and Gen. Staff Coll., 1952, Armed Forces Staff Coll., 1956, U.S. Army War Coll., 1959; m. Elizabeth Wood Chaney, 1975; children—Diane T. Knowles Buchwald, Katherine T. Knowles Buck, Rebecca T., Richard J., Stanley W. Crosby III, Steven Chaney. Commd. 2d lt. U.S. Army, 1942, advanced through grades to lt. gen., 1970; exec., bn. comdr. 96th F.S. Bn., Far East Command, 1950-51; student, then instr. Command and Gen. Staff Coll., Ft. Leavenworth, Kan., 1951-55; chief budget and plans br. Office Dep. Chief of Staff, Personnel, U.S. Army, Washington, 1956-58; chief Establishments Br., Hdqrs. U.S. Army Element, SHAPE, 1959-60, mil. asst. Office Chief of Staff, Hdqrs. SHAPE, 1960-62; comdg. officer 3d U.S. Army Missile Command, Ft. Bragg, N.C., 1962-63; div. arty. comdr., asst. div. comdr. 11th Air Assault Div., Ft. Benning, Ga., 1963-65; asst. div. comdr. 1st Cav. Div., (airmobile), Ft. Benning, Vietnam, 1965-66; chief of staff II Field Force, Vietnam, 1966; comdg. gen. 196th Light Inf. Brigade, Vietnam, 1966-67; comdg. gen. Task Force Oregon, Vietnam, 1967; asst. dep. chief of staff for mil. operations U.S. Army, Washington, 1967-70; asst. to chmn. Joint Chiefs of Staff, Washington, 1970-72; comdg. gen. I Corps Group, U.S.-Republic of Korea, Korea, 1972-73; dep. comdr. 8th Army, Korea, 1973-74; ret., 1974; mgr. support services Northrop, Saudi Arabia, 1978-79; now owner, operator The General's Store, Roswell, N.Mex. Commr. Conquistador council Boy Scouts Am., mem. Nat. council. Decorated D.S.M. with 3 oak leaf clusters, Silver Star, Legion of Merit with two bronze oak leaf clusters, D.F.C. with bronze oak leaf cluster, Bronze Star with V device and oak leaf cluster, Air medal with 25 oak leaf clusters, Purple Heart, Vietnam Nat. Order 5th Class, Vietnam Gallantry Cross with 2 bronze palms, Vietnam Armed Forces Honor medal 1st Class, Order of Nat. Security Merit Guk-Seon medal (Republic of Korea). Mem. Roswell C. of C., Ret. Officers Assn. (pres. council of chpts. N.Mex.). Club: Rotary (state rep. dist. 57). Home: PO Box 285 Roswell NM 88201

KNOWLTON, DEBORAH ANN, educator, real estate salesman; b. Long Beach, Calif., Mar. 8, 1949; d. John Albert and Patricia Ann (MacDonald) K. B.A. in Spanish, U. Calif.-Davis, 1972; M.A. in Ednl. Adminstrn., Calif. State U.-Long Beach, 1981. Cert. elem. and secondary tchr., bilingual cross-cultural tchr., adminstr., Calif.; lic. real estate salesperson, Calif. Tchr. math Santiago High Sch., Garden Grove, Calif., 1972—, Sat. sch. and attendance supr., 1983—, acting asst. principal, 1983—. Treas. Bridgecreek Villas Homeowners Assn.; docent Rancho Los Almitos; adult sponsor YWCA, 1973. Mem. Nat. Council Tchrs. of Math., Calif. Mat. Council, Orange County Math. Assn., Am. Assn. Tchrs. of Spanish and Portuguese, Calif. Assn. TESL, NEA, Calif. Tchrs. Assn. Garden Grove Edn. Assn., Assn. for Supervision and Curriculum Devel., Girls' League Advs. Assn. of So. Calif. (newsletter editor, sec., pres.), AAUW (mem. telephone com.), Cal Aggie Alumni Assn., Calif. State U.-Long Beach Alumni Assn., Phi Delta Kappa, Phi Kappa Phi, Kappa Delta Pi, Pi Lambda Theta. Republican. Roman Catholic. Club: Santiago Faculty. Home: 12518 Montecito St Seal Beach CA 90740 Office: Santiago High School 12342 Trask Ave Garden Grove CA 92643

KNOX, CHARLES ROBERT, football coach; b. Sewickley, Pa., Apr. 27, 1932; s. Charles McMeehan and Helen (Keith) K.; B.A., Juniata Coll., 1954; postgrad. Pa. State U., 1955; m. Shirley Ann, Aug. 2, 1952; children—Christeen, Kathy, Colleen, Chuck. Asst. football coach Wake Forest Coll., 1959-60, U. Ky., 1961-62, N.Y. Jets, 1963-66, Detroit Lions, 1967-72; head football coach Los Angeles Rams, 1973-78, Buffalo Bills, 1978-82, also v.p. football ops.; head football coach Seattle Seahawks, 1983—. Lutheran. Club: Big Canyon Country. Address: Seattle Seahawks 5305 Lake Washington Blvd Kirkland WA 98033*

KNOX, JOHN THERYLL, lawyer, former state legislator; b. Reno, Sept. 30, 1924; s. Ernest B. and Jean (Monat) K.; A.B., Occidental Coll., 1949; J.D., Hastings Coll. Law, 1952; m. Jean Henderson, Dec. 27, 1949; children—John Henderson, Charlotte, Mary. Admitted to Calif. bar, 1953, in pvt. practice at Richmond; mem. Calif. Assembly from Richmond, from 1960, speaker pro tem, from 1976, mem. Ways and Means com.; now ptnr. Nossaman, Guthner, Knox & Elliott, San Francisco. Mem. Contra Costa County Dem. central com., 1955-60; trustee Occidental Coll., Hastings Coll. Law. Served with USAAF, 1943-45. Mem. Am., Contra County, Richmond bar assns., Sigma Alpha Epsilon, Phi Delta Phi. Moose, Lion. Home: 229 Bishop Ave Richmond CA 94801 Office: 100 The Embarcadero San Francisco CA 94105

KNOX, NAPHTALI HERZL, urban planning cons.; b. St. Paul, June 4, 1933; s. Marcus and Esther Leah (Barron) K.; B.Arch. with distinction, U. Minn., 1955; M.City Planning, U. Pa., 1957; m. Marian Osheroff, June 29, 1958; children—Aliza, Charles Ethan. Chief advance planning City of Des Moines, 1959-60; sr. planner Livingston and Blayney, San Francisco, 1960-63; univ. community planner U. Calif. Statewide, Berkeley, 1963-66; dir. phys. planning and constrn., asst. v.p. U. Chgo., 1966-72; dir. planning and community environ. City of Palo Alto (Calif.), 1972-81; pres. Naphtali H. Knox & Assos., Inc., Palo Alto, 1981—; housing bond coordinator Santa Clara County, 1982—; sec.-treas. Soc. Coll. and Univ. Planning, 1971-72; chmn. archtl. adv. com. City of Mill Valley (Calif.), 1966. Chmn. Marin Council Civic Affairs, Marin County (Calif.), 1965; bd. dirs. Santa Clara County (Calif.) Comprehensive Health Planning Assn., 1974-75, Palo Alto Housing Corp., 1982—, Forum on Community and Environ., 1982—. Served as officer USAF, 1957-59. Mem. Am. Inst. Cert. Planners (sec.-treas. Calif. chpt. 1964-65, nat. bd. examiners 1970-78), Am. Planning Assn. Author papers in field. Home: 1025 Forest Ave Palo Alto CA 94301 Office: 420 Florence St Suite 300 Palo Alto CA 94301

KNOX, ROBERT LEE, economist, educator; b. Enid, Okla., Jan. 15, 1932; s. Beryl LeRoy and Doris Ethel (Ulrey) K.; m. Mary Frances Kern, Aug. 16, 1958; children—Shelly Lee, Cynthia C. B.S. in Commerce, Okla. State U., 1954, M.S. in Econs., 1958; Ph.D. in Econs., U. N.C., 1963. Asst. prof. econs. Coll. William and Mary, Williamsburg, Va., 1961-63; asst. prof. econs. Ariz. State U., Tempe, 1963-66, assoc. prof., 1966-71, prof., 1971—; cons. antitrust econs. Chmn. Ariz. State Health Planning Council, 1973-75. Served to capt. USAF, 1954-57. Mem. Am. Econ. Assn. Contbr. articles to profl. jours.

KNUDSEN, CONRAD CALVERT, forest products co. exec.; b. Tacoma, Oct. 3, 1923; s. Conrad and Annabelle (Callison) K.; B.A., U. Wash., 1948, LL.B., 1950; postgrad. in law (fellow), Columbia U., 1951; m. Julia Lee Roderick, Nov. 22, 1950; children—Calvert, Elizabeth Page, Colin Roderick, David Callison. Partner firm Bogle, Bogle & Gates, Seattle, 1951-61; exec. v.p. Aberdeen (Wash.) Plywood & Veneer Inc., 1961-63, also dir.; pres., chief adminstrv. officer, vice chmn. bd. Evans Products Co., Portland, Oreg., 1963-68; sr. v.p. corp. growth Weyerhaeuser Co., Tacoma, 1969-76; pres., chief exec. officer MacMillan Bloedel Ltd., Vancouver, B.C., Can., 1976-80, chmn., chief exec. officer, 1980—; also dir.; dir. Celupal, S.A., Spain, Cascade Corp., Portland, Can. Imperial Bank of Commerce, Toronto, Ont., Castle & Cooke, Inc., Honolulu, Koninklijke Nederlandse Papierfabrieken N.V., Maastricht, Netherlands, Physio-Control Corp., Washington, Rainier Bancorp./Rainier Nat. Bank, Seattle, Termicold Corp., Portland, Safeco Corp., Seattle, W. Fraser Timber Co. Ltd., Vancouver; partner Knudsen Erath Winery, Dundee, Oreg.; propr. Knudsen Vineyards, Dundee. Served with U.S. Army, 1942-46. Mem. Am. Bar Assn., Wash. State Bar Assn. Clubs: Arlington, Multnomah Athletic, Racquet (Portland); Vancouver, Vancouver Lawn Tennis and Badminton, Terminal City (Vancouver); Rainier, Seattle Tennis, Univ. (Seattle); Vintners (San Francisco). Office: MacMillan Bloebel Ltd 1075 W Georgia St Vancouver BC V6E 3R9 Canada*

KNUDSEN, RALPH GERALD, freight co. exec.; b. Portland, Oreg., Mar. 13, 1946; s. Harold Otto and Helen Louise (King) K.; B.S., Lewis and Clark Coll., 1968; m. Mar. 15, 1969; children—Dustin Heath, Wendi Danielle. Sales rep., PBA Inc., Dallas, 1973, sales mgr., 1974-76, dist. mgr., Chgo., 1976-78, regional sales mgr., Denver, 1978; pres., chmn. Pacific Cargo Carriers, Inc., Seattle, 1979—. Pres., Vashon Island Youth Baseball; elder Vashon Island United 1st Presbyterian Ch. Served to capt. USMC, 1968-72; Vietnam. Mem. Small Bus. Assn. Wash., VFW Vashon. Republican. Clubs: Vashon Island Sportsmen's (trustee), Ducks Unlimited, Pioneer Athletic. Home: Vashon Island WA 98070 Office: 18900 Des Moines Way S Seattle WA 98148

KNUDSON, GENE D., lumber and paper company executive; b. 1916. B.S., Oreg. State U., 1939. Chief forester Bur. of Land Mgmt., Dept. Interior, 1940-46; cons. Mason, Bruce & Girard, Cons. Foresters, 1947-49; chief forester, mgr. logging Willamette Industries Inc., Portland, Oreg., 1949, v.p., 1956, exec. v.p., 1964, pres., chief operating officer, 1970, also chief exec. officer, now chmn. bd., dir. Office: Willamette Industries Inc 1300 SW 5th Ave Portland OR 97201*

KNUDSON, JOHN ARTHUR, JR, park administrator; b. Louisville, July 9, 1947; s. John Arthur and Katherine Helen (Bartelme) K.; B.A., San Diego State U., 1975; m. Carolyn Carlena Phelps, Mar. 22, 1975; children—Molly Carlena, Peter John. Biol. aid U.S. Fish and Wildlife Service, Kenai Nat. Moose Range, Kenai, Alaska, 1975; park ranger Wasatch Mountain State Park, Midway, Utah, 1976, Rockport Lake State Park, Wanship, Utah, 1976-78; park supt. Goblin Valley State Res., Green River, Utah, 1978-80, Edge of the Cedars State Hist. Monument, Blanding, Utah, 1980—. Mem. San Juan County Devel. Bd.; leader 4-H. Mem. Western Interpreters Assn., Blanding C. of C. (dir.), San Juan County Travel Council.

KNUDSON, MELVIN ROBERT, management consultant, business executive; b. Libby, Mont., Oct. 27, 1917; s. John and Serina (Bakken) K.; B.S. in Wood Chemistry, Oreg. State U., 1942; m. Melba Irene Joice, Mar. 5, 1946; children—Mark Bradley, Kevin Marie, Kari Lynne. Mgr. quality control J. Neils Lumber Co., Libby, Mont., 1946-55; mgr. research and devel. St. Regis Paper Co., Libby, 1955-65, div. dir. tech. devel., Tacoma, Wash., 1965-69, div. dir. short and long-range planning, 1969-70; exec. v.p. Property Holding and Devel. Co., Tacoma, 1970-75; exec. v.p. and gen. mgr. U.S. Computers, Inc., Tacoma, 1975-79; corp. mgmt., orgn., univ. governance and adminstrn. cons., 1979—; owner Knudson Travel, Tacoma, 1981—; dir. Property Holding and Devel. Co., U.S. Computers; adv. bd. Coll. Engring., Wash. State U., 1967—, chmn., 1971-73. Trustee 1st Luth. Ch., Libby, 1948-56, chmn., 1954-56; trustee Sch. Dist. #4, Libby, 1964-65; trustee Christ Luth. Ch., Tacoma, 1966-71, com. chmn.; trustee Greater Lakes Mental Health Clinic, 1969-73, com. chmn., 1970-73; bd. regents Pacific Luth. U., Tacoma, 1969—, chmn., 1976-81; mem. Steilacoom Improvement Com., 1971-73; chmn. Pacific Luth. U. Pres. Search Com., 1974-75; dir. Wauna Dance Club, 1976-79; dir. Pacific Luth. Univ. "Q" Club, 1976—; bd. dirs. Tenzler Library, Tacoma, 1980—, Crime Stoppers, 1981—. Served to lt. col. F.A., Paratroops, U.S. Army, 1941-46. Mem. Wash. Realtors Assn., Wash. Securities Sales, Am. Governing Bds., Center for Study of Democratic Institutions. Republican. Clubs: Tacoma Country and Golf, Normana Male Chorus (Norwegian Singers Assn. Am.). Patentee high-temperature wood-drying process; developer domestic natural gum. Home: 6928 100th St SW Tacoma WA 98499 Office: 1103 A St Suite 200 Tacoma WA 98402

KNUTH, STEPHEN BRIAN, electrical engineer; b. Montery Park, Calif., Sept. 28, 1946; s. Eldon L. and Marie O. (Parrat) M.; B.S. summa cum laude in Elec. Engring., UCLA, 1973, M.S. in Engring., 1975; m. Sue Lynne Kozeliski, Jan. 30, 1971; children—Sean Brian, Kevin Edward. Mem. tech. staff Hughes Aircraft Co., Culver City, Calif., 1973-74; design engr. Labtest Equipment Co., Los Angeles, 1974-75; mgr. hardware devel. Computer Automation Inc., Irvine, Calif., 1975-79; v.p. engring. Phone-Mate, Inc., Torrance, Calif., 1979—. Served with USAF, 1965-68; Vietnam. Hughes fellow, 1973-75. Mem. Tau Beta Pi. Home: 22431 Atomo Mission Viejo CA 92691 Office: 325 Maple Ave Torrance CA 90503

KNUTSON, THOMAS EVERETT, pharmacist, business executive; b. North Fond du Lac, Wis., June 24, 1939; s. Walter Everett and Myrtle Genevieve (Weber) K.; student U. Wis., 1957-58; B.S., N.D. State U., Fargo, 1962, M.A., 1963; m. Judith Kay Samuelson, May 24, 1962; children—Cheryl, Daniel, Deborah, Thomas. Pharmacist, St. Alexius Hosp., Bismarck, N.D., 1962-63; mem. faculty Mary Coll., Bismarck, 1963-65; instr. pharmacology, Williston, N.D., 1965-81; chief pharmacist Good Samaritan Hosp., Williston, 1965-75, Bethel Luth. Home for Aged, 1965-81; pres. Biotomics, Inc., Issaquah, Wash., 1977—; v.p. Turpin Enterprises, 1982—; owner VR Bus. Brokers, Spokane, 1983—. Mem. Am. Pharm. Assn., N.D. Pharm. Assn., Nat. Assn. Retail Druggists (cert. fitter). Republican. Methodist. Clubs: Lions, Elks, Moose, Oddfellows, Sportsman's. Home: 5719 N Division St Spokane WA 99207 Office: 6616 Post St Spokane WA 99207

KOBAYASHI, CHARLOTTE CHIYO, import-export executive, educator, consultant; b. Olaa, Hawaii, Sept. 2, 1942; d. Ginzo and Yukie (Horike) Kobayashi; m. Robert G. Brooke, Sept. 9, 1967; 1 dau., Marissa Rika; m. 2d, Paul Anthony Braga, June 15, 1980. B.Ed., U. Hawaii, 1964, postgrad. 1966-68; M.Ed., Loyola U., Chgo., 1970; postgrad. Ind. U., 1965. Resident asst. East West Ctr. U. Hawaii, Honolulu, 1966-67, head resident, 1967-68; Head Start coordinator Leeward Dist. Hawaii, Honolulu, 1968-69; asst. ednl. cons. Erikson Inst. Early Childhood Edn., Chgo., 1969-70; tng., tech. assistance coordinator OEO, State of Hawaii, Honolulu, 1970-71, program specialist, 1971-73, ind. cons., Micronesia, 1971-72; adult basic edn. coordinator Far West Lab. Ednl. Research and Devel., San Francisco, 1973-74, staff tng. field agt. gen. assistance ctr., 1974-75; gen. mgr. Soken Trading Inc., Sausalito, Calif., 1975-78, exec. v.p., mgr., 1978—. OEO fellow, 1969; recipient outstanding community service award Hawaii Head Start, 1973. Mem. Nat. Assn. Edn. of Young Children, Women's Entrepreneur. Buddhist. Editor: Mystery of Japanese Plums, 1978, Mystery of Japanese Reishi, 1978. Office: Soken Trading Inc 591 Redwood Hwy Suite 2125 Mill Valley CA 94941

KOBAYASHI, CHRIS, TV producer-writer; b. Tokyo, Nov. 18, 1949 (parents Am. citizens); d. Kan and Sadae (Suehiro) Tagami. Producer, writer, host Sta. KTVU, San Francisco, 1974-81; exec. dir. Minorities and Women's Telecommunications Network, 1980—; nat. coordinator Nat. Regional Pub. Telecommunications Consortium, 1981-82; propr. Joint Prodns. Inc., 1980—; mem. fouding bd. Bay Area Video Coalition, Japantown Art and Media Workship, Asian Am. TV Services; freelance videographer; cons. in field. Grantee Calif. Arts Council, 1979. Mem. Media Alliance, AFTRA, Nat. Assn. Broadcast Employees and Technicians (co-coordinator film apprenticeship program for minorities and women). Contbr. poetry to anthologies. Address: 298 Coleridge St San Francisco CA 94110

KOBLIN, RONALD LEE, real estate devel. and bus. exec.; b. Santa Monica, Calif., Nov. 28, 1946; s. Bernard Lewis and Sadie Irene K.; student U. Oreg., 1965, U. Ariz., 1967; B.A., Calif. State U., Northridge, 1969, postgrad., 1970-71; postgrad. U. So. Calif., 1971. Field advt. rep. Procter & Gamble, 1969; urban planner cities of Compton and Simi Valley, Calif., 1970-72; dir. planning and constrn. Nat. Med. Enterprises, Beverly Hills, Calif., 1972-74; dir. planning and devel. So. Counties Mgmt. Co., Beverly Hills, 1974-75, v.p./cons. planning and devel., 1978-79; mgmt. cons. Gottfried Cons., Inc., Los Angeles, 1975-76; exec. v.p. David D. Brill, Inc., Los Angeles, 1976-78, vice chmn. bd. dirs., 1978—; founder, pres., vice chmn. bd. dirs. Art Showcases, Inc., Glendale, Calif., 1976—; cons. The Concept Implementation Co., Notary public County of Los Angeles, 1977—; active Los Angeles County Mus. Art. Recipient Outstanding Service award City of Simi Valley, 1972. Mem. Am. Planners Assn., Am. Mgmt. Assn., Urban Land Inst. Office: PO Box 4618 Glendale CA 91202

KOBZA, DENNIS JEROME, architect; b. Ullysses, Nebr., Sept. 30, 1933; s. Jerry Frank and Agnes Elizabeth (Lavicky) K.; B.S., Healds Archtl. Engring., 1959; m. Doris Mae Riemann, Dec. 26, 1953; children—Dennis Jerome, Diana Jill, David John. Draftsman, designer B.L. Schroder, Palo Alto, Calif., 1959-60; sr. draftsman, designer Ned Abrams, Architect, Sunnyvale, Calif., 1960-61, Kenneth Elvin, Architect, Los Altos, Calif., 1961-62; partner B.L. Schroder, Architect, Palo Alto, 1962-66; pvt. practice architecture, Mountain View, Calif., 1966—. Served with USAF, 1952-56. Mem. C. of C. (dir. 1977-79), AIA (chpt. dir. 1973), Constrn. Specifications Inst. (dir. 1967-68), Am. Inst. Plant Engrs., Nat. Fedn. Ind. Bus. Orgn. Club: Rotary (dir. 1978-79). Home: 3840 May Ct Palo Alto CA 94303 Office: 2483 Old Middlefield Way Mountainview CA 94043

KOCH, ELMER LEONARD, physician; b. Indpls., Apr. 1, 1917; s. Chris and Emma (Lange) K.; m. Geraldine T. Rea, June 7, 1942 (dec. Nov. 1971); children—Robert L., Byron D., Barbara Joanne: m. 2d, Betty Ann Pollard, Nov. 25, 1972; adopted children—Mary Ann Koch, Frank Koch. A.B., Ind. U., 1939, M.D., 1949. Electro-chemist Allison Div. Gen. Motors, 1940-45; intern St. Vincents Hosp., Indpls., 1949-50; practice medicine specializing in family practice, Danville, Ind., 1950-78, Benson, Ariz., 1978-82, Prescott Valley, Ariz., 1982—; med. dir. Ind. Boy's Sch., 1954-78; med. adviser Selective Service Bd. 30, Ind., 1954-73; mem. staff Hendricks County Hosp., Danville, Ind., chief staff, 1973-74; asso. staff Meth. Hosp., St. Vincents Hosp., Indpls.; staff Benson Hosp., St. Joseph Hosp., Tucson, Yavapai Community Hosp., Prescott, Ariz.; med. cons. Cochise County (Ariz.) Bd. Health, 1981-82; med. examiner Cochise County, 1979-82; mem. Hendricks County Bd. Health, 1969-78. Bd. dirs. Benson Hosp., 1979-80. Fellow Am. Acad. Family Practice; mem. AMA, Ariz. Med. Soc., Cochise County Med. Soc. (v.p. 1978-79). Acacia. Presbyterian. Clubs: Masons (K.T.), Rotary (pres. Danville 1968-69, Benson 1980-81, Lonesome Valley 1982-83). Home: 1037 Hyland Circle Prescott AZ 86301 Office: 8201 Jaque Dr Prescott Valley AZ also 866 Hwy 89 NW Chino Valley AZ Died Aug. 16, 1983.

KOCH, GEORGE BYRON, research co. exec.; b. Chgo., Nov. 5, 1946; s. George Oscar and Patricia LaVay (McCormick) K.; B.S. in Physics, Elmhurst (Ill.) Coll., 1968; m. Victoria Lynn Cole, May 3, 1979; 1 son, George August. Asst. chief engr. Aaron-Stevens Corp., Chgo., 1968-69; v.p. Tomorrow, Inc., Los Angeles, 1969-70; pres. Koch Research and Devel. corp., San Francisco, 1970—; dir. Guidance Industries Corp. cons. Bank of Am., FHLB, Mem. Am. Phys. Soc., AAAS, Navy League of U.S., Am. Conservative Union, Internat. Platform Assn., Four Sigma Soc. Republican. Episcopalian. Club: Commonwealth Club of Calif. Former editor. Jour. of Four Sigma Soc.; contbr. articles on sci. and philosophy to mags. and anthologies; patentee ednl. devices, furniture, energy storage, computer peripherals, med. equipment. Office: PO Box 2510 San Francisco CA 94126

KOCH, HARVEY NATHANIEL, real estate devel. co. exec.; b. Bklyn., Mar. 31, 1921; s. Selig and Blanche (Sternberg) K.; B.A., NYU, 1941, J.D., 1946; m. Phyllis Vera Schynert, Oct. 31, 1943; children—Andrea, Lizbeth, Joel. Pres., Western States Land Corp., Los Altos, Calif., 1977—; pres. H.N.K. Investment Corp., 1978—; chmn. bd. Atcor. Chmn. Assessment Appeal Bd., Santa Clara County, 1979-83; chmn. Jewish Community Relations Council, 1980-81; bd. dirs. San Francisco Jewish Welfare Fedn., 1980—; pres. Congregation Beth Am, Los Altos Hills, Calif., 1970-72. Served with AUS, 1942-45. Recipient David Ben Gurion award State of Israel. Club: B'nai B'rith (founder Palo Alto lodge). Home: 26810 Palo Hills Dr Los Altos Hills CA 94022 Office: 960 San Antonio Rd Los Altos CA 94022

KOCH, HOWARD WINCHEL, producer, director; b. N.Y.C., Apr. 11, 1916; m. Ruth Pincus; children—Melinda, Howard W. Runner on Wall St.; asst. cutter, asst. dir. 20th Century Fox; asst. dir. Eagle, Lion, MGM; freelance 2d unit dir.; producer Aubrey Schenck Prodns.; exec. producer Frank Sinatra Enterprises, 1961-64; v.p. charge prodn. Paramount

Pictures Corp.; dir. films Big House U.S.A.; producer films The Black Sleep, Sergeants Three, The Manchurian Candidate, Come Blow Your Horn, None But the Brave, The Odd Couple, Star Spangled Girl, Last of the Red Hot Lovers, On a Clear Day You Can See Forever, Once Is Not Enough; producer-dir. Badge 373. Mem. Acad. Motion Picture Arts and Scis. (bd. govs.), Dirs. Guild Am., Producers Guild Am. Office: Paramount Pictures Corp 5451 Marathon St Hollywood CA 90038*

KOCH, SHARON LEE, sales executive; b. C.Z., Sept. 9, 1947; d. Daniel William and Dorine Evelyn (Weaver) Koch. B.A. in Internat. Relations, U. So. Calif., 1969. Exec. sec. Mitsubishi Internat. Corp., Los Angeles, 1970-73; order clk. sales aviation systems div. RCA, Van Nuys, Calif., 1973-74; internat. sales adminstr. Del Mar Avionics, Irvine, Calif., 1974—. Cert. internat. exec. export mgmt. Mem. AAUW, Internat. Mktg. Assn. Orange County. Home: 4200 Park Newport Newport Beach CA 92660 Office: 1601 Alton Ave Irvine CA 92714

KOCHIN, LEVIS ABRAHAM, economics educator; b. Phila., July 7, 1943; s. Milton S. and Phyllis Adair (Levis) K.; m. Rochelle Schleifer, June 29, 1969; children—Michael, Israel, Ethlyn. B.S., Temple U., 1965; Ph.D., U. Chgo., 1975. Acting asst. prof. U. Western Ont., 1969-71, economist Fed. Res. Bank N.Y., N.Y.C., 1971-73; asst. prof. econs. U. Wash., 1973-79, assoc. prof., 1979—; vis. sr. lectr. U. Tel Aviv, 1982—, vis. economist Bank of Israel, 1982—. NDEA fellow, 1966-68; Hoover Inst. fellow, 1978-79; NSF grantee, 1981-82. Contbr. articles to profl. jours. Home: 7236 29th Ave NE Seattle WA 98115 Office: Dept Economics U Wash Seattle WA 98195

KOCKINOS, CONSTANTIN NEOPHYTOS, physicist, mathematician, consultant, researcher; b. Cairo, Egypt, Oct. 14, 1926; s. Dimitri and Irene (Sovrani) K.; came to U.S., 1947, naturalized, 1955; m. Jean Freeman Lincoln, Aug. 12, 1952; (div. 1962); 1 son, Marc Demetrius. B.A. in Physics, U. Calif.-Berkeley, 1950, B.A. in Math. with honors, 1954, M.A. in Math., 1956; Ph.D., Stanford U., 1974. Instr. U. Calif.-Berkeley, 1958-62; sr. scientist E.G.G., Nev. test site, 1962-64; research mathematician Stanford (Calif.) Research Inst., 1964-72; vis. prof. Aristotelian U., Thessaloniki, Greece, 1974-76; vis. prof. San Jose (Calif.) State U., 1976-79; mem. sci. staff Lockheed Missile and Space Div. Inc., Sunnyvale, Calif., 1979—; mem. U.S. Senatorial Bus. Adv. Bd.; cons. and researcher in field. Fellow Explorers Club; mem. Internat. Platform Assn., Naval Inst., Am. Math. Soc., Am. Math. Assn., Tensor, Planetary Soc., Sigma Xi, Pi Mu Epsilon. Republican. Greek Orthodox. Contbr. articles to profl. jours. Home: 2121 Creeden Ave Mountain View CA 94040 Office: Dept 81 10 B154 Lockheed Missile & Space Co Inc PO Box 504 Sunnyvale CA 94086

KOCMOND, WARREN CHARLES, atmospheric scientist; b. Berwyn, Ill., Oct. 4, 1939; s. Charles Roy and Elizabeth E. (Houdek) K.; B.S. in Math., U. Ariz., 1962; M.S. in Meteorology, Pa. State U., 1964; m. Judith Helen Higgins, Oct. 10, 1958; children—Warren Charles, Michael D. Research asst. Pa. State U., 1962-64; head atmospheric scis. sect. Calspan Corp., Buffalo, 1964-76; research prof. Atmospheric Scis. Center, Desert Research Inst., Reno, 1976-77, exec. dir., research prof., 1977—; sci. adv. com. cloud physics NASA; cons. Univ. Space Research Assn. Mem. Am. Meteorology Soc., AAAS, Sigma Xi, Sigma Pi Sigma. Contbr. articles profl. jours. Patentee in field. Home: PO Box 3440 Incline Village NV 89450 Office: Desert Research Institute Atmospheric Sciences Center PO Box 60220 Reno NV 89506

KODANI, JAMES KATSUMA, accountant; b. Hilo, Hawaii, Nov. 12, 1941; s. Asawo and Toyoko (Asano) K.; m. Susan Harada, Dec. 28, 1962; children—Christine, Kelly. B.S. in Bus., U. Colo., 1963. C.P.A., Hawaii. Supervising sr. Peat, Marwick, Mitchell & Co., Honolulu, 1963-70; mgr. Shigeji Sato, C.P.A., Honolulu, 1970-75; pvt. practice, Honolulu, 1975-79; ptnr. Wikoff, Kodani & Holt, Honolulu, 1979-81; dir. Wikoff, Kodani & Co., C.P.A.s, Inc., Honolulu, 1981—. Mem. Am. Inst. C.P.A.s, Hawaii Soc. C.P.A.s. Buddhist. Clubs: Honolulu, Kiwanis (Honolulu). Office: 733 Bishop St Suite 1200 Honolulu HI 96813

KODIS, MARY CAROLINE, retail and restaurant cons.; b. Chgo., Dec. 17, 1927; d. Anthony John and Callis Ferebee (Old) K.; student San Diego State Coll., 1945-47, Latin Am. Inst., 1948. Controller, div. adminstrv. mgr. Fed. Mart Stores, 1957-65; controller, adminstrv. mgr. Gulf Mart Stores, 1965-67; budget dir., adminstrv. mgr. Diana Stores, 1967-68; founder, treas., controller Handy Dan Stores, 1968-72; founder, v.p., treas. Handy City Stores, 1972-76; sr. v.p., treas. Handy City div. W.R. Grace & Co., Atlanta, 1976-79; founder, pres. Hal's Hardware and Lumber Stores, 1982—; retail and restaurant cons., 1979—. Treas., bd. dirs. YWCA Watsonville. Recipient 1st Tribute to Women in Internat. Industry, 1978. Republican. Home and Office: 302 Wheelock Rd Watsonville CA 95076

KODL, DAVID ALAN, mechanical engineer; b. Rouses Point, N.Y., Jan. 15, 1955; s. William and Margaret (Sabe) K. B.S.M.E. with honors, Union Coll., Schenectady, N.Y., 1976; postgrad. San Diego State U., 1979-80. Researcher, Union Coll., Schenectady, 1975-76; project engr. Mobil Chem. Co., Macedon, N.Y., 1976-78; process engr. Spin Physics Inc., San Diego, 1978-80; staff engr. Ampex Corp., Redwood City, Calif., 1980—; cons. in packaging field. Mem. ASME, Am. Vacuum Soc., Sigma Xi. Club: In-Skiers (San Mateo, Calif.). Home: 1101 Woodside Rd Apt 7 Redwood City CA 94061 Office: 401 Broadway MS 22-04 Redwood City CA 94063

KODZOFF, ANITA GARNICK, realtor, union official; b. Ft. Collins, Colo. Mar. 18, 1904; d. Frank Louis Garnick and Clara Ella (Werner) G.; m. George V. Kodzoff, Dec. 3, 1955 (dec., 1979); m. 2d, Harlan D. Olsen, Sept. 25, 1982. Grad. Alaska Territorial Normal Sch. Sec. treas. Local 672, Am Fedn. Musicians, Local 672 AFL-CIO, Juneau, Alaska, 1942—; mem. Alaska Ho. of Reps., 1947-49; mem. Alaska Senate, 1949-53; bailiff, law librarian Superior Ct., Juneau, 1959-69; ptnr. Kodzoff Acres Trailer Parks, Juneau, 1955-79, owner, operator, 1979—. Recipient Citizenship award Am. Legion, 1963. Democrat. Presbyterian. Clubs: Legis. Wives, Alaska, Wash. Athletic (Seattle); Order Eastern Star, Am. Legion Aux., Women Moose, Pioneers Alaska, Emblem, Alaska Native Sisterhood. Home: 107 W 1st St Juneau AK 99801

KOELLING, RICHARD WILLIAM, financial planner; b. New Haven, Mar. 1, 1935; s. William Norman and Elsie Agnes (Bruns) K.; m. Betty Louise Hemler, June 13, 1961; children—Karyn S., Richard William, Steven M., Christopher S. B.S., Syracuse U., 1956; postgrad. Air U., 1963, 72, Indsl. Coll. Armed Forces, 1973-74. Commd. 2d lt. U.S. Air Force, 1956, advanced through grades to lt. col.; air ops. staff officer Hdqrs. 22AF, Travis AFB, Calif., 1969-73, chief MAC Command Post U-Tapao Thailand, 1973-74, chief Hdqrs. 22AF CP, Travis AFB, 1974-75, sr. maintenance officer 60 FLD Mx Sqdn., 1975-77, chief combat support 60 MIL. ALFT. Wing, 1977-80; ret., 1980; div. mgr. Waddell & Reed, Inc., Fairfield, Calif., 1980—. Pres., Towne Point Civic Assn., Dover, Del., 1965-66. Decorated Air Force Commendation medal, Meritorious Service medal. Mem. Vacaville C. of C. Democrat. Clubs: Lions, Masons, Vacaville Softball Players Assn. Home: 1942 Forest Ln Vacaville CA 95688 Office: 1122 Western St Suite 204 Fairfield CA 94533

KOELZER, WILLIAM, marketing consultant; b. Lansing, Mich., May 25, 1942; s. Charles Robert and Lois Audrey K.; m. Kathi Winter; children—Jacqueline, Shelley. A.A., Orange Coast Coll., 1965; B.A., San Jose State U., 1968. Editor, Mich.-Out-of-Doors, Lansing, 1968, Otsego County Herald Times, Gaylord, Mich., 1968-69, Mich. North, 1968-69; v.p. Cochrane, Chase, Livingston & Co., Inc., 1969-75; pres. Golf Rush Advt., Eureka, Calif., 1977-78; owner, operator Gold Rush Ice Cream Co., Arcata, Calif., 1977-78; v.p. Basso & Assocs., Newport Beach, Calif., 1979-80; pres. Koelzer & Assocs., Irvine, Calif., 1980-83; v.p., co-owner Travel Reps., Inc., Santa Ana, Calif., 1983—; U.S. del. to First China Internat. Tourism Conf., 1983. Campaign mgr. Hank Happleton for County Supr., Eureka, 1976; media chmn. Orange County Holiday Project, 1981-82. Served with USN, 1961-63. Mem. Pub. Relations Soc. Am. (accredited mem.; 2 Prism awards 1982). Democrat. Club: 552. Author: Scuba Diving: How to Get Started, 1965; sr. editor Marketing Problem Solver, 1973. Home: 620 9th St Huntington Beach CA 92648 Office: 435 S Broadway Santa Ana CA 92701

KOENIG, JOAN FOSTER, real estate broker; b. Harrisburg, Ill., Feb. 15, 1930; d. William Jennings and Adria May Foster; B.S., Miami U., 1951; M.A., Ariz. State U., 1967; m. Alan Eastman Disbrow, June 26, 1978; children—William R., Theodore J. Airline stewardess Am. Airlines, Inc., 1951-52; research investigator Procter & Gamble Co., Cin., 1952-53; co-owner, v.p. Koenig Aviation, Inc., Casa Grande, Ariz., 1953-69; real estate sales assoc. Ed Post Realty, Scottsdale, Ariz., 1978-79; real estate broker Ariz. Devel. Corp., Casa Grande, from 1980; now owner, broker Koenig Real Estate. Bd. govs. Casa Grande Town Hall, 1972-75; bd. dirs. Hoemako Hosp. Aux.; vice-chmn. Pinal County Democratic Com., 1972-76, dist. 6 chmn., 1972-76, mem. state exec. com., 1972-76; pres. West Pinal County Dem. Women's Club, 1975, 83. Recipient Women's Flight Achievement award Internat. Flying Farmers, 1964. Mem. AAUW, Women's Council Realtors, Casa Grande Valley Cotton Wives, Casa Grande Panhellenic (pres. 1970), Mortar Board, Kappa Kappa Gamma. Democrat. Episcopalian. Home: Route 1 Box 469 Casa Grande AZ 85222 Office: PO Box 432 Casa Grande AZ 85222

KOENIG, JUNE HOFFMAN, health care corp. exec.; b. Oakes, N.D., June 30, 1943; d. Walter Frederick and Alice Mae (Obenchain) Hoffman; A.A., W. Valley Jr. Coll., Saratoga, Calif., 1980. Various clerical and secretarial positions, 1962-71; med. sec. II, Profl. Group-VMC, Inc., San Jose, Calif., 1971-78, asst. to bus. mgr., 1978-82, asst. adminstr., 1982—; mem. med. adv. com., regional occupational program Met. Adult Health Program, San Jose, 1978-79. Mem. Nat. Assn. Female Execs. Office: 751 S Bascom Ave San Jose CA 95128

KOETHER, BILLIE GLEN, elec. engr.; b. Clifton, Tex., Oct. 26, 1940; s. Willie and May Belle K.; B.S., U. Wash., 1962; m. Janet Carolyn Walker, Dec. 20, 1959; children—Kathryn Lynn, Kristine Roberta. Asso. reliability engr. Boeing Airplane Co., Seattle, 1962-64; reliability engr. Honeywell, Inc., Seattle, 1964-71, prin. reliability engr., 1971-73, prin. devel. engr., 1973-82, sr. prin. devel. engr., 1982—, VLSIC designer, 1980—. Loaned exec. King County (Wash.) United Way, 1975; sr. warden St. Luke's Episcopal Ch., Seattle. Office: 5303 Shilshole Ave NW Seattle WA 98107

KOFF, JOAN HANNAH, psychologist; b. N.Y.C., Feb. 22, 1946; d. Norman H. and Ruth (Sass) Warembud; m. Irwin Koff, June 5, 1966; children—Emily, Gabriel. B.A., CCNY, 1966; M.A., George Washington U., 1969, Ph.D., 1971. Lic. psychologist, Hawaii. Pvt. practice clin. psychology, Kahuku, Hawaii, 1975—; lectr. Hawaii Sch. Profl. Psychology; cons. Hawaii Ctrs. for Ind. Living. Mem. Am. Psychol. Assn., Hawaii Psychol. Assn., Phi Beta Kappa, Psi Chi. Office: Kahuku Hosp Kahuku HI 96731

KOFRANEK, JAN JAROSLAV, architect; b. Prague, Czechoslovakia, Oct. 1, 1939; came to U.S., 1969, naturalized, 1974; s. Jan and Marie (Baresova) K.; M.S., U. Prague, 1962; m. Marcela Zakova, Mar. 29, 1969. Project architect Prague Project Inst., 1963 68, Cooka Architects, Vienna, Austria, 1968; job capt. John Graham Co., Seattle, 1970-73; project architect Whimberly, Whisenand, Allison, Tong & Goo, Honolulu, 1973-74; v.p. Campbell Assocs., Seattle, 1974-79; prin., owner Kofranek Architects, Mercer Island, Wash., 1979—; asst. prof. Coll. Architecture, Prague, 1965. Mem. AIA (Residences award 1976, 77, 81). Club: Bellevue Athletic. Designer solar-heated office bldgs., Washington, 1978, passive solar homes, 1978, 79, 82. Address: Kofranek Architects 4140 Holly Ln Mercer Island WA 98040

KOGA, ROKUTARO, astrophysicist; b. Nagoya, Japan, Aug. 18, 1942; came to U.S., 1961, naturalized, 1986; s. Toyoki and Emiko (Shinra) K. B.A., U. Calif.-Berkeley, 1966; Ph.D., U. Calif.-Riverside, 1974. Research fellow U. Calif.-Riverside, 1974-75; research physicist Case Western Res U., Cleve., 1975-79, asst. prof., 1979-81; physicist Aerospace Corp., Los Angeles, 1981—. Mem. Am. Phys. Soc., Am. Geophys. Union, IEEE, N.Y. Acad. Scis., Sigma Xi. Contbr. articles to profl. confs.; research on gamma-ray astronomy, solar neutron observation, space scis. Home: 8028 Airlane Ave Los Angeles CA 90045 Office: Aerospace Corp Space Scis Lab PO Box 92957 Los Angeles CA 90009

KOGOVSEK, RAY PETER, congressman; b. Pueblo, Colo., Aug. 19, 1941; s. Frank L. and Mary E. (Blatnick) K.; A.B. in Bus. Adminstrn., Adams State Coll., Alamosa, Colo., 1964; m. Eulice A. Kroschel, June 27, 1964; children—Lisa Marie, Toni Rae. Chief dep. clk. Pueblo County (Colo.), 1964-73; mem. Colo. Ho. of Reps., 1969-70, Colo. Senate, 1971-78; mem. 96th-97th Congresses from 3d Colo. Dist., 1979—. Democrat. Roman Catholic. Prime sponsor Small Claims Ct. in State of Colo., 1976. Home: 1627 Horseshoe St Pueblo CO 81001 Office: 430 Cannon House Office Bldg Washington DC 20515

KOHEN, JANET ANN, sociology educator; b. Brooklyn, Iowa, Jan. 3, 1941; d. Harvey T. and Catherine A. (Walsh) Spading; m. Richard David Kohen, June 14, 1965 (dec.); children—Elizabeth, Jessica. B.A., U. Iowa, 1962, M.A., 1965, Ph.D., 1972. Research dir. Seattle Atlantic Street Ctr., 1965-69; asst. prof. sociology U. Mass.-Boston, 1972-79; vis. prof. sociology U. Mich., 1980; assoc. prof. Women's studies San Diego State U., 1980—; cons. in field; editorial review, textbooks. NIH fellow, 1962-65; Russell Sage Found. grantee; NIH postdoctoral fellow, 1979-80. Mem. Am. Sociol. Assn., Soc. Study Social Problems, Am. Psychol. Assn., Nat. Women's Studies Assn., Pacific Sociol. Assn. Contbr. articles to profl. jours. Home: 5150 Manchester Rd San Diego CA 92115 Office: Dept Women's Studies San Diego State U San Diego CA 92182

KOHLMANN, HENRY GEORGE, corporation executive, lawyer; b. Lincoln, Nebr., Oct. 20, 1939; s. John Henry Kohlman and Lottie Louise (Marzok) Kohlman Linch; m. Ramona Marie Turinia, Aug. 17, 1968; children—Tina Maria, Henry George, Elizabeth Eileen. A.A., Coll. San Mateo, 1965; B.S.E.E., San Jose State Coll., 1971; J.D., Hastings Sch. Law, U. Calif., 1974. Bar: U.S. Patent Office 1972, Calif. 1974. Engring. asst. Lockheed Missles and Space, Sunnyvale, Calif., 1966-69; computer procedures analyst Varian Assocs., Palo Alto, Calif., 1969-70; computer cons. Lockheed Missles and Space, Sunnyvale, 1973; sole practice, San Mateo, Calif., 1974-77; patent counsel McDonnell Douglas Corp., Long Beach, Calif., 1977-79; chief counsel Microdata Corp., Newport Beach, Calif., 1979—. Served with USNR, 1958-60. Mem. Calif. State Bar Assn., Orange County Bar Assn., San Francisco Bar Assn., IEEE, Eta Kappa Nu, Tau Beta Pi. Democrat. Developer patentability of computer software, technical idea exchange. Office: 4000 MacArthur Blvd Suite 9000 Newport Beach CA 92660

KOHN, ROBERT SAMUEL, JR., real estate consultant; b. Denver, Jan. 7, 1949; s. Robert Samuel and Miriam Lackner (Neusteter) K.; B.S., U. Ariz., 1971; 1 son, Randall Stanton; m. 2d, Eleanor B. Kohn; adopted children—Joseph Robert, Andrea Rene. Asst. buyer Robinson's Dept. Store, Los Angeles, 1971; agt. Neusteter Realty Co., Denver, 1972-73, exec. v.p., 1973-76; pres. Project Devel. Services, Denver, 1976-78, pres., chief exec. officer, 1978—; pres. Kohn and Assocs., Inc., 1979—. Mem. Bldg. Owners and Mgrs. Assn. (pres. 1977-78, dir. 1972-78, dir. S.W. Conf. Bd. 1977-78), Denver Art Mus., Denver U. Library Assn., Central City Opera House Assn., Inst. Real Estate Mgmt. Republican. Jewish. Club: Newport Beach Athletic. Home: 1961 Port Nelson Pl Newport Beach CA 92660

KOJIAN, VARUJAN HAIG, conductor; b. Beirut, Mar. 12, 1945; came to U.S., 1956, naturalized, 1965; s. Haig Awak and Anouche (Der-Parseghian) K.; student (1st prize) Paris Nat. Conservatory, 1953-56; diploma Curtis Inst. Music, 1959; student U. So. Calif., 1964. Asst. concertmaster and asst. condr. Los Angeles Philharm., 1965-71; asso. condr. Seattle Symphony, 1972-75; prin. guest condr. Royal Opera, Stockholm, 1973-80; music dir. Utah Symphony, Salt Lake City, 1980-83, Chautauqua (N.Y.) Symphony, 1981—; faculty dept. music U. Utah, Salt Lake City, 1980-83. Recipient 1st prize Internat. Conducting Competition, Sorrento, Italy, 1972; decorated Order of Lion (Finland), 1975, also by govts. Greece, 1956, Iran, 1955, Lebanon, 1956. Office: 123 W South Temple St Salt Lake City UT 84101

KOKEN, JACK LYLE, comptroller; b. Yakima, Wash., Mar. 6, 1931; s. Raphael A. and Clara A. (Ames) K.; student So. Oreg. State Coll., 1966-67; m. Faye Marie O'Mohundro, Sept. 3, 1950; children—Pamela Sue, Laura Dianne Koken Connor. Owner, operator Faye Fabrics Drapery and Upholstery Shop, 1952-56; office and sales mgr. Lithia Motors, Ashland, Oreg., 1956-60; non-foods supr. Oreg. Food Stores, Klamath Falls, 1960-64; bus. mgr., sec.-treas. Dodge Center, Inc., Medford, Oreg., 1964-69; sec.-treas., comptroller, dir. Lithia Motors, Inc., Lithia Chrysler-Plymouth, Inc., Valley Lincoln-Mercury, Valley Chevrolet, Inc., Lithia Ins., Inc., Lithia Leasing, Inc., Medford, 1969-81; sec., treas., comptroller, dir. Coastal Dynamics, Inc.; partner, dir. Lithia Properties, Ltd.; dir. Medford State Bank. Trustee, chmn. fin. com. Judson Bapt. Coll.; treas. Ashland Area Christian Crusade, Billy Graham Evangelistic Assn., 1969; mem. citizens adv. council Oreg. Dept. Motor Vehicles, 1978; treas. 1st Bapt. Ch. of Ashland. Mem. Oreg. Automobile Dealers Assn. (treas., dir.), Nat. Automobile Assn., Oreg. Automobile Assn., Oreg. Bankers Assn. Republican. Home: 3680 Dodson Dr Medford OR 97501 Office: 360 E Jackson St Medford OR 97501

KOLB, JAMES ANTHONY, science educator; b. Berkeley, Calif., May 31, 1947; s. James DeBruler and Mary Evelyn (Thomas) K.; m. Mary Catherine Eames, Aug. 29, 1949; 1 son, Thomas James. B.A., U. Calif.-Berkeley, 1970, M.S., 1972. Secondary sci. tchr. Hayward Unified Sch. Dist., 1972-77; project developer Marine Sci. Project: For SEA, Ednl. Service Dist. 114, Port Townsend, Wash., 1978-81; dir. Marine Sci. Ctr., Poulsbo, Wash., 1981—. Bd. dirs. Indianola Land Trust, 1980—. Nat. Diffusion Network curriculum dissemination grantee U.S. Dept. Edn., 1982-83; Wash. Dept. Edn. career edn. grantee, 1983; ESEA Title IV-C curriculum devel. testing grantee, 1978-81. Mem. Nat. Marine Edn. Assn., Nat. Sci. Tchrs. Assn., Wildlife Soc., Assn. Supervision and Curriculum Devel., N.W. Assn. Marine Educators. Democrat. Roman Catholic. Club: Indianola Community (chmn. 1979—). Author: Marine Science Career Awareness, 1978; Marine Science Activities, Grade 2, 1979; Marine Science Activities, Grade 6, 1979; Marine Biology and Oceanography, Part II, Grades 0-12, 1980; Marine Biology and Oceanography, Grades 7-8, 1981. Home: PO Box 211 Indianola WA 98342 Office: 17771 Fjord Dr NE Poulsbo WA 98370

KOLB, JAMES E., accountant; b. Burbank, Calif., Nov. 20, 1946; s. James L. and Jeanne Kolb. B.S., Calif. State U.-Northridge, 1974. C.P.A., Calif. Fin. analyst Aseptic Thermal Inc., North Hollywood, Calif., 1973; sr. systems analyst Arthur Andersen & Co., Los Angeles, 1974-78, v.p., chief fin. officer, dir. The Petersen Co., Hollywood, Calif., 1979; corp. controller Knapp Communications, Los Angeles, 1980; ptnr. Rendon & Kolb, Culver City, Calif., 1981-82; ptnr. Lamb Bushman Perras & Co., Los Angeles, 1982—. Served with U.S. Army, 1970-72. Decorated Air medal (21), Bronze Star. Mem. Am. Inst. C.P.A.s, Los Angeles Soc. C.P.A.s, Culver City Jaycees. Office: 11661 San Vincente Blvd Suite 304 Los Angeles CA 90049

KOLB, KEN LLOYD, writer; b. Portland, Oreg., July 14, 1926; s. Frederick Von and Ella May (Bay) K.; B.A. in English with honors, U. Calif., Berkeley, 1950; M.A. with honors, Calif. State U., San Francisco, 1953; m. Emma LaVada Sanford, June 7, 1952; children—Kevin, Lauren, Kimrie. First short story pub. Esquire mag., 1951; contbr. fiction and humor to nat. mags. and anthologies; numerous teleplays produced on nat. network TV; plays include: She Walks in Beauty (Writers Guild award for best half-hour drama), 1956; novels include: Getting Straight, 1967, The Couch Trip, 1970, Night Crossing, 1974; movies include: Seventh Voyage of Sinbad, 1957, Snow Job, 1972; Ken Kolb Collection established Boston U. Library, 1969; minister Universal Life Ch.; tchr. creative writing Feather River Coll., 1969. Foreman Plumas County Grand Jury, 1970; chmn. Region C Criminal Justice Planning Commn., 1975-77. Served with USNR, 1944-46. Mem. Writers Guild Am., Authors Guild, Mensa, Phi Beta Kappa, Theta Chi. Home and Office: Box 22 Hwy 70 Cromberg CA 96103

KOLB, ROBERT NOEL, personnel agy. exec.; b. Hamilton, Ohio, Dec. 24, 1925; s. Allen Thomas and Margaret Hallie (Strickler) K.; B.Sc., Ohio State U., 1949; m. Sally Ann Redington, May 5, 1951; children—Kristine, Robert, Gretchen. Labor negotiator Trailmobile Inc., Cin., 1952-56; sr. indsl. relations rep. Kaiser Aluminum & Chem. Corp., W.Va., 1956-59; labor relations mgr. Latrobe (Pa.) Steel Co., 1959-61; mng. cons. Koppers Co., Puerto Ordaz, Venezuela, 1961-64; owner, mgr. Kolb Personnel Agy., Bakersfield, Calif., 1964—; corp. mem. Blue Cross of So. Calif., Los Angeles, 1974—. Active Greater Bakersfield Conv. Bur., 1964 , chmn., 1969-70. Served with USAAF, 1944-46. Mem. Nat. Assn. Personnel Cons., Calif. Assn. Personnel Cons. (fin. chmn. 1973-74). Republican. Presbyterian. Clubs: Bakersfield Rotary, Masons, Shriners. Home: 4900-5 Nordic Dr Bakersfield CA 93309 Office: Kolb Personnel Agy 1415 18th St Bakersfield CA 93301

KOLBE, KATHRYN WONDERLIC, publisher; b. Evanston, Ill., Dec. 7, 1939; d. Eldon F. and Winifred E. Wonderlic; B.S. in Journalism, Northwestern U., 1961; children—Karen, David. Vice pres. E.F. Wonderlic & Assocs., Inc., Northfield, Ill., 1962—; editor, pub. Think Inc., ednl. materials, Phoenix, 1976—; pres. Resources for Gifted Inc., Phoenix, 1974—; chmn. Problem Solving Systems, 1980—; spl. edn. instr. Ariz. State U.; cons. in field, 1973—; co-founder, pres. Ariz. Assn. Gifted and Talented, 1975-76; chmn. Scottsdale (Ariz.) Citizens Com. Gifted Children, 1974—. Bd. dirs. Upward Found., 1977-78, Phoenix Children's Theater, 1974-75; trustee Phoenix Country Day Sch., 1977-78; mem. exec. com. Small Bus. Council Ariz., 1983; mem. Phoenix Local Devel. Corp. Named Small Bus. Person of Yr. in Ariz., SBA, 1982. Mem. Nat. Assn. Gifted Children, Nat. Council Critical and Creative Thinking, Nat. Direct Mail Assn., Am. Assn. Pubs., Am. Mgmt. Assn., Phoenix C. of C. (exec. com. 1983). Author: Nonsense and Common Sense About the Gifted, 1978; designer ednl. games Mind's Eyes, 1980, Logi-Sticks, 1980. Office: 3421 N 44th Pl Phoenix AZ 85018

KOLBERT, JACK, museum adminstr.; b. Perth Amboy, N.J., Apr. 25, 1927; B.A., U. So. Calif., 1948, M.A., 1949; Ph.D., Columbia U., 1957; m. Ruth Katz, Aug. 15, 1951; children—Harry, Shelley. Instr. Romance langs. Wesleyan U., Middletown, Conn., 1954-55; chmn. dept. Romance langs. U. Pitts., 1959-65, asst. prof., 1955-59, asso. prof., 1959-63, prof., 1963-65; prof. Romance langs. U. N.Mex., 1965-77; pres. Monterey (Calif.) Inst. Internat. Studies, 1977-80; dir. devel. and membership services Calif. Acad. Scis., San Francisco, 1980—; adj. prof. public adminstrn. U. San Francisco, 1981—; vis. prof. Pomona Coll., Claremont, Calif., 1970-71; cons. in field. Pres., Albuquerque City Council, 1973-77. Decorated knight Nat. Order Merit, officer Acad. Palms (France); Fulbright fellow, 1953-54, 63-64, Ford fellow, 1964-65. Mem. MLA, Am. Assn. Tchrs. French, France-U.S. C. of C., San Francisco World Affairs Council. Clubs: Commonwealth (San Francisco); Pebble Beach Beach and Tennis, Carmel Valley Country. Author: Edmond Jaloux Critique Litteraire, 1962; also French lang. handbooks; co-author: L'Art de Michel Butor, 1970; contbr. articles, revs. to profl. jours. Home: 2210 Jackson St San Francisco CA 94115 Office: Calif Acad Scis San Francisco CA 94118

KOLENDER, WILLIAM BARNETT, police chief; b. Chgo., May 23, 1935; s. David Solomon and Esther (Dickman) K.; student San Diego City Coll., 1963; B.A. in Pub. Adminstrn., San Diego State U., 1964; children—Michael, Myrna, Joy, Randie, Dennis. With San Diego Police Dept., 1956—, chief of police, 1976—; tchr. U. Calif., San Diego, 1971—, San Diego State U., 1972—; mem. Commn. on Peace Officers Standards and Tng. Calif.; bd. dirs. Police Exec. Research Forum. Mem. exec. com. San Diego County council Boy Scouts Am.; mem. Mayor's Crime Control Commn.; pres. Boys' Clubs of San Diego. Served with USN, 1953-55. Named Alumnus of Year San Diego State U., 1973, Outstanding Young Man of Year San Diego, 1970, Man of Yr., Irish Congress of So. Calif., 1981, Man of Yr., Charter 100 Profl. Women's Club, 1981; recipient Mayor's Award for Human Relations and Civil Rights City of San Diego, 1972, Human Relations Award Am. Jewish Com., 1975, Diogenes award San Diego chpt. Public Relations Soc. Am., 1978, Histadrut award Am. Trade Union Council, 1981, Equal Opportunity award San Diego Urban League, 1981. Mem. Calif. Police Chiefs Assn., Calif. Police Officers Assn., Internat. Assn. Chiefs Police. Republican. Jewish. Club: San Diego Rotary. Home: 4035 Tambor Rd San Diego CA 92124 Office: 801 W Market St San Diego CA 92101

KOLER, THOMAS EDWARD, engineering geologist; b. Eugene, Oreg., Nov. 16, 1950; s. Robert Donald and June Melva (Rogers) K.; B.S. in Earth Sci., Portland State U., 1977, M.S. in Geology, 1980; m. Margaret Lorraine Connor, Sept. 25, 1976. Engring. geologist U.S. Forest Service, Olympic Nat. Forest, DuPont, Wash., 1979—; geology tchr. Oreg. Correctional Inst., 1979; tchr. geology St. Martins Coll., 1983. Served with USAF, 1971-73. Mem. Geol. Soc. Am., Am. Assn. Petroleum Geologists, Assn. Engring. Geologists, AAAS, Sigma Xi. Author publ. in field. Home: 4520 31st Ave NE Olympia WA 98506 Office: PO Box 466 DuPont WA 98327

KOLKER, HAL, entertainment arena executive, sports marketing executive; b. Buffalo, Oct. 4, 1949; s. Benjamin and Rose (Lippes) K.; student U. So. Caliif., 1969-72. Exec. asst. Neil Diamond, Los Angeles, 1972-74; cons. Norman Lear Tandem Prodns., Los Angeles, 1974-76; pres. Century City Sound, Los Angeles, 1976-77; pres. Budget Rent-A-Car, San Diego, 1976-78; v.p. San Diego Clippers NBA Basketball Club, Inc., 1978-80; v.p. San Diego Entertainment Inc., operator San Diego Sports Arena, 1980—; pres. Spectator Mktg. Corp., San Diego, 1983—; cons. Paramount Pictures Corp.; Bob Speck Sports Prodns.; exec. producer Bill Walton Show, 1979-80. Campaign chmn. George C. Hardie for 46th Dist. Assembly Calif., 1976. Mem. Am. Mgmt. Assn., Am. Mktg. Assn. Office: 701 B St Suite 400 San Diego CA 92101

KOLKER-VOGT, NANCY MARIA, financial and business consulting company executive; b. Sumatra, Indonesia, Aug. 5, 1931; came to U.S., 1956, naturalized, 1961; d. Johan Frederich Heinrich and Petronella Maria (Vanderlely) Vogt; m. John Herman Kolker, July 23, 1956; children—Hans, Mike, Bill. B.A. in Home Econs., Lausanne-Suise, 1952; A.A., Fullerton Coll., 1970; B.A. in Mgmt. Info. Systems, Calif. State U.-Fullerton, 1982. Owner, mgr. Nannette's Photo Studios, La Habra, Calif., 1960-77, La Habra Capital Research, 1980—; cons. in field. Mem. Am. Mgmt. Assn., Profl. Photographers Am., Am. Bus. Women's Assn., La Habra C. of C., NOW. Republican. Roman Catholic. Office: PO Box 2847 La Habra CA 90631

KOLKOWICZ, ROMAN, political science educator, academic administrator, consultant; b. Poland, Nov. 15, 1929; came to U.S., 1949, naturalized, 1955; s. William and Edwarda (Goldberg) K.; m. Helene S. Can, Feb. 13, 1955; children—Susan, Lisa, Gabriella. B.A., U. Buffalo, 1954; M.A., U. Chgo., 1958, Ph.D., 1964. Sr. staff mem. Rand Corp., Santa Monica, Calif., 1961-66, Inst. Def. analysis, Washington, 1966-70; asst. prof. polit. sci. UCLA, 1970—, dir. Ctr. Internat. Strategic Affairs, 1974—; cons. to govt., others. Chmn. fgn. policy platform Calif. Dem. Party, 1972, 76. Served with U.S. Army, 1954-56. Ford Found. grantee, 1975-83; Rockefeller Found. grantee, 1975-77. Mem. Am. Polit. Sci. Assn., Internat. Sociol. Assn., Internat. Polit. Sci. Assn. Author: Soviet Military-Communist Party, 1967; Soldiers, Peasants, Bureaucrats, 1982; National Security and International Stability, 1983; Arms Control and International Security, 1983; Soviet Calculus of War, 1983. Home: 153 Jacan Way Pacific Palisades CA 90272 Office: Dept Polit Sci UCLA Los Angeles CA 90024

KOLPAS, SIDNEY J., educator; b. Chgo., Oct. 19, 1947; s. Irving and Molly Lou (Lubin) K.; B.A. in Math., Calif. State U.-Northridge, 1969, M.S., 1972; Ed.D. in Math. Curriculum and Instrn., U. So. Calif., 1978; m. Laurie Ann Puhn, June 27, 1971; children—Michelle, Allison. Tchr., Luther Burbank Jr. High Sch., Burbank, Calif., 1970-80, John Burroughs Sr. High Sch., Burbank, 1980—; educator, software cons. Tandy Corp., 1979—; speaker, cons. Recipient Bank Am. Fgn. Lang. award, 1965; Rotary scholar, 1966. Mem. Nat. Council Tchrs. Math., NEA, Calif. Scholastic Fedn. (life), Phi Delta Kappa, Phi Eta Sigma, Alpha Mu Gamma. Author: Topics in Mathematics, 1972; Model III TRSDOS/Disk Basic, 1982; also computer courses. Home: 12001 Salem Dr Granada Hills CA 91344 Office: 1920 Clark Ave Burbank CA 91506

KOLSTAD, ALLEN CHRIS, rancher, state senator; b. Chester, Mont., Dec. 24, 1931; s. Henry B. and Mabel W. (Webb) K.; student Concordia Coll., 1949-51; m. Iva M. Matteson, Sept. 2, 1951; children—Cedric, Chris, Cheryl, Corrine. With Chester (Mont.) Implement Co., 1951-76, pres., 1972-76; with Kolstad Grain Co., Lothair, Mont., 1953-74, pres., 1969-74; owner, mgr. Kolstad Farms, Chester, Mont., 1960—; mem. Mont. State Senate, 1975—, senate pres. pro-tem, 1979-83. Liberty County Republican chmn., 1973-75. Lutheran. Clubs: Rotary, Elks, Masons, Eagles. Home: PO Box 648 Chester MT 59522 Office: PO Box 51 Ledger MT 59456

KOLTAI, LESLIE, coll. ofcl.; b. Hungary, Apr. 6, 1931; came to U.S., 1956; s. Nicholas and Maria (Deutch) K.; B.A., U. Budapest, 1954; M.A., UCLA, 1961, Ed.D., 1967; LL.D., Pepperdine U., 1975; L.H.D., U. Judaism, 1978; m. Katherine Koltai, May 10, 1953; children—Steve, Marian, Robert. Asst. prof. U. Budapest, 1954-56; instr. Los Angeles City Schs., 1958-60; asso. prof., chmn. dept. Pasadena City Coll., 1960-67, asst. to supt., 1965-67, dir. institutional research, 1969-72; chancellor Los Angeles Community Coll. Dist.; lectr. UCLA, 1973—; vis. prof. Sch. Edn., U. So. Calif. mem. Carnegie Nat. Panel for Study Am. High Sch.; chmn. nat. task force for study assoc. degree Am. Assn. Community and Jr. Colls. Bd. dirs. Carnegie Found. on the Advancement of Teaching; mem. Los Angeles County Bus. Labor Council; Nat. Commn. on Strengthening Presdl. Leadership; trustee Ednl. Resources Info. Ctr., UCLA. Mem. Am. Council on Edn. (commn. on internat. edn., adv. council Ednl. Record), Assn. Governing Bds., Internat. Assn. Univ. Presidents (mem. N.Am. council), Assn. Governing Bds. Univs. and Colls. (mem. adv. council of pres.), League for Innovation in the Community Coll., Am. Mgmt. Assn., Los Angeles C. of C. (mem. exec. com. on edn.). Office: 617 W 7th St Los Angeles CA 90017

KOMARKOVA, VERA, researcher, ecologist; b. Pisek, Czechoslovakia, Dec. 25, 1942; d. Jiri Ruzicka and Tatana (Tomaskova) Ruzickova; M.Sc., Charles U., Prague, Czechoslovakia, 1964; Ph.D., U. Colo., 1976; divorced; 1 son, Mipam Moudry. Research assoc. Inst. Arctic and Alpine Research, U. Colo., Boulder, 1977—, asst. prof. dept. environment, organismic and population biology, 1979—. Mem. Ecol. Soc. Am., AAAS, Internat. Soc. for Vegetation Sci., Am. Inst. Biol. Scis., Am. Alpine Club (mem. expeditions com.), Explorers Club, Sigma Xi. Author: Alpine Vegetation of the Indian Peaks Area, Front Range, Colorado Rocky Mountains, 2 vols., 1979. Contbr. articles to profl. jours. Office: INSTAAR Box 450 U Colo Boulder CO 80309

KOMDAT, JOHN RAYMOND, data processing consultant; b. Brownsville, Tex., Apr. 29, 1943; s. John William and Sara Grace (Williams) K.; m. Linda Jean Garrette, Aug. 26, 1965 (div.). Student U. Tex., 1961-65. Sr. systems analyst Mass. Blue Cross, Boston, 1970-74; pvt. practice data processing cons., San Francisco, 1974-80, Denver, 1981—; mem. CODASYL End User Facilities Com., 1974-76. Served with U.S. Army, 1966-70. Mem. Assn. Computing Machinery, Denver Downtown Democratic Forum. Office: PO Box 3075 Denver CO 80201

KOMERS, RONALD WARD, personnel adminstr.; b. Los Angeles, May 3, 1944; s. Thomas Frank and Helene Marguerite (Lefevre) K.; B.A., Calif. State U., Long Beach, 1968; M.S. in Psychology, Iowa State U., 1970; m. Rhea L. Perkins, Nov. 17, 1965; children—Ward Thomas, Kara Marie. Personnel analyst Calif. State Personnel Bd., Sacramento, 1970-73; chief employment San Bernardino County, Calif., 1973-77; personnel dir. Clackamas County, Oregon City, Oreg., 1977—; dir. Creative Personnel Assos.; instr. mgmt. U. Calif. State, Golden Gate U., U. Redlands, Portland Community Coll. Mem. Nat. Assn. Counties, Am. Psychol. Assn., Internat. Personnel Mgmt. Assn., Am. Soc. Personnel Adminstrn., Nat. Public Employer Labor Relations Assn. Republican. Home: 6609 Palomino Circle West Linn OR 97068 Office: 902 Abernathy Rd Oregon City OR 97045

KOMERSKA, SALLY ARLENE, microbiologist; b. Mpls., Dec. 16, 1930; d. Helmer William and Esther Ingeborg (Reinertsen) Kestila; student Pa. State U., 1949-51, U. Pitts., 1951-52, Montefiore Hosp. Sch. Med. Tech., Pitts., 1952-53; B.S., U. Ariz., 1970, M.S., 1979; m. Robert James Komerska, Aug. 19, 1955; 1 son, Steven. Med. technologist Sch. Public Health, U. Pitts., 1953-54, Pima County Hosp., 1954-55, Thomas-Davis Clinic, 1955-60; free-lance med. technologist St. Joseph's Hosp., Tucson, 1962-63; weekend supr., microbiologist St. Joseph's Hosp., Tucson, 1962-63; med. technologist Thomas-Davis Clinic, Tucson, 1966-68, head microbiologist, 1970—, lab. supr., 1974—; bd. dirs., sec. St. Joseph's Hosp. Credit Union, 1977-78. Den mother Cub Scouts, 1971-73; mem. Altar Guild, Our Savior's Luth. Ch., 1975-78; active Heard Mus., Phoenix, Mus. No. Ariz., Flagstaff. Mem. Am. Soc. Clin. Pathologists (asso.), Am. Soc. Med. Tech. (pres., merit award 1972), Am. Soc. Microbiology, Assn. M.B.A. Execs., Nat. Assn. Female Execs., Ariz. Med. Lab. Assn. (pres. Tucson chpt.). Republican. Lutheran. Mem. profl. adv. panel Med. Lab. Observer mag., 1980—. Home: 3804 E Calle DeSoto Tucson AZ 85716 Office: Alvernon at 5th St Tucson AZ 85726

KOMINEK, EDWARD GEORGE, environmental engineer; b. Chgo., Apr. 11, 1916; s. Edward and Mae (Batista) K.; m. Elizabeth Barbara Tomaszewski, Sept. 28, 1942; children—Maribeth Kominek Drennan, Janet Kominek McDougall, James. B.S., U. Chgo., 1937, M.B.A., 1949. Registered profl. engr., Ill., Ohio, Ariz. Chemist, Infilco, Inc., Chgo., 1937-44; quality control mgr. Houdaile Hershey, Decature, Ill., 1944-45; mgr. indsl. waste ops., sales mgr., v.p. sales Infilco, Inc., Tucson, 1946-63; v.p. sales Alvey Ferguson Co., Cin., 1963-66; mgr. indsl. waste sales Eimco, Salt Lake City, 1966-80; supervisory environ. engr. Fluor Engrs., Irvine, Calif., 1980—. Bd. dirs. College Park Home Owners Assn., Irvine, Calif. Mem. Am. Water Works Assn., Am. Inst. Chem. Engrs., Water Pollution Control Fedn., Beta Gamma Sigma. Republican. Contbr. articles to profl. jours.; patentee in field. Home: 3671 Myrtle St Irvine CA 92714 Office: Fluor Engrs Inc 2801 Kelvin Ave Irvine CA 92714

KOMM, RICHARD ARNOLD, ednl. and clin. psychologist; b. St. Louis, Oct. 6, 1932; s. Bernard J. and Annette C. K.; A.B., Washington U., St. Louis, 1957, M.A. (Van Blarcom scholar), 1958; Ed.D., U. San Francisco, 1978; m. Mary Roth, May 5, 1960 (div.); 1 son, Richard Leigh. Counselor, tchr. Parkway Sch. Dist., St. Louis, 1958-60; clin. psychol. intern VA, St. Louis, 1961-64; dir. Madison County (Ill.) Coop. Sch. Psychology Program, 1964-68; psychologist Sacramento County (Calif.) Probation Dept., 1969; sr. psychologist San Francisco Unified Sch. Dist., 1969-80; psychologist pediatric Assessment Clinic, San Francisco Gen. Hosp., 1976-80; asst. prof. ednl. psychology U. San Francisco, 1973-81; pvt. practice psychology, San Francisco, 1980—; cons. psychologist Mt. St. Joseph and St. Elizabeth's Infant Hosp., San Francisco, 1969—. Pres. So. Ill. Psychologist Orgn., 1968. Served with USAF, 1951-55. Lic. clin. and ednl. psychologist, Calif. Mem. Am. Psychol. Assn., Psychologist Assn. San Francisco (pres., 1979), Calif. Psychol. Assn., Calif. Lic. Ednl. Psychologists Assn., Phi Beta Kappa, Kappa Delta Pi, Phi Delta Kappa. Club: Marines Meml. (San Francisco). Speaker in field profl. confs., U.S. and Eng. Office: 3022 Fillmore St San Francisco CA 94123 also 1137 2d St Santa Monica CA 90403

KOMOTO, SHIRLEY A., corp. bus. and project planner; b. Tokyo, July 21, 1950 (parents Am. citizens); d. Yasuro and Irene (Fujimoto) K.; B.A., Calif. State U., Long Beach, 1973, M.P.A., 1976; postgrad. U. So. Calif. Mgmt. cons. various cos., Los Angeles County, 1970—; NIMH fellow Asian Am. Mental Health Tng. Center, 1972-75, HUD fellow, 1974; program coordinator Orange County/Long Beach Health Consortium, Inc., Irvine, Calif., 1975-76; program analyst dept. ob-gyn Charles R. Drew Postgrad. Med. Sch., Los Angeles, 1976-79; sr. project planner WED Enterprises div. Walt Disney Prodns., Glendale, Calif., 1979-80, sr. bus. adminstr., adminstr., 1980-82, bus. devel. analyst, 1983—. Mem. Los Angeles Olympic Organizing Com., Cultural and Fine Arts Commn.; bd. dirs. T.H.E. Clinic for Women, 1982—, Asian/Pacific Women's Network, 1983—; vice chmn. Asian Pacific Family Outreach, 1979-80; chmn. Long Beach Pioneer Project, 1972-73, mem., 1970—; mem. Long Beach Commn. on Econ. Opportunities, 1972. Recipient community service award Los Angeles County Dept. Health Services, 1976. Mem. N.Am. Soc. Corp. Planners, So. Calif. Assn. Corp. Planners, World Future Soc., Travel and Tourism Research Assn. Democrat. Co-author: Source Book on Perinatal and Other Health Indicators, 1978; contbr. articles on edn. study and plans to profl. publs., papers to confs. Office: 1401 Flower St Glendale CA 91201

KON, CHUCKRIT SOLOMON, dentist; b. Bangkok, Thailand, Jan. 24, 1950; came to U.S, 1970; s. Vui Leong and Sui Len (Hee) K.; m. Wendy Sugiono, June 12, 1977; 1 son, Ryan Christopher. B.A. in Chemistry, Loma Linda U., 1973, D.D.S., 1980. Med. technologist Loma Linda (Calif.) Community Hosp., 1975-77; pvt. practice dentistry Kon & Sugiono Profl. Dental Corp., Colton, Calif., 1980—; lectr. in field. Recipient Loma Linda U. Oral Surgery award, 1980. Mem. Tri-County Dental Assn., ADA, Calif. Dental Assn., Acad. Gen. Dentistry, Seventh-day Adventist. Home: 2314 N Euclid Ave Upland CA 91786 Office: 191 West H St Colton CA 92324

KONARSKI, ELIZABETH LOUISE, shopping center manager, lecturer, educator; b. Oneida, Wis., Aug. 5, 1938; d. Francis and Evelyn Mary (Hill) Coonen; m. James Roy Konarski, Apr. 21, 1933; children—Scott Alan, Lee Ann. B.S. in Elem. Edn., U. Wis., 1960; M.Ed. in Curriculum and Instrn., U. Wash., 1960-73; mgr. Gillman Village shopping ctr., Issaquah, Wash., 1973—; guest lectr. U. Wash., Seattle U. N.W. regional del. White House Conf. Small Bus., 1980; mem. Trade Mission People's Republic. China, 1980; counselor SBA minority bus. pilot program; bd. dirs. Western Wash. Small Bus. Conf., 1980, King County United Way, 1983-85; co-chmn. women's adv. bd. Bellevue Community Coll; bd. dirs. King County East Conv. and Visitors Bur., 1979—. Mem. Women and Bus., Inc. (pres. 1982), Internat. Council Shopping Ctrs., Nat. Assn. Female Execs., Women's Managerial and Profl. Network, The Fashion Group, Seattle C. of C. (dir.), Issaquah C. of C., Ind. Bus. Assn., Gilman Village Mchts. Assn. (founder), Assn. Women in Fashion Related Mgmt. (hon.). Office: Gilman Village Issaquah WA 98027

KONDO, CHARLES YOSHIKI KALANI, clinical psychologist; b. Honolulu, Mar. 15, 1941; s. Yoshio and Kiyoko (Sugiyama) K.; m. Judy Bean; m. 2d, Shirley Fitzwater, Feb. 24, 1947; children—Douglas Gavin, Nicholas Tyson. B.A. in Psychology (NSF scholar), U. Hawaii, 1966; M.A. in Physiol. Psychology (Neurobehavioral Sci. fellow), U. Iowa, 1970; Ph.D. in Clin. Psychology (NIMH fellow), U. Ky., 1979. Lic. psychologist, Iowa, Utah. Research asst. dept. psychiatry U. Iowa Sch. Medicine, Iowa City, 1970-75; intern in psychology VA Med Ctr., Iowa City, 1977-79, staff psychologist, Salt Lake City, 1979—; research asst. prof. dept. psychology U. Utah, asst. prof. Sch. Medicine; cons. Stress Mgmt. Lab. dept. psychiatry So. Ill. U., Springfield; cons. Holy Cross Hosp., Salt Lake City, Catholic Community Services, Salt Lake City; Asian Am. rep. Human Goals Com. VA Med. Ctr., Salt Lake City, 1980—. Mem. Am. Psychol. Assn., Utah Psychol. Assn. Contbr. articles to profl. jours. Office: Psychology Service VA Med Ctr Salt Lake City UT 84148

KONDO, YOSHIO, mus. ofcl.; b. Kaeleku, Maui, Hawaii, Oct. 26, 1910; s. Kamazo and Tatsumi (Kurashima) K.; B.A., U. Hawaii, 1940, M.A., 1947; Ph.D., Harvard U., 1955; m. Kiyoko Sugiyama, Nov. 7, 1932; 1 son, Charles. Asst. in malacology Bishop Mus., Honolulu, 1934-47, malacologist, 1948-80, malacologist emeritus, 1980—, also mem. expdns. to S., W., E. Pacific, 1934-70. Guggenheim fellow, 1953, 54; NSF grantee, 1965-70. Mem. Am. Malacological Union, Soc. for Study of Evolution, Soc. for Systematics, Sigma Xi. Contbr. articles to profl. jours. Home: 809A Isenberg St Honolulu HI 96826 Office: 1355 Kalihi St Honolulu HI 96819

KONDRASUK, JOHN (JACK) NORTON, management consultant, educator; b. Eau Claire, Wis., Jan. 23, 1942; s. Frank Mathew and Ruth Ann (Norton) K.; m. Rosemary F. Moneta, Nov. 6, 1965. Student Coll. St. Thomas, 1960-61; B.S., U. Wis.-Eau Claire, 1964; M.A., U. Minn., 1966, Ph.D., 1972. Personnel adminstr. Honeywell, Mpls., 1968-69; instr. U. Minn., Mpls., 1969; mgmt. edn. specialist Control Data, Mpls., 1969-71; mgmt. cons., Mpls., 1971-73; psychologist Persona Corp., Portland, Oreg., 1973; cons. Rohrer Hibler & Replogle, Portland, 1973-74; asst. prof. mgmt. U. Portland, 1974-80, asst. to pres. for planning, 1980-81, assoc. prof., 1980—; planning and mgmt. cons., 1974—. U. Portland grantee, 1977-82. Mem. Acad. Mgmt. (editor div. newsletter 1980-81), Am. Psychol. Assn., Portland Psychol. Assn., Am. Soc. Personnel Adminstrn. (accredited personnel diplomate 1981—), Pacific N.W. Personnel Assn. (cert. recognition 1979) Am. Soc. Tng. and Devel. (v.p. Oreg. chpt.). Author: MBO: A System of Implementing and Reviewing, 1981; contbr. articles to profl. jours.; developed, copyrighted achievement test. Home: 4187 SW Greenleaf Dr Portland OR 97221 Office: U Portland Portland OR 97203

KOO, ALVIN RUSSELL, public relations and marketing executive; b. Honolulu, Sept. 13, 1945; s. James I. S. and Gladys Y. Koo; m. Charlotte Suzuki, Aug. 5, 1967; children—Leianne, Nicole. B.A., U. Hawaii, 1970. Accredited pub. relations practitioner. Editor, Sun Press Papers, 1970-72; reporter, editor Pacific Bus. News, 1972-74; account exec. Fawcett McDermott Cavanagh, Inc., Honolulu, 1974-75; dir., v.p. pub. relations, Aloha Airlines, Inc., Honolulu, 1975-82; owner, pres. Koo & Shiraki, Honolulu, 1983—. Pres. St. Louis Heights Community Assn., 1983; mem. Hawaii host com. U.S. Olympic Com., 1981-82. Served with Air N.G., 1967-73. Recipient John M. Thornton Meml. award, Honolulu Propeller Club, 1973; Pub. Relations News Gold Key award, 1981. Mem. Pub. Relations Soc. Am., Soc. Am. Travel Writers.

KOOGLER, RUSSELL LEWIS, security specialist; b. Zanesville, Ohio, Sept. 12, 1938; s. Emerson L. and Betty J. (DeSantel) King; student Sacramento Jr. Coll., 1972-74; B.Police Sci. and Bus., Fullerton Coll., 1975; m. Sue Ann Hicks, Dec. 10, 1982; 1 dau. by previous marriage, Patricia Louise. Fed. police officer U.S. Postal Inspectors, Los Angeles, 1967-77; owner Koogler & Asso., Pvt. Investigators, Phoenix, 1979—; loss prevention dist. mgr. K-Mart Corp., Covina, Calif.; spl. agt. Internat. Police Congress, Washington. Tchr., instr. CPR and first aid and disaster courses ARC, Santa Ana, Calif., 1971-78, disaster chmn., 1976-78. Served with Signal Corps, U.S. Army, 1961-64. Recipient awards, ARC 1973, 74, 75, Freedom Train award, 1976. Mem. Internat. Assn. Credit Card Investigators, Ariz. Retail Investigators Assn., Credit Data of Am., Internat. Consumer Credit Assn., Cole's Directory Service Greater Phoenix, Alpha Gamma Sigma, Calif. State Assn. EMT's. Contbr. articles to profl. jours. Address: 662 E Cobblestone Ln Midvale UT 84047

KOOKEN, JOHN F., banker; b. Denver, Nov. 1, 1931; s. Duff A. and Frances P. (Couch) K.; m. Emily Howe, Sept. 18, 1954; children—Diane, Carolyn. M.S., Stanford U., 1954, Ph.D., 1961. With Security Nat. Bank, Security Pacific Corp., Los Angeles, 1960—, controller, 1967-72, sr. v.p., 1972-81, exec. v.p., 1981—; instr. U. So. Calif., 1962-67. Pres., dir. Children's Bur. Los Angeles, 1981; bd. dirs. United Way Los Angeles, 1982. Served to lt. (j.g.) USN, 1954-57. Mem. Fin. Execs. Inst. Office: 333 S Hope St Los Angeles CA 90071

KOONCE, JOHN PETER, investment co. exec.; b. Coronado, Calif., Jan. 8, 1932; s. Allen Clark and Elizabeth (Webb) K.; B.S., U.S. Naval Acad., 1954; postgrad. U. So. Calif., 1957, U. Alaska, 1961, U. Ill., 1968-69; M.S. in Ops. Research, Fla. Inst. Tech., 1970; postgrad. Claremont Grad. Sch., 1970; m. Marilyn Rose Campbell, Sept. 21, 1952; children—Stephen Allen, William Clark, Peter Marshall. Indsl. engr. Aluminum Co. Am., Lafayette, Ind., 1954-56; electronic research engr. Autonetics Div. N.Am. Aviation, Downey, Calif., 1956-57; systems field engr. Remington Rand Univac, Fayetteville, N.C., 1957-59; project engr. RCA Service Co., Cheyenne, Wyo., 1959-60, project supr., Clear, Alaska, 1960-62, project supr., Yorkshire, Eng., 1962-64, re-entry signature analyst, Patrick AFB, Fla., 1964-66; mem. tech. staff TRW Systems Group, Washington, 1966-68; mgr. ops research systems analysis Magnavox Co., Urbana, Ill., 1968-69; tech. advisor, EDP, to USAF, Aerojet Electro Systems Co., Azusa, Calif., Woomera, Australia,

1969-72; investment exec. Shearson Hammill, Los Angeles, 1972-74; investment exec. Reynolds Securities, Los Angeles, 1974-75; v.p. investments Shearson Hayden Stone, Glendale, Calif., 1975-77; v.p. accounts Paine, Webber, Jackson & Curtis Inc., Los Angeles, 1977-81; v.p. nat. tax shelter sales Wedbush Noble, Cook, Inc., Los Angeles, 1981-82; pres. Argo Fin. Corp., Santa Monica, Calif., 1982—; tchr. investments Citrus Coll., Azusa, Calif., Claremont (Calif.) Evening Sch. Vice pres. Claremont Republican Club, 1973, pres., 1974; chmn. Verdugo Hosp. Assocs., 1979. Recipient Merit cert. RCA, 1966. Mem. Nat. Assn. Security Dealers, So. Calif. Options Soc., Navy League, Naval Acad. Alumni Assn. Clubs: Kiwanis, Masons. Contbr. articles to bus. jours. Home: 3718 Chevy Chase Dr Flintridge CA 91011 Office: 1661 Lincoln Blvd Santa Monica CA 90404

KOOPMANS, VEL I., personnel administrator; b. Valparaiso, Ind., Dec. 23, 1935; d. C. Earl and Alma E. (Wiemuth) Ohlfest; m. John S. Koopmans, Apr. 3, 1954; children—Susan Koopmans Geise, Kenneth. Student San Jacinto (Calif.) Jr. Coll., 1975-77, Palomar Coll., San Marcos, Calif., 1973-75, Citrus Belt Law Sch., Riverside, Calif., 1976-77, Western States Law Coll., San Diego, 1975-76. Engaged in secretarial work, 1953-68; propr. Koopmans TV & Appliance Ctrs., Escondido and Poway, Calif., 1968-76; adminstrv. asst. Western Municipal Water Dist., Riverside, Calif., 1977-80; exec. sec. City of Roseburg (Oreg.), 1980-81; personnel mgr. Kyle Tech. Corp., Roseburg, 1981—. Mem. C. of C. Republican. Office: Kyle Tech Corp 3500 NW Stewart Pkwy Roseburg OR 97470

KOPELS, DANIEL MARC, advertising agency company executive, graphic designer; b. N.Y.C., Dec. 12, 1945; s. Samuel Lee and Ethel C. (Binder) K.; m. Marva Hanaan, Oct. 6, 1974; 1 son, Samuel Lee. B.S. in Advt., U. Fla., 1968. Promotion mgr. Sta. WFTV-TV, Orlando, Fla., 1968-69; v.p., co-founder Vatican II Advt. Co., Los Angeles, 1969-71; ptnr., creative dir. Bue/Kopels Advt., Los Angeles, 1971-73; v.p., dir. Markham Products, Inc., Los Angeles, 1973—; pres., prin. Danny Kopels Advt., Los Angeles, 1973—. Recipient numerous awards in field. Club: South Bay Yacht Racing (Venice, Calif.). Office: Danny Kopels Advt 6300 Wilshire Blvd Los Angeles CA 90048

KOPENHAVER, JOSEPHINE YOUNG, painter, educator; b. Seattle, June 9, 1908; d. George Samuel and Blanche Cecilia (Castle) Young; A.B., U. Calif., 1928; M.F.A. (scholar 1936-37), U. So. Calif., 1937; spl. student Claremont Grad. Sch., 1951, 67, Chouinard Art Inst., 1946-47, Otis Art Inst., 1954-55; m. Ralph Witmer Kopenhaver, Apr. 11, 1931. Prof. art Chaffee Jr. Coll., Ontario, Calif., 1946-47, Los Angeles City Coll., 1948-73, Woodbury U., Los Angeles, 1973-76, summer sessions Calif. State U., Los Angeles, 1950, Pasadena City Coll., 1949, Otis Art Inst., Los Angeles, 1959, Pasadena Art Inst., 1948; profl. painter, exhibiting artist, 1933—; work included in exhibits museums and pvt. galleries U.S. and Mex., 1933—, including Hatfield Galleries, Los Angeles; art juror. Winner first award in oil, Los Angeles Art Festival, 1936, various art awards. Mem. Los Angeles Art Assn., Nat. Water Color (past rec. sec.), Audubon Artists, Artists for Econ. Action, Calif. Tchrs. Assn. Clubs: Los Angeles Athletic, Zeta Tau Alpha. Office: PO Box 10666 Glendale CA 91209

KOPF, JOHN OSCAR, systems programmer, sr. scientist; b. Kings County, N.Y., Feb. 21, 1938; s. Oscar Emil and Elizabeth (Lauel) K.; m. Margaret E. Rutherford, Sept. 9, 1961; children—Elizabeth Tracy, Eric David. B.A., U. Conn., 1960, M.A., 1962; Ph.D., Mich State U., 1968. Programmer, E. O. Lawrence Lab., Berkeley, Calif., 1968-73; systems programmer, sr. scientist, Tymshare, Inc., Cupertino, Calif., 1973—. Active Boys Scouts Am., 1976—. Mem. Assn. Computing Machinery. Clubs: West Valley Live Streamers; (Cupertino); Nautical Research Guild (San Francisco); Soc. Folk Harpers and Craftsmen; Soc. Ancient Numismatists.

KOPP, CLAIRE B., developmental psychologist, educator; b. N.Y.C., July 8, 1931; d. Gerson J. Bernstein and Martha J. Stavisky; m. Eugene H. Kopp, Sept. 31, 1950; children—Carolyn, Michael, Paul. B.S., NYU, 1951; M.S., U. So. Calif., 1961; Ph.D., Claremont Grad. Sch., 1970. Lic. psychologist, Calif., 1975. Lectr. psychology UCLA, 1973; Calif. Poly. U., Pomona, 1968-69, Calif. State U.-Los Angeles, 1974; asst. researcher, pediatrics, psychology UCLA, 1971-76, assoc. prof. Grad. Sch. Edn., 1977-82, lectr., 1982—; cons. Cultural Heritage Found., 1980—. Fellow Am. Psychol. Assn., Am. Occupational Therapy Assn.; mem. Soc. Research in Child Devel., Am. Assn. Mentally Deficient, AAAS. Author: The Child Development in a Social Context, 1982; contbr. articles to profl. jours.

KOPULSKY, ANDREW ALLEN, educator; b. Biloxi, Miss., Oct. 18, 1951; s. Sam and Louise (Rothschild) K.; m. Bella Jean Siegel, Oct. 23, 1952; B.A. in Religious Studies, Calif. State U.-Fullerton, 1974; M.A. in Edn., U. Judaism, 1982, M.A. in Teaching, 1980. Tchr. Judaic and secular studies Emanuel Community Day Sch., Beverly Hills, Calif., 1978-82; dir. edn. Kehillat Ma'arav, Los Angeles, 1981-82; dir. Jewish Studies Inst. Day Sch., Anaheim, Calif., 1982—. Mem. Coalition for Alternatives in Jewish Edn., Assn. Supervision and Curriculum Devel., Regligious Edn. Assn., Jewish Educators Assn. Orange County. Developer religious school curricula. Home: 1753 W Crestwood Ln Anaheim CA 92804 Office: Jewish Studies Institute Day School 1770 W Cerritos Ave Anaheim CA 92804

KORAL, ROD LEE, instruments manufacturing company executive; b. Los Angeles, Nov. 8, 1949; s. Ben B. and Mabel M. (Miller) K.; m. Pat A. Gomez, Aug. 11, 1973; children—Jeffrey, Jennifer, Gregory. A.A. in Liberal Arts, Santa Ana Coll., 1970; B.A. in Bus. Adminstrn., Chapman Coll., 1972. C.P.A. Gen. mgr. Advanced Telecommunications, Santa Ana, Calif., 1974-76; communications cons. City of Anaheim (Calif.), 1976-78; mem. staff corp. employee relations Beckman Instruments, Inc., Fullerton, Calif., 1978—. Active March of Dimes, Boy Scouts Am., Nat. Search and Rescue Assn.; bd. dirs. ARC; founder Saddleback Search and Rescue Team; cons. Fed. Emergency Mgmt. Agy., U.S. Olympic Com.; bd. dirs. Rescue Coordination Ctr. Recipient Disting. Service award Jaycees, 1972; cert. of appreciation Orange County Sheriffs Dept., 1976. Mem. Am. Soc. Safety Engrs. Republican. Club: Lions. Contbr. articles to profl. jours.

KORALEK, LESLIE JAMES, psychologist, consultant; b. Newark, Sept. 5, 1949; s. Adolph Hugo and Anita Sonja (Popper) K.; m. Susan Lee Manning, Aug. 16, 1980. M.A. in Clin. Psychology, Psychol. Studies Inst., Palo Alto, Calif., 1979, Ph.D. in Clin. Psychology, 1983. Alcohol counselor Starting Point, Hayward, Calif., 1979-80, asst. dir., Santa Clara, Calif., 1981; pvt. practice psychology, Cupertino, Calif., 1981-82; counselor Ctr. for Alcohol Treatment, Medford, Oreg., 1982-83; alcohol therapist Care Unit, Medford, 1983—; cons. alcoholism to FAA. Jewish.

KORB, LAWRENCE JOHN, metallurgist; b. Warren, Pa., Apr. 28, 1930; s. Stanley Curtis and Dagna (Pedersen) K.; B.Chem.Engring., Rensselaer Poly. Inst., Troy, N.Y., 1952; m. Janet Davis, Mar. 30, 1957; children—James, William, Jeanine. Sales engr. Alcoa, Buffalo, 1955-59; metall. engr. N. Am. Rockwell Co., Downey, Calif., 1959-62; engring. supr. metallurgy Apollo program Rockwell Internat. Co., Downey, 1962-66, engring. supr. advanced materials, 1966-72, engring. supr. metals and ceramics space shuttle program, 1972-83; mem. tech. adv. com. metallurgy Cerritos Coll., 1969-74. Served with USNR, 1952-55. Registered profl. engr., Calif. Mem. Am. Soc. Metals (chmn. aerospace activity com. 1971-76; judge materials application competition 1969, handbook com. 1978-83). Republican. Author articles, chpts. in books. Home: 251 Violet Ln Orange CA 92669 Office: 12214 Lakewood Blvd Downey CA 90241

KORCHIN, SHELDON JEROME, psychology educator; b. N.Y.C., Sept. 8, 1921; s. Solomon and Sally (Levine) K.; m. Sylvia Judith Brecher, June 16, 1942; children—Ellen, Jonathan, Marc. B.A., Bklyn. Coll., 1942; M.A., Clark U., 1943; Ph.D., Harvard U., 1946. Lic. psychologist, Calif.; diplomate Am. Bd. Profl. Psychology, Instr. psychology Harvard U., Cambridge, Mass., 1946-47; instr. psychology Princeton (N.J.) U., 1947-48; clin. psychologist VA, Phila., 1947-50; dir. psychology lab. Michael Reese Hosp. and lectr. U. Chgo., 1950-59; prof. psychology U. Calif.-Berkeley, 1963—; cons. Mem. ACLU, Am. Psychol. Assn. (Disting. Contbn. award 1978), Western Psychol. Assn., AAAS. Jewish. Author: Modern Clinical Psychology, 1976; (with others) Anxiety and Stress, 1956; (with E.E. Jones) Minority Mental Health 1982; contbr. articles to profl. jours.

KORENEFF, CONSTANTINE, cons.; b. Shangahi, China, Nov. 3, 1932; s. Constantine Gabriel and Pauline (Korchak) K.; came to U.S., 1949, naturalized, 1954; B.A., Stanford U., 1954; Ph.D., Columbia Pacific U., 1981; m. Barbara Ann Jackson, Sept. 21, 1974; children by previous marriage—Aldine, Alan, Alisa. Vice-pres. tech. devel. Computer Econs. Corp., San Francisco, 1969-71; cons., San Francisco, 1971; mgr. indsl. applications Hewlett-Packard, Cupertino, Calif., 1972-74; research dir. Kaiser Permanente Med. Center, Santa Clara, Calif., 1974—; mem. faculty Columbia Pacific U., Mill Valley, Calif., 1981—; bd. dirs. Kaiser Fed. Credit Union, 1975—, pres. bd. dirs., 1978-80. Served with U.S. Army, 1954-57. Mem. Soc. Advanced Med. Systems. Republican. Home: 1653 Cervato Circle Alamo CA 94507 Office: 900 Kiely Blvd Santa Clara CA 95051

KORF, HAROLD EDWARD, librarian; b. Osakis, Minn., Oct. 28, 1925; s. Herman R. and Elizabeth (Reller) K.; B.A., U. Calif., Berkeley, 1949, B.L.S., 1953; m. Evelyn Parson, Nov. 11, 1959. Librarian, Free Library of Phila., 1953-57; asso. humanities librarian Stanford (Calif.) U. Library, 1957-60; with Golden Gate U., San Francisco, 1960—, dir. libraries, 1963—, asso. prof. humanities, Libraries Assn., Am. Soc. Info. Sci., AAUP. Unitarian. Home: 1549 Beach St San Francisco CA 94123 Office: 536 Mission St San Francisco CA 94105

KORF, VICTOR WILLIAM, transp. engr., state ofcl.; b. Portland, Oreg., Nov. 25, 1931; s. Victor William and Grace Elizabeth (Folk) K.; m. Florence Vivian Finnell, Feb. 13, 1954; children—Dana, Dale, Nancy. B.S. in Civil Engring., Wash. State U., Pullman, 1953. Engr., designer Wash. Dept. Hwys., 1956-63, asst. dist. advance planning engr., 1963, project engr., 1963-65, dist. access design engr., 1965-67, asst. state location engr., 1967-68, dist. location engr., 1968-73, dist. engr., 1973-75; dep. sec. transp. Wash. Dept. Transp., 1975—; adv. bd. St. Martins Coll. Engring., Olympia, Wash., 1981—. Mem. exec. bd. Boy Scouts Am. Mem. ASCE (pres. Tacoma sect. 1981), Am. Pub. Works Assn. Clubs: Rotary, K.C. Home: 2609 60th Ct NW Olympia WA 98502 Office: Dept Transp Hwy Adminstrn Bldg Olympia WA 98504

KORN, WALTER, writer; b. Prague, Czechoslovakia, May 22, 1908; came to U.S., 1950, naturalized, 1956; s. Bernard and Clara (Deutsch) K.; m. Herta Klemperer, Dec. 24, 1933. Dr.Comm., Charles U., Prague, 1938; postgrad. London Sch. Econs., 1949-50; cert. systems and procedures Wayne State U., 1957. Dir. mktg. Kosmos Works, Prague, 1934-39; contract mgr. Cantie Switches, Chester, Eng., 1941-44; dir. UNRRA, U.S. Zone Occupation, Germany, 1945-47; country dir. Orgn. for Rehab. and Vocational Tng., Geneva, 1948; contract mgr. Royal Metal Mfg. Co., N.Y.C., 1951-55; bus. mgr. J. Community Ctr., Detroit, 1956-59; dir. adminstrn. JDC United Jewish Appeal, Tel Aviv, 1960-64; exec. asst. Self Help/United Help, N.Y.C., 1965-69; housing mgmt. cons. Exec. Dept. Div. Housing and Community Renewal, State N.Y., N.Y.C., 1970-76; lectr. housing for aged and housing fin., 1958-74; lectr. Brit. Allied Council, Liverpool, Eng., 1942-44. Nat. field rep. United Jewish Appeal, 1968—; mem. Vols. for Internat. Tech. Assistance, 1968-71. Served to capt. Czechoslovakian Army, 1938. Mem. Acad. Polit. Sci., Acad. Polit. and Social Sci., Am. Judicature Soc., Internat. Platform Assn., Amnesty Internat. Clubs: Princeton of N.Y.; Commonwealth of Calif.; Press (San Francisco); Sierra, Masons. Author: On Hobbies, 1936; Earn as You Learn, 1948; The Brilliant Touch, 1950; Modern Chess Openings, 12th edit., 1982; American Chess Art, 1975; America's Chess Heritage, 1978; Moderne Schach Eroeffnungen I and II, 1968, 75.

KORNBERG, ARTHUR, biochemistry educator; b. N.Y.C., Mar. 3, 1918; B.S., CCNY, 1937, LL.D., 1960; M.D., U. Rochester, 1941, 1962. Intern in medicine Strong Meml. Hosp., Rochester, N.Y., 1941-42; mem. staff NIH, Bethesda, Md., 1942-52; prof., head dept. microbiology Med. Sch., Washington U., St. Louis, 1953-59; prof. biochemistry Stanford Sch. Medicine, 1959—, chmn. dept., 1959-69. Recipient Paul-Lewis award in enzyme chemistry, 1951; co-recipient Nobel prize in medicine, 1959. Office: Dept Biochemistry Stanford Med Sch Stanford CA 94305

KORNBERG, JAMES PHILIP, physician; b. St. Louis, May 4, 1947; s. Sanford and Elinor K.; m. Sally E. Weissman, June 11, 1969; children—Mariah, Jamie, Terra. B.S. in Aero. and Astronautical Engring., M.I.T., 1969, M.S., 1970; Sc.D. in Environ. Health Sci. and Engring., (Gen. Electric fellow), Harvard U., 1974; M.D., Dartmouth Coll., 1976. Diplomate Am. Bd. Preventive Medicine. Engr., McDonnell Douglas Corp., St. Louis, 1967; cons. environ. engring., air pollution control, New Eng., 1972-77; intern Mary Imogene Bassett Hosp., Cooperstown, N.Y., 1976-77, resident in occupational medicine Harvard Sch. Public Health, 1978; sr. staff cons. occupational medicine and environ. health Arthur D. Little, Inc., Cambridge, Mass., 1977-78; pres. COHBI Corp. (Comprehensive Occupational Health for Bus. and Industry), Leominster, Mass., 1978-79, Boulder, Colo., 1980—; med. adviser Colo. Mining Assn. cons. med. dir. to numerous cos. in Rocky Mountain area; expert witness occupational medicine and toxicology, fed. and state jud. system; sr. aviation med. examiner FAA. Recipient Physicians Recognition award AMA, 1979, 82. Mem. AMA, Am. Occupational Med. Assn., Boulder County Med. Soc., Colo. Med. Soc., Mass. Public Health Assn., Rocky Mountain Acad. Occupational Medicine (dir. 1981-84), Sigma Xi, Phi Eta Sigma, Sigma Gamma Tau. Contbr. articles to profl. jours. Home: 506 Skytrail Rd Jamestown Star Route Boulder CO 80302 Office: 1777 Conestoga St #A Boulder CO 80301

KORNBLUH, WALTER, office supply executive; b. N.Y.C., Oct. 3, 1931; s. Murray and Rose (Silverman) K.; m. Joan Ann Elkin, Dec. 17, 1954; children—Mark, David, Julie. B.S., U. Pa., 1952. C.P.A. Sr. acct. Ernst & Ernst, N.Y.C., 1956-60; treas. Sports Arenas, Inc., Great Neck, N.Y., 1960-66; mng. ptnr. MDJ Investment Plan, Los Angeles, 1967-70; pres. Galaxie Nat. Corp., Los Angeles, 1971-80; pres., chmn. bd., chief exec. officer Marathon Office Supply, Inc., Los Angeles, 1980—. Treas. Fair Housing Council San Fernando Valley, 1980-83; bd. dirs. Fair Housing Congress, Los Angeles, 1982-83. Served with USCG, 1952-56. Mem. Am. Inst. C.P.A.s, Fin. Execs. Inst., Los Angeles Soc. C.P.A.s. Office: 10323 Santa Monica Blvd #D Los Angeles CA 90025

KORNELL, HANNS J., champagne producer; b. Ger., Jan. 14, 1911; s. Paul and Paula (Schoenberger) K.; m. Marilouise P. Rossini, Nov. 20, 1958; children—Paula L., Peter Hanns. Pres., Hanns Kornell Champagne Cellars, St. Helena, Calif., 1952—. Recipient numerous awards from Los Angeles County Gar, Calif. State Fair and internat. competitions. Mem. Wine Inst. Clubs: Elks, Rotary. Address: Hanns Kornell Champagne Cellars Box 249 St Helena CA 94574

KOROBKIN, GEORGE ALFRED, social agy. cons.; b. Springfield, Mass., July 2, 1929; s. Harry I. and Esther (Bessin) K.; B.S., Springfield Coll., 1954; M.S.W., U. Conn., 1956; m. Hannah Rose Riesenfeld, June 14, 1954; children—Debra, Miriam, Adam. Asst. exec. dir. Jewish Community Center, Denver, 1958-65; exec. dir. Jewish Community Center of S. Jersey, Cherry Hill, N.J., 1965-69, Jewish Community Center of Tidewater, Norfolk, Va., 1969-78; dir. Western services Nat. Jewish Welfare Bd., Phoenix, 1978—; mem. field faculty Denver U., Rutgers U., U. Conn., Va. Commonwealth U.; tng. cons. VA, Hampton, Va.; guest lectr. Hebrew Union Coll. Sch. Jewish Communal Service (Los Angeles); exec. com. Jewish Community Relations Council, 1979—. Recipient Community Service awards, Camden, N.J., 1969, Tidewater Jewish Community Center, 1978; cert. Acad. Cert. Social Workers. Mem. Nat. Assn. Social Workers, Assn. Jewish Center Workers, Am. Camping Assn. Author membership manual and handbooks for Jewish Community Ctrs., 1982. Editor: A Survey of Personnel Practices in the Center Field, 1978; The Use of Micro Computers in Jewish Center Operations, 1980. Office: 5039 N 19th Ave Phoenix AZ 85015

KORP, PATRICIA ANNE MUNN (MRS. VINCENT KORP), pub. affairs ofcl.; b. Lincoln, Nebr., Nov. 15, 1942; d. Theodore R. and Elizabeth Anne (Olson) Munn; B.S., U. Wyo., 1967, M.A., 1974; m. Vincent LeRoy Korp, Jan. 15, 1965; children—Kathleen Anne, Karen Lee. Women's editor Sheridan (Wyo.) Press, 1964-66; pub. info. and research asst. Wyo. Dept. Edn., 1967-69; dir. pub. relations and communications, editor Wyo. Edn. Assn., 1969-71; coordinator info. services Mountain Plains Edn. and Econ. Devel. Program, Glasgow Air Force Base, Mont., 1972-73; contbg. editor to The Forum, 1972-73; asst. to exec. sec. Wyo. Youth Council, 1974; pub. affairs officer Bur. Land Mgmt., Rawlins, Wyo., 1975-76, Cheyenne, Wyo., 1976—. Sec., Seton Catholic High Sch. Athletic Assn., 1981—. Recipient All-Am. award Ednl. Press Assn. Am., 1971; 43 awards Wyo. Press Women Writing Contests, 1970-72, 76-81; 1st pl. award Nat. Fedn. Press Women, 1980. Mem. Wyo. Press Women (treas. 1981—), Nat. Fedn. Press Women, Sigma Delta Chi, Pi Delta Epsilon, Alpha Chi Omega. Democrat. Roman Catholic. Club: Quota. Home: Box 10272 Cheyenne WY 82001 Office: PO Box 1828 Cheyenne WY 82001

KORZILIUS, PHYLLIS JEAN, real estate broker; b. Kalamazoo, Oct. 28, 1937; d. Orin Cevilla and Marie (Groenheide) Westra; m. Bruce Patrick Korzilius, Aug. 15, 1958 (div.); 1 son, Erik Vonn. Student Calvin Coll., 1955-57; B.A. cum laude, Kalamazoo Coll., 1959; M.A., Western Mich. U., 1960. Lic. real estate broker, Calif. Product mgr. The Upjohn Co., Kalamazoo, 1960-73; mktg. mgr. Riker Labs div. 3-M Co., Northridge, Calif., 1973-75; pvt. practice real estate broker, Laguna Beach, Calif., 1976—; gen. ptnr. Regent Realty/Regent Real Estate Sch., Laguna Niguel, Calif., 1977-82; owner, operator Hillie McCormack Realty, Laguna Beach, 1982—. Mem. Nat. Assn. Realtors, Phi Beta Kappa. Home: 24382 Los Serranos Dr Laguna Niguel CA 92677 Office: 1000 North Coast Hwy Laguna Beach CA 92651

KOS, PAUL JOSEPH, artist; b. Rock Springs, Wyo., Dec. 23, 1942; s. Paul A. and Bertha A. (Potochnik) K.; student Georgetown U., 1961-62; B.F.A., San Francisco Art Inst., 1965, M.F.A., 1967; m. Marlene Rossi, Sept. 21, 1963; children—Gregory, Jennifer. Asst. prof. art U. Santa Clara (Calif.), 1969-78; instr. San Francisco Art Inst.; exhibited in Paris Biennale, 1977, Bienal de Sao Paulo, 1973, 75, San Francisco Mus. Modern Art, 1977, Castelli Gallery, N.Y.C., 1975, 76. Trustee, San Francisco Art Inst., 1973-76, 80—. Address: PO Box 299 Soda Springs CA 95728

KOSIK, NANCY MAY, hotel executive; b. Cicero, Ill., Apr. 17, 1945; d. Peter J. and Cecelia (Longawa) Nega; m. Fred J. Kosik, July 26, 1969. Adminstrv. asst. Am. Coll. Testing Program, 1970-71; instr. dept. journalism, dept. secretarial adminstrn. N.Mex. State U., 1977-80; co-owner F.J. Kreative Advt. Agy., Las Cruces, N.Mex., 1976-80, part-time instr. U. Nev., Reno, 1980; with conv. sales dept. Harrah's Hotels, Reno, 1980-81; mng. mgr. Tropicana Hotel and Country Club, Las Vegas, 1981—. Judge, State of Nev. Spelling Contest. Mem. Am. Soc. Tng. and Devel. Author office procedures manuals. Office: Tropicana Hotel and Country Club 3801 Las Vegas Blvd S Las Vegas NV 89109

KOSKI, ELSA LAVERNE, educator, nurse, adolescent pregnancy consultant; b. Red Lodge, Mont., Feb. 23, 1929; d. Edgar Max and Elma Matilda (Prinkki) Gruel; m. Walfred Conrad Koski; children—Mark, Maureen. Nursing diploma, Carroll Coll., 1950; B.S. cum laude in Gen. Studies, So. Oreg. State Coll., 1976. Pediatric supr. St. James Hosp., Butte, Mont., 1951; night supr. Barrett Hosp., Dillon, Mont., 1951; asst. hosp. adminstr. Stillwater Meml. Hosp., 1952; pvt. duty nurse Josephine Meml. Hosp., Grants Pass, Oreg., 1952-53; clinic staff nurse ob-gyn Grants Pass Clinic, 1963-66; health tchr. Grants Pass High Sch., 1968—, adviser Future Med. Workers Club; adolescent pregnancy cons. Task force mem. health edn., home econs. edn. Seaside Health Team, Heart Health Edn.; bd. dirs. Josephine County March of Dimes, Am. Cancer Soc.; vital signs nurse instr. ARC; elder Bethany Presbyterian Ch. Recipient Health Conf. Coordinator Regional award March of Dimes, 1971. Mem. Grants Pass Edn. Assn., Oreg. Edn. Assn., NEA, Phi Delta Kappa, Delta Kappa Gamma. Democrat. Office: Grants Pass High Sch 522 NE Olive St Grants Pass OR 97526

KOSKINEN, SULO MATIAS, electronics company executive b. Vaasa, Finland, Sept 15, 1922; s. William and Emma (Ollus) K.; student Kansan Valistus Seura Inst., 1941-45, Cleve. Inst. Radio Electronics, 1949-51; m. Anna Miriam Linnakallio, Aug. 4, 1946; children—Jarmo, Pirjo, Ellen; came to Can., 1951, naturalized, 1956. Product mgr. Chisholm Industries, 1952-56; dir. engring. Anaconda Electronics Ltd. (formerly Tele Signal Electronics), Vancouver, B.C., Can., 1956-75, also dir.; pres. Koskinen Electronic Lab., Ltd. Pres., Finnish Can. Rest Home Assn., 1964—, Finnish Kalevava Bros., Vancouver, 1964—; treas. Loyal Finns in Can., 1962-75. Served with Finnish Air Force, 1941-44. Mem. IEEE, Soc. Cable TV Engrs., Internat. Soc. Hybrid Microelectronics. Club: Finlandia (pres. 1978-79) (Vancouver). Contbr. articles to tech. jours. Patentee in field (3). Home: 5390 Frances St Burnaby BC V5B 1T5 Canada

KOSKY, WILLIAM BERNARD, assn. exec.; b. Linden, N.J., Oct. 31, 1930; s. William B. and Anna E. (Eckel) K.; B.A. in Journalism, St. John's U., Jamaica, N.Y., 1965. Editor, pub. Staten Islander Mag., N.Y.C., 1959-61; pub. relations exec. ARC, N.Y.C., 1966; dist. exec. Boy Scouts Am., N.Y.C., 1970-73, mktg., sales dir., Dallas, 1978, dir. Western Distribution Ctr., Sunnyvale, Calif., 1980—; cons. in field. Served with USMC, 1950. Recipient Pelican award, Boy Scouts Am., 1970, St. George medal, 1971, others. Mem. Am. Mgmt. Assn., Direct Mail Mktg. Assn. Republican. Roman Catholic. Clubs: Decathlon, Order of the Arrow. Contbr. articles to profl. jours. Home: 7375 Rollingdell Dr Apt 39 Cupertino CA 95014 Office: 120 San Gabriel Dr PO Box 556 Sunnyvale CA 94086

KOSLOV, JUDITH WILMA, mathematics educator; b. Bklyn., Apr. 19, 1948; d. Joseph and Muriel (Heller) K.; B.A., SUNY, 1970; M.S., U. Wis., 1973; M.M. Utah State U., 1977; Ph.D., U. Colo., 1982. Research analyst Div. Health, State of Wis., Madison, 1973; with VISTA, Madison, 1973-74; human resource planner Mayor's Office, Madison,

1974-75; instr. math. Utah State U.-Logan, 1975-77; instr. math. U. Colo-Denver, 1977-82, asst. prof., 1982—. Mem. Inst. Math. Stats., Am. Statis. Assn., Assn. for Women in Math., Caucus for Women in Stats. Office: U Colo 1100 14th St PO Box 102 Denver CO 80202

KOSMONT, LARRY J., city manager; b. N.Y.C., Sept. 22, 1951; s. Serge and Juliette (Esteves) K.; B.A., SUNY-Binghamton, 1973; M.P.A., U. So. Calif., 1978. Adminstrv. asst. City of Santa Monica (Calif.), 1975-78; asst. city mgr. City of Seal Beach (Calif.), 1978-80; city mgr. City of Bell Gardens (Calif.), 1980—; part-time prof. U. So. Calif., 1982—. Treas., Rio Hondo Boys Club, 1982—; mem. Orange County Selective Services Bd., 1982—. Mem. Internat. City Mgmt. Assn., Am. Soc. Pub. Adminstrn., Mcpl. Fin. Officers Assn., Calif. Urban Econ. Devel., Urban Land Inst.

KOSOWER, EVIE MARGOLIS, educator, consultant; b. N.Y.C., May 16, 1934; d. Samuel and Marion (Nelson) Margolis; children—Erika, Vicki. B.A. in Humanities, U. Calif.-Berkeley, 1956; M.A. in Edn. Psychology, Calif. State U.-Northridge, 1972; Ed.D. in Edn. Mgmt., U. of La Verne, 1979. Cert. in adminstrv. services, life cert. in teaching, Calif. gen. elem. Tchr. Los Angeles Unified Sch. Dist., 1964-72; ednl. assoc. Found. Early Childhood Edn., Los Angeles, 1972-76; program devel. specialist Tchr. Corps, U. So. Calif., Los Angeles, 1977-79, dir. Cardiovascular Health Edn. Project, 1979-81; pvt. practice orgn. and ednl. consulting, Beverly Hills, Calif., 1981—; lectr. in field. Mem., past chmn. proposal rev. team Am. Heart Assn., Los Angeles. Mem. Am. Soc. Tng. and Devel., Orgn. Devel. Network. Author ednl. materials; contbr. articles to profl. jours.

KOST, RICHARD STEPHEN, trade assn. exec.; b. San Diego, Oct. 18, 1947; s. Ned Franklin and Helen Lucille (Mahaffey) K.; student U. Wyo., 1965, 66, 67, N.W. Community Coll., Powell, Wyo., 1967; children—Jaylene Elaine, Richard Stephen. Engr. dept. hwy. State of Wyo., 1967-68; ptnr. Slyko Enterprises, 1968-69; v.p. Wyo. Janitorial Supply, Inc., 1969-70; pres. United Companies, Laramie, Wyo., 1970; ptnr. Kost Bros. Pub., Berthoud, Colo., 1971-73; v.p. Aviation Maintenance Pubs., Basin, Wyo., 1973-78; pres. Aviation Maintenance Found., 1972—, Ednl. Fund, 1974—, Aviation Specialists, Basin, 1978—; sr. ptnr. ASI Devel. Co., Basin, 1978—; gen. ptnr. The Factory Showroom, furniture wholesaler, 1981—; dir. mktg. and sales Bus. Computer Network, Inc., Basin, 1982—; mktg. cons. Frontier Services Co., Denver; v.p. internat. services Aviation Maintenance Pubs., 1983—. Treas., chmn. fin. Big Horn County (Wyo.) Republican Central Com., 1976—, chmn. central com., 1979—. Clubs: Lions, Elks, Eagles. Contbr. articles to profl. jours. Office: 117 S 4th St Basin WY 82410 Mailing Address: PO Box 739 Basin WY 82410

KOSTERS, JEAN WESTON, sales representative; b. American Falls, Idaho, Jan. 16, 1935; d. Roy Alan and Marian Anita (Cathro) Weston; B.S., U. Idaho, 1956; M.A. in Counseling, Ariz. State U., 1968; student Def. Lang. Inst., Va., 1969; m. Howard C. Kosters, July 20, 1968; children—Paula Kay, Mary Jean. Tchr., Dover Spl. Sch. Dist., Del., 1963-66, Clark AFB, Philippines, 1961-63, Albuquerque Public Schs., 1959-61; counselor Ariz. Boys Ranch, 1967; counselor and career devel. coordinator Community Action Program, 1967-68; art tchr. art Brindisi Dependent Schs., San Vito Air Sta., Italy, 1969-74; supr., master tchr. Vacaville (Calif.) public schs., 1974-78; sales rep. Adventures in Achievement, Inc., Irvine, Calif., 1978-79; Calif. cons. for Bowmar/Noble Pubs., Los Angeles, 1979-80; area mgr. Scholastic Inc., Pleasanton, Calif., 1980-83; sales rep. Riverside Pub. Co., Glendale, Calif., 1983—. Mem. mental health adv. bd. Solano County (Calif.), 1977-78; coordinator PTA Council Cultural Arts, 1974-78. Recipient Sustained Superior Performance award Dept. Def. Overseas Schs., 1973. Mem. Women's Nat. Book Assn., Calif. Bus. Women's Network, Nat. Assn. Female Execs., Nat. Assn. Profl. Saleswomen, Women in Mgmt., AAUW (area rep. 1976-78), Delta Kappa Gamma. Home: 913 Calle Miramar Redondo Beach CA 90277 Office: 1763 Gardena Ave Glendale CA 91204

KOSTKA, WILLIAM JAMES, JR., public relations exec.; b. Mpls., Oct. 17, 1934; s. William James and Dorothy (Parmenter) K.; B.A. in Journalism, U. Colo., 1956; m. Cynthia Gleason, Apr. 6, 1974; children—Cheryl Elizabeth, Wendy Dorelle, Jennifer Anna, William James III. Chmn., pres. William Kostka & Assos., Denver, 1964—; nat. news bur. chief Martin Marietta Corp., Balt., 1961-64; reporter Rocky Mountain News, Denver, 1958-61; mem. faculty U. Colo., Boulder, 1975—. Served with U.S. Army, 1956-58. Named Outstanding Grad. in Journalism, U. Colo., 1977. Mem. Public Relations Soc. Am., Denver Advt. Fedn., Colo. Press Assn. Clubs: Denver Press, Nat. Press, Denver Country, University Mt. Vernon Country. Home: 13955 E Hamilton Dr Aurora CO 80014 Office: 1407 Larimer Sq Denver CO 80202

KOSTON, GARY MICHAEL, lawyer, real estate broker, educator; b. San Diego, Jan. 27, 1954; s. Bernard Emery and Georgia Lola (Downs) K.; m. Crystal Fay Jones, Jan. 19, 1980. B.A., U. Redlands, 1976; J.D., U. of Pacific, 1979. Bar: Calif. 1979. Sole practice, San Marcos, Calif., 1979—; adj. prof. Nat. U., Vista, Calif.; real estate broker. Active Republican Club Vista. Mem. State Bar Calif., San Marcos C. of C. (dir.). Clubs: Rotary (v.p.), Jaycees (sec.). Contbr. article to legal jour. Office: 910 W San Marcos Blvd Suite 205-B San Marcos CA 92069

KOTESKEY, FREDERICK WILLIAM, English educator, writer; b. Detroit, Oct. 1, 1926; s. William and Ethel Barbara (Oesterle) K.; m. Evelyn Maxwell Biggers, Dec. 27, 1955; 1 son, Robert William. B.J., U. Mo.-Columbia, 1949; A.B., Calvin Coll., 1953; postgrad. U. Birmingham Extra Mural Div., Stratford-Upon-Avon (Eng.), 1958; M.A., U. No. Colo., 1960. Cert. life tchr., Colo. With advt. dept. J.L. Hudson Co., Detroit, 1950-52; tchr. Grand Rapids (Mich.) Central High Sch., 1953-55, Greeley (Colo.) High Sch., 1955-57, 59-63, Hanau (Germany) Am. Sch., 1957-59; mgr. Denver Dry Goods Co., Greeley, Colo., 1963-68; tchr. Arapahoe High Sch., Littleton, Colo., 1968-73, Evergreen (Colo.) High Sch., 1973-80, Dennison Fundamental Sch., Lakewood, Colo., 1980-83; yearbook and/or newspaper advisor; lectr. in field; ghost writer Denver bus. community. Active pub. relations The Little Theatre of Rockies, U. No. Colo. Served with infantry U.S. Army, World War II. Title III grantee edn. research and curriculum devel. Arapahoe High Sch., 1967-68. Mem. Nat. Writers Club, Rocky Mountain Writers Guild, Council Basic Edn., Assn. Supervision and Curriculum Devel. Republican. Contbr. articles in field to profl. jours.; poems, plays, stories to newspapers, mags. and anthologies. Home: 800 Washington Apt 601 Denver CO 80203

KOTICK, NURIT MIDLER, consumer packaged goods product executive; b. Haifa, Israel, Oct. 3, 1954; d. Benjamin and Esther (Chemtob) Midler; m. Ronald Lee Kotick, June 17, 1979. Cert., Chase Profl. Center, 1976; A.Bus., Metro. Sch. Bus., Chgo., 1973. Paralegal, Atlantic Richfield Corp., Los Angeles, 1976-78; assoc. product mgr. Carnation Co., Los Angeles, 1978-81; product mgr. Knudsen Corp., Los Angeles, 1981—. Rotary scholar, 1972. Mem. Am. Mktg. Assn. Office: 231 E 23rd St Los Angeles CA 90011

KOTLAREK, EUGENE ROBERT, industrial equipment company executive; b. Duluth, Minn., Mar. 31, 1940; s. George S. and Mable (Murtley) K.; m. Barbara A. DeCaigny, Sept. 21, 1963; children—Brian, Debra. B.A., U. Minn., 1963; M.B.A., U. Denver, 1976. Mktg. mgr. Brunswick Corp., Chgo., Tulsa, 1970-72; mktg. mgr., gen. mgr. Kellwood Co., Detroit and St. Louis, 1972-74; mktg. mgr. AMF/Head Ski Co., Boulder, Colo., 1974-78; prin. E.R. Kotlarek & Assoc., Denver, 1978-81; regional mgr. Makita U.S.A. Co., Denver, 1981—; instr. Regis Coll., Denver, 1983—. Mem. U.S. Olympic Ski Games Com., 1968-71; coach U.S. World Ski Team, 1970. Served with USAFR, 1961-67. Named to Nat. Ski Hall of Fame, 1982. Mem. Fedn. Internat. de Ski. Mem. World Ski Team, 1958, 1966, U.S. Olympic Ski Team, 1960, 1964. Address: 4611 W 89th Way Westminster CO 80030

KOTTLOWSKI, FRANK EDWARD, econ. geologist; b. Indpls., Apr. 11, 1921; s. Frank Charles and Adella (Markworth) K.; student Butler U., 1939-42; A.B., Ind. U., 1947, M.A., 1949, Ph.D., 1951; m. Florence Jean Chriscoe, Sept. 15, 1945; children—Karen Kottlowski Harvey, Janet Kottlowski Jenkins, Diana Kottlowski Schoderbek. Party chief Ind. Geology Survey, Bloomington, summers 1948-50; fellow Ind. U., 1947-51, instr. geology, 1950; adj. prof. N.Mex. Inst. Mining and Tech., Socorro, 1970—; econ. geologist N.Mex. Bur. Mines and Mineral Resources, 1951-66, asst. dir., 1966-68, 70-74, acting dir., 1968-70, dir., 1974—; chmn. N.Mex. Mine Safety Adv. Bd., 1973—; mem. N.Mex. Coal Surface Mining Commn., 1973—; chmn. com. on disposal of excess spoil NRC; geologic cons. Sandia Corp., 1966-72. Mem. Planning Commn., Socorro, 1960-68, 71-78; mem. N.Mex. Energy Resources Bd.; sec. Socorro County Democratic Party, 1964-68. Served to 1st lt. USAAF, 1942-45. Decorated D.F.C., Air medal. Fellow Geol. Soc. Am. (councilor 1980-82, exec. com. 1981-82); mem. Am. Assn. Petroleum Geologists (dist. rep. 1965-68, editor 1971-75, disting. service award 1981), Assn. Am. State Geologists (v.p. 1983-84), Soc. Econ. Geologists, AAAS, AIME, Am. Inst. Profl. Geologists, Am. Commn. Stratigraphic Nomenclature (sec. 1964-68, chmn. 1968-70), Sigma Xi. Clubs: Rotary; Cosmos (Washington). Author: Measuring Stratigraphic Sections; contbr. articles on mineral resources, stratigraphy and areal geology to tech. jours. Home: 703 Sunset Dr Socorro NM 87801 Office: NM Bur Mines NM Tech Socorro NM 87801

KOUNTZ, CARL ARTHUR, semicondr. equipment co. mgr.; b. Fresno, Calif., Dec. 30, 1943; s. Richard Charles and Anna (Silva) K.; B.S. cum laude in Indsl. Tech., Calif. State U., Chico, 1973; m. Carol Sue Jenkins, May 18, 1974; children—Brenda, Germano, Anna. With Fairchild Semicondr Co., Mountain View, Calif., 1973-79, purchasing specialist, 1975-77, mgr. equipment purchasing, 1977-79; purchasing mgr. Cobilt Div., Computervision Corp., Santa Clara, Calif., 1979-82; v.p. mfg. L.R.C., Santa Clara, Calif., 1982—; lectr., condr. seminars on negotiations, purchasing law. Served with submarine service USN, 1961-69. Recipient Outstanding Sr. award Calif. State U., 1973. Mem. Purchasing Mgmt. Assn., Am. Prodn. and Inventory Control Soc. Home: 4013 Ambrose Ct San Jose CA 95121 Office: 5403 Betsy Ross Dr Santa Clara CA 95050

KOUPAL, JOYCE ANN, organization executive, political consultant; b. Sacramento, Mar. 7, 1932; d. Cecil Wallace and Elizabeth Louise (De Ree) Nash; m. Edwin Augustus Koupal (dec.); children—Cecil Edwin, Christine Ann, Diane Marie. Exec. dir. People's Lobby, Inc., Los Angeles, 1976—; exec. dir. The Printing Press, Los Angeles, 1977-81; polit. cons., San Rafael, Calif., 1981—. Mem., Los Angeles County Energy Commn., 1975-76. Co-author (with Faith Keating): Success Is Failure Analyzed, 1976. Office: 2315 Durant Ave Berkeley CA 94704

KOURILSKY, MARILYN LEDERMAN, college administrator, teacher educator; b. Los Angeles, Mar. 13, 1941; d. Charles and Ruth Lederman; m. Gregory Kourilsky, July 7, 1967; 1 dau., Shari. B.A in Econs., UCLA, 1961, M.A. in Econs., 1963, Ph.D. in Communications (Cognate Econs.), 1968. Tchr. social sci., Los Angeles, 1963-66; instr. UCLA Grad. Sch. Edn., 1968-74, asst. prof., 1974-82, assoc. prof., 1982—, prof., 1982—, dir. tchr. edn., 1982—; dir. Ctr. Econ. Edn.; cons. econ. edn. Recipient Willard Eccles Disting. Professorship, 1975-76; UCLA Disting. Teaching award, 1976; Excellence in Econ. Edn. award Nat. Freedom Found., 1979. Mem. Am. Ednl. Research Assn., Am. Econs. Assn., Phi Beta Kappa, Phi Gamma Mu. Author: Understanding Economics: Overview for Teachers, Experiences for Students, 1983; Mini-Society: Experiencing Real-World Economics in the Elementary School Classroom, 1983; contbr. articles to profl. jours. Creator Kourilsky Experience-based Education Programs (KEEP) including Mini-Society, Kinder-Economy, and Max-Economy. Office: UCLA Dept Education 210 Moore Hall Los Angeles CA 90024

KOURY, MARY JEAN, wholesale liquor company executive; b. Las Vegas, N.Mex., Sept. 15, 1932; d. Joe G. and Frances (Malouff) Maloof; m. M. David Koury, May 9, 1959; children—Cynthia, Nanette, Jeanine, David, George. Student U. Colo., 1950-52. With Maloof Cos., Albuquerque, 1952—, v.p., 1970—; dir. First Nat. Bank, Albuquerque. Active parochial sch. fundraising. Roman Catholic. Club: Lioness. Office: Maloof Cos 523 Commercial St NE Albuquerque NM 87103

KOUTZ, KENNETH HUNT, safety specialist; b. Berkeley, Calif., Aug. 26, 1945; s. Ernest Henry and Loya (Hunt) K.; B.S., cert. secondary teaching Calif. State U., Hayward, 1970; M.S.S., U. So. Calif., 1981; m. Jean Loux, Sept. 6, 1969. Chmn. dept. sci. Larkspur (Calif.) Sch. Dist., 1970-79; hazardous materials rep., hazardous waste rep., respiratory protection rep., machine guarding rep., safety engring. rep. U.S. Naval Supply Center Safety Office, Oakland, Calif., and Navy Public Works Center, San Francisco, 1979—; laser safety officer; NAVOSH fund coordinator. Mem. Am. Soc. Safety Engrs., Fed. Safety Council, NEA, Nat. Safety Council, Assn. Fed. Safety Profls. Democrat. Roman Catholic. Home: 1507 Trestle Glen Rd Oakland CA 94610 Office: Naval Supply Center Safety Office Code 06 Oakland CA 94625

KOVACH, MICHAEL JOHN, pharmacist, consultant; b. Akron, Ohio, Oct. 1, 1938; s. Mike and Barbara (Chaut) K.; m. Gertrude Elaine Pollock, Aug. 2, 1969; children—Michael John, Sarah Elizabeth. Student Kent State U., 1956-58; B.S. in Pharmacy, Ohio State U., 1961. Asst. mgr. Maple Valley Drug Co., Akron, Ohio, 1966-75; pvt. practice clin. pharmacy, cons. to nursing homes, cons. ostomy, Albuquerque, 1975-83; tech. mfg. pharmacist Albuquerque VA Med. Ctr., 1983—; mem. profl. adv. bd. Albuquerque Childbirth Edn. Assn. Vice pres. Parent Faculty Club, Albuquerque, 1980-81, pres., 1981-82. Served with USPHS, 1961-66. Mem. Ohio State Pharm. Assn., N.Mex. Pharm. Assn., Am. Pharm. Assn. Republican. Lutheran. Home: 1021 California SE Albuquerque NM 87108

KOVACS-FIGUEROA, CARLOS, mining corp. ofcl.; b. Otuzco, Peru, Feb. 24, 1932; came to U.S., 1957, naturalized, 1979; s. Zoltan Kovacs and Esperanza Figueroa; B.S. in Phys. Chemistry, Trujillo U., Peru, 1954, Chem. Engr., 1955; M.S., Stanford U., 1961; m. Elvira Barrientos-Peredo, Sept. 22, 1962; children—Zoltan, Gisela, Diana. Metallurgist, No. Peru Mining Co., Peru, 1956-59; asst. test engr. Phelps Dodge Corp., Ajo, Ariz., 1961-67, concentrator engr., Tyrone, N.Mex., 1972-74, asst. supt. concentrators, Morenci, Ariz., 1974—; asst. dir. research and devel. So. Peru Copper Corp., Peru, 1968-72. Served to 2d lt. CAP, 1979-80. Seagrams research grantee, 1960. Mem. Soc. Mining Engrs. of AIME (chmn. Clifton-Morenci sect.). Democrat. Roman Catholic. Club: Clifton-Morenci Rotary. Contbr. articles to profl. publs. Home: 3 Park Ave Clifton AZ 85533 Office: Phelps Dodge Corp Morenci AZ 85540

KOVARIK, JOSEPH LEWIS, thoracic surgeon; b. Omaha, Sept. 16, 1927; m. Delores Marie Casey, June 20, 1953; children—Jane Ann, Patricia Marie, Karen Rose, Joseph Edward, James John, Kenneth Michael. B.S., U. Nebr., 1950, M.D., 1950. Diplomate Am. Bd. Surgery, Am. Bd. Thoracic Surgery. Intern U. Ill. Research and Ednl. Hosps., Chgo., 1950-51; resident St. Francis Hosp., Peoria, Ill., 1951-53, Presbyn. Hosp., Chgo., 1953-55, Chgo. State Tb Sanitarium, Chgo., 1955, VA Hosp., Hines, Ill., 1955; fellow in thoracic and cardiovascular surgery Rush-Presbyn.-St. Luke's Med. Ctr., Chgo., 1957; practice medicine specializing in thoracic surgery, Denver, 1957—; mem. staff Presbyn. Med. Ctr., 1957—, St. Joseph's Hosp., 1957—, Mercy Med. Ctr., 1957—; asst. clin. prof. surgery U. Colo. Sch. Medicine, Denver, 1965-76, assoc. clin. prof., 1976—; cons. in surgery Colo. State Hosp., Pueblo, 1961-80; cons. in thoracic surgery VA Hosp., Albuquerque, 1961-66; vice chmn. Denver Areawide Comprehensive Health Planning Council, 1973-76; mem. med. tech. adv. com. Denver Regional Council of Govts., 1970-73; vice chmn. St. Anthony's Hosp., Denver, 1968; v.p. Colo. div. Am. Cancer Soc., 1979-81, pres., 1981, chmn. profl. edn. com., 1977-79, mem. exec. com., 1965—; mem. surg. rev. com. Blue Cross/Blue Shield of Colo., 1981—; mem. profl. edn. com. Colo. Heart Assn., 1966-69; v.p., chmn. med. adv. com. Colo. Cystic Fibrosis Assn., 1964-75; mem. cancer com. Colo./Wyo. Regional Med. Program, 1968-70. Bd. dirs., chmn. profl. adv. com. Community Homemakers Service, 1964-69. Mem. AMA, Colo. Med. Soc., Denver Med. Soc. (pres. 1969-70, chmn. bd. trustees 1970-71), Denver Cath. Physicians Guild (pres. 1965-66), Colo. Trudeau Soc. (pres. 1968-69), Am. Coll. Chest Physicians (pres. Colo. chpt. 1970-71), Hines Surg. Assn., Denver Acad. Surgery, Am. Thoracic Soc., Southwestern Surg. Congress, Western Surg. Assn., Am. Assn. Thoracic Surgery, Samson Thoracic Surg. Soc., ACS (pres. Colo. chpt. 1976-77, gov. 1979—). Contbr. articles to profl. jours. Address: 1633 Fillmore St Denver CO 80206

KOVNER, JOEL WYATT, banker; b. N.Y.C., May 19, 1941; s. Sidney J. and Natalie (Lieberman) K.; B.A., Cornell U., 1963; M.P.H., UCLA, 1964, Ph.D., 1968; postgrad. Harvard U., 1975-79; m. Virginia Samuels, June 17, 1965; children—Chloe, Emily, Noah. Mem. faculty UCLA, 1968; economist Kaiser Found. Health Plan, Los Angeles, 1969-72, dir. med. econs., 1972-79, v.p., 1979-81; mgr. planning and support services Kaiser-Permanente Med. Care Program, Los Angeles, 1979-81; now chmn., chief exec. officer First Profl. Bank, N.A., Los Angeles; cons. in field. Mem. Am. Public Health Assn. (chmn. med. care 1980-81), Health Info. Soc. (pres. 1971-72), Ops. Research Soc. Jewish. Contbr. articles to profl. jours. Home: 15912 Alcima Ave Pacific Palisades CA 90272 Office: 606 Broadway Santa Monica CA 90401

KOVSCHAK, ANTHONY ANDREW, JR., economic geologist; b. San Diego, Oct. 5, 1948; s. Anthony Andrew and Nellie Pearl (Shupert) K.; m. Catherine Marie Green, Oct. 14, 1972; children—Anthony Clayton, Michael Paul. Student U. Calif.-San Diego, 1966-67, San Diego State U., 1967-68; B.S. in Geology, U. Tex.-Arlington, 1971, M.S. in Geology, 1973. Jr. geologist So. Union Gas Co., Dallas, 1971; with Union Carbide Corp., 1975—, mgr. exploration Colo. plateau ops., Uravan, 1977-81, regional geologist new bus. ventures, Grand Junction, Colo., 1981-82, in charge precious metal exploration in Chile and Mexico, 1982—, on internat. tech. loan Union Carbide, South Africa, 1978, Mobil Oil Co. fellow, 1971; Sigma Xi grantee-in-aid, 1971. Mem. Soc. Econ. Geologists, Soc. Mining Engrs. of AIME, Sigma Xi, Sigma Gamma Epsilon. Methodist. Contbr. articles and chpts. to profl. publs. Home: 597 Rambling Rd Grand Junction CO 81503 Office: PO Box 1029 care Union Carbide Grand Junction CO 81501

KOWALEK, JON W., art museum ofcl.; b. Swarthmore, Pa., Dec. 11, 1934; s. John W. and Anna C. (Partyka) K.; B.S., Kutztown (Pa.) State Coll., 1956; M.Art Edn., Pa. State U., 1960; M.F.A., Cranbrook Acad. Art, 1963. Asst. dir. Flint (Mich.) Inst. Arts, 1963-65; dir. Ft. Lauderdale (Fla.) Mus. Art, 1966-67; dir. galleries U. South Fla., Tampa, 1968-69; dir. Tacoma Art Mus., 1969—. Guest lectr. Kunstgewerbeschule, Zurich, Switzerland, 1965-66, Wash. State Conf. Arts, Seattle, 1970; mem. Capitol art project com. Wash. State Arts Com., 1970; mem. Tacoma-Pierce County Arts Commn., 1973-74; mem. Wash. Gov.'s Advisory Com. Arts, 1977; mem. ofcl. arts group to China, 1978. Recipient Excellence in Visual Arts award Tacoma-Pierce County Civic Arts Commn., 1974. Mem. Assn. Art Mus. Dirs., Am. Assn. Museums, Wash. Arts Consortium (pres. 1978-79), Western Assn. Art Museums (v.p. 1971-72). Author publs. in field, including: Arts of China; producer TV series The Art Scene, Art Up Close, 1978. Home: 818 N 10th St Tacoma WA 98403 Office: 12th and Pacific Ave Tacoma WA 98402

KOWALKE, RONALD LEROY, educator, artist; b. Chgo., Nov. 8, 1936. Student U. Chgo., 1954-56, Art Inst. Chgo., 1954-56; B.A., Rockford Coll., 1959; M.F.A., Cranbrook Acad. Art, 1960. Group show: Seven Am. Printmakers, Amsterdam, Netherlands, 1967; represented in permanent collections: Mus. Modern Art, N.Y., Met. Mus. Art, N.Y.C., Library Congress, Washington, Nat. Gallery, Washington. Instr. design No. Ill. U., 1960-61; instr. drawing, design and printmaking U. Hawaii, 1969—. U. Hawaii grantee, 1970, 71. Mem. Honolulu Printmakers (adv. bd. 1970—). Office: University Hawaii Dept Art 1801 University Ave Honolulu HI 96844

KOWNACKI, WANDA MARIA, hospital planner; b. N.Y.C., Apr. 23, 1954; d. Stanislaw and Wanda Alexandra K. B.A. in Sociology, U. Calif.-San Diego, 1975; M.Pub. Policy, U. Calif.-Berkeley, 1978. Asso., Mgmt. Analysis Center, Palo Alto, Calif., 1978-79; dir. planning Peninsula Hosp. Med. Ctr., Burlingame, Calif., 1980—. Bd. dirs. Lowiczanie Folk Dance Ensemble, 1981-82. Mem. No. Calif. Health Care Mktg. Assn., Soc. Hosp. Planning of Am. Hosp. Assn. Office: 1783 El Camino Real Burlingame CA 94010

KOZIAK, JULIAN G.J., Canadian provincial minister; b. Edmonton, Alta., Can., Sept. 16, 1940; s. John H. and Maria (Woytkiw) K.; m. Barbara Lee Melnychuk, Aug. 19, 1961; children—Leanne M., Donald I., Deborah, Susan, Julian P.N. B.A., U. Alta., 1962, LL.B., 1963. Called to Alta. bar; created Queen's Counsel. Ptnr. firm Kosowan & Wachowich, Edmonton, 1964-75; mem. Legis. Assembly, Edmonton-Strathcona, 1971—; minister of edn. Govt. of Alta., 1975-79, minister consumer and corp. affairs, 1979-82, minister mcpl. affairs, 1982—. Mem. Law Soc. Alta. Mem. Progressive Conservative Assn. Ukranian Catholic. Office: 224 Legislature Bldg Edmonton AB T5K 2B6 Canada

KOZIE, DANIEL WALTER, otolaryngologist; b. Chgo., Dec. 29, 1944. S. Daniel Paul and Helen Marie (Biegaj) K.; m. Emily Anne Witt, Sept. 11, 1976; children—Ryan Dane, Adam Timothy. B.S. in Biology, U. Wis., 1967; M.D., Loyola U., Chgo., 1971. Intern, U. Oreg. Hosps., Portland, 1971-72; resident in gen. surgery St. Luke's Hosp., Milw., 1972-73; resident in otolaryngology U. Wash. Hosps., Seattle, 1973-76; practice medicine specializing in otolaryngology, Auburn, Wash., 1978—; mem. staff Auburn Gen. Hosp., Valley Gen. Hosp., Children's Orthopedic Hosp.; clin. instr. otolaryngology U. Wash. Served to maj. USAF, 1976-78. Fellow ACS, Am. Acad. Otolaryngology, Am. Acad. Facial Plastic and Reconstructive Surgery; mem. AMA, Auburn C. of C. Republican. Roman Catholic. Office: 125 3d St NE Suite 201 Auburn WA 98002

KOZLAK, JEANNE BARBARA, nursing educator, consultant, researcher; b. Torrington, Conn., Feb. 6, 1946; d. John Andrew and Mary Elizabeth (Gernat) K. R.N., Grace New Haven Sch. Nursing, 1963-66; B.S., So. Conn. State U., 1972; M.S. in Nursing, Yale U., 1974. Staff nurse Yale-New Haven Hosp., 1966-69; staff nurse Conn. Mental Health Ctr., New Haven, 1969-70; camp nurse Camp Quinnebaug, Danielson, Conn., 1970; staff nurse Conn. Mental Health Ctr., 1971-73; staff nurse Yale Psychiat. Inst., New Haven, 1974-75; assoc. prof. nursing Humboldt State U., Arcata, Calif., 1975—; educator, cons. Coll. Redwoods

Eureka, Calif., 1978—; cons. Butler Valley Inc., Arcata, 1982—. Mem. Humboldt County Mental Health Adv. Bd., 1979-81, vice chmn., 1981-82, chmn., 1982—; bd. dirs. Humboldt County Assn. for Retarded, Eureka, Calif., 1982—. NIMH trainee, 1972-74; Citizen Ambassador, People to People Internat., 1983. Mem. Am. Nurses Assn., Am. Orthopsychiat. Assn., Sigma Theta Tau, Psi Chi. Democrat. Roman Catholic. Author articles in field. Home: C 4564 Valley West Blvd Arcata CA 95521 Office: Humboldt State University Department Nursing Arcata CA 95521

KOZLOFF, JUDITH BONNIE, lawyer; b. St. Louis, Mar. 4, 1926; d. Isador and Ruth (Gould) Friedman; B.S., Northwestern U., 1947; J.D., U. Denver, 1968; m. Lloyd M. Kozloff, June 16, 1947; children—James S., Daniel I., Joseph H., Sarah R. Law clk. Mr. Justice Day, Colo. Supreme Ct., Denver, 1969-70; admitted to Colo. bar, 1969, Calif. bar, 1981; assoc. firm Holland & Hart, Denver, 1970-73; sec., gen. counsel Affiliated Bankshares Colo., Boulder, 1973-78; atty. Mountain States Tel.&Tel. Co., Denver, 1979-80, Pacific Tel.&Tel. Co., San Francisco, 1981—. Recipient award Pacific Telephone Employees for Women's Affirmative Action, 1981. Mem. ABA, Colo. Bar, Calif. Bar Assn. Home: 1750 Grant Ave San Francisco CA 94133 Office: 140 New Montgomery St San Francisco CA 94105

KRACHMAN, HOWARD E(LLIS), engineering executive; b. Phila., June 12, 1938; s. Albert and Sarah (Linetsky) K.; m. Betty A. Gurtoff, Feb. 28, 1974; children—Adam, Gower, Alexis. B.S. in Mech. Engring., Drexel U., 1961; M.S. in Mech. Engring., U. So. Calif., 1967; diploma Von Karman Inst., Brussels, Belgium, 1964. Assoc. engr. Douglas Aircraft Co., Santa Monica, Calif., 1961-63; mem. tech. staff TRW, Redondo Beach, Calif., 1963-70; dir. engring. Developmental Scis. Inc., City of Industry, Calif., 1970—. Von Karman fellow NATO, 1963. Mem. AIAA, ASME, Assn. for Unmanned Vehicle Systems, Pi Tau Sigma, Tau Beta Pi. Office: 15757 E Valley Blvd City of Industry CA 91744

KRAFT, DONALD B., advertising executive; b. Seattle, Mar. 20, 1927; s. Warren Earl and Beulah (Bowman) K.; m. Mary Jo Erickson, Dec. 20, 1973; children—Daniel, Karen, Berkeley, Erika. B.A. in Journalism, U. Wash., Seattle, 1948. Pres. Kraft Advt. Agy., 1948-54; v.p. Honig-Cooper Co., 1954-59; pres. Kraft Smith, Inc., 1959—. Served in U.S. Navy, 1945-46. Mem. Am. Assn. Advt. Agys. (sec.-treas.), Affiliated Advt. Agys. Internat. (internat. pres.). Republican. Methodist. Clubs: Rotary of Seattle (past pres.), Seattle Seafair (past prime minister), Rainier, Athletic, Overlake Golf & Country. Office: 200 1st W Seattle WA 98119

KRAFT, JOHN MICHAEL, research plant pathologist; b. Gary, Ind., July 14, 1938; s. John and Mildred Margarita-Freda (Kuehl) K.; m. Jeanne Whaley, Feb. 1, 1964; children—Christina Marie, David John. B.S., Ariz. State U., 1960; M.S., U. Minn., 1962; Ph.D., U. Calif.-Riverside, 1966. Technician U.S. Forest Service, 1957-58; research asst. U. Minn.-St. Paul, 1960-62; research asst. U. Calif., 1962-66; research plant pathologist Agr. Research Service, U.S. Dept. Agr., 1967-82; supervisory research plant pathologist, research leader, 1982—; assoc. plant pathologist Wash. State U. Mem. Am. Soc. Agronomy, Am. Soc. Plant Pathologists, Nat. Pea Improvement Assn., Sigma Xi, Beta Beta Beta. Home: Route 1 Box 1175 A Grandview WA 98930 Office: IAREC PO Box 30 Prosser WA 99350

KRAGULAC, OLGA GOLUBOVICH, interior designer, consultant; b. St. Louis, Nov. 27, 1937; d. Jovica Todor and Milka (Slijepcevich) Golubovich. A.A., U. Mo., 1958; cert. in design UCLA, 1979. Interior designer William L. Pereira Assocs., Los Angeles, 1977-80; assoc. Reel & Grobman Assocs., Los Angeles, 1980-81; pvt. practice comml. interior design, Los Angeles, 1981-82; assoc. Kaneko & Laff Assocs., Los Angeles, 1982—; design cons. Atlantic Richfield Co., Los Angeles, 1982—; bd. dirs. Self Cleaning Environments, Inc. Mem. Calif. Chamber Symphony Soc. (invitation, ticket com. 1980-81); vol. Proposition 1 Westside Rep. Council, 1971. Recipient Carole Eichen Design award U. Calif., 1979. Mem. Am. Soc. Interior Designers, Inst. Bus. Designers, Phi Chi Theta, Delta Sigma Phi. Republican. Serbian Eastern Orthodox.

KRAHENBIL, KARL, former nursing home exec.; b. Neudorf, Sask., Can., June 8, 1909; s. Rudolf and Dorothy (Volz) K.; student Concordia Coll., Edmonton, Alta., 1924-30, Concordia Sem., St. Louis, 1930-34; m. Theresia Schweitzer, Oct. 11, 1937; children—Marvin, Sylvia Laforme, Dorothy Schuler, Verne, Lois Schlitz, Sharon Herman. Ordained to ministry Lutheran Ch.-Mo. Synod, 1934; minister Luth. Chs., Wordsworth and St. Walburg, Sask., 1934-38; owner hatchery, St. Walburg and Estevan, Sask., 1938-50; minister Luth. Ch., Middle Lake, Sask., 1950-61; chmn. bd. dirs. Bethany Pioneer Village, Middle Lake, 1956-61, exec. dir., 1961-76. Vice pres. Man.-Sask. dist. Luth. Ch.-Mo. Synod, 1952-62. Village councilor, 1940-44; pres. Bd. Trade, 1966-74; chmn. Park Authority, 1967-71, 75—; sch. trustee, 1969-74. Recipient Centennial medal in recognition of valuable service to nation, 1967; Art Sihvon Meml. award for disting. service to elderly of Sask., 1978; Sask. Regional Parks Assn. award, 1982. Mem. Sask. Assn. Housing and Nursing Homes (pres. 1961-63). Editor: The Canadian Lutheran, 1971-77. Address: Box 186 Middle Lake SK Canada

KRAIN, LAWRENCE STIRLING, physician; b. Chgo., Sept. 1, 1942; s. Irving and Sylvia June K.; B.A., Northwestern U., 1962; M.D., U. Ill., 1966; M.P.H., U. Calif., Berkeley, 1969. Asst. clin. investigator Hines (Ill.) VA Hosp., 1963; engaged in cancer research, 1964-69, dermatology research UCLA Med. Center, 1969-70; exec. coordinator Nat. Coop. Clin. Melanoma Project, Harvard Med. Sch., Boston, 1973; chief VD Control Div., City of Chgo., 1974-75; chmn. dept. community medicine Oak Forest (Ill.) Hosp., 1976-77; pres. Lawrence S. Krain, M.D., Anaheim and La Mirada, Calif., 1977—, Psoriasis Control Clinics, Inc., 1979—; co-dir. Prepaid Med. Group, Los Angeles, 1979—; mem. staff Brotman Meml., La Mirada Community, La Habra Community, Garfield and Tustin Community hosps. Served with USNR, 1963-68. Diplomate Am. Bd. Dermatology, Am. Bd. Family Practice, Am. Bd. Preventive Medicine. Democrat. Contbr. articles to profl. jours., chpt. to book. Home: 11728 Wilshire Blvd Los Angeles CA Office: 11860 Wilshire Blvd Los Angeles CA 90025

KRAJEWSKI, JEFFREY JAMES, accountant, financial broker, consultant; b. East Chicago, Ind., Apr. 30, 1957; s. Raymond Joseph and Marie Helen (Almason) K.; m. Cynthia Jean White, Feb. 6, 1982. B.S. in Acctg., Calumet Coll., 1979. Controller Rand McNally & Co., Hammond, Ind., 1977-82; acct., broker, cons. Roy M. Charles & Assocs., P.A., Scottsdale, Ariz., 1982—. Club: K.C. Office: Roy M Charles & Assocs 7204 E Camelback Rd Scottsdale AZ 85251

KRAMER, ANNE PEARCE, writer, communications executive, educator, film company executive; B.A. magna cum laude, U. So. Calif., M.A., 1965, Ph.D., 1972; m. Stanley Kramer (div.); children—Larry David, Casey Lise. Gen. exec. asst. to producer/dir. Stanley Kramer Prodns., prodn. exec., story editor, casting dir., dialogue dir.; sr. lectr. cinema, comparative lit. U. So. Calif., Los Angeles; acting asst. prof. comparative lit. and film Calif. State U.-Long Beach; pres. Cathexis 3, Los Angeles; story editor, v.p. creative affairs Castle Hill Prodns., Inc., Los Angeles, 1978-80; story analyst Columbia Pictures, 1980-81, story editor, 1981—; creative collaborator Clifton Fadiman, Ency. Brit. Films; communications cons. KPFK Radio, govt., other orgns. Bd. dirs. Model UN; expert witness on censorship for Los Angeles Dist. Atty.; nurses aide ARC, Children's Hosp.; former pres. Recovery Found. for Disturbed Children; former ednl. cons., instr. Camarillo State Mental Hosp. Mem. MLA, AAUP, Women in Film, Delta Kappa Alpha, Phi Kappa Phi, Pi Beta Phi. Club: Encino Tennis. Author: Neo-Metamorphoses - A Cyclical Study, Comparative Transormations in Ovidian Myth and Modern Literature, 1972; Interview with Elia Kazan, 1974; Focus on Film and Theatre; co-author: Directors at Work, 1970.

KRAMER, CARVETH HILTON, art director, painter, educator; b. N.Y.C., June 5, 1943; s. Ben and Etta Kramer; m. Ina Saundra, July 5, 1963; children—Darren, Bradley, Tammara. Student Sch. Visual Arts, 1962. Sr. designer Redbook Mag., N.Y.C., 1972-73; art dir. McCall's Mag., N.Y.C., 1973-78, Psychology Today Mag., N.Y.C., 1978-82, Krames Communications, Daly City, Calif., 1982—. Recipient Gold Medal award Soc. Illustrators, N.Y.C., 1982; Gold Medal, Silver Medal award Soc. Publs., Designers award Art Dirs. Club. Mem. Soc. Publs. Designers. Represented in permanent collection Mus. Modern Art, Mus. Salvation Army, N.Y.C. Office: Krames Communications 3215-G Serramonte Plaza Daly City CA 94015

KRAMER, GERALD HOLMES, political science educator; b. Washington, Nov. 6, 1938; s. Alwin D. and Mary (Holmes) K.; m. Marguerite M. Nusslé, July 11, 1960; children—Alan, Eric, Phillip, Marc. B.S., MIT, 1959, Ph.D., 1965. Asst. prof. U. Rochester (N.Y.), 1963-66, assoc. prof., 1966-68; assoc. prof. Yale U., 1968-73, prof., 1973-81; prof. polit sci. Calif. Inst. Tech., Pasadena, 1981—. Ctr. Advanced Studies in Behavioral Scis. fellow, 1973-74. Fellow Am. Acad. Arts and Scis.; mem. Am. Polit. Sci. Assn. (Pi Sigma Alpha award 1968), Econometric Soc., Pub. Choice Soc. (pres. 1978-80). Contbr. articles to profl. jours. Office: Div Humanities and Social Services Calif Inst Tech Pasadena CA 91125

KRAMER, GORDON, mechanical engineer; b. Bklyn., Aug. 1937; s. Joseph and Etta (Grossberg) K.; B.S., Cooper Union, 1959; M.S., Calif. Inst. Tech., 1960; m. Ruth Ellen Harter, Mar. 5, 1967; children—Samuel Maurice, Leah Marie. With Hughes Aircraft Co., Malibu, Calif., 1959-63; sr. scientist Avco Corp., Norman, Okla., 1963-64; asst. div. head Batelle Meml. Inst., Columbus, Ohio, 1964-67; sr. scientist Aerojet Electrosystems, Azusa, Calif., 1967-75; chief engr. Beckman Instrument Co., Fullerton, Calif., 1975-82; prin. scientist McDonnell Douglas Microelectronics Co., 1982-83, Kramer and Assocs., 1983—; cons. Korea Inst. Tech. NSF fellow, 1959-60. Mem. IEEE. Democrat. Jewish. Home: 16141 Malaga Ln Huntington Beach CA 92647 Office: 16141 Malaga Ln Huntington Beach CA 92647

KRAMER, GORDON EDWARD, mfg. co. exec.; b. San Mateo, Calif., June 22, 1946; s. Roy Charles and Bernice Jeanne (Rones) K.; B.S. in Aero. Engring., San Jose State Coll., 1970; m. Christina Hodges, Feb. 14, 1970; children—Roy Charles, Charlena. Purchasing agent Am. Racing Equipment, Brisbane, Calif., 1970-71, asst. to v.p. mktg., 1971-72; founder, pres. Safety Direct Inc., hearing protection equipment, Sparks, Nev., 1972—; dir. Hodges Transp., Condor Inc. Mem. Am. Soc. Safety Engrs., Safety Equipment Distributors Assn., Indsl. Safety Equipment Assn., Nat. Assn. Sporting Goods Wholesalers, Nat. Sporting Goods Assn., Nev. State Amature Trapshooting Assn. (dir. 1978-79), Pacific Internat. Trapshooting Assn. (Nev. pres. 1979-80, 80-81). Republican. Methodist. Club: Rotary. Office: 23 Snider Way Sparks NV 89431

KRAMER, GREGORY KENT, food service administrator; b. Boston, Mar. 8, 1952, s. George William and Dorothy M. (Flynn) K., B.Ed., U. Miami (Fla.)., 1975, M.Ed., 1977. Asst. mgr. Univ. Rathskeller Inc., U. Miami, 1975-77, mgr., 1977-81; dining room mgr. Hialeah and Gulfstream Parks, Fla., 1981—; food service adminstr. Candlestick Park, San Francisco, 1982—; mem. Alcohol Awareness Task Force. Mem. Am. Personnel and Guidance Assn., Am. Coll. Personnel Assn., Nat. Restaurant Assn., Western Restaurant Assn., Assn. Coll. Unions Internat., Nat. Assn. Student Personnel Adminstrs., Order of Omega, Phi Epsilon Kappa, Tau Kappa Epsilon (chpt. advisor, dir.). Roman Catholic. Home: 365 Talbot Ave Apt T-6 Pacifica CA 94044 Office: care Harry M Stevens Inc Candlestick Park San Francisco CA 94126

KRAMER, HENRY HERMAN, chemist; b. N.Y.C., Aug. 19, 1930; s. Henry and Anna Marie (Bendhaak) K.; m. Carol Schlamp, Aug. 16, 1959; children—Paul Henry, Scott David, Pamela Ann. B.A. in Chemistry, Columbia U., 1952, M.A. in Chemistry, 1953; Ph.D. in Phys. Chemistry, Ind. U., 1960. Research scientist Union Carbide Corp., Tuxedo, N.Y., 1960-65, group leader corp. research devel., 1965-67, project mgr. nucleonics research corp. research devel., 1967-73, sr. group leader corp. research and devel., 1973-76, mgr. nuclear product tech. Med. Products div., 1976-78; v.p. research and devel. Medi-Physics, Inc., Emeryville, Calif., 1978—; mem. staff dept. nuclear medicine Johns Hopkins Med. Instns., 1965-66. Served with M.C., AUS, 1953-55. Recipient IR 100 award, 1969, 75. Mem. Am. Chem. Soc., AAAS, Am. Nuclear Soc., N.Y. Acad. Scis., Soc. Nuclear Medicine, Am. Coll. Nuclear Physicians, Atomic Indsl. Forum, Internat. Assn. Radiopharmacology. Republican. Lutheran. Contbr. articles profl. jours. Patentee in field.

KRAMER, JAMES, painter; b. Columbus, Ohio, Oct. 24, 1927; s. James Joseph and Louise (Eireman) K.; m. Barbara Peters, Apr. 11, 1959; children—Susan Kramer Erickson, Joan Kramer Busick. Student Cleve. Sch. Art, 1945-48, Western Res. U., 1948, Ohio State U., 1948-50. Archtl. practice Ohio and Calif., 1950-70; painter, 1970—; exhbns. include: Calif. Arts Club, Am. Watercolor Soc., Mainstreams U.S.A., N.Mex. Mus. Fine Arts, Albuquerque Mus. Fine Art, Artists of Am., Denver, Nat. Acad Western Art, Oklahoma City; condr. workshops and demonstrations in watercolor. Recipient Robert Wolfe Meml. prize Columbus Gallery of Fine Arts, 1949; 2d and 3d prizes Monterey County Fine Arts Exhibit, 1968-69; Best of Show and Popular prize Mother Lode Nat. Art Exhibit, 1972; Gold medal Calif. Art Club, 1973, Silver medal, 1974. Mem. Nat. Acad. Western Art. Reviewed in numerous profl jours. Address: Santa Fe NM 87501

KRAMER, JOHN KARL, forensic diagnostician; b. Bedford, Ind., Dec. 2, 1947; s. William Russell and Florence Eva (Black) K.; m. Jan Camalita Strange, Oct. 9, 1982. B.A., Hanover Coll., 1972; M.S., Butler U., 1974; Ed.D., U. No. Colo., 1978. Behavioral therapist maximum security Central State Hosp., Indpls., 1972-75; dir. Jefferson County Diagnostic Unit, Lakewood, Colo., 1978—. Mem. Am. Psychol. Assn., Am. Personnel and Guidance Assn., Colo. Assn. Probation Officers, Colo. Juvenile Council. Office: Jefferson County Diagnostic Unit 7675 W 14th Ave Lakewood CO 80215

KRAMER, MARVIN LEWIS, communications and computers consultant; b. Cleve., Jan. 16, 1931; s. Edward Aaron and Alma Zoe (Gaskill) K.; m. Edith Mae Nash, Nov. 25, 1949; children—Stuart C., Gregory B., Mark H. B.S. in Chemistry, George Washington U., 1951, postgrad., 1951-52; M.S. in Elec. Engring., U. Ill., 1963. Lic. comml. balloon pilot, FAA. Commd. lt. U.S. Air Force, 1952; advanced through grades to col., 1972; dep. dir. communications SAC, Offutt AFB, Nebr., 1973-75; vice comdr. Strategic Communication Area, Offutt AFB, 1975-77; dir. communications NORAD, Peterson AFB, Colo., 1977-79, dep. comdr. for strategic def. forces, 1979-80; ret., 1980; pvt. practice communication, computer, command and control cons., Colorado Springs, Colo., 1980—. Decorated Bronze Star, Meritorious Service medal, Legion of Merit with oak leaf cluster. Mem. IEEE, Eta Kappa Nu, Alpha Chi Sigma. Jewish. Lodge: Elks. Home and Office: 1030 Doyle Pl Colorado Springs CO 80915

KRAMER, MARY EVERIST, orthoptist; b. Bancroft, Iowa, Dec. 12, 1911; d. Francis Joseph and Gertrude Antoinette (Budde) K.; grad. St. Joseph's Sch. Nursing, Sioux City, Iowa, 1933; student Iowa U., 1936, George Washington U. Sch. Medicine, 1939-42; m. William Perry Reeves, Jan., 1939. Instr. orthoptics George Washington U. Sch. Medicine, 1944-53; orthoptics cons. Am. Optical Co., Southbridge, Mass., 1952-55; med. orthoptist Ophthalmic Lab., Phoenix, 1956—. Mem. Am. Assn. Cert. Orthoptists. Roman Catholic. Author: Clinical Orthoptics, 1949, 2d edit., 1953. Home: 24 E Hanover St Phoenix AZ 85014 Office: 323 Park Central N Med Bldg 555 W Catalina Dr Phoenix AZ 85013

KRANC, LISA RACHEL, marketing executive; b. Bklyn., Sept. 19, 1953; d. Sam and Sara Deborah (Korcarz) K. A.B. cum laude in Am. Studies, Brandeis U., 1975; M.B.A., Columbia U., 1977. Brand asst. Clorox Co., Oakland, Calif., 1977-79, asst. brand mgr., 1979-80, brand mgr., 1980—. Co-chmn. Brandeis U. Alumni Admissions Council; mem. Nat. Abortion Rights Action League. Jewish. Home: 1645 Filbert St Apt 203 San Francisco CA 94123 Office: PO Box 24305 Oakland CA 94623

KRANNICH, RICHARD STEPHEN, sociology educator, consultant; b. Akron, Ohio, Feb. 6, 1952; s. Eugene Albert and Dorothy Eileen (Leach) K.; m. Marilyn Kay, May 17, 1975; 1 son, Jesse Michael. Student Mich. State U., 1970-72; B.A. in Sociology, Kent State U., 1974; M.S., Utah State U., 1976; Ph.D., Pa. State U., 1980. Instr. sociology Pa. State U., 1978-80; asst. prof. sociology Utah State U., 1980-83, assoc. prof., 1983—. Cons. on social impacts of grazing mgmt. proposal for Schell Resource Area, Nev. Bur. of Land Mgmt., Bio/West, Inc., 1981-82. NSF research fellow, 1977-80; Utah Agrl. Expt. Sta. grantee, 1981-84, 82-85. Mem. Am. Sociol. Assn., Rural Sociol. Soc., Utah Sociol. Soc. Contbr. articles to profl. jours. Home: 350 Panoramic Dr Hyrum UT 84319 Office: Dept Sociology Utah State U Logan UT 84322

KRANTZ, IRWIN WILLIAM, business executive; b. Bklyn., Aug. 1, 1926; s. Jacob and Rose (Bernstein) K.; m. Esther Berger, June 20, 1948; children—Ellen, Robert. B.S. in Indsl. and Labor Relations, Cornell U., 1948; M.A. in Econs., UCLA, 1950; accredited personnel exec. Research technician Calif. Dept. Indsl. Relations, San Francisco, 1949-50; personnel asst., labor relations rep. Am. Airlines, N.Y.C., 1951-58; mgr. personnel adminstrn. plastics div. Mobil Chem. Co., 1959-62, div. mgr. employee relations, Macedon, N.Y., 1962-69, co. mgr. employee relations, N.Y.C., 1969-71; v.p. employee relations Potlach Corp., San Francisco, 1972—; adv. dir. Blue Cross of Calif. Served as aviation cadet USAF, 1945; to 2d lt. USAFR, 1950-51; Korea. Mem. Am. Soc. Personnel Adminstrs. Contbr. articles to profl. jours. Office: PO Box 3591 San Francisco CA 94119

KRANZ, THOMAS FRANCIS, lawyer; b. Los Angeles, Mar. 18, 1939; s. Frank George and Eileen (Savage) K.; A.B., Stanford U., 1959; LL.D., U. Calif., Berkeley, 1964; M.A., UCLA, 1973; m. Travis Barton; children—Alexander Barton, Francis Elliott. Admitted to Calif. bar, 1965, U.S. Supreme Ct. bar, 1971; dep. public defender Los Angeles County, 1966-68; mem. firm Alexander, Inman and Fine, Los Angeles, 1968-71, partner firm, 1972-75; spl. counsel and dep. dist. atty. Los Angeles County, 1975-76; partner firm Alexander, Inman, Tanzer & Wedemeyer, Beverly Hills, Calif., 1977—. Chmn. community adv. bd. Sta. KCET, Public TV, Los Angeles, 1979-81; trustee Calif. Inst. Arts, Valencia, Calif., 1980-82; v.p. Los Angeles Master Chorale, Los Angeles Music Center, 1979-81; mem. Los Angeles County Economy and Efficiency Commn., 1979-82; mem. 1984 Olympics Citizens Adv. Com., Los Angeles. Served with U.S. Navy, 1959-61. Mem. Los Angeles County Bar Assn., State Bar Calif. Roman Catholic.

KRASNER, OSCAR JAY, educator; b. St. Louis, Dec. 3, 1922; s. Benjamin and Rose (Persov) K.; B.S. in Public Adminstrn., Washington U., St. Louis, 1943; M.A. in Mgmt. with honors, U. Chgo., 1950; M.S. in Quantitative Bus. Analysis, U. So. Calif., 1965, D.B.A. in Mgmt., 1969; m. Bonnie Kidder, June 1, 1944; children—Bruce Howard, Glenn Evan, Scott Allan, Steve Leland, Michael Shawn, Bettina Jeanine. Mem. staff Exec. Office of Sec., U.S. Dept. Navy, 1944-56; supervising cons. Bus. Research Corp., Chgo., 1956-57; mem. staff flight propulsion div. Gen. Electric Co., Cin., 1957-61, mgr. VTOL project planning, 1959-61; exec. adviser long range planning space div. N.Am. Rockwell Corp., Downey, Calif., 1962-64, dir. tech. resources analysis exec. offices, 1964-70; pres. Solid State Tech. Corp. Calif., 1968-70; prof. mgmt. Pepperdine U., Los Angeles, 1970—; pres. Rensark Assos., 1976—; cons. Active community orgns.; bd. dirs. Long Beach (Calif.) Jewish Community Center, 1969-70. Served with Anti-Aircraft, AUS, 1942-44. Mem. Am. Acad. Mgmt., M.B.A. Internat. (chmn. 1976-77), AIAA, AAAS, World Future Soc., Assn. Venture Founders (bd. govs.), Beta Gamma Sigma. Home: 4709 Autry Ave Long Beach CA 90808 Office: 3415 Sepulveda Blvd Los Angeles CA 90034

KRASNOV, VLADISLAV GEORGIEVICH, educator; b. Perm, USSR, Feb. 24, 1937; came to U.S., 1965, naturalized, 1976; s. George and Ekaterina (Lykhin) K.; grad. Moscow U., 1960; M.A., U. Wash., 1968, Ph.D., 1974; m. Hiroko Tsuzuki, Dec. 14, 1970; children—Vera Carina, George Eric. Instr., U. Tex., Austin, 1971-74; asst. prof. So. Meth. U., Dallas, 1974-78; assoc. prof., head of Russian studies Monterey (Calif.) Inst. Internat. Studies, 1978—; assoc. Hoover Inst., Stanford, 1978—, vis. scholar, 1982-83; lectr. U. Lund (Sweden), 1963-65; postdoctoral fellow U. Chgo., 1966; vis. prof. Hokkaido U., Sapporo, Japan, 1980-81. Mem. Am. Assn. Advancement Slavic Studies, Am. Assn. Tchrs. Slavic and East European Langs., Assn. Russian-Am. Scholars, Delta Tau Kappa. Author: Solzhenitsyn and Dostoevsky, 1980. Contbr. articles to profl. publs. Office: Monterey Institute of International Studies 425 Van Buren St Monterey CA 93940

KRASNOW, DAVID, optometrist; b. Worcester, Mass., Sept. 8, 1947; s. Leonard and Helen K. B.A. in Biology, La Verne Coll., 1969; B.Sc. in Physiol. Optics, Los Angeles Coll. Optometry, 1971; O.D., So. Calif. Coll. Optometry, 1973; postgrad. U. So. Calif., 1972-74. Practice optometry, Los Angeles, 1973—; pres., mng. dir. London/Pacific Trading Co., Los Angeles and London, 1977—; cons., lectr. Capricon Lens Co. Ltd., London; lectr. Am. Hydron, N.Y.C.; mem. faculty Pa. Coll. Optometry; clin. investigator Igel Optics, London. Recipient Mayor's award City Los Angeles, 1972; named to Outstanding Young Men Am., U.S. Jaycees, 1980; cert. community coll. tchr., Calif. Fellow Am. Acad. Optometry. Office: 11850 Wilshire Blvd Suite 102 Los Angeles CA 90049

KRATZBERG, GEORGIA CLAUDINE, home economics educator; b. Hutsonville, Ill., May 13, 1932; d. George Dewey and Sarah Helen (Mayfield) Kratzberg. B.S. in Home Econs., Wheaton Coll., 1955; M. Home Econs., Oreg. State U., 1963. Tchr. home econs. Parma (Idaho) High Sch., 1953-57, Eagle Valley High Sch., Richland, Oreg., 1957, Medford (Oreg.) Sr. High Sch., 1958-61; faculty home econs. Clark Community Coll., Vancouver, Wash., 1962-64; faculty, dept. chmn. home econs. U. Puget Sound, Tacoma, 1964-76; assoc. prof., dir. home econs. George Fox Coll., Newberg, Oreg., 1976—. Kellogg Found. fellow, 1977, 80. Mem. Am. Home Econs. Assn., Oreg. Home Econs. Assn., Nat. Council Adminstrs. Home Econs., Home Econs. Edn. Assn., Oreg. Nutrition Council, Newberg Viewfinders, Delta Kappa Gamma. Republican. Baptist. Reviser Food Study Manual (by Helen Charley), 2d edit., 1978. Office: George Fox Coll 414 N Meridian St Newberg OR 97132

KRAUS, JAMES LEROY, tax consultant; b. Breckenridge, Minn., July 16, 1940; s. Glen and Lorraine (Stai) K.; m. Dorcas Evelyn Evans, June 18, 1966; children—James Everett, Jerri Lynn. Student U. N.D., 1961, LaSalle Ext. U., 1964-67. Asst. gen. mgr. Dakota Tastee-Freez Inc., Carrington, N.D., 1962-64; counselor Hanna Boys Ctr., Sonoma, Calif., 1964-65; acct. Trask & Squier, San Francisco, 1965-66; treas., controller Seaboard Paper Co., San Francisco, 1966-75; div. controller Graphic Arts div. Bell Industries, Sunnyvale, Calif., 1975-76; owner James Kraus, Tax Cons., Ukiah, Calif., 1977—. Bd. dirs. Vigilantia, Inc., 1975-79. Served with USN, 1958-61. Named Lion of Yr., Mendocino Lions, 1979, 80. Mem. Nat. Inst. Credit (nat. dir.), Nat. Assn. Credit and Fin. Mgmt., Shalom Arabian Horse Assn. Republican. Roman Catholic. Clubs: Lake Mendocino Lions, Commonwealth, San Francisco Comml., Elks. Address: 684 Orchard Ave Ukiah CA 95482

KRAUS, JEFFREY MILES, safety engineer; b. Los Angeles, Feb. 3, 1953; s. Samuel and Naomi (Cholden) K. B.S., Calif. State U.-Northridge, 1975. Cert. safety profl.; registered sanitarian. Loss control rep. Fireman's Fund Ins. Co., Los Angeles, 1976-79; loss prevention specialist Gt. Am. Ins. Co., Los Angeles, 1979-80; dir. safety services Bayly, Martin and Fay, Inc., Los Angeles, 1980—. Mem. Contract Services Adminstrn. Trust Fund, Calif. State Hazardous Waste Site Inspection Com. Mem. Am. Soc. Safety Engrs., Am. Indsl. Hygiene Assn., Nat. Fire Protection Assn., Assn. Gen. Contractors, Calif. Environ. Health Assn. Home: 1343 19th St #1 Santa Monica CA 90404 Office: 3200 Wilshire Blvd Los Angeles CA 90010

KRAUS, PANSY DAEGLING, editor; b. Santa Paula, Calif., Sept. 21, 1916; d. Arthur David and Elsie (Pardee) Daegling; A.A., San Bernardino Valley Jr. Coll., 1938; student Longmeyer's Bus. Coll., 1940; grad. gemologist diploma Gemological Assn. Gt. Britain, 1960, Gemological Inst. Am., 1966; m. Charles Frederick Kraus, Mar. 1, 1941 (div. Nov. 1961). Clk., Convair, San Diego, 1943-48; clk. San Diego County Schs. Publs., 1948-57; mgr. Rogers and Boblet Art-Craft, San Diego, 1958-64; part-time editorial asst. Lapidary Jour., San Diego, 1963-64, assoc. editor, 1964-69, editor, 1970—; lectr. gems, gemology local gem, mineral groups; gem & mineral club bull. editor groups. Mem. San Diego Mineral & Gem Soc., Gemol. Soc. San Diego, Gemol. Assn. Great Britain, Mineral. Soc. Am., Epsilon Sigma Alpha. Editor, layout dir.; Gem. Cutting Shop Helps, 1964; The Fundamentals of Gemstone Carving, 1967; Appalachian Mineral and Gem Trails, 1968; Practical Gem Knowledge for the Amateur, 1969; Southwest Mineral and Gem Trails, 1972; revision editor Gemcraft (Quick and Leiper), 1977; contbr. articles to Lapidary Jour. Home: 6127 Mohler St San Diego CA 92120 Office: 3564 Kettner Blvd San Diego CA 92101

KRAUS, WILLIAM HOWARD, city manager; b. Cleve., Nov. 9, 1938; s. Howard George and Gaynor Butler K.; m. Barbara Jane Saujkowsky, Aug. 31, 1941; children—Jennifer Anne, Jeffery William, Jonathan Scott; B.A., U. Calif.-Riverside, 1960; M.P.A., U. So. Calif., 1967; M.A., Occidental Coll., 1970; D.P.A., U. So. Calif., 1975. Asst. city mgr. Redlands (Calif.), 1964-67; city mgr. Beaumont (Calif.), 1967-69, Los Alamitos (Calif.), 1969-73; city adminstr. Norwalk (Calif.), 1973—; prof. Calif. State U.-Long Beach, Calif. State Coll.-Fullerton, part-time 1974—. Served with USNR, 1962-64. Coro Found. intern, 1960-61. Mem. Am. Soc. Pub. Adminstrn. (pres. chpt. 1981), Internat. City Mgmt. Assn., Western Govtl. Research Assn. Democrat. Club: Rotary. Assoc. editor Critique, 1976—.

KRAUSE, ERNST HENRY, aerospace industry consultant; b. Milw., May 2, 1913; s. Ernst and Martha (Strege) K.; m. Constance Fraser, June 29, 1939 (dec. Nov. 1972); children—Margaret Bird McCormick, Katharine Louise, Carol Marjorie, Susan Fraser; m. 2d, Betty Lou Davis, Apr. 7, 1974. B.S. in Elec. Engring., U. Wis., 1934, M.S. in Physics, 1935, Ph.D. in Physics, 1938. With Naval Research Lab., Washington, 1938-54, assoc. dir. research, 1951-54; dir. research Lockheed Aircraft Corp., Van Nuys, Calif., 1954-55; pres., chmn. Systems Research Corp., Van Nuys, 1955-56; v.p., dir. Aeronutronic Systems, Inc., 1956-59; dir. tech. staff Aeronutronic div. Ford Motor Co., 1959-62; with Aerospace Corp., El Segundo, Calif., 1962—, sr. v.p. devel., 1968-78, mgmt. and tech. cons., 1978—. Pres. World Affairs Council of Inland So. Calif., 1968-69. Recipient Disting. Civilian Service award USN, 1956. Fellow Am. Phys. Soc., AIAA (assoc.); mem. Sigma Xi, Tau Beta Pi. Home: 1919 Glenwood Ln Newport Beach CA 92660

KRAUSE, MARCELLA ELIZABETH MASON (MRS. EUGENE FITCH KRAUSE), educator; b. Norfolk, Nebr.; d. James Haskell and Elizabeth (Vader) Mason; B.S., U. Neb., 1934; M.A., Columbia, 1938; postgrad. summers U. Calif. at Berkeley, 1950, 51, 65, Stanford, 1964, Creighton U., 1966, Chico (Calif.) State U., 1967; m. Eugene Fitch Krause, June 1, 1945; 1 dau., Kathryn Elizabeth. Tchr., Royal (Nebr.) pub. schs., 1930-32, Hardy (Nebr.) pub. schs., 1933-35, Omaha pub. schs., 1935-37, Lincoln Sch. of Tchrs. Coll., Columbia, 1937-38, Florence (Ala.) State Tchrs. Coll., summer 1938, Tchrs. Coll., U. Nebr., 1938-42, Corpus Christi (Tex.) pub. schs., 1942-45, Oakland (Calif.) pub. schs., 1945-83. Bd. dirs. U. Nebr. Womens Faculty Club, 1940-42; mem. Nebr. State Tchrs. Conv. Panel, 1940-; mem. U. Nebr. Reading Inst., 1940; speaker Iowa State Tchrs. Conv., 1941; reading speaker Nebr. State Tchrs. conv., 1941; lectr. Johnson County Tchrs. Inst., 1942; chmn. Reading Survey Corpus Christi pub. schs., 1943; chmn. Inservice Reading Meetings Oakland pub. schs., 1948-57. Mem. Gov.'s Adv. Commn. on Status Women Conf., San Francisco, 1966; service worker ARC, Am. Cancer Soc., United Crusade, Oakland CD; Republican precinct capt., 1964—; v.p. Oakland Fedn. Rep. Women. Ford Found. Fund for Advancement Edn. fellow, 1955-56; scholar Stanford, 1964; Calif. Congress PTA scholar U. Calif., 1965. Mem. Nat. Council Women, AAUW (dir.), Calif. Tchrs. Assn., Oakland Mus. Assn., Ladies Grand Army Republic, 1960 Ruth Assn., Martha Assn. (pres. East Bay chpt. 1979), Sierra DAR (regent), Eastbay DAR Regents Assn. (pres.), Nebr. Alumni Assn., Grand Lake Bus. and Profl. Women, Internat. Platform Assn., Eastbay Past Matrons Assn., P.E.O., Pi Lambda Theta (pres. No. Calif. chpt.), Alpha Delta Kappa. Methodist. Mem. Order Eastern Star (past matron). Contbr. articles to profl. jours. Home: 5615 Estates Dr Oakland CA 94618

KRAUSS, GEORGE, educator; b. Phila., May 14, 1933; s. George (dec.) and Bertha (Reichelt) K.; B.S. in Metall. Engring., Lehigh U., 1955; M.S., Mass. Inst. Tech., 1958, Sc.D., 1961; m. Ruth A. Oeste, Sept. 10, 1960; children—Matthew, Jonathan, Benjamin, Thomas. Metallurgist Superior Tube Co., Collegeville, Pa., 1956-63; prof. metallurgy and materials sci. Lehigh U., Bethlehem, Pa., 1963-75; Amax Found. prof. phys. metallurgy Colo. Sch. Mines, Golden, 1975—. Metall. cons. to various firms, 1965—. Recipient NSF Postdoctoral fellowship, Max Planck Inst. Fur Eisenforschung, 1962-63. Registered profl. engr., Colo., Pa. Fellow Am. Soc. Metals; mem. Am. Inst. Metall. Engrs., Electron Microscopy Soc. Am., AIME, Sigma Xi. Author: Principles of Heat Treatment of Steel, 1980. Contbr. numerous articles to profl. jours. Home: 3807 S Ridge Rd Evergreen CO 80439 Office: Metall Engring Dept Colo Sch of Mines Golden CO 80401

KRAUSS, MICHAEL EDWARD, linguist; b. Cleve., Aug. 15, 1934; s. Lester W. and Ethel (Sklarsky) K.; m. Jane Lowell, Feb. 16, 1962; children—Ethan, Alexandra, Isaac. B.A., U. Chgo., 1953; B.A., Case Western Res. U., 1954; M.A., Columbia U., 1955; Cert., U. Paris, 1956; postgrad. Dublin Inst. for Advanced Studies, 1956-57; Ph.D., Harvard U., 1959; postgrad. U. Iceland, 1959-60. Prof. Linguistics U. Alaska, Fairbanks, 1960—; vis. prof. linguistics MIT, Cambridge, Mass., 1969-70. Author books and articles on Alaskan Indian and Eskimo langs. Address: Alaska Native Language Center Univ Alaska Fairbanks AK 99701

KRAUTER, LAURENCE GALE, mechanical design educator; b. Dickinson, N.D., Sept. 23, 1941; s. John J. and Gladys Helen (Ouellette) K.; m. Pamela Jean Kelly, Jan. 14, 1977; children—Lance, Jeffrey, Crystal, Matthew. B.A., San Jose State Coll., 1970, M.A., 1971. Research librarian H.M. Gousha Map Co., San Jose, Calif., 1964-66; designer Gen. Electric Co., San Jose, Calif., 1966-72; supr. design/drafting dept. Aeroject Corp., Marine Facility, Tacoma, 1972-74; instr. mech. design Clover Park Vocat. Tech. Inst., Lakewood, Wash., 1974—. Served with AUS, 1961-63. Mem. Am. Vocat. Assn., Wash. Edn. Assn. Roman Catholic. Home: 433 Buena Vista Fircrest WA 98466 Office: 4500 Steilacoom Blvd SW Tacoma WA 98499

KRAVITZ, ELLEN KING, music educator; b. Fords, N.J., May 25, 1929; d. Walter J. and Frances M. (Prybylowski) Kokowicz; B.A., Georgian Ct. Coll., 1964; M.M., U. So. Calif., 1966, Ph.D., 1970; m. Hilard L. Kravitz, Jan. 9, 1972; stepchildren—Kent, Kerry, Jay. Tchr. 7th and 8th grade music Mt. St. Mary Acad., North Plainfield, N.J., 1949-50; cloistered nun Carmelite Monastery, Lafayette, La., 1950-61; instr. Loyola U., Los Angeles, 1967; asst. prof. music Calif. State U., Los Angeles, 1967-71, assoc. prof., 1971-74, prof., 1974—, founder Friends of Music, 1976; mem. Schoenberg Centennial Com., 1974; assoc. Los Angeles Music Center, Seattle Wagner Festival; guest lectr., 1969—. Recipient award for masters thesis U. So. Calif., 1966. Mem. Am. Musicol. Soc., Los Angeles County Museum of Art, Roy Harris Soc., Friends of Arnold Schoenberg Inst., Mu Phi Epsilon, Pi Kappa Lambda. Editorial bd. Jour. Arnold Schoenberg Inst., Los Angeles, jour. editor Vol. I, No. 3, 1977, Vol. II, No. 3 (Schoenberg as Artist), 1978; co-author: Catalog of Schoenberg's Paintings, Drawings, and Sketches. Home: 402 Doheny Rd Beverly Hills CA 90210 Office: Calif State U Los Angeles 5151 State University Dr Los Angeles CA 90032

KRAVITZ, JOSEPH HENRY, geologist, government agency official; b. Nanticoke, Pa., Aug. 14, 1935; s. Joseph Henry and Julia Gertrude (Zimniski) K.; B.S. in Geology, Syracuse U., 1957; M.S. in Geology, George Washington U., 1975, M.Phil. in Geology, 1977, Ph.D. in Geology, 1983; m. Prudence Ann Bullock, Nov. 27, 1965; children—Joseph Henry III, Jonathan James. Research asst. dept. geology Yale, New Haven, 1961-64; research geologist Lamont Geol. Obs. of Columbia U., Palisades, N.Y., 1964-65; oceanographer Naval Oceanographic Office, Washington, 1965-71, head geol. lab., 1971-77, head oceanographic labs., 1977-78; sr. geologist Outer Continental Shelf Environ. Assessment Program, NOAA, Boulder, Colo., 1978-80, dir. marine ecosystems analysis div., 1980-81; sr. staff scientist office Marine Pollution Assessment, NOAA, Rockville, Md., 1982—; research asso. Inst. of Arctic and Alpine Research, U. Colo., 1981—; pres. Exploration Assocs. Ltd., 1981—; mem. sedimentation com. Water Resources Council, U.S., 1968-69; mem. Am. Oceanographic expedition Kara Sea, 1965; chief scientist Ocean Bottom Survey, Kane Basin, 1969. Served as 1st lt., USAF, 1957-60. Fellow Arctic Inst. N.Am., Geol. Soc. Am.; mem. Am. Inst. Profl. Geologists, Research Soc. Am. (chmn. Kaminski award com. Washington chpt. 1972), Soc. Econ. Paleontologists and Mineralogists, Delta Kappa Epsilon. Republican. Roman Catholic. Club: Explorers. Contbr. numerous articles to profl. jours. Pioneer in ocean bottom photography No. Barents Sea, 1966. Home: 91 Spyglass Dr Littleton CO 80123 Office: NOAA Rockville MD 20852

KRAVITZ, STEVEN HUGH, public relations specialist; b. Charleston, W.Va., Feb. 2, 1953; s. Louis Jacob and Hilda B. (Dennis) K.; B.A. with honors in Journalism and Govt., U. Ariz., 1974, postgrad. 1974-76. News and feature reporter Charleston (W.Va.) Gazette, 1976-78; staff asst. Mayor's Office of Fed.-State Programs, Charleston, 1978-79, staff assoc., 1979-80, sr. staff assoc., 1980-81; dir. communications United Way of Greater Tucson, 1981—; (chmn. bd. dirs. Tucson Community Cable Corp., 1983—; mem. Tucson Cable Communications Adv. Commn., 1982-83. Mem. communications com. United Way, Charleston, 1979-81; mem. exec. com. Job Corps Community Relations Council, Charleston, 1978-81. Recipient Eugene Pulliam Journalism scholarship, 1972-74. Mem. Pub. Relations Soc. Am. (v.p. So. Ariz. chpt.), Tucson Press Club (bd. dirs., orchid award 1981). Jewish.

KRCMAR, JANET A. DIXON (MRS. LUDWIG LEOPOLD KRCMAR IV), librarian; b. Morehead, Minn., June 9, 1936; d. Minet Lafayne and Anabel (Lee) Dixon; B.A., Los Angeles State Coll., 1955; D.Litt. (hon.), Hamilton State U., 1973; m. James Columbus Adams, Aug. 16, 1954 (div. Sept. 1961); children—Kirk, Corey, Kimberleigh, Nancie; m. 2d, Ludwig Leopold Krcmar IV, Dec. 27, 1964. Dir. Tanglewood Sch. for Girls, Canoga Park, Calif., 1956-58; librarian Riker Labs., Northridge, Calif., 1958-62; head librarian Thompson-Ramo-Wooldridge, Canoga Park, 1962-64, Bunker-Ramo Corp., Canoga Park, 1964—. Mem. Los Angeles City Schs. Career Guidance Bd., 1965-68; project chmn. Calif. Industry-Edn. Bd., 1966-68; pres. San Fernando Council Industry-Edn., 1970; sec.-treas. Los Angeles County Industry-Edn. Council, 1971-73, Calif. State exec. bd., 1976-79. Master adv. com. Los Angeles Trade Tech. Coll., 1966-77, Los Angeles Valley Coll., 1973-78. Mem. Am. Soc. for Info. Sci. (publs. chmn. 1966-72, pres. 1973, nat. awards chmn. 1976-77, nat. councilor-at-large 1978-80), Spl. Libraries Assn. (sci. tech. chmn. 1967-69, pres. 1977), Am., Calif. library assns., Assn. of Computing Machinery, Simi Valley Art Assn. (pres. 1976), Am. Fedn. of Minerologists, Phi Delta Phi, Alpha Psi Omega, Mu Phi Epsilon. Club: Sierra. Home: 1529 Kane Ave Simi CA 93065 Office: Arete Assocs 5445 Balboa Blvd Encino CA 91316

KREBILL, GERALD WAYNE, electronics company marketing executive; b. Montrose, Iowa, June 21, 1938; s. Roy William and Hilda Marie (Anderson) K.; m. Margaret Anne Rupert, Mar. 29, 1940; children—Michael Wayne, Gregory Todd, Bradley Dean, Staci Lynn. B.A., U. No. Iowa, 1960; M.B.A., Pa. State U.-Capital Campus, 1970. Tech. writer Bendix Corp., Davenport, Iowa, 1963-65; product mgr. McCoy Electronics, Mt. Holly Springs, Pa., 1965-70; div. sales mgr. TRW, Burlington, Iowa, 1970-73; field account mgr. TRW, Waltham, Mass., 1973-77; div. sales mgr. Dale Electronics, Norfolk, Nebr., 1977-81; dir. mktg. Ultronix, Grand Junction, Colo., 1982—. Republican. Mem. Christian Ch. Club: Masons. Office: PO Box 1090 Grand Junction CO 81502

KREBS, WILLIAM NELSON, geologist; b. Santa Monica, Calif., Sept. 4, 1948; s. Adolph and Jeanne D. (Nelson) K.; student Santa Monica City Coll., 1966-67; B.S. in Geology, UCLA, 1970; Ph.D., U. Calif., Davis, 1977. Research asst. U. Calif., Davis, 1971-73, teaching asst. gen. and hist. geology, 1974-77; micropaleontologist Amoco Prodn. Co. Denver, 1978—. Recipient Antarctic Service medal, 1979. Mem. Paleontol. Soc. Am., Soc. of Econ. Paleontologists and Mineralogists, L'Alliance Francaise, Hist. Denver, Friends of Mozart, Sigma Xi. Republican. Contbr. articles on Antarctic marine diatom ecology, micropaleontology, lacustrine diatom micropaleontology to sci. jours. Home: 1321 E 10th Ave Apt 9 Denver CO 80218 Office: Amoco Prodn Co Amoco Bldg Denver CO 80202

KREDITOR, ALAN, urban, regional planner, educator; b. N.Y.C., May 2, 1936; s. Maurice and Rachel (Baron) K.; B.Arch., Pratt Inst., 1959; M. City Planning, U. Pa., 1961; diploma in Engring. (hon.), U. Mex., 1973; m. Marcia Francine Green, June 14, 1959; children—Juliet Tamar, Eoin Lyle, Garrett Paul, Claudia Marya. Chief project planner Boston Redevel. Authority, 1961-63; pres. African Area Affiliates and Am. Assistance Group, Boston, 1962-64; dir. planning Worcester (Mass.) Redevel. Authority, 1963-64; UN adv. to rep. of Ireland and vis. lectr. U. Coll. Dublin, 1964-66; mem. faculty Sch. Urban and Regional Planning, U. So. Calif., Los Angeles, 1966—, dir., 1970-76, asso. dean Center Public Affairs, 1974-76, dir. environ. lab. Gerentology Center, 1974-76, coordinator coastal zone mgmt. U. So. Calif. Sea Grant Program, 1976—, dean Sch. Urban and Regional Planning, 1982—; cons., adv. Irvine Co., TRW, Westinghouse Corp., State of Mex., Emirate of Bahrain. Research grantee HEW, HUD, U.S. Dept. Transp., State of Calif., Ford Found., Nat. Endowment for the Arts. Mem. Am. Planning Assn. (nat. edn. devel. com. 1978—), Am. Inst. Certified Planners (gov. 1975-78), Regional Sci. Assn., Internat. Assn. Urban and Regional Research and Edn., AAUP. Democrat. Episcopalian. Contbr. articles, monographs, reports to profl. jours. Home: 888 Winston Ave San Marino CA 91108 Office: VKC 351 U Park U So Calif Los Angeles CA 90089

KREFTING, PAUL ANTHONY, foreign trade executive; b. Seattle, Oct. 4, 1946; s. Albert Roland and Artance Elizabeth (Nyberg) K.; m. Judith Lee Scott, Aug. 19, 1967; children—Sonja Jean, Adam Paul. B.A. with high honor, Calif. State U.-Los Angeles, 1968; M.A., U. Wash., 1972. Pre-doctoral teaching assoc. U. Wash., 1968-72; co-founder, v.p., chmn. bd. China Products N.W. Inc., Seattle, 1972—. Bd. dirs. Wash. State China Relations Council. Mem. Phi Kappa Phi. Club: Seattle World Trade (bd. dirs., sec. 1981-82). Home: 17164 30th Ave NE Seattle WA 98155 Office: 9750 3d Ave NE Seattle WA 98115

KREIDLER, MYRON (MIKE) BRADFORD, optometrist, state representative; b. Tacoma, Sept. 28, 1943; s. Lyell Chandler and Bendicta (Leland) K.; m. Lela A. Lopez, June 10, 1967; children—Kelli, Michael, Lora. B.S., Pacific U., 1967, D. Optometry, 1969; M.P.H., UCLA, 1972. Optometrist Group Health Cooperative of the Puget Sound, Olympia, Wash., 1972—; dir. First Community Bank, Lacey, Wash., 1979—. Bd. dirs. N. Thurston Sch. Dist., 1973-77; Democratic state rep. 22nd dist. Wash., 1977—; mem. Wash. State Centennial Commn., 1982—; mem. human services com. Nat. Conf. State Legislators, 1981—. Named Legislator of Yr., Alliance for Children, Youth and Families, 1983. Mem. Am. Optometric Assn., Am. Acad. Optometry. Mem. United Ch. Christ. Clubs: Rotary, Elks, Masons. Home: 129 San Mar Dr NE Olympia WA 98506

KREIGER, BRUCE DENNIS, lawyer; b. N.Y.C., Dec. 9, 1943; s. Sam and Sylvia (Stern) K.; B.A., City U. N.Y., 1965; M.B.A. (fellow), U. Calif., Berkeley, 1968, J.D., San Francisco, 1971; m. Lin Falk, Jan. 12, 1975; 1 son, David Aaron. Admitted to Calif. bar, 1972; law clk. U.S. Atty.'s Office, San Francisco, 1970-71; atty. investigator Nat. Assn. Securities Dealers, San Francisco, 1972-74; with office of gen. counsel Dean Witter & Co., Inc., San Francisco, 1974-77; asst. gen. counsel Shaklee Corp., San Francisco, 1977—; instr. Hastings Coll. Law. Mem. nat. adv. bd. Calif.-in-the-Capitol; mem. White House Task Force on Employment of Youth in Govt., 1968; adminstrv. asst. TV Program Operation Goverment, 1967; intern Ho. of Reps., 1967-68; mem. Pres.'s Exec. Exchange Program; spl. counsel to U.S. trade rep. Exec. Office of Pres., 1981-82; guest speaker govt., profl. and pvt. groups. Chmn. Com. on Internat. Investments, Calif. Council Internat. Trade. Recipient award for oral presentation in Moot Ct. Competition, 1971. Mem. Bar Assn. San Francisco, Am. Bar Assn. Democrat. Jewish. Contbr. articles to profl. jours. Home: 1163 Trestle Glen Oakland CA 94610 Office: 444 Market St San Francisco CA 94111

KREIMEYER, VICKI RUTH, librarian; b. Enterprise, Oreg., Jan. 25, 1947; d. Victor L. and Doreen Isabelle (Lewis) Kreimeyer. B.A. in English, Lewis and Clark Coll., 1969; M.L.S., U. Mich., 1970; postgrad. Portland State U., 1984—. Library work-study scholar U. Mich., Ann Arbor, 1969-70; acquisitions librarian Lewis and Clark Coll., Portland, Oreg., 1970-77, reference librarian, 1977-79, acting library dir., 1980-81, asst. dir. pub. services, 1981—. Pres. On the Green Homeowners Assn., Beaverton, Oreg., 1980-81; mem. Oreg. Repertory Singers, Portland, 1976—, bd. dirs. 1977-78. Mem. Assn. Coll. and Research Libraries (pres. Oreg. chpt. 1982-83), Pacific Northwest Library Assn. (pres. 1983-84), ALA, Oreg. Library Assn., NOW. Democrat. Presbyterian. Office: Lewis and Clark Coll Portland OR 97219

KREINBRING, JEFFREY COLE, medical center information systems administrator; b. Pasadena, Calif., Dec. 14, 1945; s. Paul Morton and Brooke Jane (Hawkins) K.; B.A., U. Calif., Santa Barbara, 1967; M.B.A., Claremont Grad. Sch., 1969; m. Diana Lynn Hessler, July 29, 1978. Hosp. adminstrv. asst. Lark Ellen Hosp., West Covina, Calif., 1974; systems and communications analyst Huntington Meml. Hosp., Pasadena, Calif., 1975-77; installation dir. Shared Med. Systems Corp., El Segundo, Calif., 1977-78; asst. dir. info. systems St. Joseph Med. Ctr., Burbank, Calif., 1978-81; dir. computer info. systems St. Mary Med. Ctr., Long Beach, Calif., 1981—. Served with USAF, 1969-74. Cert. in data processing Inst. for Cert. Computer Profls. Mem. Electronic Computing Health Oriented Data, Data Processing Mgmt. Assn., Hosp. Mgmt. Systems Soc., Hosp. Info. Systems Sharing Group, TRS-80 Microcomputer Users Group. Contbr. articles on microcomputer use to profl. publs.; actor, community theater, Westover AFB, Mass., 1971-73, Monrovia, Calif., 75-77. Home: Huntington Beach CA Office: St Mary Med Ctr 1050 Linden Ave Box 887 Long Beach CA 90801

KREIS, RICHARD CLARK, educator; b. Columbus, Ohio, July 24, 1955; s. Robert James and Mary Anna (Ruehrmund) K. B.A., U. Calif.-Davis, 1977; M.A., Calif. State U.-Sacramento, 19-. Tchr. math. Galt (Calif.) High Sch., 1978—. Mem. Galt Fedn. Tchrs. (pres. 1982-83) Math. Assn. Am., Nat. Council Tchrs. Math, Calif. Math Council, Council Basic Edn., Calif. Fedn. Tchrs., Am. Fedn. Tchrs. Office: 145 N Lincoln Way Galt CA 95632

KREITER, KATHERINE TAYLOR, quality engineer; b. Chgo., Oct. 27, 1954; d. Thomas Joseph Taylor and Constance Marie (Canezaro) Taylor Lind; m. Steven William Kreiter, June 30, 1974. B.A. in Bus. Adminstrn., Evergreen State Coll., 1983. Raw materials analyst Johnson & Johnson, Park Forest, Ill., 1975-78; quality engr. ITT Rayonier, Shelton, Wash., 1978-82; program asst. surplus commodities State of Wash., 1983—; mgr., foundr. Shelton Merchandising Cooperative. Mem. Am. Soc. Quality Control.

KREJCI, ROBERT HENRY, aerospace engineer; b. Shenandoah, Iowa, Nov. 15, 1943; s. Henry and Marie Josephine (Kubicek) K.; m. Carolyn R. Meyer, Aug. 21, 1967; children—Christopher S., Ryan D. B.S. with honors in Aerospace Engring., Iowa State U., Ames, 1967, M.Aerospace Engring., 1971. Commd. 2d lt. U.S. Air Force, 1968; advanced through grades to capt., 1978; served with systems command Space Launch Vehicles Systems Program Office, Advanced ICBM program officer; research asso. U.S. Dept. Energy Lawrence Livermore lab.; dept. mgr. advanced tech. programs Wasatch div. Thiokol Corp., 1978—. Decorated A.F. commendation medal, Nat. Def. Service medal. Mem. AIAA, Planetary Soc. Home: 885 N 300 E Brigham City UT 84302 Office: Thiokol Corp PO Box 524 Brigham City UT 84302

KREMPEL, ROGER ERNEST, city ofcl.; b. Waukesha, Wis., Oct. 8, 1926; s. Henry and Clara K.; m. Shirley Ann Gray, June 16, 1948;

children—John, Sara, Peter. Student Ripon Coll., 1944, Stanford U., 1945; B.C.E., U. Wis.-Madison. 1950. Registered profl. engr., Wis., Colo.; diplomate Am. Acad. Environ. Engrs. Asst. city engr., Manitowoc, Wis., 1950-51; city engr. dir. pub. works, Janesville, Wis., 1951-75; dir. water utilities, Ft. Collins, Colo., 1975-79, dir. pub. works, water utilities, 1979—. Served with U.S. Army, 1944-46. Fellow ASCE; mem. Water Pollution Control Fedn., Am. Water Works Assn., Am. Pub. Works Assn., Nat. Soc. Profl. Engrs., Wis. Soc. Profl. Engrs. Office: 300 LaPorte Ave PO Box 580 Fort Collins CO 80522

KRENK, CHRISTOPHER JOSEPH, social worker; b. Eugene, Oreg., Jan. 20, 1949; s. Marvin Aaron and Mary (Staton) K.; B.S., U. Oreg., 1971; cert. integrative adminstrn. U. Wash., 1976; M.S.W., 1977; m. Nellie Jo Babcock, July 3, 1977. Groupworker, Lane County (Oreg.) Youth Care Centers, 1971-72, program dir., 1972-75; group specialist Echo Glen Children's Center, Snoqualmie, Wash., 1976; day treatment specialist Luther Child Center, Everett, Wash., 1976-77; dir. program services Christie Sch., Marylhurst, Oreg., 1977-83; pvt. practice clin. social work, 1983—; mem. adv. bd. Tri-County Youth Corsortium; coordinator Pvt. Agy. Middle Mgrs. Mem. Clackamas County (Oreg.) Youth Network, 1979-81. HEW grantee, 1975-77; registered clin. social worker, Oreg. Mem. Nat. Assn. Social Workers, Am. Assn. Psychiat. Services to Children, Oreg. Assn. Child Care Workers (adv. bd.), Acad. Cert. Social Workers. Democrat. Home: 18585 SW Kristi Way Lake Oswego OR 97034 Office: Lake Oswego Counseling Assocs 425 W 2d St Lake Oswego OR 97034

KRENKEL, NOELE, psychologist, educator, real estate broker; b. San Francisco, Dec. 21, 1943; d. Harry Nichols and Daisy Genevieve (Ashton) Krenkel. B.A., U. Calif.-Berkeley, 1964; M.A., San Francisco State U., 1968; Ph.D. in Social and Research Psychology, U. So. Calif., 1972. Cert. elem. tchr., Calif.; cert. community coll. tchr., adminstr. Curatorial asst. de Young Mus. Art Sch., San Francisco, 1969-71; researcher San Francisco Unified Schs., 1971-76, 77-79; adminstr. U. San Francisco, 1976-77; assoc. head Field Service Ctr., U. Calif.-Berkeley, 1979-80; prof. grad. div. Antioch U., San Francisco, 1981—; lectr. grad. div. San Francisco State U., 1978—; broker Mason-McDuffie Real Estate, Inc., Berkeley, 1979—; researcher gifted edn. San Francisco Schs.; cons. Calif. Dept. Edn.; founder Ageing Concerns. AAUW grantee, 1978. Mem. Am. Psychol. Assn., Calif. Psychol. Assn. Clubs: Commonwealth of Calif., Eastern Star. Home: 45 Valdez San Francisco CA 94112 Office: 1442 A Walnut Suite 279 Berkeley CA 94709

KRESA, KENT, aerospace company executive; b. N.Y.C., Mar. 24, 1938; s. Helmy and Marjorie (Boutelle) K.; m. Joyce Anne McBride, Nov. 4, 1961; 1 dau., Kiren. B.S. in Aeros. and Astronautics, MIT, 1959, M.S. in Aeros. and Astronautics, 1961, Aeros. and Astronautics Engr., 1966. Sr. scientist Research and Advanced Devel. div. AVCO, Wilmington, Mass., 1959-61; staff mem. Lincoln Lab., MIT, Lexington, 1961-68; dep. dir., strategic tech. office Def. Advanced Research Projects Agy., Washington, 1968-73, dir. tactical tech. office, 1973-75; v.p., mgr. Northrop Research and Tech. Ctr., Hawthorne, Calif., 1975-76; v.p., gen. mgr. Ventura div. Northrop Corp., Newbury Park, Calif., 1975-82, group v.p. aircraft group, Los Angeles, 1982—; cons. Recipient Arthur D. Flemming award MIT, 1975; Meritorious Civilian Service medal Dept. Def., 1975; Meritorious Public Service citation Dept. Navy, 1975. Mem. Am. Def. Preparedness Assn., Assn. of Unmanned Vehicle Systems (hon. trustee), Navy League, Assn. U.S. Army, Soc. Flight Test Engrs., Nat. Space Club, AIAA. Office: Northrop Corporation 1800 Century Park E Century City Los Angeles CA 90067

KRESSEN, DAVID PENFIELD, educator, educational administrator; b. West Newton, Mass., June 10, 1926; s. Frank M. and Dorothy Penfield (Norton) Sleeper; m. Joyce Reeves, Aug. 20, 1950; children—Stephen, Carolyn Pinto, Norton Parker. B.A., Pomona Coll., 1949, Ed.M., Harvard U., 1950. Math. tchr., jr. adminstr., St. John's Sch., Houston, 1950-58; tchr. math. Poly. Sch., Pasadena, Calif., 1958-81, dir. middle sch., 1961-81, asst. headmaster, dir. admissions, 1958- , dir. computer edn., tchr. computer programming, 1981—; instr. computer literacy for tchrs., Pasadena City Coll.; conf. workshop leader. Past pres. Pasadena Arts Council, Pasadena Symphony Assn., Neighborhood Church. Served with Signal Corps, U.S. Army, 1944-47. Engl Trust grantee. Mem. Nat. Council Tchrs. Math., Calif. Math. Council, Computer-using Educators, Assn. for Supervision and Curriculum Devel., Internat. Council Computers in Edn., Assn. Computer Tchrs. (founding pres.), Smithsonian Assn. Republican. Mem. Unitarian Universalist Assn. Author: Teach Your Computer to Think In BASIC, 1983. Office: Polytechnic School 1030 E California Blvd Pasadena CA 91106

KRETZ, CHARLES CLARENCE, water treatment plant operator; b. Wheatland, Wyo., Feb. 17, 1929; s. Charles Carl and Jessie Viola (Locke) K.; widower; children—Ronald D., Bonnie Marie, Carl Mack. Water treatment plant operator Bd. of Pub. Utilities, Cheyenne, Wyo., 1952—. Served with USN, 1947-51. Mem. Am. Water Works Assn., Wyo. Wastewater Pollution Control Assn. Clubs: AMVETS, Nat. Campers' and Hikers' Assn. Club: Moose. Home: 600 E 3d St Cheyenne WY 82007

KREWSON, CHARLES NORMAN, diversified industries exec.; b. Williamsport, Pa., Nov. 22, 1927; s. George Norman and Harriet DeHart (Cawley) K.; B.S., Wharton Sch., U. Pa., 1951; m. Pamela Lee Hudson, June 6, 1953; children—Charles Norman, Patricia, Robert, Katherine, Douglas. With Gen. Electric Co., various locations, 1951-71; v.p. mktg. and internat. devel. Talley Industries, Inc., Mesa, Ariz., 1971-79; pres. Comml. Products Group, 1976-79; group v.p. Gen. Time Corp. subs. Talley Industries, Mesa, 1972, pres., 1973-79, also dir.; chmn., dir. Eastern Time Ltd., Hong Kong, Westclox Can. Ltd., GT Investment Ltd., Can.; chmn., pres. Antilles Industries, Inc., C. N. Krewson Assocs., Inc., Scottsdale, Ariz., 1979—; pres., dir. Talley Internat. Sales Corp.; dir. Industria Relojera Mexicana S.A. Adv. bd. Fiesta Bowl, 1977—; treas. Valley Presbyn. Ch., Scottsdale. Served with USN, 1943-44. Mem. U.S. C. of C., Nat. Security Indsl. Assn., Am. Def. Preparedness Assn., Phi Gamma Delta, Beta Alpha Psi. Mason (Shriner). Clubs: Arizona (Phoenix); Mountain Shadows Country. Paradise Valley Country, Rotary (Scottsdale). Home: 4138 E Lakeside Ln Scottsdale AZ 85253

KRIEG, ELIZABETH LYNN, conservation planner; b. Santa Monica, Calif., Sept. 6, 1949; d. John Edwin and Mazie (Mendenhall) K. A.B., U. Calif.-Santa Cruz, 1971; M.S., U. Calif.-Berkeley, 1978. Sr. research asst. Environ. Quality Lab., Calif. Inst. Tech., Pasadena, 1972-76; conservation planner Pacific Gas & Electric Co., San Francisco, 1979-82, supr. regulatory activities, residential conservation services, 1982—; cons. Fed. Energy Adminstrn., 1979. NSF fellow, 1978; Ford Found. fellow, 1977. Mem. Pacific Coast Gas Assn., Pacific Coast Electric Assn., Am. Horse Show Assn., Concord Mt. Diablo Trail Ride Assn. (v.p. 1983). Republican. Office: 77 Beale St Room A-1126 San Francisco CA 94106

KRIEGER, BENJAMIN WILLIAM, paper co. exec.; b. Cin., July 7, 1937; s. William Anthony and Catherine Regina (McDevitt) K.; A.A., U. Cin., 1965; grad. Advanced Mgmt. Program, Harvard U., 1980; m. Rosemary George, Apr. 12, 1958; children—Gregory, Kenneth, Catherine. Sales and asst. sales mgr. Chatfield Paper Corp., Cin., 1956-67; gen. sales mgr. Union Paper & Twine Co. div. Mead Corp., Cleve., 1967-69, v.p., 1969-75, gen. mgr. and pres., 1975-78, pres., Mich. area mgr. Beecher Peck & Lewis Co. div., Detroit, 1978-81; v.p. Dixon Paper Co., Denver, 1981—; pres. Cleve. Graphic Arts Council, 1975; mem. nat. adv. bd. Mead Papers, 1971-73; chmn. nat. adv. bd. Gilbert Paper Co., 1973-75; mem. packaging div. adv. council Reynolds Metals; mem. distbr. council 3M Co. Trustee, pres. North Hills Assn., 1974-75; active United Appeal Fund drive, Jr. Achievement, Greater Cleve. Growth Assn. Mem. Wholesale Distbrs. Assn., Newcomen Soc., Buckeye Paper Trade Assn., Craftsman Internat., Sales and Mktg. Execs., Cleve. Advt. Club, Cleve. Graphic Arts Assn., Advt. Prodn. Club, Jr. C. of C., Hon. Order Ky. Cols., Assn. Ohio Commodores. Republican. Roman Catholic. Clubs: K.C., Pine Lake Country, Renaissance, Fairlane, Hiwan Country, Boca Teeca Country. Home: 2431 Hearth Dr Evergreen CO 80439 Office: 410 Raritan Way Denver CO 80217

KRIENKE, CAROL BELLE MANIKOWSKE (MRS. OLIVER KENNETH KRIENKE), realtor; b. Oakland, Calif., June 19, 1917; d. George and Ethel (Purdon) Manikowske; student U. Mo., 1937; B.S., U. Minn., 1940; postgrad. UCLA, 1949; m. Oliver Kenneth Krienke, June 4, 1941; children—Diane (Mrs. Robert Denny), Judith (Mrs. Kenneth A. Giss), Debra Louise (Mrs. Ed Paul Davalos). Demonstrator, Gen. Foods Corp., Mpls., 1940; youth leadership State of Minn. Congl. Conf., U. Minn., Mpls. 1940-41; war prodn. worker Aerosearch Mfg. Co., Los Angeles, 1944; tchr. Los Angeles City Schs., 1945-49; realtor DBA Ethel Purdon, Manhattan Beach, Cal., 1949; buyer Purdon Furniture & Appliances, Manhattan Beach, 1950-58; realtor O.K. Krienke Realty, Manhattan Beach, 1958—. Manhattan Beach bd. rep. Community Chest for Girl Scouts U.S.A., 1957; bd. dirs. South Bay council Girl Scouts U.S.A., 1957-62, mem. Manhattan Beach Coordinating Council, 1956-68; mem. Long Beach Area Childrens Home Soc. (v.p., 1967-68, pres. 1979; charter mem. Beach Pixies, 1957—, pres. 1967; chmn. United Way, 1967); sponsor Beach Cities Symphony, 1953—. Mem. DAR (citizenship chmn. 1972-73, v.p. 1979, 83—), Colonial Dames XVIII Century (charter mem. Jared Eliot chpt. 1977, v.p., pres. 1979-81, 83—), Friends of Library, Torrance Lomita Bd. of Realtors, South Bay Bd. Realtors, Nat. Soc. New England Women (Calif. Poppy Colony), Internat. Platform Assn. Republican. Mem. Community Ch. (pres. Women's Fellowship 1970-71). Home: 924 Highview Manhattan Beach CA 90266 Office: 1726 Manhattan Beach Blvd Manhattan Beach CA 90266

KRIM, ARTHUR B., lawyer, motion picture company executive; b. N.Y.C., 1910. B.A., Columbia U., 1932. Bar: N.Y. 1932. Mem. Philips, Nizer, Benjamin & Krim, N.Y.C., 1932; pres. United Artists, 1951, chmn. bd., 1969-78; chmn. bd. Orion Pictures Co. (formerly Filmways, Inc.), Los Angeles, 1978—. Recipient Jean Hersholt Humanitarian award, 1974. Office: Orion Pictures Co 1875 Century Park E Los Angeles CA 90067*

KRIPPAEHNE, WILLIAM WONN, JR., comml. real estate and property mgmt. co. exec.; b. Portland, Oreg., Feb. 27, 1951; s. William and Marion K.; B.A. with honors, Oreg. State U., 1973, M.B.A., 1976; postgrad. McGeorge Sch. Law, U. Pacific, 1973-74; m. Michelle Joan Knoph, Apr. 8, 1978. Indsl. leasing and sales broker The Gilley Co., Portland, 1976-78, v.p., mgr., Seattle, 1978-79, sr. v.p., gen. mgr. The Gilley Co. subs. Cushman & Wakefield, Inc., Seattle, 1979-81; sr. v.p., br. mgr. Cushman & Wakefield of Wash., Inc., Seattle, 1981-83; pres., chief exec. officer Fisher Properties Inc., Seattle, 1983—. Mem. planning com., chmn. subcom. on Westlake Mall, Downtown Seattle Devel. Assn.; mem. Seattle Corp. Council Arts, Corvallis Mayor's Revenue Resource Com., 1971-72; chmn. Seattle Landmarks Preservation Bd.; chmn. fin. com. Maple Leaf Luth. Ch.; trustee Pacific N.W. Ballet; initiator, dir. city affairs task force Associated Students Oreg. State U., 1970-73, mem. exec. cabinet; editorial bd. dirs. Community Relations Tabloid; polit. analyst Corvallis Citizens for System Devel. Charge, 1972, Benton County Home Rule Charter Info. Com., 1972; initiator, dir. Benton County Land Use Planning Symposium. Lic. in real estate, Wash., Oreg.; lic. broker, Wash. Mem. Nat. Assn. Realtors, Nat. Realtors Mktg. Inst., Nat. Assn. Office and Indsl. Parks, Bldg. Owners and Mgrs. Assn. Seattle (trustee, fin. adv. com.), Seattle-King County Bd. Realtors, Oreg. Assn. Realtors, Portland Bd. Realtors (program chmn. 1970-77), Seattle C. of C., Oreg. State U. Alumni Assn. (dir.), Blue Key, Phi Kappa Phi. Clubs: Rainier (membership com.), Wash. Athletic (Seattle). Home: 4502 NE 38th St Seattle WA 98105 Office: 3317 Seattle First Nat Bank Bldg Seattle WA 98154

KRIPPNER, STANLEY CURTIS, psychologist; b. Edgerton, Wis., Oct. 4, 1932; s. Carroll Porter and Ruth Genevieve (Volenberg) K.; B.S., U. Wis., 1954; M.A., Northwestern U., 1957, Ph.D., 1961; m. Lelia Anne Harris, June 25, 1966; children—Caron, Robert. Speech therapist Pub. Schs., Warren, Ill., 1954-55, Richmond (Va.) Pub. Schs., 1955-56; grad. asst. Psychoednl. Clinic, Northwestern U., 1957-60; dir. Child Study Center, Kent (Ohio) State U., 1961-64; dir. dream lab. Maimonides Med. Center, Bklyn., 1964-73; faculty chmn. Saybrook Inst., San Francisco, 1973—; vis. prof. U. P.R., 1972, Calif. State Coll., Sonoma, 1972-73, U. for Life Scis., Bogota, Colombia, 1974; Hon. v.p. Albert Schweitzer Cultural Assn., Mexico City; bd. dirs. Nat. Found. for Gifted and Creative Children, Nat. Assn. for Gifted Children, Acad. Religion and Psychical Research; mem. adv. bd. A.R.E. Clinic, Central Premonitions Registry, Found for Mind Research. Recipient Service to Youth award YMCA, 1959; citation of merit Nat. Assn. for Gifted Children, 1972, Nat. Assn. Creative Children and Adults, 1975; cert. of recognition Office of Gifted and Talented U.S. Office Edn., 1976. Fellow Am. Soc. Clin. Hypnosis; mem. Am. Soc. for Psychical Research, N.Y. Soc. Clin. Psychologists (asso.), Am. Acad. Social and Polit. Sci., AAAS, Am. Ednl. Research Assn., Am. Personnel and Guidance Assn., Am. (pres. div. 32 1980-81), InterAm. psychol. assns., Assn. Humanistic Psychology (pres. 1974-75), Assn. Transpersonal Psychology, Assn. for Psychophysiol. Study Sleep, Biofeedback Soc. Am., Council for Exceptional Children, Coll. Reading Assn., Internat. Soc. for Gen. Semantics, Menninger Found., Nat. Soc. for Study Edn., Parapsychol. Assn. (pres. 1982-83), Soc. Clin. and Exptl. Hypnosis, Soc. for Sci. Study Religion, Soc. for Sci. Study Sex, World Future Soc. Author: (with Montague Ullman) Dream Telepathy, 1973; Song of the Siren: A Parapsychological Odyssey, 1975; (with Alberto Villoldo) The Realms of Healing, 1976; Human Possibilities, 1980; editor: Advances in Parapsychological Research, Vol. 1, 1977, Vol. 2, 1978, Vol. 3, 1982; Psychoenergetic Systems, 1979; co-editor: Galaxies of Life, 1973; The Kirlian Aura, 1974; The Energies of Consciousness, 1975; Future Science, 1977; editorial bd. or adv. bd. Gifted Child Quar., Jour. Am. Soc. Psychosomatic Dentistry and Medicine, Internat. Jour. Paraphysics, Jour. Humanistic Psychology, Jour. Transpersonal Psychology, Jour. Psychophys. Systems, Jour. Indian Psychology; contbr. articles to profl. jours. Home: 79 Woodland Rd Fairfax CA 94930 Office: Saybrook Inst 1772 Vallejo St San Francisco CA 94123

KRISHNAN, PALANIAPPA, research agricultural engineer, consultant; b. Kanadukathan, Ramnad District, Tamilnadu, India, Apr. 25, 1953; came to U.S., 1974; s. Lakshmanan and Umayal (Thenappan) K.; 1 child, Prashanth. B.Tech. with honors, Indian Inst. Tech., 1974; M.S., U. Hawaii, 1976; Ph.D., U. Ill., 1979. Registered profl. engr., Ill. Grad. research asst. dept. agrl. enging. U. Hawaii, Honolulu, 1974-76; research asst. dept. agrl. enging. U. Ill., Urbana, 1976-79, research assoc., 1979-80; research agrl. engr. Oreg. Satate U., Corvallis, 1980—; cons. to seed conditioning industry. Recipient A.C. Pandya trophy Indian Inst. Tech., 1973-74; Hunter fellow, U. Ill., 1977-78; Research Council grantee, 1981. Mem. Am. Soc. Agrl. Engrings., Soil Sci. Soc. Am., Nat. Soc. Profl. Engrs., Oreg. Soc. Profl. Engrs., Sigma Xi, Gamma Sigma Delta, Alpha Epsilon. Club: Oreg. State U. Table Tennis. Author tech. publs. Home: 3930 NW Witham Hill Dr Apt 23C Corvallis OR 97330 Office: Agrl Engring Dept Oreg State U Corvallis OR 97331

KRITZ, ERIC WALTER, wine/spirits marketing executive; b. N.Y.C., Apr. 17, 1943; s. Karl and Friedl (Goldschmidt) K. B.A., CCNY, 1964. With Fromm and Sichel Inc., San Francisco, 1967—, product mgr., 1980—. Served to 1st lt. U.S. Army, 1965-67. Home: 3524 Kerner Blvd San Rafael CA 94901 Office: Fromm & Sichel Inc 655 Beach St San Francisco CA 94109

KROC, RAY A., restaurant co. executive, former baseball club executive; b. Chgo., Oct. 5, 1902; ed. Oak Park (Ill.) pub. schs.; m. With Lily Tulip Cup Co., 1923-41, sales mgr., until 1941; with Mult-A-Mixer Co., 1941-55; pres. McDonald's Corp., Chgo., 1955-68, chmn., 1968-77, sr. chmn., 1977—; chmn., pres., treas. San Diego Padres Baseball Team, 1974-79, dir., 1974—. Served in Ambulance Corps, World War I. Office: care San Diego Padres PO Box 2000 San Diego CA 92120*

KROEGER, HENRY, Canadian provincial government official; b. Moscow, USSR, Mar. 28, 1918; came to Can., 1926; s. Henry Kroeger; m. Cleona Elora Kelts, Apr. 9, 1939; children—Thomas Brent, Brian Harvey, Debora Anna. Pres. Kroeger Bros. Farm Equipment Ltd., 1944—; mem. Legis. Assembly Alta. (Can.), Edmonton, 1975—, minister for transp., 1979—. Progressive Conservative. Mem. United Ch. Canada. Lodge: Rotary (past pres. Stettler). Office: 419 Legis Bldg Edmonton AB T5K 2B7 Canada*

KROEKER, LEONARD PAUL, psychologist, researcher, cons., educator; b. Borden, Sask., Can., Apr. 25, 1939; came to U.S., 1967, naturalized, 1973; s. Nicholas Jacob and Elizabeth (Knelsen) K.; m. Ann Marie, Sept. 5, 1960; children—Nancy Yvonne, Lisa Michelle. B.A., U. B.C. (Can.), Vancouver, 1960, M.A., 1967; Ph.D., U. Wis.-Madison, 1971. Tchr. physics Vancouver Sch. Bd., 1961-67; head cons. Expt. Design Lab, U. Wis., 1967-70; asst. prof. psychology U. Ill.-Chgo., 1971-74, assoc. prof., 1974-76; research psychologist Navy Personnel Research and Devel. Ctr., San Diego, 1976—; cons. LPK Assocs.; mem. faculty dept. psychology San Diego State U. Recipient Outstanding Performance citation USN, 1977, 78, Superior Performance award, 1979, 80. Mem. Am. Statis. Assn., Am. Psychol. Assn., Psychometric Soc., Western Psychol. Assn. Club: South Western Yacht (San Diego). Contbr. articles to profl. jours.; designer, creator USN enlisted personnel assignment system. Office: Navy Personnel Research and Devel Center San Diego CA 92152

KROENKE, IRVIN MILTON, mechanical engineer; b. Hepler, Kans., Jan. 22, 1931; s. Herbert Ernest and Hilda Sophia (Reith) K.; m. Nelda Vanelle Deterling, Nov. 30, 1957; children—Cary Lynn Kroenke Martinez, Debra Kay Kroenke Neugebauer, Paul Eric. B.S. in Mech. Engring., Kans. State U., 1953. With Beech Aircraft Corp, Boulder, Colo., 1953—, sr. project engr., program devel., 1981—. Served with U.S. Army, 1954-56. Recipient Apollo Achievement award NASA, 1969. Mem. AIAA, Am. Def. Preparedness Assn. Republican. Lutheran. Home: 3143 Fern Pl Boulder CO 80302 Office: PO Box 9631 Boulder CO 80301

KROES, ROBERT JAMES, university administrator; b. Racine, Wis., Dec. 3, 1935; s. Stephen A. and Ann (Dolata) K.; m. Katherine P. Zukowski, Jan. 25, 1958; children—Elizabeth, R. Christopher, Lisa, Andrew, Mark, Kevin, Amy, Michael. B.S.E.E., Marquette U., 1960; M.B.A., U. Santa Clara, 1965. Various enging. positions, Wis., N.Y. and Calif.; with Aerospace Corp., 1965-69; dir. info. systems and computing U. Calif. Santa Barbara, 1969- , asst. vice chancellor, 1975-83, vice-chancellor, 1983—; cons. and lectr. in field. Mem. Am. Econ. Assn., Nat. Assn. Coll. and Univ. Bus. Officers, C. of C. Contbr. to profl. jours. Home: 994 Saint Mary's Ln Santa Barbara CA 93111 Office: U Calif Cheadle Hall Santa Barbara CA 93106

KROGH, CONNIE KAY, marketing company executive; b. Dickinson, N.D., May 2, 1949; d. Clarence Milo and Virginia Bell (West) Krogh; m. Robert Joseph Wirt, Aug. 29, 1981; 1 dau., Margeaux Sian. B.S. in Home Econs., N.D. State U., Fargo, 1972. Dir. sales McGuires Inn and Restaurant, Arden Hills, Minn., 1975-78; nat. sales mgr. food service United Wild Rice, Inc., Grand Rapids, Minn., 1978-79, sales mgr. Western region, Mill Valley, Calif., 1979-81; pres. Swandigo Mktg., Venice, Calif., 1981—; cons. Calif. wild rice growers, 30 Minute Meals. Recipient Pres.'s award Sales and Mktg. Execs., 1978, Order of Bell, 1978. Republican. Lutheran. Editor: Sales and Marketing Executive Newsletter, 1976-78, also dir., 1976-78, 80-81. Address: 859 Commonwealth Venice CA 90291

KROGH, LYNN MILLER, aircraft charter exec.; b. Pomona, Calif., Sept. 3, 1952; s. Lynn Vernon and Virginia Raye (Woodruff) K.; A.S., Mt. San Antonio Coll., 1973; B.S. magna cum laude, Ariz. State U., 1975. Flight instr. Brackett Air Service, Pomona, Calif., 1975-76; jet charter pilot Exec. Aviaton, Long Beach, Calif., 1976-79, dir. operations, 1977-79; instr. Mt. San Antonio Coll., Walnut, Calif., 1975-79; co-founder, v.p. Internat. Jet Aviation Services, Long Beach, and Denver, 1979—; pilot Continental Airlines, Los Angeles, 1977—; mfmg. cons. Mem. adv. bd. Aeronautics Dept., Mt. San Antonio Coll., 1979—. Recipient Dedicated Achiever award, City of Scottsdale (Ariz.), 1973-74; Scholastic Excellence award, Ariz. State U., 1974-75. Mem. Aircraft Owners and Pilots Assn., Airline Pilots Assn., Alpha Eta Rho. Republican. Baptist. Club: Mt. San Antonio Coll. Flying (pres. 1972-73). Author: Air Carrier Ops. Manual, 1979, Air Carrier Tng. Manual, 1979.

KROGMAN, ROBERT JOSEPH, mil. aerospace mktg. exec.; b. Ashton, Iowa, June 19, 1934; s. Martin H. and Iola M. (Huseman) K.; student Compton Coll., 1956-57; children—Kristine, Kirk, Kenneth. With Hughes Aircraft Co., Fullerton, Calif., 1960—, div. mktg. mgr. mil. electronic support field, 1976—; tchr. night sch., 1959-62. Former chmn. Westminster Merit Commn. Served with USCG, 1952-55. Mem. Tech. Mktg. Soc. Am., Nat. Security Indsl. Assn. Home: PO Box 2035 Fullerton CA 92633

KRONBERG, GENE MAN, insurance marketing executive; b. Sunbury, Pa., Oct. 16, 1919; s. Max L. and Lillian (Man) K.; m. June Strauss, Sept. 25, 1971; children by previous marriage—Rhonda, Bradley, LoriBeth. B.S., Pa. State U., 1941. C.L.U., 1960. Entered ins. bus., 1953; pres. Qualified Programs Co., subs. Gene M. Kronberg Co., Inc., San Mateo, Calif. Mem. Mounted Patrol San Mateo County. Served to 1st lt. AUS, 1942-45. Mem. Million Dollar Round Table, Top of the Table, 8 Million Dollar Forum. Mem. Am. Soc. C.L.U.s (pres. Peninsula chpt. 1969, 80), Peninsula Estate Planning Council (founder), Leading Life Ins. Producers No. Calif. Jewish. Club: Mensa. Contbr. articles ins. trade jours. Office: One Edwards Ct #202 Burlingame CA 94010

KRONE, FRANK W., dairy and restaurant industry manager; b. Billings, Mont., Dec. 19, 1928; s. Henry C. and Karen E. (Nymen) K.;

m. Shirley Ann Maser, Aug. 29, 1950; children—Frank William, Linda Susan, Sharen Elizabeth. B.A., U. Colo., 1950; postgrad. U. Denver, 1954. Sales mgr. Meadow Gold Dairies, Denver, 1953-64; v.p. Kings Food Host USA, Lincoln, Nebr., 1964-71; sales mgr. Home Dairies, Nampa, Idaho, 1971-72; asst. sec./gen. mgr. Dairymen's Creamery Assn., Caldwell, Idaho, 1972—; exec. com. Western Dairymen's Coop.; chmn., exec. v.p. Associated Dairies; past dir. Consol. Dairy Products; treas. Coop. Dairy Farmers; mem. agrl. consulting council U. Idaho. Served as lt. USN, 1950-53. Decorated Nat. Def. medal. Named to Beatrice Foods Pres.'s Honor Club, 1963. Mem. Ret. Officers Assn., Sales and Mktg. Execs., Nat. Milk Producers Fedn. (dir.). Club: Crane Creek Country. Methodist. Home: 525 E Braemere Rd Boise ID 83702 Office: 520 Albany St Caldwell ID 83605

KRONICK, NORMAN MARKS, real estate investments co. exec.; b. Los Angeles, Sept. 19, 1928; s. Harry Bates and Rosina Morris K.; B.B.A., U. Ga., 1949; m. Josephine Taylor, Apr. 4, 1956. Sec., Nat. Co., Inc., Honolulu, 1954-79, pres., 1979—, also dir.; pres., dir. Norman Kronick Inc., Honolulu, 1975—, Olinda Country Estates, Inc., Honolulu, 1976—, Nat. Co. Inc. Served with AUS, 1951-53. Mem. Honolulu Bd. Realtors, U. Ga. Alumni Assn. Democrat. Jewish. Home: 3605 Manamana Pl Honolulu HI 96822 Office: 965 F North Nimitz Hwy Honolulu HI 96817

KRONOWITZ, ELLEN LINDA, educator; b. N.Y.C., July 15, 1945; d. Maurice H. and Beatrice K.; B.A. magna cum laude, Queens Coll., City U. N.Y., 1966; M.A., Columbia U., 1969, Ed.M., 1974, Ed.D., 1976. Tchr. elem. schs., N.Y.C., 1966-70, Agnes Russell Sch. of Tchrs. Coll., Columbia U., 1970-73; instr. Preservice Tchr. Edn. Program, Columbia U., 1973-74; instr. early childhood div. Bklyn. Coll., City U. N.Y., 1974-76; program devel. specialist Tchr. Corps Project, N.Y. U., 1976-78; assoc. prof. elem. edn. Calif. State Coll., San Bernardino, 1978—; cons. Rialto (Calif.) Unified Sch. Dist., 1980, Tchr. Corps Projects, Fordham U., Bank St. Coll. Edn., N.Y. Bd. Edn. Bilingual Tchr. Corps Project, 1973-74; condr. workshops. Fulbright awardee, 1982. Mem. Assn. Supervision and Curriculum Devel., Nat. Council Social Studies, Calif. Assn. Profs. Elem. Edn., Calif. Council Edn. of Tchrs., Calif. Assn. Colls. for Tchr. Edn., Foothill Reading Council, Fulbright Alumni Assn., Calif. Council Social Studies, Phi Beta Kappa, Kappa Delta Pi. Contbr. articles to profl. jours. Home: 200 E 30th St San Bernardino CA 92404 Office: California State College San Bernardino CA 92407

KROPOTOFF, GEORGE ALEX, civil engineer; b. Sofia, Bulgaria, Dec. 6, 1921; s. Alex S. and Anna A. (Kurat) K.; came to Brazil, 1948, to U.S., 1952, naturalized, 1958; B.S. in Civil Engring., Inst. Tech., Sofia, 1941; m. Helen M., July 23, 1972. With Pacific Car & Foundry Co., Seattle, 1952-64; structural engr. Tucker, Sadler & Bennett A-E, San Diego, 1964-74; research engr. Gen. Dynamics-Astronautics, San Diego, 1967-68, Engring. Sci., Inc., Arcadia, Calif., 1975-76; cons. Incomtel, Rio de Janeiro, Brazil, 1976; asso. Bennett Engrs., structural cons., San Diego, 1976-82; project structural engr. Hope Cons. Group, San Diego and Saudi Arabia, 1982—. Registered profl. engr., Calif. Mem. ASCE, Structural Engrs. Assn. San Diego, Soc. Am. Mil. Engrs., Soc. Profl. Engrs. Brazil. Republican. Orthodox. Home: San Diego CA

KRUCHEK, THOMAS FRANCIS, psychiatrist; b. Montgomery, Minn., Aug. 15, 1922; s. Joseph and Nettie (Washa) K.; B.S., Coll. St. Thomas, 1944; M.D., Creighton U., 1946; m. Esther Kelly, Feb. 17, 1950; 1 son, Joseph. Intern, St. Mary's Hosp., Mpls., 1946-49; resident VA Hosp., Ft. Lyon, Colo., 1948-49, Norristown (Pa.) State Hosp., 1949-50, U. Pitts., 1953-54; practice medicine specializing in psychiatry, Chgo., 1954-62, Phoenix, 1962—; mem. staff St. Joseph's Hosp., chmn. dept. psychiatry, 1973-76; mem. staff Camelback Hosp., chief staff 1965-66; mem. staff Good Samaritan, St. Luke's, Dr.'s hosps., Phoenix, Scottsdale (Ariz.) Community/Hosps.; clin. instr. psychiatry Stritch Sch. Medicine, Chgo., 1955-62; prof. psychology St. Procopius Coll., Lisle, Ill., 1954-62; pres. Thomas F. Kruchek, M.D., Ltd. Served to capt. M.C., AUS, 1951-53. Diplomate Am. Bd. Psychiatry and Neurology. Fellow Am. Psychiat. Assn., Royal Soc. Health; mem. AMA, Am. Psychotherapy Assn., Maricopa County Med. Soc., Ariz. Psychiat. Soc. (treas. 1968-69, pres. 1970-71), Phoenix Psychiat. Council, Chgo. Neurol. Soc., Am. Group Psychotherapy Assn., Acad. Psychosomatic Medicine, Acad. Religion and Mental Health, Ariz. Med. Assn. Home: 4921 Prickly Pear Ln Paradise Valley AZ 85253 Office: 350 W Thomas Rd Phoenix AZ 85013

KRUEGER, JAMES, lawyer; b. N.Y.C., Oct. 27, 1938; s. Carl and Ida (Levey) K.; B.A., UCLA, 1960; LL.B., Loyola U., Los Angeles, 1965; m. Merry Michael Hill, July 5, 1967; children—Melissa Carlton, James Michael. Bar: Hawaii 1966, U.S. Dist. Ct. Hawaii 1966, U.S. Ct. Appeals (9th cir.) 1967, U.S. Tax Ct. 1974, U.S. Supreme Ct. 1982. Assoc., Padgett, Greeley, Marumoto & Akinaka, Honolulu, 1967-72; pres. James Krueger Law Corp., Wailuku, Maui, Hawaii, 1972; lectr. Calif., Wash., Nev. trial lawyers assns., Assn. Trial Lawyers Am., Western Trial Lawyers Assn.; spl. counsel County of Maui, 1974. Fellow Internat. Soc. Barristers, Internat. Acad. Trial Lawyers; mem. Assn. Trial Lawyers Am. (gov., 1976—, state committeeman 1975-76, constl. revisions com. 1977-80, nat. exec. com. 1979-80, 81—, amicus curiae com. 1979-80, fed. liaison com. 1980-81, nat. vice chmn. profl. research and devel. com. 1980-81, nat. vice-chmn. publs. dept. 1982-83, nat. vice-chmn. edn. policy bd. 1983-84; speaker convs., instr. Nat. Coll. Advocacy), Western (gov. 1975-78, 79-80, v.p. 1977-78, pres. 1978-79, speaker convs.), Hawaii (speaker convs.), Calif. (speaker convs.) trial lawyers assns., Hawaii Acad. Plaintiffs Attys., Melvin M. Belli Soc. (trustee), Am. Coll. Legal Medicine, Am. Soc. Law and Medicine, Am. Soc. Hosp. Attys., Pitts. Inst. Legal Medicine, ABA (com. on trial techniques 1974-76, nat. vice chmn. com. on medicine and law 1977—, sect. tort and ins. practice 1977-81), Hawaii, Fed., Maui County (pres. 1975) bar assns., Phi Alpha Delta. Democrat. Jewish. Clubs: Outrigger Canoe (Honolulu); Transpacific Yacht (Los Angeles); Maui Country. Contbr. articles to profl. jours. Home: Olinda Maui HI 96768 Office: 2065 Main St PO Box T Wailuku Maui HI 96793

KRUGER, ROBERT ALAN, research, engineering and computer company executive; b. Oklahoma City, Dec. 4, 1935; s. Charles Herman and Flora Blanche (Watson) K.; m. Donna Kaye Powell, Jan. 11, 1958; children—Laura Kaye Kruger Naughton, R. Alan, Paul C., Clint D. B.S. in M.E., MIT, 1957, Ph.D. in M.E., 1961; postgrad. Cambridge U., 1958. Sr. engr. Convair-Gen. Dynamics, 1961-62; group leader Gen. Atomic, La Jolla, Calif., 1962-67; pres. Systems Sci. and Software, La Jolla, 1967-76; chief exec. officer, chmn. Horizons Tech., Inc., San Diego, 1977—. Standard Oil Calif. fellow, 1956; NSF fellow 1957, 59, 60; Proctor & Gamble fellow, 1959. Mem. AIAA, ASME, Sigma Xi, Tau Beta Pi. Home: 2640 Saint Tropez Pl La Jolla CA 92037 Office: 7830 Clairemont Mesa Blvd San Diego CA 92111

KRUKAR, MILAN, transportation economist; b. Montreal, Que., Can., Feb. 5, 1933; s. Adam and Katherine (Pajtas) K.; children—Barbara J., Johannette, Louis E., Michael R., Mark A. B.Eng., McGill U., Montreal, 1956; B.S. in Civil Engring., U. Wash., 1962, M.S., 1964; postgrad in economics Wash. State U., 1970-72, 75-76. Cert. Prof. Engr., Quebec, 1956. Sr. mining engr. Cerro de Pasco Corp., Peru, S.A., 1956-60; civil engr. Wash. State Hwy. Dept., Seattle, 1962; assoc. civil engr. hwy. research civil engring. dept. Wash. State U., Pullman, 1964-74, research engr., 1977-79; sr. econ. analyst planning dept. Wis. Dept. Transp., Madison, 1974-75; economist environ. sect. Oreg. Dept. Transp., Salem, 1979, sr. transp. economist planning-hwys., 1980—; cons. Active Salem Art Assn., 1980—. Mem. Am. Econ. Assn., Transp. Research Forum, Que. Order Profl. Engrs., Transp. Research Bd. (past coms.). Lutheran. Contbr. numerous articles to profl. jours. Home: 1180 Satara Ave NW Salem OR 97304 Office: 513 Transportation Bldg Salem OR 97310

KRUMME, GUNTER, geography educator; b. Dortmund, Germany, Sept. 18, 1937; s. Erich and Margarete (Hoevelmann) K.; m. Ursel E. Streich; children—Heidi, Lars. Abitur, Stadtgymnasium Dortmund, 1957; Dipl. oec. publ., U. Munich, 1962; Ph.D. in Geography, U. Wash., 1966. Temp. lectr., U. Coll. London, 1964; asst. prof. U. Hawaii, 1966-68, Columbia U., 1968-70; assoc. prof. geography U. Wash., 1970-79, prof., 1980—; research econ. geography and regional econs. Served with Bundeswehr, 1957-58. Mem. Am. Econ. Assn., Regional Sci. Assn., Assn. Am. Geographers. Contbr. chpts. to books, articles to profl. jours.

KRUPP, EDWIN CHARLES, astronomer; b. Chgo., Nov. 18, 1944; s. Edwin Frederick and Florence Ann (Olander) K.; B.A., Pomona Coll., 1966; M.A., UCLA, 1968, Ph.D. (NDEA fellow, 1970-71), 1972; m. Robin Suzanne Rector, Dec. 31, 1968; 1 son, Ethan Hembree. Astronomer, Griffith Obs., Los Angeles Dept. Recreation and Parks, 1972—, dir., 1976—; mem. faculty El Camino Coll., U. So. Calif., extension divs. U. Calif.; cons. in ednl. TV, Community Colls. Consortium; host teleseries Project: Universe. Mem. Am. Astron. Soc., Astron. Soc. Pacific, Los Angeles Soc. History of Astronomy, Sigma Xi. Club: Explorers. Author: In Search of Ancient Astronomies, 1978 (Am. Inst. Physics-U.S. Steel Found. award for Best Sci. Writing 1978); Echoes of the Ancient Skies, 1983; Archaeoastronomy and the Roots of Science, 1983. Editor in chief Griffith Observer, 1974—. Office: Griffith Observatory 2800 E Observatory Rd Los Angeles CA 90027

KRYGIER, EARL ELDON, marine biologist; b. Portland, Oreg., Mar. 27, 1946; s. John Joseph and Irene Catherine (Alcock) K.; B.S., Oreg. State U., 1970, M.S., 1974; m. Barbara Jean Radmilovich, Dec. 27, 1966; 1 son, Earl Ellwood. Researcher, marine biology Oreg. State U., Corvallis, 1972-80; dir. KEE Biol. Cons., 1977—; program dir. Logbook Program Alaska Trollers Assn., Juneau, 1981—. Asst., Boy Scouts Am., 1977-79. Sea grant traineeship, 1970-72. Mem. Pacific Estuarine Research Soc., Nat. Shellfish Assn., Am. Fishieries Soc., Crustacean Soc., Sigma Xi. Republican. Mem. Ch. Nazarene. Contbr. articles to profl. jours. Office: Alaska Trollers Assn 205 N Franklin St Juneau AK 99801

KRYSTINIK, KATHERINE BELL, statistician, geological and geophysical statistical consultant; b. Westerly, R.I., Oct. 17, 1955; d. Vernon Dutton and Frances Ellen (Leete) Bell; m. Lee Franklin Krystinik, June 6, 1981. B.A. in Math., Middlebury Coll., 1977; M.A. in Stats., Princeton U., 1979, Ph.D. in Stats., 1981. Research and teaching asst. Princeton U., 1977-81; statis. analyst Princeton/Dept. Energy Resource Estimation and Evaluation Project, 1978-79; statistician, mem. tech. staff Bell Telephone Labs., Murray Hill, N.J., 1979, 80; cons. statis. lab., dept. stats. Princeton U., 1980-81; statis. cons. O'Connor Research, Denver, 1982-83; statistician U.S. Geol. Survey, Denver, 1983—; ind. developer new statis. methodologies. Recipient George H. Catlin award, Middleburn Coll., 1977. Mem. Am. Statis. Assn., Rocky Mountain Sect. Soc. of Econ. Paleontologists and Mineralogists, Nat. Soc. Econ. Paleontologists and Mineralogists, Am. Assn. Petroleum Geologists, Phi Beta Kappa. Author in field. Office: US Geol Survey PO Box 25046 MS 971 Denver CO 80225

KRYSTUFEK, ZDENEK, political scientist, educator; b. Prague, Czechoslovakia, May 11, 1920; s. Maxmilian and Karla (Klirova) K. J.D., Prague U., 1948, Ph.D., 1963; J.S.M., Stanford U., 1971. Research fellow Czechoslovak Acad. Scis., Prague, 1954-68; prof. polit. sci. and jurisprudence U. Colo., Boulder, 1973—. Mem. Am. Assn. Philosophy Law and Social Philosophy, Am. Soc. Legal History, Internat. Sociol. Assn., Am. Polit. Sci. Assn., Czechoslovak Soc. Arts and Scis. Author: Historical Foundations of Legal Positivism, 1967; The Soviet Regime in Czechoslovakia, 1981; contbr. articles to profl. publs. Home: 805 29 St Boulder CO 80303 Office: U Colo Boulder CO 80309

KUBAT, ALVIN RUSHFELDT, psychologist; b. Hopkins, Minn., June 29, 1942; s. Alvin Rushfeldt and Jeanette Lucile (Berg) K. B.A., U. Miss., 1970; M.A., Western Mich. U., Kalamazoo, 1972; Ph.D., U. Utah, 1974. Lic. psychologist, Calif. Psychologist Salt Lake City Bd. Edn., Columbus Community Ctr., 1972-74; pvt. practice Asent Co., Oxnard, Calif., 1974-81; psychologist Calif. Dept. Health, Camarillo State Hosp., 1977-78; sr. psychologist Tri-Counties Regional Ctr., Oxnard, 1978-80; psychologist Casa Colina Hosp. Rehabilitative Medicine, Pomona, Calif., 1981; pvt. practice with Claremont (Calif.) Family and Psychol. Services, 1981, pvt. practice Psychol. Services, Thousand Oaks, Calif., 1981—. Served in USAF, 1965-68. Mem. Am. Psychol. Assn., Ventura County Psychol. Assn. Contbr. articles to profl. jours. Home: 976 Calle Angosta Thousand Oaks CA 91360

KUCK, MARIE ELIZABETH BUKOVSKY, ret. pharmacist; b. Milw., Aug. 3, 1910; d. Frank Joseph and Marie (Nozina) Bukovsky; m. John A. Kuck, Sept. 20, 1945 (div. Nov. 1954). Ph.C., U. Ill., 1933. Pharmacist and tchr. Am. Hosp., Chgo., 1936-38, St. Joseph Hosp., Chgo., 1938-40, Ill. Masonic Hosp., Chgo., 1940-45; chief pharmacist St. Vincent Hosp., Los Angeles, 1946-48, St. Joseph Hosp., Santa Fe, 1949-51; dir. pharm. services St. Luke's Hosp., San Francisco, 1951-75; pharmacist Mission Neighborhood Health Center, San Francisco, 1968-72. Mem. drug utilization rev. com. San Francisco County-Blue Shield, 1974-75. Recipient Bowl of Hygein award Calif. Pharm. Assn., 1966. Mem. No., Calif. (legis. chmn. aux. 1967-69, chmn. fund raising luncheon 1953-75), Nat., Am., No. Calif. (pres. 1955-56, pres. San Francisco aux. 1965-66, editor ofcl. publ. 1967-70) pharm. socs., Am. Pharm. Assn. (pres. No. Calif. br. 1956-57, hon. pres. aux. 1975), Calif. Council Hosp. Pharmacists (organizer 1962, sec.-treas. 1962-66), Am. Soc. Hosp. Pharmacists, Assn. Western Hosps. (gen. chmn. hosp. pharmacy sect. Conv. San Francisco 1958), Internat. Pharmacy Congress (U.S. del. Brussels 1958, Copenhagen 1960), Fedn. Internationale Pharmaceutique, Pharmacists Soc. San Francisco (pres.-elect 1981, pres. 1982-83, Pharmacist of Yr. 1978), Lambda Kappa Sigma. Home: 2261 33d Ave San Francisco CA 94116

KUCZUN, ANN MARIE, artist; b. Springfield, Mass., Sept. 25, 1935; d. Theodore B. and Mary L. (Rzeszutek) Yamer; m. Sam Kuczun, June 21, 1959; children—Theodore, Kyle. B.S., Bay Path Jr. Coll., 1954. Editor trade mag. John H. Breck, Inc., Springfield, 1954-56; copywriter, actor commls. Sta. WWLP-TV, Springfield, 1956-58; editor/designer co. mag. Buxton, Inc., West Springfield, Mass., 1958; advt. asst. Gibney & Barrecca, Inc., Springfield, 1958-59; freelance illustrator U. Colo., Boulder, 1982-83; painter, printmaker, Boulder, 1966—. Bd. dirs. Boulder Ctr. Visual Arts, 1973-75; mem. Boulder C. of C. Cultural Affairs Council, 1978. Orthodox Catholic. Home and Office: 930 Miami Way Boulder CO 80303

KUDO, EIGO H., accountant; b. Lima, Peru, Sept. 4, 1933; came to U.S., 1944; s. Rokuichi and Yoshiko K.; m. Elsa Higashide, Aug. 8, 1959; children—Eimi, Tami. B.S., U. Ill., 1961; C.P.A., Ill., Hawaii, N.C., La. Mgr. Arthur Andersen & Co., Chgo., Tokyo, 1961-71; dir. internat. ops., The Marmon Group, Chgo., 1971-74; ptnr. Touche Ross & Co., Tokyo, Honolulu, 1975—; cons. in field. Mem. Mayor's Oahu Traffic Safety Council; trustee Japan Am. Soc. of Honolulu; mem. Honolulu Acad. Arts. Served as cpl. U.S. Army, 1954-56. Mem. Am. Inst. C.P.A.s, Hawaii Soc. C.P.A.s, Honolulu Japanese C. of C. (dirs.). Club: Hawaii Econ. Study. Home: 5265 Lawelawe Pl Honolulu HI 96821 Office: Touche Ross/Tohmatsu Awoki & Co 733 Bishop St Suite 2000 Honolulu HI 96813

KUDO, FRANKLIN TY, computer company executive; b. Honolulu, Oct. 3, 1950; s. Charles T. and Fujie (Hayakawa) K.; B.S., U. Colo., 1972; M.B.A., U. Wash., 1974; cert. mgmt. systems analysis Inst. Advanced Tech., Control Data Corp., 1977; cert. in advanced real estate U. Hawaii, Hawaii Real Estate Commn.; m. Lei Yukie Hirano, Aug. 6, 1978; 1 child, Lindsey. Sr. acct. Peat, Marwick, Mitchell & Co., C.P.A.s, Honolulu, 1974-78; sr. v.p., controller Aloha Motors, Inc., Honolulu, 1978-83; pres., treas. Virtul Mgmt. Services Corp., 1983—. Budget dir. Hawaii campaign Carter/Mondale, 1976; fin. chmn. Democratic State Conv. Hawaii, 1977-78, 79-80. C.P.A., Hawaii. Mem. Hawaii Soc. C.P.A.s, Am. Soc. C.P.A.s. Democrat. Home: 4126-3 Keanu St Honolulu HI 96816 Office: 711 Kapiolani Blvd Suite 100 Honolulu HI 96813

KUEBER, ANTHONY JOSEPH, ret. warehousing exec.; b. Aneta, N.D., Sept. 20, 1902; s. Jacob and Mary C. (Bichler) K.; student Dunwoody Inst., 1924-25, Minnesota Coll., Mpls., 1926-27; m. Julia Valeria Kueber, Nov. 26, 1929; children—Jacqueline Lois, Janis Valeria, Robert Anthony. Mgr., L.P. Dolliff Lumber Co., 1928; promotional sales engr. Jones & Laughlin Steel Corp., Chgo., 1929-38; founder Steel Warehousing Corp., pres., gen. mgr., 1938-64; v.p., dir. Jessop Steel Co., Washington, Pa., 1959-64; pres., dir. Jessop Steel of Calif., Santa Fe Springs, 1959-64; v.p. Eastern Stainless Steel Corp., Balt., 1964-70; dir. Cochrane Chase & Co., Newport Beach, Calif., 1968-76. Village trustee LaGrange Park, Ill., 1947-51. Mem. Am. Steel Warehouse Assn. (pres. Central States chpt. 1943, 44, 47. Knight of Malta. Clubs: Serra; Executives, Union League (Chgo.); LaGrange (Ill.) Country; Chicago Golf (Wheaton, Ill.); Hacienda Golf (pres. 1974-75) (La Habra, Calif.). Home: 2164 N Papaya Dr La Habra Heights CA 90631

KUECHLER, HENRY NORBURY, III, bus. exec.; b. San Francisco, Mar. 15, 1938; s. Henry Norbury and Mary Elizabeth (Stewart) K.; B.S., U. Calif.-Berkeley, 1960; m. Alice C. Dias, Mar. 14, 1981; children—Henry N., Mary North, Thomas Dias, Alair Dias, Gregory Dias. Pres., Knob Hills Mines, Inc., Menlo Park, Calif.; pres., dir. Reclaimed Island Lands Co., Menlo Park, Knob Hill Oil & Gas Co., Menlo Park; dir. Cola Petroleum, Fed. Coca Cola Co., Beau Coup Oil & Gas Co., Booth-Bricker Fund. Bd. dirs. North Delta Water Agy.; trustee Reclamation Dists. 2060, 2062; mem. Atherton (Calif.) Planning Commn., 1973-80. Served with USN, 1960-62. Mem. Delta Water Users Assn. (dir.), Calif. Flood Central Valley Flood Control Assn. (dir.). Republican. Presbyterian. Clubs: Pacific-Union, Sonoma County Trailblazers, Frontier Boys, Rancheros Visitaderos, Big C Soc., Burlingame Country, Engrs. of San Francisco; Boston of New Orleans. Office: 1143 Crane St Suite 200 Menlo Park CA 94025

KUEHL, DENNIS WALTER, school administrator, draft horse breeder; b. Luverne, Minn., Jan. 14, 1944; s. Walter R. and Esther L. (Jessen) K.; m. Jean Kay Bos, May 12, 1948; children—Brady Dennis, Cody Gene. A.A., Worthington (Minn.) State Jr. Coll., 1967; B.S. in Math., Bemidji State Coll., 1970; M.A. in Math., U. No. Colo., 1976; postgrad. Colo. State U., 1978-80. Cert. adminstr. Colo. Dept. Edn., 1981. Tchr. jr. high sch. math. Fairfax (Minn.) High Sch., 1970-72, Bill Reed Jr. High Sch., Loveland, Colo., 1972-81; asst. prin. Conrad Ball Jr. High, Loveland, 1981—; supt. Nat. Western Stock Show Draft Horse Show, Denver, 1983—; cons. Colo. State Dept. Edn.; instr. interpersonal communications workshop Northwest Regional Lab. Served with USN, 1962-64. Mem. Assn. Supervision and Curriculum Devel., Mountain and Plains Draft Horse and Mule Assn. (pres. 1979, 80, 82, 83). Democrat. Lutheran. Developed math programs and teacher workshops for area. Office: 2660 N Monroe Loveland CO 80537

KUEHLER, LINDA LEE, accounting executive; b. Los Angeles, Feb. 28, 1956; d. Loel C. and Edith K. (Allegrezza) Lindgren; m. Richard Earl Kuehler, Aug. 23, 1980. B.A. in Bus. Adminstrn., Whittier Coll., 1978. Accounts payable clk. Baker Packers div. Baker Internat., Commerce, Calif., 1979, capital asset clk., 1979-80, acctg. coordinator 1980-82, acctg. supr. 1982—. Mem. Nat. Assn. Female Execs. Democrat.

KUEHN, DAVID LAURANCE, music educator, university administrator; b. San Marcos, Tex., Oct. 26, 1940; s. Albert August and Esther (Peschka) K.; m. Susan Eileen Travis, June 8, 1963; children—Michael Paul, Barbara Loring. B.Mus., N.Tex. State U., 1962; M.S. in Music Edn., U. Ill., 1964; assoc. diploma Royal Coll. Music, London, 1965; licentiate diploma Guildhall Sch., London, 1965; D.Mus. Arts, Eastman Sch. Music, U. Rochester, 1974. Asst. dir. bands U. Wis., Eau Claire, 1965-67; faculty Sch. Music, North Tex. State U., Denton, 1967-75, asst. dean Sch. Music, 1975-80; prof., chmn. dept. music Calif. State U., Long Beach, 1980—. Fulbright fellow, London, 1964-65. Mem. Nat. Assn. Coll. Wind and Percussion Instrs., Tubists Universal Brotherhood Assn., Calif. Music Execs. Assn. Presbyterian. Composed three books of vocalists transcribed for tuba, 1969-70. Office: Dept Music Calif State Univ Long Beach Long Beach CA 90840

KUEHN, LUCILLE, bank official; b. N.Y.C., May 26, 1924; d. David Henry and Hildagarde (Margulies) Maisel; children—Susan, Robert, David. B.A. cum laude, U. Minn., 1948; M.A., U. Calif.-Irvine, 1966. Program coodinator dept. urban affairs U. Calif.-Irvine, 1964-70, dir. program devel., 1970-72; community relations officer Am. State Bank, Newport Beach, Calif., 1979—; cons. U.S. Office Edn., Cochrane Chase & Co. Mem. Newport Beach City Council, 1974-78; trustees Newport Harbor Art Mus., South Coast Repertory Theater; bd. dirs. Mental Health Assn. Orange County, Planned Parenthood Assn. Orange County; pres. Town Hall Forum Orange County. U.S. Office Edn. fellow, 1971; recipient Orange County YWCA achievement award, 1982. Mem. Women in Bus., Newport Harbor C. of C. (Silver Anchor award 1979). Office: 500 Newport Ctr Dr Suite 910 Newport Beach CA 92660

KUEHNEGGER, WALTER, medical engineering company executive, educator; b. Graz, Austria, Aug. 8, 1928; s. Vincent and Vilma Ludmilla (Riegler) K.; came to U.S., 1955, naturalized, 1961; m. Susy Margarita Zarth, Aug. 23, 1961; 1 adopted dau., Elvira Susy. Ph.D. in Aero. Engring., U. Graz, 1948; A.M.I.E.T. in Aero. Engring., Brit. Inst. Engring. Tech., London, 1951; postgrad. courses in aerospace medicine; cert. in orthotics Northwestern U., 1973. Diplomate Am. Bd. Orthotics and Prosthetics. Head bioengring. lab. Northrop Space Labs., Hawthorne, Calif., 1962-66; dir. Kaman Work Scis. Lab., Bethesda, Md., 1966-68; dir. bioengring. lab. Litton Washington Research Ctr., Bethesda, 1968-69; dir. Camp Orthotic Research Clinic, Jackson, Mich., 1969-73; v.p. Orthodyne Inc., Gt. Falls, Va., 1973-81; former assoc. prof. dept. orthopedic surgery Howard U. Med. Sch., Washington; mem. vis.

faculty Northwestern U. Med. Sch., 1972-81; pres. Orthopaedics Internat., Inc., Tucson, 1981—; lectr. biomechanics Am. Acad. Orthopaedic Surgeons; cons. VA, N.Y. Prosthetic Ctr. Mem. Am. Aerospace Med. Assn., Am. Coll. Sports Medicine, Am. Acad. Orthotists and Prosthetists (charter; rep. to Am. Acad. Orthopaedic Surgeons), Am. Assn. Orthotists and Prosthetists, Internat. Soc. Prosthetics and Orthotics, Soaring Soc. Am. Mem. editorial staff Med. Orthopaedie-Technik, 1975—; patentee in field; introduced orthometry (subdiscipline for measurement techniques in orthopedics). Address: 8190 E Brookwood Dr Tucson AZ 85715

KUH, DAVID MICHAEL, banker; b. Los Angeles, May 16, 1944; s. Michael Edward and Eileen Claire (Egerer) K.; m. Theresa Ann Petersen, Jan. 21, 1967; children—Anne Marie, Tina Eileen. B.B.A., U. Hawaii-Manoa, 1967. With Central Pacific Bank, Honolulu, 1969—, asst. br. mgr., 1971-78, asst. v.p. mktg. dept., 1979—. Pres., Ewa Estates Community Assn., 1971-72; treas. Central/Leeward unit Am. Cancer Soc., 1982-83; mem. dept. edn. Speakers Bur., 1978—. Served with USNR, 1962-69. Named Citizen of Day, Sta. KGU, July 7, 1973. Mem. Ewa Beach Jaycees (pres. 1977-78; Gold Key award 1977-78), Honolulu Jaycees (v.p. 1974-75; Silver and Bronze Key awards 1974-77), Honolulu Press Club, C. of C. Hawaii, Honolulu Advt. Fedn. (treas.), Am. Inst. Banking, Hawaii Bankers Assn. (pub. relations and edn. com.), Moiliili Bus. and Profl. Assn. (dir. 1973-79), U. Hawaii Alumni (life), Alpha Phi Omega (life). Lodge: Elks (orgnl. com.). Office: Central Pacific Bank 220 S King St 3d Floor Honolulu HI 96813

KUHL, NORMAN E., brewery executive; b. Billings, Mont., June 23, 1940; s. Sidney Marvin and Valborg (Straatveit) K.; m. Nancy Jo Fitch, June 24, 1961; children—Michael John, Jodine Louise. B.S., U. Denver, 1963, M.S., 1967. Mem. transp. dept. Adolph Coors Co., Inc., Golden, Colo., 1963-67, warehouse mgr., 1967-76, v.p. packaging div., 1978—. Mem. Internat. Material Handling Soc., Packaging Inst. Republican. Lutheran. Clubs: Lakewood Country: Denver Athletic.

KUHN, FRANKLIN HOWARD, advertising agency executive; b. Escondido, Calif., Nov. 28, 1947; s. Franklin Kinset and Margaret Ellen (Johnson) K.; A.A., No. Va. Community Coll., 1975; B.F.A., La Salle Inst., 1971. Owner, mgr. B & K Studios, Ltd., Reston, Va., 1974-79; pres. founder Studio 3 & Assocs., Escondido, Calif., 1980—. Served to sgt. U.S. Army, 1967-73. Republican. Lutheran. Designed typeface used in major polit. campaign, 1968; author major funding proposal for U.S. Olympic Amateur Cycling Team. Office: Studio 3 & Assocs 10324 Meadow Glen Way E Escondido CA 92026

KUHN, JEAN GERLINGER, civic worker; b. Dallas, Oreg., Dec. 6, 1910; d. George Theodore and Irene Strang (Hazard) Gerlinger; B.A., U. Calif., Berkeley, 1932; m. Robert C. Kirkwood, Aug. 30, 1933 (dec.); children—Anne Kirkwood Millis, Robert C., Jean Kirkwood Casey, John Hazard; m. 2d, Charles B. Kuhn, June 15, 1968. Numerous vol. activities in various orgns., San Francisco, Sacramento, Saratoga and San Jose, Calif.; bd. dirs. San Francisco Found., 1969-79, Addiction Research Found., 1977—, Filoli Center, 1978—, Montalvo Center for the Arts, Saratoga, 1970—, World Affairs Council of No. Calif., 1968—; chmn. bd. dirs. Pacific Med. Found., 1981—, Community Found. of Santa Clara County, 1975—; mem. bd. visitors Stanford U. Law Sch., 1979—, Pacific Med. Center. Mem. Order St. John of Jerusalem, Kappa Kappa Gamma. Republican. Episcopalian. Club: Town and Country of San Francisco.

KUHN, SARAH SAPPINGTON, theatre dir., filmmaker; b. Marshall, Mo., July 20, 1935; d. William Darwin and Virginia Ethlyn (Caton) Sappington; student Kansas City (Mo.) Jr. Coll., 1953-55, U. Mo., Kansas City, 1955-57, UCLA, 1968-69, Calif. Inst. of the Arts, 1970-72; m. George Mason Kuhn, Aug. 17, 1957; children—George Robert, William Lawrence; m. 2d, Michael John Ahnemann, June 17, 1973. Filmmaker, 1968—; founder, artistic dir. Los Angeles Feminist Theatre, 1970-77, pres., 1973—; founder Sarsaku Prodns., 1973; producer ednl. films; prod. The Sirens for Calif. Internat. Women's Yr., 1977. Bd. dirs. Women's Center, 1970, bd. lady mgrs. Women's Bldg., 1973, mem. Women's Strike for Peace, Another Mother for Peace. Mem. Women's Inst. For Freedom of Press, Women Against Violence Against Women, Los Angeles Feminist Coalition, Women in Film (award Luncheon chairwoman 1978), Women in Theatre, ACLU, Amnesty Internat., Am. Film Inst., Los Angeles Coalition for Equal Rights Amendment, NOW (dir. Los Angeles 1970), Nat. Women's Polit. Caucus (founding mem. Los Angeles), Adult Drama Assn., DAR. Script and film in Women's Polit. History Collection, Smithsonian Instn. Address: 8700 Skyline Dr Los Angeles CA 90046

KUKLA, EDWARD RICHARD, rare books librarian, lecturer; b. Detroit, Jan. 31, 1941; s. Stanley Frank and ClaraBelle (Morton) K. A.B., Wayne State U., 1962; A.M., U. Mich., 1963, M.L.S., 1973. Teaching fellow U. Mich., Ann Arbor, 1963-66; asst. instr. Mich. State U., 1970-72; media mobile librarian State Library Mich., 1972; asst. librarian rare books and manuscripts Greenfield Village and Henry Ford Mus., Dearborn, Mich., 1974-78; rare books librarian Wash. State U., Pullman, 1979—; educator, lectr. rare books, history of books and printing, book collecting. Recipient Mich. Jr. Acad. Sci., Arts, and Letters membership, 1958. Mem. ALA, Assn. Coll. and Research Libraries, U. Mich. Sch. Library Sci. Alumni Assn., Wash. Library Assn., Phi Beta Kappa, Sigma Delta Pi, Beta Phi Mu. Clubs: Book of Wash., Pullman Stamp, U. Mich. Union. Author: Un estudio critico sobre Altazor de Vincente Huidobro, 1963; The Scholar and the Future of the Research Library Revisited, 1973; The Struggle and the Glory: A Special Bicentennial Exhibition, 1976. Home: NW 225 Timothy St Apt 2 Pullman WA 99163 Office: Wash State U Libraries Pullman WA 99164

KUKLIN, SUSAN BEVERLY, law librarian, educator, researcher; b. Chgo., Nov. 25, 1947; d. Albert and Marion (Goodman) K. B.A. with high honors, U. Ariz., 1969; M.L.S., Ind. U., 1970, J.D., U. Ariz., 1973; LL.M. in Taxation, DePaul U., 1981. Bar: Ariz. 1973, Ill. 1980. Asst. city prosecutor City of Phoenix cts., 1974; dep. county atty. Pima County, Ariz., 1975; polit. sci./law librarian, asst. prof. No. Ill. Univ., DeKalb, 1976-78; head law librarian, assoc. prof. law U. S.D. Sch. Law, Vermillion, 1978-79; dir. law library, asst. prof. law, DePaul U., Chgo., 1979-83; law librarian Santa Clara County, San Jose, Calif., 1983—; tchr., legal researcher, writer; sec., bd. trustees Santa Clara County Law Library, 1983. Mem. Am. Assn. Law Libraries (cert.), No. Calif. Assn. Law Libraries, Santa Clara County Bar Assn., Phi Delta Phi, Phi Beta Kappa, Phi Alpha Theta, Phi Kappa Phi, Alpha Lambda Delta. Contbr. articles in field, book reviewer profl. jours. Office: Santa Clara County Law Library 191 N 1st St San Jose CA 95113

KULDA, RICHARD JOSEPH, engineer; b. Boston, Feb. 13, 1922; s. Joseph William and Alice Anna Kletecka; m. Mary Ellen Washburn, Oct. 21, 1950; children—Gregory Paul, Mary Claire Stets, Peter John, Susan Ann, Robert Eric, Daniel John, Martha Gail, Derek Stewart. B.S. in Aero. Engring., MIT, 1943, M.S., 1947. Aerodynamicist N.Am. Aviation Co., 1947-48; engr. Northrop Corp., 1948-52; engr. Computer Research Corp., 1952-55; with Robertshaw Fulton Aircraft Controls, 1955-58, Plasmadyne Corp., 1958-61; mktg. mgr., researcher Gianini Controls Corp. (now Conrac), 1961-63; mktg. mgr. Hughes Aircraft, 1963-68; mgmt. cons., 1968—; prin. Teek Metals Co. Founding mem. Orange Park Assn. Served A.C., U.S. Army, 1943-46. Mem. AIAA. Republican. Roman Catholic. Patentee aircraft stability augmentation systems.

KULHAVY, RAYMOND WILLIAM, psychologist, educator; b. San Diego, Dec. 20, 1940; s. Lumir Oldrich and Virginia Dawn (Walker) K.; m. Linda Claire Caterind, June 25; children—Lori, Nicole. A.B., Calif. State U.-San Diego, 1967, M.A., 1968; Ph.D., U. Ill., 1971. Cert. psychologist, Ariz. Psychologist, U.S. Navy, 1967-68, vis. research scientist, 1975; staff psychologist Inst. for Personality and Ability Testing, Champaign, Ill., 1968-71; mem. faculty Ariz. State U., Tempe, 1971—, disting. research prof., 1981—; cons. Recipient Palmer O. Johnson Meml. Research award Am. Ednl. Research Assn., 1973. Mem. Am. Psychol. Assn., Am. Ednl. Research Assn., Psychonomic Society. Author books; contbr. numerous articles to profl. jours. Office: 325 Payne Hall Ariz State U Tempe AZ 85281

KULINSKY, PAUL NELSON, mining company official; b. Salt Lake City, Feb. 22, 1947; s. Carl P. and Leah M. (Nelson) K.; m. Gayle A. Harper, Mar. 9, 1967; children—Wendy A., Heather D., Robyn K. B.A., U. Wyo., 1969; A.A., Sheridan (Wyo.) Coll., 1967. Cert. secondary tchr., Wyo. Tchr. high sch. English, coach Sch. Dist. 1, Kemmerer, Wyo., 1969-77; engring. aide, employee relations mgr. FMC Corp.-Skull Point Mine, Kemmerer, 1977—; mine health and safety instr.; jr. high sch. basketball coach. Mem. Kemmerer City Council, 1976-80; dir. Wyo. Safety Council, 1980—; mem. Joint Powers Bd., 1980. Mem. Mountain States Employers Council, Wyo. Ofcls. Assn. Republican. Mormon.

KULLAS, DANIEL ALBERT, oil gas drilling company executive; b. Balt., Aug. 15, 1946; s. Albert John and Joyce May (Gladue) K.; B.S. in Applied Math., U. Colo., 1969; M.B.A., U. Denver, 1983; m. Jean Stuart Hench, June 24, 1978; children—Heather Jean, Stephen Albert. Systems engr. Martin Marietta Aerospace, Denver, 1969-74; sr. systems analyst Sci. Applications, Inc., Englewood, 1974-80; computer systems mgr. Exeter Co., Denver, 1980—. Recipient NASA Letter of Commendation, 1978; cert. in data processing, Inst. Certification of Computer Profls., 1981. Mem. Data Processing Mgmt. Assn., Computer Security Inst., Prime Users Group, Digital Equipment Computer Users Soc., Phi Kappa Psi. Office: PO Box 17349 Denver CO 80217

KULP, ELVIN LOYAL, agronomist; b. Colfax, Wash., Nov. 9, 1936; s. Nardin I. and Nellie E. Kulp; B.S. in Agronomy, Wash. State U., 1959, M.S. in Agronomy, 1961; postgrad. (NDEA fellow), U. Idaho, 1968; postgrad. (Farm Found. scholar) U. Ariz. Extension Sch., 1971; m. Mary O. Ingham, Apr. 11, 1957; children—Dawn, Nathan, Vangie, Kerry. Area agt. in agronomy Wash. State U. Coop. Extension, 1961-66, 81—, asst. prof. agronomy Coop. Extension, 1966-73, asso. prof., 1973-80, prof., 1980—. Mem. Am. Soc. Agronomy, Nat. Assn. County Agrl. Agts. (Disting. Service award 1973), Am. Registry Cert. Profls. in Agronomy, Crops and Soils, Wash. State Weed Assn. (pres. 1976), Wash. State Pest Control Cons. Assn. (pres. 1978), Wash. Extension Agts. Assn. (pres. 1980). Home: Route 1 816 F NW Ephrata WA 98823 Office: Grant County Courthouse Ephrata WA 98823

KULP, JOHN LAURENCE, company executive, consultant; b. Trenton, N.J., Feb. 11, 1921; s. John J. and Helen K. (Gill) K.; m. Helen M. Masterson, June 17, 1944; children—Ruth Elizabeth Kulp Scott, Ellen B. Kulp Schroeder, John L., Jr., James E. B.S., Wheaton Coll., 1942; M.S., Ohio State U., 1943; M.A., Ph.D. in Chemistry, Princeton U., 1945; fellow Columbia U. 1945-47; NSF sr. postdoctoral fellow in geochemistry Oxford (Eng.) U., 1958-59. Prof. geochemistry Columbia U., 1945-65; dir. Lamont Geochemistry Lab., 1955-65; pres. Isotopes, Inc., N.Y., 1965-67, Teledyne Isotopes, N.Y., 1967-75; v.p. R & D, Weyerhaeuser Co., Tacoma, 1975—; dir. Herman Miller Co. Bd. dirs. Am. Nat. Metric Council, So. Forestry Research Ctr.-N.C. State U., Coll. Mines and Earth Resources Adv. Council-U. Idaho; mem. indsl. panel sci. and tech. NSF; Scis., cons. U.S. Air Force, USPHS, AEC, U.S. Army Advanced Research Projects Agy., Fed. Radiation Council, NRC, others. NSF fellow 1959. Fellow Geol. Soc. Am., Geochem. Soc., Mineralogical Soc., N.Y. Acad. Scis.; mem. Nat. Acad. Scis., Am. Chem. Soc., Am. Phys. Soc., AAAS (Newcomb Cleveland award 1951), Am. Assn. Petroleum Geologists, Am. Geophys. Union, Soc. Am. Foresters, Am. Forestry Hist. Soc., Sigma Xi, Sigma Pi Sigma. Contbr. numerous articles to sci. jours. Office: Weyerhaeuser Co Tacoma WA 98477

KULSTAD, GUY CHARLES, public works official; b. Bend, Oreg., Feb. 28, 1930; s. John Marlyn and Annie Mildred (Boyd) Kulstad Ibison; B.S. in Civil Engring., U. Calif. at Berkeley, 1958; m. Bonnie Jane Sherman, Aug. 28, 1955; children—Anne Marie Kulstad Hurst, Mark, Alice. Engring. aide county rd. dept., Los Angeles, 1951, asst. civil engr., 1953-58; dir. pub. works, Benicia, Calif., 1958-59; dep. dir. pub. works, Solano County, Calif., 1959-65; dir. pub. works, Humboldt County, Calif., 1965—; gen. mgr. gen. Humboldt Bay Wastewater Authority 1975, 82—. Mem. coop. edn. adv. bd. Humboldt State U.; mem. communications com. United Way of Humboldt County. Served with AUS, 1951-53. Recipient Outstanding Service award North Bay chpt. Calif. Soc. Profl. Engrs., 1964, Boss of the Year award Arcata Jaycees, Recognition award Humboldt Toastmasters; Registered profl. engr., Calif., Oreg., Wash.; registered traffic engr., Calif.; registered land surveyor, Oreg.; cert. community coll. instr., Calif. Fellow ASCE; mem. Nat. Soc. County Engrs., Nat. Soc. Profl. Engrs., Am. Congress Surveying Surveyor award Humboldt chpt. Calif. Land Surveyors Assn., 1981. Oreg.; cert. community coll. instr., Calif. profl. engr., Calif., Oreg., Wash.; registered traffic engr., Calif.; registered land surveyor, Oreg. Fellow ASCE; mem. Nat. Soc. County Engrs., Nat. Soc. Profl. Engrs., Am. Congress Surveying and Mapping, Calif. Land Surveyors Assn. (Ann. award Humboldt chpt. 1981), Am. Mgmt. Assn. Clubs: Commonwealth of Calif., Sons of Norway, Toastmasters Internat. Author profl. dissertations. Office: 1106 2d St Eureka CA 95501

KUNISAKI, DENNIS MASASHI, fin. exec.; b. Los Angeles, Mar. 15, 1950; s. Leo Masashi and Grace Hideko (Kido) K.; B.S. in Bus. Adminstrn., Calif. State U., 1975; m. Ellen S. Kanda, June 25, 1976. Sales rep. Pacific Mut., Burbank, Calif., 1975-76; field underwriter Mut. of N.Y., Los Angeles, 1976—; trust officer Calif. First Bank, 1979—; dir. Little Tokyo Towers, Inc., 1979—. Gov., Pacific S.W. Dist., Japanese Am. Citizens League, 1981. Mem. Los Angeles Life Underwriters Assn., Zeta Beta Tau. Home: PO Box 521 Monterey Park CA 91754 Office: 616 W 6th St Los Angeles CA 90017

KUNKLER, J. L., geochemist; b. Okmulgee, Okla., May 23, 1921; s. Roscoe George and Mattie Jewel (Bryant) K.; B.S., Okla. State U., 1947; student U. N.Mex., 1955-61. With Stanolind Oil & Gas Co., Tulsa, 1947-48; geochemist U.S. Geol. Survey in N.Mex., 1948-82; cons. hydrologist, 1982—. Served with USMC, 1943-46. Mem. N.Mex. Geol. Soc. Author, patentee in field. Home: 116 Cmo de las Crucitas Santa Fe NM 87501

KUNZ, DONALD LEE, aerospace engineer; b. Geneva, N.Y., Oct. 19, 1949; s. Clarence Edwin and Mildred May (Kerr) K. B.S., Syracuse U., 1971; M.S., Ga. Inst. Tech., 1972, Ph.D., 1976. Research scientist Aeromechanics Lab., U.S. Army Research and Tech. Labs., Moffett Field, Calif., 1976—. Recipient ECAC Medal of Merit, Syracuse U., 1971. Mem. Am. Helicopter Soc., AIAA, Sigma Xi, Tau Beta Pi, Pi Tau Sigma, Phi Kappa Phi. Contbr. articles to profl. jours. Office: Mail Stop 215-1 Moffett Field CA 94035

KUNZE, JAY FREDERICK, engineering company executive; b. Pitts., Feb. 24, 1933; s. John Frederick and Thelma (Goetz) K.; m. Kristine Kissner, Nov. 28, 1981; children—John, Richard, Robert. Leader solar eclipse expedition, Labrador and Arabia U. Pitts., 1954-55; research asst. Carnegie Inst., 1953-58; nuclear engr. Gen. Electric, Idaho Falls, Idaho, 1954-58, mgr. ops. and analysis, 1958-62; assoc. prof. mech. engring., dir. nuclear engring. program U. Utah, Salt Lake City, 1962-69; mgr. reactor technology Aerojet Nuclear Co., Idaho Falls, 1969-70; mgr. geothermal projects and advanced energy programs EG&G, Idaho Falls, 1970-73; v.p., gen. mgr. Energy Services, Inc., Idaho Falls, 1973-78, pres., gen. mgr., 1982—; U.S. rep. for geothermal energy direct-heat-applications to Internat. Energy Agy. and Com. for Concerns of Modern Soc. of NATO, 1974-77. Unit commr. Teton Peaks council Boy Scouts Am., Idaho Falls, 1982—. Fellow Am. Nuclear Soc.; mem. Geothermal Resources Council, ASHRAE, Nat. Soc. Profl. Engrs., Sigma Xi, Tau Beta Pi, Phi Kappa Phi. Mormon. Clubs: Rotary, Astronomy. Patentee fluidized bed nuclear reactor. Home: Route 4 Box 224 Idaho Falls ID 83402 Office: 2 Airport Plaza Idaho Falls ID 83402

KUNZEL, HERBERT, corporate executive, lawyer; b. Los Angeles, Aug. 15, 1908; s. Herman and Regina (Schwartz) K.; m. Minerva Griswold, May 23, 1947; children—Ridge, Daphne, Kurt, Charles. A.B., U. So. Calif., LL.B., 1934. Bar: Calif. 1935. Ptnr. Luce, Forward, Kunzel & Scripps, San Diego, 1935-53; pres. Solar Turbines, San Diego, 1947-73; pres., reorgn. trustee Westgate Calif. Corp., San Diego, 1973-82; chmn., chief exec. officer, pres. Itel Corp., San Francisco, 1982—, dir.; dir. Energy Factors Inc. Bd. dirs. Scripps Clinic and Research Found. Served with USNR, 1942-46. Decorated Bronze Star. Mem. Calif. Bar Assn., ABA, Sigma Chi. Clubs: Bankers (San Francisco); La Jolla (Calif.) Country, San Diego Yacht. Lodge: Rotary. Office: One Embarcadero Ctr Suite 2900 San Francisco CA 941111

KUO, PING-CHIA, historian, educator; b. Yangshe, Kiangsu, China, Nov. 27, 1908; s. Chu-sen and Hsiao-kuan (Hsu) K.; A.M., Harvard U., 1930, Ph.D., 1933; m. Anita H. Bradley, Aug. 8, 1946. Prof. modern history, Far Eastern internat. relations Nat. Wuhan U., Wuchang, China, 1933-38; editor China Forum, Hankow and Chungking, 1938-40; counsellor Chinese Nat. Mil. Council, Chungking, 1940-46 and counselor Chinese Ministry Fgn. Affairs, Chungking, 1943-46; top-ranking dir. Dept. Security Council Affairs, UN, N.Y.C., 1946-48; asso. prof. history So. Ill. U., Carbondale, 1959-63, prof., 1963-72, chmn. dept. history, 1967-71, prof. emeritus, 1972—; pres. Midwest Conf. Asian Studies, 1964. Sr. fellow Nat. Endowment Humanities, 1973-74. Mem. Am. Hist. Assn., Assn. Asian Studies. Club: Commonwealth (San Francisco). Author: A Critical Study of the First Anglo-Chinese War, with Documents, 1935; Modern Far Eastern Diplomatic History (in Chinese), 1937; China: New Age and New Outlook, 1960; China (in Modern World Series), 1970; contbr. to Ency. Britannica, articles to profl. publs. Home: 8661 Don Carol Dr El Cerrito CA 94530

KUPER, DANIELA F., advertising agency executive, copywriter, lecturer, creative director; b. Chgo., June 18, 1950; d. Harry W. and Anne F. K.; m. Jesse L. Drennen III (div.); children—Judah, Sahra. B.A., So. Ill. U., 1971. Asst. creative dir., account exec., copy dir. Griff Advt., Boulder, Colo., 1978-82; pres., account exec., copy dir. Kuper Advt., Inc., Boulder, 1982—; lectr. TV and colls. Exec. bd., pres. Fundraising Attention Homes, Inc. Recipient Alfie award Denver Advt. Fedn., 1983. Mem. Denver Advt. Fedn., Boulder C. of C., ACLU.

KUPERSMITH, JOAN LESLIE, lawyer; b. N.Y.C., Jan. 30, 1953; d. Seymour and Ruth (Schechner) K.; B.A., N.Y. U., 1973; J.D., New Eng. Sch. Law, 1976. Admitted to N.Y. bar, 1977, D.C. bar, 1978, Fla. bar, 1978, Calif. bar, 1980; legal intern Mass. Atty. Gen.'s Office, 1974-75; reporter, cons. Bur. Nat. Affairs, Washington, 1975-76; trademark atty. U.S. Patent and Trademark Office, Washington, 1976-79, mem. U.S. Trademark Assn. lawyers adv. com., 1979-82; asso. firm Fulwider, Patton, Rieber, Lee & Utecht, Los Angeles, 1979—; mem. adv. com. on trademark affairs Dept. of Commerce, 1979—. Recipient spl. achievement awards Dept. of Commerce/Patent and Trademark Office, 1978. Mem. Am. Bar Assn., Women Lawyers Assn. Los Angeles, U.S. Trademark Assn. (asso.; membership com. 1982—), Assn. Bus. Trial Lawyers, Trademark Soc. (pres. 1978-79), Phi Alpha Delta. Co-editor: Los Angeles Patent Law Assn. Newsletter, 1980; contbr. articles to profl. jours. Home: 612 S Barrington Ave Los Angeles CA 90049 Office: 3435 Wilshire Blvd Los Angeles CA 90010

KURCH, WILLIAM DAVID, union exec.; b. Honolulu, Aug. 2, 1944; s. Michael and Joan Elizabith (O'Leary) K.; m. Colleen Christina, Dec. 1, 1969; children—Derek, Leah, Colleen Christina, William David; m. 2d, Fay Dora Roxenberg, Oct. 25, 1981. Student U. So. Calif., 1963-66; D.D., Hebrew Union Sem., 1966. Profl. entertainer, 1960—; union agt., organizer local 5 Hotel Workers Union, Honolulu, 1971-79; with local 555 Culinary and Service Employees Union, Honolulu, 1979—, pres., exec. officer, 1981—; chmn. Hawaii Entertainment Trades Council; exec. officer Hawaii Entertainers and Profls. Union. Active Mental Health Assn. Hawaii, Cystic Fibrosis Found., Aloha United Way; cantor Emanuel Temple, Honolulu. Mem. Hotel Workers Union, Teamsters Union, Am. Guild Variety Artists (Hawaii rep.), Musicians Union of Am. Fedn. Musicians. Democrat. Club: Press (Honolulu). Office: 2305 S Beretania St Suite 203 Honolulu HI 96826

KURIHARA, DON SUNAO, educational specialist; b. Honolulu, June 18, 1949; s. Tsugio and (Kaoru) K.; m. Kathleen (Ching) Dec. 3, 1973; children—Jonathon, David. B.E., U. Hawaii, 1971, M.Ed., 1979. Guidance counselor Dept. Army Civilian, Honolulu, 1973-78, edn. services specialist, 1979-81, supervisory edn. services specialist, 1981—. Mem. Am. Personnel and Guidance Assn., Hawaii Personnel and Guidance Assn.

KURISU, RUTH PATRICIA, utility company executive, consultant; b. Phillipsburg, N.J., May 26, 1950; d. Lawton Hughes and Grace Truell (Banks) Faunce; m. Willis Gilbert Frick, July 31, 1971; m. 2d, Verne Yoshiki Kurisu, Sept. 5, 1981. B.S. in Chemistry, Ursinus Coll., 1971; postgrad. Calif. State U.-Long Beach, 1976-78; cert. in electric power engring. UCLA, 1981. Cert. quality engr., Am. Soc. Quality Control. Chemist, Filtrol Corp., Los Angeles, 1972-73; test technician ENDEVCO, San Juan Capistrano, Calif., 1975; chemist Thiokol/Dynachem Corp., Tustin, Calif., 1975-78; quality assurance engr. So. Calif. Edison Co., San Clemente, 1978-81, sr. project adminstr. San Onofre Units 2 and 3, Rosemead, 1981—; cons. instr. Coastline Community Coll.; speaker in field. Recipient Woman of Achievement award Los Angeles YWCA, 1983. Mem. Nuclear Records Mgmt. Assn. (com. records turnover). Republican. Lutheran. Home: 29851 Millpond Ct San Juan Capistrano CA 92675 Office: PO Box 800 Rosemead CA 91770

KURMEL, LARRY DALE, financial exec.; b. Omaha, July 15, 1943; s. John George and Marjorie Louise (Retynski) K.; B.A. in Polit. Sci., Calif. State U., Sacramento, 1966; postgrad. U. Mich.; m. Ruth Elizabeth Ewing, Aug. 12, 1966; children—Claire Meredith, Lee Lindsey. Dir. elderly housing Sacramento Housing Authority, 1968-72; dir. mgmt. Conifer Devels., Inc., Tacoma, Wash., 1972-73; with Calif. Dept. Housing and Community Devel., also Office Gov. Calif., 1973-75; asst. sec. Calif. Dept. Bus., Transp. and Housing, 1975-77; sr. v.p. govt. affairs Calif. Savs. and Loan League, 1977-81; pres. Larry Kurmel & Assocs., 1982—; cons., tchr. in field. Served with USAR, 1962-65; col. Calif. N.G. Mem. Nat. Assn. Housing and Redevel. Ofcls. Club: Del Norte Swim and Tennis. Address: 4455 Park Green Ct Sacramento CA 95821

KURODA, YASUMASA, political scientist, educator, researcher; b. Tokyo, Apr. 28, 1931; came to U.S., 1951, naturalized, 1968; s. Shohei and Take (Ishii) K.; m. Alice Kuroda, Mar. 21, 1961; children—Kamilla,

Kamil. Student Waseda U., Tokyo, 1951; B.A., U. Oreg., 1956, M.A., 1959, Ph.D., 1961; postgrad. Princeton U., 1962. Instr. govt. Mont. State U., 1960-62, asst. prof., 1962-64; asst. prof. polit. sci. U. So. Calif., 1964-66; vis. assoc. prof. UCLA, 1965-66; assoc. prof. polit. sci. U. Hawaii, Manoa, 1966-72, prof., 1972—; cons. Frost & Sullivan of N.Y. Mem. exec. bd. Japanese Am. Citizens League, Hawaii, 1981—; chmn. U.S. Com. on Justice for Palestinians, 1982-83. Recipient citation for service Hawaii State Legislature, 1982; NSF fellow, 1962, Rockefeller Found. grantee, 1963-64. Mem. Am. Polit. Sci. Assn., Internat. Polit. Sci. Assn., Middle East Inst., Arab-Am. U. Grads., Asian Studies Assn. Author: Reed Town, Japan, 1974; Chihotoshi no kenryokukozo, 1976; (with Alice K. Kuroda) Palestinians without Palestine, 1978; (with others) Honolulu Residents and Their Attitudes in Multi-Ethnic Comarative Perspective: Towards a Theory of the American National Character, 1980. Office: University of Hawaii at Manoa Department of Political Science Honolulu HI 96822

KUROIWA, PAUL MASA, human resources cons.; b. Spokane, Wash., Aug. 31, 1947; s. George M. and Haru K.; B.S. in Bus. Mgmt., Lewis and Clark Coll., Portland, Oreg., 1969; M.Ed. in Adult Edn., Seattle U., 1974, Ph.C. in Ednl. Leadership, m. Anita Lynn Smith, Feb. 1, 1976; 1 son, Dustin Paul. Employment counselor Wash. Employment Security, 1966-71; vocat. counselor Seattle Public Schs., 1971-72; dir. Seattle Summer Youth Program, 1972; human relations specialist Seattle Public Schs., 1972-74; vis. lectr. Georgetown U., 1974; dir. ethnic studies Central Wash. U., 1974-76; cons. Impact Communications, Seattle, 1976-77, Osoro & Assos., Seattle, 1977-81; mgmt. cons., 1981—; acad. humanist Wash. Humanities Commn. Bd. dirs. Japanese Am. Citizens League, 1972-74, Asian Am. Edn. Assn., 1974. Mem. Am. Soc. Tng. and Devel., Nat. Assn. Edn. of Young Children, Nat. Asian and Pacific Am. Edn. Assn., Author: Confluent Theory of Values—Vision and Change, 1979; Asian American: The Invisible Students, 1976; Teacher Attitudes and Behaviors as a Socializing Agent, 1975; Human Resource Development for Speakers of Languages Other than English, 1979; Multi-Cultural In-Service Education, 1974. Home: 2509 E Denny Way Seattle WA 98122

KURTIK, NANCY DALENE, advertising agency executive; b. Oklahoma City, Jan. 10, 1946; d. Ralph Dale and Wanda Claudean (McMahan) Sexson; m. Jerome Joseph Kurtik, May 1, 1976; children—Teri Amber, Toni Lynn. Student Peperdine U., 1965-66, 70, Citrus Coll., 1970, West Los Angeles Coll., 1975. Supr. tour acctg. Continental Airlines, Los Angeles, 1971-73, staff accountant, revenue acctg., 1974, specialist tour sales planning and mktg., 1975-79; dir. mktg. Bernard Marko & Assos., Hawthorne, Calif., 1979-82; owner/founder Palm Desert Resort Rentals, 1983—. Mgr. Bobby Sox Softball, El Segundo, Calif., 1978; me. Council for Children's Religious Edn., El Segundo, 1978-79; mgr. Little League Baseball, Hawthorne, Calif., 1979, mem. Republican Presdl. Task Force. Recipient Xerox Profl. Selling Skills Course award, 1978; Public Service award Little League Baseball, 1980. Mem. Am. Mgmt. Assn. Mem. Ch. of Christ. Designer, publisher numerous airline tour brochures. Home and office: 77-565 Edinborough Palm Desert CA 92260

KURTZ, DON PHILLIP, drug and alcohol counselor, clergyman; b. Akron, Ohio, Oct. 31, 1928; s. Ray Elias and Grace Mildred (Stryker) K.; m. Karen Delecean, Aug. 3, 1962; children—Elizabeth Kurtz Morrison, Don Phillip, Ray B. B.A. in Psychology, Eastern Wash. U., 1979, M.S. in Counseling, Marriage and Family, 1981. Lic. pastor, Am. Lutheran Ch.; chem. dependency counselor, Mont. Enlisted U.S. Army, 1945, advanced through grades to master sgt., 1965, ret., 1968; marriage and family counselor Lutheran Social Service, Spokane, Wash., 1979-80; lay exec. dir. Luth. Marriage Encounter, Billings, Mont., 1976-79, drug and inpatient counselor, 1980—, adminstrv. group facilitator, trainer; pastor Broadview Luth. Ch., 1982—. Mem. Am. Personnel and Guidance Assn., Am. Mental Health Counselors Assn.

KUSHIBAB, ADELAIDE SERGOTT, nursing educator; b. Glen Lyon, Pa., Feb. 27, 1925; d. Joseph John and Joanna (Klaban) Sergott; R.N. diploma, Kings County Hosp. Sch. Nursing, Bklyn., 1946; postgrad. Ariz. State U., 1961-79, No. Ariz. U., 1964-80; m. Joseph Peter Kushibab, Oct. 11, 1947; children—Linda, Peter. Staff nurse Kings County Hosp., 1946-47, Jennings Hosp., Detroit, 1947; pvt. duty nurse Presbyn. Hosp., Phila., 1947-49; office nurse, Phoenix, 1949-51; gen.-duty nurse Good Samaritan Hosp., Phoenix, 1956-63; instr. in practical nursing, nursing assts. Area Vocat. Center, Phoenix, 1963—, clin. coordinator med. arts program. Registered profl. nurse, Ariz., N.Y. State; cert. vocat. tchr., Ariz. Mem. Nat. League Nursing, NEA, Ariz. Edn. Assn., Classroom Tchrs. Assn., Am. Vocat. Assn., Ariz. State Vocat. Assn., Health Occupations Edn. Ariz. Democrat. Roman Catholic. Club: St. Thomas the Apostle Sodality. Office: 315 N 5th St Phoenix AZ 85004

KUTCHINSKY, LEIGH ELENA, public health epidemiologist, educator; b. N.Y.C., Aug. 4, 1947; B.S., U. Calif., Berkeley, 1976, M.P.H., 1977, Ph.D., M.D., 1978; children—Buddy, Tad, Scott, Yaakov. Epidemiologist, Contra Costa (Calif.) VD Program, 1973-75; lectr. U. Calif., Berkeley, 1976-77; epidemiologist Colo. Dept. Health, Denver, 1977—; asst. prof. U. Colo. Med. Center, 1977—; pres. Medi-Search, Inc.; co-founder West Contra Costa Clinic; childbirth and Lamaze instr. Brighton Hosp. Chairperson, Contra Costa Childcare Adv. Bd., 1973-75; mem. Joint Strategy Action Com. on Medi-Cal Reform, 1975-77, Com. on Access to Health Care, 1975-78, Med. Com. for Human Rights, 1968—, U. Calif. Acad. Affairs Council, 1975-77. Chmn. issues com. Adams County Democratic Women's Caucus; mem. exec. bd. Adams County. Calif. State fellow, 1976-78, Regents fellow, 1976-78; A-CC/AMA scholar, 1975-76; HEW trainee, 1976-78. Mem. Am. Pub. Health Assn., Am. Med. Women's Assn., Colo. Pub. Health Assn., Am. Trauma Soc., Colo. Holistic Health Network, Am. Acad. Polit. Sci., EST, Mensa, Phi Beta Kappa, Alpha Gamma Sigma (Gold Pin award). Democrat. Jewish. Club: Am. Kennel. Research on herpes virus. Home and office: 2490 Channing Way Apt 503 Berkeley CA 94563

KUTSKO, JACQUELYN PATTI, educator, writer; b. Akron, Ohio, Mar. 27, 1945; d. Pete and Carolyn (Naglic) Patti; B.A., U. Akron, 1967; M.Ed., Colo. State U., 1983; m. James Andrew Kutsko, June 10, 1967; 1 son, James Andrew. Tchr. bus. N.E. High Sch., Pasadena, Md., 1967, Athens-Draughon Bus. Coll., Athens, Ga., 1967, McAuley High Sch., Cin., 1971-72; tchr. bus., coordinator Scarlet Oaks Joint Vocat. Sch., Cin., 1972-73; instr. bus. Barnes Bus. Coll., Denver, 1974-76; pres., owner Finishing Touches, Englewood, Colo., 1976-78; bus. and med. office cons., 1976-78; tchr. bus. Smoky Hill High Sch., Aurora, Colo., 1976—; lectr. profl. groups. Mem. Med. Office Asst.'s Adv. Bd., Community Coll. Denver, 1976. Mem. NEA, Nat. Bus. Edn. Assn., Mountain Plains Bus. Edn. Assn., Colo. Vocat. Assn., Colo. Educators For and About Bus., Cherry Creek Tchrs. Assn., Am. Vocat. Assn., U.S. Figure Skating Assn. Club: Denver Figure Skating. Author: Broncos: From Striped Socks to Super Bowl and Beyond, 1980; Houghton-Mifflin Typewriting-Keyboard Mastery and Applications, 1st and 2d yr. texts. Home: 8378 E Jamison Circle S Englewood CO 80112 Office: 16100 E Smoky Hill Rd Aurora CO 80015

KUWAYAMA, GEORGE, curator; b. N.Y.C., Feb. 25, 1925; s. Senzo and Kuma K.; m. Lillian Yetsuko Yamashita, Dec. 1972; children—Holly, Mark, Jeremy. B.A., Williams Coll., 1948; M.A., Inst. Fine Arts, U. Mich., 1956. Curator of Oriental art Los Angeles County Mus., 1959-69; sr. curator Far Eastern art, 1969—; lectr. U. So. Calif., UCLA, Calif. State U.-Northridge. Served with U.S. Army, 1944-46. Mem. Am. Oriental Soc., Assn. Asian Studies. Democratic. Methodist. Author numerous scholarly articles on Oriental and Far Eastern art. Home: 1417 Comstock Los Angeles CA 90024 Office: 5905 Wilshire Blvd Los Angeles 90036

KUYER, JOHN BRAND, aerospace and architectural consultant; b. The Hague, Holland, Jan. 21, 1928; s. John and Elisabeth (Zweegman) K.; Architect, Tech. Inst., Arnhem-Holland, 1953; postgrad. Brit. Inst. Engrng. Tech., London, Eng., 1953-55, Acad. Computer Tech., 1968-70; m. Nancy J. Goldberg-Williams, June 6, 1981; children by previous marriage—Yolanda Wilbeth, Ronald Pierre; stepchildren—Kevin R., Michael B. Came to U.S., 1958, naturalized, 1963. Archtl. designer, Holland, 1950-53; indsl. facilities designer, Can., 1953-58; indsl. facilities engr., cons. aero space industry, Los Angeles County, 1963—, archtl. cons. contracting firms, 1958—; lectr. arch. projects for various civic groups, youth orgns. Mem. com. Boy Scouts Am., El Segundo, 1964-68. Served with Holland Army, 1948-50. Mem. Am. Inst. Bldg. Design (bd. dirs. Los Angeles chpt. 1960-63), Am. Inst. Indsl. Engrs. (v.p. Los Angeles chpt. 1980—), Soc. Am. Mil. Engrs., Internat. Platform Assn. Club: Windjammers' Yacht (Marina del Rey, Calif.). Address: 8025 Redlands St #1 Playa del Rey CA 90291

KUYPER, DONALD MELLEMA, telephone co. exec.; b. Pasadena, Calif., June 27, 1933; s. Jacob and Frances Elizabeth (Seaman) K.; B.E.E., Rensselaer Poly. Inst., 1955; M.B.A., Harvard U., 1962; m. Verna Joan Emery, Aug. 16, 1958; children—Kurt, Neil, Scott. Elec. engr. Philco Corp., Phila., 1953-54, Bell Telephone Labs., N.Y. and N.J., 1955-61; project adminstr. RCA, Burlington, Mass., 1961-62; def. communications coordinator Hawaiian Telephone Co., Honolulu, 1962, dial adminstr., 1964-66, plant extension engr., 1966, plant extension div. engr., 1966, dir. govt. communications, 1966-69, v.p. ops. staff, 1969-71, v.p. service, 1971-72, v.p. personnel, 1972-78, pres., 1978—; v.p. mktg. and customer service Gen. Telephone Co. of Ill., 1977. Mem. exec. bd. Aloha council Boy Scouts Am.; bd. dirs. Aloha United Way, Oahu Devel. Conf.; bd. dirs., pres. Downtown Improvement Assn. Served to lt. USN, 1956-60. Mem. Armed Forces Communications and Electronics Assn., Assn. U.S. Army, Ind. Telephone Pioneer Assn., Naval Res. Assn. Clubs: Rotary, Pacific (Honolulu); Oahu Country; Masons. Office: Hawaiian Telephone Co PO Box 2200 Honolulu HI 96841

KUZMA, JAN WALDEMAR, biostatistics and epidemiology educator; b. Warsaw, Poland, Apr. 24, 1936; s. William and Elizabeth M. K.; m. Kay Humpal, Sept. 1, 1963; children—Kim, Kari, Kevin. B.A. in Math. and Physics, Andrews U., 1959; M.S. in Biostats., Columbia U., 1961; Ph.D. in Biostatistics, U. Mich., 1963. Dir. clin. trials unit UCLA Health Scis. Computing Facility, 1963-67; asst. prof. preventive medicine and pub. health Loma Linda (Calif.) U., 1963-67; Applied Stats. Tng. Inst. instr. Nat. Center Health Statis., Washington, 1972-80; chmn. dept. biostats./epidemiology Loma Linda U., 1967—, dir. Survey Research Service, 1972—, prof. biostatis., 1973—. Named Outstanding Educator Am., 1972. Am. Public Health Assn. fellow, 1969. Mem. Biometrics Soc., Am. Statis. Assn., Soc. Epidemiol. Research, Am. Pub. Health Assn., AAAS, Sigma Xi, Delta Omega Soc. Seventh-day Adventist. Contbr. articles to profl. jours. Office: Dept Biostats and Epidemiology Loma Linda Univ Loma Linda CA 92350

KWAN, BENJAMIN CHING KEE, ophthalmologist; b. Hong Kong, July 12, 1940; s. Shun Ming and Lurk Ming (Lai) K.; came to U.S., 1959, naturalized, 1969; B.S., St. Louis U., 1963; M.D., Washington U., 1967; m. Catherine Ning, Aug. 29, 1964; children—San San, David Daiwai. Intern, U. So. Calif. - Los Angeles County Med. Center, 1967-68; resident ophthalmology Barnes Hosp., Washington U. Med. Center, St. Louis, 1968-69, 71-73; practice medicine specializing in ophthalmology, chief ophthalmology dept. So. Calif. Permanente Med. Group, Harbor City, 1976—; attending physician Harbor Gen. Hosp., Torrance, Calif., 1974—, UCLA Med. Center, 1977—; asst. clin. prof. UCLA, 1980—. Served with U.S. Army, 1969-71. Recipient Physician Recognition award AMA, 1976; diplomate Am. Bd. Ophthalmology. Mem. Am. Acad. Ophthalmology, Pacific Coast Oto-Ophthal. Soc., Chinese Physicians Soc. So. Calif. (pres.). Roman Catholic. Contbr. articles in field to profl. jours. Home: 6327 Tarragon Rd Rancho Palos Verdes CA 90274 Office: 1050 W Pacific Coast Hwy Harbor City CA 90710

KWAN, KIAN MOON, sociologist, educator; b. Kwangtung, China, June 15, 1929; s. J.C. Kwan and Tak Quon Mar; m. Grace Chu-Yeng Lo, Dec. 30, 1961; children—Joseph H., Gregory L., Christie F. B.A. magna cum laude, Far Eastern U. (Phillipines), 1952; M.A., U. Calif.-Berkeley, 1954, Ph.D., 1958. Instr. Ohio U., Athens, 1958-61, asst. prof., 1961-65, chmn. dept. sociology and anthropology, 1963-65; assoc. prof. Calif. State U., Northridge, 1965-69, prof. sociology, 1969—, chmn. dept. sociology, 1969-71; vis. prof. U. Hawaii, Manoa, 1972-73. Mem. Am. Sociol. Assn. Democrat. Roman Catholic. Authur: (with Tamotsu Shibutani) Ethnic Stratficiation: A Comparative Approach, 1965. Home: 17408 Mayall St Northridge CA 91395 Office: 18111 Nordhoff St Northridge CA 91330

KYLE, ROBERT TOURVILLE, electrical engineering consultant; b. Deadwood, S.D., Jan. 15, 1910; s. Robert Doughty and Mellanie Irene (DeTourville) K.; B.E., Johns Hopkins U., 1931; M.B.A., Northeastern U., 1965; m. Colette Hart, May 29, 1937; 1 son, Robert H. Gas engr., Iroquois Gas Corp., Buffalo, 1934-45; br. mgr. Gen. Controls Co., Cleve., 1945-47; v.p. Gas Machinery Co., Cleve., 1947-59; with Commonwealth Services, N.Y.C., 1959-61; v.p. Bay State Gas Co., Boston, 1961-74; cons. in engring., San Diego, 1974—. Pres., Bernardo Home Owners Corp., San Diego; v.p. Ctr. Continuing Edn., Community Council San Diego. Mem. Johns Hopkins U. Alumni Assn. (pres. Cleve.), Am. Gas Assn., Pacific Coast Gas Assn., Nat. Soc. Profl. Engrs. Club: Rotary. Contbr. articles to profl. jours. Address: 18024 Sencillo Dr San Diego CA 92128

KYLE, WILLIAM DENNIS, restaurant owner; b. Vita, Man., Can., Dec. 24, 1941; came to U.S., 1963; s. William Ronald and Irene Anne (Opocensky) K.; student United Coll. (Man., Can.), 1960-61, UCLA, 1968-69; m. Donna Faye Chase, Sept. 19, 1964; children—Darren James, Kristin Deann, Ryan William. Salesman, Squibb-Beechnut Inc., Los Angeles, 1963-66, spl. accounts sales rep., 1966-68, dist. sales mgr. So. Calif., 1968-72; div. sales mgr. Central Plains States, Life Savers, Inc., Kansas City, Mo., 1972-73; pres. Kyle Enterprises, Inc., Twin Falls, Idaho, 1973—, Kyle Inc., Burley, Idaho, 1978—; owner, operator McDonald's Restaurants, Twin Falls, 1973—, Burley, 1979—; state rep. McDonald's Regional Operators adv. bd., 1975-78; pres. McDonald's So. Idaho Advt. Co-op, 1978-79. Chmn. YMCA Advanced Gift Fund drive, 1979. Recipient Outstanding Performance award March of Dimes, 1977; named Optimist of Yr., 1977-78; various awards McDonald's Corp., 1977-80. Mem. Twin Falls C. of C. (dir. 1978-81), Burley C. of C., McDonald's Restaurant So. Idaho Advt. Co-op., Young Family Christian Assn. Clubs: Twin Falls Blue Lakes Country, Sojourney, Optimists (dir. 1974-76, 77-78, honor club pres. 1976-77, lt. gov. Pacific N.W. dist. 1978-79, dist. youth activities chmn. 1980-81, Disting. Lt. Gov. award 1979), Twin Falls Flying. Office: 219 2d St N Twin Falls ID 83301

KYLLO, THEODORE ROBERT, govt. ofcl.; b. Richmond, Calif., June 29, 1946; s. Charles Benjamin and Lillian Louise (Madron) K.; diploma in acctg. LaSalle Extension U., 1978; m. Sharon Ann Bridges, May 27, 1972. Explosives worker, operator Naval Ammunition Depot, Hawthorne, Nev., 1967-72; explosives operator U.S. Naval Torpedo Sta., Keyport, Wash., 1977-79, explosives operator leader, 1979-82, explosives insp., 1982—; pres. Kyllo Income Tax Bookkeeping, Hawthorne, 1974-77; v.p. SK Enterprises, Hadlock, Wash., 1979—; owner Valves Unltd., 1981—. Mem. Am. Numis. Assn., Collectors of Numis. Errors. Democrat. Address: PO Box 479 200 Randolph St Hadlock WA 98339

LAANANEN, DAVID HORTON, engineer, research and development manager; b. Winchester, Mass., Nov. 11, 1942; s. Joseph and Helen Katherine (Horton) L.; m. Mary Ellen Storck, Sept. 9, 1967; children—Gregg David, Ellen Kaye. B.S. in Mech. Engring., Worcester Poly. Inst., 1964; M.S. in Mech. Engring., Northeastern U., 1965, Ph.D., 1968. Engr. Dynamic Sci. Co., Phoenix, 1972-74; asst. prof. mech. engring. Pa. State U., 1974-78; mgr. research and devel. Simula Inc., Tempe, Ariz., 1978—. Served to lt. USN, 1968-72. Recipient outstanding teaching award Pa. State U., 1977. Mem. Soc. Automotive Engrs., ASME, AIAA. Contbr. articles to sci. jours. Office: Simula Inc 2223 S 48th St Tempe AZ 85282

LABEN, ROBERT COCHRANE, educator; b. Darien Center, N.Y., Nov. 16, 1920; s. Victor L. and Ruth (Cochrane) L.; m. Dorothy Lobb, Nov. 29, 1946; children—John V., Robert J., Elizabeth Laben Cunningham, Catherine L. B.S., Cornell U., 1942; M.S., Okla. State U., Stillwater, 1947; Ph.D., U. Mo., Columbia, 1950. Research and teaching asst. Okla. State U., U. Mo., 1946-50; instr. animal husbandy, asst. animal husbandman Calif. Expt. Sta., U. Calif.-Davis, 1950-64, prof. animal sci., geneticist, 1964—, dir. Computer Ctr., 1964-69, master advisor in animal sci., 1970—, vice chmn. dept. animal sci., 1977—. Elder, deacon Presbyn. Ch.; hunter safety vol. instr. Calif. Dept. Fish and Game, 1962—; committeeman Golden Empire council Boy Scouts Am., 1955-65. Served to capt. F.A., AUS, 1942-46. Decorated Bronze Star, Purple Heart with cluster; recipient Outstanding Advisor award U. Calif. Coll. Agr., 1982. Mem. Am. Dairy Sci. Assn., Am. Soc. Animal Sci., Biometric Soc., Am. Genetic Assn., Sigma Xi, Alpha Zeta. Republican. Contbr. sci. papers on dairy cattle breeding and genetics to profl. jours. Home: 502 Oak Ave Davis CA 95616 Office: Dept Animal Sci U Calif Davis CA 95616

LABER, MARIAN ROBERTA OPPENHEIM, real estate broker and developer; b. Hanford, Calif., Jan. 18, 1918; d. Leon and Isabelle (Estrada) Oppenheim; student San Francisco City Coll., 1966, Golden Gate Coll., 1969; m. Lawrence E. Laber, Feb. 22, 1941 (dec.); children—Lawrence E., Pamela, Deborah (Mrs. Thomas McDermott), James Harrison. Telephone operator Pacific Tel. & Tel. Co., 1936-39, instr., 1940-42; mgr. office Press Wireless, Washington, 1942-43; owner Marian Lawrence, children's shop, San Francisco, 1945-48; owner, mgr. San Bruno 5-10, San Francisco, 1947-50; girl Friday, Lampley Realty, San Francisco, 1968-72, owner, real estate broker, from 1972; now with Land Mgmt. Services, San Francisco; owner Marian Laber Real Estate. Active Boy Scouts Am., Girl Scouts U.S.A., Campfire Girls; pres. local PTA, 1954-55. Treas. bd. dirs. Drew Coll. Prep. Sch. Mem. ARC, Am. Cancer Soc., San Francisco Real Estate Bd., Calif. Real Estate Assn. Roman Catholic (pres. ch. group 1950-51). Home: 2235 Laguna San Francisco CA 94122 Office: 1070 Howard St San Francisco CA

LABINGER, ALBERT L., business executive; b. 1933; B.A., UCLA, 1955; married. Pres., Bekins Bldg. Maintenance, 1964-77; pres., chief exec. officer Bekins Bldg. Services Group, 1977-78; exec. v.p., chief operating officer, The Bekins Co., 1978, pres., chief operating officer, 1979-81, pres., chief exec. officer, 1981—, also dir. Office: Bekins Co 777 Flowers St Glendale CA 91201

LA BONTÉ, C(LARENCE) JOSEPH, entertainment co. exec.; b. Salem, Mass., Sept. 23, 1939; s. Arthur and Alice Bella (Lecombe) LaB.; B.S., Northeastern U., 1966, A.M.E., 1968; M.B.A. with distinction (Baker scholar), Harvard U., 1969; m. Donna Marie Chiaradonna, Aug. 2, 1959; children—Linda Jean, Joseph Michael. With H.P. Hood & Sons, Boston, 1958-63; project engr., mktg. coordinator Market Forge Co., Everett, Mass., 1963-67; with ARA Services, Inc., Phila., 1969-79, v.p. Food Services Co., 1971-72, pres. Western Co., Los Angeles, 1972-76, exec. v.p. ARA, Phila., 1976-79; pres., chief operating officer, dir. Twentieth Century-Fox Film Corp., Beverly Hills, Calif., 1979—. Nat. bd. dirs. Big Bros. Am., 1970-74, Los Angeles Philarm. Assn., 1980—; vis. bd. dirs. Northeastern U., 1974—; mem. Harvard Bus. Sch. Fund, 1971—. Recipient Brown award Harvard Bus. Sch. Mem. Harvard Bus. Sch. Assn. (dir. So. Calif. chpt.), Husky Assos. Northeastern U. Clubs: Philadelphia Country, Down Town, Vesper; Bankers (San Francisco). Office: 20th Century Fox Box 900 Beverly Hills CA 90213*

LABORDE, GENIE ZYLKS, psychologist, artist; b. Borger, Tex., Feb. 19, 1928; d. Floyd Weber and Molsie Lee (Lowery) Zylks; B.A., La. State U., 1948; M.A., Tulane U., 1970; Ph.D., U. Calif., Santa Barbara, 1977; m. John Peter Laborde, July 2, 1949 (div. 1974); children—John Tracy, Cliffe Floyd, Gary Lee, John Peter, Adrienne; m. 2d, George Davis Griffin, Feb. 21, 1981. Dir., Confluent Edn. Research and Devel. Center, 1973-77; research dir. Berkeley (Calif.) Inst. Psychol. Research, 1977—; partner Grinder, Laborde, Hill Communication Excellence Seminars; partner VAK Newsletter; Communication Excellence Seminars N.Y. and Calif.; communication cons., precision trainer, cert. practitioner of neurolinguistic programming, Palo Alta, Calif., 1980—; seminar leader, confluent edn., gestalt and introject awareness; tchr. classes San Andreas Health Council; condr. creativity confs.; painter; works exhibited Santa Barbara, 1980. Mem. mgmt. council San Andreas Health Council, 1978; bd. dirs. Lomi Farm Inst. of Hawaii, 1977. Mem. Am. Psychol. Assn., Assn. Humanistic Psychology. Author: (with others) Tranquilizers for His Cup, 1961; editor: Around the World the YPO Way, 1964; contbr. chpt. to book. Home and Office: 1431 Webster St Palo Alto CA 94301

LA BOUNTY, HUGH ORVICE, university administrator; b. Chgo., Sept. 22, 1927; s. Hugh Orvice and Dorothy (Cooper) La B.; B.A., U. Redlands, 1950, M.A., 1951; Ed.D., UCLA, 1961; m. Gwen Evans, Sept. 5, 1950; children—Brian, Mark, Kim, Paul, Eric. Mem. faculty Citrus Coll., Azusa, Calif., 1950-53; mem. faculty dept. social scis. and history Calif. State Poly. U., Pomona, 1953—, v.p. acad. affairs 1967-77, pres., 1977—; cons., Tanzania, Greece, United Arab Emirates. Served with USNR, 1945-46. Mem. Inland Valley World Affairs Council (dir.), Pomona C. of C. (dir.). Author: Government of California, 1957. Office: Calif State Polytechnic Univ 3801 W Temple Ave Pomona CA 91768

LACEY, NANCY CAROLINE, city adminstr.; b. Sonora, Calif., Feb. 4, 1931; d. Earl Leonard and Lucile Debra (Ness) Larsen; m. Robert Roy Rowland, Apr. 7, 1951; children—Rob Roy, Nancy Lee Barnes, Katherine; m. 2d, John Allan Lacey, June 26, 1982. A.A., Saddleback Coll., Mission Viejo, Calif., 1982. Cert. profl. sec. Sec., Irvine (Calif.) Unified Sch. Dist., 1971-74, adminstrv. asst. supt., 1974-80; city clk. Irvine, 1980—. Mem. Internat. Inst. Mcpl. Clks., City Clks. Assn. Calif. Club: Soroptimist Internat. (Irvine). Office: 17200 Jamboree Rd Irvine CA 92713

LACEY-BOYD, BONNIE C(LAUDINE), heavy industrial cleaning company official; b. Salem, Oreg., Feb. 8, 1939; d. Theodore and Katie (Becker) Dalke; student Mt. Hood Community Coll., m. Neil R. Boyd; children—Carl, Cynthia Boyd DeMarco, Catherine, Rhonda. Sec., State of Oreg., 1972-73; lab. technician Truitt Bros., Salem, 1965-72; Oreg. compliance officer OSHA, Coos Bay and Salem, 1973-75; tng. officer Oreg. Workers' Compensation Dept., Salem, 1975-76; safety cons. State Accident Ins. Fund, Portland, Oreg., 1976-78; loss control/safety dir.

Crosby & Overton, Portland, 1978—; mem. Oreg. Gov.'s Safety Conf. Steering Com., Portland Shipyard Safety Council, Portland Labor/Mgmt. Safety Coordinating Com. Sec., Western's Internat. Citizen Band Assn., Salem, 1963-68; den leader Cub Scouts Salem council Boy Scouts Am., 1964-67; vol. tchr.'s aide Shaw (Oreg.) Elem. Sch., 1965-68. Mem. Am. Soc. Safety Engrs. (sec. Portland chpt. 1977-83, 2d v.p. 1983-84), Nat. Safety Mgmt. Soc. (sec. Portland chpt. 1975-76, pres. chpt. 1976-77). Republican. Baptist. Home: 8750 SE 155th #35 Portland OR 97236 Office: 5420 N Lagoon Portland OR 97217

LACHAPELLE, CAROLE, executive secretary; b. Los Angeles, May 16, 1941; d. Clay David Key and Jean Lee (Waldie) Key Zuetel; m. Rogers E. Crane, Dec. 17, 1960; m. 2d, Frank J. LaChapelle, Oct. 11, 1975; children—Steven Scott, Shawn Marie. A.A., Santa Monica Coll., 1975. Cert. profl. sec., Calif. With System Devel. Corp., A. Burroughs Co., Camarillo, Calif., 1960—; exec. sec. II Office of Chmn. and Pres., 1975—; notary pub. State of Calif. Recipient Outstanding Sec. of So. Calif. award Inst. Profl. Secs. Internat., 1982. Mem. Profl. Secs. Internat. (v.p. 1982-83), Nat. Notary Assn. Republican. Methodist. Office: 5151 Camino Ruiz Camarillo CA 93010

LACHER, STEPHEN PAUL, accountant; b. Norfolk, Va., Dec. 27, 1949; s. Sol and Ruth (Breskin) L.; 1 dau., Leslie. B.S., San Diego State U., 1973. C.P.A., Calif. Staff acct. Levin, Cooper, Spiegel & Co., C.P.A.s, 1973-76, Frankel & Lodgen, C.P.A.s, 1976-78; ptnr. Frankel, Lodgen, Lacher & Golditch, Encino, Calif., 1979—. Mem. Am. Inst. C.P.A.s, C.P.A. Soc. Calif.

LACHMAN, ALAN BARRY, dermatologist; b. New Haven, Nov. 26, 1935; s. Sander E. and Goldye (Cummins) L.; A.B., Haverford Coll., 1957; M.D. magna cum laude, U. Md., 1962; m. Margaret F. Wisneiwski, Nov. 16, 1963; children—Timothy Alan, Lisa Ann, Patrick Alan, Elizabeth Ida. Intern, U. Md., Balt., 1962-63; resident U Oreg., Portland, 1965-66, resident in dermatology, 1966-69, clin. asst. prof., 1969-81; practice medicine specializing in dermatology, Portland, 1969—; mem. staff U. Oreg. Health Scis. Center, St. Vincent's Hosp., Cedar Hills Psychiat. Hosp. Served to sr. asst. surgeon USPHS, 1963-65. Diplomate Am. Bd. Clin. Hypnosis, Am. Bd. Dermatology. Mem. AMA, Oreg. Med. Assn., Washington County Med. Soc., Oreg. Dermatology Soc., Pacific NW Dermatology Soc., Pacific Dermatology Assn., Am. Soc. Clin. Hypnosis, Alpha Omega Alpha. Republican. Home: 2630 NW 144th Ave Beaverton OR 97006 Office: 1585 SW Marlow Ave Portland OR 97225

LACK, FRED SEVIER, III, motorcycle and jet ski accessory manufacturer; b. Los Angeles, Oct. 4, 1947; s. Fred S. and Ruth Munro (Reynolds) L.; m. Barbara Ann Bell, June 19, 1971 (div.); 1 dau., Kelly Suzanne. B.S. in Mktg., U. So. Calif., 1970. Account mgr. Mattel, Inc., Hawthorne, Calif., 1971-72; owner Fredmark Distbg. Co., Inglewood, Calif., 1972-76; nat. sales mgr. Filter Dynamics, Inc., Santa Ana, Calif., 1976-78; account mgr. Flecto Co., Oakland, Calif., 1978-80; owner Fred S. Lack III and Assocs., Culver City, Calif., 1981—. Mem. Internat. Jet Ski Boating Assn., Sigma Alpha Epsilon. Republican. Presbyterian. Office: Fred S Lack and Assocs 5900 Canterbury Dr Suite A107 Culver City CA 90230

LACY, LEE MARVA LOU, educator; b. Longview, Tex., Dec. 28, 1942; d. Louis and Grace Tecumseh (Davis) Armstrong; B.S. in Math., Prairie View (Tex.) A&M U., 1965; M.A. in Secondary Math. Edn. (grantee Roosevelt Sch. Dist. 1977-78), Ariz. State U., 1978; m. Troy Lee Lacy, June 20, 1965; children—Corwyn Enrico, Aimee Siubhan, Gardenia Catriona. Tchr. math. schs. in Tex., Nebr., Md. and Ariz., 1965-68, 69-77; sr. gen. edn. instr., counselor Washington Jobs Corps, 1968; tchr. math., spl. tchr. for gifted C.O. Greenfield Jr. High Sch., Phoenix, 1978-82; math and gifted resource tchr. T.B. Barr Sch., Phoenix, 1982—; faculty assoc. Prairie View A&M U., 1981-83; vis. math. tchr. South Mountain Community Coll., Phoenix, 1982—; workshop leader, cons. in field. Vol., Arthritis Found., Leukemia Soc.; v.p., trustee sanctuary choir First Instl. Bapt. Ch., Phoenix. Mem. Nat. Council Tchrs. Math., NEA, Assn. Supervision and Curriculum Devel., Ariz. Edn. Assn., Ariz. Assn. Tchrs. Math., Roosevelt Classroom Tchrs. Assn., Ariz. State U. Alumni Assn., Delta Sigma Theta Alumnae. Baptist. Home: 416 E Greenway Dr Tempe AZ 85282 Office: 2041 E Vineyard Rd Phoenix AZ 85040

LADAR, JERROLD MORTON, lawyer; b. San Francisco, Aug. 2, 1933; s. Samuel A. and Sylvia F. L.; A.B., U. Wash., 1956; LL.B., U. Calif., Berkeley, 1960; m. Joyce B. Ladar, June 23, 1956; children—Jonathan, Jeffrey. Admitted to Calif. bar, 1961, U.S. Supreme Ct. bar, 1973; law clk. U.S. Dist. Judge Albert C. Wollenberg, San Francisco, 1960-61; asst. U.S. atty. San Francisco, 1961-70, chief criminal div. U.S. Atty.'s Office, 1968-70; instr. law San Francisco Law Sch., 1962—; lectr. continuing edn. of bar U. Calif.; mem. faculty Hastings Coll. Law, U. Calif., 1981—. Trustee, Tamalpais Union High Sch. Dist., 1968-77, chmn. bd., 1973-74. Cert. specialist in criminal law, Calif. Fellow Am. Bd. Criminal Trial Lawyers; mem. Bar Assn. San Francisco (editor reports 1974-76), Marin County Bar Assn., Am. Bar Assn., State Bar of Calif (disciplinary referee pro-tem 1975-77, chmn. exec. com. criminal law sect. 1983-84, editor Criminal Law Newsletter 1981—). Office: 507 Polk St Suite 310 San Francisco CA 94102

LADD, ALAN, JR., motion picture executive; b. Los Angeles, Oct. 22, 1937; s. Alan and Marjorie Jane (Harrold) L.; m. Patricia Ann Beazley, Aug. 31, 1959 (div.); children—Kelliann, Tracy Elizabeth, Amanda Sue. Student U. So. Calif. Agt., Creative Mgmt., Los Angeles, 1963-69; producer The Walking Stick, London, 1969, Severed Head, London, 1969, Tamlin, London, 1970, Villian, Zee, London, 1971; exec. producer Fear Is the Key, London, 1971; v.p. prodn. 20th Century Fox, Los Angeles, 1973-74, pres., 1976-80; sr. v.p. World Wide Prodn., 1974-76; pres. The Ladd Co., Burbank, Calif., 1980—. Served with USAF, 1961063. Mem. Found. Motion Picture Pioneers, Filmex. Office: 4000 Warner Blvd Burbank CA 91522

LADD, DONALD MC KINLEY, JR., lawyer; b. Huntington Park, Calif., Oct. 24, 1923; s. Donald McKinley and Rose (Roberts) L.; B.A., Denison U., 1945; J.D., Stanford U., 1950; m. Eleanor June Martin, June 29, 1951; children—Donald, Richard, Cameron. Admitted to Calif. bar, 1950; asso. firm Anderson McPharlin & Conners, Los Angeles, 1951; legal staff Union Pacific RR, Los Angeles, 1953-56; sr. dep. prosecutor City of Pasadena (Calif.), 1956-58; with Office of Dist. Atty., Santa Clara County, Calif., 1958—, asst. dist. atty., 1971—. Served to capt. USMCR, 1943-46, 51-52. Certified criminal law specialist Calif. Mem. Bay Area Prosecutors Assn., Calif. State Bar, Calif. Dist. Attys Assn., Stanford Law Alumni Assn., Blue Key, Omicron Delta Kappa, Phi Alpha Delta. Clubs: Marines Meml., Am. Commons. Home: 1034 Golden Way Los Altos CA 94022 Office: 70 W Hedding St San Jose CA 95110

LADERMAN, HARVEY ROSS, real estate devel. co. exec.; b. Los Angeles, Apr. 13, 1934; s. Morris Henry and Rose (Mellion) L.; B.A. in Econs., Stanford U., 1956, M.B.A., 1958; m. Jacklyn B. Smith, Aug. 1, 1970; children—Scott, Mark, Gregory. Vice pres. Realtech, Los Angeles, 1968-73, AMFAC Mortgage, Los Angeles, 1973-75, United Realty Trust, Beverly Hills, Calif., 1976-78; pres. Laderbel, Inc., Beverly Hills, 1978-81, Laderman Corp., Beverly Hills, 1981—; cons. infield. Pres. Fathers Club, St. Martin Tours Sch., 1979-81; pres. Webb Sch. Alumni Assn., 1977-79, mem. exec. com., 1974-80; bd. dirs. Holy Family Services, 1979; mem. Parish Council, St. Martin of Tours, 1980-82. Served with U.S. Army, 1958-61. Club: Bel Air Bay. Home: 705 S Westgate Ave Los Angeles CA 90049 Office: 9701 Wilshire Blvd Beverly Hills CA 90212

LADMAN, JERRY R., economist, educator; b. Sioux City, Iowa, Dec. 30, 1935; s. Harry L. and Amy I. (Swearingen) L.; m. Mary E. Ladman, June 4, 1960; children—Jeffrey, James, Michael. B.S., Iowa State U., 1958, Ph.D., 1968. Placement officer, Coll. Agr., Iowa State U., Ames, 1963-65, research asst., 1965-67; asst. prof., Ariz. State U., 1967-72, assoc. prof., 1972-78, prof. econs., 1979—, dir. Ctr. for Latin Am. Studies, 1976—; program asst. Ford Found., Mexico City, 1971-72; vis. prof. Nat. Sch. Agr., Chapingo, Mex., 1965-67, 71-72, Ohio State U., 1979; vis. scholar Stanford U., 1975. Chmn. Troop Com. Boy Scouts Am., Tempe, Ariz., 1976—; bd. dirs. Friends of Mexican Art, 1977—. Served to capt. USAR, 1958-65. Fulbright lectr., Ecuador, 1974. Mem. Am. Econ. Assn., Am. Agrl. Econ. Assn., Latin Am. Studies Assn., Pacific Coast Council Latin Am. Studies (treas. 1977—), Rocky Mountain Council Latin Am. Studies (bd. dirs. 1976—), Phoenix Com. Fgn. Relations, Ariz.-Mex. Commn. (bd. dirs., 1982—), Assn. Borderlands Scholars (pres. 1983—), PROFMEX (dir. 1983—). Author: The Development of Mexicali Regional Economy, 1975; United States-Mexican Energy Relationships: Realities and Prospects, 1981; Modern Day Bolivia: The Legacy of the Revolution and Prospects for the Future, 1982; contbr. articles to profl. jours, chpts. to books. Home: 1201 E Loyola Dr Tempe AZ 85282 Office: Ctr Latin Am Studies Ariz State U Tempe AZ 85287

LADNER, JUDITH SLEPPY, sch. adminstr.; b. Salt Lake City, Apr. 9, 1940; d. George S. and Bertha Annetta (Garrett) Sleppy; B.A., U. No. Colo., 1962; M.A., San Jose State U., 1976; Ed.D., U. Pacific, 1979; m. R.L. Ladner, Jr., Dec. 23, 1968. Tchr. Union Sch. Dist., San Jose, Calif., 1962-76, intermediate and jr. high sch. tchr., 1968-76, coordinator media services, 1976-77; tchr. Colegio Nueva Granda, Bogota, Colombia, 1967-68; prin. Alta Vista Sch., Los Gatos, Calif., 1977-80; asst. supt. Mountain View (Calif.) Sch. Dist., 1980—. Bd. dirs. United Way; bd. mgrs. YMCA. Mem. Assn. Calif. Sch. Adminstrs., AAUW, Assn. Calif. Sch. Adminstrs. (chmn. state conf.; regional pres. elect), Women Leaders in Edn. (sec.), Delta Kappa Gamma (chpt. pres. 1978-80), Phi Delta Kappa. Republican. Methodist. Home: 1025 Robinhood Ct Los Altos CA 94022 Office: Mountain View Sch Dist 220 View St Mountain View CA 94041

LAFFERTY, JUDITH ANN, counselor; b. LeMars, Iowa, July 19, 1939; d. Andrew R. and Elizabeth Eleanora (Tritz) L. B.A., U. Albuquerque, 1969; M.S., Calif. State U., 1971; Ph.D., Calif. Grad. Inst., 1975; postgrad. U. So. Calif., 1978-80. Lic. counselor, Calif. Psychotherapist, Andrus Vols., Gerontology Ctr., U. So. Calif., Los Angeles, 1978-82; analyst Disability Evaluation Bur., Calif. State Dept. Social Services, Los Angeles, 1971-81, Ops. Assessment, Calif. Dept. Social Services, 1981—; tchr. Interagy. Council of Aging, Cath. Archdiocese of Los Angeles, 1981—. Mem. home visitors program Cath. Welfare Bur., 1981-82. USPHS trainee, 1970-71. Mem. Am. Psychol. Assn., Am. Gerontol. Soc., Western Gerontol. Soc., Am. Rehab. Counselor Assn., Calif. Rehab. Counselor Assn., Calif. Psychol. Assn., Los Angeles County Psychol. Assn., Am. Gerontol. Soc. Democrat. Roman Catholic. Contbr. articles to profl. jours. Home: 2339 N Catalina St Los Angeles CA 90027 Office: 107 S Broadway Room 7005 Los Angeles CA 90027

LAFFOON, KAREN LOU, educator; b. Phoenix, Jan. 9, 1941; d. Ruby Lewis and Mary Elizabeth (Brown) L. B.A., San Diego State U., 1965, M. Ed., 1980. Cert. secondary, spl. edn. tchr. Calif. Substitute tchr. San Diego city schs., 1965-67; tchr. National City (Calif.) Jr. High Sch., 1967—, multi-cultural faire chmn., 1970-72. Soloist First Congregational Church San Diego, 1967-72. Mem. Nat. Assn. Tchrs. Singing, Sweetwater Edn. Assn., Calif. Tchrs. Assn., Nat. Tchrs. Assn., Sigma Alpha Iota. Author: The History of National City, 1981. Home: 3426 Belle Isle Dr San Diego CA 92105 Office: 1701 D Ave National City CA 92050

LAFKAS, PETER MICHAEL, mktg. co. exec.; b. Greece, Nov. 1, 1928; s. Michael D. and Helen M. (Poulos) L.; student UCLA, 1952-54; diploma St. Mary's Hosp., Long Beach, Calif., 1957; m. Zimika P. Ylahaki, Sept. 8, 1968; children—Michael P., Peter T. Pres. Primo Inc., Hong Kong, from 1967, Delta Oil and Gas Inc., Saigon, from 1970, Marquis Internat. Co. Inc., Reno, from 1974; owner P.M.L. Mktg., Long Beach, Calif., 1970—. Served with AUS, 1950-52; Korea. Decorated Bronze Star, Combat Inf. Badge. Mem. Am. Registry Radiologic Technologists, Ahepa. Republican. Greek Orthodox. Home: 861 Hillside Dr Long Beach CA 90816 Office: 141 E Broadway Long Beach CA 90802

LA FLASH, GEORGE WINTHROP, physician; b. Worcester, Mass., June 3, 1920; s. George Robert and Elizabeth B. (Worden) La F.; B.S., Wesleyan U., 1947; M.D., Columbia U., 1951; m. Kasandra Svensson Edin, Aug. 15, 1964; 1 dau., Joanell. Intern, St. Luke's Hosp., N.Y.C., 1951-52, resident in medicine, 1952-53; practice medicine, specializing in family medicine, Long Beach, Calif., 1953-68, occupational and indsl. medicine, 1968—; chief physician McDonnell Douglas Space Systems Center, Huntington Beach, Calif., 1968-73; med. dir. and partner occupational and indsl. medicine Avenue Med. Group, Santa Fe Springs, Calif., 1973—; co-owner med. partner Stadium East Med. Group, Orange, Calif., 1979—; sr. med. aviation examiner FAA. Served with M.C., USAAF, 1941-46. Diplomate Nat. Bd. Med. Examiners. Fellow Am. Soc. Contemporary Medicine and Surgery; mem. Am. Occupational Med. Assn., Am. Coll. Preventive Medicine, AMA (Physicians Recognition award 1979, 80, 83), Calif. Med. Assn., Orange County Med. Assn., Internat. Coll. Applied Nutrition, Aerospace Med. Assn., Orthomolecular Med. Soc. Home: 738 Elizabeth Dr Orange CA 92667 Office: 1215 W Katella Ave Orange CA 92667

LAFLASH, JUDSON CLINTON, def./aerospace marketing exec.; b. Mashpee, Mass., May 19, 1924; s. George Robert and Elizabeth Bancker (Worden) LaF.; B.A. Syracuse (N.Y.) U., 1949, postgrad., 1949-51; postgrad. Fgn. Service Inst., 1951, Northrop U., 1975; m. Jeannette Raymond, Jan. 17, 1951; children—Mark Steven, Christopher Raymond. Journalist, Syracuse Herald-Jour., 1949-51; fgn. service officer, press officer, pub. affairs officer U.S. Fgn. Service, Dept. State, Turkey, Greece, Washington, 1951-55; pub. info. officer Ramo-Wooldridge Corp., Los Angeles, 1955-58; dir. pub. relations/advt. Tamar Electronics and Operations Research Corps., Santa Monica, Calif., 1958-62; head advanced tech. mktg. Hughes Aircraft Co., El Segundo, Calif., and Canoga Park, Calif., 1962-73; sr. marketing mgr. fgn. mil. and NATO sales planning Rockwell Internat., Anaheim, Calif., 1973-74; mktg. mgr. Systems Devel. Corp., Santa Monica, 1974-77; pres., chmn. bd. Govt. Mktg. Cons. Woodland Hills, Calif., 1977—; v.p. mktg. Optonics, Inc., El Segundo; West Coast rep. Zung Advt. and Public Relations, Washington lectr., pub. speaker def. bus. devel.; cons. Honeywell Co., Boeing Co., Motorola Co.; dir. Wilburn Controls Corp. (Ill.). prof. mktg. Grad. Sch., Northrop U.; mem. faculty UCLA Extension. Served with AUS, 1943-46; ETO. Mem. Am. Astron. Soc., Am. Inst. Aeros. and Astronautics (sr.), Nat. Space Club, Aviation/Space Writers Assn., Phi Kappa Tau. Author: Prospectus 74-An Assessment of International Markets and Priorities, 1974; The Proposal: Document of Decision, 1978, also numerous govt. mktg. monographs and tech. reports. Home and office: 23113 Dolorosa St Woodland Hills CA 91367

LAFLEUR, JAMES KEMBLE, business executive; b. Los Angeles, Apr. 23, 1930; s. Herbert L. and Janet (Read) LaF.; m. Helene deCrais, May 4, 1964; children—Kathleen, Michele, Juliet. B.S., Calif. Inst. Tech., 1952; M.B.A., Pepperdine U., 1980. Lic. profl. engr. Calif. Design engr. Boeing Airplane Co., Seattle, 1952; devel. engr. AiResearch Garrett Corp., Los Angeles, 1952-56; pres. Dynamic Research Inc., Los Angeles, 1957-59; pres., chmn. bd. LaFleur Corp., Torrance, Calif., 1960-65; pres., chmn. bd. Indsl. Cryogenics Inc., Los Angeles, 1966-71; pres., chief exec. officer, chmn. bd. GTI Corp., San Diego, 1975—. Mem. ASME (chmn. nuclear cycles com. Gas Turbine Div. 1973-75), Soaring Soc. Am. Republican. Episcopalian. Clubs: Univ., Duquesne (Pitts.), Renaissance (Detroit), Lakeside Golf. Patentee turbomachinery and close cycle gas turbines, cryogenics equipment. Author: Research and Development Partnership: A Financial Breakthrough for Inventors and Small Businesses; contbr. articles to profl. jours.

LAFLEUR, LAWRENCE EUGENE, research chemist; b. Everett, Wash., Sept. 18, 1951; s. Eugene Harvey and Marie Margarett (Longborg) LaF. B.S. summa cum laude, U. Puget Sound, 1975; M.S., U. Oreg., 1977. Lab. technician U.S. Oil & Refining Co., Tacoma, 1972-75; research asst. U. Oreg., Eugene, 1975-77; research chemist Nat. Council Paper Industry for Air and Stream Improvement, Corvallis, Oreg., 1977-83, organic analytical program mgr., 1983—; environ. cons. forest products industry, 1979—. Recipient Student Affiliate award Am. Chem. Soc., 1975; La Pore award U. Puget Sound, 1974. Mem. Am. Chem. Soc., Am. Soc. Mass Spectrometry, AAAS, Assn. Ofcl. Analytical Chemists, Phi Kappa Phi. Home: 1237 NW 23d Apt 6 Corvallis OR 97330 Office: NCASI 720 SW 4th St PO Box 458 Corvallis OR 97339

LAFLEUR, MYRNA WEBER, educator, author; b. Arcola, Sask., Can., Oct. 17, 1941; d. Francis John and Christina May (Kramer) Weber; m. Lawrence Harrison LaFleur; 1 dau., Danielle Simone. R.N., Regina Grey Nuns Hosp., 1962; Ed.B. in Vocat. Edn., No. Ariz. U., 1977. Nurse, St. Joseph's Hosp., Comox, B.C., 1962-63, Children's Hosp., San Francisco, 1963; dir. staff devel. Doctors Hosp., Phoenix, 1964-70; program dir., instr. Maricopa Tech. Community Coll., Phoenix, 1970—; health care cons. Mem. Am. Vocat. Assn., Nat. Assn. Health Occupation Tchrs., Health Occupations Edn. Assn. (Creativity award 1981), Nat. Assn. Health Unit Clks.-Coordinators (founder, pres. 1981), Ariz. Health Unit Clks.-Coordinators Assn. (founder, pres. 1980), Maricopa County Community Coll. Dist. Faculty Assn., Women in Higher Edn. Ariz., Nat. Council Staff, Program and Orgn. Devel. Co-author: Unit Clerking in Health Care Facilities, 1979; Medical Service Coordinator Clinical Evaluation Handbook, 1980; contbr. articles to profl. jours. Home: 709 W Seldon Ln Phoenix AZ 85021 Office: 108 N 40th St Phoenix AZ 85034

LAFORTUNE, GAIL C., educational administrator; b. Oakland, Calif., June 19, 1930; d. Horace Radley and Celia Leona (Marchus) LaF. B.A., Pomona Coll., 1952; M.A., Calif. State U.-Sacramento, 1972. Tchr., choir dir. Bret Harte Sch., Sacramento, 1953-66; tchr., choir dir. Sutterville Sch., Sacramento, 1966-81, vice prin., 1981—; dir. elem. honor choir Sacramento City Schs., 1980; dir. youth choir Westminster Ch., Sacramento, 1977-80. Recipient honor service award PTA, 1962, 71. Mem. Music Educators Nat. Conf., NEA, Internat. Soc. Music Educators, Assn. for Supervision and Curriculum Devel., Sierra Club, Phi Delta Kappa, Delta Kappa Gamma, Alpha Delta Kappa, Pi Lambda Theta. Republican. Presbyterian. Office: 4967 Monterey Way Sacramento CA 95822

LA GANGA, THOMAS S., clin. chemist; b. Caldwell, N.J., July 23, 1927; s. James and Josephine (Messina) La G.; A.B., Drew U., 1951; M.S., Rutgers U., 1966, Ph.D., 1967; m. Shirley S. Plog, Aug. 5, 1976; children—Claire, Steve, Laurie, Shelly, Annie. Chief technologist Essex County Sanatorium, Verona, N.J., 1951-62; clin. chemist Princeton (N.J.) Hosp., 1967-69; asst. dir. endocrinology Bio-Sci. Labs., Van Nuys, Calif., 1969-79, adminstr. quality assurance, 1979—. Served with USAAF, 1945-47. Med. technologist, Am. Soc. Clin. Pathologists. Mem. Soc. Endocrinology (U.K.), N.J. Acad. Sci., Radioligand Soc., Sigma Xi. Contbr. sci. writings to profl. publs. Office: 7600 Tyrone Van Nuys CA 91405

LAGREEN, ALAN LENNART, association executive; b. Burbank Calif., May 20, 1951; s. Lennart Franklin and Mary Lillian (Cassara) LaG.; m. Wendy Diane Gilmaker, June 28, 1975; 1 dau., Cara Diane. B.A. in Journalism, U. So. Calif., 1975. Pub. relations asst. Dames and Moore, cons. engrs., Los Angeles, 1972-75; asst. pub. Orange County Illustrated, Newport Beach, Calif., 1975; membership mgr., Toastmasters Internat., Santa Ana Calif., 1975-79, mgr. dist. adminstrn and programming, 1979—. Asst. campaign mgr. Royce for State Senate 1982; mem. bd. Young Ams. for Freedom, 1972-75; active Citizens for Rail Calif., Nat. Assn. R.R. Passengers. Mem. Pub. Relations Soc. Am., Meeting Planners Internat., Am. Soc. Assn. Execs. (sect. dir. 1976-77). Republican. Mem. Reformed Ch. Contbr. to Passenger Train Jour. Office: Toastmasters International 2200 N Grand Ave Santa Ana CA 92711

LAI, WAIHANG, educator; b. Hong Kong, Jan. 7, 1939; s. Sing and Yu-ching (Wong) L.; came to U.S., 1964; B.A., Chinese U. Hong Kong, 1964; M.A., Claremont Grad. Sch., 1967; m. Celia Cheung, Aug. 13, 1966. Asst. prof. art Maunaolu Coll., Maui, Hawaii, 1968-70; instr. art Kauai (Hawaii) Community Coll., 1970—. Vis. prof. art Ariz. State U., Tempe, summer 1967. Mem. Am., Kauai (pres. 1974—) watercolor socs., Phila. Watercolor Club, Kauai Oriental Art Soc. (pres. 1981—). Author: The Chinese Landscape Paintings of Waihang Lai, 1966; The Watercolors of Waihang Lai, 1967. Home: PO Box 363 Lihue HI 96766 Office: Kauai Community Coll Lihue HI 96766

LAIDLAW, CAROLE ZAVALA, consulting firm executive, educator; b. Los Angeles, Aug. 31, 1938; d. Alexander Charles and Virginia E. (Ross) Zavala; m. David M. Laidlaw, Aug. 8, 1959 (div.); children—Marc, Brian. B.A., UCLA, 1963; postgrad. U. Calif.-Irvine, 1977-78, U. San Francisco, 1979-80. Life diploma for teaching, 1974, and gen. adminstrn. cert., 1976, Calif. Tchr. Los Angeles Pub. Schs., 1963-70; adminstr. gifted programs Capistrano Unified Sch. Dist. (Calif.), 1970-77; prin. R.H. Dana Sch., Capistrano, 1978-80; cons. State of Calif. Dept. Edn., 1980; pres. CZ Assocs. Cons., Laguna Beach, Calif., 1983—; fund devel. specialist Children's Home Soc.; cons. to sch. dists. Calif. Mem. Cable TV Task Force City of Laguna Beach; co-chmn. Alt. Edn. Task Force, Laguna Beach; bd. dirs. Laguna Beach Free Clinic, Laguna Beach Arts Alliance. Recipient scholarship CORO Women's Program Pub. Affairs, 1980; named Outstanding Young Woman, Glendale Community Coll., 1959. Mem. Assn. Calif. Sch. Adminstrs., Calif. Assn. for Gifted, Delta Kappa Gamma. Democrat. Author: Serena, 1976; Teaching Gifted Children Literature in Grades 4-6, 1978; (with E. Palo) The Lifeworks Equation—a Model for Career Change, 1982. Home: 1045 Catalina St Laguna Beach CA 92651

LAIDLAW, HARRY HYDE, JR., entomology educator; b. Houston, Apr. 12, 1907; s. Harry Hyde and Elizabeth Louisa (Quinn) L.; B.S., La. State U., 1933, M.S., 1934; Ph.D. (Univ. fellow, Genetics fellow, Wis. Dormitory fellow, Wis. Alumni Research Found. fellow), U. Wis., 1939; m. Ruth Grant Collins, Oct. 26, 1946; 1 dau., Barbara Scott Laidlaw Murphy. Teaching asst. La. State U., 1933-34, research asst., 1934-35; prof. biol. sci. Oakland City (Ind.) Coll., 1939-41; state apiarist Ala. Dept. Agr. and Industries, Montgomery, 1941-42; entomologist First Army, N.Y.C., 1946-47; asst. prof. entomology, asst. apiculturist U. Calif.-Davis, 1947-53, asso. prof. entomology, asso. apiculturist, 1953-60, prof. entomology, apiculturist, 1960-74, asso. dean Coll. Agr., 1960-64, prof. entomology emeritus, apiculturist emeritus, 1974—;

coordinator U. Calif.-Egypt Agrl. Devel. Program, AID, 1979-83. Rockefeller Found. grantee, Brazil, 1954-55, Sudan, 1967. Trustee, Yolo County (Calif.) Med. Soc. Scholarship Com., 1965-83. Served to capt. AUS, 1942-46. Recipient Cert. of Merit, Am. Bee Jour., 1957; Spl. Merit award U. Calif.-Davis, 1959; Merit award, Calif. Central Valley Bee Club, 1974; Merit award Western Apicultural Soc., 1980; NIH grantee, 1963-66; NSF grantee, 1966-74. Fellow AAAS; mem. Am. Genetics Assn., Am. Inst. Biol. Scis., Am. Soc. Naturalists, Am. Soc. Zoologists, Entomol. Soc. Am. (C.W. Woodworth award Pacific br. 1981), Genetics Soc. Am., Internat. Bee Research Assn., Nat. Assn. Uniformed Services, Ret. Officers Assn., Scabbard and Blade, Sigma Xi (treas. Davis chpt. 1959-60, v.p. chpt. 1966-67), Alpha Gamma Rho (pres. La. chpt. 1933-34, counsellor Western Province 1960-66). Democrat. Presbyterian. Club: Commonwealth (San Francisco). Author books, the most recent being: Instrumental Insemination of Honey Bee Queens, 1977; Contemporary Queen Rearing, 1979; author slide set: Instrumental Insemination of Queen Honey Bees, 1976. Home: 761 Sycamore Ln Davis CA 95616 Office: Dept Entomology U Calif Davis CA 95616

LAIDLAW, ROBERT MEYER, ethnologist; b. Norwood, Mass., May 26, 1951; s. William Robert and Amy Marie (Meyer) L.; B.A., Calif. State U., Fullerton, 1973; B.A. in Anthropology, B.A. in Philosophy and M.A. in Anthropology, Calif. State U., Fullerton, 1975; postgrad. Northwestern U., U. Calif. (Riverside); m. Margaret Mary Welty, July 17, 1976. Lectr., Calif. State U., Fullerton, 1975; spl. research dir. Calif. Dept. Edn./HEW, 1977; instr. extension univ. U. Calif., Riverside, 1977-80; research ethnologist Dept. of Interior, Sacramento, 1980—; chmn. Native Am. policy com. Soc. Calif. Archeology. Mem. Am. Anthrop. Assn., N.Y. Acad. Scis., S.W. Anthrop. Assn., AAAS, Sigma Xi, Phi Kappa Phi. Author/editor books on anthropology, resource mgmt. policy and govtl. relations. Contbr. articles to profl. jours.

LAITONE, EDMUND VICTOR, mechanical engineer; educator; b. San Francisco, Sept. 6, 1915; s. Victor Severinen and Alina (Hintikka) L.; m. Dorothy E. Bishop, Sept. 1, 1951; 1 dau., Victoria Dorothy. B.S., U. Calif.-Berkeley, 1938; M.A., Stanford U., 1944, Ph.D., 1960. Aero. engr. NACA, Langley Field, Va., 1939-41, Moffett Field, Calif., 1941-45, Cornell Aero. Lab., Buffalo, 1945-47; prof. mech. engring. U. Calif.-Berkeley, 1947—, chmn. extension engring. dept., 1979—; cons. engr. Hughes Aircraft Co., 1948-49, Douglas Aircraft Co., 1950-51, TRW, 1956-57, Office Naval Research, 1961-72; exchange prof. Moscow U., 1964; vis. fellow Balliol Coll., Oxford U., 1968. Fellow AIAA (assoc.). Contbr. numerous articles to profl. jours. Office: Dept Mech Engring U Calif Berkeley CA 94720

LAKE, BRUCE MENO, applied physicist, construction executive; b. Los Angeles, Nov. 22, 1941; s. Meno Truman and Jean Ivy (Hancock) L.; B.S.E., Princeton U., 1963; M.S., Calif. Inst. Tech., 1965, Ph.D., 1969. Mem. tech. staff advanced instrumentation dept. TRW Corp., Redondo Beach, Calif., 1969-73, head exptl. hydrodynamics sect., 1973-81, asst. mgr. fluid mechanics dept., 1977-81, mgr. fluid mechanics dept., 1981—; v.p. Site-Mixed Concrete Corp., Fontana, Calif., 1978—. Ford Found. fellow, 1964-65. Mem. Am. Phys. Soc., AIAA, Democrat. Contbr. articles to profl. jours. Office: One Space Park Redondo Beach CA 90278

LAKE, KEVIN BRUCE, physician; b. Seattle, Jan. 25, 1937; s. Winston Richard and Vera Emma (Davis) L.; B.S., Portland State U., 1960; M.D., U. Oreg., 1964; m. Donelda Crocker, Jan. 27, 1962; children—Laura, Kendrick, Wesley. Intern, Marion County Gen. Hosp. and Ind. Med. Center, Indpls., 1964-65; resident U. Oreg. Hosps. and Clinics, 1968-70; fellow in infectious and pulmonary diseases, 1970-71; fellow in pulmonary diseases U. So. Calif., 1971-72, instr. medicine, 1972-75, asst. clin. prof., 1975-79, asso. clin. prof., 1979—; dir. med. edn. and research La Vina Hosp., 1972-75; dir. respiratory therapy Methodist Hosp., Arcadia, Calif., 1975—; mem. staff Los Angeles County/U. So. Calif. Med. Center, Santa Teresita Hosp., Duarte, Calif., Huntington Meml. Hosp., Pasadena, Calif.; attending physician, mem. med. adv. bd. Foothill Free Clinic, Pasadena. 2d v.p. bd. mgmt. Palm St. br. YMCA, Pasadena, 1974, 1st v.p., 1975, chmn., 1976-78, met. bd. dirs., 1976—; bd. dirs. Mendenhall Ministries, La Vie Holistic Ministries, Hastings Found. co-pres. PTA, Allendale Grade Sch., Pasadena, 1975-76; deacon Pasadena Covenant Ch., 1976-79. Served to lt. U.S. Navy, 1965-68. NIH grantee, 1971-72. Fellow A.C.P., Am. Coll. Chest Physicians; mem. Am. Thoracic Soc., Calif. Thoracic Soc., Oreg. Thoracic Soc., Trudeau Soc., Am. Soc. Microbiology, N.Y. Acad. Scis., Calif. Med. Assn., Los Angeles County Med. Assn. Democrat. Contbr. articles to profl. jours. Home: 875 S Madison St Pasadena CA 91106 Office: 111 Congress St Suite C Pasadena CA 91105

LAKERS, LYNN ANN, accountant, tax consultant; b. Chgo., Mar. 3, 1948; d. Raymond W. and Julia M. (Gutschick) Stamer; A.A., Chabot Community Coll., Hayward, Calif., 1976; B.S., M.B.A., Calif. State U., Hayward, 1978; m. Patrick J. Lakers (div.). Audit clk. Bekins Van Lines, Hillside, Ill., 1966-67; buyer Adolph Plating Co. Inc., Chgo., 1968-70; storage mgr., payroll master Bekins Moving & Storage Co., Oakland, Calif., 1970-72; tax seasons staff H&R Block, Castro Valley, Calif., 1975-77; pvt. practice acctg., Hayward, 1978; pres. L.A. Lakers & Assos. Inc., Hayward, 1978—, Boulder City, Nev., 1978—, dir. various small bus. corps.; cons. in field; enrolled to practice before IRS. Vice-chmn. Boulder Parks and Recreation Commn., 1982, chmn., 1983. Mem. So. Nev. Assn. Tax Consultants (pres.), Boulder City C. of C., Nat. Assn. Enrolled Agts., Nat. Assn. Income Tax Practitioners (dir., 1st v.p.), Nat. Notary Assn., Nev. Recreation and Park Soc., U.S. C. of C., Internat. Platform Assn., Boulder City Mus. and Hist. Assn. (treas.), Home: 795 Marita Dr Boulder City NV 89005 Office: 806 Buchanan Blvd #102 Boulder City NV 89005

LAKSHMANAN, C. (LUX), agronomist, consultant; b. Quilon, India, Jan. 5, 1928; s. Kuncheen Cochera Panicker and Nani Amma Mechi; m. Chithra Muliyil, Oct. 19, 1933; children—Rayan, Hari. Ph.D., Ohio State U., 1962. Cert. agronomist, crop scientist, soil scientist. Postdoctoral fellow Ohio State U., Columbus, 1962-64; tech. assistance expert Internat. Atomic Energy Agy., Vienna, Austria, 1964-68; sect. head research and devel. Hunt Wesson Foods, Fullerton, Calif., 1968-77; dir., chief agronomist Inter-Am. Labs. (No. Calif.), Davis, 1977-80; dir. Calif. Agr. Cons. Service, Davis, 1980—; agr. cons. and researcher. Active East India Assn. No. Calif. Recipient Research and Devel. Merit award Hunt Wesson Foods, Fullerton, 1974. Mem. Soil Sci. Soc. Am., Am. Soc. Agronomy, Crop Sci. Soc. Am., Nat. Alliance Ind. Crop Cons. Hindu. Club: Tennis. Contbr. sci. papers and tech. reports to publs. Home: 4400 El Macero Dr Davis CA 95616 Office: 803 Russell Blvd Suite 6A Davis CA 95616

LALL, CHANDER PARKASH, civil engr.; b. Mianwali, Pakistan, Apr. 6, 1932; s. Inder Mohan and Daropadi (Chawla) L.; B.S.C.E., U. Colo., Boulder, 1960; B.S. in Indsl. Engring., U. Wash., Seattle, 1960, postgrad., 1960; came to U.S., 1949, naturalized, 1960; m. Olga Maria Bonilla, Sept. 3, 1977; children by previous marriage—Anne Cherie, Neil Mohan, Kris Insley. Engr., Boeing Commercial Airplane Co., Renton, Wash., 1957-72, field service engr., 1972-74; supr. constrn. Alyeska Pipeline Co., Fairbanks, Alaska, 1975-77; owner, mgr. Lall Enterprises (now Lall Corp.), Bellevue, Wash., 1977—; owner Westwood Travel, Seattle, 1981—. Mem. Seattle Profl. Engring. Employees Assn. Republican. Clubs: Toastmasters (awards) (Renton, Wash.); Scuba Diving, Ski. Home: 4710 Somerset Ave SE Bellevue WA 98006 Office: 4710 Somerset Ave SE Bellevue WA 98006

LALLY, THOMAS PATRICK, plastics company executive; b. Belfast, No. Ireland, May 23, 1950; s. Thomas Joseph and Maureen (Rowan) L. B.S. in Chemistry, Manchester U., 1971, M.S. in Chemistry, 1972, Ph.D. in Chemistry, 1974. Research chemist Courtaulds, U.K., 1974-77; project mgr. research and devel. Raychem Ltd., 1977-80, product devel. mgr. Mil. Electronics div. Menlo Park, Calif., 1980—. Roman Catholic. Home: 100 E Middlefield Apt 6A Mountain View CA 94043 Office: 300 Constitution Dr Menlo Park CA 94025

LAM, DAVID JAMES, health psychologist; b. Hong Kong, June 2, 1949; s. Victor Yuen-Fong and Jean Marilyn (Mah) L.; A.B., Stanford U., 1970; M.A., U. Hawaii, 1972, Ph.D. in Psychology, 1975; m. Flora Sen-Fong Inn, July 7, 1973; children—Geoffrey, Nicholas. Program coordinator Chinatown Child Devel. Center, San Francisco, 1976-77, dir., 1977-79; cons. psychologist Calif. Dept. Mental Health, San Francisco, 1979—; cons., tchr. in field. Bd. dirs. Chinatown Community Children's Center, 1977-80. Mem. Am. Psychol. Assn., Asian-Am. Psychol. Assn., Sigma Xi, Phi Kappa Phi. Author works in field; contbr. articles to profl. jours. Office: 2340 Irving St Suite 108 San Francisco CA 94122

LAMAR, MARY GAYE, theatre dir.; b. Colorado Springs, Colo., Oct. 19, 1951; d. Bernard Johnston and Mary Ellen (Hardy) Lamar; B.A., U. Colo., 1973, M.A., 1978; postgrad. Denver U. Communications, group dynamics instr., Denver area, 1972-73; with Denver Public Sch. System, 1973—, arts mgmt./theatre dir., 1973—. Vol., Colo. Arts and Humanities Council as lectr., workshop coordinator, 1974-75. Cert. bicultural/bilingual instr. Mem. Am. Theatre Assn., Women in Theatre, Nat. Council Tchrs. English, Nat. Assn. Female Execs., Colo. Assn. Sch. Execs. Author: Celebration (rock musical), 1979; Bob, The Unicorn (children's fantasy), 1981; dir., designer, producer profl. and ednl. theatrical prodns. including Godspell, 1974, Guys and Dolls, 1975, My Fair Lady, 1976, Carousel, 1977, Music Man, 1978, Celebration!, 1979, Annie Get Your Gun, 1980, Jesus Christ Superstar, 1982, Grease, 1982. Home: 11224 E Harvard Dr Aurora CO 80014 Office: 2960 N Speer Blvd Denver CO 80211

LA MARCHE, JUDITH ANN, psychologist, consultant; b. Oak Park, Ill., May 11, 1947; d. Austin White and Margaret (Bryant) La M.; m. Paul Newcomb Lydolph, June 8, 1968 (div.); children—Paul Newcomb, Tamara Bryant. B.A. in Psychology, U. Wis.-Madison, 1968, M.S. in Curriculum and Instrn., 1970; postgrad in psychology, Utah State U., 1983—. Tchr. history Milton (Wis.) Union High Sch., 1968-69, Irving Crown High Sch., Carpentersville, Ill., 1969-70; instr. Harper Coll., Palatine, Ill., 1977-79, Coll. of Lake County, Grayslake, Ill., 1978-79; cons. Hoffman Estates (Ill.) Youth and Family Services, 1979-80; dir. info. referral Helpline, Utah State U., Logan, 1980-81; clin. psychology intern Salt Lake City VA Med. Ctr., Salt Lake City, 1981-82, research asst. neuropsychology lab., 1982—; panelist, speaker, facilitator; counselor Utah State Counseling and Testing Ctr., 1980. Mem. Inter-Agy. Council, 1980-81, human resources council Bear River Assn. Govts., 1980-81, Logan Hospice, 1980-81; adv. bd. The Growing Place, 1980-81, Voluntary Action Ctr., 1980-81, Kid's Country Presch., 1979-80; pres. United Meth. Women's Assn., 1977-78. Mem. Am. Personnel and Guidance Assn., Am. Psychol. Assn., Delta Delta Delta. Office: 151A 500 Foothill Blvd Salt Lake City UT 84148

LAMB, ANN-MARIE, management consultant; b. Hartford, Conn., Feb. 21, 1931; d. James Joseph and Josephine Julia (Gleason) L. Student Marquette U., 1948-49; B.A., Trinity Coll., Washington, 1952. Sr. analyst U.S. Office Mgmt. and Budget, Washington, 1966-73; mgr. planning, analysis Atlantic Richfield Co., Los Angeles, 1974-76; ind. mgmt. cons., Los Angeles, 1976—. Bd. dirs. YWCA, Washington, 1970-73, Los Angeles, 1979—. Roman Catholic. Club: Athletic (Los Angeles). Address: 234 S Figueroa St Los Angeles CA 90012

LAMB, FLOYD A., state senator, rancher; b. Alamo, Nev., Sept. 3, 1917; children—Laurelie Lamb Turley, Marsha Lamb Bingham, Monte Carroll, Melodee. Former pres., chmn. bd., chmn. exec. com. Nev. Nat. Bank; mem. Nev. Senate from 3d dist., 1957—, mem. Legis. Commn., 1961-66, chmn., 1963-64, chmn. interim fin. com., 1977-83, mem. joint com. on fin. affairs, 1961, 65-66, pres. pro tem, 1969, 71, 73. Past mem. Nev. State Racing Commn. Democrat. Mormon. Office: Nat Bank Bldg PO Box 18415 Las Vegas NV 89114

LAMB, GORDON WILMUR, accountant; b. Bremerton, Wash., Jan. 29, 1945; s. Wilmur F. and Muriel L. (Keldgord) L.; m. Nancy M. Bowmer, Aug. 29, 1970; children—Aaron, Sara, Cory, Abbey. B.A., Wash. State U., 1970. C.P.A., Wash. Staff acct. Robert B. Miller, C.P.A. (now Presnell, Gage & Co.), Clarkston, Wash., 1971-72; staff acct. Ray Smeltz, C.P.A., Pullman, Wash., 1972-76, mng. ptnr. Smeltz & Lamb, C.P.A.s, Pullman, 1976—; dir. numerous small corps. Served with USNG, 1966-72. Mem. Am. Inst. C.P.A.s, Wash. Soc. C.P.A.s, Pullman C. of C. (dir. 1979-81). Republican. Congregationalist. Club: Rotary (Pullman), Masons, Shriners. Office: Smeltz and Lamb 204 Old Nat Bank Bldg Pullman WA 99163

LAMB, GREGORY GEORGE, energy research executive; b. Ogden, Utah, Nov. 30, 1946; s. LeDoan F. and Dora (Wright) L.; B.S. in Indsl. Engring., San Jose (Calif.) State U., 1971; M.B.A. in Fin. and Ops. Mgmt., U. Santa Clara (Calif.), 1973; m. Maryrose Burriesci, Sept. 3, 1977, children—Kelli Erin, Jonathan Gregory. Fin. analyst/budget adminstr., corp. staff Western Devel. Labs., Ford Aerospace Corp., Palo Corp., Calif., 1971-73; planning systems analyst corp. staff, 1973-76; asst. to dir. research advanced fossil power systems Electric Power Research Inst., Palo Alto, 1976-78, mgr. fin. and adminstrn. fossil fuel and advanced systems div., 1978-79, sr. asst. to v.p. for research and devel., 1979-82, sr. planning ops. adminstr., planning and evaluation div., 1983—; exec. sec. Advanced Fossil Power Systems Task Force, 1977-79. Mem. Indsl. Mgmt. Soc. (chpt. pres. 1970), Am. Inst. Indsl. Engrs., Iota Tau Sigma (pres., charter mem.). Republican. Mem. Ch. Jesus Christ of Latter-day Saints (elder). Home: 12515 Blue Meadow Ct Saratoga CA 95070 Office: 3412 Hillview Ave Palo Alto CA 94303

LAMB, WILLIS EUGENE, JR., physicist, educator; b. Los Angeles, July 12, 1913; s. Willis Eugene and Marie Helen (Metcalf) L.; B.S., U. Calif., 1934, Ph.D., 1938; D.Sc., U. Pa., 1953, Gustavus Adolphus Coll., 1975; M.A., Oxford (Eng.) U., 1956; M.A., Yale, 1961; L.H.D., Yeshiva U., 1965; m. Ursula Schaefer, June 5, 1939. Mem. faculty Columbia, 1938-52, prof. physics, 1948-52; prof. physics Stanford, 1951-56; Wykeham prof. physics and fellow New Coll., Oxford U., 1956-62; Henry Ford 2d prof. physics Yale, 1962-72, J. Willard Gibbs prof. physics, 1972-74; prof. physics and optical scis. U. Ariz., Tucson, 1974—; Morris Loeb lectr. Harvard, 1953-54; cons. Philips Labs., Bell Telephone Labs., Perkin-Elmer, NASA. Vis. com. Brookhaven Nat. Lab. Recipient (with Dr. Polycarp Kusch) Nobel prize in physics, 1955; Rumford premium Am. Acad. Arts and Scis., 1953; Research Corp. award, 1955; Guggenheim fellow, 1960-61; recipient Yeshiva award, 1962. Fellow Am. Phys. Soc., N.Y. Acad. Scis., hon. fellow Inst. Physics and Phys. Soc. (Guthrie lectr. 1958), Royal Soc. Edinburgh; mem. Nat. Acad. Scis., Phi Beta Kappa, Sigma Xi. Office: Dept of Physics U Ariz Tucson AZ 85721

LAMBERT, JANET PRUITT, ednl. adminstr.; b. Sharpsville, Pa., Nov. 10, 1930; d. Clarence Paul and Hazel Gladys (Palmer) McCracken; B.S., Oreg. Coll. Edn., 1952; M.S., So. Oreg. Coll., 1957; Ed.D., Oreg. State U., 1977; m. May 28, 1983; children—Marion, Randall. Tchr. public schs., Roseburg, Oreg., 1952-55, Ashland, Oreg., 1955-56; tchr., supr. student tchrs., asst. prof. Campus Sch., So. Oreg. Coll., Ashland, 1956-63; resource tchr. public schs., Ashland, 1963-68; instr. part time Oreg. State U., Corvallis, 1968-72, instr. div. continuing edn., 1972-73; asst. prof., Lewis and Clark Coll., Portland, Oreg., 1973-74; project coordinator Title I Salem (Oreg.) Public Schs., 1975-81, reading coordinator, 1981—; cons. in field. Mem. Internat. Reading Assn. (pres. Capitol Council br.), Assn. Adminstrv. Personnel, Assn. Supervision and Curriculum Devel., Western Coll. Reading Assn., Oreg. Reading Assn. (dir.), Assn. Student Tchrs., Phi Kappa Phi, Phi Delta Kappa, Delta Kappa Gamma. Democrat. Methodist. Home: 549 Hansen Ave S Salem OR 97302 Office: PO Box 12024 Salem OR 97309

LAMBERT, NADINE MURPHY, psychology educator; b. Ephraim Utah; d. Rulon E. and Maude Molla (Nielsen) Murphy; m. Robert E. Lambert, Dec. 29, 1956; children—Laura Allan, Jeffrey. A.B. in Psychology, UCLA, 1948; M.A. in Edn., Los Angeles State U., 1955; Ph.D. in Psychology, U. So. Calif., 1965. Sch. psychologist Los Nietos (Calif.) Sch. Dist., 1952-53, Bellflower (Calif.) Unified Sch. Dist., 1953-58; research cons. Calif. Dept. Edn., 1958-64; mem. faculty U. Calif.-Berkeley, 1964—, prof., 1976—; dir. sch. psychology program, 1964—; cons. Dept. of Justice, 1977-79. Fellow Am. Orthopsychiat. Assn., Am. Psychol. Assn. (disting. service award 1981, div. 1984—); mem. Calif. Assn. Sch. Psychologists and Psychometrists (pres., 1962-63), NEA, Am. Edn. Research Assn., Am. Assn. Mental Deficiency, Nat. Acad. Practice. Author: School Version Adaptive Behavior Scale; Moral Development and Socialization; contbr. articles to profl. jours. Office: Sch Psychology Program Education Sch Edn U Calif Berkeley CA 94720

LAMBRECHTS, MICHAEL ELISABETH, mktg. exec.; b. Antwerp, Belgium, Sept. 21, 1919; came to U.S., 1962, naturalized, 1969; s. Ludovicus Egidius and Anna (Andreassen) L.; Tech. Engr., Antwerp, 1945; Elec. Engr., U. Paris., 1947; m. Maria Johanna Hedrich, May 28, 1970. Engr., Colectric, West Africa, 1947-55; regional mgr. Comelco, West Africa, 1955-60; tech. mktg. engr. ITT Europe, 1960-62; mktg. mgr. Latin Am. ITT New York, 1962-66; mktg. mgr. satellite groundsta. Hughes Aircraft, 1966-68, tech. dir. Latin Am., 1968-71; mgr. Spain, 1971-75, regional dir. Western Europe, 1975-79, dir. market devel. groupd systems, Bonn, W. Ger., 1979—. Served with Engr. Corps, Belgium Army, 1939-42. Mem. Air Force Assn., Navy League, Tech. Mktg. Soc. Am. Club: Am. Bus. Men, Am. Embassy. Home: 41 Delbergrunweg 5330 Konigswinter 41 West Germany Office: 121 Godesberger Allee 5300 Bonn West Germany also Box 92919 Hughes Internat C-2-B181 Los Angeles CA 90009

LAMDIN, WILLIAM DUNGAN, JR., real estate broker, rancher; b. Balt., July 12, 1928; s. William Dungan and Eleanor Hardey (Clarke) L.; m. Patricia Killough, Aug. 20, 1955; children—Kathleen Archbold, Hastings, William, Meredith Cartwright, Elizabeth, Eleanor. B.A., Princeton U., 1950; M.S. U. Md., 1969. Salesman, Reuben Donnelley Corp., Balt., 1954-55; advt. Shriver Co., Balt., 1955-63; mgmt. cons. Alexander Proudfoot, Chgo., 1963-64; social worker Univ. Hosp., Balt., 1965-71; rancher, Meeteetse, Wyo., 1971—; real estate broker Yellowstone Agy., Cody, Wyo., 1979—. Trustee, Meeteese Sch. Dist., 1975-81, chmn., 1977-79. Served to lt. U.S. Army, 1950-53, Korea. Mem. Nat. Assn. Realtors, Farm and Land Inst. Episcopalian. Home: Two Cabin Ranch Meeteetse WY 82433 Office: Yellowstone Agy 1714 Stampede Cody WY 82414

LAMEIRO, GERARLD FRANCIS, computer company executive; b. Paterson, N.J., Oct. 3, 1949; s. Frank Raymond and Beatrice Cecilia (Donley) L.; B.S., Colo. State U., 1971, M.S., 1973, Ph.D., 1977. Sr. scientist Solar Energy Research Inst., Golden, Colo., 1977-78; asst. prof. mgmt. sci. and info. Colo. State U., Fort Collins, 1978-82, lectr. dept. computer sci., 1983—, lectr. dept. mgmt., 1983—; pres. Successful Automated Office Systems, Inc., Fort Collins, 1982—; dir. Solar Energy Design Corp. Am. Colo. Energy Research Inst. fellow 1976, NSF fellow 1978. Mem. Assn. for Computing Machinery, Nat. Computer Graphics Assn., IEEE. Roman Catholic. Contbr. articles in mgmt. and tech. areas to profl. jours. Home: 1112 Constitution Ave Fort Collins CO 80521 Office: Successful Automated Office Systems Inc Drake Executive Plaza Suite 210 2625 Redwing Rd Fort Collins CO 80526

LAMEMAN, TULLY, association executive; b. Home-Red Mesa, Utah, Feb. 15, 1939; s. Jack and Elsie (Adakaitso) L.; m. Nancy Tina Tsosie, Aug. 15, 1969; children—Stanford, Christina, Virginia Anne, Tully. B.S., Ariz. State U., 1969. Agr. coordinator San Juan Resource Devel. Council, Blanding, Utah, 1969-71; extension agt. Utah State U., Montezuma Creek, 1971-72; agr. dir. Utah Navajo Devel. Council, Blanding, 1972-75, adminstrn. asst., 1975-77, exec. dir., 1977—; program coordinator, extension agt. Utah State U., 1971-72; farm tng. coordinator, tchr. animal sci. Navajo Community Coll., 1975. Mem. sch. bd., vice chmn. San Juan Sch. Dist., 1970-72; chmn. bd. Utah Navajo Devel. Council Credit Union, 1978-83; bd. dirs. mem. Utah Housing Coalition, 1982—; mem. Br. Coll. Adv. Council; vice chmn. Navajo Health Systems Agy., 1981—; mem. Southeast Utah Pvt. Industry Council for Job Tng. Partnership Act. Mem. Nat. Indian Edn. Assn. Republican. Mem. Ch. Jesus Christ of Latter-day Saints. Home: PO Box 655 Blanding UT 84511 Office: PO Box 908 Blanding UT 84511

LAMM, FRANKLIN CHARLES, bus. exec.; b. Reading, Pa., Jan. 9, 1945; s. John Herman and Helen Rosa (Stamm) L.; student Chulalongkorn U., Bangkok, 1967-68, La Escuela de Agricultura y Cria, Venezuela, 1968; B.A., St. Olaf Coll., 1968; M.A., U. No. Colo., 1973; m. Marion Isabella Banks, Sept. 24, 1968; children—Tammy Michelle, Shattuck Franklin, Robin Julie. Child care worker Northwood Treatment Ctr. for Emotionally Disturbed Children, Duluth, Minn., 1965-66; vol. Peace Corps, Campiarito, Venezuela, 1968-71; assoc. headmaster Vershire (Vt.) Sch., 1971-72; learning disabilities specialist Sch. Dist. #51, Grand Junction, Colo., 1973-78; investment property locator Mesa Properties Ltd., Grand Junction, 1978-79; pres., proprietor, dir. Energy Belt Enterprises, Grand Junction, Colo., 1980—; pres. Energy Belt Property Mgmt., Energy Belt Farm and Ranch, Energy Belt Devel., Inc., Energy Belt Investments, Inc. Chmn. N.W. Citizens Task Force, Mesa County, Colo., 1979—; scoutmaster Boy Scouts Am., 1980-82. Mem. Kappa Delta Pi. Republican. Mem. Ch. Jesus Christ Latter-Day Saints. Address: 2587 G 1/2 Rd Grand Junction CO 81501

LAMM, RICHARD D., gov. Colo.; b. Madison, Wis., Aug. 3, 1935; s. A.E. and Mary (Townsend) Lamm; B.B.A., U. Wis., 1957; LL.B., U. Calif., 1961; m. Dorothy Vennard, May 11, 1963; children—Scott Hunter, Heather. Admitted to Calif. bar, 1961, Colo. bar, 1962. C.P.A., Ernst & Ernst, Denver, 1961-62; atty. Colo. Anti-Discrimination Commn., Denver, 1962-63; atty. Jones, Meikeljohn, Kilroy, Kehl & Lyons, Denver, 1963-65; pvt. practice law, Denver, 1965-74; gov. Colo., 1975—; mem. exec. com. Nat. Govs. Assn., also chmn. task force synthetic fuels, chmn. human resources com., mem. energy, environment com.; assoc. prof. law U. Denver, 1969. Pres. Denver Young Democrats, 1963-64; v.p. Colo. Young Dems., 1964-65; mem. Denver Mayor's South Platte River Com.; mem. Colo. Ho. of Reps., 1966-75, asst. minority leader, 1971-75. Served as 1st lt. U.S. Army, 1957-58. C.P.A., Calif., Colo. Mem. Conservation Found., Denver Center for Performing Arts, Center for Growth Alternatives, Central City Opera House Assn. Address: Governor's Mansion 400 E 8th Ave Denver CO 80203

LAMME, DENNIS WAYNE, broadcasting executive; b. Trenton, Mo., Mar. 19, 1955; s. John Robert and Earlene Marie (Trump) L.; m. Cindy Kay Wright, July 30, 1977; children—Kelly Marie, Jacob Fremont, Kristen Kay. B.S., Northwest Mo. State U., 1976. Account exec. Sta. KKJO, St. Joseph, Mo., 1976-77; gen. mgr. Sta. KVMT-FM, Vail, Colo., 1977-78; sta. mgr. Sta. KYEZ-FM, Salina, Kans., 1978; account exec. Sta. WRMN, Elgin, Ill., 1978-79; v.p., corp. sales Brewer Broadcasting Co. (Stas. KUAD, KSGR, KKBG) Windsor, Colo. and Hilo, Hawaii, 1979—. Chmn. bd. dirs. Thompson Valley Preschool, 1982-84. Mem. Mktg. Advt. and Communications Assn., Am. Advt. Fedn., Am. Mgmt. Assn., Am. Film Inst., Alpha Epsilon Rho. Republican. Presbyterian. Home: 3829 Logan Ave Loveland CO 80537 Office: PO Box 117 Windsor CO 80550

LAMONICA, JOHN, food executive; b. Bklyn., Apr. 26, 1954; s. Lou and Alda (Merola) L. B.S. in Acctg., Bklyn. Coll., 1977. With N.S.L. Enterprises, 1982—; with Anielzos Pizza, 1979—, Lamonicas N.Y. Pizza, 1980—; restaurant cons. Republican. Club: Beverly Hills Gun. Office: 10925 Weyburn Ave Los Angeles CA 90024

LAMPERT, ELEANOR VERNA, employment devel. specialist; b. Porterville, Calif., Mar. 23; d. Ernest Samuel and Violet Edna (Watkins) Wilson; student in bus., fin. Porterville Jr. Coll., 1977-78; grad. Anthony Real Estate Sch., 1971; student Laguna Sch. of Art, 1972, U. Calif.-Santa Cruz, 1981; m. Robert Mathew Lampert, Aug. 21, 1935; children—Sally Lu Winton, Lary Lampert, Carol R. John. Bookkeeper, Porterville (Calif.) Hosp., 1956-71; real estate sales staff Ray Realty, Porterville, 1973; sec. Employment Devel. Dept., State of Calif., Porterville, 1973—, orientation and tng. specialist CETA employees, 1976-80. Sec., Employer Adv. Group, 1973-80; mem. U.S. Senatorial Bus. Adv. Bd., 1981-82; charter mem. Presdl. Republican Task Force, 1981-82. Recipient Merit Cert., Gov. Pat Brown, State of Calif., 1968. Mem. Lindsay Olive Growers, Sunkist Orange Growers, Am. Kennel Club, Internat. Assn. Personnel in Employment Security, Nat. Wildlife Fedn., Nat. Rifle Assn., Friends of Porterville Library. Club: Internat. Sporting and Leisure.

LAMPHERE, PETER HARRY, marketing executive; b. Albany, N.Y., Sept. 15, 1943; s. Peter B. and Ethel (Runge) L.; student Pacific Luth. U., 1964-68; B.A., UCLA, 1980; m. Linda Jane Holt, Oct. 18, 1968; children—Peter Timothy, Cynthia Lynn, Pamela Louise. Sales engr. Gen. Electric Co., Los Angeles, 1968-72, export sales mgr., 1972-77; export sales/product mgr. Thermador/Waste King div. Norris Industries, Los Angeles, 1977-80; dir. sales/mktg. Natter div. Fairchild Industries, Temple City, Calif., 1980-83, mktg. and sales cons., 1983—; mem. faculty Mt. San Antonio Coll., Walnut, Calif., 1974-80. Served with USN, 1962-64. Decorated Purple Heart. Mem. Assn. Inst. Kitchen Dealers. Republican. Christian Ch. Club: Elks. Address: 3013 Blandford Dr Rowland Heights CA 91748

LANCASTER, SAMMIE LOUISE, educator; b. Jena, La., Apr. 30, 1942; d. Samuel Benard and Louise (Greer) W.; B.S., So. U., 1966; M.Ed., U. Nev., 1975; m. Robert Lancaster, Jr., Sept. 30, 1966; 1 son, Darryl Louis. Tchr., sec. Pinecrest High Sch., Winnfield, La., 1966-67, Jonesville, La., 1967-68; sec. I, Concentration Employment Program, Las Vegas, Nev., 1968-69; pre-employment analyst Holmes & Harver Inc., Las Vegas, 1969-70; tchr. bus. edn. Cashman Jr. High Sch., Las Vegas, 1970—, also girls basketball coach; instr. Clark County Community Coll., Las Vegas, 1977-78. Fin. sec., sec. sr. usher bd. Mt. Ararat Bapt. Ch., Las Vegas, 1979-81. Recipient Good Apple award Las Vegas Tchrs. Center, 1980. Mem. Am. Vocat. Assn., Nev. Edn. Assn., So. Nev. Bus. Edn. Assn., Delta Sigma Theta (corr. sec. 1979-81). Democrat. Club: Order Eastern Star. Home: 7032 Michael Collins Pl Las Vegas NV 89128 Office: 4622 W Desert Inn Rd Las Vegas NV 89102

LANDA, ESTHER ROSENBLATT, civic worker; b. Salt Lake City, Dec. 25, 1912; d. Simon and Sylvia Gertrude (Liberman) Rosenblatt; B.A., Mills Coll., 1933, M.A., 1937, H.H.D. (hon.), 1980; LL.D. (hon.), U. Utah, 1978; H.L.D. (hon.), Westminster Coll., 1982; m. Jerome Joseph Landa, Sept. 26, 1943; children—Carol Leslie, Howard Simon, Terry Ellen. Public relations Mills Coll. (Clif.), 1934-39, Bennington (Vt.) Coll., 1941; account exec. Constance Hope Assos., N.Y.C., 1941-42; info. specialist various agys. U.S. Govt., 1942-43; cons. burs. Community Devel. and Indian Services, U. Utah, 1962-65; dir. women's programs U. Utah, 1965-71; nat. pres. Nat. Council Jewish Women, 1975-79; mem. Pres.'s Adv. Com. Women, 1978-80, Pres.'s Commn. for Nat. Agenda for 80's, 1979-80; mem. Salt Lake City Bd. Edn., 1958-70, Utah State Bd. Edn., 1970-74; sec.-treas. Nat. Assn. State Bds. Edn., 1973-74; pres. Salt Lake County Community Action Program, 1968-70; pres. LWV Salt Lake City, 1956-58; chairperson task force on equal opportunity for women Nat. Jewish Community Relations Adv. Council, 1977-83; bd. dirs. Council of Jewish Fedns. N.Am.; mem. planning com. White House Conf. on Children, 1970; Utah del. White House Conf. on Families, 1980; U.S. del. World Conf. UN Decade for Women, Copenhagen, 1980. Named to Salt Lake Council of Women Hall of Fame, 1958; hon. life mem. PTA, 1963; recipient Libety Bell award Utah Bar Assn., 1963; Utah Woman of Year, AAUW, 1965; Woman of Year, B'nai B'rith, 1965; Man of Year in Utah Edn., Phi Delta Kappa, 1967; Civil Rights Worker of Year award NAACP, 1968; Disting. Service award Utah Sch. Bds. Assn., 1969, 72; U. Utah Alumni Merit award, 1976; Disting. Woman award U. Utah, 1978; Susa Young Gates award Nat. Women's Polit. Caucus, 1979; Citation Utah chpt. NCCJ, 1980. Mem. Nat. Council Jewish Women, LWV, NOW, Nt. Women's Polit. Caucus, ACLU, Phi Beta Kappa, Delta Kappa Gamma. Democrat. Jewish. Clubs: Hadassah, B'nai B'rith Women, ORT. Author Pres.'s column Nat. Council Jewish Women Jour., 1975-79. Home: 5006 S 1034 E Salt Lake City UT 84117 Office: 1130 Kennecott Bldg Salt Lake City UT 84133

LANDE, JAMES AVRA, internat. bus. exec.; b. Chgo., Oct. 2, 1930; s. S. Theodore and Helen C. Lande; B.A., Swarthmore Coll., 1952; J.D., Columbia U., 1955; m. Ann Mari Gustavsson, Feb. 21, 1959; children—Rebecca Susanne, Sylvia Diane. Admitted to N.Y. bar, 1958, Calif. bar, 1967; atty. NASA Ames Research Center, Moffett Field, Calif., 1967-70; house counsel Syntex Corp., Palo Alto, Calif., 1970-73; dir. contracts dept. Electric Power Research Inst., Palo Alto, 1973-80; dir. contracts adminstrn. Lurgi Corp., Belmont, Calif., 1981—; adj. prof. U. San Francisco Sch. Law, 1972-73; lectr. U. Santa Clara Sch. Law, 1968—; pres. Syntex Fed. Credit Union, 1971-72. Served with U.S. Army, 1955-57. Mem. Am. Bar Assn. Contbr. articles to profl. jours. Home: 1330 33d Ave San Francisco CA 94122 Office: One Davis Dr Belmont CA 94002

LANDER, ROBERT JOSEPH, educator; b. Erie, Pa., June 6, 1935; s. Frank Joseph and Kathryn Myrtle (Welsh) L.; m. Maryanne Rita Buffomante, Aug. 22, 1959; children—Deborah, Maribeth, Patricia. B.S., Gannon U., 1959; postgrad. U. Puget Sound, 1971; M.A., U. No. Colo., 1976. Commd. 2d lt., U.S. Army, 1959, advanced through grades to maj., 1967, ret., 1980; health planner Colo. Dept. Health, 1980-82; asst. prof. health care mgmt. Met. State Coll. Denver, 1982—; adj. prof. bus. adminstrn. Regis Coll., 1979; adj. asst. prof. Park Coll., 1976-78, Webster Coll., 1976-80. Decorated Bronze Star medal, Army Commendation medal with oak leaf cluster. Home: 8211 Reed Ct Arvada CO 80003 Office: 1006 11th St PO Box 33 Denver CO 80204

LANDERS, NEWLIN JEWEL, water systems and septic tanks co. owner; b. North Salem, Ind., July 10, 1906; s. DeLoy and Pearl (Paige) L.; student Skadron Contractors Sch., 1963; m. Vernette Trosper, May 2, 1959; children—Lawrence, Marlin. Formerly with Howard Hughes Multi-Color Lab., Hughes Devel. Co., Paramount Motion Picture Studios; owner, mgr. Landers Machine Shop, Bell Gardens, Calif., 1940-41; ptnr. Selwyn-Landers Co., Los Angeles, 1942-54; owner Havasu Landing, Needles, Calif., 1955, Navajo Tract, Apple Valley, Calif., 1957—; owner, mgr. Landers Water Co. (Calif.), 1958-79. Mem. Landers Vol. Fire Dept., 1963—. Recipient plaque for search and rescue service Yucca Valley Sheriffs' Rangers, 1972; plaque Landers Vol. Fire Dept., 1981; named Founding Father of Landers, 1981. Clubs: 94, Landers Garden, Landers Assn., Moose. Home: 905 Landers Ln Landers CA 92284 Office: 1105 Landers Ln Landers CA 92284

LANDERS, VERNETTE TROSPER (MRS. NEWLIN LANDERS), educator, author; b. Lawton, Okla., May 3, 1912; d. Fred Gilbert and LaVerne Hamilton (Stevens) Trosper; A.B. with honors, U. Calif. at Los Angeles, 1933, M.A., 1935, Ed.D., 1953; m. Paul Albert Lum, Aug. 29, 1952 (dec. May 1955); 1 son, William Tappan; m. 2d, Newlin Landers, May 2, 1959; children—Lawrence, Marlin. Tchr. secondary schs., Montebello, Calif., 1935-45, 48-50, 51-59; prof. Long Beach City Coll., 1946-47; asst. prof. Los Angeles State Coll., 1950; dean girls Twenty Nine Palms (Calif.) High Sch., 1960-65; dist. counselor Morongo (Calif.) Unified Sch. Dist., 1965-72, coordinator adult edn., 1965-67, guidance project dir., 1967; clk.-in-charge Landers (Calif.) Post Office, 1962-82; ret., 1982 Vice-pres., sec. Landers Assn., 1965—; sec. Landers Vol. Fire Dept., 1972—; life mem. Hi-Desert Playhouse Guild, Hi-Desert Meml. Hosp. Guild. Bd. dirs., sec. Desert Emergency Radio Service. Recipient internat. diploma of honor for community service, 1973; Creativity award Internat. Personnel Research Assn., 1972; cert. of merit for disting. service to edn., 1973; named Soroptimist of Year, 29 Palms Soroptimist Club, 1969; poet laureate Center of Internat. Studies and Exchanges, 1981, diploma of merit in letters U. Arts, Parma, Italy, 1982, other awards and certs. Fellow Internat. Acad. Poets (life); mem. Am. Personnel and Guidance Assn., Internat. Platform Assn., Nat. Ret. Tchrs. Assn., Montebello Bus. and Profl. Women's Club (pres.), Nat. League Am. Pen Women, Leonardo Da Vinci Acad. Internat. Winged Glory diploma of honor in letters 1982), Landers Area C. of C., Desert Nature Mus., Phi Beta Kappa. Clubs: Soroptimist (sec. Twenty Nine Palms 1962); Whittier (Calif.) Toastmistress (pres. 1957); Homestead Valley Women's (Landers). Author: Impy, 1974, Talkie, 1975; Impy's Children, 1975; Nineteen O Four, 1976; Little Brown Bat, 1976; Slo Go, 1977; Owls Who and Who Who, 1978; Sandy, The Coydog, 1979; The Kit Fox and the Walking Stick, 1980; contbr. articles to profl. jours., poems to anthologies. Home: 905 Landers Ln Landers CA 92284

LANDGRAF, MARY ELIZABETH NORTON (MRS. DAVID L. LANDGRAF), librarian; b. San Francisco, Aug. 7, 1937; d. Thomas Bernard and Marjorie (Milota) Norton; student San Francisco Coll. Women, 1955-58; A.B., San Francisco State Coll., 1960; M.L.S., U. Calif. at Berkeley, 1962, postgrad., 1962-63; m. David L. Landgraf, June 10, 1963; children—Robert Thomas, Lisa Marjorie. Librarian, San Francisco Pub. Library, 1958-59, 60-63; research asst. U. Calif. Grad. Sch. Librarianship, Berkeley, 1962, reviser, 1963-64; librarian San Francisco Pub. Library, 1969—. Trustee Homestead Valley Nursery Sch., 1969; bd. dirs. Sunset Community Edn. Center, 1978-83. Mem. Am., Calif. library assns., No. Calif. Tech. Processes Group (sec.-treas. 1963-64), Assn. Coll. Research Libraries, Alumni Assn. U. Calif. Library Schs., Alumnae of Sacred Heart, Beta Phi Mu. Democrat. Clubs: U. Calif. Women's Faculty (Berkeley); Viking Ski; Sausalito Cruising. Home: 173 Alpine St San Rafael CA 94901

LANDGRAFF, RONALD WILLIAM, high technology scientist; b. Wilmington, Del., Dec. 21, 1940; s. Theodore F. and Grace (Higden) L.; m. Mary Ann Garver, Aug. 28, 1963; children—Laura, Thomas, Ronald William. B.S.E.E., Villanova U., 1962; M.S.E.E., U. Del., 1964; Ph.D. in Elec. Engring., Northwestern U., 1970. Successively staff engr., sect. head project mgr. Hughes Data Systems Div., Culver City, Calif., 1970-76; project mgr. advanced systems group Systems Engring. Labs., Ft. Lauderdale, Fla., 1976-78; assoc. new ventures TRW Electronics and Def., Los Angeles, 1978-82, mgr. Tech. Research Ctr., 1982—; conf. presenter. Mem. Assn. Computing Machinery, IEEE, IEEE Computer Soc., Tau Beta Pi, Sigma Pi Sigma. Home: 26608 Lightfoot Pl Rancho Palos Verdes CA 90274 Office: 2525 E El Segundo Blvd El Segundo CA 90045

LANDHOLM, WALLACE MARVEN, ophthalmologist; b. N. Platte, Nebr., Sept. 8, 1933; s. Marven K. and Alma L. (Phillips) L.; B.A., U. Nebr., 1956, M.D., 1959; m. Marcia Greenlee, 1955; children—James, Ceryl. Intern, San Bernardino (Calif.) County Hosp., 1959-60; resident in ophthalmology State U. Iowa Hosp., 1963-65; practice medicine specializing in ophthalmology, Newport Beach, Calif., since 1967; mem. staff Hoag Meml. Hosp.; asst. clin. prof. U. Calif. Med. Sch., Irvine; fellow intraocular lens implants Pacific Hosp., Long Beach, Calif., 1976. Served to capt. M.C., USAF, 1960-63. Decorated Air medal; diplomate Am. Bd. Ophthalmology. Mem. AMA, Soc. Eye Surgeons, Am. Acad. Ophthalmology, Am. Intraocular Implant Soc., Newport Beach C. of C., Alpha Omega Alpha. Lutheran. Club: Balboa Bay (Newport Beach). Office: 320 Superior Ave Newport Beach CA 92663

LANDIS, CHARLES, night club exec., real estate developer; b. Mpls., July 21, 1917; s. Morris and Mollie (Landau) L.; B.A., U. Minn., 1940; m. Florence Regina Alsobrook, Aug. 1, 1950; children—Steven, Todd, Jan, Tim. Pres., Largo, Inc., Los Angeles, 1957—; pres. Chas. Landis Enterprises, Los Angeles, 1967—, Clan Record Co., 1969—, Starlight Hotels, Inc., 1968—, Lanvan Artists Prodns., Ltd., Los Angeles, Largo, Inc., Los Angeles and Sacramento, C.L. Record Corp., Monterey Park, Calif., Wilshire-Westlake Bldg. Co., Los Angeles, Chuck Landis Country Club, Inc., Reseda, Calif., 1978—, Country Club Investment Co., Beverly Hills, Calif., 1978—, Trademart Shopping Center, Northridge, Calif., 1981—, Hidden Hills Devel. Co. (Calif.), 1981—, Northridge Trademart Co., 1981—, Todd's Restaurants, Woodland Hills, Calif., 1982—; sec., treas. Roxy Theatre Corp., Los Angeles; chmn. bd. Mission Bldg. Enterprises, 1969—; owner, developer Monterey Park Mall; sec. Franklin Plaza Assos., Las Vegas, Nev., 1968-72. Hon. mayor City of West Hollywood (Calif.). Mem. Night Club Owners of Am. (pres. 1960-64). Home: 7509 March Ave Canoga Park CA 91304 Office: 5371 Topanga Canyon Blvd Woodland Hills CA 91364

LANDIS, RICHARD GORDON, retired multi-industry executive; b. Davenport, Okla., Apr. 5, 1920; s. John W. and Venna L. (Perrin) L.; m. Leota Beth Throne, Nov. 6, 1943; children—Gary P., Dennis M., Kay E. B.A. in Social Sci., LaVerne Coll., 1942; postgrad. Claremont Grad. Sch., 1948; LL.D. (hon.), U. LaVerne, 1981. With Del Monte Corp., San Francisco, 1942—, mgr. Eastern ops., 1964-65, v.p. Pacific Coast ops., 1966-68, v.p. U.S. prodn., 1968-69, group exec. v.p., 1969-71, dir., 1970—, pres., chief operating officer, 1971-81, chief exec. officer, 1977-81, chmn. bd., 1978-81, merged with R.J. Reynolds Industries, Inc., Winston-Salem, N.C., 1979, pres. Pacific, 1981-83, ret., 1983; dir. Crocker Nat. Corp., Crocker Nat. Bank, Potlatch Corp., SRI Internat. Bd. dirs. Kaiser Found. Hosps., Kaiser Found. Health Plan, Tax Found.; bd. regents U. of Pacific; pres.' adv. council, trustee U. LaVerne, U. Calif. Sch. Bus.; v.p. Bay Area council Boy Scouts Am.; adv. council Nat. 4-H Found. Named Calif. Mfr. of Yr., Calif. Mfrs. Assn., 1981. Mem. Conf. Bd., Blyth-Zellerbach Com., Harold Brunn Soc. Med. Research. Clubs: Pacific Union, Bohemian, St. Francis Yacht (San Francisco); Claremont Country (Oakland, Calif.). Office: Box 7218 San Francisco CA 94120

LANDIS, TERESA LYNN, financial executive; b. Merced, Calif., Jan. 3, 1951; d. Roger Rugene and Patricia Ann (Dick) Landis. B.A. in Accounting and Bus. Adminstrn., San Diego State U., 1973. Sr. staff acct. Ely, Guess & Rudd, Anchorage, 1974-76; corp. controller, bus. mgr. South Central Realty, Inc., Seattle, 1977-79; sr. tax ptnr. Ekanger & Assocs., C.P.A.s, Bellevue, Wash., 1979-81; corp. controller The Pace Corp., Bellevue, 1981-83; pres. Landis Assocs. Tax and Fin. Services, Inc., Bellevue, 1983—; bus. cons., lectr. in field. Mem. Wash. State Tax Cons. (pres. Bellevue chpt.), Internat. Assn. Fin. Planners, Nat. Assn. Tax Cons., Nat. Assn. Accts., Nat. Assn. Pub. Accts., Assn. Women Execs. Mem. Ch. of Christ. Author: How Does Your Money Grow? ... Guidelines for Financial Growth, 1983. Home: 2506 30th Ave S Seattle WA 98144 Office: 2826 Martin Luther King Jr Way S Seattle WA 98008

LANDON, ROBERT WILLIAM, law enforcement official; b. Rawlins, Wyo., Dec. 14, 1932; s. William Walter and Anna Mae (Shaffer) L.; m. Evelyn Elsie Olson, June 11, 1955; children—Lisa, Ronald. B.A., U. Puget Sound, 1972, M.P.A., 1973; LL.B., LaSalle U., 1960. With Wash. State Patrol, Olympia, 1953-81, chief, 1977-81; chief Mont. Hwy. Patrol, Helena, 1981—. Served with USN, 1950-53. Mem. Internat. Assn. Chiefs of Police, Am. Assn. Motor Vehicle Adminstrs., Wash. Assn. Sheriffs and Police Chiefs, Mont. Chiefs Assn., Phi Alpha Alpha. Lutheran. Contbr. articles on law enforcement to profl. jours. Office: Montana Highway Patrol 303 N Roberts Ave Helena MT 59620

LANDRUM, LARRY JAMES, computer engineer; b. Santa Rita, N.Mex., May 29, 1943; s. Floyd Joseph and Jewel Helen (Andreska) L.; m. Ann Marie Hartman, Aug. 25, 1963 (div.); children—Larry James, David Wayne, Andrei Mikhail, Donal Wymore; m. 2d, Mary Kathleen Turner, July 27, 1980. Student N.Mex. Inst. Mining and Tech., 1961-62, N. Mex. State U., 1963-65; A.A. in Data Processing, Eastern Ariz. Coll., 1971; B.A. in Computer Sci., U. Tex., 1978. Tech. service rep. Nat. Cash Register, 1966-73; with ASC super-computer project Tex. Instruments, Austin, 1973-80, product engr., 1975-78, operating system programmer, 1978-80; computer engr. Ariz. Pub. Service, Phoenix, 1980—; instr. computer fundamentals Eastern Ariz. Coll., 1972-73. Mem. Assn. Computing Machinery, Mensa, Phi Kappa Phi. Methodist.

LANDRUM, MARGO WADSWORTH, business executive, writer; b. Washington, Dec. 16, 1940; d. Joseph Rogers and Genevieve Frances (Folse) Wadsworth; m. James F. Landrum, June 9, 1962; children—Courtney Anne, Jay, Colin. B.A. in English, St. Mary's Dominican Coll., New Orleans, 1964. Freelance writer, 1970—, contbr. to nat. publs., newsletters; owner, mgr. Rent-A-Writer, San Jose, Calif., 1977—; pres. MS. BS. Inc., San Jose, 1981—; cons. and lectr, in field. Mem. Nat. Assn. Profl. Saleswomen, Media Alliance, Women in Communications, South Bay Pub. Relations Roundtable, San Jose C. of C., Women in Bus. Home: 6631 Mt Royal Dr San Jose CA 95120 Office: 1610 Blossom Hill Rd Suite 9 San Jose CA 95124

LANDRY, ALAN EDWARD, marketing executive, consultant, real estate developer; b. Escondido, Calif., May 14, 1953; s. Allen Edward and Madeline May (Gibson) L.; m. Lisa Ann Edgerley, May 30, 1981. B.A. in English, Chico State U., 1976, B.A. in Mass Communications, 1977. Cert. real estate agt., Calif. Editor Rancher Publs., Vista, Calif., 1977-80; v.p. mktg. Calif. Avocado Commn., Irvine, 1979—; exec. v.p. mktg. Whitworth-Landry Corp., Irvine, 1983—; cons. sales, mktg., investment counseling, real estate devel. Vice-pres. Lake Forest Oaks Homeowners, 1977. Mem. Alpha Sigma Phi. Republican. Founder Avocado Grower Mag. Home: 24891 Woodside El Toro CA 92630 Office: 17620 Fitch Irvine CA 92714

LANDSBURG, DAVID LEE, college administrator, communication consultant; b. Allegan, Mich., May 17, 1945; s. Keith Roger and Cora Augusta (Landenberger) L.; m. Saundra Kaye Hagemann, June 14, 1969; children—Laura Kaye, Erin Lee. B.A., Albion Coll., 1967; M.A., Mich. State U., 1968; Ph.D., U. Mich., 1975. Instr., Western Mich. U., Kalamazoo, 1968-69; asst. prof. Shaw U., Raleigh, N.C., 1969-71; dir. community service Westark Community Coll., Ft. Smith, Ark., 1972-76; dean, acting pres. Worthington (Minn.) Community Coll., 1976-78; exec. dean Pima Coll., Tucson, 1978—; managerial cons. communication for bus. and industry. Active Bus. Referral Club; Minn. Foster Parents Assn. NSF fellow, 1967; Midwest Community Coll. Leadership Fund grantee, 1974; U. Mich. Horace Rackham Sch. grantee, 1974; recipient Nat. Council Community Services Man of Yr. award, 1976. Mem. Am. Soc. Tng. and Devel., Nat. Council Community Services, Omicron Delta Kappa, Delta Sigma Rho. Democrat. Methodist. Contbr. articles to profl. jours. Office: 8202 E Poinciana Tucson AZ 85730

LANDSMAN, MERVYN, accountant; b. Los Angeles, June 24, 1930; s. Alec and Jennie (Schwimer) L.; m. Faith Anne Inselbuch, Nov. 6, 1960; children—David, Stephen, Mark. B.S., UCLA, 1953. C.P.A., Calif. Acct., Bay & Bay C.P.A.s, 1953, Lefkowitz, Berke, Parker & Freedman C.P.A.s, 1956-58; ptnr. Landsman, Frank and Sinclair C.P.A.s, Beverly Hills, Calif., 1958-72; corp. officer Landsman, Frank and Sinclair, An Accountancy Corp., 1972—. Served to 1st lt. USAF, 1954-56. Mem. Am. Inst. C.P.A.s, Calif. Soc. C.P.A.s, Phi Beta Kappa, Phi Sigma Delta. Home: 11241 Dona Isabel Dr Studio City CA 91604 Office: Landsman Frank & Sinclair 9595 Wilshire Blvd Suite 811 Beverly Hills CA 90212

LANE, E(DNA) JOYCE, county official; b. Avenell, Calif., Mar. 23, 1937; d. Edward Joseph and Grace Anita (Patterson) Tork; A.A., Lane Community Coll., 1974; m. Donald Robert Lane, Jan. 7, 1956; 1 son, David Anthony Tork. Police matron City of Springfield (Oreg.), 1960-63, ct. clk./adminstrn., 1965-72; data entry supr. Dept. Assessment & Taxation, Lane County, Eugene, Oreg., 1975-76, revenue div. mgr., 1976—, mem. devel. com. for uniform tax statements Oreg. Dept. Revenue, 1979—. Pres., Moffitt PTA, Springfield, Oreg., 1968-69, sec., 1967-68; sec. City Council PTA, 1968-69; United Way vol. Lane County, Oreg., 1975-81; pres. St. Alice Parish Council, Springfield, 1979-81, chmn. fin. and budget commn., 1970-72, 73-75, bd. dirs., 1969-72, 73-75, 79-81; alt. to bd. Lane Council Govts., 1977-79; bd. dirs. Lane County Econ. Improvement Commn., 1978—; bd. dirs. Willamalane Park and Recreation Dist., 1975-83, chmn. bd., 1977-78, 81-82; bd. dirs., treas. Lane County Econ. Improvement Assn., 1981—; chmn. bd. Willamalane Park and Recreation Dist., 1977-78, bd. dirs., 1975-78, 81-82. Mem. Oreg. Assn. County Tax Collectors (coordinator devel. com. for uniform, statewide magnetic tape payment program 1978—, 1st v.p. 1979-80, pres. 1980-81, mem. devel. com. for uniform tax statements 1979-81), Oreg. Park and Recreation Soc., Nat. Park and Recreation Soc., Oreg. Women for Timber, Oreg. Assn. Park and Recreation Dists., Altar Soc. Roman Catholic. Club: Zonta (treas. chpt. 1982-83). Home: 1081 L St Springfield OR 97477 Office: Lane County Courthouse 125 E 8th Ave Eugene OR 97401

LANE, JOSEPH FRANCIS, financial executive; consultant; b. N.Y.C., Oct. 18, 1948; s. Joseph Francis and Patricia Elizabeth (Clark) L. B.A., Hofstra U., 1971; postgrad. Central Mich. U.-Honolulu, 1975. Enrolled agt., IRS. Revenue officer IRS, Bklyn., 1971-72, mgmt. intern, Washington, 1972-73, mgmt. analyst, San Francisco, 1973-75, br. chief, div. chief, Honolulu, 1975-78, div. chief, Hartford, Conn., 1978-80, asst. div. chief, N.Y.C., 1980; pres., founder Cypress Group, Inc., Palo Alto, Calif., 1980—; dir. Internat. Congress on Energy, Resources and Environment, First U.S.-China Conf. Energy, Resources and Environment, Rann Inc., MacDonald Engring. Corp., Am. P.C. Labs, Inc. Bd. dirs. Palo Alto Citizens Cable Coop., 1982-83. Recipient Spl. Achievement award in

Improving Dept. Ops., IRS, 1972, 78, Dir.'s award for Div. Accomplishments, 1980. Mem. Internat. Assn. Fin. Planners, Nat. Assn. Enrolled Agts., Inst. Cert. Fin. Planners. Democrat. Roman Catholic. Club: Decathlon (Santa Clara, Calif.). Co-author: Small Business Management: A Practical Approach, 1983. Home: 75-23 San Antonio Rd Palo Alto CA 94303 Office: Cypress Group 525 University Ave Suite 820 Palo Alto CA 94301

LANE, MEREDITH ANNE, botanist; b. Mesa, Ariz., Aug. 4, 1951; d. Robert Ernest and Elva Jewell (Shilling) L.; m. Donald W. Longstreth, Apr. 6, 1974. B.S., Ariz. State U., 1974, M.S., 1976; Ph.D., U. Tex., 1980. Teaching asst. Ariz. State U., 1973-76, U. Tex., 1976-80; asst. prof. dept. environ., population and organismic biology U. Colo., Boulder, 1980—. SRIF fellow, 1981; recipient Cooley award, 1982. Mem. AAAS, Am. Soc. Plant Taxonomists, Bot. Soc. Am., Internat. Assn. Plant Taxonomists, Southwestern Assn. Naturalists, Ariz./Nev. Acad. Sci., Calif. Bot. Soc., Torrey Bot. Club, Sigma Xi, Beta Beta Beta, Phi Kappa Phi. Office: Dept Environmental Population and Organismic Biology U Colo Boulder CO 80309

LANE, PAUL JEFFREY, psychologist; b. Haverhill, Mass., Apr. 16, 1953; s. John P. and Pauline G. (Sable) L. B.S. summa cum laude in Psychology, U. Mass., 1975; M.S. in Clin. Psychology, Fla. State U., 1977, Ph.D. in Clin Psychology, 1979. Lic. psychologist Calif. Postdoctoral clin. psychology intern U. So. Calif. Sch. Medicine, Los Angeles, 1978-79; asst. clin. prof. psychology dept. psychiatry and behavioral scis. UCLA, 1980-81; cons. psychologist personnel dept. Los Angeles County Occupational Health Service, 1980—; clin. psychologist Kaiser-Permanente Med. Care Program, Lomita, Calif., 1979—; cons. Brentwood VA Hosp., 1982-83; cons., lectr. in field of psychology and criminology. Phi Kappa Phi disting. scholar, 1972-75; Mass. Commonwealth scholar, 1971-75; USPHS fellow, 1975-78; Am. Psychol. Assn. student travel scholar, 1977; recipient U. So. Calif. Sch. Medicine dept. psychiatry research award, 1979. Mem. Am. Psychol. Assn., Western Psychol. Assn., Calif. State Psychol. Assn., Assn. Advancement Psychology, Phi Beta Kappa, Phi Eta Sigma. Contbr. articles to profl. jours. Office: Kaiser Permanente 2081 Palos Verdes Dr North Lomita CA 90717

LANE, RONALD WALTER, museum executive; b. Glendale, Calif., Feb. 10, 1939; s. Walter Milton and Dorathea Ann (Cook) L.; A.A., Mt. San Antonio Coll., 1959; B.S., Calif. State U.-Fullerton, 1976; children—Barbara Ann, Leonard Ronald. Co-founder, gen. mgr. Lane's Mus. of World Wars, Buena Park, Calif., 1976—. Served as officer USAF, 1960-68, USAFR, 1968-82. Mem. Res. Officers Assn., Calif. Assn. Museums, Calif. Hist. Group. Home and office: 8700 Stanton Ave Buena Park CA 90620

LANE, SYLVIA, economist; b. N.Y.C., May 26, 1916; m. Benjamin Lane, Sept. 2, 1939; children—Leonard, Reese, Nancy. A.B., U. Calif.-Berkeley, 1934, M.A., 1936; postgrad. Columbia U., 1937; Ph.D., U. So. Calif., 1957; postgrad. (fellow), UCLA, 1963, U. Chgo., 1965, 68. Asst. prof. U. So. Calif., Los Angeles, 1947-60; assoc. prof. econs., fin. San Diego State U., 1961-65; assoc. prof. fin., assoc., dir. Ctr. for Econ. Edn., Calif. State U.-Fullerton, 1965-69, chmn. dept. fin., 1967-69; vis. prof. U. So. Calif., summer, 1967; prof. agrl. econs. U. Calif.-Davis, 1969-82, prof. emeritus, 1982—; research economist U. Calif.-Berkeley, 1982—; prof. U. Mo., summer, 1974; vis. scholar Stanford U., 1975-76; vis. prof. U. Calif.-Berkeley, 1979; project economist Los Angeles County Welfare Planning Council, 1956-59. Del., White House Conf. on Food and Nutrition, 1969; mem. Pres.'s Summit Conf. on Inflation, 1974; mem. adv. com. Ctr. for Bldg. Tech., Nat. Bur. Standards, 1975-79; bd. dirs. Am. Council Consumer Interests, 1973, Consumers Union, 1974-76. Ford Found. fellow, 1963, 65; U. Chgo. fellow, 1968; recipient Disting. Service award Omicron Delta Epsilon, 1975. Mem. Am. Econs. Assn., Western Econ. Assn. (past mem. exec. com.), Am. Council on Consumer Interests (dir.), Am. Real Estate and Urban Econs. Assn. (dir.), Am. Agrl. Econs. Assn. (dir.), Omicron Delta Epsilon (chmn. bd. trustees). Author: Personal Finance, 1963, 4th edit. 1980; contbr. articles to profl. jours. Office: Dept Agrl and Resource Econs U Calif Berkeley CA 94720

LANER, MARY RIEGE, sociology educator, researcher, writer; b. Chgo., Dec. 9, 1927; d. Frederick J. Granicher and Mary (Holasek) Vognsen. A.B. in Sociology, U. Chgo., 1966; M.A. in Sociology, U. N.Mex., 1969; Ph.D. in Sociology, Va. Poly. Inst. and State U., 1976. Research and adminstrv. asst. U. Chgo., 1962-67; grad. teaching asst. sociology U. N.Mex., 1967-69; instr. sociology No. Ariz. U., 1969-73; grad. teaching asst. sociology Va. Poly. Inst. and State U., 1973-76; asst. prof. sociology Ariz. State U., 1976-80, assoc. prof., 1980—; conf. presenter; leader, panelist workshops. Faculty grantee Ariz. State U., 1979, 78; recipient cert. of teaching excellence Va. Poly. Inst. and State U., 1974-75, 75-76, Outstanding Faculty Woman award Associated Women Students of No. Ariz. U., 1971-72. Mem. Am. Sociol. Assn., Nat. Council Family Relations, Pacific Sociol. Assn. (adv. council 1980-81, sec.-treas. 1978-81), Soc. Personality and Social Psychology, Soc. Study of Social Problems, AAUP (treas. No. Ariz. State U. chpt. 1971-72), Alpha Kappa Delta. Author: (with Ronald A. Hardert, Leonard Gordon and Mark Reader) Confronting Social Problems, 1984; editor: Courtship, Marriage, Divorce: The Contemporary American Scene, 1983; The Pairing Process: A Reader in the Sociology of Courtship from NCER Journals, 1979; assoc. editor Deviant Behavior: An Interdisciplinary Jour., 1979-82; cons. editor Jour. Homosexuality, 1978—; contbr. articles to profl. jours. Office: Dept of Sociology Arizona State University Tempe AZ 85287

LANEY, JACK STEWART, museum director; b. Tarrington, Wyo., Oct. 18, 1920; s. John Carl and Harriet Eliza (Stewart) L.; B.S., U.S. Naval Acad., 1940; B.S. in Aero Engring., U.S. Navy Postgrad. Sch., 1951; M.S. in Aero. Engring., U. Minn., 1952; M.A. in Counseling, U.S. Internat. U., 1974; m. Alma Edith Neuhausen, Oct. 21, 1944; children—Jack Terry, Marjorie Doll. Commd. ensign U.S. Navy, advanced through grades to capt.; comdg. officer Patrol Squadron 40, Air Test and Evaluation Squadron 1; comdr. Fleet Air Wing 10; dep. comdr. Operational Test and Evaluation Force; chmn. dept. sci. U.S. Naval Acad., Annapolis, Md., chief staff to comdt. 11th Naval Dist., San Diego, ret.; now dir. San Diego Hall of Sci. and Reuben H. Fleet Space Theater and Sci. Center, San Diego. Pres. Family Service Assn. San Diego County, 1980-81; sec., treas. San Diego Inter-Mus. Promotion Council, Inc., 1979-81. Decorated Legion of Merit, Meritorious Service medal, Bronze Star. Mem. Internat. Planetarium Soc., Space Theater Consortium, Inc., U.S. Naval Acad. Alumni Assn., Assn. Naval Aviation, Ret. Officers Assn. Republican. Presbyterian. (elder). Office: 1875 El Prado Balboa Park San Diego CA 92101

LANG, KATHERINE ANNE, counseling psychologist; b. Mpls., Jan. 22, 1947; d. Howard James and Barbara Anne (Bennett) L. B.A., Smith Coll., 1969; M.A., Bethel Theol. Sem., 1973; M.Ed., U. Mo.-Columbia, 1978, Ph.D., 1982. Tchr. English as 2d lang., kindergarten Am. Sch., Barcelona, Spain, 1970-71; mem. campus ministry Univ. Reformed Ch., East Lansing, Mich., 1973-76; counselor Univ. Counseling Ctr., U. Mo.-Rolla, 1978-79; coordinator Ctr. for Student Vol. Action, U. Mo.-Columbia, 1979-81; counseling psychologist U. Calif.-Davis, 1982—. Mem. Am. Psychol. Assn., Am. Personnel and Guidance Assn., Am. Coll. Personnel Assn., Christian Assn. Psychol. Studies. Office: Counseling Ctr U Calif Davis CA 95616

LANG, NEVALON BEAULAH, business college adminstrator; b. Seattle, Nov. 29, 1933; d. Arthur Roy and Beulah Etta (Dasher) Thompson; m. Alfred Wayne Lang, Feb. 19, 1965; children—Linda Egland, Janice Lang Blaine. B.S., Lewis and Clark State Coll., Lewiston, Idaho, 1970; postgrad. Ariz. State U., Calif. State U.-Los Angeles. Cert. vocat. edn., Calif. Bookkeeper, Idaho 1st Nat. Bank, Lewiston, 1952-53; sec. Boeing Aircraft, Seattle, 1953-56, State of Alaska, Soldatna, 1960-62; note teller Rainier Bank, Clarkston, Wash., 1962-65; dir., owner Valley Bus. Coll., Lewiston, 1970—; owner, mgr. several apts., Lewiston. Mem. Pacific Northwest Bus. Schs. Assn. (sec.-treas.), Wash. Bus. Edn. Assn., Idaho Bus. Edn. Assn., Am. Bus. Edn. Assn., Wash. Vocat. Assn., Am. Vocat. Assn., Lewiston C. of C. (3d v.p.). Methodist. Club: Jet Set Travel (Seattle). Office: Valley Bus Coll 507 Thain Lewiston ID 85301

LANG, THOMPSON HUGHES, newspaper pub.; b. Albuquerque, Dec. 12, 1946; s. Cornelius Thompson and Margaret Miller (Hughes) L.; student U. N.Mex., 1965-68, U. of Americas, Mexico City, 1968-69; m. Kimberley M. Lang, Mar. 1980. Advt. salesman Albuquerque Pub. Co., 1969-70, prodn. dept. asst., 1970-71, pres., gen. mgr., treas., dir., chmn. bd., 1971—; pres., treas., dir., chmn. bd. Jour. Pub. Co., Albuquerque, 1971—; pres., dir. Masthead Internat., 1971—; pres. Magnum Systems, Inc., 1973—; pres., treas., dir. Jour. Center Corp., 1979—. Mem. H.O.W. Orgn. Home: 1615 Park St SW Albuquerque NM 87104 Office: 7th and Silver SW Albuquerque NM 87102

LANGAN, LEON VERDIN, consulting engineer; b. St. Louis, July 29, 1932; s. Leon Verdin and Mary Caroline (Gross) L.; B.A. in Geology, U. N.Mex., 1953; M.S. in Mineral Sci., Stanford U., 1957; m. Karine Bowlen, Nov. 15, 1969; children—Oliver, Susan; children by previous marriage—Christopher, Kathryn, Mari: stepchildren—John, James. Geologist, AEC, Grand Junction, Colo., 1954; research asst. Stanford Research Inst., Menlo Park, Calif., 1956-57; div. sales mgr. Varian Assocs., Palo Alto, Calif., 1957-67; pres. Environ. Measurements, Inc. San Francisco, 1968—. Vice pres., bd. dirs. Hayward (Calif.) Vesper Hosp., 1980—; chmn. SanFRANCEcisco Festivals, 1979—. Served with AUS, 1954-56. Mem. Soc. Exploration Geophysicists, European Assn. Exploration Geophysicists, AAAS, Air Pollution Control Assn., Greek Ontological Devel. Soc., San Francisco Wine and Food Soc., Guardsmen. Republican. Roman Catholic. Club: Commonwealth (San Francisco). Patentee in field. Home: 2660 California St San Francisco CA 94115 Office: 215 Leidesdorff St San Francisco CA 94111

LANGDON, THELMA PERSE, civic worker; b. Pueblo, Colo., May 15, 1925; R.N., Minequa Sch. Nursing, Pueblo, 1946; m. J. Ray Langdon, 1947; 5 children. Mem. Alaska Post-Secondary Commn., 1978—; mem. Alaska Bd. Edn., 1975-78, 78-82, pres., 1978-80; del., chmn. S. Central region White House Conf. Children and Youth, 1970; mem. Alaska PTA, 1958—, pres., 1971-75, mem. nat. bd. mgrs., 1971-75; mem. Alaska Med. Assn. Aux., 1958—, pres., 1970; bd. dirs. nat. AMA Aux., 1974-76; pres. Anchorage Med. Soc. Aux., 1960; v.p. Big Bros. Anchorage, 1978; mem. Providence Hosp. Aux., Anchorage, 1958—, hon. life mem., 1974—; bd. dirs. Anchorage Mental Health Assn., 1968-70, Alaska Mental Health Assn., 1970-73; mem. bd. Office Child Advocacy, Office Gov. Alaska, 1971-74, sec.-treas., 1973-74; citizen mem. health edn. curriculum com. Anchorage Sch. Dist., 1969-74.

LANGE, CLIFFORD E., library director b. Fond du Lac, Wis., Dec. 29, 1935; s. Elmer H. and Dorothy Brick (Smithers) L.; student St. Norbert Coll., 1954-57; B.S., Wis. State U., 1959; M.S.L.S. (Library Services Act scholar), U. Wis., 1960, Ph.D. (Higher Edn. Act fellow), 1972; m. Janet M. LeMieux, June 6, 1959; children—Paul, Laura, Ruth. Head extension dept. Oshkosh (Wis.) Pub. Library, 1960-62, head reference dept., 1962-63; asst. dir. Jervis Library, Rome, N.Y., 1962; dir. Eau Claire (Wis.) Pub. Library, 1963-66; asst. dir. Lake County Pub. Library, Giffith, Ind., 1966-68; asst. prof. Sch. Library Sci., U. Iowa, 1971-73; dir. Wauwatosa (Wis.) Pub. Library, 1973-75; asst. prof. U. So. Calif., 1975-78; state librarian N.Mex. State Library, Santa Fe, 1978-82; dir. Carlsbad (Calif.) City Library, 1982—. Served with U.S. Army, 1958. Mem. ALA, Calif. Library Assn. Home: 3780 Garfield St Carlsbad CA 92008 Office: 1250 Elm Ave Carlsbad CA 92008

LANGE, JAMES DUBOIS, clinical psychologist; b. Oceanside, Calif., 1945; s. Rollo DuBois and Delores Helen (Zundel) L.; m. Janice Sue Stormer, 1971; 1 son, Brandt Stormer. B.A., U. Wis., 1972; M.A., Dalhousie U., Halifax (N.S., Can.), 1974, Ph.D., 1979. Lic. clin. psychologist Wis.; cert. clin. psychologist Ariz. Clin. intern Brown U., Providence, 1977; program coordinator Vietnam Vets. Ctr., Providence, 1979-81; clin. psychologist Camelback Hosps. Counseling Ctr., Scottsdale, Ariz., 1981—. Served with U.S. Army, 1966-69; Vietnam. Dalhousie U. scholar, 1973-75. Mem. Am. Psychol. Assn., AAAS. Contbr. articles to profl. jours. Home: PO Box 2601 Scottsdale AZ 85252 Office: Camelback Hosps Counseling Ctr 6411 E Thomas Rd Scottsdale AZ 85251

LANGE, PAUL MARTIN, educator; b. Racine, Wis., Apr. 5, 1940; s. Einar Martin and Laura Ovidia (Bergesen) L.; B.S in Bus. Adminstrn., Northwestern U., 1962; M.A., Mankato State Coll., 1968; J.D., U. Minn., 1965. Admitted to Minn. bar, 1966; with firm Farrish Zimmerman, Johnson & Manahan, Mankato, 1965-68; prof. bus. adminstrn., chmn. dept. fin. and industry Calif. State U., Fresno, 1968—. Partner, Lange & McLeod Enterprises, Fresno, 1972—; pres. Lange & Assos. Mortgage Bankers Am. fellow, 1971; Am. Risk and Ins. Assn. fellow, 1972; Chgo. Merc. Exchange fellow, 1973; Innovative Instrn. research grantee, 1974, 79; Calif. Real Estate Endowment Fund grantee, 1981. Mem. Am., Minn. bar assns., Am. Risk and Ins. Assn., Fresno Estate Planning Council, Am. Soc. C.L.U.s, Western Bus. Law Assn. (pres. 1978-79), Am. Bus. Law Assn. (v.p. 1982-83), Calif. State U. Fresno Faculty Assn. (pres. 1973-74), Delta Sigma Pi, Gamma Eta Gamma, Pi Sigma Epsilon, Beta Gamma Sigma (pres. 1974-75). Author: Real Estate Principles and Practices, California Supplement, 1977. Home: 7101 N Monte Fresno CA 93711

LANGEL, CHARLES ALFRED, manufacturing engineer; b. Vandalia, Ill., Apr. 2, 1940; s. David Alfred and Minnie Gwendollyn (Morgan) L.; m. Sally Edith Schumacher, Sept. 21, 1968; 1 dau., Karen Edith. B.S. in Natural Sci., Greenville Coll., 1963. Research technician Chevron Research Co., Richmond, Calif., 1968-69; electronic technician Recortec Inc., Mountain View, Calif., 1969-71; test engr. Western Elec. Co., Dublin, Calif., 1971-74; sr. electronic technician Searle Cardio-Pulmonary, Hayward, Calif., 1974-77; mfg. engr. Varian Assos., Palo Alto, Calif., 1977—. Served with USN, 1964-68. Mem. Soc. Mfg. Engrs. Club: Masons (San Leandro, Calif.). Home: 563 McKinley Ct San Leandro CA 94577 Office: 611 Hansen Way D-161 Palo Alto CA 94303

LANGER, JAMES STEPHEN, physicist, educator; b. Pitts., Sept. 21, 1934; s. Bernard F. and Liviette (Roth) L.; m. Elinor Goldmark Aaron, Dec. 21, 1958; children—Ruth, Stephen, David. B.Sc., Carnegie Inst. Tech., 1955; Ph.D., U. Birmingham (Eng.), 1958. Asst. prof. physics, to prof. Carnegie-Mellon U., 1958-82, asso. dean Mellon Coll. Sci., 1971-74; prof., permanent mem. Inst. Theoretical Physics, U. Calif-Santa Barbara, 1982—; cons. Guggenheim fellow, 1974-75. Fellow Am. Phys. Soc., Am. Acad. Arts and Scis.; mem. Fedn. Am. Scientists, AAAS, Com. Concerned Scientists (v.p. physics). Contbr. numerous articles to profl. jours. Home: 1130 Las Canoas Ln Santa Barbara CA 93105 Office: Inst Theoretical Physics U Calif Santa Barbara CA 93106

LANGFELD, MARILYN IRENE, art director, graphic designer; b. St. Louis, Apr. 28, 1951; d. Norman Max and Celeste (Brown) L. Student, Vanderbilt U., 1968-70; B.A. cum laude, Sonoma State U., 1978-80. Printer, Sojourner Truth Press, Altanta, 1971-73; carpenter apprentice Housebuilders Union, Atlanta, 1973-74; self employed housebuilder, Perry, Me., 1974-75; graphic artist Cuthberts Printing, San Rafael, Calif., 1976-77; graphic Designer Community Type & Design, Fairfax, Calif., 1977-80; owner, graphic designer Langfeld Design Assocs., San Francisco, 1980—. Mem. People Speaking Adv. Bd., 1979—. Sonoma State scholar, Bank of Sonoma County, 1979-80; Vanderbilt U. scholar, 1968-69, 69-70. Mem. Bookbuilders West, San Francisco Women in Advt., Western Art Dirs. Club. Art Dirs. and Artists of Sacramento, Petaluma Area C. of C. Democrat. Jewish. Office: 379A Clementina St San Francisco CA 94103

LANGHANS, EDWARD ALLEN, educator; b. Warren, Pa., Mar. 11, 1923; s. Allen Milton and Frances Allen L.; B.A., U. Rochester, 1948, M.A. in English, 1949; M.A. in Theatre, U. Hawaii, 1951; Ph.D. in Theatre, Yale U., 1955. Asst. prof. drama U. Tex., Austin, 1955-57; asst. prof. drama, theatre U. Hawaii, Honolulu, 1957-64, asso., 1964-71, prof., chmn. dept., 1971—; vis. prof. Tufts U., 1968-69; research prof. George Washington U., 1975-76. Bd. dirs. Honolulu Theatre for Youth, 1958-63, Hawaii Theatre Council, 1965-70, Hawaii Theatre Festival, 1978-81. Served with USAF, 1942-47; Decorated Air Medal, D.F.C. Nat. Endowment for Humanities grantee, 1975-76; Folger Shakespeare Library fellow, 1970-73. Mem. Am. Theatre Assn., Soc. Theatre Research, Am. Soc. Theatre Research, Malone Soc. Author: (with Philip Highfill and Kalman Burnim) A Biographical Dictionary of Actors, Actresses, Musicians, Dancers, Managers, and Other Stage Personnel in London, 1660-1800, 16 vols., 1973—; Five Restoration Theatrical Adaptations, 1980; Restoration Promptbooks, 1981; dir., designer numerous plays. Office: Dept Drama and Theatre U Hawaii Honolulu HI 96822

LANGLEY, CAROL MARY, exec. search cons.; b. Detroit, Mar. 22, 1945; d. Edson Carnegie and Ethel Helen (Hulett) L.; student Wayne State U., Detroit, Detroit Coll. Bus., Henry Ford Community Coll., Dearborn, Mich., U. Mich., Dearborn, U. Colo., Denver. Bus. mgmt. asst. to exec. and dep. dirs. Metro Fund and S.E. Mich. Council Govts., Detroit, 1967-70; asst. to exec. dir. and policy bd. dirs. Denver Regional Council Govts., 1970-80; mgr. Income Realty & Mgmt., 1980; adminstrv. asst. Davis Oil Co., 1980; adminstr. employment Home Petroleum Corp., 1981-82; pres. Langley & Assocs., Englewood, Colo., 1982—. Notary public, Colo.; lic. ins. agt., Colo.; CPS. Mem. Nat. Entrepreneurs Assn. Home: 7592 S Rosemary Circle Englewood CO 80112 Office: PO Box 4195 Englewood CO 80155

LANGLEY, GARY ALFRED, association executive; b. Livingston, Mont., Oct. 29, 1946; s. Alfred Cameron and Victoria Ann (Ricci) L.; B.A., U. Mont., 1969; m. Pamela Jane Patrick, Oct. 22, 1972; children—Jefferson Patrick, Kari Jane. Reporter, Livingston (Mont.) Enterprise, 1964-65; copy editor Spokane (Wash.) Spokesman-Review, 1969; reporter, asst. city editor, asst. editorial page editor Missoula (Mont.) Missoulian, 1969-72; bur. chief Mont. Lee Newspapers State Bur., Helena, 1972-77; dir. communications Mont. Stockgrowers Assn., Helena, 1977-81; owner Langley Public Relations Cons., Helena, 1979—. Mem. Am. Soc. Assn. Execs., Mont. Soc. Assn. Execs., Western Environ. Trade Assn., Mont. Mininy Assn. (exec. dir. 1981—), Last Chance Press Club, Sigma Delta Chi. Republican. Lutheran. Clubs: Mont. Editor, The Pick and Shovel Jour., 1980—. Home: 4315 Hwy 12 W Helena MT 59601 Office: PO Box 132 Helena MT 59601

LANGONI, RICHARD ALLEN, civil engineer; b. Trinidad, Colo., Aug. 7, 1945; s. Domenic and Josephine (Maria) L.; A.Applied Sci., Trinidad State Jr. Coll., 1966; B.S., Colo. State U., 1968; M.A., U. No. Colo., 1978; m. Pamela Jill Stansberry, Aug. 19, 1972; children—Kristi, Kerri. Civil engr. Dow Chem. Co., Golden, Colo., 1968-71; dir. public works City of Trinidad, 1971-74; civil engr. Clement Bros. Constrn. Co., 1974-75; instr. Trinidad State Jr. Coll., 1975-78; dir. public works City of Durango (Colo.), 1978-82; asst. dist. design engr. Colo. Dept. Hwys., Durango, 1982—; owner Great Expectations. Registered profl. engr. Colo., N.Mex. Mem. Nat. Soc. Profl. Engrs., ASCE, Am. Public Works Assn., Water Pollution Control Fedn., Profl. Engrs. Colo., Nat. Ski Patrol, Durango C. of C., Phi Theta Kappa, Chi Epsilon. Home: 2911 Holly Ave Durango CO 81301 Office: 6th and Railroad Durango CO

LANGOWSKI, THEODORE STEPHEN, constrn. co. exec.; b. Sopris, Colo., Oct. 9, 1923; s. Charles Eugene and Edith (Skufca) L.; A.A. in Engring., Trinidad State Jr. Coll., 1946; m. Frances Veltri, June 3, 1950; children—Theodore John, Rose Ann. Gen. supt. Walsky Constrn. Co., Topeka, 1959-65; gen. foreman AA Constrn. Co., Colorado Springs, Colo., 1965-73; with Highland Constrn., Colorado Springs, 1966; gen. supt. G.E. Johnson Constrn. Co., Colorado Springs, Austin, Tex. and Broomfield, Colo., 1966—, L.R. Johnson Constrn. Co., Colorado Springs, 1981-83, Ritchie Constrn. Co., 1983—. Active, Boy Scouts Am. Served with M.C., AUS, 1943-46. Democrat. Roman Catholic. Club: KC. Home: 1615 Howard Ave Colorado Springs CO 80909

LANGPAAP, ELEANOR MADELINE, hospital administrator; b. San Francisco, Apr. 9, 1922; d. Otto Bismarck and Emilie Marie Louise (Euvrard) Langpaap; A.B., U. Calif., Berkeley, 1943, M.P.H., 1962. Statistician Oakland (Calif.) City Health Dept., 1943-45; x-ray technologist Drs. Garland, Hill & Mottram, San Francisco, 1946-48; research asst. Pack Med. Group, N.Y.C., 1948-49; pub. health analyst, bus. mgr. Santa Barbara County (Calif.) Health Dept., 1949-54, dept. asst., 1954-60; with Santa Clara County Health Dept., 1954-60; adminstrv. asst. building and construction program Childrens Hosp. of Los Angeles, 1963-65, adminstrv. asst. physician in chief, 1965-67, asso. adminstr., 1967-68; project adminstr. Calif. Regional Med. Program, U. Calif., Davis, 1968-71, asst. to dean, 1971-73, spl. asst. to chancellor, 1972-73; asso. dir. hosps. and clinics Sacramento Med. Center of U. Calif., 1973-74, exec. asso. dir., 1974-75; adminstr. Eskaton Am. River Hosp., Carmichael, Calif., 1975—. Mem. Am. Coll. Hosp. Adminstrs., Am., Calif. Hosp. assns., Hosp. Council No. Calif., U. Calif. Berkeley Alumni Assn., Sacramento Sierra Hosp. Assn. (dir. 1973—), Assn. Western Hosps. (dir.). Republican. Episcopalian. Office: 4747 Engle Rd Carmichael CA 95608

LANGSTON, ELIZABETH RICKS, clinical psychologist; b. Brady, Tex., June 22, 1946; d. Glenn Hall and Alice Glenn (Young) Ricks; m. Daniel Leppin Hoke, Apr. 5, 1969; m. 2d, Jerome Lee Longston, June 13, 1975; 1 son, Larson Jerome. Student Tex. Christian U., Ft. Worth, 1964-65; B.S. in Speech Pathology, S.W. Tex. State U., San Marcos, 1968; M. in Ednl. Psychology, U. Tex.-Austin, 1969. Lic. psychologist, counselor, Tex. Supr. testing lab. div. psychology Southwestern Med. Sch., Dallas, 1969-70; psychologist Callier Communications Disorder Ctr., Dallas, 1970-73; sch. counselor Los Alamos schs., 1973-74; psychologist Santa Fe (N.Mex.) Ind. Sch. Dist., 1974-76; assoc. psychologist DeWitt-Lauaca Spl. Edn. Coop., Cuero, Tex., 1976-78; staff psychologist Gulf Bend Mental Health Mental Retardation Ctr., Victoria, Tex., 1978-79; mental health cons. Santa Fe Indian Health Service, 1979-82; assoc. sch. psychologist Kerrville (Tex.) Ind. Sch. Dist., 1982—; dir. Family Ctr., Inc., Dallas, 1971-73; group therapy grant Taos Pueblo Day Sch., 1981-82; family therapy cons. Picuris Holistic Ctr., Picuris Pueblo, N.Mex., 1981-82; cons. psychologist Poreer Meml. Hosp., Listen Found., Denver, 1976-79; instr. psychology Richland Community Coll., Dallas, 1972-73; cons. therapist Rape Crisis Line,

Women's Ctr., Santa Fe, 1974-76; admissions com. Blue Bonnet Youth Ranch, Yoakum, Tex., 1977-79. Mem. Am. Psychol. Assn., Chi Omega, Alpha Chi, Sigma Alpha Eta, Psi Chi. Democrat. Episcopalian. Club: Eastern Star. Home: 356 Spur St 100 Kerrville TX 78028 Office: 1035 Barnett St Kerrville TX 78028

LANNEN, VERNON T., state senator, security supervisor; m. Judy Ahartz; children—Shawn, Kimberly. Student Kellogg High Sch. Security supr. Bunker Hill Co., Kellogg, Idaho; mem. Idaho State Senate. Democrat. Office: Idaho State Senate Boise ID 83720*

LANNING, WAYNE LAWRENCE, psychologist, educator; b. Grand Rapids, Mich., June 2, 1941; s. John and Hattie (Kooienga) L.; m. Delaine E. Huber, Aug. 23, 1962; children—Jeffrey, Kimberly, Amy, Matthew. B.A., Calvin Coll., Grand Rapids, Mich., 1962; M.A., Mich. State U., East Lansing, 1964; Ed.D., Western Mich. U., Kalamazoo, 1970. Lic. counseling psychologist, Ind. Counselor, Holland (Mich.) Christian Schs., 1964-68; counseling psychologist, Ind. U., 1970-79; prof. counselor edn., U. Wyo., 1979—; vis. assoc. prof. Boston U., 1976-77; lectr., cons. in sports psychology. U. Wyo. research grantee, 1981. Mem. Am. Psychol. Assn., Am. Personnel and Guidance Assn., Internat. Soc. Sports Psychology, Assn. Counselor Edn. and Supervision. Presbyterian. Contbr. articles to profl. jours. Home: PO Box 3562 Laramie WY 82071 Office: PO Box 3374 Coll Edn Laramie WY 82071

LANSDOWNE, KAREN MYRTLE, educator; b. Twin Falls, Idaho, Aug. 11, 1926; d. George and Effie Myrtle (Ayotte) Martin; B.A. in English with honors, U. Oreg., 1948, M.Ed., 1958, M.A. with honors, 1960; m. Paul L. Lansdowne, Sept. 12, 1948; chilren—Michele Lynn, Larry Alan. Tchr., Newfield (N.Y.) High Sch., 1948-50, S. Eugene (Oreg.) High Sch., 1952; mem. faculty U. Oreg., Eugene, 1958-65; asst. prof. English, Lane Community Coll., Eugene, 1965—; cons. Oreg. Curriculum Study Center. Rep., Cal Young Neighborhood Assn., 1978—; mem. scholarship com. First Congl. Ch., 1950-70. Mem. MLA, Pacific N.W. Regional Conf. Community Colls., Nat. Council Tchrs. English, U. Oreg. Women, AAUW (sec.), Jaycettes, Pi Lambda Theta (pres.), Phi Beta Patronesses (pres.), Delta Kappa Gamma. Co-author: The Oregon Curriculum: Language/Rhetoric, I, II, III and IV, 1970. Office: 4000 E 30 St Eugene OR 97405

LANSTROM, SIGVARD WILLHELM, steel engr.; b. Youngstown, Ohio, Sept. 24, 1934; s. Carl Thure and Harriett S. (Swanson) L.; B.S. in Elec. Engring., Carnegie-Mellon U., 1956; m. Mary Edith Winegeart, May 29, 1958; children—Elizabeth Louise, Kendall Thure. With U.S. Steel Corp., Pittsburg Works, Calif., 1956—, gen. foreman tin finishing maintenance, 1967-75, asst. supt. maintenance, utilities and engring., 1975-76, asst. supt. cold reduction, 1976-78, works maintenance engr., 1978-79, supt. maintenance and utilities, 1979-81, sr. process engr., 1981—, sec. union-mgmt. joint apprenticeship com., 1973-75; instr. Los Medanos Community Coll., Pittsburg, 1980—. Mem. adult com. Am. Field Service, Antioch, Calif., 1969-71, chmn. home selection com., 1970-71; mem. Carnegie-Mellon Admissions Council San Francisco Bay Area, 1970—; mem. operating com. Solano/Contra Costa Jr. Achievement. Served to 1st lt. Signal Corps, AUS, 1956-58. Registered profl. engr., Calif. Mem. IEEE (program com. Bay area sect. 1968), Assn. Iron and Steel Engrs. (chmn. San Francisco sect. 1972-73 chmn. Western conf. 1972, 73, 74, 76, 78, 82, nat. dir. 1974), Nat. Soc. Profl. Engrs., Antioch C. of C. (dir. 1978-83, pres. 1981-82). Methodist (adminstrv. bd. 1971-82, chmn. 1977-82 trustee 1974-76). Clubs: Ambassadors, Antioch Delta Kiwanis, U.S. Steel Pittsburg Work Supts. Home: 3223 View Dr Antioch CA 94509 Office: US Steel Pittsburg Works PO Box 471 Pittsburg CA 94565

LANTOS, TOM, congressman; b. Budapest, Hungary, Feb. 1, 1928; student U. Wash.; Ph.D. (B'nai B'rith Hillel Found. scholar), U. Calif., Berkeley, 1953; married. Prof. econs. San Francisco State U., mem. 97th-98th Congresses from Calif. 11th dist. Mem. Millbrae Bd. Edn. Jewish. Democrat. Office: 1707 Longworth House Office Bldg Washington DC 20515

LANTZ, DENNIS EARLE, lawyer; b. Chgo., Apr. 15, 1938; s. Lawrence Lee and Vida Lenore (Conner) L.; m. Meridee Fell, Feb. 14, 1978; children—Lawrence Christian, Raymond Earle, Christine Denise, David James. B.S. in Gen. Engring., U. Ill., 1959; M.B.A., Calif. State U., 1969; J.D., Western State U., 1976. Bar: Calif. 1977. Dist. mgr. Constrn. Machinery div. Harnischfeger Corp., 1959-62; program/new product mgr. Aerojet & N.Am., 1962-66; controller, mgr. budgets and fin. planning Teledyne Systems Co., 1966-67; mgr. acctg. Sunnyland Juice Co., DiGiorgio Corp., 1967-68; mgmt. cons. City of Long Beach (Calif.), 1968-75; tax cons., 1968—; cons. Freeman & Freeman, 1976-77; gen. mgr. Retirement Plan Data Service, Whittier, Calif., 1974-76; sole practice, Geyersville, Calif., 1977—; cons. in field. Recipient Sierra Club Outings Leadership award, 1976. Mem. ABA, Calif. Bar Assn., Sonoma County Bar Assn. Clubs: Dry Creek Valley Assn., Sierra (chpt. chmn. 1978-79, nat. council sec. 1978-79, nat. mountaineering com. chmn. 1972—, nat. tng. chmn. 1972—). Editor Ill. Technograph, 1956-59; contbr. articles to profl. jours. Office: 128 North St Healdsburg CA 95441

LANTZ, ELIZABETH MARY, civic worker; b. Rawlins, Wyo., Feb. 13, 1915; d. Anthony and Margery (Walker) Stratton; student Lindenwood Coll., 1932-33; B.S., U. Wyo., 1936; m. Everett Delmer Lantz, Mar. 5, 1938; children—Phillip Edward, Keith William, George Everett, Barbara Elizabeth. Sec. to U. Wyo. Librarian, 1936-38. Pres. Ivinson Meml. Hosp. Aux., 1977-79, P.T.A., 1958-59; corr. sec., chaplain P.E.O.; pres. Kappa Kappa Gamma, 1934-36, alumnae pres., 1953-55, pres. house corp., 1956-52, 56-68, 76—; sec. Kiwivians, 1951; pres. Episcopal Women, 1966-69, 73-74, St. Anne's Guild, 1976-81, 82—; mem. vestry Episc. Ch., 1971-74; election bd. judge, 1965—; den mother Cub Scouts, 1947-49; registration chmn. Gov.'s Youth Conf., 1976, 78, 80, Youth Legis. Forum, 1977, 79; hostess statehouse briefing seminar Internat. Year of the Child, 1979. Mem. Phi Gamma Nu. Republican. Club: Rep. Women's. Home: 1614 Garfield St Laramie WY 82070

LANTZ, TERRY LEE, housing and personnel director; b. Los Angeles, Sept. 9, 1945; s. Jack Virgil and Pauline Marguarite (Gardes) L.; children—Todd Ryan, Trent Jonathan. B.A. in Polit. Sci., Calif. State U.-Fullerton, 1968, M.P.A., 1972. Adminstrv. asst. to city mgr., Temple City, Calif., 1969-71; community services coordinator City of Stanton (Calif.), 1971-72; adminstrv. asst. to city mgr., Garden Grove, Calif., 1972-76; personnel dir. City of Garden Grove, 1976—, housing dir., 1981—; cons. in field. Mem. So. Calif. Personnel Mgmt. (dir.), Orange County Personnel Dirs. (chmn.), Internat. City Mgrs. Assn., Internat. Personnel Mgmt. Assn., Am. Soc. Pub. Adminstrn. Address: 11391 Acacia Pkwy Garden Grove CA 92640

LANYI, JANOS KAROLY, biochemist, educator; b. Budapest, Hungary, June 5, 1937; s. Istvan and Klara (Rosthy) L.; student Eotvos Lorand U. Scis., Budapest, Hungary, 1955-56; B.S., Stanford, 1959; M.A., Harvard, 1961, Ph.D., 1963; came to U.S., 1957, naturalized, 1962; m. Carol Ann Giblin, Sept. 15, 1962; children—Clara Aileen, Sean Renton, Gabriella. Postdoctoral fellow Stanford Sch. Medicine, 1963-65; Nat. Acad. Scis. resident research asso. NASA-Ames Research Center, 1965-66, sr. scientist Moffett Field, Calif., 1966-80; prof. physiology and biophysics U. Calif., Irvine, 1980—; vis. fellow Cornell U., 1976. Recipient NASA medal for exceptional sci. achievement, 1977; H. Julian Allen award for best sci. paper Ames Research Center, 1978; Alexander von Humbolt award for sr. U.S. scientists, W. Ger., 1979-80. Mem. Am. Soc. Biol. Chemists, Biophys. Soc., Am. Soc. Microbiology, Phi Beta Kappa, Sigma Xi. Office: Dept Physiology and Biophysics U Calif Irvine CA 92717

LAPERRIERE, ARTHUR JOSEPH LOUIS, ecologist; b. Acushnet, Mass., July 13, 1942; s. Arthur J.L., Jr., and Yvonne Irene (Frennette) LaP.; B.A., U. Mass., 1964; C.P.Q., U. Okla., 1966; postgrad. U. Md., 1966-67; M.S., Iowa State U., 1971; Ph.D. (NASA fellow), U. Alaska, 1976; m. Lynn Louise Dannacher, Apr. 30, 1976; children—Monique, Colleen, Arthur, Paul. Research asst. Iowa State U., 1969-71; research fellow U. Alaska, 1971-74, research assoc., 1975-77; dir. Ecosystem Monitor, 1974-77; coordinator nat. wetland inventory U.S. Fish and Wildlife Service, Anchorage, 1977-81; pres. Ind. Seafoods, Ltd., 1981-83; sr. environ. scientist Ott Water Engrs., 1983—. Served with USAF, 1964-69. NASA/Alaska Dept. Fish and Game research grantee, 1975-77; U.S. Fish and Wildlife Service/U.S. Nat. Park Service research grantee, 1976-77; Sierra Found. research grantee, 1976-77. Mem. Iowa Acad. Sci., Am. Soc. Photogrammetry, Wildlife Soc., Alaska Conservation Soc., Sigma Xi, Gamma Sigma Delta. Club: Elks. Contbr. articles profl. jours. Office: 4790 Business Park Blvd Bldg D Suite 1 Anchorage AK 99503

LA PIERRE, SHARON DALE, artist, art educator; b. San Francisco, Mar. 1, 1945; d. George L. La Pierre and Maybelle F. (Swanson) L. B.A., Calif. State U.-San Jose, 1966; M.A. in Woven Textiles, Calif. State U.-San Diego, 1970. Cert. jr. coll. tchr., Calif. Owner, designer Basket Studio, Denver, 1970—; instr. fiber dept. Arapahoe Community Coll., Littleton, Colo., 1971-76; instr. weaving and design, U. Colo., Boulder, 1972, 1980; dir. fiber and design dept. Community Coll. Denver, Red Rocks, 1975-82, dir. gallery, 1982—; pres. Genre Communications Ltd.; artist-in-residence fibers design U. No. Colo., Greeley, 1978; instr. arts Colo. Women's Coll., Denver, 1981; lectr.; dir. workshops; exhbns. include Denver Art Mus., 1972; art ctrs. in Colo., N.Y., Nebr. Active NOW, San Diego, 1971. Recipient 1st place award Midwest Weavers Conf., 1973; Colo. Council Arts and Humanities grantee, 1978. Mem. Am. Soc. Interior Design, Handweavers Guild Am., Am. Crafts Council. Republican. Christian Scientist. Author: Design and Creativity; Drawing Out the Creative Potential by Understanding Design, 1979; You Can Design: An Adventure in Creating, 1983; contbr. articles in field. to publs.

LAPLANTZ, DAVID MILTON, art educator, jeweler; b. Toledo, Ohio, June 12, 1944; s. Milton N. and Bernice L. (Merle) LaP.; m. Shereen F. Buckland, Feb. 7, 1970. B.S., Bowling Green (Ohio) State U., 1962-66; M.F.A., Cranbrook Acad. Art, Bloomfield Hills, Mich., 1969. Instr. art Inst. Am. Indian Arts, Santa Fe, 1967-68, Flint (Mich.) Community Jr. Coll., 1968-69, Colo. State U., Fort Collins, 1969-70, San Diego State U., 1970-71, Calif. Coll. Arts and Crafts, summer 1979, Bowling Green State U., summer 1981, Arrowmont Sch. Arts and Crafts, Gatlinburg, Tenn., summer 1981; prof. art Humboldt State U., Arcata, Calif., 1971-77, 78—; vis. lectr. numous colls., univs., workshops; group shows: St. Paul Art Ctr., 1970, Mus. Contemporary Crafts, N.Y.C., 1975, Tex. Tech U., 1977, U. Ariz. Mus. Art, 1977, Phoenix Art Mus., 1977, Marietta Coll., 1979, E.B. Crocker Art Gallery, Sacramento, 1979, Am. Craft Mus., N.Y.C., 1980, Wash. State U. Mus. Art, Pullman, 1981, Renwick Gallery, Washington, 1982, others; works represented in permanent collections St. Paul Art Ctr., Colo. State U., Mad River Community Hosp., Arcata, Calif., Bowling Green State U., Genoa (Ohio) Area Pub. Library, Arrowmont Sch. Arts and Crafts, Am. Craft Mus., N.Y.C., Schmuckmuseum Pforzheim, Germany, Nat. Mus. Am. Art, Smithsonian Instn., Washington, Cranbrook Acad. Art, also pvt. collections. Recipient Outstanding Prof. award Humboldt State U., 1981, numerous other prizes and awards. Mem. Soc. N.Am. Goldsmiths, Am. Craft Council. Contbr. articles to art publs. Home: 899 Bayside Cutoff Bayside CA 95524 Office: Dept Art Humboldt State Univ Arcata CA 95521

LAPLANTZ, SHEREEN, artist; b. Glendale, Calif., Feb. 9, 1947; d. Charles Francis and Grace Elaine (Matthiesen) Buckland; m. David Milton LaPlantz, Feb. 7, 1970. B.A., Calif. State U., 1968; postgrad. Cranbrook Acad. Arts, 1968-69. One woman shows: Trident Lounge Gallery, Calif. State Coll., Los Angeles, 1968, Nelson Hall Gallery, Calif. State U., Humboldt, Arcata, 1973, The Woolmark, Eureka, Calif., 1976, Gallery 234, U. Wyo., Laramie, 1979, West Nebr. Art Center, Scottsbluff, 1980, Murray (Ky.) State U., 1983; group shows include: Colo. State U., Fort Collins, 1970, Humboldt Fed. Savs., Arcata, Calif., 1975, Behind-the-Brewery Gallery, LaCrosse, Wis., 1975, Coll. of Wooster, Ohio, 1978, Art, Inc., Anchorage, 1980, The Hand & The Spirit, Scottsdale, Ariz., 1981, Elizabeth Fortner Gallery, Santa Barbara, Calif., 1981, Handweavers of Los Altos, Calif., 1981, 83; represented in permanent collections: Mendocino (Calif.) Art Center, Murray State U., Arrowmont Sch. Crafts, Gatlinburg, Tenn.; organizer lectrs. and workshops in basket weaving. Mem. Am. Crafts Council, Handweavers Guild Am. Author: Plaited Basketry: The Woven Form, 1982; contbr. articles in field to profl. jours. Office: Fiber Studio 899 Bayside Cutoff Bayside CA 95524

LAPOE, WAYNE GILPIN, insurance company executive; b. Waynesburg, Pa., July 13, 1924; s. James Lindsay and Mary (Gilpin) LaP.; B.A., Pa. State U., 1947; m. Margaret Louise Clark, Feb. 21, 1953; children—Deborah Jean, Marqui Lynne. Personnel, sales Armstrong Cork Co., Lancaster, Pa., Chgo., San Francisco, 1947-53; personnel dir. Safeco Ins. Group, 1953-63, v.p., 1963—; v.p. Gen. Ins. Co. of Am., 1963—, Safeco Ins. Co. of Am., 1963—, Safeco Life Ins. Co., 1963—, First Nat. Ins. Co. of Am., Seattle, 1963—, Safeco Nat. Ins. Co., St. Louis, 1972—; v.p. Safeco Corp., 1976-80, sr. v.p., 1980—. Mem. White House Conf. Children and Youth, 1960. Bd. dirs. Ind. Colls. of Wash. Served to capt. USAF, 1943-46, and 1951-52. Decorated D.F.C., Air Medal with three oak leaf clusters. Mem. Steamship Hist. Soc. Am.; Am. Polit. Items Collectors (past pres.), Am. Aviation Hist. Soc., Nat. Trust for Historic Preservation, Phi Kappa Tau. Republican. Home: 11986 Lakeside Pl NE Seattle WA 98125 Office: Safeco Plaza Seattle WA 98185

LA PORTE, WILLIAM BRUCE, educational administrator, consultant; b. Los Angeles, July 13, 1925; s. William Ralph and Lura Estella (Adams) L.; m. Virginia Lee Andrew, June 4, 1949; children—Dean Bruce, Diane Lee, Dan Andrew. Student U. So. Calif., 1943-51; B.A., U. Calif.-Santa Barbara, 1953; M.S., Calif. State U.-Fullerton, 1965. Tchr. auto, machine, metal, welding El Rancho High Sch., 1953-57; coordinator indsl. edn. Whittier Union High Sch. Dist., 1957-59, coordinator adult vocat. edn., 1957-61, coordinator career edn., 1967-74; tchr. auto, drafting Pioneer High Sch., 1959-67, chmn. indsl. arts dept., 1959-61, 63-67, curriculum coordinator, 1960-63; instr. Rio Hondo Coll., 1963-64; prof. Calif. State U.-Los Angeles, 1973, 75-77; dir., sec. to bd. dirs. Tri-Cities Regional Occupational Program Dist., Whittier, Calif., 1974—; mem. Calif. State Vocat. Edn. Sch. Dist. Rev. Team, 1974, chmn., 1975-76; cons. in field. Bd. dirs. East Whittier YMCA, 1978—; pres. North Hills Home Owners Assn., 1979-80, 81-82, v.p., 80-81; bd. dirs. San Gabriel Valley Area Health Edn. Ctr. Served with USAAF, 1944-45. Named Hon. Plymouth Trouble Shooter Chrysler Corp., 1978. Mem. Am. Indsl. Arts Assn., Am. Vocat. Assn. (legis. com. for Calif., 1975-77), Assn. Calif. Sch. Adminstrs., Calif. Assn. Regional Occupational Ctrs. and Programs (v.p. 1976-77, pres. 1978-79, chmn. membership com., bd. dirs., legis. com. 1979—), Calif. Assn. Vocat. Edn., Calif. Assn. Work Experience Educators, Calif. Council Indsl. Arts Suprs. (pres. 1970-71), Calif. Indsl. Edn. Assn. (pres. 73-74, legis. com. 74-77), Cal Adminstr. Vocat. Edn. and Practical Arts (pres. 72-73), Los Angeles County Indsl. Edn. Assn. (pres. 68-69), Pico Rivera C. of C. (legis. com.), Santa Fe Springs C. of C. Indsl. League (v.p. 73-74, bd. dirs. 73-76), Whittier Area C. of C. (edn. com.), Alpha Phi Omega (pres. 1952-53), Epsilon Pi Tau. Methodist. Club: East Whittier Lions. Home: 882 Elkridge St Brea CA 92621 Office: Tri-Cities Regional Occupational Program Dist 9401 S Painter Ave Whittier CA 90605

LARAMEE, ROBERT JOSEPH, educator; b. Attleboro, Mass., Mar. 16, 1939; s. Roland Joseph and Rita Eva (Desautel) L.; B.A., Calif. State Coll., Long Beach, 1966; M.A., Calif. State Coll., Bakersfield, 1979. Tchr. English, Arvin High Sch., Bakersfield, Calif., 1967—, chmn. English dept., 1976—; tchr.-cons. Bay Area Writing Project, 1977—; dir. Visalia Writing Project, 1978, Eastern Sierra Writing Project, 1979, Kern/Eastern Sierra Writing Project, 1980—; cons. in field. NDEA grantee, 1968; summer fellow U. Calif., Berkeley, 1977. Mem. Nat. Council Tchrs. English, Assn. Supervision and Curriculum Devel., NEA, Calif. Assn. Tchrs. English (chmn. Yosemite conf. 1980-81), Calif. Tchrs. Assn. Home: 2821 St Mary's St Bakersfield CA 93305 Office: PO Box 518 Arvin CA 93203

LARAMIE, BERNARD CHARLES, television producer; b. Rochester, N.Y., July 11, 1949; s. Charles Henry and Margaret Ruth (Dragoon) L.; m. Janis Gabbert, June 11, 1978. A.A.S., Rochester Inst. Tech., 1969. Vice-pres. prodn. The Videography Co., Culver City, Calif., 1973-75; v.p. prodn. and post prodn. Sullivan & Assocs., Los Angeles, 1975-81; pres. Amalgamated Tapeworks, North Hollywood, Calif., 1981—; cons./tchr. The Convergence Corp., Irvine, Calif., 1981. Mem. Editors Guild, Soc. Motion Picture and TV Engrs., Acad. TV Arts and Scis., Dirs. Guild Am. Republican. Home: 10847 Otsego St Los Angeles CA 91601

LARK, RAYMOND, artist; b. Phila., June 16, 1939; s. Thomas and Bertha (Lark) Crawford; student Phila. Mus. Sch. Art, 1948-51; B.S., Temple U., 1961; student Los Angeles Trade Tech. Coll., 1961-62. One-man shows at Gov.'s Mansion N.Y. State, 1967, Lyzon Galleries, Nashville, 1967, Emerald Gallery, Hollywood Beach, Fla., 1969, Nader's Art Gallery, Port-au-Prince, Haiti, 1969, Phillip E. Freed Art Gallery, Chgo., 1969, Charles W. Bowers Meml. Mus., Santa Ana, Calif., 1968, Wayup Galleries, Hermosa Beach, Calif., 1967, Dalzell Hatfield Galleries, Los Angeles, 1970-75, Arthur's Gallery of Masterpieces and Jewels, Beverly Hills, Calif., 1971, Dorothy Chandler Pavillion Music Center, Los Angeles, 1974, Honolulu Acad. Arts, 1975, UCLA, 1983, numerous others; exhibited in group shows at Calif. Mus. Sci. and Industry, 1962, Cape Cod Art Assn., Inc., Hyannis, Mass., 1968, San Diego Mus. Art, 1967, Stanford (Calif.) Mus. Art, 1968, Smithsonian Instn., 1971, N.J. State Mus., Trenton, 1972, Guggenheim Mus., 1975, Met. Mus., 1976, La Galerie Mauffe, Paris, 1977, Portsmouth (Va.) Mus., 1979, Ava Dorog Galleries, Munich, W. Ger., 1979, Accademia Italia, Parma, 1980, Ames Art Gallery and Auctioneers, Beverly Hills, Calif., 1980, Galleria d'Arte, Caglairi, Naples, Italy, 1982, Internat. Ctr. Contemporary Art, Paris, 1983, others; represented in permanent collections at Library of Congress, Washington, Ont. Coll. Art, Toronto, Mus. African & African Am. Art. and Antiquities, Buffalo, Carnegie Inst., Pitts., numerous others; ednl. dir. Victor Bus. Schs., Los Angeles, 1969-71; cons. on exec. recruitment Gen. Employment Enterprises, Los Angeles, 1970; pub. relations exec. Western States Service Co., Los Angeles, 1968-70; owner, mgr. Raymond Lark's House of Fine Foods, Los Angeles, 1962-67; exec. sec. to v.p. Physicians' Drug & Supply Co., Phila., 1957-61; lectr. Los Angeles Trade Tech. Coll., 1973, Compton (Calif.) Coll., 1972, numerous others. Recipient proclamations from Pres. Nixon, 72, Pres. Ford, 1975, Pres. Carter, 1977, Gov. Brown, 1979; gold medal Accademia Italia, 1980, numerous other gold medals and best of show awards. Mem. Art West Assn. (pres. 1968-70), Internat. Platform Assn. Address: PO Box 8990 Los Angeles CA 90008

LARKIN, ROBERT LEE, data systems co. exec.; b. Kingsport, Tenn., Jan. 4, 1939; s. Carl Arthur and Pauline Sarah (Reynolds) L.; B.S.M.E., Calif. State U., Long Beach, 1964, B.S. in Indsl. Mgmt., 1967; M.B.A., U. So. Calif., 1969; div.; children—Robert Lee, Sheila Ann. Designer, quality control engr. N.Am. Rockwell, Downey, Calif., 1962-66; quality control engr. Philco-Ford Corp., Newport Beach, Calif., 1966-70, chief insp., 1966-67, sect. supr., 1967-70; mgr. quality control Century Data Systems, Anaheim, Calif., 1970-71, mgr. mfg., 1971-72, mgr. mfg. engring., 1972-75, project mgr. info. systems, 1975-81, materials mgr., 1981—. Pres., Anaheim YMCA GRA-Y Program, 1974-75; chmn. Cypress (Calif.) Spring Festival, 1972-73; bd. dirs. Cypress Little League, 1972-75; pres. Cypress Pony Baseball League, 1977-79. Named Cypress Man of Yr., 1979. Mem. Am. Prodn. and Inventory Control Soc. Republican. Home: 5451 Twin Lakes Dr Cypress CA 90630

LARKS, LEONARD, optical engr.; b. Chgo., Apr. 29, 1937; s. Saul David and Golda (Gezuk) L.; B.A., U. Calif. at Los Angeles, 1957; O.D., Los Angeles Coll. Optometry, 1961; m. Eleanor Judith Glukes, June 14, 1959; children—Caryn, Deena. Practice optometry Glendale, Calif., 1961-64, Los Angeles, 1962-64; bio./med., optical engr./scientist Hycon Mfg. Co. Monrovia, Calif., 1964-69; optical-lens designer engr. design, devel. interplanetary telescopes Jet Propulsion Lab., Calif. Inst. Tech. at Pasadena, 1969-78; cons. in optical design, interplanetary optical design, 1978—; optometrist So. Calif. Permanente Med. Group, West Covina, 1978—. Chief data processing observer Los Angeles County Dem. Party, 1967-75, mem. County Dem. Central Com., 1968-72, committeeman, chmn. 49th assembly dist. Delegation, 1968-70. Recipient Younger Lens award Los Angeles Coll. Optometry, 1961, NASA Group Achievement award for Mariner Venus/Mercury 1973 project TV Subsystem Devel. Team, 1974, for Viking Mars 1976 project Orbiter Design and Devel. Team, 1977, for Voyager Sci. Instrument Devel., Imaging Instrument 1981. Mem. Am. Inst. Physics, Optical Soc. Am., Optical Soc. So. Calif. Contbr. articles profl. jours. Patentee in field. Home: 1028 Blue Dr West Covina CA 91790 Office: So Calif Permanente Med Group 1249 Sunset West Covina CA 91720

LA ROCQUE, MARILYN ROSS ONDERDONK, communications executive; b. Weehawken, N.J., Oct. 14, 1934; d. Chester Douglas and Marion (Ross) Onderdonk; B.A. cum laude, Mt. Holyoke Coll., 1956; postgrad. N.Y. U., 1956-57; M. Journalism, U. Calif. at Berkeley, 1965; m. Bernard Dean Benz, Oct. 5, 1957 (div. Sept. 1971); children—Mark Douglas, Dean Griffith; m. 2d, Rodney C. LaRocque, Feb. 10, 1973. Jr. exec. Bonwit Teller, N.Y.C., 1956; personnel asst. Warner-Lambert Pharm. Co., Morris Plains, N.J., 1957; editorial asst. Silver Burdett Co., Morristown, 1958; self-employed as pub. relations cons., Moraga, Calif., 1963-71, 73-77; pub. relations mgr. Shaklee Corp., Hayward, 1971-73; pub. relations dir. Fidelity Savs., 1977-78; exec. dir. No. Calif. chpt. Nat. Multiple Sclerosis Soc., 1978-80; v.p. public relations Cambridge Plan Internat., Monterey, Calif., 1980-81; sr. account exec. Hoefer-Amidei Assocs., San Francisco, 1981-82; dir. corp. communications, dir. spl. projects, asst. to chmn. Cambridge Plan Internat., Monterey, Calif., 1982—; instr. pub. relations U. Calif. Extension, San Francisco, 1977-79. Mem. exec. bd., rep-at-large Oakland (Calif.) Symphony Guild, 1968-69; co-chmn. pub. relations com. Oakland Museum Assn., 1974-75; cabinet mem. Lincoln Child Center, Oakland, 1967-71, pres. membership cabinet, 1970-71, 2d v.p. bd. dirs., 1970-71. Bd. dirs. Calif. Spring Garden and Home Show, 1971-77, Dunsmuir House and Gardens, 1976-77; mem. Calif. State Republican Central Com., 1964-66; v.p. Piedmont council Boy Scouts Am., 1977. Mem. D.A.R. (chpt. regent 1960-61, 66-68), U. Calif. Alumni Assn., Women in Communications, Public Relations Soc. Am. (chpt. dir. 1980-82; accredited), Calif. Hist. Soc., San Francisco Mus. Soc., Nat. Trust for Historic Preservation, Smithsonian Assocs., Monterey Peninsula Symphony Assn., Monterey

Peninsula Mus. of Art Assn. Clubs: Commonwealth of Calif.; Contra Costa Press; Mount Holyoke Coll. Alumnae; East Bay Press; East Bay Women's Press, Women in Communication, AAUW. Author: Maestro Baton and His Musical Friends, 1968; Happiness is Breathing Better, 1976. Address: 121 Alta Mesa Ct Moraga CA 94556

LA ROWE, MILES HART, counselor, educator; b. Glendive, Mont., Mar. 2, 1948; s. Mark Lee and Mary Elizabeth (Fountain) La R.; m. Elizabeth Nickerson, June 7, 1970; children—Meighan, Margaux. B.S., Denver U., 1970; M.A., U. Who., 1973; postgrad. U. No. Colo., 1980-83. Instr. No. Catskill Occupational Ctr., Grand Gorge, N.Y., 1970-72; counselor, instr. Laramie County Community Coll., Cheyenne, Who., 1973—. Moderator, deacon First Congregational Ch. Mem. Am. Coll. Personnel Assn., Am. Personnel and Guidance Assn., Wyo. Personnel and Guidance Assn. Home: 1816 E 19th Cheyenne WY 82001 Office: 1400 E College A 137 Cheyenne WY 82007

LARSEN, CHONITA GIBBS, psychologist; b. Salt Lake City, July 5, 1923; d. Leo Vernon and Eugenia (Malloy) G.; m. Nason Ernest Newport, May 1, 1948; children—Nason Dana, Tiare Newport Brown, Rebecca; m. 2d, Jack Lucas Larsen, Aug. 17, 1971. B.A., Occidental Coll., 1947; M.A., Antioch U., 1980; Ph.D., Columbia Pacific U., 1981. Cert. marriage and family counselor, Hawaii. Pvt. practice counseling Kalffian Sandplay Therapist, Honolulu, 1977—; staff psycho therapist Kula Kokua Treatment Ctr. for Psychotic and Emotionally Disturbed Children. Mem. adv. bd. Acad. of Pacific, Honolulu; mem. children's team State of Hawaii Mental Health Clinic. Mem. Internat. Congress Sandplay Therapists of Zurich, Switzerland, Internat. Transpersonal Psychol. Assn., Humanistic Psychol. Assn., Hawaii Psychol. Assn., Am. Psychol. Assn. Home: 3707 Diamond Head Rd Honolulu HI 96816

LARSEN, JANICE MAUREEN, hosp. ofcl.; b. Cambridge, Eng., Sept. 27, 1934; d. Fred James Harvey and Olive Edna May (Bates) Boreham; ed. public schs.; children—Wanda Jenny, Wayne Blyth, David Lee, Sharon Gay. Came to U.S., 1956. Tissue culturist cancer research, radiotherapeutic dept. Cambridge U., 1949-55; lab. asst. Intercommunity Hosp., Fairfield, Calif., 1966-74; clk. personnel dept. Intercommunity Hosp., Fairfield, 1975-76, personnel asst., 1976-78, personnel services coordinator, 1978—. Mem. allocations com. United Way, 1977-79, vice chmn., 1979-80, chmn., 1980-83. Mem. Calif. Hosp. Assn., Am. Soc. Hosp. Personnel Adminstrn. Lutheran. Home: 167 El Cerrito Way Vacaville CA 95688 Office: 1800 Pennsylvania Ave Fairfield CA 94533

LARSEN, JEAN MAYCOCK, educator; b. Provo, Utah, Feb. 23, 1931; d. Lawrence S. and Lorna (Booth) Maycock; B.S., Brigham Young U., Provo, 1953, M.S., 1960; Ph.D., U. Utah, 1972; m. A. Dean Larsen, Feb. 14, 1958; children—David Lawrence, Paul Joseph, Ann, Charlotte. Tchr. schs. in Oreg. and Utah, 1953-55, 57-58; mem. faculty Brigham Young U., 1960—, assoc. prof. family scis., 1976—, coordinator early childhood edn. program, 1980—. Mem. Nat. Assn. Edn. Young Children, Assn. Childhood Edn. Internat., Utah Assn. Edn. Young Children (past pres., chmn. adv. bd.), Am. Ednl. Research Assn., Soc. Research Child Devel., Phi Kappa Phi. Republican. Mormon. Author curriculum materials in field; also research. Home: 2678 North 880 East Provo UT 84604 Office: 1319-A SFLC Brigham Young U Provo UT 84602

LARSEN, KIM ANN, marketing executive; b. N.J., May 17, 1956; d. Joseph Richard and Letitia (Merola) L. B.A. in Econs., Northwestern U., 1977, M. Mgmt., 1979. Assoc. product mgr. juices, drinks, tomato products Libby, McNeill & Libby, Inc., Chgo., 1979-80, product mgr. fruits, nectars, tomato products, 1980-81; mktg. mgr. Capri Sun, Shasta Beverages Inc., Hayward, Calif., 1982—; lectr., guest speaker. Northwestern U. scholar, 1974-75. Mem. Internat. Fund Animal Welfare, Union Concerned Scientists. Mem. Assn. M.B.A. Execs., Alpha Lambda Delta.

LARSEN, MARJORIE SUSAN, business executive; b. Reedley, Calif., July 12, 1916; d. William and Elizabeth Susan (Ario) L.; A.B., U. Calif., Berkeley, 1938; M.A., Coll. Pacific, 1947. Tchr., Orestimba High Sch., Newman, Calif., 1940-46; tchr., adminstr. Stockton (Calif.) Unified Sch. Dist., 1946-72; owner Bee Beauty Salon and Gift Shop, Stockton, 1967—; self-employed real estate asso., Stockton, 1971—. Recipient Others award Salvation Army, 1971, Disting. Service award Calif. Assn. Health, Phys. Edn. and Recreation, 1973, Susan B. Anthony award Women's Community Council, 1978; also various certs. of appreciation; named to Sports Hall of Fame, Tracy, Calif., 1983; life mem. PTA. Mem. Nat. Ret. Tchrs. Assn., Calif. Tchr. Assn. (life), Stockton Ret. Tchrs. Assn., Stockton Bd. Realtors, Delta Kappa Gamma. Republican. Club: Pacific Women's (pres. 1978-80). Author: Speed-a-way, A New Game for Boys and Girls, 3 edit., 1970 (also teaching film). Home: 1754 Middlefield St Stockton CA 95204 Office: 1904 Country Club Blvd Stockton CA 95204

LARSEN, ROBERT PAUL, extension service adminstr.; b. Provo, Utah, Dec. 1, 1926; s. Ariel E. and Vera A. (Austin) L.; m. Lorna Anderson, Sept. 10, 1948; children—Nanette K., Peggy Ann Rinehart, Mark B., Cynthia Bennett. B.S., Utah State U., 1950; M.S., Kans. State U., 1951; Ph.D., Mich. State U., 1955. Asst. prof. to prof. hort. Mich. State U., 1955-68; supt., horticulturist Tree Fruit Research Ctr., Wash. State U., Wenatchee, 1968-82; v.p. univ. extension Utah State U., Logan, 1982—. Vice pres. North Central Washington council Boy Scouts Am., 1978-82. Served with U.S. Mcht. Marine, 1945-46; Q.M.C., U.S. Army, 1951-53. Recipient Outstanding Extension Specialist award Mich. State U., 1967; Profl. Spokesman award Farm Chems. Mag., 1975; Outstanding Horticulturist award Mich. Cherry Growers Council, 1982. Fellow Am. Soc. Hort. Sci. (pres. 1975-76); mem. Internat. Soc. Hort. Sci., AAAS, Am. Inst. Biol. Sci. Mormon. Club: Rotary. Contbr. articles to profl. jours.; columnist Am. Fruit Grower Mag., 1967—. Office: Extension Service UMC 49 Utah State Univ Logan UT 84322

LARSEN, ROGER DOUGLAS, safety engineer; b. Redfield, S.D., May 7, 1935; s. George Albert and Jean Evelyn (Utne) L.; m. Elizabeth Jane Miller, July 7, 1957; 1 son, Steven Douglas. Student in bus. U. Oreg., 1955, in engring. U. Wash., 1955-57. Structural design draftsman/flight test analyst Boeing Co., Seattle, 1957-61, system safety supr., Seattle, Minet, N.D., Huntsville, Ala. and New Orleans, 1961-64, chief profl. personnel, Seattle, 1965-70; dir. health and safety Crown Zellerbach Corp., San Francisco, 1970—; cons. health and safety. Chmn. safety and health com. Am. Paper Inst.; mem. health and safety com. Calif. Mfrs. Assn. Served With U.S. Army, 1958-59. Mem. Nat. Safety Mgmt. Soc., Am. Soc. Safety Engrs., Am. Indsl. Hygiene Soc. Republican. Office: One Bush St San Francisco CA 94119

LARSEN, TIMOTHY GORDON, health facility administrator; b. Susquehanna, Pa., Aug. 20, 1944; s. Norman James and Margarete Anne (Wunsch) L.; children—Erik Cristopher, Heather Luise. B.A. summa cum laude, Fla. Atlantic U., 1965; M.A. (NDEA fellow), Vanderbilt U., 1968; M.B.A., Pepperdine U., 1978; Doctor honoris causa, 1981; cert. hosp. adminstrn. U. So. Calif., 1980; Ph.D., Bedford U., 1981. Commd. 2d lt. USAF, 1968, advanced through grades to capt., 1971; aircraft comdr. March AFB, Calif., 1972-75; assoc. prof. aerospace studies Loyola Marymount U., Los Angeles, 1975-76, U. So. Calif., Los Angeles, 1976-78; admissions counselor Air Force Acad., USAF Res., 1978—; asst. mgr. Lincoln Pacific Mktg. Corp., Long Beach, Calif., 1978-79; dep. dir. Social Rehab. Agy., Los Angeles, 1979-81; adminstr. Colima Internal Medicine, Whittier, Calif., 1981-82, Diamond Bar (Calif.) Med. Center, 1982—; asst. clin. prof. health service adminstrn. U. So. Calif., 1981—. Bd. dirs. YMCA, Diamond Bar, 1982—. Maj. USAF Res. Decorated D.F.C., Air medal (3); Commendation medal (2), Republic Vietnam Campaign medal, Republic Vietnam Cross of Gallantry with palm. Mem. Am. Acad. Polit. and Social Sci., Med. Group Mgmt. Assn., Hosp. Fin. Mgmt. Assn., Assn. Western Hosps., Internat. Police Assn., Assn. Mental Health Adminstrs., Am. Mgmt. Assn., Air Force Assn., Soaring Soc. Am., Calif. Wildlife Fedn. Home: 21155 Running Branch Rd Diamond Bar CA 91765

LARSON, BRENT THEODORE, broadcasting exec.; b. Ogden, Utah, Sept. 23, 1942; s. George Theodore and Doris (Peterson) L.; m. Tracy Ann Taylor; children—Michelle, Brent Todd. Account exec. Sta. KINS, Eureka, Calif., 1967-69; owner, mgr. Sta. KAIN, Boise, Idaho, 1969-77; owner, operator radio Stas. KXA, Seattle, 1975-83, KYYX, Seattle, 1980-83, KCKO, Spokane, Wash., 1978—, KUUZ, Boise, 1976—, KOOS, North Bend, Oreg., 1980-82, KODL, The Dalles, Oreg., 1974—, KKWZ, Richfield, Utah, 1980—, KSVC, Richfield, 1980—; v.p. Casey Larson Fast Food Co., Oreg. and Idaho, 1976—; pres. Brentwood Properties, Ogden, 1977—, First Nat. Broadcasting Corp., Idaho, 1970—, Gt. Am. Radio Corp., Wash., 1977—, Gold Coast Communications Corp., Oreg., 1980—, Sevier Valley Broadcasting Co., Inc., Utah, 1980—, Brent Larson Group Stas., Western U.S., 1969—; partner Larson Tours and Travel, Burley, Idaho, 1977—. Bd. dirs. Met. Sch., 1981—. Served with U.S. Army, 1962-63. Mem. Am. Advt. Fedn., Nat. Assn. Broadcasters, Nat. Radio Broadcasters Assn., Wash. Broadcasters Assn., Oreg. Broadcasters Assn., Idaho Broadcasters Assn., Utah Broadcasters Assn., Citizens for Responsible Broadcasting (dir.). Republican. Mormon. Home: 4014 Beus Dr Ogden UT 84403 Office: KXA-KYYX 1305 3d Ave Seattle WA 98101

LARSON, CHARLES LESTER, television writer-producer, author; b. Portland, Oreg., Oct. 23, 1922; s. Charles Oscar and Ina May (Couture) L.; student U. Oreg., 1940; m. Alice Mae Dovey, Aug. 25, 1966; 1 stepson, Wyn Donovan Malotte. Contract writer MGM Studios, Culver City, Calif., 1943-46; freelance mag. writer, 1941-51; asso. producer TV program Twelve O'Clock High, 1964; producer TV programs The FBI, 1965-68, The Interns, 1970-71, Cade's County, 1971-72; exec. producer TV program Nakia, 1974; producer CBS Tuesday Night Movie, Crime Club, 1973; co-creator TV series Hagen, 1979-80. Recipient Spl. award Mystery Writers Am., 1974. Mem. Writers Guild of Am. West, Producers Guild, Mystery Writers Am., Authors League Am. Democrat. Author: The Chinese Game, 1969; Someone's Death, 1973; Matthew's Hand, 1974; Muir's Blood, 1976; The Portland Murders, 1983. Home: 2422 SW Broadway Dr Portland OR 97201

LARSON, DEBRA J. MICKEY, market research consultant; b. Rochester, Pa., Nov. 15, 1951; d. Delbert Leorn and Frances (White) Mickey; B.S. in Public Mgmt., U. Ariz., 1975, postgrad. in mktg., 1981—; m. James Lawrence Larson, June 21, 1975. Adminstrv. asst. dept. of transp. Public Transp. div. City of Tucson, 1975-78; mgr. services Ariz. Drug Control Dist., Tucson, 1978-79, dir. adminstrv. services, 1979-81; market research cons. Fontana Group, 1982—. Mem. transp. adv. com. City of Tucson. Mem. Am. Soc. for Public Adminstrn. (exec. com. So. Ariz. chpt.), Am. Mgmt. Assn., Ariz. Polit. Women's Caucus, Chi Omega. Democrat. Presbyterian. Clubs: Woman's Programming Round Table, So. Ariz. Exec. Women's Council (2d v.p.). Home: 1507 E Lind Rd Tucson AZ 85719 Office: 2200 E River Rd Tucson AZ 85718

LARSON, IRVING, real estate appraiser, consultant; b. Bell Station, Oreg., Sept. 8, 1913; s. Walter I. and Lulu C. L.; B.B.A., U. Oreg., 1939; postgrad. Portland State U., Lewis and Clark Coll.; m. Jennie E. Jackson, Feb. 3, 1939; children—Judy, Diane. Asst. fin. officer VA Hosp., Portland, Oreg., 1947-52; auditor U.S. Fish and Wildlife Service, 1952-56; auditor Fed. Hwy. Trust Fund, 1957-75; real estate broker, Tigard, Oreg., 1975—; real estate appraiser Oreg. Dept. Vets. Affairs, 1977-81. Served with AUS, 1944-46. Mem. Assn. Govt. Accts., Am. Soc. Profl. Cons., Tigard C. of C. Address: 11720 SW 68th Ave Tigard OR 97223

LARSON, JAMES RICHARD, hosp. adminstr.; b. Sheridan, Wyo., Apr. 24, 1945; s. Theodore Jennings and Frances Marian (Dorr) L.; B.S., U. Wyo., 1968; M.P.H., UCLA, 1970; m. Cathy June Sieweke, Aug. 26, 1965; childreRichard Arnold, Tanya Lynn, Grant Theodore. Adminstrv. resident Valley Presbyn. Hosp., Van Nuys, Calif., 1969-70; asst. adminstr. Daniel Freeman Hosp., Inglewood, Calif., 1970-74; asso. adminstr. Little Co. of Mary Hosp., Torrance, Calif., 1974—; Mem. Am. Coll. Hosp. Adminstrs., Health Care Execs. So. Calif. (pres. 1979-80). Democrat. Roman Catholic. Clubs: Lions (club pres. 1978-79, zone chmn. 1980-81) (Torrance); Elks (Sheridan, Wyo.). Home: 11652 Paseo Bonita Los Alamitos CA 90720 Office: 4101 Torrance Blvd Torrance CA 90503

LARSON, JEFFRY HALE, family relations educator, therapist; b. Salt Lake City, Feb. 26, 1949; s. Hale J. and Donna A. L.; m. Diana Jean Spear, Aug. 11, 1972; children—Geoffrey Hale, Dillon Jay. B.S., Brigham Young U., 1971, M.S., 1974; Ph.D., Tex. Tech. U., 1980. Grad. teaching asst. dept. sociology Fla. State U., Tallahassee, 1977-78, research asst., 1977-78; part-time instr. dept. home and family life Tex. Tech. U., Lubbock, 1978-80; human devel. extension specialist Iowa State U., Dubuque, 1980-81; asst. prof. family relations, dir. marriage and family therapy program Mont. State U., Bozeman, 1981—; pvt. practice marriage and family therapy, Bozeman, 1981—. Bd. dirs. Dubuque Families in Action, Parents Without Ptnrs., Dubuque. Served to lt. USCG, 1974-77. Grantee Iowa State U., 1980, Mont. State U., 1983, Tex. Tech. U. Mem. Nat. Council on Family Relations, Am. Assn. for Marriage and Family Therapy (clin. mem.), Am. Personnel and Guidance Assn., Am. Home Econs. Assn. Mormon. Author: Personal Development Program Series for 4-H Leaders (10 parts), 1981; Teaching Values to Children and Teenagers, 1980; (with J.O. Anderson and A. Morgan) The Effective Stepparenting Program: Group Leader's Manual, 1981; (with J.O. Anderson and A. Morgan) Building Family Strengths, 1981; (with R. W. Alvord) Preliminary Survey of Problems Related to Low Academic Performance, 1974; contbr. articles to profl. jours.

LARSON, MARVIN ARTHUR, structural engr.; b. Chico, Calif., May 15, 1917; s. Charles Coyle and Lula Edna (Dysert) L.; A.B., Stanford U., 1938, M.S., 1947, Engr., 1948; m. Edna Mae Cassell, Apr. 27, 1946; 1 son, Charles Richard. Mining engr., Mont., Colo., N.Mex. and Alaska, 1935-41; Constrn. supt. U.S. Engr. Dept., Alaska, 1941-43, Morrison Knudsen Co., 1948-51; structural engr. cons., San Francisco, 1951-70; supervising structural engr. Kaiser Engrs. Co., Oakland, Calif., 1970-82; instr. Engr. Sch., Ft. Belvoir, Va., 1944-46. Pres., Young Republicans San Mateo County (Calif.), 1957; mem. Rep. Central Com., San Mateo County, 1957-58. Served with C.E., AUS, 1943-46. Named Civil Engr. of Year, Bay Area Engring. Council, 1957. Mem. ASCE, Am. Concrete Inst., Structural Engrs. Assn., Calif., Earthquake Engring. Research Inst., Mensa, Sigma Xi, Tau Beta Pi. Contbr. articles to profl. publs. Home: 345 Birchwood Dr Moraga CA 94556 Office: PO Box 23210 Oakland CA 94623

LARUE, ROLAND (RON) DE ARV, hotel advertising and public relations executive, consultant, artist; b. Tacoma, Wash., Sept. 8, 1932; s. DeArv F. and Goldie M. (Elliott) LaR.; m. Dava Lee Adam, Dec. 30, 1931; children—Linda, Scott, David. Student N.D. State Sch. Sci., 1951, U. Wash., 1955, Burnley Sch. Art, 1958. Audio visual supr. Boeing Aerospace, 1955-60; merchandising mgr. wood products group Weyerhaeuser Co., 1960-72; with Westin Hotels, Seattle, 1972—, dir. advt. and pub. relations, 1983—. Served with USAF, 1951-55. Recipient various advt. and pub. relations awards. Mem. Mktg. Communications Execs. Internat. (pres. 1981-82, chmn. exec. com. 1983—), Am. Hotel and Motel Assn. (past chmn. pub. relations adv. bd.), Soc. Am. Travel Writers, Internat. Advt. Assn., Seattle Advt. Fedn., Pub. Relations Soc. Am. (past assoc. rep.), Nat. Yellow Pages Service Assn. (adv. bd.). Office: Westin Hotels Westin Bldg Seattle WA 98121

LARZELERE, ROBERT EARL, psychologist, educator, editor; b. Greensburg, Pa., Apr. 3, 1945; s. John Harrold and Mary Alice (Mark) L.; m. Rosalie Busey Ash, Dec. 16, 1972; children—Lisa, William. B.A., Wabash Coll., Crawsfordville, Ind., 1967; student Columbia Bible Coll., Columbia, S.C., 1967-68; M.S., Ga. Tech. Inst., 1975; Ph.D., Pa. State U., 1979. Asst. prof., head psychology dept. Bryan Coll., Dayton, Tenn., 1977-79; asst. prof. psychology dept. counseling, clin. psychology, Western Conservative Bapt. Sem., Portland, Oreg., 1980-82; assoc. prof. psychology Rosemead Sch. Psychology, Biola U., La Mirada, Calif., 1982—; assoc. editor, Jour. Family Issues, 1980-83, Jour. Psychology and Theology, 1980—. Served with U.S. Army, 1968-71. NIMH fellow, 1976-77, 1979-80. Mem. Am. Psychol. Assn., Nat. Council Family Relations, Am. Sociol. Assn., Soc. Research Child Devel., Christian Assn. Psychol. Studies. Republican. Baptist. Contbr. articles to profl. jours. Home: 15051 Cullen St Whittier CA 90603 Office: Rosemead Sch Psychology 3800 Biola Ave La Mirada CA 90639

LA SALLE, RODNEY LEWIS, architect; b. Merced, Calif., May 21, 1950; s. Lewis Noah and Eleanor Theresa (Baldasare) La S.; B.Arch., Calif. Polytech. State U., 1973; children—Amy Louise, Jeanne Louise. Draftsman, carpenter Lewis N. La Salle, gen. contractor, Merced, Calif., summers 1964, 66-68, part time 1970-73; draftsman Larsen Ohlinger and Jones, Merced, summers 1969-71, 1969-70; draftsman Bunnell Constrn. Co., San Luis Obispo, Calif., 1971-73 part time; draftsman, later architect Larsen Ohlinger and Jones, Merced, 1973-76; partner, architect La Salle and Morgan, Merced, 1977-81; owner LaSalle & Assos., Merced, 1981—. Adviser, Merced County Regional Occupational Program, 1977—; chmn. design rev. bd. Redevel. Agy. City of Merced, 1978-81; pres. Merced Vocat. Indsl. Clubs Found. Recipient Hon. Mention award No. Calif. Home Show, 1968, Outstanding Personal Service award Stadium, 76, 1976, Appreciation award Merced County Regional Occupational Program, 1976, Outstanding Service award Vocat. Indsl. Clubs Am., 1978; registered profl. architect, Calif. Past mem. AIA (past dir. Sierra Valley chpt.). Democrat. Presbyterian. Clubs: Elks; Sunrise Toastmasters (charter, ednl. v.p. 1980) (Merced). Mentioned in New Glass, 1976. Home: 3318 M St Apt 6 Merced CA 95340 Office: La Salle & Assos PO Box 1085 Merced CA 95341

LASATER, LANE, psychologist; b. Falfurrias, Tex., Nov. 3, 1946; s. Tom Miller and Mary Caroline (Casey) L.; m. Nancy Larson, Dec. 30, 1978. B.A., Princeton U., 1968; M.A., Ohio State U., 1973; Ph.D., U. Colo., 1979. Clin. psychologist Community-Univ. Health Care Ctr., Mpls., 1979-80; clin. psychologist Pastoral Care Ctr., Boerne, Tex., 1980-81; clin. psychologist Comprehensive Psychol. Services, Boulder, Colo., 1982—. Mem. Am. Psychol. Assn. Home: 1340 Norwood Boulder CO 80302 Office: 2709 Pine Boulder CO 80302

LASITER, JACK BRINKLEY, utility holding co. exec.; b. Ft. Smith, Ark., July 20, 1930; s. Brinkley Cyrus and Ruth Leona (Wear) L.; B.S., Pepperdine U., Los Angeles, 1954, M.B.A., 1975; m. Julia Clara Simmons, June 16, 1957; 1 son, Paul Brinkley. With Aerophysics Devel. Corp., Santa Barbara, Calif., 1956-57, Kibbee, Peterson & Co., C.P.A.'s, Hollywood, Calif., 1957-58; with So. Calif. Gas Co., Los Angeles, 1958—, audit coordinator, 1978—; audit support supr. Pacific Lighting Corp., Los Angeles, 1980—. Served with U.S. Army, 1954-56. Cert. internal auditor. Mem. Inst. Internal Auditor (chmn. scholarship com. Los Angeles chpt. 1980-81), Town Hall Calif. Republican. Mem. Ch. of Christ. Home: 1330 N Valley Home Ave La Habra CA 90631 Office: 810 S Flower St Los Angeles CA 90017

LASKA, MARK SROL, dentist; b. Pitts., Apr. 26, 1945; s. Sol and Lena Irene (Berman) L.; m. Joan Margaret Dunlap, Dec. 16, 1973; chlildren—Shawn Renee, Shelia Marie, Shaye Michael. Student UCLA, 1966; D.D.S., U. So. Calif., 1970. Cert. dentist, Calif. Dentist, Group Dental Service, Los Angeles, 1970-81, head dentist, 1973-81, dental dir., 1980-81; dental assoc. S. Jay Welborn, D.D.S., Pasadena, Calif., 1981-82; pvt. practice dentistry, Los Angeles, 1981—. Bd. dirs. Laughlin Park Homeowners Assn., 1980—, pres., 1981; bd. dirs. Hollywood Los Feliz Jewish Community Ctr., 1979—; mem. citizens adv. com. Los Angeles 1984 Olympic Games, Dental Commn. Mem. ADA (com. on dental care), Los Angeles Dental Soc., Calif. Dental Assn., Acad. Gen. Dentistry, Alpha Omega, Zeta Beta Tau. Office: 3460 Wilshire Blvd Suite 104 Los Angeles CA 90010

LASKER, JOHN NICHOLAS, systems analyst; b. Kansas City, Mo., June 26, 1938; s. John and Mary Helen (Miller) L.; B.S. in Distbn. Logistics, Weber State Coll., 1975; M.S. in Human Resource Mgmt., U. Utah, 1977; m. Delores Fern Ashton Melton, Dec. 21, 1961; children—Patricia Gale, Kathleen Dawn, Deanna Marie. Spray painter Chevorolet div. Gen. Motors Corp., Leeds, Mo., 1959-61; mail carrier U.S. Post Office, Kansas City, Mo., 1957-59, 60-61; quality control technician Hercules Powder, Inc., Bacchus, Utah, 1961-66; indsl. engr. technician, systems analyst Supply Directorate, Air Force Logistics Command, Hill AFB, Utah, 1966-76; systems analyst, br. chief Data Systems Automation Center, Def. Logistics Agy., Ogden, Utah, 1976—; chairperson Mission IS Distbn. Identification Com., 1973-75. Mem. Davis County Master Plan Devel. Com., 1977-78. Recipient 3 outstanding performance awards Air Force Logistics Command Supply Directorate, 1973-76, Sustained Superior award, 1982. Mem. Soc. Logistics Engrs. (chair Ogden chpt. 1975-76). Democrat. Roman Catholic. Clubs: Second St. Snappy Shutters, Good Sam. Office: DSAC DF DDOU Ogden UT 88407

LASKER, MARTIN, ednl. services co. exec.; b. Winnipeg, Man., Can., June 17, 1946; came to U.S., 1951, naturalized, 1959; s. Saul and Tillie (Shenkarow) L.; B.S., UCLA, 1968; M.P.A., U. So. Calif., 1973; m. Jill Ellyn Abelson, Jan. 25, 1970; children—Jodi Claire, Zachary Adam. Asst. adminstr. Cedars-Sinai Med. Center, Los Angeles, 1973-77; hosp. adminstr. Hyatt Med. Enterprises, Encino, Calif., 1977-78; exec. v.p., sec.-treas. Hosp. Learning Centers, Inc., North Hollywood, Calif., 1978—; nat. cons. on mgmt. by objectives and employee appraisal systems. Mem. Am. Coll. Hosp. Adminstrs., Am. Soc. Health Manpower Edn. and Tng., Am. Hosp. Assn. Democrat Jewish. Home: 5155 Teesdale Ave North Hollywood CA 91607 Office: 6240 Laurel Canyon Blvd Suite 100 North Hollywood CA 91606

LASKO, ALLEN HOWARD, pharmacist; b. Chgo., Oct. 27, 1941; s. Sidney P. and Sara (Hoffman) L.; B.S. (James scholar), U. Ill., 1964; m. Janice Marilynn Chess, Dec. 24, 1968; children—Stephanie Paige, Michael Benjamin. Staff pharmacist Michael Reese Hosp. and Med. Center, Chgo., 1964-68; clin. pharmacist City of Hope Med. Center, Duarte, Calif., 1968-73; chief pharmacist Monrovia (Calif.) Community Hosp., 1973-74, Santa Fe Meml. Hosp., Los Angeles, 1974-77; pvt. investor, 1977—. Recipient Roche Hosp. Pharmacy Research award, 1972-73. Mem. Magic Castle, Flying Samaritans, Mensa, Rho Pi Phi. Jewish. Author books: Diabetes Study Guide, 1972; A Clinical Approach to Lipid Abnormalities Study Guide, 1973; Jet Injection Tested

As An Aid in Physiologic Delivery of Insulin, 1973. Home: 376 N Hill St Monrovia CA 91016

LASKOW, GREGORY BLAISE, army officer, psychologist; b. Phila., Sept. 7, 1947; s. John Joseph and Catherine Marie (Robison) L.; m. Barbara Anne Otherski, June 14, 1969; 1 son, Jason Gregory. B.S., U. Scranton, 1969, M.S., 1971; Ph.D., Tex. Tech U., 1974. Commd. 2d lt. U.S. Army, 1971, advanced through grades to maj., 1980; intern in psychology William Beaumont Army Med. Ctr., El Paso, 1973-74, dir. intern tng. for pre-doctoral clin. psychologists, 1975-77; psychologist 82d Airbourne div. Fort Bragg, N.C., 1978-80; chief psychology service Letterman Army Med. Ctr., San Francisco, 1980—. Decorated Army Commendation medal, Meritorious Service medal. Fellow Inter-Univ. Seminar on Armed Forces and Soc.; mem. Am. Psychol. Assn., Assn. for Advancement Psychology, Assn. U.S. Army, Nat. Register of Health Service Providers in Psychology. Home: 328-B Infantry Terr Presidio of San Francisco CA 94129 Office: PO Box 95 Letterman Army Med Ctr Presidio of San Francisco CA 94129

LASORDA, TOM CHARLES, profl. baseball team mgr.; b. Norristown, Pa., Sept. 22, 1927; s. Sam and Carmella (Covatto) L.; student pub. schs., Norristown; m. Joan Miller, Apr. 14, 1950; children—Laura, Tom Charles. Profl. player with Bklyn. Dodgers, 1954-55, Kansas City A's, 1956; with Los Angeles Dodgers, 1956—, mgr., 1977—. Served with U.S. Army, 1945-47. Los Angeles Dodgers winner Nat. League pennant, 1977, 78; 2d Nat. League mgr. to win pennant first two yrs. as mgr. Mem. Profl. Baseball Players Am. Roman Catholic. Club: Variety of Calif. (v.p.). Office: Los Angeles Dodgers 1000 Elysian Park Ave Los Angeles CA 90012*

LASSMAN, JOSEPH, radiologist; b. Chgo., Mar. 5, 1930; s. Albert I. and Anna P. (Draznin) L.; B.S., U. Ill., 1951, 52, M.D., 1955; m. Adrienne Ruth Berman, Aug. 29, 1954; children—Mark Bennett, Mindy Joy. Intern and resident in radiology and nuclear medicine, Cook County Hosp., Chgo., 1955-56, 58-62; attending physician Olive View Med. Center, Los Angeles County Med. Center, 1962-67; chief dept. radiology and nuclear medicine, N. Hollywood (Calif.) Hosp., 1963-73; Riverside Hosp., N. Hollywood, 1973—, pres. med. staff Riverside Hosp., 1977-78. Served to capt. USAF, 1956-58. Mem. Am. Coll. Radiology, Am. Bd. Radiology, Am. Coll. Nuclear Medicine (charter), Am. Coll. Nuclear Physicians (charter), Radiologic Soc. N.Am., Am. Soc. Ultrasound in Medicine, Soc. Nuclear Medicine, Calif. Med. Assn., Los Angeles County Med. Assn., Am. Fellowship of Physicians in Israel, Phi Delta Epsilon. Clubs: Am. Jewish Com., Am. Red Magen David Adom for Israel, U. Ill. Med. Alumni Assn. Office: 12629 Riverside Dr North Hollywood CA 91607

LASTER, LEONARD, physician, educator, university president; b. N.Y.C., Aug. 24, 1928; s. Isaac and Mary (Ehrenreich) L.; m. Ruth Ann Leventhal, Dec. 16, 1956; children—Judith Eve, Susan Beth, Stephen Jay. A.B., Harvard U., 1949, M.D., 1950. Diplomate Am. Bd. Internal Medicine, also Sub-Bd. Gastroenterology, Nat. Bd. Med. Examiners. Intern, resident in medicine Mass. Gen. Hosp., Boston, 1950-53; fellow in gastroenterology Mass. Meml. Hosp., 1953-59; vis. investigator Pub. Health Research Inst., N.Y.C., 1953-54; commd. lt. USPHS, 1954, advanced through grades to asst. surgeon gen. (rear adm.), 1971; mem. staff Nat. Inst. Arthritis, Metabolic and Digestive Diseases, NIH, Bethesda, Md., 1954-73, chief digestive and hereditary diseases br., 1969-73; spl. asst., then asst. dir. human resources President's Office for Sci. and Tech., 1969-73; exec. dir. assembly life scis., also div. med. scis. Nat. Acad. Scis.-NRC, 1973-74; resigned, 1973; v.p. acad. affairs and clin. affairs Med. Ctr., also dean Coll. Medicine, prof. medicine Downstate Med. Ctr., SUNY, Bklyn., 1974-78; pres. Oreg. Health Scis. U., Portland, 1978—, prof. medicine Sch. Medicine, 1978—; dir. Tektronix Inc., Standard Ins. Co. Bd. dirs. Found. Advanced Edn. Scis., Bethesda, 1965-69, Bedford Stuyvesant Family Health Ctr., Bklyn., 1976-78, Med. Research Found. Oreg., 1978—, Oreg. Symphony, 1979—, Oreg. Contemporary Theatre, 1981—, United Way, Portland, 1980—; pres. Burning Tree Elem. Sch. PTA, Bethesda, 1972-73; mem. adv. bd. Columbia Pacific council Boy Scouts Am., 1980—. Fellow ACP; mem. Am. Assn. for Study Liver Diseases, Am. Fedn. Clin. Research, Am. Gastroent. Assn., Am. Soc. Biol. Chemists, Am. Soc. Clin. Investigation, Assn. Am. Med. Colls. (council deans 1974-78), Multnomah County Med. Soc. (trustee), Portland Acad. Medicine, Marine Biol. Lab. Corp., Portland C. of C. (dir.), Phi Beta Kappa, Sigma Xi, Alpha Omega Alpha. Clubs: Cosmos (Washington); Harvard (N.Y.C.); University, City, Arlington, Downtown Rotary (Portland). Mem. editorial bd. various med. jours.; contbr. articles on gastrointestinal disease, inborn errors metabolism, devel. biology to med. jours. Home: 1863 SW Montgomery Dr Portland OR 97201 Office: 3131 SW Sam Jackson Park Rd Portland OR 97201

LASTRA, BARRY NORMAN, petroleum company executive; b. Santa Monica, Calif., Nov. 18, 1938; s. Joseph B. and Dorothy J. (Miller) L.; A.A., Diablo Valley Coll., 1975; m. Nancy L. Lastra, Dec. 15, 1956; children—David, Dian, Dennis. Salesman, Standard Stas., Inc. (Standard Oil Co. of Calif.), Santa Barbara, 1957-58, asst. mgr., 1958-60, mgr., 1960-64; retail rep. Standard Oil Co. of Calif., San Jose, 1964-65, automotive service rep., Los Angeles, 1965-68, retail sales specialist, San Francisco, 1968-70, mktg. tng. coordinator, 1970-76; sr. adv. personnel devel. Chevron USA, Inc., San Francisco, 1977-81, mgr. corp. contbns., 1981—; mem. com. on tng. and devel. for refining Am. Petroleum Inst., 1980—. Mem. adv. bd. United Way of Bay Area, 1977-78. Mem. Nat. Soc. Sales Tng. Execs. (honor award 1978, dir. 1979-81), Am. Soc. Personnel Adminstrn. (diplomate tng. and devel.). Republican. Office: Chevron USA Inc 575 Market St San Francisco CA 94105

LATHAM, CAROL, educator; b. Salt Lake City, Dec. 18, 1948; d. William James and Jennie Mae (Rasmussen) Latham. A.S., Snow Coll., 1969; B.S., Utah State U., 1971, M.Ed., 1979; cert. ednl. adminstrn. Brigham Young U., 1981. Tchr., Ch. Jesus Christ Latter-day Saints Indian Elem. Sem., Uintah County, Utah, 1971-73; day camp counselor Ch. Jesus Christ Latter-day Saints Social Services, Roosevelt, Utah, 1973; tchr. home econs. West Jr. High Sch., Roosevelt, 1971-81, vice prin., 1980, tchr. Todd Elem. Sch., 1981-82; chpt. 1 reading supr. Uintah Sch. Dist., Vernal, Utah, 1982—; demonstration tchr. reading Utah Office Edn., 1981-83, mem. Supt.'s Adv. Council, 1977-79. Utah Normal scholar, 1967-71; recipient Creative Teaching award Supt. Uintah County, 1979. Mem. Internat. Reading Assn., Utah Reading Assn., Phi Upsilon Omicron. Office: 635 W 200 S Vernal UT 84078

LATHAM, DENNET WALDRON, architect; b. Kansas City, Mo., May 24, 1950; s. Raymond Waldron and Arline Elizabeth (Downs) L.; m. Claire Elizabeth Kamm, June 1, 1974. A.B., Princeton U., 1972; M. Arch., U. Pa., 1976. Lic. architect, Oreg. Draftsman Linscott-Haylett & Assocs., Kansas City, Mo., 1969; draftsman Kaplan & Gaunt, Red Bank, N.J., 1973-74, 1977; assoc., tech. mgr., specifications writer SRG Partnership P.C., Portland, Oreg., 1977—. U. Pa. Grad. Sch. Fine Arts Dales travel scholar, 1976. Mem. AIA, Constrn. Specifications Inst. Club: Oreg. Road Runners. Office: 520 SW Yamhill Suite 231 Portland OR 97204

LATHAM, GARY PHILLIP, psychologist; b. Halifax, N.S., Can., Nov. 16, 1945; came to U.S., 1967; s. William Phillip and Hope Elizabeth (Marshall) L.; B.A., Dalhousie U., 1967; M.S., Ga. Inst. Tech., 1969; Ph.D., U. Akron, 1974; m. Sharon Lee Bridgwater, Sept. 6, 1969; children—Bryan, Brandon. Staff psychologist Am. Pulpwood Assn., Atlanta, 1969-71; mgr. human resources research Weyerhaeuser Co., Tacoma, Wash., 1973-76; pres. G.P. Latham P.S. Inc., Seattle, 1976—; research assoc. U. Wash., Seattle, 1976—. Bd. dirs. Conbela Vocat. Rehab. Center, Seattle, St. James Sch., Seattle. Fellow Am. Psychol. Assn., Can. Psychol. Assn.; mem. Acad. Mgmt. Author: (with K.N. Wexley) Increasing Productivity through Performance Appraisal, 1981, Developing and Training Human Resources in Organizations, 1981; contbr. 100 articles to profl. jours. Home: 15260 Maplewild Ave Seattle WA 98166 Office: Bus Sch U Wash Seattle WA 98195

LATHAM, WILLIAM IGNATIOUS, JR., air force officer; b. El Paso, Tex., June 17, 1948; s. William Ignatious and Martha Jane (Stark) L.; m. Tricia Lildella Caraway, July 5, 1969; children—William Ignatious III, Joshua Luke. B.A., U. Tex.-El Paso, 1970; postgrad. Utah State U., 1974-75. Commd. 2d lt. U.S. Air Force, 1970, advanced through grades to maj., 1982; helicopter rescue pilot Da Nang Airfield (Vietnam), 1972-73; instr. pilot Combat Crew Tng. Sch., Hill AFB, Utah, 1973-76; instr. pilot for German Air Force fighter pilots, Sheppard AFB, Tex., 1976-78, wing chief flight ops br. 80th Flying Tng. Wing, 1978-81; dep. comdr. for ops. Detachment 8, 37th ARRS, Vandenberg AFB, Calif., 1981—. Music dir., edn. dir. Calvary Bapt. Ch., Ogden, Utah, 1977-79; young adult tchr. 1st Bapt. Ch., Wichita Falls, Tex., 1977-79; active Democratic election campaign, 1969. Decorated Air medal (7), Meritorious Service medal, Air Force Commendation medal (2); Humanitarian Service medal (Dept. Def.); named Outstanding Officer of Yr., 1550th Flying Tng. Squadron, Hill AFB, 1974. Mem. Air Force Assn., Internat. Brotherhood Magicians, Tex. Assn. Magicians, Wizards of Wichita Falls, Order of Daedalians, Pi Sigma Alpha. Club: Vandenberg AFB Officers Open Mess. Home: 652 Korina St Vandenberg AFB CA 93437 Office: Detachment 8 37th ARRS/DO Vandenberg AFB CA 93437

LATHE, ADRIAN JOYCE, food co. exec.; b. Cleve., June 5, 1927; s. John H. and Marion Joyce Lathe; B.B.A., Case Western Res. U., 1950; m. Charlia Jack, June 3, 1950; children—Charles, Douglas, Timothy. With SCM Corp., and predecessors, 1950-78, group v.p., 1969-78; cons. edible oils, 1978-81; pres. Agricom Internat., San Francisco, 1981—. Served with AUS, 1945-47. Republican. Office: 633 Battery St San Francisco CA 94111

LATHROP, JOYCE KEEN, civic worker; b. Los Angeles, Nov. 25, 1939; d. William Lavern Trewin and Therese (Wenig) Keen; student Russell Sage Coll., 1957-58, Goucher Coll., 1958-59; B.A., U. So. Calif., 1961; m. Mitchell Lee Lathrop, June 29, 1959 (div. 1977); children—Christin Lorraine, Alexander Mitchell, Timothy Trewin Mitchell. Dir., Assistance League Glendale, 1964-70, Pasadena (Calif.) Sr. Center, 1966-68; dir. jrs. Los Angeles Orphanage Guild, 1968-74, pres., 1974-75, treas., 1972-73, v.p., 1973-74; mem. Symphonians Los Angeles Philharmonic Orch., 1969-73, Opera Assos., Music Center, 1965-78, Aux. Hosp. Good Samaritan, Los Angeles; bd. dirs. Mus. Sci. and Industry Council Calif., 1979—, pres., 1981-82, chmn. bd., 1983—; bd. dirs. Los Angeles Music Center Opera Assn., 1973-74, Aux. Pasadena Sr. Center, 1975—; mem. nat. council Met. Opera, N.Y.C., 1970-77, mem. Met. Assos., 1977—. Recipient vol. service award Huntington Meml. Hosp., Pasadena, 1967; decorated officer Mil. and Hospitaller Order St. Lazarus of Jeruslalem. Episcopalian. Clubs: Goucher of So. Calif. (treas. 1966-67, sec. 1964-66) (Los Angeles); Valley Hunt (Pasadena). Home: 1375 Inverness Dr Pasadena CA 91103

LATHROP, KIMBALL LANE, lawyer; b. Los Angeles, Oct. 5, 1948; d. Warren Joseph and Louise (Scheu) Lane; m. Mitchell Lee Lathrop, May 9, 1981. Student San Diego State U., 1967-70; J.D., Loyola U., Los Angeles, 1973. Bar: Calif. 1973, N.Y. 1983, U.S. Supreme Ct. 1979. Assoc. Seltzer, Caplan, Wilkins & McMahon, San Diego, 1973-77; asst. counsel Solar Turbines Internat., San Diego, 1977-79; assoc. Macdonald, Halsted & Laybourne, Los Angeles and San Diego, 1979-80, Rogers & Wells, N.Y.C. and San Diego, 1980—; adj. prof. labor law Western State U. Sch. Law, 1978-80. Nat. patron Met. Opera, N.Y.C., 1981—, mem. nat. council, 1981—. Mem. ABA, Calif. Bar Assn., San Diego County Bar Assn., State Bar Calif. (standing com. on profl. responsibility and conduct 1980—, arbitrator Superior, Mcpls. cts. San Diego County 1978—), San Diego State U. Alumni Assn. (dir. 1978-82). Republican. Roman Catholic. Club: Charter 100 (pres. 1983—). Contbr. articles to profl. jours. Mem. staff Loyola U. Los Angeles Law Rev., 1971-72, assoc. editor, 1972-73. Office: Rogers & Wells 101 W Broadway San Diego CA 92101 also 200 Park Ave New York NY 10166

LATHROP, MITCHELL LEE, lawyer; b. Los Angeles, Dec. 15, 1937; s. Alfred Lee and Barbara (Mitchell) L.; m. Kimball Ann Lane; children—Christin Lorraine, Alexander Mitchell, Timothy Trewin Mitchell. B.Sc., U.S. Naval Acad., 1959; J.D., U. So. Calif., 1966. Admitted to D.C., Calif. bar, 1966, U.S. Supreme Ct. bar, 1969, N.Y. bar, 1981; dep. counsel Los Angeles County, Calif., 1966-68; with firm Brill, Hunt, DeBuys and Burby, Los Angeles, 1968-71; ptnr. firm Macdonald, Halsted & Laybourne, Los Angeles and San Diego, 1971-80; sr. ptnr. Rogers & Wells, N.Y.C., San Diego, 1980—; asst. presiding referee, chmn. rev. dept., mem. exec. com. Calif. Bar Ct.; lectr. law Advanced Mgmt. Research, Inc., Practicing Law Inst, N.Y., Continuing Edn. of Bar, State Bar Calif., ABA. Western regional chmn. Met. Opera Nat. Council, Council 1971-81, mem. exec. com., 1971—. Trustee Honnold Library at Claremont Colls.; bd. dirs. Music Center Opera Assn., Los Angeles, sec., 1974-80, San Diego Opera Assn., 1980—. Capt. JAG Corps, USNR. Mem. ABA, N.Y. Bar Assn., Fed. Bar Assn., Fed. Bar Council, Calif. Bar Assn., D.C. Bar Assn., San Diego County Bar Assn. (chmn. ethics com. 1980-82, bd. dirs. 1982—), Assn. Bus. Trial Lawyers, Assn. So. Calif. Def. Counsel, Los Angeles Opera Assos. (pres. 1970-72), Soc. Colonial Wars in Calif. (gov. 1970-72), Order St. Lazarus of Jerusalem, Friends of Claremont Coll. (dir. 1975-81, pres. 1978-79), Friends of Huntington Library, Am. Bd. Trial Advocates, Judge Advocates Assn. (dir. Los Angeles chpt. 1974-80, pres. So. Calif. chpt. 1977-78), Internat. Assn. Ins. Counsel, Brit. United Services Club (dir. Los Angeles 1973-75), Mensa Internat., Calif. Soc., S.R. (pres. 1977-79), Phi Delta Phi. Republican. Clubs: California (Los Angeles); Valley Hunt (Pasadena, Calif.); Metropolitan (N.Y.C.). Home: 706 Stafford Pl San Diego CA 92107 Office: 101 W Broadway 20th Floor San Diego CA 92101 also 200 Park Ave New York NY 10166

LATIMER, DOUGLAS HAMILTON, magazine publisher; b. Istanbul, Turkey, Dec. 19, 1937; s. Frederick Palmer and Rebecca (Haigh) L.; m. Rosemarie Yule, Sept. 17, 1966; 1 dau., Allison Yule; m. 2d Karen Whitney, Dec. 24, 1975; children—Katherine Whitney, Jonathan Hamilton. B.A., Princeton U., 1962. Coll. textbook salesman McGraw Hill Pub. Co., various locations U.S., 1962-64; engring. editor, 1965; editor-in-chief bus., econs. and engring., 1966; v.p., pub. Coll. div. Harper & Row, Pubs., N.Y.C., 1967, group v.p. higher edn. group, 1968-77, dir., 1968-77; pres., pub., chmn. Latimer Pubs., Inc., 1977—; pres., pub. Women's Sports Publs., Inc., Palo Alto, Calif., 1977—, chmn. bd. dirs., 1977—. Served with AUS, 1958-60. Home: 40 W Summit Dr Redwood City CA 94062 Office: 318 Town and Country Village Palo Alto CA 94301

LAU, BUONG PECK, physician; b. Singapore, Nov. 27, 1932; s. Tiong King and Lik Hon (Ding) L.; came to U.S., 1952, naturalized, 1970; B.S., Randolph Macon Coll., 1955; M.D., Med. Coll. Va., 1959; m. Judith Tien, June 1, 1962; children—Laura Ginn, Estelle Tsui. Intern, Washington Hosp. Center, 1959-60, resident in radiology, 1960-62; resident in radiology U. Calif. San Francisco Med. Center, 1962-64, instr. radiology, 1964-65, asst. prof., 1965-66; fellow in radiotherapy U. Tex.-M.D. Anderson Hosp., Houston, 1966-67; asso. prof. radiology Med. Coll. Va., Richmond, 1967-68; chief radiotherapist Los Angles County Harbor Gen. Hosp., 1969-70; head radiation therapy and nuclear medicine Med. Clinic Inc., Fresno, Calif., 1970—; head radiation oncologist Visalia Radiation Therapy Med. Clinic, 1972—; head radiation therapy and nuclear medicine Valley Med. Center, 1972—. Bd. dirs. Am. Cancer Soc., 1970-74, 77-78, 80-81. Diplomate Am. Bd. Radiology. Mem. AMA, Pam Am. Med. Assn., Am. Coll. Radiology, Calif. Radiol. Soc., Am. Soc. Therapeutic Radiologists, N.Y. Acad. Scis., Radiol. Soc. N.Am., Phi Beta Kappa. Contbr. articles to profl. jours. Home: 5331 N Sequoia Dr Fresno CA 93711 Office: 1201 E Herndon St Suite 101 Fresno CA 93710 also 317 S Locust St Visalia CA 93277

LAU, EDWARD P., biochemist; b. Hong Kong, Nov. 17, 1949; came to U.S., 1967, naturalized, 1980; s. Stephen H. and Lai K. Lau; B.A. in Chemistry, Central Wash. State Coll., 1970, M.S. in Chemistry, 1972; Ph.D. in Chemistry, U. Wyo., 1977; m. Claudia Wong, July 18, 1976. Research asst. U. Wyo., Laramie, 1973-77; research assoc. U. Colo., Boulder, 1977-80, research scientist in applied molecular genetics, 1981—; scientist Schwarz/Mann Radiochems., Orangeburg, N.Y., 1980. Am. Cancer Soc. Instl. grantee, 1979. Mem. Am. Chem. Soc., AAAS, N.Y. Acad. Sci., Sigma Xi. Contbr. reports to sci. jours. Office: 2045 32d St Boulder CO 80301

LAU, HENRY, mech. engr.; b. Hong Kong, Feb. 4, 1941; came to U.S., 1963; s. Mon Ngok and Julia Ha (Seto) L.; B.S., U. Tenn., 1966; M.S., Duke U., 1969, Ph.D., 1973; m. Bing Y. Sin, June 6, 1970; 1 son, Ryan. Research assoc. Duke U., Durham, N.C., 1973-74; project engr. Ayres & Hayakawa Energy Mgmt., Los Angeles, 1974-77; tech. dir. Ayres Assocs., Los Angeles, 1978—; energy cons. Lawrence Berkeley Lab., U. Calif., 1976—, Calif. Energy Commn., 1981—, Rockwell Internat., 1982. Research grantee Dow Chem. Co., 1965, U.S. Army, 1969, ASHRAE, 1973. Registered profl. engr., Calif. Mem. ASME, ASHRAE, Sigma Xi, Phi Kappa Phi, Tau Beta Pi, Pi Tau Sigma. Contbr. articles in field to profl. jours. Home: 1948 Crest Dr Los Angeles CA 90034 Office: 1180 S Beverly Dr Los Angeles CA 90035

LAU, IRENE OI LIN, bank executive, import company executive; b. Canton, China, Mar. 24, 1950; d. Kin Hon and Wai Ching (Lee) Yee; m. Danny Lau, Mar. 14, 1971 (div.); Student San Francisco City Coll., 1977—. Asst. mgr. Violet's Fashions, Hong Kong, 1967-68; teller Bank of Am., San Francisco, 1969-78, unit supr., 1978-80, shift supr., 1980-81, asst. v.p., 1981—; v.p. merchandising Silky Way, Inc. of Calif., 1979-81, pres., 1981—. Bilingual election officer Election Bd., San Francisco, 1981-82. Mem. Nat. Assn. Female Execs., Nat. Retail Mcht. Assn. Democrat. Club: Postal Commemorative Soc. Columnist for Chinese Community newspaper.

LAU, LAWRENCE JUEN-YEE, economics educator; b. Guizhou, China, Dec. 12, 1944; came to U.S., 1961, naturalized, 1974; s. Shai-Tat and Chi-Hing (Yu) L.; B.S. with great distinction, Stanford U., 1964; M.A., U. Calif.-Berkeley, 1966, Ph.D., 1969. Mem. faculty dept. econs. Stanford (Calif.) U., 1966—, prof. econs., 1976—; dir. Bank of Canton of Calif., 1980—; vice chmn. Bank of Canton of Calif. Bldg. Corp., 1981—; pres. EcoMetrics, Inc., 1979—; cons. World Bank, others. Fellow Econometric Soc. Author: (with D.T. Jamison) Farmer Education and Farm Efficiency, 1982; contbr. articles to profl. jours. Office: Dept Econs Stanford U Stanford CA 94305

LAUBE, ROGER GUSTAV, financial planner; b. Chgo., Aug. 11, 1921; s. William C. and Elsie (Drews) L.; ed. Roosevelt U., 1938-42; LL.B., John Marshall Law Sch., 1950; postgrad. Northwestern U., 1960, trust div. Pacific Coast Grad. Sch. Banking, 1962-64; m. Irene Mary Chadbourne, Mar. 30, 1946; children—David Roger, Philip Russell, Steven Richard. With Chgo. Title & Trust Co., 1938-42, 48-50; with Nat. Bank Alaska, Anchorage, 1950-72, mgr. mortgage dept., 1950-56, organized 1st trust dept. in Alaska, 1956, v.p., trust officer, mgr. trust dept., 1956-72, v.p., trust officer, mktg. dir., mgr. estate and fin. planning div. Bishop Trust Co. Ltd., Honolulu, 1972-82; exec. v.p. Design Capital Planning Group, Inc., Tucson, 1982-83; pres., chief exec. officer Advanced Capital Devel., Inc., 1983—; charter mem. Anchorage Estate Planning Council, 1960-72, pres., 1960-62; mem. Hawaii Estate Planning Council, 1972—, v.p., 1978-79, pres., 1980. Charter mem. Anchorage Community Chorus, 1947-48, 50-70, pres., 1959-60; pres. Gideons Internat., Anchorage, 1957-72, Honolulu, 1972-82, Tucson, 1982—; mem. adv. bd. Faith Hosp., Glennallen, Alaska, 1960—; sec.-treas. Alaska Baptist Found., 1955-72; mem. bd. Alaska Festival Music, 1960-72; mem. bd. advisers Salvation Army, Anchorage, 1961-72, chmn., Anchorage, 1969, Others award, 1971, bd. advisers, Honolulu, 1972-82, Tucson, 1983—, chmn. bd., Honolulu, 1976-78. Mem. exec. com. capital fund drive Hawaii Bapt. Acad. Served with AUS, 1942-48, asst. staff Judge Adv., Alaskan Command, 1946-48. Mem. Am. Inst. Banking (instr. trust div. 1961—), Am. Bankers Assn. (mem. legis. council trust div. 1961-72), Nat. Assn. Life Underwriters (asso.), Internat. Assn. Fin. Planners (treas. Honolulu chpt. 1980-82), Am. Assn. Handbell Ringers, Sabino Townhouse Assn. (pres. 1983—). Baptist (exec. com. conv. 1959-61, dir. music Chgo. 1938-42, 48-50, Anchorage 1950-72, Hawaii 1972-82, Tucson 1982—; chmn. trustees Anchorage 1950-72, Hawaii 1972-74). Home: 7115 E Sabino Vista Circle Tucson AZ 85715 Office: 1580 N Kolb Rd Suite 200 Tucson AZ 85715

LAUBER, MIGNON DIANE, food processing co. exec.; b. Detroit, Dec. 21; d. Charles Edmond and Maud Lillian (Foster) Donaker; student Kelsey Jenny U., 1958, Brigham Young U., 1959; m. Richard Brian Lauber, Sept. 13, 1963; 1 dau., Leslie Viane. Owner, operator Alaska World Travel, Ketchikan, 1964-67; founder, owner, pres. Oosick Soup Co., Juneau, Alaska, 1969—. Treas., Pioneer Alaska Lobbyists Soc., Juneau, 1977—. Mem. Bus. and Profl. Women, Alaska C. of C. Libertarian. Club: Washington Athletic. Home: 321 Highland Dr Juneau AK 99801 Office: PO Box 1625 Juneau AK 99802

LAUDAN, CHARLES JOSEPH, sales executive; b. Chgo., Apr. 17, 1948; s. Edward Florian and Roberta Lee (Doolan) L.; B.S. in Aero. Engring., Parks Coll. Aero. Tech., St. Louis U., 1969; m. Vickie Ann, June 22, 1973; children—Laurie Ann, John Edward Charles. Sales rep. Dictaphone Corp., San Bernardino, Calif., 1977-80, br. sales mgr., 1980-82; nat. sales mgr. TA Mfg., Glendale, Calif., 1982—. Served with USAF, 1970-76; Vietnam, Korea. Roman Catholic. Office: 375 W Arden St Glendale CA 91203

LAUDENSLAGER, WANDA LEE, speech pathologist; b. San Jose, Calif., July 22, 1929; d. Victor Vierra and Florence Lorene (Houck) Silveira; A.A., Coll. San Mateo, 1960; B.A., San Jose State U., 1962, M.A., 1965; m. Leonard E. Laudenslager, Apr. 26, 1952; children—Leonard E. II, Dawn Marie. Speech pathologist Newark (Calif.) Unified Sch. Dist., 1962-65, dist. coordinator speech, hearing and lang. dept., 1965—; trainer student tchrs. Certified in supervision, teaching, speech, standard designated services, Calif.; lic. real estate broker, gen. bldg. contractor, audiometrist, speech pathologist, Calif.; lic. speech pathologist, Calif.; cert. clin. competence in speech pathology Am. Speech, Lang. and Hearing Assn. recipient Crown Zellerbach Found. award, 1961; hon. life mem. Calif. Congress Parents and Tchrs., Inc. Mem. Phi Kappa Phi, Alpha Gamma Sigma, Pi Lambda Theta, Kappa Delta Pi. Home: 37733 Logan Dr Fremont CA 94536 Office: 5715 Musick Ave Newark CA 94560

LAUDERDALE, PAT L., social scientist, educator; b. Cache, Okla., Oct. 19, 1948; s. T.E. and Almeta (Cantrell) L. M.S. in Psychology, U. Tex., 1969; postgrad. (Woodrow Wilson fellow) Princeton U., 1968; Ph.D. in Sociology, Social Psychology, Stanford U., 1975. Vice-pres. Corad Inc., El Paso, Tex., 1967-69; vis. asst. prof. U. Calif.-Santa Cruz, 1973-74; assoc. prof. U. Minn., Mpls., 1974-80; prof. justice studies, adj. prof. law Ariz. State U., Tempe, 1980—; research dir. Ctr. for Study of Justice; research cons. Nat. Inst. Justice. Alumni ambassador Stanford U., 1977-79; mem. Cuban Cultural Ctr., 1979. Recipient Disting. Teaching award U. Minn., 1979; Research and Travel award Cuba, Office of Internat. Programs, 1980. Mem. Phi Beta Kappa, Omicron Delta Kappa. Club: Non-nuclear Future (Washington). Author: A Political Analysis of Deviance, 1980; (with James Inverarity) Law and Society, 1983.

LAUDIEN, MARK LOUIS, engring. cons.; b. N.Y.C., Aug. 22, 1943; s. Paul and Brandla (Merkin) L. B.S.C.E., N.Y. U., 1966; M.S.C.E., U. So. Calif., 1970. With Rockwell Internat., 1966-68, 71-73; sr. engr. Litton Ship Systems, 1968-70; sr. engr. R.M. Parsons, Los Angeles, 1970-71, Bechtel, Norwalk, Calif., 1973-74, Control Data Corp., Los Angeles, 1974-77; prin. cons. McDonnell Douglas Automation Co., Los Angeles, 1977-81; corp. engring. specialist Lear Siegler, Inc., Santa Monica, Calif., 1981—. Mem. ASCE, ASME. Home: 550 S Barrington Ave 126 West Los Angeles CA 90049 Office: 2850 Ocean Park Blvd Santa Monica CA 90406

LAUER, HUGH CONRAD, computer scientist, engr.; b. Phila., Nov. 11, 1942; s. Wilbur W. and B. Lucille (Niswander) L.; m. Ruth Ellen Caseino, Aug. 17, 1968; children—Will, Jennifer, Alison, Arthur. B.S. in Math., Antioch Coll., 1965; M.S. in Math., Carnegie-Mellon U., 1967, Ph.D. in Computer Sci., 1972. Lectr., U. Newcastle-upon-Tyne (Eng.), 1971-75; computer scientist System Devel. Corp., Santa Monica, Calif., 1976-77; cons. mem. programming staff, staff scientist, area mgr. Xerox Corp., Palo Alto, Calif., 1977-81, project mgr. office system devel., 1981—. Cub Scout leader Boy Scouts Am. Mem. Assn. Computing Machinery, IEEE, IEEE Computer Soc. Democrat. Unitarian. Contbr. articles to tech. jours. Patentee in field. Office: 3333 Coyote Hill Rd Palo Alto CA 94304

LAUFENBERG, FRANCIS, supt. schs.; b. Rock Island, Ill., Aug. 5, 1921; s. August J. and Jane (Higgins) L.; student St. Ambrose Coll., 1940-41; B.S., U. Calif., Santa Barbara, 1948; M.Ed., U. So. Calif., 1950, Ed.D., 1958; m. Frances Lee Windsor, Oct. 22, 1944; children—Lawrence Windsor, Linda Lea. Tchr., Los Angeles pub. schs., 1948-50, adminstr., 1950-58; asst. supt. Oxnard (Calif.) City Schs., 1958-60; asst. supt., asso. supt., dep. supt. Long Beach Unified Sch. Dist., 1960-78, supt., 1978—; asso. supt. Long Beach City Coll., 1960-70. Lectr. U. So. Calif., Calif. State Coll., Long Beach. Served to maj. USMCR, 1942-46. Mem. Assn. Calif. Sch. Adminstrs., Delta Tau Delta, Phi Delta Kappa. Episcopalian. Kiwanian. Home: 2625 Hillcrest Ave Orange CA 92667 Office: 701 Locust Ave Long Beach CA 90813

LAUGHLIN, LOUIS GENE, banker; b. Santa Barbara, Calif., Sept. 20, 1937; s. Eston A. and Cornelia Helen (Snively) L.; student Pomona Coll., 1955-58; B.A., U. Calif., Santa Barbara, 1960; postgrad. Claremont Grad. Sch., 1966-70, Sch. Bank Mktg., U. Colo., 1974-75, Grad. Sch. Mgmt., U. Calif.-Irvine, 1983. Mgr., Wheeldex-Los Angeles Co., 1961-62; v.p. Warner/Walker Assos., Inc., Los Angeles, 1962; cons. Spectra-Sound Corp., Los Angeles, 1964-65; rep. A.C. Nielsen Co., Chgo., 1962-64; research analyst Security Pacific Nat. Bank, Los Angeles, 1964-67, asst. research mgr., 1967-68, asst. v.p., 1968-72, v.p., mgr. market info. and research div., 1972-76, v.p. research adminstrn., pub. affairs/research dept., 1976-82, v.p. govt. relations dept., 1982—; mem. Nat. Conf. on Fin. Services, 1982—; mem. policy council Nat. Conf. on Competition in Banking, 1978-79, 81. Sec. econs. Town Hall of Calif., 1966. Mem. Am., Western econ. assns., Nat. Assn. Bus. Economists, Am. Mgmt. Assn., Issues Mgmt. Assn., Bank Mktg. Assn., Los Angeles C. of C. (food and agr. adv. com. 1981), Packard Automobile Classics, Packard Internat., Corvair Soc. Am. Office: Security Pacific Plaza 333 S Hope St Los Angeles CA 90071

LAUGHLIN, RICHARD LEE, school district administrator; b. Pendleton, Oreg., May 31, 1934; s. Marshall E. and Sylvia K. (Kirby) L.; m. Janet L. Rothenberg, June 11, 1955; children—Debra Mathews, James. B.S., Portland State Coll., 1958; M.Ed., Oreg. State U., 1962; Ed.D., U. Wyo., 1973. Tchr. pub. schs., Milwaukee, Oreg., 1961-64; curriculum coordinator Colegio Nueva Granada, Bogota, Colombia, 1964-66; counselor pub. schs., Portland, Oreg., 1966-71, 73-76; teaching asst. U. Wyo., Laramie, 1971-73; prin. Lincoln County (Oreg.) Sch. Dist., Newport, 1976-80; supt. Crook County (Oreg.) Sch. Dist., Prineville, 1980—. Bd. dirs. Crook County United Way. Mem. Confedn. Oreg. Sch. Adminstrs., Oreg. Assn. Sch. Execs., Nat. Assn. Sch. Adminstrs., C. of C. (mem. conf. com.), Phi Kappa Phi. Democrat. Episcopalian. Club: Kiwanis. Home: 401 S Fairview St Prineville OR 97754 Office: Crook County Sch Dist 1390 SE 2d St Prineville OR 97754

LAUGHLIN, WINSTON MEANS, soil scientist, researcher; b. Fountain, Minn., May 2, 1917; s. Laurence Losson and Stella Valerie (Means) L.; m. Dorothy Florence Fuleihan, June 7, 1947; children—Ellen Valerie Taylor, Laurence Means, Keith Daniel, Brian Nave. B.S., U. Minn., 1941; M.S., Mich. State U., 1947, Ph.D., 1949. Registered profl. agronomist, soil scientist. Labor foreman Muck Expt. Sta., Mich. State U., East Lansing, 1941-42, research soil scientist Agrl. Research Service, U.S. Dept. Agr., Palmer, Alaska, 1949—. Served with C.E., U.S. Army, 1943-45. Mem. Am. Soc. Agronom, Soil Sci. Soc. Am., Internat. Soil Sci. Soc., Am. Sci. Affiliation, AAAS, Am. Inst. Biol. Scis., Potato Assn. Am., Internat. Peat Soc. Presbyterian. Contbr. articles to profl. jours. Home: Star Route D Box 9965 Palmer AK 99645 Office: Box AE Palmer AK 99645

LAUGHNAN, DON FRANCIS, wood treatment and finish consultant; b. Spring Green, Wis., Mar. 18, 1915; s. Thomas Raphael and Lillian Anna (Hutter) L.; m. Laura Ann Nolden, May 25, 1940; children—Karen Ann, Steven Thomas, Michael Jon, Joel James. B.S. in Chemistry, U. Wis., 1938. With paint research sect. U.S. Forest Products Lab., Madison, Wis., 1936-40, 41-59, sect. chief, sr. chemist, 1950-59; prodn. engr. trade sales dept. Pittsburgh Plate Glass Co., Milw., 1940-41; sr. specialist treatments and finishes for wood Simpson Timber Co., Seattle, 1959-79; pres. Laughnan Cons., Inc., Bellevue, Wash., 1979—; mem. Joint Coatings-Forest Products Com., 1961-79. Mem. Forest Products Research Soc., Fedn. Socs. for Coatings Tech. Republican. Roman Catholic. Home and Office: 12526 SE 15th St Bellevue WA 98005

LAUNER, ROBERT DAVID, data processing executive; b. N.Y.C., May 10, 1951; s. Arthur and Eileen Ilona (Steingeisser) L.; B.S.E.E., UCLA, 1973. Computer lab. instr. U. So. Calif., 1969-70; computer programmer I, Sch. Engring., UCLA, 1972-75; computer systems engr. Electronic Data Systems Corp., San Francisco, 1975-80; dir. data processing Summit Workshops, Inc., Redwood City, Calif., 1980—; tchr. computer programming Los Angeles Sch. Dist., 1970-71. Los Angeles Council of Engrs. and Scientists scholar, 1970-71, 71-72; Inst. for Advancement of Engring. scholar, 1970-71. Mem. IEEE, Am. Soc. Engrs. and Architects, Engring. Soc. of UCLA. Contbr. articles to profl. jours. Office: 386 Main St Redwood City CA 94063

LAURAE, DAVID BRUCE, accountant; b. San Jose, Calif., Aug. 31, 1948; s. Donald Burt and Vera Meriam (Lawrence) L.; m. Patricia Mae Buckland, Aug. 5, 1973; m. 2d, Geryl Lynn Vonhof, Aug. 22, 1982; children—April Lynn Thompson, James David. B.S. in Bus. Adminstrn., San Jose State U., 1972. C.P.A., Wash. Gen. ptnr. LauRae Lighting, Mountain View, Calif., 1973-76; acct. Whitaker, Lipp & Healea, Longview, Wash., 1976-77, Deming & Assocs., Redmond, Wash., 1977-80; owner, prin. David B. LauRae, C.P.A., Kirkland, Wash., 1980—; owner, designer LauRae Products, wood products, Woodinville, Wash., 1977—; dir. John's Pork Chop Sandwich, Inc. Mem. Am. Inst. C.P.A.s, Wash. Soc. C.P.A.s, Kirkland C. of C. Lodge: Lions (Longview, Wash.). Office: 505 Market St Suite 102 Kirkland WA 98033

LAUSON, SAMUEL KENT, energy company executive, orthodontist; b. Billings, Mont., Feb. 16, 1945; s. Spencer Norman and Marjorie (Dove) L.; D.D.S., U. Iowa, 1971; cert. in grad. periodontics U.S. Air Force Med. Center, 1972; M.S. in Orthodontics, St. Louis U., 1975, Assoc. in Religious Sci., 1981. Pvt. practice orthodontics, Englewood, Colo., 1975-76; asso. pub. Colo. Outdoor Guide Mag., Lakewood, 1978; founder, pres. Sun Energy Systems, Inc., Denver, 1978-80, Diversified Energy Systems, Inc., Englewood, 1980—, chief exec. officer, 1980—; dir. Am. Solar Energy Corp., 1977-78; condr. seminars in interceptive orthodontics. Served as capt. Dental Corps, USAF, 1971-73. Honored as Disting. Alumni, Nat. Belimi award ceremonies, Billings Sr. High Sch., 1977; Cert. of Recognition, Colo. Dept. Health, 1980; Cert. of Appreciation, Metro. Denver Dental Soc., 1977; Vocat. Edn. award, Columbine High Sch., 1980. Mem. Am. Soc. Preventive Dentistry, Orthodontic Research Found. St. Louis, Delta Sigma Delta. Republican. Religious Sci. Ch. Clubs: Rocky Mt. Dental Study, Columbine Study, Lowry Nickerson Investors. Contbr. articles to profl. jours. Home: 12419 E Amherst Circle Aurora CO 80014 Office: 4800 E Happy Canyon Rd Denver CO 80237

LAUTH, ROBERT EDWARD, geologist; b. St. Paul, Feb. 6, 1927; s. Joseph Louis and Gertrude (Stapleton) L.; student St. Thomas Coll., 1944; B.A. in Geology, U. Minn., 1952; m. Suzanne Janice Holmes, Apr. 21, 1947; children—Barbara Jo, Robert Edward II, Elizabeth Suzanne, Leslie Marie. Wellsite geologist Columbia Carbon Co., Houston, 1951-52; dist. geologist Witco Oil & Gas Corp., Amarillo, Tex., 1952-55; field geologist Reynolds Mining Co., Houston, 1955; cons. geologist, Durango, Colo., 1955—. Served with USNR, 1944-45. Mem. N.Mex., Four Corners (treas., v.p., pres., symposium com.) geol. socs., Rocky Mountain Assn. Geologists, Am. Inst. Profl. Geologists, Am. Inst. Mining, Metall. and Petroleum Engrs., Am. Assn. Petroleum Geologists, Helium Soc., N.Y. Acad. Sci. Am. Assn. Petroleum Landman, Soc. Econ. Paleontologists and Mineralogists, The Explorers Club. Republican. Roman Catholic. K.C. Clubs: Durango Petroleum (dir.), Denver Petroleum, Elks. Author: Desert Creek Field, 1958; (with Silas C. Brown) Oil and Gas Potentialities of Northern Arizona, 1958, Northern Arizona Has Good Oil, Gas Prospects, 1960, Northeastern Arizona; Its Oil, Gas and Helium Prospects, 1961; contbr. papers on oil and gas fields to profl. symposia. Home: 2020 Crestview St PO Box 776 Durango CO 81301 Office: 555 S Camino del Rio Durango CO 81301

LAVE, CHARLES ARTHUR, economics educator; b. Phila., May 18, 1938; s. Israel and Esther (Axlerod) L.; 1 dau., Rebecca. B.A., Reed Coll., 1960; Ph.D., Stanford U., 1968. Mem. faculty, U. Calif.-Irvine, 1966—, prof. econs., chmn. dept. econs., 1978—; vis. prof., vis. scholar Hampshire Coll., 1972, Stanford U., 1974, MIT, 1982, Harvard U., 1982. Trustee Reed Coll., 1978-82. Served with USAF, 1967. Dept. Energy grantee, 1975-83; Dept. Transp. grantee, 1977-81. Mem. Am. Econ. Assn., Econometric Soc., AAAS, Soc. for Applied Anthropology, Transp. Research Bd. Author: An Introduction to Models in the Social Sciences, 1975 (with James March); Energy and Auto Type Choice, 1981; Education and Cognitive Development, 1979, others. Address: Dept Econs Univ Calif Irvine CA 92717

LAVINE, MARY ANN, personnel consultant; b. Austin, Minn., June 15, 1935; d. Leslie Ted and Alice Seneva (Erie) Young; m. Lyndon B. Petersen, Aug. 22, 1954 (dec.); children—Elizabeth Hilton, Penny; m. 2d, Maurice Charles Lavine, Aug. 21, 1969; 1 dau., JoAnne. B.A. in Edn., Ariz. State U.-Tempe, 1973, M.A., 1979. Program developer, instructional team leader Washington Elementary Dist. 6, Phoenix, 1973-81; cons. home health care personnel Referral Services, Inc., Phoenix, 1982—. Mem. Glendale Community Council; past dept. comdr., state pres. Disabled Am. Vets. Aux. Mem. Am. Soc. Tng. and Devel., Nat. Council Social Studies, Ariz. Assn. Personnel Cons. (assoc.), Midtowners Bus. and Profl. Women's Club, Glendale C. of C., Kappa Delta Pi, Pi Lambda Theta. Presbyterian.

LAVINE, THOMAS GAYLORD, real estate investment co. exec.; b. Los Angeles, Sept. 16, 1945; s. Lee A. and Ethel C. L.; B.S., U. So. Calif., 1967; M.B.A., UCLA, 1969; m. Beau Berlinski, May 20, 1972; children—Suzette Alyssa, Michelle Lee. Vice-pres. West Coast Community Exchange, 1971-73; exec. v.p., dir. Lago Calc, Inc., 1972-73; mng. dir. World Trade Co. N.V., 1973—; pres. Wilshire Properties, Los Angeles, 1967—; chief exec. officer GMG Capital Enterprises, Inc., Beverly Hills, Calif., 1980—. Mem. adv. bd. Internat. Orphans Inc., Children's Village U.S.A. Mem. Nu Beta Epsilon. Club: Masons. Office: 9301 Wilshire Blvd Beverly Hills CA 90211

LAW, EDWIN B., construction consultant; b. Ft. Worth, Aug. 19, 1924; s. Allan B. and Josephine (Parks) L.; student Tex. A. and M. Coll., 1940-42; B.S. in Archtl. Engring., U. Tex., 1949; m. Margaret Ellen Russell, May 29, 1948 (div.); children—Patrick E., Michael M., Gregory P., Katherine A., James R.; m. 2d, Carol J. Settimo, 1979; 1 stepson, P.J. Engr., J.M. Odom Constrn. Co., Austin, Tex., 1947-49; estimator J.W. Bateson Constrn. Co., Dallas, 1949; chief estimator Von Frellick Inc., San Angelo, Tex., 1949-50, Frank E. Blaser Bldg. Co., Wichita, Kans., 1950-52; chief engr. Dondlinger & Sons Constrn. Co., 1953-59; chmn. bd., chief exec. officer Law Co., Inc., 1959-83; cons. Aragon West, Inc., Scottsdale, Ariz., 1983—. Organizer, dir. Civic Progress Citizens Assn., 1957-63; organizer Citizens for Commn.-Mgr. Plan, 1959; pres. Greater Downtown Wichita, 1963-64; chmn. Wichita-Sedgwick County Met. Area Planning Commn., 1962-63; chmn. Bd. Zoning Appeals, 1962-63; bd. dirs. local USO, 1957, NCCJ, United Fund of Wichita and Sedgwick County, Inc. Registered profl. engr., Kans. Named Kans. Outstanding Jaycee by Jr. C. of C., 1958-59. Served to capt., USMC, 1942-46, 52-53. Mem. Nat., Ariz., Kans., Wichita assns. profl. engrs., Assoc. Gen. Contractors (nat. dir., pres. Kans. builders chpt. 1974-75), Cons. Constructors Council Am., Sigma Nu. Republican. Roman Catholic. K.C. (4 degree). Clubs: Desert Highlands Fairfield Continental Country (Flagstaff, Ariz.); Phoenix Country.

LAWER, BETSY, banker; b. Anchorage, July 27, 1949; d. Daniel Hon and Betty Jane (Puckett) Cuddy; m. David A. Lawer, June 9, 1972; 1 dau., Sarah Anne. B.A. in Econs., Duke U., 1971; postgrad. Calif. State U.-Sacramento, 1974-75. With First Nat. Bank of Anchorage, 1974—, now v.p. mktg. div., dir. Mem. Anchorage Symphony Opera Womens League; active Am. Diabetes Assn., Alaska State Troopers Safety Bear Program, Neighborhood Watch, Municipality of Anchorage Employee Sponsored Pass Program. Mem. Am. Inst. Banking, Bank Adminstrs. Inst., Alaska Council Econ. Edn. (past treas., mem. exec. com.), Advt. Fedn. Alaska, Pub. Relations Soc. Am., Alaska C. of C. Clubs: Anchorage Woman's, Press. Office: First Nat Bank of Anchorage PO Box 720 Anchorage AK 99510

LAWLER, JUDY ANN, data processor; b. West Bend, Wis., Aug. 4, 1944; d. Alexander John and Elsie Frieda (Zumach) Boettcher; m. Michael Francis Lawler, Jan. 28, 1968 (div.); children—Timothy Shane, Alisandra Michelle. B.S., U. Ariz. Tucson, 1966, M. Ed., 1967. Systems engr. IBM Co., Phoenix, 1967-71; systems mgr. Kaibab Industries, Phoenix, 1972-78; pres. System/3 Assocs. S.W. Inc., Scottsdale, Ariz., 1975-79; data processing mgr. Marathon Steel, Phoenix, 1978-82; data processing mgr. Ariz. Mail Order, Inc., Tucson, 1982—; instr. N. Am. Coll. of Data Processing, Phoenix, 1980-81. Sec. bd. dirs. COMMON (Nat. IBM Small Systems Users Group). Lutheran. Contbg. editor Small Systems World, 1979-81. Office: 3740 E 34th St Tucson AZ 85713

LAWRENCE, DAVID ANTHONY, educator; b. Saginaw, Mich., Aug. 1, 1951; s. Cecil Anthony and Bernadine Bernice (Symkowiak) L. A.A. in Architecture, Orange Coast Coll., 1971; B.A. in Indsl. Arts, Calif. State U.-Long Beach, 1973; M.A. in Secondary Curriculum, U. San Francisco, 1978. Standard secondary teaching credential, community coll. credential, adminstrv. services credential, Calif. Tchr. indsl. arts Villa Park (Calif.) High Sch., 1975—; dist. dept. chmn. indsl. arts Orange (Calif.) Unified Sch. Dist., 1981—; tech. instr., architecture and engring. Santa Ana (Calif.) Coll., 1976—; cons. archtl./engring. drawing to Calif. Dept. Edn. Recipient Hats Off award Orange Unified Sch. Dist., 1982; Epsilon Pi Tau scholar, 1971-75. Mem. Am. Vocat. Assn. (Calif. chmn. indsl. arts div. 1981—), NEA, Calif. Indsl. Edn. Assn., Calif. Assn. Vocat. Educators, Epsilon Pi Tau (sec. 1973—). Roman Catholic. Home: 768 N Grand Ave Orange CA 92667 Office: 18042 E Taft Ave Villa Park CA 92667

LAWRENCE, DEAN GRAYSON, lawyer; b. Oakland, Calif.; d. Henry C. and Myrtle (Grayson) Schmidt; A.B., U. Calif.-Berkeley, 1934, J.D., 1939. Admitted to Calif. bar, 1943, U.S. Dist. Ct., 1944, U.S. Ct. Appeals, 1944, Tax Ct. U.S., 1945, U.S. Treasury Dept., 1945, U.S. Supreme Ct., 1967; asso. Pillsbury, Madison & Sutro, San Francisco, 1944, 45; gen. practice Oakland, 1946-50, San Jose, 1952-60, Grass Valley, 1960-63, 66—; county counsel Nevada County, 1964-65. Nevada County Bd. Suprs., 1969-73, chmn., 1971. Sec. Nev. County Humane Animal Shelter Bd., 1966—; state humane officer, 1966—; pres. Nev. County Humane Soc., 1974—, mem. Humane Soc. U.S., Fund for Animals; bd. dirs. Nevada County Health Planning Council, Golden Empire Areawide Health Planning Council, 1974, 75; mem. Nevada County Democratic Central Com., 1980—, sec., 1982—. Mem. Bus. and Profl. Women's Club, AAUW, State Bar Calif., Phi Beta Kappa, Sigma Xi, Kappa Beta Pi, Pi Mu Epsilon, Pi Lambda Theta. Episcopalian. Office: PO Box 66 Grass Valley CA 95945

LAWRENCE, ERNEST S., psychologist and psychoanalyst; b. N.Y.C., Apr. 12, 1920; m. Gerda Lawrence, Aug. 31, 1947; children—David, Annette; m. 2d, Anne Lawrence Nov. 4, 1974; 1 son, James F. Ph.D., U. So. Calif., 1953. Lic. psychologist, Calif.; diplomate Am. Bd. Profl. Psychology. Pvt. practice psychotherapy and psychoanalysis, Los Angeles, 1955—; dir. tng., supr. psychoanalysis Los Angeles Inst. Psychoanalytic Studies, 1977—; cons. Didi Hirsch Community Mental Health Ctr., 1970—, Wright Inst., 1975—. Served with U.S. Army, 1941-45. Elected to Nat. Acads. Practice, 1982. Mem. Am. Psychol. Assn. (pres. elect div. psychoanalysis 1982), Calif. Psychol. Assn. (pres. 1970-71). Office: Suite 923 1100 Glendon Ave Los Angeles CA 90024

LAWRENCE, JEROME, playwright, director, educator; b. Cleve., July 14, 1915; s. Samuel and Sarah (Rogen) L. B.A., Ohio State U., 1937, D.H.L. (hon.), 1963; D.Lit., Fairleigh Dickinson U., 1968; D.F.A., Villanova U., 1969; D.Letters, Coll. of Wooster, 1983. Reporter Wilmington (Ohio) News-Jour., 1937; editor New Lexington (Ohio) Daily News, 1937; with Sta. WOSU, Columbus, Ohio, 1934-37, Sta. KMPC, Beverly Hills, Calif., 1938-39; with CBS, Hollywood, Calif., 1939-41, CBS, N.Y.C., 1941-42; ptnr. playwrights Lawrence & Lee, 1942—; playwright, dir. numerous prodns.; actor The Life and Times of Paul Muni, Inherit the Wind, Auntie Mame, Mame, The Night Thoreau Spent in Jail, First Monday in October, The Gang's All Here, Jabberwock, The Crocodile Smile, Look Ma, I'm Dancin', Only in America, The Incomparable Max, numerous other works; traveler, specialist, lectr. U.S. State Dept.; lectr. Ohio State U., Baylor U., NYU; advisor coms. in theatre, broadcasting and edn.; founder, pres. Am. Playwrights Theatre. Founder, served to sgt. Armed Forces Radio, 1942-45. Recipient Peabody award, 1946, 48; Lifetime Achievement award Am. Theatre Assn., 1979; Ohioana Library prize (4), Nat. Thespian Assn., 1979; Dir.'s prize, 1980; N.Y. Press Club award, 1942; Moss Hart Meml. award, 1973; U.S. State Dept. medal, 1968; Pacific Pioneer Broadcasters award, 1981; Donaldson award, 1955; numerous other awards for contbns. to theatre. Mem. Acad. Motion Picture Arts and Scis., Dramatists Guild (council), Writers Guild Am. (founder, council), Players Club of N.Y., Phi Beta Kappa, Sigma Delta Chi. Democrat. Collections of manuscripts and recs. of Lawrence and Lee at Library and Mus. of Performing Arts, N.Y.C., Harvard U.'s Widener Library, Ohio State U., Kent State U. office: 21056 Las Flores Mesa Dr Malibu CA 90265

LAWRENCE, MARY CAROLE, art retailer; b. Oregon City, Oreg., Mar. 18, 1944; d. Richard Franklin and Mary Virginia (Poljnar) Pitts; m. Gary D. Lawrence, June 13, 1971; children—Brad, Brent, Angela. B.S. in Home Econs., Oreg. State U., 1966. High sch. home econs. tchr. West Linn, Oreg., 1966-70; co-owner (with husband), mgr. Lawrence Galleries, Portland, Sheridan and Salishan, Oreg., 1977—; sec. bd. dirs. Art Focus Inc., Lawrence/Lawrence Inc. Mem. Omicron Nu, Phi Kappa Phi. Republican. Episcopalian. Office: 913 SW Broadway Portland OR 97205

LAWRENCE, RICK L., architect; b. Loveland, Colo., Jan. 15, 1954; s. Virgil Walter and Twila Lea (Brown) L.; B.Arch., U. Idaho, 1977; m. Terri Ann Clayton, Apr. 7, 1979; 1 dau., Shandra Denise. Archtl. draftsman The Neenan Co., Ft. Collins, Colo., 1977-78, George R. Fullen, architect, Englewood, Colo., 1978; archtl. draftsman, archtl. job capt. Victor Huff & Assos., Aurora, Colo., 1978-81; project architect Bourn and Dulaney Architects, Englewood, 1981-82; project architect Urban Design Group, Denver, 1982—. Registered architect, Colo.; cert. NCARB. Mem. AIA, Nat. Bldg. Mus., Cousteau Soc., Greenpeace, Nat. Geog. Soc. Office: 1400 Market St Suite 300 Denver CO 80202

LAWRENCE, SUSAN PATRICIA, financial services co. exec.; b. St. Louis, July 4, 1942; d. George Oscar and Ethel May (Gwen) Bland; m. Edmond Peter FitzWilliam III, Dec. 27, 1962 (div. June 1978); 1 son, Patrick Brian; m. 2d Thomas Lee Lawrence, Sept. 2, 1982. A.A., William Woods Coll., 1962. Lic. ins. broker, Mo. Adminstr. asst. Sherwood Industries div. Brunswick, St. Louis County, Mo., 1962-66; assoc. First Capitol Savs. & Loan Assn., St. Charles, Mo., 1967-77; client retention services James E. Frick Inc., St. Louis, 1977-79; sales rep. Reed, Roberts Assocs., Los Angeles, 1979-82; regional mgr. Hamilton Taft & Co., Los Angeles, 1982—. Mem. Nat. Assn. Profl. Saleswomen, Nat. Assn. Female Execs. Inc. Republican. Episcopalian. Clubs: Toastmasters, Scottish Terrier of Calif., Nat. Breed, Welsh Terrier. Home: PO Box 3111 Culver City CA 90230 Office: 11222 LaCienega Blvd Suite 535 Los Angeles CA 90304

LAWS, RUFINA MARIE MAGOOSH, educator, consultant, counselor, hypnotherapist; b. Mescalero, N.Mex., Sept. 21, 1944; d. Gibson and Magdalena (Magoosh) Fatty; B.S. in Edn., Eastern N.Mex. U., 1968; M.A. in Edn., Ariz. State U., 1976; children—Cynthia Marie Fairbanks, John Lowell Fairbanks. Elementary tchr. Tularosa (N.Mex.) Mcpl. Sch.

System, 1967-68, tchr., 1977-78, 79-80; residential supr. Las Cruces (N.Mex.) Open Door Center, 1978-79; elementary tchr., Bur. Indian Affairs, Acomita Day Sch., Albuquerque area, 1969-70; tchr. counselor Bur. Indian Affairs, Ft. Apache Agency, Phoenix (Ariz.) Area, 1972-75; pres. Learning Concepts, 1980—; cons. United Mgmt. System, Inc. of Ariz., 1980—; pvt. practice, 1980—; youth addiction counselor Phoenix Indian Center, Inc., Phoenix, 1981; cons. Advanced Learning Network, Mankato, Minn. Native Am. program coordinator Parents Anonymous of Ariz., 1982. Mem. Am. Personnel Guidance Assn., Nat. Assn. Female Execs., Ariz. Soc. Profl. Hypnotists, Soc. Accelerated Learning and Teaching, Internat. Platform Assn., NEA, AAUW, Congress Am. Indians, Am. Assn. Profl. Hypnotists. Home: 2628 N 71st St Scottsdale AZ 85257

LAWSON, HARRY HANNON, psychologist, educator, cons.; b. Hayneville, Ala., June 14, 1936; s. John C. and Zeola B. (Bradley) L.; m. Laura M. Steele, Sept. 17, 1961; children—Shenita, Cassandra. B.A. in History magna cum laude, Chapman Coll., 1973; Ph.D. in Clin. Psychology (Am. Psychol. Assn. fellow), U. Ariz. 1979. Cert. psychologist, Ariz. Enlisted in U.S. Air Force, 1954; to service in Netherlands, 1956-59, Vietnam, 1965-66; ret., 1974; coordinator fin. aid and student activities Victory Valley Community Coll., 1974-75; intern in psychology U. So. Calif. Med. Ctr., 1978-79; psychologist Palo Verde Mental Health Clinic, Tucson, 1979—; assoc. faculty Pima Community Coll., 1979—. Bd. dirs. Tucson chpt. NAACP. Decorated Air Force Commendation medal, Comdt.'s award. Mem. Am. Psychol. Assn., Assn. Black Psychologists, So. Ariz. Psychol. Assn. Democrat. Author: College-Bound Blacks: How to Succeed in College, 1983. Home: 2051 W Brichta Dr Tucson AZ 85745 Office: 2051 W Brichta Dr Tucson AZ 85745

LAWSON, JAMES RICHARD, devel. engr.; b. Salamanca, N.Y., Nov. 27, 1934; s. Arthur Edward and Velma (Helby) L.; A.S., SUNY, 1955; m. Joyce Rebecca Kame, Apr. 24, 1954; children—Jerry Richard, Jamie Robert. Lab. asst. Westinghouse Co. Scholarship Program, Bath, N.Y., 1952-53; shop asst. A.S. Wickstrom Co., 1954-55; application and market engr. Clark Bros. Co., Olean, N.Y., 1957-66; with Solar Turbines Internat., San Diego, 1966—, now sr. devel. engr. Mem. 44th Dist. Congl. Adv. Com. Served with U.S. Army, 1955-57. Republican. Presbyterian. Home: 6283 Lake Lomond San Diego CA 92119 Office: 2200 Harbor Dr San Diego CA 92138

LAWSON, NEIL HENRY, oil company executive; b. Springfield, Mass., Nov. 21, 1934; s. Henry Way and Cecelia Marie (Choinere) L.; B.S. in M.E., U. Vt., 1958; m. Priscilla Flora Conover, July 1, 1960; children—Dean, Kent, Dawn. Constrn. and maintenance supr. Shell Oil Co., Syracuse, N.Y., 1958-62, dist. engr., 1962-63, asphalt sales rep., Savannah, Ga., 1963-68, N.Y., Conn., R.I., 1968-69, head office rep., 1969-72, dist. mgr., San Francisco comml. sales dist., 1972-82, dist. account mgr. asphalt sales, 1983—. Sustaining mem. Republican. Nat. Com.; fin. dir., chmn. Boosters Club, Contra Costa Christian High Sch., 1980-81. Registered profl. engr., N.Y., Ga., S.C., Tex. Mem. Nat. Soc. Profl. Engrs., Calif. Soc. Profl. Engrs., Sigma Alpha Epsilon. Republican. Presbyterian. Clubs: Commonwealth, Round Hill Golf and Country. Home: 2132 Dunblane Ct Walnut Creek CA 94598 Office: PO Box 250 San Ramon CA 94583

LAXALT, PAUL, senator; b. Reno, Aug. 2, 1922; s. Dominique and Theresa (Alpetche) L.; student Santa Clara U., 1940-43; B.S., LL.B., Denver U., 1949; m. Jackalyn Ross, June 23, 1946 (div.); children—Gail, Sheila, John, Michelle, Kevin, Kathleen; m. 2d, Carol Wilson, Jan. 2, 1976; 1 dau., Denise. Admitted to Nev. bar, 1949; practice in Carson City; partner firm Laxalt, Ross & Laxalt, 1954-62; dist. atty. Ormsby County, 1951-54; city atty. Carson City, 1954-55; lt. gov. Nev., 1962-66, gov. Nev., 1967-70; sr. partner Laxalt, Berry & Allison, Carson City, 1970-74; U.S. senator from Nev., 1975—. Pres. Ormsby House Hotel and Casino, Carson City, 1972-74. Mem. ABA, Am. Legion, VFW. Club: Eagles. Office: 323A Russell Senate Office Bldg Washington DC 20510

LAY, S. HOUSTON, lawyer, diplomat, educator; b. Virden, Ill., Jan. 31, 1912; s. Samuel Houston and Pearl (Jones) L.; A.A., Blackburn Coll., 1931, A.B., U. Ill., 1936, J.D., 1937, LL.M., Columbia U., 1938, m. Eleanore Erikson, Sept. 9, 1939; 1 son, Samuel Houston III. Admitted to Ill. bar, 1937, U.S. Supreme Ct. bar, 1950, D.C. bar, 1952; sr. atty. Office of Gen. Counsel, REA, Dept. Agr., 1938-42; dep. asst. legal adviser adminstrn. and fgn. services Dept. State, 1946-50; chief adminstrv. law sect. Office of Gen. Counsel, Office of U.S. High Commr. Germany, Frankfort and Bonn, 1950-51, dir. law com. and legis. affairs div., 1951-53, asst. gen. counsel, 1953-54; dep. dir., then acting dir. Office of Spl. Consular Services, Dept. State, 1954-55; counsel mut. security affairs, NATO officer Am. embassy, Athens, Greece, then sr. insp. Fgn. Service Inspection Corps, Dept. State, 1955-58; head team to survey ops. Visa Office, Dept. State, 1961-62; dir. internat. affairs and legal profession program Am. Bar Found., 1962-67; partner firm Rose, Stansbury, Albright, Mason and Lay, Chgo. and Washington, 1964-67; prof. Calif. Western Sch. Law, San Diego, 1967—, dir. Inst. Study of Internat. Law, 1974—; disting. vis. prof. McGeorge Sch. Law, U. Pacific, 1974-75. Served from lt. (j.g.) to comdr. USNR, 1942-46. Mem. Inter-Am., Am., Fed., Ill., Chgo. bar assns., Am. Soc. Internat. Law, Fgn. Law Assn., Am. Inst. Aeros. and Astronautics, World Peace Through Law Center, Chgo. Council Fgn. Relations, Am. Fgn. Service Assn., Am. Acad. Polit. and Social Sci., Phi Alpha Delta, Phi Rho Pi. Author: (with Howard Taubenfeld) The Law of Activity in Space, 1970; New Directions in the Law of the Sea, Vols. 1-4, 1973, Vols. 5-10, 1977; Multivolume New Dimensions in International Air Law, 1981; Direct Broadcast Satellites, 1981; contbr. articles to profl. jours. Home: 5930 Folsom Dr La Jolla CA 92037 Office: Calif Western Sch Law 350 Cedar St San Diego CA 92101

LAYCOX, JACK WILLIAM, painter, designer; b. Auburn, Placer County, Calif., Apr. 11, 1924; s. William Harper and Florence Marion (Colt) L.; m. Jayne Amason, Oct. 21, 1949. B.F.A. San Francisco State U., 1948; postgrad. Inst. Allende, Mex., 1978. Designer, art dir. Bacon Am. Corp., Muncie, Ind., 1948-63; designer Mission-Regency Cards, N.Y.C., 1964-67; commd. work includes: calendar series, Gen. Tire Internat. Corp., Akron, Ohio, 1972, 73, 76, poster series, Delta Airlines, 1978-82; owner, fine artist, Jack Laycox Galleries, Carmel, Calif., 1970—; art instr. Sunset Studio 15, Carmel, Sunset Cultural Ctr., Carmel. Bd. dirs. Monterey Peninsula Cypressaires Chorus. Recipient Best of Show award Diablo Pagent Arts, 1961; 2d award Watercolor Soc. Western Artists Ann., 1963; Champion Papers award, 1976; DeAnza Expdn. award, 1976; Degree of Honor award Soc. Western Artists, San Francisco, 1978. Mem. West Coast Watercolor Soc., Soc. Western Artists. Republican. Club: Monterey Peninsula. Author: Dramatic Paintings from Familiar Scenes, 1972; produced Jay Laycox Lithography Series, 1976, Laycox Fine Arts Lithographs, 1980. Home: PO Box 5054 Carmel CA 93921 Office: Jack Laycox Galleries PO Box 5054 Carmel CA 93921

LAYDEN, DAVID ARTHUR, accountant; b. Providence, Oct. 17, 1945; s. Thomas Addin and Mary Elizabeth (Hoey) L. B.B.A., Sacred Heart U., 1967. Acct., Dictaphone Corp., Bridgeport, Conn., 1967-69, City of Bridgeport, 1969-80; fin. dir. City of Gillette (Wyo.), 1980—. Mem. Am. Mgmt. Assn., Nat. Assn. Accts., Mcpl. Fin. Officers Assn., Mcpl. Treas. Assn., Wyo. Assn. Mcpl. Clks. and Treas. Roman Catholic. Clubs: Moose K.C. bus (treas. 1981—). Office: City of Gillette 301 S Gillette Ave Gillette WY 82716

LAYDEN, FRANCIS PATRICK, professional basketball team manager; b. Bklyn., Jan. 5, 1932. Ed., Niagara U. Head coach and athletic dir. Adelphi-Suffolk Coll., Niagara U., Niagara Falls, N.Y., 1968-76; asst. coach Atlanta Hawks, 1976-79; gen. mgr. Utah Jazz, Nat. Basketball Assn., 1979—. Bd. dirs. Utah Prevention of Blindness, Utah Spl. Olympics, Utah chpt. Multiple Sclerosis. Served to 1st lt. U.S. Army. Office: Utah Jazz The Salt Palace 100 SW Temple Suite 206 Salt Lake City UT 84101*

LAYMAN, DONNA JEAN, retail exec.; b. Buffalo, June 10, 1948; d. Harold Charles and Jeanne May (Detrich) Critoph; B.A., Parsons Coll., 1970; m. John William Layman, Aug. 9, 1969; 1 dau., Amy Ruth. Trouble shooter Hugh Johnson Brokerage Firm, Buffalo, 1967; tchr. spl. edn., public schs., Fairfield, Iowa, 1969-70; tchr., public schs., Peoria, Ariz., 1970-71; sales rep. Amigo Inc., Glendale, Ariz., 1977, disability counselor, 1977—, area mgr. Ariz., Nev., Utah, 1978—. Vol., Phoenix Gen. Hosp., 1974—; jr. vol. coordinator Ariz. Hosp. Assn. Council, 1976-79; leader Ariz. Campfire Girls, 1977-81; mem. Mayor's Com. on Employment of Handicapped, 1980-81. Mem. Multiple Sclerosis Soc. Office: 19617 N 43d Ave Glendale AZ 85308

LAYMAN, THOMAS A., economist; b. San Antonio, May 12, 1951; s. Wilburn E. and Martha Ann L. B.A. magna cum laude, Vanderbilt U., 1973; Ph.D., U. N.C., 1979. Vis. instr. dept. econs. N.C. State U., Raleigh, 1976-78; asst. prof. dept. econs. Ariz. State U., Tempe, 1978-79; v.p., internat. economist Crocker Nat. Bank, San Francisco, 1979—; lectr. Korean Bankers Program, U. Wash., Seattle, 1980-83. State Farms Cos. Found. fellow, 1973-74; Julian Price fellow, 1973-74; Chgo. Bd. Trade Found. fellow, 1977-78. Mem. Am. Econ. Assn., So. Econ. Assn., Nat. Assn. Bus. Economists, World Affairs Council San Francisco. Office: Dept Econs Crocker Nat Bank 1 Montgomery St West Tower San Francisco CA 94104

LAYSER, EARLE FRANKLIN, forester, biologist, ecologist; b. Lebanon, Pa., Dec. 14, 1939; s. Earle F. and Elsie M. (Reichard) L.; B.S. in Forest Sci. (teaching asst. 1964-65), U. Mont., 1965; M.S. in Botany and Plant Ecology (teaching asst. 1965-66, research fellow 1969-70) SUNY, Syracuse, 1970; postgrad. Wash. State U., 1970-71; m. Sandra Lee Simons, June 9, 1963; children—Brett Eric, Ryon Earle. With Pa. Dept. Forestry and Waters, Slate Run, 1961; seasonal timber technician U.S. Dept. Agr., Forest Service, Mont., 1962, Pa., 1965, smoke jumper, 1963-64; forester Intermountain Lumber Co., Missoula, Mont., 1966-67; herbarium curator asst. Wash. State U., Pullman, 1970-71; with U.S. Dept. Agr., Forest Service, 1970-80, resource br. chief Bridger-Teton Nat. Forest, Wyo., 1977-80; owner, mgr., cons. Land Mgmt. Services, Jackson, Wyo., 1980—; v.p. IMEC/Intermountain Mineral and Energy Cons., 1982—; mem. working group, chmn. forest ecosystems Idaho State Natural Areas System, 1975-76; mem. N.Mex. Environ. Council, 1977; mem. U.S. Dept. Agr. Forest Services task force on Middlesnake River Dam Proposal, 1975, Nat. Forest Mgmt. Act, 1977. Served with USN, 1957-60. Recipient U.S. Dept. Forest service cash award, 1975; Am. Motors nat. conservation award, 1977; lic. real estate salesman, Wyo.; cert. silviculturist, ecologist, wildlife biologist. Mem. Soc. Am. Foresters, Ecol. Soc. Am. cert. profl. ecologist AAAS, Nat. Audubon Soc., Nat. Wildlife Fedn., Am. Forestry Assn., Sigma Xi. Clubs: Elks, Toastmasters (ednl. v.p. 1972). Contbr. articles on bryology, plant taxonomy, ecology wildlife, and forestry to profl. jours. Address: PO Box 2116 Jackson WY 83001

LAYTON, HARRY CHRISTOPHER, artist, lectr.; b. Safford, Ariz., Nov. 17, 1938; s. Christopher E. and Eurilda (Welker) L.; L.H.D., Sussex Coll., Eng., 1967; D.F.A. (hon.), London Inst. Applied Research, 1972; D.D. (hon.), St. Matthew U., Ohio, 1970, Ph.D. (hon.), 1970; m. Karol Barbara Kendall, July 11, 1964; children—Deborah, Christopher, Joseph, Elisabeth, Faith, Aaron, Gretchen, Benjamin, Justin, Matthew, Peter. Lectr. ancient art Serra Cath. High Sch., 1963-64, Los Angeles Dept. Parks and Recreation, summer 1962, 63, 64; interior decorator Cities of Hawthorne, Lawndale, Compton, Gardena and Torrance (Calif.), 1960-68, one-man shows paintings, Nahas Dept. Stores, 1962, 64; group shows include: Gt. Western Savs. & Loan, Lawndale, Calif., 1962, Gardena (Calif.) Adult Sch., 1965, Serra Cath. High Sch., Gardena, 1963, represented in permanent collections: Sussex Coll., Eng., Gardena Masonic Lodge, Culver City-Foshey Masonic Lodge, Gt. Western Savs. & Loan; paintings include: The Fairy Princess, 1975, Nocturnal Covenant, 1963, Blindas Name, 1962, Creation, 1962. Elder Ch. of Jesus Christ of Latter-day Saints, Santa Monica, Calif., 1963—. Mem. Gardena Valley Art Assn., Centinella Valley Art Assn., Internat. Soc. Artists, Internat. Platform Assn., Am. Security Council, Soc. for Early Historic Archaeology, Am. Councilor's Soc. of Psychol. Counselors, Am. Legion, Alpha Psi Omega. Republican. Clubs: Masons (32 deg.), Shriners, K.T. Home: 3932 McLaughlin Ave Los Angeles CA 90066

LAZAR, RUBIN MANUEL, lawyer; b. Montreal, Que., Can., Nov. 21, 1928; s. Isaac and Celia (Maron) L.; came to U.S., 1939, naturalized, 1946; student UCLA, 1945-46, 48; J.D. cum laude, Loyola U., Los Angeles, 1951; m. Serene Sperling, Dec. 24, 1950; children—Mark B., David J., Robin. Admitted to Calif. bar, 1952; law clk. to judge U.S. Dist. Ct., 1951-52; pvt. practice, Beverly Hills, 1952—; partner Silver & Lazar, P.C., 1956—; lectr. continuing edn. series Calif. State Bar, 1962—. Vice chmn. attys. div. United Jewish Welfare Fund, 1962-63; pres. Adat Ari El (formerly Valley Jewish Community Center and Temple), 1969-70; v.p. Los Angeles Hebrew High Sch., 1971-76; patron U. Judaism. Recipient William Tell Aggeler award and Bur. Nat. Affairs award Loyola U. Sch. Law, 1951. Fellow Am. Acad. Matrimonial Lawyers; mem. Am. Judicature Soc., Calif. (past com. chmn.), Los Angeles, Beverly Hills bar assns., Am. Arbitration Assn. (arbitrator), Phi Delta Phi, Pi Kappa Delta. Mem. B'nai B'rith (pres. Los Angeles 1959). Home: 3920 Longridge St Sherman Oaks CA 91423 Office: 1901 Ave of Stars Suite 1451 Los Angeles CA 90067

LAZARUS, STEVEN S., management consultant, educator, computer scientist; b. Rochester, N.Y., June 16, 1943; s. Alfred and Ceal H. (Rothstein) L.; m. Elissa Camen, Apr. 20, 1945; children—Michael R., Stuart G., Jean I. B.S., Cornell U., Ithaca, N.Y., 1966; M.S. in Engring., Poly. Inst. N.Y., 1967; Ph.D. in Bus. Adminstrn., U. Rochester, 1974. Asst. prof. prodn. mgmt. Dartmouth Coll., Hanover, N.H., 1973-74; sr. analyst Spectrum Research, Inc., Denver, 1974-76; asst. prof. Coll. Bus. Adminstrn., U. Denver, 1976-79; pres. Mgmt. Systems Analysis Corp., Denver, 1976—; sr. scientist, dir. Denver office JRB Assocs., Englewood, Colo, 1979—; instr. Grad. Sch. Mgmt., U. Rochester, 1967-69; instr. dept. econs. Monash U., Melbourne, Australia, 1971-72; instr. U. Phoenix, 1983—; assoc. prof. Colo. State Coll., Denver, 1983—; adj. assoc. prof. internat. studies U. Denver, 1984—; cons. to hosp., 1974—. Mem. Colo. Health Care Policy Adv. Bd., 1977-79. NDEA fellow, 1968-71. Mem. Ops. Research Soc. Am., Inst. Mgmt. Scis. Contbr. articles to jours., publs. Home: 7023 E Eastman Ave Denver CO 80224 Office: 40DTC W 7935 E Prentice Ave Englewood CO 80111

LAZICH, GILBERT STEVAN, ednl. adminstr.; b. Detroit, July 20, 1926; s. Steven P. and Anna (Mamula) L.; B.A. in History and Slavic Area Studies, U. Mich., Ann Arbor, 1952. M.Ed. in Ednl. Adminstrn. and Supervision, Wayne State U., Detroit, 1968, Ed.D., 1974; m. Lis Hellgren Jørgensen; children—Nils H., S. Peter, Lis Anne, Julia. Tchr., elem. sch. prin., Warren, Mich., 1957-68; instr.-coordinator student teaching Wayne State U., 1968-69; Charles S. Mott fellow, Flint, Mich., 1969-70; asst. supt. curriculum and instrn. Niles (Mich.) Community Schs., 1970-74; asst. supt. instrn. Interboro Sch. Dist., Prospect Park, Pa., 1974-80; instr. ednl. adminstrn. and supervision Bever Coll., Glenside, Pa., 1980; with Dept. Instrn., Coordinative Services, Office of Santa Clara County Supt. Schs., San Jose, Calif., 1980—. Adv. council Nationalities Service Center; bd. dirs. South Valley Symphony. Mem. Mich. Assn. Elementary Sch. Prins. (exec. council 1965-69), Pa. Assn. Supervision and Curriculum Devel. (pres. Delaware Valley region 1979), Am. Ednl. Research Assn., Assn. Calif. Sch. Adminstrs., Calif. Assn. Compensatory Edn., Nat. Community Edn. Assn., Pa. Assn. Fed. Program Coordinators (v.p. 1978-80). Cert. in elem. and secondary edn., Mich.; cert. sch. adminstr., Pa.; cert. in gen. edn., adminstrn., Calif. Home: 1310 Meadow Ct Morgan Hill CA 95037 Office: 100 Skyport Dr San Jose CA 95115

LE, SON MINH, philosophyer, educator; b. Ninh Binh, Vietnam, Jan. 16, 1945; came to U.S., 1964, naturalized, 1977; s. Chuyen Van and Tuyet Thi (Dinh) L.; B.A. (Presdl. scholar 1964-67), Fordham U., 1967; M.A., Antioch Coll., 1968; Ph.D., Ohio State U., 1971; m. Mary Kai Ming Cheung, Apr. 6, 1969 (dec., 1977); children—Trang M., Dao M., Tri Minh; m. 2d, Marilyn Matsumura, Aug. 9, 1980. Instr. philosophy Franconia Coll., 1968; instr. philosophy Antioch Coll., 1968; instr. Ohio State U., 1968-71, research asst., 1971-74; research asst. U. So. Calif. Med. Center, 1974-75; prof. philosophy Mission Coll., Santa Clara, Calif., 1975—. Mem. U.S. Congressional Adv. Bd. Mem. Am. Philos. Assn., Am. Assn. Advancement of Humanities, Assn. Symbolic Logic, Soc. Health and Human Values, Center for Study of Values, Am. Acad. Polit. and Social Sci. Office: 3000 Mission College Blvd Santa Clara CA 95054

LEA, WAYNE ADAIR, elec. engr., linguist; b. Helena, Mont., Jan. 16, 1940; s. Robert Klondike and Genevieve May (Best) L.; B.S.E.E., Mont. State U., 1962, M.S.E.E., 1964; S.M. in Linguistics, E.E., M.I.T., 1966; Ph.D., Purdue U., 1972; m. Gayle Harriet Johnson, Aug. 6, 1976; 1 dau., Kathy; children by previous marriage—Wayne, David, Christopher, Linda; stepchildren—Daniel Podratz, Kimberly Podratz. Research assoc. Electronics Research Lab., Mont. State Coll., Bozeman, 1962-64; NSF fellow M.I.T. Research Lab. Electronics, Cambridge, 1964-66; mathematician, project leader NASA Electronics Research Center, Cambridge, 1966-70; grad. instr., researcher Purdue Research Found., West Lafayette, Ind., 1970-72; prin. systems design engr. Sperry Univac, St. Paul, 1972-77; research linguist, research engr. Speech Communications Research Lab., Los Angeles, 1977-81; adj. assoc. prof. linguistics U. So. Calif., Los Angeles, 1978—; dir. Speech Sci. Pubs., Santa Barbara, Calif., 1979—; sr. research scientist Signal Tech. Inc., 1981—; prin. investigator Dept. Def. contracts, 1972—; cons. in field. Recipient gold medal Mont. Soc. Engrs., 1961; NSF grantee, 1978—. Mem. Acad. for Forensic Application of Communication Scis. (chmn. 1978—), IEEE (sr.), Am. Assn. Phonetic Scis., Internat. Soc. Phonetic Scis., Missile, Space and Range Pioneers, Acoustical Soc. Am., Sigma Xi, Phi Eta Sigma, Tau Beta Pi. Author: Trends in Speech Recognition, 1980; Computer Recognition of Speech, 1982; Voice Analysis on Trial, 1983; Selecting, Designing and Using Speech Recognizers, 1983; contbr. articles to profl. jours. Home: 889 Sanford Ct Santa Barbara CA 93111 Office: 5951 Encina Rd Goleta CA 93117

LEACH, JOHN FRANK, printing and forest products company executive; b. New Ross, Wexford, Ireland, Mar. 11, 1921; s. John Reginold and Evelyn Muriel (Ard) L.; came to U.S., 1921, naturalized, 1926; B.S. in Indsl. Mgmt., Wayne U., 1950; m. Lee Marie Serre, Dec. 1, 1945; children—John Michael, Suzanne Lee Leach Born. Apprentice tool and die maker Ford Motor Co., Dearborn, Mich., 1934-38, various mfg. positions, 1938-50, prodn. mgr. Cleve. engine plant, 1950-54; dir. mfg. Studebaker-Packard Corp., Detroit, 1954-56; v.p. mfg. Bunker-Ramo Corp. (formerly Amphenol Electronics Corp.), Chgo., 1956-59, div. pres., 1959-63, group exec., 1963-68, exec. v.p., chief operating officer, 1968-72; pres., chief exec. officer, chmn. Arcata Corp., Menlo Park, Calif., 1972-82, vice chmn., 1983—, also dir.; dir. Nat. Safe Depository, Tymshire, Inc., SRI Internat. Council, Consol. Freightways Corp., Fiming Tractor & Equipment Co., Union Bank. Bd. dirs. Bus. Sch., U. Calif.-Berkeley, Calif. C. of C. Served to 2d lt. USAAF, 1943-45. Recipient medal of honor Electronic Industries Assn., 1972. Clubs: University, Palo Alto, Menlo Country, Sunset Ridge Country. Home: 121 Sheridan Way Woodside CA 94062 Office: 3000 Sand Hill Rd Bldg 2 Suite 140 Menlo Park CA 93025

LEACH, ROBERT ALLAN, JR., financial consultant; b. Arlington, Wash., Jan. 4, 1950; s. Robert Allan and Mary (Bruce) L.; B.S., U. Wash., 1972; m. Kathleen Ann Gasper, Feb. 19, 1977. Sales researcher Sta. KIRO, Seattle, 1972-73; v.p., sales mgr. Everett Transmission & Rubber Co. (Wash.) 1973-75; v.p. sales Vernon Publs., Inc., Seattle, 1975-80; ptnr., v.p. Gail, Bachert, Leach & Assocs., Seattle 1980-82; fin. cons. Foster & Marshall/Am. Express, Lynnwood, Wash., 1982—. Mem. Seattle C. of C. South Snohomish County C. of C. Republican. Club: Everett Golf and Country. Home: 14200 Cascadian Way Everett WA 98204 Office: 18710 33d St W Lynnwood WA 98036

LEACH-CLARK, MARY AGNES, educator, counselor of handicapped; b. Wichita, Kans., Aug. 5, 1931; d. Frank N. and May Jean (Hollow) Leach; m. Courtney Clark, June 12, 1954 (div.); children—David Courtney, Bruce Colin, Anne Clark Nelson, Jeffrey Charles. B.S. in Edn., U. Kans., 1954; M.Ed. in Counseling, Wichita State U., 1978. Lic. counselor, Kans., Colo. Tchr. gifted Dist. 110, Overland Park, Kans., 1954-56; activity dir. Booth Meml. Hosp., Wichita, 1978; tchr. personal and social adjustment classes, Wichita, 1979-80; therapist Aidance Devel. Programs, 1980-82, counselor, 1982—; instr. Community Coll., Greeley, Colo., 1983; art curriculum coordinator Creative Arts Ctr., Greeley, 1983—. Mem. AAUP, Am. Mental Health Counselors, Amer. Personnel and Guidance Assn., Kans. Mental Health Counselors, Kans. Personnel and Guidance Assn., Internat. Platform Assn., Kans. Author's Club, Alpha Chi Omega. Office: Box 2354 Greeley CO 80631

LEACHMAN, SKIP, pharmacist; b. Winnipeg, Man., Can., June 30, 1943; came to U.S., 1956, naturalized, 1961; s. Harry and Shirley L.; B.S. in Pharmacy, Oreg. State U., 1969; m. Judy B. Baer, May 6, 1973. Asst. dir. pharmacy Drs. Hosp., Lakewood, Calif., 1972-77; dir. pharmacy Garfield Med. Center, Monterey Park, Calif., 1977-82; asst. dir. pharmacy Hosp. of Good Samaritan, Los Angeles, 1982-83; with Family Health Program Long Beach, Calif., 1983—; instr. clin. pharmacy U. So. Calif., 1982-83; pharmacy cons. Internat. div. Nat. Med. Enterprises, Los Angeles, 1980—; organizer, cons. seminars; mgmt. cons. Oreg. State U. Health Professions grantee, 1965-69. Mem. Am. Soc. Hosp. Pharmacists, Am. Pharm. Assn., So. Calif. Soc. Hosp. Pharmacists (bd. dirs., vice chmn. com. for profl. affairs). Home: 5210 Canton St Long Beach CA 90815

LEADBETTER, JOHN EMERSON, engineering consultant; b. Garden City, Mo., Aug. 28, 1912; s. Adelbert and Hallie Fern (Headington) L.; m. Dolores Mae Kindschi, Aug. 8, 1937; 1 dau., Linda Rae Leadbetter Gabriele. Student U. Okla., 1930-32. With extension tng. div. Diesel Engring. Sch., Los Angeles, 1934-37; extension div. dir. Aero Industries Tech. Inst., Los Angeles, 1937-42; gen. supr. indsl. relations div. Northrop Aircraft, Inc., Hawthorne, Calif., 1942-53; asst. gen. mgr. Northrop Aero Inst., Inc., Hawthorne, 1953-54; pres. Assoc. Aero Sci. Labs., Inc., Hawthorne, 1954-68; tech. cons. Calif. Legislature, Sacramento, 1969-70; engring. cons., Tahoe, Calif., 1971—. Bd. dirs. Centinela Valley YMCA, 1963-64; bd. trustees El Camino (Calif.) Jr. Coll., 1964-69, pres. bd., 1966-67. Mem. Hawthorne C. of C. Republican. Lodges: Rotary (dist. chmn. 1959-60, pres. Hawthorne chpt. 1958-59), Elks. Co-author: Sketch-Easy Training Course in Three-D, Free Hand Sketching, 1956. Home and Office: PO Box 17905 South Lake Tahoe CA 95706

LEAGUE, VINCENTE CONRAD, management company executive; b. Indpls., June 28, 1947; s. Jonah Bemouth and Thelma Ruth (Pride) L.; student Butler U., 1965-68; B.A. in Pub. Adminstrn., Chgo. State U., 1976. Dir. in charge outreach Soul Ark Youth ministry, Indpls., 1970-71; project dir. Community Orgn. Program, Eastside Indpls., 1971-72; asst. dir. Region 5 Alcohol & Drug Abuse Tng. Center, Chgo., 1972-78; project dir. Region 8 Tng. and Devel. Center, Oakland, 1978—; exec. dir. A.H. Tng. & Devel. Systems, Inc., Oakland, Calif., 1981—; prin. Calif. Wine Country, Napa, Calif., 1981—; cons. numerous orgns. Bd. dirs. Person Edn.-Devel. Edn., Mpls., 1981—; chmn. bd. dirs. Grantsmanship Center, Los Angeles, 1974-81. Mem. Am. Soc. Tng. and Devel., Nat. Mgmt. Assn. (bd. dirs. 1983—), Nat. Assn. Prevention Profls. (pres., co-founder Eugene Oreg., co-conv. coordinator 3d ann. conv. 1980). Author: Developing Successful Programs, 1978, rev. edit., 1983; Funding Handbook, 1981; Management: A Guide for Prevention Programs, 1982; Inside Napa Valley, 1982. Home: 151 Lakeside St Apt 302 Oakland CA 94612 Office: 100 Webster Suite 206 Oakland CA 94607

LEAKE, DONALD LEWIS, oral and maxillofacial surgeon; b. Cleveland, Okla., Nov. 6, 1931; s. Walter Wilson and Martha Lee (Crow) L.; A.B., U. So. Calif., 1953, M.A., 1957; D.M.D., Harvard U., 1962; M.D., Stanford U., 1969; m. Rosemary Dobson, Aug. 2O, 1964; children—John Andrew Dobson, Elizabeth, Catherine. Intern, Mass. Gen. Hosp., Boston, 1962-63, resident, 1963-64; postdoctoral fellow Harvard U., 1964-66; practice medicine specializing in oral and maxillofacial surgery; asso. oral surgery Children's Hosp. Med. Center, Boston, 1966-69; asso. prof., dental dir., chief oral surgery Harbor-UCLA Med. Center, Torrance, 1970-74, prof., 1974—; asso. dir. Dental Research Inst., UCLA, 1979-82, dir., 1982—; cons. Long Beach (Calif.) Meml. Hosp., Long Beach Community Hosp., St. Mary's Hosp., Long Beach, Sepulveda (Calif.) VA Hosp., Martin Luther King Hosp., Los Angeles, 1972—. Recipient 1st Prize award with greatest distinction oboe and chamber music Brussels Royal Conservatory Music, 1956. Fellow ACS, Am. Coll. Dentists; mem. So. Calif. Acad. Oral Pathology, Internat. Assn. Dental Research, Am. Assn. Oral and Maxillofacial Surgeons, So. Calif. Soc. Oral Surgeons, Med. Research Assn. Calif., AAAS, European Assn. Maxillofacial Surgeons, Brit. Assn. Oral Surgeons, ASTM, Soc. Biomaterials, Internationale Gesellschaft fur Kiefer-Gesichts-Chirurgie, Phi Beta Kappa, Phi Kappa Phi. Club: Harvard of Boston. Contbr. articles to profl. jours. Home: 2 Crest Rd W Rolling Hills CA 90274 Office: Harbor-UCLA Med Center 1000 W Carson St Torrance CA 90509 also 701 E 28th St Suite 415 Long Beach CA 90806

LEAPTROTT, JOHN J., JR., accountant; b. Savannah, Ga., May 27, 1950; s. John J. and Jeanette M. (Ek) L.; m. Marsha S. Engle, June 9, 1973; 1 son, Jeffrey R. B.S., Oreg. State U., 1972. C.P.A., Oreg. Assoc. Kohnen, Larson & Co., Roseburg, Oreg., 1975-83; sole practice acctg., 1983—. Served to capt. Air N.G., 1968-77. Mem. Am. Inst. C.P.A.s, Oreg. Soc. C.P.A.s. Republican. Clubs: Kiwanis (past treas. Roseburg), Elks. Office: 1600-2 NE Vine St Roseburg OR 97470

LEAR, NORMAN MILTON, writer, producer, director television and films; b. New Haven, July 27, 1922; s. Herman and Jeanette (Seicol) L.; m. Frances A. Loeb, Dec. 7, 1956; children—Ellen Lear Reiss, Kate B., Maggie B. Engaged in pub. relations, 1945-49; comedy writer for TV, 1950-54; writer, dir. TV and films, 1954-59; writer, producer, dir. for TV and films, 1959—; writer, producer films: Come Blow Your Horn, 1963, Divorce Am. Style, 1967, The Night They Raided Minsky's, 1968; writer, producer, dir. film: Cold Turkey, 1971; creator, producer TV shows: TV Guide Awards Show, 1962, Henry Fonda and the Family, 1963, Andy Williams spls., also Andy Williams series, 1965, Robert Young and the Family, 1970; developer TV shows; creator All in the Family, 1971; creator, developer Maude, 1972—; co-developer TV show Sanford and Son, 1972; developer Good Times, 1974, The Jeffersons, 1975, Hot L Balt., 1975, Mary Hartman, Mary Hartman, 1976, The Dumplings, 1976, One Day at a Time, 1976, All's Fair, 1976, A Year at the Top, 1977; co-creator All that Glitters, 1977; creator Fernwood 2 Night, 1977; developer The Baxters, 1979, Palmerstown, 1980; creator, developer I Love Liberty, 1982. Pres. ACLU Found. So. Calif., 1973—; bd. dirs. People for Am. Way. Served with USAAF, 1941-45. Decorated Air medal with 4 oak leaf clusters; named one of top ten motion picture producers Motion Picture Exhibitors, 1963, 67, 68, Showman of Yr., Publicists Guild, 1971, Assn. Bus. Mgrs., 1972, Broadcaster of Yr., Internat. Radio and TV Soc., 1973, Man of Yr. Hollywood chpt. Nat. Acad. TV Arts and Scis., 1973; recipient Emmy awards for All in the Family, 1970-73, Peabody award for All in the Family, 1978, Gold medal Internat. Radio and TV Soc., 1982. Mem. Writers Guild Am., Dirs. Guild Am., AFTRA. Office: 1901 Ave of Stars Los Angeles CA 90067

LEARAKOS, THEODORE JAMES, mortgage banker; b. Tucson, Nov. 6, 1954; s. James Theodore and Georgette (Vakaros) L.; m. Kathleen Ann Keitch, Sept. 6, 1980. A.A. in Food Service (Scholar), Orange Coast Coll., 1976; B.A. in Mktg. and Merchandising, Calif. State U.-Fullerton, 1978; cert. of completion Am. Airlines Traffic Sch., Los Angeles, 1980. Lic. real estate agt., Calif. Account exec. Hughes Ad House, Newport Beach, Calif., 1975-80; gen. mgr. Ultimate Travel Agy., Tustin, Calif., 1980-81; advt. mgr. Lyco Food Products Co., Santa Fe Springs, Calif., 1980—; loan officer Equity Converters, Newport Beach, 1983—. Active Balboa Bay Club, Newport Beach, 1978—. Mem. Tustin Jaycees. Greek Orthodox. Club: Orange Baseball Assn. (Orange). Office: Equity Converters 4041 MacArthur Blvd Suite 170 Newport Beach CA 92660

LEARNED, ELEANOR MARIE (MRS. G.H. LEARNED, JR.), mineral museum curator; b. San Francisco, Jan. 10, 1913; d. Charles Milton and Eleanor Olivia (Johannesen) Bauer; m. George Harold Learned, Jr., Oct. 31, 1937; children—Ann Holley McWhirk, Richard Arthur. Student E. Contra Costa Jr. Coll., 1953. Typist, Western States Life Ins. Co., 1930-33; cost acct. Calif. Packing Corp., 1933-37, acct., 1965-69; sr. info. clk., acting curator div. mines and geology, State Mineral Mus., San Francisco, 1970-80, curator, 1980—; cons.; instr. mineral identification and micromounting. Recipient Golden Bear award Calif. Fedn. Mineral. Socs., San Francisco, 1976. Mem. Mineral. Soc. Am., Calif. Assn. Mus., Calif. Acad. Scis., San Francisco Gem and Mineral Soc. Republican. Presbyterian. Club: P.E.O. Contbr. articles to profl. jours. Office: Calif Div Mines and Geology Ferry Bldg Room 2022 San Francisco CA 94111

LEARNER, JUDITH, broadcasting company executive; b. Pitts., Apr. 14, 1936; d. Harry and Anne Kleinberg; children—Howard, Steven. Student Chatham Coll. for Women, 1953-55, Pa. State U., 1955-56; B.A., U. Wis., 1972. Appeared in The Trial, 1963, Anne of a Thousand Days, 1966; Copy dir., disc. jockey Sta. WISN, Camden, N.J., 1965-67; asst. producer Les Crane Show, KTTV, Los Angeles, 1967-68; anchor woman, dir. public affairs Sta. WISC-TV, Madison, Wis., 1972-75; media buyer Ed Libov Assocs., Los Angeles, 1976-78; asst. dir. public affairs div. First Interstate Bank, Los Angeles, 1978-79; advt. supr. First Interstate Bank Corp., Los Angeles, 1979-80; dir. creative services Sta. KABC, Los Angeles, 1980—; actress various TV and stage prodns., 1960's and 70's. Named Phila. Woman of Yr., Mayor James Tate, 1963; recipient Outstanding Service award Leukemia Council, 1977; Coro Found. fellow, 1978. Mem. Women in Bus., Women in Communications, Women in Pub. Affairs, Pub. Relations Soc. Am., Nat. Leukemia Broadcast Council, Coro Found. Assocs.

LEASE, JANE ETTA, librarian; b. Kansas City, Kans., Apr. 10, 1924; d. Joy Alva and Emma (Jaggard) Omer; B.S. in Home Econs., U. Ariz., 1957; M.S. in Edn., Ind. U., 1962; M.S. in L.S., U. Denver, 1967; m. Richard J. Lease, Jan. 16, 1960; children—Janet (Mrs. Jacky B. Radifera), Joyce (Mrs. Robert J. Carson), Julia Lease Marvin, Cathy (Mrs. Edward F. Warren); stepchildren—Richard Jay II, William Harley. Newspaper reporter Ariz. Daily Star, Tucson, 1937-39; asst. home agt. Dept. Agr., 1957; homemaking tchr., Ft. Huachuca, Ariz., 1957-60; head tchr. Stonebelt Council Retarded Children, Bloomington, Ind., 1960-61; reference clk. Ariz. State U. Library, 1964-66; edn. and psychology librarian N.Mex. State U., 1969-71; Amway distbr., 1973—; cons. solid wastes, distressed land problems reference remedies, 1967; ecology lit. research and cons., 1966—; ind. observer 1st World Conf. Human Environment, 1972. Mem. NEA, N.Mex. Edn. Assn., P.E.O., D.A.R., N.Mex. Rifle and Pistol Assn., Las Cruces Story League. Methodist (lay leader). Address: 2145 Boise Dr Las Cruces NM 88001

LEASE, RICHARD JAY, former police officer, educator, consultant; b. Cherokee, Ohio, Dec. 10, 1914; s. Harold and Mabelle (Fullerton) L.; m. Marjorie Faye Stoughton, Sept. 2, 1939 (div. Apr. 1957); children—Richard Jay II, William Harley; m. Jane Etta Omer, Jan. 16, 1960; stepchildren—Janet Radifera, Joyce Garson, Julia Marvin, Catherine Warren. Student Wittenberg U., 1932-33; B.A., U. Ariz., 1937, M.A., 1961; postgrad. Ind. U., 1950, 60, Ariz. State U., 1956, 63-64, 67—; grad. So. Police Inst., U. Louisville, 1955. Grad. asst. U. Ariz., 1937-38; with Tucson Police Dept., from 1938, advanced from patrolman to sgt., also served as safety officer Pima County Sheriffs Dept., Tucson, 1953, patrol supr., 1953-55, investigator, 1955-56; tchr. sci. pub. schs., Tucson, 1957-59; lectr. dept. police adminstrn. Ind. U., 1960-65; asst. prof. police sci. N.Mex. State U., Las Cruces, 1965—; cons. law enforcement problems HEW, 1960, Indpls. Police Dept., 1962, police sci. dept. Harrisburg Community Coll., 1967, Phoenix Police Dept., 1968—; adviser police tng. programs various small city police depts., Ind., 1960-63, Indpls., 1962; mem. oral bd. for selection chief in Bateville, Ind., 1962, oral bd. for selection sgts. and lts. Las Cruces Police Dept., 1966—; participant numerous FBI seminars. Active youth work, philanthropy among Am. Indians in S.W.; founder awards for outstanding ROTC cadets N.Mex. State U., 1967; founder Wiltberger ann. awards Nat. Police Combat Pistol Matches; scoutmaster Yucca council Boy Scouts Am., 1966—. Served to 1st lt. USMCR, 1942-45; PTO. Fellow Am. Acad. Forensic Scis. (sec. gen. sect.); mem. Internat. Assn. Chiefs Police, Internat. Assn. Police Profs., Brit. Acad. Forensic Scis., Can. Soc. Forensic Sci., Am. Soc. Criminology, Ret. Officers Assn., Assn. U.S. Army (2d v.p. 1969—), NEA, N.Mex. Edn. Assn., N.Mex. Police and Sheriffs Assn., Internat. Crossroads, Nat. Rifle Assn. (benefactor mem.), Sigma Chi. Club: Masons, Shriners, Elks. Author: (with Robert F. Borkenstein) Alcohol and Road Traffic: Problems of Enforcement and Prosecution, 1963; cons. editor: Police; research and publs. on chem. tests for intoxication, correlation of reading disabilities and delinquency, psychol. errors of honest witnesses. Home: 2145 Bois Dr Las Cruces NM 88001

LEAVITT, DANA GIBSON, corp. exec.; b. Framingham, Mass., Dec. 4, 1925; s. Luther C. and Margaret (Gibson) L.; B.A., Brown U., 1948, student Harvard Bus. Sch., 1954-55; m. Frances Smith, Apr. 12, 1952; children—Margaret Gibson, Jonathan. Home office rep. Aetna Life Ins. Co., Boston also Long Beach, Calif., 1949-54; v.p., sec.-treas., exec. v.p. North Am. Title Ins. Co., Oakland, Calif., 1955-64; pres. Transam. Title Ins. Co., Oakland, 1964-72; v.p. Transam. Corp., 1969-71, group v.p., 1971-77, exec. v.p., 1977-81; pres. Leavitt Mgmt. Co.; dir. Syntex Corp., Pritchard Services Corp. N.Am., Inc. Regional Chmn. Brown U. Fund, 1969-72. Bd. dirs. Children's Hosp. Med. Center, 1969-72, Children's Hosp. Med. Center Found., 1969-72; trustee Lewis and Clark Coll., Portland, Oreg., 1972-75; trustee Brown U., Providence, R.I., 1973-78, emeritus, 1978—. Served with USMCR, World War II. Mem. Delta Kappa Epsilon. Republican. Clubs: Brown U. Club No. Calif., Pacific Union, Harvard Bus. Sch. of No. Calif., Orinda Country, Bohemian, Napa Valley Country. Home: 1100 Union St San Francisco CA 94109 Office: 1738 Union St San Francisco CA 94123

LEAVITT, LOIS HUTCHEON, consumer and homemaker educator; b. Whiterocks, Utah, Nov. 6, 1920; d. Arthur James and Ada E. (Peterson) Hutcheon; m. Jack William Leavitt, June 19, 1943; children—VaLoy, Joyce, LaJean. B.S., Brigham Young U., 1943, postgrad. 1955-83. Cert. vocat. home econs., secondary edn. tchr. Utah. Tchr. consumer and homemaking edn. Spanish Fork (Utah) High Sch., 1943-45, Roosevelt (Utah) High Sch., 1945-47, Union High Sch., Roosevelt, 1954—; advisor Future Homemakers Am. chpt. Named Outstanding Utah Home Econs. Tchr., Utah Cowbells of Utah Cattlemen's Assn. Mem. Am. Home Econs. Assn., Utah Home Econs. Assn. (Home Econs. Tchr. of Yr. 1982), Navhet Vocat. Assn., Uavhet Vocat. Assn., Am. Vocat. Assn., Utah Vocat. Assn., Bus. and Profl. Women (pres., sec.). Mormon. Home: Box 234 Neola UT 84053 Office: Union High School PO Box 400 Roosevelt UT 84066

LEBARON, DONALD RAY, mechanical engineer; b. American Fork, Utah, May 20, 1951; s. Donald Ralph and Rae Marie (Jerling) L.; m. Susan Christine Parkin July 14, 1976; children—Julianne, Ray Michael. B.S.M.E., Brigham Young U., 1976, M.M.E., 1977. Engr. AiResearch (Garrett), Phoenix, 1977-79; sr. engr. Hercules Inc., Magna, Utah, 1979—. Mem. ASME. Republican. Mormon. Home: 3502 W Piera Circle West Jordan Utah 84084 Office: Hercules Inc Magna UT 84044

LEBBOS, BETSEY WARREN, lawyer; b. Brockton, Mass., Dec. 14, 1944; d. Richard Carter and Madeleine Lydia (Snow) Warren; student U. Madrid (Spain), 1964-65; B.A., Tufts U., 1966; J.D., Northeastern U., 1971; 1 dau., Aida Madeleine. Admitted to Mass. bar, 1971, Calif. bar, 1975; individual practice family law, San Jose, Calif., 1971—; faculty Peninsula Law Sch. Mem. Am. Bar Assn., Mass. Bar Assn., Calif. Bar Assn., Calif. Queen's Bench, Calif. Trial Lawyers Assn., Santa Clara Women Profls. (pres., 1977-78), Santa Clara Women Lawyers. Contbr. articles to legal publs. Home: 6580 Northridge Dr San Jose CA 95113 Office: 111 W Saint John St Suite 330 San Jose CA 95113

LEBEDEFF, NICHOLAS BORIS, cons. co. exec.; b. Hollywood, Calif., Apr. 16, 1944; s. Boris Paul and Alexandra Esidorovna (Koshell) L.; B.B.A., Loyola U., Los Angeles, 1967; M.B.A., U. So. Calif., 1970; m. Judith Leah Moffett, Nov. 22, 1969; children—Christina, Christopher. Budget and adminstrv. analyst City of Los Angeles, 1967-73; mgr. budget and fiscal ops. Van de Kamp's Holland Dutch Bakers div. Gen. Host Corp., Los Angeles, 1973-74; mgr. fin. planning and analysis dept. U.S. Borax and Chem. Co., Los Angeles, 1974-75; pres. NBL Assos., Los Angeles, 1976—, Micro-Software, Inc., Los Angeles, 1977—, Planning Systems Group, Los Angeles. Bd. dirs. Friends of Ft. Ross, Am. Med. and Ednl. Services in Africa; mem. Calif. State Citizen's Adv. Com. on Ft. Ross, 1975—. Mem. So. Calif. Corp. Planners, Planning Execs. Inst., Am. Mgmt. Assn., British Interplanetary Soc., U. So. Calif. Alumni Assn., Commerce Assos. Republican. Mem. Orthodox Ch. Am. Home: 123 S Arden Blvd Los Angeles CA 90004 Office: Planning Systems Group Inc 21243 Ventura Blvd Suite 110 Woodland Hills CA 91364

LEBIEN, ROBERT FRANK, bank executive; b. Indpls., Aug. 2, 1934; s. Alfred John and Elfrieda M. (Oppliger) L.; m. Sara Jane Spradling, Nov. 10, 1957; children—Mark Darrel, Michael Robert. B.A., Butler U., 1956; M.B.A., Ind. U., 1961. With Security Pacific Bank, 1961—, asst. v.p. investment dept., 1964-68, v.p., dep. mgr. investment dept., 1968-79, sr. v.p., adminstr. internat. money mgmt. dept., 1979—; dir. Security Pacific Fin. Futures, Inc., Security Pacific Australia, Ltd.; mem. fgn. exchange com. Fed. Res. Bank N.Y. Club: North Ranch Country.

LEBLANC, MAURICE ARTHUR, rehab. engineer; b. Long Beach, Calif., Oct. 10, 1938; s. Maurice A. and Irene A. (Palladine) LeB.; m. Ingrid T. Uhlig, Dec. 23, 1967; 1 son, Branden N. B.S.M.E. cum laude, Stanford U., 1960, M.S.M.E., 1961; postgrad. in Prosthetic-Orthotics, UCLA Med. Sch., 1966; cert. prosthetist Calif. Staff specialist prosthetic-orthotic program UCLA Med. Ctr., 1965-68; staff engr. com. prosthetics research and devel. Nat. Acad. Scis., Washington, 1969-74; dir. research Rehab. Engring. Ctr., Children's Hosp., Stanford, Palo Alto, Calif., 19—; lectr., cons. in field. Served to lt. USN, 1961-65, test engr. Polaris Submarine Program, 1962-65. Recipient John Hopkins Nat. Search Applications Personal Computing Aid to Handicapped regional award, 1981. Mem. ASME, Am. Acad. Orthotists and Prosthetists, Internat. Soc. Prosthetics and Orthotics, Rehab. Engring. Soc. N.Am. (founding mem.). Contbr. numerous articles to profl. jours. Office: 520 Willow Road Palo Alto CA 94304

LEBLANC, WHITNEY JOSEPH, JR., TV producer, writer, theatre designer, dir.; b. Memphis; s. Whitney Joseph and Lucy (Chambliss) LeB.; B.A., So. U., 1954; M.A., U. Iowa, 1958; children—Jelynne, Michael, Rosalynde, William. Designer, mgr. Karamu, Cleve., 1959; designer Lincoln U., summers 1959, 60; dir., designer Antioch (Ohio) Coll., 1959-64, Howard U., 1964-65; dir., stage designer Towson (Md.) State Coll., 1965-69; producer, dir. TV series Our Street, 1969—; designer Center Stage, Balt., 1965—; founder, dir. Action Arts, Balt., 1968; producer, dir. Theatre U. and Elizabeth Walton Dance Co., Balt., 1968—; now asso. producer Good Times; producer, dir. series Up & Coming; pres. LeBlanc Prodns. Served with AUS, 1955-56. Recipient Ohio State award, 1972. Mem. Nat. Assn. Ednl. Broadcasters, Am. Ednl. Theatre Assn., Alpha Phi Alpha. Democrat. Roman Catholic. Author (plays) The Killing of An Eagle, Dreams Deferred. Home: 8 Orinda Vista Dr Oakland CA 94605

LEBLOND, RICHARD EMMETT, JR., performing arts adminstr.; b. Cin., Nov. 14, 1924; s. Richard E. and Mildred (Ziegler) LeB.; B.A. in Sociology, U. Cin., 1950, M.A., 1950; Ph.D. in Sociology, U. Mich., 1968; children by previous marriage—Helen LeBlond Banister, Richard Emmett, Anne W., Laurence Z. Instr. sociology U. Mich., Ann Arbor, 1955-57; instr. Temple U., Phila., 1957-62, asst. prof., 1962-66; assoc. prof., chmn. dept. sociology Rider Coll., Trenton, N.J., 1966-73; pres., gen. mgr. Pa. Ballet, Phila., 1973-75, San Francisco Ballet, 1975—; guest lectr. profl. confs. and orgns.; mem. dance adv. panel N.J. State Arts Council. Bd. dirs. San Francisco Bay Area Dance Coalition, San Francisco Arts Advocates, San Francisco Visitors and Conv. Bur., Garden State Ballet, Newark. Served with USN, 1943-46. Mem. Assn. Am. Dance Cos. (dir. 1966—, pres.), Am. Arts Alliance (dir.), Calif. Assn. Dance Cos. (dir.), Calif. Confedn. of Arts (pres.), AAUP. Office: San Francisco Ballet 378 8th Ave San Francisco CA 94121*

LECHMAN, SANDRA ELAINE, govt. ofcl.; b. Meadville, Pa., Nov. 13, 1947; d. John Robert and Dorothy M. (Heimbeucher) Clements; m. Gary J. Lechman, May 1, 1971; children—Heather, Christopher. A.A. in Bus., New Castle (Pa.) Bus. Coll., 1967. With U.S. Govt., 1967—, Indian programs community devel. rep., Denver, 1980—. Bd. dirs. Point So. Homeowners Assn., 1980-82. Recipient Outstanding Performance award USAF, 1970, HUD, 1982. Mem. Nat. Fedn. Fed. Employees (pres. 1980-82). Roman Catholic. Office: 1405 Curtis St Denver CO 80231

LECHNER, THOMAS ALLEN, educator, accountant, economist; b. Princeton, N.J., Aug. 8, 1949; s. Hans Henry and Rosemarie Clara (Allen) L.; m. Judith Helen Henkels, Feb. 26, 1977 (div.); m. Judith Leilani Pedersen, July 2, 1983. B.A. in Econs., Carleton Coll., 1971; M.S., Iowa State U., 1981. Acct. Arthur Andersen & Co., Chgo., 1977-81; asst. prof. acctg., Chapman Co., Orange, Calif., 1981—, dir. Summer Youth Program of Free Enterprise Inst., Chapman Coll.; fin. cons. Treas. Common Cause, Ill., 1979-81, mem. state bd., exec. com., 1977-81. Mem. Am. Acctg. Assn., Nat. Acctg. Assn., Am. Inst. C.P.A.s, Am. Econ. Assn., Nat. Tax Assn., Tax Inst. Am., Carleton Coll. Alumni Assn. (dir. 1979-80, mem. So. Calif. area steering com. 1981—). Democrat. Home: 16 Dragonfly Irvine CA 92714 Office: Chapman Coll Sch of Bus Orange CA 92666

LE CLAIR, RONALD ARTHUR, physician, med. microbiologist, med. co. exec.; b. Plainfield, Conn., Mar. 15, 1933; s. Ivan William and Edith Mary (Johnson) Le C.; B.S., U. Tenn., 1960, M.S., 1961; M.P.H., UCLA, 1968, Dr.P.H., 1968; M.D., Universidad Autonoma de Ciudad Juarez (Mex.), 1978. Dir. health lab. services Sch. Public Health, UCLA, 1968-71; chief clin. microbiology VA Hosp., Sepulveda, Calif., 1971-73; dir. labs. Clin. Standards Labs., Carson, Calif., 1973—; dir. Bio-Stat Labs., Inc., Carson, 1973—; postgrad. physician Los Angeles County-U. So. Calif. Med. Center, 1979-80; vis. prof. infectious diseases Universidad Del Noreste, Tampico, Mex., 1975; cons. tropical medicine Dispensaire de l'Oeuvres des Pupilles de St. Antoine, Port-au-Prince, Haiti, 1980—. Active Big Bros. Am., 1966-71. Served with USAF, 1950-55. Recipient award for pub. service Mayor City of Tampico, 1975. Postdoctoral fellow Sch. Pub. Health U. Calif., 1968-71. Mem. Internat. Acad. Preventive Medicine, Am. Soc. Microbiology, Med. Soc. Study Venereal Diseases, Am. Venereal Disease Assn., Royal Soc. Health, VFW. Episcopalian. Author: The Comprehensive Desk Reference of Veterinary Pharmaceuticals and Biologicals, 1976. Contbr. articles to profl. publs. medicine, sci., researcher infectious diseases, clin. microbiology. Home: PO Box 5570 Santa Monica CA 90405 Office: 12579 Venice Blvd Los Angeles CA 90066

LE COMPTE, GARÉ, psychologist; b. Chgo., Sept. 15, 1937; s. Edward Winston Groshell and Clair Agnew LeCompte; B.A., U. Wash., 1959, M.A., Am. U., 1967, Ph.D., 1970; Ph.D., Case-Western Res. U., 1979; m. Dorothy Joan Bookhamer, Jan. 28, 1961; children—Michele, Nicole, Andre. Nat. def. analyst U.S. Govt., Washington and Boston, 1960-62; vis. prof. Syrian U., Damascus, 1962-63; research coordinator spl. projects Gen. Dynamics Corp., Groton, Conn., 1964-67; sr. research scientist, dir. social sci. research Conn. State Research Commn., Hartford, 1967-71; dir. research N.Y.-Pa. Health Mgmt. Corp., Binghamton, N.Y., 1971-73; dean, prof. behavioral sci. Ohio Coll. Podiatric Medicine, Cleve., 1973-80; exec. dir. Acad. Ambulatory Foot Surgery, 1980—; pvt. practice behavioral treatment of stress disorders, 1980—; clin. affiliate Mgmt. of Stress Response Clinic, U. Wash., 1981—; bd. dirs. Inst. Middle Eastern and N. African Affairs, Highgate Social Research Center; mem. faculty U. Hartford (Conn.), 1967-71. Mem. Am. Psychol. Assn., Am. Pub. Health Assn., Assn. Advancement Behavior Therapy, AAAS (resource group of handicapped scientists), Found for Sci. and Handicapped, Episcopalian. Contbr. articles on health and mental health service systems to profl. jours. Home: 10826 Kulshan Rd Woodway Edmonds WA 98020 Office: 21206 72d Ave W Edmonds WA 98020

LEDBETTER, CARL SCOTIUS, counselor, educator; b. Pyatt, Ark., Aug. 19, 1910; s. James Oliver and Lillie Belle (Wall) L.; student Phillips U., Enid, Okla., 1930-32; A.B., Ky. Christian Coll., 1937; A.B., Butler U., 1939, M.A., 1940; M.A., U. Redlands, 1967; postgrad. Claremont Grad. Sch., 1961-64, Mankato (Minn.) State Coll., 1970-73, Calif. State

Coll., 1974-76; m. Ruth Slocum Weymouth, June 20, 1948; children—Carla Sue Ledbetter Holte, Carl Scotius, Charles Stephen, Craig Slocum, Candace Sybil Ledbetter Heidelberger, Christa Sharyn Ledbetter Sanders. Ordained to ministry Christian Ch., 1933; student pastor, Huntington, W.Va., 1935-36, Russell, Ky., 1936-39, Atlanta, Ind., 1939-40; mem. editorial staff Standard Pub. Co., Cin., 1940-41; commd. 1st lt. U.S. Army, 1941; advanced through grades to col., 1961; command chaplain Augsburg (W. Ger.) area, 1950-53; div. chaplain 3d Inf. Div., 1953-55; dep. army chaplain 6th U.S. Army, 1955-58; command chaplain 5th Region Army Air Def. Command, 1959-61; ret., 1961; dean men U. Redlands, 1961-69; dir. counseling, v.p. acad. affairs Lea (Minn.) Coll., 1969-74; rehab. counselor J.O.B. Work Activities Ctr., Hesperia, Calif., 1976-80, dir., 1980—; adj. prof. psychology and religion Chapman Coll., 1976—. Recipient award of merit Boy Scouts Am., 1967, Silver Beaver award, 1969. Mem. Am. Personnel and Guidance Assn., Nat. Vocat. Guidance Assn., Am. Rehab. Counselors Assn., Alpha Phi Gamma, Phi Delta Kappa, Pi Ch, Pi Gamma Mu, Alpha Phi Omega. Democrat. Club: Masons. Home: 611 Juniper Ct Redlands CA 92373 Office: 17292 Eucalyptus St Hesperia CA 92345

LEDBETTER, DONALD HENRY, mfg. co. ofcl.; b. St. Louis, Aug. 27, 1948; s. Henry Patrick and Mary Willetta (Blaise) L.; B.A. in Indsl. Psychology, St. Louis U., 1971; M.B.A. in Personnel and Indsl. Relations, Central Mo. State U., 1977; postgrad. U. Mo. Law Sch., Kansas City, 1978; m. Helen Briggs, Sept. 15, 1973; 1 dau., Jamie Kristin. Indsl. relations rep. Consol. Aluminum Corp., Madison, Ill. 1972-73; mgr. manpower planning Whitaker Cable Corp., North Kansas City, Mo., 1973-78; personnel dir. Nordson Corp., Amherst, Ohio, 1978-81, Megatek Corp., San Diego, 1981—; speaker lectr. on EEO/AAP to mfrs. and personnel groups, 1975—. Accredited exec. in personnel Personnel Accreditation Inst. Mem. Am. Soc. for Personnel Adminstrn., Am. Soc. for Tng. and Devel., Personnel Mgmt. Assn. Greater Kansas City (v.p. fin., treas. 1978), Personnel Mgmt. Asso., San Diego, Am. Mensa Ltd. Author: (booklets) The Employment Application Explanation, 1978, The Engineering Professional/Technical Classification Plan, 1981. Office: 3985 Sorrento Valley Blvd San Diego CA 92121

LEDENDECKER, CONSTANCE LUCILE, interior designer; b. Indpls., Feb. 17, 1923; d. William Henry and Dorothy Lucile (Johnson) Keller; m. Richard Humphreys Martin, Nov. 10, 1942; children—Stephen Richard Martin, Kathryn Constance Martin. m. 2d, William Henry Ledendecker, Dec. 26, 1971. Student Butler U., Indpls., 1940-42, Memphis Art Acad., Tenn., 1959-62, Musee D'Arts Decoratif, Paris, 1979. Interior designer Kimbrough, Inc., Memphis, 1962-63; ptnr. Wessie Davis Interiors, Coronado, Calif., 1964-66; prin. Constance Martin Interiors, Riverside, 1966-68, La Canada, 1968—; cons. in field. Mem. Am. Soc. Interior Designers (pres. Pasadena chpt., nat. chmn.), La Canada Hist. Soc., Pasadena Playhouse Restoration, Delta Gamma. Republican. Episcopalian. Clubs: La Canada Thursday (La Canada, Calif.) Contbr. design work to profl. jours. Address: 4376 Beulah Dr La Canada CA 91011

LEDERER, EUGENE GERALD, lawyer; b. N.Y.C., Apr. 20, 1933; s. Leo Michael and Anna (Bender) L.; B.S. summa cum laude, U. Ariz., 1954; LL.B., UCLA, 1961; m. Bette Jean Good, Sept. 7, 1963; children—Michael Lee, Deanna Lynn. Admitted to Calif. bar, 1961, individual practice law, Los Angeles, 1964—; lect. Calif. Continuing Edn. of Bar Served to 1st lt. AUS, 1955 57. C.P.A., Calif.; cert. tax specialist, Calif. Mem. Am. Bar Assn., Calif. Bar Assn., Los Angeles County Bar Assn., Beverly Hills Bar Assn., Calif. Soc. C.P.A.s. Republican. Jewish. Contbr. articles to profl. jours. Office: 1880 Century Park East Suite 615 Los Angeles CA 90067

LEDWIN, ANA GRACIELA, psychological consultant; b. Buenos Aires, June 26, 1951; came to U.S., 1979; d. Roberto and Ester (Hochcajt) Ledwin; 1 dau., Eleonora S. M.A. in Psychology, Universidad Kennedy, 1974; Ph.D. in Psychology, U.S. Internat. U., 1982. Cert. psychol. asst., Calif. Pvt. practice psychology, Buenos Aires, 1974-79, psychologist Sunrise Community Counseling Center, Los Angeles, 1979-80; psychol. cons. La Calle Psychol. Services, Santa Ana, Calif., 1980—; childbirth educator. Mem. Am. Psychol. Assn., Calif. Hispanic Psychol. Assn., Am. Soc. Psychoprophylaxis in Obstetrics.

LEE, ALBERT YIN-PO, economist; b. China, Sept. 1, 1930; s. Lan Ken and Weis Wee; m. Linda Shief-mei, Feb. 23, 1962; children—Min-wei, Angel, Finny. Ph.D. in Econs., So. Ill. U., Carbondale, 1970. Asst. prof. econs. Calif. State Coll.-Stanislaus, Turlock, 1970-73, assoc. prof., 1973-77, prof. 1977—; assoc. prof. U. Pacific, Stockton, Calif., 1977; prof. Golden Gate U., San Francisco, 1980—. Mem. Am. Econs. Assn., Western Econs. Assn. Contbr. articles to profl. jours. Home: 1225 Estate Dr Turlock CA 95380 Office: 800 Monte Vista Turlock CA 95380

LEE, BRIAN DALVIN, pediatric dentist; b. Berkeley, Calif., Dec. 23, 1942; s. David Alvin and May (Hum) L.; student U. Calif., Berkeley, 1960-62; D.D.S., U. Calif., San Francisco, 1966; M.S.D., Ind. U., 1970; m. Dorlene Sandria Yee, Aug. 13, 1966; children—Lisa Ann, Jonathon Everett. Practice pediatric dentistry, Foster City, Calif., 1972—; guest lectr. U. Calif. Sch. Dentistry; clin. instr. Ind. U. Sch. Dentistry; dental examiner Calif. Bd. Dental Examiners. Served as capt. Dental Corps, U.S. Army, 1966-68. Decorated Army Commendation medal with oak leaf cluster; Crippled Children's fellow, 1968-70. Fellow Am. Acad. Pedodontics; mem. Am. Bd. Pedodontics (diplomate; examiner), Am. Soc. Dentistry for Children, Calif. Soc. Dentistry for Children, Calif. Soc. Pediatric Dentists, ADA, Calif. Dental Assn., Golden Gate Pedodontic Study Club, Foster City C. of C. Club: Lions (Foster City). Contbr. articles to profl. jours. Home: 198 Flying Mist Isle Foster City CA 94404 Office: 1289 E Hillsdale Blvd Foster City CA 94404

LEE, BYRON JEN, lawyer, accountant; b. Los Angeles, Feb. 25, 1942; s. Frank York and Suzy (Inn) L.; B.S., U. Notre Dame; M.B.A., UCLA; J.D., Loyola U., Los Angeles; m. Akemi Ichiho. Mem. firm Zazueta, Osterhout & Co. C.P.A.s, Los Angeles, 1965—; admitted to Calif. bar; prin. firm Byron Jen Lee, Los Angeles, 1974—; adj. asso. prof. med. econs. and legal medicine Coll. Osteo. Medicine of Pacific, 1978—. Chmn., CSC, City of Montebello, Calif., 1980. Mem. Am. Assn. Atty.-C.P.A.'s (dir. 1975—, v.p. 1980), Calif. Assn. Atty.-C.P.A.'s (dir. 1975—, pres. 1979), Am. Inst. C.P.A.'s, Calif. Soc. C.P.A.'s, Am. Bar Assn., State Bar of Calif., Los Angeles County Bar Assn., Japanese Am. Bar Assn. Greater Los Angeles Area, So. Calif. Chinese Lawyers Assn. Club: Rotary. Editor: Atty.-C.P.A., 1979-80. Home: Montebello CA Office: Suite 200 1800 Century Park East Los Angeles CA 90067

LEE, CHARLES JAMES, financial executive; b. San Francisco, July 19, 1925; s. Charles H. and Eugenia C. (Mangan) L.; m. Jean Egan, June 1, 1949; children—Kevin, Dennis, Moira, Terri, Sheila. B.S., U. San Francisco, 1949; Exec. Devel. Program, Cornell U., 1959. C.P.A., Calif., 1954. With Price, Waterhouse & Co., 1949-56, Tidewater Oil, 1956-64; v.p., controller Occidental Petroleum, 1964-69, v.p., treas., 1970-72; v.p. fin. Bergen Brunswig, 1972-74; sr. v.p. fin. Natomas Co., San Francisco, 1974—, also dir.; dir. Mattel, Inc., Bergen Brunswig Corp. Trustee U. San Francisco; mem. adv. bd. Sch. Bus., U. Santa Clara. Served with AUS, 1943-46. Mem. Fin. Execs. Inst., Am. Inst. C.P.A.s, Am. Petroleum Inst. Republican. Roman Catholic. Clubs: Bankers, St. Francis Yacht (San Francisco). Office: 601 California St San Francisco CA 94108

LEE, C(HARLES) NICHOLAS, language and literature educator; b. Washington, July 27, 1933; s. Charles Foster and Frances Cornelia (McAllister) L.; m. Mollie Kathleen Boivin; children—Alison, Christopher, Jennifer, Bronwyn. B.A., U. Md., 1956, M.A., 1958; student (Adenauer scholar) Ludwig-Maximilians U., Munich, W.Ger., 1953-54, (Fulbright fellow) U. Paris, 1955-56; Ph.D., Harvard U., 1964, postgrad. (NDEA fellow), 1967, Am. Council Learned Socs. fellow, 1975-76. Instr., U. Md., 1956-60; asst. prof. Bucknell U., 1963-65; asst. prof. U. Colo., Boulder, 1965-66, assoc. prof., 1966-74, prof., 1974—, chmn. dept. Oriental and Slavic langs. and lits., 1981-82, chmn. dept. Slavic langs. and lit., 1982—, dir. NDEA Title VI Slavic and East European Studies Inst., 1967-69. Mem. Am. Assn. Tchrs. Slavic and East European Langs., Western Slavic Assn., Rocky Mountain MLA, Colo. MLA. Episcopalian. Author: The Novels of Mark Aleksandrovic Aldanov, 1969. Home: 1276 Harrison Ct Boulder CO 80303 Office: Campus Box 279 Dept Slavic Langs and Lits U Colo Boulder CO 80309

LEE, CHARLIE, T., rancher, banker; b. Alamogordo, N.Mex., June 28, 1928; s. Don T. and Charlotte T. Lee; student N.Mex. Western U., 1947-50; m. Jean Emily Althaus, May 28, 1949; children—Linda Jean, Don L. Owner, Hat Ranch Inc., Alamogordo, 1950—; dir. Security Bank & Trust; dir. Fed. Land Bank of Las Cruces, 1974-81, chmn., 1979-80. Mem. Nat. Public Lands Council-N.Mex. Livestock Bd., 1979-80; state senator Lincoln and Otero Counties, Dist. 39. Recipient Honor award for outstanding service NEA, 1977; Man of the Yr., Progressive Farmer Mag., 1978; Cattleman of the Yr., N.Mex. Cattle Growers Assn., 1981; Father of the Yr., N.Mex. Cowbelles, 1976. Mem. N.Mex. Cattle Growers Assn. (pres. 1974-76), Nat. Cattlemen's Assn. (bd. dirs. 1972-76), Alamogordo C. of C., Otero County Farm Bur. Republican. Presbyterian. Home: 2520 Yale St Alamogordo NM 88310 Office: PO Drawer 149 Alamogordo NM 88310

LEE, CHI WON, plant geneticist, horticulturist; b. Yesan, South Korea, Feb. 14, 1943; came to U.S., 1971; s. Dae-Bok and Mu-Ye (Kang) L.; B.S., Kon-kuk U., Seoul, 1970; M.S. (David Ross fellow 1974), Purdue U., 1974, Ph.D., 1977. Research asst., then research asso. horticulture Purdue U., 1972-77; asst. prof. plant sci. U. Ariz., Tucson, 1977—. Served with Korean Army, 1964-67. Mem. Am. Soc. Hort. Sci., Internat. Soc. Hort. Sci., Tissue Culture Assn., Ariz. Soc. Electron Microscopy and Microbeam Analysis, Am. Soc. Plant Physiologists, Sigma Xi. Methodist. Author articles in field. Home: 6819 E Scarlett St Tucson AZ 85710 Office: Plant Scis Dept U Ariz Tucson AZ 85721

LEE, CHI-HANG, biochemist; b. Vinh Long, South Viet-Nam, Jan. 1, 1939; came to U.S., 1955, naturalized, 1972; s. Thieu-Ban and On-Phuong (Ip) L.; B.A., So. Ill. U., 1960; Ph.D., Rutgers U., 1966; m. Mee-Han Chan, Sept. 19, 1964; children—Maurice, Irving. Sr. chemist, sr. research specialist Gen. Foods Corp., Tarrytown, N.Y., 1967-78; sr. research scientist RJR Foods, Winston Salem, N.C., 1978-80; mgr. food biochemistry Del Monte Corp., Walnut Creek, Calif., 1980—; vis. prof. King's Coll., 1973-77. Mem. exec. council Am. Sci. Affiliation, 1979-83, pres., 1982. Recipient Chms. award Gen. Foods Corp., 1977; Rutgers U. research fellow, 1962-66. Mem. Am. Chem. Soc., Am. Sci. Affiliation. Editor: Ambassadors Mag., 1962-63, 76-80; patentee in field. Office: 205 N Wiget Ln Walnut Creek CA 94598

LEE, CHIN-TIAN, horticulturist, educator; b. Taiwan, June 22, 1940; came to U.S., 1967, naturalized, 1977; s. Pou-Tong and Wu-May (Young) L.; B.S., Nat. Taiwan U., 1964, M.S., 1967; M.S., U. Wis., 1969, Ph.D., 1971; m. Shu-Teh Kuo, June 22, 1969; children—Corinna, Frances. Grad. research asst. Nat. Taiwan U., 1965-67; grad. research asst. U. Wis., 1967-71, biologist, 1971-74; asst. prof. horticulture U. Guam, Mangilao, 1974-80, asso. prof., 1980—; cons. Guam Dept. Parks and Recreation, South Pacific Commn. Served to 2d lt. China Air Force, 1964-65. L.F. Chao fellow, 1965-66; Youth Anti-Communist and Nat. Salvation Corps fellow, 1963-64; U.S. Tropical Agrl. research grantee, 1979-80, 80—; U.S. Pesticide Impact Assessment research grantee, 1979 80. Mem. Am. Soc. Hort. Sci., Am. Soc. Agronomy, Am. Soc. Hort. Sci. in Tropical Regions. Mem. Christian Ch. (Disciples of Christ). Contbr. articles to profl. jours. Home: 136 Bengbing St Dededo GU 96912 Office: Coll Agr and Life Scis U Guam UOG Sta Mangilao GU 96913

LEE, CURTIS DON, business executive; b. Ada, Minn., Mar. 4, 1934; s. Lawrence Theodore and Alphild Theodora (Engstrom) L.; m. Nancy Colleen Olson, Oct. 16, 1955; children—Kathleen Rego, Richard, Larry. B.S. in Commerce, U. N.D., 1955, M.S. in Econ., 1971. Commd. 2d lt. U.S. Army, 1955; advanced through grades to col., 1977; ret., 1979; staff mgr. Servco Pacific Inc., Honolulu, 1980, asst. v.p., 1981, v.p., asst. group mgr., 1982—. Mem. Hawaii State Hwy. Safety Council. Decorated Legion Merit with 1 oak leaf cluster, meritorious service medal with 1 oak leaf cluster, army commendation medal with 2 oak leaf clusters. Mem. Am. Soc. Mil. Comptrollers, Sigma Chi Alumni, Ret. Officers Assn. Democrat. Presbyterian. Office: 2828 Paa St Honolulu HI 96819

LEE, CURTIS HOWARD, cons. engr.; b. San Francisco, June 7, 1928; s. Lum Quong and Kum Ho (Lee) L.; B.S. with honor, Calif. State Poly. Coll., 1952; postgrad. McGeorge Coll. Law, 1964-67; children—Roberta, Sabrina, Kristina. Mech. engr. Buonaccorsi & Assos., cons. engrs., San Francisco, 1953-57, Eagleson Engrs., cons. engrs., San Francisco, 1957-59; 60-63; chief engr. C.S. Hardeman, San Francisco, 1959-60; spl. project engr. A.E. D'Ambly, cons. engrs., Phila., 1963-64; self-employed as cons. engr., Sacramento, 1964-67; chief engr. George W. Dunn & Assos., cons. engrs. San Diego, 1967-69; prin. Dunn-Lee-Smith-Klein & Assos., National City, Calif., 1969—. Mem. Accrediting Commn. of Assn. of Ind. Colls. and Schs., 1970-76; mem. adv. panel Calif. State Bldg. Standards Commn., 1971-76; mem. San Diego City Bd. Bldg. Appeals, 1974-79; mem. Chula Vista City Bd. Appeals, 1980—. Served with AUS, 1947-48. Registered profl. engr., Ariz., Calif., Colo., Fla., Ga., Wash., Nev., N.Mex., Ohio, Oreg., Pa., Tex. Mem. Am. Arbitration Assn. (mem. nat. panel 1969—, regional adv. bd. 1977—), Am. Acad. Forensic Scis., Am. Cons. Engrs. Council (mem. Calif. mech.-elec. cons. engrs. com. 1972-80), Nat. Soc. Profl. Engrs. (pres. San Diego chpt. 1972-73, state dir. 1973-74, nat. dir. 1974-76), Am. Soc. Heating, Refrigeration and Air Conditioning Engrs., ASME, Am. Soc. Plumbing Engrs. (charter pres. San Diego chpt. 1970, nat. 3d v.p. 1970-72), Constrn. Specifications Inst. (dir. San Diego chpt. 1974-75, pres. 1976-77, Inst. com. 1978—), Am. Soc. Profl. Estimators, Am. Soc. Quality Control, Archeol. Inst. Am., Instrument Soc. Am., Internat. Solar Energy Soc., Internat. Assn. Plumbing and Mech. Ofcls., Nat. Fire Protection Assn. Office: 1003 Plaza Blvd National City CA 92050

LEE, DAVID SEN-LIN, computer company executive; b. Pei Ping, China, June 23, 1937; came to U.S., 1956, naturalized, 1970; s. Wen-Chi and Li-Ping (Wong) L.; B.S.M.E., Mont. State U., 1960; M.S.M.E., N.D. State U., 1962; m. Chi-Ming Wan, Jan. 8, 1966; children—Eric, Gloria, Randy. Engr., NCR, Dayton, Ohio, 1962-64; mgr. Singer, San Leandro, Calif., 1964-69; mgr. Diablo Systems, Hayward, Calif., 1969-73; exec. v.p. Qume, San Jose, Calif., 1973-81, pres., 1981—, chmn., 1981—, also dir.; dir. Envision. Recipient Entrepreneur award Harvard Bus. Sch. Assn. of No. Calif., 1979; ASTM award, 1962. Mem. Chinese Inst. Engrs. (v.p. 1981, pres. 1982), Asian Bus. League (dir. 1981), Tau Beta Pi, Pi Tau Sigma. Inventor daisy-wheel printer, 1971. Home: 14000 Tracy Ct Los Altos Hills CA 94022 Office: 2350 Qume Dr San Jose CA 95131

LEE, DICK, income tax consultant, b. Boston, Feb. 12, 1926; s. Bartholomew F. and Anna (Marrow) L.; m. May Foss, Nov. 28, 1974; children—Andrew, Linda, Warren, Ramsy. B.S., Northeastern U., 1949; M.S., Boston Coll., 1950; B.S., Johns Hopkins U., 1955; M.B.A., U. So. Calif., 1960. With Lintion Industries, 1956-57; with Hughes Aircraft Corp., Los Angeles, 1957-68, program mgr., 1958-65, corp. diversification mgr., 1965-68; cons. Advanced Mgmt. Corp., Brentwood, Calif., 1968; fin. and income tax cons., Pacific Palisades, Calif., 1968—. Served with USMC, 1943-45. Mem. Mensa, Research Inst. Am., Phi Rho Alpha. Libertarian. Author: How to Pay Zero Income Tax-Legally. Contbr. articles to profl. jours. Address: 1085 Ravoli Dr Pacific Palisades CA 90272

LEE, DOMINIC (SHI FONG), civil, mechanical and electrical engineer; b. Hong Kong, Apr. 21, 1942; came to U.S., 1962, naturalized, 1973; s. Thomas T.H. and Theresa K.M. (Ho) L.; B.S. in Elec. Engring., U. Mo., 1968, M.S. in Elec. Engring., 1971, M.S.M.E., 1976, M.S. in Aerospace Engring., 1976, postgrad., 1979-81; postgrad. in civil engring. U. Alaska, 1979-81; m. Freddie Sue, Sept. 9, 1968; children—Chris, Marian, Benji, Julie. Sr. elec. engr. U. Mo. Med. Center, 1968-70; process plant engr. 3M Co., 1970-71; instr. engring. Lincoln (Mo.) U., 1971-75, dir. engring. program, 1973-75; chief engr. Ellerbe Assos. of Mo., Columbia, 1975-77; sr. engr. Crews McInnes & Hoffman Cons. Engrs., Anchorage, 1977-78; chief mech. engr. Ellerbe Alaska, Anchorage, 1978-80; pres., chief exec. officer Little Susitna Co., Anchorage, 1980—, chmn. bd., 1981—; pres. L.A. Investment Inc., ABL Constrn. Inc.; chmn. bd. Alaska Nat. Homes Inc. Commr. Plumbing Code Bd. Appeals, Columbia, Mo., 1975-77; sec. Alaska Soc. Minority Profls., 1979-83. Named Hon. Knight of St. Patrick, Coll. Engring., U. Mo., 1967. Mem. Am. Welding Soc., ASHRAE, ASME, IEEE, Mo. Soc. Profl. Engrs. (dir. 1976-77, Young Engr. of Yr., 1977, Alaska Soc. Profl. Engrs., Am. Cons. Engrs. Council. Republican. Clubs: Optimists (chmn. membership 1979-80); Commonwealth North (Anchorage). Contbr. articles to profl. jours. Home: SRA 924 Anchorage AK 99502 Office: 821 N St Anchorage AK 99501

LEE, DOUGLAS CRAIG, beverage distribution executive; b. San Francisco, June 28, 1945; s. Joseph Stanley and Janet (Chan) L.; m. Kay Hatamiya, Sept. 14, 1974. B.A., U. Calif.-Berkeley, 1966, M.B.A., 1969. Account exec. Benton and Bowles Advt., N.Y.C., 1970-72; sr. mktg. mgr. E & J Gallo Winery, Modesto, Calif., 1972-77; v.p., gen. mgr. RC Cola Co., Sacramento, 1977-81; pres. Affiliated Beverages, Inc., Salinas, Calif., 1981—; instr. various Calif. colls.; cons. in field. Mem. Am. Mktg. Assn., Salinas C. of C. Office: Affiliated Beverages Inc 881 Vertin Ave Salinas CA 93901

LEE, ELEANOR, state senator, business executive; b. Elgin, Ill., July 17, 1931; d. Earl H. and Catherine (Goldback) Selle; m. David H. Lee, 1951; children—Virginia Boylan, Phyllis Kenworthy, Marica. B.A., Evergreen State Coll. Bus. mgr. Fairman B. Lee Co., Inc., Burien, Wash.; formerly mem. Wash. Ho. of Reps., now mem. Wash. State Senate. Recipient Service award CAP, Women Helping Women award Soroptomists, Service award Lake Burien PTA. Mem. Nat. Order Women Legislators, Elected Wash. Women, Am. Legis. Exchange Council, C. of C. Club: Soroptomists. Republican. Home: PO Box 66274 Burien WA 98166 Office: Washington State Senate Olympia WA 98504

LEE, EUGENE WILLIAM, mgmt. cons. co. exec.; b. Livingston, Calif., July 25, 1927; s. Forrest William and Irene Jeanette (Ingols) L.; S.T.M., San Francisco Theol. Sem., 1952; diploma Spanish Lang. Inst., Costa Rica, 1954-55; postgrad. N.Y. U., Columbia U., 1958-59; M.B.A., U. So. Calif., 1970; m. Jeanne Marie Rice, Aug. 20, 1950. Ordained to ministry Presbyterian Ch., 1952; pastor Trinity Presbyn. Ch., San Anselmo, Calif., 1950-54; communication cons. Nat. Council of Chs., Latin Am., 1961-66; gen. mgr. Mgmt. Center of Mex., Mexico City, 1970-72, Pyramid Films, Santa Monica, Calif., 1973-74; v.p. Am. Mgmt. Assn., San Francisco, 1975-77; mgr. W.A. Golomski & Assos., San Francisco, 1977—. Bd. dirs. Calif. League for the Handicapped, 1978—. Met. YMCA, San Francisco, 1979—. Mem. Am. Soc. for Tng. and Devel. Republican. Clubs: Commonwealth, San Francisco Rotary. Office: W A Golomski & Assos 681 Market St San Francisco CA 94105

LEE, FRANCIS DUANE, consulting engineer; b. Leavenworth, Wash., Jan. 11, 1940; s. Warren Tingley and Dorothy Lucille (Simmons) L.; m. Marian Marie Peter, June 8, 1965; children—Joseph Duane, Daniel Bryant. B.S. in Engring., Ariz. State U., 1966, M.S. in Engring., 1968. Registered profl. engr. Oreg., Wash., Idaho. Design engr. Williams and Ellis, Phoenix, 1963-68; project mgr., design engr. Stevens, Thompson and Runyan, Portland, Oreg., Boise, Idaho, 1968-74; office mgr. H.G.E. Inc., Portland, 1974-75; pres. Lee Engring. Inc., Oregon City, Oreg., 1975—; lectr. in field. Chmn. Clackamas Dist. Boy Scouts Am., com. chmn. Troop 183; mem. vestry St. Paul's Episcopalian Church. Mem. Am. Water Works Assn., Water Pollution Control Fedn., Am. Pub. Works Assn., Nat. Soc. Profl. Engrs., Am. Cons. Engrs. Council. Republican. Club: Oregon City Lions (past pres.); Elks. Office: 708 Main St Suite 202 Oregon City OR 97045

LEE, GLENN RICHARD, university dean; b. Ogden, Utah, May 18, 1932; s. Glenn Edwin and Thelma (Jensen) L.; B.S., U. Utah, 1953, M.D., 1956; m. Pamela Majorie Ridd, July 18, 1969; children—Jennifer, Cynthia. Intern, then resident in internal medicine Boston City Hosp., 1956-58; USPHS clin. asso. Nat. Cancer Inst., 1958-60; postdoctoral research U. Utah Med. Sch., 1960-63, mem. faculty, 1963—, prof. internal medicine, 1973—, dean, 1978—. Markle Found. scholar, 1965; grantee NIH, 1977-83. Mem. ACP, Am. Soc. Hematology, Am. Soc. Clin. Investigation, Western Assn. Physicians, AMA, Am. Inst. Nutrition. Mormon. Co-author: Clinical Hematology, 8th edit., 1981; contbr. to articles med. jours. Office: 50 N Medical Dr Salt Lake City UT 84132

LEE, GWENDOLYN MARLENE DAVIS, educator; b. Yoakum, Tex., Dec. 7, 1934; d. Theodore Roosevelt and Callie Juanita (Butler) Davis; children—Bettye Janiece, Peter Scott. B.S.Ed., Prairie View A&M U., 1957; postgrad. Ariz. State U., 1958-60, San Jose State U., 1961-62, La Verne U., 1967, 71, Claremont Grad. Sch., 1969-70; M.A. in Edn., U. Redlands, 1977. Tchr. 4th grade Roosevelt Sch. Dist., Phoenix, 1957-60; tchr. pub. schs., Hanford, Calif., 1964-65; elem. sch. tchr. Pomona (Calif.) Unified Sch. Dist., 1966—, mem. math field day planning com. for grades 4-8, 1982-83; cons. Chalk Talks, math. competition program. Lee C. O'Neal scholar, 1955-57; tchrs. preparation in edn. scholar. Mem. NEA, Calif. Tchrs. Assn., Pomona Tchrs. Assn., Foothill Reading Council. Methodist.

LEE, J. CRAIG, public relations director, consultant; b. Phoenix, Sept. 9, 1953; s. James Rudolph and Bertha Odell (Craig) McIlroy; m. Bertha Hiskey, Feb. 18, 1977; children—Brandon, Rachele, Stacey. B.A. in Communications, Brigham Young U., 1978. Adminstrv. asst. pub. relations Brigham Young U., Provo, 1976-77, asst. dir. performance scheduling, 1977-80, asst. dir. pub. relations, 1980-82, dir. hosting services, 1982—; ptnr. Darais, Bowie and Lee, pub. relations cons. firm. Bd. dirs. Utah Valley Indsl. Devel. Assn., 1980—, Utah County Travel Council. Mem. Pub. Relations Soc. Am., Council for Advancement and Support of Edn., Orem, Utah C. of C. (dir. 1980-82, v.p. pub. relations 1982—). Republican. Mormon. Office: Brigham Young University Hosting Ctr Provo UT 84602

LEE, JANET WASHBURN, stockbroker; b. Tucson, Apr. 2, 1953; d. Benton Charles and Thelma Louise W.; B.A.E. in Communication Arts,

Ariz. State U., 1976. Piece parts buyer, Motorola Phoenix, 1976-78; mgr. employer communication, Honeywell, Phoenix, 1978-80; human resources cons., Phoenix, 1980; stockbroker Boettcher & Co., Phoenix, 1981-82; stockbroker Kidder, Peabody & Co., Inc., 1982—; condr. seminars. Advisor, Honeywell Polit. Action Com., 1979-80; mem. adv. council Center for Exec. Devel., Ariz. State U.; chmn. celebrity tennis tournament Spina Bifida Assn., 1983. Mem. Internat. Assn. Bus. Communicators, Purchasing Mgmt. Assn., Am. Soc. Tng. and Devel., Nat. Assn. Female Execs., Nat. Fedn. Bus. and Profl. Women (Young Careerist 1978-79; Woman of Year 1981). Republican. Clubs: Phoenix Ski, Exec. Home: 4330 N 19th Dr Phoenix AZ 85015 Office: 2929 E Camelback #220 Phoenix AZ 85016

LEE, JAR JUEH, elec. engr.; b. Kwangtung, China, Oct. 1, 1945; came to U.S., 1968, naturalized, 1978; s. Han Yuen and Li Chin (Mai) L.; B.S., Nat. Taiwan U., 1967; Ph.D., Case Inst. Tech., 1973; m. Mu Lien Ho, Sept. 25, 1971; children—Henry K., Brenda A. Research asst. Case Inst. Tech., 1968-73; research asso. Cornell U., Ithaca, N.Y., 1973-74; research engr. GTE Sylvania, Inc., Needham, Mass., 1974-77; mem. tech. staff Rockwell Internat., Anaheim, Calif., 1977-82; group head Hughes Aircraft Co., Fullerton, Calif., 1982—; also spl. antennas designer communications and radar systems, 1978—; cons. in field; free-lance tech. translator. Served with Chinese Navy, 1967-68. Mem. IEEE, Antennas and Propagation Soc. Soc. Contbr. articles to profl. jours., chpts. to books. Home: 24 Christamon St E Irvine CA 92714 Office: B600/D141 Hughes Aircraft Co PO Box 3310 Fullerton CA 92634

LEE, JERALD KEITH, city official; b. Laramie, Wyo., Feb. 16, 1938; s. Raymond Amos and Lenore Pauline (Baumgardner) L.; B.S., U. Utah, 1960; M.P.A., U. So. Calif., 1971; m. Barbara Clarene Taylor, June 7, 1960; children—Christine, Lisa, Heather. Staff asst. Pacific Telephone Co., 1963-64; budget officer Los Angeles Fire Dept., 1964-72; chief negotiator Los Angeles City Adminstrv. Officer, 1972-80; gen. mgr. El Pueblo de Los Angeles State Hist. Park, exec. asst. to gen. mgr. Dept. Recreation and Parks City of Los Angeles, 1980—; mem. faculty Los Angeles City Coll., 1972, East Los Angeles Coll., 1975; cons. Ryland Research Co., 1979. Bd. dirs. Friends of Los Angeles Maritime Mus., 1981, Soc. Preservation Drum Barracks; mem. adv. com. Riverside Elem. Sch.; mem. enrichment com. Riverside Schs. Served to lt. (s.g.) USN, 1960-63. Mem. Calif. Pub. Employers Labor Relations Assn. Mem. Ch. Jesus Christ of Latter-day Saints. Home: 5220 Mary Ellen Ave Van Nuys CA 91401 Office: 200 N Main St Room 1330 Los Angeles CA 90012

LEE, JOHN FRANCIS, international management consulting company executive, author; b. Boston, Sept. 19, 1918; s. Michael Francis and Catherine Mary (Arrigal) L.; m. Helene Zinka Comes, May 13, 1946 (div.); children—Anne-Marie Lee Dorman, Robert Paul, Virginia Louise Lee Linden, Jacqueline. S.B., The Citadel, 1947; S.M., Harvard U., 1948; Sc.D., U. London, 1968; Litt.D. (hon.), U. Malaga, 1972. Registered profl. engr., Maine, D.C. Asst. prof. to assoc. prof., U. Maine, Orono, 1948-52; Broughton disting. prof. engring. N.C. State U., Raleigh, 1952-61; pres. SUNY-Stony Brook, 1961-62; special advisor, cons. NSF, 1962; pres., chief exec. officer Internat. Devel. Services, Inc., Washington, 1962-71; pres., chief exec. officer Promotorco, S.A. (Europe), Luxembourg, 1971-79; pres., chief exec. officer, Intercontinental Mgmt. Cons., Inc., Torrance, Calif., 1979—; dir. internat. firms; vis. prof. Calif. State Univ. system. Participant White House Conf. Internat. Cooperation, 1965; ambassador ICEM-Argentina Negotiations; participant State Dept. Foreign Policy Conf., 1970-71. Served to maj. U.S. Army, 1941-45. Decorated Bronze Star, Purple Heart; order Southern Cross (Brazil), Order Bernardo O'Higgins (Chile) chevalier Legion D'Honeur (France); named Ambassador of Good Will, State of N.C., 1961. Mem. Am. Foreign Service Assn., IEEE, AIAA, Optical Soc. Am., Soc. Photo-optical Instrumentation and Engring., Internat. Soc. Hybrid Microelectronics, Sigma Xi, Tau Beta Pi, Pi Tau Sigma. Unitarian. Clubs: Cosmos, International (Washington); Jockey (Paris). Author: Theory and Design of Steam and Gas Turbines, 1954, 2nd edit., 1961; co-author: Thermodynamics, 1955, 2nd edit., 1962; Statistical Thermodynamics, 1963, 2nd edit., 1973; others; contbr. articles to profl. jours. Home: 6702 Los Verdes Dr #2 Rancho Palos Verdes CA 90274 Office: 3838 Carson St MS 110 Torrance CA 90503

LEE, JOHN P., hospital administrator; b. Portland, Oreg., Apr. 29, 1942; s. Patrick and Margaret Ann (Molahan) L.; m. Feb. 27, 1965; children—Kevin, Kelly, Jason. B.B.A., U. Portland, 1964, M.B.A., 1973; M.P.A. in Hosp. Adminstrn., UCLA, 1970. Asst. adminstr. fin. and gen. adminstrn. Good Samaritan Hosp. and Med. Center, Portland, 1970-75; dep. adminstr., St. Vincent's Hosp. and Med. Center, Portland, 1975-79; adminstr. Providence Med. Center, Portland, 1979—. Served to capt. Med. Service Corps, USAF, 1964-68. Fellow Am. Coll. Hosp. Adminstrs., Hosp. Adminstrv. Mgmt. Assn. Office: 4905 NE Glisan St Portland OR 97213

LEE, JONG HYUK, accountant; b. Seoul, Korea, May 6, 1941; came to U.S., 1969, naturalized, 1975; s. Jung Bo and Wol Sun Lee; B.A., Sonoma State U., Rohnert Park, Calif., 1971; M.B.A. in Taxation, Golden Gate U., San Francisco, 1976; m. Esther Kim, Jan. 24, 1970. Cost acct., internal auditor Foremost-McKesson Co., San Francisco, 1971-74; sr. acct. Clark, Wong, Foulkes & Barbieri, C.P.A.s, Oakland, Calif., 1974-77; pres. J.H. Lee Accountancy Corp., Oakland, 1977—; instr. Armstrong Coll., Berkeley, Calif., 1977-78. Bd. dirs. Korean Residents Assn., 1974, Multi-service Center for Koreans, 1979; chmn. caucus Calif.-Nev. ann. conf. United Methodist Ch., 1977; commr. Calif. State Office Econ. Opportunity, 1982-86. Served with Korean Marine Corps, 1961-64. C.P.A., Calif. Mem. Am. Inst. C.P.A.s, Nat. Assn. Asian Am. C.P.A.s (dir.), Am. Acctg. Assn., Nat. Assn. Accountants, Internat. Found. Employee Benefit Plans, Calif. Soc. C.P.A.s, San Francisco C. of C., Korean Am. C. of C. Democrat. Club: Lions. Author tax and bus. column Korea Times, 1980. accountant; b. Seoul, Korea, May 6, 1941; came to U.S., 1969, naturalized, 1975; s. Jung Bo and Wol Sun Lee; B.A., Sonoma State U., Rohnert Park, Calif., 1971; M.B.A. in Taxation, Golden Gate U., San Francisco, 1976; m. Esther Kim, Jan. 24, 1970. Cost acct., internal auditor Foremost-McKesson Co., San Francisco, 1971-74; sr. acct. Clark, Wong, Foulkes & Barbieri, C.P.A.s, Oakland, Calif., 1974-77; pres. J.H. Lee Accountancy Corp., Oakland, 1977—; instr. Armstrong Coll., Berkeley, Calif., 1977-78. Bd. dirs. Korean Residents Assn., 1974, Multi-service Center for Koreans, 1979; chmn. caucus Calif.-Nev. ann. conf. United Methodist Ch., 1977; commr. Calif. State Office Econ. Opportunity, 1982-86. Served with Korean Marine Corps, 1961-64. C.P.A., Calif. Mem. Am. Inst. C.P.A.s, Nat. Assn. Asian Am. C.P.A.s (dir.), Am. Acctg. Assn., Nat. Assn. Accountants, Internat. Found. Employee Benefit Plans, Calif. Soc. C.P.A.s, San Francisco C. of C., Korean Am. C. of C. Democrat. Club: Lions. Author tax and bus. column Korea Times, 1980. Home: 180 Firestone Dr Walnut Creek CA 94598 Office: 369 13th St Oakland CA 94612

LEE, KRISTINE SNYDER, marketing executive; b. Chgo., Sept. 16, 1952; d. Stanley Eugene and Doris Mae (Rieke) Snyder; m. Robert Bruce Lee, Feb. 6, 1982. A.S., Bennett Coll., 1972. Saleswoman, then mgr. Carson Pirie Scott and Co., Chgo., 1969-73; list mgr. Leewards Creative Crafts, Elgin, Ill., 1973-76; mktg. mgr. Holiday Gifts, Wheat Ridge, Colo., 1976-79; dir. list mgmt. Ambassador Internat., Tempe, Ariz., 1979—. Active Jr. Achievement, Inc. Mem. Direct Mktg. Assn., Direct Mktg. Club of So. Calif., Chgo. Assn. Direct Mktg., New Eng. Mail Order Assn., Women's Direct Response Group, Direct Mktg. Assn. N. Tex., Corp. Bus. and Profl. Women, Phoenix Direct Mktg. Club. Republican. Methodist. Office: Ambassador International 711 West Broadway St Tempe AZ 85282

LEE, LARRY TODD, aerospace engr.; b. Wood Lake, Minn., Jan. 26, 1941; s. Arthur Oander and Alma Katharina (Todt) L.; B.S., U. Minn., Mpls., 1964, M.S., 1966; m. Karen Jean Hokenson, June 15, 1966. Mem. tech. staff dynamics TRW Systems, Redondo Beach, Calif., 1966-73; asst. dept. mgr. dynamics J. H. Wiggins Co., Redondo Beach, 1973-79; staff engr. dynamics TRW Electronics and Defense Sector, Redondo Beach, 1979—. Treas., Com. for Preservation Tule Elk, 1980—. Mem. AIAA, Sigma Gamma Tau, Tau Beta Pi. Club: Sierra (Conservation Service award 1979). Office: 1 Space Park Redondo Beach CA 90278

LEE, MARGARET KYRLE, coll. adminstr.; b. Fort Collins, Colo., June 18, 1925; d. Charles Vincent and Elizabeth Margaret (Lamb) L.; B.A., U. Wyo., 1957, M.Ed., 1963; postgrad. Ill. State U., 1967, Colo. State U., 1974, Walden U., 1981. Tchr., Niobrara County Sch. Dist., Lusk, Wyo., 1945-62, prin. elementary sch., 1962-65, elementary guidance counselor, 1965-66; dean of women, instr. edn., counselor Eastern Wyo. Coll., Torrington, 1966—. Mem. Wyo. Personnel and Guidance Assn., AAUW, Delta Kappa Gamma. Methodist. Club: Order of Eastern Star. Home: 3135 Alta Vista Torrington WY 82240 Office: 3200 W C Torrington WY 82240

LEE, MARTIN LAURENCE, pharmaceutical company executive; b. London, June 8, 1953; came to U.S., 1957, naturalized, 1962; s. Victor and Edie (Lefcovitch) L.; m. Marilyn Ina Arbetman, Dec. 12, 1976; 1 son, Eliot. B.A., UCLA, 1974, M.S. in Biostats., 1976, Ph.D. in Biostats., 1979. Statistician dept. epidemiology UCLA, 1975; sr. statistician dept. gastroenterology Sch. Medicine, UCLA, 1976-79; research biostatistician Hollywood Presbyn. Med. Ctr., Los Angeles, 1978-79; sr. biostatistician Hyland Therapeutics div. Travenol Labs., Inc., Los Angeles, 1979-81, mgr. clin. devel., 1981—; lectr. stats. Calif. State U.-Los Angeles, Calif. State U.-Northridge, 1976-79; vis. lectr. biostats. UCLA, 1979—. Recipient Disting. alumni award UCLA Sch. Pub. Health Alumni Assn., 1979. Regents' fellow, 1977-79; USPHS trainee, 1976-77. Fellow Royal Statis. Soc.; mem. Am. Statis. Assn., Am. Soc. for Quality Control, Biometric Soc., Soc. for Clin. Trails, Phi Beta Kappa. Democrat. Jewish. Home: 6836 Lasaine Ave Van Nuys CA 91406 Office: 444 W Glenoaks Blvd Glendale CA 91202

LEE, MICHAEL DAVID, television and motion picture producer; b. San Francisco, Dec. 30, 1950; s. John Git and Ruth Marian (Chow) Wong. B.A. in Broadcast Communications, San Francisco State U., 1973; M.B.A. in Mgmt., Golden Gate U., 1983. Lic. real estate broker, Calif.; lic. life and disability agt., Calif. Producer ABC-TV, San Francisco, 1975-77; pres. Media Inc., San Francisco, 1977—; pres. On-Air Auctions Inc., San Francisco, 1981—; pres. Ind. Video News Inc., San Francisco, 1981—; gen. mgr. Cable TV Channel 8, Pacifica, Calif.; tchr. TV dept. Coll. of San Mateo (Calif.); mem. adv. bd. Gateway Savs. and Loan Assn. Bd. dirs. Asian Bus. League. Mem. Screen Actors Guild, AFTRA, Nat. Acad. TV Arts and Scis. Clubs: Mensa, Commonwealth (Calif.). Author: Success-A Guide to Creating Your Own, 1982; movie producer The Kill Squad, 1981; movie co-producer The Clonus Horror, 1979. Office: PO Box 16065 San Francisco CA 94116

LEE, PETER CHING-YUNG, social worker; b. China, July 25, 1947; came to U.S., 1972; s. Chang Shing and Lin Fon L.; B.A., Tunghai U., Taiwan, 1971; M.S.W., U. Hawaii, 1974; M.P.H., U. Calif.-Berkeley, 1977, D.S.W., 1980; m. Tria Yang, Apr. 11, 1979. Psychiat. social worker Diamond Head Mental Health Center, Hawaii, 1973-74; counselor treatment facilities for youth and children, Hawaii, 1972-74; counselor Oakland (Calif.) Center Retarded Children, 1975-76; teaching asso. U. Calif.-Berkeley, 1975-77; asst. prof. social work San Jose State U., 1977-80, asso. prof., 1980—, dir. Joint Center for Human Service Devel., 1983—; dir. Asian Community Mental Health Services, Oakland; dep. gen. sec. Sino-Am. Conf. Social Welfare Devel.; cons. dept. health Taiwan Provinical Govt., 1983—; cons. Kaohsiung Mental Hosp. (Taiwan), 1983—. Bd. dirs. Santa Clara unit Am. Cancer Soc., research grantee, 1977-78; v.p. Pacific Neighbors Inc.; Mental Health Service Assessment grantee, 1979-80; Kaiser Found. fellow, 1974-75; Charles Fish scholar, 1975-76; Kaiser Found. fellow, 1974-75. Mem. Am. Public Health Assn., Caucus Asian Am. Health Workers, Council Social Work Edn., Nat. Assn. Social Workers. Author: Psychosocial Impact of Cancer: An Evaluation of Rehabilitation Service for Cancer Patients, 1980; cons. editor Jour. Community Devel., 1980—; editor Procs. Sino-Am. Conf. Social Welfare Devel., 1981. Office: School of Social Work Washington Sq San Jose State University San Jose CA 95192

LEE, POLLY JAE STEAD (PALI KEALOHALANI KI LOA LEE), librarian, author; b. Toledo, Nov. 26, 1929; d. Jonathan Everett Wheeler and Ona Katherine (Grunder) Stead; student U. Hawaii, 1945-47; m. Richard H.W. Lee, Apr. 7, 1945 (div. 1978); children—Lani Lee Lee, Karin Lee Robinson, Ona Lee Yee, Laurie Lee Lam, Robin Louise Lee Halbert. Cataloger and processor U.S. Army Air Force, 1945-46; with U.S. Weatern Bur. Film Library, New Orleans, 1948-50, FBI, Wright-Patterson AFB, Dayton, Ohio, 1952, Ohio Wholesale Winedealers, Columbus, Ohio, 1956-58; with Coll. Engring., Ohio State U., Columbus, 1959; tech. manual writer Annie Whittenmyer Home, Davenport, Iowa, 1960; with Grand Rapids (Mich.) Pub. Library, 1961-62; dir. Waterford (Mich.) Twp. Libraries, 1962-64; acquisition librarian Pontiac (Mich.) Pub. Libraries, 1965-71, dir. East Side br., 1971-73; librarian Bishop Mus., Honolulu, 1975—. Chmn. Oakland County br. Multiple Sclerosis Soc., 1972-73, co-chmn. Pontiac com. of Mich. area bd., 1972-73; sec. Ohana o Kokua, 1979-83, Paia-Willis Ohana, 1982—; bd. dirs. Detroit Multiple Sclerosis Soc., 1971; mem. Mich. Area bd. Am. Friends Service Com., 1961-69, Recipient Mother of Yr. award Quad City Bus. men, Davenport, Iowa, and Moline, Ill., 1960. Mem. Internat. Platform Assn. Author: Mary Dyer: Child of Light, 1973; Giant: Pictorial History of the Human Colossus, 1973; History of Kaneohe Bay Area, 1976; Na Po Makole—History of the Night Rainbow, 1981; 1981; Mo'olelo O Na Pohu Kaina, 1983; to Aloha and Honolulu mags., 1982, also various other publs. Office: Atherton Halau Bishop Museum PO Box 19000-A Honolulu HI 96819

LEE, RANDALL BRUCE, association executive; b. Berwyn, Ill., Oct. 30, 1946; s. Oswen Grelly and Kathryn Jeannette (Rietema) L.; student U. Ga., 1964-65, Community Coll. Denver, 1970-71; m. Mary Catherine Otte Myers, Oct. 25, 1980; children—Christy Lynn, Rhett Brian. With engring. support services dept. Western Electric Co., Aurora, Colo., 1966-71; mng. editor Communications, also TV Communications, Englewood, Colo., 1971-73; asst. exec. dir. Am. Soc. Bariatric Physicians, Englewood, 1973-76, exec. dir., 1976—; mng. editor Obesity and Bariatric Medicine, 1973—; adminstr. Obesity Found., 1980—. Del., Colo. Republican Conv., 1976; Rep. precinct committeeman, 1976-80. Served with USAR, 1966-68; Vietnam. Recipient Presdl. citation Am. Soc. Bariatric Physicians, 1979. Mem. Am. Soc. Assn. Execs., Colo. Soc. Assn. Execs. (dir. 1981, sec.-treas. 1982-83, v.p. 1983-84), Nat. Model R.R. Assn. (Vol. award 1980; conv. chmn. 1977), Denver HO Model R.R. Club (dir. 1982—, sec. 1982-83), Am. Assn. Med. Soc. Execs. Office: 5200 S Quebec St Englewood CO 80111

LEE, ROBERT ANDREW, librarian; b. Washington, Dec. 7, 1923; s. Frederic Edward and Edna (Stewart) L.; B.A. in English, Oberlin (Ohio) Coll., 1947; M.L.S., U. So. Calif., 1966. Jr. cataloger Columbia U. Law Library, 1950-51; reference librarian N.Y. Daily Mirror, 1952-54; researcher for Dore Schary, MGM, Culver City, Calif., 1955; with Universal City Studios (Calif.), 1955—, research librarian, 1960-69, head research dept., 1969—. Served with AUS, 1943-46. Decorated Bronze Star with oak leaf cluster. Mem. Acad. Motion Picture Arts and Scis. (gov. 1973-75), Acad. TV Arts and Scis., Am. Film Inst., Los Angeles Internat. Film Exposition, Spl. Libraries Assn. Author articles in field. Home: 2212 Cahuenga Blvd Apt 104 Los Angeles CA 90068 Office: 100 Universal City Plaza Universal City CA 91608

LEE, RONALD DEMOS, demographer, economist, educator; b. Poughkeepsie N.Y., Sept. 5, 1941; s. Otis Hamilton and Dorothy (Demetriacopoulou) L.; m. Melissa Lee Nelken, July 6, 1968; children—Sophia, Isabel, Rebecca. B.A., Reed Coll., 1963; M.A., U. Calif.-Berkeley, 1967; Ph.D., Harvard U., 1970. Postdoctoral fellow Nat. Demographic Inst., Paris, 1970-71; asst. prof. to prof. U. Mich., Ann Arbor, 1971-79; prof. demography and econs. U. Calif.-Berkeley, 1979—; cons. in field; with Peace Corps., Ethiopia, 1963-65. NIH fellow, 1965-67; NSF fellow, 1968-69; SSRC fellow, 1970-71; NIH grantee, 1973—. Mem. Population Assn. Am., Am. Econ. Assn., Internat. Union Sci. Study of Population. Democrat. Author: Econometric Studies of Topics in Demographic History, 1978; Population Patterns in the Past, 1977; contbr. articles to profl. jours. Home: 2933 Russell St Berkeley CA 94705 Office: Grad Group in Demography 2234 Piedmont Ave Berkeley CA 94720

LEE, ROXANE LILLIAN, retail clothing company executive; b. Bayport, Minn., Oct. 20, 1929; d. William M. and Myrna M. (Carlson) Swanson; m. Harold M. Lee, Jan. 18, 1952; children—David, Heidi, Cynthia. A.A. in Merchandising, U. Minn., 1951. Asst. buyer Baker Co., women's clothing, Mpls., 1950-51; buyer Lillian Shop, ready-to-wear, Petersburg, Alaska, 1952-54; mdse. mgr. Leonard Hopkins, mfrs. rep., Petersburg, 1956-67; founder, pres. Lee's Clothing, Inc., Petersburg, 1969—. Bd. dirs. Petersburg Little Norway Com., 1964-81; mem. Alaska Commn. on Status of Women, 1978-83. Recipient Norwegian-Am. Outstanding Citizen award Little Norway Com., 1981; cert. for service on Alaska Gov.'s Commn. on Status of Women, 1983. Mem. Petersburg Bus. and Profl. Women's Club, Petersburg C. of C. (pres. 1975), NOW. Democrat. Lutheran. Club: Pioneer of Alaska (Petersburg). Home: 202 2d St Box 747 Petersburg AK 99833 Office: 305 Main St Petersburg AK 99833

LEE, S. WHITFIELD, business executive; b. Lawton, Okla., Jan. 7, 1944; s. M. Stanley and Geraldine Lee; m. Christina Calvert, Sept. 2, 1966; children—Adrienne, Whitfield, Alexandra. B.A., Harvard U., 1966; M.B.A., Wharton Sch., Fin., U. Pa., 1969. Chmn. bd. IML Freight, Inc., Salt Lake City, 1976—; dir. Mobile Billboard, Factran Fin. Service Corp., Yankee Oil Co. Trustee, Rowland Hall, St. Mark's Sch. Office: IML Freight Inc 2175 S 3270 W Salt Lake City UT 84119

LEE, THEODORE BO, lawyer, real estate developer; b. Stockton, Calif., Dec. 28, 1932; s. Wong Bo Lee and Daisy Lum; m. Doris Shoong, June 14, 1959; children—Gregory T.H., Ernest T.H. B.A., Harvard U., 1954; LL.B. U. Calif.-Berkeley, 1959; M.B.A., 1966. Bar: Calif., 1960. Temporary asst. lectr. U. Singapore, 1960-61; assoc. Fong, Miho, Choy & Robinson, Honolulu, 1961-62; asst. vice chancellor East-West Ctr., U. Hawaii, Honolulu, 1962-64; individual practice law, San Francisco, 1966-82; dir., pres. Urban Land Co., San Francisco, 1972—; dir., mem. exec. com. Nat. Dollar Stores, San Francisco, 1969-72; assoc. Nat. Housing Partnership. Contbr. articles to profl. jours. Bd. dirs. Harvard Alumni Assn., Boalt Hall, U. Calif. Bus. Sch. Devel. Fund. U. Calif.-Berkeley internat. legal fellow, 1959. Mem. ABA, Urban Land Inst., Internat. Council Shopping Ctrs. Club: Rotary (San Francisco). Home: 837 Mason St San Francisco CA 94108 Office: 44 Montgomery St San Francisco CA 94104

LEE, TSU-YUM RICHARD, mech. engr.; b. Szechuan, China, Feb. 28, 1942; came to U.S., 1968, naturalized, 1976; s. F.P. and Chi (Ni) L.; B.S., Chung-Yuan Coll., Taiwan, 1966; M.S. in Chem. Engring., Purdue U., 1970, Ph.D. in Mech. Engring., 1977; m. Caroline K. Liu, Sept. 20, 1969; children—Dickson, Christopher. Teaching asst. Fu-Jen Cath. U., Taiwan, 1967-68; research asst., teaching asst. dept. chem. engring. Purdue U., West Lafayette, Ind., 1968-70; asst. researcher, Center for Info. and Numerical Data Analysis and Synthesis, Purdue U., 1970-77, asst. sr. researcher, 1977; mech. engr. Civil Engring. Squadron, U.S. Air Force, Abilene, Tex., 1977-79, Naval Civil Engring. Lab., Port Hueneme, Calif., 1979—. Served to 2nd lt. Army of Republic of China, 1966-67. Registered profl. engr., Tex. Mem. Am. Inst. Chem. Engrs., ASME, Sigma Xi. Christian Ch. Contbr. articles to profl. jours.; author: Thermal Expansion-Nonmetallic Solids, 1978, Vol. 13 of TPRC Data Book Series, Purdue U. Home: 3287 Heatherglow St Thousand Oaks CA 91360 Office: Code L63 Naval Civil Engring Lab Port Hueneme CA 93043

LEE, YONG TSUN, lawyer; b. Shanghai, China, June 12, 1952; s. Kwong Cheong and Ching So (Lee) L.; came to U.S., 1970, naturalized, 1973; student Orange Coast Coll., 1971-72, So. Calif. Coll., 1970-71; J.D. and B.S. in Law, Am. Coll. Law, 1978; children—Mia, Erin, Jennifer, Christin, Candice. Lab. instr. math. Orange Coast Coll., Costa Mesa, Calif., 1971; mgr. Shanghai Pine Garden, Balboa Island, 1973-78; admitted to Calif. bar, 1978; practice law, Costa Mesa, 1979—. Mem. Am. Bar Assn., Orange County Bar Assn. Democrat. Roman Catholic. Office: 720 W 19 St Costa Mesa CA 92627

LEE, YUAN CHUEN, pollution control company executive; b. Chengtu, China, Nov. 18, 1913; s. T.F. and Y.S. Lee; B.S., Calif. Inst. Tech., 1938. With Consol. Vultee Corp., Downey, Calif., 1941-46, U. So. Calif., Los Angeles, 1946-47; mgr. space tech. div. Aerojet Gen. Corp., Azusa, Calif., 1947-60; pres. Astropower Corp., Newport Beach, Calif., 1960-63; dir. power systems Lockheed Millies and Space Div., Sunnyvale, Calif., 1963-69; pres. Environics, Huntington Beach, Calif., 1969-76; pres. Eneron Corp., Costa Mesa, Calif., 1976—. Mem. Am. Rocket Soc., Combustion Inst., Inst. Aero. Scis. Patentee vapor control system, oxides of nitrogen reduction. Home: PO Box 51 Palm Springs CA 92263 Office: 3100 Airway Costa Mesa CA 92626

LEECING, WALDEN ALBERT, educator; b. Glendale, Calif., Sept. 6, 1932; s. Horace Walden and Leona Belle (Dudek) L.; B.A. U. Redlands, 1954; M.A., Stanford, 1956, postgrad., 1973—; m. Elizabeth Joan Miller, Aug. 16, 1958; children—Jeffrey Scott, Brian Walden. Tchr., El Rancho High Sch., Whittier, Calif., 1957-59, Santa Ana (Calif.) High Sch., 1959-66; from instr. to asso. prof. lang. arts Chabot Coll., Hayward, Calif., 1967—, chmn. speech dept. Vice-pres. Santa Ana Community Players, 1964-66; asst. organist San Ramon Valley Ch., 1968—. Mem. Nat. Council English Tchrs., AAUP, No. Calif. Forensics Assn., Am. Guild Organists, Stanford Alumni Assn. (life). Republican. Conglist. Author: The Santa Ana Community Players: 1920-1927, 1956; (with James Armstrong) The Curious Eye, 1970; Viva la Causa! A Historiographic Survey of Chicano Studies Programs at Five Bay Area Colleges and Universities. Home: 697 Paradise Valley Ct S Crow Canyon Country Club San Ramon CA 94583 Office: Chabot Coll 25555 Hesperian Blvd Hayward CA 94545

LEEDS, ANDREW (MACK), psychologist, consultant; b. Cleve., May 25, 1949; s. Maurice A. and Alice Joy (Rich) L.; m. Laura Strohm, Sept. 8, 1968, m. 2d, Deborah Diane Taylor-Fench, Feb. 9, 1979. B.A. in Psychology with honors, U. Calif.-Santa Cruz, 1972; M.A. in Clin. Psychology, Goddard Coll., 1975; postgrad. Internat. Coll., 1981-83.

Lic. marriage and family therapist, Calif., 1978. Pvt. practice clin. psychology, Santa Cruz, 1975-79; program coordinator Sentient Systems, Santa Cruz, 1977-79; pvt. practice Ctr. for Holistc Psychology and Edn., Beverly Hills, Calif.; 1980-83; pvt. practice, dir. psychol. services, LifePlus, Santa Monica, Calif., 1983—; cons. in stress mgmt.; psychosomatic therapy trainer. Bd. dirs. Lomi Sch. Found., Marin County, Calif., 1978-82; mem. Santa Cruz Mental Health Adv. Bd., 1978-79; active Physicians for Soc. Responsiblty. Mem. Am. Psychol. Assn. Contbr. articles to profl. jours. Home: Apt 22 303 California Ave Santa Monica CA 90403 Office: LifePlus 1547 9th St Santa Monica CA 90401

LEEGARD, ARLIE LONGSWORTH, mfg. co. exec.; b. Webster, S.D., Dec. 31, 1919; s. ALbert and Ida Olivia (Engebretson) L.; m. Bernice Loretta Chessey, Aug. 16, 1941; children—Bruce Michael, Mark Jeoffrey, Bonnie Jean, Nancy Jean. Dist. mgr. Colgate Palmolive Co., Mpls., 1939-48; v.p., gen. mgr. Nesbitt Fruit Products, Inc., Los Angeles, 1948-66; pres. Instl. Marketeers, San Jose, Calif. and Memphis, 1966—; adviser to instl. grocery trade. Served to lt. (j.g.) U.S. Maritime Service 1944-45. Recipient Nugget award Nugget Distbrs. Inc., 1969, Nifda award, 1972; Pitts. Corning award, 1974, 75, 76, 77, 78, 79. Mem. Am. Mktg. Assn., Pitts. Corn Producers Club. Republican. Baptist. Clubs: Masons, Scottish Rite, Shriners. Developer various food improvements in restaurant operation. Office: 1880 Dobbin Dr San Jose CA 95133

LEE-MERROW, SUSAN WARREN, computer co. exec.; b. Regensburg, Germany, Nov. 1, 1947 (parents Am. citizens); d. Robert Vernon, Jr., and Cynthia Baldwin (Warren) Lee; A.A., Foothill Coll., 1976; B.A. with distinction, San Jose State U., 1978; m. Norman Dennis Lane, 1982; children by previous marriage—Justin Rufus, Victoria Lee. Coordinator program devel. Mental Research Inst., Palo Alto, Calif., 1978-80; human resource analyst Inpsych, Cupertino, Calif., 1980-81; new products mgr. Automated Simulations, Mountain View, Calif., 1981-83; producer Electronic Arts, San Mateo, Calif., 1983—; cons. Mental Research Inst. Mem. Computer-User Educators, Assn. Ednl. Data Systems, Alpha Kappa Delta, Alpha Gamma Sigma. Contbr. chpts. in books. Home: 31422 Brae Burn Ave Hayward CA 94544 Office: 2755 Campus Dr San Mateo CA 94402

LEES, SALLY K., manufacturers representative; b. Wichita, Kans., Apr. 17, 1926; d. August R. and Dena H. (Ellis) Krehbiel; B.A., Kans. U., 1947; m. Milton H. Lees, Nov. 16, 1969; children—Mary Catherine Kellett, Molly Ann Wantuch. Mfrs. rep. children's wear, San Francisco, 1959—; pres. Sally Lees Inc. Mem. Children's Wear Assn. (dir. 1973-79). Mem. Kappa Kappa Gamma. Republican. Presbyterians. Club: Peninsula Golf and Country (San Mateo, Calif.). Home: 141 W Bellevue San Mateo CA 94402 Office: 833 Market St Suite 604 San Francisco CA 94103

LEES, SHIRLEY ANN, communications/librarian specialist; b. Acushnet, Mass., Mar. 19, 1928; d. Walter Edward and Edna Frances (Reed) Mellor; m. Robert Alfred Lees, Mar. 14, 1928; children—Mark, John. A.A. with honors in English, Chaffey Community Coll., 1976; B.A. cum laude in English and Humanities, Calif. State Poly. U., 1978. Reporter, editor Standard Times, New Bedford, Mass., 1946-50; bookkeeper various firms, Los Angeles, 1950-55; reporter Progress Bull., Pomona, Calif., 1955-70; libararian various schs. and libraries in Pomona Valley, 1970-78; family sect. editor Progress Bull., Pomona, 1978-81; communications and library specialist Aerospace div. Perkin-Elmer Corp., Pomona, 1981—. Pres. YWCA of Pomona Valley, 1981-82, bd. dirs., 1979-81; pres. Claremont Rep. Women's Club, 1965, 66. Mem. Spl. Libraries Assn., Press Club So. Calif. (v.p. 1982-83, bd. dirs. 1981-82), Soroptimist Internat. Pomona. Republican. Roman Catholic. Club: Hi-Nooners Toastmasters (Pomona). Office: Perkin-Elmer Corp Aerospace Div 2771 N Garey Ave Pomona CA 91767

LEFEBRE, FREDERICK HERMAN, financial services company executive; b. Grand Rapids, Mich., July 17, 1919; s. Fred J. and Harmanna (Stuitje) LeF.; m. Garretta J. Bierlink, July 26, 1949; children—Tony, Joni, Lori, Tim. Student Calvin Coll., 1939-41. Commd. 2d lt. U.S. Air Force, 1942, advanced through grades to col., 1952, ret., 1970, with IRM, 1971—, sr. v.p., Alamo, Calif., 1980—. Elder, council v.p. Christian Ref. Ch., 1972-75, 81—. Decorated D.F.C., Air medal. Republican. Mem. Ret. Officers Assn. Club: Rotary. Home: 48 Cuesta Way Walnut Creek CA 94596 Office: 1443 Danville Blvd Alamo CA 94507

LEFEBURE, TAM LEO, securities corporation executive; b. Cedar Rapids, Iowa, Nov. 13, 1939; s. Leo Tamblyn and Meryl (Frederick) LeF.; B.S., U. Ariz., 1962, M.S., 1964; m. Diana Reyes, Oct. 4, 1969; children—Colleen, Bryan. Bank examiner FDIC, 1965-69; asst. v.p. Lloyds Bank, San Francisco, 1969-74; internat. bank examiner loan rev. Wells Fargo Bank, San Francisco, 1975; pvt. investor, San Francisco, 1976-79; pres. Cooper-Keanworthy, Inc., San Francisco, 1979—. Mem. Info. Assn. Fin. Planning. Clubs: Elks, Masons, Porsche of Am. Home: 11 Highland Ct Larkspur CA 94939 Office: Cooper-Kanworth Inc 601 California St San Francisco CA 94108

LEFEBVRE, D'ARGENCÉ, RENÉ-YVON, educator, museum ofcl.; b. Plouescat, France, Aug. 21, 1928; s. Marc Lefebvre d'Argencé and Andrée Thierry; student U. Sorbonne, Paris, 1946-51, Cambridge U. (Eng.), 1951-52; m. Ritva Anneli Pelanne, Sept. 7, 1955; children—Chantal, Yann, Luc. Came to U.S., 1962. Curator, Musée Cernuschi, Paris, 1953-58; mem. Ecole Française d'Extrême-Orient, 1954—; curator Blanchard de la Brosse Mus., Saigon, 1954-56, Louis Finot Mus., Hanoi, 1954-56; Quai d'Orsay grant Taiwan, 1959-62; prof. art history U. Calif. at Berkeley, 1962-65; curator Asiatic collections de Young Museum, San Francisco, 1964-65, dir. Avery Brundage Collection, 1965-68, dir., chief curator Asian Art Mus. of San Francisco, 1969—; pres. French-Am. Bilingual Sch. of San Francisco, 1976-79, v.p., 1979—; trustee Asian Art Found., 1979—, Fondation Beaudry, 1977—; v.p. Chinese-Am. Sch., 1981—; mem. adv. council Marin Cultural Center, 1981—. Served with Free French Forces, World War II. Decorated médaille de la Reconnaissance Française, chevalier de l'Ordre National du Mérite (France); chevalier de l'Etoile du Nord (Sweden); recipient Order of Merit, Avery Brundage Found., 1968; Order Cultural Merit (Korea). Mem. Soc. Asian Art (adv. com. San Francisco 1964), French-Am. Bilingual Sch. (pres. San Francisco 1976-79). Roman Catholic. Contbr. to publs. in field. Home: 16 Midhill Dr Mill Valley CA 94941 Office: Asian Art Museum Golden Gate Park San Francisco CA 94118

LEFOND, ANNE MAY, real estate broker; b. Ashland, Wis., Apr. 26, 1917; d. Charles and Anna (Erickson) Newman; B.A. cum laude, Northland Coll., Ashland, 1939; M.L.S., U. Wis., 1940; m. Stanley J. Lefond, Dec. 26, 1946; children—Dennis C., Robert E. Reference librarian Colgate U., Hamilton, N.Y., 1945-46, U. Mich., Ann Arbor, 1949-52; librarian Euclid (Ohio) Public Schs., 1953-66; sales asso. Lloyd C. Helgager Co., Woodland Hills, Calif., 1967-70; broker New Eng. Realty Co., Westport, Conn., 1970-72; broker-mgr. Crown Realty Co., Evergreen, Colo., 1972-75; broker-asso. Junction Realty Co., Evergreen, 1976—; v.p. Indsl. Minerals, Inc., Evergreen, 1976—. Mem. Evergreen Bd. Realtors (dir.), Colo. Assn. Realtors, Nat. Assn. Real Estate Brokers, Nat. Inst. Real Estate Brokers. C. of C. Lutheran. Clubs: Hiwan Country, Swedish of Denver. Home: 29983 Canterbury Circle Evergreen CO 80439 Office: PO Box 1867 Evergreen CO 80439

LE FONTAINE, JOSEPH RAYMOND, publisher, writer; b. Buffalo, Apr. 6, 1927; s. Joseph Romeo and Charlotte Henrietta (Bertrand) LeF.; m. June Roberta Aldred, June 22, 1944 (div. 1976); children—Stephen, Bruce, David, Suzanne Le Fontaine Conley. B.S.M.E., Rochester Inst. Tech., 1949. Design engr. Nat. Engrng. Co., Los Angeles, 1950-52, Houston Fearless Corp., Los Angeles, 1952-54; chief engr. Koehler Aircraft Products Co., Los Angeles, 1955-58, Skyvalve, Inc., Los Angeles, 1959-65; dir. research and devel. Snap Tite, Inc., Erie, Pa., 1965-67; dir. research and devel. Scoville Fluid Products, Wake Forest, N.C., 1967-69; nat. sales mgr. Western Precipitation Co., Los Angeles, 1969-72; rare book dealer, Los Angeles and N.Y.C., 1972-76; writer, pub., Vashon Island, Wash., 1976—; books include: A Directory of Buyers: Old Books and Paper Americana, 1978; Turning Paper to Gold: The Paper Miners Manual, 1982; (as Joseph H. Raymond) The Investors Guide to Rare Books, 1978, You Can Write Yourself a Fortune, 1979; International Book Collectors Directory, 1983; editor, pub. The InvestArt Almanac, 1975-77, Graphic Arts Collector, 1975-76, Information Marketers Newsletter, 1978-79; tchr. writing seminars. Served with AUS, 1944-46; ETO. Mem. Com. Small Mag. Editors and Pubs., Nat. Writers Club. Ind. Cons. Am. Republican. Episcopalian. Office: PO Box 872 Vashon Island WA 98070

LEFORGEE, REX SLOAN, accountant; b. Kansas City, Kans., Feb. 22, 1939; s. John Calvin and Eleanor (Sloan) L.; m. Cheryl Kempke, Sept. 3, 1966; children—Jason, Shelby, Paul. B.S., Kans. State U., 1961. C.P.A., Idaho. Acct., Kennedy & Coe, C.P.A.s, Salina, Kans., 1962-68; controller Kit Mfg. Co., Caldwell, Idaho, 1968-72; mng. ptnr. Leforgee, Rogers & Evans, C.P.A.s, Twin Falls, Idaho, 1972—. Served with USAR, 1961-67. Mem. Am. Inst. C.P.A.s, (council), Idaho Soc. C.P.A.s (past pres.). Lutheran. Clubs: Rotary (pres.), Blue Lakes Country. Home: 1779 Falls Ave E Twin Falls ID 93301 Office: 864 Filer St Twin Falls ID 83301

LEFTIN, HARRY PAUL, chemical research director; b. Beverly, Mass., Oct. 23, 1926; s. Eli Moses and Annie (Davidoff) L.; m. Selma Muriel Gordon, July 22, 1954; children—Lori Beth, Debra Joy, Alyson Ruth. A.B., Boston U., 1950, Ph.D. in Chemistry (Research Corp. fellow, 1951-54), 1955. Research fellow Mellon Inst., Pitts., 1954-59, research chemist, 1959-60, supr. chem. research, 1960-67, sr. research assoc., 1967-73, research mgr., 1973-81; assoc. dir. research M.W. Kellog Co., Houston, 1981—; adj. prof. chemistry Farleigh Dickinson U., Rutherford, N.J., 1960-75; dir. Adventure Personnel Inc. Mem. bd. visitors dept. chemistry Boston U.; Served with U.S. Army, 1944-45, USAR, 1945-48. Recipient Disting. Alumni award Boston U., 1975. Fellow Am. Inst. Chemists; mem. Am. Chem. Soc., Catalysis Soc. No. Am., Sigma Xi. Club: Knights of Pythias. Assoc. editor: Catalysis Reviews; contbr. articles in field to profl. jours. Office: 16200 Park Row Houston TX 77084

LEGEND, MOLLY, artist; b. Chgo., Apr. 30, 1927; d. Jack and Bessie (Yedwalsky) Schulman; m. Albert Sol Singer, July 23, 1945 (dec.); m. 2d, Mark Legend, Mar. 13, 1975. Student Chgo. Art Inst., 1940-44, Chouinard Art Sch., 1950-53, UCLA, 1955-76. Artist in oils and acrylics, 1952—, specialist in custom made Egyptian paintings and hieroglyphics, Los Angeles, 1978—; one-woman shows: All-State Savs. & Loan, Prudential Savs. & Loan, 1980-81, Los Angeles; group shows in Westwood, Beverly Hills, San Francisco, San Jose, Walnut Creek, Palm Springs and Palm Desert, Calif.; represented in numerous pvt. collections U.S. and abroad. Mem. Orange Art Assn., Cerritos Art Assn., South Bay Art Assn., Am. Nat. Theatre Assn., Artist Equity Assn. Office: PO Box 24446 Los Angeles CA 90024

LEGG, LORRAINE OLIVERO, forest products company executive; b. Chgo., Oct. 12, 1939; d. John C. and Gisella M. (Nomellini) Olivero; B.A., U. Calif., Berkeley, 1960; J.D., Lincoln U., 1967; m. Kenneth G. Legg (div.). Vice pres. Transam. Mortgage Co. Calif., San Francisco, 1960-67, Fed. Nat. Mortgage Assn., Washington, 1967-70; with Boise Cascade Corp., Boise, Idaho, 1970—; sr. v.p., gen. mgr. Boise Cascade Home & Land Corp., 1972-80, dir. real estate and risk mgmt., 1979-80, treas., 1980—, v.p., 1982—; dir. L.B. Nelson Corp., Menlo Park, Calif., Terteling Mktg., Inc., Boise, Liquidity Funds for Thrifts, N.Y.C. Pres. Women's Forum West, 1978-79; 1970-79, bd. dirs. Boise Civic Opera, 1982—. Mem. Fin. Execs. Inst., Treas. Club San Francisco. Democrat. Roman Catholic. Editor-in-chief Lincoln Law Rev., 1966-67. Office: 1 Jefferson Sq Boise ID 83728

LEGO, JAREN CAMPBELL, broadcasting executive; b. Cin., May 6, 1954; d. Arlie and Leila (Combs) Campbell. m. John Raymond Lego, May 24, 1978. B.A. in Communicative Arts and Scis., DePauw U., 1976; cert. radio mktg. cons. Radio Advt. Bur. Account exec., Sta. KERE Radio, Denver, 1976-78, Sta. KDLR Radio, 1978-80, KPPL Radio 1980-81; v.p., gen. sales mgr., then gen. mgr., Sta. KKBZ Radio, Santa Paula Calif., 1981—. Active Republican Nat. Com. Mem. Advt. Club Ventura (Calif.) County. Republican. Home: 1070 Creek Rd Ojai CA 93023 Office: Sta KKBZ 15115 Faulkner Rd Santa Paula CA 93060

LEGOY, SHIRLEY MCDONOUGH, accountant; b. Tonopah, Nev., Mar. 18, 1929; d. James Joseph and Marie McDonough; B.S., U. Nev., 1950, M.B.A., 1976; m. Leo Robert LeGoy, Feb. 18, 1950; children—Leo Robert, James Michael, Philip Richard. Staff acct. Elmer Fox & Co., Reno, Nev., 1967-75, Barnard & Hildahl, C.P.A.s, Reno, 1975-77; prin. Shirley M. LeGoy, C.P.A., Reno, 1977; partner Samon, LeGoy & Co., C.P.A.s, Reno, 1978—. Chmn. continuing profl. edn. com. State Bd. Nev. Accountancy, 1977-79; mem. Nev. State Bd. Equalization, 1978; treas. Mary Gojack for Senate campaign, 1980, Congress campaign, 1982. Mem. Am. Inst. C.P.A.s, Nev. Soc. Public Accts. Republican. Club: Soroptimist Internat. Home: 1245 Washington St Reno NV 89503 Office: 216 Mount Rose St Reno NV 89509

LE GRANDE, HARRY, university administrator; b. San Bernardino, Ca., July 16, 1953; s. George Tyree and Ruby C. (Shannon) LeG.; m. Denise Marthee Florence, Jan. 2, 1978; 1 dau., Mychal Etienne. B.A., U. Calif.-Irvine, 1975; M.Ed., Oreg. State U., 1978. Dir. housing, asst. dean students Pacific U., Forest Grove, Oreg., 1978-80; area coordinator U. Wash., Seattle, 1980-81; asst. dir. housing and child care U. Calif.-Berkeley, 1981—. Recipient Outstanding Service award U. Calif.-Irvine, 1975. Mem. NW Coll. Personnel Assn. (sec. 1979-80, pres.-elect 1980-81), Nat. Assn. Student Personnel Adminstrs., Assn. Coll. and U. Housing Officers Internat. (presented minority issues in housing conf., Tampa, Fla., 1982), Calif. Assn. U. and Housing Officers (program, housing internship and nominating coms. 1982-83), Am. Coll. Personnel Assn., Am. Personnel and Guidance Assn., Sigma Chi. Democrat. Office: U Calif-Berkeley 2401 Bowditch St Berkeley CA 94720

LEHMAN, EDGAR RUSSELL, life insurance company executive; b. Los Angeles, Aug. 15, 1933; s. Phillips D. and Louise (Bachelor) L.; m. Sonja Jean Park, Aug. 12, 1961; children—David, Mary. B.A., U. So. Calif., 1955; diploma magna cum laude Biola U., 1957. With Pacific Mut. Life Ins. Co., Newport Beach, Calif., 1956—, asst. v.p., 1971, 2d v.p., 1972-82, v.p., 1982—. Trustee Biola U., 1966—, chmn., 1982—. Mem. Life Office Mgmt. Assn. (dir. and chmn. human resources council). Republican. Contbr. articles to mgmt. jour. Office: Pacific Mut Life Ins Co 700 Newport Center Dr Newport Beach CA 92660

LEHMAN, GEORGE HENRY, aviation safety consultant; b. Cin., June 15, 1921; s. Clarence Henry and Goldie (Gellman) L.; student Glendale Coll., 1948-51, U. So. Calif., 1956, U. Ariz., 1967; m. Bernice Denos, Apr. 3, 1948; children—Cathy, Laura, Howard. Flight test engr. Lockheed Aircraft, Burbank, Calif., 1940-53; engr. flight test, systems safety engrng. Rockwell Internat., Downey, Calif., 1953-79, ret., 1979; prin. forensic engr. Teledyne Engrng. Services, Costa Mesa, Calif., 1979-80; engrng. specialist Northrop Corp., 1980—; cons. aviation safety, La Habra, Calif., 1971—. Served with USN, 1944-50. Recipient Apollo Achievement award NASA, 1962. Registered profl. engr., Calif. Mem. System Safety Soc. Club: Masons. Office: PO Box 723 La Habra CA 90631

LEHMAN, JAMES ALDEN, economics educator; b. St. Charles, Ill., Oct. 20, 1947; s. Harold Richard and Elsie (Landis) L.; m. Kay Laura Behrens, Aug. 25, 1973. B.A., Davidson (N.C.) Coll. 1973; M.A. in Econs., Duke U., 1976, Ph.D., 1981. Instr. econs. Duke U. 1975-77, 80-81; instr. Kobe (Japan) U., 1977-80; asst. prof. Pitzer Coll., Claremont, Calif. 1981—. Thomas J. Watson fellow 1973-74; Calvin B. Hoover fellow 1974-75. Mem. Am. Econs. Assn. Democrat. Presbyterian. Office: Dept Econs Pitzer Coll Claremont CA 91711

LEHMAN, RICHARD HENRY, congressman; b. Sanger, Calif., July 20, 1948; s. Henry and Elaine Lehman; m. Patricia Kandarian, Aug. 28, 1971. Ed. Fresno (Calif.) City Coll., Calif. State U.-Fresno, U. Calif.-Santa Cruz. Adminstrv. asst. to mem. Calif. Assembly, 1969-76; mem. 31st Calif. Assembly, 1976-82; mem. 98th Congress from 18th Calif. Dist. Mem. Calif. N.G., 1970-76. Democrat. Lutheran. Office: 1319 Longworth House Office Bldg Washington DC 20515

LEHMAN, WILLIAM FRANCIS, agronomist; b. Montgomery, Minn., Apr. 25, 1926; s. William Earnest and Mary Ann (Washa) L.; m. Betty Helen Drysdale, Aug. 5, 1950; children—William D., Barbara H. B.S., Wartburg Coll., Waverly, Iowa, 1950; postgrad. U. Ariz., 1951-52; M.S., U. Minn., 1956, Ph.D. 1956. Jr. agronomist U. Calif.-Davis, 1956-58, asst. agronomist, 1958-64, assoc. agronomist, 1964-74, agronomist, 1974—. Served with U.S. Army, 1944-46. Mem. Am. Soc. Agronomy, Crop Sci. Soc. Am., Am. Soc. Agronomy, Am. Genetic Assn. Contbr. articles to profl. jours.

LEIDIGER, LYNDA JEAN, communications specialist, writer; b. Milw., Dec. 20, 1952; d. J. Kilian and Shirley J. (Fruhner) Leidiger; m. John B. Kafka, Feb. 29, 1976. B.A., U. Wis.-Madison, 1975. Prodn. asst., Automobile Club of So. Calif., Los Angeles, 1976-78, communications specialist, 1978—; free lance fiction writer, 1976—; stories pub. Playboy, 1979, McCall's, 1983. Winner Internat. Imitation Hemingway Competition, Harry's Bar & Am. Grill, 1983; best new fiction contbr. award Playboy, 1979. Mem. Internat. Assn. of Bus. Communicators.

LEIFERER, CHARLES EDWARD, judge; b. Raton, N. Mex., Feb. 27, 1927; s. Calvin J. and Allie Amelia (Hyden) L.; B.A., U. Colo., 1950, LL.B., 1952; student Jud. Coll., Reno, 1976-77; m. Nita Jean Gilbert Harre, Sept. 7, 1948; children—Michael, Clifford, Charlita Jo. Asso. firm Leunartz & Walrod, Sterling, Colo., 1953-54; individual practice law, Eagle, Colo., 1954-60; judge adminstrv. law, public utility commr. State of Oreg., Salem, 1960—; lectr. in field. Exec. bd. Cascade Area council Boy Scouts Am., 1970—, recipient Silver Beaver award, 1973; mem. Marion County Search and Rescue, Inc. Served with USAAF, 1944-47. ICC practitioner. Mem. Colo. (bd. govs. 1956-60), Oreg. (chmn. adminstrv. law com. 1974) bar assns., Am. Legion, Oreg. Guides and Packers Assn. Methodist.

LEIGH, EMILY ANN, banker; b. Hilmar, Calif., Apr. 12, 1926; d. Sarafin S. and Maria R. Morais; m. Keith B. Leigh, Apr. 8, 1976; children—Daniel, Larry, Maryann. Bookkeeper, Bank of Newman (Calif.), 1943-50; with Bank of Am., Turlock, Calif., 1956-78; with Golden Valley Bank, Hilmar, Calif., 1978—, now v.p., mgr.; dir. CIA Fin. Corp. Mem. Hilmar C. of C. (past pres.). Democrat. Roman Catholic. Club: Soroptimist (v.p.) (Turlock, Calif.). Home: 2505 Teresa Ct Turlock CA 95380

LEIGHNINGER, DAVID SCOTT, cardiovascular surgeon; b. Youngstown, Ohio, Jan. 16, 1920; s. Jesse Harrison and Marjorie (Lightner) L.; m. Margaret Jane Malony, May 24, 1942; children—David Allan, Jenny. B.A., Oberlin Coll., 1942; M.D., Case Western Res. U., 1945. Intern Univ. Hosps. of Cleve., 1945-46, resident, 1949-51, asst. surgeon, 1951-68; research fellow in cardiovascular surgery research lab. Case Western Res. U. Sch. Medicine, Cleve., 1948-49, 51-55, 57-67, instr. surgery, 1951-55, sr. instr., 1957-64, asst. prof., 1964-68, asst. clin. prof., 1968-70; resident Cin. Gen. Hosp., 1955-57; practice medicine specializing in cardiovascular surgery, Cleve., 1957-70; pvt. practice medicine specializing in cardiovascular and gen. surgery Edgewater Hosp., Chgo., 1970-82, staff surgeon, also dir. emergency surg. services, 1970-82; staff surgeon, also dir. emergency surg. services Mazel Med. Ctr., Chgo., 1970-82; emergency physician Miner's Hosp., Raton, N.Mex., 1982—, No. Colfax County Hosp., Raton, 1982—; assoc., courtesy, or cons. staff Marymount Hosp., Cleve., Mt. Sinai Hosp., Cleve., Geauga Community Hosp., Chardon, Ohio, Bedford Community Hosp (Ohio), 1957-70. Tchr. tng. courses in CPR for med. personnel, police, fire and vol. rescue workers, numerous cities, 1950-70. Served to capt., M.C., AUS, 1946-48. Recipient Chris award Columbus Internat. Film Festival, 1964, numerous other award for sci. exhibits from various nat. and state med. socs., 1953-70; USPHS grantee, 1949-68. Fellow Am. Coll. Cardiology, Am. Coll. Chest Physicians; mem. AMA, N.Mex. Med. Assn., Colfax County Med. Assn., Ill. Med. Assn., Chgo. Med. Assn., U. Cin. Grad. Sch. Surg. Soc. Contbr. numerous articles to med. jours., chpts. to med. texts; spl. pioneer research (with Claude S. Beck) in physiopathology of coronary artery disease and CPR; developed surg. treatment of coronary artery disease; achieved 1st successful defibrillation of human heart, 1st successful reversal of fatal heart attack; provided 1st intensive care of coronary patients. Home: PO Box 408 Fort Garland CO 81133

LEIGHTON, FREEMAN BEACH, geologist; b. Champaign, Ill., Dec. 19, 1924; s. Morris Morgan and Ada Harriet (Beach) L.; B.S. in Engrng. Geology, U. Va., 1946; M.S. in Geology, Calif. Inst. Tech., 1949, Ph.D. in Geology, 1951; m. Wanda J. Downey, Feb. 19, 1946; children—Jamie, Stephen, Richard, Roger. Chmn. dept. geology Whittier (Calif.) Coll., 1951-72; pres. Leighton & Assocs., Irvine, Calif., 1960—. Bd. dirs. City of Hope, 1980. Served to ensign USNR, 1946-46. Recipient Claire P. Holdredge award Nat. Assn. Engrng. Geologists, 1967. Mem. Assn. Engrng. Geologists, Am. Geol. Inst., Geol. Soc. Am., AAAS, Am. Assn. Petroleum Geologists, Am. Inst. Profl. Geologists, Sigma Xi. Republican. Methodist. Clubs: Branner, Whittier U. Author: Landslides and Hillside Development, 1966; Bluebird Canyon Landslide, Laguna Beach, 1979-82. Home: 22042 Arcos St Mission Viejo CA 92691 Office: 1151 Duryea Ave Irvine CA 92714

LEIGHTON, HENRY ALEXANDER, physician; b. Manila, Philippines, Nov. 12, 1929 (parents U.S. citizens); s. Raymond Harry and Theola Marie (Alexander) L.; B.A. in History, U. Calif., Berkeley, 1952, M.P.H., 1971; M.D., U. Calif., San Francisco, 1956; m. Helga Maria Hell, Jan. 17, 1970; children—Alan Raymond, Henry Alexander, Michael Ballinger, John, Marni, Tammy Ballinger. Intern, So. Pacific Gen. Hosp., San Francisco, 1956-57; resident in surgery Brooke Gen. Hosp., Ft. Sam Houston, Tex., 1960-62; commd. 2d lt., U.S. Army, 1957, advanced through grades to col., 1971; div. surgeon 8th Inf. Div., Germany, 1964-66; comdr. 15th Med. Bn., Vietnam, 1966-67; instr. Med. Field Service Sch., San Antonio, 1968-70; resident preventive medicine, Ft. Ord, Calif., 1971-72, chief preventive medicine, 1973-76; chief preventive medicine U.S. Army Europe, 1976-79; ret., 1979; chief occupational health MEDDAC, Ft. Ord, 1981—; cons. preventive medicine U.S. Army Res. Europe. Neighborhood commr. Boy Scouts Am., 1964-66; bd. dirs. Regional Am. Lung Assn., 1980—, treas., 1981. Decorated Air medal with oakleaf cluster, Bronze Star, Legion of Merit, Meritorious Service Medal; diplomate Am. Bd. Preventive Medicine. Fellow Am. Coll. Preventive Medicine; mem. Am. Public Health Assn., Am. Occupational Med. Assn., AMA, Assn. Mil. Surgeons, Ret. Officers Assn., Assn. U.S. Army, Theta Xi. Clubs: Masons, Shriners. Salinas CA 93908 Office: Occupational Health USAMEDDAC Fort Ord CA 93941

LEIGHTON, JACK RICHARD, company executive, educator; b. Boise, Idaho, May 10, 1918; s. Ralph Waldo and Lucia (Strub) L.; student U. Wash., Seattle, 1938-39; B.S., U. Oreg., 1941, M.S., 1942, Ph.D., 1954; postgrad. U. Iowa, 1950; m. Helen Louise Wirtenberger, July 24, 1942; 1 son, James Carl. Dir. phys. edn. and athletics Montpelier (Idaho) High Sch., 1941-42; exec. asst. phys. medicine rehab. service Vancouver (Wash.) VA Hosp., 1946-50; assoc. prof. phys. edn. Pa. State U., State College, 1952-53; dir. div. health, phys. edn., recreation and athletics Eastern Wash. U., 1953-81, assoc. prof., 1953-56, prof., 1955-81, pres. Leighton Flexometer Co. Com. secondary sch. health and phys. edn. Idaho Dept. Edn., Boise, 1942; cons. state adv. com. on school activity and phys. edn. Wash. Dept. Pub. Instrn., Olympia, 1954-55, mem. com. phys. edn. curriculum guide, 1957-58. Served with AUS, 1942-46. Fellow Am. Coll. Sports Medicine (mem. Am. necrology com. 1955-58, chmn. fitness sect. 1960-61, mem. research council, com. study purpose and propose revisions of structure and procedures of gen. div. 1960-61; mem. N.W. dist. honor awards com. 1955-57, 76-79, chmn., 1976-77, constitution com. 1957-60, chmn. research sect. 1957-58, v.p. phys. edn. 1957-58, chmn. fitness sect. N.W. dist. 1963-64, pres. N.W. dist. 1971-72); mem. Wash. Assn. Health, Phys. Edn. and Recreation (mem. phys. fitness steering com. 1955-57, constitution com. 1957-58, chmn. tchr. tng. sect. 1956-57, chmn. phys. fitness steering com. 1957-59, v.p. Eastern dist. 1957-58, pres. 1959-60), Am. Congress Rehab. Medicine, N. Am. Soc. for Psychology of Sport and Phys. Activity (exec. bd. 1964-66), Nat. Rehab. Assn. (mem. Western states regional planning com. 1949), Am. Corrective Therapy Assn. (chmn. accreditation council 1978-79), Spokane United Sch. Groups (Eastern Wash. U. rep. 1957-60), Phi Delta Kappa, Phi Epsilon Kappa. Author: Physical Education for Boys, 1942; Objective Physical Education, 1946; Progressive Weight Training, 1961, Fitness, Body Devel., and Sports Conditioning Through Weight Training, 1983. Assoc. editor Research Quart. Am. Assn. Health, Phys. Edn. and Recreation, 1960-63. Editor Jour. Assn. for Phys. and Mental Rehab., 1963-67; asso. editor Jour. Health, Phys. Edn. and Recreation, 1967-68; editorial bd. Am. Corrective Therapy Jour., 1972-79. Contbr. articles and chpts. to profl. publs. Patentee instrument to measure range of joint motion. Home: E 1321 55th St Spokane WA 99203

LEINO, DEANNA ROSE, educator; b. Leadville, Colo., Dec. 15, 1937; d. Arvo Ensio Leino and Edith Mary (Bonan) Leino Malenck. B.S. in Bus. Adminstrn., U. Denver, 1959, M.S. in Bus. Adminstrn., 1967; postgrad. Community Coll. Denver, U. No. Colo., Colo. State U., U. Colo., Met. State Coll. Cert. tchr., vocat. tchr., Colo. Tchr. Jefferson County Adult Edn., Lakewood, Colo., 1963-67; tchr. bus., coordinator coop. office edn., Jefferson High Sch., Edgewater, Colo., 1959—; instr. Community Coll. Denver, Red Rocks, 1967-81, U. Colo. Denver, 1976-79, Parks Coll. Bus., 1983; dist. adviser Future Bus. Leaders Am. Active City of Edgewater Sister City Project Student Exchange Com.; pres. Career Women's Symphony Guild; treas. Phantoms of Opera, 1982—; active Opera Colo. Assocs., I Pagliacci; ex-officio trustee Denver Symphony Assn., 1980-82. Recipient disting. service award Jefferson County Sch. Bd. 1980; Jefferson High Sch. Wall of Fame 1981. Mem. NEA (life), Colo. Edn. Assn., Jefferson County Edn. Assn., Colo. Vocat. Assn., Am. Vocat. Assn., Colo. Educators for and about Bus., Profl. Secs. Internat., Career Women's Symphony Guild, Profl. Panhellenic Assn., Colo. Congress Fgn. Lang. Tchrs., Delta Pi Epsilon, Phi Chi Theta, Beta Gamma Sigma, Alpha Lambda Delta. Republican. Roman Catholic. Club: Tyrolean Soc. Denver.

LEIPOLD, WAYNE H., mechanical engineer; b. Buffalo, Jan. 19, 1938; s. Hugo C. and Pearl L. (Fisher) L.; m. Barbara J. Wilson, Dec. 17, 1960; children—Mark, Karen. B.S, U. Buffalo, 1958, M.S., 1962. Registered profl. engr., N.Y., Ariz. With Cornell Aero. Lab., Buffalo, 1958-67, research electronics engr., 1965-67; sr. electronics design engr. Delevan Electronics div. Am. Precision Ind., East Aurora, N.Y., 1967-71; with Airco Speer Electronics, Nogales, Ariz., and Airco de Mexico Nogales, Mexico, 1971-72; prodn. engr. West Cap div. San Fernando Electric, Tucson, 1973, Rogers Corp., Chandler Ariz., 1973-74; with Phelps Dodge Corp., Douglas Reduction Wks., Douglas, Ariz., 1974—, tech. services dept. head, 1979—; instr. U. Buffalo, 1962-65, Cochise Coll., Douglas. Mem. Republican Com., Pirtleville, Ariz., 1982. Mem. IEEE, AIME, Nat. Soc. Profl. Engrs., Air Pollution Control Assn. Presbyterian. Address: Drawer E Douglas AZ 85607

LEIRAN, WAYNE JARVIS, insurance executive; b. Thief River Falls, Minn., Oct. 4, 1938; s. Edry Jewel and Anna Bertine (Hegrenes) L.; m. Irene Gwendolyn Morris, June 24, 1942; children—Kim, Joni, Dawne, Bryan. B.S. B.A., U. N. Dak., 1960. Cert. Life Office Mgmt. Assn., 1979. Acct., Gen. Mills, Mpls., 1960-62; with Empire Life Ins. Co. Am., Dallas, 1962-68; comptroller Los Angeles Life Ins. Co., 1968-71; chief acct. Exec. Life Ins. Co., Beverly Hills, Calif., 1971-73; sr. v.p. fin. Comml. Bankers Life Ins. Co., Newport Beach, Calif., 1973—. Mem. Ins. Acctg. and Stats. Assn. Republican. Lutheran. Clubs: Elks. Office: 1401 Dove St Suite 550 Newport Beach CA 92660

LEITCH, CLARENCE MERVIN, barrister; b. Creelman, Sask., Can., Jan. 13, 1926; s. Peter Harold and Martha Ann (Walker) L.; m. Margaret Joyce Morris, Apr. 17, 1954; children—Hugh Campbell, Margaret Jan, Catherine Anne, James Harold. B.A., U. Alta., 1951, LL.B., 1952. Called to Alta. bar, 1953, created queen's counsel, 1968; Mem. firm Macleod Dixon, Calgary, Alta., Can., 1952-71, 1983—; atty. gen. Province of Alta., 1971-75, provincial treas., 1975-79, minister energy and natural resources, 1979-82; dir. Can. Pacific Enterprises Ltd., Chieftain Devel. Co. Ltd. Served with Royal Can. Navy, 1943-45. Mem. Can. Bar Assn., Calgary Bar Assn., Law Soc. Alta. Conservative. Clubs: Calgary Golf and Country, Mission Hills Country. Office: Macleod Dixon 324 8 Ave SW Suite 1500 Calgary AB T2P 2Z2 Canada

LEM, RICHARD DOUGLAS, painter; b. Los Angeles, Nov. 24, 1933; s. Walter Wing and Betty (Wong) L.; B.A., UCLA, 1958; M.A., Calif. State U.-Los Angeles, 1963; m. Patricia Ann Soohoo, May 10, 1958; 1 son, Stephen Vincent. Exhibited in one-man shows at Gallery 818, Los Angeles, 1965; group shows at Lynn Kottler Galleries, N.Y.C., 1973, Palos Verdes Art Gallery, 1968, Galerie Mouffe, Paris, France, 1976, numerous others; represented in permanent collections; writer, illustrator; Mile's Journey, 1983. Served with AUS, 1958-60. Mem. UCLA Alumni Assn. Address: 1861 Webster Ave Los Angeles CA 90026

LEMAY, BARRY WILLIAM, financial planner; b. Berkeley, Calif., Apr. 23, 1945; s. Remi Bernard and Barbara Evelyn (LeM.); m. Charlotte Ellen Butler, Nov. 1, 1969; 1 dau., Monique Francoise. Cert. fin. planner, Coll. for Fin. Planning, 1977. With Investors Diversified Services, San Jose, Calif., 1969-74; fin. planner Belmont Reid & Co., San Jose, 1974-76; owner Ambar Fin. Group, Campbell, Calif., 1976—. Past pres. St. Lucy's PTA, 1982-83. Mem. Internat. Assn. Fin. Planning, Inst. Cert. Fin. Planners. Republican. Roman Catholic. Club: Kiwanis (past pres. S. San Jose 1976). Home: 1852 Dry Creek Rd San Jose CA 95124 Office: 340 E Hamilton Ave Campbell CA 95008

LEMCKE, HARLAND FRITZ, safety engr.; b. Hecla, S.D., Jan. 12, 1918; s. Dick Johnston Wihlm and Rosa Clara (Lahman) L.; student Flandreau Vocat. Sch., 1937-41; m. Verna Jo Gray, July 26, 1946; children—Richard Harland, Douglas Dean. Machinist, Kaiser Steel Corp., Fontana, Calif., 1946-47; auto machinist U.S. Naval Hosp., Norco, Calif., 1947-48; engr., salesman comml. forgings Corona Clipper Co. (Calif.), Corona 1948—. Scoutmaster, Boy Scouts Am., 1960-70; agt. Little League players, 1965-72. Served with U.S. Army, 1941-46; ETO, PTO. Decorated Silver Star (2). Recipient Safety Design award Nat. Safety Council and Hartford Ins. Co., 1980. Cert. tchr. numismatics, Calif. Mem. Am. Soc. Safety Engrs. Democrat. Club: Corona Coin (pres. 1964—). Patentee trencher tooth, safety equipment design; contbr. articles on numismatics to profl. jours. Home: 946 Via Bernardo St Corona CA 91720 Office: 14200 E 6th St Corona CA 91720

LEMERY, EUGENE FRANKLIN, social worker; b. Lockwood, Mo., Sept. 17, 1927; s. John Nelson and Ann (Black) L.; m. Noreen Mary Paulson, Aug. 12, 1961; children—Mary Christine, Mark Eugene. B.A, U. Calif.-Berkeley, 1952; M.S.W., U. Utah, 1963. Cert. social worker, S.D. With Alaska Div. Pub. Welfare, 1959-63, dist. rep., Fairbanks, 1963-65; commd. corps officer Indian Hosp., USPHS, Pine Ridge, S.D., 1965-66; cons. Nev. Dept. Pub. Welfare, Carson City, 1966; psychiat. social worker Mo. Div. Mental Health, Springfield, 1967-75; social worker VA Med. Ctr. Hosp., Hot Springs, S.D., 1975-82, chmn. Internat. Yr. of Disabled Persons com., 1981; social worker Community Counseling Ctr., Ft. Richardson, Alaska, 1982—. Hot Springs mayor's rep. for Internat. Yr. of Child, 1979. Served with AUS, 1946-47. Recipient letter of commendation Gov. of Alaska, 1979. Mem. Acad. Cert. Social Workers, Nat. Assn. Social Workers, S.D. Mental Health Assn., Commd. Officers Assn. USPHS. Lutheran. Lodges: Kiwanis (v.p. 1978-79), Elks (Hot Springs); Masons. Home: 5020 Loveland Circle Eagle River AK 99557 Office: Community Counseling Center 172-D Infantry Brigade Fort Richardson AK 99505

LEMESSURIER, MARY JEAN, provincial government official; b. Montreal, Que., Can., June 12, 1929; m. Ernest Dawes LeMessurier, May 22, 1953; children—Willa Jamieson, Jill, Tim, Andrew. B.A. in Phys. Edn., McGill U.; grad. technician in hematology Royal Victoria Hosp. Founding mem. Alta. Council for Internat. Agys., 1973; past pres. Can. Save the Children Fund; v.p., then pres. Miles for Millions, 1973-77; mem. Legis. Assembly Province of Alta., 1979—, now minister of culture. Progressive Conservative. Office: 131 Legislative Bldg Edmonton AB T5K 2B6 Canada

LEMIRE, DAVID STEPHEN, school counselor; b. Roswell, N.Mex., May 23, 1949; s. Joseph Armon and Jeanne (Longwill) L.; B.A., Linfield Coll., 1972, M.Ed., 1974; Ed. S., Idaho State U., 1978; now postgrad. in counselor edn. U. Wyo., Laramie. Sch. counselor, psychol. technician Goshen County Sch. Dist. 1, Torrington, Wyo. Cert. sch. counselor, student personnel worker, psychology instr., Calif. Mem. Assn. Poetry Therapy, Nat. Council for Creative Therapies, Am. Personnel and Guidance Assn. Past editor WPGA Jour.; cons. editor WCRA Jour. Contbr. articles to profl. jours. Address: PO Box 2326 Evanston WY 82930 also Uinta County Sch Dist Davis Middle Sch

LEMMY, LEMMY, painter, printmaker, consultant, arts researcher; b. Ipoh, Perak, West Malaysia, Jan. 7, 1940; s. Aummryn Saw and Lymmpoon Lymm. Student U. Oreg., 1956-59; B.A., San Francisco State U., 1964; student Centre de Gravure Contemporaine, Geneva, 1969-70. Designer, Pinney Archtl. Constrn., San Francisco, 1960-62; arts cons., painter, printmaker, sculptor; commns. include: Bank of Calif., San Francisco, 1967, Abegg Mus., Riggisberg/Bern, Switzerland, 1974, Hess Holding Coops., Bern, 1976, Firma Rohm Gmbh, Darmstadt, Ger., 1980, 82; arts juror and lectr. Artist-in-residence, Centre de Gravure Contemporaine, Geneva, 1971, 74, 76. Mem. Associated Art Council N.Y.C., Nat. Soc. Lit. and the Arts, Stanford Com. for Art. Buddhist. Office: PO Box 1083 Menlo Park CA 94025

LEMUS, GEORGE, educator; b. Del Rio, Tex., Apr. 14, 1928; s. Leopoldo and Ines (Suarez) L.; student U. Nacional Autónoma de México, 1946-48; B.A., U. Tex., 1952, M.A., 1956, Ph.D., 1963; m. Carmen Garcia, Aug. 6, 1957; children—Agnes Marie, Sarita Ann, Henry Edward, Robert Leopold, William Anthony. Tchr. pub. high sch., Aberdeen, Idaho, 1953-54; teaching fellow U. Tex., Austin, 1955-57; instr. USAF Lang. Sch., Lackland AFB, Tex., 1957-58, Loyola U., Los Angeles, 1958-60; asst. prof. Spanish, San Diego State U., 1960-64, assoc. prof., 1965-68, prof., 1968—, dir. summer program, 1964, 65, chmn. Latin Am. Studies Com., 1963-66, grad. adv. Latin Am. Studies Program, 1966-70; vis. prof. U. Colo., summer 1968. Sec.-treas. Pacific Coast Council Latin Am. Studies, 1964, mem. governing bd., 1967-69. Direccion General de Relaciones Culturales fellow, Madrid, 1957; Del Amo Found. fellow, 1970. Mem. Am. Assn. Tchrs. Spanish and Portuguese, Assn. Latin Am. Studies, Real Sociedad Bascongada de los Amigos del País, Sigma Delta Pi, Alpha Mu Gamma. Democrat. Roman Catholic. Author: Francisco Bulnes: su vida y sus obras, 1965. Contbr. articles to profl. jours. Home: 5730 Lance St San Diego CA 92120

LENDARIS, GEORGE GREGORY, systems scientist, educator; b. Helper, Utah, Apr. 2, 1935; s. Gregory George and Argie (Xenakis) L.; B.S. with honors, U. Calif., Berkeley, 1957, M.S., 1958, Ph.D., 1961; m. Irene Kokinos, July 26, 1958; children—Miriam, Dorothy. Sr. staff scientist, project mgr. Gen. Motors Def. Research Labs., Goleta, Calif., 1961-69; prof., chmn. faculty Oreg. Grad. Center for Study and Research, 1969-71; prof. systems sci. Portland (Oreg.) State U., 1971—; cons. in field. Mem. Oreg.' Gov.'s Tech. Adv. Com., 1970-72, Oreg. State Senate Task Force on Econ. Devel., 1972-73, Multnomah County Econ. Devel. Adv. Commn., 1977-79, Econ. and Fin. Adv. Panel, Portland Energy Commn., 1980. Named Archon, Greek Orthodox Patriarchate of Constantinople, 1982; NSF fellow, 1960-61; Nat. Acad. Scis. Sr. postdoctoral fellow, 1973-74. Fellow IEEE (Citation for work in optical diffraction patterns for image analysis 1982); mem. Pattern Recognition Soc., Assn. Transpersonal Psychology, Soc. Gen. Systems Research, Systems, Man and Cybernetics Soc., Control Systems Soc., Sigma Xi. Greek Orthodox. Clubs: Greek Civic, AHEPA, Pan Cretan Assn. Am. Mem. editorial bd. Internat. Jour. Gen. Systems, Systems Research Jour.; contbr. articles to profl. jours. Home: 10655 SW Wedgewood St Portland OR 97225 Office: PO Box 751 Portland OR 97207

LENDVAY, GLENDA LOUISE FITE, personnel adminstrator; b. Henryetta, Okla., Oct. 14, 1946; d. Elvin Glenn and Bettie Louise (Carlton) F.; B.S. in Elem. Edn., Okla. State U., 1968. Sec. to v.p. Bank & Trust Co., Tulsa, 1968-71; adminstrv. asst. to new accounts supr. Cities Service Oil Co., Tulsa, 1971-73, sec. to credit card center asst. mgr., legis. coordinator, systems and programming coordinator, 1973-74; sec. to pres. and owner, bookkeeer, receptionist WRP Lumber Corp., Sedro Woolley, Wash., 1974-75; personnel asst. Homequity, 1975-76, personnel adminstr., Wilton, Conn., 1976-77, regional mgr., mgr. adminstr., San Mateo, Calif., 1977-82. Mem. Bay Area Personnel Assn., Am. Soc. Personnel Adminstrn., Am. Mgmt. Soc., Internat. Assn. Personnel Women. Republican. Home: 611 Weatherly Pl San Ramon CA 94583

LENHART, BOB GENE, grain company engineer; b. Wren, Ohio, Aug. 7, 1932; s. Orval M. and Rose N. (Elzey) L.; student Purdue U., 1956-62; m. Deloris M. Werling, June 21, 1953; children—Deborah, Kristi, Kim, Nancy. Engr., Central Soya Co., Inc., Ft. Wayne, Ind., 1956-66, maintenance engr., Gibson City, Ill., 1966-67, Ft. Worth, 1967-69; chief engr. Hayes & Stolz Co., Ft. Worth, 1969-70; engr. Continental Grain Co., Chgo., 1970-74, regional engr. Pacific Coast Region. Tacoma, 1974-81, regional ops. engring. mgr. Pacific Coast region, Portland, Oreg., 1981—. Served with U.S. Army, 1953-55. Mem. IEEE Grain Elevator and Processing Soc. Lutheran. Home: 19900 Roan Circle West Linn OR 97068 Office: Continental Grain Co 200 Market Bldg Suite 1050 Portland OR 97201

LENNON, JOHN AUZERAIS, merchandising and management consultant; b. San Francisco, July 22, 1911; s. Milton Byrne and Aimee (Auzerais) L.; A.B., U. San Francisco, 1933; student Harvard U., 1933-34; m. Marie Slamar, Oct. 1, 1974; children—Barbara Ann Lennon Hobbs, John Anthony. Cons. to furniture industry, San Rafael, Calif., 1954-82; mem. staff Retail Home Furnishings Assn., Chgo., 1955-59; pres. J. A. Lennon Co., San Rafael, 1959. Served with USAAF, 1942-45. Republican. Roman Catholic. Club: Lions. Chief contbg. editor Professional Furniture Merchant, 1970-82. Address: 60 Marinita Ave San Rafael CA 94901

LENSSEN, JOHN L., lawyer; b. Norwalk, Conn., July 19, 1936; s. Nicholas F. and Edith L. (Barratt) L.; m. Diane L. Lenssen; children—Andrew, Nicholas; A.B. Dartmouth Coll., 1958; LL.B., Stanford U., 1964. Bar: Calif. 1965, N. Mex. 1964. With Cadwell, Lenssen, Mandel & Jesmer, Santa Fe, 1973—. Served with USMC, 1958-61.

LENT, BERKELEY, chief justice state supreme court; b. Los Angeles, Sept. 22, 1921; s. Oscar Paul and Lucile (Berkeley) L.; student Occidental Coll., 1945, Reed Coll., 1948; J.D., Willamette U., 1950; m. Joan Kay, Dec. 27, 1968; children—Patricia Lee Lent Brandt, Deirdre Jan, Eric Berkeley, Terry Ann. Admitted to Oreg. bar, 1950; asso. editor Bancroft-Whitney Law Pub. Co., San Francisco, 1950; with Office Gen. Counsel, Bonneville Power Adminstrn., 1950-51, 52-53; individual practice law, Coos Bay, Oreg., 1951-52, Portland, Oreg., 1970-71; asso. firm Peterson & Pozzi, Portland, 1953-56; partner Peterson, Pozzi & Lent, Portland, 1957-59, Peterson & Lent, Portland, 1959-62, Peterson, Lent & Paulson, Portland, 1962-64, Lent, York, & Paulson, Portland, 1964-67, Lent, York, Paulson & Bullock, Portland, 1967-70; circuit ct. judge for Multnomah County, Portland, 1971-77; assoc. justice Oreg. Supreme Ct., Salem, 1977—, chief justice, 1982-83; mem. Oreg. Ho. of Reps., 1957-65, minority whip, 1965; mem. Oreg. Senate, 1967-71, majority leader, 1971. Served with USNR, 1942-45. Mem. VFW. Democrat. Club: Elks. Contbr. articles to law jours., chpts. to books. Office: Supreme Ct Bldg Salem OR 97310

LENTES, DAVID EUGENE, corp. exec.; b. Spokane, Dec. 14, 1951; s. William Eugene and Ellen Elsie L.; A.A., Spokane Falls Community Coll., 1972; B.B.A., Gonzaga U., 1975; m. Debra Kay White, May 19, 1973; children—Janette Adele, Damon Arthur. Vice-pres. Dellen Wood Products, Inc., Spokane, 1972—, also dir.; v.p. Custom Computer Services, Inc., Spokane, 1980—; mng. partner Com-Lease, 1980—, Len-Lease, 1980—; v.p., dir. DWP Trucking, Inc., 1982—, Sentel Corp., 1983—, BDR Investment Corp., 1983—; dir. Custom Computer Services, Inc. Treas., Dishman Hills Natural Area Assn., 1970—; elder Bethany Presbyn. Ch., 1980—. Mem. Assn. Wash. Bus., Nat. Fedn. Ind. Businessmen, Am. Fedn. Bus., Spokane C. of C., Timber Products Mfrs. Republican. Office: Bldg 18 Spokane Indsl Park Spokane WA 99216

LEO, ROBERT JOSEPH, association executive, consultant; b. Paterson, N.J., Nov. 24, 1939; s. Dewey J. and Jean (Bianco) L.; m. Margaret Elena Ingafu, Aug. 5, 1962; children—Christopher, Nicholas. B.A. in Speech, Temple U., 1960, M.A., 1962; Ph.D., U. Wash., 1968. Instr. Monmouth Coll., West Long Branch, N.J., 1962-64; spl. asst. to chancellor Dallas County (Tex.) Community Coll. Dist., 1968-71, dir. spl. services and gov. relations, 1971-76; assoc. exec. dir. League for Innovation in the Community Coll., Los Angeles, 1976-80, exec. dir., Dallas, 1980-82; gen. mgr. Los Angeles Jaycees, 1982—; founding pres. Nat. Council Resource Devel., adj. assoc. prof. East Tex. State U., 1975-76; chmn. Tex. Health Planning Council. Recipient Disting. Service award Oak Cliff Jaycees, 1973; Spl. Recognition award Nat. Council Resource Devel., 1981; named Significant Contbr. to Fair Housing, Greater Dallas Housing Opportunity Ctr., 1973. Mem. Am. Soc. Tng. and Devel., Am. Soc. Assn. Execs., Nat. Council Resource Devel., AAAS, Fgn. Policy Assn., Am. Youth Soccer Orgn. Roman Catholic. Clubs: Porter Valley Country, Los Angeles Athletic. Author articles in field. Home: 11934 Gerald Ave Granada Hills CA 91344 Office: Jr Chamber of Commerce 404 S Bixel St Los Angeles CA 90017

LEODOLTER, WALTER, aerospace engineer; b. Doellach, Austria, Aug. 25, 1931; s. Viktor and Hildegard (Pierer) L.; m. Liselotte Leodolter, June 10, 1961; 1 son, Gerhard. B.S.E.E., Poly. Coll., Graz, Austria, 1956. Design engr. Vogel and Noot, Wartberg, Austria, 1956-60; staff engr. structural design Helman Aircraft, Cairo, 1960-67; engr. scientist structural design Boeing Vertol, Phila., 1967-68; sr. engr. scientist structural design Douglas Aircraft, Long Beach, Calif., 1968-80, unit chief advanced tech. structural design, 1980—. Mem. AIAA. Patentee superplastic forming/diffusion bonding process. Home: 26823 Hyte Rd Rancho Palos Verdes CA 90274 Office: 3855 Lakewood Blvd M/S 36-53 Long Beach CA 90846

LEONARD, ANTHONY CHARLES, investor, manager; b. N.Y.C., June 11, 1937; s. Richard Anthony and Elizabeth (Peach) L.; m. Katherine Warner Oakley, Mar. 8, 1975; children—Sarah Elizabeth, Anthony Charles, Richard Rial. A.B., Harvard U., 1959, M.B.A., 1966. Securities analyst Mellon Bank, Pitts., 1959-64; treas., sec., mktg. v.p., gen. mgr., plant supt. Gen. Interiors Corp., Lewisburg, Pa., N.Y.C., 1966-71; asst. to pres. Suburban Propane Gas Corp., Morristown, N.J., 1971-75, v.p., 1975-82; pres. Plateau, Inc., Albuquerque, 1980-82; ptnr. The Leonard Co., 1982—. chmn., YMCA, Albuquerque, 1983; co-fin. chmn. Com. to Reelect Manuel Lujan to U.S. Ho. of Reps., 1981-82; sr. warden St Mark's Ch., Albuquerque, 1982-83. Republican. Episcopalian. Office: PO Box 6253 Albuquerque NM 87197

LEONARD, FRANK EDWARD, II, resort exec.; b. Rexburg, Idaho, Dec. 29, 1949; s. Edward Cyrus and Lois (Sherrard) L.; B.A. in Journalism, Drake U., 1972; degree in Advt./Research, Mich. State U., 1974; m. Georgia Louise Leonard, Aug. 31, 1976; children—Frank E. III, Sarah Catherine. Dir. devel. United Cerebral Palsy Nat. Assn., Des Moines, 1974-75; exec. dir. United Cerebral Palsy of Ill., Peoria, 1975-76; v.p., gen. mgr. Glen Eden Inc. Four Season Resort, Steamboat Springs, Colo., 1976—; cons. in field. Bd. dirs. Routt County Bd. Appeals. Pres., North Routt County Fire Dist., Steamboat Springs, Colo.; bd. dirs., 1st v.p. Steamboat Springs C. of C. Democrat. Roman Catholic. Club: Rotary. Home: 455 12th St Steamboat Springs CO 80477 Office: PO Box 812 Clark CO 80428

LEONARD, GEORGE PERRY, contracting engr.; b. Stillwater, Minn., Dec. 19, 1904; s. William Henry and Orlinda Elizabeth (Gilmore) L.; A.B., Macalester Coll., 1927, LL.D., 1975; m. Wilma Fox, Dec. 24, 1931; children—Barbara Robben, Thomas George (dec. 1975), Mark George. Gen. supt. Martin Wunderlich Co., Jefferson City, Mo., 1928-44, exec. v.p. Wunderlich Contracting Co., Omaha, 1944-66; pres. Bakers Beach Apartments Co., San Francisco, 1952-66; pres. Stinson Beach (Calif.) Water Co., 1956-74; v.p. Consol. Lands, San Bruno, Calif., 1955-69. Vice pres. Marin Symphony Assn., 1973-77, Inverness Music

Festival, 1974-79. Mem. Marin County Planning Commn., 1971-73. Bd. dirs. Marin Sr. Coordinating Council, 1975-77; trustee Macalester Coll., 1960—, also chmn. high winds com.; bd. regents St. Mary's Coll., Moraga, Calif., 1976—; bd. dirs. Marin Property Owners Assn.; mem. godfathers club St. Vincent's Sch. for Boys; chmn. constrn. div. United Crusade San Mateo County (Calif.), 1958. Recipient Golden Beaver Award Nat. Assn. Heavy Constrn. Contractors, 1963; Centennial medal Macalester Coll., 1974, Pacesetter award, 1976; Outstanding Citizen award Macalester Coll. Alumni Assn., 1965; Service award Marin Sr. Coordinating Council, 1974. Fellow Am. Soc. C.E. (life mem.); mem. Wherry Housing Assn. (nat. pres. 1962-66, dir.). Home: End of Avenida Las Baulinas Stinson Beach CA 94970 Office: Stinson Beach CA 94970

LEONARD, HARRY A., investment company executive, commerical property developer; b. Pebble Beach, Calif., Dec. 21, 1911; s. Harry B. and Henrietta (McKee) L.; m. Maxine Harbolt, June 21, 1941; children—Sydney, Sally. B.S., U. Oreg., 1935. With Securities Arbitrage, Manila, P.I., 1944-50; now pres. H.A. Leonard Co.; chmn. bd. Nortam Fin. Corp. Served to comdr. USNR, 1941-44. Clubs: El Dorado Country; Beach and Tennis (Pebble Beach). Address: Viscaino Rd Box 753 Pebble Beach CA 93953

LEONARD, KENNETH EARL, economics educator; b. Glendale, Calif., Apr. 11, 1947; s. James O. and Blanche E. (Klingarmen) L.; m. Marcia F. Lowber, June 8, 1970; children—Shawna, Kimberly. B.A., U. La Verne, 1969; M.Ed., Eastern Wash. U., 1974; Ph.D., U. Wash., 1982. Tchr., Fullerton (Calif.) Unified Sch. Dist., 1970-71; asst. prof., dir. Ctr. Econ. Edn., Whitworth Coll., Spokane, Wash., 1973-76; assoc. dir. Wash. State Council Econ. Edn., Seattle, 1977-78, exec. dir., 1978—; asst. prof. econs. Seattle Pacific U., 1978—; speaker; cons. to small bus. Recipient Award for Excellence in Pvt. Enterprise Edn., Freedoms Found. at Valley Forge, 1978; Newsmaker of Tomorrow award, Seattle, 1978; Nat. award for Teaching of Reasoning, Joint Council Econ. Edn., 1982. Mem. AAUP, Nat. Council Social Studies, Assn. Supervision and Curriculum Devel., Nat. Assn. Affiliated Econ. Edn. Dirs., Wash. State Council Social Studies. Club: Rotary. Baptist. Office: Seattle Pacific U Seattle WA 98119

LEONARD, LEO DONALD, ednl. sociologist; b. Salt Lake City, Nov. 23, 1938; s. Leo Bradford and Florence (Robbins) L.; B.S., U. Utah, 1961, student U. Wash., 1961-62, 64-65; M.S., Utah State U., 1967, Ed.D., 1969; m. Marilynn Rae Hoyt, Jan. 2, 1962; 1 son, Richard Corey. Acting head King County Dept. Mental Health and Adoptions, Seattle, 1962; dir. programs and youth Snoline YMCA, Seattle, 1962-64; instr. Shorecrest High Sch., 1967-68, Roy (Utah) High Sch., 1966-67; instr. ednl. methods Utah State U., 1968-69; prof. edn. U. Toledo, 1969-80; dean Sch. Edn., U. Portland (Oreg.), 1979—; univ. coordinator Catholic Diocese of Toledo Curriculum Devel. Project, 1970-75; coll. dir. Canadian Dissemination Project, 1971-74; bd. dirs. Internat. Tchrs. Edn. Council, 1970—; mem. Nat. Task Force on Health Edn. in Tchr. Edn., 1983— Bd. dirs. Toledo Symphony Orch., 1970-79; trustee Choral Arts Soc. Portland, Tucker Maxon Sch., Open Meadows Learning Ctr. Fellow Internat. Tchr. Edn. Council, 1971—; Fulbright scholar, Africa, 1967; grantee U.S. Office Edn-Tchr. Corps, 1970, many others. Mem. Am. Assn. Individual Guided Edn., Am. Edn. Research Soc., Comparative Edn. Soc. U.S., Comparative Edn. Soc. Can., Am. Assn. Colls. of Tchr. Edn. (pres. state council deans of edn. 1983—), Marine Corps League (commandant Portland detachment 1983-84), Phi Kappa Phi, Phi Alpha Theta, Phi Delta Kappa. Author: (with Robert T. Utz) The Building Skills for Competency Based Teaching, 1974, The Foundations of Competency Based Education, 1975, A Competency Based Curriculum, 1971, La Enseñanza como Desarrollo de Competencias, 1979; (with others) 7 instructors guides for individually guided edn.; contbr. articles to profl. jours. Office: Sch Edn U Portland 5000 Willamette Blvd Portland OR 97203

LEONARD, ROBERT KENNETH, advertising agency executive; b. Cin., July 27, 1953; s. Edmund B. and Marie Catherine (Arnold) L.; M. Linda Wentz, Apr. 17, 1976. Profl. studies Cin. Art Acad., 1971-72; B.A., Morehead State U., 1973; M.A., Pepperdine U., 1978. Account exec. J. Walter Thompson Co., San Francisco, 1980-82, Ketchum Communications, San Francisco, 1982-83, Foote, Cone & Belding/Honig, San Francisco, 1983—. Served to capt. USMC, 1975-79. Recipient first degree Black Belt in Japanese Karate. Mem. Am. Advt. Fedn., Marine Corps Res. Officer Assn., San Francisco Advt. Club. Democrat. Episcopalian. Lodge: Order De Molay. Home: 1255 Detroit Ave Townhouse 1 Concord CA 94520 Office: 55 Francisco St San Francisco CA 94119

LEONE, PATRICIA BUDER, research engineer; b. St. Louis, Oct. 18, 1947; d. Evatt Edward and Mary Catherine (Solich) Buder; m. David Michael Leone, Sept. 19, 1981. Student Fairleigh Dickinson U., 1967-69; B.S. magna cum laude, St. Louis U., 1971; M.S., MIT, 1973. Research asst. MIT, Cambridge, 1971-73; UCAR fellow, Nat. Center for Atmospheric Research, Boulder, Colo., summers, 1971, 72; research meteorologist SRI, Internat., Menlo Park, Calif., 1973-81; research engr. Lockheed Missiles & Space Co., Sunnyvale, Calif., 1981—. Univ. Corp. for Atmospheric Research fellow, 1971-72; Sloan fellow, 1972-73. Mem. Am. Meteorol. Soc. (chmn. N.C. 1978-79), Nat. Mgmt. Assn., Sigma Xi, Phi Zeta Kappa, Pi Mu Epsilon. Contbr. articles to profl. jours. Home: 1569 McKendrie St San Jose CA 95126 Office: 1111 Lockheed Way B/562 0/62A1 Sunnyvale CA 94086

LEONG, GORDON KOCK KEON, elec. engr.; b. Honolulu, Nov. 29, 1938; s. Henry Hon Hung and Alice D.Z. (Chock) L.; B.S.E.E., U. Calif., Berkeley, 1961; M.S., Stanford U., 1965, Ph.D., 1969; m. Elaine U. Leong, Feb. 11, 1961; children—Keith, Karen. Mem. tech. staff GTE Sylvania, Mountain View, Calif., 1962-67, project mgr., 1967-73, sect. head, 1973-76, engring. mgr., 1978—, dir. research and devel., 1977-78. Asst. scoutmaster Boy Scouts Am., 1971—, scout commr., 1979; advisor Jr. Achievement. Mem. IEEE, Sigma Xi, Eta Kappa Nu. Episcopalian. Clubs: Hawaiian, Leong Soong Duck Tong. Home: 599 Utica Ct Sunnyvale CA 94087 Office: Box 188 Mountain View CA 94087

LEONG, LAWRENCE YET CHIEN, laboratory director; b. Honolulu, Aug. 22, 1946; s. Kam Man and Alma Yuen Hoy (Chang) L. B.A., Lawrence U., 1968; M.S., U. Calif.-Berkeley, 1970, Ph.D., 1974. Assoc. Pub. Health U. Calif.-Berkeley, 1969-71; lectr. U. Calif.-Irvine, 1974-79; sr. chemist James M. Montgomery Cons. Engrs. Inc., Pasadena, Calif., 1974-75, lab. dir., 1976-82, lab. dir., v.p., 1983—. Mem. Am. Water Works Assn., Water Pollution Control Fedn., Am. Soc. Microbiology, AAAS, Assn. on Water Pollution Research and Control, Am. Chem. Soc., Am. Soc. Testing and Materials. Democrat. Contbr. numerous articles to profl. jours. Office: J M Montgomery Engrs 555 E Walnut St Pasadena CA 91101

LEONG, LEONARD KWOCK PING, construction company executive; b. Honolulu, May 30, 1947; s. Wally Wah Hong and Betty Wai Lan (Au) W.; B.S. in Civil Engring., U. Hawaii, 1970; m. Sherrilynn S.J. Wong, Dec. 5, 1970; children—Paul K.M., Janelle S.E., Jonathan K.I., Kristen K.L. Vice pres. Royal Contracting Co., Ltd., Honolulu, 1970—, also dir. Mem. Hawaii Environ. Quality Commn., 1981-84. Mem. Am. Assn. Cost Engrs. Episcopalian. Office: 677 Ahua St Honolulu HI 96819

LEOPOLD, IRVING HENRY, ophthalmologist, medical educator; b. Phila., Apr. 19, 1915; s. Abraham and Dora (Schlow) L.; m. Eunice Robinson, June 24, 1937; children—Ellen Robinson, John. Student, Pa. State U., 1934; M.D., U. Pa., 1938, D.Sc., 1943. Intern, Hosp. of U. Pa., 1938-40, fellow, instr. ophthalmology Hosp. U. Pa. U. Pa. Med. Sch., 1940-45, assoc., 1945-54; research investigator chem. warfare OSRD, 1941-45; successively assoc., asst. prof., assoc. prof. U. Pa. Grad. Sch. Medicine, 1946-55, prof., head dept. ophthalmology, 1955-64, chief dept. ophthalmology Grad. Hosp., 1955-61; dir. research Wills Eye Hosp., 1949-64, attending surgeon, 1952-64, med. dir., 1961-64, cons. surgeon, 1965—; chmn. sci. adv. com. Allegan Pharms, 1974, exec. v.p., 1975; prof., chmn. dept. ophthalmology Mt. Sinai Sch. Medicine, 1965—; dir. dept. ophthalmology Mt. Sinai Hosp., N.Y.C., 1964-75; prof. chmn. dept. ophthalmology U. Calif.-Irvine, 1975—; clin. prof. ophthalmology Coll. Physicians and Surgeons, Columbia, U., 1964-66; cons. opthalmologist St. Joseph's Hosp., 1959-65, Albert Einstein Med. Ctr., 1959-65; Proctor lectr. U. Calif.-San Francisco, 1962; Gifford Meml. lectr., Chgo., 1967; Edwin B. Dunphy lectr. Harvard U. Cambridge, Mass., 1968, 75; Walter Wright lectr. U. Toronto, 1969, Richardson Cross lectr. Royal Soc. Medicine, 1970, Doyne Meml. lectr. Ophthalmology Soc. U.K., 1971; DeSchweinitz Meml. lectr., Phila., 1972; Jules Stein Lectr. UCLA, 1974; Bedell lectr., Phila., 1975; Cons. Chem. Warfare Service, U.S. Army, 1943-52, 81—, surgeon gen. USPHS, 1953—, FDA, HEW, 1963. Chmn. ophthalmology panel U.S. Pharmacopeia, 1960-70, mem. revision panel, 1970—; chmn. panel drug efficancy in ophthalmology, Nat. Acad. Sci.-NCR, 1966-67; mem. tng. grant com. USPHS, 1952-58, mem. spl. sensory study sect. research record diseases and blindness, 1954-58; mem. field investigating com. Nat. Inst. Neurol. Diseases and Blindness, 1959-61, mem. neurol. project com., 1961-63, chmn. vision research tng. com., 1967-68. Trustee Seeing Eye Guide, 1965-74. Recipient Zentmayer award, 1945, 49; Honor award Am. Acad. Ophthalmology, 1955; Edward Lorenzo Holmes citation and award, 1957. Diplomate Am. Bd. Ophthalmology (chmn. bd. 1971-72, chmn. visual scis. study sect. 1968-70, mem. subcom. impaired vision and blindness 1967-69, task force on ocular pharmacology, 1967-69, cons. 1975-79). Mem. N.Y. Acad. Medicine, Am. Ophthal. Soc. (Verhoeff Meml. lectr. 1973, Lucien Howe medal 1974), N.Y. Opthal. Soc., Am. Acad. Opthalmology and Otolaryngology (chmn. drug com. opthalmology 1963-74; Edward Jackson Meml. lectr. 1965), Assn. Research Opthalmology (trustee, chmn., Friedenwald medal 1960), Nat. Soc. Preventive Blindness (dir., v.p., exec. com.), ACS, AAAS, Art Alliance Phila., John Morgan Soc., Coll. Physicians Phila., Am. Diabetes Assn., AMA (chmn. residency rev. com. opthalmology 1970-72), N.Y. Acad. Sci., Pan Am. Assn. Opthalmology, Pan. Pacific Surg. Assn., N.Y. State Med. Soc., N.Y. County Med. Soc., Phila. Med. Soc., Calif. Med. Assn., Orange County Med. Assn., Sigma Xi, Alpha Omega Alpha. Clubs: Med. Biochemist, Vesper, Alpha (Phila.), Newport Beach Tennis, Big Canyon Country, Balboa Bay (Newport Beach); Century Country, Princeton (N.Y.C.). Editor in chief: Survey of Opthalmology, 1958-62, cons. editor, 1962—; mem. editoral bd. Am. Jour. Diabetes, 1956-73, Investigative Opthalmology, 1961-74, Am. Jours. Opthalmology, 1965—. Home: 1484 Galaxy Dr Newport Beach CA 92660 Office: U Calif Calif Coll Medicine Ophthalmology Dept Irvine CA 92717

LEPAK, REVA LORENE, marketing executive; b. Denver, Jan. 5, 1942; d. Kenneth Charles and Frances Thelma (Voorhees) Burt; B.S., U. Colo., 1967; children—Renza Gayle, Regina Liesl. Tchr. spl. edn. Boulder Valley (Colo.) Sch. System, 1967-74; adminstrv. asst. to v.p. mktg. Central Bank for Coops., 1974-76; market mgr. Residential Products Mktg. Div., Johns-Manville Sales Corp., Denver, after 1976; pres. Christy Metals & Mfg., Inc.; dir. Fortune Wall Systems, Inc. Recipient Merit award Johns Manville Corp., 1978. Mem. Am. Bus. Women's Assn., LWV, Friends of Library. Republican. Office: PO Box 4272 Fremont CA 94539

LEPERA, LEONARD J., real estate corr.; b. Gilroy, Calif., Feb. 16, 1941; s. Louis and Louisa (Carpignano) L., B.S., U. Calif., Berkeley, 1966, M.B.A. (fellow), 1967; m. Meriel Mura, Feb. 3, 1973. Rep. Pacific Mut. Life Ins. Co., Los Angeles, 1969-70, supr., 1970-71, mgr., 1971-73, dir., 1973-74, asst. v.p., 1974-76, 2d v.p., 1976-77, v.p., 1977-80; partner Property Corrs., Newport Beach, Calif., 1980—. Mem. Alpha Kappa Psi (life). Home: 3592 South Mall Irvine CA 92714 Office: Property Corrs Pacific Mutual Plaza 840 Newport Center Dr Suite 670 Newport Beach CA 92660

LEPIE, ALBERT HELMUT, chemist; b. Malapane, Germany, Aug. 6, 1923; s. Albert and Emilia (Zachlod) L.; M.S., Tech.U. Aachen (Germany), 1958; Ph.D., Tech. U. Munich, 1961. Research chemist German Inst. Research Aeros., Munich, 1961-63, Naval Propellant Plant, Indian Head, Md., 1963-64, Naval Weapons Center, China Lake, Calif., 1964—; chmn. mech. properties panel Interagy, Chem. Rocket Propulsion Group, 1977—. Fellow Am. Inst. Chemists; mem. Am. Chem. Soc., AAAS, China Lake Astronom. Soc., Sigma Xi. Research in damage and failure of polymeric materials. Office: Naval Weapons Center Code 3858 China Lake CA 93555

LEPOFF, WAYNE ALBERT, business executive, accountant; b. Santa Monica, Calif., July 12, 1951; s. Samuel O. and Rebecca (Auerbach) L.; m. Deborah M. Baldwin, May 5, 1954; 1 dau., Karissa Anne. B.B.S. with honors, U. Calif.-Berkeley, 1973; postgrad. in acctg. UCLA, 1974-76. C.P.A., Calif. Sr. acct. Berglund & Assocs., Los Angeles, 1977-79; v.p. fin. Western Security Systems & Services, Torrance, Calif., 1979-80, exec. v.p., 1980-81, pres., 1981—; tech. adviser Palos Verdes Estates Police. Recipient J. Edgar Hoover award Nat. Assn. Chiefs of Police, 1982. Mem. Amer. Inst. C.P.A.s, Calif. Soc. C.P.A.s, Am. Soc. Indsl. Security, Nat. Assn. Chiefs of Police. Democrat. Home: PO Box 8361 Van Nuys CA 91409 Office: Western Security 18411 S Crenshaw Blvd Torrance CA 90504

LEPORE, ALBERT RALPH, educator; b. San Diego, Apr. 13, 1920; s. Luigi and Jeanne (Robin) L.; m. Margaret Ashby, Sept. 25, 1924; children—Jeanne Robin Thomas, Lawrence R. B.A. (DAR scholar), San Diego State U., 1942; M.A., Tchr.'s Coll., Columbia U., 1949, Ph.D., 1960. Tchr., San Diego City Schs., 1946-48; asst. prof. edn. San Francisco State U., 1951-59; prof., head div. edn., dean coll., Calif. State U.-Hayward, 1959—; cons. to public schs. trustee St. Rose Hosp., Hayward, 1972—. Served to capt. inf. U.S. Army, 1942-46. Decorated Silver Star. Recipient Community Service award Calif. State U. Affiliates, 1982, Citizen of Yr. award Hayward Lions, 1982. Mem. Piaget Soc., AAAS, Am. Psychol. Assn., Phi Delta Kappa. Democrat. Research on instructional TV. Home: 2614 Lancaster Rd Hayward CA 94542 Office: Calif State U Hayward CA 94542

LEPORE, EVANGELISTA NICOLA (E. NICK), safety and facilities engring. cons.; b. Newark, Aug. 25, 1933; s. Evangelista and Angelina (Casale) L.; student Rutgers U., U. Ariz. Pres., Lepore & Bollen, Inc., Bloomfield, N.J., 1955-61; safety and facilities engring. mgr. Kitt Peak Nat. Obs., Tucson, 1961-69, 70-78; cons. safety, loss control, facilities engr., 1978—; asst. obs. mgr. Cerro Tololo Interam. Obs., La Serena, Chile, 1969-70; bd. dirs. S.W. Safety Congress. Served with U.S. Army, 1955-56. Cert. internat. hazard control mgr., sr. level; cert. instr. for voluntary compliance U.S. Dept. Labor. Mem. Am. Soc. Safety Engrs. (pres. So. Ariz. chpt. 1978-79), Internat. Hazard Control Mgrs. Republican. Roman Catholic. Responsible for archtl. design and engring. McGraw-Hill Observator Dome and support bldgs. Kitt Peak Nat. Obs. and Mountain Site, 1975. Home and Office: 2644 N Balboa Ave Tucson AZ 85705

LERCH, STANFORD EARL, lawyer; b. Newberrytown, Pa., Aug. 24, 1933; s. Mizpah Earl and Julia Elizabeth (Smith) L.; J.D., U. Ariz., 1961; m. Isabella Middleton Barnwell, June 2, 1959; children—Susan, Bradley, Michael. Admitted to Ariz. bar, 1961, since practiced in Phoenix; partner firm Jones Hunter & Lerch, P.A., Phoenix, 1964-79, pres., 1974-79; partner firm, v.p. Harrison, Myers, Singer & Lerch, P.C., Phoenix, 1979; now v.p. Harrison & Lerch, P.C.; evaluator legal services program OEO, 1967-68. Maricopa County chmn. Young Citizens for Johnson-Humphrey, 1964; mem. Planning Task Force for Democratic Party Reorgn. in Maricopa County, 1965-66; Dem. state committeeman, 1962-64. Bd. dirs. Maricopa County Legal Aid Soc., 1964-70, Maricopa County Cancer Soc., 1967-68; bd. visitors Ariz. State U. Law Sch., 1974—; mem. youth and govt. com. Ariz. YMCA, 1966-78; mem. jud. selection adv. com. City of Phoenix, 1974-78. Recipient A. Louis Slonaker award as outstanding alumnus U. Ariz., 1970. Fellow Am. Bar Found.; mem. Am. Bar Assn. (council young lawyers sect. 1966-68, dir. 1968-69; ho. of dels. 1969-79, 79—, chmn. retirement com. 1974-75, council family law sect. 1976-78, sec. 1978-79, chmn. family law sect. 1981-82), State Bar Ariz. (chmn. young lawyers sect. 1965-66, chmn. bankruptcy sect. 1968-72, treas., v.p., gov. 1973-77, Fed. Bar Assn. (nat. council 1974—), U. Ariz. Alumni Assn. (dir. 1971-77), 20-30 Internat. (internat. pres. 1970-71), Phi Delta Theta, Delta Sigma Rho, Phi Alpha Delta, Blue Key. Episcopalian. Club: Phoenix Country. Bd. editors Fair Share mag. Home: 2102 Encanto Dr SW Phoenix AZ 85007 Office: 650 N 2d Ave Phoenix AZ 85003

LERMAN, CAROLYN, dietitian; b. Colville, Wash., Sept. 21, 1926; d. Louis S. and Reine G. (Grinsfelder) Strauss; children—Steven, David, Mitchell. B.A., Mills Coll., 1948. Cert. dietitian. Dietitian, San Francisco Convalescent Center, 1971-72, Marriott In-Flite, Millbrae, Calif., 1972-73; staff dietitian San Francisco Gen. Hosp., 1973-76; chief dietitian Mt. Zion Hosp., San Francisco, 1976—; counselor 2 dietetic traineeships. Mem. Clin. Dietitians of the Bay Area (chief). Home: 15 Poncetta Dr Apt 329 Daly City CA 94015 Office: 1600 Divisadero San Francisco CA 94115

LERMAN, CHARLES ALBERT, consulting psychologist, therapist, educator; b. Buenos Aires, Argentina, Sept. 10, 1949; s. Bernardo and Cecilia (Gevirtz) L. B.A., Bklyn. Coll., 1971, M.S., 1975; Ph.D. in Psychology, U. Tex., 1979. Lic. psychologist, Calif., Tex.; lic. sch. psychologist, N.Y. Staff psychologist U. Tex., Austin, 1979-80; staff psychologist Claremont Coll. Counseling Ctr., 1980-81; asst. dir. consultation and edn. U. So. Calif. Counseling services, 1981-83, assoc. dir., 1983—; mem. adj. faculty Calif. Sch. Profl. Psychology, 1981—; mem. adj. faculty Calif. State Coll., San Bernadino, 1980, U. San Francisco Organizational Behavior program; pvt. practice cons. psychologist, Santa Monica, Calif., 1982—. Mem. Am. Personnel and Guidance Assn., Am. Coll. Personnel Assn., Am. Soc. for Tng. and Devel., Orgn. Devel. Network, Los Angeles County Psychol. Assn., Nat. Registry Health Service Providers, Phi Kappa Phi. Office: University Southern California Counseling Center 857 W 36th Place Los Angeles CA 90089

LERMAN, EILEEN R., lawyer; b. N.Y.C., May 6, 1947; d. Alex and Beatrice (Kline) L.; B.A., Syracuse U., 1969; J.D., Rutgers U., 1972; M.B.A., U. Denver, 1983. Admitted to N.Y. State bar, 1973, Colo. bar, 1976; atty. FTC, N.Y.C., 1972-74; corp. atty. RCA, N.Y.C., 1974-76; corp. atty. Samsonite Corp. and consumer products div. Beatrice Foods Co., Denver, 1976-78, asso. gen. counsel, 1978—, asst. sec., 1979—; dir. Legal Aid Soc. of Met. Denver, 1979-80. Bd. dirs. Colo. Postsecondary Ednl. Facilities Authority, 1981—, HMO Colo., Am. Jewish Com.; mem. Leadership Denver, 1983. Mem. Colo. Women's Bar Assn. (dir. 1980-81), ABA, Colo. Bar Assn., Denver Bar Assn., Am. Corp. Counsel Assn. (dir. young lawyers div.), Rutgers U. Alumni Assn. Club: Soroptimist. Home: 1018 Fillmore St Denver CO 80206 Office: 11200 E 45th Ave Denver CO 80239

LERMAN, HANNAH, psychologist, feminist therapist; b. N.Y.C., Mar. 7, 1936; d. Ephraim and Lillian (Harris) Lerman. Ph.D., Mich. State U., 1963. Lic. psychologist Calif.; cert. sex therapist. Psychologist, Topeka (Kans.) State Hosp., mem. faculty Menninger Sch. Psychiatry, 1963-66; psychologist, asst. prof. psychiatry Los Angeles-U. So. Calif. Med. Center, 1966-70; dean student and acad. affairs Calif. Sch. Profl. Psychology, Los Angeles, 1970-73; pvt. practice clin. psychology, Los Angeles, 1973—. Recipient Gardner Murphy award CCNY, 1957. Mem. Am. Psychol. Assn., Calif. State Psychol. Assn., Los Angeles County Psychol. Assn., Los Angeles Soc. Clin. Psychologists, Soc. Sci. Study Sex, Am. Assn. Sex Educators, Counselors and Therapists, Am. Group Psychotherapy Assn., Los Angeles Group Psychotherapy Assn., Group Psychotherapy Soc. So. Calif., Assn. Women in Psychology. Contbr. numerous articles to profl. jours. Home and Office: 1543 S Oakhurst Dr Los Angeles CA 90035

LERNER, SHELDON, plastic surgeon; b. N.Y.C., Mar. 3, 1939; s. Louis and Lillian L.; A.B. with honors, Drew U., Madison, N.J., 1961; M.D., U. Louisville, 1965. Intern, resident Albert Einstein Coll. Medicine, Bronx-Mcpl. Hosp. Center, 1965-73; practice medicine, specializing in plastic surgery Plastic Cosmetic and Reconstructive Surgery Center, San Diego, 1973—. Served with USPHS, 1968-70. Mem. AMA, Am. Soc. Plastic and Reconstructive Surgeons, Calif. Med. Soc., San Diego County Med. Soc., San Diego Internat. Plastic Surgery Assn. Clubs: Masons, Shriners. Office: 3399 1st Ave San Diego CA 92103

LEROY, DAVID HENRY, lieutenant governor Idaho; b. Seattle, Aug. 16, 1947; s. Harold David and Lela Fay (Palmer) L.; B.S. in Bus., U. Idaho, 1969, J.D. (Am. Trial Lawyers scholar), 1971; LL.M., N.Y. U., 1972; m. Helen LaVonne Transue, Aug. 5, 1972. Student intern U.S. Ho. of Reps., Washington, 1967; Law clk., bailiff Idaho 4th Dist. Ct., Boise, 1969; Legal asst. Legal div. Boise Cascade Corp., 1970; admitted to Idaho bar, 1971, N.Y. bar, 1973, U.S. Supreme Ct. bar, 1976; asso. firm Rothblatt, Rothblatt, Seijas & Peskin, N.Y.C., 1971-73; dep. prosecutor Ada County Prosecutor's Office, Boise, 1973-74, pros. atty., 1974-78; atty. gen. Idaho, Boise, 1978-82; lt. gov. Idaho, 1983—; law lectr. State Bar Assn., Boise State U., Idaho Prosecutors Assn.; mem. Idaho Task Force on Child Abuse, 1975, Idaho Supreme Ct. Commn. on Sentencing, Juvenile Law and Corrections, 1975-77, Ada County Council on Alcoholism, 1976. Student body pres. U. Idaho, 1967-68; legal counsel Young Republicans, 1974-77; del. Rep. Nat. Conv., 1976, 80; chmn. Idaho state campaign Pres. Ford Com., 1976, co-chmn. Reagan Campaign, 1980; mem. Duke U. Forum on Presdl. Nominations, 1981; div. chmn., bd. dirs. United Fund, 1974-77. Mem. U.S. Supreme Ct. Bar Assn., Idaho Bar Assn., Nat. Dist. Attys. Assn. (chmn. energy com. 1981-82), Western Conf. Attys. Gen. (chmn. 1981-82), Idaho Pros. Attys. Assn., Am. Trial Lawyers Assn., Idaho Trial Lawyers Assn., Nat. Assn. Attys. Gen., Blue Key, Sigma Alpha Epsilon, Pi Omicron Sigma. Presbyterian. Clubs: Intercollegiate Knights; Silver Lance. Author: Manual of Legal Forms for Social Work in Idaho, 1974; Handbook of Idaho Criminal Complaints, 1976. Contbr. articles to Legal jours. Office: Lt Gov's Office Boise ID

LESCHAK, LINDA ANN, medical group executive; b. Coral Gables, Fla., Jan. 19, 1951; d. Henry S. and Dorothy L. (Hindman) Sherrill; student U. Ariz., 1969-70, Pima Coll., 1972-74; m. Paul B. Leschak, Aug. 23, 1980; 1 son, Paul M.B. Office mgr. Clark Office Products, Tucson, 1968-71; bus. mgr. Southwestern Surgery Assocs., Ltd., Tucson, 1971—. Mem. Med. Group Mgmt. Assn., Ariz. Med. Group Mgmt. Assn. (pres. 1980). Office: 5402 E Grant Rd Bldg B5 Tucson AZ 85712

LESIEUR, HELEN ELAINE, foundation public relations executive; b. Coffeyville, Kans., Feb. 16, 1920; d. Frank R. and Grace (Koon) LeS. B.S. in Edn., S.E. Mo. State Coll., 1943; student in art Washington U., St. Louis, 1943-44; student in bus. adminstrn. Northwestern U., 1945-46. Dir. Mcpl. Concerts Bur., Houston, 1950-52; free-lance theatrical publicist, Chgo., 1952-54; pub. relations account exec. Aaron D. Cushman & Assocs., Chgo., 1954-60; pub. relations dir. Ill. chpt. Arthritis Found., 1960-61, pub. relations dir., v.p. pub. relations So. Calif. chpt., Los Angeles, 1961—. Mem. Pub. Relations Soc. Am. (sec. Los Angeles Area Chpt. 1971-73), Soc. Fund Raisers, Publicity Club (pres. 1966-67), Women's Ad Club, Internat. Assn. Bus. Communicators, Los Angeles Soc. Pub. Relations Counselors. Home: 5709 Fallsgrove St Los Angeles CA 90016 Office: 4311 Wilshire Blvd Los Angeles CA 90010

LESKE, REINHOLD HERMAN, safety engineer; b. Sheboygan, Wis., Mar. 28, 1929; s. George William and Martha (Killig) L.; B.S. in Mining Engring., U. Wis., 1957; m. Anna J. Mangrum, May 15, 1982; children—Randall Lee, Sandra Jean, Lynn Belue, Frank Mangrum. Corp. safety engr. Bethlehem (Pa.) Steel Co., 1968-73; indsl. relations mgr. Hecla Mining Co., Casa Grande, Ariz., 1974-77; safety dir. N. Am. Coal Co., Cleve., 1977; safety dir. Exxon Minerals Co., Casper, Wyo., 1977—; mgr. safety AMOCO Minerals Co., Englewood, Colo., 1980—. Served with USN, 1948-52. Registered profl. engr., Pa. Mem. AIME, Am. Soc. Safety Engrs. Republican. Lutheran. Home: 7931 S Adams Way Littleton CO 80122 Office: 7000 S Yosemite St Englewood CO 80155

LESLIE, WILLIAM METHVEN, JR., public affairs executive; b. Richmond, Va., Aug. 22, 1935; s. William Methven and Marion Ellen (Tibbs) L.; m. Josephine Ann Canterbury, Nov. 22, 1963; children—William Methven III, Eric Parker, Ryan Shannon; stepchildren—Stephen Canterbury, Stanley Howard. Student Occidental Coll., 1954-56; B.A. in Econs., San Francisco State U., 1961; M.B.A., Golden Gate U., 1974, postgrad. 1978—. With Standard Oil Co. Calif., San Francisco, 1960-76, pub. affairs mgr. western ops., Los Angeles, 1976; pub. affairs mgr. Chevron U.S.A., La Habra, Calif., 1977—. Pres.-elect So. Calif. Consortium Industry Edn. Councils, 1983-84; bd. dirs. Calif. Lyric Grand Opera, 1983; life mem. Jr. Chamber Internat. Senators Calif.; mem. Los Angeles County Youth for Vol. Action, community liaison com. Chaffey Coll., Los Angeles Mayor Bradley Consensus 2000 subcommittee air pollution, environ. concerns, and water resources San Fernando Valley; past pres. indsl. div. San Francisco Recreation and Park Dept., 1974-76, bd. religious edn. Piedmont Community Ch., 1971-73; past nat. dir. U.S. Jaycees, 1969-70. Served with U.S. Army, 1956-58. Recipient Outstanding Dist. Gov. in State award Calif. Jaycees, 1969; Outstanding Pub. Relations Program in U.S. award Nat. Arbor Day Found., 1973; honored by Calif. Legislature Resolution 24, Joint Rules Com., 1983; honored by Calif. Legislature Resolution 14, Assembly Rules Com., 1983; honored by Bd. of Suprs. Proclamation, County of Riverside (Calif.), 1983; honored by Bd. of Suprs. Resolution, County of San Bernardino (Calif.), 1983. Mem. Calif. Hist. Soc., Commonwealth Club Calif. (sec. bus. econs. sect.), Constl. Rights Found., Los Angeles Area C. of C., Los Angeles Pub. Affairs Officers Assn., Nev. Citizens for Priv. Enterprise, Pasadena C. of C., (vice chmn. energy com. 1983—), San Diego C. of C., San Fernando Valley Pub. Relations Roundtable (pres. 1983-84), Town Hall Calif., Pub. Relations Soc. Am. (sec. S. Pacific dist. 1982-83). Republican. Baptist. Club: Sierra. Office: Chevron U S A Inc 1201 S Beach Blvd La Habra CA 90631

LESSLER, RICHARD SIGMUND, marketing and management consultant; b. Lynbrook, N.Y., Aug. 26, 1924; s. William S. and Minnie (Gold) L.; m. Evelyn S. Sobotka, Aug. 31, 1952; children—Michael Jay, Jonathan Peter, Daniel Stephen. B.A. in Exptl. Psychology, U. N.C., 1943; M.B.A., Columbia U., 1948; postgrad. NYU, 1948-52. Research assoc. CBS, 1948-49, Dancer-Fitzgerald-Sample, Inc., 1949-55; v.p., dir. mktg. services Grey Advt. Inc., N.Y.C., 1955-72, chmn. bd., 1967-72; chief operating officer U.S.A. McCann-Erickson Inc., N.Y.C., 1972-79; vice chmn. bd. Interpublic Group of Cos., Inc., N.Y.C., 1979-80, exec. cons., 1980-82; mgr. western region Canter, Achenbaum Assocs. Inc., Patagonia, Ariz., 1982—; prof. mktg. and advt. U. Ariz., 1980-83. Served to lt. USN, 1943-46. Mem. Phi Beta Kappa, Beta Gamma Sigma. Author: Advertising Media, 1957; Advertising Management, 1962. Home: RL Ranch PO Box 181 Patagonia AZ 85624 Office: Canter Achenbaum Assocs Inc PO Box 768 Patagonia AZ 85624

LESTER, JOHN CLAYTON, life ins. co. exec.; b. Cheyenne, Wyo., Sept. 26, 1940; s. Arthur C. and Harleen E. (Gorman) L.; B.B.A., Wichita State U., 1965; m. Ruth A. Whatley, Nov. 21, 1959; children—John Clayton, Connie Sue. Office supr. State Farm Fire & Casualty Co., Greeley, Colo., 1965-69; agt. Equitable Life Assurance Soc., Greeley, 1969-70, dist. mgr., then agy. mgr., Denver, 1970-78, regional agy. v.p., 1978—. Served with USN, 1958-61. C.L.U., 1977. Mem. Am. Soc. C.L.U.s. Republican. Home: 5840 Goldsmith Dr Englewood CO 80111 Office: Orchard Place IV Suite 210 5990 S Syracuse St Englewood CO 80111

LESTER, WILLIAM ALEXANDER, JR., chemist, educator; b. Chgo., Apr. 24, 1937; s. William Alexander and Elizabeth Frances (Clark) L.; B.S., U. Chgo., 1958, M.S., 1959; postgrad. Washington U., St. Louis, 1959-60; Ph.D., Cath. U. Am., 1964; m. Rochelle Diane Reed, Dec. 27, 1959; children—William Alexander III, Allison Kimberleigh. Phys. chemist Nat. Bur. Standards, Washington, 1961-64; asst. dir. Theoretical Chemistry Inst., U. Wis., Madison, 1965-68, lectr. dept. chemistry, 1966-68; research staff mem. IBM Research Lab., San Jose, Calif., 1968-75, mgr., 1976-78; mem. tech. planning staff IBM T.J. Watson Research Center, Yorktown Heights, N.Y., 1975-76; dir. Nat. Resource for Computation in Chemistry, Lawrence Berkeley Lab., Berkeley, Calif., 1978-81, asso. dir., staff sr. scientist, 1978-81, faculty sr. scientist, 1981—; prof. chemistry U. Calif. at Berkeley, 1981—; cons. NSF, 1976-77, 80-83; mem. U.S. nat. com. Internat. Union Pure and Applied Chemistry, 1976-79; mem. chemistry research evaluation panel Air Force Office Sci. Research, 1974-78; chmn. Gordon Conf. on Atomic and Molecular Interactions, 1978; mem. NRC panel for chem. physics of Nat. Bur. Standards, 1980-83; mem. com. to survey chem. scis. Nat. Acad. Scis., 1982—. Recipient alumni Achievement award in sci. Cath. U. Am., 1983. Mem. Nat. Orgn. Black Chemists and Chem. Engrs. (Percy L. Julian award), Am. Chem. Soc. (sec.-treas. Wis. sect. 1967-68, chmn. div. phys. chemistry 1979, treas. div. computers in chemistry 1974-77), Am. Phys. Soc., Nat. Inst. Sci., Sigma Xi. Mem. editorial bd. Jour. Phys. Chemistry, 1979-81, Jour. Computational Chemistry, 1980—, Internat. Jour. Quantum Chemistry, 1979—, Computer Physics Communications, 1981—. Office: Dept Chemistry Berkeley CA 94720

LESTER, WILLIAM WALTER, real estate exec.; b. Santa Clara, Calif., July 17, 1916; s. William Walter and Ethel Viola (Gerrans) L.; student San Jose (Calif.) State U., 1935-38, U. Calif., Davis, 1938-40, U. Santa Clara, 1941, Columbia U., 1942; m. Hazel Marie Barnes, Mar. 6, 1944; children—Stanley, Marie, William, III, George, Russell. Vice pres., treas. Vallco Park, Ltd., 1964—; owner Lester & Lester, orchard, Cupertino, Calif., 1940—; dir. Orchard Supply Bldg. Corp. Mem. Santa Clara County Planning Commn., 1956-64, Cupertino Public Safety Commn., 1971-75; bd. dirs. Santa Clara County Water Dist., 1965-66; pres. Calif. History Center Found., 1979—. Served to lt. USNR, World War II. Named Man of Year, Cupertino C. of C., 1981. Mem. Internat. Council Shopping Centers, Am. Inst. Plant Engrs., Western Water Assn., Farm Bur. Fedn., Council Calif. Growers, U.S. C. of C., Calif. C. of C., Cupertino C. of C. Clubs: Chancellors (U. Calif., Davis), Commonwealth of Calif., Masons. real estate exec.; b. Santa Clara, Calif., July 17, 1916; s. William Walter and Ethel Viola (Gerrans) L.; student San Jose (Calif.) State U., 1935-38, U. Calif., Davis, 1938-40, U. Santa Clara, 1941, Columbia U., 1942; m. Hazel Marie Barnes, Mar. 6, 1944; children—Stanley, Marie, William, III, George, Russell. Vice pres., treas. Vallco Park, Ltd., 1964—; owner Lester & Lester, orchard, Cupertino, Calif., 1940—; dir. Orchard Supply Bldg. Corp. Mem. Santa Clara County Planning Commn., 1956-64, Cupertino Public Safety Commn., 1971-75; bd. dirs. Santa Clara County Water Dist., 1965-66; pres. Calif. History Center Found., 1979—. Served to lt. USNR, World War II. Named Man of Year, Cupertino C. of C., 1981. Mem. Internat. Council Shopping Centers, Am. Inst. Plant Engrs., Western Water Assn., Farm Bur. Fedn., Council Calif. Growers, U.S. C. of C., Calif. C. of C., Cupertino C. of C. Clubs: Chancellors (U. Calif., Davis), Commonwealth of Calif., Masons. Home: 10650 Linnet St Cupertino CA 95014 Office: 10050 N Wolfe Rd Suite SW 2-106 Cupertino CA 95014

LETENDRE, LORIN, pub. co. exec.; b. Mpls., Feb. 21, 1947; s. Douglas N. and Lola E. (Atwater) L.; A.B., U. Calif., Santa Barbara, 1968; M.A., 1969; m. Karen Barkley List, June 1, 1980; children—Dana Andre, Jason Michel. Instr. polit. sci. Santa Barbara City Coll., 1969-71; prof. polit. sci. San Diego Community Colls., 1971-73; with CTB/McGraw-Hill, Monterey, Calif., 1973-80, dir. new ventures, 1979-80; sr. v.p., gen. mgr. Cons. Psychologists Press, Inc., Palo Alto, Calif., 1980—. Mem. Am. Personnel and Guidance Assn., Council Exceptional Children, Am. Mgmt. Assn., Am. Soc. Tng. and Devel. Author: Understanding American Politics Through Fiction, 1973, 2d edit., 1977. Office: 577 College Ave Palo Alto CA 94306

LEUNG, KOK MING, research physicist; b. Hong Kong, Feb. 17, 1951; s. Sang and Sin Wan (Cheung) L.; B.S., U. Mo., 1973; Ph.D., U. Wis., 1979. Teaching asst. U. Wis., 1973-76, research asst., 1976-79; research physicist dept. physics U. Calif., Santa Barbara, 1979—. Mem. Am. Phys. Soc., Sigma Xi, Sigma Pi Sigma. Contbr. articles to profl. jours. Home: 6584 El Greco Rd Goleta CA 93117 Office: Dept Physics U Calif Santa Barbara CA 93106

LEUSCHNER, LUCILLE MARY, ret. librarian; b. Beloit, Wis., Sept. 25, 1911; d. Charles Herbert and Rose Anna (Connell) Kline; student Beloit Coll., 1929-31; student U. Wis. at Madison, 1933-34, certificate in L.S., 1940; m. Robert Earl Leuschner, Nov. 1, 1947; children—Robert Charles, William Richard, Anne (Mrs. Leonard Edward Collins). Library staff Beloit Pub. Library, 1934-44; librarian Norfolk Naval Hosp., Portsmouth, Va., 1944-46, VA Hosp., Tomah, Wis., 1947-48; head librarian Tomah Pub. Library, 1953-57; mem. staff Agnews State Hosp. library, San Jose, Calif., 1958-77, sr. librarian charge med. library, 1965-75; part-time med. staff librarian Alexian Bros. Hosp., San Jose, 1978-80. Bd. dirs. Coop. Info. Network, 1972-74; co-chmn. Med. Library Consortium Santa Clara County, 1976-77. Sec. bd. dirs. Santa Clara County Mental Health Assn. Mem. Calif. Library Assn. (pres. hosp. and instns. library div. 1969-70), Med. Library Assn., No. Calif. Med. Library Group. Author chpt. in book. Home: 1970 Minna Way San Jose CA 95124

LEV, OVADIA EZRA, researcher, engr., educator; b. Baghdad, Iraq, Mar. 28, 1938; came to U.S., 1966; s. Ezra and Mazal (Murad) L.; B.S., Technion, Haifa, Israel, 1962; M.S., Columbia U., 1967, D.Eng. Sci., 1971; m. Amilia Sweiry, Dec. 7, 1962; children—Roneet, Anat, Tsafreer. Structural engr. Weidenfeld Consulting, Tel-Aviv, Israel, 1962-64; constrn. engr. Mekoroth Water Co., Tel-Aviv, 1964-65; chief field supr. Van Hassel en DeKoning, Dead Sea Works, 1965-66; project engr. Weidlinger Assos., N.Y.C., 1971-73; asst. prof. U. Ill., Urbana, 1973-77; mgr. dept. advanced design and devel. Merritt Cases, Inc., Redlands, Calif., 1977-81; sect. head facilities dept. TRW System Group, San Bernardino, Calif., 1981—; cons. Sargent and Lundy, Chgo., 1976, Constrn. Engring. Research Lab., U.S. Army, 1975; instr. grad. courses Calif. State U., Fullerton. NSF research grantee, prin. investigator Geometric Optimization, 1978; registered profl. engr., Calif. Mem. ASCE (chmn. com. on optimization, 1978-82, public sec. com. on electronic computation of structural div., 1980—). Contbr. articles to nat. and internat. jours. Office: TRW PO Box 1310 San Bernardino CA 92402

LEVCHUK, GEORGE, mechanical-aeronautical consulting engineer; b. Poland, Nov. 27, 1907; s. Ioan Basili and Nadia Kornilia (Ferencewich) L.; came to U.S., 1949, naturalized, 1952. M.E., Warsaw (Poland) Inst. Tech., 1938, M.S., 1969; Ph.D., Kensington U., 1982. Polish State aircraft factory designer, 1932-38; engr. Polish Airlines, 1938-39; prototype shop mgr. Turkish Air League, 1941-48; impact extrusion engr. Victor Metal Industries, Bklyn., 1949-50; engr. Chase Aircraft Co., Trenton, N.J., 1950-53; designer N.Am. Aviation Corp., 1953-60; mathematician-designer U.S. Steel Corp., 1960-61; re-entry flow engr. Hughes Aircraft Corp., 1962-63; aerodynamicist Aeronutronics-Ford subs. Aeronutronic, Newport Beach, Calif., 1965-66; research scientist Calif. Inst. Tech., Pasadena, 1967-70; B-1 structures engr. Rockwell Corp., Inglewood, Calif., 1970-72, shuttle stress engr., 1973-77; stress engr. McDonnell Douglas Corp., St. Louis, 1978-81; mech.-aero. cons. engr., Downey, Calif., 1982—. Served to lt. Polish Air Force, 1939-41. Mem. AIAA.

LEVENTER, TERRI (AKRISH), clinical psychologist; b. N.Y.C., Sept. 13, 1922; d. David and Stella Akrish; m. Seymour E. Leventer, Aug. 20, 1949 (div.); children—David, Jerry. B.A., Hunter Coll., 1944; M.A., N.Y. U., 1951; Ed.D., UCLA, 1969. Lic. psychologist, Calif. With Northridge Hosp., 1970-77; staff mem. Woodland Hills Community Ch. Human Relations Center, 1972—; pvt. practice, psychology, 1972—; cons. Valley Hot Line, San Fernando Valley, Calif., 1971—; adminstr. coordinator Holistic Network, San Fernando Valley. Mem. Am. Psychol. Assn., Calif. Psychol. Assn., San Fernando Valley Psychol. Assn. (pres. 1980), Group Psychotherpy Assn. So. Calif., Calif. Psychol. Health Plan, Council for Nat. Register of Health Service Providers in Psychol. Democrat. Unitarian Universalist. Contbr. article to profl. jour., 1976.

LEVICK, DOUGLAS GUINNESS GWYNNE, III, business executive; b. Durham, N.C., Oct. 14, 1935; s. Douglas G.G. and Virginia Carver (Lenz) L.; m. Virginia Reed, Aug. 15, 1964; children—Carolee, Deborah, Reed. B.S.E., Princeton U., 1954; M.B.A., Harvard U., 1962. Controller, IBM-Europe, Paris, 1972-76, dir. fin. analysis IBM, Armonk, N.Y., 1976-77; v.p. fin. Millipore Corp., Bedford, Mass., 1977-80; sr. v.p. fin. Amdahl Corp., Sunnyvale, Calif., 1981—; dir. Comdisco Corp., Rosemont, Ill. Served to lt. (j.g.) USN, 1958-60. Mem. Fin. Executives Inst. Clubs: Round Hill (Greenwich, Conn.); Country (Brookline, Mass.); Princeton (N.Y.C.). Home: 10 Sargent Ln Atherton CA 94025 Office: Amdahl Corp 1250 E Arques Ave Sunnyvale CA 94086

LEVIN, ALVIN IRVING, educator; b. N.Y.C., Dec. 22, 1921; s. David and Frances (Schloss) L.; B.M. in Edn., U. Miami (Fla.), 1941; M.A., Calif. State U., Los Angeles, 1955; Ed.D. with honors, UCLA, 1968; m. Beatrice Van Loon, June 5, 1976 (div. 1981). Composer, arranger for movies, TV, theater Allied Artists, Eagle-Lion Studios, Los Angeles, 1945-65; tng. and supervising tchr. Los Angeles City Schs., 1957-65, adult edn. instr., 1962-63; research specialist Los Angeles Office Supt. Edn., 1965-67; asst. prof. ednl. research Calif. State U., Los Angeles, 1968; asst. prof. elem. edn. Calif. State U., Northridge, 1969-73; founder, pres. Alvin Irving Levin Philanthropic Found., 1973—; ordained to ministry Ch. of Mind Sci., 1975; founder, pres. Divine Love Ch.-An Internat. Metaphys. Ch., 1977—, Meet Your New Personality, A Mind Expansion Program, 1975-77. Bd. overseers Calif. Sch. Profl. Psychology, 1974—; gen. chmn., producer Fiftieth Anniversary Pageant of North Hollywood Park, 1977. Recipient plaque State of Calif., 1977. Mem. Nat. Soc. for Study Edn., AAUP, Am. Statis. Assn., Internat. Council Edn. for Teaching, Los Angeles World Affairs Council, Internat. Platform Assn., North Hollywood C. of C. (dir. 1976—), Phi Delta Kappa. Author: My Ivory Tower, 1950; (music-drama) Happy Land, 1971; Symposium: Values in Kaleidoscope, 1973; America, America! (TV series), 1978-79; (docu-drama) One World, 1980; compiler and contbr. U.S. Dept. Edn. reports; Adult Counseling and Guidance, 1967, Parent Child Presch. Program, 1967, English Classes for Foreign Speaking Adult Profls., 1967. Home: 8612 Jellico Ave Northridge CA 91325

LEVIN, DANIEL PETER, real estate developer; b. Syracuse, N.Y., Jan. 14, 1949; s. Philip Morris and Mary Stephanie (Spoljaric) L.; m. Janie Lee Lignon, May 29, 1971; children—Hannah, Rogers. A.B., Harvard U., 1970; M.B.A., U. Chgo., 1976. With NMUN, N.Y.C., 1970-71; mgr. Food Exporting, Atlanta, 1971-73; loan officer, First Chgo. Citibank, Chgo., 1973-77; v.p. Rexall Drug Co. (Ross Hall Corp.), Palo Alto, Calif., 1977-79; ptnr. Lincoln Property Co., Foster City, Calif., 1979—; instr. bus. fin. San Francisco State U., 1978-82. Mem., bd. dirs. San Mateo County Devel. Assn. Mem. Redwood City C. of C. (dir.). Club: Harvard (sec., dir.) (San Francisco). Home: 115 Cole St San Francisco CA 94117 Office: 212 Lincoln Center Dr Foster City CA 94404

LEVIN, MARTIN HOWARD, computer consultant, former air force officer; b. Hazleton, Pa., Feb. 9, 1941; s. Benjamin and Selma Louise (Rosen) L.; B.S. in Bus. Adminstrn., Pa. State U., 1962; M.S. in Retailing, N.Y. U., 1963; m. Rosa Bernardina Fernandez Rosado, Aug. 15, 1965; children—Maya Ann, Richard Benjamin. Commd. 2d lt. U.S. Air Force, 1963, advanced through grades to maj., 1973; comdr. 825th Services Squadron, Little Rock AFB, Ark., 1968-69; commissary officer Anderson AFB, Guam, 1969-72; comdr. 635th Services Squadron, U-Tapao, Thailand, 1972-73; services staff officer Hdqrs. 15th Air Force, SAC, 1973-75; camp comdr. Anderson AFB Indochina Refugee Camp, 1975; dep. comdr. Korea Regional Exchange, Seoul, 1975-78; chief USAF Acad. Cadet Dining Hall, 1978-79; dir. housing and services Aerospace Def. Command, Colorado Springs, Colo., 1979-80; services requirements mgr. SAC, 1980-83; ret., 1983; course dir., instr. Am. Inst. Profl. Edn., Madison, N.J., 1982—; cons. microcomputer applications and edn., 1982—; instr. Pikes Peak Community Coll., Colorado Springs, 1980-82. Decorated Air Force Commendation medal with 3 oak leaf clusters, Meritorious Service medal, Joint Service Commendation medal. Jewish. Home and Office: 5850 Escapardo Way Colorado Springs CO 80917

LEVIN, NORMAN, health care executive; b. Mpls., Sept. 8, 1930; s. Henry and Anna (Sedransky) L.; A.A., U. Minn., 1950; B.B.A., St. Mary's U., 1956; m. Karen Hochfeld, Nov. 24, 1962; children—Adrienne, Adam, Jason, Alison, Seth. Pres., Western Health Facilities, Inc., Seattle, 1963-73; exec. v.p. Villa Care, Inc., Issaquah, Wash., from 1973, now pres.; pres. Wash. Pharm. Services, Inc., Mercer Island, 1974—, Seattle Med.-Surg. Group, Redmond, Wash., 1982—; mem. Bd. Examiners, Nursing Home Adminstrs., 1970-73; mem. Nursing Home Adv. Council, Wash., 1980-83; Pres., Iowa chpt. Am. Nat. Theatre and Acad., 1959-61; sec.-treas. Seattle Beer Sheva Sister City Com., 1977—; chmn. Care Polit. Action Com., Issaquah, 1980-83. Served with USAF, 1951-53. Fellow Am. Coll. Nursing Home Adminstrs. Jewish. Club: B'nai B'rith (pres. 1958-59). Office: 9311 SE 36th Mercer Island WA 98040

LEVINE, ARTHUR STEPHEN, real estate devel. co. exec.; b. Toronto, Ont., Can., Mar. 22, 1941; s. Philip and Lilian (Hoffman) L.; came to U.S., 1978; B.A., U. Toronto, 1963; B.Arch., Dalhousie U., 1970; postgrad. Pepperdine U.; m. Claudia Lea Barritt, June 23, 1977. Land devel. officer Cadillac Fairview Corp., Toronto, 1974-77; project mgr. L.B. Nelson Corp., Menlo Park, Calif., 1978-79, Daon Corp., Newport Beach, Calif., 1979; mgr. land devel. and land acquisition, mgr. ops. Broadmoor Homes, Dublin, Calif., 1980-81; investment mgr. Genstar Investment Housing, 1981-82; dir. devel. Empire Savs. and Loan, Riverside, Calif., 1982—. Bd. dirs. Grand Ballet Classique, San Francisco, 1978, Temple Isaiah, Newport Beach, 1979, Youth Services Assn., Newport Beach, 1981—. Recipient award Canadian Housing Design Council, 1974. Mem. Royal Archtl. Inst. Can., Ont. Assn. Architects, Homebuilders Council Calif. Jewish. Club: University Athletic. Home: 303 Marguerite Ave Apt D Corona del Mar CA 92625 Office: 7724 California Ave Riverside CA 92504

LEVINE, GENE NORMAN, sociology educator; b. Medford, Mass., May 15, 1930; s. Joseph Michael and Jennie (Herman) L. B.A. summa cum laude, Boston U., 1952; Ph.D., Columbia U., 1959. Research assoc. Bur. Applied Social Research Columbia U., N.Y.C., 1954-64; project dir. UN Research Inst. Social Devel., Geneva, 1964-67; prof. sociology UCLA, 1965—. Mem. Am. Jewish Com. Fellow Inst. Contemporary Jewish Life U. of Judaism; mem. Am. Sociol. Assn., Pacific Sociol. Assn., Am. Assn. for Pub. Opinion Research, Assn. for Social. Study of Jewry, Phi Beta Kappa. Author: Workers Vote, 1960; Inducing Social Change in Developing Communities, 1967; The Japanese American Community, 1981; Social Structure and Mass Communications, 1983. Office: Dept Sociology UCLA Los Angeles CA 90024

LEVINE, JOHN WARREN, lawyer, real estate broker; b. Los Angeles, Mar. 21, 1954; s. Phillip H. and Shirley G. L. B.A., Brandeis U., 1975; J.D., Loyola U.-Los Angeles, 1978. Bar: Calif. 1978. Assoc., Prince & Beck (now Prince, Littenberg & Warren), Los Angeles, 1978-80, Richards, Watson, Dreyfuss & Gershan, Los Angeles, 1980-83; v.p. La Canada Flintridge Devel. Corp., Los Angeles, 1980—. Co-chmn. Party Heavers Fundraising Charity. Recipient Letter of Commendation, Mayor Tom Bradley, 1978. Mem. ABA, Friends of the Earth, Solar Lobby, NOW, Los Angeles County Bar Assn., La Canada Bd. Realtors. Jewish. Office: Suite 3800 333 S Hope St Los Angeles CA 90071

LEVINE, MARILYN ANNE, artist; b. Medicine Hat, Alta., Can., Dec. 22, 1935; d. Herman Rutherford and Annie Louise (Waldo) Hayes; came to U.S., 1973; m. Sidney Levine, Sept. 30, 1959 (div. 1982). B.Sc., U. Alta. (Can.), 1957, M.Sc., 1959; M.A., U. Calif.-Berkeley, 1970, M.F.A., 1971. Teaching fellow dept. chemistry U. Alta., 1957-59; chemist I, Geol. Survey of Can., Ottawa, Ont., 1959-61; instr. chemistry Campion Coll., U. Sask., 1962-64; sessional instr. ceramics U. Regina, 1966-69; vis. instr. art U. Calgary, 1968-71; sessional instr. ceramics U. Regina, 1971-73, visual arts, 1972-73; lectr. art U. Calif.-Davis, 1973; vis. instr. art U. Sask., 1973; asst. prof. art U. Utah, Salt Lake City, 1973-76; vis. lectr. sculpture U. Calif.-Berkeley, 1975-80; vis. lectr. art Calif. State U.-Hayward, 1981; one woman shows include Univ. Art Mus., Berkeley, 1971, Hansen Fuller Gallery, San Francisco, 1971, Bernard Danenberg Galleries, N.Y.C., 1973, Norman McKenzie Art Gallery, U. Regina, 1974, O.K. Harris Gallery, N.Y.C., 1974, Morgan Gallery, Kansas City, 1974, Peal House Galleries, 1975, Hansen Fuller Gallery, 1975, O.K. Harris Gallery, 1976, 79, 81, Inst. Contemporary Art, Boston, 1981, Galerie Alain Blondel, Paris, 1981; Astier Faure Gallery, Los Angeles, 1983; exhibited in group shows at Montreal Mus. Fine Arts, 1970, Sharp Focus Realism, Sidney Janis Gallery, N.Y.C., 1972, Indpls. Mus. Art, 1972, David Stuart Galleries, Los Angeles, 1972, San Francisco Mus.

Modern Art, 1972, Musee d'Art Moderne de la Ville de Paris, 1973, Alta. Coll. of Art Gallery, 1973, Clay-Whitney Mus. Am. Art, 1974, Fendrick Gallery, Washington, 1975, Kunstreserent der Stadt Darmstadt, Germany, 1975, Mus. Contemporary Art, Chgo., 1976, Renwick Gallery, Washington, 1976, Ackland Meml. Art Center, Chapel Hill, N.C., 1977, Australian Nat. Gallery, Canberra, 1977, The San Francisco Mus., 1978, Everson Mus. Art, Syracuse, N.Y., 1978, U. So. Calif. and Denver Art Mus., 1979, Albuquerque Mus., 1979, Danforth Mus., 1980, San Diego Mus. Art, 1980, Palm Springs Desert Mus., 1982, San Jose Mus. Art, 1982, Kanazawa Exhibition, Japan, 1982, many others; permanent collections incl.: Confedn. Art Gallery and Mus., Charlottetown, P.E.I., Internat. Mus. Ceramics, Faenza, Sheridan Coll. Sch. Design, Toronto, Montreal Mus. Fine Arts, Nat. Mus. Modern Art, Kyoto and Tokyo, Va. Mus. Fine Arts, U. Sask., Norman McKenzie Art Gallery, Utah Mus. Fine Arts, William Rockhill Nelson Gallery Art, Australian Nat. Gallery, Indusmin Collection, Toronto, Oakland Mus., Everson Mus. Art, San Francisco Mus. Modern Art, Glenbow Mus., Calgary, Purdue U., many others. Numerous articles to profl. jours.

LEVINE, MELDON EDISES, congressman, lawyer; b. Los Angeles, June 7, 1943; s. Sid B. and Shirley B. (Blum) L.; m. Jan Greenberg, June 23, 1950; 1 son, Adam Paul. A.B., U. Calif.-Berkeley, 1964; M.P.A., Princeton U., 1966; J.D., Harvard U., 1969. Bar: Calif. 1970, D.C. 1972. Assoc. Wyman, Bautzer, Rothman & Kuchel, 1969-71; legis. asst. U.S. Senate, Washington, 1971-73; mem. Leveine Krom & Unger, Beverly Hills, Calif., 1973-77; mem. Calif. Assembly, 1977-82; mem. 98th Congress from 27th Calif. Dist., 1983—. Mem. governing bds. So. Calif. chpts. Anti-Defamation League, Am. Jewish Com., Am. Jewish Congress, NAACP Legal Def. Fund; mem. nat. governing bds. U. of Judaism, City of Hope, U. Calif. Alumni Council. Mem. Calif. Bar Assn., Los Angeles Bar Assn. Author: The Private Sector and the Common Market, 1968; contbr. articles to publs. Office: US Congress Washington DC 20515

LEVINE, MICHAEL, public relations co. exec., publisher, author; b. N.Y.C., Apr. 17, 1954; s. Arthur O. and Virginia (Gaylor) L.; student Rutgers U., 1972-73, UCLA, 1978-79; m. Darlene Mancuso, Jan. 14, 1977. Pres., Michael Levine Presents, Inc., Fort Lee, N.J., 1973-78; pub. TV News Mag., Hollywood, Calif., 1977—; pres. Michael Levine Pub. Relations, Hollywood, 1979—, Sunset Merchandising Mail Order Co., Inc., 1978—; campaign dir. Media for Brown, 1978. Mem. Calif. Gov.'s State Mental Hosps. adv. bd.; active ERAmerica. Recipient Am. Cancer Soc. cert. merit, 1976. Mem. Universal Autograph Collectors, Polit. Memorabilia Orgn., Hollywood C. of C. (dir.). Jewish. Author: How to Reach Anyone Who's Anyone, 1980; author syndicated column Spotlites, 1976—. Office: 967 N La Cienega Blvd Los Angeles CA 90069

LEVINE, MORRIS HAROLD, radiologist; b. Lowell, Mass., Nov. 4, 1905; s. Max and Bertha (Richard) L.; m. Frances Ida Jacobs, Oct. 31, 1937; children—Stanley Bryant, Marshall Andrew, Leonard Jordan, Lawrence Elliot. B.S., Tufts U., 1928, M.D., 1934. Diplomate Am. Bd. Radiology. Gen. intern St. Luke's Hosp., Pittsfield, Mass., 1934-35; path. intern Montefiore Hosp., N.Y.C., 1935-36, asst. resident, 1936-37; resident in radiology Mt. Alto (Wash.) Hosp., 1940-42; resident Jewish Hosp., Cin., 1946-47; mem. staff VA Hosps. in Marion, Ill., 1942-43, Huntington, W.Va., 1943-46, Newington, Conn., 1947, Hartford, Conn., 1947-48; chief radiology Nat. Jewish Hosp., Denver, 1948-67; radiologist Colo. Gen. Hosp., Denver, 1948-52; radiologist Gen. Rose Meml. Hosp., Denver, 1952-69; chief radiol. services VA Hosp., Vancouver, Wash., 1969—; cons. in field; assoc. prof. radiology U. Colo., 1949-69. Served to major AUS, 1943-46. Fellow Am. Coll. Radiology (pres. Colo. chpt.); mem. soc. Nuclear Medicine, Rocky Mountain Radiol. Soc. Home: 1200 E Evergreen Blvd Vancouver WA 98661 Office: VA Med Center Vancouver WA 98661

LEVINE, MYRON LOUIS, optometrist; b. Los Angeles, Nov. 21, 1930; s. Jack and Jennie (Berman) L.; m. Nancy Lou Stiegler Gambet, Aug. 15, 1953; children—Jeffrey Dean, Bradley Allen, Steven Mitchell. B.S., Pacific U., 1953, O.D., 1954. Lic. optometrist, Calif., Nev. Pvt. practice optometry, West Los Angeles, 1954-60, group practice, Beverly Hills, Calif., 1960-81, partnership practice, Los Angeles, 1982—; mem. staff Mt. Sinai Optometric Clinic, 1960-63, Queen of Angels Hosp., 1964—, Santa Marta Hosp., 1964—, contact lens clinic, 1982; lectr. various profl. groups. Recipient Los Angeles Service award, Dist. 4 Chain Maker award, Past Pres. Service award, B'nai B'rith. Mem. Los Angeles Optometric Assn. (Award of Merit 1966), Am. Optometric Assn. (charter mem. contact lens sect., multidisciplinary practice sect.). Democrat. Jewish. Clubs: Masons, B'nai B'rith (past pres.). Contbr. articles to profl. jours. Home: 10587 Holman Ave Los Angeles CA 90024 Office: 840 S Robertson Blvd Los Angeles CA 90035

LEVINE, REEVA MILLER, painter; b. Hollywood, Calif., Nov. 23, 1912; d. Bernard and Rose (Schuman) Torf; m. Maurice Miller, 1932; m. 2d, Raphael Levine, Apr. 20, 1959; children—David Miller, Stuart Miller. Student Santa Monica City Coll., UCLA. Art dir. Camp Ben Swig, Union Am. Hebrew Congregations Inst., 1952-58; numerous invitational exhibitions and one-man shows, 1948-82; group shows, 1962-67; numerous pub. commissions, paintings and portraits 1948-75; work represented in pub. collections, 1944-51. Recipient first prize, Santa Monica Art Assn., 1947, second prize, 1948; named artist of Yr. Music and Art Fdn., Seattle, 1970. Mem. Artists Equity Assn. (Wash. chpt.). Jewish. Club: B'Nai B'rith. Created cover and illustrations for Wild Branch on the Olive Tree, Holy Mountain. Address: 16 Skagit Key Bellevue WA 98004

LEVINGER, JEFFREY EMMET, computer cons.; b. Bklyn., June 21, 1941; s. Herbert R. and Selma L.; B.S., M.I.T., 1963; postgrad. in edn. Harvard U., 1963; m. Mary Lucretia Duncan, Feb. 5, 1972; children—David Taylor Fox, Leah Rebecca. Tchr. math. public schs. San Lorenzo, Calif., 1963-64; systems cons. Ill. Inst. Tech. Research Inst., Chgo., 1964-67, Levinger Assocs., Chgo., 1967-69; dir. project mgmt. Western Ops., Inc., 1969-71; pres. Levinger Assocs., San Francisco, 1971—; instr. tech. writing DeAnza Community Coll., 1980—. Cert. in data processing. Mem. Am. Mgmt. Assn., Data Processing Mgmt. Assn., Assn. Systems Mgmt. Author computer guides. Home: 300 Sussex St San Francisco CA 94131 Office: 57 Post St Suite 503 San Francisco CA 94104

LEVINGS, DAVID STEVEN, bank ofcl.; b. Marion, Ohio, Mar. 12, 1948; s. Robert Eugene and IvaLoo Jean (Sewell) L.; A.A. in Banking and Fin., 1982; m. Elvia Garcia, Mar. 14, 1971; children—Troy Steven, Todd David. With Valley Bank Nev., Las Vegas, 1971—, mgr. computer ops., 1979-80, mgr. communications, 1980—. Active local Cub Scouts Am. Served with USAF, 1967-71; Vietnam. Mem. Am. Inst. Banking. Address: PO Box 15427 Las Vegas NV 89114

LEVINSKY, JANET BETH, designer and retailer; b. Indianapolis, Nov. 1, 1947; d. Samuel and Dora (Shuster) Levinsky; m. Marc Stein Prigozen, Mar. 16, 1980. B.F.A., U. Colo., 1969, M.F.A., 1971. Designer Wright, Porteous & Lowe, Indpls., 1970; design mgr. Witkin Homes, Denver, 1970-73; designer and sales staff Foliage Services, Inc., Denver, 1973-75; mgr. design ctr., Mission Viejo Co., Mission Viejo Calif., and Denver, 1975-76; store mgr. Dancewear Showcase, Denver, 1976-78; bus. mgr. Colo. Conservatory Ballet, Denver, 1976-78; owner, operator Denver Dance Shop, Denver, 1978—; freelance designer. Mem. exec. Bd. Coll. Contemporary Dance; mem. Children's Diabetes Guild, Jr. Symphony Guild, Denver Ballet Guild; sponsor David Taylor Dance Theatre. Mem. Am. Soc. Interior Designers, Nat. Landscape Inst., Nat. Soc. Interior Designers. Home: 4530 S Verbena Unit 336 Denver CO 80237 Office: Denver Dance Shop 8101 E Belleview Ave Denver CO 80237

LEVINSON, ELAD, human resources development executive, consultant; b. N.Y., Mar. 1, 1947; s. Paul and Ruth (Jacobs) L.; m. Susan Irene Covey, Dec. 23, 1981; 1 dau., Sarah Covey. B.A. in Psychology, San Francisco State U., 1968; M. Social Work with honors, Adelphi U., 1970. Lic. clin. social worker, Calif. Program dir. United Jewish Community Ctr. Camp Tawonga, San Francisco, 1968-71; dir. human resources, tng. & devel. David Marcus & Co., Sausalito, Calif., 1975-76; alcoholism therapist Sequoia Hosp., Redwood City, Calif., 1976-79; pres. Levinson Assocs. Cons. Organizational & Human Resource Devel., Palo Alto, Calif., 1979—; mgr. human resources devel. Stanford U. Hosp., Palo Alto, 1981—; dir. State of the Art Stress Mgmt. Consultants, Palo Alto, 1976—; lectr. Stanford U., U. Santa Clara, U. Calif.-Santa Cruz, San Jose, San Francisco State U. Mem. adv. bd. dirs. Pegasus Project An Alcoholism Outpatient Service, Stanford U. Alcoholism Clinic. Mem. Am. Soc. Tng. Devel., Orgn. Devel. Network, Bay Area Assn. Soc. Hosp. Mgmt. Educators and Tng. Buddhist. Author publs. in field. Home: 1160 California Ave Palo Alto CA 94306 Office: 160 California Ave Palo Alto CA 94306

LEVITZ, JOEL JACOB, community developer; b. Phila., Jan. 4, 1935; s. Milton and Sophia (Kurtz) L.; B.S., CCNY, 1958; M.A., Sacramento State Coll., 1964; postgrad CCNY, 1959-60, Columbia U., 1960-61, U. Denver, 1961-62; Ed.D., Temple U., 1973; m. Karen R. Bell, Sept. 17, 1977; children—Michael Seth, John, Susan, Robin, Michael Kimball. Tchr. emotionally disturbed children Hawthorne (N.Y.) Cedar Knolls, 1958-60; tng. supr., tech. rep. Am. Machine & Foundry, Stamford, Conn., 1960-62; engring. psychologist Aerojet Gen. Corp., Sacramento, 1962-64, Philco Ford, Willow Grove, Pa., 1964-66; program mgr. ednl. systems Burroughs Corp., Ardmore, Pa., 1966-70; dir. spl. support serviced Federal City Coll., Washington, 1970-71; v.p. mktg., Ill. and Ariz. ops. Environ. Devels., Inc., 1971-78; pres. Executive Homes Inc., Denver, 1977—, Calvan Properties Inc., 1978—, Paragon Realty (USA) Ltd., 1979—; pres. The Levitz Group, 1982—; mem. U.S. Senatorial Bus. Adv. Com. Mem. Human Factors Soc. (exec. council at large 1966-67), Am. Psychol. Assn., (asso.), Nat. Assn. Homebuilders, Nat. Assn. Realtors, Psi Chi, Phi Delta Kappa, Phi Theta Tau. Home: 3670 S Helena Way Aurora CO 80013 Office: 14001 E Iliff Ave Aurora CO 80014

LEVY, ALAN DAVID, real estate exec.; b. St. Louis, July 19, 1938; s. I. Jack and Natalie (Yawitz) L.; grad. Sch. Real Estate, Washington U., 1960; m. Abby Jane Markowitz, May 12, 1968; children—Jennifer Lynn, Jacqueline Claire. Property mgr. Solon Gershman Inc., Realtors, Clayton, Mo., 1958-61; gen. mgr. Kodner Constrn. Co., St. Louis, 1961-63; regional mgr. Tishman Realty & Constrn. Co., Inc., N.Y.C., 1963-69, v.p., Los Angeles, 1969-77; exec. v.p., dir. Tishman West Mgmt. Corp., 1977—; dir. Metro-Plex Airline, Dallas; guest lectr. on real estate mgmt. to various forums. Mem. devel. com. Los Angeles County Mus. Art. Mem. bldg. owners and mgrs. assns. Los Angeles (dir.), N.J. (co-founder, hon. dir.), Inst. Real Estate Mgmt. (cert. property mgr.), Urban Land Inst., Internat. Council Shopping Centers. Contbr. articles on property mgmt. to trade jours. Home: 541 Loring Ave Los Angeles CA 90024 also 10960 Wilshire Blvd Los Angeles CA 90024

LEVY, DAVID, television producer/writer, novelist; b. Phila.; s. Benjamin and Lillian (Potash) L.; m. Lucile Alva Wilds (div.); children—Lance Lee, Linda Gorman. B.S. in Econs., U. Pa., 1934, M.B.A., 1935. Vice-pres., assoc. dir. radio-TV dept. Young & Rubicam Inc., N.Y.C., 1938-59; v.p. network programs and talent NBC-TV, N.Y.C., 1959-61; ind. TV producer/writer, cons., Los Angeles, 1961—; creator, exec. producer The Addams Family, The Pruitts of Southhampton, Sarge, Name That Tune, Face The Music; pres. Wilshire Prodns. Inc., Beverly Hills, Calif., 1972—; cons. Sandy Frank Prodns.; dir. Golden Orange Broadcasting, Anaheim, Calif. Served as lt. USNR, 1944-46. Mem. ASCAP, Producers Guild Am., Writers Guild Am., Caucus Producers, Writers and Dirs. (steering com., sec.). Republican. Author: The Chameleons, 1964; The Gods of Foxcroft, 1970; The Network Jungle, 1976. Home and Office: 214 1/2 Spalding Dr Beverly Hills CA 90212

LEVY, DAVID HOWARD, astronomy educator, planetarium manager; b. Montreal, Que., Can., May 22, 1948; s. Nathaniel Lewis and Edith (Pailet) L. B.A., Acadia U., Wolfville, N.S., Can., M.A., 1972; M.A., Queen's U., Kingston, Ont., 1979. Astronomy instr. various children's camps, 1966-80; coordinator and tchr. edn. activities Kingston Centre, Royal Astron. Soc. Can., 1977—; floor mgr. Flandrau Planetarium, Tucson, 1980—. Recipient Royal Astronomical Soc. Can. medal, 1980; recipient Riverside Telescope Conf. merit award 1980. Mem. Am. Astron. Soc., Tucson Amateur Astronomy Assn. (pres. 1980-82), Am. Assn. of Variable Star Observers, Assn. of Lunar and Planetary Observers, Royal Astron. Soc. Can. (hist. com. 1980-82; Messier certificate 1981), Astron. Soc. of the Pacific, Pi Lambda Theta. Developer edn. programs in astronomy for children. Home: Route 7 Box 414 Tucson AZ 85747

LEVY, DAVID STEVEN, coll. adminstr.; b. Los Angeles, Mar. 9, 1955; s. Henry and Gloria Grace (Barouh) L.; B.A., Occidental Coll., 1977; M.A., 1979. Asst. dir. fin. aid Calif. State Coll., San Bernardino, 1978-79; fin. aid counselor Calif. State U.-Northridge, 1979-80; assoc. dir. student fin. aid Calif. State U.-Dominguez Hills, 1980-82; dir. fin. aid Occidental Coll., Los Angeles, 1982—; mem. Title IA Adv. Com. Calif., 1977—. Mem. life-long learning com. Calif. Postsecondary Edn. Commn., 1980—. Richter fellow Princeton U., 1976; Calif. State U. adminstrv. fellow, 1981—. Mem. Mortar Board Alumni Assn. (pres. 1977—), Calif. Assn. Student Fin. Aid Adminstrs., Western Assn. Student Fin. Aid Adminstrs., Nat. Assn. Student Fin. Aid Adminstrs., Phi Beta Kappa, Delta Phi Epsilon, Psi Chi, Phi Alpha Theta, Sigma Alpha Epsilon. Jewish. Co-editor Calif. Student Aid Commn. Student Aid Workbook, 1977—. Home: 3522 Henrietta Ave LaCrescenta CA 91214 Office: 1600 Campus Rd Los Angeles CA 90041

LEVY, HAROLD, optometrist; b. N.Y.C., Aug. 14, 1914; s. Gustave and Lena (Goldstein) L.; m. Lillian Epstein, Dec. 1939; children—Barbara Gale, Peggy Jane; m. 2d, Katherine Rains, Jan. 1960; m. 3d Jane Marie Pruenal, June, 1972. Student CCNY, 1931-34; B.S., Columbia U., 1936; O.D., Ky. State Coll. Optometry, 1943. Lic. optometrist, Colo. Practice optometry, Denver, 1945—. Recipient Brotherhood award Denver Indian Community, 1980. Mem. Nat. Eye Research Found. (fellow in orthokeratology, cert. diplomate contact lens), Am. Optometric Assn., Colo. Optometric Assn., Internat. Orthokeratological Soc. Home: 6908 W Nova Dr Littleton CO 80123 Office: Dr Harold Levy 620 E Colfax St Denver CO 80203

LEVY, HAROLD P., public relations cons.; b. Trinidad, Colo., Mar. 8, 1907; s. Phan and Fannie (Akerman) L.; A.B., U. Wash., 1929; m. Alice Klund, Sept. 8, 1938. Reporter, Seattle Union Record and Seattle Post-Intelligencer, 1926-29; reporter, editor Seattle Times, 1929-34; resident writer Henry St. Settlement, N.Y.C., 1934-35; dir. publicity Nat. Conf. Social Work, Columbus, Ohio, 1935-39; research asso. Russell Sage Found., N.Y.C., 1939-45; nat. dir. public relations Commn. Community Interrelations, N.Y.C., 1945-47; founder, pres. Harold P. Levy Public Relations, Los Angeles, 1947—; faculty U. Calif. Extension, 1947-49. Bd. dirs. Tb and Health Assn. Los Angeles County, 1958-64, pres., 1962-63; bd. dirs. Calif. Orgn. Public Health Nursing, 1949-52, Pasadena Symphony Orch., 1981—. Mem. Public Relations Soc. Am. (charter; nat. dir. 1954, chpt. dir. 1950-54), Sigma Delta Chi. Clubs: Assocs. of Calif. Inst. Tech., Athenaeum. Author: Public Relations for Social Agencies, 1956; Building a Popular Movement, 1944; A Study in Public Relations, 1943; contbr. articles to profl. jours. Address: 2980 Edgewick Rd Glendale CA 91206

LEVY, LESLIE GARY, podiatrist; b. N.Y.C., Nov. 15, 1954; s. William and Natalie Rose (Weltz) L.; A.S. in Chemistry, Nassau Community Coll., 1974; B.S. in Biology, SUNY, Stony Brook, 1976; D.P.M., Calif. Coll. Podiatric Medicine, 1979. Intern, resident under Lyman H. Wilson, D.P.M., Orange County, Calif., 1979-80; pvt. practice podiatric medicine, Los Angeles, 1980—; vol. physician Haight-Ashbury Free Med. Clinic, San Francisco, 1978-79; team physician Kennedy High Sch., Granada Hills, Calif., 1981—; instr. Diabetic Clinic, Holy Cross Hosp., Mission Hills, Calif., 1981—. Mem. Am. Podiatry Assn., Calif. Podiatry Assn., Los Angeles County Podiatric Assn., Am. Acad. Podiatric Sports Medicine, Am. Public Health Assn., San Fernando C. of C. Club: North San Fernando Valley Rotary. Home: 16750 Cassen St Granada Hills CA 91343 Office: 11600 Eldridge St Suite 104 Lake View Terrace CA 91342

LEVY, LOUIS ALAN, neurol. surgeon; b. N.Y.C., Feb. 26, 1939; s. Leon S. and Ina (Eisenberg) L.; B.A., U. Calif., Santa Barbara, 1962; M.D., U. So. Calif., 1964; m. Johanna Antoinette; children—Lori Anne, Jennifer Elizabeth, Robert Louis, Alan Edward. Intern, Los Angeles County Gen. Hosp., 1964-65; resident gen. surgery Los Angeles County Harbor Gen. Hosp., 1965-66; resident neurol. surgery Los Angeles County, Univ. So. Calif. Med. Center, 1970-73; pvt. practice medicine specializing in neurol. surgery, Reno, Nev, 1974—; mem. staff Washoe Med. Center, St. Mary's Hosp.; cons. Reno VA Hosp. Diplomate Am. Bd. Neurol. Surgery. Fellow ACS. Home: 864 Marsh Ave Reno NV 89509 Office: 1000 Ryland St Reno NV 89502

LEVY, RUTH JACOBS (MRS. WOLFGANG E. LEVY), clinical psychologist; b. N.Y.C., Apr. 5, 1915; d. Edward Jacobs and Rose (Gell) J.; m. Wolfgang E. Levy, Feb. 11, 1934; children—Reuben E., Edna J., Ralph D. B.A., N.Y.U., 1934; M.A., Columbia U., 1937, Ph.D. in Psychology, 1940; J.D., Lincoln U., San Jose, Calif., 1972. Diplomate Am. Psychol. Assn. Clin. psychologist CCNY, 1934-40, U. Wash., Seattle U., 1940-56, Santa Clara County Hosp., San Jose City Health Dept., 1956-75; pvt. practice clin. psychology, Saratoga, Calif., 1975—. Fellow Am. Psychol. Assn.; mem. Sigma Xi. Contbr. numerous articles to profl. jours. Home: PO Box 813 Saratoga CA 95071

LEWIN, DEREK JOHN, internat. relocation mgmt. exec.; b. Stamford, Conn., Jan. 19, 1943; s. Helmut Louis and Elizabeth (Broder) L.; B.A., U. Colo., 1964; postgrad. Wharton Sch., U. Pa., 1976; children—Nancy, Daniel. Mgr., Hertz Corp., Denver, 1964-67; dir. corp. mktg. Homequity, Inc., Wilton, Conn., 1967-72; pres. Van Relco, Inc., Denver, 1973-82, Intergroup Mgmt. Co., Denver, 1982—. Mem. Employee Relocation Council, Internat. Real Estate Fedn., Internat. Inst. Valuers. Home: 99 Benthaven Pl Boulder CO 80303 Office: 1125 17th St Denver CO 80202

LEWIN, MELVYN MATTHEW, psychologist; b. Los Angeles, Mar. 29, 1940; s. Edwin and Minnie Ruth (Kluger) L.; student U. Calif., Santa Barbara, 1958-59; B.A., UCLA, 1959-62; M.S., U. So. Calif., 1970, Ph.D., 1976; m. Ingrid Keyne, Jan. 7, 1968; 1 dau., Alexa-Sascha Allegra Keyne. Coordinator recreation program Five Acres, Altadena, Calif., 1967-69; sch. psychologist Torrance (Calif.) Unified Sch. Dist., 1969-77; marriage, family and child counselor Marriage, Family & Child Counselor Corp., Palos Verdes Estates, Calif., 1977-78; staff devel. couns., Palo Verdes Estates, 1973—; prin., clin. psychologist Psychol. Corp., Palos Verdes Estates, 1978—; instr. Marymount Palos Verdes Coll., 1973-74. Treas., Abalone Cove Landslide Assn., 1978—. Served with AUS, 1962-66. Mem. Am. Psychol. Assn., Calif. Psychol. Assn. Home: 6778 Alta Vista Dr Rancho Palos Verdes CA 90274 Office: 716 Yarmouth Rd Palos Verdes Estates CA 90274

LEWIS, ALLEN MARTIN, educator; b. Louisville, Jan 25, 1942; s. Aren Arnold and Bertha (Brodsky) L.; m. Judy Heller, Sept. 13, 1963; 1 dau., Rebecca Rose. B.S. in Bus. Adminstrn., Calif. State U.-Hayward, 1965; M.S. in Computer Sci., U. London, 1975. Programmer, systems analyst, software specialist Poly. Central, London, 1973-75, Fresno (Calif.) State U., 1975-77, Ariz. State U., Tempe, 1977-78; chmn. dept. data processing Truckee Meadows Community Coll., Reno, 1978—. Mem. Nat. Soc. Profs. (pres. chpt.), Data Processing Mgmt. Assn., Assn. Systems Mgmt. Presenter papers at profl. convs. Office: Truckee Meadows Community Coll Dept Data Processing 7000 Dandini Blvd Reno NV 89512

LEWIS, ANNA ELIZABETH, writer; b. Salisbury, N.C., Oct. 24, 1946; d. Samuel Clee and Ruth Geraldine (Weaver) Laster, Sr.; A.A., Stratford Coll., 1966; postgrad. Wake Forest U., 1966-67; m. Jesse Ray Lewis, Jr., Mar. 14, 1970; children—Mary Elizabeth, Laura Ellen. Reporter, advt. saleswoman, photographer Myrtle Beach (S.C.) Sun News, 1967-70, spl. feature writer, 1972-76; prodn. mgr., writer Valley Inquirer newspaper, Ridgecrest, Calif.; freelance writer. Organizer, bd. dirs. Grand Strand Humane Soc., Myrtle Beach, 1969-70; bd. dirs. New Hanover Humane Soc.; mem. Animal Shelter Constrn. team City of Ridgecrest; vol. Services for the Aging. Mem. Beta Sigma Phi. Democrat. Episcopalian. Home: 214 W Wilson St Ridgecrest CA 93555 Office: 619 W Ridgecrest Blvd Ridgecrest CA 93555

LEWIS, BETTY ANN, writer, historian; b. Fresno, Calif., June 1, 1925; d. Roy William and Dorothy Fredricka (Porter) Bagby; m. Monte Randall Lewis, Jan. 11, 1946; children—Christine, Marci, Mike, Kelly. Student Hartnell Coll. Author: Victorian Homes of Watsonville, 1974; Walking and Driving Tour of Historic Watsonville, 1975; Highlights in the History of Watsonville, 1975; Watsonville Memories That Linger, 1976; Monterey Bay Yesterday, 1977; Watsonville Yesterday, 1978; Watsonville Memories That Linger, Vol. II, 1980; speaker, cons., researcher radio programs. Mem. Watsonville Library Bd., 1982-85. Recipient SCOPE award, 1977, 78; San Jose State U.-Sourisseau Acad. research grantee. Mem. Nat. League Am. Pen Women, Theatre Historians, Calif. Conf. Hist. Socs. (v.p. 1982), Pajaro Valley Hist. Assn. (pres. 1980-81; Hubert Wyckoff Meml. award 1979), Santa Cruz Soc. Hist. Preservation. Republican. Presbyterian (elder). Club: Watsonville Woman's. Office: 420 E Main St Suite 204 Mansion House Watsonville CA 95076

LEWIS, BRIAN THOMAS, computer scientist, researcher; b. Bogota, Colombia, Sept. 26, 1951; s. John Bagley and Pearl (Olen) L. B.S. in Math., U. Wash., 1973, M.S. in Computer Sci., 1975, Ph.D. in Computer Sci., 1979. Teaching asst., dept. math. U. Wash., 1974-75; research assoc. dept. computer sci., 1975-79; cons. mem. devel. staff, Xerox Corp., Palo Alto, 1979—. Nellie Martin Carman scholar, 1969-73. Mem. ACM, IEEE, Phi Beta Kappa, 1973. Contr. articles to profl. jours. and tech. reports. Home: 2420 Laura Ln Mountain View CA 94043 Office: Xerox Corp 3333 Coyote Hill Rd Palo Alto CA 94304

LEWIS, CARETHA FRANCES, business administrator, educator; b. Orange, N.J., Mar. 18, 1948; d. Charles and Ruby (Grasty) L. Student Rutgers U.; B.S. in Bus. Adminstrn., U. Redlands, 1981. Fin. analyst Warner-Lambert Co., Morris Plains, N.J., 1973-78; human resource analyst Hughes Aircraft Co., Los Angeles, 1978-81; instr. Barbizon Charm Sch., N.Y. and N.J., 1973-78; placement dir. Control Data Inst., Los Angeles, 1978-83, fiscal adminstrv. officer, Anaheim, Calif. 1983—; lectr. in field. Vol. Arthritis Found. Drive, 1981, Big Sisters, Los Angeles, 1982, Orphans Clothes Drive, 1982. Recipient Performance award Hughes Aircraft Co., 1980; Great Opportunity award Terry Cole Ministries, 1981. Mem. Assn. Computer Machinery, NAACP, Calif. Assn. Fiscal Aid Adminstrs., Nat. Assn. Female Execs. (network dir. 1982). Coordinator fashion shows combining drama and art.

LEWIS, DAVID EDWIN, trust banker; b. Los Angeles, Aug. 16, 1945; s. Edwin Norbert and Marie Lucy (Concenia) L.; m. Bonne Ann Ostroff, June 8, 1968. B.S. in Bus. Adminstrn. and Instl. Mgmt., U. Nev., 1968; A.A.S. in Money and Banking, Western Nev. Community Coll., 1976, A.A.S. in Law Enforcement, 1977; cert. Am. Inst. Banking, 1970-75; honor grad. Pacific Coast Banking Sch., U. Wash., 1982. Salesman, Sears, Roebuck & Co., Reno, 1968; asst. cashier Pioneer Citizens Bank of Nev., Reno, 1970-74, asst. cashier, ops. officer Moana Lakeside br., 1974-75, asst. mgr., loan officer Moana-Lakeside br., 1975-76, trust officer, Reno, 1976—. Active YMCA, Reno, 1979-83; mem. Fleischmann Scholarship Com. Reno/Sparks Campus, Western Nev. Community Coll., 1976-78. Served with U.S. Army, 1968-70. Mem. Estate Planning Council, Am. Inst. Banking, (pres. Sierra Nevada chpt. 1977-78, mem. No. Nev. Dist. Council 1978-80, Nev. state chmn.-elect 1981). Republican. Roman Catholic. Club: Lions. Home: PO Box 3023 Reno NV 89505 Office: PO Box 2351 Reno NV 89505

LEWIS, ELMORE WINFRED, JR., physician; b. N.Y.C., Aug. 24, 1929; s. Elmore Winfred and Therese Marie (Kelly) L.; A.B. cum laude, Princeton U., 1951; M.D., N.Y. U., 1956; m. Bernadine Esther Pietraschke, Sept. 13, 1958; children—Lisa Marie, Julie Therese. Intern, U.S. Naval Hosp., Camp Pendleton, Calif., 1956-57; resident Bellevue Hosp., 1959-61; practice medicine specializing in pediatrics, Downey, Calif., 1962—; physician, bd. dirs. Gallatin Med. Group Inc., 1962—, chief exec. officer, 1980-81; mem. staff Downey Community Hosp., chmn. dept. pediatrics, 1968-71; mem. staff Children's Hosp. Los Angeles; clin. prof. U. So. Calif. Med. Sch., 1978—. Served to lt. comdr. M.C., USNR, 1956-59. NIH fellow, 1961-62; diplomate Am. Bd. Pediatrics. Fellow Am. Acad. Pediatrics; mem. Calif. Med. Assn., Los Angeles County Med. Assn., Los Angeles Pediatric Soc., Sigma Xi. Republican. Roman Catholic. Clubs: Princeton (N.Y.C.); Marines Meml. (San Francisco). Office: 10720 S Paramont Blvd Downey CA 90241

LEWIS, FARRELL WALTER, clin. psychologist; b. Winslow, Ariz., Feb. 9, 1925; s. Walter L. and Ann (Hatch) L.; B.S. in Psychology magna cum laude, Brigham Young U., 1966, M.A. in Sch. Psychology, 1968, Ph.D. in Clin. Psychology, 1971; m. Irene Whiting, June 24, 1946; children—Lynette (Mrs. Stephen Peterson), Karen, Peggy (Mrs. John Kennedy), Kristine (Mrs. Hal Holladay), DeeAnn, Stephen. Intern clin. psychology Patton (Calif.) State Hosp., 1969-70; postdoctoral fellow clin. child psychology Devereux Found., Devon, Pa., 1971-72; asst. prof. child devel. Brigham Young U., Provo, Utah, 1972-74, adj. assoc. prof. psychology, 1974—; adminstrv. dir. Timpanogos Community Mental Health Center, Provo, 1974-76, dir. children and youth services, 1974-77, dir. community clin. services, 1977-80, dir. outpatient services, 1980—. Dir. Civil Def., Navajo County, Ariz., 1960-63; mem. Human Resources Taskforce Utah County, Utah, 1975-76; mem. Mountain Lands Assn. Govts. Task Force for Children's Services, 1976-77, mem. profl. adv. council Div. Mental Health, 1976—, mem. quality assurance council, 1978—. Served with AUS, 1943-46. Named valedictorian Coll. Social Sci., Brigham Young U., 1966, outstanding grad. student Grad. Sch., 1971, recipient James E. Talmadge award, 1966. Diplomate Am. Acad. Behavioral Medicine. Mem. Am., Rocky Mountain, Utah (dir. 1978-80, pres.-elect 1982, founder div. psychologists in public service 1979, pres. 1981) psychol. assns., Am. Soc. Clin Hypnosis, Nat. Acad. Neuropsychologists, Utah Assn. Mental Health Program Dirs. (pres. 1976-77), Holbrook (Ariz.) C. of C. (pres. 1960), Ariz. Hwy. 66 Assn. (pres. 1959), Nat. Soc. Sons of Utah Pioneers (v.p. 1982), Phi Kappa Phi. Club: Rotary. Home: 722 E 2620 N Provo UT 84604 Office: 1161 E 300th N Provo UT 84601

LEWIS, FRANCIONE NEWELLENE JOHNSON, educator; b. Berkeley, Calif., July 9, 1937; d. Alfred Newell Johnson and Paulene Loyola (Speese) Jones; B.A., San Francisco State U., 1959, M.A., 1978; postgrad. Union for Experimenting Colls. and Univs., 1980—; children—Ahlerman Van, Frederic Paul. Tchr., McClymonds High Sch., Oakland, Calif., 1962-69; program asst. Far West Lab., San Francisco, 1969-76, asst. dir. responsive edn. program, 1976-78, dir. responsive edn. program and responsive multicultural basic skills project, 1978—; cons. in field. Bd. dirs. Berkeley Youth Alternatives, 1973-76; dir. Consumer Coop., 1977; chairperson Black history Bay Area Jack and Jill of Am., Inc., 1980. Mem. Assn. Supervision and Curriculum Devel., Nat. Assn. Edn. Young Children, Phi Delta Kappa. Office: 1855 Folsom San Francisco CA 94103

LEWIS, GERALD JORGENSEN, judge; b. Perth Amboy, N.J., Sept. 9, 1933; s. Norman Francis and Blanche Myrtle (Jorgensen) L.; A.B. magna cum laude, Tufts U., 1954; J.D., Harvard, 1957; m. Laura S. McDonald, Dec. 15, 1973; children—Michael D.G., Mark J. Admitted to Calif. bar, 1962, D.C. bar, 1957, N.J. bar, 1961; atty. Gen. Atomic, La Jolla, Calif., 1961-63; mem. firm Haskins, Lewis, Nugent & Newnham, San Diego, 1963-77; lectr. bus. law San Diego State Coll., 1961-62, Calif. Continuing Edn. of Bar, 1971, 76; tchr. evidence law Western State U. Coll. Law, 1977—; city atty. City of Del Mar, Calif., 1963-74, City of Coronado, Calif., 1971-77; spl. counsel San Diego County Comprehensive Planning Orgn., 1972, San Diego Air Pollution Control Dist. Hearing Bd., 1974-76; judge Ramona Jud. Dist., 1976; gen. counsel Calif. Soc. Anesthesiologists, 1968-77, San Diego County Med. Soc., 1976-77; judge protem San Diego County Superior Ct., 1975-76; judge El Cajon Municipal Ct., 1977-78, Superior Ct. of Calif., San Diego County, 1978—. Mem. exec. bd. Western State U. Coll. Law. Served to lt. comdr. USNR, 1958-61. Mem. Nat. Inst. Municipal Law Officers, San Diego County City Attys. Assn., Calif., San Diego County bar assns., Am. Arbitration Assn. (panel of arbitrators), Calif. Judges Assn. Rotarian. Clubs: Cuyamaca (San Diego); La Jolla Country. Home: 6505 Caminito Blythefield La Jolla CA 92037 Office: San Diego County Courthouse San Diego CA 92101

LEWIS, GREGORY WILLIAMS, govt. research scientist; b. Seattle, Mar. 3, 1940; s. Delbert Srofe and Eileen Juliann (Williams) L.; B.S., Wash. State U., 1962, M.A., 1965, Ph.D., 1970; postgrad. U. Wash., 1963-65; m. Stephanie Marie Schwab, Sept. 18, 1966; children—Jeffrey Williams, Garrick Peterson. Teaching asst. Wash. State U., 1965-66, research asst., 1966-69; commd. 2d lt. U.S. Army, 1967, advanced through grades to capt., 1968; research psychophysiologist, head vision electrophysiology sect. Army Med. Research Lab., Fort Knox, Ky., 1970-74; resigned, 1975; head Biotech. Lab., Command and Support Systems, 1980—; project dir. Navy Personnel Research and Devel. Center, San Diego, 1974—, research group leader, security systems, 1981—; research cons., 1970—. Bd. dirs., pres. Mesa View Homeowners Assn., 1980-82. Recipient Navy Superior Quality Research awards, 1977, 78. Fellow Internat. Orgn. Psychophysiology; mem. N.Y. Acad. Scis., Soc. Neurosci., Assn. for Research in Vision and Ophthalmology, Soc. for Psychophysiol. Research, Chemometrics Soc., Human Factors Soc., AAAS, Sigma Xi, Alpha Kappa Delta, Psi Chi, Delta Chi. Republican. Contbr. articles to profl. jours. Home: 8583 Hydra Ln San Diego CA 92126 Office: Navy Personnel Research and Devel Center San Diego CA 92152

LEWIS, JAMES JOSEPH, retired naval officer; b. Harrisonville, Mo., Dec. 24, 1940; s. Samuel Theron and Pharis Zelda (Haynes) L.; m. Paula Jean Crose, Aug. 12, 1962; children—Lisa Lynne, Laura Lee, Lyndsey Anne. B.A., William Jewell Coll., 1962; M.B.A., U. San Francisco, 1975; M.S., Naval Postgrad. Sch., 1976. Commd. ensign, U.S. Navy, 1963, advanced through grades to comdr., 1978; inventory mgmt. officer USS White Plains, San Francisco, 1969-71; staff Naval Supply Ctr., Oakland, Calif., 1971-75, supply officer USS Tarawa, San Diego, 1977-79, dir. aviation dept. Naval Supply Ctr., Oakland, 1979-82; ret., 1982; ops. mgr. Pinne, Garvin, Herbers & Hock Inc., 1982—. Founding pres. Homeowners of Inverness Park, San Ramon, Calif., 1981-82. Clubs: Mensa, Sigma Nu.

LEWIS, JAMES LUTHER, banker; b. Bridgeport, Ohio, Sept. 29, 1912; s. William Luther and Gwen (Evans) L.; grad. Mercersburg Acad., 1931; B.A., Yale, 1935; m. Mary Anne Glen, Oct. 26, 1943; children—William Luther II, Gwendolyn. Salesman, asst. sales dist. mgr. Chgo. Pneumatic Tool Co., 1935-43, asst. to pres., 1946-55; v.p. adminstrn. and sales dir. Van Norman Industries, Inc., 1956; pres. Insuline Corp. of Am.; v.p. Norris Thermador Corp., Los Angeles; dir. Firth Sterling, Inc.; chmn. bd. Am. Savs. & Loan Assn., Reno, 1965—, Sierra Fin. Corp., 1968—. Served as lt. USNR, 1943-46. Decorated Purple Heart. Clubs: Yale (N.Y.C.); Prospector's (Reno). Home: 7755 Lakeside Dr Reno NV 89511 Office: 67 W Liberty St Reno NV 89501

LEWIS, JANE ELIZABETH, psychologist; b. Inglewood, Calif., Apr. 2, 1950; d. Robert Turner and Jane Frances (Badham) L.; student Am. Coll., Paris 1970; B.A., Occidental Coll., Los Angeles, 1971; M.S., Calif. State U.-Los Angeles, 1974; Ph.D., U.S. Internat. U., San Diego, 1977. Psychol. asst. Cortical Function Lab., Los Angeles, 1973-74; sch. psychologist Placentia Unified Sch. Dist., 1974-79; clin. psychologist Rancho Los Amigos Hosp., Downey, Calif., 1979-80; psychologist, Culver City, Calif., 1980—; cons. Landmark Ednl. Center, 1979-81, Sr. Center, Long Beach, Calif., 1980. Mem. Am. Psychol. Assn., Calif. State Psychol. Assn., Los Angeles County Psychol. Assn. Office: 9808 Venice Blvd Penthouse Suite Culver City CA 90230

LEWIS, JAY LESLIE, clinical psychologist; b. N.Y.C., Feb. 20, 1951; s. Harold Alan and Miriam Ruth (Fellman) L. B.A., Queens Coll., 1972; M.A., Ariz. State U., 1975, Ph.D., 1978. Lic. psychologist, Ariz., Tex. Fellow in clin. psychology U. Tex. Health Sci. Center, Dallas, 1975-76; staff psychologist Terrell (Tex.) State Hosp., 1976-77, supervising psychologist and dir. tng. 1978-80; psychology assoc. Adobe Mountain Sch., Phoenix, 1978; pvt. practice psychology, Phoenix, 1980—. Mem. Am. Psychol. Assn. Office: 3930 E Camelback Rd Suite 205 Phoenix AZ 85018

LEWIS, JERRY, U.S. congressman; b. Oct. 21, 1934; B.A., UCLA, 1956; married; children—Jerry, Jennifer, Jeff and Dan (twins). Life ins. underwriter; field rep. for former U.S. Rep. Jerry Pettis; mem. Calif. State Assembly, 1968-78, vice chmn. rules com., chmn. subcom. on air quality; mem. 96th-98th Congresses from 37th Calif. dist. Mem. San Bernardino Sch. Bd. Named One of Outstanding Young Men, Calif. Jaycees, 1970. Office: 326 Cannon House Office Bldg Washington DC 20515*

LEWIS, JERRY L., real estate co. exec.; b. Hillsboro, Oreg., Feb. 24, 1941; s. William Robert and Naomi (Knoff) L.; B.A., U. Oreg., 1963; m. Kathleen J. Rowe, Jan. 20, 1962; children—Cindy, Sally, Amy. Sales mgr. Xerox Corp., San Francisco, 1967-70; broker Coldwell, Banker & Co., San Francisco, 1970-74; exec. v.p. Dohemann & Co., San Rafael, Calif., 1974-76; v.p. World Savs. & Loan Assn., Oakland, Calif., 1978-80; pres. Cal-Pacific Devel. Corp., San Rafael, 1976—; v.p., br. mgr. Cushman & Wakefield, Inc., Oakland, Calif., 1983— dir. PLM, Inc., Triadic Oil Corp.; founder Comml. Bank of San Francisco, 1973. Mem. adv. bd. Mount Hermon Assn., 1975—; chmn. bd. dirs. Valley Christian Sch., 1978—; deacon Valley Baptist Ch., 1979—; com. mem. Marin County Young Life, 1979—. Mem. Beta Theta Pi. Republican. Club: Elks. Home: 18 Mt Diablo Circle San Rafael CA 94903 Office: Cal-Pacific Development Corp 1346 4th St San Rafael CA 94901

LEWIS, JOHN CALVIN, retirement community exec.; b. Monterey Park, Calif., May 10, 1932; s. Charles Simmons and Ruth Dickinson (Weed) L.; B.S. in Mktg., U. So. Calif., 1953; postgrad. in econs., U. N.Mex., 1956; m. Ann Taylor Rohlffs, Aug. 27, 1977; children—Jill P., John Calvin, Melissa B., Peter D., Carolyn B., Joy E. Founder, pres., chief exec. officer Western Propane, Inc., Portland, Oreg., 1960-76, now cons. engr.; pres., chief exec. officer, dir., chmn. exec. com. Panorama Corp. of Wash., Lacey, 1977—; gen. mgr. Panorama Partnership; pres. Lease-Line Ltd., Calvin Co. Adminstrv. and fin. bd. United 1st Methodist Chs.; active United for Wash., Young Ams. for Freedom; trustee Oreg. Mus. Sci. and Industry; bd. dirs., pres. Thurston County Taxpayers Assn.; bd. dirs., mem. steering com. Thurston County Econ. Devel. Bd. Served to lt. col., USAF, 1954-60. Mem. Nat. Liquified Petroleum Gas Assn. (Ancient Gasser award, H. Emerson Thomas Safety award 1970), Assn. of Wash. Bus., Res. Officers Assn. (life), Smithsonian Fellows (charter), Air Force Assn. (life), U. So. Calif. Alumni (life), Nat. Rifle Assn. (life), Aircraft Owners and Pilots Assn. (dir.), Olympia C. of C. (chmn. bus. and indsl. devel. com.), Lacey C. of C., Internat. Comanche Soc., Commanche 400 Assn. (chief), Nat. Search and Rescue Assn., Internat. Bush Pilots Assn., Wash. Pilots Assn., Oreg. Pilots Assn. (dir.), Seattle Aircraft Owners and Pilots Assn. (dir.), Alaska Bush Pilots, Izaak Walton League, Pierce Arrow Soc. Republican. Methodist. Clubs: Olympia Country and Golf, Tumwater Valley Athletic, Multnomah Athletic, Ranier, Baja Bush Pilots, Knife and Fork, Evergreen Gun, Pacific Indians, Fort Lewis Officers, McChord AFB Officers, Panorama Supper, Order of Daedalians, Ducks Unltd. Home: 5047 Cooper Point Rd NW Olympia WA 98502 Office: 150 Circle Dr Lacey WA 98503

LEWIS, JOHN CLIFFORD, water quality and waste water engineering educator; b. Portland, Oreg., Nov. 13, 1944; s. Clifford August and Emmeline (Eschler) L.; m. Patricia Jo Ranton, Nov. 25, 1966; children—Cameron Fielding, Corey Eryn. Student Linfield Coll., 1962-63; B.S. in Chemistry, Portland State U., 1971; M.S. in Civil and Sanitary Engring., U. Idaho, 1979. Registered profl. engr., registered sanitarian, Oreg. Environ. chemist air pollution researcher Reynolds Metals Co., Troutdale, Oreg., 1967-71; cons. san. engr., lab. dir. Straam Engrs., Portland, 1971-81; instr., chmn. dept. water quality and waste water engring. Clackamas Community Coll., Oregon City, Oreg., 1981—; mem. Engrs. Coordinating Council (Oreg.); mem. environ. services adv. com. Oreg. Dept. Higher Edn.; mem. cross connection control adv. com. Oreg. Dept. Health. Served to capt. M.C., USAR, 1966—. Recipient Excellence of Design award Cons. Engrs. Council Oreg., 1974; Western Kraft research grantee, 1978. Mem. Water Pollution Control Fedn., Am. Water Works Assn., Nat. Environ. Health Assn., Am. Chem. Soc., ASCE, Tau Beta Pi. Presbyterian. Club: Palisades Park Community. Author papers in field. Address: 2325 Greentree Rd Lake Oswego OR 97034

LEWIS, JOHN WILSON, polit. scientist, educator; b. King County, Wash., Nov. 16, 1930; s. Albert Lloyd and Clara L. Seeman; A.B. with highest honors, UCLA, 1953, M.A., 1958, Ph.D., 1962; m. Jacquelyn Clark, June 19, 1954; children—Cynthia, Stephen, Amy. Asst. prof. govt. Cornell U., 1961-64, assoc. prof., 1964-68; prof. polit. sci. Stanford U., 1968—, William Haas prof. Chinese politics, 1972—, dir. arm control and disarmament program, 1972—1972-83, dir. Ctr. Internat. Security and Arms Control, 1983—, dir. N.E. Asia-U.S. Forum on Internat. Policy; chmn. Joint Com. on Contemporary China, Social Sci. Research Council, Am. Council Learned Socs., 1976-79; bd. dirs., former vice chmn. Nat. Com. on U.S.-China Relations; cons. U.S. Senate Select Com. on Intelligence, 1977-81; chmn. Com. on Advanced Study in China of Com. on Scholarly Communication with People's Republic of China, 1979-82. Mem. Phi Beta Kappa. Author: Modernization by Design, 1969; editor: Peasant Rebellion and Communist Revolution in Asia, 1974; contbg. author: China's Quest for Independence, 1980. Home: 541 San Juan St Stanford CA 94305 Office: 320 Galvez St Stanford U Stanford CA 94305

LEWIS, LAWRENCE GUY, software consultant; b. Logan, Utah, July 28, 1941; s. Russell Guy and Helen (Allred) L.; B.A., U. Utah, 1965; Ph.D., Ind. U., 1969; m. Barbara Anderson, Dec. 19, 1964; children—Michael Guy, Andrea, Christian James, Samuel Russell. Postdoctoral fellow CUNY, 1969-70; asst. prof. math. U. Utah, Salt Lake City, 1970-73; mgr. licensee ops. IRECO Chemicals, Salt Lake City, 1974-77, dir. mgmt. info. systems, 1977-82, dir. corp. planning and budgeting, 1980-82; owner LGL Cons. Services, 1982—; pres. Software First, Inc., 1983—. Assoc. instr. U. Utah, 1981—. Mem. Data Processing Mgmt. Assn. (pres.), Nat. Prime Users Group (pres.), Planning Execs. Inst., AAAS. Contbr. papers in abstract math. analysis to profl. jours. Home: 3200 Terrace View Circle Salt Lake City UT 84109 Office: Software First Inc University Club Bldg Suite 1200 Salt Lake City UT 84111

LEWIS, LEE, fire chief; b. Bozeman, Mont., Mar. 25, 1938; s. Gene and Elva (Leavitt) L.; m. Diana Shepherd, Mar. 4, 1983; children—Shelly, Lita, Brian, Frank. Student Mont. State U., 1958-59. With Bozeman (Mont.) Fire Dept., 1962—, dep. chief, 1980-82, fire chief, 1982—. Bd. dirs. United Way; chmn. local unit ARC, 1975-78. Served with AUS, 1955-58. Mem. Western Fire Chiefs Assn. (Mont. state v.p.), Mont. Fire Chiefs Assn. (past pres.), Mont. Fire Prevention Assn. (past pres.), Mont. Arson Assn. (dir.), Am. Legion. Clubs: Masons, Elks. Home: 16 E Aspen St Bozeman MT 59715 Office: PO Box 640 Bozeman MT 59715

LEWIS, LEONARD J., lawyer; b. Rexburg, Idaho, Jan. 10, 1923; s. Jack and Hannah (Beesley) L.; B.S., U. Utah, 1947; J.D., Stanford U., 1950; m. Lois Ann Cannon, Sept. 3, 1947; children—Leslie Ann, John, James C., Janet. Admitted to Utah bar, 1950; mem. firm Van Cott, Bagley, Cornwall & McCarthy, Salt Lake City, 1950—, pres., 1975—, now chmn.; dir. Fed. Resources Corp., Temple St. Investment Co., Am. Ins. and Investment Corp., Centennial Devel. Co., also venture capital activities. Mem. bd. visitors Stanford U. Law Sch., 1979-80. Served with U.S. Army, 1941-43. Mem. Am. Bar Assn., Am. Trial Lawyers Assn., Salt Lake County Bar Assn., Internat. Bar Assn., Utah Bar. Assn. (past chmn. ct. adminstrv. com.). Clubs: Salt Lake Country, Alta, University, Petroleum, Hamilton Racquet. Home: 910 Donner Way Apt 701 Salt Lake City UT 84108 Office: 50 S Main St Suite 1600 Salt Lake City UT 84144

LEWIS, LINDA JANE, educator; b. Derry, N.H., Apr. 5, 1951; d. Carl S. and Evelyn M. (Demaree) Lewis; B.A. in Math., UCLA, 1977, M.Ed., 1980. Ednl. therapist Acad. Therapy and Counseling, Sherman Oaks, Calif., 1978-79; dir. ABC Ednl. Devel., Newbury Park, Calif., 1980—; staff research assoc. Neuropsychiat. Inst., UCLA, 1977-81. Mem. Assn. Supervision and Curriculum Devel., Calif. Assn. Ednl. Therapists, Pi Lambda Theta. Home: 1581 Glenbrock Ln Newbury Park CA 91320

LEWIS, LOUISE MILLER, educator, art gallery dir.; b. St. Louis, Dec. 4, 1940; d. Hugh M. and Jeanne Eugenie (Vical) Miller; m. Guy R. Lewis, Nov. 26, 1966; 1 son, Kevin. B.A., U. Calif.-Berkeley, 1963; cert. Sorbonne U., Paris, 1964; M.A., U. N.Mex., 1966, M.A., 1972. Asst. dir. U. N.Mex. Art Mus., 1966-72; asst. dir. Art Gallery, Calif. State U.-Northridge, 1972-80, dir., 1980—, asst. prof. art history, 1972-78, assoc. prof., 1978—; lectr. in field. Mem. Phi Beta Kappa. Contbr. articles on art to profl. jours. Office: Art History Dept Calif State U Northridge CA 91330

LEWIS, MADGE KATHARINE, psychologist, psychotherapist, educator; b. Rhosllanerchrugog, Wales; d. Hugh Iorwerth and Claudia Ellen (Williams) Lewis. B.A., U. So. Calif., 1938, M.A., 1940; Ph.D., U. Chgo., 1959. Lic. Psychologist, Calif., 1960. Counselor, Long Beach (Calif.) Public Sch. System, 1948-54; research assoc., psychotherapist Counseling Center, U. Chgo., 1956-60; counselor Counseling Center and Health Center, San Francisco State U., 1960-80, prof. counseling and psychology, 1960—; pvt. practice psychotherapy. Served with WAVES, 1945-46. Mem. Nat. Register of Health Service Providers in Psychology, Am. Psychol. Assn., Calif. Psychol. Assn., San Francisco Psychol. Assn. (sec., 1962-64, 70-71), Am. Acad. Psychotherapy, No. Calif. Group Psychotherapy Soc. (council mem. 1964-67; sec. 1968-69), Am. Musical Soc., Welsh Am. Soc. No. Calif., English Speaking Union. Co-author, articles in profl. books. Home: 355 Serrano Dr 12 K San Francisco CA 94132 Office: San Francisco State U Counseling Dept 1600 Holloway San Francisco CA 94132

LEWIS, MARILYN ANNETTE, child and family therapist; b. Nauvoo, Ill., May 14, 1952; d. Morgan William and Genevieve Marie (Pilkington) I. B.S., Marycrest Coll., 1974; M.S.Ed. in Guidance and Counseling, Western Ill. U., 1978. Residential counselor St. Mary's Acad., Nauvoo, 1977-79; mental health counselor Hancock County Mental Health Ctr., Carthage, Ill., 1979-80, Community Mental Health Ctr. of Fulton-McDonough Counties, Canton, Ill., 1980-81; staff counselor Ill. State U. Student Counseling Ctr., Normal, Ill., 1982; child and family therapist No. Wyo. Mental Health Ctr., Sheridan, 1982—. Mem. Am. Personnel and Guidance Assn., Am. Coll. Personnel Assn. Roman Catholic. Office: 1221 W 5th St Sheridan WY 82801

LEWIS, NORMAN, author, educator; b. N.Y.C., Dec. 30, 1912; s. Herman and Deborah (Nevins) L.; B.A., CCNY, 1939; M.A., Columbia U., 1941; m. Mary Goldstein, July 28, 1934; children—Margery, Debra. Instr., lectr. CUNY, 1943-52; assoc. prof. English, NYU, 1955-64; instr. Compton (Calif.) Coll., summers 1962-64. UCLA extension, 1962-69; prof. English, Rio Hondo Coll., Whittier, Calif., 1964—, chmn. communications dept., 1964-75, pres. acad. senate, 1966-68, chmn. curriculum com., 1967-68. Author: (with Wilfred Funk) Thirty Days to a More Powerful Vocabulary, 1942, rev. edit., 1970; Power with Words, 1943; How to Read Better and Faster, 1944, rev. edit., 1978; The Lewis English Refresher and Vocabulary Builder, 1945; Better English, 1948; Word Power Made Easy, 1949, rev. edit., 1978; The Rapid Vocabulary Builder, 1951, rev. edit., 1980; How To Get More Out of Your Reading, 1951; Twenty Days to Better Spelling, 1953; The New Roget's Thesaurus in Dictionary Form, 1961, rev. edit., 1978; Dictionary of Correct Spelling, 1962; Correct Spelling Made Easy, 1963; Dictionary of Modern Pronunciation, 1963; New Guide to Word Power, 1963; The New Power With Words, 1964; Thirty Days to Better English, 1964; The Modern Thesaurus of Synonyms, 1965; RSVP-Reading, Spelling, Vocabulary, Pronunciation, elementary texts I-III, 1966, coll. edit., 1977; See, Say and Write, I and II, 1973; Instant Spelling Power, 1976; RSVP for College English Power, Books II and III, 1978; Instant Word Power, 1981, rev. edit., 1982; RSVP with Etymology, Book I, 1980, Book II, 1981, Book III, 1982, RSVP Books I-III rev. 2d edits., 1982-83; also numerous articles nat. mags.

LEWIS, NORMAN N. RICHARD, public relations/advertising executive; b. N.Y.C., Aug. 13, 1925; s. David and Jeanne (Miller) L.; m. Margaret Alderson Bowman, Dec. 3, 1962; children—Ian, Richard; m. 2d, Sandra Kay Weatherly, Dec. 17, 1970. B.S., Ohio U., 1950. Reporter Ala. Post Advocate, 1953-54; news bur. chief Auto Club So. Calif., 1954-57; account exec. Fallon & Co., Los Angeles, 1957-60; pres. Lewis/Coffin/Assocs., Los Angeles, 1960—. Served to 1st lt. U.S. Army, 1950-53. Decorated Bronze Star. Mem. Public Relations Soc. Am. (accredited), Soc. Mktg. Profl. Services (dir. So. Calif. chpt.), Nat. Assn Real Estate Editors. Clubs: Jonathan, Mountain Gate Country, Los Angeles Press. Office: 801 N La Brea Ave Los Angeles CA 90038

LEWIS, RALPH MILTON, devel. co. exec., accountant, lawyer; b. Johnstown, Pa., Nov. 9, 1919; s. Morris and Sarah (Galfond) L.; A.A., Los Angeles City Coll., 1939; B.S., UCLA, 1941; postgrad. U. So. Calif., 1944-49; m. Goldy Sarah Kimmel, June 12, 1941; children—Richard Alan, Robert Edward, Roger Gordon, Randall Wayne. Prin., Ralph M. Lewis, C.P.A., Los Angeles, 1945-55; admitted to Calif. bar, 1952; individual practice law, Los Angeles, 1953-55; chmn. bd. Lewis Homes, Upland, Calif., Lewis Constrn. Co., Inc., Upland, Lewis Bldg. Co., Inc., Las Vegas, Nev., Republic Sales Co., Inc.; dir., v.p. Kimmel Enterprises, Inc.; mng. partner Lewis Homes of Calif., Lewis Homes of Nev., Western Properties, Upland, Foothills Investment Co., Las Vegas, Republic Mgmt. Co., Upland; dir. Gen. Telephone of Calif.; adv. bd. Security Pacific Nat. Bank Inland Div.; mem. Calif. Gov.'s Task Force on Home Bldg. and Constrn. Industry, 1967; instr., lectr. in field. Pres. bd. trustees Citrus Community Coll., Azusa, Calif., 1967-73; mem. Calif. Commn. Housing Community Devel., 1965-67; mem. dean's council UCLA Grad. Sch. Architecture and Urban Planning. Recipient Builder of Year award Bldg. Industry Assn. Calif., 1970; Gold Nugget design awards Pacific Coast Builders Conf., 1969-70; humanitarian award NCCJ, 1979. Licensed real estate broker, gen. bldg. contractor. Mem. Am. Bar Assn., Calif. Soc. C.P.A.'s, Nat. Assn. Home Builders (dir.), Calif. Builders Council (dir.), Bldg. Industry Assn. Calif. (dir., past pres.). Contbr. articles to profl. jours. Home: 2120 Vallejo Way Upland CA 91786 Office: PO Box 670 Upland CA 91786

LEWIS, RICHARD BOND, advertising executive; b. Atkinson, Nebr., Apr. 14, 1925; s. Monte Claire and Lulu Pearl (Bond) L.; m. Carol Ann Bigglestone, Nov. 23, 1948; children—Eric, Shannon, Carrie. Student U. Ariz., 1946-49; B.A., Art Center Coll. Design, 1953. Art dir., account exec. Hal Stebbins Inc. advt. agy., Los Angeles, 1953-64; account exec. Buxton Advt., Pasadena, Calif., 1964-65; account mgr. McCann-Erickson advt. agy., Los Angeles, 1965-71; pres. Richard Bond Lewis & Assocs., West Covina, Calif., 1971—. Bd. dirs. Vis. Nurses Assn., W. Covina; commr. West Covina Personnel Dept.; del. Pacific S.W. conf. United Methodist Ch., 1979-82. Served to staff sgt. U.S. Army, 1945-46. Recipient Camp Fire Girls special service award, 1979, West Covina resolution award for service, 1982. Mem. West Covina C. of C. (com. mem. of year 1971, 72, 76, pres. 1981-82), Art Dirs. Club Los Angeles, West Covina Hist. Soc. (dir.), Lambda Chi Alpha. Republican. Club: Kiwanis. Home and office: 1112 W Cameron Ave Covina CA 91790

LEWIS, ROBERT, naval officer, educator; b. Duncan, Okla., Aug. 8, 1929; s. Birt L. and Katherine Mae L.; B.A., Naval Postgrad. Sch., 1966; M.A., George Washington U., 1975, Ed.S., 1977; m. Margaret Louise Kunick, Sept. 4, 1955; children—Deborah Lee, Robert John, Ronald Birt. Commd. ensign U.S. Navy, 1952, advanced through grades to capt., 1973; fighter pilot, 1952-73; dir. aviation safety programs Naval Safety Center, Norfolk, Va., 1973-78, dir. Aviation Safety Sch., 1978-81; dir. aviation safety programs Naval Postgrad. Sch., Monterey, Calif. Decorated Bronze star, Air medals (10). Mem. Am. Soc. Safety Engrs., Internat. Soc. Air Safety Investigators. Home: Quarters N Naval Postgrad Sch Monterey CA 93940 Office: Dir Aviation Safety Programs Naval Postgrad Sch Monterey CA 93940

LEWIS, ROY V., behavioral researcher; b. Ross, Calif., Apr. 18, 1943; s. Stanley V. and Velma Lois L.; B.A., San Francisco State U., 1968; M.P.A., U. So. Calif., 1977; m. Melissa Linda Thomas, June 22, 1968; children—Carrie Ann, Kingsley Corey. Correctional officer Calif. State Dept. Corrections, San Quentin, 1968; research trainee Calif. State Dept. Social Welfare, 1968-69, jr. social research analyst, 1969-70, asst. social research analyst, 1970-73; assoc. social research analyst Calif. Youth Authority, 1973-76, research analyst II, Sacramento, 1976-83; research analyst II Calif. Dept. Justice, 1983—. Served with U.S. Navy, 1964-66. Mem. Am. Soc. Criminology, Nat. Council on Crime and Delinquency, Calif. Assn. Criminal Justice Researchers, Phi Kappa Phi. Republican. Contbr. articles to profl. jours. Author: (with Ted Palmer) An Evaluation of Juvenile Diversion, 1980. Office: 4241 Williamsbourg Dr Sacramento CA 95823

LEWIS, SAMELLA SANDERS, art historian, artist, curator; b. New Orleans, Feb. 27, 1924; d. Samuel and Rachel (Taylor) Sanders; m. Paul Gad Lewis, Dec. 22, 1948; children—Alan Stephen, Claude Anthony. B.S., Hampton Inst., 1945; M.A., Ohio State U., 1948, Ph.D., 1951; postgrad. U. So. Calif., 1964, 65, 68. Instr. art Hampton (Va.) Inst., 1945-47; asst. prof. art Morgan State U., Balt., 1949-52; prof. art Fla. A&M U., Tallahassee, 1953-58, SUNY-Plattsburgh, 1958-68; coordinator edn. Los Angeles County Mus. Art, 1969-70; prof. art history Scripps Coll., Claremont Colls., Calif., 1978—; chairperson Clark Humanities Mus.; curator Mus. of African Am. Art, Santa Monica, Calif.; represented in permanent collections: Va. Mus. of Art, Balt. Mus. Art, High Mus.-Atlanta, Palm Springs Mus. Ford Found. fellow, summers 1965, 81-82. Mem. Nat. Conf. of Artists, So. Calif. Art History Assn., Soc. for Asian Studies. Author: Black Artist on Art, I and II, 1969-75; Art: African American, 1978; The Art of Elizabeth Catlett, 1983. Home: 259 W Radcliffe Dr Claremont CA 91711 Office: Scripps Coll Claremont CA 91711

LEWIS, SANDRA JOYCE, association executive; b. Seattle, Jan. 5, 1943; d. Arthur O. and Rose Ann (Caplan) Epstein; m. David Charles Lewis, Sept. 12, 1964; 1 son, Kent Jason. B.S. in Preventive Medicine, U. Wash., Seattle, 1965, M.S.W., 1970. Cert. secondary tchr., Wash. Caseworker, Wash. State Dept. Social and Health Services, 1965-68; sr. social worker Ruth Sch. for Girls, 1970-71; social services coordinator Seattle-King County Dept. Pub. Health, 1971-78; exec. dir. Multiple Sclerosis Assn. King County, Seattle, 1978—; student placement instr. U. Wash. Grad. Sch. Social Work. Mem. Wash. Gov.'s Com. Employment of Handicapped; vol. Wash. State Spl. Olympics. Recipient Vol. Coordinator award United Way of King County, 1980, 81, 82. Mem. Nat. Assn. Social Workers, Am. Pub. Health Assn., Nat. Abortion Rights League, U. Wash. Alumni Assn. (past pres. Grad. Sch. Social Work alumni). Club: Soroptimist (v.p. 1983-84). Office: 6869 Woodlawn Ave NE Seattle WA 98115

LEWIS, SHIRLEY JEANE, educator; b. Phoenix, Aug. 23, 1937; d. Herman and Leavy (Hutchinson) Smith; A.A., Phoenix Community Coll., 1957; B.A., Ariz. State U., 1960; M.S., San Diego State U., 1975, M.A., 1983; M.A., Azusa Pacific U., 1982; Ph.D., U. So. Calif., 1983; m. Edgar Anthony Lewis, June 25, 1966 (div. May 1980); children—Edgar Anthony, Roshaun, Lucy Ann. Recreation leader Phoenix Parks and Recreation Dept., 1957-62; columnist Ariz. Tribune, Phoenix, 1958-59; tchr. phys. edn. San Diego Unified Schs., 1962—; adult educator San Diego Community Colls., 1973—, instr. psychology, 1977—; community counselor S.E. Counseling and Cons. Services, and Narcotics Prevention and Edn. Systems, Inc., San Diego, 1973-77; counselor educator, counselor edn. dept. San Diego State U., 1974-77; marriage, family, child counselor Counseling and Cons. Center, San Diego, 1977—; inservice educator San Diego Unified and San Diego County Sch. Dists., 1973-77; lectr. in field. Girl Scout phys. fitness cons., Phoenix, 1960-62; vol. community tutor for high sch. students, San Diego, 1963; sponsor Tennis Club for Youth, San Diego, 1964-65; troop leader Girl Scouts U.S.A., Lemon Grove, Calif., 1972-74; vol. counselor USN Alcohol Rehab. Center, San Diego, 1978. Named Woman of Year, Phoenix, 1957, One of Outstanding Women of San Diego, 1980; recipient Phys. Fitness Sch. award and Demonstration Sch. award Pres.'s Council on Phys. Fitness, Taft Jr. High Sch., 1975; Delta Sigma Theta scholar, 1957-60; Alan Korrick scholar, 1956; certified tchr., Calif. Mem. NEA, Calif. Tchrs. Assn., San Diego Tchrs. Assn., Assn. Marriage and Family Counselors, Am. Personnel and Guidance Assn., Calif. Assn. Health, Phys. Edn. and Recreation, Am. Alliance of Health, Phys. Edn. and Recreation, Delta Sigma Theta. Democrat. Baptist. Contbr. articles to profl. jours. Home: 1226 Armacost Rd San Diego CA 92114 Office: 2630 B St San Diego CA 92102

LEWIS, WILLIAM LEROY, educator; b. Krebs, Okla., Feb. 1, 1908; s. Thomas J. and Mary (Tamar) L.; A.B. magna cum laude, Oklahoma City U., 1930; M.A., U. Mich., 1936; postgrad. Northwestern U., summers 1937, 39; Litt.D. (hon.), Midwestern U., 1951; m. C. Marguerite Garber, June 16, 1937; children—Sylvia Thomas, David Catherine Linda. Instr., Wichita (Kans.) State U., 1930-35, Duke U., Durham, N.C., 1935-43; sec. N.C. Bankers Assn., Raleigh, 1943-44; nat. ednl. dir. Am. Inst. Banking, N.Y.C., 1944-64; asso. prof. Kingsborough Community Coll., N.Y.C., 1964-66, asst. to pres. Acad. Council, 1965-66; mem. staff Found. for Edn. in Econs., 1947-53, sec., 1953-62; spl. lectr. Stonier Grad. Sch. Banking, Rutgers U., 1947-57; dir. spl. courses Tex. Christian U., Ft. Worth, 1966-73; disting. vis. prof. San Diego State U., 1973-74, prof., 1974—; guest speaker and U.S. del. to Internat. Banking Summer Sch., St. Andrews U., Scotland, 1958. Mem. Am. Acad. Polit. Sci., Adult Edn. Assn., Nat. Assn. Tchrs. Speech, Am. Econ. Assn., Tau Kappa Alpha, Pi Kappa Delta, Pi Gamma Mu, Lambda Chi Alpha. Republican. Methodist. Clubs: Univ. (N.Y.); Faculty (San Diego). Contbr. numerous articles on banking to jours.; editor Tak-heel Banker, 1943-44. Home: 6254 Cabaret St San Diego CA 92120 Office: Coll Bus San Diego State U San Diego CA 92182

LEWIS, WILLIAM THOMAS, real estate analyst; b. Cleve., Feb. 14, 1947; s. Robert Martin and Margaret Josephine Mulh) L.; B.A., Columbia U., 1969; B.S. in Arch., Ohio State U., 1972. Designer, George S. Rider Assos., Cleve., 1972-73, Louis Marino & Assos., 1973-74, Greenwin, Inc., Toronto, Ont., 1974-78; archtl. project coordinator Bank of Am., San Francisco, 1979, real estate analyst, 1979—; design cons., owner William T. Lewis Assos., San Francisco, 1979—. Real estate agt., Calif. Home: 750 Opera Plaza 601 Van Ness Ave San Fracisco CA 94102 Office: 560 Davis St San Francisco CA 94111

LEWISON, MARC ALAN, accountant; b. Akron, Iowa, Apr. 10, 1953; s. Curtis L., Jr. and May Lou (McKee) L.; m. Robin A. K. Kullman; children—Taylor E., Barclay J. B.S. in Bus. Mgmt., U. S.D., 1975. C.P.A., Iowa. Auditor Arthur Andersen & Co., Denver, 1976-77; acct., mgr. Petro-Lewis Corp., Denver, from 1977, now adminstrv. mgr. western region, Bakersfield, Calif. Bd. dirs. Pendulum Ministries, Denver. Mem. Am. Inst. C.P.A.s, Petroleum Accts. Soc. (council). Republican. Club: Laurel Glen Tennis (Bakersfield). Home: 7109 Margaret Ct Bakersfield CA 93309 Office: Suite 300 5500 Ming Ave Bakersfield CA 93309

LEWITZKY, BELLA, choreographer; b. Los Angeles, Jan. 13, 1916; d. Joseph and Nina (Osson) L.; student San Bernardino Valley (Calif.) Jr. Coll., 1933-34; m. Newell Taylor Reynolds, June 22, 1940; 1 dau., Nora Elizabeth. Co-founder, co-dir. Dance Theatre, Los Angeles, 1946-50; founder, dir. Dance Assos., Los Angeles, 1951-55; founder, 1966, since artistic dir. Bella Lewitzky Dance Co., Los Angeles; chmn. contemporary dance dept. U. So. Calif., Idyllwild, 1956-72, adv. panel, 1972—; founder Sch. Dance, Calif. Inst. Arts, 1969, dean, 1969-72; vice chmn. dance adv. panel Nat. Endowment Arts, 1974-77, mem. artists-in-schs. adv. panel, 1974-75; mem. Nat. Adv. Bd. Young Audiences, 1974—, Joint Commn. Dance and Theater Accrediation, 1979—; com. mem. Am. chpt. Internat. Dance Council of UNESCO, 1974—; bd. dirs. Am. Arts Alliance, 1977—, Arts, Edn. and Americans, 1978—; trustee Calif. Assn. Dance Cos., 1976-81; trustee Center for Music, Drama and Art, Lake Placid, N.Y., 1982—, Nat. Found. Advancement in the Arts, Miami, Fla., 1982—, mem. Calif. Arts Council, 1982—. choregrapher, 1948—. Recipient ann. award Dance mag., 1978, Dir.'s award Calif. Dance Educators Assn., 1978; grantee Mellon Found., 1975, 81, Guggenheim Found., 1977-78, Nat. Endowment Arts, 1969—. Author in field.

LEYDA, JEAN CRAVENS (MRS. VIRGIL WILLIAM LEYDA), author, editor, club woman; b. Granby, Mo., Jan. 15, 1903; d. William A. and Lois (Harmon) Cravens; A.A., Stephens Coll., 1920; B.A., Mt. Holyoke Coll., 1923; M.A. in English Lit., U. Wis., 1930; m. Virgil William Leyda, Aug. 10, 1945; 1 foster son, Leonard Breckler. Tchr. English, Freeport (Ill.) High Sch., 1923-26, head English dept., 1926-27; head English dept. Mishawaka (Ind.) High Sch., 1929-45, dir. English, Mishawaka Jr. and Sr. High Schs., 1938-45; co-author lit. anthologies Scott, Foresman Co., Chgo., 1940-50, editorial staff, after 1945; now ret. Pres., Chandler (Ariz.) Woman's Club, 1954-55, chmn. community service com., 1961-63, hon. life mem.; edn. chmn. Ariz. Fedn. Women's Clubs, 1955-57. Mem. founding adv. bd. Chandler Pub. Library. Recipient alumnae achievement award Stephens Coll., 1956. Former mem., past pres. Ind. Council Tchrs. English. Mem. Ind. Ret. Tchrs. Assn., Nat. Ret. Tchrs. Assn., DAR, Colonial Dames 17th Century, PEO, Phi Theta Kappa. Democrat. Presbyn. (trustee 1951-53, life elder). Mem. Order Eastern Star, Daus. of Nile. Club: Desert (past pres.). Author: (with others) Enjoying Life through Literature, 1951; Exploring Life through Literature, 1951. Address: 400 N Hartford St Chandler AZ 85224

LEYDET, FRANÇOIS GUILLAUME, author; b. at Neuilly-sur-Seine, France, Aug. 26, 1927; s. Bruno and Dorothy (Lindsey) L.; A.B., Harvard, 1947, postgrad. Bus. Sch., 1952; postgrad. Johns Hopkins Sch. Advanced Internat. Studies, 1952-53; Bachelier-es-lettres-philosophie, U. Paris (France), 1945; m. Patience Abbe, June 17, 1955 (div.); step children—Catherine Abbe Geissler, Lisa Amanda O'Mahony; m. 2d, Roslyn Carney, June 14, 1970; step-children—Walter E. Robb IV, Rachel R. Avery, Holly H. Prunty, Mary-Peck Harris. Came to U.S., 1940, naturalized, 1956. Bd. dirs. Acad. World Studies; bd. advisers Research Ranch, Elgin, Ariz., Am. Wilderness Alliance; past dir. Marin County Planned Parenthood Assn., Planned Parenthood Center Tucson. Served to 1st lt. French Army, 1947-48. Mem. Nat. Parks Assn., Wilderness Soc., Sierra Club, Nat. Audubon Soc., World Wildlife Fund, Am. Mus. Natural History, Union Concerned Scientists, Environ. Def. Fund, Friends of the Earth, Ariz.-Sonora Desert Mus., Ariz. Hist. Soc., Common Cause, People for Am. Way, Western Writers Am., Western River Guides Assn. Clubs: Harvard (San Francisco). Author: The Last Redwoods, 1963; Time and the River Flowing: Grand Canyon, 1964; The Coyote: Defiant Songdog of the West, 1977. Editor: Tomorrow's Wilderness, 1963; regular contbr. to Nat. Geog. mag. Address: 183 Oak Ave San Anselmo CA 94960

LEZAK, MURIEL DEUTSCH, neuropsychologist; b. Chgo., Aug. 26, 1927; d. Lester L. and Sylvia (Friedman) Deutsch; m. Sidney I. Lezak, June 26, 1949; children—Anne D., David J., Miriam L. Ph.B., U. Chgo., 1947, A.M., 1949; Ph.D., U. Portland, 1960. Diplomate Am. Bd. Profl. Psychology. Staff psychologist Community Child Guidance Clinic, Portland, Oreg., 1949-53; chief psychologist Clackamas County Child Guidance Clinic, Oregon City, Oreg., 1959-61; counselor, asst. profl. ednl. psychology Portland (Oreg.) State Coll., 1961-63; clin. neuropsychologist VA Med. Center, Portland, 1966—; assoc. prof. neurology and psychiatry Oreg. Health Scis. U., Portland, 1968—; adj. prof. psychology U. Oreg., Eugene, 1980, 82; adj. scientist Neurol. Scis. Inst., Good Samaritan Hosp. and Med. Center, Portland, 1980—. Mem. nat. adv. bd. Nat. Head Injury Found.; mem. adv. council Family Survival Project for Brain Damaged Adults, San Francisco. Pfizer travelling fellow Clin. Research Inst., Montreal, 1981. Mem. Am. Psychol. Assn., Internat. Neurol. Soc. (dir. 1978-81), Am. Bd. Clin. Neuropsychology (dir., treas.), Am. Assn. State Psychology Bds. (mem. exam. com.), Oreg. Psychol. Assn. (chmn. ethics com. 1968-69), Oreg. Neuropsychiat. Soc., Portland Psychol. Assn. (pres. 1972-73). Club: Mazamas Mountaineering (mem. research com. 1972-78); Multnomah Athletic (Portland, Oreg.). Author: Neuropsychological Assessment, 1976, 2d edit., 1983. Home: 1811 SW Boundary St Portland OR 97201 Office: Psychology Service VA Med Center 3710 SW USVAH Rd Portland OR 97207

LHOTKA, BONNY PIERCE, artist; b. Hinsdale, Ill., July 14, 1942; d. Earl Frances and Adeline A. (Zaransky) Pierce; m. Joseph D. Lhotka, June 15, 1963; children—Douglas, Gregory. B.F.A., Bradley U., Peoria, Ill., 1964. Tchr. Workshops Internat. Soc. Artists, Foothills Art Center, Golden, Colo., Colo. Watercolor Soc., Colo. Artists Workshops; one-woman shows: Wyo. State Art Gallery, Cheyenne, 1980, Carson-Sapiro, 1981, Art Spirit Gallery, Boulder, Colo., 1981, Gallery A, Taos, N.Mex., group shows: Nat. Acad. Design, 1977, 79, 81, Am. Watercolor Soc., Allied Artists Am., others. Mem. Nat. Watercolor Soc. (awards 1974, 76, 78) Audubon Artists (awards 1976, 81), Nat. Soc. Painters in Casein and Acrylic, Rocky Mountain Water Media Soc. Home: 5011 Ellsworth Pl Boulder CO 80303

LHYLE, KATHLEEN GILLMER, hospital executive, nurse; b. Long Beach, Calif., Nov. 14, 1945; d. Arthur Kenneth and Betty Jane (Akers) Gillmer; m. Rodney Kent Lhyle, Jan. 10, 1968 (div.); children—Marcke Townsend, J. Paige. B.S.N., U. Wash., 1967; M.A., No. Ariz. U., 1982; postgrad. Ariz. State U., 1982—. R.N., Calif., Mich., Ariz. Nursing supr., clin. instr. ob-gyn Sinai Hosp., Detroit, 1969-71; clinic supr., instr., cons. M.M. Greenberg, M.D. and M.A. Treger, M.D., LaMesa-San Diego, 1971-72; nursing supr. Paradise Valley Unified Sch. Dist., Phoenix, 1974-77; nurse Surgicenter, Inc., Phoenix, 1978-80; corp. dir. staff tng. and devel. Cambelback Hosps., Inc. and Mental Health Ctr., Phoenix, 1980—; mem. adj. faculty No. Ariz. U., 1982—; mem. adv. council Ariz. State U. Served with USNR, 1966-67; Viet Nam. Mem. Am. Psychol. Assn., Ariz. Nurses Assn., Am. Soc. Tng. and Devel., Am. Edn. and Research Assn., Nat. Soc. Performance and Instrn., Central Ariz. Consortium for Tng. and Instrn., Ariz. Nursing Educators, Pi Beta Phi.

LI, SHING TED, electronics engr.; b. Fukien, China, Aug. 15, 1938; came to U.S., 1964, naturalized, 1972; s. Li Ming Fa and Chang Feng Yu; diploma in Elec. Engring., Taipei Inst. Tech., China, 1958; M.S. in Elec. Engring., U. Tenn., 1965; Ph.D., Ga. Inst. Tech., 1974; m. Florence Lengpo Lee, Dec. 30, 1966. Asst. engr. Taiwan Power Co., Taipei, 1958-59, 61-64; design engr. Eastern Engring. Co., Atlanta, 1965-69; electronics engr. Naval Ocean Systems Center, San Diego, 1974—. Served to 2d lt. Nationalist Chinese Army, 1959-61. Recipient Sustained Superior Performance award Naval Ocean Systems Center, 1977-78. Mem. IEEE, Sigma Xi, Pi Mu Epsilon. Registered profl. engr., Ga., Taiwan. Contbr. articles to profl. jours. Office: Naval Ocean Systems Center Code 8112 271 Catalina Blvd San Diego CA 92152

LIANG, LOUIS H., elec. engr.; b. Shanghai, China, May 3, 1944; came to U.S., 1964, naturalized, 1973; s. P.C. and Maisie (Lee) L.; B.A. in Engring. Scis., U. Calif., San Diego, 1969, M.S. in Engring., 1971. Research engr. Heliodyne Corp., Van Nuys, Calif., 1969; sr. mfg. engr. Nat. Semicondr., Santa Clara, Calif., 1972-77; sr. engr. Monolithic Memories Inc., Sunnyvale, Calif., 1977; mgr. PolySwitch mfg. Raychem Corp., Menlo Park, Calif., 1977—; pres. TM Enterprises, Campbell, Calif., 1974—; semicondr. mfg. cons. Mem. IEEE, Sigma Zeta. Contbr. articles on lasers and laser Raman spectroscopies to profl. jours. Office: 300 Constitution Dr Menlo Park CA 94025

LIATSOS, HELENE KAREN, travel systems company manager; b. Lamia, Greece, Feb. 1, 1951; came to U.S., 1951; d. John and Maria (Priovolos) L. B.A., Fairleigh Dickinson U., 1973; postgrad. Fordham U., 1976. With TWA, Inc., N.Y.C., 1974-80; ops. mgr. Travellers Internat. Tour Operators, Los Angeles, 1981; western rep. Corp. Meetings and Incentives mag., Los Angeles, 1981-82; sales mgr. Sheraton-Universal Hotel, Los Angeles, 1982; dist. sales mgr. Cardillo Travel Systems, Inc., Los Angeles, 1983—. Mem. Nat. Assn. Female Execs., Hellenic-Am. C. of C. (com. tour and travel). Republican. Greek Orthodox. Office: 5710 Hannum Ave Culver City CA 90230

LIBBY, PERRY BENJAMIN, water company owner; b. Westfield, Iowa, Aug. 25, 1936; s. Perry and Mary (Connelly) L.; m. Pauline Kay Orr, Sept. 3, 1971; children—Steven Wesley, Janice Louise. Student U. Nebr., Omaha, 1973-74. Foreman wastewater plant City of Blair (Nebr.), 1974-77; supr. water dept. City of Gillette (Wyo.), 1977-80; owner Libbys O & M Service Co., Gillette, 1980—; faculty Casper Coll., 1978-81. Served with USN, 1954-57, USAF, 1959-63. Recipient Wyo. Plant Ops. Merit award Rocky Mountain Pollution Control Assn., 1979; William D. Hatfield award Water Pollution Control Fedn., 1980. Mem. Am. Water Works Assn., Water Pollution Control Fedn., Nat. Safety Council, Wyo. Water Quality Pollution Control Assn. Address: 1304 Rawhide Dr Gillette WY 82716

LIBERMAN, ALAN DOUGLAS, clin. psychologist; b. Seattle, Apr. 30, 1947; s. Martin and Florence Harriet (Katz) L.; B.A., Calif. State U.-Northridge, 1969; M.S., Calif. State U.-Los Angeles, 1971; Ph.D., Calif. Sch. Profl. Psychology, 1976; m. Susan Tess Friedman, Dec. 17, 1972; 1 dau., Dana. Vocat. rehab. counselor Calif. Dept. Rehab., 1971-73; sch. psychometrist San Diego City Schs., 1975-76; psychol. intern San Diego Center for Children, 1974-75; pre- and postdoctoral psychology intern Mesa Vista Hosp., San Diego, 1975-77; clin. and cons. psychologist in pvt. practice, 1977—; staff clin. psychologist Calif. Dept. Health, Garden Grove, 1977—, also clin. psychologist Brea Neuropsychiat. Hosp., 1978—; dir. psychol. services Med. Sq. Counseling Center, 1977—; instr. Rancho Los Amigos Learning Labs., Calif. Dept. Vocat. Rehab., Social Security Adminstr.; chmn. com. psychotherapeutic methods Met. State Hosp., 1978-79, mem. ethics com., 1980—; cons. Care Manor Hosp. Lic. psychologist, marriage, family and child counselor, sch. psychometrist, Calif; cert. Nat. Health Service Providers in Profl. Psychology. Mem. Am. Psychol. Assn., Calif. Psychol. Assn., Assn. Advancement Psychology, Orange County Psychol. Assn., Orange Soc. Clin. Hypnosis, Calif. Assn. Marriage, Family and Child Counselors, Orange County Soc. Marriage, Family and Child Counselors, Met. Psychol. Assn. Republican. Jewish. Research in geriatrics. Office: 1125 E 17th St Suite N-453 Santa Ana CA 92701

LIBERMAN, ROBERT PAUL, psychiatry educator, researcher, writer; b. Newark, Aug. 16, 1937; s. Harry and Gertrude (Galowitz) L.; m. Lee Susman, Apr. 12, 1961; children—Peter, Sarah, Danica, Nathaniel, Annalisa; m. Janet Marilyn Brown, Feb. 16, 1973. A.B. summa cum laude, Dartmouth Coll., 1959, diploma in medicine with honors, 1960;

M.S. in Pharmacology, U. Calif.-San Francisco, 1961; M.D., Johns Hopkins U., 1963. Diplomate Nat. Bd. Med. Examiners, Am. Bd. Psychiatry and Neurology; cert. community coll. instr., Calif. Intern Bronx (N.Y.) Mcpl. Hosp.-Einstein Coll. Medicine, 1963-64; resident in psychiatry Mass. Mental Health Ctr., Boston, 1964-68; postdoctoral fellow in social psychiatry Harvard U., 1966-68, teaching fellow in psychiatry, 1964-68; mem. faculty group psychotherapy tng. program Washington Sch. Psychiatry, 1968-70; with Nat. Ctr. Mental Health Service, Tng. and Research, St. Elizabeths Hosp., also mem. NIMH Clin. and Research Assocs. Tng. Program, Washington, 1968-70; asst. clin. prof. psychiatry UCLA, 1970-72, assoc. clin. prof., 1972-73, assoc. research psychiatrist, 1973-76, research psychiatrist, 1976-77, prof. psychiatry in residence, 1977—; adj. faculty mem. Antioch Coll. West/U. Without Walls, 1971-73; lectr. Calif. Luth. Coll., 1973-74; cons. div. mental health and behavioral scis. edn. Sepulveda (Calif.) VA Hosp., 1975-80; cons. in psychiatry to hosps.; practice medicine specializing in psychiatry, Reston, Va., 1968-70, Thousand Oaks, Calif., 1977—; staff psychiatrist Fairfax Hosp., Falls Church, Va., 1968-70, Ventura County Mental Health Dept., 1970-75; staff psychiatrist Ventura County Gen. Hosp.; mem. med. staff UCLA Hosp.; dir., prin. investigator study of schizophrenia Mental Health Clin. Research Ctr., NIMH, 1977—; chief rehab. medicine service Brentwood div. Los Angeles VA Med. Ctr., 1980—; dir. clin. research unit Camarillo State Hosp., 1970—; dir. Rehab. Research and Tng. Ctr. Mental Illness, 1980—. Bd. dirs. Lake Sherwood Community Assn., 1978—, pres., 1979-81; mem. Conejo Valley Citizens Adv. Bd., 1979-81. Served as surgeon USPHS, 1964-68. Research grantee. Mem. Assn. Advancement Behavior Therapy (exec. com. 1970-72, dir. 1972-79), Am. Psychiat. Assn., Phi Beta Kappa. Author: (with King, DeRisi and McCann) Personal Effectiveness: Guiding People to Assert Their Feelings and Improve Their Social Skills, 1975; A Guide to Behavioral Analysis and Therapy, 1972; (with Wheeler, DeVisser, Kuehnel and Kuehnel) Handbook of Marital Therapy: An Educational Approach to Treating Troubled Relationships, 1980; mem. editorial bd. Jour. Applied Behavior Analysis, 1972-78, Jour. Marriage and Family Counseling, 1974-78, Jour. Behavior Therapy and Exptl. Psychiatry, 1975—, Behavior Therapy, 1979—, Assessment and Inververntion in Devel. Disabilities, 1980—; assoc. editor Jour. Applied Behavior Analysis, 1976-78, Schizophrenic Bull., 1981—; contbr. over 150 articles to profl. jours., chpts. to books. Home: 528 E Potrero Rd Thousand Oaks CA 91361 Office: 11301 Wilshire Blvd Suite 691/B 117 Los Angeles CA 90073

LICHTENSTEIN, SARAH, research psychologist; b. Seattle, May 12, 1933; d. Frank Lewis Curtis and Eunice Florence (Morris) C.; (div.) children—David, Eric Nathan. B.A. with honors, Swarthmore Coll., 1955; M.A., U. Mich., 1958, Ph.D. in Math. Psychol., 1962. Human factors scientist Systems Devel. Corp., Santa Monica, Calif., 1962-63; cons. Rand Corp., Santa Monica, 1964-66; research supr. So. Ill. U., 1964-66; research assoc. Oreg. Research Inst., Eugene, 1966-76; research assoc. Decision Research, br. Perceptronics, Inc., Eugene, 1976—; adj. prof. U. Oreg., 1972—; editorial bd. Acta Psychologica & Organizational Behavior and Human Performance, 1976; com. mem. Lead in the Human Environ., NRC, Nat. Acad. Scis. Active with Nat. Women's Polit. Caucus. Fellow Am. Psychol. Assn., Western Psychol. Assn. Author: (with B. Fischoff, P. Slovic, S. Derby, R. Keeney) Acceptable Risk, 1981; contbr. articles to profl. jours., books' chpts. Home: 1650 Kona St Eugene OR 97403 Office: Decision Research 1201 Oak St Eugene OR 97401

LICKISS, EDWIN EMMETT, fin. planner; b. Oakland, Calif., Sept. 19, 1947; s. Edwin E. and Norma A. (Hayden) L.; m. Marilyn L. Whelton, Sept. 13, 1969; children—Jennifer, Michael, Thomas. B.A., Calif. State U., 1970, M.A., 1972; Cert. Fin. Planner, Coll. for Fin. Planning, 1979. Tchr. for deaf Concord, Calif., 1971-74; prin., gen. agt. life and disability ins. Orinda (Calif.) Fin. Group, 1974-81; founder Danville (Calif.) Fin. Group, 1981—; registered securities rep., 1976—. Bd. dirs. San Ramon (Calif.) Home Owners Assn., 1976-77; mem. Parish Council, St. Joan of Arc Ch., San Ramon, 1980—, mem. liturgy com., 1982—. vol. interpretor for deaf, 1971—. Mem. Nat. Assn. Securities Dealers, Internat. Assn. Fin. Planners, Inst. Cert. Fin. Planners. Roman Catholic. Club: Commonwealth. Office: 55 Oak Ct Danville CA 94526

LIDICKER, WILLIAM ZANDER, JR., zoologist, educator; b. Evanston, Ill., Aug. 19, 1932; s. William Zander and Frida (Schroeter) L.; B.S., Cornell U., 1953; M.S., U. Ill., 1954, Ph.D., 1957; m. Naomi Ishino, Aug. 18, 1956 (div. Oct. 28, 1982); children—Jeffrey Roger, Kenneth Paul. Instr. zoology, asst. curator mammals U. Calif., Berkeley, 1957-59, asst. prof., asst. curator, 1959-65, assoc. prof., asso. curator, 1965-69, assoc. dir. Mus. Vertebrate Zoology, 1968-81, acting dir., 1974-75, prof. zoology, curator mammals, 1969—. Bd. dirs. No. Calif. Com. for Environ. Info., 1971-77; mem. steering com. Internat. Theriological Council, UNESCO, 1978—. NSF fellow, 1963-64; Miller prof., 1967-68; numerous research grants. Fellow AAAS, Calif. Acad. Scis.; mem. Am. Soc. Mammalogists (dir., 1967—, 2d v.p. 1974-76, pres. 1976-78), Am. Soc. Naturalists, others. Club: Berkeley Folk Dancers (pres. 1969). Contbr. articles to profl. jours. Office: Mus of Vertebrate Zoology U Calif Berkeley CA 94720

LIE, KIAN JOE, medical parasitologist; b. Indonesia, Nov. 25, 1916; s. Siong Pin and How Nio (Tio) L.; came to U.S., 1960, naturalized, 1978; Ph.D., U. Indonesia, 1941, M.D., 1943; D.T.M.H., London Sch. Hygiene and Tropical Medicine, 1950; m. Luan Eng Injo, Apr. 18, 1948; children—Tiong, Tony. Lectr. pathology U. Indonesia Med. Sch., 1943-47; asst. research microbiologist Inst. Tropical Hygiene, Leyden, Netherlands, 1947-50; prof. parasitology and gen. pathology U. Indonesia, 1950-60; research parasitologist Hooper Found., U. Calif., San Francisco, 1960—, adj. prof. parasitology, 1978—. Recipient Eykman medal Dutch Soc. Tropical Medicine, 1948. Mem. AAAS, Am. Soc. Parasitologist, Am. Soc. Tropical Medicine and Hygiene, Soc. Invertebrate Pathology. Author numerous papers in field. Home: 30 Lansdale St San Francisco CA 94127 Office: Dept Epidemiology and Internat Health Univ Calif San Francisco CA 94143

LIEB, GERARD JOSEPH, accountant; b. N.Y.C., May 6, 1949; s. Hilmar Otto and Ethel Margaret (Mitchell) L.; m. Trudy Patton Bigham, July 24, 1946; 1 son, Geoffrey. B.A. cum laude, Boston Coll., 1971; M.B.A., NYU, 1975. C.P.A., Calif., Oreg. Sr. acct. Clarence Rainess & Co., Beverly Hills, Calif., 1975-78; mgr. Weissbrod, Ozur & Radder, C.P.A.s, Beverly Hills, 1978-80; tax mgr. Yergen & Meyer, C.P.A.s, Portland, Oreg., 1980-83, ptnr., 1983—. Mem. Am. Inst. C.P.A.s, Calif. Soc. C.P.A.s, Oreg. Soc. C.P.A.s. Republican. Club: Columbia-Edgewater Country (Portland). Lodge: Sertoma (Beaverton and Milwaukie, Oreg.). Home: 19030 SW Lisa Dr Aloha OR 97006 Office: Yergen and Myer CPAs 4640 SW Macadam St Suite 100 Portland OR 97202

LIEBEGOTT, NANCY JEAN, accountant; b. Jamaica, N.Y., June 25, 1944; d. John Arthur and Dorathea (Cron) Diemer; m. Charles Herbert Liebegott, Oct. 26, 1968; B.A. in Acctg., Queen's Coll., 1968; postgrad. West Coast U., 1981—. Sr. cost acct. Hazeltine Corp., Little Neck, N.Y., 1968-69; full charge bookkeeper Jewels by Martinez, Inc., N.Y.C., 1971-72; sr. cash reconciliation acct. ABC, N.Y.C., 1972-73; acct., office mgr. F.T. Andrews, Inc., Fullerton, Calif., 1973—. Mem. AAUW, Nat. Assn. Female Execs. Republican. Clubs: Sierra (Los Angeles); Canyon Explorers (treas. Fullerton, Calif.). Office: F T Andrews Inc 1343 W Valencia Dr Fullerton CA 92633

LIEBERMAN, FREDRIC, music educator, ethnomusicologist; b. N.Y.C., Mar. 1, 1940; s. Stanley and Bryna (Mason) L.; Mus.B., U. Rochester, 1962; M.A. in Music, U. Hawaii, 1965; Ph.D. in Music, UCLA, 1968. Asst. prof. music Brown U., Providence, 1968-75; assoc. prof. U. Wash., Seattle, 1975—, dir. Sch. Music, 1981—; Panelist Nat. Endowment for the Arts, 1977-80; mem. King County Arts Commn., 1977-80. Mem. Soc. Ethnomusicology, Soc. Asian Music, Internat. Council Traditional Music. Editor: Ethnomusicology, 1978-80; author: Chinese Music: An Annotated Bibliography, 1970, 2d edit., 1979; A Chinese Zither Tutor, 1983; contbr. articles to prof. jours; author numerous poems and compositions. Office: Sch Music Univ Wash Seattle WA 98195

LIEBERMAN, MYRON ALLEN, chemist, chess fedn. exec.; b. Hollywood, Calif., Sept. 3, 1941; s. Louis A. and Frances (Klausner) L.; A.A., Glendale City Coll., 1961; B.S. in Chemistry, Ariz. State U., 1965, M.S. in Chem. Engring., 1970; m. Rachel Esther Barchas, Mar. 7, 1964; children—Lawrence Allen, Linda Corlene. Section mgr. ion physics and material standards Motorola, Inc., Phoenix, 1963-75; dir. Motorola Credit Union of Ariz., 1975—; tchr. semi-conductor processing Mesa (Ariz.) Community Coll., 1975-76; cons., tutor in chemistry, physics, math. and chess orgn., 1970—. Pres., Motorola Chess Club, 1964—; nat. chess tournament dir., 1966—; tchr. chess City of Tempe, Ariz., 1974-75; regional v.p. U.S. Chess Fedn., 1977-78, mem. exec. com., 1978—, nat. sec., 1978-81, treas., 1981—, meritorious service award, 1981; chief organizer U.S. Open Championship, 1978, U.S. Class Championship, 1980, U.S. Sr. Open, 1981, editor policy bd. newsletter, 1978-81; organizer Ariz. Nat. Chess League Team, 1978—. Project dir. Tempe Community Council's Needs Assessment Project, 1978-79. Recipient Motorola Profit Sharing Council Service award, 1972, Dean Haddon award Reaction Research Soc., 1959, Motorola Press Club awards, 1967-73. Mem. Assn. U.S. Chess Journalists, Ariz. Chess Assn. (pres. 1978—). Contbr. articles on solid state chemistry to profl. publs. Home: 1444 W 6th St Tempe AZ 85281 Office: United States Chess Fedn 186 Route 9W New Windsor NY 12550

LIEBERMAN, PAUL, aero. engr., engring. research co. exec.; b. Bklyn., Dec. 25, 1932; s. Benjamin and Frances (Firestone) L.; B.S. in Aero. Engring., N.Y. U., 1954; M.S. in Aero. Engring., Princeton U., 1956; Ph.D. in Applied Mechanics, Ill. Inst. Tech., 1964; children by previous marriage—Naomi Ruth, Leah, Micah Benjamin. Engr., Bell Aircraft Corp., Buffalo, N.Y., 1954; sr. scientist Ill. Inst. Tech. Research Inst., Chgo., 1957-69, project engr. devel. of instrumentation; sr. project mgr. TRW, Redondo Beach, Calif., 1969-81; v.p. systems engring. Nat. Tech. Systems, Saugus, Calif., 1981—. Served to 1st. lt. USAF, 1955-57. Guggenheim fellow, 1954-55. Mem. Sigma Xi. Jewish. Contbr. numerous articles on thermodynamics, applied mechanics and air force systems to profl. jours.; author reports in field. Home: 19815 Mildred Ave Torrance CA 90503 Office: 26525 Golden Valley Rd Saugus CA 91350

LIEBERSON, STANLEY, sociologist, educator; b. Montreal Que., Can., Apr. 20, 1933; s. Jack and Ida (Cohen) L.; m. Patricia Ellen Beard, June 1, 1960; children—Rebecca, David, Miriam, Rachel. M.A., U. Chgo., 1958, Ph.D., 1960. From instr. to asst. prof., assoc. dir. Iowa Urban Community Research Ctr., U. Iowa, Iowa City, 1959-61; from asst. prof. to prof. U. Wis., Madison, 1961-67; prof. U. Wash., Seattle, 1967-71, dir. Ctr. Studies Demography and Ecology, 1968-71; prof., assoc. dir. Population Research Ctr., U. Chgo., 1971-74; prof. sociology U. Ariz., Tucson, 1974—; Claude Bissel disting. vis. prof. U. Toronto, Can., 1979-80. Recipient Colver-Rosenberger Ednl. prize, 1960; Guggenheim fellow, 1972-73. Mem. Am. Sociol. Assn. (Disting. Contbn. Scholarship award 1982), Internat. Population Union, Population Assn. Am., Pacific Sociol. Soc. Author: (with others) Metropolis and Region, 1960; Ethnic Patterns in American Cities, 1963; Language and Ethnic Relations in Canada, 1970; (with others) Metropolis and Region in Transition, 1970; A Piece of the Pie, 1980; Language Diversity and Language Contact, 1981; editor: Explorations in Sociolinguistics, 1967. Home: 3520 N Prescott Pl Tucson AZ 85715 Office: U Ariz Dept Sociology Social Science Bldg Tucson AZ 85721

LIEBERT, ARTHUR GERALD, casino operator; b. St. Louis, Jan. 15, 1924; s. Samuel and Mae (Rich) L.; student Ill. Wesleyan U., Bloomington, 1942-43; m. Judith Wishne, Sept. 2, 1945; children—Sheri Seigel, Sandra Ewan, Mark Liebert, Ptnr., Liebert Realty Co., St. Louis, 1946-66; pres., owner Rainbow Club and Casino, Henderson, Nev., 1966—; owner Lucky Club, Henderson, 1973-74; pres. owner Nev. Hotel, Las Vegas, 1979-80. Bd. dirs. Jewish Fedn., 1976—; pres. Jewish Family Services Agy. Las Vegas, 1979-80; active United Way, Boy's Club. Mem. C. of C. Office: 122 Water St Henderson NV 89015

LIEBL, GARY E., corporate executive; b. Mpls., Nov. 13, 1941; s. Warren H. and Lillian L. (Beaublen) L.; m. Kay Dodge; 1 dau., Nicole Caroline. B.S. in Psychology, Loyola U.-Los Angeles, 1964; M.B.A. U. So. Calif., 1968. Sr. systems analyst Vons Grocery Co., El Monte, Calif., 1957-68; v.p. mktg. MSI Data Corp., Costa Mesa, Calif., 1968-76; pres. Microdata Internat. corp., Irvine, Calif., 1977-81, pres., chief exec. officer Microdata Corp., 1981—. Mem. World Trade Center Assn. (dir. Orange County chpt.), Young Presidents Orgn., Am. Electronics Assn., Internat. Mktg. Assn., Am. Mgmt. Assn. Office: PO Box 19501 Irvine CA 92743

LIENTZ, BENNET PRICE, educator; b. Hollywood, Calif., Oct. 24, 1942; s. Beverly Price, Jr. and Josephine Anne (Palen) L.; B.A., Claremont Men's Coll., 1964; M.S., U. Wash., 1966, Ph.D., 1968; m. Martha Jane Benson, Aug. 29, 1964; children—Bennet Price, Andrew, Charles. Sr. research scientist, br. head System Devel. Corp., Santa Monica, Calif., 1968-70, cons., 1972-73; asst. prof., asso. prof. systems engring. U. So. Calif., Los Angeles, 1970-73; prof., vice chmn. Grad. Sch. Mgmt., also acad. asst. to chancellor, dir. Office Adminstrv. Info. Services, UCLA, 1974—, curriculum chmn., 1975—, vice chmn. computers and info. systems, 1980—; cons. Jet Propulsion Lab., 1972-73, Atlantic Richfield Co., 1974, Calif. Fed. Savs. and Loan, 1974, Security Pacific Nat. Bank, 1978—. Grantee NASA, 1969-71, Office Sci. Research-USAF, 1970-73, Office Naval Research, 1973—; research fellow U. Wash., 1966-67. Mem. Operations Research Soc. (sec.-treas. Western region 1971—), Am. Statis. Assn. (treas. 1972-74), Am. Math. Soc., Inst. Math. Statistics, EDP Auditors Assn., Operations Research Soc. (student affairs com. 1971-77). Presbyn. (chmn. Mariners group 1972-76). Author: Computer Applications in Operations Analysis, 3d printing, 1975; Systems in Action, 1978; Effective Business Communications, 1979; Software Maintenance Management, 1980; Introduction to Distributed Systems, 1981; also numerous articles in profl. jours. Contbg. editor Data Process, 1974—; editorial bd. Computer Networks, 1975—. Home: 229 21st Pl Santa Monica CA 90402 Office: Grad Sch of Mgmt U of Calif Los Angeles CA 90025

LIFF, JOAN SURCKLA, data processing company executive; b. Cleve., Aug. 29, 1941; d. John and Ann (Vasiluk) Surckla; B.B.A. with honors, Nat. U., 1980. Employment counselor Cleve. Employment Agy., 1959; tech. asst. Gould (Clevite Corp.), Cleve., 1960-65; staff asst. data systems div. Sanders Assos., Nashua, N.H., 1966-68; exec. sec. Gen. Dynamics Corp., Rochester, N.Y., 1968-70, supr. adminstrv. and documentation services Western Data Center, San Diego, 1980—. Recipient Extraordinary Achievement award Gen. Dynamics Corp., 1982. Mem. Internat. Word Processing Assn. (dir. 1981—), Nat. Mgmt. Assn. (mgr. awards 1979). Club: Order Eastern Star. Home: Apt 133 5440 Baltimore Dr La Mesa CA 92041 Office: Western Data Systems Center Gen Dynamics Corp PO Box 80847 San Diego CA 92138

LIGHT, FRANK R., agricultural products company executive; b. 1928. Pres., Acme Fast Freight Inc., 1946-72; v.p., contractor Alexander & Baldwin; pres., chief exec. officer Sun-Diamond Growers of Calif., Stockton, 1980, also dir.; pres. Sunsweet Growers Inc., Sun-Maid Growers of Calif. Inc., Diamond Walnut Growers Inc. Office: Sun-Diamond Growers of Calif 1050 S Diamond St PO Box 1727 Stockton CA 92501*

LIGHT, IVAN HUBERT, sociology educator; b. Chgo., Nov. 3, 1941; s. Ivan H. and Lily Ann (Shulz) L.; m. Leah Lazarovitz, June 15, 1966; children—Matthew A., Nathaniel E. B.A. magna cum laude, Harvard U., 1963; Ph.D., U. Calif.-Berkeley, 1969. Asst. prof. sociology UCLA, 1968-74, assoc. prof., 1974-79, prof., 1979—. NSF grantee, 1976-79, 83—; U.S. Dept. Labor grantee, 1967-68. Mem. Am. Sociol. Assn., AAUP, Internat. Sociol. Assn., U. Calif. Faculty Assn., Internat. Assn. for Prejudice and Peace Research (charter mem.), Sierra Club. Democrat. Club: Claremont Democratic. Author: Ethnic Enterprise in America, 1972; Cities in World Perspective, 1983. Home: 819 Marymount Ln Claremont CA 91711 Office: Dept Sociology UCLA 405 Hilgard Ave Los Angeles CA 90024

LIGHT, ROBERT MERWIN, broadcasting association executive; b. Denver, June 23, 1918; s. Louis and Sally (Conn) L.; m. Margaret Colville Dodgson, Oct. 2, 1943; 1 son, Robert Louis; m. Julie Fraser Giguere, Dec. 10, 1953; children—Jonathan Fraser, Lisa Karen. Student pub. schs., Denver, N.Y.C. Actor theater, radio, N.Y.C., 1934-39; contract player Warner Studios, Hollywood, Calif., 1935-37; writer, dir. radio programs for ABC, NBC, Los Angeles, 1939-42; tchr., exec. dir. AFTRA, Los Angeles, 1946-49; writer Alan Ladd Radio Show, Abbott Kimball Co. Advt., Los Angeles, 1949-53; dir. promotion and advt. RKO Gen., Western Div., Los Angeles, 1953-59; pres. So. Calif. Broadcasters Assn., Hollywood, 1959—; lectr., tchr. UCLA, U. So. Calif., Los Angeles City Coll., London U. Mem. Los Angeles County Hwy. Safety Commn.; mem. adv. council So. Calif. Assn. Govts. Served to lt. col. Armed Forces Radio, 1942-46; ETO. Decorated Bronze Star; recipient honors Los Angeles County Bd. Suprs., Los Angeles City Council. Mem. Hollywood Radio & TV Soc., Los Angeles Ad Club, Am. Advt. Fedn., So. Calif. Theatre Assn. (v.p.). Office: 1800 N Highland Ave Suite 609 Hollywood CA 90028

LIGHTCAP, EDWARD JOHN, fin. auditor; b. Dubuque, Iowa, Apr. 12, 1954; s. Albert Wallace and Eunice Irene (Strelesky) L.; B.B.A., U. Iowa, 1976; student DePaul U., 1978-79, U. Portland, 1981—; m. Valerie Ann Wing, June 11, 1977. Staff auditor Price Waterhouse & Co., Chgo., 1977-80, fin. auditor, 1977-78, tax sr., 1978-80; with Pacific Power & Light, 1980—, sr. fin. auditor corp. fin. group, 1980—. C.P.A., Iowa. Mem. Am. Inst. C.P.A.'s, Oreg. Soc. C.P.A.'s. Roman Catholic. Clubs: Toastmasters Internat., K.C. Home: 12375 Mt Jefferson Terr Lake Oswego OR 97034 Office: 920 SW 6th St Suite 1400 Portland OR 97204

LIGHTER, FREDERICK JOHN, ethologist, ecologist; b. Seattle, May 15, 1942; s. Eli and Ruth G. (Link) L.; B.A., Whitman Coll., 1964; B.S., U. Wash., 1966; Ph.D., U. Hawaii, 1977. Instr. biometry U. Hawaii, 1974; instr. natural scis. Honolulu Community Coll., 1975-77; cons. environ. studies Honolulu Zoo, 1978-80; project coordinator Environ. Monitoring Center, Pacific Sci. Center, Seattle, 1979-80; cons. Mus. of History and Industry, Seattle, 1981; naturalist Seattle Aquarium, 1981-82, coordinator mktg. programs, 1982—. Bd. trustees, exec. sec. Friends of Honolulu Zoo, 1975-78; mem. exec. bd. Scientists-Citizens Organized for Policy Issues, 1980. Served with U.S. Army, 1967-69. NSF trainee, 1969-72. Mem. Ecol. Soc. Am., Am. Soc. Zoologists, AAAS, Animal Behavior Soc., Sigma Xi. Contbr. articles to profl. jours. Co-editor: Contrasts in Behavior, 1978. Home: 834 NE 100th Seattle WA 98125

LII, KEH-SHIN, statistician, educator; b. Szechuan, China, May 19, 1945; came to U.S., 1971; s. Chuan-shuen and Wen-Yu Lo L.; m. Maritha Ming-Shi Liu, Sept. 4, 1973; children—Joanne, Stella, Jessica, John. B.S. in Math., Nat. Taiwan Normal U., 1969; M.A. in Math., U. Calif.-San Diego, 1973, Ph.D. in Math., 1975. Teaching asst. Nat. Taiwan Normal U., 1968-71; teaching/research asst. U. Calif.-San Diego, 1971-75; asst. prof. Northwestern U., Evanston, Ill., 1975-78; asst. prof. stats. dept. U. Calif.-Riverside, 1978—. Served to 2d lt. Army Republic of China, 1969-70. NSF grantee, 1976-78. Mem. Inst. Math. Stats., Am. Statis. Assn., Time Series Analysis and Forecasting Soc. (dir.). Contbr. articles to profl. jours. Home: 315 Maravilla Dr Riverside CA 92507 Office: Dept Stats U Calif Riverside CA 92521

LIJPHART, AREND, political science educator, author; b. Apeldoorn, Netherlands, Aug. 17, 1936; s. Anthonius and Mathilde Theodora (d'Angremond) L.; m. Eva Tamm, Aug. 10, 1959 (div.); children—Antony Sune, Anna Margaretha. B.A., Principia Coll., 1958; M.A., Yale U., 1959, Ph.D., 1963. Instr. polit. sci. Elmira (N.Y.) Coll., 1961-63; asst. prof. U. Calif-Berkeley, 1963-68, assoc. prof., 1968-69; prof. internat. relations U. Leiden (Netherlands), 1968-78, dept. chmn., 1972-74, 76-78; vis. prof. govt. Harvard U., Cambridge, Mass., 1970; vis. research fellow Inst. Advanced Studies, Australian Nat. U., Canberra, 1971-72; prof. polit. sci. U. Calif.-San Diego, 1978—. Netherlands Inst. Advanced Study fellow, 1974-75. Mem. Am. Polit. Sci. Assn. (ethnic and cultural pluralism award 1979), Internat. Polit. Sci. Assn., Royal Netherlands Acad. Scis., Com. Polit. Sociol., Internat. Studies Assn. (v.p. 1976-77), European Consortium Polit. Research (exec. com. 1977-78), Internat. Council on Future of Univ. Author: The Trauma of Decolonization: The Dutch and West New Guinea, 1966; The Politics of Accomodation: Pluralism and Democracy in the Netherlands, 1968; Verzuiling, pacificatie en kentering in de Nederlandse politiek, 1968; Democracy in Plural Societies: A Comparative Exploration, 1977; editor: World Politics: The Writings of Theorists and Practitioners, Classical and Modern, 1966; Conflict and Coexistence in Belgium: The Dynamics of a Culturally Divided Society, 1981; and others; contbr. numerous articles and chpts. to profl. publs.; mem. several editorial bds. profl. jours. Office: Dept Polit Sci Q-060 U Calif San Diego La Jolla CA 92093

LIKENS, JAMES DEAN, economist, consultant; b. Bakersfield, Calif., Sept. 12, 1937; s. Ernest LeRoy and Monnie Jewel (Thomas) L.; m. Janet Sue Pelton, Dec. 18, 1965 (div.); children—John David, Janet Elizabeth. B.S. in Econs., U., Calif.-Berkeley, 1960, M.B.A., 1961; Ph.D. in Econs., U. Minn., 1970. Asst. prof. econs. Pomona Coll., Claremont, Calif., 1969-75, assoc. prof., 1975-82, prof. econs., 1982—. Mem. Western Econ. Assn., Am. Econ. Assn., Indsl. Orgn. Soc., Health Econs. Research Orgn. Author: (with Joseph LaDou), Medicine and Money, 1977; contbr. articles to econ. jours. Office: Dept Economics Pomona Coll Claremont CA 91711

LILJEKRANS, ALAN EDWARD, systems management executive, accountant; b. Duluth, Minn., Apr. 29, 1944; s. Axel Enander and Bertha (Goeppinger) L.; m. Wendy L. Jensen, Nov. 30, 1974; children—Heidi, Kirsten, Jon, Amy. B.A., U. Minn.-Duluth, 1966. C.P.A. Data processing programming analyst various cos., 1966-77; cons. Price Waterhouse, Denver, 1977-80; dir. info. systems planning Am. TV and Communications, Denver, 1980—. Mem. Am. Inst. C.P.A.s, Colo. Soc. C.P.A.s, Assn. Systems Mgmt. Office: Am TV and Communications 160 Inverness Dr W Englewood CO 80112

LILLY, HERBERT JOSEPH, JR., design engr.; b. Maywood, Calif., June 22, 1931; s. Herbert Joseph and Beatrice Mary (Schmitz) L.; Aero. Engr., Northrop U., 1959; m. Carol Diana Thrush, June 24, 1964; children—Wayne Joseph, Eric John. Design engr. N.Am. Aviation, Downey, Calif., 1959-64; lead engr. Ocean Systems div. Rockwell Internat., Long Beach, Calif., 1964-72, sr. design engr. Satellite Systems div., Seal Beach, Calif., 1972-76, sr. lead engr. shuttle ops. Downey, Calif., 1976—. Served with USNR, 1951-55. Mem. Nat. Rifle Assn. (life), Am. Def. Preparedness Assn. Republican. Roman Catholic. Club: Elks. Patentee on offshore oil prodn. Home: 25616 Via Viento Mission Viejo CA 92691 Office: 12214 Lakewood Blvd Downey CA 90241

LILLY, JAMES ALEXANDER, construction executive; b. Bluefield, W.Va., Sept. 1, 1918; s. Clifford Abraham and Eva Acre (Dinwiddie) L.; Engr., Bluefield Coll., 1938; B.S.M.E., Va. Poly. Inst. and State U., 1940; children—James Alexander, Pamela, Robert Clifton, Anne Martha. Engr. Ingersoll Rand Co., N.Y.C., 1940-42; engr., gen. supt. George M. Brewster & Son Co., Bogota, N.J., 1945-49; engr. W.S. Bellow Constrn. Co., Houston, 1949-50; engr., supt. McKenzie Constrn. Co., San Antonio, 1950-54; project mgr. Whittle Constrn. Co., Dallas, 1954-59; with Morrison-Knudsen Co., Inc., Boise, Idaho, 1959—, gen. mgr. Vietnam, 1965-68, v.p., gen. mgr. Morrison-Knudsen Internat. Co., Inc., 1968-71, v.p. splty. div., 1971-72, v.p. domestic ops., 1972-73, exec. v.p. domestic ops., 1973-76, exec. v.p. N. Am. ops., 1976—, dir., 1973—; pres., chief exec. officer, dir. M-K Nat. Corp.; pres., dir. Morrison-Knudsen of Fla., Inc.; v.p., dir. Emkay Fin. Co., Inc.; v.p. Emkay Devel. Co.; dir. Internat. Engring. Co. Inc. Mem. Va. Poly. Inst. Ednl. Found. Served with USMCR, 1942-45. Decorated D.F.C. with stars, Air medal with oakleaf clusters. Mem. Acad. Mgmt., ASCE, Soc. Am. Mil. Engrs., ASME, Am. Inst. Constructors, Am. Inst. Chem. Engrs., Soc. Mining Engrs. of AIME, Am. Underground-Space Assn., Assn. Energy Engrs., Alaska Pipeline Builders Assn., AAAS, Am. Forestry Assn., Deep Founds. Inst., Fusion Energy Found., Nat. Acad. Scis., Am. Wind Energy Assn., IEEE, Mining and Reclamation Council Am., N.Y. Acad. Scis., Brit. Tunnelling Soc., Internat. Tech. Inst., Soc. Chem. Industry, Assn. U.S. Army, Sunsat Energy Council, Am. Nuclear Soc., Moles, Beavers (dir., Golden Beaver award 1980), Nat. Trust Historic Preservation, Nat. Audubon Soc., Nat. Geog. Soc., Smithsonian Assos., Newcomen Soc. N. Am., Nat. Hist. Soc., Met. Mus. Art, Internat. Platform Assn., Idaho Historic Preservation Council, Collectors Guild, Boise Gallery Art, Boise Philharmonic Assn., Tau Beta Pi, Pi Tau Sigma. Episcopalian. Clubs: Arid, Carlton, Laramie Country, Ground Hog, Hillcrest Country; International (Washington). Home: 3232 Catalina Ln Boise ID 83705 Office: One Morrison-Knudsen Plaza Boise ID 83729

LIM, LUCY, culture foundation administrator, art historian, writer; B.A., U. Mich., 1962; M.A., UCLA, 1970; postgrad. Inst. Fine Arts, N.Y.U., 1982—. Research asst. Brit. Mus., London, 1965; asst. to dir. UCLA Art Gallery, 1966-67; free-lance writer for nat. mags., 1975-80; exec. dir. Chinese Culture Found. of San Francisco, 1981—; writer Chinese Art. Am. Council Learned Socs. fellow, 1975-76; Am. Oriental Soc. fellow, 1976-77; Lit. Program fellow, 1978; NEA grantee, 1978; NEA fellow, Mus. Profl. fellow, 1982. Mem. Coll. Art Assn. Contbr. articles on Chinese art to profl. jours. Office: Chinese Culture Found 750 Kearny St San Francisco CA 94108

LIM, TERI SANAYE, food products company manager; b. Santa Monica, Calif., Sept. 20, 1951; d. John Shizuo and Suzuko (Shimoide) Yamamura; m. Richard Du Lim, Aug. 5, 1978. B.A. magna cum laude, UCLA, 1972, secondary sch. teaching credential, 1973, M.B.A., 1978. Instr., Los Angeles Unified Sch. Dist., 1975-76; mktg. mgr. Purex Corp., Carson, Calif., 1978-80; product mgr. Hunt-Wesson Foods, Inc., Fullerton, Calif., 1980-81, Knudsen Corp., Los Angeles, 1981—. Mem. Phi Beta Kappa.

LIM, VICTOR ALLEN, optometrist; b. San Francisco, May 14, 1944; s. Allen and Lilly (Chow) L., m. Camille Chan, Apr. 22, 1967; children—Matthew, Brett. B.A., U. Calif.-Berkeley, O.D., 1970. Lic. optometrist, Calif., 1970. Optometrist San Bruno (Calif.) Med.-Optical Clinic, 1970-72; ptnr. pvt. practice Lim and Schrader, 1972—. Mem. City of Davis (Calif.) Personnel Bd.; mem. adv. bd. Yolo County (Calif.) Drug and Alcohol Abuse Commn., Los Ricos Community Coll. Mem. Am. Optometric Assn., Calif. Optometric Assn., Sacramento Valley Optometric Assn., C. of C. (Man of Year 1979), U. Calif. Optometry Sch. Alumni. Democrat. Roman Catholic. Clubs: Chinese Fellowship of Davis (past pres.), Kiwanis (past pres.). Home: 4022 Almond Ln Davis CA 95616 Office: 1109 Kennedy Pl Davis CA 95616

LIMA, PAUL EDWIN, mfg. co. exec.; b. Boston, July 17, 1945; s. Fortunato Roosevelt and Mary Louise (Machado) L.; B.S., U.S. Mil. Acad., 1967; M.A., Boston U., 1971; postgrad. U. Puget Sound, 1972-74, U.S. Army Command and Gen. Staff Coll., 1977-80, Exec. Program U. Va., 1982; m. Maria Elena Leon, June 8, 1967; children—Paul E., Antonio M., Pedro A. With PACCAR, Inc., Bellevue, Wash., 1974—, sales adminstr. for internat. group, 1975-77, adminstrv. asst. to chmn., 1977-78, adminstrv. asst. to pres., 1978-79, spl. asst. to pres., 1979-80, dir. Latin Am. ops., 1981—; dir. Kenworth Mexicana S.A. de C.V., Kenpar S.A. de C.V. Bd. dirs. Booster Program, U. Puget Sound Sch. Law, 1977—; exec. com. Am. GI Form, State of Wash., 1977-78; dir. Hispanic Heritage program, 1977-78; bd. dirs. El Comite, 1976-77. Served with U.S. Army, 1967-72; maj. USAR, 1972—. Decorated Bronze Star with oak leaf cluster, Meritorious Service medal with two oak leaf clusters, Air medal, Army Commendation medal with oak leaf cluster; recipient cert. of achievement Nat. Civil Affairs Assn., 1977. Mem. Motor Vehicle Mfrs. Assn. U.S., Soc. Internat. Devel. Republican. Roman Catholic. Home: 14268 128th Ave NE Kirkland WA 98033 Office: PO Box 1518 Bellevue WA 98009

LIN, CHWEN-HAO, structural engr.; b. Taiwan, Oct. 22, 1949; s. Chuan-Hsiang and Tsai-Hwei (Chao) L.; came to U.S., 1975; B.S. in C.E., Nat. Taiwan U., 1973; M.S. in C.E., U. Calif., Berkeley, 1976, postgrad., 1976-77; m. Jean Lung; 1 son, Christopher Cheyih. Civil engr. Raymond Internat., Inc., San Francisco, 1977-78; research structural engr. R & D div. Vetco Offshore, Inc., Ventura, Calif., 1979-80; mem. tech. staff Energy Systems Group, Rockwell Internat., Canoga Park, Calif., 1980-81; sr. engr. Pipeline & Prodn. Facilities div. Bechtel Petroleum, Inc., San Francisco, 1981—; cons. engr. offshore structures, marine pipelines, subsea prodn. systems. Registered profl. engr., Calif.; Sigma Xi Research grantee, 1977. Mem. ASCE, Sigma Xi. Home: 2636 Monte Cresta Dr Belmont CA 94002 Office: 50 Beale St San Francisco CA 94105

LIN, JUANG LU, elec. engr.; b. Changhua, Taiwan, Dec. 1, 1934; came to U.S., 1963, naturalized, 1973; s. Lin Shen Chuang and Li En; B.S., Nat. Taiwan U., 1956; M.S., Mich. State U., 1964, Ph.D., 1967; m. Shiah Chiang Su, Sept. 16, 1965; children—George Huei-Che, Albert Hueihsien. Elec. engr. D.B. Hank & Co., Taipei, Taiwan, 1959-63; asst. prof. elec. engring. Wash. State U., Pullman; sr. specialist research engr. Boeing Aerospace Co., Seattle, from 1972, now prin. engr. Mem. IEEE (sr.), Internat. Sci. Radio Union, Sigma Xi. Contbr. articles on electromagnetic theory, radiation and scattering to profl. jours. Home: 225 173d Pl NE Bellevue WA 98008 Office: Boeing Aerospace Co Seattle WA 98124

LIN, LAWRENCE SHUH LIANG, mental health executive; b. China, July 5, 1938; s. Wan Chow and Inn Chi Lin; came to U.S., 1967, naturalized, 1979; LL.B., Soochow U., 1963; M.B.A., Pepperdine U., 1970; m. Grace Yu, July 31, 1966; children—Ray, Lester. Spl. project acctg. supr. Motown Records, Hollywood, Calif., 1975; chief accountant Elektra/Asylum/Nonesuch Records, Beverly Hills, Calif., 1976-77, United Artists Music Pub. Group, Hollywood, 1977-80; controller-adminstr. Pasadena (Calif.) Guidance Clinics, 1980—. Mem. Nat. Accountants Assn. Mem. Christian Assembly Ch. Office: 66 Hurlbut St Pasadena CA 91105

LIN, TZ-HONG, chemist; b. Taiwan, Jan. 30, 1934; s. Tsai-Shin Lin and A-wu Chang; B.S., Nat. Taiwan U., 1956; M.S., N.Mex. Highlands U., 1964; Ph.D., U. Calif., Berkeley, 1969; m. Kay Yu, July 31, 1969; children—Alan L., Brian Y. Postdoctoral fellow La. State U., Baton Rouge, 1969-71; research scientist, project mgr., mgr. research, assoc. dir. research and devel. Medi-Physics Inc., Emergyville, Calif.,1971—. Mem. Am. Chem. Soc., Soc. Nuclear Medicine, Chinese Chem. Soc. Patentee in radiopharmaceuticals. Home: 765 Ondina Dr Fremont CA 94539 Office: 5855 Christie Ave Emeryville CA 94608

LIND, BRUCE ELVIN, land devel. co. exec.; b. Twin Falls, Idaho, June 25, 1941; s. Wyland Herman and Helen Eileen (Bailey) L.; B.S., Utah State U., 1967, B.S. in Bus. Edn., 1968, M.S. in Mktg., 1969; m. Norma Jean Kitchen, Sept. 19, 1966; children—Billie Jean, Bonita, Ben, Katy, Tyler, Tara, Corbin. Product mgr., wholesaler Boise Cascade Corp. (Idaho), 1968-70; asst. to nat. sales mgr. Trus-Joist Corp., Boise, 1970-71; founder, pres. A.M.R. Corp., Idaho Falls, Idaho, 1971—, chmn. bd., 1972—. Mem. Delta Phi Kappa. Club: Lions. Office: 2630 N Yellowstone St Idaho Falls ID 83401

LIND, MARSHALL LEE, state education commissioner; b. Appleton, Wis., June 1, 1936; s. Darwin F. and Elsie R. (Blohm) L.; B.S., U. Wis., 1958; M.Ed., U. Mont., 1965; Ph.D., Northwestern U., 1969; m. Lois Ann Zimmerman, Nov. 22, 1958; children—Peter, Elizabeth, Jeffry. Jr. high sch. tchr., Bunduel, Wis., 1959-61; tchr., adminstr. Bur. Indian Affairs, Alaska, 1961-67; supt. Kodiak Island (Alaska) Borough Sch. Dist., 1969-71; commr. edn. State of Alaska, Juneau, 1971—. Vis. prof. Northwestern U. Bd. dirs. Agy. for Instrnl. TV, N.W. Regional Ednl. Lab. Served with U.S. Army, 1958-59. Mem. Am. Assn. Sch. Adminstrs., NEA, Phi Delta Kappa. Methodist. Rotarian. Office: Dept Edn State Office Bldg Pouch F Juneau AK 99811*

LINDAL, SIR WALTER, construction executive, b. Elfros, Sask., Can., Jan. 31, 1919; s. August Jacobson and Ingeborg (Torfason) L.; student U. Ottawa, 1938-39; m. Isobel Mary Rendall, July 12, 1941; children—Robert W., Douglas F., Martin J., Bonnie G. Salesman, retail lumber, 1939-41; pres. Colonial Homes Ltd., Toronto, 1945-62; pres., chmn. bd. Lindal Cedar Homes, Seattle, 1962-75, chmn. bd., sec., 1981—. Served to capt. Can. Army, 1941-45. Recipient Can. R & D in Housing award, 1974; Excellence in Housing Design award HUD, 1981. Mem. Nat. Assn. Home Mfrs. Republican. Presbyterian. Club. Wash. Athletic. Patentee (22). Home: 1120 8th Ave #1702 Seattle WA 98101 Office: 4300 104th Pl Seattle WA 98178

LINDAUER, LAWRENCE LOUIS, educator, biologist; b. Rifle, Colo., June 2, 1939; s. Louis and Edna M. (Wurtz) L.; m. Roberta K. Wright, Dec. 22, 1963; children—Kevin L., Kelly R. B.S., Colo. State U., Ft. Collins, 1962; M.S., U. No. Colo., Greeley, 1968; Ph.D., Rutgers U., 1971. Tchr. asst. Rutgers U., New Brunswick, N.J., 1969-71; dir. Keystone (Colo.) Environ. Edn. Center, 1975-77; cons. environ. edn. Keystone Sci. Sch., 1977—; adj. asst. prof. U. Colo., Denver, 1979—; tchr. Denver Pub. Schs., 1962—; program chmn. Colo. Sci. and Health Conf., 1983; cons. environ. edn., sci. curricula. Mem. exec. bd. Bear Valley Improvement Assn., 1979-82; active Boy Scouts Am. NSF Ecology Tng. grantee, 1970-71; recipient Outstanding Tchr. award Tchrs. Award Found., 1975. Mem. Colo. Biology Tchrs. Assn. (pres. 1973-76), Nat. Assn. Biology Tchrs. (chmn. papers sect. conv. 1976), Am. Inst. Biol. Scis., Am. Assn. Sci. Suprs., Nature Conservancy. Democrat. Contbr. articles to profl. publs. Home: 3039 S Depew St Denver CO 80227 Office: 2650 Eliot St Denver CO 80211

LINDBERG, CARL ALBERT, consultant, planner, geographer; b. St. Paul, Mar. 17, 1944; s. Carl Albert and Helen Louise (Shaw) L.; m. Karen Marie Hoffman, June 29, 1968; children—Eric Carlson, Kristofer Mathew. B.G.S., U. Nebr., 1969; M.A., St. Louis U., 1974; postgrad. U. Nebr., U. Mo., Seattle Internat. U. City planner, University City, Mo., 1971-74; program mgr., Lucas County, Ohio, 1974-75; planning dir. City of Lincoln City (Oreg.), 1975-78; prin. cons. Lindberg & Assocs., Federal Way, Wash., 1978—; instr. Linn-Benton Community Coll. Bd. dirs. Lincoln County Sch. Bd., 1979-80; mem. curriculum com. U. Oreg., 1978-79; careers seminar leader, mem. Laity in Ministry Com. Lutheran Ch., 1983. Served with USAF, 1965-69. NDEA fellow, U. Nebr., 1970-71. Mem. Am. Soc. Tng. and Devel., Community Devel. Soc., Am. Planning Assn., Gamma Theta Upsilon. Club: Rotary (Lincoln City, Oreg.). Author: Beaches and Dunes Handbook for the Oregon Coast, 1978. Office: 30012 11th Pl S Federal Way WA 98003

LINDBERG, LAWRENCE AARON, school administrator; b. Seattle, Oct. 2, 1925; s. Gerald Ole and Florence Catherine (Sigrist) L.; m. Barbara Jean Whitehead, June 9, 1950; children—Arne Jay, Helen Lorraine; m. 2d, Heidi Jane Klippert, Oct. 25, 1975; stepchildren—Kristin Marie Sternkopf, Peter Vanroe Sternkopf. Student Olympic Coll., 1945-46; B.A., Central Wash. W., 1949; M.A. Columbia U., 1952; postgrad. Stanford W., 1957-64, Fresno W., 1962, U. Wash., 1975-78. Jr. high sch. tchr. Highline Sch. Dist, Seattle, 1949-51; cons. Agnes Russell Ctr., Tchrs. Coll., Columbia U., 1951-52; prin. Renton (Wash.) Sch. Dist., 1952-56; dir. personnel Oxnard (Calif.) Sch. Dist., 1958-61; supt. Weaver Union Sch. Dist., Merced, Calif., 1961-64; dir. instrn. Marin County Schs., Corte Madera, Calif., 1964-70; supt. Sausalito (Calif.) Sch. Dist., 1970-73; supt. schs. Snoqualmie Valley (Wash.) Sch. Dist., 1973—; instr. U. Calif.-Berkeley, Dominican Coll. Bd. dirs. Louise A. Boyd Marin Mus. Sci., 1962-64; chmn. Marin County delegation Gov.'s Conf. on Children, 1970. Served with U.S. Army, 1943-45. Recipient citation for patriotism Am. Legion, 1981. Mem. Wash. Assn. Sch. Adminstrs. (pres. Metro Region), Sch. Supts. Assn. King County (pres. 1982), Supts. Assn. Seamont Interscholastic League Wash. (pres. 1981), Am. Assn. Sch. Adminstrs., Phi Kappa Sigma, Phi Delta Kappa, Kappa Pi. Republican. Co-author: Water Pollution, 1972; Air Pollution, 1973; Noise Pollution 1974.

LINDBLAT, WILLIAM J., utility company executive; b. 1929. B.S. in Elec. Engring., U. Calif.-Berkeley, 1951. Project engr. Pacific Gas & Electric Co., 1954-76; v.p. engring. and constrn. Portland (Oreg.) Gen. Electric Co., 1977, pres., 1980, also dir. Served to lt. USN, 1951-54. Office: Portland Gen Electric Co Inc 121 SW Salmon St Portland OR 97201*

LINDE, HANS ARTHUR, justice Oreg. Supreme Ct.; b. Berlin, Apr. 15, 1924; s. Bruno C. and Luise (Rosenhain) L.; came to U.S., 1939, naturalized, 1943; B.A., Reed Coll., 1947; J.D., U. Calif., Berkeley, 1950; m. Helen Tucker, Aug. 13, 1945; children Lisa, David Tucker. Admitted to Oreg. bar, 1951; law clk. U.S. Supreme Ct. Justice William O. Douglas, 1950-51; atty. Office of Legal Adviser, Dept. State, 1951-53; individual practice law, Portland, Oreg., 1953-54; legis. asst. U.S. Sen. Richard L. Neuberger, 1955-58; asso. prof., prof. U. Oreg. Law Sch., 1959-76; asso. justice Oreg. Supreme Ct., Salem, 1977—; Fulbright lectr. Freiburg U., 1967-68, Hamburg U., 1975-76; cons. ACDA, Dept. Def.; mem. Adminstrv. Conf. U.S., 1962-76. Mem. Oreg. Constl. Revision Commn., 1961-62; mem. commn. on vice presdl. selection Democratic Nat. Com., Com., 1973. Served with U.S. Army, 1943-46. Mem. Am., Oreg. bar assns., Am. Law Inst. (council), Order of Coif, Phi Beta Kappa. Author: (with George Bunn) Legislative and Administrative Processes, 1976; editor-in-chief Calif. Law Rev., 1949-50. Office: Oreg Supreme Ct Salem OR 97310

LINDEBORG, RICHARD ANDREW, science editor, union official; b. Lansing, Mich., Dec. 24, 1946; s. Robert Gustav and Margaret Eloise (Isley) L.; m. Susan McCreight, Mar. 30, 1970. B.A., N.Mex. Highland U., 1968, M.S. Syracuse U., 1973; student Dartmouth Coll., 1964-65; student Syracuse u., 1974. Acting chmn. dept. communication Baker U., Baldwin, Kans., asst. prof. journalism, 1974-76; adminstrv. tech. U.S. Dept. Agr. Forest Service, Santa Fe Nat. Forest, Pecos, N.Mex., 1976-78, sci. editor, Rocky Mountain Forest and Range Expt. Sta., Fort Collins., Colo., 1979—; pres. local 1950, Nat. Fedn. Fed. Employees, 1980—; nat. v.p. Forest Service Council; instr. journalism Colo. State U., 1980, cons. speech research to pres. 1981-82. Bd. dirs. Larimer Choral Soc., vice chmn. Community Devel. Block Grant Program, Fort Collins, 1981; bd. dirs. Santa Fe County Red Cross, 1977-78; active ACLU. Served with US Army, 1968-71. Decorated Bronze Star, Army Commendation medal, Vietnam campaign medal, two oak leaf clusters. Recipient Forest Service Achievement awards, 1978, 81; John Ben Snow Research Asst., 1971-74. Mem. Soc. Profl. Journalists, Sigma Delta Chi. Democrat. Presbyterian (deacon). Club: Opera 100, Fort Collins. Contbr. articles in communications to publs. Office: 240 W Prospect St Fort Collins CO 80526

LINDEMANN, CHARLES THOMAS, JR., aviator; b. Denver, Aug. 7, 1928; s. Charles T. and Mildred E. (Westblade) L.; student Colo. Coll., 1946-48; m. Adrienne Krafft, Oct. 17, 1950; children—Patricia Ann, Michael, Paula, Janet. Aircraft pilot Western Airlines, Denver, 1957—, capt., 1967—, accident investigator, 1982; Mont. area safety coordinator, 1972-74; Denver area safety coordinator, 1974; mem. working group aero. charts, 1976—, chmn. rescue and fire com., 1982—; mem. Stapleton Internat. Airport Masters Plan Adv. Com., 1976—. Served with USN, 1948-55; Korea. Recipient Charles Pfizer Co. Award of Merit, 1980, Safe Assn. Service award, 1981. Mem. Denver Regional Council of Govts. (mem. aviation tech. adv. com. 1979—), Nat. Fire Protection Assn. (mem. com. on aircraft rescue and fire fighting 1976—), Internat. Fedn. Airline Pilots Assns. (aerodrome ground aids working group), Airline Pilots Assn. (Air Safety Outstanding Service award 1981), Beta Theta Pi. Democrat. Clubs: Masons, Hiwan Golf. Contbr. articles on aircraft accidents and safety to profl. publs. Home: 31218 Kings Valley West Conifer CO 80433 Office: Stapleton Airport Denver CO 80207

LINDEMANN, JAMES EARL, psychologist; b. Lansford, Pa., May 11, 1927; s. John Abner and Mary Elizabeth (Lesher) L.; m. Sally Jean Hart, Aug. 29, 1953; children—John, Kathryn, Ann Wilkins, Barbara. B.S. (Pa. Senatorial scholar), Pa. State U., 1950, M.S., 1951, Ph.D., 1954. Clin. psychologist, coordinator counseling psychology VA Hosp., Perry Point, Md., 1954-60; chief psychol. services VA Hosp., Salisbury, N.C., 1960-63; assoc. prof. med. psychology Oreg. Health Scis. U., Portland, 1963-72, prof. med. psychology, crippled children's div., 1972—; pvt. practice psychology, Salisbury, N.C., 1960-63, Portland, 1963—; cons. Oreg. Vocat. Rehab. Div. Served with USN, 1945-46; PTO. Recipient Service to Man award Portland Sertoma Clubs, 1971. Fellow Am. Psychol. Assn. (council rep. 1974-79, 82—, pres. div. 1982); mem. Oreg. Psychol. Assn. (pres. 1967-68, Spl. Appreciation award 1979), AAUP, Sigma Xi, Psi Chi. Club: Mazamas (Portland, Oreg.). Author: Interviewing skills, 1971; Psychological and Behavioral Aspects of Physical Disability, 1981. Home: 25371 NE Butteville Rd Aurora OR 97002 Office: Crippled Children's Div Oreg Health Scis U PO Box 574 Portland OR 97207

LINDEN, MARGARET JOANNE, librarian; b. Berkeley, Calif., d. Arthur William and Johanna Gesina (Zuydhoek) Dickie; m. Roy J. Linden, Jan. 6, 1965; A.B., Swarthmore Coll., 1960; M.L.S., U. Calif.-Berkeley, 1962. Librarian, Hans Kelsen Grad. Social Scis. Library, U. Calif.-Berkeley, 1962-66, librarian Giannini Found. Agrl. econs., 1966-70; social scis. librarian Idaho State U., 1970-71; librarian Standard Oil Co. Calif., San Francisco, 1971-74, asst. chief librarian, 1974-77, mgr. corp. library, 1978—. Mem. Spl. Libraries Assn., Calif. Library Assn. Office: 225 Bush St Room 1410 San Francisco CA 94104

LINDEN, STEPHEN JEFFREY, data processing engr.; b. Los Angeles, Feb. 20, 1956; s. William John and Joan Marlene (Robinson) L. B.S. in Bus. Adminstrn., Calif. State U.-Los Angeles, 1979; M.B.A. in Mgmt. Info. Systems, U. So. Calif., 1980; M.B.A. in Telecommunications Mgmt., Golden Gate U., 1983. Cert. data processor. Computer operator Calif. Inst. Tech., Pasadena, 1978-80; mgmt. cons. data processing Ross Systems, Inc., Los Angeles, 1980-81; data processing engr. Minicomputer Engring. Ctr., Pacific Tel. & Tel., Pasadena, 1981—. Office: Pacific Telephone & Telegraph 177 E Colorado Blvd Pasadena CA 91105

LINDENMEYER, THOMAS HOWARD, ecologist; b. Merridian, Miss., Nov. 27, 1944; s. Paul Henry and Carol Virginia (McCartney) L.; m. Kerry K. Crawford, Dec. 17, 1976; 1 dau., Anna Kristine. B.S., San Francisco State U., 1972; cert. ecologist, 1981. Sr. biologist Environ. Sci. Assocs., Foster City, Calif., 1972-81; environ. co-ordinator East Bay Regional Park Dist., Oakland, Calif., 1981—; instr. Cogswell Coll., San Francisco, 1981. Served with USN, 1965-69, Vietnam. Decorated Purple Heart. Mem. Ecol. Soc. Am., Am. Inst. Biol. Scis., Calif. Acad. Scis. Democrat. Contbr. articles in field to profl. jours. Office: 11500 Skyline Blvd Oakland CA 94619

LINDER, CLYDE AMIEL, mayor, former air traffic controller; b. Ft. Lupton, Colo., July 25, 1921; s. Henry Julius and Charlotte (McCoy) L.; m. Norma Victoria Hale, Mar. 20, 1947; children—Gordon, Kathryn, Kent, Cheryl, Rosalyn, Garth, Ramona. B.S. in Agrl. Engring., Utah State Agrl. Coll., 1950. Cert. secondary sch. tchr., Utah; cert. air traffic controller. Farmer, Colo. until 1941; surveyor, engr. Soil Conservation Service, USDA, Logan, Utah, 1956-57; high sch. tchr. Hyrum, Utah, 1951-56; air traffic controller Salt Lake City Air Route Traffic Control Ctr., 1957-79; mayor City of Millville (Utah), 1982—; instr. air traffic control, 1971-73. Mem. Millville Town Council, 1980-82; chmn. Planning and Zoning Commn. Served with USAAF, 1942-46. Mem. Am. Soc. Agrl. Engrs., Air Traffic Control Assn., NEA (life). Mormon. Author: (with Norma Linder) The Descendants of Joseph and Margaret Linder, 1972.

LINDGREN, HENRY CLAY, psychology educator, writer; b. Sacramento, Apr. 12, 1914; s. Henry August William and Bertha (von Breymann) L.; m. Fredrica Lippman, June 12, 1935; 1 dau., Loretta Zoe. A.B., Stanford U., 1934, A.M., 1935; Ph.D., 1942. Tchr. music Intermediate Sch., Hilo, Hawaii, 1935-37; sales engr. T.K. Barker Co., San Francisco, 1937-40; tchr. lang. Brown Mil. Acad., Pacific Beach, Calif., 1941-42; veterans counselor San Francisco City Schs., 1945-46; adminstr. advisement and guidance VA, San Francisco, 1946-47; prof. psychology San Francisco State U., 1947—; Fulbright lectr. in ednl. psychology Pedagogical Inst. U. Rome, 1956-57; ednl. psychology cons. UNESCO U. Sao Paulo, Brazil, 1962-63; vis. prof. psychology Am. U., Beirut, Lebanon, 1964-65, 68-70; Disting vis. prof. Am. U., Cairo, 1980. Served to lt. comdr. USNR, 1942-45. Fellow Am. Psychol. Assn., AAAS; mem. Calif. Personnel & Guidance Assn. (pres. 1955-56). Democrat. Unitarian. Author: (with R.W. Watson) Psychology of the

Child and the Adolescent, 4th edit., 1979; Educational Psychology in the Classroom, 6th edit., 1980; Great Expectations: Psychology of Money, 1980; (with J.H. Harvey) An Introduction to Social Psychology, 3d edit., 1981; Leadership, Authority and Power Sharing, 1982. Home: 120 Lansdale Ave San Francisco CA 94127 Office: Dept Psychology San Francisco State U San Francisco CA 94132

LINDHEIM, ELAINE LAVIS, psychometrician, educational evaluator; b. Los Angeles, Sept. 25, 1942; d. Salvo and Stella (Amado) Lavis; m. Richard David Lindheim, Dec. 22, 1963; children—Susan Patricia, David Howard. B.A., Stanford U., 1963; M.Ed., UCLA, 1978, Ed.D., 1983. Secondary teaching credential, Calif. Tchr., program adminstr., guidance counselor Los Angeles City Schs., 1964-75; dir. test devel. IOX Assessment Assocs., Cilver City, Calif., 1975-83; cons. testing and measurement. Mem. Am. Ednl. Research Assn., Nat. Council on Measurement in Edn., Assn. Tng. and Devel., Phi Beta Kappa.

LINDHOLM, RICHARD WADSWORTH, economist, educator; b. Mankato, Minn., June 11, 1913; s. Theodore E. and Elizabeth S. (Swanson) L.; B.A., Gustavus Adolphus Coll., 1935; M.A., U. Minn., 1938; Ph.D., U. Tex., 1942; m. Mary M. Trunko, Sept. 11, 1948; 1 son, Richard Theodore. Tchr. Souris (N.D.) Jr. High Sch., 1935, Worthington (Minn.) High Sch., 1938-39; mem. Minn. Income Study, 1939-40; instr. Coll. St. Thomas, 1940-41, U. Tex., 1941-42; asst. prof. Tex. A&M Coll., 1942, Ohio State U., 1946-48; asso. prof. Mich. State U., 1948-50, prof., 1950-58; dean, Coll. Bus. Adminstrn., U. Oreg., 1958-67, founding dean Grad. Sch. Mgmt. and Bus., 1967-71, prof. finance, 1971—, dean emeritus, 1979—; fiscal economist Fed. Res. Bd., 1950-51, 64-65; econ. cons. 1st Nat. Bank Oreg., 1961-69; mem. Mich. Employment Com., 1954; sr. tax adviser, cons. econ. devel. ICA, Saigon, Viet-Nam, 1955-57; bus. tax cons. Mich. Legislature tax study, 1958; coordinator econ. adv. group in Korea, 1959-61; nat. com. Taxation, Resources and Econ. Devel.; tax com. to increase exports U.S. Dept. Commerce, 1965-74, mem. Ways and Means Com., 1975, 79; mem. Lincoln Inst. Land Policy, 1976. Chmn. Chinju-Eugene Lister City Com., 1961. Tax cons. to Gov. of Oreg., 1970-72; adviser Dept. State, 1972-75. Served from pvt. to capt., AUS, 1942-45; ETO. Decorated 5 battle stars. Fulbright lectr., Pakistan, 1952. Mem. Am. Econ. Assn., Nat. Tax Assn. (bd. dirs.), Am. Finance Assn., Pi Beta Delta, Beta Gamma Sigma (research scholar 1975-76), Pi Gamma Mu. Author: The Corporate Franchise as the Basis of Taxation, 1944; Taxation in Ohio, 1946; Public Finance of Air Transportation, 1948; Introduction to Fiscal Policy, 2d edit., 1955; (with others) Public Finance and Fiscal Policy, 2d edit., 1958; Money and Banking, 3d edit., 1969; Money and Finance, 1951; Taxation of the Trucking Industry, 1951; Principles of Money and Banking, 1954; Money and Banking and Economic Development in Free Viet-Nam, 1957; (sr. author) Our American Economy, 1958, 4th edit., 1969: (with others) The Tax System of Michigan with Recommendations, 1958; Economic Development Policy, 1964; (with others) A Description and Analysis of Oregon's Fiscal System, 1971; Taxation of Timber Resources, 1973; New Tax Directions for the United States, 1975; Value Added Tax and Other Tax Reforms, 1976; Money Management and Institutions, 1978; Financing and Managing State and Local Government, 1979; Economics of VAT, 1980; editor, contbr. Viet-Nam—The First Five Years, 1959; Property Taxation—U.S.A., 1967; Property Taxation and the Finance of Education, 1974; Property Tax Reform, 1977; Henry George and Sun Yat-Sen, 1977; Land Value Taxation, 1982. Contbr. articles to jours. in field. Home: 2520 Fairmount Blvd Eugene OR 97403

LINDLEY, FRANCIS HAYNES, lawyer; b. Los Angeles, May 25, 1899; s. Walter and Florence (Haynes) L.; student Williams Coll., 1916-17; A.B., Harvard U., 1922; student U. So. Calif. Law Sch., 1923-26; LL.D., Claremont Grad. Sch.; m. Grace N. McCanne, Sept. 6, 1930; children—Francis Haynes, Walter. Admitted to Calif. bar, 1926, since practiced in Los Angeles; partner Chapman, Frazer, Lindey & Young, 1953-64; former dir. Safeco Co., Great Basins Petroleum Co., O. T. Johnson Corp., Compania Contratists de Costa Rica, Bolsa Corps.; dep. city atty. Los Angeles, 1927-36, asst. city atty., 1936-42, 45-46. Pres., Town Hall, 1952; dir. Christmas Seal Fund, 1950-52; former bd. dirs. Los Angeles Children's Bur.; mem. U.S. Regional Loyalty Bd., 1949-53; mem. Los Angeles Com. Fgn. Relations, Los Angeles Bd. Power and Water Commrs., 1965-67; v.p., trustee Hosp. Good Samaritan Med. Center; pres. Haynes Found., 1937-77, chmn. bd. trustees, 1977—; past pres. Friends Claremont Colls.; hon. trustee Claremont Univ. Center, Whittier Coll., Honnold Library Soc. of Claremont Colls.; bd. dirs., Hosp. Council So. Calif., 1970-76, English Speaking Union Los Angeles br. Mem. Am. Bar Assn. (chmn. sect. municipal law 1951-52), Los Angeles Bar Assn., Phi Delta Phi. Republican. Clubs: California, Lincoln, Men's Garden (Los Angeles); Harvard (So. Calif.). Home: 639 S June St Los Angeles CA 90005 Office: 530 W 6th St Los Angeles CA 90014

LINDLY, CHARLES ALBERT, educational adminstration educator; b. Anselmo, Nebr., Feb. 12, 1930; s. James Lewis and Ethel (Williams) L.; m. Marilyn Marie Eck, Aug. 10, 1952; children—Stephen, Catherine, Elizabeth, Daniel. B.A., Kearney State Coll., 1952; M.A., U. No. Colo., 1957, Ed.D., 1961. Jr. high tchr., Minden, Nebr., 1953; high sch. tchr., coach, Hemingford, Nebr., 1954-58; high sch. prin., Berthoud, Colo., 1959-60; dir. secondary edn., asst. supt., supt. schs., Rapid City, S.D., 1961-75; prof. ednl. adminstrn. U. Wyo., Laramie, 1975—; state dir. North Central Assn., 1975-83. Mem. adv. bd. Salvation Army; active Big Bros. Served with USNR, 1950-59. Recipient Outstanding Grad. award Kearney State Coll., 1964; Service award Rapid City C. of C., 1975; Spl. Recognition to Alumni award U. No. Colo., 1980; Dedicated Service award Salvation Army, 1981. Mem. Am. Assn. Sch. Adminstrs., Nat. Assn. Secondary Sch. Prins., Assn. Supervision and Curriculum Devel. Presbyterian. Club: Rotary (Laramie). Home: 1067 Colina Dr Laramie WY 82070 Office: U Wyo Laramie WY 82071

LINDMAN, ELISABETH JACOBSEN (LISSE J WILSON), interior designer, consultant; b. Nyborg, Denmark, June 18, 1911; came to U.S., 1918, naturalized, 1932; d. Hans Christian and Ellen Maria Elisabeth La Cour (Siegumfeldt) Jacobsen; m. Guy Childers Wilson, June 18, 1936 (dec.); children—Richard Guy, Ellen Celia Wilson Ekedal; m. 2d, Bertram Herman Lindman, Aug. 10, 1974. B.A., U. Wash., 1934; student Art Ctr. Sch., Los Angeles, 1934; postgrad. U. Calif.-Riverside, 1970. Interior designer Robinson's, Los Angeles, 1934, Hildebrandt Interiors, Hollywood, Calif., 1935; sec., treas. Wilson Equipment Co., Redlands and Colton, Calif., 1954-66; interior designer Gibboney Interiors, Redlands, 1969, Robinson's, Santa Barbara, 1970; interior designer and originator interior design dept. Haywards, Santa Barbara, Calif., 1970; mem. adv. com. Santa Barbara City Coll.; career adviser U. Calif.-Santa Barbara. Bd. dirs. Trust for Hist. Preservation, Santa Barbara; chmn. scholarship com. Am. Scandinavian Found., Santa Barbara. Mem. Am. Soc. Interior Designers. Club: Ret. Officers Santa Barbara. Office: Haywards 1025 Santa Barbara St Santa Barbara CA 93101

LINDO, BERNICE ZINNET, educational consultant, public speaker; b. Bklyn., Oct. 21, 1937; d. Louis and Dora (Stackel) Richman; m. Allen Gross, June 14, 1959 (div.); m. 2d, George Lindo, Aug. 27, 1969; 1 dau., Lisa Rachel; m. 3d, Jess Samuels, July 16, 1976 (dec.). B.A. cum laude in Edn., Bklyn. Coll., 1959; M.A. with honors in Reading, Calif. State U.-Los Angeles, 1971; postgrad. U. Calif.-Riverside, 1973-75; Ph.D. in Psychology, U.S. Internat. U., San Diego, 1977. Cert. tchr., N.Y., Conn., Calif., Israel. Various teaching positions, 1959-64; Miller-Unruh reading specialist Lawndale (Calif.) Unified Schs., 1967-69; instr. English, reading, Tel Aviv, 1969-70; Miller-Unruh reading specialist Compton (Calif.) Unified Schs., 1970-74; instr. reading lab (evening session) Compton Jr. Coll., 1971-74; instr. edn. Pepperdine U., Los Angeles, 1972-78; instr. dept. humanities UCLA, 1974—; tng. and devel. trainer assertive discipline courses. Ednl. TV, Canter & Assocs., 1978-81, Calif. State U.-Fullerton, 1978-79, U. La Verne (Calif.), 1979-81, U. Hawaii, 1980—; instr. dept. arts mgmt. tng. bus. health and indsl. corps., UCLA, 1980—; instr. nationwide presentations assertiveness tng. Schaffer Publs., Inc., Torrance, Calif., 1982—; program coordinator dept. humanities, Learning Resources Ctr., extension div., UCLA, 1974-76; regional dir. Calif. Community Colls. Tutorial Assn., 1977-78; adminstrv. dir. Learning Resources Ctr., Glendale (Calif.) Coll., 1976-78; pres., chmn. bd. Lindo Ednl. Corp., Beverly Hills, 1978—; ednl. cons.; bd. advisors Cert. Planners Am. Mem. Nat. Assn. Female Execs., Reading Specialists Calif. (life). Mem. Sci. of Mind Ch. Club: Millionaire's (Brentwood, Calif.). Author: Instant Phonics Kit, 1971; Black Ghetto Dialect Textbook, 1972; Instant Record Keeper for Individualized Reading, 1973; Instant Contracts for Prescriptive Teaching, 1973; The Assertive Parent Kit, 1981, Hosted Impact Radio Show, 1976. Office: Box 5090 Beverly Hills CA 90210

LINDQUIST, JUDITH ANN, hospital administrator, free-lance writer; b. Brockton, Mass., Nov. 12, 1947; d. Gordon Robert and Ellen Elsie (Carlson) Lindquist; m. Odell Handcox, Apr. 24, 1969; m. Lawrence Sena, Sept. 26, 1981. Student Wheaton Coll., 1965-67; B.A. magna cum laude in Philosophy, U. Mich., 1969; M.A. in Far Eastern Studies, Sophia U., Tokyo, 1975. Editor, Pacific Stars & Stripes, Tokyo, 1975-77; promotion mgr. Los Angeles Times, 1978-82; assoc. dir. community relations Torrance (Calif.) Meml. Hosp. Med. Ctr., 1982—; cons. Shueisha Pub. Co. Mem. Pub. Relations Soc., Am., NOW. Democrat. Unitarian. Contbr. feature articles to Japan Times, Home Mag., popular mags.

LINDSAY, CHARMAINE CAROL, educator; b. Rock Springs, Wyo., Dec. 13, 1929; d. Oscar Wayne and Irene Ilah (Wakkila) Matson; m. Roy L. Lindsay, Aug. 21, 1949; children—Gregory M., Alison C., Wade W., Lisa A. Student, Linfield Coll., 1947-50; B.A., Portland State Coll., 1964; M.S.T., Portland State U., 1973. Lang. arts tchr., dept. chmn., tchr. evaluator Tigard (Oreg.) Sr. High Sch., 1968—, dept. chmn., tchr. evaluator, 1972—, tchr. lang. arts, 1968—. Chmn., Lloyd Johnson Meml. Scholarship Com., 1982—; alumni rep. Linfield Coll. Bd. Trustees, 1973-79. Mem. NEA, Assn. Supervision and Curriculum Devel., Nat. Council Tchrs. English, Oreg. Council Tchrs. English, Oreg. Edn. Assn., Tigard Edn. Assn., Delta Kappa Gamma. Democrat. Methodist. Office: 9000 SW Durham Rd Tigard OR

LINDSAY, J. ARTHUR, industrial relations executive; b. Okemah, Okla., Mar. 19, 1930; s. Frank E. and Margaret E. (Barnes) L.; m. Katherine Sherman, Dec. 16, 1949 (div. 1960); children—Karen K., Brian G.; m. 2d, Willa B. Flowers, July 28, 1962; 1 son, Darrin C. B.B.A., U. Ga., 1955; M.B.A., San Francisco State U., 1968. Personnel mgr. Firemans Fund Ins. Co., Oakland, Calif., 1960-68, Argonaut Ins. Co., San Francisco, 1970-73; v.p. indsl. relations Soule' Steel Co., San Francisco, 1974-78; pres. Federated Employers, San Francisco, 1979—, Lindsay Oil Properties-Art Realty & Investments, Alameda, Calif., 1968—; gen. ptnr. Arjay Well Servicing Co., Cherryville, Kans., 1980—. Served to sgt. U.S. Army, 1948-52. Mem. Am. Soc. for Personnel Adminstrn., Nat. Soc. Pub. Accts., Nat. Assn. Real Estate Brokers, Delta Mu Delta. Club: San Francisco Commonwealth. Writer, editor, pub. newsletters and reference materials in field. Home: 1166 Otis Dr Alameda CA 94501 Office: Federated Employers 582 Market St Suite 412 San Francisco CA 94104

LINDSAY, LAURENCE DUANE, foods co. exec.; b. Heber City, Utah, June 14, 1935; s. Ray and Grace Virginia (Murdock) L.; B.S., Brigham Young U., 1971; m. Shirley Ann Lee, Aug. 2, 1957; 1 son, Stanley Duane. Mem. new products devel. staff Haig Berberian Inc., Modesto, Calif., 1966-68, mgr. quality assurance, 1974-80, with Funsten Nut div., 1977—; mgr. quality assurance S&W Tree Nuts, Inc. div. S&W Fine Foods, 1980-81; dir. quality assurance research and devel. Sun-Diamond Growers Calif., 1981—; supr. Wilkinson Center, Brigham Young U., Provo, Utah, 1969-71; asst. supr., food div. Salt Lake City-County Health Dept., 1971-74. Com. chmn. scout troop Boy Scouts Am. Served with anti-aircraft U.S. Army, 1954-56. Registered sanitarian. Mem. Inst. Food Technologists, Am. Soc. for Microbiology, Dried Fruit Assn. (sci. adv. bd.). Republican. Mormon. Home: 2517 Killarney Way Modesto CA 95355

LINDSEY, JACK B., business exec.; b. Taft, Calif., Nov. 20, 1925; student Fresno State Coll., 1943-44; B.Applied Sci. in Elec. Engring., U. Calif., at Berkeley, 1946; M.B.A., Stanford U., 1950; m. Jean Catherine O'Brien, Jan. 24, 1948 (dec. Mar. 1983); children—Daniel Lee, David Allan. Mktg. mgr. Carnation Co., Los Angeles, 1950-59; asst. to pres. Microdot, Inc., electronics, South Pasadena, Calif., 1959-61; pres. Lindsey-Westwood Assos., mgmt. cons., Los Angeles, 1961-64; v.p. mktg. Early Calif. Foods, Inc., Los Angeles, 1964-69, pres., 1971-74; v.p. Early Calif. Industries, Inc., Los Angeles, 1964-74; dir., 1964-75; pres., pub. Clarke Pub. Co., Portland, 1969-71; pres., chief exec. officer Sun Harbor Industries, San Diego, 1974-77, Point Adams Packing Co. (Oreg.), 1974-75, Sun Harbor-Caribe, Inc., P.R., 1974-77; chmn. bd., chief exec. officer Lindsey-Westwood Assocs., mgmt. cons., 1977—; chmn. Sun Belt Energy Corp., Sun Belt Mgmt. Service, Inc. Legis. sec. to gov. of Calif., 1966-67; chmn. Favorite Son Com., 1968; alt. del. Republican Nat. Conv., 1968; candidate for Congress, 1969; mem. President's Round Table. Served to lt. (j.g.) USNR, 1943-47. San Francisco Advt. Club grantee, 1948. Mem. IEEE, Order of Golden Bear, Pres.'s Assn., Stanford Alumni Assn., Gamma Delta. Christian Scientist. Club: San Diego Yacht. Home: 1594 Hacienda Dr El Cajon CA 92020

LINDSEY, JAMES FRANCIS, educator; b. San Francisco, Feb. 28, 1923; s. Lawrence S. and May I (Shintaffer) L.; m. Catherine Elizabeth Penn, Aug. 10, 1945; children—Mary Wood, Barbara Eding, Margaret Koster, Patricia, Terry. B.A., San Francisco State U., 1945, M.A., 1952; Ed.D., U. Calif.-Berkeley, 1966. Teaching, administrv. credentials, Calif. Tchr. pub. schs., Calif., 1945-50; prin. elem. schs., Hopland, Calif., 1950-54, Marysville, Calif., 1954-59, Citrus Heights, Calif., 1959-66; prof. edn. Calif. State U.-Chico, 1966—; vis. prof. Christchurch Tchrs. Coll., N.Z., 1980-81, St. Patrick's Coll., Dublin, 1983-84. Mem. AAUP, Internat. Reading Assn., Assn. Supervision and Curriculum Devel., Phi Delta Kappa. Republican. Roman Catholic. Club: Butte Creek Country. Contbr. articles to profl. jours. Home: 24 Pebblewood Pines Chico CA 95926 Office: Edn Dept Calif State U Chico CA 95929

LINDSEY, WILLIAM FUSSELL, newspaper association executive; b. Rocky Mount, N.C., Mar. 22, 1923; s. Robert Penn and Wallolah (Fussell) L.; B.A. Westminster Coll., 1948; B.S., U. Colo., 1950; m. Gwen R. Caverly, Dec. 28, 1948; children—Charles Penn, Rebecca Ruth. Jr. acct. Redecker, Stanley & Alhberg, Denver, 1950-52; with Colo. Press Service, Denver, 1952-64; sec.-mgr. Colo. Press Assn., Denver, 1964—; Served with USAAF, World War II. Decorated D.F.C., Air medal with six oak leaf clusters. Mem. Newspaper Assn. Mgrs. (pres. 1978), Nat. Newspaper Assn. (dir. 1978), Nat. Editorial Assn., Soc. Profl. Journalists, Advt. Club Denver, Colo. C. of C., Denver Press Club, Delta Tau Delta. Home: 405 Baseline at Gregory Canyon Boulder CO 80302 Office: Press Bldg 1336 Glenarm Pl Denver CO 80204

LINDSTEDT-SIVA, KAREN JUNE, marine biologist, oil company executive; b. Mpls., Sept. 24, 1941; d. Stanley L. and Lila (Mills) Lindstedt; m. Ernest Howard Siva, Dec. 20, 1969. Student U. Calif.-Santa Barbara, 1959-60, U. Calif.-Davis, 1960-62; B.A., U. So. Calif., 1963, M.S., 1967, Ph.D., 1971. Asst. coordinator Office Sea Grant Programs, U. So. Calif., 1971; environ. specialist So. Calif. Edison Co., Rosemead, 1971-72; asst. prof. biology Calif. Luth. Coll., 1972-73; sci. advisor Atlantic Richfield Co., Los Angeles, 1973-77, sr. sci. advisor, 1977-81, mgr. environ. scis., 1981—. Trustee, Bermuda Biol. Sta. for Research. Recipient Calif. Mus. Sci. and Industry Achievement award, 1976; research grantee. Mem. Soc. Petroleum Industry Biologists (pres. 1976-80), AAAS, Marine Tech. Soc., Phi Beta Kappa, Sigma Xi, Phi Kappa Phi. Clubs: Conejo Valley Audubon Soc., Calif. Native Plant Soc. Contbr. articles to sci. jours. Office: 515 S Flower St Los Angeles CA 90071

LINDSTROM, ANITA INGER, psychologist; b. Ranea, Sweden, May 7, 1940; came to U.S., 1972; d. Helge Eugene and Alice (Gunborg) Broms; B.Ed., U. Lulea, 1962; M. Ednl. Psychology, U. Stockholm, 1972; Ph.D. in Counseling Psychology, Profl. Sch. for Humanistic Studies, San Diego, 1982. Tchr. various pub. schs., Sweden, 1962-71; resource tchr. Taby Schs., Ellagard, Sweden, 1965-69, ednl. program designer, 1969-71; program specialist for developmental disabilities Bd. Edn., Stockholm, 1971; sch. psychologist Taby Sch., 1972; exchange visitor UCLA Neuropsychiat. Inst., 1972-73; psychologist Children's Hosp. Regional Center, Los Angeles, 1973-75, St. John's Hosp., Kennedy Regional Center, Santa Monica, Calif., 1974-75, N. Los Angeles County Regional Center, Van Nuys, Calif., 1975-77, Exceptional Children's Found., Los Angeles, 1975-78; pvt. practice psychology, marriage, family and child counselor, Newhall, Calif., 1978—; cons. in field. King Gustav VI Found. grantee, 1972. Mem. Am. Psychol. Assn., Calif. Psychol. Assn., Calif. Soc. for Hypnosis in Family Counseling, Calif. Assn. for Marriage, Family and Child Therapists, Newhall C. of C. Home: 17349 Boswell Pl Granada Hills CA 91344 Office: 23560 Lyons Ave Suite 205 Newhall CA 91321

LINDSTROM, FREDERICK BURGESS, sociologist, educator; b. Palmer, Mass., June 8, 1915; s. Frederick Gerald and Ruth Hazel (Burgess) L.; m. Laura Johnson, Sept. 9, 1946; children—Naomi, Frederick J., Isaac. A.B., U. Chgo., 1938, A.M., 1941, Ph.D., 1950. Instr. sociology U. Mass., Amherst, 1951-53; asst. prof. Ariz. State U., Tempe, 1953-59, assoc. prof., 1959-66, prof., 1966—, assoc. chmn. dept., 1981—. Served with U.S. Army, 1943-46. Mem. Am. Sociol. Assn., Population Assn. Am. Pacific Sociol. Assn., Western Social Sci. Assn., AAUP, Visual Sociol. Assn. Contbr. articles to profl. jours. Home: 1024 Maple Ave Tempe AZ 85281 Office: Department Sociology Arizona State University Tempe AZ 85287

LINDSTROM-TITUS, KAREN MAE, home economics educator/administrator; b. Covina, Calif., May 29, 1940; d. Fritz and Frances Irene (Hayden) Lindstrom; m. Richard Gaige Titus, Feb. 9, 1979. A.A. in Home Econs., Fullerton Coll., 1960; B.A. in Home Econs., U. Calif.-Santa Barbara, 1962; M.A. in Textiles, San Jose State Coll., 1969. Home econs. tchr. Schurr Jr. High Sch., 1962-64; home economist Dept. Water and Power Anaheim (Calif.), 1964-70; home econs. tchr. Anaheim High Sch., 1964-66; home econs. prof. Fullerton (Calif.) Coll., 1966-73, div. chmn., 1973—; bridal cons., editor consumer publ. Mem. Commn. Tchr. Prep. and Licensing; mem. adv. com. J.C. Penney; mem. child care bd. Fullerton Coll.; fin sec. Christian Women's Assn.; mem. home econs. edn. adv. com. Calif. State U.-Long Beach; mem. So. Calif. Council Against Health Fraud; mem. Calif. Community Coll. Occupational Program Evaluation System; active 4-H. Recipient Martha Schope Meml. award Martha Schope Found., 1960; Kiwanis scholar, 1960. Mem. Orange County Home Econs. Assn. (pres. chpt.), Calif. Home Econs. Assn., Am. Home Econs. Assn., Internat. Fedn. Home Econs., Calif. Vocat. Assn., Assn. Calif. Community Coll. Adminstrs., Western Region Coll. Tchrs. Home Mgmt. and Family Econs. Fullerton Coll. Speakers Bur., Faculty Women's Assn. (past pres.), Am. Assn. Women in Community and Jr. Colls. Club: Job's Daughters. Home: 17437 Olive Tree Circle Yorba Linda CA 92686 Office: Fullerton Coll 321 E Chapman Ave Suite 1005 Fullerton CA 92634

LINDVIG, ELISE KAY, school psychologist; b. Sidney, Mont., Feb. 10, 1952; d. William F. and Katheryn E. (Taylor) L. B.A. in Psychology with honors, U. Mont., 1974, sch. psychology cert., 1982; M.S. in Clin. Psychology with high honors, U. Idaho, 1979, postgrad., 1983—. Ins. sec. John W. Strizich, M.D., Helena, Mont., 1970-71; work-study clk., Forestry Service, U. Mont., 1971-72; lab. technician Primate Lab., U. Mont., 1972-74; asso. coordinator Mont. Dept. Community Affairs, Glendive, 1974-75; grad. teaching asst. dept. psychology U. Idaho, 1975-77; various positions including farm labor, parts sales, and music areas, 1977-79; sch. psychologist Dist. #3, Hamilton, Mont., 1979—; asst. mgr. Moscow (Idaho) Moose Lodge, 1975-77. Vol. worker with handicapped, charitable orgns., animals, vocatl and instrumental music. Mem. Am. Psychol. Assn. (assoc.), Mont. Assn. Sch. Psychologists. Republican. Roman Catholic. Clubs: Moose Aux., Eagles' Aux. Author: Nutrition and Mental Health, 1979; Grade Retention, 1982; contbr. articles to profl. jours. Home: PO Box 1358 Hamilton MT 59840

LINEHAN, KATHLEEN SCHOONMAKER, psychologist; b. Ellenville, N.Y., Apr. 18, 1951; d. Clifford Benjamin and Grace (Marek) Schoonmaker; m. Steven Robert Linehan, Sept. 22, 1973; 1 dau., Sara Bryn. B.S., St. Lawrence U., 1972; M.S., Memphis State U., 1976, Ph.D., 1979. Lic. psychologist, Calif. Psychology intern VA Med. Ctr. and Stanford U., Palo Alto, Calif., 1979-80; clin. psychologist Stress and Pain Control Med. Ctr., Palo Alto, 1981—. Mem. Am. Psychol. Assn., Phi Beta Kappa, Sigma Xi. Contbr. articles to profl. jours. Home: 2721 Midtown Ct Apt 210 Palo Alto CA 94303 Office: 525 University Ave Suite 910 Palo Alto CA 94301

LINES, PAUL ANDERSON, oral surgeon; b. Phoenix; s. Ruskin R. and Jeana Priscilla (Allred) L.; D.D.S., Loma Linda U., 1969; M.S. in Orthodontics, Washington U., St. Louis, 1971; m. Cynthia Maerz, Sept. 19, 1973; children—James Wyatt, Trevor William, Justin Heath. Resident oral surgery U. Nurnberg, Erlangen, W.Ger., 1973-74, Kantonsspital Luzern (Switzerland), 1972-73; U. Mo., Kansas City, 1974-76; practice dentistry specializing in oral and maxillofacial surgery, Tempe, Ariz.; mem. faculty (part-time) dept. oral and maxillofacial surgery U. Mo., Kansas City, from 1976, now asst. prof. (part-time); oral surgeon Univ. Med. Center, U. Ariz. Tempe. Cert. oral surgery Kanton Hosp., Lucerne, Switzerland. Fellow Am. Assn. Oral and Maxillofacial Surgeons; mem. ADA, Am. Assn. Orthodontics, Central Ariz. Dental Soc., Pacific Coast Soc. Orthodontics, Ariz. State Dental Assn. Mormon. Contbr. articles to profl. jours. Home: 223 E Concorda Tempe AZ 85282 Office: 2415 S Rural Rd Suite B Tempe AZ 85282

LINGLE, CHARLES PHILIP, aerospace engr.; b. Springfield, Mo., Oct. 21, 1931; s. Charles Philip and Helen Elizabeth (Ryan) L.; B.S. in Aero. Engring., M.I.T., 1957; M.B.A., Calif. State U., 1974; m. Lenore Ruth Anderson, June 12, 1954; children—Charles Phillip, Victoria Lenore. System engr. Consol. Systems Corp., Monrovia, Calif., 1961-63; mem. tech. staff Rockwell Internat., Downey and Seal Beach, Calif., 1963-75; engring. mgr. Swedlow Inc., Garden Grove, Calif., 1977-79; mem. tech. staff Jet Propulsion Lab., Calif. Inst. Tech., Pasadena, 1979-82, Northrop Electronics, Hawthorne, Calif., 1982—. Served with USAF, 1951-52. Contbr. articles to profl. jours. Office: 3740/N3 2301 W 120th St Hawthorne CA 90250

LINHART, YAN BOHUMIL, biologist, educator; b. Prague, Czechoslovakia, Oct. 8, 1939; m. Bohumil and Olga (Kabesova) L.; m. Muriel Valesca, Aug. 6, 1966; 1 son, Nikolas Bohumil. B.S., Rutgers U., 1961; M.F., Yale U., 1963; Ph.D., U. Calif.-Berkeley, 1966. Asst. prof. U. Colo., Boulder, 1971-77, assoc. prof., 1978-82, prof., 1983—; cons. Denver Water Bd., Colo. Energy Research Inst. Rutgers U. Fgn. Student scholar, 1957-61; C.B. Wood scholar, 1961-62, Yale U. fellow, 1962-63; U. Colo. Faculty fellow, 1983-84; NSF grantee 1975-78, 78-80, 81-84. Mem. AAAS, Assn. Tropical Biology, Botanical Soc. Am., Soc. Study Evolution, Soc. Am. Foresters, Am. Soc. Naturalists. Author numerous articles and book chpts. for profl. publs. Office: Dept Biology U Colo Boulder CO 80309

LINKE, CURTIS GLENN, manufacturing executive; b. Columbus, Ind., Nov. 17, 1942; s. Glenn S. and Emma (Reinking) L.; m. Carol J. Eynon, Jan. 4, 1964; children—Tod, Natalie. B.S. in Bus. and Journalism, Ind. U., 1964. Public relations supr. Procter & Gamble, Cin., 1965-69; accounts supr. Ruder & Finn, Chgo., 1969-70; asst. pub. relations dept. mgr. Container Corp. Am., Chgo., 1970-74; dir. pub. affairs Consol. Foods, Chgo., 1974-78; v.p. corp. relations Manville Corp., Denver, 1978—. Bd. dirs. Jr. Achievement. Mem. Jefferson County Hist. Soc. (dir.), Leadership Denver, Denver C. of C., Pub. Relations Soc. Am. (accredited, Silver anvil award 1979, 83), Nat. Investor Relations Inst. Lutheran. Club: Hiwan Golf (Evergreen, Colo.). Office: Ken-Caryl Ranch PO Box 5108 Denver CO 80217

LINN, BRIAN JAMES, lawyer; b. Seattle, July 8, 1947; s. Bruce Hugh and Jeanne De V. (Weidman) L.; m. Renee Diane Mousley; children—Kelly, Kareem, Kari. B.A. in Econs., U. Wash., 1972; J.D., Gonzaga Sch. Law, 1975. Bar: Wash. 1975. Mng. atty. Legal Services for Northwestern Pa., Franklin, 1975-76; staff atty. The Nat. Ctr. for Law and the Handicapped, U. Notre Dame Law Sch., South Bend, Ind., 1976-78; sole practice, Seattle, 1978—; lectr. Seattle U. Chmn. civil and legal rights subcom. Gov.'s Com. on Employment of the Handicapped; mem. Wash. State Devel. Disabilities Planning Council, 1980—; trustee Community Service Ctr. for the Deaf and Hard of Hearing, Seattle, 1982—. Served with U.S. Army, 1967-69; Vietnam. Mem. Wash. State Bar Assn., Washington State Trial Lawyers Assn., Omicron Delta Epsilon. Democrat. Methodist. Hon. editor DePaul Law Rev., 1978; contbr. articles to profl. jours. Home: 21211 21st Ave S Seattle WA 98188 Office: Brian Linn 245 SW 152d St Seattle WA 98166

LINN, STUART MICHAEL, biochemist; b. Chgo., Dec. 16, 1940; s. Maurice S. and Pauline Linn.; children—Matthew S., Allison D., Megan S. B.S. with honors in Chemistry, Calif. Inst. Tech., 1962; Ph.D. in Biochemistry, Stanford U., 1967. Asst. prof. dept. biochemistry U. Calif.-Berkeley, 1968-72, assoc. prof., 1972-75, prof., 1975—. Helen Hay Whitney fellow, 1966-68; John Simon Guggenheim fellow, 1974-75. Mem. Am. Soc. Biol. Chemists, Am. Soc. Microbiologists, AAAS. Mem. editorial bd. Nucleic Acids Research, 1974—, Jour. Biol. Chemistry, 1975—; contbr. articles to profl. jours. Office: Dept Biochemistry U Calif Berkeley CA 94720

LINSDAY, RICHARD H., insurance agent; b. Oak Park, Ill., Oct. 30, 1947; s. Herbert Robert and Margaret Deliah (Boyer) L.; B.S. in Bus., No. Ill. U., DeKalb, 1969; C.L.U., 1977; m. Laura Jane Brink, June 16, 1979. Brokerage rep., then mgr. Aetna Life Ins. Co., Los Angeles, 1972-78; brokerage mgr. Mfrs. Life Ins. Co., Los Angeles, 1978—, pres. Linsday Fin. Ins. Services, Inc. (formerly Richard H. Linsday & Assocs., Ltd.), Los Angeles, 1975—; tchr. adult edn. estate planning. Coordinator, W. Los Angeles Spl. Olympics, 1978-79. Served with USMCR, 1969-72; Vietnam. Recipient cert. public service Joseph Kennedy Found., 1979. Mem. Nat. Assn. Life Underwriters (v.p. W. Los Angeles chpt. 1980, pres. 1982-83, Philip Grosser Meml. award 1982), Am. Soc. C.L.U.s, Wilshire Estate Planning Council (v.p. 1981, pres. 1982-83), Calif. Assn. Life Underwriters (trustee region 6), Cert. Fin. Planners Assn. Methodist. Author articles in field. Home: 5540 Vista Canada Pl La Canada CA 91011 Office: 3731 Wilshire Blvd Los Angeles CA 90010

LINSKY, RONALD BENJAMIN, natural resources consultant; b. Los Angeles, June 16, 1934; s. Walter Frank and Helen Pearl (Goodlin) L.; B.S., U. So. Calif., 1962, M.S., 1962; m. Patricia L. Shaffer; children—Bryan Howard, Todd Eric. Tchr., Huntington Beach (Calif.) Union High Sch. Dist., 1962-67; dir. Floating Lab. program Orange County Dept. Edn., 1967-70; dir. Sea Grant Instl. program U. So. Calif., Los Angeles, 1970-75; dir. Sea Grant Coll. program U. Hawaii, Honolulu, 1975-77, assoc. dean marine programs, 1975-77; head aquaculture research and devel. Coll. Tropical Agr., U. Hawaii, 1977-78; owner Ron Linsky and Assocs., marine and coastal resources devel. and mgmt.; marine cons., 1978—; chief tech. adviser UN Devel. Program; chief exec. officer Inst. Marine Affairs, Chaguaramas, Trinidad and Tobago, W.I., 1980-82; mem. Santa Ana region Calif. Water Quality Bd., 1970-75; mem. sci. and statis. com. Western Regional Fish Mgmt. Council, 1977; adv. council Nat. Ocean Industry Assn.; cons. UN Devel. Programme; mem. Newport Beach Environ. Quality Citizens Adv. Com. Served with U.S. Army, 1954-56. Recipient Premi Tridentd' Ora award Italian Govt., 1971. Mem. Marine Tech. Soc., Nat. Marine Educators Assn. (hon.), Newport Harbor Area C. of C. Editorial bd. Coastal Zone Mgmt. Jour., 1975-80, Marine Edn. Jour., 1976-80. Address: PO Box 1764 Newport Beach CA 92663

LINTON, FREDERICK MELVIN, paper company executive; b. Stanton, Mich., Aug. 6, 1932; s. Clarence and Clelia (Tow) L.; m. Peggy Jensen, May 27, 1954; children—Michael, Melinda, Meg. B.A., Mich. State U., 1959, M.A., 1960. Tchr., San Diego, 1960-66; asst. to pres. Am. Cement, Los Angeles, 1968-69; cons. Peat Marwick & Mitchell, Los Angeles, 1968-69; sr. v.p. Shareholders Capital Corp., Los Angeles, 1970-71; pres., chief exec. officer Boyden Assocs., Inc., N.Y.C., 1971-74; founder, pres. Delta Group, Inc., Newport Beach, Calif., 1974—; pres. Universal Paper Goods, Los Angeles, 1983—. Bd. dirs. Indsl. League Orange County, Good Will Industries; former pres. bd. govs. Econ. Literacy Council Calif. Served with USAF, 1954-59. Recipient Bus. and Industry award Calif. Mus. Sci. and Industry, 1974; Bus. Achievement award Calif. Assembly, 1974; Community Service to U. Calif.-Irvine, Calif. Assembly and U. Calif.-Irvine Alumni, 1978. Republican. Episcopalian. Clubs: Internat., Balboa Bay, UCI. Home: 2706 Vista Umbrosa Newport Beach CA 92660 Office: 369 San Miguel Dr Suite 180 Newport Beach CA 92660 also 7171 Telegraph Los Angeles CA 90040

LINTZ, DAVID ROGER, architect; b. Deer Lodge, Mont., Jan. 6, 1952; s. William Ralph and Mildred Iolanthe (Moote) L.; m. Joan Andre Raynal, Aug. 27, 1977. B.Arch. with distinction, Mont. State U., 1975; M.B.A. with distinction, U. Portland, 1981. Architect-in-tng. A-E Partnership, Billings, Mont., 1974; asst. faculty mem. Rhode Island Sch. Design, Providence, 1975; assoc. planner Washington County Planning Dept., Hillsboro, 1975-77; bldg. supt., project mgr. Tektronix, Inc., Beaverton, Oreg., 1977-80, constrn. project mgr. major projects, 1980—; project devel. cons. Mem. camp com. Columbia River council Girl Scouts U.S.A.; trustee Oreg. Sch. Arts and Crafts; Mem. AIA (Mont. chpt. scholar 1974, sch. medal 1975), Nat. Trust Hist. Preservation, Phi Kappa Phi, Beta Gamma Sigma, Delta Phi Delta. Republican. Christian Scientist. Club: West Hills Racquet (Beaverton). Office: Tektronix Inc PO Box 500 D/S Y6-028 Beaverton OR 97077

LINVILLE, WILLIAM RAYMOND, educator; b. Sioux City, Iowa, Oct. 8, 1930; s. Raymond John and Mary Anastasia (Kelly) L.; B.A., Calif. State U., 1957, M.A., 1963; Ph.D., U. Hawaii, 1982. Faculty, Calif. State U., Los Angeles, 1963-69, Los Angeles City Coll., 1969-79; lectr. Leeward Community Coll., Honolulu, 1979—; instr. English and Am. studies U. Hawaii, Honolulu. Mem. Am. Studies Assn. Author: Poems, 1957; Almagest, 1963; The Hawk, the Oak, and the Animals, 1971; Three Sides of Seeing: A Semantic Primer, 1977; Helena Blavatsky: Aquarian. Age Theosophy, 1982. Home: 3009-A Manoa Rd Honolulu HI 96822

LIONAKIS, GEORGE, architect; b. West Hiawatha, Utah, Sept. 5, 1924; s. Pete and Andriani (Protopapadakis) L.; student Carbon Jr. Coll., 1942-43, 46-47; B. Arch., U. Oreg., 1951; m. Iva Oree Braddock, Dec. 30, 1951; 1 dau., Deborah Jo. With Corps Engrs., Walla Walla, Wash., 1951-54; architect Liske, Lionakis, Beaumont & Engberg, Sacramento, 1954—. Mem. Sacramento County Bd. Appeals, 1967—, chmn., 1969, 75, 76; pres. Sacramento Builders Exchange, 1976. Served with USAAF, 1943-46. Mem. AIA (pres. Central Valley chpt., 1972—), Constrn. Specifications Inst. (pres. Sacramento chpt., 1962; nat. awards, 1962, 63, 65), Sacramento C. of C. (code com., 1970—). Rotarian (pres. East Sacramento 1978-79). Prin. works include Stockton (Calif.) Telephone Bldg., 1968, Chico (Calif.) Main Telephone Bldg., 1970, Mather AFB Exchange Complex Sacramento, 1970, Base Chapel Mather AFB, Sacramento, 1970, Woodridge Elementary Sch., Sacramento, 1970, Pacific Telephone Co. Operating Center Modesto, Calif., 1968, Sacramento, 1969, Marysville, Calif., 1970, Red Bluff, Calif., 1971, Wells Fargo Banks, Sacramento, 1968, Corning, Calif., 1969, Anderson, 1970, Beale AFB Exchange Complex, Marysville, 1971, Cosumnes River Coll., Sacramento, 1971, base exchanges at Bergstrom AFB, Austin, Tex., Sheppard AFB, Wichita Falls, Tex., Chanute AFB, Rantoul, Ill., McChord AFB, Tacoma, Wash., health center Chico State U., Sacramento County Adminstrn. Center, Sacramento Bee Newspaper Plant. Home: 160 Breckenwood Way Sacramento CA 95825 Office: Liske Lionakis Beaumont & Engberg 10 Fullerton Ct Sacramento CA 95825

LIPKIN, MARY CASTLEMAN DAVIS (MRS. ARTHUR BENNETT LIPKIN), former psychiat. social worker; b. Germantown, Pa., Mar. 4, 1907; d. Henry L. and Willie (Webb) Davis; student grad. sch. social work U. Wash., 1946-48; m. William F. Cavenaugh, Nov. 8, 1930 (div.); children—Molly C. (Mrs. Gary Oberbillig), William A.; m. 2d, Arthur Bennett Lipkin, Sept. 15, 1961 (dec. June 1974). Nursery sch. tchr. Miquon (Pa.) Sch., 1940-45; caseworker Family Soc. Seattle, 1948-49, Jewish Family and Child Service, Seattle, 1951-56, psychiat. social worker Stockton (Calif.) State Hosp., 1957-58; supr. social service Mental Health Research Inst., Fort Steilacoom, Wash., 1958-59; engaged in pvt. practice, Bellevue, Wash., 1959-61. Former mem. Phila. Com. on City Policy. Former diplomate and bd. mem. Conf. Advancement of Pvt. Practice in Social Work. Mem. Acad. Cert. Social Workers, Nat. Assn. Social Workers, Internat. Conf. Social Work, Menninger Found., Union Concerned Scientists, Physicians for Social Responsibility, Center for Sci. in Pub. Interest, Jr. League, Seattle Art Mus., Asian Art Council, Wing Lake Mus., Bellevue Art Mus., Pacific Sci. Center, Western Wash. Solar Energy Assn., Nature Conservancy, Wilderness Soc., Mcpl. League of Seattle-King County, Sierra Club, Am. Symphony Orch. League, Phila. Art Alliance, Common Cause, ACLU, Pa. Acad. Fine Arts. Clubs: Cosmopolitan, Cricket (Phila.); Women's University (Seattle). Home: 8230 SE 33d Pl Mercer Island WA 98040

LIPMAN, JEANNE E., business educator; b. Billings, Mont., Apr. 29, 1948, d. Harry and Esther Ann (Niss) L., m. David Michael Barnes, Oct. 22, 1982. A.B.A., Denver U., 1968; B.A., Bradley U., 1971; M.A., U. No. Colo., 1977; postgrad. Ariz. State U., 1982 . Type A teaching cert. and vocat. credential, Colo. Tchr., YWCA, Peoria, Ill., 1969-71; sec. Honeywell Inc., Denver, 1971-72; adminstrv. asst. Majestic Savs. Assn., Denver, 1972-73; tchr. Arickaree Schs., Anton, Colo., 1973-75; asst. prof. bus. U. No. Colo. Lab. Sch., Greeley, 1975—, chmn. dept., 1978-82. Mem. Nat. Bus. Edn. Assn., Am. Vocat. Assn., Phi Delta Kappa, Delta Pi Epsilon. Democrat. Jewish. Office: University of Northern Colorado Laboratory School Greeley CO 80639

LIPOFSKY, MARVIN BENTLEY, art educator, artist; b. Elgin, Ill., Sept. 1, 1938; s. Henry and Mildred (Hyman) L.; 1 dau., Lisa Beth. B.F.A. in Indsl. Design, U. Ill., 1961; M.S., M.F.A. in Sculpture, U. Wis., 1964. Instr. design U. Wis., Madison, 1964; asst. prof. design U. Calif.-Berkeley, 1964-72; prof., chmn. glass dept. Calif. Coll. Arts and Crafts, Oakland, 1967—; guest instr. Haystack Mountain Sch., Deer Isle, Maine, 1967, 73, San Francisco Art Inst., 1968, Hunterdon Art Ctr., Clinton, N.J., 1973, Pilchuck Sch. Glass, Stanwood, Wash., 1974; one-man shows: Richmond (Calif.) Art Ctr., 1965, Contemporary Crafts Assn., Portland, Oreg., 1966, Glass from Berkeley, Marvin Lipofsky and his students Anneberg Gallery, San Francisco, 1966, Crocker Art Gallery, Sacramento, Calif., 1967, San Francisco Museum Art, 1967, Mus. Contemporary Crafts, N.Y.C., 1969, U. Ga., Athens, 1969, Utah Mus. Fine Arts, U. Utah, Salt Lake City, 1969, Calif. Coll. Arts and Crafts, 1970, Stedelijke Mus., Amsterdam, Holland, 1970, Galerie de Enndt, Amsterdam, 1970, Baxter Art Gallery, Calif. Inst. Tech., Pasadena, 1974, AO Gallery, Tokyo, 1975, Yaw Gallery, Birmingham, Mich., 1976, 78, Gallery Marronnier, Kyoto, Japan, 1979, U. Del., Newark, 1979, Greenwood Gallery, Washington, 1980, SM Gallerie, Frankfurt, W.Ger., 1981, Galerie L. Hamburg, W.Ger., 1981, Betsy Rosenfield Gallery, Chgo., 1982; vis. artist, critic Gerriet Rietveld Academie, Amsterdam; vis. artist Atheneium Sch. Art and Design, Helsinki, Finland, 1970, UCLA, 1973, Pilchuck Sch. Glass, 1977, 81, Sommervail, Battle Mountain Glass Symposium, Vail Colo.; vis. prof. Bazalel Acad. Art and Design, Jerusalem, 1971. Nat. Endowment for Arts fellow, 1974, 76. Mem. Glass Art Soc. (pres. 1978-80, jour. editor Glass Art Soc. Jour. 1976-80).

LIPOW, MYRON, computer software engineer; b. Newark, Apr. 12, 1928; s. Sidney Samuel and Aline (Ackerman) L.; m. Susan-Lee Landisman, Aug. 27, 1950; children—Martin Edward, Stephen Kenneth. B.S. in Math., Calif. Inst. Tech., 1949; cert. quality, reliability engr., Am. Soc. Quality Control, 1972. Statistician Aerojet-Gen. Corp., Azusa, Calif., 1949-50, devel. engr., 1951-55, reliability engr., 1956-58; reliability sect. head TRW Systems Group, Redondo Beach, Calif., 1958-60, dept. mgr., 1961-67, product assurance mgr., 1967-71, sr. staff engr., 1972-79, subproject mgr. software product assurance, Electronics and Def., 1979—; cons. in field. Recipient TRW good neighbor award, 1973. Assoc. fellow AIAA; sr. mem. IEEE (Computer Soc., Reliability Soc.), Math. Assn. Am., AAAS. Jewish. Club: Los Verdes Men's. Co-author: Reliability: Management, Methods, and Quality, 1978; Characteristics of Software Quality, 1978; Software Reliability: A Study in Large Project Reality, 1978. Office: TRW Electronics and Defense One Space Park Dr Redondo Beach CA 90278

LIPP, DONALD RALPH, interior designer; b. Bonners Ferry, Idaho, June 8, 1935; s. Claude Alfred and Anna May (Belden) L. B.A., U. Wash., 1960. Jr. designer Western Contract Furnishers, San Francisco, 1960-63; designer Albers-Gruen Assoc., San Francisco, 1963-67; v.p., treas., chief designer Store Planning Assocs., San Francisco, 1967—. Served in U.S. Army, 1956-57. Mem. Am. Soc. Interior Designers, Inst. Store Planners. Democrat. Office: 135 Post San Francisco CA 94108

LIPP, JEROME FRANCIS, retail company real estate executive; b. Omaha, Aug. 2, 1922; s. Maurice Herbert and Rose (Newman) L.; m. Elizabeth Anne Miller, Dec. 31, 1960; children—Jonathan, Lawrence, Jennifer. A.A., Sacramento City Coll., 1942; student U. Calif., 1942-43; B.S., U. Ariz., 1947. Chief land agt. Sacramento Redevel. Agy., 1956-59, exec. dir., 1959-61; v.p. Hale Bros. Assocs., Sacramento, 1961-63; mgr. properties Broadway Hale Stores, 1963-71; pres. Carter Hawley Hale Properties, Los Angeles, 1971—. Served with USNR, 1943-45. Mem. Urban Land Inst., Internat. Council Shopping Centers. Club: Stock Exchange (Los Angeles). Home: 245 Country Club Dr San Gabriel CA 91775 Office: 550 S Flower St Los Angeles CA 90071

LIPPE, PHILIPP MARIA, neurosurgeon, educator; b. Vienna, Austria, May 17, 1929; s. Philipp and Maria (Goth) L.; came to U.S., 1938, naturalized, 1945; m. Gail B. Busch, 1977; children by previous marriage—Patricia Ann Marie, Philip Eric Andrew, Laura Lynne Elizabeth, Kenneth Anthony Ernst. Student Loyola U., Chgo., 1947-50; B.S. in Medicine, U. Ill. Coll. Medicine, 1952, M.D. with high honors, 1954. Rotating intern St. Francis Hosp., Evanston, Ill., 1954-55; asst. resident gen. surgery VA Hosp., Hines, Ill., 1955, 58-59; asst. resident neurology and neurol. surgery Neuropsychiat. Inst., U. Ill. Research and Ednl. Hosps., Chgo., 1959-60, chief resident, 1962-63, resident neuropathology, 1962, postgrad. trainee in electroencephalography, 1963; resident neurology and neurol. surgery Presbyn.-St. Luke's Hosp., Chgo., 1960-61; practice medicine, specializing in neurol. surgery, San Jose, Calif., 1963—; instr. neurology and neurol. surgery U. Ill., 1962-63; clin. instr. surgery and neurosurgery Stanford U., 1965-69, clin. asst. prof., 1969-74, clin. assoc. prof., 1974—; staff cons. in neurosurgery O'Connor Hosp., Santa Clara Valley Med. Center, San Jose Hosp., Good Samaritan Hosp., Los Gatos Community Hosp., El Camino Hosp. (all San Jose area); founder, exec. dir. Bay Area Pain Rehab. Center, San Jose, 1979—; clin. adviser to Joint Commn. on Accreditation of Hosps.; mem. dist. med. quality rev. com. Calif. Bd. Med. Quality Assurance, 1976—, chmn., 1976-77. Served to capt. USAF, 1956-58. Diplomat Am. Bd. Neurol. Surgery, Nat. Bd. Med. Examiners. Fellow ACS; mem. AMA (Ho. of Dels. 1981—), Calif. Med. Assn. (Ho. of Dels. 1976-80, sci. bd., council 1979—, sec. 1981—), Santa Clara County Med. Soc. (council 1974-81, pres.-elect 1977-78, pres. 1978-79), Chgo. Med. Soc., Congress Neurol. Surgeons, Calif. Assn. Neurol. Surgeons (dir. 1974—, v.p. 1975-76, pres.-elect 1976-77, pres. 1977-79), San Jose Surg. Soc., Am. Assn. Neurol. Surgeons (dir. 1983—), Western Neurol. Soc., San Francisco Neurol. Soc., Santa Clara Valley PSRO (dir., v.p., dir. quality assurance 1975—), Fedn. Western Socs. Neurol. Sci., Internat. Assn. for Study Pain, Am. Pain Soc. (founding mem.), Alpha Omega Alpha, Phi Kappa Phi. Contbr. articles to profl. jours. Pioneered med. application centrifugal force using flight simulator. Office: 2100 Forest Ave Suite 106 San Jose CA 95128

LIPPIT, VICTOR DAVID, economics educator; b. Bklyn., Apr. 16, 1938; s. Jules and Rose (Regenbogen) L.; m. Noriko Mizuta, Dec. 6, 1963; children—Akira M., Seiji M., Yukio M., Tamiko M., Takuro M. B.A., Harvard U., 1959; M.A. in Econs., Yale U., 1963, Ph.D. in Econs., 1971. Instr. econs. Fordham U., 1968-71; asst. prof. to assoc. prof. econs. U. Calif.-Riverside, 1971—; Fulbright lectr., Pakistan, 1982. Fulbright research fellow Tokyo U., 1972-73; Social Sci. Research Council and Am. Council Learned Socs. research grantee, 1975-76; Japan Found. fellow, 1978-79. Mem. Am. Econ. Assn., Union Radical Polit. Econs., Assn. Evolutionary Econs. Author: Land Reform and Economic Development in China, 1974; editor: (with Mark Selden) The Transition to Socialism in China, 1982; contbr. articles to profl. jours., Ency. of Japan.

LIPPITT, ELIZABETH CHARLOTTE, writer; b. San Francisco; d. Sidney Grant and Stella Lippitt; student Mills Coll., U. Calif.-Berkeley. Writer, performer own satirical monologues; contbr. articles to 85 newspapers including N.Y. Post, Los Angeles Examiner, Orlando Sentinel, Phoenix Republic. Recipient Congress of Freedom award, 1959, 71-73, 77, 78; writer on nat. and polit. affairs for 85 newspapers including Muncie Star, St. Louis Globe-Democrat, Washington Times, Utah Ind., Jackson News. Mem. Commn. for Free China. Mem. Nat. Assn. R.R. Passengers, Nat. Trust for Hist. Preservation, Am. Security Council, Internat. Platform Assn., Am. Conservative Union, Nat. Antivivisection Soc., Free Afghanistan Com. Clubs: Metropolitan, Olympic, Commonwealth. Pop singer, recorder song album Songs From the Heart. Home: 2414 Pacific Ave San Francisco CA 94115

LIPPOLD, ROLAND WILL, surgeon; b. Staunton, Ill., May 1, 1916; s. Frank Carl and Ella (Immenroth) L.; B.S., U. Ill., 1940, M.D., 1941; m. Margaret Cookson, June 1, 1947; children—Mary Ellen Lippold Davey, Catherine Anne Lippold Rolf, Carol Sue Lippold Webber. Intern, Grant Hosp., Chgo., 1941-42, resident in surgery, 1942-43, 47-48; resident in surgery St. Francis Hosp., Evanston, Ill., 1946-47; fellow in pathology Cook County Hosp., Chgo., 1947-48, resident in surgery, 1949-50; pvt. practice specializing in surgery, Chgo., 1950-53, also asst. in anatomy U. Ill., 1950-53; pvt. practice specializing in surgery, Sacramento, 1953-68; chief med. officer No. Reception Center-Clinic, Calif. Youth Authority, Sacramento, 1954-68, chief med. services, 1968-79; cons. in med. care in correctional instns.; cons. Calif. State Personnel Bd. Chmn. Calif. Expn. Hall of Health, 1971-72. Served to comdr. M.C., USNR, 1943-73; PTO. Diplomate Am. Bd. Surgery. Mem. Sacramento Surg. Soc., Sacramento County Med. Soc., Calif. Med. Assn., AMA, Assn. Mil. Surgeons U.S., Am. Occupational Med. Assn., Am. Heart Assn., Audubon Soc., Sacramento Hist. Soc. (life). Republican. Lutheran. Contbr. monthly articles to Sacramento Medicine, 1957-58. Home: 1811 Eastern Ave Sacramento CA 95825

LIPPS, SANDRA DEANNE, personnel executive; b. McMinnville, Tenn., May 19, 1946; d. Gordon Alvin and Mildred Marie (Fults) McGinnis; m. Bruce Wayne Robbins, Aug. 30, 1968; children—David Aaron, Shannon Lynn; m. Bernard David Lipps, July 19, 1981. B.S. in Polit. Sci., Brigham Young U., 1968. Cert. tchr., Calif. Tchr. English, St. Mary's Sch., Whittier, Calif., 1968-70; tchr. adult edn. Montebello (Calif.) Adult Sch., 1976—; pres. Lipps Service, Santa Monica, Calif., 1976—; cons., tchr. in field. Mem. Calif. Assn. Personnel Cons., Calif. Assn. Ind. Schs., Nat. Assn. Ind. Schs., Calif. Tchrs. Assn. Republican. Mormon. Office: 1630 Euclid St Santa Monica CA 90404

LIPSON, EUGENE, pediatrician; b. Pitts., Feb. 18, 1935; s. Albert and Betty (Tivorofsky) L.; B.S., U. Pitts., 1957, M.D., 1961; m. Diana Galletti, Mar. 8, 1981; children by previous marriage—Steven, Sheryl, Susan, Trudi, Michelle. Intern, Tripler U.S. Army Hosp., Honolulu, 1961-62; resident in pediatrics Children's Hosp., Oakland, Calif., 1964-66; practice medicine, specializing in pediatrics, Concord, Calif., 1966—; mem. staff Mt. Diablo Hosp., John Muir Hosp., Los Medanos Hosp., Delta Hosp., Children's Hosp., Oakland; med. cons. Contra Costa County Hosp., Infant Hearing Assessment, Antioch Unified Sch. Dist. lectr. in field. Served with M.C., U.S. Army, 1962-64. Mem. AMA, Calif. Med. Assn., Alameda Contra Costa Med. Assn., East Bay Pediatric Soc., Am. Philatelic Assn., Concord C. of C. Jewish. Club: Concord Century. Contbr. articles to med. jours. Office: 2485 High School Ave Suite 111 Concord CA 94520 also 3737A Lone Tree Way Antioch CA 94509

LIPSTONE, HOWARD H., television production executive; b. Chgo., Apr. 28; s. Louis R. and Ruth B. (Fischer) L.; m. Jane A., Apr. 7, 1957; children—Lewis, Gregory. B.A. in Cinema, U. So. Calif., 1950. Asst. to gen. mgr. Sta. KTLA, Los Angeles, 1950-54; film and program dir. Sta. KABC-TV, Los Angeles, 1954-63; exec. asst. to pres., exec. producer Selmur Prodns. Inc. subs. ABC-TV, 1963-69; exec. v.p. Ivan Tors Films, Inc., 1969-70; pres. Alan Landsburg Prodns., Inc., Los Angeles, 1970—. Mem. Soc. Motion Picture and TV Engrs., Acad. TV Arts and Scis., Motion Picture Acad. Arts and Scis. Office: 11811 Olympic Blvd Los Angeles CA 90064*

LIRMAN, IRVING ROBERT, engr.; b. Chgo., Dec. 14, 1922; s. Max and Dora (Piatigorsky) L.; student U. Ill., 1945-48; B.S. in Chemistry, Calif. State Coll., Los Angeles, 1963; m. Sonia P. Lirman, Feb. 14, 1943; children—Mark L., Glenn R., Daryl S. Engr., Pacific Semiconductors, Inc., Culver City, Calif., 1958-60; semiconductor project engr. Micro Systems, Inc., Pasadena, Calif., 1960-66; mem. tech. staff TRW Systems, Inc., Redondo Beach, Calif., 1966-68; mem. tech. staff microelectronics div. Teledyne Systems Co., Los Angeles, 1968-70; product mgr. semiconductor div. Micron Instruments, Inc., Los Angeles, 1970—. Served with U.S. Navy, 1943-45. Mem. Instrument Soc. Am., Am. Chem. Soc., Calif. State Coll. Alumni Assn. Jewish. Inventor devel. of planar diffused silicon devices technique using photolithography approach; developed etched silicon strain gages. Home: 1516 Palisades Dr Pacific Palisades CA 90272 Office: 1519 Pontius Ave Los Angeles CA 90025

LIS, ELAINE WALKER, nutritionist; b. Denver, Apr. 25, 1924; d. Charles Alonzo and Marjorie (Macomber) Walker; A.B. in Biology, Mills Coll., Calif., 1945; Ph.D. in Nutrition, U. Calif., Berkeley, 1960; children—Richard, Janina, Victoria. Postdoctoral research fellow U. Calif., Berkeley, 1960-62; lectr. Portland (Oreg.) State U., 1964-68; nutritional cons. U. Oreg. Health Scis. Center, Portland, 1964-68, prof. nutrition Crippled Childrens Div., 1968—, prof. pub. health and preventive medicine, 1981—. Served to lt. Med. Service Corps, USNR, 1951-54. Mem. Soc. Nutrition Edn., Am. Home Econs. Assn., AAUP (chpt. pres. 1974), Am. Assn. Mental Deficiency (chairperson nutrition and dietetics div.), Nutrition Today Soc., Oreg. Nutrition Council, Oreg. Public Health Assn., Sigma Xi, Iota Sigma Pi. Contbr. articles to sci. jours. Home: 7950 SW Crestline Dr Portland OR 97219 Office: 707 SW Gaines Rd Portland OR 97201

LIS, YVONNE, mktg. exec.; b. Amsterdam, N.Y., June 14, 1957; d. Charles John and Rose Emily Lis; B.S. cum laude, SUNY, Albany, 1978; M.B.A., San Francisco State U., 1979; m. William D. Greenroad, Oct. 6, 1979. Adminstrv. asst. Office Lt. Gov. N.Y. State, Albany, 1975-78; price adminstrn. supr. Intel Corp., Santa Clara, Calif., 1979-80, corp. planner, 1980-81, customer mktg. engr., 1981-82; product mktg. mgr. Shugart Assocs., Sunnyvale, Calif., 1982—. Mem. Am. Mktg. Assn., Assn. M.B.A. Execs. Roman Catholic. Home: 651 E McKinley Ave Sunnyvale CA 94086 Office: 475 Oakmead Pkwy Sunnyvale CA 94086

LISH, VIRGINIA ANN (HEAD), curriculum educator; b. Rupert, Idaho, Apr. 19, 1931; d. James Floyd and Mary Jane (Becker) Head; m. Arnold Richard Lish, Dec. 18, 1955 (dec.); 1 son, Eric Temocx. Student So. Idaho Coll. Edn.; B.A. in English, U. Idaho-So. Branch, 1956; postgrad. U. Ariz.; M.A. in Curriculum and Adminstrn., Calif. State U., 1974. Cert. elem., secondary sch. tchr., Idaho, Ariz., Calif.; supr., adminstr., Calif.; reading specialist. Elem., secondary tchr. Idaho, Ariz., Calif., including Navajo Indian Reservation schs., 1950-69; curriculum cons., lang. specialist, reading specialist Ceres (Calif.) Sch. Dist., 1969-73, curriculum coordinator, projects dir., 1973—; curriculum cons.; inservice seminar leader. Bd. dirs. Women's Resource Center. Named Creative Tchr. U.S. Office Edn., 1978, Nat. Career Educator, 1974; exemplary Developer Demonstrator, 1983, grantee, 1979-81. Mem. Internat. Reading Assn., Assn. Calif. Sch. Adminstrs., Am. Assn. Sch. Adminstrs., Assn. Curriculum and Supervision, Phi Delta Kappa. Democrat. Club: Soroptomist Internat. (Ceres).

LISHEY, ROBERT F., environmental health and safety engineer, consultant; b. Los Angeles, Jan. 6, 1949; s. Robert J. and Catherine (Townsend) L.; m. Alice Butler, Sept. 5, 1970; children—Robert, Allison. B.S. in Health and Safety, Calif. State U., 1975. Cert. hazard control mgr. Loss control rep. Hartford Ins. Group, Los Angeles, 1976-77; loss control cons. Fremont Indemnity Co., Los Angeles, 1977-78; environ. health and safety engring. adminstr. Hughes Aircraft Co., Tucson, 1978-81; adminstr. accident prevention and occupational health HITCO div. ARMCO, Gardena, Calif., 1981-83. Served with U.S. Army, 1968-71. Recipient Safety Profl. Achievement Recognition award, 1982. Mem. Am. Soc. Safety Engrs. (exec. bd. Los Angeles chpt. 1980-82). Democrat. Methodist. Club: So. Area Boys.

LISK, JAMES BURTON, retired architect; b. Hankinson, N.D., May 2, 1919; s. Levi Edgar and Alvina Minna (Kramer) L.; A.B., N.W. Nazarene Coll., 1941; postgrad. U. Ill., 1965, 66, U. Wash., 1964, summer 1966; m. Doris Lenora Snyder, May 30, 1942; children—Jamelyn Doris, Susan RoJean. Active architecture, Boise, Idaho, 1948-53, Yakima, Wash., 1953-57; instr. engring., Columbia Basin Coll., Pasco, Wash., 1958-75, instr. architecture, 1975-78; pvt. practice architecture, Winnemucca, Nev., 1978-79; architect Morrison-Knudsen, Boise, 1978-82, sr. architect, 1981-82. Active Pasco Planning Commn., 1974-78. Recipient various scholarships NSF, OCD. Mem. Guild for Religious Architecture. Club: Kiwanis. Home: 1411 Lake Lowell Ave Nampa ID 83651

LISSY, DAVID JEROME, photographer; b. Oak Park, Ill., July 6, 1950; s. Alfred E. and Eleanoretta (Mathews) L.; m. Carol Melissa Mather, Oct. 9, 1977; children—Brooke Melissa, Joel David. B.A. in Polit. Sci., No. Ill. U., 1972. Photographer, John Russell Photography Co., Aspen, Colo., 1976-79, Norm Clasen Photography, Aspen, 1979-80; freelance photographer David Lissy Photography, Aspen, 1980—. Mem. Am. Soc. Mag. Photographers (cert.), Rocky Mountain Ski Writers, Assoc. Photographers Internat., U.S. Ski Writers (cert.). Contbr. photography to numerous popular mags. Office: David Lissy Photography PO Box 11122 Aspen CO 81612

LIST, KEN W., organ builder, musician; b. Indpls., June 2, 1939; s. Kenneth Noel and Charlotte Edith (Wey) L. Student Jordan Coll. Music, Butler U., 1957-60, Battell Sch., Yale U., 1959. Asst. to pres., voicer Schlicker Organ Co., Buffalo, 1963-74; gen. mgr. Lawrence Phelps & Assocs. Organ Builders, Erie, Pa., 1974-79; tonal dir. Rodgers Organ Co. div. CBS Mus. Instruments, Hillsboro, Oreg., 1979—; classical music broadcaster Sta. WQLN-FM, Erie, Pa., 1975-78; harpsichordist with chamber groups and orchs., solo performances. Served with U.S. Army, 1962-63. Mem. Am. Guild Organists, Hillsboro Community Arts, Smithsonian Instn., Phi Mu Alpha Sinphonia. Democrat. Episcopalian. Contbr. articles to profl. jours. Installed largest electronic organ in world in Shinji Shumeikai, Japan. Home: 2526 NE Grant St Hillsboro OR 97123 Office: 1300 NE 25th Ave Hillsboro OR 97123

LISTER, ANTHONY, real estate and mortgage broker; b. N.Y.C., Oct. 21, 1931; student Wilkes Coll., Fairleigh Dickinson U., San Jose City Coll., NYU, Foothill Coll., Los Altos Hills, Calif., West Valley Coll.; m. Susan Chason, Aug. 11, 1957; children—Diane, William David. Employed in chem. industry and lighting supply, 1955—; with Lister Industries, Inc., San Jose, Calif., 1966—, pres., 1966—; mem. San Jose Real Estate Bd. Football and boxing coach Jr. Olympic Boxing Ofcl. and judge, Police Athletic League, San Jose, 1968—; advisor to city ops. and fin. com.; advisor Campbell chpt. DeMolay, 1969—; mem. Vol. Fire Dept., 1957—, sec. dept.; former bd. dirs. Santa Clara County Epilepsy Soc., Loma Prieta, Inc. Served with USMCR, 1950-62. Republican. Clubs: Commonwealth of Calif., Elks, Masons (32 deg.). Home: 109 Crows Nest Dr Boulder Creek CA 95006 Office: PO Box 94 Boulder Creek CA 95006

LISTON, ALBERT MORRIS, educator, adminstr.; b. Carlinville, Ill., Aug. 6, 1940; s. Joseph Bostick and Hazel Marie (Smalley) L.; A.B. in Econs., U. Calif., Davis, 1963; M.A. in Govt., Calif. State U., Sacramento, 1970; m. Phyllis Clayton, Feb. 27, 1967 (div. July 1970). Research analyst Ombudsman Activities Project polit. sci. dept. U. Calif., Santa Barbara, 1970-72; asst. prof. polit. sci. dept. Calif. State U., Fullerton, 1973-79. Served to lt. Supply Corps, USN, 1963-66. Mem. Am. Polit. Sci. Assn., Am. Soc. for Public Adminstrn., Town Hall of Calif., Kappa Sigma, Phi Kappa Phi. Democrat. Contbr. chpt. to Executive Ombudsmen in the United States, 1973. Office: Box 691 Laguna Beach CA 92652

LIT, ESTELLE MARKS, educator; b. N.Y.C., Apr. 11, 1921; d. Maurice Z. and Jeanette (Lessinger) Marks; A.B., U. Calif., 1942; M.S. in Edn. (Educare scholar), U. So. Calif., 1950, Ed.D., 1973; m. Mark David Lit, Nov. 7, 1943; children—Bonnie, Jeff. Tchr., counselor, dept. chmn. Los Angeles Unified Sch. Dist., 1944-77, coordinator sch.-community relations, 1960-62, tchr. trainer, 1964-65; asst. prof. secondary edn. Calif. State U., Los Angeles, 1970—; asst. dir. NSF project, 1974-76; dir. Tchrs. Teach Tchrs. project of NEA, United Tchrs. of Los Angeles, 1976-78; dir. U.S.A. Global Interdependence project, 1979-82. Bd. dirs. Northridge Civic Assn., 1978-81. Recipient Hilda Maehling award NEA, 1982. Mem. Calif. Council Social Studies (past v.p.), So. Calif. Social Scis. Assn. (past pres.), Nat. Council Social Studies (chmn. urban edn. com. 1981), Phi Delta Kappa, Pi Lambda Theta. Democrat. Jewish. Contbr. in field; designer master's degree program in global interdependence edn. Home: 18233 Bermuda St Northridge CA 91326 Office: 5151 State University Dr Los Angeles CA 90032

LITCHFIELD, PETER MACINTYRE, seminar design executive; b. Detroit, Aug. 17, 1941; s. Edward Harold and Ann Muir (Macintyre) L. B.A., U. Mich., 1963; M.A., San Diego State U., 1969; Ph.D., U. Portland, 1971. Asst. prof. psychology Calif. Poly. State U., San Luis Obispo, 1970-74, assoc. prof. psychology, 1974-81; dir. Proseminar Inst., San Francisco, 1978-82; pres. Symposia Prodns., Inc., San Francisco, 1977-82, chmn., 1983—; exec. dir. Profl. Sch. Biofeedback Tng., San Francisco, 1982—; coordinator behavioral medicine splty. Ph.D. program in clin. psychology Rosebridge Inst., 1983—. Bache Fund NSF grantee, 1960; Calif. Poly. State U. grantee, 1973-74. Mem. Am. Psychol. Assn., AAAS, Aircraft Owners and Pilots Assn. Democrat. Contbr. articles to profl. jours.

LITIZZETTE, STANLEY VICTOR, lawyer; b. Helper, Utah, Aug. 25, 1920; s. Victor E. and Vera A. (Bottino) L.; B.A. magna cum laude, Notre Dame U., 1942; J.D., Georgetown U., 1949; A.A. (hon.), Coll. Eastern Utah, 1981; m. Edith Breznick, June 16, 1956; 1 son, Stanley Lawrence. With identification div. FBI, Washington, 1942; admitted to D.C. bar, 1949, Utah bar, 1949, U.S. Supreme Ct., 1977; since in pvt. practice at Helper, Utah; city atty. Helper, 1954-76; gen. counsel, dir. Helper State Bank, 1957-78. Chmn. bd. trustees Price River Water Improvement Dist., 1960-78; chmn. Carbon County Planning Commn., 1968-72; bd. dirs. Carbon Hosp., 1958-73. Served with USAAF, 1943-45. Mem. Eastern Utah Bar Assn. (pres. 1953, 1968, 74), Am. Bar Assn., Assn. Trial Lawyers Am., Am. Legion. Roman Catholic. Clubs: Elks, KC. Home: 26 S Main St Helper UT 84526 Office: 30 S Main St Helper UT 84526

LITROWNIK, ALAN JAY, psychologist, educator; b. Los Angeles, June 25, 1945; s. Irving and Mildred Mae (Rosin) L.; m. Hollis Merle, Aug. 20, 1967; children—Allison Brook, Jordan Michael. B.A., UCLA, 1967; M.A., U. Ill., Champaign-Urbana, 1969, Ph.D., 1971. Psychologist Ill. Dept. Mental Health, Decatur, 1970-71; asst. prof. psychology San Diego State U., 1971-75, assoc. prof., 1975-78, prof., 1978—, chmn. dept. psychology, 1981—; cons. San Diego County Dept. Edn. Program Evaluation, 1975-81; project dir. Self-Concept and Self-regulatory Processes in Developmentally Disabled Children and Adolescents, 1975-78. U.S. Office Edn. grantee, 1975-78, 80-81. Mem. Am. Psychol. Assn., Assn. Advancement Behavior Therapy. Research, publs. in field; contbr. chpts to books. Office: Dept Psychology San Diego State U San Diego CA 92182

LITTELL, JEFFREY D., real estate advisor, consultant; b. Lansing, Mich., June 23, 1954; s. Edward G. and Alice (Woodruff) L.; B.S. in Bus., U. So. Calif., 1976. With Norris Beggs & Simpson, Los Angeles, 1976-79, Westfield Devel. Co., Irvine, Calif., 1979-82; owner, operator The Littell Co., Irvine, 1982—; guest lectr. Orange Coast Coll. Recipient Sr. Recognition award U. So. Calif., 1976. Democrat. Episcopalian. Club: Newport Harbor Yacht (Newport Beach, Calif.). Office: 18662 MacArthur Blvd Suite 200 Irvine CA 92715

LITTERAL, EMMETT BRYAN, physician; b. Vinita, Okla., Oct. 30, 1898; s. Isaac Nathaniel and Mary (Sellers) L.; A.B., George Washington U., 1925, M.D, 1929; m. Harriet Faries, July 26, 1929 (dec.); m. 2d, Christine Phillips Nicholson, May 17, 1964. Commd. 1st lt. U.S. Army, 1929, advanced through grades to col., 1955; gen. rotating intern Walter Reed Hosp., Washington, 1929-30, psychiatry and gen. medicine ward officer, 1930-31, chief dept. neuropsychiatry, 1953-55; asst. post surgeon, Ft. Hamilton, N.Y., 1932-34; resident psychiatry St. Elizabeth's Hosp., Washington, 1934-35; asst. supt. Corozal Mental Hosp., Corozal, Panama, C.Z., 1935-37, acting supt., 1937; ward officer neuropsychiat. sect. Letterman Gen. Hosp., San Francisco, 1938-39, asst. chief, 1939-41, chief, 1942, 46-53; postgrad. Langley Porter Clinic, San Francisco, 1946; psychoanalysis trainee San Francisco Psychoanalytic Inst., 1948-50; comdg. officer 80th Gen. Hosp., Camp White, Oreg., New Guinea, Philippines, 1942-45; asst. supt., chief psychiat. service and neurology service Agnews State Hosp., San Jose, Calif., 1956-68, neurol. and teaching cons., 1968-72; staff psychiatrist and cons. Rehab. Mental Health Services, San Jose, 1968-83. Med. and psychiat. cons. Rehab. Planning Com., Santa Clara. Decorated Legion of Merit, 1947; recipient certificate of merit Walter Reed Army Med. Center, 1955. Diplomate Am. Bd. Psychiatry and Neurology. Fellow A.C.P., Am. Psychiat. Assn., Am. Geriatrics Assn., mem. Am. Acad. Neurology, AAAS, Mil. Order World Wars, Am., Calif. med. assns., Santa Clara County med. socs., San Francisco Neurology Soc., No. Calif., Psychiat. Soc., Soc. St. Elizabeth's Hosp. Republican. Contbr. articles to med. jours. Home: 2910 Pruneridge Ave Santa Clara CA 95051

LITTLE, BONITA CLAUDENE, home economics educator; b. Greenville, Tex., Aug. 21, 1952; d. Claude Edward and Bonnie Bell (Poteet) Little. Student Bethany Nazarene Coll., 1970-71; B.S. in Vocat. Home Econs. Edn., East Tex. State U., 1974, M.S. in Home Econs., 1979. Cert. tchr. vocat. home econs. edn., Tex. Tchr., coordinator Home Econs. Coop. Edn., Wolfe City (Tex.) Ind. Sch. Dist., 1975-78; asst. instr. home econs. East Tex. State U., Commerce, 1978-79, adj. instr., 1981; prof. home econs. edn. N.W. Nazarene Coll., Nampa, Idaho, 1981—; lectr. in field. Recipient Henson-Kickernick scholarship, East Tex. State U., 1972. Mem. Am. Home Econs. Assn., Idaho Home Econs. Assn., Am. Vocat. Assn., Idaho Vocat. Assn., Home Econs. Edn. Assn. Nazarene. Office: NW Nazarene Coll Nampa ID 83651

LITTLE, CONNIE FAY, computer scientist; b. Hayti, Mo., Oct. 19, 1950; d. Charles Quincy and Mary Alice (Calhoun) Mack; m. Harold Stevens (dec.); m. 2d, Wynile D. Little, May 23, 1975. B.S., Ind. State U.; postgrad. Golden Gate U. Statis. asst. J. I. Case, Terre Haute, Ind., 1973-74; programming technician Lawrence Livermore Nat. Lab., 1978-79, computer scientist, 1979—. Served with U.S. Army, 1975-78. Mem. Assn. Systems Mgmt., Soc. Women Engrs., No. Calif. Council Black Profl. Engrs., Nat. Council Negro Women, Alpha Kappa Alpha. Baptist.

LITTLE, DAVID, state senator, rancher; b. Emmett, Idaho, Jan. 31, 1918; s. Andrew and Agnes (Sproat) L.; m. Geraldine Laidlaw, Sept. 9, 1941; children—James, Judith, Bradley. B.S. in Edn., U. Idaho-Moscow, 1941. Cattle rancher, farmer, Emmett, Idaho, 1941—; mem. Idaho Ho. of Reps., 1970-72; mem. Idaho Senate, 1972—; dir. Albertson's Inc., Boise, Idaho. Republican nat. committeeman for Idaho. Presbyterian. Club: Kiwanis. Office: PO Box 68 210 W Main St Emmett ID 83617

LITTLE, GORDON A., health physicist, consultant; b. Portland, Oreg., July 7, 1930; s. Thomas Gordon and Mary Catherine (Haberly) L. B.S., Lewis and Clark Coll., 1952; student Oreg. State U., 1964-66. Engr., Gen. Electric Co., Richland, Wash., 1952-55, specialist, 1957-64; health physicist U. Calif-Berkeley, 1966-76, reactor health physicist, 1976—. Charter mem. Diablo Folk Dancers, Powder Hounds Ski Club. Served with AUS, 1955-57. Radiol. Health fellow, 1964. Mem. Health Physics Soc. (charter; dir., pres. No. Calif. chpt.), AAAS, Am. Nuclear Soc., Am. Soc. Safety Engrs. Home: 1625 Richmond St El Cerrito CA 94530 Office: EH&S Office 481 Cowell Hosp Berkeley CA 94720

LITTLE, JACK MILTON, real estate and investment exec.; b. Mt. Clemens, Mich., Feb. 1, 1922; s. Milton R. and Arline E. (Armstrong) L.; B.S. in Acctg., Fla. So. Coll., 1952; m. Maidie Jo Wood, Aug. 31, 1946; children—Jill Elizabeth, Jeffrey Alonzo, Jeri A. Ins. adminstrn./gen. auditor Aerojet-Gen. Corp., 1957-68; v.p. fin. and adminstrn. Digital Logic Corp., Anaheim, Calif., 1968-69; pub. acctg. practice, Orange, Calif., 1970-77; pres., dir. Myglo Corp., Laguna Hills, Calif., 1977—; exec. v.p., dir. Blanco Investments & Land, Ltd., Laguna Hills, 1977—, also dir.; dir. Orange Coast Video Co.; part-time instr. Biola Coll., La Mirada, Calif., 1970-75. Treas. Redford Republican League, 1955-56; v.p. Rescue (Calif.) Elem. Sch. Bd., 1965-66. Served to capt. USAAF and USAF, 1943-53. Decorated Air medal with 4 oak leaf clusters. Profl. acct., Calif. Mem. Soc, Calif. Accts. (past chpt. dir.). Republican. Mem. Evang. Ch. Club: Masons. Home: 712 E Riverdale St Orange CA 92665 Office: PO Box 1 East Irvine CA 92650

LITTLEFORD, WILMA LEE, real estate broker; b. Guilford, Mo., Oct. 11, 1932; d. Alvin and Georgia Irene (Weatherman) Gillett; m. Leland E. Taylor, Jan. 10, 1952; children—Irene E., Charles E.; m. Ronald James Littleford, Apr. 19, 1961; 1 son, Gene A.; stepchildren—Randy, Dennis, Laurie, Ronald. Student Las Vegas Real Estate Sch., 1968. Cert. real estate specialist. With Norman Kaye Real Estate, Las Vegas, Nev., 1969—, mgr., 1978-80, broker, 1980—; faculty Las Vegas Bd. Realtors. Named Salesman of Yr., Norman Kaye Real Estate, 1979, 80, 82. Mem. Las Vegas Bd. Realtors, Beta Sigma Phi. Republican. Home: 6600 Pickford Ln Las Vegas NV 89107 Office: Norman Kaye Real Estate 1019 S Decatur Las Vegas NV 89107

LITTLER, CHARLES A., artist, educator; b. Montrose, Colo., Jan. 31, 1928; s. Paul L. and Dorothy (Armstrong) L.; m. Cora Clifford (div.); m. 2d, Pat A. Dolan, Dec. 26, 1981; children—Steven, Selina. B.A., U. N.Mex., 1949; student Hans Hofmann Sch. Art, 1950-52; M.F.A., Alfred U., 1957. Instr. Alfred (N.Y.) U., summer 1957, Brown U., Providence, summer 1959; instr. U. Ariz., Tucson, 1958-83; co-founder RubyLee, Trail Mix, art collaborative, creator permanent site sculptures and Park Art; represent in permanent collections. Founder Rancho Linda Vista Oracle, Ariz., 1968, pres., 1968-79, trustee, 1979—. Recipient of numerous mus. awards. Democrat. Home: OM Star Rt #2360 Orcacle AZ 85623

LITTMANN, MARK EVAN, science writer, astronomy educator; b. St. Louis, Dec. 8, 1939; s. Lewis E. and Muriel Jane (Stein) L.; B.S., M.I.T., 1961; M.A. (fellow), Hollins Coll., 1962; Ph.D. (fellow), Northwestern U., 1969; m. Peggy Anne Owens, Dec. 14, 1980; 1 dau., Beth Ann. Dir., Hansen Planetarium, Salt Lake City, 1965-83; staff meteorologist Sta. KCPX-TV, Salt Lake City, 1971-72; sci. reporter, 1971-73; drama and dance reviewer Salt Lake Tribune, 1966-67; adj. assoc. prof. physics, mem. faculty honors program U. Utah; Disting. vis. scholar Westminster Coll. Nat. Endowment for Humanities grantee, 1976, 80, 81; grantee Am. Chem. Soc., 1977, 79, 83, NSF, 1979, Rockwell Internat. Corp., 1978, AAAS, 1979, 83, NASA grantee, 1976, 80. Mem. AIAA, Am. Astron. Soc., Internat. Planetarium Soc. (service award 1982). Jewish. Author: The People, 1976; Footsteps, 1978; The Universe of Dr. Einstein, 1980; Springtime of the Universe, 1980; Skywatchers of Ancient Mexico, 1981; The Dawn of Astronomy, 1983; author, dir., producer numerous planetarium programs; contbr. articles in field to profl. jours.

LITTRELL, ROBERT THOMAS, educator; b. Winfield, Kans., Nov. 6, 1926; s. Harold Hubert and Winifred (Davis) L.; B.S., U. Nebr., 1950, M.A., 1951, Ed.D., 1957; m. Shirley Clinkenbeard, Sept. 8, 1946; children—Gloria Ann, Allison; m. 2d, Agnes Cummings, Feb. 4, 1967; 1 son, Stephen Robert. Prin. pub. sch., Blue Hill, Nebr., 1951-53; dir. elementary edn., jr.-high edn. and tchr. edn. for the Govt. of Am. Samoa, Pago Pago, Samoa; also Tutuila, Samoa, 1953-55; counselor-trainer U. Nebr., Lincoln, 1956-57, research asst., 1955-56; test officer Long Beach State Coll., 1957-65, coordinator instnl. research, 1959-65, asst. prof., 1957-60, asso. prof. psychology, 1960-64, prof., 1964-71, dir. instl. research, 1971—; ltd. pvt. practice counseling and hypnotherapy; tax-shelter cons. Stout-Hall and Assocs., South Pasadena, Calif; dir. Coll. and Univ. Research Enterprises, Inc., Long Beach; ednl. cons. State Farm Ins. Co., Santa Ana, Calif., 1960-64. Served with USMCR, 1943-46. Decorated Purple Heart. Mem. Am. Psychol. Assn., Calif. Assn. Instl. Research (exec. com.), Psi Chi, Phi Delta Kappa, Phi Kappa Phi. Mason. Contbr. articles to profl. jours. Home: 1900 E Ocean Blvd Apt 916 Long Beach CA 90802 Office: 1250 Bellflower Blvd Long Beach CA 90840

LIU, ANTONY AN-KUO, research and cons. co. exec.; b. China, Sept. 7, 1947; came to U.S., 1971, naturalized, 1979; s. Jose S.H. and Ai-I (Lei) L.; Ph.D., Johns Hopkins U., 1976; m. Linda L., June 22, 1973; children—Eileen, Eric. Research scientist Dynamics Tech., Inc., Torrance, Calif., 1976—. Whitehead fellow, 1971-76. Mem. Am. Phys. Soc., Am. Geophys. Union, Sigma Xi. Home: 2814 El Dorado St Torrance CA 90503 Office: Dynamics Technology Inc 22939 Hawthorne Blvd Suite 200 Torrance CA 90505

LIU, CHI TSIEH, research material engr.; b. Honan, Republic of China, Aug. 8, 1939; came to U.S., 1964, naturalized, 1973; s. Mo En and Da Jen (Wang) L.; B.S., Chen-Kung U., 1962; M.S., Columbia U., 1966, grad. in engring., 1969; Ph.D., Va. Poly. Inst. and State U., 1975; m. Lien-Yu Chang, Jan. 30, 1965; children—Patricia Meng-Fu, Jeffrey Chia-Perng, Micheal Chia-Hsiang. Research asst. civil engring. Columbia U., N.Y.C., 1964-68; stress analyst Fairchild Republic Co., Farmingdale, N.Y., 1968-72; research asst. engring. sci. and mechanics dept. Va. Poly. Inst. and State U., Blacksburg, Va., 1973-75; aerospace engr. Naval Ordnance Sta., Indian Head, Md., 1975-77; research mech. engr. engring. mechanics div. Office of Research, U.S. Dept. Transp., Washington, 1977-78; aerospace engr. Naval Engring. Support Office, Naval Air Sta., Alameda, Calif., 1978-80, NASA Ames Research Center, Moffett Field, Calif., 1980-81; research material engr. Air Force Rocket Propulsion Lab., Edwards AFB, Calif., 1981—; tech. cons. to Naval Air System Command, 1979. Recipient Fairchild Industries Service Recognition award, 1973. Mem. AIAA, Sigma Xi, Phi Kappa Phi. Contbr. articles on fatigue and structural engring. to profl. publs.; research on structural reliability and exptl. mechanics. Home: 2607 Bridle Ln Walnut Creek CA 94596 Office: Air Force Rocket Propulsion Lab Edwards AFB CA 93523

LIU, DIOMEDES, shipping co. exec.; b. Pyapon, Burma; came to U.S., 1960, naturalized, 1971; s. Saik Yain and Annie (Lee) L.; B.S.E.E., U. Pitts., 1965, M.S.E.E., 1968, M.S.I.E., 1972; m. Angela Tien. Various engring. and mgmt. positions Auburn & Assos., Pitts., Swindell-Dressler Co., R.T. Patterson Co., Pitts., 1965-69; lectr., researcher U. Pitts., Point Park Coll., Community Coll. Allegheny County, 1969-72; mgmt. positions Sea-Land Service, Inc., Elizabeth, N.J., 1972-79; dir. terminal and cargo Am. President Lines, Inc., Oakland, Calif., 1980—; officer, dir. Port Progress, Inc., of N.J. Active Transp. Research Bd., also Nat. Acad. Scis. Registered profl. engr., Calif., Del., N.J., Pa.; lic. gen. contractor, Calif. Mem. Sigma Xi. Patentee in field. Researcher in port planning and devel. Office: 1950 Franklin St Oakland CA 94612

LIVERMORE, KELLEN E., educator; b. Las Cruces, N.Mex., May 10, 1948; d. Marlin M. and Lola Mae (Engle) L.; m. Douglas C. Benko, Oct. 2, 1975; 1 dau., Julie Skye Livermore. B.A. in English, U. N.Mex., 1970, M.A., 1981. Clerical specialist Sch. Law U. N.Mex., Albuquerque, 1973-75, acad. advisor 1976-80, career advisor, 1980-83, coordinator coop. edn., 1983—; legal sec. firm Jones, Gallegos, Snead & Wertheim, P.A., Santa Fe, 1975; staff asst. Regional Med. Program, Albuquerque, 1976; mgmt. and orgnl. devel. cons., trainer. Bd. dirs. Tranquillo Pines Water Users Coop., 1980-83, v.p., 1981-82. Recipient recognition award U. N.Mex., 1983, five yr. service award, 1981. Mem. Am. Soc. Tng. and Devel. (v.p. communications, cert. of appreciation, Albuquerque chpt. 1983), N.Mex. Coll. Placement Assn., Profl. Orgn. Women. Democrat. Home: Star Route Box 197-H Tijeras NM 87059 Office: Mesa Vista 2110 U NMex Albuquerque NM 87131

LIVESAY, GARY FREDERIK, accountant; b. San Rafael, Calif., Sept. 28, 1952; s. Donald Sterling and Jacqueline Marie (Larsen) L.; m. Joanne Miller, June 28, 1975; 1 son, Brent Sterling. B.S., Lewis and Clark Coll., 1974. C.P.A., Oreg. Audit mgr. Coopers & Lybrand, Eugene, Oreg., 1973-82; chief fin. officer Eugene TV Inc., 1982—; prof. acctg. U. Oreg., 1977-81. Treas., Goodwill Industries Lane City, 1981—; chmn. bd. Halfway House Services Inc., 1980-82, bd. dirs., 1983—. Mem. Am. Inst. C.P.A.s, Oreg. Soc. C.P.A.'s (pres. chpt. 1980-81). Clubs: Town, Oregon Track (Eugene). Home: 2837 Morgan Ct Eugene OR 97401 Office: Eugene TV Inc PO Box 1313 Eugene OR 97440

LIVINGSTON, DAVID GLENN, investment banker; b. Van Wert, Ohio, Oct. 28, 1933; s. Glenn Herbert and Helen Ida (Gilliland) L.; m. Joyce Bricker, Aug. 28, 1955; children—Laura Ann, Linda Joy, David B., Douglas G. A.B. in Econs., U. Mich., 1955, M.B.A., 1956. Credit analyst, loan officer No. Trust Co., Chgo., 1956-59; with Western Bancorp., 1958-70, asst. v.p. United Calif. Bank, San Francisco, 1959-62, exec. v.p. Bank N.Mex., Albuquerque, 1962-70; chmn. bd. dirs. First Nat. Bank, Albuquerque, 1970-75; pres. David Livingston & Assocs., Inc., Albuquerque, 1975—; chmn., N.Mex. Pacific Investment Corp., Albuquerque, 1979—; dir. South China Foods Ltd., Mac Farms, Inc., Amco Services, Inc. Past pres., bd. dirs. Albuquerque YMCA; hon. bd. dirs. Chaparral council Girl Scouts U.S.; past pres., bd. dirs. Assn. Commerce and Industry N.Mex.; past chmn. Albuquerque Needs Com.; pres. bd. trustees Manzano Day Sch., Albuquerque, past bd. dirs. Santa Fe Opera, United Way of Albuquerque, N.Mex. Symphony, Albuquerque Acad. Clubs: Albuquerque Petroleum, Albuquerque Country, Tennis, Exec. Sports. Home: 1730 Lafayette Dr NE Albuquerque NM 87106 Office: 501 Tijeras NW Albuquerque NM 87102

LIVINGSTON, JOSEPH CALVIN, JR., accountant, tax consultant; b. Quincy, Fla., July 28, 1955; s. Joseph C. and Irma K. Livingston; m. Josephine M. Bruins, Aug. 19, 1973; children—Damian, Tracy. Student Talahassee Comml. Coll., 1972-74, Chaffey Coll., 1975-78. Enrolled agt. U.S. Treasury Dept. Cost acct. Purex Corp., City of Industry, Calif., 1978-79; staff acct. Acme Acctg., Upland, Calif., 1979-82; founder, ptnr. Livingston & Assocs., Upland, 1982—. Mem. Calif. Soc. Enrolled Agts. (dir.), Nat. Soc. Pub. Accts. Home: 8551 Avalon Ct Alta Loma CA 91701 Office: 715 N Mountain Ave Suite E Upland CA 91786

LIVINGSTON, PATRICIA ANN (PAT MURPHY), manufacturing company executive; b. Manila, July 30, 1934; d. Marion Michelin and Phoebe (Nelson) Karolchuck; B.A., Reed Coll., 1955; m. Johnston R. Livingston, Sept. 4, 1965; adopted children—Henry, Ann, Jane, David. With George Washington U. Office Human Resources Research, 1955-58; asst. sec.-treas. Bus. Equipment Mfg. Assn., N.Y.C., 1958-60; fin. writer N.Y. Post, 1961-62, Chgo. Daily News, 1962-66; fin. columnist Dallas Morning News, 1966-71, also syndicated by Newsday, 1968-69; v.p. fin. Enmark Corp., Denver, 1971—; also dir. Trustee, Colo. Women's Coll., 1979—, U. Denver, 1982—; mem. exec. bd. U. Denver Theatre Assn., 1978—. Episcopalian. Club: Denver. Home: 869 Vine St Denver CO 80206 Office: 5070 Oakland St Denver CO 80239

LIVINGSTON, PETER MYER, educator, artist. B.A., Brigham Young U., 1956; M.F.A., U. Utah, 1959; summer student Harry Sternberg and Joseph Hirsch. One-man show Glass and Light, Salt Lake Art Ctr., 1980; group shows include Light, Motion, Space, Walker Art Ctr., Mpls., 1967, Some More Beginnings, Bklyn. Mus., 1968, Art and Tech., High Mus. Art, Atlanta, 1969, Art of the 60s, Denver Art Mus., 1970, Kinetic Light Show, Phoenix Art Mus., 1973, Utah Valley Sculptors Invitational, Springville Art Mus., 1979; represented in permanent collections at Colorado Springs Fine Arts Ctr., Denver Art Mus., U. Nev., Las Vegas, Phoenix Art Mus., Salt Lake Art Ctr.; assoc. prof. chmn. dept. art U. Nev., Las Vegas, 1962-72; art gallery dir. Brigham Young U., Provo, Utah, 1972-78, prof. art, 1972—. Recipient Best in Show for Ars Moriendi, Spring Art Roundup, 1965, 2d prize for painting Utah State Inst. Fine Arts Exhbn., 1974. Mem. Western Assn. Art Mus. (regional rep., 1974-78), Am. Assn. Art Mus., Utah Mus. Assn. Office: Dept Art Harris Fine Arts Center Brigham Young University Provo UT 84602

LIVINGSTON, SALLY LOU, human relations consultant; b. Herington, Kans., Oct. 23, 1932; d. Harry Francis and Laura Frances (Montgomery) Duke; m. Addison Hugh Livingston, Sept. 2, 1951 (div.); children—Michael, Barbara, David, Margaret Anne. Student U. Kans., 1950, Wichita U., 1951, Coll. San Mateo, 1973; B.A. in Urban Studies, San Francisco State U., 1975. Chair, Call for Action, Sta. KABL, San Francisco, 1969-73, regional dir. Call for Action, Washington, 1970-73; intern Kramer Blum & Assocs., San Francisco, 1974-75; women's program staff assoc. CORO Found., San Francisco, 1975; founder, prin. MAINSTREAM Planning Assocs., Foster City, Calif., 1975—; dir. Williams Concept/ACTIVATE!, Foster City, Business Woman mag. Past dir. Organize Tng. Ctr., San Francisco; mem. steering com. Bay Area Orgn. Pres. Council San Mateo; mem. steering com. San Mateo County Women's Found. Recipient Outstanding Contbn. award Golden Gate chpt. Tng. and Devel., 1976, 80; Excellence in Leadership award Women Entrepreneurs, 1982; Women for Women award San Mateo chpt. Soroptimists, 1983. Mem. Women Entrepreneurs Bay Area (pres. 1982), San Mateo Exec. Women's Roundtable (founder), Organizational Devel. Network. Democrat. Mem. Disciples of Christ Ch. Columnist San Francisco Examiner Career Series, 1980-83; founder, pub. VENTURING newsletter, 1980-83; author: A Handbook for Quality Circles and Team Building: The MAINSTREAM Model, 1981. Home: 866 Cortez Foster City CA 94404

LIVINGSTON-LITTLE, DALLAS EUGENE, historian; b. Ravalli, Mont., Sept. 25, 1916; s. Onlie Vane and Laura (Livingston) L.; B.A., Wash. State U., 1936; M.A., U. Ala., 1938; Ph.D., U. So. Calif., 1961. Tchr. high sch., Idaho, 1940-42; history instr., student activities coordinator Narbonne High Sch. and Los Angeles City Coll., 1946-55, student activities coordinator, chmn. dept. history, 1955-57; prof. Calif. State U., Northridge, 1968-69; placement dir. Los Angeles Valley Coll., 1957-76, prof. history and placement dir. emeritus, 1976—. Active Valley Committee for Employment of Handicapped. Served to capt. AUS, 1942-46. Mem. Res. Officers Assn. (pres. chpt. 1982), Personnel and Indsl. Relations Assn., Am. Hist. Assn., Calif. Hist. Soc., Hist. Soc. So. Calif., AAUP, Western Hist. Assn., Calif. Community Coll. Placement Assn., Western Writers Am., Los Fiesteros De Los Angeles, Kappa Sigma, Phi Alpha Theta. Democrat. Presbyn. Author: An Economic History of North Idaho, 1800-1900, 1964; The Mexican War Diary of Thomas B. Tennery, 1970; also numerous articles on Western history and Indians. Editorial bd. Jour. of West. Home: 15284 Rayneta Dr Sherman Oaks CA 91403 Office: 5800 Fulton Ave Van Nuys CA 91401

LIVSEY, ROBERT CALLISTER, lawyer; b. Salt Lake City, Aug. 7, 1936; s. Robert Francis and Rosezella Ann (Callister) L.; B.S., U. Utah, 1962, J.D., 1965; LL.M., NYU, 1967; m. Renate Guertler, Sept. 3, 1962; children—Scott, Rachel, Daniel, Benjamin. Bar: Utah 1965, Calif. 1967. Clk. to Hon. Alan J. Crockett, Utah Supreme Ct., 1965; lectr. in comml. law and acct. Haile Sellasie U., Addis Ababa, Ethiopia, 1965-66; spl. asst. to chief counsel for IRS, 1977-79; assoc. Brobeck, Phleger & Harrison, San Francisco, 1967-75, mem. firm, 1975—; mem. taxation law adv. com. Calif. Bd. Legal Specialization; adj. prof. U. San Francisco Law Sch., 1969-76. Served with USAF, 1955-58. Mem. ABA (chmn. real estate syndications subcom.), Calif. Bar Assn. (chmn.-elect taxation sect., exec. com.), San Francisco Bar Assn. (chmn. taxation com. 1982), Calif. Soc. C.P.A.s, Am. Inst. C.P.A.s, Am. Law Inst., Order of Coif, Beta Gamma Sigma. Research editor U. Utah Law Rev., 1964-65; grad. editor Tax Law Rev., 1966-67. Home: 128 LaSalle Piedmont CA 94610 Office: One Market Plaza San Francisco CA 94105

LIZARDI, LINDA CAROL, mfg. co. exec.; b. San Diego, Calif., Aug. 27, 1954; d. Francisco Martinez and Jesse Marie (Comer) L. Student San Diego State U., 1972-73; B.A., Calif. State U., Fresno, 1976. Community coordinator March of Dimes, Fresno, 1976; sec. Blue Thumb Co., Los Angeles, 1977, advt. mgr., salesperson, 1977-78, mgr. advt. and sales, 1978-79, pres., 1979—. Active Big Sisters of Los Angeles. Mem. Exhibit Designers and Producers Assn. (pres. elect Western chpt.), Women in Bus., Press Forum Los Angeles, Fresno Alumni Assn., AAUW, NOW. Home: 14823 Leadwell St Van Nuys CA 91405 Office: 5247 San Fernando Rd W Los Angeles CA 90039

LIZUT, NONA MOORE PRICE, state health ofcl.; b. Quay, N.Mex., Aug. 8, 1923; d. Charley W. and Alba Moore; student N.Mex. State U., 1941-42; m. Charles P. Price, Jr., 1944; 1 son, Charles P. III; m. 2d, William J. Lizut, May 27, 1970. Sec., N.Mex. State Health Dept., Santa Fe, 1942-44: sec. environ. div., 1951-68; adminstrv. sec. environ. div. N.Mex. Health and Social Services Dept., Santa Fe, 1968-74, adminstrv. asst. to dep. dir., 1974-78; adminstrv. asst. to dep. sec. N.Mex. Health and Environ. Dept., Santa Fe, 1978-82, adminstr. health services div., 1982—. Mem. N.Mex. Water Pollution Control Assn. (life, adminstrv. officer 1956-71), N.Mex. Pub. Health Assn. (sec.-treas. 1962-68, pres. elect 1969), Nat. Secs. Assn. (v.p., program chmn. rec. sec., corr. sec.), Santa Fe C. of C. (women's div.). Club: Capitol City Bus. and Profl. Women's (v.p., program chmn.). Home: 1408 Santa Rosa Dr Santa Fe NM 87501 Office: 735 St Michaels Dr Santa Fe NM 87503

LLEWELLYN, MARCUS DELANEY, civic worker; b. Chgo., Oct. 6, 1925; s. Clifford Delaney and Dity Simpson Llewellyn; student Calif. State U., 1946; m. Mamie McKay, June 15, 1956 (div.); children—Diane, Frank. Supr., Moonlite Maintenance, Los Angeles; dir. Llewellyn's Bldg. Maintenance; asst. dir. 7th Step Found., Los Angeles; founder, dir. Americans Helping People, Los Angeles. Served with USAF, 1942-46. Democrat. Roman Catholic. Office: 1207 Plymouth Blvd Los Angeles CA 90019

LLOYD, DONALD FLETCHER, public works director; b. Portland, Oreg., Sept. 18, 1921; s. Arthur E. and Gertrude (Ward) L; m. Helen Elizabeth Oswald, Oct. 30, 1943; children—Diane Bertsch, W. Scott. Student Regis Coll., Denver, 1965; B.C.E., Oreg. State U., 1950. Registered profl. engr., Idaho, 1954, Oreg., 1958. Engr., mgr. North Roseburg (Oreg.) San. Dist., 1950-52; engr. CH2M Hill, Oreg. and Utah, 1952-58; city engr. City of Idaho Falls, 1958-62; dir. pub. works, 1962—. Pres. Eagle Rock Sch. PTA, 1960-61; bd. dirs., sec. ARC, 1977-81; commr., sec. Flood Control Dist. 1 of Idaho, 1978—; mem. adv. bd. Pollution Control, 1983. Served to sgt. AC, U.S. Army, 1942-46. Recipient Meritorious Service award for Teton Dam Disaster, Gov. of Idaho, 1965; Silver Beaver award Boy Scouts Am. Mem. Am. Pub. Works Assn., Am. Water Works Assn., Idaho Soc. Engrs., Nat. Soc. Profl. Engrs. Contbr. papers to profl. confs. and jours. Office: 380 C St PO Box 220 Idaho Falls ID 83402

LLOYD, GLEN ASHTON, architect; b. Salt Lake City, Dec. 6, 1928; s. George Careless and Leah (Ashton) L.; m. Sylvia Knight, Oct. 8, 1959; children—Brian G., Warren K., Daniel G., Allison M., Karen L. Student U. Utah, 1948, 51-54; B. Arch., U. Wash., 1956. Lic. architect, Utah. With archtl. firms, Seattle, 1956-57; chief planner Utah State Bldg. Bd., Salt Lake City, 1958-63; prin. Glen Lloyd Architects, Salt Lake City, 1963-78; architect Lloyd & Butler Architects, Salt Lake City, 1978—. Chmn. N.E. Regional Council Neighborhood Assns., Salt Lake City, 1982—; mem. Days of '47 com., Salt Lake City, 1978—; mem. Salt Lake City Bd. Edn., 1971-72; bd. dirs. Great Salt Lake Council Boy Scouts Am., 1972-79. Mem. AIA, Nat. Council Architectural Registration Bds., Council Edn. Facilities Planners, Sons of Utah Pioneers (nat. pres. 1982-83). Mormon. Home: 70 Dorchester Dr Salt Lake City UT 84103 Office: 511 E 3d S Salt Lake City UT 84102

LLOYD, JOHN BRADFORD, JR., marketing executive; b. Colorado Springs, Colo., Jan 1, 1940; s. John Bradford and Jessie Doris (Smith) L.; m. 2d Pamela Sue Peak, July 6, 1980; children—Patricia, John III, Brendan. B.S., U. Colo., 1963. Asst. mgr. Decol's Inc., Los Alamos, N.Mex., 1964-69; dist. sales mgr. EPOI, Inc., San Francisco, also N.Y.C., 1969-79; dir. mktg. Abrahamson and Assocs., Denver, 1979-80; corp. mktg. dir. Adams, Inc., 1980-81; gen. mgr., Rocky Mountain ADS, Inc., Denver, 1981—. Recipient various sales awards. Club: Associated Railroads of Colo. (Denver). Home: 145 W Midway Blvd Broomfield CO 80020 Office: Rocky Mountain Ads Inc 400 W Colfax Ave Denver CO 80204

LLOYD, JUDSON FRANK, physician; b. N.Y.C., Dec. 2, 1934; s. Frank Sidney and Julia (Wester) L.; B.A., Western Wash. State U., 1956; M.D., Siriraj Med. Sch., Bangkok, Thailand, 1962; m. Russana M. Lloyd; children—Kathryn Anne, Pamela Patricia, Mark Alan, Jeffrey Frank. Intern, Siriraj Med. Sch. Hosp., Bangkok, 1962-63; acting dir. Ben Houei Sai Loas Hosp. of Thomas A. Dooley Found., 1962; resident in surgery Mt. Carmel Hosp., Columbus, Ohio, 1962-63, Mpls. VA Hosp., 1964-66, Virginia Mason Med. Center, Seattle, 1968-69, Watts Hosp., Durham, N.C., 1969-70; staff surgeon Natchez (Miss.) Charity Hosp., 1970; pvt. practice, Belzoni, Miss., 1970-71; staff physician Medgar Evars Comprehensive Health Center, Fayette, Miss., 1971-72, med. dir., 1972-73; owner Christian Clinic, Natchez, 1973-79; med. dir. Programa de Salud de No. Colo., Gill, 1979; mem. staffs Natchez Charity, Jefferson County hosps.; clin. instr. dept. family medicine Med. Sch., U. Miss., 1977-79; physician IV Fort Logan Med. Center, Denver, 1979-80; pvt. practice Longmont, Colo., 1979—. Pres., Montebello Elementary and Jr. High Sch. PTA, Natchez, 1973-74; trustee S.W. chpt. Miss. ACLU, 1974-76; bd. dirs. Miss. chpt. Am. Cancer Soc., 1975-76; founder mem. bd. dirs. Natchez YMCA, 1975-77, v.p., 1977-78, pres., 1978-79; adv. AJF Improvement Corp., Natchez; home health adviser Adams County Pub. Health Dept., 1975-79. Mem. Longmont Human Relations Commn., 1981—, Longmont Coalition for Women, 1979-81. Served in M.C., U.S. Army, 1966-68; Vietnam. Diplomate Am. Bd. Family Practice. Fellow Am. Acad. Family Practice; mem. AMA (Physicians Achievement certificate 1968, 72, 76, 80), Nat., Miss. med. assn., Miss. Med. and Surg. Assn. (trustee 1977-79), Colo. Acad. Family Practice, Mile High Med. Soc. Am. Coll. Emergency Physicians (charter mem.), Christian Med. Soc., Miss. Thoracic Assn., Miss. Found Med. Care, NAACP. Democrat. Presbyterian. Contbr. articles to profl. publs. Home and Office: Suite D 1380 Tulip St Longmont CO 80501

LLOYD, RICHARD ALAN, psychiatrist; b. Detroit, Nov. 17, 1939; s. Emlyn and Ethel Lucile (Walker) L.; B.A., U. Mich., 1961; M.D., Stanford U., 1966; m. Mollyanne Weber, Dec. 20, 1966; children—Dawn Marie, Jennifer Ellen, Adam Michael, Anwylyd Elizabeth. Intern, Stanford U. Med. Center, 1966-67; resident in psychiatry and fellow child psychiatry UCLA Neuropsychiat. Inst., 1967-71; med. dir. Mental Health Services Mariposa County (Calif.), 1972-74; staff psychiatrist Mental Health Services Merced County (Calif.), 1972-73; dir. Merced County Mental Health, 1973-74; practice medicine specializing in child, adolescent and adult psychiatry, Merced, 1974—; mem. staff Mercy Hosp., Merced, Merced Community Med. Center; dir. counseling program Catholic Community Merced; cons. in field. Vice chmn. bd. trustees St. Luke's Day Sch., Merced, 1974-82; mem. Our Lady of Mercy Sch. Bd., Merced, 1979-81. Served with M.C., USAF, 1971-72. Diplomate Am. Bd. Psychiatry and Neurology. Mem. AMA, Am. Psychiat. Assn., Am. Soc. Clin. Hypnosis, Internat. Soc. Hypnosis, Central Calif. Psychiat. Soc., Calif. Med. Assn., Merced-Mariposa Med. Soc. (pres. 1982). Republican. Roman Catholic. Clubs: Merced Rotary (pres. 1983-84, dir.), KC. Contbr. articles to profl. jours. Office: 2039 Canal St Merced CA 95340

LOBB, CHARLES WILLIAM, electronics co. ofcl.; b. Kansas City, Mo., Dec. 10, 1932; s. Lloyd W. and Urazelle M. (Huhn) L.; B.E.E., U. Minn., 1955; M.S. in Elec. Engring., U. So. Calif., 1968; m. Charlotte Jane Carter, Aug. 9, 1961; children—Carolyn Jane, Patricia Ann. Mem. engring. research and devel. staff Gen. Mills, Inc., Mpls., 1955-56; mem. tech. staff Hughes Aircraft Co., Culver City, Calif., 1958-68, group head, 1968-71, sect. head, 1971-78, dept. mgr., 1978-80, corp. dir., 1980—, instr. electronics, 1967-78; lectr. UCLA, 1982; cons. Calif. Commn. Indsl. Innovation, 1982—; asst. dir. Tech. Edn. Center, Culver City, 1980—. Mem. adv. council Sch. Continuing Edn., U. So. Calif., 1982-83. Served as capt. USAF, 1956-58. Recipient Air Def. Command Commendation, 1964; Hughes fellow, 1966-68. Mem. IEEE, Am. Radio Relay League, Quarter Century Wireless Assn., Calif. Engring. Found., Am. Soc. Engring. Edn. Contbr. articles on computers to profl. publs. Home: 1843 244th St Lomita CA 90717 Office: Hughes Aircraft Co PO Box 1042 El Segundo CA 90245

LOBDELL, ROBERT CHARLES, newspaper executive, lawyer; b. Mankato, Minn., Jan. 1, 1926; s. Darwin Norman and Hilda Cecelia (Peterson) L.; m. Nancy Marion Lower, July 12, 1952; children—Teresa Lobdell Johnson, Robert John, William Scott, James Marston. A.B., Stanford U., 1948, LL.B., 1950. Bar: Calif. 1951, U.S. Supreme Ct. 1964. Atty., corp. officer Youngstown Sheet and Tube Co. (Ohio), 1952-65; asst. gen. counsel, asst. sec. Times Mirror Co., Los Angeles, 1965-70, v.p., asst. sec., 1970—; v.p., gen. counsel Los Angeles Times, 1970—. Sec., trustee Pfaffinger Found., Los Angeles Times Fund. Served with USAAF, 1944-45; to lt. USAR, 1951-52. Mem. Los Angeles County Bar Found. (dir.), Inst. for Corp. Counsel (chmn. gov.), Lawyers Adv. Council, Constl. Rights Found., ABA, Calif. Bar Assn., Los Angeles County Bar Assn., Am. Soc. Corp. Secs. Episcopalian. Club: University (Los Angeles). Co-editor: So. Calif. Conf. on Media and Law, 1977.

LOBERG, ROBERT WARREN, artist, educator; b. Chgo., Dec. 1, 1927; s. Merton Irving and Ruth Meldred (Mahon) L. Numerous one-man shows including: Artist's Gallery, N.Y.C., 1959, Oakland Jewish Community Ctr., 1960, Staempfli Gallery, N.Y.C., 1962, Henry Gallery, U. Wash., 1968, Calif. Coll. Arts and Crafts, 1969, Berkeley (Calif.) Art Ctr., 1977, San Jose Mus. Art, 1978, Sun Gallery, Hayward, Calif., 1983; 2-man show: Walnut Creek (Calif.) Civic Arts Ctr., 1983; group shows: Ithaca Coll. Mus. Art, 1968, San Francisco Art Festival, 1963-79, Oakland (Calif.) Mus., 1977, San Francisco Mus. Modern Art, 1979, Gallery Paule Anglim, San Francisco, 1980, 81, numerous others; works represented in permanent collections: Art Inst. Chgo., San Francisco Art Commn., Portland (Oreg.) Art Mus., Henry Gallery, U. Wash., Seattle, Oakland Art Mus., Gallery of Modern Art, Washington, North Truro (Mass.) Art Gallery, Naples (Fla.) Art Gallery, Synanon House, Oakland, Calif. Coll. Arts and Crafts, Security Pacific Nat. Bank, Los Angeles, Itel Corp., also pvt. collections; lectr. art U. Calif.-Berkeley, 1955, 56, 59, 65, instr. in art. 1965; instr. painting and drawing Calif. Coll. Arts and Crafts, Oakland, 1961-63, lectr. in art, 1981; instr. painting and drawing, San Francisco Art Inst., 1963-66; vis. faculty dept. art U. Wash., Seattle, 1967-68; instr. art Acad. Art Coll., San Francisco, 1970; lectr. art Contra Costa Coll., San Pablo, Calif., 1971, U. Caif.-Davis, 1971-72; pvt. instr., 1972-79. Bd. dirs. Artists Council, San Francisco Art Inst., 1963-65. Served with USMC, 1946-47. Recipient numerous awards including Fine Arts Merit award San Francisco Art Festival, 1976; Nat. Endowment for Arts fellow, 1982, 83. Contbr. articles to art publs. Home: 2020 Vine St Berkeley CA 94709

LOBUE, ANGE JOSEPH, psychiatrist, communications cons., med. services adminstr.; b. New Orleans, Aug. 12, 1937; s. Joseph V. and Augustine (Palmintier) L.; B.S. in Pharmacy, U. Miss., 1960; M.D., La. State U., 1964; M.P.H. in Health Services Adminstrn., UCLA, 1969; m. Susan Bailey Flaherty, Feb. 28, 1976. Intern in medicine and surgery So. Pacific Meml. Hosp., San Francisco, 1964-65; resident in gen. preventive medicine UCLA, 1968-72, resident in psychiatry Neuropsychiat. Inst., 1969-72; practice medicine specializing in psychiatry, Los Angeles, 1972—; sr. public health physician Venice Youth Clinic, Los Angeles Dept. Health, 1969-70; vis. scholar dept. preventive medicine St. Thomas Hosp. and Ministry Health, London, 1969, dept. psychiatry U. Edinburgh (Scotland), 1969, Fed. Inst. Medicine, U. Belgrade (Yugoslavia), 1969, spl. asst. to adminstr., HSMHA, health services HEW, Washington 1970; asst. to pres. N.Y.C. Health and Hosps. Corp., 1970-71; asst. clin. prof. dept. psychiatry UCLA, 1972—; asso. dir. health info. and services Roche Lab. div. Hoffmann-LaRoche, Inc., Long Beach, 1977—; mem. med. staff Century City Hosp., chmn. dept. psychiatry, 1973-77; mem. med. staff Bauer Hosp., St. Mary's Med Center, Long Beach, Cedars-Sinai Med Center, Los Angeles New Hosp., Meml. Hosp. Med. Center, Long Beach, Pacific Hosp., Long Beach, Los Alamitos Hosp., Westwood Hosp., Los Angeles; guest lectr. Columbia U. Sch. Public Health, N.Y.C., 1970; planning coordinator Calif. Commn. Regional Med. Programs, 1967; med. dir. Central City Drug Abuse Program, 1975-77; lectr., condr. seminars on communications, health services mgmt., psychiatry. Alt., Mayor's Organizational Task Force on Comprehensive Health Planning, N.Y.C., 1970-71. Served to capt. M.C., U.S. Army, 1965-67; Vietnam. Diplomate Am. Bd. Psychiatry and Neurology; registered pharmacist, Tex. Fellow Royal Soc. Health, Am. Geriatrics Soc. (founding), Acad. Psychosomatic Medicine; mem. AMA, World, Calif., Los Angeles County med. assns., Am. Coll. Preventive Medicine, Am., World psychiat. assns., AAAS, Am. Soc. Adolescent Psychiatry, Am. Acad. Clin. Psychiatrists, So. Calif. Psychiat. Soc.,

Biofeedback Soc. Am., Biofeedback Research Soc., Am. Soc. Clin. Pharmacology and Therapeutics, AMA, Calif. Soc. Treatment of Alcoholism and Other Drug Dependencies, Physicians Drug Council So. Calif. Soc. Adolescent Psychiatry, Western Pharmacology Soc., UCLA Alumni Assn., Delta Omega. Contbr. numerous articles to profl. jours.; co-editor Psychiatry and the Media Newsletter, 1982—. Office: 2429 Pacific Ave Long Beach CA 90806

LOCK, EUGENE RAYMONG (GENE), advertising executive; b. Jefferson City, Mo., June 6, 1943; s. Harry Paul and Ann Jeannette (Reinkemeyer) L.; m. Susan Ann Heinen, May 18, 1967. B.A. in Journalism, Lincoln U. Mo., 1965; M.A. in Advt., Pub. Relations, U. Mo., 1973. Account exec., copywriter C.O. Bogges Advt. Agy., Sacramento, 1973-75; pres., chief exec. officer Lock Agy., Inc., Sacramento, 1975—. Mem. pub. relations com. Sacramento chpt. ARC. Served to maj. USAF, 1965-73; Vietnam. Decorated Air medal with 7 clusters. Mem. Sacramento Assn. Advt. Agys. (treas.), Sacramento C. of C. (mil. affairs com.), Sacramento Advt. Club. Home: 7061 Wilshire Circle Sacramento CA 95822 Office: 3009 F St Sacramento CA 95816

LOCKART, BARBETTA, counselor, educator, researcher, writer; b. Sacramento, Calif., Feb. 28, 1947; d. Bernard Elwood and Naomi Joyce (Wilson) L.; m. Michael Stanley Ray, Dec. 29, 1982. A.A. in English, Southwestern Coll., Chula Vista, Calif., 1974; B.A., San Diego State U., 1975; M.A. in Edn. Adminstrn., N.Mex. State U.-Las Cruces, 1979, M.A. in Counseling and Guidance, 1981. Sec., interim coordinator, tchr. Indian Edn. Project, Palm Springs (Calif.) Unified Sch. Dist., 1976-79; outreach counselor Tecumseh House/Boston Indian Council, 1980-81, asst. dir., 1981; acad. counselor, coordinator native Am. affairs Eastern N.Mex. U., Portales, 1981-82; ind. researcher in field of counseling, Albuquerque, 1982—; speaker in field of community edn., alcoholism, urban native Am. women. Rockefeller Found. fellow, 1978-79; Nat. Inst. Edn. fellow, 1979-80. Mem. Nat. Edn. Assn., Am. Indian Higher Edn. Council, Am. Personnel and Guidance Assn., N.Mex. Personnel and Guidance Assn. Author: Resolving Discipline Problems for Indian Students: A Preventative Approach, 1981; contbr. articles to profl. jours.

LOCKHART, JAMES BLAKELY, diversified services company executive, lawyer; b. N.Y.C., May 27, 1936; s. Edgar L. and Margaret Evelyn (Blakely) L.; m. Ruth Douglas, Oct. 30, 1976; children—Marc Blakeley, Diallo Williams. B.S. in Bus. Adminstrn., Boston U., 1957; J.D., 1959. Bar: Ill. 1963. Asst. corp. counsel City of Chgo.; ptnr. Rivers, Lockhart, Clayter & Lawrence, Chgo., 1965-71; v.p., gen. counsel, sec. Budget Rent A Car, Chgo., 1971-78, sr. v.p. legal affairs, sec., 1978-79; v.p. pub. affairs Transam. Corp., San Francisco, 1979—. Chmn. bd. dirs. Sta. KQED, Sta. KQED-TV; chmn. bd. dirs. Bay Area Urban League; mem. exec. com. Downtown Assn. San Francisco; mem. steering com. St. Mary's Coll. Exec. Symposium. Served to capt. U.S. Army, 1960-63. Mem. Pub. Affairs Council (dir.), Calif. Roundtable (dep.), ABA, Nat. Bar Assn., Ill. Bar Assn., San Francisco C. of C. (chmn. pub. affairs com.). Clubs: World Trade, Commonwealth of Calif., Moraga Country, San Francisco Tennis. Office: Transam Corp 600 Montgomery St 24th Floor San Francisco CA 94111

LOCKHART, KORALJKA, opera magazine editor, public relations administrator; b. Dubrovnik, Yugoslavia, May 30, 1932; came to U.S., 1965, naturalized, 1971; d. Zvonimir Peter and Lina (Kukuljica) Krstic; m. Keith M., Lockhart, July 26, 1966 (div. 1979). Student Music Sch., Dubrovnik, 1941-51, U. Zagreb (Yugoslavia), 1951-55. Music dir. Sta. KKHI-AM-FM, San Francisco, 1965-70; press rep. San Francisco Opera, 1970-74, mag. editor, pub. relations dir., 1981—; acting pub. relations dir. San Francisco Symphony, 1979-80; dir. promotion Com. for Arts and Lectures, U. Calif., Berkeley, 1974-78; cons. in field. Author: San Francisco Opera: The Adler Years, 1953-81, 1981; Opera Calendar, 1980-81. Home: 289 Lexington Rd Kensington CA 94707 Office: War Meml Opera House San Francisco CA 94102

LOCKNANE, MICHAEL SCOTT, accountant; b. Seattle, Oct. 3, 1945; s. Charles Scott (dec.) and Verbenia Alice (Francis) L.; student Everett Jr. Coll., 1963-65; B.B.A. in Acctg., Boise (Idaho) State U., 1973; m. Carol Raie Todhunter, Oct. 14, 1967; children—Kristina, Cindy, Mindy. Owner acct. Locknane Acctg., Nampa, Idaho, 1974—. Treas. Majors & Minors, Nampa, 1975—, Nampa Countryman's Club, 1979—; campaign chmn. Nampa Area United Way, 1982. Served with USAF, 1966-69. Recipient President award plaque Idaho Assn. Public Accts., 1980. Mem. Idaho Assn. Public Accts. (pres.), Nat. Soc. Public Accts. (fed. taxation com.). Presbyn. Clubs: Majors and Minors; Elk. Home: Route 3 Box 3668 Nampa ID 83651 Office: PO Box 996-1712 9th St S Nampa ID 83651

LOCKWOOD, BARBARA JORDAN, nurse, adminstr.; b. Landshut, W. Ger., Aug. 23, 1948; d. Bob Ernest and Christa Barbara (Tilgner) Jordan; B.S., U. Colo., 1970, M.S., 1973. Nurse, Denver Gen. Hosp., 1970-72; nurse Med. Personnel Pool, Denver, 1973; flight nurse St. Anthony Hosp. System, Denver, 1973-75, flight nurse supr., 1975-76, mgr. critical care services, 1976-79, systems dir. nursing service, 1979-81, asst. exec. dir. nursing services, 1981—; resource person on trauma and emergency care. Vol. nurse Comitis Crisis Center, 1971-73; instr. various nursing orgns. Mem. Am. Acad. Med. Adminstrs., Am. Coll. Med. Adminstrs.; Am. Assn. Critical Care Nurses, Nat. League Nursing, Colo. League Nurses (sec. 1982-84), Sigma Theta Tau. Democrat. Lutheran. Contbr. chpt. to Critical Care Nursing, 1977; contbr. articles to profl. jours. Office: 4231 W 16th Ave St Anthony Hosp Denver CO 80204

LOCKWOOD, COURTNEY DANA, public relations professional; b. San Bernardino, Calif., Oct. 9, 1951; d. Carleton W. and Jeane M. (Plumb) L.; m. David Mikio Kabashima, Jan. 1, 1976; 1 son, Gregory Ryan Kabashima. A.B., Occidental Coll., 1972; profl. designation in Pub. Relations, UCLA, 1978. Account coordinator J. Walter Thompson, Los Angeles, 1974-75; pub. relations dir. San Fernando (Calif.) Valley council Girl Scouts U.S.A., 1975-78; pub. relations specialist Calif. Computer Products, Anaheim, Calif., 1978-79; account supr. Harshe-Rotman & Druck, Inc., Los Angeles, 1979-81; group supr. The Bohle Co., Los Angeles, 1981—. Mem. Pub. Relations Soc. Am. (accredited), Publicity Club Los Angeles (v.p., outstanding pub. relations program award 1980). Office: The Bohle Co 1901 Ave of the Stars Suite 450 Los Angeles CA 90067

LOCKWOOD, JO ANN CECELIA, seminar director; San Francisco, Mar. 2, 1931; d. Bruno and Edna M. (Dal Porto) Del Debbio; m. Robert L. Lockwood, June 3, 1950; 1 son, Kenneth J. Student Healds Coll., San Francisco, 1949-50. Exec. sec. Social Security Adminstrn., San Francisco, 1951-53, cons. firms, San Francisco, 1967-71; seminar dir. U.S. Dental Inst., San Francisco and Orange County, Calif., Seattle and Calgary, Alta., Can., 1972—. Roman Catholic. Office: US Dental Inst 346 Littlefield Ave S San Francisco CA 94080

LODGE, MICHAEL JOSEPH, culinary educator, catering service exec.; b. Bklyn., Sept. 7, 1955; s. Damian Michael and Virginia Yolanda (Tummennilli) Lagennusa; m. Deanna Kay Lindeman, June 5, 1978. A.A., Culinary Inst. Am., 1976; student Colo. State U., 1981-82. Chef, Walt Disney Prodns., Orlando, Fla., 1971-79, Sheraton Denver Tech. Ctr., 1979-80; culinary educator Aurora Pub. Schs. Tech. Ctr., Aurora, Colo., 1980—; pres. Profl. Catering Services, Inc., Aurora, 1979—. Mem. Colo. Edn. Assn., Am. Edn. Assn. Republican. Roman Catholic. Office: 500 Buckley Rd Aurora CO 80011

LOEB, ROGER MARTIN, computer services co. exec.; b. Chgo., July 27, 1941; s. Martin Bernard and Dorothy Grace (Walker) L.; B.S. in Math., U. Wis., 1964; m. Mileah Lynnore Harrington, July 16, 1977; children—Roger Gregory, Remy Mileah. Successively programmer, systems analyst, systems programmer, dir. research and devel. Neodata Services Co., Boulder, Colo., 1965-75; mktg. rep. Computer Scis. Corp., Mountain View, Calif., 1975-76; pres. Creative Profits Co., Sunnyvale, Calif., 1976-77; v.p. data processing Neodata Services Group, A.C. Nielsen Co., Boulder, 1977—. Home: 3457 Iris Ct Boulder CO 80302 Office: 1255 Portland Pl Boulder CO 80302

LOEBLICH, HELEN NINA TAPPAN, geologist, educator; b. Norman, Okla., Oct. 12, 1917; d. Frank Girard and Mary Pearl (Jenks) Tappan; m. Alfred Richard Loeblich, Jr., June 18, 1939; children—Alfred Richard III, Karen Elizabeth Loeblich McClelland, Judith Ann Loeblich Covey, Daryl Louise Loeblich Valenzuela. B.S., U. Okla., Norman, 1937, M.S., 1939; Ph.D., U. Chgo., 1942. Instr. geology Tulane U., 1942-43; geologist U.S. Geol. Survey, 1943-45, 47-58; mem. faculty UCLA, 1958—, prof. geology, 1966—, vice chmn. dept., 1973-75; research assoc. Smithsonian Instn., 1954-57. Guggenheim fellow, 1953-54; recipient Woman of Sci. award UCLA Med. Aux., 1982, Cushman award for research Cushman Found. for Foraminiferal Research, 1982. Fellow Geol. Soc. Am. (councilor 1978-81); mem. Paleontol. Soc. (medal for paleontology 1982), Soc. Econ. Paleontology and Mineralogy (councilor, paleontology 1975-77, best paper award 1957, hon. membership awardee 1978), Phycol. Soc. Am., Internat. Phycol. Soc., Soc. Protozoologists, AAUP, Internat. Paleontol. Assn., Marine Biology Assn. U.K., Am. Micros. Soc., Palaeontographical Soc., Phycol. Soc. Gt. Britain, Am. Inst. Biol. Scis., Phi Beta Kappa, Sigma Xi. Author: (with Alfred Loeblich, Jr.) Treatise on Invertebrate Paleontology, Pt. C, Protista 2, 2 vols., 1964; Paleobiology of Plant Protists, 1980; contbr. numerous articles to profl. jours., U.S. govt. publs. and encys.; assoc. editor Cushman Found. Foraminiferal Research, 1950-51; mem. editorial bd. Palaeogeography, Palaeoclimatology, Palaeoecology, 1972-82. Home: 11427 Albata St Los Angeles CA 90049 Office: Dept Earth and Space Sci UCLA Los Angeles CA 90024

LOEBNER, EGON EZRIEL, physicist; b. Plzen, Czechoslovakia, Feb. 24, 1924; s. Emil and Josephine (Koeser) L.; came to U.S., 1947, naturalized, 1952; B.A. in Physics, U. Buffalo, 1950, Ph.D. in Physics, 1955; m. Sonya S. Sajovics, June 18, 1950; children—Gary Emil, Benny Joseph, Mindy Sue. Draftsman, Danek & Co., Bolevec, Czechoslavakia, 1941-42, asst. to chief engr. Terezin Waterworks, 1942-44; sr. engr. Sylvania Electric Products, Inc., Buffalo and Boston, 1952-55; mem. tech. staff RCA Labs., Princeton, N.J., 1955-61; mgr., research specialist H.P. Assos., Palo Alto, Calif., 1961-65; dept. head, research adviser Hewlett-Packard Labs., 1965-74, lab. assoc., 1976-77, mgr. data base mgmt. systems dept., 1977-80, mgr. cognitive interface dept., 1980—; counselor sci. and technol. affairs U.S. embassy, Moscow, 1974-76; lectr. Stanford U., part-time 1968-74; lectr. U. Calif. at Santa Cruz, 1972-74. Mem. N.J. Commn. on Radiation Protection, 1960-62; mem. lay adv. com. on math. Unified Palo Alto Sch. Dist., 1964-66. Bd. dirs. Jewish Center, Princeton, 1957-59. Fellow Phys. Soc. London; mem. Am. Phys. Soc., IEEE, Am. Optical Soc., Nat. Calif. socs. profl. engrs., AAAS, Sigma Xi, Assn. for Computing Machinery, Cognitive Sci. Soc., N.Y. Acad. Scis., Calif. Acad. Scis., Sigma Alpha Mu. Democrat. Jewish. Club: Palo Alto Hills Golf and Country, Commonwealth. Research in physics, chemistry, electronics, metalurgy, psychology, biophysics, cybernetics, math., sci. policy and linguistics data processing. Patentee in optoelectronics. Home: 2934 Alexis Dr Palo Alto CA 94304 Office: 1501 Page Mill Rd Palo Alto CA 94304

LOEFFLER, RICHARD HARLAN, manufacturing company executive; b. Kansas City, Mo., Sept. 15, 1929; s. Sidney A. and Lily L. (Cowell) L.; children—Kimberly Anne, Mellissa Anne. B.A., U. Mo., 1949; M.B.A., Pepperdine U., 1975. Ptnr., Foristall Co., Los Angeles, 1957-65; pres. Beverly Hills Film Corp. (Calif.), 1963-66; v.p. Buttes Gas & Oil Co., Oakland, Calif., 1965-66; v.p. TRE Corp., 1966-72, pres., chief operating officer, dir., 1976—; pres. Simplex Industries, Inc., Adrian, Mich., 1972-76, also chief exec. officer; dir. Standard Brands Paint Co. Served with U.S. Army, 1950-53. Home: 10308 Briarwood Dr Los Angeles CA 90024 Office: 9460 Wilshire Blvd Beverly Hills CA 90212

LOESCH, RONALD JOHN, newspaper publisher; b. Erie, Pa., Aug. 3, 1952; s. Claude F. and Phyllis J. (Loftis) L.; m. Anne M. Tice, Aug. 6, 1977; 1 dau., Jennifer Anne. Student U. Wis., 1970-73. With prodn. dept. Ketchikan (Alaska) Daily News, 1973-76; owner, pub. Petersburg (Alaska) Pilot, 1976—. Mem. Nat. Newspaper Assn., Sigma Delta Chi. Baptist. Clubs: Rotary, Elks. Office: Petersburg Pilot PO Box 930 Petersburg AK 99833

LOEWE, MAX, food company executive; b. N.Y.C., Dec. 19 1916; s. Gerhard and Rose (Weiss) L.; m. Vivienne Brown, Feb. 9, 1941; children—Gregory D., Allan P. B.S., U. Conn., 1939. Sr. microbiologist Conn. Bur. Labs., Hartford, 1939-44; sect. head Birdseye div. Gen. Foods Co., Boston, 1947-52; tech. dir. Star-Kist Foods, Inc., Terminal Island, Calif., 1952-82, Star Kist tech. cons., 1982—; cons. FAO; mem. Calif. Fisheries Tech. Adv. Com. Served with U.S. Army, 1944-47. Mem. Nat. Food Processors Assn., Pacific Fisheries Technologists, Nat. Planning Fisheries Policy Conf., Food Processors Inst., U.S. Nat. Marine Fishery. Republican. Jewish. Patentee in field. Home: 8032 Rosina St Long Beach CA 90808 Office: Star-Kist Foods Inc 582 Tuna St Terminal Island CA 90731

LOEWENBERG, STEPHEN PETER, mktg. exec.; b. Chgo., May 21, 1937; s. Sydney Bernard and Jeanette Shirley (Braverman) L.; student Ohio U., 1958, N.Y. U., New Sch. Social Research, Harvard Grad. Sch. Bus.; m. Nancy Louise Hug, Oct. 23, 1970; children by previous marriage—David Sydney, Amy. With McCann-Erickson, N.Y.C., 1958-60; asst. advt. dir. Beaunit Fibers, N.Y.C., 1960-64; merchandising mgr. PPG Industries, N.Y.C., 1964-69; mgr. market devel. Ladies Home Jour., N.Y.C., 1969-71; pres. Stephen Loewenberg & Asso., N.Y.C., San Francisco, 1971—; prof. mktg. N.Y. Inst. Advt. Served with USN, 1955-57. Address: #4-15th Ave San Francisco CA 94118

LOEWY, OLIVIA ROCHELLE, personnel adminstrator; b. Calif., Nov. 14, 1946; d. Peter and Annette (Cohen) Markin; m. Aaron David Loewy, June 14, 1970. B.A., UCLA, 1969; M.A. in Ednl. Psychology, Calif. State U.-Northridge; postgrad. U. So. Calif. Cert. marriage, family and child counselor, Calif. Dir. Full Circle Guidance Clinic, Glendale, Calif., 1977-80; cons., trainer Western region U.S. Dept. Labor, 1980—, U.S. Office Personnel Mgmt., 1982—; co-founder Personal Dimensions, Glendale, Calif.; hon. academic appointee Calif. Sch. Profl. Psychology. Mem. Am. Soc. Tng. and Devel., Calif. Assn. Marriage and Family Therapists. Writer numerous fed. funded grant proposals. Home: 11019 Hortense St North Hollywood CA 91602 Office: 417 Arden Ave Glendale CA 91203

LOFSTROM, MARK D., public relations official, arts administrator, writer; management consultant; b. Mpls., May 11, 1953; s. Dennis E. and Dorothy Dee (Schreiber) L. B.A. in Art History, Carleton Coll., 1976. Editorial asst. CANTO: A Rev. of Arts, Andover, Mass., 1977-78; pub. relations asst. Honolulu Acad. Arts, 1979, pub. relations rep., 1980—; sec., dir. Arts Council Hawaii; Mem. Am. Assn. Mus., Pub. Relations and Communications Mgmt. Com., Hawaii Mus. Assn. (editor newsletter), Pub. Relations Soc. Am., Historic Hawaii Found., Nat. Trust for Historic Preservation, Hawaii Lit. Arts Council. Editor mag. on preservation; contbr. articles on current exhbns.; organizer artists and writers exhbn., 1981. Home: 60 E Beretania St Apt 1108 Honolulu HI 96817 Office: Honolulu Acad Arts 900 S Beretania St Honolulu HI 96814

LOGAN, DEBORAH JEAN, cons.; b. Modesto, Calif., Mar. 14, 1952; d. Robert Bruce and Joyce Modean (Sullivan) McFarland; B.A., Calif. State U., 1974; m. W.A. Logan, Sept. 20, 1980. Ops. supr. Am. Nat. Bank, Bakersfield, Calif., 1977-79, loan officer, 1979, regional utility exec. Sacramento, 1979, 1st. v.p., tng. coordinator, Bakersfield, 1980-82; cons. Human Resources Dimensions, 1982—. Mem. Am. Soc. Tng. and Devel., Am. Inst. Banking. Clubs: Little Sisters of the Seven Stars, Soroptimists (vp 1979, rec. sec. 1979). Office: 5401 Business Park S Suite 201 Bakersfield CA 93309

LOGAN, GENE ADAMS, sculptor; b. Kickapoo, Kans., June 14, 1922; s. Frank William and Myrtle (Hundley) L.; B.S., S.W. Mo. State U., 1949; cert. in phys. therapy Med. Coll. Va., 1951; M.S., U. Ill., 1952; Ph.D., U. So. Calif., 1960; M.F.A., U. Kans., 1967; m. Elsie E. Ozal, Jan. 24, 1943 (dec. June 1977); children—Diane Candace, Mark Adams; m. 2d, Elayne Russell Hampton, Sept. 1, 1978. One-man shows: Ankrum Gallery, Los Angeles, 1970, 71, 72, 75, 78, 82, El Camino Coll., Torrance, Calif., 1973, Pioneer Mus. and Haggin Galleries, Stockton, Calif., 1977, Zantman Art Galleries, Ltd., Carmel, Calif., 1979, Townhouse Gallery, New Orleans, 1980, Crowther of Syon Lodge Sculpture Garden, London, 1981; group shows include: Los Angeles Mcpl. Art Show, 1957-60, 62, NAD Ann., N.Y.C., 1961, Nat. Orange Show, San Bernardino, Calif., 1963, 72, 73, Maxwell Galleries, San Francisco, 1973, Invitational Exhbn. San Bernardino County Mus., 1976, Van Doren Gallery, San Francisco, 1976, Crowther of Syon Lodge, Ltd., London, 1980, Laguna Beach (Calif.) Mus. Art, 1982; represented in permanent collections: El Camino Coll. Sculpture Garden, Torrance, Ring Bros. Corp., Santa Monica, Calif., Westmont Industries, Santa Fe Springs, Calif., Chase Nat. Ins. Co., Springfield, Mo., City of La Mirada (Calif.), also pvt. collections. Served with USN, 1942-45. Recipient cash award Los Angeles Mcpl. Art Show, 1957, Medal award, 1962; 1st prize All-Calif. Invitational Exhbt., 1960, 61; 1st prize Gold Medal award Calif. State Fair, 1962; Best of Show, La Mirada Festival of Arts, 1972, honorable mention, 1973. Home 1299 Greenvale Circle Upland CA 91786 Office: 1551 W 13th St Suite 215 Upland CA 91786

LOGAN, LEE ROBERT, orthodontist; b. Los Angeles, June 24, 1923; s. Melvin Duncan and Margaret (Seltzer) L.; B.S., U. Calif., Los Angeles, 1952; D.D.S., Northwestern U., 1956, M.S., 1961; m. Corki Nadler, June 20, 1975; children—Fritz, Dean, Scott, Gigi, Chad, Casey. Gen. practice dentistry, Reseda, Calif., 1958-59; practice dentistry specializing in orthodontics, Northridge, Calif., 1961—; pres. Lee R. Logan D.D.S. Profl. Corp.; mem. staff Northridge Hosp., Tarzana Hosp. Served to lt. USNR, 1956-58. Diplomate Am. Bd. Orthodontics. Fellow Internat. Acad. Nutrition; mem. Am., San Fernando Valley dental assns., Am. Assn. Orthodontists, Pacific Coast Soc. Orthodontists (dir., pres. so. sect. 1974-75, chmn. membership 1981—), Found. Orthodontic Research (charter mem.), Calif. Soc. Orthodontists (chmn. peer rev. 1982), G.U. Black Soc. (charter mem.), Angle Soc. Orthodontists (pres., bd. dirs. 1982—, chmn. membership com. 1982—), Xi Psi Phi. Club: U.S.C. Century. Contbr. articles to profl. jours. Home: 4830 Encino Ave Encino CA 91316 Office: 18250 Roscoe Blvd Northridge CA 91324

LOGAN, THOMAS JACKSON, museum director, Egyptologist; b. San Francisco, Feb. 14, 1942; s. John A. and Jeanne S. (Smith) L.; m. Virginia Baksa, Nov. 1, 1980; children—Sean, Margaret, Thomas. A.A., Foothill Coll., Los Altos Hills, Calif., 1963; B.A. in History, U. Calif.-Berkeley, 1965; postgrad. U. Chgo., 1970. Instr., lectr. Egyptian history, art and archaeology, summers 1959-72; coordinator, instr. adj., depts. history and archaeology Hunter Coll., N.Y.C., 1972-76; adj. assoc. prof. fine arts N.Y. U., N.Y.C., 1979-81; assoc. curator Egyptian dept. Met. Mus. Art, N.Y.C., 1974-81; dir. Monterey (Calif.) Peninsula Mus. Art, 1981—; bd. dirs. Monterey Conf. Ctr. Art Commn.; trustee Caesarea World Monument. U. Chgo. fellow, 1967, 68-69; Patricia R. and Edmundo Lassale Fellow in Egyptology, 1969-70; Oriental Inst. fellow, 1970-71; Met. Mus. profl. travel stipend grantee, 1976. Mem. Am. Hist. Assn., Am. Research Ctr. Cairo, Egypt Exploration Soc. London, Calif. Assn. Mus. (bd. dirs.), Central Coast Art Assn., Phi Alpha Theta. Club: U. Chgo. Archaeology (pres. 1967-68). Contbr. publs. to profl. jours. Home: 24798 Santa Rita St Carmel CA 93923 Office: 559 Pacific St Monterey CA 93940

LOGSDON, DONALD FRANCIS, JR., educator; b. Chgo., Mar. 7, 1940; s. Donald Francis and Wilma Theresa (Wax) L.; m. Nancy Colette Graham, Dec. 14, 1963; children—David Kenneth, Valory Joie, Cynthia Lenore, Donald Christopher. B.A. in Biology, Northwestern U., 1961; M.S. in Biology, Trinity U., 1970; Ph.D., Colo. State U., 1975; LL.B., LaSalle Extension U., 1972; M.A. in Edn., Chapman Coll., 1982; B.S. in Med. Lab. Services, Thomas A. Edison Coll., 1982; A.A., A.S., SUNY, 1973; Radioisotope technician Argonne (Ill.) Nat. Lab., 1961-63; commd. 2d lt. U.S. Air Force, 1963, advanced through grades to maj., 1973, lt. col. USAFR, 1978—; health physicist Brooks AFB, San Antonio, 1963-65; intern clin. lab. Lackland AFB, San Antonio, 1965-66; chief clin. lab. Luke AFB, Ariz., 1966-67; chief radioisotope clinic USAF Sch. Aerospace Medicine, San Antonio, 1967-70; assoc. prof. U.S. Air Force Acad., 1970-75; chief U.S. Air Force Environ. Health Lab., 1975-78; dir. Sacramento Area Residence Edn. Ctr., 1978—; assoc. prof. Chapman Coll., Am. River Coll. Decorated Air Force Commendation medal. Mem. AAAS, Soc. Armed Forces Med. Lab. Scientists, Sigma Xi, Phi Delta Kappa. Democrat. Contbr. book revs. and articles to profl. jours.

LOHMAN, GUY MARING, info. systems analyst; b. St. Louis, July 16, 1949; s. Ira H. Jr. and Louise M. Lohman; B.A., Pomona Coll., 1971; M.S., Cornell U., 1975, Ph.D., 1977. Teaching asst. Sch. Ops. Research, Cornell U., Ithaca, N.Y., 1972-75; asso. ops. research analyst Atlantic Richfield, Los Angeles, summers, 1973, 74; database adminstr. Cornell Law Assn., Cornell U., Ithaca, 1975-76; sr. engr. Jet Propulsion Lab., Pasadena, 1976-79, acting group supr., 1977-79, mem. tech. staff End-to-End Info. Systems Tech. Devel. Group, 1979-81, group supr. Advanced DBMS Engring. Group, 1981-82; mem. research staff IBM Research Lab., San Jose, Calif., 1982—; instr. safety/systems mgmt. U. So. Calif., Los Angeles, 1978-79. Served to capt., USAR, 1972. Cornell U. fellow, 1975-76. Mem. Assn. for Computing Machinery (spl. interest group on mgmt. of data, vice chmn. San Gabriel Valley chpt. 1979-81, publicity chmn. 1981-82), IEEE Computer Soc., Internat. Conf. on Very Large Data Bases (internat. publicity chmn. 1982), Phi Beta Kappa, Sigma Xi. Clubs: Jet Propulsion Lab. Ski (pres. 1979-80), Jet Propulsion

Hiking, Sierra. Contbr. articles to and referee for profl. jours. Office: K55-281 IBM Research Lab 5600 Cottle Rd San Jose CA 95193

LOHR, GEORGE EMORY, supreme ct. justice; b. Gary, S.D., Oct. 31, 1931; s. Earl Leon and Gladys Cleora (Thomas) L.; B.S., S.D. State U., 1953; J.D., U. Mich., 1958; m. Paula Jean Brewer, Dec. 11, 1955; children—Scott, Karen, Sarah. Admitted to Colo. bar, 1958, Calif. bar, 1968; asso. to partner firm Davis, Graham & Stubbs, Denver, 1958-68; counsel law dept. Janss Corp., Thousand Oaks, Calif., 1968-69; gen. counsel Snowmass Corp., Snowmass Village, Calif., 1969-70; counsel Real Estate Affiliates, Inc., Aspen, Colo., 1970-71; judge 9th Jud. Dist. of Colo., 1972-79; justice Colo. Supreme Ct., Denver, 1979—. Served with USAF, 1953-55. Mem. Am. Bar Assn., Colo. Bar Assn., Denver Bar Assn. Office: 2 E 14th Ave Denver CO 80203

LOKEY, NORMA ELNORA, savings and loan executive; b. Berlin, Md., June 13, 1921; d. George William and Mary Esther (Birch) Pruitt; m. Gordon Hugh Lokey, Apr. 7, 1943; children—William Duff, James Kelso. Student Buckingham Bus. Sch., 1936-38, Ariz. State U., 1964-65; grad. Inst. Fin. Edn., 1966. Office mgr. Stickland's Better Stores, Berlin, Md., 1938-45; asst. sec., treas. Denver Fed. Savs. & Loan, 1946-52; office agt. Home Ins. Agy., Albuquerque, 1953-55; treas. First Thrift Assn., Albuquerque, 1955-57; asst. br. mgr. Silver State Savs. & Loan, Denver, 1957-59; exec. sec. First Fed. Savs. & Loan Assn. Ariz., Phoenix, 1960-66, asst. corp. sec., 1966-73, corp. sec., 1973—; instr. Inst. Fin. Edn., Phoenix. Mem. Phoenix Inst. Fin. Edn. (past pres.), Exec. Women Internat. (past pres.). Republican. Methodist. Home: 6457 W Bethany Home Rd Glendale AZ 85301 Office: First Fed Savs & Loan Assn 3003 N Central Ave Phoenix AZ 85012

LOLLI, ANDREW RALPH, industrial engineer, former army officer; b. Seatonville, Ill., Oct. 15, 1917; s. Joseph Fredrick and Adolfa (Fiocchi) L.; student Armed Forces Staff Coll., 1950, Nat. War Coll., 1957, N.Y. Inst. Fin., 1971; B.S., Dickinson Coll., 1952; postgrad. Fordham U., 1952; m. Mary H. Tatsapaugh, Jan. 14, 1983. Enlisted in U.S. Army, 1940, advanced through grades to maj. gen., 1960; chief plans and priorities Allied Forces So. Europe, 1952-56; comdr. Air Def. units, N.Y. and San Francisco, 1957-60; comdr. XX U.S.A. Corps, 1961-62, XV, 1962-63, comdr. Western NORD Region, Hamilton AFB, Calif., 1963-66; ret., 1966; exec. asst. Hughes Aircraft Co., Fullerton, Calif., 1967; dir. gen. services State of Calif., Sacramento, 1967-70; v.p. Sigmatics, Newport Beach, Calif., 1970-73, Intercoast Investments Co., Sacramento, 1975-76; pres. Andrew R. Lolli Assos. Inc., San Francisco, 1973—, Lolman Inc., San Francisco, 1976—; pres. bd. trustees Commonwealth Equity Trust, 1974—; vice chmn. Calif. Pub. Works bd., 1967-69; mem. adv. panel Nat. Acad. Scis. and Engring. in Research, Washington, 1968-70; mem. fed., state and local govt. adv. panel Fed. Gen. Services, Washington, 1968-69. Bd. dirs. Columbia Boys Park Club, San Francisco, Lab. for Survival, San Francisco. Decorated D.S.M., Legion of Merit with oak leaf cluster, Bronze Star with oak leaf cluster; named Man of Year, Italian Sons of Am., 1964. Mem. Nat. Assn. Uniformed Services, Assn. U.S. Army, Ret. Officers Assn. Roman Catholic. Clubs: Presidio San Francisco, Golf. Developed short notice inspection system for army air def. missiles, 1960. Home: 1050 North Point San Francisco CA 94109 Office: 286 Jefferson St San Francisco CA 94133

LOMAWAIMA, HARTMAN HENRY, university administrator; b. Winslow, Ariz., Nov. 11, 1949; s. Harvey and Elsa Neva (Setima) L.; m. Tsianiana Carr, Apr. 15, 1980. S.B., No. Ariz. U. with honors, 1971; Ed.M., Harvard U., 1972; postgrad. Stanford U., 1980. Counselor, Phoenix Coll., 1970-71; teaching asst. social scis. Harvard U., Cambridge, Mass., 1971-72; asst. dean grad. studies Stanford U., 1975-80; asst. to dir. Lowie Mus. of Anthropology, U. Calif.-Berkeley, 1980—, instr. dept. anthropology, 1982—. Bur. Indian Affairs fellow, 1968, 69; Harvard Grad. fellow, 1971; Am. Indian Grad. fellow, 1973, 74. Mem. Nat. Indian Edn. Assn., AAUP, Council on Anthropology and Edn., Mus. Stores Assn., Epsilon Pi Tau, Phi Delta Kappa. Author: The Minority Report, 1974; American Indian Community Colleges, 1977. Office: 103 Kroeber Hall U Calif Berkeley CA 94720

LOMBARD, CARYN ANDERSON, telecommunications company executive; b. Rochester, Minn., June 1, 1942; d. Bruce Murat and Caroline (Brown) Anderson; m. Russell Joseph Lombard, Jr., July 24, 1971; 1 son, Christian Murat. B.A., Stanford U., 1963; M.B.A., San Francisco State U., 1977. Asst. product mgr. Castle & Cooke, 1972-74; account exec. N.Y. Times Info. Service, 1976-78; consumer promotion mgr. MJB Co., 1978-80; sales promotion mgr. Calif. Canners & Growers, 1980-82; account exec. maj. accounts Pacific Telephone Co., San Francisco, 1982—; mktg. cons. Chmn. Mayor's Women's Advt. Com., 1980-82; exec. com. Mayor's Econ. Devel. Council, 1980-81; pres. Freends of Commn. on Status of Women, 1981-83; founding mem. Bay Area Women's Coalition; mem. Internat. Visitors Ctr. Bay Area, Embarcadero Ctr. Forum. Mem. Women in Advt. (dir. 1976-79), Women in Telecommunications, Merchandising Execs. Club (dir. 1980-82). Clubs: San Francisco Tennis, Les Amis du Vin, Commonwealth of Calif. (exec. com. internat. relations sect.).

LOMBARD, PATRICIA MAY, arts administrator, pianist, composer; b. Newark, Dec. 17, 1954; d. William Gabriel, Sr., and Patricia May (Brown) L. B.A., Bucknell U., 1977; postgrad. Manhattan Sch. Music, N.Y.C., 1978. Account exec. John O'Donnell Co., Fin. Devel./Pub. Relations, N.Y.C., 1979-80; gen. mgr. Anchorage Symphony Orch., 1980-82; exec. dir. Visual Arts Center of Alaska, Anchorage, 1983—. Bd. dirs. Alaska Arts Alliance, 1981—; mem. adv. com. Anchorage Performing Arts Ctr. 1981—. Recipient Creative Achievement award Pa. chpts. Phi Beta Kappa, 1977. Office: 614 Warehouse Ave Anchorage AK 99501

LOMBARDI, ROBERT PAUL, publishing company executive; b. Bklyn., Dec. 14, 1952; s. Philip J. and Edith J. (Pasquariello) L.; m. Susan Krause, Sept. 8, 1979; 1 dau., Meghan Anne. B.A. in Advt., U. Ill., 1975. Advt. mgr. Summit Sentinel, Dillon, Colo., 1977-78, gen. mgr., 1979-81; gen. mgr. The Entertainer, Dillon, 1978-79; pres., pub. Summit Pub. Co., Inc., Dillon, 1981—. Recipient Best Ad of Yr. awards, Gen. Excellence award Colo. Press Assn., 1980, 81. Mem. Colo. Press Assn. (mem. postal audit, circulation coms., bd. dirs. 1983—, awards for photo journalism, personal columns, advt. excellence), Summit County C. of C. Democrat. Roman Catholic. Developer seminar on newspapers in edn. for elem. children.

LOMEN, DAVID ORLANDO, mathematician, educator; b. Decorah, Iowa, May 11, 1937; s. Erlin Reuben and Ellen Dorthea (Jensen) L.; m. Constance Sylvia Trecek, Dec. 25, 1961; 1 dau., Catherine Ellen. B.A., Luther Coll., 1959; M.S., Iowa State U., 1962, Ph.D., 1964. Research asst. Socony Mobil Research Lab., Duncanville, Tex., summer 1960; design specialist Gen. Dynamics/Convair Co., San Diego, 1963-66; asst. prof. math. U. Ariz., Tucson, 1966-69; assoc. prof., 1969-74, prof., 1974—; vis. scientist dept. applied math. and theoretical physics U. Cambridge (Eng.), 1972-73; vis. scientist Inst. voor Cultuurtechniek en Waterhuishouding, Wageningen, The Netherlands, summer 1978; vis. prof. U. Oslo, 1980; cons. in field. Bd. dirs. Tucson chpt. Cystic Fibrosis Found., 1975-80. Recipient Creative Teaching award U. Ariz. Found., 1978; Marshall Fund Research award Am. Assn., Norway, 1980. Mem. Am. Math Soc., Soc. Indsl. and Applied Math., Soil Sci. Soc. Am. Geophys. Union, European Geophys. Soc., Consortium for Math. and Application. Lutheran. Club: Nordmanns Forbundet. Research in math. modeling of water flow in soils and developing math. lessons for computer aided instrn. Contbr. numerous articles and research reports to Applied Math. Home: 6945 E Blue Lake Dr Tucson AZ 85715 Office: Math Dept U Ariz Tucson AZ 85721

LONDON, BILLIE, hospital training and development director, consultant; b. Langley, Va., Sept. 21, 1944; d. William Vernon and Frances Lee (Ransone) L.; 1 dau., Celeste K. B.S. in Psychology, Calif. Western U., 1979. Editor, analyst Policy & Procedure, U. Calif.-San Diego, 1972-75, mgr. Organizational Cons. Service, 1975-80; cons. Billie London & Assocs., Del Mar, Calif., 1980-82; dir. organizational and profl. devel. Watsonville (Calif.) Community Hosp., 1982—; mgmt. career devel. seminars. Campaign mgr. Del Mar City Council election, 1972, 74, mem. 5 yr. plan com., Del Mar, low income housing com., Del Mar. Mem. Am. Soc. Tng. and Devel., Organizational Devel. Network. Democrat. Unitarian. Home: 160 Oakdale Dr Aptos CA 95003 Office: PO Box 310 Watsonville CA 95076

LONDON, JOE, acctg. supr.; b. Oklahoma City, Mar. 7, 1921; s. Charles Leigh and Laura (McSwain) L.; student U. Okla., 1940; BBA., Woodbury U., Los Angeles, 1948; m. Valerie Joyce Tilcock, Jan. 21, 1955; children—JoAnn, Julie. Adminstrv. positions, mem. customer staff So. Calif. Gas Co., Los Angeles, 1948-60, mem. internal audits staff, 1960-80, supr. accounts payable, 1980—. Served with USAAF, 1942-45; ETO. Mem. EDP Auditors Assn., Inc. (pres. Los Angeles chpt., internat. treas.-dir.), EDP Auditors Found. for Edn. and Research (nat. treas.-trustee), Inst. Internal Auditors, Soc. for Advancement Mgmt. (past v.p. Los Angeles chpt.), Pacific Coast Gas Assn., Am. Gas Assn. Democrat. Office: So Calif Gas Co 810 S Flower St Los Angeles CA 90017

LONDON, MARY ELLEN, ednl. cons. and coordinator; b. Hutchinson, Kans., Apr. 3, 1927; d. Chester Iaasic and Edna Louise (Anderson) Lewis; grad. in Fine Arts/Edn., Kans. U., 1949; M.A. in Early Childhood Edn., Goddard Coll., 1973; postgrad. Froebel Inst., London, 1972; Ph.D., Golden State U.; m. Lewis London, Sept. 30, 1967; 1 son by previous marriage, Richard Norman Batie. Design engr. Boeing, Wichita, Kans., 1952-59; supr., trainer Parent Child Guidance Center Head Start, Los Angeles, 1968-74, Fedn. Head Start trainer, supr., 1974-78; exec. dir. Assistance League Day Nursery-Kindergarten, 1982—; pvt. practice cons. early childhood edn., Los Angeles, 1971—; exec. dir. Assistance League Day Nursery-Kindergarten; dir. Creative Environment Learning Center, Los Angeles, 1971-73; cons. Early Childhood Edn. Study, Newton, Mass., 1970; instr., asst. prof. Long Beach (Calif.) State U., 1975-77; asst. prof. early childhood edn. Pepperdine U., Los Angeles, 1975-78, Calif. State U.-Los Angeles, 1980—, Pacific Oaks Coll., 1981—, LaVerne (Calif.) U., 1975—; field coordinator state pre-sch. career incentive program Inst. for Profl. Devel.; Child Devel. Consortium rep., Washington, 1976—; adv. bd. on follow through Graham Elem. Sch.; advisory bds. on early childhood edn. S.W. Coll., Valley City Coll., Compton Coll., Los Angeles City Coll., Dominguez Hills U., Calif. State U. Long Beach; adv. bds. Harbor Coll., El Camino Coll.; cons. assessor Urban Inst., Region IX ACYF-HEW, 1979—. Recipient awards Kans. Regional Art Exhibit, 1944, Head Start, 1968, 75, efficiency economy award Lockheed, 1962; tchr. tng. cert. OEO, 1966; supervision of year trophy Head Start, 1974, 78. Mem. So. Calif. Assn. for Edn. Young Children (Los Angeles v.p., 1976-78, 83-85), Calif. Assn. for Edn. Young Children (chmn. Internat. Yr. of Child, 1978-79), Nat. Assn. for Edn. Young Children (governing bd., public policy task group, Washington, 1977—, local coordinator conf., Anaheim, 1976), Alpha Kappa Alpha (Black Heritage chmn., 1977-79, 25 year medalion, 1979, community service award, 1979, exhibit award, 1979), Black Women's Forum Los Angeles, Exec. Female. Methodist. Club: Hollywood Wilshire Soroptimist (v.p.). Artist, organist, dress designer; participant art exhibit, Oakland, Calif., 1965; author: Creative Environment Learning Center, 1973. Home and Office: 1235 Stearns Dr Los Angeles CA 90035

LONDON, RAY WILLIAM, clinical, consulting and medical psychologist; b. Burley, Idaho, May 29, 1943; s. Loo Richard and Maycelle Jerry (Moore) L.; A.S., Weber State Coll., 1965, B.S., 1967; M.S.W., U. So. Calif., 1973, Ph.D., 1976. Congressional asst., U.S. Ho. of Reps., 1964-65; research asso. Bus. Advisors, Inc., Ogden, Utah, 1965-67; dir. of counseling and consultation services, Meaning Found., Riverside, Calif., 1966-69; mental health and social service liaison San Bernardino (Calif.) County Social Services, 1968-72; clin. trainee VA Outpatient Clinic, Los Angeles, 1971-72; clin. trainee Childrens Hosp. Los Angeles, 1972-73, clin. fellow, 1973-74; clin. tng. Reiss Davis Child Study Center, Los Angeles, 1973-74, Los Angeles County U. So. Calif. Med. Ctr., mem. psychotherapist, Benjamin Rush Neuropsychiat. Center, Orange, Calif., 1973-75; clin. psychology intern Orange County Mental Health, 1976-77; clin. psychologist Orange Police Dept., 1976-80; pvt. practice psychotherapy, Santa Ana, Calif., 1974—; postdoctoral fellow U. Calif., Irvine, 1978; vis. lectr. U. So. Calif., Los Angeles, 1973, U. Redlands (Calif.), U. Calif., Riverside, Calif. State Coll., San Bernardino, 1970-76; faculty U. So. Calif., UCLA; pres. bd. govs., Human Factors Programs, Ltd., 1976—; clin. faculty U. Calif. at Irvine Med. Sch.; cons. St. Joseph Orange, 1973—, Neophron, Inc., Anaheim, 1975—, various public schs. and hosps., So. Calif., 1970—; presenter nat. and internat. lectrs. and workshops. Diplomate Am. Acad. Behavioral Medicine, cert. sex therapist, diplomate in clin. hypnosis Am. Bd. Psychol. Hypnosis, Am. Bd. Psychotherapy, Internat. Bd. Medicine and Psychology; lic. marriage, family and child counselor, clin. social worker, clin. psychologist, Calif. Fellow Royal Soc. Health, Soc. for Clin. Social Work (dir.), Internat. Bd. Medicine and Psychology (pres. 1980—, dir.); mem. Am. Assn. Social Psychiatry, Internat. Soc. Social Psychiatry, Am. Assn. of Marriage and Family Therapy, Am. Psychology-Law Soc., Biofeedback Soc. Am. Am. Assn. Sex Educators Counselors and Therapists, Am. Calif., County psychol. assns., Am. Soc. Clin. Hypnosis, Am. Orthopsychiat. Assn., Soc. Behavioral Medicine, Am. Group Psychotherapy Assn., AAAS, Acad. Psychosomatic Medicine, Internat. Soc. Hypnosis, Soc. for Clin. and Exptl. Hypnosis, Am. Soc. Psychosomatic Dentistry and Medicine, N.Y. Acad. Scis., Phi Delta Kappa, Delta Sigma Rho, Tau. Kappa Alpha, Pi Rho Phi, Lambda Iota Tau. Assoc. editor Australian Jour. Hypnotherapy and Hypnosis; editorial cons. Internat. Jour. Clin. and Exptl. Hypnosis; editor Medicine and Psychology newsletter; contbr. chpts. to books, articles to profl. jours. Office: 1125 E 17th St Santa Ana CA 92701

LONERGAN, THOMAS FRANCIS, III, criminal justice cons.; b. Bklyn., July 28, 1942; s. Thomas Francis and Katherine Josephine (Roth) L.; B.A., Calif. State U., Long Beach, 1966, M.A., 1973; M.P.A., Pepperdine U., 1976; postgrad. U. So. Calif.; m. Irene L. Kaucher, Dec. 14, 1963; 1 son—Thomas F. Dep. sheriff Los Angeles County Sheriff's Dept., 1963-68; U.S. Govt. program analyst, 1968—; fgn. service officer USIA, Lima, Peru, 1970-71; dep. sheriff to lt. Los Angeles Sheriff's Office, 1971-76, aide lt. to div. chief, 1976-79; dir. Criminal Justice Cons., Downey, Calif., 1977—; cons. Public Adminstrv. Service, Chgo., 1972-75, Nat. Inst. Corrections, Washington, 1977—, Nat. Sheriff's Assn., 1978, 79; tchr. N. Calif. Regional Criminal Justice Acad., 1977-79. Mem. Air Force Assn., U.S. Naval Inst., U.S. Strategic Inst., Nat. Jail Assn., Nat. Jail Mgrs. Assn., Nat. Sheriff's Assn., Am. Polit. Sci. Assn., Zeta Beta Tau. Democrat. Roman Catholic. Author: California-Past, Present & Future, 1968; Training-A Corrections Perspective, 1979; AIMS-Correctional Officer; Liability-A Correctional Perspective; Liability Law for Probation Administrators; Liability Reporter; Probation Liability Reporter. Study Guides.

LONES, ELAINE AVERY, computer software exec.; b. Richfield, Utah, Nov. 18, 1940; d. Gilbert and Wanda (Washburn) Avery; B.A. in Math., San Diego State U., 1963; children—Loren, Lance. Systems analyst U. Calif., San Diego, 1964-69; owner, operator L&L Systems, computer software firm specializing in devel. of software for mortgage banking industry, San Diego, 1969—. Active Boy Scouts Am., Girl Scouts U.S.A. Mem. IEEE. Home: 3429 Hill St San Diego CA 92106 Office: PO Box 7513 San Diego CA 92107

LONETREE, GEORGIA L., rehabilitation counselor; b. Portage, Wis., Sept. 22, 1946; d. Edward and Minnie I. (Decorah) L.; children—Lucinda J., Aaron E. Yazzie. B.S. in Vocat. Rehab., U. Wis.-Stout, 1976, postgrad., 1976-77; M.S. in Vocat. Rehab. Counseling, U. Wis., 1981, postgrad., 1981-82. Team tchr. U. Wis.-Stout, 1976, Native Am. coordinator ednl. and cultural enrichment program, 1977-78; statewide specialist Indian edn. and community programs U. Wis. Extension, 1978-79; sec. to tribal atty. Wis. Winnebago Bus. Com., Madison, 1980; rehab. counselor intern Waisman Ctr. Mental Retardation and Human Devel., U. Wis., 1981, project evaluator Madison Indian parent com., 1981-82; vocat. evaluator, edn. coordinator Project Hogan Naa Nish, Navajo Vocat. Rehab. Program, Tuba City, Ariz., 1982—; instr. rehab. edn. Navajo Community Coll., Tsaile, Ariz. Vocat. adv. com. Tuba City High Sch., 1982; treas. Wisconsin Dells chpt. Native Am. Ch., 1979-80; sec.-treas. Ho-Chunk Housing Authority, Wis. Winnebago Bus. Com., Nekoosa, 1979-80; past officer, mem. Native Am. Awareness Club, U. Wis.-Stout, 1972-76. Continuing edn. scholar Dells Indian Club, Inc., 1982; Am. Indians into Grad. Edn. fellow, 1981-82; Advanced Opportunity fellow, 1980-81; recipient Am. Indian Scholarship award, 1976, Chancellor's award for high acad. achievement, 1975. Mem. Am. Rehab. Counseling Assn., Am. Personnel and Guidance Assn. Home: PO Box 2442 Tuba City AZ 86045

LONEY, JAMES OWEN, mus. adminstr.; b. Champaign, Ill., June 4, 1944; s. James William and Francis Irene (Mix) L.; m. Rosemary Ann Loney, Aug. 6, 1966; 1 dau., Heather. B.S., Ind. State U., Terre Haute, 1967; M.F.A., Temple U., 1973; postgrad. Harvard U., 1979. Mem. sculpture and design faculty Tyler Sch. Art, Elkins Park, Pa., 1973-74; acting dir., curator edn. S.E. Ark. Arts and Sci. Center, Pine Bluff, Ark., 1974-77; exec. dir. Muncie (Ind.) Children's Mus., 1977-80; exec. dir. Kidspace, Pasadena, Calif., 1980—; cons., grants rev. NEH, Washington, 1980—, Inst. Mus. Services, Washington, 1978—. Mem. exec. com. Pasadena Arts Council, 1981—; mem. youth com. Planet Fest, Calif. Inst. Tech. and Jet Propulsion Lab., 1981. Mem. Am. Assn. Mus., Assn. Youth Mus., Western Assn. Mus., So. Calif. Mus. Educator's Assn. Sculpture represented in permanent collections Swope Gallery, Terre Haute, Inc., Ind. State U., Terre Haute, Cheltenham (Pa.) Art Ctr., Ark. Art Ctr. Little Rock, Ball State U. Mus., Muncie, Ind. Home: 1309 N Chester Ave Pasadena CA 91104 Office: 390 S El Molino Ave Pasadena CA 91101

LONG, ALFRED O., insurance agent; b. Dayton, Ohio, July 26, 1938; s. George Orlan and Florence Elizabeth (Dale) L.; m. Marilyn Rae Sensenbaugh, Apr. 5, 1958; children—Mark E., Marcia E. B.S. in Mech. Engring., Gen. Motors Inst., 1961. Engr., Inland Mfg., Dayton, Ohio, 1956-61; engr. McDonnell Douglas, St. Louis, 1961-68; sales mgr. Gilmore Industries, Cleve., 1968-74; pres. Long Ins. Services, Inc., Anaheim, Calif., 1974—, Bridge Fin. Services, Anaheim, 1974—. Scoutmaster, Orange Empire council Boy Scouts Am., 1970-78; backpacking instr. Girl Scouts Am., 1976-78; trustee Anaheim Citizens Against Violent Crime Reward Fund, 1980-82; pres. Anaheim Police Officer Hon. Assn., 1981-82. Served with AUS, 1956-65. Mem. Nat. Assn. Life Underwriters, Orange County Employee Benefit Council, Orange County Life Underwriters Assn., Anaheim C. of C., Million Dollar Round Table. Republican. Lutheran. Clubs: Kiwanis, Exchange. Patentee six wheel scrambler all-terrain vehicle. Office: 621 S Harbor Blvd Anaheim CA 92805

LONG, CORINNE O'KANE, educator; b. N.Y.C., Oct. 5, 1933; d. John Adam and Mary Magdelyn (Danz) Siegmund; m. Robert Fredrick O'Kane (dec.); children—Karen Anne, Laura Julia; m. 2d, Glen Carl Long, Jan. 3, 1980. B.S., SUNY, 1954, M.A., U. Santa Clara, 1973. Tchr., Valley Stream, N.Y., 1954-57, Fitchberg, Mass., 1957-58, Monterey, Calif., 1963, 70-83, W.Ger., 1963-65, Ft. Rucker, Ala., 1967, Levenworth, Kans., 1969; tchr. reading lang. arts Patton Sch., Ft. Ord, Calif., 1983—; tchr. grad. courses Chapman Coll.; program reviewer State of Calif.; test writer Calif. Edn. Dept. Mem. Childrens' Home Soc., 1979-82. Mem. Calif. Tchrs. Assn., NEA, Internat. Reading Assn., AAUW, Delta Kappa Gamma. Episcopalian. Club: Racquet (Monterey).

LONG, DONNA DEANE, savings and loan executive; b. New Orleans, Jan. 31, 1946; d. Deane Snyder and Roselle Esther (Farabaugh) L.; m. Louis Howard Knierim, Sept. 15, 1979. B.A. in Math., San Diego State U., 1967; M.B.A., Nat. U., 1980. Systems engr. IBM, Los Angeles, 1967-70; systems analyst San Diego Fed. Savs. & Loan Assn. (name changed to Gt. Am. Fed. Savs. Bank 1982), 1970-74, asst. v.p., mgr. loan systems and tng., 1974-77, v.p., dir. tng. and devel., 1977—. Vice chmn. bd. dirs. Greater San Diego Industry-Edn. Council, 1979—; bd. dirs. San Diego City Ballet, 1982-83; v.p. fin. Calif. Ballet Assn., 1980-81; alternate mem. San Diego Pvt. Industry Council, 1983; mem. adv. bd. County Dept. Edn. Adopt-A-Sch. Program. Recipient Dir.'s award Calif. Ballet Assn.; Vol. Service award Carnation Co., 1981; Salute to Bus. award Industry-Edn. Council, 1983; San Diego Woman of Achievement award, 1983. Mem. Am. Soc. Tng. and Devel. (dir. 1980—), Charter 100. Office: Great American Federal Savings and Loan Assn 600 B St San Diego CA 92183

LONG, ELAINE MARGARET CHISHOLM, nutritionist, dietitian, educator; b. Santa Barbara, Calif., Dec. 21, 1947; d. Kenneth James and Margaret Esther (Oien) Chisholm; m. James Allen Long, July 22, 1972; children—Matthew, Andrew. Student Whittier Coll., 1966, 1968; B.S. in Biochemistry, Calif. State Poly. U., 1970; M.S. in Nutrition, Iowa State U., 1974. Registered dietician. Research asst. Sansum Clinic Research Found., Santa Barbara, Calif., 1970-71; research fellow Iowa State U., 1971-74; asst. dietitian St. Lukes Hosp., Boise, Idaho, 1974-75; asst. prof. home econs. Boise State U., 1975-80, chmn. dept., 1980-82, assoc. prof. community health, 1982—; nutrition cons. Idaho Dept. Edn., Boise, 1979—; relief dietitian Elks Rehab. Hosp., Boise, 1981—. Recipient Outstanding Tchr. award Boise State U. Alumni Assn., 1978; NSF fellow, 1969; NDEA fellow, 1970; Nutrition Edn. Tng. grantee, 1979, 80, 82-83. Mem. Am. Dietetic Assn. (Young Dietitian of Yr. 1977), Soc. Nutrition Edn., Ctr. for Sci. in Pub. Interest, Idaho Dietetic Assn., Phi Kappa Phi. Home: 9520 Hackamore St Boise ID 83109 Office: Boise State U 1910 University Blvd Boise ID 83725

LONG, GEORGE STEVENSON, JR., photographer; b. Indpls., June 12, 1923; s. George Stevenson and Hazel (Walker) L.; m. Marjorie Claire Carper, May 9, 1947; children—Steve, Bob, Timothy, Joan. Student Navy Photographic Sch., Pensicola, Fla. Photographer, UPI, Los Angeles, 1951-61; photographer Steve Hannigan, Sun Valley, Calif., 1948-51; owner Sheedy and Long Photography, 1961-75; owner Long Photography, Los Angeles, 1975—. Served in USN, 1943-46. Mem. Profl. Photographers Am., Los Angeles Press Photographers. Presbyterian. Work appears in Sports Illustrated (17 years), Time, Life, Fortune, Nat. Geog., U.S. News & World Reports. Home: 7514 Otto St Downey CA 90240 Office: 1265 S Cochran Ave Los Angeles CA 90019

LONG, J. SCOTT, sociology educator; b. Elgin, Ill., Nov. 5, 1951; s. J. Henry and Mildred L. (Fogelsanger) L.; m. Valerie Lynn Derrickson, June 23, 1973; 1 dau., Megan Marie. B.A., Juniata Coll., Huntingdon, Pa., 1973; M.A., Cornell U., 1975, Ph.D., 1977. NIMH postdoctoral fellow Cornell U., 1977-78; asst. prof. sociology Wash. State U., 1978-82, assoc. prof. sociology and program in stats., 1982—; statis. cons., researcher. Recipient Social Sci. Research award Juniata Coll., 1973; NIMH trainee Cornell U., 1973-77; NSF research grantee. Mem. Am. Statis. Assn., AAAS, Soc. Social Study of Sci., Am. Sociol. Assn. Contbr. articles and book revs. to profl. jours. Home: NW 2225 Yates St Pullman WA 99163 Office: 247 Wilson Hall Dept Sociology Wash State U Pullman WA 99164

LONG, JOSEPH M., retail drug chain company executive; b. 1912. Grad. U. Calif., 1933. Asst. to city mgr. City of Berkeley (Calif.), 1933-36; with Safeway Stores Inc., 1936-37; with Longs Drug Stores Inc., Walnut Creek, Calif., 1938—, pres., chief exec. officer, 1946, chmn. bd., chief exec. officer, 1975, chmn. bd., dir., 1977—. Office: Longs Drug Stores Inc 141 N Civic Dr PO Box 5222 Walnut Creek CA 94596*

LONG, RICHARD LOUIS, JR., chemical engineer, educator; b. Kansas City, Mo., June 5, 1947; s. Richard Louis and Alta Marie (Giddens) L. B.A., Rice U., 1969, Ph.D., 1973. Registered profl. engr., Tex., N. Mex. Research engr. E. I. DuPont, Orange, Tex., 1973-78; asst. prof. chem. engring. Lamar U., 1978-81, N.Mex. State U., Las Cruces, 1981—; cons. in field; mem. steering com. U.S. Senatorial Bus. Adv. Bd., 1982. Served to 1st lt. USAR, 1976-78. Recipient Research award Sigma Xi, 1973. Mem. Am. Inst. Chem. Engrs. (v.p. Rio Grande sect. 1982), Am. Chem. Soc. Methodist. Author student communications guide; contbr. articles to profl. jours. Office: Dept Chem Engring N Mex State U Box 3805 Las Cruces NM 88003

LONG, ROBERT MERRILL, retail drug company executive; b. Oakland, Calif., May 19, 1938; s. Joseph Milton and Vera Mai (Skaggs) L.; student Brown U., 1956-58; B.A., Claremont Men's Coll., 1960; m. Eliane Quilloux, Dec. 13, 1969. With Longs Drug Stores Inc., Walnut Creek, Calif., 1960—, dir., 1968—, pres., 1975—, also chief exec. officer. Mem. Nat. Assn. Chain Drug Stores (vice chmn., dir.). Office: Long's Drug Stores Inc 141 N Civic Dr Walnut Creek CA 94596

LONG, ROGER BRUCE, agricultural economist; b. Mpls., Feb. 19, 1934; s. Richard Benjamin and Lenore Madeline L.; m. Genevieve Ann Frisk, June 13, 1959; children—Kristen, Dana, Elenore, Benjamin. B.S., U. Minn., 1955, M.F., 1959, Ph.D., 1963. Asst. prof. N.Mex. State U., Las Cruces, 1963-66; mem. faculty dept. agrl. econs. U. Idaho, Moscow, 1966—, prof., 1973—; vis. prof. U. Alta., Edmonton, 1970-72. Served to capt. USAF, 1955-58. Mem. Am. Econ. Assn., Am. Agrl. Econs. Assn., Am. Water Resources Assn. Lutheran. Author: The Primary and Secondary Impacts of a Water Resource Development Project, 1980; The Economic Structure of Blaine County Idaho, 1981. Home: 1453 Alpowa Moscow ID 83843 Office: Dept Agrl Econs U Idaho Moscow ID 83843

LONG, STEPHEN CARREL MIKE, lawyer; b. Roswell, N.Mex., Sept. 22, 1951; s. R.E. (Mike) and Evelyn Marie (Row) L.; B.B.A. with honors, N.Mex. State U., 1973; J.D., U. N.Mex., 1977; m. Barbara Lowe, July 19, 1980; 1 dau., Jennifer Lynn. Bar: N.Mex. 1977. Pres. firm Stephen C.M. Long, P.A., Albuquerque, 1977—. Chmn. bd. dirs. Christian Profl. Counseling Services, Inc., Albuquerque, 1980—; sustaining mem. Nat. Republican Com., 1980—. Served with N.Mex. N.G. Mem. ABA, Christian Legal Soc., Am. Trial Lawyers Assn., N.Mex. Trial Lawyers Assn., Delta Theta Phi, Albuquerque Bar Assn. Republican. Baptist. Editor: Nat. Resources Jour., 1976-77; contbr. articles to profl. jours. Home: 1217 June St NE Albuquerque NM 87110 Office: Western Bank Bldg Suite 1600 Albuquerque NM 87102

LONG, STEPHEN D., accountant; b. Salmon, Idaho, Aug. 18, 1949; s. Philip R. and Lorene I. (Holman) L.; m. Linda K. Gockley, Aug. 30, 1969; children—; Lori, Darrell, Bradley. Ministerial degree Conquerors Bible Coll., 1970; B.S. in Bus. Adminstrn., U. Albuquerque, 1973. C.P.A. Staff acct. Ernst & Whinney, Boise, Idaho, 1973-74; corp. tax. acct. Albertson's, Inc., Boise, 1974-76; prin. S.D. Long C.P.A., Ontario, Oreg., 1977—; seminar presenter Treasure Valley Community Coll. Mem. Am. Inst. C.P.A.s, Idaho Soc. C.P.A.s, Ontario C. of C., Fruitland C. of C. (dir.). Republican. Club: Ontario Kiwanis (past pres.). Office: 1289 SW 6th Ave Suite 405 Ontario OR 97914

LONG, TERRY LEE, financial analyst; b. Lancaster, Pa., Apr. 16, 1951; s. Fred Eshelman and Martha Ada (Breneman) L. B.S., Millersville State Coll., 1973; M.A., Boston U., 1977. Acctg. mgr. Container Corp. Am., Cleve., 1977-78, plant controller, Boston, 1978-80; budget mgr. Mary's Help Hosp., Daly City, Calif., 1980—. Served with U.S. Army, 1973-77. Mem. Hosp. Fin. Mgmt. Assn. Republican. Office: 1900 Sullivan Ave Daly City CA 94015

LONG, WILLIAM ELLIS, hydrologist; b. Minot, N.D., Aug. 18, 1930; s. Fred Ellis and Meda (Becker) L.; B.S. in Geology, U. Nev., 1957; M.Sc. in Geology, Ohio State U., 1961, Ph.D. in Geology, 1964; m. Katherine Marie Costigan, Sept. 11, 1971; children—William Ware, Brooke Ellis. Research asso. Antarctic exploration and research Ohio State U., 1959-64; geologist Tenneco Oil Co., 1964-65; prof. geology Alaska Meth. U., 1965-76; planner Matanuska-Susitna Borough, 1976-77; hydrologist, chief water resources sect. Alaska Div. Geol. and Geophys. Surveys, Anchorage, 1977—; mem. Calif. Himalayan Expdn., 1954, Am. Antarctic Mountaineering Expdn., 1966-67; participant 1st ascent of Vinson Massif, Antarctica, 1966; scientist, explorer, Mapper 5 Antarctic expdns. Served with USAF, 1951-55. Recipient Antarctic Service medal, 1960; La Gorce medal for exploration Nat. Geog. Soc., 1967; Long Gables and Long Hills in Antarctica named in his honor. Mem. Geol. Soc. Am., Am. Assn. Petroleum Geologists, Am. Inst. Profl. Geologists, Alaska Geol. Soc., Alaska Ground Water Assn., Explorers Club, Am. Alpine Club, Am. Morgan Horse Assn., Am. Horse Show Assn., Alaska Hunter-Jumper Assn., Alaska Morgan Horse Assn., U.S. Dressage Assn. Republican. Methodist. Contbr. articles on Antarctic geology to profl. jours. and periodicals. Home: Moose Creek Ranch PO Box 1831 Palmer AK 99645 Office: Alaska Div Geol and Geophys PO Box 2116 Eagle River Anchorage AK 99577

LONGBRAKE, WILLIAM ARTHUR, banker; b. Hershey, Pa., Mar. 15, 1943; s. William Van Fleet and Margaret Jane (Barr) L.; m. Martha Ann Curtis, Aug. 23, 1970; children—Derek Curtis, Mark William, David Robert, Dorothy Eleanor Lois. B.A., Coll. of Wooster, 1965; M.A., U. Wis., 1968, M.B.A., 1969; D.B.A., U. Md., 1976. Jr. asst. planner Northeastern Ill. Planning Commn., Chgo., 1966; instr. Coll. Bus. and Mgmt., U. Md., 1969-71, lectr., 1976, 79-81; fin. economist FDIC, Washington, 1971-75, sr. planning specialist Office Corp. Planning, 1975-76, spl. asst. to chmn., acting controller, 1977-78; assoc. dir. div. banking research Office Comptroller of Currency, Treasury Dept., Washington, 1976, dep. dir. econ. research and analysis div., 1976-77; dep. comptroller for research and econ. programs, 1978-81, acting sr. dep. comptroller for policy, 1981-82, sr. dep. comptroller for resource mgmt., 1982; exec. v.p. Wash. Mut. Savs. Bank, Seattle, 1982—; small bus. cons. Mem. College Park (Md.) Citizen's Adv. Com. on Code Enforcement, 1973-74, cons., 1975. Recipient Kenneth E. Trefftz prize Western Fin. Assn., 1971, cert. of recognition William A. Jump Meml. Found., 1978. Mem. Am. Econs. Assn., So. Econs. Assns., Am. Fin. Assn., Eastern Fin. Assn., Fin. Mgmt. Assn. (dir. 1978-80), Coll. of Wooster Alumni Assn. (pres. Washington chpt. 1976). Presbyn. (trustee 1973-75, chmn. 1975, elder, 1979—, clk. 1980-81). Assoc. editor Fin. Mgmt., 1974-78; mem. editorial adv. bd. Issues in Bank Regulation, 1977—, Jour. Econs. and Bus., 1980—; contbr. articles to profl. jours. Home: 939 18th Ave E Seattle WA 19812 Office: 1101 2d Ave Seattle WA 98101

LONGFELLOW, LAYNE ALLEN, psychologist; b. Jackson, Ohio, Oct. 23, 1937; s. Hershel Herman and Opal Edna (Pursley) L.; B.A. magna cum laude with honors in Psychology, Ohio U., 1959; M.A. (Woodrow Wilson fellow, NSF fellow) Univ. Mich., 1961, Ph.D., 1967; postgrad. (NIMH fellow) Center for Studies of the Person, 1968-70. Asst. prof. psychology Reed Coll., Portland, 1967-68; asst. prof. psychology Prescott (Ariz.) Coll., 1970-71, chmn. dept., 1971-72, acad. v.p. 1972-74; dir. exec. seminars The Menninger Found., Topeka, 1975-78; co-dir. Center for Mgmt. of Stress, Los Angeles and Santa Barbara, Calif., 1978-80; internat. lectr, cons., 1978—; dir. Wilderness Exec. Seminars, Banff Centre, Alta., Can., 1978—; sr. asso. Health Edn. Inst., Phoenix Bapt. Hosp., 1980-81; pres. Lecture Theatre, Inc., Phoenix, 1981—; adj. faculty Union Grad. Sch. and Humanistic Psychology Inst., 1974—. Bd. dirs. Prescott Center Coll., 1976-81; bd. dirs. Am. Inst. Productivity and Creativity, 1981-82. Mem. Am. Psychol. Assn., Nat. Speakers Assn., Assn. for Humanistic Psychology, ACLU, Phi Beta Kappa, Beta Theta Pi. Composer: Ten Songs, 1969; Uncommon Festival of Christmas, 1974; author, creator: Body Talk, 1970; The Feel Wheel, 1972; Stress, The American Addiction, 1982; From Adolescence to Middlescence, 1983; Leadership, Power and Productivity in the '80s, 1983; (TV documentary) The Mountain Waits, 1983. Office: 2432 W Peoria Ave Suite 1010 Phoenix AZ 85029

LONGLEY, BERNIQUE (MRS. JAMES A. ORR), painter, muralist, sculptor; b. Moline, Ill., Sept. 27, 1923; d. Eli James and Effie Marie (Coen) Wilderson; grad. Art Inst. Chgo., 1945; postgrad. Instituto de Allende, Mex., 1971; Santa Fe Sch. Arts and Crafts, 1975; m. James Alexander Orr, Apr. 15, 1968; 1 dau., Bernique Longley Glidden. One-woman shows: Mus. N.Mex., 1947, 50, 52, 53, Little Shop, Santa Fe, 1952-58, Maurice Appleman Gallery, Denver, 1953-54, Van Dieman Lilienfield, N.Y.C., 1953, Rotunda-City Paris, San Francisco, 1955-56, Sanger-Harris Gallery, Dallas, 1968, Lars Laine, Palm Springs, Calif., 1963-69, Gallery A, Taos, 1966-69, Cushing Galleries, Dallas, 1977, Gov.'s Gallery, N.Mex. State Capitol, 1978, Santa Fe East, Austin, Tex., 1979, Woman's Bank of Denver, 1982; group shows include; Art Inst. Chgo., 1946, 48, Denver Art Mus., 1948-49, Mus. N.Mex., 1952, 53, 68, also Summer Gallery, Santa Fe, Blair Gallery, Santa Fe, Santa Fe Festival Arts, 1977-81, St. John's Coll., Santa Fe, others; retrospective exhbn. Santa Fe (N.Mex.) East, 1982; executed murals La Fonda del Sol restaurant, N.Y.C., home Alexander Girard, Santa Fe, 1960; represented in permanent collections of Red Skelton, Greer Garson, Mark Harris, Tex. Instruments, Dallas, First Nat. Bank Denver, Santa Fe Hilton Hotel, Dome Oil Exploration Co., San Francisco, Coll. Santa Fe, Mus. N.Mex., Santa Fe, Coll. Santa Fe, Colorado Springs Fine Arts Center, others; operator Summer Gallery, Santa Fe, 1973—. Bryan Lathrop fgn. traveling fellow, 1945. Mem. Art Inst. Chgo. Alumni Assn. Home: 427 Camino Del Monte Sol Santa Fe NM 87501

LONGLEY, KARL EMERY, civil engineer, educator; b. Porterville, Calif., May 14, 1937; s. John Raymond and Paula Louise (Mauser) L.; m. Friedel Anni Hagenlocher, June 28, 1979; B.S. in Civil Engring., U. N. Mex., 1960; M.S. in Engring., D.Sc., John Hopkins U., 1974. Registered profl. engr., Calif., Md., Tex. Jr. civil engr. State of Calif., 1960; commd. 2d lt., U.S. Army, 1960, advanced through grades to lt. col.; engr. U.S. Mary Med. Dept.; served in Germany, Korea, Vietnam, and Panama, 1960-81, ret., 1981; adj. assoc. prof., U. Tex.-San Antonio, 1977-81; cons. engr. Strauss and Roberts, Inc., 1981-82; prof. Calif. State U.-Fresno, 1982; ptnr. Hanna, Longley and Assocs., Fresno, 1982. Decorated Bronze Star, Meritorious Service medal with cluster, Commendation medal with two oak leaf clusters. Mem. ASCE, Am. Acad. Environ. Engrs., Am. Water Works Assn., Water Pollution Control Fedn. (service award 1982); Internat. Assn. Water Pollution Research, Am. Soc. Microbiology. Episcopalian. Contbr. articles to profl. jours. Home: 4106 Nicholas Dr Visalia CA 93291 Office: Dept Civil Engineering Calif State U Fresno CA 93740

LONGLEY, WILLIAM HENDERSON, advertising executive; b. Grosse Pointe, Mich., Aug. 2, 1951; s. John H. and Winifred (Hughes) L.; m. Candace Marion Perkins, Apr. 30, 1983. Student Hillsdale Coll., 1970-72; B.A., U. Ariz., 1976. Western mktg. mgr. 13-30 Corp., Knoxville, Tenn., 1978-80; western advt. mgr. Esquire mag., Los Angeles, 1980-82, group advt. dir., 1982—. Active Benedict Canyon Assn. Mem. Los Angeles Advt. Club, Bugatti Owners Club. Republican. Presbyterian. Office: Esquire Mag 2049 Century Park E Suite 830 Los Angeles CA 90067

LONGMAN, ALICE JEAN, nurse; b. Bklyn., Oct. 15, 1929; d. Walter Niblo and Alice May (Lager) L.; B.S., Coll. Mt. St. Vincent, N.Y.C., 1951; M.A., N.Y. U., 1957, postgrad., 1965-66, 69-70; M.Ed., Columbia U., 1972, Ed.D., 1974. Staff nurse Mercy Hosp., Rockville Centre, N.Y., 1951-53, St. Luke Hosp., Pasadena, Calif., 1952, Nassau County Dept. Health, Mineola, N.Y., 1953-57; supr. Manhasset (N.Y.) Vis. Nurse Service, 1957-59; instr. State U. Coll., Plattsburgh, N.Y.C., 1959-63, asst. prof., 1964-66, acting asso. dir., 1966-67; asst. dir. nursing adv. service Nat. League for Nursing-Nat. Tb and Respiratory Disease Assn., N.Y.C., 1967-71, dir., mem. staff dept. test constrn., 1971; instr. Bellevue Sch. Nursing, Hunter Coll., N.Y.C., 1971; instr. dept. nursing Herbert H. Lehman Coll., Bronx, N.Y., 1972, adj. lectr. bilingual program, 1972-73; instr. nurse edn. Pace U., N.Y.C., 1973; asso. prof. U. Ariz., Coll. Nursing, Tucson, 1974—; staff nurse People-to-People Health Found, Project HOPE, Trujillo, Peru, 1963-64, participant delegation to S. Am., 1979. Vol. blood pressure readings, 1975, Am. Cancer Soc., others. USPHS trainee, 1971-73; recipient Mary Opal Wolanin award, 1978. Mem. Am. Nurses Assn., Ariz. Nurses Assn. (chmn. com. on resolutions 1977-79), Nat. League for Nursing (vice chmn. bd. rev. for accreditation ednl. programs 1981—), Am. Assn. Higher Edn., AAUP, Assn. for Supervision and Curriculum Devel., Oncology Nursing Soc., Columbia U. Nursing Edn. Alumni Assn., Sigma Theta Tau. Contbr. articles to profl. jours. Office: Coll Nursing U Ariz Tucson AZ 85721

LONGSHORE, JAMES FREDERICK, aircraft manufacturing company executive; b. Arkansas City, Kan., Oct. 1, 1934; s. Fred and Rita Longshore; B.S.E.E., U. Mo.-Rolla, 1956; M.S.E.E., U. Ill., 1957; m. Janet Conkle, Oct. 19, 1980; children—James Steven, Deborah Kay. Various positions McDonnell Douglas Astronautics Co., St. Louis, 1957-67; sr. project engr. HARPOON flight controls, 1970-74; mgr. tech. integration McDonnell Douglas Corp., St. Louis, 1974-75, dir. tech. planning corp. engring. and research, 1975-78; dir. flight systems engring. Douglas Aircraft Co., Long Beach, Calif., 1978—. Fellow AIAA (assoc.); mem. IEEE, Eta Kappa Nu, Tau Beta Pi, Phi Kappa Phi. Home: 6600 Warner Ave Apt 50 Huntington Beach CA 92647 Office: Douglas Aircraft Co Mail Code 36-49 3855 Lakewood Blvd Long Beach CA 90846

LONGSTROM, COLLEEN KAY, school administrator; b. Tyler, Minn., Dec. 31, 1941; d. Ellsworth Marvin and Shirley Maxine (Willfong) Swanson; m. Jerry Eugene Longstrom, Nov. 26, 1960; children—Jeffrey Eugene, Gregory Michael. B.S. in Home Econs., U. Minn., 1963; M.A. in Edn. Adminstrn. and Supervision, Ariz. State U., 1977; postgrad. No. Ariz. U. Home economist Minn. Women's Prison, Shakopee, 1965-67; tchr. home econs. Delano (Minn.) High Sch., 1967-68; tchr. Glendale (Ariz.) Elem. Sch. Dist., 1969-77; adminstr., asst. prin. Glendale Elem. Sch. Dist., 1977—. Mem. NEA, Ariz. Sch. Adminstrs. Assn., Nat. Assn. Elem. Sch. Prins., Phi Delta Kappa. Home: 4921 W Laurie Ln Glendale AZ 85302 Office: 5535 N 67th Ave Glendale AZ 85301

LONIDIER, FRED, art educator, artist; b. Lakeview, Oreg., 1942; s. Sampson Bill and Sigrid (Brodine) L. A.A., Yuba Coll., 1962; B.A. in Sociology, San Francisco State Coll., 1966; M.F.A., U. Calif.-San Diego, 1972. Teaching asst. in visual arts U. Calif.-San Diego, 1970-72, instr. summer session, 1970-72, U. Calif. extension, 1972, part-time lectr., 1972-74, assoc. prof., 1981—; one man shows: Long Beach Mus. of Art, 1976, Whitney Mus. Am. Art, N.Y.C., 1977, Houston Ctr. for Photography, 1983, also others; group shows: Museum Folkwang, Essen W.Ger., 1980-81, 5. Wiener Internationale Biennale, Austria, 1981, Midland Group Postal Exhibit, Nottingham, Eng., 1972, Galerie La Bertesca, Genoa, Italy, 1974, San Francisco Mus. Modern Art, San Francisco Art Inst., 1976, Los Angeles Inst. Contemporary Art, 1977, 78, Fundacao Rio, Brazil, 1982, Galerie ImZwinger St. Wendel, W.Ger., 1982, Kunscentrum De Gele Rijder, Arnhem, Holland, 1982, R.I. Sch. Design, 1982, Santa Barbara Contempory Arts Forum, 1982-83, So. Ill. U., 1983, Carleton Coll., 1983, Smith Coll., 1983, Kunst Per Post, Utrecht, Holland, 1983, numerous others in U.S., Can., Europe; represented in permanent collections Long Beach Mus. Art, Oakland Mus., also others; panelist, panel coordinator S.W. Labor Studies Conf., Calif. State U.-Northridge, 1982; activist Artists Advance, Social and Pub. Arts Resource Ctr. retreat, Venice, Calif., 1982. Regents fellow U. Calif.-San Diego, 1971-72; Nat. Endowment for Arts fellow, 1980-81, 82; U. Calif.-San Diego Acad. Senate Research grantee, 1975-76, 78-80, 81, 82; Ford Found. grantee, 1977, 1981. Photographs published in numerous profl. jours.; contbr. articles to profl. jours. in field. Address: Visual Arts Dept B-027 U Calif San Diego LaJolla CA 92093

LONIE, DAVID DONALD, JR., real estate developer; b. Bay City, Mich., Nov. 16, 1924; s. David Donald and Ellen Marie (Lind) L.; B.S., U. Oreg., 1947; m. Virginia Mae Peterson, Oct. 18, 1947; children—Stephen Peter, Diane Cynthia, Thomas Edward, Nancy Madeline. Printing salesman Statesman Publishing Co., Salem, Oreg., 1947-48; asst. prodn. mgr. Joseph R. Gerber Advt., Portland, Oreg., 1948-50; editor N. Lincoln County News Guard, Lincoln City, Oreg., 1950-51; asst. advt. mgr. First Nat. Bank Oreg., Portland, 1951-53; with pub. relations dept. Portland Gen. Electric Co., 1953-55; sales mgr. sta. KPTV, Portland, 1955-57; owner Lonie Co., pub. relations, Portland, 1957-72; propr. Lonie Co., real estate devel., Honolulu, 1972—; pres. Oreg. Advt. Club, 1956. Served with USNR, 1943-46. Mem. Hawaii C. of C. (vice chmn. planning com.), Hawaii Hotel Assn., U. Oreg. Alumni Assn. (past pres.). Republican. Presbyterian. Clubs: Portland Golf, Arlington (Portland); Oahu Country, Honolulu Press, Outrigger Canoe, Plaza (Honolulu); Shriners. Home: 1216 Riverside Dr Reno NV 89503 Office: PO Box 10837 Reno NV 89510

LONKY, MARTIN LEONARD, electronics company executive; b. N.Y.C., Jan. 5, 1944; s. Hyman and Irene (Feldman) L.; B.S. in Physics, Rensselaer Poly. Inst., 1964; M.S., U. Del., 1967, Ph.D., 1972; m. Jean Williams, June 14, 1981. Teaching fellow U. Del., Newark, 1970-72; presdl. intern Land Warfare Lab., Aberdeen, Md., 1972, ops. research analyst, 1973; fellow engr. Westinghouse Electric Corp., Balt., 1975-78, supervisory engr., 1978; mgr. phys. sci. Questron Corp., El Segundo, Calif., 1978-81; supr. I.R. Tech. Group, JPL/Caltech., Pasadena, Calif., 1981; mgr. NH & S component electronics Northrop Electronics, Hawthorne, Calif., 1981—. Mem. Electrochem. Soc., IEEE, Am. Phys. Soc. Clubs: Mt. Scopus Lodge, Masons. Contbr. articles to profl. jours. Patentee in field. Home: 26214 Athena Ave Harbor City CA 90710 Office: Northrop Electronics Div 2301 W 120th St Hawthorne CA

LOOMIS, JOHN BROLAN, economist, educator; b. North Hollywood, Calif., Aug. 23, 1953; s. Charles Douglas and Frances Helen (Lombard) L.; m. Jayne Cullen July 27, 1974; 1 dau., Kelly Marie. B.A. in Econs., Calif. State U.-Northridge, 1975, M.A., 1977. Instr. econs., Los Angeles Valley Coll., Van Nuys, 1977; regional economist, U.S. Bur. Land Management, Moab, Utah, 1977-80; economist U.S. Fish and Wildlife Service, Ft. Collins, Colo., 1980—; faculty affiliate dept. econs., Colo. State U., 1981—; instr. various govt. agys. Litton Data Systems scholar, 1975-76; recipient Wall St. Jour. award, 1973. Mem. Am. Econs. Assn., Assn. Environ. and Resource Economists. Contbr. articles to profl. jours. Office: US Fish and Wildlife Service 2627 Redwing Rd Fort Collins CO 80526

LOOMIS, STEVEN ARTHUR, optometrist; b. Butte, Mont., Oct. 19, 1955; s. Harrison Barnard and Dorothy Lorena (Stark) L.; m. Kathy Christenberry, Dec. 30, 1977; children—Harrison Boyd, Ashley Chris. Student Mont. State U., 1973-75; B.S., Pacific U. 1977, O.D., 1979. Lic. optometrist, Oreg., Colo. Intern Madigan Army Med Ctr., Tacoma, Wash., 1978; staff optometrist Kaiser-Permanente Med. Care Facility, Denver, 1979-81; practice optometry, Littleton Colo., 1981—. Mem. Am. Optometric Assn., Colo. Optometric Assn. Office: 6505 W Ottawa Pl Suite 4 Littleton CO 80123

LOONEY, RALPH EDWIN, newspaper editor; b. Lexington, Ky., June 22, 1924; s. Arville Zone and Connie Elizabeth (Boyd) L.; B.A., U. Ky., 1948; m. Clarabel Richards, Dec. 7, 1944. Successively proof reader, photographer, chief photographer, sports writer, reporter Lexington Leader, 1943-52; reporter Albuquerque Tribune, 1953-54; reporter, copy editor, chief copy editor St. Louis Globe-Dem., 1955-56; city editor Albuquerque Tribune, 1956-68, asst. mng. editor, 1968-73, editor, 1973-80; editor Rocky Mountain News, Denver, 1980—. Founder, mem. N.Mex. Motion Picture Commn., 1967-76; bd. dirs. Albuquerque Indsl. Devel. Service, 1971-80; bd. advisors Lovelace Med. Center, Albuquerque, 1976-80. Recipient Robert F. Kennedy Journalism award, 1970; N.Mex. Medal of Merit, 1968; George Washington Honor medal Freedoms Found., 1969; 18 E.H. Shaffer awards for editorial writing, reporting and photography N.Mex. Press Assn., 1964-80. Mem. N.Mex. Press Assn. (state pres. 1976), Colo. Press Assn. (bd. dirs.), Newspaper Comics Council, Sigma Delta Chi (state pres. 1960). Methodist. Author: Haunted Highways, the Ghost Towns of New Mexico, 1969; contbr. articles to mags. including Atlantic, Nat. Geog., Nat. Observer, others; contbr. photographs to profl. publs. Office: 400 W Colfax St Denver CO 80204

LOONEY, ROBERT EDWARD, educator, economist; b. San Jose, Calif., June 6, 1941; s. Edward Donald and Virginia Ella (McCracken) L.; m. Anne Cochrane Craven, Dec. 31, 1943; children—Catherine, Virginia. Ph.D., U. Calif., 1969. Devel. economist Stanford Research Inst., 1969-71; asst. prof. U. Santa Clara, 1971-77; prof. Monterey (Calif.) Inst. Internat. Studies, 1977-79; assoc. prof. Naval Postgrad. Sch., 1979—; econ. cons. govts. of Iran, Saudi Arabia, Mex., Panama. Internat Labor Office grantee, 1981-82. Mem. Am. Econ. Assn., Royal Econ. Soc., Econometric Soc. Republican. Roman Catholic. Author: Economic Development of Iran, 1973; Economic Development of Panama, 1976; Mexico's Economy, 1978; Income Distribution Policies, 1975; World Inflation, 1979; Iran at the End of the Century, 1977; Saudi Arabia's Growth Potential, 1982; Mexico's Growth Alternatives, 1983. Home: 3 Sommerset Rd Monterey CA 93940 Office: Naval Postgraduate Sch Monterey CA 93940

LOORAM, JAMES FRANCIS XAVIER, management consultant; b. N.Y.C., Jan. 25, 1940; s. James Francis Xavier and Mary Harden L.; m.

Mary Bellacosa, June 30, 1962; children—Patrick, Mark, Mary Frances, Sean Meaghan. B.S., U.S. Mil. Acad., 1961; Ph.D., NYU, 1975. Commd. 2d lt. U.S. Army, 1961, advanced through grades to lt. col., inf., 1975; dir. tng. U.S. Army Orgn. Devel. Ctr., 1977-78; chief U.S. Army Mgmt. Cons. Div., 1978-81; prof. psychology and leadership U.S. Mil. Acad., West Point, N.Y., 1971-74; ret., 1981; mem. grad. faculty Pepperdine U., Malibu, Calif., 1978-80, Golden Gate U., San Francisco, 1977-80; pres. Looram & Assocs., Pacific Grove, Calif., 1981—. Decorated Bronze Star, Joint Service Commendation medal, Meritorious Service medal; Vietnamese Cross of Gallantry. Mem. Am. Acad. Mgmt., Mgmt. Inst. Monterey (dir.). Mem. editorial bd. Vision-Action. Home: 226 Willow St Pacific Grove CA 93950 Office: Looram & Assocs 532 Abrego St Monterey CA 93940

LOPER, GERALD MILTON, plant physiologist, researcher; b. Sykesville, Md., Jan. 7, 1936; s. Clark Milton and Anna Belle (Carey) L.; m. Virginia Evelyn Peiffer, Feb. 3, 1962; children—David Milton, Timothy Paul. B.Sc. in Agr., U. Md., 1958; M.Sc., U. Wis.-Madison, 1959, Ph.D. in Agr. and Biochemistry, 1961. Research agronomist Agrl. Research Service, USDA, Brookings, S.D., 1962-67, research plant physiologist, Tucson, Ariz., 1967—, supervisory research plant physiologist, 1978—, research leader crop pollination research unit, 1978—. Served with Army N.G., 1961-67. Mem. Am. Soc. Agronomy, Bot. Soc. Am., Soc. Plant Growth Regulation, Sigma Xi. Republican. Mem. Pentecostal Ch. Office: 2000 E Allen Tucson AZ 85719

LOPER, JAMES LEADERS, pub. broadcasting co. exec.; b. Phoenix, Sept. 4, 1931; s. John D. and Ellen Helen (Leaders) L.; B.A., Ariz. State U., 1953; M.A., U. Denver, 1957; Ph.D., U. So. Calif, 1967; m. Mary Louise Brion, Sept. 1, 1955; children—Elizabeth Margaret, James Leaders. Asst. dir. Bur. Broadcasting, Ariz. State U., Tempe, 1953-59; news editor, announcer KTAR Radio, Phoenix, 1955-56; dir. Ednl. TV, Calif. State U.-Los Angeles, 1960-64; v.p. Community TV So. Calif., Los Angeles, 1962-63; asst. to pres. KCET Pub. TV, Los Angeles, 1963-65, sec., 1965-66, dir. ednl. services, 1964-65, asst. gen. mgr., 1965-66, v.p., gen. mgr., 1966-69, exec. v.p., gen. mgr., 1969-71, pres., gen. mgr., 1971-76, pres., chief exec. officer, 1977-82; chmn. mgmt. edn. program for pub. broadcasters Harvard U. and Nat. Assn. Ednl. Broadcasters, 1977; dir. Western Fed. Savs. & Loan. Bd. dirs. Los Angeles Civic Light Opera Assn., 1975—; chmn., dir. The Performing Tree, Los Angeles, 1975—; trustee Poly. Sch., Pasadena, 1977-82; bd. dirs. Calif. Confedn. of Arts, 1977-78; mem. adv. bd. UCLA Arts Mgmt. Program, 1975—; mem. alumni/alumnae adv. council Ariz. State U., Tempe, 1977-80; mem. adv. bd. Coll. Continuing Edn., U. So. Calif., 1978—; mem. Los Angeles World Affairs Council, 1974—, Los Angeles Town Hall, 1974—; mem. exec. bd. Art Center/Coll. Design, Pasadena, Calif. Recipient Disting. Alumnus award Ariz. State U., 1972; Alumni award of Merit, U. So. Calif., 1975; Govs. award Hollywood chpt. Nat. Acad. TV Arts and Scis., 1975; Alumni Achievement award Phi Sigma Kappa, 1975. Mem. Young Pres. Orgn., Pacific Pioneer Broadcasters (dir. 1973-80), Western Ednl. Soc. Telecommunications (pres.), Assn. Calif. Pub. TV Stas. (pres.), Sigma Delta Chi, Phi Sigma Kappa, Alpha Delta Sigma, Pi Delta Epsilon. Clubs: Valley Hunt (Pasadena); Bel-Air Bay, 100, Sunset, 100, California (Los Angeles). Contbr. articles to profl. jours.; contbr. to ETV: The Farther Vision, 1967, Broadcasting and Bargaining: Labor Relations in Radio and Television, 1970. Home: 735 Holladay Rd Pasadena CA 91106

LOPER, WARREN EDWARD, computer specialist; b. Dallas, Aug. 2, 1929; s. Leon Edward and Belva (Fannin) L.; student So. Meth. U., 1945-46, Baylor U., 1947, Dallas Coll., 1948; B.S. in Physics, U. Tex. at Austin, 1953, B.A. in Math with honors, 1953; m. Ruth M. Wetzler, June 17, 1967; 1 dau., Mary Katherine Loper. Commd. ensign U.S. Navy, 1953, advanced through grades to lt., 1957; physicist U.S. Naval Ordnance Test Station, China Lake, Calif., 1956-61; operational programmer U.S. Navy Electronics Lab., San Diego, 1962-64; project leader, systems programming br., digital computer staff U.S. Fleet Missile Systems Analysis and evaluation Group, Corona, 1964-65, sr. systems analyst digital computer staff U.S. Naval Ordnance Lab., Corona, 1965-69; head systems programming br. Naval Weapons Center, Corona Labs, 1969; computer specialist compiler and operating systems devel. Code 5200, Naval Electronics Lab. Center, San Diego, 1969-76, project leader in devel. CS-4 Navy programming lang., 1970-75, head langs. and operating systems br., 1976-77; project leader langs., operating systems and graphics Naval Ocean Systems Ctr., San Diego, 1977—; Navy rep. on tech. subgroup Dept. Def. High Order Lang. Working Group, 1975-80. Mem. IEEE, Assn. Computer Machinery. Democrat. Roman Catholic. Lodge: K.C. Home: 6542 Alcala Knolls Dr San Diego CA 92111 Office: Naval Ocean Systems Center Code 8315 271 Catalina Blvd San Diego CA 92152

LOPEZ, ANTHONY, social work educator, consultant; b. San Juan, P.R., July 12, 1943; s. Antonio and Octavia (Cordero) L.; m. Lorraine Mata, July 29, 1967; children—Anthony III, Teresa, Orlando. B.A. in Sociology and Theology, So. Calif. Coll., 1971; M.S.W., U. So. Calif., 1973; postgrad. U. Denver, 1976—. Psychiat. social worker U. So. Calif. Med. Ctr., 1973-74, dir. tng. substance abuse program, 1974-76; intergovtl. relations coordinator III, drug abuse program Denver Regional Council Govts., 1978-79; instr./coordinator human services program Community Coll. Denver-Aurora, Denver, 1979—; cons. in field. NIMH grantee, 1971-73; Council Social Work Edn. grantee, 1976-78. Mem. Nat. Assn. Social Workers, Nat. Orgn. Human Service Educators, Coalition Spanish-Speaking Mental Health Orgns., Nat. Orgn. Puerto Ricans Social and Drug Abuse Workers, Chicano Alliance, Hispanic Democratic Caucus. Mem. Assembly of God Ch. Home: 630 S Dayton St B-14-A-107 Denver CO 80231 Office: 1111 W Colfax Denver CO 80204

LOPEZ, BARBARA BOYLE, advertising executive; b. Detroit, Mar. 28, 1943; d. James Joseph and Daisy Irene (Porter) Boyle; div.; 1 dau., Yvette Emma. Account exec. various Los Angeles advt. agys., 1969-74; pres., co-creative dir. Cozad & Lopez Advt., Los Angeles, 1974-77; chief exec. officer BLA Corp. advt. and exec. search, Los Angeles, 1977—; lectr. in field. Mem. Los Angeles Advt. Women (past pres.), Western States Advt. Agys. Assn. (bd. dirs., 1979-81), Am. Advt. Fedn. (dir. 1979). Club: Los Angeles Athletic. Office: 12021 Wilshire Blvd Suite 500 Los Angeles CA 90025

LOPEZ, CARLOS URRUTIA, educator; b. Concepcion, Chile, Oct. 6, 1932; came to U.S., 1953, naturalized, 1960; s. Hernan M. and Mila M. (Urrutia) L.; B.H., U. Chile, 1953; B.S. in Econs., U. Santa Clara, 1958; M.A., U. Calif., Berkeley, 1959; Licenciado, U. Chile, 1965; m. Eveleen K. Johnston, June 21, 1958; children—Lawrence, Andrea, Elena. Instr., U. Santa Clara, 1959-61; from instr. to prof. humanities Menlo Coll., Menlo Park, Calif., 1961—, Trustees Disting. prof. humanities, 1975—; soccer coach U. Santa Clara, 1958-61, Menlo Coll., 1961—. Nat. Endowment Humanities grantee, 1972; Sourisseau Acad. grantee, 1973. Mem. Chilean Acad. History, Am. Assn. Tchrs. Spanish and Portuguese, Latin Am. Studies Assn., Congress Latin Am. History, Am. Assn. Soccer Coaches. Republican. Roman Catholic. Club: Club de la Union (Santiago, Chile). Author seven books including: Historia de la Marina de Chile, 1969; We Were Forty-Niners, 1976; contbr. numerous articles profl. jours. Office: Menlo College Menlo Park CA 94025

LOPEZ, CESAR, JR., manufacturing company official; b. Veracruz, Mexico, Oct. 18, 1946; came to U.S., 1955, naturalized, 1966; s. Cesar and Silvia (Zamorano) L.; B.S. in Physics, Calif. State U., Los Angeles, 1969; M.B.A./M.S. in Bus. Adminstrn., UCLA, 1972; postgrad. (doctoral fellow) Rand Grad. Inst., 1972-74. Project engr. Hughes Electron Dynamics Div., Torrance, Calif., 1969-72; exec. asst. to v.p. nat. security div. Rand Corp., Santa Monica, Calif., 1972-74; sr. mktg. specialist Northrop Corp., Hawthorne, Calif., 1974-78; mgr. fin. and adminstrn. comml. div. Hughes Helicopters, Culver City, Calif., 1978—; faculty Calif. State U., Los Angeles, 1976-78. Mem. World Affairs Council, Am. Mktg. Assn., Am. Mgmt. Assn. Democrat. Roman Catholic. Contbr. articles to profl. jours. Office: Hughes Helicopters Centinela and Teale Sts Culver City CA 90230

LOPEZ, MELITON, supt. schs.; b. Los Aldamas, Nuevo Leon, Mex., Mar. 15, 1934; came to U.S., 1946, naturalized, 1960; s. Antonio Cantu Lopez and Felipta Cantu Garcia; B.A. in Polit. Sci., U. Tex., 1958; M.S. in Edn., Calif. State U., Fullerton, 1968; Ph.D. in Ednl. Adminstrn./Curriculum Leadership, Wayne State U., 1972; m. Ida Diane Griffin, Sept. 2, 1961; children—Carlos Antonio, Dolores Maria, Vanesa Rebeca, Sonya Elisa. Elem. sch. tchr., Hemet, Calif., 1960-64, jr. high and sr. high tchr., 1964-68, high sch. counselor, 1968-70; coordinator, dir. spl. and bilingual edn. programs Riverside County (Calif.) Schs., 1970-71; asso. prof. U. Calif., Santa Cruz, 1971-73, U. Pacific, Stockton, Calif., 1973-75; asst. supt. curriculum Chula Vista (Calif.) City Sch. Dist., 1975-81; supt. schs. Laguna Salada Sch. Dist., Pacifica, Calif., 1981—; cons. Calif. State Dept. Edn., Sacramento, 1968-80; mem. faculty U. Calif., Riverside, 1968-70, San Diego State U., 1975-80, U. San Diego, 1978-79, Pepperdine U., 1979; evaluator, auditor Headstart, Follow-Thru, Title VII, Job Corps, U.S. Office Edn., 1968-75. Mem. Econ. Opportunity Policies Bd., Riverside County, 1965-68; mem. Focus on Complete Utilization Schs. Com., 1975; mem. integration task force San Diego City Schs., 1978-80. Served with U.S. Army, 1958-60. NDEA fellow U. Tex., 1962; Mott Found. fellow, 1970-71; Nat. Endowment Humanities fellow U. Calif., San Diego, 1978, NSF fellow Stanford U., 1979. Mem. Assn. Mex.-Am. Edn., Assn. Supervision and Curriculum Devel., NEA, League United Latin-Am. Citizens, Assn. Calif. Sch. Adminstrs., Sigma Delta Pi, Pi Kappa Pi. Democrat. Roman Catholic. Club: Marriage Encounter. Home: 732 Rockaway Beach Ave Pacifica CA 94044 Office: 375 Reina Del Mar Pacifica CA 94044

LOPEZ, RALPH JOHN, interior designer; b. Chgo., May 6, 1941; s. Ralph Joseph and Hope (Herrera) L.; B.A., Loyola U., Los Angeles, 1964; postgrad. UCLA, 1975, 77. Furniture buyer J. W. Robinsons, 1964-65, Gimbel Bros., Phila., 1965-67; clothing buyer J. C. Penney's, Los Angeles, 1967-68; mem. adminstrv. staff Los Angeles County-U. So. Calif. Med Center, 1968-82; owner R. J. Lopez Interiors, Los Angeles, 1972—; mem. Interior Design Adv. Bd., 1978. Mem. sta. KCET, Pub. Broadcasting; mem. performing arts council Mus. Contemporary Art. Mem. Los Angeles County Mus. Art, Acad. Polit. Sci., World Affairs Council. Roman Catholic. Office: 6000 Whitworth Dr Los Angeles CA 90019

LOPEZ, RAUL ALBERTO, museum consultant b. Los Angeles, May 8, 1937; s. Jorge and Herminia Ignacia (Ramirez) L.; A.A., Los Angeles City Coll., 1964; B.A., UCLA, 1966, M.A., 1969; m. Sylvia Doris Schmid, June 25, 1960; children—Raul E., Andrea I. Curator, Mus. of Cultural History, UCLA, 1967-78; dir. Riverside (Calif.) Mcpl. Mus., 1978-82; mem. nat. mus. services bd. Dept. Edn., Washington, 1977-81; chmn. bd. Family Group Homes, 1976-80. Ford Found. fellow, 1966-68; Nat. Endowment Humanities fellow, 1972-75. Mem. Am. Assn. Museums. Democrat. Office: 3772 Orange St Riverside CA 92501

LOPEZ, RHODA LEBLANC, sculptor; b. Detroit, Mar. 16, 1912; d. Leo William and Rhoda Ann (Schell) LeBlanc; m. Felix Carlos Lopez, May 28, 1933 (dec. 1953); children—Carol Lopez Wiffong, Jon Carlos. Student Wayne U., Detroit, Cranbrook Art Acad., 1949-50, Scripps Coll., 1953. Instr., Potters Guild, Ann Arbor, Mich., 1950-59; med. artist U. Mich. Med. Sch., 1953-59; instr. ceramics LaJolla Mus. Art, U. Calif.-San Diego, 1960-78; founder, dir. Clay Dimensions, San Diego, 1969—; lectr., cons. in field; commd. works include Meml. Wall Unitarian Ch., San Diego, 1978, panels Juvenile Hall, San Diego, mural Home Fed. Savs. and Loan Assn., San Juan Capistrano, mural People's Bank S.D. Mem. African arts com. San Diego Fine Arts Gallery; active Folk Art Mus., La Jolla, Friends of Internat. Ctr. U. Calif.-San Diego. Mem. Am. Bus. Women's Assn. Unitarian-Universalist. Address: 1020 Pacific Beach Dr San Diego CA 92109

LOPOUR, MARTHA JEANETTE, business exec., former county govt. ofcl.; b. El Paso, Tex., Nov. 18, 1937; d. Clarence Oren and Martha Belle (Denerson) Shirey; student N.Mex. Jr. Coll.; m. David Lee LoPour, July 6, 1956; children—Melissa Dianne, David Gregory. Dep. tax assessor Lea County Tax Assessor's Office, Lovington, N.Mex., 1957-61, dep. appraiser-tax assessor, 1968-76, data processing coordinator, 1976-81; owner LoPour Ltd., 1982—; v.p. LoPour Storm Windows & Doors. Sec., Lovington Democratic Women, 1980, rec. sec., 1981; Lovington bd. dirs. March of Dimes Found., 1962, 78; bd. dirs. Lovington Blood Services; mem. Youth Ctr. Council, sponsor, 1981-82. Recipient cert. of nobility N.Mex. Sec. State, 1980. Mem. Beta Sigma Phi (pres. 1981). Baptist. Home and office: 802 W Gore St Lovington NM 88260

LOPP, GEORGE RAYMOND, trading company executive; b. Columbus, Kans., Oct. 4, 1930; s. Charles Benjamin and Iva Lorene (Evans) L.; m. Bernice Gill, July 23, 1950; children—Sherry Ann Ord, Brenda Rae Brownell, David Lynn. Student No. Ariz. U., U. Ariz. With Babbitt Bros. Trading Co., 1948—, mgr. lumber dept., Holbrook, Ariz., 1955-65, mgr. Wholesale div., Flagstaff, 1965-73, v.p. supr. Wholesale div., 1973—, also dir., mem. exec. com., v.p., dir. subs., also supr. home center ops.; dir. 1st Interstate Bank of Ariz. Bd. dirs. Petrified Forest Mus. Assn., 1963, Flagstaff United Fund, Flagstaff Sign Code Com., 1968, No. Ariz. Health Care Found., 1978; trustee Holbrook Community Ch., 1964; pres. bd. trustees Flagstaff Community Hosp., 1976; bus. adv. council Coll. Bus. No. Ariz. U.; Named Outstanding Man of Yr., City of Holbrook (Ariz.), 1964. Mem. Ariz. Lumber and Builders Supply Assn. (bd. dirs., exec. com., chmn. legis. and govtl. affairs com., pres. 1972), Flagstaff C. of C. (pres. 1970, econ. devel. com.) Beta Gamma Sigma. Clubs: Holbrook Rotary (pres. 1965), Rotary Internat. (bd. dirs. 1977), Elks, Flagstaff Townjacks, No. Ariz. U. Century. Home: 2024 N Crescent Dr Flagstaff AZ 86001 Office: PO Box 1328 Flagstaff AZ 86002

LOPRESTI, RONALD B(ASIL), educator, composer; b. Williamstown, Mass., Oct. 28, 1933; s. Basil and Jane D. (Moon) LoP.; m. Marjorie Ann Beverly, Nov. 28, 1952; children—Ronald, Laurence, Leonard, Nina, Grant, Alicia. B.M., Eastman Sch. Music, 1955, M.M., 1956. Tchr. theory Tex. Tech. Coll., Lubbock, 1959-60; Ford Found. composer in residence Winfield (Kans.) Pub. Schs., 1960-62; asst. prof. music Ind. (Pa.) State Coll., 1962-64; prof. composition and theory Ariz. State U., Tempe, 1964—. Recipient Spl. Serge Koussevitsky award, 1955; Percussion award Eastman Sch. Music, 1956; awards Coll. Band Dirs., 1957, Syracuse U. Festival of Arts, 1962; Writer awards ASCAP, 1963-82. Mem. ASCAP, Nat. Golden Key Soc. (hon.). Composer: The Masks, 1955; Pageant Overture, 1956; Suite for 5 Trumpets, 1960; Kansas Overture, 1960; Elegy for a Young American, 1964; Tundra, 1967.

LORBEER, VIRGINIA L., educator: b. Denver, May 31, 1941; d. Earl C. and Alice L. (Schlemeyer) L.; B.S. in Bus. Edn. and English, Ft. Hays State U., 1963; M.A. in Secondary Sch. Adminstrn., U. Colo., 1973: postgrad. U. No. Colo., 1977-79. Tchr. bus. edn., sponsor pep club and cheerleaders, Manual High Sch., Denver, 1964-81, student activities dir., 1975-76, hon. cadet sponsor; tchr. bus. edn., dir. Student activities Montbello High Sch., Denver, 1981—; tchr. bus. edn. Opportunity Sch., Night Sch., Denver Public Schs., 1964—; passenger relations agt. Trans World Airlines, Stapleton Airport, 1976—; speaker on sch. spirit, self discipline: part-time model; judge nat. and local cheerleaders. Mem. Nat. Assn. of Cheerleaders, Colo. Edn. Assn., Colo. Bus. Edn. Assn., Sigma Kappa. Featured in article on work with cheerleaders Rocky Mountain News, 1972, 76; contbr. articles on sch. spirit to publs. Home: 13965 E Oxford Pl Aurora CO 80014 Office: 5000 Crown Blvd Denver CO 80239

LORCH, BARBARA RUTH, sociology educator; b. Pendleton, Oreg., Sept. 30, 1924; d. George Washington and Ruth Irene (Spangler) Day; m. Robert Stuart Lorch, Dec. 19, 1964; 1 son, John Day. B.S. in Psychology, Wash. State U., 1946, M.A. in Sociology, 1947; Ph.D., U. Wash., 1956. Instr. sociology Ariz. State U., Tempe, 1947-48, Bowling Green State U., 1948-50; asst. prof. sociology U. Ariz., Tucson, 1952-53; acting instr. sociology U. Wash., Seattle, 1953-56; asst. prof. U. Mont., Missoula, 1956-58, assoc. prof., 1958-59; asst. prof. sociology Calif. State U.-Long Beach, 1959-61, assoc. prof. sociology, 1961-65, prof. sociology, 1965-69; prof. sociology U. Colo., Colorado Springs, 1969—, chmn. dept., 1969-73. Mem. Am. Sociol. Assn., Internat. Sociol. Assn., Western Social Sci. Assn., Phi Beta Kappa, Phi Kappa Phi, Pi Lambda Theta, Alpha Kappa Delta, Psi Chi, Delta Delta Delta. Reviewer (20) books; contbr. articles to profl. jours. Office: U Colo PO Box 7150 Colorado Springs CO 80933

LORD, ERNEST RAYMOND, architect; b. Pa., Dec. 14, 1930; s. Ernest and Elizabeth Amanda (Snedeker) L.; m. Bette Lou Best, Feb. 19, 1952; children—Richard, Carol Davidson, Kenneth, Steven. Registered architect, Calif., Ariz. Draftsman U.S. Air Force, Edwards AFB, Muroc, Calif., 1949-52, Standard Oil Co. Exploration, Bakersfield, Calif., 1952-53, Ernest L. McCoy Architects, Bakersfield, 1953-54; draftsman Stuhr & Hicks Architects, Bakersfield, 1954-59, chief draftsman, 1960-62; architect Roy Dowley and Assocs. Architects, Hollywood, Calif., 1962; project architect Hope Cons. Group Architects and Engrs., San Diego, 1962-68; dir. prodn., 1968-77, v.p., 1972-77, pres., San Diego office, 1978-80, exec. v.p., sec., 1981—. Bd. dirs. San Diego Taxpayers Assn., 1980-82, v.p., 1983; bd. dirs. Cedar Community Ctr., 1976—. Served to staff sgt. USAF, 1948-52. Mem. AIA (honor award San Diego Stadium, project architect, 1979), Constrn. Specifications Inst., Constrn. Mgmt. Assn. Am., Am. Concrete Inst. Republican. Methodist. Clubs: Rotary, San Diego. Home: 3456 Baker St San Diego CA 92117 Office: 401 W 'A' St San Diego CA 92101

LORD, JACK, actor, artist, writer, producer, director; b. N.Y.C., Dec. 30, 1930; s. William Lawrence and E. Josephine (O'Brien) Ryan; B.S. in Fine Arts, NYU, 1954; m. Marie de Narde, Apr. 1, 1952. Exhbns. include: Corcoran Gallery, Washington, NAD, Whitney Mus., Bklyn. Mus., Met. Mus. Art, N.Y.C., Library of Congress, Bibliotheque Nationale, Paris; represented in permanent collections: Met. Mus. Art, Mus. Modern Art, Bklyn. Mus., Fogg Mus., Santa Barbara Mus. Art, Cin. Art Mus., Fine Art Gallery, San Diego, Chouinard Art Inst., Los Angeles, Free Library of Phila., DePauw U. Art Mus., Brit. Mus., London, Atkins Mus. Art, Kansas City; appeared in Broadway plays including: Traveling Lady (Theatre World award 1954), Cat on a Hot Tin Roof; motion picture performances include: Court Martial of Billy Mitchell, Williamsburg-The Story of a Patriot, Tip on a Dead Jockey, God's Little Acre, Man of the West, The Hangman, True Story of Lynn Stuart, Walk like a Dragon, Doctor No; leading roles in TV prodns. including: Constitution series Omnibus, Playhouse 90, Goodyear Playhouse, Studio One, U.S. Steel Hour; TV appearances include Have Gun Will Travel, Untouchables, Naked City, Rawhide, Bonanza, Americans, Route 66, Gunsmoke, Stagecoach West, Dr. Kildare, Greatest Show on Earth; starring role in Stoney Burke series and Hawaii Five-O series; creator TV shows Tramp Ship, Yankee Trader, McAdoo, The Hunter series; writer screenplay Melissa, 1968; creator, dir., producer M Station: Hawaii (TV film); dir. Death with Father, How to Steal a Masterpiece, Honor is an Unmarked Grave, Top of the World, Why Won't Linda Die, Who Said Cops Don't Cry; pres. Lord and Lady Enterprises, Inc. Recipient St. Gauden's artist award, 1948, Fame award, 1963; others; named to Cowboy Hall of Fame, 1963. Office: 1999 Kahala Ave Honolulu HI 96816 also care J W Hayes 132 S Rodeo Dr Beverly Hills CA 90212

LORD, MICHAEL PHILLIP, city official; b. Los Angeles, June 24, 1943; s. Kenneth Phillip and Floriene Dunn (Loomis) L.; m. Barbara Metz, Nov. 20, 1982; children—Matthew, Susan, Kenneth, Sarah. B.S. in Civil Engring., Calif. State U., 1969. Estimator, Robert E. McKee, Inc., 1969-70; constrn. engr. Guy F. Atkinson Co., 1970-72; tech. services div. mgr. Water Dept., City of Garden Grove (Calif.), 1972-75; engring. services mgr. Dept. Pub. Works and Devel., City of Garden Grove, 1975-77; fin. dir. Santa Margarita Water Dist., Mission Viejo, Calif., 1977—. Mem. steering com. Yes on 9 (Peripheral Canal) Orange County, Calif. Served with U.S. Army, 1966. Mem. Calif. Soc. Mcpl. Fin. Officers, Am. Water Works Assn. Republican. Home: 538 Nantucket Ct Leucadia CA 92024 Office: 2610 Marguerite Pkwy Mission Viejo CA 92691

LORD, SAMUEL, banker; b. Steel County, Minn. Sept. 24, 1929; s. Samuel and Mary-Louise (Lyon).; m. Jette Jacobsen, Dec. 31, 1966; children—Samuel, Anne-Marie. A.B. cum laude, Amherst Coll., 1951; J.D., U. N.Mex., 1954; grad. Stonier Grad. Sch. Banking,Rutgers U., 1962, Advanced Mgmt. Program, Harvard U., 1965. Bar: Minn. 1954, N.Y. 1957, Wash. 1977. Vice pres. Citibank N.A. also Citicorp, N.Y.C., 1954-76; sr. v.p., sec. Rainier Bancorp, Seattle, 1976—; dir. Lord Corp., Erie, Pa.; mem. thesis panel examiners Stonier Grad. Sch. Banking; adv. com. corp. debt financing project Am. Bar Found. Trustee Am. Scandinavian Found., N.Y.C., 1971—, treas., 1974-76. Mem. ABA, Wash. Bar Assn., Assn. Bar City of N.Y., Am. Soc. Corp. Secs. Clubs: Rainier (Seattle); Wing Point Golf and Country (Bainbridge Island, Wash.). Home: PO Box 10537 Bainbridge Island WA 98110 Office: Rainier Bancorp PO Box 3966 Seattle WA 98124

LORENZ, GARY WAYNE, computer company executive; b. Norfolk, Nebr., Jan. 18, 1949; s. Erwin William and Marjorie Joyce (Fuesler) L.; B.S. with honors, Calif. State Poly. U., Pomona, 1971; m. Linda Marie Phillips, Jan. 12, 1974; children—Adam Phillip, Lisa Elisabeth, Jonathan David. Co-owner Amsec Co., Long Beach, Calif., 1972-74, div. mgr. Amsec div. R.D. Products, Inc., 1974—, v.p. R.D. Products, Inc., 1979-82; v.p., div. mgr. Griffin Tech. Inc., Rancho Dominguez, Calif., 1982—. Patentee self-clocking magnetic encoder. Mem. IEEE, Sigma Pi Alpha. Republican. Home: 13156 Acoro Pl Cerritos CA 90701 Office: 17621 Susana Rd Rancho Dominguez CA 90221

LORENZO, FRANCISCO A., airline company executive; b. N.Y.C., 1940. B.A., Columbia U., 1961; postgrad. Harvard U. Grad. Sch. Bus. Adminstrn., 1963. Pres., chief exec. officer Tex. Air Corp., Houston; chmn. bd. Continental Airlines, 1982—; dir. Tex. Internat. Airlines, N.Y. Airlines, Inc., Elsinore Corp., McCormick Oil & Gas Co. Office: Tex Air Corp 4040 Capital Bank Plaza Houston TX 77002*

LORNE, SIMON MICHAEL, lawyer; b. Hampton, Eng., Feb. 1, 1946; came to U.S., 1952, naturalized, 1961; s. Henry Thomas and Daphne Mary (Brough) L.; A.B. cum laude, Occidental Coll., 1967; J.D. magna cum laude, U. Mich., 1970; m. Patricia Ann Coady, Aug. 12, 1967; children—Christopher, Michele, Allison, Nathan James, Katrina. Admitted to Calif. bar, 1971; assoc. firm Munger, Tolles & Rickershauser,

Los Angeles, 1970-72, ptnr., 1972—; vis. assoc. prof. law U. Pa., 1977-78, acting dir. Ctr. Study of Fin. Instns., 1977-78. Mem. Los Angeles Mayor's Com. on Internat. Trade Devel., 1979-81; bd. dirs., sec. Los Angeles Internat. Trade Devel. Corp., 1982—; mem. adv. com. to U.S. Senator S.I. Hayakawa on Internat. Trade, 1979-82; bd. govs. Econ. Literacy Council Calif., 1981—. Served with USMCR, 1967-68. Mem. Los Angeles Area C. of C. (exec. com., internat. commerce com., leadership mission to People's Republic of China, 1980), ABA, Los Angeles County Bar Assn. (exec. com. bus. and corps. law sect., 1st vice chmn. 1983-84). Republican. Roman Catholic. Clubs: Jonathan; Stock Exchange. Office: Munger Tolles & Rickershauser 612 S Flower St Los Angeles CA 90017

LORZ, LUCY URSULA, sheetmetal company executive; b. Lewiston, Idaho, Sept. 24, 1931; d. George Wesley Phillips and Arta Thelma (Oylear) Greer; m. Kenneth Adrain Lorz, July 30, 1928; children—Delores Kay Sanders, Beverly Jean Smith, Barbara Helen Wammack, Sherry Lynn Sanborn. Office mgr., field supr. gen. contractor's office, Fairbanks, Alaska, 1972-76; owner, mgr. Clearwater Heating & Sheetmetal, Fairbanks, 1974—.

LOSCHEN, LESLIE ROBERT, accounting educator; b. LeRoy, Kans., Sept. 14, 1923; s. Peter Thomas and Theta Myrle (Bussert) L.; m. Mary Jane Rigney, Apr. 9, 1963. Student Central Wash. Coll., 1941-43; A.B., Whitman Coll., 1944; postgrad. U. London Sch. Econs., summer 1952; M.B.A., Harvard U., 1949; Ph.D., U. Wash., 1963. CPA, Wash; cert. mgmt. acct. Instr. bus. adminstrn. Coll. Puget Sound, Tacoma, 1950-51; State Dept. exchange prof. Am. U., Beirut, Lebanon, 1951-52; asst. prof. acctg. U. So. Calif., Los Angeles, 1954-59, lectr. acctg., 1963-64, assoc. prof., 1964—; asst. prof. acctg. San Diego State Coll., 1960-63; vis. prof. U. Cape Town, 1971, U. Wash., 1979; vis. prof. bus. Loyola Marymount U., Los Angeles, 1981-82. Served to lt. (j.g.), Supply Corps, USNR, 1943-46. Mem. Am. Acctg. Assn., Fin. Execs. Inst., Nat. Assn. Accts., Phi Kappa Phi, Beta Gamma Sigma, Beta Alpha Psi. Author: (with others) An Introduction to Financial Control and Reporting in Multinational Enterprises, 1973; contbr. to Managerial Cost Accountants Handbook, 1979. Home: 21 Gaucho Dr Rolling Hills Estates CA 90274 Office: Sch Acctg U So Calif Los Angeles CA 90089

LOSER, THOMAS JOHN, personnel administrator, vocational education administrator; b. Cornwall, Pa., Mar. 15, 1944; s. Carl Walter and Margaret Rose (Chernick) L.; m. Blanche Elizabeth Hammer, Dec. 30, 1944; children—Tim, Carl, Julieane. B.A., Adams State Coll., 1969; M.Ed. in Vocat. Edn. Adminstrn., Colo. State U., 1973, Ph.D., 1976. Drafting technician Buell Engring., Lebanon, Pa., 1965-67; vocat. drafting instr. San Luis Valley Area Vocat. Sch., Monte Vista, Colo., 1970-72; job devel. specialization, mgr. adult edn. and spl. programs, Larimer County Voc-Tech Ctr., Ft. Collins, Colo., 1973-79; personnel adminstr. Desktop Computer div. Hewlett-Packard Co., Ft. Collins, 1979—; mgmt. tchr.; mem. High Tech Ad Hoc State Com. Colo. State Bd. Community Colls. and Occupational Edn. fellow. Mem. Am. Soc. Personnel Adminstrs., Am. Soc. Tng. and Devel. Democrat. Roman Catholic. Office: Hewlett Packard Co 3404 E Harmony Rd Fort Collins CO 80525

LOTT, DAVIS NEWTON, advertising agency executive, publisher; b. San Antonio, May 8, 1913; s. James and Sissilla (Davis) L.; m. Arlene Marion Peterson Nov. 1, 1942; children—Vicki Arlene, Christy Sue, Laurie Ann. B.S., Northwestern U., 1935; post-grad. UCLA. With Better Homes and Gardens, Des Moines, Iowa, 1935-36; with Abbott, Labs., North Chicago, Ill., 1936-37; copywriter J. Walter Thompson, Chgo., 1938-39; owner and pres. Lott Advt. Agy., Los Angeles, 1939-41, 46—; owner Lott Pub. Co., Los Angeles, 1948—; pres. USA Corp., Marina del Ray, Calif.; pres. Western Publs., Santa Monica, Calif.; pub. Am. Buyers Rev., Am. Carwash Rev., Am. Personal Protection Rev.; dir. spl. projects Microlert Systems Internat. Past bd. dirs. Los Angeles Library Assn. Served to comdr. USNR, 1941-46, 1951-52, World War II, Korea. Named Assoc. Dean of Candy Industry, Nat. Candy Wholesalers Assn., 1974. Author: Rules of the Road, 1942; Emergency Shiphandling Manual, 1943; Collision Prevention, 1947; Treasure Trail, 1944; Star Spangled Broadcast, 1950; Mystery of Midnight Springs, 1954; Dodge City Justice, 1957; The Inaugural Addresses of the American Presidents, 1964; The Presidents Speak, 1965; See How They Ran 1972; The Presidents Illustrated, 1976; Jimmy Carter-And How He Won, 1976; co-author: (with Bruce Greenland) musical comedy The Music Room, 1982. Home: 13222 B Admiral Ave Marina del Rey CA 90291 Office: PO Lockbox 9669 Marina del Rey CA 90291

LOTWALA, BHUPENDRA TULSIDAS, hospital finance executive; b. Bombay, India, Dec. 12, 1944; came to U.S., 1967; s. Tulsidas Jadavjee and Jaya Tulsidas L.; m. Harshada Pranjivan Popat, Apr. 15, 1973; children—Raj, Dhir. B.Commerce, U. Bombay, 1966; M.B.A., Pace Coll., 1971. Acct., Computer Applications, Inc., N.Y.C., 1968-70; asst. controller Meml. Hosp., Phoenix, 1973-79; controller Desert Hosp., Palm Springs, Calif., 1979—. Mem. Hosp. Fin. Mgmt. Assn. (dir. Ariz. 1977-78), Healthcare Fin. Mgmt. Assn. Office: 1150 N Indian Ave Palm Springs CA 92262

LOUDEN, JAMES E., trust co. exec.; b. Ft. Wayne, Ind., June 13, 1944; s. Paul Hackett and Berniece Isabelle (Spurgeon) L.; B.S., Ind. U., 1966, J.D., 1969; m. Marlene A. Springer, Aug. 27, 1965; children—Jason, Barrett, Kane Stanton. Admitted to Ill. bar, 1969, Ariz. bar, 1979; with First Nat. Bank Chgo., 1969-78, v.p., 1977-78; pres. First Chgo. Trust Co. Ariz., Scottsdale, 1978—; mem. faculty U. Wis. Grad. Sch. Banking, 1973—. Mem. ABA, State Bar Ariz., Maricopa County Bar Assn., Scottsdale Bar Assn., Valley Estate Planning Council (dir. 1980-82). Author articles in field, chpts. in books. Office: 7501 E McCormack Pkwy Scottsdale AZ 85258

LOUDEN, KENNETH HAROLD, clin. psychologist; b. Calgary, Alta., Can., May 27, 1928; s. Charles Harold and Margaret Emma (Mackay) L.; B.A., U. Alta., 1951; M.Div., Fuller Theol. Sem., 1954; Ph.D., Fuller Grad. Sch. Psychology, 1974; m. P. Joan Havell, June 7, 1958; children—Carol Anne, David. Mem. Staff Inter-Varsity Christian Fellowship of Can., 1954-66, regional dir., 1958-64; gen. dir. Pioneer Camps of Can., Pacific region, 1964-66; mem. staff Rosemead (Calif.) Counseling Service, 1967-77, dir., 1973-77; partner, dir. counseling services Med. Resources Inst., Inc., San Jose, Calif., 1977-80; sr. ptnr. Counseling Resources, Inc., San Jose, 1980; pvt. practice Psychotherapy Assocs., Los Gatos, Calif.; cons. Trans World Radio; mem. faculty Rosemead Grad. Sch. Psychology, 1973-77. Mem. Am. Psychol. Assn., Can. Psychol. Assn., Christian Assn. Psychol. Services, Calif. State Psychol. Assn., Santa Clara County Psychol. Assn., Psychology and Law Assn. Mem. Evang. Free Ch. Research affect of father absence on child devel. Home: 1047 Vuelta Olivos Fremont CA 94538 Office: 5150 Graves Ave Bldg 1 San Jose CA 95129

LOUGHARY, JOHN WILLIAM, psychologist, educator; b. Omak, Wash., Nov. 6, 1930; s. William Ernest and Margaret Genevieve (Bagan) L.; children—Kathleen, Kevin, Patrick, Rebecca, Kelly, Keenan. B.S., U. Oreg., 1952; M.A., U. Iowa, 1956, Ph.D., 1958. Lic. psychologist, Calif., Oreg. Mem. faculty U. Oreg., Eugene, 1962—, prof. counseling psychology, 1966—, assoc. dean Coll. Edn., 1974-78; pres. United Learning Corp., Eugene, 1970—; cons. in field. Mem. Am. Psychol. Assn., Oreg. Psychol. Assn. Author: Producing Workshops and Seminars, 1979; Helping Others Help Themselves, 1979; Career and Life Planning Guide, 1976; This Isn't Quite What I Had in Mind, 1978; Career Survival Skills, 1974; Man Machine Systems in Education, 1966; Counseling in Secondary Schools, 1961. Home: 591 Lochmoor Pl Eugene OR 97405 Office: Counseling Dept U Oreg Eugene OR 97403

LOUGHEED, E. PETER, lawyer, legislator; b. Calgary, Alta., Can., July 26, 1928; s. Edgar and Edna (Bauld) L.; B.A., U. Alta., 1951, LL.B., 1952; M.B.A., Harvard, 1954; m. Jeanne Estelle Rogers, June 21, 1952; children—Stephen, Andrea, Pamela, Joseph. Admitted to Alta. bar, 1955, sec. Mannix Co., Ltd., 1956-58, gen. counsel, 1958-59, v.p., 1959-60, dir., 1960-62; pvt. practice law, 1962-67; leader Progressive Conservative Party Alta., 1965—; mem. Alta. Legislative Assembly, leader of Opposition from Calgary West constituency, 1967—; elected premier of Alta., 1971—, pres. exec. council. Mem. Anglican Ch. Office: 307 Legislature Bldg Edmonton AB T5K 2B7 Canada

LOUGHLIN, THOMAS RICHARD, wildlife biologist; b. Santa Monica, Calif., July 19, 1943; s. Francis Charles and Adele Marjorie (Judy) L.; m. Nancy Ann MacTernan, Mar. 20, 1971; children—John Thomas, Michael Andrew. B.A., U. Calif.-Santa Barbara, 1972; M.A., Humboldt State U., 1972; Ph.D., UCLA, 1977. Biol. cons. Terra Scan, Eureka, Calif., 1973-74; research specialist Nat. Marine Fisheries Service, NOAA, Washington, 1977-80, acting chief research and mgmt., 1980-81, task leader Bering Sea ecosystem project, Seattle, 1981—. Served with U.S. Army, 1966-69; Vietnam. Decorated Air Medal, Purple Heart. Recipient U.S. Dept. Commerce outstanding performance award, 1979; U. Calif. Regents grantee, 1976; U.S. Marine Mammal Commn. grantee, 1975-77. Mem. Am. Soc. Zoologists, Am. Inst. Biol. Scis., Am. Soc. Mammalogists, Western Soc. Naturalists. Republican. Contbr. articles to profl. jours., chpts. to books. Office: Nat Marine Mammal Lab 7600 Sand Point Way NE Seattle WA 98115

LOUGHMILLER, DONALD RAY, educational administrator; b. Twin Falls, Idaho, Nov. 30, 1944; s. Lawrence Walter and Mabel Pauline (Foster) L.; m. Gail Lee Arford, Sept. 5, 1965; children—Tamara Lynn, Sandra Dawn. B.S., U. Idaho, 1967; M.A.T., Colo. State U., Fort Collins, 1973. Tchr., coach, Monroe (Wash.) Sch. Dist., 1967-70; tchr., coach, athletic dir. Nampa (Idaho) Sch. Dist., 1970-76, vice prin. West Jr. High Sch., 1976-81, asst. prin. Nampa Sr. High Sch., 1981—, dir. Summer Sch., 1983. Mem. Nat. Assn. Secondary Sch. Prins., Am. Assn. Sch. Adminstrs. Mem. Ch. Nazarene.

LOUIE, ANDY FONG, hosp. adminstr.; b. Kwongtung Province, China, Nov. 1, 1932; came to U.S., 1950, naturalized, 1950; s. William and Helen (Lew Choy Ying) L.; student Boise Jr. Coll., 1956-57; B.S., Idaho State U., 1962; postgrad. Boise State U., 1974-75, U. Colo., 1978; m. Helen F. Fung, Aug. 2, 1964; 1 son, Michael. Pharmacist, Sav-More Drug, Boise, Idaho, 1962-63, Thrifty Drug, Boise, 1963-66, Ford Drug Store, Boise, 1966-67; pharmacy cons., mgr. Casa Loma Convalescent Center, Payette, Idaho, 1971-74; pharmacy cons. Malheur Meml. Hosp., Nyssa, Oreg., 1972-74; pharmacy and purchasing dir. Holy Rosary Hosp., Ontario, Oreg., 1967-75, asso. hosp. adminstr., 1975—, acting adminstr., 1980. Sec., treas. Cub Scout Pack 94, Ore-Ida council Boy Scouts Am.; founder, bd. dirs. Treasure Valley Area Health Consortium. Served with U.S. Army, 1955-57. Mem. Hosp. Fin. Mgmt. Assn., Western Hosp. Improvement Program of IHA (dir.), Oreg. Emergency Med. Services Task Force, Am. Mgmt. Assn., Am. Pharm. Assn., Am. Soc. Hosp. Pharmacists, Oreg. State Hosp. Pharmacists Assn., Idaho Soc. Hosp. Pharmacists, Idaho Capitol Soc. Pharmacists. Club: Optimist (founder, sec., treas., Ontario, 1970). Home: 3822 Star Valley St Boise ID 83709 Office: 315 SW 9th St Ontario OR 97914

LOUISE, MELINDA, career consultant, vocational rehabilitation counselor; b. Tacoma, Nov. 19, 1947; d. John David and Ramona Joyce (Frazier) Wefler. B.A. in Women's Studies, Antioch U./West, 1978; M.A. in Career and Life Planning, Goddard Coll., 1980. Owner, pvt. cons. bus., 1979—, ML Enterprises, Santa Monica, Calif., 1982—; cons., tchr., lectr.; leader workshops and seminars. Mem. Nat. Career Devel. Project, Mar Vista Bus. and Profl. Women's Club, South Coast Bus. Network, Ventura County Profl. Women's Network. Author: Leaving the Clerical Track: A Feminist Analysis, 1980. Office: ML Enterprises 2269 32d St Santa Monica CA 90405

LOUVAU, GORDON ERNEST, mgmt. cons., educator; b. Oakland, Calif., May 29, 1928; s. Ernest and Ella Meta (Meins) L.; student U. Calif., 1946-49; postgrad. Calif. State U., Hayward, 1975-77; M.B.A., John F. Kennedy U., 1980; m. Ramona Jean Weigel, Oct. 13, 1946; children—John Pierre, Tanya Lissette, Charles Frederic. Accountant, Oakland, 1950-59; asst. controller U.S. Leasing, Inc., San Francisco, 1960-61; pres. Louvau Systems Co., Oakland, 1962-66; v.p., gen. mgr. Prescolite div. U.S. Industries Co., San Leandro, Calif., 1966-68; cons. acctg. systems, Oakland, 1969—; vis. prof. acctg. U. S.Africa, 1970-71; dir. Inst. Research and Bus. Devel., asst. prof. acctg. Calif. State U. at Hayward, 1972-80; asst. dean., asso. prof. mgmt., dir. acctg. programs J.F. Kennedy U., 1969—. Cert. in mgmt. acctg. Mem. Nat. Assn. Accts. (dir. 1972-74), Am. Acctg. Assn. Republican. Club: Athenian-Nile Oakland. Author: Financial Management of the Clinical Laboratory, 1974; Management and Cost Control Techniques for the Clinical Laboratory, 1977; Computers in Accountant's Offices, 1981. Home: 25 Selborne Dr Piedmont CA 94611 Office: 3661 Grand Ave Oakland CA 94610

LOVAAS, JUDITH JEAN BARKER, nurse; b. Rochester, N.Y., Jan. 1, 1939; s. Alfred Ralph and Alberta Jean (Miller) Barker; B.S., U. Rochester, 1960, M.S., 1963; m. Arvin Lovaas, Aug. 17, 1963; children—Steven, Perri. Staff nurse Boston Children's Hosp., 1961-62; instr. Genesee Hosp. Sch. Nursing, Rochester, 1962-63; instr. practical nursing Larimer County Vo-Tech Center, Ft. Collins, Colo., 1976-81, coordinator practical nursing program, 1981-83; health educator Colo. State U. Health Ctr., 1983—; mem. Larimer County Bd. Health, 1975—, pres., 1978, 82-83. Mem. Ft. Collins bd. zoning appeals, 1974-75, Ft. Collins Downtown Renewal Commn., 1974-76. Mem. Am. Vocat. Edn. Assn., Colo. Vocat. Edn. Assn. (pres. health occupations div. 1981-82), Am. Coll. Health Assn., Am. Nurses Assn., LVW. Republican. Lutheran. Home: 304 E Myrtle St Fort Collins CO 80524 Office: 4616 S Shields St Fort Collins CO 80522

LOVATT, ARTHUR KINGSBURY, JR., mfg. co. exec.; b. Ventura, Calif., Mar. 12, 1920; s. Arthur Kingsbury and Flora (Mercedes) L.; B.S., U. So. Calif., 1941; M.B.A., Queens U., 1943; m. Juanita Gray, Feb. 1, 1946; children—Sherry Lynn, Tim Arthur. Leaseman, Shell Oil Co., Los Angeles, 1946-51; dir. indsl. relations Willys-Overland Motors, Inc., Los Angeles, 1952-55; asst. to pres. and gen. mgr. Pastushin Aviation Corp., Los Angeles, 1955-57; pres. Lovatt Assos., Los Angeles, 1957-66; chemn. bd., pres., gen. mgr. Lovatt Tech. Corp., Santa Fe Springs, Calif., 1966—, also dir.; chmn. bd. Lovatt Sci. Corp., Santa Fe Springs; dir. Lovatt Industries, Inc., others. Mem. Calif. Republican State Central Com., 1964—; state adviser U.S. Congl. Adv. Bd. Served with U.S. Army, 1943-45. Mem. Am. Legion (post comdr. 1946), AAAS, Nat. Space Inst., Am. Soc. Metals, Los Angeles C. of C., U. So. Calif. Alumni Assn. (life), Nat. Hist. Soc. (founding assoc.), N.Y. Acad. Scis., Internat. Oceanographic Found., Smithsonian Assos., Am. Ordnance Assn. Club: Masons (past master, Shriner). Inventor, developer tech. processes. Home: 13649 E Valna Dr Whittier CA 90602 Office: 12120 Altamar Pl Santa Fe Springs CA 90670

LOVE, BRUCE WAYNE, lawyer; b. Minster, Ohio, Aug. 29, 1945; s. Sam Sanford and Evelyn Jeannette (Strosnider) L.; m. Kathleen Ann Felix, Aug. 29, 1970; children—Amy Christina. B.A., San Diego State U., 1968; J.D., U. San Diego, 1971. Bar: Calif. 1972. Assoc. Freeman, Harris & Love, National City, Calif., 1972-73; sole practice, National City, 1973—. Mem. Calif. Bar Assn., San Diego County Bar Assn., San Diego County S. Bay Bar Assn., Calif. Family Law Cert. Specialists, San Diego Bar Assn., C. of C. Democrat. Roman Catholic. Club: Kiwanis. Office: 345 E 8th St National City CA 92050

LOVE, (CATHERINE JANE) REEVE, vocational educator; b. N.Y.C., Oct. 18, 1944; d. Claude Rolf and Mary Sue (Jaynes) L. B.A., Duke U., 1965; M.A., U. Tex., 1971; postgrad. U. N.Mex., 1980—. Ednl. tech. writer S.W. Ednl. Devel. Lab., Austin, Tex., 1968-73; tchr. high sch. English, Am. Sch. Found., Mexico City, 1973-74; media technologist/tech. writer Ednl. Devel. Corp., Austin, 1974-75; tng. specialist Ctr. for Pub. Sch. Ethnic Studies, U. Tex., Austin, 1975-76; edn. cons. Intercultural Devel. Research Assn., San Antonio, 1976-80; lectr. Navajo tchr. edn. devel. program, dept. elem. edn. U. N.Mex., Albuquerque, 1980-81, assoc. dir. sex desegregation tng inst., dept. secondary and adult tchr. edn., 1981-82, assoc. dir. Vocat. Edn. Equity Center, 1982—; participant various nat., internat. ednl. confs., 1977—; cons. Tex. Edn. Agy., 1974-75, Air Force Human Resources Lab., Lackland AFB, 1975, U.S. Dept. Edn., 1983—, others. Nat. Merit scholar, 1961-65; Tinker Found./U. N.Mex. research grantee in Latin Am. 1982; Dolores Gonzales Meml. fellow U. N.Mex., 1982-83, title VII Bilingual fellow, 1982—, Millicent A. Rogers Found. fellow, 1982—; Mellon Found. Inter-Am. Field Research grantee, 1983. Mem. Nat. Assn. for Bilingual Edn., N.Mex. Assn. for Bilingual Edn., Internat. Transactional Analysis Assn., Latin Am. Studies Assn., Coalition of Environ. Voters, Phi Beta Kappa, Theta Alpha Phi. Democrat. Contbr. articles in field to profl. lit. Home: 824 Quincy St NE Albuquerque NM 87110 Office: Dept Secondary and Adult Tchr Edn U N Mex Albuquerque NM 87131

LOVE, HAROLD OREN, lawyer; b. Indpls., May 27, 1909; s. Roscoe A. and Clara (Evans) L.; A.B. magna cum laude, Butler U., 1933; J.D., U. Mich., 1936; m. Sara Elizabeth Scherling, June 12, 1937; children—Robert Evans, Barbara Lynn. Admitted to Ind. bar, 1930, Mich. bar, 1936, since practiced in Detroit; mem. firm Love & Kipp, 1937-40, Love & Miel, 1943-46, Love & Snyder, 1946-50, Love, Snyder & Lewis, 1950—; dir., officer numerous corps.; pres., pub. Tombstone Epitaph; pres. Historic Tombstone Adventures. Exec. v.p. Archives of Am. Art; bd. dirs. Tucson Mus. Art; past mem. Detroit Art Commn. Former chmn., treas. 14th Congl. Republican Com.; former mem. Wayne County Rep. Com.; v.p. Detroit City Plan Commn., 1940, pres. 1941-42; mem. Regional Planning Com.; mem., pres. Grosse Pointe Woods Planning Commn., Grosse Pointe Woods Charter-Com.; mem. Wayne County Bd. Suprs. Bd. dirs. Detroit Symphony Orch., Inc.; bd. govs. Players; trustee Detroit Adventure. Served from lt. (j.g.) to lt. USNR, 1943-45. Mem. Am. (past chmn. retirement and security sect.), Mich., Detroit bar assns., Fine Arts Soc., Soc. Contbrs. to Detroit Symphony Orch. (pres.), Detroit Hist. Soc., Friends Grosse Pointe Library, Detroit Inst. Arts Founders Soc., Greater Detroit Bd. Commerce, Phi Delta Theta, Tau Kappa Alpha, Phi Kappa Phi, Kappa Delta Rho. Presbyn. Clubs: Lawyers (U. Mich.); Mich., Indian Village (bd. govs.), University, Country of Detroit; Skyline Country (Tucson). Author: Business as Usual, 1951; Tax Free Profits for your Family, 1954; More for your Money, 1957. Contbr. articles to mags., periodicals. Home: 6545 N St Andrews Dr Tucson AZ 85718 Office: 3d and Fremont Tombstone AZ 85638

LOVE, JOHN A., cement manufacturing company executive, former governor. B.A., U. Denver, 1938, LL.B., 1941. Bar: Colo. Practiced law, 1945-62; gov. State of Colo., 1962-73; dir. Office of Energy Policy, 1973-74; sr. v.p., pres., chief operating officer Ideal Basic Industries, Inc., Denver, 1974, pres., chief exec. officer, 1975—, now chmn. bd., also dir.; dir. Frontier Airlines, United Banks of Colo., Johns-Manville Corp., Gt. Western Life Assurance Co. Served to lt. commdr. USN, 1942-45. Office: Ideal Basic Industries Inc 950 17th St Colo Nat Bank Bldg Denver CO 80202*

LOVE, SANDRA RAE, info specialist; b. San Francisco, Feb. 20, 1947; d. Benjamin Raymond and Charlotte C. Martin; B.A. in English, Calif. State U., Hayward, 1968; M.S. in L.S., U. So. Calif., 1969; m. Michael D. Love, Feb. 14, 1971. Tech. info. specialist Lawrence Livermore (Calif.) Nat. Lab., 1969—. Mem. Spl. Libraries Assn. (sec. nuclear sci. div. 1980-82, chmn. 1983-84), Beta Sigma Phi. Democrat. Episcopalian. Office: Lawrence Livermore Nat Lab Library PO Box 5500 Livermore CA 94550

LOVE, SYDNEY FRANCIS, management consultant; b. Winnipeg, Man., Can., June 10, 1923; s. Francis Henry and May Eliza (Smith) L.; m. May Kikue Abe, June 20, 1979; children—Rodney, Kevin, Brian. B.A.Sc., U. Toronto, 1947, M.A., 1948; M.A.Sc., U. Waterloo, 1970. Supr. applications engring. Can. Gen. Electric, Toronto, 1952-59; mgr. TV engring. Electrohome, Kitchener, Ont., 1959-66; pres. Designectics Internat., Inc., Waterloo, 1967-79; pres. Advanced Profl. Devel., Inc., Los Angeles, 1979—. Served with Royal Can. Air Force, 1942-44. Brit. Am. fellow, 1967; Can. Mortgage and Housing Corp. fellow, 1968-70. Mem. IEEE (sr., sect. chmn. 1966), Project Mgmt. Inst., Assn. Profl. Engrs. Ont. Author: Mastery and Management of Time, 1978; Planning and Creating Successful Engineered Designs, 1980; Project Management, 1976. Office: 5519 Carpenter Ave North Hollywood CA 91607

LOVE, WILLIAM HENRY, aerospace engineer; b. New London, Conn., Sept. 4, 1934; s. William Henry and Mona Ann (Jenkins) L.; m. Karen White, July 27, 1957; children—Kirsten, Alyssa, Jennifer, Darrel B.S., San Diego State U., 1957, H.S. in Aerospace Engring., 1971. Sr. aerodynamics engr. Gen. Dynamics/Convair Aerospace Labs., San Diego, 1957-76, pre-design and sr. project engr. Cruise Missile Project office, 1976-78, engring. chief systems verification, 1978-79, acting dir. systems engring., 1979-81, engring. mgr. systems devel., 1979-81; chief engr. Ground Launched Cruise Missile Trainer project, 1981—; instr. San Diego State U. Assoc. fellow AIAA (outstanding contbn. 1974, outstanding contbn. San Diego community 1982, past sect. chmn.). Republican. Methodist. Contbr. articles to profl. jours. Office: Gen Dynamics/Convair PO Box 80847-MZ 53 6000 San Diego CA 92138

LOVELACE, DENNIS JOSEPH, cons.; b. Pierre, S.D., June 18, 1940; s. Marcus Joseph and Joyce Clara (Lemar) L.; A.A., U. Md., 1976; B.A., U. Md., 1977; M.S., U. So. Calif., 1979; m. Han Soon Chung, Nov. 29, 1974; children—Deborah, Darlene. Joined U.S. Army, 1958, advanced through grades to master sgt., 1976, personnel mgr. Saigon, Viet Nam, 1970-71, Pentagon, Washington, 1971-72, Seoul, Korea, 1972-77, Fort Lewis, Wash., 1977-78; ret., 1978; pvt. mgmt. cons., Reno, 1979—; internal mgmt. systems cons. Asian Devel. Bank, Manila, 1980—; part-time instr. Lassen Coll., Western Nev. Community Coll., Chapman Coll. Decorated Meritorious Service medal, Army Commendation medal with 2 oak leaf clusters; life Calif. community coll. instr. credentials in bus. and indsl. mgmt. Mem. Am. Planning Assn., Assn. Systems Mgmt. (profl.), Am. Mgmt. Assn., Am. Soc. Profl. Consultants, Internat. Platform Assn., U. So. Calif. Gen. Alumni Assn. (life). Club: Masons. Contbr. article in field to profl. jour. Home and Office: PO Box 6475 Reno NV 89503

LOVELACE, JACQUELINE ANNE, publishing corporation executive; b. Albuquerque, June 16, 1949; d. William Randolph and Mary Easter (Moulton) L. m. Lynn Richard Johnson, July 2, 1982. Student

Mills Coll., 1967; B.A., U. Colo., 1970. Press sec. U.S. Senate Interior Com., Washington, 1972-75, Reelection for Congressman Tim Wirth, Denver, 1975-76; editor Titsch Pub. Inc., Denver, 1976-79; pres./pub. Lovelace Corp., Denver, 1979—. Active Jr. League Denver, 1981—, Denver Symphony 1980—, Alliance for Contemporary Art, 1979—; mem. fin. com. Campaign for Rep. T. Wirth, 1978. Recipient trophy for outstanding journalism White Stag, 1980; Maggie award for best new city and met. mag. Western Pubs. Assn., 1982. Democrat. Presbyterian. Club: Kansas City. Home: 2100 E 7th Ave Denver CO 80206 also 310 W 49th Wornall Plaza Suite 508 Kansas City MO Office: Lovelace Corp Suite C-207 1410 Grant St Denver CO 80203

LOVELACE, JON B., investment mgmt. co. exec.; b. Detroit, Feb. 6, 1927; s. Jonathan Bell and Marie (Andersen) L.; A.B. cum laude, Princeton, 1950; m. Lillian Pierson, Dec. 29, 1950; children—Carey, James, Jeffrey, Robert. Personnel asst. Pacific Finance Co., 1950-51; with Capital Research & Mgmt. Co., Los Angeles, 1951—, treas., 1955-62, v.p., 1957-62, exec. v.p., 1962-64, pres., 1964-75, 82—, chmn. bd., 1975-82, also dir.; vice chmn. Capital Group, Inc.; chmn. bd. Am. Mut. Fund, Inc., 1968—; pres., dir. New Perspective Fund, Inc.; chmn. bd. Investment Co. Am.; chmn. bd., dir. Capital Research Co. Trustee, Claremont McKenna Coll., chmn., 1973-76; trustee Calif. Inst. Arts, Santa Barbara Med. Found., J. Paul Getty Mus.; vice chmn., bd. fellows Claremont U. Center. Mem. Council on Fgn. Relations. Clubs: Princeton, University (N.Y.C.); Sierra; Calif. (Los Angeles). Home: 800 W 1st St Los Angeles CA 90012 also 780 El Bosque Rd Santa Barbara CA 93108 Office: 333 S Hope St Los Angeles CA 90071

LOVELL, EMILY KALLED (MRS. ROBERT EDMUND LOVELL), journalist; b. Grand Rapids, Mich., Feb. 25, 1920; d. Abdo Rham and Louise (Claussen) Kalled; student Grand Rapids Jr. Coll., 1937-39; B.A., Mich. State U., 1944; M.A., U. Ariz., 1971; m. Robert Edmund Lovell, July 4, 1947. Copywriter, asst. traffic mgr. Sta. WOOD, Grand Rapids, 1944-46; traffic mgr. KOPO, Tucson, 1946-47; reporter, city editor Alamogordo (N.Mex.) News, 1948-51; Alamogordo corr., feature writer Internat. News Service, Denver, 1950-54; Alamogordo corr., feature writer El Paso Herald-Post, 1954-65; Alamogordo news dir., feature writer Tularosa (N.Mex.) Basin Times, 1957-59; co-founder, editor, pub. Otero County Star, Alamogordo, 1961-65; newscaster KALG, Alamogordo, 1964-65; free lance feature writer Denver Post, N.Mex. Mag., 1949-69; corr. Electronics News, N.Y.C., 1959-63, 63-69, Sierra Vista (Ariz.) corr. Ariz. Republic, 1966; free lance editor N.Mex. Pioneer Interviews, 1967-69; asst. dir. English skills program Ariz. State U., 1976; free-lance editor, writer, 1977—; sec., dir. Star Pub. Co., Inc., 1961-64, pres., 1964-65. 3d v.p., publicity chmn. Otero County Community Concert Assn., 1950-65; mem. Alamogordo Zoning Commn., 1955-57; mem. founding com. Alamogordo Central Youth Activities Com., 1957; vice chmn. Otero County chpt. Nat. Found. Infantile Paralysis, 1958-61; charter mem. N.M. Citizens Council for Traffic Safety, 1959-61; pres. Sierra Vista Hosp. Aux., 1966; pub. relations chmn. Ft. Huachuca chpt. ARC, 1966. Mem. nat. bd. Hospitalized Vets. Writing Project, 1972—. Recipient 1st Pl. awards N.Mex. Press Assn., 1961, 62. Pub. Interest award Nat. Safety Council, 1962. 1st Pl. award Nat. Fedn. Press Women, 1960, 62; named Woman of Year Alamogordo, 1960. Editor of Week Pubs. Aux., 1962, adm. N.Mex. Navy, 1962, col. a.d.c. Staff Gov. N.Mex., 1963, Woman of Yr., Ariz. Press Women, 1973. Mem. N.Mex. (past sec.), Ariz. (past pres.) press women, N.Mex. Fedn. Womens Clubs (past dist. pub. relations chmn.), N.Mex. Hist. Soc. (life), N.Mex. Fedn. Bus. and Profl. Womens Clubs (past pres.), Pan Am. Round Table Alamogordo, Theta Sigma Phi (past nat. 3d v.p.), Phi Kappa Phi. Democrat. Moslem. Author: A Personalized History of Otero County, New Mexico, 1963; Weekend Away, 1964; Lebanese Cooking, Streamlined, 1972; A Reference Handbook for Arabic Grammar, 1974, 77; contbg. author: The Muslim Community in North America, 1983. Home: PO Box 7152 Stockton CA 95207

LOVELL, KAY L., wholesale music company official, b. Blanding, Utah, Apr. 16, 1943; s. LaForge A. and Louise (Peterson) L.; student Utah State U., 1961-62; B.S. in Accounting, Brigham Young U., 1967; m. Jane Dixon, June 3, 1966; children—Debora, Cynthia, Tamara, Russell Edward Justin. Acct. Am. Oil Co., Salt Lake City, 1967-71; auditor, Casper, Wyo., 1971-72; auditor Kaman Corp., Colorado Springs, Colo., 1972-78; dir. fin. Coast Wholesale Music Co., San Carlos, Calif., 1978—, C. Bruno & Son, Wheeling, Ill., 1981-82. Bd. dirs. Vista Grande West Recreation Assn., 1976-78; com. chmn. Pikes Peak council Boy Scouts Am., 1974-78, com. mem. Santa Clara council, 1979—; bishop Ch. of Jesus Christ of Latter-Day Saints. Mem. Nat. Assn. Accts. Republican. Home: 2418 Lacey Dr Milpitas CA 95035 Office: 200 Industrial Way San Carlos CA 94070

LOVELL, WILLIAM STUART, research and devel. co. exec., lawyer; b. Oak Park, Ill., Apr. 23, 1933; s. John Herbert and Frances Sizer (Rogers) L.; B.S., Portland State U., 1959, B.A., 1959; M.A., Princeton U., 1962, Ph.D., 1963; J.D., Willamette U., 1971; m. Margaret Mary Ramaley, Aug. 4, 1967; children—Theodore, David, Jennifer, James. Chemist, Chipman Chem. Co., Portland, Oreg., 1957-58; teaching asst. Portland State U., 1958-59; research asst. Princeton U., 1961, 62-63, McKay research fellow, 1961-62; chem. physicist Nat. Bur. Standards, Boulder, Colo., 1963-68; patent abstractor, Chem. Abstracts Service, Columbus, Ohio, 1968-70; asst. prof. chemistry Oreg. Coll. Edn., Monmouth, 1968-72; admitted to Oreg. bar, 1972; dep. dist. atty. Polk County Dist. Atty.'s Office, Dallas, Oreg., 1972-77; individual practice law, Monmouth and Salem, Oreg., 1977-81; patent mgr. Oreg. State U., 1981—. pres. Advanced Projects Corp., Monmouth and Salem, 1979-81. Served with USAF, 1950-54; now lt. comdr. USNR, 1967—. Mem. Am. Chem. Soc., AAAS, Oreg. Bar Assn., Licensing Execs. Soc., Theta Delta Phi. Democrat. Roman Catholic. Contbr. articles in field to profl. jours. Home: 357 E St Independence OR 97351 Office: Research Office Oreg State U Corvallis OR 97331

LOVETERE, DON PAUL, pharm. co. mktg. exec.; b. Richmond, Va., Sept. 2, 1942; s. Arthur and Mary (Hanly) LoV.; B.S., U. Conn., 1964; M.B.A., San Francisco State U., 1971; m. Shari Colvin, May 13, 1972; children—Scott Keiffer, Sara Hanley. Product mgr. Barnes Hind Pharms., Sunnyvale, Calif., 1972-74; product mgr. Health Application Systems, Burlingame, Calif., 1974-76; sales mgr. Fibreboard Corp., San Francisco, 1976-77; mgr. market planning and research Cooper Labs., Mountain View, Calif., 1977-80, dir. mktg., 1980—. Served as capt. U.S. Army, 1964-66. Mem. Med. Mktg. Assn., Am. Mktg. Assn., Am. Mgmt. Assn. Home: 11262 Palos Verdes Ct Cupertino CA 95014 Office: 455 E Middlefield Rd Mountain View CA 94043

LOVETT, ROBERT ELIOT, management consultant; b. Washington, Feb. 14, 1926; s. Eliot Callender and Helen Lucetta (Thompson) L.; m. Glenna Beatrice Bartlett, Jan. 26, 1957; children—Sharon, Laura Lee, Robert Eliot. A.B., U. Mich., 1948; M.B.A., N.Y.U., 1950; Ph.D., U. So. Calif., 1965. Fin. rep. Jour. of Commerce, N.Y.C., 1948-49; pub. relations adminstr. N.Y.U., 1949-51; buyer Gladding & McBean, 1951-53; customer service cons., 1953-54; v.p., treas., mktg. dir. Boylhart, Lovett & Dean, Inc., 1954-76; pres. Nat. Research Center, 1966-76; ptnr. BLD Mgmt., 1960-76; pres., dir. Voice in Pasadena, Inc., Los Angeles, 1964—; pres., chmn. Robert E. Lovett, Inc., Laguna Beach, Calif., 1976—; officer, dir. KRLA, Inc., Los Angeles, 1972-76; dir. Higgins, Marcus & Lovett, Inc., Los Angeles, 1979—; dir. C.W. Driver, Los Angeles, 1970—; dir. workshops on Mng. for Results, 1979—; lectr. mktg. and mgmt. U. So. Calif., UCLA, Calif. State U.-Fullerton, 1954-79. Past mem. Calif. State Toll Bridge Authority, Orange County Citizens' Direction-Finding Commn.; registered mem. Pasadena Tournament of Roses Assn. Served with U.S. Army, Chem. Corps, USAAF, 1944-46. Mem. Am. Mktg. Assn., Nat. Assn. Realtors. Republican. Christian Scientist. Club: Jonathan (Los Angeles). Contbr. articles in field to profl. jours. Home: 396 Myrtle St Laguna Beach CA 92651 Office: PO Box 1483 Laguna Beach CA 92651

LOW, BENSON P., clinical psychologist, educator; b. Los Angeles, July 15, 1951; s. Fon and Fung (Lee) L.; m. April Diane Wong, April 29, 1978. B.A. with honors, UCLA, 1973, M.A. in Theology, 1976; Ph.D. in Clin. Psychology, Fuller Theol. Sem., Pasadena, Calif., 1979. Lic. psychologist, Wash., 1980. Dir. research and evaluation, clin. child psychologist Seattle Mental Health Inst., 1979-81; chief psychologist Seattle Children's Home, 1981—; cons. Seattle Mental Health Inst.; clin. instr. U. Wash.; practicum instr. Seattle U. Am. Psychol. Assn. minority fellow, 1976-77; Wash. Dept. Social and Health Services grantee, 1980-81. Mem. Am. Psychol. Assn., Soc. Psychol. Study of Social Issues, Assn. Advancement of Behavior Therapy. Contbr. articles to profl. jours. Office: 2142 10th Ave W Seattle WA 98119

LOW, DAVID WILLIAM, applied mathematician; b. Denver, Sept. 27, 1939; s. George W. and Jean A. (McDowell) L.; A.B., UCLA, 1963, Ph.D., 1971; M.S., Calif. State U., Northridge, 1968; m. Isabel Rivera Estrada, Aug. 7, 1976; children—Michael Scott, Christine Louise, Jennifer Elizabeth. Flight test engr. Lockheed Calif. Co., 1963-64; systems engr. IBM, Los Angeles, 1964-66; instr. Calif. State U., Northridge, 1966-67; computer sci. cons. LDV, Inc., Los Angeles, 1967-68; teaching and research asst. U. Calif., Los Angeles, 1968-71; staff mem. IBM Los Angeles Sci. Center, 1971-80, project mgr., 1981—. Mem. Ops. Research Soc. Am., Inst. Mgmt. Sci., Soc. Indsl. and Applied Math. (chmn. So. Calif. chpt.), ASHRAE (chmn. computer applications tech. com.). Contbr. articles to profl. jours. Office: IBM Corp 9045 Lincoln Blvd Los Angeles CA 90045

LOW, DON R., educator, consultant, counselor; b. Urbana, Mo., Feb. 6, 1935; s. Jewel Claude and Ada Leona (Payne) L.; m. Dolores Lynette Hamilton, May 23, 1957; children—Mark Hamilton, Deanne Marie. B.S. in Edn. and Biology, S.W. Mo. State U., 1956; M.S. in Biology, U. Mo., 1963; Ed.D. in Curriculum Instrn., U. So. Calif., 1973. Tchr. biology Mt. Vernon (Mo.) High Sch., 1956-58, Ferguson/Florissant High Sch., St. Louis, 1960-61, tchr. biology, counselor Whittier (Calif.) High Sch., 1961-71, Orange Coast Coll., Costa Mesa, Calif., 1971—. Mem. adminstrv. council First United Meth. Ch.; campaign mgr. candidate local sch. bd.; rep. Whittier Area Council Chs.; mem. citizens adv. bd. City of La Habre (Calif); speakers bur. Orange Coast Coll. Served with U.S. Army, 1958-60. Orange Coast fellow, 1974, 77, 78, 80-81; NSF grantee 1980-81; NSF awardee. Mem. NEA, Calif. Tchrs. Assn., Assn. Sch. Counselors (v.p. 1977-78, bd. dirs. 1977-80), Am. Personnel and Guidance Assn., Nat. Assn. Advisors to Health Professions, Whittier Secondary Edn. Assn. (bd. dirs. 1969-71), Nat. Assn. Sch. Counselors (state del. 1974-76, bd. dirs. 1976-78, pres. 1977-78). Democrat. Methodist. Home: 2140 Vista Dorado Newport Beach CA 92660 Office: Orange Coast Coll 2701 Fairview Rd Coast Mesa CA 92626

LOW, WALTON H., hydrologist; b. Sacramento, Apr. 3, 1951; s. John K. and Ping L.; m. Diane F.; 1 son, James A. Medina. B.S., U. Calif.-Davis, 1974. Hydrologist, U.S. Geol. Survey, Boise, Idaho, 1975—. Served with USAFR, 1970-76. Mem. Am. Geophys. Union, Geochem. Soc. Am., Nat. Water Well Assn., Idaho Soc. Profl. Geologists. Author U.S. Geol. Survey reports. Office: 230 Collins Rd Boise ID 83702

LOWE, B(EVERLEY) JAMES, nuclear company executive, engineer; b. Keyser, W. Va., June 4, 1929; s. Frank Devries and Edna Louise (Harkins) L.; m. Marjorie Roeber, Oct. 22, 1953; children—Steven Alan, Paul Clifton, Kimberley Ann, Pamela Ellen; m. 2d, Suzette Diedel, Jan. 30, 1982. A.B., Columbia U., 1951; M.S. in Naval Architecture, Naval Engr., MIT, 1958. Registered profl. engr., Md. Commd. officer U.S. Navy, 1951-65; constrn. officer Mare Island Naval Shipyard, 1958-61; staff comdr. submarine force U.S. Atlantic Fleet, 1961-63; sr. site rep. at Westinghouse Astronuclear, AEC, 1965-77; mgr. programs, engring. dir. Oceanic div. Westinghouse Electric Corp., Annapolis, Md., 1965-78; v.p. quality control Naval Products div. UNC Nuclear Industries, Inc., Richmond, Wash., 1979-80, v.p. mktg., 1980—, pres., gen. mgr. Systems & Services div., 1980—; mem. exec. bd. Gov.'s Sci Adv. Council, State of Md., 1973-78. Bd. dirs. Am. Oceanic Orgn., 1975-78. Mem. Am. Def. Preparedness Assn., Soc. Naval Architects and Marine Engrs., Mil. Order CARABAO, Phi Gamma Delta. Roman Catholic. Club: Meadow Springs Country. Home: 1917 Fairway Dr Richland WA 99352 Office: UNC Systems & Services Div UNC Nuclear Industries Inc 2900 George Washington Way Richland WA 99352

LOWE, HELEN WINONA, educator; b. Weaverville, Calif., Feb. 21, 1936; d. Walter William and M. Winona (Starkey) Heffington; B.S., Tex. Woman's U., Denton, 1959; M.B.A., N. Tex. State U., Denton, 1965; children—Walter Richard, William Davis. Instr., Midwestern State U., Wichita Falls, Tex., 1962-65, Angelo State U., San Angelo, Tex., 1967-69; asst. prof. bus. edn. N.Mex. Highlands U., Las Vegas, 1972-75, Sul Ross State U., Alpine, Tex., 1977-79, founder Bus. Awards Program, 1978; asst. prof. bus. Eastern Oreg. State Coll., 1979—, also coordinator secretarial sci. bus. edn.; cons., guest lectr. in field. Adv. counsel for bus. and office edn. curriculum Oreg. Dept. Edn. Hon. mem. Nat. Secs. Assn., Phi Chi Theta. Mem. Nat. Bus. Edn. Assn., Am. Mgmt. Assn., Am. Vocat. Assn., AAUP, Southwestern Adminstrv. Services Assn. (charter), Am. Records Mgmt. Assn., Nat. Assn. Female Execs., Nat. Assn. Bus. Tchr. Educators, Oreg. Bus. Edn. Assn. (chmn. legis. com.), Western Bus. Edn. Assn. Republican. Methodist. Clubs: Gourmet, Women's of Am., Garden. Author papers in field. Office: Sch Profl Studies La Grande OR 97850

LOWE, JAMES HENRY, JR., transit co. exec.; b. Tulsa, Nov. 9, 1933; s. James Henry and Olivia Margaret L.; B.S., Okla. U., 1959; M.S., N.Y. U., 1967; M.B.A., Golden Gate U., 1980; Ph.D., Hamilton State U., 1974; m. Latrecia Ann Hampton, June 5, 1971; children—Kai M., Anika O. Sr. systems analyst Union Carbide, N.Y.C., 1969; cons. E.F. Shelley and Co., N.Y.C., 1969-72; sr. systems analyst Okla. U. Health Sci. Center, Oklahoma City, 1972-76; dir. info. systems A. C. Transit, Oakland, Calif., 1979—; part-time tchr. Oakland Unified Sch. Dist., 1977—. Chmn. Black Polit. Assembly, NAACP, Oklahoma City, 1974-76, legal redress chmn., 1975-76. Served with USN, 1952-56. Mem. Data Processing Mgmt. Assn., Am. Mgmt. Assn. Democrat. Home: 2590 Maraschino Ct Union City CA 94587 Office: 508 16th St Oakland CA 94612

LOWENBERG, TIMOTHY JOSEPH, lawyer; b. Ft. Madison, Iowa, Sept. 16, 1946; s. Calvin Wilbur and Mary Ellen (Driscoll) L.; m. Mary Ann Lowenberg, Aug. 28, 1968; 1 dau., Catherine Malia. B.A., U. Iowa, 1968; J.D., U. Iowa, 1971. Bar: Wash. 1976. Asst. atty. gen. for higher edn. insts. Office of Atty. Gen., Olympia, Wash., 1976-77; ptnr. Schweinler & Lowenberg, Tacoma, Wash., 1977—; adj. prof. law U. Puget Sound, Tacoma, 1983—, prof. legal process, 1975-76, prof. edn. law, 1977—; lectr. labor law Tacoma Community Coll., Pacific Luth. U., Ft. Steilacoom Community Coll., 1977—, U.S. Office of Personnel Mgmt., 1977—; spl. asst. atty. gen. for litigation State of Wash., 1979-80. Bd. dirs. Tenzler Meml. Library, Tacoma. Served to lt. col. USAF, 1972-76. Decorated Air Force Commendation medal. Mem. Tacoma Pierce County Bar Assn., Iowa Bar Assn., Wash. Bar Assn., ABA, Wash. Trial Lawyers Assn., Assn. Trial Lawyers Am. Episcopalian. Club: Rotary. Office: 950 Fawcett Ave S Suite 211 Tacoma WA 98402

LOWENSTEIN, DANIEL HAYS, lawyer, educator; b. N.Y.C., May 10, 1943; s. Nathan and Elizabeth (Corn) L.; m. Sharon Yagi, Feb. 14, 1970; children—Aaron, Nathan. A.B., Yale U., 1964; LL.B., Harvard U., 1967. Bar: N.Y. 1968, Calif. 1969. Staff atty. Calif. Rural Legal Assistance, 1968-71; dep. sec. State of Calif., 1971-75; 1st chmn. Calif. Fair Polit. Practices Commn., 1975-79; law prof. UCLA, 1979—; cons. on freedom of Info. Legislation, Province Que., Can., 1979. Bd. dirs. Common Cause; v.p. Calif. for Nonsmokers' Rights; counsel to House Democrats of Calif., 1981-82. Draftsman Calif. Polit. Reform Act, 1974. Office: UCLA Law Sch 405 Hilgard Los Angeles CA 90024

LOWERY, DENNIS JOSEPH, advertising and promotion executive; b. St. Helena, Calif., July 5, 1933; s. Joseph Lambert and Alna Vivian (Herndon) L.; m. Alma Sue Watkins, Mar. 14, 1953; children—Daniel, Kimberly. B.A., U. Colo., 1955. Mng. editor Morning Sun, Grand Junction, Colo., 1955-60; city editor Flagstaff (Ariz.) Daily Sun, 1960; mgr. publs. Uranium Inst. Am., Grand Junction, 1961-62; owner Lowery Advt., Grand Junction, 1963-66; promotion mgr. Dixson Inc., Grand Junction, 1966-68, group v.p., 1969-81; pres. Creative Concepts Colo. Inc., Grand Junction, 1981—.

LOWREY, ELEANOR BLODWYN LANE, educational administrator; b. Mpls.; d. George Emerson and Eunice Blodwyn (Owen) Lane; student Macalester Coll., 1942-44, U. Minn., 1944-45; B.S., U. Denver, 1965, Ed.D., 1973; m. Jack B. Lowrey, Sept. 15, 1945; children—Susan, Gretchen, Georgia, John, David. Tchr., Fort Logan Mental Health Center, Denver, 1965-67; ednl. specialist Jefferson County Schs., Lakewood, Colo., 1968-71, coordinator spl. edn., learning disabilities, behavioral disorders, 1973-80, asst. dir. spl. edn., 1980—; facilitator and cons., 1982—; mem. bd. Gifted and Talented Colo., 1977-78. Bd. dirs. Indian Hills (Colo.) Water Dist., 1973—. Mem. Children with Learning Disabilities, Colo. Assn. Gifted and Talented, Council Exceptional Children (pres.), Soc. Learning Disabilities and Remedial Edn., Council Exceptional Children (dir.), Assn. Supervision and Curriculum Devel., Phi Delta Kappa, Kappa Delta Pi. Home: Box 977 Indian Hills CO 80454 Office: 3115 Kipling St Lakewood CO 80227

LOWRY, ALBERT JAMES, management consultant; b. Thunder Bay, Ont., Can., Apr. 14, 1927; s. M.B.A., Ph.D., Calif. Western U.; m. Darlene Patience, 1962; children—Lark, Lane, Adrian, Asher, Justin. Dir., owner Edn. Advancement Inst., Reno, Nev. Mem. Inst. Real Estate Mgmt., Realtors Inst. Office: 50 Washington St Apt 101 Reno NV 89503

LOWRY, LARRY LORN, management consulting company executive; b. Lima, Ohio, Apr. 12, 1947, s. Frank William and Viola Marie (Bormuth) L.; m. Jean Carroll Greenbaum, June 23, 1973; 1 dau., Alexandra Kristin. B.S. in Elec. Engring., MIT, 1969, M.S. in Elec. Engring., 1970; M.B.A., Harvard U., 1972. Mgr. Boston Cons. Group, Boston, 1972-74, Menlo Park, Calif., 1974-80; v.p. Strategic Mgmt. Group, Booz, Allen & Hamilton, Inc., San Francisco, 1980—. Western Electric fellow, 1966-69; NASA fellow, 1969-70; W.T. Grant fellow, 1971-72. Mem. Tau Beta Pi, Eta Kappa Nu, Sigma Xi. Presbyterian. Home: 137 Stockbridge Ave Atherton CA 94025 Office: 555 California St San Francisco CA 94104

LOWRY, MIKE, congressman; b. St. John, Wash., Mar. 8, 1939; s. Robert and Helen L., B.A., Wash. State U., 1962; m. Mary Carlson, Apr. 6, 1968; 1 dau., Diane. Chief fiscal analyst, staff dir. Wash. Senate Ways and Means Com., 1969-73; govtl. affairs dir. Group Health Coop. of Puget Sound, 1974-75; mem. King County (Wash.) Council, 1975-78; mem. 96th-98th Congresses from 7th Dist. Wash. Chmn. King County Housing and Community Block Grant Program, 1977. Mem. Wash. Assn. Counties (pres. 1978). Democrat. Office: 1206 Longworth House Office Bldg Washington DC 20515

LOWTHER, FRANK EUGENE, research physicist; b. Orrville, Ohio, Feb. 3, 1929; s. John Finger and Mary Elizabeth (Mackey) L.; m. Elizabeth E. Koons, Apr. 21, 1951; children—Cynthia E., Victoria J., James A., Frank Eugene. Grad. Ohio State U., Columbus, 1952. Scientist missile systems div. Raytheon Corp., Boston, 1952-57, Gen. Electric Co., Syracuse, N.Y., and Daytona Beach, Fla., 1957-62; mgr. ozone research and devel. W.R. Grace Co., Curtis Bay, Md., 1972-75; sr. engring. assoc. Linde div. Union Carbide Corp., Tonawanda, N.Y., 1975-79; chief scientist, Purification Sci. Inc., 1979-81; chief scientist, Atlantic Richfield-Energy Conversion and Materials Lab, 1981—. Recipient Inventor of Yr. award Patent Law Assn. and Tech. Socs. Council, 1976. Assoc. fellow AIAA; mem. IEEE (sr.). Club: Masons. Patentee in field of ozone tech., plasma generators, solid state power devices, internal combustion engines, electro-desorption, thermoelectrics, virus and bacteria disinfection systems. Home: 10341 Canoga Ave Apt 47 Chatsworth CA 91311 Office: 20711 Prairie St Chatsworth CA 91311

LOYE, DAVID ELLIOT, forecaster, social psychologist; b. Palo Alto, Calif., Apr. 25, 1925; s. Percival Elliot and Winifred (Sanders) L.; m. Billy Henslee, May 12, 1950 (div. 1977); children—Jenella, Kathryn, David Christopher, Jonathan. B.A., Dartmouth Coll., 1948; M.A., New Sch. Social Research, N.Y.C., 1967, Ph.D., 1974. Acct. exec. Cunningham & Walsh, Inc., N.Y.C., 1961-66; profl. assoc. Ednl. Testing Service, Princeton, N.J., 1967-73; vis. lectr. Princeton U., 1973-74; research dir. Program on Psychosocial Adaptation and the Future, UCLA, 1974-80, research psychologist, 1974—; co-dir. Inst. Futures Forecasting, Carmel, Calif., 1980—. Chairperson Troop 50, Boy Scouts Am., Princeton, 1969-71; chairperson pub. relations com. Family Service Agy., Princeton, 1972-74; co-chairperson Vol. for Anderson for Pres., Monterry County, Calif., 1980; bd. dirs. Monterry Peninsula chpt. ACLU, 1981—. Recipient Anisfield-Wolf Found. award, 1971. Mem. Am. Psychol. Assn., World Futures Soc., Soc. Psychol. Study of Social Issues (chairperson Los Angeles chpt. 1975-76). Democrat. Author: The Healing of a Nation, 1971; The Leadership Passion: A Psychology of Ideology, 1977; The Knowable Future: A Psychology of Forecasting, 1978; The Sphinx and the Rainbow: Brain, Mind and Future Vision, 1983; developer tests: The IMP and MCP Profiles, 1975-80. Office: Institute for Futures Forecasting 25700 Shafter Way Carmel CA 93923

LOYOLA, VINCENT MIJARES, chemist; b. Snyder, Tex., Feb. 24, 1949; s. Casimiro Cordova and Francisca (Mijares) L.; B.S., Angelo State U., 1973; Ph.D., N.Mex. State U., 1977; Postdoctoral fellow Purdue U., West Lafayette, Ind., 1977-79; mem. tech. staff Sandia Nat. Labs., Albuquerque, 1979—. Mem. Am. Chem. Soc., AAAS, Smithsonian Instn., Sigma Xi, Gamma Sigma Epsilon. Democrat. Roman Catholic. Home: 11809 Holiday Ave NE Albuquerque NM 87111

LOZANO, IGNACIO EUGENIO, JR., newspaper publisher, editor, former ambassador; b. San Antonio, Jan. 15, 1927; s. Ignacio Eugenio and Alicia (Elizondo) L.; m. Marta Eloisa Navarro, Feb. 24, 1951; children—Leticia Eugenia, Jose Ignacio, Monica Cecilia, Francisco Antonio. B.A. in Journalism, U. Notre Dame, 1947. Asst. pub. La Opinion, Los Angeles, 1947-53, editor, pub., 1953-76, 77—; pres. Lozano Enterprises, Inc., 1958-76; ambassador to El Salvador, 1976-77; dir. Bank of Am. NT & SA, Pacific Lighting Corp., Walt Disney Prodns. Trustee Orthopaedic Hosp., Occidental Coll., Monterey Inst. Internat. Studies; bd. dirs. Community TV So. Calif., Santa Anita Found., Nat. Park Found., Youth Opportunities Found.; mem. Los Angeles Council

Internat. Visitors, Nat. Park Found., So. Calif. Bldg. Funds, Youth Opportunity Found., Pres.'s Com. on Arts and Humanities; trustee Museum Contemporary Art. Mem. Calif. Press Assn., Catholic Press. Council So. Calif., World Affairs Council Orange County, Inter Am. Press Assn. (chmn. exec. com., dir.), Los Angeles World Affairs Council (dir.), Los Angeles Philharmonic Assn. (dir.), NCCJ (dir. So. Calif. region), Calif. Newspaper Pubs. Assn., Los Angeles Boys' Club, Sigma Delta Chi. Clubs: Greater Los Angeles Press, Calif., Transpacific Yacht, Los Angeles Country (Los Angeles); Santa Ana Country, Newport Harbor Yacht, Balboa de Mazatlan. Address: 1436 S Main St Los Angeles CA 90015

LU, KUO HWA, biostatiscian, educator; b. Antung, Liaoning, China, Jan. 7, 1923; s. Pei San Lu and I Chen Sun; came to U.S., 1947, naturalized, 1960; m. Catherine Collins, July 7, 1973; children—Randolph S., Conway K., Nancy L., Cliff B. B.S., Nat. Central U., Chungking, China, 1945; M.S., U. Minn., 1951, Ph.D., 1951. Research fellow U. Minn., 1952-56; assoc. prof. stats. Utah State U., 1956-60; assoc. prof. biostats. U. Oreg. Health Sci. Center, 1960-63, prof., chmn. dept. biostats., 1963—, dir. statis. lab., 1967—; prof. med. psychology, adj. prof. med. genetics Oreg. Health Scis. U., Portland, 1970—. Mem. Am. Statis. Assn., Biometric Soc., Math. Assn. Am., Internat. Assn. Dental Research, Sigma Xi. Democrat. Office: Biostats Oreg Health Sci U 611 SW Campus Dr Portland OR 97201

LUA, MICHELLE ANN, auditor; b. Paradise, Calif., Feb. 14, 1950; d. Raymond Elhart and Betty Dean (Thomas) Lua. B.A., Gonzaga U., Spokane, 1972; postgrad. San Jose State U., Sacramento State U., Santa Rosa Jr. Coll. Cert. secondary tchr., Alaska. Secondary tchr., Alaska and Calif., 1972-74; office auditor IRS, Santa Rosa, Calif., 1974-78, first-line mgr., 1978—. Named Disting. Performer, IRS, 1982, recipient sustained Superior Performance award, 1979-80. Mem. Kappa Delta Pi, Gamma Pi Epsilon. Office: 777 Sonoma Ave Santa Rosa CA 95404

LUBATTI, HENRY JOSEPH, physicist; b. Oakland, Calif., Mar. 16, 1937; s. John and Pauline (Massimino) L.; A.A., U. Calif., Berkeley, 1957, A.B., 1960; M.S., U. Ill., 1963; Ph.D., U. Calif., Berkeley, 1966; m. Catherine Jeanne Berth Ledoux, June 29, 1968; children—Karen E., Henry J., Stephen J.C. Research asso. Faculty Scis., U. Paris, Orsay, France, 1966-68; asst. prof. physics M.I.T., 1968-69; asso. prof., sci. dir. visual techniques lab. U. Wash., 1969-74, prof., sci. dir. visual techniques lab., 1974—; vis. lectr. Internat. Sch. Physics, Erice (Sicily) Italy, 1968, Herceg-Novi (Yugoslavia) Internat. ch., 1969, XII Cracow Sch. Theoretical Physics, Zapokane, Poland, 1972. Alfred P. Sloan research fellow, 1971-75. Fellow Am. Phys. Soc.; mem. Sigma Xi, Tau Beta Pi. Contbr. numerous articles on high energy physics to profl. jours. Office: U Wash Visual Techniques Lab Physics FM-15 Seattle WA 98195

LUBCKE, HARRY RAYMOND, patent counsel; b. Alameda, Calif., Aug. 25, 1905; s. Charles Henry and Ellen Lubcke; B.S., U. Calif., Berkeley, 1929, postgrad., 1930; children—Joan Lubcke Serlian, Christine Lubcke Canary. Dir. TV, Don Lee Broadcasting System, Hollywood, Calif., 1930-51; pvt. practice patent counsel, Hollywood, 1952—; dir. sta. KSFO-TV, Oakland-San Francisco, 1956-62. Patron, Los Angeles County Mus. Art, 1980, Los Angeles World Affairs Council, 1979; mem. com. Windsor Sq.-Hancock Park Hist. Soc. Mgr. prime contracts to USN, U.S. Army, World War II. Recipient TV Pioneer award, Pacific Pioneer Broadcasters, 1966, Diamond Circle, 1980. Fellow AAAS, Soc. Motion Picture and TV Engrs., IEEE; mem. ABA, Los Angeles Patent Law Assn. (gov., 1974), Acad. TV Arts and Scis. (pres., 1949-50), Soc. TV Engrs. Hollywood (founding pres., 1946), Phi Beta Kappa, Sigma Xi, Tau Beta Pi, Eta Kappa Nu. Republican. Presbyterian. Contbr. articles to publs.; patentee in field. Office: 2443 Creston Way Hollywood CA 90068

LUBECK, MARVIN JAY, physician; b. Cleve., Mar. 20, 1929; s. Charles D. and Lillian (Jay) L.; A.B., U. Mich., 1951, M.D., 1955, M.S., 1959; m. Arlene Sue Bitman, Dec. 28, 1955; children—David Mark, Daniel Jay, Robert Charles. Intern, U. Mich. Med. Center, 1955-56, resident ophthalmology, 1956-58, jr. clin. instr. ophthalmology, 1958-59; practice medicine, specializing in ophthalmology, Denver, 1961—; mem. staff Rose, Children's, Mercy, St. Luke's hosps.; asso. clin. prof. U. Colo. Med. Center; cons. ophthalmologist State of Colo. Served with U.S. Army, 1959-61. Diplomate Am. Bd. Opthalmology. Fellow ACS; mem. Am. Acad. Ophthalmology, Denver Med. Soc., Colo. Ophthalmol. Soc., Am. Intraocular Lens Implant Soc. Home: 590 S Harrison Ln Denver CO 80209 Office: 3865 Cherry Creek N Dr Denver CO 80209

LUBY, LARRY WALTER, psychologist; b. Inglewood, Calif., Feb. 6, 1945; s. Louis William and Helen Martha (Kuklenski) L.; B.A., Calif. State U., Dominguez Hills, 1969; M.A., Pepperdine U., 1971, credential in sch. psychology, 1973; Ph.D., U.S. Internat. U., 1980. Psychologist Hermosa Beach (Calif.) Sch. Dist., 1972-73, Laguna Beach (Calif.) Sch. Dist., 1973-74, La Habra (Calif.) Sch. Dist., 1974-75, Saddleback Unified Sch. Dist., Laguna Hills, Calif., 1975—; pvt. practice psychol. counseling, Laguna Beach, Calif., 1978—; oral commr. Calif. State Bd. Behavioral Sci. Examiners, 1978; instr. psychology Compton Coll., 1972-73, Saddleback Coll., 1974—, Chapman Coll., 1975—. Served with M.C., U.S. Army, 1966-68. Licensed ednl. psychologist, marriage, family and child counselor, Calif.; certified sch. psychologist, pub. sch. adminstr., community coll. instr., Calif. Mem. Am. Psychol. Assn., Calif. Assn. Sch. Psychologists, Calif. Psychol. Assn., Calif. Assn. Marriage and Family Therapists, Orange County (Calif.) Assn. Ednl. Psychologists, Psi Chi. Democrat. Roman Catholic. Research with mentally gifted and learning disabled students. Home: PO Box 551 South Laguna CA 92677 Office: Saddleback Unified Sch Dist 25631 Diseno Dr Mission Viejo CA 92675

LUCAS, DONALD LEO, private investor; b. Upland, Calif., Mar. 18, 1930; s. Leo J. and Mary G. (Schwamm) L.; B.A., Stanford U., 1951, M.B.A., 1953; m. Lygia de Soto Harrison, July 15, 1961; children—Nancy Maria, Alexandra Maria, Donald Alexander. Asso. corporate finance dept. Smith, Barney & Co., N.Y.C., 1956-59; gen., ltd. partner Draper, Gaither & Anderson, Palo Alto, Calif., 1959-66; pvt. investor, Menlo Park, Calif., 1966—; chmn. bd. Oracle Corp., Inc., Menlo Park, Tri-Data Corp., Mountain View, Calif.; dir. Data Card Corp., Mpls., HBO & Co., Atlanta, ICOT Corp., Mountain View, Liconix, Mountain View, Robinton Products, Inc., Sunnyvale, Calif., Tracor, Inc., Austin, Tex. Chmn. bd. regents Bellarmine Coll. Prep., 1977—; regent emeritus U. Santa Clara, 1980—. Served to 1st lt., AUS, 1953-55. Mem. Stanford U. Alumni Assn., Stanford Grad. Sch. Bus. Alumni Assn., Zeta Psi. Clubs: Commonwealth (San Francisco); Stanford Buck; Vintage (Palm Springs, Calif.); Menlo Country (Woodside, Calif.); Menlo Circus (Atherton, Calif.). Home: 224 Park Ln Atherton CA 94025 Office: 3000 Sand Hill Rd Menlo Park CA 94025

LUCAS, GEORGE KAWEKIU MANU, insurance company executive; b. San Francisco, Feb. 26, 1948; s. George Kawekiu and Ruth (Slight) L.; 1 son, George III. Student U. Hawaii, 1965-69, Brigham Young U., Honolulu Bus. Coll., Hawaii Pacific Coll. Programmer, C. Brewer, Hilo, Hawaii, 1969-76; systems analyst Hawaiian Ins. Co., Honolulu, 1976-79, data processing mgr., 1979-82, dep. dir., mgr. ops., 1982—. Served with USNG, 1966-72. Mem. Assn. Systems Mgmt. (past pres., v.p. 1983). Office: Hawaiian Ins Co 190 S King Suite 650 Honolulu HI 96813

LUCAS, JOHN EDWARD, public relations executive; b. Miami, Fla., Sept. 22, 1953; s. Joseph Stephen and Madeline Mary (Lubert) L.; m. Christine Ann Listug, Aug. 14, 1982. B.A. in Journalism, U. Calif., 1977. Staff writer Daily Californian, Berkeley, 1976; staff reporter Novato (Calif.) Advance, 1977-78; exec. asst. Bldg. Industry Assn. No. Calif., Novato and San Francisco, 1978-79; pub. relations writer David W. Evans, Inc./Calif., San Francisco, 1979-81, editorial services mgr., 1981-82, dir. pub. relations, 1982—; co-founder, coordinator Bay Area Pres.'s Council Communications Orgns. Mem. Pub. Relations Soc. Am. (No. Calif. chpts. Hon. Achievement award in feature news release 1982, chmn. membership San Francisco chpt. 1983—), Internat. Assn. Bus. Communicators, Soc. Tech. Communication. Democrat. Roman Catholic. Club: Calif. Alumni of Bay Area Young Blues. Contbr. numerous articles for clients in industry trade publs. Office: 22 Battery St San Francisco CA 94111

LUCAS, KENNETH LEE, manufacturing executive; b. Des Moines, Aug. 25, 1947; s. Emil Lee and Geneva Mary Ann (Krause) L.; m. Reiko Murotane, Nov. 14, 1970; children—Kenneth Lee II, Mikael Lee. B.A., Drake U., 1974, M.B.A., 1975. Vice pres., dir. sales and mktg. Directory Service Co., Boulder, Colo., 1975-80; pres., chmn. bd., chief exec. officer McCoy Industries Inc., Denver, 1980—. Served with USN, 1967-71. Mem. Phi Alpha Alpha. Republican. Home: 1452 Franklin Ct Louisville CO 80027 Office: 1201 Distel Dr Lafayette CO 80026

LUCAS, MALCOLM MILLAR, federal judge; b. Berkeley, Calif., Apr. 19, 1927; s. Robert and Georgina M. (Campbell) L.; student U. Calif. at Los Angeles, 1946-47; B.A., U. So. Calif., 1950, LL.B., 1953; m. Donna Joan Fisher, June 23, 1956; children—Gregory, Lisa. Admitted to Calif. bar; practiced law with firm Lucas, Deukmejian & Lucas, Los Angeles, 1955-67; judge Los Angeles County Superior Ct., 1967-71; judge U.S. Dist. Ct. for Central Calif., Los Angeles, 1971—. Trustee Los Alamitos Sch. Dist., 1963-71, pres. bd., 1964-65. Served with USNR, 1945-46. Mem. Am., Calif., Los Angeles County, Long Beach (past gov.), bar assns., Am. Trial Lawyers Assn., Internat. Acad. Trial Judges, Legion Lex. Office: 312 N Spring St Los Angeles CA 90012

LUCAS, SUZANNE, statistician; b. Baxter Springs, Kans., Jan. 16, 1939; d. Ralph Beaver and Marguerite (Sansocie) L.; div.; children—Patricia Sue Jennings, Neil Patric Jennings. B.A. in Math., Calif. State U.-Fresno, 1967, M.A. in Ednl. Theory, 1969; M.S. in Stats., U. So. Calif., 1979. Asst. to dir. NSF Inst., Calif. State U.-Fresno, 1968; tchr. math. secondary schs. Fresno City Schs., 1968-78; statistician corp. indsl. relations Hughes Aircraft Co., Los Angeles, 1979-80, personnel adminstr. space and communications group, 1981-82, mem. tech. staff math., 1982—; lectr. in biostats., research asst. U. So. Calif., 1978-79. Mem. Soc. Women Engrs., Am. Statis. Assn., Am. Psychol. Assn., U. So. Calif. Alumni Assn. Office: Hughes Aircraft Co PO Box 92919 Bldg S-50 Mail Station X334 Los Angeles CA 90009

LUCAS, WILLIAM GEORGE, financial executive; b. Sheridan, Wyo., Dec. 1, 1931; s. George and Mona Mable (Bell) L.; m. Billie Ann Lucas, Dec. 27, 1952; children—Debra Gail, Marcia Ann. B.S. in Civil Engring., U. Wyo., 1957, M.B.A., 1976. Profl. engr., Wyo., 1965. Supt. Taggart Constrn. Co., Cody, Wyo., 1958-59; supt., chief engr. Wyo. Hwy. Dept., Cheyenne, 1959-77; pres. Rocky Mountain Fed. Savs., Cheyenne, 1977—; dir. Indsl. Devel. Assistance, Cheyenne, Wyo. Indsl. Devel. Corp., Wyo. Savs. Service Corp.; dir., pres. Rocky Mountain Capital Corp. Chmn. Wyo. Hwy. Users Fedn., 1981; campaign chmn. Laramie County United Way, 1979; chmn. Dean's Adv. Council, U. Wyo., 1981; trustee Laramie County Hosp., 1978-80; bd. dirs. Cheyenne Credit Bur. 1979—. Served to capt. U.S. Army, 1953-56. Mem. Cheyenne C. of C. (dir.), Wyo. Engring. Soc., U.S. League Savs. and Loans, Savs. and Loan Assns. Wyo. Republican. Presbyterian. Clubs: Cheyenne Country, Masons. Home: 1950 Cheshire Dr Cheyenne WY 82001 Office: 2020 Carey Ave Cheyenne WY 82001

LUCAS, WILLIAM JASPER, transp. exec.; b. Red Oak, Okla., June 13, 1926; s. Raymond Haskell and Carrie P. (Butler) L.; student Okla. State U., 1946-48, St. Michaels U., 1954, U. N.Mex., 1974; m. Martha Joye Hines, Aug. 29, 1948; children—Mark William, Bret Raymond, Kurt Jonathan, Lane. Terminal mgr. Santa Fe Storage & Transfer Co. (N.Mex.), 1952-60; mgr. traffic and sales Dalton Transfer & Storage, Albuquerque, 1960-68; exec. v.p. H-K Moving & Storage, Albuquerque, 1968-77, pres., treas., 1977—, also cons.; rate and traffic cons. N.Mex., 1961—, ICC, 1961—; mil. and govt. affairs com. Mayflower Transit Co., 1978—; guest lectr. art U. N.Mex., 1977—. Sponsor Albuquerque Boys Club, 1970—. Served with Horse Cavalry, U.S. Army, 1944-46, adj. gen. dept., 1950-52. Mem. Am. Soc. Traffic and Transp., Assn. Interstate Commerce Practitioners, Nat. Def. Exec. Res., Soc. for Photog. Edn., Albuquerque C. of C. Republican. Unitarian. Club: Tennis of Albuquerque. Contbr. articles to profl. jours.; show photographs, U. N.Mex. Fine Arts Center, 1977, 1983, also others. Office: H-K Moving & Storage 3300 2d St NW Albuquerque NM 87107

LUCE, GORDON COPPARD, savs. and loan exec.; b. San Diego, Nov. 21, 1925; s. Edgar Augustine and Carma (Coppard) L.; B.A., Stanford U., 1950, M.B.A., 1952; postgrad. Ind. U. Sch. Savs. and Loan, 1959; m. Karon Turnbow, Sept. 3, 1955; children—Kelly, Randy, Andrew. Chmn. bd. Gt. Am. Fed. Savs. and Loan Assn. (formerly San Diego Fed. Savs. and Loan Assn.), 1969—, chief exec. officer, 1969—, also dir.; chmn. bd. Fin. Scene, Inc.; dir. Pacific S.W. Airlines, Fed. Home Loan Bank Bd., San Francisco, Intermark, Inc. Sec. of bus. and transp., mem. gov.'s cabinet State of Calif., 1967-69; chmn. Calif. Hwy. Commn., 1967, Calif. Toll Bridge Authority, 1967-68; mem. advisory com. Mktg. Program for Indsl. Devel.; advisory bd. U. So. Calif. Center for Study Financial Instns. Mem. bd. electors Internat. Aerospace Hall of Fame; past chmn. San Diego Econ. Devel. Corp.; mem. Exchange Group; trustee San Diego Mus. Art, Sea World Research Inst.; bd. dirs. San Diegans, Inc.; bd. overseers Hoover Instn. on War, Revolution, Peace at Stanford U.; trustee U. So. Calif.; vice chmn. Hosp. of Scripps Clinic, La Jolla, Calif.; chmn. Republican State Central Com. of Calif., 1973-74; mem. Pres.'s Commn. on Housing, 1981, chmn. subcom. on pvt. sector financing and housing; mem. Pres. Reagan's Housing Policy Task Force, 1981; mem. Republican nat. Com., 1973-75; del. Rep. Nat. Conv., 1964, 68, 72; del. UN 37th Assembly, 1982. Served with inf. U.S. Army, 1944-46. Decorated Bronze Star; recipient Headliner of Year award San Diego Press Club, 1975, 79; Cabrillo Heritage award, 1980; Diogenes award Public Relations Soc. Am., 1980, others. Mem. Calif. Savs. and Loan League (past pres.), Calif. State C. of C. (past dir.), San Diego C. of C. (v.p.) Food and Wine Soc. of La Jolla, U.S. League Savs. Assns. (dir.), NCCJ (honoree San Diego region 1977), San Diego Mktg. Soc. (Mktg. Man of Year award 1976), Am. Bus. Conf., Lambda Alpha. Episcopalian. Clubs: El Dorado Country, San Diego Yacht, Univ. of San Diego, Cuyamaca of San Diego; La Jolla Beach and Tennis. Office: 600 B St San Diego CA 92183

LUCE, WILLARD RAY, JR., educator, writer; b. Price, Utah, Sept. 18, 1914; s. Willard Ray and Rachel (Olsen) L.; B.S., Brigham Young U., 1947; m. Celia Geneva Larsen, June 3, 1940; children—Willard Ray, Loretta Luce Evans. Elementary sch. tchr., San Juan County, Utah, 1938-43; phys. edn. tchr. San Juan High Sch., Blanding, Utah, 1943-44; elementary sch. tchr., Orem, Utah, 1944-45; instr. journalism Brigham Young U., Provo, Utah, 1946-47; elementary sch. tchr., Orem, Utah, 1948-54, 56-73; ret. Recipient 1st pl. juvenile book div. award (with Celia Luce) Utah State Div. Fine Arts, 1978. Mem. Utah Edn. Assn., NEA, League of Utah Writers (state pres. 1948-49, treas. 1950-54). Mem. Ch. of Jesus Christ of Latter Day Saints. Contbr. articles, photos to various mags. and newspapers; author: (with Celia Luce) Sutter's Fort, Empire on the Sacramento, 1969; (with Celia Luce) Jim Bridger, Man of the Mountains, 1966; (with Celia Luce) Timmy and the Golden Spike, 1963; Birds that Hunt, 1970; The Red Stallion, 1961; Jerry Lindsey, Explorer to the San Juan, 1958; (with Celia Luce) Utah Past and Present, (with Celia Luce) 1958; Lou Gehrig, Iron Man of Baseball, 1970; (with Celia Luce) UTAH!, 1975. Address: 710 N 600 St W Provo UT 84601

LUCENTE, ROSEMARY DOLORES, ednl. adminstr.; b. Renton, Wash., Jan. 11, 1935; d. Joseph Anthony and Erminia Antoinette (Argano) L.; B.A., Mt. St. Mary's Coll., 1956, M.S., 1963. Tchr. pub. schs., Los Angeles, 1956-65, supr. tchr., 1958-65, asst. prin., 1965-69, prin. elem. sch., 1969—; cons., lectr. Dr. William Glasser's Educator Tng. Ctr., 1968—; nat. workshop leader Nat. Acad. Sch. Execs. and Am. Assn. Sch. Adminstrs. Recipient Golden Apple award Stanford Ave. Sch. PTA, Faculty and Community Adv. Council, 1976, resolution for outstanding service South Gate City Council, 1976. Mem. Nat. Assn. Elem. Sch. Prins., Assn. Calif. Sch. Adminstrs. (charter), Assn. Elem. Sch. Adminstrs. (vice-chmn. chpt. 1972-75, exec. bd., exec. com. 1972-80), Los Angeles Elem. Prins. Orgn. (v.p. 1979-80), Pi Theta Mu, Kappa Delta Pi (v.p. 1982-84), Delta Kappa Gamma. Democrat. Roman Catholic. Home: 6501 Lindenhurst Ave Los Angeles CA 90048 Office: Encino Elem Sch 16941 Addison St Encino CA 91316

LUCERO, AILEEN FAY, sociologist; b. Las Vegas, N.Mex., July 11, 1950; d. Juan Carlos and Yvonne Rae (Kueffer) Lucero. B.A. in Sociology, U. Colo., 1973, Ph.D., 1980. Vis. asst. prof. Chicano studies program Wash. State U., Pullman, 1979, NIMH postdoctoral trainee dept. sociology, 1980-82; applied sociologist adj. Centro de las Familias, S.W. Denver Community Mental Health Services Inc., 1982—. Recipient Nat. Research Service award HUD, 1980-82; Ford Found. fellow, 1976-79; Minority Grad. fellow U. Colo., 1974-76. Mem. Am. Sociol. Assn., Western Social Sci. Assn., Southwestern Sociol. Assn. Contbr. chpts. and articles to profl. publs. Home: 2730 Tennyson St Denver CO 80212 Office: Southwest Denver Community Mental Health Services Inc 205 Knox Ct Denver CO 80219

LUCEY, JACK, painter, art educator; b. San Francisco, Feb. 11, 1929; s. John and Julia (Casey) L.; m. Charlotte Marie Wyckoff, July 28, 1956; children—John, Robert, Michael. A.A. in Painting and Design, Indian Valley Colls., 1975; B.A. in Vocat. Edn., San Francisco State U., 1976. Artist, draftsmen Shell Oil Co., San Francisco, 1952-56; owner, illustrator Jack Lucey/Art & Design, San Rafael, Calif., 1956—; art dir. Ind. Jour. Newspaper, San Rafael, 1956—; instr. illustration Coll. Marin, Kentfield, Calif., 1975—; instr. Acad. Art, San Francisco, 1976-77. Mem. Adv. Bd. Marin Community Colls., Contra Costa Regional Occupational Program. Served with USMC; Korea. Recipient 1st place award Indsl. Graphic Internat., San Jose, Calif., 1978; 1st place awards Editor and Pub. Ann., 1970-79; Editorial award State of Calif. Hwy. Patrol; 1st place award Calif. Newspapers Assn., 1983. Mem. Soc. Western Artists, Coll. Art Assn. Am., San Francisco Soc. Communicating Arts, Artists in Print, North Bay Advt. Communicating. Roman Catholic. Club: Art Dirs. Work published in numerous profl. jours. Home: 84 Crestwood Dr San Rafael CA 94901 Office: 24 Belvedere St San Rafael CA 94901

LUCHETTI, MELVIN LOUIS, educator; b. Stockton, Calif., Dec. 1, 1934; s. Louis John and Lena Mary (De Barbieri) L.; B.E.E., U. Santa Clara, 1956; postgrad. San Jose State U., 1961-64, 66-69, 71-74, U. Calif. at Santa Cruz, 1970, 72; M.A., U. San Francisco, 1976. Electronics engr. Sylvania Electric Co., Sunnyvale, Calif., 1958-61; tchr. Santa Clara (Calif.) Unified Schs., 1964—; tech. cons. Organ Concert, Notre Dame Cathedral, Paris, 1969, Annunciation Cathedral, Stockton, 1963-70; electronic music cons. Cathedral of St. John the Divine, N.Y.C., 1970, St. Mary's Cathedral, San Francisco, 1971, 77, 80, U. Calif., Berkeley, 1974, Stanford, 1974, Grace Cathedral, San Francisco, 1975, World Library Publs., 1972—; lectr. in field. Co-founder, bd. dirs. Automatic Music Found., San Francisco, 1974—. Served with Ordnance Corps, AUS, 1956-58. Mem. Automatic Musical Instruments Collectors Assn. Internat. (co-founder 1963, dir. 1970-72, chmn. research com. 1970-72, chmn. tech. com. 1970—, chmn. hist. com. 1972—, Silver Appreciation of Service award 1974). Dir., editor, narrator film: They All Laughed When I Sat Down At The Piano, But When It Began to Play; editor, compiler: Technicalities, Vol. I, 1972, Vol. II, 1975, Vol. III, 1978, Vol. IV, 1981; Video Tapes Technicalities, Vols. I-II, 1981, Vols. III-IV, 1982, Vols. V-VI, 1983; co-author, pub: Wear Comfortable Shoes and Bring a Sack Lunch, 1977. Home: 3449 Mauricia Ave Santa Clara CA 95051 Office: 3250 Monroe St Santa Clara CA 95051

LUCIER, JOHN PRICE, management consultant; b. Cambridge, Mass., Mar. 30, 1932; s. Howell John and Mildred (Price) L.; m. Shirley Haynes, Sept. 13, 1969; children—Sara, John F., Molly. A.B., Columbia Coll., 1953, M.S., 1959. Assoc., Robert Heller & Assocs., Cleve., 1961-64; v.p. Booz-Allen & Hamilton, Inc., San Francisco, 1964-70; v.p. mktg. Shareholders Capital Corp., Los Angeles, 1970-72; with ITT, N.Y.C., 1973-74; v.p. Foster & Assocs., San Francisco, 1975-79; pres. Lucier Assocs., San Francisco, 1980—. Served with USNR, 1953-55. Club: St. Francis Yacht. Home: 2006 Bush St San Francisco CA 94115 Office: 649 Mission St San Francisco CA 94105

LUCKE, THOMAS WILLIAM, goverment official; b. Bellevue, Iowa, Oct. 21, 1940; s. Robert J. and Esther (Ernst) L.; m. Louise Zimmer, Aug. 23, 1970; children—Anne, David, Robert. B.A., Loras Coll., 1963; M.A., U. Colo., 1965; J.D., U. Iowa, 1971. Bars: Iowa 1971, Colo. 1973, U.S. Supreme Ct. 1979. With Nat. Park Service, 1970—, staff Mesa Verde Nat. Park, Colo., 1970-71, Buffalo Nat. River, Ark., 1972-73, Ft. Larned Nat. Historic Site, Kans., 1974-75, chief Div. Environ. Coordination, Santa Fe, N.Mex., 1980—; Peace Corps vol., Nepal, 1966-68; tchr. park planning and environ. legislation, Egypt, 1981. Mem. Iowa Bar Assn., Colo. Bar Assn., ABA, Audubon Soc. Democrat. Roman Catholic. Contbr. articles to profl. jours. Address: 2596 Avenida de Isidro Santa Fe NM 87501

LUCKHARDT, ROBERT LOUIS, agronomist; b. Tarkio, Mo., Aug. 15, 1916; s. Harry Alan and Susie Valentine (Sloss) L.; B.S., U. Tulsa, 1937; M.S., U. Nebr., 1941; postgrad. U. Okla., 1936, U. Miami (Fla.), 1945-47, U. Calif., Irvine, 1965; m. Doris Mae McMurtry, Oct. 8, 1941; children—Carol Ann (Mrs. Elmo Moore, Jr.), Mary L., Helen Mae. With U.S. Bur. Fisheries, Stanford (Calif.) U., 1938-39, 40-41; range surveyor Soil Conservation Service, Pleasanton, Tex., 1939-40, Grass Range, Mont., 1941-42; meteorologist Pan Am. Airways, Miami, Fla., 1943-46; instr. U. Miami (Fla.), 1945-47; agronomist Agriform Co., Santa Ana, Calif., 1948-53; supr. agr. tech. services Union Chem. Div., Los Angeles, 1953-80; cons., 1980—. Recipient Golden Flipper award, N.W. Plant Food Assn., 1978; named Man of the Year, Calif. Fertilizer Assn., 1959, 77; certified profl. soil specialist. Mem. Calif. Fertilizer Assn., Am. Soc. Agronomy (honoree Calif. sect. 1981), AAAS. Methodist. editor Solution Sheet, 1953, Planet N Abstracts, 1970-78, Chemistry Review for Fieldmen, 1971; author: Urea Manual for Fieldmen, 1977. Home and Office: 248 E 20 St Costa Mesa CA 92627

LUCOFF, KATHY ANN, fine arts cons.; b. Los Angeles, Ja. 28, 1953; d. Marvin and Lolly Ruth (Blaugrund) L.; student San Diego State U., 1970-72; B.F.A., Calif. Coll. Arts and Crafts, Oakland, 1974; postgrad. in mus. studies Calif. State U., Long Beach, 1974-76. Asst. dir. L.A. Louver Gallery, 1975-78; instr. art edn. Santa Monica (Calif.) Coll., 1976-77; owner, operator Kathy Lucoff Fine Arts, Los Angeles, 1978—; art critic Sta. KABC; freelance writer; art cons. to architects, interior designers, corps., banks. Home and Office: 806 N Alfred St Los Angeles CA 90069

LUDEKE, KENNETH LEROY, agronomist, research consultant; b. Holdrege, Nebr., Mar. 9, 1945; s. Harvey William and Darlene M. (Olson) L.; m. Anne M. B.S. in Agronomy, U. Ariz., 1968, M.S. in Agronomy, 1973, Ph.D. in Agronomy and Plant Genetics, 1976. Cert. profl. agronomist. Field equipment operator Anaconda Mining Co., Tucson, 1965-68; lab. scientist U. Ariz., Tucson, 1964-68; tech. field rep. Shell Oil Co., Lubbock, Tex., 1968-70; research agronomist Cyprus Mining Co., Tucson, 1971-77; chmn. open-pit mining session Commn. on Surface Mining and Reclamation, Nat. Acad. Scis., Washington, 1978-80; research and devel. assoc. Monsanto Chem. Co., San Diego, 1977-79; research cons. Ludeke Corp., San Diego and Phoenix, 1979—; tech. advisor Nat. Petroleum Council, Washington, 1980-81; environ. coordinator Union Oil Co. Calif., Grand Junction, 1980-81; v.p. research and devel. Natural Fibre Industries, San Diego, 1982—; v.p. research and devel. S.W. Desert Farms, Inc., 1980—; tchr. agrl. internship program; dir. World Mining, World Mining and World Coal. Served with USMCR, 1963-65; USAR, 1975-78. Recipient Govs'. Highest award Protecting Ariz. Environ. 1975. Republican. Invented and trademarked products for protecting environment disturbed by mankind; contbr. chpt. to textbooks, numerous articles to profl. jours. Home: 12894 Caminto de las Olas Del Mar CA 92014 Office: 1st Interstate Tower 3550 N Central Ave Suite 906 Phoenix AZ 85012

LUDEMAN, BART LEE, banker, cons.; b. Pueblo, Colo., Mar. 27, 1930; s. Rudolph C. and Lois E. (Irwin) L.; B.S. in Advt. and Journalism, U. Colo., 1952, M.P.A., 1952. Asst. dir. placements U. Denver, 1957-62; various managerial positions Lloyds Bank Calif., Los Angeles, 1962-73, dir. human resources devel., 1973-80, v.p., 1975—; pres. Bart Ludeman Assocs., 1980—; dir. Leaseby Inc., Practical Mgmt. Assocs., Inc., mem. Calif. Consortium for External Degree in Banking, 1975-76; dir. LeaseBy, Practical Mgmt. Assocs. Served with USAF, 1952-56. Mem. Am. Soc. for Tng. and Devel. (Gordon Bliss award 1976, nat. pres. 1978), Calif. Bankers Assn. (dir. 1976-78), Nat. Industry/Edn. Coop. (bd. dirs.), Calif. Coop. Edn. Assn. (dir. 1979, pres.-elect 1977), Nat. Ednl. Work Assn. Republican. Episcopalian. Office: 1656 E Burnett Signal Hill CA 90806

LUDLUM, MARGARET DEBORAH, economist; b. Washington, Feb. 1, 1944; d. Robert Phillips and Ruth Althea (Smith) L.; divorced; 1 son, Jeffrey Hashimoto. B.A. in Econs. magna cum laude, Cornell U., Ithaca, N.Y., 1965; M.A. in Econs., Columbia U., 1970, Ph.D. in Econs., 1979. Mgmt. trainee Prudential Ins. Co., Newark, 1965-66; researcher Nat. Econ. Research Assocs., N.Y.C., 1967; instr. U. Detroit, 1972; instr. Shoreline Community Coll., Seattle, 1975; instr. Seattle U., 1976; instr. U. Puget Sound, Seattle Campus, 1977; economist Seattle Water Dept., 1978—. Treas. Boy Scout Troop 177, 1982—. AAUW fellow, 1974-75. Mem. Am. Econ. Assn., Phi Beta Kappa. Republican. Unitarian. Home: 3214 NE 97th St Seattle WA 98115 Office: Seattle Water Dept 821 2d Ave Seattle WA 98104

LUDWICK, JOHN HOYER, lawyer; b. Carthage, Mo., June 1, 1945; s. Arthur Lee and Jean Catherine (Hoyer) L. Student U. Wash., 1963-65; B.S., U. Puget Sound, 1968; J.D., Willamette U., 1974. Bar: Wash. 1974, U.S. Dist. Ct. Wash. 1975. Asst. atty. gen. State of Wash., 1974-75; assoc. Murray, Dunham & Waitt, Seattle, 1975-76; ptnr. Fitch & Ludwick, Seattle, 1976—. Served to 1st lt. USAR, 1968-71. Decorated Bronze Star, Commendation Medal with oak leaf cluster. Mem. Seattle-King County Bar Assn., Wash. State Bar Assn., ABA, Am. Soc. Hosp. Attys., Wash. State Soc. Hosp. Attys. (trustee). Presbyterian. Club: Bellevue Athletic.

LUDWIGSEN, KRISTINA RAHBEK, clinical psychologist, air force officer; b. Jacksonville, Fla., July 10, 1945; d. Hans B. and Elizabeth J. (Dunne) L.; B.A., Eckerd Coll., 1967, M.A., Emory U., 1969, Ph.D. (USPHS fellow), 1972. Asst. prof. psychology U. Dayton (Ohio), 1972-79; psychol. cons. Dayton State Hosp., 1972-75, Adolescent Inpatient Service, Cin., 1975-76; adj. asst. prof. psychology U. Cin. Med. Center, 1975-76; asst. clin. prof. dept. psychiatry Wright State U. Sch. Medicine, Dayton, 1976-79; commd. capt. U.S. Air Force, 1979; chief psychologist Behavioral Medicine Clinic, USAF Hosp., Hill AFB, Utah, 1979-82, chief of Clinic, 1981-82; chief psychologist USAF Regional Hosp., March AFB, Calif., 1982—; psychol. cons. to U.S. Army, 1980-81; mem., sec. Tri-Service Health Psychology Com., 1981—. Decorated Air Force Commendation medal; named Outstanding Contbr. to Air Force Clin. Psychology, 1981. Mem. Am. Psychol. Assn., Air Force Soc. Clin. Psychologists (sec. 1980-83), Assn. Adv. Psychology. Democrat. Unitarian. Editor, The Forum newsletter, 1980-83. Office: Behavioral Medicine Clinic USAF Regional Hosp March AFB CA 92518

LUEBKE, WILLIAM ROBERT, JR., astronomy educator; b. Boulder, Colo., Sept. 3, 1947; s. William Robert and Robin (Nevine) L.; B.A. with honors, U. Calif., Berkeley, 1969; M.S. (NASA trainee), U. Chgo., 1971; m. Margaret Fluvog, Sept. 6, 1969; children—Eric, James. Instr., Modesto (Calif.) Jr. Coll., 1974—, prof., 1976—. Mem. Internat. Planetarium Soc., Am. Astron. Soc., NEA, Astron. Soc. of Pacific, Sierra Club, Vesper Soc., Yosemite Faculty Assn. (pres. 1983—), Sigma Xi. Republican. Lutheran. Clubs: Ducks Unltd., Commonwealth. Contbr. articles to profl. jours. Office: Modesto Jr Coll Modesto CA 95350

LUECHAUER, HELYN CATHERINE ANDERSON, dentist; b. Oakland, Calif., Aug. 13, 1921; d. Virgil Vinson and Lillian (Hickox) Anderson; m. Jarvis H. Luechauer, Feb. 26, 1944. Student Pacific Union Coll., 1939-43, Fresno State Coll., 1960-62; D.D.S., U. Calif.-San Francisco, 1966; postgrad. in nutrition chemistry UCLA Sch. Pub. Health, 1974-77. Practice dentistry, Hollywood, Calif., 1966—; asst. clin. prof. UCLA Sch. Dentistry, 1967-77; mem. Calif. Bd. Dental Examiners, 1977—, Calif. Com. Dental Auxs., ADA Joint Commn. Nat. Bd. Exams; lectr. nutrition and holistic dentistry. Mem. Friends of Hollywood; active Presbyn. Med. Ctr. Fellow Am. Coll. Dentists, Acad. Gen. Dentistry, Internat. Acad. Dental Studies; mem. ADA, Calif. Dental Assn., Los Angeles Dental Assn., Am. Acad. Oral Medicine, Am. Assn. Women Dentists (editor, past pres.), Internat. Acad. Preventive Medicine, Internat. Coll. Applied Nutrition, Internat. Acad. Preventive Medicine, Internat. Coll. Applied Nutrition, Internat. Acad. Metabology, Internat. Acad. Microendocrinology, Holistic Dental Assn., Orthomolecular Med. Soc., Far West Med. Assn., NOW, Nat. Women's Polit. Caucus, Nat. Women's Health Network. Republican. Congregationalist. Home: 3347 Charleston Way Hollywood CA 90068 Office: 3169 Barbara Ct Hollywood CA 90068

LUEPKE, GRETCHEN, geologist; b. Tucson; d. Gordon Maas and Janice (Campbell) L.; student U. Colo., summer 1962; B.S., U. Ariz., 1965, M.S., 1967. Geologist, U.S. Geol. Survey, Menlo Park, Calif., 1967—. Registered geologist, Oreg. Mem. Soc. Econ. Paleontologists and Mineralogists, Geol. Soc. Am., Bay Area Mineralogists (chmn. 1979-80), Ariz. Geol. Soc., Peninsula Geol. Soc., History of Earth Soc., Sigma Xi. Editor: Stability of Heavy Minerals in Sediments (vol. 81 of series Benchmark papers in Geology); contbr. articles on heavy mineral analysis to sci. jours. Office: US Geol Survey 345 Middlefield Rd Menlo Park CA 94025

LUETGER, CHARLES LINDBERGH, motor common carrier co. exec.; b. Burlington, Iowa, Oct. 29, 1927; s. Louis Edward and Flossie Ella (McDaniel) L.; B.S.B.A., Century U., 1980, M.B.A., 1982; m. Katheryn Anne Kennedy, Feb. 14, 1950; children—Theresa, Steven, Timothy, Matthew. With BN Transport, Inc., Burlington, Iowa, 1946-49, Galesburg, Ill., 1949-73, v.p. mgmt. services, Denver, 1973-78, v.p. adminstrn., 1978-83, v.p. mktg. and traffic, 1983—; exec. v.p., gen. mgr. Hart Motor Express, Inc., St. Paul, 1978-80; also dir. v.p. BNT Terminals, Inc., also dir. Mem. Am. Mgmt. Assn., Adminstrv. Mgmt. Soc., Assn. Computer Users, Am. Trucking Assn. (mgmt. services com.), Am. Mktg. Assn., Nat. Council Phys. Distbn. Mgmt. Home: 4171 S Verbena St Denver CO 80237 Office: 6775 E Evans Ave Denver CO 80222

LUH, BOR SHIUN, food technologist; b. Shanghai, Kiangsu, China, Jan. 13, 1916; s. Tsung Fong and King Yin (Chen) L.; came to U.S., 1946, naturalized, 1958; B.S., Chiao Tung U., Shanghai, 1938; M.S. in Food Sci., U. Calif., Berkeley, 1948, Ph.D. in Agrl. Chemistry, 1952; m. Bai Tsain Luh, Nov. 23, 1940; children—Jane Luh Chien, Janet S. Luh Seastrom. Chemist, MaLing Canned Foods Co., Ltd., Shanghai, 1941-46; research asst. U. Calif., Berkeley, 1948-51; jr. specialist U. Calif., Davis, 1952-56, jr. food technologist, 1956-57, asst. food technologist, 1957-63, asso. food technologist, 1963-69, food technologist, 1969—; prof. Pahlavi U., Shiraz, Iran, 1977-78. Recipient various research grants. Mem. Am. Chem. Soc., Inst. Food Technologists, Am. Assn. Cereal Chemists, Am. Oil Chemists Soc., AAAS, N.Am. Soc. Phytochemistry, Chinese Inst. Engrs. U.S.A. (chmn. food processing sect. 1968, 76), Sigma Xi. Author: (with J.G. Woodroof) Commercial Fruit Processing, 1975, Commercial Vegetable Processing, 1975, Rice: Production and Utilization, 1980. Home: 1215 Enreka Ave Davis CA 95616 Office: Dept Food Sci U Calif Davis CA 95616

LUIK, REIN, communications equipment company executive; b. Harku, Estonia, Aug. 21, 1936; came to U.S., 1950, naturalized, 1956; s. Peeter and Alide (Talo) L.; m. Marje Palm, Aug. 14, 1965; children—Kristi Aime, Riina Maie. B.S. in Mech. Engring., U. Wash., 1962; postgrad. (NDEA fellow), Ill. Inst. Tech., 1963-64; Ph.D., Stanford U., 1973. Research engr. WDL div. Philco Ford Corp., Palo Alto, Calif., 1962-69, mgr. antenna integration sect. WDL div. Aeronutronic Ford Corp., Palo Alto, 1969-72, mgr. antenna substems engring. dept. WDL div. Ford Aerospace & Communications Corp., Palo Alto, 1972-76; pres., dir. TIW Systems Inc., Sunnyvale, Calif., 1976—, dir. TIW Systems Ltd., Toronto, Ont., Can., 1976—. Mem. AIAA, IEEE, Estonian League of West Coast (pres. 1973-75, chmn. organizing com. Estonian Festival 1975), Sigma Xi. Republican. Lutheran. Office: TIW Systems Inc 1284 Geneva Dr Sunnyvale CA 94086

LUJAN, MANUEL, JR., congressman; b. San Idlefonso, N.Mex., May 12, 1928; s. Manuel and Lorenzita (Romero) L.; B.A. in Bus. Adminstrn., Coll. Santa Fe, 1950; student St. Mary's (Calif.) Coll., 1946-47; m. Jean Kay Couchman, Nov. 18, 1948; children—Terra Kay Everett, James Manuel, Barbara Frae Browne, Robert Jeffrey. Engaged in ins. bus., Santa Fe and Albuquerque, 1948—; mem. 91st-97th congresses from 1st N.Mex. Dist., mem. interior and insular affairs, water and power resources coms., energy and environment subcom., mem. sci. and tech. com., sci. energy research and prodn. subcom., investigations and oversight subcom. Office: 1323 Longworth Office Bldg Washington DC 20515*

LUK, KING SING, engring. co. exec., educator; b. Canton, China, Sept. 1, 1932; came to U.S., 1954, naturalized, 1964; s. Yau Kong and Liang Yu L.; B.S., Calif. State U., Los Angeles, 1957; M.S. in Civil Engring., U. So. Calif., 1960; Ph.D. with distinction, UCLA, 1971; m. m. Kit Ming Wong, July 14, 1957; children—Doris, Stephen, Eric, Marcus. Chief engr. R.E. Rule Inc., 1958-60; pres. King S. Luk & Assos., Inc. Cons. Engrs., Los Angeles, 1960—; prof. civil engring. Calif. State U., Los Angeles, 1960—, chmn., 1968-74; commr. Calif. Seismic Safety Commn.; dir., corp. exec. officer Mechanics Nat. Bank, Cathay Pacific Inc., Luk & Lum, Inc., Concord Assos., Inc. NSf fellow, 1966, 70. Fellow ASCE; m. Structural Engrs. Assn. So. Calif. Author: Civil Engineering Reviews, 1964; contbr. articles in field to profl. jours. Research in reinforced concrete and earthquake engring. Home: 5525 Huntington Dr N Los Angeles CA 90032 Office: 5151 State University Dr Los Angeles CA 90032

LUKE, TERRI KATHERINE, public relations executive; b. Chgo., Oct. 4, 1948; d. Walter and Eleanor Soltysinski; children—Dennis W., Nicole Therese; m. 2d, Edwin L. Luke, Jr., Oct. 18, 1980. B.A. in Journalism, Ariz. State U., 1975. Spl. projects pub. relations Gov.'s Office, Phoenix, 1975-76; coordinator campaign hdqrs. Tony Mason Congress, 1976; dir. pub. relations Phoenix and Valley of the Sun Conv. & Visitors Bur., 1977; owner Butner & Assoc. Pub. Relations (now Terri Luke Communications), Phoenix, 1978—; mem. State of Ariz. Women's Commn., 1976-79. Mem. Nat. Assn. Female Execs., Phoenix Press Club, Phoenix C. of C. Democrat. Roman Catholic. Office: PO Box 34316 Phoenix AZ 85067

LUM, GERALD HOONG WUN, architect, interior designer, educator; b. Honolulu, Feb. 21, 1948; s. Norman B.Y. and Rita K.M. (Wong) L.; divorced. B.Arch. with honors, U. Ill., 1971; M.B.A., U. Hawaii, 1979; cert. Hawaii, 1973, Alaska, 1976, Calif., 1979; Tex., 1980, Nat. Council Archtl. Registration Bds., 1975. Instr. archtl. tech. Champaign County (Ill.) Urban League, Urbana, 1969; project designer Everett I. Brown Co., Honolulu, 1971-73; prin. Gerald Lum Assocs., Honolulu, 1973-80; pres. Lum & Okita, Inc. (named changed to Gerald Lum, Inc.), Honolulu, 1980—; vis. lectr. Coll. Arts and Scis., U. Hawaii, Honolulu, 1975-76, instr., 1976-77, vis. lectr. Sch. Architecture, U. Hawaii 1981—. Active Hist. Hawaii Found., 1980—. Bates scholar, 1967-70. Edmund J. James scholar, 1970. Mem. AIA (cert. 1973, membership chmn. chpt. 1975, chmn. task force transp. 1977), Am. Soc. Interior Designers (cert. 1977, dir. chpt. 1980—), Constrn. Specifications Inst. Congregationalist.

LUM, HAROLD CHAN KONG, broom mfg. co. exec.; b. Honolulu, June 19, 1925; s. Kam Oot (Young) L.; A.A., Armstrong Coll., 1949, B.B.A., 1951; m. Sue N. L. Tong, Sept. 28, 1952; children—Colin G.C., Brian G.W., Lianne K.L. Pres., H.B.F. Inc., 1966—. Committeeman Aloha Pack 201 Cub Scouts, Boy Scouts Am., 1966-72. Served with AUS, 1946. Recipient award Outstanding Employers of the Handicapped, 1972. Mem. Lum's Soc. (pres. 1968), Hawaii Ballroom Dance Assn. (auditor chpt.). Home: 912 Alewa Pl Honolulu HI 96817 Office: 1017 N King St Honolulu HI 96817

LUM, HERMAN TSUI FAI, supreme ct. associate justice; b. Honolulu, Nov. 5, 1926; s. Kan Pun and Helen (Tom) L.; student U. Hawaii, 1945-46; J.D., U. Mo., 1950; m. Almira Ahn, June 17, 1949; children—Forrest K., Jonathan K. Bar: Hawaii 1950. Asst. pub. prosecutor City and County of Honolulu, 1950-52; chief atty. Hawaii Ho. of Reps., Honolulu, 1955, chief clk., 1956-61; ptnr. firm Suyenaga, Sakamoto & Lum, Honolulu, 1956-61; U.S. atty. Dist. of Hawaii, Honolulu, 1961-67; circuit judge 1st Jud. Circuit, Honolulu, 1967-80, sr. judge Family Ct., 1971-76; assoc. justice Supreme Ct. of Hawaii, Honolulu, 1980—; chmn. supervisory bd. State Law Enforcement and Juvenile Delinquency Planning Agy., 1977, mem., 1969—. Chmn. Mental Health Council, 1975, Western Interstate Commn. Higher Edn., 1971-76; trustee Honolulu Med. Group Research and Edn. Found., 1980. Served with U.S. Navy, 1945-46; with U.S. Army, 1952-54. Named Disting. Alumnus, U. Mo., 1980. Mem. Jr. Bar Assn. (pres. 1957), Am. Bar Assn., Bar Assn. Hawaii, Fed. Bar Assn. Hawaii (pres. 1963). Office: Supreme Ct 417 S King St Honolulu HI 96813

LUM, JEAN LOUI JIN, nurse educator; b. Honolulu, Sept. 5, 1938; d. Yee Nung and Pui K. (Young) L. B.S., U. Hawaii-Manoa, 1960; M.S. in Nursing, U. Calif.-San Francisco, 1961; M.A., U. Wash., 1969, Ph.D. in Sociology, 1972. Registered nurse, Hawaii. From instr. to prof. Sch. Nursing, U. Hawaii, Manoa, Honolulu, 1961—, acting dean, 1982, dean, 1982—; project coordinator Analysis and Planning Personnel Services, Western Interstate Commission Higher Edn., 1977; extramural assoc. div. Research grants NIH, 1978-79. Mem. mgmt. adv. com. Honolulu County Hosp., 1982-85; mem. exec. bd. Pacific Health Research Inst., 1980-85; mem. health planning com. East Honolulu, 1978-81. Recipient nurse of yr. award Hawaii Nurse's Assn., 1982; USPHS grantee, 1967-72. Mem. Am. Nurses Assn., Council Nurse Researchers, Nat. League for Nursing, Western Council Higher Edn. for Nurses, Western Soc. for Researchers in Nursing, Am. Sociol. Assn., Pacific Sociol. Assn., Assn. for Women in Sci., Hawaii Pub. Health Assn., Phi Kappa Phi, Sigma Theta Tau, Alpha Kappa Delta, Mortar Bd., Delta Kappa Gamma. Episcopalian. Contbr. papers to profl. jours. Office: Sch Nursing U Hawaii at Manoa Webster 416 2528 The Mall Honolulu HI 96822

LUMBY, MALCOLM EUGENE, JR., public relations executive, educator; b. Rome, N.Y., June 2, 1938; s. Malcolm Eugene and Henrietta (Zcah) L. A.A., Pasadena City Coll., 1970; B.A., Calif. State U.-Los Angeles, 1971; M.S., So. Ill. U., 1972, Ph.D., 1974, postgrad. UCLA, 1979. Minister, Internat. Assn. Bible Students, Ghana, also Calif., La., N.C., N.Y., 1957-68; student instr. Sch. Journalism, So. Ill. U., Carbondale, 1972-74; pubis. coordinator, speech trainer Automobile Club So. Calif., Los Angeles, 1975-79; v.p. pub. relations First Interstate Bancorp, Los Angeles, 1979—; pub. relations instr. UCLA, 1978-79; instr. Grad. Sch. Bus. and Fin., Golden Gate U., Los Angeles, 1981—. Bd. dirs. Pasadena (Calif.) Heritage, 1982—. Mem. Assn. for Edn. Journalism, Internat. Assn. Bus. Communicators (golden quill award 1982), Pub. Relations Soc. Am. (prism award 1981), Soc. Profl. Journalists, Town Hall of Calif., Sigma Delta Chi. Republican. Club: Toastmasters (Century City pres. 1979, gov. Los Angeles area 1980). Contbr. articles to profl. jours. Office: First Interstate Bancorp 707 Wilshire Blvd Los Angeles CA 90017

LUNA, DENNIS R., lawyer; b. Los Angeles, Aug. 21, 1946; B.S. in Petroleum Engring., U. So. Calif., 1968, M.S. in Petroleum Engring., 1969, M.B.A., 1971; J.D., Harvard U., 1974. Admitted to Calif. bar, 1974; asso. firm McCutchen, Black, Verleger & Shea, Los Angeles, 1974-81, partner, 1981—. Registered profl. petroleum engr., Calif. Mem. Soc. Petroleum Engrs., Am. Bar Assn., State Bar of Calif. Office: 600 Wilshire Blvd Los Angeles CA 90017

LUNA, MICHELE ANNE, nurse; b. N.Y.C., Jan. 18, 1941; d. Charles and Anna Mae (Holtje) Barnett; student Citrus Jr. Coll., 1968-69, Los Angeles Trade Tech. Coll., 1971-72; A.A. in Nursing, UCLA, 1974, pediatric nurse practitioner, 1974; B.A., U. Redlands, 1976; M.B.A. in Health Care Adminstrn., bus. Golden Gate U., 1981; m. John Luna, Jr., Sept. 3, 1966; children—Michael, Stephanie, Andrea. Nurse, Glendora Community Hosp., 1969-70; mobile intensive care nurse St. Jude Hosp., Fullerton, 1972-75; nurse practitioner, project head start Charles R. Drew Postgrad Sch. Medicine, Compton, Calif., 1974-75; dir. nurses Santa Teresita Hosp., Duarte, Calif., 1975-76; dir. edn. Fountain Valley Community Hosp., Fullerton, Calif., 1976-77, dir. nurses, 1977-80; dir. med.-surg. nursing Anaheim (Calif.) Meml. Hosp., 1980-81, exec. dir. quality hosp. staffing, 1981—; instr. mgmt. devel.; lectr. Nat. U., Irvine, Calif.; lectr. stress mgmt., women in bus., other topics. Fellow Nat. Assn. Pediatric Nurse Assos.; mem. Calif., Am. nurses assns., Nurses Council Orange County (dir.), Nat. Assn. Pediatric Nurse Assos. and Practitioners, Am. Hosp. Health Edn. and Tng. Soc., Am. Soc. Law and Medicine, Nat. League Nurses, Orange County Long Beach Edn. Consortium. Club: Am. Nurses Found. Century. Home: 916 Miramar Laguna Beach CA 92651

LUND, DALE A., sociology educator, researcher; b. Salt Lake City, Apr. 18, 1951; Elden A. and Pearl A. Lund; m. Patty Rawlings, June 26, 1975; children—Matthew, Angela. B.S. in Psychology, U. Utah, 1973, M.S. in Sociology, 1976, Ph.D. in Med. Sociology, 1979. Instr. dept. sociology N.D. State U., 1975-76; teaching fellow, assoc. instr. dept. sociology U. Utah, 1976-79; asst. prof. dept. sociology Valdosta State Coll., 1979-80; vis. asst. prof. dept. family and consumer studies U. Utah, 1980-81; project dir., research asst. prof., assoc. dir. Research Gerontology Ctr., Coll. Nursing U. Utah; cons., workshop leader in field. Mem. target 5 com. Utah div., Am. Cancer Soc., 1978-79; chmn. target 5 task force Valdosta, Ga. div., Am. Cancer Soc., 1979-80; chmn. smoking cessation and health promotion com., Utah div. Am. Cancer Soc., 1980—, mem. exec. com., bd. dirs., 1980—; campaign worker Utah Democratic Party. Recipient Outstanding Tchr. award Dept. Sociology, U. Utah, 1978, 79. Mem. Gerontol. Soc. Am., Am. Sociol. Assn., Pacific Sociol. Assn., Am. Arthritis Found. (allied health professions sect.). Author: Human Development, 1981; contbr. articles, reports on health issues to profl. jours., profl. meetings. Home: 2776 S 2475 E Salt Lake City UT 84109 Office: Coll Nursing U Utah Salt Lake City UT 84112

LUND, ROBERT KIRSTINE, architect; b. Mpls., Oct. 14, 1920; s. Einar A. and Kirstine J. (Christenson) L.; m. Carol Joy Bruggeman, Aug. 30, 1953; children—Robert C., Josh C. B. Arch., Mont. State U., Bozeman, 1950. Registered architect, Mont., Wyo. Chief estimator Carson Constrn. Co., Helena, Mont., 1950-53, supt. constrn., McGrath, Alaska, 1952; ptnr. Hoiland & Lund Architects, Great Falls, Mont., 1953-63; architect R.K. Lund, Great Falls, 1964-67; ptnr. Amundson Beer Lund & Ptnrs., Architects-Engrs.-Planners, Great Falls, 1967-77; ptnr. Amundson Lund & Ptnrs., Architects, Great Falls, 1978—. Mem. council Boy Scouts Am., 1954-67; chmn. City-County Beautification Com., Great Falls, 1964-70; v.p. Forward Great Falls program, 1971-75; pres. S.W. Home Owners, 1954-74; bd. dirs. Salvation Army. Served to capt. USAF, 1943-46. Decorated Bronze Star (2). Mem. AIA (spl. design award Mont. chpt. 1969), Great Falls Soc. Architects (pres. 1962), Mont. Tech. Council (pres. 1971-73). Republican. Episcopalian. Clubs: Lions, Elks. Home: 1724 Alder Dr Great Falls MT 59404

LUND, STEVE, agronomist, research administrator; b. Exeland, Wis., Dec. 3, 1923; s. Robert Henry and Annie Belle (McHenry) L.; m. Gracemary Henrietta Bernskoetter, Jan. 29, 1946; children—Steve, John R., Thomas A., Cynthia M., Lisa A. B.S., Clemson Coll.; M.S., U. Wis.-Madison, 1951, Ph.D., 1953. Extension agronomist Clemson Coll., 1953-54; asst. research specialist Rutgers U., New Brunswick, N.J., 1954-57, assoc. research specialist, 1957-62, research prof., 1962-75, chmn. dept. soils and crops, 1971-75; supt. and prof. Oreg. State U., Columbia Basin Agrl. Research Ctr., Pendleton, 1975—. Served to 1st sgt. U.S. Army, 1943-46. Mem. Crop Sci. Soc. Am., Am. Soc. Agronomy, Western Soc. Crop Sci., Sigma Xi, Alpha Zeta, Phi Kappa Phi, Phi Eta Sigma. Club: Rotary. Office: Columbia Basin Agrl Research Ctr PO Box 370 Pendleton OR 97801

LUNDBERG, BERNARD JOHN, industrial arts educator; b. Milbank, S.D., Mar. 5, 1938; s. Elvie Emanuel and Mary Josephine (Gruzka) L.; m. Sally Ann Hope, Dec. 27, 1960; m. 2d, Donna Jean Gibson, June 10, 1975; children—Cindy, Glenda. B.S., Gen. Beadle State Tchrs. Coll., 1960; M.Ed., Oreg. State U., 1964. Lic. gen. contractor, Oreg. Machine operator, spiker Great Northern R.R., 1954-56; tchr., coach Colman High Sch., Colman, S.D., 1961, Bonanza (Oreg.) High Sch., 1961-70; tchr. Lost River High Sch., Merrill, Oreg., 1970-76; indsl. arts tchr. Brixner Jr. High Sch., Klamath Falls, Oreg., 1976—; cons. small schs.

program indsl. arts and small schs. devel. assistance team. Mem. U.S. Senatorial Club, Klamath Falls, 1983. Mem. NEA, Oreg. Edn. Assn., Am. Vocat. Assn., Am. Indsl. Arts Assn., Oreg. Vocat. Assn., Oreg. Indsl. Arts Assn. (named Indsl. Arts Tchr. of Yr. 1970), ARRL (life, lic.), Klamath Basin Amateur Radio Orgn., Epsilon Pi Tau. Republican. Lutheran. Clubs: Elks (Madison, S.D. and Klamath Falls). Home: 515 Delta St Klamath Falls OR 97601

LUNDBERG, CRAIG CARL, management and organization educator; b. Seattle, Sept. 7, 1932; s. Carl A. and Estelle R. (Booth) L.; m. V. Signe Erickson; children—Kim Lundberg-Bruner, Erica; m. 2d, Jenna K. Sockel. B.B.A., U. Wash., 1954; M.B.A., 1957; Ph.D., Cornell U., 1966. Asst. prof. Wharton Sch., U. Pa., Phila., 1966-69; dir. research, chmn. sch. bus. So. Meth. U., Dallas, 1969-73; prof., chmn. sch. bus. Oreg. State U., Corvallis, 1973-79; dean sch. mgmt. SUNY-Binghamton, 1979-82; prof., chmn. dept. mgmt. and orgn. Sch. Bus. Adminstrn., U. So. Calif., 1982—; cons. in field. Recipient Marshall Dimock award Am. Soc. Pub. Adminstrn., 1975; Best Paper award Eastern Acad. Mgmt., 1981; Ford Found. fellow, 1959-60. Fellow Acad. Mgmt.; mem. Am. Sociol. Assn., Soc. Applied Anthropology, Organizational Behavior Teaching Soc., Phi Kappa Phi. Editor: Exchange, 1983; contbr. articles to profl. jours. Home: 3568 Mountain View Pasadena CA 91107 Office: Sch of Bus U So Calif Los Angeles CA 90080

LUNDBERG, DAVID ALAN, electronics manufacturing executive; b. Two Harbors, Minn., Apr. 5, 1947; s. Darrell Jay and Catherine Anne (Johnson) L.; divorced, 1 son David Darrell. A.A., San Diego Mesa Coll., 1973; postgrad. U. Calif.-Santa Barbara, 1973-74; B.B.A., Nat. U., San Diego, 1978. Test technician Elgar Corp., San Diego, 1974-76; quality control supr. Action Instruments Co., Inc., San Diego, 1976-77, night supr. 1977-78, prodn. control mgr., 1978-81, new products mgr., 1981—. Served with USAF, 1966-70. Mem. Am. Prodn. and Inventory Control Soc., Over-the-line Players Assn. Democrat. Roman Catholic. Home: 3140 Clairemont Dr San Diego CA 92117 Office: 8601 Aero Dr San Diego CA 92123

LUNDBERG, MERLE FRANKLIN, city ofcl.; b. Cedar Rapids, Iowa, May 23, 1926; s. Carl Oscar and Addie Lena (Reed) L.; B.S., U. Calif., Berkeley, 1950, M.B.A., 1956; m. Patricia Leslie, July 12, 1953; children—Michael Allen, Jeffrey Brian, James Robert, John Eric. Auditor, Haskins & Sells, C.P.A.'s, Los Angeles, 1952-57; asst. controller Earle C. Anthony, Inc., Los Angeles, 1957-60; sec.-treas. So. Calif. Water Co., Los Angeles, 1960-70; acctg. cons., Los Angeles, 1971-72; controller City of Beverly Hills (Calif.), 1972-75; dir. fin. Irvine (Calif.) Ranch Water Dist., 1975-77; dir. fin. City of Manhattan Beach (Calif.), 1977—. Troop treas. Boy Scouts Am., 1964-66, troop com. chmn., 1966-68; tribe chief Indian Y Guides, 1973-74; bd. mgrs. Wayfarers Chapel Portuguese Bend, Calif., 1964—, chmn. bd., 1979—. Served with USNR, 1944-46. C.P.A., Calif. Mem. Am. Inst. C.P.A.'s, Calif. Soc. C.P.A.'s, Mcpl. Fin. Officers Am., Calif. Soc. Mcpl. Fin. Officers. Republican. Mem. New Jerusalem Ch. Am. and Can. Office: 1400 Highland Ave Manhattan Beach CA 90266

LUNDBLAD, GERALD THOMAS, management consultant, educator; b. San Jose, Calif., Oct. 8, 1945; s. Lauren Alfred and Doris Ruth (Perterson) L.; B.A. in Econs., U. Calif.-Berkeley, 1967. C.P.A., Calif. With audit dept. Touche Ross & Co., San Francisco, 1973-78, cons., 1981—; fin. officer Universal Chems. Inc., Sacramento, 1978-81; instr. sch. bus. Calif. State U., Sacramento, 1980—. Pres. bd. dirs. Martin Luther Towers, San Francisco, 1973-80; treas., bd. dirs. Hayward (Calif.) Vesper Hosp., 1979—. Mem. Am. Inst. C.P.A.s, Calif. Soc. C.P.A.s. Republican. Lutheran. Club: Sutter (Sacramento). Home: PO Box 15757 Sacramento CA 95852 Office: Touche Ross & Co PO Box 25-4747 Sacramento CA 95825

LUNDELL, JOHN HARRY, aerospace engineer; b. Chgo., Oct. 13, 1927; s. Harry Paul and Elsie O. (Sundell) L.; m. Alleta Coralyn Davis, Aug. 21, 1953; children—Karen, John, Keith. B.S.M.E. (Pure Oil fellow), Northwestern U., Evanston, Ill., 1951; Engr. (grad. fellow), Stanford U., 1955. Research engr. NACA, 1955-58; research scientist NASA, Moffett Field, Calif., 1958-81, asst. chief thermo and gas dynamics div., 1982—. Elder Presbyterian Ch.; mem. No. Calif. dist. Fed. Grand Jury; mem. pub. service com. Santa Clara County Med. Soc.; pres. Pajaro Dunes Assn. Served as cpl. AUS, 1946-47, Mem. AIAA, Sigma Xi. Contbr. articles to profl. jours. Home: 18951 Ansley Pl Saratoga CA 95070 Office: NASA Ames Research Ctr Moffett Field CA 94035

LUNDFELT, CHARLES EDWARD, fire chief, educator; b. N.Y.C., Mar. 7, 1944; s. Charles Edward and Marie Clotilde (Reilly) L.; m. Abigail Jane Cheney, Aug. 21, 1966 (div. 1973); 1 child, Christian August; m. 2d, Cathi Laird Carr, Mar. 9, 1973. Student, U. Alaska, 1965, Tanana Valley Community Coll., 1979—. Cert. paramedic Los Angeles County; cert. fire fighter program instr., Alaska. Owner, supt. Dunrite Constrn. Systems, Fairbanks, Alaska, 1974-80; fireman, paramedic Clear AFS Fire Dept., Anderson, Alaska, 1980-81; fire chief Chena Goldstream Fire Dept., Fairbanks, 1978-81; fire chief North Star Vol. Fire Dept., Fairbanks, 1981—; fire service instr. State of Alaska Dept. Edn., Fairbanks, 1981—. Pres., Greater Fairbanks Headstart Assn., 1974-75. Served to sgt. U.S. Army, 1966-69, Vietnam. Mem. Alaska Fire Chiefs' Assn. (sec.), Internat. Assn. Five Service Instrs., Tanana Valley Community Coll. Fire Sci. Adv. Bd. Democrat. Quaker. Author: (procedure manual) North Star Volunteer Fire Department, 1983. Home: PO Box 81349 College AK 99708 Office: North Star Vol Fire Dept SR 70116 Fairbanks AK 99701

LUNDGREN, TERRY DENNIS, sociologist; b. Chgo., Mar. 3, 1941; s. George and Elsie Elizabeth L.; m. Carol Ann Schulz, Nov. 27, 1963. B.S., Ill. State U., 1964; M.A., Ohio State U., 1966, Ph.D., 1976. Instr. sociology Central Mich. U., Mt. Pleasant, 1968-70; asst. profl. sociology Eastern N.Mex. U., Portales, 1976-77, assoc. sociology, 1977-80, chmn. dept. behavorial and social scis., 1978-80; systems analyst Anchor Nat. Life Ins., Phoenix, 1980—. Mem. Am. Sociol. Assn., Am. Statis. Assn., Southwestern Sociol. Assn. Republican. Contbr. articles and photography to popular mags. and profl. jours. Office: Anchor Nat Life Ins Co Camelback at 22d St Phoenix AZ 85016

LUNDQUIST, VIOLET ELVIRA, developmental disabilities consultant; b. Bristol, Conn., Jan. 28, 1912; d. Otto Nimrod and Mabel Elvira (Lindeen) Ebb; diploma music Augustana Coll., Rock Island, Ill., 1932; postgrad. mgmt. systems U. Mo., 1969; m. Vernon Arthur Lundquist, May 14, 1935; children—Karen Ebb, Jane Christine. Tchr. music, public schs., Olds, Iowa, 1932-35; editor Warsaw (Mo.) Times, 1935-45, Anthon (Iowa) Herald, 1945-57; field dir. Iowa Heart Assn., Des Moines, 1957-66; exec. dir. S.E. Iowa Community Action Program, Burlington, 1966-74; adminstrn. dir. S.E. Ariz. Govts. Orgn. Community Services, Bisbee, Ariz., 1975-77; statewide advocate developmentally disabled adults, 1977-80; adminstr. Arizona City Med. Center, part time, 1979-80; now cons. Bd. dirs. Central Ariz. Health Systems Agy., 1979—; chmn. Arizona City Home and Property Owners Assn., 1979-80; Cons. Dist. V, Ariz. Developmental Disabilities Council, 1981—; mem. Ariz. Dist. V Human and Legal Rights Com. Recipient Carol Lane award Nat. Safety Council, 1956; USPHS scholar, Columbia U., summers 1963, 64; cert. vocat. rehab. adminstr. Mem. Nat. Soc. Community Action Program Dirs. (dir. 1966-74), Iowa Fedn. Press Women, Nat. Rehab. Assn. Lutheran. Clubs: Zonta (pres. chpt. 1982-83, dir. Ariz., Utah, Nev. area 1984—), Women of Moose. Recipient 1st place awards Nat. Fedn. Press Women, 1952, 53, 55, 57. Home and Office: 609 W Cochise St Arizona City AZ 85223

LUNDSTEN, JOHN MERTON, real estate executive, bank officer; b. Rockford, Ill., July 17, 1940; s. Merton Robert and Beatrice Pearl Bergholt. B.S. in Zoology and Music, U. Ill., 1963, M.S. in Edn., 1967. Lic. gen. contractor, 1980, real estate salesperson, 1980. Bldg. mgr. Tishman Realty, N.Y.C., 1965-69; project mgr. Ogden Devel. Corp., N.Y.C., 1969-73; v.p., gen. mgr. Fredrick G. Krapf, Inc., Wilmington, Del., 1974-76; v.p., Thomas L. Karsten Assocs., Los Angeles, 1976-82, exec. v.p., 1982—. Mem. Pension Real Estate Assn. (dir. 1983—), Phi Kappa Phi, Omicron Delta Kappa. Contbr. articles to profl. jours. Office: 10960 Wilshire Blvd Suite 2224 Los Angeles CA 90024

LUNDY, MURIEL LEE, educational administrator; b. Wheeling, W.Va., May 1, 1937; d. Mae H.L. B.S. in Edn., Kent State U., 1959; M.Ed., Boston U., 1968; Ed.D., U. N.C., 1978. Cert. prin., supt., Ariz. Tchr., Rocky River, Ohio, 1959-61, Dept. Def., Europe, 1961-64; tchr. coordinator, Newton, Mass., 1964-68; prin., 1968-72; edni. specialist Ednl. Services Inst., Inc., Cin., 1972-73; staff devel. specialist, Winston-Salem, N.C., 1973-75; instr. Jefferson Coll., Greensboro, N.C., 1976; cons. The Ednl. Ctr., Greensboro, 1976-78; assoc. supt. curriculum and instrn. Franklin County Dept. Edn., Columbus, Ohio, 1978-81; asst. supt. curriculum and instrn. S. Washington County Schs., Cottage Grove, Minn., 1981-82; curriculum specialist lang. arts, Phoenix, 1982—. Mem. Assn. Supervision and Curriculum Devel., Internat. Reading Assn., Ariz. Assn. Sch. Adminstrs., Ariz. Assn. Supervision and Curriculum Devel. Contbr. articles to profl. jours. Office: 8610 N 19th Ave Phoenix AZ 85021

LUNGREN, DANIEL EDWARD, congressman; b. Long Beach, Calif., Sept. 22, 1946; s. John Charles and Lorain Kathleen (Youngberg) L.; m. Barbara Kolls, Aug. 2, 1969; children—Jeffrey Edward, Kelly Christine, Kathleen Marie. A.B. cum laude, Notre Dame U., 1968; postgrad. U. So. Calif. Law Sch., 1968-69; J.D., Georgetown U., 1971. Bar: Calif. 1972; Staff asst. Sen George Murphy, Sen. William Brock, 1969-71; spl. asst. to co-chmn. Republican Nat. Com., dir. spl. programs Rep. Nat. Com., 1971-72; assoc. Ball, Hunt, Hart, Brown & Baerwitz, Long Beach, 1973-78, ptnr., 1978; mem. 96th and 97th Congresses from 34th Calif. Dist., 98th Congress from 42d Calif. Dist. Mem. Rep. State Central Com. Calif., 1974—; co-chmn. Nat. Congressional Council, 1977-78; bd. dirs. Long Beach chpt. ARC, Boy's Club. Recipient Good Samaritan award Los Angeles Council Mormon Chs., 1976; named one of Calif.'s 5 Outstanding Young Men, Calif. Jaycees, 1981. Mem. ABA, Los Angeles County Bar Assn., Long Beach County Bar Assn. Republican. Roman Catholic. Office: 555 E Ocean Blvd Long Beach CA 90802 also 328 Cannon House Office Bldg Washington DC 20515

LUNT, OWEN RAYNAL, biologist, educator; b. El Paso, Tex., Apr. 8, 1921; s. Owen and Velma Adel (Jackson) L.; m. Helen Hickman, Aug. 8, 1953; children—David Payne, Carol, Janet Lunt Tanner. B.A., Brigham Young U., 1947; Ph.D., N.C. State U., Raleigh, 1951. Cert. profl. agronomist/soil scientist. Agronomist Am. Smelting and Refining Co., El Paso, Tex., 1947; lectr. N.C. State U., Raleigh, 1950; asst. prof. UCLA, 1951-57, assoc. prof., 1957-63, prof. biology, 1963—, acting dir. lab. biomed. and environ. scis., 1965-68, dir., 1968—; spl. cons. IAEA, Kenya, E. Africa, 1983; cons. in field. Served as electronic technician USN, 1944-56. Recipient Brigham Young U. Dist. Alumnus award, 1973. Fellow Am. Soc. Agronomy, Soil Sci. Soc. America, Am. Nuclear Soc., Sigma Xi. Republican. Mormon. Contbr. articles to profl. jours. Home: 1200 Roberto Ln Los Angeles CA 90077 Office: 900 Veteran Ave Los Angeles CA 90024

LUNZER, JEAN HUDSON, travel writer/editor; b. Seattle, Sept. 14, 1916; d. William Edward and Dora Orlette (Lobaugh) Hudson. B.A. in Journalism, U. Wash., 1938. Reporter, soc. editor, gen. assignment reporter/news Tacoma Times, 1938-47; women's news editor San Mateo (Calif.) Times, 1947-48; women's news reporter, home fashions editor, editor Weekender mag., Seattle, 1948-71; travel writer/editor Seattle Post-Intelligencer, 1971—. Bd. dirs. Steamer Va. V Found., Seattle, 1978-81. Recipient numerous awards Wash. Press Assn.; Service to Tourism award Korea Nat. Tourism Corp., 1981. Mem. Soc. Am. Travel Writers, Am. Newspaper Guild, Wash. Press Assn., Nat. Press Women, Sigma Delta Chi. Office: 521 Wall St Seattle WA 98102

LUPSHA, PETER ANTHONY, polit. scientist, educator; b. Hempstead, N.Y., Dec. 14, 1938; s. Frank X. and Sylvia K. (Bollinger) L.; B.A., Okla. State U., 1961; M.A., U. Calif., Berkeley, 1963; Ph.D. (NSF fellow), Stanford U., 1967; children—Audrey, Arthur, Maria Remedios. Asst. prof. Yale U., New Haven, Conn., 1967-72; assoc. prof. polit. sci. U. N.Mex., Albuquerque, 1972—, dir. div. govt. research, 1973-74, faculty adv. Jewish Student Union, 1976-77; cons. Mayor's Office, City of Boston, 1968, reorgn. of govt., Cambridge, Mass., 1969, reorgn. govt., Shelton, Conn., 1970; mem. Albuquerque Com. on Fgn. Relations, 1977—. Bd. dirs. N.Mex. Council on Crime and Delinquency, 1979—. Ford Found. grantee, 1970-71, U. N.Mex. Faculty research grantee, 1976-77. Mem. Am. Polit. Sci. Assn., Acad. of Criminal Justice Scis., Am. Soc. Public Adminstrn., Southwest Criminal Justice Educators, Internat. Network for Social Network Analysis, Latin Am. Studies Assn., Soc. for the Study of Anthropology and Law, Western Polit. Sci. Assn. (mem. exec. council 1979, pres. 1983-84), Latin Am. Studies Assn., Nat. Rifle Assn., N.Mex. Sport Shooting Assn. Contbr. articles on organized crime, polit. violence and urban politics to lit. and scholarly jours.; mem. editorial rev. bd. Jour. Police; contbr. poems to popular publs. Office: Dept Polit Sci Univ of New Mexico

LUSTECK, CLAUDIA ANN DUFEK, home economics educator; b. Phoenix, Sept. 2, 1948; d. John Allen and Teresa Magdolin (Lazok) Dufek; m. Ronald James Lusteck, Nov. 30, 1968; 1 son, Ryan Alexander. B.S., U. Ariz., 1971; M.Ed., 1974. Cert. home econs. tchr. Tchr. high schs. Tucson Unified Sch. Dist., 1971—; tchr. adult edn. program Pima (Ariz.) Community Coll., 1974-75; workshop facilitator; lectr. in field. Mem. Am. Home Econs. Assn., Ariz. Home Econs. Assn. (Tchr. of Yr. 1981), Am. Vocat. Assn. Ariz. State Vocat. Assn., Ariz. Assn. Vocat. Home Econs. Educators, Pi Lambda Theta. Author: Activity Guide for Good Food, 1982; Activity Guide for Housing Decisions, 1983. Office: Palo Verde High Sch 1302 S Avenida Vega Tucson AZ 85710

LUTER, JOHN, journalist, educator; b. Knoxville, Tenn., Jan. 17, 1919; s. John T. and Bertha M. (Carver) L.; B.A., St. Mary's U., 1939, postgrad. Coll. Law, 1939-42; postgrad. (Time Inc. fellow) Sch. Advanced Internat. Studies, 1945; m. Mary Jane Hickey, Sept. 10, 1948 (dec. 1966); 1 dau., Linda; m. 2d, Yvonne Spiegelberg, Oct. 1966 (div. 1971); m. 3d, Nan Hoyt Lawrence, July 19, 1974. Reporter, San Antonio Light, 1939-42, Washington (D.C.) Star, 1942-44; corr. Washington bur. Time Mag., 1944-45; war corr. in Pacific, Time and Life mags., 1945, fgn. corr., southeast Asia, 1945-46, Japan, 1946-47, Israel, 1948-49, Italy, 1949-54, asst. editor internat. edit. Life, 1954-56; TV reporter, writer CBS News, 1957-58; assoc. editor Newsweek mag., 1958-61; radio news commentator WQXR and QXR-FM network, 1960-61; coordinator Advanced Internat. Reporting Program, Columbia U. Grad. Sch. Journalism, N.Y.C., 1961-72; dir. Maria Moors Cabot program, 1961-74; mem. staff Bank St. Coll. Edn., N.Y.C., 1973-74; cons. Center for Inter Am. Relations, 1972-74; pres. Gamma Prodns., 1965-68; chmn. adv. screening com. on communications Sr. Fulbright Program, 1970-73; prof., chmn. journalism U. Hawaii, Honolulu, 1974—; mem. Honolulu Community Media Council, 1975—, vice chmn., 1978-81, chmn., 1982—. Chmn. internat. relations com. N.Y.C. Protestant Council, 1968-71; bd. dirs. UN Assn. of N.Y.C., 1973-74; trustee Overseas Press Club Found., 1962-72, chmn., 1964-65. Recipient Disting. Alumnus award St. Mary's U., 1962, Disting. Service award Overseas Press Club Am., 1965. Mem. Assn. Edn. Journalism, Am. Soc. Journalism Sch. Adminstrs., Am. Assn. Schs. and Depts. Journalism, Overseas Press Club Am. pres. 1960-62, (life bd. govs.), Soc. Profl. Journalist, Honolulu Com. on Fgn. Relations. Club: Outrigger Canoe (Honolulu). Home: 2442 Halekoa Dr Honolulu HI 96821 Office: 208 Crawford Hall U Hawaii Honolulu HI 96822

LUTHER, JOHN STAFFORD, biology educator, consultant; b. Los Angeles, April 5, 1943; s. John Andrew and Marcia (Stafford) L.; divorced; 1 son, David. B.A., Beloit (Wis.) Coll., 1965; M.A., Calif. State Coll.-Hayward, 1968. Mem. faculty dept. biology Merritt Coll., Oakland, Calif., 1968-70; mem. faculty Coll. of Alameda (Calif.), 1970—, chmn. sci. and math. div., 1973-75; cons. Environ. Impacts Reports, 1972—; leader natural history trips, 1978—. Mem. Oakland (Calif.) Mus. Assn., 1972—; mem. Ednl. Use Adv. Com., East Bay Regional Park Dist., 1981—. Mem. Western Field Ornithologists (pres. 1978-81, dir. 1975—), Calif. Bird Records Com. (sec. 1976-81), Sierra Club, Nat. Audubon Soc., Golden Gate Audubon Soc., Nature Conservancy, Cooper Ornithol. Soc., Point Reyes Bird Obs. Contbr. articles to Western Birds. Home: 6511 Exeter Dr Oakland CA 94611 Office: Coll of Alameda 555 Atlantic Ave Alameda CA 94501

LUTIN, DAVID LOUIS, real estate devel. and finance cons.; b. East Hartford, Conn., Apr. 18, 1919; s. Solomon and Esther (Newman) L.; A.B., Ohio No. U., 1946; M.B.A., Syracuse U., 1949; m. Dorothy Marmor, Dec. 3, 1944; children—Gary, Marnie (Mrs. George Wittig). Housing economist and field rep. HHFA, Washington, 1950-57; dir. urban renewal City of Brookline, Mass., 1957-58; cons. on urban renewal and housing Com. for Econ. Devel., N.Y.C., 1958-59; propr. David L. Lutin Assocs., real estate devel. and fin. cons., Rye, N.Y., 1959-73, 75—; v.p. real estate and mortgages Am. Bank and Trust Co., N.Y.C., 1973-75. Research assoc. Albert Farwell Bemis Found., M.I.T., 1951-52. Served to capt. AUS, 1942-46. Decorated Purple Heart. Mem. Am. Econ. Assn., Nat. Planning Assn., Mortgage Bankers Assn., Urban Land Inst., Am. Planning Assn., Am. Statis. Assn., Nat. Assn. Home Builders. Contbr. articles and reports on econs., housing and urban devel. to profl. jours. Home and office: 11419 N Century Ln Scottsdale AZ 85254

LUTSKY, SHELDON JAY, marketing consultant, writer; b. New Kensington, Pa., Jan. 13, 1943; s. Hyman I. and Rose S. (Schwartz) L.; B.S., Kent State U., 1967; postgrad. U. Colo., 1969-70. Chemist B.F. Goodrich, Akron, Ohio, 1966; with United Bank of Denver, 1968-75; founder Mountain States Ski Assn., pub. Mountain States Recreation, Denver, 1976-81; pres. Lutsky and Assocs., Denver, 1981—; instr. penny stocks Denver U. Recipient Burr Photog. Achievement award Kent State U., 1965. Mem. Denver C. of C., Denver Conv. Bur., Nat. Ski Writers Assn., Rocky Mountain Ski Writers Assn., Rocky Mountain Fin. Writers Assn. (pres. 1982—). Developer Slope Scope, ski slope evaluation system. Home: 4807 S Zang Way Morrison CO 80465 Office: Lutsky & Assocs 2124 S Dayton St Denver CO 80231

LUTVAK, MARK ALLEN, computer co. mktg. exec.; b. Chgo., Feb. 9, 1939; s. Joseph Issac and Jeanette Nettie (Pollock) L.; m. Gayle Helene Rotofsky, May 24, 1964; children—Jeffrey, Eric. B.S. in Elec. Engring., U. Mich., 1962; M.B.A., Wayne State U., Detroit, 1969. Sales rep. IBM Corp., 1962-64; successively sales rep., product mktg. mgr., corp. product mgr. Burroughs Corp., Detroit, 1964-76; mgr. product mktg. Memorex Corp., Santa Clara, Calif., 1976-80, product program gen. mgr., 1980-81; dir. product mktg. Personal Computer div. Atari, Inc., Sunnyvale, Calif., 1981—; prof. Applied Mgmt. Center, Wayne State U., 1967-72, Walsh U., Troy, Mich., 1974-76, West Valley Coll., Saratoga, Calif., 1977-78. Trustee, pres. brotherhood Temple Emanuel, San Jose, Calif., 1979-80. Mem. IEEE, Soc. Applied Math., Alpha Epsilon Pi (life). Home: 1311 Peralta Ct San Jose CA 95120 Office: Atari Inc PO Box 50047 San Jose CA 95150

LUTZ, DAVID JOHN, psychologist; b. Denver, Sept. 20, 1953; s. Joseph Herbert and Eleanor Josephine L.; m. Ellen Scott McLean, Aug. 8, 1978. B.A., U. Kans., Lawrence, 1975, M.A., 1978, Ph.D., 1980. Asst. prof. psychology Calif. State Coll.-San Bernardino, 1980—; cons. in field. Mem. Am. Psychol. Assn., Western Psychol. Assn., Assn. Advancement Psychology. Republican. Home: 1165 E Alexander Ave San Bernardino CA 92404 Office: Dept Psychology Calif State Coll San Bernardino CA 92407

LUTZ, LOUISE MARIE, transportation company executive; b. Chgo., Aug. 17, 1949; d. Louis S. and Susan (Perksta) Mattis; m. John F. Lutz, Jr.; 1 dau., Nicole Eileen. B.A., Calif. State U., 1971, postgrad. 1971-73. With Ampex Corp., Redwood City, Calif., 1971-73, Consol. Freightways, San Francisco, 1973-74, Allied Van Lines, San Francisco, 1974-75; with United Parcel Service, San Francisco, 1975—, personnel supr., Oakland, 1976-78, safety mgr., 1979, employment mgr., 1980—; exec. on loan New Oakland Com., 1981. Recipient Cert. of Achievement, Human Devel. Seminars, Inc., 1981. Mem. Nat. Assn. Female Execs., Assn. Personnel Profls. Oakland, Calif. Unemployment Ins. Council. Home: 968 Pizarro Ln Foster City CA 94404 Office: 8400 Pardee Dr Oakland CA 94621

LYALL, JOHN FRANCIS, personnel dir.; b. Hunnington Park, Calif., July 9, 1940; s. Glen and Shirley May (Henderson) G.; B.A. in Social Scis., U. Calif., Humboldt, 1963; M.A. in Am. Lit., Calif. Western U., San Diego, 1966; 1 son, Jeffrey Jason IV. Tchr., San Diego Unified Sch. Dist., 1966-71; cons. various sch. dists., 1971-73; personnel dir. gen. services dept. City of Seattle, 1973-79; personnel dir. Seattle Public Library, 1979—; instr. personnel mgmt. City Coll. Seattle, 1975-80. Bd. dirs. San Diego Urban League, Rainier Vista Health Clinic, 1978-80, Neighborhood Health Center, 1980—. Served with Army N.G., 1964-71. Mem. Am. Soc. Personnel Adminstrn., Am. Mgmt. Assn., Seattle Mgmt. Assn., Wash. Library Assn. Republican. Home: 2816 31st Ave S Seattle WA 98144 Office: 1000 Fourth Ave Seattle WA 98104

LYBARGER, SAMUEL ALBERT, safety engineer; b. Albuquerque, June 30, 1948; B.S., U. 1970; postgrad N.Mex. Highlands U., 1970, U. Houston, 1979-80; M.E., U. Nev., Las Vegas, 1980—; m. Judith Kay Johnson, July 14, 1973. Tchr., coach Morairty (N.Mex.) Mcpl. Schs., 1972-73; dir. safety programs ARC, Albuquerque and Metairie, La., 1973-75; safety insp. Zapata Offshore, Houston, 1975-76; safety rep. Mundy Service Co., Houston, 1976-80; sr. safety engr. Reynolds Elec. & Enging. Co., Las Vegas, 1980—; instr. Clark County Community Coll.; safety cons. So. Calif. div. ARC. Instr. trainer 1st aid, CPR, Water safety, lifeguard tng. ARC. Mem. Am. Soc. Safety Engrs. (div. liaison constrn.), Am. Soc. Tng. and Devel., Internat. Rescue and 1st Aid Assn., Commodore Longfellow Soc. Home: 1101 Woodbridge Dr Las Vegas NV 89108 Office: PO Box 14400 Las Vegas NV 89114

LYDDON, CAROLEE MAE, rehabilitation center administrator; b. Linneus, Mo., Mar. 31, 1935; d. Charles R.M. and Cecile Blanche (Cordray) Buswell; m. Dale Harry Lyddon, Oct. 26, 1951; children—Deborah Vaday, Phillip, Stephen, Kevin. Cert. specializing tng. of severely retarded; cert. Quality Assurance Inst., Nebr. Plan for Client Evaluation. Owner, mgr. comml. orchard, Parkdale, Oreg., 1966-72;

with Columbia Gorge Rehab. Ctr., Hood River, Oreg., 1973—, mgr. benchwork dept., 1978-81, gen. mgr. Hood River br., 1981-82, exec. dir., 1983—; mem. Spl. Olympics Com., 1983—. Mem. Republican Precinct Com., 1972-73; bd. dirs. Parkdale Community Ctr., 1971-75. Mem. Am. Assn. Nurserymen, Nat. Hort. Therapy Assn., N.W. Assn. Rehab. Industries, Nat. Assn. Rehab. Facilities, Oreg. Assn. Nurserymen. Baptist. Home: 945 Pear Blossom Rd Hood River OR 97031 Office: 2940 Thomsen Rd Hood River OR 97031

LYDICK, LAWRENCE TUPPER, judge; b. San Diego, June 22, 1916; s. Roy Telling and Geneva (Lydick) L.; A.B., Stanford, 1938, LL.B. (Crothers law scholar), 1942; postgrad. (Sigma Nu exchange scholar), U. Freiburg, Germany, 1938-39, Harvard, 1943, Mass. Inst. Tech., 1943-44; m. Gretta Grant, Aug. 7, 1938; children—Gretta Grant, Lawrence Tupper; m. 2d, Martha Martinez, Oct., 1969; 1 son, Chip. Admitted to Calif. bar, 1946, since practiced in Los Angeles; dir. disputes div., 10th region Nat. War Labor Bd., San Francisco, 1942-43; asst. to pres., gen. counsel U.S. Grant Export-Import, Ltd., Los Angeles, 1946-48; asso. Adams, Duque & Hazeltine, Los Angeles, 1948-53, partner, 1953-71; U.S. dist. ct. judge Central Dist. Calif., 1971—. Served from ensign to lt. USNR, 1943-46. Mem. Am., Calif., Los Angeles bar assns., Sigma Nu. Republican. Conglist. Clubs: Commonwealth (San Francisco). Home: 549 Camino Verde South Pasadena CA 91030 Office: US Court House Los Angeles CA 90012

LYELL, EDWARD HARVEY, educator; b. San Francisco, Nov. 11, 1944; s. Aubrey Sheridan and Ila Mae (Franklin) L.; B.A., San Francisco State U., 1968, M.B.A., 1970; D. Bus. Adminstrn., U. Colo., 1977; 1 son, Kelly; m. Judith Belnap; stepchildren—Erin, Heather Creagh. Asst. dean research San Francisco State U., 1968-70, part-time faculty mem., 1969-70; part-time faculty mem. U. Colo., 1970-76, 78, Community Coll., Denver, 1973-74, Met. State U., 1977; dir. policy analysis Colo. Commn. on Higher Edn., 1973-76; asst. prof. Grad. Sch. Public Affairs, asso. dir. info. sci./genetic resources U. Colo., Boulder, 1978-79; asst. prof. bus. and econs. Colo. Coll., Colorado Springs, 1979-81; asso. prof. bus. Met. State Coll., Denver, 1981—; pres. Colo. Planning and Mgmt. Systems, Inc., Boulder. Scoutmaster Boy Scouts Am., 1977-83; del. Boulder County Democratic Conv., 1976, 78, 80, 82, Colo. Dem. Conv., 1976, 80, 82; mem. issues com. Colo. Dem. Com., 1981—; mem. Colo. Gov.'s Sci. and Tech. Adv. Council. Mem. AAAS, Am. Assn. Higher Edn., Am. Econ. Assn., Am. Ednl. Research Assn., Am. Mktg. Assn., World Future Soc. Quaker. Author: Eucation Evaluation and Assessment System for You, 1972; contbr. articles to profl. jours. Office: Mgmt Dept Bus Sch Met State Coll 1006 11th St Denver CO 80204

LYETH, MUNRO L(ONGYEAR), banker; b. N.Y.C., Oct. 28, 1915; s. J.M. Richardson and Judith (Longyear) L.; A.B., Harvard U., 1937, LL.B., 1940; m. Josephine Clifford Good, June 28, 1939, m. 2d, 1963 (dec. 1967); children—Munro L., Judith; m. Marian Neal Rubey, Feb. 17, 1968; stepchildren—William B. Rubey, Jr., Marian S. Mitchell, Robert N. Rubey, Christina C. Rubey. Asso. Spence, Windels, Walser, Hotchkiss & Angell, 1940-41; trust officer U.S. Nat. Bank of Denver, 1946-52; pres., dir. Cherry Creek Nat. Bank, 1952—, chmn. bd., 1961-74, hon. chmn. bd., 1974—; ltd. ptnr. Lyeth Winery and Vineyard, Geyserville, Calif.; dir. Cyclo Mfg. Co., Longyear Realty Corp. Bd. dirs. Central City Opera House Assn., Music Assos. of Aspen. Served as comdr. USNR, 1941-46. Fellow Aspen Inst. Humanistic Studies; mem. Newcomen Soc. N.Am. Clubs: Denver, Denver Country; Garden of the Gods (Colorado Springs, Colo.). Home: 556 S Elizabeth St Denver CO 80209 Office: PO Box 1560 Aspen CO 81612

LYKE, GERALD MARK, educational administrator; b. Seattle, Dec. 3, 1953; s. Gerald L. and Peggy B. (Rogers) L.; m. Joan Rheinhardt, Aug. 20, 1978. B.A., U. Wash.-Seattle, 1976; M.Ed., Seattle U., 1982. Cert. tchr., Alaska. Tchr. Chatham sch. dist. pub. schs., Angoon, Alaska, 1976-80; field services coordinator Tlingit and Haida Central Council, Juneau, Alaska, 1980—. NSF grantee, 1978. Mem. Assn. Supervision and Curriculum Devel., Seattle U. Alumni Assn., U. Wash. Alumni Assn. Lutheran. Home: 9696 Moraine Way Juneau AK 99801 Office: Tlingit and Haida Central Council One Sealaska Plaza Suite 200 Juneau AK 99801

LYKOSH, WALTER MICHAEL, business executive; b. Perth Amboy, N.J., Nov. 4, 1947; s. Stephen Joseph and Ann (Bucsok) L.; B.S., Monmouth Coll., 1970. Accountant, Peat Marwick, Mitchell & Co., Los Angeles, 1970-74; v.p. fin. Knightsbrigde Properties, Inc., Los Angeles, 1974-75, Concentric Internat. Assos., Inc., Los Angeles, 1976-78; bus. mgr. Asso. Bus. Mgmt., Ltd., Los Angeles, 1978—; dir. Concentric Internat. Assos., Inc., Cal Burgers, Inc., Leon Block Co. Ltd., Illingworth, Morris & Co. U.S.A., Ltd., Hunt & Winterbotham, Ltd., L & C Pub., Inc., Profl. Securities, Inc. C.P.A., Calif. Mem. Am. Inst. C.P.A.'s, Calif. Soc. C.P.A.'s, Internat. Council Shopping Centers, Nat. Assn. Securities Dealers. Republican. Roman Catholic. Clubs: Pips Internat., Century West. Home: 2559 Hutton Dr Beverly Hills CA 90210 Office: 1801 Century Park E Suite 1850 Los Angeles CA 90067

LYLE, DUNCAN CAMPBELL, insurance executive; b. Copperhill, Tenn., Jan. 6, 1929; s. Oscar Kenton and Nora Roxanna (Watson) L.; m. Glenna June Loomis, Mar. 28, 1953; children—Steven Kenton, Susan Gail, Leslie Ann. Student, U. Tenn., 1947-50; B.A. in Econs., Calif. State U., 1972; postgrad. U. So. Calif. Cert. safety profl. Commd. officer U.S. Air Force, 1951, advanced through grades to lt. col., 1971, ret., 1973; loss control supr. CG/Aetna Ins. Co., Sacramento, 1981—; tchr. safety classes Sacramento Safety Council. Decorated Bronze Star, Air Force Commendation medal. Mem. Am. Soc. Safety Engrs. (pres. 1979), Ret. Officers Assn. Republican. Baptist. Club: Toastmasters. Home: 6830 Silverthorne Circle Sacramento CA 95842 Office: 2255 Watt Ave Suite 280 Sacramento CA 95825

LYLE, JIMMIE GRANT, interior designer, educator; b. Dalhart, Tex., Nov. 17, 1931; s. Julius Fred and Audrey Theresa (Shaffer) L.; div.; children—Stewart, Gina, Dineh, Seth. B.A. in Philosophy, U. Wichita, 1954. Design dir. Robert Morry, Inc., 1957-58; free-lance designer, 1958-63; design dir. Contract div. Ebasco Industries, San Francisco, 1963-67, Belmuth Corp., Los Angeles, 1967, Sampson West Coast, Los Angeles, 1968, Tom MacDonald & Assocs., Vancouver, Wash., 1969-70; design dir., bus. mgr. John Masquelier & Assocs., San Francisco, 1970-71; ptnr. Pacific Design Group, Campbell, Calif., 1972—; instr. San Jose (Calif.) State U., 1979—. Mem. Campbell Bd. Permit Appeals. Served to capt. USAF and USAFR, 1955-65. Mem. Am. Soc. Interior Designers. Designs include hotels, restaurants, offices; designer stained glass windows, ceramics, ceramic murals, wood murals, tapestry; painter; represented in permanet collections: Fidelity Savs. & Loan Ski Resort, North Star, Calif.; Sarkiss K. Noravian & Assocs., Santa Clara, Calif., U. Wichita (Kans.), also pvt. collections. Home: 150 W Rincon A Campbell CA 95008 Office: 150 E Campbell Suite 203 Campbell CA 95008

LYLES, ELIZABETH VENEMANN, construction company executive, educator; b. Denver, Oct. 18, 1911; d. Henry Gerald and Elizabeth Frey (Doughty) Venemann; m. William Murray Lyles, Mar. 30, 1933 (dec. May 1965); children—William M., Mary Elizabeth, Gerald V. B.S., Purdue U., 1933, M.S., 1934. Lic. secondary tchr., Calif. Substitute tchr. High schs., Ind., Calif., 1933-45; gen. office work Macco-Robertson Co., Avenal, Calif., 1940-42; co-founder W.M. Lyles Co., Fresno, Calif., 1945, sec., treas., dir., 1945-65, pres., dir., 1965—; co-owner Lazy L Aberdeen Angus Ranch, Monterey County, Calif., 1954—. Triennial del. Episc. Churchwomen, Diocese San Joaquin, 1961, 64, pres., 1963-66; dep. gen. conv., 1973, 76, 79, 82; trustee Coalinga Coll., 1963-67; bd. dirs. Fresno-Madera chpt. ARC, 1975-78; bd. dirs., mem. adv. bd. Sequoia council Boy Scouts Am., 1978—; bd. govs. Purdue Found., 1981—. Fellow Rotary Internat., 1974; named One of Alpha Xi Delta's Women of Achievement in Bus., 1968; recipient Bishop's Cross, 1972, Alpha Xi Delta Alumna of Yr. award, 1979, Citizenship award Purdue U. Alumni Assn., 1980. Mem. AAUW (charter pres. Avenal br. 1946-67), Purdue U. Alumni Assn. (regional dir. 1971-75), Fresno C. of C. (dir. 1974-77, chmn. edn. com. 1977, 78), Daus. Am. Colonists, DAR, Gen. Soc. Mayflower Desc. Republican. Episcopalian. Clubs: Zonta (charter pres. Fresno 1971), Order Eastern Star. Home: 4672 N Wishon Ave Fresno CA 93704 Office: 1210 W Olive Ave Fresno CA 93728

LYMAN, JACK, energy company executive; b. Salt Lake City, July 20, 1949; s. John Reynolds and Helen Marie (Borden) L.; m. Susan Ramsey Bernick, Nov. 17, 1973; children—John Ramsey, Margaret Ellen. B.S. in Indsl. Engring., U. Utah, 1972, M.Engring. Adminstrn., 1977. Registered profl. engr., Utah. Sales engr. McNalley Pittsburg Mfg. Co., (Kans.), 1974; indsl. engr. Thiokol Corp., Brigham City, Utah, 1975-77; energy conservation specialist Utah Office Energy, Salt Lake City, 1977-79; dir., 1979-81; dep. dir. Utah Dept. Natural Resources, Salt Lake City, 1981-82; dir. external affairs White River Shale Oil Corp., Salt Lake City, 1982—; chmn. Western State Energy Bd., 1981-82; dir. Western Solar Utilization Network, 1979-82; v.p. Uintah Natural Resource Assn., 1982—; mem. Tri-State Consortium for Energy Related Tng., 1982—. Mem. civil engring. adv. bd. Utah State U., 1982—. Served with USAR, 1969-75. Mem. Am. Inst. Indsl. Engrs., Pub. Relations Soc. Am. Democrat. Office: 115 S Main St Suite 500 Salt Lake City UT 84111

LYMAN, JOHN (HENRY), engineering, applied science and psychology educator, consultant; b. Santa Barbara, Calif., May 29, 1921; s. Oren Lee and Clara Augusta (Young) L.; children—John Harnish, Wendy Elizabeth. B.A. in Math. and Psychology, UCLA, 1943, M.A., 1950, Ph.D. in Exptl. Psychology, 1951. Lic. psychologist, Calif. With Lockheed Aircraft Co., Burbank, Calif., 1940-44; chief human engring. sect. U.S. Army Q.M. Climatic Research Lab. (on leave from UCLA), 1952-53; prof. engring. and applied sci. UCLA, 1950—, prof. psychology, 1956—, chmn. engring. systems dept., 1977—, head biotech. lab., 1958—; cons. to govt. and industry; vis. prof. bioengring. Tech. Inst., Delft, Netherlands, 1965; spl. cons. Nat. Acad. Sci., 1973. VA, U.S. Army, USAF, USN, USPHS, NSF, NIH, NASA grantees, 1952—. Fellow Human Factors Soc., (pres. 1967-68), AAAS, Am. Psychol. Assn.; mem. Biomed. Engring. Soc. (pres. 1980-81), Am. Soc. Engring. Edn., IEEE, Systems, Man and Cybernetics Soc., Engring. in Medicine and Biology Soc., Sigma Xi, Tau Beta Pi. Mem. editorial bds. Jour. Cybernetics, Bull. Prosthetics Research; founding mng. editor Human Factors, 1958-63, Annals Biomed. Engring., 1971-76; contbr. sci. articles to profl. lit. Home: 3512 Beverly Ridge Dr Sherman Oaks CA 91423 Office: UCLA BH7619 Los Angeles CA 90024

LYMAN, ORLANDO HAMMOND, retired museum director; b. Hilo, Hawaii, Nov. 19, 1903; s. Levi Chamberlain and Nettie Eugenia (Hammond) L.; m. Helen Irene Maxson, June 12, 1936. Student U. Mass., 1925-26, Columbia U., 1926; B.S. in Sugar Tech., U. Hawaii, 1927. Mgr. Maui ops. Hawaiian Sugar Planters Expt. Sta., 1926-36, mgr. Hawaii ops., 1936-67; pres., dir. Lyman House Meml. Mus., Hilo, 1967-83; dir. Hawaii Electric Light Co.; v.p. Realty Investment Co., 1940-77. Pres. bd. trustees Hilo Boarding Sch., 1940-65; pres. Homelani Cemetery, 1938-80; exec. officer Office Food Prodn., Island of Hawaii, World War II. Mem. Hawaii Island C. of C. Republican. Congregationalist. Clubs: Hilo Yacht, Hilo Rotary (past pres.). Home: PO Box 514 Hilo HI 96720 Office: 276 Haili St HI 96720

LYNCH, CHARLES ALLEN, business executive; b. Denver, Sept. 7, 1927; s. Laurence J. and Louanna (Robertson) L.; m. Linda Bennet, June 14, 1952; children—Charles Allen Jr., Tara O'Hara, Casey Alexander. B.S. in Indsl. Adminstrn., Yale U., 1950. Dir. mktg. fabrics and finishes dept. E.I. duPont De Nemours, Wilmington, Del., 1950-69; v.p., group pres. mfg. SCOA Industries, Columbus, Ohio, 1969-72; exec. v.p., group exec. consumer services group W.R. Grace Co., N.Y.C., 1972-78; chmn. bd., chief exec. officer Saga Corp., Menlo Park, Calif., 1978—; dir. Indsl. Indemnity Co., John Blair & Co. Chmn. Calif. Roundtable; vice chmn. Bay Area Council; dir. Industry Edn. Council Calif.; bd. dirs. San Francisco YMCA, also mem. nat. bd. trustees; trustee Hill Sch.; mem. Conf. Bd.; mem. corp. Joslin Diabetes Ctr.; exec. bd. Youth Tennis Found. No. Calif. Served with USN, 1945. Republican. Roman Catholic. Clubs: Ponte Vedra Beach and Tennis (Fla.); Menlo Circus (Atherton); Coral Beach and Tennis (Bermuda); Menlo Country (Redwood City). Office: 1 Saga Ln Menlo Park CA 94025

LYNCH, CHARLES THOMAS, communications educator; b. Waterbury, Conn., Oct. 10, 1918; s. Charles Thomas and Sara (Carroll) L.; student U. Ala., 1935-37, Mich. State U., 1960; B.A., Western Mich. U., 1963, M.A., 1966; Ph.D., So. Ill. U., 1972; m. Helen Victoria Kaliss, Aug. 4, 1941; children—C. Thomas, III, Jean, Christopher. Announcer, producer, writer various radio stas., Conn., Fla., Pa., Mich., 1938-49; program dir., exec. producer Fetzer Broadcasting Co., Kalamazoo, 1949-67; asst. prof. radio-TV, sta. mgr. Sta. WSIU, So. Ill. U., 1967-74, assoc. prof., chmn. dept. radio-TV, 1974-79; gen. mgr. Sta. WSIU-TV, Carbondale, 1978-79, Sta. WUSI, Olney, Ill., 1978-79; prof., chmn. dept. radio-TV-film Calif. State U.-Northridge, 1979—; dir. broadcasting Sta. KCSN, Northridge, Calif., 1981—. Pres., Kalamazoo Area PTA Council, 1960-61, Kalamazoo Civic Players, 1962-64, Community Theatre Assn. Mich., 1963-65, Am. Cancer Soc., Kalamazoo, 1965-67. Recipient Broadcast Preceptor award Broadcast Industry Conf., 1976. Mem. Nat. Acad. TV Arts and Scis., Am. Film Inst., Broadcast Edn. Assn., Ill. News Broadcasters Assn., Hollywood Radio and TV Soc., Pacific Pioneer Broadcasters (dir. 1983—), Sigma Delta Chi, Alpha Epsilon Rho, Phi Kappa Phi. Author various documentaries, spl. broadcast programs; contbr. articles to profl. jours. Home: 9565 Reseda Blvd Apt 226 Northridge CA 91324 Office: Radio-TV-Film Dept Calif State U Northridge CA 91330

LYNCH, DELL MARIE RYAN (MRS. JAMES MERRIMAN LYNCH), civic worker, writer, artist; b. Scranton, Pa.; d. Cornelius James and Alice Wall (Burke) Ryan; B.A., Manhattanville Coll., 1922; m. James Merriman Lynch, Apr. 6, 1926 (dec. Feb. 1982); 1 son, Nathaniel Merriman. Exhibited in group shows Pala Art Show, Showcase of Arts, Bank Am. Exhibit, Fireside Restaurant Exhibit, Country Squire Exhibit; one-woman show Woman's Club, 1979; publicity chmn. Santa Barbara County Med. Aux., 1947-48; co-chmn. Garden sect. Palomar Meml. Hosp. Aux., 1958-61; bd. mem. Friends of Leonell Strong Cancer Found., 1969-70; v.p. Friends of Pala Indian Mission Sch., 1967-72, Friends of Escondido Library, 1972-73; chmn. Showcase of Arts Gallery, 1967-68; project chmn. Exceptional Girl Scouts U.S.A., 1957-58. Recipient award for over 20 yrs. vol. service Palomar Meml. Hosp., 1981; hon. mention state poetry award Women's Club, 1980. Mem. Felicita Found. (life), Escondido Hist. Soc. (life), Palomar Meml. Hosp. Aux. (life), Friends of Escondido Library (life), Chaparral Poets, AAUW (life; area rep. for cultural interests 1964-65, courtesy chmn. 1968-77, cultural interests chmn. 1977-78, creative writing chmn. 1978-81, cert. of appreciation 1977-78). Clubs: Woman's (chmn. creative writing 1977-81, creative writing chmn. 1977—, cert. of appreciation 1977-78, 1st place poetry, writing contest 1978, 1st, 2d, 3d places poetry, 1979, 3 1st place awards for poetry, 2d place for prose 1980, 1st place and 2d place for poetry 1981), Escondido Garden (therapy co-chmn.). Author: Bright Orbits (poetry), 1975. Home: 810 Omar Dr Escondido CA 92025

LYNCH, FRANK WILLIAM, aerospace executive; b. San Francisco, Nov. 26, 1921; s. James Garfield and Med (Kelly) L.; m. Marilyn Leona Hopwood, June 24, 1950; children—Kathryn Leona, Milly Louise. A.B., Stanford U., 1943. Research engr. Boeing Airplane Co., Seattle, 1948-50; mgr. engring. dept. Northrop Corp., Hawthorne, Calif., 1950-57; div. v.p. engring. Lear-Siegler Corp., Anaheim, Calif., 1957-59; v.p. engring. Nortronics div. Northrop Corp., Los Angeles, 1959-61, v.p., gen. mgr. Electronics Systems div., 1961-62, v.p., gen. mgr. Electro-Mech. div., 1962-74, sr. v.p. ops. corp. hdqrs., 1974-78, sr. v.p., group exec. Tactical and Electronic Systems Group, 1978-82, pres., chief operating officer, 1982—. Served to 1st lt. U.S. Army, 1942-46. Mem. IEEE, AIAA, Assn. U.S. Army, Am. Def. Preparedness Assn., Armed Forces Communications and Electronics Assn. Clubs: Regency (Los Angeles); Balboa Yacht (Newport Beach, Calif.). Office: Northrop Corp 1800 Century Park E Los Angeles CA 90067

LYNCH, GREGORY WILLIAM, wildlife biologist; b. Columbus, Ohio, Mar. 2, 1946; s. Merrill Woodrow and Helen Louise (Haywood) L.; B.S., U. Idaho, 1974; M.S., Tex. A&M U., 1977; m. Pamela Hartley, Apr. 1, 1967. Caesar Kleberg research asst. Tex. A&M U., College Station, 1974-77; biologist wildlife research, U.S. Fish and Wildlife Service, Twin Falls, Idaho, 1977-80; biologist U.S. Forest Service, Afton, Wyo., 1980—. Served with USAF, 1966-70. Mem. Sigma Xi, Phi Sigma, Xi Sigma Pi. Methodist. Club: United Meth. Men. Contbr. writings to profl. publs. in field, poetry to mag. Home: PO Box 954 Afton WY 83110 Office: PO Box 338 Afton WY 83110

LYNCH, JAMES EDWARD, association executive; b. Butte, Mont.; s. Earl Joseph and Marie Elizabeth (Garrels) L.; A.B., Carroll Coll., 1961; postgrad. Calif. State U., 1976, Santa Clara U., 1975, Mills Coll., 1977; m. Cathy Coupe, Jan. 1, 1963; children—Mike, Colleen, Doug. Asst. mgr. Butte (Mont.) C. of C., 1960-62; ins. adjuster GAB, Chico, Calif., 1962-64, mgr. claims office, Bishop, Calif., 1964-65; asst. mgr. Butte (Mont.) Sash & Door Co., 1965-68; claims rep. Calif. Farm Ins., Chico, 1968-74; exec. v.p., gen. mgr. Chico (Calif.) C. of C., 1974—. Vice chmn. bd. govs. Chico Community Meml. Hosp., 1977—; bd. dirs. Chico Community Scholarship Program Assn., 1978—. Mem. Am. C. of C. Execs., Calif. Assn. C. of C. Execs. (dir. 1978-82), Superior Calif. C. of C. Execs. (dir. 1977-82). Clubs: Rotary, Exchange. Office: Chico Chamber of Commerce PO Box 3038 Chico CA 95927

LYNCH, MRS. PHILIP (HELEN COON LYNCH), polit. worker, civic worker; b. David City, Nebr., May 27, 1896; d. Frank Ross and Bertha (Wilcox) Coon; student pub. and pvt. schs.; m. Philip Raymond Lynch, May 22, 1917. Mem. N.Mex. Library Commn., 1957-65; pres. Retarded Children's Assn. of Grant County, N.Mex., 1957-60, finance chmn. LWV 1959. Bd. mem. Episcopal Revolving Fund of South West Diocese, 1958-59; dir. Nat. Library Week for N.Mex., 1959; mem. small library project A.L.A.; adviser to Welfare Dept. N.Mex. on books for aging, mem. bd. Humane Soc., 1972—; pres. bd. Grant County Mus., 1973—; mem. bd. Econ. Opportunity, Grant County; mem. Silver City Commn. on Aging, 1974—; life mem. bd. dirs. Silver City Mus. Del. Rep. Nat. Conv., 1960; pres. Grant County Rep. Women, 1955-59, finance chmn. Grant County Rep. Party, 1961-63; 2d v.p. N.Mex. Federated Rep. Women, 1957-59; mem. Rep. State Central Com., 1960—. Named Citizen of Year Grant County C. of C. 1978; recipient Civic Works award Town of Silver City, 1983. Mem. Women's Aux. Am. Inst. Mining, Metall. and Petroleum Engrs. (head library com. S.W. N.Mex), S.W. N.Mex. Hist. Soc., Grant County Archeol. Soc. Club: Women's (Silver City). Home: 313 W 10th St Silver City NM 88061

LYNCH, PAUL VINCENT, safety engr.; b. Bklyn., Apr. 11, 1932; s. John Andrew and Mary Catherine L.; B.A., St. Anselm's Coll., Manchester, N.H., 1954; postgrad. Fordham U. Law Sch., 1958-59, U. N.H., 1969-71; m. Muriel Dubuc, Jan. 25, 1956; children—David, Marianne. Corp. ins. specialist Allied Chem. Corp., 1959-66; asst. to dir. risk mgmt. Am. Metal Climax, Inc., N.Y.C., 1966-68; lectr. risk mgmt., adminstr. safety U. N.H., Durham, 1969-71; asso. prof. safety N.H. Vocat.-Tech. Coll., 1971-75; pres. Lynch Assocs., Inc., cons., Pittsfield, N.H., 1972-75; regional safety officer GSA, 1976-79; safety mgr. for Calif., U.S. Bur. Land Mgmt., Sacramento, 1979—; v.p. N.H. Safety Council, 1972-74; instr. safety mgmt. Am. River Coll., Sacramento, 1975-76. Active, Boy Scouts Am., 1962—, membership chmn., mem. exec. bd. Golden Empire Council, 1978—. Served with U.S. Army, 1955-57. Recipient Silver Beaver award Boy Scouts Am., 1977. Mem. Am. Soc. Safety Engrs. (pres. Sacramento chpt. 1981-82; regional v.p.; nat. long range planning com.; chmn. legis. affairs com.), Am. Indsl. Hygiene Assn. Author, editor govt. publs. Office: Federal Bldg 2800 Cottage Way Sacramento CA 95825

LYNCH, ROBERT BERGER, lawyer; b. LaCrosse, Wis., June 10, 1931; s. Jan P. and Eve (Berger) L.; B.S., U.S. Merchant Marine Acad., 1955; J.D., U. of the Pacific, 1967; m. Ann Godfrey, May 30, 1980; 1 son, Jan Fredrick. Sr. engr. Aerojet Gen. Corp., Sacramento, Calif., 1955-61, proposal mgr., 1961-63, asst. contract adminstrn. mgr., 1963-66, contract adminstrn. mgr., 1967-70; admitted to Calif. bar, 1969, U.S. Supreme Ct. bar, 1972; individual practice law. Rancho Cordova, Calif., 1969—; instr. bus. law Solano Community Coll., 1977-79, San Joaquin Delta Coll., 1978-79. Active various charity fund-raising campaigns in Sacramento Calif., 1966-68; mem. mission com. St. Clements Episcopal Ch., Rancho Cordova, Calif., 1967-68; trustee Los Rios Community Coll. Dist., Calif., 1971-79. Fellow Brit. Interplanetary Soc.; mem. Am. Bar Assn., Fed. Bar Assn., Sacramento County Bar Assn., Assn. of Trial Lawyers of Am., Calif. Trial Lawyers Assn., IEEE, Mensa. Home: 10615 Coloma Rd Rancho Cordova CA 95670 Office: 2840 Cordova Ln Rancho Cordova CA 95670

LYNCH, SHARON KAY, toxicologist, criminalist; b. Mitchell, S.D., Oct. 16, 1945; d. William Ellsworth and Gertrude Marie (Maguire) Schwank; B.A., UCLA, 1969; M.S., Calif. State U., Los Angeles, 1972; m. Nathaniel Merriman Lynch, May 20, 1967; 1 son, James Ernest. Toxicologist, Los Angeles County Office Chief Med. Examiner-Coroner, 1970-73; criminalist Los Angeles County Sheriff's Dept., 1973-76; chief criminalist Laramie County Sheriff's Dept., Cheyenne, Wyo., 1977-80; criminalist San Diego Police Dept., 1980—. Diplomate Am. Bd. Forensic Toxicology. Mem. Am. Acad. Forensic Sci., Am. Chem. Soc., Internat. Assn. Forensic Toxicologists, Internat. Assn. Identification, Calif. Assn. Criminalists, Calif. Assn. Toxicologists. Democrat. Roman Catholic. Office: 801 W Market St San Diego CA 92101

LYNCH-STAUNTON, FRANK C., lt. gov. Alta. (Can.); b. Pincher Creek, N.W.T., Alta., Can., Mar. 8, 1905; student Can. Coll., Calgary, 1919-22; B.A. Sc., U. Alta., 1927, LL.D. (hon.), 1980; m. Monica Adam, Sept. 21, 1929 (dec. Sept. 1976); children—Betty Lowe, Marina Field, Hugh. With Imperial Oil Co., 1927-28; lt. gov. Province of Alta., Edmonton, 1979—; Founding mem. Community Auction Sales (dir.). Served as maj. Militia and Army Reserves, 1934-42. Office: Office of the Lieutenant Governor Legislative Bldg Edmonton AB T5K 2B6 Canada

LYND, NANCY HELLMAN, tech. writing co. exec.; b. Bklyn., Nov. 10, 1944; d. Al and Esther Deborah (Kleinspiec) Hellman; B.S., N.Y. U., 1965; M.A., Calif. State U., Northridge, 1973, postgrad., Fullerton, 1978-79, Dominguez Hills, 1977-78; m. William Lynd, July 3, 1973; children—Allyn David Herman-Lynd, Barry Howard Herman-Lynd. Secondary sch. tchr., N.Y., La., Calif., 1965-67; free lance ghost writer, 1968-72; tchr. Calif. State U., Northridge, 1972-73; programmer/tech. writer Logicon/Intercomp, Inc., Torrance, Calif., 1974-76; pres. Lynd Assos., Santa Ana, Calif.; now pres. Twist-Text, Inc. Active Women for Polit. Action, Orange County Music Center, Inc., South Coast Repetorary Theater. Mem. NOW (treas. Palos Verde 1974-76, consciousness raising leader), Am. Bus. Women's Assn., Nat. Women's Network. Jewish. Office: 1232A S Village Way Santa Ana CA 92705

LYND, WILLIAM, computer company executive; b. Boston, Nov. 24, 1942; s. Joseph Mearle and Alice (Campbell) L.; A.A., Menlo Coll., 1963; B.S. in Indsl. Mgmt., U. Calif., San Jose, 1965; B.S. in Elec. Engring., Lawrence U., 1965; M.B.A., Pacific Northwestern U., 1968; M.S., Bruckner U., 1969, Ph.D., 1969; m. Nancy Helman Herman Lynd, July 3, 1973; children—Allyn David, Barry Henry, Bradford Joseph. Project analyst U. Calif., 1962-64, salesman Control Data Corp., Palo Alto, 1964-67; regional mgr. DPF & G Co., Westwood, Calif., 1967-71; v.p. sales, founder Logicon Intercomp, Torrance, Calif., 1971-75; dir. mktg./sales MacAro div. MacDonald Douglas Co., Carson, Calif., 1975-77; founder, 1977, then exec. v.p. MRP, Inc., Santa Ana, Calif., 1977-80; pres. M-Systems, Santa Ana, 1980—, also dir.; dir. CIT, Inc., Santa Ana; lectr. U. Calif., Irvine, 1979-80, Saddleback Coll., 1977-79. Scoutmaster Boy Scouts Am. Mem. Am. Prodn. and Inventory Control Soc. (cert.). Home: 11321 Cielo Pl Santa Ana CA 92705 Office: 4501 Birch Newport Beach CA 92660

LYNDS-CHERRY, PATRICIA GAIL, psychologist; b. Woodlake, Calif., Feb. 7, 1950; d. Edgar David and Frances Jean (Eberle) Lynds; m. Albert L. Cherry, Nov. 13, 1982. B.A., Calif. State U.-Fresno, 1972; M.A., U. Nebr., 1975, Ph.D., 1977; postdoctoral study U. Calif.-Davis, 1978-81. Registered sch. psychologist, Calif. Project coordinator System Multicultural Pluralistic Assessment II, U. Calif.-Davis, 1979-80; psychologist Sacramento County Office Edn., 1980-81, Kings County Schs., 1981—; also cons. Mem. Am. Psychol. Assn., Calif. Assn. Sch. Psychologists and Psychometrists. Contbr. articles to profl. jours. Home: 460 W Deodar Dr Lemoore CA 93245 Office: Kings County Supt of Schs Govt Ctr Hanford CA 93230

LYNN, ELIZABETH MEAGHER, educator; b. Oshkosh, Wis.; d. Joseph E. and Gertrude J. (DeYoung) Meagher; m. Lowell A. Lynn (dec. 1981). B.A., Marygrove Coll., 1960; M.A., Villanova U., 1962; M.Ed., Columbia U., 1971; Ph.D., Ind. U., 1974. Chem. sales corr. Westvaco, 1963-65; tchr. English, Phila. Bd. Edn., 1965-66; film prodn. coordinator Marathon Internat. Prodns., 1966; broadcast editor Nat. Assn. Broadcasters Code Authority, 1966-67; writer CBS-TV's 21st Century, Nat. Citizens Com. Pub. Broadcasting, 1967-68; lectr. CCNY, 1968-71; assoc. instr. Ind. U., 1971-74; instr. Cuyahoga Community Coll., Cleve., 1974-75; sr. research assoc. Case Western Res. U., Cleve., 1975-76; communications cons., profl. lectr., Cleve., 1976-77; staff assoc.-tng. Standard Oil Co. (Ohio), Cleve., 1977-82; adj. assoc. prof. Sch. Bus. Adminstrn., U. So. Calif., 1982—; speaker and cons. corps.; reviewer profl. manuscripts ERIC, Wadsworth and Addison-Wesley Pub. Co. Columbia U. fellow, 1969-71; Nat. Inst. Edn. grantee, 1974; Ind. U. grantee, 1973-74; CUNY grantee, 1968; Villanova U. grantee, 1960-62. Mem. Am Arbitration Assn., Am. Soc. Tng. and Devel., Speech Communication Assn., Am. Bus. Communications Assn., Internat. Communication Assn., Central States Communications Assn., Alpha Psi Omega, Lambda Iota Tau, Pi Lambda Theta. Author: Improving Classroom Communication, 1976; contbr. articles to profl. jours. Office: Bus Communication Dept Sch Bus Adminstrn U So Calif Los Angeles CA 90089

LYON, DAVID WILLIAM, research and development executive; b. Lansing, Mich., Mar. 26, 1941; s. Herbert Reid and Mary Kathleen (Slack) L.; m. Catherine McHugh Dillon, July 8, 1967. B.S., Mich. State U., 1963; M.S. in City and Regional Planning, U. Calif.-Berkeley, 1966, Ph.D., 1972. Regional economist Fed. Res. Bank. Phila., 1969-71; research dir. human and econ. resources The N.Y.C.-Rand Inst., 1972-75, v.p., 1975; sr. economist The Rand Corp., Santa Monica, Calif., 1975-77, dep. v.p., 1977-79, v.p. domestic research div., 1979—; dir. Coll. Environ. Design Council, U. Calif.-Berkeley, 1979—. Mellon fellow in city planning, 1966-68; Econ. Devel. Adminstrn. grad. fellow, 1966. Mem. AAAS, Am. Econ. Assn. Club: Riviera Tennis, Pacific Palisades, Calif. Contbr. articles to profl. jours. Office: 1700 Main St Santa Monica CA 90406

LYON, JOHN DAVID, lawyer, energy company executive; b. Tulsa, Feb. 16, 1937; s. Buford Carl and Mary Louise (Cochrane) L.; m. Melinda Mitchell, June 16, 1972. B.A., U. Chgo., 1955; J.D., Harvard U., 1960. Bar: N.Y. 1961, Calif. 1974. Assoc., Paul, Weiss, Rifkind, Wharton & Garrison, 1961-65; with Tosco Corp. and predecessor firm The Oil Shale Corp., Los Angeles, 1965—, v.p., gen. counsel, 1979-75, exec. v.p., 1975—, dir., 1979—, chief operating officer Oil Shale div., 1980-82, chief operating officer Comml. Devel. div., 1982—; pres. Lion Oil Co., 1976-77. Served with USAR, 1960-66. Mem. State Bar Calif., Los Angeles County Bar Assn., Assn. Bar City N.Y. Office: 10100 Santa Monica Blvd Los Angeles CA 90067

LYON, KEITH GEOFFREY, systems engineer; b. Springfield, Ill., Dec. 31, 1951; s. Wolcott Norbert and Marjorie Ann (Ingham) L.; B.S., Eastern Ill. U., 1973; Ph.D., Iowa State U., 1978. Teaching asst. Iowa State U., 1973-75; head tennis coach, 1975-77; research asst. Ames Lab., U.S. Dept. Energy, 1975-78; sr. project engr. Hughes Aircraft Co. Space and Communications Group, Los Angeles, 1978—. Mem. Sigma Xi, Sigma Pi Sigma. Home: 8828 Pershing Dr #302 Playa del Rey CA 90293 Office: PO Box 92919 Los Angeles CA 90009

LYON, MARTHA SUE, naval officer, research engineer; b. Louisville, Oct. 3, 1935; d. Harry Bowman and Erma Louise (Moreland) Lyon. B.A. in Chemistry, U. Louisville, 1959; M.Ed. in Math., Northeastern Ill. U., 1974. Cert. tchr. Ill., Ky. Research assoc. U. Louisville Med. Sch., 1959-61, 62-63; commd. ensign, USNR, 1965, advanced through grades to comdr., 1983; instr. instrumentation chemistry Northwestern U., Evanston, Ill., 1968-70; tchr. sci., chemistry, gifted math. Waukegan (Ill.) pub. schs., 1970-75; phys. scientist Library of Congress, Washington, 1975-76; research engr. Lockheed Missiles & Space Co., Sunnyvale, Calif., 1976-77; instr., assoc. chmn. dept. physics U.S. Naval Acad., Annapolis, Md., 1977-80; analyst Systems Analysis Div., Office of Chief of Naval Ops. Staff, Washington, 1980-81; comdg. officer Naval Res. Ctr., Stockton, Calif., 1981—; Grantee Am. Heart Assn., 1960-62, NSF, 1971, 72. Mem. Soc. Women Engrs., Am. Statis. Assn., Am. Soc. Photogrammetry, Internat. Conf. Women in Sci. Engring. (protocol chair), Mensa, Zeta Tau Alpha, Delta Phi Alpha. Club: Order of Eastern Star. Developer processes used in archival photography, carbon-14 analyses; presenter of papers at profl. cons.

LYONS, CHERIE ANN, educational administrator, author; b. Denver, Dec. 15, 1948; d. Clair Leroy and Mary Margaret (Benner) Case; m. David Greer Lyons, Aug. 22, 1970; children—Michael Greer, Andrea Christine. B.S., U. Colo., 1971, M.A., 1975. Prof. tchr. cert., adminstr. cert. Colo. Dept. Edn. Tchr. English, Cherry Creek Schs., 1971-76; tchr. English, health edn. Jefferson County Schs., Lakewood, Colo., 1971-76, curriculum writer, 1975-78, project dir. career edn., 1976-81, staff devel. specialist, 1981—; cons., 1976—; dir. Sch. Team Approach to Substance Abuse Prevention, Jefferson County. Mem. Jefferson County Task Force Youth and Drugs; mem. Lakeshore Homeowners Assn. Mem. Jefferson County Edn. Assn., Colo. Edn. Assn., NEA, Colo. Lang. Arts Soc., Nat. Council Tchrs. English, Nat. Staff Devel. Council, Assn. Supervision and Curriculum Devel., Phi Delta Kappa. Democrat. Episcopalian. Club: 300 - Women's Investment (Denver). Author: The Writing Process: A Program of Composition and Applied Grammar, Book 12, 1982. Home: 8041 Lamar St Arvada CO 80003 Office: Jefferson County Schs 1209 Quail St Lakewood CO 80215

LYONS, DANIEL JOE, graphics executive; b. Williamsport, Pa., Nov. 17, 1942; s. Clair E. and Theor A. (Young) L. Student Rochester Inst. Tech., 1962. With Edgerton, Germeshausen & Grier, Las Vegas, Nev., 1963-65; prodn. mgr. Milton Standard Pub. Co. (Pa.), 1965-66; asst. prodn. mgr. Las Vegas Review-Jour., 1967-71, bus. mgr., 1971-74; owner Apperception, Ltd., Las Vegas, 1971-76; graphic communications mgr. City of Las Vegas, 1976-81; print services mgr. Clark County Community Coll., North Las Vegas, 1981—; founder, chmn. bd. Optigraphics, Inc., Las Vegas, 1980—; lectr. in field. Mem. supervisory com. Clark Vocat.-Tech. Ctr., 1967-74; active multimedia programs United Way, 1972-73; publicity dir. Las Vegas Stars Semi-Profl. Hockey Team, 1978-79; bd. dirs. Nev. State Soccer Assn., 1979; graphics chmn. Nat. League of Cities Host Com., 1979. Mem. In-plant Printing Mgmt. Assn., Nat. Micrographics Assn., Am. Records Mgmt. Assn., Soc. Photo-Optical Instrumentation Engrs., Calif. Assn. Reprodn. Services. Republican. Methodist. Clubs: Kiwanis, Toastmasters, Masons, Shriners, DeMolay (Legion of Honor). Author: In Your Own Image, 1975. Home: 2125 Glen Heather Way Las Vegas NV 89102 Office: 3200 E Cheyenne Ave North Las Vegas NV 89030

LYONS, JEROME MICHAEL, industrial relations executive; b. Chgo., Mar. 24, 1937; s. John A. and Mary S. Lyons; B.A. in Psychology, Loyola U., Los Angeles, 1965, M.Ed., 1972; M.B.A., Pepperdine U., 1976; m. Barbara; children—David, Diana, Mary, Toni, Kevin, Casey. Credit mgr. Neighborhood Fin. Corp., Elmwood Park, Ill., 1960; controller Aldens Corp., Chgo., 1961; personnel rep. Hyland Labs. div. Baxter Labs., Los Angeles, 1965-67; dir. indsl. relations VSI Corp., Pasadena, Calif., 1967-73; v.p. adminstrn. Cherry Textron, Cherry div. Textron Inc., Santa Ana, Calif., 1973—; instr. wage adminstrn. U. Calif., Irvine, 1978—; instr. bus. and labor law Loyola U., Los Angeles, 1981—; mem. indsl. relations bd. Calif. Inst. Tech., Pasadena, 1970-72. Mem. Orange County (Calif.) adv. bd. United Way, 1973-75; bd. dirs. YMCA, Santa Ana, 1974-76; mem. adv. bd. Chapman Coll. Served with U.S. Army, 1958-60. Mem. Am. Soc. Personnel Adminstrn., Personnel Indsl. Relations Assn., Nat. Alliance Businessmen (pres. commn. 1977-78, adv. bd. 1977-79), DAV (pres. 1978), Calif. Jaycees, Santa Ana C. of C. (v.p.), Mchts. and Mfrs. Assn., Big Bros. Orange County. Republican. Club: Kiwanis. Home: 18212 Bayberry Irvine CA 92715 Office: 1224 E Warner Ave Santa Ana CA 92707

LYONS, JERRY LEE, industrial hygienist; b. Ogden, Utah, Mar. 26, 1943; s. Ray and Clara Lucille (Merrill) L.; m. Pauline Pilgrim, May 24, 1974; children—Sausha Lyn, Sharesa Lea. Student Idaho State U., 61, Boise State U., 1970-73; A.S. in Microbiology, Tex. A&M U., 1982. Patrolman Idaho State Police, Idaho Falls, 1966-69; microbiology supr. J.R. Simplot Co., Heyburn, Idaho, 1969-76, lab. technician, indsl. hygienist, 1977—. Adviser Jr. Achievement, 1978-79. Served with USAF, 1961-65. Mem. Am. Indsl. Hygiene Assn. (air pollution com., pres. Idaho sect.), Am. Soc. Safety Engrs. Club: Toastmasters. Home: 695 El Rancho Pocatello ID 83201 Office: PO Box 912 Pocatello ID 83204

LYTLE, DENNIS JOSEPH, soil scientist; b. Sheridan, Wyo., Nov. 7, 1953; s. Reno and Gertrude Irene (Joslyn) L.; m. Marilyn Kay Bryant, June 12, 1976. A.S., Sheridan Coll., 1974; B.S., U. Wyo., Laramie, 1976. Lab. technician U. Wyo., 1974-76; soil scientist State of Wyo., Rawlins, 1976-77; soil scientist Soil Conservation Service, U.S. Dept. Agr., Rawlins, 1977-78, Yreka, Calif., 1978-80, supervisory soil scientist, Yuba City, Calif., 1980—. Mem. Soil Sci. Soc. Am., Soil Conservation Soc. Am., Alpha Zeta. Democrat. Methodist. Home: 1668 Tamarack Dr Yuba City CA 95991 Office: 1511 Butte House Rd Suite B Yuba City CA 95991

MA, ABRAHAM CHIH-KANG, control engr.; b. Canton, China, Apr. 21, 1949; came to U.S., 1974; s. Yen-Chang and Lan-Yin (Wei) M.; B.S., Nat. Tsing Hua U., Shin-Chu, Taiwan, 1972; M.S.M.E., U. Notre Dame, 1976; M.S. in Control Engring. U. Wis., Madison, 1978. Control system engr. Bendix Corp., South Bend, Ind., 1979-80, Bechtel Petroleum, Inc., San Francisco, 1980—; cons. engring. Cert. engr. in tng., Ind. Mem. IEEE, ASME. Contbr. articles to profl. jours.; patentee in field. Home: 5020 Anaheim Loop Union City CA 94587

MAAG, JOHN CLYDE, instrument company executive; b. Defiance, Ohio, Sept. 12, 1949; s. Albert James and Elizabeth Theresa (Eck) M.; children—Douglas, Andrea. B.S. in Acctg., St. Joseph's Coll., 1971. C.P.A., Ind. Acct. Coopers & Lybrand, Ft. Wayne, Ind., 1971-78; internal auditor Consol. Foods Corp., Chgo., 1978; corp. acctg. mgr. Bowmar Instrument Corp., Ft. Wayne, Ind., 1978-80, corp. controller, Newbury Park, Calif., 1980—, treas., 1982—. Mem. Am. Inst. C.P.A.s, Ind. Assn. C.P.A.s. Roman Catholic. Club: Elks. Home: 1036 Hendrix Ave Thousand Oaks CA 91360 Office: 850 Lawrence Dr Newbury Park CA 91320

MAAS, SALLY ANN, journalist; b. Portage, Wis., Apr. 10, 1947; d. Franklin Arthur and Mabel Gladys (Engen) Maas; m. Robert A. Marshall, Aug. 3, 1973. B.S. in Journalism, U. Wis., 1969. Reporter, The Paper, Oshkosh, Wis., 1969-70; feature writer The Press, Binghamton, N.Y., 1970-71; feature writer The Press-Enterprise, Riverside, Calif., 1971-76, lifestyle editor, 1976-83, feature editor, 1983—. Recipient Outstanding Woman of Achievement award Bus. and Profl. Women's Club, 1981. Mem. Soc. Newspaper Designers, Women in Communications, LWV, Sigma Delta Chi. Club: Twin Cities Press (past pres.). Home: 26925 Ladera Redlands CA 92373 Office: 3512 14th St Riverside CA 92501

MABEY, EDWARD MILO, ins. agy. exec.; b. Bountiful, Utah, Feb. 26, 1919; s. Charles Rendell and Afton (Rampton) M.; student U. Utah, 1936-38, 40, San Francisco Trade Sch., 1941-42, U. Tenn., 1944; m. Edrice Louise Haslam, July 23, 1940 (div.); children—James Edward, Afton Louise Mabey Wettstein, Charlynn Edrice Mabey Scharlow; m. 2d, Gun Sundberg, Aug. 27, 1979; 1 dau., Amanda Gun. Book salesman, mgr. Edward Brown & Sons Gen. Ins. Co., Oakland, Calif., 1940-41; pres., dir. Western Gen. Agy., Inc., Salt Lake City, 1947-81; pres. Brother Christopher Inc. Western Underwriters, Inc.; chmn. bd., dir. Investment Mgmt. Corp.; pres., chmn. bd. Western Indsl. Shares, Inc.; chmn. bd. Bountiful State Bank, 1965-68; pres., dir. Western Holding Corp., 1973—; mng. dir. Internat. Guaranteed Fund, Ltd.; dir., owner-developer Oakridge Improvement Co., Farmington, Utah; mng. dir. Bahamian Investment Mgmt. Ltd.; dir. Natural Resources, Inc., New Hemisphere Life Ins. Co., Victoria Falls Enterprises, Inc., Bayview Park Devel. Co., Woods Cross, Utah, Zions First Nat. Bank, Bountiful, Foursquare Fund, Boston. Exec. dir. Utah Opera Co., 1979, pres., 1980-82, chmn. bd., 1982—. Served with USNR, World War II. Mem. Intercollegiate Knights, Beta Theta Pi. Republican. Mem. Ch. Jesus Christ of Latter-day Saints. Clubs: Ambassador, Oakridge Country (dir.). Address: 780 E South Temple Salt Lake City UT 84110

MABIE, RUTH MARIE, realtor; b. Pueblo, Colo., Feb. 7; d. Newton Everett and Florence Ellen (Porter) Allen; student San Diego State U., 1957-60, Grossmont Jr. Coll., 1970-71, U. Calif., San Diego, 1970, 72; M.B.A., La Jolla U., 1980, Ph.D., 1981; m. Richard O. Mabie, Nov. 29, 1946; 1 son, Ward A. Mgr., LaMont Modeling Sch., San Diego, 1962; tchr. Am. Bus. Coll., San Diego, 1964-66; fashion modeling, 1960-72; owner, broker Ruth Mabile Realty, San Diego, 1972—; asst. v.p. Skil-Bilt, Inc., 1976—; dir. Mabie & Mintz, Inc. Bd. dirs. Multiple Sclerosis Dr., 1971—. Mem. San Diego Bd. Realtors, Nat. Assn. Female Execs. Republican. Home: 4481 Palo Verde Terr San Diego CA 92115 Office: 6280 Riverdale St San Diego CA 92121

MACAPINLAC, JOSEPH PINEDA, savings and loan executive; b. Pampanga, Philippines, Mar. 3, 1943; s. Eleuterio G. and Marina S. (Pineda) M.; came to U.S., 1960, naturalized, 1969; B.B.A., U. San Francisco, 1963; M.B.A., Golden Gate U., 1966; postgrad. Exec. Devel. Sch., U. Ga., 1976-77; m. Aurora C. Cunanan; children—Joseph, Josephine. With Standard Oil Co. Calif., San Francisco, 1964-74, material requisition clk., 1966-67, project asst., 1967-70, cost engring. technician, 1970-74; mgr. main office Island Fed. Savs. & Loan Assn., Honolulu, 1974-75, mgr. main office and bus. devel. dept., 1975-77, mgr., asst. v.p. br. adminstrn., 1977, mgr., v.p. br. adminstrn., 1978; mgr., v.p. br. adminstrn. First Fed. Savs. & Loan Assn., Honolulu, 1978-79, mgr., v.p. bus. devel., 1979; founder, pres., chief exec. officer People's Savs. and Loan Assn., Honolulu, 1979—. Adviser, Jr. Achievement, San Francisco, 1973-74, Honolulu, 1975-76; sect. chmn. Aloha United Way, Hawaii, 1978-79; founder Filipino Am. Youth Council, 1972, adviser, 1973; bd. dirs. Am. Cancer Soc., Balik-Bahay Project; exec. bd. Aloha council Boy Scouts Am.; fin. chmn. Internat. Filipino Garden; mem. Honolulu Planning Commn., Philippine Cultural Found.; organizer Philippine Med. Assn. Named Boss of Year, Am. Bus. Women's Assn. Hawaii, 1975; recipient Calif. Leadership award Calif. Jaycees, 1972, also others. Mem. Inst. Fin. Edn., Small Bus. Mgmt. Assn., Sales and Mktg. Execs., Honolulu Exec. Assn. (dir. 1977-78), Hawaii Jaycees (named Outstanding Regional Dir. 1977), Filipino Hist. Soc. of Hawaii, Hawaii C. of C., Kalihi Bus. Assn. (dir.), Filipino C. of C. (dir.), Ateneo Alumni Assn. (dir.) U. San Francisco Alumni Assn. (pres. Hawaii). Roman Catholic. Home: PO Box 25055 Honolulu HI 96825 Office: 1188 Fort Street Mall Honolulu HI 96813

MACARUSO, MARILYNN LOUISE, pipe mfg. co. exec.; b. Mpls., Dec. 28, 1932; d. Edward Dexter and Floy Adelaide (Abbs) Smith; student Frances Shimer Coll., 1949-50; m. Ralph B. Macaruso, Oct. 13, 1962; 1 son, Stephen David. Personnel mgr. Continental Can Co., Santa Ana, Calif., 1964-71; sec.-treas. Colby Plastic Converters, Inc., Anaheim, Calif., 1971—, Brenco Sales, Inc., Anaheim, 1975—, Bradley Specialties, Inc., Anaheim, 1979—; dir. Colby Plastic Converters, Inc., Brenco Sales, Inc. Republican. Episcopalian. Home: 18103 Yosemite Ct Fountain Valley CA 92708 Office: 1335 Allec St Anaheim CA 92805

MACBETH, (BARBARA) LOUISE, psychologist, educator, researcher; b. Fresno, Calif., Mar. 12, 1944; d. Francis Scott and Leona Anne (Carlson) Thompson; m. Paul Robert Macbeth, Dec. 20, 1969 (div.); m. 2d, Andrew Christensen, May 7, 1983. B.A. cum laude, Calif. State U.-Fresno, 1967; M.A., U. Oreg., 1970, Ph.D., 1975. Lic. psychologist, Calif. Teaching asst. U. Oreg., Eugene, 1967-69, vis. asst. prof., 1972-73; research asst. Oreg. Research Inst., Eugene, 1969-72; predoctoral intern in clin. psychology Ingleside Mental Health Center, Rosemead, Calif., 1973-74; postdoctoral fellow in child/adolescent clin. psychology Los Angeles County-U. So. Calif. Med. Ctr., 1974-75, clin. psychologist, asst. clin. prof. psychiatry, 1975—; pvt. practice clin. psychology. Mem. Am. Psychol. Assn., Assn. for Women in Psychology, U. So. Calif. Med. Faculty Women's Assn., Western Psychol. Assn., Calif. Psychol. Assn., NOW. Research, publs. and presentations on measurement of ability to delay gratification, birth-order characteristics, feminist therapy and women's groups, clin. supervision, and assessment adolescent psychopathology. Office: 1937 Hospital Pl Los Angeles CA 90033

MACBRIDE, THOMAS JAMISON, judge; b. Sacramento, Mar. 25, 1914; s. Frank and Lotta (Little) MacB.; A.B., U. Calif.-Berkeley, 1936, LL.B., 1940; m. Martha Harrold, Nov. 7, 1947; children—Peter, Thomas Jamison, David, Laurie. Admitted to Calif. bar, 1940; dep. atty. gen. State of Calif., 1941-42; practiced in Sacramento, 1946-61; U.S. dist. judge for Eastern Dist. Calif. Sacramento, 1961—, chief judge, 1967-79, sr. judge, 1979—; mem. U.S. Fgn. Intelligence Surveillance Ct., 1979-80; mem. U.S. Temporary Emergency Ct. Appeals, 1982—. Pres., Town Hall, Sacramento, 1952; pres. N.E. area YMCA, Sacramento, 1960, bd. dirs., 1956-68; mem. Nat. Commn. Reform Fed. Criminal Laws; mem. U.S. Jud. Conf., 1975-78, chmn. Criminal Justice Act Com., 1979—. Mem. Calif. Ho. of Reps., 1955-60. Bd. dirs. KVIE Ednl. TV. Founding mem. League to Save Lake Tahoe. Served to lt. USNR, 1942-46. Mem. ABA, U. Calif. Alumni Assn. (v.p. 1955, 60), Phi Delta Phi, Kappa Sigma. Democrat. Clubs: Masons (33 deg., Shriner KCCH), Rotary (pres.), University (pres. Sacramento 1953), Sutter, Comstock (bd. dirs., treas., pres. 1975-76) (Sacramento); Senator Outing. Home: 1800 Rockwood Dr Sacramento CA 95825 Office: US Courthouse Sacramento CA 95814

MACCALLUM, (EDYTHE) LORENE, pharmacist, consultant; b. Monte Vista, Colo., Nov. 29, 1928; d. Francis Whittier and Bernice Viola (Martin) Scott; m. David Robertson MacCallum, June 12, 1952; children—Suzanne Rae MacCallum Homiak and Roxanne Kay (twins), Tracy Scott, Tamara Lee MacCallum Johnson, Shauna Marie. B.S. in Pharmacy, U. Colo., 1950. Registered pharmacist, Colo. Pharmacist Presbyterian Hosp., Denver, 1950, Corner Pharmacy, Lamar, Colo., 1950-53; research pharmacist Nat. Chlorophyll Co., Lamar, 1953; relief pharmacist, various stores, Delta, Colo., 1957-59, Farmington, N.Mex., 1960-62, 71-79, Aztec, N.Mex., 1971-79; mgr. Med. Arts Pharmacy, Farmington, 1966-67; cons. pharmacist Navajo Hosp., Brethern in Christ Mission, Farmington, 1967-77; sales agt. Norris Realty, Farmington, 1977-78; pharmacist, owner, mgr. Lorene's Pharmacy, Farmington, 1979—; tax cons. H&R Block, Farmington, 1968; cons. Pub. Service Co., N.Mex. Intermediate Clinic, Planned Parenthood, Farmington, mem. N.Mex. Bd. Pharmacy. Advisor Order Rainbow for Girls, Farmington, 1975-78. Mem. Nat. Assn. Bds. Pharmacy (com. on internship tng.), Nat. Assn. Retail Druggists, N.Mex. Pharm. Assn. (mem. exec. council 1977-81). Presbyterian. Club: Order Eastern Star (Farmington). Home: 1301 Camino Sol Farmington NM 87401 Office: 901 W Apache Farmington NM 87401

MACCOLLAM, JOEL ALLAN, church association executive, consultant; b. Albany, N.Y., Dec. 19, 1946; s. Allan and Edith Jacqueline (Jones) M.; m. Jann Scherer, May 3, 1975; children—Jessica, Jordan. B.A., Hamilton Coll., 1968; M.Div., Gen. Theol. Sem., 1972; postgrad. Columbia U., UCLA. Ordained priest Episcopal Ch., 1972; Asst. minister St. John's Ch., Troy, N.Y., 1972-73; assoc. rector St. John's Ch., Oneonta, N.Y., 1973-74; rector St. Stephen's Ch., Schuylerville, N.Y.,

1974-78; assoc. rector St. Mark's Ch., Glendale, Calif., 1978-79; dir. pub. relations Door of Hope Internat., Glendale, 1981-82; v.p. program devel. United Community Chs. of Am., Glendale, 1982—; cons. for polit. and non-profit groups. Mem. Pub. Relations Soc. Am., Nat. Soc. Fund Raising Execs. Author: The Weekend that Never Ends, 1972; The Way Doctrine, 1978; Carnival of Souls, 1979. Home: Box 977 Glendale CA 91209 Office: United Community Chs of Am Box 90 Glendale CA 91209

MACCORQUODALE, PATRICIA LEE, sociology educator; b. Denver, Aug. 20, 1950; d. Donald Willard and Zoe (Newman) MacCorquodale. B.A., Carleton Coll., 1972; M.S., U. Wis.-Madison, 1974, Ph.D., 1978. Lectr. sociology U. Wis.-Madison, 1976-78; asst. prof. sociology U. Ariz., Tucson, 1978—; chmn. planning, evaluation coms. Womens Studies Implementation grant NEH, 1981-84; co-dir. NSF Women in Sci. Career Workshop, 1981. Nat. Inst. Edn. grantee, 1979-82. Mem. Am. Sociol. Assn., Pacific Sociol. Assn., Western Social Scis. Assn., Soc. Study Social Problems. Author: (with J. Delamater) Premarital Sexuality, 1979; contbr. articles to profl. jours. Office: Dept Sociology U Ariz Tucson AZ 85721

MACCULLOUGH, ANN WINSLOW, food service planning and design consulting company executive; b. Washington; d. Joseph E. and Agnes B. Winslow; m. Craig C. MacCullough, Jan. 5, 1963; children—Sharin, Andrew. Student State Tchrs. Coll., Towson, Md. Exec. sec. GAO, Washington, 1957-64, Design Premiums, Inc., Continuous Curve Contact Lenses, Inc., Zapata Ocean Resources and Travelodge-Trusthouse Forte, San Diego; officer, bus. mgr., adminstrv. asst. Mac Cullough Brown Assocs., San Francisco and San Diego, 1980—. Dir. canteen service Bethesda (Md.) Naval Med. Hosp., ARC, 1961-62; treas. Jaycee Wives, Bethesda, 1969-70; chmn. com. Parkwood Elem. Sch. PTA, 1973, 74, 75; chmn. ch. com., Kensington, Md., 1973, 74, 75; sec. Parkwood Civic Assn., 1975-76; mem. San Carlos (Calif.) Protective Assn., 1980; mem. San Carlos Area Council, 1980, 81, 82, 83; 1st v.p., 1981-82, pres., 1982-84; key area supr. campaign for Mayor of San Diego, 1983; mem. San Carlos Friends of Library; mem. central bd. San Diego Friends of Library. Clubs: Kenwood Golf and Country (Bethesda); San Carlos Swim and Racquet (San Diego); Porsche of Am.

MACDONALD, AONGHAIS EWAN, advertising agency executive; b. Glasgow, Scotland, Dec. 22, 1941; came to U.S., 1976; s. Aonghais and Marjorie Bell (Cameron) M.; m. Helen Isobel Campbell, July 18, 1970; children—Katherine, Calum. M. Econs., U. Edinburgh, 1964. With Leo Burnett Co., London, 1966-68, Madrid, Spain, 1968-70, Johannesburg, S. Africa, 1970-71, 74-76, mng. dir., Lisbon, Portugal, 1971-74, account supr., Chgo., 1976-80, vice chmn., London, 1980-81; sr. v.p., mgmt. dir. McCann-Erickson Inc., San Francisco, 1981—. Served with Royal Naval Res., 1960-63. Recipient Mary Erskine prize U. Edinburgh, 1964. Presbyterian. Home: 2663 Filbert St San Francisco CA 94123 Office: McCann-Erickson Inc 201 California St San Francisco CA 94111

MACDONALD, DIANE CHARMAINE, advertising company executive; b. N.Y.C., June 28, 1953; d. Bryan J. and Elizabeth Ann MacD. B.A., U. Calif.-Santa Barbara, 1976. Asst. product mgr. Sunshine Biscuits Inc., N.Y.C., 1978-80; assoc. product mgr. Carnation Co., Los Angeles, 1980-81; account exec. Dailey & Assocs., Los Angeles, 1981—; instr. for mentally retarded Alpha Tng. Ctr., Santa Barbara, 1976-77. Club: Los Angeles Advertising. Office: Dailey & Assocs 3055 Wilshire Blvd Los Angeles CA 90010

MACDONALD, JOHN BERNARD, dept. store exec.; b. Jerome, Ariz., Mar. 14, 1923; s. John Bernard and Martha Marie (Wilson) MacD.; B.S.C., U. Santa Clara (Calif.), 1949, grad. student bus. mktg., 1968-70; s. Velma Dolores Keller, Feb. 10, 1952; children—Jack, Michael, Debra, Gregory. Trainee, mdse. mgr. Montgomery Ward & Co., Calif., Utah and Oreg., 1949-54; store mgr. Spiegel's, Calif., 1954-59; with J.M. McDonald Co. div. Wickes, Santa Monica, 1959—, store mgr., Santa Clara, San Jose, Calif., 1959-70, v.p. sales, mem. exec. com., Hastings, Nebr., 1970-75, v.p. for advt. and sales promotion, 1975-76, vice chmn. and sales promotion officer, office of pres., 1976-79, store mgr., Visalia, Calif., 1979—. Bd. dirs. Better Bus. Bur. Santa Clara, 1965-68; mem. bd. distributive edn. com. San Jose (Calif.) High Sch., 1968; hon. dir. Santa Clara Philharm., 1965; adv. com. San Jose City Coll., 1967-68. Served with USNR, 1942-46. Named Nat. Retailer of Yr., Brand Name Found., 1968; recipient Coopers Nat. Jockey award merit, San Jose, 1968. Mem. Alumni Assn. U. Santa Clara. Democrat. Roman Catholic. Home: 833 S Linwood Visalia CA 93277

MACDONALD, LACHLAN PETER, author, publisher; b. Lake Linden, Mich., Apr. 21, 1929; s. Sydney Gilbert and Irene Esther (Schick) MacD.; M.A. in History, U. Chgo., 1957; m. Karen Louise Reinecke, Dec. 14, 1974; children—Lawrence, Roderick, Gordon, Craig. Pub., Padre Prodns., San Luis Obispo, Calif., 1974—; owner Book Link Distbrs., 1982—, Padre Systems, 1983—; lectr. in field. Chmn. promotional coordinating com. City of San Luis Obispo, 1970-78. Served with U.S. Army, 1950-52. Recipient Olga and Paul Menn Fiction award, Chgo., 1956; MacDowell Colony fellow, 1956; U. N.H. grantee, 1956; U. Utah grantee, 1960. Editor, pub.: Publishing in the Output Mode, 1981; author: Uncommon Guide to San Luis Obispo County, 1977; The Hunter and Ohter Stories, 1984. Office: PO Box 1275 San Luis Obispo CA 93406

MACDONALD, MYRON PHILIP, computer executive; b. Kelso Wash., June 18, 1937; s. Wayne A. Poutt and Ila J. Hill; m. Nancy L. Hamner, Mar. 9, 1962; children—Martin, Mitchell. Diploma, Multnomah Sch. Bible, 1958, Th.B., 1971. Computer specialist IBM, San Jose, Calif., 1963-66; systems specialist Lockheed Missiles & Space Co., Sunnyvale, Calif., 1966-70; mgr. systems Singer Co., San Leandro, Calif., 1970-74; mgr. systems devel. Nat. Semiconductor, Santa Clara, Calif., 1974-83; chief exec. officer Datrek Corp., Cupertino, Calif., 1983—; computer sci. cons. Fremont Sch. Dist. Served with AUS, 1959-61. Office: 21050 McClellan Rd Suite 1 Cupertino CA 95014

MAC DONALD, NORVAL WOODROW, safety engr.; b. Medford, Oreg., Dec. 8, 1913; s. Orion and Edith (Anderson) MacD.; grad. high sch. Los Angeles; student U. So. Calif., 1932-34; m. Elizabeth Ann Clifford, Dec. 8, 1937; children—Linda (Mrs. Bob Comings), Peggy (Mrs. Don Lake), Kathleen. Safety engr. Todd Shipyards, San Pedro, Calif., 1942-44, Pacific Indemnity Ins. Co., San Francisco, 1944-50; with Indsl. Indemnity Co., San Francisco, 1950—, area safety engring. mgr., 1951—; area safety mgr. Beaver Ins. Co., 1976—. Tchr. adult evening classes U. San Francisco, 1960-63, Golden Gate U., 1969—. Registered profl. safety engr., Calif. Mem. Am. Soc. Safety Engrs. (pres., 1958-59), Engrs. Club San Francisco. Methodist. Mason. Club: Las Posas Country (Camarillo, Calif.). Contbr. articles to profl. jours. Home: 1710 E Shoreline Camarillo CA 93010 Office: 100 California St San Francisco CA 94111

MACEDON, GEORGE G., marketing executive; b. Tucson, Ariz., July 31, 1940; s. George G. and Victoria G. (Zuccala) M.; m. Chiquita Archer, Oct. 23, 1982. B.S., Ariz. State U., 1966, M.S.W., 1968. Owner restaurants, Phoenix, El Paso, 1968-73; mfr.'s rep., 1972-75; sales mgr. Western states Broadmoor Industries, 1975-77; nat. sales mgr. Sampo Corp. of Am., Elk Grove Village, Ill., 1977-80; v.p. sales and mktg. Bohsei USA, Chatsworth, Calif., 1981-82; pres. Progressive Mktg., Tempe, Ariz., 1982—. Republican. Roman Catholic. Home: 2335 W Nopal Ave Mesa AZ 85202 Office: 228 S Clark Dr Suite 102 Tempe AZ 85281

MACELWEE, MRS. IRVIN REED, civic worker, club woman, business exec.; b. Stevens Point, Wis.; d. Joseph Victor and Jeannette M. (Gasche) Collins; B.E., U. Wis., Stevens Point; postgrad. Carroll Coll.; B.Lit. Sci., U. Wis., Madison; m. Irvin Reed MacElwee, Dec. 29, 1927; children—Marilyn Jean Macelwee Throckmorton, Donald Beall. Dir. Fibremold, Inc., Woburn, Mass. Apptd. to 1960 Assay Commn. Mem. bd. Phila. Cancer Dr., 1954-64; hon. pres. St. Christopher's Hosp. Auxiliary, 1957-61. Mem. advisory com. Phila. Com. on Alcoholism. Pres. Pa. Council Republican Women, 1960-62; pres. Rep. Women Pa., 1954-60; mem. bd. Nat. Fedn. Rep. Women, 1960-64, mem. exec. bd., 1962-64; alternate del. Rep. Nat. Conv., 1972, 76. Mem. bd. Soc. Retarded Children, March of Dimes, Phila., Women's Soc. Prevention Cruelty to Animals; active Tucson Symphony, 1978-82. Recipient Plaque for citizenship work in Swarthmore, Lions Club, 1966, Alumni Achievement award, Wis. State U., 1969. Mem. D.A.R. (Phila. chpt. regent 1956-59, state program chmn. 1957-67), Am. Acad. Polit. and Social Scis., Los Angeles Mus. Art, Daus. 17th Century, Colonial Dames Am., Needlework Guild Am. (dir. Swarthmore br. 1935-79), Woman's Med. Coll. Aux., Sons and Daus. Pilgrims, Soc. Preservation Old Landmarks, AAUW, Am. Contract Bridge Assn., Nat. Geog. Soc., U. Wis. Phila. Alumni Assn. (v.p. 1958-61, 64-69), Internat. Platform Assn., Emergency Aid Am., Smithsonian Assocs., Strawberry Mansion and Com. of 1926, Delta Zeta (dir. eastern region 1926-34). Presbyterian. Clubs: Players of Swarthmore; Nat. Travel; Union League; Springhaven Golf (Wallingford, Pa.); Capitol Hill (Washington). Home: 861 Camino del Monte Green Valley AZ 85614

MACENSKI, ALLEN GEORGE, industrial hygiene engineer, educator, consultant; b. Hibbing, Minn., Jan. 1, 1947; s. Alec and Jennie (Chica) M.; m. Marcia Lynn Jacobson, Jan. 28, 1968; m. 2d Paul Jean Kornbluth, April 1, 1977; children—Todd Devin, Tasha Marie, Trevor William. B.S., Calif. State U., 1970, M.S., 1972; J.D., Northrop U., 1982. Safety and indsl. hygiene cons. Employers Ind. Co., Los Angeles, 1970-72; environ. health, safety engr. TRW Space and Def. Systems, Redondo Beach, Calif., 1972-74; mgr. environ. health and safety Hughes Aircraft Co., Los Angeles, 1974-83, corporate indsl. hygienist, 1983—; part-time faculty mem. Calif. State U., U. So. Calif.; cons. bus., pub. orgns. Industry br. pres. Los Angeles coastal cities unit Am. Cancer Soc.; vice chmn. San Fernando Valley council Mental Health Assn., 1971-73. Recipient William H. Cameron award Nat. Safety Council, 1977, 78, 79. Mem. Bd. Cert. Safety Profls. Am., Am. Indsl. Hygiene Assn., Am. Soc. Safety Engrs., Inst. Environ. Scis., Am. Pub. Health Assn. Democrat. Author: (with David Pepitone) Prudent Practices for Storing Industrial and Laboratory Chemicals, 1983. Office: PO Box 1042 Bldg C2 Mail Sta B171 El Segundo CA 90245

MACGREGOR, DONALD LANE, banker; b. Duluth, Minn., June 21, 1930; s. Donald Lane and Julia (Waldo) MacG.; m. Mary Jo Rouse, Sept. 27, 1959; children—Jeffrey Lane, Steven Scott, John Rouse. Student Carleton Coll, 1948-51; B.S. in Econs., Macalester Coll, 1956. Asst. cashier, 1st Nat. Bank Mpls., 1956-61; v.p. United Calif. Bank, San Francisco, Los Angeles, 1961-69, San Francisco, 1971-72; pres. Ormand Industries, Inc., Dallas, Los Angeles, 1969-70; pres., chief operating officer, dir. Am. Security Bank, Honolulu, 1972—; dir., past pres. Bancard Assn. Hawaii, Inc. Bd. dirs. Aloha council Boy Scouts Am., 1974—; trustee, chmn. fin. com. Hawaii Loa Coll., past pres.; active Hawaii Army Mus Soc., Aloha United Way. Served to capt. USAF, 1951-55. Decorated D.F.C. with oak leaf cluster. Mem. Hawaii Bankers Assn., Western Ind. Bankers. Clubs: Rotary, Pacific, Outrigger Canoe (Honolulu). Office: 1314 S King St Honolulu HI 96814

MACHAMER, ROY JOHN, electronics company executive; b. Tower City, Pa., Feb. 4, 1934; s. John Aaron and Margaret Naomi (Shaffer) M.; m. Lois Ann Moyer, Mar. 26, 1955 (div. 1976); children—Mark Gene, Renee Elizabeth Crooks. B.S. in Physics, Pa. State U., 1960. With HRB-Singer, 1958-67, mgr. Western ops., State College, Pa. and San Jose, Calif., dir. advanced systems and research planning Friden div. Singer Co., Palo Alto, Calif., 1967-69; founder, pres. Office Communications, Inc., Sunnyside, Calif., 1970-74; founder, pres. Good Buddy Co., Reno, Nev., 1976-80; v.p. subs. Triad Holding Co. SA, 1974-75; v.p. research and devel. Atari, Inc. div. Warner Communications, Milpitas, Calif., 1981—. Served with USN, 1952-56. Mem. Sigma Pi Sigma. Patentee in field. Home: 1961 Avenide de Las Rosas Santa Clara CA 95050 Office: 1501 McCarthy Blvd Milpitas CA 95035

MACHETANZ, FRED, artist, educator; b. Kenton, Ohio, Feb. 20, 1908; s. Fred and Ella Margaret (Traeger) M.; m. Sara Burleson Dunn, June 25, 1918; 1 son, Traeger. A.B., Ohio State U., 1930, M.A., 1935; postgrad. Chho. Art Inst., 1930-32, Art Students League, 1946; D.F.A. (hon.), U. Alaska, 1973. Painter, 1935—; writer, illustrator books; lectr. on Alaska; tchr. art U. Alaska, summers 1962-72. Served to lt. comdr. USN, 1942-45. Decorated Bronze Star; recipient silver medal Cowboy Hall of Fame wild animal competition, 1979; named Alaskan of Yr., 1977; Artist of Yr., Am. Artist mag., 1981. Mem. Explorers Club, Soc. Animal Artists. Stone lithograph collection in U. Alaska and Frye Mus., Seattle; Author (with lithographs) Panuck Eskimo Sled Dog, 1939, On Arctic Ice, 1939, Alaskan Paintings of Fred Machetanz, 1977, Oil Paintings of Fred Machetanz, 1980, Fifty Lithographs of Fred Machetanz, 1983; Wildlife Artists at Work, 1982. Home and Office: High Ridge PO Box 2589 Palmer AK 99645

MACHIDA, GERALD KIYOYUKU, state senator; b. Puunene, Hawaii, Sept. 23, 1937; s. Seichi and Mildred Yuriko (Hazuma) M.; B.S. in Mech. Engring., U. Hawaii, 1959; m. Eleanor M. Suzuki, June 20, 1959; children—Roxanne, Keith. Mem. Hawaii Ho. of Reps., 1974-79, Hawaii Senate, Honolulu, 1979—. Mem. Hawaii Heart Assn., 1970—, Maui Adult Edn. Adv. Council, 1975—, Maui Mental Health Assn., 1974—, Maui United Way, 1968—. Mem. Kahului Town Assn. Democrat. Clubs: Haleakala Lions; Waiehu Golf. Office: Room 218 State Capitol Honolulu HI 96813

MACHIRAJU, NAGABHUSHAN RAO, public health executive, consultant; b. Sompalli, India, Dec. 1, 1947; s. Subba Rao and Suryakantam (Kasinathuni) M.; m. Savithri, July 31, 1974. B.Com., Osmania U., India, 1966; M.P.H., Calif. State U., 1971. Registered internat. cons. Internat. Cons. Found. Asst. supr. div. vocat. edn. UCLA, 1971-74; dir. tng. Algorithms in Systems, Inc., Northridge, Calif., 1974-79; v.p. ICVT, Culver City. Calif., 1979—; lectr. Chapman Coll., 1979—. Mem. Am. Pub. Health Assn., Internat. Cons. Found. Author: Conversations With Doers, 1972. Office: 5805 Uplander Way Culver City CA 90230

MACIEL, RONALD JOHN, lawyer, motion picture producer; b. Hanford, Calif., Nov. 25, 1943; s. John Joaquin and Ludrie Virginia (Mendes) M.; m. Shirley May Lucchesi, July 8, 1967; 1 dau., Virginia. B.S., UCLA, 1966; J.D., Loyola U., Los Angeles, 1973. C.P.A.; cert. specialist in taxation law, Calif. Agt., IRS, Los Angeles, 1966-76; sole practice law, Glendale, Calif., 1976-79, Hanford, 1980—; pres., dir. RJM Prodns., RJM Electronics, Inc. Pres., dir. Port o' Call, Lemoore, Calif., O Fundo de Alivio Portugues; elder Lemoore Community Bible Ch. Served with USMCR, 1962-68. Mem. ABA, Kings County Bar Assn., Christian Legal Soc., Am. Assn. Atty. C.P.A.s, Am. Inst. C.P.A.s. Calif. Soc. C.P.A.s. Club: Kings County Cabrillo. Office: 521 N Redington St Hanford CA 93230

MACK, BRENDA LEE, public relations consultant, sociologist; b. Peoria, Ill., Mar. 24; d. William James and Virginia Julia (Pickett) Palmer; A.A., Los Angeles City Coll., 1969; B.A. in Sociology, Calif. State U., Los Angeles, 1980; m. Rozene Mack, Jan. 13, 1960 (div.); 1 son, Kevin Anthony. Ct. clk. City of Blythe, Calif., 1962; partner Mack Trucking Co., Blythe, 1961-64; ombudsman, sec. bus facilities So. Calif. Rapid Transit Dist., Los Angeles, 1974-81; pres. Brenda Mack Enterprises, Los Angeles, 1981—. Bd. dirs. Narcotic Symposium, Los Angeles, 1968. Served with U.S. WAC, 1960-61. Home: 8749 Cattaraugus Ave Los Angeles CA 90034 Office: PO Box 5942 Los Angeles CA 90055

MACK, DIANA TRIMBLE, interior designer; b. Nampa, Idaho, Apr. 24, 1953; d. Shelley Dell and Iris Joaquine Trimble; B.F.A., U. Idaho, 1976; m. John Frederick Mack, Aug. 30, 1978. Interior designer Showroom One, Boise, Idaho, 1976-77, Don Gile Architects and Planners, Boise, 1977; pres. Trimble & Assocs., Boise, Idaho, 1977-83, Dundas Office Interiors, Boise, 1983; mgr. interior design dept. Lombard-Conrad Architects, Boise, 1983—. Mem. Sales Mktg. Execs., Kappa Kappa Gamma. Republican. Roman Catholic. Club: Crane Creek Country. Office: 1221 Shoreline Ln Boise ID 83706

MACK, EDWIN BRYCE, banker; b. Honolulu, Feb. 19, 1942; s. Joseph and Maurine (Phillips) M.; m. Sandra Jo Scott, Dec. 31, 1976; children—Jamie Lynn, David Bryan. Student U. Ariz., 1959-63; B.S. in Fin., U. Houston, 1976. Loan officer Tex. Commerce Bank, Houston, 1968-71; v.p. Meyerland Bank, Houston, 1971-74; pres., chief exec. officer Navigation Bank, Houston, 1974-75, City Commerce Bank, Santa Barbara, Calif., 1977—. Bd. dirs. Las Positas Park Found., New Directions Found.; mem. Santa Barbara Parking Commn., 1980—. Mem. Santa Barbara C. of C. (dir.). Republican. Presbyterian. Clubs: Rotary, La Cumbre Country, Santa Barbara Yacht, University. Office: 915 State St Santa Barbara CA 93102

MACK, ROBERT LEONARD, hospital engineer; b. Watertown, S.D., July 12, 1929; s. Nicholas Peter and Eleanor (Heyn) M. Plant supt. Alexian Bros. Hosp., St. Louis, 1962-64, San Jose, Calif., 1964-70; adminstrv. engr. San Jose Hosp. and Health Ctr., 1970—. Bd. dirs., pres. Home Helpers, Inc., San Jose. Mem. Am. Soc. Hosp. Engring., Calif. Soc. Hosp. Engring., Nat. Fire Protection Assn. Office: 675 E Santa Clara St San Jose CA 95112

MACK, RONALD BRAND, dentist; b. San Francisco, Feb. 20, 1948; s. Edward Semmel and Susan Tabor (Brand) M.; m. Barbara Hamilton, June 16, 1973; children—Joshua Hamilton, Aaron Edward. B.S., U. Calif.-Davis, 1969; D.D.S., U. Pacific, 1973; cert. pediatric dentistry Ind. U., 1975. Practice dentistry specializing in pedodontics, San Francisco, 1975—; instr., mem. staff, Oakland (Calif.) Children's Hosp., 1976-82; instr. gen. practice residency Mt. Zion Hosp., San Francisco, 1978—. United Cerebral Palsy clinical fellow, 1973, 74; G.R. Baker fellow, 1975. Fellow Am. Acad. Pedodontics, Acad. Dentistry for the Handicapped; mem. San Francisco Dental Soc., Bay Area Dental Guidance Council for the Disabled (co-founder, 1977), U. Pacific Sch. Dentistry Alumni Assn., Calif. Dental Assn., Calif. Soc. Pediatric Dentists (bd. dirs. 1979-81), Calif. Soc. Dentistry for Children (pres. 1981-82), ADA, Am. Acad. Pedodontics, Am. Soc. Dentistry for Children, Ind. U. Pedodontic Alumni Assn. (bd. dirs. 1981—), Acad. Dentistry for the Handicapped, Am. Med. Joggers Assn., Nat. Running and Fitness Assn., Internat. Assn. Dentistry for Children, Internat. Assn. Dentistry for the Handicapped. Sr. editor, contbg. author: Essentials of Clinical Pediatric Dentistry; contbr. articles to profl. jours., chpts. to books. Home: 52 Madrone Ave San Francisco CA 94127 Office: 800 Santiago St San Francisco CA 94116

MACK, SHUN FEI, corporation executive, consultant; b. Canton, China, Mar. 12, 1921; s. Ming-Hing and Shen-Chuen M.; m. Alice D. Luu, July 12, 1978; children—Stephen T., Phyllis, Fontaine, Samson. B.A., Nat. Sun Yat Sen U., 1944; postgrad. St. Louis U., 1955-58. Lic. realtor, Calif. Pres. Marvels Realty, San Francisco, 1974—; chmn. bd. Magnum Internat. Fin. Group, 1982—, Magnum Internat. Devel. & Investment (U.S.), Inc., San Jose, Calif., 1982—; dir. Internat. Agrl. Services, Inc., San Francisco; dir. various corps. Served to capt. Chinese Air Force, 1946. Mem. San Francisco Bd. Realtors, Bankcard Holders of Am., Smithsonian Instn. Taoist. Author: Understanding South East Asia, 1949.

MACK, ZELLA EDITH, writer, real estate investor; b. Jonesville, Mich.; d. George Melvin and Edith Mae (Brown) Kennedy; m. Frank Patrick Mack, Sept. 15, 1945. B.A. in Polit. Sci., U. Calif.-Berkeley, 1944. Cert. legal asst. Nat. Assn. Legal Assts. Legal sec. various law firms, San Francisco, Boston and Sacramento, 1939-52, Calif. Atty. Gen.'s Office, Sacramento, 1952-63; aide to assoc. justice Calif. Ct. Appeals Third Dist., Sacramento, 1963-77; free-lance writer, Sacramento, 1977—; tchr. legal secs., legal assts. Mem. exec. bd. Camellia Soc. Sacramento. Mem. Calif. Writers Club, Nat. Assn. Legal Assts., Inc., Nat. Fedn. Paralegal Assns., Sacramento Assn. Legal Assts. (assoc.), Sacramento Apt. House Assn., Legal Secs. Inc., Sacramento Legal Secs. Assn., Am. Camellia Soc. Roman Catholic. Club: Sutter Lawn Tennis (Sacramento). Author: California Paralegal's Guide, 1977, 2d edit., 1982, columnist daily newspaper; contbr. various mags. Home and Office: Sacramento CA 95816

MACKAY, ALEXANDER RUSSELL, physician; b. Bottineau, N.D., Oct. 8, 1911; s. Alexander Russell and Eleanor (Watson) M.; B.S., Northwestern U., 1932, M.D., 1936; M.S. in Surgery, U. Minn., 1940; m. Marjorie Andres, July 16, 1941; children—Andrea, Alexander Russell. Intern, Med. Center, Jersey City, 1935-37; fellow in surgery Mayo Clinic, Rochester, Minn. 1937-41; practice medicine specializing in gen. surgery, Spokane, Wash., 1941-82, semiret., 1982; staff Deaconess, Sacred Heart hosps., Spokane. Served from lt. to capt., M.C., AUS, 1942-45. Diplomate Am. Bd. Surgery. Fellow A.C.S.; mem. Spokane Surg. Soc., N. Pacific Surg. Assn., Alpha Omega Alpha, Phi Delta Theta, Nu Sigma Nu, Phi Beta Kappa. Home: E 540 Rockwood Blvd Spokane WA 99202

MACKAY, ROBIN, aerospace mfg. co. exec.; b. Montreal, Que., Can., Mar. 27, 1931; s. Agret Albert and Marie Florence (Bruneau) M.; came to U.S., 1956, naturalized, 1964; B.A. in Math. and Econs., McGill U., Montreal, 1952, postgrad., 1952-53; m. Valerie Wilde Mackay, May 22, 1954; children—Heather Ann, Wendy Elizabeth, Trevor Duncan. Sales engr. Boeing Co., Seattle, 1958-64; dir. indsl. power market devel. Garret Corp., Los Angeles, 1964—. Mem. Am. Gas Assn. Clubs: Calif. Yacht, Redondo Beach Power Squadron (comdr. 1977). Contbr. articles to profl. jours.; patentee nutating nozzle, 1959, uninterruptible power system, 1977, solar-powered turbine system, 1981. Home: 6626 Locklenna Ln Rancho Palos Verdes CA 90274 Office: 9851 Sepulveda Blvd Los Angeles CA 90009

MACKBY, M. JUDSON, surgeon, educator; b. N.Y.C., Jan. 15, 1914; s. Jules C. and Selma Rose (Marbe) M.; m. JoAnne Jicka, Oct. 10, 1965; children—Peter Judson, Jenifer, Jo Ellen. B.A., Columbia U., 1934; M.D., SUNY, 1938. Diplomate Am. Bd. Surgery. Intern Bklyn. Hosp., 1938-40; resident Univ. Hosp., N.Y.C., 1940-42; Bowen-Brook fellow in surgery N.Y. Acad. Medicine, 1945-46; practice medicine specializing in gen. and thoracic surgery, San Francisco, 1955—; attending surgeon Children's Hosp., Presbyn. Hosp., French Hosp.; cons. surgeon San Francisco Gen. Hosp.; clin. asst. prof. surg. U. Calif. Med. Sch., San Francisco, 1964—; dir. 1st Nat. Bank of Marin. Served to lt. comdr., M.C., USNR, 1941-45. Fellow ACS; mem. Soc. for Surgery Alimentary Tract, Pan Pacific Surg. Soc., Pan. Am. Med. Soc. Republican. Presbyterian. Club: Rafael Racquet (San Rafael, Calif.). Author: (monograph) Surgical Treatment of Portal Hypertension, Bleeding Esophageal Narices and Ascites; contbr. articles on surg. to med. jours. Home: Box 824 Ross CA 94957 Office: 595 Buckingham Way San Francisco CA 94132

MACKER, PAUL KENNETH, professional basketball team executive; b. Denver. B.S., Loyola U., Los Angeles. Dir. pub. relations N.Am. Aviation, Inc., 1941-46, TWA, 1947-49, Philippine Airlines, 1950-53; pub. relations cons. Ampex Corp. in 1950's; pres. P.K. Macker & Co., 1954-60; sr. v.p. Communications Council, Inc., 1960-61; pub. Philippine Herald, 1961-67; pres. Inter-Island Broadcasters Corp., Philippines, 1961-67, Mindinao Radio Network, Philippines, 1961-67; commr., pres., chmn. Nat. Profl. Soccer League, 1967-69; pres. Internat. Corp. Counselors, Inc., from 1969; exec. v.p., chief exec. officer Golden State Warriors, NBA, Oakland, Calif., 1972-73, 80—. Recipient Durward Howes award, 1946. Exec. dir. Olympic Games, Swuaw Valley, 1960. Office: Golden State Warriors Oakland Coliseum Arena Oakland CA 94621*

MACKEY, BRUCE ERNEST, statistician; b. Akron, Ohio, Feb. 9, 1939; s. James P. and Virginia R. (Penrose) M.; m. Carol R. Llewellyn, Aug. 25, 1961; children—Sharon, Ann; m. Nancy K. Smith, Oct. 17, 1970. B.S., Akron U., 1961; M.S., Cornell U., 1964, Ph.D., 1966. Statistician, U.S. Dept. Agr., Beltsville, Md., 1966-69, Berkeley, Calif., 1969—; cons. Mem. Am. Statis. Assn. Author: (with Richardson and Hejl) Statistically improved animal tests for vaccine effectiveness, 1968; (with James B. Hoy) Culex tarsalis: sequential sampling as a means of estimating populations in California rice fields, 1978; (with James T. MacGregor) The micronucleu test; statistical design and analysis. Mutation research, 1979. Home: 1200 Peralta Ave Berkeley CA 94706 Office: 800 Buchanan St Berkeley CA 94710

MACKEY, DONALD R., veterinarian, livestock industry consultant; b. La Salle, Colo., July 6, 1919; s. Raymond E. and Mary F. (Pumphrey) M.; m. Ruth L., Sept. 6, 1941; children—Donald Jack, Lawrence Ray. B.S., Colo. State U., D.V.M., 1942. Registered veterinarian, Colo., 1942. Owner, operator Mackey's Veterinary Service, 1942—. Recipient T-Bone Club Award for Outstanding Service to the Livestock Industry, 1970. Mem. Profl. Veterinary Supply (pres.), Colo. Veterinary Med. Assn. (past pres.), Colo. State Veterinary Soc., Am. Veterinary Assn., Am. Assn. Bovine Practitioners, Agrl. Cons. Soc., Nat. Fedn. Ind. Businessmen. Republican. Presbyterian. Clubs: Elks, Lions, T-Bone, Greeley, Colo. Contbg. editor Feedlot Mgmt., Dairy Herd Mgmt. Home: 4704 13th St Greeley CO 80631 Office: 4704 13th St PO Box 57 Greeley CO 80632

MACKEY, JOHN DICKERSON, stockbroker; b. San Francisco, Dec. 8, 1930; s. John William and Norinne Dickerson Buck M.; m. Madeleine Gill, Apr. 9, 1950; children—Sheila, John, Lisa, Brent. B.S., U. Nev., 1953; M.A. in English, U. So. Calif., 1965. Stockbroker, Eastman Dillon, San Francisco, 1956-69; mng. ptnr. Henry F. Swift & Co., San Francisco, 1969—; mem. faculty Coll. of Marin, 1967-70. Trustee, Marin Community Coll. Dist., 1977-81, pres., 1979-81. Served with U.S. Army, 1954-56. Named Trustee of Yr., Marin Sch. Dist., 1981. Mem. Nat. Assn. Security Dealers, San Francisco Bond Club. Democrat. Baptist. Clubs: Le Cercle de l'Union, Mchts. Exchange, Elks, Marin Rod and Gun. Columnist Ind. Jour., 1982—. Home: 110 Diablo Dr Kentfield CA 94904 Office: 433 California St San Francisco CA 94104

MACKEY, WILLIAM KEMPER, JR., banker; b. Mansfield, Ohio, Jan. 7, 1932; s. William K. and Isabelle R. (Robinson) M.; m. Gretchen Franz, Jan. 3, 1936; children—Robin, Scott K., Perrin. B.S. in Bus. Adminstrn., Boston U., 1959; postgrad. Nat. Trust Sch., 1963-65. With Old Colony Trust Co., First Nat. Bank Boston (name changed to Bank of Boston Trust Co. of Ariz., 1979), Phoenix, 1959—, asst. trust officer, 1965-67, trust officer, 1967-70, v.p., 1970-79, pres., 1979—. Served with U.S. Army, 1952-55. Mem. Am. Inst. Banking, Ariz. Bankers Assn. (chmn. trust com. 1981-82), Central Ariz. Estate Planning Council (dir.), Phoenix Soc. Fin. Analysts, Phoenix C. of C. (chmn. retirement com.). Clubs: Arizona Country (Phoenix); Arizona; Madison Beach (Conn.). Home: 2007 E State Ave Phoenix AZ 85020 Office: Bank of Boston Trust Co of Arizona 2525 E Arizona Biltmore Cir Suite 119 Phoenix AZ 85016

MACKIN, DOROTHY MAE, hotel executive, writer, play producer; b. Hayden, Colo., July 16, 1917; d. Earl Glen and Ruth Lillian (Stacy) Mabee; m. Wayne S. Mackin, Mar. 5, 1946; children—Stephen Kirk, Susan Diane Mackin Lever, Jeffrey Wayne. Student pub. schs., Salamanca, N.Y. Sec., payroll clk. London Gold Mine, Alma, Colo., 1936-37; sec., saleswoman, buyer, officer mgr. Nobel Merc. Co., Denver, 1937-39; owner Intermountain Food Brokerage Co., Denver, 1939-43; co-owner, mgr., producer, dir. Imperial Hotel and Imperial Players, Cripple Creek, Colo., 1946—; guest dir. Star Bar Players, Colorado Springs, Colo., 1982. Trustee, pres. Cripple Creek Dist. Mus. Recipient (with Wayne Mackin) Larry Tijari Drama award, 1967; Gov.'s Hospitality award, 1981. Mem. Internat. Platform Assn., Rocky Mountain Writers Guild. Episcopalian. Club: Balboa (Mazatlan, Mex.). Author: The Imperial, 1977; Melodrama Classics: Six Plays and How To Stage Them, 1982.

MACKINNON, PEGGY LOUISE, public relations executive; b. Florence, Ariz., June 18, 1945; d. Lacy Donald and Goldie Louise (Trotter) Gay; m. Ian Dixon Mackinnon, Oct. 20, 1973. B.A., San Jose State U., 1967. Cert. secondary tchr., Calif. Copyright clk., Australian Broadcasting Commission, Sydney, 1969-70; edn. officer Ormond School, Sydney, 1970-72; tchr. Belconnen H.S., Canberra, Australia, 1972-73; mktg. mgr. Roadtown Wholesale Ltd., Brit. Virgin Islands, 1975-80; v.p., dir. publicity and mktg. Hill & Knowlton, Inc., Denver, 1981—. Mem. Pub. Relations Soc. Am. Home: 3855 S Monaco St Pkwy Apt 102 Denver CO 80237 Office: 909 17th St Suite 505 Denver CO 80202

MACKRO, JAY AUGUST, computer company official; b. Bridgeport, Conn., Mar. 15, 1949; s. August V. and Virginia A. (Winspur) M.; B.S.M.E., M.S.M.E., M.I.T., 1972; M.B.A., Stanford U., 1977. Analytical engr. Digital Equipment Corp., Maynard, Mass., 1972-75; tech. services mgr. Tandem Computers, Cupertino, Calif., 1977-80, ops. planning mgr., 1980—. Mem. Stanford U. Alumni Assn. Club: M.I.T. No. Calif. Office: 10300 N Tantau Ave Cupertino CA 95014

MACLAREN, GRANT WOODWARD, merchant; b. Vancouver, B.C., Can., June 18, 1933; s. Grant Oswald and Elizabeth Eleanor (Sanders) MacL.; grad. U. B.C.; chartered accountant; m. Sherrill Maxwell, May 17, 1962; children—Nicola Eleanor, Michelle Maxwell, Grant Douglas, Monique Elizabeth. With Price Waterhouse Co., chartered accountants, Vancouver; with Woodward Dept. Stores Ltd., Vancouver, store mgr., now pres., chief operating officer, also dir.; dir. Hastings West Investment Ltd., Chancellor Reins. Co. of Can. Ltd. Woodward Stores Ltd., Peter Cundill Fund. Trustee Lester Pearson Coll. Pacific; bd. dirs. Heart Found., Edmonton Centre, Project 200. Mem. Chartered Accountants Assn. Clubs: Vancouver, Shaughnessy Golf and Country. Home: 1529 W 35th St Vancouver BC V6M 1H1 Canada Office: 101 W Hastings St Vancouver BC V6B 1H4 Canada

MACLAY, DONALD TRACY, communications consultant; b. Buffalo, Mar. 20, 1933; s. Donald Edwin and Barbara (Tracy) M.; m. Caroline Ann Pedersen, Dec. 23, 1967; children—Nelson Donald, Tracy Anne, Craig Aksel. B.Mech. Engring., Cornell U., 1956; postgrad. exec. program Stanford U., 1977. Engr., plant mgr. Warren Wire Co., Pownal, Vt., Santa Barbara, Calif., 1959-63; plant mgr. Gen. Cable Corp., Santa Barbara, Calif., 1963-65; cons., assoc., v.p. Booz Allen & Hamilton, Los Angeles, Australia, Thailand, Korea, 1965-77; gen. mgr. Thai Zinc, Inc., Bangkok, 1977-78; pres. Tel-Max, 1977—; communications cons. and western sales orgn. for Via Titus, Inc., Los Angeles, 1977—, v.p., 1979—. Chmn., Santa Monica Unified Spl. Com. for Sch. Desegregation, 1978-79; chmn. troop com. Boy Scouts Am., 1980-82; bd. dirs. Point Dume Property Owners, 1980-81, Point Dune Community Ctr. Assn., 1982—. Republican. Office: 1801 Ave of the Stars Suite 201 Los Angeles CA 90067

MACLEAN, CHARLES CHALMERS, III, architect; b. N.Y.C., June 24, 1937; s. Charles Chalmers and Lee Selden (Howe) MacL.; B.A., Yale U., 1960, B.Arch., 1963; m. Barbara Ann Weathers, Dec. 6, 1974; children—Eric, Heather. Architect, Paul Rudolph Architect, N.Y.C., 1965-66, Pedro Mirranda & Assos., San Juan, P.R., 1966-69, Nicolas Quintana & Assos., San Juan, 1969-74, Taylor Pearson & Assos., Phoenix, 1974-77; pres. Charles C. MacLean, III, Architect Ltd., Phoenix, 1977—; lectr. in field. Lic. architect, V.I. and various states, including Ariz., Calif, N.Y. Mem. AIA, Nat. Council Archtl. Registration Bds. Episcopalian. Club: Ariz. Biltmore. Mem. design team: Roberto Clemente Coliseum, P.R.; other designs include: Shea Scottsdale (Ariz.) Center (winner Nat. Mall Monitor's Center of Excellence award), Park Santa Fe Plaza, Flagstaff, Ariz., Ariz. Heart Inst., Phoenix, Jack Londen Office Complex, Phoenix, Southwest Corp. Center, Tempe, Ariz., Scottsdale Fin. Center, Tempe City Ctr., Biltmore Fin. Ctr., Phoenix. Home: 2102 E Marshall Ave Phoenix AZ 85016 Office: 3930 E Camelback Rd Suite 101 Phoenix AZ 85018

MACLEAN, CHARLES RICHARD, credit bur., collection agy. exec.; b. Selma, Calif., Aug. 17, 1934; s. Robert Dale and Anna Belle (Benner) M.; student Willamette U., 1951-52; m. Joanna Acklen, Mar. 9, 1972; children by previous marriage—Linda Susan, Shawn Marie (dec.), Marta D. Surveyor, Oreg. State Hwy. Dept., 1952-55; with Stevens Equipment Co., Salem, Oreg., 1955-58; with S. C. Johnson & Son, Racine, Wis., 1958-71; pres. Central Oreg. Collections, Inc., Bend, Oreg., 1971—; pres. Credit Info. Services of Central Oreg., Inc., Bend, 1980—, Medallion Mktg. of Pacific Northwest, 1981—; dir. Assoc. Oreg. Industries, Consumer Credit Counseling Service of Central Oreg., Inc., Am. Collectors Assn., Inc., ACA Enterprises, Inc., Mpls. Co. advisor Oreg. Bus. Week, 1980, curriculum chmn., 1981. Mem. Oreg. Collectors Assn., Am. Collectors Assn. (pres. 1982-83), Med.-Dental Hosp. Bur. Am., Assoc. Credit Burs. Inc., Bend C. of C., Redmond C. of C., C. of C. of U.S. Western Collectors Conf. Republican. Methodist. Clubs: Bend Golf and Country, Bend Rotary, Elks. Home: 1670 NE Northview Dr Bend OR 97701 Office: 316 NW Greenwood St Bend OR 97701

MACLEISH-JENSEN, LINDA, management consulting firm executive; b. Wiesbaden, Germany, Apr. 11, 1951; d. Thomas Robert and Gisela Elizabeth (Gonnerman) MacLeish; m. Stephen Anton Jensen, Oct. 4, 1981. A.A. in Bus. Adminstrn. cum laude, Wesley Coll., 1974; B.S. in Bus. Adminstrn. cum laude, Del. State Coll., 1980, postgrad., 1982—. Clk.-typist Del. State Fire Sch., 1971-73, sec., 1973-76, adminstrv. asst., 1976-78, adminstrv. officer, 1978-81; pres., propr. Linda MacLeish-Jensen Assocs., Phoenix, 1981—; tech. asst., cons. U.S. Fire Adminstrn., 1976—. Bd. dirs., chmn. pub. relations com. YWCA of Maricopa County; mem. reproductive choice com. LWV. Mem. Am. Soc. Tng. and Devel., Internat. Soc. Fire Service Instrs. Roman Catholic. Contbr. articles to profl. jours.

MACLEOD, JOHN, basketball coach; b. New Albany, Ind., Oct. 3, 1937; s. Dan J. and Ann Elizabeth (Welch) MacL.; m. Carol Ann McGroder, Jan. 18, 1974; children—Kathleen, Matthew. B.A. in History, Bellarmine Coll., Louisville; M.A. in History and Phys. Edn., Ind. State U., Terre Haute, 1965. Coach high schs., Ky. and Ind.; coach U. Okla.; now head coach Phoenix Suns Nat. Basketball Assn. team; active hon. coach Ariz. Spl. Olympics. Active Soc. for Blind. Served with USAR, 1959-60. Named Coach of Year, Nat. Basketball Assn., 1980. Mem. Nat. Basketball Assn. Coaches Assn. (treas.). Office: 2910 N Central Ave Phoenix AZ 85012

MACMANUS, DONALD H., state senator; b. Des Moines, 1928; student Drake U.; grad. Am. Inst. Art, Mpls.; m. LaVerna MacManus; children—Jon, Margery, Lynn, Christopher. Exec. dir. Rocky Mountain Food Dealers Assn.; mem. Colo. Senate, vice chmn. legis. audit com. 51st Gen. Assembly. Mem. adv. bd. Colo. Hwy. Safety Div.; mem. adv. bd. Adams County Salvation Army; past pres. Adams County Young Democrats; past sec. Adams County Dem. Central Com. Served with U.S. Army. Mem. Colo. Soc. Assn. Execs. Democrat. Office: 1015 Kipling Lakewood CO 80215*

MACMILLAN, ROBERT SMITH, electronics engr.; b. Los Angeles, Aug. 28, 1924; s. Andrew James and Moneta (Smith) M.; B.S. in Physics, Calif. Inst. Tech., 1948, M.S. in Elec. Engring., 1949, Ph.D. in Elec. Engring. and Physics cum laude, 1954; m. Barbara Macmillan, Aug. 18, 1962; 1 son, Robert G. Research engr. Jet Propulsion lab. Calif. Inst. Tech., Pasadena, 1951-55, asst. prof. elec. engring., 1955-58; asso. prof. elec. engring. U. So. Calif., Los Angeles, 1958-70; mem. sr. tech. staff Litton Systems, Inc., Van Nuys, Calif., 1969-79; mgr. systems engring. Litton Data Command Systems, Agoura, Calif., 1979—; treas., v.p. Video Color Corp., Inglewood, 1965-66. Cons. fgn. tech. div. USAF, Wright-Patterson AFB, Ohio, 1957-74, Space Tech. Labs., Inglewood, Calif., 1956-60, Space Gen. Corp., El Monte, Calif., 1960-63. Served with USAAF, 1943-46. Mem. IEEE, Am. Inst. Physics, Am. Phys. Soc., Sigma Xi, Tau Beta Pi, Eta Kappa Nu. Research in ionospheric, radio-wave, propagation; very low frequency radio-transmitting antennas; optical coherence and statist. optics. Home: 350 Starlight Crest Dr La Canada CA 91011 Office: 29851 Agoura Rd Agoura CA 91301

MACMILLAN, THOMAS FERGUSON, educator, cons.; b. Burbank, Calif., Apr. 13, 1939; s. Robert Neil and Florence Eleanor (Ferguson) MacM.; B.A. in Philosophy and Lang. Arts, San Francisco State Coll., 1960, M.A. in Lang. Arts, 1961; Ed.D. in Higher Edn. and Counseling, U. Calif., Berkeley, 1969; m. Leota Ann MacDonald, Feb. 7, 1960; children—Aaron, James, Graham. Mem. faculty in counseling Napa Coll., 1961-68; project dir. NORCAL Research Group, 1968-70; adminstrv. dean, research and student services, Santa Barbara (Calif.) City Coll., 1970-73; dean of students, acting dean of instrn., mem. faculty dept. humanities, Mendocino Coll., Ukiah, Calif., 1973—; sr. staff cons. Center for Edn. and Manpower Resources, 1978—, also chmn. bd. dirs. Chmn. plan devel. com. No. Calif. HSA Bd.; mem. bd. mgrs., exec. com. Am. Baptist Chs. of West, 1982-83. Served with USCGR, 1957-65. Mem. Calif. Tchrs. Assn. (chpt. pres.), Calif. Jr. Coll. Assn. (chmn. research and devel. commn.), NORCAL Research Group (steering com.). Republican. Clubs: Masons (master Abell Lodge 146, 1979), Ukiah Rotary. Contbr. articles to profl. publs. Home: 1900 Mosswood Rd Ukiah CA 95482 Office: PO Box 3000 Ukiah CA 95482

MACNAUGHTON, ANGUS ATHOLE, diversified industry exec.; b. Montreal, Que., Can., July 15, 1931; s. Athole Austin and Emily Kidder (MacLean) MacN.; student Lower Can. Coll., Montreal, 1947-48, McGill U., 1949-54; m. Penelope Bower Lewis, Mar. 2, 1957; children—Gillian Heather, Angus Andrew. Auditor, Coopers & Lybrand, Montreal, 1949-55; accountant Genstar Ltd., Montreal, 1955, asst. treas., 1956-61, treas., 1961-64, v.p., 1964-70, exec. v.p., 1970-73, pres., 1973-76, vice chmn., chief exec. officer, San Francisco, 1976-81, chmn., pres., chief exec. officer, 1981—; dir. Canadian Pacific Enterprises Ltd., Sun Life Assurance Co. of Can., Can. Permanent Mortgage Corp., Dart Containerline Inc., Canadian Comml. Corp. Bd. govs. Lakefield Coll. Sch. Mem. Fin. Execs. Inst., Tax Execs. Inst. (past pres. Montreal chpt.), Que. Inst. Chartered Accts. Clubs: Pacific Union, World Trade (San Francisco); Mount Royal, Montreal Badminton and Squash, St. James (Montreal); Toronto. Office: 4 Embarcadero Center San Francisco CA 94111

MACPHERSON, BARRY LEE, psychologist; b. Lamar, Colo., Oct. 26, 1946; s. Wallace Alexander and Lillian (Rowe) M. A.A. in Psychology, Los Angeles Harbor Coll., 1967; M.A. in Ednl. Psychology, Calif. State U.-Long Beach, 1971. Cert. sch. psychologist, Calif.; lic. ednl. psychologist, Calif.; lic. marriage family child therapist, Calif. Teaching asst. Seal Beach Sch. Dist., 1970; psychometric asst. Savannah Sch. Dist., 1971; sch. psychology intern Long Beach (Calif.) Unified Sch. Dist., 1971; dist. psychologist Newport-Mesa (Calif.) Unified Sch. Dist., 1972, psychologist spl. edn., 1980; ednl. psychologist, marriage/family/child therapist in pvt. practice, 1977—; oral commr. ednl. psychologist lic. bd. Recipient WHO award Calif. Tchrs. Assn., 1980. Mem. Newport/Mesa Psychol. Assn. (pres. 1980-82), Am. Psychol. Assn., NEA, Calif. Assn. Ednl. Psychologists, Orange County Assn. Ednl. Psychologists, Newport/Mesa Tchrs. Assn.. Home: 515 35th St Newport Beach CA 92663 Office: 425 East 18th St Costa Mesa CA 92627

MACQUEEN, PATRICIA LOUISE, architectural firm administrator; b. Johnson City, N.Y., Sept. 15, 1940; d. Leonard William and Marjorie Mae (Lott) Coy; m. James Aldelbert MacQueen, Feb. 21, 1962; 1 son, Vincent William. Student Ventura Community Coll. Lic. notary pub., Calif. Office clk. L.G. DeFelice & Sons, Whitney Point, N.Y., 1964-69; gen. office staff R.W. Rudy, Johnson City, 1970-74; bookkeeper, sec. Robert Martin & Assoc., Ventura, Calif., 1974-76; bookkeeper C.E. Miller, Port Huenene, Calif., 1977-79; acctg. mgr., clerical supr., adminstrv. asst. W. John Kulwiec AIA, Camarillo, Calif., 1979—. Mem. Nat. Notary Assn., Nat. Assn. Exec. Secs. Home: 3015 W Wooley Rd Apt D Oxnard CA 93030 Office: 330 N Wood Rd Suite D Camarillo CA 93010

MADDEN, FLORENCE DURKEE, elementary educator; b. American Falls, Idaho, June 11, 1918; d. Frederick Daniel and Eva Elaine (Barnard) Durkee; m. David E. Madden, Mar. 7, 1940; children—Michael F., David T. B.A., U. Utah, 1939; student Idaho State U., U. Idaho, Brigham Young U., U. Colo., 1969-82. Cert. tchr., Idaho. Tchr. Parrish Kindergarten, American Falls, Idaho, 1967-71; tchr. Cassia-Power Dist. 381, American Falls, 1971—. Active ARC, Service to Mil. Families, Power County, Idaho. Named Tchr. of Yr., Dist 381, 1978. Mem. Idaho Edn. Assn., American Falls Tchrs. Assn., Delta Kappa Gamma. Republican. Presbyterian. Club: P.E.O. Sisterhood. Home: 708 Falls Ave American Falls ID 83211 Office: PO Box 316 American Falls ID 83211

MADDEN, MARSHA SHERRILL, employment agency executive; b. San Diego, Nov. 10, 1943; d. Vernon Shirley and Helen Betty (Taylor) M.; divorced; children—Lisa Anne Hurdiss, Kelli Eileen Cox, Charity Lynne Cox. Student UCLA, 1975, 80, Anchorage Community Coll., 1981-83. Personnel asst. Ins. Services Orgn., Los Angeles, 1974-75; customer service rep. Hughey and Phillips, Inc., Burbank, Calif., 1976; owner Ledger Line, resume service, Anchorage, Alaska, 1977—; ptnr., mgr. Quest, Inc., placement agy., Anchorage, 1980—; ptnr. Madden-Markey & Assocs., Anchorage, 1983—; mem. career planning faculty Anchorage Community Schs.; workshop facilitator Alaska Pacific U., Anchorage. Stage mgr. Theater Guild. Mem. Am. Soc. Tng. and Devel., Personnel Assn., Assn. Profl. Placement Services (founder, past pres.), Nat. Personnel Women. Club: Toastmasters Internat. (pres. Aurora 1983, publicity dir. Yukon council). Office: 6160 Old Seward Hwy Suite 212 Anchorage AK 99503

MADDEN, PAUL R., lawyer; b. St. Paul, Nov. 13, 1926; s. Ray Joseph and Margaret (Meyer) M.; student St. Thomas Coll., 1944; A.B., U. Minn., 1948; LL.B., Georgetown U., 1951; m. Rosemary R. Sorel, Aug. 7, 1974; children—Margaret Jane, William, James Patrick, Derek R. Sorel, Lisa T. Sorel. Admitted to Ariz., Minn., D.C. bars; asso. firm Hamilton & Hamilton, Washington, 1951-55; legal asst. to commr. S.C., Washington, 1955-56; law clk. Lewis & Roca, Phoenix, 1957, asso., 1957-59, partner, 1959—; asso. gen. counsel Blood Systems, Inc., Scottsdale, Ariz.; dir. Pacific Standard Life Co., Davis, Calif. Sec. Minn. Fedn. Coll. Republican Clubs, 1947-48; chmn. 4th dist. Minn. Young Rep. Club, 1948; nat. co-chmn. Youth for Eisenhower, 1951-52; mem. Ariz. Rep. Com., 1960-62; bd. dirs., chmn. Found. for Sr. Adult Living, Inc., Phoenix; bd. dirs., past pres. Jr. Achievement Central Ariz., Inc.; bd. dirs., chmn. bd. Found. for Sr. Adult Living, Phoenix. Served with USNR, 1946-48. Mem. Am., Ariz., Maricopa County, Fed. bar assns., Phoenix Soc. Financial Analysts, Internat. Assn. Ins. Counsel, Fedn. Ins. Counsel, Nat. Health Lawyers Assn., Am. Soc. Hosp. Attys., Nat. Assn. Bond Lawyers, Ariz. Assn. for Indsl. Devel., Phi Delta Phi. Clubs: Lawyers, Arizona (dir.) (Phoenix); The Barristers (Washington). Home: 3732 E Pierson St Phoenix AZ 85018 Office: 100 W Washington Phoenix AZ 85003

MADDEN, RICHARD BLAINE, forest products company executive; b. Short Hills, N.J., Apr. 27, 1929; s. James L. and Irma (Twining) M.; B.S., Princeton, 1951; J.D., U. Mich., 1956; M.B.A., NYU, 1959; m. Joan Fairbairn, May 24, 1958; children—John Richard, Lynn Marie, Kathryn Ann, Andrew Twining. Admitted to Mich. bar, 1956, N.Y. bar, 1958; gen. asst. treas.'s dept. Socony Mobil Oil Corp., N.Y.C., 1956-57, spl. asst., 1958-59, fin. rep., 1960; asst. to pres. Mobil Chem. Co., also dir. Mobil Chems. Ltd. of Eng., 1960-63; exec. v.p., gen. mgr. Kordite Corp., also v.p. Mobil Plastics, 1963-66, v.p. Mobil Chem. Co., N.Y.C., 1966-68, group v.p., 1968-70, asst. treas. Mobil Oil Corp., 1970-71; chmn. Mobil Oil Estates Ltd., 1970-71; pres., chief exec. to chmn., chief exec. officer Potlatch Corp., San Francisco, 1971—; dir. Pacific Gas and Electric Co., Del Monte Corp., AMFAC, Inc. From lectr. to adj. asso. prof. fin. N.Y.U., 1960-63. Bd. dirs. Am. Paper Inst.; trustee, chmn. Am. Enterprise Inst.; bd. govs., v.p., exec. com. San Francisco Symphony; bd. dirs. San Francisco Opera Assn.; mem. distbn. com. San Francisco Found. Served to lt (j.g.) USNR, 1951-54. Mem. N.Y., Mich. bar assns. Roman Catholic. Clubs: University (N.Y.C.); Pacific Union (San Francisco); Lagunitas (Ross, Calif.). Office: Potlatch Corp PO Box 3591 San Francisco CA 94119

MADDEN, SARA LEE, educator; b. Spearville, Kans., Mar. 24, 1928; d. Delbert Dewey and Arva Alene (Clark) Imel; m. Gerald Houk, Sept. 1948 (dec. Dec. 1972); 1 son, Robert Dewey; m. 2d, Donald Madden, Dec. 28, 1967 (dec. July 1979). B.S. in Bus. Adminstrn./Edn., U. Wichita, 1964. Cert. tchr., Calif. Sec., Office of Vets. Affairs, Salina, Kans., 1949-50; sec. engring. dept. Kans. State Coll., Manhattan, 1951-52; exec. sec. Transport Co. of Tex., Kwajalein, M.I., 1958-61; tchr. Wichitan High Sch. West, Wichita, Kans., 1964; tchr. bus. and office edn. Franklin High Sch., Stockton, Calif., 1964—, chmn. dept., 1967—;

tchr. adult edn. San Joaquin Delta Community Coll., Stockton, 1965-82; mem. Adv. Com. for Vocat. Edn., mem. Adv. Com. for Regional Occupational Ctr. Mem. Nat. Bus. Edn. Assn., NEA, Calif. Bus. Edn. Assn., Western Bus. Edn. Assn., Am. Vocat. Assn., Calif. Assn. Vocat. Edn., Stockton Tchrs. Assn., Kappa Delta Pi. Republican. Home: 3503 Harpers Ferry Dr Stockton CA 95209 Office: 300 N Gertrude Ave Stockton CA 95205

MADDOX, GRACE BERYL, economist, former govt. ofcl.; b. Hayward, Wis.; d. McPherson C. and Grace (Bailey) Maddox; student U. So. Calif., 1926-27, U. Calif. at Los Angeles, 1927-28; A.B., Am. U., 1954, M.A. in Econs., 1958. With various U.S. govt. agys., 1937-67; staff of U.S. mem. Internat. Mil. Tribunal, Nuremberg, Germany, 1945-46; Near East polit. analyst CIA, Washington, 1947-51, East European economist, Washington, 1952-56; economist FTC, Washington, 1956-67; researcher in field industry and finance. Recipient Superior Service award FTC, 1961, 67. Mem. Am. Econ. Assn., D.A.R. (Mission Canyon chpt.), Phi Delta Gamma. Contbr. articles to govt. publs. Home: 5796 Encina Rd Apt 5 Goleta CA 93117

MADDOX, ROBERT ALAN, atmospheric scientist; b. Granite City, Ill., July 12, 1944; s. Robert Alvin and Maxine Madeline (Elledge) M.; m. Rebecca Ann Speer, Dec. 27, 1967; children—Timothy Alan, Jason Robert. Student Purdue U., 1962-63; B.S., Tex. A&M U., 1967; M.S. in Atmospheric Sci., Colo. State U., 1973, Ph.D. in Atmospheric Sci., 1981. Meteorologist, Nat. Weather Service, Hazelwood, Mo., 1967; research meteorologist Geophys. Research & Devel. Corp., Ft. Collins, Colo., 1975-76; research meteorologist Atmospheric Physics and Chemistry Lab., NOAA-Environ. Research Labs., Boulder, Colo., 1976-79, meteorologist Office Weather Research and Modification, 1979-82, program mgr. weather analysis and storm prediction, 1982-83, dir. weather research program, 1983—; participant numerous sci. workshops; tchr. weather analysis, forecasting, mesoscale phenomena; presenter workshops on mesoscale analysis and heavy precipitation forecasting Nat. Weather Service Forecast Offices; cons. in field. Served to capt. USAF, 1967-75. Decorated Air Force Commendation medal with oak leaf cluster; recipient Superior Performance award NOAA, 1981. Mem. AIAA, (atmospheric environ. tech. com.), AAAS, Am. Meteorol. Soc., Nat. Weather Assn. (award for outstanding contbns. to operational meteorology 1981), Phi Kappa Phi, Chi Epsilon Pi. Contbr. articles to profl. publs. Office: NOAA/ERL OWRM RX8 325 Broadway Boulder CO 80303

MADDUX, JAMES TOLBERT, JR., pathologist; b. Water Valley, Miss., May 31, 1933; s. James Tolbert and Annelle (Perkins) M.; med. certificate U. Miss., 1955; M.D., Jefferson Med. Coll., Phila., 1957; m. Helen Delores Glisson, June 15, 1957; children—Carol Denise, Susan Diane, James Tolbert. Intern, Charity Hosp., New Orleans, 1957-58; resident VA Hosp., Phila., 1960-64; dir. Gulf Coast Dist., Miss. State Health Dept., Bay St. Louis, 1958-60; staff mem. VA Hosp., Phila., 1960-64; asso. dir. clin. labs. Rowan Meml. Hosp., Salisbury, N.C., 1964-66; dir. clin. labs. St. Patrick Hosp., Missoula, Mont., 1966—; asso. med. examiner Dept. Justice, State of Mont., 1981—; bd. dirs. Western Mont. Center for Med. Tech.; faculty mem. dept. microbiology U. Mont.; cons. in field. Bd. judges Mont. Sci. Fair; bd. dirs. Big Bros. Missoula, 1971-72; mem. Mont. Found. for Med. Care, 1977—. Diplomate Am. Bd. Pathology. Fellow Coll. Am. Pathologists; mem. Am., Mont. (chmn. lab. com. 1970-71, 1971-72), Western Mont. med. assns., Mont. Soc. Pathologists (v.p., 1968-69). Republican. Episcopalian. Club: Rotary. Home: 3925 Fox Farm Rd Missoula MT 59802 Office: 500 W Broadway Missoula MT 59801

MADDY, KEITH THOMAS, public health official, veterinarian; b. Knoxville, Iowa, Oct. 28, 1923; s. Aura H. and Helen E. (Rankin) M.; D.V.M., Iowa State U., 1945; M.P.H., U. Calif., Berkeley, 1954, postgrad., 1959-60; m. Colleen Jo-Anne Barlow, Nov. 30, 1946; children—Kathleen, Donald, Dana, Danille, Lori, Duane. Assoc. prof. vet. medicine U. Nev., Reno, 1945-47; vet. meat inspector U.S. Dept. Agr., Los Angeles, 1948-51; practice vet. medicine specializing in small animal practice, Berkeley, Calif., 1953-54; public health service officer USPHS, 1954-70, epidemiologist, Phoenix, 1954-59, chief exptl. epidemiology sect. div. air pollution, Washington, 1960-61, asst. br. chief, 1961-62, scientist adminstr. Nat. Inst. Allergy and Infectious Diseases, NIH, Bethesda, Md., 1962-64, Nat. Heart Inst., 1964-69, chief pulmonary diseases br., Nat. Heart and Lung Inst., NIH, Bethesda, 1969-71; staff toxicologist div. pest mgmt. Calif. Dept. of Food and Agr., Sacramento, 1972—; cons. to EPA, Idaho Dept. Agr., Ariz. Dept. Health, Nat. Research Council of Can., Dept. Labor, WHO, Nat. Inst. Occupational Safety and Health Adminstrn. Served with U.S. Army, 1943-45, 51-53. Mem. Am. Vet. Med. Assn., Calif. Vet. Med. Assn., Sacramento Valley Vet. Med. Assn., Intermountain Vet. Med. Assn., Am. Public Health Assn., Soc. for Occupational and Environ. Health, Commd. Officers Assn. of USPHS, AAAS, Am. Coll. Toxicology, Am. Coll. Vet. Toxicology, Am. Coll. Vet. Microbiology, Am. Bd. Vet. Public Health. Republican. Methodist. Contbr. over 100 articles on toxicology and comparative medicine to profl. publs.; contbg. editor books on occupational illness due to pesticides. Home: 1413 Notre Dame St Davis CA 95616 Office: 1220 N Sacramento CA 95814

MADDY, KENNETH LEON, state senator, lawyer; b. Santa Monica, Calif., May 22, 1934; s. Russell T. and Anna M. (Balzer) M.; m. Beverly Ann Chinello, 1957; children—Deanna G., Donald P., Marilyn M. B.S., Fresno State Coll., 1957; J.D., UCLA, 1963. Ptnr., Chinello, Chinello, Maddy & Shelton, Fresno, Calif., 1963—; mem. Calif. State Assembly from Dist. 30, 1971-78, now mem. Calif. State Senate. Del. Republican Nat. Conv., 1976, 80. Served to 1st lt., USAF, 1957-60; capt. Res. Mem. Calif. Bar Assn., Jaycees, Fresno C. of C., Blue Key, Sigma Nu, Phi Delta Phi. Club: Rotary. Republican. Home: 1221 Van Ness Ave Fresno CA 93721 Office: California State Senate Sacramento CA 95814

MADERA, JOSEPH J., bishop; b. San Francisco, Nov. 27, 1927; ed. Domus Studiorum of the Missionaries of the Holy Spirit, Coyoacan, D.F., Mexico. Ordained priest, Roman Cath. Ch., 1957; ordained coadjutor bishop of Fresno (Calif.), 1980, bishop of Fresno, 1980—. Office: PO Box 1668 1550 N Fresno St Fresno CA 93717*

MADILL, EDWIN JOSEPH, cons., former fgn. service officer; b. Charlevoix, Mich., Feb. 19, 1911; s. Robert G. and Elaine J. (Orlowski) M.; student Georgetown U., 1929-32, Columbus U., 1936-37, 41-42; grad. U.S. Army War Coll., 1957; Breveted Brig. Gen., 1972; m. Margaret A. Shea, May 9, 1934; children—Margaret Ann Madill Baptie, Mary Paula Madill Jarrett, Edwin Joseph and Michael Shea. Tax analyst Mich. Tax Commn., 1933-34; asst. supt. HOLC, 1934-36; successively acct., tech. adviser, classification agt., personnel dir. Office of Treas., Treasury Dept., 1936-45; asst. dir. Office Contract Settlement, Exec. Office of Pres., 1945-46; spl. adminstrv. cons., 1946; mgmt. analyst Dept. State, 1946-48; mem. civil service com. expert examiners, 1948; spl. liaison officer to Brit. and Can. govts. on emergency planning problems, 1947-56; spl. rep. Dept. State to Paris, 1948, 50, Rome and London, 1949, Philippines, Thailand and India, 1949, Rome and Geneva, 1950, Panama, France, Germany, Austria, Italy, 1952, France, Italy, Saudi Arabia, E. Africa, 1953, Italy, 1954, Italy, Austria, France, Eng., Ger., Spain, Greece, Turkey, Lebanon, 1955; spl. asst. to adminstr. Bur. Security and Consular Affairs, Dept. State, 1955-56; spl. coordinator to Italy, Lebanon, Syria, Jordan, Israel, Cyprus, Egypt, Iraq, 1956-57; U.S. consul, Calgary, Alta., Can., 1957-63, dean Calgary Consular Corps, U.S. consul, Auckland, N.Z., 1963-64, ret., 1964; cons. public relations adminstrn. and mgmt. engrng. Hon. mem. Canukeena Club, Lord Strathcona's Horse, The Queen's Own Rifles, King's Own Armored Regt., H.M.C.S. Tecumseh; hon. chief Sarcee Tribe. Clubs: Ranchmen's (Calgary); Royal N.Z. Yacht Squadron; Auckland; Northern, KC, Rotary, Elks. Author: Position Classification in the Federal Service, 2d edit., 1945; Manual on Emergency Procedures and Practices, 1950, edits. 1952-56; History of Emergency Planning, 1957; Genealogy of Five Families, 1977; The Madill Chronicles, 3 vols., 1983. Home: 5630 E Calle Del Paisano Phoenix AZ 85018

MADLAING, ART GABOT, real estate broker, fin. planner; b. Binalonan, Pangasinan, Philippines, Aug. 18, 1947; s. Emilio Baguilat Madlaing and Elena Gabot; Sampayan A.A. in Forestry (scholar), U. Philippines, 1967; cert. fellowship Christian Writers Courses, 1972, Calif. Sch. Real Estate, 1977; m. Virginia Jimenez; children—Wynema Joy, Darlene Vi. Asst. regional info. officer Bur. Forestry, Manila, 1968-75, community editor Forum Philippines, San Francisco, 1976; account exec. (pres.'s club awardee) Putnam Fin. Services; owner/broker Am. Bankers Realty; cooperating broker Roland Land Investment Co., Inc., 1982-83; mgr., notary public, pres., corp. broker Internat. Realtors Corp., San Francisco, 1978-79; dist. mgr. Fil-Am Enterprises; pub. Filipino dist. mgr. Am. Brokers Ins. Group. Mem. Calif. Assn. Realtors, Nat. Assn. Realtors, Nat. Notary Assn., San Francisco Bd. Realtors, Zeta Beta Rho. Clubs: Bagino-Californians (sec. 1980-83), Toastmasters Internat., Jaycee (life; press relations officer 1978, vol. editor The Informer). Author: A Plea for Christian Unity, 1974; Focus Philippines, 1975; Binalonan-A Town to Watch, 1975; real estate columnist Philippine News, 1982, Calif. Examiner, 1983. Home: 730 Madrid St San Francisco CA 94112 Office: 345 Gellert Blvd Penthouse Daly City CA 94015

MADOFF, JEREMY WILLIAM, psychologist; b. Los Angeles, July 30, 1951; s. Milton and Ruth Madoff; m. Jan Rosenbaum, July 11, 1976. B.A. in Psychology, U. Calif.-Berkeley, 1972; M.A. in Psychology, San Jose U., 1976; Ph.D. in Profl. Psychology, Calif. Sch. Profl. Psychology, San Diego, 1980. Lic. psychologist, marriage, family and child counselor, Calif. Postdoctoral psychology intern Southwood Mental Health Ctr., Chula Vista, Calif., 1980-81; treatment counselor Family Stress Ctr., Chula Vista, 1982—; pvt. practice, San Diego. Mem. Am. Psychol. Assn., Calif. Psychol. Assn. Home: 8011 Paseo Del Ocaso La Jolla CA 92037

MADSEN, DOUGLAS FRED, banker; b. Salt Lake City, Feb. 11, 1942; s. Marion J. and Marguerite B. Madsen; m. Kathleen McCarthy Riter, June 16, 1967; children—Maureen R., Christine M. B.S., U. Utah, 1965; M.B.A., Harvard U., 1967. Corp. fin. assoc. Blyth & Co., Inc., N.Y.C., 1967-73; 1st v.p. corp. fin. Blyth Eastman Dillon & Co., Inc., Los Angeles, 1973-79; exec. v.p. Capital Markets, First Interstate Bancorp., Los Angeles, 1979—; dir. several First Interstate affiliates. Trustee Chandler Sch.; bd. dirs. Hathaway Home for Children. Served with USAR, 1960-65. Mem. Fin. Execs. Inst., Los Angeles Soc. Fin. Analysts, Harvard Bus. Sch. Assn. So. Calif. (dir.), Town Hall, Lincoln Club. Republican. Presbyterian. Clubs: Calif., Annandale Golf, Duckville Gun. Office: First Interstate Bancorp 707 Wilshire Blvd Los Angeles CA 90017

MADSEN, JOHN WILLIAM, educator; b. Soda Springs, Idaho, Sept. 29, 1928; s. John P. and Dortha M. (Wood) M.; B.A. with honors, U. Chgo., 1950, M.A. in English, 1954; postgrad. Washington U., St. Louis, 1955-60, (fellow), U. Mich., 1956, U. Calif., Berkeley, 1960-62, U. Mo., 1970-72, Idaho State U., 1976-77; m. Ann Johnson, Aug. 8, 1967; 1 son, Peter. Asst. supr. night emergency staff ARC, Chgo., 1949-55, social worker, St. Louis, 1957-69, San Francisco, 1960-62, case corr. Midwest area, 1957-69; grad. asst. dept. English, Washington U., St. Louis, 1955-59; tchr. Whitfield Sch., St. Louis, 1956-60; instr. freshman composition So. Ill. U., East St. Louis, Ill., 1959-60; tchr. elem. sch. Oakland, Calif., 1961-62; asst. editor series publs. U. Calif. Press, Berkeley, 1963-64; instr. lit. survey courses, composition and linguistics Idaho State U., Pocatello, 1964-68; chmn. lang. arts dept. Sheridan (Wyo.) Coll., 1968-69; instr. adult basic edn., 1970; tchr. St. Louis Bd. Edn., 1971-76; counselor Alcoholic Rehab. Center, Pocatello, 1977; chmn. social work activities ARC, Bannock County, Idaho, 1977-79, employment counselor Ch. of Jesus Christ of Latter-day Saints, Boise, 1980-81, supr. group reading manuscripts in German, French and Latin, 1980-81; tchr. Head Start, Boise, Idaho, 1981—; writer TV programs, St. Louis, 1952-60; founder Iota mag., Idaho State U., 1964, editor, 1964-68. Served with USN, 1946-48. Council of Learned Socs. fellow, 1957. Mem. MLA, Linguistic Soc. Am., Nat. Council Tchrs. English, Basic Edn. Assn., Assn. for Supervision and Curriculum Devel., Nat. Assn. Social Workers. Democrat. Mormon. Contbr. articles on linguistics and edn. to various publs.; editor U. Chgo. Press, 1951-53, Hunting and Fishing News, 1971. Address: PO Box 3502 Boise ID 83703

MADSEN, LINDA GAIL, real estate company controller; b. Cleburne, Tex., Dec. 7, 1942; d. Raymond Woodrow and Georgialee (Stephens) M.; student Tex. Lutheran Coll., 1961-62, El Camino Coll., 1964-69. Jr. accountant Inglewood Wholesale Electric Co. (Calif.), 1962-66; office mgr. Christensen Orthopedic Co., Redondo Beach, Calif., 1966-71, Dryterior Inc., Lawndale, Calif., 1971-72; controller, corp. officer Patraco Inc., Gardena, Calif., 1973-74; chief fin. officer, dir. Head Shampoo, Inc., Carson, Calif., 1974-80; controller, office mgr. Cloverleaf Group Mgmt. Inc., real estate/property mgmt., Los Angeles, 1980—. Mem. Christian Bus. and Profl. Women's Council (treas. 1978-80), Nat. Assn. Female Execs., Nat. Notary Assn. Democrat. Lutheran. Home: 3724 Spencer St Apt 319 Torrance CA 90503 Office: 1801 Century Park E Suite 500 Los Angeles CA 90067

MADSEN, M(EAD) HERBERT, accountant; b. Milw., Apr. 12, 1926; s. Mead Herbert and Bernita Alma M.; B.B.A. with honors, U. Wis., 1950; C.P.A., U. Ill., 1956; m. Helen Towers, Apr. 22, 1961; children—John G., Marc H., Kent R. Mgr., Ernst & Whinney, 1950-76; treas., controller Nelson Irrigation Corp., Walla Walla, Wash., 1976—. Bd. dirs. Walla Walla County United Way, 1977-81; chmn. bd. trustees First Ch. of God, Walla Walla, 1981-82. Served with USNR, 1944-46. Mem. Ill. Soc. C.P.A.s, Risk and Ins. Mgmt. Soc., Inc. Mem. Ch. of God Anderson, Ind. Club: Union League (Chgo.). Home: 1952 Carl St Walla Walla WA 99362 Office: Rt 4 Box 169 Airport Rd Walla Walla WA 99362

MADSEN, ROY PAUL, educator, film animator, artist, sculptor; b. Chgo., July 7, 1928; s. Helmer Johan and Esther Nicola (Ellingsen) M.; B.F.A., U. Ill., 1951; M.A., U. So. Calif., 1963, Ph.D. in Communications, 1966; m. Barbara Jean Tozier, Sept. 6, 1952; children—Sally Dawn, Mark Hunter, Kristie Sue. Film animator Kling Studios, Chgo., 1951-54; artist, 1954-64; lectr. cinema U. So. Calif., 1961-63; film producer, lectr. Syracuse U., 1963-66; prof. film dept. telecommunications and film San Diego State U., 1966—; media cons. Dept. Justice, Dept. State, USIA, maj. corps.; USIA speaker, 24 countries. Huntington Hartford fellow, 1955-56; recipient Stacey prize, 1958; Hollywood Screen Dir.'s Guild fellow, 1960; recipient Jessie E. Lasky award, 1962. Mem. Univ. Film Assn., Soc. Motion Picture and TV Engrs., Internat. Assn. Film Animators, Cinema Circulus, Am. Film Inst., Sierra Club, Nat., Internat. wildlife assns. Republican. Presbyterian. Club: The Westerners. Author: Animated Film, Concepts, Methods, Uses, 1969; Impact of Film, 1973; editor: The Artist and The Real World, 1980. Home: 6431 Lake Adlon Ct San Diego CA 92119 Office: Telecommunications and Film Dept San Diego State U San Diego CA 92182

MADSEN, WILLIAM DANIEL, public affairs executive; b. Denver, Apr. 28, 1913; s. Emil Thomas and Mabel Wessel M.; B.S., Colo. State U., 1939; m. Mary Evelyn O'Connor, Jan. 11, 1947; children—William Daniel, Karen Elaine. Asst. to supt. Swift & Co., Denver, 1939-42; adj. Colo. Wing CAP, 1942-46; pres. Rocky Mountain Air Shows, 1946-53; air photo instr. U.S. Air Force, Lowry AFB, 1953-58; charter mgr. Vest Aircraft Co., Denver, 1958-62; pub. affairs specialist U.S. Air Force, USAF Acad., Colorado Springs, 1962—; tchr. photography Pikes Peak Community Coll., 1974—. Bd. dirs. Alumni Found., Colo. State U. Served with USAF, 1942-44. Named Sr. Mem. of Yr., CAP, 1981, recipient Brewer Meml. Aerospace award, 1982; named to Colo. Aviation Hall of Fame, 1982; Crown Circle award Nat. Congress on Aerospace Edn., 1983. Mem. Cross and Cockade, Aerospace Historians, OX-5 Aviation Pioneers, Aircraft Owners and Pilots Assn., Comml. Pilots Assn., Air Force Assn., Profl. Photographers Assn., Colo. Pilots Assn., Colo. Aviation Hist. Soc. (pres. 1979—), Colo. Aviation Assn. (pres. 1982), Colorado Springs Press Assn., Colorado Springs C. of C. (visitors promotion com.), Sigma Chi, Alpha Lambda Epsilon. Episcopalian. Clubs: Denver Pilots, Colo. Silver Wings. Editor, pub: The Aircraft Bluebook, 1958-63. Home: 1327 Kern St Colorado Springs CO 80915 Office: Room 3132 Stapleton Internat Airport Denver CO 80207

MAESTRE, JOSE MARIA, marketing, ednl. and mgmt. cons.; b. Allentown, Pa., Nov. 1, 1929; s. Jose Maria and Anna Ingeborg (Linde) M.; B.A. in English cum laude, Rutgers U., 1960; postgrad. Temple U., 1962-65; postgrad. in marketing and finance U. Calif. at Berkeley Extension, 1968, in marketing U. Golden Gate, San Francisco, 1968-71; M.A. in Bilingual Vocat. Edn., U. San Francisco, 1979, postgrad. in multicultural vocat. edn., 1979—; m. Theodora Joan Racin, Sept. 11, 1962; children—Lauren Margaret, Rebekka, Gwynnd Delaen. Accounting clk. Johns Manville Products Corp., Manville, N.J., 1947-56; supr. publs. Electro-Mech. Research, Princeton, N.J., 1957-65; product mgr., advt. mgr. Warner-Lambert Pharm. Co., Richmond, Calif., 1965-67; asst. to v.p. mktg. Pacific Press & Shear Corp., Oakland, Calif., 1968; mgr. mktg. services Lex Computer Systems, Palo Alto, Calif., 1969-71; nat. mktg. mgr. Concord Communications Systems, Farmingdale, N.Y., 1972-73; pres. Learning Tools, Inc., Oakland, Calif., 1971-79; owner P.M. Prodns., Oakland, 1971—; v.p. Inst. Community Relations Research, 1978—; instr. mktg. for small bus. Downtown Community Coll., San Francisco, 1980—; instr. computer literacy Mission Community Coll. 1978—; San Francisco, U. San Francisco, 1978-79; ednl. cons. minority bus. edn. projects, 1975-77; cons. migrant edn. Calif. Office Edn., 1976-77. Mem. adv. bd. Oakland Bi-Lingual Edn. Project, 1971-72. Served with AUS, 1951-53. Recipient Advt. award Reinhold Pub. Co., 1966. Mem. Internat. Tape Assn. (mem. adv. bd. 1972), Internat. Inst. Gen. Semantics, Rutgers Alumni Assn., Designed (with wife) proprietary math manipulatives; created 5 x 13 wall mural art deco motif commissioned by Shoong Found. and installed Paramount Theatre Arts; developer, condr. proprietary program Presentation Techniques for Minorities in Job Acquisition and Career Devel., 1980; contbr. articles on mktg. to tech. jours. Home: 6986 Park Blvd Oakland CA 94611

MAEWEATHER, KAREN SUE, telephone co. exec.; b. Indpls., Oct. 19, 1949; d. James W. and Katie L. (Segraves) Tanner; B.S. in Mktg., Calif. State U., Los Angeles, 1975; M.B.A., Pepperdine U., 1978. With Gen. Telephone of Calif., Santa Monica, 1969—, mgmt. devel., 1973-74, personnel research mgr., 1974-77, bus. strategies mgr., product mgr. residential services and direct sales, 1977-81, mktg. planning dir., 1981—. Mem. Am. Mktg. Assn., Personnel Women of Los Angeles, Internat. Assn. Personnel Women) bd. dirs. Los Angeles chpt.), Personnel and Indsl. Relations Assn. (bd. dirs.). Democrat. Baptist. Condr. research project on Flextime, 1976. Home: 2032 Brentwood Dr West Covina CA 91792 Office: 100 Wilshire Blvd Santa Monica CA 90401

MAFFINI, MARTHA WAHL LEEMAN, educator; b. Hartford, Conn., Jan. 20, 1939; d. William Fritz and Virginia (Yenney) Wahl; B.S., U. Vt., 1961; M.Ed., Boston U., 1965; postgrad. Clarke Sch. Deaf, Smith Coll.; m. Richard Orvo Leeman, Apr. 4, 1970 (dec. Mar. 1975); children—Harry William, Amy Rachel; m. 2d, William L. Maffini, July 8, 1982, 1 dau., Cara Suzanne. Elem. sch. tchr., Scotia, N.Y., 1961-64, tchr. speech Central Inst. Deaf, St. Louis, 1965-66; supr. lang. problem classes Horace Mann Sch. Deaf, Boston, 1966-69; tchr. hearing impaired Haman Elem. Sch., Santa Clara, Calif., 1970-74, Wilson Intermediate Sch., Santa Clara, 1975-81, Buchser Jr. High Sch., 1981—; master tchr., cons. in field. Coordinator, St. Andrew's Youth Choirs, 1980-83; active Cub Scouts, Brownies. HEW fellow, 1964-65. Mem. Am. Speech and Hearing Assn., Alexander Graham Bell Assn., Am. Heritage Soc., Campbell (Calif.) Hist. Soc., Alpha Delta Pi. Episcopalian. Author papers in field. Home: 65 S Milton Ave Campbell CA 95008 Office: Santa Clara Unified Sch Dist Lawrence Sta Rd Santa Clara CA 95050

MAGALLANES, CARLOS B., state hosp. ofcl.; b. Oxnard, Calif., Nov. 29, 1931; s. Florentino and Guadalupe Maria (Banales) M.; A.A., Ventura Coll., 1952; student UCLA, 1972; B.A. in Public Adminstrn., U. San Francisco, 1980; m. Josephine Vigil, Apr. 13, 1960; children—Carlos Martin, Maria Josephina, Anna Maria. Psychiat. technician Camarillo State Hosp., Oxnard, 1958-73, sr. psychiat. technician, 1973-76, affirmative action coordinator, staff services analyst, 1976-78, chief central program services, 1978—. Served with AUS, 1953-55. Office: Camarillo State Hosp Box A Camarillo CA 93010

MAGARY, JAMES FREDERICK, educator, psychologist; b. St. Clair, Mich., Apr. 26, 1933; s. Carey A. and Ethel E. (Douglass) M. A.B., U. Mich., 1954; M.A., Wayne State U., 1956; Ph.D., Ind. U., 1960. Diplomate Am. Bd. Profl. Psychology. Asst. prof. U. So. Calif.-Los Angeles, 1960-64, assoc. prof., 1964-70, prof., 1970—; vis. prof. Jersey City State U., 1962-63, U. Mich., Ann Arbor, 1972-73, U. Washington; Fulbright prof. U. Singapore, 1968-69; cons., researcher. Regents Alumni scholar U. Mich., 1950. Mem. Am. Psychol. Assn., Council on Exceptional Children, Am. Assn. Mental Deficiency, NEA. Unitarian. Author: Exceptional Child, 1960; School Psychological Services, 1968; Piagetion Theory and the Helping Professions, 1978, 80, 83. Home: 1016 S Gramercy Pl Los Angeles CA 90019 Office: 601 Phillips Hall U So Calif Los Angeles CA 90007

MAGEE, DOUGLAS THOMAS, oil company executive; b. Man., Can., Aug. 14, 1921; s. Arthur Rugless and Sarah Alice (Young) M.; m. Habel Hinds, Sept. 31, 1951; children—Susan Elizabeth, Douglas Neil; 1 stepson, Philip Cox. B. Mining Engrng., McGill U., 1949; M.Sc. in Petroleum Engrng., Stanford U., 1951. Engr., Chevron Standard, 1951-56; chief engr., mgr. prodn. Chevron de Venezuela, 1956-63; dist. supt. Standard Oil of Tex., 1963-67; asst. to v.p. Chevron Standard, 1967; mng. dir. Caltex Petroleum Indonesia, 1968-72; mng. dir., chmn. West Australia Petroleum, 1972-74; v.p., dir. Western Ops. Inc., 1974-76; regional v.p. exploration, land and prodn. Western region Chevron U.S.A., Inc., San Francisco, 1977—; dir. Long Beach Oil & Devel. Co. Adv. council Calif. Poly. State U. Served with RCAF, 1941-45. Decorated D.F.C. Mem. Alaska Oil and Gas Assn. (dir.). Clubs: San Francisco Stock Exchange, Moraga Country, Masons.

MAGEE, JAMES ALLEN, lawyer; b. Pensacola, Fla., May 14, 1940; s. Allan E. and Clara Diana (Rotter) M.; m. Dianne Mullane, Oct. 25, 1941; children—Caroline Elizabeth, Margaret Mullane. B.A., Yale U., 1962; J.D. with honors, U. Mich., 1966. Bar: N.Y., 1967, Calif. 1979. Assoc., Donovan Leisure Newton & Irvine, N.Y.C., 1967-73, ptnr.,

1973—, mng. partner Los Angeles office, 1979—. Mem. dirs. council Orthopaedic Hosp., Los Angeles; founding dir. Hollywood Presbyn. Med. Ctr. Found. Mem. ABA, Calif. State Bar Assn., Assn. Bar. City N.Y., Los Angeles County Bar Assn., Los Angeles Area C. of C. Republican. Episcopalian. Clubs: N.Y. Yacht, Circumnavigators (N.Y.C.); Calif. (Los Angeles). Home: 1590 Lombardy Rd Pasadena CA 91106 Office: Donovan Leisure Newton & Irvine 333 S Grand Ave Suite 4100 Los Angeles CA 90071

MAGEE, THOMAS JOSEPH, physicist; b. Bogalusa, La., May 11, 1940; s. Joseph Newton and Hazel Della (Reeves) M.; B.S., Tulane U., 1962, B.A., 1962, Ph.D., 1970; m. Karen Loushin, June 22, 1974; children—Sean Thomas-Andrew, Kimberleigh Elizabeth. Elec. engr. Lockheed Electronics Co., Houston, summer 1966; research engr. Boeing Co., New Orleans, 1963-66; research asso. Air Force Cambridge Research Labs., Bedford, Mass., 1970-71; sr. physicist Stanford Research Inst., Menlo Park, Calif., 1971-77; mgr. solid state physics Advanced Research and Applications Corp., Sunnyvale, Calif., 1977—. Mem. Am. Phys. Soc., Sigma Xi, Sigma Pi Sigma. Democrat. Contbr. articles to profl. jours. Patentee solid state devices. Office: 1223 E Arques Ave Sunnyvale CA 94086

MAGEE, WAYNE EDWARD, biochemistry educator; researcher; b. Big Rapids, Mich., Apr. 11, 1929; s. William Fredrick and Elsie E. (Gifford) M.; m. Nannette A. Pierce, June 11, 1951; children—Lawrence, William, John. B.A. magna cum laude in Chemistry, Kalamazoo Coll., 1951; M.S. in Biochemistry, U. Wis., 1953, Ph.D. in Biochemistry, 1955. Scientist, then sr. scientist Upjohn Co., Kalamazoo, 1955-71; adj. prof. biology Western Mich. U., 1970-71; prof. life sci. Ind. State U., 1971-74; prof. biology, head div. allied health and life sci. U. Tex.-San Antonio, 1975-80, prof., 1980-81; prof. biochemistry, head dept. bacteriology and biochemistry U. Idaho, 1981—. Wis. Alumni Found. grad. fellow, 1951-52; NSF predoctoral fellow, 1952-55; Mem. AAAS, Am. Chem. Soc., Am. Inst. Biol. Sci., Am. Soc. Biol. Chemists, Am. Soc. Microbiology. Contbr. articles and abstracts to profl. jours., chpts. in books. Research on phospholipid membranes, liposomes as drug carriers, immune modulation, monoclonal antibodies. Home: 472 Ridge Rd Moscow ID 83843 Office: Dept Bacteriology and Biochemistry U Idaho Moscow ID 83843

MAGGARD, WOODROW WILSON, JR., mgmt. cons.; b. Quincy, Ill., Feb. 5, 1947; s. Woodrow Wilson and Claire Lorene (Lyons) M.; B.A., Brigham Young U., 1971; M.P.A., Consortium of Calif. State U., 1978; m. Linda Margaret Davis, Dec. 30, 1967; children—Jared Isaac, Erin Leigh-Taylor, Solveig Kirsten, Christian Heinrich, Anica May. Div. mgr. Sears, Roebuck & Co., Provo, Utah and Ventura, Calif., 1967-74; adminstrv. officer County of Ventura (Calif.), 1974-78; founding partner Maggard, Maughan, Gress and Assos., Ventura, 1976—; founder Intermountain Property Services, Ventura, 1974—; v.p. econ./bus. devel. Dineh Coops., Inc., Chinle, Navaho Nation, Ariz., 1978-80; dir. econ. devel. City of Scottsdale (Ariz.), 1980-81; exec. dir., chief exec. officer Fairbanks Devel. Authority (Alaska), 1981—. Instr. real estate econs./appraisal Oxnard (Calif.) Coll., 1975-78; instr. bus. Utah Tech. Coll., Provo, 1978. Active Boy Scouts Am.; high priest Ch. of Latter-Day Saints. Recipient Dixwell Pierce award, 1975; cert. rev. appraiser. Mem. Am. Soc. Public Adminstrn., Internat. Right-of-Way Assn. (internat. property mgmt. com.), Nat. Assn. Rev. Appraisers (sr.), Nat. Council on Urban Econ. Devel., Urban Land Inst., Acad. Polit. Sci., Internat. Platform Assn., United Indian Planners., Phi Alpha Theta. Democrat. Club: Rotary. Contbr. articles to profl. jours. Home: 312 Farewell Fairbanks AK 99701 Office: Fairbanks Devel Authority Suite 514 First Nat Center 100 Cushman Fairbanks AK 99701

MAGILL, MICHAEL JAMES PONSONBY, economist, educator; b. Bradford-on-Avon, Eng., Nov. 17, 1942; s. J.H. Magill. B.A., Cambridge U., 1964; Ph.D., Brown U., 1970. Asst. prof. Ind. U., 1968-75, assoc. prof., 1976-77; Milton Friedman fellow U. Chgo., 1977; assoc. prof. Northwestern U., 1977-78, Stanford U., 1978-79; assoc. prof. econs. U. So. Calif., Los Angeles, 1979-81, prof., 1981—, also assoc. dir. Modelling Research Group. NSF grantee, 1976—. Mem. Econometric Soc., Am. Math. Soc., Am. Econ. Assn., Omicron Delta Epsilon. Author: On a General Economic Theory of Motion, 1970.

MAGLEBY, MCRAY, JR., graphic designer; b. Coalville, Utah, July 23, 1941; s. McRay and Florence (Demming) M.; m. Dianne Disorbio, June 26, 1965; children—Michelle, Justin. B.F.A., U. Utah, 1966. Designer, Bailey and Montague, 1966; art dir. Circuit & Eddington, 1967; mem. faculty Brigham Young U., Provo, Utah, 1969—, also dir. graphics; prof. U. Utah. Served with Air N.G., 1963-69. Recipient Gold and Silver award N.Y. Art Dirs., named Designer of Year, 1982. Mem. Salt Lake Art Dirs. (dir.). Office: 221 Brigham Young Univ Provo UT 84602

MAGLIARO, MICHAEL JOHN, JR., health care management consultant; b. Mt. Vernon, N.Y., July 8, 1948; s. Michael J. and Josephine (Di Marie) M.; m. Kathleen Maule, June 12, 1970; 1 son, Matthew Evert. B.B.A., Fla. Atlantic U., 1971, M.B.A., 1972; M.S., U. Ala., 1974. Grad. asst., instr. mgmt./mktg. Fla. Atlantic U., Boca Raton, 1971-72; adminstrv. resident Bapt. Med. Centers, Birmingham, Ala., 1973-74; pres. Med. Group Mgmt. Services, Inc. and adminstr. Simon-Williamson Clinic, P.A., Birmingham, 1974-77; adminstr. Rees-Stealy Med. Group, San Diego, 1977-82; pres. Michael J. Majliaro, Jr., Inc., Health Care Mgmt. Cons., San Diego, 1982—; adj. clin. prof. San Diego State U., 1980; cons. in field. Bd. dirs. Calif. Ballet, 1982—. Mem. Med. Group Mgmt. Assn., Am. Coll. Clinic Adminstrs., Med. Group Mgmt. Assn. Ala. (past pres.), Phi Kappa Phi. Republican. Presbyterian. Office: PO Box 201134 San Diego CA 92101

MAGNER, FREDRIC MICHAEL, financial services exec.; b. N.Y.C., June 27, 1950; B.A. in Internat. Studies, U. S.C., 1971, M.B.A., 1972, M.S. in Acctg., U. So. Calif., 1976; m. Rachel Sherrill Harris, May 14, 1972. Asst. mktg. rep. I.B.M., Los Angeles, 1976-77, assoc. mktg. rep., 1978-79, mktg. rep., 1979; mgr. project adminstrn. Western Bancorp Data Processing Co., Los Angeles, 1980-81; v.p., mgr. project devel. First Interstate Services Co., Los Angeles, 1981-82; v.p. First Interstate Bancorp, Los Angeles, 1982-83; sr. v.p. First Interstate System, Inc., 1983—. Served to capt. USAF, 1972-76. Cert. mgmt. acct. Mem. U. So. Calif. M.B.A. Alumni Assn., Assn. M.B.A. Execs., U. So. Calif. Alumni Assn. Home: 2200 Pine Ave Manhattan Beach CA 90266 Office: Box 54068 Los Angeles CA 90054

MAGNER, MARTIN, producer, dir. stage, TV, radio; b. Stettin, Germany, Mar. 5, 1910; s. Max and Zerlina (Silberstein) M.; M.A., U. Berlin (Germany), 1928; came to U.S., 1939, naturalized, 1945; m. Marion Palfi, June 6, 1951. Actor, Hamburger Kammerspiele, Hamburg, Germany, 1928-29; producer, dir. Nuremberg, Breslau, Berlin, Vienna, Prague, 1929-38; stage dir. Chgo. Opera Co., 1940-41, San Francisco Opera, 1972; producer, dir. NBC, Chgo. and N.Y.C., 1942-49, CBS, N.Y.C., 1950-63; instr., artist in residence drama and music U. Chgo., 1941, Northwestern U., 1942-43, Adelphi Coll., N.Y., 1948, Canisius Coll., Buffalo, 1958; artistic dir. New Theatre, Inc., Los Angeles, 1977—. Recipient several documentary awards AMA; Spl. award for maintaining consistently high standards Los Angeles Drama Critics Circle, 1975. Mem. Dirs. Guild Am. Home: 1282 S Burnside Ave Los Angeles CA 90019

MAGNER, RACHEL HARRIS, banker; b. Lamar, S.C., Aug. 5, 1951; d. Garner Greer and Catherine Alice (Cloaninger) Harris; B.S. in Fin., U. S.C., 1972; postgrad. U. Calif., Los Angeles, 1974, Calif. State U., 1975; m. Fredric Michael Magner, May 14, 1972. Mgmt. trainee Union Bank, Los Angeles, 1972-75, comml. loan officer, 1975-77; asst. v.p. comml. fin. Crocker Bank, Los Angeles, 1978, asst. v.p., factoring account exec. subs. Crocker Comml. Services, Inc., 1978-81; v.p., sr. mktg. rep. comml. services div. Crocker Nat. Bank, Los Angeles, 1981-82, v.p., sr. account mgr. bus. banking div., 1982—. Mem. Los Angeles Bank Creditmen's Assn., NOW, Wilshire Women's Bus. and Profl. Assn., Los Angeles Women's Profl. Bank Assn., Professions and Fin. Club, Textile Profl. Club. Home: 2200 Pine Ave Manhattan Beach CA 90266 Office: 2029 Century Park E Suite 3590 Los Angeles CA 90069

MAGNESS, ROBYN CHERI, paralegal assistant; b. Montebello, Calif., May 9, 1951; d. William and Marie A. (Kochman) Roux; m. Darrel L. Magness, Aug. 31, 1975 (div.), A.A., Phoenix Coll., 1971; B.S. in Edn., No. Ariz. U., 1973, M.A., 1974. Cert. secondary sch. tchr., jr. coll. instr., Ariz. Tchr. Flagstaff (Ariz.) pub. schs., 1973-76, Carefree Daycare Ctr., 1975-76; instr. Yavapai Coll., Flagstaff, 1976; paralegal asst., office mgr. Community Legal Services, Phoenix and Glendale, Ariz., 1977—. Bd. dirs. Little Candle Communities, Inc., Mem. Ariz. Paralegal Assn., Glendale C. of C. Roman Catholic. Club: Soroptimist Internat. Home: 5702 N 19th Dr Phoenix AZ 85015 Office: Community Legal Services 5540 West Glendale Ave Suite C105 Glendale AZ 85301

MAGNUS, LAVELLE GRABER, ret. sch. prin.; b. Ottumwa, Iowa, Jan. 3, 1920; d. Harold Wordworth and Opal (Funk) Graber; B.Ed., Chgo., Tchrs. Coll., 1942; M.A., Long Beach State U., 1956; m. Gordon Eugene Magnus, June 4, 1960 (dec.); 1 son, Larry Coffman; stepchildren—Joyce McQuade, Jack Magnus, Clark Magnus. Tchr. pub. schs., Chgo., 1942-44, Little Lake Sch. Dist., Norwalk, Cal., 1944-45; tchr. Lynwood (Cal.) Sch. Dist., 1947-65, elem. sch. prin. 1965-76. Mem. NEA (life), Nat. Assn. Elem. Sch. Prins. Assn. Calif. Sch. Adminstrs., AAUW, DAR (past regent, past dist. dir., state rec. sec.), Republican Women, Freedoms Found. at Valley Forge, Smithsonian Assocs. Methodist. Clubs: Universe, Eastern Star (Past Matrons club), Gethsemane White Shrine. Home: 1221 Oakmont Rd 178-B Seal Beach CA 90740

MAGOON, JOHN HENRY, JR., airline executive; b. Honolulu, Dec. 2, 1915; s. John H. and Juliet (Carroll) M.; student U. Calif. at Berkeley, 1933-35; m. Adele Whitlock, Oct. 28, 1939; 1 dau., Sara. Pres., Hawaiian Linen Supply, Ltd., 1941-60; pres., dir. Hawaiian Securities & Realty, Ltd., Honolulu, from 1955; pres. Hawaiian Airlines, Inc., Honolulu, from 1964, now chmn. bd., chief exec. officer; dir. Hawaiian Trust Co., Ltd., Castle & Cooke, Inc., Magoon Bros., Ltd., Magoon Estate, Ltd., Magoon Devel. Corp., Magoon Land Corp., First Ins. Co. Hawaii, Ltd., Cox Broadcasting Corp., Atlanta; mem. adv. com. to bd. dirs. New Eng. Mut. Life Ins. Co., Boston. Mem. Territorial CSC, 1948-53; bd. govs. Iolani Sch.; pres. bd. trustees Kapiolani Hosp.; bd. dirs. Hawaii Visitors Bur. Mem. C. of C. Hawaii (dir.), Phi Kappa Psi. Clubs: Outrigger Canoe, Pacific, Oahu Country, Waialae Country, Diamond Head Tennis; Met. (Washington). Office: Hawaiian Airlines Inc Honolulu Internat Airport Honolulu HI 96820*

MAGOWAN, PETER A., supermarket chain executive; b. 1942. Student Johns Hopkins U. Sch. Advanced Internat. Studies; grad. Stanford U., Oxford U. With Safeway Stores, Inc., Oakland, Calif., 1968—, real estate negotiator, 1968, various mgmt. positions, Washington, regulation mgr. internat. div., v.p., mgr. west coast retail divs., 1976, chmn. bd., chief exec. officer, 1979. Mem. adv. council Johns Hopkins U. Sch. Advanced Internat. Studies. Office: Safeway Stores Inc 4th and Jackson Sts Oakland CA 94660*

MAGUIRE, EVERETT WILLIAM, JR., lawyer; b. San Bernardino, Calif., Jan. 2, 1928; s. Everett Henry and Edith Marie (Droscha) M.; m. Nancy Lee Grant, Oct. 7, 1951; children—Nanette Eileen, William Everett, Constance Sue. A.A., San Bernardino Valley Coll., 1948; B.S. in Civil Engring., U. Calif., 1950; J.D., U. Calif.-Los Angeles, 1957. Registered civil engr., Calif., 1955; bar: Calif. 1958, U.S. Dist. Ct. (so. dist.) Calif. 1977, U.S. Dist. Ct. (cen. dist.) Calif. 1958, U.S. Dist. ct. (ea. dist.) Calif. 1974, U.S. Dist. Ct. (no. dist.) Calif. 1973, U.S. Ct. Appeals (9th cir.), 1963, U.S. Supreme Ct., 1975. Asst. hwy. engr., div. hwys. Calif. Dept. Pub. Works, San Bernardino and Los Angeles, 1948-57, sr. trial atty., div. contracts and rights of way, 1958-65; assoc. Grant & Popovich, Beverly Hills, Calif., 1966-68; ptnr. Shapiro & Maguire Law Corp., Beverly Hills, 1968—. Bd. mgrs. Palisades-Malibu YMCA, 1971—; trustee Pacific Palisades Methodist Meml. Found., 1979—, Pacific Palisades Meth. Ch., 1983—. Served with C.E., U.S. Army, 1950-52. Mem. ABA, State Bar Calif., Santa Monica Bar Assn., Los Angeles County Bar Assn., ASCE, Soc. Am. Mil. Engrs., Am. Legion. Club: Masons (Santa Monica). Office: Shapiro & Maguire Law Corp 8383 Wilshire Blvd Suite 310 Beverly Hills CA 90211

MAGUIRE, JOHN DAVID, educator, university president; b. Montgomery, Ala., Aug. 7, 1932; s. John Henry and Clyde (Merrill) M.; A.B. magna cum laude, Washington and Lee U., 1953, Litt.D. (hon.), 1979; Fulbright scholar, Edinburgh (Scotland) U., 1953-54; B.D. summa cum laude, Yale, 1956, Ph.D., 1960; postdoctoral research, Yale U. and U. Tubingen (Germany), 1964-65, U. Calif.-Berkeley, 1968-69, Silliman U., Chinese U., Hong Kong, 1976-77; m. Lillian Louise Parrish, Aug. 29, 1953; children—Catherine Merrill, Mary Elizabeth, Anne King. Acting chaplain Washington and Lee Univ., 1952-53; acting dir. Internat. Student Center, New Haven, 1956-58; asst. in instrn. systematic theology Yale Div. Sch., 1958-59; mem. faculty Wesleyan U., Middletown, Conn., 1960-70, asso. provost, 1967-68; vis. lectr. Pacific School Religion, 1968-69; pres. State U. N.Y. Coll. at Old Westbury, 1970-81; pres. Claremont (Calif.) U. Center and Grad. Sch., 1981—. Mem. Conn. adv. com. U.S. Commn. Civil Rights, 1961-66; participant White House Conf. on Civil Rights, 1966; permanent trustee and dir. Martin Luther King Center for Social Change, Atlanta, 1968—; pres., bd. dirs. Nassau County Health and Welfare Council, 1971-78; trustee Inst. Internat. Edn., United Bd. for Christian Edn. in Asia; bd. dirs. Assn. Am. Colls., China Inst. Am. Recipient Julia A. Archibald High Scholarship award Yale Div. Sch., 1956; Day fellow Yale Grad. Sch., 1956-57, Kent fellow, 1957-60; Howard Found. postdoctoral fellow Brown U. Grad. Sch., 1964-65; Fenn lectr., 7 Asian countries, 1977; recipient Conn. Prince Hall Masons' award outstanding contbs. human rights in Conn., 1965; E. Harris Harbison Gt. Tchr. prize Danforth Found., 1968. Mem. Soc. Religion Higher Edn. (bd. dirs. 1967—, pres. 1974-81), Hazen Theol. Discussion Group, Phi Beta Kappa, Omicron Delta Kappa, Democrat. Author: The Dance of the Pilgrim: A Christian Style of Life for Today, 1967; also numerous articles. Office: Office of President Claremont Univ Center and Grad Sch Claremont CA 91711

MAGUIRE, THOMAS ELDON, accountant; b. Piqua, Ohio, Mar. 7, 1952; s. Frederick Edward and Lois Jean (Englert) M.; m. Laura Marie Grew, Oct. 18, 1975; children—Steven, David. B.B.A., U. Notre Dame, 1974. C.P.A., Ill., Ariz. Agt., IRS, Chgo., 1974-77; tax specialist Bolan, Vassar & Barrows, Phoenix, 1977-78; ptnr. Main Hurdman, Phoenix, 1978—. Mem. Central Ariz. Estate Planning Council, Am. Inst. C.P.A.s, Ariz. Soc. C.P.A.s. Republican. Roman Catholic. Clubs: Rotary, Arizona (Phoenix). Office: Main Hurdman 201 N Central Ave Suite 2000 Phoenix AZ 85073

MAH, RICHARD, materials scientist; b. N.Y.C., Nov. 24, 1947; s. Foochu and Yu-Ou (Chen) M.; B.S., U. Ill., 1968, M.S. in Metall. Engring., 1970; m. Mary Angela Santogrossi, June 27, 1970; children—Emily Mary, Stephanie Jean. Materials engr. Dow Chem. U.S.A., Midland, Mich., 1970-71, sr. research engr., Golden, Colo., 1971-75; sr. research engr. C.F. Braun & Co., Alhambra, Calif., 1975-76; dep. group leader, project mgr. Los Alamos Nat. Lab., 1976—. Registered profl. engr., Calif. Mem. Am. Soc. Metals. Home: 525 Paul Pl Los Alamos NM 87544 Office: PO Box 1663 MS 770 Los Alamos NM 87545

MAHAFFY, LORRENCE ALGER, JR., retired naval officer; b. Coffeyville, Kan., Aug. 5, 1940; s. Lorrence Alger and Mary Jewell (Robb) M.; m. Geraldine Rose Odom, June 25, 1982; children by previous marriage—Lorrence Scott, Jon Paul, Wendy Suzanne; stepchildren—Juliann, Jeff. B.S., U. Kans., 1963; M.S., Naval Postgrad. Sch., 1974. Commd. ensign U.S. Navy, 1963, advanced through grades to comdr., 1978; ops. analysis officer U.S. 6th Fleet, Naples, Italy, 1968-70; navigator, ops. officer in U.S.S. Entemedor, New London, Conn., 1970-72, in U.S.S. Ulysses S. Grant, Charleston, S.C., 1974-77, Amphibious Sqdn. 5, San Diego, 1977-79, exec. officer in U.S.S. Ft. Fisher, San Diego, 1979-81, ops. officer in U.S.S. Long Beach, Bremerton, Wash., 1981-83; mem. faculty U. S.C., 1975-77. Mem. Tau Beta Pi, Sigma Gamma Tau, Sigma Tau. Methodist. Club: Carousel Dance.

MAHAN, JACK LEE, JR., real estate developer, behavioral scientist; b. Springfield, Mo., Oct. 2, 1941; s. Jack L. and Verna Jane (Wright) M.; A.A. in Psychology, Palomar Coll., 1961; B.A. in Exptl. Psychology, San Diego State U., 1964, M.A. in Exptl. Psychology, 1966; postgrad. in Sociology, Internat. Grad. Sch. U. Stockholm, 1966-67; Ph.D. in Human Behavior (Dr. Edwin T. Olson scholar), U.S. Internat. U., 1970; M.B.A., Nat. U., 1978, M.B.A. in Real Estate Mgmt., 1979; m. Ronna Clair Ward, June 27, 1964. Psychology aid sect. tuna behavior U.S. Bur. Comml. Fisheries, La Jolla, Calif., 1962-63, psychologist, 1963-64; teaching asst. in psychology San Diego State U., 1964; research psychologist Naval Med. Neuropsychiat. Research Unit, San Diego, 1965-66, 67-69, research psychology personnel tng. research lab., 1969; research psychologist U. Stockholm, 1966-67; Nobel Laureate programs officer Salk Inst., La Jolla, 1969-70; trainee devel. officer Peace Corps, Hawaii, 1971; exec. v.p., sec. bd. dirs. JAMACO Community Developers, Inc., Escondido, Calif., 1971-73; prin. Mahan & Assos., Archtl. Research and Behavioral Planning, Escondido, 1974—; v.p. Mahan Custom Homes, Inc., Escondido, 1978—, Jack L. Mahan, Jr. Co., real estate devel., 1977—, Milestones Awards Co., 1979—; instr. Palomar Coll., 1974—; mem. faculty Calif. Sch. Profl. Psychology, 1976—. Mem. Escondido Planning Commn., 1975-77; mem. San Diego Mayor's Task Force on Urban Design, 1975—; bd. dirs., pres. Escondido Regional Arts Council. Recipient letter of commendation UN FAO Hdqrs., Rome, 1964. Mem. Am. Psychol. Assn., AIA (Spl. award Urban Design 1976), UN Assn. for U.S., San Diego Zool. Soc., Environ. Design Research Assn., Assn. Study Man-Environment Relations, Calif. Assn. Realtors, World Future Soc. (pres. 1970-71). Contbr. articles to profl. publs. Home: 1982 Craigmore Ave Escondido CA 92027 Office: 401-E East Valley Pkwy Escondido CA 92025

MAHER, EDWARD PATRICK, management consultant, marriage/family therapist; b. Birmingham, Ala., May 22, 1937; s. Glennon Edward and Mary Elizabeth (Botts) M.; B.A./B.S., U. Minn., 1960, M.Ed., 1965; m. Constance Catherine Schorr, Oct. 12, 1973; children—Heather Siobhan, Maura Helene. Tchr., coach pub. schs., Excelsior, Minn., 1961-66; trainer adult vols. for youth programs K.C., New Haven, 1966-70; exec. v.p. Action Display, Inc., Mpls., 1970-72; mgr. Sanford Rose Assos., Mpls., 1972-73; sales mgr. Progress Assn., Mpls., 1973-76; owner, dir. Power Action Tng., HOPE Unltd., La Mesa, Calif. 1976—; faculty U. Calif. Extension, San Diego, 1980—. Named Jr. C. of C. Outstanding Young Man, 1965. Cert. alcoholism counselor. Mem. Calif. Assn. Marriage and Family Therapists (chmn. profl. edn. 1979—, pres. edn. found. 1983-84), Am. Soc. Tng. and Devel., Calif. Assn. Alcoholism Counselors, Nat. Assn. Alcoholism Counselors. Home: 4383 Rous St San Diego CA 92122 Office: 7373 University Ave Suite 208 La Mesa CA 92041

MAHER, JOHN FRANCIS, investment banker; b. Berkeley, Calif., Apr. 25, 1943; s. Edward J. and Emilia (Radovan) M.; B.S., Menlo Coll., 1965; M.B.A. (Joseph Wharton fellow), U. Pa., 1967; m. Helen Stillman, March 20, 1976; children—Michael Stillman, Helen Cathline; children by previous marriage—E. John, Elizabeth Ann. First v.p. Blyth Eastman Dillon, Inc. and gen. partner Eastman Dillon Union Securities Co., N.Y.C., 1967-73; exec. v.p. fin. adminstrn. Great Western Fin. Corp., Beverly Hills, Calif., 1973-76, now dir.; exec. v.p. Blyth Eastman Dillon, Los Angeles, 1976-79; mng. dir. Lehman Bros. Kuhn Loeb Inc., 1979—. Bd. dirs. ARC, Big Bros. of Greater Los Angeles, YMCA of Met. Los Angeles; trustee St. John's Hosp. and Health Center Found. Clubs: Bel Air Bay, Calif., Los Angeles Country. Office: 515 S Figueroa St Los Angeles CA 90071

MAHER, KEVIN EDWARD, project engr.; b. N.Y.C., July 13, 1949; s. Edward Stephen and Margaret (Jackson) M.; B.S. in Physics, U. Mo., St. Louis, 1971; M.S. in Physics, U. Wis., Madison, 1973. Product devel. engr. Spectra-Physics, Mountain View, Calif., 1975-76, mfg. engr., 1976-78, sr. engr., 1978-79, project engr., 1979-80; project engr. Coherent Inc., Palo Alto, Calif., 1980-83; lead engr. Videodisk div. McDonnell Douglas Electronics Co., Palo Alto, 1983—. Mem. Optical Soc. Am., Soc. Photo-Optical Instrumentation Engrs. Home: 200 Mariposa Ave Mountain View CA 94041 Office: 1057 E Meadow Circle Palo Alto CA 94304

MAHER, LEO THOMAS, bishop; b. Mt. Union, Iowa, July 1, 1915; s. Thomas and Mary (Teberg) M.; ed. St. Joseph's Coll., Mountain View, Calif., also St. Patrick's Sem., Menlo Park, Calif. Ordained priest Roman Cath. Ch.; asst. pastor in San Francisco, 1944-47; sec. archbishop of San Francisco, 1947-61; chancellor Archdiocese San Francisco, 1956-62, dir. vocations, 1957-62, archdiocesan consultor, 1959-62; apptd. domestic prelate, 1954; bishop Santa Rosa, Calif., 1962-69; 3d bishop of San Diego, 1969—; prior Western Lieutenancy of Knights and Ladies of Holy Sepulchre. Bd. dirs. Soc. Propagation of Faith, Youth's Director. Cath. Youth Orgn.; chmn. bd. trustees U. San Diego. Del. Ecumenical Council, Rome, Italy, 1962, 63, 64, 65. Home: 2031 Sunset Blvd San Diego CA 92103 Office: Diocesan Office Alcala Park San Diego CA 92110

MAHER, PETREA ANN, magazine editor, writer, artist; b. N.Y.C., June 18, 1933; d. William Randolph Hall and Anna Petrea (Swenson) H.; m. James J. Maher, May 7, 1955; children—James Scott, William Clay, Jon Paul. Student N.Y. State Tchrs. Coll.-Potsdam, 1951-52. Profl. water skier, Cypress Gardens, Fla., 1953-54; editor-in-chief Refunder's Digest, Santa Barbara, Calif., 1979—. Mem. Scripps Inst. Oceanography (sr. docent 1973-76), Oceanids. Club: Santa Barbara Yacht. Editor Extra Income Mag. Home: 740 Monte Dr Santa Barbara CA 93110

MAHILUM, PAULITA MELCHOR, extension home economist; b. Surigao City, Philippines, Oct. 10, 1935; d. Sotero and Claudia (Rendon)

Melchor; m. Benjamin Comawas Mahilum, July 26, 1956; children—David, Lourdes, Ma Junever, Lyman, Jorge, Don. B.S. in Home Econs., Central Mindanao U., Musuan, Bukidnon, Philippines, 1958; M.S. in Homes Econs. Edn., Okla. State U., 1969, Ed.D. in Home Econs. Edn., 1971. Vocat. tchr. Negros Occidental Nat. Agrl. Sch., Kabankalan, Negros Occidental, Philippines, 1959-61; high sch. tchr. U. So. Mindanao, Kabacau, North Cotabato, Philippines, 1962-66; instr. coll., 1966-71, asst. prof., 1971-73; assoc. prof., guidance counselor U. Eastern Philippines, Catarman, No. Samar, 1973-74; assoc. prof., chmn. dept. home sci. Visayas State Coll. of Agr., Baybay, Leyte, Philippines, 1974-76; lectr. food sci. Coll. Agr. U. Hawaii, Hilo, 1980-81; tchr. English, St. Joseph High Sch., Hilo, 1981; county extension home economist Hawaii Inst. of Tropical Agr. and Human Resources, U. Hawaii, Honolulu, 1982—. Altrusa Internat. grantee, 1968-69; Philanthropic & Ednl. Orgn. scholar, 1969-71; recipient Grad. Excellence award Okla. State U., 1969, 70, Presdl. Honor award 1970. Mem. AAUP, NEA, Am. Home Econs. Assn., Hawaii Home Econs. Assn., Internat. Fedn. of Home Economists, U. Hawaii Profl. Assembly, Nat. Assn. Extension 4-H Agts., Hawaii Assn. Extension Home Economists (chairperson profl. improvement com.), Omicron Nu, Phi Kappa Phi. Roman Catholic. Contbr. articles to profl. jours. Home: Gen Delivery Kamuela HI 96743 Office: PO Box 335 Honokaa HI 96727

MAHLER, DAVID, chem. co. exec.; b. San Francisco; s. John and Jennie (Morgan) M.; Ph.C., U. So. Calif., 1932; children—Darrell, Glenn. Pres., United Drug Co., Glendale, Calif., 1934-37, Blue Cross Labs., Inc., Saugus, Calif., 1937—. Active Fund for Animals, Friends of Animals, Com. for Humane Legislations; patron Huntington Hartford Theatre, Hollywood, Calif. Mem. Packaging and Research Devel. Inst. (hon.), Anti-Defamation League, Skull and Daggar, Rho Pi Phi. Office: 26411 N Golden Valley Rd Saugus CA 91350

MAHMOUDI, HODA, sociology educator; b. Tehran, Iran, Oct. 24, 1948; came to U.S., 1959; s. Jalil and Badri (Behnam) M.; m. Richard W. DaBell, June 21, 1975; 1 child, Bijan DaBell. B.A. in Psychology, U. Utah, 1972, M.A. in Edn. Psychology, 1973; Ph.D. in Sociology, 1979. Instr. sociology dept. U. Utah, Salt Lake City, 1976-79; asst. prof. sociology Westminster Coll., Salt Lake City, 1979-81, prof., 1981—; acting dir. Middle East Library, U. Utah, 1978-79. Mem. Am. Sociol. Assn., Pacific Sociol. Assn., Western Social Sci. Assn. Bahai. Contbr. chpts. to books, articles to profl. jours. Office: Westminster Coll 1840 South 1300 E Salt Lake City UT 84105

MAHONEY, JAMES CHARLES, quality engineer; b. Buffalo, Sept. 28, 1950; s. James Joseph and Margaret (Cromwell) M.; m. Beverly Jean Nagel, Jan. 19, 1974; 1 dau., Mya Sioban. B.S., SUNY-Buffalo, 1977. Quality engr. Naval Air Rework Facility, Alameda, Calif., 1977-81, aircraft maintenance engr., 1981-82; quality engr. Systron Donner, Concord, Calif., 1982—; tchr. in field. Pres. Solano County Apt. Assn.; mem. Benicia Library Bd. Served with USAF, 1969-73. Mem. AAAS, Am. Soc. Quality Control. Developer quality assurance info. systems, quality report formats. Office: 935 Detroit Ave Concord CA 94518

MAHONEY, PATRICK FRANCIS, naval officer; b. Norwalk, Conn., Jan. 13, 1941; s. Joseph Francis and Catherine (McCue) M.; m. Karyl Ann Sager, May 27, 1967; children—Sean, Kerryn, Kelleigh. A.B., Bradley U., 1963; M.A., U. No. Colo., 1978. Commd. U.S. Navy, 1963, advanced through grades to comdr., 1978; ops. officer Sqdn. 33, 1977; comdg. officer Helicopter Anti-Submarine Sqdn., 37, 1978-79; air strike officer, comdr. Cruiser Destroyer Group One, 1980-82, staff mem. to comdr. Naval Air Force, Pacific Fleet, 1982—. Decorated Air medal (2); recipient award for outstanding leadership San Diego Jr. C. of C., 1974. Mem. Am. Helicopter Soc., U.S. Naval Inst., Navy Helicopter Assn., U.S. Coast Guard Aux., Acad. Polit. Sci. Republican. Roman Catholic.

MAHONEY, THOMAS WREN, banker; b. Holyoke, Mass., Nov. 26, 1928; s. John F. and Mary V. (McNamara) M.; m. Elizabeth A. Mueller, May 16, 1981; children by previous marriage—Terese Ann, Thomas Wren, Daniel M., Gregory M., Kathryn H., Jason E. M.B.A., U. Chgo., 1964. Dir. fin. communications/research United Bank Denver; v.p.-mgr. Hawaii Bancorp Leasing, Honolulu, 1971-72, pres., 1972-73; sr. v.p. Bank of Hawaii, Honolulu, 1981—; pres. Bancorp Leasing of Hawaii, 1982—, Bancorp Fin. of Hawaii, 1982—, Bancorp Bus. Systems of Hawaii, 1982—. Vice pres., mem. exec. com. Hawaii Opera; bd. dirs. Vietnam Vets. Leadership Program; planning cons. Hawaii Visitors Bureau; active Goodwill Industries. Served to maj. USAF, 1949-69. Decorated Air medal, Air Force Commendation medal. Mem. Am. Bankers Assn. (exec. mktg. com.), Bank Mktg. Assn., Nat. Assn. Accts. Roman Catholic. Clubs: Plaza, Press. Home: 72 Makaweli St Honolulu HI 96825 Office: PO Box 2900 Bank of Hawaii Honolulu HI 96846

MAHONY, ROGER MICHAEL, bishop; b. Hollywood, Calif., Feb. 27, 1936; s. Victory James and Loretta Marie (Baron) M. A.A., Our Lady Queen of the Angels Sem., 1956; B.A., St. John's Sem. Coll., 1958, B.S.T., 1962; M.S.W., Cath. U. Am., 1964. Ordained priest, Roman Catholic Ch., 1962; asst. pastor St. John's Cathedral, Fresno, Calif., 1962; in residence St. Genevieve's Parish, Fresno, 1964, adminstr., 1964-67, pastor, 1967-68; in residence St. John's Cathedral, Fresno, 1968-73, rector, 1973-80; ordained bishop, 1975; titular bishop of Tamascani and aux. to bishop of Fresno, 1975-80; vicar gen. Diocese of Fresno, 1975-80, chancellor, 1970-80; Diocesan dir. Cath. Charieies and Social Service, Fresno, 1964-70; exec. Cath. Welfare Bur., Fresno, 1964-70, Infant of Prague Adoption Service, 1964-70; chaplain St. Vincent de Paul Soc., Fresno, 1964-70; mem. faculty Fresno State U. extension div., 1965-67; sec. U.S. Cath. bishops ad hoc com. on farm labor Nat. Conf. Cath. Bishops, 1970-75; chmn. com. pub. welfare and income maintenance Nat. Conf. Cath. Charities, 1969-70; dir. West Coast regional office Bishops Com. Spanish-Speaking, 1967-70; chmn. Calif. Assn. Cath. Charities Dirs., 1965-69; trustee St. Patrick's Sem. Archdiocese of San Francisco, 1974-75; bishop of Stockton (Calif.), 1980—. Mem. Urban Coalition of Fresno, 1968-72, Fresno County Econ. Opportunities Commn., 1964-65, Fresno County Alcoholic Rehab. Com., 1966-67, Fresno City Charter Rev. Com., 1968-70, Mexican-Am. Council Better Housing, 1968-72, Redevel. Agy. City of Fresno, 1970-75; dir. Fresno Community Workshop, 1965-67; trustee St. Agnes Hosp. Named chaplain to His Holiness Pope Paul VI, 1967; named Young Man of Yr., Fresno Jaycees, 1967. Mem. Canon Law Soc., Nat. Assn. Social Workers. Office: Diocese of Stockton Chancery Office 1105 N Lincoln St Stockton CA 95203*

MAHR, THOMAS ANTHONY, air force officer; b. Bethlehem, Pa., Apr. 23, 1949; s. Anthony John and Kathleen (Faulkner) M.; m. Lou Ann Gurney, Jan. 14, 1972 (div.). B.S. in Internat. Affairs, U.S. Air Force Acad., 1971; M.A. in Mass Communications, U. Denver, 1977. Commd. 2d lt. U.S. Air Force, 1971, advanced through grades to maj., 1980; dep. chief info. Carswell AFB, Tex., 1971-74; chief pub. affairs div. Hdqrs. 13th Air Force, Clark Air Base, Philippines, 1974-76; chief plans, policy and security rev. br. Office Pub. Affairs, Hdqrs. SAC, Offutt AFB, Nebr., 1977-80, exec. officer, 1980-81, student Air Command and Staff Coll., Maxwell AFB, Ala., 1981-82, chief plans and resources div. Office Pub. Affairs, U.S. Air Force Acad., Colorado Springs, Colo., 1982—. Named Disting. Grad., Air Force Inst. Tech., U. Denver, 1977, Squadron Officers' Sch., 1979, Air Command and Staff Coll., 1982. Mem. Pub. Relations Soc. Am. (accredited), Air Force Assn. Republican. Methodist. Home: 3173 Dublin Blvd Colorado Springs CO 80198 Office: Pub Affairs US Air Force Academy CO 80840

MAIBAUM, MATTHEW, cons. psychologist, writer; b. Chgo., Aug. 14, 1946; s. Richard Walter and Sylvia (Kamion) M.; A.B., U. Calif.-Berkeley, 1969; M.P.A., UCLA, 1970; Ph.D., Calif. Sch. Profl. Psychology, 1975; Ph.D. in Polit. Sci., Claremont Grad. Sch., 1980. Psychologist, State of Calif., 1976-78; faculty U. Redlands (Calif.), 1976, 77, Sch. Pub. Health, UCLA, 1978-79; pvt. practice cons. psychology, Los Angeles, 1978—; grad. student tutor, 1974—; author novels: Sanity, 1975; Hope Is the Waking Man's Dream, 1979; contbr. articles on mental health sociology, prejudice, social conflict, minorities to publs.; cons. in field; mem. adv. bd. Pico-Robertson Sr. Service Ctr., 1973-74, Furthermore Found. Clinic, Los Angeles, 1975—. Co-recipient best paper award Calif. State Psychol. Assn., 1975. Mem. Am. Psychol. Assn., Authors League Am., Dramatists Guild, Internat. Social Sci. Hon. Soc., Amity Circle, Sigma Xi. Home: 826 Greentree Rd Pacific Palisades CA 90272

MAIER, CORNELL C., aluminum and chem. co. exec.; b. Herreid, S.D., Jan. 12, 1925; s. Phillip and Ann Riedlinger M.; B.S. in Engring., U. Calif., Berkeley, 1949. With Kaiser Aluminum & Chem. Corp., Oakland, Calif., 1949—, v.p., gen. mgr. European region Kaiser Aluminum Internat., 1963-68, v.p., gen. mgr. Mill Products div. parent co., 1969, v.p., gen. mgr. N.Am. aluminum ops., 1969-70, exec. v.p., 1970-72, gen. mgr. in charge day-to-day ops., 1971-72, pres., 1972-82, chief exec. officer, 1972—, chmn. bd., 1978—, also dir.; dir. Anglesey Aluminum (London) Metal Ltd., Comalco Industries (Australia) Pty. Ltd., Volta Aluminum Co. Ltd., Bank Am. N.T. and S.A., BankAm. Corp.; dir., dep. chmn. Fed. Res. Bank San Francisco; mem. industry adv. council U.S. Dept. Def. Trustee, Nat. Urban League; mem. Pres.' Task Force on Pvt. Sector Initiatives. Served with USAAF, 1943-45. Mem. U.S. Council Internat. Chambers Commerce, Calif. C. of C. (bd. dirs.), Bus. Roundtable, Alliance to Save Energy (bd. dirs.). Internat. Primary Aluminum Inst., Aluminum Assn. Clubs: Round Hill Country, Alamo. Home: 565 Bellevue Ave Oakland CA 94610 Office: Kaiser Aluminum & Chem Corp Kaiser Center 300 Lakeside Dr Oakland CA 94643*

MAIER, WILLIAM DAVIES, photojournalist; b. San Diego, June 27, 1946; s. Louis Arthur and Jeane Olive (Davies) M.; m. Diane Marie Butler, May 30, 1972; children—William T., Honora J., Heather M. Student Grossmont Coll., 1978, San Diego State U., 1978-81. Freelance photojournalist, San Diego, 1975—. Bd. dirs. Child Nutrition Program San Diego, 1981-82, chmn. bd., 1981-82; bd. dirs. San Diego chpt. Oceanic Soc., 1981-82; mem. program com. Peninsula YMCA, 1980. Mem. Internat. Assn. Bus. Communicators (bd. 1978-79, Excellence in Photography award 1979), Nat. Assn. Press Photographers, Navy League San Diego, Calif. Press Photographers. Republican. Roman Catholic. Club: Point Loma Kiwanis. Office: PO Box 7053 Ocean Beach CA 92107

MAIERSPERGER, WALTER PAUL, aeronautical engineer; b. Bklyn., May 26, 1916; s. Paul Martin and Marie (Schmidt) M.; m. Evelyn Louise Stearns, Apr. 24, 1945. B.M.E., CCNY, 1939. Served to 2nd lt. U.S. Army, 1937-38; served to lt. col. USAF, 1939-59; pilot, engring. officer U.S. Army Air Corps, 1939-47; service engr. Trans World Airline, 1947; chief of aircraft spl. projects sects., Wright Field, 1947-53; dir. research and devel. projects aircraft br. Office Dep. Chief Staff for Research and Devel., Hdqrs. U.S. Air Force, 1953-57; liaison for research and devel in 7 states and Navy Bur. Aeros., 1937-39, project mgr. aerial recovery sect. All Am. Engring. Co., Wilmington, Del., 1959-63, sr. engr. Research Analysis Corp., McLean, VA., 1964-70. Decorated D.F.C. Mem. AIAA. Contbr. numerous articles in field of flight tech. and history to profl. jours. Home: 25420 Telarana Way Carmel CA 93923

MAIL, PATRICIA DAVISON, public health educator; b. Kamloops, B.C., Can., Dec. 10, 1940; came to U.S., 1943, naturalized, 1959; d. George Allen and Constance Lamotte (Davison) M. B.S., U. Ariz., 1963; M.A., 1970; M.S., Smith Coll., Northampton, Mass., 1965; M.P.H., Yale U., 1967. Instr. Green Fields Prep. Sch., Tucson, Ariz., 1967-68; pub. health educator USPHS Indian Health Service, Parago Reservation, 1970-72, Seattle, 1972-79, chief health edn. br., Portland, 1979—; instr. alcohol studies program Seattle U., 1974-78. Mem. The Dorian Group, Seattle, 1974—. NDEA scholar, 1968-70. Mem. Am. Pub. Health Assn. (recipient Early Career award 1979), Soc. Pub. Health Edn., Am. Anthrop. Assn., Soc. Applied Anthropology, AAAS, Soc. Med. Anthropology. Republican. Episcopalian. Author: Tulapai to Tokay: An Annoted Bibliography, 1980; contbr. articles to profl. jours. Home: 2500 S 370th St Apt 265 Federal Way WA 98003 Office: 4735 E Marginal Way S Suite 1470 Seattle WA 98134

MAIN, ROBERT GAIL, communications and training cons., producer, television and film educator, former army officer; b. Bucklin, Mo., Sept. 30, 1932; s. Raymond M. and Inez L. (Olinger) M.; B.S. magna cum laude, U. Mo., 1954; grad. with honors, Army Command and Gen. Staff Coll., 1967; M.A. magna cum laude in Communications, Stanford U., 1968; Ph.D., U. Md., 1978; m. Anita Sue Thoroughman, Jan. 31, 1955; children—Robert Bruce, David Keith, Leslie Lorraine. Commd. 2d lt. U.S. Army, 1954, advanced through grades to lt. col., 1968; various command and staff assignments field arty., 1954-64; sr. instr. and div. chief Pershing missile div. U.S. Army Arty. and Missile Sch., Ft. Sill, Okla., 1964-66; mem. faculty U.S. Army Command and Gen. Staff Coll., 1968-70; chief speechwriting and info. materials div. U.S. Army Info. Office, 1971, chief broadcast and film div., 1972-73; dir. def. audiovisual activities Office of Info. for Armed Forces, 1973-76, ret., 1976; prof., grad. adv. Sch. Communications, Calif. State U., Chico, 1976-83; sr. v.p. Grant & Main, Inc., instrnl. developers. Decorated Legion of Merit, Meritorious Service medal, Commendation medal with oak leaf cluster, combat Inf. Badge; Vietnamese Cross of Gallantry; recipient Freedom Found. awards, 1972, 73, 74; Bronze medal Atlanta Film Festival, 1972; Best of Show award Balt. Film Festival, 1973; Creativity award Chgo. Indsl. Film Festival, 1973; Cine gold award Internat. Film Producers Assn., 1974. Mem. Assn. for Ednl. Communications Tech., Am. Soc. of Curriculum Developers, Nat. Assn. Ednl. Broadcasters, Phi Eta Sigma, Alpha Zeta, Phi Delta Gamma, Omicron Delta Kappa, Alpha Gamma Rho. Mem. Christian Ch. Author: Radio Station Handbook, 1973; contbr. articles on audiovisual communications to profl. publs.; producer army info. films, army radioseries, 1972-73.

MAINE, RICHARD EDWIN, aerospace engineer; b. Louisville, Oct. 20, 1951; s. Reuben E. and Nancy Willis (Boston) M.; m. Trindel Ann Engelmann, June 16, 1974; 1 son, Altair Trindel. B.S. in Aero. Engring., Purdue U., 1973; M.S. in System Sci., UCLA, 1976. Engring. trainee NASA Flight Research Ctr., Edwards, Calif., 1970-73, aerospace engr., 1973-74; cons. Optimization Software Inc., Los Angeles, 1974-76; owner Stochastic Control Software, Los Angeles, 1974-76; aerospace engr. NASA Dryden Flight Research Ctr., Edwards, 1976—. NASA Dryden Outstanding tech. paper award, 1977, 81; NASA Invention and Contbns. Bd. award, 1978; Spl. Achievement award NASA, 1981. Mem. AIAA (outstanding paper award of Atmospheric Flight Mechanics Conf. 1978, Outstanding. Tech. Contbn. award Antelope Valley sect. 1978), Aircraft Owners and Pilots Assn., Planetary Soc. Libertarian. Contbr. articles to profl. jours. Home: 2827 W Ave N-8 Palmdale CA 93550 Office: PO Box 273 Edwards CA 93523

MAINES, CLIFFORD BRUCE, insurance company executive; b. Tacoma, Aug. 14, 1926; s. Clifford McLean and Ida Vera (Wardall) M.; student Central Coll., Fayette, Mo., 1944-45, U. Mich., 1945-46; B.S., U. Wash., 1948, LL.B., 1949, J.D., 1949; m. Mary Jean Marshall, Sept. 4, 1948; children—Molly, Janet Lynn. Admitted to Wash. bar, 1950; mem. legal staff Safeco Corp., Seattle, 1950-62, asso. gen. counsel, 1962-66, gen. counsel, 1966-68, v.p., gen. counsel, 1968-74, sr. v.p., 1974-81, pres., 1981—, dir., 1977—; exec. v.p., chief operating officer, dir. Gen. Ins. Co. Am., 1974-77, pres., 1977-81, now dir.; exec. v.p. 1st Nat. Ins. Co. Am., 1974-77, pres., 1977-81, now dir.; exec. v.p. Safeco Ins. Co., 1974-77, pres., 1977-81, now dir.; dir. Safeco Life Ins. Co.; exec. v.p. GSL; Served with USNR, 1944-46. Mem. Mcpl. League, Am., Wash., Seattle-King County (past trustee) bar assns., Wash. Ins. Council (past pres.), Pacific Coast Casualty and Surety Execs. (exec. com.), Beta Theta Pi. Methodist (past chmn. bd.). Clubs: Washington Athletic, Broadmoor Golf, Seattle Golf, Lions (Seattle). Office: Safeco Corp Safeco Plaza Seattle WA 98185

MAIONE, ORLANDO THOMAS MATTIO, architect; b. Astoria, N.Y., Oct. 19, 1935; s. Attilio and Teresa (Cosenza) M.; B.Arch. (univ. award 1954, univ. sculpture purchase prize 1956, 57), U. Notre Dame, 1958; B.Psychology, U. San Francisco, 1970. Archtl. intern Eggers and Higgins, N.Y.C., 1954-62; with various archtl. and engring. firms in Calif., 1962-69; resident architect Foothill/De Anza Community Coll. Dist., Los Altos Hills, Calif., 1970-72; facilities architect Am. Savs. and Loan Assn. No. Calif., Redwood City, 1972-73; architect, prodn. coordinator, regional graphics coordinator Kaiser Found. Hosps., Oakland, Calif., 1973-79; staff architect Stanford U. Hosp. Med. Center, Palo Alto, Calif., 1979-82; freelance archtl. cons., 1983—; mem. visual arts jury Palo Alto City Council, 1976—, chmn., 1981—; trustee, pres. bd. trustees Triton Mus. Art, Santa Clara, Calif., 1975—. Founder, com. chmn. local archtl. Explorers Post, Boy Scouts Am., 1977-80. Served with Intelligence Corps, U.S. Army, 1958-61. Recipient Photography award Masonry Inst., 1977. Mem. AIA (chpt. dir. 1973-78, Calif. council dir. 1979; cert. of appreciation Santa Clara Valley chpt. 1974-76), Am. Assn. Hosp. Planning, Nat. Writers Club, San Francisco Archtl. Heritage, Nat. Trust Historic Preservation, Internat. Scuba Divers Assn., Italian-Am. Heritage Found., Museo Italo Americano, Palo Alto Hist. Assn., Internat. Platform Assn. Republican. Roman Catholic. Clubs: Press of San Francisco, U. Notre Dame Alumni (pres. 1981) (San Jose, Calif.). Author articles, columns. Home: 1736 Oak Creek Dr Apt 414 Palo Alto CA 94304

MAITZEN, DOLORES ANN, educator; b. Chgo., Nov. 2, 1952; d. Joseph Thomas and Angeline G. (Butz) Svacik; student John Robert Powers Modeling Sch., 1975-76; B.S., Ill. State U., 1973; M.S., Chgo. State U., 1976; m. Robert H. Maitzen, Jr., Apr. 15, 1978. Tchr., Josephinum High Sch., Chgo., 1973-75, Queen of Peace High Sch., Burbank, Ill., 1976-79; coordinator H.E.R.O. and tchr. home econs. North High Sch., Phoenix Union Dist., 1979-81; asst. prof. Ariz. State U., 1981—. Mem. Ariz. Assn. Vocat. Home Econs. Educators (state membership chmn. 1981—), Am. Vocat. Assn., Ariz. Vocat. Assn. (sec. 1983-84), Am. Home Econs. Assn., Ariz. Home Econs. Assn. (profl. awards chmn., profl. recognition award 1982, 83, 84, Elem.-Secondary Adult Edn. award 1982), Ill. State U. Alumni Assn., Ariz. State U. Women's Faculty Assn., Ariz. State Home Econs. Adv. Council, Nat. Restaurant Assn., Chgo. State U. Alumni Assn., Alpha Gamma Delta, NEA, Ariz. Edn. Assn. Club: Young Ladies of St. Joseph Ch. Home: 3702 E Dahlia Dr Phoenix AZ 85032 Office: Dept Home Econs Ariz State U Tempe AZ

MAJHANOVICH, STEVE, state senator; b. Rock Springs, Wyo., Jan. 20, 1926; s. Bob and Mary (Ivankovich) M.; m. Caroline Shipley Wilde, 1948; 1 dau., Carole Ann. Student Coll. of St. Thomas, 1943-45. Mem. Wyo. Ho. of Reps., 1965-72, Wyo. State Senate, 1973—. Adv. bd. Southwestern Wyo. Jr. Coll.; mem. Rock Springs city council, 1950-58. Served as ensign, USNR, 1943-46; PTO. Mem. Sweetwater County Conservation Assn., C. of C. Democrat. Roman Catholic. Clubs: Elks, Exchange. Home: 1412 Clark St Rock Springs WY 82901 Office: Wyoming State Senate Cheyenne WY 82002

MAJOVSKI, LAWRENCE VLADIMIR, clin. psychologist; b. Portland, Oreg., July 3, 1945; B.A., Reed Coll., 1967; M.Div., Western Sem., 1971; Ph.D., Fuller Grad. Sch. Psychology, 1975; children—Alisa Michelle, Kristin. Clin. psychology intern Kaiser-Permanente Hosp., 1975-76; U.S./USSR biomed. exchange scientist, Moscow, 1976-77; NIH postdoctoral fellow dept. psychology and psychiatry UCLA, 1977-79; asst. prof. psychology Fuller Grad. Sch. Psychology, 1979-80; dir. med. psychol. services Huntington Meml. Hosp., Pasadena, 1980—, dir. neurobehavioral research Huntington Inst. Applied Med. Research, 1980—. Diplomate Am. Bd. Profl. Psychology. Mem. Am. Psychol. Assn., Western Psychol. Assn., Calif. Psychol. Assn., Soc. Neuroscis., Internat. Neuropsychol. Soc., Nat. Acad. Neuropsychology, AAAS. Presbyterian. Club: University. Home: 387 Wenham Rd Pasadena CA 91107 Office: 130 S Euclid St Pasadena CA 91101

MAK, STANLEY MING, radio station executive; b. Chengtu, Szechwan, China, Feb. 17, 1949; came to U.S., 1969, naturalized, 1976; s. Fung and Siu Fun (Mil) M.; m. Suzanne Debra Phelps, June 9, 1971; children—Justin S., Kristin S.L. B.A., Eastern Wash. State U., 1972. Account exec. Sta. KREM, Spokane, Wash., 1972-75, Sta. KING, Seattle, 1975-76, Sta. KORL, Honolulu, 1976-77, Sta. KING-TV, Seattle, 1977-79; sales mgr. Sta. KINK, Portland, Oreg., 1979-82, gen. mgr., 1982—. Mem. Oreg. Assn. Broadcasters, Nat. Assn. Broadcasters. Club: Willamette Athletic (Portland). Office: Sta KINK 1501 SW Jefferson St Portland OR 97201

MAKOWSKI, PETER EDGAR, hosp. exec.; b. Milw., Nov. 21, 1953; s. Edgar Leonard and Patricia Mae (Nock) M.; m. Cynthia Renee Edgerly, Apr. 7, 1979. B.A. in Polit. Sci., Whittier Coll., 1976; M.P.H., UCLA, 1980. Adminstrv. intern Calif. Hosp. Med. Center, Los Angeles, 1977, unit mgr. emergency dept., 1977-78; adminstrv. resident Presbyn. Intercommunity Hosp., Whittier, Calif., 1979-80, adminstrv. dir. support services, 1980-82, v.p. ambulatory/spl. services, 1982—. Mem. Am. Hosp. Assn., Am. Coll. Hosp. Adminstrs. (student assoc.), Health Care Execs. So. Calif., Med. Group Mgmt. Assn., UCLA Hosp. Adminstrn. Alumni Assn., Nat. Honor Soc. Republican. Roman Catholic. Club: Whittier Host Lions. Home: 1308 Calle Galante San Dimas CA 91773 Office: 12401 E Washington Blvd Whittier CA 90602

MALACHOWSKI, MICHAEL JON, biophysicist, educator; b. Chgo., Sept. 4, 1945; s. Thaddeus and Natalie Constance (Kryczewski) M. A.B. in Physics, U. Calif.-Berkeley, 1968, Ph.D. in Biophysics, 1978. Engr., Coherent Radiation Labs., Palo Alto, Calif., 1966-67; v.p. Centurian Enterprises, Berkeley, 1968-72; research assoc. Lawrence Berkeley Labs., 1973-77; NRC fellow U. Western Ont., London, Can., 1977-80; instr. Peralta Coll., Oakland, Calif., 1980—, San Francisco Coll., 1980—; assoc. NASA Ames Research Ctr. NIH biophysics tng. grantee, 1972-76; Calif. Dept. Agr. grantee, 1980-81. Mem. Am. Acad. Scis., AAAS, Am. Chem. Soc., Am. Inst. Biol. Scis., Radiation Research Soc., Electron Microscope Soc. Am., Airplane Owners and Pilots Assn., Tau Kappa Epsilon. Author: Cellulose Conversion Handbook, 1980; Biomass Conversion Handbook, 1983; contbr. articles to profl. jours. Office: PO Box 9315 Berkeley CA 94709

MALCOLM, DAVID ROBERT, university administrator; b. Green Lake, Wis., Jan. 11, 1926; s. David Donald and Esther Victoria (Moen) M.; B.S., Winona State Coll., 1949; M.S., Wash. State U., 1951, Ph.D.,

1954; m. Shirley S. Worner, June 18, 1949. Instr. entomology Iowa State U., 1954; instr. biology Portland State U., 1954-56, asst. prof., 1956-59, asso. prof., 1959-66, prof., 1966-69, acting head dept. biology, 1961-62, asst. dean grad. studies, 1967-69; prof. biology, chmn. dept. biology Pacific U., 1969-76, chmn. div. sci. and math., 1969-76, now dean Coll. Arts and Scis., 1976-83, v.p. devel. and univ. relations, 1983—. Served with USAAF, 1944-45. Mem. Am. Inst. Biol. Sci., Am. Arachnological Soc., Sigma Xi. Contbr. articles to profl. jours. Office: Pacific Univ Forest Grove OR 97116

MALCOLM, GERALD LINDBURG, elec. co. exec.; b. Genola, Utah, Dec. 18, 1927; s. John Leo and Rhoda (Steele) M.; student U. Utah, Salt Lake City, 1957-59; m. Edith Jackson, Oct. 4, 1952; children—Guy David, Roger Allan, JoAnn, Tracy Dale, Gerald Leo, Edith Christine. Electrician, Excel Neon Sign Co., Salt Lake City, 1946-48; owner, operator Malcolm Electric Co., Santaquin, Utah, 1948-52; journeyman electrician Dept. Army, Dugway Proving Grounds, Utah, 1952-60; sr. constrn. foreman A, Thiokol Chem. Corp., Tremonton, Utah, 1960-62; electrician leader VA Med. Center, Salt Lake City, 1962-73, constrn. mgr., 1973-81; owner, operator Malcolm Electric Co., Salt Lake City, 1965—; instr. Utah Tech. Coll., Salt Lake City, 1974-76; lectr. in field. Active Soil Conservation, Utah County, U.S. Dept. Agr., 1950-51. Master electrician, Utah, also elec. contractor license. Mem. Ch. Jesus Christ Latter-Day Saints. Home: 1549 S 1300 W Salt Lake City UT 84104 Office: 1549 S 1300 W Salt Lake City UT 84104

MALCOLM, JAMES CURTIS, JR., accountant; b. San Diego, Jan. 17, 1926; s. James Curtis and Mildred Evelyn (Turner) M.; B.S., Pepperdine U., 1950; postgrad. U. So. Calif., UCLA, San Diego State Coll.; children—Daniel L., David J., James Curtis, III. Internal auditor Hughes Aircraft Corp., 1950-54; civilian auditor gen. USAF, 1954-57; propr. Malcolm Accountancy Corp., La Jolla, Calif., 1960—; instr. Southwestern Coll., Chula Vista, Calif., 1959-69, Mesa Coll., San Diego, 1967-69; head bus. dept. San Diego City Coll., 1966—. Served with USNR, 1942-46. Pub. acct., Calif.; enrolled agt. IRS. Mem. Inst. Enrolled Agts. (past pres.), Calif. Inst. Enrolled Agts. (past pres.), Los Angeles Inst. Enrolled Agts. (past pres.), San Diego Inst. Enrolled Agts. (past pres.) Western Pension Council, Nat. Soc. Public Accountants. Club: Shriners. Home: 625 3d Ave Chula Vista CA 92010 Office: 7744 Fay Ave Suite 201 La Jolla CA 92037

MALEADY, ANTOINETTE KIRKPATRICK, author, publisher; b. Powell, Wyo., Dec. 9, 1918; d. Sherman S. and Beatrice E. (Chrisman) Kirkpatrick; B.S., W.Va. Wesleyan Coll., Buckhannon, 1940; M.L.S., U. Calif., Berkeley, 1968; m. Thomas J. Maleady, Sept. 21, 1954; 1 dau., Sarah Ann. Various clerical positions, 1940-44; asst. billet mgr. USAF, Tokyo, 1946-48; consular clk. Dept. State, 1948-54; pres. Chulainn Press, Inc., San Anselmo, Calif., 1975—. Served with USN, 1944-45. Mem. Am. Recorder Soc., Choral Dirs. Assn., Music Library Assn., Western Book Pubs. Assn., Assn. Recorded Sound Collections, Pvt. Libraries Assn., Press Club of San Francisco. Home: 1040 Butterfield Rd San Anselmo CA 94960 Office: PO Box 770 San Anselmo CA 94960

MALECHA, MARVIN J., architect, educational administrator; b. Lonsdale, Minn., June 26, 1949; s. George Jacob and Barbara Ann (Lamac) M.; m. Cynthia Marie Miller, Aug. 8, 1970; children—Peter John, Michelle Marie. B.Arch., U. Minn., 1973; M.Arch., Harvard U., 1974. Designer, Wallace and Mundt Architects, Edina, Minn., 1969-73, Hugh Stubbins and Assocs., Cambridge, Mass., 1973-76; instr. Cambridge Urban Awareness Program, 1973-76, Boston Archtl. Ctr., 1974-76; instr. design Calif. Poly. U., Pomona, 1976-77, asst. prof., 1978, assoc. prof., 1979-82, dean Sch. Environ. Design, 1982—, asst. chmn. dept., 1978, chmn. dept., 1979-82; coordinator La Verne (Calif.) Architecture and Research Team, 1976—; cons. in field. Mem. steering com. Architects for Social Responsibility; mem. art and liturgy com. Our Lady Of Assumption Ch., Claremont, Calif. Rotch Travelling scholar, 1980; Ellerbe Archtl. award Boston Soc. Architects, 1972; Henry Adams award A.I.A., 1973. Mem. AIA (dir. Los Angeles chpt.), Soc. Am. Registered Architects. Author: The Fabric of Architecture, 1982; contbr. articles to profl. jours. Office: 3801 W Temple Ave Pomona CA 91768

MALEK, LEONARD, film editor, writer; b. N.Y.C., Oct. 2, 1928; s. Joseph and Sadie (Skolnick) M.; m. Zena B. Chaitman, July 9, 1949; children—Shana Elaine, Aviva Beth. B.A., UCLA, 1957. Asst. editor TV shows and films including: I Dream of Jeannie, The Monkees, The Ironhorse, The Brady Bunch, Paper Moon, SWAT, Long Ride Home, Red Badge of Courage, Hustling; editor B.J. Lange Presents, Cosette-Sugarman Prodns., Los Angeles, 1971, Charlie's Angels, Spelling-Goldberg Prodn., 1976, Eight is Enough, Lorimar Prodns., 1980, Light on Synanon, Tomorrow Entertainment, 1982; script writer Al Ruddy-Sam Peckinpaugh Prodns., Maynor Enterprises, Artisan Lodge, 1968-71; free lance film editor and script writer, Los Angeles, 1968—. Mem. Motion Picture Editors Guild, Writers Guild of Am. Home: 3650 S Bentley Ave Los Angeles CA 90034

MALIWANAG, MANUEL PEYTON, electronics company executive, chemical engineer; b. Manila, Philippines, Nov. 1, 1941; s. Primo Guia and Cora Y. (Peyton) M.; m. Cora Esguerra, June 6, 1964; children—Maria Theresa, Ricardo Roberto. Chem. Engr., Mapua Inst. Tech., Manila, 1962; M.B.A., UCLA, 1969. Asst. to pres. Findlay Millar Corp., Philippines, 1966-67; mgr. process engring. Mica Corp., Culver City, Calif., 1967-73; v.p. ops. Lamination Tech., Inc., Santa Ana, Calif., 1973-76; chmn. bd., pres. Century Laminators, Inc., Santa Ana, 1976—, Century Travel, San Francisco, 1980—, Circuit Diagnostics, Santa Ana, 1981—, Century Phoenix, 1982—; chmn. bd. Century Norcal, San Jose, Calif., 1980—; mng. ptnr. M.E.'s Assocs., C.A.M. Engring. Assocs. Republican. Roman Catholic. Office: 1225 Knollwood Circle Anaheim CA 92801

MALKOFF, JUDY D., psychotherapist; b. Altoona, Pa., Apr. 8, 1933; d. Joseph L. and Edna R. (Brett) Sherman; m. Jack Malkoff, Dec. 19, 1954; children—Laurie, Robbie, Gregg, Scott. B.S., Pa. State U., 1954; M.S. in Counseling, Youngstown State U., 1976. Cert. interactional psychotherapist, Ariz. Assertiveness tng. leader YWCA, Altoona, 1977-79; therapist Family Service Agy., Scottsdale, Ariz., 1980-81, CIGNA Health Plan, Phoenix, 1981—; group leader assertiveness tng. Paradise Valley Community Edn. Program, Phoenix, 1979. Vice pres. LWV, Youngstown, Ohio. Mem. Am. Personnel and Guidance Assn., Am. Mental Health Counselors Assn., Assn. Specialists in Group Work, Ariz. Personnel and Guidance Assn.

MALLENDER, WILLIAM H., diversified manufacturing company executive; b. 1935. A.B., Yale U., 1957; LL.B., U. Mich., 1960. Assoc. Donovan, Leisure, Newton & Irvine, 1961-69; v.p. Gibraltar Research & Mgmt. Co. Inc., 1969-70; v.p. GAC Investments Inc., 1970-71; v.p., sec., gen. counsel Talley Industries Inc., Mesa, Ariz., 1971, exec. v.p., now sec., gen. counsel, pres. and chief exec. officer, 1981-83, chmn., chief exec. officer, 1983—, also dir. Office: Talley Industries Inc 3500 N Greenfield Rd Mesa AZ 85205*

MALLER, JUDY BATMAN, public relations counselor; b. Bridgeport, Conn., Jan. 3, 1939; d. Homer C. and Margaret (Evvard) Batman; m. Jonathan Cromwell, June 11, 1960; 1 dau., Kimberly Anne; m. 2d, John Morton Maller, June 24, 1971. B.A., Manhattanville Coll., 1960; M.S., UCLA, 1967. Vice pres. Penney & Bennett, Inc., Los Angeles, 1968-71; account supr. Laurence Laurie & Assocs., Los Angeles, 1971-72, 73-81; dir. pub. relations Charles Luckman Assocs., Los Angeles, 1972-73; owner, managing counselor Judy Maller Pub. Relations Counsel, Los Angeles, 1981—. 1st v.p., chmn. exec. and fin. com., Crippled Children's Soc. of So. Calif., 1982—, bd. dirs., 1972—, dir. of program planning, 1972-82; pres. Gold Diggers for Crippled Children, 1978. Recipient Lulu award Los Angeles Advt. Women, 1970. Mem. Pub. Relations Soc. Am., Nat. Assn. Real Estate Editors. Office: Judy Maller Pub Relations Counsel 1108 Somera Rd Los Angeles CA 90077

MALLINCKRODT, MARTHA GRAVES (MRS. CHARLES O. MALLINCKRODT), club woman; b. Louisville, Dec. 2, 1905; d. Allison and Ellen (Monks) Graves; student N.Y. Sch. of Applied Design for Women, 1924, U. Louisville, 1924; m. Charles Olcott Mallinckrodt, Oct. 3, 1934; children—Charles Olcott, Ellen Louise. Active Jr. Service League, Summit, N.J., 1941-51, Girl Scouts Am. and Boy Scouts Am., 1945-46, 49-55; dir. Hobby Show Palos Verdes Woman's Club, 1953-54, asst. dir., 1954-55; dir. Sr. Assembly of Palos Verdes Estates, 1953-54; dir. Palos Verdes Community Arts Assn., 1957-59; founding mem. Palos Verdes Surf-Writers, 1957, treas., 1957, asst. v.p. program adviser, 1958, 59; hospitality chmn. Palos Verdes Peninsula chpt. Am. Assn. for UN, 1958-59; vol. staff Children's Hosp., Los Angeles, 1958—; mem. Mayor's Citizens Com., Los Angeles, Calif., 1964. Mem. Jr. League Newport Harbor, Assistance League Laguna Beach, IEEE, Laguna Hills Art Assn., Los Angeles County Mus. Art, Saddleback Hist. Soc., Leisure World Astronomy Club, Antiques Soc. Orange County. Clubs: Ebell of Laguna Hills; Old Treasures (chmn. treasure mart 1965). Home: 3193 A Via Buena Vista Laguna Hills CA 92653

MALLON, JOHN LAWRENCE, II, railroad exec.; b. Seattle, Jan. 25, 1946; s. John Thomas and Alice (Archibald) M.; B.A. in Econs., Seattle U., 1971; A.A. in Real Estate, Shoreline Community Coll., 1977; M.B.A. candidate U. Puget Sound, 1979—. Various positions Bank Calif., Seattle, 1966-67; auditor Best Western Motel, Seattle, 1969-73; acct. Burlington No. R.R., Seattle, 1973-74, supr. acctg., 1974, mgr. acctg., 1975, dir. adminstrn. natural resources, 1976-81, dir. fin. services, 1981—; resource exec. Plum Creek Timber Co., Inc.; cons. taxes. Served with USMC, 1967-69. Mem. Am. Mgmt. Assn., Internat. Platform Assn., Am. Forestry Assn. Republican. Roman Catholic. Clubs: Grays Harbor Golf and Country, Bellevue Golf. Home: 2665 168th Ave SE Bellevue WA 98008 Office: First Interstate Bank Bldg Seattle WA 98104

MALLORY, DANIEL HENRY, optometrist; b. Washington, May 5, 1954; s. Herbert Dean and Dorothy Marie (Graber) M.; m. Kerry Kathleen Flanigan, May 29, 1981; 1 dau., Aimee Ranai. B.S. in Biol. Scis., U. Calif.-Irvine, 1977; O.D., So. Calif. Coll. Optometry, 1981. Pvt. practice optometry, Ridgecrest and Lake Isabella, Calif., 1982—. Methodist. Club: Rotary. Office: PO Box 2953 5109-B Lake Isabella Blvd Lake Isabella CA 93240

MALM, DONALD BURNELL, marketing executive; b. Erie, Pa., Nov. 12, 1933; s. John Sigurd and Manghild Svea (Johnson) M.; m. Janice Helen Driscoll, June 6, 1964; children—Barbara Jan, Dion John. B.S. in Journalism, Northwestern U., 1956. Traffic mgr. Young & Rubicam, N.Y.C., 1962-64; advt. and sales promotion mgr. Royal Typewriter Co., N.Y.C., 1964-69; advt. mgr. Plus Products, Irvine, Calif., 1969-75; owner DBM Advt., San Clemente, Calif., 1975-80; v.p. mktg. Radiance Products Inc., City of Industry, Calif., 1980—. Served with AUS, 1955-58. Montgomery Ward scholar, 1956. Mem. Mensa. Republican. Methodist.

MALM, ROYCE ELLIOTT, musician; b. Los Angeles, Nov. 22, 1929; s. Albin Nils and Mildred Elizabeth (Aden) M.; Mus.B., U. So. Calif., 1952, M.Mus. in Composition, 1954; m. Ruth Emilie Eggert, Dec. 1, 1962; 1 dau., Lorraine Elise. Tchr. public schs. in Calif., 1957—; tchr. secondary choral music and music appreciation Burbank (Calif.) Unified Sch. Dist., 1964—; mem. Burbank Symphony Assn., 1971—, pres., 1975-78, exec. dir., 1979—; dir. ch. choirs, 1953-73; v.p. Burbank Community Concerts Assn., 1973-75, Symphony League Los Angeles County, 1978—, Performing Arts Fedn. Burbank, 1977-78. Composer: Reflections, 1980; others. Served with AUS, 1954-56. Mem. Music Educators Nat. Conf., NEA, Burbank Tchrs. Assn., Calif. Tchrs. Assn., Choral Conductors Guild Calif., So. Calif. Vocal Assn., Pro Musica Sana, Sir Thomas Beecham Soc., Pi Kappa Lambda, Phi Mu Alpha. Democrat. Presbyterian. Home: 924 Tufts Ave Burbank CA 91504 Office: 420 S Mariposa St Burbank CA 91506

MALMAN, RUTH CHERYL, lawyer; b. Cin., July 8, 1953; d. Saul and Florence D. (Deutsch) M.; B.A. with distinction, U. Mich., 1974; J.D., U. Denver, 1978; m. Michael B. Opatowski, July 22, 1978. Law clk. Denver Dist. Ct., 1977; researcher Alaska Atty. Gen's Office, Anchorage, 1977; admitted to Colo. bar, 1978; ptnr. firm Malman & Malman, P.C., Denver, 1978—. Vol. tchr. Colo. Women's Correctional Facility, 1978, Denver Free U., 1979; bd. dirs. Family Builders by Adoption, 1979—. Cert. tchr., Mich. Mem. Am. Bar Assn., Colo. Bar Assn., Denver Bar Assn., Colo. Women's Bar Assn., Colo. Criminal Def. Bar Assn. Address: 1544 Pearl Denver CO 80203

MALMSTADT, HOWARD VINCENT, university dean; b. Marinette, Wis., Feb. 17, 1922; s. Guy August and Nellie (Rusch) M.; B.S., U. Wis., 1943, M.S., 1948, Ph.D., 1950; m. Carolyn Gay Hart, Aug. 3, 1947; children—Cynthia Sue, Alice Ann, Jonathan Howard. Postdoctoral research asso. U. Wis., 1950-51; mem. faculty U. Ill., 1951—, prof. chemistry, 1961-78, emeritus, 1978—, dir. electronics insts., 1960-74; dean sci. and tech., v.p. acad. affairs Pacific and Asia Christian U., Kona, Hawaii, 1978—; Fulbright-Hays disting. prof., Romania, 1978; cons. to govt. and industry. Served as officer USNR, 1943-46. Recipient award in edn. Instrument Soc. Am., 1970, Outstanding Analytical Chemist award Pitts. Conf. Analytical Chemistry and Applied Spectroscopy, 1978, ISCO award contbns. biochem. instrumentation, 1980; Guggenheim fellow, 1960; grantee NSF, 1965-78, NIH, 1975-80. Mem. Am. Chem. Soc. (award instrumentation 1963, award analytical chemistry 1976, award for excellence in teaching 1984), Optical Soc. Am., Soc. Applied Spectroscopy, Am. Assn. Clin. Chemists. Author textbooks, articles in field; adv. bds. profl. jours. Patentee sci. instruments. Home: 75-5786 Niau Pl Kailua-Kona HI 96740 Office: PAC Univ Box YWAM Kailua-Kona HI 96740

MALMSTROM, LAURIE SUZANNE, marketing executive; b. Salt Lake City, Oct. 7, 1949; d. Wayne W. and Claire F. (Ford) M.; divorced; children—Hollie, Jennifer. Student U. Utah, 1969-73. Writer, producer Sta. KTVX-TV, Salt Lake City, 1975-76; advt. dir. Castletons Advt., Salt Lake City, 1976-77; account exec. Ross Jurney Advt., Salt Lake City, 1977-78; franchise mktg. supr. Burger King Inc., San Francisco region, 1978-81; account supr. Dailey and Assoc., San Francisco, 1981; field mktg. mgr. Jack-in-the-Box div. Foodmaker Inc. (Ralston Purina), San Diego, 1981—; cons. in field. Mem. Salt Lake City Young Democrats; active Utah gov.'s campaign for re-election, 1974. Office: PO Box 783 San Diego CA 92112

MALMUTH, MASON STUART, statistician; b. Coral Gables, Fla., Nov. 13, 1951; s. Joseph Arnold and Doris (Brown) M. B.S. in Math., Va. Poly. Inst. and State U., 1973, M.S. in Math., 1975. With U.S. Census Bur., 1975-82, acting chief quality assurance and evaluations br., 1981; statistician reliability group, advance system div. Northrop Corp., Pico Rivera, Calif., 1982-83, sr. ops. analyst, 1976—. Mem. Am. Statis. Assn. Democrat. Home: 5250 Bindewald Rd Torrance CA 90505

MALONE, DENNIS MICHAEL, lawyer; b. Ithaca, N.Y., Dec. 8, 1947; s. Donald Bernard and Mary Elizabeth (Banfield) M.; B.A., Colo. Coll., 1969; J.D., U. Colo., 1973; m. Carol Jeanne Cimino, Dec. 28, 1968; 1 son, Patrick Michael. Admitted to Colo. bar, 1973; dir. tuition classification U. Colo., 1973-74; partner firm Garlutzo & Malone, Trinidad, Colo., 1974-76; pvt. practice, Trinidad, 1976—. Mem. 3d Dist. Jud. Nominating Commn., 1978—. Mem. Am. Trial Lawyers Assn., Am. Bar Assn., Comml. Law League Am., Colo. Bar Assn., Colo. Trial Lawyers Assn., So. Colo. Bar Assn. (pres. 1982-83), Trinidad C. of C. (pres. 1980). Roman Catholic. Author: Colorado Tuition Classification Handbook, 1973. Home: 219 W Baca St Trinidad CO 81082 Office: Suite 209 First Nat Bank Bldg Trinidad CO 81082

MALONEY, JOHN GERALD, mechanical engineer; b. Orange, Calif., June 18, 1940; s. John Francis and Dorothy (Toney) M.; m. Barbara Maria Anderson, July 18, 1964. B.S. in Engring., Loyola U., Los Angeles, 1963; M.S.M.E., U. So. Calif., 1966; M.B.A., Calif. State U.-Fullerton, 1976. With Apollo Project, Rockwell Internat., Downey, Calif., 1962-63; with Gen. dynamics, Pomona, Calif., 1963-83, engring. specialist in structural dynamics, 1976-83; staff scientist Brunswick Def., Costa Mesa, Calif., 1983—. Fellow AIAA (assoc.); mem. Soc. Automotive Engrs., Tau Beta Pi. Club: Diamond Bar Lions.

MALONY, HENRY NEWTON, JR., psychologist; b. Birmingham, Ala., May 17, 1931; s. Henry N. and Amie (Milligan) M.; m. Suzanna Davis, Nov. 23, 1953; children—Laurence E., Allen D., Michael N. B.A., Birmingham-So. Coll., 1952; M.Div., Yale U., 1955; M.A., Peabody Coll., Vanderbilt U., 1961, Ph.D., 1964. Lic. psychologist, Calif. Ordained to ministry Methodist Ch., 1953; pastor chs., 1955-59; chaplain Davidson County Hosp., Nashville, 1959-61; psychologist Frankfort (Ky.) State Hosp., 1964-65; prof. psychology Tenn. Wesleyan Coll., 1965-69; prof., dir. program in integration of psychology and theology Grad. Sch. Psychology, Fuller Theol. Sem., Pasadena, 1969—. Served with Army N.G., 1957-64. Mem. Am. Psychol. Assn., Western Psychol. Assn., Calif. Psychol. Assn., Christian Assn. for Psychol. Studies, Am. Assn. Pastoral Counselors. Democrat. Author: Current Perspectives in the Psychology of Religion, 1978; Understanding Your Faith, 1979; Wholeness and Holiness, 1983; Living The Answers, 1981; Christian Conversion, 1982; others.

MALOOF, GILES WILSON, mathematics educator; b. San Bernardino, Calif., Jan. 4, 1932; s. Joseph Peters and Georgia (Wilson) M.; m. Mary Anne Ziniker, Sept. 5, 1958 (dec. Oct. 1976); children—Mary Jane, Margery Jo. B.A., U. Calif. at Berkeley, 1953; M.A., U. Oreg., 1958; Ph.D., Oreg. State U., 1962. Petroleum reservoir engr. Creole Petroleum Corp., Venezuela, 1953-54; mathematician electronics div. research dept. U.S. Naval Ordnance Research Lab., Corona, Calif., 1958-59; asst. prof. math. Oreg. State U., Corvallis, 1962-68, research assoc. dept. oceanography, 1963-68, vis. prof. math., 1977-78; prof. math. Boise (Idaho) State U., 1968—, head dept., 1968-75, dean grad. sch., 1970-75; project dir. Dept. Energy Citizens' Workshop Energy Environment Simulator for Eastern Oreg., No. Nev. and Idaho, 1976—. Served with Ordnance Corps, AUS, 1954-56. Recipient Carter award, 1963, Mosser prize, 1966, Oreg. State U. Mem. Math. Assn. Am., Am. Math. Soc., Soc. Indsl. and Applied Math., Northwest Coll. and Univ. Assn. for Sci. (dir. 1973—), Northwest Sci. Assn. (trustee 1977-80), Sigma Xi, Pi Mu Epsilon, Phi Kappa Phi. Editor Ida. Council of Tchrs. of Math. Newspaper, 1971-73. Home: 1400 Longmont Ave Boise ID 83706

MALORRUS, FARLEY MARTIN, astrologer; b. St. Louis, Aug. 11, 1948; s. Fred Max and Beatrice (Cuttler) M. B.A. in Speech, Drama and English, Central Meth. Coll., Fayette, Mo., 1970; postgrad. in English, UCLA, 1974, in Astrology, 1974-76. Pvt. practice astrology, Culver City, Calif., 1975—; ship's astrologer, lectr. Sun Princess, Queen Elizabeth 2, Sitmar, Cunard, Princess and Carnival Cruise Lines, 1980—; columnist Redondo Beach (Calif.) Community Network News, 1982—; dir., host astrology series for cable TV, 1983; appearances on TV and radio. Address: PO Box 2988 Culver City CA 90230

MALOSH, JAMES BOYD, mechanical engineering educator, consultant; b. Licking, Ill., July 30, 1943; s. John Andrew and Nadean Gertrude (Crandall) M.; m. Sandra Sue Bowne, June 22, 1963 (div. 1971); children—Jeffrey, Brian, Ronald; m. 2d, Helen Fay Kangas, Oct. 22, 1973; 1 dau., Melanie. B.S.M.E., Wayne State U., 1966; M.S. in Engring. Mechanics, Mich. Tech. U., 1969, Ph.D. in Engring. Mechanics, 1980. Registered profl. engr., Mich., Ohio, Pa., Alaska. Acoustical engr. Walker Research Lab., Grass Lake, Mich., 1969-70; research assoc. Mich. Tech. U., Houghton, 1970-75; sr. research engr. U.S. Steel Research Labs., Monroeville, Pa., 1975-80; prin. research scientist Battelle Meml. Labs., Columbus, Ohio, 1980-81; assoc. prof. mech. engring. U. Alaska, Fairbanks, 1981—; acoustical cons. Arctic Designers, Fairbanks, Cowper & Madson Attys., Fairbanks; prin. investigator Alaska Dept. Transp. Wayne State U. Bd. Govs. scholar, 1966; NSF trainee, 1968, 70, 71. Mem. ASME, Nat. Soc. Profl. Engrs., Soc. Automotive Engrs., Acoustical Soc. Am., Sigma Xi, Tau Beta Pi, Pi Tau Sigma. Lutheran. Patentee automotive silencer, blast furnace stove burner to reduce pulsations. Home: 717 Chandalar U Alaska Fairbanks AK 99701 Office: Dept Mech Engring U Alaska Fairbanks AK 99701

MALOTT, JAMES RAYMOND, JR., lawyer; b. Globe, Ariz., Feb. 23, 1917; s. James Raymond and Edith Mary (Spencer) M.; student U. Ariz., 1934-36; A.B., Stanford U., 1938, J.D., 1941; m. Carol Hover, Sept. 9, 1939; children—James Spencer, Lucinda; m. 2d Barbara Farr, Feb. 20, 1949; m. 3d Ruth Austin, Jan. 18, 1975. Admitted to Ariz. bar, 1940, Calif. bar, 1941; dep. county atty. Gila County, Ariz., 1943; asso. law firm Morris and Malott, Globe, Ariz., 1945—, sr. partner, 1967—; mem. Ariz. Bd. of Bar Govs., 1955-60, v.p., 1959-60. Served with USAAF, 1943-45. Mem. Am. Bar Assn., Am. Coll. Probate Counsel (fellow), Am. Judicature Soc. Clubs: Elks, Lions, Masons (Shriner). Home: 1220 Skyline Dr Globe AZ 85501 Office: 1450 South St Globe AZ 85501

MALSAM, MARGARET HULA, public relations specialist, free-lance writer, marketing consultant; b. Enid, Okla., Aug. 15, 1937; d. William B. and Mary M. (Lovci) Hula; m. George R. Malsam, Aug. 26, 1957; children—Mike, Mark Paul, Mary. B.A., Okla. State U., 1959; M.A., U. Colo., 1983. Free-lance writer, 1960—; advt. copywriter Holiday Gifts, Denver, 1963-75; pub. relations specialist Adams County Sch. Dist. 14, Commerce City, Colo., 1975-78, Dist. 12, Northglenn/Thornton, Colo., 1978-83; cons. pub. relations Malsam Mktg., 1983—. Recipient Ann. Communications award Colo. Press Women, 1980, 81, 82, 83; Freedoms Found. scholar, 1982. Mem. Nat. Sch. Pub. Relations Assn., Colo. Sch. Pub. Relations Assn., Colo. Press Women Assn., Nat. Press Women Assn. Republican. Roman Catholic. Contbr. over 100 articles to nat. mags., profl. jours. Home: 3333 W 55th Ave Denver CO 80221

MALSON, THOMAS JOHN, plant engr.; b. Fountain Springs, Pa., Oct. 26, 1950; s. Thomas Edward and Yvonne Jean (Baranowska) M.; A.A., Sacramento City Coll., 1970; B.S. in Indsl. Tech., Calif. Poly. State U., 1973; m. Grace Elizabeth Holson, Apr. 28, 1973; 1 dau., Grace Yvonne. Maintenance planner and supr. Firestone Tire & Rubber Co., Salinas, Calif., 1973-79, tech. asst. sect. plant engring., Akron, Ohio, 1979-80; maintenance coordinator Guardian Industries Corp., Kingsburg, Calif., 1980; plant engr. Holz Rubber Co., Lodi, Calif., 1980-81; facilities design engr. Aerojet Strategic Propulsion Co., Sacramento, 1981—. Served with USMC, 1971. Recipient cert. achievement Firestone Tire & Rubber Co. Mgmt. Seminar, 1979. Mem. Am. Inst. Plant Engrs.

Democrat. Roman Catholic. Office: Hwy 50 and Hazel Ave Sacramento CA 95813

MALTBY, HAZEL FARROW, weaver; b. San Francisco, Dec. 26, 1917; d. Richard Harry and Effie Isabelle (Hardin) Johnstone; student San Francisco State Coll., 1935-36; m. Jack Allen Maltby, Nov. 11, 1974; children—Charlene Sue McAuley, Claudia Jane Polzl. Tchr.-lectr. weaving Foothill Community Coll., Los Altos, Calif., De Anza Coll., Cupertino, Calif., 1973-74, Nat. Conf. Handweavers, San Francisco, 1974; pvt. tchr., 1970—; one-woman exhbns. include Menlo Park Civic Center, libraries and banks in Palo Alto, Woodside, Los Altos, San Jose, Calif., 1972-75, also exhibited San Jose Fine Art Mus., Triton Mus., San Jose, Calif. Art Festival, Nat. Conf. Handweavers, No. Calif. Handweavers Conf., Bay Area Arts and Crafts, Internat. Weaving exhbn., others; author: Painting Warps, 1974; group exhbns. include Los Vegas Art League, 1971, Tex. Fine Arts League, 1974, Internat. Weaving Exhbn., Kouvola, Finland, 1977; commd. to do 6 large tapestries Epiphany Episc. Ch., San Carlos, now weaving tapestries for indsl. firms. Mem. Palo Alto Art Club (v.p.), Trampornus Weaving Guild (past pres.), Handweavers Guild Am., Bay Area Arts and Crafts Guild, Loom and Shuttle Weaving Guild, Calif. PTA (hon. life; past pres. San Carlos). Clubs: Order Eastern Star, Order Jobs Daus. Address: 118 Plazoleta St Los Gatos CA 95030

MALTIN, FREDA, univ. adminstr.; b. Calgary, Alta., Can., June 4, 1923; d. Meyers Wolfe and Ida (Kohn) Rosen; came to U.S., 1958; diploma Garbutt's Bus. Coll., Calgary, 1942; m. Manny Nayton Maltin, Aug. 25, 1950; 1 son, Richard Allan. Various secretarial and bookkeeping positions, 1951-61; mem. adminstrv. staff U. So. Calif., 1961—, adminstrv. asst. Center for Futures Research, Grad. Sch. Bus. Adminstrn., 1981—. Mem. Exec. Women Internat. Club: U. So. Calif. Staff (charter). Office: U So Calif Brl 401 University Park Los Angeles CA 90007

MALTZMAN, IRVING MYRON, experimental psychology educator; b. Bklyn., May 9, 1924; s. Israel and Lillian (Mass) M.; m. Diane Maltzman, Aug. 14, 1949; children—Sara, Kenneth, Ilaine. B.A., NYU, 1946; Ph.D., U. Iowa, 1949. From instr. to prof. psychology UCLA, 1949—, chmn. dept. psychology, 1970-77. Home: 11260-22B Overland Ave Culver City CA 90230 Office: Dept of Psychology UCLA Los Angeles CA 90024

MAMIN, ESTHA LEE GINSBERG (BEBE), real estate broker; b. Dallas; d. Jacob B. and Hinda (Bernstein) Ginsberg; B.A., U. Tex., 1945; student Lumbleau Sch. Real Estate, 1955-56; children—Cynthia Anne, Victoria Lynn, H. Jonathon, Marshall Timothy. Research asst. Cancer Lab., U. Tex. Med. Coll., Galveston; biochemist, pathology lab. James Walker Meml. Hosp., Wilmington, N.C., Tex. Children's Hosp., Dallas, 1946-47, research asst., pathology dept. Harvard Med. Coll., 1947-48; med. technologist, bus. mgr. med. office, Pasadena, Calif., 1948-56; real estate salesman H.H. Armistead Co., Pasadena, 1956-64, broker, Mamin Co., Pasadena, 1964—. Mem. Pasadena Bd. Realtors (edn. com. 1966, mem. com. 1967, sec. women's council, 1967). Calif. Real Estate Assn., Nat. Assn. Real Estate Bds., Los Angeles County Med. Aux. (com. chmn. 1962), League Women Voters, Pasadena Civic League, AAUW, Los Angeles World Affairs Council. Clubs: Officers Wives, Curtain Raiser; Town Hall (Los Angeles). Home: 161 S Oak Knoll Ave Pasadena CA 91101

MAMMEN, BETTY JUNE, artist, consultant, art gallery executive; b. Joplin, Mo., July 23, 1927; d. Harry Leroy and Bessie Pearl (Watson) Wetherell; m. Robert Mammen, May 16, 1947; children—Cary Douglas, Nancy Lynn Emmons. Student Los Angeles City Coll., 1946-47. Profl. artist, Los Angeles, 1962-74; owner, artist, Ladera Gallery, Los Angeles, 1970-73; mgr., dir. Savage Galleries, Scottsdale, Ariz., 1975-81; owner, dir. Mammen Gallery II, Scottsdale, 1981—; oil paintings in permanent pvt. and corp. collections; art cons. Elder Presbyn. Ch., Phoenix, 1977—; troop leader Angelus council Girl Scouts U.S.A., 1965-72. Mem. Phoenix Art Mus. Republican. Home: 10611 N 35th St Phoenix AZ 85028 Office: 4151 N Marshall Way Scottsdale AZ 85251

MAMMEN, GEORGE, tax service and bus. mgmt. co. exec.; b. Los Angeles, Feb. 3, 1930; s. Elmer George and Marie Leona (Bonker) M.; student Mt. Sac Jr. Coll., Walnut, Calif., 1975-76; married; children—Anthony, Gary, Tina, Steven, Janette, Donna. Constrn. worker, 1942-49; various positions with various cos., 1958-77; prin. G Mammen & Assocs., bus., investment, bookkeeping, income tax and audit advisers, Covina, Calif. Served with U.S. Army, 1949-58. Republican. Home: 4837 Brightview Dr Covina CA 91722 Office: G Mammen & Assocs 536 W Arrow Hwy Suite 204 Covina CA 91722

MAN, GUY KEE, mechanical engineer; b. Kowloon, Hong Kong, May 27, 1951; s. Hon Kwong and Sau Ching (Luk) M.; B.S., U. Redlands, 1974; M.S., Stanford U., 1975, M.E., Ph.D., 1979; m. Debra Y. K. Ching, Dec. 15, 1979. Sr. engr. guidance and control sect. Jet Propulsion Lab., Calif. Inst. Tech., Pasadena, Calif., 1979-82, tech. group leader, guidance and control analysis group, guidance and control sect., 1982—; cons. dynamics, automatic control and seismic analysis, 1982—. Registered profl. engr., Calif. Mem. AIAA, ASME, Calif. Soc. Profl. Engrs., Nat. Soc. Profl. Engrs., Sigma Xi. Contbr. tech. articles to various publs. Home: 20113 Cassia Ct Cerritos CA 90701

MANAHAN, MICHAEL LARRY, community relations adminstr., land devel. exec.; b. Los Angeles, Nov. 6, 1923; s. John Robert and Gertrude Jane (Nelson) M.; student Calif. State U.-Los Angeles, 1942-43; profl. cert. pub. relations UCLA, 1980; m. Ruth Virginia Crosby, May 15, 1949; children—Mark Steven, Stacy Anne. Sales supr. Farmers Ins. Group, Ind., Wis. and Mich., 1949-56, dist. agy. owner, Los Angeles, 1957-64; pres. Manahan & Eggers, Inc., Corona del Mar, Calif., 1965-69; mgr. community relations the Irvine Co., Newport Beach, Calif., 1969—. Pres. Orange County Industry/Edn. Council, 1976; chmn. U. Calif.-Irvine Pub. Relations Council, 1976; bd. Coastline Regional Occupation Program, 1973-76; bd. dirs. Irvine Master Chorale, 1976, Salvation Army Orange County, 1972-76, Orange County United Way, 1976, Orange County chpt. Nat. Council Alcoholism, 1982—; pres. Boys Club Harbor Area, 1971. Recipient Spirit award Irvine Women's Club, 1972, civic leadership award Salvation Army, 1976, Silver Anchor award Newport Harbor C. of C., 1976; Community Leadership award Girl Scouts U.S.A., 1977; Chancellor's citation for merit U. Calif. at Irvine, 1978; Nat. Silver Keystone award Boys Clubs Am., 1982. Mem. Pub. Relations Soc. Am. (accredited, pres. chpt. 1980), U. Calif. Interfaith Found. (pres. 1973). Republican. Methodist. Clubs: Corona del Mar Kiwanis (pres. 1972), Masons (master 1965), Shriners, Orange County Press, Merced Toastmasters (pres. 1953). Office: 550 Newport Center Dr Newport Beach CA 92663

MANCHESTER, MARGARET KIMMAN, nurse, educator; b. Pierz, Minn., Oct. 25, 1940; d. Arnold B. and Edith J. (Wolf) Kimman; divorced; children—Brian, Julie. Grad. St. Gabriel's Sch. Nursing, 1962; B.S. in Nursing, U. Nev., 1976, M.S., 1979. Staff nurse various hosps. Minn., Nev., N.C., 1962-70; self-employed pvt. duty nurse, Las Vegas, Nev., 1974-80; instr. nursing Clark County Community Coll., Las Vegas, 1976-80, coordinator Lic. Practical Nurse program, 1980—. Served to capt. Nurse Corps, USAF, 1966-68. Mem. Am. Nurses Assn., Am. Personnel and Guidance Assn., Am. Assn. Women in Community and Jr. Colls. Home: 5203 Reeder Circle Las Vegas NV 89119 Office: 3200 E Cheyenne N Las Vegas NV 89030

MANCINA, WILLIAM PETER, computer systems exec.; b. Eveleth, Minn., June 27, 1924; s. Anthony and Victoria (Marra) M.; B.S., U. Minn., 1948, M.S., 1952; M.A., Stanford U., 1954; m. Doris L. Olson, Aug. 28, 1948; children—Dean William, Mark Allan. Instr., athletic dir. East High Sch., Duluth, Minn., 1949-52; asst. prof. U. Minn., 1952-56; mgr. systems integration and testing TRW, Redondo Beach, Calif., 1956—. Served to capt. USAAF, 1942-46. Mem. Assn. Computing Machinery, Am. Def. Preparedness Assn. Home: 6082 Shields Dr Huntington Beach CA 92647 Office: 1 Space Park Redondo Beach CA 90278

MANCINI, FRANK PETER, engineering manager; b. Chicago Heights, Ill., Feb. 20, 1938; s. Frank May and Elsie Wilhelmina (Brueggert) M.; m. Gladista Dae Moritz, Dec. 27, 1975; children—Peter, Lance. B.S., Ariz. State U., 1961, M.S., 1972, Ph.D., 1977; M.A., U. Ariz., 1964. Cert. profl. engr., Ariz., Ill.; cert. energy mgr. Research engr. Motorola, Phoenix, 1964-67; research assoc. Ariz. State U., Tempe, 1967-71; research engr. Ariz. Transp. Research Ctr., 1971-77; assoc. dir. engring. Ariz. Solar Energy Commn., Phoenix, 1977—; adj. prof. Phoenix Coll. Mem. Ariz. Humane Soc., 1982—. NASA fellow, 1967; Fed. Hwy. Adminstrn. Research grantee, 1972-75; Dept. Energy Research grantee, 1977-82. Mem. Nat. Soc. Profl. Engrs., Ariz. Soc. Profl. Engrs., Ill. Soc. Profl. Engrs., Am. Statis. Assn., Assn. Energy Engrs. Roman Catholic. Club: Ariz. Basenji (Phoenix). Author: Dissipative and Non Dissipative Stochastic Processes, 1983; Large Range Magnification Optical, 1972, Ariz. Dept. Transp., Materials Division; Air Sunditioning (solar powered cooling device for automobiles, 1983). Office: 1700 W Washington 502 Phoenix AZ 85007

MANCINO, JOHN GREGORY, tea co. exec.; b. N.Y.C., Nov. 14, 1946; s. John D. and Carmela A. Mancino; B.A., Colgate U., 1968. Chief appraiser Rusciano Appraisers & Cons., N.Y.C., 1968-70; v.p. Pisces Prodns., Boulder, Colo., 1971-73; v.p. ops. Celestial Seasonings Inc., Boulder, 1973—, also dir.; dir. Spruce St. Mktg.; ptnr., dir. Computer Connection, Inc., Mr. Software, Inc.; ptnr. First Nat. Investment. Home: Mount Mead Boulder CO Office: 1780 55th St Boulder CO 80301

MANDEL, BARBARA S., marketing consultant, advertising agency owner; b. Chgo., Aug. 8, 1953; d. Sherman I. and Phyllis (Greenberg) Mandel; m. Hal E. Stephens, Sept. 18, 1981. B.A. with honors in Advt. and Pub. Relations, U. Ill., 1975. Mktg. asst. United Banks Wis., Madison, 1975-76; advt. mgr. CUNA Supply affiliate Credit Union Nat. Assn., Madison, 1976-78; mktg. dir. Los Angeles Water & Power Employees Credit Union, 1978-79; owner Mandel & Co., San Diego, 1979—; owner mgmt. seminar co., electronic funds transfer service, casualty ins. agy.; cons. nursing dept. U. Calif. Extension, San Diego Nutritionist Assn. Active San Diego Symphony Assn.; bd. dirs. San Diego Pops. Mem. Am. Mktg. Assn. (San Diego best promotion award 1982); San Diego Ad Club. Office: Mandel & Co 5665 Oberlin Dr Suite 200 San Diego CA 92121

MANDEL, FLORENCE JASLOW, chamber of commerce exec.; b. Mt. Clemens, Mich., Aug. 21; d. Samuel and Sarah (Strauchler) Jaslow; m. Max Mandel, July 2, 1944; children—Barbara Nadine, Charlene Debra, Sandra Kathy. Student UCLA Extension, Mission Coll., 1974-76, U.S. C. of C. Inst. Mgmt., 1979-83. Exec. sec. U.S. Maritime Commn., N.Y.C., 1943-44; exec. mgr. Leonard Jacobs Inc., N.Y.C., 1941-43; exec. mgr. Pacoima (Calif.) C. of C., 1976-79, Reseda (Calif.) C. of C., 1979-80, Panorama City (Calif.) C. of C., 1979-81 (merged with Sepulveda (Calif.) C. of C., 1982), Panorama City-Sepulveda C. of C., 1982—. Pres. Pacoima Community Coordinating Council, 1974-76, Verdugo Hills Hebrew Ctr. Sisterhood, 1979-81; bd. dirs. Mid-Valley Community Police Council; troop leader, Brownie leader, troop organizer Girl Scouts U.S.A., 16 yrs.; chmn. United Way. Named Woman of Yr., Verdugo Hills Hebrew Ctr., 1982; recognition from Los Angeles County Bd. Suprs., YWCA, Foothill div. Los Angeles Police Dept., mayor of Los Angeles, citations from city, state and govt. ofcls., various others. Mem. So. Calif. Assn. C. of C. Execs., Calif. C. of C. Exec. Mgrs. Assn., Mission Hills C. of C. (hon.). Jewish. Clubs: Soroptimist San Fernando Valley, Panorama City Woman's (hon. life), Sizzler, Pacoima Woman's. Home: 9137 Patrick Ave Arleta CA 91331 Office: 14600 Roscoe Blvd Suite 201 Panorama City CA 91402

MANDEL, LEON, III, author; b. Chgo., July 31, 1928; s. Leon and Edna H.; student Cornell U., 1946-54, Columbia U., 1950, Hastings Coll. Law, 1960; m. Olivia Eskridge, June 12, 1953; children—Leon, Olivia. Salesman, Brit. Motors Co., Burlingame, Calif., 1957, sales mgr., Salinas, Calif., 1958-59, gen. mgr., 1959; owner, sales mgr. Vallejo Sports Cars (Calif.), 1960; editor Belmont (Calif.) Courier Bull., 1963, Competition Press, San Francisco, 1964-67; mng. editor Car and Driver mag., N.Y.C., 1967; editor, 1968-71, sr. editor, 1971-72; pub. Autoweek, Reno, 1972-75; sr. editor Motor Trend mag., Los Angeles, 1978—; auto editor KTVN-TV, Reno, 1976—; instr. mag. journalism Truckee Meadows Community Coll., 1980; cons. SRI Internat. Author: Speed With Style, 1974; Driven, 1977; Murder So Real (pseudonym Al Bird), 1978; Fast Lane Summer, 1981; William Fisk Harrah, 1982; American Cars, 1982. Address: 3450 San Mateo Ave Reno NV 89509

MANDEL, RAY ALLEN, psychologist; b. Santa Cruz, Calif., Sept. 7, 1948; s. Robert James and Wilma Audrey (Tallman) M.; m. Pamela Krouse, Nov. 18, 1971; m. Darla Marie Mann, Mar. 4, 1978; children—Clarisa, Simon, Abigail. B.A., Humboldt State U., 1982, postgrad., 1983—. Ordained minister Am. Evangelistic Assn., 1978. Asst. dir., sch. psychologist I'SOT, Inc., Canby, Calif., 1983—. Chmn. Juvenile Justice and Delinquency Prevention Commn., Modoc County, Calif., 1980-81. Mem. Nat. Sch. Psychology Assn.; Am. Personnel and Guidance Assn. Home: PO Box 125 Canby CA 96015

MANDEL, ROBERT MICHAEL, international affairs educator, researcher, consultant; b. Washington, Oct. 30, 1949; s. Philip and Alice Grace M.; m. Annette Kelley, Aug. 1, 1981. A.B., Brown U., 1972; M.A., Yale U., 1974, M. Phil., 1975, Ph.D., 1976. Dir. research Admissions Office, Yale Law Sch., 1973-76; summer intern CIA, 1974-75; asst. prof. Lewis and Clark Coll., Portland, 1976-82, assoc. prof., 1982—. Active World Affairs Council Oreg., 1978—. Yale U. fellow 1972-76; Yale Councilium Internat. Studies Dissertation grantee 1975-76; Lewis and Clark Coll. research grantee 1980-82; recipient Rookie of Yr. award Lewis and Clark Coll. 1977, Faculty of Yr. 1979. mem. Am. Polit. Sci. Assn., Internat. Studies Assn. Quaker. Reviewer Am. Polit. Sci. Rev., Internat. Studies Quart., Jour. Conflict Resolution; contbr. chpt. to book, articles to profl. jours. Home: 19300 SW Anderson St Aloah OR 97007 Office: Lewis and Clark Coll PO Box 96 Portland OR 97219

MANDEL, WILLIAM, accountant, real estate executive; b. Newark, Feb. 27, 1955; s. Morris and Ida (Schindel) M.; m. Diane Lupinacci, July 19, 1980. B.S. in Bus. Adminstrn., Fairleigh Dickinson U., 1976. C.P.A., Calif., N.J. Jr. acct. J.C. Cohn & Co., Newark, 1975-80, sr. acct., 1980; treas. The Naiman Co., San Diego, 1980—. Mem. Calif. Soc. C.P.A.s, N.J. Soc. C.P.A.s. Republican. Jewish. Office: 4115 Sorrento Valley Blvd San Diego CA 92121

MANDELL, STEPHEN ELLIOT, mgmt. cons., real estate syndicator; b. Bklyn., Apr. 28, 1944; s. Herman and Estelle (Minchenberg) M.; B.S. in Mech. Engring., N.Y. U., 1965, M.B.A., 1978, Ph.D./ABD, 1978; M.S. in Mgmt. Sci., Stevens Inst. Tech., 1971; m. Barbara Cooper, Dec. 31, 1971; children—David Herman, Iris Morrisa. Engr. in tng. Combustion Engring. Inc., Windsor, Conn., 1965-66; project engt. Bendix Corp., Teterboro, N.J., 1966-67; successively project engr., mgmt. cons., chief mgmt. scientist U.S. Army Material Command, Dover, N.J., 1967-76; mgr. ops. Operating Group Citibank, N.A., N.Y.C., 1976-77, mgr. fin. ops. Investment Mgmt. Group, 1977-78; dir. NE Health Survival, Inc., Maplewood, N.J., 1977—, Health & Survival Inc., Modesto, Calif., 1980—; founder, pres. Morgan/Tech. Corp., 1979—; cons. in field. U.S. Army fellow, 1971-73. Mem. Inst. Mgmt. Scis., Assn. Computing Machinery, Omega Rho (nat. sec.), Beta Gamma Sigma (past pres.). Clubs: Game Point Racquet, Scuba. Home: Box 6097 Modesto CA 95355 Office: 1700 McHenry Village Way Suite 10 Modesto CA 95350

MANDEVILLE, GILBERT HARRISON, consulting engineer; b. Bklyn., July 6, 1910; s. Gilbert Spier and Minnie (Ross) M.; m. Mildred Schwagerman, June 20, 1936; 1 dau., Terry Melinda. B.S., Seattle U., 1953. Exec. dir., v.p. Leo O. Daly Co., Seattle, 1952-57; ptnr., cons. engr. Mandeville & Berge, Architects and Engrs., Seattle, 1957—; dir., sec.-treas. Riverfront Assocs.; dir. Bruce Second & James, U.S. Devel. Co., Bruce-Glenwood; ptnr. Broadway Village, Inc. Bd. dirs. Evergreen Safety Council, 1966—; chmn. Seattle City Planning Commn., 1960-62; chmn. Puget Sound Regional Planning Council, 1960-62. Served to lt. comdr. USN. Registered profl. engr., Wash., R.I., Alaska. Fellow ASCE, IEEE; mem. Am. Soc. Planning Ofcls., Am. Arbitration Assn. (chmn. constrn. panel Seattle sect. 1973—). Presbyterian. Clubs: Wash. Athletic, Seattle Engring. Home: 13041 42d Ave NE Box 652 Seattle WA 98125 Office: 500 Union St Seattle WA 98101

MANDIBERG, MYRTLE, psychologist; b. N.Y.C., July 1, 1918; d. Samuel and Sadie (Friedman) M. B.A., Bklyn. Coll., 1938; M.A., U. Pa., 1940. Intern, Wayne County Gen. Hosp., Eloise, Mich., 1940-41, psychologist, 1941-42; head tchr. Nursing Sch., Detroit Bd. Edn., 1942-44; psychologist Detroit Recorder's Ct. Psychopathic Clinic, 1944-49; psychotherapist Devereux Ranch Sch., Santa Barbara, Calif., 1949-51; supr. Reiss-Davis Child Study Center, Los Angeles, 1959-62; adj. lectr. psychology UCLA, 1978—; coordinator profl. services Los Angeles Child Devel. Center, 1979—; pvt. practice psychology, Los Angeles, 1951—. Mem. Am. Psychol. Assn., Calif. Psychol. Assn., Los Angeles County Psychol. Assn., Assn. Child Psychoanalysis. Home and Office: 1470 Glendon Ave Los Angeles CA 90024

MANDL, WILLIAM JOHN, computer products mfg. co. exec.; b. Los Angeles, Apr. 8, 1939; s. Bernard William and Theresa (Rodia) M.; B.E.E., Calif. State U., Los Angeles, 1962; M.S.E.E., U. So. Calif., 1964; m. Mary Louise Mullins, Nov. 6, 1976; children—Kathryn Ingrid, Stephen William, Joseph William. Research engr. Rockwell Internat., Downey, Calif., 1960-64; sr. research engr. RCA, Van Nuys, Calif., 1964-67; sr. engr. Litton Systems, Woodland Hills, Calif., 1964-69; v.p. mktg. Macrodata, Woodland Hills, 1969-76; mgr. new products mktg. EMM, Chatsworth, Calif., 1976-78; founder, pres. Hometech, Brea, Calif., 1978—; asst. prof. engring. Calif. State U., Los Angeles, 1964-67. Republican. Roman Catholic. Home: 8303 Faust Canoga Park CA 91304 Office: 266 Viking Way Brea CA 92621

MANDLER, GEORGE, psychologist; b. Vienna, Austria, June 11, 1924; came to U.S., 1940, naturalized, 1943; s. Richard and Hede (Goldschmied) M.; B.A., N.Y. U., 1949; M.S., Yale U., 1950, Ph.D., 1953; postgrad. U. Basel (Switzerland), 1947-48; m. Jean Matter, Jan. 19, 1957; children—Peter Clark, Michael Allen. Asst. prof. Harvard U., 1953-57, lectr., 1957-60; prof. U. Toronto (Ont., Can.), 1960-65; prof. psychology, dir. Center for Human Info. Processing, U. Calif., San Diego, 1965—, chmn. dept. psychology, 1965-70; fellow Center for Advanced Study in Behavioral Scis., 1959-60; vis. fellow Oxford (Eng.) U., 1971-72, 78; hon. research fellow Univ. Coll., London U., 1977-78, 82—. Served with U.S. Army, 1943-46. J.S. Guggenheim fellow, 1971-72. Fellow AAAS; mem. Am. Assn. Advancement Psychology (trustee), Psychonomic Soc. (chmn. governing bd. 1983), Am. Psychol. Assn. (pres. div. exptl. psychology 1978-79, pres. div. gen. psychology 1982-83, mem. Council Reps. 1978-81), Soc. Exptl. Psychologists, Fedn. Behavioral, Psychol. and Cognitive Scis. (pres. 1981), AAUP, Authors Guild. Author books, the most recent being: Mind and Emotion, 1975; German edit., 1980; contbr. articles and revs. to profl. jours.; editor Psychol. Rev., 1970-76. Home: 1406 La Jolla Knoll La Jolla CA 92037 Office: Dept Psychology U Calif at San Diego La Jolla CA 92093

MANDLES, MARTINN HEROE, corporate exective; b. Tacoma, Nov. 1, 1940; s. Aaron Hirsh and Maxine (Bennigson) M.; m. Dayna Lindstrom, Aug. 3, 1968; div.; 1 dau., Melanie Dayan. B.S. Stanford U., 1964. Registered profl. engr. Asst. to pres. Microdot Inc., Los Angeles, 1969-72; v.p. Am. Bldg. Maintenance Industries, Los Angeles, 1972—. Trustee, Jewish Big Bros. Assn., Los Angeles. Served to lt. comdr. USN, 1964-69; Vietnam. Mem. Century City C. of C. (dir.). Republican. Jewish. Club: Marina City (Marina del Rey, Calif.). Home: 4626 Maytime Ln Culver City CA 90230 Office: Am Bldg Maintenance Industries 9831 W Pico Los Angeles CA 90035

MANDRA, YORK T., geology educator; b. N.Y.C., Nov. 24, 1922; s. Raymond and Irene (Farruggio) M.; m. Highoohi Kechijian, Jan. 26, 1946. B.A., U. Calif.-Berkeley, 1947, M.A. in Paleontology. 1949; Ph.D. in Geology, Stanford U., 1958. Instr. to assoc. prof. geology San Francisco State U., 1950-63, prof., 1964—, head geology sect., chmn. dept., 1960-67; vis. prof. U. Aix-Marseille, 1959, Syracuse U., summer 1963, U. Maine, summer 1969, U. Calif.-Santa Barbara, summers 1972—; research assoc. U. Glasgow, 1959, Calif. Acad. Scis., 1966—; vis. scientist N.Z. Geol. Survey, fall 1970. Pres., David S. Sohigian Found., 1975—. Served with USAAF, 1942-46. Teaching fellow Danforth Found., 1958; teaching fellow NSF, 1959, research grantee, 1967-77. Fellow Calif. Acad. Scis., Geol. Soc. Am., AAAS; mem. Nat. Assn. Geology Tchrs. (pres. Far Western sect. 1953-54, 73-74 Robert Wallace Webb award 1977), Paleontol. Soc., Soc. Econ. Mineralogists and Paleontologists, Soc. for Environ. Geochemistry, and Health, AAAS. Contbr. numerous articles to sci. publs.

MANERA, ELIZABETH S., educator; b. Atlanta, Nov. 27, 1929; d. Isaac Aaron and Roberta (Roberts) Sturgis; m. Paul A. Manera, Jan. 3, 1959. B.S., Towson State U., 1951; M.A., Ariz. State U., 1962, Ed.D., 1967. Tchr. Towson (Md.) Schs., 1951-53, St. Louis Schs., 1955-57; dir. Girl Scouts Camp, Glendale, Calif., 1956, Phoenix, 1957-59; research asst. to asst. dean Ariz. State U., Tempe, 1960-61, grad. tchrs. asst. phys. edn., 1961-62, instr. phys. edn., 1962-63, vis. lectr. secondary edn., 1967-73, asst. prof. secondary edn., 1973—; vis. lectr. secondary edn. U. Mo., 1967; tour instr. Coll. Abroad, Europe, 1972; cons. in field. Leader Ariz. Cactus Pine Girl Scouts, U.S.A., Phoenix, 1973. Mem. NEA, Am. Coll. and Univ. Faculty Assn., Ariz. Classroom Tchrs., Ariz. Edn. Assn., Assn. Supervision and Curriculum Devel., AAUW, AAUP, Am. Assn. Tchr. Educators (chmn. editorial bd. jour.), World Council Curriculum and Instr., Phi Delta Kappa, Delta Kappa Gamma, Pi Lambda Theta. Contbr. articles to profl. jours. Home: 8316 N 53d St Scottsdale AZ 85253 Office: Dept Secondary Education Ariz State Univ Tempe AZ 85287

MANGAN, MARGARET JENE, educational administrator; b. Clintonville, Wis., Feb. 7, 1928; d. Fred and Helen (Rosinski) Fumelle; m. James E. Mangan, June 16, 1951 (div.). B.S., Wis. State U.-Stevens Point, 1949; M.S., U. Wis., 1958. Tchr. public schs., Phillips, Elkhart Lake, Kiel and Sheboygan, Wis., 1949-60; tchr. Garden Grove (Calif.) Unified Sch. Dist. 1960-61; tchr. Anaheim (Calif.) Union High Sch. Dist., 1961-65, counselor, 1965-68, asst. prin., 1968-79, sr. high prin., 1979-80, dir. instructional services, 1980—. Mem. Assn. Calif. Sch. Adminstrs., Assn. Supervision and Curriculum Devel., Council Exceptional Children, Anaheim Secondary Sch. Adminstrs. Assn., PTA, So. Counties Women Mgrs. in Edn., U. Wis. Alumni Assn. Republican. Roman Catholic. Home: 1303 N Paradise Ct Anaheim CA 92805 Office: 501 Crescent Way Anaheim CA 92803

MANGAN, TERENCE JOSEPH, police chief; b. Utica, N.Y., Feb. 17, 1938; s. Lawrence and Eloise (Roth) M.; m. Charlotte Mauss, June 19, 1971; children—Sean, Megan. B.A., St. Mary's Coll., Norwalk, Conn., 1961; M.A., St. Albert's Coll., 1965; postgrad. in Pub. Adminstrn., Adminstrn. Justice, U. So. Calif., 1972-76; Grad. FBI Nat. Acad. Cert. Wash. State Criminal Justice Tng. Commn., Calif. Peace Officers Standards and Tng. Commn. With Seaside (Calif.) Police Dept., 1968-72; with Lakewood (Calif.) Police Dept., 1972-76, chief, dir. community safety, to 1976; chief Bellingham (Wash.) Police Dept., 1976—; mem. Wash. State Criminal Justice Tng. Commn., Gov.'s Adv. Bd. Criminal Justice, Mgmt. Adv. Group Organized Crime and Narcotics Enforcement; lectr. FBI Acad. Pres., Assumption Parish Council; bd. dirs. United way, Whatcom County, Calif.; mem. archdiocesan steering com. 1982 Ann. Catholic Appeal. Recipient Disting. Service award City of Seaside, 1972; citation U.S. Secret Service, 1969; Congressional Com. Internal Security, 1971; Disting. Service award City of Lakewood, also Wash. Assn. Sheriffs and Police Chiefs, 1978-81; Law Enforcement Officer of Yr. award Wash. VFW, 1980; Community Service award Wash. Toastmasters Internat., 1980; Pres. award Pacific Lutheran U., 1981. Mem. Internat. Assn. Chiefs Police, Nat. Council Crime and Delinquency, Wash. Assn. Sheriffs and Police Chiefs (dir.), Internat. Peace Arch Law Enforcement Council. Roman Catholic. Office: Police Dept Hdqtrs 210 Lottie St Bellingham WA 98225

MANGELS, JOHN DONALD, banker; b. Victoria, B.C., Can., Apr. 14, 1926; s. August and Marguerite E.M. (parents Am. citizens); B.A. in Bus. and Econs., U. Wash., 1950; Grad. Sch. Credit and Fin. Mgmt., Stanford U., 1961; m. Mary Ann Hahn, Nov. 25, 1954; children—Susan, Meg, John Donald. With Rainier Nat. Bank and affiliates, Seattle, 1950—, vice chmn. Rainier Bancorp., 1975—, pres. Ranier Nat. Bank, 1976—. Bd. dirs. Downtown Seattle Assn., Corp. Council for Arts, United Way of King County. Served with USAAF, 1944-46. Mem. Wash. Soc. C.P.A.s, Assn. Res. City Bankers, Robert Morris Assos. Presbyterian. Clubs: Rainier, Broadmoor Golf, Bellevue Athletic. Office: One Rainier Sq PO Box 3966 Seattle WA 98124

MANGIARELLI, RICHARD DONALD, solar energy co. exec.; b. Providence, Apr. 23, 1940; s. Santo and Jennie (Granieri) M.; student Tulane U., 1954-55; B.A., U. Conn., 1959; M.B.A., Pepperdine U., 1975; m. Lou Ann Williams, Apr. 2, 1964; children—Donnie, Lisa, Maria, Gina. Cons. bus. ins., pension profit sharing plans, San Diego, 1964-68; pres., founder Profl. Athletes Mgmt. Co., San Diego, 1969—, So. Calif. Solar; chmn. bd. Dynasty Resources, Inc.; chief exec. officer Solalso, Inc.; profl. football player, 1959-60; dir. Ice Vendors Am.; guest lectr. Saddleback Coll. Served to lt. col. USMC, 1962-65. C.L.U., Calif. Mem. Bldg. Contractors Assn., Assn. Profl. Appraisers, NFL Alumni Assn., Nat. Football League Player Agts. Assn., Marine Corps Res. Officers Assn. Republican. Roman Catholic. Club: Atlas Health. Home: PO Box 250 Rio Senda Rancho Santa Fe CA 92067 Office: 11211 Sorrento Valley Rd San Diego CA 92121

MANGUM, WILLIAM THOMAS, mgmt. cons. co. exec.; b. Memphis, Dec. 7, 1931; s. Cary and Jennie (Matthews) M.; A.A., Santa Monica Coll., 1952; B.S., U. So. Calif., 1954; children—Stacy, Christopher. With Psychol. Research Corp., N.Y.C., 1952-54; employee relations specialist Beckman Instruments, Inc., Fullerton, Calif., 1954-55; dir. personnel, asst. gen. mgr. Fairchild Camera & Instruments Corp., Los Angeles, 1955-60; partner Deane-Thomas Co., Los Angeles, 1960-64; pres. Thomas Mangum Co. Inc., Los Angeles, Calif., 1965—; cons. dir. TMI Mgmt. Inc., 1965—; prof. indsl. relations Whittier Coll., 1958-60. Bd. dirs. La Habra Heights Community Devel. Com., 1970-73; mem. Los Angeles County Rep. Central Com., 1960-68. Mem. IEEE, AIAA, U. So. Calif. Personnel and Indsl. Relations Assn. (pres., 1961-62), Assn. Computing Machinery, Personnel Indsl. Relations Assn., Am. Ordnance Assn., Ops. Research Soc., Old Crows Assn. Contbr. articles to profl. jours. Home: 2181 El Cajonita La Habra Heights LA 90631 Office: 1145 W 6th St Los Angeles CA 91731

MANI, KURIAN KOTHAPPALLYL, research aerodynamics engr.; b. Kottayam, Kerala, India, Dec. 23, 1946; came to U.S., 1974; s. Mani and Saramma (Chacko) K.; B.E. with honors, Govt. Engring. Coll., Jabalpur, India, 1968; M.Tech., Indian Inst. Tech., Madras, 1970; Ph.D., Ga. Inst. Tech., 1977; m. Jaya Kurian, Oct. 24, 1970; 1 dau., Seira. Aerodynamics engr. Indian Space Research Orgn., Trivandrum, India, 1970-74; postdoctoral fellow Ga. Inst. Tech., Atlanta, 1977-78; asst. research scientist, 1978-79; sr. aerodyn. engr. Lockheed-Calif. Co., Burbank, 1979—. Mem. AIAA, Contbr. articles to profl. jours. Home: 21952 Marjoram Ct Saugus CA 91350 Office: Dept 7552 Bldg 63-3 Plant A-1 PO Box 551 Lockheed Calif Co Burbank CA 91520

MANIBUSAN, ROY CRUZ, school administrator, educator; b. Agana, Guam, July 17, 1939; s. Jesus Leon Guerrero and Engracia Garcia (Cruz) M.; m. Zenaida Lopez Galura; children—Adrian, Jessica, Rowena. B.A. in Sociology, U. Guam, 1969; M.A. in Couseling and Psychology, Ball State U., 1973; postgrad. U. Ark., 1973-74, U. Nev.-Las Vegas, 1977-83. Cert. edn. adminstrn., counselor. Served as enlisted man U.S. Air Force, 1958-69, commd. 2d lt., 1969, advanced through grades to capt., 72; ret., 1980; prin. St. Christopher Sch., North Las Vegas, Nev., 1979—; adj. instr. psychology, sociology and counseling Nicholls State U., Thibodaus, La., Park Coll., St. Louis, Clark County Community Coll., Las Vegas, 1975—. Mem. Nat. Assn. Elem. Sch. Prins., Nat. Cath. Edn. Assn., Assn. Supervision and Curriculum Devel., AAUP. Republican. Roman Catholic. Club: K.C.

MANICHE, BARBARA LANE, office services company executive; b. Malvern, Ark., July 18, 1942; d. Oliver C. and Valerie (Jones) Lane; m. Firmino A. Maniche, Sept. 16, 1967 (div.); 1 dau., Stephanie Alise. A.A. in Bus. Adminstrn., Golden Gate U., 1980, postgrad., 1981-82; cert. St. Mary's Paralegal Program, 1981. Payroll and personnel clk. Del Monte Corp., San Francisco, 1966-69, payroll tax clk. indsl. relations dept., 1969-72, sec. pub. affairs dept., 1972-74, payroll tax acct., 1974-81; owner, mgr. Maniche's Clerical Services, Oakland, Calif., 1982—. Edn. dir. Oakland LWV; Mem. Nat. Assn. Female Execs., Nat. Notary Assn. (Notary Pub. Commn. 1982—), Oakland C. of C. Address: 4817 Brookdale Ave Oakland CA 94619

MANIERI, MICHAEL JOSEPH, industrial hygienist, safety engineer; b. Jersey City, Dec. 16, 1951; s. Michael Joseph and Lucille (De Luca) M. B.S., N.Y. Inst. Tech., 1973; M.S. in Indsl. Hygiene, Wayne State U. Sch. Medicine, 1976. Indsl. hygienist, research analyst SRI Internat. (formerly Stanford Research Inst.), Menlo Park, Calif., 1976-77; corp. indsl. hygienist Employees Benefits Ins. Cos., San Jose, Calif., 1977-80; assoc. indsl. hygienist Calif. Dept. Occupational Safety and Health, San Jose, 1980-81; corp. mgr. indsl. hygiene safety AVANTEK, Inc., Santa Clara, Calif., 1981—. Mem. Am. Electronics Assn., Am. Indsl. Hygiene Assn. (symposium com. No. Calif. sect. 1983), Am. Soc. Safety Engrs., Peninsula Indsl. Bus. Assn., Bay Area Electronics Safety Group, Soc. Bio-Med. Scis., Tau Epsilon Phi. Roman Catholic. Clubs: U.S. Ski Assn., EBI Cos. Softball. Contbr. articles to profl. jours. Home: 100 Glen Eyrie Ave Apt 5 San Jose CA 95125 Office: 481 Cottonwood Dr Milpitas CA 95035

MANION, MARLENE SCHAEFER, tax accountant, financial consultant; b. Steger, Ill., Aug. 25, 1932; d. Nicholas Peter and Lyda Matilda (Larsen) Schaefer; m. Russell K. Moreton, Aug. 17, 1950; m. 2d, James T. Manion, Apr. 23, 1977; children—Nanci Jimenez, Russell, L. Desiree LaVertu. Student Orange Coast Coll., 1959-60, NYU, 1969. Cert. enrolled agt., IRS. Pvt. practice income tax preparation, fin. cons., Laguna Hills, Calif., 1963—. Pres. El Toro chpt. Am. Field Service. Mem. Nat. Soc. Pub. Accts., Accreditation Council of Accountancy, Nat. Assn. Enrolled Agts., Calif. Soc. Enrolled Agts. Republican. Office: Suite 201 25255 Cabot Rd Laguna Hills CA 92653

MANION, MARTHA LISA, librarian, bibliographer; b. San Francisco, Feb. 2, 1949; d. Roy R. and Maxine F. (LeDoux) M.; m. Ronald Allen Powell, Feb. 8, 1975. B.A. cum laude, San Jose State U., 1971, M.A., 1974; M.L.S., U. Calif.-Berkeley, 1976. Cert. tchr., Calif. Research asst. Univ.-Wide Library Automation Project, Berkeley, Calif., 1976; reference librarian Santa Clara County Library, Sunnyvale, Calif., 1977; asst. librarian Sci. and Engring. Library, San Jose (Calif.) State U., 1977-80; librarian Mt. View Research Ctr., Stauffer Chem. Co. (Calif.), 1980—. Mem. Spl. Libraries Assn., San Francisco Bay Area Online User's Group, Pi Lambda Theta, Beta Phi Mu, Kappa Delta Pi. Author: Writings about Henry Cowell: An Annotated Bibliography, 1982. Office: Mt View Research Ctr Stauffer Chem-Co 1195 W Fremont Ave Sunnyvale CA 94087

MANKIEWICZ, ANGELA CONSOLO, computer systems designer/manager, consultant; b. Bklyn., May 26, 1944; d. Michael and Josephine (Comande) Consolo; m. Richard Chester Mankiewicz, Feb. 25, 1972. B.A. in Rhetorical Theory, Calif. State U.-Los Angeles, 1966, postgrad. 1966-67. Tng. co-ordinator, systems analyst United Mchts. and Mfrs., Los Angeles, 1966-72; cons. data processing, Los Angeles; sr. systems analyst Proto Tool Co., Los Angeles, 1973-75; tech. services mgr. Pacific Stock Exchange, Los Angeles, 1976-77; project leader Warner Bros., Burbank, Calif., 1977-79; project mgr. micro-systems Xerox Computer Services, Los Angeles, 1979—. Mem. Assn. Systems Mgmt., Am. Prodn. and Inventory Control Soc., Bus. and Profl. Women's Fedn., Data Processing Mgmt. Assn., ACLU, NOW. Office: Xerox Computer Services 5310 Beethoven St Suite MA-33 Los Angeles CA 90066

MANLY, PHILIP JAMES, health physicist; b. Cin., Apr. 12, 1944; s. Richard Samuel and Marian (LeFevre) M.; B.S., M.I.T., 1967; M.S., Rensselaer Poly. Inst., 1971; m. Jean Angela Maron, Mar. 25, 1967; children—Charlotte, Frederick, Peter, Elizabeth. Shift radiol. control dir. Pearl Harbor Naval Shipyard, 1971-72, head radiol. tech. div., 1972-74, sr. health physicist, 1974-75, head radiol. support div., 1975-78; pres. Gamma Corp., Wahiawa, Hawaii, 1978—; symposium chmn. 13th Midyear Topical Symposium, Honolulu, 1979. Diplomate Am. Bd. Health Physics. Mem. Health Physics Soc. (founder, chpt. 1st pres. 1977, symposia com. 1980-82), Am. Nuclear Soc., AAAS, Sigma Xi. Home: PO Box 430 Wahiawa HI 96786 Office: 649 California Ave Suite 102 Wahiawa HI 96786

MANN, GORDON LEE, JR., ins. broker; b. Taylor, Tex., May 5, 1921; s. Gordon L. and Ruth (Kirkpatrick) M.; student U. Calif. at Los Angeles, 1939, Sch. Law, Loyola U., Los Angeles, 1961. Claims mgr. Traders and Gen. Ins. Co., Los Angeles, 1948-52, Fireman's Fund Am. Ins. Cos., 1952-70; account exec., claims cons. Behrendt-Levy Ins. Agy., 1970-72; asst. div. mgr. Argonaut Ins. Co., Los Angeles, 1972-78; v.p. Frank B. Hall & Co., Los Angeles; 1978—. Served to lt. USNR, 1946. Recipient Meritorious Pub. Service citation Dept. Navy, 1965; Nat. Scroll of Honor, Navy League, 1968. C.P.C.U. Mem. Am. Soc. C.P.C.U.'s (pres. Los Angeles chpt. 1972, gen. chmn. nat. conv. 1970), Navy League U.S. (nat. dir. 1963-75, v.p. for adminstrn. 11th region 1974-75, pres. Los Angeles council 1962, state pres. 1965), Am. Legion (past comdr.) Nat. Soc. Colonial Wars (gov. Calif. soc. 1967, nat. dep. gov. gen. 1969), Children Am. Revolution (past nat. com. chmn.), S.R., Mil. Order World Wars, Men of All Saints' Soc. (past pres.), Naval Order U.S. Republican. Episcopalian (past vestryman). Clubs: Masons, Los Angeles; American (London). Speaker and writer on ins. and patriotic subjects. Home: 435 S Curson Ave Los Angeles CA 90036 Office: 3200 Wilshire Blvd Los Angeles CA 90010

MANN, NANCY LOUISE, statistician; b. Chillicothe, Ohio; d. Everett Chaney and Pauline Elizabeth Robbins; B.A., UCLA, 1948, M.A., 1949, Ph.D. (NIH fellow 1959-62), 1965; m. Kenneth Douglas Mann, June 19, 1949; children—Bryan Wilkinson, Laurie Ellen. Mem. tech. staff, then sr. scientist Rocketdyne div. Rockwell Internat. Co., 1962-75, project mgr. reliability and stats. Sci. Center, Thousand Oaks, Calif., 1975—; research prof. biomath. UCLA, 1978-81; Disting. vis. prof. Bucknell U., 1974; adv. com. Bur. Census, 1974-77; bd. advisers U.S. Naval Postgrad. Sch., Monterey, Calif., 1979-82; adv. com. nuclear regulatory research Nuclear Regulatory Commn., 1980-82; mem. panel nonstandard distbns. Nat. Acad. Scis., 1980-82, chmn. subpanel phys. applications, 1980-82. Recipient Silver Medallion award So. Calif. YWCA, 1977; grantee Nat. Inst. Drug Abuse, 1979-81. Fellow Am. Statis. Assn. (pres. So. Calif. chpt. 1970-71, chmn. council 1976); mem. Internat. Statis. Inst., Sigma Xi, Pi Mu Epsilon, Delta Delta Delta. Co-author: Methods for Statistical Analysis of Reliability and Life Data, 1974; editorial bd. Communications in Stats., 1973—; editorial adv. bd. Statis. Computation and Simulation, 1977—; contbr. articles to profl. jours. Home: 1870 Veteran Ave Los Angeles CA 90025 Office: Biomath U Calif Los Angeles CA 90024

MANN, NIKKI JEAN, business communications educator; b. Columbus, Ohio, Sept. 16, 1951; d. Kenneth F. and Jeanne E. (Wagner) Mann; m. Robert K. Jones, June 26, 1976. B.S. summa cum laude, Ohio State U., 1974, M.A., 1978, postgrad., 1978-79. Cert. tchr. bus. edn., English, psychology, N.Mex. Sec. Buckeye Union Ins. Co., Columbus, 1969-74; instr. Madison Local Sch. Dist., Groveport, Ohio, 1974-76; instr. Albuquerque Tech.-Vocat. Inst., Albuquerque, 1979—; developer, presenter of seminars to businesses in Albuquerque and throughout N.Mex. Mem. Assn. Profl. Writing Consultants, Assn. for Supervision and Curriculum Devel., Nat. Council Tchrs. English, Nat. Soc. for Performance and Instrn., Pi Lambda Theta. Home: 3050 Blake Rd SW Albuquerque NM 87105 Office: 525 Buena Vista Albuquerque NM 87106

MANN, STUART MARK, optometrist; b. Berkeley, Calif., Dec. 5, 1949; s. Frank Phillip and Camille Audrey (Thompson) M.; m. Judith Ann Ross, July 27, 1980; 1 dau., Rachel. B.S., Pacific U., 1973, O.D., 1974; postgrad. Coll. Notre Dame, Belmont, Calif., 1977—. Gen. practice optometry, San Carlos, Calif., 1974—. Named Calif. Young Optometrist of Yr., 1977—; recipient Recognition award Am. Optometric Assn., 1980, 81, 82. Fellow Coll. Optometrists Vision Devel.; mem. Am. Optometric Assn., Calif. Optometric Assn. (sports vision sect., contact lens sect.), ACLU. Democrat. Jewish. Clubs: Kiwanis, San Carlos. Home: 1548 Crestwood Dr San Mateo CA 94403 Office: 1234 Cherry St San Carlos CA 94010

MANNEL, CHARLES HOWARD, ednl. adminstr.; b. Balt., Feb. 5, 1929; s. Charles and Kathleen Agnes (McCrea) M.; B.P.A., U. Md., 1957; B.S. in Edn., U. Minn., 1958, M.A., 1965; m. Rose Janice Schumann, Feb. 26, 1953; children—Charles Howard, Laura Kay, Kurt John. Tchr. Balt. public schs., 1957-58, Duluth (Minn.) public schs., 1959-61; with Investors Diversified, Inc., 1961-62; faculty U. Minn., Duluth, 1962-64; placement dir. U. Minn., Duluth, 1965-67; dir. placement U. Minn., Mpls., 1967-69, asst. dean programs and adminstrn., 1969-73, dir. student services and alumni, 1973-76; dir. career services Am. Grad. Sch. of Internat. Mgmt., Thunderbird campus, Glendale, Ariz., 1976-81, v.p. corp. relations, 1981—; cons. in field; cons. Personnel Decision Inc., 1968—. Active fund raising, YMCA, Boy Scouts Am., Indian Guides; mem. CAP, 1967-76, regional dir. aerospace edn. N.Central Region, 1971-76. Served with USAF, 1950-54. Decorated Air Force Commendation medal, Meritorious Service medal; recipient Outstanding Faculty Staff award U. Minn., 1964, 67; Frank G. Brewer award Nat. Recognition Aerospace Edn., 1975; Frank B. Kokesh award for student service, 1976. Mem. Aircraft Owners and Pilots Assn., Air Force Res. Assn., Midwest Coll. Placement Assn., Rocky Mountain Coll. Placement Assn., Western Coll. Placement Assn., Coll. Placement Council. Republican. Methodist. Clubs: Scottish Rite, Kiwanis. Contbr. articles to profl. jours. Home: 4633 W Frier Dr Glendale AZ 85301 Office: Am Grad Sch Internat Mgmt Thunderbird Campus Glendale AZ 85306

MANNELLY, KATHY OLSON, associate dean consultant, lecturer; b. Lawrence, Mich., Jan. 24, 1945; d. William Edward and Marjorie Ellen Olson; m. 2d Patrick Kevin Mannelly, Apr. 9, 1980; stepchildren—Brian, Michael. A.B., Grand Rapids Jr. Coll., 1971; B.S. in Psychology, Grand Valley State Coll., 1973; postgrad. Pacific Luth. U., 1982. Lic. social worker, Mich. Coordinator edn., coordinator Sunrise Program, Project REHAB, Grand Rapids, Mich., 1974-75, supr. employee assistance resource, 1975-77, v.p. personnel and mktg., 1977-78; program analyst Dept. Mgmt. and Budget, State of Mich., Lansing, 1978-80; dir. coop. edn., govtl. grants officer Pacific Luth. U., Tacoma, 1980—; trainer, cons. Dymaxion Corp., Lansing, Profl. Update, Sahurst, Wash., 1975-82; lectr. in communications. Recipient various awards. Mem. Am. Soc. Tng. and Devel., Coop. Edn. Assn., Nat. Assn. Female Execs., Assn. for Cons., Commn. for Coop. Edn., South Sound Womens Network. Office: Pacific Luth Univ Tacoma WA 98447

MANNING, AL(CIE) G(WYN), author; b. Houston, June 19, 1927; s. Alcie Gwyn and Marjorie (Powell) Limke; B.S. summa cum laude UCLA, 1950; M.Religious Sci., Inst. Religious Sci., Los Angeles, 1958; D.D., Coll. Divine Metaphysics, Indpls., 1959; m. Fannie Mary, Jan. 1, 1972; children—Michael G., Richard R. Controller, v.p. Aetna Maintenance Co., Los Angeles, 1954-60; controller, sec. Susquehana Scis. Inc., Pasadena, 1960-63; v.p. fin. Kinelogic Corp., Pasadena, 1963-66; exec. v.p. R. L. Smith Engring., Inglewood, Calif., 1966-69; pres. E.S.P. Lab., Los Angeles, 1967—; pvt. accounting practice, 1956—; author: The Miraculous Laws of Universal Dynamics, 1964; Helping Yourself with E.S.P., 1966; Helping Yourself with Psycho-Cosmic Power, 1968; Helping Yourself with White Witchcraft, 1972; The Miracle of Universal Psychic Power, 1974; The Magic of New Ishtar Power, 1977; Miracle Spiritology, 1975; Helping Yourself With The Power of Gnostic Magic, 1979; Moon Lore and Moon Magic, 1980; Eye of Newt in My Martini, 1981; Rainbows Falling on My Head, 1982; Your Golden Key to Success, 1982. Served with USN, 1945-46, 52-54. C.P.A., Calif. Contbr. articles to jours. Office: 7559 Santa Monica Blvd Los Angeles CA 90046

MANNING, CAROL ANN, ins. co. exec.; b. Chgo., Nov. 26, 1942; d. Gernon S. and Anne M. B.S., Marquette U., 1964. Assigned risk supr. Zurich-Am. Ins. Co., Chgo., 1964-65, chief rate clk., 1965-66, large lines underwriter, 1966-69, processing supr., 1969-72, processing and services mgr., 1972-73, sr. devel. specialist, tng. and manpower devel. dept., 1973-75, dir. product devel., 1975, prodn. mgr., Los Angeles, 1975—; sales mgr. Northbrook P. & C., Brea, Calif., 1980—; v.p. Turner Real Estate and Investments, Inc., 1981—; dir. Bear Valley Springs Resort Devel. Asst. to campaign mgr. Jack Shaffer for Congress, 1976. Mem. Orange County Field Assn., AAUW, Bus. and Profl. Women's Club, Tehachapi C. of C. Home: 519 East F St Tehachapi CA 93561 Office: 326 Tehachapi Blvd Tehachapi CA 93561

MANNING, DARRELL V., state official; b. Preston, Idaho, July 17, 1932; s. Virgil and Olive Ann (Jenks) M.; B.S., Utah State U., 1955; m. Rochelle Cole., June 4, 1954; children—David Scott, Michael Allen. Vice pres. Mannings, Inc., Pocatello, Idaho, 1960-71; dir. Idaho Aeros. Dept., Boise, 1971-74; dir. Idaho Transp. Dept., Boise, 1974—; mem. Idaho Ho. of Reps., 1961-68, minority floor leader, 1965-68; mem. Idaho Senate, 1970-71. Served with USAF, 1955-60. Mem. Am. Assn. State Hwy. and Transp. Ofcls. (pres. 1977-78), Western Assn. State Hwy. and Transp. Ofcls. (pres. 1980-81), Internat. Northwest Aviation Council (dir.), Nat. Conf. State Rail Ofcls. (v.p. 1979), Nat. Assn. State Aviation Ofcls. (regional v.p.). Mem. Ch. Jesus Christ of Latter-day Saints. Office: PO Box 7129 Boise ID 83707

MANNING, DAVE MARTIN, state senator; b. Chippewa Falls, Wis., Feb. 28, 1897; s. Jackson and Amelia (Hogan) M.; grad. U. Mont.; m. Ruth Clark, Jan. 21, 1920; children—Shirley Mouat, Vivian LaSalle, David Martin. Engaged in contracting business, Hysham, Mont.; mem. Mont. Ho. of Reps. 1933-40, speaker; mem. Mont. Senate, 1941—, minority leader, pres. pro tem; acting gov. of Mont. Recipient Disting. Colleague award dept. civil engring. U. Mont., 1978. Democrat. Roman Catholic. Longest legis. tenure in any state.

MANNING, EMMA LEE, educator; b. Neodesha, Kans., July 11, 1940; d. Daniel Hall and Ida (Newton) Forbes; m. Albert Darrell Manning, Feb. 12, 1982. B.S., Kans. State U., 1962; M.S. in Curriculum and Supervision, Emporia State Teachers Coll., 1970, postgrad. in adminstrn., 1974-76. Art tchr. pub. schs., Columbus, Kans., 1962-64, Topeka, 1964-66, Wichita, Kans., 1968-69, Washington, 1975-76; home econs. tchr., Dept. Def. Dependent Schs., W.Ger., 1966-68, art tchr., Okinawa, 1969-75, 76-79, asst. prin. Amelia Earhart Intermediate Sch., Kadena AFB, Okinawa, 1979—. Mem. Nat. Assn. Secondary Sch. Prins., Assn. for Supervision and Curriculum Devel., NEA (life), Phi Delta Kappa. Democrat. Methodist. Office: Amelia Earhart Intermediate Sch APO San Francisco 96239

MANNING, JANE ANN, college public information director; b. Wichita Falls, Tex., Mar. 22, 1947; d. Preston L. and Sadie Mae Manning. B.S. in Journalism, Tex. So. U., 1969; M.A., Columbia U., 1970. City reporter Press and Enterprise, Riverside, Calif., 1973-74; prof. dept. journalism Tex. So. U., Houston, 1974-79; dir. pub. info. Riverside (Calif.) City Coll., 1979—; instr. U. Calif.-Riverside, 1982—. Commr., Riverside Community Relations Commn.; bd. dirs. Community Action Assn. Recipient outstanding journalist award Riverside Community, 1973; outstanding service award United Way, 1981. Mem. NAACP, AAUW (pub. relations chmn.), Pub. Relations Soc. Am. (dir.), Soc. Profl. Journalists. Editor: Riverside, Riverside, Riverside, 1983. Home: 3597 Pine St Riverside CA 92501 Office: 3800 Magnolia Ave Riverside CA 92506

MANNING, JARUE STANLEY, educator; b. Indiana, Pa., Sept. 25, 1934; s. Jay Henry and Ruth (Stanley) M.; m. Gretchen Helen Franzmann, Jan. 30, 1960; 1 dau., Andrea. A.A., City Coll. San Francisco, 1958; B.A., San Francisco State Coll., 1962; Ph.D., U. Calif.-Berkeley, 1969. NIH fellow Nat. Cancer Inst., U. Calif.-Bekeley, 1969-70; asst. prof. dept. agrl. bacteriology U. Calif.-Davis, 1971-76, assoc. prof., 1976-82, prof., 1982—. Mem. Am. Soc. Microbiology, Soc. Invertebrate Pathology. Contbr. articles to profl. jours. Office: University of California Dept Agrl Bacteriology Davis CA 95616

MANNING, RICHARD EDWARD, state senator, former firefighter, businessman; b. Gt. Falls, Mont., July 25, 1926; s. Edward Berkley and Nellie Elizabeth (Richards) M.; m. Josephine Elvera Nilson, June 27, 1952; children—Colleen Diann Manning Mathison, Edward Emmanuel, Rhonda LuRae. Student schs., Gt. Falls. With Gt. Falls Fire Dept., 1952-76; mem. Mont. Ho. of Reps., 1979, 81; mem. Mont. Senate, 1982—; lobbyist for firemen, 1963-76. Sec. Mont. State Firemen's Assn., 1965-76, Gt. Falls Fire Dept. Relief Assn., 1956-67. Served with U.S. Army, 1944-46. Democrat. Mem. Unity Ch. Club: Moose. Office: Mont Senate 810 7th Ave N Great Falls MT 59401

MANNING, TERESA MARY, computer analyst; b. Lincoln, Nebr., Mar. 16, 1947; d. James F. and Rosemarie (Weller) Manning. B.A. in Spanish and English, Mt. St. Scholastica Coll. (now Benedictine Coll.), 1969; postgrad. U. Wash., Seattle, 1974-77; cert. computer programming North Seattle Community Coll., 1978. Cert. tchr., Colo., Wis. Tchr. Spanish pub. schs., Pueblo, Colo., 1969-71, chmn. dept. fgn. lang., 1970-71; tchr. Spanish, English pub. schs., Eau Claire, Wis., 1972-74; programmer/analyst Boeing Computer Services, Seattle, 1978-80, program mgr., 1980-81; systems analyst Salt River Project, Phoenix, 1981—. Recipient Cost Improvement award Boeing Computer Services, 1980, Spl. Achievement award, 1981. Mem. NOW, Nat. Assn. Female Execs. Democrat. Home: 505 W Baseline Rd #1096 Tempe AZ 85283 Office: Salt River Project DFIS Project PO BOx 1980 Phoenix AZ 85001

MANNING, TIMOTHY CARDINAL, archbishop; b. Cork, Ireland, Oct. 15, 1909; s. Cornelius and Margaret (Cronin) M.; came to U.S., 1928, naturalized, 1945; student St. Patrick's Sem., Menlo Park, Calif., 1928-34; D.C.L., Gregorian U., 1938. Ordained priest Roman Catholic Ch., 1934; asst. pastor Immaculate Conception Ch., Los Angeles, 1934-35; consecrated bishop, 1946; aux. bishop and chancellor Roman Cath. Archdiocese of Los Angeles, from 1946; 1st bishop of Fresno, 1967-69; titular bishop of Capri, 1969-70; arch bishop of Los Angeles, 1969—; created cardinal, 1973. Address: 1531 W 9th St Los Angeles CA 90015*

MANNIX, BERNICE LENA, banker; b. Deer Lodge, Mont., June 23, 1922; d. Jens M. and Lena (Markelson) Hansen; B.A. in Bus. Adminstrn., U. Mont., 1944; m. William (Ted) Mannix, Apr. 3, 1945; children—Katherine M., Mary D., Margaret V., Teresa M. Teller Deer Lodge Bank & Trust Co., 1944-45, mem. acct. dept., 1967-69, installment loan sec., 1969-76, asst. cashier, 1976-78, asst. v.p., 1978-81, real estate loan officer, trust officer, escrow officer, 1978—, asst. v.p., auditor, 1981—; bookkeeper Mannix Feed, Deer Lodge, 1948-63; bookkeeper Barmont Sales, Deer Lodge, 1966-67. Leader 4-H, Deer Lodge, 1961-71, sec. Powell County council, 1965-68, pres., 1969-71; sec. Powell County (Mont.) Mus. and Arts, 1974-77, v.p., 1978-81, pres., 1982; chpt. mother State Future Homemakers Am., 1965-66; active hosp. aux., community chorus; Mem. Nat. Assn. Bank Women (chmn. Rocky Mt. group 1977, State membership chmn. 1982-83). Republican. Roman Catholic. Clubs: Woman's (sec. 1957-58, pres. 1959), Am. Legion Aux., Deer Lodge Golf. Home: 708 Milwaukee Ave Deer Lodge MT 59722 Office: PO Box 599 Deer Lodge MT 59722

MANNIX, GARY WAYNE, engineer, water utility executive; b. N.Y.C., Nov. 29, 1946; s. Jesse Paul and Florence Aluilda (Dahlen) M.; m. MaryLou Sayatovic, Mar. 8, 1968; children—Sheila Ann, Paul Joseph. B.S., Mont. Coll. Mineral Sci. and Tech., 1969, M.S. in Engring. Sci., 1974. Class 1 water treatment and distbn. lic., Mont. Engr. Butte (Mont.) Water Co., 1973-76, supt., 1976-83, v.p., ops. mgr., 1983—; guest coll. lectr. Served to lt. USN, 1969-71, USNR, 1964-80. Mem. Am. Water Works Assn. (chmn. Mont. sect.). Club: Courtrooms Racquet & Health (Butte). Home: 1625 A St Butte MT 59701 Office: Butte Water Co 124 W Granite St Butte MT 59701

MANOUKIAN, NOEL EDWIN, state supreme ct. chief justice; b. Livingston, Calif., Jan. 1, 1938; s. Hagop H. and Rose (Boranian) M.; B.A., U. of Pacific, Stockton, Calif., 1960; LL.B., J.D., U. Santa Clara (Calif.), 1964; m. Louise Marie Andresakis, 1969; children—Jacqueline Marie, Joseph Edwin. Admitted to Nev. bar, 1964; law clk., bailiff to judge Washoe County (Nev.) Dist. Ct., 1964-65; dep. dist. atty., Douglas County, Nev., 1965-66; assoc. firm Manoukian & Manoukian, Carson City, 1965-70; individual practice law, Carson City, Lake Tahoe and Carson Valley area, 1971-74; judge 1st Jud. Dist. Ct., Carson, Churchill, Douglas, Lyon and Storey counties, 1974-76; judge 9th Jud. Dist. Ct., Douglas and Lyon counties, 1976-77; justice Nev. Supreme Ct., Carson City, 1977—, now chief justice; vice chmn. Nev. Small County Allocation Com. for Distbn. Fed. Funds, 1974-77; mem. Nev. State Personnel Adv. Com. Vice chmn. bd. dirs. Nev. div. Am. Cancer Soc., 1970, chmn. bd., chmn. exec. com., 1973-74, state chmn. pub. edn. com., hon. life mem. Am. Cancer Soc., 1978, Noel E. Manoukian Pub. Edn. award Nev. div., 1978—; active Nev. Area council Boy Scouts Am. Recipient Lawyer of Year award Santa Clara Law Sch., 1978; named Lawyer of Year, City of Hope, Las Vegas, 1978. Mem. Am. Bar Assn., Nev. Bar Assn., Am. Judicature Soc., Nev. Dist. Judges Assn. (chmn. bd., pres. 1975-77), Nev. Crime Commn., NCCJ, Blue Key. Democrat. Roman Catholic. Clubs: Minden (Nev.) Rotary (past pres.); Las Vegas Breakfast, Exchange, Kit Carson Toastmasters. Contbr. articles to mags. and newspapers. Office: Nev Supreme Ct Capitol Complex Carson City NV 89710

MANRIQUE, LUIS ALBERTO, agronomist; b. Huancayo, Peru, Dec. 26, 1948; s. Prospero and Thelma (Canchari) M.; came to U.S., 1977; B.S., U. Lima, 1969, M.S., 1972; Ph.D., U. Hawaii, 1981. Agronomist, Benchmark Soils Project, U. Hawaii, Honolulu, 1978—. Mem. Am. Soc. Agronomy, Internat. Soc. Tropical Root Crops, Soil Sci. Soc. Am., Gamma Sigma Delta. Home: 1717-204 Makiki St Honolulu HI 96822 Office: University of Hawaii Benchmark Soils Project 3190 Maile Way Honolulu HI 96822

MANSELL, WILLIAM BLOOD, educational administrator; b. Salt Lake City, Aug. 27, 1939; s. Lawrence William and Esther Lowella (Hadlock) M.; m. Helen Annette Welch, June 8, 1962; children—William Richard, Marcia Anne, Michael Welch, Diane Jane, Gregory Andrew, Katherine Esther. B.S., U. Utah, 1965, M.Ed., 1971. Cert. tchr., Utah; cert. adminstr., Utah. Tchr. Mill Creek Elem., Granite Sch. Dist., Salt Lake City, 1965-79; adminstr. Western Hills Elem., Kearns, Utah, 1979—. Chmn. local dist. Salt Lake City Republican party, 1977-78. Recipient award Latter Day Saints Blood Bank, 1983. Mem. Granite Assn. Elem. Sch. Prins., Granite Assn. Suprs. and Adminstrs., Utah Assn. Elem. Sch. Prins., Nat. Assn. Elem. Sch. Prins. Mormon.

MANSFIELD, GEORGE CAMPBELL, III, newspaper exec.; b. Honolulu, Oct. 26, 1937; s. George Campbell and Thelma Helene M.; B.S., U. Hawaii, 1964; m. Carol Ann Schweiss, Jan. 14, 1965; children—George Campbell IV, Karen Marie. Account exec. Hawaii Newspaper Agy., 1964-67; advt. mgr. first Hawaiian Bank, Honolulu, 1967-68; account mgr. Lennen & Newell, Inc., Honolulu, 1968-73; mktg. officer Hawaii Thrift & Loan, Inc., Honolulu, 1973-74; advt. dir. Community Publs. Inc., Kaneohe, Hawaii, 1974-75; advt. dir. Hawaii Press Newspapers, Inc., Honolulu, 1975—; gen. partner Maidu Park, 1980—; cons. sales mktg. Bd. dirs. Leeward Cancer Soc., 1975-78; coach Hawaii Kai Youth Baseball, 1979-80. Served with AUS, 1959-61. Mem. Honolulu Advt. Fedn. (dir. 1977-78), Honolulu Press Club, Honolulu Exec. Assn. Lutheran. Club: Rotary. Home: 710 Koko Isle Circle Honolulu HI 96825

MANTELL, SUZANNE, interior designer, lecturer; b. Rochester, N.Y., June 22, 1928; d. Louis Levinson and Sarah (Jacobson) L.; m. Stanley Mantell, July 7, 1951; children—James, Douglas, Andrew. B.A., Syracuse U., 1950; postgrad. in interior design San Jose State U., 1969-72, Stanford U., 1969-74. Sr. designer Macy's, Palo Alto, Calif., 1972—; lectr. San Jose State U. Mem. com. for art Stanford U. Mem. Am. Soc. Interior Designers (cert.), Mus. Soc. San Francisco. Democrat. Jewish. Club: Fremont Hills (Los Altos). Contbr. articles to profl. jours. Office: Macy's Stanford Palo Alto CA 94304

MANTES, THEODORE ROOSEVELT, mfg. co. exec.; b. Soladad, Calif., Nov. 14, 1904; s. William John and Mary Elizabeth (Smith) M.; E.E., Poly. Coll. Engring., 1926; m. Muriel R. Morgan, May 19, 1940; 1 dau., Muriel Gwendolyn. With Fairbanks Morse & Co., San Francisco, 1926-31, Murry Jacobs Co., 1931-33; pres., gen. mgr. Mantes Scale Co., 1933-69; co. rep. to Nat. Scale Men's Assn., Nat. Controls, Inc., 1972—. Established Muriel R. Mantes Scholarship Fund, Yuba Community Coll., Marysville, Calif., 1979. Mem. Nat. Scale Men's Assn. (hon.). Republican. Clubs: Mason, Commonwealth. Patentee in field. Home: Palo Alto CA Office: Mantes Scale Co div National Controls Inc 810 E San Carlos Ave San Carlos CA 94070

MANVILLE, ROBERT D., hospital administrator; b. Des Moines, Mar. 20, 1924; s. Elbert Charles and Mabel Lucille Manville; m. Marian S. Robertson, June 11, 1948; children—Michael Dean, Mindy Lee. B.A., Grinnell Coll., 1949. Loss auditor Continental Ins. Co., Chgo., 1949; field dir., rep. Am. Nat. Red Cross, Ill., Tex., Okla. and Mich., 1950-53; with Meml. Hosp. of Natrona County, Casper, Wyo., 1953, now adminstr. Served to lt. U.S. Army, 1943-46. Mem. Am. Coll. Hosp. Adminstrs., Wyo. Hosp. Assn. Republican. Presbyterian. Club: Masons.

MANWARING, ALAN VAR, candy company executive; b. Rexburg, Idaho, Dec. 18, 1931; s. David Heber and Sarah Zella (Hart) M.; B.S., Brigham Young U., 1956; postgrad. Utah State U., 1960-63; m. Florence Whitworth, Nov. 20, 1956; children—Kerry Alan, Michelle, Karen, Shauna, Brian. Purchasing trainee Gen. Electric Co., Richland, Wash., 1956-59; buyer Thiokol Chem. Co., Brigham City, Utah, 1959-64; purchasing agt. Burroughs Corp., Pasadena, Calif., 1965-67; mgr. prodn. control Modern Plastics Co., Los Angeles, 1967-69; v.p. Manwaring Constrn., Inc., Rexburg, Idaho, 1969-80, pres., 1980—; owner Mom's Kandy Kitchen, Rexburg, 1981—. Mem. Retail Confectioners Internat. Republican. Mormon. Club: Rotary. Home: 295 Apache Ave Rexburg ID 83440 Office: 290 N 1st E Resburg ID 83440

MANWARING, CAROL CANDIE, educator; b. Springville, Utah, Sept. 28, 1919; d. Kenneth P. and Zina (Childs) Condie; m. William Randolph Kreth, May 13, 1945; children—Carol Ann Peterson, Thomas K.; m. 2d, Wilford M. Manwaring; 1 son, John W. B.S., Brigham Young U., 1941; postgrad. U. Utah, 1969-70, Utah State U., 1974. Tchr. high schs., Utah, Idaho, Nev., 1941-50; tchr. Springville (Utah) High Sch., 1950-59, tchr. homemaking, 1976—; tchr. Spanish Fork (Utah) Jr. High Sch., 1962-76; tchr. sewing programs; demonstrator profl. and amateur groups. Mem. adv. com. Utah Valley Symphony Orch. Mem. NEA, Utah Edn. Assn., AAUW, Utah Assn. Vocat. Home Econs. Tchrs., Am. Vocat. Assn., Utah Vocat. Assn. Republican. Mormon Clubs: Federated Music, Literary, Haffen Dallin Service, Lady Lions. Home: 121 N 1300 E Springville UT 84663 Office: Springville High Sch 1205 E 900 S Springville UT 84663

MANWELL, EDMUND RAY, lawyer; b. Yuba City, Calif., June 23, 1942; s. Edmund T. and June K. (Christiansen) M. A.B., U. Calif.-Berkeley, 1964, J.D., 1967. Bar: Calif. Ptnr., Manwell & Manwell, Marysville, Calif., 1967-68, Brobeck, Phleger & Harrison, San Francisco, 1968-81, Lasky, Haas, Cohler & Munter, San Francisco, 1981-82; sr. ptnr. Manwell & Wes, San Francisco, 1982—; dir. Dreyer's Grand Ice Cream, Inc., Leisure Enterprises, Inc.; lect. N.Y. Law Jour., Rutter Group Seminars. Mem. ABA, State Bar Calif., Order of Colf. Republican. Presbyterian. Clubs: Olympic, Presidio Golf, Moraga Country. Co author: Attorney's Guide to California Real Estate Syndicates, 1978; bd. contbrs. Equipment Leasing Newsletter. Office: Manwell & Wes 425 California St Suite 1301 San Francisco CA 94104

MANZO, ANTHONY JOSEPH, painter; b. Saddle Brook, N.J., Apr. 25, 1928; s. Michael and Jennie (Spinneli) M.; m. Ruth Hendricks, Jan. 27, 1956; children—Kathleen, Joanne. Student NAD, N.Y.C., 1946-49, Phoenix Sch. Design, N.Y.C., 1955-58; studied privately with Salvatore Lascari, 1945-65. Freelance comml. illustrator, 1956-59; painter and sculptor, 1958—; instr. pvt. art classes Renaissance Sch. Art, N.J. Served with U.S. Army, 1950-52. Recipient Ray A. Jones award N.J. Painters and Sculptors Soc., 1976. Am. Artist Profl. League fellow. Mem. Salmagundi Club. Roman Catholic. Address: Box 2708 Taos NM 87571

MANZO, CLAUDETTE KINTZ, reading specialist; b. New Brunswick, N.J., Apr. 14, 1932; d. M.C. and Mary (O'Hara) Kintz; B.A. in Edn., Pacific Luth. U., 1960; M.A. in Edn., Ariz. State U., 1970; postgrad. No. Ariz. U., 1979-82; m. J.B. Manzo, May 23, 1950; children—Patricia, Margaret, Pamela. Elem. tchr., Los Angeles, 1962-64, Gila Bend, Ariz., 1964-67; dir. reading Littleton (Ariz.) Sch. Dist., 1967—; master tchr. adv. Ariz. Dept. Edn. Mem. Internat. Reading Assn., NEA, Ariz. Edn. Assn., Pi Lambda Theta, Phi Delta Kappa. Club: Lioness.

MAPELLI, ROLAND LAWRENCE, cattle co. exec.; b. Denver, June 10, 1922; s. Herman and Della (Borelli) M.; student Regis Coll., 1959-61; m. Neoma Robinson, Apr. 1942; children—Terralyn Mapelli DeMoney, Geraldine Mapelli Petersen. Vice pres. Monfort of Colo., Inc., Greeley, 1969-76, sr. v.p., 1976—, chmn. bd., 1971—; pres. Monfort Food Distbg. Co., Greeley, 1969—; owner, operator Mapelli Farms, Eaton, Colo., 1974—; chmn. bd. Denver Union Stock Yards Co., 1969-70; dir. Intrawest Bank, Greeley, Intrawest Fin. Corp., Denver. Mem. Gov.'s 100-Man Local Affairs Commn., 1962-66; div. chmn. 1962 Mile High United Fund campaign; mem. Colo. Bd. Agr.'s Frozen Food Provisioners Bd., 1967-71; mem. Colo. Agrl. Adv. Com., 1966-73; chmn. Denver Off-Street Parking Commn., 1960-72; mem. Denver City Council, 1955-59; mem. Colo. Ho. of Reps. (to fill vacancy), 1961; mem. Colo. Senate, 1962-66; state fin. chmn. Democratic Party, 1963-66; mem. adv. bd. Ft. Logan Mental Health Center, 1961-64; bd. dirs. North Denver Civic Assn., 1955-65, Better Bus. Bur., 1966-69; mem. bd. ambassadors Loretto Heights Coll., 1960-65; adv. bd. St. Anthony's Hosp., 1960-65; bd. dirs., exec. com. Nat. Western Stock Show, 1966—. Served to 2d lt. USAF, 1942-45; ETO. Recipient Knute Rockne award for outstanding civic achievement, 1961. Mem. Colo. Meat Dealers Assn. (pres. 1968-69), Colo. Cattlemen's Assn., Colo. Cattlefeeders Assn., Colo.-Wyo. Restaurant Assn., Nat. Assn. Meat Purveyors. Roman Catholic. Home: 18979 Weld County Rd 78 Eaton CO 80615 Office: PO Box G Greeley CO 80632

MAPLE, M. BRIAN, physicist, educator; b. San Diego, Nov. 20, 1939; s. Merrill and Evelyn May (Hayes) M.; B.S., San Diego State Coll., 1963, A.B., 1963; M.S., U. Calif., San Diego, 1965, Ph.D., 1969; m. Margaret Eleanor Boland, Feb. 2, 1962. Asst. research physicist U. Calif., San Diego, 1969-75, assoc. research physicist, 1975-79, lectr. physics, applied physics, info. scis., 1972, asst. adj. prof. physics, 1973-75, acting asso. prof., 1975-77, assoc. prof., 1977-81, prof., 1981—; assoc. research physicist Inst. Theoretical Physics, U. Calif., Santa Barbara, 1980; vis. scientist U. Chile, Santiago, 1971, 72; vis. prof. Instituto de Fisica Jose Balseiro, San Carlos de Bariloche, Argentina, 1974. Air Force Office Sci. Research grantee, 1971, 72; NSF grantee, 1973-78, ERDA grantee, 1975-78; Dept. Energy grantee, 1978—. Mem. Am. Phys. Soc., AAAS, Am. Vacuum Soc., Calif. Catalysis Soc. Contbr. articles to profl. jours. Home: 2675 Boca Raton St Del Mar CA 92014 Office: Dept Physics U Calif San Diego La Jolla CA 92093

MAPLETHORPE, WILLIAM SPRAGUE, insurance agency executive; b. Easton, Wash., Oct. 19, 1924; s. William Lemuel and Mina Belle (Sprague) M.; m. Barbara Jean Eversole, Apr. 4, 1948; children—Bari Maplethorpe Jost, Bonita Louise, William Bruce. Student Oreg. State U., 1942-43, Miami U., Oxford, Ohio, 1943-44; B.S. in Bus. Adminstrn., U. Oreg., 1947. Co-agt. Sta. PGL, Eugene, Oreg., 1947-50, sta. mgr., Corvallis, Oreg., 1950-51; with GMAC, 1951-66; spl. collection mgr., credit supr. Standard Ins. Co., 1966-67, life ins. agt., 1967-68; ins. agt. FIG, 1968-69; account exec. Alexander & Alexander; now mgr. Ins. Assocs. Inc., Sherwood, Oreg. Active Oreg. div. Am. Cancer Soc., also state crusade chmn., 1980-81, treas., 1982-83; mem. Steering Com. to Elect Roy Rogers County Commr., Washington County, Oreg., 1983; chmn. Citizen of Yr. Com., Sherwood, 1983. Served to comdr. USNR. Mem. Ind. Agts. Assn. Oreg. (pres. Washington County chpt. 1980-82), Ind. Agts. Assn. U.S., Ind. Agts. Assn. Washington County, Naval Res. Assn. (life), Navy League (life), Ret. Officers Assn. (life). Democrat. Baptist. Clubs: Rotary (dist. gov. 1974-75, chmn. zone cons. team youth service 1983-84), Masons, Order Eastern Star. Home: Route 5 Box 79-D Sherwood OR 97140 Office: 45 NW Washington St Sherwood OR 97140

MAPP, MITCHELL JEROME, state ofcl.; b. Chgo., Dec. 19, 1947; s. Mitchell Lee and Mildred Junita (Collums) M.; B.Arch., B.A. in Sociology, Idaho State U., 1975; m. Mabel Lynn Blackwell, Aug. 25, 1973; children—Mitchell Jason Adam, Matthew Alan Russell. Asso. planner City of Pocatello (Idaho), 1974-80; space planning supr. Bur. Architecture, Div. Public Works, State of Idaho, Boise, 1980-82; design rev. analyst, City of Boise, 1982—; v.p. The Music Connection, 1983—. pres. N.W. Planning, Boise. Pres., S.E. Idaho Planning Assn., 1979-80; chmn. Bannock County Census Com., 1980. Mem. Historic Preservation Assn., Am. Planning Assn., Kappa Alpha Psi. Office: 150 N Capitol Blvd Boise ID 83702

MARABLE, ELAINE MARJORIE, county public information officer; b. Cin., June 10, 1931; d. Harold Courtney and Margaret Elder (Campbell) Brauer; m. Ronald Burl Marable, Feb. 9, 1952; children—Michael David, Blyth Michelle Marable Bennett, Paula Carrie. B.S. in Bus. Adminstrn., U. Redlands, 1981; pub. relations profl. cert. U. Calif.-Riverside, 1981. Society editor Compton (Calif.) Herald Am., 1950-55; editor newsletters, free-lance photographer Long Beach (Calif.) Ind. Press-Telegram, 1951-55; ops. supr. dist. service office Allstate Ins. Co., Ontario, Calif., 1961-66; feature writer, photographer Daily Press, Victorville, Calif., 1967; reporter-photographer San Bernardino (Calif.) Sun, 1968-78, bur. chief, 1974-78; pub. info. officer County of San Bernardino, 1978—; owner, operator Careerlines, cons., resume service, career devel. Recipient award for spl. events, photography and newsletter Nat. Assn. Counties, 1981, First Place Feature Story award, Second Pl. Spl. Events, Newsletter award 1982. Mem. Pub. Relations Soc. Am. (sec. Calif. Inland Empire chpt.). Republican. Club: Bus. and Profl. Women's.

MARAVICH, MARY LOUISE, realtor; b. Fort Knox, Ky., Jan. 4, 1951; d. John and Bonnie (Balandzic) M. A.A. in Office Adminstrn., U. Nev., Las Vegas, 1970; B.A. in Sociology and Psychology, U. So. Calif., 1972. Adminstrv. asst. dept. history U. So. Calif., Los Angeles, 1972-73; asst. personnel supr. Corral Coin Co., Las Vegas, 1973-80; Realtor, Americana Group div. Better Homes and Gardens, Las Vegas, 1980—. Mem. Nev. Assn. Realtors (cert. realtors inst.), Las Vegas Bd. Realtors, Nat. Assn. Realtors, Nat. Assn. Female Execs. Office: Americana Group Realtors 3300 S Jones St Suite 101 Las Vegas NV 89102

MARCELYNAS, RICHARD CHADWICK, manufacturing company manager; b. New London, Conn., Aug. 21, 1937; s. Anthony F. and Elizabeth A. (Chadwick) M.; m. Betty F. Forray, July 1, 1961; children—Michael R., Thomas R. B.A. in Bus. Adminstrn., U. Wash., 1961; postgrad. Seattle U., 1971-72. Mgmt. trainee, installation foreman Pacific Bell, Fullerton, Calif., 1964-65; cost acct. Scott Paper Co., Everett, Wash., 1965-68; asst. v.p. personnel and adminstrn. Nat. Pub. Service Ins. Co., Seattle, 1968-77; mgr. indsl. relations Heath Tecna Precision Structures Inc., Kent, Wash., 1978—; cons., lectr. Active youth soccer and Jr. Achievement programs. Served to maj. USMCR, 1961-77. Decorated commendations for bravery and tech. expertise, 1962, 63, 64; recipient Seattle Pacific N.W. Personnel Mgrs. Assn. Bd. Dirs. award, 1975. Mem. Am. Soc. Personnel Adminstrs., Pacific N.W. Personnel Mgrs. Assn. (past pres. Tacoma chpt.), Am. Soc. Safety Engrs. Republican. Roman Catholic. Lodge: Elks. Office: 19819 84th Ave S Kent WA 98032

MARCHAND, SONJA SPENCER, business educator, administrator, consultant; b. El Paso, Tex., Sept. 23, 1938; d. Lawrence Carlyle and Joy Ellen (Wilson) Spencer; m. Robert Marchand, Dec. 22, 1962; 1 son, Paul. B.A., U. Tex., 1958, M.A., 1960. Supr. tech. publs. AMF, Santa Barbara, Calif., 1961-62; tech. planning staff mem. Litton Industries, Beverly Hills, Calif., 1962-66; dir. devel. Johns Hopkins U., Balt., 1967-71; pres. S. S. Marchand Assoc., Los Angeles, 1971-72; dir. devel. Joint Ctr. for Polit. Studies, dir. Bur. Bus. Services and Research, Calif. State U., Northridge, 1974—. Mem. Valley Industry Commerce Assn. (exec. com.), San Fernando Valley Regional C. of C. (bd. dirs.), Beta Gamma Sigma, Alpha Mu Gamma. Democrat. Episcopalian. Office: Calif State U 18111 Nordhoff St Northridge CA 91330

MARCHANT, GARY REED, management and engineering consultant; b. Peoa, Utah, June 7, 1934; s. Gilbert Reed and Mary Afton (Harding) M.; m. Janiece Ottosen, Dec. 13, 1956; children—Jalane, Gary Lamont, Sharie Sue, Julie Ann, Evan Reed, Roy Allen, Jane, Wendie. B.S.E.E., Brigham Young U., 1959; Ph.D., U. Utah, 1967. Lic. profl. engr., Utah. Research scientist NASA Ames Research Ctr., Moffat Field, Calif., 1959-62; instrumentation engr. Thiokol Chem., Brigham City, Utah, 1962-63; project engr. Sperry Utah Co., Salt Lake City, 1963-64; lectr. engring. adminstrn. U. Utah, Salt Lake City, 1964-68; dept. mgr. instrumentation and control Kennecott Minerals Co., Salt Lake City, 1967-81; pres. G. Reed Marchant & Assocs., mgmt., motivational and engring. cons., Salt Lake City, 1982—. Mem. Davis county (Utah) Bd. Edn., 1970-76; sec. Utah State Engring. Registration Bd., 1978-82. Served to capt. USAF, 1959-62. NSF trainee, 1964-67. Mem. Instrument Soc. Am. (dir. 1976-79, mem. internat. exec. bd., 1980-82), IEEE (sr.; Outstanding Community Service award, 1974), AIME, Cons. Engrs. Council Utah, Utah Engrs. Council, Am. Cons. Engrs. Council. Republican. Mormon. Contbr. numerous articles to tech. pubns. Office: PO Box 538 North Salt Lake UT 84054

MARCHI, GARY MICHAEL, futurist, business-market development consultant; b. San Francisco, Feb. 25, 1953. Cert. B.L. Internat. Corp. Bus. Sch., Aervoe/Dynamin Corp. Bus. Sch., San Francisco, 1974. Bus. and market devel. cons. Califa Corp., San Francisco, fund raising cons. Leo Fund Raising Services div., 1972-73; owner, operator, bus.-market devel. advisor Spirit of the Future Unltd., San Francisco, 1974—, pub. relations, promotion advisor Media Network Systems div., San Francisco, 1979—; founder, dir. Spirit of the Future Creative Inst., 1976—; planning cons. Mem. Venture Devel. Assn. (co-founder, pres., 1981—), Creator-producer FUTURE CONSUMER, weekly radio and TV documentary series, 1979—; creator various creative thinking and logic systems. Office: PO Box 40296 San Francisco CA 94110

MARCHI, JON, investment brokerage exec.; b. Ann Arbor, Mich., Aug. 6, 1946; s. John Robert and Joan Trimble (Toole) M.; student Claremont Men's Coll., 1964-65; B.S., U. Mont., 1968, M.S., 1972; m. Mary Stewart Sale, Aug. 12, 1972; 1 dau., Aphia Jessica. Sec., treas. Marchi, Marchi & Marchi, Inc., Morris, Ill., 1968-69; account exec. D. A. Davidson & Co., Billings, Mont., 1972-75, asst. v.p., office mgr., 1976-77, v.p. mktg. and adminstrn., Great Falls, Mont., 1977—; sec., dir. D. A. Davidson Realty Corp., Great Falls, 1978—, chmn. research com., 1980, also v.p. mktg., research and spl. products; dir. Big Sky Airlines, Billings; chmn. Mont. Gov.'s Subcom. for Venture Capital Devel. Served with U.S. Army, 1969-71. Mem. Securities Industry Assn., Great Falls C. of C. (chmn. energy com.), Episcopalian. Clubs: Rotary, Glacier Racquet, Leadership Great Falls, Ski, Mont., Helena Wilderness Riders. Home: 1926 Cherry Dr Great Falls MT 59404 Office: D A Davidson & Co 8 3d St N Great Falls MT 59401

MARCKWARDT, HAROLD THOMAS, assn. exec.; b. Chgo., May 4, 1920; s. Herman and Carrie (Polachek) M.; A.B., U. So. Calif., 1949, A.M., 1953; M.S., U. Calif., 1970, postgrad., 1970—; m. Patricia Ann Hoffman, Apr. 7, 1945; children—Craig, Diana, Brad, Glenn. Tool and machinery designer Douglas Aircraft, Santa Monica, Cal., 1939-43; playground leader County Los Angeles, 1946-47; community program dir. Hollywood (Calif.) YMCA, 1947-51, dir. community program and bldg., 1952-55; exec. dir. Westchester YMCA, Los Angeles, 1955-63; area dir. Nat. Council YMCA, 1963-66, pres. Western Center Assos., Los Angeles, 1966—. Exec. dir. Calif. Youth and Govt. Statewide Com., 1965, del. seminar UN, 1959. Colliver lectr. U. Pacific, 1965. Trainer, Leadership Devel. Camp, Los Angeles, 1959; mem. Mayor's Steering Com., 1973-75, chmn. Mayor's Facilitators com. Conf. Children, Youth and Sr. Citizens, 1974; mem. employment and tng. subcom. Los Angeles County Task Force, 1977; mem. Task Force on Equity for Women in Employment, 1976-77. Served to 1st lt., USAAF, 1943-46, USAF, 1950-52. Recipient One of Hollywood's Top Ten Young Men award, 1954. Mem. Am. Soc. Tool Engrs. (charter mem.), Pacific Southwest Area YMCA Assn. Profl. Dirs. (pres. 1963-66), Orgn. Devel. Network, Airplane Owner's and Pilots Assn., Am. Soc. Tng. and Devel. (v.p. 1979, pres. 1980), Assn. for Humanistic Psychology. Democrat. Author: The Leader Makes The Difference, 1968; Leading Discussion Groups, 1972; How to Make Executive Decisions About Training, 1976; 16 Steps to the Job You Want, 1979; The Quality Circles Kit, 1982. Home: 4216 Colbath Sherman Oaks CA 91423 Office: Suite 2 11326 Magnolia Blvd North Hollywood CA 91601

MARCOTTE, GIRARD NOEL, mfg. co. exec.; b. Kankakee, Ill., Dec. 25, 1931; s. Arshall George and Isabelle Bertha (Girard) M.; B.B.A., Loyola U., Los Angeles, 1955; postgrad. Sacramento State U., 1963, U. Calif., San Francisco, 1968, Canada Coll., 1973, Coll. San Mateo, 1977; M.B.A., Pepperdine U., 1980; m. Marlene J. Hague, Sept. 14, 1957; children—Denise, Dorene, Steven, Renae. Dept. mgr. J. C. Penney Co., Whittier, Calif., 1955-56; sr. ops. control analyst Aerojet Gen. Corp., Sacramento, 1956-67; corp. officer Crocker Nat. Bank, San Francisco, 1967-74; adminstr. operating regulations Nat. BankAmericard, Inc., San Francisco, 1974-76; with Shaklee Corp., San Francisco, 1976—, mgr. corp. policies and procedures, 1979—. Pres. P.T.A., 1962; com. chmn. Boy Scouts Am., 1970; campaign chmn., treas. San Mateo County, Calif., 1979. Mem. Am. Mgmt. Assn., Soc. Advancement of Mgmt., Am. Radio Relay League, Nat. Rifle Assn. (sharpshooter), Loyola Alumni Assn., U. Calif. Alumni Assn., Pepperdine Alumni Assn., Order of Forresters, Order of Arrow. Democrat. Roman Catholic. Home: 1457 Murchison Dr Millbrae CA 94030 Office: 444 Market St San Francisco CA 94111

MARCUM, DANIEL BRUCE, farm advisor; b. Selma, Calif., Sept. 29, 1947; s. Lester P. and Dorothy (Davenport) M.; m. Deborah Ellis, June 19, 1976; children—Jeffrey, Mary Jane. Ph.D., U. Calif.-Davis, 1980. Farm advisor, 1976—. Served with U.S. Army, 1970-71. Mem. Am. Soc. Agronomy. Baptist. Club: C. of C.

MARCUM, DANIEL WOODROW, lawyer; b. Logan, W.Va., Nov. 19, 1947; s. Woodrow and Sadie Marcum. B.A. cum laude in Polit. Sci., Brigham Young U., 1971; J.D., U. Utah, 1976; LL.M. in Taxation, U. Fla., 1976. Bar: Utah 1974, W.Va. 1975. Assoc. Senior & Senior, Salt Lake City, 1975-78; sole practice Salt Lake City and Logan, W.Va., 1978—; dir. bar rev. courses, Utah and Idaho. Active Primary Children's Hosp. Deferred Gifts Com., Salt Lake Estate Planning Council, Utah Opera Co. Planned Giving Com. Mem. ABA (real property, taxation, probate and trust law sect.), Utah State Bar (taxation sect.), W.Va. State Bar. Republican. Mormon. Club: Bonneville Knife and Fork Internat. Contbr. article to legal publ. Office: 1200 Beneficial Life Tower Salt Lake City UT 84111

MARCUM, ROBERT DEAN, educational administrator, religious educator; b. Driggs, Idaho, Dec. 23, 1945; s. R. LaVerne and Ruth (Daniels) M.; m. Susan Janene Andreasen, Aug. 31, 1946; children—Erica, Bryant, Aaron, Cameron, Jared, Matthew, Brandon. B.A., Brigham Young U., 1972; M.Ed. in Curriculum and Supervision (Mormon Ch. grantee), Idaho State U., 1982. Tchr., Mormon Ch. Edn. System, Arimo, Idaho, 1972-74, tchr., prin., regional coordinator, Nampa, Idaho, 1974-75, tchr., St. Anthony, Idaho, 1975-77; tchr., prin., regional coordinator Snake River Sem., Blackfoot (Idaho) region, 1977-83; prin., tchr. Western Sem., Mormon Edn. System, Las Vegas, Nev., 1983—; coach football, basketball Snake River High Sch., Blackfoot, 1977-81. Bd. dirs., treas. Snake River Sch. Dist. Bd. Mem. Idaho Sch. Bd. Assn., Nat. Sch. Bds. Assn., Assn. Supervision and Curriculum Devel. Home and Office: 405 Estella Ave Las Vegas NV 89107

MARCUS, PHILLIP RONALD, industrial engineer; b. Newark, Aug. 4, 1947; s. Samuel and Sophie (Hackmeyer) M. B.S. Indsl. Engring., N.J. Inst. Tech., Newark, 1969, postgrad., 1972-73; M.B.A., Seton Hall U., South Orange, N.J., 1971; postgrad., Montclair State Coll., 1973-75, A.F. Inst. Tech., Dayton, Ohio, 1982. Mgr. bd. edn., Newark, 1970-79; dir. GRT Vending Inc., Bloomfield, N.J., 1979-82; chief indsl. engring. Castle (Calif.) AFB, 1982—; lectr. Mercy Coll., Dobbs Ferry, N.Y., 1982. Chmn. Newarkers for Good Govt., 1973-82; vice chmn. Essex Residents for Effective Govt., 1973-78; chmn. Com for Thorough and Efficient Bd. Edn., 1975-82. Named Man of Yr., Newarkers for Good Govt., 1979, 81. Mem. Am. Inst. Indsl. Engrs., ASME, Soc. Am. Mil. Engrs., AIAA, Assn. M.B.A. Execs. Jewish. Contbr. numerous articles to newspapers and mags.

MARCUS, ROBERT, aluminum company executive; b. Arlington, Mass., Feb. 24, 1925; s. Hymen David and Etta (Arbetter) M.; A.B., Harvard U., 1947; M.B.A., U. Mich., 1949; M.Ed., Tufts U., 1950; children—Lawrence Brian, Janie Sue, Clifford Scott, Emily. Market analyst Govt. Commodity Exchange, N.Y.C., 1952-54; mkt. research analyst Gen. Electric Co., 1954-55; corp. mkt. analyst Amax Inc., N.Y.C., 1955-62, staff mkt. mgr. aluminum group, 1962-65, pres. internat. aluminum div., 1965-70, v.p. 1970-71; exec. v.p. Amax Pacific Corp., San Mateo, Calif., 1971-72; exec. v.p. Alumax Inc., San Mateo, from 1972, now pres., chief exec. officer; dir. Advanced Memory Systems, 1973-76, Alumax Inc., Intalco, Eastalco; trustee World Affairs Council, 1974—. Served with USN, 1943-46. Mem. Bankers Club San Francisco, Harvard Club N.Y. Office: Alumax Inc 400 El Camino San Mateo CA 94402

MARCUS, SAMUEL WESLEY, automotive aftermarket company executive; b. Chgo., Aug. 8, 1947; s. Alex A. and Deloris J. Marcus; children—Brian L., Jeff G. B.S., B.A., U. Colo., 1970; grad. exec. mgmt. mktg. program Cornell U., 1979. Comml. rep. Mountain State Tel & Tel. Co., Denver, 1965-69; with Miles Labs., 1970-79, mgr. sales planning, Elkhart, Ind., 1974-75, mgr. mil. mktg. and sales planning, 1976-79; v.p. Lifestyle Industries, Inc., Elkhart, 1980-81; dir. sales and mktg. AccraPac, Inc., Elkhart, 1981; dir. mktg. Cragar Industries, Inc., Compton, Calif., 1981—. Vol. fundraiser on-air auctioneer Sta. WNIT-TV, Elkhart, 1975-78. Recipient Pub. Service award Pub. Broadcasting Service, 1975, 76, 78. Mem. Nat. Am. Logistics Assn. (nat. chmn. subcom. of commissary com., mem. bd. mgrs. Chgo. chpt.), Nat. Assn. Tobacco Distbrs. (Henry Gunst, Sr. exec. mgmt. award 1976), Am. Mgmt. Assn. Author: Vitamin Space Management System, 1978; contbr. articles to profl. jours.; producer, author industry tng. films and tapes. Home: 323 Emerald Bay Laguna Beach CA 92651 Office: 19007 S Reyes Ave Compton CA 90221

MARCUSON, RICHARD LAWRENCE, biostatistician, mathematician; b. Springfield, Mass., May 27, 1945; s. Milton and Barbara May (Strunk) M.; B.A., Clark U., 1967; M.A., Ind. U., 1969, Ph.D. in Math., 1972. Lectr. math. dept. So. Ill. U., Carbondale, 1973; vis. asst. prof. math. U. Alta., Edmonton, Can., 1973-75; biostatistician McNeil Labs., Inc., Ft. Washington, Pa., 1976-77; sr. fellow biostats. dept. U. Wash., Seattle, 1977-79; research assoc. Sch. Medicine, Stanford U., 1979-80; sr. biostatistician Linus Pauling Inst. Sci. and Medicine, Palo Alto, Calif., 1981—; assoc. dir. data mgmt. Stanford Heart Disease Prevention Program, 1979-80. Mem. Am. Math. Soc., Am. Stats. Assn. Contbr. articles to profl. jours. Home: 3207 Alma St Palo Alto CA 94306 Office: Linus Pauling Inst of Sci and Medicine 440 Page Mill Rd Palo Alto CA 95306

MAREE, ANDREW MORGAN, 3D, investment advisor; b. Detroit, Mar. 9, 1927; s. Andrew Morgan, Jr. and Elizabeth Lathrop (Cady) M. B.A., Claremont Men's Coll., 1949; M.B.A., U. Chgo., 1950; J.D., Whittier Coll., 1982; m. Wendy Patricia Haymes, Dec. 20, 1980; children by previous marriages—Andrew Morgan, Samantha Marguerite Haymes. Investment analyst Mfrs. Hanover Bank & Trust Co., N.Y.C., 1951; pres. A. Morgan Maree Jr. & Assocs., Los Angeles; dir. Carson Estate Co., Four Star TV, 1955-65, Mid Am. Minerals Corp., Oklahoma City, 1962-64. Served with USNR, 1944-46. Mem. Los Angeles County Bar Assn., Acad. Motion Picture Arts and Scis., Nat. Assn. Accts., Delta Kappa Epsilon. Club: Players. Office: A Morgan Maree Jr & Assos 6363 Wilshire Blvd Suite 600 Los Angeles CA 90048

MARESCA, JOSEPH WILLIAM, JR., phys. oceanographer; b. Tampa, Fla., Feb. 5, 1946; s. Joseph William and Mary (Cueto) M.; B.S. in Civil Engring., Lehigh U., 1968; M.S., Stanford U., 1969; M.S. in Oceanic Sci., U. Mich., 1973, Ph.D., 1975; m. Noreen Mary Angiola, June 27, 1970; children—Michele Eileen, Craig Robert. Sr. oceanographer, program mgr. SRI Internat. (formerly Stanford Research Inst.), Menlo Park, Calif., 1975—. Served with C.E., U.S. Army, 1969-72. NSF trainee, 1972-74; NDEA Title IV fellow, 1974-75. Mem. Marine Tech. Soc., Am. Geophys. Union, Sigma Xi, Tau Beta Pi, Chi Epsilon. Roman Catholic. Contbr. articles to profl. jours. Home: 780 Fife Way Sunnyvale CA 94087 Office: SRI Internat 333 Ravenswood Ave Menlo Park CA 94025

MARGERUM, J(OHN) DAVID, chemist; b. St. Louis, Oct. 20, 1929; s. Donald Cameron and Ida Lee (Nunley) M.; A.B., S.E. Mo. State Coll., 1950; Ph.D., Northwestern U., 1956; m. Virginia Bolen, June 5, 1954; children—John Steven, Kris Alan, Julie Ellen. Research chemist Shell Oil Co., Wood River, Ill., 1954-55; chief spectroscopy sect. U.S. Army QMR&E Center, Natick, Mass., 1957-59; research specialist Sundstrand Corp., Pacoima, Calif., 1959-62; with Hughes Aircraft Co., Malibu, Calif., 1962—, sr. scientist, head, chemistry sect., 1967—. Served with U.S. Army, 1955-57. Recipient Holley medal ASME, 1977. Fellow AAAS; mem. Am. Chem. Soc., Electrochem. Soc., Soc. for Info. Display, Inter-Am. Photochem. Soc., Sigma Xi. Democrat. Unitarian. Contbr. articles to profl. jours. Patentee in field. Home: 5433 Rozie Ave Woodland Hills CA 91367 Office: 3011 Malibu Canyon Rd Malibu CA 90265

MARGOLES, MICHAEL STUART, orthopedic surgeon; b. Milw., Aug. 14, 1942; s. Sidney Regal and Sylvia (Posner) M.; student San Jose State U., 1961-63; B.A., U. Calif., Berkeley, 1965; M.D., U. Calif., Irvine, 1969; m. Michelle Stratton Church, July 2, 1967; children—Shaynah Stratton, Honey Elizabeth. Intern, Hosp. for Joint Disease and Med. Center, N.Y.C., 1969-70, resident in orthopedic surgery, 1970-74; practice medicine specializing in orthopedic surgery and pain therapy, San Jose, Calif., 1977—. Diplomate Am. Bd. Orthopedic Surgery. Fellow Am. Acad. Neurol. and Orthopedic Surgeons; mem. Santa Clara County Med. Soc., Calif. Med. Assn., Internat. Assn. Study of Pain, Am. Pain Soc., Phi Delta Epsilon. Home: 5018 New Trier Ave San Jose CA 95136 Office: Cambrian Park Plaza 14438 Union Ave San Jose CA 95124

MARGOLIN, CYNTHIA RAE, psychologist, educator; b. Los Angeles, Aug. 19, 1941; d. Samuel Isaac and Pearl Victoria (Grody) M.; children—Kevin, Meegan. B.A., U. Calif.-Berkely, 1963; M.A., U. Minn., 1965, Ph.D., 1966, Research assoc., instr. U. Minn., 1966-68; asst. prof. Stanford U., 1968-69; prof. San Jose (Calif.) State U., 1969—, coordinator women's studies, 1982—, dir. counseling services, 1982-83. NIMH fellow, 1963-66; NSF fellow, 1966; Calif. State U. adminstrv. fellow, 1981-82. Mem. Soc. for Research in Child Devel., Calif. Women in Higher Edn., Am. Psychol. Assn., NOW, Phi Beta Kappa. Contbr. articles to profl. jours. Office: Psychology Dept San Jose U San Jose CA 95192

MARGOLIN, ELIAS L., science educator, engineering consultant; b. N.Y.C., Aug. 13, 1921; s. Irving and Dora (Weinberg) M.; m. Frances Mongin, Mar. 12, 1944; children—Janice, John, Carol, Paul. B.S. in Chem. Engring., CCNY, 1942; M.S. in Mech. Engring., U. Pa., 1948; postgrad. Ohio State U., 1948-52; M.A., San Diego State U., 1983. Registered profl. engr., Ohio. Project engr. USAF, Dayton, Ohio, 1948-53; sr. thermodynamics engr. Convair Co., San Diego, 1955-61; research specialist N.Am. Aviation Co., Downey, Calif., 1962-66; prof. tech. math. and sci. San Diego City Coll., 1967—; adj. prof. profl. engr. exam rev. U. Dayton; dir. Acad. Edn., Family, Group and Individual Therapy, La Jolla, Calif. Troop leader Boy Scouts Am., La Jolla, 1975-78; bd. dirs. Republicans of La Jolla, 1980—. Served with U.S. Army, 1944-46. Fellow AAAS; mem. Am. Inst. Chem. Engrs., AIAA, Am. Assn. Individual Investors. Contbr. articles to profl. jours. Home: 887 La Jolla Rancho Rd La Jolla CA 92037 Office: 1313 12th Ave San Diego Ca 92101

MARGOLIS, ESTHER LUTERMAN, court management analyst; b. Pitts., Jan. 12, 1939; d. Nathan and Belle (Fogel) Luterman; B.S., Ariz. State U., 1976, M.S., 1978; m. Herbert Marvin Margolis, Apr. 15, 1962; children—Ruth Lys, Judith Lyn. Statistician, court planners office Ariz. Supreme Ct., 1976-77; planner Ariz. Dept. Corrections, 1979; adminstrv. asst. planning and research bur. Phoenix Police Dept., 1979-83; mgmt. analyst Adminstrv. Office of Cts., San Francisco, 1983—; instr. Phoenix Community Coll., 1980-82. Mem. textbook selection com. Roosevelt Sch. Dist., Phoenix, 1975; chmn. bd. YMCA, South Mountain br., 1977-81; bd. mgrs. Phoenix and Valley of the Sun YMCA, 1978-81; pres. bd. dirs. Do it Now Found., 1978-80; bd. dirs. Boys' Clubs Phoenix, 1982-83; mem. Mayor's Women's Issues Com., 1982-83. Mem. Am. Soc. Public Adminstrn., Am. Soc. Criminology, Nat. Council Crime and Delinquency, Nat. Assn. Women in Criminal Justice, Profl. Women for Kennedy. Editor ann. report Phoenix Police Dept., 1979-81. Office: State Bldg Room 3154 350 McCallister St San Francisco CA 94102

MARGOLIS, HAROLD JULES, psychologist; b. Los Angeles, Oct. 12, 1933; s. Abraham and Pauline (Finestein) M.; m. Hannah Francine Ontman, Mar. 10, 1962; children—David, Jonathan, Joel. B.A., U. So. Calif., 1956, Ph.D., 1971; M.A. Calif. State U.-Los Angeles, 1961; postgrad. U. Iowa, 1962-64. Lic. psychologist Calif. Sch. psychologist Sioux City (Iowa) Schs., 1964-66; clin. psychologist mental health sect. Los Angeles Unified Sch. Dist., 1966-71; lectr. psychology dept. State U. Calif.-Los Angeles, 1972-74; pvt. practice clin. psychology, Los Angeles, 1964—; community mental health psychologist Los Angeles County Dept. Mental Health. Troop leader Boy Scouts Am., 1979—. Served with U.S. Army, 1957-62. B'nai Brith fellow, 1955-57; Wallace Labs. research grantee, 1962; OEO research grantee, 1966. Mem. Am. Psychol. Assn., Calif. Psychol. Assn., San Fernando Valley Psychol. Assn. Jewish. Contbr. articles to profl. jours. Home: 3168 Benedict Canyon Dr Beverly Hills CA 90210 Office: 8101 Sepulveda Blvd Van Nuys CA 91406

MARGOSIAN, LUCILLE K. MANOUGIAN, artist, educator; b. Highland Park, Mich.; d. George Krikor and Vera Varsenig (Jernukian) Manougian; B.F.A., Wayne State U., 1957, M.A., 1958; postgrad. Calif. State U., Fresno, 1959-60, U. Calif. at Berkeley, 1960-61; m. Ervin M. Margosian, Oct. 28, 1960; children—Rebecca L., Rachel L. One-man show at Jackson's Gallery, Berkeley, 1961; exhibited in group shows at Detroit Art Inst., 1958, Oakland (Calif.) Art Museum, 1961, Wayne State U. Community Arts Center, Detroit, 1965, San Francisco Ann. Art Festivals, 1967, 68, 69, Jack London Square Arts Festival, Oakland, 1969, 70, Judah L. Magnes Meml. Mus., Berkeley, 1970, Kaiser Center Gallery, Oakland, 1970, Oakland Mus. Changing Gallery, 1969, Olive Hyde Art Center, Fremont, 1971, 73, Richmond (Calif.) Art Center, 1972, Villa Montalvo Galleries, Saratoga, Calif., 1976, others; faculty Peralta Community Colls., Laney campus, Oakland, 1967—, prof. art, 1970—, chmn. dept., 1982—. Charter mem. univ. art mus. council U. Calif., Berkeley, 1965—. Recipient Cert. of Disting. Achievement, Am. Legion, 1950, Best of Show 1st prize 5th Ann. Textile Exhbn., Fremont, Calif., 1973, Merit award City of Fremont, 1973, Merit award Zellerbach Bldg. Gallery, San Francisco, 1975. Mem. Calif. Art Edn. Assn., Oakland Museum Assn., Richmond Art Center, Women of Wayne, Wayne State U. Alumni Assn., East Bay Watercolor Soc., Internat. Platform Assn., Am. Fedn. Tchrs., Peralta Fedn. Tchrs. Office: Laney Coll Art Dept 900 Fallon St Oakland CA 94607

MARGULIES, CAL, interior designer; b. Los Angeles, May 29, 1932; s. Henry David and Anna (Wolfstone) M.; m. Harriet Dolores Mathews, June 17, 1951; children—Susan Denise Miyamoto, Laura Diane Morgan, Catherine Lynn. A.A., Los Angeles City Coll., 1956; student Calif. State U.-Los Angeles, 1956-60, Calif. State U. Poly., 1979-80. Cert. Nat. Council Interior Design, 1974. Interior designer, sales mgr., gen. mgr. Miller Desk div. Household Internat. Corp., Los Angeles, 1956-67; gen. mgr. Cannel & Chaffin, Inc., Los Angeles, 1968-69; pres. Custom Industries Inc., Covina, Calif., 1969-77, Corp. Interiors, Inc., Los Angeles, 1977-79, Corona Pacific Designs, Irvine, Calif., 1979-81; prin. Cal Margulies & Assocs., Costa Mesa, Calif., 1979-81, Margulies, Bentley & Assocs., 1981—; instr. Interior Designers Guild, 1982—, Sch. Interior Design, 1982—. Pres., bd. dirs. Hope House for Multiple Handicapped, 1965-80; bd. dirs. San Gabriel Valley YMCA, 1972; pres. Covina Republican Club, 1968; mem. Capital Improvements Com. Covina, 1970. Mem. Sales and Mktg. Execs. Internat. (Outstanding Achievement award 1971, Merit award 1972), Am. Soc. Interior Designers, Inst. Bus. Designers. Republican. Seventh-day Adventist. Clubs: Acad. Magical Arts and Scis., Masons, Kiwanis (Kiwanian of Yr. 1964, Outstanding Leadership award 1967; pres. 1965). Contbr. designs to various jours. Office: 2915C Red Hill Ave #101 Costa Mesa CA 92626

MARIANI, MARLENE KAY, health agy. exec.; b. Endicott, N.Y., Aug. 20, 1941; d. Sterling A. and Helen M. (Verbanic) Reinhart; A.A.S., Broome Community Coll., 1961; B.S., Grand Canyon Coll., 1980; m. Aug. 1, 1964; children—Michael, Mark, Christine, Anthony. Exec. sec. IBM, Vestal, N.Y., 1961-65; adminstrv. asst. Central Ariz. Health Systems Agy., Phoenix, 1973—, personnel adminstr., 1975-77, public info. and edn. coordinator, 1979-80, acting exec. dir., 1980—. Active Young Democrats. Named Outstanding Employee, Central Ariz. Health Systems Agy., 1975; named Citizen of Yr., Ariz. chpt. DAR, 1980. Mem. Am. Soc. for Tng. and Devel., Ariz. Affirmative Action Assn., Ariz. Action for Congress. Democrat. Roman Catholic. Contbr. articles to profl. jours. Home: 8130 N 33 Dr Apt 1 Phoenix AZ 85021 Office: 1820 W Washington Phoenix AZ 85007

MARICICH, SUZANNE AYOTTE, public relations counsel; b. New Haven, Sept. 11, 1941; d. Harold Paul and Edwina Kathryn (Damutz) Ayotte; m. Tom J. Maricich, Aug. 29, 1964; children—Mark, Janet, David. B.A., Albertus Magnus Coll., 1963; M.A., Moorhead (Minn.) State U., 1971. Coordinator pub. relations Children's Village-Family Service, Fargo, N.D., 1973-75; dir. pub. relations Southeast Mental Health & Retardation Ctr., Fargo, 1974-75, St. Mary Med. Ctr. Bauer Hosp., Long Beach, Calif., 1976-79, Hoag Meml. Hosp. Presbyn., Newport Beach, Calif., 1979—. Recipient ACE award So. Calif. Bus. Communicators, 1979; Editors Workshop award, 1982. Mem. Women in Communications, Internat. Assn. Bus. Communicators (Silver Six award region 6, 1982), Am. Acad. Hosp. Pub. Relations (Scott Webster award 1981-82, MacEachern award 1977-78, 81), So. Calif. Hosp. Pub. Relations Soc. (Golden Advocate award 1983), Pub. Relations Soc. Am. (PROTOS awards 1981-82). Office: 301 Newport Blvd Newport Beach CA 92663

MARINE, JAMES BUCHANAN, advertising and public relations counsel; b. N.Y.C., Mar. 22, 1925; s. James S. and Helen M. (Buchanan) M.; m. Vera Lewis, Sept. 5, 1948; children—Nancy, Leslie Ann Marine Robinson, Julie, Helen. B.A. in English, Yale U., 1947. Newspaper reporter Pueblo (Colo.) Chieftain, 1947-48, Dayton (Ohio) Herald, 1948-49; account exec. Carl Byoir & Assocs., N.Y.C., 1949-59; asst. publicity dir. Mut. of N.Y., N.Y.C., 1959-62; pub. relations dir. The Bowes Co., Los Angeles, 1963-71, pres., chief exec. officer, Brown, Keefe, Marine, Bowes, Los Angeles, 1971—; polit. commentator Sta. KPOL, Los Angeles, 1964-75. Served to lt. USNR, 1943-46; PTO. Mem. Western States Advt. Agys. Assn. (dir. 1971—, past pres). Republican. Office: 3435 Wilshire Blvd Los Angeles CA 90010

MARINER, JAMES LLOYD, science educator, consultant; b. Kansas City, Kans., Dec. 5, 1937; s. R.E. and Elizabeth (Smith) M.; m. Anne Pederson, Aug. 20, 1959; children—Paul Edwin, Sarah Lynne, Peter Douglas. B.S. in Biol. Sci., Kans. State U., 1959; B.S. in Edn., U. Kans., 1961; M.S., in Biology, Emporia State U., 1967. Cert. secondary edn. Peace Corps vol., tchr. scis. St. Augustine's Coll., Cape Coast, Ghana, 1962-63; tchr. Lincoln Rural High Sch. (Kans.), 1963-66, Whiteman Sch., Steamboat Springs, Colo., 1967-68; tchr., chmn. dept. sci. Fountain Valley Sch., Colorado Springs, Colo., 1968—; mem. Title IV Adv. Council, Denver, 1978-82. Mem. Widefield Sch. Dist. No. 3 Bd., Security, Colo., 1975—, pres., 1982—. Served with USNG, 1960-66. NSF grantee, 1966-67. Mem. AAAS, Nat. Assn. Biology Tchrs. (dir.

1976-80), Colo. Biology Tchrs. Assn. (dir. 1975-77), Lincoln Jaycees, Nat. Speleological Soc., Cum Laude Soc. (hon.). Author: Understanding Ecology, 1975; An Introduction to Genetics and Evolution, 1977; Human Reproduction and Development, 1979; co-author: Biology, 1981. mem. editorial bd. Nat. Assn. Biology Tchrs., 1972-76, 82—; contbr. articles to profl. jours. Office: Fountain Valley School Colorado Springs CO 80911

MARINO, MARLENE, financial training officer; b. Los Angeles, July 26, 1953; d. Armand Richard and Rose Catherine (Azzara) M.; m. Andrew Victor Wiedensohler, Oct. 27, 1973 (div.); 1 son, Christopher Andrew. A.A. in Sociology, W. Los Angeles Coll., 1973; student Calif. State U.—Dominguez Hills, 1979-81. Teller, new hire instr., br. mgr. Marina Fed. Savs. and Loan, Los Angeles, 1972-76; internal auditor to tng. specialist Hughes Aircraft Employee Fedn. Credit Union, Los Angeles, 1978-81; tng. officer SAFE Fed. Credit Union, North Highlands, Calif., 1981—. Active Alma Soc. Mem. Am. Soc. Tng. and Devel. Republican. Roman Catholic. Club: Am. Taekwondo Assn. (Sacramento). Office: 4636 Watt Ave North Highlands CA 95660

MARINOU, ROSALIND LEE, retail manager, retail systems consultant; b. San Diego, Jan. 12, 1952; d. Larry and Marjorie (Mekas) Crandall. B.A., U. San Diego, 1975; postgrad. U. San Francisco, 1980—. With splty. stores, La Jolla, Calif., 1971-76; store mgr. I. Magnin, San Francisco, 1976-78, floor mgr., 1978-80, buyer, 1980-82; store mgr. McDermott's Co., San Francisco, 1980-82; cons. retail info. systems Lazor Systems Co., Sunnyvale, Calif., 1982; mgr. gen. merchandising Just Closets, San Rafael, Calif., 1983—; cons. retail software, computing systems. Active De Jung Mus., San Francisco, Mus. Modern Art, San Francisco. Mem. Assn. M.B.A. Execs., Nat. Assn. Female Execs. Democrat.

MARIONI, TOM, artist, museum director; b. Cin., Mar. 21, 1937; s. John and Jenny (Geiss) M.; (div.); children—Marino, Anthony, Miles. Student Cin. Art Acad., 1955-59. Founder Mus. Conceptual Art, San Francisco, 1970, dir., 1970—. Served with U.S. Army, 1960-63. Guggenheim fellow, 1981-82, Nat. Endowment for Arts fellow, 1980. Home: 2015 Del Norte Berkeley CA 94707 Office: 75 3rd St San Francisco CA 94103

MARKARIAN, LOUSANDER ARPIAR, furniture company executive; b. Moush, Armenia, Oct. 9, 1908; came to U.S., 1911, naturalized, 1926; s. Arpiar and Siranoush (Bedrosian) M.; m. Madeline Moradian, June 1, 1935; children—Claudia June, Linda Louise, Sandra Lou. A.A., Fresno State Coll., 1965. Ptnr. Sun Maid Furniture Co., Fresno, Calif., 1923—. Pres., People to People. Republican. Clubs: Sister Cities, Elks, Toastmasters, Optimist, Fig Garden Golf, Triple X Fraternity, Armenian Gen. Benevolent Union. Home: 1426 Echo Ave Fresno CA 93728 Office: 1296 N Wishon Ave Fresno CA 93728

MARKER, MARC LINTHACUM, lawyer, leasing corporation executive; b. Los Angeles, July 19, 1941; s. Clifford Harry and Voris (Linthacum) M.; m. Sandra Yocum, Aug. 29, 1965; children—Victor, Gwendolyn. B.A. in Econs. and Geography, U. Calif.-Riverside, 1964; J.D., U. So. Calif., 1967. Bar: Calif. 1971, U.S. Tax Ct. 1972, D.C. 1977. Asst. v.p., asst. sec. Security Pacific Nat. Bank, Los Angeles, 1970-73; chief counsel, sec. Security Pacific Leasing Corp., San Francisco, 1973—; pres. Security Pacific Leasing Services Corp., San Francisco, 1977—; sec., dir. Voris, Inc., 1973—; dir. Refiners Petroleum Corp.; lectr. in field. Served with USCGR, 1966—. Mem. ABA, Calif. Bar Assn., San Francisco Bar Assn., Am. Assn. Equipment Lessors. Republican. Lutheran. Club: University Los Angeles. Home: 41 Lakeside Dr Corte Madera CA 94925 Office: 4 Embarcadero Ctr Suite 1200 San Francisco CA 94111

MARKHAM, REED B., univ. exec.; b. Alhambra, Calif., Feb. 14, 1957; s. John Frederick and Reeda Margaret (Bjarnson) M. student Georgetown U., 1974; A.S., SUNY, 1980, B.S., 1981; A.A., Brigham Young U., 1980, B.A., 1981, M.A., 1982, M.P.A., U. So. Calif., 1983. Archtl. office adminstr. Markham & Markham Corp., Provo, Utah, 1973-76, exec. sec., 1980; editing adminstr. Mountainwest Mag., Provo, 1978-79, v.p. Student Devel. Assn., Brigham Young U., 1979, pres., 1980-82; jud. intern to chief justice U.S. Supreme Ct., 1980; public relations adminstr.; adminstr. N.Y. State Nat. Family Week, 1977; asst. Nat. ARC Month, 1978, Genealogy Week, 1978; public communications adminstr. N.Y. Hill Cumorah Pageant, 1978; mem. nat. devel. and nat. student adv. bd. Nat. Soc. Internships and Exptl. Edn., 1981-83. Mem. adv. bd. Am. Security Council; mem. Nat. Republican Com. Recipient awards, including Nat. Exploration award TRW Corp., 1976, Nat. Slogans USA award Washington Post, 1976; named 1 of Top 10 Nat. Collegiate Debators, Nat. Debate Assn., 1976, Nat. Cross Exam. Debate Assn., 1979, others; Hinckley scholar, 1980; Barrett scholar, 1981; Kaltenborn scholar, 1982; Civitan Internat. scholar, 1982; Whitten scholar, 1982; Warner scholar, 1982. Mem. Internat. Invention Devel. Assn., New Eng. Geneal. Soc., Am. Forensic Assn., Nat. Geneal. Soc., Am. Soc. Internat. Law, Assn. Coll. Unions Internat., U.S. Supreme Ct. Hist. Soc., Nat. Forensic League (Degree of Distinction 1975), Nat. Speech Communications Assn., Western Speech Communication Assn., Nat. Peace Speech Assn., Georgetown Philademic Soc., Utah Hist. Soc., Intercollegiate Studies Inst., Nat. Center for Study of Presidency, Utah Geneal. Assn., Western N.Y. Geneal. Assn., Brigham Young U. Alumni Assn., Eng. Heraldry Soc., Sigma Alpha, Delta Tau Kappa Alpha, Alpha Phi Omega, Phi Kappa Phi, Tau Kappa. Mormon. Author: (with Stan Miller) Especially For Mormons, 1978; Effective Speechwriting: A 20th Century Viewpoint, 1983.

MARKLE, FRANCENE LOUISE, interior designer; b. Oakland, Calif., May 3, 1938; d. Francis William and Cora Frances (Hedemark) Silver; m. Jack Lee Markle, Feb. 1, 1958; children—Gregory Alan, Cynthia Diane, Samantha Anne. B.A. in Interior Design, San Jose State U., 1973. Interior designer Capri Carpet & Interiors, Cupertino, Calif., 1970-73; W & J Sloane, San Jose 1973-80; prin. Francene Markle Interiors, 1980—; cons. in field. Mem. Am. Soc. Interior Designers, Los Gatos C. of C., Saratoga Contemporary Artists Club. Kappa Alpha. Republican. Methodist. Office: 348 N Santa Cruz Ave Los Gatos CA 95030

MARKOVITZ, RICHARD TYLER, motion picture marketing executive; b. Phila., June 9, 1951; s. Victor Seymour and Anita (Rosenthal) M.; m. Deborah Phyliss Robins, July 18, 1982. B.A. in English, Trinity Coll., 1973. Account exec. Spiro & Assocs., Advt. Agy., Phila., 1973-75; publicist Columbia Pictures, Universal Studios, Phila., 1976-77; account exec. Grey Advt. Co., N.Y.C., 1977-78; account supr. D'Arcy, MacManus & Masius Co., Los Angeles, 1979-80; dir. advt. RASTAR Prodns., Burbank, Calif., 1980-82; v.p. internat. mktg. Lorimar Inc., Culver City, Calif., 1982—; lectr. in field. Mem. Acad. Motion Pictures Arts and Sci. Club: Harmony (N.Y.C.).

MARKS, BRUCE, artistic director, choreographer; b. N.Y.C., Jan. 23, 1937; s. Albert and Helen (Kosersky) M.; student Brandeis U., 1954-55, Juilliard Sch., 1955-56; m. Toni Pihl Petersen, Jan. 27, 1966; children—Erik Anthony, Adam Christopher, Kenneth Rikard. Prin. dancer Met. Opera, 1956-61, Am. Ballet Theatre, 1961-72, Royal Swedish Ballet, 1963, Festival Ballet, London, 1965, Royal Danish Ballet, 1971-76; artistic dir. Ballet West, Salt Lake City, 1976—; choreographer Eliot Field Ballet Co., 1970, Royal Danish Ballet, 1972-73, Netherlands Dance Theatre, 1974, Ballet West, 1976—; prof. U. Utah, 1981—; mem. dance adv. panel Nat. Endowment for Arts, 1979, chmn. internat. selection com., 1979, chmn. dance adv. panel, 1981. Artistic fellow Aspen Inst. for Humanistic Studies, 1979. Office: Box 11336 Salt Lake City UT 84147

MARKS, IAN DANIEL, computer system cons.; b. N.Y.C., July 27, 1939; s. Samuel and Beatrice (Kahn) M.; m. Anne Carthew Marcus, 1966; m. Margaret Anne Duncanson, May 22, 1971. B.S., Calif. Inst. Tech., Pasadena, 1961; postgrad. Calif. State U.-Northridge, 1975-80. Assoc. engr. Lockheed Missiles Space Co., Sunnyvale, Calif., 1961-62; programming group leader AiResearch Mfg. Co., Los Angeles, 1962-65; systems analyst Astrodata, Inc., Anaheim, Calif., 1965-69; computer systems cons. Compata, Inc., Woodland Hills, Calif., 1969-76; v.p. tech. dir. Zeta Systems, Inc., Woodland Hills, 1976—; inst. computer sci. Calif. State U.-Northridge, 1976-77. Mem. IEEE, ACM. Office: 6430 Variel Ave Suite 203 Woodland Hills CA 91367

MARKS, MILTON, state senator; b. San Francisco, July 22, 1920; s. Milton and Olita M. (Meyer) M.; B.A., Stanford U., 1940; LL.B., San Francisco Law Sch., 1949; m. Carolene Wachenheimer, Aug. 14, 1955; children—Carol, Milton, Edward David. Mem. Calif. Assembly, from 1959; judge mcpl. ct., San Francisco, from 1967; mem. Calif. Senate, 1968—, chmn. coms. local govt., select com. on maritime industry, com. on disabled. Bd. dirs. Nat. Council on Alcoholism, Calif. League for Handicapped, St. Anthony's Dining Room, Mex. Am. Polit. Assn., Chinese-Am. Citizens Alliance. Served with U.S. Army, World War II. Recipient numerous awards including: Bronze Key award Nat. Council on Alcoholism; Man of Yr. award Council for Civic Unity of San Francisco Bay Area, 1973; Legislator of Yr. award Calif. Assn. Physically Handicapped, 1973; Consumer Legislator of Yr. award, 1981; Calif. Preservation award, 1982; Legislator of Yr. award Students of Calif. State Univ. System. Mem. Am. Legion, VFW. Republican. Jewish. Clubs: Lions, Press Club (San Francisco). Office: 350 McAllister St Room 2043 San Francisco CA 94102

MARKS, ROBERT JACKSON, II, electrical engineer; b. Sutton, W.Va., Aug. 25, 1950; s. Robert Jackson and Lenore (Hersman) M.; B.S.E.E., Rose-Hulman Inst. Tech., 1972, M.S.E.E., 1973; Ph.D.E.E., Tex. Tech. U., 1977; m. Connie Lynn Jewett, July 27, 1974; 1 son, Jeremiah Jackson. Reliability engr. Naval Weapons Support Center, Crane, Ind., 1974-75; research asst. Tex. Tech. U., 1975-77; asst. prof. elec. engring. U. Wash., Seattle, 1977-82, assoc. prof., 1982—; cons. applied physics lab. U. Wash., 1978-79; cons. APPA Systems Inc., 1981-82. NSF grantee, 1979-81. Mem. IEEE (sr.), Optical Soc. Am., Soc. Photo-optical Instrumentation Engrs., Sigma Xi, Eta Kappa Nu. Republican. Contbr. articles on holography, optical info. processing, linear systems, Shannon sampling theory, statis. detection theory to profl. jours. Home: 16515 Ashworth Ave N Seattle WA 98133 Office: U Wash Elec Engring Dept FT 10 Seattle WA 98195

MARKS, THOMAS, clinical psychologist; b. Balt., Mar. 24, 1953; s. Joseph Harold and Esther Marks. B.A., U. Calif.-Santa Barbara, 1976; M.A., Calif. Sch. Profl. Psychology, Los Angeles, 1978, Ph.D., 1980. Clin. dir. Psychol. Testing Service, Santa Barbara, 1982—; pvt. practice psychology, Santa Barbara and Conrad, Mont., 1982—; head services Powdera County-North Central Mont. Community Mental Health Ctr., Conrad, 1983—; cons. to attys. and non-profit orgns. Mem. Am. Psychol. Assn. Author computerized interpretation system for Minnesota Multiphasic Personality Inventory. Office: PO Box 1453 Conrad MT 59425

MARKS, THOMAS LELAND, newspaper executive; b. Boise, Idaho, May 1, 1944; m. James Aaron and Pearl (O'Neil) M.; m. Catherine C. Gray, June 21, 1963; children—Trudi Jensen, Todd Thomas. Student UCLA, 1965, Boise State U., 1973-74, U. Idaho, 1975. Cert. tchr. Idaho, 1973-75. Advt. salesman Idaho Statesman, Boise, 1963-69, Los Angeles Times, 1969-70; advt. mgr. Roseville (Calif.) Press Tribune, 1970-73; gen. mgr. Welles Dept. Store, Boise, 1973-75; mktg. dir. Boise Schs., 1976-79; pub. The Valley News, Meridian, Idaho, 1979—; advisor Idaho State House Edn. Com., 1979, Boise State U., 1979-80, Boise schs., 1977-80. Chmn. Meridian Cancer Drive, 1983. Named Meridian Mchts. Assn. Mcht. of Yr., 1981, 82. Mem. Idaho Newspaper Assn., Idaho Advt. Assn., Meridian C. of C. (publicity chmn. 1981-83), Boise Edn. Assn., Idaho Edn. Assn., NEA, Nat. Newspaper Assn. Republican. Congregationalist. Club: Kiwanis (pres. 1982-83) (Meridian). Office: 714 E 1st St PO Box 365 Meridian ID 83642

MARKSBURY, OLLIE ORVILLE, bookkeeping and tax service exec.; b. Ft. Scott, Kans., Aug. 22, 1919; s. Charles Lester and Nelle Mae (Wheeler) M.; student Ind. U., 1946-47, Mont. U., 1951, also UCLA; m. Eleanore Martha Poppe, Feb. 26, 1960; children—Jeffrey, Gregory; 1 stepson, Edmund Dilliard. Staff accountant Ernst & Ernst, 1947; sr. auditor State of Calif. Div. of Corp., 1947-50; pres. Marksbury Bookkeeping & Tax Service, Inc., Yucaipa, Calif., 1952—; sec. H.V.S., Inc., H.V.S. Domestic Water, Inc. Served with USAAF, 1942-47, with USAF, 1950-52; capt. CAP. Decorated D.F.C., Air Medal, 2 Bronze Stars; enrolled to practice before IRS; lic. comml. and instrument pilot. Mem. Aircraft Owners and Pilots Assn., Silver Wings, Nat. Assn. Accountants, VFW (sr. vice comdr. 1976-77), Air Force Assn. (sec. Covina squadron 1960), Soc. Preservation Dixieland Jazz. Republican. Lutheran. Clubs: Kiwanis (pres. 1976-77), Eagles, Elks. Home: 280 Slack Pl Calimesa CA 92320 Office: 33733 Yucaipa Blvd Suite 5 Yucaipa CA 92399

MARLATT, WILLIAM EDGAR, meteorology educator; b. Kearney, Nebr., June 5, 1931; s. Clifford H. and Queenie B. (Williams) M.; B.A., Nebr. State Coll., 1956; M.S., Rutgers U., 1958, Ph.D., 1961; m. Patricia J. Olson, May 29, 1956; children—Stuart W., Valerie A. Research asst. meteorology Rutgers U., 1956-58, research assoc., asst. prof. meteorology, 1958-61; asst. prof. dept. atmospheric sci. Colo. State U., Ft. Collins, 1961-65, asso. prof., 1965-69, prof., 1969—, assoc. dean Grad. Sch., 1967-68, prof., head dept. earth resources, 1970-75, prof., 1975—; vis. prof., acting dept. head dept. environ. scis. and engring. ecology Colo. Sch. Mines; sr. scientist Environ. Resources Assn., Houston, 1969-70; owner, head Marlatt & Assocs., Ft Collins, 1972—; founder, mem. governing bd. Colo. Solar Corp., Denver, 1980—. Served with USN, 1951-54. Mem. Internat. Biometeorology Soc., Council Agr. and Sci. Tech., Am. Meteorol. Soc., AAAS, Sigma Xi, Gamma Sigma Delta, Lambda Delta Lambda. Mem. Christian Ch. Home: 3611 Richmond Dr Fort Collins CO 80526 Office: Earth Resources Dept Colo State U Fort Collins CO 80523

MARLENEE, RONALD CHARLES, Congressman; b. Scobey, Mont., Aug. 8, 1935; student Mont. State U., U. Mont., Reisch Sch. Auctioneering; m. Cynthia Tiemann; children—Sheila, Casey, Allison. Farmer, rancher; mem. 96th-98th Congresses from 2d Mont. Dist. Mem. Mont. Stockgrowers Assn., Daniels County Farm Bur., Daniels Fair Assn., Mont. Beef Performance Assn., Mont. Grain Growers Assn. Republican. Lutheran. Lodges: Masons, Lions. Office: 409 Cannon House Office Bldg Washington DC 20515

MARLETT, D(E OTIS) L(ORING), real estate exec.; b. Indpls., Apr. 19, 1911; s. Peter Loring and Edna Grace (Lombard) M.; B.A., M.A., U. Wis., 1934; postgrad. Northwestern U., 1934-39, Harvard (Littauer fellow in econs. and govt.), 1946-47; m. Ruth Irene Pillar, Apr. 10, 1932 (dec. Feb. 1969); children—De Otis Neal, Marilyn Ruth; m. 2d, Marie Manning Ostrander, May 1, 1970 (dec. Apr. 1982); m. 3d, Peggie P. Whittlesey, Jan. 15, 1983. Staff Ill. Commerce Commn., 1934-39; lectr. econs. and pub. utilities, Northwestern U. (part time), 1936-39; staff mem. Bonneville Power Adminstrn., U.S. Dept. Interior, 1939-45, asst. adminstr., 1945-52; acting adminstr. Def. Electric Power Adminstrn., 1950-51; asst. to v.p., also gen. mgr. Dicalite and Perlite divs. Gt. Lakes Carbon Corp., 1952-53, v.p., also gen. mgr. Mining and Mineral Products div., 1953-62, v.p. Property Investment dept., 1962-81; pres., chief exec. officer, dir. Del Amo Energy Co., Great Lakes Properties, Inc., dir., v.p. Rancho Palos Verdes Corp., G.L.C. Bldg. Corp.; gen. mgr. Palos Verdes Properties. Former mem. Calif. State Mining Bd., Western Gov.'s Mining Adv. Council. Bd. govs. Western div. Am. Mining congress, chmn., 1962-63. Past dir. United Cerebral Palsy Assn., Los Angeles County; bd. dirs., co-chmn. So. Calif. region NCCJ, nat. trustee; trustee City of Hope; past pres., dir. Los Angeles area council Boy Scouts Am., past chmn. relationships com., past pres. Sunshine area, pres. Western region, past mem. nat. relationships com., field support com., mem. nat. ops. group com., exec. bd., exec. com.; incorporator, pres. Torrance Meml. Hosp. Med. Center Health Care Found., 1980—; mem. UN Assn. Recipient Disting. Service medal Dept. Interior, 1952; decorated knight Order of Crown (Belgium). C.P.A., Wis. Mem. Fin. Execs. Inst., Los Angeles World Affairs Council, Wis. Alumni Assn., So. Calif. Choral Music Assn., Perlite Inst. (past pres., dir.), Am. Inst. Mining and Metall. Engrs., Los Angeles C. of C. (past dir., chmn. mining com.), Mining Assn. So. Calif. (past pres., dir.), Calif. Mine Operators Assn. (past dir.), Bldg. Industry Assn. So. Calif., Regional Plan Assn. So. Calif., Town Hall, Phi Kappa Phi, Beta Gamma Sigma, Phi Beta Kappa, Beta Alpha Psi. Democrat. Clubs: Rotary, Calif., Portuguese Bend (pres.), Rolling Hills Country. Author articles and reports on pub. utility regulation, operation and mgmt. Home: 32759 Seagate Dr #104 Rancho Palos Verdes CA 90274 Office: Suite 220 Del Amo Exec Plaza 3838 Carson St Torrance CA 90503

MARLEY, BERT W., state senator, educator; m. Betty Jane Marley; 5 children. A.B. in History and Edn., M.A. in Polit. Sci., Brigham Young U.; Ph.D. in History, U. Utah. Prof. history Idaho State U.; former mem. Idaho Ho. of Reps.; now mem. Idaho State Senate. Adv. bd. Idaho State Hist. Records; mem. Idaho State Council Devel. Disabilities. Mem. Idaho Hist. Soc. (trustee), VFW, Am. Legion. Democrat. Mormon. Office: Idaho State Senate Boise ID 83720*

MARLOW, ROBERT ALLEN, family physician; b. Brighton, Colo., Mar. 13, 1948; s. Herbert Allen and Ima Jean (Campbell) M.; B.A. in Math. and Gen. Studies cum laude, U. Colo., 1970, M.D. magna cum laude, 1974; m. Iva Loraine Warren, Aug. 14, 1971; children—Courtney Paige, Kimberly Nicole. Intern, U. Colo. Med. Center, Denver, 1974-75, resident in family practice, 1974-77, asst. prof. family medicine and preventive medicine, 1977-78; practice medicine specializing in family practice, Sterling, Colo., 1978—; partner N.E. Colo. Family Medicine Assos., P.C.; mem. staff Logan County Hosp.; asst. clin. prof. family medicine and preventive medicine U. Colo. Health Scis. Center. Mem. Colo. Lt. Gov.'s Health Manpower Recruitment and Placement Consortium, 1979-80. Recipient Joseph and Regina Glaser Med. Student Research award U. Colo. Med. Sch., 1974; Boetteher Found. scholar, 1966-70. Fellow Am. Acad. Family Physicians; mem. Colo. Acad. Family Physicians (exec. bd.), N.E. Colo. Med. Soc., Colo. Med. Soc., Christian Med. Soc., Logan County C. of C., Phi Beta Kappa, Alpha Omega Alpha. Republican. Baptist. Home: 1307 Evans St Sterling CO 80751 Office: 1405 S Eighth Ave Sterling CO 80751

MARMILLION, VALSIN ALBERT, public relations manager; b. Houma, La., Apr. 16, 1951; s. Norman J. and Lillian M. B.A., Northwestern State U., 1972. Mem. staffs Sen. Allen J. Ellender, Sen. Elaine S. Edwards and Congressman Burt Talcott, Washington, 1972-73; adminstrv. asst. to Congressman John Breaux, Washington, 1973-81; mgr. pub. info. programs Atlantic Richfield Co., Los Angeles, 1981—. Chmn., Los Angeles Lend-A-Hand, 1982-83, Los Angeles Bus. Vols. for Arts Theatre Survey, 1982, pres. Fedn. Am. Nat. Spectators, 1982-83, Leadership Seminars Am., Inc., 1975-83. Mem. Los Angeles C. of C. Home: 8455 Fountain Ave #628 Los Angeles CA 90069 Office: ARCO 515 S Flower St AP 1625 Los Angeles CA 90071

MARNELL, ANTHONY AUSTIN, II, architect; b. Riverside, Calif., Mar. 30, 1949; s. Anthony Austin and Ida Marie (Comforti) M.; B.Arch., U. So. Calif., 1972; m. Sandra Jean Graf, June 24, 1972; children—Anthony, Alisa. Architect, draftsman firms in Calif. and Nev., 1969-72; project coordinator Zuni Constrn. Co., Las Vegas, Nev., 1973-74; office mgr., architect Corrao Constrn. Co., Inc., Las Vegas, 1974-82; chmn. bd. Marnell Corrao Assos., Las Vegas, 1976—; pres. Marinelli Internat., Inc., 1978—, A.A. Marnell II, Architect, 1980—, Air Continental Jet Charter, Inc., 1980—; sec.-treas. F & M Importing, 1981—; mem. ethics com. Nev. Bd. Architects, 1974; prin. works include: additions to Caesar's Palace Las Vegas, Maxim Hotel, Sundance Hotel, additions to Desert Inn and Sands Hotel (all Las Vegas), Caesar's Boardwalk Regency, Atlantic City, others. Mem. Nat. Council Archtl. Registration Bds., Post Tensioning Inst. Roman Catholic. Office: 4495 S Polaris Ave Las Vegas NV 89103

MARON, MILFORD ALVIN, judge; b. Chgo., Jan. 21, 1926; s. Martin and Anna (Newman) M.; B.A. cum laude, U. So. Calif., 1949, M.A., 1953, LL.B., 1954, LL.M., 1958; m. Esther Kass, Dec. 24, 1966; children—Steven, Dean, Melissa, Adam. Admitted to Calif. bar, 1955; dep. commr. corps. Calif. Div. Corps., Los Angeles, 1955-57; trial counsel SEC, Los Angeles, 1957-61, Calif. Div. Labor Law Enforcement, 1961-63; adminstrv. law judge Calif. Office Adminstrv. Hearings, Los Angeles, 1963—. Served with AUS, 1944-46. Mem. Bar Assn. Calif. Democrat. Jewish. Office: 314 W 1st St Los Angeles CA 90012

MAROTTA, LAWRENCE JOSEPH, communications executive; b. N.Y.C., Apr. 22, 1954; s. Joseph Leo and Rosario Jeanette (Guastella) M.; m. Elizabeth Shanov, July 22, 1978. B.A., Fordham U., 1975; M.B.A., NYU, 1982. Supr. program ops. ABC Radio, N.Y.C., 1975; asst. to dir. corp. quality control ABC Inc., N.Y.C., 1975-79, asst. dir. corp. quality control, Hollywood, Calif., 1979—. Pres. Olivetree Homeowners Assn. Mem. Hollywood Radio and TV Soc. Office: ABC-TV 4151 Prospect Ave Hollywood CA 90027

MARQUARDT, TERRY TYRONE, optometrist; b. Alamogordo, N.Mex., Nov. 20, 1949; s. Oscar Henry and June Lavonne (Weaver) M.; m. Karen Fay Thompson, Dec. 30, 1977; children—Phillip, Kristina, Tyrone, Todd. B.S., U. N.Mex., 1970; O.D., So. Coll. Optometry, 1974; lic. optometrist. Assoc. Drs. Marquardt & Marquardt, Alamogordo, 1974-78; pvt. practice optometry, Ruidoso N.Mex., 1978—; low vision cons. N.Mex. Services for the Blind, N.Mex. Sch. Visually Handicapped, 1975-76. Coach Seratoma Little League Basketball. Bausch & Lomb Contact Lens Research fellow 1973. Mem. Am. Optometric Assn., Optometric Extension Program Found., Council on Sports Vision, Republican. Lutheran. Club: Rotary (dir. 1980). Home: PO Box 3596 Ruidoso NM 88345 Office: Dr TT Marquardt Sierra Professional Ctr 123 Mescalero Trail Ruidoso NM 88345

MARQUEZ-OROZCO, RICARDO, architect, football coach; b. Mexico City, Mexico, Sept. 3, 1948; came to U.S., 1977, naturalized, 1981; s. Flavio and Amalia (Orozco Mendez) Marquez de la Fuente; m. Mary Joel Machrol, Mar. 22, 1980. B.Arch., U. Mexico, 1975; grad. in solar tech., Ariz. State U., 1980. Football coach U. Mexico, 1975-77; architect TORACT, Mexico City, 1975-77; football coach Ariz. State U., Tempe, 1978-79, 80—; architect/planner Gilbert Honanie, Inc., Tempe, 1978—;

asst tchr. U. Mexico Coll. Arch., 1976-77. Named Coach of Yr., U. Mexico, 1976; Dubois Orgn. scholar, 1978-79. Mem. AIA (assoc.), Constrn. Specifications Inst., ASHRAE. Roman Catholic. Author: Como Organizar un Equipo de F.B.A., 1980. Home: 17044 Armour Circle Fountain Hills AZ 85268

MARR, LUTHER REESE, motion picture company executive; b. Kansas City, Mo., June 23, 1925; s. Luther Dow and Aileen (Shimfessel) M.; m. Christelle Lois Taylor, July 12, 1956; children—Michelle Lois, Stephen Luther, Christelle Elizabeth, A.B., UCLA, 1946; J.D., U. So. Calif., 1950. Bar: Calif. 1951. Mem. firm Hasbrouck and Melby, Glendale, Calif., 1951-54; atty. Disney Prodns., Burbank, Calif., 1954—, corp. sec., 1957, also officer, dir. subs. Sec., Disney Found., Burbank, 1957, Calif. Inst. Arts; trustee, v.p., gen. counsel Le Lycee Francais de Los Angeles, 1964—. Served to ensign USNR, 1946-47. Mem. Am. Soc. Corp. Secs., ABA, State Bar Calif., Los Angeles County Bar Assn., Phi Beta Kappa, Phi Alpha Delta. Republican. Methodist (lay leader 1969—). Home: 2323 Via Saldivar St Glendale CA 91208 Office: 500 S Buena Vista St Burbank CA 91503

MARRA, P(ETER) GERALD, manufacturers representative firm executive; b. Cranbrook, B.C., Can., June 29, 1940; came to U.S., 1964, naturalized, 1973; s. John and Angela Rose Marra; B.Sc., U. B.C., 1963, postgrad., 1963-64; m. Eileen Elizabeth Sowerby, Feb. 11, 1967; children—Amber Eileen, Anne-Marie Geraldine. Computer engr. Canadair Ltd., Montreal, Que., 1962-63; research engr. Boeing Corp., Seattle, 1964-68; hardware specialist Computer Sci. Corp., Toronto, Ont., Can., 1969; pres., gen. mgr. D.I.S.C., Seattle, 1970-74; sales mgr. Hayes Tech. Co., Seattle, 1975; owner, pres. Marra & Assocs., Bellevue, Wash., 1976—; cons. small bus., 1970—. Republican party platform chmn. King County, 1976-78, legis. dist. chmn., 1978; pres., dir. fundraising for U. B.C., Friends of U. B.C., 1975—; asst. chmn. archery com. Wash. State Sportsmen's Council, 1980, chmn., 1981-83, chmn. big game com. 1981—; mem. Mt. Rainier Wildlife Com., 1981-83. IBM scholar, 1964. Mem. U. B.C. Alumni (pres. Seattle, Pacific N.W. chpt. 1974—). Club: Cedar River Bowman Archery. Home: 1739 172d Pl NE Bellevue WA 98008

MARRIOTT, DAVID DANIEL, Congressman; b. Bingham, Utah, Nov. 2, 1939; s. Raymond D. and Gladys (Steuri) M.; B.S., U. Utah, 1967; m. Marilynn Tingey, Sept. 19, 1965; children—David Russell, Jon Michael, Katherine Nicole, Lindsay. Gen. agt. Guardian Life Ins. Co. of Am.; pres. Marriott Assos., Salt Lake City, 1968-76; mem. 95th-98th Congresses from 2nd Utah Dist.; ranking Republican, House Select Com. on Children, Youth and Families; mem. mining, forest mgmt. and Bonneville Power Adminstrn. Subcom. Coach, Little League Baseball, 1969-76. Served with Air N.G., 1958-63. C.L.U. Mem. Million Dollar Roundtable, Chartered Life Underwriters (past pres. Utah chpt.), Mountain States Pension Conf. (past dir.), Salt Lake City C. of C., Estate Planning Council, Nat. Fedn. Ind. Businesses. Republican. Mormon. Club: Salt Lake Exchange. Contbr. articles to profl. jours. Home: Salt Lake City UT 84108 Office: Longworth House Office Bldg Washington DC 20515

MARSANICO-BYRNE, LINDA, psychotherapist; b. Queens, N.Y., Nov. 24, 1946; d. Thomas Robert and Agnes (Gianatiempo) Marsanico; m. Robert F. Stolp, Jan. 17, 1964; 1 son, Tom; m. Luke Martin Byrne, Oct. 22, 1971; 1 dau., Leigh. B.S. in Psychology, Ramapo Coll., 1979; M.Ed. in Human Devel. Counseling, Peabody/Vanderbilt U., 1981; postgrad. Loughborough U. (Eng.), 1981—. Therapist, Arapahoe House, Englewood and Sheridan, Colo., 1982—, Southwest Mental Health Ctr., Denver, 1982—. Mem. Am. Personnel and Guidance Assn., Brit. Psychol. Soc. Office: Arapahoe House 3530 W Lehigh Ave Sheridan CO 80016

MARSELLA, ANTHONY JOSEPH, psychology educator; b. Cleve., Sept. 12, 1940; s. Steven and Antonia Luparello; m. Joy Ann Marsella, June 20, 1963; children—Laura Joy, Gianna Malia. B.A., Baldwin-Wallace Coll., 1962; Ph.D., Pa. State U., 1968. Assoc. prof. psychology U. Hawaii, Honolulu, 1969—; psychologist Hawaii State Hosp., 1969-70, U. Hawaii Med. Sch., 1970-71; cons. Hawaii Job Corps, Queens Med. Ctr., WHO; bd. dirs. Waikiki Drug Clinic, 1973-75, Inst. Behavior Scis., 1972—. Gen. Motors Corp. fellow, 1958-62; Fulbright-Hays fellow, 1967-68; NIMH research fellow, 1968-69; grantee Founds. Fund for Research in Psychiatry, 1968, NIMH, 1969, Internat. Liaison Council Korean Research, 1972, WHO, 1974-76. Mem. Am. Psychol. Assn., Hawaii Psychol. Assn., World Fedn. Mental Health, Internat. Assn. Cross-Culture Psychology, Assn. for Advancement Psychology, Soc. Intercultural Edn., Tng. and Research. Author monographs; contbr. articles to profl. jours., chpts. to books. Home: 161 Hanapepe Loop Honolulu HI 96825 Office: Dept Psychology U Hawaii Honolulu HI 96822

MARSH, BILLY WAYNE, missile and space co. exec.; b. Cross Plains, Tex., Nov. 19, 1926; s. Thomas Marvyn and Carrie (Gaines) M.; B.S. in Aero. Engring., Tex. A. and M. U., 1948; M.S. in Aero. Engring., U. Mich., 1949; postgrad. Stanford U., 1961-62; m. Helena Isbell, July 31, 1948; children—Judith Carolyn, Leslie Ann, Curtis Wayne, William Kenton. Mathematician, Gen. Dynamics Co., Fort Worth, 1948; aerodynamicist McDonnel Douglas Co., El Segundo (Calif.) div., 1949-51; project aerodynamicist Marquardt Aircraft Co., Van Nuys, Calif., 1951-54; aerodynamic group supr. Lockheed Missiles & Space Co., Sunnyvale, Calif., 1954-55, asst. mgr. aerodynamics, 1955-59, mgr. satellite test center tech. ops., 1959-62, mgr. aero-mechanics, 1962-64, mgr. advanced reentry systems, 1964-71, program mgr. space systems div., 1971—; instr. UCLA Extension, 1951-54. Coach, Little League, 1962-67. Served with USN, 1945-46. Mem. Nat. Mgmt. Assn., AIAA, Aircraft Owner and Pilots Assn. Home: PO Box 980 Los Altos CA 94022

MARSH, RICHARD CHARLES, psychologist; b. Los Angeles, Jan. 20, 1942; s. Lazar William and Miriam Rose (Marr) M.; A.B. in Psysiology, U. Calif., Berkeley, 1964; M.S. in Bioengring. and Neuroanatomy, Purdue U., 1970; postgrad. U. Md., 1966-67; M.S. in Physiology, UCLA, 1969; Ph.D. in Psychology, Utah State U., 1971; m. Sandra Marian Combs, Sept. 27, 1975; children—Shuan Eric, Alexander Dendry, Andrew Tatanka. Postdoctoral fellow in neuroscis. Brain Research Inst., UCLA, 1971-72; prof. psychology Eastern Ky. U., Richmond, 1972-74; staff psychologist Los Angeles County Mental Health Service, 1974-76; pvt. practice psychology, Beverly Hills, Calif., 1976—; psychologist Problem Back Clinic, San Fernando Valley, 1977-79; project dir. Medper Project, Beverly Hills, 1979—; cons. various med. corps., ins. cos., lawyers. Lic. marriage family and child counselor and psychologist, Calif. Mem. Am. Psychol. Assn., Assn. for Advancement of Psychology. Clubs: Optimist Internat., Nat. Buffalo Assn. Honored speaker Purdue U. Neurology Group, 1973; contbr. articles to profl. publs.

MARSH, RICHARD NORMAN, electrical engineer; b. Hartford, Conn., June 22, 1946; s. Norman Frank and Virginia E. (Corey) M.; m. Gertrude Margarette Hart, Dec. 12, 1971. B.S.E.E., Sacramento State Coll., 1966. With Lawrence Livermore Nat. Lab., Livermore, Calif., 1966—, computer systems engr. calibration and measurements Standards Lab., 1966-79, tech. coordinator prompt diagnostics nuclear test research and devel. labs., 1979-82, sr. elec. engr. tech. coordinator, 1982—. Mem. noise abatement com. City of Livermore, 1977. Served with U.S. Army, 1969-72. Mem. Audio Engring. Soc., Soc. Audio Cons., No. Calif. Audio Soc. Republican. Home: 5424 Sunflower Ct Livermore CA 94550 Office: PO Box 808 Livermore CA 94550

MARSHALL, ARTHUR K., lawyer, judge, author; b. N.Y.C., Oct. 7, 1911; s. Louis and Fanny M.; B.S., CCNY; LL.B., St. John's U.; LL.M., U. So. Calif., 1952; m. Mary Jane Ratliff, June 26, 1948; 2 children. Admitted to N.Y. bar, 1937, Calif. bar, 1947; pvt. practice, N.Y.C., 1937-43, Los Angeles, 1947-50; atty. VA, Los Angeles, 1946-50; tax counsel, State Bd. Equalization, Sacramento, 1950-51; inheritance tax atty., State Controller, Los Angeles, 1951-53; commr. Superior Ct. Los Angeles County, 1953-62; judge Mcpl. Ct., Los Angeles judicial district, 1962-63, judge Superior Court, Los Angeles, 1963-81, supervising judge probate dept., 1968-69, assoc. judge appellate dept., 1973-76, presiding judge appellate dept., 1976, Ct. Appeal (by assignment), judge pro tempore, 1981—; acting asst. prof. wills, estates and real property UCLA, 1954-59; grad. faculty U. So. Calif., 1955-75; lectr. Continuing Edn. of Bar. Served with AUS, 1943-46; lt. col. Res. Named Judge of Year, Lawyers Club of Los Angeles County, 1975. Fellow Am. Bar Found.; mem. Santa Monica Bar Assn. (past pres.), Westwood (past pres.), Los Angeles Bar Assn. (created 1st Arthur K. Marshall Probate and Trust award), State Bar Calif. (exec. com. adviser estate planning and probate sect. 1974—), Am. Judicature Soc., Am. Legion (past comdr.), Internat. Acad. Estate and Trust Law (founder, 1st pres., now chancellor), U. So. Calif. Law Alumni Assn. (past pres.), Phi Alpha Delta (justice Alumni chpt.). Clubs: Lawyers; Naval and Mil. (London). Author: Joint Tenancy Taxwise & Otherwise, 1953; Branch Courts, 1959; California State and Local Taxation, Forms & Text, 3d edit., 1977, supplement, 1980; California Probate Procedure, 4th edit., 1979, supplement, 1980; Guide to Procedure Before Trial, 1975, supplement, 1980; (with others) Survey of California Law, 1953, 54, Family Law, 1956, Civil Procedure Before Trial, 1957. Home: Los Angeles CA 90012 Office: 523 W 6th St Los Angeles CA 90014

MARSHALL, BEVERLY KAYE, petroleum landman, oil and gas consultant; b. Bozeman, Montana, Nov. 29, 1953; d. Peter and Winifred Irene (Sluys) Broekema; m. Milton Douglas Marshall, Mar. 21, 1981 (div.). Student Mont. State U., 1976; B.S. with honors in Mktg., U. Colo., Denver, 1982, postgrad. in Fin., 1982—. Asst. to adminstr. Manhattan (Mont.) Christian Sch., 1970-72; asst. to fin. mgr. Elba Systems Corp., Denver, 1972-75; land analyst, petroleum landman Tex. Pacific Oil Co., Denver, 1977-80; petroleum landman, Denver, 1981—. Vol. Am. Cancer Soc. Cystic Fibrosis; active Arapahoe (Colo.) Young Republicans. Recipient Valedictorian award Manhattan Christian High Sch., 1972. Mem. Denver Assn. Petroleum Landmen, Am. Assn. Petroleum Landmen, Nat. Assn. Female Execs., Beta Gamma Sigma. Methodist. Office: PO Box 2383 Denver CO 80201

MARSHALL, CONSUELO BLAND, judge; b. Knoxville, Tenn., Sept. 28, 1936; d. Clyde Theodore and Annie (Brown) Arnold; B.A., Howard U., 1958, LL.B., 1961; m. George Edward Marshall, Aug. 30, 1959; children—Michael Edward, Laurie Ann. Admitted to Calif. bar, 1962; atty. City of Los Angeles, 1962-67; asso. mem. firm Cochran & Atkins, Los Angeles, 1968-70; commr. Los Angeles Superior Ct., 1971-76; judge Inglewood Mcpl. Ct., 1976-77, Los Angeles Superior Ct., 1977-80, U.S. Dist. Ct. Central Dist. Calif., Los Angeles, 1980—. Mem. adv. bd. Richstone Child Abuse Center. Research fellow Howard U. Law Sch., 1959-60. Mem. State Bar Calif., Calif. Women Lawyers Assn., Calif. Assn. Black Lawyers, Calif. Judges Assn., Black Women Lawyers Assn., Los Angeles County Bar Assn., NAACP, Urban League, Beta Phi Sigma. Mem. Ch. Religious Science. Contbr. articles to profl. jours.; notes editor Law Jour. Howard U. Office: US Courthouse 312 N Spring St Los Angeles CA 90012

MARSHALL, DENNIS LEHR, gen. contractor, home bldg. exec.; b. Denver, Feb. 13, 1943; s. Howard Leonard and Gloria Elise (Larkin) M.; student LaSalle Extension U., 1963; m. Jeanette Burnett, Aug. 28, 1960; children—Randy Lee, Donna Jean. Carpenter foreman Ray Delcamp Gen. Contractor, Denver, 1960-64; sub contractor Marshall Constrn., Denver, 1965-67; with Vantage Builders Wheat Ridge, Colo., 1967—, creator Vantage Custom Homes, 1968, pres., 1970—; founder Vantage Enterprises, 1973. Mem. Bd. Review, Jefferson County, 1972-83; coach Little League Football, 1969-77; mem. Residential Energy Com., 1979-82, chmn. Codes and Standards Com.; gov.'s appointee Colo. State Housing Bd. Recipient Builder of Year award Home Builders Assn. Met. Denver, 1977, 78; Outstanding Service award Colo. Assn. Home Builders, 1978. Mem. Nat. Assn. Home Builders (bd. dirs.), Colo. Assn. Home Builders (bd. dirs.), Home Builders Assn. Met. Denver (past pres.). Republican. Baptist. Club: Beech Areo; Toastmaster. Home: 1051 S Foothill Dr Lakewood CO 80228 Office: Vantage Enterprises 3805 Marshall St Wheat Ridge CO 80033

MARSHALL, DWIGHT ALAN, university dean; b. Bedford, Iowa, Mar. 7, 1929; s. William Daniel and Ruth Eva (Thompson) M.; B.A., U. No. Iowa, 1951, M.A., 1954; children—Deborah Ann (Mrs. Thomas Barnett), Diane Annette. Supervisory investigator intelligence agy., U.S. Govt., Munich, Germany, 1954-57; prin. high sch., 1957-59; personnel mgr. Harrahs Co., Reno, Nev., 1959-61; new bus. coordinator Lockheed Corp., Sunnyvale, Calif., 1961-66; dean continuing edn. U. Nev., Las Vegas, 1966—; founder Center for United Campus Ministry; MX cons. to cities and legislators; team leader, accreditation visitor Am. Assn. Trade and Tech. Schs.; mem. accrediting commn. Nat. Assn. Trade and Tech. Schs., 1977—; grant and contract cons. on edn. and aerospace; co-producer, reviewer Learning Resource Series for physicians, educators and students pub. by Am. Lung Assn.; rev. mgr. Avline citations for lay edn. of chest diseases Nat. Library Medicine (through Am. Lung Assn. and Am. Thoracic Soc.). Served with CIC, AUS, 1951-53. Mem. Am. Vocat. Assn. (chmn. armed forces com. 1970-73), Nat. Univ. Continuing Edn. Assn. (bd. dirs., mem. exec. com. 1983-84), Nev. Lung Assn. (pres. 1975-76), Am. Lung Assn. (dir. 1976—), Phi Delta Kappa. Methodist (chmn. administrv. bd.). Mason. Office: U Nev 4505 Maryland Pkwy Las Vegas NV 89154

MARSHALL, JOHN CARL, art educator; b. Pitts., Feb. 25, 1936; s. Thomas William and Francis Rose (Diana) M.; m. Margaret J. Neff, Aug. 22, 1959; children—David, Joel. B.F.A. in Silversmithing and Design, Cleve. Inst. Art, 1965; M.F.A., Sch. Art, Syracuse U., 1967. Instr. figure drawing Cleve. Inst. Art, 1964-65; instr. Sch. Art, Syracuse (N.Y.) U., 1965-68; asst. prof., 1968-70; assoc. prof. U. Wash., Seattle, 1970-75, chmn. metalworking dept., 1970-75, prof. 1975—. Mem. Am. Crafts Council (Wash. chpt. rep. 1974-75), Soc. N.Am. Goldsmiths (founding mem.), N.W. Designer Craftsmen, Goldsmiths. Numerous commissions for colls., chs. and founds. Home: 23312 Robinhood Dr Edmonds WA 98020 Office: Dept Art U Wash Seattle WA 98195

MARSHALL, JOHN FOSTER, psychobiologist; b. Boston, Sept. 5, 1948; s. Edwin Rowe and Barbara H. (Foster) M.; B.A., Williams Coll., 1970; Ph.D., U. Pa., 1973; postgrad. Karolinska Inst. (Sweden), 1974-75; m. Christine Elizabeth Vereb, Dec. 24, 1977. Asst. prof. depts. psychology and psychiatry U. Pitts., 1973-77; asst. prof. dept. psychobiology U. Calif., Irvine, 1977-81, asso. prof., 1981—; lectr. Summer Tng. Inst. for Scientists in Neurology and Mental Illness, Irvine, 1978; mem. neurobiology rev. panel NSF, 1980—. Mem. Fogarty Center Task Force on Obesity and the Am. Public, Bethesda, Md., 1977. Alfred P. Sloan research fellow, 1980-82. Mem. Soc. for Neurosci., Brain Neurochems. and Behavior Soc., AAAS, Sigma Xi, Phi Beta Kappa. Contbr. articles on neurosci. and psychobiology to sci. publs. Office: Psychobiology Dept U California Irvine CA 92717

MARSHALL, JOSEPHINE RETTMAN, insurance auditor; b. Dallas, July 24, 1937; d. Robert Henry and Sophie Elizabeth (Barnard) R.; m. Charles Roy Foord, Oct. 2, 1971 (dec. Mar. 1974); m. 2d, Alden Edgar Marshall Jr., June 26, 1976. B.S. in Bus. Adminstrn., North Tex. State U., 1962. Sr. audit reviewer Fireman's Fund Ins. Group, Dallas, 1962-65; premium audit supr. Hartford Ins. Group, San Francisco, Reno and Los Angeles, 1965-75; regional premium audit mgr. C.G./Aetna Ins. Co., Los Angeles, 1975-82; controller designate Argonaut Ins. Co., Fullerton, Calif., 1982—; fin. planner, audio visual editor, planner; mktg. researcher, forecaster; fashion model. Active Los Angeles County Mus. Art, San Francisco Ballet, Am. Heart Assn.; organizing com. Reno Air Show. Recipient Hartford Ins. Group Spl. Achievement award, 1971, C.G./Aetna Ins. Co. Affirmative Action award, 1982. Mem. Nat. Soc. Ins. Premium Auditors (charter), Colonial Dames Am., Fashion Models Internat., Ins. Auditors Assn. West (1st v.p., Achievement Recognition award 1983), Calif. Ins. Audit Mgrs. Assn., Internat. Environ. Edn. for Whale Protection. Republican. Roman Catholic. Club: Toastmistress Internat. Contbr. material to profl. publs. Office: 801 E Chapman Ave Suite 108 Fullerton CA 92631

MARSHALL, L. B., medical technologist; b. Chgo., Feb. 10; s. Gillman and Ethel (Robinson) M.; B.S., U. Puget Sound; postgrad. San Francisco State U., City Coll. San Francisco; Sc.D.; m. Esther Wood, Sept. 28, 1961; 1 dau., Lelani. Pres., Community View Med. Labs. Med. Group Inc., San Francisco, 1964—; founder pres. Rolls Royce Limousine Service, San Francisco, 1973—. Served with U.S. Army, 1947-53. Decorated Bronze Star, Med. Combat Badge. Recipient certificate of appreciation Pres. Nixon, 1973, Urban League, 1973, Calif. Dept. Human Resources, 1973. Mem. Am., Calif. assns. med. technologists, NAACP (life). Clubs: Oyster Point Yacht, Commonwealth. Author poetry. Home: 765 Point San Pedro Rd San Rafael CA 94901 Office: 786 Haight St San Francisco CA 94117

MARSHALL, MAUREEN GRETA, management company executive; b. Yorkshire, Eng., Aug. 14, 1921; d. George Cyril and Greta Beatrice (Hall) Stevenson; came to U.S., 1952; B.A. with distinction, U. Calif. at Berkeley, 1969, M.A., 1970; m. Sherwood Barnett Marshall, Nov. 1, 1952; 1 dau., Virginia Maureen Marshall Lang. Vice pres. Alameda (Calif.) Convalescent Hosp., 1968-70, Sonoma (Calif.) Convalescent Hosp., 1970-74; gen. ptnr. Valley View Lodge, Walnut Creek, Calif., 1974-82; exec. v.p. SAV Service Corp., Walnut Creek, 1975—; pres. Tri-County Supply Inc., Walnut Creek, 1978—; v.p. Kristina Odysseys, Ltd., Del., 1979. Served with Canadian Women's Army Corps, World War II. Mem. San Francisco Women's Artists (pres. 1977-79), Phi Beta Kappa. Episcopalian. Paintings exhibited at Calif. Inst. Art, Mus. Modern Art, San Francisco, Worth Ryder Gallery, San Francisco, U. Calif. at Berkeley, San Francisco Art Commn. Gallery, St. Mary's Coll., Moraga, Calif., Internat. Ctr. for Contemporary Art, Paris, 1983, also at juried shows. Office: care Seiler & Co 44 Montgomery St Suite 1000 San Francisco CA

MARSHALL, ROBERT LEONARD, electronics co. exec.; b. Kansas City, Mo., Feb. 20, 1924; s. Conrad H. and Grace K. (Raney) M.; m. Sonia D. Nyberg, Apr. 11, 1953; children—Barbara E., William K. Student San Diego State Coll., 1941-43; B.S. in Mech. Engring., U. Tex., Austin, 1947; postgrad. U. Pitts., 1947-48, UCLA, 1948-52. Sales engr. Westinghouse Electric Corp., Pitts. and Los Angeles, 1947-56, Weston Electric Inst. Co., Los Angeles, 1956-55; with Consol. Electrodynamics Co., Pasadena, Calif., 1957-59; owner, mgr. Dyna Sales Co., Los Angeles, 1959—, Dynaservice Co., Los Angeles, 1960—. Served to lt. USN, 1943-46. Mem. IEEE, Instrument Soc. Am., Electronics Reps. Assn., Nat. Electronic Distbrs. Assn., Am. Mgmt. Assn., Mfrs. Agts. Nat. Assn. Republican. Methodist. Club: Los Angeles Athletic. Office: 1020 S Atlantic Blvd Los Angeles CA 90022

MARSHALL, ROBERT VANCE, hospital administrator; b. Ft. Riley, Kans., July 29, 1944; s. Lloyd Claude and Phyllis Jacqueline (Massey) M.; 1 son, William Lloyd. B.A., Tex. Christian U., 1967; M.H.A., Washington U., 1976. Adminstrv. resident Deaconess Hosp., Evansville, Ind., 1975-76; asst. adminstr. West Suburban Hosp., Oak Park, Ill., 1976-78; asst. adminstr. Lawrence (Kans.) Meml. Hosp., 1978-79; asst. adminstr. St. Luke's Hosp., Denver, 1979—. Chmn. United Way Campaign, 1981; mem. Mile High Child Care Consortium, 1981—; Denver Partnership Gilpin Sch. Task Force, 1982—. Served with U.S. Army, 1969. Mem. Am. Coll. Hosp. Adminstrs., Denver Area Young Health Care Adminstrs. (steering com.), Sigma Phi Epsilon. Republican. Home: 1134 Lafayette Apt 2 Denver CO 80218 Office: St Luke's Hosp 601 E 19th Ave Denver CO 80203

MARSHALL, STEPHEN WHITNEY, geneticist; b. Twin Falls, Idaho, July 10, 1942; s. Joseph Walden and Florence Lucy (Sinclair) M.; m. Ruth McKinney, May 30, 1964; children—Nicholas Scot, Paul James. B.S. in Biology, Coll. Idaho, 1964; M.S. in Botany, U. Idaho, 1966, Ph.D. in Plant Genetics, 1971. Teaching and research asst. U. Idaho, Moscow, 1966-70; research fellow Wash. State U., Pullman, 1970-71; dir. research Crookham Co., Caldwell, Idaho, 1971-76, v.p. research, 1976—. Contbr. articles to sci. jours. Mem. Gov.'s STAR com. Mem. Nat. Sweet Corn Breeders Assn. (pres. 1982), Sigma Xi, Phi Sigma, Gamma Sigma Delta. Club: Kiwanis. Home: 1515 Everett Caldwell ID 83605 Office: PO Box 520 Caldwell ID 83605

MARSOLEK, L. GENE, manufacturer's representative; b. Denver, Apr. 2, 1942; s. Paul Robert and Tillie Marie (Richter) M.; m. Judith Kay Busch, Dec. 26, 1970; 1 son, Eric Lee. Student U. Colo., 1965. Mgr. Marsolek's Hardware & Appliance Store, 1961-65, 67-68; mfr.'s rep. John Brickell Co., Denver, 1970-74; owner, pres. L. Gene Marsolek Co., Inc., Denver, 1975—. Served with Colo. Air N.G., 1965-69; Korea. Mem. Assoc. Rep. of Mfrs. Presbyterian. Clubs: El Jebel Mariners, Shriners, Masons. Home: 6314 S Monaco Ct Englewood CO 80111 Office: L Gene Marsolek Co Inc 2186 S Holly St Suite 206A Denver CO 80222

MARSOLEK, PAUL ROBERT, hardware and appliance co. exec.; b. Grand Island, Nebr., June 9, 1916; s. Thomas J. and Cecelia (Hebda) M.; m. Tillie M. Richter, Oct. 22, 1937 (dec. 1971); children—Herbert, Gene, Paul Robert; m. 2d, Lorraine M. Long, July 1, 1972; stepchildren—David E Neil, Carol Ann Jones. Gen. mgr. Rudolph's Foot Comfort Store, Denver, 1936-44, Dr. Scholls Foot Confort Shop, Denver, 1939-44; owner, pres. Marsolek's Hardware and Appliance Co., Denver, 1943—. Deacon, Central Christian Ch., Denver; pres. E. Denver Civic Assn. Mem. Mountain States Hardware and Implement Assn. (past pres.), Am., Rocky Mountain, Colo., Wyo. numis. assns., Denver Press Club (life), Internat. Assn. Shrine Yacht Clubs (treas.). Republican. Clubs: Optimists (past pres.), Elks, Masons. Home: 1970 Union Dr Lakewood CO 80215 Office: 2606 E Colfax St Denver CO 80206

MARSONETTE, MADELEINE MACARTHUR, museum director; b. Chinook, Mont., Jan. 18, 1924; d. Finlay and Isabella (Thompson) MacArthur; m. Luverne G. Marsonette, May 1, 1954; children—Roger L., Shirley J. Clk. of Dist. Ct., Blaine County, Chinook, Mont., 1967-77; co-owner, bookkeeper Valley Lumber Co., Chinook, Mont., 1980-83; mgr. Blaine County Mus., Chinook, 1982—. Mem. Mont. State Hist. Soc., Mont. Oral History Assn., Blaine County Hist. Soc., VFW Aux. Democrat. Presbyterian. Home: 808 Illinois PO Box 1176 Chinook MT 59523 Office: 501 Indiana PO Box 927 Chinook MT 59523

MARSOOBIAN, EDWARD FRED, educator; b. Chgo., Sept. 28, 1919; s. Paul and Rose M.; A.S., Compton Coll., 1965; B. Vocat. Edn., Calif. State U., Los Angeles, 1967, M.A. in Indsl. Edn., 1968; Ph.D. in Indsl. Edn. (scholar), Tex. A&M U., 1975; m. Regina Eshkonian, June 24, 1962; children—Melissa, Rachelle, Danny, Paul. Communication officer, lt. Lynwood (Calif.) Police Dept., 1946-57; communication engr. Los Angeles City Fire Dept., 1958-63; dean Calif. Tech. Trade Sch., Long Beach, 1965-69; prof. electronics Calif. State U., Los Angeles, 1968—; dir. bio-med. tng. program Space div. N.Am. Rockwell, Downey, Calif., 1971, cons., 1966-71. Pres. Bd. Edn., Mesrobian Elem. and High Sch., Pico Rivera, Calif., 1971-74. Served with U.S. Army, 1940-45; PTO. Decorated Bronze Star. Mem. Am. Vocat. Assn., IEEE (sr.), Calif. Assn. Indsl. Tech., Community Coll. Electronics Faculty Assn., Calif. Indsl. Edn. Assn., Phi Delta Kappa (Man of Year 1974), Am. Legion. Democrat. Roman Catholic. Club: Elks. Contbr. articles to textbooks. Office: California State University 5151 State University Dr Los Angeles CA 90032

MARSTON, MICHAEL JAN, urban econ. cons.; b. Oakland, Calif., Dec. 4, 1936; s. Lester Woodbury and Josephine (Janovic) M.; B.A., U. Calif. at Berkeley, 1959; postgrad. London Sch. Econs., 1961-63; m. Alexandra Lynn Geyer, Apr. 30, 1966. Vice pres. Larry Smith & Co., San Francisco, 1964-72, exec. v.p. urban econ. div., 1964-72; chmn. bd. Keyser Marston Assos., Inc., San Francisco, 1973—; gen. partner The Sequoia Partnership, 1979—; pres. Marston Vineyards and Winery, 1975—, Marston Assos., 1982—. Chmn., San Francisco Waterfront Com., 1966—; bd. dirs., mem. exec. com. San Francisco Planning and Urban Research Assn., 1964—; trustee Cathedral Sch. for Boys, 1981—; v.p. Presidio Heights Assn. of Neighbors, 1981—; v.p., bd. dirs. People for Open Space, 1972—; mem. Gov.'s Issue Analysis Com. and Speakers Bur., 1966; mem. speakers bur. Am. embassy, London, 1961-63; v.p., bd. dirs. Democratic Forum, 1968-72; v.p., trustee Youth for Service. Served to lt. USNR. Mem. Urban Land Inst., Order of Golden Bear, Lambda Alpha, Sigma Chi. Clubs: Vintners, Commonwealth. Home: 3375 Jackson St San Francisco CA 94118 Office: 230 California St San Francisco CA 94111

MARTELLO, MICHAEL EDWARD, lawyer; b. Quantico, Va., Dec. 14, 1941; s. Salvatore Frank and Vivian Patricia M.; B.S. in Acctg., Fairleigh Dickinson U., 1965; M.B.A. in Taxation, Pace U., 1969; J.D., Seton Hall U., 1979; LL.M. in Taxation, NYU, 1983; m. Marie Gloria Inzalaco, Dec. 23, 1962; children—Michael, Matthew, Michele, Marc. Bar: N.J. 1980. Tax acct. Worthington Corp., 1962-66, Martin Marietta Corp., 1966-68, Abex Corp., N.Y.C., 1968-69; asst. tax mgr. Foster Wheeler Corp., Livingston, N.J., 1969-71, tax mgr., 1971-77, dir. taxes, 1977-81, corp. tax counsel, 1981-82; asst. controller and mgr. taxes Bechtel Corp., San Francisco, 1982—. Mem. ABA, N.J. Bar Assn., Tax Execs. Inst. Roman Catholic. Home: 1732 Oro Valley Circle Walnut Creek CA 94596 Office: 50 Beale St San Francisco CA 94105

MARTH, SELDEN BOLIVAR, psychologist; b. Dallas, Sept. 30, 1924; s. Frederick Christian and Martha Eason (Anderson) M.; student So. Meth. U., 1942-43; B.A., U. Tex., Austin, 1945; M.Div., Yale U., 1949; Th.D., So. Calif. Sch. Theology, 1962; m. Charlene Joyce Tucker, June 28, 1975; 1 dau., Shelley; stepchildren—Susan, Michael. Ordainedto ministry United Methodist Ch., 1947; minister Meth. chs., Conn. and Ill., 1947-56; pastoral counselor 1st Congregational Ch., Los Angeles, 1957-63; pvt. practice psychotherapy, Claremont, Calif., 1959—; pres. Nautilus Tapes, Inc. Mem. Am. Psychol. Assn., Calif. State Psychol. Assn., Group Psychotherapy Assn. So. Calif. (dir.), Phi Beta Kappa, Alpha Kappa Delta. Democrat. Methodist. Producer library of hypnotherapy tapes, 1979; writer newspaper column What's On Your Mind, Ont. Daily Report. Home: 1938 Abbie Way Upland CA 91786 Office: 433 W Arrow Hwy Claremont CA 91711

MARTIN, ALICE LOUISE MCCLURE, purchasing exec.; b. Ottumwa, Iowa, Mar. 23, 1926; d. Floyd Edgar and Lena Olive (Shepherd) McClure; student Iowa State Coll., 1946-47; m. George Kenneth Martin, Oct. 19, 1947, 1 son, Douglas Bruce. Draftsman, engring. dept. Ottumwa Iron Works (Iowa), 1944-46, order receiver John Morrell & Co., Ottumwa, 1946-50; clk. prodn. control Proto Tool div. Ingersoll-Rand Co., Portland, Oreg., 1970-72, steel inventory planner, 1972-77, steel buyer, 1978—. Mem. Clackamas County Election Bd., 1961-70; pres. women's assn. Oak Hills Presbyn. Ch., 1965-66. Mem. Nat. Assn. Female Execs., Inc., Sigma Kappa. Republican. Presbyterian. Home: 5332 SE El Centro Way Portland OR 97222 Office: 10330 SE 32d Ave Portland OR 97222

MARTIN, BOYD ARCHER, educator; b. Cottonwood, Idaho, Mar. 3, 1911; s. Archer Olmstead and Norah Claudine (Imbler) M.; student U. Idaho, 1929-30, Pasadena Jr. Coll., 1931-32, UCLA, summer 1934, B.S., U. Idaho, 1936, A.M., Stanford, 1937, Ph.D., 1943; m. Grace Charlotte Swingler, Dec. 29, 1933; children—William Archer, Michael Archer. Research asst. Stanford U., 1936-37, teaching asst., 1937-38; instr. polit. sci. U. Idaho, 1938-39; acting instr. polit. sci., Stanford U., 1939-40; John M. Switzer fellowship, summer, 1939-40; chief personnel officer, Walter Butler Constrn. Co., Farragut Naval Training Center, summer, 1942; instr. polit. sci., U. Idaho, 1940-43; asst. prof. polit. sci., 1943-44, asso. prof. polit. sci., 1944-47, prof. and head dept. of social sci., asst. dean Coll. Letters and Sci., U. Idaho, 1947-55, dean 1955-70, dean emeritus, 1973—, Borah disting. prof. polit. sci., 1970-73, now emeritus, dir. Bur. Pub. Affairs Research, 1955-73, dir. Inst. Human Behavior, 1970—; vis. prof. polit. sci. Stanford U. summer 1946, 52; vis. prof. polit. sci. U. Calif., Berkeley, 1962-63, with Center for Study Higher Edn., 1962-63. Attended UN Conf., San Francisco, Great Plaines, UNESCO Conf., Denver, 1947. Chmn. Wm. Edgar Borah Found. for Outlawry War, 1948-55; mem. Commn. to Study Orgn. Peace, 1955-66; mem. Ida. Constl. Revision Commn.; mem. N.W. Conf. Higher Edn., 1960-67, chmn., 1966-67; mem. Inter-Am. Coordinating com. Partners Alliance for Progress; mem. bd. Am. Assn. Partners Alliance for Progress. Mem. Idaho Assn. Presidents and Deans (chmn. liberal arts colls.), Am. Polit. Sci. Assn. (mem. exec. council 1951-53), Western (pres. 1950), Pacific N.W. (pres. 1961-62) polit. sci. assns., Nat. Municipal League, Am. Soc. Pub. Adminstrn., Fgn. Policy Assn., UN Assn., AAUP, Phi Beta Kappa, Alpha Phi Omega, Kappa Delta Pi, Pi Sigma Alpha, Phi Gamma Mu. Author: The Direct Primary in Idaho, 1947; (with Sidney Dancombe) Recent Elections in Idaho (1940-70), 1972; also articles on polit. sci. to revs.; co-author: Introduction of Political Science, 1950; Rocky Mountain Politics, 1962; Western Politics, 1962; Politics in the American West, 1969; Idaho Voting Trends: Party Alignment and Percentage of Votes for Candidate, Parties and Elections, 1890-1974, 1975. Co-editor: State and Local Government in Idaho: A Reader, 1970. Contbr.: Strengthening the United Nations, 1958. Home: 1314 Walenta Dr Moscow ID 83843

MARTIN, CAROL ANNE, federal administrator; b. Los Angeles, Nov. 7, 1935; d. Larry C. and Florrie Amelia (Schofield) Larsen; m. Philip DePons Martin, June 11, 1965, (dec. 1965); children—Richard D., Ronald P. B.A., Occidental Coll., 1957; M.A., U. Ariz., 1980. Tech. typist and records clk. Consol. Electrodynamics, Pasadena, Calif., 1959-61; adminstrv. clk. Tuzigoot Nat. Monument, Clarkdale, Ariz., 1965-67, supt., 1971-74; adminstrv. officer Custer Battlefield Nat. Monument, Crow Agency, Mont., 1967-71; chief Western Archeol. and Conservation Ctr., Tucson, 1974—; research assoc. Ariz. State Mus., U. Ariz. Fulbright fellow, Innsbruck, Austria, 1957-58; recipient Spl. Achievement awards Nat. Park Service, 1966, 69, 76. Mem. So. Ariz. Fed. Execs. Assn. (v.p. 1980, co-chmn. combined fed. campaign 1980, pres. 1981, 82), Pacific Sci. Assn., Am. Assn. Mus., Internat. Council Mus., Fulbright Alumni Assn., Soc. for Applied Anthropology, Phi Beta Kappa, Beta Sigma Phi. Author: (with William E. Brown) People of the Stone Villages, 1973. Office: PO Box 41058 Tucson AZ 85717

MARTIN, CHARLES HENRY, market research firm executive; b. Houston, Aug. 31, 1931; s. Vaiden Cosby and Minilie (Hurt) M. m. Sydney Helen Decker, Jan. 1951 (div.); 2 sons, 1 dau.; m. 2d Jean Krieg, Sept. 6, 1968. B.A., B.J., U. Tex.-Austin, 1956, M.A., 1972, Ph.D. in Communications, 1974. Pub. relations rep. Norfolk and Dedham Ins. Co., Dallas, 1956-60; account exec. Troxell and Assocs., Houston, 1961-63; advt. cons., Houston, 1963-68; reseach assoc. U. Tex.-Austin, 1970-73; prof. U. Ga., Athens, 1974-78. Pepperdine U., Malibu, Calif., 1979-81; market research cons. Calif. Communications Cons., Los Angeles, 1981—. Served as staff sgt. USAF, 1951-55. Mem. Am. Mktg. Assn., Advt. Club Los Angeles, Sales and Mktg. Execs. Assn., Los Angeles C. of C. Author: Advertising, 1979; contbr. articles to profl. jours. Home: 2807 Burkshire Ave Los Angeles CA 90064 Office: Calif Communications Cons 8425 W 3d St Suite 204 Los Angeles CA 90048

MARTIN, DOUGLAS RICHARD, educational administrator; b. Wadena, Minn., Oct. 16, 1940; s. Richard Oskar and Myrtle Jessie (Carter) M.; m. Anita Jo Friedrichs, June 29, 1963; children—Richard Norman, Jennifer Elizabeth. B.A., Concordia Coll., 1963; M.A., U. So. Calif., 1969, Ed.D., 1974. Tchr., adminstrv. intern Los Angeles Unified Sch. Dist., 1963-71, adminstrv. dean, 1971-73; vice prin. Paso Robles (Calif.) Pub. Schs., 1973-79; prin. Lindsay (Calif.) Unified Sch. Dist., 1979-82; supt. Esparto (Calif.) Unified Sch. Dist., 1982—. Scoutmaster, dist. commr., council tng. chmn. Boy Scouts Am., 1979—. Recipient Kiwanis Disting. Pres.'s award, 1977; IDEA fellow, 1982. Mem. Assn. Calif. Sch. Administrs., Assn. Supervision and Curriculum Devel., Phi Delta Kappa. Republican. Lutheran. Clubs: Esparto (Calif.) Lions; Kiwanis. Home: 584 Mountain Circle Lindsay CA 93247 Office: 600 Yolo Ave Esparto CA 95627

MARTIN, FRANCES FRANKLIN, civic worker, club woman; b. Gary, W.Va., May 3, 1915; d. John Thomas and Mabel (Marion) Franklin; student Concord Coll., 1935; A.B., Fairmont State Coll., 1942; M.A., Chapman Coll., 1963; m. Wayne S. Martin, Nov. 25, 1937; children—Carolyn Noel (Mrs. Maynard William Gurnsey, Jr.), Marilyn Curtis. Tchr. pub. schs., McDowell County, W.Va., 1935-39; exec. dir. Girl Scouts U.S.A., Fairmont, W.Va., 1954-59. Retarded Children's Council. Fairmont, 1960-61; counselor Anaheim, Cal., 1962-63; special-ist Edn. Retarded Children, Sparks, Nev., 1963—. First v.p. Fairmont Woman's Club, 1953-55; dist. dir. W.Va. Garden Club, 1959-61; pres. Fairmont Music Club, 1952-55, Marion County (W.Va.) Garden Council, 1954-56, Marion County council Girl Scouts U.S.A., 1952-54. Mem. Nev. Tax Commn., 1972-76; mem. Gov.'s Council on Children and Youth, 1975. Named Woman of Year Beta Sigma Phi, 1955; recipient nat. certificate of recognition for spl. class tchrs. of handicapped, 1971, Distinguished Service award Washoe County Tchrs. Assn., 1973. Mem. Nat., Nev. edn. assns., Nat., Nev. assns. retarded children, Phi Delta Kappa. Republican. Presbyn. Home: 1019 La Rue Ave Reno NV 89509 Office: Marvin Picollo Sch for Mentally Retarded Reno NV

MARTIN, FRANK, insurance company executive; b. Los Angeles, Dec. 7, 1954; s. Flaviano and Antonia Romero. B.A. (Calif. State, Occidental Scholastic fellow), Occidental Coll., 1977. Trainee, State Farm Ins. Cos., Salem, Oreg., 1979, comml. underwriter, Salem, 1980—. Fellow Ins. Inst. Am. Clubs: Toastmasters Internat., Occidental Soccer. Home: 2341 State St Salem OR 97301 Office: State Farm NW Regional Office 4600 25th Ave Salem OR 97313

MARTIN, FRED KENNETH, JR., solar energy company executive; b. Fresno, Calif., Nov. 21, 1942; s. Fred K. and Emma B. (Balmer) M.; m. June 5, 1976; children—Kenneth Martin, Mario Martin. A.A., Fresno City Coll., 1964; B.E.E., Fresno State Coll., 1966. With Travelers Corp., San Jose Calif. and Hartford, Conn., 1967-72, regional sales dir., prodn. mgr., 1972-75; with Fafco Inc., Menlo Park, Calif., 1976—, nat. comml. sales mgr., 1971-78, gen. mgr., Bay Area Distbn. Co., 1978, pres., 1979—; dir., v.p. Solar Energy Sales, Inc.; pres., chmn. bd. Martin & Mickle Ins. and Fin. Corp., 1983—; advisor Pacific Gas & Utility Co., Calif. Energy Commn. Served with USMCR, 1960-68. Mem. Calif. Solar Energy Soc., Calif. Solar Industries Assn., Calif. Insulation Contractors Assn. (div., chmn. govtl. affairs, chmn. polit. action com.), Internat. Solar Energy Soc. Republican. Lutheran. Office: 740 N Mary Ave Sunnyvale CA 94086

MARTIN, GREGORY CLARKE, civil engr.; b. Jamaica, N.Y., Mar. 12, 1944; s. Paul Joseph and Margaret Elizabeth (Steigler) M.; B.E., Cooper Union U., 1965; M.S., U. Ill., 1967, Ph.D., 1971; M.B.A., St. Mary's Coll., 1983; m. Theresa Gaglio, Aug. 27, 1966; children—Joseph, Kimberly, Dana Joyce. Sr. research engr., mgr. applied tech., dir. dynamics research Assn. Am. R.R.s, Chgo., 1971-77; rehab. planner, asst. dir. rail and equipment tech., dir. mech. engring. Conrail, Phila., 1977-79; v.p. engring. rail div. Itel Corp., San Francisco, 1979—. U. Ill. fellow, 1967-68. Mem. ASCE, ASME, Am. Mgmt. Assn., Chi Epsilon, Phi Kappa Phi. Club: Toastmasters (Concord, Calif.). Home: 2335 Holly Oak Dr Danville CA 94526 Office: 55 Francisco St San Francisco CA 94133

MARTIN, HARRY (JOE), JR., advt. and pub. relations exec.; b. Detroit, July 19, 1931; s. Harry M. and Irene Louise (McClung) M.; B.A., Mich. State U., 1957; m. Linda Garn, Feb. 15, 1976; children—Monique, Michael, Jeffrey. Asst. advt. mgr. Gate City Sash & Door Co., Ft. Lauderdale, Fla., 1955-56; advt. brand mgr. Coca Cola Co., 1958-59; founder, pres. Martin Advt., Inc., Tustin, Calif., 1960—; mem. adv. bd. Eldorado Bank. Pres., Tustin area Republican Assembly, 1967-68. Mem. Pub. Relations Soc. Am., Western States Advt. Assn. Am., Nat. Assn. Home Builders, Bldg. Industry Assn., Sales and Mktg. Council. Office: 18141 Irvine Blvd Tustin CA 92680

MARTIN, J. DAVID, real estate development company executive; b. Columbus, Ga., July 11, 1955; s. C. C. and Dollyie M. M.; B.S. in Mktg. and Fin., U. N. Ala., 1977; M.B.A., Golden Gate U., 1980; m. Margaret Parris Martin, Feb. 11, 1978. Real estate lender Central Bank of Ala., 1977-79; real estate mgr. Union Bank, San Jose, Calif., 1979-81; v.p., prin. C.P.S. Comml. Real Estate Co., Pleasanton, Calif., 1980—. Mem. Mortgage Bankers Assn., Nat. Assn. Indsl. and Office Parks, Assn. South Bay Brokers, Bay Area Mortgage Assn., Phi Gamma Delta. Home: 201 Montair Dr Danville CA 94526 Office: 4637 Chabot Dr Suite 300 Pleasanton CA 94566

MARTIN, JEAN CLARK, program director, music educator; b. Mercer, Pa., May 30, 1921; s. Frederick Milton and Nelle (Reilly) Clark; m. Lawrence K. Martin, Aug. 17, 1946 (div.). B.S., Grove City Coll., 1943; M.S., Columbia U., 1951; postgrad. Stanford U., 1951-55. Program dir. Stanford U., Calif., 1969—; pvt. tchr. piano. Served to lt. j.g. USN, 1943-46. Mem. Music Tchrs. Nat. Assn., Assn. Coll. Unions Internat., Stanford Alumnae Assn. Episcopalian. Home: 1571 Madrono Palo Alto CA 94306 Office: Stanford Univ PO Box 6508 Stanford CA 94305

MARTIN, JOANNE, psychologist, educator; b. Salem, Mass., Sept. 25, 1946. A.B., Smith Coll., 1968; Ph.D. in Social Psychology (Franklin Reynolds fellow 1972-76, Sigma Xi dissertation grantee 1976-77), Harvard U., 1977. Project mgr. McBer & Co. (formerly Behavior Sci. Ctr. of Sterling Inst.), Cambridge, Mass. and Washington, 1969-72, dir. govt. mktg., 1972; teaching asst. Sloan Sch. Mgmt., MIT, 1971, guest lectr. dept. psychology, 1976; departmental advisor, tutor, teaching asst., research asst. Harvard U., 1972-76, guest lectr., various courses, 1976; asst. prof. organizational behavior Grad. Sch. Bus. and dept. sociology Stanford U., 1977-81, assoc. prof., 1981—; cons. in field, 1972-76. Bus. and Profl. Women's Found. Lena Lake Forrest research fellow, 1977-78. Mem. Am. Psychol. Assn. (Div. Indsl. and Organizational Psychology Dissertation award 1978), Western Psychol. Assn., Acad. Mgmt., Soc. Psychol. Study Social Issues, Soc. Organizational Behavior. Contbr. chpts., articles to profl. publs. Office: Grad Sch Bus Stanford U Stanford CA 94305

MARTIN, JOSEPH, JR., lawyer; b. San Francisco, May 21, 1915; s. Joseph and Helen (Jackson) M.; B.A., Yale, 1936, LL.B., 1939; m. Ellen Chamberlain, July 5, 1946; children—Ellen C. Myers, Luther M. Greene. Admitted to N.Y. bar, 1940, Calif. bar, 1946; assoc. Cadwalader, Wickersham & Taft, N.Y.C., 1939-41; ptnr. Wallace, Garrison, Norton & Ray, San Francisco, 1946-55; ptnr. Pettit & Martin, San Francisco, 1955-70, sr. ptnr., 1973—; gen. counsel Fed. Trade Commn., Washington, 1970-71; U.S. rep. Geneva Disarmament Conf., 1971-76; mem. Pres.'s Adv. com. for Arms Control and Disarmament, 1974-78; vis. fellow Stanford U. N.E. Asia-U.S. Forum on Internat. Policy, 1980—. Pres. San Francisco Pub. Utilities Commn., 1956-60; Republican Nat. committeeman Calif., 1960-64; dir. Nat. Fair Campaign Practices Com., 1965—; dir. Arms Control Assn., 1977—; treas. Rep. Party Calif., 1956-58; bd. dirs. Patrons of Art and Music, 1959-63; bd. dirs. Palace Legion of Honor, 1958-70, pres., 1963-68. Served to lt. comdr. U.S. Navy, 1941-46. Recipient Disting. Honor award U.S. Arms Control and Disarmament Agy., 1973; Outstanding Service citation FTC, 1973; lifetime achievement award Legal Assistance to Elderly, 1981. Fellow Am. Bar Found.; mem. Calif. State Bar, N.Y. State Bar, D.C. Bar Assn. Clubs: Pacific-Union (San Francisco); Burlingame Country; Yale of New York. Home: 2580 Broadway San Francisco CA 94115 Office: 600 Montgomery St San Francisco CA 94111

MARTIN, JOSEPH JOHN BAXTER, telecommunications exec.; b. Rochester, N.Y., Aug. 19, 1943; s. Joseph J. and Merrylin Louise B. (Baxter) M.; B.A., DePauw U., 1965; M.A., Monterey Inst. Internat. Studies, 1971; M.B.A. in Internat. Bus., Golden Gate U., 1980, M.B.A. in Telecommunications Mgmt., 1981; m. Giselle Paris, Dec. 23, 1977. Tchr. math. and history Clay County (Fla.) Bd. Edn., 1967-69; ins. cons., broker Jefferson Standard Life Ins. Co., San Francisco, 1972-74, Home Life N.Y., 1974-76, Allstate/Lloyds of London, San Francisco, 1976-77; communications cons. and sales rep. ITT Terryphone Unit, ITT, San Francisco, 1977-78; telecommunications cons. and sales engr. No. Calif. Telephone Co., Richmond, 1978; telecommunications mgmt. specialist automated data and telecommunications service, region 9, GSA, San Francisco, 1978-82; telecommunications sales/systems cons. ROLM Corp., Santa Clara, Calif., 1982—; faculty lectr. Golden Gate U., 1980—. Pres., No. Calif. Council on Internat. Relations, 1970-71; mem. Nat. Republican Congl. Com., 1981—, Rep. Presdl. Task Force, 1982—. Mem. Telecommunications Assn., TransWorld Radio, Christian Broadcasting Network, Internat. Platform Assn., Oakland World Trade Club, Beta Theta Pi. Republican. Club: Golden Gate Tennis. Home: 182 Caldecott Ln Oakland CA 94618 Office: USG/GSA ADTS 525 Market St San Francisco CA 94105

MARTIN, JUNE JOHNSON CALDWELL, journalist; b. Toledo, Oct. 6; d. John Franklin and Eunice Imogene (Fish) Johnson; A.A., Phoenix Jr. Coll., 1939-41; B.A., U. Ariz., 1941-43, 53-59; student Ariz. State U., 1939, 40; m. Erskine Caldwell, Dec. 21, 1942 (div. Dec. 1955); 1 son, Jay Erskine; m. 2d, Keith Martin, May 5, 1966. Free-lance writer, 1944—; columnist Ariz. Daily Star, 1956-59; editor Ariz. Alumnus mag., Tucson, 1959-70; feature writer, fashion editor, book editor Ariz. Daily Star, Tucson, 1970—. Panelist, co-producer TV news show Tucson Press Club, 1954-55, pres., 1958. Mem. Tucson Civil Def. Com., 1961. Worker campaigns of Samuel Goddard, U.S. Rep. Morris Udall, Ariz. Gov. Raul Castro. Recipient awards Nat. Headliners Club, 1959, Ariz. Press Club award, 1957-59, Am. Alumni Council, 1966, 70. Mem. Jr. League of Tucson, Ariz. Press Women, Tucson Press Club. Pi Beta Phi. Democrat. Methodist. Contbg. author: Rocky Mountain Cities, 1949, World Book Ency., 1975—. Bd. dirs., editorial bd. Clarior, women's issues newspaper. Contbr. articles and stories to mags. Home: PO Box 2631 Tucson AZ 85702 Office: PO Box 26807 Tucson AZ 85726

MARTIN, MERLE PHILLIP, educator; b. San Francisco, Dec. 30, 1936; s. Lorne Phillip and Irene Estworthy (Marshall) M.; B.S., U. Calif., Berkeley, 1958; M.S., Stanford U., 1964; children—Elizabeth, Charles, Stephen, David. Commd. 2d lt. USAF, 1959, advanced through grades to maj., 1971; sta. Hdqrs. Tactical Air Command, Hampton, Va., 1964-67, Anchorage, 1967-71; separated, 1971; asso. prof. quantitative systems U. Alaska, 1971-74; mgr. tech. ops. Alaska Ct. System, Anchorage, 1974-81; lectr. Sch. Bus. Adminstrn., Tex. A&M U., 1981—; lectr. U. Alaska, 1974-81, Chapman Coll., 1974-81; instr. Anchorage Community Coll., 1974-80; cons. in field. Served as lt. col. Air N.G., 1971-78. Decorated Air Force Commendation medal; cert. in data processing. Mem. Data Processing Mgmt. Assn. (chpt. pres. 1974). Baha'i Faith. Contbr. articles to profl. jours., poetry to mags. Home: 303 Cooner Apt F College Station TX 77840

MARTIN, PAUL, history educator; b. Paducah, Ky., Mar. 25, 1941; s. William Paul and Polly (Kissinger) M.; m. Dolores Ester Aragon, Feb. 17, 1973; children—Eliza Maria, Christina Teresa. B.A. in History, Calif. State U.-Fullerton, 1969; M.A. in Edn., N.Mex. State U., 1983. Teaching intern N.Mex. State U., Las Cruces, 1982—; farmer, Las Nutrias, N.Mex., 1977-79; tchr. St. Mary's Sch., Belen, N.Mex., 1975-77; hydrological technician Middle Rio Grande Conservancy, Albuquerque, 1979-81; instr. curriculum and instrn. N.Mex. State U., Las Cruces, 1982—. Mem. Concerned Citizens of Dona Ana County. Served with USAF, 1962-66. Mem. Assn. Supervision and Curriculum Devel., Phi Kappa Phi. Democrat. Presbyterian. Home: 401 Dona Ana Sch Rd Las Cruces NM 88005 Office: Box 3N N Mex State U Las Cruces NM 88003

MARTIN, RICHARD FRANCIS, mfg. co. exec.; b. Newburgh, N.Y., Mar. 19, 1920; s. Roland Francis and Marion (Hall) M.; m. Phyllis Norton, Nov. 21, 1951; children—Richard Francis, Pamela Gilmore,

William F., Thomas S. B.S. in Bus. Adminstrn., Syracuse U., 1949. With Fairmont Foods Co., Omaha and Phila., 1951-69, adminstrv. v.p. Eastern Div., 1964-69; with Martin Mgmt. Services, Denver, 1969-72, pres., 1969-72, part-time, 1972—; exec. v.p. adminstrn. Tanner Co., Phoenix, 1972—, dir., 1980—; dir. Tanner S.W., Inc. Trustee Hahnemann Hosp. and Coll., Phila., 1965-69; mem. Valley Forge (Pa.) Park Commn., 1964-69; chmn. bd. Met. YMCA, 1981-82. Served with USN, 1942-46. Mem. Ariz. Gen. Contractors (chmn. edn. com.), Soc. Tng. and Devel., Am. Soc. Personnel Adminstrn. Republican. Methodist. Clubs: Rotary, Phoenix Execs. (treas., dir.), Toastmasters (internat. dir. 1965-67). Office: PO Box 20128 Phoenix AZ 85036

MARTIN, ROBERT EDWARD, JR., forester; b. Flint, Mich., Jan. 9, 1931; s. Robert Edward and Sarah Catharine (Royal) M.; B.S., Marquette U., 1953; B.S., U. Mich., 1958, M.S., 1959, Ph.D., 1963; m. Patricia Ann Meyer, Nov. 7, 1953; children—Steven Francis, Michael Philip, Kathleen Marie. Research forester So. Forest Fire Lab., 1960-63; asst. prof. forestry Va. Poly. Inst., Blacksburg, 1963-67, asso. prof., 1967-70, prof., 1970-71; prof., project leader fire sci. program U. Wash., Seattle, 1971-75; project leader, supervisory research forester Silviculture Lab., U.S. Forest Service, Bend, Oreg., 1975-82; prof. wildland fire mgmt. U. Calif.-Berkeley, 1982—; adj. prof. Oreg. State U., 1978—, U. Wash., 1971—. Served with USN, 1953-56. Mem. Soc. Am. Foresters, AAAS, Forest Products Research Soc., Sigma Xi. Clubs: Toastmasters, Oreg. Nordic. Home: 75 Chadbourne Way Oakland CA 94619 Office: U Calif Berkeley CA 94720

MARTIN, SALLY CROCKETT, city ofcl.; b. Lowell, Mass., June 20, 1936; d. Harry Baxter and Sally Dexter Crockett; B.A., U. Colo., 1975; m. Harry B. Martin; children—Pam, Cynthia, Shelley. Mem. nat. adv. bd. Nat. Women's Polit. Caucus, 1979-81; field dir., Lamm/Dick campaign, 1982; sr. analyst econ. devel. Colo. Gov.'s Office; legis. intern Colo. State Legislature, 1976; mem. Colo. Commn. on Women, 1979; commr. Boulder Urban Renewal Authority, 1979—; dir. Eldorado Heights Treatment Facility, 1979—; founder, pres. Boulder County Women's Polit. Caucus, 1978-79; bd. dirs. Boulder LWV, 1975-76; vice chmn. Boulder County Democratic Party, 1979—; chmn. Boulder Urban Renewal Authority, 1982-83. Home: 305 Fox Dr Boulder CO 80303 Office: 770 Grant St Denver CO 80302

MARTIN, SANDRA LEE, official, human resources consultant; b. Denver, Dec. 24, 1949; d. James Edward and Sophie (Conti) M. Student Colo. State U., 1968-69; A.A., B.A. with honors, Metro State Coll., 1976; M.P.A., U. Colo.-Denver, 1979; cert. in bus. mgmt., U. Denver, 1982—. Cert. human service worker Nat. Com. Human Services Workers. Data Coordinator Jefferson County Mental Health Ctr., Lakewood, Colo., 1973-78; citizen advocacy coordinator Colo. Assn. Retarded Citizens, Denver, 1978-79; dir. human resources City of Arvada (Colo.), 1979—; cons. stress mgmt., volunteerism, orgnl. devel. Mem. human devel. policy commn. Internat. City Mgmt. Assn., 1982. Bd. dirs. Jefferson County Mental Health Ctr., 1982—; chmn. nominations com. Assn. Retarded Citizens Colo., 1982—; v.p. Assn. Retarded Citizens Jefferson County, 1980-82; pres. Family Tree Bd., 1981-82. Selected speaker White House Regional Conf. Volunteerism, San Francisco, 1981. Mem. Nat. Conf. Social Welfare, Am. Soc. Profl. Exec. Women, Profl. Women in Pub. Sector, U.S. Conf. Mayors, U.S. Conf. Human Services Ofcls. Democrat. Roman Catholic. Author: Your City Volunteer Program: 5W's and H, 1982.

MARTIN, WILLIAM CHARLES, lawyer; b. Shenandoah, Iowa, May 25, 1923; s. J. Stuart and Chloe Irene (Anderson) M.; m. Marilyn Forbes, Oct. 18, 1947 (div. 1979); children—Ann, James; m. 2d, Kathryn Ann Fahr, Sept. 17, 1979. B.A., U. Iowa, 1946, J.D., 1947. Bar: Iowa 1947, Oreg. 1948. Sr. ptnr. Martin Bischoff, Templeton, Biggs & Ericsson, Portland, Oreg., 1951—; mem. Oreg. Bd. Bar Examiners, 1966-69; instr. Lewis and Clark Coll. Law, 1973-75. Bd. dirs. Eastmoreland Gen. Hosp., Portland, 1960—, chmn., 1978-81; mem. Lawyers Com. for Civil Rights Under Law, Jackson, Miss., 1965—; bd. dirs. Lake Oswego (Oreg.) Pub. Library, 1981—, chmn., 1982—. Served to 1st lt. USAAF, World War II. Mem. Iowa State Bar, Oreg. State Bar, ABA, Phi Delta Phi, Sigma Nu. Democrat. Presbyterian. Clubs: University (Portland); Mt. Park Tennis, Oswego Lake Country, Portland Heights. Home: 3915 S Shore Blvd Lake Oswego OR 97034 Office: 2908 First Interstate Tower Portland OR 97701

MARTIN, WILLIAM WAYNE, controller; b. Dickson, Tenn., Sept. 1, 1948; s. William W. and Bessie (Batey) M.; m. Brenda Anne Sullivan, Feb. 18, 1968; children—Kathy Lynette, Deborah T., Sharon R.; m. 2d Ericka Helene Bridges, Mar. 30, 1979. B.S. in Acctg., Austin Peay State U., 1971. C.P.A., Tenn. Sr. acct. Tenn. Pub. Service Commn., Nashville, 1971-75; revenue requirements mgr. Continental Telephone Service Corp. (name changed to Contel Service Corp.), Eastern Region, Dulles, Va., 1979, asst. v.p. revenue requirements, Western Region, Bakersfield, Calif., 1979-81, asst. v.p., controller, 1981—. Vice pres. Plaza Girls Bobby-Sox Softball League, 1981, pres., 1982. Mem. Am. Inst. C.P.A.s, Am. Mgmt. Assn. Republican.

MARTIN, YOLANDA MAY, software systems specialist, data processor; b. Hull, Ill., May 28, 1945; s. James Wesley and Doll (Farnsworth) M.; B.S. in Math., U. Mo., Kansas City, 1969; postgrad. Rochester (N.Y.) Inst. Tech., Am. Grad. Sch. Internat. Mgmt., 1979-80; spl. student Thunderbird Sch. Mgmt., 1979; m. Lyle L. Borrowman, 1964 (div. 1975); children—Rhonda Suzanne, Eric Todd, Carl Edward. Programmer, AT&T Co., Kansas City, Mo., 1969-74, Xerox Corp., Rochester, 1974-76; sr. data base analyst, data adminstrn. Am. Express Credit Card Co., Phoenix, 1976-80; software systems specialist CAPEX, Phoenix, 1980-82; sr. assoc. programmer/ptnr. IBM GPD IMS Systems Support, Tucson, 1982—; data processing cons. INTEL, Austin, Tex., 1982. Vol. adult probation aide Maricopa County Adult Probation Dept. Mem. Assn. Computing Machinery, Assn. Systems Mgmt. (v.p. activities 1980), Data Processing Mgmt. Assn. Ariz. Council Engring. and Sci. Assns. (chmn. edn. com. 1982—), Mensa, Intertel. Clubs: So. Ariz. Hiking, IBM Tennis, IBM Ski. Home: PO Box 17090 Tucson AZ 85731 Office: IBM Dept 82L Bldg 031 GPD 9000 S Rita Rd Tucson AZ 85744

MARTINELL, WILLIAM LAWRENCE, wood preserving co. exec.; b. Savanna, Ill., Oct. 16, 1922; s. Lawrence Constance and Mary Margaret (Pieruccini) M.; m. Betty Joan Croker, June 14, 1947; children—Laura Lynn, Patricia Elayne, Karen Ann, William L., Robyn Leigh. B.S. in Indsl. Mgmt., Ga. Inst. Tech., 1947. Plant mgr., v.p. procurement So. Wood Preserving Co., Atlanta, 1947-69; v.p. ops. So. Wood Piedmont Co., Spartamburg, S.C., 1970-77, exec. v.p., dir., 1978-80; pres., chief operating officer, J.H. Baxter & Co., San Mateo, Calif., 1980—, also dir. Served to lt. USN, 1942-46. Mem. Am. Wood Preservers Assn., Ry. Tie Assn. (pres. 1979-80), So. Pressure Treaters Assn. (pres. 1977-78), Western Wood Preservers Inst. Republican. Roman Catholic. Clubs: San Mateo Rotary, East Point, Ga. Rotary (pres. 1966-67), K.C. Office: PO Box 5902 San Mateo CA 94402

MARTINEZ, ALEJANDRO MACIAS, clinical psychologist; b. Mexico City, Mar. 28, 1951; s. Octaviano Garcia Martinez and Esperanza Macias de Martinez; m. Deidre Alexis LeMelle, July 3, 1971; children—Fernando Octavio, Dacia Leticia. B.A., Harvard U., 1969; M.A. in Psychology, U. Mich., 1975, Ph.D. in Clin. Psychology, 1980. Psychology intern Washtenaw County Community Mental Health Ctr., Ypsilanti, Mich., 1974-76, U. Mich. Counseling Ctr., Ann Arbor, 1977-78; research asst. Inst. Social Research, U. Mich., 1977-79; staff psychologist Cowell Student Health Ctr., Stanford (Calif.) U., 1979—; cons., instr. in field. Mem. Am. Psychol. Assn., Bicultural Assn. Spanish Speaking Therapists and Advs. Democrat. Roman Catholic. Contbr. articles to profl. jours. Office: Cowell Student Health Ctr Stanford U Stanford CA 94305

MARTINEZ, ALEX G., state senator; b. 1926. Ed. St. Michael's Coll., Coll. Santa Fe. Agt. for A.T. & S.F. Ry.; mem. N.Mex. Ho. of Reps., 1963-66, N.Mex. State Senate, 1967—. Served with U.S. Army, 1943-45; PTO. Decorated Purple Heart with 2 oak leaf clusters. Mem. Am. Legion, VFW, Order Purple Heart, YMCA (dir.). Democrat. Roman Catholic. Club: Kiwanis. Home: 1949 Hopi Rd Santa Fe NM 87501 Office: New Mexico State Senate Santa Fe NM 87503

MARTINEZ, KARL ALLEN, venture capital investments co. exec., development exec.; b. Sugar City, Colo., June 6, 1949; s. Paul and Eleanor Martinez; student Met. State Coll., Denver, Regis Coll., Denver; m. Virginia Mary Sanchez, Nov. 4, 1978; children—Karie, DeWayne, Evette. Agt., IRS, 1973-80; pres., asst. exec. dir. El Dorado-Denver Industries Inc., 1980—; v.p. Villa Central Devel. Corp., El Dorado Devel. Co., Inc., Denver Central, Inc., tax mgmt. cons. Served with USAR, 1968-70. Mem. Am. Mgmt. Assn., Am. G.I. Forum, Assn. Hispanic Employment Coordinators. Democrat. Roman Catholic. Home: 1240 E 85th Pl Denver CO 80229 Office: 4142 Tejon St Denver CO 80211

MARTINEZ, MATTHEW GILBERT, congressman; b. Walsenburg, Colo. Feb. 14, 1929; s. Matthew Joseph and Helen (Hayes) M.; m. Elvira Yorba, Jan. 7, 1950; children—Matthew, Diane, Susan, Michael, Carol Ann. Student Los Angeles Trade Tech. Coll. Mem. Calif. Sold Waste Mgmt. Bd., 1977-80; mem. Monterey Park (Calif.) City Council, 1974-80; mem. Calif. Assembly, Sacramento, 1980-82; mem. 97th Congress from 30th Calif. Dist. Served with USMC. Recipient spl. award for service Monterey Park Boys Club, 1979. Mem. VFW, Hispanic Am. Democrats, Nat. Assn. Latino Elected Ofcls., Am. Legion. Lodge: Rotary (Rotarian of Yr. Monterey Park, Paul Harris fellow).

MARTINEZ, ROY, ins. agt., former supt. schs.; b. Taos, N.Mex., May 27, 1930; s. Eduardo D. and Elma (Flores) M.; B.A., N.Mex. Highlands U., 1956, M.A. in Ednl. Adminstrn., 1963, postgrad. 1964-77; postgrad. U. Calif. Extension, San Diego, 1969, Chapman Coll., 1974, U. N.Mex., 1978-81; IDEA fellows program Antioch U., 1979; m. Betty, Apr. 7, 1951; children—Christina, Paul, Charles. Tchr. social studies and English, Vaughn (N.Mex.) pub. schs., 1956-58, also adv. yearbook; tchr. math. and English Taos (N.Mex.) Jr. High Sch., 1958-62; tchr. English, Taos High Sch., 1962-66, counselor, 1965-66, also adv. yearbook; dir. spl. services Taos Mcpl. Schs., 1966-68, asst. prin. Taos High Sch., 1968-71, dir. fed. projects, 1971-78, supt. schs., 1978-81; agt. Prudential Ins. Co., 1981—; Exec. dir. Boys' Club of Taos Valley, Inc., 1965-80; dir. Neighborhood Youth Corps, Taos, 1971-75. Served with U.S. Army, 1950-52; Korea. Named Taos Citizen of Year, 1962. Mem. NEA (life), Vaughn Edn. Assn., Taos County Edn. Assn. (pres. 1957-58), N.Mex. Council on Edn., Am. Assn. Sch. Adminstrs., Nat. Assn. Neighborhood Youth Corps Dirs., Taos Mcpl. Edn. Assn. (pres. 1964-65). Democrat. Roman Catholic. Club: Optimist (Internat. President's Heritage award 1976, pres. 1971-74, 78-80). Contbr. curriculum guides to local sch. dist. Home: PO Box 1193 Los Cordovas Route Taos NM 87571 Office: PO Box 1886 Taos NM 87571

MARTING, VIRGINIA EMILY, management information services executive; b. Calcutta, India; d. Frederick William Casper and Harriet Agnes Marting. B.S., U. Cape Town; M.S., U. Cambridge; M.A., UCLA. Mng. dir. V.E. Marting & Assocs., Johannesburg, S. Africa; group computer sec. Anglo Am. Corp., Johannesburg; corp. dir. mgmt. info. services Engelhard Minerals & Chems. Corp., N.Y.C., 1978-80, Computer Scis. Corp., El Segundo, Calif., 1981—. Mem. Internat. Fedn. Info. Processing (past nat. rep. gen. assembly), Internat. Fedn. Univ. Women (research fellow), Bus. and Profl. Women (hon. life v.p.), Computer Soc. S. Africa (past pres.), Assn. Computing Machinery. Episcopalian. Clubs: Soroptimist, Toastmasters. Contbr. articles to profl. jours. Office: 650 N Sepulveda Blvd Suite E340 El Segundo CA 90245

MARTINI, EMIL P., JR., drug company executive; b. Teaneck, N.J., 1928; grad. Purdue U., 1950. With Bergen Brunswig Corp., 1952—, pres., mgr. Bergen Drug Co. div., 1956-69, pres., chief exec. officer parent co., from 1969, also chmn. bd.; dir. Bro-Dart Industries, Beverly Hills Bancorp. Office: Bergen Brunswick Corp 1900 Ave of Stars Los Angeles CA 90067

MARTINI, LUC JEAN ROGER, electrical engineer; b. Anzegem, Belgium, May 13, 1944; came to U.S., 1957, naturalized, 1960; stepson Robert S. and Adrienne Irma (Caes) Chaney; B.S. in Elec. Engring., Capitol Inst. Tech., Kensington, Md., 1973. Field service engr. electro-optical systems Westinghouse Electric Corp., Balt., 1973-76, test engr. radar systems, 1976-78; project engr. airborne instrumentation lab. Boeing Aerospace Co., Seattle, 1978-80, tech. instr. E-3A radar system, 1980—; tchr., instr. in field. Vol., Lang. Bank Seattle, 1978—, Children's Orthopedic, also Valley Gen. hosps. (both Seattle). Served with USAF, 1963-67. Mem. IEEE, Brit. Archaeol. Soc., Geothe Inst. (Italy), Sigma Beta (pres. chpt. 1972). Roman Catholic. Home: 20500 244th St SE Maple Valley WA 98038 Office: BAC Plant II Marginal Way S Seattle WA 98124

MARTINI, ROBERT FRANK, aircraft company executive; b. Somerville, Mass., Mar. 21, 1928; s. Robert C. and Phyllis (Ferri) M.; student Northeastern U., 1949-52; B.S., Stanford U., 1954; cert. bus. mgmt. UCLA, 1966; M.B.A., Loyola Marymount U., 1978; m. Mary Jane Conner, June 25, 1955; 1 son, James Robert. Staff engr. Instrumentation Lab., M.I.T., Cambridge, 1955-57; group leader Lockheed Missile and Space Co., Sunnyvale, Calif., 1957-61; lab. mgr. Hughes Aircraft Co., Culver City, Calif., 1961—. Mgmt. adv. Jr. Achievement program, Culver City, 1967. Served with USN, 1946-48. Mem. IEEE, Am. Mgmt. Assn., M.B.A. Alumni Assn. Loyola Marymount U. (dir. 1981-83). Republican. Roman Catholic. Club: Hughes Management. Home: 7886 Truxton Ave Los Angeles CA 90045 Office: PO Box 92426 Los Angeles CA 90009

MARTINI, STEVEN MARK, accountant, business consultant; b. N.Y.C., May 15, 1957; s. Mario and Edna (Gross) M. B.S. in Acctg., Ariz. State U., 1979; postgrad. Golden Gate U., 1981—. C.P.A., Calif. Staff acct. Bash, Gesas & Co., Beverley Hills, Calif., 1979-81; sr. acct., mgr. Tanner & Mainstain, Los Angeles, 1981—; active Vol. Income Tax Assistance. Vol. various diabetic funds; treas. Commodore Homeowners Assn. Mem. Calif. Soc. C.P.A.s, Am. Inst. C.P.A.s. Democrat. Jewish.

MARTINSON, STEVEN LEROY, health services adminstr.; b. Kansas City, Kans., Aug. 18, 1949; s. Clarence and Ruth Marie (Newland) M.; A.B., U. Minn., Duluth, 1971; M.S.W., Fla. State U., 1974; m. Kathleen Ann Peterson, Feb. 14, 1971; children—Eric Beowulf, Matthew Tor. Assistantship, Fla. State U., 1972-74; psychiat. social worker Kern View Community Mental Health Center, Bakersfield, Calif., 1974-75, mental health planning analyst, 1975-76, substance abuse program coordinator, 1976—; participant 1st Ann. Needs Assessment Conf., 1977, Ohio Drug Studies Inst., 1979. Kern County Mental Health Services bldg. grantee, 1975. Mem. Assn. Calif. Drug Abuse Program Coordinators. Democrat. Lodges: East Bakersfield Optimist, Eagles. Contbr. articles to profl. publs. Home: 3311 Camellia Dr Bakersfield CA 93306 Office: 1960 Flower St Bakersfield CA 93305

MARTYN-GODFREY, BARRY (BARRY MARTYN), jazz musician; b. Egham, Surrey, Eng., Feb. 23, 1941; came to U.S., 1972; s. John Richard and Kathleen Elizabeth (Armstrong) G.; student pvt. schs., Surrey; children—Emile Wesley, Benjamin Blue. Numerous appearances as band leader, singer and jazz drummer with own band, Europe and U.S., 1955-72; bandleader The Legends of Jazz, 1973—, tours of Europe, Can. and U.S., 1973—; rec. artist Crescent Jazz; headliner, mus. dir. show 1000 Years of Jazz, 1979—; producer jazz shows internationally; writer and lectr. on New Orleans jazz. Mem. Am. Fedn. Musicians. Episcopalian. Office: 22217 Dolorosa St Woodland Hills CA 91367

MARTZ, DONALD LEROY, physicist; b. Claremore, Okla., Apr. 13, 1934; s. Lester Leroy and Irene (Croy) M.; student Calif. State U., 1957-59, B.S. in Physics, 1963; m. Betty Jean Jordan, Aug. 21, 1959; children—Kelly Ann, Steven Eric. Mem. tech. staff Space Gen., El Monte, Calif., 1962-63; sr. research scientist Heliodyne Corp., Los Angeles, 1964-69; prin. research scientist KMS Tech. Center, Los Angeles, 1970-73; mgr. threat analysis Aerospace Corp., El Segundo, Calif., 1973-78, dir., sr. staff engr., 1979—; guest lectr. UCLA, 1962-64, M.I.T. Lincoln Lab., 1979-81. Served with USMC, 1953-56. Mem. Am. Indian Sci. and Engring. Soc., Am. Inst. Physics, AAAS. Home: 30332 Via Borica Rancho Palos Verdes CA 90274 Office: 2350 E El Segundo Blvd El Segundo CA 92957

MARUSKA, JOHN HANS, marketing and management consultant; b. Trenton, N.J., Feb. 5, 1946; s. John Howard and Ruth Anne (Peterson) M.; B.S., N.Mex. State U., 1968; M.A., U. N.Mex., 1976; diploma Am. Inst. Banking, 1972; M.A., N.Mex. Highlands U., 1981; m. Evelyn D. Martinez, Sept. 3, 1966; children—Jacquelyn, Kristin. With Fed. Land Bank, Albuquerque, 1971-72, Valley Nat. Bank, Espanola, N.Mex., 1972-73; with N.Mex. Parks and Recreation Commn., Santa Fe, 1973—, dir. Bur. Planning and Devel., 1975—; propr. Magnum Enterprises, cons.; chmn. La Acequia de Los Chicos Irrigation Commn., 1978; mem. N.Mex. Soil and Water Conservation Commn., 1981-83; past mem. N.Mex. Coal Surface Mining Commn. Chmn. adv. bd. Embudo (N.Mex.) Presbyn. Hosp., 1972-75. Served with USN, 1969-71. Mem. Nat. Recreation and Park Assn., N.Mex. Park and Recreation Assn., N.Mex. Solar Energy Assn. Democrat. Roman Catholic. Club: Rotary (dir. Espanola 1971-73). Home: PO Box 118 Velarde NM 87582 Office: 2720 Carlisle Blvd NE Suite D Albuquerque NM 87110

MARVIN, ROY MACK, foundry executive; b. Aberdeen, Wash., May 4, 1931; s. Merrill McKinley and Jennie Marie (Larsen) M.; m. Diane Valeri MacKenzie, Nov. 21, 1955. A.S., Grays Harbor Jr. Coll., 1951; B.B.A., Lewis and Clark Coll., 1954. C.P.A., Oreg. Acct. Pope, Loback, McFaddin & Co., Portland, Oreg., 1953-59; controller Ranch Homes, Inc., Beaverton, Oreg., 1959-61; controller Precision Castparts Corp., Portland, 1961-67, treas., dir., 1967-70, v.p. fin., 1970-80, v.p. adminstrn., 1980—. Mem. Clackamas County Econ. Devel. Commn.; bd. dirs. Physicians Assn. Clackamas County. Served as spl. agt. CIC, U.S. Army, 1954-56. Mem. N. Clackamas County C. of C. (past pres.), Nat. Assn. Accts. (past pres. Portland chpt.), Oreg. Soc. C.P.A.s, Am. Inst. C.P.A.s, Planning Execs. Inst. (past pres. Portland chpt.). Republican. Presbyterian. Office: 4600 SE Harney Dr Portland OR 97206

MARVIN, WILLIAM LAWRENCE, traffic engineer; b. Chgo., Feb. 19, 1925; s. Charles H. and Ruth (Ahlgren) M.; m. Geraldine G. Armstrong, Feb. 12, 1949; children—Pamela Ann Wurster, Nels William, Kevin Charles. B.C.E., U. Mich., 1949; Cert. Hwy. Traffic Engring., Yale U., 1950. Registered profl. engr., Mich., Wis., Minn., Iowa, N.Y., Ariz. Engr. traffic ops. Mich. State Hwy. Dept., 1949-62; dir. dept. traffic engring. Wis. div. Am. Automobile Assn., 1962-76; traffic engr. Automobile Club of N.Y., N.Y.C., 1976-78; dir. planning Town of Paradise Valley, Ariz., 1978-79; city traffic engr. City of Glendale (Ariz.), 1979—. Fellow Inst. Transp. Engrs.; mem. Nat. Soc. Profl. Engrs. Club: Elks. Home: 4913 W Eva St Glendale AZ 85302 Office: PO Box 1556 Glendale AZ 85311

MARVIT, YAYOE (GAIL), social worker, administrator; b. Gila River, Ariz., May 12, 1943; d. Gilbert Masao and Alice Tsukiye (Yoshimoto) Kuramitsu; 1 son, Joshua Kamehameha Masao. B.A. in Art, Calif. State U.-San Jose, 1965; M.S.W., Boston Coll., 1970. Lic. clin. social worker, Oreg. Dir. dept., art instr. Kailua High Sch., Honolulu Acad. Arts, 1965-67; med.-psychiat. social worker Queens Med. Ctr., Kaiser Med. Ctr. Multiple Sclerosis Soc., Honolulu, 1970-77; group therapist Alcohol Treatment, Eugene, Oreg., 1977-78; nephrology social worker, group therapist alcohol treatment, 1978-82; dir. dept. med. social work Sacred Heart Hosp., Eugene, 1978—; cons. in field. Bd. dirs. ARC. Mem. Soc. for Hosp. Social Work Dirs. Democrat. Jewish. Co-editor, pub.: The Black Sheep Newsletter Cookbook, 1982. Home: 1010 Polk Eugene OR 97402 Office: PO Box 10905 Eugene OR 97440

MARX, AUSTIN FREDERICK, electronics co. exec.; b. Chgo., May 31, 1927; s. Elmer William and Gertrude (Derrough) M.; B.S., Mass. Inst. Tech., 1949, M.S., 1950; m. Marlene Banister, July 12, 1958 (div.); children—John Banister, Kathy Derrough. Sr. tech. editor Motorola, Inc., Chgo., 1952-53; govt. contract adminstr., govt. sales rep. Stewart-Warner Electronics, Chgo., 1953-57; Eastern regional computer mgr. Beckman Instruments, Richmond, Calif., 1957-60; mktg. mgr. Computer Measurements Co., San Fernando, Calif., 1960-61; mgr. sales planning Hewlett-Packard Co., Palo Alto, Calif., 1961-65, mgr. corporate planning and econs., 1965—. Vice-chmn. registration Internat. Conf. on Planning, 1975. Mem. bd. campus ministry Stanford, 1964-70, chmn. finance com., 1966-70. Bd. dirs., exec. com., finance com. Herbert Hoover Meml. Boys' Club, 1974—; mem. Los Trancos Woods Community Marching Band, 1979—; regent Cogswell Coll., 1975—, mem. planning com.; chmn. long-range planning com. Santa Clara County United Way, 1976, mgmt. assistance program, 1982—; bd. dirs., treas. Am. Youth Hostels Central Calif. Council, 1982—; bd. dirs. Alviso Community Child Devel. Ctr., 1982—. Served with USNR, 1945-46, 51-52. Mem. Peninsula Mktg. Assn. (chmn. edn. adv. com. 1966-67, dir. 1967-68, pres. 1968-69), Corp. Planners Assn. (sec. 1969, pres. 1970, dir. 1971), WESCON (chmn. registration 1969), AAAS, World Future Soc., N.Am. Soc. for Corporate Planning, Nat. Assn. Bus. Economists, IEEE, Instrument Soc. Am., Inst. Noetic Scis. (dir., treas. 1979—), Strategic Mgmt. Soc. (founding mem.), Calif. C. of C. (econ. adv. council 1979—), Sigma Xi, Tau Beta Pi (pres. San Francisco Peninsula Alumnus chpt. 1972), Eta Kappa Nu, Sigma Chi, Presbyn. (ruling elder 1973—, v.p. trustees, chmn. mission dept. 1973-74). Home: 2453 Mosswood Lane Santa Clara CA 95051 Office: 3000 Hanover St Palo Alto CA 94304

MARX, DONALD LAWRENCE, air force officer; b. Gary, Ind., Jan. 30, 1942; s. Harold Edward and Hazel E. (Small) M.; B.S.E.E., Purdue

U., 1964; M.S. in Systems Mgmt., U. So. Calif., 1977; m. Ruth Helen Davidson, Aug. 31, 1963; children—Patti Lee, Donald Lawrence. Commd. 2d lt. U.S. Air Force, 1964, advanced through grades to col., 1982; fighter and interceptor pilot, 1966-68; forward air controller, 1968-69; instr. pilot, 1970-72; air ops. staff officer, 1972-74; USAF exptl. test pilot, 1974-78; aerospace research flight test officer Peterson AFB, Colo., 1978-81; chief weapons div. Hdqrs. Space Command, 1981—; dep. dir. Sec. of Def. Directed Study-Strategic Def. 2000; pres., owner Marcraft Industries. Decorated Air Force Cross, Silver Star, Bronze Star, Air Force Commendation medals; Cross of Gallantry (Vietnam). Mem. Soc. Exptl. Test Pilots, Air Force Assn., IEEE. Republican. Methodist. Contbr. articles to profl. jours. Home: 13925 Wyandott Rd Colorado Springs CO 80908 Office: Space Command/XPAW Peterson Air Force Base CO 80914

MARX, NICKI DIANE, sculptor, painter, photographer; b. Los Angeles, Oct. 3, 1943; d. Donald F. and Ruth H. (Ungar) M. Attended U. Calif.-Riverside, 1961-65, U. Calif.-Santa Cruz, 1971. One-person shows include: Phoenix Art Museum, 1975, Palm Springs Desert Mus., 1977, Bank Am. World Hdqrs., San Francisco, 1979, Bruised Reed Gallery, Montery, Calif., 1981, Weston Gallery, Carmel, Calif., 1981, Kirk De Gooyer Gallery, Los Angeles, 1982; exhibited in invitational and competitive exhibits; represented in permanent collections: IBM, Bank Am., Cedars-Sinai Hosp., Los Angeles, Calif. Farm Bur. Fedn., Sherman Fairchild Sci. Ctr., Stanford (Calif.) U., Univ. Mus. Ariz. State U., Tempe, Also pvt. collections; gallery representation: Weston Gallery, Carmel, Kirk De Gooyer Gallery. With Life Yard Project; trustee Save Our Shores. MacDowell Colony fellow, N.H., 1975. Mem. Artists Equity, Am. Crafts Council. Office: 417 Cliff St Santa Cruz CA 95060

MARYLANDER, STUART JEROME, hosp. adminstr.; b. Oakland, Calif., Nov. 13, 1931; s. Philip and Lilyan (Wolf) M.; M.P.H. in Hosp. Adminstrn., U. Calif. at Berkeley 1956; m. Judith Rosenblatt, June 3, 1956; children—Steven Mark, Grant. Research asst. med. care adminstrn. Sch. Pub. Health, U. Calif. at Berkeley, 1955-56; adminstrv. resident Mt. Zion Hosp., San Francisco 1956-57; asst. adminstr. Cedars of Lebanon Hosp., Los Angeles, 1957-62; adminstr. Mt. Sinai Hosp. div. Cedars-Sinai Med. Center, Los Angeles, 1963-64, adminstrv. dir. center, 1964-66, asso. exec. dir. and adminstrv. dir., 1967-71, exec. dir., 1971-74, exec. v.p., 1974-78, pres., 1979—; instr. Sch. Pub. Adminstrn., U. So. Calif., 1965-69. Bd. dirs. Blue Cross of So. Calif., 1976—, Commn. Adminstrv. Services to Hosps., 1967-76; bd. dirs. Hosp. Council So. Calif., 1968-76, pres., 1975-76. Served with AUS, 1953-55. Fellow Royal Soc. Health, Am. Pub. Health Assn., Internat. Hosp. Fedn., Am. Coll. Hosp. Adminstrs.; mem. Am. Hosp. Assn. (rep. to ho. of dels. 1983-85), Assn. Am. Med. Colls. (assembly 1977-82, exec. council 1979-82), Calif. Hosp. Assn. (trustee 1974-80, chmn. 1979), Council of Teaching Hosps. (mem. adminstrv. bd. 1977-82, chmn. 1980-81), Sigma Alpha Mu. Home: 3644 Ballina Cyn Rd Encino CA 91436 Office: 8700 Beverly Blvd Los Angeles CA 90048

MARYOTT, RICHARD MEANS, quality assurance engr.; b. Phila., Nov. 21, 1928; s. George Ulysses and Eugenia (Means) M.; Asso. in Tech., Temple U., 1955; student U. Hawaii, 1965—; m. Joyce Lemomi Lum, Dec. 24, 1951 (div. Mar. 1983); children—Barbara Lynn, Richard Lee, Carol Lynn; m. 2d, Ida Garo, May 1983. Field tech. rep. Engring. Research Corp., ACF Electronics, Riverdale, Md. and Gen. Precision Co., Binghamton, N.Y., 1955-65; field service rep., quality assurance engr., mgr. Naval Edn. and Tng. Center, Def. Dept., Pearl Harbor, 1965—; profl. practice field engr. rep., Japan, 1955-57, Los Alamitos, Calif., 1958-60, Hawaii, 1960—; concert violinist, 1933-55; night sch. instr. electronics Temple Tech. Inst., 1954-55; FAA cert. flight instr., owner small bus. in Hawaii; night club performer, rec. artist. Chief flight instr., chief check pilot, dep. comdr ops. safety and tng. officer, hdqrs. flight ops. officer and chief check pilot, flight encampment ground/flight instr. CAP, 1971—, head accident investigation bd. Hawaii Wing, 1973; accident prevention counselor FAA, 1972—, recipient cert. of competency, 1972, cert. of merit, 1972, award of merit, 1973, Flight Proficiency Safety award, 1973-74, 75-76, 77-78. Charter mem. Republican Presdl. Task Force. Served with USN, 1940-52. Recipient cert. exemplary performance Def. Dept., 1974. Mem. Soaring Soc. Am. (instr. 1973—), Gen. Aviation Council Hawaii, Hawaii Soaring Assn. (Service and Achievement in Soaring award 1974), Honolulu Astron. Soc., Planetary Soc., Internat. Platform Assn., Parachute Club Am., Nat. Assn. Flight Instrs., Aloha Sky Divers, Siu Lum Pai Kung Fu Club Hawaii, Parachutists Over Phorty Soc., Order Quiet Birdmen, Am. Theatre Organ Soc., Nat. Rifle Assn. Editor: Wing Up, 1972; contbr. articles nat. publs.; star Ursa Major 22 registered as Stella Richard Maryott, 1981. Home: 40-A Ekolu Pl Wahiawa HI 96786 Office: NAVTRAEQUIPC-EN FEO Pearl Harbor Box 526 Pearl Harbor HI 96860

MARZULLO, ANDREW BRADFORD, product engineer; b. San Pedro, Calif., Aug. 14, 1950; s. Ralph Anselmo and Calista (Washburn) M. Student El Camino Community Coll., 1968-73. Quality control analyst Mattel Toys Inc., Hawthorne, Calif., 1970, reliability technician, 1971-75, reliability test technician, 1977, reliability engr., 1977-82, supr. reliability test lab., 1982, sr. product integrity engr., 1982—; gas turbine test technician, Garrett AiResearch, 1975-77. Democrat. Clubs: Century, Torrance/South Bay YMCA. Designer test methods for devel. and prodn. toys. Office: 5150 Rosecrans Ave M S 314-1 Hawthorne CA 90250

MASDEN, FRANK DOLAN, JR., accountant; b. Kansas City, Mo., Aug. 3, 1931; s. Frank Dolan and Allee (Young) M.; m. Barbara Jeanette Schall, Oct. 13, 1962; children—John Andrew, Jeanette Allee, James Elmer, Jayne Evaline. A.A., Kansas City Met. Jr. Coll., 1950; B.S., Central Meth. Coll., 1952; M.A., U. Mo., Columbia, 1955. C.P.A., Mo., Ariz. Staff acct. Touche Ross & Co., C.P.A.s, Kansas City, Mo., 1952-55, 55-59, sr. acct., Denver, 1959-60; asst. to credit mgr., supr. receivables, mgr. spl. acctg. projects Vendo Co., Kansas City, Mo., 1961-67; mgr. gen. acctg., mgr. cost acctg. Misco div. Howmet Corp., Muskegon, Mich., 1967-71; founder, pres. Masden & Green P.C., Lake Havasu City, Ariz., 1972—; mem. res. faculty Mohave Community Coll., 1975—; mem. adv. bd. 1st Fed. Savs., Lake Havasu City, 1982—. Bd. dirs. Community Coll. Campus Found., 1979—; chmn. Charter Writing Com. Lake Havasu City, 1982; chmn. Bond Election and Sch. Consol. Citizen Com., 1978-79. Served with U.S. Army, 1952-54. Recipient Merit award Boy Scouts Am., 1980; named Citizen of Yr., C. of C. Lake Havasu City, 1981. Mem. Am. Inst. C.P.A.s, Am. Assn. Accts., Republican. Presbyterian. Club: Rotary. Home: 2725 Empress Ct Lake Havasu City AZ 86403 Office: 2240 McCulloch Blvd Lake Havasu City AZ 86403

MASICH, ANDREW EDWARD, museum director; b. Yonkers, N.Y., Feb. 7, 1955; s. Edward John and Mary Alexandra (Gibson) M.; m. Deborah Jean Niermeyer, Dec. 27, 1978; 1 son, Matthew Andrew. B.A., U. Ariz., 1977. Curator, Ariz. Hist. Soc., Tucson, 1978, dir. Century House Mus., Yuma, 1978—; chmn. Yuma Crossing Cultural Alliance, 1980-83; pres. Yuma Crossing Corral of the Westerners, 1980-82. Fellow Co. Mil. Historians; mem. Am. Assn. State and Local History, Am. Assn. Mus., Soc. Hist. Archaeology, Westerners Internat., Phi Beta Kappa, Phi Kappa Phi. Club: Calif. Vol. Cavalry Co. A (Tucson). Home: 1490 6th Ave Yuma AZ 85364 Office: 240 Madison Ave Yuma AZ 85364

MASKALL, MARTHA JOSEPHINE, data processing recruiter; b. Kearny, N.J., Mar. 30, 1945; d. Charles Edgar and Mathilda Comba M.; B.A. in Biology, Stanford U., 1966; M.A., Duke U., 1969; m. Edward C. Page, Apr. 4, 1981. Programmer-analyst Leasco Systems and Research, Bethesda, Md., 1969-70; systems analyst Mitre Corp., McLean, Va., 1970-71; data base adminstr. Armco Steel, Ashland, Ky., 1972-74; cons., project mgr. Rand Info. Systems, San Francisco, 1974-78; mgr. systems devel. fleet services div. Itel Corp., San Francisco, 1978-79; Datacom sales rep. ADR, San Francisco, 1980-81; systems engr. Four-Phase Systems, Sacramento, 1981-83; data processing recruiter Mgmt. Recruiters, Sacramento, 1983—; coordinator data base series info. sci. seminars Golden Gate U., 1979-80. Mem. citizens adv. com. on wastewater mgmt., 1977-78. NDEA fellow, 1966-68. Mem. Data Processing Mgmt. Assn. (program dir. 1980, 82, sec. 1983), Nat. Assn. Female Execs., Am. Mgmt. Assn., NOW. Democrat. Home: 8456 Hidden Valley Circle Fair Oaks CA 95628 Office: 2316 Bell Executive Ln Suite 100 Sacramento CA 95825

MASLACH, CHRISTINA, psychologist, educator; b. San Francisco, Jan. 21, 1946; d. George James and Doris Ann (Cuneo) M.; m. Philip George Zimbardo, Aug. 10, 1972; children—Zara, Tanya. B.A. magna cum laude, Radcliffe Coll., 1967; Ph.D., Stanford U., 1971. Prof. psychology U. Calif.-Berkeley, 1971—. Recipient Henry Guze research award, Soc. Clin. and Exptl. Hypnosis, 1980. Mem. AAAS, Am. Psychol. Assn., Soc. Exptl. Psychology. Author: (with P. Zimbardo, E. Ebbesen) Influencing Attitudes and Changing Behavior, 1977; (with Ayala Pines) Experiencing Social Psychology, 1979; Burnout: The Cost of Caring, 1982. Office: Psychology Dept U Calif Berkeley CA 94720

MASLAN, NEAL LYLE, hosp. mgmt. co. exec.; b. Richmond, Va., Sept. 22, 1940; s. Bernard and Anne M.; B.A., U. Va., 1962; M.P.H., Yale U., 1964; m. Wyllie Lugo, Mar. 20, 1976; children—Jonathan Carter, David Asher. Exec. v.p. Cenco Corp., also Cenco Hosp. and Convalescent Homes Corp., Chgo., 1971-72; exec. v.p. Hyatt Med. Enterprises, Inc., Encino, Calif., 1973-82; group v.p., corp. dir. hosp. support services Am. Med. Internat., 1982-83, sr. v.p., dir. Western div., 1983—; dir. Hyatt Med. Mgmt. Services, Inc.; pres. bd. dirs. Med Center Tarzana (Calif.); vis. lectr. UCLA. Served with Med. Service Corps, AUS, 1964-66. Fellow Am. Coll. Nursing Adminstrs.; mem. Am. Acad. Med. Adminstrs., Fedn. Am. Hosps., Alliance for Health Care Cost Containment (steering com.), United Hosp. Assn., Calif. Hosp. Assn., Calif. C. of C. (health care cost com.). Republican. Office: 601 S Valencia Ave Brea CA 92621

MASON, BRUCE BONNER, political science educator, consultant; b. Cleburne, Tex., Dec. 19, 1923; s. Joseph Lee and Daisy (Bonner) M.; m. Jacqueline Tenery, Dec. 13, 1946; 1 son, Douglas Lee. B.S., N. Tex. State U., 1947; M.A., Tex. Christian U., 1949; Ph.D., U. Tex., 1952. Mem. faculty Northwestern State U., 1952-53; mem. faculty Memphis State U., 1953-54; mem. faculty U. Fla., Gainesville, 1954-58, assoc. prof., 1957-58; mem. faculty U. Ill., Urbana, 1958-60; mem. faculty Ariz. State U., Tempe, 1960—, prof. polit. sci., 1963—; prof., adviser Nat. Chengchi U., Taipei, Taiwan, 1963-64; expert Inst. Pub. Adminstrn., Accra, Ghana, 1966-67; cons. local govt. adminstrn.; cons. on elections ABC-TV, 1962—. Pres. Community Mental Health Services, 1980-82; pres. Max Connolly Meml. Trust, 1980—. Recipient Provost's Research award Ariz. State U., 1981. Mem. Am. Polit. Sci. Assn., Am. Soc. Pub. Adminstrn., Western Polit. Sci. Assn., Am. Legion. Democrat. Unitarian. Author: Constitutional Government in Arizona, 1963, 7th edit., 1982; A Guide to the Arizona Constitution, 1982; contbr. articles to profl. jours. Office: Dept Polit Sci Ariz State U Tempe AZ 85287

MASON, DAVID MALCOLM, chemical engineering educator; b. Los Angeles, Jan. 7, 1921; s. David Malcolm and Anna (McKelvy) M.; B.S., Calif. Inst. Tech., 1943, M.S., 1946, Ph.D., 1947; m. Honora Elizabeth MacPherson, Sept. 12, 1953. Design chem. engr. Standard Oil of Calif., 1943-46; instr. chem. engring. Calif. Inst. Tech., Pasadena, 1949-52, resident group supr. applied chemistry Jet Propulsion Lab., 1952-55; assoc. prof. chem. engring. and chemistry, Stanford U., 1955-59, chmn. div. chem. engring., 1955-60, prof. chem. engring. and chemistry, 1959—, chmn. dept. chem. engring., 1960-72, assoc. dean undergrad. studies, 1973-77, David M. Mason lectr. chem. engring., 1975—, assoc. dean engring. for student—faculty affairs, 1979-82; cons. in field. Served with USN, 1943-46; PTO. NSF fellow, Imperial Coll., London, 1964-65; recipient Disting. Alumni award Calif. Inst. Tech., 1966. Fellow Am. Inst. Chem. Engrs.; mem. Am. Chem. Soc., Electrochem. Soc., AAAS, Am. Soc. Engring. Edn., Sigma Xi, Tau Beta Pi. Republican. Contbr. articles to profl. jours. Home: 148 Doud Dr Los Altos CA 94022 Office: Dept Chem Engring Stanford U Stanford CA 94305

MASON, DEAN TOWLE, physician, med. educator; b. Berkeley, Calif., Sept. 20, 1932; s. Ira Jenckes and Florence Mable (Towle) M.; A.B., in Chemistry, Duke, 1954, M.D. (1st in class), 1958; m. Maureen O'Brien, June 22, 1957; children—Kathleen, Alison. Intern Osler Med. Service, Johns Hopkins Hosp., 1958-59, med. resident, 1960-61; med. resident Duke Med. Center, 1959-60; clin. assoc. cardiology br. Nat. Heart Inst., 1961-63, asst. sect. chief cardiovascular diagnosis, sr. investigator and attending physician, 1963-68; prof. medicine and physiology, chief sect. cardiovascular medicine U. Calif. at Davis Sch. Medicine, 1968—; cons. Letterman Gen. Hosp., Travis AFB Med. Center. Cons. research and tng. grants Nat. Heart and Lung Inst., VA; chmn. cardiovascular drugs U.S. Pharmacopeia Com. of Revision, 1970-75. Served as sr. asst. surgeon USPHS, 1961-63. Recipient Research award Am. Therapeutics Soc., 1965; Theodore and Susan B. Cummings Humanitarian award Am. Coll. Cardiology and State Dept., 1972, 73, 75, 78; Med. Sch. Faculty Research award U. Calif., 1978; Disting. Alumni award Duke U. Sch. Medicine, 1979; named Outstanding Prof., Med. Sch. Class 1972, U. Calif. at Davis. Diplomate Am. Bd. Internal Medicine (mem. bd. cardiovascular diseases subspeciality), Fellow ACP, Am. Coll. Cardiology (pres. 1977-78), Am. Coll. Chest Physicians, Royal Soc. Medicine, Am. Heart Assn. (councils clin cardiology, circulation, arteriosclerosis); mem. Am. Soc. Clin. Investigation, Am. Physiol. Soc., Am. Soc. Pharmacology and Exptl. Therapeutics (Exptl. Therapeutics award 1973), Am. Fedn. Clin. Research, Cardiac Muscle Soc., Am. Assn. U. Cardiologists, Western Assn. Physicians, Western Soc. Clin. Research (pres. 1974-75), N.Y. Acad. Scis., Phi Beta Kappa, Alpha Omega Alpha. Author: Congestive Heart Failure; Advances in Heart Disease, 3 vols.; Cardiac Emergencies; Echocardiography and Nuclear Cardiology; editorial bd. Jour. Clin. Investigation, Circulation, Am. Jour. Cardiology, Chest, Clin. Pharmacology and Therapeutics, Heart and Lung, Cardiovascular Nursing, Circulation Research, Jour. Electrocardiography, Angiocardiology, Catheterization and Cardiovascular Diagnosis, Drugs, Jour. Cardiovascular Pharmacology; Editor Clin. Cardiology; editor-in-chief Am. Heart Jour. contbr. over 1000 articles in cardiovascular medicine to profl. jours. Home: 3015 Country Club Dr El Macero CA 95618 Office: Sect Cardiovascular Medicine Univ Calif Sch Medicine Davis CA 95616

MASON, KATHERINE MOLER, social services administrator; b. Martinsburg, W.Va., Mar. 8, 1935; s. D. Grove and Katherine (Hirst) M.; m. Howard Merritt, July 7, 1956; children—Katherine, Virginia, Ellen. B.S. in S.W., W.Va. U., 1956; M.S.W., U. Utah, 1971; postgrad. U. Utah, 1973-75. Group worker YWCA, Washington, 1956-59; child welfare worker Utah Div. Family Services, 1965-71, program specialist, 1971-74, cordinator mental retardation program, 1974-76; dept. dir. Office Family, Children and Adult Services, Dept. Social and Health Services State of Wash., Olympia, 1976-78, asst. dir. program and adminstrn. div. developmental disabilities, 1979-80; asst. dir. Santa Clara County Dept. Social Services, San Jose, Calif., 1980-82; adminstr. client services San Andreas Regional Ctr., San Jose, 1982—. Mem. AAUW (dir. San Jose br. 1981-83), Am. Pub. Welfare Assn. (dir. 1980-82, nat. membership chairperson 1980-82, regional membership chairperson 1975-80). Democrat. Episcopalian. Contbr. in field. Home: 1096 Prevost Ct San Jose CA 95125 Office: 1270 S Winchester Blvd San Jose CA 95150

MASON, NAOMI ANN, interior designer; b. Kansas City, Kans., Mar. 11, 1934; d. Hugh Frederick and Lottie Elizabeth (Granstrom) Guilford; m. Ronald Anthony Mason, June 28, 1954; children—Teresa, Sheryl, Christina, Ronald Anthony. A.A., Kansas City (Mo.) Jr. Coll., 1954; B.A. in Home Econs., Calif. State U.-Long Beach, 1981. Sec., Kansas City Gas Co. (Mo.), 1954-55, Hughes Aircraft Co., Culver City, Calif., 1957-59; owner Mason Interiors, Orange, Calif., 1980—. Mem. Am. Soc. Interior Designers, Omicron Nu Soc. Republican. Lutheran. Co-host weekly TV program A Slice of Orange, 1982—.

MASON, PEGGY, petroleum company executive; b. Mt. Vernon, Wash., Aug. 31, 1932; d. James Geddes and Margaret (McNaught) Murray; m. Donald Kent Hill, Mar. 26, 1960; 1 son, Harry James; m. 2d, Mort Devol Mason, Mar. 5, 1976. Student U. Alaska, 1981—. Accredited personnel mgr. Personnel Accreditation Inst. Dir. adminstrn., personnel Alaska Pacific Assurance, Anchorage, 1974-77; asst. to pres. Alaska Gen. Alarm Co., Anchorage, 1978-79; personnel mgr. Tesoro Alaska Petroleum Co., Anchorage, 1979—. Bd. dirs. Cook Inlet Native Assn. Pvt. Industry Council; mem. Job Service Employers Com.; bd. dirs. BNA Personnel Policies Forum; mem. Am. Cancer Soc., 1968-72; sec., treas. Kings Lake Camp, Inc., Anchorage, 1967-78; bd. dirs. McLaughlin Youth Ctr. Adv. Bd., Anchorage, 1971-73; mem. Tesoro Polit. Action Com., 1981-82. Mem. Anchorage Personnel Assn. (pres.), Pacific NW Personnel Mgmt. Assn. (bd. dirs.), Am. Soc. Personnel Adminstrn., Am. Assn. for Affirmative Action.

MASON, ROBERT HAL, business and management educator; b. Durango, Colo., Jan. 16, 1929; s. Edison and Rhea Lucretia (Easterling) M.; m. Marilyn Kay Humphreys, Apr. 13, 1958; children—Karl Craig, Kristin Denise. B.S., Colo. State U., 1955, M.S., 1957; Ph.D. (Stanford Sloan fellow 1962-63, Standard Oil fellow 1964), Stanford U., 1966. Indsl. economist Stanford Research Inst., Menlo Park, Calif., 1957-66; asst. prof. Grad. Sch. Mgmt., UCLA, 1966-69, assoc. prof., 1969-73, prof. internat. bus. and bus. policy, 1973—; cons. to various govt. agys., pvt. orgns. Co-chmn. clearing house task force, mayor's office subcommittee internat. trade, Los Angeles, 1975-78; mem. task force on internat. bus. edn. Am. Council Edn., 1977; mem. task force on internationalization of curriculum Assembly of Collegiate Schs. of Bus., 1978. Served with U.S. Army, 1951-53. IBM fellow, 1977-78; NSF awardee, 1978-81. Mem. Am. Econ. Assn., Western Econ. Assn., Acad. Mgmt., Acad. Internat. Bus. (editorial bd. Jour. Internat. Bus. Studies) Phi Kappa Phi, Alpha Zeta, Betta Gamma Sigma. Democrat. Author: (with R.R. Miller, D.R. Weigel) The Economics of International Business, 1975; editor: International Business in the Pacific Basin, 1978; contbr. articles to profl. jours.

MASON, ROBERT LEWIS, educational administrator; b. Burns, Wyo., July 3, 1929; s. Lewis George and Jessie O. (Dougherty) M.; m. Margaret Wright, Dec. 26, 1948; children—Lewis, Gary, Donald, Marie. B.S., U. Wyo., 1951, M.S., 1955; Ed.D., U. Wash.-Seattle, 1968. Tchr., Cheyenne (Wyo.) high schs., 1951-53; grad. asst., U. Wyo., Laramie, 1954-55, instr. summers, 1955, 56, 57, 60, field coordinator, 1960-62; tchr., coach testing coordinator Laramie (Wyo.), high schs., 1955-60; staff Big Bend Community Coll., Moses Lake, Wash., 1962—, dean student services, dir. agrl. tng., 1966—. Active United Way of Moses Lake, pres. Bi-Centennial Commn. Mem. NEA, Am. Personnel and Guidance Assn., Nat. Wrestling Coaches Assn., Wash. Assn. Community Coll. Adminstrs., Moses Lake C. of C. Clubs: Sons of Norway, Kiwanis, Masons. Author: A History of Wrestling in the Mountain State Conference, 1951; The Legal Relationship between Washington Colleges and their Students, 1968. Home: Route 4 Box 245 Moses Lake WA 98837 Office: Big Bend Community College Moses Lake WA 98837

MASON, WILLIAM A(LVIN), psychologist, educator, researcher; b. Mountain View, Calif., Mar. 28, 1926; s. Alvin Frank and Ruth Sabina (Erwin) M.; m. Virginia Joan Carmichael, June 27, 1948; children—Todd, Paula, Nicole, Hunter. B.A., Stanford U., 1950, M.A., 1952, Ph.D., 1954. Asst. prof. U. Wis., Madison, 1954-59; research assoc. Yerkes Labs. Primate Biology, Orange Park, Fla., 1959-63; head dept. behavioral sci. Delta Primate Research Ctr., Tulane U., Covington, La., 1963-71; prof. psychology, research psychologist, U. Calif.-Davis, 1971—, cons. USPHS, 1968-75; leader behavioral biology unit Calif. Primate Research Ctr., Davis, 1972—; bd. dirs. Jane Goodall Inst., 1979—, Karisoke Research Ctr., 1980—. Served with USMC, 1946-48. USPHS spl. fellow, 1963-64. Fellow Am. Psychol. Assn. (pres. Div. 6 1982), AAAS, Animal Behavior Soc.; mem. Internat. Primatological Soc. (pres. 1976-80, 81—), Internat. Soc. Devel. Psychobiology (pres. 1971-72, Best Paper of Yr. award 1976), Sigma Xi. Contbr. numerous chpts., articles to profl. publs.; editorial bd. Animal Learning and Behavior, 1973-76, Infant Behavior and Devel., 1976—, Internat. Jour. Primatology, 1980—. Home: 1380 MacDonald Ct Dixon CA 95620 Office: Dept Psychology U California Davis CA 95616

MASON, WILLIAM HENRY, podiatrist; b. Pasadena, Calif., Nov. 18, 1949; s. Jack Edral and Josephine Ann (Popple) M.; B.A., Whittier Coll., 1972; Dr. Podiatric Medicine, Calif. Coll. Podiatric Medicine, 1976; m. Susan Carole Boster, Dec. 29, 1972. Clin. instr. dept. podiatric medicine Calif. Coll. Podiatric Medicine, San Francisco, 1977-78; chief podiatric medicine, Reynolds Army Hosp., Fort Still, Okla., 1977-78, staff podiatrist, 1976-78; pvt. practice podiatry, Rohnert Park, Calif., 1978—; sec. podiatric sect. Warrack Med. Center Hosp., Santa Rosa, Calif., 1980-81. Active 20-30 Club. Served with Med. Dept., U.S. Army, 1976-79. Diplomate Nat. Bd. Podiatry Examiners. Mem. Am. Podiatry Assn., Redwood Empire Div. Calif. Podiatry Assn., Am. Assn. Hosp. Podiatrists, Am. Coll. Foot Surgeons (asso.), Am. Soc. Podiatric Dermatologists, Am. Podiatric Circulatory Soc., Sonoma State U. Athletic Assn. (bd. dirs.), Alpha Gamma Kappa. Republican. Episcopalian. Clubs: Rotary; High-12; Mason (Shriner). Contbr. articles to profl. jours. Office: 6920 Commerce Blvd Suite 108 Rohnert Park CA 94928

MASS, SANDRA ANN, computer manufacturing executive; b. Ann Arbor, Mich., July 1, 1953; d. Edward Leon and Lorraine Mass. B.S. in Info. and Computer Sci., U. Calif.-Irvine, 1978. Systems analyst Logic-Share, Inc., Irvine, Calif., 1974-76; project leader Positive Systems, Inc., Los Angeles, 1976-78; tech. dir. Info. Systems Cons., Los Angeles, 1978-79; v.p. ops. Mancom Corp., Los Angeles, 1979-82; dir. applications software Sci. Data Systems, Inc., Venice, Calif., 1982—. Mem. Internat. Word Processing Assn., Computer Security Inst. Office: 344 Main St Venice CA 90291

MASSARO, DOMINIC WILLIAM, psychologist, educator; b. Youngstown, Ohio, Feb. 5, 1941; s. William P. and Anita L. (Zarlengo) M.; m. Karen Thuesen, July 6, 1968. B.A., UCLA, 1965; M.S., U. Mass., Amherst, 1966, Ph.D., 1968. Asst. prof. psychology U. Wis.-Madison, 1970-73, assoc. prof., 1973-76, prof., 1976-80; prof. psychology U. Calif.-Santa Cruz, 1980—. NIMH fellow, 1968-70, 1975; Guggenheim fellow, 1973. Mem. Am. Psychol. Assn., Psychonomic Soc., Internat. Reading Assn. Author: Experimental Psychology and Information Processing, 1975; Understanding Language, 1975; Letter and Word

Perception, 1980. Office: Program in Experimental Psychology U Calif Santa Cruz CA 95064

MASSARO, KAREN THUESEN, ceramist, educator; b. Copenhagen, Oct. 23, 1944; d. Jens and Amalie (Andersen) Thuesen; m. Dominic William Massaro, July 6, 1968; 1 son, Andrew. B.S. in Edn., SUNY-Buffalo, 1966; M.F.A., U. Wis., 1972. Pvt. studio work, 1972—; vis. instr. ceramics U. Wis., Madison, 1976, lectr. dept. art, 1978; mem. vis. faculty Scripps Coll., Claremont Calif., 1980; vis. artist John Michael Kohler Arts Ctr. 8 Artists in Industry co-sponsored by Kohler (Wis.) Co. and Nat. Endowment for Arts, 1976, Ohio State U., Columbus, 1977, artist/industry program Kohler Co., 1979. Nat. Endowment for Arts Fellowship grantee, 1976-77; Wis. Arts Bd. grantee. Mem. Nat. Council Edn. in Ceramic Arts (chairperson exhbns. 1978-80). Photos of ceramic work in publs, including: Whiteware, 1974; Ceramica Viva, 1979; Porcelain Traditions and New Visions, 1981. Home: 617 Arroyo Seco Santa Cruz CA 95060

MASSART, KEITH GEORGE, mech. engr., constrn. cons.; b. Merrill, Wis., Apr. 30, 1916; s. William Wallace and Mayme (Johnson) M.; B.S. in Mech. Engring., U. Wash., 1941; m Helen Eileen Benson, Nov. 14, 1941; children—Carol Ann (Mrs. James A. Kent), Eileen Bernice (Mrs. Thomas B. Fargher). Mechanic, Tropicair Stoker Co., Seattle, 1934-37; design engr. Isaacson Iron Works, Seattle, 1946-49; from engr. to v.p. The Massart Co., Seattle, 1949-81; owner Keith G. Massart and Assos., Seattle, 1981—; ptnr. Massart Investment Co., Seattle, 1954—; dir. Queen City Savs. & Loan Assn., Seattle, 1975-82. Vice pres. bd. advisers Wash. Sch. Bldg. Systems Project, 1976. Served to capt. AUS, 1941-46. Decorated Bronze Star. Registered profl. engr., Wash. Mem. Wash. Soc. Profl. Engrs., ASHRAE (pres. Puget Sound chpt. 1961, dir. at large 1976-79), Seattle Mech. Contractors Assn. (pres. 1959, 65), West Seattle YMCA. Club: Rotary. (dir. Ballard club 1974-75). Home and office: 5520 SW Lander Pl Seattle WA 98116

MASSELL, THEODORE BENEDICT, vascular surgeon; b. Boston, May 26, 1907; s. James Hirsch and Regina Goldie (Chaloff) M.; A.B., Harvard, 1926, M.D., 1931, A.M., 1934; m. Helen C. Weinberg, Dec. 5, 1930 (d. Dec. 1971); m. 2d, Margaret A. Hansen, Mar. 17, 1973; 1 dau., Diane Massell Toberman. Practice medicine specializing in surgery, Worcester, Mass., 1937-41; chief vascular surgery Birmingham VA Hosp., Van Nuys, Calif., 1946-49; practice medicine specializing in vascular surgery, Los Angeles, 1950—; cons. Calif. Dept. Health, 1973-78; chief vascular surgery Cedars-Sinai Med. Center, 1955-71; asst. prof. surgery Coll. Med. Evangelists, 1947-57; ind. med. examiner Workmen's Appeal Bd., 1975—. Served to maj. AUS, 1942-46. Mem. Internat. Cardiovascular Soc., Am. Coll. Angiology (past pres.), Internat. Coll. Angiology (past v.p.), Phi Beta Kappa, Alpha Omega Alpha. Clubs: Harvard, Beach. Asso. editor Angiology, 1967-70. Contbr. articles to med. jours. Home: 4822 Van Noord Ave Sherman Oaks CA 91423 Office: 9735 Wilshire Blvd Beverly Hills CA 90212

MASSETTI, CECILIA ANN, school psychologist, consultant; b. Madera, Calif., May 24, 1954; d. Fred Carroll and Evelyn Marie (Bergon) Massetti. B.S., St. Mary's Coll., 1976, M.A., 1977; M.A. in Edni. Adminstrn., U. San Francisco, 1981 Counselor Woodland (Calif.) Joint Unified Sch. Dist., 1978; intern psychologist Sacramento Med. Ctr., 1978-79; sch. psychologist Madera County Dept. Edn., 1979—, cons., coordinator, 1982—; trainer human devel. tng. inst. programs; chmn. Madera County spelling championships. Chmn. Madera County Acad. Decathlon; mem. St. Joachin's Parish Council, 1982—. Mem. Calif. Assn. Sch. Psychologists, Assn. Calif. Sch. Adminstrs., Madera Hist. Soc., Assn. Supervision and Curriculum Devel., AAUW. Republican. Roman Catholic. Home: 8256 Road 26 Madera CA 93637 Office: Madera County Dept Education 28123 Ave 14 Madera CA 93638

MASSEY, CAROLYN ANNE, business executive; b. St. Louis; d. Leonard and Iselena Anne Savage. B.S., Edgewood Coll.-St. Mary's Coll., 1970. Head nurse U. Chgo., 1975; clin. specialist Michael Reese Hosp., Chgo., 1976; br. mgr. Kimberly Services Inc., Overland Park, Kans., 1979-80, regional dir., 1980, regional mgr., 1981—, ops. cons., 1982—. Mem. Nat. Assn. Female Execs. Buddhist. Office: 8500 W 110th St Suite 600 Overland Park KS 66210

MASSICK, JAMES WILLIAM, heavy equipment mfg. co. exec.; b. Seattle, Jan. 19, 1932; s. Peter James and Annetta Jean (Dormier) M.; B.S., U. Wash., 1954; M.B.A., UCLA, 1966; m. Joyce Allair Puckey, Apr. 7, 1973; children—Scott, Christopher, Kit, Timothy, Nina, Sally, John, Jill. Constrn. engr. Kaiser Engrs., Oakland, Calif., 1957-60; project mgr. Ralph M. Parsons Co., Los Angeles, 1960-65; engring. mgr. Weyerhauser Co., Tacoma, 1965-68; ops. mgr. Western Gear Corp., Everett, Wash., 1968-70; pres. Truckweld Equipment Co., Seattle, 1970—; dir. Truckweld Corp., Puget Sound Lease Co., Pacific N.W. Utility & Supply Co., Truckweld Utilities, Inc., Big Bud Tractors, Inc. Served to capt. USNR, 1950, 54-57. Decorated Navy Cross, Silver Star, Legion of Merit, Purple Heart. Mem. ASCE, Soc. Am. Mil. Engrs., Seattle C. of C., Mcpl. League, Theta Delta Chi. Episcopalian. Club: Overlake Golf and Country. Patentee in field. Home: 11451 SE 326th Pl Auburn WA 98002

MASSIER, PAUL FERDINAND, aerospace scientist, mechanical engineer; b. Pocatello, Idaho, July 22, 1923; s. John and Kate (Arki) M.; m. Miriam Parks, May 1, 1948; children—Marilyn Massier Schwegler, Paulette Massier Holden; m. 2d, Dorothy Hedlund, Sept. 12, 1978. B.S.M.E., U. Colo., 1947; M.S.M.E., MIT, 1949. Engr., Pan Am Refining Corp., Texas City, Tex., 1948; design engr. Maytag Co., Newton, Iowa, 1949-50; research engr. Boeing Co., Seattle, 1950-55; research engr. Jet Propulsion Lab., Pasadena Calif., 1955-58, research group supr., 1958-81, mgr. direct heating and conversion, exec. asst. thermochem. research and systems sect., 1980—. Served to sgt. AUS, 1943-46. Recipient Group Achievement award in basic noise research NASA, 1981, Apollo Achievement award, 1969. Mem. AIAA, Sigma Xi. Tau Beta Pi, Sigma Tau, Pi Tau Sigma. Congregationalist. Contbr. articles to tech. jours. Home: 1000 N 1st Ave Arcadia CA 91006 Office: 4800 Oak Grove Dr Pasadena CA 91109

MASSOPUST, CARL FRANK, manufacturing consultant; b. Manitowoc, Wis., Oct. 28, 1919; s. Hugo Anton and Anna Mary (Auermiller) M.; B.Ch.E., Marquette U., 1942; m. Mary Geraldine Stamm, June 16, 1942; children—James, John. Mfg. devel. engr. RCA Victor div. Radio Corp. Am., Camden, N.J., 1942-44; cons. Gregory Blessing Assos., N.Y.C., 1944-46; v.p. Elgctronic Processing Co., N.Y.C., 1945-46; dir. research and devel. Plastics Group, GATX, Chgo., 1946-59; corp. group v.p. Dart Industries, Inc., Los Angeles, 1960-82; cons., 1982—. Pres. St. Martin of Tours Parish Council, Los Angeles, 1978-79. Mem. Soc. Plastics Engrs., Soc. Plastics Industry, Am. Soc. Engring. Edn., Sigma Phi Delta, Tau Beta Pi, Pi Mu Epsilon. Club: Calif. Yacht. Office: 3340 Ocean Park Blvd Suite 3077 Santa Monica CA 90405

MASTERMAN, CHARLES WILLIAM, communications executive; b. St. Paul, Apr. 20, 1924; s. Carl George and Ruby Matilda (Johnson) M.; m. Patricia M. Walsh, June 23, 1945; children—William, Julia. Sr. Bus. Cert. U. Minn. Extension Sch., 1959. With printing and purchasing dept. Weyerhaeuser Sales Co., St. Paul, 1942-48; advt. mgr. Rilco Laminated Products, Inc., St. Paul, 1948-62; merchandising mgr. Weyerhaeuser Co., Tacoma, 1962-66, advt. and sales promotion mgr., 1966-82, mgr. mktg. communications, 1982—; mem. trade promotion and advt. com. Red Cedar Shingle & Handsplit Shake Bur. Club: Weyerhaeuser Employees 20 Yr. (pres.). Home: 921 Forrest Park Dr Tacoma WA 98466 Office: Weyerhaeuser Co Tacoma WA 98477

MASTERS, LANCE ALAN, marketing, strategic planning educator, consultant; b. Erie, Pa., July 20, 1947; s. William R. and Ruth (Kirkpatrick) M.; m. Coleen Toole Bohart, Sept. 17, 1967; 1 son, George K.; m. 2d, Betty Hart, June 10, 1974. B.A. with honors in Econs., U. Calif.-Riverside, 1973; M.B.A., Calif. State U.-San Bernardino, 1977; Ph.D., Claremont Grad. Sch., 1983. Mgr. western region Arby's Inc., Denver, 1968-73; controller Ryder Systems, Riverside, Calif., 1973-76; mktg. planning mgr. Fleetwood Enterprises, Riverside, 1976-79; corp. dir. mktg. Butcher Boy Food Products Co., Riverside, 1979-81; asst. prof. adminstrn. Calif. State Coll.-San Bernardino, 1981—; vis. prof. U. Calif.-Riverside, 1981—; pres. Mgmt. Masters, Riverside, 1981—; cons. in field. Vol. cons. United Way, Riverside, 1982. Mem. Nat. Assn. Bus. Economists, Am. Mktg. Assn., Ops. Research Soc. Am., Western Mktg. Educator's Assn., Mktg. Sci. Assn., Western Social Sci. Assn. Club: Lions (past sec., dir.) (Riverside, Calif.). Author: The Practice of Marketing Control, 1983; Marketing in the Not-for-profit Enterprise, 1982; Improving Communications Effectiveness, 1982. Home: 2619 Kayjay St Riverside CA 92503 Office: Dept Bus Adminstrn Calif State Coll San Bernardino 5500 College Pkwy San Bernardino CA 92407

MASTERS, WALLACE ELLSWORTH, manufacturing executive; b. Cottage Grove, Ore., June 4, 1937; s. Roy Franklin and Sonia (Hackstead) M.; m. Shirley Ileen Murrey, June 27, 1959; children—Gregory, Nancy. B.S. in Engring., Oreg. State U., 1959. Indsl. engr. Boeing Co., Seattle, 1959-63; prodn. mgr., Tektronix, Inc., Beaverton, Oreg., 1963-78; producibility engring. mgr. Electro Sci. Industries, Portland, Oreg., 1978-80, mfg. mgr., 1980-82, v.p. mfg., 1982—. Republican. Presbyterian. Co-author article for profl. jour. Office: 13900 N W Sience Pk Dr Portland OR 97229

MASTRACCO, VINCENT P(AUL), foods industry marketing manager, educator; b. Little Falls, N.Y., Apr. 3, 1951; s. Paul H. and Ursule A. (Rich) M. A.A., Am. River Coll., 1971; B.A. in Journalism, Calif. State U.-Sacramento, 1976. Asst. info. officer Calif. Dept. Boating and Waterways, 1973-75; account exec. Sta. KMUV-TV, Sacramento, 1975, Sta. KGMS-KSFM, Sacramento, 1976, Sta. KXOA, Sacramento, 1976-77; concert promoter Jetty Prodns., Pismo Beach, Calif., 1979; account exec., copywriter, pub. relations dir., producer Kemper Advt., Sacramento, 1977—; part time instr. Bauder Coll., Sacramento, 1979—; account exec. DJMC Advt., San Francisco, 1981; regional field mktg. mgr. Denny's Restaurants and Sam's Hof Braus, Sacramento, 1981—; instr. pub. relations Am. River Coll., Sacramento; instr. advt. and mktg. for restaurant industry U. Calif-Davis extension, 1983.

MASURSKY, HAROLD, geologist; b. Ft. Wayne, Ind., Dec. 23, 1923; s. Louis and Celia (Ochstein) M.; B.S. in Geology, Yale U., 1943, M.S., 1951; D.Sc. (hon.), No. Ariz. U., 1981; 4 children. With U.S. Geol. Survey, 1951—, chief astrogeologic studies br., 1967-71, chief scientist Center Astrogeology, Flagstaff, Ariz., 1971-75, sr. scientist, 1975—, lunar orbiter Surveyor Projects, 1965-67; team leader, prin. investigator TV experiment Mariner Mars, 1971; co-investigator Apollo field geol. team Apollo 16 and 17, also mem. Apollo orbital sci. photog. team, Apollo site selection group; leader Viking landing site staff, dep. team leader orbiter visual imaging systems Viking Mars, 1975; mem. imaging sci. Voyager (Jupiter, Saturn), 1977, chmn. mission ops. group Venus Pioneer, 1978, co-chmn. mission operational group Galileo, 1981, mission ops. leader, radar team Venus Radar Mission, 1981—; mem. Space Sci. Adv. Com., 1978-81, solar system exploration com., 1980-83, Space Sci. Bd., 1981—; sec. Coordinating Com. of Moon and Planets; mem. U.S./USSR Plan Exchange, 1972-81. Served with AUS, 1943-46. Fellow Geol. Soc. Am. (asso. editor bull.), AAAS, Am. Geophys. Union, Internat. Astron. Union (commns.), Am. Astron. Assn., Com. Space Research (v.p. Com. D.). Asso. editor Geophys. Research Letters, Icarus. Address: US Geol Survey 2255 N Gemini St Flagstaff AZ 86001

MATAN, LILLIAN KATHLEEN ARCHAMBAULT, designer, educator; b. Boston, Aug. 18, 1937; d. George Frances and Lillian May (Herbert) Archambault; B.S., Seton Hill Coll., 1960; postgrad. U. Tex., 1972, Tex. A&I, 1971, Towson (Md.) State U., 1973, Rudolph Schaeffer Sch. Design, 1977-80, San Francisco State U.; m. Joseph Anthony Matan, Aug. 6, 1960; children—Maria, Meg, Tony, Lizabeth, Joan. Tchr. home econs., Surrattsville, Md., 1961-62; ednl. cons. Head Start, Frederick County, Md., 1971-72; head dept. home econs. Brunswick (Md.) High Sch., 1971-72, tchr. adult edn., 1972-73; designer Dudley Kelly & Assos., San Francisco, 1977-82. Chmn. Seconds to Go, resale shop Convent of Sacred Heart, San Francisco, 1975-76. Mem. Marin County LWV, Ecumenical Housing Assn., Women in Design, Am. Home Econs. Assn., Assn. Home Economists in Bus., Calif. Home Econs. Assn., Ross Valley Ecumenical Housing Assn. Democrat. Home: PO Box 1140 Ross CA 94957 Office: 1045 Sansome St San Francisco CA 94111

MATAR, ADEL FAHMY, thoracic surgeon; b. Giza, Egypt, Jan. 18, 1929; s. Abdelhamid Fahmy Matar Affandi and Nabila Hanem; came toto U.S., 1968, naturalized, 1974; M.B., B.Ch., Kasr-El-Aini Cairo, U., 1951; m. Maureen Kelley, May 23, 1963; children—Tarek, Adam. Rotating intern Kasr-El-Aini Hosps., 1952-53; med. officer Egyptian Ministry Public Health, 1953; resident supr. registrar Agouza Hosp., Cairo, 1953-56; med. officer Brit. Hosp., Moascar, 1956; surg. house officer orthopedics and casualty Royal Cornwall Infirmary, Truro, Eng., 1957-58; jr. house med. officer Blood Transfusion Service, Oxford, 1958-59; sr. house officer neurosurg. unit Frenchay Hosp., Bristol, 1959-60, Locum sr. house officer plastic surgery, 1960, sr. house officer regional thoracic and cardiac unit, 1960-61; surg. registrar Wexford County (Ireland) Hosp., 1962; surg. registrar thoracic and cardiac unit Western Health Instns. Bd., Galway, Ireland, also surg. tutor Univ, Coll. Med. Sch., Galway, 1962-65; surg. registrar Inst. Cardiology, Nat. Heart Hosp., London, 1965-66; sr. thoracic surg. registrar Harefield Hosp., 1966-67; research fellow Cardiovascular and Thoracic Found., Laurention U., Sudbury, Ont., Can., 1967-68; internat. fellow St. Vincent Hosp.-U. Oreg. Med. Sch., Portland, 1968-69; chief resident gen. surgery St. Vincent Hosp., 1969-70; resident cardiac surgery U. Oreg. Hosps., 1970-72; dir. intensive care unit Emanuel Hosp., Portland, 1972-76, chmn. dept. cardiology/cardiac surgery, 1980—; clin. instr. U. Oreg. Med. Sch., 1972-76; asst. prof. cardiopulmonary surgery U. Oreg. Health Sci. Center, 1980—. Diplomate Am. Bd. Surgery, Am. Bd. Thoracic Surgery. Fellow Am. Coll. Chest Physicians, Royal Coll. Surgeons Eng.; mem. Soc. Cardiovascular and Thoracic Surgeons Gt. Britain and Ireland, Am. Heart Assn., A.C.S., Soc. Critical Care Medicine, Soc. Thoracic Surgeons, Am. Coll. Cardiology, Oreg. Med. Assn., Oreg. Thoracic Soc., Oreg. Assn. Respiratory Therapy (med. adv.), Oreg. Heart Assn., Oreg. Soc. Critical Care Medicine (pres. 1977), Multonomah County Med. Soc. (chmn. tel-med. com. 1980), Portland Surg. Soc. Club: Multnomah Athletic (Portland). Author articles in field. 1966-67; research fellow Cardiovascular and Thoracic Found., Laurention U., Sudbury, Ont., Can., 1967-68; internat. fellow St. Vincent Hosp.-U. Oreg. Med. Sch., Portland, 1968-69; chief resident gen. surgery St. Vincent Hosp., 1969-70; resident cardiac surgery U. Oreg. Hosps., 1970-72; dir. intensive care unit Emanuel Hosp., Portland, 1972-76, chmn. dept. cardiology/cardiac surgery, 1980—; clin. instr. U. Oreg. Med. Sch., 1972-76; asst. prof. cardiopulmonary surgery U. Oreg. Health Sci. Center, 1980—. Diplomate Am. Bd. Surgery, Am. Bd. Thoracic Surgery. Fellow Am. Coll. Chest Physicians, Royal Coll. Surgeons Eng.; mem. Soc. Cardiovascular and Thoracic Surgeons Gt. Britain and Ireland, Am. Heart Assn., A.C.S., Soc. Critical Care Medicine, Soc. Thoracic Surgeons, Am. Coll. Cardiology, Oreg. Med. Assn., Oreg. Thoracic Soc., Oreg. Assn. Respiratory Therapy (med. adv.), Oreg. Heart Assn., Oreg. Soc. Critical Care Medicine (pres. 1977), Multonomah County Med. Soc. (chmn. tel-med. com. 1980), Portland Surg. Soc. Club: Multnomah Athletic (Portland). Author articles in field. Office: 2800 N Vancouver Ave Suite 242 Portland OR 97227

MATAS, MYRA DOROTHEA, interior designer, consultant; b. San Francisco, Mar. 21, 1938; d. Arthur Joseph and Marjorie Dorothy (Johnson) Anderson; m. Michael Richard Matas Jr., Mar. 15, 1958; children—Michael Richard III, Kenneth Scott. Cert. interior design, Canada Coll.; cert. interior design, Calif. Owner, operator Miquel's Antiques Co., Millbrae, Calif., 1969-70, Miguel's Antiques & Interiors Co., Burlingame, Calif., 1970-79, Country Elegance Antiques & Interiors Co., Menlo Park, Calif., 1979—, La France Boutique Co., 1979—; mgr. La France Imports, Inc., 1982—; instr. interior design dept. Canada Coll. Mem. Nat. Home Fashion League, Am. Soc. Interior Designers (asso.), Menlo Park C. of C. Contbr. articles in field to profl. jours. Office: 200 Kansas St San Francisco CA 94103

MATAYOSHI, HERBERT TATSUO, mayor; b. Hilo, Hawaii, Nov. 21, 1928; s. Zenko and Midori (Shiraishi) M.; m. Mary Yuriko, Feb. 9, 1951; children—Jerold, Ronald, Eric, Kathryn. B.S., U. Mich., 1950; postgrad. Temple U.; M.B.A., U. Hawaii, 1980. Mem. Hawaii County Bd. Suprs., 1962-68, Hawaii County Council, 1968-74, chmn., 1970-72; mayor County of Hawaii, Hilo, 1974—; v.p., treas. Camp Cable TV; mgr. Francis I. duPont & Co., Hilo; owner-mgr. Hilo Investors Service. Chmn. Am. del., mem. exec. com. Japan-Am. Conf. Mayors and C. of C. Presidents; chmn. County Hosp. System Com.; vice chmn. state adv. bd. Comprehensive Health Program; chmn. Hawaii Econ. Devel. Dist. Com.; gov.'s steering com. Hawaii State Conf. on Employment; vice chmn. supervisory bd. Hawaii Law Enforcement and Juvenile Delinquency Planning Agy.; chmn. CETA Consortium of Hawaii; dir. Natural Energy Lab. of Hawaii; mem. Japanese C. of C. and Industry of Hawaii; past pres. Hui Okinawa. Democrat. Congregationalist. Clubs: Y Men's, East Hawaii Kiwanis (past pres.), U. Hawaii at Hilo Athletic Booster, Hilo Rotary (hon.). Office: 25 Aupuni St Hilo HI 96720

MATEJU, JOSEPH FRANK, state instn. adminstr.; b. Cedar Rapids, Iowa, Oct. 18, 1927; s. Joseph Frank and Adeline Clara (Smid) M.; B.A., U. N.Mex., 1951; M.A., N.Mex. State U., 1957. Sr. juvenile probation officer San Diego County, Calif., 1958-64; adminstrn. Villa Solano State Sch., Hagerman, N.Mex., 1965-67; state coordinator Mental Retardation Planning, Dept. Hosps. and Instns., Santa Fe, N.Mex., 1969-70; adminstr. Los Lunas (N.Mex.) Hosp. and Tng. Sch., 1968-69, 1970—. Bd. dirs. Archdiocese of Santa Fe Sch. System, Mountain Plains Regional Center for Services to Deaf Blind Children. Served with USAAF, 1946-47. Fellow Am. Assn. Mental Deficiency (chmn. state chpt.), Am. Coll. Health Care Adminstrs. (state pres.); mem. Nat. Assn. Supts. in Residential Facilities for Mentally Retarded, Assn. Mental Health Adminstrs. (cert.), Nat. Assn. Retarded Children, Albuquerque Assn. Retarded Citizens (adv. bd. mental health devel. disabled program), N.Mex. Hosp. Assn., Pi Gamma Mu. Home: 405 Fontana Pl NE Albuquerque NM 87108 Office: PO Box 208 Los Lunas NM 87031

MATHEIS, MARIANNE AGNES, systems and procedures analyst, human resources development specialist; b. Germany, July 22, 1944; came to U.S., 1952; d. Robert S. and Anna M. (Braun) Pohl; m. Thomas A. Matheis, Mar. 20, 1965; 1 dau., Christine A. Student Sawyers Sch. Bus., 1962-64; B.S. cum laude, Calif. State U.-Dominguez Hills, 1981, M.S.A., 1983. Loan asst. Crocker Bank, Los Angeles, 1962-65; exec. sec. Aerospace Corp., Los Angeles, 1966-78, div. adminstr., 1978-80, staff devel. asst., 1980-81, staff devel. assoc., 1981-81, systems, procedures analyst, 1982—; pres. Career Dimensions, Human Resources Devel. Cons. Firm, 1982—; seminar leader, instr. career mgmt., conflict mgmt., listening skills courses. Recipient Bank Am. award for Bus., 1962; named Woman of Yr., Aerospace Corp., 1975. Mem. Am. Soc. Tng. Devel. (bd. dirs.), Am. Soc. Engring. Edn., Am. Bus. Women's Assn., Career Devel. Adult Edn. Network, Performax Internat. (cert. 1983), So. Calif. Cons. Services. Democrat. Roman Catholic. Home: 1137 W 164th St Gardena CA 90247 Office: Aerospace Corp PO Box 92957 M3/443 Los Angeles CA 90009

MATHER, ELDON HUBERT, fin. exec.; b. Upland, Calif., Oct. 16, 1925; s. Wiley Wells and Glenn Vivian (Shaw) M.; B.S., U. Calif., Berkeley, 1950; M.B.A., Golden Gate U., San Francisco, 1975; m. Anne Leslie Swigart, Dec. 6, 1959; children—Timothy, Richard, Stephen. Acct., Herbert Thielmeyer C.P.A., San Mateo, Calif., 1950-54; internal auditor Crown Zellerbach Corp., 1954-57, audit supr., 1957-62, tax acct., San Francisco, 1962-73, mgr. tax acctg. tech., 1973—; adj. prof. Golden Gate U. Served with AUS, 1944-46. C.P.A., Calif. Mem. Am. Acctg. Assn., Am. Inst. C.P.A.s, Tax Execs. Inst., Calif. Soc. C.P.A.s. Republican. Methodist. Club: Marin Mavericks Sq. Dance. Home: 21 Prince Royal Passage Corte Madera CA 94925 Office: 1 Bush St San Francisco CA 94104

MATHER, KEITH BENSON, physicist, university administrator; b. Adelaide, Australia, Jan. 6, 1922; came to U.S., 1961; B.Sc. in Elec. Engring., U. Adelaide, 1942, M.Sc. in Physics, 1944; D.Sc. (hon.), U. Alaska, 1968; m. Betty Tossell Ralph, July 18, 1946; children—Elizabeth Sharman, Bernita Kaye. Physicist-in-charge Mawson Sta., Antarctica, 1957; lectr. in physics Melbourne (Australia) U., 1958-61; asso. research geophysicist Geophys. Inst., U. Alaska, Fairbanks, 1961-62, assoc. prof. 1962-63, asst. dir. inst., 1963, dir. inst., prof. physics, 1963-76, vice chancellor for research and advanced study, 1976—. Mem. Am. Geophys. Union, AAAS, Inst. Physics, Phys. Soc. (London), Australian Inst. Physics, Archaeol. Inst. Am., Nat. Council Univ. Research Adminstrs. Author: Experiments in Physics for First Year Students, 1951; (with P. Swan) Nuclear Scattering, 1958. Office: U Alaska Fairbanks AK 99701

MATHESON, DONALD MILLS, physician; b. Boston, Apr. 30, 1944; s. Daniel and Isabella (Mills) M.; m. Suzanne Couture, Aug. 15, 1970; children—Angus, Colin. B.A., Harvard, 1966; M.D., Stanford U., 1972. Intern Sacramento Med. Ctr., 1972-73; resident in family practice U. Calif.-Davis, 1972-74; founder, ptnr. Baechtel Creek Med. Clinic, Willits, Calif., 1974—; clin. lectr. preventive medicine Stanford U. Active ecology groups. Mem. Physicians for Social Responsibility. Democrat. Contbg. author: American Health Empire, 1970. Office: 1245 S Main St Willits CA 95490

MATHESON, IVAN MACK, state senator; b. Cedar City, Utah, Nov. 9, 1926; s. Owen and Sarah E. (Webster) M.; student Oreg. State Coll., 1944-45; m. Etta Louise Warren, July 21, 1948; children—Carolyn, Elma, Angela, Renee, Ivan James. Painter Lunt Motor, Cedar City, Utah, 1948-61; dairy farmer, Cedar City, 1961—; chmn. bd. Matheson Dairy Corp., Cedar City, 1978—; Iron County commr., 1963-76; mem. Utah Senate, 1977—, mem. natural resources com., 1977—, chmn. agrl. and health com., 1980—. Chmn. bd. Valley View Med. Center, 1963-75; chmn. public land com. Western Conf. State Legislators, 1980-81. Served with U.S. Army, 1944-46. Named Outstanding County Ofcl. Utah, 1976. Mem. Five County Assn. Mormon. Office: 265 E Midvalley Rd Cedar City UT 84720

MATHESON, SCOTT, gov. Utah. Office: State Capitol Bldg Salt Lake City UT 84114

MATHEWS, CHARLES ANDERSON, electronics co. exec.; b. Cardiff, Wales, Feb. 23, 1938; came to U.S., 1969; s. Mervyn Charles and Bertha Annie (Farrow) M.; B.Sc., Imperial Coll. Sci., London, 1960; m. Stephanie Rose, Aug. 30, 1980. Project dir. ITT, London, 1965-69; asst. controller ITT Gilfillan, Van Nuys, Calif., 1969-71; dir. ops. ITT Cannon Electric, Santa Ana, Calif., 1971-73; dir. tech. services Plessey Co., Ltd., London, 1973-76; v.p. Plessey, Inc., Plessey Trading Corp., Plessey Materials Corp., pres., dir. Plessey Peripheral Systems Inc., Irvine, Calif., 1976—; dir. Plessey France S.A., Plessey Verkauf A.G., Italian Peripheral Systems S.p.A. Home: 11781 Westlake Blvd Westlake Village CA 91361 Office: 17466 Daimler Irvine CA 92714

MATHEWS, LINDA MCVEIGH, journalist; b. Redlands, Calif., Mar. 14, 1946; d. Glenard Ralph and Edith Lorene (Humphrey) McVeigh; m. Thomas Jay Mathews, June 15, 1967; children—Joseph, Peter. B.A., Radcliffe Coll., 1967; J.D., Harvard U., 1972. Gen. assignment reporter Los Angeles Times, 1967-69, Supreme Ct. corr., 1972-76, corr., Hong Kong, 1977-79, China corr., Peking, 1979-80, op-ed page editor, 1980-81, dep. nat. editor, 1981—; corr. Wall St. Jour., Hong Kong, 1976-77; lectr.; freelance writer; books include: (with others) Journey Into China, 1982; One Billion: A China Chronicle, 1983. Mem. Women's Legal Def. Fund, 1972-76; co-founder, pres. Hong Kong Montessori Sch., 1977-79; docent Pasadena Heritage, 1982—. Mem. Fgn. Corrs. Club Hong Kong, Am. Soc. Newspaper Editors. Office: Los Angeles Times Times Mirror Sq Los Angeles CA 90053

MATHEWS, LISA ESSA, educator; b. Modesto, Calif., Nov. 19, 1955; d. Mark Newvia and Elizabeth (Warda) Essa; m. Rick Mathews, Aug. 16, 1980. B.A., U. Pacific-Stockton, 1977, M.A. in Curriculum and Instrn. Reading, 1980. Cert. tchr., Calif. Tchr. primary grades Delhi (Calif.) Elem. Sch. Dist., 1978-80; reading clinic tutor San Joaquin Delta Community Coll., Stockton, Calif., 1980; tchr. primary grades Hayward (Calif.) Unified Sch. Dist., Femmes Club scholar, 1973; U. Calif. Optometry Alumni Assn. scholar, 1973; Jobs Daughters scholar, 1974. Mem. Internat. Reading Assn., Calif. Tchrs. Assn., Hayward Unified Tchrs. Assn. Democrat. Episcopalian. Club: Internat. Order Jobs Daughters (past honored queen 1973-74, Bethel, 263, Modesto, Calif. Home: 1960 Clay Apt 109 San Francisco CA 94109

MATHEWS, MICHEL ANTHONY, management consultant; b. Oakland, Calif., June 3, 1947; s. Walter Cleo and Vivian (Hughes) M.; A.A., Laney Coll., 1968; B.S., U. Kans., 1970; teaching credential Calif. State U., Hayward, 1973; M.S. (Ednl. fellow), Holy Names Coll., 1976; children—Anthony, Ticey. Cons., Bur. Ednl. and Cultural Affairs, Washington, 1973-74; instr. Peralta Community Coll. Dist., Oakland, 1974-75; tchr. Sacramento Unified Schs., 1976-78; adminstr. CETA Program, Oakland, 1978-81; v.p. mgmt. cons. firm, Oakland, 1981—. State Dept. grantee, 1973-74. Mem. Employment and Tng. Assn. Calif., Am. Vocat. Assn., Nat. Employment and Tng. Assn., Calif. Assn. Vocat. Edn., Am. Mgmt. Assn., AAU. Democrat. Roman Catholic. Home: 1127 E 23d St Oakland CA 94606 Office: 333 E 8th St Oakland CA

MATHEWS, PATRICK JOHN, publishing executive; b. Sydney, Australia, Apr. 1, 1946; came to U.S., 1973; s. Patrick John and Kathleen Mary (Munroe) M.; m. Debbie Ponomarenko, Jan. 7, 1971; children—Lawrence, Christian. Degree in Mktg., Ultimo Coll., Sydney, 1965. Advt. exec. USP Needham, Sydney, 1966-70; mktg. dir. Far East Travel Ctr., London, 1970-74; dir. advt. Brit. Caledonian Airways, N.Y.C., 1974-79; dir. Continental Airlines account Benton & Bowles Advt., Los Angeles, 1979-81; west coast mgr. Travel & Leisure Mag., Am. Express Pub., Beverly Hills, Calif., 1981—. Recipient African Travel Assn. award for outstanding achievement in promoting travel to Africa 1977; Clio award 1975. Mem. Pacific Area Travel Assn. (dir. Allied Assoc. Council, 2d vice chmn. So. Calif. chpt.), Travel Research Assn., Los Angeles Advt. Club, Am. Soc. Travel Agts., Am. Travel Assn. Roman Catholic. Club: L'Ermitage (Beverly Hills). Contbr. articles to travel mags. Home: 22653 Michale St Canoga Park Los Angeles CA 91304 Office: 8383 Wilshire Blvd Suite 212 Beverly Hills CA 90211

MATHEWS, R. MARK, psychologist, educator; b. Topeka, Kans., Apr. 12, 1953; s. Ralph C. and Dorthy C. (Quiggle) M.; m. Stephanie A. Scheffler, June 15, 1976. B.G.S., U. Kans.-Lawrence, 1974, M.A. in Human Devel., 1975, Ph.D. in Child and Devel. Psychology, 1980. Research assoc. Ctr. Pub. Affairs, U. Kans., 1976-80; asst. prof. psychology U. Hawaii, Hilo, 1980—; program evaluation cons. Life Care of Hilo, 1982—. Grantee Kans. Bd. Regents, 1979-80, HEW, 1979-80, Hawaii Bd. Regents, 1981-82. Mem. Am. Psychol. Assn., Assn. for Advancement Behavior Therapy. Co-author (with S. B. Fawcett) Matching Clients and Services: Information and Referral, 1981; contbr. articles to profl. jours. and chpts. to books. Office: Dept Psychology U Hawaii Hilo HI 96720

MATHIAS, BETTY JANE, real estate investment company executive, communications consultant; b. East Ely, Nev., Oct. 22, 1923; d. Royal F. and Dollie B. (Bowman) M.; student Merritt Bus. Sch., 1941, 42, San Francisco State U., 1941-42; 1 dau., Dona Bett. Asst. publicity dir. Oakland (Calif.) Area War Chest and Community Chest, 1943-46; various positions in public relations Am. Legion, Oakland, 1946-47; asst. to public relations dir. Central Bank of Oakland, 1947-49; public relations dir. East Bay chpt. of Nat. Safety Council, 1949-51; propr., mgr. Mathias Public Relations Agy., Oakland, 1951-60; gen. assignment reporter and teen news editor Daily Rev., Hayward, Calif., 1960-62; free lance public relations and writing, Oakland, 1962-66, 67-69; dir. corp. communications Systech Fin. Corp., Walnut Creek, Calif., 1969-71; v.p. corp. communications Consol. Capital companies, Oakland, 1972-79, v.p. community affairs, Emeryville, Calif., 1981—; v.p., dir. Consol. Capital Realty Services, Inc., Oakland, 1973-77; v.p., dir. Centennial Adv. Corp., Oakland, 1976-77; communications cons., 1979—; bd. dirs. Oakland YWCA, 1944-45, ARC, Oakland, So. Alameda County chpt., 1967-69, Family Ctr. Children's Hosp. Med. Center No. Calif., 1982—; adult and publs. adv. Internat. Order of the Rainbow for Girls, 1953-78; communications arts adv. com. Ohlone (Calif.) Coll., 1979—, chmn., 1982; pres. San Francisco Bay Area chpt. Nat. Reyes Syndrome Found., 1981—; bd. dirs., sec. Equestrian Ctr. of Walnut Creek, 1983—. Recipient Grand Cross of Color award Internat. Order of Rainbow for Girls, 1955. Mem. Women in Communications (dir. 1979-83), Nat. Assn. of Real Estate Editors, East Bay Press Club, East Bay Women's Press Club (pres. 1960-61, 83-84). Club: Order Eastern Star (publicity chmn. Calif. state 1955). Editor East Bay Mag., 1966-67, Concepts, 1979—. Office: 1900 Powell St Suite 1000 Emeryville CA 94608

MATHIEUX, OLIVIER CHARLES, optical products distbn. exec.; b. Lyon, France, July 4, 1942; came to U.S., 1965, naturalized, 1969; s. Pierre P. and Anne (Blehaut) M.; M.Communications Scis., Inst. des Relations Publiques, Paris, 1965; M.B.A., Northwestern U., 1969; m. Lucia M. Warslewski, Aug. 20, 1966; children—Geoffroy, Douglas. Account exec. Compton Advt., Chgo., 1965-68; with A.T. Kearny, mgmt. cons., Chgo. and Paris, 1969-72; mktg. dir. Feudor, Lyon, 1972-76; mktg. and sales dir. Am. continent Essilor Internat., Paris, 1977-79; pres. subs. Multi Optics Corp., Foster City, Calif., 1979—; dir. Amsa Co., Mexico City. Served with French Army, 1963-64. Mem. French Am. C. of C., Am. Mgmt. Assn. Club: Chantilly (France) Golf. Office: 1153D Triton Dr Foster City CA 94404

MATHIS, VIOLETTE ELEANOR, sauna and hydrotherapy mfg. exec.; b. Kouts, Ind., Feb. 14, 1933; d. Benjamin John and Elnora (Egli) Kaufmann; student Kellberg Inst. Phys. Therapy, 1952-53, No. Bapt. Sem., 1954-55, U. Calif., 1955-57; m. Cleo Donald Mathis, Nov. 5, 1961. Youth dir. 1st Bapt. Ch., Garden Grove, Calif., 1955-57; pvt. practice phys. therapy, Long Beach Calif., 1957-59; owner Rita LeRoy franchise, Long Beach, 1959-60; partner Otto C. Klaye Real Estate Investments, Encino, Calif., 1960-61; co-founder, exec. v.p. Vico Products Mfg. Co. Inc., South El Monte, Calif., 1961—; cons. sauna and hydrotherapy to archtl. and mech. engring. firms. Mem. Bldg. Industry Assn. Republican. Composer designer tech. manuals in field. Home: 609 Howard St Montebello CA 90054 Office: 1808 Potrero St South Elmonte CA 91733

MATHUS, THOMAS BURTON, safety engr.; b. Benton, Ill., Mar. 7, 1920; s. Claude William and Edna Elizabeth (Shanks) M.; B.S., St. Louis U., 1948; student Washington U., St. Louis, 1937-38, Mo. Inst. Accountancy, 1940-42; m. Wilma Fulton, Oct. 2, 1948; children—Edward, David, William, Anne. With Am. Surety Co., 1948-54, Consol. Mut. Ins. Co., Cleve. and San Francisco, 1954-73, Eldorado Ins. Co., Palo Alto, Calif., 1973-74; regional engr. N.W. terr. Harbor Ins. Co., San Francisco, 1974—. Fin. dir. Mt. Diablo council Boy Scouts Am., 1975-77; active Antioch Little Theatre. Served with USAAF, 1942-45; PTO. Cert. profl. engr., Calif., safety profl. Mem. Am. Soc. Safety Engrs., Ins. Engrs. Assn. No. Calif., Bay Area Fire Forum, Nat. Fire Protection Assn. Club: Masons. Home: 3002 Longview Rd Antioch CA 94509 Office: 50 California St San Francisco CA 94111

MATLACK, GEORGE MILLER, radiochemist; b. Pitts., June 14, 1921; s. Allyn Wolcott and Mildred Narcissa (Miller) M.; A.B., Grinnell Coll., 1943; M.S., State U. Iowa, 1947, Ph.D., 1949; m. Meredith Mildred Madsen, Sept. 4, 1943; children—Nancy Christine, Martin, Allyn. Prin. chemist Iowa Geol. Survey, Iowa City, 1943-46; research asst. State U. Iowa, 1946-49; sect. leader Los Alamos Sci. Lab., 1949—, now assoc. group leader. Pres. Los Alamos Choral Soc., 1961-62, Los Alamos Sinfonietta, 1967-69. Fellow Am. Inst. Chemistry, AAAS; mem. Am. Chem. Soc., Am. Nuclear Soc., N.Y. Acad. Scis., Iowa Acad. Scis. Mem. United Ch. of Los Alamos. Clubs: Masons, Eastern Star. Contbr. articles profl. jours. Home: 254 San Juan Dr Los Alamos NM 87544 Office: PO Box 1663 MS-G740 Chemistry Div Los Alamos NM 87545

MATLOCK, PHILIP VAL, radiologist; b. Columbus, Ohio, Feb. 4, 1929; s. Val N. and Irma C. (Bowen) M.; B.Sc., Ohio State U., 1951, M.D., 1956; m. Diane R. Deshler, Mar. 20, 1947; children—Sheryl D., Philip Val, Susan R., Sally I, Regina M. Intern, Univ. Hosps., Columbus, 1956-57; asst. physician Kings County Gen. Hosp., Hanford, Calif., 1957-59; resident in radiology City of Hope Med. Center, Duarte, Calif., 1960-62; fellow in radiology Los Angeles Tumor Inst., 1962-63; practice medicine specializing in radiology, Arcadia, Calif., 1963—. Diplomate Am. Bd. Radiology. Mem. Am. Coll. Radiology, N.Am. Radiol. Soc., Los Angeles County, Calif., Am. med. assns. Office: 117 E Live Oak St Arcadia CA 91006

MATNEY, JERRY ALVUS, sch. adminstr.; b. Decatur, Tex., Oct. 19, 1932; s. Clyde Alvus and Audrey Faye (Minor) M.; A.A., Santa Ana Coll., 1958; B.A., Calif. State U., 1960, L.B., 1961; postgrad. Chapman Coll., 1961-63; m. Nedra Doreen Files, Feb. 18, 1956; children—Dee Ann, Brett Alvus. With Marine Aircraft Corp., Newharp, Tex., 1952-53; corrections counselor Orange County Probation Dept., Orange, Calif., 1959-61; adminstr. Orange County Dept. Edn., Santa Ana, Calif., 1961—; dir. Juvenile Ct. Schs. Orange County, 1973—. Chmn. West Orange County Red Cross Campaign, 1975; pres. Huntington Townhouse Assn., 1964-66; trustee Fountain Valley Sch., 1965-68, pres., 1966-68; v.p. Home Owners Mut. and Exec. Council, Huntington Beach, Calif., 1967-68; councilman City of Huntington Beach, 1968-76, mayor, 1973-74. Served with USMC, 1953-56. Recipient Disting. Service award Huntington Beach Jaycees, 1968; Thom McAnn award NEA, 1968; commendation Calif. Assembly, 1976. Mem. Juvenile Court Sch. Adminstrs. Calif. (pres. 1977-79), Internat. Correctional Edn. Assn., Assn. Calif. Sch. Adminstrs., Phi Delta Kappa. Huntington Beach C. of C. Republican. Methodist. Clubs: Fountain Valley Boys Club of America (dir.); Huntington Beach Host Lion (v.p. 1971-73); Santa Ana Moose. Home: 1421 Arch Ln Huntington Beach CA 92648 Office: 15252 Victoria Ln Huntington Beach CA 92647

MATOWIK, DEENA, accountant; b. Anchorage, Dec. 8, 1952; d. James Joseph and Charlotte (Page) M. B.A. in Music, U. Calif., 1975. Corp. acctg. supr. R.L. Kautz & Co., Los Angeles, 1976-79; payroll mgr. Nat. Med. Enterprises, Los Angeles, 1979—; cons. in field. Mem. Am. Payroll Assn., Nat. Assn. Female Execs. Republican. Office: 11620 Wilshire Blvd Suite 940 Los Angeles CA 90025

MATSEN, JEFFREY ROBERT, lawyer; b. Salt Lake City, Nov. 24, 1939; s. John Martin and Bessie (Jackson) M.; B.A. cum laude, Brigham Young U., Provo, Utah, 1964; J.D. with honors, UCLA, 1967; m. Susan Davis, July 27, 1973; children—Gregory David, Melinda Kaye, Brian Robert, Jeffrey Lamont, Kristin Sue, Nicole. Admitted to Calif. bar, 1968, also U.S. Supreme Ct., U.S. Tax Ct., D.C. Ct. Appeals bars; practice in Los Angeles, 1968, Newport Beach, 1971—; mng. partner firm Davidson & Matsen, 1978—; prof. law Western State U. Coll. Law, Fullerton, Calif., 1969—; instr. Golden Gate U. Grad. Taxation Program, 1978—. Served as capt. USMCR, 1968-71. Decorated Navy Commendation medal. Mem. Am. Bar Assn., State Bar Calif. (certified taxation specialist), Order of Coif. Mormon. Author: Business Planning for California Closely-Held Enterprises. Contbr. articles to legal jours. Office: 4000 MacArthur Blvd Suite 600 Newport Beach CA 92660

MATSON, DONNA MARIE, educational television producer; b. Los Angeles; d. John Churchill Matson and Mary Evalena (Satterthwaite) Matson. B.A., U. Calif.-Santa Barbara, 1952; M.A., Calif. State U.-Los Angeles. Life time cert., teaching credential, Calif. Tchr., journalist, lectr., 1953-67; v.p. Western Video Industries, Los Angeles, 1967-70; pres. Western Instructional Television, Inc., Los Angeles, 1970—. Mem. Nat. Assn. Ednl. Broadcasters, (bd. dirs.), Assn. Ednl. Communications and Tech., Dir.s Guild Am., Acad. for TV Arts and Scis., Oceanic Soc. Produced more than 700 TV programs for PBS stas. Office: Western Instructional Television Inc Suite 570 1438 W Gower St Los Angeles CA 90028

MATSON, GEORGE ALLEN, precision forge consultant; b. Duluth, Minn., Nov. 27, 1940; s. George Martin and Lucille May (Adette) M.; m. Judith A. Wyneken, June 16, 1969; children—Gregory, Christopher. Cert. in tool engring., Santa Ana (Calif.) Coll., 1961. With Aluminum Forge Co., Santa Ana, 1959-78, quality control mgr., 1974-76, sales engr., chief engr., 1969-78; pvt. practice aluminum forging cons., Carnelian Bay, Calif., 1978—. Mem. Soc. Mfg. Engrs., Am. Soc. Metals. Republican. Lutheran. Home and Office: PO Box 417 Carnelian Bay CA 95711

MATSUDA, FUJIO, university president; b. Honolulu, Oct. 18, 1924; s. Yoshio and Shimo (Iwasaki) M.; m. Amy M. Saiki, June 11, 1949; children—Bailey Koki, Thomas Jenji, Sherry Noriko, Joan Yuuko, Ann Mitsuyo, Richard Hideo. B.S. in Civil Engring., Rose Poly. Inst., 1949; D.Sc., MIT, 1952; D.Engring. (hon.), Rose Human Inst. Tech., 1975. Research engr. MIT, 1952-54; asst. prof. U. Ill., Urbana, 1954-55; asst. prof. engring. U. Hawaii, Honolulu, 1955-57, assoc. prof., 1957-62, chmn. dept. civil engring., 1960-63, prof., 1962-63, dir. engring. research ctr., 1962-63, v.p. bus. affairs, 1973-74, pres., 1974—; dir. Hawaii Dept. Transp., Honolulu, 1963-73; v.p. Park & Yee, Ltd., Honolulu, 1956-58; pres. SMS & Assocs., Inc., 1960-63; pvt. practice structural engring., 1958-60; dir. C. Brewer & Co., Ltd., Hawaiian Electric Co., UAL, Inc., United Air Lines. Mem. Bd. Water Supply, Honolulu, 1963-73; mem. Airport Ops. Council Internat., 1963-73; pres. Pacific Coast Assn. Port Authorities, 1969; ex-officio bd. dirs. Research Corp. U. Hawaii, East West Ctr., Stadium Bd.; bd. dirs. Aloha United Way, 1976-79; mem. Hawaii Inst. Electronic Research; mem. Army Sci. Bd., Dept. Army, 1978-80, Army Civilian Adv. Group, 1978—. Served with AUS, 1943-45. Recipient Honor Alumnus award Rose Poly. Inst., 1971; Disting. Service award Airport Ops. Council Internat., 1973; Disting. Alumnus award U. Hawaii, 1974; named Hawaii Engr. of Yr., 1972. Mem. ASCE, Japanese-Am. Soc. Honolulu (trustee 1976—), Social Sci. Assn., Western Coll. Assn. (exec. com. 1977-84, pres. 1980-82), Nat. Acad. Engring., Nat. Soc. Profl. Engrs., Sigma Xi, Tau Beta Pi, Beta Gamma Sigma. Home: 2234 Kamehameha Ave Honolulu HI 96822 Office: 2444 Dole St Honolulu HI 96822

MATSUDA, RALPH S., fin. counselor; b. Kohala, Hawaii, Sept. 16, 1925; s. Kamasuke and Masu Matsuda; student Honolulu Bus. Coll., 1948-49; m. Sue Hayashi, Jan. 20, 1968; children—Johanna S., Alan T., Glenn R., Earle S. Vice-pres. Exec. Life Ins. Co., Hawaii, 1964-66; pres., gen. agt. Investors Adv. Services, Inc., Honolulu, 1967-74; v.p. Am. Savs. & Loan Assn., Honolulu, 1975-80; sr. v.p., dir. Progressive Investment Corp., Honolulu, 1980—; faculty mem. Coll. for Fin. Planning; advisor in retirement planning. Served with U.S. Army, 1951. Cert. fin. planner. Mem. Inst. Cert. Fin. Planners, Internat. Assn. Fin. Planners. Clubs: Honolulu, Plaza. Office: Suite 1177 1580 Makaloa St Honolulu HI 96814

MATSUDAIRA, KAZUAKI, internat. banker; b. Tokyo, Apr. 1, 1927; came to U.S., 1963; d. Chokichi and Fumiko (Tanahashi) Nakashige; B.A. in Polit. Sci. and Econs., Waseda U., Tokyo, 1951; m. Renko Matsudaira, Apr. 25, 1961. With fgn. exchange dept. Sumitomo Bank, Ltd., Tokyo, 1951-54, asst. mgr. fgn. dept., 1958-63; with acctg. dept. Sumitomo Bank Calif., San Francisco, 1954-58; with internat. div. Crocker Nat. Bank, San Francisco, 1963—, internat. banking officer, 1971-74, asst. v.p., 1974-77, v.p. internat. div., 1977—. Mem. Japanese C. of C. No. Calif., Japan Soc. No. Calif. Buddhist. Clubs: Bankers of San Francisco, Calif. Golf. Home: 302 27th Ave San Francisco CA 94121 Office: 1 Montgomery St San Francisco CA 94104

MATSUI, ROBERT TAKEO, congressman; b. Sacramento, Sept. 17, 1941; s. Yasuji and Alice (Nagata) M.; A.B. in Polit. Sci., U. Calif.-Berkeley, 1963; J.D., U. Calif.-San Francisco, 1966; m. Doris Kazue Okada, Sept. 17, 1966; 1 son, Brian Robert. Legal intern Calif. State Dept. Water Resources, Sacramento, 1966; admitted to Calif. bar, 1967; practice law, Sacramento, 1967-78; mem. Sacramento City Council, 1971-78; mem. 96th Congress from 3d Calif. Dist., 1979—, mem. com. on ways and means. City rep. Sacramento Area CD and Disaster Council, 1972-. Campaign chmn. Congressman John E. Moss re-election campaign, 1972, 74, 76; mem. Calif. Democratic Central Com., 1973-74, 75-76, 77-78. Named Young Man of Year, Jaycees, 1973, recipient Disting. Service award, 1973. Mem. Sacramento Japanese Am. Citizens League (pres. 1969), Sacramento Met. C. of C. (dir. 1976). Clubs: 20-30 (pres. 1972), Rotary (Sacramento). Office: 231 Cannon House Office Bldg Washington DC 20515

MATSUKAWA, WAYNE TSUYOSHI, insurance agency executive; b. Wahiawa, Hawaii, Aug. 7, 1947; s. Robert S. and Grace T. (Mikami) M.; m. Diane L. Takiguchi, Aug. 17, 1969. B.S., Oreg. State U., 1969. C.L.U. Pres. Matsukawa Ins. Agy., Wahiawa, Hawaii, 1979—. Methodist. Club: Lions (Wahiawa, Hawaii). Office: 410 Kilani Ave Suite 210 Wahiawa HI 96786

MATSUNAGA, SPARK MASAYUKI, U.S. senator; b. Kauai, Hawaii, Oct. 8, 1916; s. Kingoro and Chiyono (Fukushima) M.; Ed.B., U. Hawaii, 1941; J.D., Harvard U., 1951; LL.D. (hon.), Soochow U., 1973, St. John's U., 1977, Eastern Ill. U., 1978, U. Md., 1979, Lincoln U., 1979; D.H.L. (hon.), Hawaii Loa Coll., 1980; m. Helene Hatsumi Tokunaga, Aug. 6, 1948; children—Karen, Keene, Diane, Merle, Matthew. Vets. counsellor U.S. Dept. of Interior, 1945-47; chief priority claimants div. War Assets Adminstrn., 1947-48; admitted to Hawaii bar, 1952; asst. pub. prosecutor city and county of Honolulu, 1952-54; practice law 1954-63; mem. Hawaii Ho. of Reps., 1954-59, majority leader, 1959; mem. U.S. Ho. Reps. 88th to 94th congresses from Hawaii; U.S. senator, 1976—, now chief dep. Democratic whip. Mem. Hawaii Statehood Delegation to Congress, 1950-54; mem. adv. com. Honolulu Redevel. Agy., 1953-54. Exec. bd. World Brotherhood, Soc. for Crippled Children and Adults; bd. chmn. Kaimuki YMCA. Served from 2d lt. to capt., inf. AUS, 1941-45; lt. col. JAG, ret. 1969. Decorated Bronze Star Medal, Purple Heart. Mem. Am., Hawaii bar assns., Criminal Procedural Rules Com., V.F.W., D.A.V. Democrat. Episcopalian. Club: Lion. Office: 109 Hart Senate Office Bldg Washington DC 20510

MATSUNAKA, HARRY HIROSHI, electronics technology educator; b. Brighton, Colo., Aug. 28, 1921; s. Suyekichi and Tsuru Matsunaka; B.E., Colo. State U., 1980; m. Tetsuko Mary Toda, Oct. 28, 1951; children—Dean, Stanley, Richard, Alan, Robert. TV technician, 1952-70; instr. electronics Morgan Community Coll., Ft. Morgan, Colo., 1970-72; instr. consumer electronics Larimer County Vocat. Tech. Center, Ft. Collins, Colo., 1973-83; rep. Mid-Am. Vocat. Curriculum Consortium. Served with AUS, 1942-45, USAF, 51-52. Decorated Combat Inf. badge. Mem. Am. Vocat. Assn., Colo. Vocat. Assn. Democrat. Lutheran. Home: 3717 S Taft Apt 233 Fort Collins CO 80526

MATSUYAMA, WAYNE SUSUMU, optometrist; b. Honolulu, Oct. 23, 1952; s. Toshio and Ellen Kimie (Hashizume) M.; m. Judy Sayeko Morimoto, June 4, 1977. Student Chaminade Coll., Honolulu, 1968-70, U. So. Calif., 1970-72, U. Hawaii, 1972-73; O.D., Ill. Coll. Optometry, 1977. Lic. optometrist, Hawaii, Ill. Ptnr. Kikawa, Terada & Matsuyama, O.D., Inc., Honolulu, 1977—. Pub. edn. chmn. Am. Cancer Soc., 1979-80; bd. mgrs. YMCA, 1982—. Mem. Hawaii Optometric Assn. (corr. sec. 1979-81, (1st v.p. 1981-82, pres. 1982-83, Man of Yr. 1981), Am. Optometric Assn. (del. to congress contact lens sect. 1982), Kaimuki Bus. and Profl. Assn. (bd. dirs. 1979-81, 2d v.p. 1982-83, co-chmn. Christmas Parade 1980-82). Club: Lions (pres.). Home: 98-1361 Koaheahe Pl Apt 112 Pearl City HI 96782 Office: Kikawa Terada & Matsuyama OD Inc 1109 12th Ave Honolulu HI 96816

MATTERN, DOUGLAS JAMES, computer engineer; b. Creede, Colo., May 19, 1933; s. John A. and Ethel (Franklin) M.; student San Jose (Calif.) City Coll., San Jose State U., 1956-58; m. Noemi E. Del Cippo, May 4, 1963. Reliability engr. Advanced Memory Systems, Sunnyvale, Calif., 1973-75, Intersil, Sunnyvale, 1975-80; sr. engr. Synerteck Corp., Santa Clara, Calif., 1980-81, Data Gen. Corp., Sunnyvale, 1981—. Co-chmn. Concerned Citizens, Palo Alto, Calif., 1965-72; sec. Gen. World Citizens Assembly, San Francisco, 1975—; dir. World Citizens Registry, San Francisco, 1976—; del. Peoples Congress, Paris, 1980—; editor World Citizen Newspaper, 1973—; co-dir. World Citizens Polit. Project, San Francisco, 1983—. Served with USN, 1951-55. Mem. Electron Microbean Analysis Soc. Am. Democrat. Contbr. articles to profl. jours. Home: 2671 Southcourt St Palo Alto CA 94306 Office: 312 Sutter St Room 608 San Francisco CA 94108

MATTEUCCI, DOMINICK VINCENT, real estate developer; b. Trenton, N.J., Oct. 19, 1924; s. Vincent Joseph and Anna Marie (Zoda) M.; B.S., Coll. of William and Mary, 1948; B.S., Mass. Inst. Tech., 1950; m. Emma Irene DeGuia, Mar. 2, 1968; children—Felisa Anna, Vincent

Eriberto. Owner, Matteucci Devel. Co., Newport Beach, Calif.; pres. Nat. Investment Brokerage Co., Newport Beach. Served with USAAC, 1943-46. Recipient NASA achievement award, 1974; registered profl. engr., Calif.; lic. gen. bldg. contractor, real estate broker. Home: 2104 Felipe Newport Beach CA 92660 Office: PO Box 8328 Newport Beach CA 92660

MATTHES, RAYMOND W., tax consultant; b. Chgo., Nov. 4, 1946; s. Hugo Walter, Jr. and Marcella (Coles) M.; B.S. in Accountancy, No. Ill. U., DeKalb, 1968; m. Lynda A. Smith, June 15, 1968; children—Julia Kristine, David Barrett. Sales rep. Coll. Life Ins. Co. Am., DeKalb, 1968; student ministries dir. Youth for Christ Internat., Wheaton, Ill., 1968-72, circulation mgr. Campus Life mag., 1972-76; controller Beechcraft West, Hayward, Calif., 1977-78; self-employed tax cons., Concord, Calif., 1978—; founder, pres. Barrett Tax Report, 1980; owner, operator Tax and Fin. Services, Concord, 1983—; controller Howell Electric Co. Fin. dir. Joni com. World Wide Pictures, Concord; chmn. Adult Christian Edn. Com., Evang. Free Ch., Walnut Creek, Calif. Recipient cert. of appreciation Faith Missionary Outreach, 1979. Mem. Nat. Assn. Accts., Fin. Execs. Christian Orgns., Youth for Christ Alumni Assn. Office: 3052 Willow Pass Rd Suite 205 Concord CA 94519

MATTHEWS, BARBARA ANN, telecommunications account exec.; b. Columbia, S.C., Oct. 16, 1951; d. William Nathan and Lilly Ruth (Harvey) M.; B.A., U. S.C., 1973, M.B.A., 1976. Public relations dir. United Way, Columbia, 1973-75; S.C. Med. Assn., Columbia, 1975-76; mng. dir. Pi Sigma Epsilon, N.Y.C., 1976-78; account exec. Pacific Telephone Co., Los Angeles 1979-83, Am. Bell/AIS, Los Angeles, 1983—. Mem. Los Angeles Transp. Club, Pi Sigma Epsilon, Delta Nu Alpha. Office: 333 S Beaudry #1200 Los Angeles CA 90017

MATTHEWS, EUGENE EDWARD, artist; b. Davenport, Iowa, Mar. 22, 1931; s. Nickolas Arthur and Velma (Schroeder) M.; student Bradley U., 1948-51; B.F.A., U. Iowa, 1953, M.F.A., 1957; postgrad. (fellow in painting) Am. Acad. Rome, 1957-60; m. Wanda Lee Miller, Sept. 14, 1952; children—Anthony Lee, Daniel Nickolas. Exhibited in one-man shows U. Wis., Milw., 1960, Brena Gallery, Denver, 1963, 65, 67, 70, 74, 76, 78, 80, Dubins Gallery, Los Angeles, 1981, Colorado Springs Fine Arts Center, 1967, Sheldon Art Gallery, U. Nebr., 1968, Denver Art Mus., 1972, James Yu Gallery, N.Y.C., 1973, 77; exhibited numerous group shows U.S., Europe, Africa, Asia; represented in permanent collections Nat. Collection Fine Arts, Washington, Denver Art Mus., Butler Inst. Am. Art, Chrysler Art Mus. others; prof. fine arts Grad. Faculty, U. Colo., Boulder, 1961—. Creative Research fellow, 1966-67. Recipient Penello d'Argento award Acitrezza Internazionale, 1958; S.P.Q.R. Cup of Rome, Roma Olimpionica Internazionale, 1959; Gold Medal of Honor, Nat. Arts Club, N.Y.C., 1969; Bicentennial award Rocky Mountain Nat. Watercolor Exhbn., 1976, others.

MATTHEWS, JACK EDWARD, real estate exec.; b. El Paso, Oct. 29, 1928; s. Jack C. and Helen (Guidry) M.; A.A., Los Angeles City Coll., 1951; postgrad. U. So. Calif., 1953; m. Willa Blaine Davis, May 29, 1948; children—Jon E., Vikki. Gen. sales mgr. Volk-McLain Co., San Diego, 1956-60; co-owner Brent-Matthews & Co., San Diego, 1960-62; v.p. Am. Savs. & Loan, No. Calif., 1962-67; sr. v.p. 1st Western Savs. & Loan, Las Vegas, Nev., 1967-69; pres. Jack Matthews & Co., Realtors, Las Vegas, 1969-80, Merrill Lynch Realty/Jack Matthews, 1981—. Sponsor big league and state championship slow-pitch softball team; active Little League; pres. Lions Club, 1975-76, named Lion of Year, 1976; state baseball chmn. Am. Legion. Served with USNR, 1946-48; PTO. Mem. Nat. Homebuilders Assn. (Realtor of Month 1974, Sales Mgr. of Year 1959), Realtors Inst. (cert. residential specialist, designation), Nat. Assn. Realtors (dir. 1978-79), Nev. Assn. Realtors (pres. 1982), Las Vegas Bd. Realtors (pres. 1976), Reno Bd. Realtors, Bay Area Sales Mgrs. Club (charter), Las Vegas Execs. Club. Democrat. Club: Las Vegas Country. Office: 3100 S Valley View St Las Vegas NV 89102

MATTHEWS, NORMAN SHERWOOD, JR., ins. co. executive; b. San Antonio, Tex., Apr. 23, 1944; s. Norman Sherwood and Alice Ann (Hathaway) M.; student Middle Tenn. State U., 1962-64, Ventura Coll., 1965, Calif. State U., 1965-66, U. Md., 1968-70; B.B.A., U. Tex., 1972; postgrad. U. Hawaii, 1977-79; m. Masayo Nakamura, Sept. 1, 1970; children—Debbie Ann, Scott Tsuyoshi. Research asst. State Farm Ins. Co., Murfreesboro, Tenn., 1963-64; inventory control analyst Minn. Mining & Mfg. Co., Camarillo, Calif., 1964-65; sr. acct. Peat, Marwick, Mitchell & Co., Honolulu, 1973-75; dir. mgmt. analysis Hawaii Med. Service Assn., Honolulu, 1975—. Served with USAF, 1966-70. Decorated Air medal with 8 oak leaf clusters. C.P.A., Hawaii; cert. internal auditor. Mem. Am. Inst. C.P.A.s, Hawaii Soc. C.P.A.s, Nat. Assn. Accts., Am. Acctg. Assn., Inst. Internal Auditors, EDP Auditors Assn., Am. Mgmt. Assn. Home: 1561 Kanunu St Apt 505 Honolulu HI 96814 Office: 818 Keeaumoku St Honolulu HI 96814

MATTHEWS, WANDA (LEE) MILLER, artist; b. Barry, Ill., Sept. 15, 1930; d. Harry Leonard and Gladys (Smith) Miller; B.F.A., Bradley U., Peoria, Ill., 1952; M.F.A., U. Iowa, 1957; m. Eugene Edward Matthews, Sept. 14, 1952; children—Anthony Lee, Daniel Nicholas. Spl. services artist U.S. Army, Ft. Riley, Kans., 1954-55; research asst. printmaking U. Iowa, 1956-57; travel in Italy and Europe, 1957-60; producing, exhibiting printmaker, Boulder, Colo., 1961—; one-woman exhbns. include Lehigh U., Bethlehem, Pa., 1973, Gettysburg (Pa.) Coll., 1973, U. Colo., 1976, U. N.D., 1976, Jane Haslem Gallery, 1982, Oxford (Eng.) Gallery, 1982, Am. Center Gallery, Belgrade, Yugoslavia, 1982; group exhbns. include USIS Gallery, Naples, Italy, 1960, Nat. Invitational Print Exhbn., Otis Art Inst., Los Angeles, 1962, 63, Brit. Internat. Print Biennale, Bradford, Eng., 1970, 79, Invitational Graphics, Minot (N.D.) State Coll., 1972, Printmaking Now, W. Tex. Mus., Lubbock, 1973, Colorprint USA, Tex. Tech U., Lubbock, 1974, 78, Nat. Invitational Print Show, Central Wash. State Coll., Ellensburg, 1975, 11th Internat. Exhbn. Graphic Art, Ljubljana, Yugoslavia, 1975, 6th, 7th, 8th Internat. Print Biennales, Cracow, Poland, 1976, 78, 80, Internat. Book Fair, Leipzig, E. Ger., 1977, New Talent in Printmaking, 1980, Associated Am. Artists, N.Y.C. and Phila., 1980, others: rep. permanent collection Nelson Gallery Art/Atkins Mus., Kansas City, Mo., Boston Pub. Library, Los Angeles County Mus., Nat. Collection Fine Arts, Washington, Phila. Mus. Art, Library of Congress, others. Tiffany grantee, 1957-58, 58-59; recipient numerous awards, 1956—, including Purchase prize Prints 1962 Nat. Exhbn., State U. Coll., Potsdam, N.Y., 1962, Prints 10th ann. print exhbn., 1970; purchase prize Dulin Nat. Print and Drawing competition Dulin Gallery Art, Knoxville, Tenn., 1968, 81, 22d ann. nat. exhbn. Boston Printmakers, 1970; purchase award Graphics '71, Nat. Print and Drawing Exhbn., Western N.Mex. U., Silver City, 1971, Soc. Am. Graphic Artists, 1979; Benton Spruance prize Print Club Phila., 1971. Mem. Calif. Soc. Printmakers, Print Club Phila. Studio: 2865 Jay Rd Boulder CO 80301

MATTHEWS, WARREN WAYNE, state supreme ct. justice; b. Santa Cruz, Calif., Apr. 5, 1939; s. Warren Wayne and Ruth Ann (Maginnis) M.; A.B., Stanford U., 1961; LL.B., Harvard U., 1964; m. Donna Stearns Matthews, Aug. 17, 1963; children—Holly Maginnis, Meredith Sample. Bar: Alaska 1965; assoc. firm Burr, Pease & Kurtz, Anchorage, 1964-69; assoc. firm Matthews & Dunn, Matthews, Dunn and Baily, Anchorage, 1969-77; justice Alaska Supreme Ct., 1977—; bd. dirs. Alaska Legal Services Corp., 1969-70. Mem. Alaska Bar Assn. (bd. govs. 1974-77), Am. Bar Assn. Office: 303 K St Anchorage AK 99501

MATTHIES, FRED JOHN, architect, engineering company executive; b. Omaha, Oct. 4, 1925; s. Fred J. and Charlotte Leota (Metz) M.; m. Carol Mae Dean, Sept. 14, 1947; children—John Frederick, Jane Carolyn. B.S. in Civil Engring., Cornell U., 1947; postgrad. U. Nebr., 1952-53. Registered profl. engr., Iowa, Nebr., Wash., Calif., Fla.; diplomate Am. Acad. Environ. Engrs. Civil engr. Henningson, Durham & Richardson, Omaha, 1947-50, 52-54; sr. v.p. devel. Leo A. Daly Co., Omaha, 1954-81, sr. v.p., dir. western region, 1982—; lectr. Mem. central com. Douglas County (Nebr.) Republican party, 1968-72; bd. regents Augustana Coll., Sioux Falls, S.D., 1976—; bd. dirs. Orange County Lutheran Hosp. Assn., Anaheim, Calif., 1961-62, Luth. Hosp., Omaha, 1978-82; mem. Dist. Export Council, 1981-83, Nebr. State Internat. Adv. Bd. Served to 1st lt. USMCR, 1943-46, 50-52. Fellow ASCE, Instn. Civil Engrs. (London); mem. Am. Water Works Assn., Nat. Soc. Profl. Engrs., Air Force Assn., Am. Legion. Lutheran. Club: Happy Hollow Country (Omaha). Contbr. articles to profl. jours. Home: 2383 Century Hills Los Angeles CA 90067 Office: Leo A Daly Co 3333 Wilshire Blvd Suite 200 Los Angeles CA 90010

MATTICE, JACK S., ecologist; b. Hobart, N.Y., Aug. 25, 1941; s. Henry B. Mattice and Kathryn S. Mattice Bellinger; m. Elizabeth Lench, June 2, 1967. B.S., SUNY-Stony Brook, 1963; Ph.D., Syracuse U., 1971. Research assoc. Oak Ridge Nat. Lab., 1972-76, research staff mem., 1976-81, project mgr. ecol. studies program Electric Power Research Inst., Palo Alto, Calif., 1981—. U.S. Acad. Scis.-Polish Acad. Scis. fellow, 1970-71. Mem. AAAS, ASTM, Am. Inst. Biol. Scis., Ecol. Soc. Am., Am. Fisheries Soc., N.Am. Benthological Soc., Internat. Soc. Limnology, Malacological Soc. of London, Sigma Xi. Contbr. articles to profl. jours. Office: 3412 Hillview Ave Palo Alto CA 94303

MATTINGLY, RAYMOND JESS, media specialist; b. St. Louis, Oct. 17, 1930; s. Jess and Ann Elizabeth (Helmich) M.; m. Lois Jane Pilley, Aug. 18, 1961; children—Diane Estelle, Michael Vincent, Vicki Sue. A.A., Grossmont Coll., 1970; B.A., LaVerne U., 1972. Joined U.S. Navy, 1946, advanced through grades to chief yeoman, 1946-66; media specialist U.S. Naval Air Force Pacific Fleet, San Diego, 1967—; dir. media services Naval Air Sta., San Diego; cons. to Navy. Recipient Navy's Outstanding Tech. Instr. award. Mem. Internat. TV Assn. (leadership award editor San Diego chpt. newsletter, pres. San Diego chpt.). Club: Men's (San Diego). Office: FASO Naval Air Station North Island San Diego CA 92135

MATTIS, NOEMI PERELMAN, psychologist, educator, b. Lodz, Poland, Oct. 16, 1936; came to U.S., 1958; d. Chaim Pinchas and Fela Estera (Liwer) Perelman; m. Daniel Charles Mattis, Nov. 9, 1958; children—Michael, Olivia. B.A., Free U., Brussels, 1955, J.D., 1958; M.A., Columbia U., 1963, Ph.D., 1973. Lic. psychologist, N.Y., Utah. Instr. French lit. Briarcliff Coll., 1960-62; psychologist Cage Teen Ctr., White Plains, N.Y., 1973-76; pvt. practice, Scarsdale, N.Y., 1976-80, Salt Lake City, 1981—; psychologist, adj. asst. prof. dept. ednl. psychology, Women's Resource Ctr., U. Utah, Salt Lake City, 1980—, clin. asst. prof. dept. psychology, 1980—. Bd. dirs. YWCA, 1980—. Mem. Am. Psychol. Assn., Utah Psychol. Assn., Soc. Psychol. Study Social Issues, Utah Psychologists in Pvt. Practice, Westchester Psychol. Assn. (past dir.), Alliance Francaise (hon.), Psi Chi, Kappa Lambda Pi, Pi Lambda Theta. Address: 299 Federal Heights Circle Salt Lake City UT 84103

MATTISON, ELISA SHERI, industrial psychologist; b. Grand Rapids, Mich., Apr. 24, 1952; d. Andrew and Lorraine R. Wierenga; m. John H. Mattison, Sept. 29, 1978. B.S. cum laude, Western Mich. U., 1974, M.A., 1979. Cons., trainer No. Inst., Anchorage, 1980; counselor, trainer Alaska Assocs. Human Devel. Inc., Anchorage, 1980-82; job devel. specialist Collins, Weed and Assocs., Anchorage, 1982—; owner Akashic Enterprises, Anchorage; mem. adj. faculty Anchorage Community Coll., 1981-82; cons. Employee Assts. Cons. Alaska, Anchorage, 1982. Mem. Am. Soc. Tng. and Devel. (v.p. Anchorage chpt.), Alaska Psychol. Assn., Alaska Rehab. Assn. Contbr. articles to profl. publs. Office: 2600 Denali Suite 501 Anchorage AK 99503

MATTLAGE, KARL PAUL, lawyer; b. Waco, Tex., Dec. 8, 1940; s. Marvin William and Ruth Edith (Hintze) M.; B.B.A., Baylor U., 1963, J.D., 1965; m. Parilee Ann Hunt, Sept. 1, 1962; children—Lara Annette, Karl Gregory, Amy Kathleen. Admitted to Tex. bar, 1965, Colo. bar, 1971; dep. dist. atty. Fourteenth Jud. Dist., Colo., 1974-75; partner firm Yegge, Hall & Evans, Denver, 1974-77, partner firm Mattlage, Maus & Lettunich, Steamboat Springs, Colo., 1977—; mem. Colo. Hwy. Legis. Rev. Com. Chmn. Routt County Democratic Party, 1975-79, chmn. 31st senatorial dist., 1975-79, chmn. 56th rep. dist., 1975-79; appointed mem. Colo. State Hwy. Commn., 1977-79; bd. dirs., v.p. Yampa Valley Coll. Found., 1979—. Served to capt. USAF, 1966-70; maj. Res. Mem. Am. Bar Assn., Tex. Bar Assn., Colo. Bar Assn. Lutheran. Club: Lions. Home: 1370 Delta Queen Rd Steamboat Springs CO 80477 Office: Suite L Routt County National Bank 320 Lincoln Ave Steamboat Springs CO 80477

MATTSON, HOMER ALPHIN, vocational education consultant; b. Braham, Minn., Apr. 29, 1922; s. Alphin E. and Ida C. (Amnell) M.; m. Joyce B. Anderson, Apr. 6, 1946; children—Brian, Drew, Lee, Faye. B.S., St. Cloud State U., 1951; M.A., U. No. Colo., 1959; Ed.D., U. Nebr., 1970. Cert. tchr., vocat. dir., Wash. Sec. treas. Mattson Builders Inc., Mpls., 1951-58; indsl. arts tchr. Omaha pub. schs., 1959-61, supr. trade and indsl. edn., 1961-69; vocat. dir. Spokane Sch. Dist. 81, from 1969—; now Peace Corps vocat. edn. adviser W.I. Ministry of Edn., St. Vincent; cons. Burroughs Corp., No. Natural Gas. Past pres., bd. dirs. Riverview Terr. Served with AUS, 1943-46. Recipient Spokane Bd. Edn. Cert. Merit, 1982. Mem. Am. Vocat. Assn., Wash. Vocat. Assn., Nat. Council Local Adminstrs., Am. Indsl. Arts Assn., Phi Delta Kappa. Author articles for profl. publs.; creator stained glass windows. Home: PO Box 14974 Spokane WA 99214 Office: N 400 Bernard Spokane WA 99201

MATTSON, JAMES ALLEN, clinical psychologist; b. Seattle, July 4, 1949; s. Glenn Arthur and Lillian B. (Schnaidt) M.; m. Charyl B. Thurber, July 22, 1972; children—Robert Charles, David James. B.S. in Psychology, U. Wash., 1971; Ph.D. in Clin. Psychology, U. Tex.-Austin, 1975. Lic. psychologist, Wash. Assoc. dir. planning and evaluation North Central Community Mental Health Ctr., Columbus, Ohio, 1975-78; exec. dir. Drug Abuse Council, Everett, Wash., 1978—; co-founder Substance Abuse Treatment Assn. Mem. Am. Psychol. Assn. Unitarian. Office: 3409 Colby Ave Everett WA 98201

MATULICH, MARILYN ALENE, sch. adminstr.; b. Spokane, Wash., Dec. 14, 1931; d. Lyndell Lloyd and Florence Genevieve (Anderson) Shields; B.A. in Edn., Wash. State U., 1954; M.A., Whitworth Coll., 1973; m. Mark Anthony Matulich, May 15, 1954; children—Robert Allan, Paul Shields, James Christopher. Dir. Pre-Sch. of Port Townsend (Wash.), 1961-63; library media specialist Spokane Sch. Dist. 81, 1967-76, asst. instructional media coordinator, 1976—. Chairperson, LWV, Spokane, 1964; drive chmn. Port Townsend Cancer Soc., 1962. Mem. AAUW, Assn. Supervision and Curriculum Devel., Wash. Library Media Assn., Assn. for Ednl. Communications and Tech., N.E. Wash. Assn. Sch. Adminstrs., Adminstrv. Women in Edn., Delta Kappa Gamma, Phi Kappa Phi, Pi Lambda Thelta. Democrat. Home: N 7231 Fotheringham Spokane WA 99208 Office: N 200 Bernard Spokane WA 99201

MATY, RONALD PAUL, mechanical design engineer; b. Harvey, Ill., Oct. 19, 1947; s. Paul Joseph and Evelyn Edna (Krugler) M.; m. Nancy Lou Kraas, Aug. 24, 1968; children—Kimberly, Kerry, Kathryn. B.A. in Physics, Central Mo. U., Warrensburg, 1970; B.S.M.E., U. Mo.-Rolla, 1970. Registered profl. engr., Fla., 1974. Sr. mech. design engr. Fla. Research & Devel. Ctr., Pratt & Whitney Aircraft Corp., West Palm Beach, 1970-77; sr. mech. design engr. Garrett Turbine Engine Co., Phoenix, 1977—. Bd. elders Gethesemane Lutheran Ch., Tempe, Ariz., 1977—, chmn. 1981, 82. Mem. ASME. Republican. Lutheran. Home: 1242 W Madero Mesa AZ 85202 Office: Garrett Turbine Engine Co 111 S 34th St Phoenix AZ 85010

MATZENAUER, JAMES OTIS, aerospace engineer; b. Tacoma, Wash., Nov. 7, 1917; s. Charles S. and Edna Alice (Otis) M.; m. Shirley McKee, Oct. 6, 1946; children—Victoria Borden, Alison Rondone, Cathy Gavriliadis. B.S. in Aero. Engring., U. Wash., 1941; postgrad. UCLA, U. So. Calif., 1947-60. Lic. mech. engr., Calif. Power plant test and devel. engr. Douglas Aircraft, Santa Monica, Calif., 1946-47; power plant devel. supr. N.Am. Aviation, Los Angeles, 1947-57; rocket engine preliminary design engr., supr. applications engring., chief engr. spl. projects Rocketdyne div. Rockwell, Canoga Park, Calif., 1957-62; mgr. advanced lunar systems studies, proposal mgr., payload integration project engr. Rockwell Space Div., Downey, Calif., 1962-79; acctg. mgr. payload integration shuttle engring. Aerospace Corp., El Segundo, Calif., 1979-81, project engr. system requirements and analysis, 1981—. Served to maj. USAFR, 1940-51. Mem. AIAA (Los Angeles tech. com.), Am. Rocket Soc., Inst. Aerospace Sci., Am. Astronautical Soc. Republican. Roman Catholic. Clubs: Aerospace, Nat. Rifle Assn. Contbr. articles to profl. jours.; patentee in field. Office: 2350 E El Segundo Blvd M5-557 El Segundo CA 90245

MAUDERLY, JOE LLOYD, vet. physiologist; b. Strong City, Kans., Aug. 31, 1943; s. Joseph Park and Violet May (Cox) M.; B.S., Kans. State U., 1965, D.V.M., 1967; m. Cheryl Gaines, Jan. 31, 1965; children—Laurie Jean, Jennifer Lynn. Physiologist, Inhalation Toxicology Research Inst., Lovelace Biomed. and Environ. Research Inst., Albuquerque, 1969-83, patho-physiology group leader, 1980—. Served with USAF, 1967-69. Mem. Am. Physiol. Soc., Am. Thoracic Soc. (program com. 1980—, Assembly Environ. and Occupational Health), Am. Soc. Vet. Physiologists and Pharmacologists, World Assn. Vet. Physiologists, Pharmacologists and Biochemists, AVMA, N.Mex. Vet. Med. Assn., AAAS. Republican. Baptist. Asso. editor Lab. Animal Sci., 1978-83; mem. editorial bd. Exptl. Lung Research, 1983—; contbr. chpts. to books, articles to profl. publs. Home: 4517 Banff NE Albuquerque NM 87111 Office: PO Box 5890 Albuquerque NM 87115

MAUDLIN, LLOYD ZELL, physicist; b. Miles City, Mont., Feb. 20, 1924; s. Lloyd Zell and Effie Lenora (Vick) M.; B.A. in Physics, U. Calif. at Los Angeles, 1949; M.S. in Physics, U. So. Calif., 1952; m. Lauralee Rose Williams, June 26, 1946; children—Craig, Lynn, Alicia, Dawn. Physicist, U.S. Naval Ordnance Test Sta., Pasadena, Calif., 1951-68; sr. physicist Naval Undersea Ctr., San Diego, 1968-77, head simulation and computer sci. dept., 1977-81; pres. Lloyd Z. Maudlin and Assos., 1981—; sr. scientist Integrated Systems Analysts Inc., National City, Calif. Pres. Gifted Children's Assn., Los Angeles, 1968-70; trustee Los Angeles City Missionary Soc., United Methodist Ch., 1961-73. Served in USAAF, 1943-46. Recipient U.S. Govt. Meritorious Civilian Service award, 1953. Mem. IEEE (pres. oceanic engring. council), Computer Soc., Soc. for Computer Simulation, Am. Ordnance Assn., N.Y. Acad. Sci., AAAS. Republican. Patentee in field. Home: 5461 Toyon Rd San Diego CA 92115 Office: Integrated Systems Analysts Inc 222 W 24th St National City CA 92050

MAUDLIN, W(ARREN) THOMAS, JR., real estate developer; b. Hollywood, Calif., July 28, 1936; s. Warren Thomas and Helen Elizabeth (Rowe) M.; B.Sc., U. So. Calif., 1959; m. Linda Dean, Dec. 28, 1961; children—Dean, Scott. Profl. football player Toronto Argonauts, 1962-63; pres., chmn. bd. Descolin, Inc., Woodland Hills, Calif., 1971—. Served to capt. USMC, 1959-61. Republican. Clubs: Jonathan, Country (Los Angeles). Office: 21241 Ventura Blvd Suite 274 Woodland Hills CA 91364

MAUGHAN, EDWIN KELLY, geologist; b. Glendale, Calif., Oct. 13, 1926; s. Thomas Adamson and Irene (Kelly) M.; B.S. with honors, Utah State U., 1950; postgrad. UCLA, 1950-51, U. Colo. Grad. Sch., 1956-57, Colo. Sch. Mines, 1977; m. Fae Lewis, June 8, 1951 (div. 1971); children—Kenneth Lewis, Gordon Lewis, Laura Anne, Evan Lewis; m. 2d, Jayne Kessler, Nov. 15, 1975. Geologist U.S. Corps Engrs., Los Angeles, 1951, U.S. Geol. Survey, Denver, 1951-67; tech adviser U.S. Geol. Survey & Agy. for Internat. Devel., Bogota, Colombia, 1967-69; geologist U.S. Geol. Survey, Middlesboro, Ky., 1969-72, Denver, 1972—. Served with USNR, 1945-46. Fellow Geol. Soc. Am.; mem. Soc. Econ. Paleontologists and Mineralogists (v.p. Rocky Mountain sect. 1983-84), Am. Assn. Petroleum Geologists, Colo. Chorale (dir. 1976-80), Men's Orgn. Denver Symphony Orch., Sigma Gamma Epsilon, Phi Kappa Phi. Mem. Ch. of Jesus Christ of Latter-day Saints (br. pres. 1968-69). Author, co-author numerous articles on Upper Paleozoic stratigraphy, paleogeography, and petroleum source rocks in northern Rocky Mountains and Great Basin; areal geology in central Mont., Wyo. and southeastern Ky.; and Cretaceous phosphorite deposits in Colombia. Home: 1317 Yank St Golden CO 80401 Office: US Geol Survey Fed Center Denver CO 80225

MAUK, THOMAS GREGORY, city manager; b. Oakland, Calif., Oct. 21, 1943; s. James R. and Constance Ivy (Nensen) Nourse; m. Rebecca V. Mauk, Mar. 18, 1968; children—Donald, Katherine, Laura, Danielle. B.B.A., Calif. State U.-Pomona, 1966; M.P.A., U. So. Calif., 1972. Adminstrv. analyst City of Los Angeles, 1967-70; asst. city adminstr. City of Montclair (Calif.), 1970-76; city mgr. City of Norco (Calif.), 1976-80, City of Whittier (Calif.), 1980—; pub. speaker; tchr. Named Man of Yr., Norco C. of C., 1977. Mem. Internat. City Mgrs. Assn., Los Angeles World Affairs Council, Town Hall of Calif. Club: Lions. Home: 10015 Santa Gertrudes St Whittier CA 90603 Office: 13230 Penn St Whittier CA 90601

MAUL, TERRY LEE, psychologist; b. San Francisco, May 6, 1946; s. Chester Lloyd and Clella Lucille (Hobbs) M.; A.B., U. Calif., Berkeley, 1967, M.A., 1968, Ph.D., 1970; student Coll. San Mateo, 1964-65; m. Gail Ann Retallick, June 27, 1970; 1 son, Andrew Eliot. Asso. prof. psychology San Bernardino Valley Coll., San Bernardino, Calif., 1970—; researcher self-actualization. Mem. Am. Psychol. Assn., AAUP (chpt. pres. 1971-73), Audubon Soc., Mensa, Nature Conservancy, Rachel Carson Council, Wilderness Soc., Sierra Club. Democrat. Author: (with Eva Conrad) Introduction to Experimental Psychology, 1981; (with Gail Maul) Beyond Limit: Ways to Growth and Freedom, 1983. Home: 6155 Bluffwood Dr Riverside CA 92506 Office: 701 S Mount Vernon Ave San Bernardino CA 92403

MAULDIN, JEAN HUMPHRIES, aviation co. exec.; b. Gordonville, Tex., Aug. 16, 1923; d. James Wiley and Lena Leota (Noel-Crain) Humphries; B.S., Hardin Simmons U., 1943; M.S., U. So. Calif., 1961; postgrad. Westfield Coll., U. London, 1977-78, Warnborough Coll., Oxford, Eng., 1977-78; m. William Henry Mauldin, Feb. 28, 1942; children—Bruce Patrick, William Timothy III. Psychol. counselor social services 1st Baptist Ch., 1953-57; pres. Mauldin and Staff, public relations, Los Angeles, 1957-78; pres. Stardust Aviation, Inc., Santa Ana, Calif., 1962—. Mem. Calif. Democratic Council, 1953-83; mem.

exec. bd. Calif. Dem. Central com., 1957—, Orange County Dem. Central Com., 1960—; mem. U.S. Congl. Peace Adv. Bd., 1981—; del. Dem. Nat. Conv., 1974, 78; pres. Santa Ana Friends of Public Library, 1973-76, McFadden Friends of Library, Santa Ana, 1976-80; chmn. cancer crusade Am. Cancer Soc., Orange County, 1974; mem. exec. bd. Lisa Hist. Preservation Soc., 1970—; lay leader Protestant Episcopal Ch. Am., Trinity Ch., Tustin, Calif. Named Woman of Yr., Key Woman in Politics, Calif. Dem. Party, 1960-80. Am. Mgmt. Assn. (pres.'s club), Bus. and Profl. Women Am., Exptl. Aircraft and Pilots Assn., Nat. Women's Polit. Caucus, Dem. Coalition Central Coms., Calif. Friends of Library (life), Women's Missionary Soc. (chmn.), LWV, Nat. Fedn. Dem. Women, Calif. Fedn. County Central Com. Mems., Internat. Platform Assn., Peace Through Strength, Oceanic Soc., Nat. Audubon Soc., Sierra Club, Nat. Wildlife Fedn., Internat. Amnesty Assn., Am. Security Council, Nat. Women's Pilot. Club: U. So. Calif. Ski, Town Hall of Calif. Author: Cliff Winters, The Pilot, The Man, 1961; The consummate Barnstormer, 1962; The Daredevil Clown, 1965. Home: 1013 W Elliott Pl Santa Ana CA 92704 also 102 E 45th St Savannah GA 31405 also 112 8th St Seal Beach CA 90740 Office: 16542 Mount Kibby St Fountain Valley CA 92708

MAUND, GAY ELIZABETH, audiologist; b. Phila.; d. Walter Thomas and Eleanor Claire (Logan) Maund. B.A., Marymount Coll., 1963-67; M.A., U. So. Calif., 1969. Lic. audiologist, Calif. Audiologist, VA Outpatient Clinic, Los Angeles, 1970—, coordinator, hearing aid program, 1978—, pub. relations officer, 1979—; part-time faculty Calif. State U.-Los Angeles, Calif. State U.-Northridge; lectr. in field. Mem. Los Angeles City Council for the Handicapped, 1982-83. Recipient VA Bronze Pin Spl. Award for Excellence in Improving Communications and Service to Pub., 1975, VA Quality Increase Performance award, 1977, Cert. of Appreciation, 1980, Spl. Contbn. award, 1982, others. Mem. Am. Speech and Hearing Assn. Address: 425 S Hill St Apt G70 Los Angeles CA 90068

MAURER, CHARLES D., clinical psychologist; b. Yuba City, Calif., March 17, 1946; s. John Paul and Catherine Ellen (Edgerton) M.; m. Carol Ann McCullough, June 14, 1975. A.B., Kenyon Coll., Gambier, Ohio, 1968; M.A., Kent State U., 1970, Ph.D., 1972. Lic. psychology, Wash. Clin. psychology intern, Akron Child Guidance Ctr., 1970-71; clin. psychology trainee Brecksville VA Hosp., 1971-72; clin. psychologist Wilford Hall, USAF Med. Ctr., San Antonio, 1972-73; staff clin. psychologist, USAF Hosp., Wiesbaden, W.Ger., 1973-74, asst. chief outpatient mental health clinic, 1973-75, chief, clin. psychology service, 1975-76; clin. instr. dept. community dentistry U. Wash., Seattle, 1976-78; cons. Seattle Mental Health Inst., 1976-78, King County Juvenile Services, Seattle, 1977—, Seattle pub. schs., 1976-77, mental health cons. Westinghouse Health Systems, 1979 81; cons. clin. psychology, delinquency prevention services program, 1977-81; instr. U. Md. overseas undergrad. program, 1974 76; guest lectr. Seattle U., 1980—; outside clin. supr. psychol. services and tng. U. Wash., 1981—. Trustee, pres. Seattle Day Nursery, 1982-83; mem. adv. bd. Nat. Council Compulsive Gambling. Served to capt. USAF. Predoctoral fellow NSF, 1969-70. Mem. Am. Psychol. Assn., Assn. Advancement of Psychology, Wash. State Psychol. Assn., N.W. Soc. for Adolescent Medicine, Council for Nat. Register of Health Service Providers in Psychology, Wash. Acad. Clin Hyponosis. Contbr. articles to profl. jours. Office: 9730-3d Ave NE Suite 202 Seattle WA 98115

MAURER, ERNEST WILLIAM, aeronautics educator; b. Lakewood, Ohio, Aug. 11, 1951; s. Ernest Edward and Cynthia Bell (Muir) M. A.A., Cuyahoga Community Coll., Ohio, 1972; B.S. in Edn., Kent (Ohio) State U., 1973, M.A. in Tech., 1976; postgrad. in higher edn. UCLA. Cert. tchr., Calif.; lic. pilot, FAA. Mechanic, service mgr., asst. store mgr., various Goodyear tire ctrs. Cleve., 1971-73; indsl. arts tchr., Lakewood (Ohio) High School, 1973-76, Fontana Junior High School, Ohio, 1976-77; prof. aeros. and indsl. edn. Coast Community Coll. Dist., Costa Mesa, Calif., 1977—; cons. to Taiwan Ministry Edn. in tchr. edn. and indsl. automation. Mem. AIAA, Univ. Aviation Assn., Flying Tchrs., Aircraft Owners and Pilots Assn., Theta Tau. Contbr. articles to profl. books and jours. Home: 7611 Rhone Ln Huntington Beach CA 92647 Office: Orange Coast Coll 2701 Fairview Rd Costa Mesa CA 92626

MAURO, ANTHONY PATRICK, engineer, computer manufacturing company executive; b. New Rochelle, N.Y.,1939; B.S., Fordham U., 1962; m. Judith Ann Zercher, July 15, 1960; children—Penny Lou, Anthony Patrick II, Marilyn Jo, Nicholas J., Michael J. Mfg. engr. RCA Power Tubes, Lancaster, Pa., 1962-64; design and devel. engr. RCA Color Picture Tube, Lancaster, 1964; mfg. engr. Gen. Electric, Milw., 1964-66, advance mfg. engr., 1966-68, mgr. mfg. engrng. med. systems div., 1971-74, mgr. tube mfg., 1974-76; asst. ops. mgr. electro-optical devices div. Amperex, North Smithfield, R.I., 1968-70, mgr. imaging devices prodn., 1970-71; mgr. mfg. word processing div. Memorex Corp., Santa Clara, Calif., 1976-77, gen. mgr. Comdata div., 1977-79, v.p., gen. mgr. precision plastics div., 1979-81; pres. Digitran of Becton, Dickinson Co., 1981-82; v.p. Data Electronic Corp., San Diego, 1982-83; exec. v.p. Evotek Corp., Fremont, Calif., 1983—. Recipient So. Calif. Edison Energy Mgmt. award, 1978, Memorex Corp. Asset Mgmt. award, 1979, So. Calif. Handicap Employment Recognition award, 1980, others. Home: 4100 Crestview Rd Norco CA 91760 Office: Evotek Inc 1220 Page Ave Fremont CA 94534

MAURO, RICHARD FRANK, lawyer; b. Hawthorne, Nev., July 21, 1945; s. Frank Joseph and Dolores D. (Kreimeyer) M.; A.B. (Francis Wayland scholar), Brown U., 1967; J.D. summa cum laude, U. Denver, 1970; m. LaVonne A. Madden, Aug. 28, 1965; 1 dau., Lindsay Anne. Comml. loan adminstr. United Bank Denver, 1968-70; admitted to Colo. bar, 1970; since practiced in Denver, with firms Dawson, Nagel, Sherman & Howard, Vancise, Freeman, Tooley & McClearn, 1970-74, Hall & Evans, 1974-81, Morrison & Foerster, 1981—; part-time prof. Met. State Coll., Denver, U. Denver Coll. Law; lectr. legal symposia. Regional dir. Brown U., 1970-76. Mem. Colo. Assn. Corporate Counsel (pres. 1975-76), Am., Colo., Denver bar assns., Am. Arbitration Assn. (panel comml. arbitrators), Order St. Ives (U. Denver). Club: Brown U. of Colo. (pres. 1976). Editor: Colorado Corporations Systems Manual; contbr. articles to legal jours. Home: 1810 Union Dr Lakewood CO 80215 Office: 2900 Energy Center 717 17th St Denver CO 80202

MAVRITTE, HAROLD EMERSON, psychiatrist, educator; b. Washington, Nov. 30, 1929; s. Eugene T. and Mildred (Chappelle) M.; m. Dolores Washington, June 20, 1947; 1 son, Richard R. B.S., Howard U., 1951, M.D., 1955; M.S. in Social Psychiatry, UCLA, 1970. Gen. practice medicine, Pasadena, Calif., 1958-65; med. cons. Los Angeles County, 1958-65, psychiat. cons. Dept. Social Services, 1968-70, regional chief Dept. Mental Health, 1970-72, dep. dir., 1972-74, dep. dir. Dept. Health Services, 1974-78, asst. dir./program chief Dept. Mental Health, 1978—; asst.-clin. prof. UCLA, 1970—; cons. in field. Served with USN, 1956-58. Mem. Am. Psychiat. Assn., So. Calif. Psychiat. Assn. (past chmn.), Black Psychiatrists Am., Black Psychiatrists So. Calif. (past chmn.), Charles Drew Med. Soc., Nat. Med. Assn., NAACP. Home: 6531 Whitworth Dr Los Angeles CA 90035 Office: 2415 W 6th St Los Angeles CA 90057

MAWHINNEY, JOHN THOMAS, state senator; b. Phila., May 27, 1937; s. James Joseph and Helen Grace (Maguire) M.; m. Margaret Jane Cybulski, June 21, 1958; children—Helen Marie, John Thomas II, Katherine Elizabeth. Student parochial schs., Phila. Enlisted USAF, 1954, advanced through grades to maj., 1966; ret., 1966; pilot, flight engr. Pan Am. Airways, 1966—, mem. flight engrs. system bd. adjustment, N.Y.C., 1974—; referee Pima County Juvenile Ct., 1977—; mem. Ariz. Senate from Dist. 12, 1979—, majority whip, 1981—, asst. majority leader, 1983—. Fire commr. Manalapan (N.J.) 1 Fire Dist., 1973; mem. Ariz. Groundwater Study Comm., 1979. Decorated Air medal with 4 oak leaf clusters. Mem. Airline Pilots Assn., Flight Engrs. Internat. Assn., Am. Legion, Mil. Order World Wars. Republican. Office: Ariz State Senate Phoenix AZ 85007

MAWICKE, PAUL DENNY, landscape architect, horticulturist; b. Park Ridge, Ill., Dec. 2, 1950; s. Albert Thomas and Dorthy (Harris) M.; B.S. in Horticulture and Landscape Architecture, Iowa State U., 1974. Project landscape architect estimator Lawrence & Ahlman, Dundee, Ill., 1974-75; landscape architect CSC Landscape Group, Chgo., 1975-76; asso. landscape architect Don Halamka Assos., Inc., Chgo., 1976; sr. landscape architect SSPF, Inc., St. Charles, Ill., 1976-77; sr. landscape architect, horticulturalist John R. Cook Assos., Rockford, Ill., 1977-79; chief designer Triad Assos., Bellevue, Wash., 1979; chief designer David Evans & Assos. Inc., Bellevue, 1979-80; dir. planning Land Planning and Mgmt., Inc., Kent, Wash., 1980-81; prin. Mawicke & Assocs., landscape architects, Seattle, 1981—. Registered landscape architect, Wash. Mem. Am. Soc. Landscape Architects, Am. Nurseryman's Assn. Democrat. Roman Catholic. Club: Beech Aero. Home: 343 NW 76th St Seattle WA 98117 Office: 343 NW 76th St Seattle WA 98117

MAXEY, CARL WOODARD, wood products mfg. co. exec.; b. Chillicothe, Mo., Feb. 26, 1926; s. Leonard and Mary Ellen (Woodard) Bryant; B.S., U. Calif., Berkeley, 1957, M.S., 1962; m. Wanda Juanita Moore, Jan. 21, 1948; children—Craig Marshall, Robbin Juanita. Lab. technician U. Calif., 1956-61; wood technologist McDade Timber Testing Co., 1961-63; corp. dir. electronic research Black Clawson Co., Everett, Wash., 1963-74; assoc. prof. forest products Oreg. State U., Corvallis, 1974-77; owner, pres. Carl Maxey Co., Corvallis, 1977—; pres. Carl Maxey So., Inc., Atlanta, Tex.; cons. wood products, 1977—. Active 4-H Clubs, 1961-63. Served with U.S. Army, 1944-48. Mem. Forest Products Research Soc. (Woodworking and Furniture award 1977). Republican. Clubs: Elks. Contbr. articles to profl. jours. Patentee helical saw, veneer patching machine, defect detector, wood scanners, others. Home: PO Box 1810 Corvallis OR 97339 Office: Carl Maxey Co PO Drawer 1810 Corvallis OR 97330

MAXEY, VALERIE KRIZ, oil service company official, communications consultant; b. Berkeley, Calif., Oct. 16, 1954; d. Leland Calvin and Rita Rose (Webber) Kriz; m. Lyle Denny Maxey, June 2, 1979. B.A. in Communication, Stanford U., 1976. Analyst parts & service div. Ford Motor Co. Pico Rivera, Calif., 1977-79; account coordinator Bozell & Jacobs, Inc., Newport Beach, Calif., 1979-81, account exec., 1981, account supr., 1981-82; corp. pub. relations mgr. Smith Internat., Inc., Newport Beach, 1982—; bd. dirs., communications advisor The Newport Found. Study Major Econ. Issues. Chmn. Stanford U. Ann. Fund, Orange County (Calif.), 1982—. Mem. Pub. Relations Soc. Am., Women in Communications, Nat. Assn. Female Execs., Soc. Petroleum Engrs., Soc. Calligraphy (Los Angeles). Office: Smith Internat Inc 4343 Von Karman Ave Newport Beach CA 92660

MAXIMOV, JUDITH B., computer co. exec.; b. Chgo., Sept. 16, 1943; d. Marshall and Helaine (Friedlen) Salzman; B.A., North Park Coll., Chgo., 1976, m. Michael J. Maximov, June 20, 1965 (div. 1983); children—Justin, Marc, Hannah. Chairwoman, Ariz. ERA Coalition, 1976-80; owner, operator Judith's Computer Works, Tucson, 1978—. Bd. dirs. Temple Emanu-El, Tucson, 1982-83; bd. dirs., fundraising chairwoman Tucson Center for Women and Children, 1982-84; state bd. dirs. NOW, 1981-82; pres. Tucson sect. Nat. Council Jewish Women, 1982-84, bd. dirs., 1980-82; pres. Women in Tucson, 1982-83; v.p. Mt. Lemmon Homeowners Assn., 1981-82, pres., 1982-83; mem. Mt. Lemmon Vol. Fire Dept., 1983-84; participant Leadership Tucson, 1981, Leadership Tucson Alumni, 1982—. Address: PO Box 675 Mount Lemmon AZ 85619

MAXON, JAMES CLARK, archaeologist, environmental education specialist; b. Alamosa, Colo., Dec. 19, 1935; s. Leo Gilbert and Mary Edith (Taylor) M.; student U.S. Mil. Acad., 1954; B.A. in Anthropology, U. Denver, 1958; M.A. in Archaeology, U. Wis., 1969; m. Sharon Kay Sullivan, Aug. 16, 1958; children—Kevin Joseph, Clark Christopher, Dianne Marie; m. 2d, Kristin Jane Lenning, Jan. 3, 1982. Archaeologist, Aztec Ruins Nat. Monument, 1958-61, Bandelier Nat. Monument, 1961-67; environ. edn. specialist Lake Mead Nat. Recreation Area, 1967-74; instr. continuing edn. U. Nev., Las Vegas, 1972—; with U.S. Bur. Reclamation, Lower Colo. River region, Boulder City, Nev., 1975—, regional archaeologist, 1976—. Pres. Nev. Environ. Edn. Council 1974—. Mem. Soc. Am. Archeology, Am. Soc. Conservation Archeology, Nev. Hist. Soc., Boulder City First Nighters. Author: Indians of the Lake Mead Country, 1971; Boating Guide to Lake Mohave, 1971; Lake Mead: The Story Behind the Scenery, 1980. Home: 870 Ave B 704 Boulder City NV 89005 Office: US Bur Reclamation Regional Office PO Box 427 Boulder City NV 89005

MAXTED, JOHN WESLEY, mechanical engineer; b. Detroit, Aug. 29, 1952; s. Wesley Leroy and Alma Lee (Grogan) M.; m. Karen Lou Webb, July 26, 1975; children—James Paul, Brian Edward. B.A. in Aerospace Engring., U. Mich., 1974, B.S. in Mech. Engring., 1974; M.S. in Engring., U. Calif.-Irvine, 1980. Cert. profl. engr., Calif. Engr. sci. specialist structures and materials McDonnell Douglas Astronautics Co., Huntington, Calif., 1974—. Mem. AIAA, Soc. Allied Weight Engrs. Roman Catholic. Home: 15551 Pelican Ln Huntington Beach CA 92649 Office: 5301 Bolsa Ave Huntington Beach CA 92647

MAXWELL, DONALD STANLEY, publishing co. exec.; b. Los Angeles, May 30, 1930; s. Harold Stanley and Margaret (Trenam) M.; student Long Beach City Coll., 1948-50; B.B.A., Woodbury Coll., 1956; m. Martha Helen Winn, Dec. 5, 1952; children—Sylvia Louise, Cynthia Lynn, Bruce Stanley, Bradley Erl, Walter James, Wesley Richard, Amy Bernice. Partner, Robert McDavid & Co., C.P.A.'s, Los Angeles, 1955-61; controller Petersen Pub. Co., Los Angeles, 1961-68, v.p. finance, 1969; controller Los Angeles Times, 1969-79, v.p., 1977-79, v.p. fin., 1979-81; asst. treas. Times Mirror Co., 1971-81; v.p., controller, 1982—. Trustee Woodbury U., 1981—. Served with AUS, 1950-52. C.P.A., Calif. Mem. Fin. Execs. Inst. (dir. 1979—; dir. Los Angeles chpt. 1968-76, chpt. pres. 1973-74), Am. Inst. C.P.A.s, Calif. Soc. C.P.A.s, Inst. Newspaper Controllers and Fin. Officers (dir. 1978-82, pres. 1980-81), Am. Horse Council, Internat. Arabian Horse Assn., Arabian Horse Assn. So. Calif. Republican. Baptist. Club: Friendly Hills Country (Whittier, Calif.). Home: 2160 Le Flore Dr La Habra Heights CA 90631 Office: Times Mirror Sq Los Angeles CA 90028

MAXWELL, JEROME EUGENE, electronics co. exec.; b. Princeton, Ill., June 2, 1944; s. Emmett Eugene and June (Erickson) M.; B.S.E.E., So. Meth. U., 1967, M.S.E.E., 1971; m. Cynthia Jane O'Connell, July 30, 1977; children—Eric Vaughn, Christina Dawn, Jeremy Emmett, Jason Daniel, Nicholas Mark. Maintainability engr. product support div. Collins Radio Co., Richardson, Tex., 1965-67; jr. engr. computer systems div., 1967-70; sr. engr. TRW Colo. Electronics, Colorado Springs, 1970-73, mgr. engring., 1973-79, mgr. program mgmt. office, 1979-81, gen. mgr. space electronics mfg. div., 1981—. Mem. adv. council U. Colo., Colorado Springs, 1973—, U. So. Colo., Pueblo, 1974-78; Weblo leader, asst. pack leader Boy Scouts Am., 1976-77; fin. chmn. Ascension Luth. Ch., 1981—; cons. to community edn. coordinator for computer systems and equipment, 1980—. Republican. Patentee in field. Home: 2108 Skye Circle Colorado Springs CO 80915 Office: 3650 N Nevada Ave Colorado Springs CO 80907

MAXWELL, LEROY MAHLON, construction company executive, consultant; b. Sheridan, Wyo., May 23, 1935; s. James Alfred and Blanche Edith (Stallings) M.; m. Joan Gierisch, Sept. 6, 1957; children—Sheree Maxwell Bench, Daniel, David, Kerri, Jonathon; m. 2d, Yvonne Akin, Sept. 13, 1975. C.E., Colo. State U., 1959. Constrn. mgr. Lloyd M. Hill, Inc., Salem, Oreg., 1968-71, Cabax Mills, Eugene, Oreg., 1971-78; owner, mgr. Maxwell Cons., Eugene, 1978-80; v.p., mgr. Gen. Constrn. Co. of Hawaii, Honolulu, 1980-82; v.p. ops. mgr. Arctic Slope/Wright Schuchart Constrn. Co., Anchorage, 1982—; cons. U.S. Forest Service. Mem. Pres.'s Republican Task Force (charter), U.S. Senatorial Club. Mem. Am. Mgmt. Assn. Republican. Clubs: Plaza (Honolulu); Elks (Eugene). Home: 1113 W Firewood Ln #700 Anchorage AK 99503 Office: Arctic Slope/Wright Schuchart Constrn Co PO Box 6223 Anchorage AK 99502

MAXWELL, MARY SUSANNA, educational psychologist, educator; b. Dallas, Mar. 28, 1948; d. Otis Allen and Emma Vee (Dunlap) M.; m. Barry L. Lutz, July 25, 1981. B.A., U. Tex., Austin, 1970, Ph.D., 1978. Lic. psychologist, Ariz. Asst. instr. ednl. psychology U. Tex., Austin, 1974-76; evaluator Tchr. Corps, Austin, 1976; adminstrv. intern S.W. Ednl. Devel. Lab., Austin, 1977; asst. prof. ednl. psychology, dir. Sch. Psychology Program No. Ariz. U., Flagstaff, 1978—. Mem. Ariz. Assn. Sch. Psychologists (exec. bd.). Home: 3330 Gillenwater Flagstaff AZ 86001 Office: Box 6002 No Ariz U Flagstaff AZ 86011

MAXWELL, SY, insurance broker; b. N.Y.C., Apr. 5, 1929; s. Jack and Stella (LeBow) M.; m. Charlotte Edelstone, Jan. 10, 1954; children—Leslie, Bruce, Robin, Tracy. B.A., U. Mich., 1950. Pres., Triangle Ins., Inc., Sherman Oaks, Calif., 1955—. Pres. 500 Club of City of Hope, 1982; sec. Ins. Council, City of Hope. Served with USNR, 1947-57. Mem. Beverly Hills Bus. and Profl. Men's Assn. (pres. 1962), Ind. Ins. Agts. and Brokers Assn. Calif. (pres. San Fernando Valley chpt. 1969-70, chmn. govt. affairs com.). Democrat. Office: 4340 Fulton Ave Sherman Oaks CA

MAY, DAVID JON, food service executive; b. Toledo, Ohio, June 2, 1937; s. Claud and Josephine Margaret (Schmidt) M.; m. Judith Ann Royer, Dec. 27, 1959; children—Kimberly Ann, Kevin Clark. B.A., Hillsdale Coll., 1959. With Saga Corp., Tempe, Ariz., 1959—, dist. mgr., Mont., Idaho, Colo., 1965-72, Nev., N.M., Ariz., So. Calif., 1972-79, Western dir. campus mktg., 1979-80, v.p. account planning and devel., 1980-81, v.p. mktg. and sales Edn. Div., Tempe, 1981-82, v.p. adminstrv. services, 1982—. Mem. Nat. Restaurant Assn., Food Service Execs. Assn., Nat. Assn. Coll. and Univ. Bus. Officers. Republican. Episcopalian. Club: Mesa Country. Contbr. articles to profl. jours. Home: 2159 E Balboa Dr Tempe AZ 85282 Office: Saga Corp 1 Saga Ln Menlo Park CA 94025

MAY, DONALD ROBERT LEE, ophthalmologist; b. Spring Valley, Ill., Nov. 26, 1945; s. Reo G. and Edna A. (Klein) M.; B.S. with honors in Liberal Arts and Scis. and distinction in Microbiology, U. Ill., 1968, M.D., 1972. Intern, Northwestern Meml. Hosps., Chgo., 1972-73; resident in ophthalmology U. Ill. Eye and Ear Infirmary, Chgo., 1973-76, ophthalmology fellow (retina and vitreous surgery), 1976-77; attending surgeon U. Ill. Eye and Ear Infirmary, Chgo., 1976-77, fellow in diabetic retinopathy study and diabetic retinopathy vitrectomy study, 1976-77; cons. Oreg. Regional Primate Research Center, Beaverton, 1979-81, Martinez (Calif.) VA Hosp., 1979—; asst. prof. ophthalmology U. Calif. Sch. Medicine, Davis, 1979-81, assoc. prof., 1981—, dir. Retina and Vitreous Service, 1979—, chmn. operating room com., 1981-83, chmn. research affairs com., 1981-84, dir. ann. research symposium, 1982, 83, ann. vitreoretinal symposium, Lake Tahoe, 1982—; clin. assoc. prof. ophthalmology U. Calif. Sch. Medicine, San Francisco; lectr. NBC News, TV, Chgo., 1976, 77, CBS News, San Antonio, 1978-79, ABC News, Sacramento, 1982—; speaker profl. confs.; invited lectr. and Surgeon People's Republic of China, 1980, 82, Japan, 1982, 83. Served to maj. M.C., USAF, 1977-79. Diplomate Am. Bd. Ophthalmology. Mem. Am. Assn. Ophthalmology, Am. Acad. Ophthalmology, Assn. Research in Vision and Ophthalmology, ACS, Sacramento County Med. Soc., AMA, Calif. Med. Assn., Alta Calif. Ophthal. Soc., World Eye Found. (bd. dirs. 1982—). Lutheran. Contbr. articles on ophthalmic surgery to profl. jours. Office: 4301 X St Room 251 Sacramento CA 95817

MAY, MARK WILLIAM, hospital administrator; b. Corning, N.Y., Aug. 16, 1955; s. William Andrew and Virginia Theresa (Bruno) M. B.S. in Health Planning and Adminstrn., Pa. State U., 1977; M.A. in Health Care Adminstrn., George Washington U., 1979. Coordinator med. staff services St. Vincent Hosp. and Med. Ctr., Portland, Oreg., 1980, dir. human resources, 1980-83, asst. adminstr./ancillary services, 1980—. Mem. Am. Soc. Personnel Adminstrs., Am. Coll. Hosp. Adminstrs. Club: Rotary (Beaverton, Oreg.). Office: 9205 SW Barnes Rd Portland OR 97225

MAY, MICHAEL WAYNE, radio sta. exec.; b. Springhill, La., Mar. 31, 1949; s. Willie Wilmer and Ethel Florene (Sigler) M.; student So. Ark. U., 1968-70, La. Tech. U., 1970-71. Prodn. dir. Sta. KKAM, Pueblo, Colo., 1973-75; quality control dir. Sta. KBOZ, Bozeman, Mont., 1975-78; music dir., dir. research, disk jockey Sta. KOOK, Billings, Mont., 1978-80; founder, operator Yellowstone Sch. Broadcasting, Billings, 1980—. Club: Elks. Author: Building with the Basics: Radio Personality Development, 1979. Home: 3600 Jansma Billings MT 59101 Office: PO Box 127 Billings MT 59103

MAYALL, BROUN HUNT, news executive; b. Oklahoma City, Jan. 21, 1908; s. Roy Winfield and Loutilla (Hunt) M.; m. Geneva Ann Holmes, June 1, 1927; children—Donald H., Russell H.; m. Melba Maurine White, Apr. 15, 1945; children—Nancy Sue May, Elizabeth Ann Mayall Straka, Sally Lou Brasher. B.A., Central State U., 1927; M.Ed., Okla. U., 1935. Registrar, Southeastern State Coll., Durant, Okla., 1927-28; registrar, dir. pub. relations Okla. Coll. for Women, Chickasha, 1928-42; nat. dir. USAF Ground Observer Corps, Colorado Springs, Colo., 1953-57; command dir. info. Air Def. Command, Colorado Springs, 1957-61; v.p. mktg. Colorado Springs Nat. Bank, 1961-74; pres. Mayall Assocs., Colo. Springs, 1974—; dir. Miller High Life News Bur. Olympic Tng. Ctr., Colorado Springs, 1982—; cons. pub. relations Nat. Carvers Mus., Sheraton Inn, Raemar Herzog Advt. Agy. Chmn. communications com. Nat. Benevolent Assn.; bd. dirs. Colo. Christian Home, 1977-81; mem. Pikes Peak council Boy Scouts Am., Pikes Peak Council Chs.; mem. Colo. Commn. on Aging, 1977—, chmn., 1979-81; mem. ofcl. bd. 1st Christian Ch. Served to col. USAF, 1942-61. Decorated Legion of Merit, Commendation medal with 2 oak leaf clusters. Mem. Pub. Relations Soc. Am., Phi Delta Kappa. Democrat. Mem. Disciples of Christ Ch. Clubs: Lions, Garden of the Gods, El Paso (Colorado Springs). Author numerous articles on sr. citizens programs and aging. Home: 2403 Constellation Dr Colorado Springs CO 80906 Office: 1750 E Boulder St Colorado Springs CO 80909

MAYEDA, CRAIG SHIGERU, farmers cooperative manager; b. Honolulu, Feb. 27, 1953; s. Jack Noboru and Helen Kazuko (Meguro) M.; m. Charmain Yim, June 21, 1980. B.S., U. Hawaii, 1975, M.S., 1978. Office supr., night auditor Ala Moana Hotel, Honolulu, 1971-79; night auditor Hyatt Regency Hotel, Honolulu, 1977-78; gen. mgr. Koolau

Farmers Coop. Ltd., Kaneohe, Hawaii, 1979—; host garden program Sta. KHVH, Honolulu. Mem. Soil and Water Conservation Bd. S. Oahu County; chmn. community affairs Kaneohe Bus. Group. Home: 2825 S King St Apt 301 Honolulu HI 96826 Office: Koolau Farmers Coop Ltd 45 580 Kamehameha Hwy Kaneohe HI 96744

MAYER, BARBARA ANN, personnel adminstr.; b. Flint, Mich., Jan. 5, 1932; d. Greer Richard and Gladys Irene (Wallace) Davis; B.A. in English, U. Mich., 1954, M.A., 1955, M.A.L.S., 1963; M.P.A., Golden Gate U., 1976; m. Robert Lyon Mayer, Mar. 1, 1968 (dec. 1974). Tech. librarian, chief tech. resources, tech. editor Western Test Range, U.S. Air Force, Vandenberg AFB Air U., 1960-69, guidance counselor, edn. services officer, chief internat. info., 1969-73, chief employee tng. devel., 1974—. Mem. Coll. Fed. Council for So. Calif., 1973-77. Mem. Calif. Women in Govt., Am. Soc. Public Adminstrn., Am. Soc. Personnel Adminstrs., So. Calif. Personnel Assn., Civilian Mgmt. Council, UCLA Alumni Assn. Home: PO Box 746 Lompoc CA 93436 Office: Vandenberg AFB CA 93437

MAYER, ERNEST, research aeronautical engineer; b. Arad, Romania, June 4, 1916; s. Henry and Adele (Popper) M.; m. Elizabeth Weiss, Feb. 6, 1943; children—Vivian F., Virginia A. B.S., CCNY, 1939; M.A., Columbia U., 1941; Ph.D., Poly. Inst. Bklyn., 1952. Instr. physics CCNY, 1939-43; research engr. Westinghouse Labs., Pitts., 1943-46; research and devel. engr. Kellogg Co., Jersey City, 1946-52; staff scientist Arde Assocs., Newark, 1952-57; tech. specialist Rocketdyne Co., Canoga Park, Calif., 1957-60; assoc. dir. Scis. Nat. Engring Sci. Co., Pasadena, Calif., 1960-68; instr. aerospace systems mgmt. U. So. Calif., Los Angeles, 1969-74; sr. scientist Hughes Aircraft Co., El Segundo, Calif., 1974—; cons. in field. Mem. Am. Rocket Soc., AIAA, Combustion Inst., Phi Beta Kappa, Sigma Xi. Contbr. articles to profl. jours. Home: 9063 E Florence Ave Downey CA 90240 Office: 2000 Imperial Hwy El Segundo CA 90245

MAYER, JULIAN RICHARD, college dean; b. N.Y.C., Feb. 12, 1929; s. William and Jean (Belmont) M.; m. June L. Burns, June 29, 1975; children—Stephen, Timothy, Donald, Jon, Lisa, Mili, James. B.S., Union Coll., 1950; M.A., Columbia U., 1951; Ph.D., Yale U., 1955. Research fellow Yale U., New Haven, 1952-54; research chemist Sterling Winthrop Research Inst., Sterling Drug Co., Albany, N.Y., 1954-61, group leader, 1961-62; asst. program dir. sci. facilities program NSF, Washington, 1962-63, staff assoc., planning directorate, 1964-66, staff assoc. univ. sci. devel. program, 1966-70; asst. dir. atmospheric scis. research center SUNY, Albany, 1963-64; lectr. George Washington U., Washington, 1969-70; spl. asst. to the pres. SUNY, Fredonia, 1970-71, dir. environ. resources center, 1971-77, research prof., 1977-78; dean Huxley Coll. Environ. Studies, Western Wash. U., Bellingham, 1978—. Mem. Am. Chem. Soc., AAAS, Sigma Xi. Mem. Christian Reformed Ch. Contbr. articles on chemistry to profl. jours. Office: Western Washington University Huxley College Bellingham WA 98225

MAYER, LAWRENCE STEPHEN, statistics educator, consultant; b. Milw., Nov. 14, 1946; s. Andrew and Goldie (Goldman) M. Student Ariz. State U., 1964-65; B.S., Ohio State U., 1967, B.A., 1968, M.S., 1969, Ph.D., 1970. Asst. prof. math. and polit. sci. Ohio State U., 1970-71; asst. prof. stats. Va. Poly. Inst., Blacksburg, 1971-73; assoc. prof. stats. and environ. studies Princeton U., 1973-79; dir. Wharton Analysis Ctr., Wharton Sch., U. Pa., 1979—; vis. scholar statis. dept. Stanford U., 1982—; med. cons. Vol. Sheriff's Dept. Maricopa County, Ariz. Mem. AAAS, Am. Statis. Assn., Am. Polit. Sci. Assn. Contbr. numerous articles to profl. jours. Home: 2131 Hanover St Palo Alto CA 94306 Office: Dept Stats Sequoia Hall Stanford U Stanford CA 94305

MAYKOWSKYJ, GEORGE, supt. schs.; b. Leuphan, Germany, Feb. 20, 1945; s. Emilian and Antonia Maykowskyj; came to U.S., 1949, naturalized, 1955; B.A. in Biology, Eastern Wash. State U., 1967; B.A. in Ed., 1970; M.A. in Public Sch. Adminstrn., U. Alaska, 1976; m. Judith Healy Green, Aug. 13, 1966; children—Michael George, Marne Antonia. Tchr., Valdez (Alaska) City Sch., 1970-72, prin. high sch., 1972-74, asst. supt., 1974-80, supt., 1980—. Served with AUS, 1967-69. Mem. Assn. Supervision and Curriculum Devel., Am. Assn. Sch. Adminstrs. Clubs: Eagles, Elks.

MAYNARD, JO HELEN, real estate executive; b. Goose Creek, Texas, Aug. 23, 1935; d. Mack M. and Lela M. (Guillory) Hayes; m. Richard L. Maynard, Aug. 5, 1955 (div.); children—Catherine, Richard. Student Sam Houston State U., 1953-54, E. Tex. State Coll., 1954, Lee Coll., Tex., 1954-55. Sales, A.C. Masterson Real Estate, Alexandria, Va., 1969-71, David Meyers Real Estate, Seattle, 1972-74; pres. Market Am., Inc., Seattle, 1975—. Recipient Saleswoman of Yr. awards. Mem. Nat. Assn. Female Execs. (dir.), Seattle C. of C., Downtown Devel. Assn. Democrat. Baptist. Club: U. Texas Exes. Home: 88 Virginia St Townhouse 20 Seattle WA 98101 Office: 2033 6th Ave Suite 707 Seattle WA 98121

MAYNARD, ROBERT CLYVE, editor, publisher; b. Bklyn., June 17, 1937; s. Samuel Christopher and Robertine Isola (Greaves) M.; student (Nieman fellow), Harvard U., 1966; m. Nancy Hall Hicks, Jan. 1, 1975; children—Dori J., David H., Alex Caldwell. Reporter, Afro-Am. News, Balt., 1956; reporter York (Pa.) Gazette and Daily, 1961-67; reporter Washington Post, 1967-72, asso. editor, ombudsman, 1972-74, editorial writer, 1974-77; editor Oakland (Calif.) Tribune, 1979—, now also publisher. Bd. dirs. Coll. Prep. Sch., Oakland; former chmn. Inst. Journalism Edn.; active Mex.-Am. Legal Def. and Edn. Fund; bd. dirs. Marcus Foster Ednl. Inst.; mem. Western regional adv. bd. Am. Press Inst. Mem. Am. Newspaper Publishers Assn. (govt. affairs com.), Am. Soc. Newspaper Editors, Nat. Acad. Scis. (assembly on behavioral scis.), Am. Bar Assn. (commn. on public understanding of law), Nat. News Council, Council Fgn. Relations. Office: 409 13th St Oakland CA 94612

MAYO, FRANK JOSEPH, charitable organization administrator; b. Tacoma, Wash., Dec. 26, 1925; s. Willis and Arvilla Marchetta (Anderson) M.; diploma Simpson Coll., 1949; postgrad. U. Calif., Los Angeles, 1965, Kennedy Sinclaire Estate Planning Sch., 1966, 72, 78; m. Ruth Rustad, July 18, 1947 (div. Sept. 1983); children—Karen Ruth, Sharon Darlene, Rebekah Kay, Deborah Jean. Ordained to ministry Christian and Missionary Alliance, 1951; pastor chs., Wolf Creek, Oreg., Boise, Idaho, Ellensberg, Wash., Dallas, Oreg., Sherman Oaks, Calif.; field rep. planned gifts Christian and Missionary Alliance, Western U.S. area, 1966-72; v.p. planned giving Le Tourneau Coll. Fund, Longview, Tex., 1972-76; planned gifts cons. Western ter. Salvation Army, Rancho Palos Verdes, Calif., 1976—; pres. Frank Mayo and Co., planned giving consultants, 1980—; v.p. So. Calif. Planned Giving Roundtable, 1981—; cons. in field. Bd. dirs. Simpson Coll. Found., 1974-79; trustee Simpson Coll., San Francisco, 1963-79. Served with USAF, 1944-46. Mem. Christian Stewardship Council (dir. 1974-79, 82—). Republican. Home: PO Box 7000 275 Rolling Hills Estates CA 90274 Office: 30840 Hawthorne Blvd Rancho Palos Verdes CA 90274

MAYO, JOHN (JACK) BLOUNT, JR., corporation public relations executive, educator, consultant; b. Richmond, Va., Jan. 9, 1938; s. John Blount and Lillian (Hargrave) M.; m. Nita Louise Kellam, May 30, 1965; children—Carolyn, Sara, John, Kathleen. B.A., U. N.C., 1960; M.A., U. Tex., 1966; M.A., Am. U., 1976. Accredited Pub. relations. Commd. ensign U.S. Navy, 1960, advanced through grades to comdr., 1975, served as pub. affairs officer, ret. 1980; prof. pub. relations, dir. pub. relations Nat. U., San Diego, 1980-82, adj. prof. pub. relations, 1982—; corp. communications dir. Robert Keith & Co. Inc., San Diego, 1983—; pub. relations cons. Mayo & Assos., San Diego. Recipient Donald M. Mackie award, Navy League N.S., 1981, publicity award North San Diego County Press Club, 1982, PR Casebook Spl. events award, 1983. Mem. Pub. Relations Soc. Am. (dir.), Nat. Acad. TV Arts and Scis., San Diego Press Club. Methodist. Club: Navy League of U.S. Author: Bulletin from Dallas: The President Is Dead, 1967 (frontispiece by Lyndon B. Johnson, Pres. U.S., preface by Frank Stanton, Pres. CBS, Inc.). Home: 17023 Cloudcroft Dr Poway CA 92064

MAYOR, ROBERTA ADRIAN, educational administrator; b. Honolulu, June 13, 1944; d. Robert David and Alice (Park) Phillips; m. Richard Lee Mayor, Dec. 17, 1965; children—Regina Helene, Robert William. B.A. in English, U. Hawaii, 1966, postgrad. 1967-75, M. in Ednl. Adminstrn., 1981. Cert. tchr., sch. adminstr., Hawaii. Tchr. English, Waipahu (Hawaii) High Sch., 1968-78, dept. chmn., 1972-75; vice-prin. Kahuku (Hawaii) High Sch., Elem. Sch., 1977, Pearl City (Hawaii) High Sch., 1978-80; prin. Waianae (Hawaii) Intermediate Sch., 1980, Waipahu (Hawaii) Intermediate Sch., 1980-82, Waianae (Hawaii) High Sch., 1982—; mem. Supt.'s Task Force on Intermediate Sch., Learning Ctrs.; mem. Leeward Dist. Civil Rights Complaint Bd. Vice-pres., Pearl City Community Assn.; mem. Waianae Mil.-Civilian Adv. Council. NEH fellow, 1981. Mem. Nat. Assn. Secondary Sch. Prins., Hawaii Assn. Secondary Sch. Prins., Assn. Supervision and Curriculum Devel. Office: 85-251 Farrington Hwy Waianae HI 96792

MAYORKAS, CHARLES ROBERT, textile co. exec.; b. Havana, Cuba, Sept. 18, 1930; s. Moises and Jane (Barth) M.; m. Anita R. Gabor; children—Helena C. Alejandro N., James B., Anthony D. A.B., Dartmouth Coll., 1951; M.B.A., 1953. Sales mgr. Indsl. div., Gen. Distbrs., Havana, 1954-57; owner Industrias Metalan S.A., Havana, 1957-60; controller Gordon Internat. Adv., Miami, Fla., 1961-63; exec. v.p. Barth & Dreyfus, Los Angeles, 1963—; pres. B&D Computer Services, Inc., Los Angeles, Mem. at large Town Hall (Calif.). Jewish. Club: Dartmouth (So. Calif.) Home: 207 S Willaman Dr Beverly Hills CA 90211 Office: 2260 E 15th St Los Angeles CA 90021

MAYRSOHN, WILLIAM, marketing executive, geologist; b. N.Y.C., June 29, 1931; s. Charles M.; M. Natalie Ruth Engerman, Feb. 6, 1953; children—Cheryl L., Valerie A. M.A., Kans. U., 1957; M.B.A., NYU, 1971. Geologist, Skelly Oil Co., Wichita, Bismarck, 1957-63; Belco Petroleum Co., N.Y.C., 1963-66; fin. analyst. Conoco Oil Co., N.Y.C., 1966-67, sr. fin. analyst Kennecott Copper, N.Y.C., 1967-74; treas. Rosario Resources, N.Y.C., 1974-77, v.p. materials, 1977-80; mgr. mktg. Minerals Div., v.p. mktg. Copper Range Div., La. Land & Exploration Co., Lakewood, Colo., 1980—; cons. in field. Mem. Am. Assn. Petroleum Geologists, AIME, Colo. Mining Assn. Home: 9241 W Hialeah Pl Littleton CO 80123 Office: 3900 S Wadsworth Blvd Lakewood CO 80235

MAYS, VICKIE M., psychologist, educator; b. Chgo., Jan. 30, 1952; d. Leonard and Ruth (Little) M. B.A., Loyola U., Chgo., 1973, M.A., 1979; Ph.D. (NIMH fellow), U. Mass., 1979. Grad. research asst. dept. psychology Loyola U., 1972; intern in psychology Ill. Drug Abuse Program, U. Chgo., 1972-73; psychology trainee Westside Vets. Hosp., Chgo., 1972-73; teaching asst. U. Mass., 1973-74, lectr. S.W. Residential Coll., 1974, counselor-tchr. Upward Bound Program, 1974, acting intake coordinator, supr. Psychol. Services Ctr., 1977, research asst., cons. Collegiate Edn. Black Students, 1978-79; cons. George Washington U. Community Relations Div., 1975-76; research psychologist UCLA, 1979, asst. prof. clin. psychology, 1979—; cons. to women's orgns., community mental health ctrs.; postdoctoral vis. scholar, NIMH fellow for Nat. Survey Black Ams. Programs, U. Mich., 1981. Recipient Career Devel. award UCLA, 1983; NIMH fellow, 1983-85. Mem. Am. Psychol. Assn., Assn. Women in Psychology, Western Psychol. Assn., Am. Psychology-Law Soc. Democrat. Office: Dept Psychology UCLA 405 Hilgard Ave Los Angeles CA 90024

MAYTHAM, THOMAS NORTHRUP, museum ofcl.; b. Buffalo, July 30, 1931; s. Thomas Edward and Lorana Margaret (Northrup) M.; B.A., Williams Coll., 1954; M.A., Yale U., 1956; 1 son, Gifford. Asst., then head dept. painting Mus. Fine Arts, Boston, 1956-67; asso. dir., then acting dir. Seattle Art Mus., 1967-74; dir. Denver Art Mus., 1974—. Mem. Am. Fedn. Arts, Assn. Art Mus. Dirs. Home: 211 Ivanhoe St Denver CO 80220 Office: 100 W 14th Ave Pkwy Denver CO 80204

MAZE, MARILYN ELIZABETH, administrator, career counselor, author, educator; b. Colorado Springs, Sept. 13, 1945; d. Robert Orra and Viola A.E. (Schultz) M. Student St. Olaf Coll., 1963-65; B.A. in Math., U. Fla., 1967; M.A. in Counseling, San Francisco State U., 1975. Computer programmer Oak Ridge Nat. Lab., 1967-69; instr. math. Marbel Coll., Philippines, 1969-71; counselor, Calif., 1975-78; user services coordinator Eureka Career Info. System, Richmond, Calif., 1978-80; counselor Career Devel. Inst., San Francisco, 1980-81; counseling instr. San Francisco State U., 1981-82; dir. Eureka Career Info. System, Richmond, Calif., 1981—. Mem. Am. Vocat. Assn., Am. Personnel and Guidance Assn., Calif. Personnel and Guidance Assn., Calif. Career and Guidance Assn., Phi Beta Kappa, Pi Lambda Theta, Phi Delta Kappa. Author: How to Select a Computer-Assisted Career Guidance System, 1983. Office: Eureka Career Info System 5625 Sutter Ave Richmond CA 94804

MAZELIS, MENDEL, plant biochemist, educator, researcher; b. Chgo., Aug. 31, 1922; s. Jacob and Anna (Brvarnick) M.; m. Noreen Beimer, Mar. 24, 1969; 1 son, Jacob Russell. B.S., U. Calif.-Berkeley, 1943, Ph.D., 1954. Jr. research biochemist U. Calif.-Berkeley, 1954-55; research assoc., instr. U. Chgo., 1955-57; assoc. chemist Western Regional Research Lab., Albany, Calif., 1957-61; asst. prof. U. Calif.-Davis, 1961-64, assoc. prof., 1964-73, prof., 1973—. Served to lt. USN, 1943-46. Mem. Am. Soc. Plant Physiologists, Am. Soc. Biol. Chemists, Biochem. Soc. London, Phytochem. Soc. N.Am., Phytochem. Soc. Europe, Inst. Food Technologists. Office: Dept Food Sci and Tech 3450 Chemistry Annex U Calif Davis CA 95616

MAZUREK, JOSEPH P., lawyer, state senator; b. San Diego, July 27, 1948; B.A., U. Mont., 1970, J.D., 1975; m. Patty Mazurek; 3 children. Admitted to Mont. bar, 1975; mem. Mont. Senate, 1981—. Served with U.S. Army, 1970-72. Mem. ABA, Beta Gamma Sigma, Phi Delta Phi, Phi Delta Theta. Assoc. editor Mont. Law Rev., 1974-75. Office: Box 1715 Helena MT 59601

MAZZA, ROBERT BRADLEY, public relations executive; b. San Luis Obispo, Calif., Mar. 23, 1948; s. Alfred and Ester Ellen (Haden) M. B.A. in Journ., Pepperdine U., 1971. Asst. press sec. to county supr. Los Angeles County, 1972-74; publicity dir. San Antonio Spurs, Am. Basketball Assn., 1974; with publicity dept. MGM-TV Studios, Los Angeles, 1976-80; owner-ptnr. Cottman/Mazza Pub. Relations, Los Angeles, 1980—; lectr. UCLA Extension, Pepperdine U. Active in publicity Los Angeles Free Clinic. Mem. Am. Mktg. Assn. (publicity chmn. chpt.), Los Angeles Advt. Club, Acad. TV Arts and Scis., So. Calif. Book Publicists. Office: 303 S Crescent Heights Blvd Los Angeles CA 90048

MAZZEI, SANDO ERNEST, school administrator; b. Tacoma, Wash., Apr. 21, 1926; s. Peter and Clara M.; m. Jean Margaret Williams, Aug. 1, 1962. B.A., U. Puget Sound, 1952, B.E., 1954, M.E., 1958; postgrad. Ohio State U., Seattle U. Tchr., 1952-58; asst. prin. Jason Lee Jr. High Sch., 1958-62; asst. prin. Stadium High Sch., 1962-65; adminstr. secondary edn., Tacoma Pub. Schs., 1965-80, dir. grants mgmt., 1980-82; cons. adminstrv. services, Tacoma, 1982—. Served with USNR, 1944-46. John Hay fellow, 1963. Mem. Wash. Edn. Assn., NEA, Phi Delta Kappa. Clubs: Kiwanis, Lakewood Racquet, Elks, Oakbrook Golf and Country. Home: 7414 Onyx Dr SW Tacoma WA 98498

MAZZEO, DANIEL PATRICK, naval officer, aerospace engring. cons., aviator, instr.; b. Brooklyn, April 18, 1949; s. Gennaro and Marie Grace (Mazzei) M.; m. Belva Faye Musick, Sept. 10, 1977; 1 son, Gennaro Warren. B.S. in Aerospace Engring., Poly. Inst. N.Y., 1971; student U.S. Naval Postgrad. Sch., Monterey, Calif., 1980-81; FAA rated transport pilot. Served as enlisted man U.S. Navy, 1969-71; commd. ensign, 1971, advanced through grades to lt. comdr., 1980; project mgr. research and devel., Naval Air Systems Command, Washington, 1973-75; jet flight instr. Naval Air Sta., Kingsville, Tex., 1975-77; aircraft comdr., VR-1, Naval Air Sta., Norfolk, Va., 1977-78, transport aircraft comdr., 1978-80; electronic warfare pilot tactical electronic warfare squadron 137, Washington, 1982—; instr. aeros.; engring. cons. Decorated Nat. Def. Service medal; Am. Inst. of N.Y.C. sci. grantee, 1973. Mem. AIAA, U.S. Naval Inst., Tailhook Assn. Roman Catholic. Contbr. articles to profl. publs.; inventor motion electrophotographic imaging machine.

MCADAMS, CHARLES MICHAEL, historian, ednl. adminstr.; b. Oceanside, Calif., May 8, 1947; s. John and Trudy Mae (Fleming) McA.; B.A., U. Pacific, 1976; M.A., John Carroll U., 1978; Ed.D. candidate U. San Francisco; m. Mary Anna Tuma, Dec. 13, 1968. Ednl. mktg. cons. Ednl. Mgmt., Inc., Berkeley, Calif., 1977-78; program coordinator U. San Francisco, 1978-80, regional mgr. Coll. Profl. Studies, 1980—; career/life planning cons. Mondragon Assos., San Francisco, 1977-82; co-dir. Croatian Info. Service, 1975—. Served with USMC, 1965-69, U.S. Army, 1971-72. Mem. Am. Assn. Univ. Adminstrs., Am. Assn. Advancement Slavic Studies, Croatian Acad. Am., Am. Soc. Tng. and Devel., Assn. Croatian Studies, Delta Tau Kappa, Phi Alpha Theta. Contbr. articles to profl. jours. Home: PO Box 254483 Sacramento CA 95865 Office: University of San Francisco 601 University Ave Sacramento CA 95825

MCADAMS, HARRY MAYHEW, broadcasting exec., state senator; b. Lorena, Tex., Aug. 12, 1916; s. William Rufus and Violet (Hutchinson) McA.; A.A., Decatur Bapt. Coll., 1936; B.S., N. Tex. State Coll., 1938; m. Gladys Crume, Apr. 2, 1942; children—James Michael, Diane Louise. Tchr. pub. schs. of Tex., 1938-41; pres., gen. mgr. Sta. KWEW, Inc., Hobbs., N.Mex., 1946—. Plains Broadcast Co., Inc., Portales, 1950-53; pres. Triple M Mining Co., Inc., 1953—; exec. v.p. Plaza Devel. Inc., 1959—; mem. N.Mex. Senate, 1970—. Mem. Hobbs Athletic Adv. Bd., Hobbs Pub. Sch. Bd. 1961—, pres., 1963—; pres. Hobbs Bd. Edn., 1962-63; lay mem. Sch. Improvement Com., 1957-58; chmn. Hobbs City Park and Recreation Bd., 1952—. Served to lt. col. USAF, 1941-46. mem. Res., now comdt. Hobbs Air Res. Unit. Decorated Air Medal with 9 oak leaf clusters, D.F.C., Presdl. citation, Purple Heart. Mem. C. of C. (pres. 1957-59). Clubs: Masons, Shriners. Home: 2112 N Fowler St Hobbs NM 88240 Office: 1515 N Dal Paso Hobbs NM 88240

MCADAMS, MARY TUMA, association executive, consultant; b. Ft. Dodge, Iowa, Jan. 16, 1948; d. Vencl Joseph and Mary Phyllis (Phillips) Tuma; m. Charles Michael McAdams, Sept. 13, 1968. B.A. summa cum laude, U. Pacific, 1971, M.A. summa cum laude, 1972; M. Pub. Adminstrn., U. San Francisco, 1984. Program coordinator San Joaquin County Mental Health Service, Stockton, Calif., 1972-78; dep. dir. Statewide PCP Project, UCLA, 1978-81; dir. edn. Vis. Nurse Assn., Sacramento, 1981—; cons. State of Calif. Am. field service exchange student to Switzerland, 1966-67. Mem. Am. Soc. Tng. and Devel., Am. Field Service, No. Calif. Council Inservice Educators, Am. Soc. Health Edn. and Tng. Republican. Author: Communicating ... Sense and Nonsense, 1975; Phencyclidine Abuse Manual, 1980.

MCADAMS, RONALD EMERSON, medical electronics co. exec.; b. Evansville, Ind., Sept. 17, 1942; s. Waldo Emerson and Alma Inez (Pierce) McA.; 1 dau., Claire Emerson. B.S., U. Evansville, 1969; M.B.A., Wharton Sch., U. Pa., 1971. Bus. analyst ARCO, 1972-74; dir. treasury Raychem. Corp., 1974-79; pres., chief exec. officer Circadian Inc., Sunnyvale, Calif., 1979—; dir. Metcal, Inc., Tasa Corp.; part-time extension tchr. U. Calif. Served with USN, 1963-67; Vietnam. Decorated Bronze Star with combat V, Purple Heart; Joseph Wharton fellow, 1969. Address: 1152 Greenwood Ave Palo Alto CA 94301

MC ALLISTER, CYRUS RAY, JR., cons.; b. Portland, Oreg., Apr. 22, 1922; s. Cyrus Ray and Edna Marion (Parks) McA.; B.A. magna cum laude, U. Minn., 1948; M.A., U. Oreg., 1951; m. Mary Ruth Carter, Sept. 28, 1953; children—Sharon Louise, Cyrus Ray III, Mark Ross. Teaching asst. U. Minn., 1948; instr. U. Idaho, 1948-50; teaching fellow, grad. asst. U. Oreg., 1950-52; analyst Dept. Def., Washington, 1952; staff mem., mathematician Sandia Corp., Albuquerque, 1952-57, cons., 1957; sr. research scientist Nuclear div. Kaman Aircraft Corp., Albuquerque, 1957-59, cons., Colorado Springs, Colo., 1959-60; cons. Hamilton Watch Co., Lancaster, Pa., 1960; pres., tech. dir. McAllister & Assos., Inc., Albuquerque, 1960-63; research dir., Booz, Allen Applied Research, Inc., Los Angeles, 1963-68; with the Aerospace Corp., 1968-72; chmn. bd. Fenmac, Inc., 1978—; cons., 1966—. Cons. mem. Joint Am. Soc. Quality Control-IEEE Task Force on Systems Reliability, 1961. Mem. citizens adv. com. Planning Dept., City of Los Angeles, 1976-77; bd. dirs. Encino Property Owners Assn., 1974-82, v.p., 1975-77, pres., 1978-79. Served with USAAF, 1940-45; ETO. Mem. Am. Meteorol. Soc., Am. Math. Soc., Soc. Indsl. and Applied Math., Math. Assn. Am., AAAS, Am. Statis. Assn., Soc. Engring. Sci., AIM, N.Y. Acad. Scis., Encino C. of C. (dir.), Phi Beta Kappa, Sigma Xi, Pi Mu Epsilon. Contbr. articles to profl. jours. Home: 4729 Libbit Ave Encino CA 91436

MC ALLISTER, GIGI (GRACE EDGAR), interior designer; b. Daytona Beach, Fla., Oct. 19, 1936; d. Wiley and Bettie (Bennett) Edgar; student Stetson U., DeLand, Fla.; m. Jack McAllister, Dec. 6, 1969. Sec. Edgar's Cement Block Co., 1956; profl. model, 1956-69; owner Poodle Parlour and Gaybrook Crossing Kennels, Fairview, Pa., 1955-68, Sch. for Dog Grooming, Breeding and Showing, Fairview, 1955-68; asst. producer TV show Children's Hour, 1965-66; interior designer, 1967—;

propr. Discount Decors, Reno, 1970—; owner Designs by Gigi, catering bus.; screen and TV actress, appearing in: Quincy, Jinx, California Split, Operation Overkill; breeder poodles, Yorkshire Terriers, Dalmations, Maltese; tchr. interior design, also dealer Horseless Carriages, Ltd., vintage automobiles. Bd. dirs. St. Vincent's Aux., Reno, 1977—. Recipient Times award for home design Times News, 1967; owner Yorkshire Terrier, champion Gaybrook Steiff Toy, winner Best of Breed, Westminster All-Breed Show, Madison Sq. Gardens, 1967. Mem. Jr. League, Nat. Thespians. Baptist. Address: Riverside Terr 1327 Jones St Reno NV 89503

MCALLISTER, JAMES C., management consultant; b. Ala., Nov. 16, 1954; s. Roy L. and Zedell (Ward) McA. B.S. in Orgn. Behavior, U. Ala., 1977. Coll. instr., fund raiser U. Ala., Tuscaloosa, 1977-78; dir. alumni affairs U. South Ala., Mobile, 1978-80; v.p. Morehead & Co., Los Angeles, 1980—. Office: 2029 Century Park E Suite 2150 Los Angeles CA 90067

MCALLISTER, LERAY L., state senator, educator; b. Anaconda, Mont., Apr. 10, 1930; s. Leland G. and Mary LuElla (Gray) McA.; m. LuJean Roper, 1954; children—Ann, Douglas, Bruce, Maria, Eric. B.S., Brigham Young U., 1957; M.S., Ariz. State U., 1959, D.B.A., 1971. Asst. prof. acctg. So. Utah State Coll., 1959-63; assoc. prof. acctg. Brigham Young U., 1963—; mem. Utah Ho. of Reps. from Dist. 36, 1975-83, Utah State Senate, 1983—. Served with C.I.C., U.S. Army, 1953-55. Mem. Am. Acctg. Assn., Beta Gamma Sigma. Republican. Mormon. Home: 296 E 1864 S Orem UT 84057 Office: Utah State Senate Salt Lake City UT 84114

MCALLISTER, PETER MICHAEL, hospital administrator; b. Glendale, Calif., Nov. 27, 1938; s. Paul Blanchard and Blanch Isabella (Kirkpatrick) M.; m. Diane Marie Williams, Feb. 4, 1961; children—Kevin, Paul, Kim, Jeannie. Student Oreg. State Coll., 1956-57; B.S., U. So. Calif. 1961. Process engr. Aeronutronic Co., Newport Beach, Calif., 1966-68; indsl. engr., plant mgr. Krasne Co., Los Angeles, 1968-69; project engr., mgr. indsl. engring. Am. Medicorps Inc., 1970-73; asst. adminstr. Sunrise Hosp., Las Vegas, Nev., 1973-75, assoc. exec. dir., 1975-82; cons. med. execs., 1982—; assoc. adminstr. North Las Vegas Hosp., 1982-83; adminstr. Community Hosp. of Huntington Park, 1983—. Served to capt. USMC, 1961-66. Decorated 21 Air medals, Purple Heart. Mem. So. Council Nev. Hosp. Assn. (chmn. 1979), Nev. Hosp. Assn. (pres. 1981-82). Home: 7435 S Rogers St Las Vegas NV 89118

MCALPINE, TERRY LYNN, public information officer; b. Lynwood, Calif., Jan. 5, 1952; d. Max N. and Mary H. (Mozingo) McA.; m. Louis A. Palmer, June 26, 1982. B.A. in Journalism, Pepperdine U., 1974. Pub. info. officer Norwalk-La Mirada Unified Sch. Dist., Norwalk, Calif., 1975—; Mem. Nat. Sch. Pub. Relations Assn., Pub. Relations Soc. Am., Norwalk-La Mirada Adminstrs. Assn., So. Calif. Sch. Pub. Relations Assn. (pres.). Home: 9602 Walthall Ave Whittier CA 90605 Office: Norwalk-La Mirada School District 12820 S Pioneer Blvd Norwalk CA 90650

MC ANALLY, DON, editor-publisher; b. Sewell, N.J., Oct. 27, 1913; s. James C. and Ina (MacLeod) McA.; grad. high sch.; m. Edith P. McKinney, Dec. 11, 1934; 1 dau., Shirley M. English. Reporter, Woodbury (N.J.) Daily Times, 1932-45; editor Owens-Ill. Co. publs. in N.J. and Ohio, 1945-47; asst. advt. mgr. Libbey-Owens-Ford Glass Co., also Libbey-Owens-Ford Glass Fibers Co., Toledo, 1947-59; editor Pacific Oil Marketer, Los Angeles, 1960-66; editor-publisher O&A Marketing News, La Canada, Calif., 1966—, The Automotive Booster of Calif., 1974—, Calif. Sr. Citizen News, La Canada, 1977—. Recipient Good Neighbor award Toledo, 1948; award Western Oil Industry, 1971; Man of Yr. award Pacific Oil Conf., 1977; awards Douglas Oil Co., 1978, Automotive Affiliated Reps., 1979. Mem. Calif. Ind. Oil Marketers Assn., OX5 Aviation Pioneers. Republican. Episcopalian. Clubs: Elks, Lions, Masquers, Gabby, Silver Dollar, Roorag (Los Angeles). Home: 4409 Indiana Ave La Canada Office: PO Box 765 La Canada CA 91011

MCANNANY, TERRY GORDON, accountant; b. Austin Minn., Apr. 14, 1937; s. Clifford James and Harriet Elaine M.; m. Arlene Renee Farris, Mar. 10, 1969 (div.); 1 dau., Shannon Renee. B.A., Mankato State Coll., 1963. C.P.A., Minn., 1968. Pvt. practice, Wheatland, Wyo., 1973—; tchr. adult edn., Wheatland. Mem. Town Council Wheatland, 1977-80, mayor, 1981-82; vol. fireman, emergency med. technician. Served with USAF, 1957-61. Recipient Dyna Med. award, 1982. Mem. Am. Inst. C.P.A.s, Wyo. Ambulance Emergency Med. Services Assn. Republican. Club: Masons. Address: 1556 Gilchrist St Box 398 Wheatland WY 82201

MCARTHUR, DAVID ALEXANDER, physicist; b. Meridian, Miss., Aug. 14, 1938; s. Robert Stainton and Kathleen (Sanders) McA.; B.S., U. Ariz., 1960; postgrad. U. Munich, 1960-61; Ph.D., U. Calif., Berkeley, 1967; m. Beverley Bogue, Sept. 16, 1961; children—Shirin Robin, Kara Kay, Paul David. With Bell Telephone Labs., Holmdel, N.J., 1967-69; with Sandia Labs., Albuquerque, 1969—, mem. tech. staff, 1969-83, disting. mem. tech. staff, 1983—. Active, N. Valley Neighborhoods Assn., Albuquerque, 1974—. Nat. Merit scholar, 1956-60; Fulbright scholar to Germany, 1960-61; Woodrow Wilson fellow, 1961-62; NSF fellow, 1962-67. Mem. Am. Phys. Soc., Ams. for Rational Energy Alternatives, Am. Nuclear Soc. Republican. Presbyterian. Research and inventions in plasma modelling, 1971-74, reactor-excited laser, 1974-76, exptl. work in nuclear reactor safety, 1977-82, others; patentee in field. Office: Div 6423 Sandia Nat Labs PO Box 5800 Albuquerque NM 87185

MCATEE, RICHARD EVERETT, alcohol fuels co. exec.; b. Springfield, Mo., Dec. 14, 1929; s. Eslie Howard and Esther Marie (Rippey) McA.; B.S., Fort Hays Kans. State Coll., 1962; M.S., U. Idaho, 1964; m. Wanda Joyce Houston, Jan. 20, 1952; children—Peggy Jo, Diana Gay, Nancy Beth. Mass spectroscopist Phillips Petroleum Co., Idaho Falls, Idaho, 1964-66, Idaho Nuclear Corp., Idaho Falls, 1966-70; sr. chemist Allied Chem. Corp., 1970-78; scientist EG&G Idaho, Inc., 1978-80, mgr. ops., 1980—. Bd. dirs. Atomic Workers Credit Union, 1971—. Served with U.S. Army, 1948-50. NDEA fellow, 1962-64. Mem. Am. Nuclear Soc., Geothermal Resource Council. Methodist. Club: Toastmasters. Contbr. articles to profl. jours. Home: 646 E 16th St Idaho Falls ID 83401 Office: EG&G PO Box 1625 Mail Stop 72 Idaho Falls ID 83415

MC ATHIE, MARYLOU, nursing cons.; b. Huron, S.D., July 9, 1927; d. John and Agnes Virginia (Mangan) McA.; diploma Oak Park Hosp. unit Loyola U., Chgo., 1948; B.S. in Nursing, DePaul U., 1954, M.S. in Nursing, 1956; Ed.D., U. San Francisco, 1980. Cons. Calif. State Dept. Health, 1961-68; dir. nursing San Joaquin Gen. Hosp., Stockton, Calif., 1960-68; regional nursing cons., spl. asst. Pacific Basin affairs USPHS, HEW, San Francisco, 1968—; ex officio mem. exec. com. Western Council on Higher Edn. for Nursing. Mem. scholarship com. San Joaquin March of Dimes, 1964-68. Recipient award HEW Region IX, 1974, commendation March of Dimes, 1968, citizen's commendation San Joaquin County, 1967, cert. of merit UCLA, 1972, cert. in leadership tng. Western Council on Higher Edn. in Nursing, U. Calif., San Francisco, 1962, cert. in pub. health nursing Calif. Dept. Pub. Health, U. San Francisco, 1964. Mem. Am., Calif. (conv. del. 1972) nurses assns., Nat., Western (chmn. com. nursing service adminstrs.) leagues for nursing, AAUW, Am. Pub. Health Assn., Western Soc. Research in Nursing, Nat. Assn. Fed. Suprs., Fed. Exec. Women's Assn., Council on Grad. Edn. in Nursing Service Adminstrn., Sigma Theta Tau. Speaker, convs., confs.; contbr. to audio and TV tapes, articles to profl. publs. Home: 8109 Arroyo Way Stockton CA 95209 Office: 50 United Nations Plaza San Francisco CA 94102

MCAULEY, LAWRENCE YOUNG, JR., engineering design and construction company executive; b. Tampa, Fla., May 16, 1943; s. Lawrence Young and Avanelle (Scofield) McA.; student U. S. Fla., 1961-63, B.S., John Quincy Adams Coll., 1965; postgrad. Ga. Inst. Tech., 1967; m. Joan G. Dibbley, Apr. 3, 1967; 1 dau., Nicole A. Mech. draftsman S. Allen Selby, Cons. Engrs., Atlanta, 1965-67; asso. Frank M. Brewer & Assos., Cons. Engrs., Atlanta, 1967-72; pres. Astro Heating and Air Conditioning Co., Inc., Atlanta, 1972-75; sr. project engr. Hosp. Bldg. and Equipment Corp., St. Louis, 1976-78; mech. project mgr. aerospace and high tech. Jacobs Architects, Pasadena, Calif., 1978—. Bd. dirs. Ashdun Hall Sch., Atlanta, 1974-75; mem. local Congressional Bd. of Advisement San Fernando Valley, Calif., 1981-83. Mem. ASHRAE, Am. Soc. Plumbing Engrs., Assn. Energy Engrs., Calif. Solar Energy Assn. Home: 11581 Blythe St North Hollywood CA 91605 Office: 251 S Lake Ave Pasadena CA 91101

MCAULIFFE, CLAYTON DOYLE, chemist; b. Chappell, Nebr., Aug. 18, 1918; s. John F. and Emma Elizabeth (Stenger) McA.; A.B., Nebr. Wesleyan U., 1941; M.S. (Univ. fellow 1941-42), U. Minn., 1942; Ph.D. (Univ. fellow 1942-43, 46-48), Cornell U., 1948; m. Irene Opal Pickering, Sept. 5, 1943; children—Carol Ann, Clifford Andrew, Douglas Clayton, Thomas Frank. Lab. asst. Nebr. Wesleyan U., 1939-41; research chemist Manhattan Project, 1943-46; cons. Dept. Agr., 1947-48; research asso. Cornell U., 1948-50; research asso. prof. N.C. State U., 1950-56; sr. research chemist Chevron Oil Field Research Co., La Habra, Calif., 1956-67, sr. research asso., 1967—; mem. steering com. petroleum in marine environ., com. energy and environ. Nat. Acad. Scis., 1972-75, mem. Ocean Scis. Bd., 1975-77; cons. in field. Grantee NSF, duPont Co., AEC. Fellow AAAS; mem. Am. Chem. Soc., Soc. Petroleum Engrs., Am. Soc. Agronomy, Soil Sci. Soc. Am., Am. Assn. Petroleum Geologists. Republican. Methodist. Author papers in field, chpts. in books. Patentee in field. Home: 1220 Frances Ave Fullerton CA 92631 Office: Box 446 La Habra CA 90631

MC AUSLAND, THOMAS DENNIS, aerospace executive; b. N.Y.C., Dec. 4, 1932; s. Thomas and Mary (Friel) McA.; B.S. in Mech. Engring., Columbia U., 1958; student CCNY, 1954-56; m. Catherine Desmoulins, Apr. 30, 1969. Project engr. W.L. Maxson Corp., N.Y.C., 1958-59; sales engr. Hazeltine Corp., Little Neck, N.Y., 1959-62; dir. European ops. Hughes Aircraft Co., Paris, 1962-68, mgr. mktg. ground systems group, Fullerton, Calif., 1968-72; dir. European ops. Litton Data Systems, Brussels, 1972-78, v.p., Van Nuys, Calif., 1978—. Mem. Nat. Democratic Club, Washington, 1980—. Mem. Am. Def. Preparedness Assn., Navy League, Electronic Industries Assn., Assn. U.S. Army, Air Force Assn. Roman Catholic. Club: Capitol Hill (Washington). Home: 4411 Portico Pl Encino CA 91316 Office: Litton Data Systems 8000 Woodley Ave Van Nuys CA 91409

MCAVOY, GARY ROBERT, communications exec.; b. Mar. 4, 1949; s. Robert Joseph and Marjorie Ann (Friend) McA. Western regional adminstr. GTE Info. Systems, Anaheim, Calif., 1974-77; chmn., chief exec. officer Aventura Sailing Assn., Inc., Dana Point, Calif., 1976—; freelance writer; newspaper columnist South Coast Beacon, 1980 82; dir. communications Nautical Heritage Mus. at Dana Point, 1982—. Trustee Dana Point Ocean Inst. Found., 1980-82. Served with U.S. Army, 1969-72. Decorated Army Commendation medal. Mem. Dana Point C. of C. (pres. 1979-80), U.S. Yacht Racing Union, Dana Harbor Assn. (pres. 1981—), So. Calif. Marina Assn., Manuscript Soc., Nat. Writer's Club, Orange County Press Club. Contbg. editor Day by Day, 1978-79. Office: 35102 Del Obispo St Dana Point CA 92629

MCBRIDE, GUY THORNTON, JR., chemical engineer, university president; b. Austin, Tex., Dec. 12, 1919; s. Guy Thornton and Imogene (Thrasher) McB.; m. Rebekah Jane Bush, Sept. 2, 1942; children—Rebekah Ann, William Howard, Ellen McBride McCarty. B.S. with distinction in Chem. Engring., U. Tex., 1940; Sc.D. in Chem. Engring., M.I.T., 1948. Registered profl. engr., Tex., La., N.Y., Colo. Instr. chem. engring. M.I.T., Cambridge, 1942-44, research assoc., 1946-48, assoc. prof. chem. engring., dean students Rice U., Houston, 1948-58; v.p. research Texasgulf Inc., N.Y.C., 1960-63, v.p. agrl. chems. div., 1963-70, dir., 1974; pres., prof. mineral engring. Colo. Sch. Mines, Golden, 1970—; dir. Hailiburton Co., Texasgulf Inc. (hon.), Hercules Inc., Kerr-McGee; mem. Colo. Gov's. Sci. Tech. Adv. Council, 1976—; mem. Nat. Pub. Lands Adv. Council. Fellow Am. Inst. Chem. Engrs.; mem. Am. Chem. Soc., Sigma Xi. Office: Colo Sch Mines Golden CO 80401

MCBRIDE, ROBERT RAY, communications exec.; b. Pocatello, Idaho, May 8, 1942; s. Robert Leroy and Leah Rose (Christiansen) McB.; B.S., U. Calif., Davis, 1965; postgrad. Golden Gate U., 1977; m. Sandra Lee Medinger, July 2, 1977. N.E. regional sales mgr. Commex Corp., Sunnyvale, Calif., 1974-75; communications coordinator ITT, Sunnyvale, 1975-76; mgr. hdqrs. communications Foremost-McKesson, Inc., San Francisco, 1976-77; corp. communications mgr. ROLM Corp., Santa Clara, Calif., 1977—; pres., prin. TELCOM Assos., Half Moon Bay, Calif., 1976-77; propr. El Gato Bit & Spur, Half Moon Bay, 1970—. Clubs: Am. Horse Show Assn. (judge), Am. Quarter Horse Assn., Calif. State Horsemen's Assn. Home: PO Box 307 Half Moon Bay CA 94019 Office: 4900 Old Ironsides Dr Santa Clara CA 95050

MCBRIDE, SUSAN MARIE, accountant; b. New Ulm, Minn., Dec. 24, 1953; d. Walter James and Grace Victoria (Nelson) Rolloff; B.A., Central Wash. State U., 1975; m. Larry Ronal McBride, Dec. 18, 1971 (div. Dec. 1975); adopted children—Michael Allen Stay, Melissa Ann Stay. Staff acct. Dolsen, Synoground, Smith & Martin, Yakima, Wash., 1975-76; office mgr. Simco Mechanical Inc., Yakima, 1976-78; state examiner IV, Office State auditor, Olympia, Wash., 1978—. Mem. Wash. Soc. C.P.A.'s. Democrat. Lutheran. Home: Route 11 Box 11400 Lot 126 Kennewick WA 99336 Office: Office State Auditor Legislative Bldg Olympia WA 98504

MC BRIDE, THOMAS FREDERICK, university dean; b. Elgin, Ill., Feb. 8, 1929; s. Thomas Wallace and Sarah Rosalie (Pierce) McB.; B.A., N.Y. U., 1952; LL.B., Columbia, 1956; m. Catherine Higgs Milton, Aug. 23, 1975; children—Matthew, Elizabeth, John, Raphael, Luke. Admitted to N.Y. State bar, 1956, D.C. bar, 1966, U.S. Supreme Ct. bar, 1963; asst. dist. atty. N.Y. County, 1956-59; trial atty. organized crime sect. Dept. Justice, 1961-65; adviser to Home Ministry, Govt. India, 1964; ofcl. Peace Corps, 1965-68; dep. chief counsel select com. on crime Ho. of Reps., 1969-70; asso. dir., staff dir. Police Found., 1970-73; asso. spl. prosecutor Watergate, 1973-75; dir. bur. enforcement CAB, 1975-77; insp. gen. U.S. Dept. Agr., Washington, 1977-81, U.S. Dept. Labor, Washington, 1981-82; assoc. dean Stanford U. Law Sch., 1982—. Served with AUS, 1946-47. Mem. D.C. Bar Assn. Co-author: Team Policing, 1973. Office: Stanford U Law School Stanford CA 94305

MCCABE, DONALD LEE, physician; b. Phila., Nov. 5, 1925; s. Joseph Grant and Agnes Muriel (Lee) McC.; student Ursinus Coll., 1944-45, Haverford Coll., 1946; D.O., Phila. Coll. Osteo. Medicine, 1950; m. Jean Smallwood, June 25, 1977; children—Geoffrey, Timothy, Karen, Ellie, Derek, Traill. Intern, Phila. Osteo. Hosp., 1950-51; resident in psychiatry Del. Valley Mental Health Found., 1973-74; individual practice medicine, specializing in gen. practice, Towanda, Pa., 1951-68, specializing in psychoanalysis, gen. medicine, Harrisburg, Pa., 1968-71; psychiatrist Harrisburg State Hosp., also Delaware Valley Mental Health Found., 1970-73; individual practice medicine specializing in gen. practice and psychiatry, 1974—; faculty Phila. Coll. Osteo. Medicine, 1971; preceptor Mich. State Osteo. Med. Coll., 1978; founder Coll. Osteo. Medicine of Pacific, 1979; cons. in field. Lic. physician Calif. Fellow Am. Public Health Assn., Acad. Psychosomatic Medicine, Am. Coll. Gen. Practitioners in Osteo. Medicine and Surgery (pres. Pa. 1968-71, nat. dir. 1970-71, pres. Calif. Soc., 1977); mem. Osteo. Physicians and Surgeons Calif. (pres. 1979) editor jour. 1975-79), Calif. Soc. Orthomolecular Medicine (founding), Am. Osteo. Assn. (Calif. del. 1978-79), Am. Coll. Neuropsychiatry, AAAS, Academie International de Lausanne, other orgns. Club: Vallejo Yacht (Calif.). Home: Sacramento CA Office: 3530 Auburn Blvd Suite 3 Sacramento CA 95821

MCCABE, JAMES LAURENCE, auditor; b. Los Angeles, Dec. 26, 1945; s. William Laurence and Frances Adel McC.; B.S. in Mktg., Chico State Coll., 1971; B.S. in Bus. Edn., Calif. State U., Chico, 1973; M.S. in Bus. Edn., Mont. State U., 1977; m. Dolores Emma, June 22, 1974; children—John Joseph, Karen Renee. Tchr. bus. edn. Gonzales (Calif.) Union High Sch., 1973-76; grad. teaching asst. Mont. State U., 1976-77; mgmt. instr. Lower Columbia Coll., 1977-78, Wenatchee Valley Coll., 1978-81; pres. Mgmt. Cons. Co., Wenatchee, Wash., 1979-81; owner, gen. mgr., dir., Inter-systems Inc., Wenatchee, 1980-81; mgr., fin. analyst U. Idaho, Moscow, 1981-82, asst. auditor, 1982—. Coordinator dance marathon Muscular Dystrophy Assn., Wenatchee, 1980. Served with U.S. Army, 1968-70; Vietnam. Recipient citation of merit Muscular Dystrophy Assn., 1980. Mem. Wash. State Mid-Mgmt. Educators Assn. (chmn. 1980-81). Republican. Clubs: Lions, Toastmasters (Outstanding Service award as speechcraft coordinator 1979). Home: 216 Cedar Ave Moscow ID 83843 Office: U Idaho Moscow ID 83843

MC CABE, RICHARD MICHAEL, aircraft co. ofcl.; b. Cambridge, Mass., Sept. 24, 1935; s. Francis Thomas and Luberta Marie (Harden) McC.; B.S. in Naval Architecture and Marine Engring., M.I.T., 1957, M.S. in Indsl. Mgmt., 1965; m. Mary Ann Kelly, Sept. 3, 1960; children—Ann Catherine, Michael Eugene, Matthew Scott, John Neil. Marine engr. Newport News (Va.) Shipbuilding and Dry Dock Co., 1957-63; propulsion engr. Douglas Aircraft Co., Long Beach, Calif., 1965-66, bus. systems analyst, 1966, bus. systems devel. mgr., 1967-80, dir. mgmt. and info. systems, 1980—; instr. human resources mgmt. Calif. State U., Long Beach, 1981-82. Chmn., vice chmn., sec. YMCA of West Orange County, 1970-79. Served with USAF, 1958-63. Mem. Soc. Naval Architects and Marine Engrs., Am. Mgmt. Assn., Douglas Aircraft Mgmt. Club. Republican. Roman Catholic. Home: 1015 Catalina Ave Seal Beach CA 90740 Office: 3855 Lakewood Blvd Long Beach CA 90846

MCCAFFERY, MICHAEL ERIN, lawyer; b. New Orleans, May 11, 1944; s. Walter M. and Clair Anita (Tankersley) McC.; m. Angie Garcia, Mar. 5, 1966; children—Michele, April. A.A., Golden West Coll., 1972; B.S.L., Western State U., 1974, J.D., 1976. Bar: Calif. 1977. Mgr., Alpha Beta Co., Huntington Beach, Calif., 1968-77; sole practice law, Westminster, Calif., 1977-79; house counsel/ops. mgr. Challenge Builders, Inc., Bakersfield, Calif., 1979-80; gen. counsel Carl N. Swenson Co., Inc., San Jose, Calif., 1980—; instr. Coastline Regional Occupational Programs, Grocery Occupations, Costa Mesa, Calif., 1975-76; legal counsel Miscellaneous Unemployed Singers in Concert, 1980-82. Served to 1st lt. U.S. Army, 1965-68. Decorated Purple Heart, Air medal, Bronze Star; Retail Clks. Union scholar, 1975. Mem. Santa Clara County Bar Assn. (chmn. labor law com. 1983), Peninsula Assn. Gen. Counsel, Associated Gen. Contractors (collective bargaining com.). Republican. Episcopalian. Office: 95 S Market St Suite 600 San Jose CA 95113

MCCAFFREY, FRANK JOSEPH, electronic mfg. co. exec.; b. N.Y.C., Feb. 18, 1923; s. Patrick J. and Catherine (Kavanagh) McC.; B.S. in Bus. Adminstrn., Hofstra U., 1958; M.B.A., San Jose State U., 1974; m. Ann M. Owens, Sept. 10, 1949; children—Ann Marie, Kathleen, Patricia Josephine, Joan Frances, Robin Elizabeth, Jill Diane. Systems Sales rep. McBee Co., N.Y.C., 1945-47, zone sales mgr., 1947-49, area sales mgr., 1950 55; dir. sales promotion and sales tng. Royal McBee Corp., N.Y.C., 1955-61, dist. sales mgr. computer services Litton Automated Bus. Services, San Francisco, 1961-65, regional mgr., 1966-67, nat. accounts mgr., 1967-69; founder, v.p. mktg. Novar Corp. div. Gen. Tel. & Elec., Mountain View, Calif., 1969, v.p. mktg. 1970-73; v.p. mktg. Trendata Corp., 1973-74; founder, v.p. mktg. AzurData Inc., 1974-78; pres., founder Winners Group, Inc., 1978—, also dir.; pres., founder Star Computer, Inc., 1980—. Served with USNR, 1943-45. Mem. Sales Honor Club, 1947-67; recipient top sales dist. award Litton Automated Bus. Systems, 1966. Mem. Nat. Assn. Accountants, San Francisco C. of C., Hosp. Fin. Mgmt. Assn. Am. Mgmt. Assn. Roman Catholic. K.C. Home: 19796 Oakhaven Dr Saratoga CA 95070 Office: 3080 Olcott St Santa Clara CA 95051

MC CAFFREY, JAMES DAVID, physician; b. Pawtucket, R.I., May 16, 1920; s. James P. and Louise E. (Cassidy) McC.; student Brown U., 1950; M.D., Washington U., St. Louis, 1952; m. Shirley A. Dulong, Feb. 15, 1952; children—James David, Roger, Elizabeth. Intern, Miami Valley Hosp., Dayton, Ohio, 1952-53; practice medicine, Dayton, 1953-59; partner Johnston Gendel Med. Clinic, occupational med. services, Anaheim, Calif., 1959-78; cons. practice medicine specializing in occupational medicine, Fullerton, Calif., 1978—; mem. staff Anaheim Meml. Hosp., 1959-81, Martin Luther Hosp., 1960-80; hosp. adminstr. Canyon Gen. Hosp., 1979-80, also chmn. bd. dirs.; pres. Canyon Gen. Hosp., Inc.; med. dir., cons. various coms. Served with Med. Adminstrv. Corps, U.S. Army, 1941-46. Lic. physician, Calif., Ohio, Mo. Diplomate Am. Bd. Preventive Medicine. Fellow Am. Occupational Med. Assn.; mem. Calif., Orange County med. assns., Am., Western (past chmn.) occupational health confs., Western Occupational Med. Assn. (past chmn.), Am. Acad. Occupational Medicine. Roman Catholic. Home: 1525 Camino Loma Fullerton CA 92633

MC CAFFREY, STANLEY EUGENE, univ. pres.; b. Taft, Calif., Feb. 26, 1917; s. Joseph Cormack and Dorothy (Bunyard) McC.; A.B., U. Calif., 1938; LL.D., Golden Gate U., 1972, Pepperdine U., 1978, Korea U., 1981; m. Beth Conolley, July 6, 1941; children—Stephen Conolley, Nancy. Personnel work Standard Oil Co. (Calif.), 1939-40; coordinator vets. affairs U. Calif. at Berkeley, 1946, v.p., exec. asst., 1957-60, exec. mgr. Alumni Assn., 1948-56; advt. mgr. Kaiser Aluminum, Oakland, Calif., 1946-48; exec. asst. to Vice Pres. U.S., 1960; pres. U. Pacific, Stockton, Calif., 1971—; pres., exec. officer San Francisco Bay Area Council, 1961-71. Mem. Vets Bd. Cal., chmn., 1956; del. Gov.'s Conf. on Children and Youth, 1956; mem. Berkeley Recreation Commn., v.p., 1957; mem. Oakland Manpower Commn., 1967-68; mem. State Commn. on Govt. Orgn. and Economy, 1966-68. Bd. dirs. Berkeley Community Chest, 1952-55, Berkeley YMCA, 1953-54, Internat. House; pres. Berkeley Service Club Council, 1954-55, pres. San Francisco Bay Area council, 1960-71; trustee Peralta Jr. Coll. Dist., 1962-68, pres., 1964-66; vice chmn. trustees Golden Gate Coll., San Francisco, 1965-71; trustee U. Calif. Alumni Found., Pacific Med. Center; bd. regents Coll. Holy Names. Served from ensign to lt. comdr., USNR, 1940-45. Decorated Silver Star, Legion of Merit. Mem. Am. Alumni Council (treas. 1952-54), Assn. Ind. Calif. Colls. and Univs. (pres. 1976-78), Ind. Colls. No. Calif. (dir.), Western Coll. Assn. (exec. com. 1975, v.p. 1977-78, pres. 1979—), Big C Soc. U. Calif. (dir. 1948-57), Internat. House Assn. (nat. exec. com.), Navy League (v.p. San Francisco council), Order of Golden Bear, Phi Beta Kappa, Pi Sigma Alpha. Conglist. Clubs: Rotary (pres.

Berkeley club 1954-55, now hon. mem., also hon. mem. Stockton club; dist. gov. Rotary Internat. 1964-65; chmn. internat. youth com. 1966-67, mem. internat. bd. dirs. 1969-71, internat. 1st v.p. 1970-71, research com. 1976, nominating com. 1976, 79, internat. pres. 1981-82); Berkeley Fellows; Family, Commonwealth of Calif. (quarterly chmn. 1955, gov.), Bohemian, St. Francis Yacht (San Francisco). Home: Presidents Home U Pacific Stockton CA 95211

MC CAIN, JAMES GORDON, lawyer; b. Charleston, S.C., Feb. 17, 1913; s. John Sydney and Katherine (Vaulx) McC.; B.A., George Washington U., 1933, LL.B., 1935; m. Mary Elizabeth Bouve, Sept. 24, 1938; children—James Gordon, Mary Bouve, Margaret Catherine. Admitted to D.C. bar, 1935; atty. FCC, 1938-41; asst. to pres. Aerojet Engring. Corp., Pasadena, Calif., 1942-44; with J.G. Boswell Co., Los Angeles, 1946-50; practiced in Corcoran, Calif., 1950—; atty. City of Corcoran, 1961—. Asst. sec., atty. Corcoran Community Found.; sec., atty. Corcoran Cemetery Dist. Mem. Am. Bar Assn. (coms. on condemnation and condemnation procedure and municipal tort liability, sects. local govt. law and corps.), Nat. Inst. Law Officers. Club: Commonwealth of Calif. (San Francisco). Home: 1421 Sherman Ave Corcoran CA 93212 Office: 1107 Norboe St Corcoran CA 93212

MCCAIN, JOHN SIDNEY, III, congressman; b. C.Z., Panama, Aug. 29, 1936; s. John Sidney and Roberta (Wright) McC.; m. Cindy Hensley, May 17, 1980; children—Douglas, Andrew, Sidney. B.S., U.S. Navy Acad., 1958; grad. Nat. War Coll., 1973. Commd. ensign U.S. Navy, 1958; dir. Navy Senate Liaison Office, Washington, 1977-81; ret., 1981; prisoner of war, Vietnam, 1967-73; mem. 98th Congress from 1st Ariz. Dist., pres. Freshmen Republicans, 1983. Active Community Assistance League. Decorated Legion of Merit, Bronze Star, Purple Heart, Silver Star, D.F.C., Vietnamese Legion of Merit. Mem. Ariz. C. of C., V.F.W., Am. Legion, D.A.V. Episcopalian. Office: 1123 Longworth House Office Bldg Washington DC 20515

MCCAIN, ROBERT VERNE, newspaper publisher; b. Seattle, Sept. 9, 1929; s. Barton Verne and LaNita Irene (Tribbet) McC.; m. Donna Mae Fields, Jan. 18, 1930; children—Roger, Janice, Earlene. B.A. in Journalism, U. Wash., 1952. Advt. mgr. Honig-Cooper Advt. Agy., Seattle, 1944-46, 48-49; nat. advt. mgr. Vancouver (Wash.) Columbian, 1953-59; pub. Newberg (Oreg.) Graphic, 1959—. Served with AUS, 1946-47. Mem. Soc. Profl. Journalists, Newberg C. of C., Sigma Delta Chi. Methodist. Club: Elks. Home: 1207 Pennington Dr S Newburg OR 97132 Office: 109 N School St Newberg OR 97132

MCCAIN, WARREN EARL, supermarket executive; b. Logan, Kans., 1925; A.A., Oreg. State U., 1948. Supr. sales Mountain States Wholesale Co., 1951-59; with Albertson's Inc., owner, operator supermarkets, 1959—, became mgr. non-foods, 1959, mgr. store, 1962, supr. merchandise, 1965, dir. intermountain region, 1967, v.p. ops., 1968-72, exec. v.p., 1972-74, pres., 1974-76, pres., chmn. bd., chief exec. officer, Boise, Idaho, 1976—, also dir.; dir. Idaho 1st Nat. Bank. Office: Albertson's Inc 250 Parkcenter Blvd Boise ID 83726

MCCALL, CHARLES EDWARD, legal investigator, consultant; b. Coalinga, Calif., Dec. 15, 1942; s. Gale Edward and Nadine Essie (Glover) M.; m. Shirley Ann Beatty, June 9, 1967; children—Karen, Patsy, Lori. A.A. in Criminal Justice, Modesto Jr. Coll., 1974; student Columbia-Pacific U., 1982—. Officer, Riverbank (Calif.) Police, 1971-74; loss prevention mgr. Montgomery Ward & Co., Modesto, Calif., 1974-78; owner and founder McCall's Legal Investigators, Oakdale, Calif., 1974—; accident investigator A.L. Gilbert Co., 1979; former instr. Modesto Jr. Coll. Active Oakdale Planning Commn., 1981—. Served with USAF, 1960-64, USAFR, 1981. Mem. Stanislaus County Safety Council, Am. Soc. Safety Engrs. (dir.). Democrat. Mem. Reformed Christian Ch. Clubs: Moose, Mason. Founder and editor Safety and Loss Prevention Newsletter, 1980.

MCCALLA, MARY ELLEN, artist, educator; b. Memphis, June 15, 1944; d. Martin Joseph and Carolyn Elizabeth (Butin) Travers. Student Okla. U.-Norman, 1962-63; B.S. in Art, Memphis State U., 1967. Cert. tchr., Tenn. Tchr., Memphis Pub. Schs., 1967-75; one woman show: The Four Pheasants, Kalispell, Mont., 1979; group shows include: Ligoa Duncan Arts, N.Y.C., 1977; represented in pvt. collections; sang with Memphis Community Choir, 1972-73. Recipient Prix de Paris, Ligoa Duncan Arts, 1977; Salon des Surindependants, Les Surindependants, Paris, 1977. Mem. NEA, Tenn. Edn. Assn., Memphis Edn. Assn., West Tenn. Edn. Assn., West Tenn. Vocal Music Edn. Assn. (treas. 1967-69), Music Educators Nat. Conf., Memphis Art Edn. Assn. (asst. sec. inservice tng. 1973-74), Art Edn. Assn., Am. Choral Dirs. Assn., Mont. Choral Dirs. Assn., Internat. Soc. Artists, Les Surindependants, Internat. Fine Arts Guild, Alpha Gamma Delta, Mu Phi Epsilon. Home: 264 Scenic Ridge Rd Kalispell MT 59901

MCCALLUM, GEORGE WALTER, state senator; b. Conrad, Mont., July 8, 1919; s. Warren and Gwen (Blackshaw) McC.; m. Verdie Nadine Armstrong, 1943; children—Janice Johnson, Anita Delong, Glenda Ueland, Debra. Student pub. schs. Area supr. J. Hofert Co., 1960-70; mem. Mont. State Senate from 27th Dist., 1971—. Chmn. Sanders County Republican Central Com., 1963-69; trustee Hot Springs High Sch.; dir. East Sanders County Hosp. Bd., Sanders County Fair Bd. Mem. Grange. Presbyterian. Lodge: Masons. Home: Niarada MT 59852 Office: Montana State Senate Helena MT 59620

MCCANDLESS, ALFRED A., congressman; b. Brawley, Calif., July 23, 1927; m. Gail W. Glass; children—Christina, Alfred A., II, Craig, Blaine, Ward. B.A. in Polit. Sci. and Pub. Adminstrn., UCLA; grad. Gen. Motors Inst., Flint, Mich. Bus. exec. Gen. Motors auto-truck dealership, Indio, Calif., 1953-75; mem. 98th Congress from Calif., 1982—. Mem. Riverside County Bd. Suprs., 1972-82, chmn. 4 yrs.; founding mem. South Coast Air Quality Mgmt. Dist., 1975-82, chmn., 1975-81; mem. Riverside County Housing Authority, chmn., 1974-82; founding mem. Sunline Transit Agy., chmn., 1977-82; mem. Coachella Valley Assn. Govts.; exec. com., dir. County Suprs. Assn. Calif., 1971-74. Mem. Indio C. of C., Greater Riverside C. of C. Republican. Lodge: Indio Rotary (past pres.). Office: 510 Cannon House Office Bldg Washington DC 20515*

MCCANN, GERALD ALOYSIUS (KEVIN COSTELLO), playwright, journalist; b. N.Y.C.; s. Aloysius Joseph and Ann (Granaghan) McC.; B.A., San Jose State U.; student Lincoln U. Law Sch.; m. Angelina Palomino, Sept. 17, 1954 (div.); children—Kevin Carlos. Editor, pub. Downtowner Weekly, Ft. Worth, 1950-51; section editor El Universal, Mexico City, Mexico, 1955, 57-59; editor, pub. Curtain Call Mag., Harlingen, Tex., 1956-57; staff KGBT-TV, Harlingen, KATR, Corpus Christi, Tex., 1959; editor CSEU Union Call, San Francisco, 1961-62, Mensa Intelligencer, Los Gatos, Calif., 1973; dir., founder Pacific Internat. Press Service, Palo Alto, Calif., columnist It Takes all Kinds, 1959—, Dateline-Mount Olympus, 1962—, Del Companario (Spanish), 1979—; 1974—. Mem. staff Remedial Phonetic Tng. Center, San Francisco, 1966—. Am. Judicature Soc., Am. Nat. Theatre Assn., Nat. Writers Club, Mensa Internat., Sindicato Nacional de Redactores de la Prensa Mexico City. Author: The Cross of Bonaventure (play) 1967; Viva la Quince Brigada; One Step Enough for Me. Contbr. short stories and articles in English and Spanish to numerous mags. Address: care Clan-na-Gael Literary Agy PO Box 2380 St James Park Sta San Jose CA 95109

MCCANN, JACK ARLAND, former construction and mining equipment company executive, consultant; b. Chestnut, Ill., Apr. 16, 1926; s. Keith Ogden and Miriam Imogene McC.; m. Marian Adele Gordon, Mar. 31, 1956; 1 son, Christopher John. A.B., Bradley U., 1950. Mgr. Washington Office, R.G. LeTourneau Inc., 1950-53; mgr. def. and spl. products Westinghouse Air Brake Co., 1958-64, mgr. nat. accounts, 1964-67, mng. dir. Belgian plant and European mktg., 1967-70; gen. sales mgr. WABCO div. Am. Standard Inc., Peoria, Ill., 1970-73, v.p. mktg., 1973-80, v.p. staff, 1980-82; ret., 1982; now cons. Served with USNR, 1944-46. Decorated chevalier Ordre de la Couronne (Belgium). Mem. Nat. Def. Transp. Assn. (life), U.S. C. of C., Am. Legion. Clubs: Bradley Chiefs; Creve Coeur, Shriners (Peoria); Union League (Chgo.). Masons.

MCCANN, TRAVIS ALEX, state human resources development official, consultant; b. Modesto, Calif., Oct. 21, 1948; s. Travis W. and Vera L. (West) M.; m. Kathy J. Moore, Mar. 2, 1969 (div.); m. 2d, Rose Ann Goldberg, Feb. 22, 1975 (div.). A.A., Cerritos Coll., 1971; B.S. in Acctg., Calif. State U.-Sacramento, 1973; postgrad. Sch. Human Resources Devel., LaJolla, 1974—. Served as enlisted man U.S. Navy, 1966-74; commd. ensign U.S. Navy, 1974; tax auditor Calif. Dept. Employment Devel., Sacramento, 1972-74; tng. officer Calif. Dept. Social Services, Sacramento, 1974—; sr. ptnr. McCann & Tashima Tng. Cons., Sacramento, 1981—; adj. prof. human and orgn. devel. U. San Francisco, 1983—. Decorated Vietnam Service medal, Cross of Gallantry (Vietnam). Mem. Am. Soc. Tng. and Devel. (Sacramento chpt.), Beta Alpha Psi, Chi Gamma Iota (pres. 1971). Club: Handball/Raquetball (Sacramento). Office: McCann & Tashima Tng Cons Suite 301 1008 10th St Sacramento CA 95814

MC CARDELL, RICHARD KEITH, nuclear engr.; b. Pocatello, Idaho, Nov. 6, 1936; s. Keith Bronson and Gladys Fern (Harris) M.; B.S., Idaho State U., 1960, M.S., 1962; m. Janet Lynn Arave, Mar. 30, 1963; children—Laurie Machelle, Bryan Keith. Reactor physicist Phillips Petroleum Co., Idaho Falls, Idaho, 1962-68; sr. physicist Idaho Nuclear Corp., Idaho Falls, 1968-72; project engr. Aerojet Nuclear Co., Idaho Falls, 1972-76, EG&G Idaho Inc., Idaho Falls, 1976—. Mem. Am. Nuclear Soc. Mormon. Contbr. articles to profl. jours. Home: Rt #4 Box #163 Rigby ID 83442 Office: Box 1625 Idaho Falls ID 83415

MC CARDLE, RANDALL RAYMOND, realtor; b. Phila., Sept. 2, 1931; s. Russell Henry and Ruth Hertha (Snyder) McC.; A.A., Orange Coast Coll., 1956; B.A., Chapman Coll., 1958, M.A., 1966; Ph.D., Western Colo. U., 1974; 1 son, Mark. Real estate broker, Newport Beach, Calif., 1953-61; founder, pres. The Real Estaters, Orange County, Calif., 1961—, Treeco Escrow Co., Inc., Costa Mesa, Calif., 1971—; founder Bank of Costa Mesa, 1972, dir. bus. devel., 1973—; also newspaper columnist, lectr., investment counselor. Fund-raising chmn. Boys' Club of Am., Harbor area, 1979-80; bd. dirs. Boys Club Harbor Area; mem. adv. com. Orange Coast Coll., 1964—, Golden West Coll., 1969—. Served with USNR, 1950-53. Recipient Appreciation award Bd. Realtors, 1967, 68, 70, 76, 80; inducted into Orange Coast Coll. Hall of Fame, 1983. Mem. Calif. Assn. Realtors (state dir. 1963-67), Calif. Assn. Real Estate Tchrs. (state dir. 1966-80), Orange County Coast Assn. (dir. 1974—), C. of C., Nat. Assn. Real Estate Appraisers, Bd. Realtors (pres. 1966-67 long-range planning com. 1981), U. So. Calif. Faculty Assn., Red Baron Flying Club. Mason (Shriner). Contbr. articles to various publs. Home: 1828 Jamaica St Costa Mesa CA 92626 Office: 1525 Mesa Verde Dr Suite 116 Costa Mesa CA 92626

MCCARRON, JOHN ASHLEY, clinical psychologist; b. Cleve., June 21, 1949; s. John Keller and Sarah (Prindle) M.; m. Tina Adrian Wisznia, Oct. 29, 1972. B.S. in Psychology, U. Houston, 1972; M.S. in Clin. Psychology, Calif. State U., 1976; Ph.D. in Clin. Psychology, Calif. Sch. Profl. Psychology, 1980. Lic. psychologist, Calif. Staff psychologist Sharp Rehab. Hosp.; pvt. practice clin. psychology, San Diego, 1982—. Bd. dirs. Bayside Settlement House, San Diego. Mem. Am. Psychol. Assn., Calif. State Psychol. Assn., Biofeedback Soc. Am., Biofeedback Soc. Calif., Colo. Hist. Assn. Democrat. Office: 6310 Alvarado Ct San Diego CA 92120

MCCARTHY, CLAIRE LOUISE, nurse administrator, clinical specialist; b. Long Branch, N.J., Jan. 22, 1947; d. James Lewis and Mildred (Seidler) Kortenhaus. R.N., Mountainside Hosp., Montclair, N.J., 1968. Staff nurse cardiology St. Lukes Hosp., Phoenix, 1970-78, supr., adminstrv. dir. cardiology, 1978-81; cardiovascular clin. specialist Advanced Cardiovascular Systems, Mountain View, Calif., 1981—; lectr. in field. Mem. Am. Assn. Critical Care Nurses, Am. Heart Assn.

MCCARTHY, FRANK MARTIN, medical educator; b. Olean, N.Y., Aug. 27, 1924; s. Frank Michael and Joan (Quinn) McC.; B.S., U. Pitts., 1943, D.D.S., 1945, M.D., 1949; M.S. in Oral Surgery, Georgetown U., 1954; Sc.D. (hon.), St. Bonaventure U., 1956; m. Julia Richmond, Nov. 24, 1949; children—Robert Lee, Joan Lee. Med. intern Mercy Hosp., Pitts., 1949-50; practice oral surgery, Los Angeles, 1954-75; teaching fellow Georgetown U., 1952-53; research fellow NIH, 1953-54; prof. oral surgery U. So. Calif. Sch. Dentistry, 1966-75, prof., chmn. sect. anesthesia and medicine, 1975—, asst. dean for hosp. affairs, 1979—; guest lectr. Loma Linda U. Sch. Dentistry, 1958—; dir. anesthesiology U. So. Calif. oral surg. sect. Los Angeles County Hosp., 1958—; course dir. postgrad dir. U. So. Calif. Sch. Dentistry, 1959—; cons. Central Los Angeles County Health Services, 1980—. Guest lectr. UCLA, 1970-74. Mem. sci. rev. panel drug interactions projects Am. Pharm. Assn., 1972-79; mem. adv. panel on dentistry, sect. on anesthetizing agts. Nat. Fire Protection Assn., 1971-79; cons. anesthetic agts. FDA, 1972-74; mem. Am. Nat. Standards Com., 1974—. Bd. councilors Sch. Dentistry, U. So. Calif., 1972-75. Served as lt. M.C., USNR, 1950-52. Fellow Internat. Assn. Oral Surgeons (founder), Am. Coll. Dentists, Internat. Coll. Dentists; mem. ADA (mem. council dental therapeutics 1967-73), AAAS, Am. Dental Soc. Anesthesiology (ad hoc com. advanced and continuing edn. 1970—, Heidbrink award 1977, dir. 1982—), Am. (chmn. anesthesia com. 1971), So. Calif. (pres. 1974) soc. oral surgeons, Calif. (com. nitrous oxide safety 1971-73, disting. service award 1977), Los Angeles County dental assns., Western Soc. Oral and Maxillofacial Surgeons (disting. service award 1980), Delta Tau Delta, Psi Omega, Phi Rho Sigma, Omicron Kappa Upsilon. Author articles oral surgery and anesthesiology. Author: Emergencies in Dental Practice, 1967, 3d edit., 1979; Medical Emergencies in Dentistry, 1982. Cons. editor, contbr. Aktuelle Zahnmedizin, Medica Verlag, 1966; editorial cons. Jour. Calif. Dental Assn., 1966-74, 80—; cons. sect. anesthesia Jour. Oral Surgery, 1972-82; cons. Jour. ADA, 1969—. Home: 480 S Orange Grove Blvd Apt 11 Pasadena CA 91105 Office: U So Calif Sch Dentistry University Park MC 0641 Los Angeles CA 90089

MCCARTHY, J. THOMAS, lawyer, educator; b. Detroit, July 2, 1937; s. John E. and Virginia M. (Hanlon) McC.; B.S., U. Detroit, 1960; J.D., U. Mich., 1963; m. Nancy Irene Orrell, July 10, 1976. Admitted to Calif. bar, 1964; asso. firm Julian Caplan, San Francisco, 1963-66; prof. law U. San Francisco, 1966—; vis. prof. law Univ. Coll., Dublin, summer 1975, U. Calif., Berkeley, 1976-77, U. Calif., Davis, 1979-80; cons. in field. Mem. Calif. Atty. Gen.'s Consumer Protection Task Force, 1970-78; adv. bd. Bur. Nat. Affairs; mem. Nat. Panel Consumer Arbitrators. Recipient Rossman award Patent Office Soc., 1979. Mem. Am. Patent Law Assn. (Watson award 1965), Licensing Execs. Soc., IEEE. Author: McCarthy on Trademarks and Unfair Competition, 2 vols., 1973; (with Oppenheim and Weston) Federal Antitrust Laws, 1981. Office: U San Francisco 2130 Fulton St San Francisco CA 94117

MCCARTHY, JOANNE ELIZABETH, educator, consultant; b. Allentown, Pa., May 6, 1943; d. Robert Franklin and Sarah Elizabeth (Knauss) Schall; m. William James McCarthy, June 21, 1969. B.A., UCLA, 1968; M.Ed., U. Rochester, 1974; M.S., U. LaVerne, 1981; M.A., Mills Coll., 1983. Elem. tchr. Centralia Sch. Dist., Buena Park, Calif., 1968-70; reading specialist elem. sch. Spencerport (N.Y.) Sch. Dist., 1973-74, Wayne Central Sch. Dist., Ontario, N.Y., 1974-75; tchr. State Demonstration Project, Pittsburg (Calif.) Unified Sch. Dist., 1977-78; English and reading tchr. Vallejo (Calif.) City Unified Sch. Dist., 1978—; staff devel. cons. Profl. Devel. Ctr. Mem. NEA, Assn. Supervision and Curriculum Devel., Calif. Assn. Tchrs. English, Nat. Council Tchrs. English, Phi Delta Kappa, Pi Lambda Theta; Nat. Audubon Soc. Author publ. in field. Home: 105 Poshard St Pleasant Hill CA 94523 Office: Vallejo City Unified School District 2833 Tennessee St Vallejo CA 94591

MCCARTHY, JOHN FRANCIS, JR., aeronautical engineer, government official; b. Boston, Aug. 28, 1925; s. John Francis and Margaret Josephine (Bartwood) McC.; m. Carmille Dian Martinez, May 4, 1968; children—Margaret I., Megan, Jamie M., Nicole E., John F. S.B., MIT, 1950, S.M. in Aero. Engring., 1951; Ph.D. in Aeros. and Physics, Calif. Inst. Tech., 1962. Supr. air/ground communications TWA, Rome, 1946-47; project mgr. Aeroelastic and Structures Research Lab., MIT, 1951-55, prof. aeros. and astronautics, 1971-78; ops. analyst Hdqrs. SAC, Offutt AFB, Nebr., 1955-59; dir., asst. chief engr. Apollo Space div. N.Am. Aviation, Inc., Downey, Calif., 1961-66; v.p. Los Angeles div./Space div. Rockwell Internat. Corp., 1966-71; dir., prof. MIT Ctr. for Space Research, 1974-78; dir. NASA Lewis Research Ctr., Cleve., 1978-82; v.p., gen. mgr. Electro-Mech. div. Northrop Co., Anaheim, Calif., 1982—; mem. Internat. Council Aero. Scis., Cologne, W.Ger., 1978—; mem. U.S. Air Force Sci. Adv. Bd., Washington, 1970-82; mem. sci. adv. group joint chiefs staff Joint Strategic Target Planning Staff, Offutt AFB, 1976-81; com. mem. Energy Engring. Bd., Assembly Engring., NRC, 1979; mem. dept. adv. bd. Rensselaer Poly. Inst.; cons. in field. Bd. govs. Cleve. Airshow; campaign chmn. Downey Community Hosp., 1968-69; chmn. Fed. Exec. Bd., Cleve., 1979-80. Served with USAAF, 1944-46. Recipient Apollo Achievement award NASA, 1969, Disting. Service medal, 1982; Meritorious Civilian Service medal U.S. Air Force, 1973, Exceptional Civilian Service medal, 1978. Fellow AIAA (dir. 1975-76), Royal Aero. Soc. (London); mem. Am. Soc. Engring. Edn. (exec. com. aerospace div. 1969-72), Nat. Acad. Engring., Am. Mgmt. Assn., Sigma Xi, Sigma Gamma Tau. Unitarian. Clubs: Cosmos; Cleve. 50; Nat. Space (gov. 1978—) (Washington). Author numerous tech. reports; patentee impact landing system. Home: 19171 Via del Caballo Yorba Linda CA 92686 Office: Northrop Electro-Mechanical Div 500 E Orangethorpe Ave Anaheim CA 92801

MCCARTHY, LEO T., lieutenant governor Calif.; b. Auckland, New Zealand, Aug. 15, 1930; s. Daniel and Nora Theresa (Roche) McC.; m. Jacqueline Lee Burke, Dec. 17, 1955; children—Sharon, Conna, Adam, Niall. B.S., U. San Francisco, 1955; J.D., San Francisco Law Sch., 1961. Bar: Calif. 1963. Mem. San Francisco Bd. Suprs., 1964-68; mem. Calif. State Assembly, 1969-82, speaker, 1974-80; lt. gov. State of Calif., 1983—. Bd. regents U. Calif.; trustees Calif. State Coll. System; chmn. Task Force Investigating Nursing Home Care; mem. World Trade Commn., Calif. Lands Commn., Calif. Emergency Council; mem. Calif. State Democratic Central Com. Served with USAF, 1951-52. Recipient Outstanding Legislator in U.S. award Nat. Council Sr. Citizens, 1972; Torch of Liberty award B'nai B'rith Anti-Defamation League, 1976. Roman Catholic. Office: Room 1028 State Capitol Sacramento CA 95814

MCCARTHY, MARY PHYLLIS MASCITTI, social worker, nun; b. Leominster, Mass., Oct. 12, 1928; d. Pelino and Anna (DiNino) Mascitti; m. Walter Joseph McCarthy, May 21, 1955 (dec.). B.A., UCLA, 1954; M.S.W., Cath. U. Am., 1963; Ph.D., Bryn Mawr Coll., 1976. Joined Order Sisters in Social Service, Roman Catholic Ch., 1959; psychometrist UCLA, 1953-55; caseworker Cath. Social Services, Vallejo, 1959-61; instr. Immaculate Heart Coll., Hollywood, Calif., 1963-65, St. Mary's Coll., Los Angeles, 1966-68; casework dir. Holy Family Adoption Service, Los Angeles, 1963-71; counselor Rosemont (Pa.) Coll., 1971-75; liaison Los Angeles Archdiocese Dept. Health and Hosps./Cedars-Sinai Med. Ctr., 1975-80; dir. Quo Vadis Family Ctr., Torrance, Calif., 1980—; social systems analyst, Los Angeles, 1976—. Mem. com. on community devel. services in child welfare Los Angeles Welfare Planning Council, 1966-71; mem. study task force services to unmarried parents Calif. Social Welfare Bd., 1968-69; local dir. Sisters of Social Service, Los Angeles, 1968-71, del., 1967, chmn. edn. commn., 1968; treas. gen. council Sisters of Social Service, 1976-78. Bd. dirs. Natural Family Planning, St. Joseph Hosp., Orange, Calif., 1981—. NIMH grantee, 1962, 71. Mem. Nat. Assn. Social Workers, Acad. Cert. Social Workers, Calif. Clin. Social Workers, Nat. Conf. Social Welfare, Internat. Conf. Social Welfare, Internat. Conf. Social Work, Los Angeles Assn. Social Workers (dir. 1967-71, chmn. div. social policy and action 1966-67), Am. Assn. Social Welfare History, Nat. Conf. Cath. Charities, Sigma Kappa. Author: Drastic Social Change of a Closed Community, 1977. Home: 1120 Westchester Pl Los Angeles CA 90019 Office: 3715 W Lomita Blvd #129 Torrance CA 90505

MCCARTHY, NANCY PATRICE, international trade association executive; b. Denver, Apr. 2, 1955; d. Thomas E. and Rita Marie (Freuen) McCarthy. B.A. in Journalism, U. No. Colo., 1977. Advt. investigator Better Bus. Bur., Denver, 1977; adminstrv. asst. U.S. Meat Export Fedn., Denver, 1977-79; communications dir. U.S. Meat Export Fedn., Denver, 1979—; freelance writer. Active steering com. Colo. Ho. of Reps. campaigns, 1980, 1982. Mem. Pub. Relations Soc. Am., Am. Soc. Assn. Execs., Nat. Assn. Farm Broadcasters, Nat. Agrl. Editors Assn. Republican. Roman Catholic. Office: US Meat Export Fedn Suite 7200 3333 Quebec St Denver CO 80207

MCCARTHY, ROBERT JOHN, lawyer; b. N.Y.C., Dec. 31, 1946; s. John Robert and Dorothy Emily (Simmons) McC.; m. Suzanne Marie Bazzano, Aug. 8, 1970; children—Brendan, Matthew, Ryan, Margaret, Robert. B.A. magna cum laude, U. Santa Clara, 1969; J.D., U. Chgo., 1972. Bar: Calif. 1972. Assoc., Cooley, Godward, Castro, Huddleson & Tatum, San Francisco, 1972-74, Broad, Khourie & Schulz, San Francisco, 1974-76; chief dep. dist. atty. City of San Francisco, 1976-80; ptnr. McCarthy & Schwartz, San Francisco, 1980—. Exec. v.p. San Francisco Housing and Devel. Corp., 1981—; bd. dirs. San Francisco Big Bros., 1982—; cabinet mem. Calif. Democratic Party, 1981—, gen. counsel, 1983—. U. Santa Clara Presdl. scholar, 1965-69; HUD fellow, 1971-72. Mem. Calif. Bar Assn., San Francisco Bar Assn. Roman Catholic. Club: Olympic (San Francisco). Office: 333 Market St 32d Floor San Francisco CA 94105

MCCARTHY, ROGER LEE, engineering company executive; b. Battle Creek, Mich., Nov. 28, 1948; s. William Howard and Eloise Erna (Maltby) M.; m. Gail Elizabeth Kendall, Jan. 6, 1979. A.B. summa cum laude, U. Mich., 1972; B.S.E., MIT, 1972, S.M., 1973, Mech.E., 1975, Ph.D., 1977. Registered profl. engr., Calif., Ariz. Engr., S.C. Johnson & Sons, Inc., Racine, Wis., 1972; project engr. Procter & Gamble Co., Inc., Cin., 1973-74; program mgr. Foster-Miller Assocs., Inc., Waltham, Mass., 1976-78; pres. Failure Analysis Assocs., Palo Alto, Calif., 1978—. Served to capt., Ordnance Corps, USAR, NSF fellow. Mem. ASME, Am. Soc. Metals, ASHRAE, Marine Hist. Soc. Mystic Seaport, Phi Beta Kappa, Sigma Xi. Republican. Roman Catholic. Office: 2225 E Bayshore Rd Palo Alto CA 94303

MCCARTHY, WILLIAM STEPHEN, architect, real estate broker; b. Montreal, Que., Can., June 8, 1951; s. William Gorman and Muriel Gladys (Jones) McC.; student Calif. Inst. Arts, 1969-71; B.Arch., So. Calif. Inst. Architecture, 1974. Designer, E. Jerome Tamen Assos., Century City, Calif., 1975-78; chief designer Flewelling-Logsdon Assos., Santa Rosa, Calif., 1978-80; prin. W. Stephen McCarthy-Design and Devel., Santa Rosa, 1980-83; ptnr. Bell, Evans, Yamamoto, McCarthy Architects, Santa Rosa and San Diego, 1983—. Address: 716 A Slater St Santa Rosa CA 95404

MCCARTIN, ROSEMARIE, educational and clinical psychologist; b. Colorado Springs, Colo., July 18, 1926; d. Emmet J. and Rula E. Raymond. B.A., Coll. Great Falls (Mont.), 1955, Immaculate Heart Coll., Los Angeles, 1960; Ph.D., U. So. Calif., 1964. Lic. clin. psychologist, Wash. Tchr., Wash., Calif., 1946-60; cons. research asst. Population Movement Project, Center for Research in Mental Retardation, Pomona Coll., 1963; asst. prof. Seattle U., 1963; assoc. prof. U. Wash., Seattle, after 1969, coordinator interdisciplinary tng. Child Develop. and Mental Retardation Center, 1973-78, prof. Coll. Edn., 1978—; cons. in field. Mem. Am. Assn. Mental Deficiency, AAUP, Am. Edn. Research Assn., Am. Psychol. Assn., Assn. Advancement Behavioral Therapies (sec. Northwest Br. 1967-69), Internat. Sch. Psychologists, Nat. Assn. Edn. Young Children, Puget Sound Psychol. Assn., Soc. Research Child Develop., Wash. Edn. Assn., Western Psychol. Assn. Democrat. Roman Catholic. Contbg. author: Early Intervention—A Team Approach, 1978; contbr. articles to profl. jours. Office: 322 Miller Hall U Wash Seattle WA 98195

MCCASHIN, ANDREW WYE, psychologist; b. N.Y.C., Nov. 10, 1940; s. Henry Andrew and Elizabeth Inskip (Wye) McC.; B.A., Am. U., 1962; M.A., Am. U., 1965; Ph.D., U. Ga., 1969; m. Judith Ann McCracken, Dec. 16, 1967; children—Alison, Daniel. Dir. tng., staff psychologist U. Mass., Amherst, 1970-75; dir. tng., coordinator planning Ventura County Mental Health Services, Ventura, Calif., 1975—; cons. Ventura Coll., 1976—; pvt. practice clin. psychology, Ventura, 1977—. Bd. dirs. Ventura County Symphony. USPHS fellow, 1968-69. Mem. Am. Psychol. Assn., Calif. State Psychol. Assn. Home: 1038 Cove St Ventura CA 93001

MCCASLIN, JOHN WEAVER, safety engineer; b. Kansas City, Mo., Dec. 22, 1917; s. John Wallace and Jane Kathryn (Weaver) M.; m. Majoria Ann Emerson, Mar. 13, 1943; children—Jane Ann, Nancy Jean, Mary Elizabeth. B.S. in Chem. Engring., U. Kans., 1939. Cert. health physicist, 1960, safety profl., 1971, indsl. safety profl., 1972. Chem. engr. Phillips Petroleum, Bartlesville, Okla., 1940, 1946-47, research safety engr., 1947-51, health safety supr., Idaho Falls, 1951-53, health and safety br. mgr., 1953-66; safety mgr. Idaho Nuclear Corp., Idaho Falls, 1966-69; safety standards branch mgr. Aerojet Nuclear, Idaho Falls, 1969-78; safety tech. support mgr. EG&G Idaho Inc., Idaho Falls, 1979-82, engring. specialist, 1982—. Served to lt. col. AC, U.S. Army, 1941-46. Mem. Am. Soc. Safety Engrs. (chmn. U. Idaho adv. com.), Health Physics Soc., Am. Indsl. Hygiene Assn. Presbyterian. Home: 1556 Falcon Dr Idaho Falls ID 83401 Office: EG&G Idaho WCB SG4 Idaho Falls ID 83415

MCCAUGHAN, ROBERT ALAN, counselor; b. Pitts., Feb. 14, 1936; s. Alan Gilbert and Kathleen (Oliver) McC.; m. Lillian Liberata, Feb. 22, 1963; children—Karen, Robert, Jr. B.G.E., U. Omaha, 1965; M.A. in Mgmt., U. So. Calif., 1969; Ph.D. in Counseling and Psychology, U. Denver, 1982. Exec. v.p. Ice Arena, Denver; tchr. workshop on communications and helping skills. Served to maj. USAF, 1960-77. Mem. AIAA, Air Force Assn., Am. Personnel and Guidance Assn. Republican. Mem. Nazarene Ch. Author: Computerized Psychological Testing: Impact on Client Expectancy, 1982. Home: 10435 W Fremont Pl Littleton CO 80127 Office: 1455 Ammons St Denver CO 80215

MCCAULEY, BRUCE GORDON, investment advisor; b. St. Louis; s. William Maurice and Evylin Adele (Halbert) McC.; student U. Mo., 1939-41, Yale U., 1944; B.S. in Engring., U. Calif. Berkeley, 1948, M.B.A., 1949, M.S. in Indsl. Engring., 1952; m. Barbara Allen Stevens, Mar. 16, 1945 (dec.); children—David S., Sharon; m. 2d, Gwen Crumpton Cummings, Nov. 25, 1967. Asst. purchasing agt. Curtis Mfg. Co., St. Louis, 1941-43; teaching asst. U. Calif.-Berkeley 1948-49, asst. prof. mech. engring., 1950-56, chmn. indsl. engring. inst., 1954-55; design engr. Standard Oil Co. of Calif., 1949-50; sr. partner McCauley & Dunmire, San Francisco, 1952-56; v.p. Shand & Jurs Co., Berkeley, 1956-58, dir., 1957-60, exec. v.p., 1958-60; asst. to pres. Honolulu Star-Bulletin, 1960-62; gen. mgr. Christian Sci. Pub. Soc., Boston, pubs. Christian Sci. Monitor, Christian Sci. Jour., Christian Sci. Sentinel, other publs., 1962-69; gen. mgr. N.Y. News, Inc., N.Y.C., 1969-74, sec., 1970-71, v.p., 1971-73, sr. v.p., 1973-75, asst. to pres., 1974-75, also dir., 1971-75; v.p. Daseke & Co., Inc., Stamford, Conn., 1975-77, sr. v.p., 1977—, mgr. West Coast office, 1978—. Dir. Better Bus. Bur., N.Y.C., 1973-77, N.Y. C. Conv. and Visitors' Bur., 1974-77. Served as capt. USAAF, 1943-46; PTO. Registered profl. engr., N.Y., Calif., Hawaii. Mem. Nat. Assn. Security Dealers (registered prin.), Am. Inst. Indsl. Engrs., ASME, Nat. Assn. Accountants, Nat. Soc. Profl. Engrs., U. Calif. Alumni Assn., Principia Alumni Assn., Sigma Xi, Tau Beta Pi, Beta Gamma Sigma, Pi Mu Epsilon. Christian Scientist. Clubs: Bankers (San Francisco); Masons (32 deg.). Home: 194 Stewart Dr Tiburon CA 94920 Office: 4780 Bank of America Center San Francisco CA 94104

MCCAULEY, MICHAEL ERLAN, engineering psychologist; b. Altadena, Calif., Oct. 16, 1944; s. Norman E. and Olive Ruby (Swenson) McC.; m. Nancy P. Pate, Dec. 30, 1970; children—Ryan Patrick, Erin Keana. A.B., U. Redlands, 1966; M.A., U. Hawaii, 1968; Ph.D., U. Calif.-Santa Barbara, 1979. Naval aerospace exptl. psychologist U.S. Navy Aerospace Med. Research Lab., Pensacola, Fla., 1968-71; research asso., project dir. Human Factors Research, Inc., Goleta, Calif., 1972-77; project mgr. Human Performance Research, Inc., Santa Barbara, Calif., 1977-80; sr. scientist Canyon Research Group, Inc., Westlake Village, Calif., 1980—; cons. in field. Served to lt. USN, 1968-71. Mem. Am. Psychol. Assn., Human Factors Soc. (chpt. pres.-elect). Lutheran. Contbr. articles to profl. jours. Address: 741 Lakefield Rd Suite B Westlake Village CA 91361

MCCHESNEY, ROBERT PEARSON, artist; b. Marshall, Mo., Jan. 16, 1913; s. John and Ruby (Pearson) Mc.; m. Mary Ellen Fuller, Dec. 17, 1949. Student Sch. Fine Arts, Washington U., 1931-34, Otis Art Inst., Los Angeles, 1936-37. One-man shows: San Francisco Mus. Modern Art, 1949, 1953, San Francisco Art Inst., 1957, Todes Art Gallery, Chgo., 1958, Reed Coll., 1959, Parsons Gallery, Los Angeles, 1960, 1961, Bolles Gallery, San Francisco, 1959, 1961, 1970, 1971, N.Y.C., 1962, 20th. Century West, N.Y.C., 1965, Lincoln Art Ctr., Santa Rosa, Calif., 1978, U. Calif.-Hayward, 1977; retrospective show San Francisco Art Commn., 1974; group shows include: Art Inst. Chgo., 1947, 1954, 1960, 1961, Corcoran Gallery, Washington, 1957, San Francisco Mus. Art Ann., 1945-60, Nordness Gallery, N.Y.C., 1964, Legion of Honor, San Francisco, 1962, 1964, Oakland Mus., 1972, 1973; represented in permanent collections: Whitney Mus. Am. Art, N.Y.C., San Francisco Mus. Art, Oakland Mus. Art, Art Inst. Chgo., Legion of Honor, Muskegon, Mich.; City of San Francisco Art commn., Washington State Art commn., mural San Francisco Social Services Bldg., 1978; instr. art Calif. Sch. Fine Arts, San Francisco, 1949-51, Santa Rosa Jr. Coll., 1957-58. Trustee San Francisco Art Inst., 1965-67. Home: 2955 Sonoma Mountain Rd Petaluma CA 94952

MC CLAIN, CHARLES KENT, city manager; b. Maud, Okla., Nov. 13, 1940; s. Charles Wesley and Dora Jean (Loney) McC.; B.A., U. Wyo., 1962; M. Pub. Adminstrn., U. Kans., 1969; m. Beverly Olive Rue, June 24, 1962. Adminstrv. asst. City of Laramie, Wyo., 1963-66; budget analyst City of Fort Worth, 1969-70; city mgr. City of Vermillion, S.D., 1970-73, City of Flagstaff, Ariz., 1973-78, City of Santa Monica (Calif.), 1979-81, City of Fremont (Calif.), 1981—. Mem. S.D. Elec. Mediation Bd., 1971-73; v.p. S.D. Municipal Elec. Assn., 1971-73; trustee Flagstaff Community Hosp., 1975—, treas., 1976, sec., 1977, pres., 1978; Vestryman Episcopal Ch. of Epiphany, 1974-76. Served to 1st lt. AUS, 1966-68. Mem. Internat., Ariz. (pres. 1977) city mgmt. assns., Am. Soc. Pub. Adminstrn., Am. Legion, VFW, Tau Kappa Epsilon. Club: Rotary. Office: 39700 Civic Center Dr Fremont CA 94538

MCCLANAHAN, MARILYN RICE, association executive, food products company executive; b. Berne, Switzerland Dec. 12, 1931; d. Carl P. and Lili (Gronna) Rice; children—Timothy, R. Bradley, W. Clinton, Sally McClanahan Hunter, William S. B.A. Brown U., 1954; student Yale Grad. Sch. Nursing, 1955-57; M.A., Calif. State U.-Sacramento; MPH, Calif. State U.-Northridge. Cert. MPH, Calif. Exec. dir. High Blood Pressure Council, Los Angeles, 1978—; pres. Diet Way Products, Inc., Van Nuys, Calif., 1979—. Office: 5820 Wilshire Blvd Suite 303 Los Angeles CA 90036

MC CLARY, DAVID MICHAEL, clergyman; b. W.Va., Aug. 29, 1943; s. Raymond Virgil and Isabelle (Moreau) McC.; Asso. degree U.S. Dept. Agr. Grad. Sch., 1969; B.A. in History and Anthropology, Am. U., 1972, M.P.A., 1975; grad. Living Word Bible Coll., 1981; postgrad. U. So. Calif. in D.C.; postgrad. Iliff Sch. Theology; m. Gaynel Kegley Frizzell, Dec. 24, 1973; 1 son, Mark Edward. Explorer, adventurer CONUS, 1964-66; cartographer U.S. Dept. Agr., 1966; geodesist gravity analyst U.S. Army Map Service, Brookmont, Md., 1967-70; statis. wage analyst U.S. Dept. Labor, Washington, 1972-73; catalog delivery analyst Sears & Roebuck Catalog, Washington, 1973-77; mgmt. analyst Boulder labs. Commerce Dept., 1977-78; flood control analyst/surveyor, Boulder, 1978-79; adminstrn. and supply staff SSG/COARNG, Longmont, Colo., 1979-81; minister Open Bible Standard Chs. Adminstrn. officer CAP, 1977-78; mil. surveyor Colo. N.G., 1977-80; co-cir. Internat. Week, Am. U., 1973. Served with U.S. Army, 1962-63. Recipient awards various govt. agencies. Mem. Am. Hist. Assn., Nat. Assn. Evangelicals, Am. Congress Mapping and Surveying, Am. Divers Assn., Am. Mgmt. Assn., Smithsonian Assocs., Nat. Geog. Soc., Am. U. Alumni, Nat. Assn. Underwater Instrs., Nat. Rifle Assn., DAV, VFW, Am. Legion, Wilderness Inst. Survival Edn. Democrat. Researcher, writer for Nat. Geog., Smithsonian, Time and various newspapers. Address: McClary Ministries PO Box 3585 Littleton CO 80161

MCCLATCHY, CHARLES KENNY, editor; b. Fresno, Calif., Mar. 25, 1927; s. Carlos Kelly and Phebe (Briggs) McC.; grad. Deerfield Acad. (Mass.), 1945; B.A., Stanford, 1950; m. Grace Kennan, Mar. 1, 1958 (div. 1968); children—Charles, Adair, Kevin. Reporter, Washington Post, 1953-55, Washington news bur. ABC TV, 1957-58, Sacramento Bee, 1958-63; asso. editor McClatchy Newspapers, Sacramento, 1963-68, exec. editor, 1968-74, editor, 1974—, pres., 1978—; mem. adv. bd. UPI. Asst. press sec. Adlai Stevenson Presdl. campaign, 1956. Served to 1st lt. AUS, 1951-53. Clubs: Sutter (Sacramento); Bohemian (San Francisco). Home: 2124 U St Sacramento CA 95818 Office: 21st and Q Sts Sacramento CA 95813

MC CLEAN, EDWARD ANTHONY, real estate exec.; b. Los Angeles, July 12, 1922; s. Mathew Wellington and Elizabeth Josephine (Moran) McC.; A.A., W. Los Angeles Coll., 1976; M.S. in Adminstrn., Calif. State U., Dominguez Hills, 1979; m. Barbara Jane Ryan, June 27, 1947; children—Margaret Mary, Mary Jane, Susan Elizabeth, Robert Edward. Regional v.p. for Los Angeles County, F.M. Tarbell Co., Realtors, 1961-79, sr. v.p., Calif., 1980—; v.p. Hartford Escrow, Inc., 1964—; sr. v.p. Austin-Tarbell Co., 1980—. Charter chmn. South Bay Housing Resource Bd., 1979; bd. dirs. Orange County Community Housing Corp., 1980—. Served with USNR, 1945-46. Named Boss of Year, Torrance Lomita Carson Jaycees, 1974. Mem. Nat. Assn. Realtors, Calif. Assn. Realtors, Inglewood Bd. Realtors, Torrance Lomita Carson Bd. Realtors (officer, dir. 1973-80, Realtor of Year 1979), Rolling Hills Bd. Realtors (dir. 1976-80), South Bay Bd. Realtors, Palos Verdes Estates Bd. Realtors, San Pedro Bd. Realtors, San Diego Bd. Realtors, Vista Bd. Realtors, Escondido Bd. Realtors, East San Diego Bd. Realtors, LaJolla Realtors Assn., Am. Mgmt. Assn., Calif. Assn. Real Estate Tchrs. Republican. Roman Catholic. Home: 27840 Via Sarasate Mission Viejo CA 92692 Office: 18062 Irvine Blvd Tustin CA 92680

MC CLEARY, HENRY GLEN, geophysicist; b. Casper, Wyo., June 4, 1922; s. Raymond McCleary and Wyoma N. (Posey) McCleary Grieve; Geol. Engr., Colo. Sch. Mines, 1948; m. Beryl Tenney Nowlin, May 28, 1950; children—Gail, Glenn, Neil, Paul. Geophysicist to party chief seismic Amoco, various locations, 1948-53; exploration mgr. Woodson Oil Co., Fort Worth, 1953-60; resident mgr. NAMCO, Tripoli, Libya, 1961-62; chief geophysicist to geophys. asso. Amoco Internat. Oil Co., 1963—, Cairo, London and Buenos Aires, 1963-71, Chgo., 1971-81, Denver, 1981—. Served with USN, 1943-46. Mem. Soc. Exploration Geophysicists, Soc. Petroleum Engrs., AAAS, Sigma Alpha Epsilon, Theta Tau. Republican. Episcopalian. Club: Adventurers. Home: 275 S Eudora Denver CO 80222 Office: Amoco Bldg 17th and Broadway Denver CO 80202

MCCLEARY, HERBERT ELWOOD, advertising executive; b. Bridgewater, Maine, Mar. 29, 1931; s. Richard James and Madeline Adora (Allen) McC.; m. Elaine Alice Nordell, July 12, 1952; children—Karen, Richard, Brian, Rhonda. B.A. in Indsl. Arts, San Diego State U., 1959. Ind. newspaper account exec., San Diego, 1962-66; advt. mgr. Mayfair Markets, San Diego, 1966-69; asst. advt. dir., Handyman Inc., San Diego, 1969-74; advt. dir. United Sporting Goods, Los Angeles, 1974-77; advt. mgr. Handy Dan/Angels, Los Angeles, 1977-78; advt. dir. Pay N Pak Stores Inc., Kent, Wash., 1978—. Served with USN, 1951-55. Republican. Home: 32520 1st Pl S Federal Way WA 98003 Office: 1209 S Central Kent WA 98031

MC CLELLAN, JACK LOVE, petroleum geologist; b. Lubbock, Tex., June 15, 1927; s. Dewey Johnstone and Anne Bertha (Howell) McC.; B.S., Tex. Tech. U., 1950, postgrad., 1950-52; m. Barbara Ann Walden, Apr. 3, 1953; children—Suzanne, Mark, Lisa. Petroleum geologist Gulf Oil Corp., Midland, Tex., 1952-54, Hobbs, N.Mex., 1955-56, Roswell, N.Mex., 1956-57, Franklin, Aston & Fair Co., Roswell, 1957-58; cons. geologist, Roswell, 1958-70; petroleum geologist McClellan Oil Corp., Roswell, 1972-76, pres., 1972—; pres. Cortez Drilling Corp., Roswell, 1966—; sec.-treas. Hondo Pipe and Supply. Mem. adv. bd. Oil Field Tng. Ctr., Eastern N.Mex. U.; bd. dirs., pres. Eastern N.Mex. Med. Center Found.; bd. dirs. Tex. Tech. U. Found., 1982—. Served with USNR, 1945-46. Mem. Am. Assn. Petroleum Geologists (cert. petroleum geologist), Ind. Petroleum Assn. (regional bd. dirs. 1974-75, public lands com. 1975—), Am. Inst. Profl. Geologists, Tex. Tech. U. Alumni Assn. (trustee, dir. 1967-70), Roswell Geol. Soc. (regional dir. 1972—), Ind. Petroleum Assn. N.Mex. (founding dir.), Gideons, Phi Delta Theta. Republican. Methodist (ofcl. bd. 1977-80, trustee 1982—). Clubs: Rotary, Masons, Shriners. Home: 3106 N Montana Roswell NM 88201 Office: 1000 Security Bank Bldg PO Drawer 730 Roswell NM 88201

MCCLELLAND, JOHN PETER, winery executive; b. N.Y.C., Aug. 17, 1933; s. Harold Stanley and Helen Lucille (Gardner) McC.; student UCLA, 1951-53; m. Ann Carolyn Campbell, Aug. 27, 1954; children—John, Kristen. With Almadén Vineyards, Inc., San Jose, Calif., 1958—, v.p. sales, then v.p. mktg., 1970-76, pres., 1976—, also gen. mgr. Served with AUS, 1954-56. Mem. Wine Inst. (chmn. public relations com. 1977—, exec. com. 1979—). Republican. Presbyterian. Office: Almaden Vineyards Inc 5130 Blossom Hill Rd San Jose CA 95118

MCCLENDON, IRVIN LEE, SR., computer systems analyst; b. Waco, Tex., June 12, 1945; s. Irvin Nicholas and Evelyn Lucile (Maycumber) McC.; m. Mary Helen Burrell Swanson, June 26, 1982; 1 son, Richard Lester children by previous marriage—Michael Boyd, Irvin Lee, Laura Ann, Paul Nicholas; stepchildren—Brenda Irene, Kevin Ray, Perry Lee. Student El Camino Coll., 1961-63, U. So. Calif., 1962-66; B.A. in Math., Calif. State U.-Fullerton, 1970, postgrad. in bus. adminstrn., 1971-76; cert. nat. security mgmt. Indsl. Coll. Armed Forces, 1974; postgrad. in religion Summit Sch. Theology, 1982—. Engring. lab. asst. Rockwell Internat. Corp., Anaheim, Calif., 1967-68, test data analyst, 1968, assoc. computer programmer, 1968-70, mem. tech. staff, 1970-82; software test analyst Auto-trol Tech. Corp., Denver, 1982-83, systems programmer A, 1983—. Sec. of governing bd. Yorba Linda Library Dist., 1972-77; trustee Ch. of God (Seventh Day), Bloomington, Calif., 1979-81, treas., 1980-81, mem. Calif. State U. and Coll. Statewide Alumni Council, 1976-77; 2d v.p. Orange County chpt. Calif. Spl. Dists. Assn., 1976, pres., 1977. Served with USAFR, 1967-71. USAF Nat. Merit scholar, 1963-67. Mem. Calif. Assn. Library Trustees and Commrs. (exec. bd., So. Calif. rep. 1976-77), Assn. Computing Machinery, Air Force Assn., Nat. Eagle Scout Assn., Calif. State U.-Fullerton Alumni Assn. (dir. 1975-77). Republican. Mem. Ch. of God (Seventh Day). Home: PO Box 33483 Denver CO 80233 Office: 12500 N Washington St Denver CO 80233

MCCLENDON, PAUL EDWARD, savings and loan executive, real estate developer; b. Albuquerque, July 28, 1936; s. Paul Monroe and Helen Louise (Miller) McC.; m. Linda Elbrecht, Nov. 29, 1949; 1 son, Christopher Paul. Student pub. schs., Albuquerque. With Four Corners Savs. and Loan, Farmington, N.Mex., 1965—, sr. v.p., 1965—, also dir.; real estate developer, 1967—. Pres., Farmington Mcpl. Schs. Bd. Edn., 1975-81; pres., bd. dirs. San Juan Coll., Farmington, 1975-81; formerly active numerous youth orgns. Mem. Am. Arbitration Assn. Club: Elks. Home: 5858 La Luz Trail Farmington NM 87401 Office: 500 W Main St Farmington NM 87401

MCCLENDON, ROBERT RAE, pharmacist; b. Tucson, Nov. 2, 1943; s. Adrian and Elizabeth (Lauck) McC.; B.S. in Pharmacy, U. Ariz. Coll. Pharmacy, 1966; m. Marsha F. Bell, Sept. 10, 1966; 1 son, Sean Robert. Asso. dir. pharmacy extension services U. Ariz., Tucson, 1966-67; staff pharmacist St. Joseph's Hosp. and Med. Center, Phoenix, 1967-70, chief pharmacist, 1970-79, dir. pharmacy, 1979—; cons. Travenol Labs., Bristol Labs., Valleylab. Mem. Am. Soc. Hosp. Pharmacists, Ariz. Pharm. Assn. (dir.), Ariz. Soc. Hosp. Pharmacists. Democrat. Methodist. Inventor I V 6500 formulator, 1979; author: Setting Up a TPN Team, 1978. Home: 7766 W Greenway Peoria AZ 85345 Office: 350 W Thomas Phoenix AZ 85013

MC CLINTOCK, ARCHIE GLENN, lawyer; b. Sheridan, Wyo., Mar. 26, 1911; s. James Porter and Martha Elizabeth (Glenn) McC.; A.B., U. Wyo., 1933, LL.B., 1935; m. Ina Jean Robinson, May 27, 1939; children—Ellery, Jeffry, Kathleen. Admitted to Wyo. bar, 1935; individual practice law, Cheyenne, 1935-73; justice Wyo. Supreme Ct., 1973-81. Mem. Wyo. Fair Employment Practices Com., 1965-71. Served with USNR, 1944-45. Mem. Wyo. Bar Assn. (pres. 1950-51), Am. Judicature Soc., Sigma Nu. Democrat. Club: Elks.

MCCLINTOCK, EVA KARIN, cosmetic executive; b. Lithuania, Mar. 23, 1938, naturalized, 1962; d. Franz and Lydia (Petrat) Slawinski; m. Ronald James McClintock, Feb. 8, 1957; children—Kurt, James, Scott. Student Salzgitter Sch. Bus. (W.Ger.), 1953-57. Dist. mgr. Avon Products, Pasadena, Calif., 1966-76; div. sales mgr. Luzier Cosmetics, Kansas City, Kans., 1976-77; dir. sales tng. Pola USA Inc., Carson, Calif., 1977-79; dir. mktg., v.p. sales Concept Now Cosmetics Inc., Santa Fe Springs, Calif., 1981-82, corp. v.p., 1982—. Den mother Cub Scouts Am., 1966-68. Recipient Pres.'s Circle award Avon, 1969, 1975. Mem. Am. Bus. Women Assn., Nat. Assn. Female Execs., We Can Women's Network. Democrat. Lutheran. Home: 5183 Melbourne Dr Cypress CA 90630

MCCLINTOCK, KAREN LYNN, advertising director; b. Los Angeles, Sept. 17, 1956; d. Frank L. and Kathryn Eleanor (Berg) McC. B.A. with honors, San Diego State U., 1978. Export adv. Sportlite mag., San Diego, 1978-81; mktg./export cons. Mountain Equipment, Inc., Fresno, Calif., 1981; dir. advt. Survive mag., Boulder, Colo., 1981—; cons. Mem. Denver Advt. Fedn., Am. Mktg. Assn. Republican. Roman Catholic. Home: PO Box 12154 Boulder CO 80302 Office: 5735 Arapahoe St Boulder CO 80303

MC CLINTOCK, THOMAS MILLER, advt. exec.; b. Boston, Feb. 15, 1927; s. Miller and Hazel (Barton) McC.; B.A., Northwestern U., 1951, postgrad., 1951-52; m. Marianne Christy, June 14, 1952; children—Thomas Miller, Virginia Christy. Dir. audience jury, radio-TV research Young & Rubicam, N.Y.C., 1952-58; media supr. Dancer Fitzgerald-Sample, N.Y.C., 1958-62; media dir. Papert-Koenig-Lois, Inc., N.Y.C., 1962-65; asso. media dir. Erwin-Wasey, Los Angeles, 1965-68; dir. sales devel. Radio KABC, Los Angeles, 1968-70; account exec. Eschen Co., Los Angeles, 1970-72; account exec., prin. Chuck Campbell Co., Los Angeles, 1972-73; pres. McClintock Assocs., Inc., 1973—; v.p. Keystone Broadcasting System, Inc., Chgo., 1983—; v.p., treas. Sound Book Press, Inc., Scarsdale, N.Y., 1958-72; pres. T. M. McClintock Prodns., Scarsdale, 1957—. Asst. scoutmaster Boy Scouts Am., 1967-73. Served with AUS, 1945-47. Episcopalian. Home: 156 Bedford Pl Thousand Oaks CA 91360 Office: 17 Topsail St Suite 4 Marina Del Rey CA 90291

MC CLISTER, MICHAEL JAMES, food wholesale distbn. co. exec.; b. Hollywood, Calif., Nov. 22, 1945; s. Perry Crawford and Pauline Gertrude (Draucker) McC.; A.A. in History, Santa Monica City Coll., 1968; student in polit. sci. San Fernando Valley State Coll., 1969-71; m. Katherine Suzanne Turgeon, Aug. 16, 1980; children—Robert Donovan, Christopher Michael, Katie Rose. Ops. mgr. Collins Foods Internat., Los Angeles, 1973-77; dir. transp. Keeler Foods/Distribuco, Santa Ana, Calif., 1977-78; dir. distbn. Proficient Food Co., Irvine, Calif., 1978-80, v.p. distbn./mktg., 1980—. Mem. Am. Mgmt. Assn., Warehousing Edn. and Research Council, Nat. Council Phys. Distbn. Mgmt. Republican. Methodist. Club: Polish Nat. Alliance (Santa Ana, Calif.). Office: 17872 Cartwright Rd Irvine CA 92714

MC CLOSKY, JOHN HOWARD, instrument and electric motor manufacturing company executive; b. Chgo., Mar. 7, 1948; s. Howard Raymond and Ethel Ingaborg (Carlson) McC.; B.A. in Econs., U. Ill., Chgo., 1973; M.B.A., Pepperdine U., 1980; m. Linda Eileen Bladh, Jan. 23, 1971; children—Evan Michael, Alisa Lyn. Planning supr. Skil Corp., Chgo., 1973-76; material planning mgr. RCA Cablevision Systems, North Hollywood, Calif., 1976-78; material mgr. Pacesetter Systems, Inc., Sylmar, Calif., 1978-79; mgr. material planning and purchasing Nordskog Industries, Van Nuys, Calif., 1978-82; materials mgr. Spectroscopy Systems div. Bausch & Lomb, 1982—. Cubmaster Pack 651, Gt. Western council Boy Scouts Am., 1980—. Served with USAF,

1966-70; Vietnam. Mem. U. Ill. Alumni Assn., Calif. State U. at Northridge Bibliog. Soc., Am. Mgmt. Assn. Home: 14022 Burton St Panorama City CA 91402 Office: 9525 DeSoto Ave Chatsworth CA 91311

MCCLOUD, JAMES N., educator; b. Knoxville, Tenn., Nov. 26, 1924; s. John Beason and Etta Mae (Seay) McC.; A.A., Pasadena City Coll., 1953, B.S. in Mech. Engring. (Airesearch scholar, 1955), Calif. Inst. Tech., 1955, M.S. in Mech. Engring. (univ. scholar), 1956; children—James Kent, Susan JoAn, David Lee. Teaching asst., Calif. Inst. Tech., Pasadena, 1956; mgr. product research and advanced engring. Skil Corp., Chgo., 1956-61; research asst., Northwestern U., Evanston, Ill., 1961; asso. dir. advanced research Sunbeam Corp., Chgo., 1962; sr. devel. engr. Airesearch, Los Angeles, 1962; staff engring. specialist Vickers Inc., Torrance, Calif., 1963-64; project engr. Preco Inc., Los Angeles, 1965-68, AMF, Santa Ana, Calif., 1968-70; v.p. Robertson Assos., Los Angeles, 1970-71; math. instr. Foothill Sch., Pasadena, 1971—; engring. instr. Ill. Inst. Tech., 1957; instr. various mgmt. courses, Marquette U., 1957-58; coll. tutor math. and physics, 1975-80. Youth dir. Glenview (Ill.) Community Ch., 1959. Recipient community service cert. for edn.; registered profl. engr. Mem. AAAS, N.Y. Acad. Scis., Profl. Engrs. Assn. (Pasadena rep., life mem. Calif. Inst. Tech., com. mem. for speakers, chmn. session speakers com., 1968-69). Club: Toastmasters Internat. (sec., Santa Ana., 1970). World patentee Skil roto hammer, dieless punch, torque control impact wrench, toothless saw blade, load dividers for railway equipment, vibratory drive for earth moving equipment. Home: 340 S Sierra Madre Blvd Apt 18 Pasadena CA 91107 Office: 3081 Foothill Blvd Pasadena CA 91107

MCCLURE, AUDREY TRUESDAIL, audiologist; b. Alhambra, Calif., Sept. 13, 1932; d. Roger Williams and Dorothy (Painter) Truesdail; B.S., U. Oreg., 1953; M.A., Calif. State U., Los Angeles, 1972; m. Roland Holmes McClure, June 22, 1952; children—Pamela Ann, Gregory Stuart. Speech pathologist HEAR Center, Pasadena, Calif., 1965-72, therapy coordinator, 1972-80; owner Love Hearing Instrument Service. Active Girl Scouts Am., Assistance League of Pasadena, 1960-67; bd. dirs. PTA, 1962-65. Mem. Am. Speech and Hearing Assn., Calif. Speech and Hearing Assn., Calif. Assn. Tchrs. of Hearing Impaired, Alexander Graham Bell Assn. Home: Apt 5 500 S Oak Knoll St Pasadena CA 91101 Office: Love Hearing Instrument Service 16 N Marengo Pasadena CA 91101

MC CLURE, CHARLES BENJAMIN, contracts engr.; b. Balt., Apr. 26, 1929; s. Charles Benjamin and Anna (Trunk) McC.; B.S. in Mech. Engring., Johns Hopkins U., 1955; postgrad. Drexel Inst., 1960-61; m. Grace Louise Wilson, Jan. 3, 1953; children—Robert C., Janet L., Scott D. Mech. engr. Bendix Radio Co., Balt., 1953-60; project engr. in electronics Martin Marietta Aerospace, Balt., 1960-61, with contract requirements dept., Denver, 1962-68, chief Viking project, 1969-76, chief contract requirements, 1976-78, mgr. contract requirements and documentation, 1979-80, mgr. configuration and data mgmt. MX Program, 1981-83; mgr. configuration and data mgmt. Strategic and Space Launch Systems Div., 1983—; mem. EIA G33 Commn. on Configuration and Data Mgmt. for Aerospace requirements. Sec.-treas. Arapahoe County Sch. Dist. 6, 1969-73, 79-81, v.p., 1975-79, pres., 1973-75; pres. S.E. Bd. Coop. Services, Englewood, Colo.; pres. bd. dirs. Arapahoe County Task Force on Youth and Drugs. Served with U.S. Army, 1951-53. Mem. Am. Philatelic Soc. Republican. Presbyterian. Club: Arapahoe Stamp. Home: 3882 E Briarwood Ave Littleton CO 80122

MCCLURE, JAMES A., U.S. senator; b. Payette, Idaho, Dec. 27, 1924; s. William Robertson and Marie Caroline (Freehafer) McC.; J.D., U. Idaho, 1950, hon. doctorate, 1981; m. Louise Marilyn Miller, Sept. 23, 1950; children—Marilyn, Kenneth, David. Admitted to Idaho bar, practiced in Payette; pros. atty., Payette County, city atty., Payette; mem. Idaho Senate, asst. majority leader, 1965-66; mem. 90th to 93d congresses from 1st Idaho Dist.; U.S. senator from Idaho, 1972—, chmn. energy and natural resources com., mem. steering com.; rules com., chmn. Rep. conf. com., interior subcom. appropriations. Mem. visitors bd. U.S. Mil. Acad.; trustee Kennedy Ctr.; bd. visitors Duke U. Sch. Forestry and Environ. Studies; bd. govs. Council Nat. Policy. Recipient Disting. Defender of Free Enterprise award U.S. Indsl. Council, 1980, Taxpayers' Best Friend award Nat. Taxpayers Union, 1981, Disting. Service award Nat. Energy Resources Orgn., 1982, Watchdog of Treasury award Nat. Assn. Businessmen, Guardian of Small Bus. award Nat. Fedn. Ind. Bus. Mem. Phi Alpha Delta. Methodist (trustee). Mason. Kiwanian. Home: 3467 N Venice Arlington VA 22207 also Payette ID 83661 Office: 361 Dirksen Senate Office Bldg Washington DC 20510

MCCLURE, MILDRED LUCILLE, hospital administrator; b. Gibson City, Ill., Apr. 3, 1923; d. Albert and Deana (Onken) Warfield; children—John, Judy, Tom. B.S. in Home Econs., U. Ill., 1944. Tchr., pub. schs., Ill., 1944-45; instr. home econs. Underwater Sound Research, Cambridge, Mass., 1946-47; instr. New Eng. Sch. Home Arts, Cambridge, 1946-47; substitute tchr. Albuquerque Pub. Sch. System, 1966-68; dir. vol. services Presbyterian Hosp. Ctr., Albuquerque, 1968—; cons. in field. Loaned exec. United Way 1982. Mem. Am. Soc. Dir. Vols., Am. Hosp. Assn., N.Mex. Hosp. Assn., N.Mex. Dir. Vols., Greater Albuquerque Vol. Assn. (dir. 1980). Republican. Clubs: PEO (pres. 1963), Zonta (pres. 1981—). Home: 3206 Linda Vista St SE Albuquerque NM 87106 Office: Presbyterian Hosp Albuquerque NM 87102

MCCLURE, PAUL THOMAS, stained glass co. exec.; b. Detroit, Feb. 18, 1943; s. Jack Cloer and Helen Maureen (Green) McC.; B.S., Calif. Western U., 1964; M.P.A., U. So. Calif., 1968, Ph.D., 1972; m. Elizabeth McCullough, Dec. 25, 1979; children—Shauna, Erin, Scott. Adminstrv. analyst Los Angeles Internat. Airport, 1966-68; policy analyst Rand Corp., Santa Monica, Calif., 1968-73; adj. prof. Golden Gate U., San Francisco, 1973—; artist/owner Am. Art Glass Co., Adelanto, Calif., 1973—. Mem. Adelanto Sch. Bd., 1973—, pres., 1976-79; mem. Adelanto Planning Commn., 1973-75, chmn., 1973-75. RAND fellow, 1972. Stained glass commns. include: Campus Hill Seventh-day Adventist Ch., Loma Linda, Calif., 10th Ave. Bapt. Ch., Los Angeles, Assembly of God Ch., Hesperia, Calif., Living Waters Chapel, Apple Valley, Calif. Office: Am Art Glass Co 15444 7th St Victorville CA 92392

MCCLURE, SCOTT DOUGLAS, manufacturing company official; b. Portland, Oreg., Dec. 15, 1950; s. C. Douglas and Ellen (Sanasak) McC.; m. Joyce Ann Sullivan, Apr. 15, 1978; children—Gregory M. Sullivan, Jordan E. Student Lane Community Coll., 1972-76, Portland State U., 1980-82. Prodn. mgr. Future Machine Corp., Portland, Oreg., 1976-78; asst. prodn. control mgr. Oreg. Metal Slitters, Portland, 1978-79; adminstr. mfg. systems Electro Sci. Industries, Portland, 1979—. Served with USCG, 1968-72. Mem. Am. Prodn. and Inventory Control Soc. (chpt. pres.). Democrat. Office: 13900 NW Science Park Dr Portland OR 97229

MCCLURE, THOMAS HARDY, computer engineer; b. Vancouver, Wash., May 2, 1938; s. David Gordon Sr. and Josephine Allie (Parker) McM.; m. Paula Irmeli Jouste, Dec. 28, 1963; children—Will, Denny, Helen, Sonja. B.S., Brigham Young U., 1966; M.A., Mich. State U., 1968; doctoral candidate U. Helsinki (Finland), 1970. Asst. prof. North Adams (Mass.) State Coll., 1972-74; computer programmer MSC Co., Salt Lake City, 1975-76, Lockheed Co., Sunnyvale, Calif., 1976-77, Signetics Corp., Orem, Utah, 1980-82; computer engr. Rockwell Internat., Clearfield, Utah, 1978-80, Vt. Yankee Nuclear Power Corp., Vernon, 1982—. Sec., Town Democratic Com., Williamstown, Mass., 1974. Mich. fellow, 1967; U. Essex (Eng.) fellow, 1974; recipient Lockheed Patent award, 1977. Mem. Digital Equipment Corp. Users Soc., ACM, Am. Statis Assn., Am. Polit. Sci. Assn., Internat. Polit. Sci. Assn., Pi Sigma Alpha. Mormon. Clubs: YMCA, Democratic. Author: Collected Poems, 1980; profl. publs. Office: Vermont Yankee Nuclear Power Corp PO Box 157 Vernon VT 05354

MCCLUSKEY, WILLIAM NORMAN, computer software co. exec.; b. Caldwell, Idaho, Apr. 25, 1933; s. William Earl and Mary Lucille (Clark) McC.; student public schs., Caldwell; m. Eutahna Gambill, June 27, 1959; children—William Dee, Tracy Lynne. With installation dept. Western Electric Co., Boise, Idaho, 1951-62; with Collins Radio Co., Cedar Rapids, Iowa, 1962-67; sales engr. Digital Equipment Corp., Denver, 1967-69; account mgr. Honeywell Info. Systems Co., Denver, 1969-74; br. mgr. Prime Computer, Inc., Phoenix, 1974-78; pres. Database Systems Corp., Phoenix, 1978—. Served with U.S. Army, 1953-55. Mem. Data Processing Mgmt. Assn., Exec. Conf. Com. (charter), Assn. Corp. Growth. Republican. Methodist. Club: Phoenix Bus. Breakfast. Home: Star Route 2 Box 974-B Cave Creek AZ 85331 Office: Database Systems Corp 1846 E Camelback Rd Phoenix AZ 85016

MC CLYMONT, HAMILTON, opera manager; b. Montreal, Que., Can., Mar. 20, 1944; s. Hamilton, Jr. and Zoe Annis (Cook) McC.; B.A., Dalhousie U., 1970. Adminstrv. dir. Toronto Arts Prodns., 1971-74; adminstr. Neptune Theatre, Halifax, N.S., 1974-76; music officer, fin. Can. Council, Ottawa, Ont., 1976-78; dir., gen. mgr. Vancouver (B.C.) Opera, 1978—. Adviser, Community Music Sch. of Greater Vancouver. Mem. Can. Music Council, Can. Conf. of Arts, Community Arts Council Vancouver (major arts liaison com.), Can. Owners and Pilots Assn. Club: Pacific Flying. Office: 111 Dunsmuir St Vancouver BC V6B 1W8 Canada*

MCCOLLOR, ROBERT LAWRENCE, engineer, physicist, consultant; b. Ocheyedan, Iowa, Feb. 20, 1922; s. Lawrence Patrick and Jennie Lee (Rumelhart) M.; m. Betty Jeanne Ebert, March 25, 1949; children—Virginia Marie, Lisa Edna Jeanne. A.S. in Mech. Engring., N.D. Agrl. Coll., Fargo, 1944; B.A. in Math. and Physics, Morningside Coll., Sioux City, Iowa, 1949; cert. Nat. Security Mgmt. Indsl. Coll. of the Armed Forces, Washington; M.S. in Mgmt. Engring., Kensington U., Glendale, Calif., 1977, Ph.D. in Physics, 1978. Registered profl. engr., Mass., N.H. Design engr. RCA Corp., Camden, N.J., 1952-54; engring. mgr. RCA, 1954-61; engring. mgr. RCA, Burlington, Mass., 1961-71, sr. engring. scientist, 1971-74; prin. engr. Support Systems Assocs., Inc., Valencia, Calif., 1975-83; sr. project engr. ManTech Internat. Corp., Valencia, 1983—. Served with U.S. Army, 1942-46. Mem. AAAS, AIAA. Contbr. articles to profl. jours. Home: 42944 Amboy St Lancaster CA 93544

MCCOMAS, JOHN LAWRENCE, safety engr.; b. Huntington, W.Va., Apr. 3, 1940; s. Lawrence Gerald and Aileen Jane (Jeffery) McC.; m. Beatrice Anne Harris, Jan. 28, 1959; m. 2d, Amalia Maria Bonnemaison, Feb. 28, 1980; children—Valerie Anne Munoz, Jeffrey Scott. B.S.M.E., Milw. Sch. Engring., 1969; M.S. with honors in Health Sci., Calif. State U., 1978. Lic. profl. engr., Calif. Loss control engr. Aetna Life and Casualty, Fresno, Calif., 1969-72; dist. mgr. Calif. Div. Indsl. Safety, San Francisco and Bakersfield, 1972-76; N. slope project engr. SOHIO/BP Constrn. Co., San Francisco, 1976-79; assoc. mgr. safety engring. Occidental Petroleum Exploration and Prodn. Co., Bakersfield, 1979-83; western regional safety engr. Cities Service Oil & Gas Corp., Bakersfield, 1983—; assoc. prof. safety and fire protection engring. Calif. State U.-Fresno; instr. safety and loss control mgmt. Bakersfield Coll. Served with USN, 1958-62. Mem. Am. Petroleum Inst. (com. safety and fire protection), Western Oil and Gas Assn. (fire, safety and health com.), Am. Soc. Safety Engrs., System Safety Soc. Republican. Presbyterian. Club: Bakersfield Racquet. Office: 5000 Stockdale Hwy Bakersfield CA 93309

MCCOMB, KARLA JOANN, curriculum consultant; b. Tacoma, July 23, 1937; d. John Frank and Lorraine Beatrice (Winters) Bohac; m. Russell Marshall McComb, Nov. 27, 1959 (div.); children—Marsha McComb Hayes, Kathleen Ann. Cert. instr. French, U. Paris, 1958; B.A., Calif. State U.-Sacramento, 1960. Cert. secondary tchr., Nev. Tchr. French and music Sacramento Waldorf Sch., 1960-62; tchr. French, Red Bluff High Sch., 1967-68; tchr. French and music Pocatello (Idaho) Schs., 1969-71; tchr., chairperson dept. Clark County Sch. Dist., 1971-76; curriculum cons. social sci., fgn. lang., profl. growth, Las Vegas, 1976—; cons. Taft Inst. Govt., Salt Lake City, 1977—, Tchr. Inservice, Follett Pub. Co., 1980-81; coordinator Nev. Close-Up Program, 1980—. Mem. Sacramento Symphony Orch., 1954-66, Nev. Humanities Com.; bd. dirs. Love All People Youth Group. Mem. Clark County Fgn. Lang. Tchrs. Assn. (pres.), Nat. Council Social Studies, Social Studies Suprs. Assn., Nev. Fgn. Lang. Tchrs. Assn. (pres.-elect), AAUW, Phi Theta Kappa, Mu Phi Epsilon, Alpha Delta Kappa. Democrat. Clubs: Vegas Valley Dog Obedience (pres.), Jackpot Obedience Assn. (pres.). Author: A Cultural Celebration, 1980. Home: 409 A N Lamb Blvd Las Vegas NV 89110 Office: 600 N 9th St Las Vegas NV 89101

MCCOMBS, BARBARA LEHERISSEY, psychologist; b. Galesburg, Ill., Nov. 30, 1942; d. Raymond Louis and Emily Marie (Schulz) Adolf; B.S., Fla. State U., 1968, M.S. (U.S. Office Edn. fellow), 1969, Ph.D., 1971; children—Heather Rae, Ryan William. Research assoc. Computer Assisted Instrn. Ctr., Fla. State U., 1969-71; unit chief human factors McDonnell Douglas Corp., Denver, 1971-82; sr. research psychologist Denver Research Inst., 1982—. Mem. Am. Psychol. Assn., Am. Ednl. Research Assn., Human Factors Soc., Assn. Devel. Computer-Base Instructional Systems. Contbr. articles to profl. jours. Home: 1050 S Monaco Pkwy Unit 66 Denver CO 80224 Office: SSRE Div 2135 E Wesley St Denver CO 80208

MC COMBS, DONALD DWAIN, real estate securities exec.; b. Eureka, Mont., Jan. 26, 1922; s. William Elmer and Olive (Schroth) McC.; student U. Calif., Berkeley, 1941-42; children—William Henry, David Christopher. Pres., McCombs Securities Co. Inc., Santa Ana, Calif., 1960—; chmn. bd. D & R Properties Inc., Santa Ana, 1970—; chmn. bd. McCombs Corp. Trustee, pres. bd. Pomona (Calif.) Unified Schs., 1966-71. Served to lt. USAF, 1942-45. Home: 30462 Paseo del Valle Laguna Niguel CA 92677 Office: 2392 E Morse Ave Irvine CA 91714

MC CONKIE, BRUCE REDD, clergyman; b. Ann Arbor, Mich., July 29, 1915; s. Oscar W. and Margaret V. (Redd) McC.; A.B., U. Utah, 1937, J.D., 1940; m. Amelia Smith, Oct. 13, 1937; children—Vivian, Joseph F., Stanford S., Mary E., Mark L., Rebecca, Stephen L., Sara J. Admitted to Utah bar, 1940; mem. firm McConkie, Boud, Summerhays & Hess, Salt Lake City, 1940-42; asst. city atty., city prosecutor Salt Lake City, 1940-42. Ordained to ministry Ch. of Jesus Christ of Latter Day Saints, 1946; ch. servicemen's coordinator, 1947-64; gen. authority of ch., 1946—, mem. First Council of 70, 1946-72; mem. council Twelve Apostles, 1972—; pres. So. Australian Mission, Melbourne, Australia, 1961-64. Mem. Bd. Edn. Ch. Jesus Christ Latter-day Saints, 1972—. Trustee Brigham Young U., Provo, Utah, 1972—, Ricks Coll., Rexburg, Idaho, 1973—, Ch. Coll. Hawaii, Laie, Oahu, 1973—. Served from 1st lt. to lt. col., M.I., AUS, 1942-46. Compiler 3 volumes of doctrines of salvation, sermons and writings of Joseph Fielding Smith, 1954, 55, 56. Author: Mormon Doctrine, 1958; Doctrinal New Testament Commentary, Vol. 1, The Gospels, 1965; vol. 2, Acts-Philippians, 1970; Vol. 3, Colossians-Revelation, 1972; The Promised Messiah—The First Coming of Christ, 1978; The Mortal Messiah—From Bethlehem to Calvary, Book I, 1979, Book II, 1980, Book III, 1980, Book IV, 1981; The Millennial Messiah, 1982. Address: 47 E S Temple St Salt Lake City UT 84184

MCCONNELL, CALVIN DALE, bishop; b. Monte Vista, Colo., Dec. 3, 1928; s. Roy and Leota Fern (Taylor) McC.; B.S., U. Denver, 1951; M.Div., Iliff Sch. Theology, 1954; S.T.M., Andover-Newton Theol. Sem., 1967; m. Mary Caroline Bamberg, Sept. 2, 1952; children—David William, Mark Andrew. Ordained to ministry United Methodist Ch.; pastor chs. in Calif. and Colo.; chaplain, asst. prof. religion Willamette U., Salem, Oreg., 1961-68; bishop of Portland (Oreg.) area, 1980—; trustee Iliff Sch. Theology, Willamette U., Alaska Pacific U., Anchorage. Club: Rotary. Office: 1505 SW 18th Ave Portland OR 97205

MC CONNELL, GERALDINE ASHLEY, pharmacist; b. Denver; d. Frederick D. and Mary (Owens) Ashley; B.S., U. Colo., 1950; m. Conrad N. McConnell, Oct. 7, 1950 (dec. Apr. 1973); 1 son, C. Peter; m. 2d, Rollins F. Christian, 1975. Pharmacist, Rocky Mountain Arsenal, Dept. Army Chem. Corps, 1951-55, VA Outpatient Clinic, Portland, Oreg., 1957-68, 73—; pharmacy mgr. Crestview Convalescent Hosp., Portland, 1968-73. Mem. community services com. Urban League of Portland, 1964-66, now mem. bd. dirs.; mem. women's bd. Reed Coll.; life mem. NAACP; pres. Portland chpt. Links Am., 1969-71; mem. Am. Revolution Bicentennial Commn. Oreg., 1973-77; appointee Gov.'s Commn. on Black Affairs, 1981. Mem. Sch. Bd. Adv. Com., Portland. Recipient Woman of Year award Portland Fedn. Women's Orgns.; bd. dirs. Young Audiences; pres. bd. dirs. Urban League Portland, 1976-77. Mem. Oreg. Soc. Hosp. Pharmacists, Alpha Kappa Alpha (award 1966, pres. 1959-61, scholarship chmn. 1957, 60, 62, 64), Jack and Jill of Am. (treas. 1966-68). Designed 1st aid kit for Chem. Corps. Home: 3640 N Winchell St Portland OR 97217 Office: 426 SW Stark St Portland OR 97204

MC CONNELL, JOHN DOUGLAS, mgmt. cons.; b. Dimboola, Victoria, Australia, May 13, 1932; s. William Thomas and Ada Maud (Gardner) McC.; came to U.S.J 1964, B.A., Melbourne U., 1954; Ph.D., Stanford U., 1967; m. Gloria Ann Revak, Oct. 12, 1968; children—Joanne Patricia, Meredith Lorraine. Asst. to mng. dir. Automotive & Gen. Industries Ltd., Melbourne, 1954-59; mgr. Eagle M.R. Service Pty. Ltd., Melbourne, 1959-64; dir. mgmt. systems SRI Internat., Washington, 1975-77, dir. mgmt. econs. Europe and Middle East, 1977-78, dir. mgmt. services group, Menlo Park, Calif., 1978-80, dir. Forest Products Ctr., 1980-83; v.p. Sungene Techs. Corp., Palo Alto, 1983—. vis. lectr. U. Bradford (Eng.); lectr. San Francisco State U. Fife gov. Royal Victorian Inst. Blind, 1957—; mem. exec. bd. Stanford Area Council Boy Scouts Am. Alfred P. Sloan Fellow, 1964-65; Gen. Electric Co. Fellow, 1966. Fellow Australian Inst. Mgmt., Advt. Inst. Australia; mem. Am. Mktg. Assn., Royal Scottish Country Dance Soc. Presbyterian. Club: Masons. Author articles. Home: 4174 Oak Hill Ave Palo Alto CA 94306 Office: 3330 Hillview Ave Palo Alto CA 94304

MC CORMAC, WESTON ARTHUR, ret. educator, ret. army officer; b. Tacoma, Mar. 5, 1911; s. Jesse Carney and Jessie (Myron) McC.; B.A., Golden Gate U., M.B.A., 1968; diploma Nat. War Coll., 1956; M.P.A., U. So. Calif., 1972; M.A., Calif. Poly. State U., 1975. m. Mary Jeanne Rapp, Sept. 5, 1940. Account exec. Merrill, Lynch, Pierce, Fenner & Beane, Tacoma, Seattle, 1929-40; commd. lt. U.S. Army, 1940, advanced through grades to col., 1946; asst. chief of staff 7th Army G 1, 1952-54; comdg. officer 35th F.A. Group, Germany, 1956-58; dep. chief of staff V Corps, 1958-60, asst. chief of staff G 1, Pacific, 1962-65; ret., 1966; prof. bus., dept. chmn. Calif. Poly. State U., San Luis Obispo, 1968-80, ret., 1980. Decorated Legion of Merit with 2 oak leaf clusters, Silver Star, Bronze Star medal, Commendation medal with oak leaf cluster. Fellow Fin. Analysts Fedn.; mem. Los Angeles Soc. Fin. Analysts. Club: San Luis Obispo Golf and Country. Home: 176 Country Club San Luis Obispo CA 93401

MCCORMACK, JAMES FRANCIS, human resource and organization development executive; b. Denver, Sept. 20, 1938; s. Charles Francis and Constance Sylvia (Brown) McC.; m. Suellen Marie Honegger, June 11, 1960; children—Kenneth, Timothy, Kevin, Kelly Ann. B.S. in Econs., Villanova U., 1960; postgrad. U. Colo., 1980—. Dist. traffic mgr. Chesapeake & Potomac Telephone Co., Washington, 1968-70, personnel mgr., cons., 1970-76; dir. mgmt. devel. service Farmbank, Denver, 1976-81, sr. dir., 1981—; cons. to bus., social service agys. Mem. Cert. Cons. Internat., Am. Soc. Tng. and Devel., Organizational Devel. Network. Republican. Roman Catholic. Home: 7815 S Elizabeth Way Littleton CO 80122 Office: Farmbank 12000 E 47th Ave Denver CO 80239

MC CORMICK, ADELE VON RÜST, psychotherapist; b. San Francisco, Dec. 11, 1929; d. George Washington and Adele E. Ryst; clin. certificate Moreno Inst., SUNY, 1968; Ph.D. in Psychology, Columbia Pacific U., 1980; m. Thomas E. McCormick, Dec. 11, 1971. Profl. actress with Warner Bros., 1958-62; appeared in films including My Enemy The Sea, 1961, Days of Wine and Roses, 1962; co-founder Charila Found., San Francisco, 1968; instr. psychiat. residents Agnews (Calif.) State Hosp., 1966-72; cons. in psychotherapy Belmont Psychiat. Center, 1972-75; founder, dir. Psychotherapy Inst., San Francisco, 1970, dir., 1970—; clin. dir. Clin. Psychotherapy Inst., 1980—; condr. clin. workshops in group dynamics and psychodrama in Switzerland, Eng., Spain, U.S., 1971-78; hon. prof. U. Madrid, 1977. Founder, exec. dir. McCormick Found., Inc., 1979. Recipient Medal of Honor, U. Madrid, 1977. Mem. Am. Personnel and Guidance Assn., Internat. Assn. Group Psychotherapy, Orthopsychiat. Soc., Am. Soc. Group Psychotherapy and Psychodrama, Friends of the Psychoanalytic Soc. Republican. Episcopalian. Contbr. articles on group psychotherapy to profl. publs. Home: 1044 Sir Francis Drake Blvd Kentfield CA Office: 671 Barberry Ln San Rafael CA 94903

MCCORMICK, FLOYD GUY, JR., educator; b. Center, Colo., July 3, 1927; s. Floyd Guy and Gladys Marie (Weir) M.; B.S., Colo. State U., 1950, M.Ed., 1959; Ph.D., Ohio State U., 1964; m. Constance P. Slane, Sept. 18, 1965; children—Angela Lynn, Craig Alan, Kim Ann, Robert Guy. Tchr. vocational agr. State Colo., 1956-62; asst. prof. agrl. edn. Ohio State U., Columbus, 1964-67; prof. agrl. edn., head dept. U. Ariz., Tucson, 1967—; vis. prof. Colo. State U., 1973. Mem. edn. in agr. and natural resources com. Nat. Acad. Sci., 1967-69; cons. in-service edn., dir. vocat. edn. Ohio Dept. Edn., 1963-64. Trustee, Nat. Future Farmers Am. Found., Washington, 1971-73. Served with USNR, 1945-46. Recipient Centennial award Ohio State U., 1970; E.B. Knight award NACTA Jour., 1980; named Hon. State Farmer Ariz., 1968, Colo., 1958, Hon. Am. Farmer, 1972. Mem. Am. Vocat. Assn. (policy com. agrl. edn. div. 1976-79, sec. agrl. edn. div. 1983—), Nat. Vocat. Agr. Tchrs. Assn. (regional outstanding service award 1974), Am. Assn. Tchr. Educators Agr. (pres. 1976-77, Disting. Service award 1978), Alpha Zeta, Alpha Tau Alpha (hon.), Gamma Sigma Delta, Phi Delta Kappa. Mason. Spl. editor Agrl. Edn. mag., 1970-74; editor Am. Assn. Tchr. Educators in Agr. Newsletter, 1975-76; co-author: Teacher Education in Agriculture, 1982, Supervised Occupational Experience Handbook, 1982; author instructional units, tech. bulls., articles in profl. jours. Home: 6933 Paseo San Andres Tucson AZ 85710

MCCORMICK, FRANK EDWARD, bank economist; b. Elmira, N.Y., Oct. 3, 1939; s. John Michael and Sara Theresa (Sweeney) McC.; m. Judith Mary Klink, July 2, 1966; children—Erin, Daniel. B.S. Villanova U., 1961; Ph.D. in Econs., U. Calif.-Berkely, 1971. Asst. prof. U. Calif.-Riverside 1971-75; economist Federal Res. Bd., Washington, 1975-79; sr. economist Bank of Am., San Francisco, 1979—. Served to lt. USN, 1961-66. ROTC scholar, 1957; Flood fellow, 1966. Mem. Am. Econs. Assn., Western Econs. Assn., Nat. Assn. Bus. Economists. Contbr. articles to profl. jours. Home: 506 Monarch Ridge Dr Walnut Creek CA 94596 Office: Bank of Am Econs Dept Box 37000 San Francisco CA 94137

MCCORMICK, HAROLD L., theatre exec., state senator; b. Florence, Colo., May 16, 1918; s. B.P. and Anna L. (Hoffman) McC.; B.S.C., U. Denver, 1940; m. Jeanne Rolfes, Jan. 8, 1941; children—Brian, Carole, Ellen. Owner, operator McCormick Theatres, Canon City, Colo.; mgr. theatre properties in Colo. and N.Mex. for Nat. Gen. Theatres, 1946-53; mem. Colo. Ho. of Reps., 1961-72; mem. Colo. Senate, 1973—, chmn. caucus, 1973-76, pres. pro tem, 1977-78. Elder, Presbyn. Ch.; trustee St. Thomas More Hosp., Canon City; candidate U.S. Ho. of Reps. from Colo. 3d dist., 1978, 80. Served to capt. USAAF, 1942-46, to col. USAF Res., to 1978. Named Legislator of Year, DAV; Citizen of Year, Jr. C. of C. Mem. Am. Legion, VFW, TROA, Omicron Delta Kappa. Republican. Clubs: Masons; Footprinters. Office: McCormick Theatres 606 Main St Canon City CO 81212

MCCORMICK, JOLEEN JOY, title company executive, escrow agency executive; b. Beeler, Kans., Apr. 18, 1933; d. Charles Austin and Evelyne Dolores (Rineley) Wood; m. Paul N. Bradford, Oct. 31, 1952; children—Paul David, James Alan, Stephen Edward; m. 2d, Gerald Eugene McCormick, Nov. 10, 1978. Typist, Chaves County, Abstract, Rowell, N.Mex., 1957-58; sec., loan officer Gessert-Sanders Abstract Co., Roswell, 1959-63; office mgr. Eddy County Abstract Co., Carlsbad, N.Mex., 1963-74, owner, pres., 1974—. Mem. Carlsbad Bd. Realtors, Artesia Bd. Realtors, Women's Council Realtors, Carlsbad Legal Secs. (past pres.), Nat. Assn. Home Builders (sec.-treas.), Nat. Assn. Female Execs., Nat. Fedn. Ind. Bus., Carlsbad C. of C., Artesia C. of C. Democrat. Baptist. Club: Does (pres. 1971).

MCCORMICK, THOMAS WILLIAM, real estate executive, accountant; b. Decatur, Ill., July 25, 1942; s. Daniel William and Veronica Juanita (Jones) McC.; B.B.A., Woodbury U., 1962; postgrad. UCLA, 1962-64; m. Linda Lee Duven, July 25, 1981; children by previous marriage—Thomas William, Laura Suzanne. With Main Lafrentz & Co. (now Main Hurdsman & Cranston, Los Angeles, 1962-66; corp. controller Retail Clks. Internat., Los Angeles, 1968-72; fin. v.p. Ring Bros. Corp., Los Angeles, 1972-76; pres., co-owner Selden Ring Corp., Los Angeles, 1976—; pres. HMI, real estate investment, Los Angeles, 1982—; real estate cons., 1980—. Officer, dir. Chatsworth Hills Acad., 1978—. Served with AUS, 1966-68. C.P.A., Calif. Mem. Am. Inst. C.P.A.s, Calif. Soc. C.P.A.s. Republican. Roman Catholic. Office: Selden Ring Corp 10960 Wilshire Blvd Los Angeles CA 90024

MCCOSH, RICHARD EDWIN, ret. cons. engr.; b. Cedar Rapids, Iowa, Oct. 22, 1917; s. John and Annie (Hromatko) McC.; B.S. E.E. in Electronics, U. Colo., 1944; postgrad. in E.E., U. Oreg., 1947-50; m. Bonnie Vinona Enderud, Feb. 19, 1944; children—Patricia McCosh Simmons, Barbara Major, Sandra McCosh Leonard, Nancy McCosh Langford, John Cantril. Asst. city engr. City of Seaside, Oreg., 1946-47; design engr. Pacific Power & Light Co., Portland, Oreg., 1947-51, system engr., elec. engr., 1953-60; sr. cons. engr. Ford, Bacon & Davis, Inc., N.Y.C., 1960-66; regional mgr. nuclear power sales Gulf Gen. Atomic Co., San Diego, 1966-73; mgr. bus. devel. power div. Daniel, Mann, Johnson & Mendenhall, Los Angeles, 1973-76; v.p. mktg. Mgmt. Analysis Co., San Diego, 1976-79, sr. cons. asso., 1979-80; cons., San Diego, 1976-80. Served with USNR, 1942-46, served to lt. comdr., 1951-53. Registered profl. engr., Oreg., N.Y., N.J., Calif. Mem. IEEE (sr.), N.W. Electric Light & Power Assn., Pacific Coast Elec. Assn., Rocky Mountain Electric League. Republican. Presbyterian (trustee, fin. sec. Valley Presbyterian Ch., Portland, 1956-59). Clubs: Electric Club of San Diego (dir., 1977-79), Mil. Order of World Wars, KP (life), Acacia, Lions Internat. (chmn. sponsoring com. Sea Scout Ship City of Roses, Boy Scouts Am., Portland, 1958-60). Author profl. govt. report, 1964. Home and Office: 5798 Bellevue Ave La Jolla CA 92037

MCCOURT, PETER EDMOND, engring. co. exec.; b. Los Angeles, June 1, 1936; s. Benjamin Arnold and Ruth (Griffin) McC. B.S. in M.E., Stanford U., 1958, M.S. in M.E., 1959; m. Suzanne Mutuberria, Sept. 20, 1958; children—Christine, John, Ben, Matthew. With energy systems group Rockwell Internat., Canoga Park, Calif., 1963—, v.p., gen. mgr. environ. and energy systems div., 1978—. Active Boy Scouts Am., 1973—. Served with USAF, 1959-63. Recipient AEC fellow, 1958-59; registered profl. engr., Calif. Mem. Nat. Mgmt. Assn., Phi Beta Kappa, Tau Beta Pi. Office: 8900 Desoto Ave Canoga Park CA 91304

MC COWN, GEORGE EDWIN, real estate and investment co. exec.; b. Portland, Oreg., July 1, 1935; s. Floyd C. and Ada E. (Stephens) McC.; B.M.E., Stanford, 1957; M.B.A., Harvard, 1962; children—Taryn, Daniel, David. With Boise Cascade Corp. (Idaho), 1963-80, gen. mgr. Housing Group, Boise, 1970-71, v.p. and gen. mgr. Boise Cascade Realty Group, Palo Alto, Calif., 1971-74, sr. v.p. Boise Cascade Realty Group, pres. Boise Cascade Home & Land Corp., Palo Alto, 1974-79, sr. v.p. Bldg. Material Group, Boise, 1976-80; chmn. Sequoia Corp., Boise Co., Vacation Internat. Ltd., The Palomar Group; chmn. policy adv. bd. Harvard-Mass. Inst. Tech. Joint Center Urban Studies; dir. Center for Real Estate and Urban Econs., U.Calif.-Berkeley; mem. Urban Land Inst.; dir. Impell Corp., Cobe Labs. Trustee, Pacific Crest Outward Bound Sch.; trustee, co-chmn. fin. com. Stanford U.; trustee Boise Futures Found. Mem. Bay Area (Calif.) Council (dir.), Young Presidents Orgn. Office: Sequoia Corp 525 University Ave Suite 1307 Palo Alto CA 94301

MC COY, FRANK MILTON, concert pianist, educator, lecturer; b. El Centro, Calif., s. Henderson C. and Annie (Lee) McC.; A.B. (Rotary scholar), San Francisco State Coll., 1949, M.A., 1960; postgrad. U. Wash., 1952-53, U. Calif. at Santa Barbara, 1957-58, U. So. Calif., 1961-65, U. Valencia (Spain), summer 1967, Walden U.; studied piano under Jean Le Duc, 1947-49, Madame Berthe Poncy-Jacobsen, 1952-53, Amparo Iturbi, 1960-62. Grad. asst. Sch. Music, U. Wash., Seattle, 1952-53; tchr. music edn. San Diego City Schs., 1953-54, El Centro Pub. Schs., 1954-57, Los Angeles City Schs.; counselor Social Service Center, Calexico, Calif., 1955-59; prof. piano and English Compton Coll., 1971-73; chmn. dept. music Portola Jr. High Sch., Los Angeles. Piano, soloist All Am. Chorus tour 1956; 1st Am. to concertize on islands of St. Pierre and Miguelon, 1960; regional rep. Robert S. Gregg Concert Assns., 1963-65; made concert tours Europe, Can., Latin Am., U.S., North Africa, Carribean, Middle East; TV appearance CBC, 1965; adjudicator piano div. Southwestern Youth Music Festival, 1964; mem. bd. adjudicators Nat. Piano Playing Auditions, 1965; music-drama critic Post-Press Newspapers; founder, chmn. Annie Lee McCoy-Chopin Meml. Piano Award, 1975—. Bd. dirs. El Centro Community Concert Assn. Recipient Leona M. Hickman award U. Wash., 1953. Mem. Music Educators Nat. Conf., Nat. Guild Piano Tchrs., Am. Guild Mus. Artists, Nat. Music Tchrs. Assn., Internat. Platform Assn., Nat. Negro Musicians, Nat. Council Tchrs. English. Author: Black Tomorrow: A Portrait of Afro-American Culture, 1976; Playlet: Music Masters, Old and New, 1966; Our American Heritage; We, Too, Are Americans, 1977; also articles. Home: 234 S Figueroa St Apt 431 Los Angeles CA 90012 Office: 18720 Linnet St Tarzana CA 91356

MCCOY, GEORGE THOMAS, construction company executive; b. Olympia, Wash., Feb. 3, 1920; s. George Thomas and Edith (Wilson) McC.; A.B., Stanford U., 1940; m. Eleanore Frates, Apr. 14, 1967; children—Sharyl, Denise, Katherine, Suzanne. With Calif. Div. Hwys., 1946-52; with Guy F. Atkinson Co., South San Francisco, 1952—, pres., chief exec. officer, from 1979, now chmn., chief exec. officer; chmn., chief exec. officer Guy F. Atkinson Co. Calif., South San Francisco. Mem. adv. bd. Project Mgmt. Inst., 1978—, San Francisco State U., 1978—. Served from ensign to lt. comdr. USNR, 1941-46. Mem. Calif. State C. of C. (dir. 1979—), Beavers. Republican. Club: Peninsula Country. Office: Guy F Atkinson Co Calif 10 W Orange Ave South San Francisco CA 94080

MC COY, LOIS CLARK, county official, magazine editor; b. New Haven, Oct. 1, 1920; d. William Patrick and Lois Rosilla (Dailey) Clark; m. Herbert Irving McCoy, Oct. 17, 1943; children—Whitney, Kevin, Marianne, Tori, Debra, Sally, Daniel. B.S., Skidmore Coll., 1942; student Nat. Search and Rescue Sch., 1974. Asst. buyer R.H. Macy & Co., N.Y.C., 1942-44, assoc. buyer, 1944-48; instr. Mountain Medicine & Survival, U. Calif. at San Diego, 1973-74; cons. editor Search & Rescue Mag., 1975; coordinator San Diego Mountain Rescue Team, La Jolla, Calif., 1973-75; exec. sec. Nat. Assn. for Search and Rescue, Inc., Nashville and La Jolla, 1975-80, comptroller, 1980-82; disaster officer San Diego County, 1980—; editor-in-chief Response! mag., 1982—; cons. law enforcement div.; Calif. Office Emergency Services, 1976-77; pres. San Diego Com. for Los Angeles Philharmonic Orch., 1957-58. Bd. dirs. Search and Rescue of the Californias, 1976-77, Nat. Assn. for Search and Rescue, Inc., 1980—; mem. Gov.'s Task Force on Earthquakes, 1981-82; chmn. Earthquake Preparedness Task Force, Seismic Safety Commn., 1982—. Recipient Hal Foss award for outstanding service to search and rescue, 1982. Mem. Am. Astronautical Soc., AIAA, IEEE, Am. Soc. Indsl. Security, Nat. Assn. for Search and Rescue, Council for Survival Edn., Mountain Rescue Assn., Nat. Jeep Search and Rescue Assn., San Diego Mountain Rescue Team, San Diego Amateur Radio Club, Sierra Club. Episcopalian. Author: Search and Rescue Glossary, 1974; contbr. to profl. jours. Office: PO Box 2123 La Jolla CA 92038

MCCOY, WILLIAM EDWARD, III, electronics engr.; b. Oakland, Calif., Jan. 9, 1939; s. William Edward and Mary Venable (Tuckerman) McC.; A.A. with honors Umpqua Community Coll., 1974; B.S. in Gen. Sci., B.S. in Math. with high scholastic honors, Oreg. State U., 1977, B.S. in Computer Sci., 1980; M.S. in Computer Sci., Calif. State U., Chico, 82. Logic designer, research asst. Hughes Aircraft Co., Culver City, Calif., 1962-64, asst. data processing analyst, Fullerton, Calif., 1964-65; programmer Bulter Publs., Hawthorne, Calif., 1966-67; data processing systems analyst Atlantic Richfield Co., Los Angeles, 1968-69, Autographics, Monterey Park, Calif., 1969-71; electronics engr. Naval Weapons Center, China Lake, Calif., 1980-81; engr. EDP applications SP Communications, Burlingame, Calif., 1981-83; engr. GTE Sprint Communications Corp., 1983—; cons. computer tech., 1971. Pres., Indian Wells Valley Pro-life Com., 1981. Served with USAF, 1956-60. Mem. IEEE (membership devel. chmn. China Lake sect. 1981-82), Assn. Computer Machinery, Soc. for Computer Simulation, AIAA, AAAS, Profl. Software Programmers Assn. (chmn. certification com.), Calif. Assn. Physically Handicapped (life mem., parliamentarian Ridgecrest chpt. 1981), Buena Park Jaycees (treas. 1964), Hawthorne Jaycees (state dir. 1966), Southside Jaycees (v.p. 1968), DAV (life), NAACP, Full Gospel Businessmens Fellowship Internat. (life, v.p. Pennicila chpt. 1983-84), Phi Kappa Phi (life). Republican. Roman Catholic. Clubs: Toastmasters (treas. China Lake 1980, sec. 1981, area gov. 1983-84, named able toastmaster), K.C. (chancellor Ridgecrest council 1980-81, dep. grand knight 1981). Patentee real time multi-input and output program controlled switch. Home: 1124 Paloma Apt 1 Burlingame CA 94010 Office: GTE Sprint Communications Corp One Adrian Ct Durlingame CA 94010

MC CRACKEN, ALICE IRENE, psychotherapist; b. Indpls., May 4, 1942; d. Neal and Palma Dorothy (Rice) Mc Cracken, B.A. with honors, Mills Coll., 1963; M.A. in Dramatic Arts (Regents fellow 1963-64), U. Calif., 1965; Ph.D. in Theatre, Tulane U., 1968; Master of Counseling, Ariz. State U., 1975; 1 dau., Tammy Maru. Head current periodical service library Ariz. State U., Tempe, 1969-70; community program specialist City of Scottsdale (Ariz.), 1971-72; women's editor Scottsdale Daily Progress, 1972-74; activities therapist Camelback Hosp., Phoenix, 1972-74, pub. relations coordinator, therapist, 1974-75, dir. pub. relations, psychotherapist, 1975-78; psychotherapist Family Service Agy., Tempe, 1978-81; pvt. practice, Scottsdale, 1981—. Served with USAR, 1976-79; counselor 438th M.P., 1976-78. Mem. Am., Ariz. personnel and guidance assns., Am. Group Psychotherapy Assn., Ariz. Group Psychotherapy Soc., Phoenix Psychoanalytic Study Group, Am. Mental Health Counselors Assn. Office: 6730 E McDowell Rd Suite 115 Scottsdale AZ 85257

MCCRACKEN, BLAIR, psychologist, administrator, author, consultant; b. Los Angeles, Nov. 12, 1933; d. Dwight Mason and Jean (Blair) McC.; 1 son, David Abrams. B.A., George Washington U., 1957; M.A., Columbia U., 1965, now postgrad. Calif. Sch. Profl. Psychology. Cert. psychol. asst., Calif.; cert. profl., Maine; cert. tchr., N.Y. State. Dir. reading OEO city-wide program for disadvantaged children, N.Y.C., 1965-66; dir. reading Chapin Sch., N.Y.C., 1966-68; prin. Lenox Elem. Sch., N.Y.C., 1968-70; univ. instr., supr. student tchrs. NYU Bklyn. Coll., 1970-71; state dir. Div. Curriculum Resources and Spl. Edn., Maine Dept. Edn., Augusta, 1972-74; psychol. cons. Title I outreach program Maine Dept. Edn., 1974-75; psychometrician, psychotherapist Mid Coast Regional Mental Health Clinic, Rockland, Maine, 1974-78; asst. dir. State Title I Div., Mass. Dept. Edn., Boston, 1979-80; dir. Women's Inst., Bay Area Found., San Francisco, 1980—; doctoral research asst. unit behavioral scis. research Kennedy-Shriver Center, Waltham, Mass., 1979-80; teaching fellow Northeastern U., 1979-80; psychotherapist Bay Area Psychol. Services, San Francisco, 1980-83; dir. admissions Vanguard Health Fedn., 1983; author books: Joey's Secret, 1971; Stars are for Storytelling, 1972; On the Edge (tchrs.' guide and pupil activity book), 1975; A Lizard to Start With, 1976; Measure Me Sky, 1979. Mem. adv. council for higher edn. U. Maine; mem. U. Maine Policy Bd., Field Services Research Ctr.; mem. Affirmative Action Commn., Maine Dept. Edn.; mem. profl. standards adv. commn. Maine Legislature; nat. del., keynote speaker Nat. Women's Conf., 1977. Recipient commendation U. Maine, 1974; Disting. Service award San Francisco Bay Area Psychol. Assn., 1982. Mem. Am. Psychol. Assn., Calif. State Psychol. Assn. (co-chmn. conv. 1983, service award 1983), Author's Guild, Soc. Children's Book Writers. Office: Marin Psychol Services 1330 Lincoln Ave San Rafael CA 94901

MCCRACKEN, JOSEPH WILLIAM, trade association executive; b. Butte, Mont., June 7, 1925; s. Thomas Lee and Phyllis Martha (Evans) McC.; B.A., U. Mont., 1948; M.P.A., Princeton U., 1950; m. Janet Seibert, Dec. 12, 1952; children—Jon Gregory, Tamsen Lyn. With Bur. Land Mgmt., U.S. Dept. Interior, Portland, Oreg., 1950-55, Office of Sec., Los Angeles, 1952-53; exec. v.p. Western Forest Industries Assn., Portland, 1955—; adv. to various govt. agys. Served with USMCR, 1943-46. Mem. Phi Delta Theta. Presbyterian. Home: 1904 SW Spring St Portland OR 97201 Office: Western Forest Industries Assn 1500 SW Taylor St Portland OR 97205

MCCRACKEN, PETE VIAU, farmer; b. Whittier, Calif., June 3, 1942; s. Melvin Barnes and Phyllis (Viau) McC.; B.S.A.E., Calif. Poly. State U., 1972; m. Meredith Ann Middlecamp, June 13, 1944; 1 son, Matthew Paul. Mgr., cons., asst. v.p. Oppenheimer Industries, Inc., Kansas City, Mo., 1975-76; v.p. Greenleaf Farms Inc., Porterville, Calif., 1977; partner Hooper & McCracken, Cons., 1978-79; pres. O.I. Farming Co., Ltd., Porterville, 1979—; agrl. cons. Chmn., Porterville Planning Commn., 1981-83. Served with USN, 1965-67. Mem. Am. Soc. Agrl. Consultants (sec.-treas. 1981-82, v.p. 1982-83). Club: Porterville-Tule Kiwanis. Office: 165 North D St Suite 3 Porterville CA 93257

MCCRARY, ELIZABETH ADELLE, aerospace software engineer, archaeologist, educator; b. Burbank, Calif., May 15, 1948; d. William Harry and Olene Adelle (Dunham) McC. B.A., UCLA, 1969, M.A., 1971, M.S., Northrup U., 1979, B.S., Calif. State U., 1983. Cert. community coll. instr., Calif. Asst. to dir. dept. inventory control U.S. Naval Supply Ctr., Long Beach, Calif., 1972-73; archaeologist U. Calif.-Santa Barbara, 1974; pub. affairs dir., archacologist Northridge (Calif.) Archaeol. Research Ctr., 1973-76; customer services rep. Wings West, Inc., Santa Monica, Calif., 1977-79; prof. Los Angeles Southwest Coll., 1973—; mem. tech. staff Hughes Aircraft Co., El Segundo, Calif., 1980—; cons. in field. Active Angeles council Girl Scouts U.S.A., Los Angeles. Mem. AIAA, AAAS. Republican. Club: PEO Sisterhood. Home: 6656 E Rosecrans Ave #S26 Paramount CA 90723 Office: Bldg S72 M/S T351 PO Box 92919 Airport Station Los Angeles CA 90009

MC CRAVEN, CARL CLARKE, health services adminstr.; b. Des Moines, May 27, 1926; s. Marcus Henry and Buena Vista (Rollins) McC.; B.S. in Elec. Engring., Howard U., 1950; M.S. in Health Services Adminstrn., Calif. State U., Northridge, 1976; m. Eva Louise Stewart, Mar. 18, 1978; 1 son, Carl B. Radiation physicist Nat. Bur. Standards, 1951-55; research engr. Lockheed Calif. Co., 1955-63; mem. tech. staff TRW Systems, 1963-72; asso. adminstr. Pacoima Meml. Hosp., Lakeview Terrace, Calif., 1972-74, v.p., 1972—; exec. dir. Hillview Community Mental Health Center, Lake View Terrace, Calif., 1974-76; asst. prof. Calif. State U., Northridge. Regent Casa Loma Coll.; chmn. bd. dirs. Lake View Med. Ctr., San Fernando Valley Girl Scout Council, Pledgerville Sr. Citizens Villa; bd. dirs., mem. budget rev. com. United Way; bd. dirs. ARC; treas. San Fernando Valley Mental Health Assn. Recipient citation Calif. Senate, 1971, Calif. Assembly, 1971, City of Los Angeles, 1971, 78. Fellow Assn. Mental Health Adminstrs.; mem. Am. Public Health Assn., Am. Mgmt. Assn., Nat. Assn. Health Services Execs., NAACP (pres. so. area Calif. conf. 1967-71, nat. dir. 1970-76). Club: North San Fernando Valley Rotary (pres.). Home: 17233 Chatsworth St Granada Hills CA 91344

MCCRAVEN, EVA STEWART MAPES, health service adminstr.; b. Los Angeles, Sept. 26, 1936; d. Paul Melvin and Wilma Zech (Ziegler) Stewart; B.S. magna cum laude, Calif. State U., Northridge, 1974, M.S., 1976; m. Carl Clarke McCraven, Mar. 18, 1978; children—David Anthony, Lawrence James, Maria Lynn Mapes. Dir. spl. projects Pacoima Meml. Hosp., 1969-71, dir. health edn., 1971-74; asst. exec. dir. Hillview Community Mental Health Center, Lakeview Terrace, Calif., 1974—, dir. Hillview Center dept. Consultation and Edn. Pres., San Fernando Valley Coordinating Council Area Assn., Sunland-Tujunga Coordinating Council; bd. dirs. N.E. Valley Health Corp., 1970-73, Golden State Community Mental Health Center, 1970-73. Fellow Assn. Mental Health Adminstrs.; mem. Am. Pub. Health Assn., Health Services Adminstrn. Alumni Assn. (v.p.), Bus. and Profl. Women, LWV. Office: 11600 Eldridge Ave Lake View Terrace CA 91342

MCCUEN, KENNETH ALAN, systems engineer; b. Tacoma, Wash., Sept. 28, 1941; s. Donald Enloe and Velma Elaine (Bayless) M.; m. Patricia McCuen, Dec. 17, 1971. B.S. in Elec. Engring., San Jose State U., 1976; postgrad. U. Santa Clara, 1978. Systems engr. Moore Systems, San Jose, Calif., 1975-77; sr. engr. Branson IPC, Hayward, Calif., 1977—. Served with USN, 1960-64. Mem. IEEE, Semicondr. Equipment Mfrs. Inst. (standards com.), Eta Kappa Nu. Democrat. Developed gas plasma chemical processing system. Home: 3165 Barletta Lane San Jose CA 95127 Office: 31172 Huntwood Ave Hayward CA 94544

MCCULLOCH, FRANK WALTER, newspaper editor; b. Fernley, Nev., Jan. 26, 1920; s. Frank Walter and Frieda (Sieke) McC.; B.A. in Journalism, U. Nev., 1941, Litt.D., 1967; m. Jakie Caldwell, Mar. 1, 1942; children—Michaele Lee McCulloch Parman, Candace Sue, David Caldwell. With UP, 1941-42, San Francisco Chronicle, 1945-46, Reno Evening Gazette, 1946-52; with Time, Inc., 1952-60, 63-72, bur. chief Time-Life News Service, Dallas, 1954-56, Los Angeles, 1957-60, China and S.E. Asia, 1963-68, N.Y.C., 1969-72, Washington editor Life mag., 1968-69; mng. editor Los Angeles Times, 1960-63; v.p. Edn. Today Co., editor-in-chief Learning Mag., 1972-75; mng. editor Sacramento Bee, 1975-80; exec. editor, dir. McClatchy Newspapers, Sacramento, 1980—. Served with USMCR, 1942-45. Mem. Am. Soc. Newspaper Editors, Sigma Delta Chi, Phi Kappa Phi, Kappa Tau Alpha, Sigma Nu. Contbr. nat. mags. Home: 1638 Del Dayo Carmichael CA 95608 Office: Sacramento Bee PO Box 15779 Sacramento CA 95813

MC CULLOCH, WILLIAM HENRY, research engr.; b. Lamesa, Tex., Mar. 28, 1941; s. W. H. and Mable Eudora (Trice) McC.; B.S. in Engring. Physics, Tex. Tech. U., 1963, M.S. in Mech. Engring., 1964, Ph.D. (NSF fellow), 1968; m. Katie Varvel Neill, July 5, 1963; children—Katie Lyn, William Neil, Carrie Leigh. Mem. staff Aerospace Nuclear Safety Directorate at Sandia Labs., Albuquerque, 1967-71, mem. staff heat transfer and fluid mechanics div., 1971-72, research engr. solar energy, Albuquerque, 1972-81, tech. mgr. nat. Solar Total Energy Program, 1975-81, project engr. hydrogen burn survival program nuclear reactor safety dept., 1981 . Mem. Ph.D. dissertation com. U. N.Mex., 1974-76. Mem. Internat. Solar Energy Soc., N.Mex. Solar Energy Assn., ASME, Sigma Xi, Phi Kappa Phi, Tau Beta Pi, Pi Tau Sigma. Baptist. Clubs: Coronado Ski. Contbr. numerous articles to profl. jours. Home: 9008 Lona Ln NE Albuquerque NM 87111 Office: Sandia Labs Albuquerque NM 87185

MCCULLOUGH, COLIN DAVID, newspaper publisher; b. Windsor, Ont., Can., Oct. 11, 1929; s. Samuel and Elizabeth (Jamison) McC.; m. Regina Maria Ratinskas, Feb. 12, 1958; 1 dau., Katharine Regina McCullough Burrell. B.A., Detroit Inst. Tech., 1951. Asst. dir. personnel relations Hiram Walker & Sons, Walkerville, Ont., Can., 1952-53; with Globe and Mail, Toronto, Ont., from 1954, fgn. corr., Peking, China, 1968-69, London, 1971-73, asst. pub., pub. Victoria (B.C.) Times-Colonist, 1979—. Bd. dirs. United Appeal, 1981; trustee Art Gallery of Victoria, 1982-83. Mem. Canadian Press (dir.), Am. Newspaper Publishers Assn., Canadian Daily Newspaper Publishers Assn. (dir. 1980-81), Commonwealth Press Union. Clubs: Victoria, Union (Victoria). Author: Insider's London, 1971; Stranger in China, 1972. Office: 2621 Douglas St Victoria BC V8W 2N4 Canada

MCCULLOUGH, HENRY FREDERICK, aircraft company manager; b. Vancouver, B.C., Can., Sept. 18, 1926 (parents Am. citizens); s. John Andrew and Beatrice Victoria (Warburton) McC.; m. Constance Agnes Van Nes, Feb. 27, 1951; children—Linda, Katherine, Cynthia, John, Pamela, Lucille. Grad., Sch. Mgmt., UCLA. Cert. quality engr., Am. Soc. Quality Control, 1966. Aircraft specialist Boeing of Can., Vancouver, 1943-45; quality control preflight insp. Boeing Co., Seattle, 1945-49, 53—, quality control chief 707-727 system test, 1955-68, quality control mgr., 1968—. Pres., commr. King County Water Dist. #107, 1965-83; charter mem. Presdl. Task Force, 1982-83. Served with USAF, 1949-53.

Decorated Air medal; recipient Silver Beaver award Boy Scouts Am., 1978; Golden Acorn, PTA, 1977; cert. Nat. Ct. of Honor for Life Saving, 1974. Fellow Am. Soc. Quality Control; mem. Am. Water Works Assn., Water Pollution Control Fedn., Boeing Mgmt. Assn. (life). Republican. Episcopalian. Clubs: Meydenbauer Bay Yacht, Newport Hills Community (past pres., dir.), Renton Fishing and Game. Home: 6808 128th Ave SE Bellevue WA 98006

MC CUNE, BAILEY BRUCE, psychologist; b. Long Beach, Calif., Sept. 12, 1931; s. Bailey Bruce and Gay (LaMar) McC.; A.A., Long Beach Community Coll., 1952; B.A., Calif. State U., 1955, M.S., 1967; Ph.D., Calif. Grad. Inst., 1974; m. Marilyn Marie Paul, Mar. 6, 1954; children—Bailey Bruce III, Bailey Ross. Tchr. Norwalk, Calif., 1955-56; dist. psychologist Tustin (Calif.) Unified Sch. Dist., 1967-69, clin. psychologist, dir. guidance and psychol. services, 1970, cons. clin. psychologist, 1974—; pvt. practice ednl. psychology, counseling and psychotherapy, Fullerton, Calif., 1973; dir., psychologist Med. Clin. Counseling Service, Fullerton, 1974—; mem. staff Esperanza Intercommunity Gen. Hosp. Instr. Pepperdine U., Los Angeles, 1968—; prof. clin. psychology Calif. Grad. Inst.; owner, pub. Prescriptive Press, Fullerton, 1970—; asst. prof. Calif. State U. at Fullerton, 1973-74; psychologist Brea Hosp. Neuropsychiat. Center, 1971—; exam commr. Bd. Behavioral Scis. Examiners, State of Calif., 1971. Mem. ednl. psychol. advisement com. Calif. State U. at Long Beach, 1972-73, mem. pupil personnel implementation adv. com. 1974. Col., Cal. State Med. Res., 1979. Served to 1st lt. inf. AUS, 1950-52. Certified Am. Examining Bd. Psychoanalysis. Mem. Am., Calif., Orange County, psychol. assns., Am. Assn. Marriage and Family Counselors, Calif. Marriage Counseling Assn., Phi Delta Kappa. Home: PO Box 331 Yorba Linda CA 92686 Office: Val-Mesa Medical Bldg Suite 106 100 E Valencia Mesa Dr Fullerton CA 92635

MCCURDY, JOHN ANDREW, JR., physician; b. Kingsville, Tex., July 17, 1945; s. John Andrew and Elizabeth (Smith) McC.; A.B. in Chemistry, Duke U., 1967; M.D., Wake Forest U., Winston-Salem, N.C., 1971; divorced; children—John Andrew, Elizabeth Anne. Intern, Letterman Gen. Hosp., San Francisco, 1971-72; resident Madigan Army Med. Ctr., Tacoma, 1972-76; practice medicine specializing in otolaryngology and facial plastic surgery, Waluku, Hawaii, 1979—; mem. staff Tripler Army Med. Ctr., Maui Meml. Hosp., Castle Meml. Hosp.; asst. clin. prof. surgery U. Hawaii Med. Sch. Served to lt. col. M.C., USAR, 1971-79. Decorated Army Commendation medal; diplomate Am. Bd. Otolaryngology. Fellow ACS, Am. Acad. Facial Plastic and Reconstructive Surgery, Am. Acad. Head and Neck Surgery. Author: The Complete Guide to Cosmetic Facial Surgery, 1981. Home: 3126 Mapu Kihei HI 96753 Office: 1063 E Main St Suite 225 Wailuku HI 96793

MCCURRAY, HOWARD AUSTIN, railroad conductor, union representative; b. Liberty, Idaho, Apr. 2, 1921; s. George Vickers and Nellie (Austin) Mc.; m. Virl Bentsen, Feb. 24, 1940; children—Linda Nelsen, LaRae Hansen, Shelly Hyldahl, Krista Hammond. Student pub. schs. Signalman, Union Pacific R.R., Salt Lake City, 1941-42, brakeman, 1946-49, conductor, 1949—; sec., treas. Brotherhood of Railroad Trainmen, Lodge 802, 1959-62, legis. rep., 1962-67, chmn. legis. bd., 1967-69, dir. state legistion, 1969—; mem. Idaho Rail Planning com., United Transp. Union. Del. state Democratic conv., 1978; mem. Gov. Cecil Andrus Idaho Tomorrow Com.; 1975-83. Served with U.S. Army, 1945-46. Mormon. Home and Office: 5010 Chinook Pocatello ID 83204

MCDANAL, LINDA LOUISE, insurance company manager; b. Manhattan, Kans., July 10, 1947; d. Robert G. and Alma A. (Rueschhoff) Mosier; m. Michael A. McDanal, June 15, 1968. Student Colo. State U., 1967. With Equitable Life Assurance Soc., Denver, 1968—, new bus. mgr., 1980—, also instr. new agts. Active Republican party, Denver Symphony. Named West Central Employee, Equitable Life Assurance Co., 1981. Roman Catholic. Home: 10075 E Caley Pl Englewood CO 80111 Office: 621 17th St Suite 710 Denver CO 80293

MCDANIEL, DAVID TERRY, nuclear engineer; b. Walnut Creek, Calif., Oct. 12, 1955; s. Terry Malcolm and Rhoda Mae (Marcks) McD.; m. Irena L. Lachicki, Mar. 10, 1979; 1 dau., Katrine. B.S. M.E. with honors, U.S. Mcht. Marine Acad., 1977; M.S. in Nuclear Engring., Rensselaer Poly. Inst., 1979; Dept. of Energy-Westinghouse cert. fusion reactor design 1980. Lic. 3d engr.; cert. U.S. Coast Guard Westinghouse Sr. Reactor Operator. Engr., officer Sea Land Service Inc., 1977; power prodn. engr. Pacific Gas & Electric Corp., 1979-82; reactor engr. Northeast Utilities, Waterford, Conn., 1982—. Served to lt. USNR, 1977—. Mem. Am. Nuclear Soc., ASME, U.S. Naval Inst. Republican. Lutheran. Author: The Design of a Gas-Cooled Fusion Reactor First Wall. Office: Pacific Gas & Electric Co Box 56 Avila Beach CA 93424

MCDANIEL, JAMES GREGORY, mech. engr.; b. St. Clair, Mich., Sept. 29, 1953; s. Richard Gregory and Rita Teresa (Kleinsmith) M.; m. Lila Lynn Heinert, Mar. 8, 1980. B.S.M.E., Mich. Tech. U., Houghton, 1975. Engring. tech. Gen. Motors Tech. Ctr., Chevrolet Engring., Warren, Mich., 1973, engring. tech. Gen. Motors Proving Grounds, Milford, 1974; shift supr. Plex Chem. Co. Union City, Calif., 1975-78; prodn. mgr. Gt. Western Chem. Co., Richmond, 1978. Mem. ASME. Republican. Catholic. Clubs: R-Ranch (Lake Berryessa, Calif.); Moose. Home: 2994 Chevy Way San Pablo CA 94806 Office: Gt Western Chem Co 860 Warf St Richmond CA 94804

MCDANIEL, PAUL NICHOLAS, investment banker; b. Springfield, Mo., Apr. 21, 1921; s. Claude Dewitt and Murillo (Nicholas) McD. B.A., Westminster Coll., 1943; student Pacific Coast Grad. Sch. Banking, 1960; A.M.P., Harvard U., 1963. With Bank of Hawaii, Honolulu, 1947—, sr. v.p. corp. bank div., 1972-78, sr. v.p., investment officer, 1978—. Mem. Hawaii CSC, 1962-70; chmn. bd. Hawaii Heart Assn., 1966-69; bd. dirs. Am. Heart Assn., 1966-69. Served to lt. (s.g.) Supply Corps, USNR, 1943-46. Republican. Episcopalian. Clubs: Oahu Country, Waialae Country (dir. 1979-81), Pacific, Outrigger Canoe (dir. 1974-79) (Honolulu); Bohemian, San Francisco Golf (San Francisco). Home: 21 Craigside St Apt 8A Honolulu HI 96817 Office: Bank of Hawaii Financial Plaza of the Pacific Honolulu HI 96802

MCDANIEL, POWELL, govt. agy. exec.; b. Gary, Ind., May 27, 1933; s. Powell and Ida (Warren) McD.; B.S., DePaul U., 1959; m. Lillian JoAnn Walker, Aug. 8, 1961; children—Kelly, Piper. Loan officer Gary (Ind.) Nat. Bank, 1961-63; loan officer Security Pacific Nat. Bank, Los Angeles, 1963-69; field rep. Gen. Motors Acceptance Corp., Los Angeles, 1966-69; minority enterprise rep. Small Bus. Adminstrn., Los Angeles, 1969-71; dep. regional dir. Minority Bus. Devel. Agy., U.S. Dept. Commerce, San Francisco, 1971—. Served with AUS, 1954-56. Mem. Internat. Council for Small Bus. Home: 47 Eastbrook Ct Clayton CA 94517 Office: 450 Golden Gate Ave San Francisco CA 94102

MCDERMOTT, DENNIS MICHAEL, association executive; b. Akron, Ohio, Jan. 9, 1947; s. Gerard J. and Irene C. (Lenz) M.; m. Margaret M. Hayden, Dec. 14, 1968 (div.); children—Martin Jerome, Kathleen Marie; m. Margaret Amberg Egan, Apr. 30, 1983. B.S. in Journalism, Kent State U., 1969, postgrad., 1973-76; postgrad. Chapman Coll., 1971-72. Reporter Akron Beacon Jour., 1967-69; conv. mgr. Am. Sch. Health Assn., Kent, Ohio, 1973-74, asst. exec. dir., 1974-77; exec. dir. Emergency Dept. Nurses Assn., Chgo., 1977-80, Oakland Bd. Realtors (Calif.), 1980—; lectr.; cons. Served with USAF, 1969-72. Mem. Am. Soc. Assn. Execs., Pub. Relations Soc. Am., Soc. Profl. Journalists/Sigma Delta Chi. Office: Oakland Bd Realtors 1528 Webster St Oakland CA 94612

MC DERMOTT, RICHARD SCHICK, govt. ofcl.; b. Las Animas, Colo., July 13, 1923; s. Raymond B. and Freda (Schick) McD.; A.B. Western State Coll., Gunnison, Colo., 1947; J.D., U. Colo., 1950; m. Dorothy E. Thompson, Jan. 6, 1952; children—Denise, Reuel, Brian, Gerald Abbott, Keith Abbott. Admitted to Colo. bar, 1951, pvt. practice. Las Animas, 1951-57; acting field solicitor Dept. of Interior, Gallup, N.Mex., 1957-59; admitted to N.M. bar, 1959; partner firm Perry & McDermott, 1959-65; chief br. of real property mgmt. Bur. Indian Affairs, Crow Indian Agy., Mont., 1965-68, real estate cons. Agua Caliente Band Mission Indians, Palm Springs, Calif., 1968-70; dir. Palm Springs Bur. Indian Affairs, 1970—. Pres. Las Animas Bd. Edn., 1955-57; v.p. McKinley County PTA Council, 1961-62; dir. U. Colo. Law Alumni Fund, 1960-62, Family Consultation Service, ARC, Big Bros.; bd. dirs. United Way of the Desert, 1977—, Palm Springs Sr. Center, 1980-81. Served with AUS, 1942-46, ETO. Mem. Am. (mem. com. improvement land title records, 1965-68), Fed. (mem. com. Indian law 1966—), Colo., N.Mex. (mem. com. to correlate mut. problems with med. soc.), McKinley County (pres. 1962) bar assns., Palm Springs C. of C. (mem. econ. devel. com. 1969-82, dir. 1973-76, 78-81), Theta Chi, Phi Alpha Delta. Methodist (trustee). Rotarian (pres. 1962-63, 75-76). Club: Knife and Fork (pres. 1964). Home: 701 Ocotillo Palm Springs CA 92262 Office: 441 S Calle Encilia Suite 8 Palm Springs CA 92262

MCDONALD, ALLAN JAMES, engineering administrator; b. Cody, Wyo., July 9, 1937; s. John William and Eva Marie (Gingras) M.; m. Linda Rae Zuchetto, Apr. 20, 1963; children—Gregory Allan, Lisa Marie, Lora Lynn, Meghan Rae. B.S. in Chem. Engring, Mont. State U., 1959; M.S. in Engring. Adminstrn., U. Utah, 1967. Engr. Wasatch div. Morton Thiokol Inc., Brigham City, Utah, 1959-67, project engr. solid rocket motor programs, 1967-74, mgr. devel. project dept., 1974-76, mgr. propellant devel. dept. 1976-79, mgr. project engring. div., 1979—; mem. Air Force Tech. Propulsion Panel, 1982—. Judge sci. fair com. Weber State Coll., 1978—; bd. dirs. St. Joseph High Sch., 1976—, trustee, 1981—, pres. 1976-79; coach Little League Football, 1972-75; coach Little League Baseball, 1971-72, pres., 1972-74; pres. CCD program St. James Catholic Ch., 1976-79. Named Outstanding Engr. of Utah, AIAA, 1971; Eastern Mont. Coll. scholar, 1955-57; Mont. State U. scholar, 1958-59. Mem. AIAA (assoc. fellow, past chmn. Utah sect., mem. solid rocket tech. com. 1979-83), Tau Beta Pi, Phi Kappa Phi, Sigma Chi. Republican. Clubs: K.C., Elks, Ogden Athletic. Patentee solid rocket, pyrotechnic systems; contbr. articles to profl. jours., publs. Home: 4050 N 900 W Pleasant View UT 84404 Office: Morton Thiokol Wasatch Div PO Box 524 m/s 260 Brigham City UT 84302

MCDONALD, CHARLES HOLMES, civil engr.; b. Charlotte, N.C., Oct. 15, 1907; s. Laban John and Lucille (Reilley) M.; student public schs., Nogales, Ariz.; m. Eunice, June, 1935; children—Malcolm Charles, Patricia Lora McDonald Driskill; m. 2d, Mary Jane, Oct. 1, 1977. With U.S. Gen. Land Office, Phoenix, 1927-30; materials engr., constrn. engr. Fed. Hwy. Adminstrn., Phoenix, 1930-63; engring. supr. materials div. City of Phoenix, 1963-74; prin. Charles Holmes McDonald, Cons. Engr., Phoenix, 1974-83. Recipient Silver medal Dept. Commerce, 1952; registered profl. engr., Ariz. Mem. Am. Soc. Inventors, Nat. Soc. Profl. Engrs., United Inventors and Scientists of Am., Nat. Acad. Scis. (mem. transp. research bd.), Am. Public Works Assn., Inst. for Transp., Mineral. Soc. Ariz., Am. Chem. Soc. (rubber div.), AAAS, Woodmen of World. Republican. Contbr. numerous articles in field to profl. jours.; patentee (14) in field of paving, U.S., Can. Home: 3130 W Pierce St Phoenix AZ 85009 Office: 2825 W Maryland Ave Phoenix AZ 85017

MC DONALD, JACK HENRY, financial executive; b. Pratt, Kans., July 16, 1910; s. John Dennis and Florence (Krieger) M.D.; A.B., U. Kans., 1933; m. Loraine Cameron; children by previous marriage—Sandra, Sara (Mrs. Christos Pagoulatos), Sally (Mrs. Richard Wahlgren), William D. Ptnr. Fink Abstract & Title Co., Fredonia, Kans., 1933-41; sec. Home Bldg. & Loan Assn., Fredonia, 1936-41; sec. Investors Savs. & Loan Assn., 1946-51, pres., 1951-63; pres., chmn. Imperial Corp. Am., San Diego, 1963-73; chmn. bd. Western Security Fin., Inc., Irvine, Calif.; ptnr. Chamorro Gardens, Agana, Guam; dir. Center City Corp., San Diego, Am. Burnham Co., San Diego, San Diego Bancorp. Bd. dirs. Tournament of Roses. Served at lt. comdr. USNR, 8th Fleet, N. Africa-Mediterranean waters, 1941-46. Recipient Golden Plate award, 1965. Mem. Nat. Savs. and Loan League (past dir.) Los Angeles County Group, Kappa Sigma. Clubs: University, Annandale Golf (Pasadena); Shady Oaks Country (Ft. Worth); California (Los Angeles); La Jolla Country, Ft. Worth. Home: 1001 Genter La Jolla CA 92037 Office: 255 Broadway Suite 900 San Diego CA 92101

MC DONALD, JEANNE GRAY (MRS. JOHN B. MCDONALD), TV producer; b. Seattle, Sept. 10, 1917; d. George Patrick and Mary Edna (Gray) Murphy; m. John B. McDonald, June 30, 1951; children—Gregory Roland Stoner, Margaret Jeanne Eve. Student Columbia U., 1940, Art Students League, 1940-43, Nat. Acad. Dramatic Art, 1945. Radio producer, commentator The Woman's Voice, Sta. KMPC, Los Angeles, 1947-50; TV producer, commentator, writer The Women's Voice, Sta. KTTV-CBS, Los Angeles, 1950-51; TV producer, commentator The Jeanne Gray Show, Sta. KNXT-CBS, Los Angeles, 1951-53; West Coast editor Home Show, NBC, Los Angeles, 1955-56; TV film producer documentaries and travelogues Virgonian Prodns., Los Angeles, 1953—. Women's chmn. Los Angeles Beautiful, 1971; mem. Women's Aux. St. John's Hosp.; trustee Freedoms Found. at Valley Forge, 1966—, founder, pres. women's chpt., Los Angeles County chpt., 1965-66, Western dir. women's chpt., 1967-68, nat. chmn., 1968-71, nat. chmn. women vols., 1973-75, hon. life mem. Recipient Francis Holmes Outstanding Achievement award, 1949, Silver Mike award, 1948; Emmy award Acad. TV Arts and Scis., 1951, Lulu award Los Angeles Advt. Women, 1952, Radio and TV Women Genii award, 1956; Geo. Washington Honor award Freedoms Found. Valley Forge, 1967, honor cert., 1972; Morale award Christians and Jews for Law and Morality, 1968; Exceptional Service award Freedoms Found., 1975; Liberty Belle award Rep. Women's Club, 1975; Leadership award Los Angeles City Schs., 1976. Mem. Am. Women in Radio and TV, Radio and TV Women So. Calif. (founder, 1st pres. 1952, hon. life mem.), Footlighters (v.p. 1958-59), Los Angeles C. of C. (dir. women's div. 1948-54, mem. exec. bd., women's div. 1954-66, pres. women's div. 1963-64, hon. past pres. women's div. 1979), Los Angeles Orphanage Guild, DAR. Clubs: Bel Air Garden, Calif. Yacht, The Muses. Author: The Power of Belonging, 1978. Home: 910 Stradella Rd Bel Air Los Angeles CA 90077

MC DONALD, JOHN JOSEPH MACALLISTER, process control co. exec.; b. Chgo., Sept. 1, 1922; s. John Joseph MacAllister and Mary Inez (O'Brien) McD.; B.S., U. Chgo., 1939; B.S. in Elec. Engring., Ill. Inst. Tech., 1940; spl. courses bus. adminstrn. Harvard, 1950-52; m. Marie Elenore Vorder, Sept. 7, 1942. Regional mgr. Consol. Electrodynamics Corp., Pasadena, Calif., 1950-52, dir. systems div., 1952-54; v.p., asst. gen. mgr. Consol. Systems Corp., Monrovia, Calif., 1954-61; v.p., gen. mgr. computer div. Packard Bell Electronics, Los Angeles, 1961-66; pres. Canterbury, Inc., Alhambra, Calif., 1966-68; gen. mgr. aircraft instrument div. Bissett-Berman Corp., Santa Monica, Calif., 1968—; v.p., gen. mgr. United Process Control Systems, Santa Fe Springs, Calif., 1970—; pres. Britt Corp., Los Angeles, 1976—. Cons. Borg-Warner Computer Control Corp. Fellow Instrument Soc. Am. (sect. pres. 1962-63, dist. v.p. 1964-65, nat. v.p. sci. and industries 1966-67). Contbr. articles to profl. jours. Home: 610 Canterbury Rd San Marino CA 91108 Office: 9419 Ann St Santa Fe Springs CA 90670

MCDONALD, JOHN RIGG, ins. exec.; b. Glasgow, Scotland, Jan. 6, 1926; s. Henry Paterson and Ethel (Smith) McD.; came to U.S., 1949, naturalized, 1954; B.S., UCLA, 1966; m. Astrid Schmidt, Mar. 1, 1967; children—Eric John, Michelle Verdugo. Supt. agencies Zurich Ins. Cos., Los Angeles, 1956-66; underwriting mgr. Stewart, Smith, Haidinger, Los Angeles, 1966-68; pres., chief exec. officer John R. McDonald Co., Inc., Los Angeles, 1968—; pres., chief exec. officer Pacific Aviation Mgrs., Inc., Los Angeles, 1979—; Lloyd's corr. Served with Brit. Army, 1944. Mem. Ins. Assn. So. Calif. (pres. 1971-72), Calif. Surplus Line Assn. (exec. com. 1970-77), Aviation Hall of Fame (charter), Western Assn. Ins. Brokers, Acad. Magical Arts. Republican. Club: Masons (32 deg.). Author articles on ins. aspect of kidnapping. Office: 3600 Wilshire Blvd Los Angeles CA 90010

MCDONALD, MARIANNE, classicist; b. Chgo., Jan. 2, 1937; d. Eugene Francis and Inez (Riddle) McD.; B.A. magna cum laude, Bryn Mawr Coll., 1958; M.A., U. Chgo., 1960; Ph.D., U. Calif., Irvine, 1975; m. Torajiro Mori, Aug. 12, 1978; children—Eugene, Conrad, Bryan, Bridget, Kirstie, Hiroshi. Teaching asst. classics U. Calif., Irvine, 1972-74, instr. Greek, Latin and English, mythology, modern cinema, 1975-79, researcher Thesaurus Linguae Graecae Project, 1979—; dir. Centrum. Bd. dirs. Am. Coll. of Greece, 1981—, Scipps Hosp., 1981—, LaJolla Country Day Sch., 1971-73; nat. bd. advisors Am. Biog. Inst., 1982—. Recipient Ellen Browning Scripps Humanitarian award, 1975; Disting. Service award U. Calif.-Irvine, 1982. Mem. Am. Philol. Assn., Am. Classical League, Philol. Assn. Pacific Coast, MLA, Am. Comparative Lit. Assn., Modern and Classical Lang. Assn. So. Calif., AAUP, Hellenic Soc., Calif. Fgn. Lang. Tchrs. Assn., Internat. Platform Assn. Republican. Buddhist; Greek Orthodox. Clubs: KPBS Producers, Hellenic Univ. (dir.). Author: Terms for Happiness in Euripides, 1978; Semilemmatized Concordances to Euripides' Alcestis, 1977; Cyclops, Andromache, Medea, 1978; Heraclidae, Hippolytus, 1979; Hecuba, 1982; Euripides in Cinema: The Heart Made Visible, 1983; contbr. numerous articles to profl. jours. Home: Box 929 Rancho Santa Fe CA 92067 Office: Thesaurus Linguae Gracae Project U Calif Irvine CA 92717

MCDONALD, MICHAEL BRIAN, economist; b. Tulsa, Jan. 1, 1948, s. William Gerald and Agnes Gertrude (Sellman) M.; m. Jane Anne Fahey, Aug. 25, 1969; 1 dau., Kelly Anne. B.A., Georgetown U., 1969; Ph.D., U. Pa., 1978. Teaching fellow, U. Pa., Phila., 1976-77; research economist Logistics Mgmt. Inst., Washington, 1977-78; assoc. dir. research Bur. Bus. and Econ. Research, U. N.Mex., 1978-81, dir., 1982—, asst. prof., 1979—. Served to capt. USAF, 1972-76. NDEA Title IV fellow, 1969-72. Mem. Am. Econs. Assn., Assn. Univ. Bus. and Econ. Research, Phi Beta Kappa. Democrat. Roman Catholic. Contbr. articles to profl. jours. Office: Bur of Bus and Econ Research U N Mex Albuquerque NM 87131

MCDONNEL, WILLIAM GEORGE, sci. instrumentation co. exec.; b. Rabat, French Morocco, May 10, 1952; came to U.S., 1953; s. Harold Albert and Anna (Yoos) McD.; B.S. in Chemistry/Biochemistry, Calif. State U., Fullerton, 1974; m. Nancy Ann Hopwood, Aug. 27, 1977; children—Melissa, Allison Roe. Product specialist Process Instruments div. Beckman Instruments, Inc., Fullerton, 1974; sr. tech. specialist ion selective electrodes Lab. Products div. Orion Research Inc., Cambridge, Mass., 1975—; speaker in field. Mem. Am. Chem. Soc., Am. Electroplaters Spc., Phi Kappa Tau. Republican. Lutheran. Home: 27412 Cenajo Mission Viejo CA 92691 Office: Orion Research Inc 840 Memorial Dr Cambridge MA 02139

MC DONNELL, EDWARD LAURENCE, real estate devel. co. exec.; b. Great Falls, Mont., May 13, 1912; s. George Edward and Clara Lucinda (Woodward) McD.; student Gonzaga U., Spokane, 1934; m. Evelyn Marie Cutz, Aug. 1, 1935; children—Thomas C., Victoria M., Virginia D. Mgr., Mont. Mustard Seed Co., Power, 1935-39; partner McDonnell Seed Co., Spokane, 1940-47; organizer, owner, mgr. E.L. McDonnell & Co., Spokane, 1947-60; pres. Trans-World Seeds, Ltd., Shelby, Mont., 1960-66; organizer, owner, mgr. Agro Supply, Billings, Mont., 1966-77; partner McBorg Properties, Billings, 1978-80, GEL Properties, Billings, 1980—; organizer, 1st pres. Pacific N.W. Pea Growers and Dealers Assn., 1949-53. Republican. Roman Catholic. Club: K.C. Author articles. Developer comml. fertilizer applicator equipment. Address: 3440 Winchell Ln Billings MT 59102

MCDONOUGH, LEAH BROOKS, psychologist; b. N.Y.C., Apr. 24, 1924; d. Nicholas and Leah (Griffin) Brooks; m. Joseph Manning McDonough, July 3, 1949; 1 dau., Susan Mar. A.B., Coll. New Rochelle, 1944; M.A., Fordham U., 1946; Ph.D., Mich. State U., 1958. Clin. psychologist V.A. Hosp., Coral Gables, Fla., 1958-61; chief cts. and corrections unit San Mateo County Mental Health, Redwood City, Calif., 1961-79, forensic psychologist, 1980—; cons., lectr. in field. Mem. Amnesty Internat., ACLU, Nat. Trust Hist. Preservation, Oceanic Soc., NOW. Mem. Am. Psychol. Assn., San Mateo County Psychol. Assn., Am. Psychology-Law Soc. Contbr. articles to profl. jours. Office: 500 Allerton St Suite 105 Redwood City CA 94063

MCDONOUGH, MARIANNE JULIA, inventory management and planning executive; b. Davenport, Iowa, July 29, 1946; d. William Michael and Margaret Mary (Lawlor) McDonough. B.A. in Textiles and Clothing, Marycrest Coll., 1968. Dept. mgr. Turnstyle, Jewel Cos., city Chgo., 1969-70, buyer, 1971-75, merchandise controller, 1975-78; dir. inventory mgmt. The GAP, San Bruno, Calif., 1979-80, v.p. inventory mgmt. and planning, 1980—. Mem. Mensa. Roman Catholic. Home: 719 Bay St San Francisco CA 94109 Office: 900 Cherry Ave San Bruno CA 94066

MC DONOUGH, THOMAS REDMOND, astrophysicist, writer; b. Boston, Oct. 4, 1945; s. Redmond Augustus and Sophie Theresa (Stankewich) McD. S.B. in Physics, M.I.T., 1966; Ph.D., Cornell U., 1973. Postdoctoral researcher Cornell U., 1973-75; resident research assoc. Jet. Propulsion Lab., Pasadena, Calif., 1976-77, cons., 1978-81; cons. Avco Embassy Pictures, Hollywood, Calif., 1981-82; coordinator search for extraterrestrial intelligence Planetary Soc., Pasadena, 1981—; lectr. in engring. Calif. Inst. Tech., 1979—, faculty lectr. summer undergrad. research fellowships, 1982. Contbr. articles, stories to popular sci. and sci. fiction mags. Recipient citation NASA, 1979; Outstanding Pro-Space Achievements award Nebraskans for Advancement Space Devel., 1982. Fellow Brit. Interplanetary Soc.; mem. Internat. Astron. Union (commn. for search for extraterrestrial intelligence 1982—), Am. Astron. Soc., Am. Phys. Soc., AIAA, Authors Guild, Sci. Fiction Writers Am., Internat. Platform Assn. Club: Toastmasters. Research, publs. in sci.

MCDOUGAL, GENEVIEVE GUERRA, government official; b. Las Cruces, N.Mex., Jan. 24, 1947; d. Augustine Arthur and Adela Miranda (Montoya) Guerra; m. Bruce Darrell McDougal, Sept. 21, 1968; children—Christina Marie, Michael Shawn. Student N.Mex. State U., 1980-83. Sales clk. Budget Shop, Stork Ctr., Las Cruces, 1963-65; sec. Home Edn. Livelihood Program, State of N.Mex., Las Cruces, 1966; with White Sands Missile Range, N.Mex., 1966—, chief mgmt. engring., work reception and systems br. Resources Mgmt. div. Facilities Engring. Directorate, 1979—. Area coordinator cookie sales Girl Scouts U.S.A.,

1979-83. Recipient numerous performance awards White Sands Missile Range, 1966-83; named Toastmistress of Yr., 1980. Mem. Assn. U.S. Army, Fed. Mgrs. Assn. Democrat. Roman Catholic. Clubs: High Noon Soccer League, Parent, Toastmistress. Home: 2025 Avalon St Las Cruces NM 88005 Office: STEWS-FE-MS White Sands Missile Range NM 88002

MC DOUGALL, GEORGE DOUGLAS, cons.; b. Indpls., July 20, 1930; s. Shirley Alton and Deborah Cleveland (Hall) McD.; student Asbury Coll., 1949-51, Mt. San Antonio Coll., 1960-61, Milw. Sch. Engring., 1977, Calif. State Poly. U., 1978; m. Maria Celia Velasquez, Aug. 4, 1956. Surveyor, Tidelands Exploration Co., Houston, 1954; with Vard, Inc., Pasadena, Calif., 1954-60, Gen. Dynamics, Pomona, Calif., 1960-62; researcher Aerojet Gen. Corp., Azusa, Calif., 1962-68; engr. Davidson Optonics, West Covina, Calif., 1968-69; mfg. mgr. Angeles Metal Systems, Los Angeles, 1969-79; cons. Fremont Gen. Corp., Los Angeles, 1979—; mem. automation research project Inst. Indsl. Relations, U. So. Calif., 1966-68; mem. research team U.S. Govt./U. So. Calif., 1979-81. Adv. bd. Automobile Club So. Calif., 1966-71; bd. dirs. St. Martha's Episcopal Sch., West Covina, Calif., 1978-81; lic. lay reader Episcopal Diocese of Los Angeles; vestryman St. Martha's Episc. Ch., West Covina, 1969-70, 77-79, 81—; mem. U.S. Congl. Adv. Bd., 1982—; gen. conv. del. Episc. Diocese of Los Angeles, 1970-78; instnl. rep. Boy Scouts Am., 1978-79, coordinator San Gabriel Valley council, 1978-79. Served with JAGC, AUS, 1951-53; Korea. Cert. in mfg. engring., Canadian Council Profl. Cert., 1977; registered profl. engr., Calif. Mem. Soc. Mfg. Engrs. (exec. council, sec. 1982; cert.), Computer and Automated Systems Assn. (charter), Nat. Soc. Profl. Engrs., Calif. Soc. Profl. Engrs., Clan MacDonald Soc. U.S. and Can. (life), Highlands Clans and Family Soc. (exec. council 1982), St. Andrews Soc. Los Angeles, SAR. Republican. Clubs: Town Hall of Calif., Masons, Shriners. Home: PO Box 848 Azusa CA 91702 Office: 1709 W 8th St Los Angeles CA 90017

MC DOWELL, JENNIFER, sociologist, composer, editor, publisher; b. Albuquerque, N.Mex. May 19, 1936; d. Willard A. and Margaret Frances (Garrison) McD.; B.A., U. Calif., Berkeley, 1957, M.L.S., 1963; M.A., San Diego State U., 1958; Ph.D., U. Oreg., 1973; m. Milton Loventhal, July 2, 1973. Tchr. English, Abraham Lincoln High Sch., San Jose, Calif., 1960-61; freelance editor Soviet field, Berkeley, Calif., 1961-63; research asst. sociology U. Oreg., Eugene, 1964-66; editor, pub. Merlin Papers, San Jose, 1969—, Merlin Press, San Jose, 1973—; research cons. sociology San Jose, 1973—; music pub. Lipstick and Toy Balloons Pub. Co., San Jose, 1978—; tchr. writing workshops; poetry readings, 1969-73; co-producer radio shows lit. and culture Sta. KALX, Berkeley, 1971-72; composer Paramount Pictures, 1982—. Recipient 8 awards Am. Song Festival, 1976-79. AAUW doctoral fellow, 1971-73; grantee Calif. Arts Council, 1976-77. Mem. Am. Sociol. Assn., Soc. for Sci. Study of Religion, Soc. for Study of Religion and Communism, Poetry Orgn. for Women, Phi Beta Kappa, Sigma Alpha Iota, Beta Phi Mu, Kappa Kappa Gamma. Democrat. Author: Black Politics: A Study and Annotated Bibliography of the Mississippi Freedom Democratic Party, 1971; Contemporary Women Poets, An Anthology of California Poets, 1977. Contbr. poems, essays, short stories, book revs. to lit. mags., 1969—; researcher women's autobiog. writings, contemporary writings in poetry, Soviet studies, civil rights movement and George Orwell, 1962—. Writer song Money Makes a Woman Free, 1976, My Love is Stronger than Life Itself, 1979, 3 songs featured in Parade of Am. Music, 1976. Office: Merlin Press PO Box 5602 San Jose CA 95150

MCDUFF, COLMAN B., clergyman, recording artist; b. LuAnn, Ark., Mar. 14; s. Clifton and Mildred Louise (Carter) McD.; stepfather James David Revils; B.A., Southwestern Assemblies of God Coll., Waxahachie, Tex., B.S.; m. Betty Joyce Hollister, June 29, 1957; children—Tammye Gayle, Melinda. Ordained to ministry South Tex. Dist. Assemblies of God., 1958; sr. pastor Full Gospel Assembly, Bell Gardens, Calif., 1977—; concert artist, TV, radio host, 1966—; exec. dir. Bell Gardens Christian Sch., 1977—; rec. artist long play albums including Colman McDuff Sings, Turn Back, My Child, The Loveliness of Christ, When I Get Up To Heaven, The Street Where the Lonely Walk, Out of My Heart and Thought. Named to Order of Ky. Cols. Mem. Colman McDuff Evangelistic Assn. (pres.), Gospel Music Assn. Office: 6262 E Gage St Bell Gardens CA 90201

MCDUFFIE, RICHARD WARNER, JR., urol. surgeon; b. Longview, Wash., June 8, 1941; s. Richard Warner and Frances Elizabeth (Alley) McD.; B.S., U. Oreg., 1965, M.D., 1967; m. Beverly Anne McMillan, Dec. 27, 1965; 1 dau., Kristine Elizabeth. Intern, St. Paul Ramsey Hosp., 1967-68; fellow in urology Mayo Clinic, Rochester, Minn., 1968-72; practice medicine specializing in urol. surgery, Eugene, Oreg., 1974—; sect. chief urology Sacred Heart Hosp., 1979-83, also sec., mem. exec. com.; mem. part-time faculty U. Oreg. Med. Sch., Portland. Bd. dirs. Willamette Sci. and Tech. Center, 1978—; bd. dirs. Friends of Library Eugene, 1976—, pres., 1980; pres. sch. bd. O'Hara Cath. Sch., 1980—; vestryman St. Mary's Episcopal Ch., Eugene, 1977-82, bd. dirs. Oreg. Pacific Econ. Devel. Corp. Served to maj. M.C., USAT, 1972-74. Diplomate Am. Bd. Urology. Fellow ACS; mem. Am. Urol. Assn., Am. Assn. Clin. Urologists, AMA, Am. Geriatric Soc., Pan Pacific Surg. Assn., Oreg. Med. Assn. (trustee, mem. exec. com.), Oreg. Urol. Soc. (pres. 1978-79), N.W. Urol. Soc., Lane County Med. Assn., Eugene Surg. Soc. (pres. 1978-79). Republican. Club: Rotary. Contbr. articles med. jours. Home: 2713 Fairmount Blvd Eugene OR 97403 Office: 677 E 12th St Suite 400 Eugene OR 97401

MCELROY, WILLIAM DAVID, biochemist, univ. chancellor; b. Rogers, Tex., Jan. 22, 1917; s. William D. and Ora (Shipley) McE.; B.A., Stanford, 1939; M.A., Reed Coll., 1941; Ph.D., Princeton U., 1943; D.Sc., U. Buffalo, 1962, Mich. State U., 1970, Loyola U., Chgo., 1970, Del. State Coll., 1971, U. Notre Dame, 1975, Calif. Sch. Profl. Psychology, 1978; D.Pub. Service, Providence Coll., 1970; LL.D., U. Pitts., 1971, U. San Diego, 1972, Fla. State U., 1973, Johns Hopkins U., 1977; m. Nella Winch, Dec. 23, 1940 (div.) children—Mary Elizabeth, Ann Reed, Thomas Shipley, William David; m. 2d, Marlene A. DeLuca, Aug. 28, 1967; 1 son, Eric Gene. War research, com. med. research OSRD, Princeton, 1942-45; NRC fellow, Stanford, 1945-46; instr. biology dept. Johns Hopkins, 1946, successively asst. and asso. prof., prof. biology, 1951-69, chmn. biology dept., 1956-69, also dir. McCollum-Pratt Inst., 1949-64; dir. NSF, Washington, 1969-71; chancellor U. Calif., San Diego, 1972-80, prof. biology, 1980—; Harvey lectr. N.Y. Acad. Sci., 1957. Mem. Sch. Bd. Baltimore City, 1958-68. Recipient Barnett Cohen award in bacteriology, 1958; Rumford prize Am. Acad. Arts and Scis., 1964; Andrew White medal Loyola Coll., Balt., 1971; Disting. Service award Stanford Athletic Bd., 1973; Pres.'s Meritorious award Am. Inst. Biol. Scis., 1973; McElroy Asteroid named by Nat. Sci. Bd. and Internat. Astron. Union Minor Planet Center, 1980. Mem. Am. Inst. Biol. Scis. (pres. 1968), Am. Chem. Soc., Nat. Acad. Sci., (council 1968-69), Am. Soc. Biol. Chemists (pres. 1963-64), Soc. Gen. Physiology (pres. 1960-61), Soc. Naturalists, Soc. Zoologists, Am. Acad. Arts and Scis., Am. Soc. Bacteriologists, Am. Philos. Soc., AAAS (pres. 1976, chmn. 1977), Sigma Xi, Kappa Sigma. Editor: Copper Metabolism (with Bentley Glass), 1950; Phosphorus Metabolism, 2 vols., 1951, 52; Mechanism of Enzyme Action, 1954; Amino Acid Metabolism, 1955; The Chemical Basis of Heredity, 1957; The Chemical Basis of Development, 1959; Light and Life, 1961; Cellular Physiology and Biochemistry, 1961; (with C.P. Swanson) Foundations of Modern Biology series, 1961-64; Biochem. and Biophys. Research Communications, 1980—; others. Author: Cell Physiology and Biochemistry, 3d edit., 1971. Office: Dept Biology Univ Calif San Diego La Jolla CA 92093

MCELWAIN, JOSEPH A., lawyer, utility company executive; b. Deer Lodge, Mont., Nov. 13, 1919; s. Lee Chaffee and Johanna (Petersen) M.; m. Mary Cleaver Witt, Mar. 8, 1945; children—Lee William, Lori Louise. B.A., U. Mont., 1943, LL.B., 1947, J.D., 1970. Bar: Mont. Sole practice, Deer Lodge, 1947-63; city atty. Deer Lodge, 1950-57, 60-63; Washington legis. counsel Mont. Power Co., Deer Lodge, 1954-63, counsel, 1963-65, asst. to pres., 1965-67, v.p., 1967-70, exec. v.p., 1970-75, pres., chief exec. officer, 1975-78, chmn. pres., chief exec. officer 1978-79, chmn., chief exec. officer, 1979—, also dir.; dir. Devel. Credit Corp., Mont., Pacific NW Power Co., First Bank System, Mont. Internat. Trade Commn., Edison Electric Inst.; mem. Mont. State Ho. of Reps., 1949-55, majority floor leader, 1951; mem. Mont. State Senate, 1962-64; state chmn. Republican Central Com., 1952-54. Trustee, U. Mont. Found., Missoula, 1958-64, 72—; mem. adv. com. Mont. Pub. Land Law Rev.; mem. Am. Power Study Team, Ger., U.S. Dept. Interior, 1972, Adv. Council Lewis and Clark Nat. Trail, U.S. Dept. of Interior, 1980—; active C.M. Russell Museum Devel. Council, 1982—; exec. bd. local council Boy Scouts Am., 1971—; active Bus. Industry Political Action Com., 1980—; co-chmn. fund-raising drive Religious Facilities Center, 1979-82; bd. dirs. Butte Jr. Achievement, 1980-82; vol. state chmn. U.S. Savs. Bonds, Mont., 1980—. Recipient Honorary Legion of Honor Degree, Internat. Supreme Council, Demolay. Mem. ABA, Mont. State, Bar Assn. Clubs: Mason, Shrine, Elks, K.P., Kiwanis. Office: 40 E Broadway Bottle MT 59701

MC ELWAIN, WARREN EDGAR, cons. engr.; b. Minot, N.D., July 7, 1934; s. Laurel Vincent and Lillian May (Randal) McE.; B.S.C.E., U. Calif., Berkeley, 1957; M.B.A., U. So. Calif., 1965; M.M.E., Calif. State U., 1979; m. Bonnie Edythe Anderson, Feb. 10, 1955; children—Sheri Lynn, Pamela Eileen, Eric Sean. With Calif. Inst. Tech., Pasadena, 1957-60, 61-69, J. Lynch, Montrose, Calif., 1960-61, Booz-Allen, Los Angeles, 1969-70, A.A. Mathews Inc., Arcadia, Calif., 1970-73, Truesdail Labs., Los Angeles, 1973-75; cons. engr., pres. Cady-McElwain Asso., Inc., Sierra Madre, Calif., 1975-82. Mem., chmn. Zoning Bd. Sierra Madre, 1968-74. Registered profl. engr., Calif. Mem. Nat. Soc. Profl. Engrs., Calif. Soc. Profl. Engrs., ASTM, Soc. for Exptl. Stress Analysis, Soc. Automotive Engrs., System Safety Soc. Presbyterian. Office: 470 W Sierra Madre Blvd Sierra Madre CA 91024

MCELWEE, DENNIS JOHN, pharm. co. exec.; b. New Orleans, July 30, 1947; s. John Joseph and Audrey(Nunez) McE.; B.S., Tulane U., 1970; m. Nancy Lu Travis, Sept. 3, 1976. Clean room and quality control analyst Sci. Enterprises Inc., Broomfield, Colo., 1975-76; analytical chemist in toxicology Poisonlab. Inc., Denver, 1977; analytical chemist, then dir. analytical quality control program Colo. Sch. Mines Research Inst., 1977-79; dir. quality control, then dir. compliance Benedict Nuclear Pharms. Co., Golden, Colo., 1979—. Author: Mineral Research Chemicals, Toxic Properties and Proper Handling, 2d edit., 1979. Home: PO Box 56 Morrison CO 80465

MCELYEA, HERMAN DOYLE, SR., natural gas distbn. co. exec.; b. Leflore, Okla., Oct. 4, 1919; s. William Thomas and Lillie Daisy (Sims) McE.; B.S. in Petroleum Engring., U. Okla., 1945 48; student in geology Internat. Corr. Schs., 1953-54; postgrad. in natural gas. engring. Tex. A. and I. U., 1958; m. Margarette Wanda Long, Nov. 24, 1945; children Carol Ann McElyea Wheeler, Herman Doyle. Field supt. S.W. Natural Gas Co., Seminole, Okla., 1936-41; engr. Arctic Cons. & Contractors, Point Barrow, Alaska, 1948-49; v.p. ops. Hobbs Gas Co. (N.Mex.), 1950—; cons. corrosion control. Democratic precinct chmn. Hobbs, 1955-60. Served with U.S. Army, 1941-45; PTO. Registered profl. engr., Calif. Mem. Nat. Assn. Corrosion Engrs., Am. Security Council (adv. bd.), Good Sam Inc. Republican. Baptist. Clubs: Kiwanis (dir. 1972—, pres. 1977, Presdl. fellow 1978-79, Outstanding Pres. award 1979), Airstream. Home: 2100 N Rojo St Hobbs NM 88240 Office: 110 S Fowler Hobbs NM 88240

MCENCROE, PAUL ROGER, restaurant executive; b. Chgo., Dec. 4, 1922; s. John James and Irene Violet (Blake) McE.; m. Donna Marie Zipprich, July 1, 1950; children—John, Andy, Linda, Anne. B.S. in Mktg., Northwestern U., 1947; postgrad. in fin. Denver U., 1964. Salesman, Burroughs Corp., Chgo., 1947-48, Snapout Forms Co., Chgo., 1948-50, Am. Seating Co., San Diego, 1951-52, Duplex Products Co., Milw., 1953-57; restaurant mgr. El Rancho Colo. Co., 1958—; condr. seminars Colo. Mountain Coll. System. Fin. chmn. Colo. Philharm., 1968-69; mem. Jefferson County (Colo.) Sch. Bd., 1969-77; adv. bd. St. Anthony Hosp. —Flight for Life,— 1973-77; mem. Lookout Mountain dist. fire protection bd., 1978-82; mem. Colo. Tourism Bd. Served with USAAF, 1943-45. Decorated Air medal; named Lakewood (Colo.) Sentinel Man of Year, 1977. Mem. Colo. Wyo. Restaurant Assn. (Disting. Service award 1981). Democrat. Office: El Rancho Rural Br El Rancho CO 80401

MCEVOY, PAMELA THOMPSON, psychotherapist; b. Forest Hills N.Y., Mar. 8, 1937; d. Reynolds Thomas and Pamela Shipley (Sweeny) McE.; div.; children—Michael B. Anderson, Candy Anderson-Nott, Kenneth Anderson, Jeffrey A. Thomas. B.A. in Criminal Justice, LaVerne U., 1976, M.S., 1980; Ph.D. in Clin. Psychology, Internat. U., 1982. Lic. marriage and family therapist, Calif. Data processing coordinator Ernest Righetti High Sch., Santa Maria, Calif., 1974-78; instr. psychology and sociology Allen Hancock Coll., 1977-78; mental health asst. Santa Barbara (Calif.) City Alcoholism Dept., 1978; gen. mgr., controller Profl. Suites, San Diego, 1978-81; therapist Chula Vista (Calif.) Counseling Ctr., 1978-82; research coordinator Mil. Family Research Ctr., San Diego, 1981-82; pvt. practice, San Diego, 1982—. Bd. dirs. San Diego Mental Health Assn., 1978-80. Calif. State scholar, 1976-77; Calif. State fellow, 1979-82. Mem. Am. Psychol. Assn., Christian Assn. Psychol. Services, Calif. Assn. Marriage and Family Therapists, Assn. Humanistic Psychology. Republican. Roman Catholic. Contbr. numerous articles to profl. jours. Home: 17452 Ashburton Rd San Diego CA 92128 Office: 5333 Mission Center Rd Suite 340 San Diego CA 92108

MC EVOY, WILLIAM RICHARD, structural engineering firm owner; b. San Jose, Calif., Oct. 31, 1949; s. William Joseph and Miriam Hazel (Blakney) McE.; B.S. in Archtl. Engring., Calif. Poly. State U., 1971. Naval architect Long Beach Naval Shipyard, Calif., 1971-73; project engr. Design & Engring. Systems, Redwood City, Calif., 1973-74; civil engr. Moore Engring. Corp., San Carlos, Calif., 1974-76; owner McEvoy Engring., San Carlos, 1976—. Lic. structural engr., Nev., Calif.; lic. civil engr., Calif. Mem. Structural Engrs. Assn. No. Calif., Am. Concrete Inst., Sierra Club, Porsche Club Am. Republican. Home: 926 Azalea Ave Burlingame CA 94010 Office: 124 El Camino Real San Carlos CA 94070

MCEWAN, ANTHONY JOHNSON, aeronautical engineer; b. Stamford, Conn., Sept. 14, 1944; s. Allerton James and Ruth Julliet (Bell) McE.; B.S.E., Princeton U., 1966; M.S. in Aero. Engring., U. So. Calif., 1970. Student engr. ONERA, Chatillon-sous-Bagneux, France, 1965; assoc. engr. aircraft div. Northrop Corp., Hawthorne, Calif., 1966-67, engr. Ventura div., 1967-69, sr. engr., 1969-74, engr. specialist, 1974-81, mgr. aerodynamics propulsion and thermal analysis, 1981-82, mgr. engring. analysis, 1982, mgr. engring. design dept., 1982—. Fellow AIAA (assoc., vice chmn. Ventura Pacific sect. 1978, chmn. 1979, nat. membership com. 1980-82); mem. Assn. Unmanned Vehicle Systems. Democrat. Clubs: Princeton (So. Calif., Los Angeles), Malibu Yacht (bd. dirs. 1981—). Contbr. articles to tech. publs. Home: 3931 Latigo Canyon Rd Malibu CA 90265 Office: Northrop Corp 1515 Rancho Conejo Blvd Newbury Park CA 91320

MCEWEN, WILLARD WINFIELD, JR., lawyer; b. Evanston, Ill., Dec. 26, 1934; s. Willard W. and Esther (Spenger) McE.; B.S., Claremont Men's Coll., 1956; J.D., Hastings Coll. Law, 1960; m. Suzanne House, Aug. 21, 1959; children—Michael, Elizabeth, Allison. Admitted to Calif. bar, 1960; dep. legis. counsel, Sacramento, 1960-61; asst. city atty., Santa Barbara, Calif., 1961-62; individual practice law, Santa Barbara, 1962—; U.S. magistrate, Santa Barbara County, 1973—; lectr. Santa Barbara Adult Edn. Program, 1970-75; judge pro tem Santa Barbara Superior Ct., 1968-72. Chmn. membership drive YMCA 1964; chmn. Citizens Adv. Com. on Sch. Dist. Tax Needs, 1965; mem. Santa Barbara City Water Commn., 1965, Recreation Commn., City of Santa Barbara, 1970-73; mem. Santa Barbara Landmarks Adv. Com., 1967-73; bd. dirs. Santa Barbara Council for the Retarded, 1962-72, gen. legal counsel, 1961—; pres. Santa Barbara County Heart Assn., 1981—. Served to capt. U.S. Army. Recipient Young Man of Yr. award Santa Barbara Jaycees, 1966. Mem. ABA, State Bar Calif., Santa Barbara County Bar Assn., Santa Barbara City C. of C. (pres. 1976-77). Club: Kiwanis (pres. 1967-68). Home: 1816 Santa Barbara St Santa Barbara CA 93101 Office: 205 E Carrillo St Suite 200 Santa Barbara CA 93101

MCFADDEN, JOAN ROBERTSON, university dean; b. Jackson County, Ind., Aug. 17, 1934; d. William Jennings Bryan and Lucy Alice (McKain) Robertson; m. Buryl L. McFadden (div.); children—Sally, Cindy. B.S., Purdue U., 1956, M.S., 1957; Ph.D., Ohio State U., 1972. Tchr. pub. schs., Greene County (Ohio), 1957-70; supr. for home econs. Ohio Dept. Edn., 1971-72; tchr. educator, head home econs. edn. Purdue U., Lafayette, Ind., 1972-75, U. Minn.-St. Paul, 1975-78; dean Coll. Family Life, Utah State U., Logan, 1978—. Bd. dirs. Logan Regional Hosp., Logan Pub. Library; chmn. nat. bd. Future Homemakers Am., 1983-84; rep. Cliffside Neighborhood Council. Mem. Am. Home Econs. Assn., Am. Vocat. Assn., Am. Ednl. Research Assn., AAUW, Bus. and Profl. Womens Club, Phi Upsilon Omicron, Omicron Nu, Phi Delta Kappa. Presbyterian (elder). Contbr. articles to profl. jours. Office: Coll Family Life UMC 29 Utah State Univ Logan UT 84322

MC FADDEN, WILMOT CURNOW HAMM, librarian; b. Lead, S.D., Oct. 30, 1919; d. William and Ingeborg (Christianson) Curnow; student S.D. State Coll., 1938-41; m. Kenneth G. Hamm, Jan. 8, 1944 (div. 1963); 1 dau., Wilmot Christine (Mrs. Charles Bice); m. 2d, John Stinson McFadden, Mar. 1965. Asst. librarian Rock Springs (Wyo.) Pub. Library, 1947-48, head librarian, 1953—. State committeewoman Democratic Party, 1952-74, also state vice chmn., del. Dem. State Conv., 1970, 72; del. Dem. Nat. Conv., 1956, 64. Mem. adv. bd. Fed. Commn. Civil Rights, 1963—; treas. Sch. Bd. Dist. 4, 1966-69, clk. dist. 1, 1969-77. Bd. dirs. State Library, Archives, Hist. Bd.; adv. bd. Western Wyo. Community Coll.; mem. Wyo. Citizens for Arts, 1977—, Wyo. Community Coll. Commn., 1983—. Recipient Nat. Grolier award Nat. Library Week, 1969, Librarian Service award Eagles Aux., 1982. Mem. Federated Woman's Club, Am. Legion Aux., Mountain Plains (exec. bd. 1967—, pres. 1972-73), ALA, Wyo. Library Assn. (chmn. conf. 1966, 70, pres. 1958-59, 72-73; Librarian of Yr. 1977, Georgia Shovlain Spl. Projects award 1980), Zonta (charter), Am. Library Trustees Assn., Wyo. Sch. Bds. Assn. (life; commendation 1979), Alpha Delta Kappa. Author: Handbook Wyoming Library Trustees. Home: 28 Cedar St Rock Springs WY 82901 Office: 400 C St Rock Springs WY 82901

MCFARLAND, ALFRED HERBERT, educator; b. Canton, Ohio, Dec. 31, 1940; s. James Sherman and Mazie Lee (Hunter) McF.; A.A., Sacramento City Coll., 1981; B.S., So. Ill. U., 1981; M.A., Calif. State U.; m. Rosamaria Johnson, Mar. 28, 1964; children—Michelle, Mia, Mendiazzab. Instr. electronics Sacramento Army Depot, 1979—. Mem. adv. com. John Still Jr. High Sch., Sacramento, 1979-80. Served with USAF, 1959-79. Decorated Air Force Commendation medal. Mem. Am. Vocat. Assn., Calif. Assn. Vocat. Edn., So. Ill. U. Alumni Assn. Club: Masons. Home: 7556 Eddylee Way Sacramento CA 95822

MCFARLAND, ELSIE JEAN, restaurant owner, vocational counselor; b. Oregon City, Oreg., June 27, 1933; d. Fred King and Ruby Dorothy (Fream) Baker; m. James McFarland, Sept. 4, 1956 (div.); children—Scott, Brett Allen, Suzanne Elizabeth. Student Westmont Coll., 1951-53; B.S., Lewis and Clark Coll., 1955; M.A. in Edn. and Sociology, U. Calif., Santa Barbara, 1969. Tchr. Suislaw High Sch., Florence, Oreg., 1956-57, Walter Johnson High Sch., 1967-68, Virginia Beach Schs., 1968-69; mgr. Caro Amico Pizzeria, Portland, Oreg., 1971-73, owner, 1973—; co-owner The Pizza Oven, Vista, Calif., 1978-81; counselor Persona Corp., Portland, 1978—, owner, pres., 1979—; owner Elsie McFarland Rentals, Portland, 1972—; vocat. counselor The Psychology Ctr., Portland, 1978—. Bd. dirs. Stop Oreg. Litter and Vandalism, 1981-82. Mem. Women Entrepreneurs Oreg. (dir. 1981-82), Restaurants of Oreg. Assn. (dir. 1982, 83), Rehab. in Pvt. Sector. Republican. Clubs: Mountain Park Singles Gourmet and Potluck Assn., PEO, Mt. Park Racquet. Home: 21 Churchill Downs Lake Oswego OR 97034 Office: 10101 SW Barbur St Portland OR 97219

MC FARLAND, NORMAN F., bishop; b. Martinez, Calif., Feb. 21, 1922; student St. Patrick's Sem., Menlo Park, Calif.; J.C.D., Cath. U. Am. Ordained priest Roman Catholic Ch., 1946, consecrated bishop, 1970; titular bishop of Bida and aux. bishop of San Francisco, 1970-74; apostolic adminstr. Diocese of Reno, 1974-76, bishop of Reno-Las Vegas, 1976—. Office: 515 Court St PO Box 1211 Reno NV 89504

MC FARLANE, SAMUEL, mfg. exec.; b. Lonaconing, Md., May 21, 1916; s. Samuel Barber and Elizabeth (Stevenson) McF.; B.S., U. Md., 1939; postgrad. Poly. Inst. N.Y., 1948-50; m. Alice Louise Beck, Oct. 7, 1944; children—Carolyn, Elizabeth Jane, Barbara Ann. Research chemist Celanese Corp. Am., Cumberland, Md., 1939-47, sect. head research, Summit, N.J., 1947-52, asst. mgr. Summit Research Lab., 1952-55, lab. mgr., 1955-57, mgr. fiber research, 1957-58; v.p., tech. dir. Onyx Oil & Chem. Co., Jersey City, 1958-60; corp. v.p. research and devel. Sun Chem. Corp. N.Y.C., 1960-68; founder, pres. ElectroPrint, Inc., Palo Alto, Calif., 1969-76; asso. mgr. U.S. ERDA, San Francisco, 1976-77; mgr. Denver office U.S. Dept. Energy, 1977-79; pres. Internat. Brands, Inc., Los Gatos, Calif., 1979-80, chmn., chief exec. officer, pres., 1980—. Fellow Am. Inst. Chemists; mem. Soc. Chem. Industry, Soc. Photog. Scientists and Engrs., Chemists Club, A.I.M., AAAS, Sci. Research Soc. Am., N.Y. Acad. Scis., Tech. Assn. Graphic Arts, Am. Chem. Soc., Sigma Xi, Alpha Chi Sigma, Alpha Rho. Presbyn. Editor: Technology of Synthetic Fibers, 1953. Contbr. articles to profl. publs. Home: 13631 Verde Vista Ct Saratoga CA 95070 Office: 100 Albright Way Los Gatos CA 95030

MCGAGH, WILLIAM GILBERT, financial executive; b. Boston, May 29, 1929; s. Thomas A. and Mary M. (McDonough) McG.; m. Sarah M. McQuigg, Sept. 23, 1961; children—Margaret Ellen, Sarah Elizabeth. B.S., Boston Coll., 1950; M.B.A., Harvard U., 1952; M.S. (Sloan fellow),

MIT, 1965. Fin. analyst Ford Motor Co., Dearborn, Mich., 1953-55; mem. staff treas.'s office Chrysler Corp., Detroit, 1955-64; comptroller, treas. Chrysler Can. Ltd., Windsor, 1965-67; staff exec. fin. Latin Am. Ops., Detroit, 1967-68; asst. treas. Chrysler Corp., Detroit, 1968-75, treas., 1975-76, v.p., treas., 1976-80; sr. v.p. fin. Northrop Corp., Los Angeles, 1980—. Served as 2d lt. USAF, 1952-53. Mem. Fin. Analysts Soc., Fin. Execs. Inst. Clubs: Detroit Athletic; Orchard Lake (Mich.) Country; Beach (Santa Monica); California (Los Angeles); Harvard (N.Y.C.). Home: 2189 Century Hill Century City Los Angeles CA 90067 Office: 1800 Century Park E Los Angeles CA 90067

MCGARVEY, DAVID CARTER, mathematician; b. East St. Louis, Ill., June 17, 1931; s. Philip Carter and Helen Cornell (Ritchie) McG.; B.A., Carleton Coll., 1953; M.A., Yale U., 1954, Ph.D., 1959; m. Judith Ann Peterson, Aug. 19, 1977; children—Scott Allen, Nancy Ann Ellerbroek; 1 stepson, Jonathan Ronning Peterson. Sr. research staff dept. econs. Rand Corp., Santa Monica, Calif., 1957-71, 80—; fgn. policy analyst Gen. Research Corp., Santa Monica, 1971-74, Pan Heuristics, Los Angeles, 1974-80; Mem. Internat. Inst. Strategic Studies, Am. Math. Soc., AIAA, Calif. Seminar on Internat. Security and Fgn. Policy, Ops. Research Soc. Am., Sigma Xi, Phi Beta Kappa. Contbr. articles to profl. jours. Home: 8756 Cadillac Ave Los Angeles CA 90034 Office: 1700 Main St Santa Monica CA 90406

MCGARVEY, FRANK STERLING, engring./constrn. co. exec.; b. Mpls., Oct. 3, 1923; s. Frank Sterling and Dorothy Lucille (Scribner) McG.; B.S. in Civil Engring., Oreg. State Coll., 1948; m. Shirley Walker, Feb. 12, 1950; children—Gwen, James, William. City engr. City of Ontario (Oreg.), 1948-50; field engr., office engr., project engr. Morrison Knudson Co., Inc., 1950-55, div. engr., Los Angeles, 1964-67, v.p. M.K., Internat., Boise, Idaho, 1970-74, pres., 1979—, chief exec. officer Morrison Knudsen Engenharia, Brazil, 1974-78; project supt. Boeing pre-flight facilities George A. Fuller Co., Moses Lake, Wash., 1955-56, project mgr. various missile base constrn. sites, 1956-61, heavy constrn. div. mgr., Los Angeles, 1962-64; gen. mgr. RMK-BRJ, Vietnam, 1967-69. Cub Scout leader Boy Scouts Am., Los Angeles, 1962-65; mem. ch. council Anglican Ch., Brazil, 1975-78. Served with USN, 1943-45. Recipient Outstanding Service award, U.S. Navy-Vietnam, 1969, Govt. of Vietnam, 1968, 69. Republican. Episcopalian. Clubs: Hillcrest Country, Arid, Elks. Home: 3517 Hillcrest Dr Boise ID 83705 Office: 2 Morrison Knudsen Plaza Boise ID 83729

MCGARVEY, JOHN JAMES, computer systems company executive, ret. naval officer; b. Yonkers, N.Y., Dec. 26, 1931; s. John Joseph and Elizabeth Marie (Flanagan) McG.; m. Patricia Ann Marsteller, May 18, 1957; children—Daniel, Sheila, Michael, John Timothy. B.S. in Acctg., Pa. State U., 1956; M.S. in Computer Systems Mgmt., Naval Postgrad. Sch., Monterey, Calif., 1966. Cert. data processor. Commd. ensign U.S. Navy, 1956, advanced through grades to comdr., 1969; dir. data systems Naval Air Systems Command, Washington, 1969-73; head logistics dept. USS Coral Sea, 1973-75; dir. EDP auditing Dept. Navy, Washington, 1975-77, ret., 1977; sr. systems designer Bay Area Rapid Transit, Oakland, Calif., 1977-78; tech. systems mgr. Am. Pres. Lines, Ltd., Oakland, 1978-79; nat. dir. profl. services Optimum Systems, Inc., Santa Clara, Calif., 1979-80; v.p. Info. Systems Group, Inc., San Leandro, Calif., 1979—; pres. Applied Systems Assocs., San Leandro, Calif., 1980—; lectr. U. Md., College Park, 1976-77, Calif. State U.-Hayward, 1978—; cons. in field. Mem. Ind. Computer Cons. Assn., Assn. Computing Machinery, Assn. Systems Mgmt., Naval Inst. Republican. Roman Catholic. Home: 8111 Phaeton Dr Oakland CA 94605

MC GAW, SIDNEY EDWIN, ednl. cons.; b. Toronto, Ont., Can., Sept. 21, 1908; s. Sidney Anson and May (Bigelow) McG.; student Fresno State Coll., 1928-31; B.S., U. Calif. at Berkeley, 1944, M.A., 1948, Ed.D., 1952; m. Clara E. Eca da Silva, June 15, 1931; children—Bruce A., Laurie A., Kathleen C. (Mrs. Richard Chylinski). Instr., counselor pub. schs., Oakland, Calif., 1941-47; asst. supr. trade and tech. tchr. tng. Calif. State Dept. Edn., 1947-50, regional supr., 1950-65; dean instrn. San Jose City Coll., 1965-74; ednl. cons., 1974—; lectr. U. Calif. at Berkeley, summers 1948-66; workshop lectr. U. Nev., summers 1955-56. Pres., Calif. League for Nursing, 1967-69; bd. dirs. Nat. League Nursing, 1967-69; chmn. edn. and tng. commn. Redwood Region Conservation Council, 1953-65. Mem. Phi Delta Kappa. Rotarian (bd. dirs. West San Jose 1969-70). Club: Commonwealth of Calif. (San Francisco). Home: 1023 Ordway St Albany CA 94706

MC GEE, FRANK CHALMERS, color consultant; b. Portland, Oreg., Aug. 25, 1927; s. George Rose and Esther (Chalmers) McG.; ed. public schs.; m. Helen Hunter, Jan. 25, 1958; children—Hunter Frank, Scott Stuart. With Moral Re-Armament, Inc., counselor, producer, actor, dir., photographer, photojournalist, Europe, Asia, Africa, Americas, 1945-65; mng. editor Pace mag., Los Angeles, 1965-70; founder, editor New Worlds of Orange County, Newport Beach, Calif., 1970-81; color cons.; guest lectr. various univs., colls.; free lance various pub., writing, photography, advt. Recipient various journalism awards for New Worlds. Republican. Presbyterian. Club: Dana West Yacht (Dana Point, Calif.). Contbr. articles and features to mags. Home: 1930 Port Dunleigh Circle Newport Beach CA 92660

MCGEE, MARK GREGORY, psychologist, educator; b. Mpls., Dec. 7, 1946; s. Theodore G. and Martha A. McGee; m. Ellen Shiplet, Aug. 8, 1977; children—Alyson, Katy, Maureen. B.A. summa cum laude, U. Minn., 1973; Ph.D. in Psychology, 1976. Teaching assoc. U. Minn., Mpls., 1974-76, coordinator undergrad. psychology, 1975-76; asst. prof. pyschology, coordinator introductory psychology Tex. A&M U., 1976-80; research fellow dept. psychiatry, U. Colo. Med. Sch., Denver, 1980-81; research psychologist, Brain Scis. Labs., Nat. Jewish Hosp., Denver, 1981—; editorial cons. NIMH fellow, 1981. Mem. Am. Psychol. Assn., AAAS, Am. Edn. Research Assn., Behavior Genetics Assn., Brain Behavioral Scis. Assn., Denver Developmental Psychobiology Research Group. Author: Human Spatial Abilities, 1979; Introductory Psychology-Reader, 1980; Psychology: Science and Applications, 1984. Home: 27848 Whirlaway Trail Evergreen CO 80439 Office: Brain Sci Labs Nat Jewish Hosp Denver CO 80206

MCGEE, PATRICIA ANN, computer mgmt. cons.; b. N.Y.C., July 22, 1939; d. Patrick James and Bridget Mary (O'Leary) Brennan; B.A., CCNY, 1961; 1 dau., Ayn Maureen. Sr. cons., analyst Western Ops., Inc., San Francisco, 1968-71; data processing mgr. R.H. Lapin & Co., San Francisco, 1971-73; project leader, systems analyst Transamerica Corp., San Francisco, 1973-74; systems analyst United Vintners, Inc., San Francisco, 1974-75; systems planner Fiberboard Corp., 1975-76; customer rep. Computer Scis. Corp., 1976-78; project mgr. Crocker Nat. Bank, 1978-80; cons. Bechtel Co., 1980, Mason-McDuffie & Co., 1980, Pacific Telephone Co., 1980-81; partner The Profls., San Francisco, 1981—; cons. Reed Risk Mgmt., 1982—. Mem. Am. Mgmt. Assn., Republican Women San Francisco, Women Entrepreneurs, World Affairs Trade Council, Profl. Women's Network, Assn. System Mgrs. Republican. Roman Catholic. Clubs: Commonwealth of Calif.; U.S. Senatorial; San Francisco Bay. Home and office: 430-10th Ave San Francisco CA 94118

MCGEE, ROBERT IRVIN, statistician; b. Lisbon, Ohio, Sept. 13, 1949; s. Irvin James and May McGee; B.A., Otterbein Coll., 1971; M.S., Miami U., Oxford, Ohio, 1973; Ph.D., Kans. State U., 1976. Vis. asst. prof. Stats. Center, N.Mex. State U., Las Cruces, 1975-76; asst. prof. Kent State U., East Liverpool, Ohio, part-time 1978-79; asst. prof. public health Sch. Public Health, U. Hawaii, Honolulu, 1979—. Mem. Am. Stats. Assn., Inst. Math. Stats., Math. Assn. Am., Sigma Xi. Democrat. Presbyterian. Club: Masons. Home: 778 Wiliwili St Apt 304B Honolulu HI 96826 Office: 1960 East West Rd Honolulu HI 96822

MC GEE, ROY JOHN, pharmacist, film critic; b. San Diego, May 2, 1932; s. Roy Charles and Maude Mildred (Pfenninger) McG.; B.S., U. Colo., Boulder, 1956; postgrad. in radiopharmacy (AEC grantee), U. So. Calif., 1974; m. Mari Rebane, June 27, 1964; children—John Tonis, Nancy Mari. Staff pharmacist Donald N. Sharp Meml. Community Hosp., San Diego, 1956-76; sr. staff pharmacist Hosp. Scripps Clinic, LaJolla, Calif., 1976—; film reviewer, columnist Reel Reviewer, Classic Film Collector, Blackhawk Digest, 1975-78, Classic Images, 1978—. Served with U.S. Army, 1956-59; Korea. Mem. Am. Film Inst., San Diego Mus. Art (life), Los Angeles County Mus. Art, San Diego Opera Assn., San Diego Hist. Soc., San Diego Zool. Soc., Am. Soc. Hosp. Pharmacists. Republican. Clubs: Masons, Shriners, Scottish Rite. Research on interferon for multiple sclerosis. Home: 3265 2d Ave San Diego CA 92103

MC GILL, BETTY ALLEN, social work cons.; b. York, S.C.; d. Carl and Johnnie Mae Allen; 1 dau., Karen Denise. Caseworker, Mecklenburg County Welfare Dept., Charlotte, N.C., 1957-59; clin. social worker VA Hosp., McKinney, Tex., 1960-61; med. social worker Los Angeles County/U. So. Calif. Med. Center, Los Angeles, 1962-63, supervising med. social worker, 1963-66; med. social work cons., Los Angeles County, 1967—. Mem. steering com. Park Hills Community Ch.; v.p. bd. dirs. Roshasharon Home for Battered Wives; bd. dirs. Delta Sigma Theta State Pre-Sch. Head Start, Angeles Mesa YWCA; mem. Women on Target; mem. community outreach com. Los Angeles County Commn. on Status of Women; vol. MOSAIC, Mus. Sci. and Industry Calif. Recipient Mayor's commendation City of Los Angeles; commendation Calif. State Assembly; resolution City Council Los Angeles. Mem. Nat. Assn. Social Workers, Child Welfare League Am., Nat. Conf. Social Welfare, AAUW, LWV, Delta Sigma Theta (pres. Los Angeles alumnae chpt. 1980—, service certs.). social work cons.; b. York, S.C.; d. Carl and Johnnie Mae Allen; 1 dau., Karen Denise. Caseworker, Mecklenburg County Welfare Dept., Charlotte, N.C., 1957-59; clin. social worker VA Hosp., McKinney, Tex., 1960-61; med. social worker Los Angeles County/U. So. Calif. Med. Center, Los Angeles, 1962-63, supervising med. social worker, 1963-66; med. social work cons., Los Angeles County, 1967—. Mem. steering com. Park Hills Community Ch.; v.p. bd. dirs. Roshasharon Home for Battered Wives; bd. dirs. Delta Sigma Theta State Pre-Sch. Head Start, Angeles Mesa YWCA; mem. Women on Target; mem. community outreach com. Los Angeles County Commn. on Status of Women; vol. MOSAIC, Mus. Sci. and Industry Calif. Recipient Mayor's commendation City of Los Angeles; commendation Calif. State Assembly; resolution City Council Los Angeles. Mem. Nat. Assn. Social Workers, Child Welfare League Am., Nat. Conf. Social Welfare, AAUW, LWV, Delta Sigma Theta (pres. Los Angeles alumnae chpt. 1980—, service certs.). Home: PO Box 43392 Los Angeles CA 90043

MCGILLIVRAY, WILLIAM ALEXANDER, chief justice; b. Calgary, Alta., Can., Oct. 14, 1918; B.A., U. Alta, 1940, LL.B., 1941. Called to Alta. bar, 1942, Sask. bar, 1965; partner firm Fenerty, McGillivray, Robertson & Co., Calgary, 1943-74; named Queen's counsel, 1957; chief justice of Alta., Calgary, 1974—. Office: Ct House 611 4th St SW Calgary AB T2P 1T5 Canada

MCGILVERY, LAURENCE, antiquarian bookseller, publisher; b. Los Angeles, May 21, 1932; s. Neil Lee and Joan (Girard) McG.; B.A., Pomona Coll., Claremont, Calif., 1954; m. Geraldine Malloy, July 5, 1955; children—Lynette, Lise, Erin, Justin. Engr., Walter Dorwin Teague Assocs., Pomona and Sunnyvale, Calif., N.Y.C., 1955-61; owner Nexus Bookstore, La Jolla, Calif., 1960-66; antiquarian bookseller, publisher, La Jolla, 1964—. Mem. adv. com. Am. Art Directory. Mem. Antiquarian Booksellers Assn., Art Libraries Soc N.Am., Art Libraries Soc Australia and N.Z., San Diego Booksellers Assn. (pres.), Dramatists Guild. Author: Artforum, 1962-68: A Cumulative Index to First Six Volumes, 1970; contbr. to other works including Allen Ginsberg, 1971, Art Nouveau, 1977, Frank Lloyd Wright, 1978, The City Lights Pocket Poets Series, 1982. Address: PO Box 852 La Jolla CA 92038

MCGINNIS, GERALD LLOYD, supermarket chain executive; b. East St. Louis, Ill., Sept. 7, 1938; s. Robert Earle and Florence Beatrice (O'Bannon) McG.; m. Earlene Basham, Sept. 19, 1959; children—Bethanie McGuire, Melanie Fritts, John. B.A., Calif. State U.-Hawyard, 1969; M.B.A., U. Calif.-Berkeley, 1970. Quality control supr. Monsanto, St. Peters, Mo., 1960-64; utilities engr. Safeway, Oakland, Calif., 1964-70, mgr. corp. real estate dept., 1973-80, mgr. real estate strategy and planning div., 1980-81, v.p., div. mgr. real estate, 1982—; cons., network mem. U. Calif.-Berkeley Found. Served with U.S. Navy, 1956-59. Mem. Nat. Assn. Corp. Real Estate Execs., Internat. Council Shopping Ctrs. Office: 201 4th St Oakland CA 94660

MCGINNIS, RICHARD ADAMS, cons. chemist; b. Douglas, Ariz., Dec. 20, 1903; s. Richard Brodhead and Alice (Adams) McG.; A.B., U. Calif., Berkeley, 1925, Ph.D., 1935; m. Olive Provis, 1933; children—Helen, Richard, Theresa, James. Research chemist, 1935-54; gen. chemist, dir. research Spreckels Sugar div. Amstar Corp., San Francisco, 1954-69; asso. editor Sugar Jour., 1971—, Sugar Tech. Revs., 1972—; adminstr., lectr. Beet Sugar Inst., Ft. Collins, Colo., 1971—; cons. chemist beet-sugar tech., San Rafael, Calif., 1970—. Fellow Am. Inst. Chemists; mem. Am. Soc. Sugar Beet Tech. (hon.; service award, 1968), U.S. Nat. Com. on Sugar Analysis (hon.), Am. Chem. Soc. (emeritus), Sigma Xi (hon.). Author: Beet-Sugar Technology, 3d edit., 1982, transl. Russian, Polish; contbr. papers to profl. publs. Home and office: 89 Crestwood Dr PO Box 1006 San Rafael CA 94915

MCGINNIS, ROBERT WILLIAM, solar energy co. exec.; b. Modesto, Calif., Oct. 31, 1936; s. George Crawford and Lola May (Provis) McG.; B.S. in Elec. Engring. with highest honors, U. Calif., Berkeley, 1962; postgrad. N.Y. U., 1962-63; m. Sondra Elaine Hurley, Mar. 1, 1964; children—Michael Fredrick, Traci Anne, Patrick William. Mem. tech. staff Bell Telephone Labs, Murray Hill, N.J., 1961-63; devel. engr., engring. mgr., product mgr., ops. mgr. Motorola Semiconductor Group, Phoenix, 1963-73, ops. mgr. for hybrid circuits group, communications div., Fort Lauderdale, Fla., 1973-76, solar ops. mgr., 1976-79; v.p., gen. mgr. Photowatt Internat., Inc., Tempe, Ariz., 1979—. Mem. Ariz. Solar Energy Commn., 1977—; chmn. photovoltaic subcom. Am. Nat. Standards Inst., 1978—; mem. coordinating council Solar Energy Research Inst. Standards, 1977—. Served with USNR, 1955-58. Mem. IEEE, Phi Beta Kappa, Tau Beta Pi, Eta Kappa Nu. Republican. Methodist. Contbr. articles in field to profl. jours. Home: 7887 Via Bonita Scottsdale AZ 85258 Office: Photowatt International Inc 2414 W 14th St Tempe AZ 85281

MC GLOTHLEN, WAYNE FRANKLIN, club exec.; b. Des Moines, Sept. 10, 1925; s. Ward Forester and Sally Ann (Lindsey) McG.; student Am. Inst. Bus., Des Moines, 1949-50, UCLA, 1961; m. Wauneta Ann Goode, May 8, 1946; children—Robert Franklin, Jo Ann, Kathy Sue, Thomas Wayne. Salesman, Home Insulation Co., Des Moines, 1946-48; office mgr. Wakonda Country Club, Des Moines, 1951-52; staff sr. accountant Harris, Kerr, Forster Co., Los Angeles, 1953-57, 63; controller Candlewood Country Club, Whittier, Calif., 1957-60; exec. asst. mgr. Mayfair Hotel, Los Angeles, 1960-61; controller Los Coyotes Country Club, Buena Park, Calif., 1961-63; asst. sec.-treas. Huntington Driftwood, Inc., Huntington Beach, Calif., 1964-65; dist. auditor Firestone Tire & Rubber Co., Akron, Ohio, 1965-66; v.p. fin. Wash. Athletic Club, Seattle, 1966-83. Chmn. fin. com. Queensgate Baptist Ch., Bothell, Wash., 1972-75. Served with USN, 1943-46; PTO. Decorated Bronze Star. Mem. Nat. Assn. Accountants, Am. Mgmt. Assn., Assn. Pvt. Pension and Welfare Plans, Am. Assn. Ret. Persons, Seattle C. of C., Phi Theta Pi. Republican. Clubs: Holiday Ramblers Recreational Vehicle, Port Susan Camping, Good Sam, Gold Bar Nature Trails Camping (pres. 1980). Home: 15512 119th Ave NE Bothell WA 98011 Office: PO Box 1709 Seattle WA 98111

MCGLYNN, D(ANIEL) JERRY, lawyer, management consultant; b. St. Louis, July 6, 1938; s. Joseph B. and Metta McGlynn; m. Jovanna Brown, Sept. 19, 1981. B.B.A., U. Notre Dame, 1960, M.B.A., 1972, J.D., 1974. Trainee, First Nat. Bank, St. Louis, 1963-64, rep., 1964-66; pres. Washington Carpet Co., St. Louis, 1966-70; exec. dir. Bicentennial Civic Improvement Corp., St. Louis, 1967-70; admitted to Calif. bar, 1974; atty. firm Peter Brekhus, San Rafael, Calif., 1976-78; pvt. practice law and mgmt. cons., San Rafael, 1978—; pro bono counsel Ross Valley Ecumenical Housing Assn., 1975—; bd. advs. Small Bus. Inst., Marin County, Calif., 1983—. Bd. dirs., pres. Mulanphy Urban Redevel. Corp., St. Louis, 1967-70; bd. dirs. St. Louis Ecumenical Housing Fund, 1969, Nat. Assn. Non-Profit Housing Orgns., 1969, Civic Employment Corp., St. Louis, 1969; pres. alumni U. Notre Dame, St. Louis, 1965, San Francisco, 1976, nat. dir., 1980-83. Named Man of Yr., U. Notre Dame Alumni, St. Louis, 1973. Mem. ABA, Calif. State Bar Assn., Marin Bar Assn., Am. Mgmt. Assn., Assn. M.B.A. Execs. Republican. Roman Catholic. Club: KC (Grand Knight 1960). Home: 825 Las Gallinas Ave 204 San Rafael CA 94903 Office: 880 Las Gallinas Ave Suite B San Rafael CA 94903

MC GONIGLE, PAUL JOHN, radio sta. exec.; b. New Castle, Pa., Sept. 29, 1942; s. John Paul and Verna Alfreda (Bailer) McG.; m. Susan L. Bimerman, Jan. 1, 1983. Student Ohio Wesleyan U., 1963, U. Va., 1968, N.C. State U., 1972. News editor WCOL, Columbus, Ohio, 1964-65; asst. mgr. WPRW, Manassas, Va., 1965-67; program dir. WEAM, Arlington, Va., 1967-69; news editor WJBK, Detroit, 1969-70; news dir. WKNR, Dearborn, Mich., 1970-71; news dir. WKIX, Raleigh, N.C., capitol chief WGHP-TV, 1971-73; news dir. KOY, Phoenix, 1973—; instr. broadcast news Phoenix Coll., Ariz. State U. Recipient Nat. Disting. Service award March of Dimes, 1967, Nat. award for outstanding pub. service in broadcast journalism Scripps-Howard Found., 1978, certs. of merit Am. Bar Assn., 1976, 78. Mem. Sigma Delta Chi, Soc. Profl. Journalists (Nat. Disting. Service award for radio reporting 1978, chpt. pres. 1981), AP Broadcasters Assn. (nat. bd.), Ariz. AP Broadcasters Assn. (pres. 1978-79, awards for spot, documentary and gen. news 1980), Radio-Television News Dirs. Assn. (radio workshop chmn.; Western regional Edward R. Murrow award 1978, 80, Western regional Spot News Reporting award 1978), Republican. Baptist. Clubs: Phoenix Press (v.p. 1979-80, v.p. found. 1982-83), Ariz. Press (sec. 1977-78, 15 awards for radio reporting 1974—). Office: KOY Radio 840 N Central Ave Phoenix AZ 85004

MCGOOKEY, LENANN, marketing and management educator; b. Castalia, Ohio, May 25, 1952; d. James Lester and Sally Light McG.; m. James Clifford Gunther, Aug. 6, 1977; 1 dau., Lindsay Erica McGookey Gunther. B.A. in Journalism magna cum laude, Bowling Green State U., 1973; M.B.A., Harvard U., 1976. Asst. buyer May Co., Los Angeles, 1976-78; mktg. rep. Xerox Computer Services, Los Angeles, 1978-80; news producer Sta. KMPC, Hollywood, Calif., 1980; news reporter/anchor Sta. KFOX, Redondo Beach, Calif., 1980; asst. prof. Chapman Coll., Orange, Calif., 1982—; freelance writer Hollywood Entertainment Radio Network, 1980-81. Active A Place for Parents, Santa Monica, Calif. Mem. Harvard Bus. Sch. Alumni Assn., NOW, Phi Kappa Phi, Alpha Lambda Delta. Home: 4306 Neosho Ave Los Angeles CA 90066 Office: 333 N Glassell Orange CA 92666

MCGOVERN, REBECCA MAPLES, chamber of commerce executive; b. West Frankfort, Ill., July 3, 1934; d. Joseph Edward and Celia Belle (Gill) McG. B.A. magna cum laude, So. Ill. U., 1956; postgrad. Boston U., 1956-57. Advt. mgr. Beacon Press., Boston, 1962-65; dir. press mktg. MIT, Cambridge, Mass., 1965-74; pres. Mariposa Enterprises, San Juan Bautista, Calif., 1974-82; mgr. San Juan Bautista C. of C., 1976—; mktg. dir. San Juan Magazette, San Juan Bautista, 1982—. Bd. dirs. El Teatro Campesino, Calif. State Hist. Park Vol. Assn., San Benito Econ. Devel. Corp., Chamber Music San Juan Found. Home: 102-104 The Alameda San Juan Bautista CA 95045 Office: 201 3d St San Juan Bautista CA 95045

MC GOVERN, WALTER T., judge; b. Seattle, May 14, 1922; s. C. Arthur and Anne Marie (Thies) McG.; B.A., U. Wash., 1949, LL.B., 1950; m. Rita Marie Olsen, June 29, 1946; children—Katrina M., Shawn E., A. Renee. Bar: Wash. 1950. Practiced law in Seattle, 1950-59; mem. firm Kerr, McCord, Greenleaf and Moen; judge Mcpl. Ct., Seattle, 1959-65; judge Superior Ct. Wash., 1965-68; judge Wash. Supreme Ct., 1968-71; judge U.S. Dist. Ct., Western Dist. Wash., 1971—, chief judge, 1975—. Mem. Am. Judicature Soc., Wash. State Superior Ct. Judges Assn., Phi Delta Phi. Office: 705 US Courthouse Seattle WA 98104*

MCGRANN, THOMAS PATRICK, steel company executive; b. Watertown, S.D., Mar. 15, 1941; s. Maurice Bernard and Margaret Amarita (Nolan) McG.; B.A., U. Minn., 1963; M.B.A., U. Chgo., 1976; postgrad. Harvard U., 1981; m. Elizabeth Aden Stiehm, Aug. 15, 1964; children—Michael, Caroline, Katherine. Sales rep. Inland Steel Co., 1967-70, asst. mgr. sales, 1971-75, mgr. sales, 1976; gen. mgr. sales CF & I Steel Corp., Pueblo, Colo., 1977-80, dir. subs. and corp. services, 1981, v.p. comml., 1982—; guest lectr. bus. and econs. Colo. Coll., Air Force Acad., 1981-82. Bd. dirs. Sangre de Cristo Arts and Conf. Ctr., 1982. Mem. Am. Iron and Steel Inst. (mem. COMPUS com.) Roman Catholic. Home: 54 Upland Rd Colorado Springs CO 80906 Office: PO Box 1830 Pueblo CO 81002

MCGRATH, LUCILLE MARIE, electronics company manager; b. Milbank, S.D., Feb. 10, 1951; d. Victor Frank and Irene Clara (Reiffenberger) Stolpman; B.A. with distinction, U. Minn., Morris, 1973; postgrad. in bus., U. Calif., Santa Barbara, 1973-76. Planning adminstrn. asst., mech. buyer, elec. buyer, Raytheon Co., Santa Barbara, Calif., 1973-76; electronic buyer, ITT Barton Instruments, City of Industry, Calif., 1976-79; sr. buyer Perkin-Elmer Memory Products div., Garden Grove, Calif., 1979-80; sr. purchasing agt. BASF, Fountain Valley, Calif., 1980; project procurement mgr. electronics and def. TRW, Redondo Beach, Calif., 1980—. Recipient Scholar of Coll. award, 1973. Mem. Purchasing Mgmt. Assn. (dir., Santa Barbara 1975-76, Los Angeles chpt. 1978—). Democrat. Home: 227 E Oak Ave El Segundo CA 90245 Office: One Space Park Redondo Beach CA 90278

MC GRATH, RICHARD WILLIAM, osteopathic physician; b. Hartford, Conn., Nov. 17, 1943; s. William Paul and Stephanie Gertrude

(Romash) McG.; B.S., St. Ambrose Coll., 1965; D.Osteo. Medicine and Surgery, Coll. Osteo. Medicine and Surgery, Des Moines, 1971; m. Mariette VanLancker, June 24, 1967; children—Shaun, Megan, Kelley. Osteo. physician Weld County Gen. Hosp., Greeley, Colo., 1971-72, Granby (Colo.) Clinic, 1972-75, Timberline Med. Center, P.C., Granby, 1975—; pres. Timberline Med. Center, 1976—, Bighorn Properties Inc., 1978—, Thia of Am. Corp., 1980—; med. coordinator/dir. regional emergency systems Colo. State Health Dept., 1978-79; mem. Colo. Comprehensive Health Planning Agy., 1975-77; assoc. prof. clin. medicine Tex. Coll. Osteo. Medicine; med. advisor Grand County Ambulance System, 1977—; vice chief staff Kremmling Meml. Hosp. Mem. steering com. to develop Colo. Western Slope Health System Agy., 1975-76, bd. dirs., 1977—; officer, police surgeon Grand Lake and Granby, 1977—; mem. parent adv. bd. Granby Sch. System, 1975-76; chmn. East Grand County Safety Council, 1974-76; dep. coroner Grand County, 1973-75; med. advisor Grand County Rescue Team, 1974-78. Recipient award Ohio State U. Coll. Medicine, 1977. Mem. AMA, A.C.S. (com. on trauma), Am. Coll. Emergency Physicians, Western Slope Physicians Alliance Assn., Colo. Union of Physicians (dir.), C. of C. of Granby, Grand Lake and Fraser Valley. Republican. Roman Catholic. Home: PO Box 706 Granby CO 80446 Office: PO Box 857 Granby CO 80446

MCGRAW, DONALD JESSE, microbiologist, writer; b. Altadena, Calif., Oct. 27, 1943; s. Jesse E. and Mary L. (Hajostek) McG.; B.S. in Biol. Scis., Calif. State Poly. Coll., Pomona, 1965; M.S., Utah State U., 1967; Ph.D. (Eli Lilly grantee 1973-74), Oreg. State U., 1976; m. Laura Lee Hansen, July 13, 1968; children—Adrienne, Holly, Rachel. Research asst. microbiology Utah State U., 1965-66, teaching asst. food and aquatic microbiology, 1966-67; grad. teaching asst. gen. biology Oreg. State U., 1970-72, instr., 1972-73; tchr. phys. and biol. scis. U.S. Bur. Indian Affairs Boarding Sch., Shonto, Ariz., 1974-75; asst. prof. biology Franklin (Ind.) Coll., 1975-78; adj. asst. prof. biology Ind. Central U., Indpls., 1977-78, Ind. U.-Purdue U., Columbus, 1978; mem. faculty Yavapai Community Coll., Prescott, Ariz., 1978-79; asso. dir. Ute Research Lab., Ft. Duchesne, Utah, 1980-81; dir., 1981-82; writer sci. books, 1982—. Served with USPHS, 1967-69. Registered microbiologist Am. Acad. Microbiology. Mem. Am. Soc. Microbiology, History of Sci. Soc., Alpha Scholastic Honor Soc. of Franklin Coll. (pres. 1976-78), Sigma Xi, Beta Beta Beta. Contbr. articles on microbiology to sci. publs.

MCGREEVY, SUSAN BROWN, museum director; b. Chgo., Jan. 28, 1934; d. Irving Leslie and Edna (Joselit) Colby; student Mt. Holyoke Coll., 1951-53; B.A. with honors, Roosevelt U., 1969; M.A., Northwestern U., 1971; m. Thomas J. McGreevy, June 16, 1973; children—Patricia Leigh Brown, Lori Alyn Brown, Cynthia Diane Brown. Curator, N. Am. Ethnology, Kansas City Mus. History and Sci., 1975-77; dir. Wheelwright Mus. Am. Indian, Santa Fe, 1978—. Mem. Am. Anthrop. Assn., Am. Assn. Museums, Am. Soc. Ethnohistory, Council Mus. Anthropology, Soc. Applied Anthropology, Mountain Plains Mus. Assn., N.Mex. Mus. Assn. Office: 704 Camino Lejo Box 5153 Santa Fe NM 87502

MCGREGOR, CAROL ANN, management education specialist; b. Ft. Wayne, Ind., Sept. 9, 1946; d. Oren and Mary Ann Culver; m. Patrick McGregory June 15, 1968 (div. 1978); 1 son, Jeffrey. B.A., Ind. U., 1968; M.B.A., Fordham U., 1977; M.A., Loyola Marymount, 1982. Systems analyst Technitron Inc., N.Y.C., 1974-76; field analyst On-Line Systems, N.Y.C., 1977-78; fin. analyst Wilshire Assocs., Santa Monica, Calif., 1979-80; mech. coordinator Engring. Dept., Gen. Telephone Co., Santa Monica, Calif., 1980—; adminstrv. dir. Psychology Dept., South Bay Free Clinic, Manhattan Beach, Calif., 1981—. Mem. Assn. Systems Mgrs. Unitarian-Universalist. Home: 3857 Bledsoe St Los Angeles CA 90066 Office: Gen Telephone Co 100 Wilshire Blvd PO Box 889 RC 3254-102 Santa Monica CA 90406

MC GREGOR, DONALD SCOTT, mortgage banker; b. St. George, Utah, Feb. 25, 1944; s. Alpine Watson and Berneice (Holt) McG.; student Dixie Coll., 1962-63; B.S., Brigham Young U., 1970; postgrad. U. Utah, 1970-71, N.Y. U., 1971-72, LaSalle U., 1972-73; m. Diane Mehew Melchin, June 1, 1967; children—Gregory, Carolyn Travis, Christopher, Sally, Timothy, Jill. Ptnr., Doolin Constrn. Co., Las Vegas, Nev., 1971; pres. McGregor Devel. Corp., St. George and Salt Lake City, 1972-75, Land Tech. Inc., St. George and Salt Lake City, 1972-76, First Am. Mortgage Corp., mortgage bankers, Salt Lake City and Vancouver, B.C., Can., 1973-77, First Am. Growth Resources, Inc., investment bankers, Salt Lake City and Vancouver, B.C., 1974-77, Vista Ambassador, Salt Lake City, 1975—; income property loan officer Western Mortgage Loan Corp., Salt Lake City, 1978—; chmn. bd. Guaranty Mortgage Corp. Am., 1978—, Fed. Fin. Corp., Salt Lake City, 1979—, v.p. Security Pacific Mortgage Corp., Salt Lake City; pres. McNeil/Mehew Group, Inc., Salt Lake City and N.Y.C.; dir. Motion Pictures Internat., Salt Lake City. Mem. Washington County (Utah) Planning Commn., 1973-74; elder Ch. of Jesus Christ of Latter-day Saints, Salt Lake City. Recipient service award Boy Scouts Am., 1974. Republican. Editor, writer Econ. Forecast, 1973-74. Home: 1569 Stonemoor Circle Salt Lake City UT 84121

MCGREW, RALPH BROWNELL, artist; b. Columbus, Ohio, Sept. 6, 1916; s. Ralph Brownell and Bertha Caroline (Horst) McG.; m. Barbara Ann Froning, Dec. 4, 1938; children—Ann Gail Eifrig, Rebecca Joan Mohler, Donna Jill Bielenberg. Student Otis Art Inst., 1936-40; Litt. D., Concordia Coll., 1981. One-man show: Laguna Beach (Calif.) Art. Mus., 1978; group shows: Artists Am. Exhbn., Denver, 1981, 82, Western Heritage Exhbns., Houston, 1981. Recipient numerous gold and silver medals, Miles Christi award, Concordia Sem., Ft. Wayne, Ind., 1982; named W. Artist of Yr., San Dimas (Calif.) Art Festival, 1980, Festival Artist of Yr., The Tucson Festival, 1983. Fellow Am. Inst. Fine Arts, Soc. Western Artists; mem. Cowboy Artists Am. Lutheran. Work published in R. Brownell McGrew, 1978. Address: PO Box 2 Quemado NM 87829

MCGREW, VIRGINIA SUZANNE, savs. and loan exec.; b. Long Beach, Calif., Sept. 11, 1948; d. Lloyd Milton and Alice Lucille (Knudsen) Chapman; student Long Beach City Coll., 1970-73, Inst. Fin. Edn. Mgmt.; m. Dan E. McGrew, 1965 (div., 1980); children—Alan Wilson, Dan Edward. Teller, Union Fed. Savs., Long Beach, 1972-73, new accounts, 1973-75, asst. br. mgr., Long Beach, 1975-77, asst. v.p., br. mgr., Pasadena, Calif., 1977-80; v.p., br. mgr. Imperial Savs. & Loan Assn., Pasadena, 1980—. Mem. adv. bd. Falcon Cable TV, 1981. Mem. Pasadena Tournament of Roses Assn., 1979—; mem. Patron Saints Fund Raising Orgn., St. Luke Hosp. Found. Mem. Women in Bus., Bus. and Profl. Women (charter treas. Pasadena chpt. 1982-84). Club: Excalibur-Knights of the Round Table (Pasadena). Home: 10744 E Hedda Pl Cerritos CA 90701 Office: 61 S Lake Ave Pasadena CA 91101

MCGUIRE, ARTHUR WILLIAM, real estate executive; b. San Francisco, July 24, 1917; s. Arthur Bradford and Alice D. McGuire; B.S., Carnegie Inst. Tech., 1938; M.B.A., Stanford U., 1949; m. Ruth Webber, May 11, 1942; children—Patricia, Nancy, William. Regional sales mgr. indsl. div. Fed. Mogul Corp., 1951-72; ptnr. Banner Homes, Woodside, Calif., 1972—. Past pres. bd. Serra Residential Center, Fremont, Calif. Served with lt. comdr. USNR, 1941-45. Republican. Congregationalist. Clubs: Sirs, Masons. Address: 9488 Godetia Rd Woodside CA 94062

MCGUIRE, JAMES CHARLES, aircraft company executive; b. St. Louis, Aug. 8, 1917; s. John Patrick and Anna Beulah (Erbar) McG.; A.B., Washington U., St. Louis, 1949, M.A. (Univ. fellow), 1953, Ph.D., 1954; m. Ingrid Elisabeth Getreu, Sept. 16, 1954. Research assoc. Ohio State U., 1953-56; research psychologist Aeromed. Lab., Wright-Patterson AFB, Ohio, 1956-59; group supr. Boeing Airplane Co., Seattle, 1959-61; dept. mgr. Internat. Electric Corp., Paramus, N.J., 1961-62; sr. human factors scientist System Devel. Corp., Santa Monica, Calif., 1962-67; v.p. Booz-Allen Applied Research, Saigon, Vietnam, 1967-72; v.p. Assoc. Cons. Internat., Saigon, 1972-75, Bethesda, Md., 1975-78; br. chief human factors Douglas Aircraft Co., Long Beach, Calif., 1978—; lectr. Nat. Def. Coll., Vietnamese Armed Forces, Saigon, 1971. Served with AUS, 1940-46. Decorated Bronze Star medal with oak leaf cluster. Mem. Am. Def. Preparedness Assn., Assn. U.S. Army, Am. Psychol. Assn., AAAS, IEEE, Human Factors Soc., Am. Assn. Artificial Intelligence, Assn. Computing Machinery, Inst. Mgmt. Scis., Computer and Automated Systems Assn., Soc. Mfg. Engrs., Ops. Research Soc. Am., Soc. Applied Learning Tech., Phi Beta Kappa, Sigma Xi. Republican. Club: Monarch Bay. Home: 23201 Mindanao Circle Laguna Niguel CA 92677 Office: 3855 Lakewood Blvd Long Beach CA 90846

MC GUIRE, MICHAEL JOHN, environ. engr.; b. San Antonio, June 29, 1947; s. James Brendan and Opal Mary (Brady) McG.; B.S. in Civil Engring., U. Pa., 1969; M.S. in Environ Engring., Drexel U., 1972, Ph.D. in Environ. Engring., 1977; m. Deborah Marrow, June 19, 1971; 1 son, David Marrow. San. engr. Phila. Water Dept., 1969-73; research assoc. Drexel U., Phila., 1976-77; prin. engr. Brown & Caldwell Cons. Engrs., Pasadena, Calif., 1977-79; water quality engr. Met. Water Dist. of So. Calif., Los Angeles, 1979—; cons. environ. engr., 1979—; instr. Temple U., Phila., 1974; cons. to subcom. on adsorbents, safe drinking water com. Nat. Acad. Scis., 1978-79. Registered profl. engr., Pa., N.J., Calif. Mem. Am. Water Works Assn. (Acad. Achievement award 1978, edn. div. chmn. 1982-83, vice chmn. Calif.-Nev. sect. water quality and resources div. 1982-83; joint tng. coordinating com. 1982-83; trustee Research Found. 1983—), Am. Chem. Soc., ASCE, Nat. Mgmt. Assn., Water Pollution Control Fedn., Assn. Bds. Certification (vice chmn. joint tng. coordinating com.), Sigma Xi, Sigma Nu, Sigma Tau. Editor: (with I.H. Suffet) Activated Carbon Adsorption of Organics From the Aqueous Phase, 2 vols., 1980; Treatment of Water by Granular Activated Carbon, 1983; Activated Carbon Treatment: Water Process Applications, 1983; contbr. articles to profl. jours. Office: Met Water Dist of So Calif 700 N Moreno Ave LaVerne CA 91750

MCHENRY, VERE A., ednl. adminstr.; b. Murray, Utah, Jan. 5, 1928; s. Samuel B. and Florence Jane (McGhie) McH.; m. Barbara Jean Oliver, July 19, 1948; children—Debra Kaye Flink, Charles Kevin, Barbara Deon, Samuel Scott. B.S., U. Utah, 1950, M.S., 1954, Ed.D., 1965; postgrad. Stanford U., 1960-61. Social studies tchr. Murray (Utah) High Sch., 1949-51, 53-54; elem. sch. prin., Murray, 1954-60; adminstrv. asst. Sunnyvale (Calif.) Sch. Dist., 1960-61; prin. jr. high sch., Murray, 1961-65; dir. curriculum Murray Sch. Dist., 1965; tchr. edn. and profl. relations Utah State Office Edn., 1965-69, adminstr., coordinator staff devel., 1969—; cons. program devel. and profl. practices. Mem. Murray City Bd. Edn., 1968-76; mem. Murray Community Council, 1970-76. Served with USAF, 1951-53, to lt. col. USAFR, 1953-81. Decorated Disting. Service medal; recipient Tchr. Educator of Year award Utah Assn. Tchr. Educators, 1981. Mem. Assn. Tchr. Educators, Nat. Assn. State Dirs. Tchr. Edn. and Cert., NEA, Utah Edn. Assn., Phi Delta Kappa. Mormon. Club: Lions. Contbr. numerous articles to ednl. jours.

MCHUGH, MARGARET ANN GLOE, psychotherapist, psychologist; b. Salt Lake City, Nov. 8, 1920; d. Harold Henry and Olive (Warenski) Gloe; B.A., U. Utah, 1942; M.A. in Edn., Idaho State U., 1964; Ph.D., U. Oreg., 1970; m. William T. McHugh, Oct. 1, 1943; children—Mary Margaret McHugh-Shuford, William Michael, Michelle. Tchr. kindergarten, Idaho Falls, Idaho, 1951-62, tchr. high sch. English, 1962-63; counselor Counseling Center, Idaho State U., Pocatello, 1964-67; instr. U. Oreg., Eugene, 1967-70; asst. prof. U. Victoria (B.C., Can.), 1970-76; therapist Peninsula Counseling Center, Port Angeles and Sequim, Wash., 1976-81; counselor/therapist McHugh & Assos., Counseling Center, Sequim, 1981—. Served with WAVES, 1944-46. Lic. psychologist. Mem. Am. Psychol. Assn., Am. Personnel and Guidance Assn., Western Psychol. Assn. Research on women in relationships, also depression and women. Home: 249 F Cameron Rd Sequim WA 98382 Office: McHugh & Assos Counseling Center PO Box 1326 336 Washington Sq Sequim WA 98382

MC HURON, CLARK ERNEST, constrn. geologist; b. Skaneateles, N.Y., Sept. 13, 1918; s. Ernest Lewis and Esther Florence (Patterson) McH.; A.B., Syracuse U., 1940; postgrad. Brown U., 1940-42; m. J. Jean Taylor, Feb. 28, 1942; children—David Clark, Gregory Ivan, Eric Jay, Barbara Marjean. Geographer, Army Map Service, Washington, 1942-44; asst. liaison geologist U.S. Bur. Reclamation, 1946-47; project geologist Boysen Dam, Wyo., 1947-50, project geologist, Palmer, Alaska, 1950-51, dist. geologist, Alaska, 1951-53; now cons. constrn. geologist, Santa Rosa, Calif.; mem. constrn. com. U.S. Com. on Large Dams. Mem. geologic hazards com. Sonoma County, 1975-76. Served to lt. (j.g.) USNR, 1944-46; PTO. Fellow Geol. Soc. Am.; mem. Assn. Engring. Geologists, Internat. Soc. Rock Mechanics, Beavers, Am. Arbitration Assn. (panel arbitrators). Republican. Clubs: Oakmont Golf, Masons. Address: 274 Mocking Bird Circle Santa Rosa CA 95405

MCINERNEY, CHARLES EDWARD, mechanical engineer; b. Globe, Ariz., Mar. 24, 1936; s. John Thomas and Lura Bessie (McBrien) McI.; m. Janice K. Frank, Aug. 1, 1964; children—Shawn Patrick, Christopher Dean. B.S. in Mech. Engring., U. Ariz., 1958. Drilling engr. Shell Oil Co., 1958-62; automotive engr. Airesearch Indsl. div. Garrett Corp., Torrance, Calif., 1962-83, head European turbocharger applications, 1979-81, mgr. central engring., 1982-83; owner McInerney's Auto Parts, Coos Bay, Oreg., 1983—. Mem. Soc. Automotive Engrs. Patentee engine turbocharger systems. Office: 140 S Schoneman Coos Bay OR 97420

MCINERNEY, WILLIAM DAVID, litigation cons.; b. Northampton, Mass., Dec. 27, 1925; s. Joseph Morgan and Mary Theresa (Mercure) McI.; student U. Rochester, 1954, Eastern Ky. U., 1972, U. Ky., 1972, 73, U. Louisville, 1975; m. Sandra Jean Schultz, June 6, 1959; children—Patricia, Eileen, William, Maura, Megan, Erin, Shannon. Archtl. hardware cons. Edward Hines Lumber Co., Skokie, Ill., 1957-64; sales engr. Prison Equipment, Herrick Pacific Corp., Hayward, Calif., 1964-68; v.p., gen. mgr. Muni-Quip Corp. div. Duncan Industries, Elk Grove Village, Ill., 1968-71; asst. dir. Nat. Crime Prevention Inst., Sch. Police Adminstrn., U. Louisville, 1971-76; mktg. and tech. cons., Anchorage, Ky., 1976-78; phys. security specialist, civil engring. lab. U.S. Navy, Port Hueneme, Calif., 1978—; expert witness in litigation involving security matters; nat. and internat. lectr. Apptd. mem. Ky. Bldg. Security Study Commn., 1975. Served with USMC, WW II and Korea. Mem. Am. Mgmt. Assn. (crimes against bus. council 1977), Associated Locksmiths of Am. (charter), Comml. and Indsl. Equipment Users Adv. Conf., Underwriters Labs. Inc., Soc. Archtl. Hardware Consultants, ASTM, Am. Soc. Indsl. Security (charter mem., cert. protection profl.), Security Equipment Industry Assn., Internat. Soc. Crime Prevention Practitioners, Internat. Assn. Chiefs of Police, Nat. Sheriffs Assn., Am. Correctional Assn., Door and Hardware Inst., Am. Legion, Order Ky. Cols. Republican. Club: Elks. Contbr. articles to profl. jours. Home: 3711 Tiller Dr Oxnard CA 93030 Office: Security Engring Div US Naval Civil Engring Lab Port Hueneme CA 93043

MCINTOSH, LOWRIE WENDELL, management consultant; b. Denver, Sept. 5, 1926; s. Lee Roy and Pearl (Jones) McI.; B.S., U. Denver, 1951; M.B.A., NYU, 1958; children—Lisa, David, Tricia. Project engr. prodn. control systems Pitney-Bowes, Inc., Stamford, Conn., 1953-58; mng. assoc. mgmt. services Arthur Young & Co., N.Y.C., 1958-65; v.p. adminstrn. No. Trust Co. of Chgo., 1965-69; corp. v.p. MIS, Lone Star Industries, Greenwich, Conn., 1969-72; pres. Informaco, Inc., N.Y.C., 1972-78, Infologics, Inc., Los Angeles, 1978—; instr., Bridgeport Engring. Inst., 1952-55; adj. prof. NYU, 1955-58. Served with USNR, 1944-46, 51-52. Registered profl. engr., Calif.; cert. records mgr. Mem. Am. Inst. Indsl. Engrs. (sr.), Fin. Execs. Inst., Soc. Mgmt. Info. Systems, Newcomen Soc. Contbr.: Ency. Sci. and Tech., 1969; Industrial Engineering Handbook, 1969. Office: 221 E Walnut St Suite 250 Pasadena CA 91101

MCINTYRE, ARLOW CARROLL, marketing executive; b. Mpls., Jan. 31, 1922; s. Harold and Agnes C. (Hill) McI.; m. Juanita Delena McBee, Aug. 17, 1946; children—Kathleen Denise, Brian Douglas, Terry Lee. B.A. cum laude, U. So. Calif., 1952. C.P.A., Calif. Auditor Touche, Niven, Bailey & Ross, Los Angeles, 1950-52; pvt. practice pub. acctg., Los Angeles, 1952-58; mktg. dir., comptroller Gainey Ceramics, La Verne, Calif., 1958—, Dragon Valves, Norwalk, Calif., 1958—; cons. in field. Served with USMC, 1940-48. Mem. Calif. Soc. C.P.A.s. Republican. Mem. Christian Ch.

MCINTYRE, CECIL WILLIS, services co. exec.; b. Boone, Iowa, Sept. 21, 1923; s. Cecil Albert and Alma (Staffsburg) McI.; student Cornell (Iowa) Coll., 1942-43; B.S.E., Drake U., 1947, M.S.W., 1951; postgrad. U. Wash., 1959; m. Ruth F. Ross, Nov. 23, 1944; children—Richard Lee, William Dennis, Douglas S. Tchr. sci., Valley High Sch., West Des Moines, 1947-55; serviceman Roto Rooter, Tacoma, 1955-56; buyer, Rhodes Camera Co., Tacoma, 1956-57; tchr. sci. Peninsula High Sch., Gig Harbor, Wash., 1957-64; mgr. Roto Rooter Service, Tacoma, 1964-69, owner, mgr., 1970—. Bd. dirs. Teen Life Internat., 1976—; mem. Wash. State Friendship Force to Korea, 1980. Served with USNR, 1943-46. Recipient Service award Christian Compassion for Children, 1980. Mem. Nat. Fedn. Ind. Bus., NEA, Peninsula Edn. Assn., Tacoma Photog. Soc. Home: 1935 50th Ave NW Gig Harbor WA 98335 Office: 4001 S 12th St Tacoma WA 98405

MC INTYRE, MAXINE, communications cons.; b. Clovis, N.Mex., Jan. 1, 1937; d. Chester Daniel and Dovie Ione (Taylor) Woltmon; B.A., Calif. State U., Sacramento, 1973, M.A., 1974; divorced; children—Janet, Lynette, Melanie, Elizabeth, Kristine, Robert II. Pres. M.B.R. Ednl. Resorces Inc., Fair Oaks, Calif., 1977—, McIntyre Enterprises, Fair Oaks, 1975—; instr. Calif. State U., Sacramento, 1974-76, Am. River Coll., Sacramento, 1974-78; mem. faculty Golden Gate U., San Francisco, 1979; tchr. police acads. and depts., criminal justice orgns., 1974—; tng. seminar instr., profl. platform speaker, 1978—. Mem. Nat. Speakers Assn., Internat. Platform Assn., Calif. Assn. Police Tng. Officers, Aircraft Owners and Pilots Assn. Co-author: (anthology) Here is Genius, 1980; (tng. manual) Build A Better You-Starting Now, 10th edit., 1980, Non-Verbal Cues as Danger Indicators to Police Officers, 1975; author articles in field. Address: 4725 Rustic Rd Fair Oaks CA 95628

MCINTYRE, ROBERT M., natural gas company executive; b. 1923. B.A., UCLA. Gen. sales mgr. So. Counties Gas Co. of Calif., 1952-70; v.p., asst. to chmn. bd. So. Calif. Gas Co., Los Angeles, 1970, sr. v.p., 1974-80, pres., 1980—, also dir. Office: So Calif Gas Co Inc 810 S Flower St Los Angeles CA 90017*

MCJUNKIN, JAMES D., hospitality industry consultant; b. Asheville, N.C., Nov. 5, 1931; s. Ambrose Milton and Lillian M. (McJunkin) Ducker. B.A. in Social Sci., Western Carolina U., 1954; postgrad. U. Calif., 1963-65. With Nat. Can Corp., Chgo., 1961-68; dir. corp. indsl. relations Rollins, Inc., Atlanta, 1968-70, ptnr., prin. Ennis & McJunkin, Los Angeles, 1970—. Served with U.S. Army, 1954-56. Democrat. Mem. Soc. of Friends. Office: 5410 W Imperial Hwy Los Angeles CA 90045

MC KASSON, ROBERT EDWARD, JR., insurance sales executive; b. Los Angeles, Feb. 3, 1945; s. Robert E. and Verda C. (White) McK.; A.A., Fullerton Coll., 1967. Salesman various life ins. cos., 1967—; pres., chmn. bd. Ind. Bankers Ins. Services, Santa Ana, Calif., 1977—. Recipient Gold medal ins. sales awards, 1976, 78; Bronze medal Investors Guaranty Life, 1979. Mem. 6 Million Dollar Forum. Club: 20-30. Featured in Nat. Underwriter, Aug. 1983. Home: 124 31st St Newport Beach CA 92660 Office: 124 31st St Newport Beach CA 92663

MC KAUGHAN, HOWARD PAUL, educator; b. Canoga Park, Calif., July 5, 1922; s. Paul and Edith (Barton) McK.; A.B., UCLA, 1945; M.Th., Dallas Theol. Sem., 1946; M.A., Cornell U., 1952, Ph.D., 1957; m. Barbara Jean Budroe, Dec. 25, 1943; children—Edith (Mrs. Daniel Skene Santoro), Charlotte (Mrs. Martin Douglas Barnhart), Patricia (Mrs. Stephen B. Pike), Barbara (Mrs. Ronald Chester Bell), Judith (Mrs. Frank L. Achilles III). Mem. linguistic research team Summer Inst. Linguistics, Mexico, 1946-52; asso. dir. Summer Inst. Linguistics, Philippines, also asso. dir. summer sessions U. N.D., 1952-57, dir. Philippine br., 1957-61; research asst. prof. anthropology U. Wash., 1961-62; research asso. prof., 1962-63; asso. prof. linguistics U. Hawaii, 1963-64, prof. linguistics, 1964—, chmn. dept., 1963-66, dir. Pacific and Asian Linguistics Inst., 1964, 1966-69, asso. dean grad. div., 1965-72, dean grad. div., dir. research, 1972-79, acting chancellor, 1979; interim vice chancellor acad. affairs, 1981-82; lectr. linguistics U. Philippines, summers, 1954, 60; Fulbright vis. prof. Philippine Normal Coll.-Ateneo Consortium, Philippines, 1977; prin. Wycliffe Sch. Linguistics, summers 1953, 61; vis. prof. Australian Nat. U., Canberra, 1970. Sr. scholar East-West Center, Honolulu, 1964; NDEA Maranao-Philippines research grantee, 1963-65; Office of Edn. Hawaii English grantee, 1965-66; NSF Jeh Language of South Vietnam grantee, 1969-70, Maranao Linguistic Studies, 1971-72, numerous other research grants. Mem. linguistic socs. Am., Philippines, Western Assn. Grad. Schs. (pres. 1978), Hawaii, Linguistic Circle N.Y., Philippine Assn. Lang. Tchrs., Hawaii Govt. Employees Assn., Phi Beta Kappa, Phi Kappa Phi. Author (with B. McKaughan): Chatino Dictionary, 1951; (with J. Forster) Ilocano: An Intensive Language Course, 1952; The Inflection and Syntax of Maranao Verbs, 1959; (with B. Macaraya): A Maranao Dictionary, 1967. Editor: Pali Language Texts: Philippines, 21 vols., 1971; The Languages of the Eastern Family of the East New Guinea Highlands Stock, 1973. Contbr. articles, chpts. to books, sci. jours. Home: 3670 Alani Dr Honolulu HI 96822

MCKAY, BRIAN, attorney general of Nevada. A.B., Colgate U., 1971; J.D., Albany Law Sch., 1974. Bar: Nev. Ptnr. Sully, McKay and Lenhard, Las Vegas, 1979-82; dep. atty. gen. State of Nev., 1975-79, atty. gen., 1982—; chmn. Young Consumers Law Edn. Project; mem. Nev. Transp. Bd. Active Boys Club, March of Dimes, Multiple Sclerosis Soc. Served with USAF. Mem. Nat. Assn. Attys. Gen. (commerce, corrections and instl. confinement and environ. control coms.). Office: Office of Atty Gen Capitol Complex Carson City NV 89710*

MCKAY, MONROE GUNN, judge; b. Huntsville, Utah, May 30, 1928; s. James Gunn and Elizabeth (Peterson) McK.; B.S., Brigham Young U., 1957; J.D., U. Chgo., 1960; m. Lucile A. Kinnison, Aug. 6, 1954; children—Michele, Valanne, Margaret, James, Melanie, Nathan, Bruce, Lisa, Monroe. Admitted to Ariz. bar, 1961; law clk. Ariz. Supreme Ct., 1960-61; assoc. firm Lewis & Roca, Phoenix, 1961-66, ptnr., 1968-74; assoc. prof. Brigham Young U., 1974-76, prof., 1976-77; judge U.S. Circuit Ct. Appeals, 10th circuit, Denver, 1977—. Mem. Phoenix Community Council Juvenile Problems, 1968-74; pres. Ariz. Assn. for Health and Welfare, 1970-72; dir. Peace Corps, Malawi, Africa, 1966-68; bd. dirs., pres. Maricopa county Legal Aid Soc., 1972-74. Served with USMCR, 1946-48. Mem. Ariz. Bar Assn., Maricopa County Bar Assn., Am. Judicature Soc., Am. Law Inst., Order Coif, Blue Key, Phi Kappa Phi. Address: US Court of Appeals 6012 Federal Bldg 125 S State St Salt Lake City UT 84138

MCKEAN, JOHN ROBERT, accountant; b. Evanston, Ill., May 30, 1930; s. Cuthbert and Mary E. (Ford) McK.; m. Mary M. Costoglus, June 17, 1956; children—John R., Pamela, Jacqueline. B.S., U. San Francisco, 1951; M.B.A., Golden Gate U., 1976. C.P.A., Calif. Controller, Hwy. Transport Inc., San Francisco, 1948-56; acct. George Kasch, C.P.A., San Francisco, 1956-58; prin. John R. McKean, C.P.A., San Francisco, 1958-73, pres., 1973—. Pres.'s ambassador U. San Francisco; pres. parish council Greek Orthodox Ch. of the Ascension, 1963-67; pres. Hearing Limited, 1964-68; bd. govs. U.S. Postal Service, 1983—. Recipient Outstanding Alumnus award Golden Gate U., 1980. Mem. Am. Inst. C.P.A.s, Calif. Soc. C.P.A.s, Nat. Acctg. and Fin. Council, Am. Acctg. Assn., Acctg. Research Assn. Club: San Francisco Commercial. Author articles in field. Home: 1596 Daily Ct San Leandro CA 94577 Office: One California St Suite 1200 San Francisco CA 94111

MCKEE, BILL EARL, mining co. exec.; b. Sidney, Mont., Dec. 28, 1916; s. Earl Linn and Frances Elizabeth (Michaels) McK.; B.S., U. Idaho, 1937; m. Natalie Parks, Aug 31, 1941; children—Jerome Storm, Maureen Katherine, Craig North. With U.S. Forest Service, 1937-40; sr. design and flight test engr. Boeing Co., 1941-46; sales engr. C.M. Lovsted & Co., Seattle, 1947-54; pres. Atlas Boiler & Equipment Co., Spokane, Wash., 1955-56; pvt. practice cons. and sales engring., Spokane, 1957-64; project engr. Hecla Mining Co., Wallace, Idaho, 1965-67, gen. supt., 1967-80; pres. M&M Engring., Inc., 1981—; vis. prof. metallurgy U. Idaho, 1982—. Chmn. bd. South Fork Coeur D'Alene Sewer Dist., 1975-79. Registered profl. engr., Idaho, Mont.; NASA fellow, 1983. Mem. Am. Inst. Mining, Metall. and Petroleum Engrs., Idaho, N.W. mining assns., Exptl. Aircraft Assn., Idaho Safe Pilots, Aircraft Owners and Pilots Assn. Republican. Episcopalian. Clubs: Spokane, Elks. Inventor child's toy. Home: Box 242 Wallace ID 83873 Office: Box 242 Wallace ID 83873

MC KEE, JOHN CAROTHERS, indsl. psychologist; b. San Diego, Apr. 25, 1912; s. John Joseph and Margaret (Giesman) McK.; B.A., U. So. Calif., 1935, M.A., 1937; Ph.D., Tulane U., 1947; m. Gladys Irene Michel, Jan. 10, 1941 (dec. Feb. 1968); children—John Michael, Hillary Barbara; m. 2d, Sara Forman, June 25, 1968; one son, Evan. Gen. mgr. Hotel Royal, La Ceiba, Honduras, 1932-33; mgmt. cons. Douglas Aircraft Co., Long Beach, Calif., 1942-67, exec. adviser, dir. operations control, 1967—, also pres. mgmt. assn. Douglas Space Systems Center; exec. adviser fin. mgmt. McDonnell Douglas Astronautics, v.p. Santa Monica Health Spot Shoe Corp., 1949—; pres. McKee Mgmt. Center, Volumetrics, Inc., Mentron Corp.; exec. v.p. Consearch Inc.; pres. McKee Mgmt. Center, Stanton, Calif., Quantek Internat. Inc.; partner McKee & Wright and Assn., Stanton; v.p. Advion Corp.; lectr. Acad. of Justice, Riverside, Calif.; cons. Space Systems Center, Huntington Beach, Calif., 1964—; cons. Hanford, Orange, Cypress police depts. (all Calif.); dir. Consultron, Inc. Pres. sports council YMCA; bd. dirs. Long Beach YMCA. Asso. dir. Mgmt. Center, Chapman Coll.; bd. dirs. McKee Wright La Verne Coll. Mgmt. Center, Cavaliers Fencing Schs., 1935—, Law Enforcement Mgmt. Center, Calif.; mgr. Stanton Bd. Trade, 1978—. Recipient Personagraph Speaker of Yr. Award, Indsl. Mgmt. Assn.; Charles R. Able citation for co. mgmt., Certificate of Merit, Amateur Fencers League Am.; named Cavalier Fencing Coach of Yr., 1982; cert. instr. Calif. Dept. Justice POST program. Mem. Internat. Platform Assn., Am. Statis. Assn. (past pres., mem. nat. council). Nat. Mgmt. Assn. (recipient Silver Knight of Mgmt., 1961, v.p. area council), Nat. Assn. Chiefs of Police, Internat. Assn. Chiefs Police, Calif. Assn. Police Tng. Officers, Fedn. Internationale D'Esgrime, Amateur Fencers League Am., A.A.A.S., C. of C. (mem. research com. of Los Angeles), Inst. Mgmt. Scis., Am. Assn. Indsl. Editors, Internat. Council Indsl. Editors, So. Cal. Indsl. Editors Assn., Nat. Assn. Bus. Economists, Orange County Econ. Roundtable (Exec. of Year award, pres.), Calif. Adminstrn. Justice Educators, Calif. Assn. Peace Officers, Phi Beta Kappa. Author: Learning Curves, Quantity-Cost Curves, Estimating Engineering Costs, Systems Analysis, Cost and Budgeting Analysis and Statistics for Non-Mathematical Managers; Zero Base Budgeting; The Fencer's Work Book; Fiscal Management. Home: 16509 Harbour Lane Huntington CA 92649 Office: McKee Wright Mgmt Center 10801 Dale St Stanton CA 90680

MCKEE, JOSEPH FULTON, engineering and construction executive; b. Placerville, Calif., Apr. 28, 1921; s. Joseph Fulton and Pearl Margarite (Varroza) McK.; m. Eva Deane Adcock, Mar. 15, 1949 (dec.); m. 2d, Sharon Lucille Ricketts Adamson, Jan. 23, 1982; children—Robert Deane, Renee E. Hackbarth. B.C.E., U. Santa Clara, 1947. Constrn. engr. Western Contracting Corp., 1947-50; supt., project engr., gen. supt. constrn. Morrison-Knudsen Co., Western U.S., 1950-54; project engr., constrn. mgr. Morocco, 1954-57, constrn. mgr., Iran, 1957-60, worldwide, 1960-65, area mgr. Australia, 1965-73, v.p. Europe, Africa, Mid-East, 1973-77, sr. v.p., Tehran, Iran, 1977-80, sr. v.p., Boise, Idaho, 1981—; project dir. Cerrejon Coal Project, Colombia, S.Am. Served to Lt. (j.g.) USN 1943-46. Mem. ASCE, Chi Epsilon, Tau Beta Pi. Republican. Roman Catholic. Office: PO Box 7808 Boise ID 83729

MCKEE, MOLLY T., software company executive; b. Kansas City, Mo., Oct. 7, 1942; d. Jack Henry and Mary Frances (Welsh) Turner; divorced; 1 son, Micah David. B.A. in Anthropology, U. Calif.-Santa Barbara, 1966, B.A. in Sociology, 1966, postgrad. in sociology, 1967. Program coordinator Job Corps, YWCA Extension Program, Oakland, Calif., 1968-70; asst. dir. People's Clinic, Boulder, Colo., 1973-76; staff asst. to Congressman Tim Wirth, Boulder-Denver, 1976-77; asst. dir. Emergency Family Assistance Assn., Boulder, 1977; adminstr., mgr. Mountain High, Inc., Boulder and Denver, 1977-80; dep. asst. Boulder Dept. Human Resources, 1980-81; mgr. adminstrn. Precision Visuals, Inc., Boulder, 1981—; dir., corp. sec. Magadel Plexi-Art Engravers; dir. The Catalyst Group. Mem. Boulder City Human Relations Commn., 1975-77, Boulder County Community Action Program, 1974-77; bd. dirs. People's Clinic, 1973-77. Mem. Boulder Area Personnel Assn., NOW, Nat. Abortion Rights League, Nat. Assn. for Female Execs. Office: 6260 Lookout Rd Boulder CO 80301

MC KEE, RAYMOND WALTER, certified public accountant; b. Joplin, Mo., Dec. 24, 1899; s. Charles Edward and Sarah Ellen (Epperson) McK.; student pub. schs., Joplin; m. Frances Ida Howe, Nov. 1, 1947; children—Michael, David, Roderick, Duncan, Malcolm, Brude. Acct., Price, Waterhouse & Co., 1923-25, Haskins & Sells, 1925-26; individual practice acctg., La Puente, Calif., 1964—; lectr. St. Louis U., 1923-24; v.p. Richfield Oil Corp., Pan Am. Petroleum Corp., 1928-30; sec. West Coast Air Transport, 1926-30; sec.-treas. West Coast div. Anchor Hocking Corp.; dir., v.p. Maywood Mut. Water Co.; pres. Cross Water Co. C.P.A., Calif. Club: Lions. Author: Accounting for Petroleum Industry, 1925; Petroleum Accounting, 1938; Book of McKee, 1959. Home and office: 738 S 3d Ave La Puente CA 91746

MCKEE, RICHARD PHILIP, advertising/broadcasting executive, consultant; b. N.Y.C., June 10, 1930; s. Joseph V. and Cornelia (Kraft) Mck.; m. Virginia C. Alicoate, Oct. 16, 1954; children—Michael, Christopher, Matthew, Teresa, Stephen. B.S.S., Georgetown U., 1952. Gen. mgr. Sta. KOB-AM & FM, Albuquerque, 1969-74; pres. Aloha Broadcasting Co., Honolulu, 1975-77; gen. mgr. Sta. KRKE AM/FM, Albuquerque, 1977-80; v.p. Summit Communications Okla. Inc., Oklahoma City, 1981; mgr. pub. info. Jacobs Engring. Group, Albuquerque, 1982; v.p. Sandia Advt., Albuquerque, 1983—; pres. Dick McKee & Assocs. Media Cons., 1974—. Commr., Bernalillo County (N.Mex.), 1974; pres. bd. trustees Bernalillo County Mental Health Ctr., 1979. Served with Signal Corps, U.S. Army, 1952-54. Named Broadcaster of Year, N.Mex. Broadcasters Assn., 1980. Mem. N.Mex. Advt. Fedn., Pub. Relations Soc. Am. Republican. Roman Catholic. Home: 9631 Village Green NE Albuquerque NM 87111 Office: Sandia Advt 3702 Matthew NE Albuquerque NM 87107

MC KEE, ROSS RAYMOND, music coll. adminstr.; b. Seattle, Aug. 2, 1914; s. Adam Elmer and Anna (Fett) McK.; grad. Manning Sch. Music, San Francisco, 1933, San Francisco Navigation Sch., 1941, U.S. Navy Sch. for Chaplains and Welfare Specialists, Coll. of William and Mary, 1943; pupil Paul Pierre Mc Neely, John Crogan Manning, Wager Swayne, Rosalyn Tureck, Ernst von Dohnany, Alexander Tcherepnine. Pianist, concerts throughout U.S.; organist, choir condr.; dir. Music and Arts Inst., San Francisco, 1934—. Served with USN, 1943-46. Mem. Music Tchrs. Assn. Calif. (sec. 1934), San Francisco Music Tchrs. Assn. (pres. 1960, 61), Am. Guild Organists, Pacific Mus. Soc., Calif. Music Execs., Nat. Assn. Schs. Music, Assn. Calif. Educators (dir. 1977—). Christian Scientist. Home: 2622 Jackson St San Francisco CA 94115 Office: Music and Arts Inst San Francisco Inc 2622 Jackson St San Francisco CA 94115

MC KEE, TIMOTHY GENE, education; b. Perrin AFB, Tex., Apr. 27, 1945; s. Earl R. and Ella Nadine (Sowder) McK.; student U. Florence (Italy), 1966, UCLA, 1969, B.A., Okla. Christian Coll., 1967; M.A., Pepperdine U., 1970, Loyola U., 1971; Ph.D., Calif. Grad. Sch. Theology, 1973; M.S., Pepperdine U., 1978, Ed.D., 1981; Ph.D., Grace Grad. Sch., 1979; postgrad. Fuller Theol. Sem., 1979—; m. Judith Rae Covalt, May 10, 1969; children—Dana Cheryl, Timothy Ray. Adult edn. tchr. Los Angeles Public Schs., 1969-70, tchr. elem. grades, 1968-70, resource guidance tchr., 1970-71; dir. youth and edn. Inglewood (Calif.) Ch. of Christ, 1971-72; instr. continuing edn. Pepperdine U., Inglewood, 1972-73; founder and adminstr. Good News Christian Acad., Los Angeles, 1973-79; adminstr. Pioneer Christian Sch., Norwalk, Calif., 1975-79; asst. prof. Grace Grad. Sch., 1978—; v.p. Mission Tng. and Resource Center, Pasadena, Calif., 1978-79, now exec. v.p.; ednl. cons., 1970—. Mem. Nat. Christian Sch. Adminstrs. Assn., Center for Law and Religious Freedom, World Future Soc., Fin. Execs. Christian Orgns., Assn. Supervision and Curriculum Devel., Inst. Mgmt. Sci., Nat. Fellowship Christian Sch. Adminstrs., Internat. Assn. Cross-Cultural Psychology, Missionary Aviation Fellowship, Soc. Intercultural Tng. and Research, World Future Soc., Speech Communication Assn., Phi Delta Kappa. Republican. Mem. Ch. of Christ. Contbg. author curriculum for books of Acts, Romans and Galatians, 1969, Genesis, 1971. Home: 4772 Raymond Dr LaVerne CA 91750 Office: 221 E Walnut Pasadena CA 91101

MCKEEL, R. BRUCE, investment banker; b. Oregon City, Oreg., Apr. 13, 1942; s. Ralph Orman and Gladys Anna (Palmer) McK.; m. Lynn E. Mackey, Feb. 14, 1976. B.A., U. Oreg., 1964. Investment banker Davis Skaggs & Co., San Francisco, 1968-73; v.p. HBE Leasing Corp., San Francisco, 1973-75; v.p. leverage leasing Equilease Corp. subs. Eltra Corp., San Francisco, 1975-77; pres., founder, dir. Qartel Corp., San Francisco, 1977-79; v.p. leverage leasing, spl. fin. project Prescott Ball & Turben, San Francisco, 1979-80; founder, chmn. bd., pres. McKeel & Co. Inc., 1980—; spl. project fin. cons. to various nat. cos., 1979—. Vice chmn. spl. gifts United Crusade, 1978. Recipient cert. distinction N.Y. Inst. Fin., 1968. Mem. Western Assn. Equipment Lessors (past officer, dir.), Am. Assn. Equipment Lessors. Republican. Episcopalian. Clubs: Olympic of San Francisco, Family, Mchts. Exchange, San Francisco Bond, Hillsborough Racquet. Home: 560 Hayne Rd Hillsborough CA 94010 Office: 500 Sansome St San Francisco CA 94111

MCKELLIPS, ANN BRANCH DASCH, communications executive; b. Lynchburg, Va., Apr. 19, 1937; d. Marion Stuart and Mary Catharine (Mitchell) Branch; m. Robert E. Dasch, June 18, 1960; children—Robert B., Valeria A.; m. James M. McKellips, Oct. 25, 1981. B.S., Towson State U., 1959. Editor-in-chief Bull. of Am. Iris Soc., 1979-81; mng. editor Stockton (Calif.) News, 1981; communications coordinator Better Bus. Bur. Mid-Counties Inc., Stockton, 1982; founder, pres. A.D. Communications; workshop, seminar instr. San Joaquin Delta Coll. Pub. relations dir. Malcolm McKnight's campaign for Congress, 2d Dist. Md., 1979. Contbr. numerous articles to various nat. and local publs.

MCKENDRICK, MAURICE NILSSON, ret. waterworks equipment company manager; b. Salt Lake City, Jan. 11, 1914; s. John Edward and Nellie (Smith) M.; B.C.E., U. Utah, 1936; m. Agnes Lucille Coles, Nov. 20, 1937; children—Agness Ann, John Charles. Rodman, U.S. Bur. Reclamation, Provo, Utah, 1936-38, asst. office engr., 1938-42; constrn. engr. Koppers Co. and George A. Fuller Co., Geneva Steel Plant (Utah), 1942-44; designer, adminstrv. asst. U.S. Army Tooele Ordnance Depot (Utah), 1945; asst. engr. sewers, engring. dept. Salt Lake City Corp., 1946-55; environ. engr. Waterworks Equipment Co., Salt Lake City, 1955-80, credit mgr., 1973-80. Registered profl. engr., Utah; recipient asso. award Nat. Inst. Credit, 1976. Fellow ASCE; mem. Utah Water Pollution Control Assn. (pres. 1963), Beta Theta Pi, Theta Tau (Intermountain Alumni pres. 1957). Clubs: Kiwanis (pres. 1967), West Side Asso. Duck (pres. 1980-81), Wasatch Gun (pres. 1979—). Home: 2589 E Commonwealth St Salt Lake City UT 84109

MCKENRY, JAMES PARIS, state ofcl.; b. Richmond, Va., Jan. 11, 1949; s. John Archibald and Natalie (Paris) McK., Jr.; B.S. in Human Relations and Organizational Behavior, U. San Francisco, 1981; M.P.A., Kennedy Sch. Govt., Harvard U., 1982; m. Michelle Martin, Dec. 4, 1976; children—Cynthia Lee, Jessica. Criminal investigator firm Opie & Lorden, Ayer, Mass., 1972-74; investment counsellor Marad Corp., Wellesley, Mass., 1974; Nev. Intergovtl. Personnel Act coordinator, exec. sec. Nev. Gov.'s Intergovtl. Personnel Adv. Com., Carson City, 1975-81; cons., writer fed. grants, 1975-81; adminstr. div. adminstrv. services Nev. Dept. Indsl. Relations, 1982—. Served with U.S. Army, 1969-72. Recipient cert. of appreciation Am. Soc. for Tng. and Devel., 1975. Mem. Nat. Soc. Public Adminstrn., Internat. Personnel Mgmt. Assn., Am. Mgmt. Assn., Cousteau Soc., Porsche Club Am. Methodist. Co-author: The Nevada IPA Experience: An Evaluation of the Impact of the Intergovernmental Personnel Act in the State of Nevada, 1978. Office: Nev Dept Indsl Relations 1390 S Curry St Carson City NV 89710

MCKENZIE, JAMES BASIL, producer; b. Appleton, Wis., May 1, 1926; s. Basil F. and Helen (Sherman) McK.; student U. Wis., 1944-45; B.A., U. Iowa, 1950, M.A., Columbia, U., 1952; m. Jeanne Bolan, 1950 (dec. 1976); children—David, Kevin, Amy, Agatha. Stage mgr. Peninsula Players Theatre Found., Inc., Fish Creek, Wis., 1946-51, press agent, 1952-54, mgr., 1955-59, producer, 1960—; press agt. Showcase Theatre, Evanston, Ill., 1954, Fred Miller Theatre, Milw., 1954; coordinator news CBS-TV, N.Y.C., 1956-57, NBC-TV, N.Y.C., 1950-52; exec. producer Conn. Theatre Found. Inc., Westport, 1959—, Am. Conservatory Theatre, San Francisco, 1968—; gen. mgr. The Celebrity Room, Palm Beach, Fla., 1964-68; stage mgr. Music Corp. Am. Indsl. Shows, 1956-60; producer Broadway plays including: The Girl in the Freudian Slip, 1968, And Miss Reardon Drinks a Little, 1971, The Secret Affairs of Mildred Wilde, 1974; co-producer various theatres including: Parker Playhouse, Ft. Lauderdale, Fla., 1971-74, Bucks County Playhouse, New Hope, Pa., 1970, 71, 74; pres. Producing Mgrs. Co., 1964-74, Lake Cinema, Inc., 1968-78; producer Dobbs Ferry (N.Y.) Playhouse, 1952-54, Lake George (N.Y.) Music Carnival, 1954. Served with USNR. Mem. League of N.Y. Theatres and Producers, Assn. Theatre Press Agts., Actors Equity Assn., Council of Stock Theatres (pres. 1964-70), Internat. Alliance Theatrical Stage Employees, League of Ind. Theatres of N. Am., Oceanic Soc., Nat. Geog. Inst., Ind. Booking Office (dir.). Club: Offshore Racing of Am. Office: 450 Geary St San Francisco CA 94102

MCKENZIE, MEREDITH CHRISTINE, television executive; b. Warren, Ohio, Nov. 1, 1952; d. William L. and Joan (Howell) Green; 1 dau., Christina Joan. M.A., Kent State U., 1980; postgrad. Ohio State U., 1977-78; B.A. cum laude, Bowling Green State U., 1975. Legal researcher Social Security Adminstrn., Columbus, Ohio, 1975-77; asst. dir. Univ. Council for Edn. Adminstrn., Columbus, 1977-79; producer/dir. Sta. WNEO-TV, Kent, Ohio, 1979-80; assoc. dir. program underwriting Sta. KCET/28, Los Angeles, 1980—. Chmn., Music & Fine Arts Com., Los Angeles, 1982-83; pres. bd. dirs. Hollywood Luth. Ch. Child Care Ctr., 1982-83; del. 8th Century of the Pacific Conf., Tokyo, 1982. Recipient Bronze award Internat. Film and Video Festival, N.Y.C., 1981; Bowling Green State U. Disting. Service award, 1975; numerous scholarships, fellowships. Mem. Women in Communication, AFTRA, Los Angeles Jaycees (dir.), Mortar Bd. Episcopalian. Club: Advertising. Program exec.: Giulini in Japan, 1983, Between Sound and Silence: The Living Arts of Japan, 1983, It's My Tomorrow, Too/You and Your Aging Parents, 1982, others. Office: 4401 Sunset Blvd Los Angeles CA 90027

MCKIBBON, CATHLEEN ANN, dietitian; b. Pueblo, Colo., Apr. 6, 1945; d. John Henry and Marie Elizabeth (Hunyada) McK.; student U. So. Colo., 1963-65; B.S. in Food Sci. and Nutrition, Colo. State U., 1968. Commd. 2d lt., USAF, 1968, advanced through grades to maj.; dietetic intern Beth Israel Hosp., 1968-69; resident in dietetics Andrews AFB; food service officer, 1970-72; chief clin. dietetics, clin. instr. USAF Dietetic Internship, 1972-74; food service officer, 1974-75; staff dietitian, renal dietitian, 1975-76; chief central tray service, 1976-77; asst. chief food prodn., procurement and service, 1977, resigned, 1977; dir. nutrition services Penrose Hosps., Colorado Springs, Colo., 1978—; instr. Dietetic Assistance Program, 1976-77; bd. dirs., 1980-83. Mem. Air NG, 1978—. Decorated Air Force Commendation medal. Mem. Am. Dietetic Assn. (registered), Am. Soc. Hosp. Food Service Adminstrs. (past pres. Colo. chpt.). Home: 4604 Winewood Village Dr Colorado Springs CO 80917 Office: 2215 N Cascade Ave Colorado Springs CO 80907

MCKINLEY, JOSEPH WARNER, hospital administrator; b. Champaign, Ill., Jan. 9, 1943; s. Lyle W. and Eloise M. (Coleman) McK.; B.S., Georgetown U., 1968; M.A., George Washington U., 1974; postgrad. U. Chgo., 1974-75. Asst. adminstr. Weiss Hosp., Chgo., 1973-75; asso. v.p. Rockford (Ill.) Meml. Hosp., 1975-79; v.p. ops. Meml. Hosp., Phoenix, 1979—. Served with U.S. Army, 1968-71. Mem. Am. Hosp. Assn., Nat. League for Nursing, Am. Coll. Hosp. Adminstrs., Ariz. Hosp. Assn. Republican. Episcopalian. Club: Ariz. Office: Memorial Hospital PO Box 21207 Phoenix AZ 85036

MCKINLEY, ROYCE BALDWIN, lawyer, executive; b. Ann Arbor, Mich., Feb. 20, 1921; s. Earle B. and Leola (Royce) M.; m. Roberta Schreck, Apr. 15, 1943; 1 dau., Martha Lee; m. 2d, Anne Breslin, July 7, 1973. Student Harvard U., 1938-40, J.D., 1948; A.B., U. Mich., 1942; LL.M., George Washington U., 1951. Lawyer, Posner, Berge, Fox & Arent, Washington, 1948-49; gen. counsel Nat. Grain Trade Council, Washington, 1950-52; counselor Ralston Purina Co., St. Louis, 1952-55; assoc. McKinsey & Co., Inc., Chgo. London, 1955-60; v.p., sec. Electro-Sci.-Investors, Inc., Dallas, 1960-63; v.p. fin., adminstrn. Space Gen. Corp., El Monte, Calif., 1963-66; asst. dir. mgmt. systems TRW, Inc., Redondo Beach, Calif., 1967-68; v.p. fin. sec., treas. Santa Anita Consol. Inc., Los Angeles, 1968-73; exec. v.p., chief operating officer, 1973-79; pres. chief exec. officer Santa Anita Realty Enterprises, Inc., Los Angeles, 1979—; dir. Santa Anita Realty Enterprises, Inc., Santa Anita Operating Co., Los Angeles Turf Club, Inc., Magnetic Head Corp., Santa Anita Devel. Corp., Robert H. Grant Corp. Served to lt. USN, 1943-46. Mem. Fin. Exec. Inst. Clubs: Calif., Rotary. Home: 262 S Orange Dr Los Angeles CA 90036 Office: One Wilshire Building Suite 2303 Los Angeles CA 90017

MCKINNEY, BETTY JO, editor, publisher; b. Maryville, Mo., July 16, 1941; d. Joseph Glen and Virginia Joy (Schubert) Thomas; m. George W. McKinney, Jan. 29, 1966. Student Tarkio Coll., 1961-63, Colo. State U., 1966, 72. Asst. dir. pub. relations, Tarkio (Mo.) Coll., 1963-65; publs. specialist Colo. State U., Ft. Collins, 1966—; pres. Alpine Publs., Inc., Loveland, Colo., 1975—. Mem. Women Bus. Owners Assn., Women's Ednl. Assn. Am., Nat. Writers Club, Rocky Mountain Book Pubs. Assn., Dog Writers Assn. Co-author: Sheltie Talk, 1976; Beardie Basics, 1978.

MCKINNEY, DAVID DUANE, lumber company executive; b. Lufkin, Tex., Nov. 4, 1947; s. Verlon David and Jacqueline Yvonne (Hughs) M. Student Chabot Coll., Hayward, Calif., 1966-68, Stephen F. Austin State U., 1969-70. Supr., Ravenswood City Sch. Dist., East Palo Alto, Calif., 1970-77; sales mgr. MacBeath Hardwood Co., San Francisco, 1977-82; v.p., dir. McKinney Hardwood Co., San Jose, Calif., 1982—. Mem. City of Sunnyvale (Calif.) Heritage Preservation Commn., 1983—. Mem. SAR, (treas. Palo Alto, Calif.), Soc. Calif. Pioneers. Republican. Episcopalian. Club: Commonwealth of Calif. (San Francisco). Lodges: Scottish Rite; Shriners. Office: PO Box 6772 San Jose CA 95150

MCKINNEY, JACK L., insurance executive; b. Madison, Mo., Jan. 22, 1932; s. Charles A. and Flossie N. (Lepper) McK.; m. Lillian A. Richner, June 5, 1954; children—Dennis L., Douglas M., Robert D. Student Southeastern Mo. State Coll., 1949-51, El Paso Community Coll., 1975, Sales Tng. Inst. Colo., 1975, U. N.D., 1960. Served with USAF, 1950-75; life ins. agt. Acad. Life Ins. Co., Colorado Springs, Colo., 1975-77, gen. agt., 1977-81, mng. gen. agt., 1981—; founder, sec.-treas. ANMAC Corp., Colorado Springs, Colo., 1977-82, v.p., ptnr., 1982—. Named Outstanding Airman of Yr., USAF, 1972. Mem. Noncommd. Officers Assn. (life; chmn. resolutions com., 1977-82), Air Force Assn. Office: 1900 E Pikes Peak Ave Colorado Springs CO 80909

MCKINNEY, VIOLET HELEN MARINES, banker; b. Crosby, Wyo.; d. George Chris and Edna Ester (Ekis) Marines; student Casper Coll.; m. Charles Edward McKinney; children—Richard Lars (dec.), Marvin Wayne. Dir. public relations First Wyo. Bank, Casper, 1969-78; public relations rep. First Interstate Bank of Casper, N.A., 1979—. Bd. dirs. Blue Envelope Health Fund, Sr. Citizen Projects, Salvation Army. Mem. Am. Inst. Banking, Wyo. Press Women's Assn., Casper Area C. of C. (dir. 1972-75). Lutheran. Clubs: Zonta, Daus. of Nile. Home: 2551 Belmont St Casper WY 82601 Office: Box 40 Casper WY 82602

MCKINNEY, VIRGINIA ELAINE ZUCCARO, ednl. adminstr.; b. San Francisco, Nov. 18, 1924; d. Salvadore John and Elaine Agnes (Shepard) Zuccaro; B.A., Calif. State U., Los Angeles, 1968; M.A., Calif. State U., Northridge, 1969; doctoral candidate Claremont Grad. Sch., 1977-; children—Joe McKinney, Walter Clifton McKinney. Official ct. reporter Los Angeles County Superior Cts., 1948-59; tchr. speech-reading, adult edn. Los Angeles Bd. Edn., 1966-71; lang., reading specialist Marlton Sch. for the Deaf, Los Angeles, 1971-79; founder, pres., dir. communication skills program Center for Communicative Devel., Inc., Los Angeles, 1969-; part-time lectr. spl. edn. Calif. State U., Los Angeles, 1971-; cons. for various univs. and programs for the hearing-impaired; mem. adv. com. for deaf Calif. Dept. Rehab., 1979—. Recipient Leadership award Nat. Leadership Tng. Program in Area of Deaf, Calif. State U., Northridge, 1974; NEA Project Life grantee, 1970, Gallaudet Coll. Center for Continuing Edn. grantee, 1974. Mem. Nat., Alexander Graham Bell assns. for deaf, Profl. Rehab. Workers with Adult Deaf, Am. Instrs. of Deaf, Nat. Registery Interpreters for Deaf, Am. Speech and Hearing Assn., Greater Los Angeles Council on Deafness (pres. 1970-71), Beverly-Hollywood (Calif.) Hearing Soc. (pres. 1967-68). Republican. Presbyterian. Developer, producer audio-visual media, including 22 films and 4 books, to aid in speechreading and auditory tng., 1963-68; participant research project with Project Life on devel. of communication skills for multiply-handicapped deaf adults, 1970; developer, pub. Toe-Hold Literacy Packet, 1973. Home: 4646 Los Feliz Blvd Apt 425 Los Angeles CA 90027 Office: 1819 W 6th St Los Angeles CA 90057

MC KNIGHT, LENORE RAVIN, child psychiatrist; b. Denver, May 15, 1943; d. Abe and Rose (Steed) Ravin; student Occidental Coll., 1961-63; B.A., U. Colo., 1965, postgrad. in medicine, 1965-67; M.D., U. Calif., San Francisco, 1969; m. Robert Lee McKnight, July 22, 1967; children—Richard Rex, Janet Rose. Intern pediatrics Children's Hosp., San Francisco, 1969-70; resident in gen. psychiatry Langley Porter Neuropsychiat. Inst., 1970-73, fellow child psychiatry, 1972-74; child psychiatrist Youth Guidance Center, San Francisco, 1974-74; pvt. practice medicine specializing in child psychiatry, Walnut Creek, Calif., 1974—; asst. clin. prof. Langley Porter Neuropsychiat. Inst., 1974—; asst. clin. prof. psychiatry U. Calif. San Francisco Med. Center. Diplomate Am. Bd. Psychiatry and Neurology. Internat. Insts. Edn. fellow U. Edinburgh, summer 1964; NIH grantee to study childhood nutrition, summer 1966. Mem. Am. Acad. Child Psychiatry, Am. Psychiat. Assn., Psychiat. Assn. No. Calif., Am. Med. Women's Assn., Internat., Diablo arabian horse assns. Breeder Arabian horses. Home: 3441 Echo Springs Rd Lafayette CA 94549 Office: 130 LaCasa Via Walnut Creek CA 94598

MCKOWN, KAREN MAY, employment and training specialist, computer analyst; b. Portland, Oreg., April 12, 1951; d. Richard B. and Doleta A. (Williams) McKown; Student City Coll., Seattle, 1976-78, USAR Acad., 1978-81, Lawrence Berkeley Labs, U. So. Calif., 1978-79. Recreation counselor Portland Job Corps, 1973-75; analyst budget Employment and Tng. Adminstrn., U.S. Dept. Labor, Seattle, 1975-77, analyst computer systems, 1977-80, specialist manpower devel. State of Oreg., 1980—; owner, operator Karens Kreations, Seattle, 1980—. Serving with USAR, 1976—. Named Young Woman of Year, Outstanding Women Assn., 1980. Mem. Am. Fed. Govt. Employees, AFL-CIO, Nat. Council Field Labor Locals, (past pres.). Clubs: Nat. Job Corps Alumni Assn. (past nat. exec. v.p.), Washington. Author manuals in field.

MCLAIN, CHARLES MANSFIELD, curriculum cons.; b. Shidler, Okla., July 21, 1929; s. Roby Earl and Thelma Grace (Watt) McL.; B.A., Okla. State U., 1951; M.A., U. No. Colo., 1957; Ed.D., Colo. U., 1970. Tchr. English Pryor (Okla.) High Sch., 1951-52, Burbank (Okla.) High Sch., 1954-55, Pawnee (Okla.) High Sch., 1955-58, Lakewood (Colo.) High Sch., 1958-77, asst. prin., 1977-79; prin. Golden (Colo.) High Sch., 1979-82; curriculum cons. Jefferson County Schs., Lakewood, 1982—. Jr. warden St. Paul's Episcopal Ch., Lakewood, Colo., 1980-82, sr. warden, 1982—. Served with U.S. Army, 1952-54. NDEA grantee, 1965. Mem. Colo. Lang. Arts Soc., Assn. Supervision and Curriculum Devel., Nat. Assn. Secondary Sch. Prins., Phi Delta Kappa. Republican. Contbr. articles to profl. jours. Home: 1337 Yank St Golden CO 80401 Office: 1209 Quail St Lakewood CO 80215

MCLARNAN, DONALD EDWARD, banker, savs. and loan assn., corp. exec.; b. Nashua, Iowa, Dec. 19, 1906; s. Samuel and Grace (Prudhon) McL.; A.B., U. So. Calif., 1930; grad. in law Southwestern U., 1933; postgrad. Cambridge U.; m. Virginia Rickard, May 5, 1939; children—Marilyn, Marcia, Roxane. Trust appraiser, property mgr. Security-First Nat. Bank, Los Angeles, 1935-54; regional dir. SBA, for So. Calif., Ariz., part of Nev., Los Angeles, 1954-61, area adminstr. for Alaska, Wash., Oreg., Idaho, Calif., Nev., Ariz., Hawaii, Guam, Samoa, U.S. Trust Ty., 1969-73; pres. Am. MARC, Inc., offshore oil drillers and mfr. diesel engines, 1961-63; pres. Terminal Drilling & Prodn. Co., Haney & Williams Drilling Co., Western Offshore Drilling and Exploration Co., 1961-63; v.p., dir. Edgemar Dairy, Santa Monica Dairy Co., 1954-70; founder, pres. chmn. bd. Mission Nat. Bank, 1963-67, Coast Fed. Savs. & Loan Assn., 1954—; cons. numerous corps. Guest lectr. various univs. Chmn. fed. agys. div. Community Chest, 1956; nat. pres. Teachers Day, 1956. Bd. councillors U. So. Calif., also nat. chmn. drug abuse program; mem. real estate adv. bd. Los Angeles City Coll.; founder, chmn., pres. Soc. Care and Protection Injured Innocent; pres. Nat. Assn. for People with Disabilities. Recipient Los Angeles City and County Civic Leadership award, 1959. Mem. Skull and Dagger, Delta Chi. Mason (K.T., Shriner). Clubs: Los Angeles, Jonathan (Los Angeles). Author articles on mgmt., finance. Home: 135 S Norton Ave Los Angeles CA 90004 Office: 1111 S Crenshaw Blvd Los Angeles CA 90019

MCLAUGHLIN, JAMES DANIEL, architect; b. Spokane, Wash., Oct. 2, 1947; s. Robert Francis and Patricia (O'Connel) McL.; B.Arch., U. Idaho, 1971; m. Willa Kay Pace, Aug. 19, 1972; children—Jamie Marie, Robert James. Project architect Neil M. Wright, Architect, AIA, Sun Valley, Idaho, 1971-74, McMillan & Hayes, Architects, Sun Valley, 1974-75; now pres., prin. James D. McLaughlin AIA, Architect Chartered, Sun Valley. Chmn., Ketchum (Idaho) Planning and Zoning Commn., Ketchum Planning Commn., Ketchum Zoning Commn.; bd. dirs. Sun Valley Planning and Zoning Commn. Served to 1st lt. U.S. Army. Registered architect, 8 states including Idaho. Mem. AIA (award of excellence for Oakridge Apts., Moscow, Idaho), Nat. Council Archtl. Registration Bds., Nat. Home Builders Assn., Ketchum-Sun Valley C. of C. (dir.). Roman Catholic. Club: Rotary. Prin. archtl. works include James West Residence, First Fed. Savs., Helm Sta. Office: PO Box 479 Sun Valley ID 83353

MCLAUGHLIN, MARGUERITE P., state representative, logging company executive; m. Bruce McLaughlin; 3 children. Owner, operator contract logging firm, Orofino, Idaho; mem. Idaho Ho. of Reps. Trustee Joint Sch. Dist. 171; pres. Orofino Celebration, Inc. Democrat. Office: Idaho State House of Representatives Boise ID 83720*

MCLAUGHLIN, ROBERT FRANCIS, lawyer; b. Mountain Home, Idaho, July 11, 1920; s. Daniel and Mary C. (Ryan) McL.; B.A., U. Idaho, 1948, LL.B., 1950, J.D., 1969; m. Patricia O'Connell, June 5, 1946; children—James D., John P., Michael R., Mary K., Elizabeth Ann. Bar: Idaho 1950, U.S. Supreme Ct., 1957, U.S. Ct. Appeals (9th cir.) 1970. Pvt. practice, 1950—; pros. atty. Elmore County, 1950-60; city atty. Glenns Ferry, 1952-54, 59-67, Mountain Home, 1962-66. Mountain Home chmn. Elmore County March of Dimes, 1950, Elmore County Boy Scout Fund Dr., 1953, Elmore County Red Cross dr., 1953; co-pres. Mountain Home PTA, 1957; chmn. Elmore County Democratic Central Com., 1954-58, 64; del. Dem. Nat. Conv., 1956-64, chmn. Idaho Dem. Conv., 1956, sec., 1952-54, platform com., 1958; mem. Kennedy-Johnson Nat. Resources Com., 1960; Dem. nominee for U.S. Senate, 1960; Elmore County Dem. state committeeman, 1964-66; chmn. Idaho Vets. Com. for Johnson-Humphrey, 1964. Served from s/sgt. to capt., inf., AUS, 1941-45 PTO. Decorated Combat Inf. Badge, others; Carnegie Inst. scholar Practising Law Inst., N.Y.C., 1957. Mem. Nat. Acad. Sci., Idaho Bar Assn. (chmn. Magistrates Manual com. for pros. attys. sect.), Idaho Pros. Attys. Assn. (pres. 1959-60, chmn. criminal code revision com. 1955), Am. Trial Lawyers Assn. (pres. Idaho chpt. 1968-70), Associated Students U. Idaho (mem. exec. bd. 1947-48), U. Idaho Law Sch. Alumni Assn. (pres. 1962-64), U. Idaho Alumni Assn. (dist. dir. 1970-74), Am. Acad. Polit. and Social Sci., Internat. Platform Assn., U. Idaho Parents Assn. (pres. 1972), Blue Key, Delta Chi, Phi Alpha Delta, Mountain Home C. of C. (sec. 1950-51), VFW, Cooties, Am. Legion, 40 and 8. Roman Catholic (parish council). Club: KC (4 deg.). Home: 875 Galena St Mountain Home ID 83647 Office: 700 N 3d East St Mountain Home ID 83647

MCLAUGHLIN, WILLIAM IRVING, space technical manager; b. Oak Park, Ill., Mar. 6, 1935; s. William Lahey and Eileen (Irving) McL.; student Calif. Inst. Tech., 1953-57; B.S., U. Calif.-Berkeley, 1963, M.A., 1966, Ph.D., 1968; m. Karen Bjorneby, Aug. 20, 1960; children—William, Margot, Walter, Eileen. Mem. tech. staff Bellcomm, Inc., 1968-71; mem. tech. staff Jet Propulsion Lab., Pasadena, Calif., 1971—; supr. terrestrial planets mission design group, 1981-83, mission design mgr. for Infrared Astron. Satellite, 1982-83, mgr. flight engring. office for Voyager/Uranus project, 1983—. Served with USMC, 1957-60. Recipient Apollo Achievement award, 1969. Fellow Brit. Interplanetary Soc.; mem. Phi Beta Kappa, Sigma Xi. Monthly columnist Spaceflight mag., 1982—. Home: 4626 Janvier Way LaCrescenta CA 91214 Office: 4800 Oak Grove Dr Pasadena CA 91109

MC LAURIN, FRANCIS WALLIN (FRANK), radio broadcasting exec.; b. Sioux Falls, S.D., Sept. 24, 1923; s. Archibald A. and Clementine B. (Wallin) McL.; student Calif. Jr. Coll., 1941-42; m. Barbara Lee Jones, May 26, 1956; 1 dau., Barbara Lyn. Announcer sta. KGGM, Albuquerque, 1946; in prodn., sta. KFXM, San Bernardino, Calif., 1947-51; gen. mgr. sta. KWRN, Reno, 1951-52; account exec. KFMB TV, San Diego, 1953-54; gen. mgr. sta. KSRO, Santa Rosa, Calif., 1954—; dir., v.p. Finley Broadcasting Co., Santa Rosa. Mem. broadcast adv. bd. UPI. Bd. dirs. Boy Scouts Am. Recipient Young Man of Yr. award, Santa Rosa Jr. C. of C., 1957. Mem. Calif. Broadcasters Assn. (dir., past chmn.), Nat. Assn. Broadcasters (dir.), Santa Rosa C. of C. (pres. 1960). Republican. Presbyn. Rotarian (pres. 1966-67). Home: 1708 Pamela Dr Santa Rosa CA 95404 Office: 627 College Ave Santa Rosa CA 95403

MCLAURIN, JAN WILLIAMS, psychologist; b. Colorado City, Tex., June 29, 1947; d. James David, Jr. and Gladys Faye (Sanders) Williams; m. Mark Vinson McLaurin, Sept. 5, 1976; 1 dau., Shana Leigh. B.S., S.W. Tex. State U., 1969; M.A., U. Houston, 1970; Ph.D., Tex. A&M U., 1976. Cert. speech pathologist. Speech pathologist, audiologist Bryan (Tex.) Pub. Schs., 1970-71; speech pathologist, audiologist A&M Consol. Ind. Sch. Dist., College Station, Tex., 1971-73; sr. research psychologist S.W. Research Inst., San Antonio, 1976-78; asst. prof. U. Alaska Sch. Nursing, Anchorage, 1981, dir. health sci. research, 1981—, assoc. prof., 1983—; cons. Mem. U. Alaska Faculty Assn.; adv. com. Scouting for Handicapped, San Antonio dist. Boy Scouts Am., 1977-78. Alpha Chi scholar, 1968; recipient Jeanne Braniff Terrell Easter Seal Soc. award, 1968; HEW fellow U. Houston, 1969-70; Univ. grad. grantee Tex. A&M U., 1974-75. Mem. Am. Psychol. Assn., Alaska Psychol. Assn. Mem. Christian Ch. Author: The Relationship of Psychosocial Stressors Locus of Control and Field Dependence to Illness Susceptibility, 1976; Alaska Analysis and Planning Project for Nursing Requirements and Resources Final Report, 1981; (with Laenger) Employability Restoration Engineering Program for Severely Handicapped, 1977. Home: 5112 Sillery Circle Anchorage AK 99508 Office: 3221 Providence Dr Anchorage AK 99508

MC LEAN, GEORGE LEONARD, tech. publs. editor; b. Camas, Wash., Apr. 18, 1922; s. George Clinton and Mary Margaret (Brantner) McL.; student psychology Reed Coll., 1951-55; grad. Edison Tech. Sch., 1957, Renton Vocat. Sch., 1967; B.A. in Journalism, Seattle U., 1970; m. Apr. 18, 1962 (div.); 1 son, George Henry. Planner research and devel. Boeing Co., Seattle, 1957-62; illustrator, art editor Milmanco Co., Renton, Wash., 1966, chief editor, 1967-68; instr. Journalism Seattle U., 1968; chief editor Volt Publ. Co., Bellevue, Wash., 1969; tech. editor Western Gear Corp., Everett, Wash., 1969-70; freelance writer, editor, Sacramento, Calif., 1970-72; supervisory tech. publs. editor Dept. Def., Keyport, Wash., 1972-79, supervisory tech. publs. editor, 1979—. Served with USN, 1942-46; ETO; USNR, 1946-54. Decorated Air medal (6), others. Recipient Nat. Newspaper Snapshot award, 1965. Mem. Soc. Tech. Communication (sr.), Mensa (life), Soc. Wireless Pioneers, Am. Def. Preparedness Assn, Internat. Clover Poetry Assn. (life), Reed Coll. Alumni Assn., Nat. Divorce Reform Assn. Club: Eagles. Home: PO Box 333 Keyport WA 98345 Office: Code 3011 Bldg 206-A NUWES Keyport WA 98345

MCLEAN-BARTOS, CAROLYN LEE, psychologist; b. Tacoma, Wash., June 16, 1932; d. Emil Victor and Audrey Medora (Yeo) Lindseth; m. Otomar Jan Bartos, June 16, 1981; children by previous marriage—Scott, Joan; stepchildren—Joe, Peter, David, Mary, James. B.A., U. Colo., 1954, M.A., 1969, Ph.D., 1975. Lic. psychologist, Colo. Post-internship cons. Wardenburg Psychiat. Staff, Boulder, 1973-74; asst. prof. dept. psychology U. Colo., Boulder, 1976—; asst. clin. prof. dept. psychiatry U. Colo. Sch. Medicine, Denver, 1977—, asst. dir. Psychology Clinic, 1972—; pvt. practice psychology, Boulder, 1978—; cons. Bur. Commerce, 1980—. Adv. bd. alcohol unit Boulder Psychiat. Inst., 1980-81. Recipient Leadership award U. Colo., 1954; NIMH fellow, 1966-70, grantee, 1972-73. Mem. Am. Psychol. Assn., Colo. Psychol. Assn. (ethics com.), Nat. Register Health Service Providers, Colo. Psychologists in Pvt. Practice, Phi Beta Kappa, Mortar Bd., Psi Chi. Home: Lee Hill Rd Boulder CO 80302 Office: 1105 Spruce St Boulder CO 80302

MCLEOD, EDWARD BLAKE, mathematics educator; b. Los Angeles, July 25, 1924; s. Edward Blake and Lillian Gertrade (Russell) M.; m. Miriam Reid, Aug. 4, 1980. B.A., Occidental Coll., 1947; M.S., Stanford U., 1948, Ph.D., 1953. Instr. U. Colo., Boulder, 1953-54; asst. prof. Oreg. State U., Corvallis, 1955-62; sr. mathematician Dynamic Sci. Corp., South Pasadena, Calif., 1963-64; assoc. prof. Calif. State U.-Long Beach, 1965-71, prof., 1972—; cons. Rocketdyne Boeing, #6 Measurement Analysis Corp., 1961-66. Served with USN, 1942-46. Mem. Am. Math. Soc., Soc. Indsl. and Applied Math., Math. Assn. Am., Am. Soc. Aeros. and Astronautics. Office: Dept Math Calif State U Long Beach CA 90840

MCLEOD, JERRY R., energy executive; b. Shreveport, La., Aug. 31, 1935; s. Harry O. and N. Odelle (Crow) McL.; m. Lynn Williams, Oct. 23, 1975; children—Mark O., Steven C. Profl. Petroleum Engr., Colo. Sch. Mines, 1957; M.B.A., Harvard U., 1965. Mgr. corp. planning Cities Service Co., N.Y.C., 1970-73, gen. mgr. exploration and prodn., Denver, 1973-76, v.p. exploration and prodn., Tulsa, 1976-77, v.p. natural gas liquids div., 1977-79; pres. Cal Gas Corp., Sacramento, 1979-82; group v.p. energy Dillingham Corp., San Francisco, 1982—. Active World Affairs Council No. Calif., 1982. Named Outstanding Young Man Am., U.S. Jaycees, 1970. Mem. Nat. LP-Gas Assn. (bd. dirs.), Soc. Petroleum Engrs., Am. Assn. Petroleum Landmen, Theta Tau. Republican. Episcopalian. Club: Sutter (Sacramento). Office: 2 Embarcadero Suite 1600 San Francisco CA 94111

MCLEVIE, JOHN GILWELL, educator; b. Masterton, New Zealand, Nov. 2, 1929; came to U.S., 1968; s. Edward Mitchell and Gwendoline Mary (Faire) McL.; B.A., Victoria U., Wellington, N.Z., 1954, M.A., 1956, Dip.Ed., 1957; Ph.D. in Curriculum, Mich. State U., 1970; m. Elaine Marianne Foote, May 7, 1955; children—Anne Jeanette, Karen Elaine, Lynne Diana. Tchr. secondary sch. Rongotai Coll., Wellington, 1953-57, Sir. William Collins Tech. Sch., London, 1957-58, Alexandra Grammar Sch., Singapore, 1958-63, St. George's Comprehensive Sch., Hong Kong, 1963-64; lectr. dept. edn. U. Hong Kong, 1964-68; mem. faculty dept. secondary edn. San Diego State U., 1970—, prof., 1976—, chairperson dept., 1978-80; integration analyst San Diego Unified Sch. Dist., 1980-81; chief of party Edn. Team, Brazilian Ministry of Edn., 1973-76. Mem. Assn. Calif. Sch. Adminstrs., Assn. Supervision and Curriculum Devel., Assn. Colls. Tchr. Edn., Phi Delta Kappa. Episcopalian. Contbr. articles to profl. jours. Home: 2440 Vista Rodeo Dr El Cajon CA 92021 Office: Dept Secondary Edn San Diego State U San Diego CA 92182

MCLURE, CHARLES E., JR., economist, educator, consultant; b. Sierra Blanca, Tex., Apr. 14, 1940; s. Charles E. and Dessie (Evans) McL.; m. Patsy Nell Carroll, Sept. 17, 1962. B.A., U. Kans., 1962; M.A., Princeton U., 1964, Ph.D., 1966. Mem. faculty William Marsh Rice U., Houston, 1965-79, prof. econs., 1972-79, Allyn R. and Gladys M. Cline prof. econs., 1973-79; exec. dir. research Nat. Bur. Econ. Research, Cambridge, Mass., 1977-78, v.p., 1978-81; sr. fellow Hoover Instn., Stanford U., 1981—; sr. staff economist Council Econ. Advs., 1969-70; cons. in field. Ford Found. fellow, 1967-68. Mem. Am. Econs. Assn., Nat. Tax Assn., Beta Theta Pi. Author: Fiscal Failure: Lessons of the Sixties, 1972; Must Corporate Income Be Taxed Twice?, 1979; co-author: Value Added Tax: Two Views, 1972, La Reforma Tributarua Colombiana de 1974, 1977; co-editor: Fiscal Federalism and the Taxation of Natural Resources, 1983; editorial bd. Nat. Tax. Jour., 1972; contbr. articles to profl. jours. Home: 250 Yerba Santa Ave Los Altos CA 94022 Office: Hoover Inst Stanford CA 94305

MC MAHAN, JOHN WILLIAM, real estate investment counselor; b. San Antonio, Aug. 4, 1937; s. John William and Lena Margaret (Coleman) McM.; A.B., U. So. Calif., 1959; M.B.A., Harvard, 1961; m. Jacqueline Mary Cardozo, Sept. 22, 1973; children—Justin, Vanessa; children by previous marriage—Cathy, Jason. Dir. feasibility studies Charles Luckman Assocs., 1961-63; founder, prin. Devel. Research Assocs., Los Angeles, 1963-70; v.p. real estate services Booz, Allen & Hamilton, N.Y.C., 1970-73; mem. faculty Stanford Grad. Sch. Bus., 1974—; founder, prin. John McMahan Assocs. Inc., San Francisco, 1976—. Mem. Am. Soc. Real Estate Counselors, Urban Land Inst., Am. Econ. Assn., Am. Inst. Planners, Am. Real Estate and Urban Econ. Assn., Am. Soc. Real Estate Counselors, Lambda Alpha, Royal Town Planning Inst. U.K. Club: Jonathan. Author: Property Development: Effective Decision Making in Uncertain Times, 1976; McGraw Hill Real Estate Pocket Guide, 1979; editor: Ency. of Urban Planning, 1973. Office: 1 Embarcadero Center San Francisco CA 94111

MC MAHON, THOMAS HENRY, corp. exec.; b. Long Island City, N.Y., Mar. 16, 1938; s. Harry and Anne (Noonan) McM.; B.A., Assumption Coll., Worcester, Mass., 1956; M.B.A., U. N.C., 1960; m. Sallie Ann Robertson, Dec. 28, 1980; children by previous marriage—Thomas Henry, Lauren, Ryan. Chief exec. officer Unitech Computer Products, 1960-70; v.p. mktg. Trivex, Inc., Irvine, Calif., 1965-70; div. v.p. Cetec Corp., El Monte, Calif., 1970-74; v.p. corp. mktg., dir. Systems Magnetic Corp., Anaheim, Calif., 1974—; sr. v.p. sales/mtg. Knudsen Mfg. Corp., 1982—; dir. Emilar Corp. Mem. U.S. Senatorial Bus. Adv. Bd., Met. Police Conf., N.Y.C.; mem. Pres. John F. Kennedy's Adv. Com., 1960-63. Served with USMC, 1956-58. Mem. Audio Engring. Soc. Am., Export Mgmt. Assn., Mfrs. and Mchts. Roman Catholic. Club: K.C., Yorba Linda Country. Home: 5295 Vista Montana Yorba Linda CA 92686 Office: 1041 N Grove St Anaheim CA 92806

MCMATH, CARROLL BARTON, JR., former coll. adminstr., ret. army officer; b. Godfrey, Wash., Sept. 18, 1910; s. Carroll Barton and Grace Jenness (Matthews) McM.; B.S., Ore. State U., 1932; M.S. (A. Olson Research scholar), N.Y. U., 1936; m. Betty Ruth Thompson, Nov. 26, 1937; children—Robert Thompson, Carol. With Sacramento Bee Newspaper, 1932-35; jr. exec. Lord & Taylor, N.Y.C., 1936-39; head dept. bus. Boise (Ida.) Jr. Coll., 1939-40; Res. officer on active duty U.S. Army, 1940-46, assigned gen. staff War Dept., 1943-45; commd. capt. regular U.S. Army 1947, advanced through grades to lt. col., assigned Joint Chiefs of Staff, 1951-53, Office Sec. of Army, 1953-55, ret., 1963; campaigns include Okinawa, Korea, Vietnam; mem. faculty U. Hawaii, Honolulu, 1964-77, asst. to dir. research, profl. adviser to faculty on research, 1964-77; faculty Indsl. Coll. of Armed Forces, Washington, 1945-46; asst. prof. retailing N.Y. U., N.Y.C., 1946-47. Mem. Assn. U.S. Army, AAAS, AAUP, Ret. Officers Assn., Honolulu Acad. Arts, Hawaiian Hist. Soc., Am. Theatre Organ Soc., Hawaii Found. History and Humanities, Scabbard and Blade, Alpha Delta Sigma, Alpha Kappa Psi, Eta Mu Pi Democrat. Elk. Club: Koa Anuenue. Home: 1624 Kanunu St PH-B Honolulu HI 96814

MC MILLAN, EDWIN MATTISON, physicist, educator; b. Redondo Beach, Calif., Sept. 18, 1907; s. Edwin Harbaugh and Anna Marie (Mattison) McM.; B.S., Calif. Inst. Tech., 1928, M.S., 1929; Ph.D., Princeton U., 1932; D.Sc., Rensselaer Poly. Inst., 1961, Gustavus Adolphus Coll., 1963; m. Elsie Walford Blumer, June 7, 1941; children—Ann B., David M., Stephen W. Nat. research fellow U. Calif. at Berkeley, 1932-34, research asso., 1934-35, instr. in physics, 1935-36, asst. prof. physics, 1936-41, asso. prof., 1941-46, prof. physics, 1946-73, emeritus, 1973—; mem. staff Lawrence Radiation Lab., 1934—, asso. dir., 1954-58; dir., 1958-73, on leave for def. research at Mass. Inst. Tech. Radiation Lab., U.S. Navy Radio and Sound Lab., San Diego, and Los Alamos Sci. Lab., 1940-45; mem. gen. adv. com. AEC, 1954-58; mem. commn. high energy physics Internat. Union Pure and Applied Physics, 1960-67; mem. sci. policy com. Stanford Linear Accelerator Center, 1962-66; mem. physics adv. com. Nat. Accelerator Lab., 1967-69; chmn. 13th Internat. Conf. on High Energy Physics, 1966; guest prof. CERN, Geneva, 1974. Trustee Rand Corp., 1959-69. Bd. dirs. San Francisco Palace Arts and Scis. Found., 1968—; trustee Univs. Research Assn., 1969-74. Recipient Research Corp. Sci. award, 1951; (with Glenn T. Seaborg) Nobel prize in chemistry, 1951; (with Vladimir I, Veksler) Atoms for Peace award, 1963; Alumni Disting. Service award Calif. Inst. Tech., 1966; Centennial citation U. Calif. at Berkeley, 1968. Faculty Research lectr. U. Calif. at Berkeley, 1955. Fellow Am. Acad. arts and Scis., Am. Phys. Soc.; mem. Nat. acad. Scis. (chmn. class I 1968-71), Am. Philos. Soc., Sigma Xi, Tau Beta Pi. Address: Lawrence Berkeley Lab Berkeley CA 94720

MC MILLAN, GEORGE MICHAEL, lawyer; b. Salt Lake City, Nov. 30, 1921; s. Verl Fayette and Eudora (Watts) McM.; student U. Utah, 1939-41; LL.B., George Washington U., 1947; m. Wilma Smith, Feb. 27, 1946; children—Nancy Gayle, Courtney Michael. Admitted to D.C. bar,

1946, Utah bar, 1947, U.S. Supreme Ct., 1959; practiced in Salt Lake City; mem. firm McKay & Burton, 1947-58, McMillan, Cannon & Browning, 1958-65; partner firm McMillan & Browning, 1965-80; of counsel firm VanCott, Bagley, Cornwall & McCarthy, 1981—; gen. counsel KUTV, Inc., Salt Lake City, 1958—, asst. sec., 1970—; gen. counsel Standard Corp. (Ogden Standard Examiner), 1953—; gen. counsel, asst. sec. Kans. State Network, Inc.; gen. counsel, dir. Nat. TeleMation, Inc., Salt Lake City, Communications Investment Corp., Salt Lake City. Mem. Salt Lake County, Utah, Fed. bar assns. Democrat. Club: Fort Douglas. Home: 960 Shirecliff Rd Salt Lake City UT 84108 Office: 50 S Main St Suite 1600 Salt Lake City UT 84144

MCMILLIAN, JAMES THOMAS, aerospace executive; b. Alhambra, Calif., Aug. 5, 1925; s. James and Mary W. (O'Hurley) McM.; m. Jean Grunland, June 27, 1953. B.E. in Civil Engring., U. So. Calif., 1951; J.D., UCLA, 1954. Engr., Calif. State Div. Hwys., Los Angeles, 1951-52, Calif. State Div. Water Resources, Los Angeles, 1953-54; patent engr. Douglas Aircraft Co., Santa Monica, Calif., 1954, asst. patent counsel, 1956-59; asst. gen. counsel, 1959-67; v.p. fin. gen. office, McDonnell Douglas Corp., St. Louis, 1967-68, corp. v.p., 1967—, dir., 1978-82; pres., dir. Mc Donnell Douglas Finance Corp., Long Beach, Calif., 1968—; pres. MDC Realty Co., Long Beach, Calif., 1974-78, now dir. Trustee, UCLA; regent Loyola Marymount U. Served with USNR, 1943-46. Mem. ABA, Calif. State Bar, Los Angeles County Bar Assn., Los Angeles C. of C., Los Angeles World Affairs Council, Nat. Def. Transp. Assn., Chi Epsilon, Tau Beta Pi. Democrat. Roman Catholic. Clubs: Bel-Air Country, The Los Angeles. Office: 100 Oceangate Suite 900 Long Beach CA 90802

MC MONIGLE, PATRICE ANN, corporate psychologist; b. Pitts., Sept. 27, 1949; d. Bernard and Anita (Bromberg) McM.; B.A. in Psychology, Radford Coll., 1971, M.A., 1972; Ph.D. in Indsl.-Orgnl. Psychology (fellow), Rice U., 1975; m. John Vaillant Gaudreau, May 19, 1973. Cons. psychologist Lifson, Wilson, Ferguson & Winick, Houston, 1975-78, Reid, Merrill, Brunson & Assos., Denver, 1979-80, Rohrer, Hibler, Replogle, Inc., 1980—; instr. Denver U., Colo. Women's Coll., Loretto Heights Coll. Mem. Am. Psychol. Assn., Colo. Indsl.-Orgnl. Psychol. Assn., Phi Kappa Phi, Colo. Whitewater Assn. Contbr. articles to profl. jours. Home: 6551 Elaine Rd Evergreen CO 80439 Office: 165 S Union Blvd Suite 414 Denver CO 80228

MCMORRIS, GRACE ELIZABETH, banker; b. Malden, Mass., Feb. 6, 1922; d. John Edward and Selma Florence (Swanson) O'Brien; B.A., Boston U., 1944; postgrad. Ariz. State U., 1962; m. William Michael McMorris, May 14, 1944 (dec.); children—Sheila Elizabeth McMorris Christenson, Michael, James, John. Clk., Parlin Meml. Library, Everett, Mass., part-time, 1938-40; clk. student post office Boston U., 1941-42; supr. classified advt. desk The Boston Post, 1942-44; substitute tchr. public schs., Randolph, Mass., 1956-57; with Valley Nat. Bank Ariz., Phoenix, 1960—, trust adminstr., 1969-73; trust officer, 1973-75, asst. v.p., 1975-78, v.p., 1978—, corporate trust mgr., 1977—. Mem. Nat. Assn. Bank Women (sec. 1974-75, dir. 1973-75), North Central Ariz. Group, Western Stock Transfer Assn. (chairperson Rocky Mountain Sunbelt Group), Stock Transfer Assn. N.Y., Am. Soc. Corp. Secs., Valbanqueras, Pi Lambda Sigma (nat. treas. 1947-48). Roman Catholic. Office: 241 N Central Ave Phoenix AZ 85004

MCMULLEN, BONNIE STARR (MRS. JAMES PATRICK MCMULLEN), economist, educator; b. N.Y.C., Dec. 20, 1951; d. Alexander Michael and Bonnie Lou (Barker) Page; m. James Patrick McMullen, June 25, 1977; children—Erin Marie, Sean Patrick. B.A., SUNY-Stony Brook, 1973; M.A. in Econs., U. Calif.-Berkeley, 1976, Ph.D., 1979. Research asst. in transp. econs., Alfred P. Sloan Found. grantee U. Calif.-Berkeley, 1976-79; asst. prof., econs., Central Mich. U., Mt. Pleasant, 1979-80; asst. prof., econs., Oreg. State U., Corvallis, 1980—, dir. Transp. Research Inst., 1980—; cons., Oreg. Log Truckers Assn. Mem. Oreg. State U. Community Orch. 1980—; mem. Emily Logan Democratic women's group, 1982. Mem. Am. Econs. Assn., Western Econs. Assn. Democrat. Contbr. articles to profl. jours. Home: 7577 NE Thousand Oaks Dr Corvallis OR 97330 Office: Dept Economics Oreg State U Corvallis OR 97331

MCMULLEN, JAMES FRANCIS, fire chief; b. Fayetteville, Ark., Apr. 18, 1939; s. Francis Otis and Lillie Jewell (Morris) McM.; m. Barbara Jean Aderton, July 19, 1958; m. 2d, Guadalupe Maria Schiele, Nov. 28, 1981; children—James Jr., Donna; stepchildren—John Flanagan, Karen Flanagan, Sharon Flanagan. A.A., Mt. San Antonio Coll., Walnut, Calif., 1967; B.A., U. Redlands, 1978. Firefighter Azusa (Calif.) Fire Dept., 1962-66; dep. fire marshal Mono, Inyo and San Bernardino Counties (Calif.), 1966-71; capt. Campbell (Calif.) Fire Dept., 1971-72; fire chief City of Victorville (Calif.), 1972-74, City of Loma Linda (Calif.), 1974-77, City of San Bernardino (Calif.), 1977-79, City of Campbell (Calif.), 1979—; ins. safety engring. mgr.; community coll. instr.; fire protection cons. Mem. Gov.'s Task Force Wild Land Fires and Conflagrations, 1981; bd. dirs. Campbell Progressive Srs., Calif. State Bldg. Standards Commn., Gov.'s Task Force on Earthquakes. Served with U.S. Army, 1957-60. Recipient cert. outstanding service San Bernardino Fire Assn., 1971, Victor Valley Coll., 1974, Victorville resolution for outstanding community service, 1974, San Bernardino exemplary service award, 1979. Mem. Santa Clara County Fire Chiefs Assn. (pres.), Calif. League Cities, Calif. Fire Chiefs Assn., Calif. Fire State Firemen's Assn., Western Fire Chiefs Assn., Internat. Assn. Fire Chiefs, Campbell C. of C. (chmn. highland games com.). Republican. Author numerous mcpl. fire protection ordinances. Office: 123 S Union Ave Campbell CA 95008

MCMURRAY, STANLEY JOSEPH, JR., business executive; b. Lewiston, Idaho, Apr. 4, 1942; s. Stanley Judson and Maxine Faye (Lathrop) McM.; student in acctg. Lewis-Clark Bus. Coll., 1965; m. Charlotte; children—Shonna, Shelli, Chad, Joe. Foreman, Potlatch Corp., Lewiston, Idaho, 1964-69; asst. mgr. Warehouse Food Market, Lewiston, 1969-72, mgr., Coeur d'Alene, Idaho, 1972-76, Spokane, Wash., 1976-78, dist. mgr., 1978-82; gen. mdse. mgr. Food and Sundries div. Costco Wholesale Club, 1983—. Served with U.S. Army, 1960-63. Rosicrucian Order. Home: 4601 121st Ave SE Bellevue WA 98006 Office: 4401 4th Ave S Seattle WA 98134

MCMURTREY, LAWRENCE JAY, hydroelectric engineer; b. Ririe, Idaho, Mar. 13, 1924; s. Lawrence Jay and Annie Eliza (Forsyth) McM.; m. Dolly Louise Hawks, Jan. 28, 1947; children—Glenn, Kathi Freeman, Gary, Lu Ann Summers, David, Jana Sifuentes. B.S.M.E., U. Colo., 1944. Lic. profl. engr., Wash. Propulsion engr. Boeing Co., Seattle, 1946-47, chief propulsion tech., 1956-58, project mgr., 1958-66, new bus. devel. mgr., 1966-71, mgr. Lunar Rover nav. system, 1971-72; instr. U. Utah, 1944-49; pres. McMurtrey Assocs., Redmond, WA, 1977—. Served with USN, 1943-46. Mem. AIAA, Am. Rocket Soc. Republican. Mormon. Patentee in field. Home and Office: 12122 196 N E Redmond WA 98052

MCNAIR, KEVIN LOFTUS, track and field coach; b. Glasgow, Scotland, Nov. 21, 1948; s. John and Margaret (Loftus) M.; m. Catherine Lambro, Aug. 4, 1973; children—Patricia, Michael. B.A., Stanford U., 1971, M.A., 1972. Cert. secondary tchr., Calif. Head track coach and asst. football coach various Calif. high schs., 1970-77; head men and women's track coach, instr. Kinesiology, sports theory and biomechanics Occidental Coll., Eagle Rock, Calif.; head track and field coach U. Calif.-Irvine, 1977—; speed devel. cons. Los Angeles Rams, 1980-81; cons. Mgmt. Sports Mktg., Inc., Newport Beach, Calif., 1981—; mem. U.S. Olympic Devel. Coaching Staff, 1984; writer, producer, announcer running and fitness program Sta. KOCM, Orange County, Calif., 1982—; lectr. Event dir. Deacon Jones Celebrity Hall Fame Games, 1982; dir. U. Calif.-Irvine Boys and Girls Track Camp, 1980—. Recipient Track and Field Pace award Stanford U., 1971; named East Bay (No. Calif.) Track Coach of Yr., Am. Motors and local press, 1974, East Bay Football Coach of Yr., 1977; Occidental Coll. Nat. Collegiate Athletic Assn. (NCAA) Div. III Cross Country Nat. Champions, 1977; Track and Field Nat. Champions, 1978; named Div. Coach of Yr. NCAA Div. III Coaches Assn., 1978; Pacific Athletic Assn. Track and Field Coach of Yr., 1981; recipient Outstanding Achievement award U. Calif. Sports Assocs., 1982. Mem. Stanford U. Block S Athletic Soc. (life), Athletic Congress, NCAA Coaches Assn. Roman Catholic. Home: 23796 Brasilia Mission Viego CA 92691 Office: Crawford Hall U Calif Irvine CA 92717

MCNALL, CLO ANN, newspaper executive; b. Goodland, Kans., July 18, 1933; d. Lloyd Cecil and Mary Alice (Haller) Wilkins; m. John Mark McNall, Oct. 19, 1951; children—Lynette, Diane, Marcie. Trainee, Gazette Telegraph, Colorado Springs, Colo., 1950-53; co-pub. Eastern Colo. Plainsman, Hugo, 1954-61, Chewelah Ind., Wash., 1966-69; editor, co-pub. Clearwater Tribune, Orofino, Idaho, 1969—. Office: PO Box 71 Orofino ID 83544

MCNALLY, JAMES HENRY, physicist; b. Orange, N.J., Dec. 18, 1936; s. James Osbourne and Edith Maude (Jones) McN.; B.Engring. Physics, Cornell U., 1959; Ph.D., Calif. Inst. Tech., 1966; m. Nancy Lee Eudaley, July 4, 1976. Staff mem., program mgr. Los Alamos Nat. Lab., 1965-74, asso. div. leader, dep. for inertial fusion, 1975-81, asst. for nat. sec. issues, 1981—; asst. dir. for lasers and isotope separation tech. AEC/ERDA, Washington, 1974-75; U.S. del. Geneva Conf. on Disarmament, 1969, 73, 74, Threshold Test Ban Treaty, Moscow, 1974. Bd. dirs. Wilson Mesa Met. Water Dist., 1976—. Mem. Am. Phys. Soc., AAAS, Internat. Inst. Strategic Studies, Sigma Xi. Home: 550 Rim Rd Los Alamos NM 87544 Office: Los Alamos Nat Lab Box 1663 Los Alamos NM 87545

MCNAMARA, CARLTON PALMER, management consultant; b. N.Y.C., Sept. 7, 1941; s. Carlton Reno and Joyce (Jarman) McN.; m. Joan K. Horne, Dec. 21, 1971; children—Carol, Susie. A.B., Colgate U., 1963; M.B.A., Columbia U., 1965; Ph.D., U. Ill., 1969. Sr. assoc. Wendell C. Walker & Assocs., 1970; mgr. Theodore Barry & Assocs., 1971-73; pres. McNamara & Co., Inc., Los Angeles, 1973—; pub. speaker. Pres. bd. dirs. Homeowners Assn.; ednl. com. St. Paul the Apostle Sch. Mem. Am. Mgmt. Pres.'s Assn. Republican. Presbyterian. Contbr. articles profl. and trade jours. Office: 9268 Robin Dr Los Angeles CA 90069

MC NAMARA, JOHN J., educator; b. Rochelle, Ill., Dec. 6, 1909; s. John and Grace (Campbell) McN.; B.E., No. Ill. U.; M.A., U. Iowa; Ph.D., Purdue U.; m. Hazel D. Dionne, Sept. 11, 1936; children—John, Denise, Carole, Michael, Terrence, Kevin. Tchr., St. Abans Acad., Sycamore, Ill., 1932-34; faculty St. Victor Coll., Kankakee, Ill., 1934-37; asso. prof. U. Detroit, 1937-43; head tng. div. Republic Aviation Corp., 1943-45; pres. M & M Cendy, Hackettstown, N.J., 1945-59; dir. M & M Mars (now Mars Inc.), McLean, Va., 1952-62; chmn. bd. Uncle Ben's Rice, Houston, 1959-62; corp. mktg. adv. Warner Lambert Pharm. Co., Morris Plains, N.J., 1966-67; prof. No. Ill. U., DeKalb, 1970-78; prof. dept. mktg. Calif. State Coll., Bakersfield, 1978-80. Calcot-Kennedy disting. prof., 1980—. Recipient Chick Evans award and service award No. Ill. U., 1971. Mem. Am. Assn. Advt. Agys. Sigma Xi, Phi Delta Kappa. Club: Stockdale Country. Contbr. articles to profl. publs. Home: 508 Malibu Ct Bakersfield CA 93309 Office: 9001 Stockdale Hwy Bakersfield CA 93309

MCNAMARA, JOSEPH DONALD, police chief; b. N.Y.C., Dec. 16, 1934; s. Michael and Eleanor (Shepherd) McN.; B.S., John Jay Coll., N.Y.C., 1968; fellow Harvard U. Law Sch., 1969-70; D.B.A. (Littauer fellow 1971-72), Harvard U., 1973; m. Rochelle Wall, Jan. 25, 1964; children—Donald, Laura, Karen. Mem. N.Y.C. Police Dept., 1956-73, dep. insp., to 1973; police chief. Kansas City, Mo., 1973-76, San Jose, Calif., 1976—; mem. adj. faculty Northeastern U., Boston, 1972, John Jay Coll., 1973, Rockhurst Coll., Kansas City, 1975-76, San Jose State U., 1980; mem. nat. adv. bd. U.S. Bur. Justice Stats., 1980; cons., lectr. in field. Served with U.S. Army, 1958-60. Recipient Disting. Alumnae award John Jay Coll., 1979, President's award Western Soc. Criminology, 1979. Mem. Internat. Assn. Chiefs Police, Major Cities Police Chiefs Assn., Police Exec. Research Forum (dir.), Calif. Police Chiefs Assn., Calif. Peace Officers Assn. Author articles in field. Office: 201 W Mission St San Jose CA 95110

MCNAMARA, STEPHEN, newspaper executive; b. Chgo., July 9, 1934; s. Robert Charles Jr. and Susan (Deuel) McN.; m. Hanne Mogensen, Feb. 21, 1960; m. 2d, Kay Copeland, June 6, 1978; children—Lise, Natalie, Kevin, Christopher, Morgan. A.B. in Am. History, Princeton U., 1955. Reporter Winston-Salem (N.C.) Jour., 1955-57; copy editor, sports writer Miami Herald, 1957-59; contbg. European editor Car & Driver, 1959; asst. news editor, exec. sports editor, Sunday editor San Francisco Examiner, 1960-66; editor, pub. Pacific Sun, Mill Valley, Calif., 1966—; pres. Marin Sun Printing Co. Inc., Pacific Sun Pub. Co. Inc., Marin Solar Village Inc., Pacific Sun Computer Systems; mng. gen. ptnr. Sunrise Investment Co.; vis. lectr. journalism San Francisco State U., 1967. Mem. innovation and planning commn. Calif. Dept. Edn. Mem. Calif. Soc. Newspaper Editors (dir. 1983—), Nat. Assn. Alternative Newsweeklies (pres. 1978-81), Sigma Delta Xi. Democrat. Clubs: San Francisco Press (1st place newspaper writing award 1967); Cap and Gown (Princeton). Home: 384 Tennessee Ave Mill Valley CA 94941 Office: 21 Corte Madera Ave Mill Valley CA 94941

MC NAUGHTON, ANDREW ROBERT LESLIE, found. exec.; b. Guilford, Eng., July 21, 1916; s. Andrew George Latta and Mable Stewart (Weir) McN.; grad. classical courses Loyola Coll., 1934; specialist in E.E. Royal Mil. Coll., 1938; postgrad. Alexander Hamilton Inst., 1938-39, McGill U., 1939; m. Jacqueline Magella (dec.). Pres. Norcan Ltd., 1946-67; partner Major & Co., 1950-55; pres. The McNaughton Found., Sausalito, Calif., 1956—, Fundación McNaughton de Mexico, 1977—; research dir. NutriSearch Found., Fenix Inc.; cons. in field. Bd. govs. Nat. Health Fedn.; bd. dirs. Israel Med. Research Found. Served with RCAF, 1939-46; chief test pilot. Decorated Air Force Cross; knight Order of Hosp. of St. John Jerusalem (Malta). Mem. Royal Soc. Medicine (Eng.) (named to Ct. of Benefactors 1970), Engring. Inst. Can., Am. Inst. Mining, Metall. and Petroleum Engrs., Canadian Aeros. and Space Inst., Canadian Test Pilots Assn., N.Y. Acad. Scis., AIAA, John Beard Research Inst., Point Reyes Bird Observatory. Club: Commonwealth (Calif.). Office: PO Box B-17 San Ysidro CA 92073

MCNEAR, DENMAN KITTREDGE, transportation company executive; b. San Francisco, July 20, 1925; s. E. Denman and Mary H. (Kittredge) McN.; B.S. in Civil Engring., M.I.T., 1948; M.B.A., Stanford U., 1950; m. Susan L. Anderson, Jan. 27, 1962; children—Denman K., Stephen A., George D. With So. Pacific Transp. Co., San Francisco, 1948—, asst. to pres., 1963-67, v.p., 1967-75, v.p. ops., 1975-76, pres., 1976-82, chmn., chief exec. officer, 1982—, also dir.; pres. St. Louis Southwestern Ry. Co., 1975—; dir. S.P. Co. Mem. corp. M.I.T., Cambridge, 1977-82. Served with USN, 1944-46. Registered profl. engr., Calif., Ariz., N.M., Tex. Mem. ASCE, Assn. Am. R.R.s (dir., exec. com.), Econ. Lit. Council Calif. (pres. 1975-78). Republican. Clubs: Bohemian, Pacific-Union, Stock Exchange. Office: So Pacific Bldg 1 Market Plaza San Francisco CA 94105

MCNEELY, E. L., merchandising cons.; b. Pattonsburg, Mo., Oct. 5, 1918; s. Ralph H. and Viola (Vogel) McN.; student Central Bus. Coll., Kansas City, Mo., 1935-36; B.A., N.E. Mo. State U., 1940; postgrad. Rockhurst Coll., 1942; m. Alice Elaine Hall, Sept. 18, 1948; children—Sandra McNeely Gessl, Gregory, Mark, Kevin. With Montgomery Ward & Co., Chgo., 1940-64, divisional mdse. mgr., 1961-64; dir. mktg. Wickes Corp., Saginaw, Mich., 1964-65, sr. v.p., 1965-69, pres., 1969-80, chmn., chief exec. officer, 1971-82; merchandising cons., 1982—; corp. dir. Dayco Corp., Dayton, Ohio, Fed.-Mogul Corp., Detroit, Pacific Tel. & Tel. Co., San Francisco, Transam. Corp., San Francisco. Chmn. San Diego Econ. Devel. Corp., 1980-81; trustee Scripps Clinic and Research Found., 1973—; mem. exec. bd. San Diego County council Boy Scouts Am., 1978—. Served to lt. (j.g.) USNR, 1942-46. Republican. Presbyterian. Clubs: Cuyamaca (San Diego); La Jolla (Calif.) Country; Metropolitan, Union (Chgo.); Saginaw (Mich.). Home: 1020 La Jolla Rancho Rd La Jolla CA 92037 Office: 7910 Ivanhoe Suite 110 La Jolla CA 92037

MCNEIL, CHRIS EDWARD, JR., lawyer; b. Juneau, Alaska, Aug. 10, 1948; s. Chris Edward and Anita Charlotte (Brown) McN.; B.A., Stanford U., 1970; M.A., Yale U., 1975; J.S.D., Stanford Law Sch., 1978; m. Mary North, Apr. 5, 1968; children—Micah Sasha, Tasha Nita. Dir., Stanford Indian Program, Stanford (Calif.) U., 1970-71; edn. coordinator Tlingit Haida Central Council, Juneau, Alaska, 1971-72; asst. to pres. Sealaska Corp., Juneau, 1978, sec., 1978—, v.p., counsel, 1982—; admitted to Alaska bar, 1979. Vice pres. T1ingit Haida Central Council, 1976-78; chmn. T1ingit & Haida Regional Housing Authority, 1977-78; chmn. T1ingit and Haida Community Council, 1980—; vice-chmn. Native Am. Rights Fund, Inc. Ford Found. fellow, 1972-75; HEW Indian Fellows program, 1976-78. Mem. Am. Soc. Corp. Secs., Alaska Bar Assn., Am. Bar Assn. Democrat. Club: Lions. Contbg. author: Alaska Native Land Claims, 1975. Home: 3241 Douglas Hwy Juneau AK 99801 Office: 1 Sealaska Plaza Suite 400 Juneau AK 99801

MC NEIL, DOUGLAS EUGENE, real estate and park development executive, university administrator, performing arts consultant; b. North Platte, Nebr., Oct. 15, 1939; s. William Bernard and Myrtle Naomi (Biehl) McN.; B.S., U. Denver, 1961, postgrad. 1962-64; 1 son, Douglas Eugene. Asso. dir. conf. div. U. Denver, 1962-65, dir. communications and pub. relations Blue Cross/Blue Shield, 1965-67, exec. dir. div. conf. coordination U. Denver, 1969-76, founder, adminstrv. sponsor All University Programs Bd., 1971-76, dir. L.T. Phipps Conf. Center; v.p., owner Western Corrosion Control, 1976—. Cons. in performing arts, 1970—, concert mgmt., 1971—, conf. planning, 1968—. Pres., founder Young Adults Symphony League, 1963-65; founding pres., chmn. Men's Symphony Assn., Denver Symphony Orch., 1968-72. Bd. dirs. Denver Santa Claus Shop, pres., 1972-74, chmn., 1974; bd. dirs. Colo. Soc. to Prevent Blindness; bd. dirs., v.p. Colo. Ballet; trustee Denver Symphony Orch. Assn., 1969-72. Mem. Western Alliance of Arts Adminstrs. (dir. 1971—), Assn. of Coll., U. and Community Arts Adminstrs. (finance com. 1968-72), Internat., Colo. hotel sales mgmt. assns., Colo. Soc. Assn. Execs., Meeting Planners Internat., Rocky Mountain Assn. Meeting Planners, Holy Name Soc., Denver Jaycees, Central City Opera Assn., Denver Art Mus., Denver Zool. Fedn., Am. Soc. Arts and Lit., Nat. Assn. Corrosion Engrs., Sigma Alpha Epsilon, Tau Kappa Epsilon, Kappa Kappa Psi. Clubs: Denver Athletic, Denver Profl. Men's. Home: 1282 Detroit Denver CO 80206 Office: 1050 17th St Suite 212 Denver CO 80265

MC NEIL, MARY, geologist; b. Boston, Oct. 2, 1917; d. Andrew and Claire (MacNeill) D'Errico; B.S., Ariz. State U., 1958; M.A., UCLA, 1963. Research asst. UCLA, 1958-60; scientist Lockheed Aircraft Corp., Burbank, Calif., 1969-70; cons. to Brazilian Govt., 1970-75; sr. staff geoscientist Bendix Field Engring. Corp., Grand Junction, Colo., 1975-80; now asso. Williams div. Jacobs Engring. Group, Lakeland, Fla. Mem. Los Angeles Sister Cities Com., Salvador, Brazil, 1960-64. Served with USNR, 1943-45. Decorated Cross of Lorraine. Mem. AIME, Am. Inst. Petroleum Geologists. Author: Brazil's Uranium and Thorium Deposits, 1979; contbr. articles to profl. jours.

MCNELLEY, JAMES E., hospital administrator; b. Paola, Kans., Apr. 2, 1925; s. Donald Boone and Luverne (Eernisse) McN.; m. Martha Ann Gregg, Dec. 1, 1950; children—Gregg Lee, Lynn Arlene, Steve Hunter. B.A., San Jose State Coll., 1948; M.H.A., Northwestern U., 1950. Adminstrv. asst. Hollywood Presbyn. Hosp., Los Angeles, 1949-50; asst. adminstr. Ind. Gen. Hosp., Elkhart, 1951-52; adminstr. Beverly Community Hosp., Montebello, Calif., 1953-58, Meml. Hosp., Glendale, Calif., 1959-71; exec. dir. Riverside (Calif.) Community Hosp.-Med Ctr., 1971—. Office: 4445 Magnolia Ave Riverside CA 92501

MC NICHOLS, RAY, judge; b. Bonners Ferry, Idaho, June 16, 1914; s. Michael T. and Catherine (Clyne) McN.; LL.B., U. Idaho, 1950; m. Mary Katherine Riley, Aug. 1, 1938; children—Michael E., Kathleen M. McNichols Dreps. Admitted to Idaho bar, 1950, practiced in Orofino, until 1964; U.S. dist. judge Dist. Idaho, Boise, 1964—. Served with USNR, 1944-47. Mem. Phi Delta Theta, Phi Alpha Delta. Democrat. Roman Catholic. Home: 550 W Fort St Boise ID 83724 Office: Federal Bldg Boise ID 83724

MCNICHOLS, ROBERT J., judge; b. 1922; grad. Wake Forest U.; LL.B., Gonzaga U. Admitted to Wash. bar, 1952; chief judge U.S. Dist. Ct. for Eastern Wash., Spokane. Office: US Dist Ct Eastern Wash PO Box 2136 Spokane WA 99210*

MCNICHOLS, WILLIAM H., JR., mayor Denver; b. Denver, Apr. 11, 1910; s. William H. and Catherine (Warner) McN.; student U. Colo., U. Ala.; m. Laverne Peterson, Oct. 25, 1947 (dec.); 1 son, Stephen Charles. Formerly in ins. bus., banker; exec. sec. to gov. Colo., 1956-62; later mgr. pub. works city and county Denver; then dep. mayor, now mayor Denver. Panel mem. White House Fellows; mem. policy com. NSF; bd. dirs., employment council Hispanic and Native Ams. Orgns., adv. bd. Children's Diabetes Found. Served with inf. AUS, World War II. Decorated Purple Heart, Combat Infantryman's Badge. Mem. Am. Legion, CAP, Am. Pub. Works Assn., Nat. League Cities (adv. council), U.S. Conf. Mayors (pres. 1978-79, mem. com. on energy and environ.). Democrat. Home: 754 Krameria St Denver CO 80220 Office: 350 City and County Bldg Denver CO 80202

MCNUTT, JAMES EDWARD, geotechnical engr.; b. Chgo., Apr. 6, 1944; s. Carmon Maurice and Jayne Mary (Coddington) McN.; B.S., Calif. State U., Los Angeles, 1968; m. Lynn McNutt, Aug. 30, 1979; children—Daniel, Michael, Nicole, Jamie. Project mgr. LeRoy Crandall & Assocs., Los Angeles, 1965-76; sr. engr. Converse Davis Dixon, Las Vegas, Nev., 1976-77; project mgr. Fugro, Inc., Long Beach, Calif., 1977-78; pres. GEG-Nev., Las Vegas, 1978-80; engring. mgr., prin. J.H. Kleinfelder & Assocs., Las Vegas, 1980—. Registered profl. engr., Ariz., Calif., Nev., Oreg., Utah Mem. ASCE, Structural Engrs. Assn. Calif., Nat. Soc. Profl. Engrs., Internat. Soc. Soil Mech. and Found. Engrs., Am. Cons. Engrs. Council, Assn. Soil and Found. Engrs. Office: 5115 S Industrial Rd Suite 605 Las Vegas NV 89118

MCOUAT, WALLACE GRAHAM, financial consultant; b. Indpls., Mar. 14, 1947; s. Robert Graham and Mary (Brittain) McO.; A.B. in Math., Ind. U., 1969, M.B.A., 1971; m. Valerie Martha Lee, Mar. 29, 1969; 1 son, Travis. Mgr., Price Waterhouse & Co., Atlanta, 1971-75, N.Y.C., 1975-76, San Francisco, 1976-77; project leader Anistics div. Alexander & Alexander, Palo Alto, Calif., 1977-78; v.p. Risk Scis. Group, Inc., San Francisco, 1978-82; pres. W.G. McOuat & Assocs., 1981—; adj. faculty U. San Francisco, 1977-78; speaker, panels, coordinator numerous profl. confs., 1976—. Mem. Marin County Energy Adv. Com., 1979-82, Marin County Planning Commn., 1982—; bd. dirs. Marin Conservation League, 1982—. Dir., Marin Citizens for Energy Planning, 1981—. C.P.A., Ind., Ga., Calif. Mem. Am. Inst. C.P.A.s (author, editor several courses), Calif. Soc. C.P.A.s, Am. Assn. Accts., Phi Beta Kappa, Pi Mu Epsilon. Contbr. articles to profl. jours. Office: 100 Laurel Ave San Anselmo CA 94960

MCPEEK, FRANK DAY, fin. exec.; b. Colliers, W.Va., Feb. 24, 1921; s. Thomas Theodore and Ruby Pearl (Snyder) McP.; B.S., U.S. Mil. Acad., 1945; M.B.A., Ariz. State U., 1966; m. Laura Mae Aldridge, June 5, 1945; children—Frank Day, Susan, Deborah, Lawrence, Kathryn, John. Commd. capt. U.S. Army, 19—; hdqrs. comdt. P.R. Army Hdqrs., 1952-54, Kmag, Korea, 1955-56, intelligence ops. and counterintelligence, Far East, 1956-59; indirect cost specialist Ariz. State U., Tempe, 1964-78, civil Defense coordinator, 1964-69; fin. officer. S.W. Biomed. Research Inst., Tempe, 1978—. mem. ch. council fin. and budget Our Lady of Mt. Carmel, 1969-74. Mem. Ret. Officers Assn., Soc. Research Adminstrs., Western Assn. Coll. and Univ. Bus. Officers. Democrat. Roman Catholic. Home: 216 E Del Rio Dr Tempe AZ 85282 Office: 123 E University Dr Tempe AZ 85281

MC PHERON, WILLIAM GRAVES, radiologist; b. McAlester, Okla., Apr. 6, 1918; s. Robert Lee and Jeannette (Kridler) McP.; student Southeastern State Coll., 1936-37; A.B., U. Okla., 1935, B.S.M., 1940, M.D., 1942; children—William, Jeannie, Donald R., Rebecca A. Intern, Touro Infirmary, New Orleans, 1942-43; fellow in radiology Cleve. Clinic Found., 1946-48; radiologist St. Paul's Hosp., Dallas, 1948-53, Bapt. Hosp., St. Dominic's Hosp., Jackson, Miss., 1953-57; chief dept. radiology Lea Regional Hosp. Served as capt. M.C., AUS, 1943-46. Fellow Am. Coll. Radiology; mem. AMA, N.Mex. Med. Soc., Soc. Nuclear Medicine, Radiol. Soc. N. Am., Am. Coll. Radiology, Am. Inst. Ultrasound in Medicine. Presbyterian. Club: Rotary. Home: 1027 Jicarilla Hobbs NM 88240 Office: PO Box 1907 Hobbs NM 88240

MCQUARRIE, MILDRED LOUISE (CHRYS), mgmt. cons.; b. Vancouver, B.C., Can., Apr. 24, 1941; s. Alexander Craig and Victoria (Dalgleish) Chrystal; student U. B.C., 1959-64, Fashion Inst. Tech. N.Y., 1968; m. Robert William McQuarrie, Dec. 27, 1971 (dec.). Buyer, dept. mgr. Hudson Bay Co., Vancouver, 1964-68; merchandiser Koret of Calif., Vancouver, 1969-71; project analyst, dept. mgr., group buyer Home Town Retail div. Crown Zellerbach, Vancouver, 1972-77; pres. McQuarrie Mgmt. Ltd., Vancouver, 1977—; founder, pres. Court Stars retail, Vancouver, 1977—; mem. faculty U. B.C., 1977-81, lectr. Can. Inst. Bankers. Mem. Commerce Alumni Assn. (pres. 1977-79), U. B.C. Alumni Assn. (bd. mgmt. 1977-79), Alpha Delta Pi. Clubs: Court House Racquet, Vancouver Lawn Tennis and Badminton. Home: 210 1855 Nelson St Vancouver BC V6G 1M9 Canada Office: 5665 West Blvd Vancouver BC V6M 3W7 Canada

MCQUIDDY, MARIAN ELIZABETH, publisher, editor; b. Los Angeles, Mar. 21, 1952; d. Arthur Robert and Aleen Frampton (Hinkle) McQ. B.J., Purdue U., 1974; postgrad. in press photography Northwestern U., 1973; postgrad. in comparative psychotherapy Webster Coll., 1981. Summer editorial intern Chgo. Daily News, 1973; new dir. Sta. KSVP, Artesia, N.Mex., 1974; police reporter, polit. editor Roswell (N.Mex.) Daily Record, 1974-77; night editor, sports and feature editor UPI, Des Moines, 1977-79; editor Mt. Vernon (Iowa) Democrat, 1979; news editor Cadillac (Mich.) Evening News, 1979-80, tchr. adult edn. Pine River High Sch., LeRoy, Mich., 1979-80; editor Portage (Wis.) Daily Register, 1980-81; pub., editor Los Lunas (N.Mex.) Village Voice, 1981—. Bd. dirs. Cadillac Area Arts Council, Community Theater, United Way, Portage. Recipient journalism award N.Mex. Press Assn., N.Mex. Farm Bur., service awards Roswell Library, Optimists, Boy Scouts Am., Portage Jaycees, Wis. Newspaper Assn. Mem. Nat. Fedn. Press Women, Women in Communications, Jr. League, Sigma Delta Chi. Methodist. Home: Box 1090 Los Lunas NM 87031 Office: 133 Hwy 85 Los Lunas NM 87031

MC QUILLIN, MAHLON (LON) BRICE, II, TV producer/dir.; b. Chgo., Apr. 3, 1950; s. Brice and Eleanor Valey (Lindskog) McQ.; A.A., Coll. San Mateo, 1970. Mem. advt. dept. San Mateo (Calif.) Times, 1970-71; audio systems mgr. Foremans Co., San Mateo, 1971-73; video systems mgr. Brooks Co., San Francisco, 1973-76; pres., gen. mgr. MicroVision Systems, San Mateo, 1976—; owner, cons. McQ Prodns.; producer, dir., editor TV programs for broadcast, corp. communications, syndication, commls.; dir. cable series Comedy Showcase; instr. Coll. of San Mateo; faculty mem. N.Am. TV Inst.; bd. dirs. San Francisco Film/Tape Council. Active Poplar Center, San Mateo. Served with USAFR, 1970-73. Winner Silver and Bronze awards Internat. Film and TV Festival of N.Y., 1979, 81, 82. Mem. Internat. TV Assn. Assn. (Golden Reel of Excellence), Soc. Motion Picture and TV Engrs., Nat. Acad. TV Arts and Scis. Author: The Video Production Guide, 1983; (with others) The Handbook of Private Television, 1982. Designer MicroVision 20 videotape editing system; editor Internat. TV News, 1975-79; contbg. editor Video Systems mag., 1978—; contbr. articles to industry publs. Office: PO Box 1676 San Mateo CA 94401

MCQUISTON, MICHAEL CHARLES, mining safety administrator; b. Nevada City, Calif., Apr. 24, 1944; s. Frank Wood and Frances (Haseltine) M.; m. Judith P. Price, Dec. 23, 1972; 1 son, Michael Scott; m. 2d, Helen Louise Sitterly, Jan. 23, 1982. A.A.S. in Indsl. Engring., Western Piedmont Community Coll., Morganton, N.C., 1972; A.A.S. in Liberal Studies, Central Ariz. Community Coll., 1975. Safety engr. Magma Copper Co., San Manuel, Ariz., 1972-77; dir. safety and environ. Smoky Valley Mining div. Copper Range Co., Round Mountain, Nev., 1978-79; supt. safety, tng. and personnel Westcoast Oil and Gas Corp., Sparks, Nev., 1979-81; site inspection controller Cementation of Am. Inc., Carlsbad, N.Mex., 1981—. Served with U.S. Army, 1968-70. Decorated Purple Heart. Mem. Am. Soc. Safety Engrs., Soc. Mining Engrs. AIME. Methodist. Home: 13982 Lear Blvd Reno NV 89506 Office: PO Box 2267 Carlsbad NM 88220

MCRAE, HAMILTON EUGENE, III, lawyer; b. Midland, Tex., Oct. 29, 1937; s. Hamilton Eugene and Adrian (Hagaman) McR.; B.S.E.E., U. Ariz., 1961, J.D., 1967; student USAF Electronics Sch., 1961-62, U. Redlands, 1962-63; m. Betty Hawkins, Aug. 27, 1960; children—Elizabeth Ann, Stephanie Adrian, Scott Hawkins. Elec. engr. Salt River Project, Phoenix, 1961; admitted to Ariz. bar, 1967, U.S. Supreme Ct. Bar, 1979; assoc. Jennings, Strouss & Salmon, Phoenix, 1967-71, ptnr., 1971—; magistrate, Paradise Valley, Ariz., 1983—; juvenile referee Superior Ct., 1983—; pres., dir. Phoenix Realty & Trust Co.; officer Indsl. Devel. Corp. Maricopa County; instr. in field; officer, dir. other corps. Elder, Valley Presbyn. Ch., Scottsdale, Ariz., 1973-75, 82—, corp. pres., 1975—; trustee, mem. exec. com. Phi Gamma Delta Ednl. Found., Washington, 1974—; trustee Upward Found., Phoenix, 1977-80; founder, trustee, pres. McRae Found., Phoenix; vol. fund raiser YMCA, Salvation Army, others. Served to 1st lt. USAF, 1961-64. Recipient various honors and awards U. Ariz., 1956-61, 64-67; named Most Outstanding Sr. in Nation, Phi Gamma Delta, 1961. Mem. ABA, Ariz. Bar Assn., Maricopa County Bar Assn., AIME, Ariz. Acad., Internat. Platform Assn., U. Ariz. Alumni Assn., Tau Beta Pi. Republican. Clubs: Phoenix Exec., Phoenix Country, Ariz., Continental Country, Clan McRae Soc. N.Am. Contbr. articles to law revs. and profl. jours. Home: 8101 N 47th St Paradise Valley AZ 85253 Office: 111 W Monroe St Phoenix AZ 85003

MC REYNOLDS, MARY BARBARA, educator; b. Los Angeles, Feb. 18, 1930; d. Clyde C. and Dorothy (Slaten) McCulloh; B.A., U. N.Mex., 1951, M.A., 1972, Edn. Specialist, 1975, postgrad., 1981—; m. Zachariah A. McReynolds, Feb. 9, 1952 (dec.); children—Gregg Clyde, Barbara, Zachariah A. Dept. sec. USAF Intelligence, Wiesbaden, W. Ger., 1953-54; tchr. Annandale (Va.) Elementary Sch., 1962-65, supr. adult edn., 1965-66; tchr. Albuquerque High Sch., 1968-75, 77—, social studies curriculum dir., 1973-75; instr. U. N.Mex., Albuquerque, 1975-76; evaluator N. Central Assn., 1970-81, dir. Cultural Awareness Workshop, 1976, 79; coordinator Sex Equality, 1979, 80. Bd. dirs. Greater U. N.Mex. Fund, 1978-79, 79-80, fund raiser, 1976-81, pres. club, 1977-80; campaign mgr. state senatorial campaign, 1976; exec. sec. Civic Assn., 1958-60; sponsor Black Student Union, 1978-80; sponsor Boys and Girls State, 1968-75. Indian research and tuition edn. grantee, 1971; grantee U. N.Mex., 1975-76, others. Mem. Assn. Supervision and Curriculum Devel., Nat. Social Studies Council, N.Mex. Social Studies Council, Phi Kappa Phi, Phi Delta Kappa, Pi Alpha Theta, Kappa Kappa Gamma. Democrat. Episcopalian. Clubs: N.Mex. Democratic Women, Air Force Officers Wives, Kappa Kappa Gamma Alumni. Condr. research in field. Home: 15 Plaza Olas Altas Albuquerque NM 87109

MC RORIE, THOMAS HENRY, III, elec. engr.; b. Raleigh, N.C., Oct. 28, 1936; s. Thomas Henry and Susie Ola (Griffin) McR.; B.E.E., U. Fla., 1961; M.B.A., Calif. State U., 1975, M.S.E.E., 1978; m. Eleanor Joyce Monck, Jan. 31, 1958; children—Thomas Hugh, James Michael, Devon Lynn. Inertial nav. systems engr. Autonetics Marine Systems div. Rockwell Internat., Anaheim, Calif., 1961—, now project engr. for anti-submarine warfare tactical data systems. Served with USNR, 1954-62. Recipient Outstanding Academic Achievement award U. Fla., 1961. Mem. IEEE. Republican. Baptist. Club: Masons. Home: 9642 Bay Meadow Dr Huntington Beach CA 92646 Office: 3370 Miraloma Ave Anaheim CA 92803

MCSWEENEY, FRANCES KAYE, psychologist, educator; b. Rochester, N.Y., Feb. 6, 1948; d. Edward William and Elsie Winifred (Kingston) McS. B.A., Smith Coll., 1969; M.A., Harvard U., 1972, Ph.D., 1974. Lectr. McMaster U., Hamilton, Ont., Can., 1973-74; asst. prof. Wash. State U., Pullman, 1974-79, assoc. prof., 1979-83, prof., 1983—; cons. in field. Woodrow Wilson fellow, Sloan fellow, 1968-69; NSF fellow, 1970-72; NIMH fellow, 1973. Mem. Am. Psychol. Assn., Western Psychol. Assn., Psychonomic Soc., Assn. Behavior Analysis, Phi Beta Kappa, Sigma Xi. Contbr. articles to profl. jours. Home: NW 90 Thomas-D Pullman WA 99163 Office: Dept Psychology Wash State U Pullman WA 99164

MCTAGGART, PENELOPE SHANE, publisher; b. Winnipeg, Man., Can., Mar. 4, 1947; d. Daniel and Tana Shane; B.A., U. Wash., 1969. Writer, Seattle Community Coll. System, 1969-70; public relations officer Embassy of Japan, San Francisco, 1971-72; public relations dir. San Francisco Ballet, 1972-76; pub. Arts and Leisure Publs., San Francisco, 1976—; v.p. THG Enterprises; dir. Exec. Publs., Inc. Bd. dirs. San Francisco Com. for Joffrey Ballet. Mem. Assn. Theatrical Press Agts. and Mgrs., San Francisco Press Club. Office: Arts and Leisure Publs 950 Battery St San Francisco CA 94111

MC VEY, MARCIA ALICE, ednl. adminstr.; b. San Jose, Calif., Aug. 31, 1934; d. Charles Thurston and Thelma (Hackett) McV.; B.A., Pomona Coll., 1955; M.A., Claremont Grad. Sch., 1959; Ed.D. (Delta Kappa Gamma scholar), U. So. Calif., 1978. Tchr., Glendora Sch. Dist., 1955-59; tchr. Covina Valley Unified Sch. Dist., 1959-65, counselor, jr. high sch., 1965-67, asst. prin. jr. high, 1967-68, prin., 1968-72, 73-79; dir. curriculum and instruction Norwalk (Calif.) LaMirada Unified Sch. Dist., 1979-83, asst. supt. Centralia Sch. Dist., Buena Park (Calif.), 1983—; ednl. cons.; mem. Calif. Dept. Edn. task force on conflict resolution in secondary schs., 1972-73. Bd. dirs. HEAR Center, Pasadena, 1976—; community vol. Pomona Coll. Assocs. Kettering IDEA fellow, 1981. Mem. Assn. Calif. Sch. Adminstrs., Calif. Assn. Gifted, Profl. Advocates for Gifted Edn., Calif. Assn. Tchrs. English, Assn. Supervision and Curriculum Devel., AAUW, Phi Delta Kappa, Delta Kappa Gamma. Contbr. articles to profl. jours. Office: 6625 La Palma Ave Buena Park CA 90620

MC VICAR, LEONARD HUGO, planning and urban design consultant; b. Winnipeg, Man., Can., May 1, 1923; s. Leonard Harold and Hedy (Eckardt) McV.; came to U.S., 1955; Diploma in Town Planning, U. Toronto (Ont., Can.), 1953; certificate in pub. adminstrn., U. Calif., Berkeley, 1963, 65. children—Lochlan, Robin, Laird. Dir. community recreation City of Fremont (Calif.), 1956-68; prin. Center for Environ. Design, Fremont, 1968-72; v.p. Ribeira & Sue Assocs., Oakland, 1972-74; pres. Townscape Inc., Los Gatos, Calif., 1974-79; pres. Pacific Urban Design, Ltd.; assoc. prof. U. Calif., Berkeley and Davis, 1963-68; spl. cons. UN. Served with Royal Canadian Navy, 1938-42. Fellow Ont. Municipal Recreation Soc.; mem. Calif. Park and Recreation Soc. (certified recreation adminstr.), Am. Inst. Planners (asso.), Am. Inst. Landscape Architects. Republican. Mem. Evangelical Free Ch. Contbr. articles to profl. jours. Home: 353 Broadway Santa Cruz CA Office: 255 N Market St San Jose CA 95110

MCWILLIAMS, JOHN GLENN, lawyer, educator; b. Columbus, Ohio, Oct. 20, 1947; s. Kenneth E. and Cora May (Uncapher) McW.; m. Jodelle Ahearn, Mar. 27, 1982; 1 son, Ian Tyson. B.S.B.A. cum laude, Ohio State U., 1969; J.D., Duke U., 1972; postgrad. U. Calif.-Berkeley, 1980. Bar: Calif. 1972. Tax mgr. Price Waterhouse & Co., San Francisco, 1972-76; assoc. prof. San Francisco State U. 1976—; 19—; of counsel firm Jonas, Mathews Dominiqueas Olsen & Grice, San Francisco, 1978—; tchr. various courses Calif. C.P.A. Found. for Edn. C.P.A., Calif. Mem. Am. Acctg. Assn., Am. Inst. C.P.A.s, Calif. Soc. C.P.A.s, Am. Bus. Law Assn. Author: Fundamentals of International Taxation, 1979. Office: 1600 Holloway San Francisco CA 94132

MC WILLIAMS, ROBERT HUGH, judge; b. Salina, Kans., Apr. 27, 1916; s. Robert Hugh and Laura (Nicholson) McW.; A.B., U. Denver, 1938, LL.B., 1941; m. Catherine Ann Cooper, Nov. 4, 1942; 1 son, Edward Cooper. Admitted to Colo. bar, 1941; Colo. dist. judge, Denver, 1952-60; justice Colo. Supreme Ct., 1961-68, chief justice, 1969-70; judge 10th Circuit Ct. Appeals, 1970—. Served with AUS World War II. Mem. Phi Beta Kappa, Omicron Delta Kappa, Phi Delta Phi, Kappa Sigma. Republican. Episcopalian. Office: US Courthouse 1929 Stout St Denver CO 80294

MCWILLIAMS, THOMAS J., equipment rental and supply co. exec.; b. Denver, June 15, 1947; s. Thomas J. and Sara Sue (Stewart) McW.; B.S. in Bus. Adminstrn., U. Colo., 1969; grad. Jones Real Estate Coll., Denver, 1980; m. Adaline Fisher Grearson, Aug. 15, 1970; 2 daus.: Molly, Lindsey. Pres. Ansafone Colo., Denver, 1972-79, East Evans Rental & Supply Inc., Denver, 1977—. Mem. Air N.G., 1970-76. Mem. Associated Gen. Contractors Am. (assoc.), Mountain States Rental Assn. (treas. 1979, sec. 1980, v.p. 1981, Phi Kappa Tau (bd. govs.). Republican. Club: Perry Park Country Home: 8668 E Easter Pl Englewood CO 80112 Office: 4845 E Evans St Denver CO 80222

MEACHAM, CRAIG LEI, police chief; b. Pasadena, Calif., Mar. 5, 1931; s. William Albert and Edna May (Hornbeck) M.; m. Carolyn June Stentz, Feb. 22, 1971; children—Alan, Pamela, Craig, Janelle, Cynthia. A.A., Rio Hondo Coll., 1964; B.A., Calif. Western U., 1976, M.A., 1976. With Whittier (Calif.) Police Dept., 1955-69, div. comdr., until 1969; cons. criminal justice Gov. Ronald Reagan, 1969-70; dep. chief West Covina Police Dept., 1970-78, chief of police, 1978—, pub. safety div. mgr., 1981—; instr. Rio Hondo Coll. Served with USAF, 1950-54. Mem. Los Angeles County Chiefs of Police Assn. (pres. 1982), San Gabriel Valley Police Chiefs Assn. (pres.), Calif. Police Chiefs Assn. (treas.), Peace Officers Assn. Los Angeles County (exec. com.), San Gabriel Valley Peace Officers Assn. (pres. 1983), West Covina C. of C. (legis. com.). Club: West Covina Lions. Office: 1444 W Garvey St West Covina CA 91790

MEACHAM, MARGIE MILLHONE, judge; b. Omaha, Feb. 4, 1930; d. Paul L. and Margaret M. (Griffith) Millhone; m. Lenard F. Meacham, Aug. 15, 1973. B.S., U. Wyo., 1952, J.D., 1954. Bar: Wyo. 1954, U.S. Dist. Ct. Wyo. 1967, U.S. Ct. Appeals (10th cir.) 1967, U.S. Supreme Ct. 1980. Law librarian, instr. U. Wyo., 1953-55; assoc. Jerry W. Housel, Cody, Wyo., 1955-56, 62-68; sole practice, Cody, 1968-73; justice of peace Carbon County, Wyo., 1974-83; mcpl. judge City of Cody, 1968-73, City of Rawlins (Wyo.), 1978-82; judge County Ct., Rawlins, 1983—; mem. Jud. Planning Com. State of Wyo., 1978—. Sec., bd. dirs. Carbon County Counseling Ctr.; bd. dirs. Wyo. Law Enforcement Acad., 1972-73; past dir. Cody Boy Scouts Am. Mem. ABA (exec. bd. council spl. ct. judges, jud. adminstrn. div.), Wyo. Bar Assn., Park County Bar Assn. (pres. 1965-66), Am. Judges Assn., Am. Judicature Soc., Nat. Assn. Women Judges (nat. membership chmn. 1982-83), Who. Judges of Ltd. Jurisdiction Assn. (pres. 1980-82). Address: 1124 8th St Rawlins WY 82301

MEAD, JERRY DALE, wine expert, writer; b. Rogers, Ark., May 14, 1939; s. Lloyd Willard and Mary Frances (Boyd) M.; m. Linda Elizabeth Gallentine, Aug. 31, 1957; children—Loretta Jean, Jerry Dion, Sean Darren. Wine expert, cons. and writer, San Francisco, 1969—; founder, nat. dir. Wine Investigation for Novices and Oenophiles (WINO). Chmn. judges panel Orange County Fair com. wine competition, chmn. wine steering com.; auctioneer KQED-TV, San Francisco, 1981, 82. Mem. Bay Area Wine Writers, Ams. for Wine. Author syndicated column Mead on Wine; pub. WINO newsletter, WINO trader; contbr. numerous articles to nat. and regional publs.

MEADOR, PAUL MAURICE, lawyer; b. Tucson, Jan. 11, 1946; s. Donald E. and Lessie (Hallmark) M.; B.A. with distinction, Ariz. State U., 1968, J.D., 1971; LL.M., George Washington U., 1976; 1 dau., Tiffany C. Admitted to Ariz. State bar, 1971, Calif. bar, 1973, U.S. Supreme Ct. bar, 1976; commd. 2d lt. U.S. Air Force, 1971, advanced through grades to capt., 1972; law clk. Chief Justice, Ariz. Supreme Ct., 1971-72; asst. staff judge advocate Sacramento Air Logistics Center, 1972-75; contracts trial atty. U.S. Air Force, Directorate of Contract Appeals, Wright-Patterson AFB, Ohio, 1976-79; ptnr. firm Meador & Herrgott, Phoenix, 1979-81; ptnr. Galasky and Meador, 1982—; lectr. law Golden Gate U., 1973-75, Inst. Fed. Law for Gen. Practitioners, Fed. Bar Assn.; Ariz. State U., 1981—; U. San Francisco Sch. Law; 1981—; Fed. Publs. Inc. 1981—. Mem. ABA (assoc. editor Public Contracts Law Jour. 1978-), Fed. Bar Assn., Nat. Contracts Mgmt. Assn. (chpt. pres. 1980-81), Phi Delta Phi, Blue Key. Home: 2735 S El Marino Mesa AZ 85202 Office: Galasky and Meador 3300 N Central Suite 1500 Phoenix AZ 85012

MEADOWS, PAUL DWAIN, oil co. exec.; b. Niotaze, Kans., Oct. 22, 1926; s. Lowell G. and Georgia (Henderson) M.; B.S., N.Mex. Inst. Tech., 1952; m. Jimmie Loree Starkey, Jan. 28, 1950; 1 dau., Paula Jean. Various engring. positions Honolulu Oil Corp., Midland, Tex., 1952-59, mgr. engring., San Francisco, 1959-61; v.p. James A. Lewis Engring., Dallas, 1961-66, Res. Oil & Gas Co., Dallas, 1966-68; pres., dir. Canadian Res. Oil & Gas Ltd., Calgary, Alta, Can., 1968-80; vice chmn., chief exec. officer Res. Oil and Gas, Denver, 1977-80; pres., chief exec. officer Meadows Energy Co., Denver, 1980—. Del., State Democratic conv. Tex., 1966. Served with USAAF, 1944-45. Mem. Am. Petroleum Inst., Ind. Petroleum Assn. Am., Am. Inst. Petroleum Engrs. Home: 44 Sedgwick Dr Englewood CO 80110 Office: 5575 DTC Pkwy Suite 310 Englewood CO 80110

MEANS, BETTY LOU, educator; b. Connellsville, Pa., Nov. 18, 1927; d. Robert Parsons and Beulah Catherine (Detwiler) McCoy; m. Robert Earl Shaw, Oct. 17, 1952; m. Albert William Means, July 12, 1959; 1 son, Donald Clayton. Student Wilson Coll., 1945-47; B.A., W.Va. U., 1950, M.A., 1957; postgrad. California State Tchrs. Coll. of Pa., Waynesburg Coll., U. Albuquerque, U. N.Mex., Laverne Coll. Cert. tchr., Pa., N.Mex. Tchr. pub. schs. Connellsville, 1955-59, Bradley Pvt. Sch., Pitts., 1959-61, Chartiers Valley Schs., Pitts., 1961-68, Albuquerque Pub. Schs., 1969—; leader career edn. workshops. Chairperson entertainment and social com. Albuquerque Ret. Tchr's. Housing Corp. Named Master Tchr., Albuquerque Pub. Schs., 1982; award for outstanding contbn. to Heart Assn., Alpha Phi. Mem. Assn. for Supervision and Curriculum Devel., AAUW. Republican. Presbyterian. Home: 1207 Robin Rd SE Rio Rancho NM 87124 Office: 1100 Hood Rd SE Rio Rancho NM 87124

MEANY, HERBERT JOHN, manufacturing company executive; b. Prescott, Ariz., Mar. 12, 1923; s. Herbert John and Alice Louise (Vallett) M.; A.A. cum laude, East Los Angeles Jr. Coll., 1949; B.S magna cum laude in Engring, U. So. Calif., 1951; children—Herbert J., Claudine Meany Moore, Deborah Meany de Santos. With NI Industries (formerly Norris Industries, then Norris-NI Industries), Long Beach, CA. 1945—, engr., 1951-53, chief engr., 1953-56, div. mgr., 1956-60, corporate v.p., 1960-67, group v.p., 1967-72, exec. v.p., 1972-75, pres., chief exec. officer, 1975—; dir. Farr Co. Councilor U. So. Calif. Grad. Sch. Bus. Adminstrn. Registered profl. engr., Calif. Served with U.S. Army, 1941-45. Mem. Elec. Industries Assn. Calif. (pres. 1963, named Man of Yr. 1973), Mchts. and Mfrs. Assn. (dir., mem. exec. com.), ASME, Newcomen Soc. Clubs: Calif., Jonathan. Office: NI Industries Inc One Golden Shore Long Beach CA 90802

MECCA, ANDREW MARK, health research adminstr.; b. Santa Monica, Calif., Jan. 11, 1947; s. Woodrow Alexander and Margret E. (Walker) M.; B.S., San Diego State Coll., 1969; M.P.H., U. Calif., Berkeley, 1974, Dr.P.H., 1978; m. Kathleen Masson, Aug. 15, 1978. Dir. program devel. Marin Open House, San Rafael, Calif., 1972-73, dir. Treatment Alternatives to Street Crime program, 1973-75; chief substance abuse Marin Community Mental Health, San Rafael, 1975-76, Marin County alcoholism adminstr., 1976—; exec. dir. Calif. Health Research Found., Belvedere, Calif., 1978—; cons. to various health programs and confs. in Calif., Ariz., Oreg., Alaska, Australia, 1972-78; guest lectr. various confs. and schs., 1970—; mem. faculty San Francisco State U. grad program in health edn., 1978—. Coach, Tigers Little League Team, 1976—; founder Youth on the Run Club, 1977; bd. dirs. San Rafael United Way, 1977-79; bd. dirs. Mt. Tamalpais Primary Sch., 1976-79, pres., 1976-79. Served to capt., U.S. Army, 1969-72; Vietnam. Decorated Bronze Star. NIH grantee, 1972-75. Mem. Am. Pub. Health Assn., Nat. Assn. of Prevention Professionals, Internat. Assn. of Prevention Professionals, Calif. State Assn. of Alcoholism Adminstrs.,

Nat. Assn. of Pretrial Services. Democrat. Episcopalian. Club: Commonwealth (San Francisco). Author: Alcoholism in America, 1979; contbr. articles to profl. jours. Home: 180 Bella Vista Belvedere CA 94920 Office: PO Box 248 Belvedere CA 94920

MECHAM, GLENN JEFFERSON, lawyer; b. Logan, Utah, Dec. 11, 1935; s. Everett H. and Lillie (Dunford) M.; B.S., Utah State U., 1957; J.D., U. Utah, 1961; m. Anna Mae Parson, June 5, 1957; children—Jeff B., Scott R., Marcia, Suzanne. Admitted to Utah bar, 1961, Supreme Ct. U.S., U.S. Ct. Appeals 10th Circuit, U.S. Dist. Ct. Utah, Utah Supreme Ct., U.S. Ct. Claims; engaged in gen. practice, Roy, Utah, 1961-65; Duchesne County atty., 1962, Duchesne City atty., 1962; city judge Roy City, 1963-66; judge City of Ogden, Utah, 1966-69; lectr.-in-law and govt. Stevens-Henager Coll., Ogden, 1963-75; asst. U.S. atty. Dist. Utah, 1969-72; ptnr. Mecham & Richards, Ogden, Utah, 1972—; mem. Bur. Justice Stats. Adv. Bd., U.S. Dept. Justice. Chmn. Ogden City Housing Authority; chmn. instl. council Utah State U.; asst. mayor City of Ogden; pres. Utah League Cities and Towns, 1981-82. Served to lt col. USAF, 1957. Mem. Weber County (pres. 1966-68), Am., Utah bar assns., Am. Judicature Soc., Weber County Bar Legal Services (chmn. bd. trustees 1966-69), Utah Assn. Mcpl. Judges (sec.), Sigma Chi, Phi Alpha Delta. Home: 1748 Victoria Ct Ogden UT 84403 Office: 2506 Madison Ave Ogden UT 84403

MECHAM, STEVEN RAY, educational administrator; b. Salt Lake City, Oct. 10, 1938; s. Milton Claudius and Marjorie (White) M.; m. Donna Jean Johnson, Jan. 22, 1943; children—Brian Paul, Allan LeRoy. A.S., Weber State Coll., 1958; B.S., U. Utah, 1963; M.A., Tchrs. Coll., Columbia U., 1965; postgrad. McGill U.; Ph.D., Laurence U., Santa Barbara, Calif., 1981. Prin., Montreal (Que.) Oral Sch., 1966-70; state dir. hearing impaired Conn. Dept. Edn., 1970-71; dir. guidance Lexington Sch. for the Deaf, N.Y.C., 1971-72; prin. Exton Elem. Jr. High Sch., Mexico City, 1972-77; coordinator spl. edn. Weber Sch. Dist., Ogden, Utah, 1977-78; prin. Roosevelt Elem. Sch., Ogden, 1978-82; asst. supt. Weber County Schs., Ogden, 1982—; instr. U. Utah, 1965-66, St. Joseph Coll., Hartford, Conn., 1970-71; adj. prof. McGill U.; instr. Tchrs. Coll., Columbia U., 1968-70; acting chmn. dept. edn. U. Americas, Mexico City, 1976-77; cons. Far West Labs., San Francisco. Bd. dirs. Instituto Mexicano Norte Americano de Relaciones Culturales, Mexico City, 1975-76; bishop Ch. Jesus Christ of Latter-day Saints. chmn. Cancer Crusade, bd. dirs. Am. Cancer Soc. Weber County. Mem. Am. Orgn. Educators of Hearing Impaired (pres.), Can. Hearing Soc. (dir.), Utah Assn. Elem. Sch. Prins., Nat. Assn. Elem. Sch. Prins., Internat. Reading Assn., Am. Assn. Sch. Adminstrs., Alexander Graham Bell Assn. Club: Rotary. Contbr. articles to profl. jours. Home: 1972 E 5875 S Ogden UT 84403 Office: 1122 Washington Blvd Ogden UT 84404

MECKEL, PETER TIMOTHY, arts administrator, educator; b. Yankton, S.D., Nov. 28, 1941; s. Myron Eugene and Cynthia Ann (Turnblom) M.; m. Louise Gloria Mudge, Sept. 8, 1962; children—Christina Louise, Christopher Mark, Moya Anne; m. Adrienne Dawn Maravich, Dec. 30, 1972. Ed. Rockford Coll., Occidental Coll. Founder, gen. dir. Hidden Valley Music Seminars, Carmel Valley, Calif., 1963—, dir. Hidden Valley Opera Ensemble, Masters Festival of Chamber Music, Master Class Series; cons. in field. Mem. Music Educators Nat. Conf. Congregationalist. Address: PO Box 116 Carmel Valley CA 93924

MEDFORD, EDWIN LLOYD, hosp. adminstr.; b. Nashville, Oct. 4, 1949; s. M.A. and Norma J. (Jensen) M.; B.B.A. in Acctg., Southwestern Adventist Coll., 1973; m. Joyce Ann Brooks, Mar. 21, 1971; 1 son, Gregory Alexander. Controller, Am. Religious Town Hall, Dallas, 1973-76; hosp. adminstr. Rusk (Tex.) Meml. Hosp., 1976-77; v.p. fin. Paradise Valley Hosp., National City, Calif., 1977-81; asst. adminstr. Centre City Hosp., San Diego, 1981; adminstr. McNamara Hosp., Fairplay, Colo., 1981—. Mem. bus. adv. council Southwestern Coll., Bonita, Calif., 1978-79. Mem. Hosp. Fin. Mgmt. Assn. Republican. Seventh-day Adventist. Office: 824 Costello Fairplay CO 80440

MEDINAS, DEANA BERNICE, nurse; b. Washington, June 3, 1945; d. William Orville and Frances Genevieve (Kerr) Carter; m. David Anthony Medinas, Feb. 12, 1967; children—William Carter, Kacie Ann. Diploma Kaiser Found. Hosp. Sch. Nursing, 1966; B.A.H.S.A., St. Mary's Coll., Moraga, Calif., 1978; M.B.A., 1981. Staff nurse II, Kaiser Permanente Med. Care Emergency Dept., Hayward, Calif., 1966-68, head nurse, 1970-71, nursing supr. Kaiser Permanente Med. Care, 1971-77, sr. indsl. engr. regional offices, Oakland, Calif., 1977-78, nursing supr. Fremont, Calif., 1978-81, nursing mgr., 1981-83, adminstrv. asst. Med. Group, Hayward, 1983—. Mem. Vintage Hills Sch. Site Council; mem. adv. com. registered nurses Ohlone Coll.; mem. adv. council Fremont/Newark Regional Occupational Program. Mem. Calif. Nurses Assn., Kaiser Permanente Med. Care No. Calif. Nursing Service Adminstrs., Am. Mgmt. Assn., Emergency Dept. Nurses Assn. Republican. Episcopalian. Club: M.B.A. Investment.

MEDSGER, THOMAS LAURENCE, art director; b. Greenport, N.Y., July 1, 1940; s. William Francis and Doris Gould (Brigden) M.; B.F.A. cum laude (Dean's medal advt. design), Pratt Inst., Bklyn., 1962. Art dir. R. Ptak, advt., Phoenix, 1962-63, Cole, Fisher, Rogow, Inc., advt., Beverly Hills, Calif., 1965-67; art dir. Frank M. Hiteshew & Assos., publishers spl. interest mags., Beverly Hills, 1967-82; art dir., asst. editor Western's World, in-flight mag., Beverly Hills, 1970-82; art dir., package designer Mattel Electronics, 1982—; guest lectr. UCLA, San Diego State U. Served with U.S. Army, 1963-65. Decorated Army Commendation medal; recipient cert. merit Soc. Illustrators Los Angeles, 1970, 72. Office: 5150 Rosecrans Ave Hawthorne CA 90250

MEDSKER, STANLEY RICHARD, petroleum mktg. co. exec.; b. Dodge City, Kans., June 2, 1931; s. Hollis L. and Dorothy K. (Miller) M.; student U. Denver, 1949-52, U. Tulsa, 1957-58; B.A., U. Colo., 1956, LL.B., 1959; m. Aldah Marie Butler, Nov. 29, 1957; children—Kathleen Lynn, Michael Scott, Kimberly Michele, Cynthia Leigh. Admitted to Colo. bar, 1959, Okla. bar, 1959; v.p., sec., gen. counsel Frontier Refining Co., Denver, 1959-66; pres. Toot-n-Moo Properties, Inc., Denver, Kansas City, Mo., 1966-69; exec. v.p. Autotronic Systems, Inc., Denver and Houston, 1969-73; pres. S-M Petroleum Properties, Inc., Vail, Colo., 1976—, also dir.; v.p., dir. Feather Petroleum Co., Grand Junction, Colo., 1977—, A. Marie Enterprises, Inc., Vail, 1977—; dir. Evergreen Oil Co. Served with U.S. Army, 1953-54. Mem. Am., Colo., Okla. bar assns., Colo. Petroleum Council, Phi Alpha Delta. Lutheran. Clubs: Denver Athletic, Denver Oilman's. Home and office: PO Box 2327 3035 Booth Falls Rd Vail CO 81657

MEDUSKI, JERZY WINCENTY, nutritionist, biochemist; b. Kalusz, Poland, Oct. 29, 1918; s. Dobieslaw Antoni and Katarzyna (Barbowska) M.; came to U.S., 1962, naturalized, 1969; M.D., Warsaw (Poland) Med. Sch., 1946; Ph.D. in Biochemistry, U. Lodz (Poland), 1951; 1 son, Jerzy Dobieslaw. Organizer, chief pharmacology labs. Polish Nat. Inst. Hygiene, Warsaw, 1945-52, organizer, head lab. of intermediary metabolism, 1952-59; asso. prof. biochemistry Warsaw Med. Sch., 1955-59; asst. prof. neurology U. So. Calif. Sch. Medicine, Los Angeles, 1973—. WHO fellow, Holland, Scotland, 1948-49; research grantee, USSR, 1956. Mem. Polish Acad. Sci. (sci. sec. biochem. com. 1952-59), Polish Med. Assn. (sci. sec. nat. bd. 1958-59), Polish Biochem. Soc. (founding mem.), Biochem. Soc. London, Chem. Soc. London, Internat. Soc. on Toxinology, AAAS, Am. Soc. Microbiology, Internat. Soc. on Oxygen Transport to Tissues, Sigma Xi. Author 3 books on biochemistry; contbr. more than 80 articles to internat. jours.; author textbook on nutritional biochemistry, 1977. Home: 1066 S Genesee Ave Los Angeles CA 90019 Office: 1411 Eastlake Ave U So Calif Sch Medicine Los Angeles CA 90033

MEEK, CARROLL LARSON, psychologist; b. Whitehall, Mont., Oct. 6, 1942; d. Leland Carroll and Doris Grace (Husband) Larson; B.A., Whitman Coll., 1964; M.S., Ind. U., Bloomington, 1966; Ph.D., U. Idaho, Moscow, 1972; m. Saul Mathew Spiro, July 31, 1982. Resident asst. Whitman Coll., Walla Walla, Wash., 1964; asst. head resident, resident asst. Ind. U., Bloomington, 1964-66; counselor, head resident U. Wis., Oshkosh, 1966-68; counselor U. Idaho, Moscow, 1968-69; psychologist Wash. State U., Pullman, 1969-82; cons. Pullman and Wash. State U. Police Depts., 1980—; psychologist in pvt. practice, 1982—. Recipient Penrose Alumni award Whitman Coll., 1978. Mem. Am. Psychol. Assn., Am. Personnel and Guidance Assn., Nat. Vocat. Guidance Assn., Am. Assn. Sex Educators, Counselors and Therapists, Am. Coll. Personnel Assn., Defenders of Wildlife, Pet/People Partnership Council, Coll. Vet. Med. Wash. State U., Cousteau Soc. Home: 2339 Wallen Rd Moscow ID 83843 Office: SE 1205 Profl Mall Blvd Pullman WA 99163

MEEK, CHARLES RONALD, community college president, agriculture educator; b. Sherman, Tex., Sept. 3, 1943; s. Marion Harold and Doris Ethyl (Keller) M.; children—Charles Ronald, II, Janyth Cheryll, Beau Joshua Keller. A.A.S., Central Tex. Coll., 1965; B.S., East Tex. State U., 1970, M.Ed., 1971, D.Ed., 1975; B. Agrl. Mgmt., Am. Tech. U., 1976. Cert tchr., Tex.; lic. pilot, Tex. Asst. instr. East Tex. State U., 1970-71; dir. agr., dir. men's dormitory Grayson County Coll., 1971-73; dir. student affairs, registrar Central Tex. Coll., 1974, adminstrv. aide to v.p., 1975-76, exec. dean Overseas Europe, 1978-80, dep. chancellor program devel. and evaluation, 1980-81; dir. adminstrv. services, registrar Am. Tech. U., 1974-75, chmn. agri-mgmt. dept., 1975-76, dean of students, 1975-77; dean mil. and vets. affairs Am. Ednl. Complex Consortium, 1976, exec. dean Ft. Hood ops., 1976-78; supt. Am. Prep. Inst., 1977-78; pres. Pueblo (Colo.) Community Coll., 1981—. Pres. Pueblo Met. Mus. Bd.; bd. dirs. Boy Scouts Am., Camp Fire Girls, Prison Vocat. Tng.; mem. Pueblo Econ. Devel. Corp. Served with USAF, 1963-66. Mem. Nat. Rehab. Assn., Colo. Vocat. Assn., Aircraft Owners and Pilots Assn., Am. Assn. Community and Jr. Colls. (Pres.'s Acad.), Pueblo C. of C. (bd. dirs.), Phi Delta Kappa, Alpha Gamma Who. Club: Rotary. Designer individualized skill tng. programs for U.S. mil. personnel. Office: 900 W Orman Ave Pueblo CO 81004

MEEK, LOYAL GEORGE, editor; b. Cedar Rapids, Iowa, Sept. 10, 1918; s. Charles William and Mina (Armstrong) M.; A.B., Coe Coll., Cedar Rapids, 1940; m. Lois Tankersley, Sept. 28, 1941; children—Jeremy, Andrew, Geoffrey, Margaret. Reporter, state editor, editorial writer Cedar Rapids Gazette, 1940-60; spl. asst. to U.S. Senator Jack Miller, 1961-62; editorial writer, then chief editorial writer Milw. Sentinel, 1962-73; editor Phoenix Gazette, 1973—. Bd. dirs. Friends of Phoenix Public Library. Service with AUS, 1942-46. Mem. Nat. Conf. Editorial Writers, Am. Soc. Newspaper Editors, Sigma Delta Chi. Club: Phoenix Press. Office: PO Box 1950 Phoenix AZ 85001

MEEKER, ARLENE DOROTHY HALLIN (MRS. WILLIAM MAURICE MEEKER), manufacturing company executive; b. Glendale, Calif., June 13, 1935; d. Haddon Eric and Martha (Randow) Hallin; grad. John Muir Jr. Coll., 1953; student Los Angeles Valley Coll., 1956-58, B.A., Whittier Coll., 1973, M.B.A., 1980; m. William Maurice Meeker, Aug. 19, 1966; 1 son, William Michael. Statewide sec. pub. relations United Republicans Calif., Los Angeles, 1964; personnel specialist Sanford Mgmt. Services, Inc., Los Angeles, 1964-66; v.p. personnel Grover Mfg. Corp., Montebello, Calif., 1966-75, pres., 1975—, dir., 1969—; dir. Brit. Marine Industries. Mem. City of Whittier Transp. and Parking Commn., 1976—, chmn. commn., 1977-79; trustee Oxford Sch., Whittier, Calif., 1982—; council mem. Los Angeles County Art Mus., 1969-80; bd. dirs. Friendly Hills Property Owners Assn. pres., 1982-83; mem. Whittier Guild, Children's Hosp.; mem. Whittier Republican Women Federated, 1977—, 1st v.p., 1981; Rep. precinct capt., 1964; mem. pres.' adv. council bus. and econs. Whittier Coll. Mem. Docian Soc. (pub. relations chmn. 1967-68), AAUW. Republican. Conglist. Club: Newport Harbor Yacht (Newport Beach, Calif.); Friendly Hills Country, Lincoln (pres. 1982—) (Whittier, Calif.). Author: Stress Differences between Male and Female Executives, 1980; columnist This Week. Home: 9710 Portada Dr Whittier CA 90603 Office: 620 S Vail St Montebello CA 90640

MEEKER, MILTON SHY, heavy duty truck mfg. co. exec.; b. Knob Noster, Mo., Nov. 9, 1933; s. David and Helen Elizabeth (Kendrick) M.; B.A., U. Calif. at Berkeley, 1955, B.S., 1959; M.B.A., U. Mich., 1963; m. Nancy Orbison, Nov. 27, 1976; 1 son, Sherwin Kendrick. With Ford Motor Co., 1959-68; dir. purchasing, mktg., research mgr. Paccar, Inc., Seattle, also Newark, Calif., 1968-71; commr. fed. supply service, commr. automated data and telecommunications, asso. dep. adminstr. GSA, Washington, 1972-75; dir. purchasing chem. group FMC Corp., Phila., 1975-77, dir. purchasing planning and adminstrn., Chgo., 1977-79; gen. sales mgr. Peterbilt Motors Co. div. Paccar, Newark, Calif., 1979-80, mktg. mgr., 1980—. Chmn., Pres.'s Com. for Purchase of Products from Blind, 1973-74; bd. dirs. Nat. Industries for the Blind. Served with U.S. Army, 1957-58. Republican. Home: 254 Almeria Ave Fremont CA 94538 Office: 38801 Cherry St Newark CA 94560

MEEKER, WILLIAM MAURICE, manufacturing company executive; b. Cropsey, Ill., May 28, 1915; s. Maurice Siebert and Clara Louise (Hood) M.; m. Arlene Dorothy Hallin, Aug. 19, 1966; children—Nancy Lee Meeker Bordier, William Michael. Student Whittier Coll., 1933-34, Lingnam U., Canton, China, 1934-35, U. Paris, 1936; B.S., U. So. Calif., 1938. Engr., Lockheed Aircraft Co., Burbank, Calif., 1938-47; mgr. Am. Die Cast Corp., San Gabriel, Calif., 1948; pres. Mode Products Corp., Alhambra, Calif., 1949-51; v.p. Grover Mfg. Corp., Montebello, Calif., 1951-55, chmn. bd., pres., 1955—, also dir.; dir. Brit. Marine Industries. Patron Huntington Hartford Theater. Mem. Los Angeles County Mus. Art, Los Angeles World Affairs Council, Alpha Epsilon Omicron, Sigma Nu. Clubs: Newport Harbor Yacht (Balboa, Calif.); Friendly Hills Country (Whittier, Calif.). Patentee in field. Home: 9710 Portada Dr Whittier CA 90603 Office: 620 S Vail Ave Montebello CA 90640

MEEKS, JAMES DONALD, librarian; b. Kansas City, Mo., May 10, 1920; s. Walter James and Mary Elizabeth (Mershon) M.; B.A. in English Lit., U. Kansas City, 1941; B.S. in Library Sci., U. Denver, 1946; M.S., Columbia U., 1951; m. Patricia Ann Lowe, Feb. 27, 1953 (div.); children—Mary, Ann, Robert. Head reference dept., then asst. library dir. Yonkers (N.Y.) Public Library, 1947-49; dir. library services USIS, Calcutta, India, 1949-50; br. asst. Bklyn. Pub. Library, 1950-51; dir. Enid (Okla.) Pub. Library, 1951-53, St. Joseph (Mo.) Pub. Library, 1953-55, Dallas Pub. Library, 1955-61; library coordinator Cherry Creek Sch. Dist., Englewood, Colo., 1962-69; instr. U. Denver, 1963-69; dir. Colo. State Library, 1969-74; mem. faculty U. Denver, 1974-75; city librarian, Eugene, Oreg., 1975—; mem. faculty U. Oreg. Sch. Librarianship; vis. prof. Grad. Sch. Library Studies, U. Hawaii, Manoa, fall 1982. Mem. Tex. Library Assn. (pres. 1960), Colo. Library Assn. (pres. 1970), Oreg. Library Assn. (pres. 1980), ALA. Served with AUS, 1942-45. Mem. Pacific N.W. Library Assn. Episcopalian. Home: 1162 Charnelton St Apt 5 Eugene OR 97401 Office: 100 W 13th Ave Eugene OR 97401

MEE-LEE, DENIS, psychiatrist; b. Brisbane, Australia, June 10, 1941; came to U.S., 1969; s. Alfred and Ora Marjorie (Hon) M.; M.B., B.S., U. Queensland, Australia, 1966; M.Sc. in Psychiatry, Ohio State U., 1971; certificate in community psychiatry Harvard U., 1972; m. Valerie Ida Brandon, Jan. 23, 1969; children—Lavonda, Denis Brandon, Matthew Byron. Intern, Townsville Gen. Hosp., Queensland, Australia, 1967-68; resident Harding Hosp., Worthington, Ohio, Ohio State U., Columbus, 1969-71; fellow Harvard U., 1971-72; instr. psychiatry Harvard U., Cambridge, Mass., 1972-73; cons. Mass. Dept. Mental Health, Boston, 1972-73; dir. center for human services New Eng. Meml. Hosp., Stoneham, Mass., 1973-76; chief psychiatrist mental health div. Hawaii Dept. Health, Honolulu, 1976-77, chief mental health div., 1977—; asso. clin. prof. U. Hawaii, Honolulu, 1976-82, asso. prof., 1982—. Mem. State Commn. on Mental Health and Criminal Justice, 1978—; mem. central com. Aloha United Way, 1978—. Mem. Am. Psychiatric Assn., Am. Public Health Assn., Am. Assn. Fgn. Med. Grads., Hawaii Psychiatric Soc., Hawaii Assn. Asian and Pacific People. Home: 2626 Ferdinand Ave Honolulu HI 96822 Office: State Dept of Health PO Box 3378 Honolulu HI 96801

MEENAN, PATRICK HENRY, state legislator; b. Casper, Wyo., Sept. 24, 1927; s. Hugh Martin and Margaret (Kelly) M.; B.S. cum laude, U. Notre Dame, 1949; m. Shirley Louise Byron, Dec. 30, 1950; children—Maurya Ann, Kevin Patrick, Michael James, Patricia Kelly. CPA Raab, Roush & Gaymon, Casper, 1949-53, partner 1960-68; asst. treas. Williston Oil & Gas Co., 1953-55; partner Meenan & Higgins, Casper, 1955-60; pres. KATI-AM & FM, Casper, 1963-81, KAWY Stero Radio, 1967-81; ptnr. Meenan, Miracle & Sherrill, C.P.A.'s, 1975-76; sec. dir. Bank of Casper, 1980—; pres. PM Enterprises, Inc., 1981—; dir. Security Bank of Glenrock; Erin Corp. Mem. CBS Radio Affiliaties, 1963—. Councilman City of Casper, 1956-65, v.p., 1961, mayor, 1962, 65; mem. Wyo. Ho. of Reps., 1969—, majority floor leader, 1983—, chmn. joint house-senate com. on corps, elections and polit. sub-divs. Pres. bd. dirs. Notre Dame Club of Wyo., 1960—; gen. chmn. Notre Dame Found., 1963—. Named Young Man of Year, Jr. C. of C., Casper, 1962; Boss of Year, 1965; Distinguished Pub. Servant award City of Casper. Mem. Am. Ist. C.P.A.'s, Notre Dame Alumni (nat. dir. 1972-75), Wyo. So. C.P.A.'s, Nat., Wyo. assns. broadcasters. Elk, K.C. Republican. Roman Catholic. Home: 3070 E 4th St Casper WY 82601 Office: PM Enterprises Inc Suite 211 Hilltop Nat Tower 300 Country Club Rd PO Box 9727 Casper WY 82609

MEGEL, GARY EDWARD, jeweler, gemologist; b. Colorado Springs, Colo., Apr. 26, 1950; s. Edward J. and LaVerne M. (Ball) M.; B.S. in Mktg./Fin., Colo. State U., 1972; grad. gemologist Gemological Inst. Am., 1973; emergency med. technician Pikes Peak Community Coll., 1981; m. D. Jeanne Williams, Sept. 2, 1978. With Megels Jewelry, Colorado Springs, 1972—, mgr., 1978—. Bd. dirs. Downtown Colorado Springs, Inc., 1977, 83—, exec. bd. dirs., 1978-80, chmn. Christmas decoration com., 1978-80; advanced and standard first aid, C.P.R. and vital signs ARC, 1981—. Fellow Gemmological Assn. Gt. Britain; mem. Gemmological Assn. Australia, Am. Gem. Soc. (cert. gemologist), Am. Numismatic Assn., Mensa. Club: Promoters (pres. 1977-78). Office: 12 E Pikes Peak Ave Colorado Springs CO 80903

MEHREN, LAWRENCE LINDSAY, investment co. exec.; b. Phoenix, May 26, 1944; s. Lawrence and Mary Teresa (Stelzer) M.; B.A., U. Ariz., 1966; M.A., U. Ariz., 1968; m. Lynn Athon McEvers, June 5, 1965; children—Lawrence Lindsay, John Eskridge. Bus. mgr. Rancho Santa Maria, Peoria, Ariz., 1968-69; traffic mgr. Glen-Mar Mfg. Co., Phoenix, 1969-70; account exec. Merrill Lynch, Pierce, Fenner and Smith, Inc., Phoenix, 1970-77, sr. account exec., 1977-78, asst. v.p., 1978-80, v.p., 1980-82; v.p. Harbor Equity Funds, Inc., 1982—. Mem. Maricopa County Citizens Action Com., Charter Govt. Com.; chmn. Madison Citizens Adv. Com., 1973-74; bd. dirs. Planned Parenthood, 1972-75, Brophy Coll. Prep. Sch., 1981—. Recipient award Ariz. Hist. Found., 1968. Mem. Nat. Securities Traders Assn., Ariz. Securities Assn., Phoenix Stock and Bond Club (dir. 1979-82), Ariz. Acad. Public Affairs, Phoenix C. of C., Inst. Cert. Fin. Planners, Internat. Assn. Fin. Planners, Phi Alpha Theta, Beta Theta Pi. Roman Catholic. Club: Phoenix Country. Home: 7215 N Central Ave Phoenix AZ 85020 Office: 2525 E Ariz Biltmore Circle Phoenix AZ 85016

MEHRING, CLINTON WARREN, civil engr.; b. New Haven, Ind., Feb. 14, 1924; s. Fred Emmett and Florence Edith (Hutson) M.; B.S., Case Inst. Tech., 1950; M.S., U. Colo., 1956; m. Carol Jane Adams, Mar. 9, 1946; children—James Warren, Charles David, John Steven (dec.), Martha Jane. Design engr., U.S. Bur. Reclamation, Denver, 1950-56; design engr. Tipton & Kalmbach, Denver, 1956-58, asst. resident engr., Quito, Ecuador, 1959-61, asst. chief design engr., Lahore, Pakistan, 1962-65, v.p., Denver, 1966-73, exec. v.p., 1973-79, pres., 1979—, also dir. Served with AUS, 1943-45. Recipient Theta Tau award as outstanding grad. Case Inst. Tech., 1950. Registered profl. engr. Wyo., Colo., Nev. Fellow ASCE; mem. Am. Cons. Engrs. Council, Colo. Soc. Engrs., U.S. Com. on Large Dams, Am. Concrete Inst., U.S. Com. Irrigation and Drainage, Sigma Xi, Tau Beta Pi, Theta Tau, Sigma Chi, Blue Key. Methodist. Home: 1821 Mt Zion Dr Golden CO 80401 Office: 1515 Arapahoe St Denver CO 80202

MEHRING, JAMES WARREN, aircraft company executive; b. Denver, June 15, 1950; s. Clinton Warren and Carol Jane (Adams) M.; B.S., Colo. State U., 1972; M.S., UCLA, 1974; Engr., Stanford U., 1981, Ph.D., 1983. Mem. tech. staff Hughes Aircraft Co., Canoga Park, Calif., 1972-74, El Segundo, Calif., 1974-77, project engr., Sunnyvale, Calif., 1977-81, sr. staff engr., 1981-83, project mgr., 1983—. Sec., Lancers Service Hon., 1970-71. Colo. State U. scholar, 1968-72; Hughes Masters fellow, 1972-74; Hughes Staff Engr. fellow, 1978-80. Mem. AIAA, IEEE, Colo. State U. Alumni Assn., ASME, Phi Kappa Phi, Sigma Tau, Tau Beta Pi. Methodist. Home: 4005 Old Mill Rd Alexandria VA 22309 Office: PO Box 92919 Los Angeles CA 90009

MEI, LEN, research engineer; b. Shaghai, China, Jan. 16, 1947; came to U.S., 1970; s. Dick and Liang-Shan (Chiang) M. B.Eng., Chiang Kung U., Taiwan, 1969; M.S., U. Ill., 1972, Ph.D., 1975. Assoc. prof. elec. engring. U. Campinas (Brazil), 1975-79; vis. assoc. prof. Stanford (Calif.) U., 1979-81; mem. sr. research staff Fairchild Semiconductor, Palo Alto, Calif., 1981—. Mem. IEEE, Am. Vacuum Soc., Am. Phys. Soc., Electrochem. Soc. Editor: Metallurgical Youth, 1966-67. Home: 1942 Silverwood Ave Mountain View CA 94043 Office: 4001 Miranda Ave Palo Alto CA 94304

MEIER, JOHN HENRY, clinical psychologist; b. Denver, Sept. 19, 1935; s. Henry Joseph and Helen Miriam Meier; m. Ann Heckendorf, Aug. 21, 1960; children—Rebecca Ann, Rita Elizabeth, Rhonda Marie. B.A. in Philosophy and English, Regis Coll., Denver, 1958; M.A. in Child Clin. Psychology, U. Denver, 1960; Ph.D. in Ednl. and Devel. Psychology, 1965. Cert. clin. psychologist Calif., Colo. Tchr., Grand County Schs., Cranby, Colo., 1958-59, Cherry Creek Schs., Englewood, Colo., 1959-61; psychotherapist, co-founder, prin. Rampart Sch., Woodland Park, Colo., 1961-62; chief sch. psychologist Littleton (Colo.) Pub. Schs., 1962-63; assoc. prof. psychology, counseling and guidance U. No. Colo., Greeley, 1963-69; dir. Learning Disabilities Project Rocky Mt. Ednl. Lab., Denver/Salt Lake City, 1967-69; dir. John F. Kennedy Child Devel. Ctr., U. Colo. Med. Ctr., Denver, 1969-75; dir. U.S. Office of Child Devel., chief U.S. Children's Bur., HEW, Washington, 1975-77; assoc. prof. pediatrics, psychiatry, clin. psychology and edn. U. Colo. Sch. Medicine, Denver, 1969-77; dir. research Childhelp USA/Internat., Beaumont, Calif., 1977—; assoc. clin. prof. med. psychology Neuropsychiatric Inst., UCLA. Fellow Am. Psychol. Assn.; mem. Calif. Psychol.

Assn., Assn. Children with Learning Disabilities, Council Exceptional Children, Am. Assn. Mental Deficiency, Child Welfare Assn. Am., Internat. Assn. Sci. Study of Mental Deficiency, Order Mark Twain, Psi Chi, Psi Upsilon. Author: The New Nursery School, 1969; System for Open Learning, 1970; Screening and Assessment of Young Children at Developmental Risk, 1973; Remote Microtraining, 1975; Developmental & Learning Disabilities, 1976; Facilitating Children's Development, 1978; contbr. numerous articles to profl. jours. Home: 103 Garden Hill Redlands CA 92373 Office: 14700 Manzanita Park Rd Beaumont CA 92223

MEIER, MATTHIAS S(EBASTIAN), historian; b. Covington, Ky., June 4, 1917; married; 5 children. B.A., U. Miami, 1948; M.A., Mexico City Coll., 1949; Ph.D. in Latin Am. History, U. Calif., Berkeley, 1954. Lectr. in U.S. history San Francisco State Coll., summers 1953-55, in U.S. and Latin Am. history Bakersfield Coll., 1955-63; asst. prof. Fresno State Coll., summer 1956, fall 1962; asst. prof. Latin Am. history U. Santa Clara, 1963-66, asso. prof., 1966-72, prof., 1972—; Fulbright lectr. Nat. U. Tucumán and Inst. Nacional de Profesorado Secundario, Buenos Aires, Argentina, 1958-59; lectr. U. Ibero-Am., summer 1965; vis. prof. San Jose State Coll., spring 1968. Served with Signal Corps, U.S. Army, 1942-46. Mem. Am. Hist. Assn., Pacific Coast Council Latin Am. Studies (pres. 1964-65, 76-77), Latin Am. Studies Assn., Conf. Latin Am. Historians, Assn. Borderlands Scholars. Author: (with Feliciano Rivera) The Chicanos: a history of Mexican Americans, 1972; A bibliography for Chicano history, 1972; editor: (with Feliciano Rivera) Readings on La Raza: twentieth century, 1973, Dictionary of Mexican American History, 1981, Borderlands Sourcebook, 1983; Bibliography of Mexican-American History. Office: Dept History U Santa Clara Santa Clara CA 95053

MEIER, PARALEE BINGHAM, publishing executive; b. Ericson, Nebr., May 31, 1931; d. William David and Violet Geniece (Benson) Bingham; m. Lyle Keith Meier, Feb. 4, 1951 (div.); children—Kathryn Mazen, John William, James Bingham. A.A., Nebr. State Coll., 1950; A.B., Calif. State U.-Chico, 1965, M.A., 1966. Teaching, reading specialist, Calif. Tchr., Pub. Schs. Trenton (Nebr.), 1950-52, Omaha, 1955-56, Chico, Calif., 1966-67; high sch. reading and English tchr., Chico, 1967-72; asst. prof. Calif. State U.-Chico, 1966-72; dir. cons. services Western region Random House Publs., N.Y.C., 1972-79; sales rep. Bowmar Noble Publs., Los Angeles, 1979-80; regional sales mgr. Raintree Publs. Group, Milw., 1979-81, regional mktg. mgr., 1981-83; exec. v.p. Cypress Pubs., Glendale, Calif., 1983—. Named Outstanding Tchr. of English, Calif., 1970. Mem. Am. Mgmt. Assn., Nat. Assn. Female Execs., Assn. Supervision and Curriculum Devel., Nat. Council Tchrs. of English (achievement contest judge 1971), Internat. Reading Assn., Calif. Assn. Tchrs. of English. Republican. Methodist. Office: 1763 Gardena Ave Glendale CA 91204

MEIER, SUSAN THERESA, educator; b. Sioux City, Iowa, Dec. 15, 1942; d. Adolph Leo and Helen Margaret (Fisher) Meier; B.A., Calif. State U.-Sacramento, 1970, M.A., 1972; Ph.D., U.S. Internat. U., 1974; divorced; children—Keith Gmeinder, Donna Sue Gmeinder. Counselor, Sacramento County Probation Dept., 1970-72, vol. Suicide Prevention Service, Sacramento, 1971-72; behavioral therapist Inst. for Smoking Control, Sacramento, 1971-72; instr. psychology San Diego Community Coll. Dist., 1973-74; psychol. and ednl. cons. Naval Postgrad. Sch., Monterey, Calif., Naval Instructional Tech. Devel. Center, San Diego, 1974-75; instr. criminal justice Calif. State U.-Sacramento, 1976, asst. prof., 1976-80, assoc. prof., 1980—; cons. Office of Edn., Santa Cruz County, 1975. Mem. San Diego County Health Edn. Commn., 1974. Recipient various fellowships, including Nat. Endowment for Humanities, 1979. Mem. Am., Western psychol. assns., Acad. Criminal Justice Scis., Am. Soc. Criminology (arrangements com. conf. 1980), Western Soc. Criminology (exec. bd. 1978-79, 82—, chmn. publicity conf. 1979, acad. membership chmn. 1981—), Psi Chi, Mensa. Home: 9709 Elmira Circle Sacramento CA 95827 Office: Div Criminal Justice Calif State U 6000 J St Sacramento CA 95819

MEIGS, JOHN LIGGET, artist, designer photographer; b. Chgo., May 10, 1916; s. John L. and b. Chgo., May 10, 1916; s. John L. and Margaret Mary (Cookley) M.; student U. Redlands, 1933-34. Newspaper reporter, Los Angeles and Honolulu, 1935-41; editor Islander Mag., 1949-50; textile designer, 1939-50; prin. archtl. design co., 1962—; one-man shows: Honolulu Acad. Arts, Santa Fe Mus., Tex. Tech. Mus., Ball Mus., Dayton Mus., Baker Gallery, Grand Central Gallery; group shows; Tex. Watercolor Soc., Am. Watercolor Soc.; represented in permanent collections; U. Tex., Roswell Mus., El Paso Mus., Tex. Tech. Mus. Exec. dir. Lincoln County Heritage Trust. Served with USN, 1942-45; PTO. Author: Peter Hurd-The Lithographs, 1968; Peter Hurd Sketchbook, 1971; The Cowboy in American Prints, 1973; Billy the Kid-Fact, Fiction, Fantasy, 1982. Address: San Patricio NM 88348

MEIKLEJOHN, ALVIN J., JR., state senator, lawyer, acct.; b. Omaha, June 18, 1923; B.S., J.D., U. Denver, 1951; m. Lorraine J. Meiklejohn; children—Pamela Ann, Shelley Lou, Bruce Ian, Scott Alvin. Mem. Colo. Senate from 19th dist., 1976—, chmn. com.; edn.; mem. Edn. Commn. of States, 1981—. Mem. Jefferson Sch. Dist. No. R-1 Bd. Edn., 1971-77, pres., 1973-77. Served to capt. U.S. Army, 1940-46; to maj. USAF, 1947-51. Mem. Am. Bar Assn., Colo. Bar Assn., Denver Bar Assn., Colo. Inst. C.P.A., Am. Inst. C.P.A., Arvada C. of C. (dir.). Republican. Clubs: Masons, Shriners. Office: 1600 Lincoln Center Bldg 1660 Lincoln St Denver CO 80264

MEIL, WALTER JOHANNES GEORGE, hotel/resort executive; b. Dornhagen, Germany, Jan. 30, 1935; came to U.S., 1963, naturalized, 1968; s. Heinrich and Margarete (Hagele) M.; m. Aug. 31, 1975; children—Bjorn, Craig, Nilsen, Colleen, Stephanie. Student pub. schs., Germany. Apprentice, ship restaurant Schinche, Germany, 1949-52; with Commis Saucier Golf Hotel, Sonnenbichl, Germany, 1952-53, Black Forrest Hotel, Germany, 1953-54, Hotel Plazer, Germany, 1954-55; asst. chef D.R. Ehrenfeld-Mederean Cruise Ship, 1955-56; corp. exec. chef Amfac Hotel & Resort, Brisbane, Calif., 1981—; mem. cooking faculty Purdue U., 1981. Culinary Art Shows grantee, 1964-76. Mem. Chef Assn. Pacific Coast, Am. Acad. Chefs, Nat. Rifle Assn. Republican. Lutheran. Office: 111 Anza Blvd Burlingame CA 94010

MEILING, JAQUE LLOYD, business administration educator; b. Provo, Utah, Sept. 5, 1937; s. John C. and Bessie I. (Iverson) M.; m. Sheila Lee, Oct. 4, 1969; children—Dennette, Neal, Nicole, Brigitte, Stacy. B.A., U. R.I., 1975; M.A., Pepperdine U., 1977, postgrad., 1978. Commd. officer U.S. Navy, 1958, advanced through grades to lt. comdr., ret., 1979; prof. Central Wash. U., 1980—; mgmt. cons. Performax Systems, Internat., 1981—; mgmt. seminar leader. Decorated Silver Star, D.F.C., Air medal with 7 gold stars, Navy Commendation Medal. Mem. Am. Soc. Safety Engrs. Republican. Contbr. articles to profl. jours.

MEISENHEIMER, THOMAS HAROLD CHARLES, gardener; b. Milw., Aug. 7, 1941; s. Harold Clarence and Dorothea Raylene (Danielson) M. Cert. in teaching of landscape tech. skills UCLA Extension, 1980. Sr. gardener Los Angeles Unified Sch. Dist., 1976-79, area gardening supr., 1979-80; sr. gardener Birmingham High Sch., Van Nuys, Calif., 1980—; tchr. gardening skills and employee devel. U.S. Govt. CETA Program, 1978-80. Pres., Men's Softball League, Burbank, Calif., 1975-79, co-organizer and ofcl. men's softball tournaments, 1977-82. Served with U.S. Army, 1964-66. Recipient Outstanding Gardening Service award Los Angeles Unified Sch. Dist., 1981, Nursery Mgmt. award, 1973, Landscape Supervision Achievement award I, 1975, II, 1976, Employee Devel. award, 1976, 77, 78. Republican. Lutheran. Club: Los Angeles City Schs. Golf. Home: 14277 Sayre St Sylmar CA 91342 Office: 8210 Orion Ave Van Nuys CA 91406

MEKELBURG, DENNIS ARNOLD, small businss owner; b. Santa Barbara, Calif., Sept. 9, 1945; s. Arnold George and Aileen Kathryn (Strong) M.; A.A.S., Northeastern Jr. Coll., Colo., 1965; m. Diana Fay Hunter, Oct. 9, 1965; children—Rhonda Lynelle, Heather Elisa. Asst. mgr. U. No. Colo. Bookstore, Greeley, 1967-70; mgr. U. So. Colo. Bookstore, Pueblo, 1970-79, dir. aux, services U. So. Colo., 1979-82; owner/operator Western Post Holes, Pueblo, 1982—. Named Outstanding Adminstr., U. So. Colo. Associated Student Govt., 1981. Mem. Nat. Assn. Coll. Stores, Rocky Mountain Skyline Bookstore Assn. (pres., trustee, mgr. of yr. 1978). Home: 4221 Blueflax Rd Pueblo CO 81001

MELAND, WANDA MARIE, counselor; b. Havre, Mont., Oct. 30, 1950; d. Sigurd Elmer and Mary Thelma (Ulven) Meland. A.A., Waldorf Luth. Jr. Coll., 1970; B.A., B.S., Eastern Mont. Coll., 1973; M.S., No. Mont. Coll., 1977. Cert. profl. in psychology, Mont. Dept. Insts.; cert. guidance, phys. edn. tchr., Mont. Alt. houseparent Yellowstone Boys and Girls Ranch, Billings, Mont., 1973-75; therapist, dir. day treatment ctr. Northcentral Community Mental Health Ctr., Havre, 1975-77; elem. counselor Chinook (Mont.) Pub. Schs., 1977—. Mem. Am. Personnel and Guidance Assn., Mont. Personnel and Guidance Assn., Am. Mental Health Counselors Assn., Mont. School Counselors Assn. Democrat. Lutheran. Club: Sons of Norway. Home: Route 1 Box 3 Chinook MT 59523 Office: Eastside School Chinook MT 59523

MELBY, ALAN KENNETH, linguist, educator; b. Murray, Utah, Mar. 25, 1948; s. Kenneth O. and Charolette (Bryner) M.; B.S., Brigham Young U., 1973, M.A., 1974, Ph.D., 1976; m. Ulla-Britta L. Sandholm, Aug. 14, 1970; children—Eric, Roland, Irene, Philippe, Yvette, Vivianne. Assoc. prof. linguistics Brigham Young U., Provo, Utah, 1977—; v.p. Mgmt. Acctg., Inc. Mem. Linguistic Soc. Am., ACM, Assn. Computational Linguistics, Linguistic Assn. Can. and U.S., Acoustical Soc. Am. Republican. Mormon. Contbr. articles to profl. jours. Home: 1223 Aspen Ave Provo UT 84604 Office: Linguistics Dept Brigham Young Univ Provo UT 84602

MELCHER, JOHN, senator; b. Sioux City, Iowa, Sept. 6, 1924; D.V.M., Iowa State U., 1950; m. Ruth Klein, Dec. 1, 1945; children—Terry, Joan, Mary, Robert, John. Practiced vet. medicine, Forsyth, Mont., 1950-69; mem. 91st-94th congresses from 2d Dist. Mont.; U.S. senator from Mont., 1976—. City alderman, Forsyth, 1953-55; mayor, Forsyth, 1955-61; mem. Mont. Ho. of Reps. from Rosebud County, 1961-62, 69; mem. Mont. State Senate, 1963-67. Served with AUS, 1943-45; ETO. Decorated Purple Heart, Combat Infantryman's Badge. Office: 730 Hart Senate Office Bldg Washington DC 20510

MELEAR, JOHN DAVID, psychologist; b. Miami, Fla., May 1, 1929; s. Cullman Clark and Lydia Pearl (Shenk) M.; m. Patricia, Mar. 4, 1950; children—Michael Scott, David Kevin, Laurie Ann. B.S., U. Miami, 1951; M.S., U. Idaho, 1953; M.Ed., Fla. Atlantic U., 1967; Ed.D., U. No. Colo., 1972. Lic. psychologist, cert. sch. psychologist, Wyo., Colo. Psychologist Palm Beach (Fla.) Sch. Dist., 1960-69; instr. U. No. Colo., 1969-72; psychologist Weld Bd. Coop. Ednl. Services, La Salle, Colo., 1972-79; psychologist Laramie County (Wyo.) Sch. Dist. 1, 1979—. Mem. Am. Psychol. Assn., Nat. Assn. Sch. Psychologists, Wyo. Psychol. Assn. Contbr. articles to profl. jours. Home: PO Box 2704 Cheyenne WY 82003 Office: 2810 House Ave Cheyenne WY 82001

MELENDY, HAROLD ARTHUR, civil engr.; b. Brockton, Mass., Oct. 24, 1920; s. Harold Arthur and Rose May (Blum) M.; B.S.C.E., Wayne State U., 1950; m. M. Dawn Olmstead, June 16, 1951; children—Kirk A., Cornealla R. Design engr. Massey-Ferguson, Detroit, 1958-64; project engr. TRW Inc., Detroit, 1964-75; chief engr. Edwards Engring., New Orleans, 1975-77; sr. devel. engr. Vlier Engring., Burbank, Calif., 1977-81; chief engr. Mayco Pump Corp., Los Angeles, 1981—. Patentee in field. Home: 9830 Reseda St Apt 319 Northridge CA 91324

MELHUISH, DONALD STEDMAN, purchasing exec.; b. Phila., Sept. 7, 1924; s. Vern Persons and Iva Maude (Stedman) M.; student Carroll Coll., 1943; B.S. in Mech. Engring., Mich. Coll. Mining and Tech., 1949; m. Dorris Jean Bourland, Jan. 7, 1951; children—David Bruce, Daniel Wayne. Engring. trainee Carnation Co., Los Angeles, Oconomowoc, Wis., Tupelo, Miss., 1949; asst. purchasing agt. Carnation Co., Los Angeles, 1950-59; purchasing agt. Gen. Milk Co. (name now changed to Carnation Internat.), Los Angeles, 1959—. Mem. bd. edn., chmn. First Bapt. Ch. West Los Angeles, 1957-60, mem. bd. deacons, 1961-63, mem. bd. trustees, 1980—, sec. bd., 1981—; scoutmaster Boy Scouts Am., Potawatomi area, Oconomowoc, Wis., 1945-47, asst. scoutmaster Crescent Bay area, Westwood dist., Los Angeles, 1966-69, scoutmaster, 1969-73, Westwood dist. tng. chmn., 1971-72, mem. Crescent Bay area tng. com., 1971-72, Westwoods dist. commr., 1972-74, recipient Wood badge, 1971, Commrs. Service award, 1974, Dist. Award of Merit, 1974. Served with USAAF, 1944-45. Lifetime cert. purchasing agt. Mem. Nat. Assn. Purchasing Mgmt., Inc. Home: 9100 Monte Mar Dr Los Angeles CA 90035 Office: 5045 Wilshire Blvd Los Angeles CA 90036

MELIA, DANIEL FREDERICK, Celtic studies and rhetoric educator, educational administrator, consultant; b. Fall River, Mass., Mar. 2, 1944; s. Daniel John and Rita Ann (Lough) M.; m. Nancy Ruth Geist, Sept. 7, 1966 (div.); m. 2d, Teresa A. Donovan, July 30, 1983. A.B. magna cum laude in English, Harvard U., 1966, M.A. in Celtic, 1970, Ph.D. in Celtic Langs. and Lit., 1972. Teaching fellow Harvard U., Cambridge, Mass., 1968-72, asst. prof. dept. Celtic, summer 1974; asst. prof. rhetoric and folklore U. Calif., Berkeley, 1972-78, assoc. prof. rhetoric and folklore, 1978—, assoc. dean Coll. Letters and Sci., 1981—, humanities faculty research fellow, 1978-79. Vis. asst. prof. English dept. UCLA, 1973; lang. cons. Harvard Grad. Prize Fellow, 1969-72; jr. summer research fellow Nat. Endowment for Humanities, 1975. Fellow Medieval Acad. Ireland; mem. Medieval Acad. Am., Medieval Assn. of the Pacific, MLA, Celtic Studies Assn. N.Am. (v.p.). Club: Harvard of N.Y.C. Author: (with D. Calder et al) Sources and Analogues of Old English Poetry, Vol. II, 1983; contbr. articles in field to publs. including Brit. Archaeological Reports, Studia Hibernica XVII, Philological Quar. Office: Dept Rhetoric Univ Calif Berkeley CA 94720

MELLO, DONALD R., state senator; b. Owensboro, Ky., June 22, 1934; s. Jack and Gladys (Jasper) M.; student U. Nev.; grad. B.F. Goodrich Co. Mgmt. Sch., Sacramento; m. Barbara Jane Woodhall; children—Donald, David. Condr., S.P. Co.; mem. Nev. Assembly from 30th Dist., 1963-, chmn. Interim Finance com., 1975-77, chmn. Legis. Commn., 1973-74, chmn. Ways and Means com., 1973-80, sr. democratic assemblyman, from 1973, sr. assemblyman, from 1977; now Nev. state senator. Mem. adv. com. Title III, Nev. Dept. Edn. Mem. Washoe County Democratic Central Com., 1968-74; mem. Pres.'s Club United Transp. Union, PTA (life). Served with USNR. Recipient Friend of Edn. award Washoe County Tchrs. Assn., 1974, Appreciation award Nev. N.G., 1973-75, Assembly Speaker's award, 1977, Appreciation award Ret. Public Employees Nev., 1979, award Clark County Classroom Tchrs., 1979; commd. hon. Ky. col.; named One of 10 Outstanding Legislators in U.S., Assembly State Govtl. Employees, 1976. Democrat. Mason, Elk. Office: Nevada State Senate Carson City NV 89710

MELLOR, CATHERINE ANN, psychologist; b. Colorado Springs, Colo., May 21, 1950; d. Virgil and Violet Louise (Morris) Koehler; m. Dennis Lee Mellor, Aug. 10, 1948. B.S., Colo. State U., 1972; M.S., Abilene Christian U., 1974; postgrad. U. Nev., 1975-81, U. Tex., San Antonio, 1974-76. Staff, Mental Health/Mental Retardation Ctr., Drug Program, Abilene, Tex., 1974; sch. psychologist Abilene Ind. Sch. Dist., 1974-75; sch. psychologist Clark County Sch. Dist., Las Vegas, Nev., 1975-81; cons. Clark County Sch. Dist., 1981—; counselor Drug Intervention program Clark County Sch. Dist., 1977—. Mem. Am. Psychol. Assn., Nev. Psychol. Assn., Nev. Personnel and Guidance Assn., Tex. Psychol. Assn., Tex. Sch. Psychologist Assn., Clark County Assn. Sch. Psychologists (sec.), Nev. Sch. Psychologists Assn., Nev. Early Childhood Assn. for Spl. Children. Republican. Mem. Ch. of Christ. Home: 6255 Elmira Dr Las Vegas NV 89118 Office: 4205 16th St Las Vegas NV 89101

MELLOR, TONY (CLINTON LEE), JR., public relations/advertising executive; b. Phila., Apr. 23, 1942; s. Clinton Lee and Catherine Eugena (Stroud) M.; m. Sandra Fay Ballenger, July 6, 1973; children—Christine Tawn, Gabriel Ballenger, Dawn Irish. B.S., U. Ariz., 1964. Salesman Sta. KGUN, ABC-TV, Tucson, 1968-74; account exec. Sta. KZAZ-TV, Tucson, 1974-76, Sta. KOLD, CBS-TV, Tucson, 1976-78; div. mgr. Uni-Lab Corp., Tucson, 1979-82; pub. relations dir. Pima County Fairgrounds, Tucson, 1982—. State bd. dirs. Ariz. Mental Health Assn.; bd. dirs. Mental Health Assn. Greater Tucson; mem. La Fiesta de los Vaqueros Rodeo Promotion Com. Mem. Internat. Rodeo Writers Club, Tucson Advt. Club, N.W. Businessmen's Club, Alpha Gamma Rho Alumni. Republican. Episcopalian. Office: 11300 S Houghton Rural Route #7 Tucson AZ 85747

MELLS, ALEXANDRA KATHRYN, lawyer; b. Los Angeles, May 30, 1950; d. Samuel and Pauline Rebecca (Kronick) M.; B.A., UCLA, 1971, cert. in litigation, 1974; postgrad. Calif. State U., 1971-73; J.D., Loyola U., 1983. Legal sec. Ingber & Levin, Beverly Hills, Calif., 1973-74; litigation paralegal Wyman, Bautzer, Rothman & Kuchel, Los Angeles, 1975-77, Loeb & Loeb, Los Angeles, 1977-83. Nat. Merit scholar, 1967; Bank of Am. Achievement award in fgn. lang., 1967. Mem. Phi Alpha Delta (treas. 1981-82, justice 1982-83, dist. judge 1983—). Democrat. Jewish. Club: Brandeis-Bardin Inst. Home: 9930 W Pico Blvd Apt 1 Los Angeles CA 90035

MELMED, RONALD MARTIN, psychiatrist; b. Middleberg, Union of South Africa, July 20, 1930; came to U.S., 1933, naturalized, 1958; s. David and Eva (Cohen) M.; student N.Y. U., 1948-50; B.A. cum laude, Lafayette Coll., 1952; M.D., Jefferson Med. Coll., 1956; m. Marilyn Cohen, May 14, 1960; children—Carey, Fran. Intern, Atlantic City Hosp., 1956-57; resident in psychiatry Manhattan VA Hosp., N.Y.C., 1957-58, Phila. Psychit. Center, 1960-62; practice medicine specializing in psychiatry, Stamford, Conn., 1962-69, Greenwich, Conn., 1964-78; med. dir. inpatient unit Stanislaus County (Calif.) Mental Health Dept., 1978—; med. dir., co-founder Fly Without Fear, N.Y.C., 1969-78; co-founder, co-dir Cardiac Comprehensive Care, Greenwich, 1977-78; founder, dir. Biofeedback and Behavior Therapy Centers Conn., Greenwich, 1976-78; mem. staff Meml. Hosp., Modesto, Calif., 1980—, Scenic Gen. Hosp., Modesto, 1981—. Served with USNR, 1958-60. Dr. Ronald Melmed Day proclaimed by Office of Bd. of Commrs. of Clark County, Nev., Oct. 24, 1977; diplomate Am. Bd. Psychiatry and Neurology. Mem. Am. Psychiat. Assn., Am. Group Psychotherapy Assn., Am. Pain Soc. (charter), Assn. for Advancement of Behavior Therapy (leader spl. interest group Biofeedback 1977-78), Biofeedback Soc. Conn. (founding; pres. 1977-78), Biofeedback Soc. Am. (chmn. Council State Socs. 1978-79, chmn. com. employment 1979-80), Biofeedback Soc. Calif., Acad. Psychosomatic Medicine, Central Calif. Psychiat. Soc., Valley Psychotherapy Assos. (founding). Jewish. Home: 3616 Sagewood Ln Modesto CA 95356 Office: 800 Scenic Dr Modesto CA 95350

MELOAN, TAYLOR WELLS, educator; b. St. Louis, July 31, 1919; s. Taylor Wells and Edith (Graham) M.; B.S., St. Louis U., 1949; M.B.A., Washington U., 1950; D.B.A., Ind. U., 1953; m. Anna Geraldine Leukering, Dec. 17, 1944 (div. Nov. 1974); children—Michael David, Steven Lee; m. 2d, Jane Innes Bierlich, Jan. 30, 1975. Vis. asst. prof. mktg. U. Okla., 1953; asst. prof. mktg. Ind. U., 1953-55, asso. prof., 1955-59; prof. mktg. U. So. Calif., Los Angeles, 1959—, chmn. dept., 1959-69, interim dean Sch. Bus. Adminstrn., 1969-71, asso. v.p. acad. adminstrn. and research, 1971-81; research adviser mktg. U. Karachi (Pakistan), 1962; vis. prof. mktg. IPSOA, Turin, Italy, 1964; disting. vis. prof. mktg. U. Witwatersrand, Johannesburg, South Africa, 1978; mktg. cons., 1953—. Bd. dirs. Council Better Bus. Burs., Inc. Served with U.S. Maritime Service, 1942-46. Mem. Am. Econ. Assn., Am. Mktg. Assn. (chpt. pres. 1957-58, 63-64, nat. publs. chmn. 1966-67), AAUP. Clubs: Univ., Rotary (Los Angeles). Co-author: Marketing Management: Policies and Decisions, 1970; author: New Career Opportunities, 1978; Innovation Strategy and Management, 1979; Home: 639 Burlingame Ave Los Angeles CA 90049 Office: U Southern Calif University Park Los Angeles CA 90007

MELONE, MARGIE RUTH, health care co. exec.; b. Shawnee, Okla., Oct. 9, 1933; d. Jonah H. and Barbara Nancy (Krause) Haze; vocat. nurse diploma Fairmont Hosp., San Leandro, Calif., 1965; postgrad. Chabot Coll., U. Calif.; m. Victor P. Melone, Apr. 26, 1952; children—Victor P., Terri R. Vocat. nurse Barrett Convalescent Hosp., Hayward, Calif., 1965-68; v.p. La-Mar Co., Hayward, 1968—, Hunt-Malone Enterprises, Hayward, 1968-78; v.p. True Care, Inc., Hayward, 1970-77, Embassy House, Walnut Creek, Calif., 1970—; pres., adminstr. Barrett Convalscent Hosp., Inc., 1968-75, owner, adminstrv. cons., 1978—; trustee Barret Rest Home, Inc.; co-chmn. Adv. Bd. Mentally Ill and Retarded, 1973. Mem. So. Alameda County Commn. Aging, Am. Health Care Assn., Alameda County Mentally Retarded Assn., Calif. Assn. Health Facilities. Clubs: Met. Yacht, Order Eastern Star. Author articles, short story, poetry. Home: 1577 Denton Ave Hayward CA 94545 Office: 1535 Denton Ave Hayward CA 94545

MELOTT, RONALD KENNETH, fire protection consultant and engineer; b. Hillsboro, Oreg., May 8, 1939; s. Quinlin W. and Alma (Doern) M.; m. Marilyn R. Volz, Feb. 3, 1961; children—Pamela S., Carla M., Daniel W. B.S. in Applied Sci., Portland State U., 1970. Registered profl. engr., Oreg., Calif., Wash. Fire fighter to staff officer Portland Fire Dept., 1961-72; chief fire prevention specialist Nat. Fire Protection Assn., 1972-77; owner, fire protection cons., fire protection engr. Melott & Assocs., Beaverton, Oreg., 1977—. Bd. govs. George H. Tryon Found.; bd. dirs. Paul Lamb Found. Served with U.S. Army, 1961-63. Mem. Soc. Fire Protection Engrs. (officer Cascade chpt.), Nat. Soc. Profl. Engrs., ASME, Internat. Assn. Fire Chiefs, Western Fire Chiefs, Oreg. Fire Chiefs, Oreg. Fire Marshals, Nat. Fire Protection Assn., Fire Marshals Assn. N.Am., Internat. Soc. Fire Service Instrs., Profl. Engrs. Oreg. Baptist. Author: (with others) NFPA Handbook on Flammable and Combustible Liquids Code, 1981. Office: 11650 SW Bel Aire Ln Beaverton OR 97005

MELOY, JOHN REID, clinical psychologist; b. Lockport, N.Y., May 7, 1949; s. John Ogden and Janet (Reid) M. B.A. in History, Coll. of Wooster, 1971; M.S.W., U. Ill., 1974; M. Divinity, McCormick Theol. Sem., 1975; Ph.D., U.S. Internat. U., 1981. Lic. psychologist, lic. clin. social worker, Calif. Clinical social worker and program coordinator Oak Park (Ill.) Family Service and Mental Health Center, 1974-77; sr. psychiat. social worker San Diego County Mental Health, Escondido (Calif.) Clinic, 1978-82; dir. Psychiat. Security Unit, San Diego County

Jail, 1982—; pvt. practice psychotherapy, 1974—; founder Family Alliance for Mentally Disabled, Escondido, 1979; vol. cons. Parents of Adult Schizophrenics, San Diego. Mem. Am. Psychol. Assn. (divs. psychoanalysis and neuropsychology), Acad. San Diego Psychologists. Democrat. Contbr. articles to profl. jours. Office: 222 West C St San Diego CA 92101

MELOY, KATHRYN DALE, educator; b. Purcel, Okla., Feb. 22, 1938; d. Alvin D. Powers and Gladys (Young) Powers Goslin; m. Jerome Simpson, Aug. 17, 1956; children—Richard, Jason B.; m. Jack E. Meloy, Jan. 1, 1981. B.S., Central State U., 1959; M.A. in Home Econs., U. N.Mex., 1969, postgrad., 1970-80, Ed.S., 1982. Cert. vocat. home econs., ednl. adminstr., N.Mex. Tchr., Piedmont, Okla., 1959-60, Edmond, Okla., 1963-65, Albuquerque, 1965-68, Urbana, Ill., 1968-69, Bernalillo, N.Mex., 1969-71; instr. home econs. U. N.Mex., Albuquerque, 1976-77, asst. dir. program specialist, 1979-80; prin. Albuquerque Pub. Sch., 1981; coordinator vocat. and acad. edn. Title IV Project, Albuquerque, 1978—; tchr. home econs. Eldorado High Sch., Albuquerque, 1971—. Active LWV; mem. Partners of the Americas, membership chmn., 1978-80. Recipient N.Mex. Home Econs. Tchr. of Yr. award, 1982; N.Mex. Vocat. Home Econs. Tchr. of Yr., 1982. Mem. N.Mex. Vocat. Assn. (pres., 1982-83), N.Mex. Home Econs. Assn. (chmn. coop. relations 1980-82), State Adv. Council Home Econs. (chmn. 1979-81), Future Homemakers Am. (nat. advisor), Albuquerque Home Econs. Assn., Vocat. Edn. Equity Council, Am. Vocat. Assn., N.Mex. Vocat. Home Econs. Tchrs. Assn., Home Econs. Edn. Assn., NEA, Okla. Edn. Assn., Albuquerque Classroom Tchrs. Assn., Phi Delta Kappa. Author: (with Norma Milanovich) VIDEOS Workshop Trainers Manual, 1978; developed curriculum for flexible modular scheduling (Exploratory Arts Program) for Indian students in basic life skills and career education. Home: 1328 Camino Equestre NW Albuquerque NM 87107

MELQUIST, WAYNE EDWARD, wildlife biologist; b. Mpls., July 28, 1947; s. Edward Woodrow and Bernice Margaret (Halverson) M.; B.S., U. Wis., 1969; M.S., U. Idaho, 1974, Ph.D., 1981. Wildlife technician U. Idaho, Moscow, 1974, research asso., 1974-75; research asso. Dept. Wildlife, 1975-82, affiliate prof. wildlife resources, 1982—; field trip chmn. Palouse Audubon Soc., 1973-74; mem. otter specialist group Internat. Union for Conservation of Nature and Natural Resources, 1980—. Served with USMC, 1969-71. Wis. Legis. scholar, 1965; Nat. Wildlife Fedn. Environ. fellow, 1977-78; R.E. Dimick award Wildlife Soc., 1979; cert. asso. wildlife biologist. Mem. Am. Ornithologists Union, Am. Soc. Mammalogists, Pacific Bird and Mammal Soc., Raptor Research Found., Wildlife Soc., Sigma Xi, Phi Sigma. Lutheran. Contbr. articles to profl. jours. Office: Dept Wildlife U Idaho Moscow ID 83843

MELSON, WILLIAM HARVEY, water treatment manager; b. San Francisco, Oct. 25, 1919; s. Charles Frank and Pauline Elizabeth (Anderson) M.; m. Janet Cecelia McLean, Apr. 12, 1948; children—David, Donald Gabrielle, Elise, Kristen. Student pub. sch., San Diego. Cert. water treatment operator, Calif. With North Marin County (Calif.) Water Dist. 1956—, dir. water quality and wastewater adult edn. teaching, 1967—. Active 4-H. Served in USMC, 1938-45. Mem. Am. Water Works Assn., Nat. Rifle Assn., Amateur Trapshooting Assn., Pacific Internat. Trapshooting Assn. Democrat. Episcopalian. Home: 420 Ridge Rd Novato CA 94947 Office: North Marin County Water Dist 999 Rush Creek Pl Novato CA 94947

MELTON, CAROL SUE, film production executive; b. Chgo., Sept. 8, 1946; d. William Joseph and Harriet Ann (Elkins) A.; 1 son, Jordan Todd. Tchr. various sch. dists., 1969-71; media coordinator Simi Valley (Calif.) Free Clinic, 1971-72; tchr. English, social studies and bus. Simi Valley Unified Sch. Dist., 1973-77; mktg. dir., gen. mgr. Design Plus, Encino, Calif., 1977-79; mktg. dir. FMS Prodns. Inc., Los Angeles, 1979-82, v.p. mktg. and distbn., gen. mgr., 1982—. Mem. Assn. Labor and Mgmt. Adminstrs. and Counselors on Alcoholism, Ind. Film Producers Am., Calif. Women's Commn. on Alcoholism, Nat. Assn. Female Execs., Phi Kappa Phi.

MELTON, JAMES ROGER, public information officer; b. Pasadena, Calif., Sept. 30, 1943; s. Orval Wayne and Muriel Joyce Melton; 1 son, Brent Orval. B.A., San Jose State U., 1966; M.A., U. San Francisco, 1978. Mng. editor The Potlatch Stody mag., Potlatch Corp., San Francisco, 1968-71; communications mgr. Western Electronics Mfrs. Assn., Palo Alto, Calif., 1971; pub. info. officer Santa Clara Valley Water Dist., San Jose, Calif., 1972—. Served with U.S. Army, 1966-68. Mem. Pub. Relations Soc. Am. (accredited in pub. relations, treas. Peninsula chpt. 1983, Silver Anvil award 1978), Internat. Assn. Bus. Communicators, San Jose State U. Journalism Alumni Assn. (dir. 1983), San Jose State U. Alumni Assn. (dir. 1978). Office: 5750 Almaden Expressway San Jose CA 95118

MELTON, LYNDEL WARREN, civil engineering consultant; b. Monterey, Calif., Aug. 22, 1952; s. Clifford Warren and N. Nadine (Whistance) M.; m. Marilyn Edwards, May 2, 1981; children—Laura Marie, Collin Alfred. B.S.C.E. magna cum laude, U. of Pacific, 1975; M.S.C.E., Stanford U., 1975. Registered profl. engr., Calif. Project coordinator Calif. Water Resources Control Bd., Sacramento, 1975-77; project engr./mktg. coordinator Black & Veatch Cons. Engrs., Walnut Creek, Calif., 1977-82; project mgr. Kennedy/Jenks Engrs., San Francisco, 1982—. Recipient spl. recognition Engring. Council Sacramento valley, 1975, Calif. Water Resources Control Bd., 1977. Mem. ASCE, Water Pollution Control Fedn., Am. Water Works Assn. Republican. Lutheran. Club: Order of DeMolay (degree chevalier 1972). Author: (with others) Technical Manual of Practice for Rehabilitation of Sewer Systems, 1983; Developing a New Water Supply: Tuolumne County and the Emigrant Wilderness Area, 1983. Office: 657 Howard St San Francisco CA 94105

MELTON, PAMELA JEAN, sales exec.; b. Fullerton, Calif., Nov. 25, 1952; d. Douglas Neal and Jean (Kahl) French; student U. No. Colo., 1970-72; B.S., Ariz. State U., 1974; m. Dennis Patrick Melton, June 22, 1974. Vice pres., sec. Westunited Realty Corp., Phoenix, 1974-76; home economist Nat. Brands Inc., Phoenix, 1976-77, wholesale maj. appliance sales rep., 1980—; home economist Noble Distbrs., Inc., Phoenix, 1977-78, ter. sales rep., home economist, 1977-80; faculty microwave cooking Rio Salado Community Coll., 1978-81. Active Chicano Awareness activities through Barrio Youth Project, 1979-80. Named Salesperson of Yr., Gibson Mfg. Co., 1979, others. Mem. Am. Home Econ. Assn., Am. Home Econ. Central Div. (sec. 1978), Home Economists in Bus. (sec. 1978, pres. 1981-82), Nat. Assn. Underwater Instrs., Ariz. State U. Alumni Assn., Les Amis du Vin, Alpha Phi. Republican. Club: Ariz. Real Estate. Home: 1537 W Tuckey Ln Phoenix AZ 85015 Office: 4633 W Polk Phoenix AZ 85043

MELTZER, ROBERT HIRAM, artist; b. New Rochelle, N.Y., Oct. 18, 1921; s. Abraham Albert and Mary C. Meltzer; B.A., So. Meth. U., 1950; postgrad. U. Hawaii, 1952-56; m. Betty Kikumi Hikiji, Jan. 26, 1957; children—Eleanor Kikumi, Abraham Chuichi. Newspaperman, Honolulu Star-Bull., 1952-54, Honolulu Advertiser, 1954-56; exhibited in one-man shows including Edward-Dean Mus., Cherry Valley, Calif., 1967—, Central Wyo. Mus., Casper, Jasper Rand Mus., Westfield, Mass., U. Wis. at Stevens Point, Brandeis U., Waltham, Mass., Stetson U., DeLand, Fla., Marywood Coll., Scranton, Pa.; exhibited group shows including Am. Watercolor Soc., N.Y., 1978, NAD, 1978, Watercolor West, Riverside, Calif., 1978, San Bernardino County (Calif.) Mus., 1978, Anchorage Fine Arts Mus., 1978, U. Hawaii, 1978, Purdue U., 1978, McCook Coll., 1978, Frye Mus., Seattle, 1978, White House, Washington, 1981; represented in permanent collections including Smithsonian Mus., Washington, Edward-Dean Mus., So. Meth. U., Dallas, Nat. Archives, Washington, San Bernardino City Hall, San Bernardino City Mus., Armed Forces Pub. Info. Officers Inst., Ft. Slocum, N.Y.; artist-in-residence Living-Learning Center, U. Redlands, 1975, 76; coordinator watercolor seminars Crafton Hills Coll.; lectr. Wenatchee Valley Coll., 1977, So. Oreg. State Coll., Jackson (Tenn.) State Coll., Southwest Watercolor Soc., others. Bd. dirs. Riverside County Art and Cultural Center, 1972-74. Served with USN, 1940-46, 50-52. Recipient Distinguished Service award Riverside County Bd. Suprs., 1974, Resolution of Commendation, San Bernardino City Council, 1980, others; NSF grantee, 1967. Mem. Am. Watercolor Soc. (Western v.p. 1976-78), Japanese Am. Citizen League (dir. Riverside chpt. 1976-79), Internat. Platform Assn. Club: Salmagundi (N.Y.C.). Subject of articles Am. Artist, Jan. 1981. Studio: 39576 Lincoln St Cherry Valley CA 92223 Address: PO Box 2132 Beaumont CA 92223

MELTZOFF, ANTONIA, psychologist; b. N.Y.C., Aug. 14, 1939; d. Samuel and Frances Elizabeth (Keene) Ratensky; m. Mark Apter Strand, Sept. 16, 1961; m. 2d, Julian Meltzoff, Oct. 16, 1976; 1 dau., Jessica Strand. B.A., Bard Coll., 1960; Ph.D. in Clin. Psychology, NYU, 1977. Lic. psychologist Calif. Instr. English lit. Bklyn. Coll., CUNY, 1968-70; intern VA Outpatient Clinic, Bklyn., 1974-76; instr. child psychology U.S. Internat. U., San Diego, 1978-79; asst. psychotherapist El Camino (Calif.) Psychology Ctr., 1979-80; staff psychologist Mercy Hosp. and Med. Ctr., San Diego, 1980—; pvt. practice psychology. Fulbright fellow comparative lit., 1960-61. Mem. Am. Psychol. Assn. Club: Dimensions. Contbr. articles to profl. jours. Office: Mercy Hosp and Med Ctr 4077 5th Ave San Diego CA 92103 also 550 Washington St San Diego CA 92103

MELVIN, PETER JOSEPH, mathematical astronomer, aerospace engineer; b. Seattle, Mar. 12, 1944; s. William Leopold and Virginia (Stevens) M.; m. Alice Sue Pfiester, May 25, 1975; children—Robert Dennis, Chloe Ann. B.A., Western Wash. State Coll., 1965; M.S., U. Ill., 1966, Ph.D., 1970. NASA trainee U. Ill., Urbana, 1966-68, instr. phys. sci., 1970-72, asst. prof., 1972-77; sr. engr. Martin-Marietta Aerospace Co., Denver, 1977-80, staff engr., 1980-83; sr. specialist engr. engring. tech. applications div. Boeing Computer Services, Seattle, 1983—. Mem. AIAA. Contbr. articles to profl. jours. Home: 10772 19th Ave SW Seattle WA 98146 Office: 565 Andover Park W Tukwila WA 98188

MENARD, MICHAEL JOSEPH, museum director; b. Saginaw, Mich., Sept. 25, 1948; s. Louis Raymond and Dorothy C. (Rable) M.; B.A., Mich. State U., 1974, M.A., 1976; m. Nora P. Webb, Apr. 3, 1971. Archivist, Mich. State Archives, 1976; mus. archivist Mus. Western Colo., Grand Junction, 1977-80, acting dir., 1978; dir. Ft. Casper Mus., Casper, Wyo., 1981—; historic preservation cons. City of Casper, 1981—; cons. new mus. com. and archives com. Colo.-Wyo. Assn. Mus., 1981—. Served with USAF, 1968-72. Mem. Soc. Am. Archivists, Am. Assn. Mus., Am. Assn. State and Local History. Contbr. articles in field to profl. jours.

MENARD, ROGER BRIGHTEN, real estate development company executive; b. San Francisco, May 12, 1941; s. Brighten Wilfred and Mary Menard; m. Mimi Lesley Platt, Dec. 21, 1968; children—Matthew Brighten, Lindsay Ann. B.S., San Jose State U., 1964; M.B.A., U. Santa Clara, 1971. Gen. bldg. contractor's lic., Calif. Constrn. loan officer Security Savs. and Loan, San Jose, Calif., 1964-66; v.p. ops. Medbak, Inc., San Mateo, Calif., 1966-68; controller, Anderson Jacobson, Inc., Sunnyvale, Calif., 1968-72; v.p. Builders Resources Corp., Menlo Park, Calif., 1972-76; pres. Raldon Housing Corp., Dallas, 1976-77, Broadmoor Homes, Dublin, Calif., 1977-83; div. pres. Pulte Home Corp., Denver, 1983—. Mem. Bldg. Industry Assn. (dir. 1978-79, chmn. How Program 1980), Nat. Assn. Homebuilders. Republican. Clubs: Los Altos Country; University of Palo Alto. Home: 23446 Toyonita Rd Los Altos Hills CA 94022 Office: Broadmoor Homes 6250 Village Pkwy Dublin CA 94566

MENARD, WESLEY ALLAN, propulsion engr.; b. Palmdale, Calif., Apr. 26, 1939; s. Julius Edmund and Margaret Marie (Smith) M.; m. Mary Jo Lewis, June 18, 1960; children—Todd E., Lori E., Mark A. B.S. in Aero. Engring., Calif. State Poly. Coll., 1961; M.S. in Engring., UCLA, 1963. With Jet Propulsion Lab., Calif. Inst. Tech., Pasadena, 1963—, mgr. solar energy conversion systems sect., 1982—; co-owner Ardus Devel. Co., Glendora, Calif.; v.p. HEG Inc., Los Alamitos, Calif.; bd. dirs. Property Funding Group Inc., Pasadena. Pres. Confraternity Christian Doctrine, Sacred Heart Parish; com. chmn. Explorer Post 419, Boy Scouts Am. Recipient NASA monetary awards, 1968, 71; named Disting. Alumnus Calif. State Poly. U. Sch. Engring., 1982. Assoc. fellow AIAA (terrestrial energy tech. com.); mem. Internat. Solar Energy Soc. (Am. sect.), Combustion Inst., Internat. Hydrogen Soc., Soc. Automotive Engrs. (Manley Meml. medal, 1977), Am. Phys. Soc., Optical Soc. Am. ASME, Sigma Xi (Caltech. chpt.), Sigma Pi Alpha. Roman Catholic. Clubs: Kiwanis of Glendora, Caltech Management. Contbr. numerous articles to tech. jours. Office: 4880 Oak Grove Dr Suite 507-228 Pasadena CA 91103

MENASCO, LAWRENCE CLIFTON, elec. engr.; b. Pachuta, Miss., Sept. 21, 1923; s. Lawrence Hayward and Lettie (Pinkham) M.; B.S. in Elec. Engring., U. N.Mex., 1953; m. Dixie Lorene Smith, Oct. 14, 1949; children—Lawrence Clifton, William Wyatt, Jeffrey Walter. With Hughes Aircraft Co., 1953—, as tech. dir. Compagnie Belge D'Electronique et D'Automation, head overseas maintenance depot, head systems installation program, tech. asst., Los Angeles, 1963-69, sr. staff engr., weapons system test, Phoenix program office, 1969—. Served with USNR, 1942-49. Mem. Sigma Tau. Home: 1590 Suffolk Ave Thousand Oaks CA 91360 Office: Hughes Aircraft Co Bldg 265 MS X-16 Canoga Park CA 91304

MENDEL, EDWARD, electronics executive; b. Hollywood Calif., Oct. 9, 1928; s. Albert and Berenice (Bowman) M.; m. Jacqueline M. Argue; children—Christine, Meredith, Mark, Alexandra. B.S., U.S. Naval Acad., 1950; M.S.E. in Aero. Instrumentation, U. Mich., 1960, Aero. and Astronautical Engr., 1960; P.M.D., Harvard U. (Sch. Bus.), 1964; grad. Indsl. Coll. Armed Forces, 1968. Commd. lt. U.S. Air Force, 1950, advanced through grades to brig. gen., 1977; served as fighter pilot, 1951-52; assigned to radar maintenance, 1954-58, test and evaluation, 1960-72, pilot tng. and logistics, 1972-79; ret., 1979; v.p. mktg. Pacific Measurements, Inc., Sunnyvale, Calif., 1979—. Decorated D.S.M., Legion of Merit, D.F.C., Bronze Star, Air medal. Mem. AIAA, Am. Def. Preparedness Assn., Assn. Old Crows. Home: 418 University Ave Los Altos CA 94022

MENDELOW, DAVID HARRIS, univ. dean; b. Bklyn., Feb. 12, 1942; s. Sydney and Marcia (Gensowit) M.; B.A. in Instnl. Mgmt., Mich. State U., 1963; M.B.A. in Health Care Adminstrn., George Washington U., 1967; m. Elaine S. Israel, Aug. 28, 1977; 1 son, Lance Richard. Affiliation adminstr. Albert Einstein Coll. Medicine, 1967-70, dir. clin. programs office, 1970-73; sr. health care cons. Arthur D. Little, Inc., 1973-77; asso. dean adminstrn. for med. sch., adminstr. clinics Stanford U., 1977-81. Bd. dirs. Big Oak Civic Assn., (Stamford, Conn.). Served with USAR, 1963-69. Mem. Am. Public Health Assn., Med. Group Mgmt. Assn., Calif. Hosp. Assn., AAAS, Am. Hosp. Assn., Am. Physicians Fellowship. Home: 654 Torwood Ln Los Altos CA 94022 Office: Stanford University Medical School M119 Stanford CA 94305

MENDELSOHN, HAROLD, social psychologist, educator; b. Jersey City, Oct. 30, 1923; s. Louis and Bessie (Yulinsky) M.; m. Irene Sylvia Gordon, Apr. 10, 1949; children—Susan, Lynn. B.S., CCNY, 1945; M.A., Columbia U., 1946; Ph.D., New Sch. for Social Research, 1956. Sr. survey analyst Dept. State, Washington, 1951-52; research assoc. Bur. Social Sci. Research, Am. U., Washington, 1952-56; assoc. mgr. mktg. communications McCann-Erickson, N.Y.C., 1956-58; assoc. dir. Psychol. Corp., N.Y.C., 1958-62; prof. dept. mass communications U. Denver, 1962—, chmn., 1970-78; trustee Colo. Med. Services Inc., 1973-78; Morton disting. vis. prof. Ohio U., 1981; cons. in field. Bd. dirs. Nat. Safety Council, 1963-69; mem. Denver Council for Pub. TV, 1970-78; mem. cancer control and rehab. adv. com. Nat. Cancer Inst., 1976-81; mem. U.S. Surgeon Gen.'s Sci. Adv. Com. on TV and Social Behavior; mem. adv. council prevention div. Nat. Inst. Alcoholism and Alcohol Abuse. Recipient Met. Life award Nat. Safety Council, 1967; Emmy award Nat. Acad. TV Arts/Sci., 1968; Gold Camera award U.S. Internat. Film Festival, 1972; Gold Eagle award Internat. Festival Film/TV, 1973, Silver award, 1974. Fellow Am. Psychol. Assn., Am. Sociol. Assn.; mem. Am. Assn. Pub. Opinion (past pres.), N.Y. Acad. Scis., Sigma Delta Chi, Omicron Delta Kappa. Club: Chgo. Press. Author: Mass Entertainment, 1966; (with D.H. Bayley) Minorities and the Police: Confrontation in America, 1969; (with I. Crespi) Polls, Television and the New Politics, 1970; (with others) Television and Growing Up: The Impact of Television Violence, 1972; (with G. O'Keefe) The People Choose a President, 1976. Contbr. articles to profl. jours. Office: Dept Mass Communications U Denver Denver CO 80208

MENDENHALL, CARROL CLAY, physician; b. Missouri Valley, Iowa, July 26, 1916; s. Clay and Maude (Watts) M.; student U. So. Calif., 1942-44, Chapman Coll., 1946-47, Los Angeles City Coll., 1947-48; D.O., Coll. Osteo. Physicians and Surgeons, 1952; M.D., Calif. Coll. Medicine, 1962; m. Lucille Yvonne Bonvouloir, June 14, 1946 (div. July 1957); 1 son, Gregory Bruce; m. 2d, Barbara Marilyn Huggett-Davis, Sept. 28, 1974. Intern, Los Angeles County Osteo. Hosp., 1952-53; gen. practice medicine, 1953—, specializing in weight control, Gardena, Calif., 1961-74, specializing in stress disorders and psychosomatic medicine, Ft. Worth, 1974-78, Santa Clara, Calif., 1978—; med. dir. Green's Pharms., Long Beach, Calif., 1956-64; v.p. Internat. Pharm. Mfg. Co., Inc., San Pedro, Calif., 1965-66; pres. Chemico of Gardena, Inc., 1964-69; staff Gardena Hosp.; tchr., lectr. biofeedback, prevention and treatment of stress, creative thought; founder, dir. Eclectic Weight Control Workshop, 1971-74, Longevity Learning, Longevity Learning Seminars, 1980; adv. bd. dirs. Los Angeles Nat. Bank. Cadre med. dir. Gardena Civil Def., 1953-54, asst. to chief med. dir., 1954-60, chief med. and first aid services, 1960-64. Served as pharmacist's mate USNR, 1944-46. Fellow Royal Soc. Health, Am. Acad. Med. Preventics; mem. AMA, Calif. Med. Assn., Santa Clara County Med. Soc., Acupuncture Research Inst. (also alumni assn.), Los Aficionados de Los Angeles (pres. 1964-66), Am. Soc. Clin. Hypnosis. Republican. Address: 255 Crestview Dr Santa Clara CA 95050

MENDEZ, CELESTINO GALO, educator; b. Havana, Cuba, Oct. 16, 1944; s. Celestino Andres and Georgina (Fernandez) M.; came to U.S., 1962, naturalized, 1970; B.A., Benedictine Coll., 1965; M.A., U. Colo., 1968, Ph.D., 1974, M.B.A., 1979; m. Mary Ann Koplau, Aug. 21, 1971; children—Mark Michael, Matthew Maximilian. Asst. prof. math. scis. Met. State Coll., Denver, 1971-77, assoc. prof., 1977-82, prof., 1982—, chmn. dept. math. scis., 1980-82. Mem. advt. rev. bd. Met. Denver, 1973-79; parish outreach rep. S.E. deanery, Denver Cath. Community Services, 1976-78; mem. social ministries com. St. Thomas More Cath. Ch., Denver, 1976-78, vice chmn., 1977-78, mem. parish council, 1977-78; del. Adams County Republican Conv., 1972, 74, Colo. 4th Congl. Dist. Conv., 1974, Colo. Rep. Conv., 1982; alt. del. Colo. Rep. Conv., 1974, 76, 5th Congl. dist. conv., 1976; del. Douglas County Rep. Conv., 1976, 78, 80, 82, mem. rules com., 1978, 80, precinct committeeman Douglas County Rep. Com., 1976-78, mem. central com., 1976-78; bd. dirs. Rocky Mountain Better Bus. Bur., 1975-79, Rowley Downs Homeowners Assn., 1976-78; mem. exec. bd., v.p. Assoc. Faculties of State Inst. Higher Edn. in Colo., 1971-73; trustee Hispanic U. Am., 1975-78; trustee Town of Parker (Colo.), 1981—, chmn. budget com., 1981—; chmn. joint budget com. Town of Parker-Parker Water and Sanitation Dist. Bds., 1982—. Recipient U. Colo. Grad. Sch. excellence in teaching award, 1965-67; Benedictine Coll. grantee, 1964-65. Mem. Math. Assn. Am., Am. Math. Soc., Nat. Council Tchrs. of Math., Colo. Council Tchrs. of Math., Colo. Internat. Edn. Assn., Asso. Faculties of State Insts. Higher Edn. in Colo. (v.p. 1971-73). Republican. Roman Catholic. Contbr. articles to profl. jours. and newspapers. Home: 10072 N Regency Pl Parker CO 80134 Office: 1006 11th St Denver CO 80204

MENDEZ, MIGUEL ANGEL, lawyer, educator; b. Brownsville, Tex., Dec. 25, 1942; s. Miguel Angel and Isaura (Longoria) M. A.A., Tex. Southwest Coll., 1963; A.B., George Washington U., 1965, J.D., 1968. Admitted to Tex. bar, 1968, Calif. bar, 1972. Law clk. U.S. Ct. Claims, Washington, 1968-69; legis. asst. U.S. Senator Alan Cranston, Washington, 1969-71; assoc. counsel Mexican-Am. Legal Def. and Edn. Fund, San Francisco, 1971-72; dep. dir. Calif. Rural Legal Assistance, San Francisco, 1972-74; dep. pub. defender Salinas, Calif., 1974-76; vis. prof. Law Sch. U. Santa Clara, Calif., 1977; assoc. prof. Stanford (Calif.) Law Sch., 1978—; cons. Nat. Inst. Trial Advocacy. Bd. dirs. Pub. Advocates, Inc., 1976—. Mem. Tex. Bar, Calif. Bar, La Raza Nat. Bar Assn. Contbr. articles to legal publs. Office: Stanford Law School Stanford CA 94305

MENESES-IMBER, SARA NATALIA, sociologist; b. Caracas, Venezuela, Dec. 28, 1944; came to U.S., 1975; d. Guillermo Meneses and Sofia Imber de Rangel; Sociologist, Universidad Central de Venezuela, 1966; M.A. in Edn., Stanford U., 1977; M.A. in Sociology (Venezuelan Ministry Edn. grantee 1975-77, Gran Mariscal de Ayacucho grantee 1977-79), 1979, Ph.D. in Edn. (Gran Mariscal de Ayacucho grantee 1979-81, Procter & Gamble dissertation grantee 1980), 1983; 1 son, Guillermo. Sociologist, head Ednl. Commn. of Caracas City Council, 1969-75; cons. Nursery Commn., 1969-71, sociologist head Adv. Commn., 1969; asst. to tech. sec. of research on socioecon. status and achievement Universidad Central de Venezuela, 1968; asst. dir. Zone IV, Venezuelan Scholarship Found. Gran Mariscal de Ayacucho, San Francisco, 1981—; officer I, Venezuelan Consulate, San Francisco, 1983—; cons. Universidad Nacional Experimental Simon Rodriguez, Venezuela, 1981. Mem. Venezuelan Assn. Sociologists and Anthropologists, Venezuelan Soc. Criminology, Stanford Alumni Assn., Latin Am. Studies Assn., Phi Delta Kappa. Office: 870 Market St Suite 665 San Francisco CA 94102

MENICUCCI, AUDREY, artist; b. Santa Rosa, Calif., Sept. 22, 1931; d. Aubrey Joseph and Elaine Ivy (Zimmerman) M. Painter, specializing in seascapes; tchr. in Sonoma and Marin counties (Calif.); condr. art workshops and demonstrations Sebastopol Art Workshop, Pallet Club, Guerneville, Calif., Artist's Round Table, Santa Rosa, Forestville Art Workshop; group shows include: San Francisco Civic Ctr. Art Show, 1964, Falkirk Mansion Cultural, San Rafael, Calif., 1980, Brevard Art Ctr. and Mus., Melbourne, Fla., 1980, Cape Cod Art Assn., Barnstable, Mass., 1981, Internat. Soc. Marine Painters, Daytona Beach, Fla., 1982; represented permanent collection Brevard Art Ctr. and Mus., Melbourne, Fla., Sausalito Hist. Soc. Recipient Sausalito Art Fest. Spinnaker award, 1973. Mem. Internat. Soc. Marine Painters. Democrat.

MENIN, LIONEL MARX, lawyer; b. Denver, June 16, 1936; s. Samuel David and Bess Polly (Rissman) M.; A.B., U. Denver, 1959, J.D., 1967; m. Martha Regina Behar, Apr. 15, 1962; children—Andrea Rochelle,

Susan Lynn. Admitted to Colo. bar, 1968; tchr. pub. schs., Denver, 1959-73; mem. firm Menin and Menin, Denver, 1968—; chmn. legal redress com. Colo. Wyo. State Conf. Brs. NAACP. Bd. dirs. Hillel Acad., 1974-75; pres. Beth Sholom Synagogue, 1976-80; v.p. Willow Creek Homeowners Assn., 1976-79; dist. capt. Democratic Party, 1976-78, Dem. committeeman, 1972-74; mem., Denver v.p. Histadrut Counsel, 1973—. Served with USAF, 1954-62. Honoree Histadrut, Denver Area Labor Council, 1981. Mem. Nat. Assn. Criminal Defense Lawyers, NEA, Colo. Edn. Assn., Denver Classroom Tchrs. Assn., Am. Fedn. Tchrs., Denver Fedn. Tchrs. (past v.p.), Arapahoe County Bar Assn., Colo. Bar Assn., Am. Bar Assn., Phi Gamma Mu, Phi Delta Kappa. Jewish. Home: 8484 E Jamison Circle N Englewood CO 80112 Office: Suite 500 Century Bank Plaza Bldg 3300 E 1st Ave Denver CO 80206

MENKIN, LAWRENCE CHRISTOPHER (KIT), leasing co. exec.; b. N.Y.C., Jan. 1, 1942; s. Lawrence and Chris (Riland) M.; student Santa Monica City Coll., 1958-60, Julliard Sch. Music, 1958, U. Calif., Los Angeles, 1960-63; m. Leslie Murdock, Apr. 5, 1968; children—Dashiell, Tascha, Ashley. News editor Radio Sta. KFRC, San Francisco, 1964-67; adminstrv. asst. Calif. Assemblyman Leo Ryan, S. San Francisco, 1967-68; news mng. editor Sta. KGO-TV, San Francisco, 1969; producer west coast news Sta. ABC-TV, Los Angeles, 1970; mgr. San Bruno (Calif.) C. of C., 1970; mgr. City of San Bruno, 1970; prin. Menkin & Assos., Santa Clara, Calif., 1971; sr. partner Am. Leasing Co., Santa Clara; owner Monte Sereno Winery; dir. Meridian Nat. Bank, Pleasant Hill. Chmn. Santa Clara Salvation Army Unit. Served with U.S. Army, 1963-64. Recipient Merit award Santa Clara Salvation Army, 1968; award United Crusade, 1969. Mem. Assn. Credit Grantors (past pres.), Internat. Assn. Fin. Planners, Am. Assn. Lessors, Credit Women Internat. (1st male pres.), Profl. Wine Soc. Santa Clara County (sec.), Santa Clara C. of C. (former pres., recipient Gavel award 1976), Bay Area Execs. (treas.). Weekly columnist Daily Comml. News, No. Calif. Electronic News, Santa Clara American, No. Calif. Indsl. News, No. Calif. Retailer; contbr. articles to trade mags. Home: 15563 Kirkorian Way Monte Sereno CA 95030 Office: 2175 De La Cruz Blvd Suite 10 Santa Clara CA 95052

MENKIN, PETER ALAN, publishing executive; b. N.Y.C., Oct. 29, 1946; s. Lawrence Abraham and Columbia (Riland) M. Columnist San Francisco Daily Comml. News, 1971-73; founder, pub., editor, mgr. Feature Assocs., San Rafael, Calif., 1977—; contbg. editor Harpers mag.; cons. Presidio Press, Novato, Calif., McCutchan Pub. Corp., Berkeley, Calif.; dir. Export Mgmt. Co. Served with USAF, 1964-69. U. Minn. Rockefeller Found. grantee, 1971. Mem. Newspaper Guild (internat. life), Calif. Newspaper Pubs. Assn., United Assn. Mfrs. Reps., Authors Club Los Angeles, Assn. Am. Export. Home: 1567 Buchanan St Novato CA 94947 Office: 3334 Kerner Blvd San Rafael CA 94901

MENLOVE, FRANCES LEE (MRS. HOWARD OLSEN MENLOVE), psychologist; b. Salt Lake City, June 4, 1936; d. Edwin Fred Anderson and Perneey Greaves (Elmer) A.; m. Howard Olsen Menlove, June 12, 1958; children—Stephen, Lynelle, Spencer, Lauren. B.S. in Psychology, Stanford U., 1958, postdoctoral research assoc., 1964-66; Ph.D. in Psychology, U. Mich., 1963; grad. Exec. Mgmt. Program, U. N.Mex., 1976. Pvt. practice psychology, Los Alamos, 1969-74; dir., Los Alamos Council on Alcoholism, 1973-74; dir. Employee Counseling Program, Los Alamos Nat. Lab., 1974-79, asst., assoc., dir. tech. support, 1979—; cons. N.Mex. Dept. Corrections; instr. Highlands U. 19 ; Danforth awardee, 1954, Woodrow Wilson fellow, 1959; named Outstanding Woman of Yr., State of N.Mex., 1972. Mem. Am. Psychol. Assn. (indsl. and occupational psychology div.), Phi Beta Kappa. Author several articles in field of behavioral modification and learning theory. Home: 2880 Arizona Los Alamos NM 87544 Office: PO Box 1663 MS A120 Los Alamos NM 87545

MENNELLA, VINCENT ALFRED, automotive and airplane co. executive; b. Teaneck, N.J., Oct. 7, 1922; s. Francis Anthony and Henrietta Vernard (Dickson) M.; B.A. in Acctg., U. Wash., 1948; m. Madeleine Olson, Aug. 18, 1945; children—Bruce, Cynthia, Mark, Scott, Chris. Sales and bus. mgmt. positions Ford div. Ford Motor Co., 1949-55; founder, pres. Southgate Ford, Seattle, 1955—, exec. v.p. Flightcraft, Inc., Seattle, 1973—; pres. Stanley Garage Door Co., 1981—. Former chmn. March of Dimes. Served to capt. USNR, 1942-45. Republican. Roman Catholic. Clubs: Rainier Golf, Seattle Tennis, Wash. Athletic, Rotary (past pres.). Home: 1400 SW 171st Pl Seattle WA 98166 Office: 14500 1st Ave S Seattle WA 98168

MENNIG, JAN COLLINS, police chief; b. Pasadena, Calif., Oct. 9, 1927; s. Christian and Lucille (Collins) M.; m. Mary Ann Harmelink, June 9, 1979; 1 dau., Lucy Marie. B.S. in Pub. Adminstrn., U. So. Calif., 1959, M.S., 1964; postgrad., U.S. Army Command and Staff Coll., 1972; postgrad. Indsl. Coll. Armed Forces, 1977; postgrad. Air War Coll., 1978. Cert. logistician, U.S. Army. With Pasadena (Calif.) Police Dept., 1950-65; with Culver City (Calif.) Police Dept., 1965—, asst. police chief, 1965-69, 76—, chief, 1970-75; cons. and lectr. in field. Chmn. Los Angeles Regional Criminal Justice Planning Bd., 1974-75; bd. mgrs. Culver Palms YMCA, chmn., 1970, 71; mem. Culver City Edn. Com., chmn., moderator, 1970. Served to col. USAR, 1944-82, World War II, Korea. Decorated Legion of Merit, others; recipient YMCA Man of Yr. award, 1971. Mem. Internat. Assn. Chiefs of Police, Fed. Criminal Investigators Assn., Los Angeles County Peace Officers Assn., Am. Soc. for Pub. Adminstrn., internat. Police Assn., Calif. Police Chiefs Assn. (past mem. exec. com.), Calif. Peace Officers Assn., Res. Officers Assn. U.S., Scapa Praetors, Pi Sigma Alpha. Republican. Clubs: Lions; Masons, Scottish Rite, York Rite, Elks (Culver City), Shriners (Pasadena). Office: PO Box 808 Culver City CA 90230

MENSINGER, PEGGY BOOTHE, mayor; b. Modesto, Calif., Feb. 18, 1923; d. Dyas Power and Margaret (Stewart) Boothe; A.B. in Polit. Sci., Stanford U., 1944; m. John Logan Mensinger, May 25, 1952; children—John B., Stewart I., Susan B. Reporter, San Francisco Red Cross Chpt. News Bur., 1944; acting mgr. Boothe Fruit Co., Modesto, Calif., 1945; asst. dir. Stanford (Calif.) Alumni Assn., 1947, exec. sec. public exercises com. Stanford U., 1949-51; mem. Modesto City Council, 1973-79, mayor, 1979—; bd. dirs. League of Calif. Cities; mem. energy and environ. com. U.S. Conf. of Mayors. Bd. dirs. Nat. council Girl Scouts U.S.A.; chmn. Citizens Com. for Internat. Students, 1965-70; pres. Modesto PTA Council, 1967-69, Modesto chpt. Am. Field Service, 1969-70, Stanislaus County Hist. Soc., 1970-71; state bd. Common Cause, 1973-75; chmn. Modesto City Cultural Commn., 1968-73, del. White House Conf. on Families, Los Angeles, 1980; chmn. Stanislaus Area Assn. Govts., 1976-77. Recipient Woman of Year award VFW Aux., 1980. Mem. Nat. League Am. Pen Women (asso.), LWV (hon.), Calif. Elected Women's Assn. for Edn. and Research, AAUW (grant honoree Edn. Found. 1978), Stanford Assos., Phi Beta Kappa, Gamma Phi Beta. Unitarian. Club: Soroptimist (hon.; Women of Achievement award 1980). Home: 1320 Magnolia Ave Modesto CA 95350 Office: 801 11th St Modesto CA 95354

MENZEL, ROBERT KENNETH, social science educator, organization development consultant; b. Reno, July 18, 1919; s. Waldemar Emil and Elise Magdalena (Syll) M.; m. Clare Ann Koenig, Aug. 27, 1944; children—Lawrence, Elizabeth Menzel Gilson, Christopher. Diploma Concordia Sem., 1944, M.Div., 1952; Th.M., Pacific Luth. Theol. Sem., 1963; Ph.D., Fielding Inst., 1978. Ordained to ministry, Lutheran Ch. Mo. Synod, 1944; pastor chs., San Francisco, 1944-46, Santa Maria, Calif., 1946-49, Mill Valley, Calif., 1949-59; asst. prof., then assoc. prof. religion, coll. relations dir. Concordia Coll., Portland, Oreg., 1959-69; dir. HUB Community Action Program, Portland, 1967-69; dir. Ctr. Human Orgn. in Changing Environments, Pacific Luth. U., Tacoma, 1969—; cons. orgn. devel. Mem. com. social concerns Portland Council Chs., 1965-69; co-founder Puget Sound Coalition, 1970-74; chmn. edn. com. Am. Cancer Soc. Mem. Am. Assn. Higher Edn., Am. Soc. Tng. and Devel., Cert. Cons. Inc., Luth. Acad. for Scholarship, Internat. Inst. Study of Systems Renewal. Democrat. Author publs. in field. Home: 805 Tule Lake Rd S Tacoma WA 98444 Office: Pacific Lutheran U Tacoma WA 98447

MENZIES, JEAN STORKE (MRS. ERNEST F. MENZIES), ret. newspaperwoman; b. Santa Barbara, Calif., Dec. 30, 1904; d. Thomas More and Elsie (Smith) Storke; B.A., Vassar Coll., 1927; M.A. in Physics, Stanford, 1931; m. Ernest F. Menzies, Oct. 20, 1937; children—Jean Storke (Mrs. Dennis Wayne Vaughan), Thomas More. Teaching asst. dept. physics Stanford U., 1927-29; instr. of physics Vassar Coll., 1929-30; tchr. math., chemistry, gen. sci. Sarah Dix Hamlin Sch., San Francisco, 1931-34; sec. to Dr. and Mrs. Samuel T. Orton, N.Y.C., 1935-36; press reporter, spl. writer Santa Barbara News-Press, 1954-63. Rec. sec. nat. YWCA, India, Burma and Ceylon, 1941-42; rec. sec., Calcutta YWCA, 1942-47, v.p., 1949-51; sec. Tri-County adv. council Children's Home Soc., Santa Barbara, 1952-54; founding dir., sec. corp. Santa Barbara Film Soc., Inc., 1960-66. Bd. dirs. Santa Barbara County chpt. Am. Assn. UN, 1954-59, Friends U. Calif. at Santa Barbara Library, 1970-74, Small Wilderness Area Preservation, 1971-79; sec. bd. trustees Crane Country Day Sch., 1955-57; trustee Mental Hygiene Clinic of Santa Barbara, 1956-60, U. Calif. Santa Barbara Found., 1974-80, Santa Barbara Mus. Natural History, 1977-81; adv. council Santa Barbara Citizens Adult Edn., 1958-62, v.p., 1960-62; bd. dirs. Internat. Social Sci. Inst., sec., 1963-68, mem. adv. bd., 1969; bd. dirs. Planned Parenthood Santa Barbara County, Inc., 1964-65, adv. council, 1966-67; trustee Santa Barbara Botanic Garden, 1967-81, hon. trustee, 1981—; trustee, Santa Barbara Trust for Historic Preservation, 1967-68, 72-77; mem. affiliates bd. dirs. U. Calif. at Santa Barbara, 1960-61, 67-70, 72-77; sec. Santa Barbara Mission Archive-Library, 1967—; mem. Santa Barbara Found., 1977-81. Mem. Santa Barbara Hist. Soc. (dir. 1957-62, founding mem. women's projects bd. 1959-63, sec. 1961-62), Channel City Women's Forum (v.p. 1969-73, bd. dirs. 1973—), Phi Beta Kappa, Sigma Xi. Club: Vassar of Santa Barbara and the Tri-Counties (1st v.p., founding com. 1956-57, 2d v.p. 1959-61, chmn. publicity com. 1961-73). Home: 2298 Featherhill Rd Santa Barbara CA 93108

MENZOR, ADONILIA JUANITA, savings and loan officer; b. Wagon Mound, N.Mex., Feb. 16, 1937; d. Jose B. and Rafaelita (Montoya) Menzor. Student N.Mex. Highlands U. Teller First Nat. Bank, Las Vegas, N.Mex., 1963-66, asst. cashier, 1966-75, cashier, 1975-76; asst. mgr. Southwest Savs. Loan Assn., Las Vegas, N.Mex., 1976-80; br. mgr., asst. v.p. First Fed. Savs. Loan Assn., Las Vegas, 1980—. Mem. San Miguel County Commn. Personnel Policy Grievance Com. Mem. Am. Bus Women's Assn., Nat. Assn. Female Execs., Inc. Democrat. Roman Catholic. Home: 7th St Ext PO Box 402 Las Vegas NM 87701 Office: 2301 7th St Las Vegas NM 87701

MEO, YVONNE COLE, artist, printmaker, educator; b. Seattle, Wash., June 5; d. Thomas A. and Lorenza (Jordan) Cole; B.A., UCLA, 1948; M.A., Calif. State U., Los Angeles, 1960; Ph.D. in African-Am. Art History, Union Grad. Sch., Ohio, 1977; Arts D. (hon.), Gt. China Arts Coll., Hong Kong, 1973; student of Glenn Lukens, Los Angeles, 1952, Maestro Jose Gutierrez, Mexico City, Mexico, 1952, Guy MacCoy, Los Angeles, 1962, 65, 68; 1 son by previous marriage, Byron Meo. Instr. ceramics, interior design, painting and drawing Fisk U., Nashville, Tenn.; tchr. stage design, ceramics and crafts secondary schs. of Los Angeles Unified Sch. Dist., 1951-67; mem. faculty art dept. Pasadena (Calif.) City Coll., 1969-70; prof. lectr. art Calif. State U., Northridge, 1969-70; instr. design, painting and art history Van Nuys (Calif.) High Sch., 1964-79; vis. prof. painting and drawing Calif. State U., Los Angeles, 1972; instr. dept. art East Los Angeles Coll., 1975-76, U.S. del. Internat. Black and African Festival of Arts and Culture, Nigeria, 1977; mem. curriculum com. Calif. State U. System, 1970; guest artist Space Symposium Brit. Interplanetary Soc., 1976, one-women shows of sculpture, paintings, prints various galleries, museums and univs. in Calif., 1965—, group shows include: Los Angeles County Art Mus., Ankrum Gallery, Taft Mus., Cin., Oakland (Calif.) Mus. Archives, also Mishima, Japan, Leipzig, Germany, Moscow, Nigeria and Mexico, 1977—; represented in permanent collections: Mus. African and African Am. Art, Buffalo, Mary McLeod Bethune Br. Library, U. So.Calif., Calif. State U., Fullerton, Oakland Mus. Archives, J&L Steel Corp., Pitts. Recipient Arc of Achievers award Calif. Inst. Tech., 1967; Gold Crown award Pasadena Art Council, 1977; numerous other art awards. Mem. Pasadena Soc. Artists, Nat. Conf. Artists, AAUW, Artists Equity Assn., League Allied Arts (Bicentennial art award 1981), Delta Kappa Gamma, Delta Sigma Theta. Contbr. articles to profl. jours.

MERA, RAYMOND DAMIAN AUGUSTO, association executive; b. Dominican Republic, Apr. 12, 1929; s. Ramon Augusto and Maria Christine (Guillen) M.; student public schs.; m. Leonor Ivonne Altamirano, Oct. 1, 1966; children—Raymond Alexis, Monique Roxanne. Spl. accounts casualty underwriter Employers Mut. of Wausau, N.Y.C., 1955-59; loss control rep. Hartford Ins. Co., Los Angeles, 1960-69; sr. loss control rep. Leatherby Ins. Cos. (now Western Employers), Fullerton, Calif., 1969-73; mgr., safety mgr. Ventura County Citrus Growers Com., Ventura, Calif., 1973—; safety cons. Calavo Growers of Calif., 1979—. Bd. dirs. Ventura County chpt. ARC, 1974-80, Ventura County Farm Bur., 1978—. Served with USN, 1948-52. Mem. Am. Soc. Safety Engrs. (co-founder Orange County chpt. 1971-72), Nat. Safety Mgmt. Soc. Registered profl. engr., Calif. Republican. Roman Catholic. Club: Toastmasters. Office: Ventura County Citrus Growers Com 5156 McGrath St Ventura CA 93003

MERCADO, LINDA ISMAEL DICKEN, business executive; b. San Francisco, June 13, 1955; d. Daniel I. and Mary F. Ismael; student public schs., Los Angeles, Clark County Community Coll., 1981, Lenz Acad. Modeling, 1983; cert. Clark County Juvenile Ct., 1980; children—Daniel, Linda; m. Jesuito Mercado, Dec. 19, 1981. Asst. mgr. Clancy Muldoon, Santa Monica, Calif., 1972-73; instr. math. and sci. Clover Elem. Sch., Los Angeles, 1974; accounts receivable supr. Advance Indsl. Fin. Co., Beverly Hills, Calif., 1974-77; asst. controller Nev. Beauty and Barber Supply Co., 1977-78; elec. designer James Glover Cons. Engrs., Las Vegas, Nev., 1978-80; owner L&R Services, Las Vegas, 1980-83; owner child care facility Little Dickens, Las Vegas, 1981—; ind. distbr. Yurika Foods Corp., 1983—; sec.-draftsperson Dinter Engring., Las Vegas, 1983—; notary public. Mem.-at-large bd. dirs. Frontier council Girl Scouts U.S., 1981—, awards and recognition coordinator, 1983, mem. personnel com., 1983—; mem. nominating com. Clark County Child Care Assn., 1983; mem. Nat. Com. for Prevention Child Abuse, 1982—; Sunday sch. tchr. for deaf. Recipient Excellence in Music award C. of C., 1969; cert. Nev. Assn. Parliamentarians; lic. child care provider. Mem. Am. Soc. Profl. and Exec. Women, Nat. Assn. Female Execs., Nat. Notary Assn., Nat. Assn. for Deaf, Am. Adventurers Assn., Am. Entrepreneurs Assn., Clark County Child Care Assn. (exec. bd. 1982—, pres. 1983—), Nev. Child Care Providers Assn. Republican. Mem. Christian Ch. Office: 2208 Santa Ynez Las Vegas NV 89104

MERCER, JOSEPH HENRY, lawyer, state senator; b. Peoria, Ill., Feb. 1, 1937; s. Maurice Dean and Dorothy Jane (Brickner) M.; B.A., U. N.Mex., 1961; J.D., Harvard U., 1964; m. JoAnn Swicegood, July 21, 1967; children—Stephen, Jennifer, Matthew. Admitted to N.Mex. bar, 1966; mem. Mercer, Lock & Keating, and predecessors, Albuquerque, 1966—; dir. Prepaid Group Legal Services Corp. of N.Mex., 1973-74, v.p., 1974-75; state rep. Dist. 24, N.Mex. State Legislature, 1975-76; mem. N.Mex. Senate from 21st Dist., 1977—, Senate minority leader, 1980—. Mem. Commn. on Uniform State Laws, 1980-83; mem. oversight com. Gov.'s Organized Crime Prevention Com. Served as 1st lt F.A., U.S. Army, 1955-58. Recipient Outstanding Service award State Bar N.Mex., 1974. Mem. Albuquerque, N.Mex. bar assns., Albuquerque Com. on Fgn. Relations (chmn. 1974-75), Am. Arbitration Assn. (N.Mex. Adv. Council), N.Mex. Jud. Council, Phi Kappa Phi, Tau Kappa Alpha. Episcopalian. Club: Kiwanis. Office: 5400 Phoenix NE Suite 100 Albuquerque NM 87110

MERCER, LLOYD JON, economics educator; b. Farnam, Nebr., Feb. 14, 1936; s. Theodore Hughes and Lulu (Waggy) M.; m. Perie Burrow Mercer, July 2, 1960; children Carolyn Alice, Janet Aileen. B.S. in Agr. Wash State U. 1958, M.A. in Agrl. Econs., 1959, M.A. in Econs., 1965, Ph.D. 1967. Asst. prof. econs. U. Calif., Santa Barbara 1966-72, assoc. prof. 1972-76, prof. 1976—. Served to capt. USAF 1959-62. Recipient Newcomen Soc. N.Am. Spl. award 1972. Mem. Am. Econ. Assn., Am. Agrl. Econs. Assn., Econ. History Assn., Western Econs. Assn., AAUP. Republican. Methodist. Author: Land Grants and the Land Grant Railroads 1982; contbr. articles to profl. jours. Home: 21 E Junipero St Santa Barbara CA 93105 Office: Dept Econs Univ Calif Santa Barbara CA 93106

MERCHANT, ROLAND SAMUEL, SR., hosp. adminstr.; b. N.Y.C., Apr. 18, 1929; s. Samuel and Eleta (McLymont) M.; B.A., N.Y.U., 1957, M.A., 1960; M.S. (USPHS fellow), Columbia U., 1963, M.S.H.A., 1974; m. Audrey Bartley, June 6, 1970; children—Orelia Eleta, Roland Samuel, Huey Bartley. Asst. statistician N.Y.C. Dept. Health, 1957-60, statistician, 1960-63; statistician N.Y. Tb and Health Assn., N.Y.C., 1963-65; biostatistician, adminstrv. coordinator Inst. for Surg. Studies, Montefiore Hosp., Bronx, N.Y., 1965-72; resident in adminstrn. Roosevelt Hosp., N.Y.C., 1973-74; dir. health and hosp. mgmt. Dept. Health, City of N.Y., 1974-76; asst. adminstr. West Adams Community Hosp., Los Angeles, 1976; spl. asst. to asso. v.p. for med. affairs Stanford U. Hosp., 1977-82, dir. office mgmt. and strategic planning, 1982—. Served with U.S. Army, 1951-53. Mem. Am. Coll. Hosp. Adminstrs., Am. Hosp. Assn., Am. Pub. Health Assn., Nat. Assn. Health Services Exec., N.Y. Acad. Scis. Home: 953 Cheswick Dr San Jose CA 95121 Office: Stanford U Hosp Stanford CA 94305

MERCURE, ROBERT LEGRAND, business executive; b. Monroe, Mich., Aug. 28, 1932; s. LeGrand J. and Nancy M. (Gattolin) M.; m. Dorothy R. Daniel, May 23, 1952; m. Patricia A. Center, Jan. 31, 1973; children—Michael R., Susan E. Student Ga. Mil. Acad., 1950-51, Auburn U., 1952-53. Pres., Mercure Steel Corp., Atlanta, 1954-60; regional mgr. Scott Graphics, Atlanta, 1960-70; pres. Technigraphics Inc., Atlanta, 1971-76; mgr. pub. utilities div. Auto Trol Corp., Denver, 1977-79; pres. Creative Capital Ltd., Larkspur, Colo., 1979—. Mem. Republican Nat. Com. Served with USAF, 1953-54. Roman Catholic. Clubs: Denver Track, Perry Park Country; Echo Hills (Larkspur). Home: 8006 S Bannock Dr Larkspur CO 80118 Office: Creative Capital Ltd 8004 S Bannock Dr Larkspur CO 80118

MERE, MANUEL HECTOR, semiconductor manufacturing company executive; b. Havana, May 13, 1945; came to U.S., 1961, naturalized, 1970; s. Manuel F. and Mercedes (Hidalgo) M.; B.S.E.E., U. Miami, 1966, M.S.E.E., 1967; M.S. in Systems Mgmt., Fla. Inst. Tech., 1970; m. Rosa Lauredo, Jan. 28, 1967; children Yvonne, Yvette, Michelle. Sr. engr. Harris Semicodr., 1967-70; engring. mgr. Nat. Semicondr., 1970-77; project mgr. IBM Corp., 1977-81; dir. mfg., ops. mgr. Xicor Corp., Milpitas, Calif., 1981—; tchr. undergrad. courses Fla. Inst. Tech., 1968-69. Chmn. personnel commn. Moreland Sch. Dist. Mem. IEEE, Am. Mgmt. Assn., Tau Beta Pi, Phi Kappa Phi, Eta Kappa Nu. Republican. Roman Catholic. Home: 6041 W Walbrook St San Jose CA 95129 Office: 851 Buckeye Ct Milpitas CA 95035

MEREDITH, JAMES HARRIS, state legislator, realty company executive; b. June 10, 1947, s. Daniel Thomas and Fannie Mae (Howell) M.; B.S. in Bus. Adminstrn., No. Ariz. U., 1972; m. Rexanne Kay Warner, May 6, 1972; children—Julisha Mae, Corinna Kay, James Warner. Owner/broker Meredith Property Mgmt. Co., Phoenix, 1972-81, Jim Meredith & Realty Assocs., Phoenix, 1982—; mem. Ariz. Ho. of Reps., 1981—; corp. officer Meredith Investments Inc. Served with Air N.G., 1968-72. Republican. Methodist. Clubs: Lions, Elks, Masons, Shriners. Home: 5034 E Lafayette Phoenix AZ 85018 Office: 2536 N 3d St Phoenix AZ 85004

MERIGAN, THOMAS CHARLES, JR., physician, med. researcher, educator; b. San Francisco, Jan. 18, 1934; s. Thomas C. and Helen M. (Greeley) M.; B.A. with honors, U. Calif., Berkeley, 1955; M.D., U. Calif., San Francisco, 1958; m. Joan Mary Freeborn, Oct. 3, 1959; 1 son, Thomas Charles III. Intern in medicine 2d and 4th Harvard med. services Boston City Hosp., 1958-59, asst. resident medicine, 1959-60; clin. asso. Nat. Heart Inst., NIH, Bethesda, Md., 1960-62, asso. Lab. Molecular Biology, Nat. Inst. Arthritis and Metabolic Diseases, NIH, 1962-63; practice medicine specializing in internal medicine and infectious diseases, Stanford, Calif., 1963—; asst. prof. medicine Stanford U. Sch. Medicine, 1963-67, asso. prof. medicine, 1967-72, head div. infectious diseases, 1966—, prof. medicine, 1972—, George E. and Lucy Becker prof. medicine, 1980—, dir. diagnostic microbiology lab. Univ. Hosp., 1966-72, dir. Diagnostic Virology Lab., 1969—, hosp. epidemiologist; mem. microbiology research tng. grants com. NIH, 1969-73, virology study sect., 1974-78, cons. antiviral substances program Nat. Inst. Allergy and Infectious Diseases, 1970—, mem. Virology Task Force, 1976-78, bd. sci. counselors, 1980—; mem. U.S. Hepatitis panel U.S. and Japan Cooperative Med. Sci. Program, 1979—; chmn. Interferon evaluation com. Am. Cancer Soc., 1978—. Recipient Borden award for Outstanding Research, Am. Assn. Med. Colls., 1973; Guggenheim Meml. fellow, 1972. Diplomate Am. Bd. Internal Medicine. Mem. Assn. Am. Physicians, Western Assn. Physicians, Am. Soc. Microbiology, Am. Soc. Clin. Investigation (council 1977-80), Am. Assn. Immunologists, Am. Fedn. Clin. Research, Western Soc. Clin. Research, Soc. Exptl. Biology and Medicine, Infectious Diseases Soc. Am., Inst. of Medicine, Nat. Acad. Scis., AMA, Calif. Med. Assn., Santa Clara County Med. Soc., Calif. Acad. Medicine, Royal Soc. Medicine, AAAS, Alpha Omega Alpha. Contbr. numerous articles on infectious diseases, virology and immunology to sci. jours.; editor: Antivirals with Clinical Potential, 1976, Antivirals and Virus Diseases of Man, 1979; Regulatory Functions of Interferon, 1980; asso. editor Virology, 1975-78; co-editor: monograph series-Current Topics in Infectious Diseases, 1975—; editorial bd. Archives Internal Medicine, 1971, Jour. Gen. Virology, 1972-77, Infection and Immunity, 1973—, Intervirology, 1973—, Virology, 1975-78, Proc. Soc. Exptl. Biology and Medicine, 1978—, Reviews of Infectious Diseases, 1979—, Jour. Interferon Research, 1980—, Antiviral Research, 1980—. Home: 148 Goya Rd Portola Valley CA 94025 Office: Div Infectious Diseases Stanford Univ Sch Medicine Stanford CA 94305

MERINEY, ANN LOUISE, interior designer, writer, lecturer; b. Indpls., Oct. 29, 1940; d. Dudley and Helen Irene Strain; m. Michael Meriney, Sept. 2, 1974; children—Trey Hoffmann, Tiffany Hoffmann. B.A. in Interior Design, Tex. Tech U., 1963. Owner, designer Ann

Hoffmann Interior Design, Abilene Tex., 1972-74; owner, pres. Ann Teriors Inc., Albuquerque, 1974—; lectr. civic women groups. Active, Republican Party. Recipient Beautification award City of Abilene (Tex.), 1971; Parade of Homes interior design award West Tex. Bd. Realtors, 1972. Mem. Internat. Soc. Interior Designers (cert.), Am. Soc. Interior Designers (cert., membership chmn.), Inst. Bus. Designers Contbr. design ideas to publs., TV news programs. Home: 4500 Glenwood Hills NE Albuquerque NM 87111 Office: Ann-Teriors Inc 3500 San Mateo NE Albuquerque NM 87110

MERIWETHER, MAGARET KATHERINE, historian; b. Lodi, Calif., July 22, 1921; d. George M. and Theresa L. (Dillonberg) Gannon; m. Richard Derling Meriwether, Nov. 18, 1945; children—Thomas Joseph, Theresa Lois. Cert. tchr. Calif. Elem. tchr., Glendale, Calif., 1943-45; docent Gamble House, Pasadena, Calif., 1969-74, organizer Greene & Greene Library, 1969-70, chmn., 1970-74; research historian Pasadena Cultural Heritage Com.; vol. reference dept. Pasadena Pub. Library, 1974—; cons. archtl. history Pasadena. Founding mem. Friends of Pasadena Pub. Library, bd. dirs., 1974-75. Recipient Pasadena Pub. Library and Cultural Heritage Com. spl. award for extraordinary service, 1982, Pasadena Heritage cert. appreciation, 1983. Mem. Gamble House Docent Council, Soc. Archtl. Historians (So. Calif. chpt.), Pasadena Heritage, Pasadena Assistance League, Alpha Chi Omega. Republican. Roman Catholic. Club: Annandale Golf (Pasadena). Author biobliographies, indexes and articles on Pasadena history and architecture. Home: 1055 Stoneridge Dr Pasadena CA 91105

MERMIGIS, STEVEN JOHN, cosmetics company sales manager; b. Kansas City, Kans., Aug. 18, 1932; s. John Steven and Thespia (Sarras) M. B.A., Stanford U., 1955. Salesman, Gen. Electric Co., Milw., 1955-58, Warner Lambert, Kansas City, 1958-61, Lever Bros. Co., El Paso, 1961-64; account mgr. Sarvis And Assocs., Creskill, N.J., 1964-73; sales mgr. Chesebrough Pond's, Inc., Greenwich, Conn., 1973—. Mem. Am. Logistics Assn. Republican. Greek Orthodox. Office: Chesebrough Pond's Inc 33 Benedict Pl Greenwich CT 06830

MERRELL, ROBERT BRUCE, oil company executive; b. Brigham City, Utah, Dec. 20, 1945; s. Elliott Hepworth and Doris (Jensen) M.; B.S. in Indsl. Engring., U. Utah, 1969, M.E.A., 1973; m. Lynne McDermott, Apr. 4, 1968; children—Melissa Ann, Jason Matthew, David Bruce. Sales rep. Shell Oil Co., 1969-70, 72-74, head office rep., 1974-75; v.p., treas., dir. Lilyblad Petroleum Co., 1975-77, dir., 1975—; dir. mktg. Pacific No. Oil Corp., Seattle, 1975—, v.p., gen. mgr., 1977, pres., chief exec. officer, 1977—, also dir. Served with USAR, 1970-71. Decorated Bronze Star. Mormon. Office: 1100 Olive Way Suite 1800 Seattle WA 98101

MERRIFIELD, JOHN THOMAS, aerospace researcher, former air force officer; b. San Antonio, Feb. 14, 1947; s. Alton Leo and Meta (Uecker) M.; B.S. in Engring. Sci., Trinity U., San Antonio, 1968; M.S. in Astronautical Engring., Air Force Inst. Tech., Wright-Patterson AFB, Ohio, 1976; postgrad. USAF Officer Tng. Sch., 1969-70, U. Mich., 1978, St. Mary's U., 1979, 80, U. Wis., 1979, Am. Inst. Profl. Edn., 1979, U. Tex., 1980; m. Sandra Lee, May 19, 1970; children—John Patrick, Kris Vaughan. Research chem. engr. Research Labs., Texaco, Inc., Port Arthur, Tex., 1968-69; commd. 2d lt. U.S. Air Force, 1970, advanced through grades to maj., 1982; aircraft comdr., instr. 41st Mil. Airlift Squadron, Charleston AFB, S.C., 1971-75, sr. controller command post 437th Mil. Airlift Wing, 1973-75; aircraft comdr. 1400 Mil. Aircraft Squadron, Randolph AFB, Tex., 1977-80; research astronautical engr. USAF Sch. Aerospace Medicine, Brooks AFB, Tex., 1977-82; flight instr., Edwards AFB, Calif., 1982—; asst. ops. officer 6512 Test Squadron, Edwards AFB, 1982—; co-owner Blue Max Ultraflight, San Antonio, 1982—; pres. Tex. Flight Research Inst., San Antonio, 1982—; project mgr., prin. investigator numerous research projects. Vol. cons. computer systems U. Tex. Inst. Texan Cultures, San Antonio, 1982—; comdr., ops. officer, pilot 19th group Tex. Wing CAP, 1978-81, project officer search and rescue eval., 1981; vol. China Grove (Tex.) Vol. Fire Dept., 1978-81. Mem. Aerospace Med. Assn., Air Force Inst. Tech. Assn. Grads., AIAA (tech. com. on gen. aviation systems), Am. Soc. Aerospace Pilots, IEEE, SAFE Assn., Exptl. Aircraft Assn., Nat. Assn. for Search and Rescue, Tex. Assn. Aerospace Tchrs., Air Force Assn., Order Daedalians. Author numerous tech. reports and papers. Address: PO Box 1458 Lancaster CA 93534

MERRIFIELD, SHIRLEY ANNE, mgmt. cons.; b. Phoenix, Nov. 8, 1948; d. Rae Allen and Mary Margaret (Smith) Echols; B.S. in Mgmt. and Info. Sci., Golden Gate U., San Francisco, 1979; m. Francis Carl Merrifield, July 14, 1978; 1 dau., Jennifer Anne. Engring. asst. Gen. Electric Co., 1969-74; engr., then engring. supr. Bechtel Inc., 1974-76; mgmt. cons. Nat. Mgmt. Inst., 1976-77; analyst, team leader Rand Info. Systems Co., 1977-78; founder, 1978, since partner Merrifield Cons. Services, Rohnert Park, Calif.; bus. columnist Sonoma County Outlook mag., 1981; dir. Datafield Co., Los Angeles; v.p. Pacific Assn. Gen. Electric Scientists and Engrs., 1973. Lobbyist, Nat. Women's Polit. Caucus, 1973; chmn. adv. com. Sonoma County Regional Occupational Program, 1980-81; bd. dirs. YWCA. Mem. Data Processing Mgmt. Assn. (chpt. v.p. 1981, pres. 1982), Women Entrepreneurs, Nat. Assn. Female Execs., Assn. Mgmt. Cons. Democrat. Home: 537 Lorraine Ct Rohnert Park CA 94928 Office: 6050 Commerce Blvd Suite E Rohnert Park CA 94928

MERRILL, CHARLES MERTON, U.S. judge; b. Honolulu, Dec. 11, 1907; s. Arthur M. and Grace Graydon (Dickey) M.; A.B., U. Calif., 1928; LL.B., Harvard, 1931; m. Mary Luita Sherman, Aug. 28, 1931; children—Julia Booth Stoddard, Charles McKinney. Admitted to Calif. bar, 1931, Nev. bar, 1932; practice in Reno, 1932-50; judge Nev. Supreme Ct., 1951-59, chief justice, 1955-56, 59; judge U.S. Ct. of Appeals, 9th Circuit, San Francisco, 1959—. Gov. State Bar Nev., 1947-50. Mem. Am. Bar Assn., Am. Law Inst. (council 1960—). Office: US Ct of Appeals PO Box 547 San Francisco CA 94101

MERRILL, DAVID WALKER, industrial psychologist; b. Plainfield, N.J., June 13, 1928; S. Miller W. and Alice (Walker) M.; m. Mary Edge Leckemby, June 15, 1951; children—David, Mark. B.A. in Psychology, Bates (Maine) Coll., 1950; M.A., U. Denver, 1955, Ph.D. in Psychology and Edn., 1957. Pres., Tracom Corp., Denver, 1979—. Served with USAF, 1950-53. Mem. Am. Psychol. Assn., Am. Personnel and Guidance Assn., Colo. Psychol. Assn., Rocky Mountain Psychol. Assn. Author: Personal Styles and Effective Performance, 1981. Contbr. articles to indsl. jours. Home: 301 Jasmine St Denver CO 80220 Office: 200 Fillmore St Suite 200 Denver CO 80206

MERRILL, ELORE MARIE (LORIE), medical center volunteer services administrator; b. Long Beach, Calif., June 30, 1934; d. John D. and Katherine Byrne (Jagerson) Herbert; m. Paul Carver Merrill, Jr.; children—Paul Todd, Richard, Andrew, Matthew. B.A. in Elem. Edn., San Jose State U., 1956. Kindergarten tchr., Palo Alto, 1956-58; asst. dir. vol. services Meml. Med. Ctr. of Long Beach, 1982—. Active Jr. League, Long Beach, 1966-82; bd. dirs. Dental Found., PTA, Family Service of Long Beach Long Beach Day Nursery. Mem. So. Calif. Assn. Dirs. Vol. Services, Am. Soc. Dirs. Vol. Services, Kappa Alpha Theta (bd. dirs. 1978-81). Republican. Presbyterian. Club: Alamitos Bay Yacht Club (Long Beach). Author: Officer Transition Workshop Manual, 1982. Office: 2801 Atlantic Ave Long Beach CA 90803

MERRILL, ISRAEL, state senator; m. Lois Merrill; 5 children. Formerly mem. Idaho Ho. of Reps.; now mem. Idaho State Senate, formerly chmn. minority caucus, mem. Senate Fin. Com. Democrat. Office: Idaho State Senate Boise ID 83720*

MERRILL, LUCETTA SWIFT, development/fund-raising/community relations executive, clinical psychotherapist; b. Fresno, Calif., Aug. 1, 1940; d. Charles and Signy Sophie (Carlson) Swift; m. Lawrence Alford Merrill, Dec. 22, 1962 (div.); children—Charlynne Marie, Melissa Jane. B.A. in Edn., Mills Coll., 1961; M.A. in Clin. Psychology, Fielding Inst., 1978. Cert. elem. tchr., Calif. Tchr., Monterey Peninsula (Calif.) Unified Sch. Dist., Mountain View (Calif.) Sch. Dist., 1961-63; pvt. practice psychotherapy, Monterey, Calif., 1973-82; devel. and community relations Moss Landing Marine Labs. (Calif.), 1982-83; prin. Merrill and Assocs., Carmel, Calif., 1983—; exec. dir. fin. com. Friends of Sam Farr (for Assemblyman), 1983—. Bd. dirs. The Lyceum of Monterey Peninsula; mem. Monterey County Juvenile Justice Commn., 1975-77, Mem. Internat. Transactional Analysis Assn., Assn. Transpersonal Psychology, Profl. Women's Network of Monterey Peninsula, Jr. League Monterey County, Nat. Women's Polit. Caucus, Monterey Bay Area Mills Club (alumnae admissions rep.), Sierra Club. Democrat. Episcopalian. Home and Office: PO Box 1835 Carmel CA 93921

MERRILL, M(ARCELLUS) S(AMUEL), inventor, devel. engr.; b. Carroll, Nebr., Aug. 7, 1900; s. George C. and Cary (Lingelbach) M.; B.S. in Elec. Engring., U. Colo., 1923, postgrad., 1936-46; m. Geraldine Robinson, Feb. 19, 1930; children—Constance Louise, M. Stanley. With engring. dept. Gen. Electric Co., Schenectady, 1923-27; mgr. and owner Merrill Axle-Wheel Service, Lakewood and Pueblo, Colo., 1928—, Merrill Engring. Labs., Denver, Pueblo, 1935—. Recipient awards U. Colo., Colo. Engring. Soc., Detroit and Colo. sects. Soc. Automotive Engrs.; inducted into Colo. Ski Hall of Fame, 1978. Mem. Soc. Automobile Engrs., Am. Soc. M.E. Presbyn. Clubs: Denver Athletic, Denver Press, Cactus, Naylor Lake, Mt. Vernon Country, Heatheridge Country. Patentee in automotive, balancing and vibration field. Home: 1201 Williams St 10C Denver CO 80218 Office: 2390 S Tejon Englewood CO 80110

MERRILL, ROBERT EDWARD, spl. machinery mfg. co. exec.; b. Columbus, Ohio, Oct. 21, 1933; s. Robert Ray and Myrna Ione (Rinehart) M.; student Ohio State U., 1954-56 M.B.A., Pepperdine U.; m. Donna Rae Bernstein, Mar. 19, 1967; children—Robert Edward, Aaron Jay, Jonathan Cyrus, Raquel Naomi. Pres., PSM Corp., San Jose, Calif., 1974—. Served with AUS, 1950-51; Korea. Mem. Soc. Mfg. Engrs., Am. Soc. Metals, Soc. of Plastics Industry. Patentee in pneumatic applications for indsl. press machinery. Home: 858 Fieldwood Ct San Jose CA 95120 Office: Box 5156 San Jose CA 95150

MERRILL, THOMAS SELFRIDGE, clinical psychologist, consultant; b. Honolulu, Feb. 17, 1940; s. William Dickey and Evelyn Merriman (Selfridge) M.; m. Kathleen Morrissey, Jan. 16, 1965; children—Lisa Lani, Kirsten Elizabeth, Kimberly Alexander. B.A., U. Colo., 1963; M.Ed., U. Hawaii, 1977; Ph.D., U. Tex., 1981. Lic. psychologist, Hawaii. Div. adminstrv. mgr. Kaiser Aluminum and Chem. Corp., Oakland, Calif., 1965-68; mktg./advt. mgr. Trans Internat. Airlines, Transamerica Corp., Alameda, Calif., 1968-70; sr. v.p. Fawcett McDermott Cavanagh Advt., Honolulu, 1970-77; pvt. practice cons., Austin and Honolulu, 1977—; clin. psychologist in pvt. practice, Honolulu, 1981—. Bd. dirs., treas. Ptnrs. in Health, Honolulu; trustee Hawaiian Mission Children's Soc. Mem. Am. Psychol. Assn., Hawaii Psychol. Assn., Tex. Psychol. Assn., Am. Group Psychotherapy Assn., Am. Soc. Clin. Hypnosis, Soc. Exptl. and Clin. Hypnosis, Running Psychologists, Am. Soc. Composers and Publishers. Club: Outrigger Canoe (Honolulu). Composer music and lyrics including Bottles & Cans, 1973. Home: 2230 Kamehameha Ave Honolulu HI 96822 Office: 1441 Kapiolani Blvd Suite 909A Honolulu HI 96814

MERRIMAN, RONALD LEWIS, accountant; b. DeKalb, Ill., Jan. 4, 1945; s. Carl E. and Geraldine (Spicer) M.; m. Kathryn Lynn Bly, June 26, 1965; children—Ronald Scott, Bradley Charles, Todd Matthew. B.S. in Acctg., No. Ill. U., 1967. C.P.A., Calif., 1969. Acct. Peat Marwick Mitchell and Co., Los Angeles, 1967—, audit ptnr., Los Angeles, 1977—. Active in fin. adv., fund raising coms. U.S. Olympic and Los Angeles Organizing Commn.; bd. dirs. Big Sisters Los Angeles, San Fernando Valley Cultural Found., Las Virgenes Edn. Found. Mem. Am. Inst. C.P.A.s, Am. Acctg. Assn., Calif. Soc. C.P.A.s. Lutheran. Clubs: Jonathan, Town Hall (Los Angeles); Calabasas (Calif.) Park Country. Office: Peat Marwick Mitchell and Co 555 S Flower St Los Angeles CA 90071

MERRITT, FRANK LEON, safety engring. cons. co. exec.; b. Danbury, Conn., May 10, 1936; s. Leon M. and Flora C. (Carlson) M.; student N.Y. U., 1968; m. Judith R. Rogers, Oct. 21, 1961 (div.); children—Linda, Kevin, Brian. Loss control rep. Hartford Ins., 1965-68; loss control dept. mgr. Pacific Ins. Co. Ltd., Honolulu, 1970-73; sr. loss control rep. Employers Ins., Wausau, Hawaii, 1974-75; pres., founder Merritt Assos. div. Mid-Pacific Claims & Engring. Services Ltd., Honolulu, 1975—; lectr. U. Hawaii System, 1975—; chmn. occupational safety and health adv. com. Honolulu Community Coll., 1975—. Registered profl. engr., Calif.; cert. safety profl. Mem. Am. Soc. Safety Engrs. (pres. Hawaii chpt. 1976-77), Nat. Safety Mgmt. Soc., System Safety Soc., Vets. of Safety. Author Merritt System. Office: 737 Bishop St Honolulu HI 96813

MERRITT, MARY ELIZABETH, fin. planner; b. Warren, Pa., Nov. 26, 1924; d. Francis Hilding and Wilma Mary (Burkett) Nelson; student Westmar Coll., 1950-52, Coll. of Desert, 1962-63, Mira Costa Coll., 1964, Cypress Coll., 1965-67; cert. fin. planner Coll. Fin. Planning, 1979; m. Milton Merritt, Aug. 9, 1947; children—Susan, Judith, Milt, Betsy. Instructional aide, Ocean View Sch. Dist., Huntington Beach, Calif., 1968; owner, mgr. Merritt Book Shoppe, Twentynine Palms, Calif., 1970-72; fin. planner Am. Pacific Securities Co., San Diego, 1972—. Methodist. Clubs: Soroptimists, Eastern Star. Office: 6150 Mission Gorge Suite 208 San Diego CA 92120

MERSEL, MARJORIE KATHRYN PEDERSEN (MRS. JULES MERSEL), lawyer; b. Manila, Utah, June 17, 1923; d. Leo Henry and Kathryn Anna (Reed) Pedersen; A.B., U. Calif., 1948; LL.B., U. San Francisco, 1948; m. Jules Mersel, Apr. 12, 1950; 1 son, Jonathan. Admitted to D.C. bar, 1952, Calif. bar, 1955; Marjorie Kathryn Pedersen Mersel, atty., Beverly Hills, Calif., 1961-71; staff counsel Dept. Real Estate State of Calif., Los Angeles, 1971—. Mem. Beverly Hills Bar Assn., Trial Lawyers Assn., So. Calif. Women Lawyers Assn. (treas. 1962-63), Beverly Hills C. of C., World Affairs Council. Club: Los Angeles Athletic. Home: 13007 Hartsook St Sherman Oaks CA 91403 Office: Dept Real Estate 107 S Broadway Los Angeles CA 90012

MERTA, PAUL JAMES, cartoonist, animator, photographer, engr., restauranteur; b. Bakersfield, Calif., July 16, 1939; s. Stanley Franklin and Mary Ann (Herman) M.; A.A., Bakersfield Jr. Coll., 1962; B.S. in Engring., San Jose State Coll., 1962. Cartoonist nat. mags., 1959—; civilian electronics engr. AirForce/Missiles, San Bernardino, Calif., 1962-65; electronics countermeasures engr., acquisition program mgr. Air Logistics Command, Sacramento, 1965—; TV film animator, owner Merge Films, 1965—; photographer, owner The Photo Poster Factory, Sacramento, 1971—; owner restaurant La Rosa Blanca, Sacramento, 1980—; producer animated films: Spaced, 1980, Grease Too, 1981; ptnr. Kolinski and Merta Hawaiian Estates, 1981—; polit. cartoonist Calif. Jour., 1958-59, Sacramento Union Newspaper, 1979—, Sacramento Legal Jour., 1979. Home: 4831 Myrtle Ave #8 Sacramento CA 95841 Office: 1005 12th St Sacramento CA 95814

MERTEL, PAUL TAFT, JR., hospital administrator; b. Mobile, Ala., Sept. 5, 1944; s. Paul Taft and Mary Martin M.; B.S. in Biology, Springhill Coll., 1966; M.P.A., U. Mo., 1974; M. Health Care Adminstrn., Baylor U., 1977. Commd. 2d lt. U.S. Army, 1967, advanced through grades to maj., 1977; chief personnel div. Munson Army Hosp., Ft. Leavenworth, Kans., 1971-75; asst. adminstr. profl. services Dewitt Army Hosp., Ft. Belvoir, Va., 1976-80; assoc. adminstr. profl. services Silas B. Hays Army Hosp., Ft. Ord, Calif., 1980-82; assoc. adminstr. Tripler Army Med. Ctr., Hawaii, 1982—. Decorated Bronze Star. Mem. Am. Coll. Hosp. Adminstrs., Am. Hosp. Assn., Young Adminstrs. Group of Nat. Capital Area. Roman Catholic. Home: 98-1739C Kaahumanu St Aiea HI 96701 Office: Box 175 Tripler Army Med Ctr Tripler Army Med Center HI 96859

MERTZ, R. JAMES, insurance loss control specialist; b. Cleve., May 10, 1951; s. William Carl and Mary Frances (Hunter) M.; m. Barbara A. Mattie, Oct. 16, 1982. B.A. in Indsl. Arts, Calif. State U., Fresno, 1975. Mgr. H.P. Metzler & Sons, Del Rey, Calif., 1973-77; loss control specialist Firemans Fund Ins., Fresno, Calif., 1977—. Served with USAR, 1971-77. Mem. Am. Soc. Safety Engrs., Central Calif. Safety Soc. (past pres.), Sigma Nu. Office: 2490 W Shaw St Fresno CA 93792

MERTZ, ROBERT LEROY, manufacturing and service company executive; b. Milw., Jan. 4, 1934; s. Joseph Stephen and Eunice Cecile (Glass) M.; m. Celine Therese Dressel, Sept. 19, 1959; children—Joan Marie, Lisa Ann, Robert Joseph. B.E.E., Marquette U., 1956; S.M., MIT, 1957; Ph.D., U. Wis., 1960. Asst. prof. elec. engring. Marquette U., Milw., 1960-64; group head system analysis AC Electronics div. Gen. Motors Corp., Milw., 1964-68; dep. mgr. Gulf Radiation Tech. div. Gulf Energy and Environ. Systems, San Diego, 1968-73; pres., chmn. bd. IRT Corp., San Diego, 1974—; cons. in field. NSF fellow, 1956-57; Bacon fellow, 1958-59. Mem. IEEE, Am. Mgmt. Assn., San Diego C. of C. Am. Electronics Assn. (dir.), Sigma Xi, Tau Beta Pi, Alpha Sigma Nu, Pi Tau Sigma, Eta Kappa Nu. Club: Kiwanis. Home: 4766 Mayita Way San Diego CA 92124 Office: 7650 Convoy Ct San Diego CA 92111

MERWIN, EDWIN PRESTON, health planning and development consultant; b. Revere, Mass., Oct. 13, 1927; s. George Preston and Edith Charlotte (Miller) M.; m. Marylynn Joy Bicknell, Nov. 3, 1979; 1 son by previous marriage, Ralph Edwin; stepchildren—Charles John Burns, Patrick Edward Burns, Stephen Allen Burns. B.S., U. So.Calif., 1955, postgrad. Law Sch., 1955-57; postgrad., San Fernando Valley State Coll., 1965-66; M.P.H. (USPHS fellow), U. Calif. at Berkeley, 1970; Ph.D., Brantridge Forest (Eng.), 1971. Tng. officer Camarillo (Calif.) State Hosp., 1961-66; asst. coordinator Mental Retardation Programs, State of Cal., Sacramento, 1966-67; project dir. Calif. Council Retarded Children, Sacramento, 1967-69; asst. dir. Golden Empire Comprehensive Health Council, Sacramento, 1970-76, health care cons., 1976-77; cons. Calif. Dept. Health, 1977-78; cons. Calif. Office Statewide Health Planning and Devel., 1978-79; chief health professions career opportunity program State of Calif., Sacramento, 1979-81; chief Health Personnel Info. and Analysis Sect., Office of Statewide Health Planning and Devel., 1981-82, asst. div. chief div. health professions devel., 1982—; tchr. Ventura (Calif.) Coll., 1962-66, Merritt Coll., Oakland, Calif., 1969; adj. prof. Golden Gate U., 1976—; lectr. continuing edn. program U. Calif. at Berkeley; instr. Los Rios Community Coll. Dist., 1982—; cons. NIMH, HEW, Calif. Assn. Health Facilities. Mem. health adv. council San Juan Sch. Dist., 1972-73; treas. Calif. Camping and Recreation Council, 1972-73. Bd. dirs., v.p. Sacramento Rehab. Facility, 1973—. Mem. Am. Assn. Mental Deficiency, Calif. Pub. Health Assn., Sacramento Mental Health Assn., Sacramento Assn. Retarded (life mem., dir.), Nat. Assn. for Retarded Children, DAV (life), Marines Meml. Assn. (life), AAAS. Contbr. articles to profl. lit. Home: 8008 Archer Ave Fair Oaks CA 95628 Office: 1600 9th St Sacramento CA 95814

MERZ, CAROL SMITH, public school administrator; b. Seattle, Sept. 29, 1942; d. Herbert Ralph and Margaret Wardell (Hill) Smith; m. Martin Daniel Merz, Aug. 23, 1964; children—Sarah Katherine, Ruth Joanna. B.A., Stanford U., 1964, M.A., 1965; Ed.D., Wash. State U., 1983. Tchr. public schs., Calif., 1965-68; instr. Columbia Basin Community Coll.-Pasco, Wash., 1971-78; adminstr. Richland (Wash.) Sch. Dist., 1979-81; prin. Edwin Markham Elem. Sch., Pasco, 1981—; cons. in field. Loan exec. United Way, Richland, 1978; vol. Girl Scouts Am., Richland, 1977-81, chmn. service area, 1978-80. Recipient Cleveland Honors award Stanford U., 1964. Mem. Wash. State Assn. Adminstrv. Women in Edn. (pres. 1981-82), N.W. Women in Ednl. Adminstrn. (exec. bd. 1978-83), N.W. Regional Ednl. Lab. (exec. bd. 1982—), Assn. Supervision and Curriculum Devel., Wash. Assn. Sch. Adminstrs., Assn. Wash. Sch. Prins., Kappa Delta Pi, Phi Delta Kappa. Democrat. Roman Catholic. Contbr. ednl. articles to profl. publs. Home: 708 Saint St Richland WA 99352 Office: Route 1 Box 600 Elm and Taylor Flats Rd Pasco WA 99301

MERZ, RUTH D., mgmt. services co. exec.; b. Phila., Oct. 29, 1945; d. William J. and Ruth E. (Edwards) M.; B.S., Wittenberg U., 1967; teaching cert. Temple U., 1967; M.A., Ind. U., 1968; postgrad. (grad. asst.) Miami U., 1968-72. Asst. dept. oncology Children's Hosp. of Phila., 1972-75; group leader Johnson & Johnson Baby Products Co., Raritan, N.J., 1975-80; dir. planning and devel. Alu Like, Inc., Honolulu, 1980—. Mem. Hawaii State Mental Health Adv. Council. Mem. AAAS, Assos. Clin. Pharmacology Profl. Soc., Nat. Congress Community Econ. Devel., Beta Beta Beta, Gamma Phi Beta (pres. Hawaii chpt.). Home: 1123 Loho St Kailua HI 96734 Office: 401 Kamakee St Honolulu HI 96814

MESCUS, PATRICIA IONA, electronics technician; b. Roadtown, Tortola, B.V.I., Sept. 14, 1956; came to U.S., 1958, naturalized, 1968; d. John Alexander and Kathleen Dorothy (Phillip) M. Student Los Angeles City Coll., 1976, Ventura Coll., 1980—. Electrician, Grumman Aerospace, Point Mugu, Calif., 1979, electronics technician range instrumentation systems dept., 1979-83; electronics technician Naval Ship Weapon Systems Engring. Sta., Port Hueneme, Calif., 1983—. Served with USN, 1975-79. Mem. Nat. Assn. Female Execs. Inc., Ventura County Navy Women's Assn. Home: 1301 W Iselin Pl Apt 4 Oxnard CA 93030 Office: Combat System Dept Code 6112 Port Hueneme CA 93043

MESKO, JOHN JOSEPH, controller; b. Jamaica, N.Y., Jan. 22, 1937; s. John Louis and Hazel Harrison (Whitler) M.; m. Constance A. Bouvier, July 21, 1973; children by previous marriage—Pam, Charlotte, Ron, Jack, June, Joseph. B.S. in Acctg. cum laude, LIU, 1969. C.P.A., Calif. Cost. acctg. mgr. Singer Co., N.Y.C., 1966-68; controller BM div. Dictaphone, Bridgeport, Conn., 1968-71; corp. controller Gen. Data

Communications, Danbury, Conn., 1971-72; corp. mgr. cost acctg. Peabody Galion Corp., Galion, Ohio, 1972-77; sec., treas., dir. Spl. Tools & Machinery Co., Los Angeles, 1977—; instr. bus. and econs. dept. Whittier Coll.; guest speaker Am. Mgmt. Assn. Served to sgt., USMC, 1955-59. Cert. mgmt. acct. Inst. Mgmt. Acctg. Mem. Nat. Assn. Accts. (Most Valuable Mem. S.E. Los Angeles chpt. 1975, chpt. pres. 1980), Inst. Mgmt. Acctg., Delta Mu Delta, Pi Gamma Mu, Alpha Sigma Lambda. Presbyterian (elder). Home: 18342 Piper Pl Yorba Linda CA 92686 Office: 4626 Pacific Blvd Vernon CA 90058

MESSANO, FRANK PETER, JR., designer, educational consultant; b. Long Beach, Calif., July 24, 1942; s. Frank Peter and Frances Rose (Pike) M.; m. Carol, July 10, 1971; children—Liza, Francesca, Frank. B.S., U. Wash., 1965. Designer, Dictaphone Co., furniture groups, Anaheim, Calif., 1965-70; dir. Ednl. Design Cons., Santa Barbara, Calif., 1970—; pres. Interior Planning Assocs. Inc., Montecito, Calif., 1978—; tng. cons. U.S. Army, 1975-77. Mem. C. of C. (Santa Barbara, Santa Maria, Bakersfield, Thousand Oaks). Patentee carpet chair. Office: 900 Knollwood Dr Montecito CA 93108

MESSEC, JOHN CHRISTIAN, accountant; b. Trenton, N.J., Oct. 9, 1942; s. John S. and Regina May (Kopp) M. B.B.A., U. Ariz., 1964, M.S. in Acctg., 1965. C.P.A., Ariz., Iowa. Staff acct. Haskins & Sells, Phoenix, 1965-67; mgr. planning Grain Processing Corp., Muscatine, Iowa, 1967-70; mgr. Touche Ross & Co., Phoenix, 1970-78; mgr. Walker & Armstrong, Phoenix, 1978-79, ptnr., 1979—. Mem. Iowa Gov.'s Economy Com., 1969. Mem. Ariz. Soc. C.P.A.s (dir. 1977-81, pres. 1980-81), Am. Inst. C.P.A.s (council 1981-82), Am. Acctg. Assn., Nat. Assn. Accts. Republican. Lutheran. Club: Elks. Home: 6052 E Vernon Scottsdale AZ 85257 Office: 2120 Valley Bank Ctr Phoenix AZ 85073

MESSICK, VELMA E. HAY (MRS. BEN MESSICK), artist; b. Bloomington, Ill.; d. Peter Pinckney and Adeline (Oldham) Hay; art student with Julydia Artzt, 1938-40, Dong Kingman, 1944, Emil Bisttram, 1945, Otis Art Inst., 1947, Chouinard Art Inst., 1948-49; m. Benjamin Newton Messick, Nov. 24, 1949; 1 dau., Caroljean McDowell Cambridge. Dir., Messick-Hay Studio Gallery, Apple Valley Calif., 1953-75, 76—; geneal. researcher, 1965—; one-woman shows: Magnolia Theatre Gallery, Long Beach, Calif., N. Long Beach Woman's Club, San Pedro (Calif.) Art Assn., Long Beach Art Assn., Pacific Coast Club Galleria, Long Beach Community Theatre Gallery, Buffum's Long Beach Gallery, E.B. Crocker City Gallery, Sacramento, Messick-Hay Studio Gallery (permanent exhibit), Long Beach, Long Beach YWCA, 1968, Pacific Coast Club Galleria, 1968, Long Beach Playhouse Studio Gallery; exhibited widely in group shows in U.S., Nat. League Am. Pen Women, 1967—; represented in permanent collections: M. Grumbacher Travel-Loan Collections, Seton Hall U., Newark, City of Hope Hosp., Springfield (Mo.) Art Mus.; executed mural for Eliza Donner Houghton Soc., Children of Am. Revolution; rep. for Ben Messick Art Works. Sec., Brawley (Calif.) PTA, 1938-40; mem. Earthquake Emergency Bd., 1938-39; fiesta chmn. children's div. Brawley C. of C., 1940; art chmn. Brawley Woman's Club, 1940-41. Recipient Key award Seton Hall U., 1958; 1st award for lecture Colonial Dames XVII Century State Conf., 1973. Mem. Long Beach Art Assn., Cultural Art Center Assn., Nat. League Am. Pen Women (rec. sec. Long Beach br. 1968-69, awards chmn. 1969-71, historian 1970-72, art chmn. 1972-74; mem. state bd. Arrangements S.W. Regional Conv. 1969; 2d award State Conf. 1971, honorable mention S.W. Conf. 1971, Calif. south state co-art chmn. 1972-74, Bicentennial chmn. Long Beach br. 1974-76), Nat. Artists and Patrons Soc., DAR (chpt. insignia chmn. 1981-82, chmn. Indian affairs Gaviota chpt. 1974-75, chpt. chmn. geneal. records 1979-80), Colonial Dames XVII Century (chmn. Roanoke Colony chpt. pub. relations 1972-75, historian 1975-76, organizing pres. Lucretia Oldham Brewster chpt. Apple Valley 1976-78, pres. 1978-79, adv. to chpt. pres. 1979-81, publicity chmn. 1976-81, registrar, chmn. chpt. resolutions, chpt. parliamentarian 1983—; heraldic frieze chmn. Calif. Soc. 1983—), Nat. Soc. Magna Charta Dames (life, historian So. Calif. div. 1974-79), Colonial Dames XVII Century (state publicity chmn. Calif. 1975-77, state vet.'s service chmn. 1979-81, state resolutions chmn. 1981-83, Gen. Soc. Mayflower Descs. (asst., rec. sec. Los Angeles Colony 1974, 75, 76, dep. gov. Inland Empire Colony 1982-84), Soc. Descs. Knights Most Noble Order Garter (hereditary life), Dames Guild St. Margaret of Scotland (hereditary life), Colonial Order Crown of Charlemagne, (hereditary life), High Desert Geneal. Soc. (charter), New Eng. Hist. Geneal. Soc., Otis Art Inst. Alumni Assn., Finley Family Assn., Colonial Soc. Ams. of Royal Descent (hereditary life), Women Descs. Ancient and Honorable Arty. Co. Mass., Clan Hay Soc. Scotland and Am. (hereditary life). Republican. Baptist. Address: 20930 Lone Eagle Rd Apple Valley CA 92307

MESSNER, KATHRYN HERTZOG, civic worker; b. Glendale, Calif., May 27, 1915; d. Walter Sylvester and Sadie (Dinger) Hertzog; B.A., UCLA, 1936, M.A., 1951; m. Ernest Lincoln, Jan. 1, 1942; children—Ernest Lincoln, Martha Allison Messner Cloran. Tchr. social studies Los Angeles schs., 1937-46; mem. Los Angeles County Grand Jury, 1961. Mem. exec. bd. Los Angeles Family Service, 1959-62; dist. atty.'s adv. com., 1965-71, dist. atty.'s adv. council, 1971-82; mem. San Marino Community Council; chmn. San Marino chpt. Am. Cancer Soc.; bd. dirs. Pasadena Rep. Women's Club, 1960-62, San Marino dist. council Girl Scouts U.S.A., 1959-68; pres. San Marino High Sch. PTA, 1964-65; bd. mem. Pasadena Vol. Placement Bur., 1962-68; mem. adv. bd. Univ. YWCA, 1956—; co-chmn. Dist. Atty.'s Adv. Bd. Young Citizens Council, 1968-72; mem. San Marino Red Cross Council, 1966—, chmn., 1969-71, vice chmn., 1971-74; mem. San Marino bd. Am. Field Service; mem. atty. gen.'s vol. adv. com., 1971-80; bd. dirs. Los Angeles Women's Philharm. Com., 1974-80, Beverly Hills-West Los Angeles YWCA, 1974—, Los Angeles YWCA, 1975—, Los Angeles Lawyers Wives Club, 1974—, Pacificulture Art Mus., 1976-80, Reachout Com., Music Center, Vol. Action Center, West Los Angeles, Calif., 1980—, Stevens House, 1980—, Pasadena Philharm. Com., 1980-83, Friends Outside, 1983—; hon. bd. dirs. Pasadena chpt. ARC, 1978-82. Recipient spl. commendation Am. Cancer Soc., 1961; Community Service award UCLA, 1981. Mem. Pasadena Philharmonic, Las Floristas, Huntington Meml. Clinic Aux., Nat. Charity League, Pasadena Dispensary Aux., Gold Shield (co-founder), Pi Lambda Theta, Pi Gamma Mu, Mortar Bd., Prytanean Soc. Home: 1786 Kelton Ave Los Angeles CA 90024

METCALF, JACK, state senator; b. Marysville, Wash., Nov. 30, 1927; s. John Read and Eunice (Grannis) M.; student U. Wash., 1944-48; B.A., B.Ed., Pacific Luth. U., 1951; m. Norma Jean Grant, Oct. 3, 1948; children—Marta Jean, Gayle Marie, Lea Lynn, Beverlee Ann. Tchr., Elma (Wash.) pub. schs., 1951-52, Everett (Wash.) pub. schs., 1952-81; mem. Wash. Ho. of Reps., 1960-64; mem. Wash. Senate, 1966-74, 80—. Chmn. Honest Money for Am. Mem. Council State Govts., Wash. Edn. Assn. (dir. 1959-61), Wash. Assn. Profl. Educators (state v.p. 1979-81, state pres. 1977-79). Republican. Club: South Whidbey Kiwanis. Office: 106A Institutions Bldg Olympic WA 98504

METHENY, TERRELL L., JR., broadcasting exec.; b. Van Buren, Ark., Aug. 22, 1934; s. Terrell L. and Leona Root M.; student U. Tulsa, 1952-55, Marquette U., 1963-64; m. Carole Ann Frazier, Sept. 12, 1981; children—Kevin, Tara. Air personality WOKY, Milw., 1960-64; v.p. programming WKLO, Louisville, 1964-68; nat. program dir. So. Broadcasting Corp., 1968; program dir. WMCA, N.Y.C., 1968-70; pres., gen. mgr. WBCS/WMKE, Milw., 1977-81; exec. v.p., gen. mgr. KUUY/KKAZ, Cheyenne, Wyo., 1981—; exec. v.p., dir. Mesa Broadcasting Group, Cheyenne and Grand Junction (Colo.). Vestryman, St. Mark's Episc. Ch. Served with U.S. Army, 1955-57. Republican. Episcopalian. Clubs: Cheyenne Country, Kiwanis. Home: 9209 Cowpoke Cheyenne WY 82009 Office: PO Box 926 Cheyenne WY 82001

METHVEN, MARGARET PETERSON, speech pathologist, school principal; b. Norfolk, Va., Dec. 24, 1918; d. Ward E. and Marguerite (Helm) Peterson; B.A., Washburn U., Topeka, 1940; M.A., U. Denver, 1960, Ed.D., 1976; m. William Charles Methven, Jan. 2, 1947: children—William Charles, Robert Ward. High sch. tchr., Burlingame, Kans., 1940-42; speech/lang. specialist Boettcher Sch. Physically Handicapped and Fairmont Sch., Denver Public Schs., 1959—, also prin. Force Elem. Sch. Mem. Am., Colo. (past treas.) speech and hearing assns., Nat. Orgn. Legal Problems Edn., Denver Elem. Prins. Assn., Kappa Delta Pi, Delta Kappa Gamma (pres. 1978-80, State Parliamentarian 1979—), Alpha Phi. Presbyterian. Office: Force Elem Sch 1550 S Wolff St Denver CO 80219

METOUR, GILDAS EUGENE, psychologist; b. Blue Canyon, Calif., Oct. 12, 1917; s. Eugene Paul and Dorothy Daisy (Koericher) M.; A.B., U. Pitts., 1937, M.A., 1938, Ph.D., 1941; postdoctoral work U. Calif., 1947-50; m. Carole Mae Carteen, Aug. 13, 1957; children—Thomas Granville, Virginia Lynn (Mrs. Peter Wade Bonnell), Leslie Annette, Heather Dorothy. Chief psychologist VA Hosp., Tucson, 1951-55; chief clin. psychology tng. VA Hosp., Sepulveda, Calif., 1955-60; chief psychology tng. Camarillo State Hosp. (Calif.), 1960-68; dir. Narcotics Addict Rehab. Act program Fed. Correctional Instn., Terminal Island, Calif., 1968-72; program dir. drug rehab. counselors tng. Suicide Prevention Center, Los Angeles, 1972-79; pvt. practice, 1979—; cons. Los Angeles County Office of Alcoholism and Alcohol Abuse, 1981—. Served as lt. comdr. USNR, 1941-45. Mem. Delta Tau Delta. Home: 15473 Milbank St Encino CA 91436 Office: 15473 Milbank St Encino CA 91436

METSCHAN, JOSEPH EMIL, insurance executive; b. Kansas City, Mo., Jan. 7, 1920; s. Emil and Hazel (Schneider) M.; m. Nedra Maxine Alumbaugh, Aug. 6, 1942; 1 son, Joseph Michael. A.A., Kansas City Jr. Coll., 1939; postgrad. Mo. U., 1940. C.L.U. Vice pres. Aurora Regional office Farmers Group, Inc., Los Angeles, 1964-67, v.p., gen. mgr. Farmers New World Life Ins. Co., 1967-69, v.p. underwriting, 1969-73, v.p. staff ops., 1973-76, v.p. field ops. Western zone, 1976-79, exec. v.p., 1979-83, pres. Farmers Group, Inc., 1983—; dir. Farmers Group, Inc., Farmers New World Life Ins. Co., Ohio State Life Ins. Co., Investors Guaranty Life Ins. Co. Served to 1st lt. USAAF, 1943-45. Decorated Croix de Guerre with 8 oak leaf clusters. Republican. Mem. Community Church. Clubs: Rotary, Wilshire Country (Los Angeles); Rancho Las Palmas (Palm Springs). Office: 4680 Wilshire Blvd Los Angeles CA 90010

METTER, GERALD EDWARD, biostatistician; b. Los Angeles, Oct. 15, 1944; s. Albert C. and Freda (Schwartzman) M.; A.B., U. Calif., Berkeley, 1966, Ph.D., 1972; postgrad. (fellow), Columbia U., 1966-67. Statistician, Nat. Communicable Disease Center, Atlanta, 1967-69; asst. prof. biostatistics Tulane U., New Orleans, 1972-73; asst. prof. statistics and human oncology U. Wis., Madison, 1973-77; biostatistician Nat. Cancer Inst., Bethesda, Md., 1977-79; dir. dept. biostatistics City of Hope Nat. Med. Center, Duarte, Calif., 1979—; lectr. dept. biomath. UCLA, 1979—; cons. Nat. Cancer Inst., Nat. Heart, Lung and Blood Inst., U.S. Forest Service, Luth. Hosp. Soc. So. Calif. Served with USPHS, 1967-69. USPHS trainee, 1969-72. Mem. Am. Statis. Assn., Biometric Soc., AAAS, Am. Soc. Preventive Oncology, Am. Soc. CLin. Oncology, Soc. for Clin. Trials, Sierra Club, Audubon Soc., Sigma Xi. Contbr. articles to profl. jours. Home: 848 W Huntington Dr Apt 27 Arcadia CA 91006 Office: City of Hope 1500 E Duarte Rd Duarte CA 91010

METTLER, MARY A., business exec.; b. Akron, Ohio, Oct. 9, 1937; d. William M. and Margaret E. (Young) M.; B.A. with distinction in Econs., Stanford U., 1959; postgrad. program in bus. adminstrn. Harvard U.-Radcliffe Coll., 1960; M.B.A., Am. U., 1962. Dir. research Ferris & Co., Washington, 1960-63; systems engr. IBM, San Francisco, 1964-68; pres. Western Ops., Inc., San Francisco, 1968-74; dir. fin. United Vintners, San Francisco, 1975-79; sr. v.p., chief fin. officer Lawrence Systems Inc., San Francisco, 1979—; dir. Lawrence Venture Capital Co. Recipient Elijah Watt Sells award, 1974. Club: Commonwealth of Calif. Home: 4462 24th St San Francisco CA 94114 Office: 340 Market St San Francisco CA 94111

METTLER, RUBEN F., business executive; b. Shafter, Calif., 1924. Student Stanford U., 1941-42; B.S.E.E., Calif. Inst. Tech., 1944, M.S., 1947, Ph.D. in Elec. and Aero. Engring., 1949; D.H.L. (hon.), Baldwin-Wallace Coll., 1980. Mem. tech. staff Hughes Aircraft Co., 1949-54; cons. Dept. Def., 1954-55; tech. supr. weapons systems Ramo-Wooldridge Corp., 1955-58; exec. v.p. to pres. TRW Space Tech. Lab., 1958-65; pres. TRW Systems Group, 1965-68; asst. pres. TRW, Inc., Redondo Beach, Calif., 1968-69, pres., chief operating officer, 1969-77, chmn. bd., chief exec. officer, 1977—, also dir.; dir. Bank Am. Corp., Merck & Co., Inc. Trustee Calif. Inst. Tech., Cleve. Clinic Found., Com. Econ. Devel.; vice chmn. Bus. Council; chmn. nat. campaign United Negro Coll. Fund, 1980-81; bd. dirs. Nat. Action Council for Minorities in Engring.; mem. Pres. Reagan's Nat. Productivity Adv. Com.; chmn. Pres.' Task Force on Sci. Policy, 1969-70. Served with USNR, 1941-46. Named Nation's Most Outstanding Young Elec. Engr., Eta Kappa Nu, 1954, Engr. of Yr., Engring. Socs. So. Calif., 1964; recipient Alumni Disting. Service award Calif. Inst. Tech., 1966, Nat. Human Relations award NCCJ, 1979. Mem. Bus. Roundtable, Nat. Alliance Bus. (chmn. 1978-79), Nat. Acad. Engring. Office: TRW Inc One Space Park Redondo Beach CA 90277

METZGER, BONNIE STUART, public relations executive; b. Hartford, Conn., Apr. 12, 1946; d. Lewis B. and Clare (Roberts) Metzger. Student pub. schs. Bristol and Newington, Conn. Ptnr., Baker Advt., San Francisco, 1972-76; promotion dir. Wenger/Michael Advt., San Francisco, 1976-78; publicist Ringling Bros. & Barnum & Bailey Circus, San Francisco, 1978-79; account exec. DJMC Advt., Los Angeles, 1979-81; owner Metzger & Co., Pub. Relations, Los Angeles, 1981—; cons. in field; lectr. in field. Featured on Merv Griffin Show, Dec. 1981. Contbr. articles to profl. jours. Office: 925 Gayley Ave Suite 7 Los Angeles CA 90024

METZGER, H(OWELL) PETER, essayist and publicist; b. N.Y.C., Feb. 22, 1931; s. Julius Radley and Gertrude (Fuller) M.; B.A., Brandeis U., 1953; Ph.D., Columbia U., 1965; m. Frances Windham, June 30, 1956; children—John, James, Lisa, Suzanne. Mgr. advanced programs Ball Bros. Research Corp., Boulder, 1968-70; research asso. Dept. Chemistry, U. Colo., Boulder, 1966-68; sr. research scientist N.Y. State Psychiat. Inst., N.Y.C., 1965-66; syndicated columnist N.Y. Times Syndicate, N.Y.C., 1972-73, NEA, N.Y.C.; sci. editor Rocky Mountain News, Denver, 1973-77; mgr. public affairs planning Public Service Co. Colo., Denver, 1977—. Cons. Environmental Instrumentation, 1970-72; dir. Colspan Environmental Systems, Inc., Boulder, Colo., 1969-72; prin. investigator USPHS grant, 1968. Pres. Colo. Com. for Environ. Info., Boulder, 1968-72; mem. Colo. gov's. adv. com. underground nuclear explosions, 1971-76; bd. dir. Wildlife-2000, 1970-72, Colo. Def. Council, 1972-74 mem. Presdl. rank rev. bd. U.S. Office Personnel Mgmt., 1981—; archivee Hoover Instn. Archives, Stanford U.; mem. Heritage Found. spl. project team on Dept. Energy mandate for Leadership: Policy Mgmt. in Conservative Adminstrn., 1980—. USPHS fellow, 1959-65. Mem. ACLU (state bd. 1968-71), Sigma Xi, Phi Lambda Upsilon. Clubs: Denver Athletic, Denver Press; Am. Alpine (N.Y.C.). Author: The Atomic Establishment, 1972. Author pamphlets; contbr. articles to jours. and newspapers. Address: 2595 Stanford Ave Boulder CO 80303

METZGER, LAWRENCE, psychologist, educator; b. Oceanside, N.Y., Jan. 9, 1933; s. Jerome and Fay (Gerber) M.; m. Martha Engle Bilsing, Dec. 24, 1970 (div.). B.A., Trinity Coll., 1955; M.S.W., U. Mich., 1970; Ph.D., Humanistic Psychology Inst., San Francisco, 1976; lic. clin. social worker Calif. Social work intern Ypsilanti (Mich.) State Hosp., 1968-69, VA Hosp., Battle Creek, Mich., 1969-70; psychiat. social worker San Francisco Dept. Pub. Health, 1970-71; tng. supr. staff devel. Alameda County Human Resources Agy., Oakland, Calif., 1971-73; psychiat. social worker Alameda County Health Care Services, Oakland, 1973-75; pvt. practice psychotherapy, Oakland, 1975—; mem. faculty U. Calif. Extension, Berkeley, Santa Cruz, Santa Barbara, San Diego, 1975—; mem. field faculty Lone Mountain Coll., San Francisco, 1976-79; dir. clin. services Vista de la Vida, Tiburon, Calif., 1979-81; staff psychologist, publicity dir. Inst. Rational Living, San Francisco, 1981; cons. in field. Mem. legis. task force unmet needs of children Nat. Assn. Social Workers, 1974; mem. San Francisco Mental Health Assn., 1975. Served with USN, 1955-57. Mem. Am. Psychol. Assn., Psychotherapy Inst., Assn. Family Therapists, Nat. Council Alcoholism (edn. com.). Contbr. articles to profl. jours. Home and Office: 5463 Manila Ave Oakland CA 94618

METZGER, ROBERT OWEN, banking consultant; b. N.Y.C., Oct. 22, 1939; s. Homer P. and Catherine Dale (Owen) M.; m. Dorothee Benkenstein, Apr. 25, 1968; 1 dau., Joelle Laurence Owen. B.S. in Econ., U. Md. Overseas Coll., 1963; P.M.D., Harvard U., 1969; Ph.D. in Bus. Adminstrn., U. Beverly Hills, 1981. Staff exec. IT&T, 1970-72; chief exec. officer Faber Merlin Ltd., Hong Kong, 1973; sr. mgr. McSweeney & Assocs., Newport Beach, Calif., 1974-75; founder, chmn., chief exec. officer Metzger, Rau & Assocs., Ltd., Tustin, Calif., 1976—; mem. faculty U. Va. Grad. Sch. Retail Banking, U. Wis. Grad. Sch. Bank Adminstrn., adj. faculty orgn. behavior U. So. Calif. Mem. Foothill Community Assn. Served with USAF, 1958-62. Mem. Inst. Mgmt. Cons., Berkshire Sch. Alumni Assn. (founder, pres. So. Calif. chpt.) Astron. Soc. Pacific. Club: Harvard Bus. Sch. So. Calif. Author: Organizational Issues to Strategic Planning in the Commerical Banking Industry, 1981; Consulting to Management, 1983; contbr. articles to profl. jours. Office: 1442 Irvine Blvd Suite 229 Tustin CA 92680

METZGER, VERNON ARTHUR, educator; b. Baldwin Park, Calif., Aug 13, 1918; s. Vernon and Nellie C. (Ross) M.; B.S., U. Calif., Berkeley, 1947, M.B.A., 1948; m. Beth Arlene Metzger, Feb. 19, 1955; children—Susan, Linda, 1 step-son, David. Estimating engr. C. F. Braun & Co., 1949; prof. mgmt. Calif. State U. at Long Beach, 1949—, founder Sch. Bus.; mgmt. cons., 1949—. Mem. Fire Commn. Fountain Valley, Calif., 1959-60; pres. Orange County Democratic League, 1967-68; mem. State Dept. mgmt. task force to promote modern mgmt. in Yugoslavia, 1977; mem. State of Calif. Fair Polit. Practices Commn., Orange County Transit Com. Served with USNR, 1942-45. Recipient Outstanding Citizens award Orange County (Calif.) Bd. Suprs. Fellow Soc. for Advancement of Mgmt. (life; dir.); mem. Acad. Mgmt., Orange County Indsl. Relations Research Assn. (v.p.), Beta Gamma Sigma, Alpha Kappa Psi, Tau Kappa Upsilon. Home: 1938 Balearic Dr Costa Mesa CA 92626 Office: 1250 Bellflower Blvd Long Beach CA 90804

METZLER, JERRY DON, nursing adminstr.; b. Mishawaka, Ind., Mar. 6, 1935; s. Gerald Donald and Cleota Christabell (Dowell) M.; m. Dorothy J. Masters, Aug. 18, 1962. B.S., Ariz. State U., 1962, M.A., 1967; B.S., San Diego State U., 1973; M.S., U. Ariz., Tucson, 1980. Sci. tchr. Washington Sch., Sanger, Calif., 1963-68; tchr. biology San Jacinto (Calif.) High Sch., 1968-70; staff nurse Maricopa County Hosp., Phoenix, 1973-76; staff nurse St. Luke's Hosp., Phoenix, 1976-77; nursing instr., dept. head Gila Pueblo Coll., Globe, Ariz., 1977-78; nurse educator, asst. dir. nursing USPHS Indian Hosp., Tuba City, Ariz., 1980—. Served with USN, 1956-60, USPHS, 1980—. Mem. Res. Officers Assn., Am. Nurses Assn., Am. Assn. Critical Care Nurses, Emergency Dept. Nurses Assn. Republican. Methodist. Club: Masons. Home: PO Box 2799 Tuba City AZ 86045 Office: USPHS Indian Hosp Tuba City AZ 86045

METZLER, ROGER JAMES, JR., lawyer; b. East Orange, N.J., Feb. 4, 1945; s. Roger James and Dorothy Marie (Clark) M.; m. Marilyn Carol Schick, Apr. 19, 1970; children—Andrea Clark, Maria Neva. B.S., Brown U., 1967; J.D. summa cum laude, U. Santa Clara, 1975; Bar: Calif. 1975. Engr., Lockheed Missile & Space Co., Sunnyvale, Calif., 1967-68; engr. Sylvania Electronic Systems, Mountain View, Calif., 1968-72; ptnr. Farrand, Malti & Cooper, San Francisco, 1975—. Mem. IEEE, ABA, Calif. Bar Assn. Republican. Roman Catholic. Office: 701 Sutter St San Francisco CA 94109

METZLER, YVONNE LEETE, travel agt.; b. Bishop, Calif., Jan. 25, 1930; d. Ben Ford and Gladys Edna (Johnson) Leete; student U. Calif., Berkeley, 1949; m. Richard Harvey Metzler, June 2, 1950; children—David Grant, Regan M., Erin E. Vocat. instr. Ukiah (Calif.) Jr. Acad., 1962-63; bookkeeper Sid Beamer Volkswagen, Ukiah, 1963-64; acct. Ukiah Convalescent Hosp., 1964, Walter Woodard P.A., Ukiah, 1964-66; asso. dir. Fashion Two Twenty, Ukiah, 1966-67, dir., Santa Rosa, Calif., 1967-71; acct. P.K. Marsh, M.D., Ukiah, 1971-72, Walter Woodard P.A. and Clarence White C.P.A., Ukiah, 1972-74; partner, travel agt. Redwood Travel Agy., Ukiah, 1973-76; owner, mgr. A-1 Travel Planners, Ukiah, 1976—; owner A-1 Travel Planners of Willits, Willits, Calif., 1979—. Commr., Ukiah City Planning Commn., 1979—, chmn., 1981-83; mem. Republican County Central Com., 1978-80. Mem. Ukiah C. of C. (1st v.p. 1980, pres. 1981-82), Mendocino County C. of C. (dir. 1981). Clubs: Soroptimist (pres. 1977-78), Bus. and Profl. Women (treas. 1977-78). Office: 505 E Perkins St Ukiah CA 95482

METZNER, RICHARD JOEL, psychiatrist, media producer, educator; b. Los Angeles, Feb. 15, 1942; s. Robert Gerson and Esther Rebecca (Groper) M.; B.A., Stanford U., 1963; M.D., Johns Hopkins U., 1967; m. Linda Susan Nordlinger, Sept. 22, 1968; children—Jeffrey Anthony, David Jonathan. Intern, Roosevelt Hosp., N.Y.C., 1967-68; resident in psychiatry Stanford U. Med. Center, 1968-71; staff psychiatrist div. manpower and tng. NIMH-St. Elizabeths Hosp., Washington, 1971-73; chief audiovisual edn. system VA Med. Center Brentwood, Los Angeles, 1973-79, chmn. VA Dist. 26 Ednl. Task Force, 1976-78; asst. prof. psychiatry UCLA Neuropsychiat. Inst., 1973-80, asso. clin. prof., 1980—, lectr. Sch. Social Welfare, 1975—; pvt. practice medicine specializing in psychiatry, Bethesda, Md., 1972-73, Los Angeles, 1973—; mem. staff Westwood Hosp., Los Angeles, St. John's Hosp., Santa

Monica, Calif.; dir. Western Inst. Psychiatry, Los Angeles, 1977—. Served with USPHS, 1968-71. Recipient 6 awards for film and videotape prodns., 1976-80; diplomate Am. Bd. Psychiatry and Neurology (cons. 1974-78, producer audiovisual exam. programs 1975-77). Mem. Am. Psychiat. Assn., So. Calif. Psychiat. Soc., Mental Health Careerists Assn. (chmn. 1972-73), AAAS, Am. Film Inst., Phi Beta Kappa. Democrat. Jewish. Contbr. numerous articles to profl. publs., 1963—; producer, writer numerous ednl. films and videotapes, 1970—; developer videoscan treatment technique in psychiatry. Home and Office: 2711 Forrester Dr Los Angeles CA 90064

MEYER, ANN JANE, psychology educator; b. N.Y.C., Mar. 11, 1942; d. Louis John and Theresa (Tikozen) M.; B.A. cum laude, U. Mich., 1964; M.A., U. Calif.-Berkeley, 1967, Ph.D., 1971. Assoc. prof., chmn. dept. human devel. Calif. State U., Hayward, 1972—. Mem. Am. Psychol. Assn., Western Psychol. Assn., Western Gerontol. Soc. Office: 28000 Carlos Bee Blvd Hayward CA 94542

MEYER, DANA JO, sales executive; b. Austin, Tex., Dec. 12, 1949; d. Arthur D. and Jo Ellen (Wischkaemper) Palmie; m. Robert Brandt Meyer, Aug. 9, 1975. Student U. Tex., 1968-72. Regional sales mgr. Holiday Inns, N.Y.C., 1973-78; dir. sales and mktg. LaJolla Village Inn, Solana Beach, Calif., 1978—. Bd. dirs. Country Friends, San Diego, 1980—. Mem. Meeting Planners Internat. (dir.), Am. Bus. Women's Assn., Nat. Assn. Profl. Saleswomen, Women in Travel, Am. Soc. Assn. Execs., Christian Bus. Women's Assn. Republican. Lutheran. Home: PO Box 691 Solana Beach CA 92075 Office: 3299 Holiday Ct LaJolla CA 92037

MEYER, DORSEY RAY, SR., farm equipment wholesale company executive; b. Omaha, Oct. 5, 1928; s. Ray R. and Carol S. (Anderson) M.; student Stockton Coll., 1946-48; m. Noma Joanne Gormsen, Aug. 3, 1946; children—Kathleen, Carol, Dorsey Ray, Constance. Order and price clk. Austin Bros., Stockton, Calif., 1948-50; rep. Towner Meyer Co. (now Meyer West), Stockton, Calif., 1950-53, sales and credit mgr., 1953-61, asst. gen. mgr., 1961-73, pres. gen. mgr., 1973—. Mem. Farm Equipment Wholesalers Assn. (1st v.p.), Tractor and Implement Club Calif. Republican. Presbyterian. Clubs: Masons, Scottish Rite. Home: 20 E Pine St Stockton CA 95204 Office: 2621 N Wigwam St Stockton CA 95208

MEYER, EVAN RAY, business consultant; b. Berkeley, Calif., July 26, 1948; s. Isaiah Simeon and Vanita (Blum) M.; m. Gay Lee Gulbrandson, Nov. 10, 1979; children—Tirzah, Leif. B.B.A., Armstrong Coll., 1978; B.A., NYU, 1978. Mgr. Beyond Repair Auto Repair Garages, Berkeley, Calif., 1969-78; pres. ERMCO, Berkeley, 1974-82; pres. Automotive Mgmt. Cons., 1975-82; service trainer Nissan Motor Corp., Walnut Creek, Calif., 1982—; cons. in field; mem. adv. bd. Bur. Automotive Repair, Calif., 1975-79. Mem. Better Bus. Bur. (arbitrator, bd. dirs. 1975-78), Automotive Service Council (pres. 1976, dir. 1977), Soc. Automotive Engrs. Democrat. Quaker. Editor: The Automotive Independent. Office: PO Box 2159 Berkeley CA 94702

MEYER, HERBERT FREDERICK REICHERT, motel executive; b. Glendale, N.Y., July 1, 1914; s. Henry Gerard and Maria Regina (Reichert) M.; m. Ellen Elizabeth Crowell, Apr. 5, 1939 (dec. Jan. 25, 1946); m. 2d, Frances Helen Lengfeld, Sept. 20, 1947; children—Diana, Barbara, Christina, Herbert Jr. B.S., Columbia Coll., 1936. With R.H. Macy and Co., N.Y.C., 1936-56, mdsg. v.p., Calif., 1956; pres. Meyer Motels Inc. (now Meyer Motels Ltd.), Redding, Calif., 1956—. Served to lt. USNR, 1942-45. Republican. Lutheran. Club: San Mateo Rotary (pres. 1968, sec. 1969-72). Home: 4480 Plumas Reno NV 89509 Office: 2059 Hilltop Dr Redding CA 96002

MEYER, IVAH GENE, social worker; b. Decatur, Ill., Nov. 18, 1935; d. Anthony and Nona Alice (Gamble) Viccone; A.A. with distinction, Phoenix Coll., 1964; B.S. with distinction, Ariz. State U., 1966, M.S.W., 1969; postgrad. U.S. Internat. U.; m. Richard Anthony Meyer, Feb. 7, 1954; children—Steven Anthony, Stuart Allen, Scott Arthur. Social worker Florence Crittendon Home, Phoenix, 1969-70; social worker Family Service of Phoenix, 1970-73; faculty asso. Ariz. State U., 1973; field supr. Pitzer Coll., Claremont, Calif., 1977—; social worker Family Service of Pomona Valley, Pomona, Calif., 1975-80; co-owner Chino (Calif.) Counseling Center, 1980—; field supr. Grad. Sch. of Social Services U. So. Calif., 1978—; dir. social service dept. Christ Anglican Ch., Pomona. Lic. clin. social worker, Calif. lMem. Nat. Assn. Social Workers, Acad. Cert. Social Workers. Republican. Roman Catholic. Home: 778 Via Montevideo Claremont CA 91711 Office: 12632 Central Ave Chino CA 91710

MEYER, J. DEAN, executive search company executive; b. St. Louis, Feb. 8, 1918; s. Joseph C. and Ros T. (Patterman) M.; m. Ruth F. Heidt, June 21, 1941; 1 son, John Dean. B.S. in Adminstrv. Engring., Purdue U., 1939. With Bendix Corp., South Bend, Ind., 1942-61, dir. sales, 1951-61; asst. dir. mktg. Martin Co., Balt., 1961-63; v.p. Menasco Mfg. Co., Burbank, Calif., 1963-73; exec. v.p. Am. Safety Equipment Corp., Encino, Calif., 1973-77, dir., 1975—; pres. J.E. Fowler & Assocs., Burbank, 1977—, dir., 1982—; dir. Flight Systems, Inc., Universal Mfg. Corp. Mem. Soc. Automotive Engrs., AIAA, Burbank C. of C., Purdue Alumni (past pres. South Bend). Club: Town Hall. Home: 2032 Hillsbury Rd Westlake Village CA 91361 Office: 255 E Orange Grove Ave Suite B Burbank CA 91502

MEYER, JAMES HENRY, univ. chancellor; b. Fenn, Idaho, Apr. 13, 1922; s. Carl A. and Anita (de Coursey) M.; B.S. in Agr., U. Idaho, 1947; M.S. in Nutrition (fellow Wis. Alumni Research Found.), U. Wis., 1949, Ph.D., 1951; m. Mary Regan, Aug. 20, 1980; children—Stephen J., Susan T., Gary C., Joan K., Teresa A. Research asst. U. Wis., 1949-51; faculty U. Calif., at Davis, 1951—, prof. animal husbandry, 1960—, chmn. dept., 1960-63, dean Coll. Agr. and Environment, 1963-69, chancellor univ., 1969—. Mem. Commn. Undergrad. Edn. in Biology. Served with USMCR, 1942-46. Recipient Am. Feed Mfr.'s award in nutrition, 1960. Mem. AAAS, Am. Soc. Animal Prodn., Western Colleges Accrediting Assn., Sigma Xi. Home: 16 College Park Davis CA 95616

MEYER, JEFFERY WILSON, chemical marketing executive; b. San Francisco, June 22, 1923; s. Wilson and Mabel Marian (Wilson) M.; m. Janet Busse, Jan. 28, 1945; children—Pamela, Elizabeth Meyer Helman. B.S., U. Calif.-Berkeley, 1948. With Wilson & George Meyer, San Francisco, 1948—, mgr. coke dept., 1952-56, v.p. agrl. dept., 1956-59, pres., dir., 1959—, chmn. bd., chief exec. officer, 1973—; fish collector for Steinhart Aquarium; dir. Barclays Bank of Calif. Past pres. Norwegian Am. C. of C.; trustee, vice chmn. Calif. Acad. Scis. Served to lt. AUS, 1942-46, 50-52; PTO. Decorated Bronze Star. Mem. Chem. Industry Council (past exec. com.), TFI-Fertilizer Inst. (dir.), IFA Internat. Fertilizer Assn. Clubs: Bohemian, Pacific Union, Cercle de l'Union, St. Francis Yacht (San Francisco); Menlo Country (Redwood City); California (Los Angeles); San Francisco Yacht (Tiburon). Home: 3880 Ralston Ave Hillsborough CA 94010 Office: 270 Lawrence Ave South San Francisco CA 94080

MEYER, JOHN WAYNE, hospital administrator; b. Baton Rouge, Apr. 2, 1947; Murtel Meyer and Audrey Lou (Clark) M.; m. Patricia Ann Rauscher, Jan. 1, 1977. B.B.A., Calif. State U. 1970; M.P.H., U. Calif., 1972. Emergency med. service coordinator Lake Winnebago Health Systems Agy., Oshkosh, Wis., 1972-75; asst. adminstr. San Pedro Peninsula Hosp., San Pedro, Calif., 1975-76; sr. planning assoc. Nat. Med. Enterprises, Los Angeles, 1977-78; dir. planning and program devel. St. Vincent Med. Ctr., Los Angeles, 1978—; instr. mgmt. programs; cons. bd. dirs. South Bay chpt. Am. Red Cross, 1975-76. Mem. Am. Coll. Hosp. Adminstrs., Soc. Hosp. Planning, So. Calif. Soc. Hosp. Planners, Assn. Western Hosps. Democrat. Contbr. articles to jours. in field. Home: 14022 Runnymede St Van Nuys CA 91405 Office: 2131 W 3rd St Los Angeles CA 90057

MEYER, JOHN WILLIAM, research scientist and engr.; b. Sacramento, Dec. 9, 1943; s. William August and Esther N. Meyer; m. Patricia Elaine Snyder, June 19, 1966; children—Jennifer Ann, Catherine Elaine. B.S.M.E., U. Calif.-Berkeley, 1966, Ph.D. in Mech. Engring., 1972. Research asst. Gas Dynamics Lab., U. Calif., Berkeley, 1966-72; research scientist Lockheed Palo Alto (Calif.) Research Lab., 1972—. Mem. AIAA, ASME, Tau Beta Pi. Club: Eichler Tennis (Palo Alto). Contbr. articles to profl. jours.; patentee in field. Home: 3124 David Ave Palo Alto CA 94303 Office: 3251 Hanover St Dept 52 33 Bldg 255 Palo Alto CA 94304

MEYER, JOSEPH JOHN, JR., ins. co. exec.; b. Somerset, Pa., May 28, 1925; s. Joseph John and Eda Agnes (Lorenz) M.; student Cornell U., 1943, U. Rochester, 1944, U. Notre Dame, 1945, George Washington U., 1946, 63; B.A., U. Hawaii, 1971; attended Staff Coll. of Armed Forces, 1958, Indsl. Coll. of Armed Forces, 1963; m. Sidney Elizabeth Donelson, June 5, 1948; children—Christine Louise Meyer Marra, Roxanne Elizabeth Meyer Shepherd, Tracy Anne. Commd. ensign U.S. Navy, 1945, advanced through grades to capt., 1966, ret., 1975; asst. v.p., gen. mgr. United Services Auto Assn., San Diego, Calif., 1975—. Bd. dirs. Armed Services, YMCA, San Diego, 1980-82. Decorated Legion of Merit with gold star, Bronze Star, Navy Commendation medal. Mem. Navy League (dir. San Diego council 1980-82), San Diego C. of C. (asst. v.p. command liaison mil. affairs 1976-81), Mil. Order World Wars, Ret. Officers Assn., Fleet Res. Assn., Poets, Naval Inst. Republican. Roman Catholic. Club: Rotary. ins. co. exec.; b. Somerset, Pa., May 28, 1925; s. Joseph John and Eda Agnes (Lorenz) M.; student Cornell U., 1943, U. Rochester, 1944, U. Notre Dame, 1945, George Washington U., 1946, 63; B.A., U. Hawaii, 1971; attended Staff Coll. of Armed Forces, 1958, Indsl. Coll. of Armed Forces, 1963; m. Sidney Elizabeth Donelson, June 5, 1948; children—Christine Louise Meyer Marra, Roxanne Elizabeth Meyer Shepherd, Tracy Anne. Commd. ensign U.S. Navy, 1945, advanced through grades to capt., 1966, ret., 1975; asst. v.p., gen. mgr. United Services Auto Assn., San Diego, Calif., 1975—. Bd. dirs. Armed Services, YMCA, San Diego, 1980-82. Decorated Legion of Merit with gold star, Bronze Star, Navy Commendation medal. Mem. Navy League (dir. San Diego council 1980-82), San Diego C. of C. (asst. v.p. command liaison mil. affairs 1976-81), Mil. Order World Wars, Ret. Officers Assn., Fleet Res. Assn., Poets, Naval Inst. Republican. Roman Catholic. Club: Rotary. Home: 16744 Valle Verde Poway CA 92064 Office: 480 Camino Del Rio S Suite 102 San Diego CA 92108

MEYER, NATALIE, state official; b. Henderson, N.C., 1930; m. Harold Meyer; children—Mary, Becky, Amy. Degree in Bus. and Edn., U. No. Iowa. Tchr. sch., Jefferson County, Colo., 5 yrs.; former leasing mgr. office complex; sec. of state State of Colo., Denver, 1982—. Vice chmn. Arapahoe County (Colo.) Republicans, 7 yrs.; mgr. Senator Bill Armstrong's 1974 Congl. campaign; exec. dir. Pres. Reagan's 1976 Colo. campaign; dir. Ted Strickland's 1978 gubernatorial race; head Phil Winn's campaign for Republican State chmn., 1978; author, dir. Colo. '80 program for Rep. Legis. Races; apptd. polit. dir. Colo. Reps., 1980; coordinated Draft Phil Winn effort; former tchr., prin. Ascension Lutheran Ch., now chmn. evangelism. Mem. AAUW. Office: Dept State 1575 Sherman St 2d Floor Denver CO 80203*

MEYER, NEIL IRWIN, neurosurgeon; b. N.Y.C., May 7, 1931; s. Gepson and Lee M.; m. Donna Jean Stitt, June 13, 1959; 1 son, Gregory Todd. A.B., W.Va. U., 1952; M.B., Chgo. Med. Sch., 1956; postgrad. Northwestern U., 1957-62. Intern New Rochelle (N.Y.) Hosp., 1956-57; resident in neurosurgery Northwestern U., Chgo., 1957-62; neurosurgeon Phila. Naval Hosp., 1962-64; attending neurosurgeon, chief of staff St. Vincent Hosp.; attending neurosurgeon Deaconess Hosp. both Billings, Mont., 1964—. Mem. Congress of Neurol. Surgeons, ACS, Mont. Med. Assn. Office: 1231 N 29th St Billings MT 59101

MEYER, ROBERT ARTHUR, JR., university dean, economics educator; b. Elmhurst, Ill., Jan. 23, 1942; s. Robert Arthur and Elizabeth Fanny (Hoffmann) M.; children—Steven, Ken, Scott, Chris. B.S. with high honors, U. Ill., 1965; Ph.D., Stanford U., 1968. Tax acct. Pure Oil Co., 1959-61; acct. Putta & Kelsey, (part-time) 1961-63; research programmer Bur. Econ. and Bus. Research, U. Ill., Urbana, 1963-65; asst. prof. econs. Purdue U., West Lafayette, Ind., 1968-73; assoc. prof. econs. U. Calif., Berkeley, 1973-77, chmn. applied econs. dept., 1975-77, assoc. dean Sch. Bus. Adminstrn., 1977—, prof., 1977—; founding ptnr. Econ. Resource Assocs., 1979—, Cargill-Meyer & Assocs., 1979—. James scholar, 1963-65; U. Ill. scholar, 1963-64, 64-65; NSF fellow, 1965-68; Purdue Research Found. grantee, 1969; Inst. Pub. Utilities grantee, 1970; Sloan Found. grantee, 1973; Purdue Research Found. grantee, 1973; Inst. Pub. Utilities faculty research fellow, 1973, grantee, 1975; Calif. Energy Resources Conservation and Devel. Commn. grantee, 1976. Mem. Am. Econ. Assn. Contbr. articles to profl. jours. Home: 6884 Chambers Dr Oakland CA 94611 Office: Sch Bus U Calif Berkeley CA 94720

MEYER, STEPHEN GEORGE, psychologist; b. Pittsburg, Kans., Aug. 23, 1942; s. Warren George and Marion (Lehman) M.; m. Ardith Lynn Williams; 1 dau., Elisa. B.S., MIT, 1964; M.A., Fuller Theol. Sem. Grad. Sch. Psychology, 1976, Ph.D., 1976. Lic. psychologist, Calif. Psychologist Hacienda Psychol. Services, Hacienda Heights, Calif., 1976-80; psychologist, assoc. dir. Associated Psychologists, Diamond Bar, Calif., 1980—. Mem. Am. Psychol. Assn., Calif. State Psychol. Assn., Calif. Perinatel Assn. Republican. Office: 23341 E Golden Springs Dr Suite 100 Diamond Bar CA 91765

MEYER, THOMAS ROBERT, TV product exec.; b. Buffalo, Apr. 20, 1936; s. Amel Robert and Mildred Lucille (Holloway) M.; student Purdue U., 1953-55, Alexander Hamilton Inst. Bus., 1960-62, West Coast U., 1969-72; m. Carol Jean Robertson, Feb. 26, 1972; children—Helen, Robyn, Sharon, Robert. Sect. chief wideband systems engring. Ground Elec. Engring. and Installation Agy., Dept. Air Force, 1960-66; product mgr., systems engr. RCA Corp., Burbank, Calif., 1966-71; systems cons. Hubert Wilke, Inc., Los Angeles, 1971-72; product mgr. Telemation, Inc., Salt Lake City, 1972-77, Dynair Electronics, San Diego, 1977—. Served with USAF, 1955-59. Decorated Legion of Merit; recipient Bronze Zero Defects award Dept. Air Force, 1966. Mem. Soc. Motion Picture and TV Engrs., Soc. Broadcast Engrs., IEEE Computer Soc., Am. Mgmt. Assn., Electronics Industry Assn., Soc. St. Paul (sr.). Republican. Episcopalian. Research and publs. on color TV tech. and optics, TV equipment and systems, application of computer to TV systems. Home: 176 E Emerson St Chula Vista CA 92011 Office: 5275 Market St San Diego CA 92114

MEYER, THOMAS VINCENT, art dealer; b. San Francisco, Calif., Dec. 28, 1943; s. Otto Ernest and Margaret (Sonder) M.; m. Constance Mae Lewallen, Apr. 7, 1979; children—Jonathan, Nina. B.S. in Bus. Adminstrn., U. Denver, 1966. Sculptor and painter, 1970-74; art dealer, 1974—. Served with USN, 1966-69. Office: 2876 California St San Francisco CA 94115

MEYER, URSULA, librarian; b. Free City of Danzig, Nov. 6, 1927; d. Herman S. and Gertrude (Rosenfeld) M.; B.A., UCLA, 1949; M.L.S., U. So. Calif., 1953; postgrad. U. Wis., 1969. Librarian, Butte County (Calif.) Library, 1961-68; asst. div. library devel. N.Y. State Library, Albany, 1969-72; coordinator Mountain Valley Coop. System, Sacramento, 1972-74; dir. library service Stockton (Calif.)-San Joaquin County Public Library, 1974—. Mem. NOW, Am. Assn. Public Adminstrs., ALA, Calif. Library Assn., Freedom to Read Found., AAUW, LWV. Club: Soroptimist Internat. Home: 6423 Monitor Pl Stockton CA 95209 Office: 605 N El Dorado St Stockton CA 95202

MEYERS, LAWRENCE CHARLES, therapist, educational administrator, educator; b. Los Angeles, Apr. 5, 1933; s. Kallman Bernard and Bettie (Abromovitz) M.; m. Reva Tackel, Mar. 22, 1956; m. 2d, Flora Bernice Heitzer, May 27, 1973; children—Nathan, Debra Meyers Kimbrell, Daniel. B.A., UCLA, 1954; M.A. in Religious Edn., Hebrew Union Coll., 1956; M.A. in History, Memphis State U., 1967; Ph.D. in Human Behavior, U.S. Internat. U., 1970, postgrad. in psychology, 1982—. Edn. dir. Temple Emanu-El, Birmingham, Ala., 1956-61, Temple Israel, Memphis, 1961-67, Temple Beth Israel, San Diego, 1967-74, Temple Israel, Westport, Conn., 1975-77, Temple Beth Sholom, Santa Ana, Calif., 1977-82; founding dir. San Diego Bur. Jewish Edn., 1967-68, San Diego Exptl. Coll. Judaism, 1971-73; asst. to dir. and sch. cons. Am. Joint Distbn. Com. in Iran, 1974-75; advisor Hillel House, Calif. State U.-Long Beach, 1978-79; instr. U. Calif.-San Diego Extension, 1971-74, dept. psychology Southwestern Community Coll., Chula Vista, Calif., 1973-74; adj. prof. ednl. psychology U. Ala., Tehran br., 1975, mental health dept. U. Bridgeport, 1975-77; tchr. psychology, Jewish history Westport Adult Edn. Dept., 1975-77; tchr., staff tng. Orange County Dept. Human Services, 1979—; mem. staff psychol. services Buena Park Police Dept., Child and Adolescent Mental Health Ctr. of Orange County. Recipient curriculum award Union Am. Hebrew Congregations/Nat. Assn. Temple Educators, 1959-63, 71, 72. Mem. Nat. Assn. Temple Educators, Am. Psychol. Assn., Am. Personnel and Guidance Assn. Democrat. Author: Teaching in the Jewish Religious School, 1967; contbr. numerous articles to periodicals. Home: 1404 N Tusin Ave Apt N-3 Santa Ana CA 92701

MEYERS, NANCY JEAN, hotel exec.; b. Spokane, Mar. 3, 1923; d. Pakie G. and Eugenia Marie (Plastino) Pieroni; student U. Wash., 1945-48, U. Idaho, 1944; m. John Meyers, Apr. 15, 1950. Fashion model Marshall Field Co., Spokane, 1952-54; office mgr. Psychiat. Clinic, Spokane, 1957-61; sec., dir. sales Olympic Hotel, Seattle, 1963-65; exec. sec. Washington Plaza Hotel (name now Westin Hotel), Seattle, 1967—, pub. relations rep., 1972-80, also adminstrv. asst. to gen. mgr. Active Cancer Soc., Heart Assn., mental health, cystic fibrosis; bd. dirs. Sandpointer Assn. Condominium, 1973-77. Mem. Exec. Women Internat. (chmn. internat. conv. 1978, pres. 1983), Pub. Relations Soc. Am. Democrat. Roman Catholic. Clubs: Variety (VIP panel 1980, 81, 82), Wash. Athletic. Editor Corp. Conversation newsletter, 1974-80; contbr. articles to profl. jours. Office: Westin Hotel 5th St at Westlake St Seattle WA 98101

MEYROWITZ, ALVIN A(BRAHAM), mgmt. exec.; b. N.Y.C., Dec. 16, 1917; s. Jacob Norman and Anne (Bader) M.; A.B., Cornell U., 1938; M.B.A., N.Y.U., 1941; law sch. George Washington U., 1948-50; m. Ruth Liberman, Feb. 1, 1942; children—Linda Jean, Jack Norman. Asso. bus. research dept. U. Newark, 1937-38; market analyst Miller Franklin Co., 1938-41; chief copper br. Office Civilian Supply W.P.B., 1941-46; dir. basic materials NHA, 1946-49; asst. dir. copper div. NPA, 1949-51; v.p. H. Kramer & Co., gen. mgr. Calif. div., El Segundo, Calif., 1951-62, v.p. H. Kramer & Co., El Segundo, 1964—; pres. Metals Refining Co., Inc., Los Angeles, 1962-64; dir. Mchts. Petroleum Co. Cons. Copper Policy, Wash., 1951-61; bd. dirs. Calif. Tech. Systems, Inc., Glendale; bd. advisers Mfrs. Bank, Los Angeles. Exec. reservist Bus. and Def. Services Adminstrn., Dept. Commerce, 1956—; vice chmn. So. Calif. Nat. Def. Exec. Res. Trustee City of Hope, Duarte, Calif. Rotarian. Mem. Am. Marketing Assn., Am. Statis. Assn. Am. Econ. Assn., Am. Ordnance Assn., A.I.M., Air Pollution Control Assn., Los Angeles, El Segundo chambers commerce, Sigma Alpha Mu. Clubs: Beverly Hills, Brentwood Country. Home: 10450 Wilshire Blvd Los Angeles CA 90024 Office: PO Box 7 El Segundo CA 90245

MEZZETTI, LEON JOSEPH, mayor, automobile dealership exec.; b. Muskegon, Mich., Oct. 28, 1920; s. Zefferino and Mary (Mateo) M.; student Western Mich. U., 1939, San Francisco Jr. Coll., 1940; m. June 27, 1942; children—Diane, Idabell, Leon, Margaret, Kimberly. With Am. Trust Co., 1948-58; pres., owner Mezzetti Volkswagon, 1958—; councilman City of Fremont (Calif.), 1974-78, mayor, 1980—. Served to capt. U.S. Army. Mem. C. of C. (pres. 1970). Democrat. Roman Catholic. Clubs: Kiwanis, Elks. Office: 39700 Civic Center Dr Fremont CA 94538*

MIANO, RICHARD JAMES, electrical manufacturing executive; b. Arlington, Mass., Dec. 13, 1936; s. Richard J. and Ruth A. (McPhail) M.; student Boston U., 1956-57, Northwestern U., 1962-63, U. Denver, 1978—, U. Pa., 1981. Dist. mgr. Thomas & Betts Corp., Seattle, 1969-74, regional mktg. mgr., San Francisco, 1974, regional mgr., Denver, 1974—. Mem. Big Bros. of Seattle, 1972-73, Denver, 1978; counselor Boy Scouts Am., 1973; active Hunger Project of San Francisco, 1977—. Served with USNR. Mem. Elec. Reps. Club of Denver, Ariz. Elec. League of Phoenix, Colo. Power Council of Denver (bd. dirs.), Rocky Mountain Elec. League of Denver, Denver C. of C. (econ. and devel. council, pres.'s club), Snake River Valley Elec. Assn., Pacific N.W. Elec. Assn. (dir.), Internat. Assn. Elec. Insps. (assoc.), Pacific Northwest Electric League (scholarship chmn. 1972-73), Southwest Elec. Reps. Club. Clubs: Vail Racquet; Brookside Tennis (Denver); N.Mex. Elec. Reps. Republican. Home: 4675 S Yosemite St Denver CO 80237 Office: 3508 Peoria St Suite 411 Aurora CO 80010

MICEK, PHYLLIS EILEEN, tax and bookkeeping co. exec.; b. Parks, Nebr., Jan. 17, 1926; d. John Carl and Mina Camilla (Brissenden) Mosser; grad. public schs., Nebr.; m. John W. Micek, July 23, 1950 (dec. 1973); children—Louis, Diane, James, John, Daniel, Ruth. Sec., Am. Commn. Co., Denver, 1943-46, County Extension Office, Benkelman, Nebr., 1948-50; sec. Morton News Co., Denver, 1955-60, accounts receivable bookkeeper, 1966-73; sec. Jamrs R. Howell & Co., Denver, 1960-66, accounts payable bookkeeper, 1974-83, office mgr., 1983—; owner, bookkeeper J. & P. Tax Service, Denver, 1962—. Republican. Clubs: Elks. Home and office: 7294 Navajo St Denver CO 80221

MICHAEL, STEPHEN WILLIAM, elec. engr.; b. El Centro, Calif., Sept. 22, 1946; s. William Eugene and Anna Mae (Lunceford) M.; A.A., Napa Coll., 1971; B.S., U. Calif. at Davis, 1973; m. Joanne Francis Frings, June 10, 1978. Product engr. Nat. Semicondr. Corp., Santa Clara, Calif., 1973-76, supervising product engr., 1976-79; mgr. div. engring. Fairchild Camera and Instrument, Mountain View, Calif., 1979—. Lt., Alameda County Underwater Recovery Unit, 1976-81; chmn. San Jose Young Reps., 1976—; active Calif. Rep. Assembly, 1976—, treas. Los Gatos-Saratoga chpt., 1978; asso. mem. Rep. State Central Com. Calif., 1977-80; mem. Santa Clara County Rep. Central Com., 1978-80; airport commr. San Jose Mcpl. Airport, 1978—, vice chmn. commn., 1981-82, chmn., 1982-83; bd. dirs. Happy Hollow Park and Baby Zoo, 1978—, treas., v.p., 1979, pres., 1982-83. Vice chmn. Santa Clara County Young Reps., 1978—; mem. Rep. State Central Com. Calif., 1980—; pres. bd. dirs. Santa Clara and Santa Cruz Counties of Campfire until 1981. Served with USCG, 1966-70. Mem. Soc.

Automotive Engring., IEEE, San Jose Jaycees (pres. 1979, internat. senator 1982), Aero Club of No. Calif., Internat. Platform Assn., Mormon. Club: San Jose Rotary. Home: 5905 Royal Ann Dr San Jose CA 95129 Office: 369 Whisman Rd M/S 19-1347 Mountain View CA 94043

MICHAELIS, JOHN UDELL, educator; b. Merino, Colo., Aug. 19, 1912; s. Richard Edward and Mary Kate (Force) M.; A.B., U. No. Colo., 1936; M.A., U. Denver, 1940; Ph.D., U. Md., 1943; m. Elizabeth Ann Rank, Oct. 5, 1935; children—John Barry, Susan Ann. Tchr. public schs., Englewood, Colo., 1936-38, prin., 1939-40; asst. supt. schs. Prince George's County (Md.) Schs., 1942; dir. tchr. edn. Fresno State Coll., 1942-45; assoc. prof. edn. U. Calif.-Berkeley, 1945-52, dir. tchr. edn., 1948-53, prof., 1953—; cons. in edn. to govts., sch. dists. Head, U.S. del. to UNESCO Conf. on History to develop internat. understanding, Summer 1951; edn. adv. U.S. AID, Lebanon, 1956, Philippines, 1960, Burma, 1968, Ecuador, 1975. Named Outstanding Alumnus in Field Edn., U. No. Colo., 1979. Mem. NEA, Am. Ednl. Research Assn., Nat. Council Social Studies, Assn. Supervision and Curriculum Devel., Nat. Council Tchrs. English, Nat. Council Geog. Edn. Democrat. Presbyterian. Club: Diablo Hills Men's Golf. Author numerous books, monographs, including: Social Studies for Children, 1956, latest edit., 1980; Prediction of Success in Student Teaching, 1953; (with Larry Hannah) Comprehensive Framework for Instructional Objectives, 1977; (with Jack Nelson) Secondary Social Studies, 1980; co-editor, co-author: The Student Teacher in the Secondary School, 1963 (NEA Outstanding Textbook 1963); editor books, including: New Trends in Curriculum and Instruction Series, 1966-69; (with Nina Gabelko) Reducing Adolescent Prejudice, 1981; co-dir. Social Studies Program, Field Ednl. Publs., 1968-74; co-dir. series: People: Cultures, Times, Places, 1976; contbr. numerous articles to profl. jours. Home: 331 Tampico Walnut Creek CA 94598 Office: Dept Edn Tolman Hall Room 4315 U Calif Berkeley CA 94720

MICHAELS, CATHERINE MARIE, museum dir.; b. Newport Beach, Calif., Mar. 13, 1953; d. Donn Owen and Marian Marie (Melandri) M.; B.F.A., U. Calif.-Irvine, 1975. Retail sales and display J.C. Penney Co., Newport Beach, 1972-77; asst. mgr. retail display Neiman-Marcus, Newport Beach, 1978-79; cons. graphics Mus. North Orange County, Fullerton, 1977-79; dir. LaHabra (Calif.) Children's Mus., 1979—. Mem. Am. Assn. Museums, Museum Educators of So. Calif., Orange County Arts Alliance, Calif. Confedn. Arts, La Habra Cultural Arts Council. Office: 301 S Euclid La Habra CA 90631

MICHAELS, PATRICK FRANCIS, broadcasting company executive; b. Superior, Wis., Nov. 5, 1925; s. Julian and Kathryn Elizabeth (Keating) M.; A.A., U. Melbourne, 1943; B.A., Golden State U., 1954; Ph.D., London U., 1964; m. Paula Naomi Bowen, May 1, 1964; children—Stephanie Michelle, Patricia Erin. War corr. CBS; news editor King Broadcasting, 1945-50; war corr. Mid-East Internat. News Service, 1947-49; war corr. MBS, Korea, 1950-53; news dir. Sta. WDSU-AM-FM-TV, 1953-54; fgn. corr. NBC, S. Am., 1954-56; news dir. Sta. KWIZ, 1956-59; commentator ABC, Los Angeles, 1959-62; fgn. corr. Am. News Services, London, 1962-64; news commentator McFadden Bartell Sta. KCBQ, 1964-68; news commentator ABC, San Francisco, 1968-70; news dir. Sta. KWIZ, Santa Ana, Calif., 1970-74, station mgr., 1974-81; pres. Sta. KWRM, Corona, Calif., KQLH, San Bernardino, Calif., 1981—. Bd. dirs. Econ. Devel. Corp., South Coast Plaza Village. Mem. Calif. Broadcasters assn., Nat. Assn. Radio Broadcasters, Am. Fedn. TV and Radio Artists, Orange County Broadcasters Assn. (pres.), Orange County Advt. Fedn., Nat. Assn. Radio and Television News Dirs. Republican. Clubs: Rotary, Balboa Bay (bd. govs.), South Shore Yacht. Home: 4521 Cortland Dr Corona del Mar CA 92625 Office: 210 Parkridge Rd Corona CA 91720

MICHAELS, RICHARD SCOTT, publishing executive; b. N.Y.C., Aug. 2, 1949; s. Hyman and Beatrice M.; m. Lauren Cohn, Oct. 20, 1979; 1 son, David. B.A. in Bus. Adminstrn. and Mktg., Kent State U., 1971. Mktg. asst. Morse Electro Co., N.Y.C., 1971-72; v.p. Kroll Assocs. Inc., N.Y.C. and San Francisco, 1972-78, pres. The Michaels Group, San Francisco, 1978—, In-Register Inc., San Francisco, 1980—. Mem. Media Alliance of San Francisco. Office: 1485 Bayshore Blvd San Francisco CA 94124

MICHALIK, EDWARD FRANCIS, constrn. co. exec.; b. Hartford, Conn., Apr. 4, 1946; s. Edward S. and Hellen A. (Sito) M.; B.B.A., Nichols Coll., Dudley, Mass., 1969; children—Marc Edward, Michael Donald. Cost engr. Wigton Abbott Corp., Plainfield, N.J., 1969-70; mgr. cost control John W. Cowper Co., Buffalo, 1970-73; fin. v.p. Titan Group Inc., Paramus, N.J., 1973-76; v.p., dir. Harrison Western Corp., Lilley Resources Corp., 1st Fin. Resources, Inc., Denver, 1980—; pres., dir. Energy Resource Systems Corp., 1983—. Mem. Associated Gen. Contractors, The Beavers, Am. Mgmt. Assn. Office: Harrison Western Corp 1208 Quail St Denver CO 80215

MICHALSEN, ROGER CHARLES, periodontist; b. Chgo., Apr. 10, 1930; s. Ole M. and Violet L. (Wernberg) M.; m. Karen Christiansen, Dec. 24, 1974; children—Richard, Lori. Student, Wright Jr. Coll., 1954, U. Ill., 1954; D.D.S., U. Ill., 1959. Lic. pvt. pilot. Resident in periodontics U. Wash., 1968-70; pres. Plexicraft Products, Chgo., 1948; pvt. practice dentistry, Chgo., 1960-68; tchr., researcher U. Ill., 1960-62; faculty U. Wash., 1968-70; pvt. practice periodontics, Mountain View, Calif., 1970-81, Redding, Calif., 1981-82, Bend, Oreg., 1982—; pres., Commuter Airline, 1978-80; chmn. dept. dentistry El Camino Hosp., Mountain View, Calif., 1976-78. Served with USN, 1950-54. Mem. Am. Acad. Periodontics, ADA, Western Soc. Periodontics, Calif. Soc. Periodontics, Calif. Dental Assn., Oreg. Soc. Periodontists, Oreg. Dental Assn., Aircraft Owners and Pilots Assn. Club: Rotary (Bend). Office: 341 NE Greenwood St Bend OR 97701

MICHEL, VICTOR JAMES, JR., librarian; b. St. Louis, Feb. 2, 1927; s. Victor James and Bernadette (Fox) M.; student St. Louis U., 1946-48; m. Margaret A. Renaud, Feb. 3, 1951; children—Dennis W., Daniel J., Catherine A., Denise M. Asst. librarian McDonnell Aircraft Corp., St. Louis, 1948-55; mgr. Anaheim (Calif.) Information Center, Electronics Ops., Rockwell Internat. Corp., 1955—; sec. Placentia Devel. Co., 1964-71. Charter mem. Placentia-Tlaquepaque Sister City Orgn., 1964—; founder, pres. Placentia chpt. St. Louis Browns Fan Club. Planning commr., Placentia, Calif., 1957-60, city councilman, 1960-70, vice-mayor, 1960-64, mayor, 1964-68. Trustee Placentia Library Dist., 1970-79, pres., 1974-79; city historian, Placentia, 1976—, city treas., 1980—; chmn. Placentia Fine Arts Commn., 1978-80. Served from pvt. to staff sgt. AUS, 1945-46. Named Placentia Citizen of Yr., 1979. Mem. Calif. Library Assn., Placentia C. of C. (v.p. 1960), Placentia Jaycees (hon. life), Calif., Orange County (pres. 1976) library assns. Democrat. Roman Catholic. Club: West Atwood Yacht (hon. yeoman emeritus with citation 1970, ship's librarian). Author: Pictorial History of the West Atwood Yacht Club, 1966; Placentia—Around the World, 1970; also articles in profl. jours. Home: 419 Somerset Dr Placentia CA 92670 Office: 3370 Miraloma Ave Anaheim CA 92803

MICHEL, WERNER, television executive; b. Petmold, Germany, Mar. 5; s. Erwin and Anne (Haas) M.; m. Rosemary Ashton, Feb. 20, 1969. Student U. Berlin, 1929-30; Ph.D. in Musicology, Sorbonne, 1933. Co-author 2 Broadway revs., 1938-40; dir. French feature films, dir. Broadcasting Voice Am., 1944-46; prodn. dir. CBS, 1946-48, chief documentaries, 1948-50; producer Ford TV Theatre, 1950-52; creator Ford 50th Anniversary Show, 1952; exec. producer Dumont TV Network, 1952-56; producer Edge of Night, 1956-58; v.p. TV, Peach McClinton Advt., 1958-62; cons. programming, comml. prodns. N.W. Ayer & Son, 1962; v.p. TV, SSC & B Advt., 1963-75; dir. programs ABC-TV, 1975-77; sr. v.p. creative affairs MGM-TV, including CHIPS, Fame, McClain's Law, 1977-82; exec. v.p., chief operating officer Guber-Peters TV, Los Angeles, 1982—. Office: 3575 Cahvenga Blvd W Suite 455 Los Angeles CA 90068

MICHELIS, JAY, broadcaster, educator, consultant; b. Livermore, Calif., Oct. 24, 1937; s. John Robert and Eileen Mary (Scullion) M. B.S. in Humanities, San Jose State U., 1959; postgrad. Stanford U., 1959. Page, NBC, Hollywood, Calif., 1959-61, page supr., 1961-63, mgr. guest relations, 1963-64, coordinator promotion, 1964, adminstr. promotion, 1964-66, mgr. promotion, 1966-70, dir. nat. promotion, 1970-72, exec. dir. nat. promotion, N.Y.C., 1972-78, v.p. talent relations, 1978-79, v.p. creative services, 1979-81, v.p. talent relations and creative services, 1981-83, v.p. corp. creative services, Burbank, Calif., 1983—; lectr. in field; bd. dirs. NBC Employees Fed. Credit Union. Dir. pub. relations com. Am. Cancer Soc. Mem. Acad. TV Arts and Scis. Democrat. Roman Catholic. Club: Am. Surfing Assn. Home: 912 Glen Oaks Blvd Pasadena CA 91105 Office: 3000 W Alameda Ave Suite 1600 Burbank CA 91523

MICHELL, GEORGIA ANN, lawyer; b. Oakland, Calif., Apr. 15, 1953; d. George Louis and Jean Ellen (Starks) M. Student UCLA, 1973-74; A.B., U. Calif.-Berkeley, 1975; J.D., U. Calif.-San Francisco, 1979. Bar: Calif. 1980. Assoc., Pillsbury, Madison & Sutro, San Francisco, 1979; with Western Energy, Fairfield, Calif., 1980; ptnr. Ganong & Michell, Walnut Creek, Calif., 1981—; legal advisor Battered Women's Alternative of Contra Costa County; chmn. East Bay chpt. Lawyers Com. Nuclear Policy, Inc.; co-chmn. East Bay chpt. Lawyers Alliance for Nuclear Arms Control. Vice pres. B'nai Shalom Sisterhood; steering com. Bus. and Profl. Women's br. Jewish Fedn. Mem. Assn. Trial Lawyers Am., ABA (vice chmn. com. on domestic violence), Calif. Trial Lawyers Assn., Contra Costa Trial Lawyers Assn., Contra Costa County Bar Assn. Republican. Jewish. Club: Orinda Country. Office: 1533 N Main St Walnut Creek CA 94596

MICHELSON, SETH GARY, biomathematician; b. Miami Beach, Fla., Aug. 29, 1950; s. Bernard and Estelle (Palay) M.; B.S., Tulane U., 1972; M.A., U. Calif.-Berkeley, 1974; M.S. in Biomath., UCLA, 1980, postgrad. 1980—; grad. 4th internat. course on computers in medicine Ettore Majoranna Center of Sci. Culture, Erice, Sicily; m. Carole Coleman, Mar. 12, 1978. Programmer/analyst Comp Sci. Corp., Sunnyvale, Calif., 1974-77; programmer/research asst. Info. Scis. Inst., Marina Del Rey, Calif., 1977-78; system programmer/analyst So. Calif. Research Inst., Los Angeles, 1978-79; biomathematician/system designer Inst. for Critical Care Medicine, Los Angeles, Calif., 1979-81; mgr. software devel. Comp-U-Med, Inc., Los Angeles, 1981-82; sr. software engr. Puritan-Bennet Corp., Los Angeles, 1982—. Vol. basketball and swimming coach Spl. Olympics, 1980. Mem. AAAS, Soc. Math. Biology, Sigma Xi. Contbr. articles to profl. jours. Office: 1973 Riverside Dr Los Angeles CA 90039

MICHENER, AUBREY WESTLAKE, JR., chem. engring. cons.; b. Chester, Pa., Apr. 21, 1921; s. Aubrey W. and Sara (Minshall) M.; B.Chem. Engring., U. Del., 1942; m. 2d, Cecilia E. Healey, June 24, 1973; 1 dau. from previous marriage—Patricia J. With Allied Chem. Corp., Morristown, N.J., 1940-80; engring. cons. Public Service Co. N.Mex., Farmington, 1980—. Mem. Am. Inst. Chem. Engrs. Republican. Patentee in field. Address: 2401 N Dustin Ave Apt 101 Farmington NM 87401

MICK, CHARLES EUGENE, corporate communications executive; b. Britt, Iowa, July 15, 1926; s. Joseph Clayton and Lena Marie (Ellingson) M. B.A., State U. Iowa, 1951. Instr. English, journalism Sr. High Sch., Cresco, Iowa, 1951-52; gen. reporter-photographer Rock Island (Ill.) Argus, 1952-54; instr. English and journalism, jr. coll. and high sch., Marshalltown, Iowa, 1954-55; corp. pub. relations mgr. Collins Radio Co., Dallas and Cedar Rapids, Iowa, 1955-62; account exec. Ted Workman Advt., Inc., Dallas, 1962; asst. dir. pub. relations, advt. mgr. Electronic Communications, Inc., St. Petersburg, Fla., 1962-63, mgr. pub. info. GTE Lenkurt Inc., San Carlos, Calif., 1963-68; pub. affairs mgr. Western states GTE Sylvania Inc., Burlingame, Calif., 1968-77; Western region mgr. pub. affairs GTE Corp., Burlingame, 1977—. Served with USAAF, 1944-46. Decorated Liberation medal (Philippines). Mem. Pub. Relations Soc. Am., San Francisco Bay Area Publicity Club. Democrat. Congregationalist. Contbr. numerous articles to profl. jours. Home: PO Box 1574 Burlingame IA 94010 Office: GTE Corp 1811 Adrian Rd Burlingame IA 94010

MICKLO, JOHN THOMAS, health services administrator; nurse; b. Fontana, Calif., Oct. 25, 1949; s. Robert Hudson and Leona Bernice (Jones) M. Student Fullerton Jr. Coll., U.S. Army Sch. of Nursing. Nurse critical care unit Century City (Calif.) Hosp., 1974-75; pvt. practice nursing, Los Angeles, 1976-77; adminstr. nursing services Upjohn Health Care Services, Los Angeles, 1977-83; adminstr. Star Med. Services, Los Angeles, 1983—; cons. in field. Served with U.S. Army, 1973-74. Recipient Upjohn Outstanding Achievement award, 1979, Baton award, 1983. Mem. Am. Nurses Assn., Am. Assn. Critical Care, Hosp. Discharge Planners So. Calif., Am. Assn. Continuity of Care Calif. Nurses Assn., Calif. Assn. Personnel Cons. (v.p.). Office: Star Med Services 3600 Wilshire Blvd Suite 1400 Los Angeles

MICKUS, MARIAN SUZANNE, financial executive; b. Chgo., July 4, 1950; d. Frank J. and Santa (Polli) Mickus; B.S. in Fin., Calif. State U., 1979; M.B.A., Loyola U., 1981. Ops. mgr. Postal Finance, Pasadena, 1968-78; asst. treas. fin. planning Fremont Gen. Corp., Los Angeles, 1982—. Mem. AAUW (cultural area rep. Pasadena), Nat. Assn. Female Execs., Los Angeles Jaycees, Town Hall Calif. Club: Los Angeles Athletic. Office: 525 S Virgil St 4th Floor Los Angeles CA 90020

MIDDLEBROOK, DAVID ARTHUR, artist, educator; b. Jackson, Mich., 1944; s. Frank and Mary (McAlpine) M.; m. Alva Marie Rosecrans; children—Jason, Aaron. B.A., Albion Coll., 1966; M.A., U. Iowa; M.F.A., U. Ky. Asst. prof. art U. Ky., Lexington, 1970-74; prof. art and ceramics San Jose (Calif.) State U., 1974—; workshop lectr. tours in South Africa, 1982, 83; vis. artist Australian Arts Council, 1980; one man shows: U. Iowa, Iowa City, 1968, Rochester (Minn.) Art Ctr., 1970, 74, Nancy Lurie Gallery, Chgo., 1974, Mills Coll. Gallery, Oakland, Calif., 1977, Nina Freudenheim, Buffalo, 1979, Quay Gallery, San Francisco, 1980, San Jose Mus. Art, 1981, Robert Mondavi Winery, Oakville, Calif., 1982, Things Gallery, Johannesburg, South Africa, 1982; group shows include: Scripps Ceramic Ann., Scripps Coll., Claremont, Calif., 1971, Ind. All Artist Craftsmen Exhbn., 1973, Nancy Lurie Gallery, Invitational Ceramic Show, Chgo., 1973, U. Ill. Sculpture of Chgo., 1974, Temple U., Phila., 1975, Berkeley (Calif.) Art Ctr., 1975, Nat. Invitational Cup Show, Smith Anderson Gallery, Palo Alto, Calif., 1976, Mus. Contemporary Crafts, N.Y.C., 1977, U. Wash., Seattle, 1978, Everson Mus. of Art, Syracuse, N.Y., 1978, Joshua Wedgewood Meml. Invitational, Phila. Mus. Art, 1980, Omaha Invitational, Contemporary Am. Ceramics, Joshland Mus., 1980, Cooper-Union Gallery, N.Y.C., 1981, Mus. Contemporary Crafts, N.Y., 25th Anniversary Show, 1981, Forgotten Dimensions, traveling show in conjuction with Internat. Sculpture Conf., San Francisco, 1982, Designers Showcase, Le Petite Trianon, San Francisco, 1982; represented by Klein Gallery, Chgo., Nina Freudenheim Gallery, Buffalo; represented in permanent collections: Davenport (Iowa) Mcpl. Gallery, Cedar Rapids (Iowa) Art Ctr., U. Iowa, U. Kans., Koehler Mus., Winona State Coll., U. Wash., Oakland (Calif.) Mus. Art, San Francisco Mus. Art, San Jose Mus. Art, Nat. Gallery Johannesburg, Nat. Conteporary Gallery, Camberra, Australia., also numerous private collections. Nat. Endowment Arts grantee, 1977; Lucy Stern vis. fellow, 1977; recipient numerous awards including: 1st prize award Arts in Other Media, Nat. Invitational, Purpee Mus., 1971; Gt. Lakes Ceramic Show, Platteville, Wis., 1969; U. Ky. Disting. Prof. award, 1971-72. Mem. Nat. Council for Edn. of Ceramic Arts. Home: 18404 Montevina Rd Los Gatos CA 95030 Office: Art Dept San Jose State U San Jose CA 95124

MIDDLEBROOK, GRACE IRENE, nurse/educator; b. Los Angeles, Mar. 5, 1927; d. Joel P. and Betty (Larson) Soderberg; dip. West Suburban Hosp., 1950; B.S. in Nursing, Wheaton Coll., 1951; M.A. in Edn., Ariz. State U., 1965, Ed.D., 1970; m. Albert William Middlebrook, July 7, 1950; children—Alberta Elizabeth, Jo Anne. Office nurse, Dr. G.A. Hemwall, Chgo., 1950-51; supr. Bates Meml. Hosp., Bentonville, Ark., 1955-58; instr. Sparks Meml. Hosp. Sch. Nursing, Ft. Smith, Ark., 1951-61; instr., coordinator med.-surg. nursing Sch. of Nursing, Good Samaritan Hosp., Phoenix, 1961-64, asst. dir. Sch. Nursing, 1964-73, dir. edn. and tng., 1968-80; corporate dir. edn. Samaritan Health Service, Phoenix, 1969—; mem. adv. com. Biosystems, Inc., 1975—. Mem. speakers bur. Sch. Career Days, 1970—. Recipient award for leadership co-op programs Phoenix Union High Sch., 1980, Sammy award Samaritan Health Service and Samaritan Med. Found., 1981. Mem. Ariz. Nurses in Mgmt. (dir. 1976—, pres. 1983—), Am. Hosp. Assn., Nat. League Nursing, Ariz. League for Nursing, Adult Edn. Assn., Pi Lambda Theta, Kappa Delta Pi, Sigma Theta Tau. Home: 4242 N 15 Dr Phoenix AZ 85015 Office: PO Box 25489 Phoenix AZ 85002

MIDDLEBROOKS, ALBERT EARL, III, shipyard executive, business consultant; b. Mare Island, Calif., July 27, 1942; s. Albert Earl and Ruth Elizabeth (Perry) M.; children—Debrath, Lisa, Albert, Tiffany, Cinamon, Rabiah, Bismillah, Ameerah; m. 2d, Nabeehah M. Smith, May 20, 1980. A.A., U. Md., 1965; postgrad. Wayne State U., 1965; B.S., U. Calif.-Berkeley, 1969; postgrad. UCLA, 1976; M.B.A., Pepperdine U., 1980. With Chrysler Corp., 1965-66, City of Phila. Jud. System, 1966-67, Todd Shipyards Corp., N.Y.C., 1967-75; with supt. indsl. relations Bethlehem Steel Corp., Terminal Island, Calif., 1975-80; chmn. bd., chief exec. officer, pres. Tri-Marine Industries, Inc., Richmond, Calif., 1980—. Mem. San Francisco. Mayor's Com. Tng. and Affirmative Action, 1970-73, Oakland (Calif.) Planning Com., 1973-75. Served with USMCR, 1960-65. Mem. Harbor Assn. Industry and Commerce, Calif. Mfg. Assn. Author: Black Business Enterprises, 1980; History of Black Americans in the Shipbuilding Industry, 1980; Shipyards and Black Shipyard Workers: A History, 1982. Office: PO Box 2541 Richmond CA 94802

MIDDLETON, ANTHONY WAYNE, JR., urologist; b. Salt Lake City, May 6, 1939; s. Anthony Wayne and Dolores Caravena (Lowry) M.; B.S., U. Utah, 1963; M.D., Cornell U., 1966; m. Carol Samuelson, Oct. 23, 1970; children—Anthony Wayne, Suzanne, Kathryn, Jane, Michelle. Intern, U. Utah Hosps., Salt Lake City, 1966-67; resident in urology Mass. Gen. Hosp., Boston, 1970-74; practice urology Middleton Urol. Assos., Salt Lake City, 1974—; mem. staff Primary Children's Hosp., staff pres., 1981-82; mem. staff Latter-Day Saints Hosp., Holy Cross Hosp.; asst. clin. prof. surgery U. Utah Med. Coll., 1977—; vice chmn. bd. govs. Utah Med. Self-Ins. Assn., 1980-81. Bd. dirs. Utah chpt. Am. Cancer Soc., 1978—; bishop Ch. Jesus Christ Latter-day Saints; vice chmn. Utah Med. Polit. Action Com., 1978-81, chmn., 1981—. Served as capt. USAF, 1968-70. Mem. A.C.S., Am. Urologic Assn., AMA, Salt Lake County Med. Assn. (sec. 1965-67, pres. liaison com. 1980-81, pres. elect 1981-83), Utah Urol. Assn. (pres. 1966-67), Salt Lake Surg. Soc. (treas. 1977-78), Phi Beta Kappa, Alpha Omega Alpha, Beta Theta Pi. Republican. Club: Univ. Contbr. articles to profl. jours. Home: 2798 Chancellor Pl Salt Lake City UT 84108 Office: 1060 E 1st S St Salt Lake City UT 84102

MIDDLETON, FRED ALEXANDER, tech. mfg. co. exec.; b. Morristown, N.J., June 27, 1949; s. Frederick A. and Carolene B. M.; B.S. in Chemistry, M.I.T., 1967-70, postgrad. in mgmt., 1970-71; M.B.A. in Fin., Harvard U., 1973; m. Carole J. Might, Dec., 1978; children—Alexander, Jennifer. Asst. to chmn. and chief exec. officer Studebaker-Worthington, N.Y.C., 1975-77; v.p. corp. planning and devel. Chase Manhattan Bank, N.Y.C., 1977-78; v.p. fin. and adminstrn., chief fin. officer, sec. Genentech, Inc., South San Francisco, Calif., 1978—. Mem. Am. Chem. Soc., Phi Lambda Upsilon, Sigma Chi. Clubs: Harvard, M.I.T. Office: Genentech Inc 460 Point San Bruno Blvd South San Francisco CA 94080

MIDDLETON, IAN JAMES, optometrist; b. Chgo., Dec. 16, 1946; s. James Bradford and Margaret Eleanor (Johnson) M.; m. Carol Lynn Robinson, Aug. 18, 1973; children—Bradford, Timothy. B.S., U. Calif.-Berkeley, 1968, O.D., 1971. Gen. practice optometry, Oakland, Calif., 1971-74, Santa Rosa, Calif., 1974-82; optometry assoc. Empire Optometric Assocs., Santa Rosa, 1982—. Chmn. bd. elders Santa Rosa Bible Ch., 1981; life mem. Lions Eye Found. Fellow Am. Acad. Optometry; mem. Am. Optometric Assn. (Optometric Recognition award 1980, 81, 82, 83), Calif. Optometric Assn., Redwood Empire Optometric Soc. (pres. 1979, treas. 1977-78), Calif. Optometric Care Found. (chmn. Redwood chpt. 1978), Execs. Assn. Sonoma County, U. Calif. Alumni Assn. (life). Club: Santa Rosa Lions (dir. 1978-80, chmn. sight conservation com. 1978-81). Office: 95 Montgomery Suite 222 Santa Rosa CA 95404

MIDDLETON, ROBERT GORDON, engineer, lecturer, author; b. Watsonville, Calif., May 31, 1908; s. Winton Gordon and Carrie (Leonard) M.; student U. Calif., 1928-31, U. Conn., 1944, N.Y. U., 1945; m. Teresa Emilson, June 29, 1940. Lectr., chief field engr. Simpson Electric Co., Chgo., 1954-57; internat. dir. tech. div. Radio Electronic TV Sch., Inc., Detroit, 1957-60. Mem. IEEE (life), Nat. Ret. Tchrs. Assn., Friends of U. Calif. at Santa Cruz Library. Club: Elks. Author 100 tech. books, the latest including: Transistor TV Servicing Guide, 1969; Transistor Color TV Servicing Guide, 1969; Tape Recorder Servicing Guide, 1970; Using Scopes in Color TV, 1970; Color-TV Waveform Analysis, 1970; Using Scopes in Transistor Circuits, 1970; Electronic Organ Servicing Guide, 1971; Audel's Television Service Manual, rev. edit., 1977; Audel's Radioman's Guide, rev. edit., 1977; Basic Electricity, 1974; Digital Equipment Servicing Guide, 1975; Handbook of Electronic Circuit Design, 1978; Handbook of Electronic System Design, 1978; Handbook of Audio Circuit Design, 1978; Acoustic Troubleshooting of Audio Systems, 1979; Understanding Microprocessors, 1980; Effectively Using the Oscilloscope, 1981; Understanding Digital Logic Circuits, 1982; Digital Logic Tests and Analysis, 1982; New Ways to Use Test Meters, 1983; contbr. articles to tech. mags. Address: PO Box 594 Santa Cruz CA 95061-0594

MIELKE, CLARENCE HAROLD, JR., hematologist; b. Spokane, Wash., June 18, 1936; s. Clarence Harold and Marie Katherine (Gillespie) M.; B.S., Wash. State U., 1959; M.D., U. Louisville, 1963; m. Marcia Rae, July 5, 1964; children—Elisa, John, Tina. Intern, San Francisco Gen. Hosp., 1963-64; resident in medicine Portland VA Hosp., 1964-65, San Francisco Gen. Hosp., 1965-67; fellow in hematology U. So. Calif., 1967-68; teaching fellow, asst. physician, instr. Tufts-New Eng. Med. Center Hosps., Boston, 1968-71; sr. scientist, dir. hematology Inst. Med. Scis., San Francisco, 1971—; chief hematology

Presbyn. Hosp., San Francisco, 1971—; asst. clin. prof. medicine U. Calif. Sch. Medicine, San Francisco, 1971-80, assoc. clin. prof., 1979—. NIH grantee, 1973—. Fellow ACP, Internat. Soc. Hematology, Am. Coll. Angiology; mem. Am. Soc. Internal Medicine, Internat. Soc. Thrombosis and Hemostasis, Am. Heart Assn., N.Y. Acad. Scis., AMA, San Francisco Med. Soc., Am. Thoracic Soc., AAAS, Internat. Soc. Angiology. Editor, Jour. Clin. Aphersis, 1981; contbr. chpts. to books, articles to med. jours. Office: Cancer Research 2200 Webster St Rm 612 San Francisco CA 94115

MIELKE, FREDERICK WILLIAM, JR., utility co. exec.; b. N.Y.C., Mar. 19, 1921; s. Frederick William and Cressida (Flynn) M.; A.B., U. Calif., 1943; J.D., Stanford U., 1949; m. Lorraine Roberts, 1947; children—Bruce Frederick, Neal Russell. Admitted to Calif. bar, 1950; law clk. to Asso. Justice John W. Shenk, Calif. Supreme Ct., 1949-51; with Pacific Gas and Electric Co., San Francisco, 1951—, exec. v.p., 1976-79, chmn. bd., chief exec. officer, 1979—, also dir.; dir. Pacific Gas Transmission Co., Alta. and So. Gas Co., Natural Gas Corp. Calif., Bd. dirs. Edison Electric Inst., 1979-82; trustee Stanford U., 1977—, Golden Gate U., 1977-79; bd. dirs. Calif. C. of C., 1979—, San Francisco C. of C., 1977-79, Ind. Colls. No. Calif., 1969-79. Served with USN, 1943-46. Mem. Am. Bar Assn., Calif. Bar Assn., Pacific Coast Elec. Assn., Pacific Coast Gas Assn., Am. Gas Assn. (bd. dirs. 1981-83). Club: Electric of San Francisco. Office: Pacific Gas & Electric Co 77 Beale St San Francisco CA 94106

MIELNICKI, RONALD PAUL, fire protection engineer; b. Syracuse, N.Y., Aug. 28, 1947; s. Eugene A. and Veronica Mielnicki; m. Mary M. Arthur, Sept. 24, 1977; children—Stephanie, Amanda, Jennifer. Student, Niagara U., 1966-67; B.A., Auburn U., 1972. Bldg. insp., Town of Owego, N.Y., 1970-72; fire protection engr. ISO Comml. Risk Services, Phoenix, 1972—; com. work Ariz. State Fire Sch. Served with USAF, 1968-69. Mem. Soc. Fire Protection Engrs., Ariz. Fire Chiefs Assn., Am. Water Works Assn., Ariz. Arson Adv. Com., Ariz. Fire Protection Assn., Ariz. Water Pollution Control Assn., Assn. Fire Fighters Ariz. Republican. Methodist. Club: Elks (Endicott, N.Y.). Office: Insurance Services Office 255 E Osborn Rd Suite 201 Phoenix AZ 85021

MIETHE, TERRY LEE, clergyman, educator; b. Clinton, Ind., Aug. 26, 1948; s. Billy and Rosemary (Procarione) M.; M.A., Trinity Evang. Div. Sch., 1973; M.Div. (scholar), McCormick Theol. Sem., 1973; Ph.D. (fellow), St. Louis U., 1976; M.A. (Babcock fellow 1980-81), U. So. Calif., 1981, Ph.D. (Miller fellow 1982-83), 1984; m. Beverly Jo Deck, June 1, 1969; 1 son, John-Hayden. Ordained to ministry Christian Ch., 1970; profl. lectr. philosophy St. Louis U., 1975-76, asst. dir. univ. honors program, 1975-76, asst. prof. dept. theol. studies, 1976-77, assoc. prof. philosophy, 1977-78; sr. engring. project analyst Burroughs Corp., 1978-79; assoc. minister First Christian Ch., Pomona, Calif., 1979-83; asst. prof. U. So. Calif., 1983—; vis. scholar Sch. Theology, Claremont, Calif., 1978-79; vis. prof. Fuller Theol. Sem., 1978, Azusa Pacific Coll., 1979, Regent Coll., Vancouver, B.C., Can., 1981, Chapman Coll., 1983. Vice-chmn. Sch. Site Council, Mountain View Sch., Claremont, 1977-79; mem. dist. adv. com. Claremont Unified Sch. Dist. Bd. Edn., 1978-79, vice-chmn., 1979-80; bd. dirs. Family Services Pomona Valley, 1979-81. Mem. Am. Philos. Assn., Evang. Theol. Soc., Am. Acad. Religion, Soc. Bibl. Lit., Evang. Philos. Soc., Nat. Assn. Student Personnel Adminstrs., Phi Beta Kappa, Phi Alpha Theta, Psi Chi, Eta Sigma Phi, Alpha Sigma Nu, Phi Delta Gamma. Author: Friedrich Nietzsche and the Death of God: The Rejection of Absolutes, 1973; The Metaphysics of Leonard James Eslick: His Philosophy of God, 1976; Thomistic Bibliography: 1940-1978, 1980; Reflections, Vol. I, 1980, Vol. II, 1982; Letters to New Christians, 1982; Aristotelian Bibliography: 1960-84, with Essays on Fundamentals of Aristotelian Scholarship, 1984; Augustinian Bibliography (1970-1980) and Thought, 1982; contbr. articles to profl. jours. Home: 3178 Florinda St Pomona CA 91767

MIEULI, FRANKLIN, professional basketball team executive; b. San Jose, Calif.; s. Giacomo M. Attended U. Oreg. From 1949 with advt. dept. San Francisco Brewing Co.; owner Mieuli & Assocs. Radio and TV Producers; part-owner San Francisco 49ers, 1954, San Francisco Giants, 1958, San Francisco Warriors, 1962; now sole owner, chmn., pres. Golden State Warriors, NBA, San Francisco. Served with USN, World War II. Office: Golden State Warriors Oakland Coliseum Arena Oakland CA 94621*

MIGDEN, CHESTER L., professional association executive; b. N.Y.C., May 21, 1921; s. Albert and Louise (Jawer) M.; B.A., CCNY, 1941; LL.B., Columbia U., 1947; m. Dina Vohl, July 22, 1944; children—Barbara, Ann, Amy. Admitted to N.Y. State bar, 1947; atty. NLRB, N.Y.C., 1947-51; various positions Screen Actors Guild Inc., Hollywood, 1952-81, nat. exec. sec., 1973-81; exec. dir. Assn. Talent Agts., Los Angeles, 1982—; v.p. Internat. Fedn. Actors, 1973-81, Calif. Labor Fedn., 1974-81, Asso. Actors and Artistes Am., 1973-81. Vice-chmn. Calif. State Film Devel. Council, 1974-78; officer, trustee Producers-Screen Actors Guild pension, welfare plans, 1960-81. Bd. dirs., sec. Motion Picture and TV Fund. Served with U.S. Army, 1942-46; PTO. Mem. Acad. Motion Picture Arts and Scis., Partnership for Performing Arts (dir. 1974-81). Democrat. Contbr. Articles to profl. jours. Home: 3539 Cody Rd Sherman Oaks CA 91403 Office: 9255 Sunset Blvd Los Angeles CA 90069

MIGLIORE, HERMAN JAMES, mechanical engineer; b. Detroit, July 13, 1946; s. Philip and Rose (Montante) M.; B.Mech. Engring. cum laude, U. Detroit, 1968, M.Engring. (Tuyere award 1969), 1969, D.Engring. (Chrysler fellow 1972), 1975. Coop. engr. Ford Motor Co., Dearborn, Mich., 1966-69; doctoral intern Chrysler Corp., Detroit, 1973-75; mech. engr. Naval Civil Engring. Lab., Port Hueneme, Calif., 1969-77; asso. prof. mech. engring. Portland (Oreg.) State U., 1977—; cons. computer aided design, nonlinear numerical methods. Mem. ASME, Am. Soc. Engring. Edn. (exec. bd. design dept.), Sigma Xi, Tau Beta Pi. Home: 4128 SW Hewett Portland OR 97221 Office: Dept Mech Engring Portland State Univ PO Box 751 Portland OR 97207

MIHALICK, CHARLES RAUTZE, JR., aluminum co. exec.; b. Ashtabula, Ohio, June 6, 1945; s. Charles R. and Mary Jane Nina (Williams) M.; B.S., Ohio State U., 1971; M.B.A., U. So. Calif., 1978; m. Lorelei Ann Lindenmayer, Oct. 31, 1964; children—Stephanie Laurel, Chad Robert. Staff auditor Coopers & Lybrand, San Francisco, 1971-73; audit sr. Hughes Aircraft Co., Los Angeles, 1973-74, head, corporate acctg., 1974-77, audit mgr., 1977-78; v.p. fin. Pioneer Aluminum, Inc., Los Angeles, 1978—, also dir. Served with U.S. Army, 1966-69. C.P.A., Calif. Mem. Am. Inst. C.P.A.'s, Calif. Soc. C.P.A.'s, Beta Alpha Psi, Beta Gamma Sigma. Democrat. Episcopalian. Home: 18862 Brasilia Dr Northridge CA 91326 Office: Pioneer AluminumInc 3800 E 26th St Los Angeles CA 90023

MIHAN, RICHARD, dermatologist; b. Los Angeles, Dec. 20, 1925; s. Arnold and Virginia Catharine (O'Reilly) M.; student U. So. Calif., 1945; M.D., St. Louis U., 1949. Rotating intern Los Angeles County Gen. Hosp., 1949-51, resident in dermatology, 1954-57; practice medicine specializing in dermatology, Los Angeles, 1957—; clin. prof. dept. medicine, dermatology and syphilology U. So. Calif. Served as lt. (j.g.) M.C., USNR, 1951-53, ret. as lt. comdr. Diplomate Am. Bd. Dermatology. Fellow ACP; mem. Internat. Soc. Tropical Dermatology, Soc. Investigative Dermatology, Pacific Dermatologic Assn. (exec. bd. 1971-74), Calif. Med. Assn. (chmn. dermatologic sect. 1973-74), AMA, Los Angeles Dermatol. Soc. (pres. 1975-76), Am. Acad. Dermatology. Office: 1245 Wilshire Blvd Los Angeles CA 90017

MIHLIK, JOSEF JOHN, real estate executive; b. Woodstock, Ont., Can., Mar. 30, 1942; s. Josef and Mary (Brinsko) M.; B.A., U. Western Ont., 1968; postgrad. Ariz. State U., evenings 1968; m. Judith Sheila Nutt, June 29, 1963; children—James John, Josef James. Came to U.S., 1966, naturalized, 1971. Staff acct. Clarkson, Gordon & Co., London, Ont., 1965, 66; sr. acct. Arthur Young & Co., Phoenix, 1966-68; controller Verco Mfg., Phoenix, 1968-69, Queen Creek Land & Cattle Corp., Phoenix, 1969-70; controller Sunshine Land & Cattle Corp., Phoenix, 1970-71, pres., 1971—; sec.-treas. Western Nat. Land Corp., Phoenix, 1971-74, pres., 1974—; pres. Republic Nat. Mortgage Corp., 1971-74, West Phoenix Properties, Inc. (formerly Litchfield Land Corp.), 1972—, Western Nat. Mortgage Corp., 1973— (all Phoenix). C.P.A., Ariz. Mem. Am. Inst. C.P.A.s, Ariz. Soc. C.P.A.s, Exec. Internat. Club, Platform Profls. Clubs: Valley of Sun Weimaraner (pres. 1972-73), Arizona (Phoenix). Home: 12202 N 60th Pl Scottsdale AZ 85254 Office: 4305 Winfield Scott Plaza Scottsdale AZ 85251

MIKALOW, ALFRED ALEXANDER, II, mcht. marine officer, deep sea diver; b. N.Y.C., Jan. 19, 1921; student Rutgers U., 1940; M.S., U. Calif., Berkeley, 1948; M.A., Rochdale U. (Can.), 1950; m. Janice Brenner, Aug. 1, 1960; children—Alfred Alexander, Jon Alfred. Owner, Coastal Diving Co., Oakland, Calif., 1950—, Divers Supply, Oakland, 1952—; dir. Coastal Sch. Deep Sea Diving, Oakland, 1950—; capt. and master research vessel Coastal Researcher I; marine diving contractor, cons. Mem. adv. bd. Medic Alert Found., Turlock, Calif., 1960—. Served with USN, 1941-47, 49-50. Decorated Purple Heart, Silver Star. Mem. Divers Assn. Am. (pres. 1970-74), Treasury Recovery Inc. (pres. 1972-75), Internat. Assn. Profl. Divers, Assn. Diving Contractors, Calif. Assn. Pvt. Edn. (no. v.p. 1971-72), Authors Guild, Internat. Game Fish Assn., U.S. Navy League, Explorer Club (San Francisco). Clubs: Masons, Lions. Author: Fell's Guide to Sunken Treasure Ships of the World, 1972; (with H.Rieseberg) The Knight from Maine, 1974. Office: 320 29th Ave Oakland CA 94601

MIKEL, THOMAS KELLY, JR, laboratory administrator; b. East Chicago, Ind., Aug. 27, 1946; s. Thomas Kelly and Anne Katherine (Vrazo) M.; B.A., San Jose State U., 1973; M.A., U. Calif.-Santa Barbara, 1975. Asst. dir. Santa Barbara Underseas Found., 1975-76; marine biologist PJB Labs., Ventura, Calif., 1976-81; lab. dir. Jacob Environ., Ventura, 1981—; instr. oceanography Ventura Coll., 1980-81. Served with U.S. Army, 1968-70. Mem. Assn. Environ. Profls., Soc. Population Ecologists. Democrat. Biol. coordinator Anacapa Underwater Natural trail U.S. Nat. Park Service, 1976; designer ecol. restoration program of upper Newport Bay, Orange County, Calif., 1978.

MIKELS, ALAN LEWIS, public relations counselor; b. Gloversville, N.Y., Mar. 19, 1943; s. Irving and Ethel M.; m. Shirley Middleton, May 3, 1975; 1 dau., Irma B.S., So. Ill. U., 1966; M.S., SUNY-Albany 1967; Ph.D., La. State U., 1970. Mem. faculty U. Pacific, Stockton, Calif., 1970—, prof. public relations, 1979—; pub. relations cons., 1975—. Bd. dirs. Childrens Home, United Way, Am. Cancer Soc.; past pres. Home Owners Assn. Grantee Ford Motor Co., 1973. Mem. Pub. Relations Soc. Am. (bd. dirs.). Contbr. articles to profl. jours. Home: 6871 Atlanta Circle Stockton CA 95209 Office: 3601 Pacific Ave Stockton CA 95211

MIKESH, DAVID LEONARD, geologist; b. Cresco, Iowa, Nov. 3, 1941; s. Leonard and Gladys (Springer) M.; B.A., U. Iowa, 1963, M.S., 1965, Ph.D., 1968. Research asso. U. Ga. Marine Inst., Sapelo Island, 1968-69; with Amoco Prodn. Co., Denver, 1970-74, Koch Exploration Co., Denver, 1974-75, TransOcean Oil, Denver, 1975-76, Webb Resources, Denver, 1976-77, Laguna Petroleum Co., Denver, 1977-80; exec. v.p. exploration and geology Mallon Oil Co., Denver., 1980—; asst. prof. geology U. Iowa, Iowa City, 1969. Mem. Am. Assn. Petroleum Geologists, Am. Inst. Profl. Geologists, Soc. Econ. Paleontologists and Mineralogists, Sigma Xi. Club: Mensa. Home: 7993 S Trenton St Englewood CO 80112 Office: 1616 Glenarm St Suite 2750 Denver CO 80202

MIKOWSKI, THEODORE JOHN, JR., civil engr., field engr.; b. Coos Bay, Oreg., Jan. 31, 1948; s. Theodore John and Alice May (Hughes) M.; B.S. in C.E., Oreg. State U., 1973. Civil engr. Peace Corps, Costa Rica, 1973-76; surveyor H.G.E., Inc., Coos Bay, 1976-77; civil engr. Mater Engring., Ltd., Corvallis, Oreg., 1977—. Served with USMC, 1968-70. Mem. ASCE, Am. Water Works Assn., Nat. Soc. Profl. Engrs., Am. Concrete Inst., Am. Soc. Photogrammetry, Profl. Engrs. Oreg. Home: Route 3 Box 772 Albany OR 97321 Office: Box 0 Corvallis OR 97339

MIKULKA, BOHUSLAV EDUARD, wood products co. exec.; b. Velka Bystrice, Czechoslovakia, Apr. 7, 1925; s. Bohuslav and Anna (Langer) M.; B.S., U. Tharandt, Eberswalde, Germany, 1942-44; postgrad. U. Brno, Czechoslovakia, 1945-48; M. Forest Engring., Hochschule fur Bodenkultur, Vienna, Austria, 1951; D.Tech. Sci., Swiss Fed. Inst. Tech., Zurich, 1955; Ph.D., Inst. Wood Tech., Munich and Braunschweig, Germany, 1955; m. Maja Doris Eimer, July 25, 1956; 1 dau., Ann Elizabeth. Came to U.S., 1955, naturalized, 1961. Research assoc. Swiss Fed. Inst. Tech., 1951-55; with Temple Industries, Inc., Diboil, Tex., 1956-65; with Evans Products Co., 1965—, dir. research and devel., mgr., Doswell, Va., 1969-71, mgr. tech. and engring. center, Corvallis, Oreg., 1971-77, dir. tech., 1977-79, v.p., dir. tech., 1979—. Mem. tech. com. Insulation Bd. Inst., 1959-60; pres. Student Assn. Brno, 1947-49, Czechoslovakia Student Assn., Zurich, 1951-55, U. Free Europe, Strasbourg, France, 1953-55. Mem. Forest Products Research Soc., Nat. Particleboard Assn. (tech. com. 1964-65), Am. Hardboard Assn. (tech. com. 1971—). Home: 2917 NW Angelica Corvallis OR 97330

MIKURIYA, TOD HIRO, physician; b. Brownsville, Pa., Sept. 20, 1933; s. Tada Fumi and Anna Susanna (Schwenk) M.; student Haverford Coll., 1951-54, Reed Coll., 1954-56, Guilford Coll., 1954; B.A., Reed Coll., 1956; M.D., Temple U., 1962; 1 son, Tada Fumi. Resident in psychiatry Oreg. State Hosp., Salem, 1963-65, Mendocino State Hosp., Talmage, Calif., 1965-66; dir. Drug Abuse Treatment Center, N.J. Neuro-Psychiatric Inst., Princeton, N.J., 1966-67; cons. research psychiatrist NIMH, Center for Narcotics and Drug Abuse Studies, Chevy Chase, Md., 1967; cons. psychiatrist Alameda County Alcoholism and Drug Abuse Programs, 1968-70; attending psychiatrist Everett A. Gladman Meml. Hosp., Oakland, Calif., 1970—; dir. research, 1970-75; dir. Mikuriya Data Systems, Mind/Body Lab., Berkeley, Calif., 1975—. Mem. adv. bd. Nat. Orgn. for Reform of Marijuana Laws, 1972; mem. steering com. Calif. Marijuana Initiative, 1972; bd. dirs. Amorphia, 1972-73; trustee FitzHugh Ludlow Library, San Francisco, 1973—; chmn. Libertarian Central Com., Alameda County, Calif., 1982. Served with M.C., U.S. Army, 1956-58. Winner, vocal soloist, Ft. Sam Houston, Tex., 1958; award Computer Faire, San Francisco for most unusual application, 1976. Mem. Biofeedback Soc. Calif. (bd. dirs. 1974-80), Calif. Med. Assn., Alameda Contra Costa Med. Assn., Am. Psychiat. Assn., N. Calif. Psychiat. Soc., East Bay Psychiat. Assn., Biofeedback Assn. Am., Am. Assn. Biofeedback Clinicans, Internat. Cannabis Alliance for Reform, Alliance for Cannabis Therapeutics. Contbr. articles to profl. jours. Office: Hotel Claremont 41 Tunnel Rd Berkeley CA 94705

MILAM, WILLIAM JEROME, mech. engr.; b. St. Paul, Jan. 16, 1924; s. James Perkins and Evelyn Verleen (McQue) M.; B.S. in Mech. Engring., U. Minn., 1948; m. Violet Gouras, Jan. 5, 1946; children—Suzanne, Billie. Mech. engr. Ellerbe & Assos., St. Paul, 1948-53, Welton Becket & Assos., Los Angeles, 1953-62, Rocketdyne div. N. Am. Aviation Co., 1962-67; chief mech. engr. Hughes Tool Co., Culver City, Calif., 1967-73; sr. plant engr. ITT Gilfillan Co., Van Nuys, Calif., 1973-78, Litton Systems Inc., Woodland Hills, Calif., 1978-79; sr. mech. engr. Lockheed Corp., Burbank, Calif., 1979—; cons. in field. Served with USAAF, 1942-44; ETO. Decorated Silver Star, Purple Heart, Air medal; recipient engring. merit award San Fernando Valley Engrs. Council, 1983. Mem. Am. Inst. Plant Engrs., DAV. Contbr. articles to profl. publs. Address: 8350 Hillview Ave Canoga Park CA 91304

MILANO, DOMINIC DAVID, journalist, musician, graphic artist; b. Chgo., Dec. 26, 1955; s. Dominic J. and Nichali (Lourik) M.; student Roosevelt U., Chgo. Mus. Coll., 1973-75; m. Leanne Van Deursen, May 26, 1977; children—Dominic Christopher, Alia Janel. Asst. editor Contemporary Keyboard, Cupertino, Calif., 1975-76, advt. dir., asst. editor, 1976-78, art dir., asst. editor, 1977-80, asst. editor, 1975—; art dir. Guitar Player Mags., Cupertino, 1980-82; cons. Moog Music, Keyboard div. Yamaha Internat., 1979—. Editor: British Rock Guitar, 1976; Folk Guitar as a Profession, 1976; Pedal Steel Handbook, 1976. Office: 20605 Lazaneo Dr Cupertino CA 95014

MILANT, JEAN ROBERT, art gallery operator; b. Milw., Dec. 27, 1943; s. Jacques J. and Virginia (Zeller) Milant. B.F.A., U. Wis., 1965; M.A., U. N.Mex., 1970. Owner, mgr. Cirrus Art Gallery, Los Angeles, 1970—; founder Mus. Contemporary Art, Los Angeles; v.p. Los Angeles Visual Arts Ctr. Named Tamarind Master Printer, Tamarind Lithography Workshop. Office: 542 S Alameda St Los Angeles CA 90013

MILBURN, JEFFREY BURGESS, health care exec.; b. Binghamton, N.Y., Oct. 15, 1946; s. Edward G. and Nancy A. (Hatch) M.; m. Joan N. Scott, 1977; 1 son, Stephen. A.S.B.A., Mitchell Coll., 1966; B.S. in Bus. Adminstrn., U. Denver, 1968; M.B.A., Northeastern U., 1976. Asst. v.p. Shawmut County Bank, Cambridge, Mass., 1971-76; v.p. comml. lending United Bank of Colorado Springs, 1976-80; assoc. adminstr. Colorado Springs Med. Ctr., 1980—. Served with U.S. Army, 1969-71. Recipient Spl. Achievement award C. of C., 1978. Mem. Colorado Springs C. of C. (dir.), Med. Group Mgrs. Assn., Robert Morris Assn. Clubs: Kiwanis (dir.), Rotary. Home: 1680 Old Stage Rd Colorado Springs CO 80906 Office: 209 S Nevada Ave Colorado Springs CO 80903

MILBURN, JUDITH ANNETTE, psychologist; b. Denison, Tex., Feb. 29, 1936; d. Henry Lynn Milburn and Edith Lorelei (Lynch) M.; divorced. B.A., Baylor U., 1958; M.Ed. La. State U., 1960; Ph.D. in counseling, U. Md., 1971. Lic. psychologist, Calif. Bd. Med. Quality Assurance, 1978. Research psychologist dept. personnel Los Angeles County Sheriffs Dept., 1970-73; instr., psychology, U. Calif.-Irvine extension, 1971; counseling psychologist, program coordinator human devel. service Calif. State U.-Long Beach, 1973-77, assoc. prof. dept. criminal justice, 1973—; instr. Ctr. Criminal Justice Tng. and Research, 1974—; pvt. practice psychology Calif., 1974—; cons. Police Found., 1973-4, Nat. Inst. Occupational Health and Safety, 1973-75. Bd. dirs. Am. Phys. Standards Research Found., Iowa city; mem. Interval House Women's Shelter, Seal Beach. Mem. Am. Psychol. Assn., Humanistic Psychol. Assn., Transpersonal Psychol. Assn., Western Psychol. Assn., Am. Assn. Correctional Psychologists, Internat. Law Enforcement Stress Assn., Phi Kappa Phi. Democrat. Mem. Ch. of Religious Sci. Home: 8400 Edinger T102 Huntington Beach CA 92647 Office: The Learning Center 1910 Old Tustin Ave Santa Ana CA 92701 also Dept Criminal Justice Calif State U Long Beach 90840

MILBY, THOMAS HUTCHINSON, physician, consultant, researcher, educator; b. South Bend, Ind., Feb. 7, 1931; s. Terry Hutchinson and Evelyn Luciel (Hecht) M.; m. Marilyn Monarch, June 1, 1953 (div. 1973); m. Rachel Natera, May 19, 1973; children—David, Steven, Nancy, Dalia. B.S., Purdue U., 1953; M.D., U. Cin., 1957, M.S., 1965; M.P.H., U. Calif-Berkeley, 1966. Diplomate Am. Bd. Preventive Medicine. Chief Bur. Occupational and Environ. Health, Dept. Health, State of Calif., Berkeley, 1962-75; sr. med. scientist SRI Internat., Menlo Park, Calif., 1975-77; med. cons. occupational and environ. medicine, Berkeley, 1977—; adj. assoc. prof. occupational medicine U. Calif.-Berkeley. Served to lt. comdr. USPHS, 1959-62. Fellow Am. Acad. Occupational Medicine, Am. Coll. Epidemiology; mem. N.Y. Acad. Sci. Contbr. articles to profl. jours. Home: 524 Woodmont Ave Berkeley CA 94708 Office: 2150 Shattuck Ave Suite 401 Berkeley CA 94704

MILDON, JAMES LEE, author, photojournalist; b. San Francisco, Jan. 5, 1936; s. James Lee and Jeannette Marie (Balandras) M.; B.A. cum laude, Calif. State U. at San Francisco, 1963; M.A., U. Nev. at Reno, 1970; m. Marie Roberta Wilson, Sept. 17, 1958; children—Laura Marie Jeannette. Owner Jim Mildon: Images, Ink, Reno, 1969—; v.p. Frank & Mildon, Assos., Reno, 1971—; mgmt. cons. Western Electric Co., 1972; devel. cons. Vacation Plan Ltd., 1971—; instr. photojournalism U. Nev., 1974—. Served with Army Security Agy., AUS, 1959-60. Mem. Profl. Photographers Assn. Am., Nat. Profl. Photographers Assn., Phi Kappa Phi, Alpha Kappa Nu, Beta Phi Gamma. Author: (with others) Portland, The City Across the River, 1972. Pub., editor, co-author: My World to Share, 1982. Illustrator: Newswriting: From Lead to 30, 1977. Address: 9135 Spearhead Way Reno NV 89506

MILES, DAVID CHARLES, food service co. mgr.; b. N.Y.C., Sept. 14, 1945; s. Harold Charles and Frances Leo M.; B.S., Pa. State U., 1967; m. Melanie Macko, June 14, 1969; children—Scott David, Michael Simon. Food service dir., area supr. Saga Corp., Balt., Washington, 1974-76, Eastern field tng. dir., 1976-79, nat. dir. mgmt. devel., Edn. div., Menlo Park, Calif., 1979-82, nat. mgmt. devel. dir. all groups, 1982—; curriculum adv. Pa. State U., S.D. State U. Bd. dirs. Civic Assn., Washington Crossing, Pa., 1977-79, Sch. Assn., Danville, Calif., 1979—. Mem. Am. Soc. Tng. and Devel., Pa. Hotel and Restaurant Soc. Home: 1274 Lawrence Rd Danville CA 94526 Office: 1 Saga Ln Menlo Park CA 94025

MILES, FRANKLIN EVERETT, adj. gen. N.Mex.; b. Tucumari, N.Mex., Jan. 4, 1923; s. John Esten and Susie Carmen (Wade) M.; B.B.A., U. N.Mex., 1950; grad. numerous service schs.; m. Patricia Maes, Dec. 13, 1973; children—Donna, John, Jeff, Larry, Carl, Karin. Joined Enlisted Res. Corps, U.S. Army, 1942, active duty as officer in PTO, 1943-46; mem. N.Mex. N.G., 1948—, commd. 1st lt., 1949, advanced through grades to maj. gen., 1975, adj. gen. N.Mex., 1974—; exec. v.p. N.Mex. Sch. Book Depository, Inc., 1957-74. Decorated Legion of Merit, Meritorious Service medal. Mem. Am. Legion, VFW, N.G. Assn., Sigma Chi. Democrat. Clubs: Kiwanis, Shriners. Office: PO Box 4277 Santa Fe NM 87501

MILES, MELVIN HENRY, research electrochemist; b. St. George, Utah, Jan. 18, 1937; s. Maurice Jarvis and Mary (Lyon) M.; grad. Dixie Jr. Coll., 1957; B.A., Brigham Young U., 1962; Ph.D. in Phys. Chemistry, U. Utah, 1966; m. Viola Joyce Cook, July 21, 1962; children—David Lyon, Jolene Carol, Melinda Marie, Samuel Jarvis. NATO postdoctoral fellow, Munich, Germany, 1966-67; research chemist Naval Weapons Center Corona Labs., Corona, Calif., 1967-69; asso. prof. Middle Tenn. State U., Murfreesboro, 1969-78; vis. scientist Brookhaven Nat. Lab., Upton, N.Y., summers, 1974, 75, Naval Weapons Center, China Lake, Calif., summers, 1971, 72, 73, 76, 77; research electrochemist Naval Weapons Center, China Lake, 1978—.

Scoutmaster, Boy Scouts Am., 1978-79. Recipient Outstanding Performance award Naval Weapons Center, 1979, 81. Mem. Electrochem. Soc. Republican. Mormon. Contbr. articles to internat. jours. Patentee in field. Office: Naval Weapons Center Code 3852 China Lake CA 93555

MILES, RALPH EARL, sr. statistician; b. San Antonio, Oct. 4, 1949; s. John and Bernice (Mapp) M.; B.A., Calif. State U., Los Angeles, 1972; M.P.H., UCLA, 1976; m. Theresa Paul Williams, Apr. 4, 1970; children—Tracy, Ahbani, Ralph Earl, Sabriya. Statistician dept. community medicine Drew Med. Sch., Los Angeles, 1973-75; statistician programmer Fanon Research and Devel. Center, Los Angeles, 1975-77, sr. statistician dept. psychiatry, 1977—, corporate dir. research and data analysis, 1977—; cons., lectr. in field. Mem. Health Sci. Minority Com., Chancelor UCLA, 1973, 74; bd. dirs. Southside YMCA. Mem. Am. Statis. Assn., Math. Assn. Am., Am. Pub. Health Assn. Democrat. Roman Catholic. Researcher pineal gland calcification, cycle phenomena, social factor in stress; also articles. Home: 440 W 62d St Los Angeles CA 90003 Office: Fanon Research and Devel Center 12714 S Avalon Blvd Suite 301 Los Angeles CA 90061

MILES, ZANE STANLEY, lawyer; b. Eagle City, Okla., Jan. 30, 1935; s. Paul McDill and Stella Sarah (McCrary) M.; J.D., U. Pacific, 1977; m. Janet K. Niebruegge, Oct. 27, 1967; children—Mark, Melissa. Reporter, sports editor Enid (Okla.) Pub. Co., 1951-54; reporter Nev. State Jour., Reno, 1958-59; editor Tahoe (Calif.) Daily Tribune, 1960; reporter, sub-editor Nev. State Jour., 1961-64; editor Fort Collins Coloradoan, 1965-68; editor Ely (Nev.) Daily Times, 1969, Aberdeen (Wash.) Daily World, 1969, Carson City (Nev.) Appeal, 1970; owner Capitol Pub. Co. and Miles Communications Co., Carson City, Nev., 1971-74; intern Nev. Supreme Ct., 1975-76; admitted to Nev. bar, 1977; individual practice law, Elko, Nev., 1977—; public defender Elko County, 1979-82. Vice chmn. Carson City Republican Com., 1973-74; chmn. Elko County Rep. Com., 1980-82, chmn. emeritus, 1982—; co-chmn. rural Elko County Heart Fund, 1977—. Served with USAF, 1954-58. Mem. Colo. AP Mng. Editors Assn. (pres. 1967), Elko County C. of C. (dir. 1980-81), Carson City C. of C. (dir. 1972-74), ABA, Nev. Bar Assn., Elko County Bar Assn., Am. Trial Lawyers Assn., Nev. Trial Lawyers Assn. (gov. 1979—). Episcopalian. Club: Lions. Office: 687 6th St Elko NV 89801

MILICI, RAYMOND BIAGIO, advertising executive; b. N.Y.C., Aug 7, 1919; s. Charles and Alfonsina (Bartoli) M.; m. Jacqueline Horvath, July 14, 1950; children—Kari Jo, Gary, Tooni. B.A., Lafayette Coll., 1943. With advt. dept. Sta. WOV, N.Y.C., 1945, Honolulu Star Bull., 1945-46; ptnr. Beam & Milici Advt. Agy., Honolulu, 1946-56; pres. Milici/Valenti Advt. Inc., 1956—, chmn., chief exec. officer, 1974—. Adviser Japan-Hawaii Econ. Council; mem. civilian adv. group U.S. Army Pacific; mem. Hawaii Environ. Council; bd. dirs. Hawaiian Music Found.; mem. exec. bd. Aloha council Boy Scouts Am. Served to capt. USMCR, 1943-45. Recipient citation Nat. Com. Jobs for Vets, 1973; pub. service award for police dept. campaign Council City and County of Honolulu, 1971; Silver medal award Am. Advt. Fedn., 1970; named Advt. Man of Yr., Honolulu Advt. Club, 1963. Mem. C. of C. Hawaii (v.p. 1972, chmn. bd. 1973), Advt. Fedn. Am. (past bd. govs. Western Region), Am. Assn. Advt. Agys., Sigma Alpha Epsilon. Clubs: Rotary (v.p. 1972, pres. 1973), Honolulu Advertising (past pres.), Honolulu Press (past dir.), Oahu Country, Waialae Country. Home: 670 Hakala Pl Honolulu HI 96816 Office: 700 Bishop St Honolulu HI 96813

MILLARD, AMOS DANIEL, educator; b. Portland, Oreg., Aug. 24, 1923; s. Amos D. and Vina C. (Simonson) M.; B.A., Northwest Coll., 1949; M.A., Winona Lake Sch. Theology, 1956; Ph.D., Calif. Grad. Sch. Theology, 1977; m. Lorna Mae Gunnarson, Aug. 27, 1948; children—Daniel Paul, Donald Wesley, David Lawrence, Dean Mark. Dean admissions, registrar, faculty mem. Northwest Coll., Kirkland, Wash., 1949—; cons. to bd. dirs. acad. master plan com. Northwest Coll., 1979-80. Mem. Am. Assn. Collegiate Registrars and Admissions Officers, Pacific Coast Assn. Collegiate Registrars and Admissions Officers, Wash. Council on High Sch.-Coll. Relations. Mem. Assembly of God Ch. Author: Learning form the Apostles, 1972, The Old Testament Historical Books, 1973. Home: 5047 114 St NE Kirkland WA 98033 Office: Northwest Coll Kirkland WA 98033

MILLARD, LAVERGNE HARRIET, freelance artist; b. Chgo., July 8, 1925; d. Lewis and Julia (Smolk) Bassmire; student Chgo. Art Inst., 1937-39; m. Samuel Costales, 1943 (div. 1957); m. Bailey Millard, Mar. 9, 1958 (div.); children—Bryan Lewis Costales, Julianne, Juanita Crump, Candace Lynn Millard. Cocktail waitress Verdis, Grant Street, Concord, Calif., 1955-61; mgr. used book shop Joyce Book Shop, Concord, 1964-79, seller art works, own prints; freelance artist, 1979—. Recipient ribbons local fairs, art shows. Republican. Copyright holder for pastel art work. Home and office: 1890 Farm Bureau Rd Concord CA 94519

MILLER, ALAN, psychologist, researcher, scientist; b. N.Y.C., Sept. 18, 1940; s. Frank and Natalie (Rosenberg) M.; m. Diane Hsu, June 1972 (div.); 1 son, Stephan Hsu. B.E.E., CCNY, 1963; M.S., U. So. Calif., 1965, Ph.D., 1977. Lic. clin. psychologist, Calif. Staff TRW, Redondo Beach, Calif., 1965-77, cons., Los Angeles, 1981—; staff psychologist Met. State Hosp., Los Angeles, 1977-79; psychologist UCLA, 1981-82; staff Westwood (Calif.) Psychiat. Hosp., 1981—; faculty Calif. State U., Los Angeles, U. So. Calif., U. Houston; media cons. stas. KNBC, KABC, KMET, KFWB; pvt. practice, Beverly Hills, Calif. Univ. affiliated program Children's Hosp. grantee, 1974; recipient NASA Achievement award 1971; Army Achievement award, 1975. Mem. IEEE, Am. Psychol. Assn. Numerous media presentations; Apollo Mission planning and activities documents; contbr. numerous articles to profl. jours.

MILLER, ALISA DOROTHY NORTON, artist; b. Wellsville, N.Y., Nov. 18, 1920; d. Oak Duke and Gladys Virginia (Dexter) Norton; student Rochester (N.Y.) Bus. Inst., 1938-41, Mt. Union Coll., Alliance, Ohio, 1960-61, West Valley Coll., Saratoga, Calif., 1977—, San Jose State U., 1981; m. Robert E. Miller, Oct. 12, 1974; children by previous marriage—Richard, Linda, Michael. Airline stewardess Colonial Airlines, N.Y.C., 1944-45; art supr. Eastman Kodak Co., Rochester, 1962-70; exec. sec. 3M Corp., Rochester, 1970-72; med. sec., asst., Los Gatos, Calif., 1972-76; portrait artist art Art Studio, Los Gatos, 1976—; one-man show: Norton Gallery, Rochester, 1972; group shows include: Glossinger Cultural Mus., Xenia, Ohio, 1964, Rosicrucian Mus., San Jose, Calif., 1981, Triton Mus., Santa Clara, Calif., 1982; represented in permanent collections: Glossinger Cultural Mus., also numerous pvt. collections. Mem. Soc. Western Artists, Nat. League Am. Pen Women. Unitarian. Home and Office: 22002 Old Santa Cruz Hwy Los Gatos CA 95030

MILLER, ARNOLD, engring. co. exec.; b. N.Y.C., May 8, 1928; s. Sam and Mina (Krutalow) M.: B.S. in Chemistry, UCLA, 1948, Ph.D. in Phys. Chemistry (Mosher fellow), 1951; m. Beverly Shayne, Feb. 5, 1950; children—Debra Lynn, Marla Jo, Linda Sue. Research phys. chemist Wrigley Research Co., Chgo., 1951; supr. phys. chemistry Armour Research Found., Chgo., 1951-54, mgr. chemistry and metallurgy dept., 1954-56; chief materials scis. dept. Borg-Warner Research Center, Des Plaines, Ill., 1956-59; dir. research Autonetics div. Rockwell Corp., Anaheim, Calif., 1959-66, dir. microelectronics ops., 1967-68; group exec. materials ops. Whittaker Corp., Los Angeles, 1968-70; pres. Theta Sensors, Inc., Orange, Calif., 1970-72; mgr. Xeroradiography div. Xerox Corp., Pasadena, Calif., 1972-75, corp. dir. research and advanced devel., Stamford, Conn., 1975-78, El Segundo, Calif., 1978-81, v.p. electronics div., 1981—; mem. civilian systems adv. group U.S. Dept. Commerce, 1959-60. lMem. vis. com. on materials sci. U. So. Calif., 1966-68. Recipient award of sci. merit Navy Bur. Ordinance and Armour Research Found., 1952, IR-100 award, 1964-69. Mem. Am. Chem. Soc., AIME, IEEE, Soc. Photog. and Instrumentation Engrs. and Scientists, Electronics Industries Assn. (past chmn. microelectronics), Phi Beta Kappa, Sigma Xi, Phi Lambda Upsilon. Mem. editorial adv. bd. Advances in Solid State Chemistry; contbr. numerous articles to profl. jours., also monographs; patentee in field. Home: 505 Westchester Pl Fullerton CA 92635 Office: Xerox Corp 701 S Aviation Blvd El Segundo CA 90245

MILLER, BARBARA STALLCUP, medical foundation administrator; b. Montague, Calif., Sept. 4, 1919; d. Joseph Nathaniel and Maybelle (Needham) Stallcup; m. Leland F. Miller, May 16, 1946; children—Paula Kay, Susan Lee, Daniel Joseph, Alison Jean. B.A., U. Oreg., 1942. Women's editor Eugene (Oreg.) Daily News, 1941-43; law clk. to J. Everett Barr, Yreka, Calif., 1943-45; mgr. Yreka C. of C., 1945-46; Northwest supr. Louis Harris and Assocs., Portland, Oreg., 1959-62; dir. pub. relations and fund raising Columbia River council Girl Scouts U.S.A., 1962-67; pvt. practice pub. relations cons., Portland, 1967-72; adviser of student publs., asst. prof. communications U. Portland, 1967-72, dir. pub. relations and info., asst. prof. communications, 1972-78, dir. devel., 1978-79, exec. dir. devel., 1979-83; assoc. dir. St. Vincent Med. Found., 1983—. Pres. bd. dirs. Vols. of Am. of Oreg., Inc., 1980—, pres. regional adv. bd., 1982—; pres. bd. dirs. Oreg. Black History Project; chmn. bicentennial youth essay contest, 1976. Recipient Presdl. Citation, Oreg. Communicators Assn., 1973, Matrix award, 1976, 80, Miltner award U. Portland, 1977. Mem. Council Advancement and Support Higher Edn. (editor regional newsletter 1975), Women in Communications (NW regional v.p. 1973-75), Nat. Fedn. Press Women, Oreg. Press Women (dist. dir.), Pub. Relations Soc. Am. (dir. local chpt.), Oreg. Fedn. Womens Clubs (communications chmn. 1978-80), Alpha Xi Delta. Unitarian. Clubs: Portland Zenith (pres. 1975-76, 81-82). Contbr. articles to profl. jours. Home: 5930 SW Meadows Rd Lake Oswego OR 97034 Office: 9205 SW Barnes Rd Portland OR 97225

MILLER, BETSY SOTZIN, hospital official, management consultant; b. Washington, Nov. 10, 1925; d. Heber A. and Ann Henretta S.; m. Jack Edward Miller, 1949; 1 son, John Allen. B.A., Stanford U., 1947. Buyer, Roos Bros., Inc., 1947-51; profl. vol., 1951-69; dir. vol. services USPHS Hosp., San Francisco, 1969-81, St. Mary's Hosp., San Francisco, 1981—. Bd. dirs. Vol. Ctr., San Francisco, 1978—, pres., 1980-82; bd. dirs. Easter Seal Soc. San Francisco, 1978-81. Mem. No. Calif. Assn. Dirs. Vol. Service (pres. 1976-77), Assn. Vol. Adminstrn., Am. Soc. Dirs. Vol. Service (dir. 1979-82, pres. 1983), Chi Omega, Stanford U. Alumni Assn. Club: Stanford Women's (San Francisco). Home: 261 Santa Paula Ave San Francisco CA 94127 Office: Saint Marys Hosp 450 Stanyan St San Francisco CA 94117

MILLER, C. HOWARD, architect, planner; b. Columbus, Ohio, Dec. 16, 1920; s. Charles Howard and Inez Ruth (Perry) M.; children—Stephen H., Martha S. (dec.). B. Arch., Ohio State U., 1943; M. Arch., MIT, 1947. Pvt. practice architecture, Denver and Arvada, Colo., 1949-53; asst. prof. U. Denver Sch. Architecture, 1947-51, acting dir., 1950-51; project architect, planner Daniel, Mann, Johnson & Mendenhall, Los Angeles, 1953-55; jr. ptnr. Richard J. Neutra and Robert E. Alexander, Los Angeles, 1955-60; pvt. practice architecture, San Francisco, 1961-68; planner HKS Inc., 1968-69; pres., treas. C. Howard Miller Assocs. Inc., Phoenix, 1970-80, M-Bar-M Corp., Reno and Carson City, Nev., 1972—; mem. Ecore Cons. Registry, Inc., Palo Alto, Calif., 1983—; sec.-treas. Policy Adv. Council, Washington, 1978—; mem. Washington Building Congress, 1980. Served with USNR, 1944-46. Mem. Am. Soc. Cons. Planners (dir.), Am. Planning Assn., AIA (nat. com. regional and urban planning 1974—), Am. Inst. Cert. Planners. Methodist. Home: PO Box 1693 Carson City NV 89702 Office: PO Box 881051 San Francisco CA 94188

MILLER, CAROLE ANN LYONS, editor, publisher; b. Newton, Mass., Aug. 1, 1943; d. Markham Harold and Ursula Patricia (Foley) Lyons; m. Francis John Tucker, Dec. 28, 1968; m. 2d, David Thomas Miller, July 4, 1978. Student Boston U., 1964; bus. cert., Hickox Sch., Boston, 1964; Cert. advt. and mktg. profl. UCLA, 1973; cert. retail mgmt. profl. Ind. U., 1976. Editor Triangle Topics, Pacific Telephone, Los Angeles; programmer Los Angeles Central Area Speakers' Bur., 1964-66; mng. editor/mktg. dir. Teen mag., Los Angeles, 1966-76; advt. dir. L.S. Ayres & Co., Indpls., 1976-78; v.p. mktg. The Denver, 1978-79; founder, editor, pub. Clockwise mag., Ventura, Calif., 1979—; owner Miller & Miller, Ventura; instr. retail advt. Ind. U., 1977-78. Recipient Pres.'s award Advt. Women of N.Y., 1974; Seklemian award 1977; Pub. Service Addy award, 1978. Mem. Advt. Women N.Y., Advt. Club Los Angeles, Ventura County Profl. Women's Network (founding), UCLA Alumni Assn. Editor: Sek Says, 1979. Home: 2554 Spinnaker Ave Port Hueneme CA 93041 Office: 1236 E Main St Ventura CA 93001

MILLER, CAROLYN JEAN, educator; b. Detroit, Sept. 23, 1939; d. John and Clara E. Miller; A.A. with honors, Pasadena (Calif.) City Coll., 1960; B.A. with high honors, U. Calif., 1962; M.A. in Edn. (Experienced Tchr. fellow), Stanford U., 1967. Tchr., Pasadena (Calif.) Unified Schs., 1962-73, discovery room tchr., 1974, lang. arts resource tchr., 1976-78, project coordinator Sch. Improvement Program, 1978-79, tchr. Saturday tutorial program, 1979-80, reading resource tchr., 1979-81, coordinator Hoffman Reading Center, 1980-81, adminstrv. mgmt. intern, 1981, project coordinator Title I and sch. improvement programs, 1981-82, curriculum resource tchr., 1982—. chmn. bd. dirs. Worthington Manor. Cert. tchr., Calif. Mem. Los Angeles Reading Assn. (dir. 1978-82), Assn. Supervision and Curriculum Devel., Calif. Reading Assn., Internat. Reading Assn., Angeles Crest Reading Assn. (charter, treas.), Calif. Math. Council. Stanford Alumni Assn., Phi Delta Kappa, Delta Kappa Gamma. Home: 1801 Fair Oaks St Apt G South Pasadena CA 91030 Office: care Pasadena Sch Dist 351 S Hudson St Pasadena CA 91109

MILLER, CAROLYN JEAN, educator; b. Okemah, Okla., June 17, 1938; d. Marvin Max and Pauline Frances (Smith) M. B.S. in Edn., Tex. Christian U., 1959; M.A. in Reading, fellowship grantee, So. Meth. U., 1967. Elem. tchr., Dallas, 1959-67, teacher specialist, summer 1967; reading specialist, spl. projects dir., reading coordinator, Title I evaluator, trainer in-service edn. Basset Unified Sch. Dist., La Puenta, Calif., 1967—, also math. coordinator. Named to Big Spring (Tex.) Hall of Fame in sports, 1979. Mem. NEA, Calif. Tchrs. Assn., Calif. Reading Specialists, Basset Teachers Assn., Assn. Supervision and Curriculum Devel., Internat. Reading Assn., Women in Ednl. Leadership, Calif. Realtors Assn., Zeta Tau Alpha. Republican. Roman Catholic. Developer diagnostic/prescriptive tests for use with reading texts. Home: 2702 S Peck Ave San Pedro CA 90731 Office: 904 N Willow Ave La Puente CA 91746

MILLER, CHARLES D., business executive; b. Hartford, Conn., 1928; grad. Johns Hopkins U.; married. Sales mgr. Yale & Towne Mfg. Co., 1955-59; asso. Booz, Allen & Hamilton, 1959-64; with Avery Internat. Corp., 1964—, group v.p., 1969-72, exec. v.p. ops., 1972-75, pres., 1975—, chief exec. officer, 1977—, also dir. Office: Avery Internat 150 N Orange Grove Blvd Pasadena CA 91103

MILLER, CHESTER WAYNE, cement and concrete technologist; b. Sullivan County, Ind., Sept. 10, 1924; s. Garrett Hobert and Geneva Blanche (Walters) M.; m. Rose Mary Sligar, Sept. 20, 1945; children—Reginald, Phyllis, James, David, Debra; m. 2d Ruth L. McCoy, June 14, 1969. B.S., Butler U., Ind., 1949; M.S., Purdue U., 1951; postgrad. in measurement and evaluation, U. Ariz., 1965. Supr. Kingan & Co., Indpls., 1951-52; lab. technician Ariz. Portland Cement Co., Phoenix, 1952-53, mix chemist, 1954-55, plant chemist, 1956-67, kiln foreman, 1965-66, combustion control, new product devel., tech. service engr., 1968-82, dir. tech. services, 1982—; concrete and concrete prodn. technician U. Colo., 1968; cons., lectr. in field. Flotilla comdr., USCG Aux., 1979-80; comdr. Rio Salado Power Squadron, 1982—. Served as pharmacist mate, USN, 1943-46. Decorated Purple Heart with 1 gold star. Mem. Am. Concret Inst. (Ariz. chpt.), Structural Engrs. Assn. Ariz., ASTM, Sigma Xi, Phi Eta Sigma. Republican. Contbr. articles to profl. jours. Home: 5325 N 61st Dr Glendale AZ 85301 Office: 2400 N Central Suite 308 Phoenix AZ 85004

MILLER, DENNIS WAYNE, financial planner, engineer; b. Inglewood, Calif., Jan. 19, 1947; s. C. R. and Bertha Irene (Higgins) M.; B.S., Calif. Poly. U., 1968. Field engr. Gen. Electric Co., overseas ops., 1968-70, El Monte, Calif., 1971-76, Western U.S. tng. coordinator, 1976-78; nat. sales mgr. Ceromet Industry Calif., 1978-80; owner, cons. Enterprise Programs, Huntington Beach, Calif., 1980—. Served with AUS, 1970-71. Mem. Am. Soc. Tng. and Devel., Internat. Assn. Fin. Planners. Republican. Address: 4161 Pierson Dr Huntington Beach CA 92649

MILLER, DONALD ARNOLD, airlines administrator; b. Onamia, Minn., Dec. 19, 1924; s. Arnold Leopold and Iola Grace (Morphew) M.; student U. Chgo., 1942; m. Barbara Louise Frisk, Mar. 9, 1968; children—Randal Lee, Garner Frisk. With Northwest Orient Airlines, 1946—, pilot instr., 1978—, supervisory check airman, 1977—. Pres. Lake Sammamish Community Club, Bellevue, Wash. Served with U.S. Navy, 1942-45. Mem. Northwest Capts. Club, Inc. (pres. 1975-76, 80—). Republican. Clubs: Washington Athletic, Issaquah Tennis. Home: 17450 SE 40th St Bellevue WA 98008 Office: Sea/Tac Airport Seattle WA 98168

MILLER, DONALD BRITTON, management consultant; b. Rochester, N.Y., Apr. 10, 1923; s. Alvin Austin and Avis (Britton) M.; B.S. in Mech. Engring., U. Rochester, 1944; M.B.A. in Mgmt., Columbia U., 1948; m. Alice Ruth Mellgard, Aug. 26, 1950 (dec. 1981); children—James Austin, Christopher Donald; m. 2d, Frances Martin Clark, Nov. 21, 1982. Telephone instrument engr. Stromberg Carlson Co., 1943-45; asst. to dean Columbia U. Sch. Engring., 1947-52; with IBM Corp., 1952-78, program mgr. human resources, 1975-78; owner Donald Britton Miller, cons., Santa Clara, Calif., 1978—; instr. Santa Clara U. Sch. Engring., 1978; prof. John F. Kennedy U., Orinda, Calif., 1978—. Fellow Soc. Advancement Mgmt. (past pres., Human Relations award 1983); mem. Am. Soc. Engring. Edn. (Disting. Service award 1978), ASME, IEEE, Acad. Mgmt., Am. Soc. Tng. and Devel., Orgn. Devel. Network. Club: Rotary (Saratoga). Author: Personal Vitality, 1977, Personal Vitality Workbook, 1977, Twice Turned Tales, 1977, Careers, 1980-81, Working With People, 1979; also articles. Home: 14600 Wild Oak Way Saratoga CA 95070 Office: 3600 Pruneridge Ave Suite 185 Santa Clara CA 95051

MILLER, DONALD C., service co. exec.; b. Fullerton, Calif., Aug. 9, 1946; s. Clifford and Tina Teresa (Mazza) M.; B.S., Calif. State Poly U., 1969; m. Jean Ann West, Dec. 26, 1967; children—Neisha Lynn, Matthew Scott. Dietetic intern Letterman Gen. Hsp., San Francisco, 1969-70; mgr. dietary services Cabrillo Med. Ctr., San Diego, 1977-80; pres. DCM Inc. food service mgmt., Chula Vista, Calif., 1980—; dir. dietary dept. Scripps Clinic and Research Found., La Jolla, Calif., 1981—. Mem. Indian Guides YMCA, 1979-81. Served to capt. USAF, 1969-77. Decorated Meritorious Service medal. Mem. Am. Dietetic Assn., Calif. Dietetic Assn., Gamma Sigma Delta. Democrat. Roman Catholic. Address: 136 Rainier Ct Chula Vista CA 92011

MILLER, ELVA RUBY CONNES (MRS. JOHN R. MILLER), civic worker; b. Joplin, Mo.; d. Edward and Ada (Martin) Connes; student Pomona Coll., part-time, 1936-56; m. John R. Miller, Jan. 17, 1934 (dec. Nov. 1968). Entertainer various night clubs, supper clubs, also Hollywood Bowl, 1967; tv appearances; rec. artist Capitol Records, 1966—, Amaret Records, 1969—; appeared in motion pictures. Active Girl Scouts U.S.A., 1933-58; hon. mem. Mayor's Com. for Sr. Citizens, Los Angeles, 1966; sustaining mem. Republican Nat. Com.; mem. Rep. Presdl. Task Force. Recipient awards including Thanks badge Girl Scouts U.S.A., 1956, Key to City, Mayor San Diego, 1967, plaque Dept. of Def. for trip to Viet Nam, 1967. Mem. Performing Arts Council, Music Center of Los Angeles County, Gen. Alumni Assn. U. So. Calif. (life). Club: Northridge Rep. Women's. Home: 9585 Reseda Blvd Northridge CA 91324

MILLER, EMERSON WALDO, government accountant; b. Green Island, Jamaica, W.I., Jan. 27, 1920; s. Adolphus Eustace and Catherine Sarah (Dixon) M.; m. Olive Claire Ford, Apr. 10, 1945; children—Cheryll, Hellena, Emerson, Oliver, Donald, Selwyn. Student U. Toronto (Ont., Can.), 1938-41, U. Calif.-Berkeley, 1950-61. Came to U.S., 1950, naturalized, 1957. Cost accountant Poierier & McLane Corp., N.Y.C., 1941-42; prin. Emerson Miller & Co., Kingston, Jamaica, 1942-49; lectr. accounting and bus. law Jamaica Sch. Commerce, Kingston, 1945-48; tax examiner, conferee Internat Revenue Service, San Francisco, 1963-64; chief financial and accounting aspects transp. and communications services programs Gen. Services Adminstrn., San Francisco, 1965-70, chief maj. segment financial mgmt. activities, 1970—; instr. govt. accounting, 1966-69. Fed. Govt. Accountants Assn. rep. mgmt. improvement com. Fed. Exec. Bd., San Francisco, 1973-74. Chmn. credit com. VARO Fed. Credit Union, San Francisco, 1969-81, treas., dir., 1981—. Recipient Disting. Service award Toastmasters Internat., 1968, Commendable Service award Gen. Services Adminstrn., 1968, Spl. Achievement award, 1969; Faithful Service award VARO-SF Fed. Credit Union, 1974. Mem. Am. Accounting Assn., Nat. Assn. Accountants, Fed. Govt. Accountants Assn. (chpt. pres.), Am. Mgmt. Assn., Financial Mgmt. Assn., Brit. Inst. Mgmt., Am. Judicature Soc., Royal Econ. Soc. (Cambridge), U. Calif. Alumni Assn., Internat. Platform Assn., Acad. Polit. and Social Sci. Clubs: Toastmasters Internat. (ednl. v.p.), (San Francisco), No. Calif. Cricket (San Anselmo); Brit. Social and Athletic (Los Angeles). Home: PO Box 471 Berkeley CA 94701 Office: 525 Market St San Francisco CA 94105

MILLER, EVANGELIN M. SCHNEIDER, lawyer, small business specialist; b. Madison, Wis., Feb. 5, 1930; d. George Jacob Henry and Amelia Christina (Winger) Schneider; student Calif. State U.-Sacramento, 1967; J.D., U. Pacific, 1970; m. W. Kenneth Miller, Sept. 3, 1950; children—Kim Miller, Walter Kenneth. Tchr., prin. Flournoy Elem. Sch., Tehama County, Calif., 1948-50; mgr. Chico Creamery (Calif.), 1950-54; statistician Pepsi Cola Belfast, San Francisco, 1954-55; office mgr., acct. Berlin Food Equipment Mfg. Co., 1955-58; admitted to Calif. bar, 1971; founder, pres. Schneider Lift Translator Co., Sacramento, 1975-82; prin. Sierra PowrQuip Assocs.; pres., dir. Angel Leasing Co. Mem. Small Po Producers of Calif., Calif. Women Lawyers, Calif. Bar Assn., Soc. Calif. Accts., Sacramento Women Lawyers (sec. 1973-74, pres. 1974-75). Republican. Clubs: San Francisco Press, Comstock, Eastern Star. Office: 3961 American River Dr Sacramento CA 95825

MILLER, FRANK R., broadcasting exec.; b. Milledgeville, Ill., July 31, 1933; s. George and Dorothy (Bower) M.; B.A., U. Iowa, 1956; m.

Eugenia Flebig, Aug. 17, 1958; children—Karen Kay, Matthew F., Andrew G. In prodn. Sta. WMT-TV, Cedar Rapids, Iowa, 1958-66; dir. broadcast ops. Sta. WAVE-TV, Louisville, 1966-72; mgr. Sta. WTVJ, Miami, Fla., 1972-77; v.p., gen. mgr., exec. producer Group W Prodns., Inc./Mike Douglas Show, Phila., 1977-80, John Davidson Show, Hollywood, 1980-81, v.p. mktg., 1981—. Chmn. bd. Community Mental Health Services Found., Miami, 1976-77; former dir. United Way, YMCA, Mental Health Assn. Served with Intelligence, U.S. Army, 1956-58; Far East. Mem. Nat. Acad. TV Arts and Scis., Nat. Assn. TV Program Execs. Clubs: Aronimink, Jockey, Maxwell Football. Office: Group W Prodns Inc 70 Universal City Plaza University City CA 91608

MILLER, FRANKLIN EMRICK, software engineer; b. Greenville, Ohio, Aug. 12, 1946; s. Rollin Linde and E. Evelyn (Emrick) M.; m. Sandra Lewis, Dec. 20, 1969; children—William Rollin, Rose Mary. B.S., Otterbein Coll., 1969; M.Ed. in Ednl. Psychology and Counseling, Wayne State U., 1975; postgrad. U. Denver. Lic. pvt. pilot FAA. Commd. U.S. Air Force, 1969, advanced through grades to capt.; space surveillance officer, Maine, 1970-71, Thule, Greenland, 1971-72; chief instr./systems analyst, Correlation Ctr., McGuire AFB, N.J., 1972-73; site space surveillance officer, Aviano, Italy, 1973-75; chief support programming unit, Colo., 1975-79; chief applications support programming, South Australia, 1979-81; ret., 1981; software engr. Aerojet Electro Systems Corp., Aurora, Colo., 1981—. Bd. dirs., Aurora Community Mental Health Ctr., 1976-79; vol. counselor Comitis Crisis Ctr., YMCA, Aurora, 1976-78. Mem. Am. Psychol. Assn., Phi Delta Kappa. Republican. Author: The Preliminary Online Rorschach Test Manual, 1980; contbr. article to profl. jour. Home: PO Box 31882 Aurora CO 80041

MILLER, FRANKLIN JAY, electronics manufacturing company executive; b. Rockford, Ill., May 20, 1943; s. Charles H. and Thelma (Rubin) M.; A.S. in Elec. Engring., Los Angeles City Coll., 1963; student Calif. State Coll., Los Angeles, 1963-66; m. Brenda Khirlla, July 10, 1976. Audio-visual technician Am. Electronic Supply, Los Angeles, 1958-64; asst. chief engr. Muzak, Inc., Los Angeles, 1965-67; sales Newark Electronic Supply, Inglewood, Calif., 1968-69; pres. Sescom, Inc., Las Vegas, 1969—. Mem. Audio Engring. Soc., Soc. Mfg. Engrs., IEEE. Office: 1111 Las Vegas Blvd N Las Vegas NV 89101

MILLER, GEORGE, congressman. Mem. 94th-98th Congresses from 7th Calif. Dist., chmn. subcom. on labor standards, select com. children, youth and families. Office: Room 2422 Rayburn House Office Bldg Washington DC 20515

MILLER, H(AYDEN) RAY, art center and museum director, educational administrator; b. Butler, Mo., Mar. 28, 1920; s. John C. and Martha Marie (Ray) M.; m. Maxine Smith, July 6, 1941; children—Connie Marlene, Mark Hayden, Scott Smith. M.A. in Art Adminstrn., Los Angeles State Coll., 1952; postgrad. U. So. Calif., 1951-52, Claremont Coll., 1962-63. Tchr. art and music, profl. musician, art tchr. Mountain View Sch. Dist., El Monte, Calif., art supr. Whittier (Calif.) City Schs., 1943-55; dir. fine arts Riverside (Calif.) City Schs., 1955-81; part time or extended day tchr., tchr. extension courses Whittier Coll., U. Calif., Riverside, Calif. State U., San Bernardino, Chapman Coll., Riverside City Coll., 1970—; dir. Riverside Art Center and Mus., 1981—; designer. Active Riverside Arts Council, Riverside Art Center, Downtown Businessmen Assn., Downtown Cultural Group, Mens Breakfast Forum. Served with M.C., U.S. Army, 1941-43. Office: 3425 Seventh St Riverside CA 92501

MILLER, H(ENRY) LAURENCE, JR., economics educator; b. Kansas City Mo., Nov. 6, 1925; s. Henry Laurence and Helen (Hurst) M.; m. Sarah Louse Marks, Aug. 20, 1947 (div. 1968); children—Henry, Catherine, Anne; m. 2d, Nancy Skeels Kupersmith, Feb. 21, 1970 (div. 1972); m. 3d, Lelanda Sue Lee, July 31, 1976 (div. 1980). A.B., U. Kans., 1947, M.A., 1948; B.A., Oxford (Eng.) U., 1950, Ph.D., Harvard U., 1956. Teaching fellow Harvard U. 1951-53; asst. prof. Smith Coll. 1953-57; from asst. prof. to assoc. prof. econs. UCLA 1957-65; Wadsworth A. Williams prof. econs. Carleton Coll. 1965-69; prof. U. Hawaii 1969—. Served with USAAF 1944-45. Rhodes scholar 1948-50; research fellow Nat. Bur. Econs. Research 1969-70. Mem. Am. Econ. Assn., Phi Beta Kappa. Contbr. articles to profl. jours.

MILLER, JAMES GRIER, psychiatrist, researcher, educator; b. Pitts., July 17, 1916; s. Earl Dalton and Mary Rebecca (Grier) M.; m. Jessie Louise Luthi, Sept. 3, 1938; children—John, Thomas. Student Columbia (S.C.) Bible Coll., U. S.C., 1933-34, U. Mich., 1934-35; A.B. summa cum laude, Harvard U., 1937, A.M., 1938, M.D. cum laude, 1942, Ph.D., 1943. Diplomate Am. Bd. Psychiatry and Neurology. Asst., tutor psychology Harvard U., 1937-38, mem. Soc. Fellows, 1938-44, intern Mass. Gen. Hosp., Boston, 1942-43; asst. resident, resident in psychiatry, 1943-44; Lowell lectr., Boston, 1944; asst. prof. clin. psychology Harvard U., Cambridge, Mass., 1946-47; chief clin. psychology sect. VA, 1946-47; prof., chmn. dept. psychology U. Chgo., 1948-55, prof. psychiatry, 1948-51; clin. instr. psychiatry U. Ill. Med. Sch., Chgo., 1952-55; lectr. Northwestern U. Med. Sch., Chgo., 1953-55; prof., dir. Mental Health Research U. Mich., Ann Arbor, 1955-67; co-founder EDUCOM (Interuniv. Communications Council), 1964, exec. dir., sec., 1964-66, v.p., prin. scientist, 1966-70, trustee, 1970-81, chmn bd., 1976, trustee emeritus, 1981—; v.p. Acad. Ednl. Devel., Washington, 1971-73; lectr. John Hopkins U., 1971-75; fellow Internat. Inst. Applied Systems Analysis, Laxenburg, Austria, summers 1973, 74; pres., prof. U. Louisville, 1973-80, pres. emeritus, 1980—; co-chmn. bd. Robert Maynard Hutchins Ctr. for Study of Dem. Instns., Santa Barbara, Calif., 1979-80, chief exec. officer, 1980, pres., 1981-82; vis. prof. psychiatry UCLA, 1981—; adj. prof. psychology U. Calif.-Santa Barbara, 1981—; chmn. bd. U. of the World, 1982—. Served to capt., M.C., U.S. Army; with OSS in U.S., ETO. Fellow Am. Psychol. Assn., Am. Psychiat. Assn., Am. Coll. Neuropsychopharmacology (charter), Am. Coll. Psychiatrists, AAAS; mem. Am. Soc. Cybernetics (charter), Soc. Gen. Systems Research (pres. 1973-74), Phi Beta Kappa, Sigma Xi. Episcopalian. Clubs: Century, Cosmos, Metropolitan (Washington); Harvard (N.Y.C.). Author: Unconsciousness, 1942; Living Systems, 1978; co-author: Assessment of Men, 1948; editor Behavioral Sci., 1956—; dept. editor in psychology Ency. Brit., 1952-58; co-editor: Drugs and Behavior, 1960; contbr. articles to sci., profl. books, jours., revs. Home: 3337 Campanil Dr Santa Barbara CA 93109

MILLER, JANE NELSON, neuropsychologist; b. Cleve., Sept. 23, 1926; d. George N. and Signe E. (Larson) Nelson; m. Robert E. Miller, Sept. 17, 1949 (div.); children—Jeffrey, Mark, Karen, Kristina. B.A., Ohio Wesleyan U., 1948; M.A., Ohio State U., 1949, Ph.D., 1972; M.S., Miami U., Oxford, Ohio, 1966. Lic. for pvt. practice, Ind.; Lic. psychologist, Calif. Dir. Bureau Testing and Guidance, Earlham Coll., 1949-52; dir. Home-Sch. Counseling Service, Richmond, Ind., 1966-70; dir. pupil personnel and spl. edn., schs. of Mishawaka, Ind., 1972-78; with Mesa Vista Mental Hosp., 1978-81; pvt. practice neuropsychology. EDPA fellow Ohio State U., 1970-72. Mem. Am. Psychol. Assn., Calif. Psychol. Assn., San Diego Acad. Psychologists, Nat. Register Health Service Providers in Psychology. Republican. Contbr. articles to profl. jours. Office: 2550 5th Ave Suite 605 San Diego CA 92103

MILLER, JEAN RUTH, librarian; b. St. Helena, Calif., Aug. 4, 1927; d. William Leonard and Jean (Stanton) M.; B.A., Occidental Coll., 1950; M.S. in L.S., U. So. Calif., 1952. Base librarian U.S. Air Force, Wethersfield, Edn., 1952-55; post librarian U.S. Marine Corps Air Sta., El Toro, Calif., 1955-63; data systems librarian Autonetics (name changed to Rockwell Internat.), Anaheim, Calif., 1963-65; chief librarian Beckman Instruments, Inc., Fullerton, Calif., 1966—; chmn. Fullerton area scholarship alumni interview program U. So. Calif., 1974—; mem. adv. commn. library technician program Fullerton Coll., 1969—. Recipient Superior Performance awards U.S. Marine Corps Air Sta., El Toro, 1957, 61. Mem. So. Calif. Assn. Law Librarians, Am. Soc. Info. Sci., Orange County (past pres.) library assns., IEEE, Spl. Libraries Assn. (pres. So. Calif. chpt. 1975-76). Republican. Author: Bibliography on Electrical Shock Hazards, 1974. Bibliography on Field Air Traffic Control, 1965. Home: 17901 E Chapman Ave Orange CA 92669

MILLER, JEFFREY L., lawyer; b. Santa Monica, Calif., May 15, 1950; s. LaVerle E. and Carmen C. (Chase) M. B.S. in Anthropology, U. Calif.-Davis, 1973; J.D., San Fernando Valley Coll. Law, 1978; LL.M. in Taxation, U. San Diego, 1983. Assoc., Sanford M. Gage, Beverly Hills, Calif., 1977-79, Myer E. Sankary Century City, Calif., 1979-80; ptnr. Miller & Riave, San Fernando, Calif., 1980-81; sole practice, San Fernando, 1982—; mem. vol. probate panel Los Angeles Superior Ct., 1981—. Mem. Calif. State Bar, Los Angeles County Bar Assn., San Fernando Valley Bar Assn., Assn. Trial Lawyers Am., Los Angeles Trial Lawyers Assn. Republican. Mem. editorial staff Rev. of San Fernando Coll. Law 1975-78; contbr. Latina Mag., 1983. Office: 563 S Brand Blvd San Fernando CA 91340

MILLER, JOHN ALBERT, university administrator, marketing educator; b. St. Louis County, Mo., Mar. 22, 1939; s. John Adam and Emma D. (Doering) M.; m. Eunice Ann Timm, Aug. 25, 1968; children—Michael, Kristin. A.A., St. Paul's Coll., 1958; B.A. with honors, Concordia Sr. Coll., 1960; postgrad. Wash. U.-St. Louis, 1960-64; M.B.A., Ind. U., 1971, D.B.A. in Mktg., 1972. Proofreader, editor Concordia Publ. House, St. Louis, 1960-62, periodical sales mgr., 1964-68; asst. prof. Drake U., 1972-74; cons. FTC, 1974-75; vis. assoc. prof. Ind. U., 1975-77; assoc. prof. U. Colo., 1977-79, prof. mktg., resident dean, 1980—; cons. and researcher govt. and industry; dir. health maintenance orgn. Active, Colorado Springs Symphony Orch. Council. Served with U.S. Army, 1962-64. U.S. Steel fellow 1970-71. Mem. Assn. Consumer Research, Am. Mktg. Assn., Am. Acad. Advt., Pikes Peak chpt. Am. Advt. Fedn. Lutheran. Club: Izaak Walton League. Author several monographs; contbr. articles to profl. jours. Home: 2905 La Estrella Ct Colorado Springs CO 80917 Office: U Colo Colorado Springs CO 80907

MILLER, JOHN CAMPBELL, lawyer; b. Las Vegas Nev., Mar. 8, 1938; s. John Randall and Elizabeth Margaret (Campbell) M.; B.S. in Math., U. Nev., 1961; M.S. in Math., U. Nev., 1963; J.D. in Law, U. Mont., 1972; m. Peggy Louise Eriksen, May 29, 1962; children—Kristin Alyce, Meghan Elizabeth. Dir. computing center, asso. prof. Mont. State U., Bozeman, 1963-69; clk. Nev. Supreme Ct., Carson City, 1972-73; partner firm Vaughan, Hull, Marfisi & Miller, Elko, Nev., 1973-77. Hoy & Miller, Reno and Elko, 1977—. IBM-Western Data Processing Center fellow, 1962-63. Mem. Soc. Mining Engrs., Mont. Data Processing Assn. (pres. 1968-69), Rocky Mountain Mineral Laws Found., Nev. Mining Assn. Home: 358 W Fir St Elko NV 89801 Office: Suite 201 Blohm Bldg Elko NV 89801

MILLER, JOHN DAVID, lawyer; b. Long Beach, Calif., Dec. 2, 1927; s. Fred and Erie M. (McLaren) M.; A.B. with distinction, Leland Stanford Jr. U., 1950, J.D., 1953; m. Barbara Lee Decker, Dec. 27, 1952 (dec. May 1972); children—Thomas Lee, Jennifer Lynne; m. 2d, Kathleen Houts, Jan. 19, 1974 (div. 1982); children—Karen Luann, Timothy John; m. 3d, Sharon Keerfoot, 1982. Admitted to Calif. bar, 1953; practiced in Long Beach, 1953—; partner Miller & Bronn (and predecessor firms), Long Beach, 1970-81, John D. Miller Profl. Corp., 1981—. Mem. Calif. Law Revision Commn., 1969-78, vice chmn., 1970-71, chmn., 1972-73. Trustee, St. Mary's Long Beach Hosp.; bd. dirs. Long Beach Boys' Clubs Found., Greater Long Beach chpt. ARC, 1978—. Served with AUS, 1946-47. Mem. Am., Long Beach (bd. govs. 1967-68, 79—), Los Angeles bar assns., The State Bar of Cal., Phi Delta Theta, Phi Delta Phi, Phi Delta Epsilon. Elk. Club: Long Beach International City (bd. dirs. 1971-72). Office: 1900 E Ocean Blvd Long Beach CA 90802

MILLER, JOHN HARRIS, mayor, resort owner; b. Lubbock, Tex., Aug. 5, 1934; s. Francis Elmer and Edith Alma (Harris) M.; m. Judy Dorrance, Feb. 3, 1957; children—John Harris, Jr., Mary Frances, Ellen Kathleen, Linda Anne. B.A. in Geology, U. Colo., 1957. With Geophys. Exploration Co., Houston, 1959; sr. clk. reservoir engring. dept. Nat. Gas Pipeline Co. Am., Amarillo, Tex., 1959-63; asst. mgr. Red River (N. Mex.) ski area, 1963-65; sr. planning engr. Molycorp., Questa, N.Mex., 1965-71; co-owner, operator Powder Puff Mountain, Red River, 1971-79 co-owner, operator Miller's Art Gallery, Miller's Crossing; charter councilman, Red River, 1971-76, mayor pro tem, 1977-78, mayor, 1978—. Mem. vestry St. James Episc. Ch., Taos, N.Mex., 1977-78; v.p. Questa Ind. Sch. Bd., 1976-77. Served to lt. (j.g.) USN, 1957-59. Mem. Red River C. of C. (past pres.), N. Mex. Geol. Soc. Republican. Clubs: Red River Jaycees (past pres.), Kiwanis (past pres.). Home: PO Box 122 Red River NM 87558 Office: Lifts West Mall Main St Red River NM 87558

MILLER, JON HAMILTON, forest products executive; b. Des Moines, Jan. 22, 1938; s. Victor George and Virginia Adelaine (Hamilton) M.; A.B. in Econs., Stanford U., 1959, M.B.A. in Mktg. and Fin., 1961; m. Sydney Gail Fernald, June 4, 1966; children—Emily, Sara. With Boise Cascade Corp. (Idaho), 1961—, exec. v.p. paper and paper products, 1974-76, exec. v.p. timber, wood products and bldg. materials, 1976-78, pres., chief operating officer, dir., 1978—; dir. First Corp. Bd. dirs. St. Luke's Hosp., Boise; mem. Boise State U. Bronco Athletic Assn. Served with U.S. Army, 1959-60. Mem. Greater Boise C. of C. (pres. 1977). Methodist. Clubs: Arid (Boise); Multnomah Athletic (Portland, Oreg.). Office: Boise Cascade Corp 1 Jefferson Sq Boise ID 83728*

MILLER, KENNETH JOHN, engineering company executive, consultant; b. Casper, Wyo., July 19, 1929; s. Jack W. and Evelyn W. (May) M.; m. Betty L. Noel, July 15, 1950; children—Michael S., Douglas E., Linda A., Steven J. B.A. in Chemistry, U. Colo., 1953. Research chemist Goodyear Tire and Rubber Co., 1953-54; lab. dir. health dept. City of Denver, 1954-62, dir. planning and water resources, water dept., 1962-79; dir. water engring. CH2M Cons. Engrs., Denver, 1979—, v.p., 1983—; dir. Water for Colo. Recipient Internat. Ambassador award People-to-People, 1977; Cert. of Appreciation, EPA, 1979. Mem. Am. Water Works Assn. (Rocky Mountain sect. past chmn. award 1974, Fuller award, past pres. award 1982), Water Pollution Control Assn., Am. Cons. Engrs. Council. Republican. Clubs: Pinehurst Country (Denver), Masons. Contbr. numerous articles to profl. jours.

MILLER, LINDA LOUISE, annuity company executive; b. Bay City, Mich., Aug. 14, 1945; d. Victor Hugo and Dolores Juanita (Martin) Floyt; B.A. in Communication Arts, Mich. State U., 1967. Speech tchr. Southfield (Mich.) Bd. Edn., 1967-68; sales rep. Revlon, Inc., N.Y.C., 1971-76; sales rep. Security First Group, Inc., Los Angeles, 1976-77, regional sales dir., Marina Del Rey, Calif., 1977—. Recipient Glen A. Holden Mgr. of Yr. award Security First Group, 1980. Mem. Nat. Assn. Female Execs. Lutheran. Home: 16727 Bosque Dr Encino CA 91436 Office: 17215 Studebaker Rd Suite 180 Cerritos CA 90701

MILLER, MAGGI FISK, management consultant; b. Mpls., Dec. 13, 1947; d. Frank Wilbur and Eleanor (Mieike) Fisk; married. B.Mus. in Vocal Performance, Capital U., Columbus, Ohio, 1970; postgrad. Ohio State U., San Diego State U. Vocal music tchr. Licking Heights Sch. System, Summit Station, Ohio, 1970-71; sec. United Jewish Fund, Columbus, 1972; sec., then charge distbn. acctg. Arthur Treacher's Fish & Chips, Columbus, 1972-76; comptroller Cooper Bus. Machines Co., Columbus, 1975-77; owner Margo Ltd., acctg., Columbus, 1977—; owner, ptnr. Da.M.E., ecol. and human needs solutions, Columbus, 1977—, Hamilton-Fisk Guild, bus. promotion, Columbus, 1977-80; ptnr. Miller-White Assocs., tax accts., Columbus, 1979—; owner, coordinating dir. The Brain Bank, mgmt. cons., Columbus, 1977—; owner Mgmt. Systems, acctg., San Diego, 1980—. Mem. Am. Mensa, P.E.O. Presbyterian. Author: The Monarchy Series, vol. 1, 1978; co-author: The Suicide Book, 1979, The Million Calorie Book, 1978; editor: Absurb Patents, 1979. Office: PO Box 2655 Chula Vista CA 92012

MILLER, MARGARET (PEGGY) ANN, insurance agent; b. Warren, Ohio, Mar. 1, 1939; d. Arthur Morgan and Harriet Elizabeth (Burrows) Duff; m. Henry Franklin Miller, June 3, 1961 (div.); 1 son, Mark Russell. Student U. Ariz., 1957-59. Inland marine underwriter Home Ins. Co., Phoenix, 1959; underwriter Messimer Ins. Agy., Williams, Ariz., 1959-62; admitting clk. Williams Hosp., 1966-67; clms. clk. Blue Cross Blue Shield, Phoenix, 1967; personal lines underwriter Beal & Assocs. Ins. counselors, Phoenix, 1967-68, comml. lines underwriter, 1968-70, comml. ins. agt., 1970—. Mem. women's com. Fiesta Bowl, 1971-80; mem. exec. bd. Jr. Achievement, Phoenix, 1977-80. Mem. Nat. Fedn. Bus. and Profl. Women's Clubs, Alpha Chi Omega. Republican. Presbyterian. Office: 5635 E Thomas St Phoenix AZ 85018

MILLER, MARTHA ELIZABETH POUND, assn. exec.; b. Phoenix, May 16, 1931; d. John Milton and Lurline Okey (Pettijohn) Pound; student Phoenix Coll., 1949-50, Ariz. State U., 1950; m. Leigh Donald Miller, Aug. 30, 1952; children—Cory MacDonald, Donna Leigh, Keith Ruskin. Office mgr. Cartmell Miller Archtl. firm, Phoenix, 1971-73; exec. sec. Charles Luckman Assos., Phoenix, 1973-75; exec. sec. Streich, Lang, Weeks, Cardon & French, Phoenix, 1975-76; adminstrv. asst. to dir. Heard Mus., Phoenix, 1976-77; exec. dir. Central Ariz. chpt. AIA, Phoenix, 1977—. Bd. dirs. Phoenix Arts Council. Mem. Am. Soc. Assn. Execs., Ariz. Soc. Assn. Execs., Nat. Assn. Female Execs. Republican. Congregationalist. Club: Toastmasters Internat. (treas.). Office: 614 E Adams St Phoenix AZ 85004

MILLER, MARVIN MERLE, office automation consultant; b. Kirkwood, Ill., Aug. 30, 1928; s. Bert Harold and Rheba Mae (Haines) M.; m. Dorothy Elizabeth Sanatel, Aug. 14, 1953; children—Michael, Patrick, Mark, Matthew. Student Portland State Coll., 1953-61. Mgr. Crown Zellerbach, San Francisco, 1955-82; cons., info. specialist, San Francisco, 1983—. Served with U.S. Army, 1948-52. Home: 991 Stimel Dr Concord CA 94518 Office: 681 Market St Suite 565 San Francisco CA 94105

MILLER, MICHAEL LEWIS, clin. psychologist, educator; b. Milwaukee, Oct. 27, 1947; s. David Manfred and Beatrice (Cohen) M. B.A., U. Calif., Berkeley, 1969, Ph.D., 1976; lic. psychologist Wash.; cert. Nat. Register of Health Service Providers, 1979. Clin. supr., dir. inservice tng. Youth Eastside Services, psychotherapist Applied Psychol. Services, Seattle, 1977-78; clin. instr. dept. psychiatry and behavioral scis. U. Wash., Seattle, 1977-79, clin. asst. prof., 1980—; pvt. practice in clin. psychology, Seattle, 1978—; cons. Dept. Youth Services, King County, Wash.; mem. exec. bd. Mental Health North Community Mental Health Ctr. Mem. Am. Psychol. Assn., Wash. State Psychol. Assn. (exec. bd., pres. King county chpt., 1980), Assn. Advancement Psychology, Soc. Adolescent Medicine, Psychoanalytic Assn. Seattle, Phi Beta Kappa. Democrat. Jewish. Contbr. articles to profl. jours. Home: 7037 18th Ave NE Seattle WA 98115 Office: 9730 3rd Ave NE Seattle WA 98115

MILLER, NORMAN, psychology educator; b. N.Y.C., Nov. 29, 1933; s. Arthur and Pearl (Dondera) M.; m. Natalie F. Brigham, 1956 (div.); 1 dau.; Carrie Ellen. A.B., Antioch Coll., 1956; M.S., Northwestern U., 1957, Ph.D., 1959. Asst. prof. Yale U., 1959-65; assoc. prof. U. Calif., Riverside, 1965-66; assoc. prof. U. Minn., 1966-68, prof., 1968-70; prof. psychology, head social psychology program U. So. Calif., Los Angeles, 1970—, chmn. dept., 1973-74, Mendel B. Silberberg prof. psychology, 1974—, dir. Program for Research on Desegregation, Social Sci. Research Inst. NIMH fellow, 1968; Jame McKeen Cattell fellow, 1975. Author: (with C. Kiesler and B.E. Collins) Attitude Change, 1970; (with H.B. Gerard) School Desegregation, 1975, also articles. Home: 17031 Bollinger Dr Pacific Palisades CA 90272 Office: 126 Denny Research Bldg U So Calif Los Angeles CA 90089

MILLER, PAUL A., utility holding company executive; b. San Francisco, Oct. 30, 1924; s. Robert W.; A.B., Harvard U., 1946; children—Robert L., Charles B., Christian F., Gordon E., Alejandro C., Juan J. Staff aide So. Calif. Gas Co., Los Angeles, 1948-52; treas., dir. Pacific Lighting Corp., San Francisco, 1952-58, v.p., treas., 1958-66, exec. v.p., 1966-68, pres., chief exec. officer, 1968-72, chmn. bd., chief exec. officer, 1972—; dir. Wells Fargo & Co., Wells Fargo Bank N.A.; trustee Mut. Life Ins. Co. of N.Y. Vice pres. bd. dirs. Calif. Civic Light Opera Assn.; bd. dirs. Los Angeles World Affairs Council, United Way, Inc., Los Angeles, Music Center Opera Assn. Los Angeles, Calif. Roundtable; trustee Am. Enterprise Inst. Washington, U. So. Calif.; bd. govs. United Way Am., Los Angeles Civic Light Opera Assn.; active Bus. Roundtable. Served with U.S. Army, 1943-46. Mem. Am., Pacific Coast gas assns., Calif. C. of C. (dir.). Clubs: Calif., Los Angeles; Pacific Union, Bohemian (San Francisco); Brook, Racquet and Tennis (N.Y.C.). Office: Pacific Lighting Co 810 S Flower St Los Angeles CA 90017*

MILLER, PAUL JAMES, banker; b. Leesburg, Fla., Jan. 14, 1932; s. Paul Alexander and Verna A. (Crumpton) M.; B.A., U. Fla., 1958, M.A., 1959; Ph.D., U. Calif., Berkeley, 1961; m. Mary Lee Meeker Hunt, Aug. 23, 1952; children—Agnes Fennelle deForest, Ethan Allen Hunt. With J. Barth & Co., San Francisco, 1962-67; v.p., dir. Jovair Corp., El Segundo, Calif., 1967-68; sec./treas., v.p., dir. McCulloch Aircraft Corp., El Segundo, 1968-69; with Dean Witter & Co., San Francisco, 1970-73; v.p. Wells Fargo Investment Advisors, San Francisco, 1973-81; v.p., sr. mgr. Crocker Investment, San Francisco, 1981-82; v.p., dir. mktg. Crocker Investment Mgmt. Corp., 1982—; pres., chmn. bd. Indian Island Inc., Redding, Calif., 1977—; guest lectr. Winthrop Sch. Bus., Winthrop Coll., 1976, Fla. Bankers Assn., 1977. Founding pres. Fla. Young Republican League, 1952-56. Served with USAF, 1950-51. Mem. Security Analysts Soc. San Francisco, Fin. Analysts Fedn., Assn. Investment Mgmt. Sales Execs., Western Pension Conf., Am. Mgmt. Assn., Internat. Found. Employee Benefit Plans, 2d Amendment Found., Nat. Rifle Assn., Helicopter Assn. Am., Am. Motorcyclist Assn., Sigma Chi, Pi Sigma Alpha, Phi Delta Phi. Libertarian. Club: W. Whight Potters Assn. Office: 44 Montgomery St San Francisco CA 94104

MILLER, RALPH HENRY, business educator, consultant; b. Berkeley, Calif., Nov. 4, 1944; s. Russell Sparks and Ruth Elizabeth (Bailey) M., m. Linnea Ann Pregler, Jan. 27, 1968 (div.); m. 2d, Nancy Sabin Root, Sept. 29, 1979. B.A. in Psychology, U. Calif.-Berkeley, 1967; M.A., San Jose State U., 1969; Ph.D. (NDEA fellow 1970-73), Claremont Grad. Sch., 1979. Cert. personnel testing, Calif. Asst. dir. Ctr. Applied Social Research Claremont (Calif.) Grad. Sch., 1973-76; lectr.

ops. mgmt. dept. Sch. Bus., Calif. State Poly. U., Pomona, 1976-79; asst. prof. ops. mgmt. dept., 1979-83, assoc. prof., 1983—; v.p. Alice Inc., Los Angeles, 1978—. Bd. dirs. Willow Sch., Rancho Cucamonga, Calif., 1980-81. Named Outstanding Educator, Calif. State Poly. U., 1982. Mem. Common Cause, Am. Psychol. Assn., Western Psychol. Assn., AAAS, Am. Inst. Decision Scis. Home: 1725 Finecroft Dr Claremont CA 91711 Office: 3801 W Temple Ave Calif State Poly U Pomona CA 91768

MILLER, RAYMOND JARVIS, university dean; b. Claresholm, Alta., Can., Mar. 19, 1934; s. Charles Jarvis and Wilma Macy (Anderson) M.; m. Francis Anne Davidson, Apr. 28, 1956; children—Cheryl Rae, Jeffrey John, Jay Robert. B.S., U. Alta., 1957; M.S., Wash. State U., 1960; Ph.D., Purdue U., 1962; postgrad. Inst. Edn. Mgmt., Harvard U., 1977. Asst. prof. N.C. State U., 1962-65, assoc., prof., 1965; assoc. prof. U. Ill., 1965-69, prof., 1969; asst. dir. Ill. Agr. Expt. Sta., 1969, assoc. dir., 1971-73, dir., assoc. dean Idaho Agrl. Expt. Sta., 1973; acting dean Coll. Agr., U. Idaho, 1979, dean, 1980—. Fed. Provincial grantee, 1954-55; Dan Baker scholar, 1954-56; Internat. Congress Soil Sci. travel grantee, 1960-61; Purdue Research Found. summer grantee, 1960. Fellow Am. Soc. Agronomy, Soil Sci. Soc. Am.; mem. Internat. Soc. Soil Sci., Clay and Clay Minerals Soc., Am. Chem. Soc., Am. Soc. Plant Physiologists, AAS, Sigma Xi, Phi Kappa Phi, Gamma Sigma Delta, Alpha Zeta. Clubs: Lions, Elks. Contbr. articles to profl. jours. Home: 1213 Highland Dr Moscow ID 83843 Office: College of Agriculture University of Idaho Moscow ID 83843

MILLER, RAYMOND WOODRUFF, soil science educator, researcher, consultant; b. St. David, Ariz., Jan. 13, 1928; s. Loyd Lewis and Della (Judd) M.; m. Joyce Udell, June 21, 1951; children—Todd Raymond, Ann Miller Hansen, Ross Stewart, Kay, Mark Robert. Student U. Wash., 1950-51; B.S. in Chemistry, U. Ariz., 1952, M.S. in Soils and Agrl. Chemistry, 1953; Ph.D. in Soils-Agronomy, Wash. State U., 1956. Cert. profl. soil scientist. Asst. prof. soil sci. Utah State U., Logan, 1956-61, assoc. prof., 1961-67, prof., 1967—; acting dept. head, 1967; sabbatical leave Rutgers U., 1968-69; researcher in Venezuela, 1969-71; cons. in Columbia, Bolivia, Senegal, Honduras, Guinea-Bissau. Regional commr. Am. Youth Soccer Orgn., 1980-81; commr. Cache Valley Soccer League, 1983. Served with U.S. Army, 1946-48. Mem. Western Soc. Soil Sci. (sec. 1965-67, pres. elect 1968, pres. 1969), Am. Soc. Soil Sci., Am. Soc. Agronomy, Soil Conservation Soc. Am. Mormon. Co-author: Soils: an Introduction to Soils and Plant Growth, 1977, 2d edit., 1983; Soils, Waters and Environment, 1980; contbr. numerous articles to profl. jours. Home: 487 E 600 S Logan UT 84321 Office: Dept Soil Sci Utah State U Logan UT 84322

MILLER, RICHARD ALAN, forest products company executive; b. Cleve., July 29, 1939; s. Joshua Spencer and Martha (Harris) M.; m. Virginia Bell McCully, June 23, 1972; children—Cynthia, Alexander. B.B.A., U. Mich., 1961, J.D. with distinction, 1964. Bar: Ariz. 1964. Assoc., Fennemore, Craig, von Ammon, Udall & Powers, Phoenix, 1964-69, ptnr., 1970-72; v.p., corp. counsel Southwest Forest Industries, Inc., Phoenix, 1972-73, v.p., corp. counsel, sec., 1974-77, v.p. gen. counsel, sec., 1977-78, sr. v.p., corp. and legal Affairs, 1979-80, exec. v.p., 1980—; dir. Apache Ry., Atlanta & St. Andrews Bay Ry.; chmn. bd. Southwest Kenworth, Inc. Bd. dirs. Boys Clubs Met. Phoenix. Mem. ABA, Ariz. Bar Assn. Club: Paradise Valley (Ariz.) Country.

MILLER, RICHARD AUSTIN, state official; b. Albany, Oreg., Feb. 1, 1923; s. Algra Pete and Lela Marceil (Buckler) M.; B.S. in Edn., Oreg. State U., 1948, M.Ed., 1959; grad. various mil. schs.; m. Mary Ann Woods, Aug. 22, 1976; children by previous marriage—David, Anne Marie, Cathy Miller Hosmer, Janie. Tchr.-coach Grants Pass (Oreg.) High Sch., 1948-49, St. Helen's (Oreg.) High Sch., 1949-53, Hillsboro (Oreg.) High Sch., 1953-54; successively tchr.-coach, dir. athletics, vice prin., prin. David Douglas High Sch., Portland, Oreg., 1954-73; adj. gen. Mil. Dept. State of Oreg., 1973—. Bd. dirs. Willamette chpt. ARC, United Way, Marion-Polk Counties, Urban League of Portland; trustee Oreg. State U. Found.; regional v.p. Army War Coll. Found.; bd. dirs. Oreg. State U. Varsity O Club, The Inn, Home for Boys; mem. Oreg. Gov.'s Telecommunications Policy Com.; chmn. State of Oreg. Employee's Cancer Crusade. Served with AUS, 1943-46; joined Oreg. N.G., 1947, advanced through grades to maj. gen., 1974, exec. officer, then dep. comdr. 41st Brigade, 1970-72. Decorated Bronze star, Legion of Merit with oak leaf cluster, Meritorious Service medal, Combat Infantryman's badge, various N.G. medals. Mem. Multnomah County Schoolmasters (pres. 1959-60), Oreg. High Sch. Coaches Assn. (pres. 1961-62), Multnomah County Adminstrs. Assn. (pres. 1967-68), N.G. Assn. U.S. (treas. 1972-76, pres. 1976-78, N.G. Assn. Oreg. (dir. 1963-64), Oreg. Secondary Sch. Prins. Assn. (exec. bd. 1971-73), Assn. Secondary and High Schs. (permanent chmn. program com. 1971-72), Inter-League Council High Schs. in Portland Met. Area (pres. 1969-73), Oreg. Sch. Activities Assn. (mem. del. assembly 1970-73), Oreg. State U. Dad's Club (treas. 1968-69), David Douglas Edn. Assn., Air Force Assn., Assn. U.S. Army (adv. dir.), Phi Delta Theta. Presbyterian. Club: Kiwanis (pres. Greater S.E. club 1968-69), Elks. Office: Mil Dept Oreg 2150 Fairgrounds Rd NE Salem OR 97303*

MILLER, RICHARD HARRY, educator; b. Los Angeles, July 20, 1942; s. Albert David and Ann Gloria (Godfarb) M.; Ph.D., UCLA, 1975. Lectr., Calif. State U., Northridge, 1970-77; assoc. prof. geology San Diego State U., 1977-81, prof., 1982—, dir. Allison Ctr. Study Paleontology, dept. geol. scis., 1978—; v.p. Critter Creations, Inc., Los Angeles, 1976—. Am. Chem. Soc. grantee, 1976-78, NSF grantee, 1980-84. Mem. AAAS, Geol. Soc. Am., Paleontol. Soc., Brit. Palaeontol. Assn., Soc. Econ. Paleontologists and Mineralogists. Home: 4678 Fargo St San Diego CA 92117

MILLER, ROBERT, investment and venture banker; b. Los Angeles, Mar. 26, 1947; s. Robert Martin and Marion Elizabeth (Mills) M.; m. Amparo Jaramillo Cortés, Nov. 6, 1978. Chmn., chief exec. officer, dir. CaliforniaGroup Internat. Ltd., Beverly Hills, Calif. Office: 9701 Wilshire Blvd Beverly Hills CA 90212 also AA34339 Bogota Colombia

MILLER, ROBERT GORDON, physician; b. Cambridge, Mass., Jan. 8, 1942; s. Gordon R. and Marjorie L. (Eaton) M.; B.S. with distinction, U.S. Naval Acad., 1963; M.D., Cornell U., 1970; m. Christine Ernst. Med. intern Children's Hosp. of San Francisco, 1970-71; resident in internal medicine U. Calif., San Diego, 1971-72; resident in neurology U. Calif., San Francisco, 1972-75; research fellow Nat. Hosp., London, 1975, U. Freiburg (W. Ger.), 1975-76; practice medicine specializing in neurology, Portland, Oreg., 1976-79, San Francisco, 1979—; asst. prof. dept. neurology U. Oreg. Health Scis. Center, Portland, 1976-79; chief neurology service Children's Hosp. of San Francisco, 1979—, dir. neuromuscular research and Neuromuscular Clinic, 1979—; asst. clin. prof. neurology U. Calif., San Francisco, 1979-82, adj. assoc. prof. neurology, 1982—. Served with USN, 1963-66. Diplomate Am. Bd. Psychiatry and Neurology. Fellow Am. Acad. Neurology; mem. Am. Assn. of Electromyography and Electrodiagnosis (mem. edn. com. 1977-79, chmn. 1979-82, dir. 1980-82, chmn. program com. 1982-83), Soc. for Neurosci., AAAS, N.Y. Acad. Scis., Am. Fedn. Clin. Research. Contbr. articles in field to med. publs. Home: 532 Throckmorton Mill Valley CA 94941 Office: 3700 California St San Francisco CA 94119

MILLER, ROBERT LEON, public relations consultant; b. Gothenburg, Nebr., Mar. 9, 1942; s. Cleo Robert and Inez Bell (Bullock) M. Student U. Nebr., 1960-61, U. Alaska, 1965, U. Hawaii, 1979. Reporter two newspapers, Nebr., 1961-66; polit. reporter, columnist, editor Anchorage Times, 1966-69; press sec. Alaska Gov. Keith H. Miller, Juneau, 1966-69; supr. pub. relations Alyeska Pipeline Service Co., Anchorage, 1970-71, mgr. pub. affairs, 1971-77; communications coordinator for Alaska Lands, Office of Gov. Jay S. Hammond, Juneau, 1979-80; freelance pub. relations cons., Anchorage, 1981—. Active community affairs; chmn. Alaska State Council on Arts; campaign mgr. Stephen C. Cowper for Gov., 1982. Served with U.S. Army, 1964-66. Mem. Pub. Relations Sco. Am. Episcopalian. Office: 550 W 7th Ave Suite 850 Anchorage AK 99501

MILLER, ROBERT WARBURTON, psychologist; b. Bellefonte, Pa., Nov. 23, 1921; s. Joseph Frederick and Mary (Warburton) M.; A.B., Pa. State U., 1942; M.A., Redlands U., 1951; Ph.D., U. So. Calif., 1957; m. Joyce Larayne Maxey, Mar. 24, 1946; children—Pamela Joyce Larayne, Robert Brent Warburton, Page Layne Warburton. Grad. mgr. Asso. Student Body, San Bernardino Valley Coll., 1946-51; lectr. U. So. Calif., Los Angeles, 1956-57; pvt. practice psychology and speech pathology, San Bernardino, Calif., 1954—; staff clin. psychologist San Bernardino County Gen. Hosp., 1968-75; dir. Mojave Valley Mental Health Services, 1970-72; cons. Grand Terrace Convalescent Hosp., 1965—, Citrus Care Convalescent Hosp., 1968—. Lectr., U. Redlands, 1958-59, Loma Linda U., 1963; mem. Calif. Licensing Com. for Speech Pathologists, 1959-61; mem. psychol. exam. com. Calif. Bd. Med. Examiners, 1970-74, chmn. subcom. legislation, 1971-73, chmn. subcom. statistics and evaluations, 1972-74; owner, supr. Tao-Teh-King Farms, 1953—; owner, adminstr. Warburton Profl. Office Bldgs., 1959-71; chmn. bd. dirs. San Bernardino and Riverside Counties Investment Corp., 1958-70; pres., dir. Colton Profl. Bldg., Inc.; pres. Avora Corp., 1973—; dir. E. Pioneer Water Co., 1972—, v.p., 1974—. Dep. sheriff San Bernardino County, 1961-68; troop com. chmn. San Bernardino Boy Scouts Am., 1964-65; mem. fruit rack com. Nat. Orange Show, 1957-64; adv. bd. San Bernardino Area Mental Health Assn., 1965, chmn. speakers bur., 1964-66; bd. dirs. San Bernardino Goodwill Industries, 1963—, exec. com. Inland Counties, 1965-71, pres., 1968-70, hon. mem. bd., 1972; v.p., then pres. bd. dirs., now trustee San Bernardino chpt. City of Hope Hosp. Served to lt. USNR, 1942-46, to lt. comdr., 1951-53; capt. Res. Recipient George Washington medal Freedoms Found. at Valley Forge, 1970, 72, 73; Distinguished Pub. Service award Inlands So. Calif. Psychol. Assn., 1976. Fellow Am. Assn. Marriage Counselors; mem. Calif., Inland (pres. 1973-74) psychol. assns., U. Redlands Fellows, Soc. Am. Mil. Engrs., San Bernardino Civic Light Opera Assn., S.A.R. (chpt. v.p. 1965-66, state pres. 1967-69, nat. trustee 1970-71, v.p. gen. 1971-73, nat. exec. com. 1972-76, nat. sec. gen. 1974-76, chmn. nat. soc. 1976-77), Nat. Congress Parents and Tchrs., Naval Res. Officers Assn. (pres. Arrowhead chpt. 1973-74), San Bernardino C. of C. (dir. 1975—), Navy League, Pi Lambda Sigma, Kappa Sigma, Tau Kappa Alpha. Methodist. Clubs: Carriage (pres. 1965-67, dir.), Wilsonian (San Bernardino), Masons. Author: (with Joyce L. Miller) Dealing With The Behavioral Problems In The Elementary School, 1968, A Therapy Guide For The Families of Adult Aphasics, 1972. Contbr. articles to profl. jours. Office: 1308 N D St San Bernardino CA 92405

MILLER, RODNEY BLAINE, advertising executive; b. Payson, Utah, June 7, 1952; s. Howard George and Renee (Johnson) M.; m. Susan Sandau, Mar. 15, 1974; 1 dau., Kate. B.S. in Journalism, Utah State U., 1975. Asst. producer Utah State U. Radio/TV Broadcasting Service, Logan, 1974-75; writer, producer, dir. sta. KMVT-TV, Twin Falls, Idaho, 1975-77; account exec., creative dir. Bitton Advt., Idaho Falls, Idaho, 1977-79; ptnr., creative dir. HM&C Advt., Idaho Falls, 1979-82; v.p. creative services Pierson & Kearney Advt., Ogden, Utah, 1982—; cons. Utah Advt. News. Recipient numerous awards for creative excellence in advt. Affiliated Advt. Agencies Internat., Art Dirs. Salt Lake City, Utah Advt. Fedn., Idaho Advt. Fedn. Mem. Am. Advt. Fedn., Idaho Advt. Fedn. Morman. Office: 1521 W 2550 S Ogden UT 84404

MILLER, ROGER JOHN, auto dealership owner; b. St. Paul, Jan. 9, 1935; s. Joseph and Dorothy (Salvatore) M.; m. Ruth M. Quayle; 1 dau., Pamela. Profl. baseball player Bklyn. Dodgers Orgn., 1955-57, St. Paul Saints, 1958-63; salesman Chevrolet, Norwalk, Calif., 1963-65, Costa Mesa, Calif., 1965-74; pres. Roger Miller Chevrolet, Riverside, Calif., 1975-78; pres. Roger Miller Imports, Riverside, 1978—; bd. dirs. So. Calif. Datsun and Honda Dealers; bd. dirs. Motor Car Dealers. Trustee Southcoast Repertoire; bd. dirs. St. Jude's Hosp., Hope Meml. Hosp., Newport Beach, Calif. Served with U.S. Army, 1953-54. Recipient Pres.'s Man of Yr. award, 1975. Clubs: Balboa Bay (bd. govs.), Victoria County (Riverside); Springs (Rancho Mirage); John Wayne Tennis, Irvine Coast Country (Newport Beach). Home: Corona Del Mar CA 92625 Office: 8330 Indiana Ave Riverside CA 92504

MILLER, RONALD THOMAS, utility co. exec.; b. Burke, Idaho, Aug. 6, 1919; s. Dale D. and Mary E. (Dunphy) M.; B.S., Oreg. State U., 1941; m. Betty Loretta Bergman, Mar. 7, 1942; children—Mary L. (Mrs. John A. Rhine, Jr.), Margaret A. (Mrs. Jan E. Monroe). Insp. fed. diking project U.S. C.E., Deer Island, Oreg., 1941; with N.W. Natural Gas Co., Portland, 1947—, chief engr., 1968-71, v.p. engring. and gas control, 1971-73, exec. v.p., 1973-75, pres., chief exec. officer, 1975— also dir., chmn. exec. com.; v.p., dir. Asso. Oreg. Industries, Blue Cross Oreg. Pres., Lake Oswego (Oreg.) P.T.A., 1963, Am. Field Service, Lake Oswego, 1966-67; bd. dirs. Portland Better Bus. Bur., Columbia-Pacific council Boy Scouts Am. Served to capt. C.E. AUS, 1942-47; PTO. Registered profl. engr., Oreg. Mem. Am. Gas Assn. (chmn. liquefied natural gas com. 1972-73, dir. 1979—), Am. Soc. M.E., Nat. Soc. Profl. Engrs., Profl. Engrs. Oreg. (award of merit 1968, chpt. sec. 1968), Pacific Coast Gas Assn. (gen. chmn. operating sect. 1972-73, dir. 1976—, 2d vice chmn. 1979—), Portland C. of C. (dir. 1979—), Alpha Sigma Phi. Republican. Roman Catholic. Clubs: Waverley Country (Portland); Arlington; Rotary. Office: Northwest Natural Gas Co 123 NW Flanders St Portland OR 97209

MILLER, RONALD WILLIAM, film executive; b. Los Angeles, Apr. 17, 1933; s. John W. and Stella M.; student U. So. Calif., 1951-54; m. Diane Marie Disney, May 9, 1954; children—Christopher, Joanna, Tamara, Jennifer, Walter, Ronald, Patrick. With Walt Disney Prodns., 1954—, co-producer, 1964-67, producer, 1967—, exec. producer, 1968-76, exec. v.p. in charge prodn. and creative affairs, 1976-80, pres., chief operating officer, 1980-83, chief exec. officer, 1983—, also dir., mem. exec. com. Served with U.S. Army, 1954-55. Mem. Acad. Motion Picture Arts and Scis., Nat. Acad. TV Arts and Scis., Motion Picture Pioneers, U. So. Calif. Assos. Republican. Episcopalian. Office: Walt Disney Prodns 500 S Buena Vista Burbank CA 91521*

MILLER, ROY FRANKLIN, mgmt. cons.; b. Salt Lake City, Feb. 3, 1912; s. Roy F. and Cassie A. Miller; B.B.A., U. Wash., Seattle, 1934; m. Lena C. Clifford, May 26, 1935; children—Roy Franklin, III, Richard C., Virginia Moody. Owner Med. Dental Hosp. Service, Pocatello, 1950; chmn. bd. Profl. Adjustment Bur., Pocatello, Idaho, 1965; chmn. bd. Kirchner Miller Agy., Inc., Pocatello, 1980; partner M & M Farms, Pocatello, 1950, Devel. Assos., Pocatello, 1967, Miller and Miller Land Devel. Co., Pocatello, 1968; past dir. S. Idaho Med. Service Corp.; chmn. bd. dirs. Blue Cross of Idaho Health Services, Inc.; mem. Eastern Idaho Council Industry and Energy. past pres. Med. Dental Hosp. Burs. Am.; past mem. Idaho Health Planning Council. Bd. dirs. Idaho Youth Ranch, Idaho Scottish Rite Found., Acacia Ednl. Found., Idaho DeMolay Found.; chmn. fin. com. Acacia Nat. Com., mem. fin. com. Central Pacific conf. United Ch. Christ; moderator Pocatello United Ch. Christ; past chmn. bd. Pocatello Library; past chmn. Bannock County Republican Party; del. Rep. Nat. Conv., 1976; bd. dirs. Idaho Youth Ranch Found. Recipient Stanley R. Mauck award Med. Dental Hosp. Burs. Am., 1970; recipient various certs. merit. Mem. Fort Hall Water Users Assn., Am. Collectors Assn. (charter mem., past dir.), Nat. Fedn. Ind. Bus., Idaho Collectors Assn. (past pres.), Idaho Assn. Commerce and Industry, Pocatello C. of C. Clubs: Pocatello Rotary, Masons (33 deg., treas.), Shriners. Home: 91 Foothill Blvd Box 1090 Pocatello ID 83204 Office: 653 E Center St Suite D Pocatello ID 83201

MILLER, RUSSELL TUTTLE, realtor; b. Spokane, Dec. 10, 1922; s. Russell Tuttle and Claudia (Lewis) M.; B.S., Mass. Inst. Tech., 1948; postgrad. Colo. Sch. Mines, 1950; m. Georgette Thioliere, Apr. 17, 1948. Pres., New World Exploration Corp., Los Angeles, 1948-56; cons. mineral engring., Los Angeles, 1956-58; pres. Tech. Mktg. Assos., Los Angeles, 1959-73; pres. Titan Realty Corp., Los Angeles, 1959—, Worldwide Properties, Ltd., Newport Beach, Calif., 1976—, Sepol, Ltd., Irvine, Calif., 1976—. Served in U.S. Army, 1942-45. Decorated Purple Heart. Mem. Am. Inst. Mining and Metall. Engrs., Am. Inst. Mining Engrs., Am. Inst. Chem. Engrs., Soc. Exploration Geophysicists. Episcopalian. Clubs: Calif. Yacht, Riviera Country, Marina City, Balboa Bay. Home and office: 2 Mandarin Irvine CA 92714

MILLER, SAMUEL LEE, real estate exec.; b. Maywood, Ill., Apr. 22, 1912; s. Samuel Lee and Clarissa (Buck) M.; Ph.B., U. Chgo., 1935; m. Sally Ann Walton, June 24, 1939 (dec.); 1 dau., Sally Ann (Mrs. David Roth); m. 2d, Irene A. Reed, 1973. Foreman mfg. Am. Can Co., Maywood, 1933-42; adminstrv. mgr. George S. May Co., San Francisco, 1942-47; gen. sales mgr. Hunt Foods and Industries, Fullerton, Calif., 1947-58; with H.M. Parker and Son, wholesale automobile parts co., 1958-68, v.p., gen. mgr., North Hollywood, Calif., 1962-68, bd. dirs., 1959-68; pres. Am. Parts Systems, Inc., North Hollywood, 1968-69, regional sales promotion mgr., 1970-71, gen. mgr., Fairfield, Calif., 1972-76; pres. Roth & Miller Realty, Inc., 1977—. Mem. Theta Delta Chi. Republican. Methodist. Mason. Home: 248 Cheyenne Dr Vacaville CA 95688 Office: 1313 E Monte Vista Vacaville CA 95688

MILLER, SAMUEL TILDEN, city ofcl.; b. Skaitook, Okla., Nov. 28, 1939; s. Samuel Archie and Maureen Hilda (Munsey) M.; A.A., Northwestern Community Coll., Powell, Wyo., 1964; student U. Wyo., 1958-60, 64-66; m. Ella Annette Boyd, Jan. 22, 1960; children—Samuel Joseph, Natalie Christine. Surveyor U.S. Bur. Reclamation, Townsend, Mont., 1960-61; roughneck Empire State Oil Co., Thermopolis, Wyo., 1961-63; surveyor W.E. Grenier, C.E., Laramie, Wyo., 1964-65, bldg. inspr., 1965-70; street supt. City of Laramie (Wyo.), 1970—; real estate appraiser, adult edn. instr., surveyor. Pres. Gem City Fed. Credit Union, 1966-68. Bd. dirs. Rocky Mountain chpt. Internat. Conf. Bldg. Ofcls. Mem. Am. Public Works Assn., Am. Inst. Real Estate Appraisers. Home: 3419 Alta Vista Dr Laramie WY 82070 Office: 1264 N 4th St Laramie WY 82070

MILLER, VESTA H., realtor; b. Stockton, Kans., Oct. 23, 1928; d. George W. and Emma Colburn; m. G. Stanley Miller, Aug. 31, 1947; children—Judy, Cindy, Shelley, Greg; B.S., Kans. State U., 1949. Tchr., Dodge City (Kans.) Jr. High Sch., 1949-54; councilwoman, Arvada, Colo., 1973—, mayor pro tem, 1975-79, mayor, 1979-81; realtor, Arvada, Colo., 1982—. Mem. Jefferson County Bd. Realtors, Arvada Hist. Soc., Denver Regional Council Govts. (chmn. 1980-82), Nat. Assn. Regional Councils (dir. 1979-82), Nat. League Cities, Denver Met. Ministries. Republican. Home: 6191 Flower St Arvada CO 80004 Office: 8001 Ralston Rd Arvada CO 80002 also 8101 Ralston Rd City Hall Arvada CO 80002

MILLER, WALTER HENRY, architect; b. Walla Walla, Wash., Apr. 25, 1932; s. Henry and Lena (Foltz) M.; B.Archtl. Engring., Wash. State U., 1959; m. Janice Irene Stevenson, Aug. 27, 1955; children—Steven Michael, Scott Adrian. Draftsman, Putnam & Dimke, Architects, Lewiston, Idaho, 1959-65, Hugh Richardson, Architect, Lewiston, 1965-70; partner Richardson Miller Architects, Lewiston, 1970-78; proprietor Walter H. Miller, Architect, Clarkston, Wash., 1979—; chmn. adv. com. drafting technologies program Lewis Clark State Coll., 1970—, chmn. Lewiston Bldg. Code Com. and Bd. Appeals, 1970—. Mem. exec. bd. Lewis Clark council Boy Scouts Am., 1969—, v.p., 1973, 74, 76, 77, pres., 1975-76. Served with U.S. Army, 1952-54. Recipient Silver Beaver award Boy Scouts Am., 1975. Mem. AIA, Wash. State Council Architects. Republican. Presbyterian. Clubs: Kiwanis, Elks, Masons, Shriners, Scottish Rite. Home: 2003 Willow St Clarkston WA 99403 Office: 744 5th St Suite 102 Clarkston WA 99403

MILLER, WARREN EDWARD, political science educator; b. Hawarden, Iowa, Mar. 26, 1942; s. John Carroll and Mildred Ovedia (Lien) M.; children—Jeffrey Ralph, Jennifer Louise. B.S., U. Oreg., 1948, M.S., 1950; Ph.D., Maxwell Sch. Citizenship and Pub. Affairs, Syracuse U., 1954; Ph.D. (hon.), U. Goteborg (Sweden), 1972. Asst. study dir. Survey Research Ctr., Inst. Social Research, U. Mich., Ann Arbor, 1951-53, study dir., 1953-56, research assoc., 1956-59, program dir., 1959-68, research coordinator polit. behavior program, 1968-70, dir. Ctr. Polit. Studies, Inst. Social Research, 1970-81, asst. prof. polit. sci., 1956-58, assoc. prof., 1958-63, prof., 1963-81, Arthur W. Bromage prof. polit. sci., 1981, adj. prof., 1982—; vis. disting. prof. polit. sci. Ariz. State U., Tempe, 1981, prof., 1982—; asst. prof. polit. sci. U. Calif.-Berkeley, 1954-56; fellow Ctr. Advanced Study in Behavioral Scis., 1961-62; exec. dir. Interuniv. Consortium for Polit. and Social Research 1962-70; vis. prof. U. Tilburg (Netheralands), 1973, U. Geneva, 1973, European U. Inst., Florence, Italy, 1979; trustee Inst. Am. Univs., 1970—. Served with USAAF, 1943-46. Recipient Disting. Alumnus award Maxwell Sch. Citizenship and Pub. Affairs, Syracuse U., 1974, Disting. Faculty Achievement award U. Mich., 1977. Fellow Am. Acad. Arts and Scis.; mem. Am. Polit. Sci. Assn. (pres. 1979-80), Internat. Polit. Sci. Assn. (council 1969-73), Midwest Polit. Sci. Assn., Internat. Soc. Polit. Psychology, So. Polit. Sci. Assn., Social Sci. History Assn. (pres. 1979-80). Author books including: (with others) The American Voter, 1960; (with T.E. Levitin) Leadership and Change: Presidential Elections from 1952-1976, 1977; (with others) The American National Election Studies Data Sourcebook, 1952-78, 1980; mem. editorial bd. Am. Polit. Sci. Rev., 1966-71, Computers and the Humanities, 1969-71; mem. editorial adv. bd. Sage Electoral Studies Yearbook, 1974—; contbr. articles to profl. publs. Office: Dept Polit Sci Ariz State U Tempe AZ 85281

MILLER, WATKINS WILFORD, soil scientist, educator; b. Hawthorne, Calif., Feb. 21, 1947; s. Paul M. and Sarah E. (Watkins) M; children—Ryan William, Jason Tally. B.S. in Soil Sci., Calif. State Poly. U., 1968; Ph.D. Soil Physics, U. Calif.-Riverside, 1973. Cert. Am. Registry Cert. Profls. in Agronomy, Crops and Soils. Soil Sci. trainee Soil Conservation Service, Coachella, Calif., 1964-68; agrl. chemist Nelson Labs., Stockton, Calif., 1968-70; research asst. U. Calif.-Riverside, 1970-73; assoc. prof. soil and water sci. U. Nev., Reno, 1973—. cons. Legis. and Research Adv. Bd. grantee; recipient outstanding tchr. award Coll. Agr., 1979. Mem. Am. Soc. Agronomy, Soil Sci. Soc., Sigma Psi, Gamma Sigma Delta. Club: Lions. Contbr. articles to profl. jours. Home: 1965 Van Ness Reno NV 89503 Office: Univ Nev Reno NV 89557

MILLER, WENDELL SMITH, chemist, cons.; b. Columbus, Ohio, Sept. 26, 1925; s. Wendell Pierce and Emma Josephine (Smith) M.; B.A., Pomona Coll., 1944; M.S., U. Calif. at Los Angeles, 1952; m. Dorothy

Marie Pagen, Aug. 18, 1949; children—William Ross, Wendell Roger. Chemist U.S. Rubber Co., Torrance, Calif., 1944; sr. chemist Carbide & Carbon Chemicals Corp., Oak Ridge, 1944-48; partner Kellogg & Miller, Los Angeles, 1949-56; patent coordinator Electro Optical Systems, Inc., Pasadena, Calif., 1956-59; v.p. Intertech. Corp. optical and optoelectronic system devel., North Hollywood, Calif., 1960-66, dir., 1966—, dir. Slim Barnard Enterprises, Hollywood, Calif., 1971—, Central Empire, Inc., Fresno, Calif. Commr., Great Western Council Boy Scouts Am., 1960-65. Served with AUS, 1944-46. Mem. Los Angeles Patent Law Assn., I.E.E.E., A.A.A.S., Sigma Xi, Phi Beta Kappa, Pi Mu Epsilon. Numerous patents in field. Home: 1341 Comstock Ave Los Angeles CA 90024

MILLER, WILLIAM ELWOOD, mining co. exec.; b. Bend, Oreg., May 9, 1919; s. Harry Adelbert and Sarah (Heyburn) M.; B.A., Stanford, 1941, M.B.A., 1947; m. Constance Alban Crosby, July 2, 1955; children—William, Constance, Harold, Mary, Sarah Crosby, Charles Crosby, Helen, Harry. Owner and operator Central Oregon Pumice Co., Bend, 1948—; pres. The Miller Lumber Co., Bend, The Miller Ranch Co., Bend. Commr., City of Bend, 1959-62, mayor, 1960. Bd. dirs. Central Oreg. Coll.; pres. Central Oreg. Coll. Found., 1956-57; dir. Central Oregon Coll. Area Ednl. Dist., 1961-65, chmn., 1964-65; bd. govs. Ore. Dept. Geology and Mineral Industries, 1971-75. Served with A.C., USNR, 1942-45. Decorated D.F.C., Air medal. Mem. Central Oreg. (v.p. 1954), Bend (pres. 1954) chambers commerce, Kappa Sigma. Republican. Episcopalian. Rotarian (dir. Bend 1955-56). Club: Bend Golf. Home: 527 NW Congress St Bend OR 97701 Office: 5 NW Greenwood Ave Bend OR 97701

MILLER, WILLIAM HOWARD, mgmt. and mktg. cons.; b. Jersey City, Mar. 6, 1933; s. William Howard and Eleanor Virginia M.; M.B.A., La Jolla U., 1980; m. Sonya M. Tharp, Oct. 17, 1958; children—Valerie, Lynn, Lori, Michael, Billy Joe. Enlisted U.S. Marine Corps, 1948, ret., 1967; instr. N.J. and Calif. police depts. in karate, judo and mob control; sales and mktg. dir. Buddy Systems, Inc., La Verne, Calif., 1964-68; dist. sales mgr. Syntex Labs., Palo Alto, Calif., 1968-75; owner, dir. Mgmt. Dynamics, Inc., San Diego, 1975—; field sales mgr. Performax Systems Internat., 1980—; pres./owner Bill Miller & Assos., Inc., cons. to mgmt., exec. search and personnel services; instr. sales and mktg., mgmt. and orgn., human relations U. Calif.-San Diego, Nat. U.; painter seascapes and landscapes, exhibited one-man show, 1971; pub. novel, 1975. Recipient Nat. Sales Mgr./Salesman/Rookie of Yr. award; All-Around Athlete and Coach of Yr. award. Mem. Am. Soc. Tng. and Devel., Internat. Platform Assn., Calif. Tchrs. Assn., Nat. Rifle Assn., Am. Security Council, Sierra Club, Wilderness Soc. Home: 12682 Pacato Circle N Rancho Bernardo CA 92128

MILLER, WILLIS LEE, rancher; b. Akron, Ohio, Feb. 3, 1921; s. William Lee and Nina Mae (Bell) M.; student U. Calif., Davis; m. Dorothy Rhea Murdy, June 22, 1945; children—William Lee, Norma Jeanne, Walter James, Dorothy Willene, Marilyn Louise, Katherine Anne, Wesley Stephen. Engaged in farming and ranching, Westminster, Calif., 1946—; owner, pres. Willis L. Miller Ranch Co., 1967—, Los Alisos Ranch Co., 1967—, Springdale Equipment Co., 1960—; dir. Riverside Asso. Fed. Land Bank, County Nat. Bank. Deacon, elder Presbyn. Ch., 1948—. Served as pilot USAAF, World War II; ETO. Decorated D.F.C. with oak leaf clusters, Air medal with 15 oak leaf clusters. Mem. Farm Bur. Republican. Address: 13070 Old Bolsa Rd Westminster CA 92683

MILLER, ZOYA DICKINS (MRS. HILLIARD EVE MILLER, JR.), civic worker; b. Washington, July 15, 1923; d. Randolph and Zoya Pavlovna (Klementinovska) Dickins; grad. Stuart Sch. Costume Design, Washington, 1942; student Sophie Newcomb Coll., 1944, New Eng. Conservatory Music, 1946; grad. Internat. Sch. Reading, 1969; m. Hilliard Eve Miller, Jr., Dec. 6, 1943; children—Jeffrey Arnot, Hilliard Eve III. Instr., Stuart Summer Sch. Costume Design, Washington, 1942; fashion coordinator Julius Garfinckel, Washington, 1942-43; fashion coordinator, cons. Mademoiselle mag., 1942-43; star TV show Cowbelle Kitchen, 1957-58, Flair for Living, 1958-59; model mags. and comml. films, also nat. comml. recs., 1956—; dir. program devel. Webb-Waring Lung Inst., Denver, 1973—. Mem. exec. com., bd. dirs. El Paso County chpt. Am. Lung Assn., 1954-63; bd. dirs., mem. exec. com. Colo. State Am. Lung Assn., 1955—, chmn. radio and TV council, 1963-68, mem. med. affairs com., 1965-72, pres., 1965-66, procurer found. funds, 1965-72; developer nat. and internat. radio ednl. productions Am. Lung Assn., 1963-68, coordinator statewide screening programs Colo., other states, 1965-72; founder, state coordinator Nov. Noel benefits for pediatrics, 1973—; mem. exec. com. Colo. Gov.'s Comprehensive Health Planning Council, 1967-76, chmn., 1973-75, chmn. Colo. Chronic Care Com., 1969-72, chmn. fund raising, 1970-72, chmn. spl. com. congl. studies on nat. health bills, 1971-72; mem. Colo.-Wyo. Regional Med. Program Adv. Council, 1969-74; mem. Colo. Med. Found. Consumers Adv. Council, 1972-75; chmn. benefit fund raising El Paso County Cancer Soc., 1963; founder, coordinator Colorado Springs Debutante Ball, 1967—; coordinator Nat. Gov.'s Conf. Ball, 1969; mem. decorative arts com. Colorado Springs Fine Arts Center, 1972-75; Recipient James J. Waring award Colo. Conf. on Respiratory Disease Workers, 1963; Zoya Dickins Miller Vol. of Year award Colo. State Am. Lung Assn., 1979, Gold Double Bar Cross award, 1980; lic. pvt. pilot, Colo. Mem. Nat. (chmn. nat. father of year contest 1956-57), Colo., El Paso County (pres. 1954, TV chmn. 1954-59) cowbelle assns. Club: Broadmoor Garden (ways and means chmn. 1967-69, civic chmn. 1970-71, publicity chmn. 1972) (Colorado Springs, Colo.). Contbr. articles, lectures health care systems. Home: 74 W Cheyenne Mountain Blvd Colorado Springs CO 80906

MILLER-TIEDEMAN, ANNA LOUISE, career education institute executive; b. Huntington, W.Va., Sept. 21, 1934; s. Elmer and Pearl (Todd) Miller; m. David V. Tiedeman, Jan. 6, 1973. B.B.A., Marshall U., 1963, M.A. in Sociology, 1967; Ph.D. in Guidance, Counseling, Group Work, Ohio U., 1973. Various positions C.&O. Ry., Huntington, W.Va., 1957-66; resident dir. Ohio U., Athens, 1967; human relations specialist Inst. for Regional Devel., Athens, 1968; housing specialist Action, Inc., Huntington, 1969; real estate salesperson Massey Realty Co., Huntington, 1968-71; assoc. ednl. devel. specialist Appalachia Ednl. Lab., Charleston, W.Va., 1970-71; writer P.J. Abbot Middle Sch., San Mateo (Calif.) City Sch. Dist., 1971-72, counselor, 1972-73; career guidance coordinator/counselor DeKalb (Ill.) High Sch., 1973-80; asst. prof. career edn. No. Ill. U., DeKalb, 1974-80; Title IX coordinator DeKalb Community Unit Sch. Dist. 428, 1979-80; research assoc. Nat. Inst. for Advancement of Career Edn., U. So. Calif., Los Angeles, 1981—, v.p. devel., 1982—, adj. asst. prof. higher and postsecondary edn. and counseling, Sch. Edn., 1981—; tutor Internat. Coll., Los Angeles, 1981—; speaker, participant workshops in field. Mem. Am. Personnel and Guidance Assn. (outstanding research award 1981), Assn. for Measurement and Evaluation in Guidance, Nat. Vocat. Guidance Assn., Internat. Women's Writing Guild. Author: (with D.V. Tiedeman) Career Development: Journey into —I— Power, 1981; contbr. chpts. to books; contbr. articles to jours., newspapers. Home: 426 S Norton #105 Los Angeles CA 90020 Office: NIACE U So Calif University Park MC-0031 Los Angeles CA 90089

MILLHAM, CHARLES BLANCHARD, computer scientist, environmental scientist, educator, consultant; b. Liberal, Kans., Nov. 1, 1936; s. Charels B. and Abbie Estella (Lawrence) M.; 1 son, Michael Blanchard. Student Carleton Coll., 1954-56; B.A., Iowa State U., 1958, M.S., 1961, Ph.D., 1962. Instr. math. Iowa State U., 1962-64, asst. prof., 1964-66; asst. prof. Wash. State U., Pullman, 1966-69, assoc. prof., 1969-74, prof., 1974, former chmn. environ. sci. and regional planning; profl. cons. Recipient citation Royal Sci. Soc. Jordan; Fulbright grantee U. Jordan, Amman, 1976-77. Mem. Soc. Indsl. and Applied Math., Math. Programming Soc., Ops. Research Soc., Am. Econ. Assn., Assn. Research Profs. Wash. State U. (founding mem., past pres.). Roman Catholic. Contbr. articles to profl. jours., chpts. to books. Home: 135 Webb St Pullman WA 99163 Office: Troy 305 Wash State U Pullman WA 99164

MILLIGAN, ALICE JUNE NELSON, educator, consultant; b. Farmington, N.Mex., June 26, 1937; d. Bailey W. and Alice (Lindsey) Nelson; 1 dau., Deborah Jean. A.A., Colo. Woman's Coll., 1957; B.S., U N.Mex., 1959; postgrad. U. Oslo, 1961, U. Guam, 1963-64; cert. in library sci. Ariz. State U., 1972. Tchr. pub. schs., Calif., N.Mex., N.C., Tex., 1959-63; ednl. cons. Govt. of Guam, 1963-65; prin. U.S. Navy Schs., Guam, 1965-68; program supr. Nat. Child Care Ctrs., Phoenix, 1969-71; tchr. 1st grade Washington Sch. Dist., 1976-81; owner Serendepity Assocs., Phoenix, 1981—. Mem. Am. Assn. Bus. and Profl. Women, NEA, Women Emerging, Ariz. Authors Assn., Nat. Spakers Assn., AAUW, Kappa Alpha Theta, Delta Tau Kappa. Republican. Mem. Science of Mind Ch. Author: The Island, 1981. Home and office: 525 E Tuckey Ln Phoenix AZ 85012

MILLIGAN, CARINA MARCIA HARGIS, family counselor, school psychologist; b. Chgo., May 31, 1955; d. Ira Clair and Geraldine Marie (Kelley) Hargis; m. Dennis Edward Milligan, Aug. 22, 1981. B.S. in Psychology and English, U. Central Ark., 1977; M.S. in Counseling and Sch. Psychology, U. Fullerton, 1980. Lic. marriage, family and child counselor, Calif., 1982. Counselor, Buena Park High Sch., Calif., 1977-78, Centralia Sch. Dist., Buena Park, 1978-80, Cornelia Connelly High Sch., Anaheim, Calif., 1980-82; marriage, family and child counselor in pvt. practice, Buena Park, 1982—. Mem. Am. Psychol. Assn., Am. Personnel and Guidance Assn., Calif. Personnel and Guidance Assn., Calif. Assn. Marriage and Family Therapists. Roman Catholic.

MILLIKEN, CHARLES CLOYD, park ranger; b. Phoenixville, Pa., Feb. 6, 1949; s. Charles Robert and Daris Mae (Kirkpatrick) M.; B.S., Geneva Coll., 1971; postgrad. U. Mont., Missoula, 1971-72; m. Marjorie D. Dennison, Oct. 2, 1971; 1 dau., Jennifer. Seasonal park ranger U.S. Nat. Park Service, Yellowstone and Everglades Nat. Parks, 1969-76; park ranger (interpretation) Bent's Old Fort Nat. Hist. Site, 1976-77, Mount Rushmore Nat. Memorial, 1977-81; park ranger, chief interpretation Chiricahua Nat. Monument, Willcox, Ariz., 1981—. Mem. Assn. Interpretive Naturalists. Republican. Presbyterian. Office: Chiricahua Nat Monument Dos Cabezas Route Box 6500 Willcox AZ 85643

MILLIKEN, WILLIAM GRAWN, JR., oil company executive; b. Traverse City, Mich., Oct. 14, 1946; s. William Grawn and Helen Marguerite (Wallbank) M.; B.A., Colo. Coll., 1973. Dir. corp. relations Youth for Understanding, Washington, 1973-77; asst. campaign mgr. Ill. Gov. James Thompson, Springfield, 1978; dir. public affairs Hamilton Bros. Oil Co., Denver, 1979-82; mgr. adminstrn. Sumatra Energy Co., Denver, 1982—. Mem. Colo. Small Bus. Council. Served with U.S. Army, 1967-68. Mem. Public Affairs Council, Nat. Investor Relations Inst. Republican. Club: Denver. Home: 700 S Jackson St Denver CO 80209 Office: 999 18th St Suite 1400 Denver CO 80202

MILLIMAN, JOAN ANN, management consultant in arts, educator; b. Glendale, Calif., Jan. 27, 1937; d. Kenneth Miles and Blanche (Christine (Fitch) M. B.A., Occidental Coll., 1959; M.A. (hon.), Cambridge (Eng.) U., 1972; Ph.D. in Musicology, U. So. Calif., 1977. Secondary tchr. English and music Los Angeles City Schs., 1960-67, adult tchr. Am. lit., 1962-65; teaching asst. dept. music history U. So. Calif., 1968-71; asst. prof. music Humboldt State U., spring 1975; tech. writer/editor Laventhol & Horwath, C.P.A.s., Los Angeles, 1978, cons. and adminstrv. supr. dept. mgmt. adv. services Leisure Time Industries Group, 1979—; lectr. div. inter-arts and cultural studies Sch. Performing Arts, U. So. Calif., 1981—; music reviewer and feature writer Star News, Pasadena, Calif., 1979-80; cons. to arts orgns., 1980—; panelist Artreach, 1980, Bus. Vols. for Arts, Los Angeles, 1981, U.S. Nat. Commn. for UNESCO, Washington, 1981. AAUW research fellow Cambridge U., 1971-73. Mem. Assn. Coll., Univ. and Community Arts Adminstrs., Am. Musicol. Soc., Am. Council for Arts, Am. Mgmt. Assn., Calif. Confedn. for Arts. Home: 901 N Ave 66 Los Angeles CA 90042 Office: 3700 Wilshire Blvd Los Angeles CA 90010

MILLINER, JO ANN, newspaper sales executive; b. Cushing, Okla., Nov. 26, 1929; d. Carlton Earl and Elsie Faye (Brown) De Graw; student advt. Internat. Corr. Schs., Scranton, Pa., 1958-60, UCLA, 1970-79, Pierce Coll., 1971, Valley Jr. Coll., 1975, Internat. Corr. Sch., Center for Degree Study, 1981—; m. Thomas Joseph Hess, July 16, 1949; children—Sherrie Lynne, Thomas Joseph III; m. 2d, Jean Samuel Clothier, May 11, 1956; 1 son, Geoffrey Vaughan; m. 3d, John William Samuel, Mar, 2, 1967 (div.); m. 4th, Royce Elwood Milliner, Apr. 2, 1983. Billing clk. typist Swift & Co., South San Francisco, Calif., 1947-49; comptroller's sec. Farmers Ins. Co., Des Moines, 1953-55; with Van Nuys Pub. Co., Valley News (now Daily News), Los Angeles, 1958—, mktg. analyst, 1973-76, adult sales account exec., 1976-81, inside retail sales mgr., 1981-82, inside sales/tele-mktg. account exec., 1983—; owner, operator Jo Ann Clothier Press Clipping Service, 1962-72. Mem. com. Marathon Run of Press, Pierce Coll., 1979. Mem. Adventures in Achievement (life), Internat. Platform Assn. Republican. Mem. Christian Ch. (Disciples of Christ). Clubs: Toastmasters; Grand Squares Square Dance (Sepulveda, Calif.). Home: 6545 Wilbur Ave Space 45 Reseda CA 91335 Office: Daily News 14539 Sylvan St Los Angeles CA 91411

MILLNER, DIANNE MAXINE, lawyer; b. Columbus, Ohio, Mar. 21, 1949; d. Charles Nelson and Barbara Rose (Johnson) Millner. A.A., Pasadena City Coll., 1969; A.B., U. Calif.-Berkeley, 1972; J.D., Stanford U., 1975. Bar: Calif. 1975. Assoc. Pillsbury, Madison & Sutro, San Francisco, 1975-80; ptnr. Millner & McGee, San Francisco, 1980—; pres., dir. Black TV Workshop of Santa Rosa, Inc. NEH fellow, 1978. Mem. Nat. Bar Assn. (Women's Div. Presdl. award 1980), Calif. State Bar Assn., Bar Assn. San Francisco, Bar Assn. No. Calif., Black Women Lawyers, Phi Beta Kappa. Office: 390 Hayes St San Francisco CA 94102

MILLS, CAROL MARGARET, trucking co. exec.; b. Salt Lake City, Aug. 31, 1943; d. Samuel Lawrence and Beth (Neilson) M.; B.S. magna cum laude, U. Utah, 1965. With W.S. Hatch Co., Woods Cross, Utah, 1965—, corp. sec., 1970—, traffic mgr., 1969—, dir. publicity, 1974—; dir. Hatch Service Corp., Nat. Tank Truck Carriers, Inc., Washington; bd. dirs. Intermountain Tariff Bur. Inc., 1978—, chmn., 1981—. Vice chmn. bd. Fund raiser March of Dimes, Am. Cancer Soc., Am. Heart Assn.; active senatorial campaign, 1976. Recipient service awards W. S. Hatch Co., 1971, 80. Mem. Nat. Tank Truck Carriers, Transp. Club Salt Lake City, Am. Trucking Assn. (public relations council), Utah Motor Transport Assn. (dir. 1982—), Beta Gamma Sigma, Phi Kappa Phi, Phi Chi Theta. Home: 77 Edgecombe Dr Salt Lake City UT 84103 Office: 643 S 800 W Woods Cross UT 84087

MILLS, CAROLINE LUCILLE, nurse, educator; b. Calgary, Alta., Can., Dec. 9, 1939; came to U.S., 1955, naturalized, 1961; s. Philip and Caroline (Lutz) Unterschultz; R.N., Nebr. Meth. Hosp., 1961; B.S.N., Whitworth Coll., 1964; M.S. in Edn., Portland State U., 1978; m. Otha Edmond Mills, Apr. 22, 1967; children—Chuck Bruce, Shannon Marie. Charge nurse Deaconess Hosp., Spokane, Wash., 1961-64; instr. nursing Sacred Heart Hosp. Sch. Nursing, Spokane, 1964-65; inservice instr. Providence Hosp., Portland, Oreg., 1965-69; day supt. Dwyer Hosp., Milwaukie, Oreg., 1969-70; instr. nursing Clackamas Community Coll., Oregon City Oreg., 1970-71; dir. nurses Oregon City Hosp., 1971-76; tchr. health careers Canby (Oreg.) High Sch., 1976—. Vol. Multiple Sclerosis Assn.; active blood drive ARC; Sunday sch. tectchr. Immanuel Luth. Ch.; vol. tchrs. death and dying seminar for local sch., 1978. Recipient various certs. of appreciation. Mem. Oreg. Vocat. Assn., Oreg. Nurses Assn. (pres. dist. 26, 1974), Health Occupations Students Am. (Oreg. adv. bd. 1977—), Oreg. Edn. Assn. Republican. Home: 6696 Cavalier Way Milwaukie OR 97222 Office: 721 4th St Canby OR 97013

MILLS, EUGENE SUMNER, college president; b. West Newton, Ind., Sept. 13, 1924; s. Sumner Amos and Lela (Weatherly) M.; A.B., Earlham Coll., 1948; M.A., Claremont Grad. Sch., 1949, Ph.D., 1952; postgrad. Harvard U., 1958-59; LL.D., N.H. Coll., 1979; m. Dorothy Frances Wildman, Oct. 22, 1945; children—David Walden, Sara Anne. Instr. psychology Whittier Coll., 1950-52, asst. prof., chmn. dept., 1952-55, assoc. prof., dept. chmn., 1955-60, prof. psychology, dept. chmn., 1960-62; prof. psychology U. N.H., Durham, 1962-79, chmn. dept., 1962-65, dean Grad. Sch., coordinator research, 1963-67, dean Coll. Liberal Arts, 1967-70, acad. v.p., 1970-71, provost, 1971-74, provost, acting pres., 1974, pres., 1974-79; prof. psychology, pres. Whittier Coll., 1979—; vis. prof. U. Victoria (B.C.), summers 1958, 60. Bd. dirs. N.H. Council on World Affairs, 1976-79, Elderhostel, Inc., 1977—; mem. Town Hall of Calif., 1979—; mem. exec. bd. Los Angeles Area council Boy Scouts Am., 1981—; trustee, Southwest Mus., 1979—. Danforth Found. grantee, 1956-57; NSF grantee, 1963-66. Fellow Am. Psychol Am. Psychol. Assn.; mem. Western Psychol. Assn., Eastern Psychol. Assn., N.H. Psychol. Assn. (pres. 1969-70, dir. 1967-70), Sigma Xi, Phi Kappa Phi, Omicron Delta Kappa. Quaker. Clubs: California, Los Angeles. Author: George Trumbull Ladd: Pioneer American Psychologist, 1969. Contbr. articles to profl. jours. Home: 13952 Summit Dr Whittier CA 90602 Office: Whittier Coll 13406 Philadelphia St Whittier CA 90608

MILLS, JAMES HENRY, art critic; b. Chaseburg, Wis., Jan. 17, 1924; s. Stephen A. and Nellie Gertrude (Natwick) M.; student Central Sch. Speech and Drama, London, 1945; B.S., U. Wis., 1947; M.F.A., Fordham U., 1953. Actor, writer, 1947-55; personnel dir. Denver Post, 1955-74; art editor Denver Post, 1974-83; art juror; lectr. Served in U.S. Army, 1943-46. Decorated Purple Heart. Mem. Denver Council Arts and Humanities, Larry Tajiri Found., Alliance for Contemporary Art, Asian Art Assn., Newspaper Personnel Relations Assn. (exec. sec. 1960-70).

MILLS, JUDITH LANELLE, county official; b. Richland, Wash., Sept. 12, 1949; d. Thomas Francis and Esther Lola (Leavell) Walsh; student Columbia Basin Coll., Pasco, Wash., 1967-68, 74-75; children—Gary William, Tamara Lynn, Rebecca Anne. Police, fire and emergency med. dispatcher City of Richland, 1972-75, 76-77; dep. sheriff, Franklin County Sheriff's Office, 1975-76; dir. Benton County Emergency Dispatch Center, Kennewick, Wash., 1977—; instr. Wash. Tng. Commn.; trustee, chmn. communications Mid-Columbia Emergency Med. Services Council. Mem. Asso. Public Safety Communication Officers (chpt. pres. 1979-81, nat. exec. com. 1981-82), Tri-Cities Mycol. Soc., Am. Mus. Natural History (assoc.), Nat. Assn. Female Execs. Clubs: Altrusa, Finley Saddle. Office: PO Box 6108 Kennewick WA 99336

MILLS, LAWRENCE, lawyer, trucking co. exec.; b. Salt Lake City, Aug. 15, 1932; s. Samuel L. and Beth (Neilson) M.; B.S., U. Utah, 1955, J.D., 1956. Admitted to Utah bar, 1956, U.S. Supreme Ct. bar, 1963; with W.S. Hatch Co. Inc., Woods Cross, Utah, 1947—, gen. mgr., 1963—, v.p., 1970—, also dir.; dir. Nat. Tank Truck Carriers, Inc., Washington, 1963—, pres., 1974-75, chmn. bd., 1975-76; mem. motor carrier adv. com. Utah State Dept. Transp., 1979; keynote speaker Rocky Mountain Safety Supervisors Conf., 1976. Del. to County and State Convs., Utah, 1970-72; v.p. Utah Safety Council, 1979-82, pres.-elect, 1982, pres., 1983; mem. Utah Gov's Adv. Com. on Small Bus. Recipient Safety Dir. award Nat. Tank Carriers Co., 1967, Trophy award W.S. Hatch Co., 1975. Mem. Salt Lake County Bar Assn., Utah Motor Transport Assn. (dir. 1967—, pres. 1974-76), Utah Hwy. Users Assn. (dir. 1981—), Indsl. Relations Council (dir. 1974—), Salt Lake City C. of C., U.S. Jaycees (life Senator 1969—, ambassador 1977—, pres. Utah Senate 1979-80), Silver Tank Club. Club: Ambassador Athletic (Salt Lake City). Contbr. articles to legal publs. Home: 77 Edgecombe Dr Salt Lake City UT 84103 Office: 643 S 800 West Woods Cross UT 84087

MILLS, PAUL CHADBOURNE, museum ofcl.; b. Seattle, Sept. 24, 1924; s. Reed C. and Lillian (Hoey) M.; student Reed Coll., 1945-48; B.A., U. Wash., 1953, M.A., U. Calif., 1961; Ph.D. (hon.), Calif. Coll. Arts and Crafts, 1971; m. Janet L. Dowd, Apr. 30, 1955; children—Katherine, Megan, Michael. Reporter, Bellevue (Wash.) Am., 1948-51; asst. curator Henry Gallery, U. Wash., Seattle, 1952-53; curator art Oakland (Calif.) Mus., 1953-70; dir. Santa Barbara (Calif.) Mus. Art, 1970-82; v.p. Western Mus. Conf., 1956, 59. Served with Signal Corps, AUS, 1942-45. Ford Found. fellow, 1960-61; Spanish-U.S. Cultural Exchange grantee, 1977, 79. Mem. Western Assn. Art Mus. (v.p. 1956-57, treas. 1971—), Assn. Art Mus. Dirs. (trustee 1972-73, 80, sec. 1973—), N. Am. Vexillogical Assn. Contbr. articles to catalogues, profl. jours. Home: 638 Las Alturas Rd Santa Barbara CA 93103 Office: 1130 State St Santa Barbara CA 93101

MILLS, SHERRY RAE, state arts program administrator, consultant; b. Colorado Springs, Colo., Apr. 3, 1940; d. Ray Edwin and Lorena M. (Ferguson) Gregory; m. Ronald Keith Mills, July 22, 1962; children—Tracy Rae, Darren Keith. B.M.E., U. Colo., 1962; M.Ed., U. Colo.-Colorado Springs, 1979. Cert. tchr., adminstr., Colo. Classroom and gen. music tchr. Harrison Sch. Dist. 2, 1962-66; summer music tchr. Colorado Springs Sch. Dist. 11, 1958-68, spl. edn. music tchr., 1976-81; arts coordinator Colo. State Arts for Handicapped, Colorado Springs, 1981—; pvt. instrumental tchr., 1962-78; music tchr. Rocky Mountain Rehab. Ctr., Colorado Springs, 1971-76; music tchr. Evang. Christian Acad., 1973-76; cons.; workshop presenter. Mem. Pikes Peak Arts Council, Colorado Springs, 1982-83. Title IV grantee, 1980-81, 81-82, 82-83; Found. for Exceptional Children grantee, 1981-82; others. Mem. Music Educators Nat. Conf., Council for Exceptional Children, Am. Assn. Mental Deficiency, Found. for Exceptional Children. Presbyterian. Contbr. articles to ednl. jours. Home: 2220 Glenwood Circle Colorado Springs CO 80909 Office: 1773 S 8th St Suite L 5 Colorado Springs CO 80906

MILLSAPS, ELIZABETH A., public relations executive, educator; b. Los Angeles, May 15, 1948; d. Paul R. Jr. and Kathryn (Griffin) Millsaps. B.A. with honors in Journalism and Polit Sci., U. Wyo., 1970; M.A. with honors in Human Resources Mgmt., U. Redlands, 1979. Press aide to congressmen Washington, 1970-72; adminstrv. asst. White House Personnel Operation, Washington, 1972-73; writer-editor pub. relations dept. NAM, Washington, 1973-75, Pres. Ford Com., Washington, Los Angeles, 1976; account exec. George Wells & Assocs. Pub. Relations, Washington, 1977; exec. asst. div. univ. relations U. Redlands (Calif.), 1977-79, instr. bus. and mgmt., 1979—; dir. pub. relations

Redlands Community Hosp., 1979—; instr. Alfred North Whitehead Ctr., U. Calif., Riverside. Bd. dirs. Inland Empire unit Am. Cancer Soc., 1981—; mem. nominating com. San Gorgonio Council Girl Scouts U.S.A., 1981—; bd. dirs. United Way of Redlands, 1982—; del. to Triennium Conv., Washington, 1982; bd. dirs., pres. YWCA of Redlands, 1981—. Mem. Pub. Relations Soc. Am., Soc. Hosp. Pub. Relations, AAUW (exec. bd. Redlands br.), Redlands C. of C. (chmn. legis. com.), Phi Kappa Pi, Pi Delta Epsilon. Republican. Episcopalian. Office: PO Box 391 Redlands CA 92373

MILOSZ, CZESLAW, poet, author, educator; b. Lithuania, June 30, 1911; came to U.S., 1960, naturalized, 1970; s. Aleksander and Weronika (Kunat) M.; M.Juris, U. Wilno (Lithuania), 1934; Litt.D. (hon.), U. Mich., 1977. Programmer, Polish Nat. Radio, 1935-39; diplomatic service Polish Fgn. Affairs Ministry, Warsaw, 1945-50; vis. lectr. U. Calif., Berkeley, 1960-61, prof. Slavic langs. and lits., 1961-78, prof. emeritus, 1978—; author books: The Captive Mind, 1953, Native Realm, 1968, Post-War Polish Poetry, 1965, The History of Polish Literature, 1969, Selected Poems, 1972, Bells in Winter, 1978; The Witness of Poetry, 1981. Recipient Prix Littéraire Européen, Les Guildes du Livre, Geneva, 1953, Neustadt Internat. prize for lit. U. Okla., 1978; citation U. Calif., Berkeley, 1978; Noble Prize in Literature, 1980; Nat. Culture Fund fellow, 1934-35; Guggenheim fellow, 1976. Mem. Polish Inst. Letters and Scis. in Am., PEN Club in Exile. Office: Dept Slavic Langs and Lits U Calif Berkeley CA 94720*

MILSTEAD, ANDREW HAMMILL, aerospace engineer, flight instructor, b. Statesville, N.C., Mar. 28, 1934; s. Andrew Dallam and Sarah Lee (Kincaid) M.; m. Jennifer Ann Pickering, Feb. 20, 1970 (div.). B.S. in Physics, U. N.C., 1956; M.S. in Physics, Ohio State U., 1957; M.A. in Astronomy, UCLA, 1964, Ph.D. in Engring., 1968. Cert. airline transport pilot, flight instr.; lic. real estate broker, Calif. Aero. research engr. NASA, Langley, Va., 1956; mem. tech. staff Douglas Aircraft Co., Santa Monica, Calif., 1958-59; assoc. engr. Space Tech. Labs., El Segundo, Calif., 1959-60; staff engr. Aerospace Co., El Segundo, Calif., 1960-70; sr. staff engr. Hughes Aircraft Co., El Segundo, 1970-71, sect. head, 1971-78, dept. mgr., 1978-81, sr. scientist, 1981—. Served with USNR, 1974—. Recipient Aerospace Co. doctoral fellowship, 1965-67. Mem. AIAA, U.S. Naval Inst., Naval Res. Assn., Aircraft Owners and Pilots Assn., Santa Monica Airport Assn. Episcopalian. Club: International Elite (Los Angeles). Contbr. articles to profl. jours. Home: 721 25th St Santa Monica CA 90402 Office: 532/C319 PO Box 92919 Los Angeles CA 90009

MILTNER, JOHN ROBERT, university official; b. Conneaut, Ohio, Sept. 6, 1946; s. Robert John and Grace Evelyn (Hall) M.; m. Carol Lee Herd, Oct. 27, 1973; children—William, Kelli, Bryan, Tiffany, Robert. B.S., Bowling Green U., 1968; M.B.A., Pace U., 1981. Cert. fundraising exec. Exploring dir. Boy Scouts Am., Toledo, 1968-72, dir. exploring, N.Y.C., 1975-76, dir. devel., 1977-79, exec. dir. devel. and communications Greater N.Y. councils, 1979-80; mktg. mgr. IBM, Toledo, 1972-73; regional mktg. mgr. Docutel Corp., Boston, 1974; dir. devel. Meml. Sloan-Kettering Cancer Ctr., N.Y.C., 1980-83; vice chancellor U. Calif.-Irvine, 1983—. Bd. dirs. Am. Humanics Found., Pace U., N.Y.C., 1977-83; mem. alumni bd. Bowling Green State U., 1983—. Mem. Nat. Soc. Fund Raising Execs. (cert.; dir. 1977—, v.p. 1979-81, pres. 1981-82, vice chmn. nat. bd. 1982—). Congregationalist. Clubs: Vertical, Princeton (N.Y.C.); Glen Ridge Country; Balboa Bay (Newport Beach, Calif.). Home: 69 Monticello St Irvine CA 92714 Office: 555 Adminstrn Bldg U Calif Irvine CA 92717

MILTON, DAVID SCOTT, writer; b. Pitts., Sept. 15, 1934; s. Si and Gertrude (Osgood) M. Writer plays, novels and screenplays; plays include: The Interrogation Room, 1966; Halloween Mask, 1966; Duet for Solo Voice, 1970; Bread, 1974; Duet, 1975, Skin (Neil Simon Playwrights award), 1980; films include: Born to Win, 1971, novels include: The Quarterback, 1970; Paradise Road (Mark Twain Jour. award), 1974; Kabbalah, 1980; Skyline, 1982; sr. lectr. in drama U. So. Calif.; field faculty advisor grad. program Goddard Coll., Plainfield, Vt. Mem. Writers Guild Am., Dramatists Guild, Authors Guild, Authors League. Home and Office: 1235 24th St Apt 1 Santa Monica CA 90404

MINAMI, ISAMU, farmer; b. Guadalupe, Calif., July 21, 1922; s. Henry Yaemon and Kuni (Yamasaki) M.; student Santa Maria (Calif.) Jr. Coll., 1942; m. Grace Misao Yamamoto, May 6, 1950; children—Sammy Yahe, Susan Kuniye. Engaged in vegetable farming, Guadalupe, 1944—; owner Security Farms, 1944—; past pres., bd. dirs. Santa Barbara County Fair Bd. Bd. dirs. Santa Maria Assn. Retarded, Boys Club Santa Maria Valley; past bd. dirs. bldg. fund Sis Sisters Hosp., Santa Maria; mem. comdr.'s liaison group Vandenburg AFB; bd. regents Santa Clara U.; mem. subcom. Calif. State Bd. Food and Agr.; mem. Santa Maria Valley Water Study Com.; bd. dirs. Marian Hosp. Found.; mem. community adv. com. Valley Community Hosp.; past mem. spl. adv. com. Senator S.I. Hayakawa of Calif. Mem. Nisei Farmers League, United Fresh Fruit Assn., Iceberg Lettuce Research Assn. (dir.), Grower-Shippers Assn. (bd. dirs., past pres.), Western Growers Assn. (dir.), Calif.-Ariz. Growers Assn. (dir.), Calif. Farm Bur. Assn., Calif. C. of C., Santa Barbara County Taxpayers Assn., Santa Maria Valley C. of C. (dir.; Citizen of Year award 1980), Santa Maria Valley Developers (dir.), Friends of Santa Barbara County, Japan Am. Soc. So. Calif., Japanese Am. Citizens League, Santa Maria Valley Farmers Assn. (past pres.). Republican. Buddhist. Clubs: Guadalupe Rotary, 36th Congl., Republican Century, Santa Maria Elks. Office: PO Box 818 Guadalupe CA 93434

MINDELL, EARL LAWRENCE, nutritionist, pharmacist, author; b. St. Boniface, Man., Can., Jan. 20, 1940; s. William and Minerva Sybil (Galsky) M.; came to U.S., 1965, naturalized, 1972; B.S. in Pharmacy, N.D. State U., 1963; Ph.D. in Nutrition, U. Beverly Hills, 1980; m. Gail Andrea Jaffe, May 16, 1971; children—Evan Louis-Ashley, Alanna Dayan. Sec.-treas. Natural Organics Inc., Los Angeles, 1971—; pres. Adanac Mgmt. Inc., 1979—; dir. Santa Monica Thrift and Loan; instr. Dale Carnegie course; lectr. on nutrition, radio and TV. Mem. Beverly Hills, Rancho Park, Western Los Angeles (dir.) regional chambers commerce, Calif., Am. pharm. assns., Am. Acad. Gen. Pharm. Practice, Am. Inst. for History of Pharmacy, Am. Nutrition Soc., Internat. Coll. Applied Nutrition, Nutrition Found., Nat. Health Fedn., Am. Dieticians Assn., Orthomolecular Med. Assn., Internat. Acad. Preventive Medicine. Clubs: City of Hope, Masons, Shriners. Author: Earl Mindell's Vitamin Bible; Earl Mindell's Vitamin Bible for your Kid; Earl Mindell's Quick and Easy Guide to Better Health; Earl Mindell's Pills and You. Contbr. articles on nutrition to profl. jours. Home: 709 N Hillcrest Rd Beverly Hills CA 90210 Office: 2020 Cotner Ave West Los Angeles CA 90025

MINER, BETTY EMERY, home economics educator; b. Buffalo, June 15, 1937; d. Frederick Earl and Lena Josephine (Moore) Emery; m. John Ronald Miner, Aug. 4, 1963; children—Saralena Marie, Katherine Alice, Frederick Gerald. B.S. in Home Econs. Edn., Kans. State U., 1959, M.S. in Foods and Nutrition, 1960. Instr. food and nutrition Cornell U., 1960-62, U. Hawaii, 1962-63; instr. home econs. Highland Park High Sch., Topeka, 1963-64; instr. foods and nutrition Kans. State U., Manhattan, 1964-66, Iowa State U., Ames, 1967-72, Oreg. State U., Corvallis, 1972—. Mem. governing bd. First Presbyn. Ch., Corvallis, 1982—. Mem. Am. Home Econs. Assn., Oreg. Home Econs. Assn., Phi Kappa Phi, Omicron Nu, Alpha Lambda Delta. Clubs: Opera Guild, Gourmet. Contbr. articles to profl. jours. Home: 3131 NW Norwood Pl Corvallis OR 97330 Office: School of Home Economics Oregon State University Corvallis OR 97331

MINER, JOHN MOREY, banker; b. Plainfield, N.J., May 24, 1922; s. Vincent Bernard and Laura Elizabeth (Morey) M.; m. Jeanne Louise Smith, 1947; children—Wendy, Forest; m. 2d, Anne Elaine Merritt, 1954; children—Kent, Kim, Grant. A.B., Princeton U., 1946. With Princeton (N.J.) Bank and Trust, 1946-48; with Fidelity Bank, Phila., 1949-78, v.p. loan adminstrn., 1960-65, exec. v.p. Nat. div., 1965-70, sr. exec. v.p., 1970-73, dir., chmn. credit policy com., 1973-78; sr. v.p., chmn. risk mgmt. com. Crocker Nat. Bank, Los Angeles, 1978—; dir. Atlantic Electric Co., Pleasantville, N.J. Served with U.S. Army, World War II, Korea. Recipient Spl. Corp. Citizenship award Phila. Tribune, 1972; named hon. alumnus U. Mich., 1944. Mem. Robert Morris Assn. Clubs: Union League (Phila.), Univ. (Los Angeles). Office: Crocker Nat Bank 333 S Grand Ave Suite 880 Los Angeles CA 90071

MINER, M(ARY) JANE, coach, school administrator; b. Provo, Utah, Aug. 5, 1949; d. Herbert Kershaw and Thelma (Smith) Miner. B.S., Brigham Young U., 1971; M.Health Edn., 1973. Tchr., coach Hillcrest High Sch., Midvale, Utah, 1971-76; asst. athletic dir., coach basketball Weber State Coll., Ogden, Utah, 1976—, head coach, 1976—; dir. Lady Wildcat Basketball Camps. Named Dist. 6 Coach Yr. Nat. High Sch. Coaches Assn., 1975; Coach Yr. Mountain Div. Intermountain Athletic Conf., 1982. Mem. Women's Basketball Coaches Assn., Nat. Assn. Coll. Dirs. Athletics. Mormon. Office: Weber State Coll Athletics Ogden UT 84408

MINETA, NORMAN Y., congressman; b. San Jose, Calif., Nov. 12, 1931; B.S., U. Calif. at Berkeley; m. May H. Mineta; children—David K., Stuart S. Owner Mineta Ins. Agy., San Jose, 1956—; mem. adv. bd. Bank Calif. 1st Bank (Bank of Tokyo of Calif.), 1961—; mem. San Jose City Council, 1967-71; vice mayor San Jose, 1969-71, mayor, 1971-74; mem. 94th-98th Congresses from 13th Calif. Dist., mem. public works and transp., intelligence, budget coms., dep. whip-at-large Dem. steering and policy com., chmn. task force on credit budget. Chmn. finance com. Santa Clara County Council Chs., 1960-62; commr. San Jose Human Relations Commn., 1962-64, San Jose Housing Authority, 1966—; precinct chmn. Community Theater Bond Issue, 1964; mem. spl. gifts com. Santa Clara County council Boy Scouts Am., 1967; chmn. visitors com. Freer Art Gallery; bd. regents Smithsonian Instn., 1979—. Sec. Santa Clara County Grand Jury, 1964. Bd. dirs. Wesley Found, San Jose State Coll., 1956-58, Pacific Neighbors, Community Council Central Santa Clara County, Japan Soc. San Francisco, Santa Clara County chpt. NCCJ, Mexican-Am. Community Services Agy.; mem. exec. bd. No. Calif.-Western Nev. dist. council Japanese Am. Citizens League, 1960-62, pres. San Jose chpt., 1957-59. Served to lt. U.S. Army, 1954-56. Mem. Greater San Jose C. of C., Nat. Cal., San Jose (dir. 1960-62) assns. ind. ins. agts., North San Jose Optimists Club (charter pres. 1956-58), Jackson-Taylor Bus. and Profl. Assn. (dir. 1963). Methodist (treas. 1962-63). Democrat. Office: 2350 Rayburn House Office Bldg Washington DC 20515*

MINGIONE, ALBERT, info. system cons.; b. Phila., Oct. 23, 1939; s. Michael and Catherine (Horwath) M.; B.A. in Math., San Jose State U., 1969; married; children by previous marriage—Tina Mingione Mangosing, Mark, Elizabeth, Paul, Monique. Computer programmer N. Am. Rockwell Co., Anaheim, Calif., 1962-63; programmer analyst Gen. Dynamics Co., Pomona, Calif., 1963-65; mgmt. info. systems mgr. Dole Co., San Jose, Calif., 1965-67; system dir. Western Ops. Co., San Francisco, 1967-71; pvt. practice info. system cons., San Jose, 1971—; mem. faculty info. sci. dept. Golden Gate U. chmn. Developmentally Disabled Commn. Santa Clara County, 1982—. Served with USAF, 1957-61. Recipient cert. in data processing Data Processing Mgmt. Assn. Mem. Assn. for System Mgmt. (pres. Santa Clara chpt. 1971, chmn. div. 21 1973-75, Outstanding Service award Santa Clara chpt. 1972, Merit award 1974, Achievement award 1977). Democrat. Roman Catholic. Home and Office: 364 Gordon Ave San Jose CA 95127

MINISCE, RICHARD ANTHONY, college dean, management consultant; b. Rochester, N.Y., Sept. 16, 1942; s. Anthony J. and Albertine C. (Elman) M.; m. Louise J. Schliessman, Aug. 14, 1971; children—Heather, Holly, Courtney, Anthony. B.S. in Sociology, St. John Fisher Coll., 1964; M.A. in Sociology, Boston Coll., 1968; postgrad. New Sch. for Social Research, 1969-72, Wash. State U., 1978-79. Asst. to area supr. Bur. Recreation, Rochester, N.Y., 1961-64; instr. sociology Kings Coll., Wilkes Barre, Pa., 1965; asst. prof. St. Lawrence U., Canton, N.Y., 1966-68; prof. Suffolk County Community Coll., Selden, N.Y., 1969-81; dean of instrn. Tillamook Bay Community Coll., Bay City, Oreg., 1981—; pres. RAM Assocs., Mgmt. Services, 1983—; chief of security, policeman, park ranger. reviewer coll. texts; cons. criminologist, sociologist. Chmn. bd. dirs., Tillamook County Vol. Bur. project; fireman, mem budget com. Bay City Vol. Fire Dept.; treas. Clatsop-Tillamook Fire Dept. Adv. Group; sr. warden, vestry St. Albans Ch., Tillamook, Oreg.; chmn. personnel com. Bay City City Council, 1983—. Named Jaycee of Yr. Canton, N.Y., 1966; recipient Kiwanis Ruby K award, 1982. Mem. Oreg. Council Instructional Adminstrs., Nat. Council Community Services and Continuing Edn., Oreg. Assn. Community Edn. Deans and Dirs., Am. Sociol. Assn., Am. Vocat. Assn., Oreg. Assn. Criminal Justice Educators, Am. Assn. Community and Jr. Colls., Nat. Council Local Adminstrs., Oreg. Community Edn. Assn. Club: Tillamook Kiwanis (dir.).

MINNICK, WALTER CLIFFORD, building materials company executive; b. Walla Walla, Wash., Sept. 20, 1942; s. Walter Lawrence and Dorothy (Waldron) M.; B.A., Whitman Coll., 1964; M.B.A., Harvard U., 1966, J.D., 1969; m. Jo Anne Oliver, June 11, 1965; children—Amy Louise, Adam Wade. Admitted to Oreg. and Wash. bars; assoc. firm Davies, Biggs, Strayer, Stoel & Boley, Portland, Oreg., 1969-70; staff asst. Domestic Council, Washington, 1971-72; dep. asst. dir. Office Mgmt. and Budget, Washington 1972-73; with Trus Joist Corp., Boise, Idaho, 1974—, v.p. div. ops., 1976-79, pres., 1979—. Mem. bus. adv. council Boise State U. Sch. Bus.; trustee Boise Futures Found. Served with U.S. Army, 1970-72. Mem. Wash. State Bar Assn., Oreg. State Bar Assn., Idaho Conservation League, Nature Conservancy, Boise Fgn. Affairs Soc., Bogus Basin Recreation Assn. Republican. Unitarian. Office: 9777 Chinden Blvd Boise ID 83702

MINNIEAR, DIANE ROBERTA, advertising executive; b. Long Beach, Calif., Feb. 24, 1941; d. Robert W. and Esther (Beckenstein) Nasworthy; m. Roger W. Minniear, Apr. 10, 1964 (div.). A.A., Long Beach City Coll., 1960; postgrad. Pacific Christian Coll., 1958-59, Minn. Bible Coll., 1961-62, Calif. State U., 1962-64. Sales exec. GTE Directories Corp., Los Alamitos, Calif., 1970-77; Yellow Pages account exec. with various advt. agys., Calif., 1977-78; ind. contractor Nat. Yellow Pages, 1978-79; mgr. nat. Yellow Pages Budget Rent A Car, Western region, 1979-82; dir. Yellow Pages advt. Transamerica Mktg. Services, Los Angeles, 1982—; Yellow Page advt. cons., sales trainer. Named GTE Yellow Pages Sales All Star, 1975. Republican. Office: Transamerica Center 1150 S Olive St Suite 2400 Los Angeles 90015

MINO, PAUL LEWIS, army officer; b. Ellwood City, Pa., Aug. 8, 1931; s. Peter and Mary Susan (Minnocci) M.; m. Loretta Marie Vaccaro, May 29, 1954; children—Tracy, Kathy, Paul, Mary, Lisa. B.S., U. Pitts., 1954; grad. Command and Gen. Staff Coll., Ft. Leavenworth, Kans., 1965. Commd. U.S. Army, 1967; advanced through grades to col., 1976; staff officer logistic plans U.S., Alaska, Germany, Vietnam, 1954-68; dir. logistics, plans and programs Joint staff level Pentagon, Washington, 1968-73; dir. material mgmt. depot and nat. inventory control point, Pueblo, Colo., 1971-76, St. Louis, 1976-79; quartermaster cons. for res. components Denver, 1979—. Mem. Woodmar Homeowners Assn. Decorated Legion of Merit, Bronze Star with oak leaf cluster, Meritorious Service medal with 2 oak leaf clusters, Army Commendation medal with oak leaf cluster. Mem. Quartermaster Assn., Assn. U.S. Army, Ret. Officers Assn. Democrat. Roman Catholic. Club: Fitzsimons Officers. Office: Army Readiness Mblzn Region VIII Fitzsimons Army Med Ctr Aurora CO 80045

MINTZ, RONALD EARL, artist, art conservator; b. Rocky Mount, N.C., Jan. 21, 1926; m. Mildred Tilson, Dec. 18, 1948; children—Richard, Robert. A.B., U. N.C., 1948, M.S., George Washington U., 1964; Ph.D., Jackson State U., 1975. Dep. commr. revenue State of N.C., Greenville, 1950-52; artist, art conservator, Washington, 1956-58, various locations, Tex., Fla., Maine, Wash., Ala., Nebr. and Calif., 1958-74; prin. firm Macropaedia Conservation, conservation hist. and artistic works, Chapel Hill, N.C., 1974-80; exhibited in one man shows, Chapel Hill, 1978, 80, Seattle, 1981, 82; exhibited in group shows, Bellevue, Wash., 1982, New Orleans, 1982-83, Palm Beach, Fla., 1982-83. Helped establish N.C. State Mus. Art, 1949-51. Served to col. USAF, 1951-74. Decorated Legion of Merit, Meritorious Service medal. Developer abstract art form technique of Chromoformism. Address: 14510 SE 167th St Fairwood Greens Renton WA 98055

MINUDRI, REGINA URSULA, librarian, consultant, lecturer; b. San Francisco, May 9, 1937; d. John C. and Molly (Halter) M. B.A., San Francisco Coll. for Women, 1958; M.L.S., U. Calif.-Berkeley, 1959. Reference librarian Menlo Park (Calif.) Pub. Library, 1959-62; regional librarian Santa Clara County (Calif.) Library, 1962-68; project coordinator Fed. Young Adult Library Services Project, Mountain View, Calif., 1968-71; dir. profl. services Alameda County (Calif.) Library, 1971, asst. county librarian, 1972-77; library dir. Berkeley (Calif.) Library, 1977—; lectr. U. San Francisco, 1970-72, U. Calif., Berkeley, 1977-81; cons., 1975—. Mem. ALA (exec. bd. 1980—, council 1979-83, Grolier award 1974), Calif. Library Assn. (pres. 1981, council 1965-69, 79-82), LWV (dir. Berkeley chpt. 1980-81). Author: Getting It Together, A Young Adult Bibliography, 1970; contbr. articles to publs. including School Library Jour., Wilson Library Bulletin. Office: 2090 Kittredge St Berkeley CA 94704

MINZNER, DEAN FREDERICK, aviation company executive; b. Winchester, Mass., July 20, 1945; s. Frederick Louis and Winifred (Hughes) M.; B.A., Franklin and Marshall Coll., 1967; M.B.A., Columbia U., 1972. Dist. exec. Greater N.Y. councils Boy Scouts Am., N.Y.C., 1972-76; sales exec. Coast Avia, Long Beach, Calif., 1976-78, Performance Aircraft, Inc., Hayward, Calif., 1978; owner, pres. Western Aviation Consultants, Inc., Hayward, 1978-82, Cal-Pacific Enterprises, Hayward, 1982—. Mem. Assn. M.B.A. Execs., Columbia U. Grad. Sch. Bus. Alumni Assn., Aircraft Owners and Pilots Assn. Office: PO Box 6206 Hayward CA 94540

MIRACLE, BRIAN FLOYD, psychologist; b. Casper, Wyo., June 9, 1933; s. Evert Arnold and Ann Alice (Nelson) M.; B.A., U. Wyo., 1959, M.A., 1964, Ed.D., 1965; m. Nancy; children—Robert Lowell, Jennifer Janet. Pvt. practice psychology, Lander, Wyo., 1965—; chmn. Wyo. State Parole Bd., Rawlins, 1971-78; dir., chmn. Copper Mountain Energy Co., Lander, 1978—; dir., treas. Orthomolecular Inc., 1981—; dir. Yellowstone State Bank, Lander, Wyo. Trustee U. Wyo., 1978—. Served with U.S. Army, 1950-52. Decorated Purple Heart. Mem. Am. Psychol. Assn., Wyo. Psychol. Assn., Wyo. Peace Officers Assn. Republican. Episcopalian. Clubs: Elks, Rotary, Masons, Shriners. Author: (with Carl Delacato) Neurological Organization and Reading, 1966. Home: 1290 S 2d St Lander WY 82520 Office: 925 Washakie St Lander WY 82520

MIRACLE, ROBERT WARREN, banker; b. Casper, Wyo.; m. Maggie; children—Mark, John. B.S. in Law, U. Wyo., 1951; diploma Pacific Coast Banking Sch., 1960. Bookkeeper Wyo. Nat. Bank, Casper, 1954-56, asst. trust officer, 1956-61, asst. v.p., trust officer, 1961-65, v.p., trust officer, 1965-66, sr. v.p., dir., 1966-67, exec. v.p., 1967-68, pres., chief exec. officer, 1968-83, vice chmn. bd., chief exec. officer, 1983—; pres., chief exec. officer, dir. Affiliated Bank Corp., Wyo., 1970—; dir. Wyo. Nat. Bank Gillette, 1974—; dir. Wyo. Nat. Bank East Casper, First Nat. Bank and Trust Co. Wyo., Cheyenne, Wyo. Bank Rawlins, Wyo. Nat. Bank Kemmerer; dir. Investment in Casper, pres. 1967-70. Bd. dirs. United Fund Natrona County, 1963-65, campaign co-chmn., 1973-78; trustee Colo. Sch. Banking, 1974—; trustee Myra Fox Skelton Found., 1963—; trustee Casper Coll. Found., 1967—, pres. 1973-75; trustee U. Wyo. Found., 1972—; chmn. Casper Downtown Improvement Assn., 1974-75; bd. dirs. Central Wyo. Fair Bd., 1974-79, pres. 1977-78; mem. exec. council Central Wyo. Boy Scouts Am. Served to capt. USMC, 1951-53. Recipient James C. Scarboro Meml. award Colo. Sch. Banking, U. Colo., 1977; Disting. Service in Bus. award U. Wyo. Coll. Commerce and Industry, 1980. Mem. Wyo. Bankers Assn. (pres. 1974-75), Am. Bankers Assn. (payment policy com. 1978, 79, governing council 1974-75), Am. Bankers Assn. (payment policy com. 1978, 79, governing council 1974-75, 81-83), Mountain States Employers Council (dir. 1979—), Rocky Mountain Oil and Gas Assn., Am. Mgmt. Assn. Casper C. of C. (pres. 1965-66, disting. service award 1981), VFW, Newcomen Soc. N.Am. Clubs: Casper Petroleum, Casper Country, Masons, Casper Mountain Lions (pres. 1960-61). Office: Affiliated Bank Corp PO Box 2799 Casper WY 82601

MIRIKITANI, CARL KUNIO, lawyer; b. Honolulu, Jan. 16, 1948; s. Carl Mamoru and Hisa (Yoshimura) M.; A.B. magna cum laude, Oberlin Coll., 1969; J.D., U. Chgo., 1972; 1 son by previous marriage, Carl Kunio II. Bar: Hawaii 1972. Law clk. to justice Supreme Ct. Hawaii, 1972; assoc. Goodsill, Anderson & Quinn, Honolulu, 1972-77; ptnr. Goodsill, Anderson, Quinn & Stifel, 1977—. Chmn. rules com. Republican Party Hawaii, 1974-77, 2d state vice chmn., 1974-77, state chmn., 1977-79; mem. Nat. Rep. Com., 1977-79; del. Rep. Nat. Conv., 1976; bd. dirs. Hawaii affiliate Am. Diabetes Assn. Mem. ABA, Hawaii Bar Assn., Order of Coif, Phi Beta Kappa. Office: 1600 Castle and Cooke Bldg Financial Plaza of the Pacific Honolulu HI 96813

MISA, KENNETH FRANKLIN, management consultant; b. Jamaica, N.Y., Sept. 24, 1939; s. Frank J. and Mary M. (Soszka) M.; B.S. cum laude in Psychology, Fairfield U., 1961; M.S., Purdue U., 1963; Ph.D. in Psychology (Fellow 1963-66), St. John's U., 1966. Staff psychologist Rohrer, Hibler & Replogle, Los Angeles, 1966-67; asso. A. T. Kearney, Inc., Los Angeles, 1968-71, sr. asso., 1972-74, prin., 1975-78, v.p., partner, 1979—. Cert. mgmt. cons.; lic. psychologist, Calif. Mem. Am. Psychol. Assn., Calif. Psychol. Assn., Los Angeles County Psychol. Assn., Am. Soc. for Tng. and Devel., Acad. of Mgmt., Indsl. Relations Research Assn. Internat. Assn. Applied Psychology, Mchts. & Mfrs. Assn., World Affairs Council of Los Angeles, Town Hall of So. Calif., Los Angeles C. of C. Clubs: Jonathan, Rancho Las Palmas Country. Home: 330 Kempton Rd Glendale CA 91202 Office: One Wilshire Bldg Suite 2501 Los Angeles CA 90017

MISAGHI, IRAJ JONATHAN, plant pathologist; b. Neireez, Iran, May 22, 1938; came to U.S., 1964, naturalized, 1974; s. Jalal and Rooha (Ahdieh) M.; M.S., Pahlavi U., Shiraz, Iran, 1964; Ph.D., U. Calif., Davis, 1969; m. Patricia Anne Taylor, Sept. 8, 1968; 1 son, Mark Christopher. Research asst. dept. plant pathology U. Calif.-Davis,

1965-69, asst. research plant pathologist, 1970-72; research asso. dept. plant pathology U. Ariz., Tucson, 1972-73; research plant pathologist U. Calif.-Davis, 1974-78, asst. prof. plant pathology, 1978-83, assoc. prof., 1983—; U.S. Dept. Agr. grantee, 1978, 1979, 1980. Iceberg Lettuce Research Adv. Bd. grantee, 1978—. Mem. Am. Phytopath. Soc., Sigma Xi. Baha'i. Author text in plant disease physiology; contbr. phytopath. articles to profl. jours. Office: Dept Plant Pathology U Ariz Tucson AZ 85721

MISCHLER, JANET KATHRYN, nursing educator; b. Boston, Sept. 30, 1939; d. Frederick Joseph and Eileen A. M. R.N., Boston City Hosp., 1960; B.S. in Nursing, Boston U., 1969; M.S., U. Calif.-San Francisco, 1970; Ed.D., U. So. Calif., 1982. Lic. R.N., Calif., Mass., Alaska; vocat. trade and tech. teaching in nursing edn. (life), Calif.; community coll. adminstr. and instr. (life), Calif. Staff nurse Boston City Hosp., 1960-64, instr. Sch. Practical Nursing, 1966-67; sr. staff nurse Boston U. Med. Ctr., 1964-66; instr. Solano Coll., Suisun City, Calif., 1971-82; asst. prof. nursing, coordinator U. Alaska, Anchorage, 1982—, also mem. adminstrv. council, curriculum com. Co-chmn. disaster preparedness com. Vallejo-Multi-Hosp., 1972-76; trustee, chmn. pub. edn. Solano-Napa County br. Am. Heart Assn., 1974-76; mem. Solano County Emergency Med. Care Com., 1973-76; mem., sec., exec. com. Anchorage Area Emergency Mgmt. Adv. Com.; mem. trauma com. Providence Hosp., 1982; mem. disaster preparedness and nursing com. Anchorage chpt. ARC, 1982—; mem. ASPCA, Humane Soc. U.S., Wild Canid Survival and Research Ctr., Sierra Club, Anchorage Fine Arts Mus. Assn., N.Am. Wildlife Park Found., Internat. Sled Dog Racing Assn., Alaska Sled Dog Racing Assn., Chugiak Dog Mushers; mem., vol. Iditarod Trail Com., Gray Panthers. Middlesex County (Mass.) Women's Med. Assn. scholar, 1957-58; Allstate scholar, 1967; HEW trainee, 1968, 69-70; U. So. Calif. scholar, summers 1978, 80, 81. Mem. Alaska Nurses Assn., Nat. League Nursing, Western Gerontol. Soc., Western Council Higher Edn., Western Soc. Research in Nursing, Phi Delta Kappa, Sigma Theta Tau. Home: PO Box 223 Chugiak AK 99567 Office: Univ Alaska Anchorage 3211 Providence Dr Anchorage AK 99508

MISCZYNSKI, DEAN JOHN, economist; b. Chgo., Aug. 29, 1946; s. George J. and Josephine M. (Kobas) M.; m. Marilyn A. Misczynski, June 22, 1968. B.A., Stanford U. 1968, M.A. 1970, also postgrad. Research economist U. Calif., 1972-76; sr. economist Calif. Gov.'s Office Planning and Research, 1976-78, dir. policy and planning 1978—. Served to capt. USAR 1970-76. Mem. Am. Econs. Assn., Phi Beta Kappa. Contbr. articles to profl. jours. Home: 1241 Perkins Way Sacramento CA 95818 Office: 1410 10th St Sacramento CA 95814

MISHKA, JOHN CHARLES, data processor, alcohol counselor; b. Ettlingen, Baden, W.Ger., Oct. 6, 1949; s. Frank Charles and Klara Amalie (Mozer) M. Student, Monterey (Calif.) Pub. Schs., U.S. Army Adj. Gen.'s Sch. Coin cons. and security expert, 1979-82; asst. mgr. info. systems orgn., Pacific Tel. & Tel., Hayward, Calif., 1982—; alcohol behavioral cons. Mem. Citizens for Better Environ. Served with U.S. Army, 1968-70. Recipient Incentive award Pacific Telephone Co., 1982. Mem. Comprehensive Care Corp. (life), Internat. Planetary Soc., Internat. Assn. Turtles. Democrat. Lutheran. Clubs: Eagles, Castro Country (San Francisco) Author: Planning Your Home Computer Purchase, 1982. Home: 124 Humboldt Rd Brisbane CA 94005

MISHRA, INDU B., research scientist; b. Kujahala, India, Feb. 10, 1938; s. Baikunthanath Mishra and Kausalya Misra; M.S., Utkal U. (India), 1959; Ph.D., U. So. Calif., 1971; m. Kanan K. Misra, Feb. 9, 1964; children—Trinayana, Jharana, Seema. Translator, Oriya Ency., 1958-59; lectr. in chemistry Ravenshaw Coll., Cuttack, India, 1959-64, 66, S.C.S. Coll., Puri, India, 1964-65; teaching asst. and research asst., lectr., postdoctoral fellow U. So. Calif., Los Angeles, 1966-72; prof. collaborator, U. Brasilia (Brazil), 1972-75; vis. asst. prof. S.D. Sch. Mines and Tech., Rapid City, 1976; NRC sr. research fellow Air Force Rocket Propulsion Lab., Edwards AFB, Calif., 1976-77; sr. research scientist, Talley Industries Ariz., Mesa, 1977—; cons. in field; OAS vis. prof. U. Wis., Madison, 1974. Served to lt. Nat. Cadet Corps, India, 1962-65. Recipient Air Force Rocket Propulsion Lab. award, 1977. Mem. Am. Chem. Soc., AAAS, Combustion Inst., Sigma Xi, Alpha Chi Sigma. Clubs: India of Phoenix (bd. dirs.), U. So. Calif. Alumni (Phoenix). Author: Practical Chemistry for Pre University, 1961; contbr. articles to profl. publs. Home: 4 High Forest Dr Carbondale IL 62901 Office: 4551 McKellips Rd Box 849 Mesa AZ 85201

MISKIMEN, JOHN ANDREW, financial cons.; b. Phoenix, Aug. 12, 1932; s. Carl W. and Violette (Phillips) M.; A.B., Harvard U., 1954; M.B.A., Golden Gate U., 1967; m. Marilyn J. Howard, Aug. 30, 1952; children—Debra L., John Andrew, Anne K. Dir. research Irving Lundborg & Co., San Francisco, 1959-65; sr. analyst Mitchum, Jones & Templeton, Inc., San Francisco, 1965-67; v.p. William Hutchinson & Co., Inc., San Francisco, 1967-72; v.p., treas. Manalytics, Inc., San Francisco, 1977-78; sr. v.p. Kelso & Co. Inc., 1978-81; pres. Corp. Procedures, Inc., 1981—. Mem. city council, San Rafael, Calif., 1967-83, Planning Commn., 1964-67. Bd. dirs. Bay Area Air Pollution Control Dist., 1968-70. Served to 1st lt. arty. AUS, 1954-56. Republican. Episcopalian. Home: 24 Dominican Dr San Rafael CA 94901 Office: PO Box 1201 San Rafael CA 94915

MITCHAM, PATRICIA HAMILTON, educator; b. El Paso, Tex., Sept. 8, 1942; d. Leverett Chandler and Annabelle (Cunningham) Hamilton; B.A., Tex. Western Coll., 1964; m. Eugene L. Mitcham III, Apr. 19, 1968; children—Shirley Dianne, Steven Craig. Teaching asst. U. Tex., El Paso, 1965-67; instr. English, Hardin Simmons U., Abilene, Tex., 1967-68; tchr. El Paso (Tex.) public schs., 1968-70, 75-79; vol. supr. Army Community Service, Fort Bliss, Tex., 1971-74; tchr. Bret Harte Sch., Los Angeles, 1979-81, Washington High Sch., Los Angeles, 1981—. Mem. Assn. for Supervision and Curriculum Devel., Assn. Calif. Sch. Adminstrs. Episcopalian. Home: 6082 Hardwick Circle Huntington Beach CA 92647 Office: 10860 S Denker St Los Angeles CA 90047

MITCHELL, ANN DENMAN, genetic toxicology research director, consultant, educator; b. Nashville, Oct. 29, 1939; d. Clarence Phillips and Annie Mary (Sprouse) Denman; m. Earl Eugene Mitchell, Feb. 28, 1969; 1 son, Benjamin Ephraim. B.A. in Biology, U. Tex.-Austin, 1960, Ph.D. in Zoology, 1971. Tchr. biology and chemistry, Fort Worth and Austin, 1961-66; research assoc. pathology Stanford U. Sch. Medicine, 1970-72, NIH fellow devel. biology, 1972-73; cell biologist and biochem. cytogenetics program mgr. SRI Internat., Menlo Park, Calif., 1973-79, dir. dept. cellular and genetic toxicology, 1979—; NSF fellow 1965, 1959; recipient gen. dynamics excellence in teaching award 1963. Mem. AAAS, Am. Soc. Cell Biology, Am. Soc. Testing and Materials, Assn. Women Sci., Environ. Mutagen Soc. (treas. 1977-80, 80-83), Genetic and Environ. Toxicology Assn., Genetic Toxicology Assn., Genetics Soc. Am., Soc. Risk Analysis, Tissue Culture Assn. Contbr. articles to sci. publs. Home: 10718 Nathanson Ave Cupertino CA 95014 Office: SRI Internat 333 Ravenswood Ave Menlo Park CA 94025

MITCHELL, BEVERLY ANNE, lab. asst.; b. Altus, Okla., May 26, 1946; d. Clarence Willard and Velma Ruth (Dorsey) Garrison; Cert. lab. asst. St. Anthony's Hosp., 1965; student Tex. Tech. U., 1968, Ariz. Western Coll., 1981—; m. Donald M. Mitchell, Aug. 19, 1966; children—Robin Page, Valerie Ruth. Lab. technician St. Anthony's Hosp., Amarillo, Tex., 1965-66, West Tex. Hosp., 1966-69, Riley Hosp., Meridian, Miss., 1970, Med. Arts Clinic, Lab., Lubbock, Tex., 1973-74; sec./receptionist Frontier Realty, Yuma, Ariz., 1980; lab. technician Younglove Lab., Yuma, 1980-81. Mem. Am. Soc. Clin. Pathologists, Beta Sigma Phi, Phi Theta Kappa. Democrat. Baptist. Clubs: Marine Officers Wives, Marine Air Weapons and Tactics Squadron-1 Officers Wives. Address: 1758 Camino Cerro Yuma AZ 85364

MITCHELL, ETHEL RENART, interior designer; b. College Point, N.Y., April 29, 1914; d. Matthias Peter and Florence Charlotte (Ghetti Renart; m. William Ralph Mitchell, June 9, 1934; children—Renart, Suzanne, Florence. Student in studio design John Morris Curtis, N.J., 1939, also Katharine Gibbs, N.Y.C.; pvt. study in Europe, Orient. Sec., designer Goebel Decorators, Phoenix, 1950-51, Coles Home Furnishings, Phoenix, 1951-56; interior designer Casa Decor, Phoenix, 1956-58, Lou Regester, Phoenix, 1958-63, interior designer Mehagian's, Phoenix, 1963—; host TV shows on interior design, 1954-56. Mem. Scottsdale Girls Club Aux. Mem. Phoenix Art Museum, Am. Soc. Interior Designers. Republican. Episcopalian. Home: 6262 E Avalon Scottsdale AZ 85251 Office: Mehagians 825 N Central Phoenix AZ 85253

MITCHELL, GARY DAVID, psychologist, primatologist, educator; b. Keene, N.H., May 4, 1940; s. John David and Pauline Leila (Parker) M.; children—Jody Lynn, Lisa Deanna, Gary David Jr. B.A., U.N.H., Durhan, 1958-63; M.A., U. Wis.-Madison, 1965, Ph.D., 1966. Mem. faculty dept. psychology, U. Calif.-Davis, 1967—, prof., 1975—. Recipient Eldon L. Johnson Creativity award U. N.H., 1962; Woodrow Wilson fellow, 1963. Mem. Am. Psychol. Assn., Am. Soc. Primatologists, Internat. Primatological Soc. Author: Behavioral Sex Differences in Nonhuman Primates, 1979; Human Sex Differences, 1981.

MITCHELL, GERALD ALEXANDER, JR., oral surgeon; b. Atlanta, Oct. 23, 1928; s. Gerald Alexander and Willa Maye (McCutchen) M.; D.D.S, Emory U., 1954; m. Rebecca Sue Boyle, May 3, 1980. Practice dentistry, Glendale, Calif., 1956-64; resident oral surgery Los Angeles County-U. So. Calif. Med. Center, Los Angeles, 1964-67; fellow anesthesiology White Meml. Med. Center, Los Angeles, 1967-68; practice oral surgery, Dana Point, Calif., 1968-69, Santa Maria, Calif., 1969—; mem. staffs U. So. Calif. Sch. Dentistry, Los Angeles County-U. So. Calif. Med. Center, Glendale Adventist Hosp., Valley Community Hosp., Marian Hosp., Lompoc Hosp. Dist., Santa Ynez Valley Hosp.; fellow gen. anesthesia Am. Dental Soc. of Anesthesiology; cons. oral surgery Vandenberg AFB, Lompoc, Calif., Fed. Correctional Instn., Lompoc. Served to maj. USAF, 1954-56. Fellow Am. Assn. Oral and Maxillofacial Surgeons; mem. No. Calif. Soc. Oral and Maxillofacial Surgeons, Western Soc. Oral and Maxillofacial Surgeons, Central Coast Dental Soc. (sec.-treas. 1980-81), Am., Calif. dental assns. Marsh Robinson Acad. Oral Surgeons. Contbr. sci. articles to profl. jours. Home: 121 E Tunnell St Santa Maria CA 93454 Office: 1414 S Miller St Suite 3 Santa Maria CA 93454

MITCHELL, JAMES GEORGE, computer scientist; b. Kitchener, Ont., Can., Apr. 25, 1943; s. James Irving and Adele Mary (Hahn) M.; m. Judith Ann Wainwright, Jan. 14, 1979; children—Laura Eden, Paul Kenneth, Scott Wainwright. Programmer, Berkeley Computer Corp. (Calif.). 1970-71; research fellow Xerox Research Cntr., Palo Alto, Calif., 1971—. Mem. Assn. Computing Machinery, Brit. Computer Soc., IEEE. Author: Interactive Programming Systems, 1979. Office: 3333 Coyote Hill Rd Palo Alto CA 94304

MITCHELL, JANET GWENDOLYN, communications company manager; b. N.Y.C., June 14, 1949; d. Roosevelt and Rosetta (Askew) Broughton; student Hartwick Coll., 1967-71, Calif. State U., 1978-79. Grad. intern Amdahl, Sunnyvale, Calif., 1978-79; tech. skills tng. instr. Siltec, Menlo Park, Calif., 1979-80, corp. employee devel. and tng. mgr., 1980, corp. communications mgr., 1980-82; mgmt. cons., 1982-83; N.W. region tng. and devel. mgr. MCI Communications, San Francisco, 1983—. Vol. probation officer, Colorado Springs, 1975. Served with U.S. Army, 1971-78. Decorated Meritorious Service medal. Mem. Am. Soc. Tng. and Devel., Internat. Assn. Bus. Communicators. Club: Colorado Springs Ski (v.p. 1975-76). Home: 1026 Trellis Ln Alameda CA 94501 Office: 340 Market St San Francisco CA 94126

MITCHELL, JOAN BEARD, sales executive; b. Chgo., Sept. 13, 1932; d. Donald Redwood and Margaret (Toombs) Beard; m. Michael Eugene Mitchell, Sept. 13, 1953; children—Michael Thomas, Donald Gregory, Nicole Margaret. B.A. in English, Calif. State U.-Fullerton, 1979; A.A., DePaul U., 1952. Pub. relations DePaul U., Chgo., 1962-64, LeMoyne Coll., Syracuse, N.Y., 1968-71; coordinator pub. relations Conklin, Labs and Bebe, Syracuse, 1972; placement assoc./art instr. Folk Art Gallery, Syracuse U., 1973-75; coordinator project equity Calif. State U.-Fullerton, 1977-78; dir. Joana Bus. Enterprises and v.p. Cyonic Systems, Inc., 1978—; art tutor, freelance writer, nutritional sales, computer sales. Facilities dir. Salt City Playhouse, Syracuse, 1972-73. Mem. AAUW, Nat. Assn. Female Execs., Beta Sigma Phi, Alpha Kappa Alpha, Mu Epsilon, Iota Nu Omega. Contbr. poetry to various pubs.; art exhibited at Folk Art Gallery, Syracuse, Psynetics, Anaheim, Calif.

MITCHELL, JOSEPH NATHAN, insurance company executive; b. Winnipeg, Man., Can., Oct. 10, 1922; came to U.S., 1931, naturalized, 1936; s. Edward D. and Anna (Copp) M.; m. Beverly Edna Henigson, Oct. 27, 1946; children—Jonathan Edward, Jan Ellen, Karin Helene. Student UCLA, 1940-42. With Beneficial Standard Life Ins. Co., Los Angeles, 1946—, dir., 1946—, now pres.; chmn. exec. com. Transit Casualty Co.; dir. Fidelity Interstate Life Ins. Co., Beneficial Assurance Co., Glacier Nat. Life Assurance Co., Vancouver, B.C., Can., Beneficial Standard Mortgage Co., Beneficial Standard Properties, Inc.; v.p. and treas. Jackson-Mitchell Pharms., Inc., Santa Barbara, Calif., Calif. Fed. Savs. and Loan Assn., Pacific Lighting Corp.; mem. internat. bd. dirs. Ampal-Am. Israel Corp., N.Y.. Mem. adv. bd., exec. bd. dirs. Los Angeles Area council Boy Scouts Am.; mem. exec. com. Performing Arts Council Music Center, vice chmn., bd. govs., 1980-81, chmn. Campaign 1981 Unified Fund; past bd. dirs. Jewish Fedn. Council of Greater Los Angeles; past exec. com., past v.p., gen. chmn. United Jewish Welfare Fund, 1962; past v.p., bd. trustees Jewish Community Found.; mem. adv. bd., past chmn. investment com.; vice chmn., bd. dirs., mem. exec. com., audit com., bldg. com., chmn. investment com. and exec. personnel com. Cedars-Sinai Med. Ctr.; gen. campaign chmn., past mem. exec. com., cabinet State of Israel Bonds; mem. Mayor's Ad Hoc Com. on Housing, 1980; mem. Dist. Atty.'s Adv. Council; bd. dirs. Los Angeles Safety Council; mem. exec. com. Invest-in-Am.; mem. Los Angeles 200 Com. (bicentennial), 1980-81, 100 Club; mem. Los Angeles Citizens' Olympic Adv. Commn.; past officer United Jewish Appeal; bd. dirs. United Way, mem. exec. com., gen. campaign chmn., 1972; past bd. dirs. exec. com. Am. Jewish Joint Distbn. Com. Served with AUS, 1942-46; ETO. Mem. World Bus. Council, Am. Technion Soc. (past nat. v.p., gov.), NCCJ (presiding chmn. 1975, co-chmn. 1976, dir.), Israel C. of C. (dir. western states), Los Angeles Area C. of C. (chmn. bd. dirs. 1980, pres. 1979). Clubs: Hillcrest Country (dir., treas. 1966-72), Los Angeles; Palm Springs (Calif.) Tennis, Tamarisk Country; Regency. Office: 3700 Wilshire Blvd Los Angeles CA 90010

MITCHELL, JOSEPH PATRICK, architect; b. Bellingham, Wash., Sept. 29, 1939; s. Joseph Henry and Jessie Delila (Smith) M.; student Western Wash. State Coll., 1957-59; B.A., U. Wash., 1963, B.Arch., 1965; m. Marilyn Ruth Jorgenson, June 23, 1962; children—Amy Evangeline, Kirk Patrick, Scott Henry. Asso. designer, draftsman, project architect Beckwith Spangler Davis, Bellevue, Wash., 1965-70; prin. J. Patrick Mitchell, AIA & Assos./Architects/Planners/Cons., Kirkland, Wash., 1970—. Chmn. long range planning com. Lake Retreat Camp, 1965—; bldg. chmn. Northshore Baptist Ch., 1980—; mem. bd. extension and central com. Columbia Baptist Conf., 1977—. Cert. Nat. Council Archtl. Registration Bds. Mem. AIA, Constrn. Specification Inst., Interfaith Forum Religion, Art and Architecture, Christian Camping Internat., Woodinville C. of C. Republican. Office: 12620 120th Ave NE Suite 208 Kirkland WA 98033

MITCHELL, JUDITH MARIE, research associate, counselor; b. Los Angeles, Oct. 1, 1950; d. Glen H. and Carla Jane (Builderback) Taylor; m. Paul Francis Mitchell, Dec. 29, 1970 (div.); 1 dau., Jennifer Ann. B.A., Calif. State U.-Northridge, 1976, M.A., 1980; postgrad. UCLA, 1980—. Research and data mgmt. asst. County Office Alcohol Abuse, Los Angeles, 1977-78; vocat. youth counselor, statis. reporter Seventh Step Found., Los Angeles, 1978-79; rehab. counselor San Fernando (Calif.) Valley Assn. for Retarded, 1979-80; vocat. counselor, V.A. Hosp., Sepulveda, Calif., 1980-81; research assoc. UCLA Sch. Medicine, Brentwood VA Hosp., Los Angeles, 1981—. Mabel W. Richards Assn. fellow, 1974-77; Calif. State U.-Northridge fellow, 1974-76; U. Women's Club fellow, 1978; UCLA fellow, 1981-83. Mem. Am. Personnel and Guidance Assn., Am. Psychol. Assn. Home: PO Box 5064 Mission Hills CA 91345 Office: Brentwood VA Hosp 10300 Wilshire Blvd Los Angeles CA 90073

MITCHELL, LYNDA KATHLEEN, education educator; b. Albuquerque, Feb. 27, 1954; d. Finis Aubrey and Helen Elizabeth (Curnutt) M. B.A. cum laude, UCLA, 1975; M.A., Calif. State U.-Northridge; Ph.D., Stanford U., 1980. Teaching research asst. Calif. State U., Northridge, 1975-77; home intervention therapist Ctr. on Child Abuse Olive View Med. Ctr., Sylmar, Calif., 1976-77; child mgmt. cons. North Los Angeles Regional Ctr., 1976-77; counselor Stanford (Calif.) U. Counseling Inst., 1977-78; teaching aresearch asst. Stanford U., 1977-80; prof. sch. edn. Calif. State U., Los Angeles, 1980—. Recipient Calif. State U. Robert V. Rainey award, 1977; Canfield scholar, 1977-80. Mem. Am. Psychol. Assn., Am. Ednl. Research Assn., Am. Personnel and Guidance Assn., Stanford Profl. Women's Assn. (Los Angeles chpt.). Contbr. articles to profl. jours. Office: Dept Counselor Edn Calif State U Los Angeles CA 90032

MITCHELL, MICHAEL JOSEPH, JR., business exec.; b. Washington, May 24, 1939; s. Michael J. and Ruth (Alexander) M.; student Everett Jr. Coll., 1960-62. Electronic tech. Boeing Co., Seattle, 1959-62, engrng. aide, 1962-64; owner-pres. The Mitchell Co. (U.S.) Ltd., Seattle, 1964-81; partner-v.p. Northwest Avionics Co., Renton, Wash., 1964-66; pres. M.J. Mitchell & Assos., Seattle, 1972-81, The Mitchell Co. (Internat.) Ltd., 1973-81, First Internat. Bus. & Fin. Mgmt. Corp., 1977—, First Internat. Pub. Corp., 1979—, First Internat. Fin. Services, Corp., 1980—, Securintel, Ltd., 1981—, First Internat. Corp., 1982—. Served with USNR, 1957-59. Mem. Seattle Fire Buffs Soc., Am. Mgmt. Assn. Democrat. Elk. Home: 2803 8th Ave W Seattle WA 98119 Office: 231 Summit Ave E Seattle WA 98102

MITCHELL, PATRICIA ANN, education educator; b. Washington, Sept. 17, 1946; d. James Garnell and Ruth Estella (Harper) Turner; m. Larry Wayne Mitchell, June 19, 1977; 1 dau., Candyce. B.S. in Edn., Morgan State Coll., 1968; M.S. in Edn. (fellow), So. Ill. U., 1970; Ph.D. (fellow), Cath. U. Am., 1978. Cert. pub. sch., jr. coll. tchr., Calif., Md. Tchr. 1st grade Prince George's County (Md.) Pub. Schs., 1968, reading specialist, 1970-77; instr. U. San Francisco, 1977-78, asst. prof. edn., 1978—. Mem. NAACP, Nat. Urban League. Mem. Am. Ednl. Research Assn., Nat. Assn. Female Execs., Internat. Reading Assn., Calif. Women in Higher Edn. Assn., Coll. Reading Assn., Alpha Kappa Alpha. Democrat. Methodist. Office: Sch Edn U San Francisco 2130 Fulton St San Francisco CA 94117

MITCHELL, RANDALL LEE, hospital foundation executive, public relations consultant; b. Elizabethtown, Ky., July 13, 1920; s. Troy Miller and Ava Elizabeth (Randall) M.; m. Carolyn Leslie, Sept. 6, 1952; children—John Leslie, Susan Lee, Jeffrey Alan, Lisa Kay. B.S., U. Ky., 1942; B. Journalism, U. Mo., 1947. Commd. 2 Lt. U.S. Marine Corps, 1942, advanced through grades to maj., 1952; occupation duty, North China, 1945, Japan and Korea, 1954-55; stationed hdqrs., Washington, 1951-53; pub. affairs officer, Camp Pendleton, Calif., 1960-63; ret. 1963; v.p. Tri-City Savs. & Loan, Oceanside, Calif., 1963-64; pres., owner Mitchell & Assocs., Oceanside, Calif., 1964—; pub. relations dir. Tri-City Hosp. Dist., Oceanside, 1976-82; exec. dir. Tri-City Hosp. Found., Oceanside, 1982—; lectr. San Diego State U.; cons. in pub. relations. Chmn., Mobile Homes Fair Practices Commn., Oceanside, 1980-81, Heritage Park Adv. Com., 1977-79; vice chmn. Oceanside Bicentennial Com., 1972-76. Decorated Purple Heart; recipient Citizen of Yr. award Oceanside C. of C. and The Blade Tribune, 1982. Mem. Pub. relations Soc. Am. (accredited), Nat. Assn. Hosp. Devel., Am. Soc. Hosp. Pub. Relations, Alpha Delta Sigma. Republican. Clubs: Oceanside Rotary (past pres.), Masons. Home: 161 Parnassus Circle Oceanside CA 92054 Office: Tri-City Hosp Found 4002 Vista Way Oceanside CA 92056

MITCHELL, REGENA L., educational administrator, organization development consultant; b. Plain City, Ohio, Dec. 8, 1948; d. William Marlow and Edna Mae (Phillips) Mitchell; m. Philip Gates, Nov. 28, 1981. B.S. in Mgmt. Sci. summa cum laude, U. New Haven, 1977; M.S. in Organizational Behavior, U. Hartford, 1979; postgrad. in mgmt. and orgn. theory Claremont Grad. Sch., 1979—; student Bowling Green State U., 1966-68. Asst. br. mgr. Huntington Nat. Bank, Columbus, Ohio, 1968-73; adminstrv. asst. to nat. product mgr. U.S. Elec. Motors, Milford, Conn., 1974-75; jr. cons. R.K. Stevens, Inc., Fairfield, Conn., 1977; lectr. U. New Haven, West Haven, Conn., 1977-79; dir. M.B.A. placement and recruiting Claremont Grad. Sch. (Calif.), 1981-83, assoc. dir. bus. adminstrn., 1983—; external cons. Kaiser Permanente Med Care Program, Los Angeles, 1981—. Recipient Returning Woman award U. New Haven, 1977; Grad. Profl. Opportunities Program fellow, 1979-82. Mem. Orgn. Devel. Network, Internat. Registry Orgn. Devel. Profls., Nat. Assn. Female Execs., Am. Soc. Tng. and Devel., Alpha Chi. Office: 10th and Dartmouth St Claremont CA 91711

MITCHELL, RIE ROGERS, psychologist, educator; b. Tucson, Feb. 1, 1940; d. Martin Smith and LaVaun (Peterson) Rogers; B.S., U. Utah, 1962, M.S., 1963; M.A., U. Calif., Los Angeles, 1969, Ph.D., 1969; m. Rex Mitchell, Mar. 16, 1961; 1 son, Scott Rogers. Tchr., Coronado (Calif.) Unified Sch. Dist., 1964-65; sch. psychologist Glendale (Calif.) Unified Sch. Dist., 1968-70; psychologist Glendale Guidance Clinic, 1970-77; prof. ednl. psychology Calif. State U., Northridge, 1970—, chmn. dept., 1976-80, acting exec. asst. to pres., 1981-82; adminstrv. fellow Calif. State U., Dominquez Hills, 1978-79; cons. psychology various sch. dists., Calif. Named U. Utah Woman of Year, 1962; licensed psychologist, Calif. Mem. Am. Psychol. Assn., Calif. Assn. Counselor Educators and Suprs. (dir. 1976-78), Western Assn. Counselor Educators and Suprs. (pres. 1980-81), Assn. Counselor Educators and Supervisors (treas. 1983-86), U. Calif. Los Angeles Doctoral Alumni

Assn. (pres. 1974-76) Pi Lambda Theta (chpt. pres. 1970-71, nat. resolutions chmn. 1971-73), Psi Chi, Mu Phi Epsilon, Pi Sigma Alpha. Contbr. articles to profl. jours. Editor UCLA Educator, 1971. Home: 22945 Paul Revere Dr Calabasas CA 91302 Office: Monterey Hall Calif State U 18111 Nordhoff St Northridge CA 91330

MITCHELL, TERENCE ROBERT, psychologist, educator; b. Chgo., Jan. 13, 1942; s. James Matlock and Mary Margaret (Hill) M.; m. Sandra Kathryn, June 14, 1970; children—Amanda, Colleen. B.A., Duke U., 1964; grad. diploma in public adminstrn. U. Exeter (Eng.), 1965; M.A. U. Ill.-Urbana, 1967, Ph.D. in Psychology, 1969. Asst. prof. mgmt. and orgn. and psychology U. Wash., 1969-72, assoc. prof., 1972-77, prof., 1977—. Named Burlington No. Scholar of Yr., 1982; Office Naval Research grantee, 1972-79; NSF grantee, 1979-82; Army Research Inst. grantee, 1979-83. Fellow Am. Psychol. Assn.; mem. Acad. Mgmt., Soc. Organizational Behavior. Author books, including: (with others) Organization Theory, 1980; People in Organizations, 1982, contbr. numerous articles to profl. publs. Home: 2514 Magnolia Blvd West Seattle WA 98199 Office: Dept Mgmt DJ-10 U Wash Seattle WA 98195

MITCHELL, TONY FRANK, fire chief; b. Tacoma, Jan. 16, 1930; s. Tony and Rose (Carino) M.; student public schs.; m. Patricia Keller, Nov. 7, 1953; children—Michael, Janyce, Linda. Firefighter, Tacoma Fire Dept., 1955-64, fire lt., 1964-66, fire capt., 1966-73, dep. chief, 1973-76, fire chief, 1976—. Served with U.S. Army, 1951-53. Mem. Wash. State Firefighters Assn., Pierce County Fire Chiefs Assn., Wash. State Fire Chiefs Assn., Internat. Assn. Fire Chiefs, Nat. Fire Protection Assn. Roman Catholic. Club: Day Island Yacht. Office: 901 Fawcett St Tacoma WA 98402

MITCHELL, WAYNE LEE, educator, social worker; b. Rapid City, S.D., Mar. 25, 1937; s. Albert C. and Elizabeth Isabelle (Nagel) M.; B.A., U. Redlands (Calif.), 1959; M.S.W., Ariz. State U., 1970, Ed.D., 1979. Profl. social worker various county, state, and fed. agencies, 1962-70, Bur. Indian Affairs, Phoenix, 1970-77, USPHS, 1977-79; asst. prof. Ariz. State U., 1979—. Bd. dirs. Phoenix Indian Community Sch., 1973-75; bd. dirs. Phoenix Indian Center, 1974—, Community Service award, 1977; mem. Phoenix Area Health Adv. Bd., 1975; mem. Community Behavioral Mental Health Bd., 1976-80; lectr. in field. Served with USCG, 1960-62. Recipient Community Service award Ariz. Temple of Islam, 1980. Mem. Nat. Congress Am. Indians, UN Assn., Nat. Assn. Social Workers, Am. Orthopsychiat. Assn., NAACP, Internat. Platform Assn., Asia Soc., U.S.-China Assn., Kappa Delta Pi, Phi Delta Kappa, Chi Sigma Chi. Congregationalist. Democrat. Contbr. articles to publs. Home: PO Box 61 Phoenix AZ 85001 Office: West Hall Ariz State U Tempe AZ 85281

MITCHELSON, MICEALA ANN, business executive; b. Rock Springs, Wyo., Sept. 16, 1938; d. Adolph and Minnie Maude (Webster) Sitzman; m. Dwayne Joseph Mitchelson, July 7, 1957; children—Rick, Dan, Lalene. Student Barnes Bus. Coll., 1956-57, Western Wyo. Coll., 1966-67. Ptnr., Mitch's Cafe, Service & Sitzman Motel, Farson, Wyo., 1972—. Clk. Bd. Edn. Dist. #1, Sweetwater County (Wyo.), 1980-83. Republican. Roman Catholic. Club: Farson-Eden Progress. Home and Office: PO Box 25 Farson WY 82932

MIX, CONNIE LEE JACOBSEN BROWER, dental hygienist, consultant; b. Audubon, Iowa, Nov. 6, 1948; d. Richard Eugene and Edna Arnvig (Faaborg) Jacobsen; m. Lowell Alan Brower, Sept. 6, 1969 (dec. Oct. 1970); m. 2d, J. Steven Mix, Apr. 2, 1978; children—Chad Jacob, Jonathan Jacob. Grad. Shoreline Dental Hygiene Sch., 1970. Registered dental hygienist, Wash. Clin. hygienist various dentists, 1970-77; hygienist dental health program Federal Way (Wash.) Sch. Dist., Wash., 1973-74; dental health cons. Wash. State Health Dept., 1977—. Mem. Downs Syndrome Congress, Oak Park, Ill., 1978. Recipient cert. outstanding service Federal Way Sch. Dist., 1974; cert. of appreciation Benton Franklin County Dental Soc., 1981. Mem. Health Edn. Alliance, Wash. Pub. Health Assn., Wash. Dental Hygiene Component. Lutheran. Contbr. articles to mags. and profl. jours. Office: Dental Health Services Mailstop LP-16 Olympia WA 98504

MIX, SHIRLEY V., banker; b. Des Moines, Nov. 27, 1934; d. Lauren Xenophen and Evelyn Marguerite (Jordan) Smith; m. Gale Lee Mix II, Aug. 13, 1967 (div.); children—Sheri Scott, Tracy Foster, Michelle Schierman. Student Boise Jr. Coll., San Jose State U., U. Idaho. Artist, advt. dir. Mercantile Stores, Inc., Boise, Idaho, 1962-65; staff writer, editor Idaho Statesman Newspapers, Boise, 1965-67; publs. editor, dir. public relations Hawaii Employers Council, Honolulu, 1968-70; staffer Lewiston (Idaho) Morning Tribune, part-time 1970-72; freelance writer Idaho Statesman, Northwest Experience Mag., Daily Idahonian, The Spokesman Rev., 1970-72; co-owner, advt. and graphics exec. Western Home Ctr., Moscow, Idaho, 1972-74; owner, Ad 1 Advt. and Public Relations, Moscow, 1974-80; public affairs officer, asst. v.p. First Security Bank Idaho, Boise, 1979—. Former mem. Moscow City Personnel Adv. Com.; chmn. Idaho Republican Conv. Moscow, 1976; mayoral candidate, Moscow, 1973; bd. dirs. Moscow Recycling Ctr.; mem. Idaho Com. for Internat. Women's Yr.; pres. Gritman Hosp. Aux., Moscow; bd. dirs. Idaho Park Found.; mem. funding drive com. YMCA; mem. Mayor's Blue Ribbon Task Force on Clean Air. Mem. Nat. Assn. Bank Advocates, Am. Inst. Banking, Idaho Press Women (past pres.), Idaho Assn. Commerce and Industry, Boise C. of C., Idaho Advt. Fedn. Recipient awards Idaho Press Women, Nat. Fedn. Press Women, 1st place direct mail award Idaho Advt. Fedn., 1978. Club: Womens Ltd., Plantation Country. Home: 3553 E 52d Ln Boise ID 83703 Office: PO Box 7069 Boise ID 83730

MIX, THOMAS NORTON, engineering representative; b. Cobleskills, N.Y., Nov. 17, 1945; s. Charles Sholtes and Margaret (Norton) M.; m. Margaret Deborah Rhoades, Feb. 13, 1971; 1 dau., Meghan Elizabeth; B.S.M.E., Rochester (N.Y.) Inst. Tech., 1968. Engr., U.S. Navy, Indian Head, Md., 1968-72; power plant engr. United Airlines, San Francisco, 1972-79; United Airlines resident rep., Boeing Co., Seattle, 1979—. Mem. AIAA, Soc. Automotive Engrs. Office: United Airlines care Boeing Box 3707 Seattle WA 98104

MIXON, ROSALIE WARD, social work cons.; b. Maysville, Mo., Feb. 17, 1908; d. Luther Thomas and Mary (Bray) Ward; A.B., Park Coll., 1929; postgrad. (Univ. scholar 1929-30, 32-35), U. Chgo., 1929-34; M.S.W., U. So. Calif., 1944; postgrad. UCLA, 1965; U. Calif., 1970; U. Calif., San Diego, 1975-76; m. John Lewis Mixon, Dec. 20, 1929; children—Rosemary Mixon Snow, John Lindley, David Lewis, Robert Nelson. Dir. med. social service Children's Meml. Hosp., Chgo., 1951-52; researcher in religious demography, 1952-58; instr. social work La Verne (Calif.) Coll., 1958-59; with Calif. Dept. Mental Hygiene, San Bernardino and Pomona, 1959-66, 69-74; Fulbright lectr., cons. psychiat. and med. social work Med. Sch., Pahlavi U., Shiraz, Iran, 1966-67; lectr. Sch. Social Work, Teheran, Iran, 1966-67; social researcher Meth. Bd. World Missions, Lima, Peru, 1968-69; pvt. practice psychiat. social work cons., Redlands, Calif., 1974—; vis. prof. social work Alaska Pacific U., Anchorage, 1978-79. Active Chgo. Community Fund Adv. Com., 1951, Claremont Community Services Com., 1960-75, Redlands A.B.L.E. Com., 1975—. Lic. clin. social worker, Calif. Mem. Nat. Assn. Social Workers, Nat. Acad. Cert. Social Workers, Register Clin. Social Workers, Soc. for Internat. Devel. Club: Browser's Book. Author: The Methodist Churches of Arizona, 1966; The Barriadas of Lima, Peru, 1969; contbr. chpt. to Choice and Change, 1966.

MIYAHIRA, RICHARD SUNAO, city administrator, architectural engineer; b. Kapaa, Kauai, Hawaii, May 11, 1937; s. Matsu and Kana (Ikehara) M.; m. Evelyn C. Ishii, Aug. 8, 1959; children—Sharon Lynne Sachiko, Valerie Ann. B.S. in Architecture, Calif. Poly. Inst., 1963; M.P.A., U. So. Calif., 1973. Cert. profl. code adminstr. Design engr. City of Orange (Calif.), 1964-70; asst. dir. bldg. and safety City of Oxnard (Calif.), 1970-73, adminstr. bldg. and safety, 1973—; instr. politics and adminstr. La Verne U.; mem. adv. com. Ventura Coll. Mem. city staff adv. com. City of Oxnard, 1973-78, mem. city community devel. com. 1979—. Mem. Internat. Conf. Bldg. Ofcls. (pres. local chpt. 1977), Calif. Bldg. Ofcls. (chmn. coms. 1975, 76, exec. dir. 1976-77, sec. 1978, pres. 1981), Calif. League Cities (adminstrn. services com. 1978-80), Nat. Acad. Code Adminstrn. (dir.), Local Govt. Mgr.'s Assn. (dir.), Phi Kappa Phi. Home: 721 Lawnwood Oxnard CA 93030

MIYASATO, JACK SADAO, archtl. engr.; b. Motobu, Okinawa, Aug. 14, 1947; s. Raymond Shigematsu and Nobuko (Teruya) M.; came to U.S., 1955, naturalized, 1969; B.S., U. Hawaii, 1972, M.B.A., 1977; Ph.D., Sophia U., 1979; grad. U.S. Army Command and Gen. Staff Coll., 1980. Pres., Jack Miyasato & Assos., Inc., Architects, Engrs., Planners, Honolulu, 1980—. Sec. Cherry Blossom Festival, 1974; mem. mayoral campaign com., 1974. Served with U.S. Army, 1969-72; Vietnam; maj. Res. Decorated Bronze Star medal, Army Commendation medal. Mem. Soc. Am. Mil. Engrs., Japanese Jr. C. of C., Res. Officers Assn. Democrat. Buddhist. Home: 717 Ahukini St Honolulu HI 96825 Office: 1225 Young St Honolulu HI 96814

MIZUGUCHI, NORMAN, businessman, state senator; b. Hilo, Hawaii, May 26, 1939; married, 1 child. B.S., Springfield Coll.; M.A., Mich. State U.; Ph.D., U. Utah. Tchr.; pres. Hawaiian Emporium, Inc.; clk. edn. com. Hawaii Senate, later sr. legis. analyst; mem. Hawaii Ho. of Reps., 1974-78, chmn. edn. com., 1976-78; mem. Hawaii Senate, 1978—, chmn. transp. com., majority floor leader. Chmn. Hawaii Democratic Platform Com.; sec. Pearl City Makule Softball League; dir. Washiawa Gen. Hosp. Mem. Navy League U.S. Office: 98-1007 Kahapili St Aiea HI 96701*

MLYNEK, JUDITH KENDALL, mfg. co. exec.; b. Duluth, Minn., Mar. 30, 1938; d. Gustav Adolf and Marjorie Mildred (Kendall) Nordin; B.S. in Mgmt., Pepperdine U., Los Angeles, 1979; m. Ken Lindley; 1 dau., Judith Kendall Lindley; children by previous marriage—Marjorie Dawn, Marie Heather. Teller, U.S. Nat. Bank, Pasadena, Calif., 1965-67; sr. acctg. clk., then asso. adminstr. Xerox Corp., Pasadena, 1967-78, fin. adminstr., 1979-80, sr. fin. adminstr., 1981—; income tax cons., 1975—. Mem. Arcadia Presbyn. Ch. Mem. Nat. Mgmt. Assn., Exec. Female, Career Guild. Clubs: Singles with Purpose, Xerox Ski. Home: 300 Leda Ln Arcadia CA 91006 Office: 300 N Halstead Ave Pasadena CA 91107

MO, SUCHOON, psychologist, educator; b. Nagoya, Japan, Apr. 19, 1932; s. Chihyun and Shinha (Shin) M.; Ph.D., U. Pa., 1968; m. Mary Madeline Lang, Aug. 13, 1958; m. 2d, Judith Carol Oslick, Dec. 26, 1970; children—Blaise, Bernard, Sage, Daisy, Clifton. Asst. prof. psychology U. Detroit, 1967-73; prof. psychology U. So. Colo., Pueblo, 1973—; cons. VA Med. Center, Ft. Lyon, Colo. Bd. dirs. Pueblo West (Colo.) Met. Dist. Mem. AAAS, Am. Psychol. Assn., Internat. Soc. Study of Time, Psychonomic Soc., Sigma Xi. Republican. Contbr. articles to profl. jours. Home: 1158 S Yerba Santa Dr Pueblo West CO 81007 Office: U So Colo Pueblo CO 81001

MOBERLY, DAVID LINDSEY, found. exec.; b. Irvine, Ky., Apr. 25, 1929; s. Earl and Blanche F. (Finney) M.; A.B. in Econs., U. Ky., 1951, M.A., 1953; Ph.D., Kent State U., 1965; m. Peggy C. Compton, Dec. 30, 1951; children—Kent, Lynn. Tchr. high sch. social studies Jefferson County Schs., Louisville, 1951-54, dean of boys, 1954-55, asst. prin., 1955-57, supt. and high sch. prin. Newbury (Ohio) Bd. Edn., 1965-66; tchr. edn. adv. AID, Tripoli and Benghazi, Libya, 1957-61, ednl. program officer, Nairobi, Kenya, 1961-62; instr. Kent (Ohio) State U., 1962-65, instr. (part-time), summer, 1972; supt. Tallmadge (Ohio) Bd. Edn., 1966-67, Warren (Ohio) city schs., 1967-71, University Heights city sch. dist., Cleveland Heights, Ohio, 1971-74, Evanston (Ill.) Twp. high sch. dist., 1974-76, Seattle sch. dist., 1976-81; pres. Seattle Found., 1981—; guest speaker numerous community churches, clubs and orgns.; numerous guest appearances on TV talk shows; U.S. del. to World Orgn. of Teaching Profession, Rome, Italy, 1958; spl. participant ABC-TV documentary on problems in edn., 1976. Mem. nat. adv. bd. Corp. for Public Broadcasting; trustee Pacific Sci. Center Found., 1976, Seattle council Boy Scouts Am., 1976—. Mem. Large City Supts. Assn., Am. Assn. Sch. Adminstrs. (resolutions com. 1971), Phi Delta Kappa, Kappa Delta Pi. Methodist. Club: Rotary. Contbr. articles to profl. publs. Home: 3045 44th Ave W Seattle WA 98199 Office: 1411 4th Ave Bldg Seattle WA 98101

MOBERLY, LINDEN EMERY, educational administrator; b. Laramie, Wyo., Jan. 4, 1923; s. Linden E. and Ruth (Gathercole) M.; B.S., Coll. Emporia, 1952; M.S., Kans. State Tchrs. Coll., 1954; m. Viola F. Mosher, Apr. 29, 1949. Tchr. sci., Florence, Kans., 1952-54, Concordia, Kans., 1954-56, Grand Junction, Colo., 1957-60; asst. prin. Orchard Mesa Jr. High Sch., Grand Junction, 1960-66, prin., 1967—. Served to sgt. USMC, 1941-46. Recipient Outstanding Secondary Prin. award Colo. Assn. Sch. Execs., 1978. Mem. NEA, Nat. Assn. Secondary Prins. (dir. 1979-83), Colo. Edn. Assn. (dir. 1968-71), Colo. North Central Assn. Colls. and Secondary Schs., Colo. Assn. Secondary Sch. Prins. (dir. 1974-77). Club: Lions.

MOCK, CAROL LYNN, education educator, administrative analyst; b. San Diego, Nov. 14, 1952; d. Stanley C. and Joan F. (Ward) Mock; m. Peter A. Meyer, June 5, 1977. B.A., U. Calif.-Santa Barbara, 1975; M.A., U. Calif.-Berkeley, 1977, Ph.D., 1983. Adminstrv. analyst U. Calif. Systemwide Adminstrn., Berkeley, 1976-78; teaching asst. U. Calif.-Berkeley, 1977-79, teaching assoc., 1981; acting asst. prof. higher edn. UCLA, 1982—; chairperson Assoc. Students U. Calif.-Santa Barbara, 1975, mem. Chancellor's Acad. Plan and Budget Rev. Com., 1974-75, Pres.'s Adv. Com. on Instructional Improvement Programs, 1974-76; mem. Pres.'s Task Force on Affirmative Action Issues in Univ. Coop. Ext., U. Calif.-Berkeley, 1979. Trustee Norton Simon Mus. Art, 1976-77. Regents' Scholar; fellow, 1975-77; Gayley fellow, Danforth fellow, 1979-81; recipient Thomas M. Storke award for excellence U. Calif.-Santa Barbara, 1975; Disting. Achievement award U. Calif.-Santa Barbara Alumni Assn., 1976. Mem. Am. Polit. Sci. Assn., Assn. Study Higher Edn., Sierra Club, Nature Conservancy, Phi Beta Kappa. First bd. regents U. Calif.-Santa Barbara, 1975-76. Office: UCLA Grad Sch Edn 405 Hilgard Ave Los Angeles CA 90024

MOCK, DAVID CLINTON, JR., physician, educator; b. Redlands, Calif., May 6, 1922; s. David Clinton and Eithel (Benson) M.; A.B., U. So. Calif., 1944; M.D., M.H.D., Hahnemann Med. Coll., 1948; m. Marcella Enriqueta Fellin, Nov. 13, 1952. Intern Hahnemann Hosp., Phila., 1948-49; resident San Mateo County Hosp., San Mateo, Calif., 1949-51, 54, VA Hosp., Oklahoma City, 1954-55; research fellow exptl. therapeutics U. Okla. Sch. Medicine, Oklahoma City, 1956-57, L.N. Upjohn fellow, 1958, dir. exptl. therapeutics unit, 1959-62, assoc. prof. medicine, 1963-72, prof., 1972—, assoc. dean med. student affairs, 1970-76, assoc. dean postdoctoral edn., 1976-82, dir. continuing med. edn., 1980—, dir. history of medicine program, 1982—. Assoc. mem. Faculty of Homeopathy, Royal London Homeopathic Hosp., Eng. Pres. Coachella Valley Fruit Co., Inc., Indio, Calif., partner Village Date Gardens Co., Coachella, Calif. Surgeon USPHS Res.; active duty, 1951-53, 81, now med. dir. Res. Fellow ACP; mem. Am. Fedn. Clin. Research, AMA, N.Y. Acad. Scis., Assn. Med. Coll. Dirs. Continuing Med. Edn., So. Med. Assn. Home: 325 8th St Coronado CA 92118 Office: 940 Stanton Young Blvd Oklahoma City OK 73104

MOCKLER, JAMES DAVID, association executive; b. Lander, Wyo., Mar. 9, 1939; s. Frank and Esther (Heyne) M.; m. Colleen Williams, June 21, 1962; children—Richard W., Lana. B.S., U. Wyo., 1961. Co-owner/operator Cattle Ranch, Dubois, Wyo., 1961-67; real estate broker, Basin, Wyo., 1968-76; exec. dir. Mont. Coal Council, Helena, 1976—. State rep. Big Horn County, Wyo., 1973-76; chmn. Joint Rev. Com., 1975-76. Mem. Am. Mining Congress, Western States Mining Council (chmn.), Western Environ. Trade Assn. (dir. 1981), Bur. Land Mgmt. (adv. council 1983). Roman Catholic. Clubs: Elks, Montana. Home: 230 S Roberts St Helena MT 59601 Office: 2301 Colonial Dr Helena MT 59601

MODIC, RICHARD VALENTINE, engineer, b. Johnstown, Pa., Feb. 14, 1937; s. Rudy and Ann Marie (Popovich) M.; m. Dolores Sophia Otolinsky, children—Dianne, Christopher, Richard Jr., Blaise. B.S., Ohio U., 1962; postgrad. Squadron Officers Sch., 1969, Command and Staff Coll., 1972-73, Air War Coll., Indsl. Coll. Armed Forces, 1975, No. Colo. U., 1977-79. Commd. 2d lt. U.S. Air Force, 1962; advanced through grades to lt. col., 1979; ret. 1981; engring. mgr. Pacific Tel. and Tel. Co., Sacramento, 1981—. Decorated DFC, Bronze Star, Air medal with 5 oak leaf clusters, Viet Nam Service medal, Vietnam Cross of Gallentry. Mem. USAF Navigator Assn. Democrat. Roman Catholic. Club: Optimist (Rancho Cordova, Calif.). Contbr. articles to U.S. Air Force publs. Home: 9591 Appalachian Dr Sacramento CA 95827

MODISETTE, BILLY RAY, behavioral scientist, research institute executive; b. Norphlet, Ark., Feb. 16, 1930; s. Clayton Stokes and Lillie Mae (Ware) M.; B.S., La. State U., 1951; B.A., U. Tex., 1955; M.S., Purdue U., 1958; postgrad. La. Poly. Inst., 1949, U. Colo., 1954. With System Devel. Corp., Santa Monica, Calif., 1958-70; sr. human factors analyst, behavioral scientist Am. Justice Inst., Marina del Rey, Calif., 1970-74; prin. scientist Angeles Research Co., Inglewood, Calif., 1974-75; sr. assoc., dir. Planning Analysis and Research Inst., Santa Monica, 1975-82, v.p., 1982—, project mgr. System Devel. Corp., Santa Monica, 1977—; former cons. Advanced Research Projects Agy., Office Sec. Def., Bell Telephone Labs., Italian Air Ministry, Criminal Justice Planning Inst., U. So. Calif., Am. Justice Inst., System Devel. Corp., Calif. Dept. Econ. Devel. Served to 1st Lt. USAF, 1951-53. Mem. Am. Acad. Polit. and Social Sci., Western Psychol. Assn., ACLU, Am. Justice Inst., Nat. Geog. Soc., Common Cause, Smithsonian Assos., Sierra Club, Nat. Audubon Soc., Human Factors Soc., Fortune Soc., World Future Soc., Phi Eta Sigma, Delta Sigma Pi, Kappa Alpha. Home: 837 Third St Santa Monica CA 90403 Office: 2500 Colorado Ave Santa Monica CA 90406

MOE, ANDREW IRVING, veterinarian; b. Tacoma, Jan. 2, 1927; s. Ole Andrew and Ingeborg (Gordham) M.; B.S. in Biology, U. Puget Sound, 1949; B.A., Wash. State U., 1953, D.V.M. 1954; m. Dorothy Clara Decker, June 25, 1950; children—Sylvia Moe McGowan, Pamela Moe Barker, Joyce. Meat cutter Art Hansen, Tacoma, 1943-48; gen. practice as veterinarian Baronti Vet. Hosp., Eugene, Oreg., 1956-57; veterinarian, regulatory Calif. Bur. Animal Health-Calif. Dept. Food and Agr. Resident veterinarian II, Modesto, Calif., 1957-64, acting veterinarian-in-charge Modesto Dist. Office (veterinarian III), 1976-77. Watersafety instr. ARC, 1958-61. Served from 1st lt. to capt., Vet. Corps., 1954-56, 62; comdr. 417th Med. Service Flight Res. (AFRES), 1963-66, 71-73; lt. col. Biomed. Scis. Corps USAF, ret., 1982. Recipient Chief Veterinarian badge, 1975. Mem. Am., Calif., No. San Joaquin (pres. 1979) vet. med. assns., Calif. Acad. Vet. Medicine (charter), Res. Officers Assn. (life), Assn. Mil. Surgeons U.S., U.S. Animal Health Assn., Sons of Norway, Theta Chi. Alpha Psi. Lutheran (del. 102d Synod 1961). Club: Masons (Illustrious Master Modesto council 1983, Allied Masonic Degrees). Home: 161 Norwegian Ave Modesto CA 95350 Office: 1800 Coffee Rd Suite L82 Modesto CA 95355

MOE, DOUGLAS EDWIN, professional basketball coach; b. Bklyn., Sept. 21, 1938. Student U. N.C. Player, Padua, Italy, Italian Basketball League, 1965-67, New Orleans, Am. Basketball Assn., 1967-68, Oakland, 1968-69, Caolina Cougars, 1969-70, Va. Squires, 1970-72; coach San Antonio Spurs, Nat. Basketball Assn., 1976-80, Denver Nuggets, 1980—. Mem. Am. Basketball Assn. All-Star Team, 1968-70, Am. Basketball Assn. Championship Team, 1969. Office: Denver Nuggets McNichols Sports Arena 1635 Clay St Denver CO 60204*

MOE, STEPHEN S., electronic and computer company executive; b. Eugene, Oreg., June 18, 1942; s. Siguald B. and Kay B. (Byrne) M.; Student U. Oreg., 1960-62, So. Oreg. Coll., 1962-63, Lane Community Coll., 1973-75. With Inter City Constrn. Co., Eugene, 1960-73, v.p., 1966-73; owner, operator Stephen Moe Co. (became Inter City Electronics, Inc. 1980), 1969-80; pres. Inter City Electronics, Inc., Springfield, Oreg., 1980—. Mem. Lane County Met. Area Planning Adv. Com.; bd. dirs. Glenwood Community Orgn.; mem. Glenwood Water Dist. Budget Com., Willamatic Park Dist. Budget Com.; chmn. Springfield Schs. Electronic Studies Adv. Com. Mem. Assoc. Gen. Contractors, Springfield C. of C., Eugene C. of C. Patentee portable traffic control system. Office: PO Box 595 Springfield OR 97477

MOE, WILLIAM MAX, air force officer; b. Alexandria, La., May 9, 1943; s. Max Eugene and Elizabeth Sharon (Light) M.; B.A., U. Ariz., 1966, M.A., 1967; postgrad. La. State U., 1974-76; m. Constance Kay Kloos, Jan. 10, 1970; children—Travis William, Jessica Lee. Commd. maj. USAF, 1979; squadron pilot, Vietnam, 1968-69, Travis AFB, Calif., 1970-72; instr., asst. prof. psychology USAF Acad., Colo., 1972-74; chief customer assistance sect. Lowry AFB (Colo.) Personnel Office, 1976-77, chief social actions program, 1977-79; chief social actions program Osan Air Base, Korea, 1979-80; chief program support div. Air Res. Personnel Center, Lowry AFB, Colo., 1980-81, chief tng. evaluation div., 1981-82, squadron comdr. 3462d Sch. Squadron, 1982; Chief Tng. Devel. and Resources br. Inter-Service Nuclear Weapons Sch., Kirtland AFB, N.Mex., 1982—. Attendee Aurora (Colo.) Action Com. for Social Services, 1977-78. Served with U.S. Army, 1961. Decorated D.F.C., Air medal with 5 oak leaf clusters, Meritorious Service medal with two oak leaf clusters, Air Force Commendation medal; U. Ariz. honors scholar, 1965-66, NDEA fellow, 1966. Fellow Inter-Univ. Seminar on Armed Forces and Soc.; mem. Air Force Assn., U. Ariz. Alumni Assn., Sigma Nu, Phi Theta Kappa. Republican. Home: 13020 Calle de Sandias NE Albuquerque NM 87111 also 227 Elm Grove Hazelwood MO 63042 Office: Kirtland AFB NM 87117

MOESER, ELLIOTT LYLE, educational administrator; b. Milw., Nov. 9, 1946; s. Lyle M. and Marion J. (Knutson) M.; m. Susan Joan Rhodes, Aug. 15, 1970; children—Aaron Paul, Matthew Edward, Adam Elias. B.S., Midland Lutheran Coll., 1969; M.A., U. Wis.-River Falls, 1972; specialist cert. U. Wis.-Milw., 1977; postgrad. U. Minn., 1977—. Cert. sch. supr., Idaho. Social studies tchr. South Milwaukee (Wis.) Jr. High Sch., 1969-72, asst. prin., 1972-74; prin. Webster Stanley Middle

Sch., Oshkosh, Wis., 1974-77; supt. schs. Somerset (Wis.) Pub. Schs., 1977-80, Blackfoot Sch. Dist. #55, Idaho, 1980—. Mem. Idaho Adv. Com. Indian Edn.; mem. planning com. Gov.'s Conf. Children and Youth, 1981. Pres., bd. dirs. Friends of Channel 10; mem. Idaho State Hist. Soc., Am. Cancer Soc. Recipient Dutch Uncle award Big Bros. and Sisters Fox River Valley, 1965. Mem. Am. Assn. Sch. Adminstrs., Idaho Assn. Sch. Adminstrs., Greater Blackfoot Area C. of C. (dir.), Assn. Supervision and Curriculum Devel., Phi Delta Kappa. Lutheran. Clubs: Blackfoot Rotary, Kiwanis (dir.). Contbr. articles to profl. jours. Home: Route 4 Box 14 Blackfoot ID 83221 Office: Blackfoot School Dist #55 440 W Judicial Blackfoot ID 83221

MOFFETT, BEN L., public relations official, free-lance writer; b. San Antonio, N.Mex., Sept. 7, 1939; s. John B. and Regina Leona (Staneart) M.; children—Bret, Pamela Moffett Thorp, Mark. B.A. in Journalism, U. N.Mex., 1966, M.A. in Speech Communication, 1975. With Albuquerque Jour., 1960-73, state editor, 1965-66, sports editor, 1966-73; asst. to regional dir. pub. affairs S.W. regional office Nat. Park Service, U.S. Dept. Interior, Santa Fe, 1973—; free-lance writer on environment, out-of-doors. Served with U.S. Army, 1961-63. Named Sports Writer of Yr., N.Mex. chpt. Nat. Sports Writers and Sportscasters Assn., 1972; Fed. Employee of Yr., N.Mex.-Albuquerque-Santa Fe Fed. Exec. Bd., 1977; recipient El Conquistador award N.Mex. chpt. Pub. Relations Soc. Am., 1978. Mem. Pub. Relations Soc. Am. (accredited), Rocky Mountain Outdoor Writers, N.Mex. Outdoor Writers (past pres.), Sigma Delta Chi. Contbr. articles on nat. parks to Readers Digest, others. Home: 2821 Camino Principe Santa Fe NM 87501 Office: Pub Affairs Nat Park Service PO Box 728 Santa Fe NM 87501

MOFFETT, FRANK CARDWELL, architect, civil engr.; b. Houston, Dec. 9, 1931; s. Ferrell Orlando and Jewell Bernice (Williams) M.; B.Arch., U. Tex., 1958; m. Annie Doris Thorn, Aug. 1, 1952 (div.); children—David Cardwell (dec.), Douglas Howard. Architect with archtl. firms, Seattle, Harmon, Pray & Detrich, Arnold G. Gangnes, Ralf E. Decker, Roland Terry & Assos., 1958-64; partner Heideman & Moffett, AIA, Seattle, 1964-71; chief architect Wash. State Dept. Hwys., Olympia, 1971-77, Wash. State Dept. Transp., 1977—; advisor Wash. State Bldg. Code Adv. Council, 1975—; instr. civil engring. tech. Olympia Tech. Community Coll., 1975-77; adv. mem. archtl. barriers subcom. Internat. Conf. Building Ofcls.; archtl. works include hdqrs. Gen. Telephone Directory Co., Everett, Wash., 1964; Edmonds Unitarian Ch., 1966; tenant devel. Seattle Hdqrs. Office, Seattle-First Nat. Bank, 1968-70; Wash. State Dept. Transp. Area Hdqrs. Offices, Mt. Vernon, Selah, and Raymond, 1973-77, Materials Lab., Spokane, Wash., 1974; archtl. barriers cons. State of Alaska, 1978. Chmn. Planning Commn. of Mountlake Terr., Wash., 1963, 64, mem., 1961-67; mem. State of Wash. Gov.'s Task Force on Wilderness, 1972-75; trustee Cascade Symphony Orch., 1971; incorporating pres. United Singles, Olympia, Wash., 1978-79. Served with USN, 1951-54. Registered architect, Alaska, Calif., Wash., profl. engr., Wash.; cert. Nat. Council Archtl. Registration Bds., U.S. Dept. Def., Fallout Shelter Analysis, environ. engring. Mem. AIA (dir. S.W. Wash. chpt. 1980-82, sec. 1983, architects in govt. nat. com. 1978—), Am. Public Works Assn., Inst. Bldgs. and Grounds, ASCE, Constrn. Specifications Inst., Am. Arbitration Assn. (invited panelist), Gen. Soc. Mayflower Descs. (gov. Wash. Soc. 1982—), Nat. Huguenot Soc. (pres. Wash. Soc. 1981-83), Olympia Geneal. Soc. (pres. 1978-80), SAR (state sec. 1982—), SCV, Sons and Daus. of Pilgrims, Order of Magna Charta. Republican. Unitarian. Clubs: Rotary Internat. (pres. Edmonds, 1969-70), Coll. of Seattle, Olympia Yacht. Home: PO Box 2422 Olympia WA 98507 Office: Transportation Bldg KF-01 Olympia WA 98504

MOFFITT, JOHN FRANCIS, art historian, art educator; b. San Francisco, Feb. 25, 1940; s. John F. and Jean P. (Petrie) M.; m. Lea Henry, June 1969. B.F.A., Calif. Coll. Arts and Crafts, 1962; M.A., Calif. State U.-San Francisco, 1963; Ph.D., Universidad de Madrid (Spain), 1966. Instr., East Carolina U., Greenville, N.C., 1966-68, Sonoma State Coll., Cotati, Calif., 1968-69; assoc. prof. art N. Mex. State U., Las Cruces, 1969—; vis. assoc. prof. art Fla. State U., 1978; vis. prof. art history Universidad de Valencia (Spain), 1981; mem. adv. screening com. Art and Art History Council for Internat. Exchange of Scholars, 1980—. Served with USAR, 1957-62. Travel grantee Hispano-Am. Exchange Council for Internat. Exchange of Scholars, 1981; research grantee, Philosophical Soc., 1982. Mem. Coll. Art Assn., Am. Soc. Hispanic Art Hist. Studies. Author: Spanish Painting, 1973; contbr. articles to profl. art jours. Home: 1104 Luna St Las Cruces NM 88001 Office: Art Dept Box 3578 N Mex State U Las Cruces NM 88003

MOFFORD, ROSE, state official; b. Globe, Ariz., June 10, 1922; student pub. schs. Sec. to Ariz. State Treas., 1941-43, to Ariz. State Tax Commr., 1943-54, to Ariz. Sec. of State, 1954-55; asst. sec. of state State of Ariz., Phoenix, 1955-79, sec. of state, 1979—. Democrat. Office: Office of Sec of State West Wing State Capitol Phoenix AZ 85007*

MOGG, DONALD WHITEHEAD, chemist; b. La Grange, Ill., Feb. 11, 1924; s. Harold William and Margaret (Whitehead) M.; B.S., Allegheny Coll., 1944; postgrad. Harvard U., 1946-47. Asst. chemist Gt. Lakes Carbon Corp., Morton Grove, Ill., 1947-48, chemist, 1948-53, research chemist, 1953-56, project supr., 1956-59, sect. head, 1959-63; sect. head Gt. Lakes Research Corp., Elizabethton, Tenn., 1963-66; research and devel. mgr. bldg. products div. Grefco, Inc., Torrance, Calif., 1966-68, corp. research and devel. mgr., 1968-72, group mgr., 1972-81, sr. research assoc., 1981-82. Served with U.S. Army, 1944-46. Mem. Am. Chem. Soc., AAAS, Phi Beta Kappa, Phi Kappa Psi. Presbyterian. U.S. and fgn. patentee in field of bldg. products. Home: 3823 Ingraham St Apt B202 San Diego CA 92109

MOGREN, EDWIN WALFRED, educator; b. Mpls., Sept. 16, 1921; s. Andrew Walfred and Ester C. (Carlsson) M.; B.S.F., U. Minn., 1947, M.F., 1948; Ph.D., U. Mich., 1955; m. Arle Mae Arnason, May 21, 1944; children—Paul Andrew, Eric William. Research asst. U.S. Forest Service, 1942, U. Minn., 1947-48; instr. to prof., dept. forest and wood scis. Colo. State U., Ft. Collins, 1948—. Served to capt. U.S. Army, 1942-46. Fellow AAAS; mem. Soc. Am. Foresters, Ecol. Soc. Am., Sigma Xi, Xi Sigma Pi, Alpha Zeta, Gamma Sigma Delta, Phi Kappa Phi. Contbr. research papers to profl. publs. Home: 1317 W Myrtle St Fort Collins CO 81521 Office: Dept Forest and Wood Scis Colo State U Fort Collins CO 80523

MOGULL, ROBERT GABRIEL, educator, researcher; b. N.Y.C., Aug. 16, 1939; s. Alexander and Shirley M.; m. Susan Lyn Mogull; children—Robin, Scott, Michael. B.A. in History, Govt., U. Conn. 1961; M.S. in Guidance Counseling, L.I. U. 1965; M.A. in Econs., SUNY-Buffalo 1967; Ph.D. in Econs., W.Va. U., 1969. Cert. tchr., N.Y. Tchr., Roslyn (N.Y.) High Sch., 1963-65; teaching fellow SUNY-Buffalo, 1965-67, W.Va. U., 1967-69; asst. prof. dept. econs. Purdue U., Calumet Campus, 1969-70; mgr. Mogull Electronics Co., N.Y.C., 1971-73; asst. prof. bus. stats. Calif. State U., 1970-75, assoc. prof. 1975-78, prof. bus. stats. and econs., 1978—. Area Studies grantee Cornell U., 1964; Regional Research Inst. W.Va. U. grantee, 1969. Mem. Am. Econs. Assn. Contbr. articles to profl. jours., statis. text. Office: Sch of Bus Calif State U Sacramento CA 95819

MOHERMAN, DARRELL WAYNE, corp. exec.; b. Ashland, Ohio, Aug. 26, 1945; s. George Austin and Mildred (Jones) M.; B.S. in Bus. Adminstrn., Ohio State U., 1967; m. Teresa Lola Baer, Sept. 14, 1973; children—Nicole Tara, Austin Andrew. Store mgr., store opener, dist. mgr. Rockower Bros., Inc., Huntingdon Valley, Pa., 1967-80, regional v.p. until 1980; regional v.p., A.L. Williams, Denver, 1980-83, sr. v.p., 1983—. Home: 1330 S Paris Ct Aurura CO 80012 Office: 5680 S Syracuse Circle Suite 300 Englewood CO 80111

MOHNEY, LEONE LAURA, microbiologist; b. Raton, N.Mex., May 29, 1935; d. Curtis Gilliam and Ruth Clara (Jillson) Mohney. B.S., U. Ariz., 1957; M.A., U. Calif.-Berkeley, 1961. Research asst. George Williams Hooper Found., U. Calif.-San Francisco, 1958-60; research assoc. Sch. Pub. Health, U. Calif.-Berkeley, 1961-77; research asst. dept. microbiology U. Ariz., Tucson, 1978-81, research asst. dept. med. and molecular microbiology Ariz. Health Scis. Center, 1981—. Mem. Am. Soc. Microbiology, Am. Inst. Biol. Scis., Assn. Women in Sci., Phi Beta Kappa, Phi Kappa Phi. Republican. Presbyterian.

MOHOLY, NOEL FRANCIS, clergyman; b. San Francisco, May 26, 1916; s. John Joseph and Eva Gertrude (Cippa) M.; grad. St. Anthony's Sem., Santa Barbara; S.T.D., Faculte de Theologie, Universite Laval, Quebec, Que., Can., 1948. Joined Franciscan Friars, 1935; ordained priest Roman Catholic Ch., 1941; tchr. fundamental theology Old Mission Santa Barbara, 1942-43, sacred theology, 1947-58; tchr. langs. St. Anthony's Sem., 1943-44; Am. adminstr. (handling affairs of the cause in U.S.) Cause of Padre Junipero Serra, 1950-55, vice postulator, 1958—; retreat master San Damiano Retreat, Danville, Calif., 1964-67. Mem. Ann. Assay Commn. U.S. Mint, 1964. Occupied numerous pulpits, assisted in several Franciscan Retreat Houses; condr. series illustrated lectrs. on cause of canonization of Padre Junipero Serra to students of all Franciscan study houses in U.S., summer 1952, also speaker in field at various clubs of Serra Internat. in U.S., Europe and Far East, on CBS, ABC broadcasts and conducted own local TV series. Exec. dir., treas. Old Mission Restoration Project, 1954-58; mem. Calif. Hist. Landmarks Adv. Com., 1962-71, Calif. Hist. Resources Commn., 1971-76, Calif. Bicentennial Celebration Commn., 1967-70; pres. Serra Bicentennial commn., 1983—. Nat. and internat. authority on mariology, Calif. history (particularly history of Father Serra). Decorated Knight comdr. Order of Isabella the Catholic. Pres. Father Junipero Serra 250th Anniversary Assn., Inc., 1964—. Named hon. citizen Petra de Mallora, 1969, Palma de Mallorca, 1976. Mem. Cath. Theol. Soc. Am., Mariol. Soc. Am., Native Sons Golden West, Associacion de los Amigos de Padre Serra, K.C. Author: Our Last Chance, 1931; Saint Irenaeus; the Father of Mariology, 1952; The California Mission Story, 1975; The First Californian, 1976; producer phonograph records Songs of the California Missions, 1951, Christmas at Mission Santa Barbara, 1953, St. Francis Peace Record, 1957; producer The Founding Father of the West, 1976. Home: St Boniface Friary 133 Golden Gate Ave San Francisco CA 94102 Office: Serra Cause Old Mission Santa Barbara CA 93105

MOHR, MARY L., marketing executive; b. Orange, N.J., Feb. 3, 1950; d. Christopher J. and Bernice S. Mohr. B.A., Gettysburg Coll., 1972; M.B.A., U. Denver, 1981, postgrad. in law, 1982—. Spl. events coordinator U. Denver, 1978-79; mktg. dir. Jewish Community Ctr., Denver, 1980-81; mktg. mgr. First Trust, Denver, 1981, v.p. mktg., 1981-82; v.p. mktg. First Retirement Mktg. Inc., Denver, 1982—; dir. Leo Fleur Inc., cons. Sta. KCFR, pub. radio, Israel. Mem. Denver Advt. Fedn., Am. Mktg. Assn., Internat. Assn. Fin. Planners. Democrat. Jewish. Club: Oxford, (Denver). Office: 444 Sherman St Denver CO 80213

MOHR, SELBY, ophthalmologist; b. San Francisco, Mar. 11, 1918; s. Selby and Henrietta (Foorman) M.; A.B., Stanford U., 1938, M.D., 1942; m. Marian Buckley, June 10, 1950; children—Selby, John Vincent, Adrianne E., Gregory P. Asst. resident in ophthalmology U. Calif. Hosp., 1942-43; pvt. practice ophthalmology, San Francisco, 1947—; mem. past pres. med. staff Marshall Hale Meml. Hosp.; mem. staff Mt. Zion Hosp., St Francis Meml. Hosp. Dir. Sweet Water Co., Mound Farms, Inc., Mound Farms Oil & Gas, Inc. Served from lt. (j.g.) to lt. USNR, 1943-46; PTO. Diplomate Am. Bd. Ophthalmology. Fellow Am. Acad. Ophthalmology and Otolarngology; mem. AMA, Calif., San Francisco med. socs., Pan-Pacific Surg. Soc., Pan-Am. Assn. Ophthalmology, Pacific Coast Oto-Ophthalmol. Soc., Pan-Am. Med. Soc. Home: 160 Sea Cliff Ave San Francisco CA 94121 Office: 450 Sutter St San Francisco CA 94108

MOISE, BETH MAXWELL, organizational behavior specialist, consultant; b. Champaign, Ill., Feb. 21, 1945; d. Harry P. and Virginia May (Jameson) Maxwell; m. Steven K. Moise, June 2, 1968; children—Adam, Grant. B.A., U. Colo., 1967, M.A., 1969; Ph.D. with distinction, U. N.Mex., 1977. With Foley's Dept. Store, 1967-68, May D & F., 1969-71; instr. U. N.Mex., Albuquerque, 1976-82; orgn. behavior specialist Mountain Bell, Albuquerque, 1981—; pvt. practice cons., 1974—; adj. prof. Sch. Bus., U. N.Mex. Bd. dirs. YWCA, 1979-81; mem. Nat. Women's Polit. Caucus, NOW, Mayor's Adv. Com. for Women in City Govt., 1979-81, Nat. Council on Alcoholism Adv. Bd., 1983. Mem. Am. Soc. Tng. and Devel., N.Mex. Personnel Assn., N.Mex. Psychol. Assn. Home: 6611 Guadalupe Trail NW Albuquerque NM 87107 Office: Mountain Bell 400 Tijeras NW Station 133 Albuquerque NM 87103

MOISE, IRWIN STERN, lawyer; b. Santa Rosa, N.Mex., Dec. 1, 1906; s. Sigmund Solomon and Rosa (Stern) M.; m. Hilda Dvorken, May 26, 1934. Student U. Colo., 1923-25; J.D., U. Mich., 1928; LL.D., N.Mex. Highlands U., 1963. Bar: N.Mex. 1928, Ill. 1960. Indisidual practice law, Tucumcari, N.Mex., 1928-33, Santa Rosa, 1933, Albuquerque, 1946-59; dep. adminstr. NRA, Washington, 1934-36; dist. judge 4th Jud. Dist., Las Vegas, 1937-43; justice N.Mex. Supreme Ct., 1959-70, chief justice, 1969-70; ptnr. firm Sutin, Thayer & Browne, Albuquerque, 1970—. Mem. N.Mex. Correction Commn., 1971-75; chmn. N.Mex. Council Nat. Council on Crime and Delinquency, 1971-73; past mem. bd. dirs. Bataan Meml. Meth. Hosp., Child Guidance Ctr., Legal Aid Soc. Served as lt. USNR, 1943-46. Mem. ABA, N.Mex. Bar Assn., Albuquerque Bar Assn. (past dir.), Am. Judicature Soc. Democrat. Jewish. Club: Albuquerque Petroleum. Lodge: Masons. Home: 4715 Marquette NE Albuquerque NM 87108 Office: 600 First Plaza Bldg Albuquerque NM 87102

MOISE, STEVEN KAHN, lawyer; b. Lubbock, Tex., July 28, 1944; s. Joseph J. and Marguerite K. Moise; B.A., U. Colo., Boulder, 1966, J.D., 1969; m. Beth Maxwell, June 2, 1968; children—Adam M., Grant S. Admitted to Colo. bar, 1969, N.Mex. bar, 1971; atty. firm Rothgerber, Appel & Powers, Denver, 1969-71; partner firm Sutin, Thayer & Browne, P.C., Albuqueruqe, 1971—; dir. S.W. Nat. Bank, Albuquerque. Bd. dirs. N.Mex. Symphony Orch., 1973-78, pres., 1977-78; bd. dirs. Presbyn. Hosp. Center Found., Albuquerque, 1978—, U. Colo. Found., 1969-79, United Way, 1979—; bd. dirs. Congregation Albert, Albuquerque, 1975—, v.p., 1979-80, pres., 1981-83; trustee Manzano Day Sch., Albuquerque, U. N.Mex. Robert O. Anderson Sch. Mgmt. Found.; mem. adv. council Robert O Anderson Sch. Mgmt. Mem. ABA, N.Mex. Bar Assn., Colo. Bar Assn., Albuquerque Bar Assn., Denver Bar Assn. Democrat. Home: 6611 Guadalupe Trail NW Albuquerque NM 87107 Office: PO Box 1945 Albuquerque NM 87103

MOLANO, RAFAEL ANTONIO, utilities exec.; b. Leon, Nicaragua, Dec. 18, 1951; came to U.S., 1969; s. Louis and Elsa (Balduizon) M.; m. Pamela Ann Balker, Mar. 6, 1981. B.S. in Elec. Engring., La. State U., 1973; M.S. with honors in Econs., U. Wyo., 1976. Fin. analyst and power requirements supr. Tri-State Generation and Transmission, Denver, 1976-79; sr. cons. Booz, Allen & Hamilton, Bethesda, Md., 1979-80; cons. Dept. Energy, San Diego, 1981; sr. analyst Pacific Gas and Electric, San Francisco, 1981—. Mem. Internat. Assn. Energy Economists, Assn. Western Econs. Home: 18 Zurich Ct Pleasant Hill CA 94523 Office: 77 Beale St San Francisco CA 94106

MOLDOVAN, JANNLEE, association executive, consultant; b. San Diego, Apr. 19, 1944; d. William Thomas and Vandalee Teresa (Matte) Long; m. Charles Kenneth Brooks, Jr., Oct. 18, 1964; 1 son, Charles Kenneth; m. 2d, Emil Moldovan, May 15, 1978; 1 son, Nicholas Alexander. Student San Diego State Coll., 1962-63, San Diego Evening Coll., 1963-65. Apprentice, San Diego Union, 1962-66; city editor Bonita Pub. Co., Montclair, Calif., 1968-72; mng. editor Highland Publs., Hacienda Heights, Calif., 1972-78; exec. dir. San Gabriel (Calif.) C. of C., 1978—. Pres. San Gabriel Community Coordinating Council; treas. Temple City Little League; mem. Selective Service Bd., Temple City. Recipient various journalism awards Twin Counties Press Club, 1970, 71; Outstanding Jr. Career Woman award Calif. Bus. and Profl. Woman's Club, 1972; Outstanding Woman in Bus. award in City of San Gabriel, Women's Div. San Gabriel C. of C., 1978. Mem. So. Calif. Assn. Chamber Execs., San Gabriel Valley Assn. Chamber Execs., San Gabriel C. of C. Women's Div., San Gabriel Hist. Assn. Republican. Episcopalian. Club: Soroptimist (v.p. Alhambra-San Gabriel). Office: San Gabriel Chamber of Commerce 534 W Mission Dr San Gabriel CA 91776

MOLINA, MARIA ELBA, savings and loan executive; b. Cananea, Sonora, Mex., Mar. 17, 1948; d. Ramon and Victoria (Acosta) Leon; came to U.S., 1946, naturalized, 1964; m. Bill G. Molina, Oct. 4, 1975. Student U. Ariz., 1962-64, 66-70, 70-71, Pima Community Coll., 1971—. Bilingual sec., adminstrv. asst. So. Ariz. Bank & Trust Co., 1964-71; asst. v.p., security officer Banco de las Am., 1971-74; asst. v.p., branch mgr. Home Fed. Savs. & Loan Assn., Tucson, 1974-75, v.p., regional mgr., 1979, v.p. community relations, bus. devel. mktg. dept., 1980—. Chmn. bd. trustees El Dorado Hosp. & Med. Ctr.; past pres. Soroptimist Internat. Desert Tucson; bd. dirs. United Way Tucson; bd. dirs. Jr. Achievement, 1979; mem. Ariz.-Mex. Commn. Office of Gov., 1978; bd. dirs. 88-Crime; chmn. fin. adv. com. Pima Community Coll., 1981; del. Ariz. Acad. Town Hall, 1979; mem. Tucson Airport Authority, 1980. Named Outstanding Civic Leader LULAC, 1975; Outstanding Young Hispanic Woman, Adolph Coors Co., 1980, Outstanding Citizen, 1981. Mem. Ariz. Bus. and Profl. Women's Club, Exec. Women Internat. (assoc.), Exec. Women's Council So. Ariz., Exec. Women's Council. Democrat. Roman Catholic. Club: Second Tuesday. Office: PO Box 2871 Tucson AZ 85702

MOLINDER, JOHN IRVING, engineering educator; b. Erie, Pa., June 14, 1941; s. Oskar and Carin (Ecklund) M.; m. Janet Marie Ahlquist, June 16, 1962; children—Timothy Scott, Karen Marie. B.S. in Elec. Engring., U. Nebr., 1963; M.S., Air Force Inst. Tech., 1964; Ph.D., Calif. Inst. Tech., 1969. Registered profl. engr., Calif. Sr. engr. in communication systems research group Jet Propulsion Lab., Pasadena, Calif., 1969-70, mem. tech. staff, deep space network systems engring. office, 1974-76, mem. tech. staff, tracking and data acquisition engring. office, 1976-79, deep space network rep., 1979-80, mgr. engring. analysis, telecommunications and data axquisition engring. office, 1980—; lectr. Calif. State U.-Los Angeles, 1970-74; asst. prof. engring. Harvey Mudd Coll., Claremont, Calif., 1970-75, assoc. prof., 1975-80, prof., 1980—, dept. chmn., 1983—. Served to capt. USAF, 1963-67. Mem. IEEE. Contbr. articles to profl. jours. Office: Harvey Mudd College Engineering Dept Claremont CA 91711

MOLLICONE, RICHARD ANTHONY, research and development executive, consultant; b. Bklyn., Feb. 18, 1935; s. Anthony Francis and Bertha Marie (Filas) M.; m. Joyce Elayne McCoy, Nov. 30, 1958. B.S., U.S. Mil. Acad., 1957; M.S. in Engring. Mechanics, Rensselaer Poly. Inst., 1965, Ph.D., 1970. Registered profl. engr., Colo., 1970. Pilot, U.S. Air Force, McClellan AFB, Calif., Yokota AB, Japan, 1957-63; assoc. prof. engring. mechanics and materials sci. U.S. Air Force Acad., Colorado Springs, Colo., 1966-71; chief Beddown planning, 7th Air Forcehdqrs., Vietnam, 1971-72; chief applications, chief tech. services div., special asst. for comdr. Materials Lab., El Segundo, Calif., 1976-77; chief advanced concepts div. Space Div., El Segundo, 1977-78; v.p., dir. western research ops. Analytic Decisions Inc., Hawthorne, Calif., 1978—; cons. space research and develop. Served with USAF to lt. col. (ret.), 1957-78. Decorated Bronze Star, Air Medal with Oak Leaf Cluster, Vietnam Gallantry Cross with Device. Mem. AIAA, Order of Daedalians, ASME, Nat. Def. Preparedness Assn. Soc., VFW, Nat. Rifle Assn., Sigma Xi, Alpha Phi Omega. Roman Catholic. Club: K.C. Contbr. articles to profl. jours. Home: 15931 Redlands St Westminster CA 92683 Office: 5155 Rosecrans Ave #307 Hawthorne CA 90520

MOLLOY, WILLIAM FRANCIS, management consulting company executive; b. Orange, N.J., June 23, 1945; s. Corneilius John and Jean Ann (Marquier) M.; m. Lorraine Madeline La Pointe, Jan. 26, 1979; children—Heather Ann, Michael Francis. B.A. in History, Stonehill Coll., 1968; M.Ed. in Counseling and Personnel Services, U. Md., 1973. Tchr., coach Mackin High Sch., Washington, 1968-69; tchr., coach, counselor Red Bank (N.J.) Cath. High Sch., 1969-70; counselor, dir. devel. DeMatha High Sch., Hyattsville, Md., 1970-75; fin. planner Waddell & Reed, Washington, 1974-75; dealer mgr. Royal Bus. Machines, Pitts., 1975-77; successively mktg. mgr., regional mgr., v.p. Western region Devel. Dimensions Internat., Los Angeles, 1977—; guest speaker, lectr. in field. Vice pres. Fox Hills Pines Home Owners Assn., 1979-80. Mem. Am. Soc. Tng. and Devel., Los Angeles C. of C. Contbr. articles to profl. publs. Home: 5950 Canterbury Dr #C-104 Culver City CA 90230 Office: 6300 W Century Blvd Suite S-340 Los Angeles CA 90045

MOLNAR, RONALD JOHN, optoelectronics engineering manager; b. Whittier, Calif., Nov. 2, 1950; s. John and Maralee Viola (Wallin) M.; m. Carole Ann Danilson, June 24, 1978; children— Kelly Elizabeth, Melanie Ann. B.S.E.E., U. Calif.-Berkeley, 1973. Product engr. Monsanto Co., Palo Alto, Calif., 1973-78; mfg. engring. mgr. Siemens-Litronix div., Cupertino, Calif., 1978—. Served with USCGR, 1969-74. Mem. IEEE, Club: Seals Booster (Oakland, Calif.). Office: 19000 Homestead Rd Cupertino CA 95014

MOLOF, MARTIN JOSEPH, research psychologist; b. N.Y.C., June 8, 1936; B.A., Bklyn. Coll., 1957; Ph.D. in Psychology, Stanford U., 1963. Assoc. social research analyst State of Calif. Youth Authority, Sacramento, 1963-69; sr. research psychologist Mentec Corp., Los Angeles, 1970; sr. behavioral sci. Am. Justice Inst., Sacramento, 1971-73 part-time research assoc., 1981-82; criminal justice statistician City of Denver Anti-Crime Council, 1973-74; lead evaluator, cons. Santa Clara County, Calif., 1974-76; system sci. The MITRE Corp., McLean, Va., 1976-81; personnel research psychologist Navy Personnel Research and Devel. Ctr., San Diego, 1983—. Mem. Evaluation Research Soc., Phi Beta Kappa. Home: 829A Beach Front Dr Solana Beach CA 92075 Office: Navy Personnel Research and Devel Ctr San Diego CA 92152

MOLOFF, PAULA FAITH BEIDES, public health administrator; b. N.Y.C., Apr. 4, 1944; d. Isidore and Molly (Percik) Beides; B.A., CUNY, 1965; M.S.W., U. Nebr., 1974; M.B.A., U. No. Colo., 1982; m. Paul Moloff, 1965; children—Andrew R., Lisa Francesca. Dir. dept. social service Bapt. Home of Nebr., Omaha, 1972-74; health and social work resource cons. Pima Health Systems, Tucson, 1975; case mgr. Child Protective Services, Tucson, 1976; social work discharge planner Kino Community Hosp., Tucson, 1976-78; pvt. practice individual and group therapy, Tucson, 1976-78; group therapist Pima County (Ariz.) Juvenile Ct., Tucson, 1976-78; div. dir. Child and Youth project Dept. Health County of Pima, 1978-80; dir. dept. health Pascua-Yaqui Tribe, Tucson, 1980-82; health program mgr. Ariz. Dept. Health Services, Ariz. Health Care Cost Containment, Systems Div., 1982—. vice chmn. Foster Care Rev. Bd., Ariz. State Supreme Ct., 1980—; practicum instr. U. Nebr., 1974, Ariz. State U., 1977—. Recipient Cert. of Recognition, World Muslim Community, Tucson, 1979. Mem. Nat. Assn. Social Workers, Acad. Cert. Social workers, Am. Public Health Assn., Vis. Nurses Assn. (dir. 1977-80). Democrat. Home: 7126 N 19 Ave #122 Tucson AZ 85021 Office: 1200 W Washington Ave Room 224 Phoenix AZ

MOLONEY, MICHAEL JAMES, commercial real estate agent; b. Washington, Aug. 18, 1944; s. Raymond Lawrence and Patricia Louise (Wilson) M.; B.A., Miami U., Ohio, 1965; M.A., U. Ariz., 1969; m. Regina Maria Marinho, June 3, 1978; children—Camile Alexandra, Sean Patrick, Daniel Marinho. Vol., Peace Corps, Chile, 1967-69; adminstrv. asst., project coordination adminstr. Tucson Model Cities Dept., 1969-75, community conservation and devel. adminstr., 1975-78, dir. housing and urban redevel., 1978-80, dir. Central Phoenix redevel., 1980-81; redevel. specialist Bookbinder Fin. Corp., Phoenix, 1981—. NDEA fellow, 1967. Mem. League United Latin Am. Citizens, Phoenix Com. Fgn. Relations, Nat. Assn. Rev. Appraisers (cert.), Urban Land Inst., Am. Planning Assn., Nat. Assn. Housing and Redevel. Ofcls., Council Urban Econ. Devel. Democrat. Mem. Soc. of Friends. Home: 836 E McLellan Blvd Phoenix AZ 85014 Office: 96 W Osborn Rd Phoenix AZ 85013

MOLTENI, BETTY PHILLIPS, painter: b. Norfolk, Va., Dec. 15, 1913; d. William Henry and Margaret (Brownley) Phillips; A.B., Coll. William and Mary, 1938; student art U. Nev., Reno, 1966-71; m. Peter G. Molteni, Jr., July 22, 1939; children—Peter G. III, Margaret Elizabeth, Christopher Phillips, Marianne Stephanie. Founder, chmn. Armed Forces Art Show Hawaii, 1962; one woman shows Artist Co-op., Reno, 1978, 81, Mother Lode Nat. Art Exhbn., Sonora, Calif., 1977, 79, Delta Art Assn. Show, Antioch, Calif., 1978; exhibited group shows Nev. Women Art Show Las Vegas, 1976, Nat. League Am. Pen Women, Salt Lake City, 1973, Sacramento, 1978, Lodi Art Ann., Acampo, Calif., 1979, Tahoe Erhman Mansion Arts Festival, 1979-80; represented in pvt. collections. Bd. dirs. Nev. Art Gallery, 1975-78; del. Sierra Arts Assembly, 1977-78, 80-81. Mem. Nat. League Am. Pen Women (v.p. 1973, treas. Reno br. 1979, pres. 1980, state pres. 1982-84), Soc. Western Artists, Latimer Art Club (art scholarship chmn., pres. 1971, treas. 1978), Carson City Alliance (charter), Nev. Artists Assn., Nev. Art Gallery, Sierra Arts Assembly, Artist Co-op. (charter, v.p. 1983), Sierra Nevada Mus. Arts Aux., Reno Philharmonic League, Cath. Daus. Republican. Roman Catholic. Home: 1130 Alpine Circle Reno NV 89509

MOLZEN, DAYTON FRANK, cons. engr.; b. Newton, Kans., Jan. 6, 1926; s. Walter N. and Ionia Maude (Gordon) M.; B.S., Kans. State U., 1950; m. Margaret Jean Hanna, Aug. 13, 1949; children—George Walter, Lucena Ann. Project engr. Kans. Hwy. Commn., Garden City, 1950-51; design engr. Wilson and Co. Engrs., Albuquerque and Salina, Kans., 1953-60; civil engr., pres. D. F. Molzen and Assos., Inc., Albuquerque, 1960-75, Molzen, Corbin and Assos., Inc., Albuquerque, 1975—. Served with A.C., AUS, 1942-45, USAF, 1951-53. Fellow Am. Cons. Engrs. Council (pres. 1964-66, nat. bd. dirs. 1981—); mem. ASCE, Am. Pub. Works Assn. Mason (Shriner, pres. Shrine Air Patrol 1970). Clubs: N.Mex. Appaloosa Horse (pres. 1971-72), Nat. Appaloosa Horse (dir. 1978—), Albuquerque Rotary. Home: Box 356 Corrales NM 87048 Office: Craddock Commerce Center 2301 Yale Blvd SE Albuquerque NM 87106

MOMMAERTS, WILFRIED FRANCIS HENRY MARIA, physiologist, educator; b. Brochem, Belgium, Mar. 4, 1917; came to U.S., 1948, naturalized, 1956; s. Henrik D. and Maria (van Damme) M.; children—Robert, Edina, Quentin. B.A., U. Leiden, Netherlands, 1937, M.A., 1939; Ph.D., U. Kolozsvar, Hungary, 1943, D. (hon.), U. Dijon, France, 1976. Mem. faculty Am. U., Beirut, 1945-48, Duke U., 1948-53, Western Res. U., 1953-56; coordinator Commonwealth Fund Med. Curriculum Expt. 1955-56; spl. fellow Univ. Coll., London, 1956; prof. medicine and physiology, dir. Cardiovascular Research Lab., UCLA, 1956—, chmn. dept. physiology, 1966—; Commonwealth Fund fellow Centre des Recherches Macromolecules, Strasbourg, 1963-64; chmn. physiology tng. com., 1967-72; Brittingham prof. biol. scis. U. Wis., 1967-68; vis. prof. Baker Inst. Med. Research, Malbourne, Australia, 1971, U. Dijon, 1973-74; apptd. Conseiller Exceptional to Inserm, France; fgn. mem. Institut Pasteur; hon. prof. U. Hong Kong, 1979; mem. Internat. Commn. Genetic Experimentation. Recipient award for contbn. to sci. knowledge Los Angeles County Heart Assn., 1967, Golden Apple teaching award UCLA Sch. Medicine, 1969, Outstanding Prof. award Sch. Dentistry, 1969-70, award of merit, 1971, Maharishi award for creativity and success in life, 1980. Mem. Am. Acad. Arts and Scis. (exec. com. Western Center sect.), Royal Belgian Acad. Medicine, Assn. Am. Med. Colls., Assn. Chmn. Dept. Physiology, Internat. Brain Research Orgn., UCLA Med. Soc., Neurophysiol. Soc., Cardiac Muscle Soc., Am. Soc. Cell Biology, Biophys. Soc., Am. Physiol. Soc., Am. Coll. Cardiology, Soc. Neurosci., Phi Beta Kappa. Adv. editor Current Topics in Bioenergetics. Office: Dept of Physiology U Calif Sch Medicine Los Angeles CA 90024

MONAGLE, JOHN JOSEPH, university dean; b. Chester, Pa., Feb. 2, 1929; s. John Joseph and Katherine (Conroy) M.; m. Elizabeth Brette Nolan, Aug. 7, 1954; children—Peter, Lisa, Cathy, John, Matthew. B.S. in Chemistry, Villanova U., 1950; Ph.D., Poly. Inst. Bklyn., 1954. Research chemist Sinclair Research Labs., Inc., 1954-56, Jackson Labs., E.I. duPont de Nemours & Co., Inc., 1956-61; asst. prof. N.Mex. State U., Las Cruces, 1961-63, prof., head dept. chemistry, 1963-67, dean Coll. Arts and Scis., 1968-70, now assoc. dean Coll. Arts and Scis., dir. arts and scis.; prof., head dept. chemistry U. Ala., Tuscaloosa, 1967-68. Bd. dirs. Ala. Community Research Center and Tech. Services Agy., 1967-68. Mem. Am. Chem. Soc. (nat. councilor 1965-66, 68, 70-77, chmn. so. N.Mex. sect. 1965), AAAS, Soc. Research Adminstrn., Nat. Council Univ. Research Adminstrs., Sigma Xi, Phi Kappa Phi, Phi Lambda Upsilon. Roman Catholic. Club: Rotary. Contbr. articles to profl. jour.; patentee. Home: 4044 Tamarisk Dr Las Cruces NM 88001 Office: Box RC New Mexico State U Las Cruces NM 88003

MONAHAN, JAMES PATRICK, sales exec.; b. Billings, Mont., Nov. 20, 1944; s. James Edward and Cecil (Sharpe) M.; student U. Mont., 1966-67; m. Kolleen A. Stocke, May 10, 1968; children—John Patrick, Alyssa Marie. Partner, mgr. Cecil's Shop, womens clothing retail, Missoula, Mont., 1966-74; salesman N.Y. Life Ins. Co., Missoula, 1974-75; owner, mgr. ACME Personnel Services, Albany, Oreg., 1975-82; sales assoc. Town & Country Mech. Contractors, Albany, 1983—. Served with U.S. Army, 1964-66. Mem. Albany Area C. of C. Roman Catholic. Clubs: Rotary, Elks. Home: 2313 Ermine Ct SE Albany OR 97321 Office: 145 N Baker Albany OR 97321

MONAHAN, JEANNETTE, hospital management development specialist; b. Dallas, May 9, 1949; d. John I. and Julia M. (Galloway) Welsh; m. Terence F. Meany, Mar. 17, 1977; 1 dau., Theresa K. Monahan. B.A. in English, U. Tex.-Austin, 1971; M.P.A., U. Colo., 1975; diploma of competency in systems renewal consultation Internat. Inst. for Study of Systems Renewal, Seattle, 1981. Intern, City of Boulder (Colo.), summer 1975, Dept. Regulatory Agys., State of Colo., Denver, summer 1976; tng. specialist Municipality of Met. Seattle, 1977-78; mgr. employee tng. and devel. U. Wash. Hosps., Seattle, 1978-82; dir. mgmt. devel. Virginia Mason Med. Ctr., Seattle, 1982—. Recipient Suggestion award Municipality of Met. Seattle, 1978. Mem. Am. Soc. for Tng. and Devel. (recipient outstanding contbn. award 1977, 78, mem. region VIII conf. planning com. 1983), Am. Soc. Healthcare Edn. and Tng. (nat. program planning com. 1982, 83). Democrat. Roman Catholic. Club: Toastmasters Internat. Contbr. articles on organizational devel. to profl. jours. Office: Virginia Mason Med Ctr 925 Seneca St PO Box 1930 Seattle WA 98111

MONARCHI, DAVID EDWARD, management scientist, information scientist, educator; b. Miami Beach, Fla., July 31, 1944; s. Joseph Louis and Elizabeth Rose (Muller) M.; B.S. in Engring. Physics, Colo. Sch. of Mines, 1966; Ph.D. (NDEA fellow), U. Ariz., 1972; 1 son by previous marriage, David Edward. Asst. dir. of Bus. Research Div., U. Colo., Boulder, 1972-75, asst. prof. mgmt. sci./info. systems, 1972-75, assoc. prof. mgmt. sci. and info. systems, 1975—; assoc. dir. Bus. Research Div., 1975—, dir. Div. Info. Sci. Research, 1982—; prin. investigator of socio-econ. environ. systems for govtl. agys., and local govt. orgns., State of Colo., also info. systems for pvt. firms, 1972-77. Mem. Gov.'s Energy Task Force Com., 1974. Mem. Inst. for Mgmt. Sci., Ops. Research Soc. Am., Am. Inst. for Decision Scis., Assn. Computing Machinery. Contbr. numerous articles on socio-econ. modeling to profl. jours. Home: 32 Benthaven Place Boulder CO 80303 Office: Grad Sch Bus Univ of Colorado Boulder CO 80309

MONE, LOUIS CARMEN, clin. social worker; b. Bklyn., July 10, 1936; s. Louis Anthony and Mildred (Guidone) M.; B.A., U. Ariz., 1962; M.S.W., Rutgers U., 1965; doctoral candidate Inst. Clin. Social Work, 1979; m. Elinor Sypniewski, Sept. 28, 1958; children—Marc, Lisa. Detention supr. Pima County Detention Home, Tucson, 1959-60; social worker N.J. Neuro-Psychiat. Inst., Princeton, 1961-63; psychiat. social worker Alcoholism Treatment Center, Roosevelt Hosp. Metuchen, N.J., 1963-66; caseworker Family Counseling Service of Somerset County, Bound Brook, N.J., 1965-67, group cons., 1965-69; prin. psychiat. social worker Raritan Bay Mental Health Center, Middlesex County Mental Health Clinic, Perth Amboy, N.J., 1966-69; social work cons. Borough of Spotswood, Spotswood (N.J.) Pub. Schs., 1967-69; pilot project dir., group therapist Heart Assn. Middlesex County, Edison, N.J., 1968-69; chief psychiat. social worker Insts. Religion and Health, N.Y.C., 1969-71; pvt. practice adolescent and adult psychotherapy, marriage and family counseling, East Brunswick, N.J., 1965-71, Del Mar, Calif., 1972-78, individual, marriage, family and child therapy, San Diego, 1973-78, La Jolla, Calif., 1978—; instr. nursing programs Rutgers U., New Brunswick, N.J., 1970; dir. profl. services Family Services Assn. San Diego, 1971-75; instr. Calif. Sch. Profl. Psychology, 1974, 76-80. Served with AUS, 1955-57. Mem. Am. Group Psychotherapy Assn., Nat. Assn. Social Workers, San Diego Group Psychotherapy Soc., Delta Chi. Club: Calif. Ensenada Yacht. Author: Private Practice: A Professional Business. Home: 12859 Via Latina Del Mar CA 92014 Office: 8950 Villa La Jolla Dr Suite 2151 La Jolla CA 92037

MONFORT, KENNETH, cattle production and meat processing company executive; b. 1928. Mem. Colo. Ho. of Reps., 1965-69; pres. Monfort of Colo. Inc., Greeley, 1969—, co-chmn., sr. v.p., 1976, pres., chief exec. officer, 1980—, also dir. Office: Monfort of Colo Inc North of Greeley PO Box G Greeley CO 80632*

MONHEISER, L. LORRAINE, accountant; b. Denver, Sept. 14, 1947; d. Kenneth E. and Jewel R. Pratt; m. William J. Monheiser, Dec. 31, 1965; children—Jeffery Michael, David William. B.S. in Bus. Adminstrn. with distinction, Colo. State U.-Ft. Collins, 1975. C.P.A., Colo. Mem. tax staff, tax sr. Touche Ross & Co., Denver, 1975-78; tax specialist Coopers & Lybrand, Denver, 1978-79, tax supr., 1979-80, tax mgr., 1980—; mem. affiliate faculty Colo. State U. Ft. Collins. Trustee, treas. Womanshcool Network, Lakewood, Colo., 1981—. Mem. Am. Inst. C.P.A.s, Colo. Soc. C.P.A.s, Denver Women's Soc. C.P.A.s. Club: 300 (Denver). Contbr. articles to profl. jours.

MONICAL, STUART DEAN, mech. engr.; b. Cin., Apr. 13, 1951; s. Robert Duane and Carol Arnetha (Dean) M.; B.S.M.E., Purdue U., 1973; m. Jeannette L. Ferrand, Oct. 1, 1978. With McFall & Konkel, Cons. Engrs., 1973-79; v.p. McFall, Konkel & Kimball Cons. Engrs., Denver, 1979—; guest lectr. U. Wyo. Mem. Am. Soc. Plumbing Engrs., ASHRAE, Nat. Fire Protection Assn., Inst. Environ. Scis. Mem. Disciples of Christ. Home: 3383 E Euclid Pl Littleton CO 80121 Office: 2160 S Clermont St Denver CO 80222

MONKS, WILLIAM WAYNE, audiologist; b. Jeannette, Pa., Sept. 15, 1926; s. William Wayne and Aline (Wazelle) M.; m. Lina Guadelupe Castro, Apr. 3, 1982; children from previous marriage—Merri Martha, Virginia Aline, William Wayne, Blake Charles, Marilee Allyn. B.A., U. No. Iowa, 1956; M.S., U. Ill., 1960; Ph.D., U. Sussex, 1974. Served with U.S. Army Air Force, 1943-45; enlisted in U.S. Air Force, 1948, advanced through grades to maj.; ret.; speech and hearing specialist pub. schs. in Iowa, Ill., Nev., Calif., 1956-62; instr. secondary schs., Garden Grove, Calif., 1962-67; asst. prof. U. Guam, 1967-68; chief dept. audiology and speech pathology Ont. Hosp. Sch., Blenheim, Can., 1971-74; audiologist state of Calif. Dept. Devel. Services, Pomona, 1974—. Mem. Am. Speech and Hearing Assn., Calif. Speech and Hearing Assn., Calif. State Employees Assn., Ret. Officers Assn., Am. Legion. Republican. Clubs: Elks, Masons, Moose. Author: The Audiological Dental and Medical Aspects of Tempromandibular Joint Arthrosis, 1974; Operant Methods of Inducing Language Acquisition in the Developmentally Disabled, 1976. Office: 3350 Pomona Blvd Pomona CA 91766

MONNIG, LINDSAY, marketing executive; b. Bronxville, N.Y., Dec. 25, 1951; s. Hugo and Lulie (Engelsmann) M. B.A., Antioch Coll., 1975. Sales corr. Holt Rinehart & Winston, Los Angeles, 1975-76; asst. to v.p. mktg. Kenyon & Eckhardt Advt., Los Angeles, 1977; assoc. dir. corp. research Knapp Communications, Los Angeles, 1977—. Mem. Am. Mktg. Assn., Mktg. Research Assn., Travel and Tourism Research Assn., Direct Mktg. Assn. Office: 5900 Wilshire Blvd Los Angeles CA 90036

MONOHAN, GERALDINE LEA, child care supr.; b. Los Angeles, Sept. 24, 1955; d. Clyde Kenneth and Geraldine Elsie (Kuschell) Mawhinney; B.S.W., Calif. State U., Long Beach, 1977. Child-care worker Maryvale, residential treatment center for girls, Rosemead, Calif., 1977-79, evening supr., 1979-82, program supr., 1982—. Cert. trainer mgmt. assualtive behavior, Calif. Mem. Nat. Assn. Social Workers Nat. Assn. Edn. for Young Child, So. Calif. Assn. Edn. for Young Child. Roman Catholic. Home: 9253 Bona Vista Ln Whittier CA 90602 Office: 7600 E Graves Ave Rosemead CA 91770

MONROE, STANLEY EDWIN, surgeon; b. Bangor, Mich., June 26, 1902; s. Samuel E. and Ella (Monroe) M.; A.B., U. Mich., 1925; M.D., U. Chgo., 1936; m. Ruth Williams, June 14, 1932 (dec. 1981); m. 2d, Flora Doss, Aug. 6, 1982. Intern, Evanston (Ill.) Hosp., 1935-36, resident surgeon, 1936-37, asst. surgeon, 1940-41; clin. asst. surgeon Northwestern U., 1938-39, instr. surgery, 1940-41; asst. to Dr. Frederick Christopher, 1937-41; chief surgery VA Hosp., Tucson, 1947-49; surgeon ARAMCO, Saudi Arabia, 1950; pvt. practice, Chula Vista, Calif., 1952-82; staff Paradise Valley Hosp., Mercy Hosp. (San Diego); founder Monroe Clinic. Served from capt. to maj. AUS, 1942-47; PTO. Diplomate Am. Bd. Surgery. Fellow Soc. for Academic Achievement, Internat. Coll. Surgeons; mem. Soc. Gen. Surgeons of San Diego, Am. Med. Writers Assn., Assn. Mil. Surgeons, Am. Soc. Abdominal Surgeons (founding), Alpha Omega Alpha, Phi Beta Pi. Author: Medical Phrase Book with Vocabulary (also Spanish edit.). Office: 2 Palomar Dr Chula Vista CA 92011

MONROE, TERRY ROBERT, fitness and health firm executive; b. Los Angeles, Mar. 27, 1950; s. Monte and Dorothy (Brown) M.; B.A., U. So. Calif., 1972; Ed.M., Harvard U., 1974, M.S., 1975, postgrad., 1975-77. Health planner Orange County Health Planning Council, Tustin, Calif., 1977-80; instr. Calif. State U.-Long Beach, 1979-80, Coastline Community Coll., Fountain Valley, Calif., 1978-81; research specialist U. Calif.-Irvine, 1980-81; dir. personal health programs Newport Beach Psychol. Assos. (Calif.), 1981; exec. dir. Powerobics: Total Fitness and Health Programs, Newport Beach, 1981—; dir. Wellness Resources, Balboa Island, Calif., 1982—. Mem. adv. bd. Health Policy Council, N.Y.C.; mem. adv. bd. Health Promotion with Elderly, U. Wash.; vice chmn. Laguna Beach Human Needs Task Force, 1978-80; mem. Calif. Health Promotion Adv. Com., 1981; mem. Calif. State Task Force on Health Edn. Standards, 1978-80. USPHS fellow, 1974-75. Fellow Soc. Pub. Health Edn.; mem. Orange County Harvard U. Alumni Assn. (treas. 1978-81). Contbg. editor: The Living Center, 1981; editor: Orange County Wellness Resource Guide, 1981-82. Home: 375 Osgood Ct Laguna Beach CA 92651 Office: 180 Newport Center Dr Newport Beach CA 92660

MONSON, DAVID SMITH, state ofcl.; b. Salt Lake City, June 20, 1945; s. Smith Weston and Dorothy (Brammer) M.; B.S. in accounting, U. Utah, 1970; m. Julianne Johnson, Feb. 4, 1971; children—David Johnson, Traci Lyn, Marianne, Kari, Smith Douglas. Accountant, Elmer Fox and Co., Salt Lake City, 1970-72; auditor State of Utah, Salt Lake City, 1972-76, lt. gov., sec. of state, 1976—. Mem. exec. com. Nat. Conf. Lt. Govs., 1978—; bd. dirs. Utah Soc. Prevention Blindness; v.p. Western Conf. Council State Govts., 1974-75; trustee Travis Found., Ballet West, 1977-81; chmn. Utah Cancer Crusade, 1979-80; unit chmn. Am. Cancer Soc., 1980-81; govt. unit chmn. United Way, 1975, 79, assoc. campaign chmn., 1981, Campaign chmn., 1982. C.P.A., Utah. Mem. Am. Inst. C.P.A.s, Utah Assn. C.P.A.s, Nat. Assn. Secs. of State. Republican. Mormon. Office: 203 State Capitol Bldg Salt Lake City UT 84114

MONSON, LARRY ALVIN, international sales company official; b. Hutchinson, Minn., Aug. 15, 1944; s. Alvin Theodore and Erma Marjorie (Peterson) M.; student U. N.D., 1963-66; m. Sheila R. Hovda, Nov. 6, 1966; children—Erik Allen, Tamara Jo. Engr. Dale Electronics, Yankton, S.D., 1966, Melpar, Inc., Falls Church, Va., 1967-69; engr., sales mgr. internat. sales Link div. Singer Co., Binghamton, N.Y., 1969—. Served with USAF, 1962-66. Mem. Assn. U.S. Army, Am. Mgmt. Assn., Acrospace Industries Assn., Nat. Aeronautical Inst. Republican. Lutheran. Home: 1761 Maysong Ct San Jose CA 95131 Office: 1077 E Arques Ave Sunnyvale CA 94086

MONSON, THOMAS SPENCER, church ofcl., publishing co. exec.; b. Salt Lake City, Aug. 21, 1927: s. George Spencer and Gladys (Condie) M.; B.S. in Marketing with honors, U. Utah, 1948; M.B.A., Brigham Young U., 1974; m. Frances Beverly Johnson, Oct. 7, 1948; children—Thomas L., Ann Frances, Clark Spencer. With Deseret News Press, Salt Lake City, 1948-64, mgr., 1962-64; mem. Council Twelve Apostles, Ch. of Jesus Christ of Latter Day Saints, 1963—, bishop, 1950-55, pres. Canadian Mission, 1959-62; pres., chmn. bd. Deseret News Pub. Co., 1977—; dir. Beneficial Life Ins. Co., Mountain States Tel. & Tel., Comml. Security Bank, Deseret Mgmt. Corp., Continental Western Life Ins. Co., Murdock Travel, Inc.; Utah bd. advisers Mountain States Tel. & Tel; pres. Printing Industry Utah, 1958; bd. dirs. Printing Industry Am., 1958-64. Mem. Utah State Bd. Regents; nat. exec. bd. Boy Scouts Am.; trustee Brigham Young U. Served with USNR, 1945-46. Recipient Recognition award Printing Industry Am., 1964; Silver Beaver, Silver Buffalo awards Boy Scouts Am. Mem. Utah Assn. Sales Execs., U. Utah Alumni Assn. (dir.), Salt Lake Advt. Club, Alpha Kappa Psi. Club: Exchange (Salt Lake City). Home: 4125 Carter Circle Salt Lake City UT 84117 Office: 47 East S Temple St Salt Lake City UT 84111

MONTAG, DAVID MOSES, computer company executive; b. Los Angeles, Apr. 30, 1939; s. Gustave and Esther (Kessler) M.; student UCLA, 1957-61; m. Beverly Edythe Bowden, Sept. 24, 1967; children—Daniel Gershon, Esther Yael, Michael Menachem. Tech. writer L.H. Butcher Co., Los Angeles, 1961; phys. sci. lab. technician East Los Angeles Coll., Monterey Park, 1961—, planetarium lectr., 1963—; partner EDUCOMP, Vernon, Calif., 1979—; pres., chief exec. officer Aquinas Computer Corp.; ednl. cons. for computer-assisted instrn. Bd. dirs. Or Chadash, Inc., Monterey Park, 1968—; v.p., bd. dirs. Coll. Religious Conf., 1968—. Mem. Assn. of Orthodox Jewish Scientists, Laser Inst. Am., AIAA. Home: 729 N Spaulding Ave Los Angeles CA 90046 Office: 1301 Brooklyn Ave Monterey Park CA 91754

MONTAG, PAUL MICHAEL, microcomputer co. exec.; b. Freehold, N.J., Mar. 27, 1945; s. Michael M. and Mary Montag; B.S.E.E., B.A., Rutgers U., 1968; M.B.A., U. Santa Clara, 1972; m. Sandra McCobin, Sept. 8, 1968; 1 dau., Pamela J. Elec. design engr. Raytheon Co., Sudbury, Mass., 1968-69; product mktg. mgr. Hewlett-Packard, Palo Alto, Calif., 1969-73; sr. sales engr. Texas Instruments, Los Angeles, 1973-75; Western regional sales mgr. Control Logic Inc., Santa Ana, Calif., 1975-77; pres. Micro-Specialists, Inc., Hollywood, Calif., 1978—; dir. Melvic Enterprises. Mem. Assn. M.B.A. Execs., IEEE, Am. Mgmt. Assn. Club: Masons. Home: 19342 Baywater Ln Huntington Beach CA 92646 Office: 535 E Main St Tustin CA 92646

MONTALVO, FANYA S., computer scientist; b. Monterrey, Nuevo Leon, Mex., Aug. 22, 1947; s. Alfonso S. and Sava (Brusilovsky) M.; B.S., Loyola U., 1969; postgrad. U. Ill., 1971-72; Ph.D. in Computer and Info. Sci., U. Mass., 1976. Research assoc. in psychology, Loyola U., 1969-71; research asst. bio-engring. U. Ill., 1971-72; research asst. in computer sci. U. Mass., 1972-76; computer scientist Lawrence Berkeley (Calif.) Lab., 1976-80; computer scientist Hewlett Packard Labs., Palo Alto, Calif., 1980—. Mem. Am. Assn. Artificial Intelligence, Cognitive Sci. Soc., Assn. Computing Machinery. Contbr. articles to Am. and Japanese profl. jours. Home: 870 Bruce St Palo Alto CA 94303 Office: Hewlett Packard Bldg 3L 1501 Page Mill Rd Palo Alto CA 94304

MONTANO, ANDREW, hospital administrator, educator; b. N.Y.C., June 15, 1929; s. Victor and Carmen Maria Rivera (LePrant) M.; m. Lillian Marie Levizon; children—Richard, Linda, Anne, Marguerite; m. 2d, Janett Welton, June 17, 1979. B.S., Calif. State Coll., Long Beach, 1957, M.A., 1960; M.P.A., Am. U., 1960; M.Ed., Nat. U., San Diego, 1974. Assoc. research chemist VA Med. Ctr., Long Beach, Calif., 1957-59, med. technologist, 1959-61, asst. to research coordinator, 1961-62, research adminstrv. officer, 1967-71; asst. chief research facilities planning VA Central Office, Washington, 1962-66, acting chief research in basic scis., 1966-67, phys. sci. adminstrv. officer, 1967; asst. hosp. dir. trainee VA Med. Ctr., Martinez, Calif., 1971-72; asst. hosp. dir. VA Med. Ctr., San Diego, 1972-79; assoc. hosp. dir. VA Med. Ctr., Miami, Fla., 1979-81; dir. Jerry L. Pettis Meml. VA Hosp., Loma Linda, Calif., 1981—; assoc. prof. Nat. U., U. Miami, 1979-81; adj. lectr. Fla. Internat. U., 1980-81; mem. faculty U. Redlands (Calif.); asst. prof. Sch. Psychiatry, Loma Linda Med. Sch., 1982—; examiner bd. behavioral scis. Calif. Dept. Consumer Affairs, 1977-79; mem. citizen adv. com. to dean sch. Social Work Service, San Diego State U., 1977-79. Recipient award for contbns. in pub. adminstrn. field Calif. Legislature, 1978. Mem. U.S. and Mex. Border Pub. Health Assn., Nat. Chicano Health Orgn., Health Care Execs. Assn. Contbr. to profl. publs. Office: Jerry L Pettes Meml VA Hosp 11201 Benton St Loma Linda CA 92357

MONTERO, DARREL MARTIN, sociologist; b. Sacramento, Mar. 4, 1946; s. Tony and Evelyn (Hash) M.; A.B., Calif. State U., 1970; M.A., U. Calif., Los Angeles, 1972, Ph.D., 1974; m. Tara Kathleen McLaughlin, July 6, 1975; children—David Paul, Lynn Elizabeth, Laura Ann. Postgrad. researcher Japanese Am. Research Project, U. Calif., Los Angeles, 1971-73, asso. head Program on Comparative Ethnic Studies, Survey Research Center, 1973-75, dir. research Japanese Am. Research Project, 1973-75; asst. prof. sociology Case Western Res. U., Cleve., 1975-76; asst. prof. urban studies, research sociologist Pub. Opinion Survey, dir. urban ethnic research program U. Md., College Park, 1976-79; assoc. prof. and dir. urban ethnic research program Ariz. State U., Tempe, 1979—; cons. research sect. Viewer Sponsored Television Found., Los Angeles, Berrien E. Moore Law Office, Inc., Gardena, Calif., 1973. Served with U.S. Army, 1966-72. Mem. Am. Sociol. Assn., Am. Assn. Pub. Opinion Research (exec. council, standards com.), Am. Ednl. Research Assn., Council of Social Work Education, Soc. Study of Social Problems, D.C. Sociol. Soc., Am. Soc. Pub. Adminstrn. Author: Japanese Americans: Changing Patterns of Ethnic Affiliation Over Three Generations, 1980: Urban Studies, 1978; Vietnamese Americans: Patterns of Resettlement and Socioeconomic Adaptation in the United States, 1979; editorial bd. Humanity and Society, 1978—. Home: 1444 W Kiva St Mesa AZ 85202 Office: Sch Social Work Ariz State U Tempe AZ 85281

MONTGOMERY, DANIEL GEORGE, lawyer; b. Oakland, Calif., Apr. 20, 1944; s. Daniel George and Helen Elizabeth (Grosskopf) M.; student (Calif. State scholar) U. San Francisco, 1966, J.D., 1974; m. Diane M. Azevedo, Nov. 15, 1974. Admitted to Calif. bar, 1975; men's hairstylist, 1967-75, also law clk. Edwin T. Caldwell, 1973-75; individual practice law, San Francisco, 1975-79; partner firm Montgomery & Goldkind, Chico, Calif., 1979-81, Montgomery & Larson, Chico, 1982—; officer, dir. Sumar Corp.; dir. Tri-Calmo Corp. Mem. San Francisco Trial Lawyers Assn., San Francisco Bar Assn., San Francisco Barristers Club, Butte County Bar Assn., Butte County Barristers. Club: Elks. Office: 1209 The Esplanade Suite 4 Chico CA 95926

MONTGOMERY, JAMES FISCHER, savs. and loan assn. exec.; b. Topeka, Nov. 30, 1934; s. James Maurice and Frieda Ellen (Fischer) M.; B.A. in Accounting, U. Calif., Los Angeles, 1957; m. Linda Jane Hicks, Aug. 25, 1956; children—Michael James, Jeffrey Allen, Andrew Steven, John Gregory. With Price, Waterhouse & Co., C.P.A.'s, Los Angeles, 1957-60; controller Conejo Valley Devel. Co., Thousand Oaks, Calif., 1960; asst. to pres. Gt. Western Fin. Corp., Beverly Hills, Calif., 1960-64; fin. v.p., treas. United Fin. Corp., Los Angeles, 1964-69, exec. v.p., 1969-74, pres., 1975; pres. Citizens Savs. & Loan Assn., Los Angeles, 1970-75; pres., chief operating officer, dir. Gt. Western Fin. Corp., also Gt. Western Savs. and Loan Assn., Beverly Hills, 1975-79, pres., chief exec. officer, 1979-81, pres., chmn., chief exec. officer, 1981—; dir. Fed. Home Loan Bank San Francisco, Petrolane, Inc.; trustee Putnam Mgmt. Co.; mem. thrift instns. adv. council Fed. Res. Bd. Served with AUS, 1958-60. Mem. Calif. C. of C. (dir.), U.S. League of Savs. Instns. (exec. com.). Office: Great Western Financial Co 8484 Wilshire Blvd Beverly Hills CA 90211

MONTGOMERY, JEFFERSON DAVIS, JR., market research consultant; b. Frenchtown, Ark., June 23, 1928; s. Jefferson Davis and Clarcie Opal (Williams) M.; B.S. in Elec. Engring., Ill. Inst. Tech., 1954; M.B.A., U. Santa Clara, 1973; m. Lois Evelyn Cummins, Mar. 14, 1947; children—Samuel Gale, Theresa Ruth, Valerie Kaye, Jeffrey Stephen. Engr., Andrew Corp., Orland Park, Ill. and Claremont, Calif., 1953-55, mktg. mgr., 1955-57, gen. mgr., 1957-63; product mgr. Varian Assos., Palo Alto, Calif., 1963-67, mgr. long range product planning, 1967-71; dir. electronic component market research Quantum Sci. Corp., Palo Alto, 1971-73; pres. Gnostic Concepts; Inc., Menlo Park, Calif., 1973-81, Electronicast Corp., Redwood City, Calif., 1981—. Councilman, City of Montclair (Calif.), 1962-63; planning commr. City of Belmont (Calif.), 1971-72. Served with USN, 1945-49. Mem. IEEE (sr.), Soc. Info. Display, Instrument Soc. Am., Soc. Photo-Optical Instrumentation Engrs., Eta Kappa Nu. Democrat. Congregationalist. Office: Electronicast Corp 40 Birch St #6 Redwood City CA 94062

MONTGOMERY, JOEL R., journalist; b. Ames, Iowa, Aug. 13, 1946; s. Joel and Maxine (Kepner) M.; B.A., Carleton Coll., 1968; postgrad. U. N.Mex., 1979-80; m. Susan Frances Connors, Sept. 4, 1976; children—Zoe Noelle, Colin Conor. Copy boy, reporter, copy editor Rocky Mountain News, Denver, 1963-66; reporter, photographer Longmont (Colo.) Daily Times-Call, 1968-69; reporter Healdsburg (Calif.) Tribune, 1969; copy editor The Albuquerque Tribune, 1972-78, asst. city editor, 1980-81, copy desk chief, 1981-82, assoc. sports editor, 1982—; English tchr. Peace Corps, Morocco, 1978. Recipient 1st Pl. award N.Mex. Press Assn., 1973. Mem. Soc. Profl. Journalists, Albuquerque Press Club, Sigma Delta Chi. Home: 3509 Calle del Monte NE Albuquerque NM 87106 Office: 717 Silver Ave SW Albuquerque NM 87102

MONTGOMERY, JOHN WARWICK, religion educator; b. Warsaw, N.Y., Oct. 18, 1931; s. Maurice Warwick and Harriet (Smith) M.; A.B. with distinction, Cornell U., 1952; B.L.S., U. Calif.-Berkeley, 1954, M.A., 1958; M.Div., Wittenberg U., 1958, M.S.T., 1960; Ph.D., U. Chgo., 1962; Docteur de L'Universite, mention Theologie Protestante, U. Strasbourg (France), 1964; LL.B., LaSalle Extension U., 1977; diploma cum laude, Internat. Inst. Human Rights, Strasbourg, 1978; m. Joyce Ann Bailer, Aug. 14, 1954; children—Elizabeth Ann, David Warwick, Catherine Ann, Librarian, gen. reference service U. Calif. Library, Berkeley, 1954-55; instr. Bibl. Hebrew, Hellenistic Greek, Mediaeval Latin, Wittenberg U., Springfield, Ohio, 1956-59; ordained to ministry Luth. Ch., 1958; head librarian Swift Library Div. and Philosophy, mem. federated theol. faculty U. Chgo., 1959-60; assoc. prof., chmn. dept. history Sir. Wilfred Laurier U., Ont., Can., 1960-64; prof., chmn. div. ch. history, history of Christian thought, dir. European seminar program Trinity Evang. Div. Sch., Deerfield, Ill., 1964-74; prof. law and theology Internat. Sch. Law, Washington, 1974-75; theol. cons. Christian Legal Soc., 1975-76; prof. Large Melodyland Christian Ctr., Anaheim, Calif., 1976-80; dir. studies Internat. Inst. Human Rights, Strasbourg, 1979-81; dean, prof. jurisprudence, dir. European program Simon Greenleaf Sch. Law, Orange, Calif., 1980—; vis. prof. Concordia Theol. Sem., Springfield, Ill., 1964-67, DePaul U., Chgo., 1967-70; hon. fellow Revelle Coll., U. Calif.-San Diego, 1970; bar: Va. 1978, Calif. 1979, U.S. Supreme Ct. 1981; Nat. Luth. Ednl. Conf. fellow, 1959-60; Can. Council postdoctoral sr. research fellow, 1963-64; Am. Assn. Theol. Schs. faculty fellow, 1967-68. Diplomate Med. Library Assn. Fellow Academie de Gastronomie Brillat-Savarin (Paris), Victoria Inst. (London), Am. Sci. Affiliation (nat. philosophy sci. and history sci. commn. 1966-70; mem. Middle Temple (London), World Assn. Law Profs., Am. Soc. Internat. Law, ABA, Internat. Bar Assn., Union Internat. des Avocats, Internat. Real Estate Fedn., Tolkien Soc. Am., Am. Hist. Assn., Soc. Reformation Research, Creation Research Soc., Tyndale Fellowship (Eng.), Am. Theol. Library Assn., Bibliog. Soc. U. Va., Evang. Theol. Soc., Internat. Wine and Food Soc., Societe des Amis des Arts (Strasbourg), Chaine des Rotisseurs (chevalier), Phi Beta Kappa, Phi Kappa Phi, Beta Phi Mu. Author: The Is God Dead? Controversy, 1966; (with Thomas J. J. Altizer) The Altizer-Montgomery Dialogue, 1967; Crisis in Lutheran Theology, 2 vols., 1967, rev. edit., 1973; Esconfiable el Christianismo?, 1968; Ecumenicity, Evangelicals, and Rome, 1969; Where is History Going?, 1969; History and Christianity, 1970; Damned Through the Church, 1970; The Suicide of Christian Theology, 1970; Computors, Cultural Change and the Christ, 1970; In Defense of Martin Luther, 1970; La Mort de Dieu, 1971; (with Joseph Fletcher) Situation Ethics: True or False?, 1972; The Quest for Noah's Ark, 1972, rev. edit., 1974; Verdammt durch die Kirche?, 1973; Christianity for the Toughminded, 1973; Cross and Crucible, 2 vols., 1973; Principalities and Powers: the World of the Occult, 1973, rev. edit., 1975; How Do We Know There Is a God?, 1973; Myth, Allegory and Gospel, 1974; The Inerrant Word of God, 1974; Jurisprudence: A Book of Reading, 1974; The Law above the Law, 1975; Como Sabemos Que Hay un Dios?, 1975; Demon Possession, 1975; The Shaping of America, 1976; Faith Founded on Fact, 1978; Law and Gospel: A Study in Jurisprudence, 1978; Slaughter of the Innocents, 1981, others; editor: Lippincott's Evangelical Perspectives, 7 vols., 1970-72; International Scholars Directory, 1973; editor-at-large Christianity Today, 1965—; films: Is Christianity Credible?, 1968; In Search of Noah's Ark, 1977; Defending the Biblical Gospel, 1981; contbr. articles to profl. jours. Address: 1 rue de Palerme Strasbourg 67000 France also 2530 Shadow Ridge Ln Orange CA 92667

MONTGOMERY, WILLIAM FREDRIC, accountant; b. Los Angeles, Aug. 25, 1921; s. Raymond R. and Cora L. (Dock) M.; student, Sawyer Bus. Coll., 1946-47; student law LaSalle U., 1948-50; m. Ave Maria T. Devine, Oct. 13, 1946; children—Ave Maria, Sarah Maria, Margaret Mary, Kathleen B., William Fredric. Accounting trainee Paul E. Bain & Asso., Pasadena, Calif., 1947-49; comptroller Diggins Enterprize Corp., 1949-53; mgr., tax cons. Bookkeepers Bus. Service Co., 1953-57; pub. accountant, tax cons. William F. Montgomery, Pub. Accountant, Sacramento, 1957—. Served with AUS, 1942-45. C.P.A., Calif. Mem. Soc. Am. Accountants, Am. Soc. Fed. Tax Accountants, Nat. Soc. C.P.A.'s, Soc. Calif. Accountants, Sacramento Exchange Club, Holy Name Soc. (treas.). Moose, Woodmen, K.C. (3 deg.) Club: Valley Hi Country. Home: 114 Northlite Circle Sacramento CA 95831 Office: 3823 V St Sacramento CA 95817

MONTHAN, DORIS BORN, writer, editor; b. Manitowoc, Wis., May 26, 1924; d. Edgar Jacob and Linda Sophia (Vogt) Born; m. Guy Monthan, Sept. 20, 1952; 1 son, William Edgar. Student U. Ariz., 1943-44, N.Y.U., 1948-49, Columbia U., 1950-51. Women's editor Tucson Daily Citizen, 1944-45; sect. editor Women's Wear Daily, N.Y.C., 1945-46; assoc. editor Simplicity Mag., N.Y.C., 1949-51; advt. mgr. Crown Sleep Shops, Pasadena, Calif., 1953-67; editor-in-chief Northland Press, Flagstaff, Ariz., 1970-72; editor Mus. Notes, Mus. No. Ariz., Flagstaff, 1972-75; tchr. writing, cons. Flagstaff Jr. High Sch., 1980-81; author: The Thief (novel), 1961; (with Guy Monthan) Art and Indian Individualists: The Art of Seventeen Contemporary Artists and Craftsmen, 1975, Nacimientos: Nativity Scenes by Southwest Indian Artisans, 1979; R.C. Gorman: The Lithographs, 1978; contbr. articles on Am. Indian art to art publs. Bd. dirs. Flagstaff Festival of the Arts, 1970-82, art cons., 1979-82; panelist Ariz. Commn. Arts, 1982—. Recipient awards Rounce and Coffin Club, 1975, Book Builders, 1975, Border Regional Library Assn., 1975. Mem. Assistance League, Kappa Kappa Gamma Alumnae Club. Democrat. Episcopalian (vestry). Address: PO Box 1698 Flagstaff AZ 86002

MONTRONE, PAUL MICHAEL, industrial company executive; b. Scranton, Pa., May 8, 1941; s. Angelo H. and Beatrice M. (Giancini) M.; m. Sandra R. Gaudenzi, May 30, 1963; children—Michele Marie, Angelo Henry, Jerome Lawrence. B.S. in Acctg. magna cum laude, U. Scranton, 1961; Ph.D. in Fin., Econs. and Ops. Research, Columbia U., 1966. Ops. analyst Office of Sec. Def., Washington, 1965-67; v.p. Penn-Dixie Industries, N.Y.C., 1967-69; exec. v.p., chief fin. officer Wheelabrator-Frye Inc., Hampton, N.H., 1970-83; exec. v.p. Signal Cos., Inc., La Jolla, Calif., 1983—, also dir. Trustee New Eng. Conservatory of Music, Marywood Coll., Scranton; overseer Boston Symphony Orch.; incorporator N.H. Charitable Fund; bd. visitors Whittemore Sch. Bus. and Econs., U. N.H. Served to capt. U.S. Army, 1965-67. Roman Catholic. Clubs: Brook, University (N.Y.C.); Bald Peak Colony (Melvin Village, N.H.). Home: Great Hill Hampton Falls NH 03844 Office: Liberty Ln Hampton NH 03842 also 11255 N Torrey Pines Rd La Jolla CA 92037

MOODY, GEORGE FRANKLIN, banker; b. Riverside, Calif., July 28, 1930; s. William Clifford and Mildred R. (Scott) M.; student Riverside City Coll., 1948-50; grad. with honors, Pacific Coast Banking Sch., 1963; m. Mary Jane Plank, Jan. 19, 1950; children—Jeffrey George, Jane Ellen Moody Fowler, John Franklin, Joseph William. Bus. officer U. Calif., Riverside, 1950-52; with Security Pacific Nat. Bank, 1953—, v.p., personnel dir., Los Angeles, 1970-71, sr. v.p. inland div. adminstrn., 1971-73, exec. v.p., 1973-78, vice chmn., from 1978, pres., chief operating officer, 1981—; dir. Music Center Operating Co. Bd. dirs. YMCA of Met. Los Angeles, Hollywood Presbyterian Med. Center, Los Angeles chpt. ARC; trustee Pomona Coll., 1981—; exec. bd. Los Angeles Area council Boy Scouts Am., 1980—. Mem. Los Angeles C. of C. (chmn. bd., dir.), Mchts. and Mfrs. Assn. (treas.), Colorado River Assn. (pres.). Republican. Presbyn. Club: Hacienda Heights Golf. Address: Security Pacific Nat Bank 333 S Hope St Los Angeles CA 90071

MOODY, HELEN FLETCHER, writer, educator; b. Palo Alto, Calif., Feb. 6, 1949; d. Dwight L. and Bobbie Jean (Naugher) M.; m. Michael James Stroud, Sept. 11, 1977; 1 dau., Amy S. Ph.D., U. Calif.-Berkeley, 1980. Founder, dir. Communications Strategies, Inc., Albuquerque, 1980—. Mem. Women in Communications, Assn. Devel. Computer-based Instructional Systems, Am. Soc. Tng. and Devel., MLA. Democrat. Episcopalian. Author: The Debate of the Rose, 1980; Writing Strategies for Professionals, 1981; Solving Problems, 1982. Office: PO Box 14773 Albuquerque NM 87501

MOODY, JAMES LAROY, theatrical lighting designer and cons.; b. Joliet, Ill., Apr. 25, 1942; s. Tom A. and Norma Jean (Story) M.; B.S., So. Ill. U., 1967; M.F.A., UCLA, 1969; m. Cheryl Rae Geleto, Aug. 28, 1968 (div. Oct. 1978); children—Scott Alexander, Kimberly Rae. Tchr. theatrical lighting UCLA, 1968-69; tech. adminstr. Berkey-Colortran Inc., Burbank, 1969-71; owner James Moody Lighting Consultants, Northridge, Calif., 1971-72; co-founder, owner Sundance Lighting, Hollywood, Calif., 1972—, pres., chmn. bd., 1975—. Served with USAF, 1961-65. Mem. Illuminating Engrs. Soc., Acad. TV Arts and Sci., U.S. Inst. Theatre Tech., Profl. Entertainment Prodn. Soc. (founding chmn. 1979, pres. 1980), Am. Soc. Lighting Dirs. (bd. dirs., award of excellence 1979, 80), Internat. Photographers (dir. photography), United Scenic Artists. Contbr. articles to profl. jours. Designer lighting for concert artists including John Denver, Billy Preston, Diana Ross, Fifth Dimension, Frank Zappa, Rod Stewart and Faces, Jackson Browne, Stevie Wonder, Captain and Tennille, Donny and Marie Osmond, Andy Gibb; also for network and syndicated TV shows. Home: 21907 Gresham St Canoga Park CA 91303 Office: 19725 Sherman Way Suite 130 Canoga Park CA 91306

MOOERS, CHRISTOPHER NORTHRUP KENNARD, phys. oceanographer, educator; b. Hagerstown, Md., Nov. 11, 1935; s. Frank Burt and Helen (Miner) M.; B.S., U.S. Naval Acad., 1957; M.S., U. Conn., 1964; Ph.D., Oreg. State U., 1969; m. Elizabeth Eva Fauntleroy, June 11, 1960; children—Blaine Hansen MacFee, Randall Walden Lincoln. Postdoctoral fellow U. Liverpool (Eng.), 1969-70; asst. prof. U. Miami (Fla.), 1970-72, asso. prof., 1972-76; asso. prof. U. Del., Newark, 1976-78, prof., 1978-79; prof., chmn. dept. oceanography Naval Postgrad. Sch., Monterey, Calif., 1979—. Served with USN, 1957-64. NSF grad. fellow, 1964-67; NATO postdoctoral fellow, 1969-70; Sr. Queen Elizabeth fellow, 1980. Mem. Am. Geophys. Union (pres.-elect oceanography sect.), Eastern Pacific Oceanographic Council (chmn. 1979—), Am. Meteorol. Soc., Acoustical Soc. Am., Challenger Soc., Oceanographic Soc. Japan, Marine Tech. Soc., AAAS, Sigma Xi. Contbr. articles to profl. jours. Home: 4 Pinehill Way Monterey CA 93940 Office: Dept Oceanography Naval Postgrad Sch Monterey CA 93940

MOON, ELVIN WARDELL, aircraft corporation executive; b. Pine Bluff, Ark., Sept. 15, 1947; s. Madison and Lee'Ester M.; B.S. in Bus. Adminstrn., U. Ark., Pine Bluff, 1971; M.B.A., Pepperdine U., 1982. Asst. produce mgr. Market Basket, Pine Bluff, 1965-67; maintenance dept. Royal Tuft Carpet Mill, 1967-69; coop. edn. student Weyerhaeuser Co., 1969-70; profl. employment rep. Rockwell Internat. Space Div., Downey, Calif., 1971-74; employment supr. Bechtel Power Corp., Norwalk, Calif., 1974-81; mgr. coll. relations Hughes Aircraft Corp., Los Angeles, 1977-81; mgr. staffing Northrop Corp., Gardena, Calif., 1981—; cons. in field. Trustee, Calif. Dem. Council, 1974-78; candidate Calif. Assembly, 1978; trustee Calif. Dem. Council Youth Motivation Task Force, 1974-79; mem. Bd. Bldg. and Safety Commrs., Los Angeles, 1983—; active community youth orgns. Recipient various awards. Mem. Western Coll. Placement Assn., So. Calif. Tech. Personnel Com., Employment Mgmt. Assn. Methodist. Home: 8924 Kitty Hawk Ave Westchester CA 90045 Office: PO Box 1338 Gardena CA 90249

MOON, MARJORIE RUTH, ofcl. State of Idaho; b. Pocatello, Idaho, June 16, 1926; d. Clark Blakeley and Ruth (Gerhart) Moon; student Pacific U., 1944-46; A.B. in Journalism cum laude, U. Wash., 1948. Reporter, Pocatello Tribune, 1944, Caldwell (Idaho) News-Tribune, 1948-50; reporter, chief Boise (Idaho) bur. Deseret News, Salt Lake City, 1950-52; owner Idaho Pioneer Statewide, Boise, 1952-55; founder, owner Garden City (Idaho) Gazette, 1954-68; partner Sawtooth Lodge, 1958-61, Modern Press, Boise 1958-61; treas. State of Idaho, 1963—. Mem. Nat. Assn. State Treasurers (sec.-treas. 1976-78, regional v.p. 1979), Western State Treasurers Conf. (past chmn.), Idaho Press Women (past pres.), Nat. Fedn. Press Women. Democrat. Conglist. Soroptomist (past pres.). Office: State House Boise ID 83720

MOONAN, RAYMOND LEWIS, aerospace company official; b. Trenton, N.J., Feb. 24, 1930; s. Raymond Xavier and Claire Mary (Ginther) M.; B.S., U.S. Naval Acad., 1953; m. Barbara Jean Payne, July 12, 1958; children—Deborah Lynne, David Allyn, Brooks, Deborah Lynne, David Allyn. Commd. ensign U.S. Navy, 1953, advanced through grades to lt., 1957 resigned, 1961; tech. mgmt. specialist Rockwell Internat., Los Angeles, 1961—. Mem. Am. Def. Preparedness Assn., Tailhook Assn. Republican. Roman Catholic. Home: 13940 Tahiti Way #226 Marina Del Rey CA 90291 Office: 201 N Douglas Douglas vice 331 Lapham St El Segundo CA 90245

MOONEY, PATRICK JOSEPH, gerontologist; b. Chgo., July 21, 1930; s. Hugh Nicholas and Dorothy (Montgomery) M.; B.Sc., Roosevelt U., Chgo., 1965; children—Mary Kimera, Michael Kevin, Mary Kathleen. Constrn. and devel. engr., Chgo., 1950-64; archtl. supt. U. Ill., Chgo., 1964-67; bus. mgmt. systems cons., Chgo. and San Diego, Calif., 1969-76; co-founder, pres. Supernutrition Research, San Francisco, 1976—, Forever Young, San Francisco, 1977—; research and teaching assoc. Am. Inst. Biosocial Research, Tacoma, 1979—; founder, dir. Inst. Human Ecology, San Francisco, 1980—; cons. balancing body chemistry for life-extension. Recipient award for outstanding contbns. to field of nutrition, Internat. Coll. Applied Nutrition, 1980. Author: Supernutrition, the Answer to Aging, Wrinkles and the Degenerative Diseases, 1978; (with Hans J. Kugler) A Computerized Diet Analysis and Health Risk Evaluation, 1979. Office: 531 44th Ave San Francisco CA 94121

MOONEY, SHERRY LYNN, substance abuse counselor; b. Morgantown, W.Va., Sept. 2, 1948; d. Harry David and Genevieve (Smith) Edwards; m. Edward Page Whittaker, June 6, 1964 (div. Mar. 1980); children—David E., Stephen S.; m. 2d, Robert Emmet Mooney, Jr., Mar. 28, 1981. A.A., Burlington County Coll., 1976; B.A., Thomas Edison Coll., 1978. Med. liaison officer Fed. Govt. Alcohol and Drug Control Program, Frankfurt, Germany, 1978-80; aftercare/family service coordinator Raleigh Hills Hosp., Redwood City, Calif., 1980—; pres. Counseling Assocs./Scholarship Services, Pleasanton, Calif., 1982—; edn. dir. Counseling Ednl. Assocs., San Francisco, 1983—. Mayor, Community Life Program, Frankfurt, Germany, 1974-76. Mem. Nat. Assn. Alcoholism Counselors, Soc. Hosp. Social Work Dirs., Calif. Assn. Alcoholism Counselors. Home: 4207 Dundalk Ct Pleasanton CA 94566 Office: 1600 Gordon St Redwood City CA 94661

MOORADIAN, GREGORY CHARLES, research physicist; b. Tampa, Fla., Sept. 5, 1947; s. Richard Dick and Lucianne (Antonian) M.; B.S., Fresno State U., 1969; M.S., U. Calif., San Diego, 1971, Ph.D., 1973; m. Marsha Eileen Sterling, Dec. 27, 1973; children—Michelle Lucienne, Michael Sterling. Laser physicist Naval Weapons Center, China Lake, Calif., 1968-69; cons. laser systems and weapons Greg Mooradian Enterprises, Del Mar, Calif., 1971-73; head laser lab., research physicist in high power laser effects Gulf Gen. Atomic, La Jolla, Calif., 1969-72; NSF Presdl. appointee, optical communications Naval Electronics Lab. Center, San Diego, 1972-73; br. head, chief staff scientist in optical communications, phenomenology and detection Naval Ocean Systems Center, San Diego, 1973—, chief staff scientist for electro-optics, chief scientist strategic laser communications program, instr. in field. Active local polit. and community activities, Del Mar. Recipient Navy Meritorious Civilian Service award, 1977, various scholarships; NSF fellow, 1969-71. Mem. Optical Soc. Am., Am. Phys. Soc., Phi Kappa Phi (nat. award 1969). Chmn., organizer confs.; contbr. papers to profl. publs. Patentee in field. Home: 13792 Mar Scenic Dr Del Mar CA 92014 Office: NOSC Code 811 271 Catalina Blvd San Diego CA 92152

MOORE, BOUDE CLISBY, electrical engineer; b. Nagasaki, Japan, Mar. 11, 1925; s. Boude Chambers and Anne (McAlpine) M.; m. Ramona Faye Smith, Oct. 4, 1944; 6 children; m. 2d, Shirley Elaine Reed, May 3, 1980; 3 children. B.S. in Elec. Engring., Calif. Inst., Tech., Pasadena, 1948, M.S., 1949. Instr. in elec. engring. Calif. Inst. Tech, 1948-49; engr. Douglas Aircraft Corp., Santa Monica, Calif., 1949—, sect. chief subs. McDonnell Douglas, Huntington, Calif., 1965—; cons. vacuum tech. and space simulation. Served with USN, 1943-46. Recipient NASA tech. award, 1980. Mem. Am. Vacuum Soc., AIAA, ASTM, IEEE, Working Group in Space Simulation, Test Lab. Mgrs. Working Group Republican. Unitarian. Contbr. 50 articles to profl. jours.; patentee in field. Home: 17776 S Palo Verde Av Cerritos CA 90701 Office: 5301 Bolsa Ave M/S 31 Huntington Beach CA 92647

MOORE, BRUCE WALLACE, county ofcl.; b. LaJolla, Calif., Feb. 23, 1937; s. George R. and Katherine E. M.; B.S., Calif. State U., Fresno, 1970, M.B.A., 1970; m. Verna Christofferson; children—Katherine, Laura, Ian. Asst. mgr. Fresno (Calif.) Flood Control Dist., 1972-73; dep. exec. dir. Fresno Housing Authority, 1973-75, exec. dir., 1975-77; exec. dir. Monterey County (Calif.) Housing Authority, 1977—. Served with Army N.G., 1959. Mem. Nat. Assn. Housing and Redevel.Ofcls. (past pres. Pacific S.W. region), No. Calif. Exec. Dirs. Assn. (past v.p.). Club: Rotary. Office: 134 E Rossi St Salinas CA 93901

MOORE, CARLETON BRYANT, educator; b. N.Y.C., Sept. 1, 1932; s. Eldridge Carleton and Mabel Florence (Drake) M.; B.S., Alfred U., 1954, D.Sc. (hon.), 1977; Ph.D., Cal. Inst. Tech., 1960; m. Jane Elizabeth Strouse, July 25, 1959; children—Barbara, Robert Carleton. Asst. prof. geology Wesleyan U., Middletown, Conn., 1959-61; mem. faculty Ariz. State U., Tempe, 1961—, now prof., dir. Center for Meteorite Studies; vis. prof. Stanford U., 1974. Prin. investigator Apollo 11-17; preliminary exam. team, Lunar Receiving Lab., Apollo, 12-17. Fellow Ariz.-Nev. Acad. Sci. (pres. 1979-80), Meteoritical Soc. (pres. 1966-68), Geol. Soc. Am., Mineral. Soc. Am., AAAS (council 1967-70); mem. Geochem. Soc., Am. Chem. Soc., Am. Ceramic Soc., Sigma Xi. Author: Cosmic Debris, 1969; Meteorites, 1971; Principles of Geochemistry, 1981. Editor: Researches on Meteorites, 1961; editor Meteoritics, Jour. Meteoritical Soc. Contbr. articles to profl. jours. Home: 507 E Del Rio Dr Tempe AZ 85282

MOORE, CHARLES WILLARD, architect, educator; b. Benton Harbor, Mich., Oct. 31, 1925; s. Charles Ephraim and Nanette Kathryn (Almendinger) M.; B.Arch., U. Mich., 1947; M.F.A., Princeton U., 1956, Ph.D., 1957; M.A. (hon.), Yale U., 1965. Architect, Mario Corbett, Architect, 1947-48, Joseph Allen Stein, Architect, 1948-49, Clark & Beuttler, Architects, 1949; asst. prof. U. Utah, 1950-52; asst. prof. architecture Princeton U., 1957-59; asso. prof. U. Calif., Berkeley, 1959-65, chmn. dept. architecture, 1962-65; chmn. dept. architecture Yale U., New Haven, 1965-69, dean, 1968-71, prof., 1971-75; prof. architecture UCLA, 1975—, head dept., 1976-77, 77-80; architect Moore Lyndon Turnbull Whitaker, Architects, 1961-64, Moore Turnbull, San Francisco and New Haven, 1964-70, Charles Moore Assos., Essex, Conn., 1970-76, Moore Grover Harper, Essex, Conn., and Moore Ruble Yudell, Los Angeles, 1976—. Served to capt. U.S. Army, 1952-54. Nat. Endowment Arts grantee, 1975; Guggenheim grantee, 1976-77. Fellow AIA. Democrat. Author: The Place of Houses, 1974; Dimensions, 1975; Body Memory and Architecture, 1977. Office: Moore Ruble & Yudell 4141 Glencoe Ave Venice CA 90291

MOORE, DAN HOUSTON, II, biostatistician, consultant; b. N.Y.C., Sept. 24, 1941; s. Daniel Houston and Eugenia Smart (Caldwell) M.; m. Patricia Ann Smith, July 9, 1966; 1 son, Derek. B.A. in Math., U. Calif.-Santa Barbara, 1963; Ph.D. in Biostats., U. Calif.-Berkeley, 1970. Research assoc. U. Pa., Phila., 1970-72; biostatistician Lawrence Livermore Lab. U. Calif., 1972—. Served to lt. U.S. Army, 1964-66. Mem. Biometric Soc., Am. Statis. Assn., Sigma Xi. Contbr. articles to profl. jours. Office: Biomedical Sci Div Lawrence Livermore Lab Livermore CA 94550

MOORE, DOROTHY MARIE, social studies educator; b. Seattle, Dec. 19, 1944; d. Sidney W. and Edith Clara (Ruddell) M. B.A., Alaska Meth. U., 1967; M.Div., So. Bapt. Theol. Sem., 1974. Cert. pub. sch. tchr., Alaska. Tchr. pub. sch., Homer, Alaska, 1967-69; missionary journeyman sch. tchr., Santiago, Dominican Republic, 1969-71; teamster Bechtel Constrn. Co. Trans-Alaska Pipeline, Valdez, 1975-77; warehouseman Alyeska Pipeline, Valdez, 1977-81; tchr. social studies Gilson Jr. High Sch., Valdez, 1981—. Mem. NEA, Delta Kappa Gamma. Club: Pioneers of Alaska (trustee, sec.). Office: Gilson Jr High Sch Valdez AK 99686

MOORE, GENE FRANKLIN, city mgr.; b. Asheville, N.C., Dec. 23, 1936; s. Samuel Franklin and Nina Lee (Buckner) M.; m. Varcy Navarra, Sept. 18, 1981; children—Joshua, Linda, Ronnie. With U.S. Air Force, 1954-74; ret., 1974; city mgr., Manassas Park, Va., 1974-77; town mgr., Bluefield, Va., 1977-78; city mgr., Kotzebue, Alaska, 1978—. Mem. Internat. City Mgmt. Assn., Am. Soc. Public Adminstrs., Am. Mgmt. Assn., Air Force Assn., VFW, Am. Legion. Club: Lions (pres. Manassas Park 1973-75). Office: PO Box 46 Kotzebue AK 99752

MOORE, GORDON E., mfg. co. exec.; b. San Francisco, Jan. 3, 1929; s. Walter Harold and Florence Almira (Williamson) M.; B.S. in Chemistry, U. Calif., 1950; Ph.D. in Chemistry and Physics, Calif. Inst. Tech., 1954; m. Betty I. Whittaker, Sept. 9, 1950, children—Kenneth, Steven. Mem. tech. staff Shockley Semicondr. Lab., 1956-57; mgr. engring. Fairchild Camera & Instrument Corp., 1957-59, dir. research and devel., 1959-68; exec. v.p. Intel Corp., Santa Clara, Calif., 1968-75, pres., chief exec. officer, 1975-79, chmn., chief exec. officer, 1979—; dir. Micro Mask Inc., Silver King Ocean Farms, Transam. Corp., Varian Assocs. Fellow IEEE; mem. Nat. Acad. Engring., Am. Phys. Soc., Electrochem. Soc. Office: Intel Corp 3065 Bowers Ave Santa Clara CA 95051

MOORE, INA MAY, artist, educator; b. Hayden, Ariz., Feb. 20, 1920; s. Jonathan Loveall and Minnie Alice (Salmon) Booth; m. Minton Inman Moore, Aug. 7, 1942. B.A., U. Ariz., 1941; M.A., Ariz. State U., 1966. Tchr. art elem. schs., Ariz., 1942-50; pvt. art instr., 1955-65; tchr. watercolor Phoenix Art Mus., 1967—, Phoenix Coll., 1978—; one-woman shows: Camelback Gallery, Scottsdale, Ariz., annually, Thompson Galleries, 1980; group shows: Ariz. Watercolor Assn., 1982, Ariz. Artist Guild, 1982, Contemporary Watercolor Exhbn., 1983; works represented in corporate and pvt. collections. Aux. mem. Don's Club of Phoenix. Recipient numerous prizes and awards for art. Mem. Ariz. Watercolor Assn. (past pres.), Ariz. Artists Guild, Contemporary Watercolor Assn., Nat. League Am. Pen Women, Alpha Rho Tau. Home: 5718 N 19th Ave Phoenix AZ 85013

MOORE, JAMES COLLINS, museum adminstr.; b. Topeka, Oct. 12, 1941; s. Albert Ora and Alice Winifred (Collins) M.; B.F.A., U. N.Mex., 1966; M.A. (Woodrow Wilson fellow), Ind. U., 1968, Ph.D. (Samuel H. Kress Found. fellow), 1974; m. Margaret Ruth Vasquez, Jan. 30, 1965; children—Daniela Ruth, Evan Albert. Asst. prof. Wichita (Kans.) State U., 1970-77; coordinator art history program Toledo Mus. Art, 1977-79; dir. Albuquerque Mus., 1979—; adj. asso. prof. art U. N.Mex. Served with Air N.G., 1964-65. Mem. Am. Assn. Museums. Club: Rotary. Condr. research 19th and 20th century Am. art; author: Harry Sternberg: A Catalog Raisonne of His Graphic Work, 1975. Office: PO Box 1293 Albuquerque NM 87103

MOORE, JAMES EDWARD, mechanical engineer, consultant; b. Okmulgee, Okla., June 15, 1943; s. James T. and Beatrice D. (Adam) M.; m. Autie Phyllis McCoin, May 27, 1967; children—Angel, Shauna, Keisha. B.S. in Chemistry, Langston U., 1965; M.S. in Environ. Sci., West Coast U., 1978. With Rachelle Labs., Long Beach, Calif., 1964-71; project mgr. McGaw Labs., Irvine, Calif., 1971-78; owner, gen. mgr., J.E.M. Engrs. and Assocs., Cerritos, Calif., 1978—. Baptist. Office: 12611 Hiddencreek Way Suite K Cerritos CA 90701

MOORE, JOHN C., JR., advertising executive; b. Chgo., Jan. 23, 1924; s. John C. and Helene F. Moore; divorced; children—Julia, Jeri, John, Marilyn. B.A in Sociology, Yale U., 1947, M.A., 1948. Mgr. advt. market research So. Calif. Gas Co., Los Angeles, 1950-70; pres. Communicus Inc., Los Angeles, 1979—; lectr. Chmn. Los Angeles Mayor's Com. Human Relations, 1965-70. Served with U.S. Army, 1943-46. Decorated Bronze Star. Mem. Advt. Research Found., Am. Mktg. Assn. Contbr. numerous articles to profl. jours. Office: Communicus Inc 11661 San Vincente Blvd Los Angeles CA 90049

MOORE, JOHN D., legal adminstr.; b. Mt. Pleasant, Iowa, Apr. 7, 1937; s. Burris P. and Esther I. (Copenhaver) M.; A.B., Muscatine Community Coll., 1961; B.B.A., Augustana Coll., 1966; postgrad. U. Iowa, 1966-68; m. Karen K. Kriegel, June 19, 1957; children—Charles A., Michael J., Susan K., David J. Office mgr. Stanley Engring., Muscatine, Iowa, 1956-64; personnel mgr. Oscar Mayer & Co., Davenport and Perry, Iowa, 1964-68; Midwest regional mgr. A. S. Hansen, Lake Bluff, Ill., 1968-73; legal adminstr. Gardner, Carton & Douglas, Chgo., 1973-78, Heller Ehrman White & McAuliffe, San Francisco, 1978—. Pres., Libertyville (Ill.) High Sch. Bd., 1974, Libertyville Ecumenical Council, 1975; bd. dirs. Libertyville YMCA, 1969-71. Recipient Muscatine Disting. Service award, 1963; named Outstanding State V.P., Iowa Jaycees, 1964; Outstanding Nat. Dir., U.S. Jaycees, 1965. Mem. Assn. of Legal Adminstrs. (regional v.p. 1977-78, nat. v.p. 1979-81, nat. pres. 1982-83), Perry C. of C. (v.p. 1967), Am. Mgmt. Assn., Adminstrv. Mgmt. Soc., Golden Gate Assn. Legal Adminstrs. Republican. Methodist. Home: 2632 Quiet Place Dr Walnut Creek CA 94598 Office: 44 Montgomery St San Francisco CA 94104

MOORE, JOHN H., oil co. exec.; b. Apache, Okla., Jan. 29, 1926; s. John G. and Beatrice (Enright) M.; B.S.M.E., U. Okla., 1945; m. Mary Horn, Feb. 1, 1947; children—Denise, Brenda Moore Sides. With Texaco, Inc., 1946-72, mgr. prodn. dept., Trinidad, W. I., 1966-68, gen. mgr. Latin Am., 1968-72; sr. v.p. Ladd Petroleum Corp., Denver, 1972-79, pres., 1979—, also dir.; dir. Am. Nat. Bank. Served with USN, 1943-46. Mem. Am. Petroleum Inst., AIME, Ind. Petroleum Assn. Am., Rocky Mountain Oil and Gas Assn. (pres.). Republican. Methodist. Clubs: Cherry Hills Country, Denver, Denver Petroleum. Office: 518 17th St Denver CO 80202

MOORE, JOHN HAMPTON, economist; b. Grand Forks, N.D., Apr. 19, 1935; s. Charles Harold and Marie (Lindberg) M.; m. Barbara Sue Corbett, Feb. 23, 1963; children—John Randolph, Matthew Corbett. B.S.E., U. Mich., 1958; M.B.A., 1959; Ph.D., U. Va., 1966. Research chemist Procter & Gamble Co., 1959-63; asst. prof. econs. U. Va., 1966-70, assoc. prof., 1970-77; assoc. dir., research prof. Law and Econs. Center, U. Miami (Fla.), 1977-80; assoc. dir. Law and Econs. Center, prof. econs. Emory U., Atlanta, 1980; assoc. dir., sr. fellow Hoover Instn., Stanford U., 1981—; mem. Nat. Scis. Bd., 1982—. NASA fellow, 1963-66; Hoover Instn. fellow, 1975-76. Mem. Am. Econs. Assn., So. Econs. Assn., Western Econs. Assn., Mont Pelerin Soc., Phila. Soc. Author: Growth with Self-Management: Yugoslav Industralization, 1952-1975, 1980; co-translator, co-editor Stalinist Planning for Economic Growth, 1933-52, 1980; contbr. articles to profl. jours. Office: Hoover Instn Stanford CA 94305

MOORE, JUANDA JEAN, statistician, consultant; b. Nacogdoches, Tex., Aug. 30, 1944; d. Sam and Bessie Lee (Ikner) Randle; m. Robert Carl Moore, June 1, 1969 (div.); 1 son, Robert Christopher. B.S., Howard U., 1966; M.B.P.A., Southeastern U., Washington, 1977. Lic. community sch. tchr., Calif. Casework coordinator Big Bros., Washington, 1969; postal clk. U.S. Postal Service, Washington, 1969; statis. clk. D.C. Recreation Dept., Washington, 1969-70, statistician IRS, Washington, 1970-77, statistician, Fresno, 1977—, program mgr. stats. of income programs, 1978—; instr. Fresno Community Coll.; cons. Auditor, mem. bd. McCardle Sch. PTA. Recipient Sustained Superior Performance award IRS, 1977. Mem. Am. Statis. Assn., Nat. Council Negro Women, Assn. Improvement of Minorities, Alliance for Arts, Am. Bus. Women's Assn., Kuumba Artists, Delta Sigma Theta. Mem. Religious Science Ch. Office: IRS 5045 E Butler Ave Fresno CA 93888

MOORE, JUDITH MARIE, nurse, b. Evanston, Ill., June 2, 1947; d. Herbert Potter and Irene Ellen (Wagner) M.; B.S., Loma Linda (Calif.) U., 1970. Mem. staff White Meml. Med. Center, Los Angeles, 1970-80, coordinator edn. tng. MacPherson Applied Physiology Lab., 1979-80; critical care nurse Critical Care Services, Inc., Los Angeles 1980; dir. health edn. and rehab. tng. St. Helena Hosp. and Health Center, Deer Park, Calif., 1981—; bd. dirs. Napa County chpt. Am. Heart Assn., 1980—; speaker in field. Mem. Am. Assn. Critical Care Nurses (CCRN), Nat. Critical Care Inst., Am. Heart Assn., Calif. Soc. Cardiac Rehab. Seventh-day Adventist. Home: PO Box 154 Deer Park CA 94576 Office: St Helena Hosp and Health Center Deer Park CA 94576

MOORE, JULIE LEE, librarian; b. Sioux City, Iowa, Sept. 11, 1941. D. Mabel M. DeRaad. B.A., U. Denver, 1962, M.S. in L.S., 1963. Prin indexer for Fed. Aid in Wildlife and Fish Restoration Library Reference Project, Denver, 1965-68; coordinator library and info. scis. Gerontology Ctr., U. So. Calif., 1969-74; wildlife info. scientist, head Julie Moore & Assocs., Riverside, Calif., 1969—; cons. Nat. Clearinghouse on Aging, 1973-74, 76. Mem. Wildlife Soc., Spl. Libraries Assn., NOW. Author: Bibliography of Wildlife Theses, 1900-1968, 1971, Cumulative Index to the Bibliography of Reported Biological Effects— of Radiofrequency Radiation Exposure, 1982, Updata Index to the U.S. Department of Agriculture Handbooks, 1982. Office: 6130 Camino Real Suite 223 Riverside CA 92509

MOORE, KATHRYN, business and tax consultant; b. Salt Lake City, Jan. 26, 1948; d. Willis Butterfield and LaVon (Taylor) Selin; m. James Benton Moore, June 28, 1967; 1 son, James Benton. Student pub. schs., Salt Lake City. Lic. tax cons., Oreg. Tax cons., bookkeeper, office mgr. Gen. Bus. Systems and Master Tax Service, Redmond, 1977-81; owner, mgr. Advanced Bus. Cons., Redmond, Oreg., 1979—; tchr. basic income tax preparation courses. Mem. Oreg. Soc. Tax Cons. (past sec. High Desert unit), Am. Soc. Notary Pubs. Mormon. Home and Office: 224 N 4th St Redmond CA 97756

MOORE, LARRY ADEN, safety engr.; b. Boise, Idaho, Nov. 23, 1947; s. Frank Aden and Helen H. (Nelson) M.; children—Robert James, Roger Irwin. A.S. in Pub. Safety, Treasure Valley Community Coll., Ontario, Oreg., 1968; B.A. in Adminstrn. Criminal Justice, Boise State U., 1974. Patrol specialist Canyon County Sheriff's Dept., Caldwell, Idaho, 1971-73; police chief City of Homedale (Idaho), 1976-78; safety engr. Morrison-Knudsen Co., Inc., Boise, 1978—; safety cons. Mem. Wheatland (Wyo.) Vol. Fire Dept., 1978-79. Served as 2d lt. U.S. Army 1973-76; Vietnam. Mem. Am. Soc. Safety Engrs., System Safety Soc., Nat. Safety Mgmt. Soc., Lambda Alpha Epsilon. Republican. Roman Catholic. Home: 2050 Magic Way Apt 103 Henderson NV 89015 Office: PO Box 224 Moapa NV 89025

MOORE, LEE COPPAGE, home economics educator, TV station administrator; b. Chelsea, Okla., Dec. 9, 1925; d. Jessie Malcolm and Florence Eliza (Glover) Coppage; m. Lester Cross Moore, Dec. 25, 1949; children—Lester Kent, Martha Liane Moore Parsley. B.S., Okla. State U., 1949; M.A., U. No. Colo., 1974. With Gulf Oil Co., 1950-51, Okla. Natural Gas Co., 1951-53; home service dir. Gas Service Co., Wichita, 1949-50; tchr. pub. schs., Oklahoma City, 1960-64; with broadcasting ctr. Sta. KRMA-TV, Denver, 1960-64; tchr. home econs. Littleton (Colo.) pub. schs., 1966—, Newton Jr. High Sch., 1966—. Named Mrs. Oklahoma City, 1956. Mem. Am. Home Econs. Assn., Colo. Home Econs. Assn. (past pres.), Colo. Home Econs. Found. (treas.), Delta Kappa Gamma, Alpha Delta Pi Alumnae. Baptist. Office: Newton Jr High Sch 4001 E Arapahoe Rd Littleton CO 80122

MOORE, LEONARD WENGERT, corporate executive, engineer; b. Independence, Iowa, Nov. 26, 1933; s. Leonard Dewey and Lillian Teresa (Wengert) M.; m. Martha Floyd Monger, June 16, 1956; children—Leonard Anthony, John Nicholas, Christopher Scott. B.S. in Elec. Engring., Iowa State Coll., 1956. Registered profl. engr., Calif. Test equipment liaison Hughes Aircraft, Culver City, Calif., 1956; project engr. Swanson Engring. Co., Inglewood, Calif., 1956-59; v.p. Ronan Engring. Co., Woodland Hills, Calif., 1959-67; project mgr. Waugh Controls, Chatsworth, Calif., 1967-68; pres., chief exec. officer Moore Industries-Internat., Inc., 1968—; pres. Moore Industries-Europe, Electromagnetics, Moore Industries Prodns. Active Republican Club; patron YMCA; mem. Pres.'s Circle, Los Angeles County Mus. Mem. Calif. Mfrs. Assn., Mchts. and Mfrs. Assn., Instrument Soc. Am. (sr.). Clubs: Regency, Mountain Gate Country, Los Angeles. Patentee in field of process instrumentation. Office: 16650 Schoenborn St Sepulveda CA 1343

MOORE, LILLIAN S., assn. exec.; b. Chgo., Oct. 26, 1911; s. Charles and Mary (Burgess) Schlagel; A.A., Los Angeles City Coll., 1934; B.A., UCLA, 1936; M.A., U. So. Calif., 1937; postgrad. N.J. State Colls., 1964-72; m. Theodore L. Moore, Dec. 20, 1941; children—Marilyn A. Ludwig, Thomas O. (dec.). Tchr. English, French, Spanish, Antelope Valley Joint Union High Sch., Lancaster, Calif., 1937-42; tchr. English, French, Meml. High Sch., Cedar Grove, N.J., 1963-76; pres. AAUW, Grand Junction (Colo.) br., 1981—, editor state div. bull., 1978-80, 81—, mem. travel team Colo. State Div., 1979-81, regional reporter Rocky Mountain Region, Grad. Woman mag., 1979-81. Active, Adopt A Grandtchr. program, Delhi, Iowa, 1979—. Address: 2855 Brittany Dr Grand Junction CO 81501

MOORE, MARVIN E(VERARD), Canadian provincial official, farmer, businessman; b. Grande Prairie, Alta., Can., Aug. 31, 1938; s. Charlie S. and Winifred L. (DeBolt) M.; m. Frances Bodeker, Feb. 20, 1959; children—Kerry, Lonny, Bernice. Student schs., Grande Prairie, Alta. Elected Provincial Council Alta., 1971, minister of agr., 1975-79, minister of mcpl. affairs, 1979-82, minister of transp., 1982—; farmer, DeBolt, Alta. Office: 423 Legislature Bldg Edmonton AB T5K 2B7 Canada

MOORE, MARY ALICE, advertising executive, artist; b. Grantsburg, Wis., Dec. 11, 1949; d. Milton Harding and Charlette Marguerite (Anderson) Muller; m. Franklin Robert Moore, Jr., Oct. 2, 1971 (div.). B.S., Western State Coll., 1971. Media buyer, prodn. artist Turk Prodns., Colorado Springs, Colo., 1975-76; account exec. R. F. Goodwin & Assocs., Colorado Springs and Pueblo, Colo., 1976-77; ptnr., account exec. Tel Moore Mktg., Colorado Springs, 1977—; guest speaker Pikes Peak Community Coll. advt. instr. Advt. bd. Nat. Little Britches Rodeo Assn.; advt. com. Nat. Sports Festival Colorado Springs; bd. dirs. Women's Resource Agy., 1982; mem. Colorado Springs Fine Arts Ctr., 1978—; pub. relations The Troupe Repertory Group, 1977-79; active Colorado Springs Music Theatre, 1977-78, fund raising and telehon Muscular Dystrophy Assn., 1977-81, St. Jude's Hosp. Telethon, 1977-78, Spl. Olympics, 1977-82; recruiter, fund raiser Jr. Achievement of Colorado Springs, 1977-82; vol. Cheyenne Village, Silver Key. Recipient Inst. Outdoor Advt. award, 1978. Mem. Pikes Peak Advt. Fedn. (pres. 1982—; Excellence in Advt. awards 1977, 78, 82; active advt. and pub. relations Pikes Peak Hospice Program 1982), Sales and Mktg. Execs. Colorado Springs (pres. 1981—), Colorado Springs Area C. of C. Republican. Lutheran. Club: Pikes Peak Civitan (pres. 1980). One-woman art shows: Colorado Springs Nat. Bank, 1971, Western State Coll., Gunnison, Colo., 1973; illustrations pub. Colorado Springs Monthly Mag. Office: 1801 N Union Colorado Springs CO 80909

MOORE, MARY FRENCH, potter, county official; ofcl.; b. N.Y.C., Feb. 25, 1938; d. John and Rhoda (Teagle) Walker French; B.A. cum laude, Colo. U., 1964; m. Alan Baird Minier, Oct. 9, 1982; children—Jonathan Corbet, Jennifer Corbet, Michael Corbet. Ceramics mfr., Wilson, Wyo., 1969—; commr. County of Teton (Wyo.), 1976—, chmn. bd. commrs., 1981, 83, mem. dept. public assistance and social service, 1976—, mem. recreation bd., 1978-81, water quality adv. bd., 1976—. Bd. dirs. Teton Sci. Sch., 1968—, vice chmn., 1979-81, chmn., 1982; bd. dirs. Teton Energy Council, 1978—; mem. water quality adv. bd. Wyo. Dept. Environ. Quality, 1979—; Democratic precinct committeewoman, 1978-81; mem. Wyo. Dem. Central Com., 1981—; mem. Gov.'s Steering Com. on Troubled Youth, 1982. Recipient Woman of Yr. award Jackson Hole Bus. and Profl. Women, 1981. Mem. Nat. Assn. County Ofcls., Wyo. County Commrs. Assn. (dir. 1977—; co-chmn. legis. com.), Jackson Hole Art Assn. (vice chmn. 1981, chmn. 1982), Pi Sigma Alpha. Home: PO Box 161 Wilson WY 83014 Office: PO Box 1727 Jackson WY 83001

MOORE, MICHAEL CRARY, mfg. exec.; b. Denver, Mar. 5, 1938; s. Thomas Edgar and Barbara Ruth (Glassco) M.; m. Ann A. Aukerman, Sept. 9, 1962; children—Mandela, Hopi, Nocole. B.A. (J. Fred Brown fellow), Yale U., 1962. Peace Corps vol., Togo, West Africa, 1962-64; area coordinator community action programs OEO, Washington and Kansas City, Mo., 1965-66; exec. dir. Denver Opportunity, 1966-68; moderator Hot Line radio program Sta. KTLN, Denver, 1968-69; program dir., sec. Great Western United Found., Denver, 1968-72; pres. Snugli, Inc., Evergreen, Colo., 1966—; cons. Nat. Study Commn. Undergrad. Edn. and Edn. of Tchrs., 1972-74; dir. Christopher G. Moore Constrn. Co., Inc., 1979-81. Bd. dirs. Colo. Children's Chorale, 1979—, sec., 1982—; bd. dirs. U. Wilderness, 1982—, Found. Urban and Neighborhood Devel., 1969-79, Denver Birth Center, 1976-79, Rocky Mountain Planned Parenthood, 1977-79, Mountain Area Planning Council, 1971-72; mem. Evergreen Chorale, 1974—, pres., 1977-79, dir., 1976-79; mem. Colo. Open Space Council, 1969—, ACLU, 1966—, Evergreen Baroque Ensemble, 1976—, Social Planning Dept. Adv. Com., 1970-74; pres. Evergreen Center for Arts, 1979, founding mem., dir., 1976-79; chmn. Jefferson County Open Space Adv. Com., 1975-77, Plan Jeffco, 1972, dir., 1974-80; chmn. Jefferson County Human Relations Council, 1971-72, citizens adv. com. Jefferson County Bd. Edn., 1969-70; gov. Metro Denver Urban Coalition, 1969-71, Metro Denver Fair Housing Center, 1969-71; Democratic precinct committeeman, 1972-74, 76-80; candidate Colo. Legislature, 1970. Colo. guide Brussell's World Fair, 1958; recipient recognition for pub. service Jefferson County LWV, 1973. Episcopalian. Club: Sierra. Home: 1150 Colorado Hwy 74 Evergreen CO 80439 Office: 1212 Kerr Gulch Rd Evergreen CO 80439

MOORE, MICHAEL JOSEPH, electronic engr.; b. Buffalo, July 11, 1935; s. Michael Joseph Kocinsky and Helen (Wegrzyn) K.; student U. Buffalo, 1952-54, M.S., 1962; B.E.E., U. Mich., 1956; student San Jose State Coll., 1959-60; m. Lucille Cuvillier, Aug. 30, 1958; children—Michael Peter, Patrice Lucille, Christopher Thomas, Gregory Paul. Electronic engr. Bell Aircraft Corp., Buffalo, 1956-57; jr. engr. Philco Corp., Palo Alto, Calif., 1959-60; asst. Calspan Corp. (name formerly Cornell Aero. Lab.), Buffalo, 1960-61, asso., 1961-63, research engr., 1963-68, head systems analysis sect., computer research dept., 1968-73, mgr. computer systems dept., Vallejo, Calif., 1973-76; pres. Dynacon Systems, Inc., Concord, Calif., 1976—. Instr. courses in logical design digital computers Martin Marietta Corp., 1962-63. Served to 1st lt. USAF, 1957-59. Registered profl. engr., N.Y. State, Calif. Mem. IEEE (sr., past chmn., past mem. exec. com. Buffalo), Assn. Computing Machinery, AAAS, Sigma Xi. Republican. Roman Catholic. Designer spl. purpose digital computers for USN and ABM Systems; designer real-time ultrasonic test signal processing systems. Author tech. manual, several Interim and Final Engring. reports. Home: 2274 Monticello Rd Napa CA 94558 Office: 2280 Diamond Blvd Suite 460 Concord CA 94524

MOORE, PHYLLIS CLARK, library director; b. Binghamton, N.Y., Jan. 31, 1927; d. John Oscar and Gladys Jeanette (Tilbury) Clark; B.A., Hartwick Coll., 1949; M.A., Syracuse U., 1952, M.S., 1954; Ph.D., U. Wis., 1971; Litt.D., Colo. State U., 1973; m. Roberts Scott Wellington

Moore, Sept. 14, 1954. Librarian-adminstr. GS-9 main reference/ Interloan Center, dir. 22 spl. services libraries met. Stuttgart, U.S. Govt. Spl. Services Europe, 1957-62; dept. Head young adult, fine arts, audiovisual, reference Yonkers (N.Y.) Pub. Library, 1962-67; dir. Hastings-on-Hudson (N.Y.) Pub. Library, 1967-68; cons. audio-visual services Westchester County (N.Y.) Library System, 1968-71; dir. Falls Church (Va.) Pub. Library, 1972-77, Alameda (Calif.) Free Library, 1978—; cons. in field; research dir. underwater sealabs, Bremerhaven, W. Ger., 1960-61; tech. adviser Community Action Program Yonkers, N.Y., 1965-68. Active Nat. Humane Soc., Recording Service for Visually Handicapped. Mem. ALA (exec. council 1975-), Internat. Oceanographic Found., Mask and Lute (pres. 1974), Calif. Library Assn., Nat. Audiovisual Assn., Nat. Health and Welfare Assn. (exec. bd.), Defenders of Wildlife (adv. council), Bay Area Library and Info. System (chairperson 1978—), DAR, Am. Film Inst., Smithsonian Instn., Audubon Soc., Nat. Trust Hist. Preservation, AAUW, Friends of Library, Conservation Soc. Am., Alpha Psi Omega, Sigma Alpha Iota, Gamma Phi Delta. Presbyterian. Clubs: Bus. and Profl. Women's, Army-Navy Country, Officers. Author: (play) Command Performance, 1975; Beneath the Sea, 1974; Blues in the Bibliotheque, 1979; A Catchy Title, 1980; Beyond the Blues, 1981. Contbr. articles to profl. publs. Home: 5625 Greenridge Rd Castro Valley CA 94546 Office: Alameda Free Library 1433 Oak St Alameda CA 94501

MOORE, PHYLLIS MAIE, mayor, real estate broker; b. Wendle, Idaho, Oct. 7, 1929; d. Gordon James and Elizabeth Dori' (Van Slyke) Staples; m. Jack Moore, Feb. 25, 1954; children—Katherine Jean Moore Earnest, Elizabeth Dori' Moore Daugherty, Jeffery lavid. Student pub. schs. Lic. real estate broker, Calif. Real estate sales rep., broker, 1972-82; mem. Napa (Calif.) City Council, 1976-80; mayor City of Napa, 1980—; chmn. Sanitation Dist.; rep. gen. assembly Assn. Bay Area Govts. Office: City Hall Napa CA 94558

MOORE, RAY AGNEW, state senator; b. Seattle, Apr. 19, 1912; s. Charles and Elsie (Agnew) M.; student U. Wash., 1930-34; m. Virginia Mary Lloyd, Sept. 14, 1973; children—Lucy Moore Hilgenoorf, Eileen Marshall Kelton (step-dau.). With Puget Power, Seattle, 1934-36, Hotpoint Co., Seattle, 1936-42, Boeing Co., Seattle, 1942-45; treas. Hartley Rogers Investments, Seattle, 1945-50; with Walston & Co., Seattle, 1950-59, Bache & Co., Seattle, 1959-69; v.p. Shearson Loeb Rhoades, Seattle, 1969-79; pres. King-Gallatin Corp., Seattle, 1975—; partner Sagemoor Farms; now mem. Wash. Senate; v.p. Security Savs. & Loan, 1968-76. Pres., Seattle Urban League, 1959-61, Wash. Mental Health Soc., 1962-65; chmn. King County Rep. Central Com., 1948-53; chmn. bd. Tech. Research Corp., 1970-80. Named Man of Yr., B'Nai B'rith, 1957; recipient spl. citation Seattle Police Officers Guild, 1981. Mem. Nat. Restaurant Assn. Democrat. Club: Seattle Tennis. Office: 109 Institutions Bldg Olympia WA 98504*

MOORE, RICHARD DIXON, radiologist; b. West Chester, Pa., Aug. 4, 1918; s. William Harvey and Helen Mason (Dixon) M.; M.D., Jefferson Med. Coll., 1944; m. Catherine Evans Lloyd, June 19, 1959; children—Susan, Richard, Christina, Michael, Anne, Patricia, David. Intern, Bryn Mawr (Pa.) Hosp., 1944; resident in radiology U. Pa., 1948-50, asso. in radiology, 1950-52; radiologist Grad. Hosp. U. Pa., 1950-52; dir. dept. radiology St. Francis Hosp., Honolulu, 1952—; asso. prof. radiology U. Hawaii Sch. Medicine, Honolulu, 1968—. Mem. Bd. Health, State of Hawaii, 1960-62; bd. dirs. Am. Cancer Soc., Hawaii div., 1960-67. Served with U.S. Army, 1945-47. Diplomate Am. Bd. Radiology. Fellow Am. Coll. Radiology; mem. Am. Roentgen Ray Soc., Radiol. Soc. N. Am., AMA (alt. del. 1959-61, del. 1962-70), Pan Pacific Surg. Assn. (treas. 1960-75), Honolulu County Med. Soc. (treas.). Club: Oahu Country. Home: 3890 Pokapahu St Honolulu HI 96816 Office: 2230 Liliha St Honolulu HI 96817

MOORE, SANDRA DERRICKSON, marketing and public relations exec.; b. Hart, Mich., Feb. 7, 1947; d. John Thomas and Doris (Van Vleck) Derrickson. Student Mich. State U., City reporter Muskegon (Mich.) Chronicle, 1967-68; city editor Portland (Oreg.) Community Press, 1970-76; owner, pres. Moore Media, Portland, 1976—; cons. mgmt. and mktg. service Clackamas County Coop. Library Network, 1979—; lectr., workshop leader. Mem. Portland/Multnomah Commn. on Aging; past bd. dirs., sec. Morrison Center for Youth/Family Services; pres. Lazuli Research Found.; media vol. Oreg. Mus. Sci. and Industry; vol. Friends of Multnomah County Library; mem. Multnomah County Task Force on Adult Protective Services. Recipient Mental Health Communicator of Yr. award Oreg. Mental Health Assn., 1972; others. Mem. Investigative Reporters and Editors, Women in Communication Oreg. Press Women, Nat. Soc. Interior Designers, Womens Network Group, Greater Portland Conv. Assn., Oreg. Library Assn. (chmn. pub. relations com.), Nat. Fedn. Press Women. Club: City (mem. com. on law enforcement and pub. safety) (Portland). Author poetry; co-producer TV documentary Tenny Hale: American Prophet, 1982. Address: PO Box 19291 Portland OR 97219

MOORE, THEODORE LYNN, environ. engr.; b. Central City, Nebr., Mar. 22, 1907; s. Charles Albert and Laura May (Mead) M.; B.S., Nebr. Central Coll., 1930; postgrad. U. Nebr., 1932-33; m. Lillian Rudd Schlagel, Dec. 20, 1940; children—Marilyn Moore Ludwig, Thomas (dec.). Instr. chemistry and physics Nebr. Central Coll. Central City, 1930-32; civil engr. Nat. Park Service, 1934-40, Atchison, Topeka and Santa Fe Ry., 1940-43; chief civil engr. U.S. Bur. Mines, 1943-51; chief environ. engr. Gibbs & Hill, Inc., N.Y.C., 1951-72; pvt. practice cons. environ. engr., West Caldwell, N.J., 1972-76, Grand Junction, Colo., 1976—; lectr. to schs. and civic groups. Mem. Am. Inst. Chem. Engrs., ASCE, Am. Water Works Assn., Royal Soc. Health, Internat. Assn. Water Pollution Research, Am. Acad. Environ. Engrs., Aircraft Owners and Pilots Assn. Contbr. articles to profl. jours. Home and Office: 2855 Brittany Dr Grand Junction CO 81501

MOORE, THOMAS GALE, economist, educator; b. Washington, Nov. 6, 1930; s. Charles Godwin and Beatric (McLean) M.; B.A., George Washington U., 1957; M.A., U. Chgo., 1959, Ph.D. in Econs., 1961; m. Cassandra Chrones, Dec. 28, 1958; children—Charles G., Antonia L. Fgn. research analyst Chase Manhattan Bank, N.Y.C., 1960-61; asst. prof. econs. Carnegie Inst. Tech., 1961-65; asso. prof., then prof. econs. Mich. State U., East Lansing, 1965-74; sr. staff economist Council of Econ. Advisers, 1968-70; hon. research fellow Univ. Coll., London, 1973-74; adjunct scholar Am. Enterprise Inst., 1971—; sr. fellow, dir. domestic studies program Hoover Instn. on War, Revolution and Peace, Stanford U., 1974—; mem. Dept. Commerce Econ. Adv. Bd., 1971-73; mem. advisory com. RANN, NSF, 1975-77. Served with USN, 1951-55; Korea. Fellow Earhart Found., 1958-59, Walgreen Found., 1959-60, Hoover Instn., 1973-74. Mem. Am., So., Western econ. assns., Mont Pelerin Soc. Club: Chevy Chase. Author: The Economics of American Theater, 1968; Freight Transportation Regulation, 1972; Trucking Regulation: Lessons From Europe, 1976; Uranium Enrichment and Public Policy, 1978; co-author: Public Claims on U.S. Output, 1973; contbr. articles, papers, reports, chpts. in books. Home: 3766 La Donna St Palo Alto CA 94306 Office: Hoover Institution Stanford Univ Stanford CA 94305

MOORE, WALTER THOMAS, engineer, scientist, business executive; b. Ft. Lauderdale, Fla., Aug. 26, 1921; s. Walter Ralph and Cora Alabama (Craighead) M.; student U. Chgo., 1947-55; m. Esther Regina Judith Cornelia Rojewski, Dec. 15, 1949; children—Evid, Naomi, Gregory Ralph, Kevin Thomas. Radio engr. Signal Corps Engring. Labs., N.J., 1942-44, 46; site mgr. Hypo Project, Dakar, Senegal, 1946-47; TV and radio engr. WBKB, WBBM, WBIK, Chgo., 1947-62; project engr. Bendix Field Engring., 1962-64; Grumman rep., sr. engr. Grumman Aerospace Corp., 1964-76; sr. engr./scientist Veda, Inc., 1976—, also pres. Cordon Lelanj, Inc., Camarillo, Calif., 1972—. Bd. trustees Dundee Twp. (Ill.) Library Bd., 1959-62; pres. Lake Marion Property Owners Assn., 1961; Democratic precinct committeeman, 1958-62. Served with USN, 1944-46, 51. Mem. Assn. Old Crows, Nat. Security Council, Internat. Brotherhood Elec. Workers, Soc. Plastics Engrs., Am. Def. Preparedness Assn. Contbr. to Jour. Space Flight, 1948-50; patentee field of solar energy. Home: 782 Mardigras Ct Camarillo CA 93010

MOORE, WILLIAM ERNEST, state senator; b. Sterling, Colo., May 24, 1929; s. George Ernest and Margaret Elizabeth (Warren) M.; B.B.A., U. Utah, 1957; m. Marilyn McFarlane, Dec. 21, 1953; children—Peggy Gail, Keith Ernest, Evan Henry, Mark Raymond, Paul William, Matthew Wade (dec.). Owner, mgr. Seagull San. Supply, Salt Lake City, 1957-64; gen. agt. Blue Cross, 1974-81, Sierra Life Ins. Co., 1964-81, Standard of Oreg., 1970-81, Surety Life Ins. Co., 1970-81, Wabash Life Ins. Co., 1977-81, Continental Gen. Life Ins., Coeur d'Alene, Idaho, 1979-81; mem. Idaho State Senate, 1980—. Pres. Kootenai County Property Owners Assn., 1978-79. Served with U.S. Army, 1951-53. Mem. North Idaho Assn. Life Underwriters (pres. 1972-73). Republican. Mormon. *

MOORE, WILLIAM JOSEPH, airline pilot, business executive; b. Banks, Oreg., Dec. 3, 1923; s. Charles Windsor and Eva Belle (Schulmerich) M.; B.S. in Aero. Engring. with honors, U. Colo., 1957; m. Mary Louise Talcott, Nov. 3, 1945; children—Jeffry Talcott, William Andrew, Colleen Louise. Commd. 2d lt. U.S. Air Force, 1944, advanced through grades to lt. col., 1964, served as navigator, meteorologist, instr. pilot, ambassador's pilot, 1944-58, test pilot, aero. engr., comdr. flight test engring. div., directorate of flight well-weather test, Wright-Patterson AFB, Ohio, 1958-63, staff officer Hdqrs. Air Force System Command, Andrews AFB, Md., 1963-65, advisor, evaluator, test pilot for procurement of aircraft and aircraft systems; served S. Pacific, Italy, Middle East, Aleutians, ret., 1965; pilot United Airlines, 1965-68, capt., 1969—; dir. Intelligent Systems, Inc., Sunnyvale, Calif.; 1st v.p., co-owner Moore Nat. Lease Co., Portland, Oreg., 1972-82, also bd. dirs. Decorated Air Medal with 2 oak leaf clusters, Purple Heart. Mem. Airline Pilots Assn., Am. Meteorol. Soc., Tau Beta Pi, Phi Delta Theta. Republican. Episcopalian. Co-author writings in field for Air Force. Home: 1546 Wistaria Ct Los Altos CA 94022 Office: Flight Operations United Airlines San Francisco International Airport San Francisco CA 94128

MOORE, WILLIS HENRY, state official; b. N.Y.C., Dec. 14, 1940; s. Carl Allphin and Mary Catherine (Moody) M.; B.A. Letters, U. Okla., 1962; M.Ed. in Adminstrn., U. Hawaii, 1971; children—Patrick Kakela, Michael Kirby, Catherine Malia. Teaching asst. dept. history U. Hawaii, 1962-64; tchr. history, Hawaiian studies and speech Hawaii Bapt. Acad., Honolulu, 1964-67; dir. edn. Bernice P. Bishop Museum, Honolulu, 1967-76; pres. Hawaii Geog. Soc., Honolulu, 1976-78, exec. sec., 1978—; mem. Hawaii Com. for Humanities, 1976—; producer, narrator film-lecture programs Nat. Audubon Soc. and travelogue forums; instr. in Hawaiian culture and Hawaiian studies Hawaii Loa Coll. and U. Hawaii system, 1970—; lectr., speaker in field; producer, narrator travel documentaries; mem. Hawaii Council for Culture and Arts. Mem. Pacific Sci. Assn., Hawaii Museum Assn. (pres. 1972-74), Pacific Area Travel Assn., Am. Guild Organists (v.p. Hawaii chpt.), Sierra Club (chmn. Hawaii chpt. 1973-75), Hawaiian Hist. Soc. Republican. Club: Honolulu Press. Contbr. articles to Honolulu Advertiser, Pacific Daily News, Guam, Pacific Mag. Office: 217 S King St Suite 308 Honolulu HI 96813

MOORHEAD, CARLOS JOHN, Congressman; b. Long Beach, Calif., May 6, 1922; s. Carlos Arthur and Florence (Gravers) M.; B.A., UCLA, 1943; J.D., U. So. Calif., 1949; m. Valery Joan Tyler, July 19, 1969; children—Theresa, Catharine, Steven, Teri, Paul. Admitted to Calif. bar, 1949; dir. Lawyers Reference Service, Glendale Bar Assn., 1950-66; practiced in Glendale, Calif., 1949-72; mem. 93d-98th Congresses from 22d Dist. Calif. Mem. Verdugo Hills council Boy Scouts Am. Mem. Calif. Assembly, 1967-72; mem. Calif. Law Revision Commn., 1969-73; pres. 43d Dist. Republican Assembly, Glendale Young Reps., 1957; mem. Los Angeles County Rep. Central Com., 1966—, Calif. Rep. Central Com., 1966—. Bd. dirs. Glendale La Crescenta Camp for Girls. Served to 1st lt. AUS, 1942-46; lt. col. Res., 1946-75. Mem. Calif., Los Angeles County, Glendale (past pres.) bar assns., C. of C. Mason (Shriner), Lion, Elk. Office: 2346 Rayburn House Office Bldg Washington DC 20515

MORAIN, MARY STONE DEWING, assn. exec.; b. Boston, Mar. 18, 1911; d. Arthur S. and Frances (Hall Rousmaniere) Dewing; student Radcliffe Coll., 1930-33; B.S., Simmons Sch. Social Work, 1934; M.A., U. Chgo., 1937; cert. social work U. So. Calif., 1941; m. Lloyd L. Morain, July 6, 1946. Social worker, Calif., N.Y.C., 1941-45; tchr. social scis. Keuka Coll., N.Y., 1945-46; v.p. LWV, Boston, 1946-53; bd. dirs., v.p. Planned Parenthood League Mass., 1948-52; bd. dirs., pres. Planned Parenthood Assn. San Francisco, 1953-60; bd. dirs. Internat. Humanist and Ethical Union, 1953-65; bd. dirs., v.p. Assn. Vol. Sterilization, 1963-77, 79—, UNESCO Assn. U.S.A., 1977—, Monterey YWCA, 1975-80, UN Assn. San Francisco, 1961-69; pres. Internat. Soc. Gen. Semantics, 1976—. Fellow World Acad. Art and Sci.; mem. Am. Assn. Social Workers. Club: Altrusa. Author: (with Lloyd Morain) Humanism as the Next Step, 1954; contbr. articles to profl. jours. Editor: Teaching General Semantics, 1969; Classroom Exercises in General Semantics, 1980. Home: PO Box 7190 Carmel CA 93921 Office: PO Box 2469 San Francisco CA 94126

MORALES, MARY LOU, business educator, real estate broker; b. San Antonio, Aug. 26, 1934; d. T. N. and Maria Angel Martinez; m. Rudy Morales, June 6, 1954; 1 dau., Jean Elizabeth. B.A., Tex. Woman's U., 1954; postgrad. Loma Linda U., 1964-67. Tchr. bus. edn., Colo., 1954-57, Calif., 1957—, Alvord Unified Sch. Dist., 1959—, Notre Vista High Sch., 1959-76, Alvord Continuation High Sch., 1976-82, La Sierra High Sch., Riverside, Calif., 1982—; instr. shorthand Riverside City Coll., 1975—. Mem. state com. Democratic party; mem. re-election com. ednl. chmn. Congressman George Brown; re-election com. Assemblyman Walter Ingalls. Mem. NEA, Assn. Sch. Curriculum Devel., Calif. Tchrs. Assn. (area polit. chmn.), Calif. Bus. Edn. Assn. Democrat. Roman Catholic. Office: 4145 La Sierra Ave Riverside CA 92505

MORAN, (BRENDA) ROSALYN (LYN), editor, author; b. County Antrim, No. Ireland, Feb. 8, 1936; d. Edward Henderson Moran and Evelyn (Orr) Desmond; student East Dulwich Inst., London, Brit. Mil. Coll. Lang., Germany, 1968-69; student dramatic art, London. Toured in repertory theater, Eng., 1952-55; sec. to gen. mgr. Luders Shipyard-Constrn. Co., Stamford, Conn., 1956-60; fgn. corr. Ice Hockey World, 1957-59, Ice Hockey News, 1959-60; staff writer, co-editor Hockey Fan, 1960-67; staff writer, asst. editor Bldg. Trade Jour., London, 1960-61; exec. sec. to dir. vocat. evaluation unit Goodwill Industries, Springfield, Mass., 1962-63; exec. med. sec. Wesson Meml. Hosp., Springfield, 1963-64; staff writer, co-editor Grice Hockey News, London, 1964-65; exec. sec. to TV dir. Lintas Advt. Agy., 1964-65; sports writer Beaver Weekly (Can. Forces in Germany), 1967-69; gen. writer Union Jack, also asst. mgr. YMCA/NATO Shops and Clubs, Germany, 1967-69; free-lance writer sports and gen. interest articles, 1960—; asst. editor Golf & Club mag., Santa Monica, Calif., 1970-71; staff writer Ulster-Am. monthly, Inglewood, Calif., 1972-77; sports editor, gen. writer (as Lyn and Rosalyn Moran) Singles Critique monthly, Los Angeles, 1972-75; exec. sec., asst. editor, mem. pub. relations staff 1st Fed. Savs., Santa Monica, 1972-75; asst. editor AcroSports, 1976-77; editor Gymnastics World, Santa Monica, 1979-80; assoc. editor, writer Internat. Gymnast mag., Santa Monica, 1977-82; cassette short story writer Narrations, Inc., Santa Clara, Calif., 1983—; author: The Young Gymnasts, 1979, 2d rev. edit., 1980; contbr. chpts. to books, including Alternative Life Styles; The Gymnastics Guide; publicist USSR Hockey Team tour, 1959-60, Polish Nat. Hockey team tour, 1967; exec. sec. to dir. Mercedes Benz/BMW Distbrs., Glasgow, Scotland, 1965-67; mgr. Ayr (Scotland) Rangers profl. ice hockey team, 1966-67; TV and radio appearances as sports authority and as expert and lectr. on North Irish politics in U.S.A., U.K., Can., Germany; lectr., researcher on Ulster affairs. Adviser U.S. nat. hockey team, 1958-60; scout Brit. ice hockey clubs, 1957-64; tchr. dramatic art YWCA, Mass., 1962-63. Mem. Authors Guild, Soc. Children's Book Writers, Soc. for Prevention Cruelty to Animals. Clubs: Mayflower of Calif.; Ulster Irish; PICAS of Calif. Home: 1712 Harper Ave Redondo Beach CA 90278

MORAN, H. DANA, aerospace engineer, research institute executive; b. Quincy, Mass., Jan. 19, 1927; s. Herbert Claude and Mildred Lorraine (Davidson) M.; m. Shirley Doreen Barnes, Nov. 5, 1955; 1 dau., Kelly Doreen. B.S. in Aero. Engring., Northrop U., 1960; M.S. in Engring. Mgmt., UCLA, 1964. Preliminary design engr. Northrop Aircraft Co., 1951-56; engring. mgr. Aerospace Industries Assn., 1956-61; program mgr. Weber Aircraft, Burbank, Calif., 1961-63; mgr. West Coast, Battelle-Columbus Labs., Los Angeles, 1963-69, program mgr., 1969-77; asst. to dir. Solar Energy Research Inst., Golden, Colo., 1977-82, mgr. industry relations, 1982—; cons. aircraft systems. Mem. Energy and Environ. Council, Denver C. of C.; pres. Foothills Art Center, Golden; bd. dirs. Industries for Jefferson County, Colo. Served with AC, U.S. Army, 1944-48. Named Outstanding Alumnus Northrop U., 1969. Fellow AAAS, AIAA (assoc.; Disting. Service award 1980); mem. Am. Solar Energy Soc., Los Angeles C. of C., Golden C. of C. Tau Beta Pi. Republican. Contbr. numerous articles to profl. publs; editor: Forecast of Aerospace Materials, Process and Testing Requirements, 1965, 59, 60, 61. Home: 1037 Dogwood Dr Golden CO 80401 Office: 1617 Cole Blvd Golden CO 80401

MORAN, THOMAS HARRY, univ. adminstr.; b. Milw., Oct. 21, 1937; s. Harry Edward and Edna Agnes Moran; B.S., U. Wis., 1964, M.A., 1972, Ph.D., 1974; m. Barbara Ellen Saklad, June 10, 1969; children—David Thomas, Karen Ellen. Dir. capital budgeting Wis. Dept. Adminstrn., 1962-64; exec. dir. Wis. Higher Ednl. Aids Bd., 1964-69; spl. cons. tax policy Wis. Dept. Revenue, 1973-74; dep. dir. Wis. Manpower Council, Office of Gov., 1974-76; v.p. bus. and fin., treas. U. Detroit, 1976-78; asso. v.p. health affairs U. So. Calif., Los Angeles, 1979—. USN fellow, 1957-59; U.S. Office Edn. research fellow, 1973. Mem. Am. Mgmt. Assn., Am. Assn. Higher Edn., Phi Kappa Phi. Home: 3245 Sawtooth Ct West Lake Village CA 93631 Office: U So Calif 349 Adminstrn Bldg University Park Los Angeles CA 90007

MORANDO, JEANNE BUTLER, savings and loan association executive; b. Crystal River, Fla., Feb. 17, 1928; d. James Taylor and Lucile (Sparkman) Butler; student St. Helen's Hall Jr. Coll., 1945, U. Oreg. Extension Center, Portland, 1949-51, San Joaquin Delta Coll., 1963-65; m. Herbert O. Hope, June 12, 1951 (dec. 1958); m. 2d, Sil S. Morando, Jan. 13, 1961; children—Marta Lucile Hope Morando, James William Hope Morando. Asst. buyer Olds & Kings Western Dept. Stores, Inc., Portland, 1948-51; gen. mgr. Hadley's Inc., Stockton, Calif., 1958-61; with World Savs. and Loan Assn., 1972-77, regional mgr., Oakland and Stockton, Calif., 1974-76, mktg. coordinator, Oakland, 1977; v.p., savs. adminstr., mktg. dir. Stockton Savs. & Loan Assn., 1977—. Bd. govs. Stockton Civic Theatre, 1967-69, chmn. public relations and publicity, mem. steering com., 1967-69, 71-72, trustee, 1982—; bd. dirs. San Joaquin County (Calif.) United Way, 1979—, Friends of Chamber Music; mem. San Joaquin County Crime Awareness and Prevention Com., 1980; trustee Friends of Chamber Music, 1983—. Lic. real estate broker, Calif. Mem. Savs. Instn. Mktg. Soc. Am. (basic mktg. sch. cert.), San Joaquin County Zool. Soc. (life). Republican. Lutheran. Club: Exec. Women (Stockton). Home: 1202 McClellan Way Stockton CA 95207 Office: 131 N San Joaquin St Stockton CA 95201

MORAY, JOHN EUGENE, research inst. exec.; b. Salt Lake City, Oct. 1928; s. T. Henry and Ella Emma (Ryser) M.; B.S., U. Utah, 1957; m. Emma Lou Romney, Dec. 26, 1952; children—Rebecca, Kevin, Cynthia Lou, Patrick. Research technician Cosray Research Inst., Inc., Salt Lake City, 1946-50; missionary Latter-day Saints Ch., N.S. and New Eng., 1950-52; pres. Cosray Research Inst., Inc., 1955—, dir. research, Decorated Army Commendation medal. Mem. AAAS, Sci. Research Adminstrn., Sigma Phi Epsilon. Club: Sugar House Kiwanis (pres. 1980-81). Author: The Sea of Energy, 1978. Home: 1919 Hubbard Ave Salt Lake City UT 84108 Office: Cosray Research Institute Inc 2505 S 4th E Salt Lake UT 84115

MORCHIN, WILLIAM CARL, electrical engineer; b. Seattle, May 26, 1936; s. John and Vera (Wasolek) M.; B.S.E.E., U. Wash., 1958; M.S.E.E., Seattle U., 1968; m. Karen E. Olen, Aug. 26, 1970; children—Dianne E., William Carl. Mgr. radar analyses and test Boeing Aerospace Co., Seattle, 1958-78; contract engr. RHO Co., Seattle, 1979—; Registered profl. engr., Wash. Mem. Aerospace and Electric Systems Soc. (radar panel 1974—), IEEE, Profl. Picture Framers Assn. Club: Eagles. Contbr. articles to profl. jours. Home: 1345 E Main St Auburn WA 98002 Office: PO Box 3999 Mail Stop 8H-51 Seattle WA 98148

MORELLI, MARGARET ELAINE, educational administrator, career counselor; b. Albany, N.Y., Nov. 25, 1943. A.A. in Bus. Adminstrn., Strayer Coll., 1971, B.S. in Bus. Tchr. Edn., 1972; M.Ed. in Counseling, Trinity U., 1974; Ph.D. in Ednl. Adminstrn., Colo. State U., 1980. Cert. ednl. adminstr., counselor, Colo. Dir. Loveland (Colo.) Community Counseling Ctr., 1974-75; instr. bus., dir. job placement Rocky Mountain Coll., Boulder, Colo., 1976-77; instr. bus. Aims Community Coll., Greeley, Colo., 1978-79, dir. vocat. guidance, 1979-81, registrar, 1981—; adj. prof. U. No. Colo.; cons. in career counseling. Active Women's Guild, Lay Ministry, Our Lady of the Mountains Catholic Ch. Served with U.S. Army, 1961-64, 66-69. HEW fellow, 1978-80. Mem. Rocky Mountain Assn. Collegiate Registrars and Admissions Officers, Am. Assn. Coll. Registrars and Admissions Officers, Am. Vocat. Assn., Colo. Vocat. Assn., Am. Legion Aux., DAV, Phi Delta Kappa, Omicron Tau Theta. Home: PO Box 1146 Eaton CO 80615 Office: PO Box 69 Greeley CO 80632

MORENG, ROBERT EDWARD, educator, poultry scientist; b. N.Y.C., Jan. 29, 1922; s. Joseph and Martha Ida (Schlosser) M.; m. Miriam Trowbridge Tittman, Aug. 12, 1950; children—George R., Nathan T., Jon C., Diane M., Michael Q., Charles C., Joseph P.H. B.S., U. Md., College Park, 1944, M.S., 1948, Ph.D., 1950. Asst. prof. N.D. State U., Fargo, 1950-55; prof. avian sci. Colo. State U., Ft. Collins, 1955-72, 78—, chmn. poultry dept., 1955-72, dir. research Coll. of Agrl. Scis., 1972-78, asst. dir. Expt. Sta., 1972—; farmer, rancher. Served with AUS, 1944-46; ETO. Decorated Bronze Star. Recipient Teaching award Poultry Sci. Assn., 1967; Disting. Service award Colo. State U., 1968; Golden Turkey award Colo. Turkey Assn., 1966, 69. Fellow AAAS,

Poultry Sci. Assn.; mem. N.Y. Acad. Sci., Soc. for Exptl. Biology and Medicine, Am. Genetics Assn., Am. Inst. Biol. Scis. Contbr. articles on stress-oriented selection in chickens and turkeys, high altitude reprodn. and gen. poultry mgmt. to profl. jours. and periodicals. Home: 6221 N Country Rd 15 Fort Collins CO 80524 Office: Dept Animal Scis Colo State Univ Fort Collins CO 80523

MORENO, JOHN A., tax consultant; b. Washington, Oct. 27, 1908; s. Aristides and Margaret Bell (Field) M.; m. Marian Stuart Groner, Nov. 25, 1933; 1 dau., Janet M. B.S., U.S. Naval Acad., 1930; M.Engring. Adminstrn., George Washington U., 1959; postgrad. Army Navy Staff Coll., 1944, San Diego State U., 1964. Commd. officer U.S. Navy, 1930, advanced through grades to capt., 1945, ret., 1960; comdg. officer USS San Jacinto, USS Floyds Bay, 1942; plans officer Utah Assault Force (Normandy), 1944, So. France Assault and Lingayen Bay Assault, 1944; asst. dir. strategic plans Joint Staff, Joint Chiefs of Staff, 1956-59; mem. faculty San Diego City Coll., 1964-74; income tax cons., mgr. H & R Block, Coronado, Calif. 1978—. Decorated Legion of Merit, Bronze Star (2). Mem. U.S. Naval Acad. Alumni Assn., George Washington U. Alumni Assn. Republican. Episcopalian. Club: Rotary. Address: 1214 Fifth St Coronado CA 92118

MORESHEAD, GORDON EDGERLY, biomedical engineer; b. Portland, Maine, Oct. 30, 1948; s. George Ashton and Phyllis Arline (Edgerly) M.; m. Janet Maxine Silliman, Oct. 23, 1976; children—Emily Phyllis, Timothy Gordon. B.S.E.E., U. Fla., 1970. Research engr. VA Hosp., Gainesville, Fla., 1970-73; biomed. engr. VA Med. Center, Salt Lake City, 1973-80, biomed. systems specialist, 1980-81, dir. Verification and Devel. Center, 1982—, chief biomed. and computer systems sect., 1981-82; cons., tchr. clin. instrumentation and computer systems design. Mem. Assn. Computing Machinery, Assn. for Advancement Med. Instrumentation. Republican. Presbyterian. Club: Hercules Flyers. Contbg. author: Intracranial Pressure (Brock and Dietz), 1972. Home: 3121 E Del Mar Dr Salt Lake City UT 84109 Office: VA Med Center 500 Foothill Dr Salt Lake City UT 84148

MORGAN, ANDREW LANE, urologist; b. Honolulu May 13, 1920; s. James Albert and Elsie Edna (Johnson) M.; B.A., Dartmouth Coll., 1942; M.D., Cornell U., 1945; m. Miriam Cleary, June 9, 1951; children—Andrew Lane, Christine, Martha, James. Diplomate Am. Bd. Urology. Intern, Lenox Hill Hosp., N.Y.C., 1945-46; resident, Queen's Med. Ctr., Honolulu, 1948-50, Yale, 1950-52; practice medicine, specializing in urology, Honolulu, 1952—; chmn. dept. surgery Queen's Med. Ctr., 1979; clin. prof. urology John Burns Sch. Medicine, U. Hawaii. Served to capt., AUS, 1946-48. Fellow ACS; mem. Am. Urol. Assn. (pres. Western sect.), Hawaii Med. Assn., Honolulu County Med. Soc. (bd. govs. 1970-76, treas. 1978-79). Episcopalian. Clubs: Plaza, Pacific (Honolulu). Home: 4022 Nuuanu Pali Dr Honolulu HI 96817 Office: 1380 Lusitana St Room 1008 Honolulu HI 96813

MORGAN, CHARLES O., hydrologist; b. Fairfield, Iowa, Nov. 28, 1931; s. Orville and Mary V. (Balderson) M.; m. Pauline Baumert, Sept. 7, 1952; children—Kenneth, John. B.A., U. Iowa, 1954, M.S., 1956. Geologist, U.S. Geol. Survey, Mich., 1956, La., 1956-63, Kans., 1963-67, hydrologist, 1967-70, Calif., 1970-77, Va., 1977-81; hydrologist Dept. Defense, San Bernardino, Calif., 1981—; U.S. AID cons. Pakistan, 1969, 70; UN cons., Turkey, 1979. Recipient Superior Performance award U.S. Geol. Survey, 1965. Mem. AAAS, Internat. Assn. Math. Geology, Geol. Soc. Am., Geotimes, Nat. Water Well Assn., Sigma Xi. Home: 5272 N Sierra Rd San Bernardino CA 92407 Office: Norton AFB Box 4408 San Bernardino CA 92409

MORGAN, CLAYTON CALKINS, physician; b. Ontario, Oreg., Oct. 9, 1927; s. Frank Theodore and Jessie Margarete (Calkins) M.; B.S., U. Oreg., 1949, M.D., 1952; m. Patricia Elaine Bolander, Dec. 19, 1947; children—Cathleen, Michael, Frank, Thomas. Intern Madigan Army Hosp., 1952-53; pvt. practice medicine, Nyssa, Oreg., 1955-59, Boise, Idaho, 1959—; chief of staff St. Luke's Hosp., 1971-73, dir., 1969-73. Pres. health sci. adv. bd., med. adviser Sch. Nursing, Boise State U. Pres. bd. dirs. Boise Ind. Sch. Dist., 1973-80, pres., 1978-80; bd. dirs. Family Practice Residency S.W. Idaho, 1975—, bd. pres., 1979-82; cons. Blue Cross of Idaho, 1977—. Served with USAF, 1952-55. Recipient Star Garnet award Idaho Hosp. Assn., 1975, A.N. Robbins Community Service award, 1980. Diplomate Am. Bd. Family Physicians. Fellow Am. Acad. Family Physicians (charter), Royal Soc. Health; mem. AMA, Idaho Med. Assn. (pres. 1981-82), Ada County Med. Soc. (past pres., dir.), Am. Hosp. Assn. (mem. ho. dels., vice chmn. com. physicians, physician mem. regional adv. bd.). Editorial adv. bd. The Hosp. Med. Staff, 1970-75. Home: 2622 Alamo Rd Boise ID 83704 Office: 6613 Ustick Rd Boise ID 83704

MORGAN, DANIEL FRANCIS, architect; b. Port Angeles, Wash., Dec. 31, 1917; B.Arch., U. Wash., 1952; m. Ardell Rustemeyer, Dec. 12, 1943; children—Kim, Kelly O., Marla Dee. Architectural draftsman Callender Engring. Co., 1953-59; architect Austin Assos., Seattle, 1959-63; with Tracey Brunstrom Co. (name changed to Olympic Assos. 1980), Seattle, 1963—, lead architect, 1969—. Served with USCG, 1940-45. Mem. AIA, Am. Soc. Military Engrs. Home: 619 Paradise Ln Edmonds WA 98020 Office: Olympic Assos 1319 Dexter Ave N Seattle WA 98109

MORGAN, DENNIS BRENT, psychologist, management consultant; b. Kansas City, Mo., Dec. 28, 1949; s. Ira Pershing and Josephine (Langworthy) M. B.S., Pittsburg (Kans.) State U., 1971, M.S., 1976; postgrad. U. Kans., 1976-77; Ph.D. in Psychology, Western Colo. U., 1978. Lic. psychologist, Mo.; diplomate Am. Bd. Psychotherapy. Pvt. practice psychology, Kansas City, Mo., 1976—; chief psychologist Sierra Vista Psychiat. Hosp., Highland, Calif., 1980; psychol. asst. Center For Active Psychology, Riverside, Calif., 1981—; mem. staff Kellogg Psychiat. Hosp., Corona, Calif., Long Beach Neuropsychiat. Inst., Charter Baywood Hosp.; mem. faculty Crystal Cathedral, Lay Ministers Tng. Center, mini-seminary, San Juan Capistrano Community Ch.; mem. staff Coll. Hosp., Cerritos, Calif., 1983—. Served with M. C., U.S. Army, 1971-72. Mem. Mo. Psychol. Assn., Am. Psychol. Assn., Internat. Council Psychologists, Calif. State Psychol. Assn., Psi Chi. Republican. Clubs: Masons (Pittsburg), York Rite (Olathe, Kans.). Office: 17747 Regency Circle Bellflower CA 90706

MORGAN, DOUGLAS HENES, oral and maxillofacial surgeon; b. Berkeley, Calif., June 4, 1926; s. Frank Mattison and Mabel (Kennedy) M.; A.B., U. So. Calif., 1949, B.S., 1950, D.D.S., 1955; m. Adrienne Atwood, July 13, 1957; children—Pamela Ann, Hillary Jean. Practice dentistry, Glendale, Calif., 1955-59, specializing in oral maxillo-facial surgery, La Canada, Calif., 1959-68, La Crescenta, Calif., 1968—; mem. staff, attending oral surgeon tchr. residents U. Calif.-Irvine Med. Center, 1967—; mem. cons. staff White Meml. Hosp., Los Angeles, 1963—; chmn. oral surgery staff Meml. Hosp., Glendale, 1966-67; founding dir. temporo mandibular joint clinic White Meml. Med. Center, Los Angeles; founder, exec. dir. Oral Health Edn. Council; past spl. lectr. temporomandibular joint Sch. Dentistry, Loma Linda U. Pres., Temporomandibular Joint Research Found.; past pres. alumni control bd. U. So. Calif. Served with Cadet Corps, U.S. Mcht. Marine, 1944-46. Recipient Disting. Service award Glendale Jr. C. of C., 1957, Outstanding Com. Chmn. award Kiwanians, 1965. Founding diplomate Am. Coll. Ambulatory Anesthesia. Fellow Am. Dental Soc. Anesthesiology (founding), Am. Acad. Craniomandibular Dysfunction; mem. So. Calif. Assn. Oral Surgeons (past pres.), San Fernando Valley Dental Soc. (dir. 1966), Assn. Seventh Day Adventist Dentists (assoc.), So. Calif. Acad. Oral Pathology, Am. Assn. Hosp. Dentists, ADA, Internat. Coll. Craniomandibular Orthopedics (founding), Blue Key, Delta Sigma Phi, Delta Sigma Delta (alumni control bd.). Republican. Conglist. (trustee). Mason. Kiwanian. Author, editor: Diseases of the Temporomandibular Apparatus; Multidisciplinary Approach. Research, publs. and patents relating to temporo-mandibular joint; producer sound-color film The Prosthesis Implant (Cine Golden Eagle award), 1977, 2d edit., 1982. Home: 1700 Lila Ln La Canada CA 91011 Office: 3043 Foothill Blvd La Crescenta CA 91214

MORGAN, GARY PATRICK, utilities administrator; b. Connellsville, Pa., Dec. 21, 1944; s. Frank John and Pauline Grace (Oglethorpe) M.; m. Linda Diane Carter, Dec. 17, 1966; 1 dau., Tanya Lea. B.S. in Elec. Engring., Va. Poly. Inst. and State U., 1967; postgrad. Sacramento State Coll., 1968-69, U. Kans., 1970-72; M.S. in Bus. Adminstrn., U. No. Colo., 1978. Elec. engr. Norfolk Naval Shipyard (Va.), 1967-68, ship supt., nuclear engr., 1972-74; chief Honest John div. Rocky Mountain Arsenal, Denver, 1974-77; tech. asst. program mgr. Region VIII, EPA, Denver, 1977-79; exec. mgr. Western Area Power Adminstrn., Loveland-Ft. Collins Area Office, Ft. Collins, Colo., 1979—; adviser Gov.'s Solid Waste Adv. Council, 1977-79. Served to maj. USAF, 1967-72; col. Air NG. Decorated Air Force Commendation medal; spl. act award EPA, 1979; sustained superior performance award Dept. Energy, 1980. Mem. Govt. Refuse Collections and Disposal Assn. (past v.p. local state chpt.). Republican. Presbyterian. Home: 2332 S Dawson Way Aurora CO 80014 Office: PO Box 3700 Loveland CO 80529

MORGAN, GWYNN MARIE, educator; b. Elko, Nev., Apr. 18, 1930; d. Herbert George and Clare Mary Morgan; m. Eugene Abts, Aug. 23, 1976 (div.); 1 dau., Sheila. B.A., No. Iowa U., 1952; postgrad. U. Oreg., Portland State Coll., State Coll. Oreg., No. Iowa U. Typist, IBM operator Minn. Mut. Life Ins. Co., St. Paul, 1946-52; tchr. high sch., Wyoming and Fairbanks, Iowa, 1952-55; girls' counselor, tchr. Lincoln Jr. High Sch., Cottage Grove, Oreg., 1964-68; tchr. high sch. Winnemucca, Nev., 1971—; instr. No. Nev. Jr. Coll., Winnemucca, 1971—. Mem. NEA, Am. Home Econs. Assn., Bus. and Profl. Women Am. Democrat. Roman Catholic. Home: PO Box 1223-26 Haskell #4 Winnemucca NV 89445 Office: Kluncey RD A Lowry High Sch Winnemucca NV 89445

MORGAN, JACK M., lawyer, state senator; b. Portales, N.Mex., Jan. 15, 1924; s. George Albert and Mary Rosana (Baker) M.; B.B.A., U. Tex., 1948; LL.B., 1950; m. Peggy Flynn Cummings, 1947; children—Marilyn, Rebecca, Claudia, Jack. Admitted to N.Mex. bar, 1950; sole practice law, Farmington, N.Mex., 1956—; mem. N.Mex. State Senate, 1973—. Served with USN, 1942-46. Mem. Am. Bar Assn., N.Mex. Bar Assn., S.W. Regional Energy Council (past chmn.). Republican. Clubs: Kiwanis, Elks. Office: PO Box 2151 Farmington NM 87499

MORGAN, JACOB RICHARD, cardiologist, ret. naval med. officer, med. educator; b. E. St. Louis, Ill., Oct. 10, 1925; s. Clyde Adolphus and Henny Ella Henrietta (Van Ramshorst) M.; B.S. in Pharmacy with highest honors, B.B.A. with high honors, U. Tex., 1953, M.D., 1957; m. Alta Eloise Ruthruff, Aug. 1, 1953; children—Elaine Louise (Mrs. Thomas P. Delovich), Stephen Richard. Commd. lt., M.C., U.S. Navy, 1957, advanced through grades to capt., 1970, ret., 1973; intern, resident internal medicine U.S. Naval Hosp., Oakland, Calif., 1957-61; internist, 1961-62; chief medicine U.S. Naval Hosp., Taipei, Taiwan, 1962-64; mem. internal medicine staff U.S. Naval Hosp., San Diego, 1964-67, fellow cardiology, 1968-69, chief cardiology, 1969-73; fellow cardiology Scripps Clinic and Research Found., La Jolla, Calif., 1967-68; asso. clin. prof. medicine U. Calif. at San Diego Med. Sch., 1970; cons. cardiology U.S. Naval hosps. at Long Beach, Calif., Camp Pendleton, Calif., Port Hueneme, Calif., Bremerton, Wash., China Lake, Calif., Twenty-Nine Palms, Calif., 1969-73; prof. medicine, asso. chmn. dept. medicine Tex. Technol. U. Sch. Medicine, 1973-75; dir. medicine R.E. Thomason Gen. Hosp., El Paso, Tex., 1973-75; dir. cardiology Paradise Valley Hosp., National City, Calif., 1976—; co-dir. postgrad. course cardiology San Diego County Heart Assn. Served as officer USNR, 1943-45, 50-53. Recipient Casimir Funk award Assn. Mil. Surgeons, 1972. Diplomate Am. Bd. Internal Medicine (cardiovascular disease). Fellow Am. Coll. Cardiology (faculty postgrad. course cardiology), A.C.P., Am. Coll. Chest Physicians, Am. Coll. Angiology, Royal Soc. Medicine, Council Clin. Cardiology of Am. Heart Assn.; mem. Am. Assn. Clin. Research, Am. Med. Writers Assn., Pan-Am. Med. Assn., Assn. Mil. Surgeons, Rho Chi, Beta Gamma Sigma. Contbr. med. jours. Home: 9881 Edgar Pl La Mesa CA 92041 Office: Paradise Valley Hosp 2400 E 4th St National City CA 92050

MORGAN, JIM LEE, business educator; b. Little Rock, Apr. 14, 1943; s. James Charles and Lois Marie (McPherson) M.; B.S., B.A., U. Ark., 1961, M.Ed., 1968; M.P.A., U. So. Calif., 1980. Asst. city mgr. City of Beverly Hills, Calif., 1972-74; dir. Human Service Planning, Simi Valley, Calif., 1975-76; prof. bus. and mgmt. West Los Angeles Coll., 1975—, pres. acad. senate, 1975—; lectr. in field. Bd. advisors U. So. Calif. Traffic Safety Center, 1974-75; bd. dirs. Beverly Hills Chamber Orch., 1973-75, West Los Angeles chpt. ARC, 1972-75; founder, hon. chmn. Ann. Festival of Arts, City of Beverly Hills, 1972-75; founding mem. Research Coordinating Forum of Ventura County, 1976—; v.p. dist. senate Los Angeles Community Coll., 1978-80; treas. Acad. Senate, Calif. Community Colls., 1980-81, fin. task force commn. Chancellor's Office, 1980—. Served to capt. USAF, 1967-72. Decorated Air Force Commendation medal; honored by Jim Lee Morgan Day, City of Beverly Hills, Apr. 14, 1974; named Air Force Systems Command Personnel Officer of the Yr., 1970. Mem. Internat. City Mgrs. Assn., So. Calif. Assn. Human Resources Dirs., Am. Soc. Planning Ofcls., Am. Mgmt. Assn., Phi Delta Kappa, Blue Key, Beta Gamma Sigma. Author: Social Planning for the City, 1975; Business of Management, 1982; Study Guide to Management, 1982; editor Community Services Newsletter, 1974-75, Customer Relations: Policy and Procedures, 1975, Human Services Directory, City of Simi Valley, 1976, Rev. mag., 1972-74. Home: 601 Avery Pl Long Beach CA 90807 Office: 4800 Freshman Dr Culver City CA 90230

MORGAN, JOSEPH WILLIAM, astronautical engineer, real estate broker; b. Decatur, Ill., July 19, 1941; s. Wallace and Martha Jane (Harkless) M.; B.S.E., (Air Force Inst. Tech. scholar), Ariz. State U., 1965; M.S., Calif. State U., Fullerton, 1970; E.M.E., U. So. Calif., 1975; A.A., Coastline Community Coll., 1979; m. Carol Ann Johnson, June 8, 1962 (div.); children—Mark, Sherri. Astron. engr. USAF Space and Missile Systems Orgn., 1965-69; staff quality assurance engr., 1970-72; asst. tech. mgr. Sidewinder Program, Naval Weapons Center, China Lake, Calif., 1972-73; staff reliability engr. Space and Missile Systems Orgn., 1973-74; mission analyst Aerospace Corp., 1977-79; ind. real estate investor, broker, exchangor, Carefree, Ariz., 1980—; sr. project engr. Gen. Pneumatics Corp., 1983—; lectr. numerical analysis and computer programming Calif. State U. (Fullerton); lectr. orbital mechanics U. So. Calif. Served to capt. USAF, 1961-69. Registered profl. engr., Calif. Fellow Brit. Interplanetary Soc.; mem. Astron. Soc. Pacific, Mensa, Nat. Assn. Realtors, Nat. Council Exchangors. Author essays on orbital mechanics, 1972-79. astronautical engineer, real estate broker; b. Decatur, Ill., July 19, 1941; s. Wallace and Martha Jane (Harkless) M.; B.S.E., (Air Force Inst. Tech. scholar), Ariz. State U., 1965; M.S., Calif. State U., Fullerton, 1970; E.M.E., U. So. Calif., 1975; A.A., Coastline Community Coll., 1979; m. Carol Ann Johnson, June 8, 1962 (div.); children—Mark, Sherri. Astron. engr. USAF Space and Missile Systems Orgn., 1965-69; staff quality assurance engr., 1970-72; asst. tech. mgr. Sidewinder Program, Naval Weapons Center, China Lake, Calif., 1972-73; staff reliability engr. Space and Missile Systems Orgn., 1973-74; mission analyst Aerospace Corp., 1977-79; ind. real estate investor, broker, exchangor, Carefree, Ariz., 1980—; sr. project engr. Gen. Pneumatics Corp., 1983—; lectr. numerical analysis and computer programming Calif. State U. (Fullerton); lectr. orbital mechanics U. So. Calif. Served to capt. USAF, 1961-69. Registered profl. engr., Calif. Fellow Brit. Interplanetary Soc.; mem. Astron. Soc. Pacific, Mensa, Nat. Assn. Realtors, Nat. Council Exchangors. Author essays on orbital mechanics, 1972-79. Home and Office: PO Box 1113 36228 N Placer Pl Carefree AZ 85377

MORGAN, LUCIAN LLOYD, aerospace engineering manager; b. Wichita Falls, Tex., Dec. 22, 1928; s. Jasper Hugh and Myrtle Irene (Huffman) M.; m. Dorothy Rea Dill, Sept. 14, 1950; children—Larry Rea, Lauri Louann. B.S. in Chem. Engring., Tex. A&M U., 1949; M.S. in Nuclear Engring., So. Meth. U., 1958; postgrad. Stanford U., 1964-65; M.S. in Systems Mgmt., U. So. Calif., 1975. Registered profl. engr., Calif., Tex. Supr. U.S. Gypsum Co., Sweetwater, Tex., 1949-50; engr. supr. General Dynamics Co., San Diego, 1950-54, asst. chief chemist, 1954-57, project nuclear engr., 1957-60, supr. propulsion and analysis, 1960-62; project leader Lockheed Missiles and Space Co., Sunnyvale, Calif., 1962-81, mgr. systems engring., 1981—. Served to capt. U.S. Army, 1952-53. Recipient NASA Pub. Service award for contbrs. to space shuttle, 1982. Mem. AIAA, Air Force Assn., Nat. Mgmt. Assn. Republican. Mem. Ch. of Christ. Home: 2029 Kent Dr Los Altos CA 94022 Office: Orgn 59-12 Bldg 593 PO Box 504 Sunnyvale CA 94088

MORGAN, NEIL, author, editor, lecturer, columnist; b. Smithfield, N.C., Feb. 27, 1924; s. Samuel Lewis and Isabelle (Robeson) M.; A.B., Wake Forest Coll., 1943; m. Caryl Lawrence, 1945 (div. 1954); 1 dau., Jill; m. 2d, Katharine Starkey, 1955 (div. 1962); m. 3d, Judith Blakely, 1964. Columnist, San Diego Daily Jour., 1946-50; columnist San Diego Evening Tribune, 1950—, asso. editor, 1977-81, editor, 1981—; syndicated columnist Morgan Jour., Copley News Service, 1958—. Served to lt. USNR, 1943-46. Recipient Ernie Pyle Meml. award, 1957, Bill Corum Meml. award, 1961, Distinguished Service citation Wake Forest U., 1966; Grand award for travel writing Pacific Area Travel Assn., 1972, 78; named Outstanding Young Man of Year San Diego, 1959. Mem. Authors Guild, Am. Soc. Newspaper Editors, Soc. Journalists and Authors, Explorers Club, Phi Beta Kappa, Omicron Delta Kappa, Sigma Delta Chi. Club: Chevaliers du Tastevin. Author: My San Diego, 1951; It Began With a Roar, 1953; Know Your Doctor, 1954; Crosstown, 1955; My San Diego 1960, 1959; Westward Tilt, 1963; Neil Morgan's San Diego, 1964; The Pacific States, 1967; The California Syndrome, 1969; (with Robert Witty) Marines of the Margarita, 1970; The Unconventional City, 1972; (with Tom Blair) Yesterday's San Diego, 1976; contbg. author: A Bicentennial Portrait of the American People, 1976; This Great Land, 1983. Contbr. non-fiction articles to Nat. Geog., Esquire, Redbook, Readers Digest, Holiday, Harper's, Travel and Leisure mags., Ency. Brit. Home: 7930 Prospect Pl La Jolla CA 92037 Office: PO Box 191 San Diego CA 92112

MORGAN, PAMELA KAY, advertising executive; b. Newton, Iowa, June 21, 1948; d. Joseph Eldred and Harriett Irene (Gardner) M. Student Marshalltown Community Coll., 1967, 68, U. No. Iowa, 1966, 68, Drake U., 1969, 71, Des Moines Area Community Coll., 1978, Met. State Coll., Denver, 1979—. Customer service corr. Am. Republic Ins. Co., Des Moines, 1969-73; advt./printing prodn. coordinator AID Ins. Services, Des Moines, 1973-77; promotion prodn. mgr. Kirke-Van Orsdel, Inc., Des Moines, 1977-78; account coordinator Hibbert/Laman, Denver, 1978—. Home: 11814 Sherman St Northglenn CO 80233 Office: Hibbert/Laman 1601 23d St Denver CO 80216

MORGAN, STEVEN MICHAEL, psychologist; b. Bronx, N.Y., June 15, 1942; s. Bernard Irwin and Sophie (Golub) M. B.A., Goddard Coll., 1974; Ph.D., Calif. Sch. Profl. Psychology, 1979. Staff psychologist Patton (Calif.) State Hosp., 1979—; clin. dir. family advocacy program USMC, 29 Palms, Calif. Campaign staff mem. Bella Abzug, 1973-74, Eldon Clingdon Reelection for Manhattan Councilman-at-Large, 1974. Mem. Am. Psychol. Assn., Nat. Registry Health Care Providers, Calif. Psychol. Assn., Psi Chi. Club: Lake Arrowhead Country. Author: Conjugal Terrorism. Office: 3102 E Highland Ave Patton CA 92369

MORGAN, SUZANNE, interior designer; b. Geneva, Sept. 3, 1932; d. John and Miriam Elizabeth (Neely) Reinhardt; div.; children—Nancy Elizabeth Greene, Jonothan Greene. Student Santa Monica (Calif.) City Coll., 1950-52; degree in interior design UCLA, 1979. Interior designer Dorothy Ball Showroom, Los Angeles, 1964-65, Twentieth Century Film Corp., Los Angeles, 1966; prin. Suzanne Morgan Interiors, Santa Monica, 1966-76; display designer Liberty House Hawaii, Honolulu, interior designer Ansteths Ltd. Showroom, Honolulu, 1981; instr. Interiors Designers Guild Coll. Mem. Am. Soc. Interior Designers (assoc.), Internat. Soc. Interior Designers. Republican. Address: 950 Kealaolu Ave Honolulu HI

MORGAN, WAYNE PHILLIP, art gallery curator; b. Dunnville, Ont., Can., Apr. 1, 1942; cert. Sch. Art, Regina Coll., 1963; B.A., U. Sask., Can., 1966; student Emma Lake Artists Workshop, Sask.; student of Jules Olitski, 1964, Lawrence Alloway, 1966, Frank Stella, 1967, Don Judd, 1968. Community resident artist parks and recreation dept. Weyburn (Sask.) Arts Council, 1967-70; curator Dunlop Art Gallery, Regina (Sask.) Public Library, 1970—; secretariat mem. Regina Arts Commn., 1979—; juror various art shows, 1970—; mem. Can. Council Explorations Jury, 1977-79. Bd. dirs. Community Arts Centre, Regina, 1970—. Mem. Western Can. Art Assn. (founding mem., dir. 1973-75), Sask. Museums Assn. (pres. 1982—, dir. 1977-79), Sask. Craft Council (founding), Can. Museums Assn., Assn. of Cultural Execs., Am. Assn. of Museums, Mus. Folk Art, Regina Arts Council. Address: 2311 12th Ave Regina SK S4P 0N3 Canada

MORGAN, WILLIAM DENMAN, photographer, educator; b. Providence, Feb. 18, 1950; s. Thruman Mycroft and Phyllis Cecil (Joelsen) M.; m. Deborah Lynn Worstell, Dec. 31, 1971. Student N.Mex. State U., Las Cruces, 1968-70, U.N. Mex., Albuquerque, 1970-71. Self-employed photographer, Gallup, 1977-79; owner, Morgan Photography Studio, 1979—; instr. photography class. Recipient awards Santa Fe Festival of the Arts, 1981; disting. print awards Profl. Photographers Assn. N. Mex., 1981; Southwest Profl. Photographers Assn. Dallas, 1981; Southwest Profl. Photographers Assn., Ft. Worth, 1982; prints accepted gen. display and traveling loan collection Profl. Photographers Am., Las Vegas, 1982. Club: Elks. Home: 2410 E Aztec E-65 Gallup NM 87301 Office: 117 A West Coal PO Box 1964 Gallup NM 87301

MORGANSTEIN, STANLEY, engineering psychologist, computer scientist; b. N.Y.C., June 4, 1940; s. Louis I. and Rose M. B.S., Bklyn. Coll., 1962; M.S., Lehigh U., 1964; Ph.D., U. Mass., 1970. With Claflin U., Orangeburg, S.C., 1970-72, William Patterson Coll. N.J., 1972-74, Binary Data Corp., Plainview, L.I., 1974-76; engr. Four Phase Corp., N.Y.C., 1976-77, European Am. Bank, L.I., 1977-80; engring. psychologist Pacific Missile Test Cen., Point Mugu, Calif., 1980—. Tuition scholar, 1962; MIT research fellow, 1965-66; Univ. fellow U. Mass., 1967-68. Mem. Am. Psychol. Assn., AIAA, Sigma Xi, Psi Chi. Home: 6250 Telegraph Rd 1104 Ventura CA 93003 Office: Code 1226 PMTC Point Mugu CA 93042

MORIKAWA, MARK GEORGE, controller; b. Milw., July 8, 1951; s. George M. and Neva M. Morikawa; B.A., Biola Coll., 1976; postgrad. Golden Gate Bapt. Theol. Sem., 1976-80, Pepperdine U., 1979—. Asst. football coach Occidental Coll., Los Angeles, 1978; tchr. Sch. of 1st Bapt. Ch. of Van Nuys, Los Angeles, 1978-80; controller Hollygrove Children's Home, Los Angeles, 1975-82; fin. dir. Centrum of Hollywood, 1982—; youth minister Immanuel Presbyn. Ch., Los Angeles, 1973-75. Mem. Am. Assn. Coll. Football Coaches, Calif. Assn. High Sch. Coaches. Democrat. Home: 18016 Denker Ave Gardena CA 90248 Office: 1753 N Winona Ave Los Angeles CA 90027

MORIMOTO, CARL NOBORU, crystallographer/computer programmer/analyst; b. Hiroshima, Japan, Mar. 31, 1942; came to U.S., 1957, naturalized, 1965; s. Toshiyuki and Teruko (Hirano) M.; B.A. in Chemistry, U. Hawaii, 1965; Ph.D., U. Wash., 1970; m. Helen Kiyomi Yoshizaki, June 28, 1969; children—Matthew Ken, Justin Ray. Research asso. dept. chemistry Mich. State U., East Lansing, 1970-72; postdoctoral fellow dept. biochemistry and biophysics Tex. A&M U., College Station, 1972-75; sr. scientific programmer Syntex Analytical Instruments, Inc., Cupertino, Calif., 1975-78; prin. programmer analyst Control Data Corp., Sunnyvale, Calif., 1978-83; mem. profl. staff Space Systems div. Gen. Electric Co., Sunnyvale, Calif., 1983—. Mem. Am. Crystallographic Assn., Assn. for Computing Machinery, Am. Chem. Soc., Sigma Xi. Baptist. Home: 4003 Hamilton Park Dr San Jose CA 95130

MORIN, RAMIRO (RAY) L., safety administrator; b. San Diego, Tex., May 25, 1947; s. Jose C. and Manuela (Lopez) R.; m. Carolyn Ann Nesbitt, Mar. 25, 1972; 1 son, Brent Thomas. A.A., Fire Sci. Tech., 1976; A.A. in Occupational Safety and Health, Littleton Coll., 1978. Cert. surface mine rescue instr. Fire fighter Fitzsimons Army Med. Center, Denver, 1974-78; safety adminstr. Carter Mining Co., Gillette, Wyo., 1978—. Tng. coordinator Powder River Mine Rescue Assn. Served as sgt., U.S. Army, 1966-73. Republican. Lutheran. Office: Carter Mining Co Box 3007 Gillette WY 82716

MORITA, JAMES MASAMI, lawyer, banker; b. Kealakekua, South Kona, Hawaii, July 18, 1913; s. Ushima and Kichi (Yamamoto) M.; B.A., U. Hawaii, 1936; LL.B., Georgetown U., 1940; grad. Stonier Grad. Sch. Banking, 1970; m. Aiko Nagakura, Jan. 12, 1957; children—Caryn Sami, Marie Michiko. Admitted to Hawaii, D.C. bars, 1940, U.S. Supreme Ct. bar, 1949; partner firm Fukushima & Morita, Honolulu, 1941-50; 1st asst. pub. prosecutor, Honolulu, 1951-52; city, county atty., Honolulu, 1953-55, spl. counsel, 1956-57; atty. Morita, Kamo & Sakai, Honolulu, 1960-70; pres. Citibank Properties, Inc.; pres., dir. CB Bancshares, Inc.; chmn. bd., chief exec. officer City Bank; pres., dir. MKG Corp.; dir. All Hawaii Investment Corp., New Otani Kaimana Beach Hotel. Nat. trustee Nat. Jewish Hosp. and Research Center/Nat. Asthma Center, 1977—; mem. Full Fare Flyers Adv. bd.; trustee Hawaii Loa Coll.; active Boy Scouts Am. Mem. Bar Assn. Hawaii, Am. Bankers Assn. (govt. relations council), Hawaii Bankers Assn. (1st v.p.), Assn. U.S. Army, Mid-Pacific, Georgetown U. alumni assns., Honolulu Japanese (dir.), Hawaii chambers commerce, Hawaii Council Econ. Edn., Japan-Hawaii Econ. Council, Japan-Am. Soc. Honolulu. Democrat. Clubs: Waialae Country, 200. Home: 810 Richards St Honolulu HI 96813 Office: City Bank Box 3709 Honolulu HI 96811

MORITA, RICHARD YUKIO, microbiology and oceanography educator, researcher; b. Pasadena, Calif., Mar. 27, 1923; s. Jiro and Reiko (Yamamoto) M.; m. Toshiko Nishihara, May 29, 1926; children—Sally Jean, Ellen Jane, Peter Wayne. B.S., U. Nebr., 1947; M.S., U. So. Calif., 1949; Ph.D., U. Calif., 1954. Postdoctorate, U. Calif., Scripps Inst. Oceanography, 1954-55; asst. prof. U. Houston, 1955-58; asst. prof., assoc. prof. U. Nebr., 1958-62; prof. microbiology and oceanography, Oreg. State U., Corvallis, 1962—; program dir. biochemistry NSF, 1968-69; cons. NIH, 1968-70; researcher in field. Served with U.S. Army, 1944-46. NSF grantee, 1962—; NIH tng. grantee, 1960-68; NASA grantee, 1967-72; Office Naval Research grantee, 1966-70; Dept. Interior grantee, 1968-72; NOAA grantee, 1975-82; Bur. Land Mgmt. grantee, 1982; recipient awards including: King Fredericux IX Medal and Ribbon, 1954, Sr. Queen Elizabeth II Fellowship, 1973-74; Hotpack Lectr. and award Can. Soc. Microbiology, 1979; Japan Soc. Advancement Sci. fellow, 1978. Fellow Am. Acad. Microbiology, AAAS; mem. Am. Soc. Limnology and Oceanography, Am. Soc. Microbiology (Found. lectr. 1975-76), Oceanographic Soc. Japan, Deep Sea Biol. Soc. (hon.), Chilean Soc. Microbiology (hon.), Sigma Xi (research award 1972), Phi Kappa Phi. Contbr. over 200 articles to sci. lit.; inventor. Office: Dept Microbiology Oreg State Univ Corvallis OR 97331

MORIZUMI, JAMES S., space scientist; b. San Francisco, Nov. 13, 1923; s. Michael and Hiroko M.; m. Hiroko Kimura, Jan. 5, 1923; 1 son, Michal. B.S. in Mech. Engring., U.Calif.-Berkeley, 1955; B.S. in Mech. Engring., U. Kumamoto (Japan), 1948; M.S. in Aeros., Calif. Inst. Tech., Pasadena, 1957; Ph.D. in Math., and Applied Physics, UCLA, 1970. Engr., Douglas Aircraft Corp., Santa Monica, Calif., 1955-60; sr. engr. TRW, Inc., Def. and Space Systems Group, Redondo Beach, Calif., 1960-81; dir. A&C hydraulic research Space Application div. Textron Corp., Irvine, Calif., 1981-82; sr. scientist Electro-Optical div., Hughes Aircraft Corp., El Segundo, Calif., 1982—. Served with U.S. Army, 19-. Gustav A. Aichar Academic scholar 1953. Mem. Sigma XI, Pi Mu Epsilon, Tau Beta Pi. Contbr. numerous articles to profl. jours. Home: 29339 Stadia Hill Ln Rancho Palos Verde CA 90274

MORONEY, MICHAEL JOHN, lawyer; b. Jamaica, N.Y., Nov. 8, 1940; s. Everard V. and Margaret (Olson) M.; B.S., Villanova U., 1962; J.D., Fordham U., 1965; hon. degree U. Guam, 1976; m. Sandra S.Y. Chun, Oct. 22, 1966; children—Sean, Megan, Matthew. Spl. agt., FBI, Memphis and Nashville, 1965-67, Cleve. and Elyria, Ohio, 1967-71, Honolulu, 1971—, prin. legal advisor U.S. Dept. Justice/FBI, Honolulu 1971—; admitted to Hawaii bar, 1974, U.S. Supreme Ct. bar, 1977, High Ct. Trust Territories bar, 1977, Guam bar, 1976; law examiner, bd. examiners Hawaii Supreme Ct., 1980—, mem. applicant rev. com., 1980—. Recipient Gov.'s award Govt. Guam, 1974, 76. Mem. Am. Bar Assn., Hawaii Bar Assn., Guam Bar Assn., Assn. Trial Lawyers Am., Honolulu Press Club. Roman Catholic. Office: 300 Ala Moana Blvd Suite 4307 Honolulu HI 96850

MOROSO, MICHAEL JOSEPH, aerospace engineer; b. Centerville, Iowa, Jan. 26, 1923; s. John and Antonietta (Sartor) M.; m. Jody Mary Scripter, June 16, 1951; children—Barbara, Michael, Robert, Philip. B.S.M.E., U. Wis., 1952. Designer Douglas Aircraft Co., Santa Monica, Calif., 1952-65; engr., scientist McDonnell Douglas launch ctr. Vandenberg AFB, Calif., 1965-70; engr., sci. specialist McDonnell Douglas Astronautics Co., Huntington Beach, Calif., 1970-76; sr. propulsion engr. Northrop Corp., Hawthorne, Calif., 1976-79; customer engr. Douglas Aircraft Co., Long Beach, Calif., 1979—. Served to lt. USN, 1943-47. Mem. advancement com. Boy Scouts Am., Santa Maria, Calif., 1966-69; Little League mgr., coach, Santa Maria, 1967-69. Assoc. fellow AIAA; mem. So. Calif. Profl. Engrs. Assn., Am. Legion (adjutant, fin. officer 1950-65), Douglas Mgmt. Club. Democrat. Roman Catholic. Home: 964 Lansing Ln Costa Mesa CA 92626 Office: 3855 Lakewood Blvd Long Beach CA 90846

MORRELL, JOHN JOSEPH, business executive; b. N.Y.C., Sept. 4, 1948; s. Joseph Michael and Phylliss Morrell; m. Joanne Woodruff, June 13, 1970; children—Jennifer, Allison. B.S. cum laude, Manhattan Coll., 1970; M.B.A. summa cum laude Tex. Christian U., 1973. Market researcher Am. Courier Corp., N.Y.C., 1970-72; sales mgr. Purolator Services Corp., Dallas, 1972-73; mktg. mgr., 1974-75, v.p. mktg. N.Y., 1975-77; v.p. sales Wycoff Co. Inc., Salt Lake City, 1977-80, pres., 1980—. N.Y. Sales and Mktg. Council fellow, 1970. Mem. Salt Lake City C. of C., Am. Trucking Assn. Roman Catholic. Club: Kiwanis. Home: 1731 E Paulista Way Sandy UT 84092 Office: PO Box 366 Salt Lake City UT 84110

MORRELL, WILLIAM JOHN, union representative; b. Ophir, Utah, Jan. 4, 1917; s. John Sabotino and Concetta (Vernucci) M.; m. Nella Morrell, July 7, 1942; children—John W., Cherie Royce. Student pub. schs., Opttir and Tooele, Utah, 1923-34. Miner, 1933-41, 43-45, 46-50; with Kennecott Copper Corp., 1950-65; rep. United Steelworkers Am., Salt Lake City, 1965-83, mem. polit. action com. Bd. dirs. Salt Lake chpt. ARC, 1979—. Served in USAF, 1941-43, 45-46. Mem. Am. Assn. Ret. Persons. Roman Catholic. Home: 9080 S Cherbourg Pl Sandy UT 84092 Office: 2150 S 300 W PO Box 15604 Salt Lake City UT 84115

MORRICE, RUTH FILL, educator, author, consultant; b. Tonawanda, N.Y., Feb. 15, 1914; d. William Louis Allen and Grace Lillian Maude (Bates) Fill; B.A., Boston U., 1942, M.A., 1943, postgrad., 1945-47; postgrad. Monterey Coll., San Jose State U., U. Calif., Santa Cruz, U. Calif., Berkeley; m. Charles Elmer Conklin, Dec. 8, 1930; 1 dau., Mary Ruth Fill Conklin Mailey; m. 2d, John Buchan Morrice, Oct. 19, 1946; children—John Fill, Christina Forbes Morrice Reynolds, Eleanor Wylde Morrice, George Niven. Asst. English dept. Boston U., 1942-47; tchr. Hinsdale (Ill.) High Sch., 1943-45, head dept. English; English instr. Coll. William and Mary, Williamsburg, Va., 1947; instr. English and creative writing Culver Stockton Coll., Canton, Mo., 1948-49; faculty English and social studies Hartnell Coll., Salinas, Calif., 1967; teaching prin., counselor Olympia Sch., San Benito County, Calif., 1969-70; spl. tchr. Pacific Grove (Calif.) United Sch. Dist., 1964-76; ednl. cons., counselor, Carmel, Calif.; free lance writer, artist; sec. to Edward Rowe Snow, 1946, 47. Dir., supt. Bible Sch., Tustin (Calif.) Congl. Ch., 1964; den mother, pack and dist. leader San Fernando Valley council Boy Scouts Am.; mem. sch. bd. Montague Sch., Los Angeles; active parent groups, Heart Fund, church and other choirs. Mem. AAUP, Coll. English Assn. (sec.-treas. 1947-48), Nat. Tchrs. Assn., Calif. Tchrs. Assn., Alpha Phi. Republican. Congregationalist. Author: The Poetry of George Santayana, 1943; A Definition of the Novel 1920 to Present, 1981, A Study of Santayana and Ruskin, 1981, ...Personal Biography, 1981; editor: A Pilgrim Returns to Cape Cod (Edward Rowe Snow), 1946-47; Photographs and Thoughts from my Journeying in the Orient, 1979. Home and Office: 3508 Trevis Way Carmel CA 93923

MORRIN, VIRGINIA WHITE, educator; b. Escondido, Calif., May 16, 1913; d. Harry Parmalee and Ethel Norine (Nutting) Rising; B.S., Oreg. State Coll., 1952; M.Ed., Oreg. State U., 1957; m. Raymond Bennett White, 1933 (dec. 1953); children—Katherine Anne, Marjorie Virginia, William Raymond; m. 2d, Laurence Morrin, 1959 (dec. 1972). Social caseworker Los Angeles County, Los Angeles, 1934-40, 61-64; acctg. clk. War Dept., Ft. MacArthur, Calif., 1940-42; prin. clk. USAAF, Las Vegas, Nev., 1942-44; high sch. tchr., North Bend-Coos Bay, Oreg., 1952-56, Mojave, Calif., 1957-60; instr. Antelope Valley Coll., Lancaster, Calif., 1961-73; ret., 1974. Treas., Humane Soc. Antelope Valley, Inc., 1968—. Mem. Nat. Aero. Assn., Oreg. State U. Alumni Assn. (life). Office: PO Box 570 Lancaster CA 93534

MORRIS, ALVIN LEE, cons. corp. exec., meteorologist; b. Kim, Colo., June 7, 1920; s. Roy E. and Eva Edna (James) M.; B.S. in Meteorology (U.S. Weather Bur. fellow), U. Chgo., 1942; M.S., U.S. Navy Postgrad. Sch., 1953; m. Nadean Davidson, Jan. 16, 1979; children—Andrew N., Nancy L., Mildred M., Ann E., Jane C. Meteorologist Pacific Gas and Electric Co., San Francisco, 1947-50; commd. U.S. Navy, 1942, advanced through grades to capt., USNR, 1962, assignments including staff, comdr. 7th Fleet, ret., 1958; dir. research Navy Weather Research Facility, Norfolk, Va., 1958-62; facilities coordinator, mgr. sci. balloon facility, Nat. Center for Atmospheric Research Boulder, Colo., 1963-75; pres. Ambient Analysis Inc., Internat. Cons., Boulder, 1975—. Treas. Home Hospitality for Fgn. Students Program, U. Colo., 1969-70. Served with USN, 1942-46, 50-58. Mem. Am. Meteorol. Soc. (cert. cons. meteorologist), Am. Geophys. Union, ASTM, Ret. Officers Assn., Nat. Fedn. Ind. Bus. Club: Boulder County Knife and Fork. Editor Handbook of Scientific Ballooning, 1975; contbr. articles to profl. jours.; convenor, editor proceedings ASTM conf. Home: 15759 Sunshine Canyon Boulder CO 80302 Office: 729 Walnut St Suite C Boulder CO 80302

MORRIS, BOURNE G., marketing consulting firm executive; b. Detroit, Jan. 5, 1937; d. Howard Thomas and Margaret McHenry (Wygant) Worden; m. Robert Ramsey Morris, Nov. 7, 1964 (div.); children—Miranda, Temple; m. 2d, Robert Eugene Buss, June 25, 1982. Student Bennington Coll., 1954-57. Copywriter, Batten, Barton Durstine & Osborn, N.Y.C., 1959-64; copy supr. Ogilvy & Mather, N.Y.C., N.Y., 1964-70, account exec., 1970-74, v.p., 1974-76, mgmt. supr., 1976-77, sr. v.p., 1977-81, head Los Angeles agy., 1978-81; pres. Bourne Morris, Inc., Reno, 1981—; vis. Reynolds prof. journalism U. Nev., Reno, 1983. Bd. dirs. Southwestern Sch. Law, Los Angeles, 1980-82, Calif. Hosp. Med. Center, Los Angeles, 1981-82; co-founder ICAN Assocs., Los Angeles, 1979. Recipient TWIN award YMCA, 1981. Mem. Western States Advt. Assn. (dir. 1980-81). Contbr. articles in field to profl. publs. Home and Office: 1815 Wendy Way Reno NV 89509

MORRIS, CAROLE SUE, housing program manager; b. Arlington, Calif., May 28, 1940; d. Aubrey and Rose Marie (Graves) Luker; m. Thomas Earl Couts, Feb. 3, 1958; children—Thomas Earl, Donnie Roy; m. 2d, Bob J. Morris, Oct. 24, 1970. Student Valley Coll., 1973. Clk.-typist, County of San Bernardino (Calif.), 1959-60, Norton AFB, Calif., 1960-62; clk. II, Exptl. Housing Allowance Program, San Bernardino, 1973-75; transition counselor Housing Authority of County of San Bernardino, 1975-78, housing mgr., 1978—. Mem. Nat. Assn. Female Execs., NOW. Office: Housing Authority of County of San Bernardino 802 N E St San Bernardino CA 92410

MORRIS, DOYLE WESLEY, accountant; b. Lexington, Okla., June 21, 1922; s. Ernest Robert and Ethel Eva (Redwine) M.; grad. Hill Bus. U., 1957; m. Bobbie Jean Carrell, May 16, 1947; children—Michelle, Kevin B. Owner, Morris Oil Co., Minco, Okla., 1952-57; salesman Goodyear Tire & Rubber Co., Oklahoma City, 1957, office mgr., 1957-60; office mgr. Artesia Alfalfa Growers Assn. (N.Mex.), 1960-73; staff Glorieta Baptist Conf. Ctr.; pvt. practice acctg., Santa Fe, Served with USNR. Mem. Am. Legion. Democrat. Baptist. Clubs: Masons, Kiwanis. Office: 53 1/2 Old Santa Fe Trail Santa Fe NM 87501

MORRIS, EFFIE LEE (MRS. LEONARD V. JONES), librarian, lectr., cons., author; b. Richmond, Va.; d. William H. and Erma (Caskie) M.; B.A., Case Western Res. U., 1945, B.L.S., 1946, M.S. in Library Sci., 1956; m. Leonard V. Jones, Aug. 25, 1971. Br. children's librarian Cleve. Public Library, 1946; children's specialist Library of the Blind, N.Y. Public Library, 1958-63; coordinator children's library services San Francisco Public Library, 1963-78; originator Dial-a-Story, Early Childhood Program, 1972—; author Harcourt Brace Jovanovich, San Francisco, 1978-79; chmn. Library of Congress Adv. Com. of Children's Librarians on Selection of Books for Blind, 1958-63, nat. adv. bd. Center for the Book, 1978—; chmn. Children's Book List, Am. Issues Forum, 1976; guest prof. Atlanta U., 1954; lectr. Case-Western Res. U., 1953-55; instr. U. San Francisco, 1974-76; pres. Channel 8, Ednl. Cable TV; cons. reading project San Francisco chpt. NCCJ, 1967—; cons. Oakland (Calif.) Public Library Study, 1974-75; lectr. children's lit. Mills Coll., 1979—. Mem. ALA Newbery Caldecott award com., 1950-56, 66-67, Laura Ingalls Wilder award com., 1953-54, 58-60; chmn. Coretta Scott King Book Award Task Force; mem. com. for Carter G. Woodson award Nat. Council Social Studies, 1973-74, 76; chmn. tech. adv. com. Nat. Aid to Visually Handicapped, 1973—; mem. library adv. bd. New Book Knowledge, 1966-76; cons. children's services Chgo. Public Library Study, 1968-69; mem. adv. com. Title II E.S.E.A., State of Calif., 1965-76, Library Sch., San Jose State U., 1972—; del. White House Conf. on Children, 1970. Mem. assoc. council Mills Coll., 1973—; bd. dirs. YWCA, San Francisco, 1968-73, Bayview Crispus Attucks Community Center, 1977—; mem. Calif. Library Services Bd., 1982—; vice chmn. Mayor's Adv. Council on Child Care, 1979—; bd. dirs. 66 Cleary Ct. Condominium Homeowners, 1981-82. Recipient E. P. Dutton-John Macrae award for advancement of library service to children and young people, 1958; Lola M. Parker award Iota Phi Lambda, 1978; Appreciation award Jewish Bur. Edn., San Francisco, 1978; Disting. Service to Librarianship award Black Caucus of ALA, 1978; Disting. Service award Calif. Librarians Black Caucus, 1978; Disting. Alumnae Sch. Library Sci., Case Western Res. U., 1979; Effie Lee Morris Hist. and Research Collection of Children's Lit., San Francisco Pub. Library, established, 1981. Mem. ALA (sec. children's library assn. 1955-56, dir. children's services div. 1963-66; council 1967-72, 75—, pres. public library assn. 1971-72), LWV, Women's Nat. Book Assn. (chpt. pres. 1968-70, nat. sec. 1974-76), Nat. Council Tchrs. English, Nat. Braille Club (pres. 1961-63), AAUW, NAACP (life), Urban League (Bay area), Calif. Library Assn. (dist. pres. 1966, pres. children's services div. 1970-72, council 1977-79), Calif. Writers Club (hon.), Internat. Reading Assn. (book selection award com.), Common Cause, Nat. Assn. Bus. and Profl. Women (pres. San Francisco chpt. 1981-82), Beta Phi Mu, Alpha Kappa Alpha. Congregationalist. Clubs: Altrusa (v.p. 1968), Commonwealth. Contbr. articles to profl. jours. Address: Apt 1009 66 Cleary Ct San Francisco CA 94109

MORRIS, ELIZABETH TREAT, phys. therapist; b. Hartford, Conn., Feb. 20, 1936; d. Charles Wells and Marion Louise (Case) Treat; B.S. in Phys. Therapy, U. Conn., 1960; m. David Breck Morris, July 10, 1961; children—Russell Charles, Jeffrey David. Phys. therapist Crippled Children's Clinic No. Va., Arlington, 1960-62, Shriners Hosp. Crippled Children, Salt Lake City, 1967-69, Holy Cross Hosp., Salt Lake City, 1970-74; pvt. practice phys. therapy, Salt Lake City, 1975—. Mem. Am. Phys. Therapy Assn., Friendship Force Utah, U.S. Figure Skating Assn. Home: 4177 Mathews Way Salt Lake City UT 84117 Office: 1261 Wilmington Ave Suite 6 Salt Lake City UT 84106

MORRIS, GARY LEE, farmer; b. Potlatch, Idaho, Aug. 10, 1928; s. Victor T. and Jennie R. (Robenson) M.; m. Ginger O. Holcomb, Nov. 19, 1949; children—Carey R., Gina Morris Burnet. Farmer, Potlatch, 1948—; supr. Latah Soil and Water Conservation Dist., 1955—; pres. Clearwater Palouse Energy Coop., 1980—. Commr., Latah County, 1975—; mem. Potlatch Sch. Bd. Named Outstanding Farmer of Idaho, Jaycees, 1959. Mem. Idaho Assn. Counties (pres.), Idaho Sch. Bds. Assn. (pres.). Presbyterian. Address: Box 565 Potlatch ID 83855

MORRIS, HENRY MADISON, III, clergyman; b. El Paso, Tex., May 15, 1942; s. Henry Madison and Mary Louise (Beach) M.; B.A. summa cum laude, Christian Heritage Coll., 1976; M.Div., Luther Rice Sem., 1977, D.Min., 1978; m. Janet Deckman, July 25, 1964; children—Henry M., Scotta Marie. Regional mgr. Integon Ins. Co., Greenville, S.C., 1969-75; ordained to ministry Bapt. Ch., 1968; pastor Hallmark Bapt. Ch., Greenville, 1969-75; asso. prof. Bible, Christian Heritage Coll., El Cajon, Calif., 1977-78, adminstrv. v.p., 1978-80; pastor First Bapt. Ch., Canoga Park, Calif., 1980—; lectr. in field. Served with U.S. Army, 1959-66. Republican. Author: Baptism: What is It?, 1977; Explore the Word, 1978; Churches: History and Doctrine, 1980. Office: 20553 Sherman Way Canoga Park CA 91306

MORRIS, JAMES DYKE, business educator, researcher, consultant; b. Meadow, S.D., Jan. 10, 1927; s. Leonard G. and Clara L. Morris; m. Sue Zanna Smith, June 4, 1959. B.S.B.A., No. State Coll., Aberdeen, S.D., 1956; M.A. in Acctg., U. N.D., 1957, Ph.D., 1961. Acct. Internat. Harvester Co., Aberdeen, 1951-57; instr., head bus. div. Black Hills State Coll., 1957-62; owner J/S Morris Farm, Meadow, S.D., 1972—; prof. bus. edn. U. Hawaii, 1967—; dir. Internat. Bus. Methods Conf., Honolulu; dir. Informational Tech. Conf., Honolulu. Served with U.S. Army, 1951-53. Mem. Pi Omega Pi, Delta Pi Epsilon, Pi Delta Kappa.

MORRIS, JOHN THEODORE, planning official; b. Denver, Jan. 18, 1929; s. Theodore Ora and Daisy Allison (McDonald) M.; B.F.A., Denver U., 1955; m. Dolores Irene Seaman, June 21, 1951; children—Holly Lee, Heather Ann, Heidi Jo, Douglas Fraser. Apprentice landscape architect S.R. DeBoer & Co., Denver, summer 1949, planning technician (part-time), 1954-55; sr. planner and assoc. Trafton Bean & Assocs., Boulder, Colo., 1955-62; prin. Land Planning Assocs., planning cons., Boulder, 1962-65; planning dir. and park coordinator Boulder County, 1965-67; sch. planner Boulder Valley Sch. Dist., 1967— also dir. planning and engring., 1967—, supr. facility improvement program, 1969—; cons. U. Colo. Bur. Ednl. Field Services, 1974. Bd. dirs. Historic Boulder, 1974-76; mem. parks and recreation adv. com. Denver Regional Council Govts., 1975—. Served with USCG, 1950-53. Mem. Am. Inst. Cert. Planners, Am. Planning Assn., Council of Ednl. Facility Planners Internat. Home: 7647 N 32d St Jamestown Star Route Boulder CO 80302 Office: 6500 E Arapahoe St Boulder CO 80301

MORRIS, JOSEPH, psychologist, educator; b. Santa Monica, Calif., Jan. 17, 1942; s. Joseph and Catherine Josephine (Wernet) M. B.A. in Psychology, U. Calif.-Berkeley, 1963; Ph.D. in Edn. and Psychology, U. Mich., 1968. Lic. sch. psychologist, Calif. Asst. prof. CCNY, 1968-70, U. Pitts., 1970-73; assoc. prof. Calif. State U.-Northridge, 1973—; cons. in field. Pres. Trainers of Sch. Psychologists, 1981-83. Mem. Am. Psychol. Assn., Internat. Council Psychologists, Nat. Assn. Sch. Psychologists, Authors Guild, Phi Beta Kappa. Club: Sierra. Author: Psychology and Teaching, 1978. Editor The International Psychologist, 1978-80. Contbr. articles to profl. jours. Office: Dept Psychology Calif State U Northridge CA 91330

MORRIS, KAY WETZEL, social worker; b. Salt Lake City, July 9, 1939; d. Nevin Frank Wetzel and Jane Rawlins Deakin; student U. Utah, 1957-59; B.A. with highest honors, U. Calif., San Jose, 1961; M.S.W. summa cum laude, Ohio State U., 1963; 1 son, Michael David. social worker children's service Napa (Calif.) State Hosp., 1963-66; pupil personnel dir. Trinity County Supt. of Schs. Office, 1967-70; founder, social worker Trinity County Mental Health Services, 1970-76; pvt. practice psychotherapy and consultation, Redding, Calif., 1967—; dir. Victor Residential Center, Inc. (Stepping Stones), 1976-81; rural services com., cons. children's service com. Calif. Conf. Local Mental Health Dirs., 1972-77; mental health cons. plan devel. com. No. Calif. Health Systems Agy., 1976-81; mem. Arthritis Rehab. Team, Redding, 1982—; speaker Women's Network, Seattle, 1981; cons. Task Force for Handicapped Children, Shasta County Supt. of Schs., 1971-74, Seattle Children's Home, 1982—, Mem.l. Hosp., Redding, 1980—; developer Trinity County Mental Health Service, 1970. Trustee Redding Elem. Sch. Dist., 1977-81; bd. dirs. Group Home Assn. Calif., 1979-80. vol. KIXE Pub. Braodcasting System; Trinity County chmn. McGovern for Pres., 1972. NIMH fellow, 1961-62. Mem. Nat. Assn. Social Workers, AAUW, Psi Chi.

MORRIS, KENN GLENN, computer co. mktg. exec.; b. Murray, Utah, Mar. 24, 1935; s. Glenn and Bertha Charlotte (Hansen) M.; B.S. in Advt. and Journalism, U. Utah, 1957; M.B.A. with honors in Internat. Mgmt., Am. Grad. Sch. Internat. Mgmt., 1973. Copywriter, Ross Jurney & Assos. Advt., Salt Lake City, 1957-59; mgmt. trainee Gen. Electric Co., N.Y.C., 1959-61; public relations specialist Litton Industries, Beverly Hills, Calif., 1961-68; mgr. graphics communications Whittaker Corp., Los Angeles, 1968-71; mgr. mktg. services Audiotronics Corp., North Hollywood, Calif., 1971-72; mgr. corp. communications Envirotech Corp., Menlo Park, Calif., 1973-74; public affairs officer Office Internat. Affairs, NASA, Washington, 1974-78; mgr. mktg. communications Pertec Computer Corp., Los Angeles, 1978-82; dir. mktg. communications Callan Data Systems, Westlake Village, Calif., 1982—. Mem. Advt. Club Los Angeles, Am. Mgmt. Assn., Assn. M.B.A. Execs., Bus. and Profl. Advt. Assn., Assn. Indsl. Advertisers, Meeting Planners Internat., Public Relations Soc. Am., Chevaliers des Tastevin. Republican. Mormon.

MORRIS, LOUISE B., interior designer; b. Hubbard, Ariz., Aug. 21, 1925; d. William Franklin and Mary Anne (Adams) Butler; m. Gilbert Lavoy Morris, June 3, 1943; children—David, Joanne, Karen Morris Grissom, Donald, Gena Morris Raban, Irene, Dwayne. Prin. Morris Draperies and Interiors, Yuma, Ariz., 1961—; lectr. in field. Precinct committeeman Yuma County Republican Party, 1961—. Mem. Am. Soc. Interior Designers (assoc.), Internat. Drapery Assn. (area bd. dirs.). Republican. Mormon. Contbr. articles on home decorating to local newspapers. Office: Morris Draperies and Interiors 888 5th Ave Yuma AZ 85364

MORRIS, MARTHA LOUISE, association executive; b. Switzerland, Apr. 17, 1919; naturalized U.S. citizen, 1939; d. Theodor August and Christine Marie (Rhigi) Ming; m. John J. Buscaglia, Apr. 17, 1942; children—John, Richard; m. 2d, George Hawser Morris, Apr. 10, 1959; 1 son, George. Bookkeeper various cos., 1950-75; bookkeeper, office mgr. Holtville C. of C. (Calif.), 1975—. Clubs: Soroptimist Internat. Holtville (1st v.p.), Imperial Valley Swiss (treas.). Home: 1553 Worthington Rd Holtville CA 92250 Office: 101 5th St PO Box 185 Holtville CA 92250

MORRIS, PATRICIA KATHRYN, educator; b. Bremerton, Wash., Dec. 6, 1939; d. George M. Thomas and Lela M. Simons; A.A. with high honors, Compton Coll., 1960; B.A. magna cum laude, Linfield Coll., 1963; M.S., Oreg. State U., 1978; m. Donald E. Morris, Aug. 2, 1963 (dec.); children—Kathryn, Daryl. Sec., So. Calif. Baptist Conv., Los Angeles, 1960-63, Linfield (Oreg.) Coll., 1961-63; tchr. Bellflower (Calif.) Unified Sch. Dist., 1963-65, Newark (Del.) Spl. Sch. Dist., 1965-66; chmn. bus./office occupations div. Kenai Peninsula Community Coll. (Alaska), 1973—. Sec., Republican Party of Alaska, 1975-82, mem. state central com., 1974-82, del. nat. conv., 1976, del. aide nat. conv., 1980. Mem. Nat. Bus. Edn. Assn., Am. Bus. Communication Assn., Am. Vocat. Assn., NEA, Central Peninsula Concert Assn. Episcopalian. Clubs: Toastmasters, Soroptomists. Home: PO Box 3152 Kenai AK 99611

MORRIS, ROBERT DONALD, metal company executive; b. Telluride, Colo., May 3, 1911; s. James Elder and Hazle Muriel (Hallett) M.; m. Helen Margaret Smith, 1930 (dec. 1933); 1 dau., Patricia Morris Bailey; m. 2d., Dorthella Annette (div. 1937); 1 dau., Katherine Ann Morris Laxact, m. 3d., Virginia Nalder, 1941; children—Sherry Morris Erwin, Don, James, Jeanie; 1 foster son, Edward Tureson. Student, LaSalle Extension Law Sch., Chgo., 1945-46. With Mizpah Mine, Tonopah, Nev., 1925-29, B&B Quicksilver Mine, Nev., 1929-30; supt. Mina Mercury Mine, Dunlap Canyon, Nev., 1931-33; mill maintenance mgr. Spreckles Sugar Co., Rhoades Salt Marsh, Nev., 1933-34, miner Nev. Mass. Mining Co., Silver Dyke, Nev., 1934-35; miner Round Mountain, Nev., 1935-36; mill foreman U.S. Vanadium Corp., Pine Creek, Calif., 1936-38; supt. Rand Co., Elko County, Nev., 1938-40; gen. supt. Basil Mine, Prescott, Nev., 1940-43; mgr. Ivanhoe Quicksilver Mine, Nev., 1942-43; mine supt. Newmont Silver Cloud Quicksilver Mine, Nev., 1943-44; mgr. Alpine Mining Co., Minden, Nev., 1944-50, operator, 1951-53; mgr. Newmont Mining Co., Grass Valley, Calif., 1950-51; developer Toiyabe Mine & Milling Co., Gabbs Valley, Nev., 1953-54; v.p., gen. mgr. U.S. Copper Co., Salt Lake City, 1954-57; chmn., gen. mgr. MM&S Exploration Co., Carson City, Nev., 1957-69; pres., gen. mgr. Bullion Monarch Co., Austin, Nev., 1969-80, chmn. bd., chief exec. officer, 1980—; cons. in field. Mem. exec. bd. Boy Scouts Am., Nev. Area Council, 1965-70, v.p., 1971-73; hon. life mem. PTA, 1969—; high priest Ch. of Jesus Christ of Latter-day Saints. Recipient Silver Statue, Boy Scouts Am., 1966. Mem. AIME (sr.), Nev. Prospectors. Democrat. Lodge: Masons. Designer flotation ore reduction plant, Austin, Nev.

MORRIS, ROBERT EARL, banker; b. Albuquerque, Apr. 19, 1937; s. Benjamin Franklin and Jessie (Timmons) M.; student U. N.Mex., 1955-58, Am. U., George Washington U.; m. Janet K. Lassman; children—Staphanie, Bonny, Robert Earl, Stephen, Craig, Yvonne. With FBI, 1958-61; with N.Mex. Savs. & Loan Assn., Albuquerque, 1962—, chief exec. officer, 1962—, pres., 1975—. Past pres. United Fund Santa Fe; mem. pres.'s council Coll. Santa Fe. Mem. League Insurer's Savs. and Loan's N.Mex. (past pres.), S.W. Savs. and Loan Conf. (past pres.), Bldg. Contractors Assn. N.Mex., Mortgage Bankers Assn., Assn. Commerce and Industry, Albuquerque C. of C., U.S. Savs. and Loan League. Democrat. Clubs: Lions (past pres.), Pres.'s of U. N.Mex. Office: 2900 Louisiana St NE Albuquerque NM 87110

MORRIS, ROBERT EMUEL, utility exec.; b. Parsons, Kans., Oct. 24, 1921; s. Harry Alfred and Eddie (Evans) M.; B.S. in Elec. Engring., Ga. Inst. Tech., 1944; m. Carolyn Benziger Morris, Oct. 5, 1946 (dec. Mar. 1968); children—Janet Morris Perez, Carolyn Wynn, Martin Blair, Kenneth, Carolyn Blair McInerney, Robert Stuart; m. 2d, Isabel M. Morris, Aug. 22, 1970. With Allis Chalmers Mfg. Co., 1940-64, regional mgr., St. Louis, 1960-62, gen. sales mgr., Milw., 1963-64; dir. sales Monsanto Co., St. Louis, 1964-65; mgr. mktg. San Diego Gas & Electric Co., 1965-69, v.p. mktg., 1969-70, sr. v.p., 1971-75, pres., 1975-81, chmn. bd., 1981—; dir. The Martin Co., Topeka. Mem. Calif. Econ. Devel. Commn.; trustee Midwest Research Inst., Kansas City, Mo., Scripps Clinic and Research Found., La Jolla, Calif. Served to 1st lt. AUS, 1944-46. Named D.C. Engr. of Yr., D.C. Soc. Profl. Engrs., 1957. Registered profl. engr., D.C. Mem. IEEE, San Diego C. of C. (dir., mem. exec. com.), Alpha Tau Omega, Tau Beta Pi, Eta Kappa Nu. Office: San Diego Gas & Electric Co 101 Ash San Diego CA 92101

MORRIS, STEPHEN MATTHEW, hosp. adminstr.; b. Denmark, Ark., June 14, 1928; s. John Harvey and Pearl (Aunspaugh) M.; student Ark. Coll., 1948-50; B.B.A., Southwestern U., 1952; M.H.A., Washington U., St. Louis, 1954; m. Euala Crow, Apr. 22, 1949; children—Craig, Ann; m. Ingrid Leitner, May 21, 1983. Adminstrv. resident Good Samaritan Hosp., Phoenix, 1953-54, adminstrv. asst., 1954-55, asst. adminstr., 1956-60, adminstr., 1960-66, pres., 1966-68; pres. Samaritan Health Service, 1968—; chmn. bd., chief exec. officer Sam Cor, Phoenix; mem. Phoenix Planning Commn., 1967-69; mem. Gov.'s Commn. for Employing Handicapped, 1967-71; mem. Ariz. Health Planning Authority, 1968-72; mem. bd. commrs. Joint Commn. Accreditation Hosps., 1974—, mem. survey procedures com., 1975, accreditation com., 1977, chmn. fin. com., 1978, mem. exec. com., 1978, joint conf. com., 1978, treas., 1978; cons. Nat. Center Health Services Research and Devel., HEW, 1966-68, 72—; mem. spl. med. adv. group VA, 1972-75. Trustee Ariz. Blue Cross, 1961-65, pres., 1963-64; mem. dean's adv. council Coll. Bus. Adminstrn., Ariz. State U., 1974-77; past pres. Phoenix Regional Hosp. Council; past v.p. Ariz. League Nursing; past bd. dirs. Vis. Nurse Assn. Phoenix; mem. Ariz. Aviation Futures Task Force. Served with USNR, 1946-48; with AUS, 1950-51. Fellow Am. Coll. Hosp. Adminstrs. (regent 1964-67, gov. 1967-71, Gerard B. Lambert award for innovative ideas patient care and costs 1971); mem. Am. Hosp. Assn. (trustee, pres. 1972, chmn. ho. of dels. 1973), Ariz. Hosp. Assn. (pres. 1963-64, trustee 1961-65, Salsbury award 1978), Ariz. Acad. Mason (Shriner), Kiwanian (past pres.). Clubs: Phoenix Hiram, Phoenix Executives (dir., past pres.), Phoenix Country, Phoenix Press (asso.), Kiva (asso.), Arizona. Home: 3053 E Claremont Phoenix AZ 85016 Office: 5500 N 24th St Phoenix AZ 85016

MORRIS, THOMAS KEITH, podiatrist; b. Salinas, Calif., Dec. 31, 1946; s. Keith Ellis and Bobbye Neil (Wilson) M.; student Saddleback Jr. Coll., 1971-73; B.S., U. Calif.-Irvine, 1974; D.P.M., Ohio Coll. Podiatric Medicine, 1978; m. Linda Rhae Antram, May 7, 1966; children—Amy Lynn, Carrie Annabett. Resident in podiatric surgery Podiatry Coll. Pitts., 1978-79; pvt. practice podiatric medicine, Laguna Niguel, Calif., 1979—. Served with USN, 1965-69; Viet Nam. Recipient Cert. of Appreciaiton, March of Dimes, 1976. Mem. Am. Podiatry Assn., Orange County Podiatry Assn., Capistrano Beach C. of C. (pres. 1983), Laguna Niguel C. of C., Am. Coll. Sports Medicine, Am. Coll. Foot Surgeons (asso.). Clubs: Lions, South Coast Runners, Laguna Niguel Business. Home: 34365 Via San Juan Capistrano Beach CA 92624 Office: 30131 Town Center Dr Suite 250 Laguna Niguel CA 92677

MORRISON, BOONE M., photographer; b. Berkeley, Calif., Jan. 28, 1941. B.A. in History, Stanford U., 1962, B.A. in Communications, 1963; Yosemite Photog. Workshops with Ansel Adams, 1971-73. Owner/founder The Foundry Gallery, Honolulu, 1969-71; instr. photography U. Hawaii-Manoa, 1969-71, instr. architecture, 1970-72; instr. photography Hawaii Photog. Workshops, 1971—; dir. Statewide Photo Exhbn., 1970, The Volcano Art Ctr., Hawaii, 1974-81; dir. The Image Found, 1973—; visual arts coordinator Artists in Schs. Program, 1974; lectr. U. Hawaii, 1980; exhibited in shows: Artists of Hawaii, 1971-75, Honolulu Acad. Traveling Exhbn., Nat. Park Service Traveling Exhbn., 1976-77, Am. Photographers and the Nat. Parks, 1981-83; represented in permanent collections at Honolulu Acad. Art, Hawaii, Bishop Mus., Honolulu, State of Hawaii Collection, U.S. Nat. Park Service, Nat. Gallery Art, Washington. Mem. Image Continuum Group.

MORRISON, CAROLYN ANN, nursing educator; b. Saginaw, Mich., Sept. 2, 1935; d. James E. and Victoria (McMullen) M. A.A., Compton Jr. Coll., 1955; R.N., Queen Angels Sch. Nursing, 1958; B.S., Chapman Coll., 1981, M.S. candidate, 1981—. R.N., Calif.; cert. tchr., Calif. Staff nurse out-patient dept. Orthopedic Hosp., Los Angeles, 1958-61, hosp. staff nurse, 1961-62; nurse-extender Dr. N.E. Diess, Downey, Calif., 1981—; staff nurse, asst. head nurse surg. dept. St. Francis Med. Ctr., Lynwood, Calif., 1964-74, asst. head nurse, unit supr. orthopedic dept., 1974—; clin. instr. Compton Community Coll., 1981—. Mem. AAUW, Nat. Assn. Female Execs., Calif. Nurses Assn., Am. Nurses Assn., Nat. Assn. Orthopedic Nurses, Am. Pub. Health Assn., Assn. Rehab. Nurses.

MORRISON, DOUGLAS WILLIAM, lawyer; b. Lovell, Wyo., Apr. 7, 1940; s. Francis Elggren and Cleo (Mickelson) M.; m. Susan Kay Bankhead, July 31, 1964; children—Steven Douglas, Heidi Sue, John William, Scott Keele, Andrew Elggren, Brian James. B.S. magna cum laude, Brigham Young U., 1964; J.D., NYU, 1968. Bar: Utah 1968, D.C. 1969, U.S. Tax Ct. 1969, U.S. Supreme Ct. 1974. Assoc., Jones, Waldo, Holbrook & McDonough, Salt Lake City, 1967-69; assoc. Wilkinson, Cragun & Barker, Washington, 1969-70; assoc. Fabian & Clendenin, Salt Lake City, 1970-71, pres., prin. Douglas W. Morrison, P.C., Provo, 1971-82; shareholder, dir. Richards, Brandt, Miller & Nelson, P.C., Salt Lake City and Provo, 1983—; asst. dean Coll. Bus. Brigham Young U., 1963-64. Missionary gulf states Ch. Jesus Christ of Latter-day Saints, 1960-62, mem. high council, 1974-76, 82—; coach Little League, Provo, 1975-76; cubmaster Boy Scouts Am., 1976; trustee Friends of Timpview, 1981-83; mem. Mormon Tabernacle Choir, 1967-69. Mem. Am. Inst. C.P.A.s, Soc. Pub. Accts., Am. Assn. Attys.-C.P.A.s, ABA, D.C. Bar Assn., Utah Bar Assn., Provo C. of C. (dir. 1979-82). Republican. Home: 556 E 4020 N Provo UT 84604 Office: 50 S Main St Suite 700 PO Box 2465 Salt Lake City UT 84110

MORRISON, EMILY KITTLE, leadership development trainer, consultant, writer; b. Indpls., Apr. 17, 1942; d. John Sloan and Elizabeth (Mills) Kittle; m. William C. Kimball, Aug. 25, 1966; children—Ann Eve, Mary Lynn; m. 2d, Charles Edward Morrison, Aug. 5, 1982. B.A., Denver U., 1964; M.A., U. Ariz., 1966. Founder, pres. Jordan Enterprises, Tucson, 1980—. Active Jr. League, Girl Scouts U.S.A., Planned Parenthood, AAUW. Mem. Am. Soc. Tng. and Devel., Nat. Speakers Assn., Internat. Platform Assn., Delta Gamma. Author: How to Get the Most Out of Being a Volunteer, 1980; Skills for Leadership, 1983. Office: PO Box 31084 Tucson AZ 85751

MORRISON, JOHN RONALD, management consultant; b. Chester, W.Va., Sept. 29, 1928; s. James Ingram and Ida Helen (Brown) M.; m. Shirley Eckberg, Sept. 12, 1953; children—Lisa Jo, Christopher D., Thomas A. B.A., Bethany Coll., 1952; M.A., U. Pa., 1957. Personnel mgr. RCA, Camden, N.J., 1952-59; mgr. indsl. relations Raytheon Co., Santa Barbara, Calif., 1959-62; mgmt. cons. Heidrick & Struggles, Los Angeles and San Francisco, 1962-68; v.p., dir. W S & Y Cons., San Francisco, 1968-73; pres. J.R. Morrison & Assocs., San Francisco, 1973—. Bd. dirs. YMCA. Served with AUS, 1946-48. Mem. Bethany Coll. Alumni Assn., Beta Theta Pi. Clubs: San Francisco Univ., St. Francis Yacht (San Francisco). Office: 555 California St San Francisco CA 94104

MORRISON, LUCILE PHILLIPS, psychologist, author; b. Los Angeles, Sept. 8, 1896; d. Lee A. and Catherine (Coffin) Phillips; A.B., Vassar Coll., 1918; M.A. in Psychology, George Pepperdine Coll., 1958; Litt.D. (hon.), Calif. Sch. Profl. Psychology, 1978; m. Wayland Augustus Morrison, Dec. 27, 1917; children—Wayland Lee, Richard Holt, Lee Allen, Keith Norman; 1 adopted dau., Patricia Lee. Intern, Am. Inst. Family Relations, Los Angeles, 1952-53, asso. counselor 1954-55, counselor, 1955-64, also v.p. bd. dirs. until 1964. Pres. (founding mem.) Duarte (Calif.) Community Service Council, 1946-48, v.p., 1948-50, health chmn., 1951-54; dir., mem. Duarte Community Center Bd., 1949-57 dir. Children's Hosp., Los Angeles, 1921-44; trustee Westminster Gardens Presbyn. Ch. U.S.A., 1953-66, hon. life trustee, 1966—; trustee mem. coms. Scripps Coll., 1930-72, chmn. edn1. policy com., 1965-70, trustee emeritus, 1972—, recipient Ellen Browning Scripps Assocs. award, 1976; constituent mem. bd. fellows Claremont (Calif.) U. Center, 1967-70; mem. adv. bd. Inst. for Antiquity and Christianity, Claremont Grad. Sch., 1968—; mem. The Founders, Music Center for Performing Arts, Los Angeles; v.p., dir. mem. staff Psychol. Guidance Center, Anaheim, Calif., 1960-63; bd. dirs. Calif. Sch. Profl. Psychology, 1973-79, exec. council, 1973, acad. commn., 1974-78. Named Woman of Yr., Marlborough Sch., Los Angeles, 1979; cert. and lic. psychologist, Calif.; lic. marriage, family and child counselor, Calif. Mem. So. Calif. Symphony Assn., N.Y. Acad. Scis., Child Study Assn. Am., Hist. Soc. So. Calif., AAUW, Acad. Psychologists in Marital Counseling, Am. (asso.), Calif. State, Western psychol. assns., Am. Assn. Marriage Counselors, Calif. State Marriage Counselors Assn., Phi Beta Kappa, Delta Kappa Gamma, Psi Chi. Club: Women's Univ. (Los Angeles). Author: Mystery Gate, 1928; The Attic Child, 1929; Blue Bandits, 1930; The Lost Queen of Egypt (Nat. Pen Women's award for fiction), 1938; co-author: Taylor-Johnson Temperament Analysis, 1967; also articles; editor: Doll Dreams (4 vols.), 1927-32; The World of Books (for Scripps Coll.), 1934. Home: 1134 Rancho Rd Arcadia CA 91006

MORRISON, MARK MURLEY, army officer; b. Bakersfield, Calif., Feb. 13, 1951; s. Robert William and Clydene (Holland) M.; 1 dau., Shannon Ellen. B.A. in Polit. Sci., UCLA, 1973, M.S. in Edn., U. So. Calif., 1977. Commd. 2d lt. U.S. Army, 1973, advanced through grades to capt., 1977; service in W.Ger.; organizational devel. cons., mgmt. trainer Comdg. Gen. Spl. Staff, Ft. Sill, Okla., 1979-81; assigned to San Francisco, 1981—. Pres. Lawton-Ft. Sill Athletic Ofcls. Assn., 1980-81. Decorated Meritorious Service medal, Nat. Def. Service medal, also others. Mem. Am. Mgmt. Assn., Am. Soc. for Tng. and Devel., F.A. Hist. Assn., Assn. U.S. Army. Home: 53 Birch Ave Corte Madera CA 94925 Office: TMDO RGPSF-US ARMR IX San Francisco CA 94129

MORRISON, MARY DYER, psychotherapist, educator; b. Boston, Apr. 5, 1927; d. Leon and Gertrude (Quinlan) Dyer; m. Robert Lloyd Morrison, Apr. 7, 1945; 1 dau., Leigh. B.A., U.N.C.-Charlotte, 1976; M.A., U. Mo., Columbia, 1977, Ph.D., 1979. Prof., Orange Coast Coll., Costa Mesa, Calif., 1980-82; pvt. practice psychotherapy, Costa Mesa, 1980—; prof. Coastline Community Coll., Fountain Valley, Calif., 1982. Mem. U. Calif. Med. Center Task Force on Aging. NIMH fellow, 1978-79. Mem. Am. Psychol. Assn., Calif. Psychol. Assn., Phi Delta Kappa. Contbr. articles to profl. jours. Home: 8566 Colusa Circle 903A Huntington Beach CA 92646

MORRISON, MARY JANE, physician, army officer; b. Bridgeport, Conn., Aug. 13, 1944; d. Charles Albion and Martha Grace (Cornell) M. B.A. in Psychology, U. Conn., Storrs, 1966; M.A. in Spl. Edn., 1968, Ph.D. in Spl. Edn., 1972; M.D. Bowman Gray Sch. Medicine, Winston Salem, N.C., 1972; M.S. Rehab. Medicine, U. Wash., 1975. Intern, residency in rehab. medicine, U. Wash., Seattle, 1972-75; commd. 1st lt. U.S. Army Med. Corps, 1973, advanced through grades to lt. col.; 1982; dir. dept. phys. medicine and rehab. Danbury (Conn.) Hosp., 1975-77; dir. phys. medicine and rehab. service Landstahl (W. Ger.) Army Regional Med. Center, 1977-80; asst. chief phys. medicine and rehab. service Fitzsimmons Army Med. Center, Aurora, Colo., 1980—; cons. in field. Mem. Aurora (Colo.) chpt. Denver Symphony Guild. Mem. Am. Acad. Phys. Medicine and Rehab., Am. Congress Rehab. Medicine, Am. Psychol. Assn., Am. Burn Assn., Arthritis Found., N.W. Assn. Phys. Medicine and Rehab., Am. Assn. Electromyography and Electrodiagnosis. Episcopalian. Club: Zonta. Contbr. articles to profl. jours. Office: Box 6254 Fitzsimons Army Med Center Aurora CO 80045

MORRISON, MARY NAPOLEON, music educator; b. Monroe, La., Oct. 11, 1936; d. Louis and Ella (Barber) Napoleon; m. Zelious Turner Morrison, Nov. 1966 (div.); 1 son, Frederick Irvin Jones. B.S., Grambling State U., 1959; M.Music Edn., N.E. La. U., 1970. Cert. secondary, elem. tchr., Calif. Tchr. music, choral dir. various schs., chs., communities in no. La., 1959-71; tchr. music Oakland (Calif.) Unified Sch. Dist., 1972—; dir. Chancel Choir, Women's Chorus, Allen Temple Baptist Ch., Oakland. Mem. NEA, Calif. Tchrs. Assn., Calif. Music Educators Assn., Music Educators Nat. Conf., Oakland Edn. Assn., Today's Artist Concerts, Bus. Profl. Women's Soc., Beta Pi Sigma. Democrat. Baptist.

MORRISON, MARY TAYLOR, business college administrator, consultant, educator; b. Vernon, Tex., Aug. 4, 1934; d. Edward Bruce and Virginia M. (Reneau) Taylor; m. George Lora Mosher, July 23, 1952; children—Gerre, Gwen; m. 2d, James Orin Morrison, Feb. 28, 1963; children—Michael, Mark, John. Student Truckee Meadows Community Coll., Reno Bus. Coll., 1961, U. Nev. Sec., Reno Bus. Coll., 1961-63, registrar, 1963-65, dir., 1965-78, owner, adminstr., 1979—; pres. MJM Colls., Inc., doing bus. as Reno Bus. Coll.; cons. in field. mem. Nev. Occupational Ladders Adv. Bd.; chmn. Nev. State Incentive Grant Bd. Mem. Reno Downtown Found. Mem. Assn. Ind. Schs. & Colls., Nat. Assn. Female Execs., Nev. Assn. Fin. Aid Adminstrs., Nev. Assn. Pvt. Schs. Author pamphlets in edn., econs., politics and fin. aid. Home: 1675 Majestic Dr Reno NV 89503 Office: Reno Business Coll 258 Wonder St Reno NV 89502

MORRISON, MURDO DONALD, architect; b. Detroit, Feb. 21, 1919; s. Alexander and Johanna (Macaulay) M.; B.Arch., Lawrence Inst. Tech., 1943; children from previous marriage—Paul L., Reed A., Anne H. Individual practice architecture, Detroit, 1949, Klamath Falls, Oreg., 1949-65, Oakland, Calif., 1965-78; partner Morrison Assos., San Francisco, 1978—; v.p. Lakeridge Corp., 1968—; chmn. Oreg. Bd. Archtl. Examiners, 1961-65, chmn., 1964. Mem. Town Council Klamath Falls, 1955-57; co-chmn. Oakland Pride Com., 1968-77. Served with USN, 1943-46. Recipient Progressive Architecture award, 1955, Alumni of Yr. award Lawrence Inst., 1965. Mem. AIA (treas. East Bay, chmn. Oakland chpt.). Presbyterian. Clubs: Commonwealth, Lake Merritt Breakfast. Architect: Gilliam County Courthouse (Progressive Architecture design award), 1955, Chiloquin (Oreg.) Elem. Sch., 1963, Legaspi Plaza hotel, Burlingame, Calif., 1982, others. Home: 311 Tideway Dr Alameda CA 94501 Office: 210 Post St San Francisco CA 94108

MORRISON, ROBERT DOUGAL, optometrist; b. Merced, Calif., Jan. 25, 1945; s. Robert Lee and Florence Rita (Squire) M.; student Ariz. State Coll., 1963-64, U. Nev., 1964-66; B.S., O.D., So. Coll. Optometry, 1969; m. Michele Borsack, Oct. 25, 1969; children—Heather Katherine, Hilary Ann, Holly Patricia, Hope Christine, Michael Dougal, Haley Louise, Eric Edward, Cameron James. Partner with Leonard W. Carpi, Las Vegas, 1969-71; pvt. practice, Las Vegas, 1971—; researcher soft contact lenses FDA, 1978-79. Fellow Nat. Eye Research Found., Internat. Soc. Orthokeratology, Am. Acad. Optometry; mem. So. Nev. Optometric Assn. (bd. execs. 1972-73, pres.), Las Vegas Execs. Assn. (dir.), Phi Theta Upsilon. Lion (dir. 1969-71). Home: 4396 Garland Ct Las Vegas NV 89121 Office: 3585 S Maryland Pkwy Las Vegas NV 89109

MORRISON, ROBERT FLOYD, psychologist, consultant, educator; b. Mpls., Oct. 30, 1930; s. Floyd William and Ruth Angeline (Foster) M.; m. Kathryn Helene Olson, Jan. 30, 1953; children—Scott Robert, Rebekah Kim, Spencer Kirk, Bennett Todd, Holly Faith; m. 2d, Anne Deneiko, Oct. 11, 1975. Student, Grinnell Coll., 1948-49; B.S., Iowa State U., 1952, M.S., 1956; Ph.D., Purdue U., 1961. Employee relations asst. Mobil Oil Co., Casper, Wyo., 1956-59; mgmt. devel. specialist Martin Co., Balt., 1962-64; personnel research mgr. Sun Co., Phila., 1964-70; assoc. prof. psychology U. Toronto (Ont., Can.), 1970-76; supervisory research psychologist Navy Personnel Research and Devel. Center, San Diego, 1976—; pres. R.F. Morris Assos., Phila., Toronto, 1966-76; adj. prof. U. So. Calif., Los Angeles, 1978—; cons. in field. Served to cpl. Signal Corps, U.S. Army, 1952-54. Mem. Am. Psychol. Assn. (James McKeen Cattell research design award, 1982), Acad. of Mgmt., Internat. Assn. of Applied Psychology, Summit Group, Sigma Xi, Psi Chi. Republican. Contbr. chpts. to books and articles to profl. jours. Home: 6132 Syracuse Way San Diego CA 92122 Office: Navy Personnel Research and Develop Center San Diego CA 92152

MORRISON, ROBERT HUGH, financial co. exec.; b. Calif., Jan. 28, 1938; s. Charles Hugh and Sarah Inez (Morrison-Rutledge) M.; A.A., Pasadena City Coll., 1958; m. Patricia L. Seefried, Apr. 2, 1980; children—Robert Hugh, Jeri L., Donna D., Debra M., James C., Shawn C. Various engring. and accounting positions, 1957-61; pres. Fin. Mgmt.

Assos., Inc., Phoenix, 1961-78, Outward Bound, Ltd., Phoenix, 1978—. Mem. Nat. Assn. Accredited Tax Accts. Republican. Club: Elks. Author books including: My Hobby As A Business, 1973; The Fraud Report, 1975; Why S.O.B.'s Succeed and Nice Guys Fail in Small Businesses, 1976; Contracting Out, The Pawns, The Moneylenders, The Rulemakers, Stalemate, How to Steal a Job, various others, 1977-78; How to Survive and Prosper in the Next American Depression, War or Revolution, 1979; Divorce Dirty Tricks, 1979; The Greedy Bastard's Business Manual, 1981; Promoter's Gold, 1981; Gambler's Gold, The New Venture Planner, 1982. Home: PO Box 4759 Santa Barbara CA 93103

MORRISON, ROGER BARRON, geologist; b. Madison, Wis., Mar. 26, 1914; s. Frank Barron and Elsie Rhea (Bullard) M.; B.A., Cornell U., 1933, M.S., 1934; postgrad. U. Calif.-Berkeley, 1934-35, Stanford U., 1935-38; Ph.D., U. Nev., 1964; m. Harriet Louise Williams, Apr. 7, 1941; children—John Christopher, Peter Hallock and Craig Brewster (twins). Geologist U.S. Geol. Survey, 1939-76; adj. vis. prof. dept. geoscis. U. Ariz., 1976-80; cons. geologist Morrison and Assocs., 1978—; prin. investigator 2 Landsat-1 and 2 Skylab earth resources investigation projects NASA, 1972-75. Fellow Geol. Soc. Am.; mem. AAAS, Internat. Assn. Quaternary Research (past mem. Holocene and pedology commns.), Am. Soc. Photogrammetry, Am. Soc. Agronomy, Soil Sci. Soc. Am., Internat. Soil Sci. Soc., Am. Quaternary Assn., Sigma Xi. Club: Colorado Mountain. Author 2 books, co-author one book; co-editor 2 books; also co-editor Catena, 1973—. Contbr. over 70 articles to profl. jours. Home and Office: 13150 W 9th Ave Golden CO 80401

MORRISON, SID, Congressman; b. Yakima, Wash., May 13, 1933; student Yakima Valley Coll., Wash. State U., 1954; married. Fruit grower; mem. Wash. Ho. of Reps., 1967-74, asst. majority floor leader, 1971-73, minority orgn. leader, 1973-74; mem. Wash. State Senate, 1975-80; mem. 97th and 98th congresses from Wash. 4th dist. Republican. Methodist. Office: 208 Cannon House Office Bldg Washington DC 20515

MORRISSETT, IRVING, economist, educator; b. Columbus, Ohio, Aug. 22, 1916; s. Irving Archer and Anna Lee (Rogers) M.; m. Elizabeth Ellen Winkleman, Feb. 14, 1948; children—Steven, Hope, Alan, Paul, Nancy; m. 2d, Martha Rodgers Bury, Aug. 12, 1975. A.B. in Econs. with honors, Swarthmore Coll., 1937; M.A. in Applied Stats., U. Calif.-Berkeley, 1952, Ph.D. in Econs. (Newton Booth fellow), 1953. Lectr. econs. and stats. Earlham Coll. and Ind. U. Extension Div., Richmond, Ind., 1947-48; teaching asst. econs. and bus. adminstrn. U. Calif.-Berkeley, U. Calif.-Davis, 1949-51, lectr., 1951-52; asst. to dir. Found Research on Human Behavior, Ann Arbor, Mich., 1953-55; Carnegie postdoctoral fellow survey techniques Survey Research Center, U. Mich., 1953-55; lectr. econs. Econs Inst., U. Colo., 1959-62; asst. prof. to assoc. prof. econs. Purdue U., 1955-67; assoc. dir. Clearinghouse for Social Studies and Social Sci. Edn., Ednl. Resources Info. Center, 1970-74, dir., 1974—; exec. dir. Social Sci. Edn. Consortium, Inc., 1964—, also prof. econs. U. Colo., Boulder, 1967—; cons. in field. Grantee NSF, Office of Edn. Fellow AAAS; mem. Am. Econs. Assn., Western Econs. Assn., Rocky Mountain Social Sci. Assn., Am. Ednl. Research Assn., Nat. Council Social Studies, Assn. Evolutionary Econs., AAUP, Internat. Soc. Ednl., Cultural and Sci. Interchanges, Colo. Council Social Studies, Phi Beta Kappa, Phi Delta Kappa. Gen. editor: Social Studies Priorities, Practices and Needs, 5 vols., 1981-82; editor: (with Ann W. Williams) Social/Political Education in Three Countries, 1981; editor, author: Social Studies in the 1980s, 1982; adv. bd. History and Social Sci. Tchr., 1980-81; contbr. articles to profl. jours. Home: 244 Fir Ln Pine Brook Hills Boulder CO 80302 Office: 855 Broadway Boulder CO 80302

MORRISSEY, ARTHUR CHARLES, executive strategic market assessment; b. Westerly, R.I., March 7, 1941; s. James H. and Ruth E. (Long) M.; m. D. Jeanie Thompson, Mar. 1967; children—Connan (Conway) L., Cassie A. B.A., Washington and Jefferson Coll., Washington, Pa., 1963; Ph.D., U.S.C., Columbia 1967. Br. chief, CIA, 1967-74, mem. intelligence community staff, 1974-75, Dept. of State, 1975-77; sr. policy analyst, White House Office of Sci. and Technol. Policy, 1977-81; strategic market assessment Martin Marietta Aerospace, 1981—. Mem. AIAA, AAAS, Am. Chem. Soc., Sigma Xi. Contbr. articles to profl. jours. Home: 355 Dexter St Denver CO 80220 Office: PO Box 179 Denver CO 80201

MORRISSEY, JOHN CARROLL, lawyer; b. N.Y.C., Sept. 2, 1914; s. Edward Joseph and Estelle (Caine) M.; m. Eileen Colligan, Oct. 14, 1950; children—Jay, Ellen, Katherine, John, Patricia, Richard, Brian, Peter. B.A., Yale U., 1937, LL.B., 1940; J.S.D., NYU, 1951; grad. Command and Gen. Staff Coll., 1943. Bar: N.Y. 1940, U.S. Supreme Ct. 1944, U.S. Dist. Ct. (so. dist.) N.Y. 1946, U.S. Dist. Ct. (ea. dist.) N.Y. 1947, D.C. 1953, Calif. 1954, U.S. Dist. Ct. (no. dist.) Calif. 1975. Assoc., Dorsey, Adams & Walker, N.Y.C., 1940-41, Dorsey & Adams, N.Y.C., 1946-50; acting counsel Office of Mil. Assistance, Dept. Def., Washington, 1950-51; counsel Research and Devel. Bd., Washington, 1951; gen. counsel Def. Elec. Power Adminstrn., Washington, 1952-53; atty. Pacific Gas & Electric Co., San Francisco, 1953-70, assoc. gen. counsel, 1970-74, v.p., gen. counsel, 1975-80; sole practice law, San Francisco, 1980—; dir. Gas Lines, Inc. Mem. Human Rights Commn. San Francisco, 1976—, chmn., 1979-81; mem. World Affairs Council San Francisco. Served to col. F.A., AUS, 1941-46. Decorated Bronze Star, Army Commendation Medal. Mem. ABA, San Francisco Bar Assn., Electric Club San Francisco, Econ. Round Table San Francisco, Legal Aid Soc. San Francisco, Calif. Conf. Pub. Utility Counsel, Pacific Coast Electric Assn., Pacific Coast Gas Assn., Phi Beta Kappa. Roman Catholic. Clubs: Commonwealth, Pacific Union, Serra, Yale (San Francisco). Home: 2030 Jackson St San Francisco CA 94109 Office: 215 Market St Suite 215 San Francisco CA 94106

MORRONE, NICHOLAS FRANCIS, insulations co. exec.; b. Phila., Feb. 17, 1934; s. Fredrick and Helen (Rizzuto) M.; B.S. in Chem. Engring., Drexel U., 1956; m. Nina Cucinotta, Nov. 8, 1958; children—Mark, Nicholas, Mary Kay. Research engr. Bentley Harris Mfg. Co., Conshohocken, Pa., 1956-59; sr. research engr. Bestwall Gypsum div. Ga. Pacific, Paoli, Pa., 1959-67; now mgr. research and devel., fiberglas bldg. and automotive insulations Johns Manville Corp., Denver. Served with U.S. Army, 1958. Mem. Am. Inst. Chem. Engrs., Am. Ceramic Soc., ASTM. Roman Catholic. Patentee water resistant gypsum bd., roof insulation bd. Home: 5284 S Perry Ct Littleton CO 80123 Office: Ken-Caryl Ranch Denver CO 80127

MORROW, CHARLES TABOR, acoustical engineer; b. Gloucester, Mass., May 3; s. Charles Harvey and Melissa Douetta (Tabor) M.; m. Julia Buxton Brown, June 4, 1949; children—Hope Elizabeth, Anne Barbara Carothers. A.B., Harvard U., 1937, M. Sc., 1938, D. Sc., 1946. Sr. project engr. Sperry Gyroscope Co., Great Neck, N.Y., 1946-51; research physicist Hughes Aircraft Co., Culver City, Calif., 1951-55; mgr. sci. and engring. relations Ramo-Wooldrige Corp., El Segundo, Calif., 1955-60; mgr. tech. relations Aerospace Corp., El Segundo, 1960-67; staff scientist Western div. LTV Research Ctr., Anaheim, Calif. and Vought Adv. Tech. Ctr., Dallas, 1967-76; cons. Dallas and Encinitas, Calif., 1976—. Fellow Acoustical Soc. Am., Inst. Environ. Scis. (Vigness award, 1971); mem. Acoustical Soc. Am., IEEE, AIAA, Am. Soc. Engring. Edn., Sigma Xi. Republican. Episcopalian. Author: Shock and Vibration Engineering, 1976; contbr. articles to profl. jours. Home and office: 1345 Cherrytree Court Encinitas CA 92024

MORROW, JAMES THOMAS, management consultant; b. Seattle, Apr. 24, 1941; s. James Elroy and Helen Margaret (Helzer) M.; B.S. in Elec. Engring., Oreg. State U., 1964; Ph.D., U. Santa Clara, 1973, M.B.A., 1966; 1 child, Shannon F. Engr., Gen. Electric Co., San Jose, Calif., 1964-66; engring. mgr. Beckman Instruments, Inc., Palo Alto, Calif., 1966-69; pres. MSA Cons., Inc., Portland, Oreg., 1969-75; asst. prof. U. Portland, 1969-75; mgr. A.T. Kearney, Inc., San Francisco, 1975-78; v.p. mktg. Pierce Pacific Mfg., Portland, 1978-79; chmn., chief exec. officer Lanco Internat., Inc., Clackamas, Oreg., 1979-81; regional mgr., v.p. Case & Co., Portland, 1981—; chmn. bd. Morley & Assocs., Inc., 1982—; dir. Accucom Data Network, Inc., Pierce Pacific Mfg., Lanco Internat., Energy Guard, Inc., G&R Devel. Co., Inc., MSA Cons., Inc., Criticare of Am., Inc., Jotek Computer Systems, Inc.; sec.-treas. Everybody's Record Co., Inc. Bd. dirs. U.S. Small Bus. Acad., Found. for Oreg. Research and Edn., Jr. Achievement. Mem. Am. Mktg. Assn., Nat. Soc. Profl. Engrs., IEEE, Am. Inst. Indsl. Engrs., Am. Production and Inventory Control Soc., Sales and Mkg. Execs. Internat. Republican. Congregationalist. Contbr. articles to profl. jours., chpts. to textbooks. Home: 8525 SW Bridletrail Ave Beaverton OR 97005 Office: 4314 Marina City Dr Suite 816C Marina del Rey CA 90291 also 9735 SW Shady Ln Suite 100 Portland OR 97223

MORROW, LARRY ALAN, research agronomist; b. Boise, Idaho, Oct. 3, 1938; s. Ralph D. and Ruby E. (Pence) M.; m. Sondra Miller; children—Kevin, Daniel, Terri, Steven. B.S. in Range Mgmt., Utah State U., 1965; M.S. in Agronomy, U. Nebr., 1971, Ph.D. in Agronomy, 1974. Biologist, Agrl. Research Service, U.S. Dept. Agr., Prosser, Wash., 1965-69, Lincoln, Nebr., 1969-74; research agronomist, Mandan, N.D., 1974-77, Pullman, Wash., 1977—. Mem Western Soc. Weed Sci., Weed Sci. Soc. Am., Am. Soc. Agronomy, Crop Sci. Soc. Am., Council for Agrl. Sci. and Tech. Home: NW 2010 Friel St Pullman WA 99163 Office: 215 Johnson Hall Pullman WA 99164

MORROW, TIMOTHY T(ITUS), importer-retailer; b. Chgo., July 4, 1911; s. Albert and Donna Carnilia (Domaini) Gazzeri (changed name from Titus T. Gazzeri to Timothy T. Morrow, May 4, 1942); privately educated; 1 dau., Collette Gail (Mrs. William Van Dree). Prodn. mgr. Critchfield & Co., Chgo., 1925-29, Buchen Co., 1929-31; art dir. Rosenow Co., 1931-36; advt. and sales promotion mgr. Transparent Package Co., 1936-40; pres. Pioneer Mfg. Co., 1940-42; account exec. Bozell & Jacobs, Inc., 1942-46; v.p. and account exec. W. W. Garrison & Co., 1946-48; established Tim Morrow Advt., 1948, pres., 1948-56, merger 1956; v.p. Henri, Hurst & McDonald, 1956-58; v.p. MacFarland Aveyard & Co., 1958-60; v.p., supervising dir., mem. bd. The Biddle Co., 1960-63; owner La Casa Rosa restaurant and mail order bus., San Juan Bautista, Calif., 1963-64; owner The Gallery Ltd., Lahaina, Maui, Hawaii. Chmn. Lahaina Improvement Com.; mem. nat. host com. Western region Exhbn. of People's Republic of China, 1980. Mem. Maui C. of C. (dir.), West Maui Businessmen's Assn., Lahaina Art Soc. (co-founder, 1st pres.), Am. Soc. Appraisors (sr. mem.), Nat. Assn. Rev. Appraisers (charter). Clubs: Lahaina Yacht, Lahaina Canoe (charter). Producer: Tin Pan Alley of the Air (won Am. Fed. Advt. award as best musical of 1945), 1945-46; Of Men in Music, 1947; television: Of Men and Music, 1949; Shirley and Bedelia, Stories in the Sand, Bible Stories, Sit or Miss, 1950-51. Home: Lahaina Maui HI 96761 Office: The Gallery Ltd Front St Lahaina Maui HI 96761

MORROW, WINSTON VAUGHAN, business exec.; b. Grand Rapids, Mich., Mar. 22, 1924; s. Winston V. and Selma (von Eglestein) M.; A.B. cum laude, Williams Coll., 1947; LL.B., Harvard, 1950; m. Margaret Ellen Staples, June 25, 1948; children—Thomas Christopher, Mark Staples. Admitted to R.I. bar, 1950; asso. atty. Edwards & Angell, Providence, 1950-57; exec. v.p., asst. treas., dir., gen. counsel Avis, Inc., and subsidiaries, 1957-61; pres., dir. Avis, Inc., 1964-75; v.p., gen. mgr. Rent A Car div. Avis, Inc., 1962-64; chmn., chief exec. officer, dir. Avis, Inc., Avis Rent A Car System, Inc., 1965-77; dir., cons. Flowtrans Internat., 1977; chmn., pres., dir. Teleflorists Inc. and subsidiaries, 1978-80; pres., dir. Ticor, Los Angeles, 1981—; chmn. bd., chief exec. officer, dir. Title Ins. & Trust Co., Ticor Printers Group, Inc., Constellation Reins. Co., Ticor Mortgage Ins. Co. vice chmn. Discover Am. Travel Orgn. Mem. Pres.' Industry-Govt. Spl. Travel Task Force, 1968; travel adv. bd. U.S. Travel Service, 1968-76; bd. dirs. Ticor Found., 1981—. Served as technician, M.C., AUS, 1943-46. Decorated Stella della Solidarieta (Italy); Gold Tourism medal (Austria). Mem. Am. Acad. Achievement, Fed., R.I. bar assns., Car and Truck Rental and Leasing Assn. (nat. pres. 1961-63), Inst. Certified Travel Agts., Phi Beta Kappa, Kappa Alpha. Clubs: Bald Peak Colony (N.H.); Racquet and Tennis, Williams (N.Y.C.); Internat. (Washington); Los Angeles Athletic. Office: Ticor 6300 Wilshire Blvd Los Angeles CA 90048

MORSE, DANIEL EDWARD, molecular biologist; b. N.Y.C., May 20, 1941; m. Aileen Dobson, 1971. B.A. cum laude, Harvard U., 1963; Ph.D., Albert Einstein Coll. Medicine, 1967; fellow in molecular genetics Stanford U., 1967-69. Asst. prof. microbiology and molecular genetics Harvard U., Boston, 1969-71, assoc. prof., 1971-73; asst. dir. Marine Sci. Inst., U. Calif., Santa Barbara, 1973-75, prof., 1975—. Mem. Am. Soc. Biol. Chemists, N.Y. Acad. Scis., Am. Soc. Exptl. Biologists, AAAS. Contbr. articles in field to profl. jours. Office: University of California Dept Biological Sciences Santa Barbara CA 93106

MORSE, HERBERT ROBERT, executive search consultant; b. Providence, Jan. 24, 1930; s. Harry and Ruth (Borden) M.; m. Linda Leonard, June 25, 1968; children—Bart R., Elizabeth K. Student St. John's Coll.; B.A., Bklyn. Coll.; M.S. in Bus., Columbia U.; diploma Harvard U. Grad Sch. Engring., MIT. Acct., Coopers & Lybrand, Arthur Young & Co.; v.p. fin. Radiation at Stanford, Inc., Palo Alto, Calif.; chief operating officer Electronics Capital Corp., San Diego; v.p. fin. Internat. Industries, Los Angeles; prin. Herbert R. Morse Co., Thousand Oaks, Calif., 1968—; chief exec. officer, dir. Transistor Spltys. Corp., Electronics Corp. Advisors, Inc., Molectro Corp., Canoga Industries, Internat. Data Products, Alloyd Corp., Copper Penny Restaurants, Internat. House of Pancakes, House of Nine, Community Cablevision Corp., Harriscope Cable Corp., Electronic Energy Conversion Corp., Nat. Semicondr. Corp., Energy Systems, Inc., Vega Corp.; lectr. Calif. Luth. Coll.; cons. dir. various corps. Active Catholic Youth Orgn., World Affairs Council, Town Hall, Midnight Mission; dir., vice chmn. San Fernando Valley Interfaith Council. Served with USAAF. Mem. Cuyamaca, Alpha Phi Tau. Unitarian. Club: West Valley Tennis. Office: 610 Westchester Ln Thousand Oaks CA 91360

MORSE, KENNETH OWEN, educator, air force officer; b. Boise, Idaho, Aug. 6, 1945; s. Alfred Smith and Adelaide Dorothy (Owens) M.; B. Gen. Studies, U. Nebr., 1972, M.S., 1975; M.P.A., U. Okla., 1980; m. Joyce Elaine Smith, Mar. 1, 1969; children—Heather Dawn, Kerrienne Robin. Commd. 2d lt. U.S. Air Force, 1965, advanced through grades to Capt., 1976; instr. Far East div. U. Md., Osan, Korea, 1976, European div. Troy State U., Sembach, W. Ger., 1977-79, European div. U. Md., Kaiserslautern, W. Ger., 1979-80; asst. prof. econs. U.S. Air Force Acad., Academy, Colo., 1980—. Decorated Air medal, Meritorious Service medal. Mem. Am. Econ. Assn., Am. Soc. Public Adminstrs. Baptist.

MORSE, LOWELL WESLEY, real estate and banking exec.; b. West Palm Beach, Fla., May 1, 1937; s. Alton and Blanche (Yelverton) M.; B.S., U. Santa Clara, 1968; grad. Def. Lang. Inst., Monterey, Calif., 1959; m. Vera Giacalone, June 22, 1958; children—Lowell Wesley, Stephen D., Michael S. Russian linguist U.S. Army Security Agy., 1957-60; asst. city mgr. City of Pacific Grove (Calif.), 1961-66; city mgr. Town of Los Altos Hills (Calif.), 1967-69; pres., chmn. Morse & Assos., Inc., San Jose, Calif., 1972—; founder, dir. Plaza Bank of Commerce, San Jose, 1979—. Served with U.S. Army, 1957-60. Club: Univ. (San Jose.). Home: PO Box 5939 Tahoe City CA 95730 Office: 4010 Moorpark Ave Suite 210 San Jose CA 95117

MORSE, PAUL CLIFFORD, JR., interior designer; b. Topeka, Kans., Oct. 12, 1947; s. Paul Cody Clifford and Bette Ann (Talbot) M. Installer, James Summers Interiors, Topeka, 1971-74; installation dir., designer, Tindall-Kennedy Inc., Topeka, 1974-78; asst. buyer, designer, dir. drapery dept. State Furniture and Carpets, Farmington, N. Mex., 1978-81; co-owner design studio, 1981—. Mem. Amer. Soc. Interior Designers (assoc.). Republican. Club: San Juan Country (Farmington). Home: 2604 E 23d St Farmington NM 87401 Office: 102 S Orchard Farmington NM 87401

MORSE, RICHARD JAY, transportation and building services company executive; b. Detroit, Aug. 2, 1933; s. Maurice and Belle Roslyn (Jacobson) M. B.A. in Psychology, U. Va., 1955; teaching credential UCLA, 1957; M.A. in Psychology, Calif. State U.-Los Angeles, 1964. With Gen. Telephone Co. Calif., Santa Monica, 1957-68; dir. tng. and devel. Bekins Co., Los Angeles, 1968-69, dir. personnel, 1969-70, dir. personnel and organizational devel., 1970-72, v.p. personnel, 1972-74, v.p. adminstrn., 1974-80, v.p. human resources, 1980—; cons. organizational devel. Active City of Hope, Am. Cancer Soc. Mem. Los Angeles C. of C., Nat. Soc. Performance and Instrn. (charter), Personnel and Indsl. Relations Assn. Los Angeles, Nat. Panel Arbitrators, Am. Soc. Tng. Devel. Republican. Jewish. Clubs: Univ. (Los Angeles); Verdugo (Glendale, Calif.). Contbr. articles to profl. jours., chpts. to books. Home: 60 Glenflow Ct Glendale CA 91206 Office: 777 Flower St Glendale CA 91201

MORSE, WILLIAM FRANCIS, clergyman; b. Western Springs, Ill., Aug. 25, 1899; s. Francis William and Phoebe A. (Kelsey) M.; student Eugene Bible U., 1920-23; Lingield Coll., 1940-41; m. Mary Quintila Shirley, Feb. 22, 1929; children—William George, Patricia Anne. Farmer Harrisburg, Oreg., 1923-26; retail salesman Chase Gardens, Eugene, 1927; mgr. Sunnyside Greenhouses, Portland, Oreg., 1928; owner, operator florist bus. Newberg, Oreg., 1928-40; mgr. relief work east end Yamhill County, Newberg, 1932-33; opened ch. Mt. Top, Newberg, 1932-40; ordained to ministry Christian Ch., 1935; pastor Ch. of Christ, Amity, Oreg., 1940-44, 48-50, Seaside (Oreg.) Christian Ch., 1944-48; organizer Wi-Ne-Ma Christian Camp, Inc., Cloverdale, Oreg., 1944, pres., 1944-69, gen. mgr., 1950-67, trustee, 1944-70; pastor Wi-Ne-Ma Christian Ch., 1951-70; research and geneal. work, 1970—; pres. Morse Soc., 1973—. Trustee Turner Meml. Home, 1946-80, trustee emeritus, 1980—; chmn. bd. trustees Oretown Cemetery Assn., 1970-78, trustee, 1979—. Mem. Newberg Park Commn., 1933-40, Sch. Bd., 1936-40; chmn. Area Agy. on Aging, Dist. 1, Tillamook-Clatsop County, Oreg., 1976-79, mem. exec. bd., 1976-82; bd. dirs. Am. Indian Evangelism Assn., 1977—. Served with U.S. Army, World War I. Mem. Nesctucca Ministers Fellowship (pres. 1966-67), Oretown Grange, Vets. World War I. Home and Office: 42880 Ocean View Dr Cloverdale OR 97112

MORTELL, BONNIE PATRICIA, international exchange administrator, educator; b. Vancouver, Wash., June 29, 1945; d. William Henry and Loretta Ellen (Ellis) Lennox; 1 son, William Robert. B.A. magna cum laude in Edn., Seattle U., 1970; postgrad. various univs., 1972—. Cert. tchr., Wash. Tchr. Lake Washington High Sch., Kirkland, Wash., 1970—, chairperson fgn. lang. dept., 1975—; Greater Seattle regional rep. Iberoamerican Cultural Exchange Program, 1972-77, asst. dir., 1977-78, internat. program dir., 1978—; pres. Internat. Exchange Network of Wash. State, 1983—. Mem. Wash. Assn. Fgn. Lang. Tchrs., Nat. Assn. Tchrs. Spanish and Portuguese, Oreg. Student Exchange Fedn., Kappa Gamma Pi. Club: Seattle Super Sonics Tennis (Bellevue, Wash.). Office: 13920 93d Ave NE Kirkland WA 98033

MORTENSEN, JAMES RICHARD, aerospace industry training manager, electrical engineer; b. Col. Juarez, Mexico, Feb. 15, 1933; came to U.S., 1936; s. Jesse William and Maria Clara (Aldaz) M.; m. Jonita Bernards, May 13, 1954; children—Jean, Deborah, Kathilee, James Rochelle, Jon, Lea, Carrie. B.S. in Elec. Engring., U. Utah, 1959. Field engr., area supr. Hughes Aircraft Co., Los Angeles, 1959-66, sr. staff engr., 1966-68, group head design requirements, Canoga Park, Calif., 1968-70; instr., tng. coordinator Litton APD, Woodland Hills, Calif., 1970-77, mgr. tng. tech., skills, mgmt. Litton G&CS, Woodland Hills, 1978—; mem. industry continuing ednl. adv. council U. So. Calif.; mem. computer tech. adv. council Pierce Coll.; mem. adv. council Los Angeles Regional Occupational Ctr. High councilor Latter-Day Saints Ch., bishop's councilor, 1974-78, edn. councilor, coordinator; scoutmaster, explorer leader, com. chmn., mem. dist. com. Boy Scouts Am., 1960-80. Served with USAF, 1951-55. Mem. Am. Soc. Tng. and Devel. Republican. Author: An Introduction to OMEGA Navigation, 1978. Home: 168 Dryden Thousand Oaks CA 91360 Office: 5500 Canoga Ave M/S 27 Woodland Hills CA 91365

MORWOOD, SHARI JEAN, information specialist; b. San Francisco, Feb. 27, 1951; d. Jesse C. and Virginia J. (Olsen) Logan; m. Richard A. Morwood, Aug. 22, 1970; children—Logan, Kelly. B.A. in English, San Jose State U., 1972, M.A. in Librarianship, 1974. Reference librarian Gen. Electric, Sunnyvale, Calif., 1975-76; supr. users' library Hewlett-Packard Co., Corvallis, Oreg., 1976-80, mgr. tech. info. ctr. portable computer div., 1980—; chmn. Library & Media Groups of Oreg. Forum, 1983. Mem. steering com. Friends of Oreg. State Library. Mem. Spl. Libraries Assn. (chmn. networking com. 1982-83; chpt. pres.-elect 1983-84), Am. Soc. Info. Sci., ACM, IEEE. Democrat. Lutheran. Club: Zonta. Contbr. in field. Home: 6955 NW Concord Dr Corvallis OR 97330 Office: Hewlett-Packard 1000 NE Circle Blvd Corvallis OR 97330

MOSBY, LELAND DARRELL, minister, counselor; b. Kansas City, Mo., Dec. 18, 1947; s. Ralph Byron and Hettie Ermine (Everett) M.; m. Marilyn Sue Jackson, June 1, 1968; children—Leland Darell, Crystal Rachelle. B.A., S.W. Baptist U., 1969; M.Div., Southwestern Bapt. Theol. Sem., 1972; D.Min., Midwestern Bapt. Theol. Sem., 1978. Ordained to ministry Baptist Ch., 1969; pastor Norfleet Bapt. Ch., Kansas City, Mo., 1972-75, Concord Bapt. Ch., St. Louis, 1975-79; sr. pastor Applewood Baptist Ch., Wheat Ridge, Colo., 1979—; counselor, cons., tchr. seminars. Mem. Am. Assn. Pastoral Counselors, Christian Assn. Psychol. Study, Am. Personnel and Guidance Assn., Am. Mental Health Counselors Assn., Colo. Mental Health Counselors Assn. Author: The Lonely Valley, A Journey through Bereavement, 1978.

MOSCONA, GEORGE CHARLES, psychologist; b. New Orleans, Apr. 20, 1943; s. George J. and Eva M. (Toups) M. B.A. in Elem. Edn. Coll. Santa Fe, 1966; M.A. in Humanistic Psychology, Goddard Coll., Plainfield, Vt., 1973. Lic. tchr., counselor Calif. Tchr. Pub. Schs. Los Alamos, 1966-68, Pub. Schs. Monterey (Calif.), 1968-72; dir. tchr. credential program U. Calif.-Santa Cruz, 1972-76; pvt. practice counseling, San Francisco, 1976—; founder The Relationship Workshop. Recipient Coll. Santa Fe Pres. Award, 1966. Mem. Am. Psychol. Assn., Assn. Gay Psychologists. Democrat. Roman Catholic. Club: Dignity Bay Area. Home and Office: 2212 Pine St San Francisco CA 94115

MOSER, DEAN JOSEPH, accountant; b. San Francisco, Apr. 5, 1942; s. Joseph Edward and Velma Ida (Cruz) M.; B.S., U. San Francisco, 1964, postgrad. Law Sch., 1964-66; postgrad. Golden Gate U., 1966-81; m. Michele Patrice Cicerone, June 16, 1963; children—Jay, Lynele, Todd. Owner, acct. DJM Bookkeeping Service, 1962-65; asst. controller Dymo Industries, Internat., Berkeley, Calif., 1965-67; mgr. taxes Arthur Andersen & Co., San Francisco, 1967-76; owner, mgr. Contadora Ltd., Novato, Calif., 1981—, Esprit Realty Co., Novato, 1981—; pres. Moser & Paul Accountancy Corp., Novato, 1981—. Asst. scout master Boy Scouts Am.; past bd. dirs. Novato Human Needs Center. C.P.A., Calif. Mem. Calif. Soc. C.P.A.'s. Republican. Roman Catholic. Club: Rotary. Office: 250 Bel Marin Keys Blvd Novato CA 94947

MOSER, JAMES EDWARD, optometrist; b. Jackson, Wyo., July 31, 1953; s. Dee and Louise A. (Merritt) M.; m. Amy Louise Harris, June 12, 1975; children—Jennie Lee, Amy Rose, Megan Louise, Sarah Elizabeth. Student Utah State U., 1971-72, 74-75; B.S., So. Calif. Coll. Optometry, 1978, O.D., 1980. Gen. practice optometry, Afton, Wyo., 1980—. Mem. Am. Optometric Assn., Wyo. Optometric Assn. Republican. Mem. Ch. Jesus Christ of Latter-day Saints. Home: PO Box 1006 Afton WY 83110 Office: 460 Washington Suite 2 Afton WY 83110

MOSES, DALE FRANCIS, educator, aerospace engineer; b. Colorado Springs, Colo., Apr. 4, 1943; s. Charles Carrol and Mildred Bernice (Rexroad) M.; B.S. in Aerospace Engring., U. Ariz., Tucson, 1969, Ph.D. in Aerospace Engring., 1981. Engr. test facility design Boeing Aircraft Co., Seattle, 1966-68; engr. design liaison Hughes Aircraft Co., Tucson, 1968-70; engr. fuel mech. design Westinghouse Nuclear Fuel Div., Monroeville, Pa., 1970-72; sr. research engr. Arnold Research Orgn., Tullahoma, Tenn., 1980-81; asst. prof. dept. aerospace engring. Tex. A&M U., College Station, 1981; assoc. prof. dept. aerospace engring. and engring. mechanics San Diego State U., 1981—. Mem. AIAA, Am. Soc. Engring. Edn., Am. Inst. Archeology. Office: Dept Aerospace Engring and Engring Mechanics San Diego State Univ San Diego CA 92182

MOSES, JAMES ANTHONY, JR., clinical neuropsychologist, educator; b. San Francisco, Feb. 25, 1947; s. James Anthony, Sr., and Lucille Marian (La Rose) M. B.A. magna cum laude, San Francisco State U., 1968; M.S., San Jose State U., 1970; M.A. U. Colo., Boulder, 1971, Ph.D., 1974. Lic. psychologist, Calif. Research asst. U. Colo., 1972-73; psychology intern Palo Alto VA Med. Center, San Francisco VA Med. Center, 1973-74; staff clin. neuropsychologist Palo Alto VA Med. Center, 1974—, coordinator psychol. assessment unit, 1976—; clin. instr. Stanford U. Med. Sch., 1975-78, clin. asst. prof., 1978—, USPHS predoctoral fellow in clinical psychol. U. Colo., 1970-71. Mem. Am. Psychol. Assn., Western Psychol. Assn., Internat. Neuropsychol. Soc., Nat. Acad. Neuropsychologists, Soc. for Personality Assessment, Psi Chi. Club: Stanford U. Self-Defense (coach); Masons, Shriners (San Francisco). Co-author books on neuropsychol. batteries; contbr. articles to profl. jours. Home: 177 Westlawn Ave Daly City CA 94015 Office: 3801 Miranda Ave Palo Alto CA 94304

MOSHER, ROBERT LEE, fiberglass company executive; b. Morrison, Ill., Feb. 21, 1940; s. Elmer L. and Blanche L. (Groharing) M.; B.S. in Civil Engring., Bradley U., 1963; M.B.A., Calif. State U.-San Francisco, 1973; m. Rosalind Ann Rhoda, Apr. 4, 1964; 1 son, Derrick Robert. With C.E., U.S. Army, San Francisco, 1963-76, chief ADP Center, 1974-76, chief office staffing and mgmt., Washington, 1976-80; asst. dir. permits and schedules Office Fed. Inspector, Washington, Irvine, Calif., 1980-81, Alaska gas conditioning facility coordinator, 1981-83; pres. Balboa Fiberglass, Inc., Mission Viejo, Calif., 1983—. Treas. Serramonte Homeowners Assn., 1973; mem. Mayor's Com. for Opening Daly City Bart Sta., 1973. Registered profl. engr., Calif. Mem. Project Mgmt. Inst. Republican. Office: 25741 Obrero Dr Suite D Mission Viejo CA 92691

MOSIER, T. H., ins. co. exec.; b. Hoxie, Kans., July 10, 1916; s. David J. and Julia (Martin) M.; B.S., Ft. Hays Kans. State U., 1939; m. Naomi L. Griffith, Sept. 21, 1939; children—Janet N. Mosier Fletcher, Margaret M. Mosier Urling, Michael T. William II. Insp., Retail Credit Co., Atchison, Kans. 1939-40; with Equitable Life Assurance Soc. U.S., Emporia, Kans., 1940—, mgr., St. Joseph, Mo., 1953-57, agy. mgr., Denver, 1957-68, asso. mgr., 1968—; pres., dir. Mosier Industries, Inc., Ecothermia, Inc.; dir. Centennial Bank of Blende. Pres., Heart Assn., Kans., 1949-50. Served to capt. AUS, 1943-46. C.L.U. Mem. Million Dollar Round Table (life), Denver Assn. Life Underwriters, Phi Sigma Epsilon. Roman Catholic. K.C. (grand knight). Clubs: Cherry Hills Country, Petroleum (Denver). Home: 2745 Flora Pl Denver CO 80210 Office: First National Bank Bldg Denver CO 80293

MOSK, STANLEY, state supreme ct. justice; b. San Antonio, Sept. 4, 1912; s. Paul and Minna (Perl) M.; student U. Tex., 1931; Ph.B., U. Chgo., 1933, student Law Sch., 1935, Hague Acad. Internat. Law, 1970; LL.D., U. Pacific, 1970, U. San Diego, 1971, U. Santa Clara, 1976; m. Edna Mitchell, Sept. 27, 1936 (dec.); 1 son, Richard Mitchell; m. 2d, Susan Jane Hines, Aug. 27, 1982. Admitted to Calif. bar, 1935, practiced in Los Angeles until 1939; exec. sec. to gov. Calif., 1939-42; judge superior ct. Los Angeles County, 1943-58; pro tem justice Dist. Ct. Appeal, Calif., 1954; atty. gen. Calif., also head state dept. justice, 1959-64; justice Calif. Supreme Ct., 1964—; vis. prof. Santa Clara U., 1981-82. Mem. Calif. Commn. Jud. Qualifications, Calif. Disaster Council, Colo. River Boundary Commn., Calif. Commn. Peace Officer Standards, Dist. Securities Commn., Calif. Commn. Ofcl. Reports of Cts., Calif. Reapportionment Commn.; Calif. chmn. Thanks to Scandinavia Fund, 1967-68; chmn. San Francisco Internat. Film Festival, 1967. Mem. Dem. Nat. Com. from Calif., 1960-64. Bd. regents U. Calif., 1940; pres. Vista Del Mar Child Care Service, 1954-58. Served with AUS, World War II. Recipient distinguished alumnus award U. Chgo., 1958. Mem. Nat. Assn. Attys. Gen. (exec. bd.), Western Assn. Attys. Gen. (pres. 1963), ALA, Los Angeles Bar Assn., Santa Monica Bar Assn., San Francisco Bar Assn., Korean Bar Assn. Am. Judicature Soc., Am. Legion, Manuscript Soc., U. Chgo. Alumni Assn. (pres. No. Calif. 1966-68), Phi Sigma Delta, Phi Alpha Delta. Mem. B'nai B'rith. Clubs: Lawyers, Town Hall (Los Angeles); Commonwealth (San Francisco); Beverly Hills Tennis. Home: 1200 California St San Francisco CA 94109 Office: State Bldg San Francisco CA 94102

MOSQUEDA, LAWRENCE JOSEPH, political science educator; b. Fort Madison, Iowa, May 1, 1949; s. Richard and Antonia (Sandoval) M.; m. Patricia Elaine Flakus, Dec. 22, 1977; 1 dau., Teresa. B.S., Iowa State U., 1971; M.A., U. Wash., 1973, Ph.D., 1979. Research asst. polit. sci. U. Wash., Seattle, 1972, teaching asst., 1972-74, undergrad. advisor, 1974-75; instr. Chicano Studies Ctr., Claremont (Calif.) Colls., 1977-79; asst. prof. polit. sci. dept. U. Colo.-Denver, 1979—; speaker profl. meetings. Mem. adv. com. Denver Immigration and Naturalization Service; mem. Latin Am. human rights com. Am. Friends Service; mem. program com., popular econs. com. Denver Am. Friends Service. League of United Latin Am. Citizens scholar, 1967; J. Allen Smith fellow, 1971; Ford Found. fellow, 1975-77. Mem. Am. Polit. Sci. Assn., Western Polit. Sci. Assn., Caucus for New Polit. Sci., Nat. Assn. for Chicano Studies, Western Social Sci. Assn. Contbr. articles to profl. jours. Home: 3158 Ames St Denver CO 80214 Office: Dept Polit Sci U Colo 1100 14th St Denver CO 80202

MOSQUEIRA, CHARLOTTE MARIANNE, dietitian; b. Los Angeles, July 26, 1937; d. Leo and Magdalene Tollefson; B.S., St. Olaf Coll., 1959; postgrad. U. Oreg. Med. Sch., 1959-60; M.A., Central Mich. U., 1980; children—Mark, Michael. Chief clin. dietitian, asst. dir. food service Queen of Angels Hosp., Los Angeles, 1968-70; asst. dir. food service Presbyn. Hosp. Ctr., Albuquerque, 1970-73; dir. food service Holy Cross Hosp., Salt Lake City, 1973-77; dir. dietetics Riverside Meth. Hosp., Columbus, Ohio, 1977-79; dir. nutrition and food service Fresno (Calif.) Community Hosp. and Med. Ctr., 1980—. Mem. Am. Soc. for Hosp. Food Service Adminstrs. (regional dir.), Am. Dietetic Assn., Calif. Dietetic Assn., AAUW. Republican. Lutheran. Club: Community Vocal Chorale.

MOSS, ARTHUR JAMES, physician; b. St. Paul, Minn., May 12, 1914; s. David and Anna (Siegel) M.; B.S., U. Minn., 1935, M.B., 1937, M.D., 1938, M.S. in Pediatrics, 1942; m. Alice Litman, Oct. 19, 1941; children—Stephanie, Patricia, Tom. Intern, Mpls. Gen. Hosp., 1937-39; pediatric fellow U. Minn. Hosps., Mpls., 1939-42, research fellow, 1941-42; practice medicine specializing in pediatrics, Los Angeles, 1946-60; health service physician U. Minn. Health Service, 1946; chmn. dept. pediatrics Los Angeles Harbor Gen. Hosp., Torrance, Calif., 1948-51, chief attending staff dept. pediatrics, 1953-61, pres. hosp. staff, 1959-60; asst. clin. prof. pediatrics UCLA, 1952-53, asso. clin. prof., 1953-57, asso. clin. prof. pediatrics (cardiology), 1957-8, clin. prof. pediatrics (cardiology), 1958-60, asso. prof. pediatrics in residence, 1960-64, prof. pediatrics (cardiology), 1964—, chmn. dept. pediatrics, 1967-77, chief div. cardiology, dept. pediatrics, 1977—, dir. Cystic Fibrosis Center, UCLA Med. Center, 1963—, chief of staff UCLA Hosp. and Clinics, 1976-78; mem. hon. staff Santa Monica (Calif.) Hosp. Med. Center, 1975—; vis. prof. U. Free Berlin, Germany, 1960, Tohoku U., Sendai, Japan, 1965, Makerere U., Kampala, Uganda, 1972, U. Utah Med. Center, Salt Lake City, 1974, La Paz Hosp., Madrid, Spain, 1975, Queen Pahlavi Heart Hosp., Tehran, Iran, 1976; lecture tours in cardiology State Dept. and Am. Coll. Cardiology, Bogota, Columbia, 1966, Lima, Peru, 1966, São Paulo, Brazil, 1966; exchange prof. St. Mary's Hosp. Med. Sch., London, Eng., 1970; guest speaker 4th Internat. Congress on Cystic Fibrosis, Grindelwald, Switzerland, 1966, Internat. Conf. Cystic Fibrosis, Jerusalem, 1976; participant 7th Internat. Cystic Fibrosis Congress, Paris, 1976. Served to maj. M.C., U.S. Army, 1942-46. Recipient Susan and Theodore Cummings Humanitarian award, 1967; UCLA pediatric housestaff teaching award, 1971; Leadership award Nat. Cystic Fibrosis Research Found., 1973; Disting. Service award Am. Jour. Cardiology, 1978; diplomate Am. Bd. Pediatrics, Am. Bd. Pediatric Cardiology. Fellow Am. Coll. Cardiology (gov. So. Calif. sect. 1970-73); mem. Am. Acad. Pediatrics (chmn. cardiac sect. 1967-68, examiner sub-bd. pediatric cardiology 1970), Am. Pediatric Soc., Western Assn. Physicians, Los Angeles Acad. Medicine, Am. Heart Assn. (council on rheumatic fever and congenital heart disease 1967-68), Calif. Soc. Pediatric Cardiology (pres. 1969-70), Western Soc. Pediatric Research, Calif. Heart Assn., Los Angeles County Heart Assn. (award of merit 1964, 65, 66), Soc. Exptl. Biology and Medicine, Am. Arbitration Assn., Calif. Med. Assn. (mem. adv. panel to sect. on pediatrics 1970—), Los Angeles County Med. Assn., Sigma Xi. Author: (with F.H. Adams) Problems of Blood Pressure in Childhood, 1962, Heart Disease in Infants, Children and Adolescents, 1968; (with G.C. Emmanouilides) Practical Pediatric Electrocardiography, 1973; contbr. numerous articles on pediatric cardiology to profl. jours.; editorial bd. Am. Jour. Cardiology, 1973-78, Jour. Tropical Pediatrics and Environ. Child Health, 1973—. Home: 2222 Ave of Stars Los Angeles CA Office: Center for Health Science Dept Pediatrics UCLA School of Medicine Los Angeles CA 90024

MOSS, CHARLES NORMAN, physician; b. Los Angeles, June 13, 1914; s. Charles Francis and Lena (Rye) M.; A.B., Stanford U., 1940; M.D., Harvard U., 1944; cert. U. Vienna, 1947; M.P.H., U. Calif.-Berkeley, 1955; Dr.P.H., UCLA, 1970; m. Margaret Louise Stakias; children—Charles Eric, Gail Linda, and Lori Anne. Surg. intern Peter Bent Brigham Hosp., Boston, 1944-45, asst. in surgery, 1947; commd. 1st lt. USAF, M.C., USAAF, 1945, advanced through grades to lt. col., USAF, 1956; Long course for flight surgeon USAF Sch. Aviation Medicine, Randolph AFB, Tex., 1948-49, preventive medicine div. Office USAF Surgeon Gen., Washington, 1955-59; air observer, med., 1954, became sr. flight surgeon 1956; later med. dir., Los Angeles div. North Am. Rockwell Corp., Los Angeles; chief med. adv. unit Los Angeles County, now ret. Decorated Army Commendation medal (U.S.), Chinese Breast Order of Yun Hui. Recipient Physicians Recognition award AMA, 1969, 72, 76, 79, 82. Diplomate in aerospace medicine and occupational medicine Am. Bd. Preventive Medicine. Fellow Am. Pub. Health Assn., AAAS, Am. Coll. Preventive Medicine, Royal Soc. Health, Am. Acad. Occupational Medicine, Western Occupational Med. Assn., Am. Assn. Occupational Medicine; mem. AMA, Mil. Surgeons U.S., Soc. Air Force Flight Surgeons, Am. Conf. Govt. Hygienists, Calif. Acad. Preventive Medicine, (dir.), Aerospace Med. Assn., Calif., Los Angeles County med. assns. Research and publs. in field. Home: 7714 Cowan Ave Los Angeles CA 90045

MOSS, ERIC OWEN, architect, educator; b. Los Angeles, July 25, 1943; s. Morton Herbert and Ruth (Miller) M.; m. Maureen Elizabeth McGuire, Sept. 25, 1969; children—Jessica Anne, Damon Matthew. B.A., UCLA, 1965; M.Arch., U. Calif.-Berkeley, 1968; M.Arch., Harvard U., 1972. Lic. architect, 1974. With Pafford Clay and Skidmore, Owings & Merrill, San Francisco, 1969-71; sr. designer William Pereira Assocs., 1972-75; prof. design So. Calif. Inst. Architecture, Los Angeles, 1974—, also bd. dirs.; founder, prin. Eric Owen Moss, Architect, Santa Monica, Calif., 1976—; lectr. in field. Recipient AIA awards; design award citation Western Regional AIA/Sunset Mag. Spl. Design award Playa del Rey Duplex, 1977, Design Awards Exhbn. Los Angeles City Hall, Pacific Design Center, Playa del Rey Duplex, 1977, Progressive Architecture Design Award Citation, Morgenstern Warehouse, 1978. Mem. AIA. Contbr. articles to profl. publs. Office: 1337 Ocean Ave Suite X Santa Monica CA 90401

MOSS, HOWARD KENNETH, mech. engr.; b. Hillsboro, Ill.; s. Henry Lee and Florence Esther (Losch) M.; student U. Mo.; B.S. in Mech. Engring., U. Ill.; m. Helen Marie Moye; children—Charles, Shirley, Kelly, Gary. Mech. engr. Am. Zinc, Lead & Smelting Co.; aero. engr. Lockheed Aircraft Co., Burbank, Calif., McDonnell Aircraft Corp., St. Louis; aero. engr. Lockheed Aircraft & Missiles Co., Marietta, Ga., 1953-59, Sunnyvale, Calif., 1959-73; mech. engr. Bechtel Corp., San Francisco, 1973, sr. engr., 1973—; sr. engr. in aircraft design, on loan, U. Calif., Berkeley, 1944-45. Registered profl. engr., Calif., Ga. Mem. ASME, Republican. Presbyterian. Designer folding aircraft chair, fuel disconnect couplings, docking mechanism, captive fastener. Home: 384 Marich Way Los Altos CA 94022

MOSS, MORTON HERBERT (MOSS HERBERT), newspaper columnist, editor, poet; b. N.Y.C., Mar. 21, 1914; s. Carl and Rose (Schnur) M.; student Columbia U., 1930-32; m. Ruth Miller, Feb. 19, 1939; 1 son, Eric. Sports writer N.Y. Post, N.Y.C., 1932-37, Internat. News Service, N.Y.C., 1937-40; sports editor, columnist Los Angeles Examiner (now Herald Examiner), 1941-61, asst. sports editor, columnist, 1962-68, TV editor, columnist, 1969-77, news wire editor, 1978-79. Mem. Nat. Acad. TV Arts and Scis., Los Angeles World Affairs Council, Greater Los Angeles Press Club, Poetry Soc. Am., Internat. Poetry Soc. Represented in Best Sports Stories, E.P. Dutton & Co., Inc., 1952, 1960, 61, 62, 64, 65, 66, 67. Author: (poetry) Sennetts from the Tortuguise, 1983; contbr. articles to various mags.; contbr. poetry to mags. Lyric, Ariz. Quar., Coastlines, Am. Poet, Global Architecture, also anthologies The Golden Year, 1960, The Various Light, 1964, Ipso Facto, 1975. Creator Simplified Five, the boxing scoring system adopted by Calif. State Athletic Commn., 1960-70. Home: 1909 N Normandie Ave Los Angeles CA 90027

MOSS, RICHARD SPENCER, university official; b. Portland, Oreg., May 26, 1949; s. Harry and Mary Louise (Ruckdeschel) M.; m. Marilyn Jean Best, June 2, 1973; children—Emily Anne, Paul Spencer, Kathryn Elizabeth, Brian Richard. A.A., Mount Hood Community Coll., 1975; B.A. in Communications, U. Portland, 1977. Publs. mgr. First Nat. Bank Oreg., Portland, 1977; mgr. employee communications Ga.-Pacific Corp., Portland, 1977-80; dir. alumni and community relations U. Portland, 1980—. Served with USN, 1969-73; Vietnam. Recipient Arnold's Admirables award The Ragan Report, 1982. Mem. Pub. Relations Soc. Am., Internat. Assn. Bus. Communicators (Gold Quill award 1979, 83; chpt. dir.), Council Advancement and Support of Edn., Portland Dahlia Soc. Republican. Episcopalian. Home: 12080 SW Tremont St Portland OR 97225 Office: U Portland 5000 N Willamette Blvd Portland OR 97225

MOSS, ROBERT DEAN, electrical engineer, retired army officer; b. Cole Camp, Mo., Mar. 14, 1939; s. Vernon Elmo and Geneieve (Wood) M.; m. Carol Lynn Sanders, Jan. 1, 1983. 1 son, Brian Todd. B.S.E.E., Mo. Sch. Mines and Metallurgy, Rolla, 1962; postgrad. U. Kans., 1967-68; grad. U.S. Army Command and Gen. Staff Coll., Ft. Leavenworth, Kans., 1975; grad. in Arabic, Def. Lang. Inst., Monterey, Calif., 1976. Commd. 2d lt. U.S. Army, 1962; advanced through grades to lt. col.; ret., 1982; radio officer, Ft. Detrick, Md., 1962-63; chief cable distbn., Hawaii, 1963-66; co-comdr. 23d inf. div. RVN, 1968; signal officer 23d div. arty., Vietnam, 1969; chief system engring. Def. Communication Agy. Stuttgart, Ger., 1969-72; comdr. Safeguard Communications, Nekoma, N.D., 1972-74; signal advisor U.S. Mil. Mission, Saudi Arabia, 1976-77; dep. dir. opns. Sec. A.F. Spl. projects, 1979-82; prin. engr. PCR, Los Angeles, 1983—. Decorated Legion of Merit, Bronze Star, Air medal, Meritorious Service with oak leaf, Joint Service commendation medal, Army Commendation medal. Mem. AIAA, Assn. U.S. Army, Armed Forces Communication Electronics Assn., Ret. Officers Assn. Club: Alumni Assn. Mo. Sch. Mines and Metallurgy.

MOSS, ROBERT WARREN, economist, consultant; b. Detroit, June 8, 1941; s. Martin Louis and Betty Jean (Kohen) M.; m. Susan Gail Helyar, May 25, 1968; children—Karen, David. B.A. in Econs., U. Mich., 1962; M.A. in Econs., Am. U., Washington, 1964; postgrad. London Sch. Econs., 1964-65. Asst. dir. research Nat. Adv. Comm. Civil Disorders, Washington, 1967-68; regional coordinator Pres.'s Council Youth Opportunity, 1968-69; spl. asst. to dir. U.S. Employment Service, Dept. Labor, 1969-71, chief div. Pub. Careers Program, 1971-72; owner —Ceres— yacht charters, Rhodes, Greece, 1973-74; owner R.W. Moss & Assocs., 1977—; cons. World Bank, UN Food and Agrl. Orgn., Govt. of India; lectr. Seattle U. School Bus. OECD fellow, 1964-65. Mem. Am. Econs. Assn., Indl. Relations Research Assn., Seattle Economists Club. Club: Seattle Athletic. Home: 2205 E Newton Seattle WA 98112 Office: 1000 Turner Way E Seattle WA 98112

MOSS, SHIRLEY ANN, chemist; b. Wilmington, N.C., Nov. 28, 1943; d. Lucas Jackson and Hazel Elizabeth (Holmes) Howard; B.S. in Chemistry, Hampton (Va.) Inst., 1964; postgrad. St. Mary's U., San Antonio, Tex., 1967, San Jose State U., 1974-75; m. Luther Phillip Moss, Apr. 16, 1966 (div. 1975); 1 dau., Janis Nicole. Biochem. research asst. Pa. Hosp., Phila., 1964-66; research chemist Sch. Aerospace Medicine Brooks AFB, San Antonio, 1966-69; asso. engr. Gen. Electric, San Jose, 1973-78, chemist, 1978—. Mem. Am. Chem. Soc., Soc. Women Engrs., Delta Sigma Theta. Democrat. Mem. Ch. of Religious Sci. Home: 2118 Canoas Garden # 27 San Jose CA 95125 Office: 175 Curtner Ave San Jose CA 95125

MOSTECKY, VACLAV, lawyer, law librarian, educator; b. Jindrichuv Hradec, Czechoslovakia, June 29, 1919; came to U.S., 1948, naturalized, 1959; s. Vaclav and Emilie (Anton) M.; B.A., U. Dijon (France), 1938; J.D., Charles U., Prague, Czechoslovakia, 1946; M.A., Columbia U., 1953; M.S., Catholic U. Am., 1953; m. Iva Eret, Sept. 28, 1946; 1 dau., Iva. Br. chief Dept. State, Washington, 1949-53; asst. prof. info. scis. Catholic U. Am., 1953-58; asst. law librarian Harvard U., 1958-69; prof. law and law librarian SUNY, Buffalo, 1969-71; prof. law U. Calif., Berkeley, 1971—; cons. to law schs., 1958-79; also lectr. Co-founder Czechoslovak Soc. Arts and Scis. in U.S., 1953. Recipient Meritorious Service award Dept. State, 1952; Ford Found. grantee, 1958-60; Am. Psychiat. Assn. grantee, 1960-61. Mem. Am. Assn. Law Schs., Am. Assn. Law Libraries, Am. Internat. Law Assn., AAUP. Roman Catholic. Author: Catalog Use Study, 1958; Russian Books in American Libraries, 1960; Youth Research Centers, 1961; Index to Treaties, 1962-68; Ann. Legal Bibliography, Harvard Law Sch., 1960-68; also articles. Home: 14 Marlin Cove Oakland CA 94618 Office: Boalt Hall U Calif Berkeley CA 94720

MOSTELLER, JAMES WILBUR, III, data processing exec.; b. Ft. Riley, Kans., June 21, 1940; s. James Wilbur, Jr., and Ruth Renfro (Thompson) M.; B.S. in Econs., Rensselaer Poly. Inst., 1962; M.B.A., Temple U., 1971; m. Sandra Josephine Stevenson, Oct. 13, 1962; children—Margaret, Steven, Michael. Data processing systems analyst, Philco-Ford, Ft. Washington, Pa., 1966-69; data processing analyst and supr., Merck Sharp & Dohme, West Point, Pa., 1969-75, dir. mgmt. info. systems KELCO div. Merck and Co., San Diego, 1975—. Bd. dirs. New Horizons Montessori Sch., Ft. Washington, Pa., 1974-75; leader youth programs North County YMCA, 1977—; mem. San Diego Research Park Com., 1978—. Served with USN, 1962-66, USNR, 1966—. Certified in data processing. Mem. Data Processing Mgmt. Assn., Assn. Systems Mgmt., Naval Reserve Assn., Beta Gamma Sigma, Sigma Alpha Epsilon (chpt. pres. 1961-62). Office: Kelco Div Merck & Co Inc 8355 Aero Dr San Diego CA 92123

MOSTOFI, KHOSROW, educator; b. Tehran, Iran, July 8, 1921; came to U.S., 1949; s. Mostafa and Nasrin (Djam) M.; B.A., U. Tehran, 1944; M.A., U. Utah, 1957, Ph.D., 1958, grad. certificate pub. adminstrn., 1965; m. Nesrin Imamverdi, Aug. 18, 1960; 1 dau., Simin S. (dec.). Instr. langs. Ministry Edn., Tehran, Iran, 1944-49; asst. U. Utah Inst. Govt., Salt Lake City, 1956-58, mem. faculty, 1960—, prof. polit. sci., 1970—, dir. Middle East Center, 1967—, dir. Am. Center for Iranian Studies in Tehran, summer 1970; instr. polit. sci. Portland (Oreg.) State U., 1958-59, asst. prof., 1959-60. Mem. Am. Inst. Iranian Studies (trustee), Ctr. for Arabic Studies Abroad (bd. dirs.), Am. Inst. Yemeni Studies (trustee), Am. Found. Islamic Studies (pres.), AAUP, Western Polit. Sci. Assn., Middle East Inst., Middle East Studies Assn., Smithsonian Instn., Pi Sigma Alpha, Phi Kappa Phi. Mem. Islam religion. Author: Parsee Nameh, rev. edit., 1969; Aspects of Nationalism: A Sociology of Colonial Revolt, 1964. Contbr. to Ency. Britannica, 1974, Studies in Art and Literature of the Near East, 1974. Home: 2481 E 13th South St Salt Lake City UT 84108 Office: Middle East Center U Utah Salt Lake City UT 84112

MOTIS, GERALD, psychiatrist; b. Phila., Nov. 9, 1934; s. Philip and Shirley (Kaplan) M.; B.A., U. Pa., 1956; M.D., Temple U., 1960; m. Barbara Marian Knight, June 3, 1966; 1 son by previous marriage, Mark Vaughn; children—Valerie Anne, Andrea Marie. Intern, So. Pacific Gen. Hosp., San Francisco, 1960-61; resident in psychiatry VA Hosp., Sepulveda, Calif., 1962-65, chief resident, 1964-65, staff psychiatrist, 1965-66, chief psychiat. edn., 1968-70; in-patient dir. Golden State Community Mental Health Center, Lake View Terrace, 1971-75, med. dir., 1974-76; practice psychiatry, Granada Hills, Calif., 1968-76; sr.

psychiatrist, dir. psychiat. intensive care unit VA Med. Center, Brentwood, 1976-80, chief evaluation and admission services, 1980-81; chief admissions/evaluation and crisis unit VA Med. Center, Sepulveda, Calif., 1981—, also med. dir. Viet Nam Combat Vets. Delayed Stress Disorder Program; clin. asst. prof. psychiatry UCLA, 1976—. Mem. exec. com. Pacoima (Calif.) Meml. Hosp., 1974-76. Mem. Dem. Nat. Com., 1968-74. Served with M.C., AUS, 1966-68. Decorated Bronze Star. Mem. Am., So. Calif. psychiat. assns., AMA, Am. Profl. Practice Assn., Variety Clubs Internat., Nat. Football Found. and Hall of Fame, Phi Beta Kappa, Alpha Omega Alpha, Phi Lambda Upsilon, Alpha Epsilon Delta, Phi Beta Pi. Jewish. Contbr. to publs. in field. Home: 18776 Kenya St Northridge CA 91326 Office: VA Hosp Sepulveda CA 91343

MOTT, JUNE MARJORIE, educator; b. Faribault, Minn., Mar. 8, 1920; d. David C. and Tillie W. (Nelson) Shifflett; B.S., U. Minn., 1943, M.A., 1948; m. Elwood Knight Mott, Oct. 18, 1958. Tchr. high schs. in Minn., 1943-46, 48-53, 54-57; script writer, Hollywood, Calif., 1953-54; tchr. English, creative writing and journalism Mt. Miguel High Sch., Spring Valley, Calif., 1957—, chmn. council English dept., 1967-68; mem. Press Bur., Grossmont (Calif.) High Sch. Dist., 1958—; scriptwriter TV prodn. Lamp Unto My Feet, Jam Dandy Corp.; free-lance writer and public relations cons. Vice chmn. polit. action San Diego County Regional Resource Center, 1980-81. Writing project fellow U. Calif., San Diego, 1978; named Outstanding Journalism Tchr., State of Calif., Outstanding Humanities Tchr., San Diego County, Tchr. of Yr. for San Diego County, 1978. Mem. Nat. Council Tchrs. English, Nat. Journalism Assn., NEA, AAUW, Assn. Supervision and Curriculum Devel., Calif. Assn. Tchrs. English, Calif. Tchrs. Assn., So. Calif. Journalism Assn., Grossmont Edn. Assn. (pres. 1978-80), Greater San Diego Council Tchrs. English, Nat. Writers Club, Am. Guild Theatre Organists, Sigma Delta Chi. Democrat. Lutheran. Club: Order Eastern Star. Author, editor in field.

MOTT, TRACY LAND, economics educator; b. Oak Ridge, Nov. 4, 1946; s. Albert Gallatin and Sara Louise (Prater) M.; A.B., Princeton U., 1968; M.Div., Union Theol. Sem. N.Y.C., 1974; Ph.D. in Econs. Stanford U., 1982. St. worker Youth Services Agy., N.Y.C., 1968-69; unemployment ins. program specialist, U.S. Dept. Labor, N.Y.C., 1970-71; fiscal officer W. Harlem Group Assistance, N.Y.C., 1972-75; asst. prof. econs. U. Colo., Boulder, 1980—. Mem. Am. Econs. Assn. Office: Dept Economics Campus Box 256 U Colo Boulder CO 80309

MOTTLEY, JACQUELINE VIRGINIA, nat. chpt. coordinator; b. St. Cloud, Minn.; d. Joseph Bernard and Eleanore (Staunton) Weisser; B.A., Coll. of St. Catherine, 1949; postgrad. U. Wash., 1950-51, Mont. State U., 1964-67; m. Rudolph Herzog, Aug. 23, 1951; children—Robert, Mark, Joseph, Thomas, Richard; m. 2d, Renwick Ferrell Mottley, June 18, 1967 (div. Sept. 1972). Tchr. art Park High Sch., Livingston, Mont., 1966-67; dir. Skadron Fashion Inst., San Bernadino, Calif., after 1969; work experience coordinator Riverside (Calif.) City Coll., 1969-74, tchr., 1974-75; dir. sales Hilton Inn, San Bernardino, 1975-78; communications coordinator 1st Congl. Ch., Los Angeles; actress in Three Penny Opera prodn., Loft Theater, Bozeman, 1964; instr. San Bernardino Valley (Calif.) Coll. Sec., Overlake div. Community Chest drive, Seattle, 1953; State of Mont. Centennial TV rep., Mont., Utah, Idaho, speaker Centennial Women's Fashions, Bozeman, 1964; chmn. for wives of overseas servicemen, Mather AFB, Calif., 1967, family services coordinator, 1967-68. Recipient 1st award in black and white photography, film and TV dept. Mont. State U., 1965; 1st pl. photography 5th Ann. Art Show, 1965; hon. mention N.W. Photography Internat., 1965; named Family Service Vol. of Year, 1969. Mem. AAUW, Edward Dean Mus., Friends of the Mission Inn, Internat. Platform Assn., Bus. and Profl. Women Los Angeles (pres. 1980-81), Ebell of Los Angeles, Parapsychology Assn. (exec. bd. Riverside), Los Angeles Advt. Women, Internat. Orphans, Mary and Joseph League. Author: Hilton Victorian Hospitality. Home: 19135 Knollwood Dr Rialto CA 92376 also West Yellowstone MT Office: Childhelp USA Internat 6463 Independence Ave Woodland Hills CA 91370

MOTTWEILER, JERRY DORAN, photographer, educator; b. Evansville, Ind., Aug. 31, 1935; s. Vernon Hugo and Mildred Ann (Martin) M.; m. Gayle Joan Boettcher, June 6, 1956; children—Steven, Roxane, Scott; B.A., Calif. State U.-Los Angeles, 1962, M.A., 1971. Life cert. gen. secondary edn., Calif. Photography tchr. John Glenn High Sch., Norwalk, Calif., chm. fine arts dept., 1974-81, tchr. high Sierra backpacking classes, 1973-77; owner ProColor Photography, Whittier, Calif., 1966-77, Robinson Studio, Downey, Calif., 1977—. Trustee, del., adult Bible instr. Free Methodist Ch.; scoutmaster Boy Scouts Am., 1970-75. Served with U.S. Army, 1958-60. Recipient photog. exhibit awards, Profl. Photographers Assn. Calif., 1980, 81, Profl. Photographers West, 1979, 80, 81; award of merit Boy Scouts. Mem. NEA, Calif. Teachers Assn., Profl. Photographers Am., Profl. Photographers Assn. Calif., Profl. Photographers West. Club: Internat. Brotherhood of Magicians. Home: 5622 Palm Ave Whittier CA 90601 Office: 8011 Stewart and Gray Downey CA 90241

MOTZKO, CHARLES ANTHONY, electronics co. exec.; b. Mason City, Wash., Oct. 4, 1939; s. Donald Hart and Marjorie Jean (Kinnune) M.; student Fla. State U., 1960-64, Calif. State U., Los Angeles, 1974-75; B.A., U. Redlands, 1982; postgrad. Grad. Sch. Mgmt., UCLA, 1982—; m. Rose Marie Anderson, Dec. 8, 1962; 1 dau., Patricia Ann. Lab. supr. Nat. Astro. Labs., 1965-67; mgr. Electro Rent, Burbank, Calif., 1967-73, products and data group mgr., 1979—; v.p., tech. dir. Comtel-NAL, Burbank, Calif., 1973-77; mgr. U.S. Instrument Rentals, San Mateo, Calif., 1977-79. Mem. State of Calif. Measurement Systems Adv. Com., 1976-77. Served with USAF, 1957-65. Registered profl. engr., Calif. Mem. Am. Soc. Quality Control, Precision Measurement Assn., Soc. Logistics Engrs. Republican. Lutheran. Home: 8377 Vine Valley Dr Sun Valley CA 91352 Office: 4209 Vanowen Pl Burbank CA 91505

MOULDS, WILLIAM JOSEPH, aero. engr.; b. Newton, Kans., Mar. 7, 1933; s. William James and Edith Marie (Cox) M.; B.M.E., U. N.Mex., 1957; M.M.E., N.Mex. State U., 1970; m. Myra Teresa Cummins, Dec. 28, 1955; children—Michael J., Robert W., Barbara L., Anne T., Patrick L., Margaret L. Engr. research lab. Allis-Chalmers Mfg. Co., Cin., 1956-57; aero. and mech. engr. U.S. Air Force Weapons Lab., Kirtland AFB, N.Mex., 1958-61, supervisory aero. engr., 1961-63, sr. aero. engr., acting chief applications br., 1969-73, chief engring. br., 1973-78, dep. chief tech. services div., 1978-79, chief tech. services div., 1979—; guest lectr. dept. physics U.S. Air Force Acad., 1970. Founder, 1st pres. Highland High Sch. Baseball Booster Club, adult advisor Boy Scouts Am.; v.p. Lobo Little League. Recipient awards for sci. achievement and service U.S. Air Force; registered profl. engr., N.Mex. Mem. Nat. Soc. Profl. Engrs., Am. Inst. Aeros. and Astronautics, Research Soc. Am., U. N.Mex. Engring. Coll. Alumni Club, Sigma Xi, Sigma Tau. Democrat. Roman Catholic. Club: Chaparral Bulldog (past pres.). Contbr. articles to profl. jours.; patentee in field of aeros. (6). Home: 316 Sierra Pl NE Albuquerque NM 87108 Office: USAF Weapons Lab SU Kirtland AFB NM 87117

MOULTRIE, FRED SILAS, accountant; b. Los Angeles, July 3, 1941; s. James Leon and Autumn Ione (Henderson) M.; B.S. in Bus. Adminstrn. cum laude, U. So. Calif., 1966; m. Carolyn Melody Combs, Dec. 29, 1963; children—Susan Toi, Autumn Ingrid. Accountant, auditor Wolveck & Berney Co., Pasadena, Calif., 1963-64; internal auditor Bekins Van & Storage, Los Angeles, 1964-66; auditor Price Waterhouse & Co., Los Angeles, 1966-68; sr. partner Fred S. Moultrie & Co., Los Angeles, 1968-71; pres., chmn. bd. Moultrie, Robinson & Terrell Accountancy Corp., Los Angeles, Berkeley, and San Diego, 1971-73; partner Alexander Grant & Co., Los Angeles, 1973-75; pres., chmn. bd. Moultrie Accountancy Corp., 1975—. Served with USMCR, 1958-61. Recipient Outstanding Service award Los Angeles Brotherhood Crusade, 1971. C.P.A., Calif., Va., La. Mem. Nat. Assn. Minority C.P.A. Firms (dir. 1972-73, v.p. 1972-73), Cal. Soc. C.P.A.'s (entertainment industry com. 1969-71), Am. Inst. C.P.A.'s, Fed. Govt. Accountants Assn., Commerce Assos., Soc. Advancement Mgmt., NAACP, Black Businessmen's Assn. Los Angeles, Nat. Assn. Black Accountants (pres., chmn. bd. 1974-75, pres. Los Angeles chpt. 1973-74), Beta Alpha Psi, Alpha Kappa Psi, Kappa Alpha Psi (pres. Beta Omega chpt. 1964). Home: 540 S Rossmore Ave Los Angeles CA 90020 Office: 6207 San Vicente Blvd Los Angeles CA

MOUNDS, LEONA MAE REED, educator; b. Crosby, Tex., Sept. 9, 1945; d. Elton Phillip and Ora Lee (Jones) Reed; m. Aaron B. Mounds Jr., Aug. 21, 1965; 1 dau., Lisa Nichelle. B.A. in Elem. Edn., Bridgewater State Coll., 1973; M.A. in Mental Retardation, U. Alaska, 1980. Cert. tchr. Alaska, Colo., Tex., Mass. Tchr., Sch. Dist. 11, Colorado Springs, Colo., 1973-75; tchr. Anchorage Sch. Dist., 1976-78, 80—, mem. math. curriculum com., reading contact tchr., mem. talent bank. Tchr. Del Valle (Tex.) Sch. Dist., 1979-80. Bd. dirs. Urban League, 1974; 1st v.p. PTA, Crosby, Tex.; del. Tex. Democratic Conv., 1980; tchr. religious edn., lay Eucharist minister St. Martin De Pores Roman Cath. Ch. Served with USAF, 1964-66. Alaska State Tchr. Incentive grantee, 1981; Ivy Lutz scholar, 1972. Mem. NEA, Anchorage Edn. Assn. (minority chmn. 1982—, mem. Black Caucus polit. action com.), Black Educators of Pikes Peak Region (pres. 1974), Anchorage Edn. Assn. (women's caucus), Assn. Supervision and Curriculum Devel., Alaska Women in Adminstrn., Council for Exception Children, NAACP.

MOWBRAY, JOHN CODE, chief justice Supreme Ct. Nev.; b. Bradford, Ill., Sept. 20, 1918; s. Thomas J. and Ellen (Code) M.; B.A., Western Ill. U., 1940, L.H.D., 1976; postgrad. U. Va., 1944, Northwestern U., 1945; J.D. cum laude, Notre Dame U., 1949; LL.D. (hon.), U. Nev., 1978; m. Kathlyn Hammes, Oct. 15, 1949; children—John, Romy, Jerry, Terry. Admitted to Nev. bar, 1949, Ill. bar, 1950; chief dep. dist. atty. Clark County, Nev., 1949-53; individual practice law, Las Vegas, 1949-53; U.S. referee in bankruptcy for Dist. of Nev., Reno, 1957-59; mem. U.S. Jud. Conf. for 9th Circuit, 1957-59; dist. judge 8th Jud. Dist. Nev., Las Vegas, 1959-67; justice Supreme Ct. Nev., Carson City, 1967—, chief justice, 1979—; faculty adviser Nat. Coll. State Trial Judges, U. Pa., summer 1967; founder pub. defender program Nev. under Ford Found. grant, 1965. Vice pres. Boulder Dam Area council Boy Scouts Am., 1960-70, bd. dirs. Nev. Area council, 1967—; pres. City of Hope, 1963-64, NCCJ, 1965-66; v.p. YMCA, 1964—. Served to maj. USAAF, World War II. Recipient Honor certificate Freedoms Found., 1963, 67; George Washington medal, 1965, 69; Silver Beaver award Boy Scouts Am., 1966; regional Equal Justice award NAACP, 1970; Gen. MacArthur Medal award Nat. SAR, 1971; Outstanding Alumnus award Western Ill. U., 1971; Mowbray Hall Western Ill. U. named in his honor, 1974. Mem. Am., Nev., Ill. bar assns., Am. Judicature Soc. Home: 1815 S 15th St Las Vegas NV 89104 Office: Supreme Court Capitol Complex Carson City NV 89710

MOXLEY, ANN WEIMER, clinical psychologist; b. N.Y.C., Mar. 14, 1946; d. Rae Otis and Ruth Adrienne (Meister) Weimer; m. James Edward Moxley, Mar. 16, 1968 (div.). B.A. with honors, U. Fla., 1967, M.S. in Psychology, 1968, Ph.D. in Clin. Psychology, 1970. Diplomate clin. psychology Am. Bd. Profl. Psychology; lic. psychologist, Calif., N.Y. Prin. psychologist Monroe Devel. Center, Rochester, N.Y., 1971-78; instr. psychology, psychiatry U. Rochester, 1973-78; coordinator No. Calif. Assessment Center for Deaf, Fremont, 1978—; pvt. practice psychology, 1973—. Mem. Am. Psychol. Assn., San Francisco Mus. Soc., U. Calif.-Berkeley Alumni Assn. Clubs: Am. Contract Bridge League. Contbr. articles to profl. jours. Home: 130 Seabridge Alameda CA 94501 Office: 39350 Gallaudet Dr Fremont CA 94501

MOYE, RENE DONALD, city official; b. Salem, Oreg., June 29, 1938; s. William A. and Harriet (Fritz) M.; m. Pamela Freeman, June 20, 1964; children—Nicole, Caje. B.S., Oreg. State U., 1963; M.S., San Francisco State Coll., 1969; student Shasta Jr. Coll., 1957-58. Recreation supr. City of Oakland (Calif.), 1964-69; supt. parks and recreation Chehalem Park and Recreation Dist., Newberg, Oreg., 1969-71; dir. parks and recreation City of San Bernardino (Calif.), 1971-74, City of Corvallis (Oreg.), 1974—; instr. park adminstrn. Oreg. State U., 1975-76. Served with AUS, 1960-62. Mem. Nat. Park and Recreation Assn., Oreg. Park and Recreation Soc. (pres. 1982), Nat. Park and Recreation Assn. (council affiliated pres.). Republican. Roman Catholic. Club: Kiwanis (pres. 1982) (Corvallis). Office: 501 SW Madison St Corvallis OR 97330

MOYER, JAMES WALLACE, physicist; b. Syracuse, Aug. 16, 1919; s. Wallace Earl and Viola (Hook) M.; A.B., Cornell U., 1938; postgrad. Rutgers U., 1938-41; Ph.D., U. Rochester, 1948; m. Nedra Blake, Sept. 10, 1940; children—Jeffry Mark, Elaine, Virginia, Julia. Insp. ordnance U.S. Army, 1941-42; physicist Radiation Lab., U. Calif., Berkeley, 1942-43; sr. physicist Tenn. Eastman, Oak Ridge, 1943-46; research asso. Gen. Electric Research, Knolls Atomic Power Lab., Schenectady, N.Y., 1948-55; cons. engr. Gen. Electric Microwave Lab., Palo Alto, Calif., 1955-57; mgr. phys. sci. Gen. Electric Tempo, Santa Barbara, Calif., 1957-60; research dir. Sperry Rand Research Center, 1960-61; research dir. Servo Mechanisms Inc., 1961-63; dir. applied research Autonetics div. N. Am. Aviation, Anaheim, Calif., 1963-65; dir. engring. Northrop Corp., Beverly Hills, Calif., 1967-70; mgr. phys. systems So. Calif. Edison, Rosemead, 1976—; cons. Nat. Bur. Standards, 1956-62; mem. panel Nat. Acad. Sci., 1967-70, 71. Mem. IEEE (sr.), Am. Phys. Soc., AAAS, Sigma Xi. Home: 500 N Baldwin Ave Sierra Madre CA 91024 Office: PO Box 800 Rosemead CA 91770

MOYER, PAUL KENNETH, insurance company executive; b. Hamburg, Pa., May 29, 1936; s. Paul Frederick and Verna (Miller) M.; B.B.A., Tex. Luth. Coll., 1962; postgrad. U. Houston, 1966; M.B.A., So. Meth. U., 1971; m. Betty Louise Scheffer, Aug. 25, 1962; children—Mark Kevin, Kayla Marie, Michael Christian. Auditor Ernst & Ernst, C.P.A.s, Houston, 1962-65; asst. to asst. treas. Gulf & Western Industries, Inc., N.Y.C., 1965-68, asst. treas., 1968-69; v.p., controller UCC Fin. Corp., Dallas, 1969-73; v.p. investment services Gulf Ins. Co., Dallas, 1973-79; sr. v.p., treas. Capitol Life Ins. Co., Denver, 1979-83, sr. v.p. corp. adminstrn., 1983—. Mem. devel. bd. Tex. Luth. Coll., 1972-78; bd. dirs. Clifton Luth. Sunset Home, 1978-79, Univ. Group, Long Beach, Calif., 1979-83. Served with USAF, 1954-58. C.P.A., Tex., Colo. Mem. Am. Inst. C.P.A.s, Nat. Assn. Accts., Tex. Soc. C.P.A.s, Colo. Soc. C.P.A.s, Fin. Execs. Inst. Lutheran. Home: 7127 S Magnolia Circle Englewood CO 80112 Office: 1600 Sherman St Denver CO 80203

MOYERS, WILLIAM TAYLOR, painter, sculptor; b. Atlanta, Dec. 11, 1916; s. William Taylor and Sally Frances (McKinnon) M.; A.B., Adams State Coll., 1939; postgrad. Otis Art Inst., Los Angeles, 1939; m. Neva Irene Anderson, Mar. 20, 1943; children—Joanne, William, Charles, John. Effects animator Walt Disney Studios, 1940; freelance illustrator for book pubs., 1945-63; author, illustrator: Famous Indian Tribes, 1954, Famous Heroes of the Old West, 1956; one-man shows: Cowboy Hall of Fame, 1973, Adams State Coll., 1971; group shows: Cowboy Artists Am., 1968-78, Mont. Hist. Assn., 1973-74; mem. bd. dirs. N.Mex. Arts and Crafts Fair, 1970-71. Elder Immanuel Presbyterian Ch., Albuquerque; bd. dirs. Adams State Coll. Found. Served to capt. Signal Corps, U.S. Army, 1942-46. Mem. Cowboy Artists Am. (recipient Gold medal 1968, 72-75, Best of Show 1975, Silver medal for sculpture 1979-80). Home and Office: 1407 Morningside Dr NE Albuquerque NM 87110

MOZLEY, ANITA VENTURA, museum curator; b. Washington, Aug. 29, 1928; d. Mario and Juanita Magruder (Lewis) Ventura; m. Robert Fred Mozley, June 23, 1967. B.A., Northwestern U., 1950. Art dir. coll. issue Mademoiselle mag., 1949; design asst. to Leo Lionni, N.Y.C., 1951-52; designer, contbg. editor, mng. editor Arts, N.Y.C., 1953-63; asst. curator San Francisco Maritime Mus., 1963-67; registrar Stanford U. Mus., 1970-78, curator photography, 1972—; lectr. in field; condr. workshops. Recipient Faricy Art prize Northwestern U., 1950; Out-of-Town scholar Art Students League, 1950-51. Mem. Friends of Photogaphy, Phi Beta Kappa. Author Mus. catalogues, essays.

MRACKY, RONALD SYDNEY, advertising executive; b. Sydney, Australia, Oct. 22, 1932; came to U.S., 1947; s. Joseph and Anna (Janousek) M; m. Sylvia Frommer, Jan. 1, 1960; children—Enid Hillevy, Jason Adam. Ed. English Inst., Praque, Czechoslovakia, 1945-47; grad. Parson Sch. Design, N.Y.C., 1953; B.A., NYU, 1953. Designer, Donald Deskey Assocs., N.Y.C., 1953-54; art dir., graphic designer ABC-TV, Hollywood, Calif., 1956-57; creative dir. Neal Advt. Assocs., Los Angeles, 1957-59; pres. Richter & Mracky Design Assoc., Los Angeles, 1959-68, Ted Bates & Co., Los Angeles, 1969-73; sr. ptnr. Sylron Internat., Los Angeles, 1973—; pres. Regency Fin. Internat., Beverly Hills, Calif., 1974-77; mgmt. dir. N.Am. Standard Advt., Tokyo and Los Angeles, 1978—; cons. Pacific Basin Govts. Bd. dirs. Dubnoff Ctr. Child Devel. & Ednl. Therapy, 1968-74; bd. dirs., trustee, chmn. exec. comm. Calif. Chamber Symphony Soc., 1973-82; exec. dir. Internat. Studies & Devel., 1977-78. Served in U.S. Army, 1954-56. Recipient nat. and internat. awards design and mktg.

MROWKA, JANE TREEBS, sound/slide producer, presentation consultant, script writer; b. Cleve., Mar. 15, 1944; d. Dan A. and Evelyn (Birtic) Treebs; m. Jack P. Mrowka, Sept. 2, 1967; children—Jeff, Molly, Andrew. Student Santa Monica Coll., 1961-63; B.A. in Geography, UCLA, 1965; postgrad. U. Hawaii, summer 1966; M.A. in Instructional Tech., U. Oreg., 1982. Tchr., Santa Monica, Calif., 1966-69; substitute tchr., Glenwood, Ill., 1974, Eugene, Oreg., 1975-78; intern Eugene Water and Electric Bd., 1982; owner, mgr. Media Spectrum, Santa Rosa, Calif., 1983—; cons. presentations and scriptwriting. Bd. dirs. Rohnert Park YMCA Day Camp, 1983; leader Camp Fire Girls, 1977; den mother Cub Scouts, 1976; fundraiser Sonoma County Jr. Orch. Symphony. Mem. Am. Soc. Tng. and Devel., Assn. Supervision and Curriculum Devel., AAUW. Clubs: Wings (Santa Rosa); Multi-Image Showcase (San Francisco). Co-founder A-V Communicators, 1983. Home: 1370 Townview Circle 105 Santa Rosa CA 95405 Office: Media Spectrum 226 Roberts Ave Santa Rosa CA 95401

MSCICHOWSKI, LOIS I., ins. agent and exec.; b. Omaha, Nov. 24, 1935; d. Edward J. and Evelyn B. (Davidson) Morrison; m. Peter A. Mscichowski, Aug. 16, 1952; 1 son, Peter Edward; m. Frederick G. Chambers, Apr. 17, 1981. Ins. clk. Gross-Wilson Ins. Agy., 1955-57; ins. sec., bookkeeper Reed-Paulsen Ins. Agy., 1957-58; office mgr., asst. sec., agent Don Biggs & Assos., Vancouver, Wash., 1958—; charter mem., mem. adv. council Safecom Mgmt. Systems. Mem. Citizens Com. Task Force, City of Vancouver, 1976, Block Grant Rev. Task Force, 1978—; chmn. adv. com. Clark Community Coll. Mem. Ins. Women of SW Wash. (pres.), Nat. Assn. Ins. Women. Roman Catholic. Club: Soroptimist (pres. elect Vancouver). Home: 8770 SW Umatilla St Tualatin OR 97062 Office: 916 Main St PO Box 189 Vancouver WA 98666

MUCHNIC, SUZANNE MUCHNIC, art critic, educator, lectr.; b. Kearney, Nebr., May 16, 1940; d. Walter Marian Ely and Erva Nell Liston; m. Paul D. Muchnic, 1963; B.A., Scripps Coll., 1962; M.A., Clarement Grad. Sch., 1963. Art instr. Weber State Coll., Ogden, Utah, 1972-73; art history instr. Los Angeles City Coll., 1974-82; editor for So. Calif., Artweek, 1976-78; art critic Los Angeles Times, 1978—. Recipient Disting. Alumna award Claremont Grad. Sch., 1982. Mem. Coll. Art Assn., Internat. Assn. Art Critics. Office: Los Angeles Times Times-Mirror Sq Los Angeles CA 90053

MUECKE, CHARLES (CARL) ANDREW, U.S. judge; b. N.Y.C., Feb. 20, 1918; s. Charles and Wally (Roeder) M.; B.A., Coll. William and Mary, 1941; LL.B., U. Ariz., 1953; m. Claire E. Vasse; children by previous marriage—Carl Marshall, Alfred Jackson, Catherine Calvert. Rep. AFL, 1947-50; reporter Ariz. Times, Phoenix, 1947-48; admitted to Ariz. bar, 1953, since practiced in Phoenix; with firm Parker & Muecke, 1953-59, Muecke, Dushoff & Sacks, 1960-61; U.S. atty. Dist. Ariz., 1961-64; U.S. dist. judge, from 1964, now chief judge. Chmn. Dist. Ct. Judges Com. for Uniform Local Ct. Rules; mem. judges com. on mandates, computer-aided transcription com., adv. com. on civil rules of Jud. Conf. Mem. Phoenix Planning Commn., 1955-61, chmn., 1960. Chmn. Maricopa County Democratic Party, 1961-62. Served to 1st lt. USMCR, 1942-45. Mem. ABA (jud. adminstrn. div.), Fed. Bar Assn., Inter-Am. Bar Assn., Internat. Bar Assn., Ariz. Bar Assn., Maricopa Bar Assn., Am. Trial Lawyers Assn., Law Soc. Ariz. State U., Dist. Judges Assn. Ninth Circuit, Fed. Exec. Assn., St. Thomas More Soc. (pres. Phoenix 1958), Phi Beta Kappa, Phi Alpha Delta, Omicron Delta Kappa. Office: 7015 US Courthouse Phoenix AZ 85025

MUELLER, DONALD DEAN, meat processing company executive; b. Columbus, Nebr., Sept. 12, 1937; s. Emil J. and Hulda (Cattau) M.; m. JoAnn Ferris, Aug. 17, 1963; children—Bradford Paul, Bartley Brandon. Student U. Nebr., 1956-58, 62-63; B.S. in Bus. Adminstrn., U. Denver, 1965. C.P.A., Colo. Staff acct. Ernst & Ernst, Denver, 1965-69; treas. Monfort of Colo., Inc., Greeley, 1969-72, group v.p. fin. services and lamb ops., 1979—; v.p. fin. Spencer Foods, (Iowa), 1972-79. Mem. Nat. Assn. Accts., Am. Inst. C.P.A.s, Clubs: Greeley Country. Republican. Lutheran. Home: 1912 27th Ave Greeley CO 80631 Office: PO Box G Greeley CO 80632

MUELLER, PAUL FREDERICK CHARLES, psychologist; b. Schenectady, Nov. 24, 1923; s. Herman William and Amanda Helena (Voss) M.; m. Virginia Schwartz, Sept. 24, 1945; children—Christian William, Lisa. A.A., Concordia Collegiate Inst., 1943; B.A., Stanford U., 1947, M.A., 1950; Ph.D. with honors, U. Wash., 1959. Psychologist trainee V.A. Clinic, Palo Alto, Calif., 1947-49; clin. psychologist N.Y. State Hosp., 1950-51; admissions officer King County Youth Service Ctr., 1952; house staff Ryther Child Ctr., Seattle, 1953; boy's supr. King County Youth Service Ctr, Seattle, 1954-56; statis. research analyst Calif. State Dept. Insts., 1956-58; assoc. social research technician Calif. State Dept. Mental Hygiene, 1958-60; sr. social research analyst Calif. State Dept. Corrections, 1960-66; chief research and stats. sect. Calif. State Dept. Rehab., 1966-75, program evaluation and stats. sect., 1975-81, stats., program evaluation and research sect., 1982—. Bd. dirs. Sacramento Com. Fair Housing, 1960-65, chmn., 1961-62; mem. State Employees for Equality, 1964-66; bd. dirs. Sacramento chpt. ACLU, 1970, Sacramento People-to-People, 1971-72; bd. dirs. Sacramento World Affairs Council, 1967-83, chmn., 1973-75, 83-84; host family Experiment in Internat. Living, 1963, 65, 70, 74; bd. dirs. Sacramento Council for Internat. Visitors, 1982-83, bd. dirs., sec., 1983-84; bd. dirs., del. Matsuyama-Sacramento Sister City Corp., 1981-83, corr. sec., 1983-84; mem. UNA/USA Assn. Sacramento, 1975-76, Sacramento Civic Eaglet Theatre, 1963-82; mem. adv. council Visions Unlimited,

1983-84. Served to 2d lt. U.S. Army, 1943-46; Japan. Recipient SIRCC Leadership Appreciation award, 1972; Sacramento World Affairs Council Spl. award, 1976. Mem. Am. Psychol. Assn., Nat. Rehab. Assn., Sacramento Statis. Assn., Sacramento Valley Psychol. Assn., Calif. Psychol. Assn., Western Psychol. Assn., Sigma Xi. Democrat. Club: Sacramento Japanese Sword. Contbr. numerous articles to profl. jours. Home: 4310 Moss Dr Sacramento CA 95822 Office: 830 K St Mall Sacramento CA 95814

MUELLER, WALTER SACK, JR., special education administrator; b. Mishawaka, Ind., Mar. 3, 1929; s. Walter Sack and Lucy Harriet (Hodson) M.; m. Patricia C. Black, July 4, 1952; children—Stevan H., Douglas A., Margarete E., Teresa Marie. B.A., San Jose State U., 1953; M.A., 1964. Cert. sch. adminstr., Wyo. Tchr., prin., Likely, Calif., 1954-59; speech therapist, Hollister, Calif., 1959-69; dir. spl. programs Campbell County Schs., Gillette, Wyo., 1969—, also asst. dir. instrn. Mem. Calif. State Republican Central Com., 1966-68; Rep. fin. chmn., Gillette, 1970-74; charter mem. Am. Field Service, 1970—; trustee Campbell County Meml. Hosp., 1978—. Served as cpl. U.S. Army, 1946-48. Mem. Calif. Tchrs. Assn., Assn. for Retarded Citizens, Nat. Autistic Soc., Council for Exceptional Children, Sigma Chi. Republican. Clubs: Lions, Gillette Golf and Country, Kiwanis. Office: Campbell County Schs 1000 W Eighth St Gillette WY 82716

MUELLER-ENGHOLM, MARY KORSTAD, ednl. cons., author; b. Seattle, May 7, 1918; d. Martin and Mary (Greene) Korstad; B.Edn. in Art, UCLA, 1940; M.S. in Art Supervision, St. Lawrence U., Canton, N.Y., 1949; postgrad. art Syracuse (N.Y.) U.; m. Walter J. Weigel (div.); 1 dau., Erica Weigel; m. 2d, Paul G. Mueller (dec.); m. 3d, Glenn Stanley Engholm. Art tchr. Chemawa Jr. High Sch., Riverside, Calif., 1944-46; asst. prof. SUNY, Potsdam, 1948-58; supr. art edn. Watertown (N.Y.) City Schs., 1962-67; cons. art edn. Bakersfield (Calif.) City Sch. Dist., 1967-78. Bd. dirs. Bakersfield Arts Council, 1975—, Sister Cities Assn., Mus. Alliance of Kern County; pres. bd. dirs. Child Guidance Clinic; former pres. Young Audiences of Kern County; community adv. Jr. League of Bakersfield. Mem. Calif. Art Edn. Assn., Greater Bakersfield C. of C. (women's div.), NEA, Delta Kappa Gamma. Author: (with others) Art for Elementary Schools, 1967; Murals: Changing the Environment, 1979. Contbr. articles to profl. publs. Cert. in supervision and teaching, Calif., N.Y. Home: 3306 Harmony Dr Bakersfield CA 93306

MUHAMMAD, RACQUEL ANNISSA, educator; b. Beggs, Okla., Sept. 3, 1932; d. John and Elnora (DuBose) Lovings; B.A., San Diego State U., 1953; diploma Alliance Francaise, Paris, 1967; M.A., U.S. Internat. U., San Diego, 1976, Ph.D., 1980; m. Amos Muhammad, Nov. 25, 1951; children—Duane Bradford, Sharon Bradford; Valerie, Shana, Sita and Amos Muhammad. Prof. English, Coll. Moderne du Sikasso, Mali, 1964-67; dir. U. of Islam 8, San Diego, 1969-75; coordinator basic adult edn. and ESL, Clark County Community Coll., N. Las Vegas, Nev., 1977; edn. cons./supr. Operation Independence Inst., Las Vegas, 1978; tchr. English as 2d lang., secondary English and English as fgn. lang. San Diego Unified Sch. Dist., 1980—; acad. cons., tutor fgn. students Rabihah Acad. Cons. and Tutoring Service, San Diego, 1979—. Mem. Am. Assn. Sch. Adminstrs., Assn. Supervision and Curriculum Devel., Calif. Tchrs. English to Speakers Others Langs., Calif. English Tchrs. Assn., NEA, San Diego Tchrs. Assn. Muslim Students Assn. U.S. and Can. Democrat. Islam. Author: (series) Social Change Through Education, 1979; The Black Muslim Movement After the Death of Elijah Muhammad, 1980.

MUIR, CRAIG ALAN, psychologist; b. Portland, Apr. 7, 1944; s. John Andrew and Tearly (Iverson) M.; B.A., Pomona Coll., 1967; M.A., U. So. Calif., 1974, Ph.D., 1976; 1 dau., Sally Rachael. Personnel officer East Los Angeles Child and Youth Clinic, Los Angeles, 1970-72; research dir. Orange County Public Service Careers Project, Santa Ana, Calif., 1971-72; adminstrv. services analyst Orange County Criminal Justice Council, Santa Ana, 1972-73; staff psychologist brain injury program Casa Colina Rehab. Hosp., Pomona, Calif., 1976-79, dir. neuropsychology service, 1979—; cons. in field. NIMH fellow, 1969-70, 72-74; mem. nat. adv. bd. Nat. Head Injury Found. Mem. Internat. Neuropsychol. Soc., Am. Psychol. Assn., Calif. Psychol. Assn. Office: 255 E Bonita Ave Pomona CA 91767

MUIR, MICHAEL BILL, logging equipment mfg. corp. exec.; b. Seward, Alaska, Jan. 25, 1941; s. William and Hazel (Hirsch) M.; B.S., Stanford U., 1963; M.B.A., Harvard U., 1966; m. Kathleen Ann Norton, Nov. 23, 1962; children—Melissa, Megan, Kimberly, Jason. Market planner Cummins Engine Co., Columbus, Ind., 1966-67, West div. off-hwy. sales mgr., San Francisco, 1967-68; v.p. Okinawa Plywood Co., Naha, 1968-71; v.p. mktg. Wash. Iron Works, Seattle, 1971-72, gen. mgr. logging equipment div., 1972-75, v.p. ops., 1975-76; pres. Wash. Logging Equipment, Inc. Auburn, 1977—. Served with AUS, 1960. Lutheran. Author: (with others) An Electronic Cash and Credit System, 1966. Home: 707 S 295th Pl Federal Way WA 98003 Office: Wash Logging Equipment Inc 3602 C St NE Auburn WA 98002

MULAR, JAMES THEODORE, union ofcl.; b. Butte, Mont., Oct. 23, 1929; s. Harry Gregory and Lena Mular; student Western Mont. Coll., 1947-48, Butte Bus. Coll., 1949-50; LL.B., LaSalle U., 1963; m. Florence Ruth Johnson, June 13, 1954; children—Mark James, Christie Balaban. With No. Pacific Ry. Co., Butte, 1949-70; passenger agt. Nat. Passenger Corp. AMTRAK, Butte, 1970-79; state legis. dir. Brotherhood Ry. and Airlines Clks., Butte, 1979—. Del., Democratic State Conv., 1975; mem. Mont. Ho. of Reps., 1975-79; registered lobbyist U.S. Congress, Mont. Ho. of Reps., 1979-81. Served with USMC, 1945-46, 50-53. Mem. AFL-CIO, Ry. Clks. Polit. League, United Comml. Travelers. Roman Catholic. Clubs: Elks, K.C. Address: 440 Roosevelt Dr Rural Route 1 Butte MT 59701

MULCAHY, BOB, state senator, retired banker; b. Winnebago, Minn., Aug. 14, 1929; m. Esther Mulcahy; 5 children. Student pub. schs. Retired banker; mem. Alaska State Senate, 1978—. Former mem. Kodiak Health Resources Council, Kodiak Alv. Fish and Game Bd., Kodiak Area Econ. Devel. and Planning Com. Served with USN, 1948-52. Mem. Am. Legion, VFW. Republican. Lodge: Elks. Office: Alaska State Senate Juneau AK 99811*

MULDER, WILLEM GERARD, trade consultant; b. Amsterdam, Netherlands, Jan. 6, 1921; came to U.S., 1957, naturalized, 1962; s. Willem Jan and Gerar dina Sara (van Delden) M.; B.Sc. in Civil Engring., High Tech. Sch., Amsterdam, 1942; M.B.A., City Univ., Seattle, 1981; m. Toyoko Fujita, Dec. 13, 1962; children—Stephen E.W., Diane S., Karin A., David J. Sales mgr. Internat. Harvester Co., Durban, South Africa, 1951-57; mng. dir. Cummins Diesel Sales Corp., Tokyo, 1957-63; v.p. Lorain Internat., San Juan, P.R., 1964-67; v.p. mktg./mfg. White Motor Internat., Cleve., 1967-70; v.p., gen. mgr. Euclid Internat. (Ohio), 1970-72; exec. v.p., gen. mgr. R.A. Hanson Co., Spokane, Wash., 1972-76; prin. Mulder and Assocs., Seattle, 1976—; v.p. internat., dir. Romac Industries, Seattle. Served with Netherlands Army, 1945-46. Mem. Assn. Netherlands Registered Engrs. Republican. Author handbook. Address: Carriage Row 108 27107 48th Pl S Kent WA 98032

MULLALLY, DANA KONTILIS, construction company executive; b. Dinuba, Calif., Oct. 4, 1951; d. Bill V. and Maxine (Stafford) Kontilis; m. David Smart Mullally, Sept. 3, 1977, (div.); children—Christopher David. B.A., Calif. State U., 1976. Asst. to pres. P.S. Tours, Anaheim, Calif., 1973-75; legal asst. Hoge, Fenton, Jones & Appel, Monterey, Calif., 1976-77; mgr. community assns. Ponderosa Homes, San Ramon, Calif., 1977—. Mem. Community Assns. Inst. (nat. trustee). Office: 3 Crow Oyn Ct San Ramon CA 94583

MULLAN, JACK W., real estate developer; b. Ft. Dodge, Iowa, Sept. 17, 1924; s. Paul B. and Florence (Zeller) M.; B.S., U. So. Calif., 1950; postgrad. U. J.W. Goethe, Frankfurt, Germany, 1953-54; Ph.D., San Gabriel U., 1970; m. Beverly Fortner, Feb. 8, 1951; children—Lori Lee, Jill Ann. Co-Pilot, United Airlines, 1951-53; mgr. Aero Exploration, Frankfurt, Germany, 1954-55; pres. Mullan Real Estate, and other real estate devel. cos., 1955—. Founding chmn. Orange County Econ. and Indsl. Conf., 1959, chmn., 1960; co-chmn. Orange County Econ. Devel. Conf., 1963; bd. dirs. Orange Coast Assn., Project "21"; mem. Orange County Met. Area Com., 1963; chmn. City Newport Beach (Calif.) Air Traffic Adv. Com., 1967-68; financial steering com. Orange County Boy Scouts Am., 1959. Trustee So. Calif. Aviation Council, pres., 1979-81. Served to capt. USAAF, 1942-46; PTO. Mem. Calif. Real Estate Assn. (dir. 1957-65, state chmn. indsl. and comml. div. 1961, regional v.p. 1962), Newport Harbor Bd. Realtors (pres. 1960), Aircraft Owners and Pilots Assn., So. Calif. Aviation Council (chmn. air mus. com. 1974-75), Delta Tau Delta. Co-developer 1st horizontal condominium devel. in Calif. Home: 2031 Mesa Dr Santa Ana Heights CA 92707 Office: 3400 Irvine Newport Beach CA 92660

MULLEN, ANITA ANNE, health physicist; b. Redfield, S.D., Mar. 11, 1933; d. Leo Leroy and Frances Mae (Cutchall) Lewis; B.S., Buena Vista Coll., 1955; student Iowa State U., 1956; m. Omer W. Mullen, Dec. 29, 1956. Radiochemistry technician Westinghouse Electric Corp., Idaho Falls, Idaho, 1958-60; analytical chemist USPHS, Las Vegas, 1960-70; research chemist EPA, Las Vegas, 1970-79, health physicist, 1979—. Mem. Am. Chem. Soc., Health Physics Soc. Contbr. articles to sci. jours. Home: 1989 N Valley Dr Las Vegas NV 89108 Office: PO Box 15027 Las Vegas NV 89114

MULLEN, KATHY ANN MARIE, entertainment and business manager; b. Bronx, N.Y., Jan. 10, 1955; d. William J. and Barbara M. (Newton) M. Student Sheldon Jackson Community Coll., 1974-76. Prodn. asst. The Boeing Co., Seattle, 1978-82; mgr. Sibco, Seattle, 1982—; dir. Entertainment Arts Resources, Seattle; cons. in field. Office: PO Box 5579 Kent WA 98031

MULLER, ROLF HUGO, chemist; b. Aarau, Switzerland, Aug. 6, 1929; came to U.S., 1957, naturalized, 1967; s. Wilhelm and Alice Louise (Schmid) M.; M.S. in Natural Sci., Fed. Inst. Tech., Zurich, Switzerland, 1953; teaching cert., 1955, Ph.D. in Natural Sci. 1957; postgrad. in chem. engring. U. Calif., Berkeley, 1960-61; m. Dorothy Leah Donaldson, July 18, 1962; children—Wilhelm Karl, Alice Barbara. Asst. in phys. chemistry Fed. Inst. Tech., 1955-56; research and devel. chemist E.I. du Pont de Nemours Co., Parkersburg, W.Va., 1957-60; research asso. dept. chem. enging. U. Calif., Berkeley, 1961-62, staff scientist Lawrence Berkeley Lab., 1962-66, prin. investigator, 1966—, asst. div. head, 1970—, staff sr. scientist, 1978—, lectr. univ. dept. chem. engring., 1966—. Mem. Electrochem. Soc. (sect. chmn. 1971, councillor 1976), Internat. Soc. Electrochemistry (div. co-chmn. 1973-77, plenary lectr. Zurich 1976), Swiss Chem. Soc., Optical Soc. Am., AAAS. Clubs: U. Calif. at Berkeley Faculty. Editor books; author articles in field. Home: 36 Highgate Rd Berkeley CA 94707 Office: Lawrence Berkeley Lab U Calif Materials and Molecular Research Div Berkeley CA 94720

MULLIGAN, J. PATRICK, estate planning exec.; b. Delta, Colo., Oct. 3, 1937; s. Milo Edward and Ruth Eloise (Benway) M.; student Adams State Coll., 1955-57; m. Janice Ada Jons, Jan. 14, 1961; children—Shawn Therese, Timothy Bryan, Theodore Simon, Thomas Patrick. With Century Geophys. Corp., Moab, Utah and Casper, Wyo., 1959-72, Western Resources Ins. Co., Casper, 1972-75, Am. Gen. Life Ins. Co., Casper, Wyo., 1975-80; founder Mulligan & Assocs., estate planning, Casper, 1981—. Served with USAF, 1957-59. Mem. Nat. Assn. Campus Ministers, Nat. Assn. Estate Planning Counsels, Nat. Assn. Life Underwriters, Nat. Assn. Charitable Estate Counselors. Republican. Roman Catholic. Home: 2318 Valley Forge Ct Fort Collins CO 80526 Office: 211 W Magnolia Fort Collins CO 80521

MULLIGAN, JOHN MICHAEL, lawyer; b. Herkimer, N.Y., Sept. 18, 1950; s. Arthur Harold and Mary Fleming (Lyng) M. B.A., Ohio No. U., Ada, 1972; J.D., Western State U., Fullerton, Calif., 1978. Bar: Calif. 1979, U.S. Dist. Ct. (no. dist.) Calif. 1981, U.S. Dist. Ct. (ea. dist.) Calif. 1980. Sole practice, Santa Cruz, Calif., 1979—. Mem. Calif. Bar Assn., Santa Cruz County Bar Assn. Roman Catholic.

MULLIGAN, ROBERT PATRICK, film dir., producer; b. N.Y.C.; s. Robert Edward and Elizabeth (Gingell) M.; B.A., Fordham U.; m. Sandy Leeds. Dir. TV shows Playhouse 90, Philco Playhouse, Suspence, 1951-60; dir., producer films To Kill a Mockingbird, Summer of 42, Same Time Next Year, Inside Daisy Clover, Up the Down Staircase, The Other, Love with the Proper Stranger, Stalking Moon. Office: William Morris Agy 151 El Camino Beverly Hills CA 90212

MULLIKIN, HARRY L., hotel management company executive; b. Hot Springs, Ark., Apr. 27, 1927; s. William E. and LaVerne (Harper) M.; m. Virginia Mullikin, Nov. 26, 1951; children—Michael, Patricia Mullikin Diers, Scott, Kelly; m. 2d, Judith Ann Mullikin, July 25, 1970. Student Wash. State U., U. Wash. With Westin Hotels, 1953—, asst. v.p., dir. food and beverage, 1961-63, v.p., mng. dir. Century Plaza, 1963-70, sr. v.p., 1970-71, exec. v.p., 1971-73, pres., 1973-77, pres., chief exec. officer, 1977-81, chmn., chief exec. officer, 1981—, also dir.; dir. UAL, Inc., United Airlines, Seafirst Corp., Seattle-First Nat. Bank. Bd. dirs. Virginia Mason Hosp.; trustee Seattle U.; mem. adv. bd. U. Wash. Grad. Sch. Bus.; mem. travel and tourism council Seattle Com. on Commerce, Sci. and Transp. Served with USAAF, 1945-48. Recipient Golden Plate award Internat. Foodservice Mfrs. Assn., 1972; Alumni Achievement award Wash. State U., 1976. Mem. Mgmt. Policy Council, Am. Hotel and Motel Assn. (resort com.). Republican. Roman Catholic. Clubs: Seattle, Rainier, Corinthian Yacht. Home: 1219 NW Elford Dr Seattle WA 98177 Office: Westin Bldg Seattle WA 98121

MULLINS, RUTH GLADYS, nurse; b. Westville, N.S., Can., Aug. 25, 1943; d. William G. and Gladys H.; came to U.S., 1949, naturalized, 1955; student Tex. Womans U., 1961-64; B.S. in Nursing, Calif. State U., Long Beach, 1966; M.Nursing, UCLA, 1973; m. Leonard E. Mullins, Aug. 27, 1963; children—Deborah R., Catherine M., Leonard III. Pub. health nurse, Los Angeles County Health Dept., 1967-68; nurse Meml. Hosp. Med. Center, Long Beach, 1968-72; dir. pediatric nurse practitioner program Calif. State U., Long Beach, 1973—, asst. prof., 1975-80, asso. prof., 1980—, health service credential coordinator Sch. Nursing, chmn. grad. yr. one, 1979—; mem. Calif. Maternal, Child and Adolescent Health Bd., 1977—. Tng. grantee HHS, Calif. Dept. Health; cert. pediatric nurse practitioner. Fellow Nat. Assn. Pediatric Nurse Assos. and Practitioners; mem. Am. Pub. Health Assn., Calif. Assn. Pediatric Nurse Practitioners and Assocs., Am. Assn. U. Faculty, Ambulatory Pediatric Assn. Democrat. Methodist. Author: (with B. Nelms) Growth and Development: A Primary Health Care Approach. Home: 6382 Heil Ave Huntington Beach CA 92647 Office: Dept Nursing 1250 Bellflower Blvd Long Beach CA 90802

MULRYAN, JAMES DONALD, mining engr.; b. Santa Maria, Calif., Apr. 1, 1929; s. Henry and Marian Abigail (Trist) M.; student Stanford U., 1946-49; Mining Engr., Colo. Sch. of Mines, 1954; m. Lois Helen Matthews, Sept. 1, 1953; children—Marian D., D. Matthew. Sr. staff engr. Cyprus Mines Corp., Los Angeles, 1965-66; quarry supt. Pfizer, Inc., Lucerne Valley, Calif., 1967-68, plant supt., Victorville, Calif., 1968-71; prodn. mgr. Cyprus Indsl. Minerals Co., Three Forks, Mont., 1971-76, mgr. mining, Ennis, Mont., 1976-79, mgr. safety and land devel., Three Forks, 1979—; adminstrv. mgr. exploration and mine devel. indsl. minerals Amoco Minerals Co., Englewood, Colo., 1979—. Served from 2d lt. to 1st lt., C.E., U.S. Army, 1955-57. Mem. Am. Inst. Mining Engrs. (chmn. Los Angeles sect. 1968-69). Club: Lions. Home: 10606 Devils Head Littleton CO 80127 Office: Amoco Minerals Co Englewood CO

MULVIN, ROBERT OTIS, mktg. cons.; b. Pasadena, Calif., Mar. 31, 1933; s. Richard Louis and Fortuna Corning (Otis) M.; student U. Colo., 1951; grad. (hon.) Mil. Lang. Inst., 1954; m. Carolyn Margaret Roden, Sept. 7, 1957; children—Carol Lynn, Susan Leah. Sales mgr. Lupton Mfg. Co., 1960-69; sales mgr. Northrop Archtl. Systems, Los Angeles, 1969-73; dir. mktg. Guaranteed Products Co., Los Angeles, 1973-77; v.p. Huntington/Pacific Ceramics, Santa Fe Springs, Calif., 1977-80; v.p., dir. mktg. Covington Technologies, Fullerton, Calif., 1980-82; internat. mktg. cons., 1982—. Pres., Americanism Athletics Found., Inc., Pasadena, Calif.; committeeman Pasadena Tournament of Roses, 1961—. Served with U.S. Army, 1953-56. Named Altadena (Calif.) Outstanding Citizen, 1969, Jr. C. of C. Outstanding Citizen, 1971. Mem. Nat. Assn. Home Builders, Am. Mgmt. Assn., Constrn. Specifications Inst., Ceramic Tile Inst., Nat. Rifle Assn. Republican. Episcopalian. Clubs: Mission Viejo Country, Exchange of Altadena (dir. 1973). Home: 24661 Venablo Ln Mission Viejo CA 92691 Office: 17811 Mitchell St Irvine CA 92714

MUMFORD, DAVID EARL, entertainment industry executive; b. Chgo., June 2, 1954; s. Earl Milham and Amm Miriam (Paulsrud) M. B.S., Northwestern U., 1976. Research analyst Katz Agy., N.Y.C., 1976-79; asst. program dir. Sta. KTLA-TV, Los Angeles, 1979-81; syndication researcher Paramount Pictures Corp., Los Angeles, 1981-82; v.p. TV research Columbia Pictures Inc., Los Angeles, 1982—. Mem. Hollywood Radio and TV Soc., Waifs Orgn., Am. Film Inst., Internat. Radio and TV Soc. Lutheran. Office: Columbia Pictures Inc 15250 Ventura Blvd Sherman Oaks CA 91403

MUMFORD, EMILY HAMILTON, med. sociologist; b. Cape Girardeau, Mo., Dec. 19, 1922; d. Barney A. and Dola (Stolzer) Hamilton; A.B., U. Tulsa, 1941; M.A., Columbia U., 1958, Ph.D., 1963. Research asst. Bur. Applied Social Research, Columbia U., N.Y.C., 1958-59; instr., maj. adv. Hunter Coll., N.Y.C., 1960-64; vis. prof. behavioral and social scis. New Coll., Sarasota, Fla., 1965-66; asst. prof. sociology in psychiatry Mt. Sinai Sch. Medicine, N.Y.C., 1966-68, asso. prof., 1968-73, cons. dept. psychiatry, 1969-71; asso. prof. sociology Grad. Center, City U. N.Y., N.Y.C., 1968-73, prof. sociology grad. program in med. sociology Lehman Coll., 1973-74; prof. psychiatry Downstate Med. Center, SUNY, Bklyn., 1974-77, spl. asst. to dean, 1976-77, cons. nat. survey renal patients, 1972, cons. med. edn., 1977, cons. edn. in ethics, 1978; prof. psychiatry and preventive medicine Med. Center U. Colo., Denver, 1977—, mem. admissions com., 1978—; assoc. cons. in sociology to sci. adv. staff St. Luke's Hosp., N.Y.C., 1961; task force on studies devel. United Hosp. Fund N.Y., 1969-71; cons. Inst. for Study of Health and Soc., Georgetown, Md., 1972; co-chmn. panel, conf. on cancer rehab. Nat. Cancer Inst., Washington, 1972; mem. colloquium Am. Assn. Med. Colls., Washington, 1974; cons. on evaluation, dept. medicine Montefiore Hosp., N.Y.C., 1977; cons. Random House, 1978; cons., site visitor psychiat. edn. br. NIMH, 1978, mem. adv. council, 1979—. Mem. adv. com. for agreements between U. Riyadh (Saudi Arabia) and U. Colo. Travel grantee Milbank Meml. Fund, 1969; grantee Commonwealth Fund, 1968-70, NIMH, 1975-76, 77, project dir. HEW, 1978. Fellow Am. Pub. Health Assn., Am. Sociol. Assn. (med. sociology sect.), Am. Psychiat. Assn. (hon.); mem. Sigma Xi. Author: Interns: From Students to Physicians, 1970; (with J. Skipper, Jr.) Sociology in Hospital Care, 1967; editor Academic Guide, 1976-77; asso. editor Jour. Health and Social Behavior, 1976—; cons. TV health series, 1976; contbr. invited book reviews to profl. publs.; reviewer manuscripts for pubs.; contbr. articles to profl. publs. Home: 6925 E Exposition Denver CO 80224 Office: 4200 E 9th Ave Box C268 Denver CO 80262

MUMMA, SHARON LEE, insurance executive; b. Visalia, Calif., Feb. 13, 1943; d. Charles J. and Gertrude J. (Horan) Stanley; m. Eric J. Mumma, Mar. 11, 1961; children—Tina, Todd, Katy. Student Coll. Sequoias, Am. Coll., Bryn Mawr, 1960-83. Legal and exec. sec., Calif., Tenn., 1964-73; adminstrv. asst. ins., State College, Pa., 1974-75; career ins. agt., registered rep., State College, 1975-78; owner, operator ins. and securities firm, Exeter, Calif., 1978—. Bd. dirs. Tulare County Econ. Devel. Corp., 1983; active various polit. campaigns. Named to Million Dollar Round Table; recipient nat. sales achievement awards, nat. quality awards. Mem. Nat. Assn. Life Underwriters, Tulare/Kings County Assn. Life Underwriters, Provident Mut. Leaders Assn., Exeter C. of C. (pres. 1982). Republican. Presbyterian. Clubs: Exeter Golf; Sequoia Racketball (Visalia). Home: 707 W Pine St Exeter CA 93221 Office: 160 N E St Exeter CA 93221

MUNDAY, CLAUDE STEPHEN, neuropsychologist, clinical psychologist; b. San Francisco, Sept. 22, 1949; s. Charles Benton and Anna Lorraine (Ehle) M.; m. Susan Emma LaRue, May 2, 1981; 1 dau., Jessica. B.A. in Psychology, U. Calif.-Berkeley, 1970; M.S. in Counseling, Calif. State U.-Hayward, 1977; Ph.D., Calif. Sch. Profl. Psychology, 1979. Lic. psychologist, Calif. Specialist, USAF Psychiat. Clinic, Tachikawa, Japan, 1970-74; counselor VA, San Francisco, 1975; counselor Office of Vets. Affairs, Calif. State U., Hayward, 1975-77; psychologist Santa Clara Valley Med. Ctr., San Jose, Calif., 1976-81; pvt. practice neuropsychology, San Jose, 1981—; cons. rehab. unit St. Francis Meml. Hosp., San Francisco; mem. adv. bd. Head Trauma Support Project, Sacramento Sci. Adv. Council; mem. adv. bd. Family Survival Project Brain Damaged Adults, San Francisco. Mem. Am. Psychol. Assn., Internat. Neuropsychol. Soc. Home: 39652 Buena Vista Terrace Fremont CA 94538 Office: 925 W Hedding San Jose CA 95126

MUNDELL, JAMES ASA, clergyman; b. Pinkstaff, Ill., Feb. 14, 1922; s. Charles Simeon and Carolyn (McBride) M.; B.A., Kans. Wesleyan U., 1948; Th.M., Iliff Sch. Theology, 1952; postgrad. U. Oreg., 1957, Portland State U., 1968, Oreg. Scarritt Coll., 1965; m. Gwenda Jane McIntosh, Sept. 5, 1948; children—Kathryn Lea, Rebecca Sue, Laurel Ann. Ordained to ministry United Methodist Ch., 1953; minister, Ely and Ruth, Nev., 1953-55, Coburg, Roseburg, Seaside and Eugene, Oreg., 1955-65; program counselor Oreg. Ann. Conf., United Meth. Ch., Portland, Oreg., 1965-70; pastor Christ Ch., Portland, 1970-77; dir. communications adult and children's Christian Edn. Media Ctr., Oreg.-Idaho Ann. Conf., United Meth. Ch., Portland, 1977-83; ednl. cons., 1977-83. Pres., Infinity Photo Arts Group, Beaverton, Oreg., 1981-82. Recipient Jason Lee award Oreg.-Idaho Ann. Conf. United Meth. Ch., 1979. Mem. Christian Educators Fellowship, United Meth. Assn. Communicators, N.W. Assn. Christian Educators. Democrat. Editor The United Methodist, 1965-70, 77-83. Home: 5420 SW 18th Ave Beaverton OR 97005 Office: 1505 SW 18th Ave Portland OR 97201

MUNDY, PETER CLIVE, psychologist; b. Trinidad, W.I., May 13, 1954; came to U.S., 1957; s. Philip Augustus and Daphne (Hyde) M.; B.A., Stockton State Coll., 1976; M.A., U. Miami, 1979, Ph.D., 1981. Research assoc. U. Miami (Fla.), 1979-81; postdoctoral fellow Clin.

Research Ctr. for Childhood Psychosis, UCLA, 1981-83; ind. research psychologist Neuropsychiat. Inst., 1983—. NIMH grantee, 1983-86. Mem. Am. Psychol. Assn. Office: Neuropsychiatric Inst UCLA 760 Westwood Plaza Los Angeles CA 90024

MUNGER, JOHN ARTHUR, banker; b. Fremont, Ohio, Oct. 6, 1934; s. Arthur J. and Mary D. (Gropp) M.; m. Helen Skok, 1959; children—Michelle, Chris, Lynn, Robin; m. 2d, Janet La Bounty, June 14, 1981. Student Ariz. State U., 1961, Mortgage Banking Sch., Stanford U. 1967, Pacific State Banking Sch. 1968. Credit mgr. Sears Roebuck & Co., Phoenix, 1958-60; with Orange County Title Co., Los Angeles, 1960-61, Dwyer Curlett Mortgage Banker Co., Los Angeles, 1961-66, First Western Bank (now Lloyds Bank), Los Angeles, 1966-72; pres. Continental Bank, 1972-82, exec. v.p., dir. Continental Bank div. Tokai Bank Calif., Alhambra, 1972—; dir. Am. Pacific Securities. Past commr. City of Claremont (Calif.) Planning Commn.; bd. dirs. UCLA, Citrus Coll. Mem. Calif. Bankers Assn. (chmn. real estate lending com.), Independent Bankers Assn. (past dir.). Club: Kiwanis, Alhambra (past pres.) Office: 333 S Garfield Ave Alhambra CA 91801

MUNGER, JOHN FRANCIS, lawyer; b. Sioux City, Iowa, Dec. 18, 1946; s. Robert Prentis and Charlotte (Watkin) M.; m. Roseann Kitzinger, Dec. 24, 1982; m. Patricia Gilkeson, July 18, 1969; children—Meredith Ellen, Hilary Katherine. B.A., Stanford U., 1969; J.D., U. Ariz., 1973. Bar: Ariz. 1974. Ptnr., Veity, Smith, Lacy, Allen & Kearns, P.C., Tucson, 1974-77, Munger & Munger, 1977—; judge pro tem Pima County Superior Ct., 1982-83; lectr. law U. Ariz., 1974-75. Chmn., Ariz. Republican Party, 1983-84; mem. Rep. Nat. Com., 1983-84; gen. counsel Pima County Rep. Central Com., 1980-83; spl. counsel Ariz. Senate Judiciary Com. for Elections Investigations, 1980-81; bd. dirs. Jr. Achievement Tucson, 1977-79, com. chmn., 1981—; bd. dirs. Goodwill Industries Tucson, 1976-77, Tucson So. Counties Mental Health Services, 1975-77; mem. vestry St. Alban's Episcopal Ch., 1974-75, 77-78, 79-80; mem. Ariz. Mexico Commn., 1975-80; bd. dirs. Ariz. Opera Co., 1977-79. Mem. ABA, Ariz. Bar Assn., Pima County Bar Assn., Order of Coif. Served with AUS, 1969-71. Club: Tucson Country. Note editor Ariz. Law Rev., 1972-73. Home: 6240 E River Rd Tucson AZ 85715 Office: 120 W Broadway 168 Tucson AZ 85701

MUÑIZ, VICTOR ANTHONY, state agency administrator; b. Los Angeles, June 13, 1945; s. Victor Emilio and Olga Anita (Rodriquez) M.; m. Alexandria Cruz, July 1, 1972; children—Allyson, Antonio, Alejandro, Andres. A.A., Cerritos Coll., 1971; B.S. in Internat. Relations, Calif. State U.-Los Angeles, 1973, M.S. in Public Adminstrn., Health and Safety, 1981. With AMF Voit, Santa Ana, Calif., 1967; with Deportive Indsl., Mex., 1969; adminstrv. asst. to pres., mgr. safety and ins. Jacob. Constructors Inc., Pasadena, Calif., 1975-83; dep. chief for safety Calif. Div. of Occupational Safety and Health, 1983—. Day chmn. Cancer Benefit Community Hosp. San Gabriel (Calif.), 1980—; mem. Calif. Republican Hispanic Council, 1982. Recipient Coll. Federal Council award for scholastic achievement, 1973. Served to sgt. USMC, 1965-81. Mem. Nat. Constructors Assn., Am. Soc. Safety Engrs. Republican. Roman Catholic. Clubs: Toastmasters Internat., La Mirada Marine Assn. Office: Jacobs Constructors Inc 251 S Lake Ave Pasadena CA 91101

MUNN, HECTOR JOHN, JR., chemist, educator; b. Index, Wash., Feb. 7, 1930; s. Hector John and Pearl Marie (Bond) M.; B.S., Seattle Pacific U., 1952; postgrad. Azusa Pacific Coll., 1954-55, Claremont Coll., 1955-56; M.S., Oreg. State U., 1960, Ph.D., 1970; m. Verna E. Rice, June 12, 1953; children—James Hector, Bruce Stewart. Tchr., Pasadena (Calif.) City Schs., 1957-58; mem. faculty George Fox Coll., Newberg, Oreg., 1958-62, 67—, registrar, 1977—. Served with U.S. Army, 1952-55. Mem. Am. Chem. Soc. (sec. Portland sect.), Oreg. Sci. Tchrs. Assn., Am. Sci. Affiliate. Quaker. Home: 1314 E North Newberg OR 97132 Office: George Fox Coll Newberg OR 97132

MUNN, WILLIAM CHARLES, II, psychiatrist; b. Flint, Mich., Aug. 9, 1938; s. Elton Albert and Rita May (Coykendall) M.; student Flint Jr. Coll., 1958-59, U. Detroit, 1959-61; M.D., Wayne State U., 1965; m. Deborah Lee Munn, 1983; children by previous marriage—Jude Michael, Rachel Marie, Alexander Winston. Intern David Grant USAF Med. Center, Travis AFB, Calif., 1965-66; resident in psychiatry Letterman Army Hosp., San Francisco, 1967-70; practice medicine, specializing in psychiatry, Fairfield, Calif., 1972—; chief in-patient psychiatry David Grant Med. Center, 1970-71, chmn. dept. mental health, 1971-72; psychiat. cons. Fairfield-Suisun Unified Sch. Dist., 1971—, Fairfield Hosp. and Clinic, 1971, Intercommunity Hosp., Fairfield, 1971—, Casey Family Program, 1980—, Solano County Coroner's Office, 1981; asst. clin. prof. psychiatry U. Calif., San Francisco, 1976—; cons. VA Hosp., San Francisco, 1976, David Grant USAF Hosp., 1976. Served to maj., M.C., USAF, 1964-72, flight surgeon, chief public health, chief phys. exam. center McGuire AFB, N.J., 1966-67. Diplomate Am. Bd. Psychiatry and Neurology (examiner). Mem. Am. Psychiat. Assn., No. Calif. Psychiat. Soc., E. Bay Psychiat. Assn. Home: 450 Ridgewood Dr Martinez CA 94553 Office: 1245 Travis Blvd Suite E Fairfield CA 94533

MUNOZ, SHARON RUTH, systems analyst; b. Los Angeles, Nov. 1, 1945; d. Roosevelt and Gladys Hortense (Preuitt) Jones; m. Henry John Munoz, Oct. 9, 1971 (div.); children—Henry John, Acheera-Hortensia Kezar. Student San Jose State Coll., 1963-66; B.A. in Sociology, Pepperdine Coll., 1968. Social worker Los Angeles County, 1968-70, systems/work measurement analyst, 1970-82; systems method analyst Beneficial Standard Life Ins. Co., Los Angeles, 1982-83; systems analyst Northrop Corp., Hawthorne, Calif., 1983—. Mem. Am. Inst. Indsl. Engrs., Assn. Systems Mgmt. Democrat. Presbyterian. Club: Pasadena Folk Dance Co-op. Office: One Northrop Ave Hawthorne CA 90250

MUNRO, ALAN ROSS, museum director; b. Mineola, N.Y., Dec. 2, 1932; s. Duncan Ross and Ethel Vance (Burdett) M.; student U. Vt., 1951-52, U. Tenn., 1959-60, Scarritt (Tenn.) Coll., 1968-69; m. Constance Francis Lozon, Sept. 26, 1951; children—Duncan, Peter, Donald, Carol, Jean, Meg. Exhibits specialists Shelburne (Vt.) Mus., 1950-56, Am. Mus. Natural History, N.Y.C., 1956-59; chief dept. interpretive art Children's Mus., Nashville, 1959-71; instr. art Fisk U., Nashville, 1970-71; dir. Alaska State Mus., Juneau, 1972—. Charter mem. Juneau chpt. Nat. Audubon Soc. Mem. Western Museums Conf., Am. Assn. Museums, Alaska Hist. Soc. Unitarian. Art work represented in pub. and pvt. collections. Office: Pouch FM Juneau AK 99811

MUNRO, RALPH DAVIES, state ofcl.; b. Bainbridge Island, Wash., June 25, 1943; s. George Alexander and Elizabeth (Troll) M.; B.A. in Polit. Sci. and Edn., Western Wash. U., 1966; m. Karen Hanson, Feb. 17, 1973; 1 son, George Alexander. Indsl. engr. The Boeing Co., 1966-68; sales mgr. Continental Host, Inc., 1969; vol. coordinator State of Wash., Olympia, 1970-71, spl. asst. to gov., 1971-76, sec. of state, 1980—; asst. dept. dir. ACTION Agy., 1970; gen. mgr. Tillicum Enterprises & Food Services, Seattle, 1977—; pres. N.W. Highlands Tree Farm, Bainbridge Island, 1975—. Mem. Nat. Assn. Secs. of State, Nat. Assn. Retarded Citizens, Wash. State Historic Mus. (dir. 1980), Wash. State Trust for Historic Preservation, Nature Conservancy. Republican. Lutheran. Clubs: Rotary (founder, pres. Youth Job Employment Center for Seattle), Olympia Highlanders Pipe Band. Office: Legislative Bldg Olympia WA 98504

MUNROE, MARY JEANNE, educator, consultant; b. Rockwell, Iowa, July 20, 1934; d. Richard Francis and Mary Maxine (Brady) Murphy; m. Richard Allen Munroe, June 14, 1958; children—Scot David, Kristen Marie, Michael Richard. B.S. with honors, Wash. State U., 1956; M.Home Econs. Edn., U. Ariz., 1974, Ed.D., 1978. Cert. secondary teaching, secondary adminstrn. Tchr./counselor, Ephrata, Wash., 1956-58, El Segundo, Calif., 1958-59, Eugene, Oreg., 1959-66, Tucson, 1966-73; prin., Tucson, 1973-76; secondary tchr., Tucson, 1976-77; ednl. county agt. Globe, Ariz., 1977-80; asst. vis. prof. secondary edn., dir. Project Mainstream, U. Ariz., Tucson, 1980—; participant North Central Accreditation Team; asst. dir. Desegregation Inst., ednl. county agt. Ariz. Tchr. Residency Program; cons. in field. Active recruitment Amigos de las Americas, 1980-83, Internat. Yr. of the Disabled Commn. Recipient various grants. Mem. Assn. Supervision and Curriculum Devel., Ariz. Assn. Tchr. Educators, Assn. Tchr. Educators, Mortar Board (advisor), Phi Delta Kappa, Phi Kappa Phi, Omicron Nu, Pi Lambda Theta. Contbr. articles to profl. publs. Home: 4442 E Blacklidge Dr Tucson AZ 85712 Office: Adminstrn Amphitheatre Sch Dist Tucson AZ 85719

MUNSCHY, DOROTHY GENEVIEVE, mfg. co. exec.; b. Manteca, Calif., Dec. 3, 1922; d. Manuel A. and Mary E. (Silva) Lopes; student Bakersfield Community Coll., 1975, Calif. State U., Bakersfield; m. Roy Charles Munschy, Jan. 31, 1942; children—Charleyne Dianne Branson, Michelle Marie O'Neal. Office mgr. Valley Wide Service Center, Bakersfield, Calif., 1966-78; real estate salesperson, Bakersfield, 1967-77; pres. Etta-Kit Enterprises, Bakersfield, 1971-82, propr. Big Foot Splty. Footwear div., 1982—, also chmn. bd. Etta-Kit Enterprises; cons. new product devel., domestic and internat. mktg. Mem. Bakersfield C. of C. Patentee in field. Office: 217 Mount Vernon Ave 3 Bakersfield CA 93307

MUNSON, ALEXANDER LEE, management consultant; b. Hempstead, N.Y., Aug. 22, 1931; s. Alexander Lawrence and Bertha Louise (Geer) M.; B.A., Amherst Coll., 1953; M.B.A., Harvard, 1960; m. Betty Sue Shideler, Dec. 14, 1957 (div. June 1978); children—Eric Lawrence, Genevieve Sue, Anna Lee. Mgmt. trainee, credit analyst Mellon Nat. Bank & Trust Co., Pitts., 1953-54; asso. Cresap, McCormick & Paget, mgmt. cons., N.Y.C., 1960-62; financial adv. internat. finance Mobil Oil Corp., N.Y.C., 1962-64, Melbourne, Australia, 1964-65, mgr. spl. projects, N.Y.C., 1965-66, mgr. treasury reports and analysis, 1966-67, treas. Mobil Latin Am. Inc., N.Y.C., 1968-70; v.p.-treas. Fairchild Camera & Instrument Co., Mountain View, Calif., 1971-72, Crown Zellerbach Corp., San Francisco, 1972-82; pres. A.L. Munson & Co., 1982—. Mem. Mayor's Fin. Adv. Com., 1976—, exec. com., 1981—; bd. dirs. San Francisco Planning and Urban Research Assn. Served to lt. USCGR, 1954-64. Recipient SBA Advocate of Yr. award, 1976. Mem. Harvard Bus. Sch. Assn. of No. Calif. (exec. v.p. 1977—, founder, chmn. minority bus. cons. group 1971-75), Financial Execs. Inst., Phi Gamma Delta. Republican. Presbyterian. Club: University. Home: 3369 Jackson St San Francisco CA 94118 Office: 1 Bush St San Francisco CA 94119

MUNSON, ANNE CLARK, personnel administrator; b. Easton, Md., Sept. 18, 1944; d. Harry Ellwood and Ellen Lenore (Chaffinch) Clark; m. Stephen Andrew Munson, Mar. 27, 1971. Student Converse Coll., 1962-63; secretarial degree Katharine Gibbs Sch., 1965. Sec. CIA, 1965; sec. to Congressmen Rogers Morton, William O. Mills, Robert Bauman, to former Vice Pres. Spiro T. Agnew, Washington, 1969-75; sec. Lillick McHose & Charles, San Francisco, 1980-81, personnel adminstr., 1981—. Republican. Episcopalian. Office: Lillick McHose & Charles Two Embarcadero Ctr Suite 2600 San Francisco CA 94111

MUNSON, JOHN BACKUS, engring. co. exec.; b. Chgo., May 1, 1933; s. Mark Frame and Catherine Louise (Cherry) M.; B.A., Knox Coll., 1955; m. Anne Lorraine Cooper, July 6, 1957; children—David B., Sharon A. With System Devel. Corp., Santa Monica, Calif., 1957—, v.p. corp. software engring., 1977-81, corp. v.p. tech. ops., 1981—; mem. U.S. Air Force Sci. Adv. Bd., 1981—; disting. visitor IEEE Computer Soc., 1981—. Served to capt. U.S. Army, 1955-57. Mem. IEEE (sr. mem.; editor Trans. on Software Engring. 1982—), U.S. Army Assn., Nat. Security Indsl. Assn. Home: 19541 Greenbriar Dr Tarzana CA 91356 Office: 2500 Colorado Ave Santa Monica CA 90406

MUNSON, LUCILLE MARGUERITE (MRS. ARTHUR E. MUNSON), real estate broker; b. Norwood, Ohio, Mar. 26, 1914; d. Frank and Fairy (Wicks) Wirick; R.N., Lafayette (Ind.) Home Hosp., 1937; A.B., San Diego State U., 1963, student Purdue U., Kans. Wesleyan U.; m. Arthur E. Munson, Dec. 24, 1937; children—Barbara Munson Papke, Judith Munson Andrews, Edmund Arthur. Staff and pvt. nurse Lafayette Home Hosp., 1937-41; indsl. nurse Lakey Foundry & Machine Co., Muskegon, Mich., 1950-51, Continental Motors Corp., Muskegon, 1951-52; nurse Girl Scout Camp, Grand Haven, Mich., 1948-49; owner Munson Realty, San Diego, 1964—. Mem. San Diego County Grand Jury, 1975-76, 80-81; charter mem. Calif. Grand Jurors Assn. Mem. San Diego Bd. Realtors. Presbyterian. Home: 3538 Esterlina Dr Fallbrook CA 92028 Office: Suite 102 2999 Mission Blvd San Diego CA 92109

MUNSON, RICHARD ALLEN, lawyer; b. Conrad, Mont., Feb. 9, 1952; s. Lawrence Elmer and Elizabeth Irene Munson; m. Sharon Kay McFarland, July 4, 1980. B.A. with honors in Philosophy, Mont. State U., 1974; J.D., U. San Diego, 1977; LL.M., U. Denver, 1979. Bar: Calif. 1977, Mont. 1977, Colo. 1978. Assoc. Aronow, Anderson, Beatty & Lee, Shelby, Mont., 1978-80, ptnr., Denver, 1981—. Mem. ABA (taxation sect., corp., banking, bus. law sect.). Democrat. Contbr. article to legal jour. Office: Aronow Anderson Beatty Lee 1512 Larimer St Suite 560 Denver CO 80202

MUNTER, PAMELA OSBORNE, psychologist; b. Santa Monica, Calif., Mar. 27, 1943; d. Eric John and Frances Margo (Dellinger) Osborne; B.A., U. Calif. at Berkeley, 1964; M.A., Calif. State U. at Northridge, 1966; M.A., Calif. State U. at Los Angeles, 1969; Ph.D., U. Nebr., 1972; m. Leo J. Munter; Aug. 2, 1970 (div. 1979); 1 son, Aaron Leonard. Instr. Calif. State U. at Northridge, 1967-69; postdoctoral intern Mendota State Hosp., Madison, Wis., 1972-73; asst. prof. Portland (Oreg.) State U., 1973-76, assoc. prof., 1976-80; pvt. practice clin. psychology, Beaverton, Oreg., 1973—; dir. admissions Oreg. Grad. Sch. Profl. Psychology, also bd. dirs. Cons. to schs. in community psychology. NSF grantee, 1970; Nebr. Sch. for Alcohol Studies grantee, 1971. Mem. Am., Oreg., Portland psychol. assns., Oreg. Acad. Profl. Psychologists, Soc. for Personality Assessment, Western Psychol. Assn. (com. on status of women). Democrat. Jewish. Cons. editor Jour. Personality Assessment. Founding editor Oreg. Psychologist. Contbr. articles to profl. jours. Home: 1970 SW Pheasant Dr Beave Office: 3800 SW Cedar Hills Blvd Beaverton OR 97005

MUNTZ, ERIC PHILLIP, aerospace engineer, radiologist, educator; b. Hamilton, Ont., Can., May 18, 1934; s. Eric Percival and Marjorie Louise (Weller) M.; m. Joyce Mitchell, May 20, 1956 (div.); m. 2d, Janice Margaret Furey, Oct. 22, 1964; children—Sabrina, Eric. B.A., U. Toronto, (Ont.), 1956, M.A., 1957, Ph.D., 1961. Group leader Gen. Electric Co., Valley Forge, Pa., 1961-69; assoc. prof. aerospace engring U. So. Calif., Los Angeles, 1969-71, prof., 1971-74, prof. depts. aerospace engineering, radiology, 1974—; cons., researcher in field. Active San Gabriel Valley Council 1978—. Served with Can. Armed Forces, 1956-61, Recipient Johnny Copp trophy, U. Toronto, 1956; named Interprovincial Rugby Football Union all-star, 1959. Fellow AIAA, mem. AAAS, Am. Assn. Physicists in Medicine. Contbr. articles to profl. jours.; patentee in field. Home: 1560 E Calif Blvd Pasadena CA 91106 Office: Dept Aerospace Engring U So Calif University Park Los Angeles CA

MUNZER, RUDOLPH JAMES, gas co. exec.; b. Mpls., Mar. 9, 1918; s. William Warren and Myrtle T. (Drysdale) M.; B.A., Stanford, 1940; m. Daphne Donohue, June 29, 1946; children—Daniel, Anne, William. Vice pres. Andrews Butane Co., Long Beach, Calif., 1946-54; with Petrolane Inc., Signal Hill, Calif., 1954—, exec. v.p., gen. mgr., 1955-57, pres., 1957-71, chmn. bd., 1971—, also chief exec. officer; trustee Cash Mgmt. Trust Am.; dir. First Am. Title Ins. Co., Bond Fund Am., Inc., Tax-Exempt Bond Fund Am., Investment Co. Am., Los Angeles, Beckman Instruments, Inc., Chubb Corp., N.Y.C. Bd. dirs. Long Beach Meml. Hosp., St. Anthony High Sch. Found., Jones Found. Served to lt. USNR, 1942-45. Mem. Calif. C. of C. (dir.), Nat. Liquefied Petroleum Gas Assn. (pres. 1960, hon. bd. dirs.). Clubs: Virginia Country (Long Beach); California (Los Angeles); Pauma Country (Pauma-San Diego County). Office: Petrolane Inc 1600 Hill St Long Beach CA 90806

MURDOCH, WILLIAM RICHARD, TV exec.; b. Salt Lake City, Oct. 19, 1931; s. David L. and Ora M. (Clark) M.; B.S., U. Utah, 1957; m. Arthell Wilkins, June 11, 1953; children—Deborah, Alison, Rosemary, Matthew. With KSL-TV, Salt Lake City, 1950—, v.p. sales and mktg., 1978-82, v.p., sta. mgr., gen. sales mgr., 1982—; faculty U. Utah, Salt Lake City, 1963-64. Pres., Forest Meadow Landowners Assn., 1974-78; v.p. Pine and Forest Meadow Landowners Assn., 1980—; bd. dirs. Salt Lake City chpt. ARC, 1980—; bishop Mormon Ch., 1968-73, mem. High Council, 1966-68, 74-79. Served with U.S. Army, 1953-55; Korea. Mem. Sales and Mktg. Execs. of Utah (pres. 1978-79). Republican. Clubs: Univ., Salt Lake Ad. Office: KSL-TV Broadcast House Salt Lake City UT 84111

MURDOCK, JOHN CAREY, insurance agent, economist; b. Blackwell, Okla., Dec. 10, 1922; s. Frank Elbert and Nannine Esther (Watt) M.; m. Nancy Jean Boardman, Oct. 15, 1949; children—John Boardman, Robert Carey. B.A., U. Okla., Norman, 1947; M.S. in Econs., U. Wis.-Madison, 1951, Ph.D. in Econs., 1955. Mem. faculty, U. Miss., Columbia, 1951-78, instr. in econs., 1951-53, prof. econs., 1958, chmn. dept. econs. 1963-65, dir. research adminstrn., 1967-71, dean grad. sch., 1967-71; owner, mgr., The John Murdock Agy. (ins., fin.), DuBois, Wyo., 1978—; pres., chmn. bd. Timbered Hills Corp., DuBois; chmn. bd. Rocky Mountain Enterprises, DuBois. vis. prof. Massey U., New Zealand, 1972-73. Bd. dirs. Urban Relocation, Columbia, 1963-65, Wyo. Council for Humanities, 1982. Served to lt. with USNR, 1942-45. U. Mo. fellow, 1957, Gulf Refining Co. fellow, 1958; NASA grantee, 1963-66; NSF grantee, 1966; recipient U. Okla. Coll. Bus. Alumni Citation, 1971. Mem. Am. Econs. Assn., History Polit. Economy Assn., Econ. History Assn., Profl. Ins. Agts. Author: (with J. Graves) Research and Regions, 1967; contbr. articles to profl. jours.

MURDOCK, JOHN WILSON, aerospace engineer; b. Cedar City, Utah, July 29, 1941; s. Wilson and Faith (Stevenson) M.; m. Sandra Evelyn Sandstrom, June 9, 1964; children—Cynthia M., John G. S.B., MIT, 1964, S.M., 1964, M.E., 1965, Sc.D., 1967. Mem. tech. staff Aerospace Corp., San Bernardino, Calif., 1967-72, El Segundo, Calif., 1972-79, engring. specialist fluid mechanics dept., 1980—; vis. lectr. Univ. Coll. London, 1979-80; cons. Calif. State U.-Long Beach. Mem. Riverside Mountain Rescue Unit, Inc., 1970-72. Aerospace Corp. advanced study grantee, London, 1979-80. Assoc. fellow AIAA; mem. ASME, Sigma Xi, Pi Tau Sigma, Tau Beta Pi. Contbr. articles to profl jours. Office: PO Box 92957 Los Angeles CA 90009

MURDOCK, STEVEN KENT, financial consultant; b. Ogden, Utah, May 5, 1946; s. Dell C. and Thea (Johns) M.; children—Margaret Ann, Kristina Thea, Chanon Lorna, Mike, Paul, Lena. A.A., Shasta Coll., 1970; B.S. in Gen. Bus., U. Ariz., 1974; postgrad. Sch. Law, Irvine U., 1974, U. Calif-Irvine, 1973-74, UCLA, 1975-76, Calif. State U.-Hayward, 1979-80. Employed by various companies, 1962-69; credit mgr. Montgomery Ward Co., 1969-75; regional mgr. Saks Fifth Avenue, 1975-76; asst. mgr. and project dir. AMFAC/Liberty House, San Francisco, 1976-78; mng. ptnr. M & M Bus. Services, Castro Valley, Calif., 1978-81; mng. ptnr. MPL Assocs., Castro Valley, 1979—; pres., chief exec. officer Business Inc., 1981—. Del. Calif. Conf. on Small Bus., 1980-82; ombudsman San Francisco dist. SBA, 1981—; bd. dirs. Boys Club of Castro Valley, 1981—; founding mem., bd. dirs. We the People, 1981—. Served with USMC, 1965-68. Decorated Purple Heart; named Boss of Yr., Credit Women of East Bay, 1977. Mem. Calif. Farm Bur., Castro Valley C. of C. (dir., pres. 1982—), Livermore C. of C. Republican. Mormon. Club: Rotary. Author: The Entrepreneurs How To Book, 1981. Home: 6421 Sunnyslope St Castro Vally CA 94546 Office: Business Inc 3601 Jamison Way Castro Valley CA 94546

MURKOWSKI, FRANK HUGHES, U.S. senator; b. Seattle, Mar. 28, 1933; s. Frank Michael and Helen (Hughes) M.; student Santa Clara U., 1952-53; B.A. in Econs., Seattle U., 1955; m. Nancy R. Gore, Aug. 28, 1954; children—Carol Victoria, Lisa Ann, Frank Michael, Eileen Marie, Mary Catherine, Brian Patrick. With Pacific Nat. Bank of Seattle, 1957-59; with Nat. Bank of Alaska, Anchorage, 1959-67, asst. v.p., mgr. Wrangell br., 1963-67, v.p. charge bus. devel., Anchorage, 1965-67; commr. dept. econ. devel. State of Alaska, Juneau, 1967-70; pres. Alaska Nat. Bank of Fairbanks, 1971-80; mem. U.S. Senate from Alaska, 1981—; mem. Fairbanks adv. bd. Alaska Airlines. Vice pres. B.C. and Alaska Bd. Trade; Rep. nominee for U.S. Congress from Alaska, 1970. Served with USCGR, 1955-57. Mem. Am., Alaska (pres. 1973) bankers assns., Young Pres.'s Orgn. (Pacific N.W. chpt.), Alaska (pres. 1977), Anchorage (dir. 1966), B.C., Fairbanks (dir. 1973-78) chambers of commerce. Clubs: Elks, Lions, Wash. Athletic. Office: US Senate Washington DC 20510

MURPHY, BLANCHE MAXINE, speech pathologist; b. Shandon, Ohio, Oct. 22, 1916; d. Elmer P. and Margaret (Hayes) Heitfield; A.A. (Rotary scholar 1954), Ventura Coll., 1954; B.A. in Speech Therapy, Los Angeles State U., 1956; M.A. in Edn., U. Santo Tomas (Philippines), 1970; M.A. in Counseling Psychology, Ball State U., 1975; m. Harry Blaisdell Murphy, Aug. 24, 1952. Tchr., Santa Paula (Calif.) Sch. Dist., 1954-55, speech therapist, 1956-57; speech therapist Oxnard (Calif.) Sch. Dist., 1957-58, Ventura County (Calif.) Schs., 1958-61, Dept. Def. Dependent Schs., Clark Air Base, Republic of Philippines, 1961-70; speech pathologist Dept. Def. Dependent Schs., European Area, Sembach, Germany, 1970-77, Dept. Def. Dependent Schs., Okinawa, Japan, 1977—; speaker edn. seminars, in-service tng. Pacific Area Command Air Force, 1963-70; condr. workshops for Am. tchrs. Am. Sch., Saigon, Viet Nam, 1963. Recipient Ofcl. commendation for outstanding performance Dept. Army, 1976, Outstanding Service and Conduct award Dept. Def. Dependent Schs., Sembach, 1976; Outstanding Contbn. award as sec. of conf. European Council Parents and Students, 1977; lic. speech pathologist State of Calif. Mem. NEA, Am. Speech and Hearing Assn. (cert. clin. competence in speech pathology 1969), Calif. Speech and Hearing Assn., Am. Personnel and Guidance Assn., Overseas Edn. Assn., Pi Lambda Theta. Episcopalian. Author: Speech Improvement for First Grade Children, 1970; Speech Improvement of the Primary School Child Through Ear Training Techniques, 1975. Home: PO Box 833 FPO Seattle WA 98773 also 1804 Parkside Terr Okinawa Japan

MURPHY, BRIAN HOYT, safety director, construction engineer; b. Virginia, Minn., Mar. 11, 1947; s. Daniel Joseph and Ruth Elinor (Hoyt)

M.; m. Carol Davenport, Jan. 4, 1974; m. 2d, Bonnie Doyle, July 2, 1978; 3 children. B.A. in Econs., Dakota Wesleyan U., Mitchell, S.D., 1969. Cert. safety profl., hazard control mgr. Ins. adjuster Gen. Adjustment Bur., Norfolk, Nebr., 1968; safety engr. Stearns Roger Corp., San Manuel and Ajo, Ariz., 1969-73, Indiana, Pa., 1973-74; safety coordinator M. M. Sundt Constrn. Co., Phoenix, 1974-78, safety dir., Tucson, 1978—; lectr. local univs.; mem. adv. bd. Ariz. Center Occupational Safety and Health, U. Ariz.; judge jr. achievement. Mem. Am. Soc. Safety Engrs., Nat. Constructors Assn. (exec. bd.), Nat. Safety Council (exec. bd.). Republican. Roman Catholic. Contbr. articles to indsl. jours. Home: 25 Ave De San Ramon Tucson AZ 85710 Office: M M Sundt Constrn Co PO Box 27507 Tucson AZ 85726

MURPHY, BRIANNE, cinematographer; b. London, Apr. 1, 1937; d. Gerald Leslie and Mary Kathleen (Nobel) M.; m. Ralph Brook, Apr. 1, 1958 (dec.). M.A., Brown U., 1952; student Neighborhood Playhouse, 1952-54. Cinematographer numerous feature films, TV movies and TV series including: Fatso, Father Murphy, Like Mom, Like Me, Before and After, Stone, Cheech & Chong-Nice Dreams, Kaz, Wonder Woman, Trapper John, Little House on the Prairie, Married, others. Recipient Emmy for cinematography Five Finger Discount (NBC Spl.), 1978; Emmy nomination for Cinematography Breaking Away (ABC Series), 1981; Acad. Award for design, concept and manufacture Misi Safety Car and Trailer, 1982. Mem. Am. Soc. Cinematographers, Internat. Alliance Theatrical and Stage Employees, Soc. Motion Picture Technicians and Engrs., Acad. Motion Picture Arts and Scis., Acad. TV Arts and Scis., Am. Film Inst. Home: 10854 Morrison St North Hollywood CA 91601

MURPHY, CARYN MARIA, marketing executive; b. San Bernardino, Calif., Apr. 27, 1957; d. Carl Douglas and Rosemary (Smith) Murphy. B.A. Baylor U., 1979. Regional telephone mktg. dir. Word Inc., Waco, Tex., 1979-81; regional mktg. dir. West Coast div. Thomas Nelson Pub., Inc., Nashville, 1981—. Republican. Office: Elm Hill Pike Nelson Pl Nashville TN 37214

MURPHY, DONALDA JEAN, aerospace manufacturing company executive; b. Troy, N.Y., Feb. 16, 1952; d. Donald Edward and Grace Lorna (Betton) M.; student Kent State U., 1970-72; A.A., Miami Dade Community Coll., 1976; student Fla. Internat. U., 1976-77. Asst. mgr. Isaly's Grocery Chain, Warren, Ohio, 1970-71; exec. sec. Robco Enterprises, Niles, Ohio, 1971-72; cost control clk. Am. Hosp. Supply Corp., Miami, Fla., 1972-74, jr. inventory analyst, 1974-76, sr. inventory analyst/planner, 1976-78; systems mfg. planner Info. Internat. Inc., Culver City, Calif., 1978-80, prodn. control supr., planning supr., 1980; co-founder, asst. dir. The Foresight Group, Encino, Calif., 1980—; prodn. control supr. Aeroquip Corp., Los Angeles, 1981-83; prodn. control mgr. Voi-Shan, Los Angeles, 1983—. Mem. Nat. Assn. Female Execs., Am. Prodn. and Inventory Control Soc., Archeol. Inst. Am. Office: 4001 Inglewood Ave Redondo Beach CA

MURPHY, FRANCIS SEWARD, journalist; b. Portland, Oreg., Sept. 9, 1914; s. Francis H. and Blanche (Livesay) M.; B.A., Reed Coll., 1936; m. Clare Eastham Cooke, Sept. 20, 1974. With The Oregonian, Portland, 1936-79, TV editor, Behind the Mike columnist, 1952-79. Archeol. explorer Mayan ruins, Yucatan, Mex., 1950—, mem. Am. Quintana Roo Expdn., 1965, 66, 68. Served with AUS, 1942-46. Democrat. Congregationalist. Clubs: City (bd. govs. 1950, 64-66); Explorers. Home: 4213 NE 32d Ave Portland OR 97211 also 1102 Tavistock 10 Tregunter Path Hong Kong

MURPHY, FRANKLIN DAVID, physician, educator, publisher; b. Kansas City, Mo., Jan. 29, 1916; s. Franklin E. and Cordelia (Brown) M.; A.B., U. Kans., 1936; M.D., U. Pa., 1941; m. Judith Joyce Harris, Dec. 28, 1940; children—Judith (Mrs. Walter Dickey), Martha (Mrs. Craig Crockwell), Carolyn (Mrs. Reese Milner II), Franklin. Intern, Hosp. U. Pa., 1941-42, instr., 1942-44; instr. medicine U. Kans., 1946-48, dean Sch. Medicine, asso. prof. medicine, 1948-51, chancellor, 1951-60; chancellor U. Calif. at Los Angeles, 1960-68; chmn. bd., chief exec. officer Times Mirror Co., 1968-81, chmn. exec. com., 1981—; dir. Ford Motor Co., Times Mirror Co., Bank of Am. Pres. Kress Found.; trustee Nat. Gallery of Art, J. Paul Getty Mus., Los Angeles County Mus. Art. Served to capt. AUS, 1944-46. Named One of Ten Outstanding Young Men, U.S. Jr. C. of C., 1949; recipient Outstanding Civilian Service award U.S. Army, 1967. Diplomate Am. Bd. Internat. Medicine. Fellow A.C.P.; mem. Phi Beta Kappa, Sigma Xi, Alpha Omega Alpha, Beta Theta Pi, Nu Sigma Nu. Episcopalian. Home: 419 Robert Ln Beverly Hills CA 90210 Office: Times Mirror Co Times Mirror Sq Los Angeles CA 90053

MURPHY, JOHN ROBERT, occupational safety and health professional, consultant; b. N.Y.C., May 5, 1945; s. John Joseph and Marie Teresa (Clementi) M.; m. Faith Ann Meakin, Nov. 22, 1969; m. 2d, Kathleen Ann Murphy, July 5, 1975; 1 son, John William. B.S. in Environ. Health, San Diego State U., 1972. Registered sanitarian and med. technologist, Calif. Research Convair Aerospace div. bioengr. Gen. Dynamics, San Diego, 1971-73; health and safety mgr. VA Med. Ctr., San Diego, 1973-82; occupational safety and health mgr. Naval Submarine Base, San Diego, 1982—; instr. indsl. hygiene; cons. stress mgmt. Served with USAF, 1965-69. Recipient award for extraordinary personal action ARC, 1967. Mem. Am. Soc. Clin. Pathologists, Assn. Fed. Safety and Health Profls., Am. Soc. Safety Engrs. Republican. Presbyterian.

MURPHY, JOHN THOMAS, lawyer; b. Pierre, S.D., July 20, 1932; s. Bernard J. and Gertrude (Loner) M.; LL.B., U. S.D., 1957; m. Rose Marie Cogorno. Admitted to S.D. bar, 1957, Calif. bar, 1962; practiced Stockton, Calif., 1965-75; atty. Office Gen. Counsel Q.M. Gen. Dept. of Army, 1957-58; asst. chief counsel Sharpe Army Depot, 1958-63, gen. counsel, 1963-65; asso. Short, Short, Scott & Murphy, and predecessor firm, 1965-68; partner Hulsey, Beus, Wilson, Scott & Murphy, Stockton, 1968-70. Sec. Golden Bear Assn. Beagle Clubs. Bd. dirs. Delta-Stockton Humane Soc., 1970-75. Mem. State Bar Calif., Assn. Trial Lawyers Am., Calif. Trial Lawyers Assn., Beta Theta Pi, Phi Delta Phi. Republican. Episcopalian. Clubs: Commonwealth, Stockton Beagler's (sec., dir.). Home: 2162 Parkridge Dr Modesto CA 95355 Office: 1104 12th St Modesto CA 95353

MURPHY, KEVIN ROBERT, computer co. exec.; b. Albany, N.Y., Mar. 5, 1942; s. Arthur Joseph and Marjorie (Ward) M.; student Holy Cross Coll., 1959-60; B.S., U.S. Mil. Acad., 1964; postgrad. Bucknell U., 1969-70; m. Joanne Maloy Howell, Sept. 6, 1964; children—Arthur, Brendan, Brian. With IBM, various locations, 1970-81, adminstrv. asst., Atlanta, 1979-80, nat. sales mgr., 1980-81; v.p. field ops. Pt 4 Data Corp., Irvine, Calif., 1981-82; v.p. sales the TRW-Fujitsu Co., Los Angeles, 1982—. Served to capt. U.S. Army, 1964-70; Vietnam. Decorated Air medal (3), Bronze Star. Mem. Assn. Grads. U.S. Mil. Acad., West Point Club So. Calif. Roman Catholic. Office: 9841 Airport Blvd Suite 620 Los Angeles CA 90045

MURPHY, LEWIS CURTIS, mayor Tucson; b. N.Y.C., Nov. 2, 1933; s. Henry Waldo and Elizabeth Wilcox (Curtis) M.; B.S. in Bus. Adminstrn., U. Ariz., 1955, LL.B., 1961; m. Carol Carney, Mar. 10, 1957; children—Grey, Timothy, Elizabeth. Admitted to Ariz. bar, 1961; individual practice law, Tucson, 1961-66; trust officer So. Ariz. Bank & Trust Co., Tucson, 1966-70; city atty. Tucson, 1970-71, mayor, 1971—. Served as pilot USAF, 1955-58. Mem. Ariz., Pima County bar assns., U.S. Conf. Mayors (trustee), Nat. League Cities, League Ariz. Cities and Towns (past pres.), Central Ariz. Project Assn. (v.p.), Ariz. Acad., Phi Alpha Delta, Sigma Chi. Republican. Presbyterian. Home: 3134 Via Palos Verdes Tucson AZ 85716 Office: PO Box 27210 Tucson AZ 85726

MURPHY, MARTHA JENKINS, public relations company executive; b. S.I., N.Y., Feb. 27, 1946; d. Edward Charles and Dorothy (Longbrake) Jenkins; 1 dau., Erin Jennifer. B.A. in Journalism, U. Ariz., 1968. Reporter, 1968-69; bur. chief. Norwich Bull., Seaport, Conn., 1969-70; pub. relations cons. Wettstein Advt., Tucson, 1972-74; coordinator pub. relations Tucson Gen. Hosp., 1974-78; dir. pub. relations Pomona Valley Community Hosp., Calif., 1978-82; dir. pub. relations U.S. Internat. U., San Diego, 1982-83; pres. Martha J. Murphy & Co., San Diego, 1983—; lectr. in field. Chmn. com. Vol. Action Ctr. Greater Pomona Valley. Recipient Order of the Horseshoe Nail, Vol. Action Ctr. Mem. Pub. Relations Soc. Am., Press Club So. Calif. (v.p., achievement award), Pomona C. of C. (chmn. communications com.), So. Calif. Soc. Hosp. Pub. Relations, Am. Soc. Hosp. Pub. Relations. Author publs. in field. Home: 7428 Eads Ave La Jolla CA 92037 Office: 4305 Gesner St San Diego CA 92112

MURPHY, MICHEAL GALE, electrician, union official; b. Vancouver, Wash., Dec. 6, 1942; s. Gale John and Doris Louise (Edwards) M.; m. Judy Lee Taylor, June 27, 1964; children—Galen, Patricia. Student Lane Community Coll., Eugene, 1965-69. Elec. apprenticeship, Eugene, 1965-69, journeyman electrician, 1969—; field rep., service mgr. Pierce Corp., Eugene, 1970-72; dir. Central/Crater Lake/Southwest Oreg. Tng. Trusts, Eugene, 1974-79; asst. bus. mgr. Local #280, Internat. Brotherhood Elec. Workers, Eugene, 1979—. Chmn. elect. Oreg. State Adv. Council for Career and Vocat. Edn.; chmn. related tng. adv. com. Oreg. Bd. Edn.; mem. Lane Community Coll. Vocat. Edn. Adv. Com. Served with U.S. Navy, 1961-63. Democrat. Mem. Ch. Jesus Christ of Latter-day Saints. Club: Elks. Home: 3845 Yorkshire St Eugene OR 97405 Office: 1126 Gateway Loop Suite 118 Springfield OR 97477

MURPHY, MILES RICHARD, research scientist; b. Malaga, Ohio, Dec. 6, 1930; s. William Mann and Martha Merle (Kemp) M.; m. Catherine Josephine Friedlund, Feb. 12, 1983. B.S. in Indsl. Engring., Ohio State U., 1960; M.Sc., Stanford U., 1970; postgrad. Calif. Inst. Integral Studies, 1977. Loftsman, N.Am. Aviation Inc., Columbus, Ohio, 1955-61; human factors specialist Philco-Ford Corp., Palo Alto, Calif., 1961-67; research scientist NASA-Ames Research Ctr., Moffett Field, Calif., 1967—; cons. and lectr. in field. Served with USAF, 1949-53, Korea. Mem. Human Factors Soc., Internat. Ergonomics Soc., Internat. Transactional Analysis Assn., Assn. Humanistic Psychologists, Am. Personnel and Guidance Assn., Calif. Assn. Marriage and Family Therapists, Tau Beta Pi, Alpha Pi Mu. Club: Toastmasters (Mountain View, Calif.). Contbr. articles to profl. jours. Home: 1690 Broadway 506 San Francisco CA 94109 Office: MS 239-2 NASA-Ames Research Ctr Moffett Field CA 94035

MURPHY, RENA M., mayor; b. Butte City, Calif., Aug. 24, 1927; d. Frank W. and Laurene C. (Adams) Brower; m. John D. Christopher Jr., Nov. 18, 1945; m. 2d, Robert E. Murphy, May 25, 1967; children—John D., Karen Patrice Caldwell. Owner, Pat Kanelos & Assos., Sacramento, 1955-60, Kanelos, Lowe & Louie, Sacramento, 1960-68; exec. v.p. Cathedral City (Calif.) C. of C., 1974-77; chmn. Cathedral City Inc. Com., 1978-81, mayor, 1981—; pres. Cathedral City C. of C., 1978, Coachella Valley Assn. Chambers Commerce, 1979; vice chmn. Coachella Valley Assn. Govts., 1982. Co-founder Cathedral City Boys and Girls Club, Cathedral City Sr. Ctr.; mem. Riverside County Local Area Formation Commn., 1982-85. Recipient Bob Allen award, Coachella Valley, 1978, Desert Peoples United Outstanding Citizen award, 1980, 81. Mem. Calif. Elected Women's Assn., League Calif. Cities (dir. Citrus Belt div., mem. revenue and taxation com.). Republican. Methodist. Clubs: Soroptomists, Auto So. Calif. (adv. bd.). Editor Ind. Auto Dealers Council News, 1958-60; contbg. writer Green Sheet Gasoline News, 1961; editor Cathedral City Courier, 1975-81. Home: 38471 Paradise Way Cathedral City CA 92234 Office: 68-625 Perez Rd Suite 16 Cathedral City CA 92234

MURPHY, RICHARD, movie writer, dir.; b. Boston; s. John Donahoe and May C. (Costello) M.; A.B., Williams Coll., Williamstown, Mass., 1936; m. Katherine Mauss, Nov. 17, 1942; children—John D. II, Edward Michael. Staff writer Literary Digest, 1936-37; screen writer, 1937-41; contract writer 20th-Century Fox, 1945-54; author screenplays: Boomerang, 1947; Deep Waters, 1948; Cry of the City, 1948; Panic in the Streets, 1950; U.S.S. Teakettle, 1951; Les Miserables, 1952; The Desert Rats, 1953; Broken Lance, 1954; Compulsion, 1959; with Columbia Picture Corp., 1954-56, author-dir. Three Stripes in the Sun, 1955, Wackiest Ship in the Army, 1961; contract writer dir. 20th Century-Fox, 1956-59, writer, dir., 1963-72; writer, dir. Columbia Pictures, 1959-62; adaptation The Last Angry Man, 1960; joint creator of Our Man Higgins TV series, 1962; creator of Felony Squad TV series, 1966-69; screenplay The Kidnapping of the President, 1980; ltd. partner Daniel Reeves Co., investment brokers, 1972—; pres. Cinecom World Enterprises Ltd., 16mm films, 1973—. Served as capt. AUS, 1942-45. Mem. Screen Writers Guild (exec. bd. 1949-51, 1st v.p. 1952), Motion Picture Industry Council, 1949-52, Motion Picture Relief (exec. bd., dir. 1953—), Mem. Motion Picture Acad. Arts and Scis. (bd. govs.; treas. 1964-68), Writers Guild Am. (treas. 1967-69, pres. screen br. 1969-71; Valentine Davies award 1969), Acad. Fgn. Film (exec. bd. 1982—), Chi Psi. Clubs: Players, Williams (N.Y.); Beverly Hills Tennis (pres. 1972-74, 76-78). Home: 345 N Palm Dr Apt 6 Beverly Hills CA 90210

MURPHY, SHARON KAY, contracts administrator; b. Albany, Ga., June 10, 1946; d. John Clarence and Virginia E. (Pollock) Howard. m. Michael Dennis Murphy, Jan. 22, 1966 (div.); children—Michael David, James Edward. Student Woodbury Bus. Coll. Exec. sec. Colonial Western Agy., Sherman Oaks, Calif., 1975-77; sales mgr. Holiday Inn, Brentwood, Calif., 1977-78; asst. to chief exec. officer, personnel mgr., facilities mgr., contracts adminstr. 1978-82; contracts adminstr. Kinergetics, Inc., Tarzana, Calif., ATE Assoc., Inc., Westlake Village, Calif., 1982—. Mem. Nat. Contracts Mgmt. Assn. (awards chmn.), Nat. Assn. Female Execs. Republican. Baptist. Home: 19005 Liggett St Northridge CA 91324 Office: 5707 Corsa Ave Westlake Village CA 91362

MURPHY, SUSAN LYNN, marketing company executive; b. Flint, Mich., Dec. 12, 1951; d. Edward Conrad and Joanne Loraine (Valentine) Arndt; children by previous marriage—Kerry Elizabeth, Kelly Michael. B.S., U. Mich.-Flint, 1974. Advt. dir. Ross Showrooms, Grand Blanc, Mich., 1971-73; asst. advt. dir. Sybra Inc., Grand Blanc, 1973-76; v.p. Marr Mktg., Grand Blanc, 1976-81; prin. Murphy Mktg. Inc., Salt Lake City, 1981—. Mem. Utah Advt. Fedn., DAR (charter Grand Blanc chpt.). Republican. Presbyterian. Office: Murphy Mktg Inc 715 E 3900 South #210 Salt Lake City UT 84107

MURPHY, THOMAS J., bishop; b. Chgo., Oct. 3, 1932; s. Bartholomew Thomas and Nellie M.; A.B., St. Mary of the Lake Sem., Mundelein, Ill., 1954, S.T.B., 1956, M.A., 1957, S.T.L., 1958, S.T.D., 1960. Ordained priest Roman Catholic Ch., 1958; rector, pres. St. Mary of the Lake Sem., to 1978; bishop of Great Falls-Billings, Mont., 1978—; asso. moderator Council Cath. Women, 1968-71; asst. dir. Cath. Family Counseling Service, 1968-71; pres. Presbyterate Senate, Archdiocese of Chgo., 1970-73, also bd. counselors; chmn. Bishop's Com. Priestly Formation, 1981—; mem. adminstrv. bd. Nat. Conf. Cath. Bishops. Mem. Nat. Cath. Edn. Assn. (dir.), Cath. Theol. Soc. Am. Author: Supernatural Perfection of Conjugal Life According to Pius XII; St. Mary of the Lake; Chicago Studies; Living Light; Spiritual Life. Office: 121 23d St S PO Box 1399 Great Falls MT 59403

MURPHY, WILLIAM EDWARD, marine pilot; b. Bakersfield, Calif., June 16, 1944; s. William Charles and Margaret Cynthia (Nutt) M.; B.S., Calif. Maritime Acad., 1966; student Navy flight tng., jet and helicopter flight tng.; m. Jeanne Marie Eikenbery, Jan. 31, 1970 (dec. Sept. 1981); children—William Brendan, Erin Eileen, Andrea Megan; m. 2d, Loraine J. Weber, Jan. 8, 1983. Marine pilot, founder., past pres., dir. S.W. Alaska Pilots Assn., Homer, Alaska, 1975-81; dir. Middle Rock, Inc.; mem. U.S. Rules of the Road Adv. Com. Served with USNR, 1966-71. Lic. master with pilotage endorsements S.W. Alaska, USCG; lic. marine pilot with endorsements for S.W. Alaska, State of Alaska; lic. air transport pilot FAA. Mem. Res. Officers Assn., Propellor Club U.S., Am. Pilots Assn. Democrat. Home: PO Box 597 Homer AK 99603 Office: PO Box 977 Homer AK 99603

MURRAY, BARBARA OLIVIA, psychologist; b. Summit, N.J., July 8, 1947; d. Archibald and Anna Cutler (Mattison) M.; student Inst. d'Etudes Francaises Pour Etrangers, France, 1965, Universite de Grenoble, France, 1968; B.A. in Psychology, Lake Erie Coll., 1969; M.A. in Clin. Psychology, Cleve. State U., 1971; postgrad. Gestalt Inst. Cleve., 1971-73; Ph.D. in Clin. Psychology, Calif. Sch. Profl. Psychology, Fresno, 1976. Mental health worker Cleve. Clinic Hosp., 1970-71, asso. psychologist, 1971-73; psychiat. intake worker Cleve. Free Clinic, 1971, group leader, 1972; cons. St. John's Coll., Cleve., 1972-73; psychology intern Fresno County Dept. Health, 1973-75, student profl. worker, 1974; mem. faculty Calif. Sch. Profl. Psychology, Fresno, 1974; psychology intern Calif. State U., Fresno, 1975, lectr., 1976-77; treatment program dir. E. Ross Clark Home for Children, Inc., Modesto, Calif., 1976-77; clin. psychologist Santa Cruz County (Calif.) Community Mental Health Services, 1977-79, dir. psychol. services, 1979-83; pvt. practice psychotherapy, Soquel, Calif., 1979—; cons. NOW, 1973-76, Community Hosp., Fresno, 1974. Storm disaster mental health profl. vol. coordinator, 1982; expert witness Santa Cruz and San Francisco counties, 1979—. Mem. Women's Studies Adv. Bd., Fresno, 1975-76. Recipient Disting. Psychologist award Calif. State Psychol. Assn., 1982. Hill scholar, 1968, Smith scholar, 1969, Fritz Perls scholar, 1970; lic. psychologist, Calif. Mem. Am. Psychol. Assn., Western Assn. Women Psychologists, Western Psychol. Assn., Calif. State Psychol. Assn. (bd. dirs. Observer 1981-83), Mid-Coast Psychol. Assn. (pres. 1981), Santa Cruz Psychology Group, Laurel Soc., Psi Chi (v.p. 1968-69), Kappa Alpha Sigma. Club: Cotuit Mosquito Yacht Contbr. articles to jours. in psychology. Home and Office: 4595 Fairway Dr Soquel CA 95073

MURRAY, BILLIE JOE, import-export co. exec.; b. Durango, Colo., Mar. 9, 1927; s. Denzel R. and Gladys Ruth (Fox) M.; M.B.A., Calif. Western U., 1980; m. Nancy Leong, Dec. 25, 1975; children—William Joseph, Richard Dale, Gladys Ruth. Commd. 2d lt., U.S. Army, 1953, advanced through grades to capt., 1960; service in W. Ger., Korea, Vietnam; ret., 1969; gen. mgr. AID/State Dept. Employees Assn., Saigon, Vietnam, 1971-75; owner, mgr. Home Cafe and Smith Market, Kingsburg, Calif., 1975-76; owner, mgr. Murray Leong Co., (Fresno, Calif., 1976-78; chmn., pres., chief exec. officer Murray-Leong Co., Inc., Fresno, 1978—; owner United Travel Service, Fresno, 1982—. Mem. Coeur d'Alene council Boy Scouts Am., 1964-65; state del. Idaho Republican Party, 1965; Rep. precinct committeeman Olympia, Wash., 1967-68. Served with U.S. Navy, 1943-49. Decorated Bronze Star, Air medal, Purple Heart, Army Commendation medal, Vietnam Service medal with four Bronze Stars, Republic of Vietnam Gallantry Cross, Armed Forces Reserve medal, others. Clubs: Masons, Shriners. Office: 1300 E Shaw #169A Fresno CA 93710

MURRAY, DENNIS RICHARD, mgmt. engring. exec.; b. Los Angeles, Mar. 14, 1946; s. Arland Richard and Bonnie Beatrice (Cobb) M.; student U. Colo., 1976-77, U. Calif., Riverside, 1979-81; m. Sarah Jane Caryle, June 15, 1977; children—Shannon, Clinton. With Dennis R. Murray Yacht Constrn., Costa Mesa, Calif., 1966-70; gen. mgr. Coastal Recreation, Inc., Irvine, Calif., 1970-75; pres. Ensa. Concepts, Newport Beach, Calif., 1975—; dir. ops. Advance Fire Protection, La Habra, Calif., 1979—. Pres., W. Orange County Homeowners Assn., 1979-80. Recipient Cert. of Appreciation, Orange Coast Coll., 1975. Mem. So. Calif. Buckskin Horse Assn. (dir. 1980-81), Am. Mgmt. Assn., Am. Quarter Horse Assn. Club: Norco Valley Riders. Designer, editor ops. manual for Hancock Labs., 1977. Home: 4004 Temescal St Norco CA 92706 Office: 1451 Lambert St La Habra CA 90631

MURRAY, JOHN JOSEPH, JR., real estate exec.; b. San Francisco, July 18, 1914; s. John Joseph and Margaret Rose (Flaherty) M.; B.A., U. San Francisco, 1937; postgrad. Golden Gate Coll., U. Calif., San Francisco; m. Hallie M. Butler, Sept. 14, 1940; children—John Joseph, Jeanne Murray Costin, Maureen Anne, William Butler. With San Francisco Daily News, 1936, Calif. Dept. Social Welfare, 1937-39, San Francisco Dept. Public Welfare, 1939-41; columnist San Francisco Monitor and The Leader, 1939-46; coordinator Bethlehem Steel Corp., San Francisco, 1941-44; pres. John J. Murray Co., Inc., contractors, San Francisco, 1945-68; exec. v.p. Peninsula Mfrs. Assn., 1968-72; sales assoc. Mindell Assocs., Realtors, San Mateo, Calif., 1972—; adv. dir. BayView Fed. Savs. & Loan Assn., 1979—; pres. San Mateo Bus. Leadership Council, 1968—; instr. real estate San Mateo Coll., 1979-83. Mem. San Mateo City Council, 1965-81, mayor, 1967-81; bd. dirs. N. Calif. Indsl. Edn. Council, 1968-72, San Mateo Conv. and Tourist Bur., 1976—; mem. San Mateo Regional Planning Com., 1968-73, Calif. Republican Control Com., 1972—. Life mem. San Mateo Real Estate Million Dollar Club; recipient various service awards, certs. of appreciation. Mem. Nat. Assn. Realtors, San Mateo County Devel. Assn., San Mateo C. of C., Calif. Assn. Realtors, San Mateo-Burlingame Bd. Realtors, Growth Policy Council San Mateo (pres.), San Mateo-Toyonaka (Japan) Sister City Assn., U. Calif.-San Francisco San Francisco Alumni Assn., Serra Internat., Ancient Order Hiberians, San Mateo County Hist. Assn. Republican. Roman Catholic. Clubs: Coyote Point Yacht, San Mateo, St. Gregory's Men's, KC, Elks. Author numerous articles in field. Home: 257 Del Mar Way San Mateo CA 94403 Office: care Mindell Assos 1106 S El Camino Real San Mateo CA 94402

MURRAY, KATHLEEN ANNE, lawyer; b. Los Angeles, Feb. 14, 1946; d. Francis Albert and Dorothy Irene (Thompson) Murray; 1 dau., Anne Murray Ladd. B.A., U. Mich., 1967; J.D., Hastings Coll., 1973. Bar: Calif. 1973. Atty. San Francisco Neighborhood Legal Assistance Found., 1973-74; staff clk. U.S. Dist. Ct. Appeals (9th dist.), 1974; asst. dir. Bd. Legal Specialization, State Bar Calif., 1974-75; sole practice, San Francisco, 1977-79; atty. Child Care Law Ctr., San Francisco, 1979—; co-founder, bd. dirs. Hastings Child Care Ctr., Inc., San Francisco Infant Sch., Inc.; bd. dirs. Pacific Primary Sch. Mem. ABA, Bar Assn. San Francisco, Nat. Assn. Edn. Young Children. Democrat. Office: 625 Market St Suite 815 San Francisco CA 94105

MURRAY, KATHLEEN ELLEN, editor; b. Chgo., Feb. 23, 1946; d. John Joseph and Marie Agnes (Stoltzman) M.; B.A., Calif. State U., Sacramento, 1973; A.A., Am. River Coll., 1968. File clk. Allstate Ins. Co., Sacramento, 1964-66; clk. typist Calif. Hwy. Patrol, Sacramento, 1968-69; copy editor Sacramento Bee, 1971—; instr. Calif. State U., Sacramento, 1975-76. Newspaper Fund intern, scholar, 1971. Club: Sacramento Press. Home: PO Box 606 Nevada City CA 95959

MURRAY, RAYMOND JOHN, copper co. ofcl.; b. Butte, Mont., Aug. 6, 1942; s. Anthony John and Florence Cecelia (Rask) M.; B.S. in Metall. Engring., Mont. Coll. Mineral Sci. and Tech., 1964, M.S. (research fellow, 1964), 1966; Ph.D. in Metallurgy, U. Idaho, 1973. Research engr. Boeing Co., Seattle, 1966-70; chief chemist, asst. quality control supr. Anaconda (Mont.) Copper Co., 1974—; instructional asst. U. Idaho, 1970-72. Home: 2125 Whitman Ave Butte MT 59701 Office: PO Box 1491 Anaconda MT 59711

MURRAY, RODERICK JOSEPH, III, food company executive; b. LaGrange, Ga., Aug. 17, 1956; s. Roderick Joseph and Mary Elizabeth (Cindrick) M.; B.S. in Health Sci., San Diego State U., 1977; m. Mirella Fragione, Oct. 17, 1982. Loss control rep. Indsl. Indemnity, Pasadena, Calif., 1978-79; transp. loss control rep. Hartford Ins. Group, Los Angeles, 1979-80; loss control specialist Carnation Co., Los Angeles, 1980—. Mem. exec. com., motor transp. div. Nat. Safety Council; mem. Nat. Com. Motor Fleet Supr. Tng. Mem. Am. Soc. Safety Engrs., Calif. Assn. Safety Edn., Pasadena Jr. C. of C. Office: 5045 Wilshire Blvd Los Angeles CA 90036

MURRAY, SPENCER JACK, hosp. adminstr.; b. Urbana, Ill., Feb. 4, 1936; s. Spencer J. and Agnes L. (Smith) M.; B.A., U. Wash., 1967, M.P.A., 1975; m. Peggy Patricia Gray, Aug. 18, 1962; children—Spencer, Derek, Brandon, Brenda. Asst. mgr. Capitol Music Co., 1963-65; graphic illustrator Boeing Co., 1965-67; employment interviewer, employment mgr., asst. to personnel dir., asst. hosp. adminstr. for personnel U. Wash. Hosp., Seattle, 1973-74, asst. hosp. adminstr. for patient care, 1975—; treas. Wash. State Hosp. Safety Council, 1979. Trustee Seattle Children's Home, Community Psychiatry Center, Seattle. Served with USNG, 1961-66. Mem. Am. Hosp. Assn. Roman Catholic. Club: Rotary. Home: 6033 NE 61st St Seattle WA 98115 Office: 1959 NE Pacific St Seattle WA 98195

MURRAY, WILLIAM DANIEL, judge; b. Butte, Mont., Nov. 20, 1908; s. James E. and Viola E (Horgan) M.; B.S., Georgetown U., 1932; LL.B., U. Mont., 1936, LL.D., 1961; m. Lulu Ann MacDonald, Aug. 24, 1938; children—William Daniel, Gael Ann, Timothy. Admitted Mont. bar, 1936; since practiced in Butte; partner firm of Emigh & Murray, 1936—; asst. U.S. atty., Butte, 1938-42; U.S. Dist. judge Dist. Mont., 1949—, now sr. U.S. dist. judge. Former chmn. bd. visitors sch. law U. Mont.; mem. bd. regents Gonzaga U.; bd. devel. Georgetown U. Served as lt. UNR, 1942-45. Recipient Barromeo award Carroll Coll., 1960; DeSmet medal Gonzaga U., 1967. Mem. Am., Mont., Silver Bow County bar assns. Bar Assn. D.C. Democrat. Roman Catholic.

MURTHA, FRANCIS BRIAN, photographer, minister; b. Bklyn., Mar. 23, 1915; s. Francis Pierre and Hazel Beatrice (Greenvault) M.; grad. high sch.; m. Helen L. Braner, July 31, 1968; children—Patricia L. (Mrs. Gary Shepard), Terry, Kevin, Jack. With North Plainfield (N.J.) Police Dept., 1936-52; chief detective bur., 1941-52; with Harolds Club, Reno, 1952-72, chief of photography, 1960-72; photographer, photo lab. technician U. Nev., Reno, from 1973, ret.; ordained minister Candlelight Gospel Mission, Reno. Pres. local 85, North Plainfield (N.J.) Patrolmen's Benevolent Assn., 1937-39, del. to N.J. Legislature, 1939-42; with Nev. wing CAP, 1953-69, dep. wingcomdr., 1964-69, Distinguished award, 1965. Served with USAF, 1942-45. Mem. Profl. Photographer of Am. (mem. nat. council 1972-76). Lion. Home: 949 Del Mar Way Reno NV 89502 Office: 655 N Virginia St Reno NV

MUSHEN, ROBERT LINTON, ophthalmologist; b. Klamath Falls, Oreg., Mar. 4, 1943; s. Samuel Albert and Beulah (Gore) M.; B.S. in Chemistry (Nat. Merit scholar), Stanford U., 1964; M.D., U. Oreg., 1968; m. Deborah Campbell, July 5, 1969; children—Melanie, Gregory, Timothy. Intern, Santa Clara Valley Med. Center, San Jose, Calif., 1968-69; resident in ophthalmology Brooke Army Med. Center, San Antonio, 1972-75; chief service Kerrville (Tex.) VA Hosp., 1975-76; mem. staff Madigan Army Med. Center, Tacoma, 1976-77; chief of staff and eye service Kadlec Hosp., Richland, Wash., 1977—; pres. Richland Eye Clinic, 1977—; cons. in field. Served with M.C., U.S. Army Res., 1969-75. Recipient award Oreg. Mus. Sci. and Industry, 1960; Nat. Eye Found. fellow, 1974-75. Mem. A.C.S., Am. Acad. Ophthalmology, Am. Intraocular Implant Soc., Soc. Eye Surgeons, AMA, Wash. Med. Assn., Wash. Acad. Ophthalmology, Benton-Franklin County Med. Soc., Alpha Omega Alpha. Republican. Co-author: Neuroanatomy Guide, 1967; contbr. articles to med. jours. Inventor bifocal trial lens. ophthalmologist; b. Klamath Falls, Oreg., Mar. 4, 1943; s. Samuel Albert and Beulah (Gore) M.; B.S. in Chemistry (Nat. Merit scholar), Stanford U., 1964; M.D., U. Oreg., 1968; m. Deborah Campbell, July 5, 1969; children—Melanie, Gregory, Timothy. Intern, Santa Clara Valley Med. Center, San Jose, Calif., 1968-69; resident in ophthalmology Brooke Army Med. Center, San Antonio, 1972-75; chief service Kerrville (Tex.) VA Hosp., 1975-76; mem. staff Madigan Army Med. Center, Tacoma, 1976-77; chief of staff and eye service Kadlec Hosp., Richland, Wash., 1977—; pres. Richland Eye Clinic, 1977—; cons. in field. Served with M.C., U.S. Army Res., 1969-75. Recipient award Oreg. Mus. Sci. and Industry, 1960; Nat. Eye Found. fellow, 1974-75. Mem. A.C.S., Am. Acad. Ophthalmology, Am. Intraocular Implant Soc., Soc. Eye Surgeons, AMA, Wash. Med. Assn., Wash. Acad. Ophthalmology, Benton-Franklin County Med. Soc., Alpha Omega Alpha. Republican. Co-author: Neuroanatomy Guide, 1967; contbr. articles to med. jours. Inventor bifocal trial lens. Home: 34 Vienna Ct Richland WA 99352 Office: 948 Stevens Dr Richland WA 99352

MUSICK, JAMES KIRBY, found. exec.; b. Lubbock, Tex., Mar. 15, 1943; s. C. Kirby and Betty Musick; B.A. in Sociology, N.Tex. State U., 1965, M.Ed. in Guidance and Counseling, 1966; m. Marshia Kay Light, Apr. 2, 1966; 1 son, Kevin Kirby. Staff psychologist, team mgr. Denton (Tex.) State Sch., 1966-69; clin. psychologist, mgr. programming Parsons (Kans.) State Hosp., 1969-74; dir. Casa Grande (Ariz.) Rehab. Center, 1974-78; regional mgr. Ariz. Found. for Handicapped, 1978-80, dep. dir., 1980, exec. dir., 1980—; exec. dir. AFH Enterprises, Inc., 1980—. Chmn. Mayor's Com. Employment of Handicapped, 1976-77; exec. council Gov.'s Com. Employment of Handicapped, 1976-77. Recipient Meritorious Service award Mayor of Casa Grande, 1977. Mem. Am. Assn. Mental Deficiency, Nat. Rehab. Assn., Dist. V Assn. Devel. Disabilities and Mental Retardation, Pinal County Assn. Retarded Citizens. Republican. Methodist. Home: 2655 S El Marino St Mesa AZ 85202 Office: 5000 S 40th St Phoenix AZ 85040

MUSIHIN, KONSTANTIN K., elec. engr.; b. Harbin, China, June 17, 1927; s. Konstantin N. and Alexandra A. (Lapitsky) M.; came to U.S., 1967, naturalized, 1973; ed. YMCA Inst., 1942, North Manchurian U., 1945, Harbin Poly. Inst., 1948; m. Natalia Krilova, Oct. 18, 1964; 1 son, Nicholas. Asst. prof. Harbin Poly. Inst., 1950-53; elec. engr. Moinho Santista, Sao Paulo, Brazil, 1955-60; constrn. project mgr. Caterpillar-Brazil, Santo Amaro, 1960-61; mech. engr. Matarazzo Industries, Sao Paulo, 1961-62; chief of works Vidrobras, St. Gobain, Brazil, 1962-64; project engr. Brown Boveri, Sao Paulo, 1965-67; sr. engr. Kaiser Engrs., Oakland, Calif., 1967-73; sr. engr. Bechtel Power Corp., San Francisco, 1973-75; supr. power and control San Francisco Bay Area Rapid Transit, Oakland, 1976-78; chief elec. engr. L.K. Comstock Engring. Co., San Francisco, 1978-79; prin. engr. Morrison Knudsen Co., San Francisco, 1979—. Registered profl. engr., Calif., Colo., N.Y., N.J., Pa., Ill., Wash. Mem. IEEE (sr.), Instrument Soc. Am. (sr.), Am. Mgmt. Assn., Nat., Calif. socs. profl. engrs., Nat. Assn. Corrosion Engrs., Instituto de Engenharia de Sao Paulo. Mem. Christian Orthodox Ch. Clubs: Am.-Brazilian, Brit.-Am. Home: 320 Park View Terr Unit 207 Oakland CA 94610

MUSOLF, LLOYD DARYL, political science educator, institute administrator; b. Yale, S.D., Oct. 14, 1919; s. William Ferdinand and Emma Marie (Pautz) M.; m. Berdyne Peet, June 30, 1944; children—Stephanie, Michael, Laura. B.A., Huron Coll., 1941; M.A., U. S.D., 1946; Ph.D., Johns Hopkins U., 1950. Mem. faculty Vassar Coll., Poughkeepsie, N.Y., 1949-59, assoc. prof. polit. sci., 1955-59; chief of party, adv. group Mich. State U., South Vietnam, 1959-61, prof. polit. sci., East Lansing, 1961-63; prof. polit. sci., dir. Inst. Govtl. Affairs, U. Calif.-Davis, 1963—; vis. prof. Johns Hopkins U., 1953, U. Del., 1954, U. Mich., 1955-56; cons. Calif. Personnel Bd., 1963-65, UN Pub. Adminstrn. Div., 1966, 68, SUNY, Albany, 1970, Nat. Acad. Pub. Adminstrn., 1970, Asian Ctr. for Devel. Adminstrn., Kuala Lumpur, Malaysia, 1975; sr. assoc. East-West Ctr., Honolulu, 1968-69. Mem. exec. bd. Citizenship Clearinghouse for So. Dist. N.Y., 1952-54; mem. Poughkeepsie (N.Y.) Zoning Bd. Appeals, 1958-59. Served to lt. USNR, 1942-45. Johnston scholar Johns Hopkins U., 1946-48; faculty fellow Vassar Coll., 1954-55; vis. scholar Brookings Instn., Washington, spring 1980; named U.S. Nat. rapporteur for Internat. Congress Adminstrv. Scis., Berlin, 1983. Mem. Am. Soc. for Pub. Adminstrn. (exec. council 1967-70), Nat. Assn. Schs. of Pub. Affairs and Adminstrn. (exec. council 1972-75, research com. div. urban affairs 1980-81), Western Govtl. Research Assn. (exec. bd. 1966-68), Am. Polit. Sci. Assn. Author: Federal examiners and the Conflict of Law and Administration, 1953; Public Ownership and Accountability-The Canadian Experience, 1959; Promoting the General Welfare-Government and the Economy, 1965; (with others) American National Government-Policies and Politics, 1971; Mixed Enterprise-A Developmental Perspective, 1972; (with Springer) Malaysia's Parliamentary System-Representative Politics and Policymaking in a Divided Society, 1979; Uncle Sam's Private Profitseeking Corporations-Comsat, Fannie Mae, Amtrak and Conrail, 1983, also monographs; contbr. chpts. to books, articles to profl. jours.; editor: (with Krislov) The Politics of Regulation, 1964; Communications Satellites in Political Orbit, 1968; (with Kornberg) Legislatures in Developmental Perspective, 1970; (with Joel Smith) Legislatures in Development-Dynamics of Change in New and Old States, 1979.

MUSSELMAN, DARWIN B., artist, art educator; b. Selma, Calif., Feb. 16, 1916; s. Laban C. and Lola Belle (Banks) N.; m. Ethel Laura Walker, Aug. 30, 1940; children—Ronald Lee, Carol Sue, Steven Earl. A.B., Fresno State Coll., 1938; postgrad., Art Center Sch., Los Angeles, 1938-39; M.F.A., Calif. Coll. Arts and Crafts, 1950; M.A., U. Calif., Berkeley, 1952. Gen. secondary and spl. secondary credentials in art, Calif. Artist, art dir. Thomas Advt. Fresno, 1939-42; artist, tchr. 1945-46; art tchr. Fresno (Calif.) High Sch., 1946-48; dir. sch. art edn. Calif. Coll. Arts and Crafts, Oakland, Calif., 1948-53; prof. art Calif. State U.-Fresno, 1953-78; portrait, landscape, still life artist; paintings represented in permanent pub. and pvt. collections throughout the U.S., including Sloan-Kettering Hosp., N.Y., Oakland Art Mus., Harvey Mudd Coll., Fresno Arts Center, Kaiser Bldg., Oakland, Coll. of Arts and Crafts. Bd. dirs., past pres. Fresno Arts Center. Recipient awards Oakland Watercolor ann. 1948, Calif. State Fair, 1950, 52, 54, 55, No. Calif. Arts, Sacramento, 1954, 56, Western painters ann. Oakland, 1954, N.Y. portrait award, 1980, 81, 82. Mem. Am. Watercolor Soc., Nat. Watercolor Soc., Portrait Inst. Republican. Christian Scientist.

MUSSELWHITE, EDWIN A., consulting company executive; b. Miami, Fla., Jan. 21, 1940; s. Thomas A. and Edna B. W.; B.S., Northwestern U., 1964; m. Susan Shanks, Dec. 15, 1962; children—Kenneth, Thomas. Mktg. rep. IBM, Chgo., 1964-68, exec. staff asst., 1968, br. sales mgr., Aurora, Ill., 1968-69; dir. profl. personnel Leasco Systems Corp., Oakbrook, Ill. 1969-70; exec. v.p. Deltak, Inc., Oakbrook, Ill., 1970-76; pres. Systems Growth Inst., Santa Cruz, Calif., 1976-82; v.p. Zenger-Miller, Inc., Cupertino, Calif., 1982—; cons. mgmt. to IBM, Gen. Electric Co., Fireman's Fund Ins. Co., Stanford U., TRW, others; guest lectr. at univs.; mem. bd. advs. Center for Orgn. and Mgmt. Devel., San Jose State U. Served as sgt. U.S. Army, 1964. Mem. Internat. Transactional Analysis Assn., Orgn. Devel. Network. Contbg. author: Everybody Wins, 1976; (with others) Interpersonal Dimensions, 1981; producer over 1000 hours of video-based instrn. in mgmt. devel, data processing and sales skills, 1973—. Office: 10061 Bubb Rd Cupertino CA 95014

MUSTACCHI, PIERO, physician, educator; b. Cairo, UAR, May 29, 1920; s. Gino and Gilda (Rieti) M.; B.S., Italian Lyceum, Cairo, 1937; postgrad. U. Florence (Italy), 1937-38; élève interne anatomy U. Lausanne (Switzerland) Sch. Medicine, 1938-39; M.D., Ch.B., Fuad 1st U., Cairo, 1946; m. Dora Lisa Ancona, Sept. 26, 1948; children—Roberto, Michael. Came to U.S., 1947, naturalized, 1952. House officer, Ch. Eng. Missionary Hosp., Cairo, 1945-47; clin. affiliate U. Calif. Med. Sch., San Francisco, 1947-48, asst. resident pathology, 1949-51, mem. faculty 1957—, asso. clin. prof. medicine and preventive medicine 1966-77, clin. prof. medicine and preventive medicine, 1977—, asso. dir. continuing edn. health sci., 1966-75, cons. Wolk Clinic, 1975—; intern Franklin Hosp., San Francisco, 1948-49; resident and sr. resident medicine Meml. Hosp. for Cancer and Allied Diseases, N.Y.C., 1951-53; with epidemiology and biometry br. Nat. Cancer Inst., Bethesda, Md., 1953-55; spl. cons. to surg. gen. Rome, 1960; cons. Calif. Compensation Ins. Fund, 1968—; med. cons. medico-legal and compensation problems Govt. Italy, 1957—; mem. environ. carcinogenesis group Cancer Inst., 1967-70; med. examiner Calif., 1960-66. Bd. dirs. Leonardo Da Vinci Soc., San Francisco, 1958. Served as sr. surgeon USPHS, 1955-57. Decorated knight, knight officer, knight comdr. Order Merit Republic Italy; chevalier Légion d'Honneur (France). Sloan Kettering Inst. for Cancer Research research fellow, 1951-53; Am. Cancer Soc. research fellow, 1949-52; hon. vice consul Italy, 1972—. Fellow A.C.P. (life), Am. Occupational Medicine Assn.; mem. Am. Assn. Cancer Research. AAAS, No. Calif. Soc. Allergy, AMA, Calif. Med. Assn., San Francisco Med. Assn., Am. Soc. Environmental and Occupational Health. Club: Villa Taverna. Editor: Family's Search for Survival, 1965; editorial bd. Ospedali d'Italia Chirurgia, 1956—, Médecine d'Afrique Noire; contbr. articles to profl. jours. Home: 3344 Laguna St San Francisco CA 94123 Office: HSW 1699 Univ Calif San Francisco CA 94143 also 3838 California St San Francisco CA 94118

MUTH, GILBERT JEROME, botanist; b. Modesto, Calif., Mar. 1, 1938; s. Douglas Leland and Margret Erma (Olander) M.; B.A., Pacific Union Coll., 1961, M.A., 1967; Ph.D., U. Calif., Davis, 1976; m. Betty Lavelle Krier, Aug. 23, 1959; children—Stephen Andrew, Jenny Adele. Sci. and math. tchr. Napa (Calif.) Jr. Acad., 1961-66; botany prof. Pacific Union Coll., Angwin, Calif., 1966—, asso. prof. biology, until 1981, prof. biology, 1981—, chmn. dept. biology, 1981—; chmn. rare plant adv. com. Dir. Dept. Fish and Game, State Calif., 1979. NSF sci. faculty fellow, 1971-72; U.S. Forest Service grantee, 1978. Mem. Calif. Native Plant Soc., Calif. Bot. Soc., Sigma Xi. Republican. Adventist. Home: 305 Sky Oaks Dr Angwin CA 94508 Office: Pacific Union Coll Biology Dept Angwin CA 94508

MUTSCHLER, HERBERT FREDERICK, librarian; b. Eureka, S.D., Nov. 28, 1919; s. Frederick and Helena (Oster) M.; B.A., Jamestown Coll., 1947; M.A., Western Res. U., 1949, M.S., 1952; m. Lucille T. Gross, Aug. 18, 1945; 1 dau., Linda M. Tchr. history, high sch., Lemmon, S.D., 1947-48; asst. librarian Royal Oak (Mich.) Library, 1952-55; head librarian Hamtramck (Mich.) Library, 1955-56; head pub. services Wayne County Library System, Wayne, Mich., 1956-59, asst. county librarian, 1960-62; dir. King County Library System, Seattle, 1963—. Library bldg. cons. Wayne County Library, 1956-62, Wash. State Library, 1966—, also to Salt Lake County Library, Utah; lectr. U. Wash. Sch. Librarianship, 1970-71. Served with AUS, 1941-45, to capt., 1950-52. Decorated Silver Star, Bronze Star with cluster, Purple Heart; named Outstanding Public Ofcl. of King County and Seattle, 1980. Mem. ALA (councilor at large 1965-69, chmn. LAD PR sect. 1969-70, chmn. PLA library cooperation com. 1969-70, chpt. councilor 1971-75, pres. library adminstrv. div. 1974-75, planning com. 1980-81), Pacific N.W., Wash. (exec. bd. 1964-65, 69-71, pres. 1967-69) library assns. Republican. Lutheran. Kiwanian. Contbr. articles to profl. jours. Home: 5300 128th Ave SE Bellevue WA 98006 Office: 300 8th Ave N Seattle WA 98109

MYERS, AL, realtor property mgmt., mayor; b. Oakland, Calif., Aug. 6, 1922; s. Alvi A. and Emma (Thoren) M.; student Oreg. Inst. Tech., 1940-41; m. Viola Doreen Wennermark, Sept. 11, 1954; children—Susan Faye, Pamela Ann, Jason Allen. Supt.'s asst. Aluminum Co. Am., Troutdale, Oreg., 1942-44; asst. mgr. Western Auto Supply Co., Portland, 1944-46; owner, operator Al Myers Auto & Electric, Gresham, Oreg., 1946-53; realtor, broker Al Myers Property Mgmt., 1954—; v.p., sec. Oreg. Country, Inc.; faculty Mt. Hood Community Coll. Chmn., Indsl. and Econ. Devel. Com. for Multonomah County, Oreg. Real Estate Ednl. Program, 1961. Mayor Gresham, Oreg., 1972—. Pres. East Multonomah County Dem. Forum, 1965—, mem. exec. com., 1958—. Served with AUS, 1943. Mem. Portland Realty Bd., Nat. Assn. Real Estate Bds., Christian Bus. Men's Com. Internat., Internat. Platform Assn., Rho Epsilon Kappa (pres. Oreg.). Mem. Evang. Ch. (trustee, treas.). Home: 935 NW Norman Ave Gresham OR 97030 Office: 995 NE Cleveland Ave Gresham OR 97030

MYERS, ARLO KENNETH, JR., psychologist, educator; b. Seattle, Nov. 15, 1922; s. Arlo Kenneth and Nettie Belle (Graden) M.; m. Barbara Jacobsen, Dec. 26, 1949; children—Roger G., Anne B., Katherine B. B.S., U. Wash., 1949; M.S., 1951; Ph.D., Yale U., 1956. Research asst., instr. Yale U., New Haven, 1956-59; asso. staff scientist Jackson Meml. Lab., Bar Harbor, Maine, 1959-61; asst. prof. psychology U. Calif.-Riverside, 1961-65, asso. prof., 1965-72, prof. psychology, 1972—. Served with Signal Corps, U.S. Army, 1943-46. Mem. Psychonomic Soc., Am. Psychol. Assn., Western Psychol. Assn., AAAS, Sigma Xi, Phi Beta Kappa. Contbr. articles to profl. jours. Home: 6041 Colonial Dr Riverside CA 92506 Office: Dept Psychology U Calif Riverside CA 92521

MYERS, CLAY, state treasurer Oreg.; b. Portland, Oreg., May 27, 1927; s. Henry Clay and Helen (Mackey) M.; B.S., U. Oreg., 1949; postgrad. Northwestern Coll. Law, 1950-52; m. Elizabeth Lex Arndt, Oct. 1, 1955; children—Richard Clay, Carolyn Elizabeth, David Hobson. With 1st Nat. Bank, Portland, 1949-53; with Conn. Gen. Life Ins. Co., Hartford and Portland, 1953-62, state mgr., 1960-62; v.p. Ins. Co. Oreg., Portland, 1962-65; asst. sec. of state Oreg., Salem, 1965-67, sec. of state, 1967-76; state treas. Oreg., 1977—; dir. Unit Drop Forge Co., Milw., Mo.-Pacific Corp., Lake Oswego, Oreg. Chmn., Senate Pres.'s Bi-Partisan Com. on Legis. Salaries, 1962; chmn. House Adv. Com. Legis. Reapportionment, 1961; mem. Oreg. Gov.'s Com. Pub. Welfare Med. Costs, 1964; mem. Multnomah County Welfare Commn., 1961-62, Oreg. Public Welfare Commn., 1962-65, vice chmn., 1963-65; chmn. Gov.'s Commn. on Youth, 1969-74. Trustee, treas. Ch. Divinity Sch. of Pacific; mem. Standing Com. on Ch. in Met. Areas; bd. overseers Lewis and Clark Coll. Served with USNR, 1945. Mem. Nat. Assn. State Treasurers pres.), Sigma Nu Phi, Lambda Chi Alpha (internat. pres. 1974-78). Republican. Episcopalian (lay reader 1956-65, dep. gen. conv. 1967, 69, 70, 73, 76, 79, 82). Mason, Elk. Clubs: City, Multnomah Athletic (Portland). Author: (with others) Population Reapportionment Initiative Constitutional Amendment, 1952. Home: 334 Wyatt Ct NE Salem OR 97301 Office: 158 State Capitol Bldg Salem OR 97310

MYERS, DAVID ALAN, clinical psychologist; b. Spokane, Wash., Oct. 5, 1943; s. Charles Albert and Gladys (Swartz) M.; B.S., U. San Francisco, 1966; M.A., U. Portland, 1970, Ph.D., 1971; m. Margaret June Travis, Nov. 30, 1963; children—Paul, Timothy, Patrick, Kathleen, Rebecca. Clin. psychology intern Portland VA Hosp., Med. Sch. U. Oreg., 1970-71; psychologist Multnomah County Diagnostic Ctr., Portland, 1971-73; chief psychologist Providence Hosp., Portland, 1973-75; pvt. practice clin. psychology, Portland, 1973—; adj. asst. prof. U. Portland Law Enforcement Program, 1972-77, Lewis and Clark Law Sch., 1979. Mem. Oreg. Gov.'s Task Force on Corrections, 1977; cons. Oreg. Jud. Coll., 1979-81; mem. adv. bd. Cath. Family Services, 1979—. Mem. Portland Psychol. Assn. (past pres.), Oreg. Acad. Profl. Psychologists (past pres.), Western Psychol. Assn., Am. Psychol. Assn., Oreg. Psychol. Assn. Roman Catholic. Office: 1220 SW Morrison Suite 808 Portland OR 97205

MYERS, GENE JAY, trainer, adult educator; b. Springfield, Mass., Apr. 19, 1931; s. Elbryn Howard and Miriam Kraybill (Bard) M.; B.A., Pa. State U., 1952; m. Norma Lee Barrett, Sept. 23, 1972. Prin., sr. trainer N.W. Social Systems, Seattle, 1969-74; mgr. tng. Westinghouse Hanford Co., Richland, Wash., 1974-78; nat. seminar adminstr. Pacific Inst., Seattle, 1978-80; instructional design and implementation specialist corp. tng. Morrison-Knudsen Co., Inc., Boise, Idaho, 1980—; pres. Gene Myers Seminars; adj. faculty Western Wash. U.; vocat. instr. Columbia Basin Coll. (Pasco, Wash.). Active Boy Scouts Am., named Commr. of Year, Inland Empire council, 1967, mem. Order of Arrow, 1968. Mem. Am. Soc. Tng. and Devel., Internat. Platform Assn. Episcopalian. Author: Old Style Sioux Costumes, 1968. Home: 3910 Buckingham Pl Boise ID 83704 Office: PO Box 7808 Central Plaza Boise ID 83729

MYERS, JOHN ROBERT, publishing company executive; b. Kansas City, Mo., Feb. 7, 1947; s. George Henry and Georgiana (Benfey) M. B.A., St. Louis U., 1969, M.A. (grad. teaching fellow 1969-71), 1971; M.B.A., So. Ill. U., 1975; postgrad. (doctoral fellow 1978-81), Calif. Am. U., 1978—; m. Kerry Brown, Apr. 29, 1978; children—Katharine Bridget, Kristin Brianne. Account mgr. Xerox Corp., St. Louis and Los Angeles, 1971-76; dir. human resources Handyman of Calif., San Diego, 1976-79; chief exec. officer, dir. Leadership Studies Prodns., Inc., San Diego, 1979—; dir. Mgmt. Video Pubs., Ltd., Toronto, Ont., Can., 1980—; prof. communications Calif. Am. U., 1980. Active, St. Louis Ambassadors, 1973-75, Boy's Club of San Diego, 1977-80. Mem. Am. Soc. Tng. and Devel., Internat. TV Assn., Soc. Motion Picture and TV Engrs. Republican. Episcopalian. Clubs: San Diego Sailing, Escondido Athletic, Beta Gamma Sigma, Alpha Sigma Nu, Phi Alpha Theta. Office: 230 W 3d Ave Escondido CA 92025

MYERS, KENT CLINTON, educator, printing executive, stockbroker, writer; b. Salem, Oreg., July 31, 1932; s. Arthur V. and Ramona O. (Moore) M.; m. Joan Marie Miller, Aug. 11, 1957; children—Sally Myers Hildebran, Laura, Jill, Jane. Student Willamette U., 1950-55, B.A. in Psychology, 1954, M.A. in Edn., 1959; D.Gen. Sch. Adminstrn., Stanford U., 1963. Tchr. jr. high sch. Albany, Oreg., 1955-56; with Psychol. Testing Services, Grays Harbor County Welfare Dept., Montesano, Wash., 1958-60; guidance cons., sch. psychologist Santa Clara County (Calif.) Schs., 1961-63; dir. Oreg. Program, Lake Oswego, Oreg., 1963-65; asst. supt. instrn. Lake Oswego Pub. Schs., 1965-81; stockbroker Omega Northwest, Portland, Oreg., 1981—; pres. Myers-Murty Printing and Pub., Inc., Portland, 1982—; part time sch. psychologist Aberdeen (Wash.) Pub. Schs., 1958-60; dir. spl. edn. and guidance Grays

Harbor County Schs., Montesano, 1958-60; mem. evaluation teams, commns., univs. and profl. orgns. Bd. dirs. Christie Sch., Marylhurst, Oreg., 1974-76, Tyron Creek State Park, 1974, 75, Christ Episcopal Ch., Lake Oswego, Oreg., 1981—, also vestryman. Served with U.S. Army, 1956-58. State amateur golf champion, 1965, 72, 81, 83, named to team of ten top amateur golfers Pacific N.W. 17 of last 18 years, capt. team, 1973—; Collins grad. scholar Willamette U.; Newhouse scholar, Stanford U.; recipient Roy H. Simmons award, Willamette U. Mem. Am. Assn. Sch. Adminstrs., Nat. Assn. Supervision and Curriculum Devel., Oreg. Assn. for Curriculum Devel. (bd. dirs. 1966-71), Nat. Assn. Secondary Sch. Prins., Nat. Assn. Elem. Sch. Prins., Confedn. Oreg. Sch. Adminstrs., Am. Ednl. Research Assn., Oreg. Assn. Sch. Execs., Phi Eta Sigma, Psi Chi, Sigma Alpha Epsilon. Club: Rotary (bd. dirs. Lake Oswego 1975-78). Author: Golf in Oregon, 1977, 2d edit., 1981; Man Ltd., and Other Poems, 1978; Slumbering Giants, 1979; contbr. articles to profl. publs.

MYERS, M(ARVIN) SCOTT, mgmt. cons.; b. Doebay, Wash., Jan. 13, 1922; s. Alvin Jefferson and Virginia Stella (Boone) M.; m. Marie Beeler, Apr. 27, 1947; m. 2d, Susan Sloat, Dec. 16, 1967; children—James Daniel, Suzanne Marie, Gary Scott, David Darius. B.S., Purdue U., 1948, M.S., 1949, Ph.D., 1951. Supr. personnel planning Hughes Aircraft Co., Culver City, Calif., 1951-54; assoc. prof. public adminstrn. U. Tehran (Iran), 1954-59; mgmt. research cons. Tex. Instruments, Dallas, 1959-72; dir. Ctr. Applied Mgmt., Santa Barbara, 1972—; vis. prof. MIT Sloan Sch. Mgmt., 1969-71. Recipient Gold medal of cooperation Shah of Iran, 1957. Mem. Am. Psychol. Assn., Sigma Xi, Tau Kappa Epsilon. Republican. Club: Santa Barbara Tennis. Author: Managing Without Unions, 1976; Managing With Unions, 1978; Every Employee A Manager, 2d edit., 1981. Home and Office: 60 El Cielito Rd Santa Barbara CA 93105

MYERS, PHILLIP FENTON, business exec.; b. Cleve., June 24, 1935; s. Max I. and Rebecca (Rosenbloom) M.; B.I.E., Ohio State U., 1958, M.B.A., 1960; D.B.A., Harvard U., 1966; m. Hope Gail Strum, Aug. 13, 1961. Staff indsl. engr. Procter & Gamble Co., Cin., 1958; sr. cons. Cresap, McCormack & Paget, N.Y.C., 1960-61; staff asso. Mitre Corp., Bedford, Mass., 1961; cons. System Devel. Corp., Santa Monica, Calif., 1963-64; corp. asst. long range planning Electronic Splty. Co., Los Angeles, 1966-68; chmn. Atek Industries, 1968-72; pres. Myers Fin. Corp., 1973—, Steel Fuels Corp., 1976-77; chmn. Amvid Communication Services, Inc., 1973-79, Gen. Hydrogen Corp. Am., 1976-79, Omni Resource Devel. Corp., 1979—; chmn., pres. Am. Internat. Mining Co., Inc., 1979—; pres. Whitehall Internat. Mgmt. Co., Inc., 1982—, Synentek Internat. Corp., 1983—; founding dir. Warner Center Bank, 1980-83; lectr. bus. adminstrn. U. So. Calif., Los Angeles, 1967-74; prof. Pepperdine U. Grad. Sch. Bus. Adminstrn., 1974-81. Trustee, treas. Chamber Symphony Soc. Calif., 1971-78; public safety commr. City of Hidden Hills (Calif.), 1977-83, chmn., 1982-83; co-chmn. budget adv. com. Las Virgenas Sch. Dist., 1983—; mem. mayor's blue ribbon fin. com., 1981—. Served to 1st lt. USAF, 1958-60. Ford Found. fellow, 1961-64. Mem. Harvard Bus. Sch. Assn. So. Calif., Ohio State Alumni Assn. Club: Harvard of So. Calif. Office: 22900 Ventura Blvd Suite 340 Woodland Hills CA 91364

MYERS, R. FRASER, travel tour mgr.; b. Washington, Apr. 14, 1941; s. Gilbert Barlow and Janet Stirrat (Clark) M.; grad. Deerfield Acad., 1958; B.A., Dartmouth Coll., 1962; M.A., Cath. U. Am., 1967. Tour mgr. Olson-Travelworld, Los Angeles, 1967—, travelling over 1.6 million miles to more than 239 countries; 44 times across Atlantic, 53 across Pacific, 122 across U.S., 9 times around world, 64 times across Equator. Served to lt. comdr. USNR, 1962-82. NSF grantee Summer Inst. Glaciol. Scis., Juneau Icefield Research Program, 1966. Fellow Royal Geog. Soc. (London); mem. Explorers Club. Apptd. U.S. Fgn. Exchange rep. to Belgium-Netherlands Antarctic Expdn., 1966. Club: Travelers' Century (Los Angeles). Home: 1223 Averill Ave San Pedro CA 90732 Office: Olson-Travelworld PO Box 92734 Los Angeles CA 90009

MYERS, REX CHARLES, history educator; b. Cleve., July 1, 1945; s. Charles Fay and Merial Whiting (Jones) M.; B.A., Western State Coll., 1967; M.A., U. Mont., 1970, Ph.D., 1972; m. Trinda Ann DeVore, June 3, 1967; children—Gary, Laura. History/polit. sci. instr. Palo Verde Coll., Blythe, Calif., 1972-75; reference librarian Mont. Hist. Soc., Helena, Mont., 1975-78; assoc. prof. history, chmn. humanities and social sci. div. Western Mont. Coll., Dillon, 1979—; cons. Grant-Kohrs Ranch Nat. Hist. Site, 1979-82; dir. Beaverhead County Mus., 1979—; Mont. State historian, 1976-77; field humanist Mont. Com. Humanities, 1979—. Mem. Dillon Centennial Com., 1980. Served with U.S. Army N.G., 1968-81. Mem. Western Writers Am., Western History Assn. (membership chmn.), Mont. Oral History Assn. (pres.). Democrat. Methodist. Clubs: Kiwanis (pres.), Masons (Dillon). Author: Marble, Colorado: City of Stone, 1970; Montana Trolleys, 1970; Symbols of Montana, 1976; Not in Precious Metals Alone, 1976; Montana: Our Land and People, 1979; Colorado Rail Annual No. 15, Montana and the West: Essays in Honor of K. Ross Toole, 1983; contbr. hist. articles to profl. jours. Home: PO Box 1323 Dillon MT 59725 Office: Div Humanities and Social Sci Western Mont Coll Dillon MT 59725

MYERS, SHIRLEY STOFLE, interior designer, cons., educator, author; b. Seattle, Mar. 5, 1921; d. Sterling Leroy S. and Grace Evelyn (Lyden) Stofle; m. Edward A. Myers, Sept. 5, 1945; children—Sterling, Melinda Myers Bingham, Marlyce. B.A. in Decorative Arts, U. Calif.-Berkeley, 1944; M.A., Calif. State U., Los Angeles, 1967. Cert. elem. secondary tchr., Calif., Instr. math., Temple City, Calif., 24 years; editor Calif. State Math. Jour., 1964-70; commr. Calif. Curriculum Commn., 1972-76; interior designer Betty Willis Interiors Co., Arcadia, Calif., 1981—; adj. prof. Calif. State U.-Los Angeles, 1964-78; Whittier Coll., 1974—. Recipient Calif. Tchrs. Assn. Demonstration Tchr. award, 1965; Alpha Delta Pi fellow, 1943; Jamieson Found. fellow, 1965; NSF grantee, 1963, 67. Mem. Am. Soc. Interior Designers, Calif. Sch. Adminstrn., Found. for Edn., PTA (life), Delta Kappa Gamma, Pi Lambda Theta, Alpha Delta Pi. Republican. Methodist. Author: Sensory Learning Approach to Mathematics, 1976; Mathematic Framework for Calif. State Dept. Edn., 1944; The Laboratory Approach to Math., 1970; contbr. articles to publs. Home: 235 N Pacific Ave Solana Beach CA 92075 Office: 650 Duarte Rd S-1 Arcadia CA 91006

MYERS, THERESE ELEANOR, office automation and software systems company executive; b. Pitts., July 1, 1944; s. Harold John and Eleanor Margaret (Schmitt) M. B.A. in Econs., Newton Coll. of Sacred Heart, 1966; M.S.I.A., Carnegie Mellon U., 1968. C.P.A., N.Y. State Mgmt. cons. Arthur Young & Co., N.Y.C., 1968-70; asst. v.p. Citicorp Leasing, Citicorp, N.Y.C., 1970-72, dir. ops. Transaction Tech., Los Angeles, 1972-74; v.p. product mgmt. Lexar, Los Angeles, 1974-79; v.p. product mgmt. Lexar Bus. Communications/AXXA subs. Citicorp, Los Angeles, 1979-81; pres. Quarterdeck Office Systems, Los Angeles, 1981—. Asst. chmn. Ednl. TV Project, Jr. League Los Angeles, 1980-81, asst. chmn. provisionals, 1981-82; pres. Hollywood Bowl Juniors, Los Angeles. Roman Catholic. Club: Bel Air Bay. Inventor office automation system for profls. Home: 1 Quarterdeck St Marina Del Rey CA 90291 Office: 2210 Wilshire Suite 117 Santa Monica CA 90403

MYERS, THERON DONALD, mechanical engineer; b. Akron, Ohio, Jan. 18, 1929; s. Theron Donald and Mabel (Kniceley) M.; m. Margaret Fukuko, June 4, 1951; children—Terry Allen, Dennis Adrian, Anthony Paul. B.S. in Mech. Engring., U. So. Calif., 1962. Registered profl. engr., Calif. Russian translator/interpreter U.S. Army, 1948-54; sr. design engr. Aerojet-Gen. Corp., Azusa, Calif., 1954-62; mgr. Ramjet Engring., Chem. Systems div. United Techs., 1962—; chmn. peer group NASA Langley hypersonic propulsion. Mem. AIAA. Contbr. articles to profl. jours.

MYERS, THOMAS A., accountant; b. Long Branch, N.J., Jan. 12, 1945; s. Arthur Louis and Gladys (Kampf) M.; m. Rose Torrez, June 19, 1976; children—Kirsten, Rhonda, Rhoda. B.S. in Math., N.Mex. Sch. Mines, 1966; B.S. in Acctg., U. No. Colo., 1977. Tax cons. Touche Ross & Co., Denver, 1977-82; producer surfing films, Honolulu, 1970-76; founding ptnr. T.A. Myers & Co., C.P.A.s, Westminster, Colo., 1980—. Mem. Am. Inst. C.P.A.s, Colo. Soc. C.P.A.s, Internat. Tax Group. Republican. Methodist. Club: Denver Athletic. Contbr. articles to profl. jours. Home: 6256 W 86th Ave Arvada CO 80002 Office: Tower 1 Suite 1000 999 18th St Denver CO 80202

MYHREN, TRYGVE EDWARD, communications executive; b. Palmerton, Pa., Jan. 3, 1937; s. Arne Johannes and Anita (Blatz) M.; m. Carol-Jane, Aug. 24, 1964; children—Erik, Kirsten, Tor; m. 2d, Victoria Hamilton, Nov. 14, 1981; 1 stepdau., Paige Hamilton. B.A. in Philosophy and Polit. Sci., Dartmouth Coll., 1958, M.B.A., 1959. Sales mgr., head salesman, unit mgr. Proctor and Gamble, Cin., 1963-65; gen. mgr. retail promotion div. Glendinning Cos., Westport, Conn., 1965-67, sr. cons., 1967-69; exec. v.p. Mktg. Continental, Westport, 1969-73; v.p., gen. mgr. CRM, Inc., Del Mar, Calif., 1973-75; v.p. mktg. Am. TV and Communications Corp., Denver, 1975-78, sr. v.p. mktg. and sales, 1978-79, exec. v.p., 1979-80; pres., 1981-82, chmn. bd., chief exec. officer, 1982—; v.p. Time Inc., N.Y.; treas., dir. NCTA; dir. Temple-Eastex, Inc., HBO. Trustee Dartmouth Assn. Gt. Divide; coach Cherry Creek Soccer Assn. Served as lt. (j.g.) USNR, 1959-62. Mem. Cable TV Adminstrn. and Mktg. Soc. (past pres.). Office: Am TV and Communications Corp 160 Inverness Dr W Englewood CO 80112

MYRICK, CLAUDE CRIMONT, county ofcl.; b. Seattle, June 9, 1918; s. Hartley Claude and Mary Louise (O'Shaughnessy) M.; student Seattle U., 1948-50, Seattle Community Coll., 1969—; m. Margurite E. Petersen, June 7, 1959; stepchildren—Richard F. Walling, Sheila M. Young. Sheet metal worker, journeyman Boeing Co., Seattle, 1940-49; sales mgr., estimator, designer Colcock Furnace Co. and Condon-King Co., 1950-60; counter clk., furnace specialist Seattle Bldg. Dept., 1962-65; sales mgr., estimator, designer Gen. Heating Co., 1965-68; mech. plan examiner King County Div. Bldg., Seattle, 1969-82; with Richard M. Stern, Cons. Engr., 1953—; tchr. Community Colls. of Everett and Seattle. Operator, Eastside Community Concerts, 1968-72; mem. nat. adv. bd. Am. Security Council. Served with USMCR, 1940. Mem. ASHRAE (mech. code com. Puget Sound chpt.), Wash. Wood Energy Assn. (founder), Internat. Conf. Bldg. Ofcls., Am. Theatre Organ Soc. Conservative. Club: Atos. Home: 704 99th Ave NE Bellevue WA 98004 Office: 500 5th Ave Seattle WA 98104

NABER, CHARLES DUANE, appraiser; b. Havre, Mont., Dec. 12, 1945; s. Charles C. and Lethia Maxine N.; B.A., No. Mont. Coll., 1967, B.S., 1971; postgrad. U. Santa Clara, 1980, U. Boulder, 1981; m. Virginia Ann Opperud, May 30, 1971; children—Lori, Brenda, Karen. Office mgr., chief appraiser Mont. State Dept. Revenue, Havre, 1971-78; chief appraiser, asst. v.p. Havre Fed. Savs. & Loan Assn., 1978-81; sec., ops. mgr. H. Earl Clack Meml. Mus., Havre, 1971—; ind. appraiser, Havre, 1981—. Bd. govs. Havre Softball Assn.; bd. dirs. United Way. Mem. Mont. Ofcls. Assn. Club: Black Butte Golf and Racketball (Havre). Home and Office: Box 1675 Havre MT 59501

NABESHIMA, ELSIE MICHIKO, medical technologist, laboratory administrator; b. Brighton, Colo., July 27, 1932; d. Frank Takeshi and Florence Yoshiko (Tsuzuki) Nakata; m. Henry T.H. Nabeshima, Dec. 3, 1955; 1 dau., Allyson. Student U. Colo., 1950-54, B.S., Sch. Med. Tech., 1955; postgrad. Central Mich. U., 1976—. Med. technologist St. Anthony Hosp., Denver, 1955, Wichita St. Joseph Hosp., Wichita, Kans., 1955-57; with O'Connor Hosp., San Jose, Calif., 1957—, mgmt. coordinator, 1971-76, adminstrv. technologist, 1976—; mem. adv. com. Calif. Dept. Health. Bd. dirs. Central Area chpt. United Way, 1980. Named to Honor Roll, Omicron Sigma, 1978, 79, 80, 81, 82, 83, recipient appreciation cert. Santa Clara County Bd. Suprs., 1980. Mem. Am. Soc. Med. Tech. (Sci. Assembly Adminstrn. award 1974, cert. appreciation 1975, 79), Calif. Soc. Med. Technologists (Outstanding Technologist of Yr. 1964, 83), Calif. Assn. Med. Lab. Technologists, O'Connor Mgmt. Club, Tri-County Adminstrv. Technologist Assn., Beta Sigma Phi (Girl of Yr. 1965, 69, 75, 83), Alpha Mu Tau. Republican. Buddhist. Author: How to write a Job Description, 1978. Home: 3825 Blossomview Dr San Jose CA 95118 Office: 2105 Forest Ave San Jose CA 95128

NABOURS, ROBERT EUGENE, cons. elec. engr.; b. Tucson, Nov. 27, 1934; s. James Oliphant and Dorothy Madelle (Brown) N.; B.S.E.E. (WEMA scholar), U. Ariz., 1957, Ph.D., 1965; M.S., Stanford U., 1959; m. Jane Brock Burnett, Feb. 27, 1954; children—Kathleen, Bradley, Gregory. Engr., Lenkurt Elec., San Carlos, Calif., 1957-58, Ackerman & Aronoff, Palo Alto, Calif., 1958; instr., research engr. U. Ariz., Tucson, 1959-62; research engr. Bell Aero Systems, Tucson, 1963-65; chief engr. Burr-Brown Research Corp., Tucson, 1965-68; cons. engr., Tucson, 1968-78; sr. v.p. Johannessen & Girand, Cons. Engrs., Tucson, 1978-80; chief elec. engr. Finical & Dombrowski, Architects and Engrs., Tucson, 1980-82; pres. Robert E. Nabours, Cons. Elec. Engrs., lectr. U. Ariz.; tech. expert elec. litigation, 1969—; Tucson, 1982—; cons. to numerous govtl. agys.; works include archtl. lighting systems design and numerous structures. Registered profl. engr., Ariz., Calif., N.Mex. Mem. IEEE, Nat. Soc. Profl. Engrs., Illuminating Engring. Soc. (design award of merit 1978, 80), Instrument Soc. Am., Am. Acad. Forensic Scis., Sigma Pi Sigma, Tau Beta Pi. Republican. Episcopalian. Clubs: VIP Breakfast, Tucson Country, Elks. Research on adaptive communications and effects of extremely low frequency electromagnetic radiation. Home: 5201 Salida del Sol Tucson AZ 85718 Office: 2200 E River Rd Suite 103 Tucson AZ 85718

NACHMAN, RICHARD JOSEPH, mgmt. edn. and mktg. exec.; b. Washington, Sept. 18, 1944; s. Joseph Frank and Rosemary A. (Anderson) N.; B.A., U. Colo., 1968; m. Nancy Ruth Hodgson, Feb. 4, 1966 (div.); children—Russell James, Kirk Leslie; m. 2d, Maria Christina Hoff, Jan. 2, 1979; 1 stepson, William. Program dir. Bur. Indsl. Relations, Grad. Sch. Bus. Adminstrn., U. Mich., Ann Arbor, 1968-70; dir. Center for Mgmt. and Tech. Programs, Grad. Sch. Bus., U. Colo., Boulder, 1970-74; pres. Mgmt. Research Corp., Boulder, 1974—, RJN & Assos., Boulder, 1977—; lectr. and cons. in mgmt. and behavioral scis. for univs. and bus., direct mktg. Bd. dirs. Human Productivity Inst., 1979-80. Mem. Am. Soc. Tng. and Devel., Direct Mail Mktg. Assn., Am. Mgmt. Assn. Republican. Contbr. articles to profl. jours. and mags. Home: 4814 W Moorhead Circle Boulder CO 80303 Office: 302 S First Ave Sandpoint ID 83864

NADEAU, WILLIAM RAYMOND, marine corps officer; b. Queens Village, N.Y.C., Jan. 30, 1952; s. Joseph Michael and Marie (LeVecchia) Norton. Ed. pub. schs. Enlisted U.S. Marine Corps, 1970, advanced through grades; top secret document control clk. Joint Chiefs Staff, Washington, 1970, intelligence asst., Cherry Point, N.C., 1973; Russian linguistic student Def. Lang. Inst., Monterey, Calif., 1975; team mem. Warsaw Pack analyst sect. 2d Marine Div., 1976; air combat intelligence analyst 1st Marine Aircraft Wing, Asian Theater, 1976; insp. instr. intelligence sect. Marine Air Res. Detachment, Norfolk, Va., from 1978; Asst. scoutmaster Boy Scouts Am., Camp Lejeune, N.C., 1976-78; mem. presdl. steering com. for Senator Howard Baker, 1980. Recipient cert. of appreciation Presdl. Inaugural Com., 1973; spl. recognition award Ctr. for Internat. Securities Studies, 1979. Mem. Am. Mgmt. Assn., Non-Commd. Officers Assn., Smithsonian Assocs., Am. Security Council (nat. adv. bd. 1979-81). Republican. Roman Catholic. Address: 108 Bravo Wonson Dr Pendleton CA

NADKARNI, ARUN ANANT, aero. research engr.; b. Bombay, India, Aug. 27, 1944; s. Anant S. and Anasooya A.; B.E., U. Coll. Engring., 1966; M.E., Indian Inst. Sci., 1968; M.S., Pa. State U., 1975; Ph.D., Old Dominion U., 1977; m. Aparna A. Sadekar, Dec. 2, 1970; 1 dau., Arti. Aerodynamics engr. Indian Space Research Orgn., Bangalore, India, 1968-72; research asst. prof. Old Dominion U., Norfolk, Va., 1977-79, asst. prof. dept. mech. engring. and mechanics, 1979-81; sr. specialist engr. Boeing Commercial Airplace Co., Seattle, 1981—; aero. research fellow NASA, 1973-76. NASA Langley Research Center research grantee, 1976-81. Mem. IEEE, AIAA, Sigma Xi, Phi Kappa Phi. Office: M/S 9R-49 Boeing Commercial Airplace Co PO Box 3707 Seattle WA 98124

NAGALINGAM, SAMUEL JEBARATNAM-SUKENDRAKUMAR, product development engineer; b. Colombo, Sri Lanka, Dec. 30, 1950; s. Chellappah Jesudasan and Pooranam (Ponnambalam) N.; m. Nirmala Ponnuthurai, Aug. 30, 1978; B.S. with honors in Physics, U. Sri Lanka, 1972; M.S. in Physics, U. Notre Dame (Ind.), 1976; M.S. in Elec. Engring., U. Ill., 1981. Asst. lectr. physics U. Sri Lanka, 1973-74; asst. instr. physics U. Notre Dame, 1974-76; research asst. U. Ill., Urbana, 1976-80; product devel. engr. Nat. Semicondr. Corp., West Jordan, Utah, 1981—. Nat. Sci. scholar U. Sri Lanka, 1969; Commonwealth scholar, 1974; recipient awards, Am. Nuclear Soc. Midwest Student Confs., 1977-78. Mem. IEEE, Inst. Elec. Engrs., London, (assoc.) Contbr. articles to profl. jours. Office: 3333 W 90th S West Jordan UT 84084

NAGATA, DONALD MITSUO, telecommunications specialist; b. Puunene, Maui, Hawaii, Oct. 29, 1932; s. Jack Tsuneo and Patsy Toyo (Morohashi) N.; E.E., Valparaiso Tech. Inst., 1958; diploma Indpls. Electronic Sch., 1957; B.S.E.E., M.S.E.E., U. Beverly Hills, 1980; m. Elizabeth Rich, Dec. 24, 1976; children—Stuart John Tsuneo, Sarah Mitsuko. Sr. systems engr. Holmes & Narver, Inc., Las Vegas, 1958-61, 63-69; telecommunications engring. technician Hawaiian Telephone Co., Kaunakaki, Molokai, 1962; project engr. ICAS, Inc., Las Vegas, 1969-70; sr. systems engr. Telcom, Inc., Las Vegas, 1970-75; engring. specialist Bechtel, Inc., San Francisco, 1975—; participant nuclear test projects AEC, 1956, 58, 62, 68, 69, 71, also Gemini 5-8 U.S. space projects; mem. Calif. Inst. Tech. Jet Propulsion Lab. team, master planning emergency command control communications system for Los Angeles Police Dept., 1974-75. Served with AUS, 1952-55. Mem. Instrument Soc. Am., IEEE, Profl. Group on Telecommunications, Armed Forces Communications and Electronics Assn., Valparaiso Tech. Inst. Alumni Assn. (life), Nat. Geog. Soc., Smithsonian Assos., Calif. Acad. Scis., Nev. Hist. Soc., Milton de Young Meml. Mus. Soc., Calif. Palace Legion of Honor, Asian Art Mus. San Francisco. Contbr. articles to profl. jours. Home: 3277 Shelby Pl Fairfield CA 94533 Office: 50 Beal St San Francisco CA 94119

NAGATA, KENNETH MASUHISA, botanist; b. Honolulu, June 26, 1945; s. Kanao and Kiyome Nagata; B.A., U. Hawaii, Manoa, 1968, M.A., 1980; m. Linda Yamada, Sept. 10, 1977. Research asst. Lyon Arboretum, U. Hawaii, Manoa, 1969-74, research asso. II, 1974—, instr. botany, 1972-74; instr. botany Chaminade U., Honolulu, 1977-78, Kapiolani Community Coll., 1978, 81; botanist Hawaiian Animal Species Adv. Commn., 1978—. Grantee U. Hawaii, 1978, Garden Club Honolulu, 1979. Mem. Soc. Econ. Botany, Hawaiian Bot. Soc., Tex. Acad. Sci., Lyon Arboretum Assn., Sierra Club, Sigma Xi. Author papers in field, co-author: Hawaii's Vanishing Flora, 1980. Office: 3860 Manoa Rd Honolulu HI 96822

NAGATA, RAYMOND SHOGO, contractor; b. Honolulu, Jan. 5, 1924; s. Keizo and Tome N.; student U. Hawaii, 1941, 46, Chgo. Tech. Coll., 1946-48; m. Betty Sanaye Sakurada, June 5, 1949; children—Steven M., Russel S., Kathleen S., Noreen R. Pres., K. Nagata Ltd., Honolulu, 1948—, K. Nagata Constrn. Inc., 1951—. Mem. Contractors Licence Bd. Commn., 1969-77. Trustee, Hawaii Carpenters Pension Trust Fund, Hawaiian Carpenter Health and Welfare Trust Fund. Served with M.I., U.S. Army, 1942-45. Mem. Gen. Contractor Assn. Hawaii (dir.). Address: 723C Umi St Honolulu HI 96819

NAGEOTTE, FRANCIS LOUIS, transportation company executive; b. Cleve., Aug. 19, 1926; s. Mark Eugene and Lenore Cecilia (O'Malley) N.; m. Kathleen Marie Sweeney, Oct. 8, 1949; children—Francis Xavier, Michael Patrick, Mary Ellen Nageotte Lemon, Judith Ann Nageotte Kieffner, Mark Edward, James Kevin, Kathleen Marie, Margaret Eileen, Joseph Paul. Student Willcox Coll. Commerce, 1946-47, Case Western Res. U., 1954-57; postgrad. Stanford U., 1967, U. Pa., 1977; D.H.L. (hon.), Miles Coll., 1982. With Greyhound Corp., Phoenix, 1947—, pres., chief operating officer, 1982—; chmn., chief exec. officer Greyhound Lines, Inc., 1979—; dir. affiliated cos.; bd. cons. Eno Found. for Transp., Inc. Served with USNR, 1944-46. Mem. Hwy. Users Fedn. (officer, exec. com.). Republican. Roman Catholic. Clubs: Ariz. Country, Plaza, Arizona (Phoenix). Office: 1906 Greyhound Tower Phoenix AZ 85077

NAGER, NORMAN RICHARD, public relations educator, writer, consultant; b. Schuylerville, N.Y., June 2, 1936; s. Max and Dora Nager; m. Petra K. Nager, Jan. 25, 1959. B.A. in Journalism, U. So. Calif., 1957, M.A., 1970, Ph.D. in Communication, 1978. Copyboy Los Angeles Daily News, 1954; publicity writer City of Los Angeles, 1955-57; reporter, photographer South Coast News, Laguna Beach, Calif., 1957; reporter Burbank (Calif.) Daily Rev., 1960-61; pub. relations writer Western home office Prudential Ins. Co. Am., Los Angeles, 1961-62; assoc. editor indsl. relations TRW, Inc. Space Tech. Labs., Redondo Beach, Calif., 1962-63; adminstrv. asst. communications to Speaker Calif. State Assembly, 1963-65, chief cons. to maj. caucus, 1965-67; dir. pub. relations Meml. Hosp. Med. Ctr., Long Beach, Calif., 1967-74; pub. relations cons., freelance journalist, instr. pub. relations and journalism U. So. Calif. and Calif. State U.-Long Beach, 1974-76; head pub. relations sequence dept. communications Calif. State U.-Fullerton, 1976—. Bd. dirs. Orange County Arts Alliance, 1982—. Served with U.S. Army, 1957-60. Recipient numerous awards in pub. relations; grantee Nat. Endowmment Humanities, 1980, Found. Pub. Relations Edn. and Research, 1983. Mem. Pub. Relations Soc. Am. (accredited; past dir. Orange County) nat. chmn. educators sect.), Assn. Edn. in Journalism and Mass Communication (nat. chmn. pub. relations div.), Found. Pub. Relations Research and Edn., So. Calif. Hosp. Pub. Relations Dirs. (past pres.), Pacific Coast Press Club (past 1st v.p.). Author: (with T. Harrell Allen) Public Relations Management by Objectives, 1984. Office: Dept of Communication California State University Fullerton CA 92634

NAGLE, RICHARD CLARK, neurol. surgeon; b. Chgo., Feb. 24, 1938; s. Richard Aloysis and Catherine Elizabeth (Clark) N.; B.S., U. Notre Dame, 1959; M.D., Loyola U., 1963; m. Alice Marie Connelly, Aug. 19, 1961; children—Alice, Catherine, Maureen, Patricia, Michael. Gen. surg. and neurosurg. resident Ill. Research and Presbyn.-St. Lukes

Hosp., Chgo., 1963-69; fellow Cook County Hosp., Chgo., 1969; practice medicine, specializing in neurol. surgery, Berkeley, Calif., 1969—; asst. clin. prof. neurosurgery U. Calif., Berkeley, 1977—; pres. med. staff Brookside Hosp., San Pablo, Calif., 1975; pres. med. staff Children's Hosp. of No. Calif., Oakland, 1980. Served to maj., USAR, 1963-70. Diplomate Am. Bd. Neurosurgery. Fellow ACS; mem. Calif. Med. Assn., Alameda-Contra Costa Med. Soc., Am. Assn. Neurol. Surgeons, San Francisco Neurol. Soc. Contbr. articles to profl. jours. Office: 3000 Colby St Berkeley CA 94705

NAGLE, ROBERT OWEN, lawyer; B. Watertown, S.D., Feb. 10, 1929; s. John Raymond and Kathleen Margaret (McQuillen) N.; B.S. in Economics, U. Wis., 1951; LL.B., U. Calif., 1957; m. Louise Emerson H'Doubler, Mar. 14, 1954; children—Robert Owen, Charles Francis, Margaret Louisa. Admitted to Calif. bar, 1957; asso. firm Morrison, Foerster, Holloway, Clinton and Clark, San Francisco, 1957-62, partner, 1962-64; gen. atty. Spreckels Sugar div. Amstar Corp., San Francisco, 1964-66, v.p., 1966-68, exec. v.p., 1968-71, v.p. parent co., N.Y.C., 1971-74, exec. v.p. Am. Sugar div., N.Y.C., 1975-76; pres., chief exec. officer Calif. and Hawaiian Sugar Co., San Francisco, 1976-82, also dir.; ptnr. firm Brobeck Phleger & Harrison, San Francisco, 1982—. Bd. dirs. Bay Area Council, San Francisco Bay Area council Boy Scouts Am.; trustee U. Calif. Berkeley Found., Wis. Alumni Research Found. Served to lt. j.g. USN, 1951-54; Korea. Decorated Air medal, Bronze Star. Mem. Am. Bar Assn., State Bar Calif., Bar Assn. San Francisco, Sugar Assn. (dir.), N.Y. Coffee and Sugar Exchange, Hawaiian Sugar Planters Assn., U. Wis. Found. Clubs: Claremont Country, Pacific Union, Mchts. Exchange of San Francisco. Office: 1 Market Plaza San Francisco CA 94105

NAGLESTAD, FREDERIC ALLEN, legis. advocate; b. Sioux City, Iowa, Jan. 13, 1929; s. Ole T. and Evelyn Elizabeth (Erschen) N.; student (scholar) U. Chgo., 1947-49; m. Beverly Minnette Shellberg, Feb. 14, 1958; children—Patricia Minnette, Catherine Janette. Pub. affairs, pub. relations, newscaster, announcer KSCJ-radio, Sioux City, Iowa, 1949-51; producer, dir., newscaster, announcer WOW-TV, Omaha, 1953-57; program mgr. WCPO-TV, Cin., 1957-58; mgr. KNTV-TV, San Jose, Calif., 1958-61; owner Results Employment Agy., San Jose, 1961-75; legis. advocate Naglestad Assos., Inc., Calif. Automotive Wholesalers Assn., Calif. Franchisee Council, Calif. Product Liability Task Force, Calif. Service Sta. Council, Calif. Assn. Ind. News Distbrs., Pest Control Operators of Calif., many others, 1969—. Pres. Calif. Employment Assn., 1970-72. Asst. concertmaster Sioux City Symphony Orch., 1945-47. Served as sgt. AUS, 1951-53. Recognized for outstanding contbn. to better employment law, Resolution State Calif. Legislature, 1971. Office: 3991 Fair Oaks Blvd Sacramento CA 95825

NAHMAN, NORRIS STANLEY, elec. engr.; b. San Francisco, Nov. 9, 1925; s. Hyman Cohen and Rae (Levin) N.; B.S., Calif. Poly. State U., 1951; M.S., Stanford U., 1952; Ph.D. in Elec. Engring., U. Kans., 1961; m. Shirley D. Maxwell, July 20, 1968; children—Norris Stanley, Jr., Vicki L., Vance W., Scott T. Electronic scientist Nat. Security Agy., Washington, 1952-55; prof. elec. engring., dir. electronics research lab. U. Kans., Lawrence, 1955-66; sci. cons., chief pulse and time domain sect. Nat. Bur. Standards, Boulder, Colo., 1966-73; prof., chmn. dept. elec. engring. U. Toledo, 1973-75; chief Time Domain Metrology, sr. scientist electromagnetic waveform metrology Nat. Bur. Standards, Boulder, 1975—; prof. elec. engring. U. Colo., Boulder, 1966—; lectr. NATO Advanced Study Inst., Castlevecchio, Italy, 1983; chmn. U.S. Nat. Commn. A, 1984—. Asst. scoutmaster Boy Scouts Am., Boulder, 1968-73, Toledo, 1973, com. chmn., Toledo, 1974-75, asst. scoutmaster, 1975-78, 81—. Served with U.S. Mcht. Marine, 1943-46, U.S. Army, 1952-55. Recipient Order Arrow award Boy Scouts Am., 1976; Ford Found. fellow in exptl. physics M.I.T., 1962. Fellow IEEE; mem. Am. Soc. Engring. Edn., Internat. Sci. RadioUnion, Sigma Xi, Sigma Pi Sigma, Tau Beta Pi, Eta Kappa Nu, Sigma Tau, Am. Radio Relay League. Inventor superconducting coaxial signal delay line, 1960. Office: 325 Broadway Boulder CO 80303

NAIMAN, RUBIN, psychologist; b. Regensberg, W. Ger., July 27, 1949; s. Charles and Mollie (Zelcer) N.; came to U.S., 1950, naturalized, 1969; B.S., U. Ariz., 1971, M.S., 1973; Ph.D., U.S. Internat. U., 1980. Regional dir. mental retardation service VA, 1973-75; dir. community services, div. mental health and retardation Desert Developmental Center, Nev., 1975-78; founder, 1978, since asso. Omega Psychology Center, San Diego; cons. in field, 1973—; mem. San Diego County Hospice; adj. faculty Calif. Sch. Profl. Psychology and San Diego City Coll. Conscientious objector. Mem. Am. Psychol. Assn. Author papers in field. Office: 336 Kalmia St San Diego CA 92101

NAKAGAKI, DAVID AKIRA, civil engineer; b. Berkeley, Calif., Oct. 14, 1954; s. George Yasuyoshi and Haruye (Yoshiwara) N; B.S. and M.S. in Civil Engring., Stanford U., 1977; postgrad. Calif. State U., 1980—. Registered profl. engr., Calif., 1979. Project engr. Los Angeles County Sanitation Dists., Whittier, Calif., 1977—, solid waste mgmt. dept., 1982—. Recipient Student award ASTM, 1976. Mem. ASCE, Am. Water Works Assn., Water Pollution Control Fedn., Tau Beta Pi, Chi Epsilon. Democrat. Methodist. Home: 21302 Wavecrest Circle Huntington Beach CA 92646 Office: PO Box 4998 Whittier CA 90607

NAKAGAWA, SUSUMU, research entomologist; b. Hilo, Hawaii, Sept. 21, 1922; s. Seichi and Matsuno (Fukumori) N.; B.S., U. Hawaii, 1949; m. Ellen Chiyoko Minaai, June 15, 1951; children—Cheryl, Linda, Colin, Kris. Sci. aide U.S. Dept. Agr., Hilo, Hawaii, 1949-50, biol. aide, 1950-52, entomologist, 1952-65, research entomologist, 1965—. Served with U.S. Army, 1944-46. Recipient Unit award for superior service Dept. Agr., 1953, 59, 64. Mem. Hawaiian Entomol. Soc., Hawaiian Acad. Sci., Entomol. Soc. Am., AAAS, Orgn. Profl. Employees, Sigma Xi. Buddhist. Clubs: 442d Vets. (pres.; dir.). Home: 1180 Mililani St Hilo HI 96720 Office: Box 917 Hilo HI 96720

NAKAHATA, TADAKA, cons. engr., land surveyor; b. Kauai, Hawaii, Nov. 24, 1924; s. Tadao and Yae (Ohta) N.; B.S. in Civil Engring., U. Hawaii, 1951; m. Clara S. Sakanashi, June 23, 1956; children—Leanne A., Holly E., Merry Y. Engr./surveyor B.H. McKeague & Assos., Honolulu, 1951-55, Harland Bartholomew & Assos., Honolulu, 1955-56, Paul Low Engring. Co., Honolulu, 1956-59, Nakahata, Kaneshige, Imata & Assos., 1959-63; owner T. Nakahata, Honolulu, 1964—; mem. Hawaii Bd. Registration of Architects, Engrs. and Land Surveyors, 1980—. Served with AUS, 1946-47. Mem. ASCE, Am. Congress Surveying and Mapping, Nat. Soc. Profl. Engrs. Mem. United Ch. of Christ. Office: Room 23 1259 S Beretania St Honolulu HI 96814

NAKAMURA, HIROMU, psychologist; b. Los Angeles, Nov. 6, 1926; s. Genjiro and Misao (Kamura) N.; A.B., U. Redlands, 1948; M.A., UCLA, 1951; Ph.D., U. So. Calif., 1973; m. Tamaye Yumiba, Mar. 27, 1955; children—Glenn Vernon, Colleen Patricia. Clin. psychology intern Massillon (Ohio) State Hosp., 1951-52; clin. psychologist Patton (Calif.) State Hosp., 1952-58; clin. psychologist Lanterman State Hosp. and Developmental Center (formerly Pacific State Hosp.), Pomona, Calif., 1958—, program dir., 1971—. Mem. Am., Calif. psychol. assns., Am. Assn. Mental Deficiency, AAAS, Am. Pub. Health Assn., Nat. Geographic Soc., Town Hall Calif., Los Angeles World Affairs Council, World-wide Acad. Scholars, Psi Chi. Presbyterian. Home: 3861 Shelter Grove Dr Claremont CA 91711 Office: PO Box 100 Pomona CA 91766

NAKAMURA, YUKIO, mechanical engineer; b. Kurume, Japan, Jan. 5, 1930; s. Jingo N.; came to U.S., 1930, naturalized, 1954. B.S.M.E., UCLA, 1951; M.S.M.E., U. So. Calif., 1956; m. Alyce Sumiko Nakamura, July 18, 1954; children—Jeffrey, Kathy, Lori, Kari. Engr., Byron Jackson Pump Co., Los Angeles, 1951, 53-56; sr. engr. N.Am. Aviation, Downey, 1956-57, 59-60; cons. Rhodes E. Rule, Los Angeles, 1975-78; engr. Airite Products, Los Angeles, 1958-59; sr. engr. specialist Aerojet Gen. Corp., Azusa, Calif., 1960-71; program mgr. Jet Propulsion Lab., Pasadena, 1971—. Served with U.S. Army, 1951-53. Recipient Tech. Brief award NASA, 1979; NSF grantee, 1974, 76. Mem. AIAA, Am. Def. Preparedness Assn. Republican. Buddhist. Home: 819 Ridgeside Dr Monterey Park CA 91754 Office: 4800 Oak Grove Dr Pasadena CA 91109

NAKANISHI, ALAN TOMIO, optometrist; b. Walnut Creek, Calif., Nov. 2, 1948; m. Rea Ginochio, 1 dau., Chanel. A.A., U. Calif., 1969, B.S. in Physiol. Optics, 1971, O.D. with honors, 1973. Practice optometry, Walnut Creek, 1973—. Mem. Japanese Am. Citizens League, 1975—, M.H. deYoung Mus. Soc., 1978—, Nirvana Found., 1978—; instr. ARC, 1978—; bd. advisors Lions Eye Found., 1978; bd. dirs. O'Hara Handicap Awareness Found., 1978, dir. pub. infor., 1978; bd. dirs. Mt. Diablo Aquarium Soc., 1980-81, v.p., 1980. Recipient DAR medal of honor, 1966. Mem. Am. Optometric Assn. (Recognition award 1980, 81, 82), Calif. Optometric Assn., Bay Area Optometric Assn. (seminar chmn. 1978—, dir. 1979—), Alameda Contra Costa Counties Optometric Soc. (bull. editor 1977-80, dir. 1978—, chmn. dept. pub. info. 1979-80, program dir. 1982—), Nat. Eye Research Found., Internat. Orthokeratology Sect., U. Calif. Alumni Assn., Am. Optometric Found., Nat. Assn. Profls., Better Vision Inst., Walnut Creek C. of C., Calif. Pub. Vision League, Calif. Optometric Polit. Action Com., Pacific Coast Assn. Magicians, Internat. Contact Lens Clinic, Council Sports Vision, Fedn. Am. Scientists, Am. Juggling Assn., U.S. Table Tennis Assn., San Francisco Underwater Photographic Soc., Kajukembo Assn. Am. Clubs: Diablo Valley Lions (bull. editor 1977-78, dir. 1976-80, chmn. sight conservation 1978—), Young Magicians, Royal Hawaiian Adventure. Office: 1871 N Main St Walnut Creek CA 94596

NAKANO, GEORGE SAKAYE, educational administrator; b. Los Angeles, Nov. 24, 1935; s. Shigeto and Sumie (Asada) N.; m. Helen Michiyo Unno, Mar. 15, 1939; children—Laurie Tamiyo Nakano and Kevin Michio. B.S. in Math., Calif. State U., 1970, M.A. in Edn., 1977. Cert. tchr., Calif. Research asst. Hughes Aircraft Co., Culver City, Calif., 1962-68, sr. research asst., 1968-71; tchr. math. Jordan High Sch., Los Angeles, 1971-74; asst. proj. dir., Inglewood (Calif.) Unified Sch. Dist., 1974-76, project dir., 1976-78; asst. prin. Centinela Sch., Inglewood, 1978-82, Worthington Sch., Inglewood, 1982—. Master ceremonies, mem. exec. planning com. 1st U.S. Nat. Kendo Championship, 1978; co-founder Gardena Pioneer Project; bd. dirs. Kendo Fedn. of U.S.A., 1970—; exec. sec. So. Calif. Kendo Fedn., 1975-79, v.p., 1981—; pres. Torrance Japanese Am. Citizens League, 1983; mem. Torrance Rose Float Assn., Torrance Sister City Assn. Served with Calif. Air N.G., 1954-60; mem. Res., 1960-62. Mem. Assn. Supervision and Curriculum Devel., Calif. Math. Council, Calif. State U. Alumni Assn., Internat. Council for Computer in Edn., Nat. Assn. Educators in Computing, Nat. Council Tchrs. Math., Torrance Hist. Soc. Democrat. Buddhist. Clubs: Charter (Torrance). Home: 22710 Elm Ave Torrance CA 90505 Office: 11101 Yukon Ave Inglewood CA 90303

NAKANO, KENNETH K(ENJI), neurologist; b. Los Angeles, Jan. 29, 1942; s. Samuel T. and Kazuko K. (Nishimine) N.; B.A., Pomona Coll., 1963; M.D., Columbia U., 1967; M.P.H., Harvard U., 1971, S.M. in Epidemiology, 1972; m. Juanita Wynne, Feb. 14, 1968; children—Kenneth K., Kim K., Kam K., Kari K. Intern, Queen's Hosp., Honolulu, 1967-68; resident fellow Harvard U. Med. Sch., 1968-71, fellow in neurology, 1968-71, asst. prof., 1973-75; resident in neurology Peter Bent Brigham Hosp., Boston, 1968-71, Children's Hosp., Boston, 1968-71, Beth Israel Hosp., Boston, 1968-71; research fellow in epidemiology Harvard U. Sch. Public Health, 1971-73; neurologist Straub Clinic, Honolulu, 1975—; cons. in field. Recipient George Thorn Teaching award Harvard U., 1974. Diplomate Am. Bd. Psychiatry and Neurology. Fellow Royal Coll. Physicians (Can.); mem. Am. Assn. Electromyography and Electrodiagnosis, Royal Soc. Medicine, Am. Assn. Neurologic and Orthopaedic Surgeons, (cert.; v.p. 1982), AMA, Am. Acad. Neurology, Am. Public Health Assn., Am. EEG Soc., Am. Med. EEG Assn., World Fedn. Neurology, Hawaii Med. Assn., Mass. Med. Soc. Author: Pediatric Neurology, 1976; Neurology of Musculoskeletal and Rheumatic Disorders, 1979; Current Neurology, 1979; Textbook of Rheumatology, 1980; Back Pain: Is There a Cure?, 1983. Home: 824A N Kalaheo Ave Kailua HI 96734 Office: 888 S King St Honolulu HI 96813

NAKANO, KENNETH RIKUJI, real estate and travel exec.; b. Hilo, Hawaii, Nov. 10, 1915; s. Genatro and Takiyo (Kawakami) N.; ed. Waseda Internat. Inst., Tokyo; polit.-economy certificate, Waseda U., 1938; Ph.D., H.H.D., St. John's Theol. Sem.; m. Ellen Nakatani, June 12, 1942; 1 dau., Judith. Chmn. Nakano Ken Realty (Tokyo) Inc.; sales coordinator, travel cons. Travel Booking, Inc.; v.p. Internat. Bus. Service Co. Ltd., Tokyo; prin. broker Central Pacific Kosan, Inc., Honolulu; dir. Hawaiian Lanes Inc., Banpo Shoji Co. Tokyo Inc. Mem. Honolulu City Traffic Commn., 1953, Honolulu City Rent Control Commn., 1957; bd. govs. Goodwill Industries, Honolulu; mem. Honolulu chpt. Nat. Crime and Delinquency. Assn.; mem. rural dist. bd. mgrs. YMCA; exec. bd. Aloha council Boy Scouts Am. Recipient Lions Internat. Charter-Monarch 25 Yr. award, 1971; certificate distinguished service strengthening ties State of Calif. and Hawaii, County of Los Angeles, 1973; lic. minister Ho. of God Ch. and Bible Sch. Inst. Mem. Honolulu C. of C., Pacific Air Travel Assn., Am. Soc. Travel Agts., Honolulu Bd. Realtors, Smithsonian Assocs. Clubs: Lions, Masons, K.T., Shriners, Honolulu Press. Home and office: PO Box 245 Waianae HI 96792

NAMES, JEAN HARRELL, cons. human resources devel.; b. Port Arthur, Tex., Dec. 20, 1935; s. George Vertus and Agnes (Thibodeaux) Harrell; B.S., U. Oreg., 1976, M.S., 1978; m. Gary P. Cross, Sept. 19, 1978; children by previous marriage—B. Christopher, Kevin Milan, Loch K. Names. Exec. sec. Dow Chem. Co., Freeport, Tex., 1955-56, U. Tex. Med. Br., Galveston, 1956-62; office mgr. physicians practice, 1969-72; owner, mgmt. cons. Human Resources Devel. and Mgmt., Eugene, Oreg., 1976—; instr. Lane Community Coll.; guest speaker confs. and civic groups; vol. services to women's prison, Jr. Achievement; tchr. public relations Lane Community Coll. Pres. Stanislaus County Med. Aux., Modesto, Calif., 1969-71; publicity dir. Modesto Symphony, 1971-72; presenter weekly TV program Ecology Action in Calif., 1972; pres. Commn. Rights of Women, Eugene. Mem. Profl. Devel. Council Oreg.; mem. Am. Soc. Tng. and Devel., AAUW. Club: P.E.O. Sisterhood. Author: (with others) Conflict and Human Interaction, 1979; Professional Development for Women, 1979. Home: 460 W 25th Ave Eugene OR 97405

NANDA, VED P., law educator; b. Gujranwala, India, Nov. 20, 1934; s. Jagan Nath and Attar (Kaur) N.; came to U.S., 1959; LL.B., U. Delhi, 1955, LL.M., 1958; LL.M., Northwestern U., 1962; postgrad. Yale U., 1962-65. Asst. prof. law U. Denver, 1965-68, asso. prof., 1968-70, prof. law, dir. Internat. Legal Studies program, 1972—, pres. faculty senate, 1977-79, trustees faculty and edn. com., 1979—; vis. prof. law U. Iowa Coll. Law, Iowa City, 1974-75, U. San Diego, 1979, Fla. State U., 1973; disting. vis. prof. internat. law Chgo. Kent Coll. Law, summer and fall 1981; cons. Solar Energy Research Inst., 1978-81, Dept. Energy, 1980-81. Co-chmn. Colo. Public Broadcasting Fedn., 1977-78; mem. Gov.'s Commn. on Public Telecommunications, 1980—. U. Delhi grad. fellow, 1956-58. Mem. World Assn. Law Profs. (sec.-gen. 1979—), UN Assn. (Colo. div. v.p. 1973-76), Am. Assn. Comparative Study of Law, Am. Soc. Internat. Law (exec. council 1969-72, 81—), Assn. Am. Law Schs., U.S. Inst. Human Rights, Internat. Law Assn., Assn. U.S. Mems. of Internat. Inst. Space Law (bd. dirs., mem. exec. com.), Order of St. Ives (pres.). Clubs: Rotary, Denver Press, Denver Athletic. Editor: Water Needs for the Future, 1977; (with M. Cherif Bassiouni) A Treatise on International Criminal Law, 2 vols., 1973; (with others) Global Human Rights, 1981; The Law of Transnational Business Transactions, 1981; World Climate Change, 1983. editorial bd. Jour. Comparative Law; adv. bd. Jour. Legal Edn. Office: U Denver Coll Law 200 W 14 Ave Denver CO 80204

NANEY, DAVID GLEN, lawyer, educator; b. Bakersfield, Calif., Apr. 21, 1952; s. Glen Tillman and Olivia Mae N.; m. Linda Diane Romero, July 19, 1975; children—David Tillman, Michael Christian. A.A., Bakersfield Coll., 1972; B.A., UCLA, 1974; J.D., Loyola U., 1977. Bar: Calif. 1977. Law clk. Engstrom and Lipscomb, Los Angeles, 1976, Roberts Farms Inc., Bakersfield, Calif., Greater Bakersfield Legal Assistance Inc., 1977; atty. firm Freeman, Freeman & Smiley, Los Angeles, 1978-80; sole practice, Bakersfield, 1980—; prof. law Bakersfield Coll.; legal adviser CAP; instr. in estate planning. Mem. scholarship com.; Bakersfield Coll.; pro-bono legal counsel TEAMM Resources Inc., also Parents with Spl. Children; active Sheets for Sheriff, Ferguson for Dist. Atty. campaigns, 1982. Mem. Kern County Bar Assn., Calif. State Bar Assn., Assn. Trial Lawyers Am., ABA, UCLA Alumni Assn., Bakersfield Coll. Alumni Assn., Phi Alpha Delta. Republican. Club: Lions (East Bakersfield). Author (with Douglas K. Freeman): How to Incorporate a Small Business, 1978. Home: 3500 Akers Rd Apt 60 Pinewood Lake Bakersfield CA 93309 Office: 1715 Chester Ave Suite 300 Bakersfield CA 93301

NANKAS, ERNEST, optometrist; b. Boston, Dec. 6, 1932; s. Morris and Pearl N.; B.S., UCLA, 1953; B.S., O.D., So. Calif. Coll. Optometry, 1957; m. Barbara Lee, Aug. 4, 1963; children—Wendy Lee, Andrew David. With Los Angeles County Health Dept., 1953-54; pvt. practice optometry, Marina del Rey, Calif., 1961—. Bd. dirs. Garrick Clinic, Calif. Vision Service Plan. Mem. Marina del Rey C. of C., Los Angeles County Optometric Soc. (dir., pres. 1974), Calif. Optometric Assn. (trustee 1974—, pres. 1979-80), Am. Optometric Assn. Republican. Clubs: Marina City, Calabassas Tennis. Office: 4716 1/2 Admiralty Way Marina del Rey CA 90291

NAPIER, DANIEL WILLIAM, industrial hygienist, safety consultant; b. Palm Springs, Calif., June 20, 1944; s. Alezander John and Eoelyn Mary (Roche) N.; children—Elizabeth Christine, Daniel William. B.S. in Bus. Adminstrn., Calif. State Coll., 1972; M.S. in Environ. Sci., Calif. State U., 1980. Cert. and indsl. hygienist, Safety profl. Cons., indsl. hygienist Calif. Casualty, Los Angeles, 1974-75; tng. cons. UCIS, Marina Del Rey, Calif., 1975-76; sr. cons., indsl. hygienist Employee Benefits Ins. Co., Santa Monica, Calif., 1976-79; sr. cons., indsl. hygienist Mission Ins., Los Angeles, 1979-81; corporate indsl. hygienist Pacific Compensation, San Bruno, Calif., 1981—. Bd. dirs. ARC. Mem. Am. Acad. Indsl. Hygienists, Am. Indsl. Hygiene Assn., Am. Soc. Safety Engrs. Democrat. Roman Catholic. Home: 4005 Cathann St Torrance CA 90503 Office: 11827 Ventura Blvd Studio City CA also 950 Elm Ave San Bruno CA

NAPIER, RICHARD STEPHEN, elec. engr.; b. Clarksburg, W.Va., May 13, 1949; s. Richard Arthur and Lois Jane (Silcott) N.; B.S. in E.E., W.Va. U., 1971; M.S.E.E., Stanford U., 1973; postgrad. Foothill Coll., Los Altos Hills, Calif.; m. Barbara Elaine Deems, June 13, 1970; 1 son, Stephen Michael. Meter tester Monongahela Power Co., Clarksburg, 1969, engring. trainee, Fairmont, W.Va., 1970, 71; mem. tech. staff Bell Telephone Lab., Holmdel, N.J., 1972-73; head synthesizer equipment sect. Watkins Johnson Co., Palo Alto, Calif., 1973—. Planning commr., City of Sunnyvale. Western Electric Fund scholar, 1970-71; lic. pvt. pilot. Mem. IEEE, Nat. Profl. Engrs., Assn. Old Crows, Eta Kappa Nu, Tau Beta Pi. Republican. Contbr. articles to profl. jours. Home: 754 Carlisle Way Sunnyvale CA 94087 Office: 2525 N 1st St San Jose CA 95131

NAPOLI, WENDY JEAN, telephone company official; b. Hopewell, Va., Aug. 17, 1955; d. Tom Richard and Nancy Laura (Amos) Richardson; m. Bob Richard Napoli, July 11, 1981; 1 dau., Kindra Marie. Student Coll. Canyons, 1983—. Clk., Gen. Telephone Co., Marina Del Rey, Calif., 1974-75, machine operator, 1975-78, data control ckl., 1978-79, data supr., 1979-81, data coordinator, 1982-83, service office analyst, 1983—; computer programmer; cons. Mem. Christian Ch. Office: 11333 Sepulveda Blvd Suite 7741 Mission Hills CA 91345

NARANJO, MICHAEL ALFRED, sculptor; b. Santa Fe, Aug. 28, 1944; s. Michael Edward and Rose (Sisneros) N.; m. Laurie Engel, Apr. 29, 1978; children—Jenna Skai, Bryn Mariah. Student Highlands U., 1964-67, under Lee Jones, Taos, N.Mex., 1969-70. One man shows Colorado Springs Fine Arts Ctr., 1982; exhibited in group shows Native Am. Cultural Ctr., Niagara, N.Y., 1981; represented in permanent collection Heard Mus., Phoenix. Mem. N.Mex. Arts Commn., 1971-73. Presented Dance of the Eagle to Pres. Nixon, Oval Office, 1971; named Blind Veteran of Yr., VA, 1973; recipient Gov.'s award State of N.Mex., 1976; Outstanding Vietnam Vet. award Gov. Bruce King/Pres. Jimmy Carter, 1979; recipient Silver medal Scottsdale Nat. Indian Arts Exhbn., 1973, Catlin Peace Pipe award, 1973, P. Tarmigan Sage Co. grand award, 1st award Scottsdale Nat. Arts Exhbn., Phoenix, 1974, 1st prize sculpture SWAIA Indian Market, Santa Fe, 1975, 77, 1st prize No. Pueblos Indian Art Show, Picuris Pueblo, N.Mex., 1978, 79, 1st prize sculpture Arts Festival Atlanta, 1981. Served with 9th Inf. U.S. Army, 1967-68. Decorated Purple Heart when blinded. Appeared on Today show NBC, 1979; subject of Michael Naranjo, The Story of an American Indian (Mary Carroll Nelson), 1975; The Sweet Grass Lives on—36 Contemporary American Indian Artists (Jamake Highwater), 1980; other books and articles.

NARCIANDI, FERNANDO M., bar, dairy products and soft-service equipment co. exec.; b. Havana, Cuba, May 30, 1947; came to U.S., 1961, naturalized, 1969; s. Mateo and Leonor Narciandi, A.A., Spokane Jr. Coll., 1966; B.S., Woodbury U., 1971; m. Consuelo Herrera, Oct. 25, 1969; 1 son, Eric. Sect. supr. Prudential Ins. Co., Los Angeles, 1969-73; audit mgr. Signal Ins. Co., Los Angeles, 1973-75, Penn Fin. Corp., Santa Monica, Calif., 1974-75; gen. mgr., controller for employee benefits cons Penn Fin. Co., 1975-76, credit and collection mgr., 1976-77; pres., dir. Yogurt Mktg. Corp. and Glacier Products of So. Calif., Garden Grove, Calif., 1977-80; pres., owner Fiesta Enterprises Inc., Miami, 1980—; cons. in field. Served with USMC, 1966-69. Decorated Purple Heart. Mem. Inst. Internal Auditors, Am. Mgmt. Assn., Soc. Advancement Mgmt., Credit Mgrs. Assn., DAV. Republican. Roman Catholic. Club: Kings Racket and Health. Office: 5411 NW 74th Ave Miami FL 33166

NARODICK, SALLY GOULD, controller; b. Clinton, Mass., June 26, 1945; d. Morris and Dorothy Gould; m. Kit G. Narodick, Apr. 11, 1970; 1 dau., Lisa. B.A., Boston U., 1962; M.A., Columbia U., 1969; M.B.A., NYU, 1973. C.P.A., Wash. Security analyst Paine, Webber, Jackson & Curtis, N.Y.C., 1971-73; security analyst Seattle-First Nat. Bank, 1973-75, mgr. asset, liability, 1975-79, mgr. loan rev., exam, 1979-80, controller, 1980—. Trustee Seafirst Found.; bd. dirs. Seattle/King

County United Way; assoc. Pacific Sci. Ctr. Recipient Outstanding Alumni award NYU; chosen Newsmaker TIME mag., 1982-84. Mem. Fin. Execs. Inst., Wash. State Soc. C.P.A.s, Seattle C. of C. (trustee, treas.). Club: Rainier (Seattle). Home: 4513 54th Ave NE Seattle WA 98105 Office: Seattle First Nat Bank PO Box 3977 (FAB-21) Seattle WA 98124

NARWITZ, JERRY RAOUL, investment banking exec.; b. Los Angeles, July 16, 1936; s. Harold L. and Audrey (Britton) N.; m. Susie H. Throop, Aug. 21, 1979; 1 dau., Jeri Ann; 1 stepdau., Rachael. Student U. Puget Sound, 1954-55; A.A., Multnomah Coll., 1956; student in bus. Harvard U., 1959. Staff mgr., field rep. Goodyear Tire & Rubber Co., Akron, Ohio, 1958-61; v.p., sales mgr. J.B. Hanauer Co., Beverly Hills, Calif., 1961-66; founder, chmn. bd., pres. J.R. Narwitz Co., Sacramento and Beverly Hills, 1966-81; chmn. bd. Data-Quote, Inc., Los Angeles, 1981—; chmn., pres., chief exec. officer Rebound House Devel. Co., Inc.; dir. Urban Counsellors, Inc., Compu-Claim Co., Econ. Data-Quote Co.; exec. producer Movie Tech Corp.; mem. Mcpl. Securities Rulemaking Bd. Active numerous election coms. Republican Party, 1962—. Recipient Meritorious Achievement proclamation and key to City San Bernardino (Calif.), 1970; citation Gov. Calif., 1972. Mem. Nat. Assn. Securities Dealers, City of Beverly Hills C. of C., Securities Industry Assn., C. of C. U.S.A., Mcpls. Fin. Officers Assn. (asso.), Calif. Assessment Bond Underwriters Assn., Sigma Chi. Episcopalian. Clubs: Arden Hills Swim and Tennis (Sacramento); Dallas Cowboys. Office: 630 Fulton Ave Suite A Sacramento CA 95825

NASH, ANN ELIZABETH, educational consultant, researcher, educator; b. Winnipeg, Man., Can., Dec. 12, 1928; d. John Wills and Margaret Agnes (Gray) Macleod; m. Richard Earl Bachtel, Dec. 19, 1947; children—Margaret Ann, John Macleod, Bradley Wills; m. 2d, Louis Philip Nash, June 30, 1978. A.B., Occidental Coll., 1947; M.A., Calif. State U.-Los Angeles, 1976. Cert. tchr., adminstr., Calif. Elem. tchr. pub. and pvt. schs. in Calif., 1947-50, 64-77; dir. Emergency Sch. Aid Act program, spl. projects, spl. arts State of Calif., 1977-80; leader, mem. program rev. team Calif. State Dept. Edn., 1981—; cons. Pasadena Unified Sch. Dist., 1981—; teaching asst., adj. prof. U. So. Calif.; cons. sch. dists., state depts. edn.; presenter workshops/seminars; mem. legis. task forces. Mem. resource allocation com. City of Pasadena; mem. Los Angeles World Affairs Council; mem. docent council Pasadena Hist. Soc.; mem. Pasadena Philharm. Com.; mem. women's com. Pasadena Symphony Assn. Emergency Sch. Aid Act grantee, 1977-81. Mem. World Council Gifted and Talented Children, Internat. Soc. Edn. Through Art, Council Exceptional Children, Am. Ednl. Research Assn., Assn. Supervision and Curriculum Devel., Nat. Art Educators Assn., Calif. Art Educators Assn., Calif. Humanities Edn. Assn., AAUW, Phi Delta Kappa, Kappa Delta Pi, Assistance League of Pasadena. Contbr. articles to publs.; writer/editor: Arts for the Gifted and Talented, 1981. Office: 732 Pinehurst Dr Pasadena CA 91106

NASH, GILLIAN LEA, public relations executive; b. Gardena, Calif., May 3, 1955; d. Walter E. and Marilyn L. (Harrer) N.; A.A. in Journalism, El Camino Community Coll., 1975; B.A. in Journalism with honors, San Diego State U., 1977. Creative dir. Braun & Co., Los Angeles, 1978-80; dir. pub. relations Transam. Occidental Life, Los Angeles, 1980-82; asst. v.p. pub. relations Transam. Occidental, 1982—; cons. Com. mem. Los Angeles Arthritis Found. Recipient Clarion award Women in Communications, 1982. Mem. Women in Communications, Pub. Relations Soc. Am., Women in Pub. Affairs, Sigma Delta Chi, Sigma Kappa. Republican. Office: 1150 So Olive St Los Angeles CA 90115

NASH, THOMAS HAWKES, III, botany educator; b. Arlington, Va., Nov. 13, 1945; s. Thomas Hawkes and Muriel (Garney) N.; B.S. in Botany, Duke U., 1967; postgrad. in biology U. Minn., summers 1967, 69; M.S. in Botany, Rutgers U., 1969, Ph.D. in Botany and Stats., 1971. Teaching asst. Rutgers U., Newark, 1967-68, asst. instr., New Brunswick, N.J., 1968-69, teaching asst., New Brunswick, 1969-71; asst. prof. botany Ariz. State U., 1971-76, assoc. prof. botany, 1976-81, prof. botany, 1981—. Mem. Tempe (Ariz.) Noise Abatement Com., 1979-81. Mem. Am. Bryological and Lichenological Soc. (v.p. 1979-81, pres. 1981-83), Internat. Assn. Lichenology (sec. 1975-81), Ecol. Soc. Am., Brit. Lichenological Soc., Biometric Soc., AAAS, Am. Inst. Biol. Scis., Orgn. Tropical Studies, Bot. Soc. Am., Ariz. Acad. Sci., Sigma Xi. Contbr. numerous articles and papers to profl. jours. Home: 1449 N McAllister St Tempe AZ 85281 Office: Dept Botany Ariz State Univ Tempe AZ 85287

NASHEM, LELAND O., exec. recruiting exec., life ins. exec., mgmt. cons.; b. Seattle; s. Oscar and Myrtle A. (Spriggs) N.; ed. U. Wash.; m. Berenice K. Kaufmann, 1926; children—Bettie Lee, Jack Lee. Pres. Nashem Furniture Co., 1926-33; sales mgr. Kaufmann Leonard Co.; with Met. Life Ins. Co., 1933-38, successively agt., asst. mgr., asst. mgr. in charge; with Acacia Mut. Life Ins. Co., 1938-48, mgr. Seattle br., 1938-40, home office mgr., asst. field v.p., Washington, 1940-43, mgr. Chgo. br. and in charge Pacific Coast brs., 1943-48; pres. Lee Nashem Agy., Ltd., N.Y.C., gen. agts. for Mut. Benefit Life Ins. Co., Newark, 1948-60, Can. Life Assurance Co., Toronto, 1960-66; pres., chief exec. officer Exec. Recruiting-Search div. affiliate Lee Nashem Cos., sec. gen. agts. and mgrs. council Can. Life Assurance Co., Toronto; chmn. exec. com., dir. Life Ins. Securities Corp.; dir. Roger Williams Life Ins. Co., Providence, Major Pool Equipment Corp. N.J., Maine Indemnity Co., Portland. Mem. Century City C. of C., Nat., Am. assns. life underwriters, Midtown Mgrs., Gen. Agts. and Mgrs. Assn. N.Y., Nat. Sales Execs. Club. Clubs: Rotary, Masons, K.T., Shriners; Westchester Country (Rye, N.Y.); Boulder Brook (Scarsdale, N.Y.); N.Y. Athletic (N.Y.C.); Hunt, Oak Brook Polo (Hinsdale, Ill.); Century City (Calif.). Home: Century Towers 2222 Ave of Stars Los Angeles CA 90067 Office: 1901 Ave of Stars Los Angeles CA 90067

NASO, VALERIE JOAN, automobile dealership executive, travel company operator, photographer, writer; b. Stockton, Calif., Aug. 19, 1941; d. Alan Robert and Natalie Grace (Gardner) McKittrick Naso; m. Peter Joralemon, May 31, 1971 (div.). Student pub. schs., Piedmont, Calif. Cert. graphoanalyst. Pres., Naso Motor Co. (formerly Broadway Cadillacs, Oakland, Calif.) Bishop, Calif., 1964—; owner, operator Wooden Horse Antiques, Bishop, 1970-82; editor, writer, photographer Sierra Life Mag., Bishop, 1980-83; freelance writer, photographer, 1975—; owner, operator Boredom Tours, Bishop, 1981—; cons. graphoanalyst. Mem. Authors Guild, Inc., Authors League Am., Am. Film Inst., Archives of Am. Art, Bishop C. of C. Clubs: Cadillac LaSalle; Wagner Soc. (N.Y.C.). Fiction, non-fiction work pub. in Horse and Horseman, Am. Horseman, Cameo Mag., Desert Mag., Sierra Life Mag. Home: 220 E 54th St Apt 9A New York NY 10022 Office: 783 N Main St Bishop CA 93514

NASON, GEORGE MALCOLM, computer systems and services co. exec.; b. Spokane, Wash., Feb. 17, 1933; s. George Malcolm and Ella (Buist) N.; B.S., Calif. State Coll. at Long Beach, 1958; m. Dolores Irene Lockinger, Oct. 7, 1951; children—George Malcolm III, Scott, Lance, Natalie. Data processor, project mgr. Gen. Motors Corp., Los Angeles, 1956-65; systems mgr. dairy div. Arden Mayfair, 1965-68; dir. systems Gallo Winery, Los Angeles, Modesto, Calif., 1968-73; dir. systems and data processing Familian Corp., 1973-74; v.p. Coldwell Banker & Co., Los Angeles, 1974-78; pres. Nason & Assos., Inc., Long Beach, Calif., 1978—. Bd. dirs. Confrat. of Christian Doctrine High Sch., Long Beach, 1969-70. Served with USMCR, 1951-54. Mem. Data Processing Mgmt. Assn. Republican. Roman Catholic. Home: 4503 Pepperwood Ave Long Beach CA 90808

NASSIF, ALEXANDER, lawyer; b. Monterrey, N.L., Mexico, Dec. 3, 1946; came to U.S., 1963, naturalized, 1973; s. Alexander Nassif Attiyeh and Sara N. B.A. in Spanish Lit., UCLA, 1971, J.D., 1976. Bar: D.C. 1979. Asst. dean of students, campus programs and activities office UCLA, 1971-72; atty. adviser, office of gen. counsel, office of sec. HHS, Washington, 1976-78; trial atty. office of solicitor Dept. Labor, Washington, 1978-80; mem. Centro Latino, Los Angeles, 1983—; cons. Bd. dirs. Attiyeh Benevolent Soc. Mem. ABA, Am. Immigration Lawyers Assn., Am. Assn. Pub. Adminstrs. Democrat. Clubs: Rotary (Los Angeles); Astara. Office: 304 S Broadway Suite 500 Los Angeles CA 90013

NATARAJAN, ENGAN VENU, industrial engineer; b. Engan, India, July 25, 1942; came to U.S., 1969, naturalized, 1976; s. Engan P. and Engan (Janaki) Venu; B.S. in Mech. Engring., U. Madras, 1968; M.S. in Indsl. Engring., U. Toledo, 1971; m. Meenakshi, June 29, 1969; children—Sai, Siva, Rathna. Methods engr. Essex Internat., 1971-73; mgmt. engr. St. Vincent Hosp., Toledo, 1973-74; sr. mgmt. engr. Mt. Sinai Med. Center, Chgo., 1974-77; dir. mgmt. engring. St. Joseph's Hosp., Stockton, Calif., 1977-79; dir. budget and mgmt. services Eisenhower Med. Center, Rancho Mirage, Calif., 1979—. Life teaching cert. Calif. Community Colls. Mem. Am. Inst. Indsl. Engrs. (sr.), Hosp. Mgmt. Systems Soc. of Am. Hosp. Assn. Home: Palm Springs CA 92260 Office: 39000 Bob Hope Dr Rancho Mirage CA 92270

NATER, CHRIS, advertising executive; b. Burbank, Calif., Feb. 19, 1948; s. Carl and Virginia (Short) N.; m. Susan Dunshee, June 14, 1970 (div. 1983). B.A. in Econs., Pomona Coll., 1970; M.B.A. in Mktg., Harvard U., 1973. Dir. mktg. strategy Moorhead Mktg., Palo Alto, Calif., 1973; product mgr. E & J Gallo Winery, Modesto, Calif., 1974-76; account exec. Foote, Cone & Belding, San Francisco, 1976-78; pres. Chris Nater & Assocs., Santa Fe, 1978—. Mem. Sangre de Cristo council Girl Scouts U.S.A.; mem. Better Bus. Bureau. Served with U.S. Army, 1970-72. Mem. No. N.Mex. Advt. Fedn. (founder, 1st pres.). Democrat.

NATHAN, GERALD DALE, psychologist, farmer; b. Norfolk, Nebr., Oct. 1, 1938; s. Raymond John and Esther Marie (Neuwerk) N. Student, Wayne State Coll., Nebr., 1956-57, Yale U., 1959-60; B.A., U. Nebr., 1966, M.A., 1968, Ph.D. (NDEA fellow), 1970. Lic. marriage counselor, Calif., 1972; cert. sex educator, 1973, sex therapist, 1975; lic. psychologist, Oreg., 1974. Cons. psychologist Calavaras County Edn. Dept., San Andreas, Calif., 1970-72; pvt. practice sex and marital therapy, lifestyle and stress mgmt., Salem, Oreg., 1972—; cons. psychologist Community Counseling Center, Salem, 1972-73; sex educator Oreg. Dept. Continuing Edn., Salem, 1972-74; cons. William Temple House, Portland, Oreg., 1974-77; vis. prof. Willamette U., Salem, 1981. Mem. Salem Community Chorus, 1978—, pres., 1980-81. Served with USAF, 1959-63. Mem. Am. Psychol. Assn., Am. Assn. Marriage and Family Therapy, Am. Assn. Sex Educators, Counselors and Therapists, Oreg. Assn. Marriage and Family Therapists (dir. 1976-77), Salem Psychol. Soc. (co-chmn. 1981-82), Common Cause, ACLU, Nature Conservancy, Union Concerned Scientists, Sierra Club. Office: 635 Church NE Salem OR 97301

NATHANSON, THEODORE HERZL, aero. engr., architect; b. Montreal, Que., Can., Apr. 20, 1923; s. Henry and Minnie (Goldberg) N.; student McGill U., 1940-42; S.B. in Aero. Engring., M.I.T., 1944; M.Arch., Harvard U., 1955. Research engr. Noorduyn Aviation Ltd., Montreal, 1944-45; stress engr. Canadair Ltd., Montreal, 1945-46; structural engr. A.V. Roe (Can.) Ltd., Malton, Ont., 1946-47; with Mies van der Rohe, Chgo., summer 1949, R. Buckminster Fuller, Forest Hills, N.Y., summer 1951; cons. engr. and architect, Montreal, Boston, Los Angeles, 1955—; mem. tech. staff Rockwell Internat., Space Transp. and Systems Group, shuttle orbiter div., advanced engring., advanced design, Downey, Calif., 1979—; lectr. architecture, McGill U., 1967-68. Fellow Brit. Interplanetary Soc.; mem. Order Engrs. Que., Order Architects Que., Soc. Am. Registered Architects, Nat. Soc. Profl. Engrs., AIAA, Royal Archtl. Inst. Can., Nat. Mgmt. Assn., Copley Soc. of Boston. Jewish. Clubs: M.I.T. of So. Calif. (bd. govs.); Can. Soc. (Los Angeles). Projects and models included in group shows: Mus. Fine Arts, Springfield, Mass., 1961, N.Y. World's Fair, 1965, Winterfest, Boston, 1966, Boston Artists' Project '70. Home: 222 S Figueroa St Los Angeles CA 90012 Office: 12214 Lakewood Blvd Downey CA 90241

NATHE, DENNIS GERHARDT, ranch exec.; b. Scobey, Mont., Dec. 12, 1938; s. Michael Henry and Saralda Sophia (Korf) N.; B.S., St. Benedicts Coll., Atchison, Kans., 1962; M.S., Creighton U., 1966; m. Della Mae Snyder, Dec. 28, 1970; children—Alycia, Michael. Pharm. detail man Lederle Labs., Am. Cyanamid Co., Omaha, 1962-64; clin. research coordinator Med. Products div. 3M Co., St. Paul, 1967; farming, ranching, Redstone, Mont., 1967—; pres. Nathe Ranch Inc., 1973—; pres. Wanmdi Kinyan, Inc., 1981—. Vice-chmn. Mont. Environ. Quality Council, 1977-79, chmn., 1979—, public mem., 1981—; Mont. State Rep., 1977—; chmn. Sheridan County Planning and Improvement Council, 1973-76; del. Economic Devel. Assn. Eastern Mont., 1973-76; chmn. Three Corners Boundary Assn., 1976-77; Democratic Precinct committeeman, 1968-76; mem. Mont. Rural Area Devel. Com., 1976—; alternate Mo. River Barge Transp. Com., 1980—; mem. Gov.'s Groundwater Task Force, 1983-85; bd. suprs. Sheridan County Conservation Dist., 1969-78; chmn. Eastern Mont. Range Improvement Com., 1973-78; chmn. Sheridan County Republican Central Com., 1980—; mem. Mont. Extension Adv. Council, 1980—, participant numerous other civic activities. Served with AUS, 1957-58. Mem. Soc. Range Mgmt., (chmn. Mont. Old West regional range program 1975-79), Durum Growers Assn., K.C. Republican. Roman Catholic. Address: Box 4 Redstone MT 59257

NATSOULAS, THOMAS, psychologist, educator; b. N.Y.C., Mar. 1, 1932; s. Anthony and Helen (Theodorou) N.; m. Popi, Jan. 18, 1953; children—Anthony, John. Ph.D., U. Mich., 1959. Instr. psychology U. Mich., 1958-59; asst. prof. Wesleyan U., 1959-62, U. Wis.-Madison, 1962-64; asst. U. Calif.-Davis, 1964-66, assoc. prof., 1966-72, prof., 1972—. Fellow Am. Psychol. Assn. Contbr. articles to profl. jours. Home: 1030 Fordham Dr Davis CA 95616 Office: 179 Young Hall Dept Psychology U Calif Davis CA 95616

NATT, THEODORE MCCLELLAND, newspaper editor, publisher; b. Portland, Oreg., Mar. 28, 1941; s. Theodore Manfred and Martha Sue (McClelland) N.; B.S., U. Oreg., 1963; postgrad. Stanford, 1966-67; M. Diane Gail Shields, Dec. 27, 1962; children—Theodore McClelland, Lorena Sue, David Morris, Morgan Sadler. Reporter, Walla Walla (Wash.) Union-Bull., 1963-64, Oregonian, Portland, 1964-65; news editor St. Helens (Oreg.) Sentinel-Mist, 1965-66; asso. editor Daily News, Longview, Wash., 1968-71, mng. editor, 1971-74, editor, asst. to pub., 1974-77, publisher, 1977—; dir., sec., exec. v.p. Longview Pub. Co., 1971—; dir., sec. Prodn. Co., Renton, Wash., 1975—; dir., sec.-treas. Port Angeles Evening News Co. (Wash.), 1971—. Mem. adv. com. Wash. Dept. Social and Health Services, 1972-74; mem. Wash. Bench, Bar and Press Commn., 1977—. Bd. dirs. United Way, Cowlitz County, Wash., 1970-75; bd. dirs., pres. Lower Columbia Mental Health Center, Longview, 1970—. Stanford U. profl. journalism fellow, 1966-67; Pulitzer prize juror, 1977, 83, 84. Recipient Pulitzer prize, 1981. Mem. Wash. Asso. Press Assn. (pres. 1974-75), Soc. Profl. Journalists, Am. Soc. Newspaper Editors, Asso. Press. Mng. Editors Assn. (v.p. 1983, pres. 1984), Washington Athletic Club (Seattle), Kappa Sigma, Sigma Delta Chi (Disting. Service award 1981). Democrat. Episcopalian. Elk. Clubs: Longview Country; Nat. Press (Washington). Home: 2341 W Hills Dr Longview WA 98632 Office: 770 11th Ave Longview WA 98632

NATTENBERG, DAVID, communications common carrier co. exec.; b. Chgo., Aug. 4, 1937; s. Philip M. and Mildred P. (Pogrund) N.; student Fresno State U., 1955-57; B.A., U. Calif., 1959; m. Judith Cohen, Jan. 25, 1945; children—Heidi, Scott, Jill. Area mgr. Common Carrier Sales Motorola, Inc., Sacramento, 1964-68; v.p. Nat. Communications Co., Sacramento, 1968-69; area mgr. Airsignal Internat., Inc., Sacramento, 1969-72; v.p., gen. mgr. Radiocall, Inc., Honolulu, 1972-79; pres. Aircall of Guam, Inc., 1979—, Medi-Page, Inc., Honolulu, 1979—, Tele-Page, Inc., Honolulu, 1979—; exec. v.p. Aircall Internat., Honolulu, 1983—. Sec., trustee Temple Emanu El; trustee United Jewish Welfare Fund; bd. dirs. Am. Youth Soccer Orgn. Served to 2d lt. U.S. Army, 1959-61. Mem. Hawaii C. of C., Hawaii Telecommunications Assn. (pres.), Armed Forces Communications and Electronics Assn. Hawaii Execs. Assn. Home: 4829 Kalmoku Way Honolulu HI 96821 Office: 629 Pohukaina St Honolulu HI 96813

NAUGHTON, ALEXANDER EDWARD, banker; b. Palo Alto, Calif., Dec. 10, 1943; s. Alexander Edward Anthony and Helen Loretta (Thomas) N.; B.A. in History, Stanford U., 1965; M.A. in History, U. Calif., Santa Barbara, 1969; B.I.M., Thunderbird Grad. Sch. Internat. Mgmt., 1970; M.B.A., Fordham U., 1973. Mgmt. trainee Chem. Bank, 1970-71; asst. sec. internat. banking office Bank of Am. Internat., N.Y.C., 1971-72, area relations officer European div., 1972-73; asst. v.p. multinat. unit Mfrs. Hanover Trust Co., N.Y.C., 1974-77, v.p., 1977-78, sr. v.p., mgr. Mfrs. Hanover Bank Internat., Los Angeles, 1978—. Mem. Los Angeles Fgn. Trade Assn., Western Internat. Trade Group, Los Angeles C. of C., Los Angeles World Affairs Council, Japan-Calif. Assn., U.S./Mex. C. of C., Stanford U. Alumni Assn. Democrat. Club: Univ. (Los Angeles). Office: 445 S Figueroa St Los Angeles CA 90071

NAURATH, DAVID ALLISON, engring. psychologist; b. Houston, Mar. 11, 1927; s. Walter Arthur and Joy Frances (Bradbury) N.; student Trinity U., 1944-47; B.A., Simpson Coll., 1948; M.A., So. Meth. U., 1949; postgrad. Tex. U., 1950, Tex. Tech. U., 1951-52, U. Denver, 1955-57; m. Barbara Ellen Coverdell; children—Kathleen, David, Cynthia, Randall. Indsl. engr. Kelly AFB, 1951; job analyst Lowry AFB, 1952-55; research psychologist maintenance lab. Air Research and Devel. Command, 1955-58, Personnel Lab., San Antonio, 1958-60, life sci. dept., Point Mugu, Calif., 1960-67; engring. psychologist Systems Engring. br. Pacific Missile Test Center, Point Mugu, 1967—, acting head, 1979-80. Served with USAAF, 1944-46. Mem. Am. Psychol. Assn., Soc. Engring. Psychologists, Human Factors Soc., Soc. Info. Display, AAAS (life), N.Y. Acad. Scis., Ventura County Psychol. Assn. Contbr. articles to profl. jours. Research on sensory and perceptual functions of flight, applications of nuclear energy to flight, inflight tng. and trainer design, human factors in computer software engring.; designer simulators. Home: 5633 Pembroke St Ventura CA 93003 Office: Code 1221 Systems Engineering Branch Systems Technology Dept Pacific Missile Test Center Point Mugu CA 93042

NAVARRETE, JUAN RICARDO, artist, educator, designer; b. Albuquerque, Nov. 15, 1942; s. Pedro and Dolores (Serda) N.; B.F.A., U. Americas, Puebla, Mex., 1970; m. Patricia Ann Stern, June 22, 1970; 1 dau., Alma Paloma Sol. Asst. dir. Mus. Sci. and History, Fort Worth, 1971; artist-in-the-schs. N.Mex. arts div. Taos public schs., 1975-77; curator Harwood Found., U. N.Mex., 1979; audio visual specialist Nat. Endowment Arts grant, 1979—; project dir. Nat. Endowment Humanities grant, 1980—; cons. Taos Pueblo Youth CETA Program; vol. N.Mex. Youth Employment Support Program; trustee Albuquerque Mus., 1974-75; adv. bd. dept. Hispanic studies Mus. N.Mex., 1973-75; founder, pres. bd. El Museo y Centro Cultural, 1973. Nat. Endowment for Arts grantee, 1981, 83. Mem. Am. Assn. Museums, N.Mex. Mus. Assn. Author: Architectural Crafts, 1982. Address: PO Box 2251 Taos NM 87571

NAVE, MICHAEL ERNEST, safety consultant, educator; b. Stockton, Calif., July 7, 1952; s. Ernest Louis and Theresa Marie (Callegari) N.; B.A. in Polit. Sci., Calif. State U., Fresno, 1975, M.S. in Health Sci. with Distinction 1978. Lectr. health, edn. and pub. stats. Calif. State U.-Fresno, 1977-78; loss control rep. Employee Benefits Ins. Co., Sacramento, 1978-80; safety cons. Wise Ins. Agts. and Brokers, Roseville, Calif., 1980-83; lectr. Calif. State U.-Fresno, 1983—. speaker Golden West Safety Congress and Expn., Nat. Safety Council, Indsl. Health and Safety Course, Mgmt. and Supr. Safety Course. Instr. ARC, CPR, first aid. Mem. Am. Soc. Safety Engrs., Calif. Agrl. Safety Coordinating Com., Central Valley Council Safety Superiors. Democrat. Office: Dept Health Sci Calif State U-Fresno Fresno CA 93740

NAVEJAS, FREDERIK CARLOS, telephone company executive; b. Fresno, Calif., Mar. 2, 1950; s. Felix and Amelia (Carrillo) N.; B.S., Calif. State U., 1976, B.A., 1978, M. Public Adminstrn., 1980. Engr., Purex Corp., Carson, Calif., 1976; plant mgr. Polyplastex United, Inc., Los Angeles, 1977-78; prodn. mgr. McDonnell Douglas Aircraft Corp., Long Beach, Calif., 1979-80; engring. mgr. Pacific Telephone & Telegraph, Inc., Los Angeles, 1980—; bus. mgmt. cons. Navejas & Assocs., Hawaiian Gardens, Calif., 1979—. City councilman City of Hawaiian Gardens, 1976-80, mayor pro tempore, 1979-80; chmn. Community Action Council, Headstart, Inc., Hawaiian Gardens, 1979—; pres. Hawaiian Gardens-East Lakewood Democratic Club, 1983—. Mem. Alpha Kappa Psi, Sigma Delta Chi. Democrat. Home: 12256 E 211th St Hawaiian Gardens CA 90716

NAWROCKI, HENRY FRANZ, aeronautical engineer; b. Pueblo, Colo., Dec. 10, 1931; s. Henry Vincent and Verna Ella (Weyand) N.; m. Marlene Charlotte Kryak, Sept. 1, 1973. B.S. in Aero. Engring., U. Colo., 1953; M.S. in Aerospace Engring., U. So. Calif., 1968. Registered powerplant designated engring. rep. FAA. Flight est planning supr. Marquardt Corp., Van Nuys, Calif., 1953-64; sr. flight test analysis engr. Lockheed-Calif. Co., Burbank and Palmdale, Calif., 1964-72; mem. tech. staff Rockwell Corp., Los Angeles, 1972-77; sr. staff specialist Canadair Ltd., Montreal, Can., and Mojave, Calif., 1977-80; asst. design mgr. Lear Fan, Ltd., Reno, 1980—; lab. asst. U. Colo.; technician Engring. Exptl. Sta., Boulder; tech. cons. installed airbreathing propulsion systems. First stand cellist Pueblo Philharm. Symphony, 1948-51; bd. dirs. Calif. Fedn. Mineral. Socs., 1959-73; recipient Zero Defects award, 1971, Collier award for B-1 bomber, 1975. Mem. Inst. Aero. Socs., Soc. Automotive Engrs., Am. Aviation Hist. Soc., Nat. Rifle Assn. (life), Reno Gem and Mineral. Soc. Republican. Contbr. articles to profl. jours. Home: 3455 Cashill Blvd Reno NV 89509 Office: 14505 Mount Anderson St Reno NV 89506

NAY, DANIEL LESTER, electronic engr.; b. Brea, Calif., Aug. 19, 1934; s. Marshall Lester and Jennie (Bergman) N.; A.A., Mt. San Antonio Coll., 1960; B.S.E.E., Stanford U., 1961, M.S.E.E., (U.S. AEC fellow), 1962; m. Dorrine Ruth Short, June 23, 1956; children—Eric Randolph, Alicia Lynn, Gregory Lewis. Technician, Convair, Pomona, Calif., 1955-60; cognizant engr. Jet Propulsion Labs, Pasadena, Calif., 1962-66; electronic engr. Tasker, Marquardt, Los Angeles, 1966-70; v.p. engring. Tru-Digital Industries, Van Nuys, Calif., 1970-71; engring. dir. Magnavox Research Labs., Torrance, Calif., 1972-73; v.p. engring. Tru-Digital, Inc., Carson, Calif., 1974-75; cons., 1975-79, pres. Findex, Inc., Torrance, 1977-81; cons., designer micro-computer hardware and software. Served with USN, 1952-55. Mem. IEEE, AIAA, Mensa, Tau Beta Pi. Republican. Baptist. Developer Sensing Autonomous Mobile, first spacecraft to Mars, 1st Doppler sonar navigation system, 1st portable bus. computer. Home: 30147 Via Borica Rancho Palos Verdes CA 90274 Office: 1745 Berkeley St Santa Monica CA 90404

NAYLOR, MARY LOU, vocational education administrator, consultant, researcher, educator; b. Los Angeles, Apr. 13, 1938; d. Donald Cameron and Juanita (Joslyn) Grant; children—Sheila, Teresa, Michelle. B.S. in Bus. Adminstrn., Calif. State U., 1978, M.A. in Vocat. Edn., 1979; postgrad. Colo. State U., 1983. Instr., Placer County Office Edn., Auburn, Calif., 1976-79; prin. adult edn. prin. Nevada Union High Sch. Dist., Grass Valley, Calif., 1979-80; coordinator Vocat. Programs Placer and Nev. Counties, Calif., 1979-82; project dir. Calif. State Dept. Edn., Vocat. Tchr. Inservice, 1979-82; assoc. prof. Calif. State U.-Sacramento, 1980-83; grad. asst., assoc. researcher Colo. State U., Ft. Collins, 1982—; adult edn. prin.; exec. bd. Calif. Regional Occupational Ctrs. and Programs. Mayor of Applegate, (Calif.), 1971. Recipient Bus. and Profl. Womens Clairol Leadership award 1975, 76, Colo. State U. fellow 1982. Mem. Calif. Assn. Regional Occupational Ctrs. and Programs, Am. Vocat. Assn., Colo. Vocat. Assn., Phi Delta Kappa. Clubs: Compassion Internat., Applegate Civic Ctr. Author Handbook for Vocational Education Inservice in California, 1982; product patentee, 1959; chemical processes patentee, 1959. Home: 318 W Prospect Rd 235 Fort Collins CO 80526 Office: Colo State U Humanities Bldg Dept Vocat Edn Fort Collins CO 80523

NAYMARK, SHERMAN, engineering executive, consultant; b. Duluth, Minn., May 12, 1920; s. David and Lena N.; m. Josephine Naymark, Apr. 9, 1942; children—Ronald L., Janet Naymark Stone; m. 2d, Raquel Heller-Newman, May 4, 1980. B.S. in Engring., U.S. Naval Acad., 1941; M.S. in Engring. and Contrn., MIT, 1946. Lic. profl. engr., N.Y., Ill., Iowa, Wis., Minn., Pa., Calif. Commd. ensign U.S. Navy, 1941, advanced through grades to capt., 1956; engring. officer; ret., 1954; sr. scientist Argonne Nat. Lab., 1948-52; reactor div. dir. AEC, KAPL Project, Schenectady, N.Y., 1952-56; engring. mgr. Gen. Electric Co., 1956-70; pres. Quadrex Corp., Campbell, Calif., 1970—; lectr. U. Va., MIT, U.S. Naval Res. Tng. Schs.; adviser U.S. del. 3d Internat. Conf. Peaceful Uses of Atomic Energy, Geneva, 1964; sr. examiner profl. engrs. State of Calif., 1960-70. Recipient Disting. Citizen award City of San Jose, Calif., 1970, Torch of Liberty award Anti-Defamation League, 1982. Fellow Am. Nuclear Soc.; mem. Am. Pub. Power Assn. (assoc.), AAAS. Democrat. Jewish. Governing bd. Nuclear Tech., 1979-82; contbr. articles profl. jours., chpts. in books. Office: 1700 Dell Ave Campbell CA 95008

NEADEAU, LESLIE LEROY, business exec.; b. Atlanta, Dec. 28, 1917; s. Mark M. and Edna H. (Pogue) N.; student Golden Gate Jr. Coll., 1935-36, San Francisco State Tchrs. Coll., 1936-38; m. Ruth E. Krings, Jan. 28, 1945; children—Marion Diane, Leslie Leroy II, Denise Diane. Vice pres. Hogan & Van Gelder Lumber Co., Inc., San Francisco, 1945-48; pres. Neadeau Wholesale Lumber Co., Inc., San Francisco, 1948-50, Big Bear Lumber Co., Inc., San Francisco, 1948-50, Mill Reps., Inc., San Francisco, 1950-63; v.p. Hedlund Lumber Sales Co., Sacramento, 1963-70; pres. Am. Lumber Species, Inc., Sacramento, 1970-78, Mountain Milling, Inc., Rocklin, Calif., 1973-77; mgr. nat. div. J.E. Higgins Lumber Co., Inc., Rocklin, 1975-77; pres. Pacific Laminates, Inc., Reno, 1974—, Internat. Gold and Diamond Exploration Co., Inc., Sacramento, also Paramaribo, Surinam, 1976—, Surinam Gold and Minerals Co., Sacramento, 1979—, Surinam S.A., 1979—, T.O.N.M. Oil and Gas Exploration Corp., Sacramento, 1979—; chief exec. officer I.G.D./P.M.C. Joint Venture (Surinam), 1979—; mng. dir. Tomsur Minerals N.V., Curaçao, Netherlands Antilles, 1980—; pres. Internat. Minerals Mgmt., Surinam, 1980—; mem. adv. bd. Equinox Movie Prodns., 1980—. Bd. elders Lutheran Ch., 1950-60. Served to capt. USAAF, 1941-45. Mem. Ducks Unltd. (dir.). Clubs: Commonwealth, Masons, Shriners. Script writer radio programs; contbr. articles on lumber industry to trade jours. Home: 872 Laverstock Way Sacramento CA 95825 Office: 105 Scripps Dr Sacramento CA 95825

NEAL, BRADFORD CARL, utility co. exec.; b. Parkersburg, W.Va., Jan. 29, 1952; s. Paul Edwin and Regina (Gallagher) N.; B.S., U. Mont., 1973; M.S., Central Mo. State U., 1977; M.B.A., U. Mo., 1978; m. Sally Jane Kranich, July 12, 1975; children—Jonathan Paul, Brian Benjamin. Staff asst. to v.p., supr. expediting BEI Services, Inc., East Orange, N.J., 1978-79; project coordinator data base systems Multitech, Inc., Butte, Mont., 1979-82; project dir. fin. systems and procedures Mont. Power Co., Butte, 1982—. Mem. computer adv. com. Silver Bow Sch. Bd. Served to capt. USAF, 1973-78. Republican. Office: 40 E Broadway Butte MT 59701

NEAL, JAMES EDWARD, lawyer, real estate developer; b. Charleston, W.Va., July 29, 1937; s. William Fredrick and Elsie Marjorie (Carte) N.; B.S., Calif. State U., Long Beach, 1961; J.D., U. Calif., San Francisco, 1964; grad. Realtors Inst., 1977; m. Carolyn Elizabeth Arnold, Mar. 30, 1971; children—Victoria Elizabeth, Christopher Charles. Admitted to Calif. bar, 1965, U.S. Supreme Ct., 1968; atty. Security Title Ins. Co., Los Angeles, 1964-65; dep. prosecutor City of Long Beach, 1965-67; sec.-treas. Golden Neal, Shuffler & Johnson, law corp., Westminster, Calif., 1967-79; prin. Neal Law Offices, Westminster, 1979—; chief exec. officer, dir. Westminster Trading Co., Inc.; judge pro-tem West Orange County Mcpl. Ct., 1971; Realtor, D.R. Saint-Malo Properties; chief fin. officer, dir. WFN Corp. Vice chmn. law revision commn. City of Seal Beach, Calif., 1970-71; chmn. community revitalization com. City of Westminster. Sec., bd. dirs. Boy's Club Westminster, 1974-77; bd. dirs. Westminster Boxing Club, 1975-77; bd. dirs. Westminster Founders' Day Assn., 1977-78. Served with inf., AUS Res., 1955-61. Lic. contractor, Calif. Mem. ABA, Calif., Orange County bar assns., West Orange County Bd. Realtors, Westminster C. of C. (v.p., dir. 1975-78), Calif. State U. Alumni Assn. (dir. 1967-74), Westminster Hist. Soc. (v.p., dir. 1976-78), UN Assn. (chpt. dir. 1966-67), Am. Rose Soc., Sigma Pi, Alpha Kappa Psi. Club: Kiwanis (dir. 1972-78, pres. 1973-74). Democrat. Home: 12632 Gilbert St Garden Grove CA 92641 Office: Liberty Bldg 8231 Westminster Blvd Westminster CA 92683

NEAL, ROBERT EUGENE, JR., financial and legal printing executive; b. Lebanon, Ind., Aug. 22, 1944; s. Robert Eugene and Ruth Winifred (Medsker) N.; A.B., Wabash Coll., 1966; postgrad. Butler U., 1967-68; m. Gretchen Ann Rolfe, June 21, 1975; children—Patricia Lee, Lisa Lyn, David Christopher. With R. R. Donnelley & Sons, Chgo., 1966-69, exec. salesman, 1968-69; with Arcata Corp., Menlo Park, Calif., 1970-76, mgr. corp. planning and devel., 1975-76; pres. Bowne & Co., Inc., 1976-83; pres. Bowne of San Francisco, Inc., 1983—; pres. Pandick, San Francisco; exec. v.p. Pandick Calif., Inc. Mem. Am. Soc. Corp. Secs., Assn. Corp. Growth, Printing Industries No. Calif. Republican. Clubs: Kiwanis, Tennis (San Francisco); Round Hill Golf and Country (Alamo, Calif.); Commonwealth of Calif. Home: 28 Bushmint Pl Alamo CA 94507 Office: 190 9th St San Francisco CA 94103

NEALE, HAOLD WATSON, professional hockey team executive; b. Sarnia, Ont., Can., Mar. 9, 1937. Grad. U. Toronto, 1960. Formerly high sch. tchr. in So. Ont.; hockey coach Ohio State U. for four seasons, then coach at Hamilton, Ont., Hockey Assn.; asst. hockey coach, then head coach Minn. Fighting Saints, World Hockey Assn., 1972-76; coach New Eng. Whalers, NHL, 1976-78, Vancouver Canucks, NHL, 1978-82, v.p., gen. mgr., 1982—. Office: Vancouver Canucks 100 Renfrew St Vancouver BC V5K 3N7 Canada*

NEARON, DAVID ARTHUR, lawyer; b. San Francisco, Jan. 12, 1941; s. Arthur David and Gladys Wilhelmina (Haneberg) N.; m. Linda Hyde Clawson, Nov. 21, 1967; children—David, Kelly, James, Kimberly. Student, U. Pa., 1958-60; B.S., U. Calif.-Berkeley, 1961; J.D., U. San Francisco, 1964; M.S. in Bus., San Jose State U., 1965. Bar: Calif. 1965. Estate tax atty. IRS, San Francisco, 1964-67; assoc. Price, Postel & Parma, Santa Barbara, Calif., 1967-69; ptnr. Anderson & Nearon, Inc., Walnut Creek, Calif., 1969-80; sole practice, Walnut Creek, 1980—; dir. ADN Corp. Served to capt. USAR, 1965-72. Mem. Calif. Bar Assn., Phi Alpha Delta. Republican. Mormon. Club: Round Hill Country (Alamo, Calif.). Author: Estate Planning for Married People, 1982; Estate Planning for Single People, 1982. Home: 111 Southview Ln Alamo CA 94507 Office: 1924 Tice Valley Blvd Walnut Creek CA 94595

NEBENZAHL, BERNARD WILLIAM, accountant; b. San Francisco, Jan. 11, 1934; s. Abraham and Regina (Gross) N.; m. Gail Jacobs, Mar. 20, 1938; children—Leanne Marie, Deborah Ann, David Aaron. B.S., U. Calif.-Berkeley, 1956, postgrad. Sch. Bus., 1956, 62-63; J.D., Hastings Coll. Law, 1966. Bar: Calif. 1966. C.P.A., Calif. Pub. acct., 1960-63; assoc. firm Rudy, Rapoport & White, San Francisco, 1966-68; assoc. Main Hurdman, San Francisco, 1968—, ptnr., 1971—; chmn. Main Hurdman's Estate and Gift Tax Specialist Com., 1981—; bd. dirs. San Francisco Estate Planning Council, 1976-83, pres., 1981-82. Bd. dirs. San Francisco Jewish Community Ctr., 1974-81, Congregation Emanu El, San Francisco, 1975-81. Served to lt. USN, 1956-59. Mem. Am. Inst. C.P.A.s (tax div. com. estate planning 1982—), Calif. Soc. C.P.A.s (state tax com. 1977-82, tax com. San Francisco chpt. 1970-81, chmn. 1979-81), ABA, San Francisco Bar Assn., San Francisco Tax Club. Clubs: Commonwealth of Calif.; World Trade (San Francisco). Contbr. articles to profl. jours. Home: 175 Castenada Ave San Francisco CA 94116 Office: Main Hurdman Two Embarcadero Ctr Suite 2500 San Francisco CA 94111

NEBIKER, RALPH ROBERT, naval officer; b. Jersey City, Sept. 30, 1943; s. Ralph Oscar and Margaret Marie (Tremmel) N.; m. Marion Ann Dieckhoff, June 18, 1966; children—Ann Marion, Linda Catherine. B.S., Stevens Inst. Tech., 1966; M.S. in Aerospace Engring., M.B.A., USN Postgrad. Sch., Monterey, Calif., 1973. Commd. ensign U.S. Navy, 1968; advanced through grades to comdr., 1979; naval flight officer, maintenance div. officer, 1968-70; officer of the deck; tactical action officer, CIC officer USS Kitty Hawk, 1974-76; asst. ops. officer, flight instr., San Diego, 1976-78; ops. officer, Yokosuka, Japan, 1978-81; staff command and control officer, comdr. U.S. Navy Air Force, U.S. Pacific Fleet, Naval Air Sta., N. Island, San Diego, 1981—. Mem. AIAA, Sigma Xi. Roman Catholic. Contbr. articles to tech. jours. Office: COMNAVAIRPAC PAC Code 35 Naval Air Station N Island San Diego CA 92135

NEEDHAM, KENNETH MAXWELL, city official; b. Las Cruces, N.Mex., July 9, 1946; s. Carl William and Merle Lucille (Ellett) N.; m. Jennie Lou Jacobi, Sept. 9, 1967; children—Kevin Scott, Jason Todd. M.C.E., N.Mex. State U., 1970. Registered Profl. Engr., N.Mex. San. engr. Bur. Indian Affairs, Gallup, N.Mex., 1974-75; dir. utilities City of Las Cruces (N.Mex.), 1975—; guest instr. N.Mex. State U. Served to capt. USAF, 1970-74. Mem. N.Mex. Soc. Profl. Engrs., Gas Research Inst. Republican. Mem. Ch. of Christ. Office: PO Box CLC Las Cruces NM 88001

NEELY, CLAYTON MARSHALL, data processing exec.; b. Tiptonville, Tenn., Aug. 14, 1945; s. Polk Marshall and Dottie Louise (Pierce) N.; A.S., Casper (Wyo.) Coll., 1967; m. Teresa Mary Neubauer, June 15, 1968; 1 son, Jason. Computer programmer Salt Creek Freightways, Casper, 1968-69; programmer, analyst Western Data Assn., Casper, 1969-71, system analyst, office mgr., treas., dir., 1972-76, gen. mgr., treas., dir., 1977-78; mgr. data processing Washington County, Oreg., 1978—. Loaned exec. United Fund, 1968; baseball coach Babe Ruth League, 1969-70, Little League, 1980-81. Roman Catholic. Home: 2582 SE Mariposa Ct Hillsboro OR 97123 Office: 150 N 1st St Hillsboro OR 97223

NEELY, GAYLE, nurse practitioner; b. Stillwater, Okla., Oct. 29, 1950; d. William Fred and Mary Glynn (Munger) Cochran; m. Richard Kent Baldwin, Jan. 28, 1971; m. 2d, Gary Wayne Neely, Jan. 23, 1982. Student, Okla. Bapt. U., Shawnee, 1967-71; B.S.N., Central State U., Edmond, Okla., 1973; cert. U. Ariz., 1980. Staff nurse neonatal ICU, U. Okla. Health Scis. Center and Children's Hosp., Oklahoma City, 1973-75; nurse Presbyn. Hosp., Oklahoma City, 1975; pub. health nurse, newborn follow up program Ariz. Dept. Health Services, 1975-77; asst. dir. nursing Westside Community Hosp., Long Beach, Calif., 1977-78; nurse newborn nursery Desert Samaritan Hosp., Mesa, Ariz., 1978-80; neonatal nurse practitioner Good Samaritan Med. Center, Phoenix, 1980-83, neonatal nurse practitioner Air Evac, Phoenix, 1983—. Mead Johnson & Co. grantee, 1980. Mem. Neonatal Nurse Practitioners Assn. Ariz., Ariz. Perinatal Trust. Office: 1111 E McDowell Rd Good Samaritan Med Center Phoenix AZ 85062

NEFF, JAMES DENNIS, materials supply company executive; b. Ft. Wayne, Ind., Aug. 24, 1937; s. James Marion and Margret Ann (Lynch) N.; m. Ann Jeanette Day, Apr. 8, 1966; children—Bryan James, Julie Ann, Sarah Lynn. Student Purdue U., 1955-57; B.S.M.E., U. Ill., 1959; M.B.A., Ind. U., 1963. Sr. market analyst Allison div. Gen. Motors Corp., Indpls., 1963-67; mgr. Merwins div. Internat. Harvester, St. Croix, V.I., 1967-68; v.p., gen. mgr. structural products div. Hexcel Corp., Dublin, Calif., 1968—; coll. instr., V.I., 1967-68. Served with U.S. Army, 1960. Mem. Soc. Advancement of Material and Process Engring., Am. Mktg. Assn., Soc. Automotive Engrs., Am. Def. Preparedness Assn. (dir.), Dublin C. of C. Home: 127 Sherburne Ct Danville CA 94526 Office: 11711 Dublin Blvd Dublin CA 94568

NEHER, RAYMOND EDWIN, soil scientist; b. McCune, Kans., Feb. 5, 1925; s. Eli Edwin and Myra Sybil (Lange) N.; B.S., Kans. State U., 1950; student Cornell U., 1965, N.Mex. State U., 1966; m. Marjorie Anne Roepke, Oct. 28, 1950; 1 dau., Elizabeth Anne. Student asst. Agronomy Dept., Kans. State U., 1946-50; soil scientist trainee U.S. Dept. Agr., Emporia, Kans., 1950, Hays, Kans., 1950, soil scientist, 1950-52; self-employed rancher, farmer, Manhattan, Kans., 1952-56; soil scientist, party leader, Mountainair, N.Mex., 1956-60, Lordsburg, N.Mex., 1960-63, Taos, N.Mex., 1963-66, Las Cruces, N.Mex., 1966-77, Truth or Consequences, N.Mex., 1977-79, area soil scientist Soil Conservation Service, U.S. Dept. Agr., Las Cruces, 1979-82; ret., 1983. Served with USNR, 1944-46. Registered Soil Scientist, soil classifier, soil specialist. Mem. Soil Conservation Soc. Am. (past pres.), Am. Soc. Agronomy, Soil Sci. Soc. Am., Soil Sci. Soc. N.Mex. (past pres.). Methodist (lay speaker). Clubs: Kiwanis, Mesilla Valley, Mesilla Valley Radio, The Singing Men of Las Cruces. Contbr. articles to Dept. Agr. and univs. Home: 1930 E Madrid Rd Las Cruces NM 88001

NEHRKORN, DAVID WILLIAM, chemist; b. St. Louis, Oct. 16, 1945; s. Raymond William and Dorothy (Edwards) N.; B.S., Grinnell (Iowa) Coll., 1967; Ph.D. (NDEA fellow 1972-74), St. Louis U., 1974. Chemist, Raychem Corp., Menlo Park, Calif., 1975-78; extension instr., course designer U. Calif., Berkeley, nights 1975-77; sr. chemist Diamond Shamrock Co., Redwood City, Calif., 1978-79; sr. chemist chem. systems div. United Technologies Corp., Sunnyvale, Calif., after 1979; now materials and processes specialist Lockheed Missiles and Space Co., Sunnyvale. Mem. Am. Chem. Soc., AAAS. Home: 718 S Grant St San Mateo CA 94402 Office: Box 504 Sunnyvale CA 94086

NEIGHBORS, WILLIAM DONALD, state supreme court justice; b. Longmont, Colo., Apr. 21, 1939; s. Donald Andrew and Myrtle Marie (Lee) N.; B.S., Colo. State U., 1961, M.A., 1962; LL.B., U. Colo., 1965; m. Bonnie Jean Ware, Dec. 27, 1961; children—Linda Ann, Alan William. Admitted to Colo. bar, 1965; asso. firm Williams, Taussig and Trine, Boulder, Colo., 1965-69; partner firm Williams, Trine and Greenstein, Boulder, 1969-71; chief trial dep. Colo. State Public Defender System, Denver, 1971-73; judge 20th Jud. Dist., Boulder, 1973-83; judge Colo. Supreme Ct., Denver, 1983—; lectr. in field. Pres., Burke Elem. Sch. Parent Tchr. Orgn., Boulder, 1970-71; chmn. parish bd. St. Thomas Aquinas Catholic Ch., Boulder, 1974-76; asst. coach Thunderbird Little League, Boulder, 1976, bd. dirs., 1977—, v.p., 1977-78, pres., 1978-79, coach, 1977. Mem. Colo. State U. Alumni Assn., St. Vrain Valley Alumni Assn. (dir. 1969-73, pres. 1972-73), Colo. Dist. Judges Assn., Am. Judicature Soc., Colo. 4-H Found. (pres. 1976—, treas. 1977-79), Boulder County Legal Services (dir. 1975-76), Am. Bar Assn., Colo. Bar Assn. (bd. govs. 1976—), Boulder County Bar Assn. (trustee 1973-78, pres. 1975-76), Am. Law Inst. Democrat. Home: 4700 Ricara Dr Boulder CO 80303 Office: 2 E 14th Ave Denver CO 80203

NEIL, SUE, truck company official; b. Columbus, Ohio, Jan. 13, 1941; d. Edgar Gordon and Marian Ida (Scheuffler) Beckemeyer; m. James G. Neil, June 28, 1968; children—James G. II, Chadwick G. B.S., Ohio State U., 1962. Personnel supr. Bloomingdale's Dept. Store, N.Y.C., 1962-64; tng. supr. United Mchts. & Mfrs., N.Y.C., 1964-66; tng. dir. Accuray Corp., Columbus, 1966-71; asst. v.p., mgr. First Interstate Bank of Wash., Seattle, 1974-79; with Kenworth Truck Co., Seattle, 1979—, mgr. employee relations Seattle factory, 1981—; instr. City U., Seattle; mem. adv. council undergrad. and grad. human resource devel. progrm Seattle U.; cons. to bus. and govt.; lectrs. Mem. Am. Soc. Tng. Devel. (pres. Wash. State chpt. 1979, regional v.p. for West Coast, 1981-82, nat. dir. 1981-82, Nat. Torch award 1981), Futurist Soc. Am., Am. Soc. Personnel Adminstrn., Mortar Bd. Home: 21711 SE 259th St Maple Valley WA 98038 Office: Kenworth Truck Co 8801 E Marginal Way S Seattle WA 98108

NEILAND, BONITA JUNE, plant ecologist, conservationist, educator; b. Eugene, Oreg., June 5, 1928; d. Herbert E. and Ann L. Miller; B.S., U. Oreg., 1949; M.S., Oreg. State U., 1951; Ph.D., U. Wis., 1954; Diploma in Rural Sci., Univ. Coll. Wales, 1952; m. Kenneth A. Neiland, Dec. 21, 1955. Instr., U. Oreg., Eugene, 1954-55; instr., asst. prof. gen. ext. div. Oreg. State System Higher Edn., Eugene, 1955-60; mem. faculty biol. scis. dept. U. Alaska, Fairbanks, 1961-75, prof., 1969—, mem. faculty Sch. Agr. and Land Resources Mgmt., 1975—, dir. instrn. and pub. service, 1978—. Bd. suprs. Fairbanks Soil Conservation Dist. Fellow AAAS; mem. Ecol. Soc. Am., Brit. Ecol. Soc., Soil Conservation Soc., Internat. Ecol. Assn., Phi Beta Kappa, Sigma Xi, Phi Kappa Phi. Contbr. articles to profl. jours. Office: Sch Agr and Land Resources Mgmt Univ Alaska Fairbanks AK 99701

NEILL, RAYMOND ARLEY, aircraft company executive; b. Aurora, Mo., June 15, 1916; s. Cluster and Bessie Alma (Gallion) C.; student Harbor Jr. Coll., Los Angeles; m. Geneva Andrews, Feb. 14, 1946; children—Marilyn, Ronald, Don, David, Judy. Prodn. supr., customer relations Longren Aircraft Co., Torrance, Calif., 1943-56; founder, pres. Neill Aircraft Co., Long Beach, Calif., 1956—, also chmn.; pres., chmn. Aero-Form, Inc., Gardena, Calif.; dir. Wilmington Savs. & Loan (Calif.). Mem. exec. fin. com. Long Beach Rescue Mission, 1980—; bd. dirs. Camp Pinecrest, Twin Peaks, Calif., 1976—; mem. fin. com. Assembly of God, Springfield, Mo., 1979; bd. dirs. Calcutta Missions of Mercy Internat., Tacoma, Wash.; regional v.p. World Missions Light-For-The Lost Lit. Program. Office: 1260 W 15th St Long Beach CA 90813

NEILL, ROBERT HAROLD, state official; b. Passaic, N.J., Feb. 9, 1930; s. William J. and Rosemary A. (Connolly) N.; M.E., Stevens Inst. Tech., 1951; M.S. (Radiol. Health fellow), Harvard U., 1962; m. Townley Biddle, July 6, 1963; 1 dau., Helen Rosemary. Mech. engr. Foster Wheeler Corp., N.Y.C., 1951-56; dir. environ. evaluation group N.Mex. Health and Environ. Dept., Santa Fe, 1978—. Served with USPHS, 1956-78. Mem. Health Physics Soc., Am. Pub. Health Assn., IEEE, Chi Phi. Home: 1056 Governor Dempsy Dr Santa Fe NM 87501 Office: PO Box 968 EEG Santa Fe NM 87503

NEILSON, JOHN WILBERT TENNANT, research company executive, consultant, educator; b. Oakland, Calif., May 9, 1944; s. Donald Wilbert Tennant and Mary Vera (Peart) N.; m. Darlene Rae Mitchell, Sept. 10, 1966; children—Sean Wilbert Tennant, Kimberly Mary. B.S. in Edn., So. Oreg. State Coll., 1969, M.S. in Gen. Studies, 1972. Registered sanitarian trainee Oreg. State Dept. Health, 1973. Dept. chmn. Days Creek (Oreg.) High Sch., 1969-70; chmn. biology dept. South Umpqua High Sch., Myrtle Creek, Oreg., 1970-75; prof. sci. Lane Community Coll., Eugene, Oreg., 1976-78; salesman Jewett Office Supply, Medford, Oreg., 1978-80, Truscott Office Products, Medford, 1978-82; pres. Neilson Research, Medford, 1976—; lab. analyst, cons. drinking water. Served with U.S. Army, 1962-65, USAR, 1976—. Mem. Am. Soc. Microbiology, Am. Water Works Assn., Assn. Ofcl. Analytical Chemists. Republican. Episcopalian. Clubs: Lions, Rotary. Author: Northwestern CB Log Book, 1976. Office: Neilson Research 2053 Bradbury St Medford OR 97501

NEIMAN, MAX, educator; b. Munich, Germany, June 17, 1946; came to U.S., 1952, naturalized, 1957; s. Benjamin and Bertha Neiman; m. Sarah Deborah Federman, Sept. 8, 1968; children—David Ethan, Joshua Alan. B.A., U. Ill., 1967; M.A., U. Wis., 1968, Ph.D., 1973. Mem. faculty U. Wis.-Milw., 1972-73; mem. faculty U. Calif., Riverside, 1973—, assoc. prof. polit. sci., 1979—. NSF fellow, 1971-72; NSF grantee, 1971-72, 79. Mem. Am. Polit. Sci. Assn. Am. Assn. Planning, Assn. Urban Land Inst. Democrat. Jewish Contbr. articles to profl. jours.

NEISWENDER, JOHN S., cdnl. adminstr.; b. Ephrata, Wash., Apr. 10, 1950; s. Jess A. and Alta Louise (Halsey) N.; A.A., LeTourneau Coll., 1970; student LaSalle U., 1972-74, Inland Empire Sch. Bible, 1973-74; m. Sharon Ann Womble, Aug. 16, 1969; children—Philip Kyle, Jodie Michelle, Heather (dec.), Jon Travis. Aviation technician, asst. LeTourneau Coll., 1968-70; bookkeeper, tchr. N.W. Christian High Sch., Spokane, Wash., 1970-72; owner Arco Service Sta., 1972-73; bookkeeper Inland Empire Sch. Bible, Spokane, 1973-74, bus. adminstr., registrar, 1974-83, treas., 1975-83; pres. Legal Action Unltd., Inc., 1981—; owner/partner Sharon & Sharon Assos., data processing and acctg. Steward, 1st Evang. Free Ch., 1972-77; cons. Christian Athletic Assn., Spokane Inside Weekly newspaper. Mem. Spokane C. of C., Christian Booksellers Assn., Nat. Assn. Tax Cons. Mem. Northview Bible Ch. Home: N 8325 Colton Pl Spokane WA 99208 Office: E 618 Baldwin Spokane WA 99207

NELLOR, JOHN HAROLD, educational adminstrator, public relations consultant; b. Kadoka, S.D., Apr. 24, 1923; s. Edward Taubman and Kittie Emma (Sharon) N.; m. Maxine Barbara Barbeau, Sept. 12, 1948; children—John David, Mary Louise, Daniel Edward, Nancy Ann. B.A., Lewis and Clark Coll., 1950, M.Ed., 1953; postgrad. U. Portland, Nova U. Newspaper reporter, Mitchell, S.D., 1940-42; tchr., Astoria, Oreg., 1950-56; city editor Astonian Budget, 1956-61; lobbyist Oreg. Edn. Assn., 1961-63; dir. pub. info. Portland (Oreg.) Pub. Schs., 1963-80, asst. to supt., 1980—; cons. Served with USAAF, 1942-45. Mem. Nat. Sch. Pub. Relations Assn. (publs. awards 1970-77), Oreg. Sch. Pub. Relations Assn., Pub. Relations Soc. Am. (accredited, past pres.

Columbia River chpt.), Phi Delta Kappa. Democrat. Methodist. Author: History of Desegregation, Portland Schools, 1980. Home: 2007 E 8th St Vancouver WA 98661 Office: 501 N Dixon St Portland OR 97227

NELSEN, EDWARD ALFRED, psychologist, educator; b. Milw., Feb. 7, 1937; s. Alfred Henry and Elva Clara (Klessig) N.; m. Suzanne Dorothy (Aubart), Sept. 5, 1959; children—David, Michael, Kathryn. B.S., U. Wis., 1959; Ph.D. in Psychology, Stanford U., 1965. Asst. prof. ednl. psychology U. Wis., Madison, 1963-68; prof., dir. research and evaluation, N.C. Central U., 1968-75; prof. ednl. psychology, assoc. dir. exptl. programs, Ariz. State U., Tempe, 1975—. Mem. Am. Psychol. Assn., Am. Ednl. Research Assn, Soc. for Research in Child Devel. Contbr. articles to profl. jours. Home: 11033 N 74th St Scottsdale AZ 85260 Office: ID Payne Lab Ariz State U Tempe AZ 85281

NELSEN, LILLIAN LOUISE, nursing adminstr.; b. Victor, Idaho, May 5, 1924; d. Paul Levere and Lillian Sarah (Kearsley) Woolstenhulme; R.N., Good Samaritan Tng. Sch. for Nurses, 1946; B.S. i,n Nursing, U. San Diego Coll. for Women, 1964; B.B.A., Nat. U., San Diego, 1976; m. Feb. 2, 1946; children—Jack, Lilly, Linda, June, Sally, Esther, Mary, Richard. Electrician helper, 1942; nurse Good Samaritan Hosp., 1947; clk.-typist, Guam, 1948; nurse St. Mary's Hosp., Long Beach, Calif., 1952-54; obstetrical nurse, night supr. Sharp Hosp., San Diego, 1955-73; supr., instr. Mission Bay and Center City Hosp., San Diego, 1973-77; adminstrv. supr. Pomarado Hosp., San Diego, 1977-82; adminstrv. supr. Centre City Hosp., San Diego, 1982—. Pres. PTA, 1954-55. Cert. CPR instr. Mem. Am. Mgmt. Assn., Nat. Assn. Female Execs., Am. Security Council. Home: 15625 Paymogo St San Diego CA 92129 Office: Centre City Hosp 120 Elm St San Diego CA 92101

NELSON, AGNES MAE, writer; b. Denver; d. Carl Oscar and Lillian Emma (Kepner) Lovestedt; student U. Nev., 1954-58; divorced; children—Robert Kepner Bryant, Clifford Henri Warnken. Part-time staff mem. Reno newspapers, 1955-59; public relations sec. Riviera Hotel, Las Vegas, Nev., 1960-61; attache Nev. State Legislature, 1959-75; sec. Nev. Dept. Vocat. Edn., 1964-65, Union Fed. Savs. & Loan Assn., Reno, 1965-66, Bank of Calif., San Francisco, 1948-49, State of Nev. Mental Health Clinic, 1971-75; mem. girls singing trio The Sparkaleers, 1955-56; appearances in mus. prodns., 1964, 66; singer Reno Civic Chorus, 1967-68, Reno Women's Chorus, 1964, Meth. Ch. choir, 1968-73; author feature articles for bicentennial publs., contbr. articles to numerous mags. and Sunday newspapers, 1956—. Mem. Nat. League Am. Pen Women (1st prize feature article Reno br. 1965, others), Nev. Press Women (41 awards), 1971-80, 2d place nat. award 1981), Nev. Poetry Soc., Calif. Writers Club, Nat. Writers Club, Nev. Self-Help Found., Nev. Corral, Westerners Internat., Women for Better Govt. Mem. Ch. Religious Sci. Club: University. Address: 520A Howard Dr Sparks NV 89431

NELSON, ANITA JOSETTE, educator; b. San Francisco, June 10, 1938; d. George Emanuel and Yvonne Louise (Borel) N. B.A., San Francisco State Coll., 1960; M.A., U. Denver, 1969. Dir. Community Ctr., Nurenberg, W.Ger., 1961-63; dir. program spl. services Community Ctr., Tokyo, 1964-66; resident counselor U. Denver, 1967-69; dir. student activities Maricopa (Ariz.) Tech. Coll., 1969-72, coach women's varsity tennis, coordinator campus activities, 1972-75; counselor, fgn. student advisor Scottsdale (Ariz.) Community Coll., 1975—. Named Phoenix Mgmt. Council Rehabilitator of Year, 1977. Mem. Nat. Assn. Women Deans, Adminstrs. and Counselors, Am. Personnel and Guidance Assn. Republican. Office: 9000 E Chaparral Rd Scottsdale AZ 85253

NELSON, ARNOLD BERNARD, animal science educator; b. Valley Springs, S.D., Aug. 26, 1922; s. Joseph Bernard and Huldah (Bernhardina) N.; m. Dorothy Millicent Larson, Aug. 3, 1943; children—James, Terry, Thomas, Barbara. B.S. in Animal Sci., S.D. State U., 1943, M.S. in Animal Sci., 1948; Ph.D. in Animal Sci., Cornell U., 1950. Asst. prof. to assoc. prof. animal sci. Okla. State U., 1950-63; prof. animal and range scis. N.Mex. State U., 1963—, head dept., 1971—. Served to 1st lt. AUS, 1943-46. Fellow Am. Soc. Animal Sci., AAAS; mem. Am. Dairy Sci. Assn., Soc. Range Mgmt., Council Agr. Sci. and Tech., Nat. Assn. Coll. Tchrs. of Agr., Latin Am. Assn. Animal Prodn., Lutheran. Home: 2010 Crescent Dr Las Cruces NM 88005 Office: Box 3 I New Mexico State Univ Las Cruces NM 88003

NELSON, BARBARA ANN, ednl. adminstr.; b. Detroit, Dec. 9, 1939; d. Theodore and Stella T. (Rokocz) Neumann; cert. dental hygiene U. Detroit, 1959; B.S. in Edn., U. Nev., Las Vegas, 1976, M.S. in Edn., 1980; m. Norman E. Nelson, June 27, 1968; children—Donald Keith, Dwayne Riley. Dental hygienist Dr. G. Dwayne Ence, Las Vegas, Nev., 1964-77; mem. faculty, coordinator dental hygiene program Clark County Community Coll., 1976—; site coordinator Health Fair '80; dist. coordinator Health Fair '81; bd. dirs. Clark County unit Am. Cancer Soc., 1981—, Clark County Health Coalition, 1981—. Campaigner Paul Laxalt for Gov. Nev., 1966, for Assemblyman Ed Kovacs, 1980. Mem. Am. Dental Hygiene Assn., Nev. Dental Hygiene Assn. (pres. 1962-63), So. Nev. Dental Hygiene Soc. (pres. 1975-76), Nev. Vocat. Assn. (v.p. 1979-81), Western Soc. Periodontology. Republican. Home: 1801 N Mallard St Las Vegas NV 89108 Office: 3200 E Cheyenne St North Las Vegas NV 89030

NELSON, BEVERLY ANN, healthcare executive; b. Los Angeles, May 10, 1939; d. Thomas J. and Avona M. (Ryan) Nelson. B.S. in Acctg., U. Calif.-Fresno, 1964; M.B.A., Boise State U., 1973. Joined Congregation of Sisters of Holy Cross; acctg. asst. Holy Cross Hosp., Salt Lake City, 1963; acctg. asst. St. Agnes Hosp., Fresno, 1964-64, dir. fin. mgmt., 1964-68, adminstrv. asst., dir. fin. mgmt., 1968-71; asst. adminstr. Holy Cross Hosp., San Fernando, Calif., 1973, adminstr., 1973-76; pres., adminstr. St. Alphonsus Regional Med. Ctr., Boise, Idaho, 1976—; regional councilor, treas. health services region Sisters of Holy Cross, 1972-75, regional councilor, treas. Western region, 1975-78; dir. Blue Cross-Blue Shield Idaho, 1977—, chmn. hosp. affairs com., 1981—. Trustee Holy Cross Hosp., Mission Hills, Calif., 1977—, sec.-treas., 1973-76, chmn. fin. com., 1978-80, mem. exec. com., 1980—; trustee Holy Cross Hosp., Salt Lake City, 1972-77, mem. exec. com., 1976-77, mem. fin. com., 1972-77, mem. exec.-fin. com. 1977-82; trustee St. Agnes Med. Ctr., Fresno, 1982—, mem. fiscal mgmt. com., 1982—; trustee Holy Rosary Hosp., Ontario, Oreg., 1981—; bd. dirs. S.W. Idaho Family Practice Residency, 1976—; alt. del. region 8 adv. bd. Am. Hosp. Assn., 1983—; bd. dirs. N.W. Catholic Healthcare Conf., 1978—, pres., 1983—; mem. exec. council Holy Cross Health System, 1979—, mem. trustee enrichment task force, 1979—; mem. adv. council Sch. Health Scis., Boise State U., 1979-81, chmn., 1980-81, bd. dirs. Univ./Community Health Scis. Assn., 1981—; mem. Idaho Health Facilities Rev. Bd., 1981—; mem. nominating com. Jefferson Awards, 1980. Recipient Disting. Citizen award Idaho Statesman. Mem. Hosp. Fin. Mgmt. Assn. (sec. Fresno council 1966), Am. Coll. Hosp. Adminstrs., Idaho Hosp. Assn. (dir. 1979—, chmn. 1980-81, chmn. council on fin. and govtl. relations 1981-82, chmn. nominating com. 1981-82, mem. council on assn. devel. 1981-84), Greater Boise C. of C. (dir. 1979-80). Club: Court House. Office: St Alphonsus Regional Med Ctr 1055 N Curtis Rd Boise ID 83706

NELSON, DELBERT ANDREW, career educator; b. Britton, S.D., Feb. 18, 1944; s. Severine Andrew and Bernadene Elizabeth (Jacobs) N.; m. Doris Carolyn Pechan, Aug. 14, 1966 (div. Jan. 1983); 1 son, Brook Andrew. B.S. in Bus. Edn., Augustana Coll., Sioux Falls, S.D., 1967. Tchr. bus. Flandreau (S.D.) Indian Sch., 1967, Newell (S.D.) High Sch., 1967-69; tchr. bus. Fremont County Sch. Dist. 1 Lander Valley High Sch., Lander, Wyo., 1969-77, tchr. Experience-Based Career Edn., 1977—. Recipient citation for outstanding environ., citizenship Fremont County Audubon Soc., 1977. Mem. NEA, Wyo. Edn. Assn., Am. Vocat. Assn., Wyo. Vocat. Assn., Nat. Experience-Based Career Edn. Assn. Lutheran. Office: 1000 Main St Lander WY 82520

NELSON, DOROTHY WRIGHT, judge; b. San Pedro, Calif., Sept. 30, 1928; d. Harry Earl and Lorna Amy Wright; A.B., UCLA, 1950, J.D., 1953; LL.M., U. So. Calif., 1956, LL.D., 1983; m. James Frank Nelson, Dec. 27, 1950; children—Franklin Wright, Lorna Jean. Admitted to Calif. bar, 1954; research asso. fellow U. So. Calif., 1953-56; instr., 1957-58, asst. prof., 1959-61, asso. prof., 1961-67, prof., 1967, asso. dean, 1965-67, dean, 1967-80; judge U.S. Ct. Appeals 9th Circuit, Los Angeles, 1980—; cons. Project STAR, Law Enforcement Assistance Adminstrn. Co-chmn. Confronting Myths in Edn. for Pres. Nixon's White House Conf. on Children, Pres. Carter's Commn. for Pension Policy, 1979. Bd. dirs. Council on Legal Edn. for Profl. Responsibility, Constnl. Right Found., Am. Nat. Inst. for Social Advancement; adv. bd. Nat. Center for State Cts., 1974. Bd. visitors USAF Acad., 1976-78; adv. bd. Elizabeth Fry Center, 1973, Jr. League Los Angeles, 1976-79; mem. Los Angeles Employee Relations Bd., 1974-79; del. Internat. Women's Conf., 1975; adv. com. Nat. Jud. Edn. Program to Promote Equality for Women and Men in Cts., 1982—; bd. dirs. Pasadena Dispute Resolution Ctr., 1982—; Los Angeles County Bar Found., 1982—; adv. com. Guardian ad Litem Program, Superior Ct. Los Angeles, 1982—; co-chmn. UN Day in Calif., 1982. Named Law Adlumnus of Yr., U. Calif. at Los Angeles, 1967, recipient Profl. Achievement award, 1969; named Times Woman of Yr., 1968; recipient U. Judaism Humanitarian award, 1973; AWARE Internat. award, 1970; Ernestine Stalhut Outstanding Woman Lawyer award, 1972; Coro award for edn., 1978; Pax Orbis award World Peace through Law Center, 1975. Fellow Am. Bar Found.; mem. State Bar Calif. (bd. dirs. continuing edn. bar commn. 1967-74), Am. Law Inst., Am. Judicature Soc. (exec. com. 1976—, dir. 1972-75, 76—, research adv. com. 1974—, editorial adv. bd. Judicature 1974—, v.p. 1977-79, chmn. bd. 1979—), Assn. Am. Law Schs. (coms.), Supreme Ct. Hist. Soc., Nat. Assn. Public Adminstrn., Am. Bar Assn. (sect. on jud. adminstrn.; chmn. com. on edn. in jud. adminstrn. 1973—, Phi Beta Kappa, Order of Coif (nat. v.p. 1974-76). Baha'i. Author: Judicial Adminstration and The Administration of Justice, 1973. Contbr. articles to profl jours. Office: 312 N Spring St Los Angeles CA 90012

NELSON, FRANKLYN LLOYD, social psychologist: b. Los Angeles, June 21, 1946; s. Jack W. and Verna Maxine (Lane) N.; B.A., Calif. State U., Northridge, 1969; M.A. (NIMH fellow), U. So. Calif., 1973, Ph.D., 1975, Ph.D., Calif. Sch. Profl. Psychology, 1983. Research asso. U.S. VA, Wadsworth Med. Center, Los Angeles, 1974-77, 80-82; sr. research asso. dept. anthropology and sociology U. Queensland, Brisbane, Australia, 1977-78; staff psychologist Inst. for Studies of Destructive Behaviors and Suicide Prevention Center, Los Angeles, 1978—; cons. Los Angeles County Drug Abuse Office, 1978-79, Community Health Services Evaluation Study, Commonwealth Sci. and Indsl. Research Orgn., Australia, 1977-78; pvt. practice clin. psychology, 1982—. Area coordinator Lifelong Learning Center, West Los Angeles Coll., 1977; coordinator community youth services Los Angeles S.W. Coll., 1976. Recipient service cert. Los Angeles S.W. Coll., 1976; NIH biomed. scis. support grantee, 1973-74. Mem. Am. Acad. Polit. and Social Scis., AAAS, Am. Psychol. Assn., Am. Sociol. Assn., Am. Assn. Suicidology, Psi Chi, Alpha Kappa Delta. Democrat. Contbr. articles to profl. jours. Office: 1041 S Menlo Ave Los Angeles CA 90006

NELSON, JACK RUSSELL, university president; b. Portland, Oreg., Dec. 18, 1929; s. George Bahn and Elsa Margaret (Hamilton) N.; B.A., Pacific Union Coll., 1952; M.B.A., UCLA, 1957, Ph.D., 1962; m. Bonita Casey, June 17, 1951; children—Richard Meredith, Ronald Gregory, Robert Geoffrey. Chief accountant St. Helena Sanitarium and Hosp., 1951-53; mgr. Modesto City Hosp., 1954-55; asso. prof. Andrews U., 1959-61; from asst. prof. to prof. U. Minn. Sch. Bus., 1961-70; asst. to pres. U. Oreg., 1966-67; prof. U. Colo., Boulder, 1970-81, exec. v.p., 1974-78, chancellor, 1977-81; pres. Ariz. State U., Tempe, 1981—. Mem. Am. Econ. Assn. Contbr. articles to profl. jours. Home: 2400 S College Ave Tempe AZ 85282

NELSON, JERRY REES, microbiologist; b. Payson, Utah, Apr. 22, 1947; s. Rees William and Fern (Worthington) N.; A.S., Dixie Jr. Coll., 1967; B.S., U. Utah, 1969, M.S., 1972, Ph.D., 1975; m. Lynda Kay Smith, June 8, 1968; children—Jeffery, Amanda. Teaching asst. U. Utah, Salt Lake City, 1969-72, teaching fellow, 1973-75, curator dept. microbiology pure culture collection, 1969-75, lab. dir., v.p. microbiol. devel. and control, 1975—. Legis. dist. chmn., 1976-77, voting dist. del., 1974, voting dist. vice chmn., 1976-77. Mem. Am. Soc. Microbiology (Intermountain chpt. pres. 1978-79), Soc. Indsl. Microbiology, Am. Public Health Assn., N.Y. Acad. Scis., AAAS, Am. Soc. Quality Control, Assn. Lab. Animal Sci., Utah Assn. Lab. Animal Sci. (pres. bd. dirs., 1977-79), Parenteral Drug Assn. Mormon. Condr. research in field. Home: 2845 E 4430 S Salt Lake City UT 84117 Office: U Utah Research Park 420 Chipeta Way Suite 280 Salt Lake City UT 84108

NELSON, JOHN L., government administrator; b. Berkeley, Calif., Nov. 15, 1932; s. John Henry and Helen Virginia (Hahn) N.; m. Jane Worthington, Apr. 27, 1956; children—John Andrew, Susan Howat. B.A. in History, U. Calif.-Berkeley, 1955; postgrad. Def. Intelligence Sch., Anacostia, Md., 1965-66. Notary Public, Wash. Mktg. rep. Hallmark Cards, Inc., Berkeley, 1957-60; commd. ensign U.S. Navy, 1955, advanced through grades to lt., 1963; intelligence officer, Vietnam, 1966-67; resigned, 1967; with HEW and successor HHS, Washington, 1967-70, staff asst., Seattle, 1970—. Ski chaperone jr. and sr. high ski sch., 1970-82, co-dir. ski sch., 1978; active in community opera, 1981-82; loaned exec. United Way King County, 1982; mem. Mercer Island Arts Commn., 1983—. Served with USN, 1955-57. Recipient various profl. and community service commendations. Mem. United Ch. Christ. Club: Mercer Island Country. Home: 7818 SE 76th St Mercer Island WA 98040 Office: HHS 2901 3d Ave Seattle WA 98121

NELSON, JOHN JOSEPH, JR., aerospace, communications co. mgr.; b. Phila., June 14, 1942; s. John Joseph and Kathleen T. (Conboy) N.; B.S. in Elec. Engring., Villanova U., 1965; M.B.A., Pepperdine U., 1975; m. Claire Brydahl, June 12, 1975; children—Kathleen Anne, John Joseph. Supr. subcontracts Ford Aerospace and Communications Co., Newport Beach, Calif., 1974-76, program mgr., 1976-81, dir. material Divad div., 1981-82, program dir., 1982—. Served to maj. USMC, 1965-74. Decorated D.F.C., Air medal with 16 oak leaf clusters. Mem. Nat. Mgmt. Assn. (dir. chpt. 1980-83), Navy League. Republican. Roman Catholic. Home: 34 Songsparrow St Irvine CA 92714 Office: Ford Aerospace & Communications Co Ford Rd Newport Beach CA 92660

NELSON, KATHLEEN ANN, sales representative; b. Glendale, Calif., Feb. 22, 1948; d. William Roy and Shirley Ann (Yock) Carr; m. Michael Arthur Nelson, Dec. 4, 1971 (div. 1983); 1 son, John Michael. Student Eastern Wash. State Coll., 1966-68. Flight attendant N.W. Orient Airlines, 1968-71; sales rep. Ideal Toys div. CBS, Bellevue, Wash., 1981—; active mem., grad. Context Tng. Corp., 1982—. Recipient Disting. Vendor award Jafco Corp., 1982. Mem. Pacific N.W. Toy Assn., Nat. Assn. Female Execs. Unitarian. Home: 12384 SE 41st Ln Bellevue WA 98006

NELSON, LAWRENCE OLAF, educator; b. Hartford, Conn., Feb. 1, 1926; s. Lawrence Olaf and Gerda Amelia Elizabeth (Hanson) N.; B.S., Central Conn. State U., 1949; M.A., U. Conn., 1953; Ph.D., Mich. State U., 1960; postgrad. Inst. for Ednl. Mgmt., Harvard U., 1971; m. Kathleen Alice Brito, Aug. 26, 1950; children—Scott Laurence, Adam Foster. Tchr. pub. schs., Stamford, Conn., 1949-52; asst. dir. U. Conn., 1952-56; asst. to pres. State Coll., Moorhead, Minn., 1956-57, dean of adminstrn., 1957-58; cons. Office of Edn., HEW, Washington, 1960; mem. faculty Purdue U., Lafayette, Ind., 1960-74, asst. to dean, 1960-62, dir., 1962-65, asso. dean, 1965-67, adminstrv. dean, 1967-74, dean Ft. Wayne Campus, 1969-70, asst. to provost, 1974; prof. ednl. adminstrn. and higher edn. U. Ariz., Tucson, 1974—, dean, 1974-81; cons. in field. Mem. planning com. Ind. Gov.'s Regional Correction Center, 1969-71; mem. adv. panel Ind. Higher Edn. Telecommunications System, 1971-74; adv. bd. Midwestern Center, Nat. Humanities Series, 1972-74; mem. Ind. Com. for Humanities, 1972-74, Tucson Com. on Fgn. Relations, 1975—; bd. dirs. Continuing Edn. for Deaf, 1975-81, Ariz. Consortium for Edn. in Social Services, 1977-81. Mem. Am. Assn. Higher Edn., Assn. Continuing Higher Edn., Nat. Assn. Student Personnel Administrators, NEA, Nat. Univ. Extension Assn. (award 1971, dir. 1978-80), Delta Chi (faculty honoree 1980), Phi Delta Kappa, Epsilon Pi Tau. Clubs: Moorhead Kiwanis (dir. 1957-58); Kiwanis Greater Lafayette (pres. 1967); Rotary (dir. 1979-80, pres. 1980-81) (Tucson). Author: Cooperative Projects Among Colleges and Universities, 1961. Home: 1330 Indian Wells Rd Tucson AZ 85718 Office: 409 Edn Bldg U Ariz Tucson AZ 85721

NELSON, MARGARET ROSE, lawyer; b. St. George, Utah, May 27, 1952; d. V. Pershing and Hattie (Jones) Nelson. B.A. magna cum laude, Brigham Young U., 1973, J.D., J. Reuben Clark Law Sch., 1976. Bar: Utah 1977, U.S. Dist. Ct. Utah 1977, U.S. Ct. Appeals (10th cir.) 1977, D.C. 1979, U.S. Supreme Ct. 1980. Mem. Aldrich & Nelson, Provo, Utah, 1977-80; law and banking tchr. Utah Tech. Coll., Provo, 1978-81, Orem, Utah, 1981; law instr. Utah State Police Acad., Salt Lake City, 1981; mem. Utah State Bd. Edn., 1983—; dep. atty. Utah County, Provo, 1977—; adv. bd. Utah Legal Services, 1977-78, trustee, 1983—; exec. com. Am. Inn of Ct. I., 1982—, mem. Utah State Juvenile Ct. Ad Hoc Com., 1981-82. State and county del., central com. mem., 1982, adv. council mem. Provo Sch. Dist., 1982; mem. Utah State Bd. Vocat. Edn., 1983—; mem. Provo Freedom Festival Children's Parade Com., 1978. Named regional semi-finalist Nat. Moot Ct. Competition, Denver, 1975. Mem. Nat. Dist. Attys. Assn., Utah Assn. Prosecutors, Women Lawyers Utah, Utah Trial Lawyers Assn., Assn. Trial Lawyers Am., Central Utah Bar Assn. (sec.-treas. 1979), LWV, Am. Judicature Soc., ABA, Nat. Assn. State Bds. Edn., Provo C. of C. (chmn. legis. action com.), Phi Kappa Phi. Republican. Mormon. Home: 210 W 800 S Orem UT 84057 Office: PO Box 357 Provo UT 84603

NELSON, MARY CARROLL, artist, author, educator; b. Bryan, Tex., Apr. 24, 1929; d. James Vincent and Mary Elizabeth (Langton) Carroll; B.A. in Fine Arts, Barnard Coll., 1950; M.A., U. N.Mex., 1963; m. Edwin Blakely Nelson, June 27, 1950; children—Patricia Ann, Edwin Blakely. One-woman shows: Santoro Gallery, San Leandro, Calif., 1960, Symbol Gallery, Albuquerque, 1966, Thor Gallery, Louisville, 1967, Amerson Gallery, Tucson, 1974; group shows include: Southwestern Watercolor Soc., Dallas, N.Mex. Watercolor Soc., Nat. League Am. Pen Women, N.Mex. State Fair; represented in pvt. collections in U.S., Germany, Eng., Australia; author: American Indian Biography Series, 1971-76; (with Robert E. Wood) Watercolor Workshop, 1974; (with Ramon Kelley) Ramon Kelley Paints Portraits and Figures, 1977; The Legendary Artists of Taos, 1980; Masters of Western Art, 1982; contbg. editor Am. Artist, 1976—; tchr. art, Ayer, Mass., 1957, Charlottesville, Va., 1957-59, Mary Frances Acad., Albuquerque, 1961-62, army overseas schs., Germany, 1963-66, army schs., Ft. Knox, Ky., 1966-68, Ft. Leonard Wood, Mo., 1968-69, Sunset Mesa Schs., Albuquerque, 1971-83. Mem. Soc. Layerists in Multi-Media (founder 1982), Albuquerque Mus. Found., Nat. League Am. Pen Women, N.Mex. Watercolor Soc. Republican. Roman Catholic. Home: 1408 Georgia St NE Albuquerque NM 87110

NELSON, MICHAEL ERNEST, safety engr.; b. Salt Lake City, Mar. 24, 1952; s. David Marcus and Connie Marie (Valone) N.; m. Vickie Ann Riley, Dec. 29, 1970; children—Shawn David, David Marcus. Student USAF Community Coll., 1970-78. Cert., Nat. Safety Council. Laborer FMC Mine, Green River, Wyo., 1978, safety technician, 1978-80, mine trainer, 1980-81; supr. safety and tng. FMC Dept. Natural Resources, Skull Point Mine, Kemmerer, Wyo., 1981—. Served with USAF, 1970-78. Mem. Am. Soc. Safety Engrs. Democrat. Mormon. Clubs: Lions, Masons. Home: 420 Pearl St Kemmerer WY 83101 Office: PO Box 750 Kemmerer WY 83101

NELSON, NANCY ELEANOR, pediatrician, educator; b. El Paso, Apr. 4, 1933; d. Harry Hamilton and Helen Maude (Murphy) N. B.A. magna cum laude, U. Colo., 1955, M.D., 1959. Intern, Case Western Res. U. Hosp., 1959-60, resident, 1960-63; practice medicine specializing in pediatrics, Denver, 1963—; assoc. clin. prof. U. Colo. Sch. Medicine, Denver, 1977—, asst. dean Sch. Medicine, 1982—. Mem. Am. Acad. Pediatrics, AMA, Denver Med. Soc. (pres. 1983-84). Home: 1265 Elizabeth Denver CO 80206 Office: 4200 E 9th Ave Denver CO 80262

NELSON, RALPH, film producer, dir., writer; b. N.Y.C.; s. Carl Leo and Edith Elsa (Lagergreen) N.; grad. high sch., Long Island City, 1933; D.H.L., Columbia Coll., 1975; m. Barbara Jean Powers, Feb. 6, 1954; children—Theodor Holm, Ralph Bahnsen, Peter Powers, Meredith, Liv. Dir. films Requiem for a Heavyweight, 1961, Lilies of the Field, 1962, Soldier in the Rain, 1963, Fate is the Hunter, 1964, Father Goose, 1965, Counterpoint, 1969, Soldier Blue, 1970; producer, dir. Duel at Diablo, 1966, Once a Thief, 1967, Charly, 1968, Tic-Tic-Tic, 1970; writer, producer, dir. Flight of the Doves, 1972, The Wrath of God, 1973, The Wilby Conspiracy, 1974, Embryo, A Hero Ain't Nothin But a Sandwich, 1976, Because He's My Friend, 1977, You Can't Go Home Again, 1978, Christmas Lilies of the Field, 1979; actor in Idiot's Delight, Taming of the Shrew, There Shall Be No Night, Romeo and Juliet; dir. numerous TV shows, 1948-60; dir. stage plays Here's Mama, 1952, The Trouble-Makers, 1953, The Man in the Dog Suit, 1957. Pres. Rainbow Prodns., Los Angeles, 1960—. Guest lectr. U. So. Calif., Los Angeles, 1968-75, UCLA, 1976, U. Mich., 1981; free-lance writer, 1942—. Trustee, Columbia Coll. Served to capt. USAAF, 1941-45, wrote Air Corps manual on aerobatics. Nat. Theatre Conf. fellow, 1947. Recipient numerous awards including Emmy award for Best TV Dir., 1956, Industry award Alpha Epsilon Rho Soc., 1961, spl. citation Edinburgh Film Festival, 1963, Medal of Gold award Italian Film Critics, 1964, Religious Drama award Nat. Catholic Theatre Conf., 1964, spl. citation Los Angeles City Council, 1964; named Outstanding Film Dir. Sorrento (Italy) Film Festival, 1970, Outstanding Dir. of Year Nat. Assn. Theatre Owners, 1968. Mem. Authors League, Writers Guild, Screen Actors Guild, Soc. Composers and Pubs., Dramatists Guild, Actors Equity, Dirs. Guild of Am. (mem. nat. bd. 1965—), Radio and TV Dirs. Guild (pres. 1950-51), Players Club of N.Y. Author: (plays) Mine Kamp, 1942; Mail Call, 1943; Angels Weep, 1944; The Wind is 90, 1945; (films) The Man in the Funny Suit, 1958; Flight of the Doves, 1970; The Wrath of God, 1971; Christmas Lilies of the Field, 1979. Office: 1900 Ave of Stars Suite 2270 Century City Los Angeles CA 90067

NELSON, RICHARD DALE, elementary educator, consultant; b. Albion, Nebr., May 25, 1925; s. Clarence McKinley and Ella Viola (Richards) N.; m. Juanita Mae Montgomery, Dec. 31, 1948; children—

Rebecca and Ruth (twins), Benjamin, Samuel. Student Boise Jr. Coll., 1947-49; B.A. in Secondary Edn., Coll. of Idaho, 1956, M.Ednl. Adminstrn., 1962; Ed.D., U. Idaho, 1973. Cert. elem., secondary tchr., adminstr., prin., Idaho. Elem. tchr. Whittier Sch., Boise, Idaho, 1952-58, Hillcrest Sch., Boise, 1958-59, elem. prin., 1958-65; asst. prin. Borah High Sch., Boise, 1965-66, prin., 1966-69; supt. Cascade (Idaho) Dist. #422, 1969-72; tchr., counselor Cascade High Sch., 1971-72; supr. desegregation and affirmative action, State Dept. Edn., Idaho, 1973-76, dir. No. Regional Office, 1976-79; assoc. prof. U. Idaho, Moscow, 1976-79; supr. Moscow (Idaho) Schs., 1979-80; elem. tchr. Franklin Sch., Boise, 1980-81, Amity Sch., Boise, 1981-83; cons. state ednl. dir. Air Force Assn., 1968-76; mem. State Supt. Fin. Com., 1969-72; gen. chmn. Air Force Assn. Ednl. Symposium, 1968. Scoutmaster, mem. troop com., instl. rep. Mountain View council Boy Scouts Am., Boise, 1956-65; mem. youth com. Boise YMCA, 1960-65, Jr. Achievement Com., Boise, 1965-66; precinct committeeman, Ada County, Idaho, 1962-63; candidate for State Supt. Pub. Instrn. Idaho, 1978. Served with USMC, World War II; to lt. col. Air N.G., 1964-79; liaison officer Idaho Adj. Gen.'s Office for Mil. Support of CD, 1979-83. Mem. So. Idaho Conf. High Schs. (pres. 1966-67), 8th Dist. Idaho Edn. Assn. (pres. 1964-65), Boise Edn. Assn. (chmn. coms.), NEA, Idaho Edn. Assn. Lutheran. Author: Public School Finance in Idaho, 1973; Idaho School Finance: A Study of Status and Values, 1973; Guidelines for Public School Affirmative Action Planning, 1975; How to Hire a Superintendent, 1977. Home: 8202 S Cloverdale Rd Boise ID 83709 Office: 10000 W Amity Rd Boise ID 83709

NELSON, ROBERT D., marketing consultant; b. Chgo., May 30, 1920; s. Fritchoff G. and Marjory (Brigham) N.; student bus. mgmt. LaSalle Extension U., 1946; m. Georgia Smith, Mar. 25, 1939; children—Roberta Diane Nelson Jasa, Sandra Dee Nelson Johnson; m. 2d, Vera Monahan, Sept. 16, 1977. Salesman, Lever Brothers Co., 1939-42, sales supr., 1942-43; product mgr. United Buyers Corp., 1943-46; pres. Count-Rite Industries, 1946-47; gen. br. mgr. C.D. Kenney Co., Indpls., 1947-48; Midwest regional mgr. Carling Breweries, 1948-51; sales promotion mgr., asst. gen. sales mgr. Oscar Mayer Packing Co., Madison, Wis., 1951-60; exec. v.p., gen. mgr. Los Angeles Times, 1960-78, also v.p. parent orgn. Times Mirror Co.; cons. mgmt. and mktg., 1978—; dir. Orange Coast Pub. Co., San Bernardindo Sun Telegram, KTTV, HML Ins. Co., Newspaper 1. Chmn., Better Bus. Bur., 1971-76; vice chmn. ARC, Los Angeles, 1964-68; chmn. Arthritis Found., 1966-70; bd. dirs. United Way, Huntington Hosp. Inst. Applied Medicine Program. Mem. Am. Mktg. Assn. (Marketer of Yr. 1975), Advt. Council (dir.), Newspaper Advt. Bur. (dir.), Republican. Clubs: Annandale Golf; Los Angeles Athletic. Home: 126 Patrician Way Pasadena CA 91105 Office: 7330 N Figueroa St Los Angeles CA 90041

NELSON, ROBERT MORRIS, management consultant; b. Spokane, Wash., Feb. 18, 1925; s. Walter Daniel and Doris (Morris) N.; m. Jane Randall Gray, Sept. 1, 1951; 1 dau., Deborah. B.A., Whitman Coll., 1950; M.A., U. Chgo., 1955. Personnel officer U.S. Navy Dept., Lawrence Berkeley Lab., Calif., 1951-67; personnel dir. Stanford Linear Accelerator Ctr. (Calif.), 1968-69; dir. personnel/employee relations Stanford U. (Calif.), 1970-71; personnel mgr. Lawrence Livermore Nat. Lab., Calif., 1972-73, Bechtel Group, San Francisco, 1973-77; pvt. practice mgmt. cons., San Francisco, 1978—; dir. Greater San Francisco Opportunities Industrialization Ctr., 1976-80. Treas. Democratic Central Com. Alameda County, 1964-68. Served to cpl. U.S. Army, 1943-46. Mem. Am. Soc. Personnel Adminstrs., Profl. Services Mgmt. Assn., Mechanics Inst. San Francisco. Club: Commonwealth (San Francisco). Office: 2230 Pacific Ave Suite 303 San Francisco CA 94115

NELSON, ROBERT THOMAS, luggage manufacturing company executive; b. Wankesha, Wis., July 2, 1943; s. Thomas N. and Vivian M. (Thurber) N.; m. Janis T. Hunt, Sept. 8, 1964; children—Julie Kirsten, Christopher Lawrence. B.A. in Radio and TV, Calif. State U.-Northridge, 1970. News dir. Sta. KRAE, Cheyenne, Wyo., 1970-72; advt. supr. Mountain Bell Co., Denver, 1972-78; v.p., gen. mgr. Metagraphics, Denver, 1978-79; dir. communications Samsonite Corp., Denver, 1979—. Served with USAF, 1963-67. Recipient George Washington Honor medal Freedom Found., 1967, Golden Mike award Am. Legion, 1971. Mem. Denver Advt. Fedn. Office: Samsonite Corp 11200 E 45th Ave Denver CO 80239

NELSON, ROSEJANE MARKHAM, management recruitment executive; b. Erie, Pa., Jan. 14, 1923; d. Frank D. and Agnes T. Wiertel; m. Frank Houpt (dec.); children—David J., Diane L.; m. 2d Tom A. Markham, Aug. 6, 1949; children—Tom A., Brad, Brooke, J. Brian; m. 3d Hugh C. Nelson, Sept. 1, 1974. Grad. in bus. Erie Bus. Coll., 1941; student Buffalo Law Sch., 1972. Prin. Rosejane Markham, real estate brokerage, Chautauqua County, N.Y., 1952-74; broker McCullough Real Estate Corp., Pa. and N.Y. State, 1972; ptnr., v.p., sec.-treas. Roth Young, Phoenix, 1977—; also artist; collector rare books. Town assessor Town of Mina (N.Y.), 1966-68, municipality bingo insp., 1970-72, town justice, 1972. Republican. Home: 514 W Townley Ave Phoenix AZ 85021 Office: 5150 N 16th St Suite 236B Phoenix AZ 85016

NELSON, SCOTT DOUGLAS, political activist, public affairs consultant; b. Watford City, N.D., Dec. 14, 1954; s. Thomas Oliver and Irene Lettie (Hoover) N.; m. Paula Sue Plamondon, Mar. 18, 1978; 1 dau., Erica Suzanne. B.A., U. Puget Sound, 1978. Free-lance comml. photographer, 1974-77; staff asst. to U.S. Rep. Norman Dicks, Tacoma, Wash., 1978-80, dist. rep., Tacoma, 1980-81; western regional dir. Democratic Nat. Com., Issaquah, Wash., 1981—; mem. polit. staff or cons. to numerous Dem. campaigns for Gov., U.S. Senate, U.S. Congress and state constl. offices, including Dick Bryan for Gov. Nev., 1982 and N.Mex. Dem. party, 1982. Bd. dirs. Puget Sound Older Workers Employment Agy., Tacoma, 1979-80, Ret. Sr. Vol. Program Pierce County, Tacoma, 1978-80; fin. chmn. Dist. 2 Boy Scouts Am., 1980. Recipient Eagle Scout award Boy Scouts Am., 1968, Pro Deo Et Patria, 1969; Nat. Merit scholar, 1973. Mem. Pub. Relations Soc. Am., Ctr. Study Dem. Instns., MENSA, Pi Kappa Delta, Sigma Nu. Lutheran. Author monographs: Juvenile Justice in Washington State, 1977; Computers in Politics—Legal an Moral Questions, 1980; others. Home: 4659 190th SE Issaquah WA 98027

NELSON, SHERRY CAROLYN, artist; b. Alton, Ill., Mar. 3, 1944; d. Phillip Garr and Pearl Lillian (Davis) Nickell; B.A., So. Ill. U., 1966; postgrad. Ind. State U., 1967-68; m. Gene Nelson, Nov. 6, 1963; children—Neil Marshall, Berit Katherine Amanda. One-woman shows: Casa del Tole, Albuquerque, 1982, Bear Mountain Guest Ranch, Silver City, N.Mex., 1982; group shows at various hotels; represented in permanent collection. Decorative Arts Collection, Inc., Newton, Kans.; pres. The Magic Brush, Inc., Anthony, Tex., 1978-83. Mem. Nat. Soc. Tole and Decorative Painters (dir., pres.-elect 1983-84, Master Tchr. award 1976), Tex. Arts Assn., W. Tex. Sage Brushes. Republican. Episcopalian. Author: Let's Paint, 1973; Tole Cooking, 1974; The Birds and a Bee, 1978; The Glass Giraffe, 1979; The Glass Giraffe II, 1980; Begin with Butterflies, 1981; The Pastel Pig, 1981; From Palette to Parrot, 1982. Home: PO Box 868 Anthony NM 88021 Office: 103 S 5th St Anthony TX 88021

NELSON, STEPHEN JOHN, environmental engineer; b. Alexandria, Minn., Mar. 31, 1951; s. Herbert Woodrow and Edith (Stigelmayer) N.; m. Kathryn Ahnstedt, June 22, 1974; children—Jared Michael, Allison Kay, Brent Allen. B.S. in Civil Engring., Washington U., St. Louis, 1973; M.S., Stanford U., 1974. Registered profl. engr., Calif. Sanitary engr. Calif. Dept. Health Services, San Bernardino, 1974-76, assoc. sanitary engr., Berkeley, 1976—. Mem. ASCE (chmn. water policy com. San Francisco sect.), Water Pollution Control Fedn., Am. Water Works Assn. (chmn. Calif.-Nev. sect. water quality and resources div.). Democrat. Mem. Evangelical Covenant Ch. Am. Contbr. articles to profl. jours. Office: 2151 Berkeley Way Room 234 Berkeley CA 94704

NELSON, WARREN HOWARD, consulting aerospace engineer; b. Mount Vernon, N.Y., Oct. 5, 1924; s. Joel Gottfried and Hildur Elizabeth (Soderstrom) N.; B.S. in Aero. Engring., Tri-State U., 1943; m. Elizabeth Frances Castle, Dec. 14, 1946; children—Susan Lynn, Linda Lorraine, Craig Lee, Peggy Louise. With NACA and NASA, Ames Research Center, Moffett Field, Calif., 1943-80, aero. engr., 1943-54, asst. chief 14-foot transonic wind tunnel, 1954-59, 3.5-foot hypersonic wind tunnel, 1959-67, exec. engr. thermo and gas dynamics div., 1967-76, chief thermo-physics facilities br., 1976-80; engring. cons., 1980—; mem. Supersonic Tunnel Assn., 1970-80. Active youth baseball, 1968-73. Served with USN, 1944-46. Recipient NASA Exceptional Service medal, 1979, NASA Group Achievement award, 1980, 81. Mem. AIAA, Alpha Sigma Phi. Republican. Lutheran. Club: Elks. Author 20 NACA reports on aero. research; designer, developer subsonic transonic, supersonic, hypersonic and high-enthalpy aero. test facilities. Address: 1030 Varsity Ct Mountain View CA 94040

NELSON, WILLARD GREGORY, veterinarian; b. Lewiston, Idaho, Nov. 21, 1937; s. Donald William and Eve Mae (Boyer) N.; div.; children—Elizabeth Ann, John Gregory. B.S. in Premedicine, Mont. State U., 1959; D.V.M., Wash. State U., 1961. Lic. veterinarian, Wash., Oreg., Idaho, Mont. Pvt. practice vet. medicine, Kuna, Idaho, 1963-66; asst. to dir. Idaho Dept. Agr., Boise, 1966-78; asst. chief Idaho Bur. Animal Health, 1978-80, chief, 1980-81; adminstr. Idaho Div. Animal Industries, 1981—; comdr. vet. detachment Idaho N.G. Kuna city councilman, 1964-68, pres. Planning and Zoning Commn., 1968-72; mem. bd. trustees Joint Sch. Dist. 3, 1970-71, pres., 1972-76. Served as capt. U.S. Army Vet Corps, 1961-63. Mem. Idaho Vet. Med. Assn., S.W. Idaho Vet. Med. Assn., U.S. Animal Health Assn., AVMA, Western States Livestock Assn. Lutheran. Club: Lions (Kuna). Office: 120 Klotz Ln Boise ID 83702

NELSON, WILLIAM BISCHOFF, educator; b. St. Louis, Apr. 14, 1940; s. A.L., Jr. and M.M.H. (Bischoff) N.; student Washington U., St. Louis, 1958-60; M.S. in Mktg., U. Ariz., 1963, B.S., 1962; m. Julianne McDevitt, Dec. 1, 1972; children—Keli Anne, William Bischoff. Field advt. rep. Procter & Gamble Co., Cin., 1962; mem. mktg. staff Ford Motor Co., Dearborn, Mich., 1963-66; instr. mktg. U. Ariz., 1966-70; prof., dept. head mktg., gen. bus. and mktg. Pima Community Coll., Tucson, 1970—. Active United Way, other civic and polit. orgns.; mem. fund raising com. St. Joseph's Hosp. Mem. Nat. Assn. Mgmt. Educators (v.p. 1973-77), Am. Mgmt. Assn., Am. Mktg. Assn. (emeritus), Point-of-Purchase Advt. Inst., Audit Bur. Circulations, Internat. Newspaper Advt. Execs., So. Mktg. Assn., Southwestern Mktg. Assn., Bus. and Profl. Advt. Assn., Tucson Mus. Art, Ariz.-Sonora Desert Mus., Ariz. Hist. Soc., Nat. Trust Historic Preservation, Nat. Bus. Edn. Assn., Acad. Mktg. Sci., Direct Mail Mktg. Assn., Am. Acad. Advertisers, Am. Film Inst., Internat. Platform Assn., NEA, AAUP, Ariz. Edn. Assn., Pima Community Coll. Edn. Assn. (bd. govs. 1972-74), Smithsonian Assos., Am. Mus. Natural History, Nat. Archives Trust, Delta Sigma Pi, Beta Gamma Sigma, Phi Kappa Phi. Roman Catholic. Club: Tucson Press. Office: PO Box 41630 Tucson AZ 85717

NELSON, WILLIAM EDWARD, lawyer; b. Los Angeles, July 16, 1926; s. Ora and Mary Frances (Bower) Parton; m. Lollie Margaret Russell, Jan. 22, 1952; children—Lindsey, Neil, Mark, Anne. B.A., Pepperdine U., 1949; J.D., Loyola U., Los Angeles, 1951. Bar: Calif. 1952. With Union Bank, Los Angeles, 1952-59; gen. mgr. Gilbert & Rothschild, Los Angeles, 1959-61; v.p., dir. fin. and adminstrn. Microdot, Inc., 1961-63; sole practice, La Jolla, Calif. and San Diego, 1963—; real estate developer, 1963—; dir. La Jolla Bancorp., Mission West Properties, La Jolla Mortgage Fund; chmn. Scripps Bank; lectr. in fin. U. Calif.-San Diego. Chmn. bd. dirs. San Diegans Inc.; past pres. La Jolla Parking and Bus. Improvement Assn.; trustee La Jolla Town Council; mem. San Diego County Econ. Commn.; U.S. bd. dirs. Am. Youth Hostels; bd. dirs. San Diego Repertory Theater, La Salle Found Earth Scis.; mem. San Diego Cts. Adminstrn. Com.; chmn. San Diego City Commn. on Parking and Transp. Served with USN, 1944-46; PTO. Mem. ABA, Calif. Bar Assn., San Diego Bar Assn., Los Angeles Bar Assn., San Diego C. of C. (bd. dirs.). Author: California Land Security and Development, 1964; Real Estate Remedies, 1982. Home: 8457 Paseo Del Ocaso La Jolla CA 92037 Office: 1020 Prospect St La Jolla CA 92037 also 525 B St San Diego CA 92101

NELSON, WILLIAM GEORGE, chemist; b. Lafayette, Colo., June 7, 1930; s. Albin Carl and Caroline Margaret (Schweiger) N.; B.A., U. Denver, 1960; NSF grad. fellow Colo. State Coll., 61, Colo. Sch. Mines, 1962, Colo. Coll., 1963; m. Helen Jean Barry, Sept. 11, 1954; children—William Albin, Diana Marie. Tchr. chemistry, chmn. sci. dept. North High Sch., Denver, 1966; asst. chief chemist Amax Co., Climax Colo., 1966-69; quality control chemist, air pollution specialist process engr. U.S. Borax & Chem. Corp., 1969-79, refinery indsl. hygienist Boron, Calif., 1979-81; chief chemist Chalco Engring. Corp., 1982—. Pres. East Kern County Resources Conservation Dist., 1978. Served with U.S. Army, 1951-53; Korea. Mem. Am. Indsl. Hygiene Assn., VFW. Roman Catholic. Home: 24342 Tamarisk St PO Box 418 Boron CA 93516 Office: Chalco Engring Corp Bldg 8451 Rocket Test Site Edwards AFB 93523

NEMETZ, NATHANIEL THEODORE, Canadian ct. chief justice; b. Winnipeg, Man., Can., Sept. 8, 1913; s. Samuel and Rebecca (Birch) N.; grad. U. B.C., 1934, hon. degree, 1975; LL.D. (hon.), U. Notre Dame (B.D.), 1972, Simon Fraser U., 1975, U. Victoria, 1976; m. Bel Newman, Aug. 10, 1935; 1 son, Peter Newman. Created King's Counsel, 1950; spl. counsel Public Utilities Commn., 1958-61; spl. counsel to cities of Vancouver, Burnaby, New Westminster, B.C., Can., 1959-63; justice B.C. Superior Ct., 1963-68, chief justice 1973-78; chief justice B.C., 1979—; justice Ct. Appeals, 1968-73; mem. Royal Commn. to investigate election irregularities, 1965; arbitrator fishing, lumber and hydro industries West Coast shipping dispute, 1973; mem. senate, chmn. bd. govs. U. B.C., 1957-68, chancellor, 1972-75; chmn. Can. edn. del. to China, 1974. Chmn. Univ. Dist. Sch. Bd., 1957-59. Named hon. fellow Hebrew U., Jerusalem, 1976; recipient award Council Christians and Jews, 1958; Great Trekker award Beth Emeth Brotherhood, 1968; Canada medal, 1967; award of distinction U. B.C. Alumni, 1975; Queen Elizabeth medal, 1977; Mem. Can. Jud. Council (exec.), Can. Bar Assn., Faculty Assn. U. B.C. (hon.). Jewish Clubs: Faculty (U. B.C.), Vancouver, University (pres., 1961-62), B'nai B'rith (Vancouver). Contbr. articles in field to profl. publs. Office: Law Courts 800 Smithe St Vancouver BC V6Z 2E1 Canada

NEMIR, DONALD PHILIP, lawyer; b. Oakland, Calif., Oct. 31, 1931; s. Philip F. and Mary (Shavor) N.; A.B., U. Calif. at Berkeley, 1957, J.D., 1960. Admitted to Calif. bar, 1961; practiced in San Francisco, 1961—. Bd. dirs. Summit Found. Mem. Am. Bar Assn., Phi Delta Phi. Club: Univ. (San Francisco). Office: One Maritime Plaza San Francisco CA 94111

NEMIRO, BEVERLY MIRIUM ANDERSON, author, educator; b. St. Paul, May 29, 1925; d. Martin and Anna Mae (Oshanyk) Anderson; student Reed Coll., 1943-44; B.A., U. Colo., 1947; children—Guy Samuel, Lee Anna, Dee Martin. Tchr., Seattle Pub. Schs., 1945-46; fashion dir. Denver Dry Goods Co., 1948-51; fashion model, Denver, 1951-58; free-lance writer, Denver, 1952—; moderator TV program Your Preschool Child, Denver, 1955-56; instr. social scis. U. Colo., Denver, 1970, U. Calif., San Diego, 1977—; free lance fashion and TV model; author; (with Donna Hamilton) The High Altitude Cookbook, 1969; The Busy People's Cookbook, 1971; Where to Eat in Colorado, 1967; Lunch Box Cookbook, 1965; Complete Book of High Altitude Baking, 1961; (under name Beverly Anderson) Single After 50, 1978; The New High Altitude Cookbook, 1980. Co-founder, pres. Jr. Symphony Guild, Denver, 1960. Address: 420 S Marion Pkwy Apt 1003 Denver CO 80209

NEPTUNE, JOHN ADDISON, chemistry educator, consultant; b. Barnesville, Ohio, Nov. 27, 1919; s. George Addison and Lola Mae (Skinner) N.; m. Ruth Elizabeth Dorsey, Aug. 24, 1947; 1 son, Benjamin. B.S. summa cum laude, Muskingum Coll., 1942; M.S., U. Wis., 1949, Ph.D., 1952. Instr. chemistry Muskingum Coll., New Concord, Ohio, 1943-44, 45-48; foreman Tenn. Eastman Corp., Manhattan Project, 1944-45; asst. prof. chemistry Bowling Green (Ohio) State U., 1949-50; instr. pharm. chemistry U. Wis.-Madison, 1952-55; asst. prof. chemistry San Jose (Calif.) State U., 1955-58, assoc. prof., 1958-61, prof., 1961—, chmn. dept., 1973—; cons. FMC Corp. and Andersen 2000. Mem. Am. Chem. Soc., AAUP. Methodist. Office: Chemistry Dept San Jose State Univ San Jose CA 95192

NERAD, CHARLES AUGUSTUS, systems analyst, counselor; b. Chgo., Apr. 9, 1948; s. August and Josephine (Vicich) N.; B.S. in Computer Sci., Northeastern Ill. U., 1978; M.S. in Exptl. Psychology, Ill. State U., 1976. Transp. mgr. Gateway Transp. Co., Chgo., 1972; social worker Traemour, Chgo., 1978; systems analyst San Diego County (Calif.), 1980-81; pvt. practice mental health and alcoholism counseling, San Diego, 1980—; computer scientist Science Applications, Inc., La Jolla, Calif., 1981-82; computer specialist U.S. Navy, Point Loma, Calif., 1982-83; computer programmer/analyst U.S. Marine Corps Med. Research Hosp., Camp Pendleton, Calif., 1983—. Coordinator, Neighborhood Alert Watch, San Diego, 1980, Civic Improvement, San Diego, 1981. Served with M.C., U.S. Army, 1966-68. Mem. Assn. Advancement Behavior Therapy, Data Processing Mgmt. Assn., Assn. Labor-Mgmt. Adminstrs. and Cons. on Alcoholism, Project Wildlife, Rancho Coastal Humane Soc., Animal Rights Coalition. Home: 465 Arroyo Seco Dr San Diego CA 92114

NERI, BARBARA THORNHILL, SR., contracts administrator; b. St. Louis, June 23, 1941; d. Roy A. and Lillian (Oliver) Thornhill; m. Raimundo J. Neri, Sept. 16, 1967. Student Wayne State U., 1960-65; B.B.A. magna cum laude, Nat. U., San Diego, 1979, M.B.A., 1981. Adminstrv. asst. Mich. Blue Cross, 1967-70; adminstrv. asst. various firms, 1970-78; asst. contract adminstr. IRT Corp., San Diego, 1978-79; contract adminstr. JAYCOR, San Diego, 1979-83; sr. contracts adminstr. Computer Scis. Corp., San Diego, 1983—. Mem. Nat. Contract Mgmt. Assn., Nat. Assn. Female Execs., AAUW. Home: 836 W Pennsylvania Ave #117 San Diego CA 92103 Office: 7110 Carroll Rd San Diego CA 92121

NES, WILLIAM DAVID, plant lipid biochemist; b. Bethesda, Md., Aug. 16, 1953; s. William Robert and Estelle Jean (Shirley) N.; B.A., Gettysburg Coll., 1975; M.S., Drexel U., 1977; Ph.D., U. Md., 1979; m. Sandra Lee Chubb, June 26, 1976; children—William Bradley, Michael David. Postdoctoral fellow U. Calif., Berkeley, 1979; supervisory research chemist Plant Physiology and Chemistry Research unit U.S. Dept. Agr., Berkeley, Calif., 1980—. Binational Agrl. and Research Devel. fellow, 1980. Mem. N.Y. Acad. Scis., Am. Oil Chemists Soc., Phytochem. Soc. N. Am., Soc. Plant Physiology, AAAS, Sigma Xi. Author: (with W.R. Nes) Lipids in Evolution, 1980; editor: (with G. Fuller and L. Tsai) Biochemistry and Function of Isopentenoids in Plants, 1984; contbr. articles to various publs. including procs. Nat. Acad. Sci. Home: 2803 Grinnel Dr Davis CA 95616 Office: 800 Buchanan St Berkeley CA 94710

NESALHOUS, MARY ANNE, educator; b. Yuma, Ariz., Sept. 6, 1937; d. Robert Francis and Anne Elizabeth (McManamy) N. B.S., U. Calif.-Davis, 1959; M.Ed., U. Redlands, 1981. Tchr. home econs. Mark Keppel High Sch., Alhambra, Calif., 1960—, also chmn. dept. consumer/family living. Hospice vol. Am. Field Service Adult Group. mem. Calif. Tchrs. Assn., NEA, Alhambra Tchrs. Assn., Calif. Home Econs. Assn. (pres. Foothill dist.), Am. Home Econs. Assn., Home Econs. Tchrs. Assn. Calif. Roman Catholic. Home: 1245 Euclid St San Gabriel CA 91776 Office: 501 E Hellman St Alhambra CA 91801

NESS, BARBARA STAMPER, public relations consultant; b. Tampa, Fla., Dec. 12, 1936; d. Robert H. and Dorothy C. (Stevens) Stamper; m. Harold J. Ness, June 23, 1956 (dec.); children—Sandra, Douglas, Rebecca. A.A., U. Fla., 1958; B.A. in Journalism, Calif. State U., 1980. Cons. internal pub. relations Luth. Ch., Westminster, Calif., 1975-79; pres. Barbara Ness Pub. Relations, Garden Grove, Calif., 1980—; cons., creator Los Angeles Jewish/Israeli Concert Series, 1982—. Mem. Calif. Christian Com. for Israel. Mem. Pub. Relations Soc. Am., Phi Kappa Phi. Club: Technion Soc. Author articles, booklets on concert series, personal stories. Office: 11151 Crosby Ave Garden Grove CA 92643

NESVADBA, MARIA MIETUS, real estate broker; b. Zakopane, Poland, Aug. 14, 1951; came to U.S., 1971, naturalized, 1977; d. Jozef and Zofia Mietus; m. George V. Nesvadba, Apr. 25, 1972; children—Patrick, Margaret. Student Music Coll., Cracow, Poland, 1970. Lic. real estate agt., Colo. Real estate broker, owner mgr. Realty World North Sub Inc., Westminster, Colo., 1979—; advt. chmn., dir. Brokers Council of Realty World Rocky Mountain Region. Recipient Young Career Women award Profl. Bus. Women's Club, 1981. Mem. North Suburban Bd. Realtors, Colo. Assn. Realtors, Nat. Assn. Realtors.

NETHERCOTT, BOYD, former real estate co. exec.; b. Oakland, Calif., Dec. 6, 1919; s. Walter Alfred and Eva Theressa (Pedersen) N.; A.A., Lassen Jr. Coll., 1941; grad. U.S. Navy Flight Sch., 1942, Naval Intelligence Sch., 1958; B.S., U. Md., 1964; postgrad. art Brigham Young U., Madrid, 1974-76; m. Dortha Lou Behunin, Oct. 17, 1942; children—Pamela, Sydney, Evan, Daniel, Jill, Anthony. Commd. ensign, aviator, U.S. Navy, 1942, advanced through grades to comdr., 1957; served in Solomon Islands, 1942-44; staff intelligence, 7th Fleet target officer, Korea, 1950-52, Naval Air Sta. adminstrn. officer, 1953-57, sr. naval officer, Berlin, 1958-61, Naval mem. Berlin Watch Com., 1958-61, sr. Naval rep. Nat. Indications Center, 1961-65; ret., 1965; dep. research and devel. Nat. Photog. Interpretation Center, CIA, Washington, 1966-69, exec. sec. under U.S. Intelligence Bd., 1969-74, ret., 1974; sales mgr. Golden West, Inc., Provo, Utah, 1977-82. Decorated Air medal. Republican. Mormon. Home: 3983 N 750 E Provo UT 84604

NETTLES, WILLIAM BENJAMIN, computer co. exec.; b. Mt. Vernon, N.Y., Oct. 31, 1942; s. Alexander and Marjorie (Robinson) N.; m. Leonie Dolores March, Jan. 29, 1966; children—Lea Denise, Lesley Dahlia, William Benjamin. Student Pace Coll., 1960-61; B.A., L.I. U., 1969; M.A., Rutgers U., 1976. With IBM, 1967—, computer programmer, San Jose, Calif. 1976—. Mem. Am. Sociol. Assn., Assn. for Computing Machinery Rutgers U. Alumni Assn. No. Calif. Democrat. Home: 7202 Alder Springs Way San Jose CA 95139

NETTO, DANIEL JULIUS, JR., engr.; b. Kotaradja, Indonesia, Feb. 21, 1931; s. Daniel Marius and Johanna Marsinah (Kartosemito) N.; B.S. equiv. Leidse Instrumentmakers' Sch., Netherlands, 1957; grad. U. Leiden (Netherlands), 1957; m. Celeste Hilda Plak, Sept. 10, 1952; children—Hedy, Jennifer, Hiddo, Perla. Optics supr. Birns & Sawyer, Hollywood, Calif., 1963-66; engring. mgr. Bach Auricon, Hollywood, 1966; engring. designer Calif. Inst. Tech., Pasadena, 1966-71; profl. staff U. So. Calif./Los Angeles County Med Center, 1971—, sr. research engr., 1971—; pres. N.T.O. Engring. Services, Los Angeles, 1978—. Mem. Soc. Motion Picture and TV Engrs., Soc. Exptl. Instrumentation (Holland), Soc. Precision Instrumentation Designers (Holland), Soc. Am. Inventors. Mem. Protestant Ref. Ch. Club: A.V.I.O. Dutch. Holder three patents in field; contbr. articles to profl. jours. Home: 153 N Vendome St Los Angeles CA 90026 Office: PO Box 1800 1200 N State St Los Angeles CA 90033

NETZEL, PAUL ARTHUR, youth and family service orgn. exec.; b. Tacoma, Sept. 11, 1941; s. Marden Arthur and Audrey Rose (Jones) N.; B.S. in Group Work Edn., George Williams Coll., 1963; m. Diane Viscount, Mar. 21, 1963; children—Paul M., Shari Ann. Program dir. S. Pasadena-San Marino (Calif.) YMCA, 1963-66; exec. dir. camp and youth programs Wenatchee (Wash.) YMCA, 1966-67; exec. dir. Culver-Palms Family YMCA, Culver City, Calif., 1967-73; v.p. met. fin. devel. YMCA Met. Los Angeles, 1973-78, sr. v.p., 1979-82, exec. v.p. devel., 1982—; pres. YMCA Employees Credit Union, 1977-80; chmn. N.Am. Fellowship of YMCA Devel. Officers, 1980-83; instr., cons., fund raiser. Pres. bd. Culver City Guidance Clinic, 1971-74; mem. Culver City Bd. Edn., 1975-79, pres., 1977-78; bd. dirs. Los Angeles Psychiat. Service; mem. Culver City City Council, 1980—, vice-mayor, 1980-82, mayor, 1982-83; mem. Culver City Redevel. Agy., 1980—; bd. dirs. Los Angeles County Sanitation Dists., 1982-83. Recipient Man of Year award Culver City C. of C., 1972. Roman Catholic. Clubs: Town Hall of Calif., Los Angeles Athletic, Rotary (Los Angeles). Office: YMCA Met Los Angeles 818 W 7th St Suite 1002 Los Angeles CA 90017

NEU, CARL HERBERT, JR., mgmt. cons.; b. Miami Beach, Fla., Sept. 4, 1937; s. Carl Herbert and Catherine Mary (Miller) N.; B.S., MIT, 1959; M.B.A., Harvard U., 1961; m. Carmen Mercedes Smith, Feb. 8, 1964; children—Carl Bartley, David Conrad. Indsl. liaison officer MIT, Cambridge, 1967-69; coordinator forward planning Gates Rubber Co., Denver, 1969-71; pres., co-founder Dyna-Com Resources, Lakewood, Colo., 1971-77; pres., founder Neu & Co., Lakewood, 1977—; lectr. Grad. Sch. Pub. Affairs, U. Colo. Denver, 1982. Mem. exec. council Episcopal Diocese Colo., 1974; mem. Lakewood City Council, 1975-80, pres., 1976; chmn. Lakewood City Charter Commn., 1982; pres. Lakewood on Parade, 1978, bd. dirs., 1978-80; pres. Classic Chorale, Denver, 1979, bd. dirs., 1978—. Served with Ordnance Corps, U.S. Army, 1961-67. Decorated Bronze Star medal, Army Commendation medal; recipient Arthur Page award AT&T, 1979; Kettering Found. grantee, 1979-80. Mem. World Future Soc., Internat. City Mgrs. Assn., Lakewood C. of C. (bd. dirs. 1983—). Democrat. Episcopalian. Contbr. articles to profl. jours. Home: 8169 W Baker Ave Lakewood CO 80227

NEUGEBAUER, GERRY, astrophysicist, educator; b. Gottingen, Germany, Sept. 3, 1932; s. Otto E. and Grete (Bruck) N.; m. Marcia MacDonald, Aug. 26, 1956; children—Carol, Lee. B.S. in Physics, Cornell U., 1954; Ph.D. in Physics, Calif. Inst. Tech, 1960. Mem. faculty Calif. Inst. Tech., Pasadena 1962—, prof. physics, 1970—; mem. staff Hale Obs., Pasadena, 1970-80; acting dir. Palomar Obs. Pasadena, 1980-81, dir. 1981—. Served with AUS, 1961-63. Recipient Exceptional Sci. Achievement medal NASA, 1972. Fellow Am. Acad. Arts and Scis.; mem. Nat. Acad. Scis., Am. Astron. Soc., Internat. Astron. Union. Contbr. numerous publs. to profl. jours. Office: Calif Inst Technology 320-47 Pasadena CA 91125

NEUMANN, ALBERT JOSEPH, II, psychologist; b. Pitts., Aug. 15, 1950; s. Albert Joseph and Marie Lucille (Wright) N.; m. Angela Jeanne Killian, Oct. 22, 1977; 1 dau., Tiffany Alys. B.A. in Psychology, Calif. State Coll., 1972; M.A. in Psychology Humboldt State U., 1974; Ph.D. in Ednl. Psychology, U. Ariz., 1981. Cert. psychologist, Ariz. Psychologist I, Caswell Retardation Ctr., Kinston, N.C., 1974-75; psychologist II, O'Berry Retardation Ctr., Goldsboro, N.C., 1976; pvt. practice, Phoenix, 1982—; cons. and assessment activities for sch. dists. Mem. Am. Psychol. Assn., Ariz. Psychol. Assn. Contbr. articles to profl. jours. Home: 3747 E Winchcomb Dr Phoenix AZ 85032

NEUMANN, ALFRED KURT, medical educator; b. Milw., July 25, 1930; s. Alfred P. and Hannah A. (Lange) N.; B.A., U. Wis., 1952, M.A., 1955; M.D., NYU, 1958; M.P.H., Harvard U., 1960; m. Charlotte Grantz, Sept. 10, 1959; children—Frederick, Peter, Daniel. Diplomate Am. Bd. Preventive Medicine. Intern, Kings County Gen. Hosp., Bklyn., 1958-59; resident in preventive medicine Mass. Dept. Pub. Health-Harvard U., 1960-62; gen. practice medicine, Marathon, Wis., 1959; pub. health physician Mass. Dept. Pub. Health, 1960-61, asst. med. dir., 1961-65; instr. Tufts U. Sch. Medicine, Boston, 1963-65; dir. Health Dept. Brookline (Mass.), 1964-65; lectr. Johns Hopkins U., Balt., 1965-68; asst. prof. UCLA, 1968-71, assoc. prof., 1972-76, prof. Sch. Pub. Health, 1977—; officer rural health project Narangwal, India, 1965-68; prin. investigator, co-dir. Danfa Comprehensive Rural Health Project, Ghana, 1970-79; cons. World Bank, WHO, UNFPA, Am. Pub. Health Assn.; chmn. Internat. Health Adv. Com., Project Concern Internat. Fellow Royal Soc. Applied Anthropology, Am. Pub. Health Assn.; mem. Wis. Acad. Sci., Arts and Letters, African Studies Assn., Delta Omega. Baha'i. Contbr. articles to profl. jours. Home: 520 20th St Santa Monica CA 90402 Office: Rm 21 245CHS Sch Pub Health UCLA Los Angeles CA 90024

NEUNER, GEORGE EMIL, system engineer, photographer, real estate broker; b. Buffalo, Feb. 24, 1933; s. George and Louise (Hader) N.; m. Donna Mae Anderson, Dec. 26, 1956 (div.); children—David George, Steven Roy, Valerie Mae. B.S.M.E., Purdue U., 1956; M.S. in Engring., UCLA, 1960. Registered profl. engr., Calif.; lic. real estate broker, Calif. Project engr. Douglas Aircraft Co., Santa Monica, Calif., 1956-59; project mgr. TRW, Inc., Redondo Beach, Calif., 1959—; owner George Photography, San Pedro, Calif. Recipient National Reliability award Ann. Reliability Symposium, 1963; Silver Snoopy award NASA, 1965. Fellow AIAA (assoc.); mem. Am. Mgmt. assn., Inst. Mgmt. Sci., Am. Soc. Quality Control, Sierra Club (chmn. Palos Verdes chpt. 1979). Republican. Lutheran. Contbr. articles to profl. jours. Office: 1 Space Park Redondo Beach CA 90278

NEURATH, CLAIRE ELEANORE, neurochemist; b. Newark, July 4, 1924; d. Augustin and Irene Marie (Kappel) Zomzely; B.S. in Chemistry and Physiology, Columbia U., 1950; M.S. in Biochemistry and Nutrition, Harvard U., 1956, Ph.D. (NIH fellow), 1958; m. Otto Neurath, Mar. 24, 1963. Research technician 1st Columbia U. Research Services, 1950-53; research technician dept. Ob-Gyn N.Y. U. Med. Sch., 1953-54, research asso., 1959-60; research biochemist Monsanto Chem. Co., St. Louis, 1960-62; asst. research biochemist UCLA Med. Sch., also mem. Brain Research Inst., 1962-70; mem. dept. biochemistry Roche Inst. Molecular Biology, Nutley, N.J., 1970-80; dir. research Queen's Med. Center, Honolulu, 1980—; adj. asso. prof. biochemistry N.J. Coll. Medicine and Dentistry, Newark, 1971-76, adj. prof. 1976-80; adj. prof. physiology and biochemistry John A. Burns Sch. Medicine, U. Haiwaii, 1980—; mem. program com. Internat. Neurochemistry Congress, 1976—; mem. merit rev. bd. neurobiology VA, 1976-79; cons., lectr. in field. Fulbright fellow, 1958-59. Mem. Am. Soc. Neurochemistry (exec. council 1980—), AAAS, Am. Chem. Soc., Am. Inst. Biol. Scis., Am. Inst. Chemists, Am. Physiol. Soc., Am. Soc. Biol. Chemists, Internat. Neurochemistry Soc., Internat. Soc. Devel. Neurosci., N.Y. Acad. Scis., Soc. Neuroscis., Sigma Xi. Author articles in field, chpts. in books; mem. editorial bds. profl. jours. Home: 46-471 Holonui Pl Kaneohe HI 96744 Office: Dept Research Queen's Med Center 1301 Punchbowl St Honolulu HI 96808

NEUSS, MANFRED JOSEPH, wine and liqueur import co. exec.; b. Cologne, W.Ger., June 13, 1930; s. Christaian and Elly (Wiegleb) N.; came to U.S., 1955, naturalized, 1965. With Hotel & Restaurant Agy. Skip, W.Ger., 1954, Hotel Harrison, Hot Springs, B.C., Can., 1955-62, Romonffo's Beverly Hills (Calif.)-Nat. Wine & Liqueur Co., 1962—; with Schieffelin Co., Los Angeles, v.p. Pacific region account devel., 1980—. Mem. N.W. Prestige Wine and Food Soc., Bacchus Soc., Wine and Food Soc. Hollywood. Republican. Lutheran. Club: Importer Wine and Spirits. Office: Schieffelin Co Suite 767 1100 Glendon Ave Los Angeles CA 90024

NEVEAU, JUDITH STOLPA, interior designer; b. Budapest, Hungary, Jan. 14, 1943; d. Julius A. And Emoke Szigety (Warga) Stolpa; m. T. Daniel Neveau, June 26, 1965. B.A. in English, U. Calif.-Riverside, 1964; M.Ed., UCLA, 1966; profl. cert. in interior design UCLA Extension, 1977. Employment assistance specialist Employment Assistance Div., Bur. Indian Affairs, Los Angeles, 1966-67, 1968-73; Social Services worker Social Services Div., Bur. Indian Affairs, Fairbanks, Alaska, 1967-68; prin. J.N. Designs, Santa Monica, Calif., 1974—. Mem. Decorative Arts Council, Los Angeles County Mus. Art; bd. dirs. Santa Monica Heritage Sq. Mus.; bd. dirs. YWCA, Los Angeles; mem. citizens adv. com. 1984 Olympics; mem. adv. bd. Santa Monica Coll.; assoc. Calif. State Republican Central Com. Named Outstanding Vol. of Yr., West Los Angeles/Beverly Hills, 1978, Woman of Yr. YWCA, Santa Monica, 1981. Mem. Am. Soc. Interior Designers, Assn. Women in Architecture, NOW. Office: J N Designs 1810 14th St Santa Monica CA 90404

NEVIL, DANA CHRISTOPHER, media company executive; b. Los Angeles, Dec. 24, 1956; s. Charles Howard and Irene D. (Fialkoff) N. B.A. in History, UCLA, 1979. Acct. exec. Sta. KORJ, Garden Grove, Calif., 1978-79; acct. exec. sta. KWOW, Pomona, Calif., 1979-80; West Coast mgr. Caballero Spanish Media, Inc., 1980—, supr. Sta. KXEM, McFarland, Calif., Sta. KNEZ, Lompoc, Calif. Active So. Poverty Law Ctr. Mem. ACLU, Ad Industry Emergency Fund, Sierra Club Office: 6464 Sunset Blvd Suite 850 Los Angeles CA 90028

NEVILLE, JAMES RUSSELL, security co. exec.; b. Kansas City, Mo., Nov. 27, 1945; s. Lloyd and Blanch (Copp) N.; m. Linda Gural, Oct. 12, 1979. Br. ops. mgr. Wells Fargo Guard Services, San Francisco, 1980-81; gen. mgr. Am. Security Systems Inc., San Mateo and Los Gatos, Calif., 1982—. Served with USMC, 1965-70. Office: 421 Terrace Way San Mateo CA 94403

NEVILLE, ROY GERALD, mgmt., chem. engring. and pollution control cons.; b. Bournemouth, Dorsetshire, Eng.; s. Percy Herbert and Georgina Lallie (Jenkins) N.; came to U.S., 1951; naturalized, 1957; B.Sc., U. London, 1951; M.Sc., U. Oreg., 1952, Ph.D., 1954; F.R.I.C., Royal Inst. Chemistry, London, 1963, D.Sc. (hon.), 1973; m. Jeanne Frances Russ, July 26, 1952; children—Laura Jean, Janet Marilyn. Research chemist Monsanto Chem. Co., Seattle, 1955-57; sr. chem. engr. Boeing Co., Seattle, 1957-58; sr. research scientist Lockheed Missiles & Space Co., Palo Alto, Calif., 1958-61; sr. staff scientist Aerospace Corp., El Segundo, Cal., 1961-63; prin. scientist Rockwell Internat. Corp., Los Angeles, 1963-67; head dept. materials Scis. Lab., Boeing Sci. Research Labs., Boeing Co., Seattle, 1967-69; sr. engring. specialist Bechtel Corp., San Francisco, 1969-73; pres. Engring. & Tech. Cons., Inc., Redwood City, Calif., 1973—. Fulbright scholar to U.S., 1951; USPHS fellowship, 1951-52, Research Corp. fellow, 1952-54; chartered chemist, London. Fellow, Royal Soc. Chemistry (London), Am. Inst. Chemists, AAAS, mem. Am. Chem. Soc., Am. Inst. Chem. Engrs., History Sci. Soc., Soc. Study Early Chemistry, Royal Instn. Gt. Britain, Research Soc. Am., Soc. Mining Engrs. of AIME, Calif. Mining Assn., Sigma Xi. Contbr. articles to numerous profl. jours. Patentee in fields of chemistry, Chem. engring. and environ. pollution control. Office: PO Box 912 San Carlos CA 94070

NEVILLES, JOHN ELLSWORTH, business machines company manager, consultant; b. Mpls., Jan. 24, 1940; s. Wilbur E. and Phillis A. N.; m. Amelia Carbajal, Feb. 2, 1959; children—John, Sonya. A.B.A., St. Philips Coll., 1974. Personnel specialist, resource planner U.S. Army, 1958-78; indsl. engr. IBM, Tucson, 1978-80, sr. recruiting specialist, 1981, mgr. quality services, 1982—; lectr. career planning. Adv. mem. Job Corps, Tucson Skills Ctr. Decorated Bronze Star. Mem. Am. Soc. Quality Control, Am. Statis. Assn., Am. Soc. Tng. and Devel., Nat. Assn. Trade Tech. Schs. (cert.), VFW, Am. Legion. Democrat. Roman Catholic.

NEVLING, HARRY REED, hosp. personnel exec.; b. Rochester, Minn., Sept. 15, 1946; s. Edwin Reid and Ruth Margaret (Mulvihill) N.; A.A., Rochester Community Coll., 1973; B.A. cum laude, U. Winona (Minn.), 1974; m. Joanne Carol Meyer, Nov. 26, 1976; 1 son, Terry John. Personnel rep. Rochester Meth. Hosp., 1974-75; dist mgr. Internat. Dairy Queen Co., 1975-76; with David Realty Corp., Littleton, Colo., 1976-83, v.p., 1979-83, gen. mgr., 1981-83; personnel dir. Longmont (Colo.), United Hosp., 1977—; cons. Front Range Community Coll. of Denver, 1983—. Dist. chmn. Am. Party, 1973-74; pres., health occupations edn. bd. St. Vrain Valley Career Devel. Center, 1979—. Served to capt. U.S. Army, 1965-72; Vietnam. Decorated D.F.C., Bronze Star with oakleaf cluster, Air medal (22); recipient Helping Hand award United Way, 1974, Outstanding Service award, 1979, cert. of appreciation, 1982. Mem. Colo. Hosp. Personnel Mgrs. Assn. (pres. 1981-82), Boulder Area Personnel Assn., Am. Soc. Hosp. Personnel Adminstrs., Am. Soc. Personnel Adminstrn., VFW (past past comdr.). Home: 1432 Brookfield Dr Longmont CO 80501 Office: 1950 W Mountain View Ave Longmont CO 80501

NEW, ROSETTA HOLBROCK, home economics educator, nutrition consultant; b. Hamilton, Ohio, Aug. 26, 1921; d. Edward F. and Mabel (Kohler) Holbrock; m. John Lorton New, Sept. 3, 1943; 1 son, John Lorton Jr. B.S., Miami U., Oxford, Ohio, 1943; M.A., U. No. Colo., 1971; Ph.D., Ohio State U., 1974. Cert. tchr., Colo. Tchr. English and sci. Monahans (Tex.) High Sch., 1943-45; emergency war food asst. U.S. Dept. Agr., College Station, Tex., 1945-46; dept. chmn. home econs. adult edn. Hamilton (Ohio) Pub. Schs., 1946-47; tchr., dept. chmn. home econs. East High Sch., Denver, 1948-59, Thomas Jefferson High Sch., Denver, 1959—; mem. exec. bd. Denver Pub. Schs. U.S. Office of Edn. grantee, 1971-73. Mem. Am. Home Econs. Assn., Am. Vocat. Assn., Ohio State U. Assn., Ohio State Home Econs. Alumni Assn., Fairfield (Ohio) Hist. Soc., Republican Club of Denver, Phi Upsilon Omicron. Presbyterian. Clubs: Daughters of the Nile, Order of Eastern Star. Office: 3950 S Holly St Denver CO 80237

NEWBERG, DOROTHY BECK (MRS. WILLIAM C. NEWBERG), portrait artist; b. Detroit, May 30, 1919; d. Charles William and Mary (Labedz) Beck; student Detroit Conservatory Music, 1938; m. William C. Newberg, Nov. 3, 1939; children—Judith Anne (Mrs. John Robert Bookwalter), Robert Charles, James William, William Charles. Trustee Detroit Adventures, 1967-71, originator A Drop in Bucket Program for talented inner-city children. Bd. dirs. Bloomfield Art Assn., 1960-62, trustee 1965-67; bd. dirs. Your Heritage House, 1972-75, Franklin Wright Settlement, 1972-75, Meadowbrook Art Gallery, Oakland U., 1973-75; bd. dirs. Sierra Nevada Mus. Art, 1978-80. Recipient Heart of Gold award, 1969; Mich. vol. leadership award, 1969. Mem. Nat. League Am. Penwomen, Sierra Art Found., Birmingham Soc. Women Painters. Presbyterian. Home: 2000 Dant Blvd Reno NV 89509

NEWBERG, WILLIAM CHARLES, stock broker, real estate broker, automotive engr.; b. Seattle, Dec. 17, 1910; s. Charles John and Anna Elizabeth (Anderson) N.; B.S. in Mech. Engring., U. Wash., 1933; M. in Mech. Engring., Chrysler Inst. Engring., 1935; LL.B. (hon.), Parsons Coll., 1958; m. Dorothy Beck, Nov. 3, 1939; children—Judith N. Newberg Bookwalter, Robert Charles, James William, William Charles. Salesman, Am. Auto Co., Seattle, 1932-33; student engr. Chrysler Corp., Detroit, 1933-35, exptl. engr., 1935-42, chief engr. Chgo. plant, 1942-45, mem. subs. ops. staff, Detroit, 1945-47, pres. airtemp. div., Dayton, Ohio, 1947-50, v.p., dir. Dodge div., Detroit, 1950-51, pres. Dodge div., 1951-56, group v.p., Detroit, 1956-58, exec. v.p., 1958-60, pres., 1960; corp. dir. Detroit Bank & Trust, Detroit, 1955-60; corp. cons., Detroit, 1960-76; realtor Myers Realty, Inc., Reno, 1976-79; owner Bill Newberg Realty, 1979—; account exec. Am. Western Securities, Reno, 1980—. Elder, St. John's Presbyterian Ch., Reno, 1976—; exec. bd. Detroit Area council Boy Scouts Am., 1955-74, Nev. Area council Boy Scouts Am., 1976—; Mich. state chmn. March of Dimes, 1967-68. Mem. Soc. Automotive Engrs., Reno Bd. Realtors, Am. Def. Preparedness Assn. (life), Automotive Orgn. Team (life), U. Wash. Alumni Assn. (life), Newcomen Soc., Franklin Inst., Alpha Tau Omega. Club: Elks. Home: 2000 Dant Blvd Reno NV 89509 Office: 100 Washington St Suite 310 Reno NV 89502

NEWBERGER, JOHN LEWIS, orgn. devel. co. exec.; b. Frankfurt/Main, W.Ger., June 30, 1922; s. Fritz and Hedwig (Levisohn) N.; came to U.S., 1940, naturalized, 1944. Student Ala. Sch. Trades, 1941-42; B.A., UCLA, 1949. Technician, Nat. Bur. Standards, 1949-52; planner N.Am. Aviation Corp., 1952-53; ptnr. Advanced Electronics Mfg. Co., Santa Monica, Calif., 1953-54; mgr. staff services Space Tech. Labs. (now TRW Systems), 1954-63; gen. dir. Info. Systems A.G., Paris and Vienna, Austria, 1963-65; owner Unas Co., Los Angeles, 1965—; seminar lectr. Am. Mgmt. Assn. Served with C.E., AUS, 1944-46. Decorated Purple Heart. Mem. UCLA Alumni Assn. Author: The Administrative Guide, 1961; developer holistic approach to orgn. Office: PO Box 69A51 Los Angeles CA 90069

NEWBERRY, CONRAD FLOYDE, aerospace engineer; b. Neodesha, Kans., Nov. 10, 1931; s. Ragan McGregor and Audra Anitia (Newmaster) N.; A.A., Independence Jr. Coll., 1951; B.Engring. in Mech. Engring. (Aero. Sequence), U. So. Calif., 1957; M.S. in Mech. Engring., Calif. State U., Los Angeles, 1971, M.A. in Edn., 1974; m. Sarah Louise Thonn, Jan. 26, 1958; children—Conrad Floyde, Thomas Edwin, Susan Louise. Mathematician, Los Angeles div. N.Am. Aviation, 1951-53, jr. engr., 1953-54, engr., 1954-57, sr. engr., 1957-64; asst. prof. aerospace engring. dept. Calif. State Poly. U., Pomona, 1964-70, asso. prof., 1970-75, prof., 1975—; staff engr. EPA, 1980-82. Registered profl. engr., Calif., Kans., N.C., Tex. Fellow Inst. Advancement Engring., Brit. Interplanetary Soc.; asso. fellow AIAA (dept. dir. edn. Region VI 1976-79), Am. Soc. Engring. Edn. (chmn. aerospace div. 1979-80, mem. div. exec. com. 1976-80, exec. com. ocean and marine engring. div. 1982-86), ASME, Nat. Soc. Profl. Engrs., Soc. Naval Architects and Marine Engrs., Air Pollution Control Assn., Am. Meteorol. Soc., Tau Beta Pi, Sigma Gamma Tau, Kappa Delta Pi. Democrat. Mem. Christian Ch. (Disciples of Christ). Home: 1556 Sheridan Ave Pomona CA 91767 Office: 3801 W Temple Ave Pomona CA 91768

NEWBY, BARBARA ANNE, educator, tennis coach; b. Moberly, Mo., Aug. 28, 1933; d. James Edgar, Jr., and Anne V. (Roof) N. B.A. in Edn., U. Mo.-Columbia, 1955. Tchr., Arvada (Colo.) Jr. High Sch., 1955-56, Harrington Elem. Sch., 1957-60, Horace Mann Jr. High Sch., 1960-67; tchr. phys. edn., dept. chmn. Hill Middle Sch., Denver, 1967—; tennis coach Thomas Jefferson High Sch.; coach Olympics of the Mind; credit union rep. Block capt. Neighborhood Crime Watch Program; vol. Leukemia Assn., Heart Assn. Named Outstanding Coach in Tennis, Denver Pub. Schs. Coaches Assn., 1981-82. Mem. AAHPER, Colo. Assn. Health, Phys. Edn. and Recreation, Coaches Assn., Nat. Assn. Female Execs., Colo. Tennis Assn., NEA, Colo. Edn. Assn., Mo. U. Alumni, Am. Soc. Tng. and Devel., Women's Internat. Bowling Congress, Denver Women's Bowling Assn., U.S. Tennis Assn. Republican. Mem. Christian Ch. Clubs: Colo. Racquet (Denver); Bowling League. Home: 15810 E Ford Pl Aurora CO 80017 Office: Hill Middle School 451 Clermont St Denver CO 80220

NEWBY, CLARENCE ROSCOE, accountant; b. Abbeville, Ala., Jan. 28, 1926; s. Carl Q. and Ossie (Weems) N.; student Tuskegee Inst., 1943-44, U. Calif. at Berkeley, 1946-47, Harms Bus. Coll., 1947; B.B.A., Golden Gate U., 1949; Internal Revenue Agts. certificate (Merit scholar), U. Mich., 1956; m. Catherine Hamilton, Nov. 8, 1946; children—Clarence Roscoe II, Nigel A. Internal revenue agt. U.S. Treasury Dept., San Francisco, 1949-51, Los Angeles, 1951-58; practice public accounting, San Bernardino, Calif., 1958—. Instr. San Bernardino Valley Coll., 1961—; chmn. San Bernardino Ann. Businessmen's Tax Conf., 1964-65; mem. adv. com. on program and cost Calif. Dept. Edn., 1969-72; mem. sch. bd. Loma Linda Acad., 1971-75. Served with USNR, 1944-46. C.P.A., Calif. Mem. Am. Inst. C.P.A.'s, Calif. Soc. C.P.A.'s. Seventh Day Adventist (elder, deacon 1950—). Home: 24665 Lawton Ave Loma Linda CA 92354 Office: 165 W Hospitality Ln Suite 26 San Bernardino CA 92408

NEWCOMB, FRANK, mfg. co. exec.; b. Port Jervis, N.Y., Mar. 21, 1936; s. Francis Elmer and Mildred Marie (Cortright) N.; A.A.S., Orange County Community Coll. with honors, 1961; B.S., U. Colo., 1977; postgrad. Colo. State U., 1981, U. Phoenix, 1982; m. Susan Louise Garner, Jan. 23, 1981; children—Adrienne, Andree (by previous marriage). Test equipment engr. IBM, Poughkeepsie, N.Y., 1963-66, mgr. core storage quality assurance, Boulder, Colo., 1966, mgr. receiving inspection, 1967, mgmt. systems adminstrn., Portchester, N.Y., 1968-69, new product adminstr., Boulder, 1970-72, project mgr. mfg., 1973-76, project mgr. quality assurance, 1977, devel. engr., quality engring. mgr., of plans and controls, 1978-79, adv. engr., quality/reliability engring., 1980—, adv. engr. early entry engring., 1982—, faculty engring., mfg. edn., also stats., quality control, 1976—. Served with USAF, 1955-59, 61-62. Recipient Orange County Community Coll. Acad. Achievement award, 1961. Mem. Am. Soc. for Quality Control (sr.), Soc. Mfg. Engrs., Nat. Rifle Assn. Republican. Baptist. Clubs: Boulder Flycasters, Trout Unltd., Elks. Contbr. articles to profl. jours. mfg. co. exec.; b. Port Jervis, N.Y., Mar. 21, 1936; s. Francis Elmer and Mildred Marie (Cortright) N.; A.A.S., Orange County Community Coll. with honors, 1961; B.S., U. Colo., 1977; postgrad. Colo. State U., 1981, U. Phoenix, 1982; m. Susan Louise Garner, Jan. 23, 1981; children—Adrienne, Andree (by previous marriage). Test equipment engr. IBM, Poughkeepsie, N.Y., 1963-66, mgr. core storage quality assurance, Boulder, Colo., 1966, mgr. receiving inspection, 1967, mgmt. systems adminstrn., Portchester, N.Y., 1968-69, new product adminstr., Boulder, 1970-72, project mgr. mfg., 1973-76, project mgr. quality assurance, 1977, devel. engr., quality engring. mgr., of plans and controls, 1978-79, adv. engr., quality/reliability engring., 1980—, adv. engr. early entry engring., 1982—, faculty engring., mfg. edn., also stats., quality control, 1976—. Served with USAF, 1955-59,

61-62. Recipient Orange County Community Coll. Acad. Achievement award, 1961. Mem. Am. Soc. for Quality Control (sr.), Soc. Mfg. Engrs., Nat. Rifle Assn. Republican. Baptist. Clubs: Boulder Flycasters, Trout Unltd., Elks. Contbr. articles to profl. jours. Home: 20955 Weld County Rd #3 Berthoud CO 80513

NEWELL, DONALD MORRIS, nuclear physicist; b. Red Lodge, Mont., Feb. 27, 1921; s. James T. and Keota (Roysdon) N.; m. Frances Christina (Nordstrom) N.; June 3, 1946; children—Ginny, Kathie, Jim, Marci, Vince, Jerry. B.S. in Chemistry, Mont. State U., 1948; postgrad. in nuclear physics Wash. State U., 1948-52, So. Meth. U., 1957-58. Research chemist Hanford atomic products operation Gen. Electric. Co., Richland, Wash. 1948-56; engr. and unit head Gen. Dynamics, Ft. Worth, 1956-61; sr. research scientist Lockheed Research Labs., Palo Alto, Calif., 1961-64; sr. engring. specialist Ford Aerospace, Palo Alto, 1964-83; cons. radiation hardening, 1983—. Served with U.S. Army, 1942-46. Mem. AIAA (space sci. com.), IEEE (nuclear and space radiation effects awards coms.), Am. Chem. Soc., Soc. Aerospace Materials and Processes Engrs. Republican. Roman Catholic. Contbr. articles to tech. jours. Home and Office: 1663 New Brunswick Ave Sunnyvale CA 94087

NEWHART, ROBERT LINCOLN, II, mgmt. and planning cons. co. exec.; b. Washington, Dec. 29, 1948; s. Robert Lindoln and Doris Ruth (McElroy) N.; A.A., Orange Coast Coll., 1969; B.S. in City and Regional Planning, Calif. Poly. State U., 1972; M.Community Planning, U. Cin., 1974; m. Joyce Anne Kessler, Aug. 5, 1967; children—Blueberry, RainBow. Asst. dir. S.E. Idaho Council of Govts., 1974-77; asso. dir. FIG project Pacific N.W. Regional Commn., Vancouver, Wash., 1977-78; mgr., cons. Dept. Health and Welfare, State of Idaho, Coeur d'Alene, 1978; pres. The Evergreen Assos., Ltd., Coeur d'Alene, 1978—; co-owner Sew What's New, Coeur d'Alene, 1978—; expert witness to U.S. Spl. Senate Com. on Aging, 1977. Chmn. San Luis Obispo Citizens Adv. Com., 1970-71. Mem. AAAS, Am. Public Health Assn., Am. Planning Assn., Am. Soc. Tng. and Devel., Gerontol. Soc., Am. Mgmt. Assn., Western Gerontol. Soc., World Future Soc., Internat. Entrepreneurs Assn. Office: 421 Sherman Ave Suite 208 Coeur d'Alene ID 83814

NEWHOUSE, IRVING RALPH, state legislator Wash.; b. Mabton, Wash., Oct. 16, 1920; s. John and Tina (Bos) N.; B.S., Wash. State U., 1943; m. Ruth M. Gardner, July 14, 1945; children—Joyce, James, Linda, Laura, Daniel, Dorothy. County agrl. extension agt., Ellensburg, Wash., 1946; farmer, Yakima County, Wash., 1947—; mem. Wash. Ho. of Reps. from 15th Dist., 1964-80, Republican floor leader, 1974-77; mem. Wash. State Senate, 1980—. Bd. dirs. Sunnyside Valley Irrigation Dist., 1961-77. Served to lt. (j.g.) USNR, 1943-46. Mem. Am. Cattlemen's Assn. (pres. Yakima County 1956-57), Am. Farm Bur. (pres. Yakima County 1960-63). Republican. Mem. Christian Reformed Ch. Club: Rotary. Home: Rt 1 Box 130 Mabton WA 98935

NEWHOUSE, JEFFREY ALLAN, accountant; b. N.Y.C., Dec. 10, 1948; s. Irv and Pola (Izbicki) N.; B.A., Queen's Coll., 1969; M.B.A., St. John's U., Jamaica, N.Y., 1976; m. Kim E. Tolley, Jan. 1, 1976; children—Sarah, Kevin. Registered rep. Dupont Walston, N.Y.C., 1971-73, sales mgr. Maspeth Operating Corp., N.Y.C., 1974-75; acct. Peat, Marwick, Mitchell & Co., C.P.A.'s, San Jose, Calif., 1976-79; ptnr. Meisser, Blas, Newhouse & Co., C.P.A.'s, Aptos, Calif., 1980-82; pvt. practice acctg. Jeffrey A. Newhouse, C.P.A., 1983—. dir. Ins. Center Santa Cruz, Inc. Served to lt. USNR, 1969-71; Vietnam. C.P.A., Calif. Mem. Am. Inst. C.P.A.s, Calif. Soc. C.P.A.s. Republican. Jewish. Lodge: Masons. Home: PO Box 1263 Aptos CA 95003 Office: 9053 Soquel Dr Suite 202 Aptos CA 95003

NEWHOUSE, WILLIAM ERWIN, SR., beer and wine wholesaler, trucking co. exec.; b. Malta, Mont., Jan. 27, 1921; s. William Arthur and Lottie O. (Bakke) N.; student U. Mont., 1940-41; m. Mary Lorann Wells, Nov. 3, 1945; children—Lottie Ann Blades, Stephanie Davis, William Erwin, Karen Kaus, Lisa Dunning. Pres., gen. mgr. Newhouse Grain Co. Inc., Shelby, Mont., 1946-63, Newhouse Inc., Shelby, 1956-64, Newhouse Cattle Co. Inc., Shelby, 1957-68, United Beverage Co., 1972—, United Trucking Co., Miles City, 1972—. Mem. citizens adv. council U. Mont.; dir. Miles City Endowment Bd., Miles Community Coll. Served to capt. USAAF, 1942-45. Decorated Air medal with 4 clusters, D.F.C., Purple Heart. Mem. Mont. Beer Wholesalers Assn. (dir. 1974-77, 79—), Mont. C. of C. (dir.). Home: 305 S Custer St Miles City MT 59301 Office: 217 N 8th St Miles City MT 59301

NEWKIRK, RICHARD THOMAS, English educator; b. Wilmington, N.C., Feb. 5, 1948; s. Lawrence Harry and Carrie Mae (Sharpless) N. B.S., N.C. Agrl. and Tech. U., 1969; M.A., So. Ill. U., 1971. Grad. teaching asst. So. Ill. U., Carbondale, 1969-71; instr. Community Coll. Balt., 1971-72; instr. Yuba Coll., Marysville, Calif., 1972—, Chapman Coll., Beale AFB, Calif., 1978—; tchr. English, dept. chmn. Gray Ave. Intermediate Sch., Yuba City, Calif., chmn. lang. arts textbook adoption com., 1980-82. Vice-pres., pres. Tchrs. Assn., 1979-82; v.p. Full Gospel Businessmen Fellowship Internat., 1980—. Served to capt. USAF, 1972-76. Grantee Bowling Green U., 1971; recipient Cert. of Appreciation, Calif.-Nev. Lions Club, 1982. Mem. NEA, Assn. Supervision and Curriculum Devel., Calif. Tchrs. Assn., Yuba City Tchrs. Assn. Democrat. Home: 1130 Queens Ave Yuba City CA 95991 Office: 808 Gray Ave Yuba City CA 95991

NEWLIN, LEO MAX, II, state park exec.; b. Kokomo, Ind., June 4, 1942; s. Leo Max and Fleta LaVaugh (Pierce) N.; B.S., Wilmington Coll., 1968; m. Frances Seme Woods, May 29, 1966; children—Heather Marie, Elizabeth Renee. Ranger, Three Island State Park, Idaho Parks and Recreation Dept., 1970; asst. mgr. Lucky Peak Recreational Area, 1971-73, mgr. Black Canyon, 1973-76, Malad George, 1976, Priest Lake, 1977-79, park mgr. Massacre Rocks State Park, American Falls, Idaho, 1979—. Advisor Friends of the Park. Recipient Burp and Brag award Idaho Parks and Recreation Dept., 1975, Beth Durham award, 1981; Assn. for Humanities in Idaho grantee, 1981. Mem. Nat. Recreational and Park Assn., Idaho Recreation and Park Soc. Mem. Bahai. Faith. Inventor picnic table lifter, park bench. Home: HC 76 Box 1010 American Falls ID 83211 Office: Massacre Rocks State Park American Falls ID 83211

NEWMAN, EDGAR LEON, historian; b. New Orleans, Jan. 21, 1939; s. Isidore and Anna (Pfeifer) N.; B.A., Yale U., 1962; Ph.D., U. Chgo., 1969; children—Jonathan, Suzanne. Asst. prof. N.Mex. State U., Las Cruces, 1969-75, assoc. prof. history, 1975—; mem. U.S. Com. Bicentennial of French Revolution of 1789. Fulbright fellow, 1965-66; Am. Philos. Soc. fellow, 1971; Nat. Endowment for Humanities fellow, 1975-76. Mem. Western Soc. for French History (pres. 1977-78), Société d'histoire de la Revolution de 1848 (mem. comité directeur), Soc. Scis. History Assn., French Hist. Studies Assn., Am. Hist. Assn. Editor: Dictionary of French History 1815-1852. Office: Box 3-H New Mex State U Las Cruces NM 88003

NEWMAN, FRED LEON, farmer, rancher; b. Holyoke Colo., Aug. 9, 1935; s. Ralph C. and Hazel Leona (Show) N.; m. Naomi Nell Neiman, June 3, 1956; children—Marc, Mica, Marla, Matthew. B.S. in Vocat. Agr., Colo. State U., 1957, M.S. in Indsl. Arts, 1961. Instr. vocat. agr. Lamar High Sch., 1961-64; instr. indsl. arts Lamer Jr. Coll., 1964-65; sales mgr., agrl. engr. Butler Ag Sales, Ft. Collins, Colo., 1965-66; farmer, rancher, Holyoke County, Colo., 1966—. Mem. Holyoke Sch. Bd., 1973-77. Mem. Colo. Wool Growers (v.p. 1980-81, dir.), Colo. Flying Farmers, Profl. Farmers Am. Methodist. Clubs: Colo. State U. Alumnae (pres. 1978), Lions, Masons.

NEWMAN, JAN HARLAN, marketing research consultant; b. Dayton, Ohio, Feb. 26, 1950; d. Roy Harlan and Pearl (Fischer) H.; m. Robert L. Newman, Jan. 9, 1972. B.B.A., NYU, 1972; postgrad. Northwestern U., 1973. Research asst. J. Walter Thompson Advt., Chgo., 1972,-74; research assoc. Nat. Analysts, Booz-Allen & Hamilton Research Assocs., Chgo., 1974-76; research supr. Lee King & Ptnr. Advt., Chgo., 1976-77; pres. The Newman Group Ltd., San Mateo, Calif., 1977—. Mem. Am. Mktg. Assn. (meritorious award). Contbr. articles to profl. jours.

NEWMAN, MICHELE MARIE, graphic artist; b. Sheridan, Wyo., Dec. 15, 1954; d. Eric Carl and Harriet Ann (Wilder) N. B.S. in Geography, Ariz. State U., 1977. Map drafter ARCO, Denver, 1977-79, exploration drafter, 1979, lead drafter geology, 1980, exploration drafting specialist technician, 1982—; exploration drafter Amerada Hess Corp., Denver, 1979; pres. treas. Petroam. Cartographics, Inc., Denver. Mem. Atlantic Richfield Civic Action Program; active Girl Scouts U.S.A. Mem. Desk and Derrick, Am. Inst. Design and Drafting, Rocky Mountain Energy Drafters, Assn. Am. Geographers, AAUW, Am. Bus. Women's Assn., Ariz. State U. Alumni Assn. Republican. Methodist. Club: Ariz. State U. Century. Contbr: Our Twentieth Century's Greatest Poems, 1982. Home: 4249 Freeport Way Denver CO 80239

NEWMAN, MORRIS, mathematician; b. N.Y.C., Feb. 25, 1924; s. Isaac and Sarah (Cohen) N.; A.B., N.Y. U., 1945; M.A., Columbia, 1946; Ph.D., U. Pa., 1952; m. Mary Aileen Lenk, Sept. 18, 1948; children—Sally Ann, Carl Lenk. Mathematician, applied math. div. Nat. Bur. Standards, Washington, 1951-63, chief, numerical analysis sect., 1963-70, sr. research mathematician, 1970-76; prof. math. U. Calif., Santa Barbara, 1976—, dir. Inst. Interdisciplinary Applications of Algebra and Combinatorics, 1980—; lectr. U. B.C., 1960, U. Cal. at Santa Barbara, 1965, Am. U., also Cath. U., U. Md. Recipient Gold medal U.S. Dept. Commerce, 1966. Mem. Am. Math. Soc. (council 1980—), London Math. Soc., Math. Assn. Am., Washington Acad. Scis., AAAS, Sigma Xi. Author: Matrix Representations of Groups, 1968; Integral Matrices, 1972; also papers in math. jours. Editor Jour. Research Nat. Bur. Standards, 1966— Math. of Computation, 1975—; asso. editor Jour. Linear and Multilinear Algebra, 1973—, Letters in Linear Algebra, 1979—. Author monographs and numerous articles in field. Home: 1050 Las Alturas Rd Santa Barbara CA 93103 Office: Dept Math U Calif Santa Barbara CA 93106

NEWMAN, MURRAY ARTHUR, aquarium executive; b. Chgo., Mar. 6, 1924; s. Paul Jones and Virginia Evelyn (Murray) N.; m. Katherine Lloyd Greene, Aug. 8, 1952; 1 dau., Susan. B.S., U. Chgo., 1949; M.S., U. Calif.-Berkeley, 1951; Ph.D., U. B.C., 1960. Curator fishes UCLA, 1951-53, U. B.C., 1953-56; curator Vancouver (B.C.) Aquarium. 1956-66, dir., 1966—. Mem. council Westwater Research Centre; mem. adv. com. Disney World Epcot Ctr., 1983; chmn. Vancouver Round Table, 1983. Served with USN, 1943-46. Decorated Order of Can.; recipient Can. Centennial medal, 1967; Harold Merliees award, 1976; Man of Yr. award City of Vancouver, 1964. Mem. Western Can. Univs. Marine Biol. Soc. (chmn. adv. com. 1981—), Can. Assn. Zool. Parks and Aquariums (pres. 1978-79), Am. Assn. Zool. Parks and Aquariums (dir. 1972-75), Internat. Union Zool. Park Dirs., N.Y. Acad. Scis. Club: Vancouver. Office: Vancouver Aquarium Box 3232 Vancouver BC V6B 3X8 Canada

NEWMAN, RICHARD EUGENE, hospital official; b. Chgo., Ill., Aug. 9, 1948; s. Burton Richard and Mary Louise (Stewart) N.; m. Carol Jean Wiseman, Aug. 22, 1970. B.A., U. Evansville, 1970, M.A. in Counseling, 1972. Career counselor U.S. Air Force, Washington, 1971-75; ednl. cons. Deaconess Hosp., Evansville, Ind., 1975-80; dir. edn. John C. Lincoln Hosp. and Health Center, Phoenix, 1980—. Mem. bd. mgmt. Paradise Valley YMCA; mem. exec. com., bd. dirs. Nat. Trauma Resource Center. Served with USAF, 1971-75. Mem. Am. Soc. Tng. and Devel., Am. Soc. Healthcare, Edn. and Tng., Ariz. Pub. Health Assn. Office: 9211 N 2nd St Phoenix AZ 85020

NEWMARK, HERBERT LAWRENCE, real estate executive, lawyer; b. N.Y.C., Nov. 9, 1924; s. Julius Barney and Augusta (Edelstein) N.; m. Jeanne Lorraine Mittleman, Nov. 2, 1952; children—Richard, Phyllis, Jerome, Mile, Janice. LL.B., Balboa U., 1952. Vice pres. Hoyt Corp., Portland, Oreg., 1953-60; chmn. bd. New Tronics, Portland, 1960-64; owner Newmark & Assocs., Portland, 1964—. Bd. dirs. Valley View Water Dist.; mem. adv. com. Reed Coll. Served to lt. USN, 1944-54. Decorated D.F.C., Air Medal. Democrat. Jewish. Clubs: Multnomah, Masons (Portland). Office: 610 SW Alder Suite 707 Portland OR 97205

NEWMARK, LEONARD DANIEL, linguistics educator; b. Attica, Ind., Apr. 8, 1929; s. Max Jacob and Sophie (Glusker) N.; m. Ruth Sylvia Broessler, Sept. 16, 1951; children—Katya, Mark. A.B., U. Chgo., 1947; M.A., Ind. U., 1951, Ph.D., 1955. Mem. faculty Ohio State U., Columbus, 1954-62; asso. prof. U. Mich., Ann Arbor, summer 1961, Ind. U., Bloomington, 1962-63; prof. linguistics U. Calif.-San Diego, 1963—; ednl. cons. Office of Edn. grantee, 1975-79. Mem. Linguistic Soc. Am., Am. Assn. Applied Linguistics, Tchrs. of English to Speakers of Other Langs. Author: Standard Albanian: A Reference Grammar for Students, 1982; Spoken Albanian, 1980; Linguistic History of English, 1963; Using American English, 1964. Office: Dept Linguistics Univ Calif-San Diego La Jolla CA 92093

NEWMARK, MILTON MAXWELL, lawyer; b. Oakland, Calif., Feb. 24, 1916; s. Milton and Mary (Maxwell) N.; A.B., U. Calif. at Berkeley, 1936, J.D., 1947; m. Marion Irene Johnson, July 31, 1941; children—Mari Newmark Anderson, Lucy Newmark Sammons, Grace Newmark Lucini. Admitted to Calif. bar, 1941; practiced law with father, San Francisco, 1940-56; pvt. practice, 1956-62, Lafayette, Calif., 1962-80, Walnut Creek, Calif., 1980— lectr. bankruptcy State Bar of Calif. Continuing Edn. Program. Mem. Alameda County Rep. Central Com., 1940-41; pres. Alameda Rep. Assembly, 1950. Served with AUS, 1942-46; lt. col. Res. ret. Mem. Am. Legion, Am., San Francisco, Contra Costa bar assns., Scabbard and Blade. Mason (Shriner). Home: 609 Terra California Drive No 6 Walnut Creek CA 94595 Office: 1620 Tice Valley Blvd Walnut Creek CA 94595

NEWPORT, EUGENE NORMAN, mayor of Berkeley (Calif.); b. Rochester, N.Y., Apr. 5, 1935; s. Leon and Bertha (Richardson) N.; m. m. Claudine Smith, Feb. 1958; 1 son, Kyle; m. Maria Luisa Vigo, Nov. 9, 1974; 1 dau., Maria Mercedes. B.A. in Bus. Adminstrn., Internat. Coll., Los Angeles, 1975. Specialist employment tng. U.S. Dept. Labor, 1971-74, 77-79; dir. youth employment services City of Berkeley, 1975-76, sr. adminstrv. analyst, 1976, mayor, 1979—; cons. Office of Research, Calif. Assembly; chmn. subcom. on edn. U.S. Conf. Mayors, mem. adv. bd., 1983-84; 1st v.p. Alameda County Mayors Conf.; co-chmn. U.S. Peace Council, del. World Peace Council; mem. regional planning commn., regional housing commn. Assn. Bay Area Govt. Bd. dirs. SANE. Served with U.S. Army, 1958-60. Mem. NAACP (life). Democrat. Office: 2180 Milvia St Berkeley CA 94704

NEWSOME, JAMES ERIC, financial consultant; b. Aguana, Guam, Jan. 28, 1955; s. James Walton and Norma (Petersen) N.; m. Iris Susan Rubenstein, Dec. 28, 1980. B.S. in Marine Transp. and Mgmt., U.S. Mcht. Marine Acad., 1976; M.B.A. in Fin., U. So. Calif., 1981. Fin. cons. Ernst & Whinney, Los Angeles, 1981—. Served to lt. j.g. USNR. Mem. Am. Econ. Assn., Fin. Mgmt. Assn. Clubs: Toastmasters, Propeller of U.S. (Los Angeles, Long Beach). Home: 1510 California St Santa Monica CA 90403 Office: Ernst & Whinney 2700 Arco Tower 5155 Flower St Los Angeles CA 90071

NEWTON, GWEN, civic, union ofcl.; b. San Antonio, Nov. 11, 1930; s. Ernest H. and Bernice (Merchant) N. Student San Diego State Coll., Los Angeles City Coll., UCLA. Secr-treas, bus. mgr. Office, Profl. Employees Internat. Union, local #30, AFL-CIO, Can. Labor Congress, Los Angeles, 1964—, trustee, sec. local's Health, Welfare, Retirement Trust Funds, 1964—; v.p. Office, Profl. Employees Internat. Union, AFL-CIO, 1965—. Founding mem. Los Angeles chpt. A. Philip Randolph Inst.; v.p. Los Angeles County Fedn. Labor, also v.p. com. polit. edn.; resource del. statis. conf. Afro-Am. Labor Inst., Nairobi, Kenya, trade union conf., Lagos, Nigeria, Freetown, Sierra Leone, 1974; v.p. Nat. Officers Council, Coaltion Labor Union Women; active NAACP, Nat. Council Negro Women. Recipient cert. recognition Calif. Senate, 1972, cert. tribute, City of Los Angeles, 1972, Father Coogan award Cath. Labor Inst. Los Angeles, 1973, honors local, county units Los Angeles unions, 1979, Spcl. award Girls Club Am., 1981. Democrat.

NEWTON, MAXINE HILL, educator; b. Hunter, Utah, Aug. 13, 1917; d. Samuel F. and Almena M. (Morriss) Hill; B.S. cum laude (Normal scholar), U. Utah, 1966, Ed.M., 1975; postgrad. Brigham Young U., 1976-80; ednl. specialist cert. Utah State U., 1980; m. George A. Newton, May 17, 1941; children—Mary Jane, George Fred. Demonstrator and sample maker Singer Sewing Machine Co., Salt Lake City, 1936-42; record clk. Kearns (Utah) Army Base, 1943-45; prin. Maxine H. Newton, dressmaker, Salt Lake City, 1945-59; mgr. sch. lunch program Monroe Elem. Sch., Granger, Utah, 1959-62; tchr. West Lake Jr. High Sch., Granger, 1966-69; tchr., chmn. home econs. and consumer studies dept., Granger High Sch., 1969—; night sch. cons., 1974-76. Utah State Fair judge, 1967-81; stylemaker judge Singer Sewing Machine, 1974-78; Sunday sch. coordinator and tchr. Ch. of Jesus Christ of Latter-day Saints, 1950-64; bd. dirs. J.C. Penny Fashion, 1973-79, chmn., 1977-79. Named Utah Vocat. Tchr. of Yr., 1979, Utah Home Econs. Tchr. of Yr., 1983. Mem. Am. Home Econs. Assn., Utah Home Econs. Assn., Am. Vocat. Assn., Utah Vocat. Assn. (dir. 1977-79), NEA, Utah Ednl. Assn., Granite Edn. Assn., Utah Assn. Vocat. Home Econs. Tchrs., Utah Council Improvement Edn., Nat. Assn. Vocat. Home Econs. Tchrs., Alpha Delta Kappa, Omicron Nu. Producer ednl. films. Adv. bd. Forecast; nat. tchrs. mag., 1981-82. Home: 3694 S 6400 West West Valley UT 84120 Office: 3690 S 3600 West West Valley UT 84119

NEYENHUIS, HUGO, safety engineer, consultant; b. Amsterdam, Netherlands, Nov. 1, 1926; s. Hugo Neijenhuis and Wilhelmino-Josephina (Marchand) N.; m. Loes Theodora Wijckelsma-Muller, June 13, 1953; children—Rudolf, Marijke, Yvonne. D.P., Netherlands Acad. Chiropody, 1954; student Volks U. Amsterdam, 1954-55; Paramedic Inst., 1955-57; B.B.A., Portland State Coll., 1966. Diplomate in Podiatry, Netherlands, Industry Medic, Netherlands; cert. hazard control mgr., product safety mgr., instr./trainer first aide. Corp. loss control safety coordinator, Fred Meyer Inc., Portland, Oreg., 1960-82; ind. cons. occupational health-safety-fire prevention bus., Portland, 1982—; mem. nat. bd. Med. Govs. Emergency Med. Planning. Instr./trainer Am. Heart Assn.; hunters safety instr. Oreg. Wildlife Commn.; instr. Nat. Rifle Assn. Served with Royal Netherlands Army, 1950-51. Recipient Landsteiner medal Royal Netherlands Red Cross. Mem. Am. Soc. Safety Engrs., Nat. Safety Mgmt. Soc. (dir.), Soc. Fire Protection Engrs., Fed. Safety Council, Nat. Fire Prevention Assn., Acad. Hazard Control Mgmt. Democrat. Home: 6019 NE Alton St Portland OR 97213 Office: 6019 NE Alton St Portland OR 97213

NG, LAWRENCE MING-LOY, physician; b. Hong Kong, Mar. 21, 1940; came to U.S., 1967, naturalized, 1977; s. John Iu-cheung and Mary Wing (Wong) N.; B.Med., U. Hong Kong, 1965, B.Surg., 1965; m. Bella May Ha Kan, June 25, 1971; children—Jennifer Wing-mui, Jessica Wing-yee. House physician Queen Elizabeth Hosp., Hong Kong, 1965-66, med. officer, 1966-67; resident physician Children's Hosp. of Los Angeles, 1967-68; resident physician Children's Hosp. Med. Center, Oakland, Calif., 1968-70, fellow in pediatric cardiology, 1970-72, now mem. teaching staff; practice medicine, specializing in pediatrics and pediatric cardiology, San Leandro, Calif., 1972—, Oakland, 1982—; chief pediatrics Oakland Hosp., 1974-77; chief pediatrics Vesper Meml. Hosp., 1977-79, treas., 1983 Active Republican Party. Diplomate Am. Bd. Pediatrics. Fellow Am. Acad. Pediatrics; mem. AMA, Calif. Med. Assn., Am. Heart Assn., Los Angeles Pediatric Soc., East Bay Pediatric Soc., Smithsonian Assos., Nat. Geog. Soc., Orgn. Chinese Ams. (dir. 1980—), Chinese-Am. Physicians' Soc. (co-founder, sec. 1980, pres. 1983), Chinese for Affirmative Action, Asian Pacific Am. Advs. of Calif., Oakland Mus. Assns. Buddhist. Club: Bay-O-Vista. Office: 433 Estudillo Ave Suite 207 San Leandro CA 94577 also 310 8th St Suite 103 Oakland CA 94607

NG, MICHAEL GUAN-YUH, cosmetic and toiletries exec.; b. Singapore, Jan. 7, 1942; s. Hee Yin and Fung May (Wong) N.; B.A. in Chemistry, U. Calif., Riverside, 1965; m. Pauline Yuen-Ling Chau, Aug. 29, 1970; children—Eric Wai-Choi, Bryant Wai-Wah. Quality control chemist Nestle Co., Salinas, Calif., 1965-66; chemist Max Factor & Co., Hollywood, Calif., 1966-70, research chemist, 1970-75, sr. research chemist, 1975-80, mgr. Hair Care Lab., Research and Devel. Div., 1980-82, mgr. Skin Care Lab., Research & Devel. div., 1983—. Mem. Soc. Cosmetic Chemists, Am. Chem. Soc. Republican. Club: San Fernando Valley Chinese (Los Angeles). Home: 11719 Monte Leon Way Northridge CA 91326 Office: 1655 N McCadden Pl Hollywood CA 90028

NGISSAH, KWESI, clin. psychologist; b. Cape Coast, Ghana, Aug. 13, 1942; came to U.S., 1969; s. Kwabina Numoukyi and Ama Annan; B.A., Calif. State U., Sacramento, 1973, M.A., 1975; Ph.D. (Disting. scholar), U. Calif., Davis, 1977; m. Beatrice Cobbinah; children—Kwamina, Aba-Yawa, Ama-Annan, Kwesi. Asst. prof. psychology Calif. State U., Sacramento, 1974-78; psychol. clinician Headstart Programs, Sacramento, Placer and Sacramento Counties, 1977-78; fieldwork supr., coordinator New Careers in Psychology Project, dept. psychology Calif. State U., Sacramento, 1975-77; program dir. undergrad. med. edn. in family practice U. Calif., Davis, 1979-81; clin. psychologist Kaiser Permanente Med. Group, Inc., Sacramento, 1981—; mem. adv. bd. com. Superior (Calif.) Area Health Edn. Center, 1980-81. Coach, Brit.-Am. Soccer Club, 1978. Recipient Meml. award Sacramento City Coll., 1971. Mem. Am. Psychol. Assn., Sacramento Valley Psychol. Assn. (pres. 1981-82), Am. Soc. Clin. Hypnosis, Sacramento Acad. Profl. and Clin. Hypnosis, AAAS, Western Psychol. Assn., Alpha Phi Alpha. Roman Catholic. Author: Cross-Cultural Studies in Attitudes Toward Mental Patients, 1975; (with others) Motivation, Race, Social Class and I.Q., Preventive Medicine and Health Promotion for Medical Students, 1980. Home: 5119 Vale Dr Carmichael CA 95608 Office: Kaiser Found Hosp 2025 Morse Ave Sacramento CA 95825

NGUYEN, QUYEN HUU, agronomist, consultant; b. Mytho, South Viet Nam, May 24, 1933; came to U.S., 1978; s. Hay Van and Bien Thi (Le) N.; m. Tu Thi Le, Oct. 20, 1961; children—Dung Tri Huu, Minh T.H. Ingenieur-es-Sciences Agronomiques, Nat. Coll. Agr., (Viet Nam), 1964, M.S., U. Wis., 1972, Ph.D., 1973. Cert. profl. agronomist. Prof., chmn. dept. agronomy U. Cantho (Viet Nam), 1973-77; asst. prof.

agronomy U. Ill., Urbana, 1977-78; soybean breeder INTSOY, Isabela Exptl. Sta., U. P.R., 1978-80; research agronomist Programme Nat. Légumineuses-Zaire, USAID/KINSHASA, Zaire, 1981—; cons. tropical internat. agr. Served with South Viet Nam Air Force, 1954. Mem. Am. Soc. Agronomy, Crops Sci. Soc. Am., Am. Soybean Assn. Roman Catholic. Home: 3545 Central Ave San Diego CA 92105 Office: USAID/KINSHASA (Zaire) Dept of State (AID) Washington DC 20523

NGUYEN, TAN VAN, agronomist; b. Hanam, Vietnam, Aug. 1, 1939; came to U.S., 1975; s. Khuong Van and Bong Thi (Hoang) N.; B.S., U. Fla., 1962, M.S., 1964, Ph.D., 1972; m. Ngu Oanh Le, Apr. 26, 1970; children—Don, Kim, Dan. Plant breeder, internat. staff cons. U. Wis., Goiania, Brazil, Interam. Inst. Agrl. Sci., Goiania, 1977-79; project asso. U. Wis., Madison, 1980; plant breeder, asst. research sta. dir. Rice Researchers, Inc., Glenn, Calif., 1981—. Mem. Am. Soc. Agronomy, Crop Sci. Soc. Am., Phi Kappa Phi, Alpha Zeta. Contbr. articles in field to profl. jours. Rice Researchers Inc Route 1 Box 398 Glenn CA 95943

NGUYEN-HUU, ANH ANDY, electronics co. exec.; b. Quang-Tri, Vietnam, Jan. 1, 1939; s. Lu and Quynh-Tran Thi (Than) N.; B.S., Saigon U., 1958; Dipl.-Ing., Tech. U. Darmstadt (W. Ger.), 1963; m. Ngoc-Giao Thi Hoang, Nov. 24, 1977; children—Bettina, Patricia, Michelle, Christine. Group leader Zuse KG, Bad Hersfeld, W. Ger., 1963-66; mgr. design and application engring. Transitron Ltd., Maidenhead, Eng., 1966-70; mgr. design engring. Fairchild Camera Instrument Corp., Mountain View, Calif., 1970-74; sr. staff engr. Teradyne, Inc., Chatsworth, Calif., 1974-75; dir. engring. Integrated Circuits Internat., Inc., Sunnyvale, Calif., 1975-78; v.p. engring. Samsung Semicondr., Sunnyvale, 1978-80; pres. NCM Corp., Santa Clara, Calif., 1980—. Bd. dirs. Internat. Youth Vol. Services, 1955-58. Republican. Buddhist. Contbr. articles to profl. jours. Office: 1500 Wyatt Dr #9 Santa Clara CA 95054

NIBLETT, CHARLES TILLMAN, real estate broker; b. Birmingham, Ala., Oct. 26, 1920; s. Edgar Marvin and Emma Marie (Nuttall) N.; m. Norma Adrienne Booth, Nov. 4, 1943; children—Linda Anne Budge, Adrienne Wilson. B.F.A., U. Ga., 1942; postgrad. U. S.C., 1951-53, U. Md., 1954-56, U. Mass., 1957-59. With Stockham Valves & Fittings, Birmingham, 1947-50; recalled to active duty as capt. U.S. Air Force, 1950, advanced through grades to col., 1968, ret., 1969; owner/broker Charles T. Niblett, Realtor, Tucson, 1970—. Bd. dirs. Pima Air Mus., 1975—, pres., 1983; mem. Com. on Employer Support of Guard and Res., 1978—; v.p. 390th Bomb Gp Meml. Mus. Found., 1981—. Served with USAAF, 1942-46; CBI. Decorated D.F.C., Air medal with oak leaf cluster, Air Force Commendation medal. Mem. Nat. Assn. Realtors, Ariz. Assn. Realtors, Tucson Bd. Realtors, Air Force Assn., Ret. Officers Assn., Order Daedalians, Tucson Metro C. of C., Lambda Chi Alpha. Republican. Clubs: Westerners, Una Noche Plateada. Address: 5837 N Paseo Ventoso Tucson AZ 85715

NIBLEY, ROBERT RICKS, lawyer; b. Salt Lake City, Sept. 24, 1913; s. Joel and Teresa (Taylor) N.; A.B., U. Utah, 1934; J.D., Loyola U., Los Angeles, 1942; m. Lee Allen, Jan. 31, 1945 (dec.); children—Jane, Annette. Acct., Nat. Parks Airways, Salt Lake City, 1934-37, Western Air Lines, Los Angeles, 1937-40; admitted to Calif. bar, 1943; asst. mgr. market research dept. Lockheed Aircraft Corp., Burbank, Calif., 1940-43; asso. firm Hill, Farrer & Burrill, Los Angeles, 1946-53, partner, 1953-70, of counsel, 1970-78; v.p., dir. Post Transp. Co. Served from ensign to lt. comdr. USNR, 1943-46. Mem. Am., Los Angeles bar assns., Phi Delta Phi, Phi Kappa Phi, Phi Delta Theta. Club: California. Home: 4860 Ambrose Ave Los Angeles CA 90027

NICE, CARTER, conductor, music director; b. Jacksonville, Fla., Apr. 5, 1940; s. Clarence Carter and Elizabeth Jane (Hintermister) N.; m. Jennifer Charlotte Smith, Apr. 4, 1983; children—Danielle, Christian. B.M., Eastman Sch. Music, 1962; M.M., Manhattan Sch. Music. Asst. condr., concert master New Orleans Philharm., 1967-79; condr., music dir. Sacramento Symphony, 1979—. Office: Sacramento Symphony 2848 Arden Suite 210 Sacramento CA 95825

NICE, WILLIAM MICHAEL, air traffic controller; b. St. Louis, Apr. 20, 1941; s. William Oliver and Dorothy Della (Stallings) N.; B.A. in Bus., U. Redlands (Calif.), 1966; M.A. in Econs., U. Okla., 1974; m. Jeanette Marie Arzdorf, June 7, 1969. Enlisted in USAF, 1967, advanced through grades to capt., 1974; service in Vietnam and W.Ger.; ret., 1974; air traffic controller Salt Lake Center, FAA, 1975-81, 299th Communications Squadron, Hill AFB, Utah, 1982—; tech. adviser Berlin Air Coordinating Com., 1972-74. Decorated Commendation medal. Home: 7563 Fieldstone Ln Salt Lake City UT 84121 Office: 299th Communications Squadron Bldg 1276 Hill AFB UT 84056

NICHOLAS, DAVID RICHARD, lawyer, state senator; b. Gillette, Wyo., Mar. 2, 1941; s. Thomas Arthur and Mary Margaret (McKean) N.; B.A., Harvard Coll., 1963; J.D., U. Wyo., 1966; m. Karen Kay Brewer, Aug. 25, 1963; children—Kristin Kay, Alexander McKean. Admitted to Wyo. bar, 1967, U.S. Ct. Mil. Appeals, 1967; partner Corthell, King, McFadden, Nicholas & Prehoda, Attys., Laramie, Wyo., 1971—; instr. polit. sci. U. Wyo., Laramie, part-time, 1977-78, 83—; mem. Wyo. Senate, Laramie, 1979—, chmn. travel, recreation and wildlife com., mem. judiciary com. Justice of Peace, Albany County, Wyo., 1977-78; bd. dirs. Salvation Army, 1971-80, Cathedral Home for Children, 1975—, Senior Center, 1975-81, Albany County Public Library, 1979-83. Served to capt. Judge Adv. Gen.'s Corps, U.S. Army, 1967-71. Mem. ABA, Albany County Bar Assn., Wyo. State Bar. Republican. Club: Rotary (pres.). Office: 221 S Second St Laramie WY 82070

NICHOLS, AGNES NIELSEN, community health representative; b. Eyak, Cordova, Alaska, Sept. 16, 1925; d. Niels Peter Nielsen and Mary (Klashnikoff) N.; m. Bert Henry Nichols, Mar. 21, 1947; children—Mary Anne, Susan Marie, Judith Lee, Rebecca Jean, Betsy Mae, Nora Genevieve, Sarah Jane, Bert Henry, Jr., Clifford Peter, Andrew John. Student Seattle Pacific Coll., 1944-45. Mem., chmn. Anchorage Service Unit Native Health Bd., 1969-81; mem., vice-chmn. Alaska Native Health Bd., Cordova, 1970-83; chmn. Native Village Eyak, 1980-83; community health rep., Cordova, Alaska, 1975, 77—; instr. Prince William Sound Community Coll., chmn. adv. bd. Bd. dirs. Bidarki Corp., Anchorage Service Unit Health Bd. Recipient Inidan Health Service award, 1979; Nat. Indian Health Bd. award, 1982; Alaska Native Health Bd. award, 1982; Chugach Natives Inc. award, 1978; Delphi Found. award, 1981. Mem. Chugach Native Assn. Inc. (sec. 1965-83). Lutheran. Home: Heney Creek-Whitshed Rd Cordova AK 99574 Office: 910 Lefevre Cordova AK 99574

NICHOLS, CHARLES FRED, county official; b. San Bernardino, Calif., Nov. 6, 1947; s. Charles Blackwell and Virginia Patricia N.; B.S.I.E., Calif. State Poly. U., 1970; M.B.A., So. Ill. U., 1975; m. Nancy Claire Parks, June 13, 1971; children—Charles Kyle, Brent Alan. Analyst intern City of Hope Nat. Med. Ctr., 1969-70; productivity analyst, San Bernardino County (Calif.), 1972—. Chmn., Rialto (Calif.) Planning Commn., 1978-82; pres. Rialto Colt League, 1972-73; loaned exec. West End and Fontana United Way, 1982. Served with USN, 1971. Recipient Nat. Assn. Counties award for Productivity advancement, 1977. Mem. Am. Mgmt. Assn., Inst. Indsl. Engrs. (sr.), Am. Assn. Pub. Adminstrs, Productivity Council of S.W. Club: Kiwanis (pres. 1978-79). Home: 147 E Madrona St Rialto CA 92376 Office: OMS 157 W 5th St San Bernardino CA 92415

NICHOLS, HORACE ROBERT, psychologist; b. Denver, May 31, 1931; s. Horace R. and Alice N.; m. Ilene L. Ritchey, June 1, 1957; children—Rebel Robert, Nikki Lynn, Tammi Lee. Ph.D., Walden U., 1978. Psychologist, Coop. Ednl. Services, Tacoma, 1962-66; psychologist, dir. sexual offender unit Western State Hosp., Ft. Steilacoom, Wash., 1967-78; psychologist Nichols Molinder Agy., Tacoma, 1978—. Served with USAF, 1951-55. Home: 437 Bowes Dr Tacoma WA 98466 Office: 3902 N 34th Tacoma WA 98407

NICHOLS, JACQUELINE BRUCE, archeologist; b. Harlan, Ky., Oct. 14, 1941; d. Jack Corum and Martha Jayne (Miracle) Bruce; B.A., Wellesley Coll., 1963; M.A., SUNY, Albany, 1977; m. David Edward Nichols, Mar. 4, 1963; children—Corinna Elizabeth, David Andrew, Patrick Edward. Tchr., Bedford (Eng.) Schs., 1963-64; dir. Archeol. Field Labs., SUNY, Albany, 1976-77, Cath. U., 1978; v.p. Gt. Basin Found. for Archeol. Research, 1979; pres. Atechiston, Inc., Albuquerque, 1980—; co-founder, editor Flintknappers Exchange, 1977; founder, pub. Contract Abstracts & CRM Archeology, 1980—. Wallace Stegner fellow, 1963-64. Mem. AAAS, Soc. Am. Archaeology, Nat. Assn. Women Bus. Owners, Soc. Archeol. Sci., Found. for Desert Archaeology (dir. 1980—). Republican. Office: 4426 Constitution NE Albuquerque NM 87110

NICHOLS, JOHN BURTON, business executive; b. Bklyn., Nov. 4, 1924; s. Arthur Beach and Georgia Davis (Smith) N.; B.A.E., Rensselaer Poly. Inst., 1945; m. Betty Jane Paulsen, May 10, 1947; children—Mark Edward, Eric Paul, Jill Martha. Sect. head Gen. Electric Co., Schenectady, 1946-52; mgr. advanced planning and research Hiller Helicopters, Palo Alto, Calif., 1952-65; dir. mktg. turbine div. Boeing Co., Seattle, 1965-66; mgr. advanced design and proposals Hughes Tool Co., Culver City, Calif., 1968-71; pres. United Tech. Industries, Oceanside, Calif., 1971-79; head Wind Energy Office, Calif. Energy Commn., 1979-80; v.p. engring. Aerolift Inc., 1980-82. Mem. Gov. Research Council San Mateo County, 1960-65. Served with USN, 1942-46. Registered profl. engr., N.Y., Calif. Fellow AIAA (asso.), Royal Aero. Soc. (asso.); mem. ASME, Am. Helicopter Soc., Inst. Strategic Studies, Sigma Xi, Tau Beta Pi, Omega Delta Phi. Republican. Presbyterian. Patentee in gas turbine and helicopter fields. Contbr. articles to profl. jours. Home: 3059 Yellowstone Ln Sacramento CA 95821

NICHOLS, RALPH, paleontologist, rancher; b. Salt Lake City, Mar. 21, 1920; s. Dewitt Lethbridge and Edwina Nelson (Yearian) N.; B.A., Mont. State U., 1942; M.S., U. Mont., 1976; m. Gayle Ann; children—Mary Ed Angell, Rachel Elizabeth, Sara Gayle. Flight instr. Johnson Flying Service, Missoula, Mont., 1943-44; cowboy various ranches in Idaho, Mont. and Fla., 1946-50; rancher, Wise River, Mont., 1950—; vis. lectr. geology U. Mont., 1976; guide, outfitter; comml. pilot airplanes and helicopters; cons. geology. Active Agrl. Stablzn. and Conservation Service, 1981—. Served with USAAF, 1944-45. Named Outstanding Cooperator, Deerlodge Soil Conservation Dist., 1977. Mem. Soc. Vertebrate Paleontology, Mont. Outfitters and Guides Assn. (past pres.), Sigma Xi, Sigma Chi. Republican. Contbr. articles on paleontology to profl. jours. Home: Lazy Three S Ranch Wise River MT 59762

NICHOLS, RICHARD ALLEN, consulting engineer; b. Ottawa, Ill., Oct. 25, 1939; s. Allen Andrew and Dorothy Eline (Madsen) N.; B.S. in Sci. Engring., Northwestern U., 1963, M.S. in Chem. Engring., 1964, Ph.D. in Chem. Engring., 1966; m. Alexandra Marie Gladdys, July 4, 1973; children—Katherine, Matthew, Richard. Design engr. Airesearch Corp., Los Angeles, 1965-66; design specialist Parker Hannifin Corp., Los Angeles, 1966-69, program mgr., Irvine, Calif., 1969-71, tech. program mgr., 1971-73; owner, cons. engr. R.A. Nichols Engring., Corona del Mar, Calif., 1973—; owner R.A. Nichols, Engr., Irvine, 1980—. Bd. dirs. Community Assn., 1980—, pres., 1981—. Walter P. Murphy fellow, 1961-64; Phillipps Petroleum fellow, 1965; registered profl. engr., Calif. Mem. Nat. Fire Prevention Assn., Air Pollution Control Assn., Sigma Xi, Alpha Delta Phi. Republican. Fundamentalist. Contbr. articles in field to profl. jours.; patentee. Office: 519 Iris Ave Corona del Mar CA 92625 also 16101 Construction Circle W Irvine CA 92714

NICHOLS, ROBERT EDMUND, banker, journalist; b. Daytona Beach, Fla., Feb. 14, 1925; s. Joe D. and Edna A. (Casper) N.; m. Diana R. Grosso; children—Craig S., Kim S., Robin K. Student San Diego State Coll., 1942-43, St. John's Coll., 1944-45, George Washington U., 1948-49. Reporter, San Diego Union, 1942-44; with Washington bur. N.Y. Herald Tribune, 1945-48, CBS, 1948-51; with Time, Inc., 1951-61, contbg. editor bus. and press, asst. edn. dir., N.Y.C., 1951-52, corr. representing Time, Life, Fortune, Sports Illus. mags., San Diego area, 1952-61; Sunday editor San Diego Union, 1952-61; fin. editor Los Angeles Times, 1961-68, mem. editorial bd., 1965-68; spl. asst. to bd. govs. Fed. Res. System, 1968-70; v.p. public relations, dir. editorial services Bank of Am., 1970-73, v.p., dir. public relations, 1973-78, v.p., dir. policy and program devel., 1978—; Writer dir. film and radio documentaries. Recipient Loeb Newspaper Spl. Achievement award, 1963, Loeb award for disting. fin. reporting, 1964. Fellow Royal Geog. Soc., Explorers Club; mem. Nat. Assn. Bus. Economists, Calif. Scholarship Fedn. (hon. life), Public Relations Soc. Am., Soc. Am. Bus. Writers (pres. 1967-68), Acad. Polit. Sci., St. John's Coll. Alumni Assn. No. Calif. (dir.), Sigma Delta Chi. Clubs: South Polar Press (Little Am. Antarctica); Press (San Francisco). Home: 38 Ord Ct San Francisco CA 94114 Office: PO Box 37000 Bank Am World Hdqtrs San Francisco CA 94137

NICHOLSON, WILLIAM JOSEPH, paper co. exec.; b. Tacoma, Aug. 24, 1938; s. Ferris Frank and Athyleen (Fesenmaier) N.; S.B. in Chem. Engring., M.I.T., 1960, S.M., 1961; Ph.D., Cornell U., 1965; M.B.A., Pacific Lutheran U., 1969; m. Carland Elaine Crook, Oct. 10, 1964; children—Courtney Coleman, Brian Barrett, Kay Seaman, Benjamin Ferrers. Sr. devel. engr. Hooker Chem. Corp., Tacoma, 1964-69, Battelle Meml. Inst., Richland, Wash., 1969-70; planning asso. Potlatch Corp., San Francisco, 1970-73, mgr. ops. research consumer products div., 1973, planning and adminstrv. mgr. paper group, 1973-75, corp. energy coordinator, 1975-81, mgr. corp. energy services, 1981—. Mem. ednl. council M.I.T., 1966-69, 71—. Registered profl. engr., Wash. Mem. Am. Chem. Soc., Am. Inst. Chem. Engrs., TAPPI, AAAS, Sigma Xi. Republican. Presbyn. Club: Commonwealth. Home: PO Box 1114 Garden Rd Ross CA 94957 Office: PO Box 7864 Two Embarcadero Center San Francisco CA 94120

NICKEL, ALFRED ADOLPH, JR., oral and maxillofacial surgeon; b. San Francisco, June 17, 1947; s. Alfred Adolph and Rosemarie N.; A.B., U. Calif., Berkeley, 1969; M.S., U. Calif., San Francisco, 1971, D.D.S., B.S., 1973; m. Anna Amelia Anker, Sept. 17, 1967; 3 children. Pvt. practice oral and maxillofacial surgery, Walnut Creek and Danville, Calif., 1979—; mem. attending staffs Moffitt Hosp., John Muir Hosp., Mt. Diablo Hosp.; lectr. U. Calif. Dental Sch., San Francisco, 1976—; co-owner Gemini Scale Models, precision brass castings trains, 1974—. Mem. Am. Soc. Oral Surgery, ADA, Calif. Dental Assn., So. Calif. Acad. Oral Pathology, No. Calif. Oral and Maxillofacial Surgeons, Contra Costa Dental Soc., Nat. Model Railroader Soc., Western Logging and Hist. Soc., Audubon Soc., Nat. Trust Hist. Preservation, Sigma Xi, Omicron Kappa Upsilon. Author articles in field. Address: PO Box 583 Alamo CA 94507

NICKEL, PHILLIP ARNOLD, biologist, educator; b. Deadwood, S.D., Oct. 10, 1937; s. August Avis and Naomi Alice (Erickson) N.; div., children—Mark Phillip, Jamie Louise. B.S., Oregon State U., 1962; M.S., Kans. State U., 1966; Ph.D., 1969. Asst. prof. biology Calif. Lutheran Coll., Thousand Oaks, 1969-73, assoc. prof., 1973—, chmn. dept., 1976—, dir. med. tech. program, 1973—. Mem. Republican Nat. Com. NIH fellow, 1966-69. Mem., Am. Inst. Biol. Scis., Am. Soc. Parasitologists, Audubon Soc., So. Calif. Parasitologists, Am. Social Health Assn., Nat. Assn. Advisors for Health Professions, Western Assn. Advisors for Health Professions. Baptist. Contr. numerous articles to profl. journals. Office: Biology Dept California Lutheran College Thousand Oaks CA 91360

NICKELSON, DOUGLAS LYNN, communications consultant; b. St. Johns, Mich., Sept. 16, 1952; s. Herbert Dee and Carol Jean (Root) Estes; student Alma Coll., 1970-71; B.A., Central Mich. U., 1974; m. Janet Sue Bishop, Oct. 9, 1976; 1 dau., Laura Lynn. Announcer WRBJ, St. Johns, Mich., 1969-72, WMHW, Mt. Pleasant, Mich., 1972; English program dir. Radio Lumiere, Port-au-Prince, Haiti, 1973; announcer, Family Life Radio Sta. WUFN, Albion, Mich., 1974, news dir., 1975, asst. mgr., 1976, mgr., 1977, mgr. Family Life Radio Sta. WUNN, Mason, Mich., 1977, also chief engr., 1977; gen. mgr. Western Bible Coll., Sta. KWBI, Denver, 1977-82; prin. Doug Nickelson Assocs., polit. communications cons., 1982—; mem. faculty Western Bible Coll. Mem. Denver Christian Broadcasters (dir.), Metro Denver Broadcasters, Colo. Broadcasters Assn., Nat. Assn. Broadcasters, Gospel Music Assn., Nat. Religious Broadcasters. Baptist. Home: 1802 S Winona Ct Denver CO 80219 Office: PO Box 9332 Denver CO 80209

NICOLAI, EUGENE RALPH, public relations consultant; b. Renton, Wash., June 26, 1911; s. Eugene George and Josephine (Heidinger) N.; student U. Wash., 1929, Whitman Coll., 1929-30; B.A., U. Wash., 1934; postgrad. Am. U., 1942; M.A., George Washington U., 1965; m. Helen Margaret Manogue, June 5, 1935; 1 son, Paul Eugene. Editor, U. Wash. Daily, Seattle, 1934; asst. city editor, writer, nat. def. editor Seattle Times, 1934-41; writer Sta. KJR, Seattle, 1937-39; writer, editor, safety edn. officer Bur. Mines, Washington, 1941-45; news dir. Grand Coulee Dam and Columbia Basin Project, Washington, 1945-50; regional info. dir. Bur. Mines, Denver and Pitts., 1950-55, asst. chief mineral reports, Washington, 1955-61, news dir. office of oil and gas, 1956-57; sr. info. officer, later sr. public info. officer Office Sec. Interior, Washington, 1961-71, staff White House Nat. Conf. on Natural Beauty, spl. detail to White House, 1971, ret.; now public relations cons., tech. editor, writer. Formerly safety policy adviser Interior Dept.; com. mem. Internat. Cooperation Year, State Dept., 1971. With George Washington U. Alumni Found.; founder, mng. dir. Josephine Nature Preserve; pres. Media Assos. Bd. dirs. Wash. State Council on Alcoholism; adv. Pierce Transit Authority. Named Disting. Alumnus, recipient Penrose award, both Whitman Coll., 1979. Mem. Wilderness Soc., No. Va. Conservation Found., Nat. Trust for Historic Preservation, Nature Conservancy, Wash. Environ. Council, Nat. Audubon Soc., Crook County (Oreg.) Hist. Soc., Washington State Hist. Soc., Emerald Shores Assn, Sigma Delta Chi, Pi Kappa Alpha. Presbyn. Mason. Clubs: George Washington U.; Purdy (pres.). Author: The Middle East Emergency Committee; editor: Fed. Conservation Yearbooks. Home: Box 573 Wauna WA 98395

NICOLAI, PAMELA JANE, city official; b. Newcastle, Pa., Oct. 4, 1946; d. Charles William and Carmen L. Gilchrist; 1 son, Peter B.A., Kalamazoo Coll., 1968; M.A. in L.S., U. Mich., 1968. Head adult services Elk Grove Village (Ill.) Pub. Library, 1972-73; reference librarian Multnomah County Library, Portland, Oreg., 1973-77; library dir. San Rafael (Calif.) Pub. Library, 1977-79; asst. to city mgr. City of San Rafael, 1979—. Bd. dirs. Montessori Children's Home of Marin, 1979-82. Mem. Mcpl. Mgmt. Assn. No. Calif. Office: 1400 5th Ave San Raefael CA 94915

NICOLAIDES, JOHN DUDLEY, aerospace and engineering consultant, educator; b. Washington, Feb. 13, 1923; s. Phidias John and Marie Rose (Kelly) N.; m. Virginia Mary Driscoll, June 9, 1945; 1 dau., Kathleen Mary. Student Rensselaer Poly. Inst., 1943-45; B.A., Lehigh U., 1946; M.S., Johns Hopkins U., 1953; Ph.D., Cath. U., 1962. Project engr. Gen. Electric Co., 1946-48; research scientist Ballistic Research Lab., Aberdeen Proving Ground, Md., 1948-53; various positions, then tech. dir. astronautics Bur. Naval Weapons, 1953-61, various positions including dir. program rev. and resource mgmt. NASA, 1961-64; chmn. dept. aerospace engring. U. Notre Dame, 1964-74; head dept. aerospace engring. Calif. Poly. State U., San Luis Obispo, 1975-79, prof. aero. and mech. engring., 1979-83; pres. A-E-R-O, 1975—; cons. to govt. and industry. Served with USNR, 1943-46. Mem. AIAA, Sigma Xi, Tau Beta Pi. Author: Missile Flight Dynamics, 1957; contbr. to space sci. sect. Ency. Brit.; designer flying machine, parafoil flying wing. Home: 2048 Skylark Ln San Luis Obispo CA 93401 Office: PO Box 1676 San Luis Obispo CA 93406

NICOLL, GAIL LOGUE, nurse adminstr.; b. Lawrenceburg, Tenn., Mar. 27, 1936; d. Hartwell Brown and Kathryn Anita (Braswell) Logue; children—Merrill G., Kenneth Neagle, Kathryn Elizabeth, Russell Andrew. A.A., Amarillo Jr. Coll., 1956; R.N., N.W. Tex. Hosp. Sch. Nursing, 1957; postgrad. Ariz. State U., 1968, 71, 73; B.A. in Counseling, Stephens Coll., 1981. Cert. emergency nurse. Emergency head nurse Central Supply/Nursing Care, Southside Dist. Hosp., Mesa, Ariz., 1960-67; supr. nursing care Physicians & Surgeons Clinic, Mesa, 1967-68; emergency nurse St. Joseph's Hosp., Phoenix, 1968-71; coordinator emergency dept., paramedic coordinator, paramedic field instr. Good Samaritan Hosp., Phoenix, 1971-79; agt. Bankers Life of Iowa, 1979-80; mgr. emergency dept. Scottsdale Meml. Hosp. (Ariz.), 1980—; mem. Ariz. Adv. Bd. for Devel. Rules and Regulations for Paramedics, 1974, oral bd. examiner; cons. Ariz. State U., U. Ariz.; dir. Valley Emergency Med. Services, 1974-76; mem. Phoenix Emergency Med. Services Adv. Council, 1974; mem. Phoenix Emergency Med. Services Commn., 1975-78, Ariz. Emergency Paramedic and Tech. Adv. Council, 1975-77. Recipient award Maricopa County Med. Soc., 1976. Mem. Emergency Dept. Nurses Assn. (charter mem., pres. Cactus Wren chpt. 1973-75, charter mem., pres. Ariz. chpt. 1975-77, nat. sci. symposium com. 1979, nat. dir., regional dir. region IX, nat. pres.-elect 1981-82, pres. 1982-83). Club: Life Saver's (Phoenix). Co-developer 1st paramedic tng. curriculum, Phoenix, 1974, 1st writer paramedic examination, Ariz. Home: 2144 E Donner Tempe AZ 85282 Office: 7400 E Osborn Rd Scottsdale AZ 85251

NICOLL, GLORIA MARGARET, interior designer, educator; b. San Francisco, Jan. 24, 1924; d. Stanley Layton and Marion (Herman) Smith; m. James Donald Nicoll, Dec. 19, 1945; children—Richard, Gregory; 2d m. Alexander Salopek, July 10, 1982. Student Coll. of San Mateo, Coll. Notre Dame, Calif., 1966; A.A. in Research and Devel. Can. Coll., 1975; A.A. in Interior Design, 1981. Sec. art dept. Redwood City (Calif.) Sch. Dist., 1963-65, testing specialist, 1965—; owner, mgr. Nicoll Interiors, 1978—. Past pres. PTA. Mem. Am. Soc. Interior Designers (assoc.), Am. Fuchsia Soc., Golden Gate Race Walkers.

NICOLOSI, JOSEPH JOHN, clinical psychologist; b. N.Y.C., Jan. 24, 1947; s. Frank and Camille (LoCaso) N.; m. Linda Ruth Ames, June 16, 1978; 1 son, Joseph. B.A., L.I. U., 1970; M.A., New Sch. Social Research, 1972; Ph.D., Calif. Sch. Profl. Psychology, 1975. Lic. psychologist, Calif. Pvt. practice clin. psychology; pres., clin. dir. Thomas Aquinas Psychol. Clinic, Encino, Calif., 1980—; lectr. in field. Recipient award Western Assn. Spiritual Dirs., 1981. Mem. Am. Psychol. Assn., Calif. Psychol. Assn., Nat. Guild Catholic Psychiatrists. Roman Catholic. Office: 16661 Ventura Blvd Ste 816 Encino CA 91436

NIDEVER, JACK EDWARD, psychologist; b. Fresno, Calif., Mar. 6, 1925; s. Elza Edward and Vella Virginia (Foley) N.; B.A., Pomona Coll., 1950; M.A., U. Pa., 1952; Ph.D., UCLA, 1959; m. Feb. 15, 1948 (div. 1976); children—Linda Christine, Clare-Marie, Melissa Adrienne. Social scientist Rand Corp., Santa Monica, Calif., 1954-56; info. analyst Gen. Electric Co., Arlington, Va., 1959; engring. psychologist IBM, San Jose, Calif., 1959-62; staff psychologist Mendocino State Hosp., 1965-66, Santa Clara Valley Med. Center, 1966-67, Agnew State Hosp., 1967-70; asso. prof. Sonoma State Coll., Rohnert Park, Calif., 1966; instr. Calif. Sch. Profl. Psychology, San Francisco, 1968-70; partner Associated Psychologists of Santa Clara (Calif.), 1968—; instr. Psychol. Studies Inst., Palo Alto. Served with AUS, 1943-46. Hinkle fellow, 1963-65. Mem. Internat. Assn. Analytical Psychology, Soc. Jungian Analysts, Am. Psychol. Assn. Republican. Club: Decathlon. Home: 18789 McFarland St Saratoga CA 95070 Office: 1066 Saratoga Ave Suite 220 San Jose CA 95129

NIEBERDING, JOSEPH EDWARD, psychologist; b. Dayton, Ohio, June 16, 1949; s. John H. and Helen T. (Meineke) N. B.S., Ohio State U., 1971; M.S., Okla. State U., 1974, Ph.D., 1975. Pvt. practice clin. psychology, Oakland, Calif., 1977—; cons. residential facilities for developmentally disabled, 1977—. NIMH fellow, 1972-74. Mem. Am. Psychol. Assn., Alameda County Psychol. Assn. (sec. 1980—). Editor: (with M. Jospe and B. Cohen) Psychological Factors in Health Care, 1980. Office: 2938 McClure St Suite 1 Oakland CA 94609

NIEBLA, ELVIA ELISA, soil chemist, educator, researcher; b. Nogales, Mex., Mar. 12, 1945; d. Fernando and Marina Elena (Verdugo) N. A.A., Fullerton Jr. Coll., 1965; B.S. in Zoology, U. Ariz., 1967, M.Ed. in Spl. Edn., 1968; Ph.D. in Soil Chemistry, 1979. Lab. tech. agrl. chemistry and soils dept. U. Ariz., Tucson, 1967-68; tchr. physically handicapped Claremont (Calif.) Sch. Dist., 1968-70; tchr. learning disabled Pomona (Calif.) Unified Sch. Dist., 1970-71; grad. research asst. soils water and engring. dept. U. Ariz., Tucson, 1971-72, research asst. II, 1972-75, research assoc., 1978-79; phys. scientist Western Archeol. and Conservation Ctr., Nat. Park Service, Tucson, 1979—. Vice-pres., Fed. Women's Program Mgrs. Interagy. Council, 1979-80. U. Ariz. fellow, 1967-68. Mem. Am. Soc. Agronomy, Soil Sci. Soc. Am., Women in Agr., Alpha Zeta, Gamma Sigma Delta, Pi Beta Phi. Club: Tucson Athletic. Contbr. numerous articles to profl. jours. Office: Western Archeol and Conservation Ctr 1415 N 6th Ave Tucson AZ 85705

NIEBOER, NANCY ANN SCHWARZ, behavioral scientist, educator; b. Kingston, N.Y., May 22, 1942; d. Ernst Joseph and Margaret Virginia (Marklin) Schwarz; m. Kourtney C. Nieboer, Feb. 1963 (div. July 1974). A.B., Hope Coll., 1964; M.Ed., Springfield Coll., 1969; Ph.D., U.S. Internat. U., 1975. Asst. editor Quinn Pub. Co., Kingston, N.Y., 1964; tchr. French, Chicopee (Mass.) Pub. Schs., 1965-69; counselor, instr. psychology Chapman Coll. Ctr., George AFB, Calif., 1970-71; edn. counselor, Edwards AFB, Calif., 1971; cons. USAF Actions Programs, Soesterberg AB, Netherlands, 1972-73; edn. coordinator U.S. Army Dist. Recruiting Commands, Cleve. and Columbus, 1976-79; program mgr. high sch. testing program U.S. Army Recruiting Command Hdqrs., Fort Sheridan, Ill., 1979-82; adj. research prof. psychology Naval Postgrad. Sch., Monterey, Calif., 1982—. Recipient Outstanding Performance award U.S. Army, 1977-81. Mem. Am. Personnel and Guidance Assn., Assn. Measurement and Evaluation in Guidance, Mil. Educators and Counselors Assn. (founding; chmn. bylaws com.), Am. Vocat. Assn. (chmn. Armed Services interest sect. of guidance div. 1980-81), Mil. Testing Assn., Ohio Personnel and Guidance Assn., Mensa. Mem. Reformed Ch. Am. Author: Army Recruiter's Guide to the High School ASVAB, 1979, 82. Office: Naval Postgrad Sch Code 54 Ng Monterey CA 93940

NIEHAUS, MERLE H., agronomist, educator; b. Enid, Okla., Mar. 25, 1933; s. Roy H. and Hazel N.; B.S., Okla. State U., 1955, M.S., 1957; postgrad. Iowa State U., 1957-59; Ph.D., Purdue U., 1964; m. Allene Rollier, Aug. 20, 1954; children—Lisa, Mark. Mem. faculty agronomy dept. Ohio Agrl. Research and Devel. Center, Wooster, 1964-78, prof., 1970-78, asso. chmn., 1975-78; prof., head crops and soils scis. dept. N.Mex. State U., Las Cruces, 1978—; cons. A.I.D., UN, FAO. Mem. Wooster (Ohio) City Sch. Bd., 1977. Recipient Profl. Excellence award Ohio Turfgrass Found., 1976. Mem. Am. Soc. Agronomy, AAAS, Crop Sci. Soc. Am., Sigma Xi, Phi Kappa Phi, Alpha Zeta. Mem. Christian Ch. (elder). Contbr. articles to profl. jours. Home: 1035 Marilissa Ln Las Cruces NM 88005 Office: Box 3Q Crops and Soils Scis Dept New Mexico

NIELSEN, DAVID EDWARD, educator; b. Pasadena, Apr. 22, 1946; s. David Stjerne and Ruth (Norvell) N.; B.A., Brigham Young U., 1971; M.A., Calif. State U., Los Angeles, 1975; m. Faye Ann Brough, June 4, 1970; children—David Thomas, Kirsten Ann, Kelli Shannon, Christopher Edward. Tchr. history San Gabriel (Calif.) High Sch., 1973; tchr. history Repetto Sch., Monterey Park, Calif., 1973—, also coach, athletic dir., mem. sch. adv. council, 1977-80. Mem. Law & Order Campaign com., Calif., 1977-80; leader Boy Scouts Am. Recipient Repetto PTA hon. services awards, 1976, 80. Mem. So. Calif. Football Ofcls., Smithsonian Instn., Nat. Hist. Soc., Calif. Hist. Soc., NEA, Calif. Tchrs. Assn., Alhambra Tchrs. Assn., Nat. Trust Hist. Preservation, Archives Assos., U.S. Olympic Soc., Nat. Geog. Soc. Democrat. Mem. Ch. Jesus Christ of Latter-day Saints. Sport editor Banyon, 1969-71. Home: 87 Cedarwood Ave Duarte CA 91010 Office: 650 Grandridge Ave Monterey Park CA 91754

NIELSEN, JAMES ARTHUR, broadcaster, Canadian provincial government official; b. Moose Jaw, Sask., Can., Aug. 6, 1938; s. Erling Oscar and Lillian (Douglas) N.; m. Edith Jean Filer, Mar. 10, 1961; children—Robert, Brent, Darin, Richard, Raymond, Christopher, Michael, Debra, Julia. Ed. pub. schs., Moose Jaw and Richmond, B.C., Can. Broadcaster, news editor, reporter, news dir., ops. mgr., open-line commentator Stas. CJVI, CFAX, CFUN, CJOR, Victoria and Vancouver, B.C., 1959-75; mem. B.C. Parliament, 1975—; minister of environ. Govt. of B.C., Victoria, 1975-78, minister consumer and corp. affairs, 1978-81, minister health, 1981—. Office: Room 346 Parliament Bldgs Victoria BC V8V 1X4 Canada

NIELSEN, JAMES WILEY, state senator; b. Fresno, Calif., July 31, 1944; s. Woodrow E. and Geraldine P. (Hudson) N.; B.S. in Agribus., Fresno State Coll.; m. Deborah Reed, Feb. 25, 1966; children—Prima Delle, Brandi, Sorrill. Farm mgr.; formerly cons. Roy Riegels Co., Woodland, Calif.; now mem. Calif. State Senate, Sacramento; lectr. bus. and farm mgmt. to various orgns. Agrl. named Agrl. Spokesman of Year, 1976; Leadership Program fellow, 1975-76. Mem. Council State Legislators, Farm Bur., Agrl. Action Com., Agrl. Leadership Assos., Native Sons Golden West. Republican. Methodist. Home: 1742 Brown St Woodland CA 95695 Office: State Capitol Sacramento CA 95814

NIELSEN, LELAND C., judge; b. Vesper, Kans., June 14, 1919; s. Carl Christian and Christena (Larson) N.; m. Virginia Garland, Nov. 27, 1958; 1 dau., Christena. A.B., Washburn U., Topeka, 1946; J.D., U. So. Calif., 1946. Bar: Calif. 1947. Practice, Los Angeles, from 1947; judge Superior Ct. Calif. San Diego County, 1968-71; judge U.S. Dist. Ct. (so. dist.) Calif., 1971—. Served to maj. USAS, 1941-46. Republican. Presbyterian. Office: US Courthouse 940 Front St Courtroom 5 San Diego CA 92189*

NIELSEN, MARTIN SENIUS, energy cons.; b. Cody, Wyo., Nov. 29, 1940; s. Senius and Mary Elizabeth (Jensen) N.; student N.W. Community Coll., 1961-62; B.S., U. Wyo., 1965; m. Judy Lee Deardorff, Dec. 27, 1975; children—Tim, Greg, Chris, Marette. Owner, mgr. N & P Supply, Cody, Wyo., 1962-67; fish culturist Wyo. Game and Fish, 1965-70; owner, operator ranch, farm, Cody, 1970—; pres. Al-Agri Renewable Resources, Inc., Cody, 1980—; bd. dirs. Shoshone River Power. Mem. North Big Horn Basin Malt Barley Growers Assn. (co-founder), Wyo. Gasohol Assn., Nat. Cattlemen's Assn., Wyo. Stockgrowers Assn., Am. Quarter Horse Assn., U. Wyo. Alumni Assn. Republican. Presbyterian. Clubs: Lions, Elks. Home: PO Box 1613 Cody WY 82414 Office: PO Box 1085 Cody WY 82414

NIELSEN, RICHARD JOHN, banker; b. Idaho Falls, Idaho, Dec. 1, 1942; s. John Oluf and Helen Adair N.; m. Claudia Evelyn Harris, July 16, 1966; children—Lisa M., Joan D., Julie J., Susan L., David R., Abby L. Student, Brigham Young U., 1961-62, U. Utah, 1964, Weber State U., 1965-69, Boise State U., 1969-73. Asst. cashier Bank Idaho, 1972-75; v.p. Bank Utah, 1975-79; exec. v.p. Golden Spike State Bank, Tremonton, Utah, 1979—; instr. econs. and fin. mgmt. Am. Inst. Banking, 1975-79. Served with Utah Air N.G., 1964. Mem. Am. Bankers Assn., Western Ind. Bankers Assn., Utah Bankers Assn. Republican. Mem. Ch. of Jesus Christ of Latter-day Saints. Home: 785 N 350 E Tremonton UT 84337 Office: 25 N Tremont St Tremonton UT 84337

NIELSEN, ROBERT STANLEY, transp. exec., state ofcl.; b. Wollongong, Australia, Feb. 16, 1921; s. John W. and Rita G. (Jacobs) N.; m. Joy E. Annetts, Oct. 21, 1943; children—Robert R., Rosemary J. Hendler. B.Ec., Sydney U. (Australia), 1950; M.A., U. Calif.-Berkeley, 1956, Ph.D., 1958. Dir. research P. & O. Lines, San Francisco, 1960-66; dir. market research Eastern Air Lines, N.Y.C., 1966-69; dir. Perth Regional Transport Study, Perth, Australia, 1970; gen. mgr. and commr. Sydney Urban Transit Systems (Australia); v.p. and chief economist DeLeuw Cather & Co., San Francisco, 1974-78; asst. sec. transp. State of Wash., Olympia, 1978—; dir. Rosemary Nielsen Enterprises Inc., Pacific Transp. & Mktg. Assos. Mem. Sydney U. Transp. Task Force, 1972, Botany Bay Foreshores Adv. Com. 1978. Served to capt. Royal Australian Air Force, 1941-45. Decorated D.F.C., D.F.M.; recipient J. C. Nichols Urban Studies award, U. Calif., 1956; Sydney Transport Excellence award New South Wales State Govt., 1974; Chartered Inst. Transport fellow, London, 1973. Mem. Nat. Assn. Bus. Economists, Inst. Transp. Engrs. Presbyterian. Clubs: RAF (London), World Trade (San Francisco), Balmain Leagues (Sydney). Author: Oil Tanker Economics, 1960; Perth Regional Transport Study, 1970; Sydney Area Transport Study, 1974; With the Stars Above, 1982. Home: 3004 Westwood Ct NW Olympia WA 98502 Office: Dept Transp Olympia WA 98504

NIELSEN, SWEN C., police chief; b. Aalborg, Denmark, Mar. 16, 1935; came to U.S., 1949, naturalized, 1955; s. Arnold C. and Anna (Olesen) N.; m. Shirlene Jones, Apr. 26, 1956; children—Richard, Bradley, Eric, Claudia. B.S., Los Angeles State Coll., 1961, M.P.A., 1971. Patrolman, spl. investigator Los Angeles Police Dept., 1958-61; chief security officer Brigham Young U., 1961-74; chief of police Provo (Utah) Police Dept., 1974—; instr. justice adminstrn. Brigham Young U. Served with AUS, 1954-56. Mem. Internat. Assn. Chiefs of Police, Nat. Dist. Attys. Assn. Mormon. Author: General Administrative and Organization Concepts for University Police, 1971. Home: 1202 East 700 South Provo UT 84601 Office: PO Box 1849 Provo UT 84603

NIELSON, HOWARD CURTIS, congressman; b. Richfield, Utah, Sept. 12, 1924; m. Julia Adams, 1948; children—Noreen, Elaine, John, Mary Lee, James, Jean, Curtis. B.S., U. Utah, 1947; M.S., U. Oreg., 1949; M.B.A., Stanford U., 1956, Ph.D., 1958. Statistician, C & H Sugar, 1949-51; research economist Stanford Research Inst., 1951-57; prof. Brigham Young U., 1957-76, 78-82; assoc. commr. Higher Edn. Utah, 1976-78; mem. Utah Ho. of Reps., 1967-74, maj. leader, 1969-70, chmn. budget audit com., speaker, 1973-74; mem. 98th Congress from Utah. Served to sgt., USAAF, 1943-46. Mem. Am. Statis. Assn., Sigma Xi, Phi Kappa Phi, Phi Beta Kappa. Republican. Mormon. Office: 1229 Longworth House Office Bldg Washington DC 20515*

NIELSON, JOSEPH LYNN, coll. adminstr.; b. Logan, Utah, May 12, 1937; s. Lafe B. and Melba (Nish) N.; B.S., U. Utah, 1962; Ed.M., U. Nev., 1967; Ph.D., U. Utah, 1970; m. Nanette C. Moore, July 19, 1963; children—Daniel L., Cynthia E., Carrie Ann, Benjamin J., Andrew L. Tchr. Am. history and social scis. Ed. W. Clark High Sch., Las Vegas, Nev., 1966-68; instr. Inst. of Religion, U. Utah, Salt Lake City, 1968-71; sch. counselor Roy Martin Jr. High Sch., Las Vegas, 1967-68; coordinator community edn. Utah State Office of Edn., Salt Lake City, 1969-78; lectr. depts. recreation and ednl. adminstrn. Brigham Young U., Provo, Utah, 1970-78; adj. asso. prof. leisure studies U. Utah, 1974—; asso. supt. schs. Ogden (Utah) Sch. Dist., 1976-77; instr. communications and community edn. Weber State Coll., Ogden, 1978—, dir. community edn., 1978—; cons. community edn. to Calif. State Office of Edn., 1975, Utah State Legislature, 1970-76, Pocatello (Idaho) sch. system, 1974-75; condr. workshops for educators and govt. ofcls., 1971-78; proposal reader U.S. Office Edn., 1976-77. Sunday sch. supt. Ch. of Jesus Christ of Latter Day Saints, Salt Lake City, 1971-73, counselor in bishopric, 1978—; bd. dirs. Kaysville (Utah) Theatre, 1980—; founder Big Bros. Utah, Inc. Served with U.S. Army, 1963-65. Mott Found. grantee, 1978—. Mem. Nat. Community Edn. Assn., Adult Edn. Assn. of Utah, Utah Community Edn. Assn. (co-founder), Nat. Assn. State Dirs. Community Edn. (co-founder, pres.), Utah Assn. Sch. Adminstrs. Republican. Contbr. articles to profl. publs.; instrumental in developing Utah state wide system of community schs. Home: 137 N Pinewood Circle Layton UT 84041 Office: 1302 Weber State College Ogden UT 84408

NIELSSON, GUNNAR PREBEN, international relations educator; b. Copenhagen, Nov. 9, 1933; s. Oluf Albrecht and Ellen Marie (Pedersen) N.; came to U.S., 1956, naturalized, 1960; m. Roberta Marie Cook, May 12, 1956; children—Lisa Karen, Christina Marie. A.A., Los Angeles City Coll., 1959; B.A. with honors in Polit. Sci., UCLA, 1961, Ph.D., 1966; M.A., U. Calif.-Berkeley, 1962. Lctr. dept. polit. sci. U. Calif., Riverside, 1966-68; vis. asst. prof. Sch. Internat. Relations, U. So. Calif., Los Angeles, 1968-69, resident prof., 1969-71, research dir. grad. programs and yr.-abroad program, 1971-75, asst. prof., 1975—. Served with Danish Army, 1954-55. Woodrow Wilson fellow, 1961, 64; Charles Fletcher Scott fellow, 1962; Atlantic and West European Studies fellow, 1965; recipient U. So. Calif. Mortar Board Disting. Tchr. award, 1983. Mem. AAUP, Am. Polit. Sci. Assn., U.S. Internat. Studies Assn., Internat. Inst. Strategic Studies (London 1969-77). Democrat. Contbr. articles to profl. jours., chpts. to textbooks. Office: Sch Internat Relations U So Calif Los Angeles CA 90089

NIETO, JUAN MANUEL, physician; b. Alpine, Tex., Sept. 24, 1949; s. Edmundo Miguel and Socorro (Herrera) N.; B.S., U. Notre Dame, 1970; M.D., U. Colo., 1974; children—Ana Raquel, Cristina Marie. Intern, Los Angeles County-U. So. Calif. Med. Center, 1974-75; physician Community Health Found., Los Angeles, 1975-77, Emergency Dept. Physicians Med. Group, Marina Del Ray, Calif., 1977-78; resident in emergency medicine Denver Gen.-St. Anthony Hosp. Systems, 1978-80; mem. staff North Colo. Med. Center, Greeley, Colo., 1980—; instr. advanced cardiac life support, 1977; bd. dirs. Nat. Chicano Health Orgn., 1971-74; adv. E. Los Angeles Hypertension Screening Program, 1978; med. adv. Weld County Ambulance Service; med. dir. Air Life; del. Colo. Med. Soc. Mem. Am. Coll. Emergency Physicians, Am. Public Health Assn., Acad. Polit. Sci. Home: 1223 S Yosemite Way Denver CO 80231 Office: Emergency Dept North Colo Med Center Greeley CO 80631

NIEVES, CARMEN LYDIA, educator; b. Bayamon, P.R., Apr. 28, 1926; d. Julio and Juana (Ojeda) Fernandez; m. Andres Nieves, Oct. 16, 1954; children—Brenda Kane, Ruben, Omel, Hector. B.S., U. P.R., 1947; M.S., Syracuse U., 1949. Cert. tchr.; cert. competency in Spanish. Tchr. home econs., P.R., 1947-48; home demonstration agt. Agr. Extension Service, P.R., 1950; nutritionist P.R. Sch. Lunch Program, 1952, TV home program, Publicidad Badillo, P.R., 1954-56; tchr. Spanish, Ft. Knox (Ky.) Nursery Sch., 1963; tchr. home econs. and Spanish, Goleta (Calif.) Valley Jr. High Sch., 1969—. Mem. Friends of Santa Barbara Community Mental Health Assn. Mem. Am. Legion Aux., Calif. Tchrs. Assn., Santa Barbara Tchrs. Assn. Democrat. Roman Catholic. Home: 5178 Kaiser Ave Santa Barbara CA 93111

NIGL, ALFRED JAMES, psychologist, cons., researcher, author; b. Oshkosh, Wis., July 30, 1949; s. Alfred Joseph and Marion Jane (Roberts) N.; m. Marie E., Mar. 2, 1968; m. 2d, Terri S. Abbott, Feb. 19, 1982; 2 sons, William Scott, Geoffrey Alan. B.A. in Psychology, U. Wis., 1971; M.A. in Clin. Psychology, U. Cin., 1973, Ph.D. in Clin. Psychology, 1975. Lic. psychologist, Wis., Calif. Clin. intern or grad. trainee Cin. Gen. Hosp., 1971, Rollman Psychiat. Clinic, Cin., 1971, U. Cin. Univ. Counseling Ctr., 1971, 73, U. Cin. Med. Ctr. Central Psychiat. Clinic, 1972, Cin. Ctr. Developmental Disorders, 1973-75, U. Cin. Crises Intervention Clinic, 1973-75, U. Cin. mental health program, 1974-75; acting dir. tng. and research, mental health program U. Cin. Student Health Program, 1974-75; cons. staff psychologist Psychol. and Mgmt. Cons. Services, S.C., Milw., 1975-76; pres. Milw. Devel. Ctr., 1975-78; chief psychologist Jackson Psychiat. Ctr., Milw., 1978-80; dir. child and adolescent services Oxnard (Calif.) Mental Health Center, 1980-81; cons., dir. biofeedback Kaiser-Permanente Healthwise, 1982—; pvt. practice psychology; cons. Calif. Regional Ctrs. for Developmentally Disabled; staff psychologist Lutheran Hosp. Milw., 1978-70, dept. psychiatry Waukesha Meml. Hosp., 1978-80; dir. biofeedback, family practice residency program Waukesha Meml. Hosp. affiliated with Med. Coll. Wis., 1980; adj. clin. prof. Grad. Sch. Pub. Health, San Diego State U., 1983—; pres. Biofeedback Soc. Wis., 1979-80. Bd. dirs. Big Bros./Big Sisters, Ventura County, Calif., 1981-82, Ventura County Rape Crisis Ctr., 1982. U. Cin. Gradn. sch. Council research grantee, 1974; Am. Psychol. Assn. Overseas travel grantee, 1982. Mem. Am. Acad. Behavioral Medicine, AAAS, Am. Psychol. Assn., N.Y. Acad. Scis., Acad. Psychosomatic Medicine, Biofeedback Soc. Am. (rep. to Council State Biofeedback Socs. 1980), Ventura County Psychol. Assn. (dir. 1982-83). Author: (with Fischer-Williams and Sovine) A Textbook of Biological Feedback, 1981; The Development of Children's Understanding of Spatial Relations, vol. 62 of European Univ. Studies-Psychology, 1981; Biofeedback and Behavioral Strategies in Pain Treatment, 1983; research, publs. in field. Office: 9834 Genesee Suite 321 La Jolla CA 92037

NIGRO, THEODORE ANTHONY, banker; b. Burson, Calif., Dec. 4, 1922; s. Frank and Mabel Mary (Hansen) N.; m. Constance Louise Vannoy, May 29, 1949; children—Gary Dean, Bruce Alan, Kathleen Ann, Roger Lee, John Robert, Judith Angela. Grad. Pacific Cost Banking Sch., U. Wash., 1963. Teller, Bank of Am., Santa Cruz, Calif., 1948-54, trust div., Salinas, Calif., 1954-60; asst. trust officer Security Bank of Nev., 1961-64, sr. v.p., trust officer, 1964—. Pres., Better Bus. Bur., 1967-68, Clayton Sch. PTA, 1968-69; bd. dirs. Salvation Army, Sierra Arts Found.; bd. dirs., treas. Nev. Humane Soc.; governing elder St. John's Presbyterian Ch.; mem. adv. bd. U.Nev. Med. Sch. Served with U.S. Army, 1943-46. Mem. Nev. Bankers Assn. (chmn. trust div. 1971-72), Reno Estate Planning Council. Republican. Clubs: Lions (treas. 1975-76), Reno Executive (dir. 1979-81). Office: Security Bank of Nev 1 E Liberty St Trust Dept 3d Floor Reno NV 89501

NIKOLAI, IRVIN, school district executive, consultant; b. Fresno, Calif., Jan. 31, 1937; s. Fred and Anna Nikolai; m. Meta Lucille Craig, Aug. 25, 1961; children—Peter Craig, Meta Ann. B.A., Stanford U., 1960, M.A., 1961; Ph.D., Ariz. State U., 1969. Cert. tchr., secondary adminstrn., supt., Ariz., tchr., gen. adminstrn., Calif. Wide receiver Oakland (Calif.) Raiders Profl. Football Team, 1960; instr. Mountain View (Calif.) High Sch., 1961-63; instr. dept. def. Yamato High Sch., Tokyo, Japan, 1963-65; research asst. Stanford U., 1965, 66; asst. prin. Poway (Calif.) Unified Sch. Dist., 1965-67; faculty assoc. Ariz. State U., 1967-69; asst. dir. S.W. Coop. Ednl. Lab., Albuquerque, 1969-72; dir. Hoffman Ednl. Systems, El Monte, Calif., 1972-75; assoc. supt. Chandler (Ariz.) Unified Sch. Dist., 1976—; cons. in field. Mem. Am. Assn. Sch. Adminstrs., Ariz. Sch. Adminstrs. Assn., Assn. Supervision and Curriculum Devel. Clubs: Phoenix Retriever, Kiwanis, Rotary, Ojo Rojo Lions (chmn. sight and hearing, dir. Chandler). Author tests and ednl. materials. Home: 1140 W Ivanhoe St Chandler AZ 85224 Office: 500 W Galveston St Chandler AZ 85224

NIKOLCHEV, RINA NIKOLOY, architect; b. Bulgaria; d. Nikola Dimitrov and Grigorina (Ivanova) N.; B.A. in Architecture, U. Calif.-Berkeley, 1978; m. Michael Sechman. With DMJM Cons., San Mateo, Calif., 1979; architect, designer Bechtel Corp., San Francisco, 1979—; ptnr. Michael Sechman & Assocs.; pvt. researcher S. Am. Archtl. Heritage, 1980-81. Calif. Alumni Assn. Alumni scholar. Office: 1519 Grant St San Francisco CA 94133

NIKU, SALAR, environmental scientist and engineer; b. Tehran, Iran, Nov. 20, 1947; s. Saleh and Sara N.; B.Sc., Tehran Poly. U., 1969; M.Sc., Stanford U., 1975, Engr. Degree, 1976; Ph.D., U. Calif.-Davis, 1979. Instr., Stanford U., Tehran Poly. U., 1969-74; cons. civil engring. firms, 1969-74; research engr. U. Calif., Davis, 1976-79; sr. project engr./mgr. Brown & Caldwell Cons. Engrs., Pasadena, Calif., 1979—. Registered civil engr., Calif. Mem. ASCE, Water Pollution Control Fedn., Calif. Water Pollution Control Assn. Contbr. articles to profl. jours. Office: 150 S Arroyo Pkwy Pasadena CA 91109

NILES, DORIS KILDALE (MRS. ARTHUR D. NILES, educator; b. Eureka, Calif., July 26, 1903; d. Alfred Walter and Laura (Peterson) Kildale; A.B., Stanford U., 1926, M.A., 1927, Ph.D., 1931; postgrad. Harvard U., 1930; m. Arthur D. Niles, Mar. 11, 1938 (dec. 1978); children—Katey Niles Walker, Malcolm A., Margaret Niles Rice, James Alfred. Teaching asst. dept. botany Stanford U., 1927-28, Ariz. State Coll., 1932, Humboldt State Coll., Arcata, Calif., 1928-45, 55-58; asso. prof. U. Calif. Extension at Davis, 1958—; curator Natural History, Coll. of Redwoods; exec. dir. Nature Discovery Vols. Mem. Calif. Acad. Scis., N.Y. Acad. Scis., Sierra Club, Phi Beta Kappa, Sigma Xi, Sigma Delta Pi, Pi Lambda Theta. Home: PO Box 307 Loleta CA 95551 Office: U Calif Extension Davis CA 95616

NILES, FRANKLIN ELVIE, physicist; b. Shawnee, Okla., Aug. 26, 1934; s. Walter Franklin and Nora Lee (Clark) N.; B.S. in Engring. Physics, U. Okla., 1956; M.A. in Physics, U. Tex., Austin, 1962, Ph.D., 1964; m. Shirley June Allen, Sept. 3, 1955; children—Mitchell Eric, Stanley Royal. Research physicist, supervisory research physicist U.S. Army Ballistic Research Labs., Aberdeen (Md.) Proving Ground, 1965-76; supervisory research physicist Atmospheric Scis. Lab., U.S. Army Electronics Research and Devel. Command, White Sands Missile Range, N.Mex., 1976—. Served with AUS, 1957-59. Recipient Research and Devel. award U.S. Army, 1970; Kent award Ballistic Research Lab., 1974. Mem. Am. Phys. Soc., Am. Geophys. Union, AAAS, Research Soc. Am., Am. Sci. Affiliation, Tau Beta Pi, Sigma Tau, Omicron Delta

Kappa, Sigma Pi Sigma, Pi Mu Epsilon, Phi Eta Sigma. Baptist. Home: 701 Lenox Ave Las Cruces NM 88005 Office: DELAS-AE Atmospheric Scis Lab White Sands Missile Range NM 88002

NILES, MICHAEL SCOTT, wholesale malt beverage co. exec.; b. Cedar Rapids, Iowa, July 10, 1946; s. Sidney Robert and Bernice Doris (Cisler) N.; B.S. in Edn., No. Ariz. U., 1969; D.Beer Mktg., Anheuser Busch, 1972; m. Hazel Dawn Prince, Apr. 12, 1974; children—Brooke Asheley, Nicholas Benjamin. With Community Beverage Co., Los Angeles, 1969—, now pres., chief exec. officer; and gen. mgr. Democrat. Presbyterian. Office: 550 S Mission Rd Los Angeles CA 90033

NILES, SUSANNE, advertising executive; b. Beatrice, Nebr., July 24, 1936; d. Otis William and Lenore Catherine (Bloodgood) Kaminska; m. Lawrence Thomas Holland, Sept. 1, 1955; m. 2d, Stephan E. Niles, Dec. 18, 1976; children—Scot Thomas, Michael Alan, Christopher William, Randal Brian. Student U. Colo., 1954-55; grad. Griffin Bus. Coll., 1956. Head bookkeeper Continental Indsl. Bank, Denver, 1958-68; media dir. Evans/Pacific Advt., Seattle, 1968-78; founder, owner Northwest Media Services, Seattle, 1978—. Fund raiser Children's Home Soc. Wash. (pres. local chpt.). Mem. Seattle Women in Advt., Seattle Advt. Fedn. (tchr. media buying seminars), Advt. Speakers Bur. Republican. Office: 1507 Western Ave Suite 600 Seattle WA 98101

NILSSON, RAYMOND, tenor, educator; b. Sydney, Australia, May 26, 1920; came to U.S., 1963; s. Leslie R. and Annie A. (Cross) N.; B.A., Sydney U., 1945; diploma New South Wales Conservatory of Music, 1946; Lic., Royal Schs. Music, 1947; m. Mildred Hartle Stockslager, Dec. 10, 1949; children—Michael John, Mary Anne, Diana Elizabeth. Prof. voice and opera San Jose (Calif.) State U., 1970—; lectr. opera U. New South Wales, Victoria (Australia) Coll. Arts, Nat. Opera Studio, London, others; Royal Opera House debut as Don José in Carmen; tenor Covent Garden, London, 1953, prin. tenor, 1953-61; San Francisco Opera debut as Lionel in Martha, 1961, prin. tenor, 1961—; guest soloist numerous concerts and operas in Europe, S. Africa, Australia, 1948-77; appeared in 10 operas BBC-TV, 1953-62; command performance for Her Majesty, Queen Elizabeth II, Festival Hall, London, 1957; created leading roles in Turn of the Screw, 1954, Our Man in Havana, 1962, The English Eccentrics, 1963, Troilus and Cressida, 1956, also leading roles in La Boheme, La Traviata, The Magic Flute, Don Giovanni, Madame Butterfly, Rosenkavalier, others; tenor soloist radio and TV broadcasts, 1946-77; recording artist Decca records, Everest records; definitive recording of Peter Grimes, with composer conducting. Served as lt. Australian Army, 1941-44; PTO. Mem. Phi Kappa Phi (cert. for disting. teaching). Clubs: Bohemian, The Family (San Francisco). Home: 1285 Middle Ave Menlo Park CA 94025 Office: Music Dept San Jose State Univ San Jose CA 95192

NIP, WAI-KIT, food technologist; b. Hong Kong, May 5, 1941; s. Chuck-Foon and Jean (Sze) N.; came to U.S., 1974, naturalized, 1981; B.S., Nat. Chung Hsing U., 1962; M.S., Tex. A&M U., 1965, Ph.D., 1969; m. Li Liu, Oct. 31, 1970; children—Jun-Yuh, Jaime. Asso. prof. Nat. Chung Hsing U., 1969-74; research asso. U. Wis., Madison, 1974-76; asst. prof. food sci. and tech. U. Hawaii, 1976-82, asso. prof., 1982—. Mem. World Mariculture Soc., Inst. Food Technologists, Am. Assn. Cereal Chemists, Am. Soc. Hort. Sci., Chinese Assn. Food Sci. and Tech., Phi Tau Sigma. Contbr. articles to profl. jours. Office: 1920 Edmondson Rd Honolulu HI 96822

NIPPA, JURGEN HEINZ, clinical engineer, consultant, b. Berlin, Jan. 9, 1938; came to U.S., 1959, naturalized, 1965; s. Heinz and Jutta J. (Carow) N.; m. Christine I. Köppen, Oct. 30, 1966; 1 son, Paul. B.S. in Physics, cum laude, U. Puget Sound, 1967; M.S. in Physics, U. Hawaii, 1969. Research physicist U. Wash. Sch. Medicine, Seattle, 1969-75; dir. biomed. engring. Tacoma Gen. Hosp., 1975—; instr. physics and math. Bellevue (Wash.) Community Coll., part-time 1969-74. Served with U.S. Army, 1960-63. Mem. Assn. for Advancement Med. Instrumentation (cert. clin. engr.), IEEE, Am. Hosp. Assn., Soc. for Photo-Optical Instrumentation Engrs., Deutsche Gesellschaft für Medizintechnik. Club: Continental (treas. 1971-79, dir.) (Seattle). Contbr. articles on med. physics and biomed. engring. to sci. jours. Home: 209 Stanford Ave Fircrest WA 98466 Office: PO Box 5277 Tacoma WA 98405

NIPPER, JAMES LUTHER, city ofcl.; b. Crisp County, Ga., Sept. 26, 1918; s. Henry Floyd and Lou Tepee (Hall) N.; student U. S.C., 1948; B.A., Ariz. State U., 1972, M.A., 1973; m. Mary Josephine Wilkes, May 11, 1948; children—James Joseph, Scott Wilkes, Lori Kathleen. Enlisted U.S. Army, 1937, commd. 2d lt., 1943, advanced through grades to maj., 1954; mil. police activities, various locations, 1948-52; security officer Hdqrs. 8th U.S.A., Seoul, Korea, 1952-53; comdg. officer Troop Command, Ft. Jackson, S.C., 1954-57; ret., 1957; gen. contractor, Columbia, S.C., 1958-65; hwy. and traffic engring. cons., 1965-70; safety engr. City of Los Angeles, 1973—. Republican party candidate for state senate N.C., 1964, chmn. Rep. party Swain County, N.C., 1964-65. Mem. Am. Soc. Safety Engrs. Episcopalian. Clubs: Sertoma (life), Mason, Shriners. Home: 42 Windjammer Ct Long Beach CA 90803 Office: City Los Angeles 1401 W 6th St Los Angeles CA 90017

NISARGAND, UMESH LAXMAN, cons. engr.; b. Ahmednagar, India, Nov. 7, 1931; s. Laxman G. and Krishnabai (Dange) N.; came to U.S., 1959, naturalized, 1968; M.M.E., Purdue U., 1960; M.B.A., Seattle U., 1975; m. Rudite Zeidaks, July 4, 1964; children—Julie R., Monica L. Specialist engr. Boeing Aircraft Co., Seattle, 1962—; prin. practice engring. UN Assos., Bellevue, Wash., 1970—. Registered profl. engr., Wash., Alaska. Mem. ASME, Common Cause, Beta Gamma Sigma. Clubs: Bellevue Athletic. Home: 14866 NE 11th Pl Bellevue WA 98007

NISHIMOTO, RICHARD YOSHIO, art director/designer; b. Chgo., June 27, 1948; s. Tateo B. and Hisako (Tanaka) N. B.A., Ill. Inst. Tech., 1972; B.A., Art Inst. Chgo., 1974. Advt. mgr./dir. product devel. Kransco Mfg., San Francisco, 1975-76; art dir./art prodn. mgr. Meltzer, Aron & Lemen, San Francisco, 1976-78; art dir. Foote, Cone & Belding, San Francisco, 1978-79; designer/art prodn. mgr. Steven Jacobs Design, Palo Alto, Calif., 1979-80; exec. bd., creative dir. Summit Workshops, Inc., Redwood City, Calif., 1980-82; v.p., creative dir., prin. Quintessential Enterprises Inc., San Carlos, Calif., 1982—; instr. U. Calif., Berkeley, 1978; conductor workshops in field; lectr. in field. Served with USMC, 1968-75. Recipient cert. of achievement and contbn. Summit Workshops Inc., 1982. Mem. Western Art Dirs., Marine Corps Assn., Peninsula Mktg. Assn., U.S. Aikido Fedn., San Francisco Ad Club. Democrat. Buddhist. Art dir./photo editor Metamorphoses Mag., 1982. Office: 2400 Pacific Ave Suite 709 San Francisco CA 94115

NISHIMURA, DENNIS DEAN, lawyer; b. Hilo, Hawaii, Apr. 13, 1950; s. Pete Hideo and Tomoe Tanioka, N.; m. Noela Maile Aloy, Dec. 27, 1975. B.A. in Polit. Sci., Whittier Coll., 1972; J.D., Calif. Western Sch. Law, 1978; LL.M. in Taxation, Washington U., St. Louis, 1979. Assoc., Altman, Dixon & Assocs., Hilo, 1979-81; prin. Altman & Nishimura, Hilo, 1981-82, Dennis Nishimura, atty., Hilo, 1982—. Pres.-elect, legal counsel Nat. Exchange Club of Hilo. Mem. ABA, Hawaii C. of C., Hilo Jaycees (legal counsel). Democrat. Episcopalian. Office: 688 Kinoole St Suite 110A Hilo HI 96720

NISHIMURA, HOWARD ISAMU, accountant; b. Seattle, Aug. 31, 1936; s. Toshimi and Marumi (Hamada) N.; student Los Angeles City Coll., 1955-57; B.S., U. Calif. at Los Angeles, 1961; m. Hideko Omura, Aug. 11, 1963; children—Derek Isamu, Julia Miyuki. Mgr., Kenneth Leventhal & Co., C.P.A.s, Los Angeles, 1961-67; partner Furuta & Nishimura, C.P.A.s, Los Angeles, 1967-76; pres. Nishimura, Kojima & Sy, Los Angeles, 1978-79; commr. City of Los Angeles Community Redevel. Agy., 1978—, treas., 1979-81, chmn., 1982—; mem. community unit for participation in housing and urban devel. City Los Angeles, 1976—; bd. dirs. Skid Row Devel. Corp., 1979—. Chmn., Little Tokyo Community Devel. Adv. Com., 1975-78; pres. So. Calif. Nisei Golf, 1974-78; mem. Nisei Week Festival Com., 1977—, chmn., 1980. C.P.A., Calif. Mem. Am. Inst. C.P.A.s, Calif. Soc. C.P.A.s, Los Angeles-Nagoya Sister City Affiliation, Japan-Am. Soc. So. Calif. (bd. dirs.). Home: 3307 Landa St Los Angeles CA 90039 Office: 500 E 4th St Los Angeles CA 90013

NISKA, MARALIN FAE, singer; b. San Pedro, Calif., Nov. 16; d. William A. and Vera Stott Dice; B.A., UCLA; postgrad. U. So. Calif., Long Beach State Coll.; m. William P. Mullen, May 23, 1970. Debut in opera, 1965; appearances: Met. Opera Nat. Co., 1965-67, N.Y.C. Opera, 1967—, Met. Opera, 1972—, Santa Fe Opera, Chgo. Opera, Tulsa Opera, Fort Worth Opera, Opera Co. Boston, Providence Opera, San Diego Opera, Riverside Opera, Toledo Opera, Dayton Opera, St. Petersburg, Miami, Maggio Musicale, Florence, Italy, Colombia, Bogota; bd. govs. Agma; bd. Young Audiences. Founder, pres. Harbor Democratic Club, San Pedro. Mem. AFTRA, SAG, Am. Guild Mus. Artists, Equity. Home: 32 Cibola Circle Route 7 109 NM Santa Fe NM 87501 Office: Tony Hartmann 250 W 57th St Suite 1128A New York NY 10019

NISSAN, SAMIR ISMAIL, educator; b. Baghdad, Iraq, Apr. 6, 1940; came to U.S., 1963, naturalized, 1973; s. Ismail and Najiba (Nano) N.; B.S., AlHikma U., 1962; M.B.A. (fellow), U. So. Calif., 1965; postgrad. Harvard Sch. of Bus., 1965-66; Ph.D. (fellow), U. Ill., 1971; m. Kathleen Becker, Jan. 25, 1969; children—Tracy Amar, Ramsey Michael, Christina Rajaa, Andrew Basim. Instr., Ind. State U., 1969-70; asst. prof. Bradley U., Peoria, Ill., 1970-73; prof. bus. adminstrn. Gov.'s State U., Park Forest South, Ill., 1973-80, chmn. div. acctg. and fin., 1979-80; prof. acctg. Calif. State U., Chico, 1980— (on leave); fin. cons. Saudi Amoudi Group, a Saudi Co., Jeddah, Saudi Arabia; also cons. C.P.A. Mem. Am. Acctg. Assn., Am. Inst. C.P.A.s, Nat. Assn. Accts., Fin. Mgmt. Assn., Am. Fin. Assn. Roman Catholic. Office: Dept Acctg and Mgmt Sci Calif State U Chico CA 95929

NISSEN, LUANN, interior designer, educator, consultant, author; b. O'Neill, Nebr., Feb. 28, 1947; d. Donald Otto Nissen and Doris Jean (Appleby) N.; m. Howard Barry Goodman, Aug. 13, 1980. B.S., U. Nebr., 1969; M.A., Iowa State U., 1972. Interior designer Leo A Daly Co., internat. architects, Omaha, 1970; asst. instr. interior design Iowa State U., Ames, 1969-71; office mgr., nat. mktg. coordinator Cedric Hartman, Inc., lighting design mfg., Omaha, 1972-73; vis. prof. design Colo. State U., Ft. Collins, 1976; assoc. prof. interior design U. Nev., Reno, 1973—; textbook reviewer in field; chmn. U. Nev. Arts Festival, 1976, 77; graphic design and publicity U. Nev. Centennial, 1974-75, Find Out Fair, 1981; mem. Speakers Bureau, 1976—; mem. planning com. Barrier Free Design workshops, Reno and Las Vegas, 1978. Author: (with Sarah K. Faulkner) Inside Today's Home, 5th edit. Mem. Washoe County (Nev.) Bicentennial Com., 1975-76; mem. Nev. Gov.'s Com. Employment Handicapped 1978; active Sierra Arts Found. Nev. Council on Arts grantee, 1975-77; Nev. Humanities Com. grantee, 1976. Mem. Am. Soc. Interior Designers, Interior Design Educators Council, Am. Assn. Housing Educators, Phi Kappa Phi, Omicron Nu. Office: 100C FHE U Nev Reno NV 89557

NISSLER, PAMELA L., librarian; b. Youngstown, Ohio, Oct. 9, 1945; d. William Marcellus and Norma Jean (Klemm) Loupe; m. Perry Stevens Nissler, Sept. 10, 1977; 1 son, Carl Christian. B.S. in Edn., Bowling Green State U., 1967; M.A. in Librarianship, U. Denver, 1970. Tchr. pub. schs., Pontiac, Mich., 1967-68, Boardman, Ohio, 1968-69; librarian Edwin A. Bemis Public Library, Littleton, Colo., 1970-75, library dir., 1975—; vis. prof. U. Denver. Bd. dirs. Friends of Littleton Library Mus., 1975—; mem. Littleton Cultural Arts Found.; mem. adv. bd. Aurarla Info. Media Tech. Program; mem. Arapahoe County Gerontol. Edn. Council. Mem. ALA, Mountain Plains Library Assn., Colo. Library Assn. (pres. 1979-80), Central Colo. Library System (pres., dir.). Home: 1579 W Briarwood Ave Littleton CO 80120 Office: 6014 S Datura St Littleton CO 80120

NIVEN, JAROLD ROTHROCK, industrial psychologist, management consultant; b. Rocky Ford, Colo., July 2, 1923; s. Harold F. and Viola Lynn Rothrock) N.; m. Elizabeth Wainner, June 12, 1948 (dec.); m. 2d, Elaine Anderson, June 22, 1963; children—Susan, John, Daniel. A.B., U. Denver, 1948; M.S., Purdue U., 1949, Ph.D., 1951. Diplomate Am. Bd. Profl. Psychology. Supr. personnel research Internat. Harvester, Chgo., 1951-56; lectr. Northwestern U., Evanston, Ill., 1952-56; mgr. then corp. dir. personnel research and mgmt. devel. The Boeing Co., Seattle, 1956—; cons. to Peace Corps, 1964-70, State of Wash., 1967-68; adviser Wash. State Legislature, 1964-67; bd. editors Personnel Psychology, 1981—. Bd. dirs. Nat. Council Aging, 1976-80; trustee Leukemia Soc., 1981—; com. chair United Way of King County. Fellow Am. Psychol. Assn., AAAS; mem. Internat. Applied Psychology Assn., Midwestern Psychol. Assn., Western Psychol. Assn., C. of C. (com. chair), Sigma Xi, Lambda Xi Alpha. Republican. Club: Wash. Athletic (Seattle). Contbr. articles to profl. jours. Office: PO Box 3707 Seattle WA 98124

NIX, BARBARA LOIS, real estate exec.; b. Yakima, Wash., Sept. 25, 1929; d. Martin Clayton and Norma (Gunter) Westfield; A.A., Sierra Coll., 1978; m. B.H. Nix, July 12, 1968; children—William Martin Dahl, Theresa Irene Dahl; step-children—Dennis Leon, Denise Lynn. Bookkeeper, office mgr. Lakeport (Calif.) Tire Service, 1966-69, Dr. K.J. Absher, Grass Valley, Calif., 1972-75; real estate sales and office mgr. Rough and Ready Land Co., Penn Valley, Calif., 1976-77, coowner, v.p., sec., 1978—, also of Wildwood West Real Estate and Lake of the Pines Sales. Youth and welfare chmn. Yakima Federated Jr. Women's Club, 1957; den mother Cub Scouts, 1959-60; leader Girl Scouts, 1961-62. Recipient Pres.'s award Sierra Coll., 1973; others. Mem. Penn Valley C. of C., Nevada County Bd. Realtors, Nat. Assn. Realtors, Nat. Assn. Female Execs., St. Mary's Coll. Aux., Sierra Nevada Meml. Hosp. Aux., Nevada County Arts Council. Democrat. Roman Catholic. Clubs: Job's Daus. (life), Lady Elks. Home: 18321 Jayhawk Dr Penn Valley CA 95946 Office: PO Box 191 Rough and Ready CA 95975

NJOKU, ENI GERALD, electrical engineer; b. Ibadan, Nigeria, May 13, 1950; s. Eni and Winifred Olive (Beardsall) N.; B.A., Cambridge U. (Eng.), 1972; M.S., M.I.T., 1974, Ph.D., 1976; m. Wynafred Anna Williams, Dec. 21, 1974 (dec. July 1981). NRC postdoctoral research asso., 1976-77; mem. tech. staff Jet Propulsion Lab., Calif. Inst. Tech., Pasadena, 1977—; sr. lectr. elec. engring. Inst. Mgmt. and Tech., Enugu, Nigeria, 1980-81. Recipient NASA Group Achievement award, 1980, 82. Mem. IEEE, Am. Geophysical Union, AAAS, N.Y. Acad. Scis., Sigma Xi. Contbr. articles to profl. jours. Home: 744 Magnolia Ave Pasadena CA 91106 Office: 168-314 Jet Propulsion Lab 4800 Oak Grove Dr Pasadena CA 91109

NOBE, KENNETH CHARLES, economist, educator; b. Venedy, Ill., Oct. 26, 1930, s. Elmer Fred and Alvine (Froeke) N.; m. Hazel McCullough, Oct. 22, 1949; children—Sandra Lee, Jeffrey, Michael. B.S., So. Ill. U., Carbondale, 1953; M.S., Cornell U., 1954, Ph.D., 1959. Chief, econs. and agrl. br. Havza Engring. Co., Lahore, Pakistan, 1964-66; assoc. prof. dept. econs. Colo. State U., Ft. Collins, 1966-69, prof., chmn. dept., 1969-83, prof., chmn. dept. agrl. and natural resource econs., 1983—; econ. cons. AID, State Dept., 1977, 82, Ford Found., 1980. Served with USAF, 1949-50. Recipient Ill. State Farmer award Future Farmers Am., 1947; Disting. Service award for adminstrv. leadership Colo. State U., 1979. Mem. Am. Econs. Assn., Western Assn. Agrl. Economists, Am. Assn. Agrl. Economists, Internat. Assn. Agrl. Economists, Soil Conservation Soc. Am. Methodist. Contbr. articles to profl. jours. Home: 3510 Terry Ridge Rd Fort Collins CO 80524 Office: Colo State U Fort Collins CO 80523

NOBLE, BARBARA ANNETTE, lawyer, rehabilitation counselor for deaf; b. Crownpoint, N.Mex., May 13, 1943; d. Charles Edmund and Annette (King) N.; B.A. in English and Psychology, UCLA, 1965; postgrad. Calif. State U., Los Angeles, 1967-68; cert. in counseling for the deaf U. Tenn., 1971; J.D., Northrop U., 1977. Bar: Calif. 1977. Disability analyst State of Calif., Los Angeles, 1965-68, rehab. counselor, 1968, rehab. counselor for the deaf and hard of hearing, 1968-78, sr. rehab. counselor for the deaf and hard of hearing, 1976-78; vol. staff atty. So. Calif. Center Law and the Deaf, 1978; dep. atty. gen. State of Calif., 1978—; cons. U.S. Postal Service, 1970-78; cons. Silent Industries, 1973-78. Mem. com. for handicapped Los Angeles City Council, 1979-82; mem. deaf adv. bd. El Camino Coll., 1976-78; mem. adv. com. Northrop U. Law Sch., 1982—. Cert. rehab. counselor. Mem. Nat. Rehab. Assn., Nat. Rehab. Counseling Assn., Greater Los Angeles Council on Deafness, Profl. Rehab. Workers with Adult Deaf, Calif. Bar, Women Lawyers Assn. Los Angeles, Assn. Dep. Attys. Gen., Los Angeles County Bar Assn., Northrop U. Alumni Assn., UCLA Alumni Assn. Office: 3580 Wilshire Blvd Suite 800 Los Angeles CA 90010

NOBLE, CHARLES EDWARD, investment counselor; b. Boston, Sept. 18, 1930; s. Charles A. and Agnes (Von Adelung) N. A.B. cum laude, Harvard U., 1952, M.B.A., 1954. Security analyst Bank of Calif., San Francisco, 1957-58; investment counselor Loomis Sayles, San Francisco, 1958—, v.p., 1968—, mgr. San Francisco Office, 1968—, also dir. Pres., Guardsmen, San Francisco, 1966; bd. dirs. San Francisco Boys Club, 1966—, pres., 1979—; bd. dirs. Laguna Honda Hosp. Vols., 1977—, pres., 1980—; trustee Thacher Sch., 1978—, Children's Hosp. of San Francisco. Served with AUS, 1955-56. Mem. Security Analysts of San Francisco, Bond Club of San Francisco. Episcopalian. Clubs: University, Bohemian, Pacific Union, San Francisco Golf. Home: 1170 Sacramento St San Francisco CA 94108 Office: 2 Embarcadero St San Francisco CA 94114

NOBLE, DAN D., state senator, banker; b. Wahoo, Nebr., 1929; student U. Colo. Sch. Banking, 1960-62, Harvard U. Sr. Bank Officers Seminar; m. Donna Noble; 5 children. With San Miguel Basin State Bank, Norwood, Colo.; mem. Colo. Senate, chmn. state affairs com. 49th and 50th Gen. Assemblies, majority leader 52d Gen. Assembly, 2d session 53d Gen. Assembly, 54th Gen. Assembly. Past mem. Colo. State U. Adv. Council; mem. Adv. Council on Grand Mesa-Uncompahgre Nat. Forest; dir. San Miguel Water Conservancy Dist.; chmn. county ARC; past trustee Colo. 4-H Found. Served with U.S. Army, 1950-52. Mem. Colo. Bankers Assn., Western Colo. Clearing House Assn. Republican. Methodist. Clubs: Masons, Elks, Lions. Office: Box 71 Norwood CO 81423

NOBLE, JOHN ROBERT, investment company executive; b. Manila, June 4, 1921; s. Frederick Handy and Suzanne (Ransley) N.; came to U.S., 1938, naturalized, 1966. m. Georgia Eleanor Faith, Nov. 21, 1942; children—David Douglas, Bonnie Priscilla Noble DeGoey, Cynthia Jean Noble Busby. B.A. magna cum laude, Colgate U., 1942. With Monsanto Chem. Co., St. Louis, 1942-44; spl. engr. Manhattan Dist., Eastman Kodak Co., Oak Ridge, 1944-46; mgr. mktg. Standard Vacuum Oil Co., Bombay, India, 1946-51; gen. ptnr. Investors Research Co., Santa Barbara, Calif., 1955—; pres. Investors Research Fund, Inc., Santa Barbara, 1959—. Bd. dirs. Santa Barbara Symphony, 1962—, also past pres. Served with U.S. Army, 1944-45. Mem. Phi Beta Kappa, Alpha Chi Sigma. Episcopalian. Clubs: Santa Barbara, Santa Barbara Yacht. Author: Behind the Scenes of Money Management, 1962; contbr. to How To Manage Mutual Funds. Office: PO Box 30 Santa Barbara CA 93102

NOBLE, RICHARD LLOYD, lawyer; b. Oklahoma City, Oct. 11, 1939; s. Samuel Lloyd and Eloise Joyce (Millard) N.; A.B. with distinction, Stanford U., 1961, LL.B., 1964. Admitted to Calif. bar, 1964; asso. firm. Cooper, White & Cooper, attys., San Francisco, 1965-67; asso., partner Voegelin, Barton, Harris & Callister, Los Angeles, 1967-70; partner Noble, Campbell & Uhler and predecessor, Los Angeles, also San Francisco, 1970—; dir. Jan-U-Wine Foods, Los Angeles, Gt. Pacific Fin. Corp., Sacramento; lectr. U. So. Calif. Tax Inst., 1970. Treas., Young Republicans of Calif., 1960-62; bd. govs. Thomas Aquinas Coll.; pub. mem. Colo. River Bd. of Calif., 1983—. Recipient Hilmer Oehlman Jr. award Stanford Law Sch., 1962. Mem. Pi Sigma Alpha, Delta Sigma Rho. Clubs: Commercial (San Francisco); Capitol Hill (Washington); Beach and Tennis (Pebble Beach); Jonathan, Stock Exchange (Los Angeles). Contbr. to profl. publs. in field. Home: 2222 Ave of Stars Los Angeles CA 90067 Office: 523 W 6th St Los Angeles CA 90014 also 650 California St San Francisco CA 94108

NOBLE, ROBERT PRICE, microcircuit engr.; b. Dennison, Ohio, Aug. 10, 1918; s. Price William and Mary Gladys (Stowe) N.; student Columbia U., 1938, Ohio State U., 1941, 42, Am. TV Inst., 1948, 49, Hofstra Coll., 1952; m. Marcella Cusack, June 27, 1940; children—Karen, Arlene, Sherry, Scott. Die maker Essex Die Co., N.Y.C., 1946; sta. engr. RCA Communications Inc., N.Y.C. and San Juan, P.R., 1946-47; med. electronics staff Burton Co., Chgo., 1948-49; communications sta. installer Ill. Central R.R., No. Div., Ill., Iowa, 1949; with Sperry Gyroscope Co., Great Neck, N.Y., 1951-54; staff asso. Sandia Nat. Labs., Livermore, Calif., 1954—; instr. Air Corps Tech. Schs., 1942—; traveling lectr. N.M. Acad. Sci., 1960-61. Served with USAAF, 1942-45, U.S. Army, 1949-51. Registered profl. engr., Calif. Mem. Internat. Soc. Hybrid Microcircuits, Nat. Soc. Profl. Engrs. Republican. Methodist. Contbr. articles to profl. jours. Home: 1085 Murrieta Blvd Apt 223 Livermore CA 94550 Office: Sandia Nat Labs PO Box 969 Livermore CA 94550

NOCITA, FRANK EDWARD, psychologist; b. Omaha, Nov. 4, 1944; s. Frank Carl and Yvonne Lorraine (Whipperman) N.; B.A., U. Nebr., Omaha, 1966; M.A. in Theology, Ph.D. in Clin. Psychology, Fuller Theol. Sem. Grad. Sch. Psychology, 1972; m. Diane Mary Hendricks, Jan. 1, 1979. Cert. hypnotherapist. Mem. clin. staff Van Nuys (Calif.) Psychiat. Hosp., 1973—, Glendale (Calif.) Adventist Hosp., 1974-80; dir. psychol. services Van Nuys Psychiat. Hosp., 1974—, mem. exec. com., 1977—; dir. psychol. services Balboa (Calif.) Therapy Center, 1980-81; owner, dir. psychol. services Toluca Lake Psychol. Services, Burbank, Calif., 1978—; mem. profl. staff St. Joseph Med. Center, Burbank, 1981—, Valley Hosp. Med. Ctr., 1983—; tchr. extension div. U. Calif.-Santa Barbara, 1970-71; asso. prof. psychology Fuller Theol. Sem., 1972-74; tchr. extension div. Calif. Luth. Coll., 1977-78; mgmt. cons. Pacific Mut. Life Ins. Co., Burbank, 1977-78. Bd. dirs. Glendale/Burbank Child Guidance Clinic, 1973-79, chmn. personnel and profl. practices com., 1974-79. Mem. Am. Psychol. Assn., Calif. Psychol. Assn., Los Angeles County Psychol. Assn., Nat. Assn. Alcoholic Counselors, Burbank C. of C., Phi Kappa Phi, Psi Chi, Alpha Kappa Delta, Phi Eta Sigma, Omicron Delta Kappa, Lambda Chi Alpha. Office: Toluca Lake Psychol Services PC Suite 202 Toluca Lake Med Center 3808 Riverside Dr Toluca Lake Burbank CA 91505

NOEDING, NICHOLAS JOHN, lawyer; b. Taos, N.Mex., Nov. 4, 1948; s. Otto Thomas and Faye Merett (Seamer) N.; m. Michelle Elizabeth Hadady, May 1, 1980; 1 son, Nicholas John. B.A., U. N.Mex., 1970, J.D., 1973. Admitted to N.Mex., bar, 1973. With Poole, Tinnin and Martin, P.C., Albuquerque, 1973—, v.p., dir., 1977—. Mem. ABA (coms. on labor, law, litigation and adminstrv. law), N.Mex. Bar Assn., Albuquerque Bar Assn. Home: 400 Laguna S W Albuquerque NM 87104 Office: PO Box 1769 Albuquerque NM 87103

NOFFSINGER, EDWARD BRALLIER, psychologist; b. Aurora, Ill., Feb. 21, 1943; s. Harold Brallier and Angeline Josephine (Sterka) N.; B.S., U. Ill., 1966, M.S., 1967; M.S., Calif. State U., San Jose, 1973; Ph.D., Calif. Grad. Inst., 1975, U. Calif., Berkeley, 1977; m. Janet Marie Carder, Aug. 5, 1972. Physicist, Xerox Corp., Rochester, N.Y., summers 1966-67; sr. devel. engr. optics lab. Bell & Howell, Lincolnwood, Ill., 1968-69; project supr. physics dept. Horizons, Inc., Cleve., 1969-71; market planner Fairchild Corp., Palo Alto, Calif., 1971; psychologist psychiatry dept. Permanente Med. Group, Santa Clara, Calif., 1973—. Mem. Am. Psychol. Assn., Calif. Psychol. Assn. Roman Catholic. Contbr. articles to physics and psychology jours. Home: 10131 Hillcrest Rd Cupertino CA 95014 Office: Kaiser Hospital Psychiatry Dept 900 Kiely Blvd Santa Clara CA 95051

NOGUCHI, HIDEO, insurance agency executive; b. Kyoto, Japan, Jan. 17, 1945; s. Tasao and Ishiko (Tsujii) N.; m. Eleanor Kazuko Horii, May 7, 1970; children—Mark H.Y., Mitchell H.Y. B.B.A., U. Hawaii, 1969. Buyer RCA Purchasing Co., Tokyo, 1969-73; ins. specialist Continental Ins. Agy., Honolulu, 1973-82; pres. Noguchi & Assocs., Inc., Honolulu, 1983—; cons. Recipient Nat. New Agt. Leadership award CNA Corp., 1974, Agt. of Yr. award Continental Ins. Agy., annually 1973-81, Key Club award CNA Co., 1975, 79-81. Mem. Nat. Assn. Life Underwriters, Honolulu Assn. Life Underwriters. Home: 3678 Woodlawn Terrace Pl Honolulu HI 96822 Office: 1600 Kapiolani Blvd Box 111 Honolulu HI 96814

NOGUERA, KENNETH JOSEPH, outdoor elec. advt. exec.; b. Oak Park, Ill., July 23, 1955; s. Faust Joseph and Teresita (Escalante) N. Profl. musician, 1973-78; quality control supr. Formost McKesson Corp., Los Angeles, 1978-79; chmn. bd., pres. Belmont Sign Co., Huntington Beach, Calif., 1979-81; chmn. bd., pres. J.H. Limon Enterprises Inc., Anaheim, Calif., 1981—; v.p. King Solomon Mining Corp., 1982—; dir. Country Club Mining Corp. of Utah. Mem. Am. Mgmt. Assn.

NOH, LAIRD, state senator, rancher; m. Kathleen Noh; children—John, Susan. B.S., U. Idaho; M.B.A., U. Chgo. Owner, mgr. Noh Sheep Co.; livestock rep. to Sec. of Agr.; mem. Idaho State Senate. Republican. Office: Idaho State Senate Boise ID 83720*

NOKES, JOHN RICHARD, newspaper editor; b. Portland, Oreg., Feb. 23, 1915; s. James Abraham and Bernice Alfaretta (Bailey) N.; B.S., Linfield Coll., 1936; m. Evelyn Junkin, Sept. 13, 1936; children—Richard Gregory, William Graham, Gail Lee Nokes Hulden, Douglas James, Kathy E. With Portland Oregonian, 1936-82, beginning as copy boy, successively reporter, night city editor, city editor, asst. mng. editor, mng. editor, 1936-74, editor, 1975-82; prof. journalism Linfield Coll., 1972—. Bd. dirs. Portland USO, 1968-72, U.S. Coast Guard Acad. Found., 1972-74, Portland Opera Assn., 1976-78; trustee Linfield Coll., 1977—; pres. Linfield Coll. Alumni Assn., 1940; pres. World Affairs Council Oreg., 1973-74. Served with USNR, 1944-46; comdr. Res. ret. Recipient Disting. Service award Portland Advt. Fedn., 1982. Mem. AP Mng. Editors Assn. (dir. 1974-80), Am. Soc. Newspaper Editors, Portland C. of C., Oreg. Newspapers Pubs. Assn. (Voorhies award 1983), Navy League (pres. Portland council 1969-71), Sigma Delta Chi (pres. Willamette Valley chpt. 1975). Republican. Methodist. Club: Multnomah Athletic (Portland). Author: American Form of Government, 1939; editor Oreg. Edn. Jour., 1943-44. newspaper editor; b. Portland, Oreg., Feb. 23, 1915; s. James Abraham and Bernice Alfaretta (Bailey) N.; B.S., Linfield Coll., 1936; m. Evelyn Junkin, Sept. 13, 1936; children—Richard Gregory, William Graham, Gail Lee Nokes Hulden, Douglas James, Kathy E. With Portland Oregonian, 1936-82, beginning as copy boy, successively reporter, night city editor, city editor, asst. mng. editor, mng. editor, 1936-74, editor, 1975-82; prof. journalism Linfield Coll., 1972—. Bd. dirs. Portland USO, 1968-72, U.S. Coast Guard Acad. Found., 1972-74, Portland Opera Assn., 1976-78; trustee Linfield Coll., 1977—; pres. Linfield Coll. Alumni Assn., 1940; pres. World Affairs Council Oreg., 1973-74. Served with USNR, 1944-46; comdr. Res. ret. Recipient Disting. Service award Portland Advt. Fedn., 1982. Mem. AP Mng. Editors Assn. (dir. 1974-80), Am. Soc. Newspaper Editors, Portland C. of C., Oreg. Newspapers Pubs. Assn. (Voorhies award 1983), Navy League (pres. Portland council 1969-71), Sigma Delta Chi (pres. Willamette Valley chpt. 1975). Republican. Methodist. Club: Multnomah Athletic (Portland). Author: American Form of Government, 1939; editor Oreg. Edn. Jour., 1943-44. Office: 1320 SW Broadway Portland OR 97201

NOKES, MARK ALAN, physicist; b. Houston, Oct. 6, 1947; s. Vernon Leslie and Frances Emma (Nichols) N.; m. Paula Marie McGowan, Nov. 23, 1974. B.A., Rice U., 1969; M.A. in Physics (NIH fellow) U. Tex., 1972; Ph.D. in Applied Physics (NIH fellow), Stanford U., 1978. Electro-optical engr. Systems Control, Inc., Palo Alto, Calif., 1977-79; ind. cons., Palo Alto, 1979; devel. engr. optoelectronics div. Hewlett-Packard Co., Palo Alto, 1979—. Bd. dirs. Briarpatch Coop., Menlo Park, Calif., 1977-81. Mem. Optical Soc. Am., AAAS, Biophys. Soc., Optical Soc. No. Calif., Phi Kappa Phi. Designer laser interferometer with fiber optical probe for measuring submicroscopic vibrations in living systems. Office: 640 Page Mill Rd Palo Alto CA 94304

NOLAN, ARTHUR FRANCIS, marketing executive; b. Warren, Ohio, Nov. 4, 1950; s. Joseph Martin Nolan and Grace Arlene (Calvin) Allison; m. Priscilla Lynn Faulk, Nov. 20, 1977; 1 dau., Marina Patrice. Student, Kent State U., 1969-70, Youngstown State U., 1971-72. Dist. supr. Pickwick Internat. Inc., Los Angeles, 1970-80, advt. mgr., 1980-81; advt. mgr. Pentax Corp., Denver, 1981—; free-lance writer, 1979—. Mem. Denver Advt. Fedn., Bus. Profl. Advt. Assn., Assn. Nat. Advertisers (co-op advt. com. 1981-82). Republican. Home: 4824 E Kentucky St Glendale CO 80222 Office: Pentax Corp 35 Inverness Dr Englewood CO 80112

NOLAN, EDWARD GILLIGAN, psychologist, educator; b. Edinburgh, Scotland, June 20, 1928; s. Patrick and Mary Helen (Gilligan) N. M.A., Edinburgh U., 1948, B.Ed., 1952; M.A., (Psychometric fellow), Princeton U., 1954, Ph.D., 1957. Instr. psychology Rutgers U., Newark, 1954-57; asst. prof. psychology U. N.Mex., 1957-62, prof. behavioral sci., 1965-68, dir. SW mgmt. devel. program, 1965-68; assoc. prof. psychology San Fernando Valley State Coll., Northridge, Calif., 1962-65; prof. organizational psychology U. San Francisco, 1968—, adj. prof. labor mgmt. sch., 1972-78; cons. Calif. Dept. Employment, 1968-75. Bd. dirs. Albuquerque Boys Club, 1960-62; mem. rehab. bd. Marin County (Calif.). Served with Brit. Army, 1950-52. Mem. Am. Psychol. Assn., Western Psychol. Assn., Sigma Xi. Democrat. Roman Catholic. Contbr. articles to profl. and bus. jours. Office: McLaren 218 U San Francisco San Francisco CA 94117

NOLAN, JANIECE SIMMONS, hosp. adminstr.; b. Fort Worth; d. James Coleman and Berenice (Johnson) Simmons; B.A., U. Tex., Austin, 1961, M.A. (fellow), 1963; Ph.D., Tulane U., 1968; M.P.H., U. Calif., Berkeley, 1975; m. Robert Lincoln Nolan, 1972; children—Sheff, Gemini Janiece. Research scientist Tex. Nuclear div. Nuclear, Chgo., Austin, 1963-65; dept. head Gulf South Research Inst., New Orleans, 1968-70; research physiologist VA Hosp., Martinez, Calif., 1970-75, asso. chief staff for research, 1972-73 and adminstrv. trainee, 1973-75; asst. adminstr. Ambulatory Care Services, Univ. Calif. hosps. and clinics, 1975-77; dir. ambulatory care services John Muir Meml. Hosp., Walnut Creek, Calif., 1977-79, asst. adminstr., 1979-80, v.p., 1980—; cons. Nat. Inst. Health, 1969-70. Mem. Contra Costa County Emergency Med. Care Com., 1980—; sect. council rep. Am. Public Health Assn., 1980—. Served to lt. comdr. M.S.C., USNR, 1973—. Decorated Meritorious Unit Commendation medal (Navy); Woodrow Wilson fellow, 1961; recipient W. Glenn Ebersole Merit award 2d pl. Assn. Western Hosps., 1975. Mem. Am. Coll. Hosp. Adminstrs., Am. Physiol. Soc., Am. Hosp. Assn., Western Gerontol. Soc., Health Care Execs. No. Calif., No. Calif. Assos. Phi Beta Kappa, Delta Gamma. Contbr. numerous articles to sci. and adminstrv. jours., including Nature, Jour. AMA. Office: John Muir Meml Hosp 1601 Ygnacio Valley Rd Walnut Creek CA 94598

NOLAN, ROBERT PATRICK, insurance executive; b. Salem, Oreg., Mar. 17, 1951; s. John W. and Helen Lucille (Hannegan) N.; B.A. in Math., U. So. Calif., 1973; teaching credential in secondary edn., 1974; m. Penny Christine Parks, June 28, 1975; 1 dau., Kellie Nicole. Tchr. secondary edn. Redondo Beach (Calif.) Sch. Dist., 1974-75; loss prevention rep. Liberty Mut. Ins. Co., Long Beach, Calif., 1975-77; loss control supr. EBI Cos., Santa Monica, Calif., 1977-80; dir. loss control UniCARE Ins. Co., Irvine, Calif., 1980-83, v.p. loss control, 1983—. Mem. Am. Soc. Safety Engrs. Home: 21582 Cabrosa St Mission Viejo CA 92691 Office: 2361 Campus Dr Irvine CA 92715

NOLAN, SHEILA KAYE, public relations executive, writer/photographer; b. Danville, Va., Aug. 26, 1955; d. Julian and Peggy Ann (Holley) N. B.A., Winthrop Coll, 1977; M. Communications, U. Wash., 1980. Pub. relations specialist Catawba Regional Planning Council, Rock Hill, S.C., 1977-78; communications specialist Berkeley-Charleston-Dorchester Council Govts., Charleston, S.C., 1978; dir. pub. relations Wash. State Dairy Products Commn., Seattle, 1981—; free-lance writer/photographer. Mem. Pub. Relations Soc. Am., Women in Communications, Advt. Club II. Presbyterian.

NOLAN, TIMOTHY JAMES, psychotherapist, cons.; b. Woodburn, Oreg., Aug. 27, 1947; s. Alford Robert and Dorothy Elaine (Rush) N.; m. Dec. 31, 1971. B.S. in Psychology, So. Oreg. State Coll., 1970, M.S., 1971; Ph.D., Internat. Coll., 1977. Cert. Am. Assn. Sex Educators, Counselors and Therapists, 1979—. Counselor, U.S. Bur. Indian Affairs, Salem, Oreg., 1971-72, supervisory counselor, 1972-73; mental health cons., dir. mental health service Choctaw Indian Nation Okla., USPHS Hosp., Talihina, 1973-75; mental health cons., dir. mental health services USPHS Clinic, Riverside, Calif., 1975-79; family therapist Community Psychol. Cons., Riverside, Calif., 1979-83, Nolan-MacAfee Counseling and Therapy, Riverside, 1982—; clinic dir USPHS, 1978-79; nat. chmn. Indian health services Mental Health Br. Data System Com., 1976-79. Served to lt. comdr. USPHS, 1973-79. Recipient awards U.S. Bur. Indian Affairs, 1971, 76, USPHS, 1974, 78. Mem. Am. Psychol. Assn., Internat. Transactional Analysis Assn., Res. Officers Commd. Corps USPHS, Assn. Marriage and Family Therapists, Republican. Clubs: Elks, Sportsman's (Corona, Calif.). Author: Native Americans and the Federal Government-A Symbiosis Affecting Mental Health, 1977, also articles. Office: Nolan and MacAfee 6809 Magnolia Ave Suite 201 Riverside CA 92506

NOLDER, HARRY LESLIE, JR., ret. demographer; b. Los Angeles, Dec. 8, 1912; s. Harry L. and Georgia (Cox) N.; student U. So. Calif., 1932-36. Adminstrv. asst. Surplus Mktg. Adminstrn., U.S. Dept. Agr., Los Angeles, Denver, San Francisco, 1941-43; chief reports and analysis Civilian Food Requirements div. War Food Adminstrn., Washington, 1944-47; regional supr. Bur. Census (11 Western states, Alaska, Hawaii), Los Angeles, 1948-56; cons. demographer and freelance writer, Los Angeles, 1956-78, ret., 1978; dir. Starr Piano Co., Refrigeration Supplies Distbr. Demographic cons., mem. U.S. del. to 1951 London Civil Def. Food Conf. Alt. mem. Los Angeles County Republican Central Com., 1958, mem. 1959-62; mem. Calif. Rep. Central Com., 1962-68. Mem. Am. Statis. Assn., AAAS, Western Govtl. Research Assn., Western History Assn., Westerners Los Angeles Corral, Hist. Soc. So. Calif., Ariz. Hist. Soc., Friends of Huntington Library, Govtl. Adminstrn. Group Los Angeles (pres. 1960-61). Address: 5540 N Entrada Quince Tucson AZ 85718

NOLE, LEE BRUCE, insurance salesman, consultant; b. Cleve., Feb. 9, 1943; s. Ted and Blanche (Ohlbaum) N.; m. Alana Hersholt, May 19, 1974; children—Lauren, Kerry, Jesse; m. 2d, Lois Peck, Jan. 24, 1982. Student UCLA, 1960-61; B.B.A., Woodbury Coll., 1963. Asst. controller J.W. Robinson Co., Los Angeles, 1964-65; asst. v.p. fin. Modern Bakeries, Inc., Culver City, Calif., 1965-69; field underwriter N.Y. Life Ins. Co., Los Angeles, 1969—, mem. agts. adv. com., 1982-83, sec. com., 1983-84; pres., prin. L. Bruce Nole & Assocs., Inc., Encino, Calif., 1979—; cons., workshop leader. Pres., B'Nai B'rith Covenant Fed. Credit Union, 1980—; mem. Beverly Hills (Calif.) Charitable Found., Medallion Group, Cedars Sinai Med. Ctr. Recipient Disting. Service award B'nai B'rith, 1973, Presdl. citations, 1975, 76, Past Pres. Designation Service Acknowledgement, 1977, Commendation Sr. Citizens Ctr. Founding, 1977; Proclamation of Service, Los Angeles County Bd. Suprs., 1977; Lifetime Group Leader award N.Y. Life Ins. Co., 1982. Mem. Life Underwriters Assn. Los Angeles Lodge: B'nai B'rith (Beverly Hills). Jewish. Office: 15760 Ventura Blvd Suite 1808 Encino CA 91436

NOLL, PAUL STANLEY, author, lecturer; b. Seattle, Nov. 27, 1931; s. Mark Daniel and Myra Lee (Crawford) N.; m. Bernice Adena, July 16, 1955; children—Chet Leland, Curt Landon. Student, U. Calif.-Berkeley, 1954. Data processing tng. dir. Pacific Telephone, San Francisco, 1953-78; pres. Paul Noll & Assocs., Springfield, Oreg., 1978—. Bd. dirs. Quality in Software and Leadership Devel., Waldwick, N.J., 1982-83; deacon First Bapt. Ch., Springfield, Oreg., 1980-83. Served with U.S. Army, 1949-52. Mem. Data Processing Mgmt. Assn. Republican. Author: Structured Programming for the Cobol Programmer, 1977; Structured Programming Cookbook, 1978; Structured ANS Cobol, Part 1, 1979, Part 2, 1980. Home and office: 750 Royaldel Springfield OR 97477

NOLLENBERGER, JAMES WALTER, consultant engineering firm executive; b. Phila., Apr. 17, 1945; s. Walter G. and Viola M. (Vehkomakki) N.; m. Jan Ann Utterback, Oct. 27, 1947; children—Nicole, Kurt. B.S., U. Iowa, 1967. Registered profl. engr., Colo., Wyo. Engr., Black & Veatch, Cons. Engrs., Denver, 1970-73, project engr., 1973-79, project mgr., 1979—; designer water, sewerage treatment facilities, 1970—. Served to 1st lt. USMCR, 1967-70. Decorated Bronze Star medal. Mem. ASCE, Am. Water Works Assn. Republican. Presbyterian. Office: Black & Veatch Suite 400 12075 E 45th Ave Denver CO 80239

NOMURA, ABRAHAM MICHAEL YOZABURO, physician; b. Honolulu, July 23, 1939; s. George G. and Kaneyo Nomura; B.S., John Carroll U., 1962; M.D., Loyola U., Chgo., 1966; M.P.H., Johns Hopkins U., 1972, Dr.P.H., 1974; m. Susan Hitomi Feb. 20, 1972; children—Liane Miyoko, Ryan Yoichi. Intern medicine Michael Reese Med. Center, Chgo., 1966-67; resident in preventive medicine Johns Hopkins Hosp., 1971-74; practice medicine specializing in epidemiology, 1974—; dir. Japan-Hawaii cancer study, Kuakini Med. Center, Honolulu, 1976—; epidemiologist Cancer Center of Hawaii, U. Hawaii, Honolulu, 1974—, prof. Sch. Public Health, 1982—. Served with USN, 1967-69. Nat. Cancer Inst. grantee, 1976—. Diplomate Am. Bd. Preventive Medicine. Assoc. editor: Am. Jour. Epidemiology, 1982—. Contbr. articles on research in gastrointestinal and breast cancer to profl. jours. Home: 486 Luakini St Honolulu HI 96817 Office: 347 N Kuakini Honolulu HI 96817

NONG, painter, sculptor; b. Seoul, Korea, Oct. 10, 1930; came to U.S., 1952, naturalized, 1958. Painter, sculptor; one-man exhbns. include: Ft. Lauderdale (Fla.) Mus. Arts, Santa Barbara (Calif.) Mus. Art and E.B. Crocker Art Gallery (Sacramento), 1965, Ga. Mus. Art, Athens, El Paso Mus. Art, 1967, Galerie Vallombreuse, Berritz, France, 1970, Nat. Mus. History, Taipei, Taiwan, Nihonbashi Gallery, Tokyo, and Shinsegye Gallery, Seoul, 1971, Nat. Mus. Modern Art, Seoul, San Francisco Zool. Garden, 1975, Choon Chu Gallery, Seoul, 1982, others; group exhbns. include: Nat. Collection Fine Arts, Smithsonian Instn. and Mus. Fine Arts, Springfield, Mass., 1961, Denver Art Mus., 1965, major salons, Paris, 1969-77, San Francisco Mus. Art, 1972; represented in permanent collections E.B. Crocker Art Gallery, Nat. Mus. History, Taipei, Musee National des Beaux-Arts, Monte Carlo, Instituto de Cultura Puertoriquena, San Juan, Nat. Gallery Modern Art, New Delhi, Asian Art Mus. San Francisco, Nat. Mus. Modern Art and Nat. Mus., Seoul, Govt. of Peru, Govt. of People's Republic of China, Santa Barbara Mus. Art, Consulate Gen. Rep. of Korea, San Francisco, Presdl. Palace, Seoul, Anchorage Hist. and Fine Arts Mus., others; chmn. Nong Corp., San Francisco. Chmn., San Francisco-Seoul Sister City Com.; mem. Asian Art Commn., City and County of San Francisco. Served with U.S. Army and USAF, 1956-60. Recipient citations State of Calif., Republic of Korea; proclamation City and County of San Francisco. Mem. Art Soc. Republic of China (hon.). Patentee chest of drawers and bldg. Home: 999 Green St #2701 San Francisco CA 94133

NOONE, SHERRY E., data processing mgr.; b. Miami, Fla., Aug. 16, 1940; d. Edward Frank and Elizabeth Martha (Shipley) Blyden; B.A., UCLA, 1970. Systems programmer TRW Def. and Space Systems, Redondo Beach, Calif., 1972-77; systems programming mgr. Transamerica Info. Services, Los Angeles, 1977—. Office: 1149 S Broadway Ave Los Angeles CA 90015

NOORDA, LEON ROY, podiatrist; b. Salt Lake City, Dec. 29, 1936; s. Hilburtus and Anna Albertina (Sieverts) N.; student U. Utah, 1960-62; B.S., Brigham Young U., 1965; B.A., Calif. Coll. Podiatric Medicine, 1966, D.Podiatric Medicine, 1969; m. Katherine Keller, Mar. 17, 1978; children—Katrina, Nicole; children by previous marriage—Mitchel, Matthew, Lorin, Jameson, Julia. Practice podiatry, Las Vegas, 1969—; chief podiatry sect. Womens Hosp., 1975—; cons. VA; mem. Nev. Bd. Podiatry, 1976—, pres., 1976-80, sec., 1980—; clin. instr. Calif. Coll. Podiatric Medicine, 1971—. Served with U.S. Army, 1963. Mem. Nev. Podiatry Soc. (pres.), So. Nev. Podiatry Assn. (past pres.). Republican. Mormon. Home: 4917 Jay Ave Las Vegas NV 89106 Office: 4660 S Eastern St Suite 107 Las Vegas NV 89109

NOOT, ARIE, marketing executive; b. Amsterdam, Netherlands, May 28, 1947; s. Arie and Antje J. (Ylst) N. B.S., Brigham Young U., 1976, M.B.A., 1976. Mktg. mgr. Proctor & Gamble, Cin., 1977, Hunt Wesson Foods, Fullerton, Calif., 1977-79, Coca Cola Foods, Houston, 1979-81; dir. mktg. Bumble Bee Seafoods, Castle & Cooke, San Diego, 1981—.

NORBERG, GUNNAR, travel agency executive; b. Kenora, Ont., Can., Feb. 4, 1907; s. Nils Albert and Thilda (Osterberg) N.; brought to U.S., 1908, naturalized, 1944; m. Barbara Drew Collins, Sept. 5, 1936 (dec. Aug. 1972); children—Eric Gunnar, Karin Collins; m. 2d, Wies H. Christiansen, June 24, 1973. Student Stanford U., intermittently 1926-31. Office boy, cashier, chief clk. operating dept. Coast div. S.P. Co., 1925-35; creator, editor College Forum mag., 1931; columnist Hearst morning papers, Pacific Coast, 1931; contbg. editor Penguin mag., 1932; asst. mng. editor Fawcett Publs., 1935-36; asso. editor Screen Guide, 1936; asst., asso., mng. editor Radio Guide, 1936-37; 1st editor Click, 1937; assoc. editor Electrical Week, 1938, Outdoor Life, 1939, Vocational Trends, 1940; owner, operator Norberg Travel Service, agy., from 1941. Sec., Carmel (Calif.) Taxpayers Assn., 1957-58; councilman City of Carmel, 1958-62, 64-68, 72-80, vice mayor, 1972-76, mayor, 1976-80; chmn. Monterey County (Calif.) Conf. Mayors, 1976-79; dir. Carmel Town Hall, 1950-52; founder chmn. Main St. League, 1961—, Monterey County Coop. Council, 1959-61; gen. chmn. Carmel 50th Anniversary Celebration Year, 1966; pres. Monterey Peninsula Republican Men's Club, 1961, 64-65; producer Shakespeare plays Carmel's Forest Theater, 1971-73; pres. Forest Theater Guild, 1972-73; v.p. Carmel Area Coalition, 1971-78. Served from pvt. to cpl. AUS, 1943-45; radio news writer Office Inter-Am. Affairs during formation of UN, 1945. Republican. Clubs: Commonwealth (San Francisco); Rotary (treas. 1954-59). Author: The Private Norberg Story, 1981; contbr. short stories and articles to popular mags.; columnist Carmel Pine Cone, 1970-75, 82-83. Home: 8th and Dolores Sts PO Box 1147 Carmel CA 93921

NORD, PAUL ELLIOTT, accountant; b. Carona, N.Y., Mar. 22, 1936; s. Abe and Rose (Guss) N.; m. Marcia B. Gross, June 13, 1965; children—Howard, Aimee, Samuel. Student U. Utah, 1952-56; B.A., LaSalle Extension Inst., 1966. C.P.A., Calif. Staff acct. Robinson, Nowell & Co. (merged with Muncy McPherson & Co., Muncy McPherson McCune Dieckman 1967), 1966-73, ptnr., 1973-81, mng. ptnr., 1981—. Served with U.S. Army, 1957-58, 61-62. Mem. Am. Inst. C.P.A.s (acctg. standards exec. com. 1979-81), Calif. Soc. C.P.A.s (chmn. sub-com. acctg. principles 1981-83), C.P.A. Assocs., Mensa. Jewish.

NORDGAARDEN, LARRY E., optometrist; b. Cut Bank, Mont., July 7, 1956; s. Earl Chester and Dorene Elizabeth (Taylor) N.; m. Carol Diane Campbell, Aug. 28, 1982. Student Mont. State U., 1974-78; B.S., So. Calif. Coll. Optometry, 1980, O.D. cum laude, 1982. Lic. optometrist, Calif., Idaho. Gen. practice optometry, Santa Barbara, Calif., 1982—. Mem. Santa Barbara Optometric Soc., Tri-County Optometric Soc., Calif. Optometric Assn., Am. Optometric Assn., Beta Sigma Kappa, Omega Delta, Phi Eta Sigma, Psi Chi, Phi Kappa Phi. Clubs: Sons of Norway, Elks (Cut Bank, Mont.). Contbr. in field. Office: 25 E Canon Perdido St Santa Barbara CA 93101

NORDHOLM, GREGORY EYNON, naval architect; b. Bethesda, Md., Aug. 16, 1952; s. Eric Gregory and Lee Ellen (Eynon) N. B.S. in Naval Architecture and Marine Engring., U. Mich., 1976. Registered profl. engr., Wash. State. Naval architect Glosten Assocs., Seattle, 1976-82; v.p., chief naval architect Jensen Maritime Cons., Seattle, 1982—. Mem. Soc. Naval Architects and Marine Engrs. (assoc.), Soc. Small Craft Designers. Co-designer 1st U.S. built, non-subsidized factory trawler; co-designer floating flipping constrn. berth. Office: 4215 21st Ave W Seattle WA 98199

NORDIN, PAUL, communication satellite system engr.; b. Kansas City, Mo., Feb. 12, 1929; s. Paul and Marguerite Edith (Desmond) N.; A.A., Riverside Coll., 1951; A.B., U. Calif., Berkeley, 1956, M.A., 1957, Ph.D. in Nuclear Physics, 1961; m. Barbara Boardman, Mar. 14, 1953 (div. Feb. 1969); children—Sandra, Paul III. Sr. scientist Aeronautronic Ford, Newport Beach, Calif., 1961-63; mem. tech. staff Aerospace Corp., San Bernardino, Calif., 1963-68, TRW Def. and Space Systems Group,

Redondo Beach, Calif., 1968-81, Las Cruces, N.Mex., 1981—. Served with USCG, 1946-48. Mem. Am. Phys. Soc., AAAS, Phi Beta Kappa, Sigma Xi. Home: 1841 Embassy Dr Apt 4 Las Cruces NM 88005 Office: TRW DSSG White Sands Ground Terminal PO Box 2827 Las Cruces NM 88004

NOREEN, TERRY GENE, health and safety consultant; b. Walla Walla, Wash., May 21, 1946; s. Arthur Sanford and Norma Jean (Slater) N.; A.S., Grossmont Coll., 1974; B.A., San Diego State U., 1976; M.S., Portland State U., 1980; m. Linda Lou Mays, May 2, 1965 (div. 1982); children—Holly, Tina, Terry Gene. Dir. data communications equipment Naval Communications Sta., San Diego, 1972-76; health and safety specialist Tidewater Barge Lines, Vancouver, Wash., 1976-82; health and safety cons. to marine and gen. industry, 1982—. Mem. Clark County Sheriff Res., 1981. Served with USN, 1963-71. Cert. hazard control mgr.; lic. tankerman U.S. Mcht. Marine. Mem. Oil Chem. and Atomic Workers Union (shop steward 1978-80, health and safety steward 1979-82), Columbia River Boatmans Union (sec. 1977-78), Portland Shipyard Safety Council, Am. Soc. Safety Engrs., Nat. Fire Protection Assn., Am. Public Health Assn., Nat. Safety Mgmt. Soc. Mormon. Home: 14917 NE 24th St Vancouver WA 98664 Office: 7622 NE 47th Ave Vancouver WA 98661

NOREM, ALLAN GORDON, aerospace engineer; b. Provost, Alta., Can., Nov. 14, 1920; s. Roy and Edith Helen (Lockhart) N.; m. Joyce Drover Young, Mar. 27, 1952; children—Eric Roy, Gary Allan, Nancy J. B.S. in Engring. Physics, U. Alta., Edmonton, 1950; M.S. Stanford U., 1951, Ph.D. in Engring. Mechanics, 1953. Mem. tech. staff Bell Telephone Labs., Murray Hill, N.J., 1953-55; chief structures dept. Aerophysics Devel. Corp., Santa Barbara, Calif., 1955-59; mem. tech. staff Inst. for Def. Analyses, Washington, 1959-61; dir. vehicle integrity subdiv. Aerospace Corp., Los Angeles, 1961—; cons. Nat. Materials Adv. Bd., 1961—. Served to capt. RCAF, 1941-46. Fellow AIAA (assoc.); mem. Inst. Environ. Scis. (sr.). Club: Los Verdes Men's Golf and Country. Home: 26229 Barkstone Dr Rancho Palos Verdes CA 90274 Office: PO Box 95085 Los Angeles CA 90045

NOREN, CLARENCE MARTIN, insurance company executive; b. Tinley Park, Ill., Sept. 15, 1921; s. Frank Martin and Hanna Elizabeth (Dalman) N.; m. Lillian Therese Strandin, Aug. 27, 1949; children—Gary M., Gregory M., Margit E. B.A., U. Wash., 1949. Copywriter, account exec. Cole & Weber Advt. Agy., Seattle, 1949-53; with Safeco Corp., Seattle, 1954—, asst. v.p. mktg. communications, 1975—. Served with USN, 1942-46, 50-52. Mem. Ins. Advt. Conf., Ret. Officers Assn., Pi Kappa Alpha, Alpha Delta Sigma. Republican. Lutheran. Clubs: Masons, Lions. Home: 3008 SW Camano Dr Camano Island WA 98292 Office: Safeco Ins Safeco Plaza Seattle WA 98185

NORFLEET, MARY ANN, psychologist, educational administrator; b. Wichita, Kans.; d. D.L. and Fern C. Warburton. B.S., U. Kans., 1964, M.S., 1965; Ph.D., U. Oreg., 1969. Staff psychologist Agnew State Hosp., San Jose, Calif., 1969-72; clin. psychologist, dir. biofeedback North County Community Mental Health Clinic, Palo Alto, Calif., 1972-80; mem. health team study group Stanford U., 1974-76; dir. clin. evaluation and research Bay Area Pain Center, O'Connor Group, San Jose, 1979-81; v.p., dean acad. affairs Palo Alto Sch. Profl. Psychology, 1978—. Fellow Am. Orthopsychiat. Assn.; mem. Internat. Assn. for Study of Pain, Psychosomatic Medicine Soc., Am. Psychol. Assn., Santa Clara County Psychol. Assn. (past pres.), Sigma Xi, Psi Chi. Clubs: 99's, West Valley Flying. Office: 555 Middlefield Rd Palo Alto CA 94301

NORGAARD, RICHARD BRUCE, economist, educator, consultant; b. Washington, Aug. 18, 1943; s. John Trout and Marva Dawn (Andersen) N.; m. Marida Jane Fowle, June 19, 1965 (div.); children—Kari Marie, Marc Anders. B.A. in Econs., U. Calif.-Berkeley, 1965; M.S. in Agrl. Econs. Oreg. State U., 1967; Ph.D. in Econs., U. Chgo., 1971. Instr. Oreg. Coll. Edn., 1967-68; asst. prof. agrl. and resource econs. U. Calif.-Berkeley, 1970-76, assoc. prof., 1976-77, 80—; project specialist Ford Found., Brazil, 1978-79; cons. Ford Found., Calif. Dept. Water Resources, Pub. Interest Econs., Ind. Petroleum Producers of Calif., Plan Sierra Dominican Republic. Active civil rights, environ. and peace orgns. Mem. AAAS, Am. Econs. Assn., Fedn. Am. Scientists, Assn. Envrion. and Resource Econs. Contbr. numerous articles to acad. jours. Home: 1198 Keith Ave Berkeley CA 94708 Office: 207 Giannini Hall U Calif Berkeley CA 94708

NORMAN, GARY REEVE, safety engr.; b. Provo, Utah, Mar. 26, 1939; s. Albert Reeve and Duluth M. (Peterson) N.; student Snow Coll., 1957-58; B.S., Brigham Young U., 1962; m. Susan Ann Bush, Sept. 22, 1959; children—Douglas, Russell, Wendi, Lauri, Nancy, Patricia, Karen, Andrea, Deanna, Richard. Health and safety engr. Lawrence Radiation Lab., Livermore, Calif., 1967-70; safety engr. Kennecott Copper Corp., Bingham Mine, Utah, 1970-71; dir. safety and security NL Industries, Salt Lake City, 1971-75; safety supr. Alyeska Pipeline Service Co., Anchorage, Alaska, 1975-77; mgr. radiation safety Exxon Nuclear Idaho Co., Idaho Falls, 1977-81; mgr. safety ops. EG&G Idaho, Inc., Idaho Falls, 1981—. Active Boy Scouts Am. Registered profl. engr., Calif.; cert. safety profl. Mem. Am. Soc. Safety Engrs., Am. Indsl. Hygiene Assn., Health Physics Soc. Republican. Mem. Ch. of Jesus Christ of Latter-day Saints. Home: Route 1 Box 355A Shelley ID 83274 Office: PO Box 1625 Idaho Falls ID 83415

NORMAN, JOHN BARSTOW, JR., designer, educator; b. Paloa, Kans., Feb. 5, 1940; s. John B. and Ruby Maxine (Johnson) N.; B.F.A., U. Kans., 1962, M.F.A., 1966; m. Roberta Jeanne Martin, June 6, 1967; children—John Barstow III, Elizabeth Jeanne. Designer and illustrator Advt. Design, Kansas City, Mo., 1962-64; asst. instr. U. Kans., Lawrence, 1964-66; art dir. Hallmark Cards, Inc., Kansas City, Mo., 1966-69; instr. dept. art U. Denver, 1969-73, asst. prof., 1973-78, assoc. prof., 1978—, Disting. prof., 1980, chmn. design dept.; design cons. Mo. Council Arts and Humanities, 1966-67; cons. designer Rocky Mountain Bank Note Corp., Denver, 1971—; one man shows include: Gallery Cortina, Aspen, Colo., 1983; commd. works include: Jedda, Saudi Arabia, Synegistics Corp., Denver, Gillette (Wyo.) Pub. Library; tech. cons. Denver Art Mus., 1974—; adv. and cons. to Jefferson County (Colo.) Sch. System, 1976—; chmn. Design and Sculpture Exhibition, Colo. Celebration of the Arts, 1975-76; design exhbn. Denver Art Mus., 1974-75; work represented in film collection Mus. Modern Art, N.Y.C. Chmn. arts and scis. adv. com. Denver public sch. system, 1976-77, chmn. arts and scis. adv. bd. career edn., 1976-77. Recipient Silver Medal award N.Y. Internat. Film and Video Competition, 1976; Design awards Council Advancement and Support of Edn., 1969, 71, 73, 76. Mem. Art Dirs. Club Denver (6 Gold medal awards 1974-82), Univ. Art Dirs. Assn. Home: PO Box 302 751 Willow Lake Dr Franktown CO 80116 Office: School of Art 2121 E Asbury St U Denver Denver CO 80208

NORMAN, JOHN EDWARD, petroleum landman; b. Denver, May 22, 1922; s. John Edward and Ella (Warren) N.; m. Hope Sabin, Sept. 5, 1946; children—J. Thomas, Gerould W., Nancy E., Susan G., Douglas E. B.S.B.A., U. Denver, 1949, M.B.A., 1972. Clk., bookkeeper Capitol Life Ins. Co., Denver, 1945-46; salesman Security Life and Accident Co., Denver, 1947; bookkeeper Central Bank and Trust Co., Denver, 1947-50; automobile salesman H.A. Hennies, Denver, 1950; petroleum landman Continental Oil Co. (name changed to Conoco Inc. 1979), Denver, 1950—. Lectr. pub. lands Colo. Sch. Mines, 1968—; lectr. mineral titles and landmen's role in oil industry Casper Coll., 1969-71. Mem. Casper Mcpl. Band Commn., 1965-71, mem. band, 1961-71, mgr., 1968-71; former musician, bd. dirs. Casper Civic Symphony; former bd. dirs. Jefferson Symphony, performing mem., 1972-75. Served with AUS, World War II. Mem. Am. (dir. at large, chmn. publs. for regional dir.), Wyo. (pres.), Denver assns. petroleum landmen, Rocky Mountain Oil and Gas Assn. (pub. lands com. 1981—). Episcopalian (mem. choir, vestryman, past dir. acolytes). Club: Elks. Home: 2710 S Jay St Denver CO 80227 Office: Conoco Inc 555 17th St Denver CO 80202

NORMAN, WILLIAM J., physician, state senator; b. Duluth, Minn., Apr. 2, 1922; M.D., Marquette U.; m. Laura; 3 children. Resident in neurology U. Minn.; practice medicine specializing in neurology, Missoula, Mont.; mem. Mont. Ho. of Reps., 1971-74, Mont. Senate, 1975—. Served with U.S. Army, World War II. Democrat. Office: 440 Connell Ave Missoula MT 59801*

NORRIS, CHALMERS GAIL, state ofcl.; b. Muncy, Pa., Aug. 17, 1931; s. Chalmers Gail and Margaret Henrietta (Shue) N.; B.S.Ed., Shippensburg State Coll., 1957; A.M. in Govt., George Washington U., 1961; m. Reiko Takeuchi, Apr. 5, 1953; 1 son, Jeffrey Allen. Tchr. social studies, pub. high sch., Middleburg, Pa., 1956-57; mgmt. intern, fin. mgmt. analyst USPHS, 1957-58; program mgmt. officer U.S. Office Edn., Washington, 1958-61, spl. asst. to dep. commr., 1963-64, chief coll. facilities br. and dir. div. coll. facilities, 1964-68; adminstrv. analyst Arlington County (Va.) Sch. Bd., 1962-63; in various planning and budget positions Pa. State U., 1968-72, dir. planning, budget officer, 1972-78; exec. coordinator Wash. State Council for Postsecondary Edn., Olympia, 1978-82; assoc. commr. Utah State Bd. Regents, Salt Lake City, 1982—. Bd. dirs. Nat. Center for Higher Edn. Mgmt. Systems, 1978—; Wash. State mem. Edn. Commn. of States, 1979-82. Served with U.S. Army, 1951-53, to lt. Med. Service Corps, 1961-62. Recipient Superior Service award Dept. HEW, 1968. Mem. State Higher Edn. Fin. Officers, Am. Assn. Higher Edn., Am. Soc. Public Adminstrn., Assn. Instl. Research, Soc. Coll. and Univ. Planning, Phi Delta Kappa. Methodist. Office: 307 E South Temple Suite 201 Salt Lake City UT 98504

NORRIS, GARY ARTHUR, traffic engr.; b. Bellingham, Wash., Mar. 7, 1950; s. James Carol and Joy Loraine (Elerding) N.; m. Dariel Lynn Brady, Aug. 12, 1973; children—James, Rebeccah, Jeffrey, Christian. Student Western Wash. U., Bellingham, 1968-70; B.C.E., U. Wash., 1973, M.C.E., 1977. Registered profl. engr., Wash. Transp. planner engring. dept. City of Seattle, 1973-74; transp. engr. City of Bellevue (Wash.), 1975-80; traffic engr. City of Renton (Wash.), 1980—. Organist, Rose Hill Presbyn. Ch. U.S. Dept. Transp., Fed. Hwy. Adminstrn. Hwy. Safety scholar, 1974-75. Mem. Inst. Transp. Engrs. (sec.-treas. Wash. sect.).

NORRIS, HAROLD GURNEY, supermarket executive; b. Chico, Calif., Sept. 10, 1938; s. Robert E. and Lillian M. (Kubic) N.; grad. high sch.; m. Betty J. Schaffer, June 1, 1974; children—Robert P., Kevin S., Kathryn M. Store dir. Albertsons Inc., Boise, Idaho, 1959-74; owner Esparto Supermarket (Calif.), 1975-77; pres., owner Foods Etc., Inc., Clearlake, Calif., 1977—; chmn. Clearlake Nat. Bank. Served with USMC, 1956-57. Named Rotarian of Yr., 1979-80. Mem. No. Calif. Grocers Assn. (dir. div.), No. Calif. Ind. Grocers Assn. Clubs: Rotary, Elks. Office: PO Box 4059 Clearlake CA 95422

NORRIS, JAMES WARLAUMONT, machinery co. exec., state senator; b. Cheyenne, Wyo., Apr. 15, 1930; s. William Arthur and Ethel (Warlaumont) N.; B.S. in Commerce, U. Wyo., 1953, LL.B., 1961. Pres., The Timberline Corp., Cheyenne, Wyo., 1956—; admitted to Wyo. bar, 1961; asso. firm Pattno & Norris, Attys., Cheyenne, 1961-63; pres. Wortham Machinery Co., Cheyenne, 1968—; mem. Wyo. Senate, 1975—. Mem. Laramie County Planning and Zoning Commn., 1964-74. Served to 2d lt. USAF, 1951-53. Mem. Am. Bar Assn., Wyo. Bar Assn., Laramie County Bar Assn., Am. Legion, VFW. Democrat. Roman Catholic. Club: K.C. Home: 3408 Carey Ave Cheyenne WY 82001 Office: PO Box 349 Cheyenne WY 82001

NORRIS, JOHN STEVEN, constrn. co. exec.; b. Chgo., Apr. 25, 1943; s. Norris Dale and Olive (Grissinger) N.; B.A., U. Ariz., 1967; B.F.T., Am. Grad. Sch. Internat. Mgmt., 1968; m. Susan Jean Armstrong, May 3, 1975; children—Lindsey Jean, Whitney Ann. Inspection officer Citicorp., Brazil, Colombia, Mexico, 1968-72, asst. cashier, N.Y.C., 1972-74; pres., gen. mgr. Phoenix Athletic Club, 1974-76; bus. mgr. Phoenix Pub. Inc., 1976-77; project mgr. Environ. Constrn. Co., Phoenix, 1977-79; pres. AGN Devel. Corp., Phoenix, 1979—, Valley View Realty, Inc.; exec. v.p., sec. RGW Investment Co., Inc. Republican. Mem. Christian Ch. Home: 1138 E Redfield Rd Phoenix AZ 85022 Office: 1130 E Missouri Suite 700 Phoenix AZ 85014

NORRIS, KENNETH STAFFORD, biologist, educator; b. Angkor Wat, Cambodia, Aug. 11, 1924; s. Robert DeWitt and Jessie Matheson Norris; m. Phyllis Mayne Strout, Feb. 28, 1953; children—Susan, Nancy, Barbara, Richard. B.A., UCLA, 1948, M.A., 1951; Ph.D., Scripps Inst. Oceanography, 1959. Curator, Marineland of the Pacific, Los Angeles, 1953-60; dir. Oceanic Inst., Hawaii, 1968-71; prof. natural history UCLA, 1968-72; dir. Coastal Marine Lab., U. Calif., Santa Cruz, 1972-74, chairperson Environ. Studies Bd., 1977-79, asso. dir. Inst. Marine Resources, 1972-76, dir. environ. field program, 1978—; founder Hawaii Environ. Simulation Lab., 1970; U. Calif. Natural Land and Water Res. System; research asso. marine mammalogy Los Angeles County Mus. Natural History, 1969—. Mem. Gov.'s Com. to Prepare a Program for Preservation of Sci. Areas, Hawaii, 1969-70. Served to lt. (j.g.) USN, 1944-47; PTO. Recipient Mercer best research award, 1963, 64, Man of Year award Am. Cetacean Soc., 1976. Fellow Calif. Acad. Scis. (Fellows medal for marine mammal studies 1977), Am. Fisheries Soc., AAAS, Los Angeles County Mus.; mem. Am. Soc. Mammalogists, Nat. Wildlife Fedn., Ecol. Soc. Am., Ocean Research and Edn. Soc. (chmn. adv. com. 1976—), Soc. Marine Mammalogy (1st internat. pres. 1982), Nat. Parks Assn., Soc. Study of Evolution, Western Soc. Naturalists, Am. Soc. Ichthyologists and Herpetologists (Stoye award 1951, bd. govs. 1965-66), Am. Mus. Natural History, Am. Inst. Biol. Scis., World Population Council, Brain Research Inst. (award 1966), Biol. Instrumentation Council, Herpetologists League (pres. 1964), Friends of Sea Otter (adv. com. 1973—), Sigma Xi. Democrat. Contbr. numerous articles on marine biology and ecology to sci. jours.; editor-in-chief First Internat. Symposium of Cetacean Research, 1966. Home: 1987 Smith Grade Santa Cruz CA 95060 Office: Environmental Field Program U Calif Santa Cruz CA 95064

NORRIS, NANCY ELIZABETH, oil company executive; b. Phoenix, Oct. 20, 1959; d. Robert Earl and Edith Amelia (Olsen) N. B.B.A. in Mktg. and Mgmt., Okla. State U., 1981. Purchasing analyst Koch Industries, Wichita, 1981-82, West Coast refined products scheduler and trader, Long Beach, Calif., 1982—. Mem. Nat. Assn. Female Execs., Delta Delta Delta. Republican. Presbyterian.

NORRIS, WILLIAM ALBERT, judge; b. Turtle Creek, Pa., Aug. 30, 1927; s. George and Florence (Clive) N.; student U. Wis., 1945; B.A., Princeton U., 1951; J.D., Stanford U., 1954; m. Merry Wright, Nov. 23, 1947; children—Barbara, Donald, Kim, Alison. Admitted to Calif. and D.C. bars, 1955; asso. firm Northcutt Ely, Washington, 1954-55; law clk. to Supreme Ct. Justice William O. Douglas, Washington, 1955-56; sr. mem. firm Tuttle & Taylor, Inc., Los Angeles, 1956-80; circuit judge U.S. Ct. Appeals, 9th Circuit, Los Angeles, 1980—; spl. counsel Pres.' Kennedy's Com. on Airlines Controversy, 1961; mem., v.p. Calif. State Bd. Edn., 1961-67. Trustee, Calif. State Colls., 1967-72; pres. Los Angeles Bd. Police Commrs., 1973-74; Democratic nominee for atty. gen. State of Calif., 1974; founding pres. bd. trustees Mus. Contemporary Art of Los Angeles, 1979—; trustee Craft and Folk Art Mus., Los Angeles, 1979—. Served with USN, 1945-47. Home: 315 S June St Los Angeles CA 90020 Office: 312 N Spring St Rm 1653 Los Angeles CA 90012

NORRISS, NORMA G., clin. psychologist; b. Bronx, N.Y.; d. Harry and Ethel Isabelle (Aaronson) Ruskin; A.A. summa cum laude, Trenton Jr. Coll., 1956; B.A. with highest honors, Rutgers Coll., 1959; A.M., Temple U., 1960, Ph.D. (fellow), 1963; m. A. Harold Norriss, Apr. 18, 1943; 1 dau., Sharon Lee Norriss White. Psychology intern Johnstone Tng. and Research Center, Bordentown, N.J., 1961-62, Drenk Meml. Guidance Center, Mount Holly, N.J., 1962, Norristown (Pa.) State Hosp., 1962-63; staff psychologist Terrell (Tex.) State Hosp., 1963-64, Los Angeles County Gen. Hosp., 1964-68; research psychologist Adolescent Suicide Attempters Project, 1966-67; cons. Loma Linda (Calif.) U. Med. Sch., 1967-69, South Bay Child Guidance Clinic, Redondo Beach, Calif., 1968-70; community mental health psychologist South Bay Mental Health Service, 1968-69; asso. clin. prof. psychiatry Loma Linda U. Med. Center, 1969-81, dir. child psychology services, 1969-77; prof. psychology Calif. State U., Los Angeles, 1966-74; pvt. practice psychotherapy, 1977—; cons. Riverside Gen. Hosp., 1970-80, various sch. dists. in Calif., 1968—; guest lectr. mental health various schs. and community orgns., 1969—; pres. adv. bd. Youth Services Center, 1975-77. Lic. psychologist, Calif.; cert. psychologist Tex. Mem. Am. Psychol. Assn., Western Psychol. Assn., Soc. for Pediatric Psychology, Los Angeles Psychol. Assn. (exec. bd. 1970-72), Psychologists in Public Service (founding pres. 1966-68). Contbr. articles on pediatric psychology to profl. publs. Home: 20560 Rancho Los Cerritos Covina CA 91724 Office: 2086 S E St Suite 103 San Bernardino CA 92410

NORSELL, PAUL ERNEST, service co. exec.; b. Salt Lake City, Jan. 28, 1933; s. Alf Raae and Florence Emily (Freer) N.; B.S. in E.E., Purdue U., 1954; M.S.E., UCLA, 1956; m. Mary Elizabeth Rynd, Sept. 2, 1958; children—Stuart, Daryl, Paula. Program mgr. advanced technology satellite and advanced syncom programs Space Systems div. Hughes Aircraft, El Segundo, Calif., 1954-64; v.p. engring. and ops. Data Systems div. Litton Industries, Inc., Van Nuys, Calif., 1964-69, pres. Litcom div. Datalog div., Bus. Telephone System div., Melville, N.Y., 1969-73, v.p. Profl. Services and Equipment group, Beverly Hills, Calif., 1973; pres., dir. EXECUDEX West Los Angeles, Inc., Paul Norsell & Assocs., Inc., Los Angeles, 1974—. Mem. exec. com., chmn. exploring div. Suffolk County council Boy Scouts Am., 1971-73; bd. mgrs. Huntington (N.Y.) YMCA, 1972-73; bd. dirs. L.I. Assn. Commerce and Industry, 1970-73. Hughes fellow, 1954-56. Mem. U.S. C. of C., Los Angeles Area C. of C., AIM, IEEE, Eta Kappa Nu. Clubs: Long Beach, Transpacific Yacht, U.S. Yacht Racing Union, U.S. Power Squadrons. Office: Suite 720 9841 Airport Blvd Los Angeles CA 90045

NORTH, DEAN THOMAS, marketing executive; b. Madison, Wis., May 2, 1945; s. Thomas Wilfred and Estelle Marguerite (Jung) N.; B.S., U. Wis., La Crosse, 1967; M.A., Central Mich. U., Hawaii Center, 1979; m. Helen Margaret Adamski, Aug. 31, 1968; 1 dau., Mara Catherine. With Zesto, Monroe, Wis., 1959-61; announcer, disk jockey, news dir. Sta. WEKZ, Monroe, 1961-66, Sta. WTMB, Tomah, Wis., 1963-67, KLEI, Kailua, Hawaii, 1970-71; bus. office mgr. Wis. Tel. Co., Madison, 1967-69; collections adminstr. Hawaiian Tel. Co., Honolulu, 1969-73, revenues and earnings adminstr., 1973-74, pricing and tariff mgr., 1974-76, mktg. promotions adminstr., 1976-82, mktg. planning administr., 1982—; owner, mgr. D & H Enterprises, Kaneohe, Hawaii, 1976-82; originator, leader The Creating Time Workshop, 1979—. Pres., Ahuimanu Home Owners Assn., 1971-72. Mem. Internat. Platform Assn., Aloha Computer Club (beginners officer 1980-81, v.p. 1981-82, pres. 1982-83). Roman Catholic. Club: Kahaluu Lions (3d v.p. 1977-78). Home: 700 Richards St #801 Honolulu HI 96813 Office: Hawaiian Tel Co PO Box 2200 Honolulu HI 96841

NORTH, DOUGLAS ALFRED, engineer; b. San Francisco, June 16, 1933; s. George Alfred and Velma May (Lattin) N.; m. Jo Ann Lashato, Aug. 8, 1969; children—Douglas G., Julie Ann. B.S., U. Calif.-Berkeley, 1960. With Chem. Systems div. Norden Systems Inc., Sunnyvale, Calif., 1960—, engr. dept. mgr., 1978—. Mem. AIAA (solid rocket propulsion com.). Home: 19091 Portos Dr Saratoga CA 95070 Office: United Technologies/Chem Systems PO Box 50015 San Jose CA 95150

NORTH, KATHRYN E. KEESEY (MRS. EUGENE C. NORTH), ret. educator; b. Columbia, Pa., Jan. 25, 1916; d. Issac and Elizabeth (French) Keesey; B.S., Ithaca Coll., 1938; M.A., N.Y. U., 1950; m. Eugene C. North, Aug. 18, 1938. Dir. music Cairo (N.Y.) Central Sch. Dist., 1938; music edn. cons. Argyle (N.Y.) Central Sch. Dist., 1939; dir. gen. music curriculum Hartford (N.Y.) Central Sch. Dist., 1939; mem. staff Del. Dept. Pub. Instrn., Dover, 1943; dir. music edn. Herricks (N.Y.) Pub. Schs., 1944-71; ret., 1971. Vis. lectr. Ithaca Coll., summers 1959, 60, 62-65, Fairleigh-Dickinson U., Rutherford, N.J., summer 1966, Albertus Magnus Coll., New Haven, summer 1968; instr. Adelphi Coll., 1954-55, Sch. Edn., N.Y.U., 1964-65. Mem. Music Educators Nat. Conf., N.E.A., N.Y. State Sch. Music Assn., N.Y. State Tchrs. Assn., Nassau Music Educators Assn. (exec. bd. 1947-58), N.Y. State Council Adminstrs. Music Edn. (chpt. v.p. 1967-68), Herricks Tchrs. Assn. (pres. 1948), Sigma Alpha Iota. Mem. Order Eastern Star. Home: 1645 Calle Camille La Jolla CA 92037

NORTHCUTT, HELENE LOUISE BERKING (MRS. CHARLES PHILLIP NORTHCUTT), artist, educator; b. Hannibal, Mo., July 6, 1916; d. Robert Stanley and Alice Lee (Adkisson) Berking; student Christian Coll., Columbia, Mo., 1932-33; B.S., U. Mo., 1939, A.M., 1940, Ed.D., 1959; m. Charles Phillip Northcutt, June 4, 1938 (dec.); children—John Berking, Francois Lee Northcutt Hedeen. Art tchr., supr. Oakwood High Sch. and Elem. Sch., 1937-39; tchr. jr. high sch. U. Mo. Lab. Sch., 1939-40; tchr. elem. art, Memphis, Mo., 1941; county fine arts supr., Ralls County, Mo., 1941-42; tchr. art high sch., Columbia, 1943-44; tchr. art jr. high sch., Hannibal, Mo., 1951-54; supr. art Ralls County Reorganized Sch. Dist. VI, New London, 1954-56; vis prof. U. Upper Iowa, 1956; instr. U. Mo., 1956-57; prof. art Eastern Mont. Coll. unit U. Mont., Billings, from 1957, now prof. emeritus, mem. grad. faculty; vis. prof. art U. B.C., Vancouver, 1965; cons. in curriculum in art edn.; cons. environ. edn., cons. on Indian edn., early childhood; exhibits fibers and paintings; state dir. Am. Art Week, Am. Artists Profl. League, 1963-65; exhibit chmn. E.M.C. Gallery Fine Arts; program chmn. Becky Thatcher council Girl Scouts U.S.A., 1946-48; bd. dirs., treas. United Christian Campus Ministry; bd. dirs. Growth Through Art. Recipient scholarship Delta Kappa Gamma, 1956-57; Nat. Press award Gen. Fedn. Women's Clubs, 1951; named Outstanding Honor Grad. U. Mo., 1968; citations for distinctive service Eastern Mont. Coll., Helene B. Northcutt Gallery named in her honor. Mem. Nat. Soc. Coll. Profs., AAUP, Mont. Edn. Assn. (past pres. Eastern Faculty unit; v.p. dept. higher edn. 1966-68, dept. pres. 1968-70) Nat., Mont. (sec. 1967-69) art edn. assns., AAUW (past chpt. pres.), Mont. Early Childhood Edn. Assn., Gen. Fedn. Women's Clubs (local past pres.), Delta Kappa Gamma (past chpt. pres., chmn. com., chmn. state world fellowship), Delta Phi Delta, Kappa Delta Epsilon. Methodist (mem. commn. higher edn. ministries, trustee Yellowstone Conf.). Club: Eastern Montana College Faculty (Billings, Mont.). Author: Creative Expression, 1964; Competency base Module-Methods and Materials,

1974; contbr. to publs. in field; reviewer, editor manuscripts on art and art edn. Home: 4505 Rimrock Rd Billings MT 59106

NORTHEN, REBECCA TYSON, orchid specialist, author; b. Detroit, Aug. 24, 1910; d. William Elisha and Elizabeth (Weems) Tyson; student Radcliffe Coll., 1930-33; B.A., Wayne State U., 1935; M.A., Mt. Holyoke Coll., 1937; m. Henry Theodore Northen, Aug. 9, 1937; children—Elizabeth Northen Lyons, Philip Tyson, Thomas Henry. Lectr. in field. Mem. Am. Orchid Soc. (gold medal 1979), Orchid Digest Corp., Garden Writers Am., Sigma Xi. Author: Home Orchid Growing, 1950, 3d edit., 1970; Orchids as House Plants, 1955, 2d edit., 1976; Miniature Orchids, 1980; (with Henry Theodore Northen) Secret of the Green Thumb, 1954; Greenhouse Gardening, 1956, 2d edit., 1973; Ingenious Kingdom, 1970. Address: 1215 Drake Circle San Luis Obispo CA 93401

NORTHROP, JOHN HOWARD, scientist; b. Yonkers, N.Y., July 5, 1891; s. John L. and Alice Belle (Rich) N.; B.S., Columbia U., 1912, M.A., 1913, Ph.D., 1915, D.Sc., 1937; D.Sc., Harvard U., 1936, Yale U., 1937, Princeton U., 1940, Rutgers U., 1941; LL.D., U. Calif., 1939; m. Louise Walker, June 1918; children—Alice Havenmeyer, John W.B. Cutting traveling fellow Columbia U., 1915; apptd. asst. Rockefeller Inst. Med. Research, 1916, asso. mem., 1922, mem. Inst., 1924-62, prof. Inst. emeritus, 1962—; Hitchcock prof. U. Calif., 1939; Thayer lectr. Johns Hopkins U., 1940, De Lamar lectr., 1937; Jesup lectr. Columbia U., 1938; prof. bacteriology, biophysics, research biophysicist Donner Lab. U. Calif., 1958-59, prof. emeritus, 1959—; mem. com. on proteins NRC cons. and ofcl. investigator to NDRC, 1942. Trustee Marine Biol. Lab., Wood Hole, Mass. Capt. C.W.S., U.S. Army, 1918-19. Recipient Stevens prize Coll. Physicians and Surgeons, Columbia, 1930; Chandler medal Columbia U., 1937; Giraud medal Nat. Acad. Sci., 1944; shared Nobel prize in chemistry, 1946; Columbia Lion award Alumni Club of Essex County, 1949; Alexander Hamilton medal Columbia U., 1961. Hon. fellow Chem. Soc. London; mem. Nat. Acad. Sci., SAR, Am. Soc. Biol. Chemistry, Soc. Gen. Physiologists, Soc. Philomathique (Paris), Am. Philos. Soc., Sigma Xi, Phi Lambda Upsilon, Kais Deutch Akad. der Naturforscher. Club: Century Assn. Author: Cyrstalline Enzymes; hon. editorial bd. Jour. Gen. Physiology and Exptl. Biology Monographs; contbg. editor Funk & Wagnall's Ency. Home: PO Box 1387 Wickenberg AZ 85358

NORTON, LINDA GAY, ednl. services firm exec.; b. St. Louis, Apr. 2, 1938; d. Warren Sidney and Dollie Mae (Allen) Brooner; student Internat. Accts. Soc., 1970; children—Diana L. Blythe, Patricia A. Evans, Duane B. Norton, Jr., Steven A. Norton. Acct., San Bernardino, Calif., 1956-58; bowling instr. Orange Bowl, Rialto, Calif., 1958-60; supr. acctg. and billing depts. Henderson Sugar Refinery, Mobile, Ala., 1960-62; acct. All Plan Fin. & Motors, San Bernardino, Calif., 1962-67; acct. Skadron Coll. Bus., div. Continuing Edn. Corp., San Bernardino, Calif., 1967, office mgr., 1968-74, coll. dir., 1974-79, pres., 1979-82; corp. v.p. Continuing Edn. Corp., Tustin, Calif., 1971-82; pres. Continuing Edn. Internat., 1982—; corp. v.p. Vedax Scis. Corp., 1982—. Home: 3267 Paseo Gallita San Clemente CA 92672 Office: 412 S Lyon St Santa Ana CA 92701

NORWALT, LORETTA MARIE HOENE, elementary school assistant principal; b. Los Angeles, June 1, 1937; d. Bernard Henry and Gladys Irene (Willadsen) Hoene; m. Robert Haddon Norwalt, Aug. 31, 1957. B.A., Loyola Marymount U., 1959; M.A., Calif. State U.-Northridge, 1972. With Los Angeles City Schs., 1959—, Title IV C dir., bilingual coordinator, Norwood St. Sch., 1977-81, asst. prin. Micheltorena St. Sch., 1981—. Mem. San Fernando Valley adv. bd. Children's Bur. Los Angeles, 1976-77. Marymount Coll. scholar, 1955-59. Mem. Assoc. Adminstrs. Los Angeles, Calif. Assn. Tchrs. English, Assn. Calif. Sch. Adminstrs., Assn. Supervision and Curriculum Devel., AAUW, Delta Kappa Gamma. Republican. Roman Catholic.

NOTHMANN, RUDOLF S., legal researcher; b. Hamburg, W.Ger., Feb. 4, 1907; came to U.S., 1941, naturalized, 1943; s. Nathan and Henrietta G. (Heymann) N. Referendar, U. Hamburg, 1929, Ph.D. in Law, 1932; postgrad. U. Liverpool Law Sch. (Eng.), 1931-32. Export, legal adviser, adviser ocean marine ins. various firms, Ger., Eng., Sweden, Calif., 1932-43, 46-47; instr. fgn. exchange, fgn. trade Extension div. UCLA, 1947-48, vis. assoc. prof., 1951; asst. prof. econs. Whittier Coll., 1948-50, assoc. prof., 1950-51; contract work U.S. Air Force, U.S. Navy, 1953-59; contract negotiator space projects, space and missile systems orgn. U.S. Air Force, Los Angeles, 1959-77; pvt. researcher in internat. comml. law, Pacific Palisades, Calif., 1977—. Served with U.S. Army, 1943-45; ETO. Recipient Gold Tape award Air Force Systems Command, 1970. Mem. Internat. Bar Assn. (vice chmn. internat. sales and related comml. trans. com. 1977-82), Am. Econ. Assn. Author: The Insurance Certificate in International Ocean Marine Insurance and Foreign Trade, 1932; The Oldest Corporation in the World: Six Hundred Years of Economic Evolution, 1949. Home: PO Box 32 Pacific Palisades CA 90272

NOTTINGHAM, CARMEN EILEEN, home economist, educator; b. Santurce, P.R., Oct. 27, 1948; d. Frederick and Carmen Irma (Nazario) Krause; m. Donald James Nottingham, June 26, 1971. B.A. in Food and Nutrition, San Diego State U., 1973, M.S. in Home Econs., 1981. Cert. in adult edn., community coll. teaching, Calif. With San Diego Gas & Electric Co. (Calif.), 1973—, home economist, 1973-76, energy advisor, 1976-79, energy adv. services supr., 1979-80, sr. conservation coordinator, 1980-81, conservation program planner, 1981—; 2d v.p. Energy Products Service Assn., 1982-83; mem. Ann. Microwave Seminar Com., 1973—; mem. Pres.'s Council, 1981—, Interagy. of Nutrition, 1979—. Mem. Am. Home Econs. Assn., Calif. Home Econs. Assn. (pres. San Diego dist. 1982-83, Outstanding Home Economist in Bus. award 1981, Outstanding Home Economist in Housing award 1983), Home Economists in Bus. (chmn. San Diego dist. 1983-84). Republican. Roman Catholic. Clubs: San Diego Gas & Electric Bicycle, Torrey Pines Ski (San Diego).

NOVAK, JOHN LEWIS, studio executive; b. Ingelwood, Calif., Nov. 14, 1946; s. Willard G. and Charlotte V. (Belden) N.; m. Iris Jeanette Mixer, Aug. 8, 1979. M.A. in Communication and Theater, Pepperdine U., 1973. Tech. dir. Univ. Theater, Pepperdine U., Los Angeles, 1970-72; actor, designer, tech. dir. His Players, improvisational theater group, Los Angeles, 1972-74; lectr., instr., tech. dir. Univ. Theatre, Pepperdine U., Malibu, Calif., 1974-80; sr. prodn. coordinator Walt Disney Prodns. subs. WED Enterprises, Glendale, Calif., 1980-83; v.p. prodn. Grosh Scenic Studios, Hollywood, Calif., 1983—. Mem. U.S. Inst. Theatre Tech., Am. Theatre, Assn., Aircraft Owners and Pilots Assn. Home: PO Box 3512 Glendale CA 91201 Office: Grosh Scenic Studios Hollywood CA 90029

NOVELL, JOHN KINGSLEY, trailer mfr.; b. Spokane, June 2, 1937; s. John Amleto and Christine Edith (Austin) N.; B.A. in Econs., Wash. State U., 1959, postgrad. in econs., 1960; m. Dorothy Karen Salsbery, Apr. 1, 1961; children—Susan Elizabeth, John Austin. Bus. mgr. Alloy Mfg. Co., 1960-61; bus. mgr. Alloy Trailers, Inc., Spokane, 1961-65, treas., 1965-70, sec.-treas., 1970-79, pres., 1979—, gen. mgr., 1973—, dir., 1973—; dir. Coeur d'Mines Co., Nowillsee Ltd., Fourstar Leasing Co., T.W. Transport, Interior Transport, Westgate Investment Co., Fleetway Leasing Co., Alloy Mfg. Co., Western Leasing Co. Bd. dirs. Goodwill Industries, 1974, O.I.C., 1979; financier Boy Scouts Am., 1979. Served with USNR, 1955-63. Mem. Idaho Motor Transport, Spokane Area C. of C. (trustee), Spokane Area Econ. Devel. Council, Assn. Wash. Bus. Roman Catholic. Clubs: Manito Golf and Country, Kiwanis (lt. gov. internat. 1969). Home: E 1215 Rockwood Blvd Spokane WA 99203 Office: PO Box 19208 Spokane WA 99219

NOWELL, GEORGE CHAPMAN, financial consultant; b. Greenwich, Conn., Aug. 28, 1946; s. Lawrence Ames and Elizabeth (Allen) N.; B.S.B.A., U. Colo., 1968; m. Kathryn Kendrick, July 8, 1967; children—Lisa, Sarah. With United Profl. Planning, Inc., Boulder, Colo., 1968-73; owner George C. Nowell Property Mgmt., 1973-75; pres., broker Realist Agencies, Inc., Boulder, 1975-79; pres. Matchmaker of Colo., Inc., 1979-80; broker, asso. The Hearth Co., Realtors, Denver, 1980-81; with Computerware Corp., Boulder, 1981-82, Info. Control Systems, Inc., Denver, 1982; exec. cons. Nat. Revenue Corp., Aurora, Colo., 1983—; tchr. investment real estate Community Coll. Denver, 1980. Treas. Boys Club Boulder, 1973-75, bd. dirs., 1971—; mem. Boulder County Citizens Budget Adv. Com., 1976-77; precinct committeeman Boulder County Republicans, 1980—. Served with U.S. Army, 1968-74. Cert. property mgr. Mem. Boulder Jaycees (dir. 1971-72, chpt. mgmt. v.p. 1979-80, named Outstanding Jaycee 1973, Jaycee of Year 1974), Colo. Jaycees, (dist. v.p. 1976-77, adminstrv. v.p. 1977-78, membership v.p. 1981-82, Impromptu Speakup winner 1973), Tau Kappa Epsilon, Alpha Kappa Psi. Presbyterian. Home: 4278 N 75th St Boulder CO 80301

NOWICKI, NORBERT JOHN, multiemployer trust fund exec., mgmt. cons.; b. Hamtramck, Mich., June 23, 1935; s. Adam Lubicz and Clara Jane (Siwanowicz) N.; B.B.A. magna cum laude; M.P.A.; m. Sara Joseph, Nov. 1, 1957; children—Renee Jaunty, Richard Ethan. Enlisted USMC, 1953; service in Middle East, 1957-59, Vietnam, 1965-66, S1/Adj., Combined Action Force, 1969-70; Japan, Morocco as adj. personnel and legal officer, ret. as capt., 1973; engaged in estate planning and real estate investing, 1974-75; exec. labor relations and Trustee & employee benefit funds Engrs. and Gen. Contractors Assn., San Diego, 1975-77; adminstr. San Diego County Constrn. Laborers Benefit Funds, San Diego, 1977—; mem. Constrn. Industry Coordinating Council, 1975-76; instr. employee benefits and social ins. Nat. U. San Diego. Chmn. energy task force San Diego Overall Econ. Devel. Program, 1975-79; mem. interfaith council com. San Diego council Boy Scouts Am., 1975—. Decorated Bronze Star, Navy Commendation medal. Mem. Internat. Found. Employee Benefit Funds, Am. Soc. Personnel Adminstrn., Adminstrv. Mgmt. Soc., Western Pension Conf., Soc. Personnel Consultants, Ret. Officers Assn. Mailing Address: PO Box 83248 San Diego CA 92138 Office: 4161 Home Ave San Diego CA 92105

NOWIK, DOROTHY ADAM, medical equipment company executive; b. Chgo., July 25, 1944; d. Adam Harry and Helen (Kichkaylo) Wanaski; m. Eugene Nicholas Nowik, Aug. 9, 1978; children—George Eugene, Helen Eugene. A.A., Columbia Coll., 1980. Sec., adminstrv. asst. to pres. Zenco Engring Corp., Chgo., 1970-71; sales rep. Medizenco USA Ltd., Chgo., 1971-73; ptnr. Pacific Med. Systems, Inc., Bellevue, Wash., 1973-76, pres., 1976—. Mem. Nat. Assn. Female Execs. Mem. Orthodox Ch. Am. Home: 2804 127th St NE Bellevue WA 98005 Office: 15055 NE Bel-Red Rd Bellevue WA 98007

NOWLING, RICHARD KENNETH, real estate developer; b. Long Beach, Calif., Apr. 25, 1950; s. Kenneth Walter and Maurine (Whaley) N.; B.A., U. of Pacific, 1972; m. Barbara A. Moore, Nov. 25, 1972; children—Ryan, Darren, Jonathan. Vice pres., regional mgr. Tanco Devel., Orange County, Calif., 1972-73; pvt. practice gen. contracting, No. Calif., 1973-76; exec. v.p. Foxx Devel., Huntington Beach, Calif., 1976-77; mng. ptnr. Barnett-Nowling, Tustin, Calif., 1977—; owner, operator So. Counties Realty and Investments, Lake Forest, 1979—; founder Orange County Builders' Workshop, 1978; pres. S.O.R.D. West Coast. Recipient award for excellence in energy efficiency So. Calif. Gas Co., 1980, 81; lic. real estate broker, Calif. Mem. Nat. Assn. Home Builders. Republican. Clubs: Rotary, St. Francis Yacht, South Shore Yacht, Internat. Yachting Fellowship Rotarians. Owner, skipper racing yacht Defiance (Winner 1981 Newport to Ensenada, Mexico, Race, So. Ocean Racing Div. Class). Office: 22865 Lake Forest Dr Lake Forest CA 92630

NOYES, HENRY PIERRE, physicist; b. Paris, Dec. 10, 1923; s. William Albert and Katharine Haworth (Macy) N. (parents Am. citizens); B.A., Harvard U., 1943; Ph.D., U. Calif. at Berkeley, 1950; m. Mary Jane Wilson, Dec. 20, 1947; children—David Brian, Alan Guinn, Katharine Hope. Staff mem. M.I.T. Radiation Lab., 1943-44; asst. prof. U. Rochester (N.Y.), 1951-55; group leader gen. research theoretical div. Lawrence Livermore Lab., 1955-62; adminstrv. head theoretical physics sect. Stanford Linear Accelerator Center, (Calif.), 1962-69, asso. prof., 1962-67, prof., 1967—; mem. internat. coms. Few Body Confs. in Nuclear and Particle Physics, 1967—; cons. Project Matterhorn, 1952, Project Orion, 1958-60. Chmn. Com. for a Direct Attack on Legality of Vietnam War, 1969-72; internat. oberserver, Tehran, Iran, 1977; mem. policy com. U.S. People's Com. on Iran, 1977—. Served with USNR, 1944-46. Fulbright scholar, Birmingham, 1950-51; Leverhulme lectr., Liverpool, 1957-58; Avco vis. prof. Cornell U., 1961; NSF fellow, 1962; Center for Advanced Study Behavioral Scis. vis. scholar, 1968-69; Nat. Humanities faculty, 1969-70; Alexander von Humboldt sr. scientist award, 1979. Fellow Am. Phys. Soc.; mem. Alternative Natural Philosophy Assn. (pres. 1979—), Philosophy of Sci. Assn., AAAS, Sigma Xi. Mem. Peace and Freedom party. Author: Report from Iran, 1977; asso. editor Annual Reviews of Nuclear Sci., 1962-77; contbr. articles to profl. jours. Home: 823 Lathrop Dr Stanford CA 94305 Office: Stanford Linear Accelerator Center PO Box 4349 Stanford CA 94305

NUGENT, MICHAEL ABRAM, manufacturing company official; b. Paterson, N.J., Sept. 6, 1946; s. Edward Robert and Elizabeth Helen (Braen) N.; m. Vivian Kathrine McCary, Feb. 2, 1972; children—Vivian Arlene, Tami Anne; m. Judith Kay Santoro, Aug. 20, 1978. B.S., U. Redlands, 1968. Cert. tchr., Calif. Tchr., basketball coach Burbank (Calif.) Unified Sch. Dist., 1971-74; adminstrv. asst. Weslock, Los Angeles, 1974-76; prodn. mgr. Terry Hinge & Hardware, Van Nuys, Calif., 1976-81, La Deau Mfg. Co., Glendale, Calif., 1981—. Vol. coach Burbank Park & Recreation Dept., 1967-75; v.p. Burbank Civitan Club, 1970-74; bd. dirs., treas. Burbank Boys Sports Fedn., 1969-72; bd. dirs., pres. Valencia Lakeshore Homeowners Assn., 1980-81. Democrat. Roman Catholic. Home: 24431 W Trevino Dr Valencia CA 91355 Office: 637 W Colorado Blvd Glendale CA 91204

NULF, MARION LEROY, accountant; b. Noble County, Ind., Jan. 3, 1942; s. Kenneth Ivan and Mabel Viola (Reed) N.; m. Helen Mary Licon, Nov. 7, 1964; children—Elizabeth R., Marion Leroy. B.B.A., Eastern N.Mex. U., 1971. C.P.A., N.Mex. Staff acct. Deason, Peters & Co., Roswell, N.Mex., 1970-77; ptnr. Nulf, Jones & Co., Roswell, 1977—. Served with USAF, 1961-66. Mem. Am. Inst. C.P.A.s, N.Mex. Soc. C.P.A.s. Democrat. Roman Catholic. Club: Sertoma.

NUNAMAKER, ROBERT ROYAL, space projects engr.; b. Rochester, Minn., July 10, 1933; s. Royal Oscar and Florence Mildred (Bratager) N.; m. Dixianne Hammersley June 12, 1955; m. 2d, Linda Gail Conrad, Jan. 22, 1977; children—Dawn Marie, Dana Lee, Steven Robert, Marc Damon. B.S.M.E., Ga. Inst. Tech., 1957. Mission ops. mgr. Pioneer project NASA Ames Research Ctr., Moffett Field, Calif., 1966-72, dep. mgr., 1973-76, study mgr. Pioneer Venus project, 1972-73, chief advanced missions office, 1975-76, chief space projects div., 1976-82, chief engr., 1982—; lectr. in field. Served to capt., inf. U.S. Army, 1956-58. Recipient Pioneer 10/11 Exceptional Service medal NASA, 1974, Pioneer Venus Exceptional Service medal, 1980. Mem. AIAA. Democrat. Lutheran. Club: Oakridge Athletic, San Jose. Home: 2592 Orinda Dr San Jose CA 95121 Office: NASA Ames Research Center Moffett Field CA 94035

NUNES, CHRISTOPHER PAUL, advertising agency executive, photographer; b. Newport, R.I., June 27, 1954; s. Manuel Arthur and Elsie Lylie (Taylor) N.; m. Phyliss Genie Agins, Aug. 31, 1951. B.A. in Journalism with honors, U. R.I., 1976; M.S. in Journalism with honors, Medill Sch. Journalism, Northwestern U., 1977. Photographer Will Barbeau Assocs., Providence, 1974; advt. rep. Provincetown (Mass.) Adv., 1976; asst. account exec. Benton & Bowles, N.Y.C., 1977-78, account exec., 1978-80; account exec. Foote, Cone & Belding/Honig, San Francisco, 1980-82, account supr., 1982—. Scripps Howard Found. scholar, 1977. Mem. Friends of Photography, Alpha Kappa Delta, Kappa Tau Alpha. Office: 55 Francisco St San Francisco CA 94119

NUNIS, RICHARD ARLEN, amusement parks exec.; b. Cedartown, Ga., May 30, 1932; s. Doyce Blackman and Winnie E. (Morris) N.; B.S. in Edn., U. So. Calif., 1954; m. June Elaine Kirk, June 13, 1954; children—Lisa Lea (dec.), Richard Dean. With Walt Disney Prodns., 1955—, mem. supervisory and mgmt. staff Disneyland, Calif., 1955-61, dir. ops., 1961-68, chmn. park ops. com., 1968-74, corporate v.p. Disneyland ops., 1968—, Walt Disney World, Orlando, Fla., 1971—, exec. v.p. Disneyland and Walt Disney World, 1972, now pres.; dir. Walt Disney Prodns.; pres. pres. Watt Disney Outdoor Recreation div.; Mem. bus. and industry adv. bd. Pres.'s Council on Phys. Fitness and Sports; mem. exec. com. Pres.'s Council for Internat. Youth Exchange; bd. dirs. Jr. Achievement, Jr. Achievement So. Calif. Mem. Nat. Alliance Businessmen, Orange County Metro (adv. bd.). Republican. Methodist. First academic All-American, U. So. Calif., 1952. Office: 1313 Harbor Blvd Anaheim CA 92803

NUNN, LESLIE EDGAR, lawyer; b. Evansville, Ind., Oct. 10, 1941; s. Lockett Charles and Alberta Lorraine (Baughn) N.; B.A., U. Evansville, 1964; J.D., U. Denver, 1967; m. Jeanette E. McGovern, June 19, 1966; children—Charles Edward, Laura Adrean, Sarah Elizabeth, John Hamilton, Susanah Lorraine. Charter pilot, flight instr., 1962-65; admitted to Colo. bar, 1967, N.Mex. bar, 1977, U.S. Tax Ct., 1978, U.S. Supreme Ct. bar, 1978; commd. lt. USAFR, 1964, advanced through grades to capt., 1968; judge adv. March AFB, Calif., 1967-69, Tan Son Nhut, Viet Nam, 1969-70, Hahn AFB, Germany, 1970-73; chief mil. affairs and civil law, 1969-73; ret., 1973; lawyer, adminstr. Navajo Tribe, 1973-76; individual practice law, Silverton and Cortez, Colo., Farmington, N.Mex., 1977-79; corp. counsel Thriftway Co., 1979-82; pres. Deer Trail Mktg. Corp., 1981—; dir. Serendipity Enterprises, Deer Trail Ranches, Inc. Mem. San Juan (N.Mex.) County Republican Com., 1978—. Decorated Bronze Star, Juez Commissionado. Mem. Colo. Bar Assn., N.Mex. Bar Assn., World Peace Through Law, World Assn. Lawyers (world chmn. law and agr. com.), San Juan County Bar Assn. Mormon. Contbr. articles to legal jours. and mags. Home: 5106 E Main Farmington NM 87401 Office: 710 E 20th St Farmington NM 87401

NUNN, MARIE LOUISE DOWNS, writer, poet; b. Chico, Calif., May 23, 1905; d. James Raymond and Louise (Larson) Downs; grad. Heald's Bus. Coll.; B.A., San Jose State U.; M.A., San Francisco State U.: postgrad. U. Calif.-Berkeley, 1956-57; L.H.D., U. Free Asia, Pakistan, 1974; Litt.D., World Acad. Arts and Culture, Taipei, Taiwan, 1981; m. L.H. Dahlgren, Jan. 24, 1927; 1 son, Raymond L.; m. 2d, Wallace E. Shields, Mar. 3, 1939 (dec. 1954); m. 3d, F. William Nunn, May 6, 1956 (dec. Sept. 1961). Various secretarial positions; writer articles for various mags., including The Gallery, Am. Collector, Western Collector, Antique Trader; contbr. poetry to publs. including Poet, Janus, Modern Haiku, Haiku Highlights, Dragonfly, Good Deeder, Mount Hermon Log, Pacifica, Swordsman, also anthologies. Sec. bd. dirs. Tb and Respiratory Disease Assn., 1969-73. Recipient Highby Meml. award; Nat. DAV award, 1955; award for writing and appearance on TV promoting Christmas seals sales, 1970, 71, 72; bronze and marble plaques Republic of China; named Internat. Woman of Yr. with laureate honors, 1975; recipient Silver Bicentennial medal, San Antonio, 1976; Bronze Medal and 2 bronze plaques World Congress Poets, 1976, bronze plaque, 1979, 81. Fellow Intercontinental Biog. Assn. (life); mem. Wash. Community Coll. Adminstrs., United Poets Laureate Internat. (bronze medal) Centro Studi e Scambi Internazionali (Silver medal), World Poets Resource Center (life), Calif. Acad. Scis., AAUW, Nat. League Am. Pen Women, World Poetry Soc. (vice chancellor, book rev. editor Poet), Nat. Writers Club, Calif. Writers, (pres. Peninsula br. 1983-84; state dir.), Smithsonian Instn., Calif. Fedn. Chaparral Poets (Robert Frost and Santa Cruz chpts., chmn. Nat. Poetry Contest 1978, 81), Santa Cruz County Geneal. Soc. (charter), Edwin Markham Poetry Soc. (judge poetry contest 1981, 82, 83), Calif., Ky. (1st place award 1974), Ill. poetry socs., Ina Coolbrith Circle, PTA (life), Calif. Writers-Peninsula (pres., bd. dirs.), Mus. Soc. San Francisco, Am. Assn. Ret. Persons, Nat. Hist. Soc., Nat. Grange, Farm Bur. Mem. Order Eastern Star. Author: Rumbling Wagon Wheels, 1974; Songs of Pacifica, 1975; A Chime for Peace, 1976; Magic Moments, 1977. Editor: Fairmonitor, monthly publ., Poet, publ. of World Poetry Soc. Address: 362 Horizon Way Pacific CA 94044

NUSBAUM, CARL, hospital administrator; b. Chgo., s. Samuel and Dora L.; B.S.C., Roosevelt U., 1949; M.H.A., Northwestern U., 1953; m. Kathryn Anne Sevebeck, Oct. 2, 1969; children—Michael, Cary, Bruce, Donna. Asst. dir. personnel Michael Reese Hosp. Med. Center, Chgo., 1948-50; adminstrv. asst. Mt. Sinai Hosp. & Med. Center, Chgo., 1950-52; asst. dir. Michael Reese Med. Center, 1952-55; exec. dir. Schwab Rehab. Hosp., Chgo., 1955-60; exec. dir. Gottlieb Meml. Hosp., Melrose Park, Ill., 1960-62; exec. v.p. Louise Burg Hosp., Chgo., 1962-64; adminstr. Northeast Community Hosps., Chgo., 1964-68, 70-75; adminstr. Pritzker Children's Hosp., Chgo., 1968-70; dir. Valley View Community Hosp., Youngtown, Ariz., 1975-79; v.p. corp. services Bapt. Hosp. and Health Systems, Phoenix, 1979-83; cons. Joint Commn. on Accreditation of Hosps., 1983—. Pres., North Shore Theatre Co., Wilmette, Ill., 1973-75, Desert Foothills Community Theater, Carefree, Ariz., 1977-81, 83—. Served with AUS, 1943-46. Lic. nursing care instn. adminstr., Ariz. Mem. Central Purchasing Assn. Ariz. (v.p. 1978-80), Am. Hosp. Assn. (life), Ariz. Hosp. Assn., Ariz. Pub. Health Assn., Ariz. Nursing Home Assn.; fellow Am. Coll. Hosp. Adminstrs. Club: Kiwanis (pres. 1981-82) (Sun City, Ariz.). Home: Box 895 Carefree AZ 85377 Office: 875 N Michigan Ave Chicago IL 60611

NUTE, J. BOYCE, publishing company executive; b. Palo Alto, Calif., Oct. 18, 1935; s. James C. and Dorothea Amy (Foster) N.; m. Margaret FitzGerald, June 27, 1959; children—James, Jennifer, Katherine, Elizabeth. B.S. in Mech. Engring., Stanford U., 1957; M.B.A., U. Santa Clara, 1963. Aero. research scientist NASA, Moffett Field, Calif., 1957-62; materials mgr. Nat. Press, Palo Alto, 1963-66, v.p., chief fin. officer, 1966-72, pres., chief exec. officer, dir. Nat. Press Pub. Corp., Palo Alto, 1972—. Bd. dirs. Children's Health Council, Palo Alto, 1979—, v.p., 1980—. Mem. Young Pres. Orgn., Printing Industries Am., Am. Assn. Pubs. Republican. Clubs: Palo Alto Kiwanis (pres., dir. 1970-72), Menlo

Country. Office: Nat Press Pub Corp 285 Hamilton Ave Palo Alto CA 94301

NYE, JEAN ELIZABETH, controller; b. Hopkins, Minn., d. John and Helga (Hanvold) Lovberg; m. Howard T. Nye, Dec. 26, 1946 (div.); children—Linda J. Nye Stickel, Paul Howard. Student U. Mont., 1944-46; B.S. in Bus., Mont. State U., 1974. Owner, mgr. hardware retail store, Kalispell, Mont., 1951-62; with various ins. agys., Bozeman, Mont., 1962-70; acct. SAFECO Ins. Co., Seattle, 1974-76, mgmt. cons. ind. ins. agys. throughout U.S., 1976-77; adminstrn. mgr. Fred J. James & Co., Spokane, Wash., 1977-79; controller, corp. treas. Parker, Smith & Feek, Inc., Seattle, 1980—. Former vice chmn. Flathead County Republican Party (Mont.); chmn. county fund drive ARC. Named Woman of Yr., Beta Sigma Phi, 1961. Lutheran. Club: PEO.

NYGREN, RONALD GRANT, safety and occupational health manager; b. Fallon, Nev., Aug. 30, 1941; s. Earl Walter and Alma Mae (Strauss) N.; m. Marilyn Ann Barnett, Dec. 23, 1962; children—Shad, Karena. A.A., Boise Jr. Coll., 1962; B.A., Calif. State U.-Los Angeles, 1967, M.A., 1969; cert. tchr. Ill. Tech. illustrator aerospace firms, Los Angeles, 1962-67; safety engr. Aetna Life and Casualty Ins. Co., Los Angeles, 1967-69; instr. occupational safety and health, Ill. State U., Normal, 1969-70; safety officer, 1970-72; safety specialist HEW, Washington, 1972-75; dep. dir. Safety and Environ. Health, USPHS, Rockville, Md., 1975-79, dir., 1979-81; safety and health mgr. U.S. Naval Air Sta., Fallon, Nev., 1981—; lectr. various schs. and univs.; adv. com. Occupational Safety and Health Curriculum. Served with Air NG, 1958-64. Recipient cert. recognition outstanding contbr. hosp./healthcare sect. Nat. Safety Council. Mem. Am. Soc. Safety Engrs., Phi Delta Kappa. Republican. Baptist. Contbr. numerous articles to jours. in field. Home: PO Box 1223 Fallon NV 89406 Office: US Naval Air Sta Fallon NV 89406

NYHAN, JOHN WILLIAM, soil scientist, consultant; b. Concord, N.H., Feb. 29, 1944; s. John Clement and Barbara Ruth N.; m. Carolyn Marie Ash, Sept. 14, 1966 (div. 1978); 1 dau., Catherine Marie. B.S. in Microbiology, U. Md., 1966; M.S. in Soil Microbiology and Agronomy, Iowa State U., 1968; Ph.D. in Soil Sci. and Radioecology, Colo. State U., 1972. Meteorol. technician U.S. Polar Ops. Project, Washington, 1962; student asst. U. Md. Livestock and San. Service Lab., 1964; microbiologist Agrl. Research Ctr., Soil and Water Conservation div., Dept. of Agr., Beltsville, Md., 1964-67; microbiologist Fed. Water Pollution Control Adminstrn., Dept. Interior, Annapolis, Md., 1967; grad. research assoc. agronomy Iowa State U., 1967-69, Colo. State U., 1969-72; soil scientist Environ. Studies Group, Los Alamos Sci. Lab., 1972—. Mem. Am. Soc. Agronomy, Crop Sci. Soc. Am., Soil Sci. Soc. Am., Ecol. Soc. Am., Am. Inst. Biol. Sci., Sigma Xi, Sigma Alpha Omicron, Gamma Sigma Delta. Contbr. articles to profl. jours. Office: Mail Stop K-495 Los Alamos National Laboratory Los Alamos NM 87544

NYHAN, WILLIAM LEO, pediatrician, educator; b. Boston, Mar. 13, 1926; s. W. Leo and Mary (Cleary) N.; student Harvard U., 1943-45; M.D., Columbia U., 1949; M.S., U. Ill., 1956, Ph.D., 1958; Ph.D. (hon.), Tokushima U. (Japan), 1981; m. Christine Murphy, Nov. 20, 1948; children—Christopher, Abigail. Intern Yale U.-Grace-New Haven Hosp., 1949-50, resident, 1950-51, 53-55; asst. prof. pediatrics Johns Hopkins U., 1958-61, asso. prof., 1961-63; prof. pediatrics, biochemistry U. Miami, 1963-69, chmn. dept. pediatrics, 1963-69; prof. U. Calif.-San Diego, 1969—, chmn. dept. pediatrics, 1969—; mem. FDA adv. com. on Teratogenic Effect on Certain Drugs, 1964-70; mem. pediatric panel AMA Council on Drugs, 1964-70; mem. Nat. Adv. Child Health and Human Devel. Council, 1967-71; mem. research adv. com. Calif. Dept. Mental Hygiene, 1969-72; mem. med. and sci. adv. com. Leukemia Soc. Am., Inc., 1968-72; mem. basic adv. com. Nat. Found. March of Dimes, 1973-81, mem. Basil O'Connor Starter grants com., 1973—; mem. clin. cancer program project rev. com. Nat. Cancer Inst., 1976-80. Served with U.S. Navy, 1944-46, U.S. Army, 1951-53. Nat. Found. Infantile Paralysis fellow, 1955-58; recipient Commemorative medallion Columbia U. Coll. Physicians and Surgeons, 1967. Mem. AAAS, Am. Fedn. Clin. Research, Am. Chem. Soc., Soc. Pediatric Research (pres. 1970-71), Am. Assn. Cancer Research, Am. Soc. Pharmacology and Exptl. Therapeutics, Western Soc. Pediatric Research (pres. 1976-77), N.Y. Acad. Sci., Am. Acad. Pediatrics (Borden award 1980), Am. Pediatric Soc., Am. Inst. Biol. Scis., Soc. Exptl. Biology and Medicine, Am. Soc. Clin. Investigation, Am. Soc. Human Genetics (dir. 1978-81), Biochem. Soc., Sigma Xi, Alpha Omega Alpha. Author: (with E. Edelson) The Heredity Factor, Genes, Chromosomes and You, 1976; (with N.O. Sakati) Genetic & Malformation Syndromes in Clinical Medicine, 1976; editor: Amino Acid Metabolism and Genetic Variation, 1967; Heritable Disorders of Amino Acid Metabolism, 1974; editorial bd. Jour. Pediatrics, 1964-78, Western Jour. Medicine, 1974—; editorial staff Med. and Pediatric Oncology, 1975—. Office: Dept Pediatrics U Calif San Diego CA La Jolla CA 92093

NYHOLM, CAROL JOYCE, association executive, social worker; b. Wenatchee, Wash., Mar. 12, 1932; d. Edward and Flora Agnes (Bray) Nyholm. B.A. in Sociology, Wash. State U., 1954; M.S.W., U. Mich., 1967. Cert. social worker. Program dir. YWCA, Long Beach, Calif., 1954-60; teenage dir. YWCA, San Diego, 1960-61; youth program YWCA Mid-Peninsula, Palo Alto, Calif., 1961-65; city wide youth program YWCA, Pitts., 1967-69, assoc. exec., 1969-72, exec. dir., 1972-77; exec. dir. YWCA, Long Beach, Calif., 1977—; Bd. dirs. South Coast Ecumenical Council, 1980-82, chmn. community action com., 1980-82; bd. dirs. Bouggess-White Scholarship Found., 1979-80; steering com. Shalom Ctr., 1979-81; mem. United Way Campaign Cabinet, 1980, council of execs., 1977—; mem. equitable salaries com. Pacific Southwest Conf. United Meth. Chs. Grace H. Dodge Merit fellow YWCA, 1965-66, Florence Allen Roblee scholar YWCA 1966-67. Named Boss of Yr. Jubilee chpt. Am. Bus. Women's Assn., 1978, Susan B. Anthony Woman of Yr., Long Beach chpt. NOW. Mem. Nat. Assn. Social Workers, Nat. Assn. Female Execs., Nat. Conf. Social Welfare. Methodist. Home: 3579 Myrtle Ave Long Beach CA 90807 Office: 3636 Atlantic Ave Long Beach CA 90807

NYLAND, LARRY LAIRD, educational administrator; b. Seattle, June 11, 1948; s. Orwald E. and Rhoda K. (Wallstrom) N.; m. Kathryn M. Montgomery, Sept. 6, 1968; children—Krystl, Kirk. B.A. in Geography, U. Wash., 1969, M.A. in Geography, 1972, Ph.D. in Edn. Adminstrn., 1981. Cert. supt., Wash., Alaska. Tchr. Peninsula High Sch., Gig Harbor, Wash., 1971-75; prin. Dillingham (Alaska) Jr. High Sch., 1975-76; supt. Railbelt (Alaska) Sch. Dist., 1976-79; asst. supt. Pasco (Wash.) Sch. Dist., 1979-82, supt., 1982—. Bd. dirs. Tri-Cities United Way; Mid Columbia Mental Health, Richland, Wash.; trustee S.E. Wash. Dental Assn. Mem. Am. Assn. Sch. Adminstrs., Pasco C. of C., Phi Delta Kappa. Club: Kiwanis. Home: 2507 Rd 60 Pasco WA 99301 Office: Pasco Sch Dist 1004 N 16th St Pasco WA 99301

OAKES, DELWIN ARTHUR, architect; b. Los Angeles, Aug. 26, 1954; s. William Jacob and Virginia (Smith) O.; B.S. in City/Regional Planning, Calif. Poly. U., San Luis Obispo, 1977, M.Arch., Calif. Poly U., Pomona, 1981; m. Michele Hygh, May 7, 1977. Environ. planner Tetra Tech, Inc., Pasadena, Calif., 1977-79; archtl. job capt. McClellan, Cruz, Gaylord, Pasadena, 1981—. Scoutmaster, Boy Scouts Am., 1977-78. Mem. AIA, Am. Planning Assn. Home: 910 Cabrillo Dr Duarte CA 91010

OAKES, PATRICIA A., historian, educator, consultant; b. Seattle, Sept. 7, 1932; d. Glenn Gordon and Florence Louise (Boyd) Oakes. B.A. in English, Wash. State U., 1953; M.Ed., U. Alaska, 1961. Cert. tchr., Alaska, Tchr., Juneau-Douglas (Alaska) Sch. Dist., 1953-56, Lathrop High Sch., Fairbanks (Alaska) Sch. Dist., 1956-61; research and publs. supr. Alaska Dept. Edn., 1966-67, instructional supr., 1967-68; prin., tchr. Alaska State operated schs., Circle City, Ruby, 1961-76; owner, operator Oakeservices, Central, Alaska, 1960—; cons. rural edn. and curriculum, regional history. Mem. Alaska State Mus. Collections Adv. Com., 1980—, chmn., 1980-82; pres. Circle Dist. Hist. Soc., 1977—; bd. dirs. Alaska Hist. Soc., 1981—. Mem. Alaska Press Women, NEA. Club: Pioneers of Alaska. Author: Alaska Voters Guidebook, 1961; contbr. articles on edn. to profl. jours.

OAKES, WILLIAM STILLMAN, JR., indsl. engr.; b. Oregon City, Oreg., May 5, 1922; s. William Stillman and Mona Elaine (Toban) O.; B.S.E.E., U. Okla., 1949; m. Elizabeth Armes, 1946 (div. 1976); children—William, Myron, Evan. Cons. engr. Gen. Electric Co., 1949-69; sr. indsl. engr. Nat. Steel and Shipbuilding Co., San Diego, 1979—. Served with USN, 1942-46. Registered profl. engr., N.Y., Calif. Mem. Am. Inst. Indsl. Engrs., Am. Soc. Mfg. Engrs., IEEE. Republican. Unitarian. Patentee in field. Home: 1130 Crest Rd Del Mar CA 92014 Office: Harbor Dr and 28th St San Diego CA

OAKESHOTT, GORDON B(LAISDELL), geologist; b. Oakland, Calif., Dec. 24, 1904; s. Philip S. and Edith May (Blaisdell) O.; B.S., U. Calif., 1928, M.S., 1929; Ph.D., U. So. Calif., 1936; m. Beatrice Clare Darrow, Sept. 1, 1929; children—Paul Darrow, Phyllis Joy Oakeshott Martin, Glenn Raymond. Asst. field geologist Shell Oil Co., 1929-30; instr. earth sci. Compton Coll., 1930-48; supervising mining geologist Calif. Div. Mines, 1948-56, dep. chief, 1956-57, chief, 1958, dep. chief Calif. Div. Mines and Geology, 1959-72; cons. geologist, 1973—;cons. State of Calif.; lectr. geology Calif. State U., Sacramento, 1972-73, Calif. State U., San Francisco, 1975. Fellow AAAS, Geol. Soc. Am., Calif. Acad. Sci., Explorers Club; mem. Seismol. Soc. Am., Nat. Assn. Geology Tchrs. (pres. 1970-71, Webb award 1981), Assn. Petroleum Geologists (hon.), AIME, Mining and Metall. Soc. Am., Peninsula Geol. Soc. (past pres.), Engrs. Club San Francisco, Geol. Soc. Sacramento, Peninsula Gem and Geol. Soc. (hon.), Assn. Engring. Geologists (hon.), Earthquake Engring. Research Inst. (past dir.). Author: California's Changing Landscapes—A Guide to the Geology of the State, 1971, 2d edit., 1978; Volcanoes and Earthquakes—Geologic Violence, 1975, Japanese edit., 1981. Contbr. articles to profl. jours. Home and Office: 3040 Totterdell St Oakland CA 94611

OAKLEY, CLARON LOUIS, editor, pub.; b. Provo, Utah, Oct. 1, 1924; s. Louis Terry and Inez (McDonald) O.; student Brigham Young U., 1943, 46-47; B.S.J., Northwestern U., 1950, M.S.J., 1951; m. Julia Hansen, June 19, 1950 (dec.); children—Ellen Elizabeth, Bradford James, Sara Julia. Co-founder, v.p., sr. v.p., editor Audio-Digest Found., 1953—; sci. info. officer Pan-Pacific Surg. Assn. Mobile, 1963-66, A.C.S. mobile S.Am. sessions, 1969—; producer AMA Audio Medical News; dir. Pac Mag Equipment Co. Active Boy Scouts Am.; trustee Audio-Digest Found.; Served to maj. AUS, 1945-46; ETO. Recipient Disting. Layman award AMA, 1982. Mem. Am. Film Inst., Nat. Acad. Rec. Arts and Scis., Med. Writers Assn., Blue Key, Sigma Delta Chi. Mem. Ch. Jesus Christ of Latter-day Saints (former bishop, incumbent counselor stake presidency). Rotarian. Contbr. articles to profl. jours. Home: 2150 Kinneloa Canyon Rd Pasadena CA 91107 Office: 1577 E Chevy Chase Dr Glendale CA 91206

OAKS, DALLIN HARRIS, justice Utah Supreme Court; b. Provo, Utah, Aug. 12, 1932; s. Lloyd E. and Stella (Harris) O.; B.A. with high honors, Brigham Young U., 1954, LL.D. (hon.), 1980; J.D. cum laude, U. Chgo., 1957; m. June Dixon, June 24, 1952; children—Sharmon Oaks Ward, Cheri Lyn Oaks Ringger, Lloyd D., Dallin D., TruAnn Oaks Boulter, Jenny June. Admitted to Ill. bar, 1957, Utah bar, 1971; law clk. to Supreme Ct. Chief Justice Earl Warren, 1957-58; with firm Kirkland, Ellis, Hodson, Chaffetz & Masters, Chgo., 1958-61; mem. faculty U. Chgo. Law Sch., 1961-71, asso. dean and acting dean, 1962, prof., 1964-71, mem. vis. com., 1971-74; pres. Brigham Young U., 1971-80; justice Utah Supreme Ct., 1981—; asst. states atty. Cook County (Ill.), summer 1964; exec. dir. Am. Bar Found., 1970-71, now fellow. Mem. Wilson council Woodrow Wilson Internat. Center for Scholars, 1973-80; bd. dirs. Pub. Broadcasting Service, 1976—, chmn., 1980—; adv. bd. Notre Dame Law Sch. Center for Constl. Studies, 1977-81; trustee Intermountain Health Care, Inc., 1974-80. Mem. ABA (com. to survey legal needs 1971-79, cons. panel on advanced legal and jud. edn. 1977-80), Am. Assn. Pres. Ind. Colls. and Univs. (pres. 1975-78), Nat. Inst. Law Enforcement and Criminal Justice (adv. com. 1974-76), Nat. Assn. Ind. Colls. and Univs. (dir. 1977-79), Order of Coif. Mem. Ch. Jesus Christ of Latter-day Saints (regional rep. 1974-80, past 1st counselor Chgo. S. Stake). Author: (with G.G. Bogert) Cases on Trusts, 1967, 2d edit., 1977; (with W. Lehman) A Criminal Justice System and the Indigent, 1968; The Criminal Justice Act in the Federal District Courts, 1969; (with M. Hill) Carthage Conspiracy: The Trial of the Accused Assassins of Joseph Smith, 1975; editor: The Wall Between Church and State, 1963; editor-in-chief U. Chgo. Law Rev., 1956-57. Home: 1225 Locust Ln Provo UT 84604

O'BANNON, NORMAN DALE, economist, educator; b. Hamilton, Tex., Feb. 10, 1930; s. Preston and Cena (Allen) O'B.; m. Joan Allen, Aug. 13, 1960; children—Allen, Derek. B.A., Tex. A&M U., 1957; M.A., U. Va., 1958; Ph.D., Tulane U., 1964. Mem. faculty U. Md., College Park, 1958-60; with Fed. Res. Bank of Atlanta, 1963-65; mem. faculty Pacific U., 1965-66; mem. faculty Lewis and Clark Coll., Portland, Oreg., 1966—, prof. econs., dept. chmn., 1975—. Served with USAF, 1950-54. Office: Dept Econs Lewis and Clark Coll Portland OR 97219

OBENCHAIN, THEODORE GUY, neurosurgeon; b. Boise, Idaho, Jan. 4, 1937; s. Artie Lorraine and Violet Josephine (Isaacson) O.; A.A., Boise State U., 1957; grad. Coll. of Idaho, 1958; M.D., U. Utah, 1962; m. Jean Arline Martinovich, Jan. 8, 1968; children—Kristin Marie, Monica Lynn, Theodore John. Intern, Bellevue Hosp., N.Y.C., 1962-63; med. fellow dept. neurology U. Minn. Med. Sch., 1966-67; resident in surgery Highland Gen. Hosp., Oakland, Calif., 1967-68; resident in neurosurgery UCLA Sch. Medicine, 1968-73; asst. prof. U. Calif., San Diego Sch. Medicine, 1973-75; practice medicine, specializing in neurosurgery, Boise, 1975-77, Escondido, Calif., 1977—; mem. staff Palomar Hosp., Pomerado Hosp., Sharp Hosp. Served with U.S. Navy, 1963-66. Mem. Am. Assn. Neurol. Surgeons, Congress of Neurol. Surgeons, Fedn. Western Socs. Neurol. Sci., San Diego Acad. Neurol. Surgeons. Contbr. articles to med. jours. Home: 16528 Corte Paulina Poway CA 92064 Office: 255 N Elm Suite 202 Escondido CA 92025

OBENDORF, CHARLES EUGENE, accountant; b. Caldwell, Idaho, Feb. 6, 1935; s. Philip Charles and Edna Mae (Chapin) O.; m. Betty Louise Coon, Aug. 5, 1960; children—Roberta, Dean, Timothy, Heidi, Steven. B.S., U. Idaho, 1978. C.P.A., Wash., Alaska. Ptnr., Johnson, Paulson & Stolz, Anchorage, Alaska, 1962-64; field treas. Sudan Interior Mission, Nigeria, 1965-69; comptroller Mukluk Freight Lines, Anchorage, Alaska, 1970-71; ptnr. Bigler, Kohler & Obendorf, C.P.A.s, Soldotna, Alaska, 1972—, mng. ptnr., 1982—. Served with U.S. Army, 1958-59. Mem. Am. Inst. C.P.A.s, Alaska Soc. C.P.A.s, Soldotna C. of C. (treas. 1982-83). Republican. Baptist. Office: Box 427 Soldotna AK 99669

OBERLE, CAROLE JO, horse breeder, cons. psychologist; b. Woodbury, N.J., Oct. 27, 1942; d. Joseph A. and Helen (Klemczak) Saunders; B.A. in Psychology, U. Del., 1966; M.A., Temple U., Phila., 1969; m. Karl Heinz Oberle, Mar. 17, 1963 (dec.); children—Kathryn Jo, Gretchen. Psychologist, Child Diagnostic and Devel. Center, Wilmington, Del., 1967-68, Alfred I. DuPont Sch. Dist., Wilmington, 1968-75; with Weidman & Co., realtors and insurors, Colorado Springs, 1975-78; propr. CJO Breeding Ranch, Colorado Springs, 1975—; affiliated with Cheyenne Mountain Zoo, Colorado Springs, 1978—, Village Seven Vet. Clinic, Colorado Springs, 1978—, Elbert County Sch. Dist. #200; cons. psychologist Ursuline Acad., Colorado Springs; sec. Wilmington chpt. Am. Fedn. Tchrs., 1975. Mem. Am. Psychol. Assn., Council Exceptional Children, Am., Rocky Mountain, Standard quarter horse assns., Sand Drifters Riding Assn., Black Forest Saddle Club, Black Forest Outhouse Race Com., Psi Chi. Home: 11150 Hungate Rd Colorado Springs CO 80908

OBERT, RICHARD PATRICK, equipment manufacturing company executive; b. Seattle, July 7, 1935; s. Albert Douglas and Ruth Naomi (Goodwin) O.; m. Judith Lee White, July 24, 1961; children—Susan Lynn Obert Whitney, Sandra Lee Obert Mayes, Julie DeeAnn. Student U. Wash., 1954, Seattle U., 1955. Cert. surveyor, U.S. Dept. Labor. Sales engr. U.S. Elec. Motors, Seattle, 1955-59, dist. mgr., Portland, Oreg., 1961-67; asst. mgr. Wash. Chain & Supply, Inc., Seattle, 1967-73; v.p. Obert Marine Supply, Inc., Seattle, 1973—; pres. Northwest Wire Rope & Equipment Co., Tacoma, 1979—. Mem. Republican Presdl. Task Force; founding mem. Bellevue Art Mus.; treas., bd. dirs. Marine Exchange Puget Sound. Served with USN, 1959-61. Mem. Soc. Port Engrs., Propeller Club U.S. Clubs: U.S. Senatorial (Washington); Overlake Golf and Country (Medina, Wash.); Bellevue (Wash.) Athletic. Home: 3630 Evergreen Point Rd Bellevue WA 98004 Office: Obert Marine Supply 3441 2d Ave So PO Box 3992 Seattle WA 98124

OBERTI, SYLVIA MARIE ANTOINETTE, rehabilitation counselor and administrator, career advisor, textile consultant; b. Fresno, Calif., Dec. 29, 1952; d. Silvio Lawrence and Sarah Carmen (Policarpo) O. A.A., Fresno Community Coll., 1974; B.A. in Communicative Disorders, Calif. State U.-Fresno, 1976, M.A. in Rehab. Counseling, 1977. Lic. vocat. cons., Calif.; cert. rehab. counselor Commn. Rehab. Counselors; cert. life tchr. community coll. Rehab. counselor intern Calif. Dept. Rehab., Fresno, 1977, vol. counselor Fresno Commn. Aging, 1976-77; rehab. counselor trainee traumatic injury ward, Fresno Community Hosp., 1976-77; sr. rehab. cons. Crawford Rehab. Services, Inc., Emeryville, Calif., 1978-80; vocat. rehab. counselor Rehab. Assocs., Inc., San Leandro, Calif., 1980-81; owner, textile cons. Rugs and Carpets of the Orient, Oakland, Calif., 1979—; adminstr., counselor Oberti & Lohr, Oakland and San Jose, Calif., 1981—, exec. dir., 1983—; cons. to industry, ins. cos., disabled; tchr. job seeking skills to the disabled. Bd. dirs. Pacific Basin Sch. Textile Arts, 1982-84; mem. NOW, 1982-83, Calif. Assn. Physically Handicapped, Inc., 1976—, Bay Area Profl. Women's Network, 1979—. HEW grantee, 1976-77. Mem. Am. Personnel and Guidance Assn., Am. Rehab. Counseling Assn., Calif. Assn. Rehab. Profls., Indsl. Claims Assn., Internat. Round Table Advancement of Counseling, Nat. Rehab. Assn., Nat. Rehab. Counseling Assn., Nat. Vocat. Guidance Assn., No. Calif. Council Self-Insurers, LWV. Office: 2444 Moorpark Ave Suite 300 San Jose CA 95128 also 3645 Grand Ave Suite 206 Oakland CA 94611

OBLOW, JOYCE LOCKWOOD, marketing executive, consultant; b. Milford, Conn., May 30, 1941; d. William Scott and Ruth Eleanor (Nourse) Lockwood; m. Allen B. Oblow, June 12, 1965; children—Scott James Kalani, Mark Richard Kainoa. Student Green Mountain Coll., 1959-61. Strategist George Ariyoshi Campaign for Gov., Honolulu, 1978; salesperson Aloha Candle and Tapa Designs, Honolulu, 1979-80; sales mgr. Kukui Nuts of Hawaii, Honolulu, 1980-81; gen. mgr. India Imports, Honolulu, 1981; mktg. dir. Ala Moana Shopping Ctr., Honolulu, 1981—; retail sales specialist Sta. KITV; small store cons. Commr. bd. vets. State of Hawaii, 1979-80; bd. dirs. Honolulu Symphony Women's Assn. Mem. Am. Mktg. Assn. (program chmn. local chpt. 1982-83), Honolulu Advt. Fedn., Sales and Mktg. Execs., Gee Yung Chinese Cultural Club. Democrat. Presbyterian. Office: KITV 1290 Ala Moana Blvd Honolulu HI 96814

OBNINSKY, VICTOR PETER, lawyer, real estate developer; b. San Rafael, Calif., Oct. 12, 1944; s. Peter Victor and Anne Bartholdi (Donston) O.; m. Clara Alice Bechtel, June 8, 1969; children—Mari, Warren. B.A., Columbia U., 1966; J.D., U. Calif.-San Francisco, 1969. Bar: Calif. 1970. Sole practice, Novato, Calif., 1970—; sec. Mahoney Co., Inc., Novata, 1976-79, pres., 1979—; arbitrator Marin County Superior Ct., San Rafael, 1979—; lectr. real estate and partnership law; dir. several corps. Bd. dirs. Calif. Young Republicans, 1968-69, Richardson Bay San. Dist., 1974-75, Marin County Legal Aid Soc., 1976-78; baseball coach, 1973—; mem. nat. panel consumer arbitrators Better Bus. Bur., 1974—; leader Boy Scouts Am., 1970—. Mem. State Bar Calif., ABA, Marin County Bar Assn., Phi Delta Phi. Russian Orthodox. Club: Commonwealth (San Francisco). Author: The Russians in Early California, 1966. Home: 6 Mateo Dr Tiburon CA 94920 Office: 100 Galli Dr Novato CA 94947

O'BRIC, MICHAEL, ednl. adminstr.; b. Mpls., Mar. 21, 1934; s. John and Anne (Olsen) O'B.; A.B., Stonehill Coll., 1956; M.A., Calif. Western U., 1965; Ph.D., U.S. Internat. U., 1971; m. Karen Mann; children—Damon, Michelle, Minda Lee, Kerry. Gen. partner Bus., 1958-62; dir. Calif. Western U., San Diego, 1962-63; tchr., supt. Fountain Valley (Calif.) Sch. Dist., 1963-76; adminstr. Bellflower (Calif.) Unified Sch. Dist., 1977—; assoc. prof. Pepperdine U., 1975—; adj. prof. U. San Francisco, 1976—, Calif. State U., Fullerton, 1982—; cons. various ednl. assns. and states. Mem. Youth Devel. and Delinquency Prevention Project, 1971-76; mem. Sch. Evaluation-Calif. Joint Legis. Com., 1973-76; chmn. adv. com. Fountain Valley Hosp., 1974-76; mem. Calif. Adv. Com. on Budgeting and Acctg., 1971. Served to capt. USMCR, 1953-59. Recipient 2 awards of merit in ednl. publs., 1971; Archtl. award AIA and AASA, 1973, 76; Gold Medal Educator of 70's; Freedom Found., 1972; named Man of Yr. award Fountain Valley Jr. C. of C., 1966; registered sch. bus. adminstr. Mem. Phi Delta Kappa. Editor: California Elementary Adminstrator, 1970-71; Research for a Developed Model of School District Decentralization for Decision Making, 1971. Contbr. to publs. in field. Home: 9062 Carrolltown Dr Huntington Beach CA 92646

O'BRIEN, DANIEL F., professional baseball manager; b. Elizabeth, N.J., Mar. 26, 1930; m. Mary Ann; children—Daniel, Lori. Student Seton Hall U.; B.S., Fla. So. Coll. Gen. mgr. Pitts. Pirates' Burlington (N.C.) affiliate, from 1955, Milw. Braves farm clubs, Boise, Idaho, Jacksonville, Fla., Louisville, Greenville, S.C.; asst. to pres. Nat. Assn. Baseball Leagues, 1964-73; v.p. and gen. mgr. Tex. Rangers, 1973-79; pres. Seattle Mariners, 1979—. Office: Seattle Mariners PO Box 4100 Kingdome Seattle WA 98104*

O'BRIEN, DANIEL JOSEPH, airplane co. exec.; b. Washington, July 16, 1925; s. William Columba, and Theresa (Mathews) O'B.; B.S. in Aero. Engring., Purdue U., 1955; m. Shirley Jean Rogers, June 2, 1954; children—Patrick, Sheila, Susan, Sharon, Peggy. Commd. 2d lt., U.S. Air Force, 1949, advanced through grades to maj., 1961; system and subsystem mgr. F-111 SPO, 1960-64; subsystem mgr. FAA Supersonic Transport Office, 1964-66; ret., 1966; conceptual design mgr. remotely-piloted systems The Boeing Co., Seattle, 1979-78, remotely-piloted vehicles systems mgr., 1978—. Decorated Legion of Merit, D.F.C. Mem .Purdue Alumni Assn., Air Force Assn., Am. Def. Preparedness Assn., AIAA, Assn. Unmanned Vehicles (charter), Sigma Xi. Roman Catholic. Clubs: Wash. Athletic, Equestrian Inst., Wash. State Horsemen, Pony of Am. Patentee in field. Home: 7632 NE 123d St Kirkland WA 98033 Office: The Boeing Co PO Box 3707 MS 40 60 Seattle WA 98124

O'BRIEN, ELIOT, newspaper publisher; b. Boston, Nov. 29, 1947; s. Lincoln and Torka (Eliot) O'B.; m. Nedra Shupe, Oct. 16, 1971; children—Cody and Riannon (twins). B.A., Coll. of Artesia (N.Mex.), 1970; postgrad. N.Mex. Highlands U., 1966-68. Advt. salesman Ukiah (Calif.) Daily Jour., 1970-71, Gallup (N.Mex.) Independent, 1972-74; classified advt. mgr. San Leandro (Calif.) Daily News, 1971-72; gen. advt. mgr. Raton (N.Mex.) Daily Range, 1974-76; circulation mgr. Farmington (N.Mex.) Daily Times, 1976-78, bus. mgr., 1978-79, asst. pub., 1979-81, pub., 1981—. Bd. dirs. Farmington Better Bus. Bur. Mem. N.Mex. Press Assn. (bd. dirs.), Chess Club, Irish Club. Clubs: San Juan Country, Elks, Rotary (Farmington).

O'BRIEN, GAIL PIERCE, financial planner, marketing executive; b. N.Y.C., Jan. 22, 1930; d. Webster Willard and Marion Elise (Rhodes) Pierce; m. Thomas Gore O'Brien, May 7, 1960 (dec.); children—Thomas Gore, Page Benedict, Sarah Webster, Peter Justin. Grad. Tobe Coburn Sch. for Fashion Careers, 1950. Exec. trainee, asst. buyer Abraham & Straus, Bklyn., 1950-52, buyer, 1952-54; buyer Hecht Co., Balt., 1954-57, Burdines, Miami, Fla., 1957-59, William Filenes, Boston, 1959-64; pres. Gail Pierce O'Brien Assocs., Santa Barbara, Calif., 1977—. Founder and chmn. Santa Barbara Concours d'Elegance, 1976-79; trustee Crane Sch., 1970-79, Lobero Theater, 1969-71. Mem. Fashion Group (N.Y.C.), Santa Barbara Assocs. Roman Catholic. Club: Birnam Wood Golf (Santa Barbara). Office: PO Box 5291 Santa Barbara CA 93108

O'BRIEN, GRACE WILHELMINA EHLIG, sch. adminstr.; Los Angeles; d. Max Carl and Janette (Rentchler) Ehlig; A.A., Pasadena City Coll., 1942; A.B., UCLA, 1944; postgrad. Riverside City Coll., 1946; M.A. in Guidance, Calif. State U. at Los Angeles, 1964, postgrad., 1954-66, 68-78; m. Louis J. O'Brien, Nov. 8, 1947; children—Carol Jean, Lawrence John, Perry Lewis. Tchr., Perris (Calif.) Union High Sch., 1945-46; tchr., counselor, psychometrist Los Angeles City Schs., 1946-66, cons. counselor, sch. psychologist Elem. Secondary Edn. Act, Edn. and Guidance program, 1966-68; head counselor, asst. prin. Garden Gate Opportunity High Sch., 1968-73; girls' vice prin. Garfield High Sch., Los Angeles, 1974-75; asst. prin. Mt. Vernon Jr. High Sch., Los Angeles, 1975-76, Gage Jr. High Sch., Los Angeles, 1976-77; prin. Garden Gate High Sch., Los Angeles, 1977-80, Johnson High Sch., 1980—; co-owner, asst. mgr. Golden State Travel Bur., Pasadena, Calif., 1954-80. Den mother chmn. Cub Scouts, 1964-66. Recipient spl. service award Boy Scouts, 1964. Mem. Sr. High Sch. Prins. Assn., Assn. Adminstrs. Los Angeles, Calif. Assn. Secondary Adminstrs., UCLA Alumni Assn., Calif. State U. at Los Angeles Alumni Assn., Phateres, Pi Lambda Theta, Chi Delta Phi, Phi Delta Kappa. Presbyterian (supt. Sunday sch. 1953-54). Home: 3880 Shadow Grove Rd Pasadena CA 91107 Office: 900 E 42d St Los Angeles CA 90011

O'BRIEN, JOHN WILLIAM, JR., investment management company executive; b. Bronx, N.Y., Jan. 1, 1937; s. John William and Ruth Catherine (Timon) O'B.; B.S., MIT, 1958; M.S., UCLA, 1964; m. Jane Bower Nippert, Feb. 2, 1963; children—Christine, Andrea, Michael, John William III, Kevin Robert. Sr. asso. Planning Research Corp., Los Angeles, 1962-67; dir. fin. systems group Synergetic Scis., Inc., Tarzana, Calif., 1967-70; dir. analytical services div. James H. Oliphant & Co., Los Angeles, 1970-72; chmn. bd., chief exec. officer, pres. O'Brien Assos., Inc., Santa Monica, Calif., 1972-77; v.p. A.G. Becker Inc., 1977-81; pres., chief exec. officer Leland O'Brien Rubinstein Assos., 1981—. Served to 1st lt. USAF, 1958-62. Recipient Graham and Dodd award Fin. Analysts Fedn., 1970. Mem. Delta Upsilon. Home: 231 Surfview Dr Pacific Palisades CA 90272 Office: 1900 Ave of Stars Los Angeles CA 90067

O'BRIEN, KELLY J., lawyer; b. Goliad, Tex., Dec. 22, 1937; d. Walter Daniel and LaVerne Inez (Lang) Hardin; m. William Joseph O'Brien, Sept. 1960 (div.); children—Cindy Lou O'Brien Browning, William Daniel. J.D., Woodland U., 1978; postgrad. U. San Diego, Oxford U., 1978, The Hague, Netherlands, 1979. Bar: Calif. 1980, U.S. Dist. Ct. (cen. dist.) Calif. 1980, U.S. Ct. Appeals (9th cir.) 1981. Practice law, Encino, Calif., 1980—; staff atty. Women's Legal Clinic, Haven Hills Battered Women's Ctr. State del. Democratic Party, 1979; mem. Dem. Circle, 1982-83; mem. Sherman Oaks Dem. Club. Recipient Achievement award Gov. Edmund C. Brown, Jr., State of Calif., 1978; achievement award The White House, Pres. Jimmy Carter, 1978; achievement award U.S. Senator S. I. Hayakawa, 1978; named Law Student Yr. YWCA, 1978; recipient Women's Polit. Affairs award Coro Found., 1979-80. Mem. ABA, Calif. State Bar Assn., Los Angeles County Bar, Assn. Trial Lawyers Am., Los Angeles Women Lawyers Assn., Calif. Trial Lawyers Assn., Los Angeles Trial Lawyers Assn., Calif. Women Lawyers Assn., San Fernando Valley Bar Assn., San Fernando Valley Women Lawyers Assn., Irish Am. Bar Assn. Calif., Coro Found. Alumni Assn., Pasadena Playhouse Alumni and Assocs., Nat. Assn. Female Execs. Methodist. Lodge: Order Eastern Star. Co-founder Women's Legal Clinic, Los Angeles. Office: 16027 Ventura Blvd 4th Floor Encino CA 91436

O'BRIEN, PHILIP MICHAEL, librarian; b. Albion, Nebr., Jan. 5, 1940; s. Lawrence J. and Mar Helen (Ruplinger) O'B.; m. Christina Bartling; children—Tara, Kirsten. B.A. in Sociology, Whittier Coll., 1961; M.S. in Library Sci., U. So. Calif., 1962, Ph.D. in Library Sci., 1974. Asst. librarian Whittier (Calif.) Coll., 1962-66, spl. collections librarian, 1974—; head bus. and social scis. dept. Chico (Calif.) State Coll. Library, 1966-67; U.S. Army librarian, Europe, 1967-70. Mem. ALA, Calif. Acad. and Research Libraries. Democrat. Clubs: Rounce and Coffin (Los Angeles); University (Whittier). Home: 11724 Dorland St Whittier CA 90601 Office: Whittier Coll Library Whittier CA 90601

O'BRIEN, RAYMOND FRANCIS, transp. and mfg. co. exec.; b. Atchison, Kans., May 31, 1922; s. James C. and Anna M. (Wagner) O'B., B.S. in Bus. Adminstrn., U. Mo., 1948; grad. Advanced Mgmt. Program. Harvard U., 1966; m. Mary Ann Baugher, Sept. 3, 1947; children—James B., William T., Kathleen A., Christopher R. Accountant-auditor Peat, Marwick, Mitchell & Co., Kansas City, Mo., 1948-52; controller-treas. Riss & Co., Kansas City, Mo., 1952-58; regional controller Consol. Freightways Corp. of Del., Indpls., also Akron, Ohio, 1958-61, pres., 1973-75, now dir., chmn.; with Consol. Freightways, Inc., San Francisco, 1961—, controller-treas., 1962-63, v.p., treas., 1963-67, v.p. fin., 1967-69, exec. v.p., 1969-75, pres., 1975—, chief exec. officer, 1977—, chmn. bd. dirs., 1979—; pres., dir. Freightways Terminal Co.; chmn., dir. Can. Freightways Ltd., Centron Ltd., CF Air Freight, Inc., CF Data Services, Inc., Consol. Metco, Inc., Freightliner Corp., Freightliner Credit Corp., Freightliner Market Devel. Corp. Mem. bus. adv. bd. U. Calif., Berkeley, Northwestern U., Chgo.; bd. regents St. Mary's Coll. of Calif. Served to 1st lt. USAAF, 1942-45. Mem. Am. Trucking Assn. (exec. com., dir.), Transp. Assn. Am. (dir.), Western Hwy. Inst. (treas.), Calif. C. of C. (dir.). Clubs: World Trade, Commonwealth (San Francisco); Palo Alto Hills Golf and Country, Congl. Country (Bethesda, Md.); Burning Tree Country. Office: Consol Freightways Inc 3240 Hillview Ave Palo Alto CA 94304*

O'BRIEN, ROBERT DONALD, industrial and agricultural products manufacturing company executive; b. Seattle, 1913. Grad. U. Wash., 1935. Chmn. Univar Corp., Seattle; dir. Puget Sound Power & Light Co., Weyerhaeuser Co., Pacific Northwest Bell Telephone Co., Univar Corp., Rainier Bancorp., Olympia Brewing Co. Office: Univar Corp 1600 Norton Bldg Seattle WA 98104*

O'BRIEN, ROBERT S., state ofcl.; b. Seattle, Sept. 14, 1918; s. Edward R. and Maude (Ransom) O'B.; grad. high sch.; m. Kathryn E. Arvan, Oct. 18, 1941. With Kaiser Co., 1938-46; owner restaurant bus., 1946-50; treas. Grant County, Wash., 1950-65; treas. State of Wash., Olympia, 1965—. Chmn. Wash. State Finance Com., 1965—, Wash. State Public Deposit Protection Commn., 1969—, Wash. State Pub. Employees' Retirement Bd., 1969-77, Law Enforcement Officers and Firefighters Retirement System, 1971-77, Wash. State Investment Bd., 1981—. Mem. Wash. State Data Processing Adv. Bd., 1967-73; mem. Gov.'s Exec. Mgmt. and Fiscal Affairs Commn., 1978-80, Gov.'s Cabinet Commn. on Tax Alternative, 1978-80. Trustee Wash. State Tchr.'s Retirement System. Recipient Leadership award Joint Council County and City Employees and Fedn. State Employees, 1970; Eagles Leadership award, 1969. Mem. Nat. Assn. State Auditors, Comptrollers and Treas. (pres. 1977), Nat. Assn. Mcpl. Fin. Officers, Nat. Assn. State Treasurers, Western State Treasurers Assn. (pres. 1970), Wash. Finance Officers Assn., Washington County Treas. Assn. (pres. 1955-56), Wash. State Assn. Elected County Ofcls. (pres. 1955-58), Olympia Area, Soap Lake (pres.) chambers commerce. Democrat. Elk (hon. life), Moose, Eagle, Lion. Clubs: Olympia Yacht; Wash. Athletic (Seattle); Empire (Spokane); Olympia Country and Golf. Office: Legislative Bldg Olympia WA 98504

O'BRIEN, ROBERT THOMAS, microbiologist, educator; b. Bismarck, N.D., Dec. 20, 1925; s. Ernest P. and Etta (Webster) O'B.; m. Beverly Ruth Asbridge, Dec. 22, 1948; children—Shawnne, Timothy, Barbara, Phillip, Mary. B.S., U. N.D., 1950, M.S., 1952; Ph.D., Wash. State U., 1956. Sr. scientist Gen. Electric Co., Richland, Wash., 1956-64, cons., Syracuse, N.Y., 1964-66; prof. dept. biology N.Mex. State U., Las Cruces, 1966—, chmn. dept. biology, 1978—; cons. food industry. Served with USAAF, 1943-46. Grantee, NSF, E.P.A., Dept. Edn., U.S. Army, Water Resources Research Inst., 1966—. Mem. Am. Soc. Microbiology, Soc. Gen. Microbiology, AAAS, Sigma Xi. Roman Catholic. Contbr. articles to profl. jours. Home: 2901 Karen Dr Las Cruces NM 88001 Office: Dept Biology New Mexico State Univ Las Cruces NM 88003

O'BRIEN, SUSAN KAY, home economist, consultant; b. Ardmore, Okla., Dec. 27, 1950; d. Royce Bryan and Blanche Joan (Hubbard) Means; m. Tommy Overton O'Brien, May 17, 1974; 1 son, Eric. B.S. in Home Econs., Baylor U., 1973. Home Service adviser Pioneer Gas Co., Lubbock, Tex., 1974-75; mgr. Am. Tea, Coffee & Spice Co., Denver, 1975-77; mgr. consumer edn./microwave Fred Schmid Appliances, Denver, 1977—; cons. Gen. Electric Co. Vol., Sewall Rehab. Ctr. Mem. Colo. Home Economists in Bus., Colo. Home Econs. Assn., Am. Home Econs. Assn., Internat. Microwave Power Inst. (cooking appliance sect.). Democrat. Office: 2405 W 5th St PO Box 17809 TA Denver CO 80217

OCCHIPINTI, CARL JOSEPH, broadcasting executive; b. New Orleans, Feb. 11, 1931; s. Victor and Anne (Maenza) O.; m. Ila M. Fanning, Nov. 22, 1939; children—Vickie, Michael, Diane. B.S., U. Wyo., 1956. Bus. and advt. mgr. Laramie (Wyo.) Newspapers, Inc., 1957-63; gen. mgr. Sta. KTVS-TV, Sterling, Colo., 1963-75; gen. mgr., v.p. Wyncco Communications, Inc., including Stas. KYCU-TV, Cheyenne, Wyo., KSTF-TV, Scottsbluff, Nebr., KTVS-TV, Sterling, Colo., 1975—; dir. CBS TV Network Affiliates, Dist. 8, Equality State Bank, Cheyenne. Dir. YMCA, former 1st v.p. Served with USAF, 1950-53. Mem. Wyo. Assn. Broadcasters Assn., Rocky Mountain Broadcasters Assn., Advt. Assn. Denver, Colo. Broadcasters Assn. (past v.p.), Am. Legion, Cheyenne C. of C. (past 1st v.p.). Roman Catholic. Clubs: Rotary, Cheyenne Country, Sterling Country, Elks. Office: 2923 E Lincolnway Cheyenne WY 82001

OCHOA, EDWARD BUSTOS, educator, consultant; b. Paso Robles, Calif., Sept. 13, 1942; s. Alfonso R. and Mary Louise (Bustos) O.; m. Olivia Martinez, Feb. 23, 1962; children—Edward P., Dianne R., Paul J. B.A. in Sociology, Calif. State Coll.-Bakersfield, 1976, M.A. in Edn., 1980. Cert. tchr., Calif. Probation officer Kern County (Calif.) Probation Dept., 1970-78; rehab. counselor Assocs. in Vocat. Mgmt., Bakersfield, 1978-80; dir. student affirmative action program Calif. State Coll.-Bakersfield, 1980—; cons. pvt. rehab. Bd. dirs. Kern County Camp Fire Council; mem. Kern County Task Force on Drug, Alcohol Abuse. Served with USMC, 1959-70. Mem. Raza Adminstrs. and Counselors in Higher Edn. Assn., Assn. Calif. Univ. Profs., United Profs. Calif., Mex.-Am. Polit. Assn. Democrat. Roman Catholic. Club: VFW. Office: Calif State U 9001 Stockdale Hwy Bakersfield CA 93309

OCHOA, EDWARD MARTIN, economist, educator; b. Buenos Aires, Argentina, Nov. 18, 1950; s. Ernesto A. and Violeta (Kimelman) O.; m. Holly D. Byers, Dec. 20, 1970; 1 son, Michael Andrew. B.A. in Physics, Reed Coll., 1973; M.S. in Nuclear Engring., Columbia U., 1976; M.A. in Econs., New Sch. for Social Research, N.Y.C., 1981, postgrad., 1981—; Radiation shielding engr. Gibbs & Hill Co., N.Y.C., 1976-77; radiation safety engr. Ebasco, Inc., N.Y.C., 1977-80; instr. econs. SUNY-Old Westbury, N.Y., 1980-81; lectr. econs. Calif. State U., Fresno, 1981—. Recipient Rasmussem Essay prize U. Utah, 1980. Mem. Am. Econs. Assn., Union Radical Polit. Economists. Contbr. papers and articles to profl. jours. Office: Dept Econs Calif State Univ Fresno CA 93740

OCHSNER, J. DONALD, rancher, state senator; b. Madison, Nebr., Oct. 25, 1919; student Mont. State U.; m. Fern Ochsner; 4 children. Rancher, Miles City, Mont.; mem. Mont. Senate, 1981—; pres. Custer County Farm Bur.; dir. dist. 5 Farm Bur. Mem. Woolgrowers, Stockgrowers. Office: Broadus Route Miles City MT 59301*

O'CONNOR, DANIEL JOSEPH, beauty supply co. exec.; b. Washington, Apr. 19, 1946; s. Daniel Joseph and Bernell Mae (Faull) O'C.; A.A., Moorpark Coll., 1971; B.S. in Bus Adminstrn., San Francisco State U., 1981; m. Cheryl Jo Cook, Sept. 4, 1976; children—David Jeffrey, Morgan Jenifer. Sales rep. Systemedia div. NCR Corp., 1973-74, systems analyst, 1974-76, sales rep. computer systems, 1977-78; sales rep. Sperry-Univac, San Francisco, 1978; pvt. practice computer programmer, Oakland, Calif., 1978-79; data processing mgr., West Coast Beauty Supply Co., San Francisco, 1979—. Served with USAF, 1966-69. Republican.

O'CONNOR, NANCY CAROLYN, space and technology company executive; b. Nurnberg, W. Ger., Dec. 31, 1948; came to U.S., 1949; d. Charles John and Sylvia Carolyn (Tint) O'C. Student U. Fla., 1965-69; B.A. in Bus. and Mgmt., Calif. State U.-Dominguez Hills, 1981, M.B.A., 1982; postgrad. Loyola Law Sch. Mgr., Dub's Nightclub and Lounge, Gainesville, Fla., 1973-74; mgr. pub. relations advt. Gt. So. Music Hall, Gainesville, 1975-76; bus. analyst Iran Project Office, Systems Engring. Integration div. TRW, Tehran, 1976-77, Redondo Beach, Calif., 1977-78; bus. adminstr. FLTSATCOM Project Office, Space and Tech. Group, TRW E&D, Redondo Beach, 1978-79, sr. bus. adminstr. Internat. Polar Solar Mission, 1980-81, mgr. fin. planning Def. Support Program, 1981—; TRW rep. to Conf. Bd.'s Congl. Assistance Program, 1983; tutor TRW Adopt-A-Sch. Program. Mem. Nat. Contract Mgmt. Assn., ABA, Phi Alpha Delta. Office: TRW E&D 1 Space Park Dr Suite R5/1090 Redondo Beach CA 90278

O'CONNOR, WILLIAM QUINLAN, real estate broker; b. Syracuse, N.Y., Sept. 2, 1920; s. William Joseph and Alice (Quinlan) O'C.; student Syracuse U., 1937, Pa. State U., 1939-40; B.A., U. So. Calif., 1947; postgrad. Calif. Poly. U., San Luis Obispo, 1967-72, Air U., 1961-63; J.D., LaSalle U., 1952; m. Georgie E. Hendrix, Nov. 30, 1943; children—William, Michael, Patrick, Casey. Parking/traffic commr. City of Arroyo Grande (Calif.), 1976-77; pres. O'Connor Realty, Arroyo Grande, 1945—; owner Arroyo Grande Bill's Place, 1952—. Comdr. CAP, 1962-66. Served with USCG, 1941-45, USAF, 1948-51. Mem. Nat. Assn. Realtors, Internat. Soc. Real Estate Appraisers, Calif. Assn. Realtors, Arroyo Grande C. of C. (dir., chmn. bd., pres.), Am. Legion, VFW, Marine Meml. Club, Schoolmasters, City of Hope. Republican. Roman Catholic. Clubs: San Luis Bay Country, Blacklake Country, KC, Elks (charter), Exchange (charter), Moose. Home: 310 W Cherry Ave Arroyo Grande CA 93420 Office: 105 Bridge St Arroyo Grande CA 93420

ODA, YOSHIO, physician; b. Papaaloa, Hawaii, Jan. 14, 1933; s. Hakuai and Usako (Yamamoto) O.; A.B., Cornell U., 1955; M.D., U. Chgo., 1959. Intern U. Chgo. Clinics, 1959-60; resident in pathology U. Chgo., 1960-62, Queen's Hosp., Hawaii, 1962-63, Long Beach (Calif.) VA Hosp., 1963-65; resident in allergy, immunology U. Colo. Med. Center, 1966-67; practice internal medicine, Los Angeles, 1965-66; practice internal medicine, allergy and immunology, Honolulu, 1970—; asst. clin. prof. medicine U. Hawaii, Honolulu, 1970—. Served to maj. M.C., AUS, 1968-70. Diplomate Am. Bd. Internal Medicine. Mem. A.C.P., Am. Acad. Allergy. Office: Piikoi Med Bldg 1024 Piikoi St Honolulu HI 96814

O'DAY, RICHARD ANTHONY, oral surgeon; b. San Francisco, Dec. 14, 1932; s. Mervyn James and Theresa (Vivaldi) O'D.; B.S., U. Santa Clara, 1954; D.D.S., U. Pacific, 1958; M.S., Mayo Grad. Sch. Medicine, 1963; m. Mary Evelyn Signer, May 25, 1957; children—Richard James, Brian Frederick. Resident oral surgery Mayo Clinic, Rochester, Minn., 1960-63; practice dentistry specializing in oral and maxillofacial surgery, Sacramento, Calif., 1964—; chief oral surgery Sutter Hosp., 1975-77; mem. staff Mercy Hosp.; sr. staff Sutter Hosp.; cons. oral and maxillofacial surgery David Grant Med. Ctr., Travis AFB; guest lectr. Yale U., 1977; vis. lectr. U. Colo. Med. Center; instr. cardiopulmonary resuscitation Am. Heart Assn. Chmn., Big Bros./Big Sisters Le Ski Event benefit, Bear Valley, Calif., 1978—; comdr. Sacramento County Sheriff's Air Squadron, 1982-83. Served to capt. Dental Corps, USAF, 1958-60. Diplomate Am. Bd. Oral and Maxillofacial Surgery (examiner 1969-76, Western region cons.). Mem. Am. (chmn. anesthesia com. 1976-79, chmn. anesthesia sect. in tng. exam. 1979-81), No. Calif. (dir.) assns. oral and maxillofacial surgeons, No. Calif. ADA, Internat. Anesthesia Research Soc., Am. Dental Soc. Anesthesiology (ethics com., examiner 1983—), Exptl. Aircraft Assn., Omicron Kappa Upsilon. Rotarian. Contbr. articles to profl. jour.; lectr. Office: 1737 Professional Dr Sacramento CA 95825

ODDEN, ALLAN ROBERT, education policy research executive; b. Duluth, Minn., Sept. 16, 1943; s. Robert Norman and Mabel Eleanor (Bjornnes) O.; m. Eleanor Ann Rubottom, May 28, 1966; 1 dau., Sarina. B.S., Brown U., 1965; M.Div., Union Theol. Sem., 1969; M.A., Columbia U., 1971, Ph.D., 1975. Tchr., curriculum developer N.Y.C. Pub. Schs., 1967-72; research assoc. Tchrs. Coll., Columbia U., 1974-75; dir. Edn. Fin. Ctr. of Edn. Commn. of the States, Denver, 1975-79, dir. edn. programs div., 1979-82, dir. policy analysis and research div., 1982—; cons. Nat. Inst. Edn., Nat. Ctr. Edn. Stats., Mcpl. Fin. Officers Assn., Ford Found., Nat. Conf. State Legislatures, Newark Urban Coalition, Satellite Acads. Program of N.Y.C. Bd. Edn., N.Y. State Gov.'s Panel Sch. Fin. Mem. Am. Ednl. Research Assn., Am. Polit. Sci. Assn., Am. Sch. Adminstrs., Am. Edn. Fin. Assn. (pres. 1979-80), Nat. Tax Assn. Editor: (with Nelda Cambron-McCabe) The Changing Politics of School Finance, 1982; contbr. articles to profl. jours., chpts. to books. Home: 1736 Grape St Denver CO 80220 Office: 1860 Lincoln St Suite 300 Denver CO 80295

ODEKIRK, DONNA GRACE BRADY, investment co. exec.; b. Ogden, Utah, July 13, 1929; d. Ira Lee and Myrtle Helen (Hedelius) Brady; student Weber State Coll., 1956; m. Heber Thomas Odekirk, Feb. 10, 1945; children—David Thomas, Donna Gaylene Odekirk Brown. Acctg. technician Treasury Dept., Ogden, 1958-63, digital computer programmer, 1963-76; gen. ptnr. Cross-T-Enterprises, Ogden, 1965-78, computer systems adminstr., 1977-79, data systems security officer, 1979-83, info. systems adminstr., 1978-82, v.p., 1978—; bd. dirs. Utah Credit Union League, Ogden chpt., 1975-82. Mem. Ogden City Urban Devel. Com., 1976. Recipient Woman of Year award Treasury Dept., 1975. Mem. Am. Bus. Women's Assn., Ninety-Nines, Internat. Assn. Women Pilots. Republican. Mem. Ch. Jesus Christ of Latter-day Saints. Home: 2170 Custer Ave Ogden UT 84401

O'DELL, MARY B., multiple association executive; consultant; writer; b. Columbus, Nebr., Aug. 28, 1930; d. Harry C. and Helen A. (Cherny) Brown; m. Robert A. O'Dell, July 26, 1955 (div.); children—Christopher, Mark, Paul. B.A. in Elem. Edn., U. Colo., 1952, Tchr. elem. pub. schs., Kirkwood, Mo., 1952-55; news editor Aurora (Colo.) Sun, 1972-76; cons. various Congl. coms., 1976—; exec. dir. Colo. Assn. Tobacco and Candy Distbrs., 1977—, Colo. Assn. Indsl. Bankers, 1982—, Colo. Consumer Fin. Assn., 1982—, Denver, 1982—; cons. pub. relations; dir. Consumer Credit Counseling Service; dir. Sec. State's Bus. Adv. Council. Pres. Aurora JayCee-ettes, 1960; citywide chmn. March of Dimes, 1961; chmn. bd. dirs. Metro Denver Sewage Disposal Dist. No. 1, 1974-76, dir., 1967—; mem. Colo. Com. on Women, 1974, Aurora Citizens Adv. Budget Com., 1980-81; bd. dirs. Home Neighborly Service; mem. Arapahoe County Republican Exec. Com., 1974-81, Aurora Rep. Women's Club, 1974-76; vice chmn. 62d state rep. dist., 1982-83. Named Colo. TAN activist of Yr., Tabacco Inst., 1980, 82; recipient J. Ernest O'Brien Meml. award Nat. Assn. Tobacco Distbrs., 1981; key to City of Aurora City Council, 1976. Mem. Colo., Soc. Assn. Execs., Am. Soc. Assn. Execs., P.E.O., AAUW, LWV, Pi Lambda Theta, Tau Beta Sigma. Presbyterian. Home: 2848 S Kenton Ct Aurora CO 80014 Office: Suite 487 2701 Alcott St Denver CO 80211

ODEM, LAURA JUANITA BURTON, personnel executive; b. Newark, Jan. 21, 1947; d. Herman L. and Iola (Brnatley) Burton; B.A., Seplman Coll., 1968; postgrad. Control Data Inst., 1970; m. Jerry Odem, Sept. 4, 1970; 1 dau., Veronica Michelle. Social worker Los Angeles County Public Social Services, 1968-70; chief personnel tng., 1970-72, personnel analyst with personnel dept., 1972-74, team leader, 1974-77, community devel. analyst, 1974-77, now personnel analyst III. Pres., Black Women's Network; mem. Inter-Alumni Council United Negro Coll. Fund. Mem. Calif. Personnel Mgmt. Assn., Am. Soc. Personnel Mgmt., Am. Soc. Public Adminstrn. Presbyterian. Home: 1222 Alvira St Los Angeles CA 90035 Office: 222 N Grand Ave Los Angeles CA 90012

O'DONNELL, CHARLES JOSEPH, grocery co. ofcl.; b. Paterson, N.J., Jan. 8, 1945; s. Joseph A. and Elizabeth A. O'D.; student Pasadena City Coll., 1963-65, 1976; engr. course Chrysler Corp., 1964; corr. courses U. Pa., UCLA, U. Oreg.; m. Sandra Kay Foster, Jan. 29, 1967; children—Brian, Dianne, Debra. Supr. stores Air Calif. Airlines, Newport Beach, Calif., 1966-68; supr. stores Jet Propulsion Lab., Calif. Inst. Tech., Pasadena, 1968-69; retail store mgr. mgmt. adv. group Thrifty Corp., Los Angeles, 1969-76; ops. mgr. Gen. Mdse. div. West Coast Grocery Co., Tacoma, 1976—; dir. Older & Wiser, Inc. Mem. King County Republican Caucus, 1980. Served with USAFR, 1964-71. Mem. Am. Mgmt. Assn., N. Am. Wholesale Grocers Assn., Gen. Mdse. Distn. Co. Presbyterian. Club: Seattle Toastmasters (ednl. v.p. 1980-81). Contbr. articles on bus. and career communications to periodicals.

O'DONNELL, JEAN, educator; b. Caldwell, Idaho, May 13, 1945; d. Miles James and Mary Elizabeth (Turner) Willcutt; B.S. cum laude, Coll. of Idaho, 1966; M.A. in Teaching, U. N.Mex., 1974; postgrad. U. Wyo., Wash. State U., Eastern Wash. State U., Central Wash. State U.; m. James Ashton O'Donnell, Dec. 19, 1965; children—Donald James, Sharon Jean. Tchr. sci. Parma (Idaho) Jr. High Sch., 1966-67; tchr. math. Albuquerque public schs., 1972-77; instr. math. prep. program U. N.Mex., Albuquerque, 1976-77; tchr. math. and sci. Kennewick (Wash.) Sch. Dist., 1977—, chmn. math., 1980—. Leader Girl Scouts U.S.A., 1979-82; chmn. ways and means com. Parent Tchr. Orgn., 1978-79. Mem. NEA, Nat. Council Tchrs. Math., Assn. for Supervision and Curriculum Devel., AAUW, Wash. Edn. Assn., Kennewick Edn. Assn. (treas.), Wash. State Math. Council (treas., workshop leader). Lutheran (council pres. 1981-82, council v.p. 1983-84). Office: Kennewick Sch Dist 6011 W 10th Pl Kennewick WA 99336

O'DONNELL, LAURENCE THOMAS, aerospace manufacturing supervisor; b. Billings, Mont., Nov. 19, 1944; s. Laurence Donald and Margaret Catherine (Huddleston) O.; m. Virginia Ann Stratton, Sept. 21, 1974; children—Virginia Katherine, Alison Michele, Margaret Erin, Christine Marie. Student U. Okla., 1963-64. Mechanic N. Am. Aviation Co., Tulsa, 1965-67; mechanic Dynalectron Co., Vietnam, Eng., U.S., 1967-74; mechanic Northrop Aircraft Co., Palmdale, Calif., 1974-75, Airesearch Co., Los Angeles, 1975-77; mechanic Rockwell Internat. Co., Palmdale, 1977-78, supr., 1978-80, sr. engr. designer, 1980-82, supr. mfg. Space Div., 1982—. NASA Snoopy award, 1980. Mem. AIAA, Nat. Mgmt. Assn. Catholic. Mem. Knights of Columbus, Elks. Home: 38950 Carolside Palmdale CA 93550 Office: 1500 E Ave M Palmdale CA 93550

O'DONNELL, ROBERT JOSEPH, psychologist; b. Cresson, Pa., July 11, 1924; s. Joseph Vincent and Marie Mabel (Tubbs) O'D.; B.A., U. Pa., 1948; M.A., U. So. Calif., 1949; Ph.D., U. Pitts., 1952; m. Merle Arlene Olson, Mar. 5, 1971. Personnel dir. Pacific Press, Los Angeles, 1952-59; dir. tng. United Calif. Bank, 1959-66; personnel dir., v.p. Western Bancorp., 1966-68; pres. Orgn. Devel., Inc., Cypress, Calif., 1968-78; prof. human resources mgmt. Calif. State U., Long Beach, 1978—; cons. ReSource, Los Angeles. Served with USAAF, 1942-45. Decorated D.F.C., Purple Heart. Mem. Am. Psychol. Assn. Democrat. Home: PO Box 937 Cypress CA 90630 Office: Calif State Univ Long Beach CA

O'DONNELL, STEPHEN CHARLES, paint manufacturing company executive; b. Bklyn., June 19, 1935; s. Stephen Vincent and Lois Grace (Northrup) O'D.; B.A., U. Notre Dame, 1957; postgrad. in bus. adminstrn. Roosevelt U., 1963-64; m. Donna Ruth Johns, Feb. 17, 1962; children—Michael, Kathleen, Peter, Stephen. Sales trainee Automatic Electric Co., North Lake, Ill., 1960-63; salesman Magnecraft Electric Co., Chgo., 1963-66; sales rep. John Gillen Co., Cicero, Ill., 1966-69; area sales mgr. Nat. Can Co., Cerritos, Calif., 1969-82; owner, operator Stay and Day Paint Materials Co., Los Angeles, 1983—. Mem. Catholic Charities Vietnamese Resettlement Com., Orange County, Calif., also Rockford, Ill. Served with U.S. Army, 1957-60. Mem. Calif. Mfrs. Assn., So. Calif. Paint and Coatings Assn., Los Angeles Soc. Tech. Coatings. Home: 606 Tangier Placentia CA 92670 Office: 363 S Mission Rd Los Angeles CA 90033

O'DONNELL, WILLIAM THOMAS, radar systems mktg. exec.; b. Latrobe, Pa., Feb. 22, 1939; s. William Regis and Kathryn Ann (Coneff) O'D.; student Eastern N.Mex. U., 1958-61; student in mktg. John Carroll U., 1961-65, Ill. Inst. Tech., 1965-66; B.S.B.A., U. Phoenix, 1982, postgrad., 1982—; m. Judith Koetke, Oct. 1, 1965; children—William Thomas and William Patrick (twins), Allison Rose, Kevin Raymond. Various sales positions Hickok Elec. Instrument Co., Cleve., 1961-65, Fairchild Semicondr., Mpls., 1965-67; Transitron Semicondr., Mpls., 1967-69; Burroughs Corp., Plainfield, N.J., 1967-71; mktg. mgr. Owens-Ill. Co., 1972-73, v.p. mktg. Pantek Co., subs. Owens-Ill. Co., Lewistown, Pa., 1973-75, v.p. mktg., nat. sales mgr., Toledo, 1975-76; mktg. mgr., nat. sales mgr. Govt. Electronics div. group Motorola Co., Scottsdale, Ariz., 1976-80, U.S. mktg. mgr. radar positioning systems Motorola Govt. Electronics Group, 1981—; gen. mgr. J. K. Internat., Scottsdale, 1980-81; cons. mktg., mgmt. Chmn., Republican Precinct, Burnsville, Minn., 1968-70; city fin. chmn., Burnsville; dir. community devel. U.S. Jaycees, Mpls., 1968-69; mem. Scottsdale 2000 Com. Served with USAF, 1957-61. Recipient Outstanding Achievement award Govt. Electronics div. Motorola Co., 1976; named to Million Dollar Club, Burroughs Co., 1969-71; hon. citizen, Donaldsville, La., 1978; others. Mem. Phoenix Execs. Club, Am. Mktg. Assn. Roman Catholic. Clubs: North Cape Yacht, Scottsdale Racquet, Toftnees Country. Home: 8432 E Belgian Trail Scottsdale AZ 85258 Office: 7402 S Price Rd Tempe AZ 85283

OE, EMILY NORENE, counselor; b. Dickinson, N.D., Nov. 12, 1942; d. Nicholas George and Eunice Norene (Wilson) O.; elem. edn. cert. Presentation Jr. Coll., Aberdeen, S.D., 1962; B.Ed., U. Alaska, 1977; M.A. in Guidance and Counseling, Gonzaga U., 1978. Child care worker Home of Good Shepherd, St. Paul, 1972-73; counselor Emmaus Sch. for Girls, King George, Va., 1973-74, summers 1975, 77; guidance dir. Immaculate Conception Sch., Fairbanks, Alaska, 1974-75, 75-76, elem. sch. counselor, 1978-80; elem. sch. counselor Fairbanks North Star Borough Sch. Dist., 1980—; child counselor Catholic Community Resources, Fairbanks, 1978-80. Mem. steering com. Big Bros./Big Sisters Am. Mem. Am. Personnel and Guidance Assn., Am. Sch. Counselors Assn., Alaska Personnel and Guidance Assn., Alaska Sch. Counselors Assn., Alpha Delta Kappa (v.p. Gamma chpt. 1981-82, pres. 1982—). Roman Catholic. Home: 1813 Carr Ave Fairbanks AK 99701 Office: PO Box 1250 Fairbanks AK 99707

OEH, GEORGE RICHARD, elec. engr.; b. Tacoma, Aug. 29, 1936; s. George Kenneth and Elsie Linnea (Ness) O.; B.S. in Elec. Engring., U. Wash., 1958, M.S. (teaching fellow 1960), 1962; m. Diane Manley, Aug. 18, 1962; children—Karen Michelle, Jason Robert. Instr., U. Wash., 1961—; advanced devel. engr., Philco-Ford Co., 1963-64; mgr. electromagnetics dept. GTE-Sylvania Co., 1964-72; mgr. sales Watkins Johnson Co., Palo Alto, Calif., 1972-82; dir. internat. ops. EM Systems, Inc., Sunnyvale, Calif., 1982—. Mem. Sunnyvale Park and Recreation Bd., 1968-69; bd. dirs. Sunnyvale Little League, 1977-78. Served with USAF, 1958-60. Mem. IEEE (chmn. San Francisco chpt. 1970-71), Electronic Def. Assn., Assn. Old Crows (past officer and dir.), Assn. Former Intelligence Officers, Res. Officers Assn. Democrat. Clubs: Western World Trade, Elks. Author papers in field. Home: 1056 Firth Ct Sunnyvale CA 94087 Office: 290 Sana Ana Ct Sunnyvale CA 94086

OELRICH, MARGARET HAZEL, counseling educator, consultant; b. Chgo., Jan. 28, 1927; d. Paul A. and Myrtle C. (Matson) Malmborg; m. Carl Oelrich, Oct. 22, 1949; 1 son, Paul Raymond. B.S., Western Mich. U., 1949. Registered occupational therapist; cert. trainer Nat. Inst. Drug Abuse. Asst. dir. occupational therapy N. Shore Health Resort, Winnetka, Ill., 1949; coordinator vol. services Latterman State Hosp., Pomona, Calif., 1953-60; dir. rehab. City of Hope Med. Ctr., Duarte, Calif., 1960-79; program coordinator, vocat. specialist II Network, Honolulu, 1979-81; lectr. Leeward Community Coll., Pearl City, Hawaii, 1981—; cons., tng. specialist, career-life counselor, 1981—; guidance counselor Army Edn. Ctr. Schofield Barracks, Hawaii, 1982—; presenter numerous lectures, workshops, seminars at various hosps., U. So. Calif., Los Angeles City Coll., Calif. Nursing Sch., Inc.; lectr. profl. groups. Bd. dirs., 2d v.p., mem. program and evaluation coms. Recreation and Edn. for Adults, Children with Handicaps; staff instr., leader family support group Ptnrs. in Health, Honolulu. Mem. Am. Personnel and Guidance Assn., Am. Arbitration Assn. (nat. panel mem.), Am. Soc. Tng. and Devel. (mem. exec. bd., chmn. chpt. devel., mem. program com. Hawaii chpt.), Nat. Rehab. Assn., Nat. Assn. Female Execs., Hawaii Assn. Parks and Recreation, Joy of Learning. Named Outstanding Health Care Adminstr. So. Calif. Occupational Therapy Assn., 1975; Counselor of Yr. award Hawaii Personnel and Guidance Assn., 1983. Contbr. articles to profl. jours. chpts. to books. Home: 469 Ena Rd #712 Honolulu HI 96815 Office: Army Educ Ctr Schofield Bks HI 96867

OELRICH, PAUL RAYMOND, airline executive; b. Kalamazoo, Mich., Aug. 12, 1950; s. Carl Milton and Margaret Hazel (Malmborg) O. Student Mt. San Antonio Jr. Coll., 1968-70, San Jose State U., 1970-73; B.S. in Bus. Mgmt., Calif. Poly. U.-Pomona, 1976. Ops. agt. Am. Airlines, Ontario, Calif., part-time 1974-75, full time, 1975-79, supr. ramp services, San Francisco, 1979-80, acting group supr., 1980-81, account exec., airfreight, Los Angeles, 1981—. Mem. Am. Mgmt. Assn., Aircraft Owners and Pilots Assn., Mercedes Benz Club N.Am. Home: 1165 Rae Ct Upland CA 91786 Office: Am Airlines 5908 Avion Dr Los Angeles CA 90009

OESTREICH, JAMES JOSEPH, campground exec.; b. Mont., May 15, 1940; s. James F. and Alice M. (Bentz) O.; student pub. schs., Missoula, Mont.; m. Molly Marie, Dec. 8, 1973; 1 son, Jeremy; children by previous marriage—Joan, Jeff, John, Jennifer. Pres., chief exec. officer Am. Campgrounds Inc., and affiliates DBA ACI Parks, Bellevue, Wash., 1970—; mem. Woodall's Nat. Campground Adv. Council; mem. chmn.'s com. U.S. Senatorial Adv. Bd., 1980-81. Mem. Nat. Campground Owners Assn. (v.p. 1980-81, mem. mgmt. com. 1980-81, chmn. edn. com., mem. regionalization com., bd. dirs. 1978—), Campground Owners Mont., Wash. Resorts and Pvt. Parks Owners Assn. (pres. 1976-77, v.p., chmn. trade show 1978-80, editor, pub. directory, recognition award 1978-80, outstanding contbn. award 1979), Idaho Campground Owners Assn., Inst. Cert. Park Operators (bd. regents 1981-82, cert. park operator), Internat. Platform Assn. Office: Box 1888 Bellevue WA 98009

OFFSTEIN, LOIS, educator; b. Plainfield, N.J., Jan. 7, 1948; d. Martin M. and Jessie (Krieger) Nathanson; B.A., William Paterson State U., 1970; M.A., Calif. State U., Los Angeles, 1975. Speech lang. and hearing specialist grades kindergarten through 12 Los Angeles County Supt. Schs., 1975-81, aphasia tchr. specialist, high schs., 1975-83; pvt. practice lang. and speech pathology, 1976—; speech-lang. pathologist Citrus Community Coll., 1983—; conf. and inservice lectr. Mem. Am. Speech and Hearing Assn., Calif. Speech Pathologists and Audiologists in Pvt. Practice, Calif. Speech and Hearing Assn., Calif. Tchrs. Assn., Mensa, Phi Kappa Phi, Delta Kappa Pi. Clubs: Theater Americana (Altadena, Calif.); Drama. Contbr. articles to Los Angeles County Supt. Schs. publs.

OFSOWITZ, PAULA JOYCE, computer pogramming executive; b. Detroit, Nov. 21, 1942; d. Samuel and Pearl (Bernstein) Ofsowitz. Student, Dade County (Fla.) Jr. Coll., 1961-62; programming cert. Control Data Instr., 1971, Inst. Advanced Tech., 1982. Programmer, Fla. Comml. Banks, Inc., Miami, Fla., 1972-73, First Fed. Savs. and Loan, Miami, 1973-77; contract programmer, Computer Dynamics, Inc., Southfield, Mich., 1977-79; tech. team leader, sr. systems programmer, tech. instr., systems engr. Four Phaze Systems, Inc., Southfield, 1979-80, Cupertino Calif., 1981—. Mem. Smithsonian Inst. Assocs. Democrat. Home: 485 Northlake Dr Apt 102 San Jose CA 95117 Office: Four Phaze Systems Inc 10700 No De Anza Blvd Cupertino CA 95014

OGDEN, MYRON WALDO, former ednl. adminstr.; b. Cambridge, Mass., July 8, 1917; s. Waldo M. and Florence (Newton) O.; B.S. in Edn., Boston U., 1949; M.S. in Spl. Edn., U. Wash., Seattle, 1966; children—David M., Darren R. Instr. history Peninsula Coll., Port Angeles, Wash., 1967-70; dir. adult edn. Neah Bay (Wash.) Schs., 1969-70, dir. spl. edn., 1973-76, ret., 1976. Rep. Sch. Community Council, 1970-76. Mem. NEA, Wash., Clallam County (past pres.) edn. assns., Pi Gamma Mu, Phi Delta Kappa. Home: Belvedere 702 35th Ave Seattle WA 98122

OGG, DAVID ROSS, interior designer, educator; b. Abilene, Tex., Feb. 1, 1937; s. Elmore Ross and Kitty May (McGlen) O. Student U. R.I., 1955-56, So. Ill. U., 1956-57, Los Angeles Trade Tech. Sch., 1965-66. Freelance motion picture and TV set designer, 1964-67; sr. designer, project coordinator Albert Parvin Dohrmann Co., Beverly Hills, Calif., 1968-72; dir. design Meml. Hosp. of Culver City (Calif.), 1972-74; sr. designer R.W. Smith & Co., San Diego, 1977—; faculty mem. Grossmont Coll., El Cajon, Calif., 1981—. Mem. dean's adv. council Sch. Fine Arts, San Diego State U., 1981—; mem. Orchids & Onions Jury, 1980; program chmn. Design Expo Trade Show, 1982. Served with USAF, 1958-62. Recipient 1st place design award Hotel and Restaurant Assn., 1970, 1st ann. Outstanding Award for Service to Breed, West Highland White Terrier Club of Calif., 1982. Mem. Am. Soc. Interior Designers (cert. 1980, design com. 1982, v.p., bd. dirs. San Diego chpt.), Inst. Bus. Designers (cert. 1982), Pure Bred Dog Judges of Am. Assn. Clubs: Del Sur Kennel (bd. dirs. 1983), El Cajon. Patentee ednl. program for pure-bred dog owners. Home: 4281 Farley Ln San Diego CA 92122 Office: 501 11th Ave San Diego CA 92101

OGG, ROBERT DANFORTH, business exec., inventor; b. Gardiner, Maine, June 10, 1918; s. James and Eleanor B. (Danforth) O.; A.A., San Francisco City Coll., 1941; student U. Calif. at Berkeley, 1946-47; m. Phyllis Idun Aasgaard, Nov. 23, 1946; children—Richard Aasgaard, Robert Danforth, James Erling; m. Nancy Foote Bechtel, Oct. 21, 1978. Utilities engr. State of Calif., 1947-49; research engr., sales mgr. Danforth Anchors, East Boothbay, Maine, and Berkeley, 1949-51, gen. mgr., Berkeley, 1951-56, pres., 1956-59, also dir.; mng. dir. Danforth div. Eastern Co., mfrs. marine products, weather instruments, electronic products, auto-pilots, Portland, Maine, 1959-79, also dir.; dir. Brewers Boatyard, West Southport, Maine, Eastern Co., Henry R. Hinckley & Co. Bd. dirs. Arlington Ave. Community Center Council Kensington, 1954-57, chmn. bd., 1956-57; trustee U. Calif.-Berkeley Found.; sr. warden St. Ann's Episcopal Ch., Windham, Maine. Served as lt. comdr. USNR, 1941-46. Mem. Nat. Marine Products Assn. (pres. 1961-63), Nat. Assn. Engine and Boat Mfrs., Am. Boat and Yacht Council, IEEE, Am. Geophys. Union, Soc. Naval Architects and Marine Engrs., Am. Soc. Naval Engrs., Portland Marine Soc., N.Am. Yacht Racing Union, Internat. Oceanographic Found., Boating Industry Assn., U.S. Naval Inst., Navy League (pres. Casco Bay Council 1968-71), Explorers Club. Elk. Clubs: Outboard Boating, Sierra (San Francisco); Card Ledge Yacht; Portland Country, Portland Yacht (Portland); N.Y. Yacht; St. Croix Country (dir. 1973—, v.p. 1976—). Author: Anchors and Anchoring; Compasses and Compassing; also contbg. author Handbook of Ocean Engring., Chapman's Piloting and Seamanship. Contbr. numerous articles to various publs. Patentee in field. Office: PO Box 160 Kentfield CA 94914

OGG, WILSON REID, lawyer, educator; b. Alhambra, Calif., Feb. 26, 1928; s. James Brooks and Mary (Wilson) O.; student Pasadena Jr. Coll., 1946; A.B., U. Calif. at Berkeley, 1949, J.D., 1952. Asso. trust Dept. Wells Fargo Bank, San Francisco, 1954-55; admitted to Calif. bar; pvt. practice law, Berkeley, 1955-78; real estate broker, cons., 1974-78; curator-in-residence Pinebrook, 1964—; research atty., legal editor dept. of continuing education of bar U. Calif. Extension, 1958-63; psychology instr. 25th Sta. Hosp., Taegu, Korea, 1954; English instr. Taegu English Lang. Inst., Taegu, 1954. Trustee World U., 1976-80. Served with AUS, 1952-54. Cert. community coll. instr. Fellow Internat. Acad. Law and Sci.; mem. ABA, State Bar Calif., San Francisco Bar Assn., Am. Arbitration Assn. (nat. panel arbitrators), AAAS, Am. Soc. Phys. Research, Calif. Soc. Phys. Study (pres., chmn. bd. 1963-65), Suomi Soc., Soc. for Phys. Research (London), Parapsychol. Assn. (asso.), Internat. Soc. Philos. Enquiry (dir. admissions 1981—), Internat. Soc. Unified Sci., Worldwide Acad. Scholars, Am. Acad. Polit. and Social Sci., Mechanics Inst., Internat. Platform Assn., Am. Legion, VFW, Am. Mensa, Lawyers in Mensa, Psychic Sci. Spl. Interest Group. Unitarian. Mason, Elk. Clubs: Faculty (U. Calif.), City Commons (Berkeley); Press (San Francisco); Commonwealth of Calif.; Town Hall Calif. Editor: Legal Aspects of Doing Business under Government Contracts and Subcontracts, 1958, Basic California Practice Handbook, 1959; contbr. numerous articles to Jour. Internat. Soc. Philos. Enquiry. Address: Eight Bret Harte Way Berkeley CA 94708

OGLESBY, DONALD EASTMAN, automatic electronic test equipment company executive; b. East Providence, R.I., Jan. 23, 1931; s. Elbert Jerome and Doris Eastman (Wixon) O.; m. Beverly Ann Erickson, June 27, 1953; children—Janet Lynn, Susan Kay, Amy J., David Eastman, Douglas Erickson. B.S.E.E., Mich. State U., 1959. Project engr. Gen. Electric Co., Binghamton, N.Y., Phoenix, 1959-64, mgr. printer products, card equipment and advanced remote terminal engring. units, 1964-66; mgr. data terminal equipment, mgr. mktg. Omnitec Corp., Phoenix, 1966-68; pres., founder, chief exec. officer Data Computing, Inc., Phoenix, 1968-71; v.p., gen. mgr. equipment div. Wabash Computer Corp., Phoenix, 1971-73; pres., founder, chief exec. officer Three Phoenix Co., 1973-82, chmn. bd., chief exec. officer, 1982—; dir. Omnitest, Ltd. (Eng.). Instr. boating safety U.S. Power Squadron; dir. Sch. Bd. Sci. Com.; mem. Sch. Bd. Com.; precinct committeeman Republican Com.; bd. dirs. Desert Mission. Served with USN, 1951-55. Mem. Am. Mktg. Assn. (award 1967), Soc. Advancement Mgmt., IEEE, Am. Electronics Assn., Am. Mgmt. Assn. Club: Thunderbird Rotary. Office: 21639 N 14th Ave Phoenix AZ 85027

O'GREEN, FREDERICK WILBERT, electronics co. exec.; b. Mason City, Iowa, Mar. 25, 1921; s. Oscar A. and Anna (Heikkinen) O'G.; student Mason City Jr. Coll., 1939-40; B.S. in Elec. Engring., Iowa State U., 1943; M.S. in Elec. Engring., U. Md., 1949; LL.D. (hon.), Pepperdine U., 1977; m. Mildred G. Ludlow, Mar. 21, 1943; children—Susan Renee O'Green, Jane Lynn O'Green Koenig, John Frederick, Eric Stephen. Project engr. Naval Ordnance Lab., White Oak, Md., 1943-55; dir. Agena D project Lockheed Aircraft Co., Sunnyvale Calif., 1955-62; v.p. Litton Industries, Inc., Beverly Hills, Calif., 1962-66, sr. v.p., 1966-68, exec. v.p., 1968-74, pres., chief operating officer, from 1974, now chmn. bd., chief operating officer, dir., 1968—; dir. Security Pacific Corp., Security Pacific Nat. Bank. Area chmn. United Crusade, 1965; mem. adv. bd. Better Hearing Inst., bd. councilors U. So. Calif. Sch. Engring. Served with USNR, 1945. Recipient Meritorious Civilian Service award U.S. Navy, 1954, Outstanding Achievement award Air Force Systems Command, 1964; Disting. Achievement citation Iowa State U., 1973; named Energy Exec. of Yr., Assn. Energy Engrs., 1980. Mem. AIM, AIAA, U.S. C. of C., Assn. U.S. Army (dir.), Phi Kappa Psi, Phi Mu Alpha. Republican. Lutheran. Office: Litton Industries Inc 360 N Crescent Dr Beverly Hills CA 90210*

OGUS, ROY CHARLES, computer engineer; b. South Africa, Dec. 3, 1946; s. Solomon Alan and Sylvia (William) O.; m. Margo Rich, Dec. 23, 1976. B.S.E.E., U. Pretoria, 1968; M.S.E.E., Stanford U., 1972, Ph.D.E.E. and Computer Sci., 1975. Sr. engr. Council for Sci. and Indsl. Research, 1968-70; research assoc. Stanford U., 1975-77; prin. engr. Xerox Corp., Palo Alto, Calif., 1977-80, mgr. hardware design, 1980—. Mem. South African Inst. Elec. Engrs., IEEE, Assn. Computing Machinery, Sigma Xi.

O'GWIN, EVELYN J., social service worker, former educational administrator; b. Baton Rouge, La., Nov. 24; d. Purity and Evelyn T. Jones; B.A., So. U., Baton Rouge, 1957, M.A., 1964; m. Alfred O'Gwin, Dec. 24, 1958; 1 son, Reginal S. Tchr. pub. schs., Morgan City, La., 1957-60, Baton Rouge, 1962-70, Las Vegas, Nev., 1970-72; tchr. corps team leader U. Nev., Las Vegas, 1972-74; kindergarten prin., West Las Vegas, Nev., 1974-76; prin. Jo Mackey Sixth Grade Center, North Las Vegas, 1976-81; officer of ct. for neglected and abused children Juvenile Ct. Service, Las Vegas, 1982—; also personal mgr. entertainer. Mem. Nat. Assn. Elem. Sch. Prins., NEA, Nev. Assn. Sch. Adminstrs., Clark County Assn. Secondary Sch. Prins., Assn. Supervision and Curriculum Devel., Clark County Elem. Sch. Prins. Assn., Am. Women in Radio and TV, Phi Delta Kappa, Gamma Phi Delta. Democrat. Roman Catholic. Club: Nat. Links. Office: 311 Alexandria St Hollywood CA

OH, JESSE JISOO, trade company executive; b. Kwangpyung, Korea, Aug. 28, 1930; s. Jongshik and Kisang (Choi) O.; 1 son, Jon Junetac. M.A., Korea U., 1966, U. So. Calif., 1974; Commd. 2d lt., arty. Army of Korea, 1950, advanced through grades to col., 1968; instr., dir. Korean Army Coll., 1963-67; asst. to asst. minister nat. def., 1967-69; ret., 1969; pres. Oceanus Corp., Torrance, Calif., 1974—, chmn. bd. Mem. Am. Polit. Sci. Assn., Korean Arty. Vets. Assn. So. Calif. (pres. 1982—). Author: The Way to become American Citizen, 1962.

OH, TAI KEUN, business educator; b. Seoul, Korea, Mar. 25, 1934; s. Chin Young and Eui Kyung (Yun) O.; came to U.S., 1958, naturalized, 1969; B.A., Seijo U., 1957; M.A., No. Ill. U., 1961; M.L.S., U. Wis., 1965, Ph.D., 1970; m. Gretchen Brenneke, Dec. 26, 1964; children—Erica, Elizabeth, Emily. Asst. prof. mgmt. Roosevelt U., Chgo., 1969-73; assoc. prof. Calif. State U., Fullerton, 1973-76, prof. mgmt., 1976—; vis. prof. U. Hawaii, 1983; mgmt. cons. Named Outstanding Prof., Sch. Bus. Adminstrn. and Econs., Calif. State U., Fullerton, 1976, 78. NSF grantee, 1968-69. Mem. Acad. Mgmt., Indsl. Relations Research Assn., Acad. Internat. Bus. Editorial bd. Acad. Mgmt. Rev., 1978-81; contbg. author: Ency. Profl. Mgmt., 1978, 83; contbr. articles to profl. jours. Home: 2044 E Eucalyptus Ln Brea CA 92621 Office: Calif State U Fullerton CA 92634

O'HALLORAN, (LAVERNE M.) KATHLEEN (MRS. JOHN R. O'HALLORAN, JR.), real estate broker; b. Laurium, Mich., Nov. 15, 1921; d. Joseph Wilfred and Della K. (Gervais) Shaffer; student Fond Du Lac Comml. Coll., 1938-40, Fresno City Coll., 1965-66; m. John Richard

O'Halloran, Jr., July 15, 1942; children—Sheila Ann O'Halloran Stoll, Gregory, Michael, Maureen O'Halloran Benelli, Sean, Margaret O'Halloran Johnson. Co-owner Hamlin Hotel, San Francisco, 1946-48, Lazy F Guest Ranch, Ellensburg, Wash., 1948-50; owner, broker Kathy O'Halloran Realty, Fresno, 1980—; pres. C & R Investments, 1974-75; broker Settlers Real Estate, Inc., Fresno, 1975—. Charter mem. Infant of Prague Adoption Agy. Aux., 1954—, sec., 1955; mem. Mayor's Com. for Community Devel., 1963-64; pres. Sacred Heart Mothers Club, 1959; pres. Calif. Citizens for Decent Lit., 1961-63, Central Calif. Citizens for Decent Lit., 1959-64; precinct chmn. Goldwater campaign, 1964; chmn. Fresno County United Republicans Calif., 1962; area coordinator Clean Campaign Ballot Initiative, 1966; candidate Fresno City Council, 1961. Mem. Fresno Bd. Realtors, Nat. Assn. Real Estate Bds. Roman Catholic. Home: 3503 N Bond St Fresno CA 93726 Office: 3503 N Bond St Fresno CA 93726

OHANNESON, GREGORY STORIE, college administrator; b. Los Angeles, Dec. 17, 1929; s. Aaram Peter and Averie Kate (Storie) O.; m. Joan Marie Delmonico, May 15, 1954; children—Kim, Beth, Jill, Erin. A.A. in Chemistry, U. Calif.-Berkeley, 1949, B.S. in Soil Sci., 1952; M.A. in Agrl. Edn., Calif. State Poly. U., 1968; Ed.D. in Vocat. Edn., UCLA, 1973. Cert. tchr., Calif. Tchr. agr. Wasco (Calif.) High Sch., 1967-70; cons. Imperial Valley Community Coll., El Centro, Calif., 1971; cons. San Diego Unified Sch. Dist., 1972; asst. dir. vocat. and adult edn. Santa Clara County Office of Edn., San Jose, Calif., 1973-74, acting dir. N. County Regional Occupational Programs, 1974-75; asst. dean vocat. edn. San Jose (Calif.) City Coll., 1975-81; asst. dean occupational services San Jose Community Coll. Dist., 1981—; mgr. occupational assistance grants. Mem. Kern County Republican Central Com., 1964-65; Served to lt. USN, 1955-57; EPDA Devel. Act grantee, 1970. Mem. Am. Vocat. Assn., Calif. Community Coll. Adminstrs. Occupational Edn., Calif. Assn. Vocat. Educators, Phi Delta Kappa. Republican. Contbr. articles to Edn. Resources Info. Ctr., numerous profl. jours. Office: 2100 Moorpark Ave San Jose CA 95128

O'HARA, GENE LESTER, health care exec.; b. Northwood, N.D., Apr. 6, 1945; s. Glenn Lester and Alice Marie (Wixo) O'H.; B.S. in Pharmacy, U. Mont., 1969; D.Pharmacy, U. Pacific, 1974; m. Linda Kirk, Aug. 8, 1970; children—Ryan, Brittney. Pharmacist, Osco Drug, Billings, Mont., 1969-70, St. Vincent's Hosp., Billings, 1970-72; prof. Purdue U. Sch. Pharmacy, West Lafayette, Ind., 1974-78; exec. dir. Mont.-Wyo. Health Resources, Billings, 1978—, v.p. Billings Deaconess Hosp., 1979—; cons. Merke, Sharpe and Dohme, Inc., 1976-77. Pres., Yellowstone County Heart Assn., 1971-72, 78; bd. dirs. Mont. Heart Assn., 1972-79—, Ind. Diabetes Assn., 1976-77; pres. Tippicanoe County Diabetes Assn., 1975-76. Mem. Am. Soc. Hosp. Pharmacists, Mont. Soc. Hosp. Pharmacists, Mont. Hosp. Assn., Nat. Rural Health Assn., Billings Jr. C. of C. (dir.). Clubs: Kiwanis, Billings Petroleum, Billings Handball Assn. (pres.). Contbr. articles to profl. jours. Office: 2813 9th Ave N Billings MT 59101

OHLSON, DANNY LOY, physiologist; b. Cherokee, Iowa, Feb. 16, 1947; s. Filmore Lloyd and Margaret Ann (Woltman) O.; B.A. in Zoology, U. Iowa, 1969; M.S. in Animal Scis., U. Idaho, Moscow, 1978. Grad. research asst., then sci. aide U. Idaho, 1971-77, research assoc. animal scis., 1978—. Mem. AAAS, Am. Soc. Animal Sci., Sigma Xi, Gamma Sigma Delta, Phi Sigma, Xi Sigma Pi. Author papers in field. Home: 1230 Mountain View Rd Moscow ID 83843 Office: Dept Animal and Vet Scis Univ Idaho Moscow ID 83843

OHMAN, JOHN MICHAEL, lawyer; b. Anaconda, Mont., Dec. 22, 1948; B.S. in Bus. Adminstrn., Creighton U., 1971, J.D., 1972; m. Susan M.; children—Brittany Michelle, Andrea Michaela. Admitted to Nebr. bar, 1973, Idaho bar, 1973, also U.S. Supreme Ct. bar, U.S. Dist. Ct. bars, U.S. Ct. Appeals bar; mem. firm Denman, Reeves & Ohman, Idaho Falls, Idaho, from 1973; now mem. firm Cox & Ohman, Chartered, Idaho Falls. Pres., Am. Cancer Soc., Bonneville County. Mem. Am. Bar Assn., Idaho Bar Assn., Nebr. Bar Assn. 7th Jud. Dist. Bar Assn., Am. Trial Lawyers Assn., Idaho Trial Lawyers Assn., Am. Judicature Soc., ICC Practioners, Smithsonian Instn., Civitan Internat., Phi Alpha Delta, Omicron Delta Epsilon, Phi Kappa Psi. Home: 190 Fieldstream Ave Idaho Falls ID 83401 Office: 185 S Capital Idaho Falls ID 83401

OISHI, NOBORU, physician; b. Kapaa, Hawaii, Nov. 11, 1928; s. Masato and Shizuyo (Watada) O.; A.B., Washington U., St. Louis, 1949, M.D., 1953; m. Violet Niimi, June 12, 1956; 1 son, Scott. Intern, Detroit Receiving Hosp., 1953-54, resident in internal medicine, 1956-58; fellow in hematology U. Rochester (N.Y.), 1958-59, instr. dept. medicine, 1958-59; practice medicine specializing in hematology and oncology, Honolulu, 1959—; assoc. prof. John A. Burns Sch. Medicine, U. Hawaii, Honolulu, 1974-79, prof. medicine, 1979—; v.p. Blood Bank of Hawaii, 1974—; dir. clin. sci. program Cancer Center of Hawaii, Honolulu, 1974—. Served with USPHS, 1954-56. Fellow ACP; mem. Am. Soc. Internal Medicine, Am. Soc. Clin. Oncology, Am. Soc. for Hematology, Am. Assn. for Cancer Edn., Am. Assn. for Cancer Research. Home: 4399 Aukai Honolulu HI 96817 Office: 1236 Lauhala St Honolulu HI 96813

O'KEEFE, GARRETT JAMES, mass communications educator, consultant; b. Detroit, Dec. 24, 1942; s. Garrett James and Marcella Grace (Fichtner) O.; m. Jane Mary Engels, Feb. 7, 1970. B.A., U. Colo., 1965; M.S. in Journalism, Iowa State U., 1967; Ph.D. in Mass Communications (NDEA fellow), U. Wis., 1970. Asst. prof. dept. mass communications U. Denver, 1970-74, assoc. prof., 1975-80, prof., chmn. dept., 1980—; communications research cons. Nat. Assn. Broadcasters grantee, 1971; U.S. Dept. Energy grantee, 1978; U.S. Justice Dept. grantee, 1981. Mem. Am. Assn. Pub. Opinion Research, Am. Psychol. Assn., Assn. Edn. in Journalism, Internat. Communication Assn., Midwest Assn. Pub. Opion Research. Author: (with H. Mendelsohn) The People Choose a President, 1976; contbr. articles to profl. jours. Office: Dept Mass Communications U Denver Denver CO 80208

O'KEEFE, THOMAS BRIAN, real estate investor, consultant, lecturer; b. San Pedro, Calif., Dec. 29, 1945; s. John Joseph and Wilma (Gessner) O.; m. Carol Ann Ranson, Aug. 28, 1970; 1 son, Peter John. Student U. Md., Munich, W.Ger., 1964-65; B.S.F.S., Georgetown U. Sch. Fgn. Service, 1968; B.I.M., Am. Grad. Sch. Internat. Mgmt., 1970, M.I.M., 1971. Lic. real estate broker, Calif. Cons. Grubbs & Ellis Co., Newport Beach, Calif., 1971-75; cons. CMC, Lausanne, Switzerland, 1976-81; owner Thomas B. O'Keefe Co., Newport Beach, Calif., 1975—; cons. N. AM. Doctor's Investment Fund, Inc., 1971-75; adv. Corp. Nat. Bank, Santa Ana, Calif., 1982—; lectr. internat. mktg. and econs. Chapman Coll., Orange, Calif., 1973—. Dir. Lyric Opera Orange County, 1983; active Newport Beach Art Mus., 1980—, Textile Mus., 1979—. Recipient Ariz. Republic most outstanding advt. campaign 1971; Inst. Real Estate Mgmt. cert. appreciation 1978. Mem. Newport Harbor-Costa Mesa Bd. Realtors, Orange County Assn. Real Estate Investment Brokers. Republican. Clubs: Aston Martin Owners (West Coast rep.) (London), Pasadena Wine and Food Soc., Les Amis du Vin (Newport Beach); Alliance Francaise (Laguna Beach, Calif.). Contbr. articles to jours. in field. Office: 5031 Birch St Suite C Newport Beach CA 92660

O'KEEFE, THOMAS JOHN, lawyer; b. Detroit, Nov. 11, 1936; s. Thomas A. and Helen (Geyman) O.; m. Lucretia Styskal, 1979 (div.); m. 2d., Katherine Mary Hommes, Feb. 14, 1981; children—Thomas Lad, Jerome David, Patricia Marie. B.B.A., Loyola U., Los Angeles, 1958; LL.B., Stanford U., 1961. Bar: Calif. 1962. Assoc. Adams, Hunt & Martin, Santa Ana, Calif., 1960-67, ptnr., 1965-67; sole practice, Santa Ana, 1967-68; assoc. O'Keefe & Recht, Inc., 1969-75; pres. Thomas O'Keefe, Inc., 1975—. Pres., dir. Shorecliffs Community Assn., 1963-64; commr. San Clemente City Planning, 1964-65; councilman City of San Clemente, 1966-68, 80-81, mayor 1974-75; chmn. Orange County Ocean and Shoreline Planning Steering Com., 1970-78; dir. Mission Valley Bank. Mem. Stanford Law Sch. Moot Ct. Bd., Orange County Barristers (pres. 1967), ABA, Calif. Bar Assn., Orange County Bar Assn., Alpha Sigma Nu, Alpha Delta Gamma, Phi Delta Phi. Clubs: Internat. Bay (sec.), Balboa Bay. Home: 35531 Camino Capistrano Capistrano Beach CA 92624 Office: Thomas O'Keefe Inc 2323 N Broadway Suite 400 Santa Ana CA 92706

OKUBO, RUBY SUMIKO, hosp. official; b. Los Angeles, May 2, 1926; d. Ben Toshimune and Susan Shizue (Konishi) O. B.S., UCLA, 1965, M.P.H., 1966. Chief med. records librarian U.S. Air Force Hosp., Lowry AFB, Denver, 1951-54; asst. dir. med. records St. Vincent's Hosp., Los Angeles, 1954-55, dir. med. records, 1955-64; systems analyst hosp. data processing UCLA Hosp. and Clinics, Los Angeles, 1966-69, sr. systems analyst, 1969-74, prin. ADP systems analyst, 1974-78, mgr. med.-adminstrv. applications hosp. data processing, 1978—. Mem. Am. Med. Records Assn., Calif. Med. Record Assn., So. Calif. Med. Record Assn. (chmn. public relations com. 1962), Am. Public Health Assn., Health Info. Soc., Internat. Fedn. Med. Record Orgns. (chmn.U.S. subcom. 1968-70), Electronic Computing Health Oriented Orgn., UCLA Sch. Public Health Alumni Assn. (dean's council). (Dean's council). Office: 10833 Le Conte Ave Los Angeles CA 90024

OLAH, GEORGE ANDREW, educator, chemist; b. Budapest, Hungary, May 22, 1927; s. Julius and Magda (Krasznai) O.; Ph.D., Tech. U. Budapest, 1949; m. Judith Agnes Lengyel, July 9, 1949; children—George John, Ronald Peter. Came to U.S., 1964, naturalized, 1970. Mem. faculty Tech. U. Budapest, 1949-54; asso. dir. Central Chem. Research Inst., Hungarian Acad. Scis., 1954-56; research scientist Dow Chem. Can. Ltd., 1957-64, Dow Chem. Co., Framingham, Mass., 1964-65; prof. chemistry Case-Western Res. U., Cleve., 1965-69, C.F. Mabery prof. research, 1969-77; prof. chemistry, dir. Inst. Hydrocarbon Chemistry, U. So. Calif., Los Angeles, 1977—; vis. prof. chemistry Ohio State U., 1963, U. Heidelberg (Germany), 1965, U. Colo., 1969, Swiss Fed. Inst. Tech., 1972, U. Munich, 1973, U. London, 1973, L. Pasteur U., Strasbourg, 1974, U. Paris, 1981; cons. to industry. Recipient Leo Hendrik Baekeland award N.J. sect. Am. Chem. Soc., 1966, Morley medal Cleve. sect., 1970. Guggenheim fellow, 1972. Fellow Chem. Inst. Can.; mem. Nat. Acad. Scis., Am. (award petroleum chemistry 1964, award synthetic-organic chemistry 1979), German, Brit., Swiss chem. socs., AAAS., Sigma Xi. Author: Friedel-Crafts Reactions, Vols. I-IV, 1963-64; (with P. Schleyer) Carbonium Ions, Vols. I-V, 1969-76; Friedel-Crafts Chemistry, 1973; Carbocations and Electrophilic Reactions, 1973; Halonium Ions, 1975; also chpts. in books, numerous papers in field. Patentee in field. Home: 2252 Gloaming Way Beverly Hills CA 90210 Office: Univ So Calif Los Angeles CA 90007

OLAH, SUSAN ROSE, artist; b. Budapest, Hungary, June 14, 1947; d. Joseph and Emma (Hupcsak) Olah; came to Can., 1957, naturalized, 1962; student Art Instrn. Sch. Mpls., 1966-69, grad. 1969. One woman shows Gallery of Roof, Regina, Sask., 1973, Galerie Mouffe, Paris, 1977, Galerie Vallombreuse, Biarritz, France, 1977; exhibited in group shows Gallery of Roof, Galerie Mouffe; tchr. art Wascana Hosp., Regina, 1969-72, art cons., 1970-72. Recipient award for painting, Mpls., 1967, Gold medal Accademia Italia delle Arti e del Lavoro, 1979, Golden Centour award Accademia Italia, 1982, others. Mem. Internat. Order of Vols. for Peace. Home: 37 Haultain Crescent Regina SK S4S 4B4 Canada

OLDEMEYER, ROBERT KING, plant breeding administrator, agricultural researcher; b. Brush, Colo., Sept. 23, 1922; s. Clarence Lester and Gayle Esther (King) O.; m. Shirley Schlessinger, May 24, 1944; children—G. Janine, Kristin K. B.S., Colo. State U., 1947; M.S., U. Wis., 1948, Ph.D., 1950. Plant breeder Gt. Western Sugar Co., Longmont, Colo., 1950-60, dir. seed devel., 1960-68, dir. agrl. research, 1968-71, mgr. seed processing and prodn., 1971-72, mgr. variety devel., 1972—. Served to lt. AUS, 1943-46. Mem. Am. Soc. Sugar Beet Technologists (meritorious service award 1977), Am. Soc. Agronomy, Am. Crop Sci. Soc., Am. Inst. Biol. Sci., Inst. Agrl. Botany, Institut International de Recherches Betteraveries. Republican. Congregationalist. Club: Rotary. Contbr. articles to profl. jours.

OLDENDORPH, JAMES EDWARD, advertising executive; b. St. Louis, July 25, 1945; s. Edward Roy and Viola S. O.; children—James Jr., Jessica Sara. B.A., U. Mo., 1967. Regional advt. mgr. Seven Up Co., 1968-70, N.Y. area mktg. mgr., 1970-71, Los Angeles area mktg. mgr., 1971-73; dir. mktg. Seven Up Bottling Cos. So. Calif., Los Angeles, 1973-78; mktg. mgr. Plus Products, Irvine, Calif., 1978-79; v.p. account services Seideman & Moiselle Advt., Encino, Calif., 1979—. Recipient Am. Mktg. Assn. So. Calif. Marsy award, 1982, Effie award, 1983. Mem. Sales and Mktg. Execs. Club Los Angeles, Am. Mktg. Assn., Los Angeles Advt. Club, U. Mo. Alumni Assn., Sigma Alpha Epsilon. Office: 16027 Ventura Blvd Suite 600 Encino CA 91436

O'LEARY, DENNIS C., museum director, sculptor; b. Evanston, Ill., Apr. 21, 1945. B.A., U. Calif.-Santa Barbara, 1968, M.F.A., 1970. Asst. dir. edn. San Francisco Mus. Modern Art, 1972-78; asst. prof., gallery dir. Mont. State U., Bozeman, 1978-81; dir. Boise (Idaho) Gallery of Art, 1981—. Ex-officio mem. Boise City Arts Council. Mem. Art Mus. Assn., Smithsonian Instn., Am. Assn. Mus. Contbr. to exhbn. catalogs. Office: 670 S Julia Davis Dr Boise ID 73802

O'LEARY, ROBERT WHITE, lawyer, health system executive; b. New Bedford, Mass., Dec. 3, 1943; s. Francis White and Eileen May (Boyle) O'L. B.S., U. Mass., 1965; M.P.A., SUNY-Albany, 1968; J.D., Suffolk U., Boston, 1973. Bar: Ill. 1978. Adminstrv. asst. N.T. State Health Dept., Albany, 1965-66; asst. dir. Hosp. Assn. N.Y. State, Albany, 1966-68; exec. v.p. Mass. Hosp. Assn., Burlington, 1968-74; pres. Ill. Hosp. Assn., Naperville, 1974-82; pres. St. Joseph Health System, Orange, Calif., 1982—; bd. dirs. Tri-State Hosp. Assembly; bd. dirs., mem. exec. com., chmn. pub. affairs com. Ill. Cancer Soc.; pres. Ill. Hosp. Joint Ventures, Inc., Ill. Hosp. Research and Ednl. Found., Ill. Provider Trust, Ill. Compensation Trust, Ill. Risk Mgmt. Services, Assn. Mgmt. Resources. Mem. Gov.'s Task Force for Reorgn. State Govt., 1972, Ill. Gov.'s Transition Task Force, 1976-77. Mem. Am. Soc. Hosp. Execs., State Hosp. Assn. Execs. Forum, ABA, Ill. Bar Assn., Chgo. Bar Assn. Roman Catholic. Home: 22701 Barlovento Mission Viejo CA 92692 Office: 440 S Batavia St Orange CA 92668

OLES, STUART GREGORY, lawyer; b. Seattle, Dec. 15, 1924; s. Floyd and Helen Louise (La Violette) O.; B.S. magna cum laude, U. Wash., 1947, J.D., 1948; m. Ilse Hanewald, Feb. 12, 1954; children—Douglas, Karl, Stephen. Admitted to Wash. bar, 1949, U.S. Supreme Ct. bar, 1960; dep. pros. atty. King County (Wash.), 1949, chief civil dept., 1949-50; gen. practice law, Seattle, 1950—; sr. partner firm Oles, Morrison, Rinker, Stanislaw & Ashbaugh, and predecessor, 1955—. Chmn. Seattle Community Concert Assn., 1955; pres. Friends Seattle Pub. Library, 1956; mem. Wash. Pub. Disclosure Commn., 1973-75; trustee Ch. Div. Sch. of Pacific, Berkeley, Calif., 1974-75; mem. bd. curators Wash. State Hist. Soc., 1983; counsel King County Republican Central Com., 1964-68, chmn. rules and order com., 1964; pres. King County Ct. House Rep. Club, 1950, U. Wash. Young Rep. Club, 1947; Wash. conv. floor leader Taft, 1952, Goldwater, 1964; Wash. chmn. Citizens for Goldwater, 1964; chmn. King County Rep. convs., 1966, 68, 76, Wash. State Rep. Conv., 1980. Served with USMCR, 1943-45. Mem. Seattle, King County, Wash., Am. (past regional vice chmn. pub. contract law sect.) bar assns., Order of Coif, Scabbard and Blade, Am. Legion, Phi Beta Kappa, Phi Alpha Delta. Episcopalian (vestryman, lay-leader). Clubs: Rainier, Seattle Yacht. Home: 5766 61st St NE Seattle WA 98105 also Cape St Mary Ranch Lopez Island WA 98261 Office: Suite 3208 1001 4th Ave Seattle WA 98154

OLESON, DONALD ANDREW, history educator, dean; b. Santa Ana, Calif., June 10, 1930; s. Maynard Joseph and Elizabeth (Stewart) O.; A.B., Occidental Coll., 1952; postgrad. U. Barcelona, 1954, Internat. U. of Santander, 1954; Ph.D., U. Madrid, 1959; M.A., Calif. State U., Long Beach, 1957; m. Yolanda Marcelina Motas Llanos, Mar. 28, 1955. Rep. in Spain and Morocco, Nat. Life Ins. of Des Moines, 1957-61; mgr. European sales Compton Pub. Co., 1958-61; from instr. to prof. history Long Beach (Calif.) City Coll., 1960—, dean div. history and social sci., 1975—; instr., lectr., prof. Calif. State U., Long Beach, 1963-70. Active Sister City Program, Valparaiso, Chile-Long Beach. Del Amo Found. fellow to Spain and Portugal, 1971. Mem. Assn. Calif. Community Coll. Adminstrs., Am. Acad. Polit. and Social Sci., Am. Hist. Assn. (Pacific Coast Br. of Latin Am. Studies), Instituto de Estudios Politicos (corr.), Phi Alpha Theta, Phi Delta Kappa, Sigma Alpha Epsilon. Author: La Integracion de las Concesiones de Tierras Hispano-Mejicanas de California en la Union Norteamirica, 1958; The Treaty of Tordesillas, 1971; The History of the United States: And the People Who Made It, 1975. Home: 16751 Baruna Ln Huntington Harbour CA 92649 Office: Div Social Science 4901 E Carson St Long Beach CA 90808

OLGUIN, ERNEST FRED, tax consultant; b. Denver, Nov. 26, 1939; s. Desiderio and Maria S. Olguin; m. Joyce Ann Moore, Oct. 31, 1941 (div.); children—Teresa Ann, Jason Andrew. A.A. in Bus. Adminstrn., Fresno City Coll., 1960; B.S., Calif. State U.-Fresno, 1963; postgrad. Calif. State U.-Long Beach. Self-employed tax cons., bookkeeper, Long Beach, Calif., 1981. Address: 341 W 21st St Long Beach CA 90806

OLGUIN, RONALD GERALD, state senator, sales representative; b. Albuquerque, Mar. 15, 1941; s. Alex G. Olguin; m. Astra Marlie Valdez, 1972; children—Roxanne, Ronald. B.S. cum laude, U. Albuquerque, 1971; postgrad. U. N.Mex., 1973. Caseworker, GATE, 1969-71; ednl. analyst City of Albuquerque, 1971-73; sales rep. Xerox Corp., 1972—; mem. N.Mex. State Senate, 1979—. Demorama winner Xerox Corp. Mem. Mid-Rio Grande OIC (dir.), Action, Inc. (dir.), Delta Epsilon Sigma. Democrat. Roman Catholic. Club: Lions. Home: 3924 La Sombra SW Albuquerque NM 87105 Office: New Mexico State Senate Santa Fe NM 87503

OLHOFT, JOHN ERNEST, constrn. engr.; b. Fallon, Nev., Oct. 28, 1943; s. Karl and Isabelle Kennedy (Oakden) O.; A.S., U. Heidelberg, 1964; student U. Alaska, 1976—; B.S.C.E., Columbia Pacific U., 1982; m. Leona Faye Montgomery, 1981; children—Jonathon Scott, Trask Montgomery. Vice-pres. Consol. Investment Corp., Kodiak, Alaska, 1967—; purchasing agt. Crowley Maritime Corp., Anchorage, 1976-77; constrn. engr. Northwestern Constrn. Inc., Anchorage, 1977-80; project engr. Doyon/Reading & Bates, Fairbanks, Alaska, 1981; insp. Miner & Miner, Cons. Engrs., Inc., Greeley, Colo., 1981; safety engr. Frank Moolin & Assocs., 1982-83; sr. quality assurance engr. Morrison-Knudsen, 1983—. Served with AUS, 1961-64. Decorated Purple Heart. Mem. Nat. Safety Mgmt. Soc., Am. Mgmt. Assn., Smithsonian Instn., Am. Legion, Mensa, Internat. Platform Assn., Am. Film Inst. Mem. Ch. Jesus Christ of Latter-day Saints. Office: 813 D St Anchorage AK 99501 also PO Box 4-2846 Anchorage AK 99509

OLIPHANT, CHARLES ROMIG, physician; b. Waukegan, Ill., Sept. 10, 1917; s. Charles L. and Mary (Goss) R.; student St. Louis U., 1936-40; M.D., 1943; postgrad. Naval Med. Sch., 1946; m. Claire E. Canavan, Nov. 7, 1942; children—James R., Cathy Rose, Mary G., William D. Intern, Nat. Naval Med. Center, Bethesda, Md., 1943; pvt. practice medicine and surgery, San Diego, 1947—; gen. partner Midway Med. Enterprises; former chief staff, now chief staff emeritus Sharp Cabrillo Hosp.; mem. staff Mercy Hosp., Children's Hosp., Paradise Valley Hosp., Sharp Meml. Hosp. Charter mem. Am. Bd. Family Practice. Served with M.C., USN, 1943-47. Fellow Am. Geriatrics Soc., Am. Acad. Family Practice, Am. Assn. Abdominal Surgeons; mem. AMA, Calif. Med. Assn., Am. Acad. Family Physicians (past pres. San Diego chpt., del. Calif. chpt.), San Diego Med. Soc., Public Health League, Navy League, San Diego Power Squadron (exec. officer), SAR. Clubs: San Diego Yacht, Cameron Highlanders. Home: 4310 Trias San Diego CA 92103 Office: Midway Med-Dental Center 3405 Kenyon St San Diego CA 92110

OLIPHANT, ERNIE LOUISE, safety educator, public relations executive, consultant; b. Richmond, Ind., Oct. 25, 1934; d. Ernest E. and Beulah A. (Jones) Reid; m. George B. Oliphant, Sept. 25, 1955; children—David, Wendell, Rebecca. Student, Earlham Coll., 1953-55, Ariz. State U., 1974, Phoenix Coll., 1974-78. Planner, organizer, moderator confs., programs for various women's clubs, safety assns., 1971—; assoc. dir. Operation Lifesaver Nat. Safety Council, Phoenix, 1978—; cons. Fed. R.R. Adminstrn.; lectr. in field.; adviser Am. Ry. Engring. Assn., Calif. Assn. Women Hwy. Safety Leaders, numerous others. Mem. R.R./Hwy. grade crossing com. Ariz. Corp. Commn.; mem. transp. and system com. Ariz. Gov.'s Commn. on Environment; mem. Ariz. Gov.'s Council Women for Hwy. Safety; mem. motor vehicle traffic safety at hwy.-r.r. grade crossings com., roadway environment com., women's div. com. Nat. Safety Council; mem. Phoenix Traffic Accident Reduction Program; task force mem. U.S. Dept. Transp. on Grade Crossing Safety. Recipient Safety award SW Safety Congress, 1973; citation of Merit Adv. Commn. on Ariz. Environment, 1974; Gov.'s award for hwy. safety, 1978; Gov.'s Merit of Recognition Outstanding Service in Hwy. Safety, 1980. Mem. Assn. R.R. Editors, Nat. Assn. Female Execs., Inc., Pub. Relations Soc. Am., R.R. Pub. Relations Assn., Nat. Acad. Scis. (dir. transp. research, planning, adminstrn. of transp. safety com., r.r.-hwy. grade crossing safety com.), Women's Transp. Seminar, Ariz. Fedn. Women's Clubs (named pres. of yr. 1968), Ariz. Safety Assn. (safety recognition award 1975), Gen. Fedn. Women's Clubs (internat. bd. dirs.), Nat. Assn. Women Hwy. Safety Leaders, Phi Theta Kappa. Republican. Quaker. Author of tech. publs.

OLIPHANT, LA VERNA DEAN, accountant; b. Red Oak, Iowa, Sept. 8, 1923; d. Arthur William and Hester Shivers (Chappell) Jones; diploma Red Oak Jr. Coll., 1942; certificate Edison Bus. Sch., 1962; m. Clarence Alvin Oliphant, July 17, 1943; children—Carol A. Oliphant Wells, Lisa Oliphant Brown, Lauren Oliphant Brown, Lynne, Vida Oliphant Sneed. With sales and distbn. of surplus property div. Quartermaster Corps, Dept. Army, 1947-58, supr. in charge, 1954-58; pvt. practice accounting, Seattle, 1958-62; accountant Stallworth Tax and Bookkeeping Service, Seattle, 1962-65; prin. La. Verna D. Oliphant, accountant, Seattle, 1965—; sec., treas. Active Mortgage & Escrow Co. Asst coach track and field Central Area Youth, 1967-73. Recipient Sustained Superior Performance award Dept. Army, 1957. Mem. Nat. Soc. Pub. Accountants, Wash. Assn. Accountants (sec.-treas. 1975-79, exec. sec. 1979—), Am. Soc. Women Accountants. Wash. Soc. Assn. Execs., Am. Bus. Women's Assn. Home: 2007 25th Ave E Seattle WA 98112 Office: 2311 E Madison St Seattle WA 98112

OLIPHANT, ROBERT THOMPSON, English language and literature educator, writer; b. Tulsa, Oct. 25, 1924; s. Stephen Duncan and Dorothy Ann (Thompson) O.; m. Lois Ann Millett, Apr. 20, 1956 (div. Apr. 1964); m. 2d Jane H. Johnson, June 26, 1965; children—Matthew Duncan, Jason Stewart. A.B., Washington and Jefferson Coll., 1942; M.A., Stanford U., 1958, Ph.D., 1962. Profl. musician, 1948-55; acting instr. Stanford U., 1955-59; asst. prof. English, Calif. State U.-Northridge, 1959-63, assoc. prof., 1964-68, prof., 1959—. Served with USAAF, 1943-46; ETO. Presbyterian. Author: Harley Latin-Old English Glossary, 1966; Earnest: A Chamber Opera, 1972; (novel) A Piano For Mrs. Cimino, 1980. Office: Dept English Calif State U Northridge CA 91330

OLIVARES, LEONARDO ERMENCIO, physicians asst.; b. Edinburg, Tex., Oct. 31, 1929; s. Juan Manuel and Gregoria (Rios) O.; student Edinburg public schs., spl. courses; grad. MEDEX Program, U. Wash. Med. Sch.; m. Lore K. Bauer, Feb. 5, 1958; 1 son, Adolfo Juan. Enlisted U.S. Army, 1948, ret., 1969; chief supply div., asst. adminstr. Edinburg Mcpl. Hosp., 1969-70; chief supply and materials Mission (Tex.) Municipal Hosp., 1970-71; physicians asst. Chewalah, Wash., 1971-75, Alaska Native Med. Center, St. George Island, 1975-78, Quinault Indian Nation, 1978-80, VA Med. Center, Ft. Lyon, Colo., 1980—; hosp. privileges St. Joseph's Hosp., Chewalah; mem. staff Alaska Native Med. Center. Fellow Am. Assn. Physicians Assts., Wash. Assn. Physicians Assts.; mem. USPHS Assn. Physicians Assts.; asst. mem. Wash. Med. Assn., Stevens County Med. Soc. Republican. Roman Catholic. Club: Continental (Seattle). Research on hypertension of Aleuit natives of St. George and St. Paul Islands. Home: PO Box 66 Fort Lyon CO 81038 Office: VA Medical Center Fort Lyon CO 81038

OLIVAS, LOUIS, educator; b. Phoenix, Mar. 14, 1947; s. Angel M. and Frances V. O.; B.S., Ariz. State U., 1970, M.B.A., 1972, Ed.D., 1978; m. Adelina Olivas, June 20, 1970; children—Louis Robert, Daniel Leonard. Tchr. bus. Alhambra High Sch., Phoenix, 1970-73; instr. bus. Scottsdale (Ariz.) Community Coll., 1973-74; tng. dir. Western Savs. and Loan Assn., Phoenix, 1974-78; employee devel. adminstr. City of Phoenix, 1978-79; asst. prof. dept. adminstrv. services Coll. of Bus., Ariz. State U., Tempe, 1979—, asst. dir. Ctr. for Exec. Devel., 1979-81, dir., 1981—; cons. in tng. and devel. to local and nat. firms. Chmn. nat. com. Savs. and Loan Tng. Assn., 1975. Served with Air N.G., 1966-81. Decorated Air Force Commendation medal; recipient outstanding service award Distributive Edn. Clubs Am., 1978; Disting. Pistol Shot badge USAF; name Master Pistol Shooter, Am. Rifle Assn; one of Three Outstanding Young Men, Phoenix, 1977. Mem. Nat. Bus. Edn. Assn., ASTD (bd. dirs., pres. chpt. 1976, chmn. nat. coms. membership 1978, chpt. services 1980, chmn. nat. conf. 1982, Torch award 1979), Am. Vocat. Edn. Assn., Am. Mgmt. Assn., Delta Sigma Pi. Democrat. Roman Catholic. Clubs: Toastmasters Internat. (v.p. Round-up chpt. 1977), Optimist (pres. Dawn Busters club 1974). Contbr. articles to profl. jours. Home: 1835 E Cornell Tempe AZ 85283 Office: Arizona State U College Business Adminstrn Tempe AZ 85281

OLIVAS, NATHAN JOSEPH, seed co. exec.; b. San Jose, Calif., Aug. 27, 1937; s. Nathan Calvin and Julia Vecinta (Lopez) O.; student Hartnell Coll., 1957; B.S., Calif. State Poly., San Luis Obispo, 1960; m. Jere Lee Steidley, Aug. 16, 1957; children—Cindy Lynn, Nathan Khristian, Nancy Elizabeth. Prodn. and research technician Pieters-Wheeler Seed Co., Gilroy, Calif., 1961-64; pres., gen. mgr. Harnish-Brinker Seed Co., Five Points, Calif., 1965-67, Quali-Sel, Inc., Salinas, Calif., 1968-82, Genecorp, Inc., Salinas, Calif., 1982—. Bd. dirs. Salinas Valley Meml. Hosp., 1983—. Mem. Am. Soc. Agronomy, Am. Seed Trade Assn., Calif. Seed Assn. (dir. 1972, 73, 74), Western Growers Assn., Grower-Shipper Assn. Central Calif. Republican. Roman Catholic. Developer seven varieties of lettuce, 1968-78. Office: Quali-Sel Inc 11 W Laurel Dr Suite 125 Salinas CA 93906

OLIVER, DIANE GORDON, clin. pathologist; b. Long Beach, Calif., July 21, 1937; s. William Clark and Mary Valerie (Voros) Gordon; m. James A. Felchlin, Oct. 3, 1975; children—Lauren M., Griffin M., Anita L., Dare Valerie Felchlin. A.B., U. Calif.-Berkeley, 1959. M.D., U. Calif.-San Francisco, 1963; Intern, San Francisco Gen. Hosp., 1963-64, resident, 1964-68; resident U. Calif.-San Francisco, 1964-68; pres. Comprehensive Health, Inc., San Francisco, 1969-77; med. dir. research Flow Gen., Inc., San Bruno, Calif., 1977—, also dir. Mem. Am. Soc. Clin. Pathologists, Coll. Am. Pathologists. Office: 1057 Sneath Ln San Bruno CA 94066

OLIVER, PAT PHILLIPS, publisher, editor, writer; b. Crown Point, Ind.; d. John Adam and Anna (Kindness) Patterson; student U. Chgo., 1941, Ind. U., 1938-40; m. Charles Everett Phillips, Jr., Sept. 17, 1941 (div.); children—Anne, Jill, Candace, Pamela; m. 2d, Eddie Oliver, Feb. 2, 1963 (dec.). Columnist, feature writer Ind. newspapers, nat. mags., 1935-40; women's editor, feature writer Burbank (Calif.) Daily Rev., 1953-57, Hollywood (Calif.) Citizen-News, 1957-63; mng. editor, exec. editor Palm Springs Life mag., 1964-79; owner, pub. Palm Springs Personages, 1982—. Mem. Theta Sigma Phi. Clubs: Desert Press, Hollywood Women's Press, Palm Springs Women's Press (founding). Office: PO Box 1004 Palm Springs CA 92263

OLIVER, ROBERT EUGENE, marketing executive; b. Bloomington, Ind., Dec. 26, 1950; s. Raymond Eugene and Dorothy Loreen (Creel) O.; m. Kathryn Koons, July 20, 1974. B.S.B.A., U. Denver, 1973. Transp. asst. So. Pacific Co., San Francisco, 1973-74; transp. supr. Amtrak, Los Angeles, 1974-75; product mgr. Teledyne Water Pik, Fort Collins, Colo., 1975-79; mgr. sales and mktg. Coors BioMed. Co., Lakewood, Colo., 1979—. Bd. dirs. Ctr. for Creative Arts, Inc., Denver, 1982-83. Mem. Sigma Iota Epsilon, Omicron Delta Kappa, Mu Kappa Tau. Republican. Roman Catholic. Contbr. articles to profl. jours.

OLIVER, ROBERT WARNER, economist, educator; b. Los Angeles, Oct. 26, 1922; s. Ernest Warner and Elnore May (McConnell) O.; m. Darlene Hubbard, July 1, 1946; children—Lesley Joanne, Stewart Warner; A.B. magna cum laude in Internat. Relations, U. So. Calif. 1943, A.M. with highest honors in Econs., 1948; Ph.D. in Econs., 1957. Messenger, Bank of America, Los Angeles, 1940; teaching asst. U. So. Calif., 1946-47, asst. prof., 1952-56; instr. Princeton U., 1947-50, instr. Pomona Coll., 1950-51; research economist Stanford Research Inst., 1956-59; assoc. prof. Calif. Inst. Tech., 1959-73, prof., 1973—; cons. Brookings Instn.; economist Economics of Urbanization div. World Bank, Washington, 1962, Missions to Indonesia and Taiwan, 1971; resident scholar Rockefeller Found. Research and Study Center, Bellagio, Italy, 1974; cons. in internat. politics, econ. theory, money and banking, urban studies OECD, Paris, France, 1979. Mem. Pasadena (Calif.) City Council, 1965-69, mem. Pasadena Planning Commn., chmn. future land use com. 1972-75; mem. awards com. Pasadena Arts Council, chmn., 1974; mem. Tournament of Roses Assn.; mem., past pres. Pasadena Beautiful Found.; mem. Pasadena Recreation Commn., Southern Calif. Assn. Govts.; bd. dirs. Pasadena-Foothill Br. Los Angeles Urban League, Foothill Area Community Planning Council, Pasadena Job Devel. Corp., Pasadena Edn. Found.; adviser Fulbright selection com., Inst. Internat. Edn.; cons. Pillsbury, Madison and Sutro, San Francisco, USPHS, Beardsley, Hufstedler and Kemble, Econs. Research Assos., San Marino High School, Los Angeles County Bd. Edn., Jet. Propulsion Lab. Served to lt. (j.g.) USNR. Danforth Found. assoc. for contbns. to undergrad. teaching; Social Sci. research grantee London Sch. Econs., 1954-55. Mem. Internat. Inst. Strategic Studies, Calif. Seminar Internat. Security, Com. on For. Relations, Am. Econs. Assn., Royal Econs. Assn., Western Econs. Assn., So. Calif. Econs. Assn. (pres., 1954, 1964-65), Phi Beta Kappa, Phi Kappa Phi, Phi Eta Sigma, Pi Sigma Alpha, Sigma Phi Epsilon. Democrat. Methodist. Club: Quinta Desert (Los Angeles). Author: An Economic Survey of the City of Pasadena, 1959; Economic Considerations in the Formulation and Repayment of California Water Plan Projects, 1958; The Role of Small Scale Manufacturing in Economic Development, 1957; International Economics Cooperation and the World Bank, 1975; contbg. author: Encyclopedia of Economics, 1981, Global Monetary Anarchy, 1981, Key Issues in International Monetary Reform, 1975, Princeton Studies in International Finance, 1971, The Economics of International Adjustment, 1971; contbr. articles to profl. jours. Home: 3197 San Pasqual Pasadena CA 91107 Office: 1201 California Blvd Pasadena CA 91125

OLIVER, STEPHEN RALPH, educational consultant; b. Seattle, Jan. 16, 1949; s. Montgomery and Anne Mary (Pagni) O. B.A., Central Wash. U., 1971. Tchr., coordinator spl. programs Tacoma Public Schs., 1971-79; orgn. devel. specialist A-H Tng. and Devel. Systems Inc., Oakland, Calif., 1979—; cons. drug abuse prevention. Bd. dirs. Comprehensive Health Edn. Found., 1978-82. Mem. Nat. Assn. Prevention Profls. (v.p.), Am. Soc. Tng. and Devel. Democrat. Lutheran. Author: (with V.C. League) Developing Successful Programs, 1983; editor: The Prevention Manual, 1983.

OLIVIER, ALBERT FRANCOIS, surgeon; b. N.Y.C., Sept. 21, 1943; s. Alphonse Francois and Clotilde (Jean Baptiste) O.; B.S., Manhattan Coll., 1966; M.D., N.J. Coll. Medicine, 1970; m. Beatrice C. Olivier, Apr. 12, 1969; 1 son, Marc. Intern, St. Elizabeth Med. Center, Dayton, Ohio, 1970-71; resident in surgery Miami Valley Hosp., Dayton, 1971-75; resident in cardiothoracic surgery Henry Ford Hosp., Detroit, 1975-77; fellow in cardiovascular surgery St. Francis Hosp., N.Y.C., 1978-79; practice medicine, specializing in cardiovascular and thoracic surgery, Mesa, Ariz., 1979—; mem. staff J.C. Lincoln Hosp., Desert Samaritan Hosp., St. Luke's Med. Center, Phoenix Meml. Hosp. Diplomate Am. Bd. Surgery, Am. Bd. Thoracic Surgery. Fellow A.C.S., Am. Coll. Chest Physicians, Am. Heart Assn., Nat. Med. Assn., Ariz. Med. Assn. (edn. com. 1983—). Roman Catholic. Author: On the Threshold (novel), 1972. Office: 1500 S Dobson Mesa AZ 85202

OLLEY, ROBERT EDWARD, economist, educator; b. Verdun, Que., Can., Apr. 16, 1933; s. Edwin Henry and Elizabeth (Reed) O.; B.A., Carleton U. (Can.), 1960; M.A., Queen's U. (Can.), 1961, Ph.D. in Econs., 1969; m. Shirley Ann Dahl, Jan. 19, 1957; children—Elizabeth Anne, George Steven, Susan Catherine, Maureen Carolyn. Vis. asst. prof. Queen's U., Kingston, Ont., 1967-68; asst. prof. econs. U. Sask. (Can.), Saskatoon, 1963-67, 68-69, assoc. prof., 1969-71, 73-75, prof., 1975—; econ. adviser Bell Can., Montreal, Que., 1971-73, 78-79, 79-81, Can. Telecommunications Carriers Assn., 1978—, Sask. Power Corp., 1980-83; econ. advisor AT&T, 1980—; dir. research Royal Commn. on Consumer Problems and Inflation, 1967-68. Bd. dirs. Can. Found. for Econ. Edn., 1974-82, Can. Gen. Standards Bd., 1977-81. Recipient Silver Jubilee medal, 1977. Mem. Royal Econ. History Soc., Royal Econs. Assn., Econ. History Assn., Am. Econ. Assn., Can. Econ. Assn., Consumers Assn. Can. (v.p. 1967-76), Can. Standards Assn. (dir., mem. exec. com. 1971—). Author, editor: Consumer Product Testing, 1979; Consumer Product Testing II, 1981; Consumer Credit in Canada, 1966; Economics of the Public Firm: Regulation, Rates, Costs, Productivity Analysis, 1983. Home: 30 Murphy Crescent Saskatoon SK S7J 2T4 Canada Office: Dept Econs and Polit Sci U Sask Saskatoon SK S7N 0W0 Canada

OLLSON, DOROTHY GORE, county administrator; b. Knox City, Tex., Jan. 15, 1924; d. Roy and Lydia Edna (Moss) Gore; m. George B. Ollson, (dene); 7, 1961 (dec.); children—Lynnette Brandon, Andrew Rogers, Georgann Hackenbracht, Greg, Marjori. Student Ariz. State U., 1940-41. With Gila County Engr.'s Office, Globe, Ariz., 1963—, research analyst, 1980—. Mem. Gila County Democratic Women's Club; mem. Globe City Council, mem. minerals extraction task force com. Clubs: Emblem 235, VFW Aux. (Globe). Home: 257 N 2d St Globe AZ 85501 Office: 1400 E Ash St Globe AZ 85501

OLMOS, MARIO GUERRA, judge; b. Nogales, Ariz., July 24, 1946; s. Fidel Ramirez and Dolores Amaro (Guerra) O.; m. Mary Louise Frampton, Aug. 18, 1974; children—Daniel Benjamin, Margaret Christine. A.A., Reedley Coll., 1966; A.B., U. Calif.-Berkeley, 1968, J.D., 1971. Bar: Calif. 1972. Staff atty. Calif. Rural Legal Assistance, 1971-74; ptnr. Olmos & Frampton, Fresno, Calif., 1974-83; justice ct. judge Parlier-Selma Jud. Dist., Fresno, 1975-83, superior ct. judge, 1983—. Mem. Calif. Judges' Assn., Calif. State Jud. Council, Inns of Ct. Soc. Calif., Phi Beta Kappa. Club: Selma Rotary. Home: 281 W San Carlos St Fresno CA 93704 Office: 1100 Van Ness Ave Room 550 Fresno CA 93721

OLMSTED, MAXINE BLAKEMORE, writer; b. Seattle, Dec. 18, 1907; d. John Flick and Cassa Geneva (Illsley) Blakemore; B.A. in Drama, U. Wash., Seattle, 1931; m. Joel Burleson Olmsted, Sept. 5, 1931; children—Cassa Blakemore, Spalding Maxine. Pub. relations dir. United Cerebral Palsy Assn. Central Ariz., 1957-59; Maricopa County and Ariz. assns. mental health, 1959-61, Ariz. Assn. Crippled Children and Adults, 1962-64, Phoenix Jewish Community Center, 1965-68, Ariz. Commn. Arts and Humanities, 1969-70; Maricopa County coordinator Ariz. Commn. Arts and Humanities for dance/movement in elementary schs., 1970-79; author histories of Phoenix and Scottsdale for photography book Phoenix: 1870-1970, 1970; also articles, stories; editor Ariz. Dance Guild News, 1974-79; leading actor in documentary film The Desert Speaks (Golden Eagle award 1978). Recipient various service citations. Mem. Screen Actors Guild (actress in residence), AFTRA, Nat. League Am. Pen Women, Ariz. Dance Guild, Ariz. Dance Arts Alliance (a founder), Artes Bellas (a founder), Phoenix Art Mus., Scottsdale Center for Arts, Ariz. Humane Soc., Ariz. Theatre Co. Encompass. Republican. Episcopalian. Address: 8531 N 11th Ave Phoenix AZ 85021

OLPIN, ROBERT SPENCER, art history educator; b. Palo Alto, Calif., Aug. 30, 1940; s. Ralph Smith and Ethel Lucille (Harman) O.; m. Mary Florence Catharine Reynolds, Aug. 24, 1963; children—Mary Courtney, Cristin Lee, Catherine Elizabeth, Carrie Jean. B.S., U. Utah, 1963; A.M., Boston U., 1965, Ph.D., 1971. Lectr. art history Boston U., 1965-67; asst. prof. U. Utah, Salt Lake City, 1967-72, assoc. prof., 1972-76, prof., 1976—, chmn. dept., 1975-82, dir. art history program, 1968-76, 83—; cons. curator Am. and English art Utah Mus. Fine Arts, 1973—. Grantee U. Utah, 1972, Utah Mus. Fine Arts, 1975, Utah Bicentennial Commn., 1975, Ford Found., 1975, Salt Lake Art Center, 1979. Mem. Archives Am. Art Smithsonian Instn., Coll. Art Assn. Am., Mid-Am. Coll. Art Assn., Utah Acad. Scis. Arts Letters, Utah Art History Assn., Assn. Historians Am. Art, Utah Heritage Found., Sigma Nu. Republican. Mem. Ch. Jesus Christ of Latter-day Saints. Author: Alexander Helwig Wyant, 1836-92, 1968; Mainstreams of American Architefture, 1973; American Painting Around 1850, 1976; Art-Life of Utah, 1977; Dictionary of Utah Art, 1980; A Retrospective of Utah Art, 1981. Home: 887 Woodshire Ave Murray UT 84107 Office: Dept Art Univ Utah Salt Lake City UT 84112

OLSEN, ALFRED JON, lawyer; b. Phoenix, Oct. 5, 1940; s. William Hans and Vera (Bearden) O.; m. Susan K. Smith, Apr. 15, 1979. B.A. in History, U. Ariz., 1962; M.S. in Acctg., Ariz. State U., 1964; J.D., Northwestern U., 1966. Bar: Ariz., 1966, Ill., 1966; C.P.A. Ariz., Ill.; cert. Tax specialist. Acct. Arthur Young & Co. C.P.A.s, Chgo., 1966-68; dir. firm Ehmann, Olsen & Lane, Phoenix, 1969-76; dir. firm Streich, Lang, Weeks & Cardon, Phoenix, 1977-78; v.p. Olsen-Smith Ltd., Phoenix, 1978—. Fellow Am. Coll. Tax Counsel, Am. Coll. Probate Counsel; mem. Central Ariz. Estate Planning Council, ABA, Am. Law Inst. (chmn. tax planning for agr.), Nat. Cattlemen's Assn. (tax com.). Bd. editors Jour. Agrl. Law and Taxation. Office: 3300 Virginia Rin Plaza 301 E Virginia Ave Phoenix AZ 85004

OLSEN, ARTHUR ROBERT, economist, educator, author; b. Bklyn., Dec. 1, 1910; s. Martin and Clara Anita (Hansen) O.; m. Helen Marie Fehleisen, June 25, 1958; 1 dau., Karen Marie Steadman. B.S., NYU, 1935, A.M., 1940, Ed D., 1942. Prin. Elwood School, L.I., N.Y., 1935-37; asst. prin., instr. No. Merrick School, L.I., 1937-43; instr. Pratt Inst., N.Y.C., 1943-44; statistician Rayonier Inc., N.Y.C., 1944-47; prof. Western Ill. U., 1947-70, now emeritus; disting. adj. prof. econs. Ariz. State U., 1981-82; economist, author Southwestern Publ. Co., Cin., 1957-82; del. U.S. Nat. Commn. UNESCO, economist S.W. Mo. Council on Econ. Edn.; bd. dirs. Ill. Council Econ. Edn.; bd. dirs. Community Edn. project, Macomb, Ill., 1957-59; past dir. and moderator WKAI Round Table of the Air. Mem. Republican Presdl. Task Force, 1982; v.p. Sun City Agrl. Club, 1982. Served with USNG, 1930-33. Recipient Alumnus of Yr. award SUNY, 1978; Joint Council Econ. Edn. fellow, 1960. Mem. NEA (life), Am. Econ. Assn., Ill. Council Social Studies (past pres.), Smithsonian Assocs., Nat. Geog. Soc., Phi Delta Kappa, Kappa Delta Pi, Omicron Delta Epsilon. Republican. Protestant. Club: Masons (33rd degree), Elks, N.Y.U., Sun City Country. Author: (with J.W. Kennedy) Economics, 9th edit., 1978; Economic Institutions, 1958; Readings on Marriage and Family Relations, 1953; Economics Transparancies, 1973; Beat the Market, 1973; contbr. articles to profl. jours. Home and Office: 9232 107th Ave Sun City AZ 85351

OLSEN, CLIFFORD WAYNE, physicist; b. Placerville, Calif., Jan. 15, 1936; s. Christian William and Elsie May (Bishop) O.; A.A., Grant Tech. Coll., 1955; B.A., U. Calif., Davis, 1957, Ph.D., 1962; m. Margaret Clara Gobel, June 11, 1962; children—Anne Katherine, Charlotte Marie. Diagnostic physicist Lawrence Livermore (Calif.) Nat. Lab., 1962—, containment scientist, 1966-77, 79-81, project leader, 1977-79, asso. program leader, 1981—; cons. Aerojet Gen. Nuclear, San Ramon, Calif., 1967-68; program chmn. 2d Symposium on Containment of Underground Nuclear Explosions. Mem. bd. convocators Calif. Luth. Coll., 1975-78; leader, pres. Holy Cross Luth. Ch., Livermore, 1978; precinct worker for county supr. Mem. AAAS, Seismological Soc. Am., Am. Chem. Soc., Gourmandes de l' Arcachoraise Nacrée et de'l Ecaille d' Argent, Sigma Xi, Alpha Gamma Sigma. Democrat. Lutheran. Club: Am. Contract Bridge League. Contbr. articles in field to profl. jours. Home: 4898 Wingate Dr Pleasanton CA 94566 Office: PO Box 808 Livermore CA 94550

OLSEN, FREDERICK L., ceramist/artist; b. Seattle, Feb. 25, 1938; s. Albert F. and Jeanette (Lee) O.; m. Ingrid A. Hammermueller; 1 son, Lee A. B.A., U. So. Calif., 1960, M.F.A., 1967. Apprentice under Tomimoto Kenkichi/Kondo Yuzo, Kyoto, Japan, 1961-63; one man shows: Sydney Australia, 1963, 64, 69, Melbourne, Australia, 1963, Adelaide, Australia, 1969, Denmark, 1965, Los Angeles, 1972, 73, 74, Seattle, 1971, 73, Portland, Oreg., 1971, Palm Springs Desert Mus., 1977, San Jacinto Gallery, 1982; numerous two man and group shows; owner Olsen Kiln Kit Co., Pinyon Crest Pottery, 1968—; condr. workshops on kiln bldg. and clay throughout U.S. Nat. Endowment grant, 1977. Author: The Kiln Book, 2d edit., 1982; editor: Studio Potter mag.; patentee Olsen Kiln Kits.

OLSEN, JOSEPH CARL, engineer, lawyer; b. N.Y.C., Sept. 28, 1927; s. Henry and Rosetta O.; tool and diemaker's apprenticeship, 1948-53; B.S.M.E., U. Wash., 1956, postgrad., 1958; postgrad. Stanford, 1960-61; M.B.A., Santa Clara U., 1963, postgrad., 1964-65, J.D., 1973; D.Sc., Calif. Western U., 1982; m. Dina Elizabeth Schotz, Oct. 26, 1954; children—Joseph Carl II, Paul Maurice. Pres., corp. counsel multi-disciplined cons. engring. firm, San Jose, Calif., 1963—; admitted to Calif. bar, assoc. firm McCready, Doyle, Thompson & Olsen, San Francisco and San Jose, Calif. Pres., Calif. Inventors' Council, 1971-73. Served with USNR, 1952-60. Registered profl. engr., Calif. Mem. ASME, Nat. Soc. Profl. Engrs., Calif. Soc. Profl. Engrs., Cons. Engrs. Assn. Calif., Engrs. Club San Jose, ABA, Am. Trial Lawyers Assn., Calif. Trial Lawyers Assn., State Bar Calif. Patentee in field. Contbr. articles to profl. jours. Office: 8 S Montgomery St PO Box 1809 San Jose CA 95109

OLSEN, KENNETH MICHAEL, manufacturing and distributing company executive; b. Coeur D'Alene, Idaho, Apr. 15, 1948; s. Howard George and Irma Dean (Harris) O.; m. Dixie Kathleen McCowan, Dec. 28, 1968; children—Glenn Michael, Kerri Michelle. B.A. in Bus. Adminstrn. with high honors, U. Wash., 1970, M.B.A., 1971. C.P.A., Wash., Idaho. Staff auditor Arthur Andersen & Co., Seattle, 1971-73, sr. auditor, Boise, Idaho, 1973-75, audit mgr., 1975-80; treas., chief fin. officer Futura Corp., Boise, 1980—, v.p., 1981—; spl. lectr. acctg. Boise State U., 1976; dir. Trailer Distbrs., Inc., Image Nat., Inc., Futura Energy Products of Calif., Futura Energy Products, Inc. Active Boise C. of C. Mem. Am. Inst. C.P.A.s, Idaho Soc. C.P.A.s, Am. Acctg. Assn., Inst. Internatl Auditors, Am. Mgmt. Assn. Republican. Club: Arid, Inc. (Boise). Home: 1014 Bergeson St Boise ID 83706 Office: Futura Corp 999 Main St Suite 1010 Boise ID 83702

OLSEN, KENNETH O., supermarket chain executive; b. 1918. Student Am. Inst. Banking, NYU. Clk., Mfrs. Trust Co., 1937-38; various positions Standard Oil Co. of N.J., 1938-40; with Von's Grocery Co., El Monte, Calif., 1946—, field supr., 1949, sales mgr., 1965, ops. mgr., 1968, v.p., gen. mgr., 1969, sr. v.p., 1971, exec. v.p., 1973, pres., chief exec. officer, 1975—, also dir. Served to maj. AUS, 1940-45. Mem. Calif. Retailers Assn. (bd. dirs.), Food Mktg. Inst. (bd. dirs.). Office: Vons Grocery Co Inc 10150 Lower Azusa Rd El Monte CA 91731*

OLSEN, ORRIE CLAYTON, consulting engineer, former aluminum company executive; b. Three Forks, Mont., May 7, 1920; s. Ole Christen and Inga Amelia (Nelson) O.; student St. Olaf Coll., 1938-40; B.Sc., U. Chgo., 1947; m. Minnie Elizabeth Krause, Jan. 29, 1949; children—Paul Kristen, Lisa Ann. Lab asst. metall. labs. U. Chgo., Chgo. and Oak Ridge, 1943-44; chemist Armour Research Found., Chgo., 1945-46; project engr. Potash Co. Am., Carlsbad, N.Mex., 1948-53; sr. research assoc. Kaiser Aluminum & Chem. Corp., San Leandro, Calif., 1953-63, process engr., cons., Oakland, Calif., 1964—; tech. dir. Standard Magnesium, Tulsa, 1963-64. Active, Heather Farm & Garden Center Assn., Walnut Creek, Calif., 1969. Mem. Am. Chem. Soc., AIME, Calif. Catalysis Club. Co-inventor sulfur conversion catalyst, 1960. Home: 990 Seven Hills Ranch Rd Walnut Creek CA 94598 Office: 300 Lakeside Dr Oakland CA 94643

OLSEN, RICHARD ARNOLD, engineering psychologist, consultant; b. Duluth, Minn., Nov. 11, 1933; s. Henry Jomar and Hjordis Elfreda (Buck) O.; m. Janet Elizabeth Telford, Feb. 2, 1963; children—Erik Charles Buck, Jacob Loren Buck; m. 2d, Beverly Boyd Harris, Jan. 19, 1980; step-children—Steven Edry Jenkins, Kathleen Elizabeth Jenkins. B.S., Union Coll., 1955; M.S., Pa. State U., 1966, Ph.D., 1970. Lic. psychologist, Pa. Mem. tech. staff ground systems group Hughes Aircraft Co., Fullerton, Calif., 1960-64; head human factors research div. Pa. Transp. Inst., Pa. State U., 1967-80, asst. prof. human factors in engring., 1969-80; human factor engr. specialist Lockheed Missiles and

Space Co., Sunnyvale, Calif., 1980—; lectr. St. Francis Coll., Loretto, Pa., 1972-73; expert witness in human factors and safety; cons. Pres., Interact, 1976-80, Parents Without Partners, State College, Pa., 1979. Served to lt. (j.g.) USN, 1956-59. Recipient Teetor Ednl. award Soc. Automotive Engrs., 1976; vis. scientist Swedish Nat. Traffic Safety Research Inst., 1977, Fed. Hwy. Adminstrn., 1979; NASA/Am. Soc. Engring. Educators fellow, 1978. Mem. Am. Psychol. Assn., Human Factors Soc., Am. Assn. Automotive Medicine, IEEE, Pa. Psychol. Assn., Calif. Psychol. Assn., Transp. Research Bd., Sigma Xi. Democrat. Unitarian (mem. ch. choir). Contbg. author: Human Factors in Health Care, 1976; Transportation and Behavior, 1981; contbr. articles to profl. jours. Home: 611 Hubbard Ave Santa Clara CA 95051 Office: Lockheed Missiles & Space Co 62-91 B 157 1111 Lockheed Way Sunnyvale CA 94086

OLSEN, ROBERT ARTHUR, educator; b. Pittsfield, Mass., June 30, 1943; s. Arthur Anton and Virginia O.; B.B.A., U. Mass., 1966, M.B.A., 1967; Ph.D., U. Oreg., 1974; m. Maureen . Joan Carmell, Aug. 21, 1965. Security analyst Am. Inst. Counselors, 1967-68; research asso. Center for Capital Market Research, U. Oreg., 1972-74; asst. prof. fin. U. Mass., 1974-75; asso. prof. fin. Calif. State U., Chico, 1975—; cons. U.S. Forest Service. Stonier Banking fellow, 1971-72; Nat. Assn. Mut. Savs. Banks fellow, 1975-76. Recipient Bus. Research award Calif. State U.-Chico, 1983. Mem. Am. Fin. Assn., Western Fin. Assn. (Trefftzs award 1974), Southwestern Fin. Assn., Fin. Mgmt. Assn., Sierra Club. Contbr. articles to profl. jours. Office: Calif State U Sch Bus Chico CA 95929

OLSEN, VIGGO NORSKOV, univ. pres.; b. Copenhagen, July 18, 1916; came to U.S., 1968; B.A., Andrews U., 1948, M.A., 1950, B.Div., 1951; Th.M., Princeton Theol. Sem., 1960; Ph.D., U. London, 1966; Th.D., U. Basel (Switzerland), 1968; m. Sept. 1949. Chmn. dept. religion, acad. dean Newbold Coll., Bracknell, Eng., 1954-59, pres., 1960-66; prof. ch. history Loma Linda (Calif.) U., 1968—, chmn. dept. religion, 1971-72, dean Coll. of Arts and Scis., provost, 1972-74, pres., 1974—. Mem. Riverside City Mgrs. Group, 1974—; mem. Inland Empire Higher Edn. Council, 1974—; mem. Inland Action Bd., 1974—. Named Disting. Faculty lectr. Loma Linda U., 1972; Andrew U. Alumnus of Yr., 1973; Am. of Yr., Am. Religious Town Hall, Inc., 1981. Mem. Brit. Ecclesiastical History Soc., Am. Ch. History Soc., Soc. for Reformation Studies, Am. Council on Edn., Am. Assn. of Presidents of Ind. Colls. and Univs. (dir. 1976—), Assn. of Ind. Calif. Colls. and Univs. Seventh-day Adventist. Author: The New Testament Logia on Divorce, 1971; John Foxe and the Elizabethan Church, 1973. Home: 24958 Huron St Loma Linda CA 92354 Office: Loma Linda U Loma Linda CA 92350

OLSHAN, NEAL HUGH, psychologist, author; b. Albany, N.Y., Jan. 9, 1947; s. Calvin V. and Sally Ruth (Tenney) O.; m. Mary M. Walker, Aug. 28, 1972; children—Sandra, Robert, Maureen. B.A., Ariz. State U., 1970, M. Counseling, 1972, Ph.D. in Psychology, 1975. Cert. rehab. counselor; cert. psychologist, Ariz.; cert. Health Service Providers in Psychology. Founder, Southwest Pain Treatment Center, dir., 1972-77; pvt. practice psychology, Scottsdale, Ariz., 1976-83; numerous appearances nat. TV shows; cons. in field. Bd. dirs. Center of Mesa Lutheran Hosp. Mem. Am. Psychol. Assn., Am. Acad. Phys. Medicine and Rehab., Am. Acad. Psychosomatic Medicine, Ariz. Psychol. Assn., AFTRA, Authors Guild, Ariz. Authors Assn. Author: Phobia Free and Flying High, 1976; Fears and Phobias—Fighting Back, 1977; Power Over Your Pain Without Drugs, 1980; Everything You Always Wanted to Know About Phobias But Were Afraid to Ask, 1981; Depression, 1982. Home: 6144 E Calle del Norte Scottsdale AZ 85251 Office: Pain Mgmt Center 3302 Miller Rd Suite E Scottsdale AZ 85201

OLSON, BONNIE WAGGONER-BRETERNITZ (MRS. O. DONALD OLSON), civic worker; b. North Platte, Nebr., May 30, 1916; d. Floyd Emil and Edith (Waggoner) O.; A.B., U. Chgo., 1947; m. O. Donald Olson, May 17, 1944; children—Pamela Lynne, Douglas Donald. Dep. clk. Dist. Ct., Lincoln County, Nebr., 1940-42; advt. researcher Burke & Assos., Chgo., 1942; contbg. newspaper columnist Chgo. Herald-Am., 1943; social worker A.R.C., Chgo., 1942-44, Sacramento, Calif., 1944, Amarillo, Tex., 1945; exec. sec. Econometrica, Cowles Commn. for Research in Econs., Chgo., 1945-47; interior designer, antique dealer. Col.; participant Chgo. Maternity Center Fund Drive, 1953; mem. Colo. Springs Community Council, 1956-58, chmn. children's div., 1956-58, mem. exec. bd., 1956-58, mem. budget com., 1957-58; mem. Colorado Springs Charter Assn., 1956-60, mem. exec. bd., 1957-59, sec., 1958; chmn. El Paso County PTA, Protective Services for Children, 1959-61; chmn. women's div. fund drive ARC, 1961; mem. League Women Voters, 1957—, mem. state children's law com., 1961-63; chmn. ad hoc com. El Paso County Citizens' Com. for Nat. Probation and Parole Survey, Juvenile Ct. Procedures and Detention, 1957-61; mem. children's adv. com. Colo. Child Welfare Dept., 1959-63, chmn., 1961; del. White House Conf. on Children and Youth, 1960, 70; sec. Citizens Ad Hoc Com. for Comprehensive Mental Health Clinic for Pikes Peak Region, 1966—; mem. Colorado Springs Human Relations Commn., 1968-71; sustaining mem. Symphony Guild, 1970-72, Fine Arts Center, 1957—; mem. Pikes Peak Mental Health Center, 1964-67; Colo. del. White House Conf. on Aging, Colo. Gov.'s Conf. on Aging, 1981. Recipient Lane Bryant Ann. Nat. Awards citation, 1971; alumni citation for pub. service U. Chgo., 1961. Mem. Am. Acad. Polit. and Social Sci., Nat. Trust Historic Preservation, Women's Ednl. Soc. Colo. Coll. (life), Council on Religion and Internat. Affairs. Episcopalian. Clubs: Quadranglar, University (Chgo.); Broadmoor Golf, Garden of the Gods (Colorado Springs). Home: 2110 Hercules Dr Colorado Springs CO 80906

OLSON, CARL BERNARD, engineering executive; b. Bellingham, Wash., Sept. 19, 1940; s. Bernard Thayer and Elizabeth Injeborg (Reykalin) O.; m. Camilla Bryant, Dec. 16, 1963; children—Lori, Eric. B.S. in Electronic Engring., Calif. State U., Poly., 1963. Lic. FCC Radiotelephone (1st class). Transmission engr. Lenkurt Electric Co., San Carlos, Calif., 1965-69; engr., cons., system engring. mgr. Motorola, Inc., Foster City, Calif., 1969-73, mgr. engring. services 1973—. Served to lt. U.S. Army, 1963-65. Mem. IEEE, Assn. Pub. Safety Communications Officers. Republican. Clubs: Peninsula Covenant (Redwood City, Calif.); Family Fitness (Foster City).

OLSON, CRAIG ARTHUR, physician; b. Dayton, Ohio, Feb. 2, 1945; s. O. Charles and M. Evelyn (Sanger) O.; m. Barbara A. Vaughan, July 27, 1968; children—Charles John, Erika Marie, Kristina Anne. B.S. in Zoology, Wash. State U., 1967; M.D. U. Wash., 1971. Intern Kaiser Found. hosp., San Francisco, 1971-72; served to maj. USPHS Indian Health Br., Toppenish, Wash., 1972-74; residency in family medicine and emergency physician, Yakima Valley Meml. Hosp., 1974-76; med. dir., emergency physician Deaconess Hosp., Spokane, Wash., 1976-82; med. dir. Minor Emergency Ctr., South Hill Med. Ctr., 1982—; chmn. City and County of Spokane Emergency Med. Service, 1981; med. dir. Spokane Ambulance Co., 1977-82; paramedic dir. Spokane County, 1977-81. Mem. Am. Coll. Emergency Physicians, Spokane County Med. Soc., Wash. State Med. Soc. Republican. Presbyterian.

OLSON, DONALD RAY, neurosurgeon; b. Edgerton, Wis., Dec. 13, 1936; s. Elmore Ray and Mildred O. (Munson) O.; B.S., U. Wis., 1958, M.D., 1961; children—Jacinta Kay, Leif Eric, Alisa Rae, Kristina Francoise, Jon Christian. Intern, Alameda County (Calif.) Hosp., 1961-62; resident gen. surgery U. Wis. Med. Sch., Madison, 1964-65, resident neurol. surgery, 1965-69; asso. staff Moffatt Hosp., San Francisco, 1971-81; mem. staff St. Mary's Hosp., Reno, 1971—, Washoe Med. Center, Reno, 1971-80, chief neurosurgery, 1974-76; cons. Pershing Gen. Hosp., Lovelock, Nev., Tahoe Forest Hosp., Truckee, Calif., Carson-Tahoe Hosp., Carson City, Nev., Nev. Mental Health Inst., Reno; instr. div. neurol. surgery U. Wis. Med. Sch., Madison, 1969-70; clin. asso. and coordinator neurol. surgery U. Nev. Sch. Med. Scis., Reno, 1971-73, clin. asso. prof. surgery, 1973-78, asso. prof. surgery, 1978-80, chief neurosurgery sect., 1978-80, clin. prof., 1980—; clin. asst. prof. neurosurgery U. Calif. Med. Sch., San Francisco, 1974-81; dir. Computerized Diagnostic Lab., Inc., Reno, 1977-81; med. coordinator Nat. Coll. State Judiciary, 1977; clin. dir. Brain Research Inst., Reno, 1974-80. Mem. Washoe County Sch. Dist. Health Council, 1977-80; bd. dirs. World Med. Found., 1973-81, Pacific World Med. Found., 1981—. Served to capt. USAF, 1962-64. Diplomate Am. Bd. Neurosurgery. Fellow ACS, Internat. Coll. Surgeons, Royal Soc. Medicine (London); mem. Am. Assn. Neurosurgeons, Western Neurol. Soc., Neurosurg. Soc. Nev., Pan Pacific Surg. Assn., Western Fedn. Neurol. Sci., Am. Assn. Med. Clinics, AMA (Continuing Med. Edn. award 1969, 72, 79, 82), Nev. Med. Soc. (del. 1974), Ripon Soc., Wis. Med. Alumni Assn., Congress of Neurosurgery, Nat. Inst. Preventive Sports Medicine (dir. 1979—), No. Epilepsy League (dir. 1972-76), Washoe County Cancer Soc. (dir. 1973-76). Contbr. articles on neurology to profl. jours. Office: 3196 Maryland Pkwy #106 Las Vegas NV 89109 also 633 N Arlington Ave #220 Reno NV 89503

OLSON, ENID CLARA THALMAN, state official, educator; b. Richfield, Utah, Mar. 10, 1923; d. John Earl and Ida Arelia (Hansen) Thalman; m. Arnold Olson, Apr. 23, 1942 (div.); 1 son, Steven Arnold. B.S. in Psychology, U. Ariz., 1971, M.S. in Child Devel. and Family Relations, 1972. Cert. community coll. instr., Ariz.; cert. educator, counselor, supr., Calif. Extension agt. Coop. Extension Service, Tucson, 1975-76; health services surveyor II Ariz. Dept. Health Services, Phoenix, 1977-79; supr. counselling and case mgmt. City of Phoenix, 1980-82; state coordinator Expanded Food and Nutrition Edn. Program, Coop. Extension Service, U. Hawaii, 1982—. Chmn. grant rev. Santa Cruz (Calif.) Comprehensive Health Planning Council, 1972-74; co-chmn. Ariz. Human Resource Commn., 1977. Mem. Hawaii Nutrition Council, Hawaii Home Econs. Assn., Psi Chi, Phi Theta Kappa, Kappa Delta Pi. Democrat. Unitarian Universalist. Club: Altrusa (pres., dir. Ambos Nogales, pres. Phoenix 1981-82, v.p. Hawaii 1983).

OLSON, GERALD THEODORE, ednl. cons.; b. Rockford, Ill., Mar. 10, 1928; s. Ernest Hjalmer and Irma Lena (Widgren) O.; B.S., U. San Francisco, 1953; M.A., San Francisco State U., 1960; M.Ed., U. So. Calif., 1964; Ph.D., U. Calif., Berkeley, 1974; m. Jean Vujovich, Aug. 28, 1949; children—Gerald Theodore, Kathleen Elaina Olson Groves, John Ernest, Carol Frances Olson Love. Counselor, tchr., dir. student activities Canyon High Sch., Castro Valley, Calif., 1964-70, also lectr. Calif. State U., Hayward, 1971-72 and instr. Chabot Coll., Hayward, 1964-73; cons. counseling and guidance Colo. Dept. Edn., Denver, 1973; cons. career edn. and guidance, ednl. services group Los Angeles County Office of Supt. Schs., 1973—. Served with USMC, 1946-49, with Army Res. and Calif. Army N.G., 1950-81. Cert. secondary sch. teaching, secondary sch. adminstrn., gen. pupil personnel services, community coll., marriage, family and child counseling, Calif.; NDEA scholar, 1963-64; NIMH trainee, 1971-72; decorated Meritorious Service medal USAR, 1981. Mem. Am., Western psychol. assns., Calif. Assn. Career Guidance, Calif. Counselor Educators Assn., Am., Calif. (editor Compass newsletter 1982-83) personnel and guidance assns., Calif. Assn. Measurement and Evaluation in Guidance (pres. 1981-82), Phi Delta Kappa. Democrat. Home: 3366 Tempe Dr Huntington Beach CA 92649 Office: 9300 E Imperial Hwy Downey CA 90242

OLSON, H. EVERETT, food products executive; b. 1906; grad. Northwestern U., 1927. With Carnation Co., Los Angeles, 1931—, treas., 1948-54, v.p. fin., 1954-63, pres., 1963-71, chmn. exec. com., 1965-71, chmn. bd., chief exec. officer, 1971—, also dir. Office: Carnation Co 5045 Wilshire Blvd Los Angeles CA 90036*

OLSON, KENNETH HARVEY, computer co. exec., cons.; b. Souris, N.D., May 7, 1927; s. Oscar L. and Clara (Haugen) O.; B.A., Concordia Coll., 1950; M.S., U. N.D., 1953; Ph.D. studies U. Minn., 1955; m. Darlene R. Gronseth, Aug. 19, 1950; children—Kenneth David, Martha C., Marie K. Math. instr. U. N.D., 1952-54; computer programming supr. Convair Co., San Diego, 1955-59; with Control Data Corp., Mpls., 1959-62, San Diego, 1962-70; v.p. Automated Med. Analysts, San Diego, 1970—; pres. Health Care Services Corp., San Diego, 1971-74; chmn. Gronseth-Olson Distbrs., San Diego, 1967-70; pres., dir. H.C.S. Corp., San Diego, 1972-75; pres. 010 Corp., San Diego, 1975—; mem. adv. bd. San Diego Nat. Bank, 1982—; cons. Data Systems Mktg., 1975—. Vice pres., trustee Calif. Prepaid Health Plan Council, 1971-74; trustee H.M.O. Assn. Am., 1974-75; mem. Nat. UN Day Com., 1975. Served with AUS, 1945-46. Mem. Assn. Computing Machinery. Republican. Lutheran (congregation pres. 1957-59). Editor: Approximations for the 1604 Computer (Hans J. Maehly), 1960. Home: 4361 Valle Dr La Mesa CA 92041 Office: 5710 Ruffin Rd San Diego CA 92123

OLSON, LAURA MAXINE, adminstrv. asst., former UN ofcl.; b. Baker, Oreg., June 16, 1927; d. Arthur Vard and Retta Belle (Mercer) Olson; B.S., U. Oreg., 1949. Line-up editor True Detective mag., N.Y.C., 1949-50; promotion writer N.Y. Herald Tribune Snydicate, writer N.Y. Herald Tribune News service, 1950-52; counsellor for women U Oreg., 1952-53; news editor Cottage Grove (Oreg.) Sentinel, 1953-54; reporter, polit. writer Roseburt (Oreg.) News-Rev., 1954-56; research asst. to U.S. rep., 1957-60; press asst. to U.S. senator, 1961-62; asst. legis. asst. to U.S. senator, 1962-65, legis. asst., 1966-68; spl. cons. population problems U.S. Senate Govt. Ops. Subcom. on Fgn. Aid Expenditures, 1965-68; head info. office Nat. Endowment for Humanities, 1968-70; chief clearing house and info. sect., population div. UN Econ. and Social Commn. for Asia and Pacific, 1970-82, chmn. staff assn., 1971-73, co-editor staff bull., 1973-74, co-chmn. staff assn. welfare com., chmn. staff council souvenir com. 1977-79, advisor, 1980-81; mem. staff U.S. Congressman Jim Weaver, dist. office, Eugene, Oreg., 1983—. Mem. Oreg. Democratic Central Com.; bd. dirs. Wayne Morse Hist. Park Corp.; mem. steering com. Fgn. Student Friendship Found., U. Oreg.; founding mem. Willamette World Affairs Council; editor Vida-McKenzie Neighborhood Watch; mem. Lane County Library Adv. Com. Recipient plaque UN Econ. and Social Commn. for Asia and Pacific, 1982. Mem. Women in Communications, Fgn. Corrs. of Thailand, Satri Sakone, Women in Internat. Orgns. (founding), Common Cause, Delta Delta Delta. Democrat. Episcopalian. Clubs: Royal Bangkok Sports, Women's Nat. Dem. Home: 45014 McKenzie Hwy Leaburg OR 97489

OLSON, MELVIN NATHAN, microbial genetics mfg. co. exec.; b. Marshfield, Wis., Apr. 10, 1932; s. Carl Frederick and Dorothy Hannah (Rowley) O.; B.A., Seattle Pacific U., 1955; M.Div., Western Evang. Sem., 1959; Ed.D., U. Portland, 1970; m. Mary Olene Olson, July 26, 1969; 1 son, Michael David. Instr., Western Evang. Sem., Portland, Oreg., 1960-62; asst. prof. psychology Cascade Coll., Portland, 1962-68, pres., 1968-71; pres. microbial genetics div. Pioneer Hi-Bred Internat., Inc., Portland, 1971—; lectr., cons. in field. Bd. fellows Seattle Pacific U., 1975—. Mem. Portland C. of C., Nat. Feed Ingredients Assn. Republican. Baptist. Clubs: City, Multnomah Athletic (Portland). Home: 2305 NW 133d Pl Portland OR 97229 Office: 3930 SW Macadam Ave Portland OR 97201

OLSON, OSCAR DONALD, banker; b. Pueblo, Colo., Feb. 9, 1917; s. Oscar and Iva (Ackerman) O.; B.A., U. Chgo., 1941, M.B.A., 1948; m. Bonnie B. Waggoner-Breternitz, May 17, 1944; children—Pamela Lynne, Douglas Donald. With No. Trust Co., Chgo., 1941-54, investment research, 1941-47, asst. personnel dir., 1947-54; with Exchange Nat. Bank, Colorado Springs, Colo., 1954-72, v.p., 1959-63, sr. v.p., 1964-66, pres., 1967-72, dir., 1963-72; pres. O.D. Olson and Assos., investments, 1972-79, Warehouses, Inc.; pres. Citizens Nat. Bank, Colorado Springs, 1976-77; Air Acad. Nat. Bank, 1966-71, also dir.; past chmn. Colo. Springs Clearing Ho.; past regional adviser Small Bus. Adminstr. Bd. dirs. Colorado Springs Symphony, Colorado Springs United Fund; mem. Urban League. Served with USAAF, 1942-45; maj. gen. Res. ret. Decorated Silver Star medal, Legion of Merit, D.F.C., Air medal, four Presdl. unit citations. Recipient Alumni citation U. Chgo., 1961. Mem. Am. Bankers Assn., Colorado Springs C. of C. (past pres.), Air Force Assn. (Man of Year award, 1960, past state chmn., nat. dir.), Newcomen Soc. N.Am., Order of Daedalians, Sigma Chi. Episcopalian. Clubs: Executive (Chgo.); El Paso, Garden of the Gods. Home: 2110 Hercules Dr Colorado Springs CO 80906

OLSON, PATRICIA HAGEY, educator; b. South Bend, Ind., Mar. 16, 1926; d. George Lee and Catherine (Blakeman) Hagey; B.S., Purdue U., 1947; M.A., Loyola U., Chgo., 1955; M.Ed., U. Ariz., 1972, Ph.D., 1975; m. Robert Anderson Olson; children—Cathy Lee, Keith Alan. Tchr. high sch. Chgo. public schs., 1949-55; tchr. Deerfield (Ill.) public schs., 1955-59; tchr. Spanish in elem. schs., English as second lang., Palatine (Ill.) public schs., 1959-63; tchr. high sch. Lake Geneva (Wis.) public schs., 1963-66; tchr. 3d grade and English as second lang., Los Angeles public schs., 1968-71; asst. dir. Title I, Picacho (Ariz.) public schs., 1971; Title I reading/lang. resource tchr. Tucson Unified Sch. Dist. 1, 1972—, instr. U. Ariz., 1973, 78. Mem. Internat. Reading Assn., Ariz. State Reading Council, Tucson Area Reading Council, Assn. Supervision and Curriculum Devel. Club: Women of Moose. Contbr. articles to dist. publs. and profl. jours. Home: 4858 Casas Serenas Dr Tucson AZ 85705

OLSON, ROY CHRISTIAN, ins. co. exec.; b. San Francisco, Oct. 29, 1945; s. Roy Christian and Anna Helen Olson; A.B., Sonoma State Coll., 1967; M.S., U. Idaho, 1970; Ph.D., U. Wash., 1972; m. Jane Carol Edwards, 1968; children—Stephanie, Matthew. Instr. U. Wash., Seattle, 1972-73; asst. prof. U. Hawaii, Honolulu, 1973-75; vis. asst. prof. Miami U., Oxford, Ohio, 1975-77; asst. actuary E.F. Hutton Life Ins. Co., La Jolla, Calif., 1977—; NSF trainee, 1971, research asst., 1971-72. Fellow Life Mgmt. Inst.; mem. Actuarial Club of Pacific States, Actuarial Club of San Diego (sec./treas. 1982-83), Math. Assn. Am., Am. Math. Soc., Soc. Actuaries, Am. Acad. Actuaries, Los Angeles Actuarial Club, Sigma Xi. Author: On the Six Conics Problem, Discrete Mathematics 10, 1974; Some Results From A-Spaces, Set Theoretic Topology, 1976. Home: 7960 Berwyn Rd San Diego CA 92126 Office: 11011 N Torrey Pines Rd La Jolla CA 92038

OLSON, SHIRLEY ANN, ednl. adminstr.; b. Portland, Oreg., Oct. 19, 1947; d. Chester Eldon and Cora Alvera (Edgell) Davis; B.A., U. Oreg., 1969, M.Ed., 1976; m. Donald Scott Olson, July 1, 1969; children—Aaron Davis. Tchr. high sch., Stuttgart, Germany, 1969-71; elem. instructional aide public schs., Eugene, Oreg., 1971-72; tchr. jr. high sch., counselor public schs., Cottage Grove, Oreg., 1972-74; curriculum adminstr., acting prin. public schs., Lebanon, Oreg., 1975-80, dir. instrn., 1980—. Recipient Disting. Educator award Oreg. State U., 1978. Mem. Assn. Supervision and Curriculum Devel., Confedn. Oreg. Sch. Adminstrs. (pres.), Oreg. Assn. Sch. Suprs., Lebanon C. of C. Home: 1522 Revere Ct S Salem OR 97302 Office: 485 S 5th Lebanon OR 97355

OLSON, THOMAS HILTON, psychologist; b. Oak Park, Ill., Nov. 5, 1945; s. Theodore F. and Georgia J. (Krenz) O.; B.S., U. Utah, 1967; M.B.A., UCLA, 1969; D.B.A., U. So. Calif., 1977; m. Kathleen Ann Kunze, Oct. 24, 1970; 1 dau., Erika Britt. Asst. prof. mgmt. Calif. State U., Northridge, 1973-76; vis. prof. adminstrn. U. Calif., Riverside, 1976-77; asst. prof. mgmt. San Diego State U., 1977-78; mgr. orgn. devel. Gen. Telephone Co. of Calif., Santa Monica, 1978-80; dir. tng. and devel. Rockwell Internat., Los Angeles, 1980—; vis. prof. orgn. behavior U. So. Calif., 1973—. Commr. bd. zoning adjustment City of Manhattan Beach (Calif.), 1977-78. Lic. indsl. psychologist, Calif. Mem. Acad. Mgmt., Am. Psychol. Assn., Human Resource Planning Soc., Orgn. Devel. Network, Personnel Testing Council So. Calif., Beta Gamma Sigma. Contbr. articles to profl. jours. Office: 2230 E Imperial Hwy El Segundo CA 90245

OLSON, WILLIAM THOMAS, educator; b. Coeur d'Alene, Idaho, May 1, 1940; s. William Anthony and Julia Glenn (Hunter) O.; B.A., U. N.Mex., 1968; postgrad. U. Va., 1968-72; m. Diana Jean Dodds, Aug. 22, 1962; children—Kristin Ann, Kira Lynn. Intelligence agt. U.S. Army, 1962-65; asso. editor Newspaper Printing Corp., Albuquerque, 1965-66; news and pub. affairs dir. KUNM-FM, U. N.M., 1966-68; news person KOAT-TV, Albuquerque, 1968; news dir. WCHV Radio, Charlottesville, Va., 1968-69; moderator, producer Radio-TV Center, U. Va., 1969-73; columnist The Jefferson Jour., Charlottesville, Va., 1972; instr. history U. Va., 1971-73; information specialist Wash. State U. Cooperative Ext. Service, Pullman, 1973-77, instr. Sch. Communications, 1976-77, asst. program dir., info. officer Wash. Energy Ext. Service, 1977-79; dir. Spokane County Head Start, 1979—; cons. United Indians of All Tribes Found., 1980—. Dir., Ryegrass Sch., Spokane, 1978—. Bd. dirs. Charlottesville-Albemarle Mental Health Assn., 1969-72; bd. dirs. Charlottesville-Albemarle chpt. ACLU, 1969-71, Spokane chpt., 1983—; mem. adv. bd. Spokane Pub. Radio, 1983—; pres. Charlottesville-Albemarle Human Relations Council, 1970-71; chairperson Pullman area chpt. ACLU, 1976-79, chmn., 1976-78; organizer U. Va. Flood Relief Com., 1969; organizer Wash.-Idaho Flood Relief Vols., 1974. Served with AUS, 1962-65. Mem. Nat. Council for Resource Devel., Nat. Head Start Dirs. Assn. (region V steering com. chmn. 1981-82, regional sec. 1980). Author TV documentary (with Ken Fielding): The Golden Years?, 1973; film (with B. Dale Harrison and Lorraine Kingdon) New Directions Out of the Culture of Poverty, 1974. Home: E 2018 14th Ave Spokane WA 99202 Office: Head Start E 7401 Mission Ave Spokane WA 99206

OLTEANU, MARY ANN, merchandising consultant; b. Detroit, Feb. 3, 1943; d. Harry and Aneta (Marginean) O.; m. James Francis Heaney, Sept. 30, 1967 (div.). B.A. with distinction in English, U. Mich., 1965. Exec. trainee merchandising J. L. Hudson Co., Detroit, 1965-66; corp. tng. coordinator various divs. J. L. Hudson Co., 1970-72; creative copywriter Enterprise Paint Mfg. Co., Chgo., 1970-72; self-employed handweaver, 1972-77; mgmt. tng., asst. store mgr. Crate & Barrel Co., Chgo., 1977-79; pres. Olteanu Design, Inc. dba Grand Design, Daly City, Calif., 1979—; merchandising, store design cons. Buck Stove & Fan Ctrs., Belmont, San Jose, Calif. Recipient Regents-Alumni scholarship U. Mich., 1961-65. Mem. Nat. Assn. Female Execs., Northbay Women's Network. Office: Olteanu Design Inc 110 Serramonte Ctr Daly City CA 94015

OLTON, ROBERT MATTHEW, computer manufacturing company executive; b. Newark, July 1937; s. Robert M. and Minnie Olton; B.S., Trinity Coll., Hartford, Conn., 1959; M.Sc., McGill U., Montreal, 1961; Ph.D., U. Calif.-Berkeley, 1961-65. Research psychologist U. Calif.-Berkeley, 1965-69, mem. faculty, 1969-78; mgr. behavior research Atari Corp., Sunnyvale, Calif., 1982—; vis. scientist Xerox Research Ctr., Palo Alto, Calif., 1977-78. Mem. Am. Psychol. Assn., AAAS, Sigma Xi. Author: (with M.V. Covington) The Productive Thinking Program, 1972. Office: Atari Corporation 1265 Borregas Ave Sunnyvale CA 94088

OLUM, PAUL, mathematician, univ. pres.; b. Binghamton, N.Y., Aug. 16, 1918; s. Jacob and Rose (Citlen) O.; A.B. summa cum laude, Harvard, 1940, Ph.D. (NRC predoctoral fellow 1946-47), 1947; M.A., Princeton, 1942; m. Vivian Goldstein, June 8, 1942; children—Judith Ann, Joyce Margaret, Kenneth Daniel. Theoretical physicist Manhattan Project, Princeton, 1941-42, Los Alamos Sci. Lab., 1943-45; Frank B. Jewett postdoctoral fellow Harvard, 1947-48, Inst. Advanced Study, 1948-49; mem. faculty Cornell U., Ithaca, N.Y., 1949-74, prof. math., 1957-74, chmn. dept. 1963-66, trustee, 1971-75; prof. math., dean Coll. Natural Scis. U. Tex. at Austin, 1974-76; prof. math., v.p. for acad. affairs, provost U. Oreg., Eugene, 1976-80, acting pres., 1980-81, pres., 1981—; mem. Inst. Advanced Study, 1955-56; on leave at U. Paris (France) and Hebrew U., Jerusalem, 1962-63. NSF fellow Stanford, 1966-67; vis. prof. U. Wash., 1970-71. Mem. adv. com. Office Ordnance Research, NRC, 1958-61. Mem. Am. Math. Soc., AAUP, Math Assn. Am., Phi Beta Kappa, Sigma Xi. Author monograph, research articles on algebraic topology. Office: Office of Pres U Oreg Eugene OR 97403

O'MALLEY, JOHN ANTHONY, medical instrument manufacturing co. executive; b. Phila., July 6, 1933; s. John J. and Grace (Winters) O'M.; m. Mary Wright, June 5, 1954; children—John Anthony, Robert D., Teresa O'M. Nippes, David M. B.S., Rutgers State U., 1959; Ph.D., U. Pa., 1963. Asst. prof. Drexel U., Phila., 1963-67; dir., v.p. research and devel. Harleco, Phila., 1969-73; v.p. chemistry Oxford Labs., Foster City, Calif., 1973-76, pres., 1977-78; dir. tech. devel. Smith Kline Clin. Labs., Sunnyvale, Calif., 1979; pres. SmithKline Instruments, Inc., Sunnyvale, 1979—; dir. Nat. Com. Clin. Lab. Standards, 1977-81. Mem. Merchantville (N.J.) Planning Bd., Zoning Bd. and City Council; bd. dirs. Little League. Served with AUS, 1954-56. Mem. Am. Assn. Clin. Chemistry, Am. Chem. Soc., Am. Soc. Clin. Chemists. Club: Lions. Author: (with F. Longo) Experiments in Chemistry, 1968; contbr. articles to profl. jours. Home: 1105 Hidden Oaks Dr Menlo Park CA 94025 Office: 485 Potrero Ave Sunnyvale CA 94086

O'MALLEY, MARY KATHERINE, publisher; b. Chgo., Oct. 25, 1937; d. Michael and Katherine (Loftus) O'M.; B.A., Mundelein Coll., 1959; children—Mark, Maura, Peter, Elizabeth. Account exec. KPBS San Diego, 1974-75; pub. The LaJolla Money Book, 1975-78; pub., owner Marvelous Menus, Larkspur, Calif., 1978—. Mem. North Bay Advt. Club (co-founder), San Francisco Bay Advt. Club, San Francisco Mag. Reps. Office: 3030 Bridgeway St Sausalito CA 94965

O'MALLEY, PETER, professional baseball club executive; b. N.Y.C., Dec. 12, 1937; s. Walter F. and Kay (Hanson) O'M.; B.S. in Econs., U. Pa., 1960; m. Annette Zacho, July 10, 1971; children—Katherine, Kevin, Brian. Dir. Dodgertown, Vero Beach, Fla., 1962-64; pres., gen. mgr. Spokane Baseball Club, 1965-66; v.p. Los Angeles Dodgers Baseball Club, 1967-68, exec. v.p., 1968—; pres. Los Angeles Dodgers, Inc., 1970—; dir. Union Oil Co.; adv. dir. Bank of Am. Mem. exec. com. Pacific Coast League, 1967-68; bd. dirs. Los Angeles Central City, Los Angeles Police Meml. Found., Los Angeles Olympic Organizing Com.; trustee Little League Found.; bd. govs. Los Angeles Music Center Performing Arts Council. Home: 1000 Elysian Park Ave Los Angeles CA 90012 Office: Dodger Stadium 1000 Elysian Park Ave Los Angeles CA 90012

O'MALLEY, ROBERT HAROLD, banker; b. Troy, N.Y., Feb. 17, 1926; s. Edward Joseph and Anna Nielsena (Clausen) O'M.; grad. UCLA Sch. Mgmt., 1977; m. Theresa Mary Kenesie, May 5, 1951; children—Roger, Pamela, Patricia, Mark, Matthew. Served as enlisted man U.S. Navy, 1943-56, commd. ensign, 1956, advanced through grades to comdr., 1968; asst. supply officer USS Northampton, 1959-61; auditor NATO, 1954-56; adv. to exec. officer Naval Supply Center, Saigon, 1963-64; liaison officer Royal N.Z. Air Force, 1964-67; ret., 1967; with Security Pacific Nat. Bank, Los Angeles, 1968-72; with Santa Clarita Nat. Bank, Newhall, Calif., 1972—, asst. mgr., 1972-75, v.p., 1977—. Active San Fernando Valley council Boy Scouts Am., 1965—, asst. dist. commr., 1969-71, recipient Nat. Merit award, 1972, Silver Beaver award, St. George emblem, 1973. Mem. Ind. Bankers Assn., VFW, Fleet Res. Assn. (founder Naples, Italy br. 1956), Alumni Assn. U. Calif. Los Angeles, Navy League U.S. (pres. 1970-72). Republican. Roman Catholic. Clubs: KC, Pine Mountain (dir., treas. 1977-81). Author: Non-Appropriated Funds Control Manual (Allied Forces So. Europe-NATO), 1955. Home: PO Box 5187 PMC Frazier Park CA 93225 Office: Santa Clarita Nat Bank PO Box 898 Newhall CA 91321

OMAN, HENRY, elec. engr.; b. Portland, Oreg., Aug. 29, 1918; s. Paul L. and Mary (Levonen) O.; B.S. in E.E., with honors, Oreg. State U., 1940, E.E., 1951; m. Earlene Mary Boot, Sept. 11, 1954; children—Mary Janet, Eleanor Eva, Eric Paul. Application engr. elec. dept. Allis-Chalmers Mfg. Co., Milw., 1940-48; research engr. Boeing Co., Seattle, 1948-65; mgr. solar power research Boeing Aerospace Co., Seattle, 1965—; tchr. continuing edn. course on advanced energy systems. Registered profl. engr., Wash.; lic. amateur radio operator. Asso. fellow AIAA; mem. IEEE (sr., bd. govs. Aerospace and Electronics Systems Soc.), Astron. Soc. Pacific, AAAS, Am. Amateur Radio Relay League. Methodist. Clubs: Seattle Mountaineers, Wash. Kayak. Asso. editor IEEE Transactions on Aerospace and Electronics Systems, 1962—; contbr. articles to profl. jours., chpt. to book. Home: 19221 Normandy Park Dr SW Seattle WA 98166 Office: MS 14-31 Boeing Aerospace Co Box 3999 Seattle WA 98124

OMDAHL, ALDON EUGENE, banker; b. Devils Lake, N.D., Oct. 1, 1921; s. Arthur Wilson and Julia S. Omdahl; m. Virginia Bennett, May 25, 1946; children—Clarke, Susan Omdahl Shaw, James. B.S. in Bus. Adminstrn., U. N.D., 1943; postgrad. U. Wis., 1954-56. Office mgr., dist. rep. Comml. Credit Corp., 1946-49; mgr. time pay dept. Red River Nat. Bank, Grand Forks, N.D., 1949-51, 1st Nat. Bank, Bozeman, 1951-52; asst. cashier Corr. Bank div. 1st Nat. Bank, Mpls., 1952-60; pres., chief exec. officer 1st Bank West Billings, Billings, Mont., 1960-82, chmn., 1982—. Bd. dirs. Rocky Mountain Coll., 1966-79; pres. United Way, 1970; session mem. 1st Presbyterian Ch., 1970-73. Served to lt. U.S. Army, 1943-46. Decorated Silver Star, Bronze Star with one oak leaf cluster, Purple Heart with one oak leaf cluster. Mem. Mont. Bankers Assn., Am. Bankers Assn., Am. Legion, VFW. Republican. Clubs: Yellowstone Country, Mesa Country, Masons, Shriners, Elks. Home: 3124 Ben Hogan Pl RD 6 Billings MT 59106 Office: First Bank W Billings PO Box 20007 Billings MT 59104

O'MEARA, MARCIAN THOMAS, priest; b. Denison, Iowa, Mar. 4, 1929; s. Clarence Joseph and Elizabeth Ruth (Hassett) O'M. B.A., Conception Sem., 1954, M.A., 1959. Ordained priest, Roman Cath. Ch., 1959; prior St. Pius X Priory, Pevely, Mo., 1969, abbot, 1972-77; chaplain dir. St. Anthony Hosp., Denver, 1977-83; dir. Permanent Diaconate, Archdiocese of Denver, 1981—, dir. Formation for Seminarians, dir. vocations, 1983—. Democrat. Address: 200 Josephine St Denver CO 80206

OMHOLT, BRUCE DONALD, product designer, mechanical engineer, consultant; b. Salem, Oreg., Mar. 27, 1943; s. Donald Carl and Violet Mae (Buck) O.; m. Mavis Aronow, Aug. 18, 1963 (div. July 1972); children—Madison, Natalie; m. 2d, Darla Kay Faber, Oct. 27, 1972; 1 son, Cassidy. B.S.M.E., Heald Coll. Engring., San Francisco, 1964. Real estate salesman R. Lea Ward and Assocs., San Francisco, 1962-64; sales engr. Repco Engring., Montebello, Calif., 1964; in various mfg. engring. and mgmt. positions Ford Motor Co., Rawsonville, Saline, Owosso and Ypsilanti, Mich., 1964-75; chief engr. E. F. Hauserman Co., Cleve., 1975-77; dir. design and engring. Am. Seating Co., Grand Rapids, Mich., 1977-80; prin. Trinity Engring., Grand Rapids, Mich., 1980-81, Rohnert Park, Calif., 1981—; cons. mfg. U.S., fgn. patentee carrier rack apparatus, motorcycle improvements, panels.

OMOKAWA, NORIAKI WAYNE, manufacturing company executive; b. Los Angeles, Dec. 13, 1947; s. Noriyoshi and Tokoyo (Harada) O. Student U. Wash., 1966-68; B.A., Occidental Coll., 1970. With Japan Air Lines, San Francisco, 1970-71; territory mgr. Schick Safety Razor Co., San Francisco, 1971-73; personnel mgr. Kanematsu-Gosho (USA), Inc., Los Angeles, 1973-77, asst. corp. dir. personnel, N.Y.C., 1978; v.p., gen. mgr. Alps Electric (USA), Inc., Los Angeles, 1979—. Home: 38 S Meridith Ave Pasadena CA 91106 Office: 19401 S Vermont Ave B-102 Torrance CA 90502

OMURA, JIMMY KAZUHIRO, elec. engr.; b. San Jose, Calif., Sept. 8, 1940; s. Shomatsu and Shizuko Dorothy (Takesaka) O.; B.S., M.I.T., 1963, M.S., 1963; Ph.D. (NSF fellow), Stanford U., 1966. Research engr. Stanford (Calif.) Research Inst., 1966-69; asst. prof. system sci. UCLA, 1969-73, asso. prof., 1973-77, prof., 1977—; cons. to industry and govt. NSF grantee, 1970—. Fellow IEEE. Author: (with Andrew J. Viterbi) Principles of Digital Communication and Coding, 1979; contbr. articles to profl. publs. Office: Boelter Hall 4531 U Calif Los Angeles CA 90024

O'NEIL, MICHAEL G., aerospace products manufacturing company executive; b. 1922; married. Grad. Holy Cross Coll.; student Harvard U. Grad. Sch. Bus. Adminstrn. With Aerojet-Gen. Corp., 1946—, chmn. exec. com., 1961-65, chmn. bd., La Jolla, Calif., 1965—, also dir.; pres., dir. Gen. Tire & Rubber Co. parent co. Aerojet-Gen. Corp. Served with USAAF, World War II. Office: Aerojet-Gen Corp 10300 N Torrey Pines Rd La Jolla CA 92037*

O'NEILL, DENNIS VINCENT, architect, computer software cons.; b. Newark, Dec. 21, 1942; s. Raymond V. and Grace O'N.; B.Arch., N.D. State U., 1967; M.Arch., U. Calif.-Berkeley, 1968. Partner, Ishimaru & O'Neill, Architects, Oakland, Calif., 1972-80; owner, mgr. O'Neill Software, San Francisco, 1980—; computer software cons. Mem. AIA, ACM, IEEE Computer Soc., Mensa. Office: 440 Davis Ct Suite 1822 San Francisco CA 94111

O'NEILL, MAUREEN ANNE, arts adminstr., city official; b. Seattle, Nov. 11, 1948; d. Robert P. and Barbara F. (Pettinger) O'N.; B.A. in Sociology cum laude, Wash. State U., 1971; M.A., Bowling Green U., 1972. Grad. asst. dept. coll. student personnel Bowling Green (Ohio) U., 1971-72; asst. coordinator coll. activities SUNY, Geneseo, 1972-75, acting coordinator coll. activities, 1975-76; regional mgr. northeast Kazuko Hillyer Internat. Agy., N.Y.C., 1976-77; mgr. public performing arts (formerly lectures and concerts) U. Wash., Seattle, 1977-81; mgr. performing and visual arts Parks and Recreation, City of Seattle, 1981—; cons. Nat. Endowment for Arts, 1980, 81; mem. edn. com. Seattle Art Mus., 1981—. Bd. dirs. Bumbershoot-Seattle Arts Festival, 1979, 80, Folklife Festival, 1982—; cantor Sacred Heart Ch., Seattle, 1982—. Mem. Nat. Entertainment and Campus Activities Assn. (dir. 1969-72, Cert. of Appreciation 1975), Western Alliance Arts Adminstrs. (v.p. 1978-80), Arts Alliance Wash. State, Allied Arts Seattle, Phi Beta Kappa, Mu Phi Epsilon, Alpha Delta Pi. Roman Catholic. Home: 310 Boston St Seattle WA 98109 Office: 100 Dexter North Seattle WA 98109

O'NEILL, RICHARD MICHAEL, pediatrician; b. San Francisco, June 11, 1923; s. Richard Michael and Marcella (Woods) O'N.; B.S., U. San Francisco, 1947; postgrad. Gonzaga U., 1943, Northwestern U., 1944; M.D., Creighton U., 1951; postgrad. U. Calif. at San Francisco, 1951-54; m. Nancy Catherine Gorman, June 19, 1948; children—Richard Michael, Kevin, Kerry Ellen, Barry. Intern, San Francisco Gen. Hosp.-U. Calif., 1951-52; sr. resident in pediatrics U. Calif. at San Francisco, 1954; practice medicine, specializing in pediatrics and pediatric allergy, San Jose, Calif., 1954—; pres. Med. staff O'Connor Hosp., San Jose, 1978—; faculty Santa Clara Valley Med. Center, O'Connor Hosp., San Jose, 1954—. Trustee Found. for Med. Care. Served with USN, 1942-46, PTO. Mead Johnson fellow U. Calif. Med. Center, 1952-53. Fellow Am. Acad. Pediatrics (sec. 1954, com. on communications and pub. info., chmn. No. Calif.), Am. Coll. Allergy, mem. Santa Clara County Med. Soc., AMA, Calif. Med. Assn., Smithsonian Assos., Am. Med. Writers Assn., Task Force on Children's TV. Democrat. Roman Catholic. Club: San Jose Swim and Racquet. Editor Calif. Pediatrician, 1974—; contbr. articles in field to med. jours. and texts. Home: 1650 Cabana Dr San Jose CA 95125 Office: 100 O Connor Dr San Jose CA 95128

O'NEILL, SALLIE BOYD, educator; b. Ft. Lauderdale, Fla., Feb. 17, 1926; d. Howard Prindle and Sarah Frances (Clark) Boyd; A.A., Stephens Coll., 1945; m. Roger H. Noden, July 8, 1945; children—Stephanie Ann Ballard, Ross Hopkins Noden; m. 2d, Russell R. O'Neill, June 30, 1967. With UCLA Extension, 1960-66, program rep., 1966-72, specialist continuing edn. dept. human devel., 1972—; pres. Learning edn. cons. to bus. Adventures, Los Angeles, 1983—; HEW Women's Edn. Equity grantee, 1976-77. Mem. Nat. Univ. Extension Assn. (Outstanding Program award div. women's edn. 1980), UCLA Assn. Acad. Women, Am. Assn. Humanistic Psychology, Women in Bus. (founding), NOW. Home: 15430 Longbow Dr Sherman Oaks CA 91403 Office: 520 S Sepulveda Los Angeles CA 90024

ONLEY, TONI, artist; b. Douglas, Isle of Man, Nov. 20, 1928; s. James Anthony and Florence (Lord) O.; m. Mary Burrows, 1950 (dec.); children—Jennifer (dec.), Lynn; m. Gloria Knight, 1961; 1 son, James Anthony; m. Yukiko Kageyama, Aug. 23, 1979. Student Douglas Sch. Fine Arts, 1942-46, Doon Sch. Fine Art, 1951, Inst. Allende Mex., 1957, London, 1963. Instr. dept. fine arts U. B.C. (Can.), 1966-76; one-man shows include: Vancouver Art Gallery, 1958, retrospective, 1978, New Design Gallery, Vancouver, 1959, 61, 62, 65, Commonwealth Inst., London, 1965, Galerie Agnes Lefort, Montreal, Que., 1965, 67, Seattle Ctr., 1967, Richard Demarco Gallery, Edinburgh, Scotland, 1968, Simon Fraser U., 1969, Graphics Gallery, San Francisco, 1969, Bau-Xi Gallery, Vancouver, 1971, 72, 73, 74, 75, 76, 77, 78, 79, 80, Albert Coll. Art, 1971, U. Alta.-Edmonton, 1971, U. Lethbridge (Alta.), 1971, Gallery 4, Alexandria, Va., 1975, Hank Baum Gallery, Los Angeles and San Francisco, 1975, Westend Gallery, Edmonton, 1976, 79, 80, Thomas Gallery, Winnipeg, Man., 1976, 78, 79, So. Alta. Art Gallery, Lethbridge, 1978, Nat. Mus. of History, Taiwan, 1978, Can. Art Gallery, Calgary, Alta., 1979, 80, Meml. U. Art Gallery, St. John's, 1978, Mt. Allison U., N.B., 1978, Art Gallery N.S., Halifax, 1978, Gallery One, Toronto, 1983, numerous others; group shows include: Art Gallery Toronto, 1960, Deuxieme Biennale de Paris, 1961, Seattle World's Fair, 1962, Nat. Gallery Can. traveling exhbn., 1962-63, Rochester (N.Y.) Meml. Art Gallery, 1963, Albright-Knox Art Gallery, Buffalo, 1963, 5th Biennale Can. Art, London, 1965, Mus. Modern Art traveling exhbn., 1963-64, Hamilton Galleries, London, 1965, Oakland (Calif.) Mus., 1969, 10th Ann. Calgary Graphics Exhbn., 1970, Seattle Art Mus. 41st Internat., 1970, Montreal Mus. Fine Arts, 1970, Can. Embassy, Washington, 1970, Gallery Marc, Washington, 1970, Pa. Acad. Fine Arts, 1971, IX Exposition Internat. de Gravure, Ljubjana, Yugoslavia, 1971, X, 1972, XI, 1973, 1st Exposition of Prints, Norway, 1972, Clune Galleries, Sydney, Australia, 1972, Segunda Bienial Americana De Artes Graficas, Cali, Colombia, 1973, Premio Internat., Biello, Italy, 1973, Carleton U., Ottawa, Ont., 1973, Fredrickstad Mus., Norway, 1973, numerous others; represented in permanent collections: Alta. Coll. Art, Can. Council Art Bank, Dalhousie U., Lambton Coll., Sarnia, Ont., Le Musée des Beaux-Arts de Montréal, Le Musée d'Art Contemporain, Montréal, Nat. Gallery Can., Provincial Archives Bldg., Victoria, B.A., Queen's U., Kingston, Ont., U. Vt., Burlington, Simon Fraser U., Sir George Williams U., Seattle Art Mus., Tate Gallery, London, U. B.C., U. Calgary, U. Victoria, Victoria & Albert Mus., London, York U, Toronto. Trustee, Emily Carr Coll. Art, Vancouver. Can. Council grantee, 1961, 63; recipient Jessie Dow award, 1960; Spring Purchase award Montreal Mus. Fine Arts, 1962; Sam and Ayola Zacks award, 1963; Can. Council sr. fellow, 1964.

ONSTINE, BURTON WARNER, political science educator; b. Spokane, Wash., July 25, 1931; s. Warner and Trudy O. B.A., Reed Coll., 1954; M.A., U. Wash., 1959; Ph.D., U. N.C., 1965. Assoc. prof. dept. polit. sci., Portland (Oreg.) State U., 1972—; pres. Inspiration Lead Co., Inc., 1974—; v.p., dir. Silverore Mines, Inc., Admiral Mining Co., Dayton-Inspiration Gold Co. Inc.; pres., dir. King of Pine Creek Mining Co.; v.p., dir. Hayden Hill Mining Co.; sec./treas., dir. Huntec Creek Mining Co. Active Oreg. Hist. Mus., Portland Art Mus. Served with USAR, 1950-58. Falk fellow, 1959-60; fellow N.Y. Center for Edn. in Politics, 1964. Mem. Am. Polit. Sci. Assn. Clubs: Aero of Oreg.; City (Portland); Elks. Author: Oregon Votes, 1974. Home: PO Box 487 Portland OR 97207 Office: Polit Sci Dept Portland State Univ PO Box 751 Portland OR 97207

ONSTOTT, EDWARD IRVIN, research chemist; b. Moreland, Ky., Nov. 12, 1922; s. Carl Ervin and Jennie Lee (Foley) O.; B.S. in Chem. Engring., U. Ill., 1944, M.S. in Chemistry, 1948, Ph.D. in Inorganic Chemistry, 1950; m. Mary Margaret Smith, Feb. 6, 1945; children—Jenifer, Peggy Sue, Nicholas, Joseph. Chem. engr. Firestone Tire & Rubber Co., Paterson, N.J., 1944-46; research chemist Los Alamos Nat. Lab., 1950—. Served with C.E., AUS, 1944-46. Fellow AAAS, Am. Inst. Chemists; mem. Am. Chem. Soc., Electrochem. Soc., N.Y. Acad. Scis., Internat. Assn. Hydrogen Energy, Rate Earth Research Confs., Izaak Walton League. Republican. Methodist. Patentee in field. Home: 225 Rio Bravo Los Alamos NM 87544 Office: MS G738 Los Alamos NM 87545

OPFERMAN, CHARLES ROBERT, architect; b. Waukegan, Ill., Dec. 8, 1951; s. Charles Robert and Constance (Tribou) O.; m. Barbara Stolowski. Student Case Western Res. U., 1970-72; B.S. with honors in Archtl. Studies, U. Wis.-Milw., 1974, M.Arch., 1981. Supt., C.M. Assocs. of Milw., Inc., 1976-77, estimator, 1977-78, v.p. ops., 1978-83; project mgr. Rosser Kitchell, Sacramento, 1983—. Mem. AIA, Soc. Am. Value Engrs. Home: 3240 T St Sacramento CA 95816 Office: 1107 9th St Suite 600 Sacramento CA 95814

OPIE, KATHLEEN, educator; b. Denver, Jan. 13, 1944; d. Alfred and Anna (Klug) Iacobucci; m. William George Opie, Dec. 12, 1963; 1 dau., Sandra Lynn. M.A. in Elem. Adminstrn., U. No. Colo., 1971. Cert. elem. adminstr., Colo. Tchr. Green Mountain Elem. Sch., Lakewood, Colo., 1966-67, Belmar Elem. Sch., Lakewood, 1967-70, Eiber Elem. Sch., Lakewood, 1971-74, Glennon Heights Elem. Sch., Lakewood, 1975, Irwin Elem. Sch., Lakewood, 1975—. Mem. Colo. Profl. Practices Commn. Mem. Colo. Lang. Arts Soc., Internat. Reading Assn., NEA, Nat. Assn. Supervision and Curriculum Devel., Colo. Council Social Studies (treas.), Nat. Council Social Studies, Pi Lambda Theta (pres. Denver chpt.), Delta Kappa Gamma. Republican. Roman Catholic. Author social studies and career edn. curricula. Home: 14331 W Virginia Dr Lakewood CO 80228 Office: 1505 S Pierson St Lakewood CO 80226

OPPEDAHL, PHILLIP EDWARD, computer company executive; b. Renwick, Iowa, Sept. 17, 1935; s. Edward and Isadore Hannah (Gangstead) O.; B.S. in Naval Sci., Navy Postgrad. Sch., 1963, M.S. in Nuclear Physics, 1971; M.S. in Systems Mgmt., U. S.C., 1978; m. Sharon Elaine Ree, Aug. 3, 1957; children—Gary Lynn, Tamra Sue, Sue Ann, Lisa Kay. Commd. ensign U.S. Navy, 1956, advanced through grades to capt., 1977; with Airborne Early Warning Squadron, 1957-59, Anti-Submarine Squadron, 1959-65; asst. navigator USS Coral Sea, 1965-67; basic jet flight instr., 1967-69; student Armed Forces Staff Coll., 1971; test group dir. Def. Nuclear Agy., 1972-74; weapons officer USS Oriskany, 1974-76; program mgr. for armament Naval Air Systems Command, Washington, 1977-79, test dir. Def. Nuclear Agy., Kirtland AFB, N.Mex., 1979-82, dep. comdr. Def.Nuclear Agy., 1982-83; pres., chief exec. officer Computer Horizons Corp., Albuquerque, 1983—. Decorated Meritorious Service Medal, S. Vietnam Disting. Service Medal, 2 Navy Unit Commendations, 2 Vietnam Service Medals. Mem. Naval Inst., Am. Nuclear Soc., Am. Def. Preparedness Assn., Aircraft Owners and Pilots Assn., Tailhook Assn. Lutheran. Author: Energy Loss of High Energy Electrons in Beryllium, 1971; Understanding Contractor Motivation and Incentive Contracts, 1977. Home: 13305 Desert Flower Pl NE Albuquerque NM 87111 Office: Computer Land of Albuquerque 2258 Wyoming NE Albuquerque NM 87112

OPPENHEIMER, FRANK FRIEDMAN, physicist; b. N.Y.C., Aug. 14, 1912; s. Julius and Ella (Friedman) O.; m. Jacquenette Yvonne Quann, Oct. 15, 1936; children—Judith, Michael; m. 2d Mildred Page Danielson, Mar. 12, 1981. B.A., Johns Hopkins U., 1933; postgrad. Cavendish Lab., Cambridge, Eng., 1933-35, Inst. di Arcetri, Florence, Italy, 1935; Ph.D., Calif. Inst. Tech., 1939. Research asst. Stanford U., 1939-41; research assoc. U. Calif. Radiation Lab., 1941-47; asst. prof. U. Minn., 1947-49; high sch. sci. tchr., Pagosa Springs, Colo., 1957-59; spl. physics tchr. Jefferson County Schs., 1959-61, inservice physics tchr., 1959-61; research asso. U. Colo., Boulder, 1959-61, asso. prof., 1961-64, prof. physics, 1964-68, prof. emeritus, 1980—; vis. scholar U. Calif.-Berkeley, 1970-72; dir. The Exploratorium, San Francisco, 1969—; mem. adv. bd. Assn. Sci.-Tech. Centers, 1972-79. Recipient Millikin award Am. Assn. Physics Tchrs., 1973; Robert C. Kirkwood award San Francisco Found., 1976; Disting. Service award San Francisco Council, Dist. Mchts. Assn., 1978; Disting. Alumni award Calif. Inst. Tech., 1979; Disting. Service award U. Colo., 1980; named to Shoong Hall of Fame, 1982. Fellow Am. Phys. Soc.; mem. Am. Assn. Museums (disting. service award 1982), AAAS. Contbr. articles in field to profl. jours. Office: 3601 Lyon St San Francisco CA 94123

ORBACH, NEVENA LONIC, marketing consultant, journalist; b. Kukljica, Zadar, Yugoslavia, May 21, 1955; came to U.S., 1961, naturalized, 1967; d. Ante and Ljubica (Gobic) Lonic; m. Stuart Joseph Orbach, Aug. 27, 1982. B.A. summa cum laude in Journalism, L.I.U., 1977. Lic. real estate salesperson, Calif. Editor-in-chief N.Y. News Service, 1974-76; editor NBC Network Radio, WRC-NBC, Washington, 1975-77; account exec. Burson-Marsteller, Pub. Relations, N.Y.C., 1977-78; news editor Burbank (Calif.) Daily Rev., 1978-80; dir. sales PIC Autio-Visual Communications, Burbank, 1980-82; co-owner Foto-Com, Multi-Media Communications, Beverly Hills, Calif., 1982—. Bd. dirs. Burbank Community Hosp. Health Care Found., 1981-82, Burbank Landlord Tenant Vol. Rev., 1981-82. Univ. scholar, 1973-77; N.Y. Deadline Club scholar, 1977; recipient N.Y. State C. of C. First prize, 1973; Friends of Earth Nat. Writing Competition award, 1973. Mem. Women in Communications (pres. chpt.), Optimates, Burbank C. of C., Sigma Delta Chi, Kappa Tau Alpha. Club: Advt. of Los Angeles.

ORDE, CURTISS JOHN, wildlife biologist; b. Green Bay, Wis., Mar. 9, 1945; s. Clifford James and Marion Luella (Fend) O.; B.S., U. Wis.-Stevens Point, 1972; M.A., U. S.D., 1976; m. Barbara Joy Michels, Nov. 3, 1973; 1 dau., Heidi Ann. State park officer Wis. Dept. Natural Resources, Waupaca, 1972; computer operator, asst. ops. mgr. Green Bay Packaging Corp., 1972-74; prodn. technologist Larsen Co., Green

Bay, 1976-78; wildlife biologist U.S. Forest Service, Greeley, Colo., 1978-80, Saratoga, Wyo., 1980—. Spl. dep. Weld County Sheriff's Dept., 1978—, v.p., 1979—. Merit badge counselor Boy Scouts Am. Served with USAF, 1963-66. Registered emergency med. technician, Wyo. Mem. Wildlife Soc., Colo. Wildlife Soc., Wyo. Wildlife Soc., Inland and Western Bird Banding Assn., Nat. Dep. Sheriffs Assn., Nat. Audubon Soc., Greeley Audubon Soc. (v.p. 1980), Sigma Xi, Phi Sigma. Author tech. articles on raptor hunting techniques and banding. Home: Saratoga WY 82331 Office: 212 S 1st St Saratoga WY 82331

ORE, FERNANDO, chemical engineer; b. Trujillo, Peru, Apr. 26, 1926; s. Jose S. and Maria Julia de O.; m. Carole Botelho, Jan. 19, 1957; children—Fernando J., Michelle. M.S.Ch.Engr., U. Wash., Seattle, 1955, Ph.D.Ch.Engr., 1969. Sect. head crystallization Kerr McGee, Whittier, Calif., 1965-69; dir. phosphates research Occidental Research Corp., Irvine, Calif., 1970—. Recipient Personal Achievement award Chem. Engr. Mag., 1978, Pres. award Hooker Chem. Co., 1978, Kirkpatrick award Am. Potash, 1963. Mem. Am. Inst. Chem. Engrs., Am. Chem. Soc., Sigma Xi. Patentee in field. Office: PO Box 19601 Irvine CA 92713

O'REILLY, JAMES MICHAEL, lawyer; b. The Dalles, Oreg., June 17, 1948; s. Henry James and Muriel Irene O'R.; m. Carin Raelene Rosenquist, Mar. 28, 1970; children—Peter James, Erin Nicole. B.A., U. Calif.-Davis, 1970; J.D., U. Pacific, 1975. Bar: Calif. 1975, Nev. 1976. Law clk. 9th Jud. Dist. Ct. State of Nev., 1975-76; assoc. firm Sheerin & Griffin, Carson City, 1976-78; ptnr. Sherrin, O'Reilly, Walsh & Keele, Gardnerville, Nev., 1978—, mng. ptnr., 1981—. Asst. chmn. Douglas County Democratic Central Com., 1978; active Nev. Area Council Boy Scouts Am., YMCA. Served with USAFR, 1970-76. Mem. ABA (sect. real property, probate and trust law), State Bar Nev., State Bar Calif. Roman Catholic. Club: Rotary. Contbr. article to legal publ. Home: PO Box 1468 Minden NV 89423 Office: PO Box 1327 Gardnerville NV 89410

O'REILLY, JOHN GERARD, computer design consultant; b. Waterbury, Conn., Nov. 12, 1953; s. John James and Marjorie Veronica (Touponse) O'R.; student Worcester Poly. Inst., 1971-74; M.S., Case Western Res. U., 1978; Ph.D., Stanford U., 1981; m. Cindy Andrea Hollasch, Aug. 28, 1982. Research assoc. Stanford U. (Calif.), 1976-79; engr. decision systems dept. Systems Control, Inc., Palo Alto, Calif., 1979-82; sr. engr. Ford Aerospace and Communications Corp., Palo Alto, 1982-83; pres. Network Design Assocs., Los Altos, Calif., 1980—. Mem. IEEE (Computer Soc.), Am. Phys. Soc., AAAS, Mensa. Republican. Author: Distributed Control, 1982; Distributed Systems: Concepts and Implementations, 1983; also numerous tech. articles. Patentee in field. Home: 766 La Prenda Rd Los Altos CA 94022

O'REILLY, VIRGINIA MAE, psychologist, consultant; b. Detroit, Apr. 28, 1927; d. George Mayo and Alice Evelyn (Hall) O'R. B.S., Barry Coll., 1949; M.S. in Math., Catholic U. Am., 1952; M.S. in Guidance and Counseling, Siena Heights Coll., 1973; Ph.D. in Clin. Psychology (Danforth fellow), Calif. Sch. Profl. Psychology, 1977; lic. psychologist. Joined Sisters of St. Dominic, Roman Catholic Ch., 1944; tchr. mat., physics, secondary and coll. levels, 1946-74; therapist House of Affirmation, Inc., Montara, Calif., 1977-79, Jesuit Inst. for Family Life, Los Altos, Calif., 1979-80; pvt. practice therapy for religious personnel, San Francisco and Saratoga, Calif., 1980-81; pres., therapist Dominican Pastoral Inst., Oakland, Calif., 1981—; cons. to hosp., sem. Bd. dirs. Jesuit Retreat Assn., Los Altos. Mem. Am. Psychol. Assn., Calif. State Psychol. Assn., Mid-Coast Psychol. Assn., Western Psychol. Assn., Nat. Guild Catholic Psychologists (assoc.). Office: 3535 Ross Suite 103A San Jose CA 95124

OREM, CHARLES REACE, former financial services company executive; b. Nashville, Aug. 23, 1916; s. Charles Reace and Helen A (Adcock) O.; m. Martha E. Haley, Oct. 24, 1945; 1 dau., Carol R. Student U. Ky., 1935-37; B.S., Columbia U., 1939; LL.B., Fordham U., 1951; postgrad. NYU, 1953; grad. Advanced Mgmt. Program, Harvard U., 1957. Bar: N.Y. 1951. Mgr. Peat, Marwick, Mitchell & Co., C.P.A.s, N.Y.C., 1952-54; tax mgr., asst. treas. Sylvania Electric Products, Inc., N.Y.C., 1955-60; tras., v.p. fin. Pickands Mather & Co., Cleve., 1961-64; v.p., controller Armour & Co., Chgo., 1964-65, fin. v.p., 1965-67, sr. v.p. fin. and adminstrn., 1967-68, pres., dir., 1968-71; pres., chief exec. officer Investors Diversified Services, Inc., 1971-80, also dir.; dir. Investors Syndicate Am., Inc., IDS Life Ins. Co., Investors Mut., Inc., Investors Stock Fund, Inc., Investors Selective Fund, Inc., Investors Variable Payment Fund, Inc., IDS New Dimensions Found, Inc., IDS Progressive Fund, Inc., IDS Growth Fund, Inc., IDS Tax-Exempt Bond Fund, Inc., IDS High Yield Tax Exempt Fund Corp., IDS Bond Fund, Inc., IDS Cash Mgmt. Fund, Inc., IDS Tax Free Money Fund. Home: 6951 E Powers Ave Englewood CO 80111

ORENSTEIN, MORTON HENRY, lawyer; b. St. Louis, Apr. 22, 1936; s. Jacob Bernard and Evelyn (Essman) O.; m. Grace E. Manning, Dec. 21, 1962; children—Jeffery M., Catherine C. B.A., Northwestern U., 1958; J.D., U. Mich., 1961. Bar: Mo. 1961, Calif. 1974. With U.S. Peace Corps, Malawi, Africa, 1962-64; staff atty. NLRB, San Francisco, 1965-70, supervising atty., 1971-76; ptnr. Voltz, Cook & Orenstein, San Francisco, 1976—; vis. prof. San Francisco State U., 1975-76. Mem. ABA, Bar Assn. San Francisco (Labor and Employment Law sect. exec. com.), State Bar Calif. Democrat. Jewish. Home: 1530 Euclid Ave Berkeley CA 94708 Office: Voltz Cook & Orenstein Suite 1300 100 Bush St San Francisco CA 94104

ORFIELD, FRANKLIN BENNETT, judge; b. Mpls., Mar. 11, 1921; s. Andrew Christian and Alpha (Bennett) O.; Alycemary Kuhn, Nov. 25, 1942; 1 son, Michael Bennett. J.D., Calif. Western Law Sch., 1949; grad. Calif. Coll. Trial Judges, 1970. Bar: Calif. Practice, San Diego, 1950-69; sr. mem. Orfield, Thompson, Bunker & Sullivan, San Diego, to 1969; apptd. judge Superior Ct. Calif., 1969—, pres. judge Superior Ct., San Diego County, 1977-78, apptd. judge San Diego Sch. desegregation case, 1981; chmn. bd. Calif. Western Sch. Law, 1982—. Served with USMC, 1942-46. Recipient Presdl. cert. Appreciation SSS, 1969; award Pub. Address Freedom's Found. Valley Forge, 1970; Judge Yr. award San Diego Trial Lawyers Assn., 1976; Spl. award Presiding Judge San Diego County Bar Assn., 1978. Mem. San Diego County Bar Assn. (pres. 1961), Calif. Judges Assn. Republican. Episcopalian. Office: County Courthouse PO Box 2724 San Diego CA 92112

ORHAM, EDWARD LEROY, electronic technologist; b. Gt. Falls, Mont., May 13, 1947; s. Robert Halverson and Roberta Marie (Bann) O.; B.Tech., Oreg. Inst. Tech., 1976; m. Carmella C. Crosthwaite, Feb. 15, 1969. Field engr. Measurex Corp., Cupertino, Calif., 1976-77; sr. elec. technologist Lawrence Livermore (Calif.) Nat. Lab., 1977—. Served with U.S. Navy, 1967-72. Mem. Am. Sportsmen, Ducks Unlimited. Republican. Roman Catholic. Office: PO Box 5508 Livermore CA 94550

ORLIK, GILBERT DAVID, association executive; b. Cin., Nov. 14, 1929; s. Edward and Madeline (Klein) O.; m. Phyllis Ruth Michelson, Sept. 18, 1949; children—Randy, Mitchel, Gregg, Jeff. B.A. in Econs., U. Cin.; M.S., U. Tex. Owner, operator Orlik's, Inc., Cin.; various positions with nonprofit assns., 1968—; former exec. dir. Jewish Community Fedn., Washington and Syracuse, N.Y.; exec. dir. San Francisco Lighthouse for the Blind, 1982—. Mem. Am. Soc. Tng. Devel., Am. Soc. Assn. Execs., Nat. Soc. Fund Raising Execs. Office: Lighthouse for the Blind 1155 Mission St San Francisco CA 94103

ORMAND, DONALD REAGAN, mfg. co. mgr.; b. St. Thomas, Ont., Can., Mar. 21, 1941 (parents Am. citizens); s. Reagan Durwood and Dorothy Junita (Boren) O.; B.S. in Physics, U. Tex., Arlington, 1964; M.S. in Mgmt. Sci., West Coast U., 1974; m. Barbara Ann Spoon, Nov. 24, 1960; children—Donald Scott, John Reagan. With Hughes Aircraft Co., Fullerton, Calif., 1966—, mgr. advanced projects staff, 1977-80, mgr. Ukadge project dept., 1980-82, mgr. FAA AAS project dept., 1982—; treas. Octug, Inc. Youth counselor, then chmn. outreach commn. United Methodist Ch., 1965-68. Mem. Tech. Mktg. Assn. Am., Hactug Computer Club. Republican. Office: 1901 W Malvern St Fullerton CA 92634

ORMROD, JEANNE ELLIS, educational psychologist, educator, researcher, consultant; b. Providence, Aug. 22, 1948; d. James Oliver and Nancy (Easton) Ellis; m. Richard Kendall Ormrod, Aug. 16, 1975; children—Christina, Alex. B.A., Brown U., 1970; M.S., Pa. State U., 1973, Ph.D., 1975. Cert. sch. pathologist, Colo. Asst. prof. psychology U. No. Colo., 1976-80, assoc. prof., 1980-82, asst. to v.p. acad. affairs, 1982—. Recipient Lucretia V. T. Simmons award Pa. State U., 1974-75; NDEA fellow, 1974-75; Colo. Commn. on Higher Edn. grantee, 1981-82. Mem. Am. Psychol. Assn., Am. Ednl. Research Assn., Nat. Assn. Sch. Psychologists. Research in test devel. Office: Dept Ednl Psychology U No Colo Greeley CO 80639

ORMSBY, LIONEL, advt. agency exec.; b. Oakland, Calif., Jan. 16, 1909; s. Edgar L. and Georgia (Council) O.; A.B., U. Calif.-Berkeley, 1934; m. Myrtez Boehmer Rush, Apr. 22, 1941; children—John Rush, Jean. Advt. prodn. San Francisco News, 1936-40; asst. account exec. McCann-Erickson, Los Angeles, 1940-42; account exec. Shaw Advt. Agy., Los Angeles, 1942-46, 56-60; account exec. Dozier-Eastman & Co., Los Angeles, 1946-56; owner Hammer & Ormsby Advt., 1960—; pub. Sales Talk, syndicated newsletter; editor Rexall Reporter, Rexall Drug Co., Trade Secrets, Bank Americard Corp.; tchr. journalism Alameda (Calif.) High Sch., 1934-36; tchr. copywriting Los Angeles City Coll., 1950-53. Chmn. publicity com. Los Angeles County Tb and Health Assn., 1955-61; vice chmn. Beverly Hills council Boy Scouts Am. Bd. dirs. Los Angeles Beautiful, Inc. Mem. Assn. Indsl. Advertisers, Sales and Mktg. Execs. Assn., Los Angeles Advt. Club (1st v.p.) Club: Town Hall of Calif. Home: 476 Hillsdale Dr Santa Rosa CA 95405

ORNSTEIN, STANLEY IRWIN, economist, educator, consultant; b. Los Angeles, Jan. 31, 1939; s. Benjamin Henry and Miriam (Ringold) O.; m. Andrea Jean Sidney, July 28, 1968. B.S. in Engring., San Diego State U., 1960, M.S. in Bus. Adminstrn., 1964; Ph.D. in Econs., UCLA, 1970. Economist, Planning Research Corp., 1968-70; asst. research economist, UCLA Grad. Sch. of Mgmt., 1970-78, assoc. research economist, 1978—. Served to lt. USMCR, 1961-67. Mem. Am. Econs. Assn., Western Econs. Assn. Jewish. Editor: (with J. Fred Weston) The Impact of Large Firms on the U.S. Economy, 1973; contbr. articles to profl. jours., bulls., chpts. to books; co-author research reports to Calif. Dept. of Alcohol, Drug Programs. Home: 4243 Murietta Ave Sherman Oaks CA 91423 Office: UCLA Los Angeles CA 90024

ORONA, ERNEST JOSEPH, real estate and constrn. co. exec.; b. Belen, N.Mex., Oct. 5, 1942; s. Joseph B. and Melinda (Sanchez) O.; B.A. in Latin Am. Affairs and Spanish, U. N.Mex., 1968; m. Margaret M. Guinan, Aug. 22, 1964; children—Mary Melinda, Marie-Jeanne. Vol. community devel. Peace Corps, Colombia, S. Am., 1962-64; instr. Peace Corps tng. U. Mo., Kansas City, summer 1964, Baylor U., Waco, Tex., summer 1965, also U. Ariz., N.Mex. State U., Las Cruces, 1966, U. N.Mex., Albuquerque, 1966; exec. dir. Mid-Rio Grande Community Action Project, Los Lunas, N.Mex., 1965-66; community devel. cons. Center for Community Action Services, Albuquerque, 1967-68; project dir. Peace Corps Tng. Center, San Diego State U., Escondido, Calif., 1968-70; propr., developer GO Realty and Constrn. Co., Albuquerque, 1970—. Mem. Albuquerque Sister Cities. Mem. Nat. Bd. Realtors, Albuquerque Bd. Realtors, Albuquerque C. of C., Albuquerque Com. on Fgn. Relations. Roman Catholic. Home: 1301 Ridgecrest SE Albuquerque NM 87108 Office: 10601 Lomas NE Suite 112 Albuquerque NM 87112

O'ROURKE, A. DESMOND, agricultural economist, researcher; b. Roslea, Northern Ireland, Dec. 15, 1938; came to U.S., 1967; naturalized, 1973; s. Andrew Paul and Kathleen (Keenan) O'R.; m. Sheila McMahon, Sept. 15, 1964; children—Gerard, Dara, Daniel. B.A. in Classics, Queens U., Belfast, Ireland, 1960; B.Comm., Univ. Coll. Dublin, 1963; M.S., U. Calif.-Davis, 1968, Ph.D., 1970. Mktg. mgr. Domas Advt., Dublin, 1960-63, Adsell Advt., Dublin, 1963-66; research officer AG Inst., Dublin, 1967; grad. asst. U. Calif., Davis, 1967-70; asst. prof. dept. agr. econs. Wash. State U., Pullman, 1970-76, assoc. prof., 1976-80, prof., 1980—; cons. in field. Vice pres. Inland Empire Swimming, Spokane, Wash., 1980-82. Kellogg Found. scholar, 1968. Mem. Am. Agrl. Econs. Assn., Western Agrl. Econs. Assn. Roman Catholic. Author: Marketing in Ireland, 1967; Changing Dimensions of U.S. Agriculture Policy, 1978. Home: NE 1045 Creston St Pullman WA 99163 Office: Washington State Univ 6210 Pullman WA 99164

O'ROURKE, JAMES SCOFIELD, IV, air force officer; b. Billings, Mont., July 25, 1946; s. James Scofield and Joan Louise (Boardman) O'R.; m. Pamela Jean Spencer, Aug. 24, 1968; children—Colleen Kerry-Ann, Molly Scofield. B.B.A., U. Notre Dame, 1968; M.S., Temple U., 1970; M.A., U. N.Mex., 1973; Ph.D., Syracuse U., 1980. Prof. communication Communication Inst. Ireland, 1970; commd. 2d lt. U.S. Air Force, 1970, advanced through grades to maj., 1970—, pub. info. officer Kirtland AFB, N.Mex., 1970-73, comdr. Am. Forces Radio & TV Stas., Goose AB, Labrador, Can., 1973-75, asst. prof. aerospace studies Syracuse U., 1975-78, assoc. prof. English, U.S. Air Force Acad., 1978—, dir. media instruction and profl. services, 1982—; sr. faculty advisor Rocky Mountain Collegiate Press Assn.; adj. assoc. prof. communications U. Colo.-Colorado Springs, 1981—. Decorated Air Force Commendation medal. Harold B. Fellows Meml. scholar, Nat. Assn. Broadcasters, 1968-70. Mem. Soc. Profl. Journalists and Broadcasters, Sigma Delta Chi. Roman Catholic. Clubs: Officers Mess, Notre Dame (pres. 1982—). Author: (with J.J. Zigerell and T.W. Portre) Television in Community and Junior Colleges: An Overview and Guidelines, 1980; The Notre Dame I Remember, 1983; editorial rev. bd. Jour. Broadcasting, 1982—; contbr. articles to profl. jours. Home: Quarters 4210A USAF Academy CO 80840 Office: Dept English USAF Academy CO 80840

ORPHAL, DENNIS LEE, physicist; b. Columbia, S.C., Aug. 28, 1942; s. John Julius and Helen Virginia (Heil) O.; m. Viki Jo Gojack, Apr. 26, 1964; children—Jonathan, David. B.A., Ohio Wesleyan U., Delaware, 1964; postgrad. U. Nev., 1970-72. Registered geophysicist, Calif. Staff mem. Los Alamos Sci. Lab., 1964-67; sr. tech. staff Environ. Research Corp., Alexandria, Va., 1967-69, sr. staff scientist, div. dir., Las Vegas, Nev., 1969-72; mgr., sr. staff scientist Physics Internat. Co., San Leandro, Calif., 1972-78; v.p., dir. Calif. Research and Tech., Livermore, 1978—; adv. panels Dept. Def., Def. Nuclear Agy., U.S. Army, USAF, NASA. Mem. Am. Phys. Soc., AIAA, Am. Geophys. Union, Seismol. Soc. Am., AAAS. Contbr. numerous articles to profl. jours.; patentee in field. Office: Calif Research and Tech Inc 4049 1st St Suite 135 Livermore CA 94550

ORR, JEAN MARY, state agency official; b. Los Angeles, Sept. 23, 1923; d. Theodore Leverne and Regina Margaret (Riley) Wallace; children—Linda Lei Pope, Terri Regina Gomes. Student Porterville, Coll., 1942. Lic. real estate salesman, Calif. Co-owner White Oaks Realty, San Carlos, Calif., 1948-58; mgr. Career Counselors, San Mateo, Calif., 1960-64; owner, mgr. Merle Norman Studio, San Carlos, 1964-67; mgr., v.p. Flight Records, San Carlos, 1973-75; owner, mgr. Flight of Fantasy, San Carlos, 1973-78; adminstrv. asst. Rucker Fuller, San Francisco, 1978-82; data base mgr. Computer Connection, San Francisco, 1983; chief Bur. Employment Agys., State of Calif., Sacramento, 1983—. Pres. State of Calif. Republican Assembly, 1981-82, conv. site chmn., 1972-80, exec. state com. Rep. Central Com., 1980—; past pres. San Mateo County Fedn. Rep. Women; speaker Coll. Notre Dame Women's Re-entry Program; chmn. San Mateo County Tri-centenniel, 1977; coordinator Heritage Faire '76, San Mateo County; vice-chmn. San Mateo County Heritage '76; chmn. San Carlos Bicentenniel, 1975-76; past nat. bd. dirs. Psoriasis Research Assn.; past pres. San Carlos Community Ch. Jr. Matrons; chmn. of San Carlos Mothers' March of Dimes; chmn. small bus. United Crusade, San Carlos; active Girl Scouts U.S.A. Named Outstanding Citizen, San Carlos, 1976. Mem. Bus. Profl. Women (Redwood City Outstanding Woman 1974). Lodges: Soroptimists, Order of Eastern Star (San Carlos). Home: 133 Garnet Ave San Carlos CA 94070 Office: 1333 Howe St Sacramento CA 95814

ORSATTI, ALFRED KENDALL, association executive; b. Los Angeles, Jan. 31, 1932; s. Alfred Paul and Margaret Elisa (Hayes) O.; m. Patricia Jean Decker, June 8, 1960; children—Scott, Christopher, Sean. B.S. in Bus. Adminstrn., U. So. Calif., 1956. Vice pres. Ror-Vic TV Prodns., 1957-58, Sabre Theatrical Prodns. Inc., 1959-60; nat. rep. AFTRA, 1960-61; nat. exec. sec. Screen Actors Guild, Hollywood, Calif., 1962—; v.p. Hollywood Film Council, Calif. State Theatrical Fedn.; v.p., exec. council Calif. State Labor Fedn.; mem. Los Angeles Film Devel. Council. Served with USNR. Office: 7750 Sunset Blvd Los Angeles CA 90046

ORSINO, DONALD EUGENE, marketing researcher; b. Plainfield, N.J., Feb. 10, 1941; s. Joseph Anthony and Mary Louise (Carson) O.; m. Lynn Deanne Hall, Feb. 25, 1966; m. Mary Jane Wayment, Apr. 10, 1982. B.S.J., Northwestern U., 1962, M.S.J., 1963. Survey supr. Field Research Corp., San Francisco, 1965-66; sr. project dir. Communications Research Ctr., San Francisco, 1966-69; account mgr. Drossler Research Corp., San Francisco, 1969-71, v.p., 1972-74; assoc. Haug Assocs., San Francisco, 1971-72; ptnr. Mktg. Research Assocs., San Francisco, 1974-78; pres. Consumer Research Assocs., San Francisco, 1978—; asst. prof. mktg. San Francisco State U., 1969-70. Served in USCGR, 1963-70. Mem. Am. Mktg. Assn., Photog. Mktg. Assn., San Francisco Advt. Club. Republican. Club: Loch Lomond Yacht (San Rafael, Calif.). Home: 315 Olema Rd Fairfax CA 94930 Office: 1738 Union St Suite 100 San Francisco CA 94123

ORTEGA, RUBEN BAPTISTA, police chief; b. Glendale, Ariz., July 17, 1939; s. Epifanio Dominguez and Clara (Baptista) O.; B.S. in Criminal Justice and Police Adminstrn., No. Ariz. U., 1980; m. Nellie Ann Alvarado, Nov. 23, 1958; children—Karen Ann, Jeffrey Randal. With Phoenix Police Dept., 1960—, police chief, 1980—; instr. Phoenix Police Regional Tng. Acad., 1969-73; cons. Juvenile Crime Prevention Task Force, Phoenix, 1975-79. Bd. dirs. NCCJ, 1979-81. Recipient Outstanding Community Service awards Am. Legion, 1979, also others. Mem. Ariz. Organized Crime Prevention Council, Ariz. Law Enforcement Office Adv. Council, Internat. Assn. Chiefs of Police. Roman Catholic. Office: 620 W Washington St Phoenix AZ 85003

ORTIZ, DORIS LORAIN, journalist; b. Dalton, Minn., Sept. 5, 1926; d. Peter Christian and Ragna (Bahle) Johnson; student Los Angeles City Coll., 1947-48, Fullerton Coll., 1962-63; m. James Leonard Ortiz, Apr. 6, 1946; 1 dau., Kimberly Anne Ortiz Bird. Mem. editorial staff Centralia (Wash.) Tribune, 1944; women's editor Huntington Park (Calif.) Bull., 1946-50, Huntington Park Signal, 1950-51, Bellflower (Calif.) Herald-Enterprise, 1951-53; copywriter Claude Leach Advt., Anaheim, Calif., 1953-60, 62-69, advt. cons., 1962-69; city editor Anaheim Gazette, 1960; women's editor Tempo Mag., 1970, Anaheim Bull., 1971-81; columnist Orange County Register, 1981—. Mem. Orange County (Calif.) Press Club. Democrat. Roman Catholic. Home: 1871 Random Dr Anaheim CA 92804 Office: 1771 S Lewis St Anaheim CA 92805

ORTIZ, JERROLD JOSEPH, recreation director; b. Alamosa, Colo., June 2, 1942; s. Solomon Jose and Cleo Louise (Maestas) O.; m. Dixie Collins, Aug. 19, 1944; children—Christy, Jill, Ryan. B.S., Calif. State U.-San Francisco, 1968; postgrad. Calif. State U.-Northridge, 1976-78. Phys. edn. dir. Columbia Park Boys' Club, San Francisco, 1967-68; dir. athletics U.S. Naval Air Sta., Alameda, Calif., 1968-70; sr. recreation supr. Rancho Simi Recreation and Park Dist., Simi Valley, Calif., 1970-79; dir. recreation, City of Orem, Utah, 1979—. Mem. adv. council athletics and phys. edn. Utah Tech. Coll., 1981-82. Served with USNR, 1962-68. Mem. Utah Recreation Assn., Calif. Park and Recreation Soc., Nat. Recreation and Park Assn., Orem Ednl. Adv. Council. Republican. Mormon. Office: 56 N State St Orem UT 84057

ORTON, EVE DOROTHY, hospital food administrator; b. San Jose, Calif., Aug. 21, 1921; d. George Alfred and Margaret Caroline (Del Ponte) Prudhomme; m. Ross J. Donald Aug. 11, 1945; m. 2d, Orville Bion Orton, Mar. 20, 1954. A.B. in Dietetics, San Jose State U. 1943. Registered dietitian. Food worker Santa Clara County Hosp. (now Santa Clara Valley Med. Center), San Jose 1943, dietitian 1947-51, sr. dietitian 1951-62, dir. nutrition and food service 1962—; dietitian Providence Hosp., Oakland, Calif., 1944. Recipient Disting. Alumni award San Jose State U. 1982. Mem. Santa Clara Inter-agy. Nutrition Council, San Jose Peninsula Dist. Dietetic Assn., Am. Dietetics Assn., Am. Hosp. Assn. Food Adminstrs. Democrat. Roman Catholic. Clubs: Zonta, Santa Clara County Bowling. Home: 4925 Bel Escou Dr San Jose CA 95124 Office: 751 S Bascom Ave San Jose CA 95128

ORUND, VALDEK JAAN, mech. engr.; b. Estonia, USSR, July 4, 1922; s. Jaan and Johanna O.; M.S.M.E., Tallinna Politehniline Instituut, 1941; came to U.S., 1950, naturalized, 1963; m. Katharina Baumstark, Aug. 13, 1966. Engr., Shaffer Tool Works, Brea, Calif., 1952-69; product engring. mgr. Rucker Co., Brea, 1969-77; chief engr. research and devel. N.L. Shaffer, N. L. Industries, Inc., Brea, 1977—. Mem. ASME, Soc. Exptl. Stress Analysis, Am. Soc. Metals, AIME. Republican. Lutheran. Patentee in field. Office: 200 N Berry St Brea CA 92621

OSAZE, JANA DENISE, psychologist; b. Beaumont, Tex., Aug. 26, 1951; d. Sol and Patricia (Stephens) White; B.A., U. So. Calif., 1973, M.A., 1976, Ph.D., 1980; student Fisk U., 1969-70; m. Zoli Aswad Osaze, July 29, 1972; 1 son, Zoli Jamal. Research asst., therapist Central City Community Mental Health Facility, 1971-74; state-wide community services coordinator Calif. Assn. for retarded, 1975-76; asso. prof. psychology Los Angeles City Coll., 1977—,chmn. dept., 1982—; bd. dirs. South Central Los Angeles Regional Center; bd. dirs. Health Services Conthuum of Los Angeles. Ford fellow, 1973-77; recipient Edn. Alumni Assn. award, 1973. Mem. Am. Psychol. Assn., Smithsonian Instn., Am. Black Psychologists, Phi Beta Kappa, Sigma Xi. Democrat. Roman Catholic. Home: 6175 Canterbury Dr Apt 103 Culver City CA 90230 Office: 855 N Vermont Ave Los Angeles CA 90029

OSBORN, JAMES ROBERT, television station executive; b. Lansing, Mich., Mar. 11, 1930; s. Robert Duke and Charlotte (Major) O.; B.A., Mich. State U., 1953; m. Nancy Ann Wells, Aug. 29, 1953; children—Scott Robert, Todd Steven, Mark Jeffrey. Account exec. sta. WMBV-

TV, Green Bay, Wis., 1954-56; account exec., gen. sales mgr. sta. WXIX-TV, Milw., 1956-58; account exec. sta. WCBS-TV, N.Y.C., 1958-59; gen. sale mgr. sta KXTV, CBS, Sacramento, 1959-61; sales mgr. ABC-TV Spot TV Sales, San Francisco, 1961-66; gen. sales mgr. sta. KABC-TV, Los Angeles, 1966-68, sta. KGO-TV, San Francisco, 1968-72; v.p., gen. mgr. sta. WXYZ-TV, Detroit, 1972-79; v.p., gen. mgr. sta. KGO-TV, San Francisco, 1979—. Bd. dirs. San Francisco Travel and Conv. Bur. Served with USN, 1948-49. Mem. Nat. Acad. TV Arts and Scis. (bd. dirs.). Home: 2 Kendell Ct Sausalito CA 94965 Office: KGO-TV 277 Golden Gate Ave San Francisco CA 94102

OSBORN, RONALD LEE, fin. cons.; b. Rushville, Nebr., May 9, 1934; s. Ova H. and Georganna H. (Peters) O.; B.S. in Bus., Chadron State Coll., 1956; M.S. in Fin. Services, Am. Coll., 1982; m. Ruth A. Katen, Aug. 12, 1954; children—Ronald Lee, Scott A., Mitchell J., Lynette S. Vice pres. Marketeers Inc., Rapid City, S.D., 1956-64; dist. asst. Equitable Life Assurance Soc., Rapid City, 1964-69, mgr., Colorado Springs, Colo., 1969-73, agt., 1973-81; exec v.p. Fin. Design Cons., Inc., Colorado Springs, 1981—. Named Agt. of Yr., So. Colo. Gen. Agy. Mgrs. Assn., 1980. Mem. Life and Qualifying Million Dollar Round Table, Colorado Springs Assn. Life Underwriters, Pikes Peak C.L.U.'s. Roman Catholic. Home: 3116 Valley Hi Ct Colorado Springs CO 80910 Office: 10 N Meade St Colorado Springs CO 80909

OSBORN, TERRELL JAN, management educator, retired air force officer; b. Anthony, Kans., Oct. 19, 1941; s. Ralph Pike and LouVelma (Pearl) O.; m. Elizabeth Lynn Stafford, June 26, 1965; 1 dau., Kristin. B.A., U. Kans., 1963; M.B.A., U. Utah, 1977; Dr.Bus.Adminstrn., U.S. Internat. U., 1980. Maj., U.S. Air Force, 1965; F-4C Phantom fighter pilot, 1965-67, F-4 instr. pilot, Davis-Monthan AFB, Ariz., 1967-70, flight examiner, Homestead AFB, Fla., 1970-72, pilot in Korea, 1973, chief safety Luke AFB, Ariz., 1974-78, chief Flight Mishap Final Eval. Br., Inspection Safety Center, Norton AFB, Calif., 1978-83, ret., 1983; asst. prof. mgmt. Embry-Riddle Aero. U., Prescott, Ariz., 1983—. Vol., United Way. Decorated D.F.C., Air medals (13); cert. safety profl.; USAF Chief of Staff Individual Safety award, 1977. Mem. Am. Soc. Safety Engrs., Internat. Soc. Air Safety Investigators, Acad. Mgmt., Assn. MBA Execs., Air Force Assn., Am. Soc. Tng. and Devel., Beta Gamma Sigma. Clubs: Daedalians, Red River Fighter Pilots Assn., Internat. Council Small Bus. Club: Kiwanis (pres.). Contbr. articles to profl. jours. Home: 950 Nottingham Dr Redlands CA 92373 Office: Embry-Riddle Aeronautical Univ Prescott AZ 86301

OSBORN, TERRY WAYNE, biochemist; b. Roswell, N.Mex., May 17, 1943; s. Woodrow Edward and Wilma Marie (Meador) O.; A.A., Ventura Coll., 1967; B.S., U. Calif.-Riverside, 1969, Ph.D., 1975. Research scientist McGaw Labs., Irvine, Calif., 1976, research scientist/project leader, 1976, research scientist/project team leader, 1976-77, group leader/sr. research scientist, 1978-79, mgr. clin. research, 1979-81, mktg. product mgr., 1981-82, mktg. group product mgr., 1982-83, dir. mktg., 1983—; faculty chemistry Riverside City Coll., 1974-76, San Bernardino Valley Coll., 1974-76. Served with U.S. Army, 1962-65. Recipient Agnes M. Toland Meml. Trust award Ventura Coll., 1966, Ventura Emblem Club award, 1967; Environ. Sci. fellow, 1970-73; Dean's Spl. fellow U. Calif., 1974-75. Mem. Am. Chem. Soc., Am. Oil Chemists Soc., Inst. Food Technologists, Sigma Xi, U.S. Ski Assn., One Mile Soc., Chi Gamma Iota, Alpha Gamma Sigma. Club: Tyrolean Ski (pres. 1972-73). Home: PO Box 46 Coto de Caza Trabuco Canyon CA 92678 Office: 2525 McGaw Ave Irvine CA 92711

OSBORN, THOMAS MONTGOMERY, educator, musician; b. N.Y.C., Apr. 21, 1934; s. James Marshall and Marie-Louise (Montgomery) O.; m. Joyce Bockel, Sept. 7, 1957; children—Carolyn L., Dorothy B. A.B., Princeton U., 1956, B.M., Yale U., 1957, M.M., 1958, D.M.A., U. So. Calif., 1964. Mem. faculty Western Wash. State Coll., Bellingham, 1964-69, U. So. Calif., 1969-71, Los Angeles Pierce Coll., 1973-80; music dir., condr., prof. music Pepperdine U., Malibu, Calif., 1980—; mus. dir., condr. Calif. State U. Northridge Youth Orch. Acad., 1977—. Former pres. San Fernando Valley Arts Council. Mem. Calif. Choral Condrs. Guild (past pres.), Am. Symphony Orch. League (past chmn. Youth Symphony Orch. div., dir.), Calif. Assn. Symphony Orchs., Condrs. Guild.

OSBORNE, ADAM, computer company executive; b. Thailand, 1940. B.S., U. Birmingham, Eng., 1961; M.S., Ph.D., U. Del., 1968. With M.W. Kellogg Co., 1961-64, Shell Devel. Corp., Emeryville, Calif., 1967-70; established Osborne & Assocs., Berkeley, Calif., 1970, pub., writer, programming cons. until 1979; established Osborne Computer Corp., Hayward, Calif., 1981, former pres., chief exec. officer, now chmn. Author numerous books in computer field, including: Running Wild: The Next Industrial Revolution, 1979; Introduction to Microcomputers, 1980; contbr. numerous articles to computer mags. Office: Osborne Computer Corp 26538 Danti Ct Hayward CA 94545

OSBORNE, B. JEAN, nurse, hospital executive; b. Reno, Aug. 14, 1927; d. Byron Wesley and Francis Emily (Beatty) Hamilton; m. Donald H. Erskine, Nov. 29, 1947; children—Byron Brent, Donald Kim; m. 2d, Richard L. Osborne, Nov. 30, 1963. Student U. Nev., 1945-46; A.A., Weber State Coll., 1963; B.S. in Nursing, U. Utah, 1966, M.S., 1974. R.N., Utah, Nev. Staff nurse, office mgr., asst. adminstr. Humboldt Gen. Hosp., Winnemucca, Nev., 1946-61; nursing supr., dir. staff devel. Cottonwood Hosp., Murray, Utah, 1964-68; project adminstr., program dir. Intermountain Regional Med. Program, U. Utah, Salt Lake City, 1968-73; dir. cancer control and screening program Utah Dept. Health, Salt Lake City, 1976-80; dir. planning Holy Cross Hosp., Salt Lake City, 1980-82; cons. HEW, Nat. Cancer Inst.; cons. in health planning and fed. grant writing Utah Dept. Health, U. Utah Coll. Nursing; mem. Utah Statewide Health Coordinating Council, 1972-81; chmn. Utah Task Force Com. on Emergency Med. Services, 1972-73; mem. Gov.'s Adv. Council on Emergency Med. Services for State of Utah, 1972-76, Salt Lake City-County Bd. Health, 1976-77; chmn. Utah Joint Project Rev. Adv. Com., 1979-83, Utah Health Service Adminstrn. Governing Bd., 1979-81. Bd. dirs. Utah YWCA, 1981—, chmn. adv. com. Home for Pregnant Teens, 1981—; mem. Utah Women's Legis. Council, 1981—. Mem. Am. Hosp. Assn., Hosp. Planning Assn., Utah Soc. Health Planning, Utah Nurses Assn. (exec. dir.). Episcopalian. Club: Order Eastern Star. Contbr. articles to profl. jours. Home: 620 East 7500 South Midvale UT 84047

OSBORNE, BARTLEY P., JR., design engineer; b. Akron, Ohio, Sept. 1, 1934; s. Bartley P. and Cordelia (Sims) O.; m. Carol Ann Eubanks, Jan. 15, 1966; children—Roxane, Ashley. B.S.M.E., Carnegie Mellon U., 1956; M.S. in Aerospace Engring., U. So. Calif., 1962. Sr. structure engr. Columbus div. Rockwell, Columbus, Ohio, 1956-66; program mgr. tactical aircraft Lockheed Calif. Co., Burbank, 1966-74, chief advanced design engr. advanced devel. projects, 1978—; staff specialist aero. and ocean vehicles Office Sec. Defense, Washington, 1974-78. Pres. Chesterfield Mews Homeowner Assn., Fairfax, Va., 1977-78. Served to 1st lt. USAR ordnance corps, 1956-64. Mem. AIAA (mgmt. tech. com. 1982—, adv. bd. nat. capitol sect. 1977-78), Am. Def. Preparedness Assn. (sci. and tech. com.), Royal Aero. Soc. Democrat. Club: Mensa. Home: 13220 Whistler Ave Granada Hills CA 91344

OSBORNE, GINGER TREDWAY (VIRGINIA ANNE TREDWAY), psychology educator; b. Los Angeles, Sept. 24, 1946; d. Harold Todd and Helen Eleanor Tredway; m. John Gregory Getz, Aug. 24, 1968; m. 2d, Thomas Joe Osborne, June 28, 1975; 1 child, Brooks. B.A. in Psychology, U. Calif.-Santa Barbara, 1968; M.A., U. So. Calif., 1971, Ph.D. in Psychology, 1978. Intern, Andrus Older Adult Center, Los Angeles, 1981-82; post-doctoral trainee Human Sexuality Program, Neuropsychiat. Inst. UCLA, 1981-82; intern dept. psychiatry U. Calif.-Irvine, 1982—; instr. psychology Santa Ana (Calif.), Coll., 1972—; editorial cons. in fields of gerontology, human sexuality. HEW dissertation grantee, 1977. Mem. Gray Panthers, NOW, Sierra Club, Common Cause, Laguna Greenbelt, South Laguna Civic Assn., Am. Psychol. Assn., Gerontol. Soc. Am. Democrat. Methodist. Home: 31651 Santa Rosa Dr S Laguna CA 92677 Office: Dept Psychology Santa Ana Coll Santa Ana CA 92706

OSBORNE, LARRY WALTER, Realtor; b. San Pedro, Calif., May 11, 1939; s. Clarence Raymond and Jeanette Marie (Sepersky) O.; student Oakland City Coll., 1957-58; B.A. in Math., San Jose State U., 1961; postgrad. So. Meth. U., 1972, San Francisco U., 1974-75, Houston U., 1976, Portland U., 1977; m. Sofia Demakopoulos, July 29, 1961; children—Sharon Ann, Valerie Marie, Margaret Elizabeth. Cost analyst Ford Motor Co., Milpitas, Calif., 1962-65; salesman Morrison Homes, Oakland, Calif., 1965-69; Realtor, Estate Pleasanton, Calif., 1969-72; pres. Osborne Real Estate Inc., Pleasanton, 1972-78; sec.-treas., Realtor, Stephen G. Palmer & Assos., Inc., Pleasanton, 1978—; pres. Osborne Real Estate Inc., 1980—; dir. Founders Title Group, Mission Valley Bancorp., Bank of Pleasanton. Trustee Valley Meml. Hosp. Served with U.S. Army, 1962. Mem. Nat., Calif. assns. Realtors, Realtors Nat. Mktg. Inst., So. Alameda Bd. Realtors, Young Home Builders, Pleasanton C. of C. (dir.). Republican. Episcopalian. Club: Masons. Home: 1159 Kottinger Dr Pleasanton CA 94566 Office: 699 Peters Ave Pleasanton CA 94566

OSBORNE, ROBERT HOWARD, educator; b. Akron, Ohio, June 29, 1939; s. Clyde and Emily Hildreth (Dailey) O.; B.S., Kent State U., 1961; M.S. in Geology, Wash. State U., 1963; Ph.D., (Bownocker fellow), Ohio State U., 1966; m. Sarah Cole Sturdy, June 26, 1966; children—Mark Duncan, Todd Stuart. Asst. prof. Univ. So. Calif., Los Angeles, 1966-70, asso. prof., 1970-80, prof. sedimentology, 1980—; vis. asso. prof. U. Ky., Lexington, 1973; cons. to various orgns., 1969—. Recipient numerous grants and contracts. Fellow Geol. Soc. Am.; mem. Internat. Assn. Math. Geology, Am. Statis. Assn., Soc. Econ. Paleontologists and Mineralogists, Am. Assn. Petroleum Geologists, Sierra Club, Sigma Xi. Clubs: Am. Whitewater Affiliation (Hagerstown, Md.); Am. Canoe Assn. (Lorton, Va.). Contbr. articles to various publs. Home: 6225 W 77th St Los Angeles CA 90045 Office: Dept of Geol Scis Univ So Calif Los Angeles CA 90007

O'SCANNLAIN, DIARMUID FIONNTAIN, lawyer; b. N.Y.C., Mar. 28, 1937; s. Sean Leo (dec.) and Moira (Hegarty) O'S.; m. Maura Nolan, Sept. 7, 1963; children—Sean, Jane, Brendan, Kevin, Megan, Christopher, Anne, Kate. A.B., St. John's U., 1957; J.D., Harvard U., 1963. Bars: N.Y. 1964, Oreg. 1965. Tax atty. Standard Oil Co. N.J., N.Y.C., 1963-65; assoc. Davies, Biggs, Strayer, Stoel & Boley, Portland, Oreg., 1965-69; dep. atty. gen. Oreg., 1969-71; pub. utility commr. Oreg., 1971-73; dir. Oreg. Dept. Environ. Quality, 1973-74; sr. ptnr. Ragen, Roberts, O'Scannlain, Robertson & Neill, Portland, 1978—; cons. Office of President-Elect, mem. Energy Transition Team, Washington, 1980-81; chmn. Oreg. State Bar com. on adminstrv. law, 1980-81. Mem. Republican Nat. Com., chmn. Oreg. Rep. Party; del. Rep. Nat. Conv., 1976, 80. Served to maj. USAR, 1955-78. Mem. Fed. Energy Bar Assn., ABA. Roman Catholic. Clubs: Arlington, Multnomah Athletic (Portland). Home: 2421 SW Arden Rd Portland OR 97201 Office: 1001 SW 5th Ave 1600 Orbanco Bldg Portland OR 97204

OSGUTHORPE, SUSAN GALE LIKINS, nurse administrator, consultant; b. Salt Lake City, July 8, 1948; d. Corwin Hale and Virginia Louise (Snyder) Likins; m. Samuel Galen Grubbs, Sept. 12, 1969 (div.); m. Steven Garn Osguthorpe, Jan. 29, 1982. B.S. in Nursing cum laude, U. Utah, 1971, M.S. in Nursing, 1981. Staff nurse Sister of the Holy Cross Hosp., Salt Lake City, 1971-73, Sister of Mercy Hosp., Buffalo, 1973, St. Joseph's Hosp., Syracuse, N.Y., 1973-74; staff nurse Holy Cross Hosp., Salt Lake City, 1974-75, supr., 1975-81, critical care nurse clinician, 1981-82, clin dir. critical care services, 1982—, mem. clin. faculty Weber State Coll., U. Utah; instr., trainer Utah Heart Assn., teaching cons. Hewlett Packard, Sorenson Research Co., Salt Lake Fire Dept.; lectr. in field. Mem. nursing edn. com. Utah Heart Assn. Named Outstanding Young Woman of Am., 1981. Mem. Am. Assn. for Critical Care Nurses (Utah chpt.), Am. Assn. for Critical Care Nurses, Sigma Theta Tau (Gamma Rho chpt., ann. research award 1982), Alpha Lambda Delta. Republican. Congregationalist. Home: 7655 S 2700 E Salt Lake City UT 84121 Office: 1045 E 1st S Salt Lake City UT 84102

O'SHEA, JOHN JAMES, oil drilling company executive; b. Cork, Ireland, June 20, 1944; came to U.S., 1961; s. John and Mary (Lyons) O'S.; m. Scarlett Garafulich, July 8, 1978. B.S., Fordham U., 1969. C.P.A., N.Y. Sr. auditor Touch Ross & Co., N.Y.C., 1969-73; mgr. corp. acctg. S.C.M. Corp., N.Y.C., 1973-78; asst. controller Global Marine Inc., Los Angeles, 1978-82, controller, Houston, 1982—. Served with U.S. Army, 1965-67. Mem. Fin. Execs. Inst., Am. Inst. C.P.A.s., N.Y. State Soc. C.P.A.s., Am. Petroleum Inst., Internat. Assn. Drilling Contractors. Home: 1111 Fleetwood Pl Houston TX 77079 Office: 10260 Westminster Houston TX 77042

O'SHELL, HAROLD EUGENE, occupational safety and health consultant; b. Altoona, Pa., Oct. 29, 1924; s. Curtis Nmi and Martha Belle (McCormick) O.; m. Natalie Patricia Reynolds, 1947; children—Cathy Diane, Tracy Dawn, Christopher Shawn. B.S. in Elec. Engring., Pa. State U., 1949. Registered profl. engr., Tex. 1955. Asst. v.p. Ins. Co. N.Am., Phila., 1949-74; dir. Internat. Safety Acad., Los Angeles, 1974-78; v.p. Esis, Inc., Los Angeles, 1978-81; v.p. Internat. Loss Control Inst., Loganville, Ga., 1981; dir. Diversified Safety Enterprises, Inc., Scottsdale, Ariz., 1982—. Pres., Daylesford, Pa. Civic Assn., 1964, 65; del. Tredyffrin Twp. (Pa.) Civic Council, 1964, 65, Tredyffrin/Easttown Twps.; bd. dirs. Pa. Sch. Dist., 1965-73, pres., 1970; bd. dirs. No. Chester County Vocat. Tech. Sch., Pa., 1967-68. Served with Signal Corps, AUS 1943-46. Mem. Nat. Fire Protection Assn. (gen. storage com. 1961-68, chmn. refrigerated storage com., 1962-64, membership com. 1967-73), Soc. Fire Protection Engrs. (engring. ed. com. 1964-66, chmn., Delaware Valley chpt. pres. 1970-72), Underwriters Labs. (fire council 1969-80), Am. Soc. Safety Engrs., U.S. C. of C. (environ. pollution panel 1970); Pa. C. of C. Safety Council (dir. exec. com. 1970-73). Republican. Baptist. Club: Moose. Home: 5101 E Calavar Dr Scottsdale AZ 85254 Office: 5101 E Calavar Dr Scottsdale AZ 85254

OSIECKI, JEANNE HELEN, chemist; b. Switzerland, Dec. 6, 1926; d. Jules Lucien and Berthe Helen (Sunier) Vuilleumier; student U. Geneva, 1948-50; B.S. (NIH grantee), Wayne State U., 1956; Ph.D., Stanford U., 1960; m. Vincent Osiecki, Sept. 5, 1952. Chemist, Stanford Research Inst., Menlo Park, Calif., 1960; research scientist Lockheed Missiles & Space Co., Palo Alto, 1961-66; sr. research chemist Synvar Research Inst., Palo Alto, 1966-71; research info. specialist Wander div. Sandoz Inc. Pharm. Co., Berne, Switzerland, 1972-75; cons. organic chemistry, Los Altos, Calif., 1976—. Ethyl Corp. fellow, 1957-59. Mem. Am. Inst. Chemists (sec.-treas. 1965-66), Am. Chem. Soc., Royal Soc. Chemistry (London), Sigma Xi, Iota Sigma Pi. Contbr. articles to profl. jours.; patentee in charge transfer complexes and stable free radicals. Address: 465 Gabilan St Los Altos CA 94022

OSTENDORF, FREDERICK OTTO, real estate executive, former county official; b. Milw., May 24, 1913; s. Frederick and Emily (Smith) O.; A.A., Glendale Coll., 1933; B.A., UCLA, 1937; M.A. in Sociology, U. So. Calif., 1949, cert. in real estate, 1954; m. Beryl Louverne Bell, May 29, 1941; children—Frederick Otto, Margaret Ann. With Los Angeles County Probation Dept., 1939-73, cons. juvenile delinquency, 1948-51, adult investigator, 1951-61, hearing officer juvenile traffic Superior Ct., 1961-63, adult supervision officer, 1964-73; owner Ostendorf Properties, LaCanada, Calif., 1959—. Cub scout commr. Boy Scouts Am., La Canada, 1952-54. Served to lt. USNR, 1942-46; lt. comdr. Res. ret. Named Outstanding Older Am., La Canada City Council-Los Angeles County Bd. Suprs., 1980. Mem. Crescenta-Canada Art Assn. (past pres.), Naval Res. Assn. (charter mem.; past pres. Rose Bowl chpt.), Alpha Kappa Delta. Clubs: Toastmasters (pres. 1967, 75, Disting. Toastmaster award 1980), Descanso Garden Guild (docent La Canada 1973-79, lectr. 1975, tour dir. 1978-79), Leisure (pres. 1980-81). Author: The Art of Retirement, 1980. Home: 1084 Inverness Dr Flintridge CA 91011

OSTER, RANDAL ALLEN, psychologist; b. Boise, Idaho, Oct. 9, 1950; s. Henry John and Vivian Corrine (Carter) O.; B.A., Linfield Coll., McMinnville, Oreg., 1972; M.S., U. Utah, 1975, Ph.D., 1979; m. Lorraine Gail Frank, Aug. 26, 1972; 1 son, David Frank. Residential mgr. Psychiat. Halfway House, Salt Lake City, 1973-75; psychology intern Granite Community Mental Health Center, Salt Lake City, 1974-76; crisis intervention specialist Jail Project, 1976-77; child custody specialist Youth Services Center, Salt Lake City, 1977-78; psychologist Salt Lake County Div. Mental Health, Salt Lake City, 1978—; pvt. practice psychology, 1980—; adj. faculty Westminster Coll., 1981—. Mem. Am. Psychol. Assn., Western Psychol. Assn., Utah Psychol. Assn., Nat. Register Health Service Providers in Psychology, Internat. Neuropsychol. Soc. Presbyterian. Contbr. articles to profl. jours. Home: 1727 S 1400 E Salt Lake City UT 84105 Office: 640 B Wilmington Ave Salt Lake City UT 84106

OSTERMILLER, JOHN VICTOR, real estate co. exec.; b. Lincoln, Nebr., Nov. 4, 1910; s. John and Louise (Bernhardt) O.; student U. Nebr., 1927-28; B.S., Colo. State U., 1932; m. Margaret Ellen Kerr, June 17, 1934; children—Karen Rea, John Kerr. Tchr. vocational agr., pub. sch. Colo., 1934-42; agrl. fieldman Great Western Sugar Co., Brush, Colo., 1942-49, asst. mgr., Brush, also Ft. Morgan, 1949-57, mgr., Longmont, Colo., 1957-63, agrl. mgr., Fort Morgan, 1963-70; N.E. Colo. asst. dist. agrl. mgr., Ft. Morgan, 1970-73, v.p. Gt. Western Sugar Export Co., 1973-75; mgr. farm and ranch dept. Crown Realty Co., Denver, 1975-78, Carriage House Realtors, Ft. Morgan, 1978—. Instr. Adult Edn., Yuma, Colo., 1935-38, Brush, 1938-42. Republican precinct committeeman, Morgan County, 1950-57, 64-74, Boulder County, 1958-63; mem. St. Vrain Valley Sch. Bd., Longmont, 1961-63. Bd. dirs. Brush Civic Club, 1944-50; bd. dirs. Ft. Morgan Heritage Found., pres. 1969-75; bd. dirs., pres. Colo. State U. Found., 1973—. Mem. Ft. Morgan C. of C. (dir. 1965-69, pres. 1968), Colo. State U. Alumni (dir. 1972—, pres. 1975-76), Am. Sugar Beet Soc. Technologists, Alpha Tau Alpha, Lamda Gamma Delta, Sigma Phi Epsilon. Presbyn. Mason, Lion. Contbr. articles to profl. jours. Home: 4 Yates Terrace Fort Morgan CO 80701 Office: 409 E Platte Ave Fort Morgan CO 80701

OSTRANDER, WILLIS FREDERICK, savings and loan association executive; b. Berkeley, Calif., Apr. 23, 1926; s. Willis Frederick and Grace (Jackson) O.; m. Nancy Majors, Jan. 2, 1950; children—Margaret, Frederick, Daphne, John. B.A., U. Calif.-Berkeley, 1948. Dealer properties rep. Signal Oil Co. div. Standard Oil Co. Calif., 1951-62; appraiser, then v.p. Twin Pines Fed. Savs. & Loan Assn., Berkeley, 1962-76, exec. v.p., 1976—. Served with U.S. Maritime Service, 1944-45. Mem. Soc. Real Estate Appraisers, Bay Area Mortgage Assn. Democrat. Roman Catholic. Clubs: Orinda Country, City Commons. Author: Hunchback and the Swan, 1979. Home: 2741 Woolsey St Berkeley CA 94705 Office: 2905 Telegraph Ave Berkeley CA 94705

OTANI, ARTHUR SEIICHI, dermatologist; b. Honolulu, Sept. 5, 1947; s. Curtis W. and Shizuyo (Esaki) O.; B.A. with honors, Stanford U., 1968; Ph.D. (NIH grantee), Stanford Med. Center, 1970; M.D., U. Calif., San Diego, 1974; m. Ellen Louise Klocke, Aug. 28, 1971; children—Laura Patricia, Marc Curtis. Intern, U. Calif., San Diego, 1974-75, resident in dermatology, 1975-78; research asso. Scripps Clinic and Research Center, 1977; practice medicine specializing in dermatology, San Diego, 1978—; owner Tierrasanta Dermatology Clinic, San Diego; asst. clin. prof. medicine U. Calif., San Diego, 1979—. Co-chmn. grounds/greenspace com. residential devel., Tierrasanta, Calif., 1975-77. Recipient Bausch & Lomb Sci. award, 1965; Pfizer Sci. award, 1971; Nelson Anderson award, 1976; diplomate Am. Bd. Dermatology. Mem. San Diego Dermatology Assn., Pacific Dermatology Assn., Sonoran Dermatology Assn., Am. Acad. Dermatology, AMA, Calif. Med. Assn., Soc. Investigative Dermatologists, Soc. Dermatol. Surgery. Contbr. articles in field to profl. jours.; patentee in field. Office: 10789 Tierrasanta Blvd Suite 115 San Diego CA 92124

OTANI, DENNIS MASATO, county health ofcl.; b. Berkeley, Calif., Feb. 6, 1951; s. Noboru and Tomoye (Hiruo) O.; student Diablo Valley Coll., 1969-71; B.S. in Microbiology, San Jose State U., 1976. Student profl. asst. Santa Clara County (Calif.) Health Dept., 1975; Sanitarian II, Kings County (Calif.) Health Dept., 1976-77, sanitarian III, 1977-78, dir. environ. health, 1978—. Served with U.S. Army, 1972-74. Registered sanitarian, Calif. Mem. Nat. Environ. Health Assn., Calif. Environ. Health Assn., Calif. Conf. Dirs. Environ. Health (sec.-treas. 1981-82, pres.-elect 1982-83, pres. 1983-84), Advs. Public Health Calif. Home: 2102 Oakwood Ct Hanford CA 93230 Office: 330 Campus Dr Hanford CA 93230

OTOSHI, TOM YASUO, elec. engr.; b. Seattle, Sept. 4, 1931; s. Jitsuo and Shina Otoshi; B.S.E.E., U. Wash., 1954, M.S.E.E., 1957; m. Haruko Shirley Yumiba, Oct. 13, 1963; children—John, Kathryn. With Hughes Aircraft Co., Culver City, Calif., 1956-61; mem. tech. staff Jet Propulsion Lab., Calif. Inst. Tech., Pasadena, 1961—; cons. Recipient NASA New Tech. awards. Mem. IEEE (sr.), Sigma Xi. Contbr. articles to profl. jours. Patentee in field. Home: 3551 Henrietta St La Crescenta CA 91214 Office: Jet Propulsion Lab 4800 Oak Grove Dr Pasadena CA 91109

OTT, WENDELL LORENZ, mus. dir.; b. McCloud, Calif., Sept. 17, 1942; s. Wendell and Rose (Jacob) O.; B.A., Trinity U., San Antonio, 1968; M.F.A., U. Ariz., 1970. Asst. dir. Roswell (N.Mex.) Mus. and Art Center, 1970-71, dir., 1971—. Chmn. Roswell Humanities Series, 1972-73. Mem. N.Mex. Assn. Museums (chmn. 1973-74), Am. Assn. Museums. Office: 100 W 11th St Roswell NM 88201

OTTLEY, JEROLD DON, conductor; b. Salt Lake City, Apr. 7, 1934; s. Sidney James and Alice (Warren) O.; B.A., Brigham Young U., 1961; M.M., U. Utah, 1967; postgrad. Hochschule fur Musik, Cologne, Germany, 1968-69; D.M.A., U. Oreg., 1972; m. JoAnn South, June 22, 1956; children—Brent Kay, Allison. Tchr., Utah pub. schs., 1961-65; grad. asst. U. Utah, 1965-67, instr., 1967-68, 71-73, asst. prof., 1973-78, adj. assoc. prof., 1978—, asst. chmn. music dept., 1974-75, chmn. music edn., 1974-75, 79-82; grad. teaching fellow U. Oreg., 1969-71; music dir. Salt Lake Mormon Tabernacle Choir, 1975—; guest condr.; trustee Master Tchr. Inst. for Arts. Served with U.S. Army, 1957-59. Recipient Honors in the Arts award Salt Lake Area C. of C., 1981; Fulbright grantee, 1968-69. Mem. Am. Choral Dirs. Assn., Am. Choral Found.,

Music Educators Nat. Conf. Mormon. Rec. artist Columbia Records. Office: 50 E North Temple Salt Lake City UT 84150

OTTO, CARL WARREN, engineering and architectural consultant; b. Seattle, Apr. 18, 1922; s. Hans Paul and Gudrun Marie (Kilian) O.; m. Gloria DeEtte Williams, June 20, 1946; children—Carlin, Gari Gene, Warren, Ruth. B.S., U.S. Naval Acad., 1946; B.C.E., Rensselaer Poly. Inst., 1948, M.C.E., 1949. With contractors, Pacific Naval Air Bases, Midway Island and Hawaii, 1941-43; served with USN, 1943-56; designer, project engr., v.p., exec. v.p., Tudor Engring. Co., San Francisco, Hawaii, Peru, 1956-73, also dir.; exec. v.p. URS/Blume, San Francisco, 1973-79; exec. v.p., then pres. Keller & Gannon, San Francisco, 1979—; dir. Keller & Gannon. Mem. ASCE, Nat. Soc. Profl. Engrs., Soc. Am. Mil. Engrs. (pres. chpt. 1977). Home: 250 Austin St Atherton CA 94025

OTTO, JOHN PAUL, lawyer; b. Waterloo, Iowa, June 14, 1930; s. Paul Stephen and Winifred Irene (Dougherty) O.; m. Brownye Lucille Rhodes, Aug. 12, 1954; m. 2d, Sue Woodruff Donohue, Nov. 21, 1974; children—John Merritt, James Kelly. Jr. coll. diploma Am. U., 1952; J.D., U. N.Mex., 1957. Bar: N.Mex. 1957, Ariz. 1961, U.S. Supreme Ct. 1964. Mem. Beenton, Baya, Otto & Festinger, Alamogordo, N.Mex., 1957-59; assoc. O'Connor, Cavanagh, Anderson, Westover, Killingsworth and Beshears, Phoenix, 1960-65; assoc. law office of Marvin Johnson, P.C., Phoenix. Served to 1st lt. U.S. Army, 1952-54. Decorated Bronze Star. Recipient N.Mex. Bar Service award, 1969. Mem. N.Mex. Bar Assn., Ariz. Bar Assn., Otero County Bar Assn. (pres. 1968), Maricopa County Bar Assn. Republican. Roman Catholic. Home: 1008 E Michigan Ave Phoenix AZ 85022 Office: 45 W Jefferson 5th Floor Phoenix AZ 85003

OTTO, WALTER DAVIS, educational adminstrator; b. Los Angeles, Apr. 8, 1936; s. James E. and Francis L. (Thrall) O.; m. Christine Linda Murray, June 20, 1962; m. 2d, Pamela Steel Huie, May 15, 1948; children—Matthew Logan, James Bradford. A.A., Pasadena City Coll., 1958; student U. Houston, 1958-59; B.A., Los Angeles State Coll., 1961, postgrad, 1962; M.S., Calif. State U.-Fullerton, 1969. Tchr., athletic dir., sports commr. Pago Pago, Am. Samoa, 1962-64; tchr. Sycamore Jr. High Sch., 1965-66; tchr., coach Westminster High Sch., 1966-69; vice-prin. Madrone Intermediate Sch., 1969-70; counselor, tchr. Hawaii Prep. Acad., 1970-71; sch./community coordinator Marina High Sch., 1971-73; tchr., coach Laguna Beach (Calif.) High Sch., 1973-79; real estate salesman, Laguna Beach, Calif., 1979-80; vice-prin. Perris Valley Jr. High Sch., Perris, Calif., 1980-81, prin., 1981-83. Sch. power mem. Laguna Beach Schs., 1979-83; active Perris Valley Swimming Pool Orgn., 1980-83. NDEA grantee Los Angeles State Coll., 1961-62; named Tchr. of Yr., Laguna Beach High Sch., 1975. Mem. Assn. Supervision and Curriculum Devel., Nat. Assn. Secondary Sch. Prins., NEA, Nat. Assn. Swim Coaches, Nat. Assn. Waterpolo Coaches, Friends of Library, Assn. Calif. Sch. Adminstrs., Calif. Tchrs. Assn., Western Riverside Adminstrs. Assn., Phi Delta Kappa.

OTTOMAN, RICHARD EDWARD, oncologist; b. Guthrie, Okla., Aug. 3, 1910; s. Adolph and Ferne (Christian) O.; student Jackson Jr. Coll., 1932-34; M.D., U. Mich., 1941; m. Mary Elizabeth Merrill, Nov. 27, 1943; 1 adopted dau., Bonnie Ann. Rotating intern Virginia Mason Hosp., Seattle, 1941-42: staff physician Birmingham VA Hosp., Van Nuys, Calif., 1946-47, resident radiology, 1947-50, asst. radiologist, 1950—; asst. radiologist to chief therapeutic radiology Long Beach (Calif.) VA Hosp., 1950-52, attending staff, 1952-56; vis. roentgenologist Los Angeles County Harbor Gen. Hosp., 1950-56; attending staff St. John's Hosp., 1950-60, affiliate cons., 1960—; cons. radiology Valley Hosp., Van Nuys, 1956—, co-dir. radiology, 1973-76; instr. radiology U. So. Calif., 1950-52, asst. prof. radiology, 1952-54, asso. prof. radiology, anatomy, 1954-61, prof., 1961-71, prof. emeritus, 1971—; vice chmn. dept. radiology UCLA, 1961-65, mem. com. departmental curriculum, 1966—; chief radiation therapy Santa Monica Hosp. Med. Center, 1971-73; cons. AEC, 1952— ; pvt. practice, 1955— ; mem. Calif. Physicians Service. Mem. Town Hall. Med. adv. com. Planned Parenthood Center. Trustee, past sec.-treas. James T. Case Radiologic Found. Served from 1st lt. to maj. M.C., AUS, 1942-46. Diplomate Am. Bd. Radiology. Fellow Am. Coll. Radiology; mem. Radiol. Soc. N.Am., Radiol. Soc. So. Calif., AAAS, Am., Calif., Los Angeles County med. assns., Am. Roentgen Ray Soc., Am. Soc. Nuclear Medicine, Nat. Geog. Soc., Phi Rho Sigma. Contbr. numerous articles to med. jours. Home: 58 Stanford Circle Vandenberg Village Lompoc CA 93436 Office: Valley Hosp Med Center Van Nuys CA 91405

OTTS, JAMES WILSON, electronics co. exec.; b. Sulligent, Ala., Jan. 21, 1938; s. Tilden Leroy and Mary Hazel (Birmingham) O.; B.A. in Mgmt., St. Mary's Coll., 1980; postgrad. Pepperdine U., 1982—; m. Emma Lee Tickel, Dec. 28, 1957; children—Michele, John, Kimberly, James. Lab. analyst Jet Propulsion Lab., Pasadena, Calif., 1962-66; project mgr. Hewlett-Packard, Palo Alto, Calif., 1966-72, mfg. mgr., 1972-76; product assurance mgr. Plantronics Corp., Santa Cruz, Calif., 1976-80; dir. mfg. engring. and quality assurance Convergent Techs., Santa Clara, 1980—. Mem. adv. bd. Cabrillo Coll., Santa Cruz, 1976-80. Served with USAF, 1955-58. Recipient Sci. team award NASA, 1965. Mem. Am. Mgmt. Assn. Republican. Club: Masons. Home: 1981 Branciforte Dr Santa Cruz CA 95065 Office: 2500 Augustine Dr Santa Clara CA 95051

OUSTERMAN, WALTER E., JR., cement company executive; b. 1930. Grad. Rutgers U.; M.B.A., Harvard U. With Kaiser Cement Corp., Oakland, Calif., 1957—, prodn. dept., 1957, asst. to v.p. ops., 1959, asst. gen. prodn. mgr., 1962, gen. prodn. mgr., 1966, v.p., gen. prodn. mgr., then v.p. internat., 1968, v.p., gen. mgr. internat. div., 1969, exec. v.p. ops., 1971, pres., chief exec. officer, 1976—, chmn. bd., dir., 1979—. Office: Kaiser Cement Corp 300 Lakeside Dr Oakland CA 94612*

OUTCALT, DAVID LEWIS, university chancellor, mathematician; b. Los Angeles, Jan. 30, 1935; s. Earl Kinyan and Alberta (Estes) O.; m. Marcia Lee Beach, July 1, 1956; children—Jeffrey David, Kevin Douglas, Gregory Mark, Eric Matthew. B.A. in Math., Pomona Coll., 1956; M.A. in Math., Claremont Grad. Sch., 1958; Ph.D. in Math., Ohio State U., 1963. Asst. prof. math. Claremont Men's Coll., 1962-64; asst. prof. to prof. math. U. Calif.-Santa Barbara, 1964-82, chmn. dept. math., 1969-72, dean instructional devel., 1977-80; vice chancellor acad. affairs U. Alaska, Anchorage, 1980-81, chancellor, 1981—. Moderator bd. trustees Humana Hosp. Alaska, 1982—; mem. exec. bd. Western Alaska council Boy Scouts Am., 1982—. USAF Office Sci. Research grantee, 1964-71; U. Calif. grantee, 1975-78; NSF grantee, 1976-79. Mem. Am. Math. Soc., Math. Assn. Am., Sigma Xi. Lodge: Rotary. Contbr. articles on math. and higher edn. to profl. jours. Home: SR7295 Skyline Dr Eagle River AK 99677 Office: 3211 Providence Dr Anchorage AK 99508

OUTLAND, GEORGE FAULKNER, educator, cons.; b. Cambridge, Mass., May 8, 1929; s. George Elmer and Virginia Margaret (Stevenson) O.; B.A., U. Calif. at Santa Barbara, 1952; M.A., San Francisco State Coll., 1957; Ed.D., U. Calif. at Berkeley, 1971; m. Carolyn Wolfe, July 12, 1953; 1 dau., Marilyn Merry. Apprentice printer, Calif., Va., 1943-52; journeyman printer, proofreader various firms Calif., D.C., 1952-65; printing tchr. Oakland (Calif.) High Sch., 1956-63, social sci. tchr., debate coach, 1961-64; vocat. coordinator Oakland Public Schs., 1964-65; dir. ednl. research and resources San Mateo (Calif.) Union High Sch. Dist., 1965-75, vocat. adviser Adult Sch., 1975-76; tchr. social sci., adminstrv. asst. Burlingame (Calif.) High Sch., 1976-77; dir. Tech. Tng. Inst., for GTE Sylvania, Tehran, Iran, 1977-78; head compensatory edn. dept. San Mateo High Sch., 1978—, Aragon High Sch., 1981—; tchr. vocat. edn. U. Calif. at Berkeley, 1966-72; tchr. program planning and budgeting systems Coll. Notre Dame, 1971-72; tchr. indsl. edn. Calif. State U., San Francisco, 1972-73; vocat. researcher U.S. Office Edn., Washington, 1962, 67, Calif. State Dept. Edn., 1963-64; ednl. cons. to U.S. Office Edn., 4 state depts. edn., also county and local sch. systems; cons. and lectr. various colls. and univs.; chmn. 4 vis. coms. accrediting commn. Western Assn. Schs. and Colls. Co-chmn. Adv. Com. on Calif. Assembly ACR 127, 1970-72. Served with USN, 1952-54; capt. Res. Recipient Honor Key, U. Calif. at Santa Barbara, 1952, Letter of Commendation Sec. of Navy, 1969, Navy Commendation medal, 1978. Mem. Am. Vocat. Assn. (life), U. Calif. at Santa Barbara Alumni Assn. (life), Am. Vocat. Edn. Research Assn. (membership sec. 1968-71), Calif. Indsl. Edn. Assn. (life), U.S. Naval Inst. (life), Naval Order U.S. (life), Naval Res. Assn. (life), Blue Jackets Assn. (life), Res. Officers Assn. (life), Phi Delta Kappa (life). Republican. Club: Commonwealth (San Francisco). Home: PO Box 214 Burlingame CA 94010

OVERHOLT, MILES HARVARD, TV exec.; b. Glendale, Calif., Sept. 30, 1921; s. Miles Harvard and Alma Overholt; A.B., Harvard Coll., 1943; m. Jessie Foster, Sept. 18, 1947; children—Miles Harvard, Keith Foster. Mktg. analyst Dun & Bradstreet, Phila., 1947-48; collection mgr. Standard Oil of Calif., Los Angeles, 1948-53; br. mgr. RCA Service Co., Phila., 1953-63, ops. mgr. Classified Aerospace project RCA, Riverton, N.J., 1963; pres. CPS, Inc., Paoli, Pa., 1964-67; mem. pres.'s exec. com. Gen. Time Corp., Mesa, Ariz., 1970-78; gen. mgr., dir. service Talley Industries, Mesa, 1967-78; v.p., gen. mgr. Northwest Entertainment Network, Inc., Seattle, 1979-81; cons., 1981—. cable cons., 1981—. Served with USMCR, 1943-46. Decorated Bronze Star, Purple Heart (two). Mem. Assn. Home Appliance Mfrs., Nat. Assn. Microwave Distbn. Service Cos. Club: Harvard (N.Y.C.). Home: 8320 Frederick Pl Edmonds WA 98020 Office: 4517 California Ave SW Suite B Seattle WA 98116

OVERSON, BRENT C., real estate executive, state senator; b. Nephi, Utah, Apr. 18, 1950; s. Fay Dean and Elda Rae (Huntsman) O.; m. Joanne Robison, Nov. 18, 1971; 3 children. A.A., U. Md., 1978; B.S. in Fin., U. Utah, 1982. Lic. real estate broker. Sales agt., office mgr. Envirowest Realty, Inc., Salt Lake City, 1978-82; dir. real estate and devel. Trailside Gen. Stores, Bountiful, Utah, 1982—; dir. Wyo. Alaska Leasing Corp.; mem. Utah Senate, 1983—. Bd. dirs. Salt Lake County Mental Health Bd.; mem. Child Abuse Rev. Com. Served with USN, 1972-78. Mem. Nat. Assn. Realtors. Republican. Mormon. Office: 506 S Main St Bountiful UT 84010

OVERSTREET, HARRY LEE, archtl. designer; b. June 20, 1938; s. Joseph and Cleo O.; student Contra Costa Coll., 1956, Calif. Coll. Arts and Crafts, 1957; children—Anthony Troy, Harry Lee. With U.S. Forest Service, Calif., 1961-64; with Overstreet Bldg. Design, Oakland, Calif., 1964-68; prin. Gerson/Overstreet, Architects, Oakland and San Francisco, 1968—. Mem. Sml. Bus. Adminstrn. regional adv. bd., 1980-82; bd. dirs. Hunters Point Boys Club, 1975—; pres. Berkeley Planning Commn., 1967-73; pres., mem. bd. adjustments City of Berkeley, 1967-73. Served with U.S. Army, 1957-60. Recipient Outstanding Planner award, Ethnic Minority Assn., 1976; Award of Merit, City and County of San Francisco, 1972. Mem. Nat. Orgn. Minority Architects (co-founder, bd. dirs. N. Calif. chpt.), NAACP, Ethnic Minority Assn. Calif. Archtl. works include: Adult Edn. Center, Berkeley, 1972, Ednl. Cultural Complex, San Diego, 1975, Cragmont Sch., Berkeley, 1978, VA Hosp., Palo Alto, 1978, San Francisco Opera House, 1978, Calif. Med. Center, Vacaville, 1982, others. Home: 3324 Wisconsin St Oakland CA 94602 Office: 57 Post St Suite 804 San Francisco CA 94104

OVERTON, ANITA FAYE, mortgage banking exec.; b. Enid, Okla., Oct. 30, 1943; d. Carl J. and Audine G. (Leser) Eisele; student Enid Bus. Coll., 1961-62, Los Angeles Valley Jr. Coll., 1963-64, Lumbleau Real Estate Sch., 1978, Lane Community Coll., Eugene, Oreg., 1981-83. 1 dau. by previous marriage, Elena Suzanne Overton. Loan processor Investor's Mortgage Service Co. Los Angeles, 1964-66, Colonial Assos., Inc., Sherman Oaks, Calif., 1967-68; office mgr. Century Mortgage Co., Los Angeles, 1968-69; office mgr. The Colwell Co., Inglewood, Calif., 1969-71, asst. sec. of corp., 1969-71; adminstrv. asst. Kassler & Co., Encino, Calif., 1971-72; supr. Crenshaw Mortgage Co., Inglewood, 1972-74; loan rep. Imperial Bank Mortgage, Inglewood, 1974; office mgr. Cal Fed Mortgage Co., Northridge, Calif., 1974-75; v.p. and corp. sec. Funders Mortgage Co., Inc., Northridge, 1975-78; v.p. and corp. sec. Funders Mortgage Co., Inc., Reseda, Calif., 1978—, also dir.; corp. sec. Funders Home Loan Co., Inc., 1978—; dir. Funders Ins. Agy., Inc.; corp. sec. Funders Ins. Co., 1978-80. Lic. income tax preparer. Mem. Nat. Assn. Female Execs., Assn. Profl. Mortgage Women, Calif. Escrow Assn., Phi Theta Kappa.

OVERTON, EDWIN DEAN, campus minister, educator; b. Beaver, Okla., Dec. 2, 1939; s. William Edward and Georgia Beryl (Fronk) O. B.Th., Midwest Christian Coll., 1963; M.A. in Religion, Eastern N.Mex. U., 1969, Ed.S., 1978; postgrad. Fuller Theol. Sem., 1980. Ordained to ministry Christian Ch., 1978. Minister, Christian Ch., Englewood, Kans., 1962-63; youth minister First Christian Ch., Beaver, Okla., 1963-67; campus minister Central Christian Ch., Portales, N.Mex., 1967-68, Christian Campus House, Portales, N.Mex., 1968—; tchr. religion, philosophy, counseling Eastern N.Mex. Univ., Portales, 1970— , campus minister, Christian Campus House, 1970—, dir., 1980—; farm and ranch partner, Beaver, Okla., 1963—. State dir. Beaver Jr. C. of C., 1964-65; pres. Beaver High Sch. Alumni Assn., 1964-65; chmn. Beaver County March of Dimes, 1966; pres. Portales Tennis Assn., 1977-78. Mem. AAUP, Internat. Platform Assn., U.S. Tennis Assn. Republican. Club: Lions. Home: 1129 Libra St Portales NM 88130 Office: 223 S Ave K Portales NM 88130

OWADES, RUTH MARKOWITZ, marketing company executive; b. Los Angeles, Sept. 2, 1944; d. David and Yonina (Graf) Markowitz; m. Joseph L. Owades, Sept. 7, 1969. B.A. with honors, Scripps Coll., Claremont, Calif., 1966; M.B.A., Harvard U., 1975; postgrad. U. Strasbourg (France), 1966-67. Exec. asst. Los Angeles Econ. Devel. Bd., N.Y.C., 1968-69; copywriter D'Arcy Advt. Co., St. Louis, 1970-71; asst. program dir. KMOX-AM Radio, St. Louis, 1971-72; assoc. producer WCVB-TV, Boston, 1972-73; mktg. project mgr. United Brands Co., Boston, 1975; mktg. dir. CML Group Inc., Concord, Mass., 1975-78; founder, pres. Gardener's Eden Inc., Boston, 1978-82; pres. Gardener's Eden, div. Williams-Sonoma Inc., Emeryville, Calif., 1982—; dir. Hellenic Breweries S.A., Athens, Greece. Recipient Bausch & Lomb award, 1962; Fulbright scholar, 1966; named student Goodwill Ambassador to Nagoya, Japan, 1960. Mem. Direct Mktg. Assn., Phi Beta Kappa. Club: Harvard (N.Y.C.). Home: 44 Macondray Ln San Francisco CA 94133 Office: 5750 Hollis St Emeryville CA 94608

OWEN, CHARLES THEODORE, journalist, association executive; b. Beech Grove, Ind., June 14, 1941; s. James Robert and Helen Maurine (Sayre) O.; m. Kathleen Rose Dellaria, Apr. 29, 1967. A.S. in Journalism, Vincennes U., 1972; B.A. in Social Sci., Chapman Coll., 1976; postgrad. Nat. U. San Diego, 1984. Served as enlisted man U.S. Marine Corps, 1959-72, commd. 2d lt., 1973, advanced through grades to capt., 1979; combat journalist/photographer, Vietnam, 1967-68; dep. dir. Joint Pub. Affairs Office, Camp Pendleton, 1976-79; dir. Pub. Affairs Office, Marine Corps Recruit Depot, San Diego, 1980-81; dir. communications and mil. affairs div. Greater San Diego C. of C., 1981-82, v.p., 1982—; adj. prof. Nat. U., San Diego. Decorated Cross of Gallantry, medal of Honor 2d class (Vietnam); recipient Thomas Jefferson award, 1981. Mem. Marine Corps Combat Corrs. Assn., Pub. Relations Soc. Am., Pub. Relations Club San Diego (dir.), Press Club San Diego, Vietnam Vets. Leadership (dir.), Am. C. of C. Execs., Sigma Delta Chi. Republican. Pub.: Newswriting Program Instruction, 1972. Office: Greater San Diego C of C 110W C St Suite 1600 San Diego CA 92101

OWEN, GARY DALE, marketing executive; b. Boise, Idaho, Oct. 3, 1936; s. John Henry Garfield and Letha Venus Zoe (Williams) O.; m. Karen Diane Owen Scott, Dec. 7, 1957; children—Kim Dawn, Scott Dale, Kurt Douglas, Kristin Deone, Michael Drew; m. 2d, Beverly Jean Bretzing, May 29, 1982. Student Boise Jr. Coll., 1958, 64, Idaho State U., 1963; B.A. (hon.) Cornell U., 1978. Notary pub., Colo. Non-food merchandiser Sundries Ctrs., Boise, 1961-68; retail grocery operator, Payette, Idaho, 1968-73; non-food operator Ryan Wholesale, Billings, Mont., 1973-75; non-food merchandiser Nat. Tea Co., Denver, 1975-76; buyer A.G. Colorado, 1976-78; pres. Gary Owen Mktg. Ltd., Denver, 1978—, Mktg. Mgmt. Inc., Denver, 1979—; monthly columnist Rocky Mountain Food Dealers mag., 1979—. Served with USAR. Mem. Colo. Food Brokers Assn. (pres. 1983), Nat. Food Brokers Assn., Denver Assn. Mfg. Reps. Republican. Mem. Ch. Jesus Christ of Latter-day Saints. Contbr. articles to trade jours. Home: 8116 S Logan Dr Littleton CO 80122 Office: 2660 Walnut St Denver CO PO Box 2798 Littleton CO 80122

OWEN, NORMAN LLOYD, educator; b. Seattle, Jan. 13, 1937; s. Fred Johannes and Helen Magnhild (Johnson) O.; B.A. in Music Edn., U. Wash., 1959; D.M.A. in Music Edn., (Allyne fellow), Stanford U., 1970; M.Ednl. Adminstrn., U. Calif., Riverside, 1978; m. Muriel Lee Keller, Aug. 19, 1961; children—Paul, Sharene. Tchr., Glacier High Sch., Seattle, 1960-65; asst. prof. music Thiel Coll., Pa., 1968-72; asst. prof. music U. Guam, 1972-75; instrnl. psychologist Courseware, Inc., San Diego, 1979-80; pres., founder Learning Horizons, San Diego, 1980—; cons.; ch. music dir. Pres. Orpheus Music Club; vol. Boys Club. NDEA fellow, 1961-62. Mem. Music Educators Nat. Conf., Internat. Platform Assn., Rep. Assocs., Rep. Bus. and Profl. Club, Phi Mu Alpha Sinfonia, Phi Delta Kappa. Republican. Mem. Unity Ch. Club: Stanford. Editor: Science of Mind Hymnal, 1976; author: Reading Made Easy, 1980; (computer software) Learning To Read: Letters, Words, Sentences; composer Christmas anthem, 1958. Home: 5924 Highplace Dr San Diego CA 92120 Office: 7151 El Cajon Blvd Suites J San Diego CA 92115

OWEN, STEVEN EARL, educator, consultant; b. San Luis Obispo, Calif., July 29, 1947; s. Leland Earl and Lucille Nancy Ann (Varda) O.; m. Janet Gail Smith, Oct. 22, 1976; children—Richard Earl, Shawn Marie. B.S., Calif. State Poly. U., 1969, postgrad., 1969-70; postgrad. Calif. State U.-Stanislaus, 1970-72; M.A.Ed., Fresno Pacific Coll., 1983. Cert. tchr., Calif. Faculty Rivera Jr. High Sch., Merced (Calif.) Sch. Dist., 1970—, tchr., 1970-79, resource tchr. curriculum devel., 1979—, mem. dist. curriculum council, 1970—, dist. sci. cons., 1983—; founder Merced/Mariposa Counties Math. Conf., 1979, chmn., 1979-83; mem. program rev. teams Calif. Dept. Edn., 1979-82; partipant Project AIMS, NSF. Mem. Calif. Tchrs. Assn., Assn. Supervision and Curriculum Devel., Calif. Math. Council (affiliate council Central sect.). Democrat. Baptist. Clubs: Breakfast, Kiwanis (Merced). Co-author: From Head to Toe, I, 1982; author profl. publs., choral readings. Office: 945 Buena Vista Ave Merced CA 95340

OWEN, WILLIAM FREDERICK, environmental engineer; b. Pontiac, Mich., July 27, 1947; s. Webster Jennings and Elizabeth Helton (Hays) O.; B.S., Mich. Tech. U., 1972; M.S., U. Mich., Ann Arbor, 1973; Ph.D. in Environ. Engring., Stanford U., 1979. Registered prof. engr., Calif., Colo., Idaho. Research engr. Neptune Microfloc, Inc., Corvallis, Oreg., 1973-75; research engr. Perry L. McCarty, Cons., Stanford, Calif., 1976-79; research asst. Stanford U., 1976-79; dir. process ops. div. Culp-Wesner-Culp, Cameron Park, Calif., 1979-82; pres. Owen Mgmt. Cons., Inc., 1982—. Served with USN, 1965-68. Dept. Energy Research grantee, 1976-78. Mem. Nat. Soc. Profl. Engrs., Water Pollution Control Fedn., ASCE, Am. Soc. Energy Engrs., Tech. Assn. Pulp and Paper Industry, Author: Energy in Wastewater Treatment, 1981. Home: 3836 Toronto Rd Cameron Park CA 95682 Office: PO Box 1577 Englewood CO 80150

OWENS, GARY, radio-TV performer, author; b. Mitchell, S.D., May 10; s. Bernard Joseph and Vennetta Florence (Clark); student (speech scholarship) Dakota Wesleyan U., Mitchell; scholarship student Mpls. Art Inst.; m. Arleta Lee Markell, June 26; children—Scott Michael, Christopher. Mem. staff Sta. KMPC, Los Angeles, 1962-82, Sta. KPRZ, 1982—; radio performer, 1955—; syndicated radio show The G.O. Special Report; host Gary Owens Soundtrack of the 60's; performer, writer Children's TV Workshop, Sesame St., Electric Co.; animated cartoons Dyno-Mutt, ABC-TV, Roger Ramjet, Penelope Pitstop, Yogi Bear's Space Race, CBS, Capt. Caveman, Scooby's All-Stars, Space Heroes, NBC, 1980; appeared in films The Love Bug, Space Ghost, Prisoner of Second Ave., Hysterical, Last of the Secret Agents, The Green Hornet; regular performer Rowan and Martin's Laugh-In, 1968-73, Games People Play, 1980; TV host Gong Show, ABC-TV; host Monty Pythons Flying Circus; Chmn. Multiple Sclerosis dr., Los Angeles, 1972; chmn., grand marshall So. Calif. Diabetes drive, 1974-80; mem. nat. com. Juvenile Diabetes Assn., Am. Diabetes Assn.; mayor of Encino (Calif.); radio-TV adv. bd. Pasadena (Calif.) City Coll.; bd. govs. Grammy awards, Emmy awards; adv. bd. Sugar Ray Robinson Youth Found.; telecommunications adv. bd. U. So. Calif. Sch. Journalism. Named Outstanding Radio Personality in U.S. 9 times, Billboard mag. poll and Nat. Gavin poll, 1962-80; World's Best Radio Personality, Billboard Internat. Radio Forum, 1977; named Among Top Two TV Announcers, Radio-TV Daily; Outstanding Citizen of Los Angeles, All-Cities Employee Assn., Man of Yr., Encino B'nai B'rith, 1978; recipient Disting. Service award Hollywood Jaycees, award Los Angeles County bd. suprs.; named to Conquistidores, also Hollywood Hall of Fame; recipient star on Hollywood's Walk of Fame, 1982; honored by mayor Los Angeles, U.S. Treasury Dept., Calif. Hwy. Patrol, Boy Scouts Am., Big Bros. Hon. mem. No. Calif. Cartoonists Assn. Author: Elephants, Grapes and Pickles, 11 edit., 1965; The Gary Owens What to Do While You're Holding the Phone Book, 3d edit., 1973; nat. columnist Radio and Records newspaper, 1978—, Daily News, 1981—. Rec. artist for MGM, ABC, Warner Bros., Epic, Decca rec. cos. Office: 6255 Sunset Blvd Suite 1920 Hollywood CA 90028

OWENS, KARIN LEE, investment counselor, lecturer; b. Blythe, Calif., June 17, 1951; d. Kennith Lee and Joy Sue (Murdock) Owens. B.A. in Sociology, Calif. State U.-Sacramento, 1974; M.A. in Counseling/Marriage/Family, U. San Francisco, 1979. Registered rep. Nat. Assn. Security Dealers; lic. agt. life/disability ins., variable annuities. Bookkeeper, Crocker Bank, Carmichael, Calif., 1971-72; saleswoman Xerox Corp., Sacramento, 1976-78; office mgr. Carolyn Evarts Curtis, M.S., Sacramento, 1978-79; account exec., investment counselor Equitec Securities Co., Sacramento, 1979—; cons., tchr., lectr. Bd. dirs. Sacramento Mental Health Assn., Multiple Sclerosis Soc. Named Rookie of Yr., Xerox Corp., 1977. Mem. Internat. Assn. Fin. Planners, AAUW, C. of C. (women's council), Sacramento Women's Network. Club: Zonta. Home: 2280 Hurley Way #44 Sacramento CA 95825 Office: Equitec Securities Co 1540 River Park Dr Suite 213 Sacramento CA 95815

OWENS, PATRICK FRANCIS, JR., educator; b. Waterbury, Conn., Feb. 25, 1935; s. Patrick Francis and Alice Augusta (Edwards) O.; student Northrop Inst. Tech., 1959, UCLA, 1971-72; m. Donna Lee Hunt, July 3, 1971; 1 son, Kirk Michael. Mechanic, Haglen Aircraft Motors, Glendale, Calif., 1959-60; Triumph Motorcycle distributor, Duarte, Calif., 1960-71; race mechanic Triumph, Duarte, 1960-66, service sch. instr., 1966-68, service mgr., 1968-71; instr. motorcycle repair Los Angeles Trade Tech. Coll., 1971—. Mem. San Gabriel Valley Taxpayers Assn., 1975-78; mem. com. to get Proposition 13 on ballot for Calif. State election, 1976-78. Served with U.S. Army, 1954-56. Recipient Cert. of Achievement, Los Angeles Trade-Tech., 1981. Mem. Calif. Vocat. Assn. (sec. 1979—), Am. Motorcyclist Assn., Am. Vocat. Assn. Republican. Roman Catholic. Club: Triumph Internat. Owners. Author: Motorcycle Mechanics Workbook, 1972, 73; contbr. articles to profl. jours. Office: 400 W Washington Blvd Los Angeles CA 90015

OWENS, VICKI LEE, communication company executive; b. Long Beach, Calif., Aug. 23, 1950; d. Robert Glenn and Mavis LaVonne Owens. A.A., Cypress Coll., 1972; B.A., U. So. Calif., 1974, M.A., 1975, postgrad., 1983—. Elem. sch. specialist and women's swim coach Cypress (Calif.) Coll., 1975-79; lectr. Calif. State U.-Long Beach, 1978-80; acting pres. Cal-Tel Constrn. Inc., 1979-80; mgr. Burnup & Sims Inc., Pomona, Calif., 1980-81; pres. Tri-Communications Inc., Huntington Beach, Calif., 1981—; officer OGS Enterprises Inc., 1978. Named Outstanding Phys. Educator, Cypress Sch. Dist., 1976; Outstanding Grad. in Phys. Edn., Cypress Coll., 1972. Mem. Internat. Communication Assn., AAHPER, NOW.

OWINGS, BENJAMIN FRANKLIN, JR., oil company executive, geophysicist; b. Little Rock, July 1, 1919; s. Benjamin Franklin and Mary Lou (Brewster) O.; m. Mary Ann Mugford, Feb. 20, 1943; children—Diann Owings Warren, Mike, Steve. B.S. in Physics, U. Tex., 1941. Seismic field party chief Nat. Geophys. Co., Dallas, 1943-50; staff geophysicist Honolulu Oil Co., 1950-54; supr. Continental Geophys. Co., Midland, Tex., 1954-56; div. geophysicist Forest Oil Corp., Midland, 1956-72; cons. geophysicist, 1972-76; mgr. Anschutz Corp., Denver, 1976-81; gen. ptnr. Banner Oil and Gas Co., Denver, 1981—. Home: 3400 Kipling Dr Wheat Ridge CO 80033 Office: Banner Oil and Gas Co 555 17th St Suite 3565 Denver CO 80202

OWNBEY, VIRGINIA KAY, architect; b. Miami, Okla., June 2, 1946; d. Hal Norwood and Mary Virginia (Williams) Buchanan; B.Arch., Okla. State U., 1970; m. Charles Lewis Ownbey, Aug. 11, 1974; children—Christine Vanessa, Wade Preston. Archtl. draftsperson Frank L. Hope & Assos., Santa Ana, Calif., 1970-73, Am. Devel. Corp., Torrance, Calif., 1973-74, J. Ward Dawson, AIA, Tustin, Calif., 1975-76; architect Archi & Tekton, Newport Beach, Calif., 1977-79; individual practice architecture, Tustin, 1979—. Lic. pilot; real estate salesperson, Okla. Nat. Endowment Arts grantee, 1969. Mem. Women's Archtl. League Orange County. Mem. Reformed Ch. in Am. Address: 489 Country Hill Rd Anaheim Hills CA 92807

OXNER, EDWIN STORY, semicondr. mfg. co. exec.; b. Chgo., Mar. 28, 1928; s. Edwin Kaulbach and Sarah Ellen (Story) O.; B.S. in Elec. Engring., Tri-State U., 1948; diploma in Near Eastern Studies, Moody Bible Inst., 1959; m. Carol Ann Rothenberg, Jan. 14, 1950; children—Cynthia Oxner Peck, Sheila Oxner Johnston, Todd, Peter. Employee, U.S. Civil Service, 1948-52; sr. research engr. Trans-Sonics, Inc., 1952-54; sr. engr. Hughes Aircraft Co., 1954-56; mem. tech. staff Armour Research Found., 1956-59; engring. supr. Varian Assocs., 1959-63; mem. tech. staff Fairchild Semicondr., 1963-64; field engring. mgr. Melabs, Palo Alto, Calif., 1964-69; application mgr. Intradyne Systems Co., Sunnyvalle, Calif., 1969-70; with Siliconix Inc., Santa Clara, Calif., 1970—, mgr. spl. projects engring., 1976-78, mem. tech. engring. staff, 1978—; tech. adv. Am. Radio Relay League, 1979—. Mem. IEEE (Sr.), Joint Electron Device Engring. Com. Author: (with others) Designing with Field-Effect Transistors, 1981; Power FETs and their Applications, 1982; Editorial rev. bd. RF Design mag.; contbr. articles to electronics jours. Patentee. Home: 1337 Glen Haven Dr San Jose CA 95129 Office: 2201 Laurelwood Rd Santa Clara CA 95054

OZANICH, CHARLES GEORGE, real estate broker; b. Fayette County, Pa. Aug. 11, 1933; s. Paul Anthony and Alma Bertha (Sablotne) O.; student Am. River Coll., Sierra Coll.; m. Betty Sue Carman, Feb. 20, 1955; children—Viki Lynn, Terri Sue, Charles Anthony, Nicole Lee. Owner, broker Terrace Realty, Grass Valley, Calif., 1971—. Mem. Grass Valley Rescue Squad, 1965-78, Grass Valley Vol. Fire Dept., 1965—. Served with USAF, 1951-55; Korea. Decorated Bronze Star with three oak leaf clusters. Mem. Neveda County Bd. Realtors (dir. 1973-74). Clubs: Masons, Shriners, Elks, Lions, Moose. Home: 15053 Chinook Ln Grass Valley CA 95945 Office: 10113 Alta Sierra Dr Grass Valley CA 95945

OZAWA, TERUTOMO, economist, educator; b. Yokohama, Japan, Jan. 17, 1935; s. Hanjiro and Tsuro (Teramura) O.; m. Hiroko Ozawa, Nov. 4, 1967. B.A., Tokyo U., 1958; M.B.A., Columbia U., 1962, Ph.D., 1966. Vis. research assoc. Center for Policy Alternatives, MIT, Cambridge, 1975-76; prof. econs. Colo. State U., Ft. Collins, 1974—; vis. scholar dept. econs. and politics Cambridge U., Eng., 1982—; cons. World Bank, UN Inst. for Tng. and Research, UN Econs. and Social Commn. for Asia and the Pacific, Orgn. Econ. Coop. and Devel. UN Center Transnat. Corps. Mem. Am. Econ. Assn. Author: Japan's Technological Challenge to the West, 1950-1974, 1974; Multinationalism, Japanese Style, 1979; contbr. articles to profl. jours. Office: Colo State U Fort Collins CO 80523

OZZELLO, JAMES MICHAEL, labor representative; b. Trinidad, Colo., Aug. 31, 1931; s. Michael and Josephine Louise (Bianco) O.; m. Shirley Louise Reid, Jan. 19, 1952; m. 2d, Carol Ann Ligon, Nov. 7, 1981; children—Kathleen Ruehlen, Mark, Thomas, Sharon, Michele Ruehlen. Student Pueblo Coll., 1956-59. Troubleman So. Colo. Power Co., Pueblo, 1959-68, bus. mgr. Internat. Brotherhood Elec. Workers, Local 667, 1968—. Bd. dirs. Bd. Coop. Edn. Services, Pueblo, 1976-80; mem. exec. com. Colo. State Democratic Party, 1974-81; chmn. state Rural Electric assns. apprenticeship program, 1976-79; 4-H leader, 1973-81; chmn. labor com. United Way, 1972. Served to sgt. USMC, 1951-54. Roman Catholic. Home: 19149 Heritage Hills Dr Brookeville MD 20833 Office: 818 E 4th St Pueblo CO 81003

PACELA, ALLAN FRED, publishing company executive; b. Chgo., Oct. 5, 1938; s. John Paul and Eleanor (Sorge) P.; B.S. in E.E., MIT, 1960, M.S., 1962; cert. small bus. mgmt. UCLA, 1968; Sc.D., Ind. No. U., 1971; m. Donna Lee Mulchaey, Nov. 25, 1961; children—Elizabeth, David, John. Sr. scientist Lear-Siegler Med. Physics Lab., Santa Monica, Calif., 1963-64; chief research scientist Physiol. Instrumentation, Beckman Instruments, Inc., Fullerton, Calif., 1964-72; pres., gen. mgr. Intersci. Tech. Corp., Brea, Calif., 1972—; editor/pub. Newsletter of Biomed. Safety & Standards, Biomed. Tech. Info. Service, Jour. Clin. Engring., Clin. Lab. Letter, Radiology Letter, Quest Pub. Co., Brea, 1970—; cons. in field. Recipient Outstanding award, Ill. Jr. Acad. Sci., 1956. Mem. Assn. for Advancement of Med. Instrumentation, IEEE. Author: Guide to Biomedical Standards, 1982, others; contbr. articles to profl. jours.; patentee in field. Address: 1351 Titan Way Brea CA 92621

PACKARD, DAVID, mfg. co. exec., elec. engr., former dep. sec. defense; b. Pueblo, Colo., Sept. 7, 1912; s. Sperry Sidney and Ella Lorna (Graber) P.; A.B., Stanford U., 1934, E.E., 1939; LL.D. (hon.), U. Calif., Santa Cruz, 1966, Catholic U., 1970, Pepperdine U., 1972; D.Sc. (hon.), Colorado Coll., 1964; Litt.D. (hon.), So. Colo. State Coll., 1973; D.Eng.(hon.), U. Notre Dame, 1974; m. Lucile Salter, Apr. 8, 1938; children—David Woodley, Nancy Ann Packard Burnett, Susan Packard Orr, Julie Elizabeth. With vacuum tube engring. dept. Gen. Electric Co., Schenectady, 1936-38; co-founder, partner Hewlett-Packard Co., Palo Alto, Calif., 1939-46, pres., 1947-64, chmn. bd., 1964-68, 72—, chief exec. officer, 1964-68; dep. sec. defense, Washington, 1969-71; dir. Caterpillar Tractor Co., 1972—, Standard Oil Co. of Calif., 1972—, The Boeing Co., 1978—. Mem. Palo Alto Bd. Edn., 1947-56; mem. President's Commn. Personnel Interchange, 1972-74, Trilateral Commn., 1973-81; chmn. bd. regents Uniformed Services U. of Health Scis., 1974-82; mem. U.S.-USSR Trade and Econ. Council, 1974; bd. dirs. Santa Clara (Calif.) County Mfrs. Group, 1978—; mem. bd. overseers Hoover Instn., 1972—, mem. com. on sci. and tech., 1975-82; bd. dirs. Nat. Merit Scholarship Corp., 1963-69, Found. for Study of Presidential and Congressional Terms, 1978—, Alliance to Save Energy, 1977—, Atlantic Council, 1972—, vice chmn., 1972-83; bd. dirs. Am. Enterprise Inst. for Public Policy Research, 1978—, Wolf Trap Found., Vienna, Va.; trustee Herbert Hoover Found., 1974—, Colo. Coll., 1966-69, U.S. Churchill Found., 1965-69; trustee Stanford U., 1954-69, pres. bd. trustees, 1958-60; mem. Com. on Present Danger, 1975-81; chmn. U.S.-Japan Adv. Commn., 1983—; chmn. Calif. Nature Conservancy, 1983—. Decorated Grand Cross of Merit, Fed. Republic of Germany, 1972; recipient numerous awards including: Medal of Honor, Electronic Industries Assn., 1974, Silver Helmet Defense award AMVETS, 1973, Washington award Western Soc. Engrs., 1975, Hoover medal ASME, 1975, Gold Medal award Nat. Football Found. and Hall of Fame, 1975, Good Scout award Boy Scouts Am., 1975, Vermilye medal Franklin Inst., 1976, Internat. Achievement award World Trade Club of San Francisco, 1976, Merit award Am. Consulting Engrs. Council Fellows, 1977, Achievement in Life award Ency. Britannica, 1977, Engring. Award of Distinction, San Jose State U., 1980. Fellow IEEE (Founders medal 1973); mem. Nat. Acad. Engring. (Founders award 1979), Instrument Soc. Am. (hon. mem.), Calif. C. of C. (dir. 1962-78), Am. Mgmt. Assn. (dir. 1956-59, v.p. Calif. 1959-69), Wilson Council, Santa Clara County Mfrs. Group (vice chmn.), Calif. Roundtable (founding vice chmn.), Bus. Roundtable Advt. Council, Bus. Council, Am. Ordnance Assn. (Crozier Gold medal 1970), Am. Electronics Assn. (co-founder, past chmn.), Sigma Xi, Phi Beta Kappa, Tau Beta Pi, Alpha Delta Phi (named Disting. Alumnus of Yr. 1970). Clubs: Bohemian, Commonwealth, Pacific Union, Engrs. (San Francisco); Exec. (Chgo.); The Links (N.Y.C.); Alfalfa, Capitol Hill (Washington); California (Los Angeles). Office: Hewlett-Packard Co 3000 Hanover St Palo Alto CA 94304

PACKARD, JOHN WILLIAM, JR., hosp. adminstr.; b. Columbus, Ohio, Dec. 21, 1945; s. John William and France Iola (Ingram) P.; B.S., Ohio State U., 1968; M.H.A., Washington U., 1975; m. Sharon Wagner, June 21, 1969; children—Mason, Megan. Adminstrv. resident Kaiser Found. Med. Center, Walnut Creek, Calif., 1975; asst. adminstr. Valley Children's Hosp., Fresno, Calif., 1975-78; adminstr. Victor Valley Community Hosp., Victorville, Calif., 1978-79; adminstr. Ontario (Calif.) Community Hosp., 1980—; with Nat. Med. Enterprises, 1978—; mem. med. adv. panel Calif. Inst. for Women. Active United Way; bd. dirs. Boys/Girls Club. Served with USAF, 1968-72. Mem. Health Care Execs. So. Calif., Am. Coll. Hosp. Adminstrs., Ontario C. of C. (dir.). Club: Rotary. Office: 550 N Monterey Ontario CA 91764

PACKARD, RONALD C., congressman, dentist; b. Meridian, Idaho, Jan. 19, 1931; s. Forrest LeRoy and Esther (Carter) P.; m. Roma Jean Sorenson, July 18, 1952; children—Chris, Debre, Jeff, Vicki, Scott, Lisa, Theresa. Student Brigham Young U., Portland State U.; D.M.D., U. Oreg., 1957. Gen. practice dentistry, Carlsbad, Calif., 1959—; officer Packard Devel. Corp., Carlsbad, 1965—; mem. 98th Congress from 43d dist. Calif.; vice chmn., dir. First Nat. Bank of North County, 1981—. Trustee Carlsbad Unified Sch. Dist., 1962-74, chmn., 1968-69, 72-74; dir. North County Transit Dist., 1978-82; mayor City of Carlsbad, 1978-82. Served to lt. USN, 1957-59. Mem. Carlsbad C. of C. (dir. 1972-76), Calif. League of Cities, San Diego Assn. Govts. (dir. 1980-82), ADA, Calif. Dental Soc., San Diego County Dental Soc. Republican. Mormon.

PACKER, MARK BARRY, lawyer; b. Phila., Sept. 18, 1944; s. Samuel and Eve (Devine) P.; B.A. magna cum laude, Harvard U., 1965, LL.B., 1968; m. Donna Elizabeth Ferguson, July 2, 1967; children—Daniel Joshua, Benjamin Dov, David Johannes. Admitted to Wash. bar, 1969, Mass. bar, 1971; assoc. Ziontz, Pirtle & Fulle, Seattle, 1968-70; ptnr. Millhouse Nelle & Packer, Bellingham, Wash., 1972-82, partner Packer & Swenson, Bellingham, 1982—; dir. various corps., trustee pension, profit-sharing plans. Mem. Bellingham Planning and Devel. Commn., 1975—, chmn., 1977-81; pres. v.p. Congregation Beth Israel, Bellingham, 1980-82; chmn. Bellingham campaign United Jewish Appeal, 1979—. Recipient Blood Donor award ARC, 1979. Mem. ABA (sec. urban, state and local govt. law, commn. land use, planning and zoning), Wash. State Bar Assn. Republican. Home: 208 S Forest St Bellingham WA 98225 Office: 322 N Commercial St Suite 402 Bellingham WA 98225

PACKWOOD, BOB, U.S. senator; b. Portland, Oreg., Sept. 11, 1932; s. Fred W. and Gladys (Taft) P.; B.A., Willamette U., 1954; LL.B., N.Y. U., 1957; LL.D. (hon.), Yeshiva U., 1982, Gallaudet Coll., 1983; m. Georgie Ann Oberteuffer, Nov. 25, 1964; children—William Henderson, Shyla. Admitted to Oreg. bar, 1957; practiced in Portland, 1958-68; mem. Oreg. Ho. of Reps., 1962-68; U.S. senator from Oreg., 1968—, chmn. commerce, sci. and transp. com., mem. fin., commerce, small bus. coms. Named Jr. 1st Citizen Portland, 1966, 1 of 3 Outstanding Young Men, 1967; Oreg. Speaker of Year, 1968; recipient Arthur T. Vanderbilt public service award N.Y. U. Law Sch., 1969; Golden Bullfrog award Nat. Assn. Businessmen, 1970; Oreg. Brotherhood award B'nai B'rith Anti-Defamation League, 1970; NW Steelheaders award, 1971; Torch of Liberty award Portland Anti-Defamation League, 1971; Oreg. Man of Year award Nat. Fedn. Ind. Businessmen, 1971; Richard L. Neuberger award Oreg. Environ. Council, 1972; Outstanding Public Service award Portland U. Judaism, 1973; Lumberman of Year award, 1974; Nat. Forest Products' Monongahela Forestry Leadership award, 1976; Jonathan Netanyahu award Am. Friends of Jonathan Inst., Jerusalem, 1978; Margaret Sanger award Planned Parenthood Fedn. Am., 1979; Leadership award Oreg. Solar Lobby/Energy Coalition, 1980; Solar Man of Yr. award Solar Energy Industries Assn., 1980; Guardian of Small Bus. award Nat. Fedn. Ind. Bus., 1980; Forester of Yr. award Western Forest Industries Assn. and N.W. Timber Assn., 1980; Golden Spike award Nat. Assn. Ry. Passengers, 1981; Tom McCall award Oreg. Assn. Broadcasters, 1981; Tree of Life award Jewish Nat. Fund, 1982; award Am.-Israel C. of C. and Industry, 1982; William A. Steiger award Nat. Venture Capital Assn., 1983; Religious Freedom award Religious Coalition for Abortion Rights, 1983; others. Office: 259 Russell Office Bldg Washington DC 20510

PADGETT, REGINALD LYNN, industrial psychologist, researcher, educator, consultant; b. Lynchburg, Va., Nov. 18, 1950; s. James Alfred and Bessie Louise (Watson) P.; m. Cathy Marie Eades, April 14, 1975 (div.); 1 dau., Natalie Lynn. B.A. in Psychology, U. Richmond, 1976; M.A. in Developmental Psychology, U. Md., College Park, 1978. Endorsement in psychology, Va., 1976. Correctional psychologist Va. Dept. of Corrections, Richmond, 1976; instr. VA Rehab. Sch. Authority, Richmond, 1976-77; family planning research specialist Capital Systems Group, Inc., Rockville, Md., 1978; sr. research assoc. Biotechnology, Inc., Falls Church, Va., 1978-79; engr. psychologist Lockheed Missiles & Space Co., Sunnyvale, Calif., 1980; indsl. psychologist Westinghouse Electric Corp., Sunnyvale 1980—; cons. Health and Human Services, Nat. Clearinghouse for Family Planning Info. Served with U.S. Navy, 1972-75. Recipient Nat. Def. Service Medal; Nat. Ruritan Citizenship awardee, 1964. Mem. Am. Psychol. Assn., Western Psychol. Assn., Human Factors Soc., Psz Chi. Democrat. Lutheran. Contbr. articles in field to profl. jours., publs.

PADILLA, CHARLES EDWARD, hospital administrator; b. Springer, N.Mex., Nov. 7, 1957; s. Ofelio and Regina Emma (Cruz) P. B.B.A., U. N.Mex., 1979; M.P.H., UCLA, 1981. Residence hall advisor U. N.Mex., Albuquerque, 1977-79, conf. dir. housing dept., 1978; personnel adminstrv. intern Lovelace Research Inst., Albuquerque, 1979; adminstrv. resident St. Joseph Med. Center, Burbank, Calif., 1980-81; budget dir. St. John's Hosp., Santa Monica, Calif., 1981—, treas., bd. dirs. St. John's Fed. Credit Union, 1982—. Vol. CPR instr. ARC, Am. Heart Assn., 1977—; mem. choir St. Charles Cath. Ch., North Hollywood, Calif., 1981—. Mem. Am. Coll. Hosp. Adminstrs. Office: 1328 22d St Santa Monica CA 90404

PADILLA, JOSE RAMON, aerospace electronics design engineer, publisher; b. Silverton, Colo., Feb. 11, 1938; s. Primitivo P. and Rosario M. (Mascareñas) P.; m. Wanda M. Schmitz, May 25, 1974; 1 son, Ramon; children by previous marriage—Patrick, Kirt, Sterling, Brook. B.S.E.E., UCLA, 1966; postgrad. U. So. Calif., 1966-69. Design engr. Collins Radio Co., Newport Beach, Calif., 1966-67; Jet Propulsion Lab, Pasadena, Calif., 1967-69; sr. design engr. Martin Marietta Corp., Denver, 1969—, project engr. Galileo Atmosphere Structure Instrument, 1978-83. Co-founder LA VOZ Hispana de Colo. newspaper. Mem. Latin C. of C. (charter; dir.), Colo. Minority Engring. Assn. (dir., charter), Soc. Hispanic Profl. Engrs. Patentee in field. Home: 668 S Logan St Denver CO 80209 Office: LA VOZ Hispana De Colo 812 Santa Fe Dr Denver CO 80204

PADULA, FRED DAVID, filmmaker; b. Santa Barbara, Calif., Oct. 25, 1937; s. Fred and Mary (Adams) P.; B.A. in Music, San Francisco State U., M.A. in Art, 1965; 1 child. One-man shows in photography at San Francisco Mus. Modern Art, Kalamazoo Inst. Arts, DeYoung Young Mus. (San Francisco), San Fernando Valley State Coll., Bekersfield Wash. State U., George Eastman House; represented in permanent collections at Kalamazoo Inst. Arts, State of Calif., George Eastman House, Crocker Art Mus., Oakland Mus. Art; artist-in-residence U. Minn., Mpls.; adj. faculty U. Calif., San Francisco Art Inst., San Francisco State U.; filmmaker Ephesus, 1965 (1st pl. award San Francisco Internat. Film Festival, recognition award N.Y. Film Festival, Chgo. Internat. Film Festival, others), The Artist Speaks, Two Photographers: Wynn Bullock and Imogen Cunningham, Little Jesus (Hippy Hill), Anthology of Boats, David and My Porch, Salmon River Run, El Capitan (grand prize, 26th Film festival International du Film D'Aventure Vecue, France; Filmfestival Internazional Montagna Esplorazione, Italy; Gold medal Festival Internat. du Film Alpine, Switzerland; Internat. Bergfilme Munchen, W. Ger.; Grand prize Banff Festival of Mountain Films, Can.; Grand prize Mountain film, Can.). Electronic music composer: Come Forth to Tell, Gregorian Chant, Clarinet Loops, Barking Dogs. Address: 47 Shell Rd Mill Valley CA 94941

PAGE, THOMAS ALEXANDER, utility exec.; b. Niagara Falls, N.Y., Mar. 24, 1933; B.S. in Civil Engring., Purdue U., 1955, M.S. in Indsl. Adminstrn., 1963; m. Evelyn Rainnie, July 16, 1960; children—Christopher, Catherine. Comptroller, treas. Wis. Power & Light Co., Madison, 1970-73; treas. Gulf States Utilities Co., Beaumont, Tex., 1973-75, sr. v.p. fin., 1975, exec. v.p., 1975-78, also dir.; exec. v.p., chief operating officer San Diego Gas & Electric Co., San Diego, 1978-81, pres., chief exec. officer, 1981—, chmn. bd., 1983—, dir., 1978—. Mem. Dane County Bd. Suprs. (Wis.), 1968-72. Served to capt. USAF, 1955-57. Registered profl. engr., N.Y. C.P.A., Wis., Tex. Home: 1904 Hidden Crest Dr El Cajon CA 92020 Office: 101 Ash St San Diego CA 92112

PAGE, THOMAS LEE, research and development manager; b. Lima, Ohio, Mar. 5, 1941; s. Harold Alan and Hazel Chole (Harris) P.; m. Wilma Louise Pfister, Aug. 24, 1963; children—Alan, Stephanie. B.A., Ohio No. U., 1963; M.A., Kent State U., 1966, Ph.D. (grad. student award), 1971; post doctoral fellow Wash. U., 1970-72. Sr. research scientist Battelle NW, Richland, Wash., 1972-77, assoc. sec. mgr. freshwater scis., 1977-79, mgr. applied ecology sect., 1979—. Mem. Am. Inst. Fish Research Biology, Am. Soc. Limnology and Oceanography, Ecol. Soc. Am., Am. Inst. Biol. Scis., AAAS, Soc. Internat. Limnology, Ohio Acad. Sci., Am. Fish Soc., NW Sci. Assn., Alaska Acad. Engring. and Sci., Sigma Xi. Office: Battelle NW PO Box 999 Richland WA 99352

PAGET, JOHN ARTHUR, mech. engr.; b. Ft. Frances, Ont., Can., Sept. 15, 1922; s. John and Ethel (Bishop) P.; B.Applied Sci., Toronto, 1946; m. Vicenta Herrera Nunez, Dec. 16, 1963; children—Cynthia Ellen, Kevin Arthur, Keith William. Chief draftsman Gutta Percha & Rubber, Ltd., Toronto, Ont., 1946-49; chief draftsman Viceroy Mfg. Co., Toronto, 1949-52; supr., design engr. C.D. Howe Co. Ltd., Montreal, Que., Can., 1952-58, sr. design engr. Combustion Engring., Montreal, 1958-59; sr. staff engr. Gen. Atomic, Inc., La Jolla, 1959-81. Mem. ASME, Am. Inst. Plant Engrs., Soc. Mfg. Engrs., Profl. Engrs. Ont., Soc. for History Tech., Inst. Mech. Engrs., Soc. Am. Mil. Engrs., Newcomen Soc., Brit. Nuclear Energy Soc. Patentee in field. Home: 3183 Magellan St San Diego CA 92154 Office: PO Box 427 Nestor CA 92053

PAGLIN, MORTON, economist, educator; b. N.Y.C., Feb. 15, 1922; s. Benjamin and Dora (Mandel) P.; m. Joan Betty Curtice, Jan. 28, 1949; children—Catherine, Mark, Laura. B.A., U. Miami, Fla., 1943; Ph.D. in Econs., U. Calif.-Berkeley, 1956. Economist inter-industry econs. U.S. Bureau Labor Statis., 1950-53; asst. prof. U. Calif.-Berkeley, 1957-61, research assoc. population and urban research, 1963-65; assoc. prof. econs. Portland (Oreg.) State U., 1961-66, prof., 1966—. Ford Found. fellow in econs., 1967-68; Hoover Instn. Stanford U. fellow, 1977-78. Mem. Am. Econs. Assn. Contbr. articles to profl. jours. Home: 3435 N W Thurman Portland OR 97210 Office: Dept of Economics Portland State U Portland OR 97207

PAGTER, CARL RICHARD, lawyer; b. Balt., Feb. 13, 1934; s. Charles Ralph and Mina (Amelung) P.; m. Linda Wolfard; children—Cameron Roger, Corbin Christopher; m. 2d, Judith Elaine Cox, May 6, 1978. Student Diablo Valley Coll., Concord, Calif., 1953; B.A., San Jose State U., 1956; LL.B., U. Calif., 1964. Bar: Calif. 1965, D.C. 1977, U.S. Supreme Ct. 1976. Law clk. Kaiser Industries Corp., Oakland, Calif., 1963-64, counsel, 1964-70, assoc. counsel, Washington, 1970-73, counsel, Oakland, 1973-75, dir. govt. affairs, Washington, 1975-76; v.p., sec., gen counsel Kaiser Cement Corp., Oakland, 1976—. Served with USNR 1957-61, comdr. Res. ret. Mem. ABA, Fed. Bar Assn., Alameda County Bar Assn., Am. Folklore Soc., Calif. Folklore Soc., Calif. Bluegrass Assn. (founder), Republican. Club: Univ. (Washington); Oakland Athletic. Author (with A. Dundes): Urban Folklore from the Paperwork Empire, 1975. Home: 1809 Meadow Ln Walnut Creek CA 94595 Office: 300 Lakeside Dr Oakland CA 94612

PAI, (GURUPUR) PUNDA, city official; b. Managlore, India, Jan. 9, 1946; came to U.S., 1972, naturalized, 1981; s. Gurupur M. and Radha M. (Shenoy) P.; m. Padmini P. Mallya, Dec. 28, 1974; children—Amar, Ajeet. B.S. in Civil Engring., Kerala U., 1969; M. Regional and

Community Planning, Kans. State U., 1974; postgrad. U. Wyo. Sch. Bus., 1982—. Registered profl. engr., Wyo. Sr. planner Greater S.W. Regional Planning Commn., Garden City, Kans., 1974-77; sr. planner City of Cheyenne (Wyo.), 1977-79, civil engr./dir. zoning, 1979-82; asst. utility dir. Casper (Wyo.) Bd. Pub. Utilities, 1982—; study group leader in urban pub. works adminstrn., Casper, 1983. Mem. Am. Water Works Assn., ASCE. Democrat. Hindu. Office: Casper Bd Pub Utilities 200 N David St Casper WY 82601

PAINE, MARSHA MATTSON, interior designer; b. Topeka, Nov. 25, 1946; d. Roy Albert and Dorothy (Mattson) M.; m. Thomas Bradley Paine, June 5, 1971. B.S., Iowa State U., 1968. Designer, Wm. Ruge and Assocs., Omaha, 1968-70; designer Dayton-Hudson Corp., Mpls., 1970-72; prin. Marsha Paine Interiors, La Jolla, Calif., 1973—; owner Nettle Creek Shop, La Mesa and La Jolla, Calif., 1973—; cons., lectr. Mem. San Diego Hist. Soc., Am. Soc. Interior Designers (pres. chpt. 1982-83). Republican. Contbr. features to mags. Office: 8657 Villa La Jolla Dr La Jolla CA 92041

PAINE, MARTHA ANN, telephone company executive; b. N.Y.C., Dec. 15, 1948; d. Richard and Marie (Daniele) Paine. B.A. in Econs., U. Denver, 1970, M.A. in Econs., 1971, M.B.A., 1981. 1971, Staff supr. ops. planning and control AT&T Long Lines, Phoenix, 1971-72, ops. supr. interstate transmission facilities, Phoenix, 1972-73, mgr. engring. planning, San Francisco, 1973-74, product mgr. Dataphone Service, Bedminster, N.J., 1975-77, ops. mgr. spl. services planning, Bedminster, 1977, mktg. mgr. nat. accounts long lines Western region, Denver, 1977-79; dist. staff mgr. market mix planning Mountain Bell, Denver, 1979-80, dist. mgr. residence mktg. ops. planning, 1980-81, dist. mgr. market mgmt. comml. sector, 1981, dist. staff mgr. divesture planning, 1981-82, asst. treas., 1983—. Mem. Colo. Cash Mgmt. Assn., Nat. Assn. Exec. Women, Assn. M.B.A. Execs., Denver Soc. Bus. Economists. Office: 931 14th St Room 1100 Denver CO 80202

PAINE, ROGER WARDE, JR., naval officer; b. Austin, Tex., Aug. 13, 1917; s. Roger Warde and Corine (Malone) P.; B.S. in E.E., U.S. Naval Acad., 1939; M.S. in Nuclear Physics, M.I.T., 1949; postgrad. Naval War Coll., 1956-57; m. Isla Rea Vaile, June 1, 1941; children—Roger Warde, III, Isla Rea Paine Moore, Barbara Jean Paine Cramer. Commd. ensign, U.S. Navy, 1939, advanced through grades to rear adm., 1967; comdr. attack carrier strike group U.S.S. Shangri-La and U.S.S. Saratoga, 1967; dir. Navy Info. Systems Div., Washington, 1968-70; comdr. Tng. Command, U.S. Pacific Fleet, 1970-73, ret., 1974; tech. cons. Los Alamos Sci. Lab., 1953—; cons. fields nuclear weaponry and missile guidance, 1953—. Mem. Am. Phys. Soc., Am. Inst. Physics, U.S. Naval Inst., Navy League U.S., Disabled Am. Vets., Submarine Vets. World War II, U.S. Golf Assn. Republican. Episcopalian. Club: Miramar Men's Golf. Editor-in-chief Joint Service Manual: The Effects of Nuclear Weapons, 1953-56. Home: 1756 Circo Del Cielo El Cajon CA 92020

PAINE, THOMAS OTTEN, technology consultant; b. Berkeley, Calif., Nov. 9, 1921; s. George Thomas and Ada Louise (Otten) P.; A.B. in Engring., Brown U., 1942, Dr. Sci. (hon.), 1969; M.S. in Phys. Metallurgy, Stanford U., 1947, Ph.D., 1949; Dr. Sci. (hon.), Clarkson Coll. Tech., 1969, Nebr. Wesleyan U., 1970, N.B. U., 1970, Oklahoma City U., 1970; Dr. Engring. (hon.), Worcester Poly. Inst., 1970, Cheng Kung U., 1978; m. Barbara Helen Taunton Pearse, Oct. 1, 1946; children—Marguerite Ada, George Thomas, Judith Janet, Frank Taunton. Research asso. Stanford U., 1947-49; with Gen. Electric Co., 1949-68, Gen. Electric Research Lab., Schenectady, N.Y., 1970-76, mgr. center advanced studies, Santa Barbara, Calif., 1963-68, v.p., group exec. power generation, 1970-73, sr. v.p. tech. planning and devel., 1973-76; dep. adminstr. NASA, 1968-69, adminstr., 1969-70; pres., chief operating officer Northrop Corp., Los Angeles, 1976-82; chmn. Thomas Paine Assocs., Los Angeles, 1982—. Trustee Occidental Coll., Harvey Mudd Coll., Asian Inst. Tech., Bangkok, Thailand; chmn., United Way Campaign, 1979-80, 80-81, Nat. Alliance Bus., 1979-81, Pacific Forum, 1980—. Served to lt. USNR, World War II. Recipient Disting. Service medal NASA, 1970; Washington award Western Soc. Engrs., 1972; John Fritz medal United Engring. Soc., 1976; Faraday medal Inst. Elec. Engrs. (London), 1976. Fellow AIAA; mem. Nat. Acad. Engring., N.Y. Acad. Scis., Am. Phys. Soc., IEEE, Inst. Strategic Studies (London), U.S. Navy Inst., Sigma Xi. Democrat. Episcopalian. Clubs: Sky, Lotos (N.Y.C.); Army and Navy, Space, Cosmos (Washington); California, Regency (Los Angeles). Author: Submarining, 1971. Contbr. articles to profl. jours. Patentee in field. Home: 765 Bonhill Rd Los Angeles CA 90049 Office: Thomas Paine Assocs 10880 Wilshire Blvd Suite 2011 Los Angeles CA 90024

PAINTER, ARIS ADELAIDE, nursing administrator; b. Waynesburg, Pa., June 19, 1938; d. John Thomas and Gretchen Alberta (Yunker) Black; m. Phillip Stephen Painter, Dec. 16, 1956; children—Karen, Cathy, Connie. A.A., Chaffey Coll., 1960; B.A., Linfield Coll., 1978. Staff med./surg. nurse Mt. San Antonio Hosp., Upland, Calif., 1964-65; staff nurse obstetrics Emanuel Hosp., Portland, Oreg., 1965; staff nurse Gresham (Oreg.) Community Hosp., 1966-66, supr., 1966-75, dir. nursing, 1975-80, asst. adminstr. patient care services, 1980—. Bd. dirs. Corrine Chamberlain Found., 1981—, Am. Cancer Soc., 1979—; mem. planning com. City of Fairview (Oreg.), 1974-75; nursing adv. com. Mt. Hood Community Coll., 1976—; sponsor Campfire Internat., 1972-80. Mem. Am. Soc. Nursing Service Adminstrs., Oreg. Soc. Nursing Service Adminstrs, Oreg. League Nursing, Portland Council Nursing Adminstrs. and Educators, Nat. League for Nursing. Home: PO Box 305 Fairview OR 97024 Office: PO Box 718 Gresham OR 97030

PAINTER, JOEL HAROLD, clinical psychologist; b. Ashland, Ohio, July 3, 1936; s. Harold Dennis and Margaret Ruth (Stone) P.; student UCLA, 1959-60, Westmont Coll., 1954-57; B.S. with honors, Old Dominion U., 1967; Ph.D., Ariz. State U., 1972; m. Saundra Sue Brunn, Nov. 28, 1958; children—Daniel Joel, Jeremy Jon. Psychology intern Phoenix VA Hosp., 1969-71; staff psychologist drug treatment program Atlanta VA Hosp., 1971-74; coordinator drug dependence treatment program spinal cord injury service Long Beach (Calif.) VA Med. Center, 1974-80; chief mental health clinic VA Outpatient Clinic, Santa Barbara, Calif., 1980—; lectr. Calif. State U., Long Beach, 1979-80. Bd. dirs. Long Beach-Harbor-S.E. unit Am. Cancer Soc., 1976-80, Santa Barbara County unit, 1980—. Com. Served with AUS, 1961-64. Decorated Army Commendation Medal. Mem. Am. Psychol. Assn., Western Psychol. Assn., Internat. Acad. Nutritional Consultants (charter), Christian Businessmen's Com. Home: 6590 Camino Venturoso Goleta CA 93117 Office: VA Outpatient Clinic 4440 Calle Real Santa Barbara CA 93110

PAINTER, MICHAEL ROBERT, landscape architect; b. Los Angeles, Jan. 27, 1935; s. John G. and Lillians (Armour) P.; m. Susan Collins, Jan. 3, 1959; children—Melissa Ann, Joshua Michael. B.S. in Landscape Architecture, U. Calif.-Berkeley, 1956; M. Landscape Architecture in Urban Design, Harvard U., 1966. Designer, Lawrence Halprin & Assocs., San Francisco, 1956-58; with John Carl Warnecke & Assocs., San Francisco, 1958-69, ptnr., 1963-69; pres. Michael Painter & Assocs., San Francisco, 1969—; works include: gravesite John F. Kennedy, Arlington Cemetery, 1966, Blair House garden, Washington, 1970, Hennepin County Govt. Center, Mpls., 1975, Hewlett-Packard Corp. Hdqrs., Palo Alto, Calif., 1981, Great Hwy./Ocean Beach Plan, San Francisco, 1981, P.T&T Corporate Adminstrv. Complex, San Roman, Calif., 1981. Chmn. urban design and open space com. San Francisco Planning and Urban Renewal Assn., 1971—; pres. Friends of Recreation and Parks, 1980. Sr. warden St. Stephens Ch., Belvedere Calif. Served with USNR, 1953-61. Recipient Barlow Meml. Design award U. Calif.-Berkeley, 1956, 1st award Am. Assn. Nurserymen, 1965, 66, 67, 72, 74. Mem. Am. Soc. Landscape Architects (v.p. No. Calif. shpt. 1970-71, Honor award 1966, 67, 70, 81, 82, Merit award 1966, 68, 81, 82). Clubs: Sierra, Olympic (San Francisco). Office: 562 Mission St San Francisco CA 94105

PAKE, GEORGE EDWARD, research exec., physicist; b. Jeffersonville, Ohio, Apr. 1, 1924; s. Edward Howe and Mary Mabel (Fry) P.; B.S., M.S., Carnegie Inst. Tech., 1945; Ph.D., Harvard U., 1948; m. Marjorie Elizabeth Semon, May 31, 1947; children—Warren E., Catherine E., Stephen G., Bruce E. Physicist, Westinghouse Research Labs., 1945-46; mem. faculty Washington U., St. Louis, 1948-56, 62-70, prof. physics, provost, 1962-69, exec. vice chancellor 1965-69, Edward Mallinckrodt prof. physics, 1969-70; mgr. Xerox Palo Alto (Calif.) Research Center, 1970—, v.p. corporate research, 1978—; prof. physics Stanford U., 1956-62. Mem. gov. bd. Am. Inst. Physics, 1957-59; bd. dirs. St. Louis Research Council, 1964-70; mem. physics adv. panel NSF, 1958-60, 63-66; chmn. physics survey com. Nat. Acad. Sci.-NRC, 1964-66. Mem. St. Louis County Bus. and Indl. Devel. Commn., 1963-66; chmn. bd. Regional Indsl. Devel. Corp., St. Louis, 1966-67, St. Louis Research Council, 1967-70; mem. President's Sci. Adv. Com., 1965-69. Bd. dirs. St. Louis Country Day Sch., 1964-70, Central Inst. for Deaf, 1965-70; trustee Washington U., 1970—, Danforth Found., 1971—, U. Rochester, 1982—. Fellow Am. Phys. Soc. (pres. 1977); mem. Am. Assn. Physics Tchrs., AAUP, AAAS, Am. Acad. Arts and Scis., Nat. Acad. Sci., Sigma Xi, Tau Beta Pi. Club: University (Palo Alto). Author: (with E. Feenberg) Quantum Theory of Angular Momentum, 1953; Paramagnetic Resonance, 1962; (with T. Estle) The Physical Principles of Electron Paramagnetic Resonance, 1973. Home: 10 Arastradero Rd Portola Valley CA 94025 Office: Xerox Palo Alto Research Center Palo Alto CA

PAKKIANATHAN, ARUL RAJ, univ. computing exec.; b. Mukuperi Madras State, India, May 15, 1936; came to U.S., 1965, naturalized, 1973; s. Moses Israel and Selvam Siromoney (Samuel) P.; B.A., Pacific Union Coll.; M.B.A., Calif. State U., San Bernardino, 1980; m. Hildha Chelliah, Sept. 14, 1964; children—Faustina Siromoney, Joy Olive. Ordained to ministry Seventh-day Adventist Ch., 1964; pastor chs., India, 1959-65; printer Pacific Union Coll., Angwin, Calif., 1967-73; computer programmer Loma Linda U. and Med. Center, 1973-79, data processing coordinator Loma Linda U., 1979-81, asst. dir. univ. computing, 1981-82; assoc. dir. univ. computing 1982—; controller, sec.-treas. Pat Rutherford Realty & Investments, Grand Terrace, Calif., 1980-81; instr. Riverside City Coll., 1981—; cons. computer systems, acctg. systems. Republican. Adventist. Designed, programmed Loma U.'s gen. ledger system. Home: 1509 Bella Vista Ct Redlands CA 92373

PAL, PRATAPADITYA, museum curator; b. Bangladesh, Sept. 1, 1935; came to U.S., 1967; s. Gopesh Chandra and Bidyut Kana (Dam) P.; M.A., U. Calcutta, 1958, D.Phil., 1962; Ph.D. (U.K. Commonwealth Scholar), U. Cambridge (Eng.), 1965; m. Chitralekha Bose, Apr. 20, 1968; children—Shalmali, Lopamudra. Research assoc. Am. Acad. of Benares (India), 1966-67; keeper Indian collections Mus. Fine Arts, Boston, 1967-69; curator Indian and Islamic art Los Angeles County Mus. Art, Los Angeles 1970—, acting dir. mus., 1979; adj. prof. fine arts U. So. Calif., 1971—; vis. prof. U. Calif., Santa Barbara, 1980. Bd. dirs. Internat. Documentation Center, San Bernardino Calif., Tibetan Found., N.Y.C.; trustee Pacific Asia Mus., Pasadena, 1981-82. JDR 3d Fund fellow, 1964, 69; NEA fellow, 1974. Mem. Asiatic Soc. (Calcutta), Asia Soc. Author: The Arts of Nepal, vol. 1, 1974, vol. 2, 1979; The Sensuous Immortals, 1977; The Ideal Image: Gupta Sculptures and its Influence, 1978; The Classical Tradition in Rajput Painting, 1978. Office: Los Angeles County Museum Art 5905 Wilshire Blvd Los Angeles CA 90036

PALACIO, ROBERT SALVADOR, sociologist, educator; b. Fresno, Calif., Oct. 17, 1945; s. Salvador Flores and Frances (Dorame) P.; m. Olivia Maria Pineda, Apr. 17, 1971; children—Ana Maria, Sylvia, Andrea. B.A., Calif. State U.-Fresno, 1971; M.A., U. Calif.-Berkeley, 1974, Ph.D., 1980. Lectr., San Jose State U., Calif., 1978-79; adj. asst. prof. Calif. State U.-Fresno, 1982—, program evaluator, 1982—; Served to sgt. U.S. Army. NIMH trainee, U. Calif.-Berkeley, 1973; Ford Found. grad. fellow, 1976. Mem. Am. Sociol. Assn., Pacific Sociol. Assn., Soc. for the Study of Social Problems, Am. Acad. Polit. and Social Sci. Home: 752 W Menlo Ave Clovis CA 93612 Office: Dept Sociology Calif State U Fresno CA 93740

PALAZZO, ROBERT PAUL, lawyer, accountant; b. Los Angeles, Apr. 14, 1952; s. Joseph Francis and Muriel P. B.A. in Econs. (named Outstanding Sr.), UCLA, 1973; M.B.A., J.D., U. So. Calif., 1976. Law clk. firm Ebben & Brown, Los Angeles, 1974-75; admitted to Calif. bar, 1976, U.S. Tax Ct. bar, 1977, U.S. Supreme Ct., 1980; asso. firm Graham & James, Los Angeles, 1975-78; partner firm Rader, Cornwall, Kessler and Palazzo, C.P.A.'s, Los Angeles, 1978-81, Palazzo & Kessler, Attys.-at-Law, Los Angeles, 1978-81; sole practice law, Los Angeles, 1981—; owner Robert P. Palazzo, C.P.A.'s, Los Angeles, 1981—; judge pro tem Los Angeles Mcpl. Ct., 1982—; pres., chmn. bd. Fin. Systems Internat. Inc.; pres., chmn. bd. Consol. Am. Oil Co. Bd. dirs. Calif. Cancer Found., pres., 1979-80, mem. bylaws com. 1982-83; alumni adviser UCLA, 1977—, mem. adv. and scholarship com., 1978—. C.P.A., Nev., Colo., Calif. Mem. Am., Los Angeles (arbitration com.), Century City (vice chmn. estate planning, trust and probate coms.), Fed. (council on taxation 1978-81), Italian-Am. (gov., treas.) bar assns., Am. Inst. C.P.A.'s, Calif. Soc. C.P.A.'s, Nev. Soc. C.P.A.'s, Am., Calif. assns. atty.-C.P.A.'s, Los Angeles Trial Lawyers Assn., Nev. State Hist. Soc., Am. Numis. Assn. (dist. rep. Carson City, Nev. 1981-82, Los Angeles 1982—), Manuscript Soc., Omicron Delta Epsilon, Beta Alpha Psi, Pi Gamma Mu, Phi Alpha Delta, Zeta Phi Eta. Club: Legion Lex (Los Angeles). Office: 10100 Santa Monica Blvd Suite 1370 Los Angeles CA 90067 also 892 E William St Carson City NV also 9/11 Kensington High St London W8 5NP England

PALENCSAR, RITA FLORINE, nurse; b. Oswego, N.Y., Dec. 1, 1927; d. Seth and Jane (Leroy) Waterman; diploma St. Mary's Hosp., Rochester, N.Y., 1948; m. Carl F. Palencsar, Sept. 6, 1949 (dec.); children—Barbara Ann, Susan Jane. Staff nurse U.S. VA, Wadsworth and Livermore, Calif., 1949-52, St. Josephs Hosp., Burbank, Calif., 1952-54; supr. Motion Picture Country House and Hosp., Woodland Hills, Calif., 1956-64; staff nurse U.S. VA Med. Center, Roseburg, Oreg., 1964-66, supr. operating room, 1966—. Cert. operating room nurse. Mem. Am. Nurses Assn., Oreg. Nurses Assn., Operating Room Nurses Assn. Republican. Roman Catholic. Home: 3325 W Shasta St Roseburg OR 97470 Office: US VA Medical Center Roseburg OR 97470

PALETTA, LOUIS, marketing executive; b. San Angelo di Cetraro, Italy, Aug. 20, 1927; s. Joseph and Concetta P.; m. Regine Wanda Nordyke, July 4, 1953; children—Mark, Renee Paletta Jacoub. B.S. in Fgn. Trade, U. So. Calif., 1955. Trainee, J.C. Penney, 1949-51; with Creftcon Industries, City of Industry, Calif., 1951—, now mktg. dir. Served with USAF, 1946-49. Mem. Am. Mktg. Assn., U. So. Calif. Bus. Assn. Democrat. Roman Catholic. Office: 900 S Ajax Ave City of Industry CA 91749

PALKE, KENNETH ALAN, newspaper editor; b. Inglewood, Calif., Sept. 30, 1948; s. Byron Park and Shirley Mae (Allen) P.; m. Susan B. Peterson, Mar. 27, 1982. B.J., Calif. State U.-Long Beach, 1975. Reporter, editor Palos Verdes (Calif.) Peninsula News, 1974-77; reporter, columnist Daily Southeast News, Downey, Calif., 1977-79; editor Polk County Itemizer, Dallas, Oreg., 1979, Salem (Oreg.) Capital Press, 1979—. Chmn. adv. bd. Chemeketa Community Coll. Journalism; mem. agr. dean's adv. bd. Oreg. State U. Served with USN, 1967-71; mem. Oreg. N.G. Decorated Vietnam Service medal. Mem. Sigma Delta Chi, U.S. Ski Writers Assn. Democrat. Baptist. Office: PO Box 2048 Salem OR 97308

PALLADINO, LUCY JO, clinical psychologist, consultant, writer; b. N.Y.C., Oct. 13, 1950; d. John Michael and Lucy Nancy (Caravella) Palladino; m. Arthur Achilles Cormanom July 1, 1979; 1 dau., Julia Lucia. B.S. summa cum laude, Fordham U., 1972; M.A., Ariz. State U., 1975, Ph.D., 1978. Cert. psychologist, Ariz., 1978. Research asso. Ariz. State Hosp., Phoenix, 1973-74; intern in clin. psychology Good Samaritan Hosp., Phoenix, 1974-76, 77-78; research assoc. Nat. Spinal Cord Injury Data Research Center, Phoenix, 1975-76; editorial asst. Rehab. Psychology, Tempe, Ariz., 1975-78; Clin. psychology fellow Southwestern Med. Sch., Dallas, 1976-77; practice clin., cons. psychologist, Tucson, 1978—; faculty lectr. psychiatry U. Ariz. Med. Sch. N.Y. State Regent scholar, 1968-72; Ariz. State U. Grad. fellow, 1975-76; NIMH fellow, 1973-75, 76-77. Mem. Am. Psychol. Assn., Soc. Psychol. Study Social Issues; So. Ariz. Psychol. Assn., Council Nat. Register Health Service Provider Psychology (cert. 1981), Phi Beta Kappa. Contbr. articles to prfl. jours. Home and Office: 6502 E Calle Altair Tucson AZ 85710

PALLASCH, THOMAS J., periodontist, educator; b. Milw., June 15, 1936; s. Joseph John and Stella (Zavis) P.; D.D.S., Marquette U., 1960; M.S. in Pharmacology, certificate in periodontics, U. Wash., 1967; m. Christine Peterson, May 14, 1977; children—Brian, Jennifer, Robert. Rotating dental intern U.S. Navy, 1960-61; asso. prof. pharmacology and periodontics, chmn. dept. pharmacology Sch. Dentistry, U. So. Calif., Los Angeles, 1967—, chmn. dept. periodontics, 1981-83, dir. oral biology grad. program, 1968-77, dir. pain and anxiety control program, 1972-76; pvt. practice periodontics Burbank, Calif., 1968—. Served with USN, 1960-64. Mem. Am. Dental Assn., Am. Assn. Dental Schs., Am. Coll. Dentists, AAAS, Delta Sigma Delta (dep. supreme grand master (1968-71), Omicron Kappa Epsilon. Author: Clinical Drug Therapy in Dental Practice, 1973; Synopsis of Pharmacology for Students in Dentistry, 1974; Pharmacology for Dental Students and Practitioners, 1980; editor, pub. Dental Drug Service Newsletter. Home: 1410 Royal Blvd Glendale CA 91207 Office: 1411 W Olive Ave Burbank CA 91506

PALLEY, MARY FLYNN, lawyer; b. Rochester, N.Y., Aug. 20, 1942; d. Leonard John and Jane Elizabeth (Seely) Flynn; m. Michael Richard Palley, June 6, 1963 (dec.); 1 son, John. B.A., UCLA, 1967, J.D., 1980. Bar: Calif. 1981; cert. Nat. Assn. Legal Assts., 1976. Jud. atty. to justice Calif. Ct. Appeals, 1980-81; assoc. Nossaman, Krueger & Knox, 1981-82; pres. Palley & Palley, Inc., Los Angeles, 1982—. Recipient Am. Jurisprudence book awards, 1978, 79, 80. Mem. Common Cause, Ams. for Democratic Action, Catholics for Free Choice, Los Angeles Women Lawyers Assn., Los Angeles County Bar Assn., Beverly Hills Bar Assn., Assn. Bus. Trial Lawyers. Democrat. Roman Catholic. Office: 3257 Earlmar Dr Los Angeles CA 90064

PALLIN, SAMUEL LEAR, ophthalmologist; b. N.Y.C., May 8, 1941; s. Irving M. and Gertrude Ann (Lear) P.; B.A., Hofstra U., 1963; M.D., SUNY, Bklyn., 1968; m. Leah Dvora Nason, Oct. 9, 1965; children—Daniel Jay, Marla Jean, Laura Jane. Intern in surgery L.I. Jewish Hosp., 1968-69; resident in ophthalmology Bklyn. Eye and Ear Hosp., 1972-75; practice medicine specializing in ophthalmology, Sun City, Ariz., 1975—; med. dir. Sight Found.; mem. staff Boswell Meml. Hosp.; lectr. on intraocular lens implant techniques. Served as flight surgeon USAF, 1969-71; Vietnam. Diplomate Am. Bd. Ophthalmology. Fellow A.C.S., Am. Acad. Ophthalmology, AMA, Ariz. Med. Assn., Maricopa County Med. Soc. Jewish. Clubs: Lions, 79ers, Kiwanis, Phoenix N.W. (dir.). Author: Eye to Eye: Understanding Eye Surgery, 1978. Office: 10503 Thunderbird Blvd Sun City AZ 85351

PALLOTTI, GREGORY JAMES, safety consultant; b. Richmond, Calif., Mar. 18, 1952; s. Charles John and Jacqueline Aintoinette P. B.S. in Engring. Aero Ops., San Jose State U., Calif., 1976. Cert. asso. safety profl. Safety cons. Reed Stenhouse, Inc., San Francisco 1982. Served to capt. USAFR 1976—. Mem. Am. Soc. Safety Engrs., Soc. Fire Protection Engrs. Republican. Roman Catholic. Home: 1666 164th Ave San Leandro CA 94578 Office: 3 Embarcadero Center Suite 2400 San Francisco CA 94111

PALM, NANCY CLEONE, medical center administrator, radiography technologist; b. Portland, Oreg., July 8, 1939; d. Oscar Emanuel and Hallie Vernice (Thurber) Palm. Student U. Oreg. Sch. Radiology, 1957; grad. Hosp. Corpswave, Hosp. Corps Sch., Great Lakes (Ill. Naval Base, 1958; grad. X-ray Tech., Sch. Radiology, Bremerton, Wash. Naval Base, 1961. Lic. radiography technologist, Oreg. Chief radiography technologist New Lincoln Hosp., Toledo, Oreg., 1961-63; sr. radiography technologist Gresham (Oreg.) Gen. Hosp., 1963-64; chief radiography technologist Neurol. Clinic, Portland, Oreg., 1965-79; head bookkeeper Rinehart Clinic, Wheeler, Oreg., 1979-80; owner, gen. mgr. San Dune Motel, Marzanita, Oreg., 1971—; adminstrn. mgr. Rinehart Found., Inc. (Nehalem Bay Med. Ctr.), Wheeler and Garibaldi, Oreg., 1980—. Sponsor Willamette council Campfire Girls, Inc., 1982—. Served with USN, 1958-61. Fellow Nat. Coll. Radiography Technologists; mem. Oreg. Med. Group Mgmt. Assn., Nat. Assn. Female Execs., Am. Registry Clin. Radiography Technologists (nat. dir. 1970-76, trustee 1972-74, sec. 71-72, pres. 72-74; Citation award 1970, Disting. Service award 1971, 73, Order of Golden Ray 1974, founder Margaret Harris Award Competition 1973). Republican. Presbyterian. Home: 423 Dorcas Lane PO Box 262 Manzanita OR 97130 Office: PO Box 268 Wheeler OR 97147

PALMER, BEVERLY BLAZEY, psychologist, educator; b. Cleve., Nov. 22, 1945; d. Lawrence E. Blazey and Mildred M. B.; m. Richard C. Palmer, June 24, 1967; 1 son, Ryan Richard. Ph.D. in Counseling Psychology, Ohio State U., Columbus, 1972. Adminstrv. assoc. Ohio State U., 1969-70; research psychologist Health Services Research Center, UCLA, 1971-77; prof. psychology Calif. State U.-Carson, 1973—. Mem. Am. Psychol. Assn. Contbr. numerous articles to psychol. and health jours. Office: California State U Dept Psychology Dominguez Hills Carson CA 90747

PALMER, BLAINE CHARLES, industrial relations executive; b. Vernal, Utah, Oct. 28, 1936; s. Heber Charles and Ethel Mary (Vernon) P.; B.S., Brigham Young U., 1963; m. Shari Combs, July 10, 1964. With Litton Industries, Woodland Hills, Calif., 1963-69, mgr. coll. relations, 1964-67, contracts planner, 1968-69; with Harrahs, Inc., Lake Tahoe, Nev., 1969-76, personnel mgr., 1970-76; corp. dir. indsl. relations Valtek, Inc., Springville, Utah, 1976-83; dir. indsl. relations precision controls div. Bourns Inc., Ogden, Utah, 1983—; adj. prof. Utah Tech. Coll. Chmn., Utah County Merit Council, 1976—; chmn. adv. council Utah Tech Coll. Served with U.S. Army, 1960-62. Mem. Personnel Assn. Central Utah (pres.), Coll. Placement Council, Rocky Mountain Placement Assn., Am. Soc. Tng. and Devel., Am. Soc. Personnel Adminstrn., Utah Assn. Civil Service Commrs. (pres.). Republican. Mormon. Home: 5221 Aztec Dr Ogden UT 84403 Office: 2533 N 1500 W Ogden UT 84404

PALMER, CURTIS H., holding company executive; b. 1908; married. LL.B., U. Calif., 1932. Bar: Calif. 1932. Practice, Oakland, Calif., 1932-35; tax counsel Calif. Equalization Bd., 1943-60; gen. counsel Alfred Hart, 1943-60; vice chmn. bd. City Nat. Bank, Beverly Hills, Calif., 1953-76; chmn. bd. Arden-Mayfair Inc., 1976—, also dir.; chmn. bd. Arden Group Inc., Los Angeles, 1978—, also dir. Office: Arden Group Inc PO Box 2256 Los Angeles CA 90040*

PALMER, FRANK ALLAN, ins. co. exec.; b. Houston, Dec. 2, 1930; s. Frank Storm and Lula Allean (Miles) P.; A.A., Orange Coast Coll., 1969; m. Patsy June Powell, Dec. 30, 1950; children—Kathleen Louise, Christopher Allen. With Ins. Co. of N.Am., 1955—, tech. supr. safety and audit, Orange, Calif., 1966-75, audit mgr. So. Calif., Los Angeles, 1975-78, dir. audit Western region, Newport Beach, Calif., 1978—. Served with U.S. Army, 1950-53. Mem. Audit Mgrs. Assn. So. Calif. (past treas.), Am. Soc. Safety Engrs. (pres. Tri-County chpt. 1973), Tri-County Auditors Assn. (pres. 1975, 81), Ins. Auditors Assn. West, Nat. Soc. Ins. Premium Auditors. Republican. Baptist. Office: 23461 S Pointe Dr Laguna Hills CA 92653

PALMER, JAMES RICHARD, artist; b. Chattanooga, Dec. 13, 1944; s. Basil and Edith Marion (Smith) P.; student Otis Art Inst., 1972-73, Santa Monica (Calif.) Coll., 1973; m. Jamie Gibbs, Apr. 14, 1973. Tchr. drawing, Mill Valley, Calif., 1977-78; juror exhibit for Mill Valley Art Guild, 1978; artist, works exhibited galleries, colls. and banks in Calif., N.Y., Ga., Kans., N.Mex., Mont., Fla., Utah, including Lynn Kottler Gallery, N.Y.C., 1976, Tapia Art Gallery, Sausalito, 1976—, Village Gallery, Fairfax, Calif., 1977, Sausalito Art Festival, 1976-77, Homestead Savs. & Home Fed. Savs., Sausalito, 1977, Citizens Savs., Terra Linda, Calif., 1977, Metes and Bounds Gallery, Sausalito, 1977, Harteman Gallery, Thousand Oaks, Calif., 1977, Miami Art Exhbn., Fla., 1976, 77, Nova Gallery, Olathe, Kans., 1976, Sculpture Gallery, San Diego, 1977, Falkirk Gallery, San Raphael, Calif., 1977, Casa de Art Gallery, Larkspur, Calif., 1976—, Bergwell Gallery, Oakland, Calif., 1977-78, Union St. Gallery, San Francisco, 1978, Atlier Clemens Gallery, Pasadena, 1979—, E & B Gallery, Santa Monica, Calif., 1980, Art Expo W, Los Angeles, 1980. Mem. Soc. Western Artists, Marin Soc. Artists, Mill Valley Art Guild, Santa Monica C. of C. Home and Office: 959 Superba Ave Venice CA 90291

PALMER, MICHAEL BARRY, psychologist; b. Detroit, Aug. 20, 1942; s. George Joseph and Roslyn (Barahal) P.; m. Susan B. Howitt, 1966; m. 2d, Rose M. Carlson, Dec. 16, 1978; children—Kelly, Ryan. B.A., Ariz. State U., 1965, Ph.D., 1970; M.A., Mich. State U., 1966. Asst. prof. U. No. Colo., Greeley, 1970-73; prof. Nova U., Ft. Lauderdale, Fla., 1973-80; pvt. practice psychology, Phoenix, 1980—; affiliate Marriage and Family Inst; adj. prof. Ariz. State U., Tempe. Treas., bd. dirs. Pastoral Counseling Ctr., Ft. Lauderdale, 1976-79; bd. dirs. Human Rights Advocacy Com., Ft. Lauderdale, 1979. Mem. Am. Psychol. Assn., Ariz. Psychol. Assn., Am. Assn. Behavior Therapists, Behavior Therapy and Research Soc. Contbr. articles to profl. jours. Home and Office: 3101 W Peoria Suite B-306 Phoenix AZ 85029

PALMER, PATRICIA L., safety engineer; b. Douglas, Wyo., July 22, 1941; d. Lawrence Leo and Sara Margaret (Fackler) Nachtman; m. Stanley Francis Palmer, Oct. 14, 1961; children—Faith, Scott, Blake. Student U. Wyo., 1961; A.A. in Applied Scis., East Wyo. Coll., 1982. Safety supr. Western Nuclear, Inc., Jeffery City, Wyo., 1973-76; engr., tng. coordinator, United Nuclear, Inc., Casper, Wyo, 1976-81; radiation safety officer, Uranium Resources, Inc., 1981-82; safety tng. coordinator Glenrock Coal Co., Wyo., 1982—; cons in field. Mem. Am. Soc. Safety Engrs. (exec. bd. Wyo. chpt.), Wyo. Registry Emergency Med. Technicians. Republican. Episcopalian. Club: Women Moose. Home: 1116 Sweetwater Rd Douglas WY 82633 Office: Glenrock Coal Co Coal Co Route Glenrock WY 82637

PALMER, RICHARD CLETUS, psychiatrist; b. Cin., May 5, 1944; s. Cletus Thompson and Mary Louise (Youmans) P.; B.S., U. Mich., 1966; M.D., Ohio State U., 1970; m. Beverly Dorothie Blazey, June 24, 1967; 1 son, Ryan Richard. Intern, Good Samaritan Hosp., Phoenix, 1970-71; resident in psychiatry Harbor Gen. Hosp., Torrance, Calif., 1971-74; fellow UCLA, Los Angeles, 1973-74; practice medicine specializing in psychiatry, Torrance, 1976—; asst. clin. prof. UCLA, 1976—; chmn. dept. psychiatry San Pedro Peninsula Hosp., San Pedro, Calif., 1981-82, 83—; mem. staffs. Torrance Meml. Hosp., Harbor Gen. Hosp. Served as lt. comdr. M.C., USN, 1974-76. Recipient Dept. Psychiatry award Ohio State Univ., 1970; diplomate Am. Bd. Psychiatry. Mem. Am. Psychiat. Assn., South Bay Psychiat. Soc. (sec.-treas.), So. Calif. Psychiat. Soc., Phi Eta Sigma. Home: 29978 Knollview Dr Rancho Palos Verdes CA 90274 Office: 3250 Lomita Blvd Suite 308 Torrance CA 90505

PALMER, TED WAYNE, chemical company executive; b. Cabool, Mo., Sept. 7, 1933; s. Roscoe Wayne and Rosa Mae (Derry) P.; B.S. in Chem. Engring., Oreg. State U., 1957; m. Elizabeth Thomas, Nov. 23, 1979; children by previous marriage—Ted Wayne, Thomas William, Laura, Alison, Mary. With Dow Chem. Co., 1957-71; founder, 1971, since chmn. bd., pres. Kalama Chem. Inc., Seattle. Mem. Young Pres. Orgn. Republican. Episcopalian. Clubs: Rainier, Seattle Athletic, Seattle Yacht, Seattle Tennis, Wash. Athletic (Seattle). Home: 8885 Woodbank Dr Bainbridge Island WA 98110 Office: 1110 Bank of Calif Seattle WA 98164

PALMER, VINCENT ALLAN, constrn. cons.; b. Wausa, Nebr., Feb. 18, 1913; s. Victor E. and Amy (Lindquist) P.; A.A., Modesto Jr. Coll., 1933; B.S. in Civil Engring., U. Calif., Berkeley, 1936; m. Louise V. Cramer, Mar. 12, 1938 (dec. June 1979); children—Margaret, Georgia, Vincent Allan; m. 2d, Hope Parker, Jan. 23, 1982. Constrn. engr. Kaiser Engrs., 1938-63, constrn. mgr., 1963-69, mgr. constrn., 1970-75, project mgr., 1975-76; project mgr. reef runway Universal Dredging Corp., Honolulu, 1975-76; pvt. practice constrn. cons., Walnut Creek, Calif., 1976—. Mem. ASCE (life), Project Mgmt. Inst., Sierra Club. Home and Office: 1356 Corte Loma Walnut Creek CA 94598

PALMER, WILLIAM JOSEPH, accountant; b. Lansing, Mich., Sept. 3, 1934; s. Harold L. and Henrietta (Yagerman) P.; B.S., U. Calif., Berkeley, 1962; m. Judith Pollock, Aug. 20, 1960; children—William, Kathryn, Leslie, Emily. With Coopers and Lybrand, 1963-80, mng. partner, Sacramento, 1976-80, chmn. constrn. industry div., 1973-80; partner, chmn. constrn. industry group Arthur Young & Co., San Francisco, 1980—; guest lectr. U. Calif., Berkeley, 1971, Stanford U. Engring. Sch., 1976; lectr. Golden Gate Coll., 1975; speaker on constrn. fin. Bd. dirs. Sacramento Met. YMCA, 1976-82, v.p., 1979-82; bd. dirs. Sacramento Symphony Found., 1977—; asst. state fin. chmn. Calif. Reagan for Pres., 1980. Served to lt. USN, 1953-59. Mem. Am. Inst. C.P.A.s (vice chmn. com. constrn. industry, 1975—), Nat. Assn. Accts. (pres. Oakland/East Bay chpt. 1972, Man of Yr. 1968), Calif. Soc. C.P.A.'s, Associated Gen. Contractors Calif., Lambda Chi Alpha. Presbyterian. Clubs: World Trade, Commonwealth (San Francisco); Del Paso Country, Sutter, Comstock (Sacramento); Rio Del Oro Tennis. Author: (with Pomeranz) Managing Construction Projects, 1975; (with Coombs) Construction Accounting and Financial Management, 1977; (with Cushman) Businessman's Guide to Construction, 1980; (with others) Mahon's Industry Guides for Accountants and Auditors in the Construction Industry, 1980; (with Cushman, Stover and Sneed) Construction Management Form Book, 1983. Home: 34 Riverbank Pl Sacramento CA 95808 Office: 555 Capitol Mall Suite 1490 Sacramento CA 95814

PALMERLEE, CHARLES SEWARD, psychologist; b. Ashland, Oreg., Feb. 27, 1919; s. Henry Seward and Grace Cynthia (Candell) P.; B.A., U. Calif.-Berkeley, 1942; M.Div. (John R. Mott fellow), Pacific Sch. Religion, 1959; M.A., U. Oreg., 1970, Ph.D., 1974; m. Joy Drobish, Nov. 30, 1947; children—Ruth H., David C., John B. Tchr. high sch., Calif., 1942-45; exec. YMCA, Calif. and Oreg., 1945-70; psychotherapist Oreg. State Penitentiary, Salem, 1973-74; dir. role-playing workshop U. Oreg., 1970-74; counseling psychologist Evelyn Berger Center for Counseling and Psychotherapy, Oakland, Calif., 1975—; co-owner, co-dir. Far View Ranch Camp for Children, Bangor, Calif., 1956—; pvt. practice psychotherapy and counseling, 1974—. Danforth Found. grantee, 1958. Mem. Am. Psychol. Assn., Calif. State Psychol. Assn., Alameda County Psychol. Assn., San Francisco Soc. Clin. Hypnosis, Am. Soc. Clin. Hypnosis, ACLU, Clergy and Laity Concerned, Friends Com. Nat. Legislation, Am. Friends Service Com. Democrat. Congregationalist. Office: 508 16th St Suite 707 Oakland CA 94612

PALMIERI, FREDERICK WILLIAM, mechanical engineer, real estate executive; b. Sacramento, Oct. 16, 1932; s. Mario and Mary (Losacco) P.; m. Billie Ruth Monsen, Sept. 2, 1952; 1 son, Frederick; m. Judy Anna Drystek, Dec. 22, 1973; children—Carey, Caroline. B.S. in Math., Stanford U., 1961, M.S. in Engring. Mechanics, 1965. Engr., cons. aerospace industry, 1961-69; dir. CTI Corp., Geneva, 1978-79; v.p. Victor Palmieri & Co., Inc., Los Angeles, 1969-73; pres. chief fin. officer PCC, Inc., Irvine, Calif., 1973—. Mem. AIAA, East Orange County Bd. Realtors, Calif. Assn. Realtors, Nat. Assn. Realtors. Democrat. Roman Catholic. Contbr. articles to profl. jours. Patentee marine instrumentation. Home: 445 Bridge View Dr Anaheim CA 92807 Office: 2081 Business Center Dr Suite 180 Irvine CA 92715

PALMQUIST, LOWELL E., hospital administrator; b. Taylor Falls, Minn., Nov. 25, 1929; s. Leonard and Gladys (Hyland) P.; m. Mona Kienitz, Apr. 21, 1955; children—David, Nancy, John. B.A., St. Olaf Coll., 1952; M.H.A., U. Minn., 1958. Asst. adminstr. Fairview Hosp., Mpls., 1962-64, adminstr., 1965-69; exec. dir. Swedish Med. Center, Englewood, Colo., 1969-81, pres., 1981—. Served with U.S. Army, 1952-54. Mem. Am. Hosp. Assn., (del. at large), Am. Coll. Hosp. Adminstrs. Assn. Western Hosps. (pres. elect), Colo. Hosp. Assn. (past chmn., dir.). Club: Rotary. Office: 501 E Hampden Ave Englewood CO 80110

PALOMAR, JULIE SILVA, vocational consultant, rehabilitation counselor; b. Santa Maria, Laguna, Philippines, Sept. 26, 1941; d. Catalino and Maria (Silva) Hernandez. M.S. in Sch. Counseling, U. LaVerne, 1978; M.Div., Bangor Theol. Sem., 1977. Cert. pvt. sch. tchr. and counselor, Hawaii; cert. coll. counselor, Calif. Missionary, Liebenzell Mission, Yap, Caroline Island, 1969-71; nursery assoc. tchr., Bangor, Maine, 1971-75; high sch. counselor, dept. chmn., Hilo, Hawaii, 1977-79; counselor Cosmopolitan Social Service Agy., Honolulu, 1979; vocat. cons., counselor Crawford Rehab. Services, Inc., Honolulu, 1979—; coordinator Leading Quality Circle Group. Vol. Am. Cancer Soc.; active YWCA, Filipino C. of C., Women's Bd. East-West Ctr. Host Family. Recipient Profl. Employee of Yr. Crawford Rehab. Services, Inc. 1981. Mem. Am. Personnel and Guidance Assn., Hawaii Personnel and Guidance Assn., Am. Sch. Counselors Assn., Am. Rehab. Counselors Assn., Nat. Rehab. Assn., Rehab. Assn. Hawaii (treas. 1983). Clubs: Philippine Women's Circle (pres. 1978), Hilo Women's. Office: Crawford Rehab Services Inc 720 Kapiolani Blvd #500 Honolulu HI 96813

PALOUTZIAN, RAYMOND FRANK, psychologist, author, cons., researcher; b. Sanger, Calif., June 6, 1945; s. Frank and Louise (Sarkisian) P.; m. Eunice Marie Lerma, Feb. 4, 1967; children—Daniel Ray, Mark Aron. B.A., Calif. State U.-Los Angeles, 1968; M.A. (NDEA IV fellow), Clarmont Grad. Sch., 1970, Ph.D., 1972. NIMH predoctoral research fellow Claremont Grad. Sch., 1969-72; acting asst. prof. Scripps Coll., The Claremont Colls., 1972-73; asst. prof., then assoc. prof. psychology U. Idaho, 1973-81; prof. Westmont Coll., 1981—; vis. scholar Stanford U., 1979-80, cons., speaker, reviewer in field. Served with Army N.G., 1963-66. Mem. Am. Psychol. Assn., Western Psychol. Assn., Soc. for Psychol. Study Social Issues, Soc. for Sci. Study Religion, Soc. for Advancement Social Psychology, Psychiatrists Interested in Religious Issues. Author: An Invitation To The Psychology of Religion, 1983; contbr., articles, chpts. to profl. publs. Office: Dept Psychology Westmont Coll Santa Barbara CA 93108

PALSHAW, JOHN LOUIS, advertising executive; b. Hartford, Conn., Apr. 15, 1932; s. Francis L. and Helen E. (Curtin) P.; B.A., Trinity Coll., Hartford, 1955; postgrad. Columbia U., 1956-57, N.Y.U., 1967; m. Judith Arlene Dattner, July 1, 1973; children—David Craig, Michael Scott, Daniel Bradley. Mgr. advt. and sales promotion Edwards Co., Norwalk, Conn., 1955-60; corp. advt. adminstr. Internat. Nickel Co., N.Y.C., 1960-63; mgr. advt. and sales promotion Westvaco Corp., N.Y.C., 1963-64; pres. ICR div. Interpublic, N.Y.C., 1965-68, Palshaw Measurement, Inc., Green Farms, Conn., 1968—; lectr. Am. Mgmt. Assn. Recipient Honor award Ohio U., 1968. Mem. Am. Mktg. Assn., Pharm. Ad Council, Nat. Agri-Mktg. Assn., Savs. Instns. Mktg. Soc. Am., Bus. and Profl. Advt. Assn., Pharm. Market Research Group. Republican. Unitarian. Author: Practical Methods of Measuring Advertising Effectiveness, 1969; columnist Fin. Mktg., Med. Mktg. and Media, B/PAA Communicator. Home: Box 272 Pebble Beach CA 93953 Office: Box 1439 Pebble Beach CA 93953

PAMPLIN, ROBERT BOISSEAU, JR., agrl. co. exec.; b. Augusta, Ga., Sept. 3, 1941; s. Robert Boisseau and Mary Katherine (Reese) P.; student in bus. adminstrn. Va. Poly. Inst., 1960-62; B.S. in Bus. Adminstrn., Lewis and Clark Coll., 1964, B.S. in Acctg., 1965, B.S. in Economics, 1966; M.B.A., U. Portland, 1968, M.Ed., 1975, LL.D. (hon.), 1972; M.C.L., Western Conservative Bapt. Sem., 1978, D.Min., 1982; D.Min., 1982; D.B.A., Calif. cert. U.; certificate in wholesale mgmt., Ohio State cert. 1970; certificate in labor mgmt., U. cert. 1972; certificate in advanced mgmt., U. Hawaii, 1975; m. Marilyn Joan Hooper; children—Amy Louise, Anne Boisseau. Pres. R. B. Pamplin Corp., Portland, Oreg., 1964—; chmn. bd., pres. Columbia Empire Farms, Inc., Lake Oswego, Oreg., 1976—; pres. Twelve Oaks Farms, Inc., Lake Oswego, 1977—; dir. Mt. Vernon Mill Inc.; lectr. bus. adminstr. Lewis and Clark Coll., 1968-69; adj. asst. prof. bus. adminstrn., U. Portland, 1973-76; lectr. in bus. adminstrn. and economics, U. Costa Rica, 1968. Mem. Nat. Adv. Council on Vocat. Edn., 1975—; mem. Oreg. State Scholarship Commn., 1974—, chmn., 1976-78; mem. Portland dist. adv. council SBA, 1973-77; mem. Rewards Review Com., City Portland, 1973-78, chmn., 1973-78; mem. bd. regents U. Portland, 1971-79, chmn. bd., 1975-79, regent emeritus, 1979—; trustee Lewis and Clark Coll., 1980—, Oreg. Epis. Schs., 1979. Named disting. alumnus, Lewis and Clark Coll., 1974; recipient Air Force ROTC Disting. Service award, USAF, 1974. Mem. Acad. Mgmt., Delta Epsilon Sigma, Beta Gamma Sigma. Republican. Episcopalian. Clubs: Waverley Country, Arlington, Multnomah Athletic, Rotary. Editor Oreg. Mus. Sci. and Industry Press, 1973, trustee 1971, 74—; editor Portrait of Oregon, 1973; co-author: A Portrait of Colorado, 1976; author (with others) Three in One, 1974, The Storybook Primer on Managing, 1974; editor (with others) Oregon Underfoot, 1975. Address: 3131 West View Ct Lake Oswego OR 97034

PAN, HUO-PING, chemist; b. Foochow, China, Feb. 13, 1921; s. Bai-ming and Won-ching (Chen) Pan; B.S. in Chemistry, Nat. S.W. Assoc. U., China, 1946; Ph.D. in Food Sci., U. Ill., 1954; m. Chiou-Wen Sha, Feb. 26, 1955; 1 son, Peno. Staff mem. div. indsl. research MIT, 1954-55, div. sponsored research, 1955-57, research assoc., 1957-58; asst. biochemist agrl. expt. sta. U. Fla., Gainesville, 1958-63, asst. research prof. Coll. Engring., 1963-64; research biochemist to research chemist Patuxent Wildlife Research Center, U.S. Fish and Wildlife Service, U.S. Dept. Interior, Gainesville, 1964-77; research chemist Denver Wildlife Research Cntr., 1977—. Recipient Outstanding Publ. award Denver Wildlife Research Cntr., 1981; Spl. Achievement award U.S. Fish and Wildlife Service, 1981. Mem. Am. Chem. Soc., Am. Inst. Biol. Scis., AAAS, Internat. Soc. for Study of Xenobiotics (charter), Sigma Xi, Phi Tau Sigma. Democrat. Patentee chromatography developing chamber. Contbr. articles to profl. jours. Home: 5295 S Jellison St Littleton CO 80123 Office: Bldg 16 Fed Center Denver CO 80225

PANAS, JEROLD, mgmt. cons.; b. Cleve., Aug. 9, 1928; s. James and Celia (Heller) P.; B.F.A., U. Pitts., 1949; postgrad. U. Pitts., 1951-53, Kent State U., 1954-55, Bowling Green State U., 1955-56; LL.D., Ricker Coll., Houlton, Maine, 1968; m. Felicity Ormond, Dec. 31, 1975; children—Deborah Ayn, Rebecca Kiel, Judyth Dru, Hillary Kristen, Joshua Ormond. Dir. mgmt. fin. Nat. Council YMCA's, Newark, 1955-64; v.p. Westminster Choir Coll., Princeton, N.J., 1965-69; v.p. John Grenzebach & Assos., Chgo., 1969-71; sr. mng. partner Jerold Panas & Partners, Inc., San Francisco, 1971—; chmn. bd., chief exec. officer Decision Research Inst., San Jose, 1976—; pub. Prime Time, 1982—. Chmn. United Way, Little Silver, N.J., 1965-67, YMCA, Red Bank, N.J., 1966-68; chmn. exec. com. Ricker Coll., 1968-74. Mem. Acad. Health Care Cons. (dir. 1975-79), Assn. Mgmt. Cons., Nat. Health Care Bd. (chmn. 1974—). Episcopalian. Author: Mega Gifts, 1983; contbg. editor Managing Schools in Hard Times, 1981. Contbr. articles to profl. jours. Home: 2504 Pacific Ave San Francisco CA 94115

PANECALDO, LORETO ANTONIO (TONY), III, business executive, political worker; b. Yuba City, Calif., June 19, 1948; s. Loreto Antonio and Marjorie Isabelle Sarmento Thayer; A.A., Yuba Coll., 1969. Floral designer and decorator, owner, gen. mgr. Tony Panecaldo III, Florist, Gridley, Calif., 1971—; councilman City of Gridley, 1976-80, mayor, 1978-80. Chmn. Butte County Republican Central Com., 1974-78; mem. Calif. Rep. Central Com., also mem. exec. com., platform com., 1978; mem. Calif. Rep. Assembly, alt. del. Rep. Nat. Conv., 1976. Mem. Butte County Hist. Soc. (dir.), Bidwell Mansion Restoration Assn., Bidwell Mansion Cooperating Assn., Gridley Art League. Christian Scientist. Clubs: Commonwealth (San Francisco), Order of Eastern Star, Order of DeMolay (life), Masons. Home: 1800 Hazel St Gridley CA 95948 Office: 560 Kentucky St Gridley CA 95948

PANETTA, LEON EDWARD, congressman; b. Monterey, Calif., June 28, 1938; B.A. magna cum laude, U. Santa Clara, 1960, J.D., 1963; m. Sylvia Marie Varni, 1962; children—Christopher, Carmelo, James. Admitted to Calif. bar, 1965; individual practice law, Monterey; legis. asst. to U.S. Senator Thomas H. Kuchel of Calif., 1966-69; spl. asst. to sec. HEW, Washington, 1969; dir. U.S. Office for Civil Rights, Washington, 1969-70; exec. asst. to mayor N.Y.C., 1970-71; partner firm Panetta, Thompson & Panetta, Monterey, 1971-76; mem. 95th-98th Congresses from 16th Calif. Dist., majority regional whip, chmn. task force on budget process, budget com., chmn. subcom. on domestic mktg., consumer relations and nutrition of agr. com.; founder Monterey Coll. Law. Trustee, U. Santa Clara Law Sch.; mem. Monterey County Democratic Central Com., 1972-76; v.p. Carmel Valley Little League; mem. parish council Our Lady of Mt. Carmel Ch., Carmel Valley. Served to 1st lt. U.S. Army, 1963-65. Recipient Lawyer of Year award, 1970; NEA Lincoln award, 1969; decorated Army Commendation medal. Roman Catholic. Author: Bring Us Together, 1971. Home: Carmel Valley CA 93924 Office: 339 Cannon House Office Bldg Washington DC 20515

PANG, LUP QUON, physician and surgeon; b. Honolulu, T.H., May 6, 1907; s. Pang See and Pang Ng See; student U. Hawaii, 1927-29; M.D., Tulane U., 1933, postgrad. student in spltv., 1936-39; m. Tita K. Y. Pang, Aug. 10, 1940; children—Duane C., Meredith K. L., Wendell K. K., Derek K. H., Malcolm K. W. Intern, Queen's Hosp., Honolulu, Ter. Hawaii, 1934-35; C.C.C. camp physician, Wahiawa, Ter. Hawaii, 1935-36; resident surgeon 1935-36; resident surgeon The Eye, Ear, Nose and Throat Hosp. of New Orleans, 1936-39; pvt. practice, Honolulu, 1939—; chief staff St. Francis Hosp., 1959, now chief otolaryngology and bronchoesophagology; courtesy staff Queen's Hosp., Children's Hosp.; clin. prof. surgery (otolaryngology) U. Hawaii; cons. otolaryngology Surgeon Gen. USAF, 1960-64, Shriners' Hosp. for Crippled Children; v.p. Fin. Factors Bldg. Corp.; dir. Fin. Factors, Ltd., Fin. Realty, Fin. Investment, Grand Pacific Life Ins. Co.; nat. cons. East-West Center Hawaii, 1970-75. Regent U. Hawaii, 1961-63; bd. visitors Tulane U., New Orleans, 1971-82. Diplomate Am. Bd. Otolaryngology. Fellow ACS (pres. Hawaii 1963); mem. Am. Coll. Allergists, Assn. Clin. Immunology and Allergy, Pacific Coast Oto-Ophthal Soc., Am. Laryngology, Rhinol., Otolaryngol. Soc., Inc., AMA, Am. Acad. Otolaryngology, Acad. Otolaryngology and Head and Neck Surgery, Honolulu County Med. Soc., Hawaii Med. Assn., Internat., Am. rhinologic socs., Am. Bronchoesophagol. Assn., Pan Pacific Surg. Assn., Am. Laryngol. Assn., Am. Acad. Otolaryngologic Allergy (pres. 1970-71), Am. Assn. for Study of Headache. Clubs: Masons, Shriners, Waialae Country. Home: 1570 Alewa Dr Honolulu HI 96817 Office: 1374 Nuuanu Ave Honolulu HI 96817

PANICKER, RAMACHANDRA MATATHIL PRABHAKARAN, materials scientist; b. Kottayam, Kerala, India, Jan. 16, 1945; s. Prabhakaran M.K. Kartha and Meenakshi Kunjamma; came to U.S., 1975; B.Sc. in Engring., Banaras Hindu U., 1969; M.S., U. So. Calif., 1977, Ph.D., 1978; m. Hema Nair, May 1, 1974; children—Sandip, Premjit. Tech. asst., materials div. Indian Space Research Orgn., Trivandrum, India, 1970-72, materials engr., 1972-74, sr. materials engr., 1974-75; tech. dir. materials research Sigmatron Nova, Thousand Oaks, Calif., 1978—. Mem. Electrochem. Soc., Soc. Info. Display, Sigma Xi. Club: Lions. Office: Sigmatron Nova 1901 Oak Terrace Ln Thousand Oaks CA 91320

PANIKKAR, RAIMUNDO, educator; b. Barcelona, Spain, Nov. 3, 1918; s. Rammuni and Carmen (Alemany) P.; Ph.D., U. Madrid, 1946, D.Sc., 1958; Th.D., U. Rome, 1961. Vice mgr. chem. factory, Barcelona, 1941-45; mem. faculty U. Madrid, 1947-50, U. Rome, 1964—, Harvard U., 1967-71; prof. philosophy of religion and comparative religions U. Calif., Santa Barbara, 1971—; libero docente U. Roma, 1964—. Recipient prize in humanities Menéndez y Pelayo, 1946; Spanish Prize of Lit., 1961. Mem. Internat. Inst. Philosophy, Teilhard Centre for Future of Man (v.p.), Indian Theol. Assn., Fondazione Internazionale per il diritto dei popoli. Roman Catholic. Author: Ontonomía de la Ciencia, 1961; El silencio del Dios, 1970; māyāMāyā e Apocalisse, 1966; The Vedic Experience, 1977; Myth, Faith and Hermeneutics, 1979; The Unknown Christ of Hinduism, 2d edit., 1981, numerous others. Home: 900 Hot Springs St Santa Barbara CA 93108 Office: Dept Religious Studies U Calif Santa Barbara CA 93106

PANTON, VERA JONES, ednl. adminstr.; b. Sanford, Fla., Mar. 2, 1915; d. Alexander Lafayette and Ara Margaret (Small) Jones; student Oakwood Coll., 1933-35; B.A. in Edn., Pacific Union Coll., 1940; M.S. in Ednl. Guidance, U. So. Calif., 1962; m. Robert Joseph Panton, Nov.

16, 1977. Tchr., Los Angeles Acad., 1940-49; with Los Angeles Unified Schs., 1949-76, tchr. spl. edn., 1949-68, attendance counselor, 1968-70, advisor spl. edn., 1970-73, programs for gifted children, 1973-74, sch. psychologist, 1974-75, spl. edn. tchr. 92d St. Sch., 1975-76; prin. Los Angeles Union 7th Day Adventist Sch., 1976—. Mem. Assn. Supervision and Curriculum Devel., Calif. Assn. Marriage and Family Therapists.

PAOLINI, BARBARA ANNE, photographer; b. San Mateo, Calif., June 30, 1936; d. Etchel Rossetti and Leonora Guanda (Powell) P.; student Northwestern U., 1954-55, Stanford U., 1955, UCLA, 1955-59. Apprentice, A. Del Carlo, San Jose, Calif., 1959-67; photographer Jafay Photographs, Denver, 1961; owner Paolini Photography Co., Denver, 1962-69, Seattle, 1981—; ptnr. Paolini & Sobel Co., Seattle, 1970-81. Recipient various photog. awards in local, regional and nat. competitions. Office: 300 Fairview Ave N Seattle WA 98109

PAOLO, DORRIS JUNE, artist; b. Poplar Bluff, Mo., Feb. 4, 1935; d. Bert A. and Gracie (Frank) Brannon; student Washington U., St. Louis, 1952-55, postgrad. in English, 1978-79; B.A., U. Ariz., 1959, postgrad. Coll. Law, 1957-58; M.A. in English, Southeast Mo. State U., 1973, M.A. in Counseling, 1977; M.A. in English, Washington U., St. Louis, 1980; m. Roberto Paolo; children by previous marriages—Charles Fredman, Daniel Fredman, Bruce Schulman. Costume designer, Stephen Foster Drama Assn., Bardstown, Ky., 1959; tchr. English, Oak Ridge (Mo.) High Sch., 1969-71; instr. English, Southeast Mo. State U., Cape Girardeau; instr. writing Oreg. State U., Corvallis, 1981—; one-woman shows Jackson (Mo.) Pub. Library, 1973, Howard Johnson's, Cape Girardeau, Mo., 1975; exhibited in group shows Reflections Gallery, 1973, Art-in-the-Park, Cape Girardeau, 1973-75, Nat. Miniature Art Show, Nutley, N.J., 1978, James P. Harlin Ann. Art Show, West Plains, Mo., 1978. Recipient 1st prize acrylics Festival Mo. Women in Arts, 1974. AAUW grantee, 1975. Mem. Creative Arts Guild (pres. 1974-76), Am. Personnel and Guidance Assn., AAUW (state bd. Mo. div., area rep. for cultural interests 1974-76), LWV. Author play: Noah Built an Ark, 1977; also poetry in anthologies. Home: 5529 Kalmia Dr NE Salem OR 97303

PAPEN, FRANK O'BRIEN, banker, state senator; b. Dec. 2, 1909; m. Julia Stevenson; 1 dau., Michele Papen-Daniel. Chmn. bd., chief exec. officer First Nat. Bank Dona Ana County, Las Cruces, N.Mex., 1971—, also dir., exec. v.p., 1957-60, pres., 1960-71; mem. N.Mex. Senate, 1969—; mem. N.Mex. Ho. of Reps., 1957-58; vice-chmn. 12th Regional Adv. Com. on Banking Practices and Policies, 1965-66; mem. Adv. Com. on Fed. Legis., 1966; mem. N.Mex. State Investment Council, 1963-67; mem. N.Mex. Dept. Devel. Adv. Council, 1967-68; mem. steering com. Edn. Commn. States; mem. Albuquerque dist. adv. council SBA; pres. N.Mex. State U. Pres. Assos. Recipient Branding Iron award N.Mex. State U.; Citizen of Year award N.Mex. Assn. Realtors. Mem. Am. Bankers Assn. (savs. bond chmn. N.Mex. 1964-66), N.Mex. Bankers Assn. (mem. exec. com. 1965-66), Las Cruces C. of C., Alpha Kappa Lambda. Democrat. Lodges: Kiwanis, KC. Office: PO Box FNB Las Cruces NM 88004*

PAPEN-DANIEL, MICHELE, psychology educator, psychotherapist; b. El Paso, Tex., Dec. 6, 1943; d. Frank O. and Julia (Stevenson) Papen; children—David Thomas, Julie Daniel, Ralph Daniel. B.A. in Secondary Edn. with honors, U. N.Mex., 1970; M.A. in Edn., Ariz. State U., 1971, M.Counseling, 1972, now Ph.D. candidate. Lic. marriage, family and child counselor, Calif. Staff psychologist, North Mountain Behavioral Inst., Phoenix, 1972-74; vis. prof. dept. psychology, Mesa (Ariz.) Community Coll., 1974-76, psychol. cons., dept. spl. services, 1974-76; grad. teaching assoc., instr. dept. secondary edn. Ariz. State U., Tempe, 1974-77; counselor, instr. dept. counseling Chaffey Coll., Alta Loma, Calif., 1977-78, dir. counseling, 1978-79, counseling and testing supr., 1980-81; marriage, family and child counselor Alta Loma Family and Psychol. Services, 1979; vis. lectr. European Grad. Ctr., U. So. Calif., 1979-80; lectr. Calif. State Coll., Fullerton, 1980-81; asst. prof. psychology U. La Verne (Calif.), 1981—, also program specialist; exec. dir. Calif. Psychoednl. Systems, Inc., 1982—; pvt. practice marriage, family and child counseling; condr. tng. workshops in field, U.S., Holland, Belgium, Germany; also lectr.; dir. First Nat. Bank of Dona Ana County, Las Cruces, N.Mex. Trustee Claremont Collegiate Sch., 1978-80; Mem. Am. Personnel and Guidance Assn., Calif. Personnel and Guidance Assn., Am. Psychol. Assn. (assoc.), Far West Philosophy of Edn. Soc., Nat. Assn. Women Deans, Adminstrs. and Counselors, Philosophy of Edn. Assn., Western Psychol. Assn., Pi Lambda Theta. Contbr. writings to profl. publs. in field; author fed. grant projects.

PAPPAS, PETE, broadcasting executive; b. Price, Utah, Sept. 2, 1937; s. John and Titika P.; m. Bessie Katsavrais, Apr. 4; children—Pete and Mike (twins). Student Bill Ogden Engring. Sch. Announcer, radio sta., Modesto, Calif.; owner, investor, developer sta. KVEG, Las Vegas, Nev., sta. KGEN, Tulare, Calif., sta. KTRB, Modesto; owner, founder sta. KBOS, Tulare, sta. KHOP, Modesto/Stockton, Calif., sta. KMPH-TV, Visalia-Fresno, Calif.; now owner, gen. mgr. stas. KTRB-AM and KHOP-FM, Modesto (The Pete Pappas Co.); ptnr. Power Investment Co.; v.p. Arnold Weibe Dodge Chrysler Auto Agy., Tulare. Past chmn. Tulare Planning Commn. Served with USN. Mem. Nat. Assn. Broadcasting, Nat. Radio Broadcasters Assn., Calif. Broadcasters Assn. (past dir.-at-large). Greek Orthodox. Clubs: Rotary, Sportsmen of Stanislaus, Elks. Office: PO Box 3839 Modesto CA 95252

PAQUE, JOHN BARRETT, insurance company executive; b. Portland, Oreg., Jan. 10, 1940; s. Frank Joseph and Maxine Elizabeth (Barrett) P.; B.S., Portland State U., 1965; J.D., Northwestern Lewis and Clark Coll. of Law, 1970; m. Catherine Jean Lynch, Sept. 8, 1962; children—Shawn, Christopher, Timothy. Advt. rep. Oregonian Pub. Co., Portland, 1959-65; asst. mgerchandising mgr. Arcoa, Inc., Portland, 1965-66; asst. claim mgr. Arcoa, Inc., 1966-67; claim examiner Consol. Freightways, Portland, 1968-74; claims/safety coordinator Employee Benefits Ins. Co., Portland, 1975-76, claim mgr., 1977, v.p. claims N.W. div., 1979-83, dir., 1979-83; regional supr. self-ins. Crown Zellerbach Corp., 1983—. Active, Jennings Lodge Little League, 1975-76; appointee Oreg. Med. Rules Com., 1977. Served to 2nd lt. Army N.G., 1960-68. Recipient Erickson Trophy award Officer Candidate Sch., 1966. Mem. Portland C. of C. (task force mem. on workers compensation 1979-80), Oreg. Self Ins. Assn., Workers Compensation Claim Assn. Roman Catholic. Clubs: Elks, YMCA. Home: 6505 SW 90th St Portland OR 97223 Office: 2404 E Mill Plain Blvd Vancouver WA 98661

PAQUETTE, MARY ELLEN, ophthalmologist; b. Tucson, Oct. 1, 1938; d. Garnet Douglas and Mascha V. (Dyck) Percy; B.Sc., U. Ariz., 1960; M.D., Stanford U., 1965; m. Robert Emmett Paquette, Nov. 1, 1975; 1 dau., Connie Marie. Intern, U. Iowa, Iowa City, 1965-66; resident in ophthalmology Stanford (Calif.) U., 1966-69; practice medicine specializing in ophthalmology; mem. staffs El Camino Hosp. Mem. Am. Acad. Ophthalmology, AMA, Calif. Med. Assn., Santa Clara County Med. Assn., Peninsula Eye Soc., Phi Beta Kappa, Phi Kappa Phi, Kappa Alpha Theta. Presbyterian. Club: Soroptimists. Home: 3355 Villa Robleda Dr Mountain View CA 94040 Office: 2500 Hospital Dr Bldg 11 Mountain View CA 94040

PARADISE, MICHAEL EMMANUEL, univ. chancellor; b. Rethymnon, Crete, Greece, Mar. 26, 1928; came to U.S., 1951, naturalized, 1961; B.Sc., Morningside Coll., 1955; M.A., U. No. Colo., 1958, Ed.D., 1962; m. Ann Ramos, Dec. 29, 1957; children—Maria, George, Andrew. Tchr. high sch., Wausa, Nebr., 1956-58; tchr. high sch., Milliken, Colo., 1968-60, prin., 1960-62; prof. math. Chadron State Coll., 1962-68, chmn. div. sci., 1963-65, dean, 1965-68; pres. Northeastern Nebr. Coll., 1968-72, Central Tech. Community Coll., 1972-79; chancellor U. Alaska, Juneau, 1979—; chmn. Nebr. Higher Edn. Facilities Commn., 1971-74, Nebr. Profl. Practices Commn., 1972-74. Mem. Nebr. Republican Central Com., 1976-78; pres. Hastings (Nebr) C. of C., 1977-78, Hastings United Way, 1978. Served with Greek Air Force, 1949-51. Recipient commendation C. of C. Norfolk (Nebr.), 1972, C. of C. Hastings, 1978, Chadron State Coll., 1968, Northeastern Nebr. Coll., 1972, Central Tech. Community Coll., 1979, U. Alaska, 1980. Mem. Am. Assn. State Colls. and Univs. (Alaska chmn.), Council North Central Community and Jr. Colls. (pres. 1977-78), Kans-Nebr. Ednl. Consortium (pres. 1971-72), Nebr. Assn. Tech. Community Colls. (pres. 1972-73), Juneau C. of C. (exec. bd.), Am.-Hellenic Ednl. Progressive Assn. Republican. Greek Orthodox. Clubs: Rotary, Masons, Shriners, Elks. Office: 11120 Glacier Hwy Juneau AK 99801

PARAISO, DAVID ROMERO, video co. exec.; b. Davao City, Philippines, June 4, 1952; came to U.S., 1974, naturalized, 1980; s. David C. and Rebecca (Ochangco) P.; Lead programmer Pan Am. World Airways, Rockleigh, N.Y., 1974-78; prin. software specialist/project mgr. Digital Equip. Corp., Somerset, N.J., 1978-80; sr. systems analyst Delta Resources, Inc., Anaheim, Calif., 1980-81; mgr. tech. services Times Mirror Videotex Services, Irvine, Calif., 1981—. Chmn. council on ministries Asbury United Meth. Ch., 1981—; dir. Filipino Caucus, Inc., So. Calif., 1981—. Recipient Digital Equip. Corp. Software Excellence award, 1979. Mem. Am. Inst. Indsl. Engrs., Digital Equipment Computer Users Soc., Network Users Assn., Data Processing Mgmt. Assn. Office: 1375 Sunflower Ave Costa Mesa CA 92626

PARARAS-CARAYANNIS, GEORGE, sci. and tech. co. exec.; b. Athens, Greece, Nov. 8, 1936; came to U.S., 1955, naturalized, 1967; s. Ambrossios and Mary (Frantzis) Pararas; B.S. in Chemistry, Roosevelt U., 1959, M.S. in Chemistry, 1963; M.S. in Oceanography, U. Hawaii, 1967; Ph.D. in Marine Scis., U. Del., 1975; m. Irene Trakis, Oct. 17, 1970; children—George, Nicole. Research chemist Joanna Western Mills Co., Chgo., 1959-63; research geophysicist Hawaii Inst. Geophysics, U. Hawaii, Honolulu, 1963-67; dir. Ocean Mining & Engring. Co., Honolulu, 1967-70; dir. Mermex S.A., Mexico City, 1970-71; oceanographer U.S. Army Corps Engrs., N.Y.C., 1971-72, U.S. Coastal Engring. Research Center, Washington, 1972-74; dir. Internat. Tsunami Info. Center Intergovtl. Oceanographic Commn., UNESCO, Honolulu, 1974—; pres. Internat. Emerald Corp., Inc., Honolulu, 1976—, House of Emeralds, Inc., Honolulu, 1980—; Tsunami advisor, cons. State of Hawaii, 1974—. Mem. Am. Geophys. Union, Marine Tech. Soc., Am. Soc. Oceanography, Internat. Oceanographic Found., Am. Acad. Cons., Internat. Union Geodesy and Geophysics, Pacific Sci. Assn., Hawaii Acad. Scis., Am. Nuclear Soc., The Tsunami Soc., Sigma Xi. Contbr. numerous articles to various publs. Home: 874 Nana-Honua St Honolulu HI 96825

PARASHAR, OM DATT, psychologist, cons.; b. Delhi, India, Sept. 15, 1939; came to U.S., 1971, naturalized, 1980; s. Ram Sawrup and Ram Davi (Vashistha) P.; m. Usha Joshi, Oct. 21, 1979; 1 son, Amish. M.A. in Philosophy, Punjab U., India, 1960; M.A. in Psychology, U. Delhi, 1965; ednl. psychology cert. Oxford (Eng.) U., 1969; M.Ed., U. Toronto (Ont., Can.), 1971; Ed.D. in Spl. Edn. (HEW fellow), U. Cin., 1973. Tchr., Mcpl. Corp. of Delhi Schs., 1957-62; research fellow Nat. Council Ednl. Research and Tng. (with HEW), New Delhi, 1963-67; spl. edn. tchr. Bucks County Sch., High Wycombe, Eng. and lectr. Wymcombe Coll., High Wycombe, 1967-70; instr. U. Cin., 1971-73; asst. prof. spl. edn. Va. Commonwealth U., 1973-79; dir., cons. psychology of mgmt. Parashar Entrepreneurs, Seal Beach, Calif., 1979—; mem. exec. com. Race Relations Commn., Eng., 1967-70; Brit. Commonwealth Edn. and Travel scholar, Can., 1970. Mem. Am. Psychol. Assn., Brit. Psychol. Soc. (asso.), Soc. Prevention of Delinquency and Other Problems in Children and Youth (pres. 1979—). Author books, most recent being: Psycho-educational Diagnosis: Identifying Learning and Behavior Problems, 1976; Parashar Behavior Rating Scale, 1976; Dictionary of Special Education, 1977; contbr. articles to profl. jours. Office: PO Box 985 Los Alamitos CA 90720

PARBURY, C(HARLES) ALAN, mangement consultant; b. Palo Alto, Calif., Aug. 13, 1947; s. Charles B. and Ethel N. Parbury; B.S.C., U. Santa Clara, 1970; postgrad. Coll. San Mateo, 1972-73; m. Sandra Wanderer, June 1978; children—Cynthia J., Holly R. Sales and ops. mgr. Grantree Corp., San Francisco, 1970-74; mgmt. cons. G.S. May, Internat., Park Ridge, Ill. and BWA, Ltd., San Francisco, 1974-78; corp. pres. Alameda Joe's Inc., Alameda, Calif., 1978-81; funding dir. Women's Profl. Golf Tour, 1981-82; sr. cons. Williams & Assocs., Walnut Creek, Calif., 1982—; sr. cons., project mgr. Gustafson Cons., Walnut Creek, 1981—; v.p. TWA Mgmt. Corp., 1983—; sec. Vector Exploration Inc., Walnut Creek, 1983—. Active Big Bros. Am.; vol. Spl. Olympics, Little League Am., United Cerebral Palsy. Mem. Am. Bus. Assn., Internat. Platform Assn., Assn. Mgmt. Consultants. Republican. Roman Catholic. Clubs: Kiwanis, Elks. Office: 800 S Broadway Walnut Creek CA

PARCELL, RAYMOND EUNICE, JR., aerospace company manager; b. Fredericksburg, Va., Sept. 22, 1930; s. Raymond Eunice and Irene (Smith) P.; B.S. in Elec. Engring., Va. Poly. Inst. and State U., 1951; M.B.A. (Harriman scholar), Columbia U., 1958; m. Winifred Patricia Slaght, Nov. 8, 1974. With Hughes Aircraft Co., Culver City, Calif., 1954-59, program mgr. Japan Hughes Internat., 1959-62, mgr. Hughes Washington Internat. office, 1962-65, mgr. Advanced Programs for Air Def., Hughes Aero. Systems Div., 1965-68, mktg. mgr. Roland Program, 1968, spl. projects mgr. Hughes Aerospace Groups, 1974-75, corp. mgr. spl. programs Hughes Aircraft Co., Culver City, 1975—; dir. Perry D. Edson, Inc., Los Angeles, Raybilron, Inc., Stanton, Va. Served with U.S. Army, 1951-53; to col. Res. Tau Beta Pi, Pi Delta Epsilon, Eta Kappa Nu, Alpha Kappa Psi. Methodist. Clubs: Calif. Yacht, Interstellar, Icarian Flying, Masons. Office: PO Box 2999 242/1 Torrance CA 90509

PARCHER, ROBERT LEE, mktg. exec.; b. Whittier, Calif., Jan. 28, 1934; s. Cloyce and Utoka (Jones) P.; A.B., U. Calif., Berkeley, 1955; M.S., Utah State U., 1956; postgrad. UCLA, 1960-63. Exec. v.p. ASI Market Research, Inc., N.Y.C., 1963-76; owner, pres. The Research Center, Torrance, Calif., 1976-81; mgr. Pacific region Nat. Family Opinion, Beverly Hills, Calif., 1981—; adj. prof. Northrop U., 1979—; instr. UCLA extension, 1978—. Mem. Am. Psychol. Assn., Am. Mktg. Assn., Mktg. Research Assn. Republican. Mem. Sci. of Mind Ch. Contbr. articles to profl. jours. Office: 8383 Wilshire Blvd Beverly Hills CA 90211

PARDEE, RONALD L., educator; b. Decorah, Iowa, Dec. 14, 1947; s. Dean and Agnes (Brannon) P.; B.S. in Engring., Calif. State Poly. U., Pomona, 1978; M.A. in Edn., Calif. State Coll., San Bernardino, 1981; m. Cynthia Ann Jones, Oct. 21, 1973. Instr., Am. Motorcyle Schs., Santa Fe Springs, Calif., 1977-78; dean trade and indsl. programs, asst. prof. engring. and mech. trades, head dept. Riverside (Calif.) City Coll., 1978—; cons., propr. Pardee Cons., 1979—. Served with USNR, 1966-71; Vietnam. Named Calif. Gt. Tchr., 1980. Mem. Soc. Automotive Engrs., Am. Vocat. Assn., Calif. Dirs. Vocat. Edn., So. Calif. Council Vocat. Edn. Adminstrs. Club: Calif. Racing. Author curriculum materials. Home: 4050 Adams St Riverside CA 92504 Office: 4800 Magnolia St Riverside CA 92506

PARENTE, ROBERT BRUCE, elec. engr.; b. N.Y.C., Sept. 10, 1936; s. Almerico Elmer and Royda (Boyd) P.; B.S. in Elec. Engring., Mass. Inst. Tech., 1959, M.S. in Engring., 1959, E.E., 1961, Ph.D., 1966; m. Rozalinda Thelma Saturnio, May 28, 1977; children—Jennifer Dee, Jessica Dale, Jacquelyn Dawn. Instr. elec. engring. Mass. Inst. Tech., Cambridge, 1959-65; asst. prof. engring. U. Calif. at Los Angeles, 1965-70; mgr. electric power systems System Devel. Corp., Santa Monica, Calif., 1970-72, dir. planning, 1973-75, dep. dir. energy devel., 1975-76; sr. cons. Theodore Barry & Assos., Los Angeles, 1976-78; propr. Parente & Assocs., mgmt. cons., 1978—; expert witness before utility commns. Res. lt. sheriff Los Angeles County Sheriff's Dept., 1970—. Registered profl. engr., Calif. Mem. IEEE, Soc. Indsl. and Applied Maths., Inst. Mgmt. Scis., Ops. Research Soc. Am., Calif. Soc. Profl. Engrs., Sigma Xi, Tau Beta Pi, Eta Kappa Nu, Hex-Alpha, Theta Chi. Author: Electric Power Pools, 1983; contbr. articles to profl. jours. Patentee in field. Office: PO Box 24-BB6 Los Angeles CA 90024

PARIS, PHILLIP SANCHEZ, educator; b. Gary, Ind., Sept. 29, 1941; s. Juan and Maria Paris-Sanchez; B.S.Fgn. Service, Georgetown U., 1963; M.A. in Internat. Relations, U. So. Calif., 1967, Ph.D. in Polit. Sci., 1973; children—Jacqueline Janine, Phillip II, David Anthony, Paul James. Fellow, instr., asst. prof. Latin Am. Studies Calif. Lutheran Coll., 1967-71; research asso., state coordinator Title I (HEA 65) Coordinating Council for Higher Edn., Sacramento, 1971-74; higher edn. specialist, planning Calif. Postsecondary Edn. Commn., Sacramento, 1974-75; div. dir. multicultural edn. Northwest Regional Edn. Lab., 1975-80; acting dir. Instituto Colegial César Chávez, 1980—; project dir. Significant Bilingual Instructional Features Study, NWREL, 1981-82, vis. prof. pub. policy and adminstrn. Calif. State U., Bakersfield, 1982—, cons. on bi-lingual/multi-cultural edn., pub. mgmt./supervision; reader Title VII, ESEA, Fund for Improvement Postsecondary Edn.; chmn. bd. dirs. Colegio César Chávez. Mem. Nat. Assn. Bilingual Educators, Nat. Assn. Public Adminstrs., Oreg. Assn. Bilingual Educators, Am. Ednl. Research Assn. Democrat. Roman Catholic. Contbg. author: Argentina: Mosaic of Discord, 1968; Political Forces in Latin America, 1970; also articles. Home: 17620 Blue Heron Rd Lake Oswego OR 97034 Office: Calif State U Bakersfield CA 93309

PARISE, CARL, mfg. exec.; b. Denver, May 16, 1921; s. Michael and Rose (Ruvo) P.; student public schs.; m. Dixie Lee Connor, Dec. 5, 1978; children by previous marriage—Michael, David, Brian. Factory rep., distbr. Kirby Co., 1950-69; pres. Parise & Sons, Reno, 1972—; pres. O.M.A.C., Sierra Elec. Motors; pres. P.&S. Plastics, Gardena, Calif. Chmn. Nev. Republican Party Fin. Com.; pres. United Taxpayers of Washoe County. Served with USNR, 1942-45. Decorated D.F.C., 3 Air Medals; recipient leading distbr. and factory rep. awards for No. Nev., Kirby Co. Inventor carpet cleaning hot water extraction systems. Home: 1990 Pheasant Ln Reno NV 89509 Office: 1575 Crane Way Sparks NV 89431

PARISH, H(AYWARD) CARROLL, JR., educator, business executive; b. Pasadena, Calif., Feb. 13, 1920; s. Hayward Carroll and Gertrude I. (Riggs) P. A.B., UCLA 1943, M.A., 1950, Ph.D., 1958. Los Angeles County Youth commr., 1938-42, pres. commn., 1938; asst. prof. naval sci. U. Calif., 1946-47, 52-53, assoc. prof., 1954, asst. dean, 1957-62, assoc. dean, 1962-76, dean, 1966-71; provost, trustee Miller Community Coll., 1971—; adj. prof. polit. sci. U. La Verne, 1976—; pres. Environ. Design Assocs., 1966—; pres. Kapa Co., 1969—; attaché Calif. State legislature, 1947; Fulbright research fellow Waseda U. Tokyo, 1958-59; engaged in property mgmt.; lectr. Asiatic Studies, U. So. Calif., 1961; collaborator Inst. Internat. Relations, Aoyama Gakuin U., Tokyo, 1960—. Mem. scholarship adv. com. Calif. State Scholarship and Loan Commn., 1964-71; cons. U.S. Office Edn., 1969-71; cons. Time-Life Books Inc. Sec. citizens ind. vice investigating com. which initiated successful recall against corrupt Los Angeles adminstrn., 1938; mem. exec. com. Los Angeles Co. Coordinating Councils, 1939-41. Served in USNR, World War II, Korea; capt., 1964; comdg. officer Naval Res. Officers Sch., 1965-68. Twice decorated for combat service Pacific area; for valor at Okinawa when ship was hit by Kamikaze plane; for meritorious service as flag-sec. to comdr. assault transport div. Decorated Order Golden Merit, Japanese Red Cross; knight grand officer Order St. John The Bapt. Am.; knight comdr. Hospitaller Order St. John of Jerusalem; knight grand cross Mil. and Hospitaller Order St. Lazarus of Jerusalem; comdr. Order of Merit; knight of honor Venerable Order of Rose of Lippe. Fellow Institut International des Arts et des Lettres (life), AAAS, Augustan Soc.; mem. Am. Legion (mem. Nat. Security Commn. 1950-53, life), Am. Polit. Sci. Assn., Founders and Patriots Am. (gov. gen. 1978-81), Soc. Colonial Wars, S.R., Internat. Polit. Sci. Assn., Assn. Asian Studies (chmn. Pacific Coast regional conf. 1967), Am. Coll. Personnel Assn. (chmn. commn.), Assn. Ind. Colls. and Schs. (com. chmn.), Coll. Scholarship Service, Com. on Fgn. Students, Navy League (life), Asia Soc., Am. Siam Soc. (pres.), Siam Soc. (life), Nat. (pres. 1971, distinguished service award 1971), Western (pres. 1970, distinguished achievement award 1971) assns. student financial aid adminstrs., Associated Japan Am. Socs. U.S. (v.p. 1979-81), Japan Am. Soc. So. Calif. (hon. officer), Phi Eta Sigma, Alpha Mu Gamma, Pi Sigma Alpha, Pi Gamma Mu (chancellor Western region, nat. honor Key 1973). Episcopalian. Clubs: Jonathan (Los Angeles); Internat. House of Japan (Tokyo), UCLA Faculty Center. Author: Canada and the United Nations, 1950. Co-author: Thailand Bibliography, 1958. Contbr. articles on internat., Far East, S.E. Asian Affairs to profl. jours. Home: 633 24th St Santa Monica CA 90402

PARK, D. G., geological company executive; b. Burley, Idaho, May 1, 1935; d. Marcus Foss and Millicent Alice (Hoover) Purcell; m. John H.S. Park, Mar. 21, 1954 (div.) children—Greg, Kelly, Mitch, Kevin. B.S., Coll. of Idaho. Adminstr. edn. program Alexander Lindsey Mus., Walnut Creek, Calif., 1974-79; adminstr. Geosat Com., Inc., San Francisco, 1979—. Office: 153 Kearny St Suite 209 San Francisco CA 94108

PARK, U. YOUNG, nuclear engineer; b. Seoul; s. M.W. and D.C. (Chang) P.; B.S., Seoul Nat. U., 1963; M.S., U. Cin., 1970; m. Linda Rugh; children—Tara, Thomas. Nuclear engr. State of Ohio, to 1978, Battelle Meml. Inst., Columbus, Ohio, 1978-81; power plant system engr. Bechtel Power Corp., San Francisco, 1981—. Lic. profl. engr. Mem. Am. Nuclear Soc., Nat. Assn. Underwater Instrs. Club: Adventurers Yacht and Sailing. Office: PO Box 3965 San Francisco CA 94119

PARK, WILLIAM ANTHONY, lawyer; b. Blackfoot, Idaho, June 4, 1934; s. William Clare and Thelma Edelweiss (Shear) P.; m. Elizabeth Jane Taylor, Aug. 26, 1961 (div.); children—Susan E., William Adam, Patricia Anne. A.A., Boise Jr. Coll., 1954; B.A. in Polit. Sci., U. Idaho, 1958, J.D., 1963. Bar: Idaho 1963. Assoc. Bickel & Park, 1963-64; sole practice, Boise, Idaho, 1964-71; atty. gen. State of Idaho, Boise, 1971-75; ptnr. Park & Meuleman, Boise, 1975-82; sole practice, Boise, 1982-83; sr. ptnr. Park & Burkett, Boise, 1983—; chmn. Idaho Law Enforcement Planning Commn., 1971-75. Del. Democratic Nat. Conv., 1968; chmn. Idaho Bicentennial Commn., 1971-77; bd. dirs. Idaho Lung Assn., 1975—, Radio Free Europe/Radio Liberty, 1977-82, Am. Lung Assn., 1978—. Served with U.S. Army, 1956-57. Recipient Disting. Service award Boise Jaycees, 1971. Mem. Boise Bar Assn., Idaho Bar Assn., Assn. Trial Lawyers Am., Idaho Trial Lawyers Assn. Episcopalian. Club: Crane Creek Country (Boise). Home: 706 Warm Springs Ave Boise ID 83702 Office: Park & Burkett 802 W Bannock Suite 601 PO Box 2762 Boise ID 83701

PARKER, ALAN, artist, educator, architectural designer, color consultant; b. Harvard, Nebr., Jan. 8, 1916; s. Harry Theodore and Olga Ione (Whiteman) P.; m. Beatrice Ford, June 27, 1940. B.F.A., U. Nebr., 1938, postgrad., 1939, 49. Art dir. Brown McDonald Co., 1940-42; archtl. designer Robert Stanton, Keeble & Rhoda, Monterey, Calif., 1950-62; educator U. Calif.-Santa Cruz, 1969, 72, 82; murals executed Monterey County Courthouse, Salinas, Calif., 1963, Monterey City Juvenile Hall, Salinas, 1960; painter and sculptor. Mem. adv. com. Monterey Planning Commn., 1967—. Served as lt. USNR, 1942-46. Recipient numerous painting prizes. Author: James Joyce, A Bibliography, 1947.

PARKER, BOBBY DOUGLAS, educator, photographer; b. Anthony, Kans., Feb. 12, 1935; s. Luther Joseph and Inez Beatrice (Lawrence) P.; m. Nelda Arlene Parker, Aug. 23, 1958; children—Steven Douglas, Gregory Allen, Kirby Lynn. Attended Kans. State U., Manhattan, 1953-56; B. Music Edn., Wichita State U., 1960, M. Music Edn., 1964; specialists in edn. cert. U. Colo., 1975; student portraits for small studio Brooks Inst. Photography, Santa Barbara, Calif., 1982; student Nikon Sch. Photography, 1980; grad. with spl. honors Modern Sch. Photography, N.Y.C., 1981, N.Y. Inst. Profl. Photography, 1982. Cert. tchr., Kans.; 3d class radio lic., Kans., Colo. Tchr. elem. vocal music Moscow (Kans.) Pub. Schs., 1960-64, jr. and sr. high sch. vocal music Sublette (Kans.) Pub. Schs., 1966-73; salesman, announcer Sta.-KLEY, Wellington, Kans., 1966-73; tchr. vocal music Jefferson County (Colo.) Pub. Sch., 1973—; instr. photography, dark-room techniques, 1981—; owner, photographer Universal Creations, Arvada, Colo., 1979—; tour guide Coors Brewery; dir. ch. choirs, 1958-75, including First United Methodist Ch., Wellington, 1966-73; choir dir. Sumner County (Kans.) Community Chorus, 1966-73; dir. prize-winning music groups in contests. Mem. Colo. Tchrs. Assn., NEA, Music Educators Nat. Conf., Am. Choral Dirs. Assn., Profl. Photographers Am. (2 Nat. award merits), Wedding Photographers Internat. (Hon. award in photography at convs. 1981, 82), Photographers Soc. Am., Phi Delta Kappa, Phi Mu Alpha. Democrat. Clubs: Masons (Wellington); Shriners (Denver). Home: 8119 Webster Arvado CO 80003 Office: 7000 W 76th Arvado CO 80003

PARKER, BRIAN PRESCOTT, forensic scientist; b. Norfolk, Va., Aug. 31, 1929; s. Milton Ellsworth and Louise Randall (Smith) P.; B.S. in Quantitative Biology, M.I.T., 1953; J.D., Northwestern U., 1957; M.Criminology, U. Calif., Berkeley, 1961, D.Criminology, 1967; m. Sonia Garcia Rosario, Dec. 23, 1960; children—Robin Marie, Augustin Keith. Research asst. U. P.R. Med. Sch., 1961; cons. P.R. Justice Dept., 1961-63; spl. asst. FDA, Washington, 1964; lectr., then asst. prof. criminology U. Calif., Berkeley, 1964-70; sr. criminalist, then sr. forensic scientist Stanford Research Inst., Menlo Park, Calif., 1971-73; prof. forensic sci. and criminal justice Calif. State U., Sacramento, 1973—; project dir. phys. evidence Dept. Justice, 1969-70. Fellow Am. Acad. Forensic Scis.; mem. Am. Acad. Polit. and Social Sci., Am. Chem. Soc., Acad. Criminal Justice Scis., Calif. Assn. Criminalists, Forensic Sci. Soc. London. Co-author: Physical Evidence in the Administration of Criminal Justice, 1970, The Role of Criminalistics in the World of the Future, 1972; asso. editor Law, Medicine, Science—and Justice, 1964. Home: 5117 Ridgegate Way Fair Oaks CA 95628 Office: 6000 J St Sacramento CA 95819

PARKER, C. WOLCOTT, II, international technology transfer, licensing consultant; b. N.Y.C., Jan. 15, 1924; s. Philip McGregor and Eleanor (Landon) P.; B.B.A., U. N.Mex., 1952; postgrad. Inst. Tecnologico de Estudios Superiores de Monterrey, 1969-72, Ariz. State U., 1978; m. Mary Helen Manias, Dec. 27, 1948; 1 dau., Cynthia Jean Parker McNeill. Owner, mgr. Interam. Importing Co., Peoria, Ill., 1952-59; sales engr. Latin Am., Beloit (Wis.) Corp., 1959-66; mktg. dir. Fabricación de Máquinas, Monterrey, Nuevo Leon, Mex., 1966-72; pres. CW Parker Mgmt. Counsel, Tempe, Ariz., 1972-81; dir. INTERCOM., Am. Grad. Sch. Internat. Mgmt., Glendale, Ariz., 1981—; vis. asst. prof. Am. Grad. Sch. Internat. Mgmt.; lectr. at grad. schs., seminars, assn. meetings, and on radio and TV. Bd. dirs. Club Serra de Monterrey, 1969-72, v.p., 1970; friend Center for Latin Am. Studies, Ariz. State U., 1972-75. Served with USN, 1941-45. Mem. Licensing Execs. Soc. (publs., edn. com.) Ariz.-Mex. Commn., Southwestern World Trade Com., Ariz. Assn. Industry (treas.), Kappa Sigma. Roman Catholic. Contbr. articles to jours. and mags. Office: PO Box 50159 Phoenix AZ 85076

PARKER, CLYDE ALVIN, psychologist; b. Ogden, Utah, Mar. 17, 1927; s. Thomas and Reka (Van Braak) P.; m. Ilene Kendell, Dec. 27, 1950; children—Thomas, Gregory, Camille, Lisa Marie. B.S., Brigham Young U., 1952; M.S., U. Minn., 1957, Ph.D., 1957; Lic. Psychologist, Utah; lic. cons. psychologist, Minn. Instr., Ogden City Schs., 1952-53; asso. prof. Brigham Young U., 1953-64, dir. counseling services, 1957-60; prof. ednl. psychology U. Minn., 1964-82; psychologist McKay Dee Hosp., Ogden, 1982—; cons. in field. Served with USN, 1945-46. Mem. Am. Psychol. Assn., Am. Personnel and Guidance Assn., Assn. Mormon Counselors and Psychotherapists. Mormon. Contbr. articles to profl. jours. Home: 6103 S 2900 E Ogden UT 84403 Office: McKay Dee Hosp Ogden UT 84409

PARKER, JOHN CARLYLE, librarian; b. Ogden, Utah, Oct. 14, 1931; s. Levi and Marrietta (Parkinson) P.; m. Janet C. Greene, May 31, 1956; children—Denise, Nathan, Bret. B.A., Brigham Young U., 1957; M.L.S., U. Calif.-Berkeley, 1958. Spl. services librarian Calif. State Coll., Humboldt, 1958-60; cataloger, reference librarian Ch. Coll. Hawaii, Laie, 1960-62, acting librarian, 1962-63; head pub. services Calif. State Coll. Stanislaus Library, Turlock, 1963—, asst. dir., 1968—; lectr. general. research and reference. Sec. Turlock Centennial Found. Bd., 1971-75; pres. Turlock Community Concert Bd., 1973-75; merit badge counselor Yosemite Council, Boy Scouts Am. Served with AUS, 1953-55. Mem. Calif. Library Assn., ALA, AAUP, Calif. Tchrs. Assn., NEA, Congress Faculty Assn., Conf. Calif. Hist. Soc., Stanislaus County Hist. Soc. (v.p., program chmn. 1972-73). Democrat. Mem. Ch. of Jesus Christ of Latter-day Saints. Contbr. numerous articles to profl. publs. Home: 2115 N Denair Turlock CA 95380 Office: 801 W Monte Vista Ave Turlock CA 95380

PARKER, JOHN FRANCIS, lawyer; b. Los Angeles, Aug. 17, 1928; s. Ignatius Francis and Helen Mary (Pierik) P.; B.A. cum laude, Loyola U. of Los Angeles, 1950; J.D., U. Calif. at Los Angeles, 1953; m. Mary Ann Kirkpatrick, Dec. 26, 1950; children—Kathleen Ann, John Patrick. Admitted to Calif. bar, 1953; with Title Ins. & Trust Co., Los Angeles, 1956-57; counsel State Compensation Ins. Fund, Los Angeles, 1957-58; asso. Herlihy & Herlihy, Los Angeles, also San Bernadino, 1958-63; individual practice of law, San Bernardino, Calif., 1963-64; mem. firm Parker & Dally, Pomona, Calif., 1964—. Chmn. bd. trustees, pres. Southwestern U., Los Angeles, 1969-75, trustee, mem. exec. com., 1975—. Served to 1st lt. AUS, 1953-56. Mem. State Bar Calif., Am., Los Angeles County, Pomona Valley, San Bernardino County bar assns. Home: 778 Via Espirito Santos Claremont CA 91711 Office: 100 Pomona Mall W #300 Pomona CA 91766

PARKER, KAREN CROMWELL, clin. psychologist; b. Stamford, Conn., Aug. 26, 1946; d. Blakeslee Barnes and Doris Grace (Knutson) P.; m. Steven Tice Hutcherson, Mar. 21, 1970; 1 dau., Halle Elizabeth; m. 2d, Ronald Marvin Klein, July 12, 1980. B.A., Lake Erie Coll., 1968; B.A. in Psychology, U. Md., 1973; M.A. in Clin. Psychology, Case Western Res. U., 1977, Ph.D. in Clin. Psychology, 1978; lic. psychologist, Calif. Psychology trainee Cleve. Clinic Found., 1975-76; psychology intern Wade Park VA Hosp., Cleve., 1976-78; health psychologist VA Hosp., Loma Linda, Calif., 1978-79, coordinator pain therapy and evaluation unit, 1979-82; dir. pain mgmt. program San Pedro (Calif.) Peninsula Hosp., 1982—; lectr. Loma Linda U. Med. Center, 1979—; clin. instr. dept. psychology Fuller Theol. Sem., 1980—. Recipient Superior Performance award J.L. Pettis VA Hosp., 1980, 82. Mem. Am. Psychol. Assn. Democrat. Episcopalian. Home: 1575 Stonewood Ct San Pedro CA 90732 Office: San Pedro Peninsula Hosp 1300 W 7th St San Pedro CA 90732

PARKER, KATHLEEN, communications company executive; b. Ortonville, Minn., May 23, 1948; d. L.R. and Barbara (Bruskin) Severin; m. John Basil Parker, May 19, 1973. B.A., Barnard Coll., 1970; M.S., Columbia U., 1973. Broadcast writer AP, N.Y.C., 1973; anchorwoman, reporter Sta. KFMB-TV, San Diego, 1973-77; pres., co-owner Pacific Communications, 1978—. Mem. U.S. Olympic Fund-Raising Com., 1983-84. Recipient Women Helping Women award Soroptimist Club, 1981; East Asian journalist fellow Columbia U., 1972-73. Mem. Nat. Assn. Broadcasters. Office: Pacific Communications PO Box 4100 South Lake Tahoe CA 95729

PARKER, KEITH ROBERT, statistical consultant; b. Meriden, Conn., May 5, 1943; s. Howard Henry and Marion (Dunlop) P.; m. Karyn Stricklett, Aug. 25, 1971; 1 dau., Sherry Lynn. B.A. in Biology, Calif. State U.-Sonoma, 1972; M.S. in Stats., U. Wash., 1976. Statistician NOAA, La Jolla, Calif., 1976-79; stats. cons., 1979—; spl. cons. Electric Power Research Inst.; lectr. stats. San Diego U., 1980-81. Served with Spl. Forces, U.S. Army, 1964-67. Decorated Bronze Star. Mem. Am. Statis. Assn., AAAS. Contbr. articles to industry bulls. Developer, implementer statis. methods used world-wide. Home: 1837 Puterbaugh St San Diego CA 92103 Office: 531 Encinitas Blvd Suite 102 Encinitas CA 92024

PARKER, KENNETH DEAN, toxicologist-criminalist; b. Menan, Idaho, Feb. 27, 1935; s. Kenneth Lewis and Bernedene R. (Nichols) P.; student U. Hawaii, 1953-55; B.S., U. Calif. at Berkeley, 1958, M. Criminology, 1960; postgrad. U. Calif. at San Francisco, 1968; m. Gay Hemmerling, June 16, 1961; 1 son, Dean Walter. Research asst. U. Calif.-Berkeley, 1957-62; toxicologist-criminalist Hine Labs., Inc., San Francisco, 1962-82; owner, dir. Probe Sci. and Tech. Investigations, 1973—. Leader Mt. Diablo council Boy Scouts Am., 1970-72. Mem. Am. Acad. Forensic Scis., Am. Chem. Soc., Internat. Assn. Forensic Toxicologists, Western Pharmacology Soc. Contbr. articles to profl. jours. Home: 2170 Pyramid Dr El Sobrante CA 94803 Office: 357 Tehama St San Francisco CA 94103

PARKER, LLOYD STUART, radiologist; b. Bklyn., Mar. 8, 1952; s. Norman and Evelyn P.; m. Susan Ross, Nov. 29, 1981. B.A. in Biology, UCLA, 1973, M.D., 1977. Diplomate Nat. Bd. Med. Examiners. Intern in internal medicine, Long Beach (Calif.) VA Hosp., 1977-78; resident in radiology Wadsworth VA Hosp., West Los Angeles, 1978-82, resident in nuclear medicine, 1982—. Mem. AMA (Physician's Recognition award 1980), Soc. Nuclear Medicine, Radiol. Soc. N.Am., Phi Delta Epsilon. Republican. Office: Wadsworth VA Hosp Wilshire and Sawtelle West Los Angeles 90073

PARKER, M. J., executive assistant; b. Bay City, Mich., Nov. 3, 1950; d. Guy R. and Virginia M. (Switala) P.; m. Daniel A. Gielda, May 9, 1970 (div.). Student Delta Coll., Golden Gate Coll., San Francisco. Lic. real estate sales rep., Mich. Relocation worker for HUD, City of Bay City, 1975-79; exec. asst. to v.p. and corp. controller Shaklee Corp., San Francisco, 1980—; bd. dirs. Shaklee Employees Fed. Credit Union Chmn. Youth in Law Day. Mem. San Francisco Jr. Assn. Commerce and Industry (mem. of yr. 1982, bd. dirs.), San Francisco Mus. Soc., San Francisco Mus. Vol. Council, Mill Valley Ctr. Performing Arts. Cal Drama Assn. Republican. Club: Commonwealth.

PARKER, ROBERT DANIEL, elec. engr.; b. Carmel, Calif., May 23, 1945; s. Robert Jessie and Edna Mae (Monch) P.; B.S. in Engring. (Nat. Merit scholar 1963), Calif. Inst. Tech., 1967; M.S. in Elec. Engring., U. So. Calif., 1969, Ph.D., 1973; m. Adrianne Catherine Doyle, Oct. 18, 1980. Engr. space scis. lab. U. Calif., Berkeley, 1965-67; research asst. U. So. Calif., 1967-72; mem. tech. staff Hughes Aircraft Co., Culver City, Calif., 1972-74, sr. staff engr., 1974—. Recipient IR-100 award, 1977, NASA Tech. Brief award, 1980. Mem. IEEE, Am. Phys. Soc., Sigma Xi. Republican. Presbyterian. Author papers in field; patentee high voltage transformer. Home: 29501 Oceanport Rd Rancho Palos Verdes CA 90274 Office: Hughes Aircraft Co PO Box 92919 Los Angeles CA 90009

PARKER, SANDRA JEAN, financial executive; b. Chgo., Aug. 7, 1940; d. Harold A. and B. Jean Densmore; student U. Oreg., 1958-60; A.A., DeAnza Coll., 1981; B.S., U. Phoenix, 1982; m. Ronald A. Parker; children—Deborah L. Olsen, Richard L. Olsen. Benefits dir. Syntex Corp., Palo Alto, Calif., 1970-77; personnel dir. Kasper Instruments Co., Sunnyvale, Calif., 1977-79, Electroscale Corp., Santa Rosa, Calif., 1979-80; mktg./sales dir. Premier Vending Co., Santa Clara, Calif., 1980-81; pvt. practice mgmt. cons., 1981-83; mgr. fin. adminstrn. Astron Research and Engring., Mountain View, Calif., 1983—. Mem. Nat. Notary Assn., No. Calif. Indsl. Relations Council, Santa Clara Valley Personnel Assn., Bay Area Personnel Assn., Nat. Assn. Female Execs., Assn. Women Accts., AAUW. Home: 19545 Miller Ct Saratoga CA 95070 Office: 975 Benicia Ave Sunnyvale CA 94086

PARKER, THEODORE CLIFFORD, electronics engineer; b. Dallas, Oreg., Sept. 25, 1929; s. Theodore Clifford and Virginia Bernice (Rumsey) P.; B.S.E.E. magna cum laude, U. So. Calif., 1960; m. Jannet Ruby Barnes, Nov. 28, 1970; children—Sally Odette, Peggy Claudette. Vice pres. engring. Telemetrics, Inc., Gardena, Calif., 1963-65; chief info. systems Northrop-Nortronics, Anaheim, Calif., 1966-70; pres. AVTEL Corp., Covina, Calif., 1970-74, Aragon, Inc., Sunnyvale, Calif., 1975-78; v.p. Teledyne McCormick Selph, Hollister, Calif., 1978-82; sr. staff engr. FMC Corp., San Jose, Calif., 1982—. Mem. IEEE, Assn. Computing Machinery, Am. Prodn. and Inventory Control Soc., Am. Def. Preparedness Assn., Central Calif. Brittany Club (pres.), Am. Brittany Club (former nat. dir.), Nat. Rifle Assn. (life), Tau Beta Pi, Eta Kappa Nu. Home: 17269 Debbie Rd Los Gatos CA 95030 Office: 1105 Coleman Ave San Jose CA 95108

PARKER, WILLIAM ELBRIDGE, consulting civil engineer; b. Seattle, Mar. 18, 1913; s. Charles Elbridge and Florence E. (Plumb) P.; m. Dorris Laurie Freeman, June 15, 1935; children—Dorris Laurie, Jane Elizabeth. B.S., U.S. Naval Acad., 1935. Party chief King County Engrs., 1935-39; exec. sec., cons. engr. State Wash., 1946-49; city engr., chmn. Bd. Pub. Works, City of Seattle, 1953-57; cons. City of San Diego, 1957; ptnr. Parker-Fisher & Assocs., 1958-66; cons. engr. Minish & Webb Engrs., Seattle, 1966-70; city engr. City of Bremerton (Wash.), 1970-76; owner Parker & Assocs., Seattle, 1976—. Served to capt. C.E.C., USNR, 1939-45, 51-53. Registered profl. engr., Wash. Mem. Am. Pub. Works Assn., U.S. Naval Inst., Pioneers of State Wash. (pres.), U.S. Naval Acad. Alumni Assn., Clubs: College (Seattle), Masons, Shriners.

PARKER, WILLIAM HARVEY, electronics engineer; b. Ft. Dix, N.J., July 23, 1946; s. Andrew Jackson, Sr., and Virginia Neill (Harvey) P.; m. Connie, Oct. 31, 1969; 1 dau., Jennifer Lee. B.S.E.E., N.C. State U., Raleigh, 1973; A.S., Chowan Coll., Murfreesboro, N.C., 1972. Registered profl. engr., Calif., 1976. Electromagnetic interference filter design engr. Genisco Tech. Corp., Rancho Dominguez, Calif., 1973-76, mgr. electromagnetic compatibility Engring. Services div., 1976—; speaker in field. Served to staff sgt., AUS, 1965-69; mem. Res. Mem. IEEE (dir. Electromagnetic Compatibility Soc. 1978-81, v.p. 1982-83), Nat. Soc. Profl. Engrs., Soc. Old Crows, Soc. Automotive Engrs. Office: 18435 Susana Rd Rancho Dominguez CA 90221

PARKER, WILLIS LAMONT, publishing cons.; b. nr. Keokuk, Iowa, Oct. 14, 1904; s. Early Spring and Charlotte Jane (Robinson) P.; student Columbia, 1922-26; m. Grace Eleanor Evans, June 23, 1930 (dec. Sept. 1976); children—Sarah Martha, Daniel Evans. With Guaranty Trust Co., N.Y.C., 1927-30; free-lance editor, N.Y.C., 1930-44; mem. editorial staff U.S. Armed Forces Inst., Washington, 1944-45; with Pitman Pub. Co., N.Y.C., 1945-51, W. W. Norton and Co., N.Y.C., 1951-59; mng. editor Chandler Pub. Co., San Francisco, 1960-71; now pub. cons. Mem. Phi Gamma Delta. Home and Office: 454 Pope St San Francisco CA 94112

PARKHURST, VIOLET KINNEY, artist; b. Derby Line, Vt., Apr. 26, 1926; d. Edson Frank and Rosa (Beauchiene) Kinney; student Sch. Practical Arts, Boston, 1941-42, Baylor U., Waco, Tex., 1943, Calif. State U., Los Angeles, 1950-51; m. Donald Winters Parkhurst, Apr. 10, 1948. Fgn. corr. 5 Brazilian mags., 1946-53; tech. illustrator, 1954-55; owner five galleries including Ports of Call, San Pedro, Calif.; artist, specializing in seascapes; work included in permanent collection of Stockholm Mus., many pvt. collections including Richard M. Nixon, Mayor of Kobe, Japan, Mayor Yorty of Los Angeles, Rory Calhoun, Barbara Rush, Jim Arness, David Rose; works exhibited one-man shows at prominent galleries; numerous paintings published. Winner 30 blue ribbons for art. Fellow Am. Inst. Fine Arts. Mem. Ch. of Religious Sci. Author: How to Paint Books, 1966; Parkhurst on Seascapes, 1972. Paintings reproduced on covers South West Art, Arizona Living; ltd. edit. prints published, also ltd. edit. plates. Address: Parkhurst Gallery Ports of Call Village San Pedro CA 90731

PARKINSON, HOWARD EVANS, insurance company exec.; b. Logan, Utah, Nov. 3, 1936; s. Howard Maughan and Valeria Arlene (Evans) P.; B.S., Brigham Young U., 1961; M.B.A., U. Utah, 1963; m. Lucy Kay Bowen, Sept. 2, 1960; children—Blake, Gregory, Dwight, Lisa, David, Rebecca. Mgmt. intern AEC, Richland, Wash., 1963-65; v.p. Belstar, Inc., Rexburg, Idaho, 1965-71, dir., 1966-76, pres., 1971-76; v.p., dir. Grand Targhee Resort, Inc., Rexburg, 1967-69; v.p. Fargo-Wilson-Wells Co., Pocatello, Idaho, 1974-76; equity qualified agt. Equitable Life Assurance So. U.S., Idaho Falls, Idaho, 1977-80, mem. nat. council sales group, 1978; dist. mgr. Mass. Mut. Life Ins. Co., Idaho Falls, 1980—; fin. cons. small bus. Bd. dirs. Little League Baseball, 1974-75; coach Little League Basketball, 1975-76; high councilman Rexburg Stake, Ch. of Jesus Christ of Latter-day Saints, 1976-77, bishop, 1977—. Recipient Bronze award Mass. Mut. Life Ins. Co.; C.L.U. Mem. Million Dollar Roundtable. Republican. Club: Toastmasters (past pres.). Home: 264 S 2d W Rexburg ID 83440 Office: 720 N Holmes Idaho Falls ID 83401

PARKS, D. C., farmer and cattle breeder, drug counselor; b. Taft, Calif., Oct. 17, 1913; s. Travis Winn and Ruby Clara; student pub. schs., Kern County, Calif.; m. Olivia Maxine Lauderdale, Dec. 22, 1942; children—Roberta C. Parks Powell, Clifford Wayne. Partner, Parks Bros., Bakersfield, Calif., 1934—, Parks Bros. Investment Co., Bakersfield, Calif., 1959—; owner, operator Parks Hereford Ranch, Bakersfield, 1933-38. Founding pres. D.C. Parks Scholarship Found., Lakeview Recreation Center; lay minister Ch. of Christ; active YMCA, Lions, Native Sons of the Golden West, 4-H Clubs, trustee World U., Tucson, 1982—; chaplain Women's Protective League of Kern County; pres. Addictive Drugs Ednl. Found.; mem. Drug Abuse Tech. Adv. Com. of Kern County. Recipient Liberty Pepperdine award Congress of Freedom, 1970-77; Founders award U., 1960; Lion of Year award S. Bakersfield Lions Club, 1964, 66; Man of Year award Native Sons of the Golden West, 1959; Farmer of Year award Kiwanis Club of Bakersfield, 1957; Calif. Gov's. award for Creative Citizenship, 1968; Am. Patriot award Am. Ednl. League, 1982; Key to City of Tulsa, 1982; named hon. citizen of Okla., 1982, many others. Mem. Kern County Hist. Soc., Internat. Platform Assn., Intercontinental Biog. Assn., Smithsonian Instn., Kern County Farm Bur., Calif. Kern County cattlemans assns., Am. Assn. Ret. Persons, Nat. Rifle Assn., Nat. Automobile Club, Nitecaps Internat. Clubs: Elks, Lions (co-chmn. drug and alcohol com.). Author: Narcotics and Addiction, 1963; Narcotics, 1965; Drug Addiction: Suicide and Murder by Degrees, 1967; Narcotics and Narcotics Addiction, 1969; Youth is the Target, 1969. Home: 2639 Belle Terr Bakersfield CA 93304

PARKS, DONALD LEE, human factors engineer, mechanical engineer; b. Delphos, Kans., Feb. 23, 1931; s. George Delbert and Erma Josephine (Boucek) P.; student Kans. Wesleyan U., 1948-50; B.S.M.E., Kans. State U., 1957, B.S. in Bus. Adminstrn., 1957, M.S. in Psychology, 1959; m. Bessie Lou Schur, Dec. 24, 1952; children—Elizabeth Parks Anderson, Patricia Parks Lavin, Donna, Charles, Sandra. Elem. tchr., 1950-51; with Kans. State U. Placement Service, 1957-59; human factors engr., systems engr. Boeing Co., Seattle, 1959—, sr. specialist engr., 1972-74, sr. engring. supr., 1974—; cons., lectr. in field; participant workshops on guidelines in profl. areas, NATO, NSF, Nat. Acad. Sci., NRC. Mem. Derby (Kans.) Planning Commn., 1961-62, chmn., 1962; del. King County (Wash.) Republican Conv., 1972; mem. sci. com. Internat. Transp. Ctr. Served with AUS, 1952-54. Mem. Human Factors Soc. (Puget Sound Pres.'s award 1969), Assn. Aviation Psychologists, ASME, Am. Psychol. Assn., Midwestern Psychol. Assn. Presbyterian. Club: Elks. Contbr. numerous articles to tech. jours., chpts. to books. Home: 6232 127th Ave SE Bellevue WA 98006

PARKS, GERALD THOMAS, JR., lawyer, business executive; b. Tacoma, Wash., Feb. 25, 1944; s. Gerald Thomas and Elizabeth (Bell) P.; m. Susan Simenstad, July 22, 1967; children—Julie, Christopher; m. 2d, Bonny Kay O'Connor, Jan. 15, 1979. B.A. in Polit. Sci., U. Wash., 1966; J.D., U. Oreg., 1969. Bar: Wash. 1969. Assoc. Graham & Dunn, 1972-77, ptnr., 1977—; sec., treas. Holaday-Parks Fabricators, Inc., 1972-78, v.p., gen. mgr. (new name Holaday-Parks, Inc.), 1978—. Active in work Seattle Art Mus. Served to lt. with USN, 1969-72. Mem. Wash. State Bar Assn., ABA. Club: Seattle Yacht. Office: 3400 Rainier Bank Tower Seattle WA 98101 also 6th Floor Lowman & Hanford Bldg 616 1st Ave Seattle WA 98104

PARKS, JAMES RUSSELL, accountant; b. Glendale, Calif., Aug. 31, 1950; s. Ted and Irene Helen (Jones) P. B.S., U. So. Calif., 1972, M.Bus. Taxation, 1975. Staff accountant Peat Marwick Mitchell & Co., Beverly Hills, Calif., 1973-76, tax. mgr., 1976-78; mng. partner Parks, Adams & Palmer, Beverly Hills, 1978—; dir. Am. Frontier Exploration, Inc.; mem. faculty Calif. State U., Los Angeles, 1976-82. Recipient Service award United Way, 1976, 77. C.P.A., Calif. Mem. Am. Inst. C.P.A.s, Calif. Soc. C.P.A.s. Office: 8075 W 3d St Los Angeles CA 90048

PARKS, RICHARD DEE, theatre dir.; b. Omaha, Aug. 29, 1938; s. Charles and Josephine Marie Rose P. B.A., San Jose State U., 1961; M.A., U. Wash., 1963; postgrad. Stanford U. Tchr. San Jose State U., 1964-65; tchr. oral interpretation Stanford U., 1965-66; tchr. San Jose State U., 1966-71, B.F.A. program U. Wash., 1971-72; dir. theatre San Jose State U., 1972-79, coordinator performance area, 1979—, coordinator auditions, 1975—, chmn. performance area, coordinator M.F.A. performance degree program, 1983—; exchange prof. Ventura Coll., spring 1982; exec. dir. Actors Symposium of Hollywood; actor, entertainer, producer; free-lance producer NBC; cons. profl. and community theatre orgns.; interim coordinator theatre arts grad. program, 1977-78; dialects coach, voice and diction tutor; research cons. Ednl. Films of Hollywood; cons. Monterey Peninsula's 4th St. Playhouse; cons., dir. Gen. Electric Sales Conf., Pajaro Dunes, 1983. Winner New Play Directing award Am. Coll. Theatre Festival Region I, 1975. Mem. Calif. Ednl. Theatre Assn. (exec. sec.-treas. 1978-80), Am. Theatre Assn., AAUP, Calif. Assn. Am. Conservatory Theatre, Am. Coll. Theatre Festival, Am. Film Inst., Dramatists Guild, Authors League Am. Episcopalian. Clubs: Brit. Am., San Jose Players. Author: How to Overcome Stage Fright, 1978; American Drama Anthology, 1979; (plays) Charley Parkhurst Rides Again!, 1978, Wild West Women, 1980, Ken Kesey's Further Inquiry, 1980; (book) Career Preparation for the TV-Film Actor, 1981; (play) stage adaptation of Tandem Prodns. Facts of Life, 1982; (teaching supplement) Calendar of American Theatre History, 1982; The Role of Myth in Understanding Amber in the Ancient World, 1983. Office: Theatre Arts Dept San Jose State University San Jose CA 95192

PARMERLEE-GREINER, GLORIA ROSALIE, educator, coordinator; b. Pueblo, Colo., Sept. 4, 1940; d. Thomas Henry Whalen and Gladys Pearl (Parker) W.; m. Roscoe Hale Parmerlee, III, July 12, 1969 (dec.); m. Floyd Dale Greiner, July 31, 1982; children—Tannya Lynn Lane, Scott Gale Lane. B.A. with honors, U. So. Colo., 1968; M.A., U. Colo., 1973; postgrad. Colo. State U., U. No. Colo., U. Colo., Colo. Sch. Mines. Tchr., Boulder, 1969-80, coordinator and tchr. teen parenting program, 1980—. Mem. Colo. Ednl. Assn., Boulder Valley Schs. Ednl. Assn., NEA, Am. Home Econs. Assn., Colo. Home Economics Assn., Am. Vocat. Assn., Colo. Vocat. Assn., Phi Beta Kappa, Delta Kappa Gamma. Presbyterian. Contbr. articles to profl. jours. and popular mags. Home: 1755 Foothills Dr S Golden CO 80401

PARNELL, GAY CAROL, clinical psychologist; b. Waco, Tex., Aug. 27, 1939; d. Dallas Martin and Rubye Louise (Milstead) Parnell; children—Dana Cathryn Reece-Friedman, Lia Gabrielle Friedman. Lic. psychologist, Calif. B.S., Baylor U., 1963; M.S., So. Meth. U., 1969; postgrad. San Jose State U., 1972-73, Stanford U., 1969, 72, U. Tex. Med. Sch., 1964-65; Ph.D., Calif. Sch. Profl. Psychology, 1976. Teaching asst. Baylor U., Waco, Tex., 1961-63; lab. supr. Hillcrest Bapt. Hosp. Lab., Waco, 1959-64, Med. Center Hosp. Lab., Tyler, Tex., 1964-65; lab. technician Parkland Hosp., Dallas, 1966-68; chmn. bd., mgr. Counseling Div., Bethesda (Md.) Free Clinic, 1970-72; research assoc. Bioassay Lab., Dallas, 1966-67, surgery dept. U. Tex. Southwestern Med. Sch., Dallas, 1968-69, VA Hosp. Cancer Ward, NIH, Bethesda, 1970-71, Viral Oncology Lab., Nat. Cancer Inst., Bethesda, 1971-72; mental health worker Santa Clara County Valley Med. Center, San Jose, 1972-74; psychol. intake worker Prana-Metro Resdl. Drug Treatment Program, San Diego, 1974-75; guest panelist Psychology of Dreams, Crosstalk, KPBS, San Diego, 1976; guest lectr. human sexuality, Calif. Sch. Profl. Psychology, San Diego, 1978, 79, Gifford Clinic, U Calif.-San Diego, 1980; instr. San Diego Mesa Coll., 1977, San Diego City Coll., 1975-77, Immaculate Heart Coll., Los Angeles, 1979, Calif. Sch. Profl. Psychology, 1981; instr./trainer Gestalt Therapy, Gestalt Inst., Amsterdam, Holland, 1980, 81; licensed psychol. asst. Drs. Miriam and Erving Polster, San Diego, 1976-77; pvt. practice clin. psychology, San Diego, 1977—; condr. workshops in field. Mem. Am. Psychol. Assn., Calif. Psychol. Assn., San Diego Search and Rescue Assn. Club: Sierra. Office: 3972 Eagle St San Diego CA 92103

PARQUE, RICHARD ANTHONY, education and training consultant; b. Los Angeles, Aug. 10, 1935; s. Joe and Helen Margaret (Muto) P.; m. Vo Thi Lan, May 1, 1975; children—Kenneth, Phat, James. B.A., Calif. State U.-Los Angeles, 1958, M.A., 1966; postgrad. U. Redlands, 1966. Cert. tchr., Calif. Tchr. Yucaipa (Calif.) High School, 1961-66; sci. edn. adv. Calif. State U. System, 1966-68; profl. devel. adminstr. McDonnell Douglas Astronautics Co., 1968-71; prin. Parque Cons. Assocs., 1971-77, 79—; corp. dir. edn. and tng. Ralph M. Parsons Co., 1977-78; adj. faculty Calif. State U.-San Diego, 1966-68, Calif. State U.-Los Angeles, 1980, UCLA, 1982. Served with USMC, 1958-61. Recipient NASA Sci. Teaching award, 1966. Mem. Am. Soc. Tng. and Devel., Organizational Devel. Network, Nat. Mgmt. Assn., Nat. Sci. Tchrs. Assn., Calif. Tchrs. Assn. Republican. Contbr. numerous articles to profl. jours. Office: PO Box 52 Downey CA 90241

PARRISH, BOBBIE RAY, ins. co. mgr.; b. Close City, Tex., July 7, 1932; s. Benjamin and Rita P.; grad. Boise State U., 1978; m. Rosemary Smith, Feb. 15, 1958; children—Leslea, Andrew, Mark. Mgr. employment and econ. devel. City of Boise (Idaho), 1971-73; mgr. loss control dept. Argonaut Ins. Co., Boise, 1973-79; dir. safety and environment Delamar Silver Mine, 1979-80; mgr. loss control dept. Md. Casualty Co., Boise, 1980—. Served to sgt. USAF, 1949-70. Decorated Air medal, Bronze Star; registered profl. engr., Idaho. Mem. Idaho Safety Council (pres.), Am. Soc. Safety Engrs. (pres. Snake River chpt.), Idaho Assn. Fire Prevention Ofcls., Idaho Arson Investigators Assn. Office: PO Box 8926 Boise ID 83707

PARRISH, JERRY CLINTON, computer specialist; b. Tulsa, Oct. 30, 1936; s. Clinton Thad and Monetta Jewel (Combs) P.; student Cochise Coll., 1974; children—Sandra R., Jerry Clinton. Sr. computer specialist U.S. Army Communications Command, Ft. Huachuca, Ariz., 1969—; communications specialist U. Calif., Los Alamos Sci. Lab., 1963-66; communications adviser U.S. Army Mobility Command, St. Louis, 1966-69. Pres., Los Casitas Homeowners Assn., 1980-83. Served with USAF, 1955-58, Res. ret. Recipient USAF Commendation medal, 1980. Mem. Armed Forces Communications-Electronics Assn., Am. Fedn. Govt. Employees (pres. 1962-67, pres. Ariz. Council 1963-68), Assn. U.S. Army, Los Alamos Jaycees (pres. 1964-65), Am. Legion, N.G. Assn. U.S. Clubs: Rotary, Moose, Chaparral Corvette (v.p. 1980-81, pub. relations dir. 1982-83). Home: 4409 C Plaza Vista Sierra Vista AZ 86535 Office: CC-OPS-TS Fort Huachuca AZ 85613

PARRISH, NORMAN CHARLES, tech. cons.; b. Los Angeles, Feb. 28, 1912; s. George Cornelius and Estella Nancy (Lay) P.; B.S.M.E., U. So. Calif., 1942, M.S., 1965; A.A. Los Angeles City Coll., 1943; m. Dorothy Dalley Caswell, Jan. 16, 1976; 1 dau. by previous marriage, Candace Cole; stepchildren—Thomas Caswell, James Caswell, Dennis Caswell. With Lockheed Missile & Space Co., Sunnyvale, Calif., 1955-60, Hughes Aerospace, El Segundo, Calif., 1960-65; research engr. tech. staff U. Calif., Lawrence Berkeley Lab., 1965-80; tech. cons. Parlin Engring. Co., Rheem Valley, Calif., 1948-65, Dept. Energy, Washington, 1975-83, Nat. Bur. Standards, 1979-82, SEC, 1979-80, U.S. Justice Dept., 1981. Chmn., Fed. Exec. Res., 1979—. Mem. ASME, Am. Soc. Metals, Soc. Automotive Engrs., Sigma Xi. Author: Micro Diaphragm Pressure Traducers, 1964; Inventors Source Book, 1978; Proceedings of Hawaii Inventors Conf., 1978; contbr. articles to profl. jours. Home: 215 Rheem Blvd Moraga CA 94556 Office: PO Box 158 Rheem Valley CA 94570

PARROTT, DENNIS BEECHER, employee benefit cons.; b. St. Louis, June 13, 1929; s. Maurice Ray and Mai Ledgerwood (Beecher) P.; B.S. in Econs., Fla. State U., Tallahassee, 1954; postgrad. Princeton U., 1964; M.B.A., Pepperdine U., 1982; m. Vivian Cleveland Miller, Mar. 24, 1952; children—Constance Beecher, Dennis Beecher, Anne Cleveland. With Prudential Ins. Co. Am., 1954-74, v.p. group ins. mktg., Los Angeles, 1971-74; sr. v.p. Frank B. Hall Cons. Co., Los Angeles, 1974—; speaker in field. Chmn. Weekend with the Stars Telethon, 1976-80; chmn. bd. dirs. United Cerebral Palsy/Spastic Children's Found. Los Angeles County, 1979-82, chmn. bd. govs., 1982—; bd. dirs. Nat. United Cerebral Palsy Assn., 1977-82, pres., 1977-79; mem. community adv. council Birmingham High Sch., Van Nuys, Calif., 1982—. Served to 1st lt. AUS, 1951-53. C.L.U. Mem. Am. Soc. C.L.U.s, Internat. Found. Employee Benefits, Employee Benefits Planning Assn. So. Calif. Republican. Presbyterian. Clubs: Los Angeles, Jonathan (Los Angeles). Office: 3200 Wilshire Blvd Los Angeles CA 90010

PARROTT, DOUGLAS HOWARD, pilot; b. Spokane, Jan. 29, 1926; s. Heston Woodford and Nellie (Easely) P.; student Gonzaga U., 1944-45, Green River U., Auburn, Wash., 1969-72; m. Shirley Ann Gerrard, Jan. 9, 1951; children—Joseph David, Donald James, Jeffrey Linn. Officer in charge U.S. Weather Bur., Meacham, Oreg., 1946-50; pres., chief pilot La Grande Air Service, Inc., 1950-53; with Northwest Airlines, Inc., 1953—, capt., 1958—; owner, operator Diamond Bar P Ranches, Roundup, Mont., 1972—. Mem. sch. bd., negotiator Roundup Sch. Dist., 1978-79. Served with U.S. Navy, 1944-46. Mem. Air Line Pilots Assn. (master chmn. 1967-69, negotiations chmn. 1980—), Am. Assn. Sch. Bd. Mems., Nat. Cattlemen's Assn., Mont. Stock Growers. Clubs: Lions, Corral of the Westerners, Masons, Shriners, Elks. Home: PO Box 266 Roundup MT 59072 Office: Northwest Airlines Inc Minneapolis-Saint Paul International Airport MN 55111

PARRY, PAUL STEWART, health care administrator; b. London, Eng., Sept. 16, 1934; s. William and Winifred (Loupa) P.; came to U.S., 1949, naturalized, 1955; B.A., U. San Fernando, 1961; M.B.A., Pepperdine U., 1978; m. Deborah Joan Backhaut, May 20, 1956; children—Alan, Susan, Joan. Pub. relations mgr. Calif. Blue Shield, Los Angeles, 1958-68; asst. dir. Calif. Med. Assn., Los Angeles, 1968-71; exec. dir. Riverside County (Calif.) Med. Assn., 1971-82, Riverside County Found. for Med. Care, 1971-82, Riverside County Profl. Standards Rev. Orgn., 1974-82; adminstrv. dir. Palms Springs (Calif.) Med. Ctr., 1982—. Chmn. Riverside County Mental Health Adv. Bd., 1974-75. Mem. So. Calif. Soc. Assn. Execs., Am. Soc. Assn. Execs., Am. Coll. Legal Medicine (asso. in sci.), Am. Assn. Med. Soc. Execs., Am. Soc. Law and Medicine, Med. Group Mgmt. Assn. Author: Front Office Manual for Medical Assistants, 1962. Home: 1012 Paseo de Marcia Palm Springs CA 92262 Office: 1695 N Sunrise Way Palm Springs CA 92262

PARRY, PETER LARSON, park superintendent; b. Morgantown, W.Va., Oct. 6, 1931; s. Vernon Frank and Roma (Larson) P.; B.S., Colo. State U., 1954; m. Joyce Glen, Mar. 7, 1957; children—Christy, Frank (dec.), Michael (dec.). Ranger, Nat. Park Service, 1956-64, supt., 1975—, supt. Arches and Canyonlands Nat. Parks, Moab, Utah, 1983—. Served with USAF, 1954-56. Recipient Spl. Achievement award Nat. Park Service, 1974. Mem. Am. Legion, C. of C. Club: Rotary. Office: Canyonlands Nat Park Moab UT 84532

PARSONESE, ANTHONY JOSEPH, SR., photographer; b. Hazleton, Pa., Feb. 19, 1939; s. Tony Fortunato and Helen Margaret (Demyon) P.; m. Anna Victoria Radosky, Nov. 4, 1961; children—Anthony Joseph, Teresa M. Eastman, Vincent G., Angela A. Grad. Central Bucks High Sch., 1957. Photographic chief U.S. Marine Corps, 1956-77; owner, operator Parsonese Photography, Escondido, Calif., 1978—. Decorated Vietnamese Cross of Gallantry. Mem. Profl. Photographers Am., Profl. Photographers Calif., VFW. Republican. Roman Catholic. Clubs: Escondido East Rotary (pres. 1982).

PARSONS, AUDREY ANNE, state official; b. Tulsa, Okla, Aug. 3, 1931; d. Nick Jay and Charlie Maude (Trout) Banks; m. Yrone Parsons, July 10, 1955 (div.); children—Celeste Parsons McCoy, Bernice Parsons Griffin, Damon. Cert. in Counseling and Related Subjects, Portland State U., 1972; cert. N.W. Bus. Coll., Portland, Oreg., 1962. Comptometor operator White Stag, Portland, 1962-64, key punch operator, 1964-66; key punch operator Fred Meyer, Portland, 1966-67; with Employment Div. State of Oreg., Portland, 1967-78, field rep. Bur. Labor and Industries Apprenticeship and Tng. div., 1978—. Mem. adv. bd. Displaced Homemakers of Oreg. Mem. Internat. Assn. Personnel in Employment Security, Black Women's Network, Clackamas County Human Relations Commn. Oreg., Oreg. State Adv. Council for Career and Vocat. Edn., Multnomah-Washington Consortium Pvt. Industry Council. Episcopalian. Office: 1400 SW 5th Ave Suite 407 Portland OR 97201

PARSONS, GAIL, accountant; b. Salt Lake City, Mar. 12, 1946; d. Paul Eugene and Virginia (Jarvis) P.; B.S. in Acctg., U. Utah, 1969; m. Carl Andersen Heyes, July 25, 1975. Staff acct. Hansen, Barnett & Maxwell, C.P.A.'s, Salt Lake City, 1969-75; controller Timberhaus Ski Shops, Inc., Park City and Snowbird, Utah, 1975-76; pvt. practice as cert. public accountant, Salt Lake City, 1976—. C.P.A., Utah. Mem. Am. Inst. C.P.A.'s, Am. Woman's Soc. C.P.A.'s, Utah Assn. C.P.A.'s. Home and office: 5641 Oakdale Dr Salt Lake City UT 84121

PARSONS, JAMES EDWARDS, JR., hotel executive, promotion/advertising firm executive; b. Santa Cruz, Calif., June 30, 1953; s. James Edwards and Wilda Roberta (Miller) P.; m. Jan Lee Hipes, Apr. 3, 1982. With Sahara Tahoe Hotel and Casino, Stateline, Nev., 1975—, publicity dir., 1978-81, pub. relations, advt. dir., 1981—, sr. editor Saharan mag., 1979-82; v.p. promotion and advt. Stay, Inc., Stateline, 1983—. Mem. South Lake Tahoe (Calif.) C. of C. Club: Reno Advertising. Home: Box 5594 3695 Tamarack St South Lake Tahoe CA 95729 Office: Sahara Tahoe Hotel and Casino Box C Hwy 50 Stateline NV 89449

PARSONS, JANICE JOHNSTON, telephone company official; b. Akron, Ohio, May 22, 1955; d. Einer A. and Illene (Harrison) Adamson; m. Douglas Lee Parsons, Sept. 10, 1977; 1 son, Joshua Douglas. B.S. with honors in Journalism, Ohio U., 1976; postgrad. U. Dayton, 1976-77. Advt. sales rep. Akron Beacon Jour., 1975-76; pub. relations mgr. Nat. Cash Register Credit Union, Dayton, Ohio, 1976-77; dir. advt. and promotions Smith Corona Mfg./Allied Energy, Dayton, 1977-78; asst. staff mgr. pub. relations Mountain Bell, Albuquerque, 1978—. Pres. bd. dirs. N.Mex. Ret. Sr. Vol. Program, 1983; mem. consumer bd. Univ. Heights Hosp., 1983. Ohio U. scholar, 1974, 75, 76, Spl. Community Service Award scholar, 1974, Grad. Journalist scholar, 1976; Tallmadge Lions Club scholar, 1973. Mem. Women In Communications (pres. profl. chpt. 1983), Mountain Bell Women in Mgmt. (v.p. 1982), N.Mex. Press Women's Assn., Albuquerque Bell Fed. Credit Union (edn. com.), Soc. Consumer Affairs Profls., Internat. Assn. Bus. Communicators, Future Telephone Pioneers Am. Home: 9713 Admiral Emerson NE Albuquerque NM 87111 Office: Mountain Bell Station 49 201 3d St NW Albuquerque NM 87102

PARSONS, ROBERTA ARLENE, ins. brokerage exec.; b. Alma, Nebr., Nov. 19, 1934; d. George Lester and Audrey Velma (Niles) Buzzard; student Valley Jr. Coll., 1971-74, Harbor Jr. Coll., 1977-80, UCLA, 1980-81; m. Jack J. Parsons, June 3, 1951; children—Monte Jay, Russel Joe. Sec., Fred S. James, Los Angeles, 1972-75; adminstrv. asst. Frank B. Hall, Los Angeles, 1975; accts. adminstr. Emett & Chandler, Century City, Calif., 1975-76; exec. sec. Hoyne Industries, Carson, Calif., 1976-77; v.p. corp. adminstrn. Keenan & Assos., Torrance, Calif., 1977—; panelist 8th Ann. Women's Employment Options Conf., Anaheim, Calif., 1981. Dir. South Bay Center Cerebral Palsy Telethon, 1975-81; bd. dirs. Fre-Way Little League, Torrance, 1977-78. Cert. profl. sec. Mem. Personnel and Indsl. Relations Assn., Inc., Profl. Secs. Internat. (pres. Torrance Del Amo chpt. 1976-77), Nat. Assn. Female Execs., Inc. Home: 23768 Sandhurst Ln Harbor City CA 90710 Office: 3715 W Lomita Blvd Torrance CA 90510

PARSONS, RODNEY HUNTER, lawyer; b. Pasadena, Calif., Feb. 4, 1947; s. Clarence Eugene and Agnes Prentice (Hunter) P.; m. Deneise Renee Trebotich, Aug. 2, 1980; children—Ryan Milan, Renee Deneise. B.A., UCLA, 1968, J.D., 1975. Bar: Calif. 1975; cert. in family law. Assoc., Manley Freid, Esq., Los Angeles, 1975-78, Robert Lawton, Esq., Brea, Calif., 1978-79; ptnr. Lether & Parsons, Brea, 1979—; lectr. law-related fields. Dir. Brea C. of C., 1979-82, pres., 1981-82, chmn. bd., 1983; pres. Miss Brea Scholarship Pageant Assn., 1983; mem. HBIC, Inc., 1982-83; hon. mem. Brea Jaycees. Mem. Calif. Bar Assn., Orange County Bar Assn. Republican. Club: Brea Rotary. Office: 2601 E Saturn St Suite 101 Brea CA 92621

PARTAIN, LARRY DEAN, solar research engr.; b. McKinney, Tex., Apr. 27, 1942; s. Archie Leon and Vergie Ann (Young) P.; B.S.E.E., U. Tenn., 1965; Ph.D. in Elec. Engring., Johns Hopkins U., 1972. Asso. prof. elec. engring. U. Del., Newark, 1971-78; engr. Engring. Research div. Lawrence Livermore (Calif.) Nat. Lab., 1978-80; sr. research engr. Chevron Research Co., Richmond, Calif., 1980—; cons. to industry. Solar Energy Research Inst. grantee, 1978-79; E.I. duPont research grantee, 1974-75. Mem. IEEE, Sigma Xi. Contbr. articles to tech. jours. Patentee microwave sensor. Office: 576 Standard Ave Richmond CA 94802

PARTINGTON, CYRUS WILLIAM, radiologist; b. Denver, July 10, 1925; s. Cyrus Brown and Margaret (Crotty) P.; B.S., La. Poly. U., 1949; M.D., U. Colo., 1949, M.S. in Radiology, 1955; m. Nancy Clair Farrell, Aug. 6, 1955; children—Anne Elizabeth, Mary Margaret, Nancy Jane, Ellen Catherine, Cyrus William Walmsley. Intern, U. Hosp., Madison, Wis., 1949-50; resident VA Hosp., U. Colo., 1952-55; practice medicine, specializing in radiology, Colorado Springs, Colo., 1955—; radiologist St. Francis Hosp., Colorado Springs, 1955-75, dir. radiology, 1975—, vice chief staff, 1964, chief staff, 1971-72; cons. radiologist USAF Clinic, Peterson Field, Colo., USAF Hosp., Colorado Springs. Bd. dirs. Regis Coll., Denver. Served with M.C., USNR, 1950-52. Cert. Am. Bd. Radiology in radiology and nuclear radiology; diplomate Nat Bd. Med. Examiners. Fellow Am. Coll. Radiology; mem. AMA, Colo., El Paso County med. socs., Radiol. Soc. N.Am., Rocky Mountain, Colo. (treas. 1960-63) radiol. socs., U. Wis. Med. Alumni Assn., Soc. Nuclear Medicine, Am. Coll. Nuclear Medicine (charter), Am. Coll. Nuclear Physicians, U. Colo. Med. Alumni Assn., Catholic Physicians Guild, Phi Kappa Phi, Nu Sigma Nu. Republican. Roman Catholic. Clubs: Rotaryan (pres. Colorado Springs 1970-71); Broadmoor Golf. Home: 30 Tanglewood Dr Broadmoor Colorado Springs CO 80906 Office: St Francis Hosp Colorado Springs CO 80903

PARTRIDGE, JOHN ALBERT, music educator, organist; b. Regina, Sask., Can., Nov. 6, 1941; s. John Desmond and Vera Christina (Stutt) P.; A.A. (Men's University Club scholar 1959, U. Sask. piano scholar 1959, 60), U. Sask., 1961, B.Ed. with distinction, 1968. Organist, choirmaster 1st Presbyn. Ch., Regina, Sask., Can., 1967—; performer Canadian Broadcasting Corp., Regina, 1978-80; performer Queen Elizabeth Spl. Concert, Regina, 1977; music specialist Regina Bd. Edn., 1969-81, coordinator of music, 1981—; choral arranger. Mem. Sask. Music Educators Assn. (sec. 1969-74), Regina Centre Royal Canadian Coll. Organists (chmn.). Mem. United Ch. Canada. Home: 2737 McCallum Ave Regina SK S4S 0P8 Canada Office: Bd Edn 1600 4th Ave Regina SK S4R 8C8 Canada

PASCOE, DONALD MONTE, lawyer; b. Des Moines, Jan. 4, 1935; s. Donald Leslie and Marjorie Lucille (Powers) P.; A.B., Dartmouth Coll., 1967; LL.B., Stanford U., 1960; m. Patricia Hill, Aug. 3, 1957; children—Sarah Lynn, Edward Llewellyn, William Arthur. Bar: Colo. 1960, Calif. 1961. Assoc. Ireland, Stapleton & Pryor, P.C., Denver, 1960-65, partner, 1966-80; exec. dir. Colo. Dept. Natural Resources, Denver, 1980-83; officer, dir. Ireland, Stapleton, Pryor & Pascoe, Denver, 1983—; mem. Denver regional panel President's Commn. on White House Fellowships, 1976-79. Chmn. Colo. Democratic Central Com., 1973-77; elder Montview Blvd. Presbyn. Ch., Denver, 1967—; trustee Whiteman Sch., Steamboat Springs, Colo., 1969-78, Cystic Fibrosis Found., 1979—, Colo. Sch. Mines, 1979—. Mem. ABA, Denver Bar Assn., Calif. Bar Assn., Am. Judicature Soc., Law Club of Denver, Psi Upsilon, Phi Delta Phi. Clubs: Denver, Cactus, Rotary. Office: 1675 Broadway Suite 2600 Denver CO 80202

PASHAYAN, CHARLES, JR., congressman; b. Fresno, Calif., Mar. 27, 1941. B.A., Pomona Coll., 1963; J.D., U. Calif., 1968; B.Litt., Oxford U., 1977. Bar: Calif. 1969, D.C. 1972, U.S. Supreme Ct. 1977. Spl. asst. to gen. counsel HEW, 1973-75; mem. 96th and 97th Congresses from 17th Dist. Calif. Served as capt. U.S. Army, 1968-70. Mem. Calif. Bar Assn., Fresno County Bar Assn., Royal Inst. Internat. Affairs, Internat. Inst. for Strategic Studies. Republican. Office: 129 Cannon House Office Bldg Washington DC 20515

PASKERIAN, CHARLES KAY, JR., plastics co. exec.; b. Medford, Mass., Mar. 18, 1933; s. Charles Kay and Gertrude (Russian) P.; B.A. in Econs., Tufts U., 1954; M.B.A., Stanford, 1959; m. Susan Eileen Poland, Jan. 4, 1958; children—Michael Charles, Matthew Wayne. Salesman kordite div. Mobil Chem. Co., Los Angeles, 1959-60; dist. sales mgr., 1960-64; Western sales mgr. Webster Ind. div. Chelsea Ind., Los Angeles, 1964-66; pres. Flexi-Pac, Inc., Santa Ana, Calif., 1966—, also dir. Pub. mem. speech pathology and audiology examining com. Calif. Bd. Med. Examiners, 1973—. Mem. bd. edn. Santa Ana Unified Sch., 1969-74, pres., 1971-72. Trustee Holy Family Adoption Service, Rancho Santiago Coll. Served to capt. USAF, 1954-58. Mem. Indsl. Devel. Assn. (dir.), Soc. Plastics Engrs., Inc., Santa Ana C. of C. (dir. 1971-74), Zeta Psi. Republican. Conglist. (chmn. bd. trustees). Mason. Home: Newport Beach CA 92661 Office: 2020 S Hathaway St Santa Ana CA 92706

PASSMORE, JAN WILLIAM, ins. co. exec.; b. Winchester, Ind., Nov. 5, 1940; s. Gale Orth and Helen Louise (Hoskinson) P.; student Nebr. State U., 1959-61; B.S., Ball State U., 1963; m. Pamela Boa, Feb. 14, 1964. With Aetna Life & Casualty, 1964-75, Western region dir., San Jose, Calif., 1972-75; broker, Sanders & Sullivan, San Jose, 1975-78, partner, 1978-80, pres., 1980-81; pres., chief exec. officer Corroon & Black/Sanders & Sullivan, San Jose, 1981—; mem. nat. adv. council INA Marketdyne, 1976—; chmn. Aetna Life & Casualty Regional Adv. Council, 1982-83. Chmn. bd. Goodwill Industries, 1978-80; pres. Boy Scouts Am., 1981-83; bd. dirs. Music and Arts Found., 1980—, Alexian Bros. Hosp. Found., 1978—, Hope Rehab., 1983—; bd. dirs. Santa Clara County United Way; mem. San Jose Trolley Commn. Named Citizen of Yr., Aetna Life & Casualty Co., 1975; INA-Marketdyne Golden Circle, 1977. Mem. Western Assn. Ins. Brokers, Nat. Assn. Ind. Ins. Agts. Republican. Methodist. Clubs: San Jose Country, Kenna, Spartan Found., Pres.'s Council San Jose State U., Masons, Aetna Life and Casualty Great Performers. Home: 10801 Miguelita Rd San Jose CA 95127 Office: 1530 The Alameda St San Jose CA 95126

PASTERNAK, DERICK PETER, internist; b. Budapest, Hungary, Apr. 21, 1941; s. Leslie Laszlo and Hedvig Eva (Hecht) P.; came to U.S., 1956, naturalized, 1962; B.A., Harvard U., 1963, M.D. cum laude, 1967; m. Nancy Jean Clark, June 6, 1969; children—Kenneth Zoltan, Katherine Renee, Sarah Marie. Intern, jr. resident Bronx Municipal Hosp., N.Y.C., 1967-69; residence in internal medicine U. Calif. Hosps., San Francisco, 1971-73; mem. staff Lovelace Med. Center, Albuquerque, 1973—, med. dir. quality assurance program, 1976-80; med. dir. Lovelace Med. Found., 1980—; pres. N.Mex. PSRO, Inc., 1980-82; clin. assoc. prof. medicine U. N.Mex. Referee U.S. Soccer Fedn. Served to capt. M.C., AUS, 1969-71. Decorated Bronze Star, Army Commendation Medal. Diplomate Am. Bd. Internal Medicine. Fellow ACP; mem. Albuquerque and Bernalillo County Med. Assn., Am. Coll Physician Execs., N.Mex. Med. Soc. (councillor), AMA, Am. Diabetes Assn. Office: 5400 Gibson Blvd SE Albuquerque NM 87108

PASTREICH, PETER, orch. exec.; b. Bklyn., Sept. 13, 1938; s. Ben and Hortense (Davis) P.; A.B. magna cum laude, Yale U., 1959; postgrad. N.Y. U. Sch. Medicine, 1959-60; m. Ingrid Eggers, June 5, 1976; children by previous marriage: Emanuel, Michael; children—Milena, Anna. Mgr., Greenwich Village Symphony, N.Y.C., 1960-63; gen. mgr. Nashville Symphony, 1963-65; gen. mgr. Kansas City Philharmonic, 1965-66; asst. mgr., mgr., exec. dir. St. Louis Symphony, 1966-78; exec. dir. San Francisco Symphony, 1978—. Bd. dirs. Laumeier Sculpture Park, St. Louis. Served with U.S. Army, 1960. Recipient First Disting. Alumnus award Yale U. Band, 1977. Mem. Am. Symphony Orch. League (dir.), Assn. Calif. Symphony Orchs. (dir.). Clubs: Yale (N.Y.C.); Bankers (San Francisco). Office: San Francisco Symphony Davies Symphony Hall San Francisco CA 94102

PATA, JAN LINZY, publisher, author; b. Culver City, Calif., Apr. 4, 1942; d. Clyde Albert and Marna Maree (Johnson) Linzy; m. Ted R. Pata, Jr., July 4, 1968 (div.); children—Buzz, Jason, Janae. Student Chico State Coll., 1959-60, U. Miami, 1964-65. Profl. lic. judge, Am. Kennel Club. Author: Pointers, Field & Show, 1983, Dog Name Book, 1983; owner-operator Pata Publs., Foresthill, Calif., 1981—; speaker breed clubs; judge dog shows. Mem. Dog Writers Assn. Am., Am. Pointer Club, Pointer Club N.W. Democrat. Office: Pata Publs PO Drawer F Foresthill CA 95631

PATRICK, H. HUNTER, lawyer; b. Gassville, Ark., Aug. 19, 1939; s. H. Hunter and Nelle F. (Robinson) P.; m. Charlotte A. Wilson, July 9, 1966; children—Michael, Colleen. B.A., U. Wyo., 1961, postgrad., 1961-62, J.D., 1966. Bar: Wyo. 1966, Colo. 1967. Sole practice, Powell, Wyo., 1966—; city atty. City of Powell, 1968—; justice of the peace Park County (Wyo.), 1970—; instr. bus. law Northwest Comm. Coll., 1968—; dir. Park County Title Ins. Agy., 1975—. Wyo. del. to Nat. Conf. Spl. Ct. Judges, 1981, 82, 83; elder Powell Presbyterian Ch. Mem. ABA, Wyo. State Bar Assn., Colo. State Bar Assn., Park County Bar Assn. (past pres., past sec.), Wyo. Assn. Judges (pres. 1973-79, editor, chmn. bench book com. 1972—), Nat. Assn. Judges, Am. Judicature Soc., Democrat. Clubs: Rotary (past pres.), Elks, Odd Fellows (Powell).

PATRICK, RONALD FRANCIS, educator, author; b. Richmond, Ind., June 19, 1950; s. William Boyd and Marilyn Dorothy P.; B.A. cum laude in Journalism, San Francisco State U., 1974; 1 son, Ronald Nicholas. Personnel mgr. Health Maintenance, Inc., San Francisco, 1974-76; v.p., sr. editor Ermine Pubs., Inc., Hollywood, Calif., 1976-79; advt. and promotion dir. Pinnacle Books, Inc., Los Angeles, 1979-82; founder, pres. The Learning Network, 1983—. Mem. Book Publicists So. Calif. Author: Beyond the Threshold, 1981; Apartment 7B, 1983. Office: 704 N Gardner St at Melrose Suite 3 West Hollywood CA 90046

PATTEN, BEBE HARRISON, clergyman, college president; b. Waverly, Tenn., Sept. 3, 1913; d. Newton Felix and Mattie Priscilla (Whitson) Harrison; D.D., McKinley-Roosevelt Coll., 1941; D.Litt., Temple Hall Coll. and Sem., 1943; m. Carl Thomas Patten, Oct. 23, 1935 (dec. 1958); children—Bebe Rebecca and Priscilla Carla (twins), Carl Thomas. Ordained to ministry Ministerial Assn. of Evangelism, 1935; evangelist in nationwide campaigns, 1933-50; founder, pres. Christian Evang. Chs. of Am., Oakland, Calif., 1944—; founder, pres. Patten Coll., Oakland, 1945—; founder program daily nationwide radio ministry The Shepherd Hour, 1934—, TV daily telecast, 1976—, nationwide telecast, 1979—; founder, pres. Acad. of Christian Edn., 1944—; pastor Christian Cathedral, Oakland, 1950—. Recipient numerous awards including: medallion for religious affairs Israeli Fgn. Ministry, 1969, medal Govt. Press Office, Jerusalem, 1971, Gentile honoree Jewish Nat. Fund, 1975, Hidden Heroine award San Francisco Bay council Girl Scouts U.S.A., 1976, medallion Ben Gurion Research Inst., 1977; named hon. fellow Bar-Ilan U., 1981; chair in social action Bar-Ilan U. established in her honor, 1981. Mem. Am. Assn. Pres.'s Ind. Colls. and Univs., Zionist Orgn. Am., Am. Jewish Hist. Soc., Am. Acad. Religion, Soc. Bibl. Lit., Am. Assn. Higher Edn., Religious Edn. Assn., Bar-Ilan U. Assn. (exec. bd.). Author: Give Me Back My Soul (in English, Japanese, Spanish and Chinese), 1973; editor-in-chief The Trumpet Call, 1953—; composer 20 Gospel Songs, 1945. Address: 2433 Coolidge Ave Oakland CA 94601

PATTERSON, DARRELL ALTON, college administrator; b. Topeka, Oct. 17, 1929; s. Abe Alton and Gladys Louise (Hopkins) P.; student Washington U., St. Louis, 1947-48; B.S. in E.E., Kans. State U., 1952; m. Marilyn Nell Phelps, Aug. 12, 1951; children—Michael Lee, David Alton, Alleyne Louise. Electronic technician The Boeing Co., 1951-52, mem. engring. dept., 1954-75, mgr., 1975-76, B-52 dep. program mgr., 1977-79; dir. phys. resources Western Baptist Coll., Salem, Oreg., 1979-81, bus. mgr., 1981—, trustee, 1975-79. Served with U.S. Army, 1952-54. Mem. Assn. Phys. Plant Adminstrs., Nat. Assn. Coll. and Univ. Bus. Officers, Assn. Bus. Adminstrs. Christian Colls. Republican. Baptist. Home: 4519 Independence Dr SE Salem OR 97302 Office: 5000 Deer Park Dr SE Salem OR 97301

PATTERSON, DAWN MARIE, educator, consultant; b. Gloversville, N.Y., July 30; d. Robert Morris and Dora Margaret (Perham) P.; m. Robert Henry Hollenbeck, Aug. 3, 1958 (div. 1976); children—Adrienne Lyn, Nathaniel Conrad. B.S. in Edn., SUNY-Geneseo, 1962; M.A., Mich. State U., 1973, Ph.D., 1977; postdoctoral U. So. Calif. and Inst. Ednl. Leadership. Librarian, Brighton (N.Y.) Central Schs., 1962-67; asst. to regional dir. Mich. State U. Ctr., Bloomfield Hills, 1973-74; grad. asst. Mich. State U., 1975-77; cons. Mich. Efficiency Task Force, 1977; asst. dean Coll. Continuing Edn., U. So. Calif., Los Angeles, 1978—; cons. Mem. AAUW, Calif. Hist. Soc., Internat. Assn. Vol. Effort, Los Angeles Town Hall, Los Angeles World Affairs Council, Pasadena YWCA. Dora Louden scholar, 1958-61; Langworthy fellow, 1961-62; Edn. Professions Devel. fellow, 1974-75; Ednl. Leadership Policy fellow, 1982-83. Mem. Am. Assn. Adult and Continuing Edn. (charter), Nat. Univ. Continuing Edn. Assn., Calif. Coll. and Mil. Educators Assn. (pres.), Los Angeles Airport Area Edn. Industry Assn. (v.p. 1983), Kappa Delta Pi, Phi Delta Kappa. Democrat. Unitarian. Club: Los Angeles Zonta. Office: 3550 S Figueroa St Suite 203 Los Angeles CA 90089

PATTERSON, JERRY MUMFORD, congressman; b. El Paso, Tex., Oct. 25, 1934; s. Levin M. and Ella M. Patterson; B.A., Calif. State U., Long Beach, 1960; postgrad. U. So. Calif.; J.D., UCLA, 1966; m. Sally Jane Sandoval 1981; children—Patrick Alan, Jane Michelle, Robert Elias. Adminstrv. asst. to city adminstr. Garden Grove (Calif.), 1960-63; Admitted to Calif. bar, 1967, engaged in pvt. practice, Santa Ana, 1967-74; councilman Santa Ana, 1969-74, mayor, 1973-74; city atty. Placentia (Calif.), 1973-75; mem. 94th-97th Congresses from 38th Calif. dist., chmn. select com. on coms., mem. banking, fin. and urban affairs com., interior and insular affairs com.; mem. exec. com. So. Calif. Assn. Govts., 1971-74; v.p. Orange County League Cities, 1971. Deacon, Congregational Ch. Served with Hosp. Corps, USCG, 1953-57. Mem. Am. Soc. Pub. Adminstrn. (chpt. pres. 1973-74), Sigma Chi, Phi Delta Phi. Democrat. Club: Toastmasters (pres.). Office: Room 2238 Rayburn House Office Bldg Washington DC 20515

PATTERSON, ROBERT WILSON, school administrator; b. San Francisco, Jan. 27, 1928; s. Robert Wilson and Anne (Hight) P.; m. Evelyn Lucille Wilde, Mar. 31, 1951; children—Robert Wilson, Martha Ann. B.S., U. Ga., 1960; postgrad. Army Command & Gen. Staff Coll., 1967, U.S. Army War Coll., 1974. Commd. pvt., U.S. Army, 1945, advanced through grades to col., 1969, ret., 1975; dir. army instruction JROTC, Phoenix Union High Sch. Dist., 1975—. Decorated Legion of Merit (5). Mem. Assn. of U.S. Army, Mil. Order World Wars, Ret. Officers Assn., C. of C. Republican. Roman Catholic. Club: Rotary. Home: 6402 E Jean Dr Scottsdale AZ 85254 Office: 2526 W Osborn Rd Phoenix AZ 85017

PATTERSON, WILLIAM NOEL, consulting engineer; b. Wooster, Ohio, Dec. 24, 1939; s. Glenn Milton and Frances Ann P.; B.M.E., Ohio State U., 1971, M.S., 1971; m. Judith Ann Rafeld, June 14, 1959; children—John W., Glenn R., Joseph L., Susan B., Edwin R. With Patterson & Sons, Inc., Ashland, Ohio, 1961-64, Patterson Machinery, Ashland, 1964-66, Automatic Welding, Inc., Ashland, 1966; mgr. product devel. Bolt Beranek & Newman, Inc., Cambridge, Mass., 1972-76; chief engr. Gardner-Denver, Inc., Denver, 1976-79; gen. mgr. Colo. ops. Woodward Assos., Inc., Lakewood, 1979-80; pres., chmn. bd. Technol. Enterprises, Inc., Littleton, Colo. Served with USN, 1959-61. Olin Matheson fellow, 1970-71. Registered profl. engr., Mass., Colo. Mem. Nat. Soc. Profl. Engrs., ASME, Soc. Automotive Engrs., Soc. Mining Engrs., Inst. Noise Control Engrs., AAU, Sigma Xi, Tau Beta Pi, Pi Tau Sigma. Contbr. articles to profl. jours. Home: 7244 S Garfield St Littleton CO 80122 Office: Tech Enterprises Inc PO Box 2397 Littleton CO 80161

PATTON, AUDLEY EVERETT, retired business executive; b. Eve, Mo., Nov. 9, 1898; s. Charles Audley and Letitia Virginia (Earhart) P.; B.S. in Indsl. Adminstrn., U. Ill., 1921, M.S. in Bus. Orgn. and Operation, 1922, Ph.D. in Econs., 1924; m. Mabel Dickie Gunnison, Aug. 5, 1930 (dec. Feb. 1976); 1 dau., Julie Ann Patton Watson; m. 2d, Mary Ritchie Key, June 24, 1977. Auditor, Mfg. Dealers Corp., Cambridge, Mass., 1921; instr. econs. public utilities U. Ill., Champaign-Urbana, 1924-25, asst. prof. econs. Coll. Commerce and Bus. Adminstrn., 1925-26; asst. to pres. Chgo. Rapid Transit Co., Chgo. South Shore & South Bend R.R. Co., Chgo. North Shore & Milw. R.R. Co., Chgo. Aurora & Elgin R.R. Co., 1926; asst. to pres. Public Service Co. No. Ill., Chgo., 1926-43, sec., 1928-52, asst. treas., 1928-44, v.p., 1943-53; v.p., dir. No. Ill. Gas Co., Aurora, 1953-54; v.p. Commonwealth Edison Co., Chgo., 1952-63, ret., 1963; asst. to pres. Presbyn-St. Luke's Hosp., Chgo., 1963-65; former v.p., dir. Big Muddy Coal Co.; past dir. Gt. Lakes Broadcasting Co., Chgo., Chgo. & Ill. Midland Ry. Co., Allied Mills, Inc., Chgo., Am. Gage & Machine Co., Elgin, Ill., HMW Industries, Inc., Stamford, Conn. Treas., Katherine Kreigh Meml. Home for Children, Libertyville, Ill., 1929-36; mem. adv. com. on pub. utilities U. Ill., 1937-40, mem. gen. adv. com., 1943-46. Bd. dirs. Am. Cancer Soc. Ill. div., 1948-76, pres., 1957-59, chmn. bd., 1959-62, mem. fin. com., 1970-76; bd. dirs. Civic Fedn. Chgo., 1945-63, v.p., 1954-63; bd. dirs. South Side Planning Bd. Chgo., 1950-58; bd. dirs., mem. exec. com. Ill. C. of C., 1957-61; trustee Kemper Hall Sch. for Girls, Kenosha, Wis., 1929-37, Highland Park (Ill.) Hosp., 1946-51, Christine and Alfred Sonntag Found. for Cancer Research, 1965-81. Recipient Am. Cancer Soc. medal, 1951. Mem. U. Ill. Found., U.S. Men's (dir. 1958-62, v.p. 1960-65), Midwest (dir. 1956-60) curling assns., OX5 Aviation Pioneers, Beta Gamma Sigma, Phi Eta, Delta Sigma Pi, Phi Kappa Phi, Delta Chi. Episcopalian. Clubs: Univ. (dir. 1944-46, treas. 1945-46), Tower (Chgo.); Exmoor Country (Highland Park, Ill.); Chgo. Curling (pres. 1956-57) (Northbrook, Ill.). Contbr. articles to profl. jours. Home and Office: 14782 Canterbury Tustin CA 92680

PATTON, DAVID WAYNE, hosp. adminstr.; b. Utica, N.Y., June 15, 1942; s. Dale Willard and Eleanor (Miller) P.; B.S., Ariz. State U., 1964; M.H.A., U. Minn., 1966; m. Karmen Louise Rames, June 12, 1965; children—Jodi Lynn, Steven Wayne. Asst. adminstr. Maricopa County Gen. Hosp., Phoenix, 1969-71; adminstr. Holy Rosary Hosp., Miles City, Mont., 1971-74; exec. dir. St. Luke's Hosp., Aberdeen, S.D., 1974-79; pres., chief exec. officer Parkview Hosp., Pueblo, Colo., 1979—. Bd. dirs. Pueblo United Way, 1980-82, Jr. Achievement Pueblo, 1982—, San Louis Valley Health Maintenance Orgn., 1982— . Served to capt. USAF, 1966-69. Fellow Am. Coll. Hosp. Adminstrs. (regent 1976-79); mem. Am. Hosp. Assn., Greater Pueblo C. of C. (bd. dirs. 1982—), Colo. Hosp. Assn. Republican. Methodist. Clubs: Pueblo Country, Rotary Internat. Home: 3120 8th Ave Pueblo CO 81008 Office: 400 W 16th St Pueblo CO 81003

PATTON, FRED, motion picture producer; b. Webb City, Mo., July 24, 1911; s. Fred William and Nellie Blanche Patton; student Oklahoma City U., 1930-33; grad. Nat. Tng. Sch. Boy Scout Execs., 1939-40; m. Ruth Eugenia Overstreet, Oct. 25, 1931; children—Eugenia Lee Patton Berlin, Marilyn Dean Patton McElliott. Asst. exec. Boy Scouts Am., Oklahoma City, 1939-44; supt. camping Philmont Scout Ranch, 1944-47; freelance photographer, 1947-52; chief info. and edn. N.Mex. Dept. Game and Fish, 1952-59; owner, mgr. Fred Patton Studios, Santa Fe, 1959—; pres., chief exec. officer Multimedia Internat. Corp., Santa Fe, 1972—. Recipient Conservation Info. Merit award, 1959, N.Mex. Sportsman of Yr. award, 1958, Leadership awards N.Mex. Pub. Relations Conf., 1959, 62, 65. Fellow Internat. Inst. Profl. Photographers; mem. N.Mex. Outdoor Writers and Photographers, Rocky Mountain Outdoor Writers and Photographers. Outdoor Writers Assn. Am., Am. Film Inst. Republican. Baptist. Clubs: Kiwanis, Masons, Shriners. Address: 1403 Seville Rd Santa Fe NM 87501

PATTON, RICHARD WESTON, mortgage banking company executive; b. Evanston, Ill., Sept. 26, 1931; s. Robert Ferry and Sue Buckley P.; B.A., Amherst Coll., 1954; m. Lynda A. Kruse, Feb. 2, 1971; 1 son, Robert Weston. Sales engr. Thermo Fax Sales Corp., Chgo., 1958-60; account exec. Nat. Mortgage Investors, Inc., Chgo., also Pasadena, Calif., 1960-66, asst. v.p., 1966-67, v.p., 1967-69, exec. v.p., 1969-73, pres., 1973—, chief exec. officer, dir., 1969—; chmn. exec. com., dir. Ocean Park Restaurant Corp., Santa Monica, Calif., 1977—; dir. Pasadena Fed. Savs. and Loan Assn., P.F.S. Corp. Bd. dirs. Pasadena Boys' Club, 1963-66; mem. steering com. Amherst Coll. Capital Fund Drive, 1963-66. Served with USMCR, 1955-58. Mem. Pasadena C. of C., Calif. Savs. and Loan Assn. League, U.S. League Savs. Assns. Clubs: Overland (sec., dir.), Kronenstadt Ski (past pres.). Office: 87 N Raymond Ave Pasadena CA 91103

PATTON, SANDRA LEE, librarian; b. Berry, Ala., Sept. 8, 1944; d.Elbert Clyde and Jakie Christine (Lindsey) P.; B.S., U. Ala., 1966; M.A. in Library Media, U. Colo., 1976. Media specialist Cross Keys High Sch., Atlanta, 1966-68; head media specialist Washington Irving Jr. High Sch., Colorado Springs (Colo.) public schs., 1968-74, acquisitions librarian Sabin Jr. High Sch., also Doherty Sr. High Sch., 1974-75, supr. library services all schs., 1975—; cons. on copyright. Mem. Gov. Lamm Re-election Com., 1978, Polit. Action Edn. Com., 1970-73; mem. fund raising com. Nat. Jewish Hosp., 1980. Mem. Assn. Ednl. Communications and Tech. (mem. membership com. sch. media specialist div., also program com. 1981-82), Colo. Assn. Sch. Librarians (pres. 1972), Colo. Ednl. Media Assn. (dir. 1980—, Harold Hill Leadership award 1980, Colo. Assn. Sch. Execs., Phi Delta Kappa (sec. 1980). Democrat. Baptist. Office: 1036 N Franklin St Colorado Springs CO 80903

PAUL, DAVID WARREN, writer, consultant, film critic, scholar; b. Cherokee, Iowa, June 30, 1944; s. Firdel William and Emma Louise (Frankenfeld) P.; m. Barbara D. Dutko, Aug. 29, 1970 (div.); m. Nancy L. Jacobs, Aug. 6, 1976 (div.). B.A., Carleton Coll., 1966; postgrad. U. Vienna, 1966; M.A., Johns Hopkins Sch. Advanced Internat. Studies, 1968; postgrad. U. Colo., 1968, Zagreb (Yugoslavia) U., 1969, Charles U., Prague, Czechoslovakia, 1971; Ph.D., Princeton U., 1973. Asst. prof. polit. sci. and internat. studies U. Wash., Seattle, 1972-82; writer, cons., film critic, scholar, Seattle, 1982—; author: The Cultural Limits of Revolutionary Politics; Change and Continuity in Socialist Czechoslovakia, 1979; Czechoslovakia: Profile of a Socialist Republic at the Crossroads of Europe, 1981, 82; Politics, Art and Commitment in The East European Cinema, 1983; contbr. chpts. to books, scholarly articles to publs. Fulbright research fellow, Hungary, Austria, 1977-78. Mem. Internat. Studies Assn., Am. Assn. for Advancement of Slavic Studies, Czechoslovak History Conf. Mem. United Church of Christ.

PAUL, GEORGE RAYMOND, Realtor; b. Chattanooga, Jan. 14, 1930; s. Burnette and Lillie (Koger) P.; A.A. in Real Estate, Grossmont Coll., 1977; m. Peggy Jean Fuller, Nov. 2, 1951; children—George Richard, Raymond Duane, Julie Diane. Served as enlisted man USN, 1948-70, advanced through grades to master chief sonarman, 1963; ret., 1970; Realtor, Santee, Calif., 1970—; mem. Santee Community Planning Group, 1970-78, chmn., 1976-77; mem. San Diego County Integrated Planning Office Adv. Bd., 1977-80. Bd. dirs. El Cajon/Santee Boys' Club, 1975-78, pres., 1979; mem. San Diego County Reorgn. Task Force, 1978; mem. Planning and Land Use Adv. Bd. County of San Diego, 1979, 80, Tech. Study Com.-Groundwater Study, 1979, Septic System/Groundwater, 1980. Named Realtor of Year, El Cajon Valley Bd. Realtors, 1974. Mem. Nat. Assn. Realtors, Calif. Assn. Realtors (nominating com. 1979, regional v.p. 1978, vice-chmn. land use and environ. com.-south 1979, dir.-at-large 1980), East San Diego County Bd. Realtors (Realtor of Yr. 1976; pres. 1976, dir. 1972-78, dir.-at-large 1979, treas. 1980-81). Democrat. Clubs: Kiwanis, Masons. Home: 1527 Eagle Ln El Cajon CA 92020 Office: 11125 Woodside Ave Santee CA 92071

PAUL, MAXINE, organizational development consultant, educator; b. Ogden, Utah, May 24, 1946; d. Owen Max and Isabella (Barcas) Porter; m. Jerome Edward Paul, Nov. 22, 1969; children—Tammy Dee, Wendy Lynn, Jerome Edward. A.A. in Child Devel., Los Angeles City Coll., 1975; cert. in orgn. design, UCLA, 1977; student Pepperdine U., 1980-81. Ins. analyst Occidental Life Ins. Co., Los Angeles, 1966-69; office mgr. Gavin & Dom Studios, Los Angeles, 1969-70; mgmt. devel. specialist Occidental Life Ins. Co., 1970-74; property mgr. Glendale Investment Corp. (Calif.), 1974-75; asst. dir. orgnl. devel. Tansam. Occidental Life Ins. Co., Los Angeles, 1976—; instr. West Los Angeles Coll., 1977-79; pres. Transam. Employees Fed. Credit Union; guest speaker; condr. seminars. Mem. PTA; chmn. personnel and tng. com. Am. Heart Assn., 1978-81, mem. mgmt. and fin. com., 1981—, Vol. Recognition award, 1981; adv. bd. Coll. Continuing Edn., U. So. Calif., 1979-81. Mem. Los Angeles C. of C., Am. Soc. Tng. and Devel. Republican. Episcopalian. Club: Los Angeles Athletic. Office: Transamerica Occidental 1150 S Olive St Suite T 518 Los Angeles CA 90015

PAULEY, LEON TRENTON, air force officer; b. Charleston, W.Va., Sept. 4, 1944; s. James Meredith and Mary Louise (Hamric) P.; B.S. in Bus. Adminstrn., W.Va. U., 1967; M.A. in Mgmt. and Public Adminstrn., Webster Coll., 1977; m. Nancy Carol Warder, May 10, 1967; children—Heather Lynn, Derek Trenton. Commd. 2d lt. U.S. Air Force, 1967, advanced through grades to lt. col., 1979; pilot in U.S. and Kunsan, Korea, 1969-70, Phu Cat, Viet Nam, 1971, U.S. and Korat, Thailand, 1972-73; wing flying safety officer Davis-Monthan AFB, Ariz., 1973-75; fighter air liaison officer to 82d Airborne Div., Ft. Bragg, N.C., 1975-78; UN mil. observer, truce supervision orgn. Middle East, 1978-80; flight comdr., life support officer 358th Tactical Fighter Tng. Squadron, chief wing scheduling 355th Tactical Tng. Wing, Davis-Monthan AFB, 1981-82; dep. chief U.S. Liaison Office Kuwait and U.S., adv. to Kuwait Air Force, 1982-84. Pres., McNair PTA, Ft. Bragg, 1973-74; jr. ch. leader 82d Airborne Div. Meml Chapel, 1977-78, founder, tchr. Sunday sch. Ch. of Scotland, Tiberias, Israel, 1979-80; Sunday sch. tchr. El Camino Bapt. Ch., Tucson. Decorated D.F.C., Air medal with 16 oak leaf clusters, UN medal, Meritorious Service medal, others; recipient cert. of appreciation U.S. Army Chaplains Corp, 1978. Mem. Am. Mgmt. Assn., Air Force Assn., VFW, Nat. Def. Preparedness Assn. Republican. Contbr. articles to profl. publs. Address: USLOK Kwait Dept State Washington DC 20520

PAULIEN, DANIEL K., planning and devel. cons.; b. N.Y.C., Sept. 17, 1944; s. Kurt E. and Gertrude (Ludwig) P.; student Union Coll., Lincoln, Nebr., 1963-66; B.A. with distinction, U. Colo., Boulder, 1967, M.A., 1968; m. Susan Ann Smith, Jan. 22, 1967; 1 dau., Pamela. Instr. speech, gen. mgr. radio sta. Wis. State U., Whitewater, 1968-69; asso. research and planning Colo. Commn. Higher Edn., Denver, 1969-71, coordinator facilities planning and research, 1971-73; ednl. program planner Auraria Higher Edn. Center, Denver, 1973-76, dir. facilities planning and utilization, 1976-78, dir. planning and student aux. services, 1978-79; pres., propr. Paulien & Assocs. (formerly Planning and Devel. Services), Denver, 1979—; instr. communication U. Colo., Denver, 1976-78; planning cons. MIRA, Inc., Boulder, 1978. Pres., Capitol Hill United Neighborhoods, Inc., Denver, 1978-80, bd. dirs., 1976-82; sec., bd. dirs. Health Support Council for Capitol Hill Srs., Inc., 1983—; trustee Historic Denver, Inc., 1979-82; mem. planning and adv. bd. Denver Center for Performing Arts, 1973-77; co-pres. Stevens Sch. PTA, 1974-75; monitor Community Edn. Council Desegregation, 1975-76. Recipient award People Let's Unite for Schs., 1975; NDEA fellow, 1967-68. Mem. Soc. Coll. and Univ. Planning, Speech Communication Assn., Am. Assn. Mental Deficiency. Democrat. Home: 1259 Steele St Denver CO 80206 Office: 2010 E 17th Ave Denver CO 80206

PAULING, LINUS CARL, chemist, educator; b. Portland, Oreg., Feb. 28, 1901; s. Herman Henry William and Lucy Isabelle (Darling) P.; B.S., Oreg. State Coll., Corvallis, 1922, Sc.D. (hon.), 1933; Ph.D., Calif. Inst. Tech., 1925; Sc.D. (hon.), U. Chgo., 1941, Princeton U., 1946, U. Cambridge, U. London, Yale U., 1947, Oxford, 1948, Bklyn. Poly. Inst., 1955, Humboldt U., 1959, U. Melbourne, 1964, U. Delhi, Adelphi U., 1967, Marquette U. Sch. Medicine, 1969; L.H.D., Tampa, 1950; U.J.D., U. N.B., 1950; LL.D., Reed Coll., 1959; Dr. h.c., Paris (France), 1948, Toulouse (France), 1949, Montpellier (France), 1958, Jagiellonian U., 1964; D.F.A., Chouinard Art Inst., 1958; others; m. Ava Helen Miller, June 17, 1923; children—Linus Carl, Peter Jeffress, Linda Helen, Edward Crellin. Teaching fellow Calif. Inst. Tech., 1922-25, research fellow, 1925-27, asst. prof., 1927-29, asso. prof., 1929-31, prof. chemistry, 1931-64, chmn. div. chemistry and chem. engring., dir. Gates and Crellin labs. Chemistry, 1936-58, mem. exec. com., bd. trustees, 1945-48; research prof. Center for Study Dem. Instns., 1963-67; prof. chemistry U. Calif. at San Diego, 1967-69; prof. chemistry Stanford, 1969-74; pres. Linus Pauling Inst. Sci. and Medicine, 1973-75, research prof., 1973—; George Eastman prof. Oxford U., 1948; lectr. chemistry several univs. Fellow Balliol Coll., 1948, NRC, 1925-26, John S. Guggenheim Meml. Found., 1926-27. Numerous awards in field of chemistry, including U.S. Presdl. Medal for Merit, 1948, Nobel prize in chemistry, 1954, Nobel Peace prize, 1962, Internat. Lenin Peace prize, 1972; U.S. Nat. Medal of Sci., 1974; Fermat medal, Paul Sabatier medal, Pasteur medal, medal with laurel wreath of Internat. Grotius Found., 1957; Lomonosov medal, 1977; Chem. Scis. award Nat. Acad. Scis., 1979. Hon., corr., fgn. mem. numerous assns. and orgns. Author several books, 1930—. Contbr. articles to profl. jours. Office: Linus Pauling Inst Sci and Medicine 400 Page Mill Rd Palo Alto CA 94306*

PAULSEN, BORGE REGNAR, agricultural cooperative executive; b. San Francisco, July 26, 1915; s. Anton and Christa (Regnar) P.; student Stanford, 1933-35; B.S., U. Calif., Berkeley, 1937; m. Beverly Ann Gephart, July 3, 1942; children—Lee Ann Paulsen Hanna, R. Anthony, Eric Dana, Carol Louise. Sec., Agrl. Adjustment Adminstrn., Yolo County, Calif., 1937-41; owner, operator Sunset Rice Dryer, Inc., Woodland, Calif., 1946—; pres. Demeter Corp. Woodland, Agrivest Corp., Woodland; pres. Crane & Cross Booles, Inc., Sacramento; dir. Wells Fargo Bank, Wells Fargo & Co.; farmer, rice grower, 1937—; mem. rice research and mktg. com. U.S. Dept. Agr., others; chmn. adv. bd. Berkeley Bank for Coops., 1976. Bd. dirs., v.p. Calif. Rice Research Found., Yuba City, Woodland Meml. Hosp., also former pres.; former pres. Sutter (Calif.) Mut. Water Co.; bd. dirs. Robert Louis Stevenson Sch., Pebble Beach, Calif., Agrl. Council Calif.; adv. bd. Calif. State U., Sacramento. Served with U.S. Army, 1941-46. Recipient Distinguished Service award Calif. Farm Bur., 1974, Outstanding Service award Woodland Meml. Hosp., 1976, Calif. Rice Industry Man of Year award, 1978. Mem. Rice Research and Mktg. Bd. Calif. (v.p.), Rice Growers Assn. Calif. (pres., chmn. bd. 1968—), Bean Growers Assn. Calif. (past pres.), Delta Kappa Epsilon. Republican. Episcopalian. Clubs: Commonwealth, Bankers (San Francisco); Rotary Woodland (former pres.); Sutter, Yolo Fliers Country, El Macero Country. Home: 202 Rancho Way St Woodland CA 95695 Office: 1021 Lincoln Ave Woodland CA 95695

PAULSEN, FRANK ROBERT, coll. dean; b. Logan, Utah, July 5, 1922; s. Frank and Ella (Ownby) P.; B.S., Utah State U., 1947; M.S., U. Utah, 1948, Ed.D., 1956; Kellogg Found. postdoctoral fellow U. Ore., 1958; Carnegie Found. postdoctoral fellow U. Mich., 1959-60; m. Marye Lucile Harris, July 31, 1942; 1 son, Robert Keith; m. 2d, Lydia Ransier Lowry, Nov. 1, 1969. High sch. prin. Mt. Emmons, Utah, 1948-51; supt. schs., Cokeville, Wyo., 1951-55; asst. prof., then asso. prof. edn. U. Utah, 1955-61; prof. edn., dean Sch. Edn. U. Conn., 1961-64; dean Coll. Edn. U. Ariz., Tucson, 1964—. Scholar-in-residence Fed. Exec. Inst., Charlottesville, Va., 1970; Disting. prof. edn. U. Bridgeport, summer 1972; dir., sec. Am. Jour. Nursing Pub. Co., 1966-80; dir. Am. Gen. Growth Fund, Am. Gen. Exchange Fund, Am. Gen. Equity Accumulation Fund, Am. Gen. Capital Accumulation Fund, all Houston. Chmn., Conn. Adv. Com. Adminstrv. Certification, 1962-64; exec. com. New Eng. Council Advancement Sch. Adminstrn., 1962-64; trustee Joint Council Econ. Edn., 1962-70; v.p., dir. Southwestern Coop. Ednl. Lab., 1965-67; bd. dirs. Nat. League for Nursing, 1967-69, mem. com. on perspectives, 1966-72; dir., chmn. exec. com. ERIC Clearinghouse on Tchr. Edn., 1968-70; bd. dirs. Tucson Mental Health Center, 1968-70, Robert A. Taft Inst. for Ariz., 1978—. Served with AUS, 1942-46; PTO. Mem. Aerospace Med. Assn., NEA, Assn. Higher Edn., Am. Assn. Sch. Adminstrs., Am. Acad. Polit. and Social Sci., John Dewey Soc., Utah Acad. Letters, Arts and Scis., Ariz. Acad., Am. Assn. Colls. Tchrs. Edn. (Conn. liaison officer 1962-64, mem. studies com. 1962-68, dir.), Ariz. Assn. Colls. Tchr. Edn. (pres. 1972—), A.A.A.S., Am. Ednl. Research Assn., Kappa Delta Pi, Pi Sigma Alpha, Pi Gamma Mu, Phi Delta Kappa. Rotarian. Author: The Adminstration of Public Education in Utah, 1958; Contemporary Issues in American Education, 1966; American Education: Challenges and Images, 1967; Changing Dimensions in International Education, 1968; Higher Education: Dimensions and Directions, 1969; also numerous articles. Home: 2801 N Indian Ruins Tucson AZ 85715

PAULSEN, GEORGE ARTHUR, physician; b. Cascade, N.H., Apr. 17, 1922; s. Levi and Benny-Marie (Nelson) P.; B.S., U. N.H., 1943; M.D., Tufts U., 1946; children—Theodore Alan, Thomas Craig, Donald Scott. Intern, Mass. Meml. Hosp., Boston, 1946-47, resident in surgery, 1946-48, 50-52; thoracic surgery tng., Los Angeles, 1952-55; asst. med. dir. LaVina Sanitorium and Hosp., Altadena, Calif., 1952-55; pvt. practice thoracic surgery, Bakersfield, Calif., 1955—; chief surgery Kern County Gen. Hosp., 1960-63, chmn. staff, 1964. Pres. Kern County Tb Assn., 1959; pres. Kern County unit Am. Cancer Soc., 1962-63; exec. com. Kern County council Boy Scouts Am., 1963—, pres. So. Sierra council, 1970-72; adv. bd. Salvation Army, 1962—; pres. Kern County Heart Assn., 1966; bd. dirs. Kern County United Fund, 1972. Served from 1st lt. to capt., USAF, 1948-50. Recipient Silver Beaver award Boy Scouts Am., 1968, Silver Antelope award, 1972. Diplomate Am. Bd. Surgery. Fellow ACS, Am. Coll. Chest Physicians; mem. Am. Thoracic Soc., Bakersfield Surg. Soc. (pres. 1965), So. Calif. Tennis-Assn. (dir.), Soc. Thoracic Surgeons (a founder), Am. Acad. Tb Physicians, Pan Am. Med. Assn. (diplomate mem.), Kern County Med. Soc. (sec.-treas. 1976), Bakersfield Tennis Patrons Assn. (pres. 1964-65). Club: Bakersfield Racquet (pres. 1961-62). Contbr. articles to profl. publs. Office: 2131 19th St Bakersfield CA 92201

PAULSEN, RICHARD WALLACE, data processing executive; b. Blue Island, Ill., Aug. 9, 1945; s. Richard Wallace and Betty Lucille (Frobish) P.; student Carson Coll., 1966-67; B.S. in Bus. Adminstrn., U. Nev., 1972, M.B.A., 1980; student law DePaul U., 1975-76; m. Mildred Stephenson Baker, July 16, 1964 (dec. 1977); children—David Charles, John Stanley, Claire Jane, Kristen Irene; m. 2d, Elizabeth Susan Riley, Nov. 24, 1978; 1 son, Richard James. Materials and testing engr. Nev. Dept. Hwys., 1964-69, computer programmer, analyst, 1969-72; computer systems analyst Nev. Dept. Employment Security, 1972-74; 2d v.p. corp. lending systems Continental Bank, Chgo., 1974-81, mgr. multiple systems depts. including Europe, Far East, S.Am. and U.S.; mgr. corp. and internat. systems div., sr. v.p. world wide data processing Wells Fargo Bank, San Francisco, 1981—; initiated EDP rehab. program Nev. State Prison-Nev. Employment Security Dept., 1972-74. Trustee, Avery Coonley Sch., Athenian Sch. Recipient Outstanding Grad. award State of Nev., 1969; cert. data processor. Mem. Soc. Mgmt. Info. Systems, Am. Inst. Banking, Omicron Delta Epsilon, Beta Gamma Sigma. Unitarian. Home: 437 St Regis Dr Danville CA 94526 Office: 525 Market St San Francisco CA 94105

PAULSON, CHET CLARENCE, sporting goods retailer, gunsmith; b. Tacoma, Oct. 4, 1914; s. Wilfred Frederick and Jennie Idella (Hegland) P.; m. Irene Olga Skreen, July 19, 1939 (dec. 1958); m. 2d, Dorothy Margaret King Knierim, Mar. 12, 1960; children—Glenn Chester, Christie Sophia; 1 stepson, Kim Phillip Knierim. Student pub. schs. Tacoma, Gunsmith, Wash. Hardware Co., Tacoma, 1937-59, Wash. Sports Shop, Tacoma, 1959-61; owner, pres. Chet Paulson, Inc., Tacoma, 1961—; hunting safety instr.; coach Jr. Rifle Club Puyallup (Wash.) High Sch. Coach jr. rifle teams, 1935-60, 4-H rifle teams, 1957-60. Holder master cards in five competitive categories; named Gov.'s All Around Champion, 1958, 59, 60. Mem. Nat. Rifle Assn. (high power com. 1958-65), Wash. State Rifle & Piston Assn., Tacoma Rifle & Revolver Club (sec. 1935-46), Tacoma Sportsmen's Club, Wash. State Sportsmens' Council, Ducks Unltd. Republican. Presbyterian. Contbr. numerous articles to sporting publs. Home: 5116 40th St E Tacoma WA 98443 Office: 935 Fawcett Ave Tacoma WA 98402

PAULSON, FRANCIS JAMES, lawyer; b. Denver, Feb. 10, 1922; s. Joseph Z. and Helen Agatha (Murphy) P.; m. Annabelle McIntire, Jan. 18, 1947; 1 son, Gregory Francis. J.D. summa cum laude, U. Notre Dame, 1946. Bar: Ill. 1947, U.S. Supreme Ct. 1959, Colo. 1974. Assoc. Pope & Ballard, Chgo., 1948-56, Braun, Johnson & Ryan, Chgo., 1948-56; ptnr. Haring & Paulson, Chgo., 1956-59, Paulson & Ketchum, Chgo., 1959-74; gen. counsel High Country Corp., Denver, 1978—; pros. atty. Village of Riverdale (Ill.), 1970-74. Recipient Good Citizenship award Mut. Trust Life Ins. Co., 1970. Mem. Colo. Bar Assn., ABA; former mem. Chgo. Trial Lawyers Assn. (pres. 1956), Chgo. Soc. Trial Lawyers, Chgo. Bar Assn., Am. Arbitration Assn. (accident claims adv. council, Chgo.). Roman Catholic. Club: Chgo. Athletic Assn. Co-author Ill. Jury Instructions, 1954. Home: 255 Monaco Pkwy Denver CO 80220 Office: 1860 Lincoln Suite 100 Denver CO 80295

PAULSON, JOAN MERRYANN, development and property manager, consultant; b. Tacoma, Oct. 30, 1951; d. Arthur Gilbert and Billie Bernice (Butler) P. B.A. in Urban Planning, U. Wash., 1983. Lic. real estate salesperson, Wash. Coordinator, liaison Pike Place Project, City of Seattle, 1972-79; constrn. and devel. coordinator Pike Place Market Preservation and Devel. Authority, 1979-82; property mgr. William J. Charles Assocs., Seattle, 1983—; resident apt. mgr. Fairmount Apts., 1979—; mem. Mayor's Task Force on 1982 Downtown Plan. Pres. Denny Regrade Community Council, 1982-83; mem. LWV, 1983—, Seattle Mcpl. League, 1981—, Allied Arts of Seattle, 1982—, Seattle Shorelines Coalition, 1981—; bd. dirs. Downtown Human Service Council, 1983. Recipient award for preservation of affordable housing Seattle Tenants Union, 1980; recipient 1st award for Denny Regrade Firm Alternative, Wash. chpt. Am. Planning Assn., 1981-82. Mem. Seattle-King County Bd. Realtors. Democrat. Contbr. articles to profl. jours. Office: William J Charles 180 Nickerson St Suite 105 Seattle WA 98109

PAULSON, RICHARD, management consultant; b. Erie, Pa., Feb. 10, 1920. 1 dau., Kathy. Field test engr. Convair-Astronautics, San Diego, 1953-63; sr. cons. Bruce Payne Assoc., Los Angeles, 1963-65; self employed mgmt. cons., Beverly Hills, Calif., 1965-72; founder, pres. O.N. Eno Co., Fresno, Calif., 1972—. Served to 1st lt. USAAF, 1943-45; ret. USAFR, 1963. Author, pub.: The ABC's of Time Study, 1978; contbr. articles on mgmt. to bus. jours., tech. articles to engring. jours., travel articles, miscl. material to mags.; songwriter; designer, inventor toys, games, restaurants, artistic, comml. projects. Office: Box 11032 Fresno CA 93771

PAULSON, RICHARD GUY, retail executive; b. Portland, Oreg., Sept. 30, 1921; s. Guy W. and Bess (Spinning) P.; student Oreg. State U., 1939-41, U. Oreg., 1941-42; B.A., U. Wash., 1943; m. Norma Lee Cunningham, Apr. 29, 1944; children—Lawrence Lee, Donald Guy, Richard, Beverly Sue, David William. With G.W. Paulson Co., Portland, 1946—, v.p., 1946-57, pres., 1957—. Served to capt. AUS, 1943-46. Mem. Portland Retail Trade Bur. (pres., chmn. bd. 1956-60), Portland C. of C. (dir., exec. com. 1956-60), Gideons, Phi Gamma Delta. Republican. Baptist. Home: 2210 NE 31st Ave Portland OR 97212 Office: 3040 NE Sandy Blvd Portland OR 97212

PAULSON, STEPHANIE, graphic designer; b. San Francisco, Dec. 24, 1953; d. Stephen Junior and Lynn Lee (Phillips) P. B.A., San Jose State U., 1975. Paste-up artist Funfinder Mag., 1975-76; prodn. mgr., designer Untold Millions Advt., San Francisco, 1976-77; art dir. Go-West Mag., Burlingame, Calif., 1977-80; ptnr., creative dir. The STEPHENZ Group, Campbell, Calif., 1980—. Named best designer San Jose State U., 1975.

PAULUS, NORMA JEAN PETERSEN (MRS. WILLIAM G. PAULUS), state ofcl.; b. Belgrade, Nebr., Mar. 13, 1933; d. Paul Emil and Ella Marie (Hellbusch) Petersen; LL.B., Willamette U., 1962; m. William G. Paulus, Aug. 16, 1958; children—Elizabeth, William Frederick. Sec. to Harney County (Oreg.) Dist. Atty., 1950-53; legal sec., Salem, Oreg., 1953-55; sec. to chief justice Oreg. Supreme Ct., 1955-61; admitted to Oreg. bar, 1962; of counsel Paulus and Callaghan, Salem, 1971-76; mem. Oreg. Ho. of Reps., 1971-76; sec. of state Oreg., Salem, 1977—; fellow Eagleton Inst. Politics, 1971. Mem. Salem Human Relations Commn., 1967-70, Marion-Polk Boundary Commn., 1970-71; trustee Willamette U., 1978—; bd. dirs. Benedictine Found. Oreg., 1980—. Recipient Golden Torch award Bus. and Profl. Women Oreg., 1971, Disting. Service award City of Salem, 1971; Abigail Scott Duniway award Women in Communications, 1979; Woman of Yr. award Oreg. Women Lawyers, 1980, 82; named to Women of Future, Ladies Home Jour., 1980. Mem. Oreg. State Bar, Nat. Soc. State Legislators (dir. 1971-72). Office: Office of Sec of State 136 State Capitol Salem OR 97310

PAVA, DAVID LAUREN, computer co. exec.; b. San Francisco, Feb. 23, 1949; s. Jacob and Esther P.; B.A., Calif. State U., San Francisco, 1972; M.B.A., St. Mary's Coll., Moraga, Calif., 1981; m. Miriam L. Para, June 5, 1983; children—Aaron, Adam. Dist. mgr. Southland Corp., Dallas, 1972-77; franchise devel. mgr. Byte Industries Inc., Hayward, Calif., 1978, chief exec. officer, 1979, pres., 1980—; speaker COMDEX, 1980, 81, 82, OEM Bus. Forum, 1980, 81; mktg. cons. logical machines, Sunnyvale, Calif. Served with USCG, 1971. Jewish. Club: Horseless Carriage Am. Home: 992 Sunnyhills Rd Oakland CA 94610 Office: 21130 Cabot Blvd Hayward CA 94545

PAVIA, CHARLES NICHOLAS, photographic frame and wall decor company executive; b. Bklyn., Apr. 16, 1946; s. Vito Angelo and Frances Jean (Abruzzo) P.; B.S. in Mktg. (Mktg. Student of Yr.), Calif. State Poly. U., 1967; M.B.A., U. So. Calif., 1968. Market planning analyst Chartpak Co., Santa Ana, Calif. and Leeds, Mass., 1968-71, product mgr., Leeds, 1972-73, dir. planning, 1973-75; mktg. mgr. Pickett Industries, Irvine, Calif., 1975-78; dir. planning and devel. Chartpak Pickett Industries, 1978-79, v.p. planning and devel., 1980-82; exec. asst. to pres. Intercraft Industries Corp., Carson, Calif., 1982-83, v.p. mktg. services, 1983—; cons. mktg. Porter & Goodmyn Design Assos., 1968-69. Served with USN, 1969-71. Mem. U. So. Calif. M.B.A. Alumni Assn., Assn. Corp. Growth (Los Angeles chpt.), Beta Gamma Sigma. Republican. Roman Catholic. Home: 6466 Horse Shoe Ln Yorba Linda CA 92686 Office: 771 E Watson Center Rd Carson CA 90745

PAVLIDES, MILLER HARRY, accountant; b. Puchachi, Turkey, Mar. 28, 1912; s. Harry and Europe P.; student Ohio State U., 1935-40, Yale U., 1944, N.Mex. State U., 1946-51; m. Mary Mavromatis, Dec. 9, 1959; children—John, Daphne. Acct., Miller H. Pavlides, Albuquerque, 1946—; sec. Mellekas Advt., Albuquerque, 1969—. Served as capt. Adj. Gen. Dept., U.S. Army, 1941-45. Decorated Bronze Star. Mem. Nat. Soc. Pub. Accts., N.Mex. Soc. Pub. Accts. Greek Orthodox. Clubs: Lions (pres.), Elks, Masons, Shriners. Home: 1519 Wellesley Dr NE Albuquerque NM 87106 Office: 3117 Silver St SE Albuquerque NM 87106

PAVLOSKY, SOL I., state official, educator; b. Denver, Feb. 2, 1935; s. Louis B. and Bertha; m. Anne Natalie Drucker, July 4, 1958; children—Robin Sue, Alan N. B.A., Calif. State U.-Los Angeles, 1958; postgrad. UCLA, 1965-72; M.P.A., Chapman Coll., 1972. Placement officer, claims adjucator Calif. Employment Devel. Dept., East Los Angeles, 1958-62, dir. manpower tng. and devel. program, 1962-72, fair employment and housing affirmative action cons., San Bernardino, 1972-79, adminstr. state program, 1979—; tchr. bus. adminstrn.; cons. community action groups; faculty pub. service inst. Cons. Desert Assn. Residential Equality; bd. dirs. Casitas Del Monte Home Owners Assn.; active Eastern Area Jewish Fedn. Council, Community Relations Com. Recipient Service award Kiwanis of San Bernardino, 1975; cert. award Youth Motivation Task Force, 1978; award of merit Internat. Yr. Disabled Youth Incentive Program, 1980. Mem. Soc. Advancement Mgmt., Am. Soc. Tng. and Devel., Mex-Am. Personnel Mgmt. Assn. (parliamentarian), Am. Soc. Pub. Adminstrn. Internat. Personnel Mgmt. Assn., Personnel Mgmt. Assn. de Aztlan, Calif. Inst. Integrated Edn. Jewish. Clubs: Soc. Preserve and Encourage Radio Drama, Variety and Comedy, Covina Toastmasters (v.p.). Author: Thoughts on Evaluation, 1980; Discipline and Discharge, 1981. Home: 1913 Ranbung Rd Covina CA 91724

PAWULA, KENNETH JOHN, artist, educator; b. Chgo., Feb. 4, 1935; s. John and Clara (Brzezinski) P.; student Northwestern U., 1956, Art Inst. Chgo., 1956; B.F.A., U. Ill., 1959; M.A. in Painting, U. Calif., Berkeley, 1962. Graphic designer Motorola, Inc., Chgo., 1959-60; grad. asst. printmaking U. Calif., Berkeley, 1961-62, asso. in art, 1962-63; archaeol. delineator for Islamic excavation Am. Research Center, Egypt, 1964-65; instr. Sch. of Art, U. Wash., Seattle, 1965-67, asst. prof., 1967-73, asso. prof., 1974—; participant artist-in-residence program of Ecole Superieure Des Beaux-Arts D'Athenes at Rhodos Art Center, Greece, 1978; cons. to Wydawnictwo Interpress, Warsaw, Poland, 1978; mem. art jury ann. painting, drawing and sculpture show Art Mus. of Greater Victoria, Can., 1971, Unitarian Art Gallery, Seattle, 1968, Cellar Gallery, Kirkland, Wash., 1968, Lakewood Artist's Outdoor Exhibit, Tacoma, Wash., 1968; participant Painting Symposium, Janow Podlaski, Poland, 1977. One-man shows of paintings include: Univ. Unitarian Fine Arts Gallery, Seattle, 1970, Polly Friedlander Gallery, Seattle, 1970, Lynn Kottler Galleries, N.Y.C., 1971, U. Minn. Art Gallery, Mpls., 1971, Art Mus. of Greater Victoria, Can., 1972, Second Story Gallery, Seattle, 1972; group shows include: Worth Ryder Gallery, U. Calif., Berkeley, 1962, Seattle Art Mus., 1964, 70, 65, 66, Frye Art Mus., Seattle, 1966, San Francisco Art Ins., 1966, Henry Gallery, U. Wash., Seattle, 1966, 67, 70, State Capitol Mus., Olympia, Wash., 1967, Attica Gallery, Seattle, 1967, 69, Sec. of State's Office, Olympia, 1968, Eastern Mich. U., Ypsilanti, 1968, Rogue Gallery, Medford, Oreg., 1968, Marylhurst Coll., Oreg., 1968, Spokane Art Mus., 1968, Cheney Cowles Mus., Spokane, 1969, Jade Gallery, Richland, Wash., 1969, Alaska U., 1970, Polly Friedlander Gallery, Mpls., 1971, Anchorage Art Mus., 1972, U. Nev. Art Gallery, 1972, Juneau (Alaska) Art Mus., 1972, Springfield (Mo.) Art Mus., 1973, U. N.D., Grand Forks, 1974, Washington and Jefferson Coll., Washington, Pa., 1975, MacMurray Coll., Jacksonville, Ill., 1976, Gallery of Fine Arts, Eastern Mont. Coll., 1976, Inst. of Culture, Janow Podlaski, Poland, 1977, Seattle Arts Commn., 1978, Polish Cultural Center, Buffalo, 1979; represented in permanent collections: San Francisco Art Mus., Seattle Art Mus., Henry Gallery, U. Wash., Seattle, Highline Coll., Midway, Wash., Marylhurst Coll., Art Mus., Janow Podlaski, Poland, Tacoma Nat. Bank, Fine Arts Gallery of San Diego. Mem. Coll. Art Assn., AAUP. Office: School of Art College of Arts and Sciences Univ of Washington Seattle WA 98195

PAXTON, DAVID OLAF, office supervisor, pilot, retired army officer; b. Socorro, N.Mex., Nov. 2, 1927; s. Emery Foster and Ruth Mildred (Bursum) P.; m. Nancy Lee Shulthiess, Nov. 23, 1950; children—Mark Emery, Deborah Chandler Antonucci, Matthew Radford; m. 2d, Nancy Nordhaus Minces, Nov. 5, 1976. Student N.Mex. Mil. Inst., 1943-45, U. N.Mex., 1946, N.Mex. A&M U., 1947-48, U.S. Armed Forces Inst., 1964-66. Lic. airline transport and comml. helicopter pilot. Cattle rancher, Socorro County N.Mex., 1943-50; commd. 2d lt. Army N.G. 1950; advanced through grades to col., 1970; served as helicopter pilot, intelligence analyst Phillipines, Okinawa, Japan, Korea, Germany, Panama, Viet Nam, and Washington, 1950-70; spl. investigator state's atty. gen. and sheriff's dept., Bernillio County, N.Mex., 1970-72; pres., owner Paxton Enterprises, Inc., Albuquerque, 1972-76; ops. supr. Health and Human Services, Social Security Adminstrn., Hobbs, N.Mex., 1974—. Co-chmn. Lea County United Way; search mission pilot, CAP. Decorated Legion of Merit with oak leaf cluster, Bronze star with 2 oak leaf clusters, Air medal with 5 oak leaf clusters, Joint Service Commendation medal, Army Commendation medal with two oak leaf clusters, Navy medal for valor, Purple Heart; recipient outstanding service citation Social Security Adminstrn., 1980. Mem. Social Security Mgmt. Assn., Aircraft Owners and Pilots Assn., N.Mex. Cattle Grower's Assn., Ret. Officer's Assn., Assn. Ret. Intelligence Officers, N.Mex. Mil Inst. Alumni Assn. (bd. govs.), Am. Legion, VFW, Am. Contract Bridge League, Dalmation Club Am. Republican. Clubs: Elks, Lea County Bridge League. Author: Owning Your First Dalmation, 1957. Home: 1318 W Taos St Hobbs NM 88240

PAYEA, NORMAN PHILIP, II, plastic surgeon; b. Detroit, May 11, 1949; s. Norman Philip and Helen Margaret (Kucera) P.; m. Jennifer Jane Charboneau, June 26, 1974 (div. Jan. 1980); 1 dau., Heather Marie. B.S., Mich. State U., 1971, M.D., 1974. Diplomate Am. Bd. Plastic Surgery. Resident in surgery Loyola U. Med. Ctr., Chgo., 1974-77; resident in plastic, reconstructive and hand surgery, McGill U. Hosp., Montreal, 1977-79; vol. MEDICO br. CARE, Peru, 1979; vis. Queen Victoria Hosp., East Grinstead, Eng., 1979, Canniesburn Hosp., Glasgow, Scotland, 1979, Institutio de Chirugia Reconstructive, Guadalajara, Mex., 1980, U. Calif.-San Francisco Hosps., 1980, Mayo Clinic, Rochester, Minn., 1980; practice medicine specializing in plastic, reconstructive and hand surgery, Tawas, Mich., 1979-81, Denver, 1981—; mem. staff St. Joseph Hosp., Tawas, Luth. Med. Ctr., Denver, Children's Hosp., Denver, U. Colo. Health Scis. Ctr. Hosp., Denver, Beth Israel Hosp., Denver, St. Anthony Hosp. Systems, Denver; asst. clin. prof. U. Colo.; hon. prof. Universidad Nacional San Luis Gonzaga de Ica. Mem. AMA, Colo. Med. Soc., Clear Creek Valley Med. Soc., Internat. Coll. Surgeons (jr.), Colo. Soc. Plastic and Reconstructive Surgeons, Am. Assn. Hand Surgery, Rocky Mountain Hand Surgery Soc., Am. Cleft Palate Assn., Am. Burn Assn. Home: 3470 N Ward Rd Denver CO 80033 Office: 2020 N Wadsworth Blvd Suite 2020 Denver CO 80215

PAYNE, ANCIL HORACE, broadcasting executive; b. Mitchell, Oreg., Sept. 5, 1921; s. Leslie L. and Pearl (Brown) P.; B.S., U. Wash., 1947; student U. Oreg., 1941-42, Willamette U., 1939-41; m. Valerie Davies, Apr. 6, 1959; children—Anne, Alison, Lucinda. Asst. to U.S. Congressman, Washington, 1949-53; mgr. Alaska Martin Van Lines, Anchorage, 1954-57, Oreg-Ltd., Portland, Oreg., 1957-60; v.p. King Broadcasting Co., Portland, 1960-72, pres., Seattle, 1972—; dir. Airborne Freight Co., Intiman Theatre. Served with USN, 1942-45. Mem. Nat. Acad. TV Arts and Scis., Phi Beta Kappa, Alpha Delta Sigma, Pi Sigma Alpha. Democrat. Episcopalian. Clubs: Monday, Rainier, Multnomah Athletic. Office: 333 Dexter Ave N Seattle WA 98109

PAYNE, DANIEL FRANKLIN, cable television company executive, football team owner; b. Los Angeles, Aug. 7, 1945; s. William Franklin and Patrician Jean (Gordon) P. Student U. Ga., 1964, U. Denver, 1965, George Washington U., 1966, UCLA, 1967, Loyola Law School, 1968; M.B.A. Calif. Western U., 1976, Ph.D. in Bus., 1978. Pres., owner Design Trust and World in Water Corp., 1969-73; gen. mgr. Arbitron Com., 1973-76; mktg. mgr. Dickinson Communications, Huntington Beach, Fountain Valley and Westminster, Calif., 1976-78; dir. franchising, gen. mgr. Six Star Cablevistion Co., Los Angeles, N.Y.C. and Chgo., 1978-81; pres., chief exec. officer Internat. Cablesystems, Inc., Beverly Hills, Calif., 1981—; owner, mgr. Am. TV Network; owner, mgr. Profl. Football of Hawaii Ltd.; cons. on mgmt.; lectr. on cable T.V. Co-founder Nat. Libertarian Party. Mem. Nat. Cable TV Assn., Calif. Cable TV Assn., Calif. Rare Fruit Growers Assn., Archtl. Preservation League (founder), Mensa. Libertarian. Home: 2251 W Silver Lake Dr Los Angeles CA 90039 also Hawaii Plantation 46-482 Hulupala Pl Kaneohe HI 96744 Office: 935 River St Honolulu HI 96817

PAYNE, DENNIS KEITH, mfrs. rep., cons. mgmt.; b. Seattle, July 13, 1944; s. James Keith and Callie Jean (Mount) P.; B.A., U. Wash., 1966; m. Leslie Joan Crawley, Dec. 11, 1971; children—Megan April, David Keith, Stefanie Joan. Editor/copywriter Boeing Co., Seattle, 1966-67; various managerial positions The Denver, dept. store, 1967-69; gen. mgr.

Tot Lines Inc., Kirkland, Wash., 1969-74; mfr.'s rep., Seattle, 1974—; mgmt. cons. mktg. apparel industry. Served with U.S. Army, 1965-66. Mem. Pacific NW Apparel Assn. Republican. Episcopalian. Clubs: Wash. Athletic, Bellevue Athletic. Office: Suite 3323 2601 Elliott Ave Seattle WA 98121

PAYNE, HARRY VERN, chief justice N.Mex. Supreme Court; b. Lordsburg, N.Mex., Aug. 13, 1936; s. Harry Vearle and Mandona (Hanchett) P.; B.A., Brigham Young U., 1961; J.D., U. N.Mex., 1964; m. Yerda Ruth Mason, June 26, 1959; children—Julie Ann, Harry Bruce, Herbert Rex, Curtis Edward, Daniel Lewis, Caroline, Thomas Mason, Sarah Dawn. Admitted to N.Mex. bar, 1964; mem. firm Hannett, Hannett & Cornish, Albuquerque, 1964-68; individual practice law, 1968-70; dist. judge 2d Jud. Dist. Ct., Albuquerque, 1971-76, presiding judge, 1973-74; asso. justice N.Mex. Supreme Ct., Santa Fe, from 1977, now chief justice. Mem. N.Mex. Gov's. Council for Criminal Justice, Albuquerque, 1971-74; mem. Kit Carson exec. council Boy Scouts Am., Albuquerque, 1973-74. Democrat. Mormon (lay ofcl. 1968—). Office: Supreme Ct Bldg Santa Fe NM 87501*

PAYNE, WINNETTE RECK, educator, reading/lang. arts cons.; b. Adams County, Colo., July 15, 1923; d. Walter and Emma (Palenshus) Reck; student U. No. Colo., 1940-42; B.A., Colo. State U., 1966, M.Ed., 1971; m. Meredith L. Payne, May 12, 1946; children—Jon Meredith, Susan Elizabeth, Margaret Ann. Tchr. English and reading Lesher Jr. High Sch., Fort Collins, Colo., 1966-74; right to read dir., reading/lang. arts coordinator Poudre R-1 Sch. Dist., Fort Collins, 1974—. Bd. dirs. Norlarco Credit Union, 1972—, chmn. bd., 1977—. Mem. Internat. Reading Assn., Colo. Lang. Arts Soc., Nat. Council Tchrs. English, Nat. Staff Devel. Council, NEA, Colo. Edn. Assn., Poudre Edn. Assn., Assn. Supervision and Curriculum Devel., Colo. Assn. Sch. Execs., Poudre Assn. Sch. Execs., Delta Kappa Gamma, Phi Delta Kappa (pres. 1981—). Episcopalian. Club: Toastmistress. Co-author: The Writing Resource Book, 1977; Vocabulary Simplified, 1981. Home: 516 S Washington St Fort Collins CO 80521 Office: Poudre R-1 School District 2407 LaPorte Ave Fort Collins CO 80521

PAYTON, VIRGINA GLOVER, school counselor; b. Dermott, Ark., Apr. 10, 1936; d. Silas F. and Wilda (Neal) Glover. children—Richard, Wilda. B.A., Philander Smith Coll., 1957, UCLA, 1962; postgrad. U. Hawaii, 1968-72; M.S. in Counseling, Western Oreg. State Coll., 1982. Cert. secondary English tchr., sch. counselor. Tchr. English, Central High Sch., Lake Village, Ark., 1952-59; tchr. 5th grade Pasadena (Calif.) City Schs. System, 1960-67; 4th grade tchr. Kealakehe Sch., Kailua-Kona, Hawaii, 1968-79; guidance proj. tchr./co-ordinator kindergarten-6th grades, 1979-81; intermediate sch. counselor Konawaena High Sch., Kealakekua, Hawaii. Mem. profl. devel. and polit. action coms., 1978-81. Mem. Tchrs. Kona Assn. (pres. 1971-72), Hawaii Tchrs. Assn. (chmn. Kona chpt.), NEA, Am. Personnel and Guidance Assn., Hawaii Counselor's Assn., Alpha Kappa Alpha. Democrat. Home: 76-6135 Plumeria Rd Kailua-Kona HI 96740

PEACHES, DANIEL, state legislator; b. Kayenta, Ariz., Sept. 2, 1940; s. Henry and Adelaide (Donald) P.; B.S., No. Ariz. U., 1967. Mem. Nat. Adv. Council Indian Edn., Washington, 1972; bd. regents Haskell Indian Jr. Coll., 1975-83; exec. staff Office of Chmn. Navajo Nation, Window Rock, Ariz., 1971-83; mem. Ariz. Ho. of Reps., 1975—. Republican. Home: PO Box 1801 Kayenta AZ 86033 Office: Ariz House of Reps Phoenix AZ 85007

PEAK, JACK PERSHING, travel agt.; b. Seattle, Sept. 13, 1918; s. Homer D. and Marguerite M. (Madigan) P.; student Alameda (Calif.) public schs.; m. Vinnie Brown, June 16, 1940; children—Vinnie, Jacqueline, Tyler. Traffic and sales rep. Pan Am. World Airways, 1936-57; with Lerios and St. Claire Travel Agencies, Palo Alto, San Francisco and San Jose, Calif., 1957-63; pres. Jack Peak Travel, San Jose and Santa Clara, 1963—; mem. adv. bds. airlines, steamship cos., community colls. Pres., Menlo Park and San Jose PTAs and Parents clubs; chmn. Menlo Park Library Bd., small bus. drive Santa Clara County United Way, Santa Clara County March of Dimes; chmn. sustaining membership drive Santa Clara County Boy Scouts Am.; bd. dirs., exec. bd. Santa Clara County Better Bus. Bur.; mem. pres.'s council San Jose State U. Lt. (j.g.) USNR, 1942-55. Recipient Albert Gallatin Cert. of Merit award, 1974. Mem. Am. Soc. Travel Agts. Republican. Clubs: San Jose County, San Jose Kiwanis (pres. 1979-80), University (pres. 1980-81) (San Jose); Masons, Shriners. Office: Jack Peak Travel 1221 Lincoln St San Jose CA 95125

PEARCE, MELVIN MICHAEL, solar energy company executive; b. La Mesa, Tex., July 13, 1943; s. Melvin Marcus and Charlotte Allyne (Garnett) P.; B.Mus. Edn., N.Mex. U., 1965; Mus.M., U. Iowa, 1967; M.S., U. No. Colo., 1975; m. Sharon Ann Roether, Oct. 4, 1964; children—John David, Steven Todd, Douglas Andrew. Tchr. music Valley High Sch., Albuquerque, 1967-71; research assoc. Colo. State Archaeologists Office, 1974-76; tchr. music and archaeology Lakewood High Sch., Jefferson County, Colo., 1971-81; owner Enpro Solar Services Corp., Littleton, Colo., 1981—. Deacon, publicity dir., Littleton Ch. of Christ, 1973—. Named Tchr. of Year, Lakewood High Sch., 1975. Mem. Internat. Solar Energy Soc., Am. Solar Energy Soc., NEA, Am. String Tchrs. Assn., Nat. Sch. Orchs. Assn., Nat. Bandmasters Assn., Nat. Assn. Jazz Educators, Colo. Archeol. Soc., Colo. Edn. Assn., Colo. Bandmasters Assn. (named outstanding band dir. Colo. 1979), Solar Energy Mfg. and Retailers, Jefferson County Edn. Assn. Contbr. articles to newspapers, mags. Home: 7633 W Elmhurst Dr Littleton CO 80123 Office: Enpro Solar Services Corp 5950 S Platte Canyon Rd Littleton CO 80123

PEARCE, STANLEY KEITH, information services executive; b. Sprague, Wash., June 13, 1928; s. Charles Henry and Edna Laura (Kindred) P.; m. Donna Mae Ince Jaynes, May 7, 1955 (div. Dec. 1971); 1 son, John Kindred. B.S., U. Wash., 1952; J.D., 1956, M. Law Librarianship, 1957. Reference librarian Los Angeles County Law Library, 1957-59; dir. info. services O'Melveny & Myers, Los Angeles, 1959—; instr. Law Library Inst., U. Calif., Berkeley, 1969; bd. councillors U. So. Calif. Library and Info. Mgmt. Sch., 1980—. Mem. Internat., Am. (dir. ann. inst. 1974, 81, exec. bd. 1977-80), So. Calif. (pres. 1967-68) assns. law libraries, Assoc. Info. Mgrs., Am. Soc. Info. Scis., Spl. Libraries Assn. Unitarian (trustee 1968-74). Author: (with Viola Bird) Order Procedures, 1960. Home: 5648 Whitsett Ave North Hollywood CA 91607 Office: 400 S Hope St Los Angeles CA 90071-2899

PEARL, JANICE MARIE, restaurant/theater owner, neurosurgeon; b. Portland, Oreg., May 24, 1932; d. William Abiel and Elva Catherine (Gleason) P.; B.A. in Music with honors, Ind. U., 1954; student in organic chemistry Columbia U., 1959; M.D., Johns Hopkins U., 1963; postgrad. in gen. surgery U. Minn.-Mayo Clinic, 1963-66; postgrad. in neurol. surgery Barrow Neurol. Inst., 1966-69; 1 dau., Cynthia Ann. Profl. opera and musical comedy singer, 1954-59; intern Univ. Hosp., Mpls., 1963-64, resident in surgery, 1964-66; resident in neurosurgery Barrow Neurol. Inst., 1966-69; chief resident Maricopa County Hosp., 1967-68; practice medicine specializing in neurosurgery, 1969-78; owner, operator Pearl's on the Channel, LaConner, Wash., 1979—; speaker med. assns.; singer spl. concerts, benefits. Recipient Gold award Ind. U., 1952; award for service Am. Legion, 1945; award Portland Symphony, 1956; winner various musical awards and San Francisco Opera Auditions, 1956; Geigy Pharm. grantee, 1961; USPHS grantee, 1964-66. Mem. John Hopkins Med. and Surg. Soc., Am. Guild Musical Artists, Mu Phi Epsilon. Republican. Contbr. articles on hypothalamus and endocrine function to profl. jours. Office: 106 S 1st St PO Box 757 LaConner WA 98257

PEARL, LAWRENCE ALVIN, optometrist; b. Balt., June 24, 1949; s. Paul K. and Ruth Jeanette (Posner) P. B.S., U. Md., 1969; O.D., U. Pa., 1973; postgrad Med. Coll., U. Ariz., 1980-82. Pvt. practice optometry, Glendale, Ariz., 1973—; cons. Warner Lambert Inc., Syntex Corp., Am. Optical Inc., Danker Wolk Inc., Johnson & Johnson, Inc., Ciba-Geigy Corp., Schering Corp.; fellow Gessell Inst., Yale U., 1975, Coll. Visual Devel., 1980. Mem. Am. Optometric Assn. (diplomate in contact lens), Central Ariz. Optometric Assn., So. Tier Optometric Assn., Beta Sigma Kappa. Office: 5132 W Northern Ave Glendale AZ 85301

PEARLMAN, MARION OLA, educational administrator, consultant; b. Mechanicsville, N.Y., Dec. 24, 1920; d. Charles Forrest and Minnie (Mayhew) McBride; m. Albert M. Pearlman, June 9, 1963; 1 son, Michael Edward. B.S., SUNY-Buffalo, 1951; M.Ed., U. Ariz., 1959. Tchr., Pierce Creek Sch., Binghamton, N.Y., 1940-42; tchr. Skaneateles, N.Y., 1942-43; vacation relief agt., reservation clk., ticket agt., auditor, supr. sales control Am. Airlines, Buffalo, 1943-48; ins. analyst Aetna Casualty and Surety Co., Buffalo, 1948-49; tchr., Lancaster, N.Y., 1949-51, University Heights, Tucson, Ariz., 1951-59; Livingston, Calif., 1959-60; cons. elem. edn. County Office Edn., Napa, Calif., supr. Alum Rock Sch. Dist., San Jose, Calif., 1961-62; supr. schs. Nogales, Ariz., 1962-63; tch. Gump Sch. for retarded, blind, emotionally handicapped, deaf, trainable and educable retarded, 1964-78; prin. Valencia Sch., Sunnyside Unified Sch. Dist. #12, Tucson, 1978-83; pvt. cons., 1983—; lectr. Kans. State Tchrs. Coll., Emporia. Mem. exec. com. Tucson House for Retarded; bd. dirs. Beacon Found. for Mentally Retarded; active PTA, PTO; del. to Ariz. State Assembly. Cert. elem. tchr. Democrat. Jewish. Mem. NEA, Ariz. Edn. Assn., Tucson Edn. Assn., Sunnyside Adminstrs. Assn., AAUW (membership com., del. to nat. conv.), Phi Delta Kappa, Pi Lambda Theta.

PEARSON, JOHN, mech. engr.; b. Leyburn, Yorkshire, U.K., Apr. 24, 1923; s. William and Nellie P.; came to U.S., 1930, naturalized, 1944; B.S.M.E., Northwestern U., 1949, M.S., 1951; m. Ruth Ann Billhardt, July 10, 1944; children—John, Armin, Roger. Research engr. Naval Ordnance Test Sta., China Lake, Calif., 1951-55, head warhead research br., 1955-58, head solid dynamics br., 1958-59, head detonation physics group, 1959-67; head detonation physics div. Naval Weapons Center, China Lake, 1967—; cons., lectr. in field; founding mem. adv. bd. Center for High Energy Forming, U. Denver. Charter mem. Sr. Exec. Service U.S., 1979. Served with C.E., U.S. Army, 1943-46. Recipient L.T.E. Thompson medal, 1965; William B. McLean medal, 1979; cert. of recognition Sec. Navy, 1975, Cert. of Commendation, 1980; Merit award Dept. Navy, 1979; cert. of commendation Sec. Navy, 1981; registered profl. engr., Calif. Fellow ASME; mem. Am. Soc. Metals, Am. Phys. Soc., N.Y. Acad. Scis., AIME, Fed. Execs. League, Sigma Xi, Tau Beta Pi, Pi Tau Sigma, Triangle. Author: Explosive Working of Metals, 1963; Behavior of Metals Under Impulsive Loads, 1954; contbr. articles to profl. publs.; patentee impulsive loading, explosives applications. Home: 858 N Primavera Rd PO Box 1390 Ridgecrest CA 93555 Office: Code 383 Naval Weapons Center China Lake CA 93555

PEARSON, JOHN VICTOR, educator; b. Long Beach, Calif., Nov. 13, 1951; s. Evert Eldon and Katherine (Booth) P.; m. Marlayne Thomas, Dec. 28, 1976; children—Rachel, Rebekah, Sarah. A.A., Long Beach City Coll., 1975; B.A. in Elem. Edn., Brigham Young U., 1976; postgrad. Utah State U., 1981-83. Cert. tchr., Utah. Tchr. Sandy (Utah) Elem. Sch., 1976-78; head tchr. Snowville (Utah) Sch., 1979-81; tchr. McKinley Elem. Sch., Tremonton, Utah, 1981—. Served to 2d lt. Utah Army N.G., 1980—. Mem. NEA, Assn. Supervision and Curriculum Devel. Mormon. Home: 684 South 100 West Tremonton UT 84337

PEARSON, RICHARD JARVIS, company executive; b. Chgo., June 3, 1925; s. Andrall E. and Dorothy M. (MacDonald) P., m. Janice Lee Pope, Mar. 1, 1951; 1 son, Douglas R. B.A., U. So. Calif., 1946; M.B.A., Harvard U., 1947. Mktg. dir. Bireleys div. Gen. Foods, 1947-55, Forest Lawn Meml. Park, Glendale, Calif., 1955-57, Revell, Inc., Venice, Calif., 1957-60; dir. mktg. Avery Label Co., Monrovia, Calif., 1960-64, v.p., gen. mgr., 1964-70; group v.p. Avery Internat., San Marino, Calif., 1970-76, exec. v.p., 1976-81, exec. v.p. and chief operating officer, Pasadena, Calif., 1981—; dir. Ameron, Inc., Monterey Park, Kerr Glass Mfg. Corp., Los Angeles, Ducommun, Inc., Los Angeles. Major employee chmn. United Way of San Gabriel and Pomona Valley; dir. San Gabriel Valley council Boy Scouts Am. Served to lt. (j.g.) USN, 1946. Republican. Presbyterian. Clubs: Annandale Golf (Pasadena); California (Los Angeles). Office: 150 N Orange Grove Blvd Pasadena CA 91103

PEARSON, VERNON ROBERT, state supreme court justice; b. Bantry, N.D., Sept. 7, 1923; s. Claude Meredith and Golda May (King) P.; m. Jean Clare Robertson, Aug. 10, 1947; children—Robert, Katharine, Stephen, David. B.A., Jamestown Coll.; J.D., U. Mich. Assoc. instr. U. Wash. Law Sch., 1951-52; atty.-adviser Office Price Stabilization, Seattle, 1952-53; ptnr. Davies, Pearson & Anderson, 1953-69; judge Div. II Wash. State Ct. Appeals, 1969-82; justice Wash. State Supreme Ct., Olympia, 1982—. Served with USN, 1943-46. Fellow ABA. Office: Temple of Justice Olympia WA 98504

PEARSON, WILLIAM DONALD, acad. adminstr.; b. Seattle, Sept. 17, 1933; s. Robert Leonard and Dorothy Evelyn P.; B.A., Walla Walla Coll., 1956, M.A. in Edn., 1964; Ph.D., U.S. Internat. U., 1973; m. Carolyn Jane MacIntyre, Dec. 23, 1956; children—Anne Marie, Douglas Edward. Jr. high sch. tchr. Spokane Jr. Acad., 1956-57, 59-62; tchr. Rogers Elem. Sch., College Place, Wash., 1962-65; jr. high sch. English tchr. Loma Linda (Calif.) Acad., 1965-67; high sch. English tchr. San Diego Acad., National City, Calif., 1967-72, prin., bus. mgr., 1972-78; chmn. edn. dept. So. Missionary Coll., Collegedale, Tenn., 1978-80; prin., bus. mgr. Fresno (Calif.) Adventist Acad., 1980—; speaker, condr. workshops. Bd. trustees Paradise Valley Hosp., 1972-78; ch. organist, minister of music Chula Vista (Calif.) Seventh-day Adventist Ch., 1972-77. Served as chaplain's asst., AUS, 1957-59. Mem. Assn. Supervision and Curriculum Devel., Am. Assn. Coll. Tchrs. of Edn., Nat. Assn. Secondary Sch. Prins., Phi Delta Kappa. Author/editor: Reading Program Materials. Home: 6585 N Callisch St Fresno CA 93710 Office: 5397 E Olive Ave Fresno CA 93727

PEASE, JEFFREY MARCUS, realtor; b. Port Washington, N.Y., June 2, 1938; s. Walter H. and Elaine (Down) P.; student Syracuse U., 1956-60; m. Mary Baldwin Clarke, Oct. 20, 1973; children—Steven Peter, Tom, Michael, Joey, Timothy. Pres. Pease Hamilton Helicopters Inc., Denver, 1965-71; broker Snowmass Am. Corp., Aspen, Colo., 1971-73; pres. Pease & Assos. Aspen, Colo., 1973—; dir., chmn. bd. Realty World Corp. Colo. and Wyo.; dir. Aspen Indsl. Bank, Colo. Nat. Bank, Glenwood, Glenwood Springs, Colo. Dir., Snowmass Water & San. Dist., Snowmass Fire Protection Dist.; bd. dirs. Pease Ranch Found. Served as pilot USAF, 1960-64. Mem. Nat., Colo. assns. realtors, Mont. Assn. Realtors, Grad. Realtors Inst. Republican. Episcopalian. Clubs: Mason (32 deg.) Shriners. Home: 2 Wildoak PO Box 5711 SV Branch Aspen CO 81615 Office: Woodbridge Complex 23 Woodbridge Rd Snowmass Village CO 81615

PEASE, JOANNE KATHRYN, city and regional planner; b. Santa Monica, Calif., Jan. 5, 1952; d. Robert Wright and Kathryn Louise (Scroggin) Pease. B.A. in Geography with honors, U. Calif.-Riverside, 1973. Planner Riverside (Calif.) County Planning Dept., 1974-77; project mgr. Phillips Brandt Reddick, Inc., Irvine, Calif., 1977-78, Planning Research Corp., Orange., Calif., 1978-80; sr. project mgr. Phillpps Brandt Reddick, Inc., Irvine, 1980-82; asst. planning dir. City of Westminster (Calif.), 1983—. Mem. Nat. Assn. Exec. Females, Am. Planning Assn. asst. dir. adminstrn. and fin., mem.-at-large Orange County sect. 1980—), Assn. Environ. Profls., Phi Beta Kappa. Democrat. Contbr. articles to profl. jours. Office: 8200 Westminster Blvd Westminster CA 92683

PEASE, OTIS ARNOLD, history educator; b. Pittsfield, Mass., July 31, 1925; s. Frederic Arnold and Ruth Otis (Ensign) P.; B.A., Yale U., 1949, Ph.D., 1954; m. Mary Gazzam Haight, Aug. 4, 1949; children—Jonathan, Catherine, Martha, Emily. Instr., U. Tex., Austin, 1953-55; mem. faculty dept. history Stanford U., 1956-66, Coe prof. history and Am. studies, 1964-66; prof. history U. Wash., Seattle, 1966—, chmn. dept. history, 1967-72; mem. Fulbright screening com. for history, Com. on Internat. Exchange of Scholars, 1974-76; public mem. Nat. Adv. Rev. Bd., 1970-74. Trustee, Stanford U., 1969—. Served with U.S. Army, 1943-45, USAAF, 1945-46. Decorated Purple Heart; Social Sci. Research Council fellow, 1962-63; Phi Beta Kappa vis. scholar, 1968-69. Mem. Am. Hist. Assn. (v.p. for the profession 1978-80), Orgn. Am. Historians, Am. Studies Assn., AAUP, Phi Beta Kappa. Democrat. Club: Scroll and Key. Author: Parkman's History, 1953; The Responsibilities of American Advertising, 1958; editor, author: The Progressive Years, 1962, Frederic C. Howe's The City, 1969. Office: Dept History U Wash Seattle WA 98195*

PEAVEY, JOHN, state senator, rancher; children—David, Karen, Tom. B.S.C.E., Northwestern U. Owner, operator range sheep and cattle ranch; mem. Idaho State Senate. Served as officer USMC. Democrat. Office: Idaho State Senate Boise ID 83720*

PEAVY, GEORGE MERRILL, veterinarian; b. Bakersfield, Calif., Dec. 19, 1949; s. Merrill Alfred and Nancy Morgan (Hening) P.; B.S., U. Calif., Davis, 1972, D.V.M., 1974. Staff veterinarian Rialto (Calif.) Animal Hosp., 1974-75, Macy & Thomas Vet. Hosp., Whittier, Calif., 1975-80, San Clemente (Calif.) Vet. Hosp., 1980—. Mem. health adv. com. U.S. Senator S. I. Hayakawa, 1977-82. Mem. AVMA, Am. Assn. Zoo Veterinarians, Am. Animal Hosp. Assn., Calif. Vet. Med. Assn., So. Calif. Vet. Med. Assn., Sigma Xi, Theta Xi. Mem. Evang. Christian Ch. Contbr. articles to profl. jours. Office: San Clemente Veterinary Hospital 1833 S El Camino Real San Clemente CA 92672

PEAY, JULIA ARMSTRONG, employment agy. exec.; b. Chgo., July 24, 1952; d. Oliver Wendell and Betty Jane (Nichols) A.; B.S. in Bus. Adminstrn., William Woods Coll., 1973; m. Gregory V. Peay, June 18, 1977; children: Juddson, Sarah. With Careers, Ltd., Denver, 1974—, v.p., 1978—. Mem. consumer complaint arbitration com. Better Bus. Bur. Denver. Mem. Denver C. of C., Alpha Phi. Republican. Presbyterian. Home: 62 Paradise Rd Golden CO 80401 Office: 1390 Logan St Suite Denver CO 80203

PECCORINI, FRANCISCO LETONA, educator; b. San Miguel, El Salvador, C.Am., Nov. 27, 1915; s. Miguel Vinerta and Julia (Letona) P.; student Colegio de Loyola, Tournai, Belgium, 1935-38, Guipuzcoa, Spain, 1938-39; Ph. Licentiate, Colegio de San Francisco Javier, Burgos, Spain, 1939-43; Ph.D., Pontifical U. Comillas, Santander, Spain, 1958; m. Teresa Samayoa; 1 stepdau., Teresa Moran Enneman. Tchr., San Jose High Sch., San Salvador, El Salvador, 1943-47; writer Estudios Centro Americanos, 1947-52, editor mag., San Salvador, 1952-55; prof. philosophy U. Deusto, Bilbao, Spain, 1956-58; prof. philosophy Nat. U., San Salvador, 1959-62; asst. prof. philosophy U. San Diego, 1963-66; asst. prof. philosophy Calif. State U., Long Beach, 1966-67, assoc. prof., 1967-72, prof., 1972—. Mem. Nat. Academia de Historia, San Salvador, Medieval Assn. Pacific, Medieval Acad. Am., Am. Philos. Assn. Author: A Method of Self-Orientation To Thinking, 1969; La Voluntad del Pueblo en la Emancipacion de El Salvador, 1972; From Gentile's "Actualism" to Sciacca's "Idea", 1981; On to the World of Freedom, 1982; contbr. articles to various publs. including Rivista Rosminiana di Filosofia e di Cultura, 1976, Giornale di Metafisica, 1976, Filosofia Oggi, 1978-82, Ultimate Reality and Meaning, 1982. Home: 10050 Los Caballos Ct Fountain Valley CA 92708 Office: Calif State U Long Beach CA 90840

PECHE, DALE CLIFFORD, painter; b. Long Beach, Calif., Nov. 28, 1928; s. George F. and Grace M. (Bond) Peachy; student Long Beach City Coll., 1944-45; B. Profl. Art, Art Center Coll. of Design, 1951; m. Marilyn Jean Wise, Aug. 30, 1968. Art dir., designer North Am. Aviation, Downey, Calif., 1956-60; art dir., propr. Graphic Directions, Fullerton, Calif., 1960-68; art dir. Publ. Service Ltd., Irvine, Calif., 1968-71, Design Vista Inc., Irvine, 1971-72. One-man shows: Challis Galleries, Laguna Beach, Calif., 1972-80, Conacher Galleries, San Francisco, 1981, 82; exhibited in group shows: Nat. Watercolor Soc., Los Angeles, 1972, 74, 75, West Coast Am. Realists, Fullerton, 1972, Inland Exhbn., San Bernardino, Calif., 1972, 77, 80, Chaffey Mus., Alta Loma, Calif., 1973, La Mirada (Calif.) Fiesta De Arts, 1973, NAD, N.Y.C., 1974, 78, Royal Acad. Arts, London, 1974, 75, 80, Palos Verdes (Calif.) Art Mus., 1974, Traditional Artists 8th Ann., San Bernardino, 1974, 77, 80, Butler Inst. Am. Art, Youngstown, Ohio, 1974, 75, Allied Artists Am., N.Y.C., 1974, 75, 77, 80, Springfield (Mass.) Art League, 1975, Grand Galleria, Seattle, 1975, Cooperstown (N.Y.) 40th Ann. Nat. Art Exhbn., 1975, Royal Hibernian Acad., Dublin, 1980; represented in permanent collections: Vatican, Rome, Glendale Fed. Bank (Calif.), also pvt. collections U.S. and abroad. Served with AUS, 1945-48. Recipient numerous awards including Indsl. Graphics Internat. award, Los Angeles, 1958-71, award N.Y. Art Dirs. Show, 1962, award Los Angeles Art Dirs., 1963-70. Mem. Nat. Watercolor Soc., Allied Artists Am., Royal Soc. Arts (London).

PECK, RAYMOND CHARLES, SR., driver and traffic safety specialist; b. Sacramento, Nov. 18, 1937; s. Emory Earl and Margaret Helen (Fiebiger) P.; m. Ella Ruth Enriquez, Sept. 5, 1957; children—Teresa M. Peck Montijo, Linda M. Peck Heisler, Margaret H. Peck Ryzak, Raymond C., Christina M. B.A. in Exptl. Psychology, Calif. State U.-Sacramento, 1961, M.A. in Exptl. Psychology, 1968. Jr. research tech. Calif. Dept. Motor Vehicles, Sacramento, 1962-63, asst. social research analyst, 1963-64, staff research analyst, 1967-71, sr. research analyst, program mgr., 1971-80, research program specialist II, 1980, acting, chief research, 1980-81, research program specialist II, 1981—; cons. to Computing and Software, Inc., Mentoris Co., Sims & Assocs., Pub. Systems, Inc., Planning Research Corp., Nat. Pub. Services Research Inst., Dunlap & Assocs., Sacramento Safety Council, Nat. Safety Council. Chmn. com. on operator regulation Transportation Research Bd., Nat. Acad. Scis., 1976-82. Recipient Met. Life award of Hon., Nat. Safety Council, 1970, Met. Life Cert. of Commendation, 1972; A.R. Lauer award Human Factor Soc., 1981; award of Hon., award of Merit Traffic Safety Evaluation Research Rev., 1983. Mem. Am. Statis. Assn., Western Psychol. Assn. Democrat. Contbr. articles to profl. jours.; editorial adv. bds. profl. jours. Home: 2667 Coleman Way Sacramento CA 95818 Office: Calif Dept Motor Vehicles 2415 First Ave Sacramento CA 95818

PECK, ROBERT SHANNON, II, real estate investment and appraising co. exec.; b. Balt., July 10, 1946; s. Clemmer Marcus and Ruth Davies P.; B.S., Menlo Sch. Bus. Adminstrn., 1972; m. Julia Ann Spaich, Dec. 14, 1974; children—Robert Shannon, Heather Jeanine, Britton Cecelia.

Foreman, Spaich Bros. Ranch; expeditor Simi Winery; in mgmt. Tandy Corp.; cons. Asso. Mgmt. Systems, Palo Alto, Calif.; pres. The White Co., Saratoga, Calif., 1979—; dir. Blackhawk Devel. Co. Served with U.S. Army, 1967-70. Mem. Calif. Real Estate Assn., Nat. Assn. Realtors, San Jose Real Estate Bd., Saratoga-Los Gatos Real Estate Bd., Santa Cruz Real Estate Bd., Santa Clara County Appraisers Assn. Republican. Office: 14583 Big Basin Way Saratoga CA 95070

PECKHAM, DONALD, computer co. exec.; b. Aberdeen, S.D., Feb. 8, 1932; s. Donald Seth and Crystal (Maytum) P.; B.S. in Elec. Engring., U. Wash., 1957; M.S. in Elec. Engring., Calif. Inst. Tech., 1958; children—Dean, Deanna Jean; m. 2d, Jeanette G. Mackenzie, June 20, 1967. Engr., Hughes Aircraft Co., Culver City, Calif., 1957-60; sr. engr. Nortronics div. Northrop Corp., Hawthorne, Calif., 1960-61; v.p. Digitek Corp., Inglewood, Calif., 1961-63, v.p., gen. mgr., Los Angeles, 1963-65; research scientist Nortronics div. Northrop Corp., Hawthorne, 1965-67; staff Decade Computer Corp., Huntington Beach, 1967-71; mgr. software Pertec Computer Corp., Santa Ana, Calif., 1971-81; mgr. software tools CXC Corp., Irvine, Calif., 1981—; instr. U. So. Calif., 1960-61. Served with USNR, 1950-54. Mem. IEEE, Assn. Computing Machinery, Tau Beta Pi. Home: 21748 Tahoe Ln El Toro CA 92630 Office: 1701 Reynolds Ave Irvine CA 92714

PECKHAM, ROBERT FRANCIS, JR., U.S. dist. judge; b. San Francisco, Nov. 3, 1920; s. Robert Francis and Evelyn (Crowe) P.; A.B., Stanford, 1941, LL.B., 1945; student Yale Law Sch., 1941-42; LL.D., U. Santa Clara; m. Harriet M. Behring, Aug. 15, 1953 (dec.); children—Ann Evelyn, Sara Esther; m. 2d, Carol Potter, June 9, 1974. Adminstrv. asst. to regional enforcement atty. OPA, 1942-43; practiced in Palo Alto and Sunnyvale, Calif., 1946-48; asst. U.S. atty., 1948-52; chief asst. U.S. atty. criminal div., 1952-53; mem. law firm, San Francisco, Palo Alto and Sunnyvale, 1953-59; judge Superior Ct., Santa Clara County, Calif., 1959-66, presiding judge, 1961-63, 66; judge U.S. Dist. Ct., 1966-76, chief judge, 1976—. Bd. visitors Stanford Law Sch., 1969-75, chmn. 1971-72; chmn. adv. com. Calif. Friends Outside, 1971—; chmn. council Stanford Law Socs., 1974-75; trustee Calif. Hist. Soc., 1974-78; mem. council Friends of the Bancroft Library, 1981—. Recipient Brotherhood award NCCJ, 1968. Fellow Am. Bar Found.; mem. Soc. Calif. Pioneers (bd. dirs. 1977—), Am. Law Inst., Jud. Conf. of U.S. (budget com.), Nat. Conf. Fed. Trial Judges (chmn.), World Affairs Council (trustee 1982—), Phi Beta Kappa. Home: 101 Alma St Palo Alto CA 94301 Office: 450 Golden Gate Ave San Francisco CA 94102

PEDERSEN, JOHN DAVID, dentist, dental group administrator; b. Lawrence, Kans., Aug. 1, 1946; s. Peter and Carol Anita (Fowler) P.; m. Mary Lee Mullen, Apr. 18, 1970; children—David Erik, Kimberlee Lund; m. 2d, Shirlee Ann Lund, Oct. 14, 1979. A.A., Glendale Coll., 1968; D.D.S., U. So. Calif., 1973. Instr. fixed prosthodontics Sch. Dentistry U. So. Calif., 1973-74; pvt. practice dentistry, Newport Beach, Calif., 1974-80, owner San Bernardino Dental Group, San Bernardino, Calif., 1980—, Riverside Family Dental Group; owner So. Calif. Ceramics, Inc., Riverside; lectr. in field of gnathology. Mem. ADA, Tri-County Dental Soc., San Bernardino C. of C. Republican. Lutheran. Contbr. article to profl. jour.

PEDERSEN, JOHN EDWOOD, psychologist; b. Urbana, Ill., July 3, 1945; s. Edwood John and Gwendolyn Jane (Rowe) P.; B.S. cum laude, Milligan Coll., 1972; M.S., Rosemead Grad. Sch. Psychology, 1974, Ph.D., 1977; m. Joy Marie Good, Apr. 16, 1966; children—Melody Ruth, Mindy Michelle. Therapist, Christian therapy unit Pomona (Calif.) Psychiat. Hosp., 1976-78; psychologist Christian Psychol. Services, Riverside, Calif., 1978—; psychol. cons. Victoria Community Ch., 1979-81. Mem. Am. Psychol. Assn., Calif. Psychol. Assn., Christian Assn. Psychol. Studies. Office: 5790 Magnolia Ave Riverside CA 92506

PEDERSEN, JOHN MARTIN, educational adminstrator; b. Racine, Wis., Sept. 29, 1932; s. Ralph Ceasar and Goldie Florence (Johnson) P.; m. Jacqueline Marie Williams, Dec. 27, 1952; children—Scott, Chris, Debra Albahrani, Susan. B.A. with distinction, U. N.Mex., 1976, M.A., 1979. Cert. tchr., guidance counselor, Ariz. Evaluator, Whiteriver Unified Sch. Dist., 1979-80, Title I coordinator, 1980-81, dir. Chpt. I, 1981—; cons. computer assisted instrn. Served to maj. USAF, 1952-72. Mem. Assn. Supervision and Curriculum Devel., Phi Kappa Phi. Republican. Presbyterian (elder). Home: 220 Solano Dr SE Albuquerque NM 87108 Office: PO Box 190 Whiteriver AZ 85941

PEDERSEN, LEO DAMBORG, engr.; b. Soroe, Denmark, June 11, 1942; s. Erik Johannes and Lilly (Joergensen) P.; M.E., Tech. U. Denmark, 1968; M.B.A., Copenhagen Sch. Econs., 1972; D. Engring., U. Calif., Davis, 1978; m. Elsbeth Wildfang, Aug. 1, 1964; children—Anne, Ulrik, Malene. Project officer Danish Bd. Maritime Works, Copenhagen, 1970-72; project leader Biotech. Inst., Kolding, Denmark, 1972-75; research engr. Western Regional Research Lab., U.S. Dept. Agr., Albany, 1975-76; research asso. U. Calif., Davis, 1976-78; dir. engring. Nat. Food Processors Assn., Berkeley, Calif., 1978—. Served with Danish Navy, 1968-70. Mem. Danish Engring. Assn., Internat. Food Technologists, Assn. Energy Engrs., Am. Soc. Agrl. Engrs. Home: 3477 Savage Ave Pinole CA 94564 Office: 1950 6th St Berkeley CA 94710

PEDERSEN, LORAYNE DIELTZ, interior designer, consultant; b. Jasper, Minn., Dec. 29, 1923; d. John Edward and Emma (Buysse) Dieltz; m. Harry Arthur Pedersen, June 15, 1945; children—Wayne, Vicki Pedersen Lowell, Gregory, Terry (dec.). Grad. Cabel's Bus. Coll., 1943, F.R.A. Interior Design Sch., 1970. Cert. tchr., Calif., 1974. Freelance interior designer, 1975-80; instr. interior design Claremont High Sch. (Calif.), San Clemente High Sch. (Calif.), 1974-79; designer Furniture Gallery, San Clemente, 1979—; adv. bd. interior design program. Saddleback Coll. Mem. Am. Soc. Interior Designers (assoc.), Democrat. Roman Catholic. Club: Soroptimist (pres. Glendora, Calif. 1973). Contbr. articles to publs. Home: 405 Ave Granada Apt 201 San Clemente CA 92672 Office: 213 Ave Del Mar San Clemente CA 92672

PEDERSEN, THELMA JEAN JORGENSON, mathematics educator; m. Kent A. Pedersen. B.S., Brigham Young U., 1955. M.S. in Math., U. Utah, 1958. Cert. secondary tchr., Utah. Tchr. math., public jr. and sr. high schs., Utah, 1958-59; instr. math. U. Utah, 1959-65; asst. prof. U. Santa Clara, 1965-72, lectr., 1972—; lectr. NSF Vis. Scientist Program, 1963-65, and active various other NSF programs, 1959-79; dir. Bay Area Women and Math. Lectureship Program, 1975-80. Mem. Am. Math. Soc., Math. Assn. Am. (lectr. women and math. lectureship program mem. panel vis. lectrs., gov. No. Calif. sect. 1981—), Calif. Math. Council, Nat. Council Tchrs. Math, Santa Clara Valley Math. Assn. (pres. 1976-77). Author: (with E. Allan Davis) Essentials of Trigonometry, 1969, 2d edit., 1973, 74; (with Kent A. Pedersen) Geometric Playthings, 1973; (with Allan Davis) Essentials of Trigonometry, 1975; (with Franz O. Armbruster) A New Twist (To Arithmetic Drill Through Problem Solving), 1979; (with Peter J. Hilton) Fear No More, An Adult Approach to Mathematics, 1983; contbr. numerous articles to profl. publs.; assoc. editor Math. Mag. Home: PO Box 26 New Almaden CA 95042

PEDERSON, PETER ORLO, fire chief; b. Los Angeles, July 2, 1934; s. Orlo G. and Idia (Wilson) P.; m. Betty Lou Pederson, Nov. 27, 1954; children—David, Chris. B.A., Calif. State U.-Long Beach, 1957; M.S., Pepperdine U., 1978. Bn. chief Los Angeles County Fire Dept., 1973-80, asst. fire chief, 1980-81; fire chief Salt Lake City Fire Dept., 1981—. Served with USN, 1952-54. Mem. Nat. Fire Protection Assn., Internat. Assn. Fire Chiefs, Western Fire Chiefs Assn., Metro Fire Chiefs Assn. Lodge: Rotary. Office: 159 E 1st S Salt Lake City UT 84111

PEERY, J. CRAIG, developmental psychologist; b. Salt Lake City, Apr. 21, 1945; s. Joseph Smith and Phyllis (Evans) P.; m. Irene Weiss, June 21, 1969; children—Joseph, Christie, Samuel. B.A., Columbia U., 1970, M.A., 1973, Ph.D., 1973. Research scientist N.Y. Psychiat. Inst. and Research Found. for Mental Hygiene, N.Y.C., 1970-73; asst. prof. family and human devel. Utah State U., Logan, 1973-80, assoc. prof., 1980; assoc. prof. family scis. Brigham Young U., Provo, Utah, 1980—; spl. asst. to chmn. U.S. Senate Labor and Human Resources Com., Washington, 1980-82; staff assoc. U.S. Senate Subcom. for Family and Human Services; dir. Cottage Program Internat.; mem. several nat. adv. panels on children, adolescents, families. Com. mem. Utah Symphony. Mem. AAAS, Soc. Research in Child Devel., Am. Psychol. Assn., Nat. Council on Family Relations, Southwestern Soc. for Research in Child Devel., Sigma Xi. Mem. Ch. Jesus Christ of Latter Day Saints. Cons. editor and contbr. articles to profl. jours; contbr. chpts. to books. Office: Brigham Young U 1000 SWKT Provo UT 84602

PEKEROL, KAYA KIRK, fire chief; b. Pasadena, Calif., Oct. 21, 1944; s. S. Mehmet and Mary Maxine (Gray) P.; m. Mary Ann Greenwold, Aug. 26, 1972; 1 son, Courtney Adam. A.A., Pasadena City Coll., 1975; B.S. in Pub. Mgmt. cum laude, Pepperdine U., 1977. Fireman Pasadena Fire Dept., 1968-74, fire insp., 1974-75, fire capt., 1975-80, adminstrv. chief, 1980-81, fire chief, 1981—. Bd. dirs. Pasadena unit ARC. Served with USNR. Mem. Calif. Assn. Fire Chiefs, Internat. Assn. Fire Chiefs. Lodge: Rotary. Office: 175 N Marengo Ave Pasadena CA 91101

PELC, ROBERT EDWARD, psychologist, bus. cons.; b. Flint, Mich., July 14, 1946; s. Jim and Mary (Maxa) P.; B.S. cum laude, Central Mich. U., 1968; M.A. (NIMH fellow), U. Denver, 1973, Ph.D., 1975; m. Sharon Lynn Walsh, Sept. 12, 1980; stepchildren—Sean, Culum, Liam. Project dir. Forensic Services Center, Denver, 1975-77; program mgr. Denver Drug Abuse Treatment Program, 1977-79; cons. and psychol. services, Denver, 1979—; adj. faculty Antioch U., 1979—; cons. Denver Dist. and Juvenile Cts.; columnist Denver Bus. World. Bd. dirs. Wilderness Experience Program, Denver, 1974-77; mem. Colo. State Bd. Psychologists Examiners, 1978-81. Served with U.S. Army, 1968-70. Lic. psychologist, Colo. Mem. Am. Psychol. Assn., Am. Soc. Profl. Cons. Contbr. articles to profl. jours. Home: 475 Kearney Denver CO 80220 Office: 1900 Wazee Denver CO 80202

PELL, ROGER MARTIN, computer service exec.; b. Camp White, Oreg., Oct. 3, 1943; s. Roger Martin and Constance Margaret (Santanello) P.; B.S., Fairleigh Dickinson U., 1965; m. Rose-Marie L. Jonasson, Feb. 19, 1976; 1 dau., Kristina Ann. Pres., Century Am. Corp., Los Angeles, 1972-74; dir. mktg. Pacific Fidelity Life, 1974-77; chmn. Romarc, Los Angeles, 1977—; co-founder, pres., chmn. bd. Ins. Agys. Systems Corp., 1981—, Romarc Rating Systems, Romarc Fin. Systems, 1982—. Mem. Republican Presdl. Task Force. Mem. Internat. Assn. Fin. Planners, Smithsonian Assos., Nat. Audubon Soc., Am. Mgmt. Assn. Author: Navigating the Computer Services Maze, 1979; Field Support System Manual, 1980; Financial Counseling Workshop, 1982. Office: 6747 Odessa Ave Van Nuys CA 91406

PELLETIER, JOSEPH ANTHONY, energy company executive; b. Chgo., Dec. 18, 1922; s. Joseph A. and Margaret A. (Liston) P.; m. Martha I. von Schrader, May 26, 1944; children—Joseph A., Norman Monica, Martha, Karen. Student Ambrose (Iowa) Coll., 1942-43; B.S. in Mech. Engring., Iowa State U., 1949. Vice pres. engring. constrn. and research No. Ind. Pub. Service Co., Hammond, Ind., 1949-72; exec. v.p. Gasco, Inc. subs. Pacific Resources Inc., Honolulu, 1972-78, pres., 1978—; v.p. Pacific Resources, Inc., 1973-74, sr. v.p., 1974, exec. v.p., 1974-79, pres., 1979—; mem. Hawaii/Pacific Dist. Export Council. Mem. exec. bd. Aloha council Boy Scouts Am.; mem. exec. bd. Hawaii chpt. ARC, chmn., 1983-84; trustee Hawaii Army Mus. Soc.; chmn. Hawaii Joint Council on Econ. Edn., 1981-83; bd. dirs. Hawaii Pacific Coll.; mem. adv. bd. Newman Ctr.; mem. transp. com. Oahu Devel. Conf. Served to 1st lt., inf., AUS, 1943-46, ETO, 1951, Korea. Recipient Silver Beaver award Boy Scouts Am., 1978. Mem. C. of C. of Hawaii (dir., mem. armed services com.), Am. Gas Assn., ASME, IEEE, Assn. U.S. Army, Navy League U.S., Pacific Coast Gas Assn. (chmn. 1983-84). Roman Catholic. Clubs: Oahu Country, Outrigger Canoe, Pacific, Plaza (Honolulu). Lodge: Rotary. Office: PO Box 3379 Honolulu HI 96842

PELTYN, ROGER MICHAEL, structural engineer; b. Bklyn., Jan. 14, 1942; s. Sidney and Elizabeth (Yendricks) P.; B.S.C.E., Pa. State U., 1963; m. Zenaida Colon, Nov. 29, 1970; children—Michael Roger, Roger Sidney. Project mgr. Fraioli-Blum-Yesselman P.C., N.Y.C., 1963-69, chief structural engr., 1970-73; assoc. Alvin Fromme & Assos., N.Y.C., 1974-76; assoc. ptnr. John A. Martin & Assocs., Los Angeles, 1976-80; ptnr. Martin & Assocs., Las Vegas, 1980—. Chmn., So. Calif. Constrn. Industry Ann. Charity Luncheon Benefiting Muscular Dystrophy Assn., 1979—. Mem. Structural Engrs. Assn. So. Calif. (chmn. public relations), Zeta Beta Tau. Projects include: Golden Nugget Hotel and Casino, Atlantic City, 1980, Wilshire House Condominiums, Beverly Hills, Calif., 1980. Contbr. article to profl. jour. Home: 2801 W Mason Ave Las Vegas NV 89102 Office: 1001 Rancho Dr S Las Vegas NV 89106

PELZ, WILLIAM EMMANUEL, advertising/storage company executive; b. Fort Wayne, Ind., Oct. 6, 1939; s. Truman and Agnes Louise (Miller) P.; B.A. in Polit. Sci., Colo. Coll., 1964; M.S., St. Francis Coll., 1969; m. Lynnette Ellen Ayers, Sept. 12, 1964; children—Marni Ellen, Anthony Ayers. Purchasing agt. Central Soya Co., Fort Wayne,Ind., 1966-68; tchr. Jefferson Jr. High Sch., Fort Wayne, 1969-70, Cheyenne Mountain Schs., Colorado Springs, Colo., 1971-74; advt.-creative dir., pres. Pelz & Miller Advt., Colorado Springs; pres., founder Phonafile of Colo., Inc., Colorado Springs.; mem. art dept. bd. dirs. Pikes Peak Community Coll., 1976-80. Basketball coach Pikes Peak Community Coll., 1974-75; bd. dirs. Boys Club, Colorado Springs, 1976-77; mem. athletic bd. Colo. Coll., 1976-77, nat. alumnae council. Served as capt. U.S. Army, 1964-66. Recipient awards Pikes Peak Advt. Fedn., Am. Advt. Fedn. Mem. Pikes Peak Advt. Fedn. Republican. Mem. Christian Ch. Home: 3915 Wakefield Dr Colorado Springs CO 80906 Office: 1555 S Nevada Colorado Springs CO 80906

PENA, FEDERICO, city official; b. Laredo, Tex., Mar. 15, 1947; s. Gustave J. and Lucilla Pena. Grad. St. Joseph's Acad. and U. Tex.-Austin. Bars: Tex., Colo. Ptnr. Pena and Pena, Denver; elected to Colo. Ho. Reps., 1978, judiciary, fin., legal services, rules coms., legis. council, Ho. Democratic leader, 1981; mayor Denver, 1983—; mem. Colo. Bd. Law Examiners; former assoc. Harvard Ctr. Law and Edn. Mem. Sloan's Lake Citizen Assn., Front Range Project Coordinating Council, Jefferson, Highlands and Sunnyside Neighborhood Assn., Rocky Flats Blue Ribbon Citizens Com.; bd. mem. Am. Lung Assn., KCFR pub. radio. Named among top 10 legislators by Denver Post, Outstanding Ho. Dem. Legislator; recipient Am. Jewish Com. Award of Appreciation, Colo. Coalition for Persons with Disabilities Grateful Appreciation award. Mem. Denver Bar Assn., Colo. Bar Assn. Office: Office of the Mayor City and County Bldg Denver CO 80202

PENA, MANUEL, JR., state senator; b. Cashion, Ariz., Nov. 17, 1924; s. Manuel and Elvira (Gomez) P.; student public schs.; m. Aurora Cruz, June 13, 1945; children—Yolanda, Mary, Henry, Steve, Patricia, Geraldine, Manuel III. Owner Pena Realty & Ins. Agy., Phoenix, 1951—; mem. Ariz. Ho. of Reps., Phoenix, 1967-72, Ariz. Senate, Phoenix, 1973—. Exec. sec. Ariz. Athletic Commn., 1964-66; commr. human relations City of Phoenix, 1967-71. Served with U.S. Army, 1945-46. Mem. Am. Legion (comdr.). Democrat. Roman Catholic. Office: 1001 N Central St Suite 505 Phoenix AZ 85004

PENDERGHAST, THOMAS FREDERICK, educator; b. Cin., Apr. 23, 1936; s. Elmer T. and Delores C. (Huber) P.; B.S., Marquette U., 1958; M.B.A., Calif. State U., Long Beach, 1967; postgrad. Nova U., 1982—; m. Marjorie Craig, Aug. 12, 1983; children—Brian, Shawna, Steven, Dean, Maria. Sci. programmer Autonetics, Inc., Anaheim, Calif., 1960-64; bus. programmer Douglas Missile & Space Center, Huntington Beach, Calif., 1964-66; computer specialist N.Am. Rockwell Co., 1966-69; asst. prof. Calif. State U., Long Beach, 1969-72; asso. prof. Sch. Bus. and Mgmt., Pepperdine U., Los Angeles, 1972—; spl. adviser Commn. on Engring. Edn., 1968; v.p. Visual Computing Co., 1969-71; founder, pres. Scoreboard Animation Systems, 1971-77; exec. v.p. Microfilm Identification Systems, 1977-79; pres. Data Processing Auditors, Inc., 1981—; data processing cons. designing computer system for fin. health and mfg. orgns., 1972—. Mem. Orange County Blue Ribbon Com. on Data Processing, 1973; mem. Orange County TEC Policy Bd., 1982—. Served to lt. USNR, 1958-60. Cert. in data processing. Mem. Users of Automatic Info. Display Equipment (pres. 1966). Home: 17261 Gothard St Unit 16 Huntington Beach CA 92647

PENDLETON, JAMES ABERCROMBIE, engring. geologist; b. Reading, Pa., Nov. 6, 1946; s. Joseph Saxton and Mary Driscoll (Vernon) P.; A.B. magna cum laude, Princeton U., 1969; M.S. (NDEA fellow), U. Colo., 1973, Ph.D., 1978; m. Nancy Marie Haffey, Aug. 2, 1969. Geol. aide Gilbert-Commonwealth, Inc., Reading, summer 1967, geologist, summer 1969; engring. geologist City of Boulder (Colo.), 1970-78, city engr., 1978-79; supervising geologist Colo. Div. Mined Land Reclamation, Denver, 1980—; cons. geology, 1970-79; dir. Bristlecone Investments, Inc. Recipient John Wesley Powell award U.S. Geol. Survey, 1979. Mem. Geol. Soc. Am., Assn. Engring. Geologists, Am. Inst. Profl. Geologists, Nat. Water Well Assn., Colo. Engring. Council (sec.), Sigma Xi. Home: Seven Hills Dr Sunshine Canyon Boulder CO 80302 Office: 1313 Sherman St Room 423 Denver CO 80203

PENDOLA, LUCILLE JOAN, ednl. adminstr.; b. Boston, Sept. 14, 1947; d. Joseph John and Lucille Amelia (Griffin) P. A.B., Manhattanville Coll., 1969; student Andover-Newton Theol. Inst., Newton Coll. Sacred Heart, Fordham U., 1971, Oakland U., 1973; M.S., U. Notre Dame, 1977; student Inst. Christian Initiation of Adults, Holy Names Coll., Oakland, 1980, Jesuit Sch. Theology, Berkley, 1981. Tchr., Convent of Sacred Heart, Greenwich, Conn., 1969-70; acting head middle sch. Newton (Mass.) Country Day Sch., 1970-71; asst. head middle sch. Acad. Sacred Heart, Bloomfield Hills, Mich., 1971-74, head middle sch., 1974-78; directress Kenwood Summer Day Camp, Albany, N.Y., summer 1973; instr. religious edn. U. Detroit, 1977-78; mem. religious edn. curriculum revision com. Archdiocese of Detroit, 1978-80; dir. religious edn. Our Lady of the Lakes Parish, Waterford, Mich., 1978-80, also trustee Our Lady of the Lakes Scholarship and Ednl. Excellence Found.; dir. religious edn. St. Paschal's Parish, Oakland, Calif., 1980-83, prin. St. Paschal's Sch., 1981—; master catechist Diocese of Calif. Mem. Assn. for Supervision and Curriculum Devel., Nat. Cath. Edn. Assn. Democrat. Roman Catholic. Office: 3710 Dorisa Ave Oakland CA 94605

PENG, JOSEPH DA-CHENG, semicondr. co. exec.; b. Shan-Shie, China, Nov. 5, 1943; came to U.S., 1968, naturalized, 1977; s. King-i and Shao P.; Ph.D., Tulane U., 1975; m. Mary Sha, June 17, 1972; 1 son, Peter D. Physicist, SRI, Menlo Park, Calif., 1974-76; sr. physicist ARACOR, Sunnyvale, Calif., 197680; mgr. research and devel. materials div. Fairchild Camera & Instrument Corp., Healdsburg, Calif., 1980—. Mem. IEEE, Electrochem. Soc., Materials Research Soc., Chinese Engring. Assn., Sigma Pi Sigma. Contbr. articles to profl. jours. Home: 1106 Doyle Pl Mountain View CA 94040 Office: Fairchild Camera and Instrument Corp 33 Healdsburg Ave Healdsburg CA 95448

PENHARLOW, GORDON LYLE, elec. engr.; b. Lackawanna, N.Y., June 17, 1941; s. Walter and Helen Ethel (Ross) P.; student East Los Angeles Coll., 1959-60, Calif. State Poly. U., 1960-63, Calif. State U., Long Beach, 1963-64; B.S. in Elec. Engring., Kensington U., 1978, M.S. in Elec. Engring., 1978; m. Barbara J. Johnston, Oct. 2, 1962; children—Kathy, Kristy, Kim. Engring. supr. N.Am. Aviation, Downey, Calif., 1960-63; mgr. configuration mgmt. Litton Systems, Van Nuys, Calif., 1963-64; DCIR div. mgr. Xerox Corp., Pasadena, Calif., 1964-68; pres. Pacific Multitech, Inc., Arcadia, Calif., 1968—; cons. Dept. Def., maj. U.S. corps.; condr. courses in configuration mgmt. USAF, NASA, U.S. Navy, U.S. Army; guest lectr. Calif. State U., Northridge; speaker Systems Mgmt. Conf., 1970; vice chmn. 26th Internat. Tech. Communications Conf., Los Angeles, 1978. Active, Arcadia Bus. Assn.; bd. dirs. Arcadia Tournament of Roses Assn.; vice chmn. Arcadia Olympic Commn. for XXIII Olympiad. Registered profl. engr., Calif. Fellow Inst. Advancement Engring.; mem. Soc. Tech. Communication (chmn. Los Angeles), Soc. Logistics Engrs., Arcadia C. of C. Republican. Chmn. editorial bd., contbr. to Technograph, 1979-80; contbr. articles to profl. jours. Office: 6 N 1st Ave Arcadia CA 91006

PENN, JANICE, nurse, educator; b. Bronx, N.Y., May 2, 1941; d. Leonard and Eva Willis (Chandler) Penn; B.S., SUNY Downstate Med. Center, 1973; M.A., NYU, 1975; Ph.D., Tex. Women's U., Denton, 1982; 1 son, Jose Gonzalez. Nurse, Albert Einstein Coll. Hosp., Bronx, 1973, Bronx Montefiore Morrisania Hosp., 1973-74, Bronx VA Hosp., 1974; mem. faculty U. Albuquerque, 1975-76; supr. Bernalillo County Med. Ctr., Albuquerque, 1975-76; mem. faculty, mem. advanced psychiat. council U. N.Mex., Albuquerque, 1976—. Mem. Am., N.Mex. nurses Assns., Sigma Theta Tau. Democrat. Home: 206 Las Marias Dr SE Rio Rancho NM 87124

PENNER, STANFORD SOLOMON, educator; b. Unna, Germany, July 5, 1921; s. Heinrich and Regina (Saal) P.; B.S., Union Coll., 1942; M.S., U. Wis., 1943, Ph.D., 1946; hon. doctorate, U. Aachen, 1981; m. Beverly Preston, Dec. 28, 1942; children—Merrilynn Jean, Robert Clark. Prof. jet propulsion Calif. Inst. Tech., 1950-63; chmn. dept. aerospace engring. and applied mechanics U. Calif., San Diego, 1964-69, prof. engring. physics, 1964—, vice chancellor acad. affairs, 1969-70, dir. Inst. for Phys. Scis., 1969-72, dir. Energy Center, 1973—; chmn. Dept. Energy Fossil Energy Research Working Group, 1978-82; chmn. U.S. Adv. Com. Internat. Inst. Applied Systems Analysis, Laxenburg, Austria, 1978-82. Recipient Numa Manson medal, 1979, Internat. Columbus prize, 1981; Guggenheim fellow, 1971-72. Fellow AIAA (Pendray award 1975, Thermophysics award 1983, Energy Systems award 1983), N.Y. Acad. Scis., Am. Acad. Arts and Scis., Am. Phys. Soc., Optical Soc. Am., AAAS; mem. Internat. Acad. Astronautics, Nat. Acad. Engring., Combustion Inst., Am. Chem. Soc., Sigma Xi. Author: Radiation and Reentry, 1968; Thermodynamics, 1968; (with L. Icerman) Energy, Volume I: Demands, Resources, Impact, Technology, and Policy, 2d edit., 1981; Energy, Volume II: Non-Nuclear Technologies, 2d edit., 1983; (wth others) Energy, Volume III: Nuclear Energy and Energy Policies, 1976; editor: Advances in Tactical Rocket Propulsion, 1968; Lithium: Needs and Resources, 1978, others; editor Jour. Quantitative Spectroscopy and Radiative Transfer, 1960—, Energy, The Internat. Jour., 1976—, others. Home: 5912 Ave Chamnez La Jolla CA 92037 Office: Energy Center B-010 U Calif San Diego La Jolla CA 92093

PENNING, DAVID COLEMAN, engineering executive, consultant; b. Birmingham, Ala., Apr. 16, 1931; s. Chester and Margaret (Coleman) P.; m. Patricia Batchelor, June 28, 1959; children—Jennifer Jean, Piper Jane. B.S. in Engring., Yale U., 1953; M.B.A., Harvard U., 1959; Cert. mfg. engr., U.S. Engring. mgr. Hewlett-Packard, Palo Alto, Calif., 1959-65; v.p. Center for Mgmt. Scis., Los Angeles, 1965-70; mgr. long-range planning Honeywell, Inc., Mpls., 1970-72; pres., dir. indsl. electronics dept. Stanford Research Inst., Menlo Park, Calif., 1972-78; with DCP Assos., Palo Alto, 1978—. Vice chmn. Young Republicans, San Mateo, Calif., 1964. Served U.S. Army, Signal Corps., 1953-55; Korea. Mem. Robotics Internat. (vice chmn. chpt.), IEEE, AIEE, Soc. Mfg. Engrs. Club: Elks. Contbr. articles to profl. jours. Home: 1970 Oakdell Dr Palo Alto CA 94025 Office: 750 Welch Rd Suite 225 Palo Alto CA 94304

PENNINGTON, JOHN DAVID, optometrist, educator; b. Puyallup, Wash., Sept. 17, 1924; s. David Franklin and Kathleen Marie (Rakestraw) P.; m. Gloria Penoyer, 1943 (div.); m. 2d, Gennie A. Gottberg, Nov. 25, 1949; children—David, James, Nancy, John. B.S., Pacific U., 1953, O.D., 1954, M.S., 1966. Lic. optometrist. Practice optometry, Enumclaw, Wash., 1954-59; Pueblo, Colo., 1959-65; teaching fellow Pacific U., Forest Grove, Oreg., 1965-66; faculty mem. Pa. Coll. Optometry, Phila., 1966-70; staff mem. Group Health Co-op. of Puget Sound, Seattle, 1970—; instr. Seattle Central Community Coll., 1972-75; council mem. Clin. Council Optometric Care; cons. Interstudy, Mpls.; speaker profl. meetings. Served with USN, 1943-46. Fellow Am. Acad. Optometry; mem. Wash. Optometric Assn., Am. Optometric Assn. (multidisciplinary practice sect., cons. interassn./interprofl. affairs adv. com.). Republican. Contbr. articles to profl. jours. Home: 205 NW 177th St Seattle WA 98177 Office: Group Health Co-op of Puget Sound 20200 W 54th St Lynnwood WA 98036

PENNINGTON, WELDON JERRY, newspaper exec.; b. Tacoma, Mar. 1, 1919; s. Bert Archie and Marguerite Lucille (Heraty) P.; B.A., U. Wash., 1941; m. Dorothy Grace Kinney, Oct. 6, 1945; children—Susan Diane Merry, Scott Brian, Sally Jane Ringman, Steven Kinney. Staff acct. Allen R. Smart & Co., C.P.A.s, Seattle, 1941-42; spl. agt. FBI, 1942-46; supervising acct. Touche Ross & Co., C.P.A.s, Seattle, 1946-51; with Seattle Times, 1951—, pres., dir., 1967-82, pres., pub., chief exec. officer, dir., 1982—; pres., dir. Walla Walla (Wash.) Union-Bull., 1971—, Times Communications Co., 1971—, Allied Daily Newspapers, 1982—, dir. Rainier Nat. Bank, Seattle, Rainier Bancorp., Paccar, Inc., Safeco Corp., Westin Hotels, Blethen Corp. Pres., Seattle-King County Community Chest, 1959-60, Seattle-King County United Good Neighbor Fund, 1962-63, Downtown Seattle Devel. Assn., 1971-72; pres. Virginia Mason Med. Found., 1980; mem. bd. Virginia Mason Hosp.; trustee Seattle Goodwill Industries; trustee, pres. Seattle Found.; pres. Corp. Council for Arts, 1980; treas. Fifth Avenue Theatre Assn., 1980, pres., 1982; chmn. adv. bd. U. Wash. Grad. Sch. Bus., 1980-81; chmn. Council Corp. Responsibility, 1982-83. Named Seattle's First Citizen of 1977 Seattle-King County Bd. Realtors. Mem. Am. Inst. C.P.A.s (Elijah Watts Sells award 1941), Wash. Soc. C.P.A.s (pres. 1951-52), Assn. Former Spl. Agts. FBI, Seattle C. of C. (pres. 1964-65), Sigma Delta Chi, Beta Alpha Psi. Clubs: Rotary (pres. Seattle 1966-67), Seattle Golf (trustee 1974-77), Rainier (pres. 1968-69), Useless Bay Golf and Country, Wash. Athletic, University; Desert Island Country (Palm Springs). Office: 1120 John St PO Box 70 Seattle WA 98111

PENWELL, JONES CLARK, real estate appraiser; b. Crisp, Tex., Dec. 19, 1921; s. Clark Moses and Sarah Lucille (Jones) P.; B.S., Colo. State U., 1949; m. A. Jerry Jones, July 1, 1967; children—Dale Maria, Alan Lee, John Steven, Laurel Anne, Tracy Lynn. Farm mgmt. supr. Farmers Home Adminstrn., Dept. Agr., 1949-58; rancher 1958-61; real estate appraiser/realty officer Dept. Interior, Tex., Calif., Ariz., Colo., Washington, 1961-78, chief appraiser Bur. Reclamation, Lakewood, Colo., 1978-80; ind. fee appraiser, cons., 1980—. Served with USN, 1940-46. Accredited rural appraiser; cert. review appraiser; recipient Outstanding Performance awards U.S. Bur. Reclamation, 1964, 75, 80. Mem. Am. Soc. Farm Mgrs. and Rural Appraisers, Internat. Right-of-Way Assn., Nat. Assn. Rev. Appraisers (regional v.p. 1978-79), Soc. Real Estate Appraisers (asso.), Jefferson County Bd. Realtors. Democrat. Presbyterian. Clubs: Elks, Rotary, Mt. Vernon Country. Author: Reviewing Condemnation Appraisal Reports, 1980; The Valuation of Easements, 1980. Home: 10100 W 21st Place Lakewood CO 80215 Office: Western Area Power Adminstrn 1536 A2511 Bldg 18 Cole Blvd Golden CO 80401

PEOPLES, MARVIS VAN, educational administrator; b. Monroe, La., Aug. 24, 1936; s. Morgan Moss and Lettice (Wright) P.; m. Mable Office, June 23, 1956; children—Reuben, Alton, Malcolm. B.S., Western Bapt. Bible Coll., 1969; M.A., Calif. State U.-Hayward, 1975, Ed.D., Nova U., 1982. Cert. elem. and secondary tchr., Calif., 1970, in supervision and adminstrn., Calif. Dir. youth work Mt. Zion Ch. Oakland, Calif., 1961-66, dir. Christian edn., 1965-70; tchr. Oakland Pub. Schs., 1970-73, resource tchr./counselor, 1973-75, asst. prin. 1975-79; summer sch. tchr./counselor Alameda County Spl. Schs., San Leandro, Calif., 1971-77; prin. Brookfield and Dag Hammarskiold Schs., Oakland, 1979—; cons. in field. Mem. instnl. rev. bd. Merritt Hosp., Oakland; bd. dirs. Big Bros. of East Bay, Inst. for Devel. Urban Educators. Recipient Outstanding Service to Youth award, youth dept. Mt. Zion Ch., 1964; Outstanding Service award United Crusade, 1974; Outstanding Service to Children & Youth award Allen Temple Bapt. Church, 1978, 79, 80; Outstanding Prin. award Brookfield Sch., 1981. Mem. Nat. Assn. Elem. Sch. Prins. Am. Ednl. Research Assn., Assn. Calif. Sch. Adminstrs., United Adminstrs. Oakland Schs., Assn. for Supervision and Curriculum Devel. Democrat. Baptist. Club: Optimist. Author: A Comparative Study of Two Elementary Schools Reading Achievement: Special Funding vs Regular Funding, 1975; The Improvement of the Voting and Election Process in Upper Elementary and Junior High Grades: Citizenship Awareness, 1980; also others. Home: 4760 Tompkins Ave Oakland CA 94619 Office: 401 Jones Ave Oakland CA 94603

PEPER, JOHN BENJAMIN, educator; b. Orlando, Fla., Sept. 7, 1932; s. Charles J. and Florence C. (Wiley) P.; m. Lauretta Baldwin, Nov. 4, 1955; children—John, Mark, Graham. B.A., Baylor U., 1955; M.Ed., Temple U., 1966, Ed.D., 1969. Tchr. English and journalism Groveland (Fla.) High Sch., 1959-61, Cherry Hill (N.J.) High Sch., 1964-66; exec. dir. Sch. Dist. of Phila., 1968-72; assoc. prof. U. Va., Charlottesville, 1972-73; asst. supt. Milw. Pub. Schs., 1973-77; supt. Anchorage Sch. Dist., 1977-81; supt. Jefferson County Schs., Lakewood, Colo., 1981—. Bd. dirs. Denver Jr. Achievement, 1981—, Colo. Safety Assn., 1982—. Served with USN, 1955-59, 61-64. Mem. Am. Assn. Sch. Adminstrs., Am., Mgmt. Assn. Republican. Presbyterian. Clubs: Masons, Shriners, Rotary. Contbr. articles to profl. jours.

PEPERZAK, MARCUS BERNARD, investment management company executive; b. Harbel, Liberia, Jan. 20, 1949; came to U.S., 1954, naturalized, 1959; s. Paul and Carla (Olman) P.; m. Cheryl A. Rheault, Dec. 20, 1970; children—Johanna, Katherin. Student Lehigh U., 1966-68; B.S., U. Calif., 1970. Exec. trainee Del Monte Corp., San Francisco, 1970-71; assoc. fin. cons. Bartle Wells Assocs., San Francisco, 1971-72; v.p. Brennan Fin. Group, San Francisco, 1972-73; pres., chief exec. officer Aurora Capital Corp., Walnut Creek, Calif. and Twin Falls, Idaho, 1973—; dir. McDonald Ins. Co., Sinclair & Co., Deures. Club: Blue Lakes Country (Twin Falls). Home: Route 3 Skyline Dr Twin Falls ID 83301 Office: 2536 Kimberly Rd Box 221 Twin Falls ID 83301

PERA, IRIS CAMPODONICO, financial analyst; b. San Francisco, Sept. 13, 1936; d. Rudolph Louis and Siria Elda (Baldocchi) Campodonico; m. Richard Ignatius Pera, May 14, 1960; children—Richard, Angelo, Carol. B.A., Dominican Coll., 1958. Dir. of Pub. affairs New Century Beverage Co., San Francisco; fin. analyst Newkirk-Sloane, San Rafael, Calif.; founder, owner The Bottom Line, San Rafael, Calif.; dir., chief fin. officer New Horizons Savs. & Loan Assn. Bd. dirs., treas. Dominican Coll. Alumni Assn.; mem. citizens adv. com. Dominican Coll.; aux. vol. Bur. of Marin. Club: Cristoforo Colombo. Home: 60 Margarita Dr San Rafael CA 94901 Office: 30 Professional Ctr Parkway San Rafael CA 94903

PERATE, HANNAH MARY, educator; b. Phila., Oct. 3, 1946; d. Frank Leo and Hannah Mary (Arnold) P. B.A., Russell Coll., 1969; M.A., Calif. State Coll., 1981. Standard tchr. credential, reading specialist tchr. credential, Calif. Tchr. St. Athanasius Sch., Mountain View, Calif., 1968, Holy Name Sch., San Francisco, 1969-72, Our Lady of Angels Sch., Burlingame, Calif., 1972-75, St. Pius X Sch., Santa Fe Springs, Calif., 1975-78, Sacred Heart Sch., Redlands, Calif., 1978-79, Wrightwood (Calif.) Elem. Sch., 1979—, sec. Sch. Site Council, journalism moderator. Mem. Republican Presdl. Task Force; mem. Nat. Right to Life Com. Mem. Internat. Reading Assn., Assn. Supervision and Curriculum Devel., Calif. State Coll. Alumni Assn., Edn. Chpt. Calif. State Coll., Nat. Rifle Assn. Roman Catholic. Contbr. short stories to Purpose, Venture; contbr. poems to various publs. Office: Wrightwood Elem Sch Box 368 Wrightwood CA 92397

PERCELL, LLOYD EDGAR, service and investment executive; b. Portsmouth, Ohio, Feb. 27, 1931; s. Selvin J. and Florence (Jones) P.; m. Constance M. Stallard, July 26, 1953; children—Richard, David, Bradley, Lisa; m. Pamela Jo Hershey, Oct. 4, 1980. Student Glandale City Coll., 1953-54, Los Angeles City Coll., 1955, UCLA, 1955-56. Prodn. engr. Collins Radio Co., Burbank, Calif., 1953-54, indsl. engr., 1954-56, Western region sales, 1956-57; gen. mgr. comml. sales Lear Corp., Santa Monica, Calif., 1957-62; chief operating officer Aerospace Assocs., Inc., Miami, Fla., 1963-65, Carco Cos., Las Vegas, Nev., 1966-73, Exec. Cos., Las Vegas, 1974—. Mem. com. So. Nev. Indsl. Found., 1967-69; spl. adv. Gov. Laxalt of Nev., 1968-70; co-host Presdl. Inauguration, Washington, 1969; adv. Nat. Jr. Achievement Program, 1955-57. Served with USMC, 1950-52; ETO. Recipient Nat. Bus. Aircraft Assn. award for Safety, 1966; AEC award for Safety, 1965; Westinghouse commendation for D.E.W. Line, 1955; U.S. Goodwill Spl. Services award, 1951; Lectr. commendation Am. Soc. Tool Engrs., 1959. Mem. Ohio Oil and Gas Assn., Nat. Bus. Aircraft Assn., Helicopter Assocs. Internat. Aircraft Fin. Assn., Nat. Assn. TV Program Execs., Assn. Local and Transport Airlines, Am. Soc. Tool Engrs., Western Electronics Mfrs. Assn., Aeros. Soc., Mortgage Bankers Assn., C. of C., Am. Power Boat Assn., Pacific Offshore Powerboat Racing Assn., Boat Owners Assn. U.S. Republican. Club: Lake Mead Yacht (charter). Patentee in field; contbr. articles to profl. jours.; pub. Aero News, 1962-64; exec. producer TV shows: Fun and Fitness, Miss Phoebe's Garden, Cosmic Frontiers, Enchanted Storybook, For Goodness Sake, Las Vegas Alive, The Joan Rivers Special, others; author: What You Need to Know About Owning a Recreational Vehicle, 1979; What You Need to Know About the Oil/Gas Business, 1980; others. Address: 2235 E Flamingo Rd Las Vegas NV 89109

PEREIRA, NINO RODRIGUES, physicist; b. Amsterdam, Netherlands, Mar. 11, 1945; came to U.S., 1973; s. Paul Aron Rodrigues and Elsa Jessurun (D'Oliveira) P.; M.S., U. Amsterdam, 1970; Ph.D., Cornell U., 1976; m. Nelly Van Den Oever, Jan. 8, 1977; children—Jan Paul, Elsa. Assoc. expert UNESCO, Asuncion, Paraguay, 1970-72; postdoctoral researcher U. Calif., Lawrence-Berkeley Lab., 1976-78; scientist Dynamics Tech., Torrance, Calif., 1978-79; pvt. practice cons., Los Angeles, 1979-80; sr. scientist Western Research Corp., San Diego, 1980-81; sr. scientist Maxwell Labs., Inc., San Diego, 1981—. Mem. AAAS, Am. Phys. Soc., Sigma Xi. Office: Maxwell Labs 9244 Balboa St San Diego CA 92123

PERITO, JOSEPH GERALD, JR., educator; b. Denver, Feb. 9, 1927; s. Joseph and Rose (Comnillo) P.; B.A. in Music Edn., Denver U., 1950, M.A., 1955; Ed.D., U. No. Colo., 1967. Tchr. music Jefferson County (Colo.) Pub. Schs., Lakewood, 1950-57, supr. music, 1957-63, research specialist, 1964-65; prin. Carmody Jr. High Sch., Lakewood, 1965-78, adminstrv. asst. in central adminstrn., 1978-81. Mem. Am. Ednl. Research Assn., Am. Acad. Polit. and Social Scis., Nat., Colo. assns. secondary sch. prins., Music Edn. Nat. Conf., Am. Choral Dirs. Assn., Am. String Tchrs. Assn., Kappa Delta Pi, Phi Delta Kappa. Home: 430 N Garrison St Denver CO 80226 Office: 1209 Quail St Lakewood CO 80215

PERKES, VICTOR ASTON, educator; b. Oakland, Calif., July 17, 1930; s. Charles A. and Helen (Marshall) P.; B.A. in Biology, San Jose State Coll., 1954, M.A., 1960; Sc.D. (fellow), Stanford, 1967; m. Barbara W. Jackson, Dec. 27, 1953; children—Mark, Kent, Allison, Emily. Sci. specialist Hillsborough (Calif.) City Schs., 1959-64; curriculum coordinator sci. Cupertino (Calif.) Schs., 1964-66; research asst. Stanford, 1965-66; vis. prof. sci. edn. U. N.C., Chapel Hill, 1968, Calif. State U., Humboldt, 1972, 77; asst. prof. sci. edn. U. Oreg., 1966-67; coordinator sci. edn. U. Calif. at Davis, 1967—; dir. NSF Programs, 1969-76, 78-82; mem. State Calif. Accreditation Com., 1968-71, assessor Com. for Tchr. Preparation; lectr. confs. Recipient Helen Heffernan Scholarship and Stanford fellowship, 1964-65. Mem. AAAS, Nat., Calif. sci. tchrs. assns., Nat. Assn. Research Sci. Teaching, Nat. Assn. Biology Tchrs. (regional chmn.), Nat. Assn. Sci. Suprs. Club: Commonwealth of Calif. Contbr. to ednl. jours. Home: 2803 Anza Ave Davis CA 95616

PERKINS, ALBERT ST. CLAIR, anesthesiologist; b. Jamaica, West Indies, Nov. 4, 1916; s. Albert William and Lucille (Hoffman) P.; came to U.S., 1944, naturalized, 1953; B.S., Western Res. U., 1947; M.D. cum laude, Loyola U., 1950; m. Phyllis Mae Walker, Feb. 17, 1942; children—Robert, Michelle. Intern, Queen of Angels Hosp., Los Angeles, 1950-51; with Jamaica Med. Service, 1951-52; gen. practice, Los Angeles, 1952-62; resident anesthesiology Los Angeles County Gen. Hosp., 1962-64; mem. anesthesia dept. Whittier (Calif.) Hosp., 1965—. Mem. Calif., Los Angeles County med. assns., Internat. Anesthesia Research Soc. Republican. Home: 1720 Fullerton Rd La Habra CA 90631 Office: 15151 Janine Dr Whittier CA 90605

PERKINS, JOSEPH JOHN, JR., lawyer; b. Pitts., Feb. 22, 1954; s. Joseph John and Joan Elizabeth (Challingsworth) P.; B.S.E., Princeton U., 1976; J.D., U. Denver, 1979. Admitted to Alaska bar, 1979; asso. firm Ely, Guess & Rudd, Anchorage, 1979—. Mem. Am. Bar Assn., Alaska Bar Assn., Anchorage Bar Assn., Rocky Mountain Mineral Law Found., Sigma Xi, Tau Beta Pi. Republican. Episcopalian. Office: 510 L St #700 Anchorage AK 99501

PERKINS, PATRICIA MAUREEN, author, public speaker, business consultant; b. Oakland, Calif., Apr. 21, 1932; d. Melvin Francis and Florence Edith Fitzgerald; div.; children—Donald, Thomas, Teresa. B.S., La Jolla U., 1980. Dir. sales and on-site logistics, coordinator Cole Assocs., La Jolla, Calif., 1978-81; co-dir. New Wave Cons., La Jolla, 1981—; public speaker on success, promotion and motivation, 1980—; author: Making The Break, 1982; How To Forgive Your Ex-Husband, 1982; facilitator U. West Fla. and U. Ariz., 1980-81. Mem. G.R.O.W., Career Women's Network, Women in Mgmt., Winners Circle Breakfast Clubs (nat. dir. 1979-80), So. Calif. Publicists. Club: Soroptomists. Office: PO Box 2203 La Jolla CA 92038

PERKINS, STERRETT THEODORE, physicist; b. Oakland, Calif., July 25, 1932; s. Frank Bernard and Mary Elizabeth (Scott) P.; B.S., U. Calif., Berkeley, 1956, M.S., 1957, Ph.D., 1965; m. Carol Louise Russell, Mar. 4, 1970; children—Charles, Pamela, Jill, Terri, Lisa, Sheila. Sr. nuclear engr. Aerojet-Gen. Corp., San Ramon, Calif., 1957-59; physicist Lawrence Livermore Nat. Lab., Livermore, Calif., 1959-60; cons. Aerojet-Gen. Corp., San Ramon, Calif., 1959-60; prin. nuclear engr., 1960-65; sr. physicist Lawrence Livermore Nat. Lab., Livermore, Calif., 1965—. Bd. dirs. Livermore (Calif.) Heritage Guild, 1975-77. Registered profl. engr., Calif. Mem. Am. Nuclear Soc., Am. Phys. Soc., Sigma Xi. Office: PO Box 808 L-71 Livermore CA 94550

PERKINS, WILLIAM CLOUGH, constrn. co. exec.; b. Pocatello, Idaho, June 22, 1926; s. William Clough and Lillian Eileen (Simmons) P.; B.S. in Civil Engring., U. Nebr., 1950; m. Jackie M. Hughes, Oct. 5, 1957; 1 dau., Dianne Kay. With Morrison-Knudsen Co., various locations, 1950-62; Latin Am. div. engr. Morrison-Knudsen Internat., N.Y.C., 1962-69, spl. assignment, Boise, Idaho, 1969-72, asst. div. mgr., then div. mgr., 1972-78, v.p. Latin Am., 1978—. Served with USMC, 1943-46. Mem. ASCE, The Moles. Republican. Club: Elks. Office: 2 Morrison-Knudsen Plaza Boise ID 83729

PERLINSKI, CAROL BRADFORD, business educator; b. Bozeman, Mont., May 29, 1954; d. Robert Lloyd and Velma Louise (Chandler) Bradford; m. Jerry K. Perlinski, Dec. 24, 1972; children—Adele Jill, Arianne Jeri. B.S. in Bus. Edn., Mont. State U., 1977, M.S. in Bus. Edn., 1981. Tchr. bus. edn. Mont. State U., Bozeman, 1976-81; tchr. bus. edn. Bozeman Sr. High Sch., 1979—, cheerleader advisor, 1982—. Program dir. Camp Fire Camp, Bozeman, 1981—, bd. dirs. Headwaters council, Bozeman, 1979—, pres., 1983—. Mem. Bozeman Edn. Assn., Mont. Edn. Assn., NEA, Mont. Bus. Edn. Assn., Nat. Bus. Edn. Assn., Mont. Vocat. Assn., Am. Vocat. Assn., Pi Omega Pi. Office: Bozeman Sr High Sch 205 N 11th St Bozeman MT 59715

PERLOFF, JEAN MARCOSSON, lawyer; b. Lakewood, Ohio, June 25, 1942; d. John Solomon and Marcella Catherine (Borngen) Marcosson; m. William Harry Perloff, Dec. 26, 1968. B.A. magna cum laude, Lake Erie Coll., 1965; M.A. in Italian, UCLA, 1967; J.D. magna cum laude, Ventura Coll. Law, 1976. Bar: Calif. 1976. Assoc. in Italian U. Calif.-Santa Barbara, 1967-70; law clk., paralegal Ventura County Pub. Defender's Office, Ventura, Calif., 1975; sole practice, Ventura, 1976-78; co-prin. Clabaugh & Perloff, A Profl. Corp., Ventura, 1979-82; sr. jud. atty. to presiding justice 2d Dist. Ct. Appeals, Los Angeles, 1982—; instr. Ventura Coll. Law, 1976-79. Bd. dirs. Santa Barbara Zool. Gardens. Mem. ABA, Calif. State Bar, Ventura County Bar Assn., Calif. Women Lawyers, Women Lawyers Ventura County, Ventura County Criminal Def. Bar Assn., Mar Vista Bus. and Profl. Women (pres. elect), Kappa Alpha Sigma. Democrat. Home: 1384 Plaza Pacifica Santa Barbara CA 93108 Office: 2d Dist Ct Appeals Wilshire Blvd Los Angeles CA

PERLOFF, JEAN MARCOSSON, lawyer; b. Cleve., June 25, 1942; d. John Solomon and Marcella Katherine (Borngen) Marcosson; m. William H. Perloff, Dec. 26, 1968. B.A. magna cum laude, Lake Erie Coll., Ohio, 1965; M.A., UCLA, 1967; J.D. magna cum laude, Ventura (Calif.) Coll. Law, 1976. Bar: Calif. 1976. Teaching asst. Italian, UCLA, 1966-67; assoc. in Italian, U. Calif., Santa Barbara, 1967-70; individual practice, Ventura, 1977-78; ptnr. Clabaugh & Perloff, P.C., Ventura, 1979-82; instr. Ventura Coll. Law, Santa Barbara Law Inst. Chancellor's teaching fellow UCLA, 1965. Mem. ABA, Calif. State Bar, Calif. Lawyers Assn., Calif. Women Lawyers, Ventura County Criminal Def. Bar (pres. 1979). Home and Office: 1384 Plaza Pacifica Santa Barbara CA 93108

PERNICHELE, ALBERT DAVID, geologist, mining market specialist; b. Staunton, Ill., Jan. 24, 1936; s. John Albert and Irene P.; m. Mary Ellen Stenso, Sept. 29, 1962; children—Gwen, Ann, Matthew, Gretchen. B.S., U. Ill., 1960; M.S. in Geology, U. N.D., 1963; postgrad. U. Utah, 1963-67. Minerals geologist Ill. Geol. Survey, 1959-60; petroleum geologist N.D. Geol. Survey, 1961-62, Amoco Minerals, 1962-65; chemist U.S. Geol. Survey, 1965-67; geologist, sr. process engr. Kennecott Copper Corp., Bingham Canyon, Utah, 1967-73; project mgr. Dames & Moore, Washington, 1973-76, dir. mining market, Salt Lake City, 1979—. Served with U.S. Army, 1954-56. Ford Found. fellow, 1964-67; recipient Peele award Am. Soc. Mining Engrs., 1972. Mem. AIME. Club: University. Home: 4964 Viewmont Circle Salt Lake City UT 84117 Office: Suite 200 250 E Broadway Salt Lake City UT 84111

PEROTTE, JAMES MICHAEL, mfg. exec.; b. Los Angeles, May 13, 1929; s. Peter Richard and Blanche Anne (Patriquin) P.; A.A. in Bus. Mgmt., Santa Barbara City Coll., 1968; m. Jeanne Bozek, Aug. 24, 1954; children—Peter Thomas, Robert James, Catherine Jeanne. Engr., Ampex, Calif., 1958-64; ops. mgr. Applied Magnetics, 1964-69; engring. mgr. Potter Inst., N.Y.C. and P.R., 1969-73; mfg. mgr. Infomag., 1973-76; co-founder, pres., chief exec. officer, dir. Magretech, Goleta, Calif., 1976—; dir. Magnetic Recovery Tech., Alternative in Magnetics. Adult leader Boy Scouts Am., 1961-64. Served with USAF, 1947-50, USN, 1951-55. Mem. Am. Electronics Assn., Calif. Assn. Ind. Bus., Nat. Fedn. Ind. Bus., Santa Barbara C. of C. Republican. Episcopalian. Office: 7300 Hollister Ave Goleta CA 93117

PEROVICH, JOHN, university president; b. Van Houten, N.Mex., Feb. 9, 1924; s. P.R. and Mary G. (Kovacevich) P.; m. June Brewer, Apr. 18, 1946. B.B.A., U. N.Mex., 1948, M.B.A., 1949. Comptroller U. N.Mex., Albuquerque, 1950-67, v.p. bus. and fin., 1967-82, interim pres., 1982, pres., 1983—; commr. Western Interstate Commn. for Higher Edn. Bd. dirs. Sandia Found., N.Mex. Med. Found., U. N.Mex. Found. Served to 2d lt. USAAF, 1943-45. Mem. Albuquerque C. of C. (dir.), Nat. Assn. State Univs. and Land Grant Colls., Nat. Assn. Coll. and Univ. Bus. Officers. Lodge: Kiwanis. Office: Univ New Mexico Albuquerque NM 87131

PERREAULT, JOHN LEO, elec. and nuclear engr.; b. Troy, N.Y., Feb. 17, 1938; s. George Henry and Gladys Loretta (Terriault) P.; B.S. magna cum laude, U. Wash., 1966; M.S., U. Calif.-Berkeley, 1969; m. Hwan Ja Choi, June 25, 1966; children—Daniel Conan, Frederick George. With Gen. Electric Co., San Jose, Calif., 1966-78, sr. engr., 1973-76, mgr. engring. support services, 1976-78; sr. engr. field service Exxon Nuclear Co. Inc., Bellevue, Wash., 1978-81; sr. staff engr. Northwest Energy Services Co., Kirkland, Wash., 1981-82, mgr. energy conservation services, 1982—. Served with Signal Corps, AUS, 1956-59. Registered profl. engr., Calif. Mem. Am. Nuclear Soc., Assn. Energy Engrs., Instrument Soc. Am., Phi Eta Sigma, Tau Beta Pi. Home: 1924 165th Ct SE Bellevue WA 98008 Office: Northwest Energy Services Co 2820 Northrup Way Bellevue WA 98004

PERRENOD, DOUGLAS ARTHUR, aerospace engineer; b. Weehawken, N.J., Sept. 13, 1947; s. George Edward and Eunice Lillian (Cohn) P. Student, Fla. Inst. Tech., 1968-72; B.A. in Astronomy, U. South Fla., 1973; postgrad. Calif. State U., 1982—. Cert. glider flight instr. FAA. Engr. trainee NASA Kennedy Space Ctr., Fla., 1969-73; constrn. engr. A-1 Constrn. Co., Half Moon Bay, Calif., 1976; quality control engr. Pelletech Corp., Fontana, Calif., 1976-77; electronics specialist Gen. Telephone Co., San Bernardino, Calif., 1977-79; aerospace engr. Rockwell Internat., Downey, Calif., 1979—; aviation cons., owner-founder Flight Unltd., Long Beach, Calif. Vol. mem. Orange County Human Services Agy., 1981—; active Big Bros. of Am., 1978. Served to capt. USAF, 1973-75. Recipient Amelia Earhart award CAP, 1968, Manned flight Apollo 11 medallion NASA, 1971, 1st Shuttle Flight award NASA, 1981, Aerospace Maintenance Officer of Yr. award USAFR, 1979; named to Engr. Honor Roll, Rockwell Internat., 1982. Mem. AIAA, Res. Officers Assn., Air Force Assn., Soaring Soc. Am., Toastmasters Internat., Speakers Bur. (Rockwell Internat.), Assoc. Glider Club of So. Calif., Long Beach Navy Aero. Club. Designer telescope mount for 1st astronomy obs. Fla. Inst. Tech., 1969. Home: PO Box 4361 Downey CA 90241 Office: 12214 Lakewood Blvd AD35 Downey CA 90241

PERRETEN, FRANK ARNOLD, eye surgeon; b. Boulder, Colo., Jan. 13, 1927; s. Arnold Ervin and Keene (Nichols) P.; B.A., U. Colo., 1948; M.D., U. Pa., 1952; m. Marilyn Ann Peterson, June 26, 1953; 1 son, Michael Peterson. Intern, St. Lukes Hosp., Denver, 1952, Denver Gen. Hosp., 1953; resident postgrad. Mass. Eye and Ear Infirmary of Harvard, 1957; practice medicine, specializing in ophthalmology, Winston-Salem, N.C., 1957-60, Denver, 1960—; mem. staff Children's, St. Joseph's, St. Luke's, Mercy, Presbyn., Luth. hosps.; cons. Brighton (Colo.) Community Hosp.; asso. prof. U. Colo., 1961—; dir. N.C. Eye Bank, 1957-60. Bd. dirs. Collegiate Sch. of Denver, Goodwill Industries. Served with USNR, 1944-46. Diplomate Am. Bd. Ophthalmology. Mem. Am. Acad. Ophthalmology and Otolaryngology, N.C., S.C. eye, ear, nose and throat socs., Colo. Ophthalmology Soc., Colo., Denver County med. socs., AMA, N.Y. Acad. Sci., Newcomen Soc., U. Colo. Alumni (bd. dirs.), Delta Tau Delta Alumni (pres.). Clubs: Lions (dir.), Denver, Cherry Hills Country (Denver). Contbr. Pediatric Ophthalmology. Home: 60 S Birch St Denver CO 80222 Office: 1801 High St Denver CO 80218

PERRIZO, JAMES DAVID, artist, educator; b. Los Angeles, Dec. 10, 1938; s. Francis John and Mary Ellen (Gaffney) P.; student Marquette U., 1957, Calif. State Coll., Hayward, 1964-66; B.A., U. Calif., Berkeley, 1967, M.A., 1969, M.F.A., 1974; m. Helene Apin Martin, Aug. 1, 1964; children—Teva Vaea, Rano Darian, Melia Tiare. Corp. pilot World Properties, Walnut Creek, Calif., 1971; airline transport pilot Bristow Helicopters, Redhill, Eng., 1974; forest fire fighting helicopter pilot Calif. Div. Forestry, 1975, 78, 83, U.S. Forest Service, Oreg. and Wash., 1976, Calif. and Ariz., 1977; capt. Century Airlines, Eureka, Calif., 1979, S.F.O. Helicopter Airline, Calif., 1982; asst. prof. art Calif. State U., Hayward, 1970-77, assoc. prof., 1977—. Prin., dir. maintenance Zoom Zoom Air, Oakland (Calif.) Airport, 1969-70; bd. dirs. New Mus. Modern Art, Oakland, 1971-73. Served with USN, 1957-62. Recipient Dean's award for sculpture U. Calif.-Berkeley, 1967. Research Found. Calif. State U.-Hayward grantee, 1976, 83. Mem. Univ. Art Mus. Council, Berkeley, ACLU. Important sculpture includes Cloud Factory, 1969, No More War 1969, Sometimes Eyes Smiles, 1972, The First and Last Men, 1973, Earth Apparition, 1973, Rock Jack Entrapment, 1977, Passing Through, 1978, Five Moon Prairie, 1982, Travelair, 1982. Home: 21305 Oceanview Dr Hayward CA 94541

PERRON, PILAR NEPOMUCENO, equal employment opportunity official, cosmetics company executive; b. Quezon, Philippines, Oct. 12, 1928; came to U.S., 1952; d. Pio Jose' and Angela (Tinio) Nepomuceno; m. Armand Thomas Perron, June 2, 1951; children—Kevin, Wayne, Deborah Perron Rogers. A.A., U. of Philippines, 1960; student U. So. Colo., 1968-69, U. Colo., 1970-72. Sec. U.S. Air Force, 1949-59; ct. reporter, 1963-65, 68-76; chief Equal Employment Opportunity and Affirmative Action Programs, U.S. Air Force Acad., Colorado Springs, Colo., 1976—; div. mgr. Lady Venus Cosmetics Co., 1971-76, owner, mgr. Colorado Springs Region, 1977—. Recipient Affirmative Action award U.S. Air Force Acad., 1977, 83; Personnel Spl. Achievement award U.S. Air Force Acad., 1979, 81; Pres.' Mgmt. award Cosmetics Internat., 1980; other award U.S. Air Force Acad. Mem. Nat. Assn. Female Execs., Bus. Opportunity Assn., Am. Businesswomen's Assn., Federally Employed Women, Altrusa Internat. (exec. bd. dirs. Colorado Springs chpt.). Democrat. Roman Catholic. Home: 3127 Escapardo Ct Colorado Springs CO 80917 Office: US Air Force Acad Colorado Springs CO 80840 also Lady Venus Cosmetics Co 1614A N Academy St Colorado Springs CO 80909

PERRY, DALE LYNN, chemist; b. Greenville, Tex., May 12, 1947; s. Francis Leon and Violet (Inabinette) P.; B.S., Midwestern U., 1969; M.S., Lamar U., 1972; Ph.D., U. Houston, 1974. Nat. Sci. Found. fellow dept. chemistry Rice U., Houston, 1976-77; Miller Research fellow dept. chemistry U. Calif., Berkeley, 1977-79; head inorganic and surface chemistry, Geosciences Group, Earth Scis. Div., Lawrence Berkeley (Calif.) Lab., U. Calif., 1979—. Recipient Sigma Xi Nat. Research award U. Houston, 1974; NSF postdoctoral fellow, Rice U., 1976-77; Miller fellow U. Calif., 1977-79. Mem. Am. Chem. Soc., Soc. Applied Spectroscopy, Coblentz Soc., Sigma Xi. Contbr. articles to profl. jours. Home: 2228 Key Blvd El Cerrito CA 94530 Office: Mail Stop 70A-1115 Lawrence Berkeley Lab Univ of Calif Berkeley CA 94720

PERRY, DAVID NILES, pub. relations co. exec.; b. Utica, N.Y., Mar. 7, 1940; s. Francis N. and Marion H. P.; B.S., Utica Coll. Syracuse U., 1962; m. Jacqueline J. Adams, Dec. 21, 1962. Pub. affairs rep. Allstate Ins. Co., Pasadena, Calif., 1966-67; dir. press relations Los Angeles C. of C., 1968; rep. pub. relations Lockheed Propulsion Co., Redlands, Calif., 1968-70; mgr. pub. relations Bozell & Jacobs Inc., Los Angeles, 1970-73, Phoenix, 1971-74; pres. David Perry Pub. Relations Inc., Scottsdale, Ariz., 1974—; cons. in field; instr. Phoenix Coll. Bd. dirs. Ariz. Gov.'s commn. Ariz. environment, 1972—, Campfire Council. Served with USNR, 1962-65. Mem. Pub. Relations Soc. Am. (accredited) (dir. Phoenix chpt. 1975—). Clubs: Phoenix Press, Ariz. Press. Office: 6819 E Diamond St Scottsdale AZ 85257

PERRY, DENZEL LAFAYETTE, feed mill and bulk plant exec.; b. Great Falls, Mont., June 3, 1936; s. Clarenc H. and Theresa A. (Anderson) P.; B.S. in Engring., Mont. State U., 1958; M.B.A., Tex. Christian U., 1971; m. Donna G. Curtis, Dec. 28, 1958; children—Clayton Loren, Michelle Renne, Curtis Dean. Rancher, Choteau County, Mont., 1961-66; program controller missile programs Boeing Co., 1966-77, also internat. ops. mgr. and analyst, new bus. mgr., analyst, Seattle; owner, mgr. Perry's Outfit, Kent, Wash., Western States Industries, Inc., Choteau, Mont., 1977—. Served with ordnance, AUS, 1959-61. Home and Office: Box 855 Choteau MT 59422

PERRY, ISABEL JOHNS, ins. co. ofcl.; b. Phoenix, Nov. 8, 1924; s. Herbert Lee and Mabel Helen (Launders) Johns; student Phoenix Coll. Bus., 1942-43; m. Harold Eugene Perry, June 22, 1946; children—William Lee, Corine Mildred. Bank clk./accounts analyst Valley Nat. Bank, 1943-44; payroll clk. Goodyear Aircraft Corp., 1944-46; bank teller/credit investigator First Nat. Bank, Phoenix, 1946-51; bookkeeper Circle K Corp., Phoenix, 1960-69, payroll adminstr., 1970-74, group plan adminstr., 1974—. Mem. Phoenix Human Relations Commn., 1982—, also mem. employment and housing coms. Mem. Phoenix Life-Accident-Health Claims Assn., V.F.W. Aux., Ariz. Hist. Soc., Phoenix Hist. Soc., Epsilon Sigma Alpha. Democrat. Presbyterian. Office: 4500 S 40th St Phoenix AZ 85040

PERRY, JOHN VAN BUREN, historian, educator; b. Aberdeen, S.D., Feb. 7, 1928; s. Van Buren and Elise (Andersen) P.; B.Sc., No. State Coll., S.D., 1954; postgrad. Law Sch., N.Y. U., 1954-55; M.A., U. Calif., Berkeley, 1959; postgrad. U. So. Calif., 1965-66. Instr. history Calif. State Univ. Fresno and Sonoma, 1963-65; asst. prof. Kern Community Coll. Dist., Bakersfield and Porterville, Calif., 1969-71; prof. social scis. and humanities Central Wyo. Coll., Riverton, 1971-75; prof. history, humanities, social scis. Lake Tahoe Community Coll., South Lake Tahoe, Calif., 1975—, pres. faculty senate, 1979-80. Pres., Lake Tahoe Community Concert Assn., 1977-79, 81-84, campaign mgr., 1979-81; pres. Arts in Action, 1973-75; del. Wyo. Council on Arts, Wyo. Council for Humanities; bd. dirs. Riverton Community Concert Assn., 1972-75, Lake Tahoe Community Concert Assn., 1975—, Assn. to Restore Tallac Sites, 1981—; bd. dirs. Lake Tahoe Cultural Arts Alliance, 1981—, treas., mem. exec. com., 1982—. Served with USN, 1946-50. Root-Tilden fellow, 1954-55. Mem. Am. Hist. Assn., Community Coll. Humanities Assn., Mus. Soc. San Francisco, Los Angeles County Mus. Art, Met. Mus. N.Y.C., Central Calif. Ednl. TV, Am. Philatelic Soc. Club: Scottish Rite. Home: PO Box 14266 South Lake Tahoe CA 95702 Office: PO Box 14445 South Lake Tahoe CA 95702

PERRY, JUDITH ANN, educator; b. Portland, Oreg., June 7, 1939; d. Robert Fredrick and Jeannette A. (Pook) Roake; m. Lee Wellington Perry, Jr., Mar. 8, 1968; 1 son, Victor Anthony. B.S., Oreg. State U., 1960; M.A.T., Reed Coll., 1966; Ph.D., U. Oreg., 1983. Cert. tchr., supr., Oreg. Tchr. Grout Sch., Portland, Oreg., 1964-65, Creston Sch., 1965-66; tchr. art Ockley Green Sch., Portland, 1965-66, Fernwood Sch., Portland, 1966-67, Glencoe Sch., Portland, 1965-73; primary tchr. Llewellyn Sch., Portland, 1973-79; instr. art edn. U. Oreg., Eugene, 1979-80; tchr. art, lang. arts, social studies, reading Mt. Tabor Middle Sch., Portland, 1980—; exhibited various coll. art shows; mem. Oreg. State Art Edn. Bd. Mem. jury Open Gallery Art Show, 1979; mem. selection com. for awards Met. Arts Commn., 1981. U. Oreg. Grad. teaching fellow, 1979-80. Mem. Oreg. Art Edn. Assn. (pres. 1977-82), Nat. Art Edn. Assn. (dir. Pacific region elem. div. 1977-79), Pacific Northwest Ski Instrs. Assn., Profl. Ski Instrs. Am. Home: 6106 SE 32d Ave Portland OR 97202

PERRY, LEE ROWAN, lawyer; b. Chgo., Sept. 23, 1933; s. Watson Bishop and Helen (Rowan) P.; B.A., U. Ariz., 1944, LL.B., 1961; m. Barbara Ashcraft Mitchell, July 2, 1955; children—Christopher, Constance, Geoffrey. Admitted to Ariz. bar, 1961, since practiced in Phoenix; clk. Udall & Udall, Tucson, 1960-61; mem. firm Carson, Messinger, Elliott, Laughlin & Ragan, 1961—. Mem. bd. edn. Paradise Valley Elementary and High Sch. Dists., Phoenix, 1964-68, pres., 1968; treas. troop Boy Scouts Am., 1970-72; mem. Ariz. adv. bd. Girl Scouts U.S.A., 1972-74, mem. nominating bd., 1978-79; bd. dirs. Florence Crittenton Services Ariz., 1967-72, pres., 1970-72; bd. dirs. U. Ariz. Alumni, Phoenix, 1968-72, pres., 1969-70; bd. dirs. Family Service Phoenix, 1974-75, Vol. Bur. Maricopa County, 1975-81, 83—, Ariz. div. Am. Cancer Soc., 1978-80, Florence Crittenton div. Child Welfare League Am., 1976-81; bd. dirs. Crisis Nursery for Prevention of Child Abuse, 1978-81, pres., 1978-80; co-chmn. Republicans to Re-elect Senator De Concini, 1982. Served to 1st lt. USAF, 1955-58. Mem. State Bar Ariz. (conv. chmn. 1972), Am., Maricopa County bar assns., Phi Delta Phi, Phi Delta Theta (pres. 1954). Republican (precinct capt. 1970). Episcopalian (sr. warden 1968-72). Clubs: Rotary (dir. 1971-76, pres. 1975-76); Arizona, Plaza. Mem. law rev. staff U. Ariz., 1959-61. Office: United Bank Bldg PO Box 33907 Phoenix AZ 85067

PERRY, MICHAEL LAWRENCE, museum administrator; b. Nampa, Idaho, Jan. 6, 1946; s. Lowell D. and Lucy (Lemon) P.; m. Sandra Miles, Dec. 13, 1968; children—Allyson, Justin, Adrienne. B.A., U. Utah, 1971, M.S., 1973. Asst. curator birds, research asst. ornithology U. Utah, Salt Lake City, 1971-73; dir. Dinosaur Natural History Mus., Vernal, Utah, 1973-81; dir. Idaho Mus. Natural History, Pocatello, Idaho, 1981—. Served with USAR, 1970-76. Recipient Student award Am. Ornithologist Union, 1972, Outstanding Pub. Service award Vernal C. of C., 1977, Outstanding Employee award Utah Div. Parks and Recreation, 1978-79; U. Utah teaching fellow, 1969-73, Bur. Land Mgmt. and Utah State Div. Wildlife Resources research grantee, 1974-75. Mem. Am. Assn. Museums, Flaming Gorge Nat. History Assn., Dinosaur Nature Assn., Western Museums Conf., Idaho Assn. Museums, Utah Museums Assn., Utah State Hist. Soc., Sigma Xi. Republican. Mormon. Club: Lions (Pocatello, Idaho). Home: 5182 Pleasant View Pocatello ID 83202 Office: Campus Box 8096 Idaho State U Pocatello ID 83209

PERRY, MILDRED EVELYN, air service company executive; b. San Diego, Dec. 31, 1918; d. Carl Nelson and Esther Mathilda (Lundgren) Swartz; m. Kenneth Roal Perry, Nov. 20, 1940 (dec.); children—Loren, Bruce Alan, Leslie Ann, Ellen Kay. Student Chico State Coll., 1935-37; B.A. with honors, Calif. State U.-Sacramento, 1973. Office mgr., asst. weather modification projects Universal Air Service, Sacramento, 1955—. Mem. Older Women's League. Address: Universal Air Service 4331 S Land Park Dr Sacramento CA 95822

PERSON, EVERT BERTIL, newspaper and radio executive; b. Berkeley, Calif., Apr. 6, 1914; s. Emil P. and Elida (Swanson) P.; m. Ruth Finley, Jan. 26, 1944. Student U. Calif.-Berkeley, 1937. Co-pub., sec.-treas. Press Democrat Pub. Co., Santa Rosa, Calif., 1945-72, editor, 1972-73, pres., pub., editor-in-chief, 1973—; sec.-treas. Finley Broadcasting Co., Santa Rosa, 1945-72, pres., 1972—; pres. Person Properties Co., Santa Rosa, 1945-70; v.p. Finley Ranch & Land Co., Santa Rosa, 1947-72, pres., 1972-79; pres. Baker Pub. Co. (Oreg.), 1957-67, Sebastopol (Calif.), Times, 1978—, Russian River News, Guerneville, Calif., 1978—; mem. nominating com. AP, 1982—. Bd. dirs. Empire Coll., Santa Rosa, 1972—, Sonoma County Taxpayers Assn., 1966-69, San Francisco Spring Opera Assn., 1974-79; chmn. Santa Rosa Civic Arts Commn., 1961-62; pres. Santa Rosa Sonoma County Symphony Assn., 1966-68, Luther Burbank Meml. Found., 1979, Santa Rosa Symphony Found., 1967—; adv. bd. Santa Rosa Salvation Army, 1959-67; commodore 12th Coast Guard Dist. Aux., 1969-70. Mem. Am. Soc. Newspaper Editors, Internat. Press Inst., Calif. Newspaper Pubs. Assn. (pres. 1981-82), Inst. Newspaper Controllers and Fin. Officers (pres. 1961-62), Navy League U.S., Calif. Broadcasters Assn., Nat. Assn. Broadcasters, Sigma Delta Chi. Episcopalian. Clubs: Press, Bohemian, St. Francis Yacht (San Francisco); Sonoma County Press; Santa Rosa Golf and Country, Santa Rosa Rotary (past pres.); Masons, Shriners. Office: 427 Mendocino Ave Santa Rosa CA 95401

PERSON, ROBERT TALLMAN, utilities exec.; b. Des Moines, Aug. 6, 1914; s. Howard A. and Caroline M. (Tallman) P.; student N.Y.U., 1932; B.S., U. N.Mex., 1936; mgmt. course U. Idaho, 1954; m. Marian Elizabeth Clark, June 6, 1936; children—Nancy Joanne (Mrs. Max Morton), Robert Tallman, Howard Clark. With sales dept. Albuquerque Gas & Electric Co., 1936-40; comml. mgr. Pueblo Gas & Fuel Co., Colo., 1940-47, v.p., gen. mgr., 1947-53; v.p. pub. relations Pub. Service Co. Colo., Denver, 1953-58, dir., 1957—, exec. v.p., 1958-59, pres., 1959-76, chief exec. officer, 1959-79, chmn., 1976—, also chmn. exec. com.; pres., dir. Cheyenne Light, Fuel & Power Co. (Wyo.), 1959-76; dir. Western Slope Gas Co. (Denver), 1959-77; chief exec. officer Fuel Resources Devel. Co., 1959-77, chmn. bd., dir., from 1977; dir. Fed. Res. Bank of Kansas City, 1971-77, chmn. bd., 1975-76. Co-chmn. Rocky Mountain region NCCJ; bd. dirs. Mountain States Employers Council, Nat. Western Stock Show; past pres. Mile High United Fund; trustee Denver Mus. Natural History. Served to lt. (j.g.) USNR, 1944-46, 50; PTO. Mem. Edison Electric Inst. (past pres.), Colo. Assn. Commerce and Industry (dir.), Rocky Mountain Elec. League (past pres.), Denver C. of C. (past pres.), Nat. Assn. Electric Cos. (past dir., chmn.), Am. Gas Assn. (past dir.), Am. Legion. Clubs: Elks, Denver Country, Denver Athletic, Denver Press, Denver. Office: Pub Service Co of Colo 550 15th St Denver CO 80202*

PERSONS, RICHARD ORIS, accountant; b. Salem, Oreg., Dec. 29, 1949; s. Robert Orris and Sigrid Junetta (Heinonen) P.; m. Jeanine Marie Simpson, Jan. 12, 1980; children—Stephen, Jennifer. B.S., Brigham Young U., 1973; M.B.A., Oreg. State U., 1976. Tax mgr. P.R. Broadcasting Co., San Juan, P.R., 1977-78; acct. Fordham & Fordham, C.P.A.s, Hillsboro, Oreg., 1979-80; pres., acct. Richard O. Persons, C.P.A., P.C., Salem, 1980—; cons. Price Waterhouse Auidtores Independientes, Sao Paulo, Brazil, 1983—. Mem. City Comm. Salem, 1982-83. Latin Am. teaching fellow Fletcher Sch. Law and Diplomacy, Tufts U., 1976-77. Mem. Am. Inst. C.P.A.s, Oreg. Soc. C.P.A.s, Nat. Assn. Accts., InterAm. Acctg. Assn. Republican. Mem. Ch. Jesus Christ Latter-day Saints. Home: 2215 NW Highland Dr Corvallis OR Office: 5024 Daniel St S Salem OR 97306

PESIN, HARRY, advertising agency executive; b. N.Y.C., Oct. 16, 1919; s. Abraham and Lena (Bachman) P.; B.B.A., CCNY, 1942; m. Betty Klein, Feb. 20, 1944; children—Arthur, Alan, Richard. Creative dir. Lester L. Wolff Advt., N.Y.C., 1946; creative dir. Rockmore Co., N.Y.C., 1947-60, v.p., 1952-60; v.p. David J. Mendelsohn, N.Y.C., 1951-63, 1st v.p., 1961-63; pres., creative dir. Pesin, Sydney & Bernard, Inc., N.Y.C., 1963—; pres. Perspective Pubs., Inc., N.Y.C., 1958—, The Incredible Press, San Diego, 1978—. Served to 2d lt. AUS, 1942-45. Recipient awards Art Dirs. Club of N.Y., 1960, 68, 70, 78, 82; Communications Arts, 1968, Am. Inst. Graphic Arts, 1970; Power of Print award Time mag., 1969; Gold Camera award, 1975; Andy award, 1978, 79, 80, 81; The One Show award, 1978, 80; Effie Gold award, 1981. Mem. Am. Soc. Mag. Photographers, Am. Soc. Photographers in Communications, Copy Club N.Y. Author: (with Alan Pesin) My Little Brother Gets Away With Murder, 1958; The Acropolis Is a Nice Place to Visit But I Wouldn't Want to Live in the Eiffel Tower, 1963; Sayings to Run An Advertising Agency By, 1966; My Father, the Cigar Smoker, 1967; Why Is a Crooked Letter, 1968; Welcome, Stranger and Partners, 1974; Sayings On Running The Human Race, 1976. Home: 6710 La Valle Plateada Rancho Santa Fe CA 92067 Office: 509 Madison Ave New York NY 10022

PETERMAN, ANEES, interior designer; b. Bombay, India, Dec. 21, 1944; d. Faizula Mohamed and Shirin Banu (Bava) Hashambhoy; m. Gary James Peterman, May 31, 1975. Cert. in interior design Kareer Poly., Bombay, 1964; cert. in fine arts Sir J.J. Sch. Art, Bombay, 1968, Pan Am. Art Sch., N.Y.C., 1971; A.S., Chamberlayne Jr. Coll., Boston, 1973. Mgr., Park-Lane Gallery, Weston, Mass., 1971-73; with Juliane Galleries of Fine Art, Toronto, Ont., Can., 1973-74; interior designer Deboer's Furniture, Toronto, 1974-79, Ridpath's Interior Design, Toronto, 1980-81, Don Huish Interiors, Vancouver, B.C., Can., 1982-83. Mem. Am. Soc. Interior Designers, Interior Designers Inst. B.C. Paintings rep. in pub. and pvt. collections, Bombay, Karachi, Pakistan, London, N.Y.C., Boston, Washington, San Francisco, Toronto, Vancouver, Paris. Office: Hallmark Interiors 1251 Cardero St Suite 1503 Vancouver BC V6G 2H9 Canada

PETERMAN, EDWARD, librarian, educator; b. Longmont, Colo., Oct. 26, 1924; s. Edward and Clara (Benson) P.; student N.W. Nazarene Coll., 1943-45; Th.B., Azusa Coll., 1947; M.Div., Nazarene Theol. Sem., 1950; M.S.L., Western Mich. U., 1962; m. Clarice Stenberg, Sept. 9, 1945; children—Edward Timothy, Merri Ann. Ordained to ministry Nazarene Ch., 1950; pastor Nazarene chs., Mich., Washington, 1950-59; librarian, prof. religion Azusa (Calif.) Pacific Coll., 1959—. Mem. ALA, Calif. Coll. and U. Faculty Assn., AAUP. Home: 2623 N Sweetbriar Dr Claremont CA 91711 Office: Hwy 66 at Citrus Ave Azusa CA 91702

PETERS, BARBARA ANN, counselor, interior designer; b. LaSalle, Ill., Sept. 26, 1938; d. Lewis H. and Virginia L. (Dare) Livengood; m. Harold O. Nuss, June 26, 1960 (div. Jan. 1967); children—Kim Kristy, Douglas Alan; m. 2d, Barry J. Peters, June 2, 1968 (div. Nov. 1981). A.A., Scottsdale Community Coll., 1981; B.S., Ariz. State U., 1982, postgrad., 1984—; diploma interior design LaSalle U., 1967. Membership sec. Assn. Ednl. Data Systems, Washington, 1972; adminstrv. asst. pres. D.C. Transit Co., Washington, 1971-73; dist. sec. Congressman Robert H. Michel, Peoria, Ill., 1975; bus. mgr. Robinson Enterprises, Peoria, Ill., 1976-78; sec. to chmn. counselor edn. Ariz. State U., Tempe, 1982-83; crisis counselor Communications Info., Phoenix, 1983—. Bd. dirs. Women in Transition, 1982. Mem. Am. Personnel Guidance Assn., Am. Bus. Women's Assn., Ariz. Assn. U. Women. Republican. Roman Catholic. Home: 8738 E Whitton Ave Scottsdale AZ 85251

PETERS, DAVID MERRITT, congressional aide; b. Honolulu, Aug. 6, 1923; s. Charles Merritt and Mollie Kananipauole (Akana) P.; m. Joan Sabin, June 1, 1953; children—Lauren Moriarty, David Jr., Diane. B.S., U.S. Mil. Acad., 1946; M.S., U. Wis., 1961; grad. U.S. Army War Coll., 1968. Commd. 2d lt. U.S. Army, 1946; advanced through grades to col.; served as staff officer and comdr. at various levels Korea, Vietnam, Japan, Allied Forces So. Europe hdqrs., Italy, Belgium, U.S. Forces Germany, airborne and spl. forces; editor Army Info. Digest, 1961-63; prof. mil.; sci. U. Hawaii, Honolulu, 1973-76, ret. 1976; exec. asst. U.S. Senator Daniel K. Inouye of Hawaii, 1976—. Trustee Queen Liliuokalani Trust, Honolulu; bd. dirs. Hawaii Visitors Bur., Friends Iolani Palace; mem. exec. bd. Aloha council Boy Scouts Am. Decorated Legion of Merit with 3 oak leaf clusters, Silver Star, Bronze medal with V, Joint Meritorious Service medal, Army Commendation medal with 3 oak leaf clusters. Mem. Assn. U.S. Army, Kamehameha Alumni Assn. Episcopalian. Club: Masons, Prince Kuhio Hawaiian Civic. Home: 1371 Kina St Kailua HI 96734 Office: 6104 Prince Kuhio Blvd Honolulu HI 96850

PETERS, EUNICE SARAH BATES LOWERY (MRS. WILLIAM J. PETERS), artist; b. Chelsea, Mass., Oct. 18, 1906; d. William Edgar and Eunice Hall (Fergusson) Lowery; grad. Famous Artists Sch.; m. William J. Peters, June 3, 1927 (dec. June 1967); children—Eunice L. Peters Harrington, William J. Exhibited in group shows: Pasadena Soc. Artists, San Gabriel Soc. Arts; one-woman sculpture show; Alhambra (Calif.) Library, 1976, Rosemead (Calif.) Regional Library, 1976; sec., dir. Trail Chem. Corp., El Monte, Calif., 1947. Mem. Pasadena Arts Council, Pasadena Artists Assn., San Gabriel Fine Arts and Culture Assn., Nat. League Am. Pen Women (treas. Pasadena br. 1966-72, achievements chmn. 1982-84), Artists and Composers (pres. Pasadena br. 1972-74, corr. sec. 1974-76, art chmn., 1976—), Composers and Artists (Pasadena br.). Home: 1315 Montery Pl San Marino CA 91108 Office: 9904 Gidley St El Monte CA 91731

PETERS, GEORGE ALFRED, lawyer, engineer; b. Boston, Nov. 24, 1924; s. George A. and Mary (Edwards) P.; m. Roberta B. Bourasso, Mar. 20, 1948; children—Cheri, Barbara J. B.A., U. Mass., 1950; M.A., Temple U., 1953; J.D., U. West Los Angeles, 1970. Bar: Calif. 1970, U.S. Supreme Ct. 1975. With Peters and Peters, Santa Monica, Calif., 1970—, sr. ptnr., 1975—. Past bd. dirs. Bd. Cert. Safety Profls. Served with C.E., U.S. Army, 1943-46, 50-53. Recipient Kraft award Human Factors Soc., 1972. Fellow AAAS; mem. Am. Soc. Safety Engrs. (past v.p., tech. awards 1971, 80), Mem. System Safety Soc. (past pres.), World Safety Orgn. (past v.p.), Am. Soc. Quality Control, ABA, Calif. Bar Assn., Soc. Automotive Engrs., Assn. Trial Lawyers Am., Phi Kappa Phi. Author: Product Liability and Safety, 1971; Source Book on Asbestos Diseases, 1980; Automotive Engineering and Liability, 1983; Safety Laws, 1983. Past editor Hazard Prevention. Contbr. articles to profl. jours. Home:

515 Ocean Ave Santa Monica CA 90402 Office: 1460 Fourth St Santa Monica CA 90401

PETERS, HENRY H., state legislator; b. Honolulu, Feb. 5, 1941; student Brigham Young U.; married; 1 child. Dir., advocate Waianae Model Cities; mem. Hawaii Ho. of Reps., 1974—, now speaker of house. Served with U.S. Army, 1967-69. Office: State Capitol Room 335 Honolulu HI 96813

PETERS, RAYMOND ROBERT, banker; b. Concord, Calif., Sept. 14, 1942; s. Robert V. and Pegi M. (Carr) P.; m. Nancy Shia; children—Angel, Ray, Matthew. B.B.A., U. Oreg., 1964. Head customer securities Bank of Am., San Francisco, 1969-71, Euro currency and fgn. exchange mgr., 1971-76, sr. v.p. treasury mgmt., 1976—; cons. on fgn. currency, offshore banking matters U.S. Fed. Res., fgn. central banks. Served to lt. USN, 1964-68. Mem. Bankers Assn. Fgn. Trade (fgn. exchange com.).

PETERS, RONALD LUTHER, architect; b. Harrisburg, Pa., 1946; s. Albert Luther and Gladys Irene (Schaeffer) P.; B.F.A. in Architecture, U. N.Mex., 1972; m. Karen June Fluckey, Jan. 25, 1969; children—Stefanie, Erin. Owner, T-Square Services, Albuquerque, 1972-73; designer George Pate & Assos., architects, Sarasota, Fla., 1973-74; partner Burns/Peters Group-Architects, Albuquerque, 1974—; sec., dir. Nash-Burns-Peters-P.A., Kirkland, Wash.; prin. works include Sunstructure Office Bldg., Albuquerque (Owens Corning Design award, 1979), Navajo Community Coll. Faculty Housing, Ariz. (HUD Design award), 1978, Kline Residence, Moriarty, N.Mex. (HUD Design award), 1978. Served with USAF, 1964-68; Vietnam. Registered architect, Calif., Wash., Ariz. Mem. AIA, N.Mex. Solar Energy Soc., Nat. Historic Preservation Soc., Amateur Softball Assn., U.S. Slow Pitch Softball Assn. Democrat. Mem. Assembly of God Ch. Home: Zamora 79 Tijeras NM 87059 Office: 8000 Pennsylvania Circle NE Albuquerque NM 87110

PETERSEN, DANIEL CARL, mgmt. cons.; b. Omaha, Mar. 4, 1931; s. John Peter and Ebba Julianna (Sorensen) P.; B.S., Iowa State U., 1952; M.S. in Psychology, U. Nebr., 1972; Ed.D. in Organizational Behavior, U. No. Colo., 1980; m. Nadyne Alley, Sept. 14, 1951; children—Susan, Patricia, Thomas. Cons., Employers Ins. of Wausau, 1954-62, tng. dir., 1962-66, mgr., 1966-67; asst. v.p. Indsl. Indemnity Co., 1967-69; dir. loss control Allstate Ins. Co., 1969-70, cons., 1970-72; dir. loss control Nationwide Ins. Co., 1972-75; dir. grad. program U. Ariz., Tucson, 1975-77; asso. prof. indsl. scis. and microbiology Colo. State U., Ft. Collins, 1977-80; mgmt. cons. in safety and organizational behavior, Tucson, 1980—; tchr. various univs. Served to 1st lt. C.E., U.S. Army, 1952-54. Registered profl. engr., Calif.; cert. safety profl., Bd. Cert./Profl. Safety Profls. Mem. Am. Soc. Safety Engrs. (v.p., dir.), Nat. Safety Mgmt. Soc. (internat. pres., dir.). Republican. Lutheran. Author: Techniques of Safety Management, 1971, rev. edit., 1978; The OSHA Compliance Manual, 1975, rev. edit., 1978; Safety Management, 1975; Safety Supervision, 1976; Safety by Objectives, 1978; Industrial Accident Prevention, 1980; Readings in Industrial Accident Prevention, 1980; Analyzing Safety Performance, 1980; Human Error Reduction, 1981; cons. editor Safety Management series, 1980—. Home and office: 3431 N Camino Suerte Tucson AZ 85715

PETERSEN, GARY LEE, oil co. exec.; b. Pocatello, Idaho, Jan. 20, 1942; s. Lee Hans and Irma Louise (Ayres) P.; student Idaho State U., 1960-62; B.S., U. Idaho, 1964, M.B.A., U. So. Calif., 1973, m. Virginia Sue Mitchell, Dec. 20, 1970; children—Erik Stephen, Dana Kristopher, Heidi Kristine. Tech. service engr. Texaco, Inc., Wilmington, Calif., 1964-73; staff engr. Texaco, Inc., Houston, 1973-75; asst. to pres./v.p. U.S. Oil & Refining Co., Los Angeles, 1975-79, pres., 1979—; dir. Bruin Carbon Dioxide Sales Corp. Mem. Am. Petroleum Refiners Assn. (dir.), Am. Petroleum Inst. Presbyterian. Clubs: Jonathan, Petroleum of Los Angeles, U. So. Calif. M.B.A.'s. Home: 4312 Fir Ave Seal Beach CA 90740 Office: 5150 Wilshire Blvd Los Angeles CA 90036

PETERSEN, GEORGE THOMAS, mgmt. cons.; b. Hummelstown, Pa., Oct. 3, 1916; s. Hjalmar Hjelm and Emma Romaine (Spangler) P.; B.S. in Aero. Engring., U. Mich., 1938; advanced mgmt. program Harvard U., 1959; D. Engring. (hon.), Tex. A&M U., 1972; D.Sc. (hon.), London Inst., 1973; m. Opal Janett Herberg, Dec. 11, 1941; children—Karen, Barbara, Teressa. Commd. 2d lt., U.S. Army, 1941, advanced through grades to col., 1953; ret., 1961; dir. research Continental Motors, Detroit, 1961-69; gen. ops. mgr. transp. systems Ford Motor Co., Dearborn, Mich., 1969-76; v.p. engring. Rayco Creative Services, Royal Oak, Mich., 1976-77; v.p. Corp. Fin. Assos., Phoenix, 1977-78; pres. George T. Petersen Assos., Inc., Sun City, Ariz., 1977—; cons. Bernard Haldane Assos.; cons. tank design Israeli, Brit. and German armies. Decorated Bronze Star with 3 oak leaf clusters, Legion of Merit with 2 oak leaf clusters (U.S.), Order Brit. Empire, Croix de Guerre (France), cert. career counselor; registered profl. engr., Mich., Ariz. Mem. Am. Mgmt. Assn., Mil. Order World Wars, Am. Def. Preparedness Assn., Assn. U.S. Army, Nat. Security Assn. (dir., past chpt. pres.), Phi Delta Theta. Phi Delta Theta. Republican. Lutheran. Clubs: Lakes (Sun City); Biltmore Country (Phoenix); Wabeek Country (Bloomfield Hills, Mich.). Developer tanks, night vision devices, variable compression ratio diesel engine, Ford automated transit system. Home: 16025 Aqua Fria Dr Sun City AZ 85351 Office: 3225 N Central St Suite 1220 Phoenix AZ 85012

PETERSEN, JOSEPH CLAINE, chemist; b. Fielding, Utah, Feb. 14, 1925; s. Claudius Neils and Jane Elma (Christensen) P.; B.S., U. Utah, 1952, Ph.D., 1956; m. Erma Irene Boam, May 25, 1949; children—Brent Claine, Claudia, Warren Lee, Anne. Chemist, Am. Gilsonite Co., Salt Lake City, 1956-61; sr. research chemist E.I. duPont Co., Wilmington, Del., 1961-64; project leader U.S. Bur. Mines, Laramie (Wyo.) Energy Tech. Center, Dept. Energy, 1964—, sect. supr. asphalt research program, 1974—; mem. adv. coms. Nat. Acad. Scis./NRC, chmn. Transp. Research Bd. coms. Served with USN, 1943-46. Mem. Am. Chem. Soc. (chmn. Wyo.), Assn. Asphalt Paving Technologists, Sigma Xi, Phi Beta Kappa, Phi Kappa Phi. Contbr. articles to profl. jours.; patentee nonwoven bonded sheets, pavement antistrip agts. Home: 1072 Colina Dr Laramie WY 82070 Office: Laramie Energy Tech Center PO Box 3395 Laramie WY 82070

PETERSEN, KEITH CRAIG, historian; b. Vancouver, Wash., Mar. 23, 1951; s. Jack Kenneth and Jeannette Dolly (Benner) P.; B.A., Wash. State U., 1973; M.A., U. Wis., 1976. Dir., Latah County Hist. Soc., Moscow, Idaho, 1977-81; hist. cons., researcher groups and govt. agys., 1979—; North Idaho coordinator Idaho State Hist. Soc., Moscow, 1981—. Nat. Endowment for Humanities research grantee, 1981-83. Mem. Am. Assn. State and Local History, Inland Empire Mus. Assn. (v.p. 1980-82), Tri-State Mus. Council (Idaho rep.), U. Idaho Library Assocs., Idaho Assn. Museums (newsletter editor, treas. 1978-82), Oreg. Hist. Soc., Phi Beta Kappa, Phi Alpha Theta. Democrat. Author: Troy, Deary and Genesee: A Photographic History, 1979; A Guide to Historical and Genealogical Resources in Latah County, 1982; Corps of Engineers Walla Walla District History, 1982; The Corps of Engineers and the Environment in the Pacific Northwest, 1983; editor: Railroad Man: A Conversation with W. J. Gamble, 1981. Office: 110 S Adams St Moscow ID 83843

PETERSEN, MAUN TYRE, management consultant; b. East Ely, Nev., Apr. 24, 1944; s. Maun Tyre and Gwen (Christiansen) P.; B.S., U. Utah, 1969; m. Margene Winegar, Sept., 1977. Constrn. auditor Kennecott Copper Corp., N.Y.C., 1970-75; pres., owner Diamond Enterprises, Salt Lake City, 1972—; v.p., dir. Internat. Constrn. Systems, Inc., Salt Lake City, 1974—; adminstrv. exec. Weyher Constrn. Co., Salt Lake City, 1975-78; v.p., dir. Domgaard Assos., Salt Lake City, 1978-80; partner Elliott-Petersen, Cons., Salt Lake City, 1980—; dir., chmn. bd. Fox Investment, Ltd., Salt Lake City. Del. to Utah Democratic Com., 1970-72. Mem. Am. Mgmt. Assn., Inst. Internal Auditors. Mormon. Home: 3014 Millcreek Rd Salt Lake City UT 84109 Office: 2137 E 3300 South Salt Lake City UT 84109

PETERSEN, ROBERT CARL, port manager; b. Portland, Oreg., Dec. 4, 1928; s. Martin Carl and Venus W. (Butcher) P.; m. Toshie Matsumoto, May 6, 1964; 1 dau., Stephanie Yumi. B.S. in Bus Adminstrn., U. Wash., 1951. With States S.S. Co., Portland, San Francisco, Tokyo, 1947-63, asst. owner's rep., Far East, 1960-63, co-owner, gen. mgr. Grenada Yacht Services Ltd., St. Georges, W.I., 1963-70; port mgr. Port of Ilwaco, Wash., 1971—. Chmn. Pacific County Regional Planning Council, 1974-79; sec. Columbia-Pacific Resource Conservation and Devel., 1981—. Served with USNR, 1948-57. Mem. Wash. Pub. Ports Assn. (chmn. marina com. 1981—), Columbia-Pacific Fisheries Ctr. (dir. 1980—), Pacific Coast Congress Harbormasters and Port Mgrs. (pres. 1980-82), Tourist Regional Info. Program S.W. Wash. (dir. 1982—). Clubs: Yokohama (Japan) Yacht; Grenada Yacht; Portland (Yacht). Designer and builder small sailing yachts. Home: PO Box 182 Ilwaco WA 98624 Office: PO Box 307 Ilwaco WA 98624

PETERSEN, ROBERT EINAR, publisher, business executive; b. Los Angeles, Sept. 10, 1926; s. Einar and Bertha (Putera) P.; m. Margie McNally, Jan. 26, 1963. Student Mont. State Coll. Founder, chmn. Petersen Pub. Co., Los Angeles, 1948—; owner Petersen Galleries, Beverly Hills, Calif., 1973—, Scandia Restaurant, West Los Angeles, Calif., 1978—. Bd. dirs. Los Angeles Library Commn., 1963-64; past pres. Hollywood bd. dirs. Boys Club Am. Served with USAF. Mem. So. Calif. Safari Club, Chief Execs. Orgn., World Bus. Council, Ducks Unltd., Game Coin, Confrerie de la Chaine des Rotisseurs, Chevaliers du Tastevin, Calif. Wine Patrons. Clubs: Catalina Island Yacht, Balboa Bay, Thalians (Los Angeles). Office: Petersen Publishing Co 8490 Sunset Blvd Los Angeles CA 90069

PETERSEN, ROLAND, painter, printmaker, educator; b. Endelave, Horsens, Denmark, 1926; came to U.S., 1928; B.A., U. Calif. at Berkeley, 1949, M.A., 1950; postgrad. Han Hoffmann's Sch. Fine Arts, summers 1950-51, S.W. Hayter's Altelier 17, Paris, 1950, 63, 70, Islington Studio, London, 1977, The Print Workshop, London, 1980; m. Sharane Havlina, Aug. 12, 1950; children—Dana Mark, Maura Brooke, Julien Conrad, Karena Caia. Tchr., State Coll. Wash., Pullman, 1952-56; mem. faculty U. Calif. at Davis, 1956—, now prof. art; exhibited one-man shows Gump's Gallery, San Francisco, 1962. Staempfli Gallery, N.Y.C., 1963, 65, 67, Adele Bednarz Gallery, Los Angeles, 1966, 69, 70, 72, 73, 75, 76, Crocker Art Gallery, Sacramento, 1965, de Young Mus., San Francisco, 1968, La Jolla Mus., 1971, Phoenix Mus., 1972, Santa Barbara Mus., 1973, USIS sponsored touring one-man exhbn., Turkey, U. Reading (Eng.), 1977, 80, Rorick Gallery, San Francisco, 1981, 82, Print Mint, Chgo., 1981, University Club, Chgo., 1982, Rorick Gallery, San Francisco, 1981, 82, 83; exhibited group shows including Calif. Palace Legion of Honor, San Francisco Art Inst., 1962, Mus. Art, Carnegie Inst., Pitts., 1964, Obelisk Gallery, Washington, John Herron Art Inst., Indpls., 1964, Pa. Acad. Fine Arts, Phila., Crocker Art Gallery, Sacramento, 1965, Art Inst. Chgo., 1965, Va. Mus. Fine Arts, Richmond, 1966, U. Ariz. Art Gallery, Tucson, 1967, Am. Cultural Center, Paris, 1971, Nat. Gallery, Washington, 1972, Otis Art Inst. Gallery, Los Angeles, 1974, Auerbach Fine Art Gallery, London, 1977, 80, Nelson Gallery, U. Calif.-Davis, 1982; represented permanent collections; de Young Mus., San Francisco, San Francisco Mus. Modern Art, Va. Mus. Fine Arts, Mus. Modern Art, N.Y.C., Phila. Mus. Art, Whitney Mus. Am. Art, Phoenix Mus., Santa Barbara Mus., Musée Municipal, Brest, France, Smithsonian Instn. Nat. Collection Fine Arts, U. Reading (Eng.), others; bd. dirs. Crocker Art Gallery, 1976-78, mem. adv. bd. Davis Art Center. Mem. adv. bd. Kala Inst., Berkeley, 1978-80. Served with USNR, 1943-45, PTO. Recipient numerous prizes and awards, 1950—; Guggenheim fellow, 1963; U. Calif. creative arts fellow, 1967, 70, 77, Fulbright grantee, 1970. Mem. Print Council Am., AAUP, San Francisco Art Assn., Calif. Soc. Printmakers (dir. 1981, 82), Nat. Soc. Lit. and Arts. Address: PO Box 1 Dillon Beach CA 94929 also care Staempfli Gallery 47 E 77th St New York NY 10021 also Rorick Gallery 637 Mason St San Francisco CA 94108

PETERSEN, RONALD GREGORY, microcomputer manufacturing company executive, income tax service company executive; b. San Francisco, Feb. 7, 1948; s. Fred K. and Ann H. (Dietrich) P.; m. Esther Louise Gutierrez, June 26, 1971; children—Jill Marie, Sarah Michelle. B.S. in Math., U. Santa Clara, 1970, M.B.A., 1976. Enrolled IRS agt. Engr., Quadrex Corp., Campbell, Calif., 1971-76; mgr. and sr. cons. Control Data Corp., San Jose, Calif., 1976-82; v.p. product planning, dir. mktg. Eagle Computer, Inc., Los Gatos, Calif., 1982—; dir. ACRI Corp. Served with N.G., 1970-76. Mem. Nat. Soc. Pub. Accts., Calif. Soc. Enrolled Agts. Lutheran. Writer Petersen On Taxes, Newsletter, 1981—. Home: 145 Piedmont Ct Los Gatos CA 95030

PETERSEN, VERNON LEROY, engring. corp. exec.; b. Mason, Nev., Nov. 3, 1926; s. Vernon and Lenora Eloise (Dickson) P.; certificate Naval Architecture, U. Calif., 1944, cert. in plant engring., adminstrn. and supervision UCLA, 1977; cert. in real estate exchanging Orange Coast Coll., 1978; children—Anne C., Ruth F. Chief, Philippines Real Estate Office, U.S. C.E., 1950-55; pres., gen. mgr. Mason Merc. Co., 1956-62; pres., gen. mgr. Mason Water Co., 1956-62; pres. Petersen Enterprises, Cons. Engrs., Nev. and Calif., Downey, 1962-79, Vernon L. Peterson, Inc., 1980—; installation mgr. Pacific Architects & Engrs., Los Angeles and Vietnam, 1969-72, facilities engr., ops. supr., acting contract mgr. Los Angeles and Saudi Arabia, 1979-82; bldg. engr. Purex Co., Inc., Lakewood, Calif., 1975-79; lectr. plant engring., various colls. in Calif., 1975—. Candidate for U.S. Congress, 1956, del. Republican state conv., 1960-64. Served with AUS, 1944-47. Fellow Soc. Am. Mil. Engrs. (life mem.; named Orange County Post's Engr. of Year 1977, founder Da Nang Post 1969, Orange County Post 1977, pres. 1978-79, Red Sea Post, Jeddah, Saudi Arabia 1980), Orange County Engr. Council (pres. 1978-79), Am. Inst. Plant Engrs. (chpt. 38 Engring. Merit award 1977-78), Soc. Women Engrs. (assoc.), AIAA. Mormon. Home and Office: 28105 Espinoza Mission Viejo CA 92692

PETERSEN, WILLIAM BERT, optometrist, psychologist; b. Dillon, Mont., Apr. 3, 1940; s. Elmer William and May (Selway) P.; student Western Mont. Coll., 1958-61; B.S., Pacific U., 1963, O.D., 1964; postgrad. Western States Coll., 1963, Pacific U., 1964-65, Creighton U., 1968, Peabody Coll., 1975-77; D.O.S. (hon.), So. Coll. Optometry, 1983. Commd. 2d lt. USAF, 1966, advanced through grades to maj., 1976; resigned, 1980; chief optometrist, Offutt AFB, 1966-70; optometrist, Thailand, 1970-71, Japan, Korea, 1971-73; chief optometrist Bolling AFB, Washington, 1972-74; chief optometrist U-TAPAO RTNB, Thailand, 1974-75, Alconbury RAF, Huntingdon, Eng., 1974-75, Holloman AFB, N.Mex., 1977-80; commd. lt. comdr. USPHS, advanced to capt., 1983, chief optometrist Navajo Area Indian Health Service, Tuba City, Ariz., 1980—; adj. prof. So. Coll. Optometry, Memphis, 1980—, So. Calif. Coll. Optometry, Fullerton, 1980—. Grad. instr. Pacific U., 1964-65. Decorated Air medal, Commendation medal; Vietnam Gallantry Cross. Fellow Am. Optometric Assn., Am. Acad. Optometry, Am. Coll. Optometric Physicians (bd. dirs. 1982—); mem. Armed Forces Optometric Soc., Assn. Mil. Surgeons U.S., Navajo Area Commd. Officers Assn. of USPHS, Navajo Area Commd. Officers Assn., Omega Epsilon Phi. Home: PO Box 2139 Tuba City AZ 86045

PETERSON, B. J., interior designer, educator; b. Portsmouth, Va., Feb. 12, 1943; d. Robert Joe Siegelman and Ethel Mae (Frary) S.; m. John F. Peterson, May 30, 1969, (div.); m. 2d, William R. Rheinschild, April 20, 1978. B.A. in Art History, Calif. State U.-San Diego, 1966. Design asst. Wessie Davis Interiors Co., Coronado, Calif., 1964-64; interior designer V.J. Lloyd Co., San Diego, 1964-66; interior designer Cannell & Chaffin, Los Angeles, 1966—; instr. UCLA. Chmn., Vol. Interior Designers Com. Profl. Women to Support Symphony; sec. Los Angeles Mus. of Art, active Los Angeles county volunteers, past bd. dirs.; active Children's Hosp., Decorative Arts Council of Los Angeles Community Design Center, Big Sisters program. Recipient profl. citation Am. Soc. Interior Designers, 1979, 81. Mem. Am. Soc. Interior Designers (past bd. mem. sec., v.p. Los Angeles chpt.). Contbr. articles in field to publs. Office: 3000 Wilshire Blvd Los Angeles CA 90010

PETERSON, BROCK DUANE, public service administrator, consultant; b. Wichita, Kans., Sept. 5, 1947; s. Darrell Duane and Jean Wasson (Asher) P.; m. Kitth A. Bandanza, Nov. 28, 1972; children—Summer Lynn, John Michael-Winston, Kymberle Michele. A.S., U. Alaska, 1978; B.S. in Bus. Adminstrn., U. Phoenix, 1983. Cert. water/wastewater treatment. Operator, Ariz. Pub. Service, Palo Verde Nuc Generation, Goodyear, Ariz., 1981—; cons. City of Goodyear. Pres. Parent/Tchr. Fellowship; mem. West Valley Assembly of God Ch. Served with U.S. Army, 1967-73. Mem. Am. Water Works Assn., Water Pollution Control Assn. Developer source tests for particulates, EPA, 1977. Home: 1105 N 8th St #12 Avondale AZ 85323

PETERSON, CARL EDWARD, bus. exec.; b. Patterson, Calif., June 21, 1938; s. Fred Carlye and Loudella (Richardson) P.; student Modesto Jr. Coll., 1955-58, Fresno State Coll., 1961; B.S., Humphrey's Coll., 1964; m. Maria Lenna Pirrone, Mar. 28, 1970; children—William Morris, Shelley Gene Boone, Kenneth Edward. Jr. acct. E. & J. Gallo Winery, Modesto, Calif., 1961-64; office mgr., acct. Fairbanks Trucking, Inc., 1964-65; cost acct. E. & J. Gallo Winery, 1965-67; div. controller George Reed, Inc., Modesto, 1967-68; controller Midcal Aluminum, Inc., Modesto, 1968—, United Packaging Co., Modesto, 1969—. Bd. dirs. Gallo Employees Fed. Credit Union, 1975-77. Mem. Sigma Chi. Club: Kiwanis. Home: 3908 Trillium Ave Modesto CA 95356 Office: 500 S Santa Rosa Modesto CA 95353

PETERSON, CRAIG MENZIES, psychologist; b. Pocatello, Idaho, March 20, 1941; s. Earl Thormod and Dorothy Elizabeth (Menzies) P.; m. Carol Ann Augustus, Mar. 20, 1980; 1 son, Craig Christopher. Student, Oreg. State U., Corvallis, 1959-62; B.S., U. Oreg., Eugene, 1964, M.S., 1968, Ph.D., 1971. Lic. psychologist, Oreg., 1977. Instr., Idaho State U., Pocatello, 1967-68; psychology intern VA Hosp., Palo Alto, Calif., 1969-71; clin. child psychologist Lane County Mental Health Clinic, Eugene, Oreg., 1972-73; clin. psychologist Fairview Hosp., Salem, Oreg., 1973-74; sch. psychologist. Vancouver (Wash.) Sch. Dist., 1975—; chmn. symposium Project Normalcy: Programming the Mentally Retarded for Social Integration, Western Psychol. Assn. Conv., 1974. U.S. Govt. Rehab. Services Adminstrn. fellow, 1964-66. Mem. Am. Psychol. Assn., NEA. Club: Mazamas Mountaineering (Portland, Oreg.). Democrat. Methodist. Home: 8901 NE 59th St Vancouver WA 98662 Office: 605 N Devine Rd Vancouver WA 98661

PETERSON, CYNTHIA JANE KITTSON, building materials company executive; b. Prosser, Wash., Nov. 24, 1948; d. Augustan and Myrna Ann (Nickisch) Kittson; A.A. with honors in Bus. Adminstrn., Columbia Basin Coll., 1975; postgrad. Wash. State U., 1975-77, Central Wash. State U., 1976-77; m. George Charles Peterson, Jan. 13, 1968. Receptionist, St. Luke's Hosp., Marquette, Mich., 1969; dep. treas. Kittitas County Treas.'s Office, Ellensburg, Wash., 1971-73; exec. sec. Frank B. Hall Ins. Co., Portland, Oreg., 1973-74; treas./controller Kennewick (Wash.) Indsl. & Elec. Supply, Inc., 1974—. Bd. dirs. Kennewick-Pasco Community Concert Assn., 1976, vol. membership dr., 1975—; exec. bd. Consumer Credit Counselling Service. Recipient Outstanding Leadership award Columbia Basin Coll., 1975. Mem. Soc. Cert. Consumer Credit Execs., Tri-Cities Credit Assn. (dir., pres. 1982-83, gen. conf. chmn. 1982; Credit Individual of Yr. 1982), Wash. State Credit Assn. (dir.), Credit Women-Internat. (pres. Tri-Cities chpt. 1979-80; chpt. Credit Woman of Yr. 1982), Internat. Consumer Credit Assn., Tri-Cities C. of C. (legis. com., dir.). Club: Soroptimist Internat. Home: 4905 W 7th Ave Kennewick WA 99336 Office: 113 E Columbia Dr Kennewick WA 99336

PETERSON, DAVID ALLEN, architect; b. Mpls., Sept. 12, 1941; s. Allen Harold and Glades Lavina Strand P.; m. Gretchen Lynn Ohlsson, Oct. 19, 1963; children—Andrew David, Aaron David, Emily Lynn. A.A., U. Minn., 1963; postgrad. Dunwoody Indsl. Inst., 1964-66. Registered architect, Wash., Minn., Alaska. Store designer Red Owl Stores, Inc., Hopkins, Minn., 1966-68; draftsman, job capt. Mastny Assocs. Architects, Wayzata, Minn., 1968-72; project capt., project mgr. Ellerbe Architects, Inc., Bloomington, Minn., 1972-78; prin. Gabbert Broweleit Peterson Architects, P.S., Seattle, 1978—. Co-pres. Neighborhood Elem. Parent, Tchr. and Student Assn. Served with U.S. Army, 1961-62. Mem. Nat. Council Archtl. Registration Bds., Nat. Assn. Indsl. and Office Parks, AIA, Lake City C. of C. Republican. Mem. Christian and Missionary Alliance Ch. Home: 5413 NE 200th Pl Seattle WA 98155 Office: 11000 Lake City Way NE Seattle WA 98125

PETERSON, DOROTHY FAYE, accountant; b. Lake Preston, S.D., Oct. 29, 1921; d. John Howard and Bertha Faye (Holm) Payne; student Merritt Bus. Coll., 1939; secretarial cert. Healds Bus. Coll., 1944; m. Lennard Martin Peterson, Apr. 15, 1950; children—Cristine Ann, Scott Martin. Analyst, U.S. Govt. Air Transport Command, Alameda, Calif., 1943-47; exec. sec., investigator Montgomery Ward, Oakland, Calif., 1947-50; tax acct. Watkins & Klee, Mendocino, Calif., 1951-61; pvt. practice tax acctg. and enrolled agt., Mendocino, Calif., 1961—. Sec. Mendocino-Little River Cemetery Dist., 1964—; fin. officer Mendocino City Community Services Dist., 1974—; trustee Mendocino Sch. Dist., 1958-61; commr. Mendocino County Civil Service Commn., 1962-65; trustee Mendocino Presbyn. Ch., 1970-74. Mem. Nat. Enrolled Agts. Assn., Nat. Soc. Accts., Calif. Enrolled Agts. Assn., Mendocino Bus. and Profl. Council (treas. 1976-80), Soroptimists Internat. of Ft. Bragg. Democrat. Presbyterian. Home: 41890 Comptche Ukiah Rd Mendocino CA 5460 Office: 10540 Lansing St Mendocino CA 95460

PETERSON, EDWIN CUTHBERT, counselor, educational administrator, adult educator; b. Sault Ste. Marie, Mich., Feb. 11, 1936; s. Edwin B. and Gladys M. (Cuthbert) P. B.S., No. Mich. U., 1958, M.A. in Sch. Adminstrn., 1965; M.S. in Guidance, U. Wis., 1962; cert. in guidance, U. Mass., 1967; cert. in urban affairs, U. So. Calif., 1972, Ed.D. in Supervision Adminstrn., 1977; cert. in resource mgmt., Indsl. Coll. Armed Forces, 1979. Edn. adviser 507th Fighter Wing, Aerospace Def. Command, Kincheloe AFB, Mich., 1958-60, 327th Fighter Wing, Truax Field, Wis., 1961-62; edn. services officer, 410th Bombardment Wing, SAC, K. I. Sawyer AFB, Mich., 1963-65; chief edn. br. 8th AF Hdqrs, Westover AFB, Mass., 1965-67; chief of edn. and tng. div. Aerospace Def. Command Hdqrs., Colorado Springs, Colo., 1967-72; chief of edn. services div., Hdqrs., Pacific Air Forces, Hickam AFB, Hawaii, 1972—. Co-chmn. 1st Community Coll. of the Air Force Adv. Panel, 1977-78; mem. Veteran's Edn. Adv. Council, Chaminade U., Hawaii, 1972-74.

Recipient Disting. Alumni award, No. Mich. U., 1981; Outstanding Service award, Community Coll. of the Air Force, 1979; Career Edn. award U.S. Civil Service Commn., 1971; Outstanding Achievement in Aerospace Edn. award, SAC, 1967, Disting Edn. Achievement award, 1966, Ednl. Achievement award, 1965. Mem. Adult Edn. Assn. U.S.A. (v.p. for programs, 1978-79, Hawaii del. 1975-77, Meritorious Service award 1979), Am. Personnel and Guidance Assn., Hawaii Personnel and Guidance Assn., Phi Delta Kappa. Home: PO Box 592 Honolulu HI 96809 Office: HQ PACAF/DPAE Hickam AFB HI 96853

PETERSON, EDWIN J., chief justice Supreme Ct. Oreg.; b. Gilmanton, Wis., Mar. 30, 1930; s. Edwin A. and Leora Grace (Kitelinger) P.; B.S., U. Oreg., 1951, LL.B., 1957; m. Anna Chadwick, Feb. 7, 1971; children—Patricia, Andrew, Sherry. Admitted to Oreg. bar, 1957; asso. Tooze, Kerr, Peterson, Marshal & Shenker, Portland, Oreg., 1957-61; mem. firm Tooze, Kerr & Peterson, Portland, 1961-77; assoc. justice Supreme Ct. Oreg., Salem, 1979-83, chief justice, 1983—. Chmn. Citizens Sch. Com., Portland, 1968-70; vice chmn. Young Republican Fedn. Oreg., 1951. Served to 1st lt. USAF, 1952-54. Mem. Oreg. State Bar (bd. examiners 1963-66, gov. 1973-76, vice chmn. profl. liability fund 1977-78), Am., Multnomah County (pres. 1972-73) bar assns., Am. Judicature Soc., Council of Bar Pres.'s, Internat. Assn. Ins. Counsel, Phi Alpha Delta, Lambda Chi Alpha. Episcopalian. Club: Kiwanis (pres. 1963). Home: 3365 Sunridge Dr S Salem OR 97302 Office: Supreme Court Salem OR 97310

PETERSON, FRANK TOBIAS, marketing consultant; b. Bklyn., June 4, 1900; s. Peter and Ellen (Weston) P.; B.A., N.Y.U., 1935; m. Marjorie Elizabeth Ross, Feb. 14, 1938. Newspaper reporter Bklyn. Daily Eagle, 1935-36; info. dir. U.S. Resettlement Adminstrn., Berkeley-Calif., 1936-37, promotion dir. San Francisco World's Fair, 1938-39; dep. mayor Los Angeles, 1939-41; exec. dir. Nat. Com. Against Persecution of Jews, Washington, 1941-45; pres. 20th Century Advt. Agy., Los Angeles, 1946-61; realtor Janss Corp., Thousand Oaks, Calif., 1961-67; commr. Oxnard Harbor Dist., Port Hueneme, Calif., 1966-70, pres., 1970-72; mktg. and pub. relations cons. Port of Hueneme, 1972-77; econ. and mktg. cons., Egg City, 1975—; cons. to Asian Village, Los Angeles. Mem. So. Calif. World Trade Center Authority, Los Angeles, 1968-72; bd. dirs. Am. Cancer Assn. Ventura County, 1969-70; trustee, also vice chancellor Union U., Los Angeles, 1979—; cons. Carter/Mondale campaign com., 1976. Mem. Ventura County Humane Soc. (pres. 1969-74). Home: 951 Warwick Ave Thousand Oaks CA 91360 Office: 246 Lombard St Thousand Oaks CA 91360

PETERSON, GEORGE ELLSWORTH, JR., financial exec.; b. Bklyn., Apr. 15, 1937; s. George Ellsworth and Marjorie (Day) P.; A.B., San Francisco State Coll., 1960. Internal auditor, plant controller Crown Zellerbach Corp., San Francisco, Miami, Fla. and Newark, Del., 1963-72; internal auditor, controller, corp. center Planning Research Corp., Los Angeles, 1972-76; controller Casa Blanca Convalescent Homes, San Diego, 1976-78, Medevac Inc., emergency med. services, San Diego, 1978-79; pvt. practice fin. cons., 1979-80; dir. internat. acctg. Welton Becket Assos., Santa Monica, Calif., 1981—. Served with U.S. Army, 1960-62. Mem. Newark C. of C. Episcopalian. Home: 8735 Delgany Ave Apt 315 Playa del Rey CA 90291 Office: 2900 31st St Santa Monica CA 90405

PETERSON, GERALD ELROY, photographer, cinematographer; b. Moroni, Utah, Feb. 11, 1933; s. Charles Elroy and Lela (Nielsen) P.; student U. Utah, 1956-60; m. Patricia Hill, June 26, 1957; children—Keven S., Gerald R., Krystal L., Patricia A., Jennifer L., Cami S., Charles R., Timothy H. Missionary, Ch. Jesus Christ of Latter-day Saints, West Central states, 1954-56, group leader high priest's quorom, 1973—; research technician, sr. photographer, high velocity lab. elec. engring. U. Utah, Salt Lake City, 1956-58; supr. photog. services Utah Research & Devel. Co., Salt Lake City, 1958-64, photog. cons., 1965-69; supr. photog. services Utah Dept. Transp., Salt Lake City, 1964—; cons. photog. facilites Artificial Heart Center, U. Utah Research Park, 1969-70. Served to chief petty officer U.S. Mcht. Marine, 1951-54. Recipient Gov.'s award State of Utah, 1967. Contbr. articles to profl. jours. Home: 3976 S Kewanee Dr Salt Lake City UT 84120 Office: 4501 South 2700 West Salt Lake City UT 84119

PETERSON, GLADE, tenor, opera company director; b. Fairview, Utah, Dec. 17, 1928; s. Golden and Mabel (Mower) P.; m. Mardean Rippon, Dec. 8, 1955; children—Leslie, Kelvin, Michelle. Student U. Utah, 1953; Litt.D. (hon.), So. Utah State Coll., 1978; student Ingenuus Bentzar, Carlos Alexander, Enrico Rosati, Ettore Verna. Debut: Pinkerton in Butterfly, NBC Opera, 1957; debut with Zurich Opera House: Chevalier des Grieux in Manon Lescaut, 1960; deput with Met. Opera, N.Y.C.: Loge in Das Rheingold, 1975; resident mem. Opernhaus Zurich, 1960-75; guest appearances with opera cos. including: Salzburg Fest and Vienna Staatsoper, Austria, Berlin Deutsche Opera, Munich Staatsoper, Stuttgart, W.Ger., La Scala, Milan, Spoleto Fest, Italy, also companies in Belgium, Can., France, Holland, Switzerland; U.S. cos.: Balt., Boston, Dallas, Houston, Phila., Pitts., Portland, San Diego, San Francisco, Santa Fe. Roles include: Don Jose in Carmen, Riccardo in Anna Bolena, Edgardo in Lucia, Faust, Canio in Pagliacci, Turiddu in Cavalleria Rusticana, Ferrando in Cosi fan Tutte, Don Otavio in Don Giovanni, Tamino in Zauberflöte, Prince in Love for Three Oranges, Rodolfo in Boheme, Cavaradossi in Tosca, Riccardo in Ballo in Maschera, Don Carlo, Ernani, Don Alvaro in Forza del Destino, Alfredo in Traviata, Walther in Meistersinger, Loge in Rheingold; also recitalist, guest with symphony orchs.; gen. dir. Utah Opera Co., Salt Lake City, 1976—; tchr., coach music and drama. Served with M.P., U.S. Army, 1951-53. Scholar, Mannes Sch. Music, 1957; Martha Baird Rockefeller Aid to Musicians scholar for study in Italy, 1960. Mem. Am. Guild Musical Artists. Mormon. Office: 50 W Second S Salt Lake City UT 84101

PETERSON, GREGOR GOSS, business executive; b. San Francisco, Sept. 4, 1932; s. Clarence Walter and Lillian Inez (Goss) P.; m. Dion Zaches, Dec. 23, 1954; children—Christopher John, Eric Walter. Student So. Meth. U., 1950-51; A.B. in Social Studies, Stanford U., 1954, M.B.A., 1959. Staff asst. controller dept. FMC Corp., San Jose, Calif., 1959-61; v.p. Sutter Hill Co., Palo Alto, Calif., 1961-66, pres., 1966-70; pres. Genstar Pacific Corp., Palo Alto, 1970-75, 78—; exec. v.p. Genstar Corp.; mem. faculty Stanford Grad. Sch. Bus., 1975-78; dir. 1st Am. Fin. Corp., 1st Am. Title Corp., Hogan Assocs., Inc., numerous Genstar affiliates. Trustee Good Samaritan Hosp., San Jose, 1977-79; bd. dirs. Family Service of Mid-Peninsula, Palo Alto, 1968-71. Served to 1st lt. inf. USMC, 1954-57. Mem. Stanford Bus. Sch. Alumni Assn. (past pres.), Soc. Fellows Aspen Inst. Humanistic Studies, Newcomen Soc. Republican. Home: 1079 Jacobsen Ln Petaluma CA 94952 Office: Four Embarcadero Center San Francisco CA 94111

PETERSON, HAROLD ALBERT, elec. engr.; b. Essex, Iowa, Dec. 28, 1908; s. John Albert and Augusta Matilda (Hultman) P.; B.S.E.E., U. Iowa, 1932, M.S.E.E., 1933; m. Marion Frances Pray, Apr. 7, 1934; children—Joye Frances (dec.), David West, Gilbert Moseley. Elec. engr. Gen. Electric Co., 1934-46; prof. elec. engring. U. Wis., 1946-75, Wis. Utilities prof. elec. power engring., 1967-75, Edward Bennett prof. emeritus, 1975—, chmn. dept. elec. engring., 1947-67; cons. on electric power systems analysis and edn. to industry, colls.; sr. Fulbright lectr. Technische Hochschule, Hannover, W. Ger., 1961; chmn. industry adv. com. on underground power transmission FPC, 1965-66. Recipient Benjamin Smith Reynolds award for outstanding teaching, 1957. Fellow IEEE (life; Edn. Gold medal 1978); mem. Am. Soc. for Engring. Edn. (life), Nat. Soc. Profl. Engrs. (life), ASME, Congress Internat. Grande Reseaux Electriques, Nat. Acad. Engring. Presbyterian. Club: Rotary. Author: Transients in Power Systems, 1951; contbr. numerous articles to profl. jours. Patentee in field. elec. engr.; b. Essex, Iowa, Dec. 28, 1908; s. John Albert and Augusta Matilda (Hultman) P.; B.S.E.E., U. Iowa, 1932, M.S.E.E., 1933; m. Marion Frances Pray, Apr. 7, 1934; children—Joye Frances (dec.), David West, Gilbert Moseley. Elec. engr. Gen. Electric Co., 1934-46; prof. elec. engring. U. Wis., 1946-75, Wis. Utilities prof. elec. power engring., 1967-75, Edward Bennett prof. emeritus, 1975—, chmn. dept. elec. engring., 1947-67; cons. on electric power systems analysis and edn. to industry, colls.; sr. Fulbright lectr. Technische Hochschule, Hannover, W. Ger., 1961; chmn. industry adv. com. on underground power transmission FPC, 1965-66. Recipient Benjamin Smith Reynolds award for outstanding teaching, 1957. Fellow IEEE (life; Edn. Gold medal 1978); mem. Am. Soc. for Engring. Edn. (life), Nat. Soc. Profl. Engrs. (life), ASME, Congress Internat. Grande Reseaux Electriques, Nat. Acad. Engring. Presbyterian. Club: Rotary. Author: Transients in Power Systems, 1951; contbr. numerous articles to profl. jours. Patentee in field. Home and office: 121 Montana Jack Green Valley AZ 85614

PETERSON, HOWARD COOPER, accountant, financial planner; b. Decatur, Ill., Oct. 12, 1939; s. Howard and Lorraine (Cooper) P.; B.S. in Elec. Engring., U. Ill., 1963; M.S., San Diego State Coll., 1967; M.B.A., Columbia U., 1969; J.D., Calif. Western Sch. Law, 1983; postgrad. NYU, 1983—. Elec. engr. Convair div. Gen. Dynamics Corp., San Diego, 1963-67, sr. electronics engr., 1967-68; gen. partner Costumes Characters & Classics Co., San Diego, 1979—; v.p., dir. Equity Programs Corp., San Diego, 1973—; pres., dir. Coastal Properties Trust, San Diego, 1979—; chief fin. officer and dir. Imperial Screens of San Diego, 1977—. C.P.A., Tex.; registered profl. engr., Calif. Mem. Nat. Soc. Public Accts., Internat. Assn. Fin. Planning, Assn. Enrolled Agts. Office: 1335 Hotel Circle S Suite 205 San Diego CA 92108

PETERSON, HOWARD GEORGE FINNEMORE, sports executive; b. Presque Isle, Maine, Mar. 23, 1951; s. George Conrad and Valeda (Finnemore) P. Student New Eng. Conservatory of Music, 1967-68, Andrews U., 1968-71, Orson Welles Film Sch., 1971-72, Loma Linda U., 1972-75. Pres., Nat. Ski Touring Operators Assn., 1977-79; exec. v.p. mktg. U.S. Ski Assn., 1979-81, exec. dir., Colorado Springs, Colo., 1981—; dir. Mountain Rescue Service, Inc. Mem. U.S. Ski Coaches Assn. (dir.), Nat. Ski Touring Operators Assn. (dir.). Author: Cross Country Citizen Racing, 1980; I Hope I Get a Purple Ribbon, 1980; Cross Country Ski Trails, 1979; Cannon: A Climber's Guide, 1972. Office: US Olympic Tng Ctr 1750 E Boulder St Colorado Springs CO 80909

PETERSON, JOSEPH LADD, airline mgr., pilot; b. Deseret, Utah, Oct. 8, 1924; s. Harry Leon and Lucille (Damron) P.; grad. U. Utah, 1950; m. Bette L. Jones, Mar. 16, 1946; children—Terry L., Randall L., Susan M. Capt., Aviateca Airlines, Guatemala, 1947-50, Carco Air Service, Albuquerque, 1950-52; capt. TWA, San Francisco, 1952—, flight mgr., 1967—. Served to lt. col. USAF, 1943-47. Decorated Air medal with cluster. Mem. Airline Pilots Assn. Republican. Presbyterian. Club: Elks. Home: 131 Pepper Ct Los Altos CA 94022 Office: Box 8383 Airport Br San Francisco CA 94128

PETERSON, JUDY DIANE, accountant; b. Tacoma, Wash., Sept. 16, 1942; d. Roger W. and Edna M. (Alexander) Van Buskirk; m. Norman C. Peterson, June 5, 1965; children—Brandon Eric, Lori Anne. B.S., U. Wyo., 1965. C.P.A., Wyo., Colo., Calif. State acct. Bob Kinnison, C.P.A., 1964-65, John Cowan, C.P.A., 1965-67; acct., office mgr. food services U. Wyo., 1967-69; acct. Auxiliary Enterprises U. Wyo., 1969-73; exec. sec. Wyo. Soc. C.P.A.s, 1974-77; pvt. practice acctg., Laramie, Wyo., 1973-79, Niwot, Colo., 1979-81; mng. ptnr. Brolyer, Peterson and Assocs., Laramie, 1978-79; tax acct. Tostevin Accountancy Corp., Monterey, Calif., 1981-82; sr. staff acct. Falge & Yance C.P.A.s, Carmel, Calif., 1982—. Co-founder, v.p. Laramie Estate Planning Council; chmn. Niwot Fund Days races; treas. Harvest Baptist Women's Fellowship. Mem. Am. Inst. C.P.A.s, Wyo. Soc. C.P.A.s, Am. Women's Soc. C.P.A.s. Clubs: Zonta, PEO, Soroptomists (treas.), Bus. and Profl. Women. Home: 23 Caribou Ct Monterey CA 93940 Office: 4th St and Junipero St Carmel CA 93921

PETERSON, KENNETH LESTER, accountant; b. Ida Grove, Iowa, May 8, 1946; s. Harry Lester and Carin P. (Johnson) P.; m. Robin Hipsher, Aug. 7, 1981. B.S. in Acctg., U. Calif.-Long Beach, 1970. C.P.A., Calif. Controller, Standard Communications Corp., Carson, Calif., 1969-72; pvt. practice acctg., Torrance, Calif., 1972—; pres., chief exec. officer PNL Bus. Ventures, Inc., Torrance, 1980—. Recipient Young Businessman award Bank of Am., 1969; Calif. State scholar, 1965-68. Mem. Jaycees (treas., state dir.). Republican. Lutheran. Club: 20-30. Office: 4001 Pacific Coast Hwy Suite 107 Torrance CA 90505

PETERSON, LEWIS, research and devel. engineer; b. San Francisco, July 5, 1937; s. Lathan Whitfield and Elizabeth Dora (Crowley) P.; m. Mildred F. Taylor, Dec. 31, 1957 (div.); children—Lewis James, Jeffrey Lee, Erika Erin; m. 2d, Sharon M. Gustafson, Aug. 24, 1975 (div.); m. 3d, Kathleen J. Safken, Mar. 21, 1980 (div.). B.S. E.E. with honors, Northrup U., 1961; M.B.A., Calif. State U.-Fullerton, 1967; M.S., U. Calif.-Irvine, 1971, Ph.D. in Engring., 1975. Project engr., design engr. Hallicrafters, Santa Ana, Calif., 1961-64; sr. devel. engr. Jet Propulsion Lab., Calif. Inst. Tech., Pasadena, 1964-65; sr. engring. specialist aeronutronics Philco-Ford, Newport Beach, Calif., 1965-68; program dir. The Aerospace Corp., El Segundo, Calif., 1968-77; v.p. engring. Gulton Data Systems, Albuquerque, 1977; mgr. ground electronics TRW, San Bernardino, Calif., 1978—; tchr. engring. courses Calif. Poly., Pomona, Northrup U., U. Calif., Irvine. Served to sgt. USMC, 1954-57. Mem. AIAA, Air Force Assn. Contbr. articles to tech. jours. Home: 2171 Aspenwood Ct San Bernardino CA 92404 Office: PO Box 1310 San Bernardino CA 92402

PETERSON, LOWELL, state senator; b. Pateros, Wash., 1921; m. Ruth Peterson (dec.); children—Lowell O., Cindee, Bart. Oil distbr.; mem. Wash. State Senate. Mem. Concrete (Wash.) city council, 1957-60, mayor, 1960-63. Served with U.S. Navy. Mem. Am. Legion. Clubs: Eagles, Elks. Democrat. Home: Box 249 Concrete WA 98237 Office: Washington State Senate Olympia WA 98504

PETERSON, LOWELL S., state senator, rancher; b. Ogden, Utah, July 20, 1937; s. Rulon P. and Naomi (Skeen) P.; m. Kathleen Shurtleff, 1959; children—Dale Lowell, Laurie, Lisa, Lorna, Douglas Shurtleff, Mary Ann, Emily. B.S., Utah State U., 1961. Pres., Bar 70 Ranches, 1966-69; mng. ptnr. Peterson Bros. Herefords, 1971, Peterson Ranching Co., 1971—, Herefordshire Home Builders, 1977—; mem. Utah Ho. of Reps. from Dist. 50, 1979-80, Utah State Senate, from Dist. 20, 1981—. Pres. Young Republicans; pres. Golden Spike Nat. Livestock Show. Mem. Utah Hereford Assn. (dir.), Phi Kappa Phi, Sigma Alpha Pi, Kappa Alpha. Republican. Mormon. Home: 4538 S 1725 W Roy UT 84067 Office: Utah State Senate Salt Lake City UT 84114

PETERSON, OTIS GRANVILLE, physicist; b. Galesburg, Ill., Nov. 17, 1936; s. Paul Gustav and Elizabeth (Granville) P.; m. Kathleen Gail Moore, Aug. 2, 1975. B.S. in Engring. Physics, U. Ill., 1958, M.S., 1960, Ph.D., 1965. Sr. staff/group leader Eastman Kodak Co., Rochester, N.Y., 1965-73; co-founder, staff scientist laser isotope separation program Lawrence Livermore (Calif.) Nat. Lab., 1973-75; research assoc./mgr. optical products Allied Chem. Corp., Morristown, N.J., 1975-79; assoc. group leader applied photochemistry div. Los Alamos Nat. Lab., 1979—. Recipient IR100 award, 1971, 80. Mem. Am. Phys. Soc., IEEE, Optical Soc. Am., Sigma Xi. Contbr. articles to profl. jours.; inventor in field. Home: 220 Kimberly St Los Alamos NM 87544 Office: Los Alamos Scientific Lab Los Alamos NM 87545

PETERSON, PAMELA JOANNE, counselor; b. Lake City, Minn., June 22, 1946; d. D.L. and Sherry Paulene (Murphy) Mills. B.A. in Sociology, U. Minn., 1972; M.S. in Rehab. Counseling, San Diego State U., 1980. Established Women's Action Service, program for low income young women in San Diego County, San Diego, 1973; established ctr. for low income minority young women, San Diego, 1974; program adminstr. Youth for Progress, San Diego, 1981, exec. dir., 1982—; instr. rehab. counseling San Diego State U.; substance abuse cons.; pvt. practice counseling. Mem. Am. Personnel and Guidance Assn., Am. Rehab. Counselor Assn. Home: 1230 23d St San Diego CA 92102 Office: Youth for Progress 1816 Logan Ave San Diego CA 92113

PETERSON, PEGGY ELIZABETH, ednl. cons.; b. Dayton, Ohio, Sept. 24, 1935; d. Reginald and Ila (Roush-Costello) Curp; B.A. with honors, Ariz. State U., 1968, M.A. with honors, 1969; m. James H. Peterson, Apr. 6, 1974; children—Brownie Kay, Keely Ann, Michael Ray, Ginger Gail, Mathew Todd. Dir., Montessori Schs., 1961-66; tchr., dir. curriculum, project dir. Am. Indian Reservation schs., 1966-72; liaison 7 state edn. tech. space satellite project, dir. early childhood edn., State of Ariz., 1972-74; pres. Expanding Devel., Inc., Evergreen, Colo., 19—; edn. cons. Mem. Nat. Assn. Young Children, Assn. Sch. Curriculum and Devel., NEA, Bus. and Profl. Women Club. Democrat. Roman Catholic. Contbr. articles to profl. jours. Office: PO Box 2226 Evergreen CO 80439

PETERSON, RALPH, motion picture company executive; b. N.Y.C., Jan. 24, 1924; s. James and Mildred (Liebowitz) P.; m. Patricia Bloom, Mar. 18, 1951; children—Jeffrey, Stacey, Beth. B.B.A., CCNY, 1948. C.P.A., N.Y., 1951. Acct., S.D. Leidesdorf, 1948-51; mgr. Peat, Marwick, Mitchell & Co., 1951-67; v.p., treas., dir., exec. com. Warner Bros., Inc., Burbank, Calif., 1967—. Dir. So. Calif. Arthritis Found. Served with U.S. Air Force, 1943-47. Mem. Am. Inst. C.P.A.s, N.Y. State Soc. C.P.A.s.

PETERSON, RAY E., state senator, educator; b. Greeley, Colo.; s. Russell and Daisy Peterson; children—Joni, Roger, Gene. B.S., Colo. State U., 1960, M.Ed., 1966; Ph.D., Ariz. State U., 1975. Extension agt. 4-H program Colo. State U., 1968-73; part owner CARD Corp. (cattle ranch), 1975—; cons. Community Sch. Devel., Colo. Dept. Edn., 1980—; mem. Colo. State Senate, 1982—. Mem. Ptnrs. of Ams., Colo. Assn. Community Educators (past pres.), Pikes Peak Adult Edn. Assn. Office: State Capitol Denver CO 80203*

PETERSON, SUSAN JEANNE, underwriter, educator; b. Sacramento, Aug. 23, 1948; d. Michael Bryte Peterson and Elizabeth Claire (Murray) Berenson. B.A. in English, Dominican Coll. San Rafael, 1972. C.P.C.U. Underwriter trainee Fireman's Fund Ins. Cos., San Rafael, Calif., 1977, underwriter, 1977-79, sr. underwriter, 1979, underwriting program mgmt. analyst, 1979-82, underwriting tech. specialist, 1982—; tchr. evening adult classes Ins. Ednl. Assn.; leader seminars in career evaluation for employees. Mem. adv. com. Dominican Coll. Citizens Ednl. Bd., San Rafael, 1982-83. Recipient Meml. award St. Catherine Marie, 1972. Mem. Soc. C.P.C.U.s, AAUW, Nat. Assn. Ins. Women (Merritt Co. Essay award 1981; Region VIII Speak-Off winner 1982; Rookie of Yr. 1982), Ins. Women Marin (pres. 1983-84). Republican. Roman Catholic. Home: 8140 Sunflower Dr Cotati CA 94928 Office: Fireman's Fund Ins Cos PO Box 777 Novato CA 94998

PETERSON, VANCE TULLIN, university administrator; b. Santa Monica, Calif., Nov. 4, 1944; s. William Tullin and Chanuth Joy (Griggs) P.; m. Anne Rose Breck, Apr. 7, 1968; children—Sara Rose, Theresa Pauline. B.A., Occidental Coll., 1966; M.S., George Washington U., 1971; Ph.D., Stanford U., 1974. Admissions counselor Occidental Coll., 1966-68; instr. Stanford U., 1972-73; researcher Carnegie Commn. Higher Edn., 1972; intern Peralta Colls., 1973-74; asst. prof. U. Toledo, 1974-77; dir. acad. relations U. So. Calif., Los Angeles, 1977-81, exec. dir. univ. relations, 1981-83; dir. devel. ops. UCLA, 1983—. Mem. Pasadena Symphony Men's Com., Town Hall Los Angeles, Episcopal Diocese Los Angeles program group on communications. Served to comdr. USNR, 1968—. Nat. Coll. Athletic Assn. Div. I track and field All American, 1965; recipient USN Am. Spirit award, 1967. Mem. Council Advancement and Support Edn., Pub. Relations Soc. Am., Publicity Club Los Angeles, Union Concerned Scientists. Club: University (Los Angeles). Contbr. articles to profl. jours.

PETERSON, WALTER EDWARD, JR., civil engr.; b. Oak Park, Ill., Aug. 8, 1935; s. Walter Edward and Marjorie Alice (Keiler) P.; B.S., U.S. Coast Guard Acad., 1958; B.C.E., Rensselaer Poly. Inst., 1963; M.S., U. So. Calif. 1974; m. Judith Ann McDowell, Dec. 9, 1961; 1 son, Michael Ross. Commd. ensign U.S. Coast Guard, 1958, advanced through grades to comdr., 1972; deck/naval engring. officer on Northwind, Seattle, 1958-60, naval engring. officer on Wachusett, Seattle, 1960-62, mech./civil engr. 9th Dist. Office, Cleve., 1963-65, indsl. mgr. USCG base, Seattle, 1965-66, mgmt. analyst 13th Dist. Office, Seattle, 1966-67, chief engr. tng. center, Alameda, Calif., 1967-71, fin. mgr. Hdqrs., Washington, 1971-75, chief civil engr., 12th Dist. Office, San Francisco, 1975-78; ret., 1978; now establishing pub. co.; expert witness, cons. in fields of statistics, mgmt. and econ. analysis; lectr. in field. Decorated Coast Guard Commendation medal; recipient Oren medal Nat. award of Soc. Am. Mil. Engrs., 1974. Mem. Internat. Oceanographic Found., Tau Beta Pi, Chi Epsilon, Phi Kappa Phi. Contbr. articles to profl. jours. Home: PO Box 696 Diablo CA 94528

PETERY, MARY ANN BAUER, manufacturing company executive; b. Portland, Oreg., June 1, 1936; d. Walter H. and Ida Mae (Hartzell) Bauer; grad. Smaller Co. Mgmt. Program, Harvard U., 1977; m. Yuergen E. Schuessler, Oct. 18, 1980; children—Melinda, Lorri. Pres., chief exec. officer Selma Pressure Treating Co. Inc. (Calif.); pres. Sierra Constrn. Supply; sec.-treas. Selma Leasing Co. Inc., 1971-77; adv. council SBA; mem. adv. council to chancellor, forest products dept. U. Calif.; mem. Fresno County Pvt. Industry Council; mem. adv. council Sch. Bus., Calif. State U., Fresno; del. White House Conf. Small Bus.; fund agt. Harvard Bus. Sch., 1979, 80, 81. Mem. Calif. Wood Preserving Assn. (past chairperson), Am. Wood Preservers Assn., Western Wood Preservers Inst. (steering com.; past chairperson Calif. group), Am. Wood Preservers Bur. (past bd. govs.), Nat. Assn. Women Bus. Owners, Nat. Small Bus. Assn., Harvard Bus. Sch. Assn., Better Bus. Bur. (dir.), Colonial Dames XVII Century, DAR. Club: Harvard. Office: PO Box 13219 Fresno CA 93795

PETILLON, LEE RITCHEY, lawyer; b. Gary, Ind., May 6, 1929; s. Charles Ernest and Blanche McKay (Egan) P.; m. Mary Anne Keeton, Feb. 20, 1960; children—Andrew G., Joseph R. B.B.A., U. Minn., 1952; LL.B., U. Calif.-Berkeley, 1959. Bar: Calif. 1960. Dep. prosecutor, city atty., San Diego, 1960; dir., v.p., treas., corp. counsel Electronics Capital Corp., San Diego, 1960-67; sec., gen. counsel Republic Tech. Fund, San Diego, 1960-67; dir. venture capital Kleiner-Bell & Co., Inc., Beverly Hills, Calif., 1968-69; v.p. Creative Investment Capital Co., Los Angeles, 1969-70; corp. counsel Harvest Industries, Inc., Los Angeles, 1970-71;

v.p., gen. counsel, dir. Tech. Service Corp., Santa Monica, Calif., 1971-78; individual practice law, Los Angeles, 1978—; co-chmn. Legal Aid Soc. Santa Monica, 1978—; dir. Apollo Lasers, Inc., Los Angeles. Bd. dirs. Greater Watts Econ. Devel. Corp., Los Angeles, 1972-74; active local Cub Scouts Am. Served to 1st lt. USAF, 1952-54. Recipient cert. of appreciation Watts City Demonstration Agy., 1975. Mem. ABA, State Bar Calif., Los Angeles County Bar Assn., Santa Monica Bay Dist. Bar Assn. (trustee 1977—). Unitarian. Contbr. articles to profl. publs., chpt. to book. Home: 1636 Via Machado Palos Verdes Estates CA 90274 Office: 9841 Airport Blvd Suite 1100 Los Angeles CA 90045

PETRACK, KENNETH MICHAEL, public relations executive, consultant, writer, speechwriter; b. Chisholm, Minn., Mar. 24, 1939; s. Michael Frank and Mayme Kathleen (Fink) P. B.A. in English, Duquesne U., 1962, M.A. in Internat. Studies of East Africa, 1965, M.A. in English, 1966. Head pub. relations and internat. performer Duquesne U. Tamburitzans, Pitts., 1957-63, adminstrv. asst., grad. asst. African Inst. Duquesne U., 1962-64, grad. teaching asst. English dept., 1964-66; adminstrv. asst. Aspen (Colo.) Inst. for Humanistic Studies, 1973; chief internal info. 6th U.S. Army, San Francisco, 1974-77, regional pub. affairs coordinator, Western U.S., 1977-83; pres. Freeman, Teilmann & Petrack Assos., Inc., Pub. Relations, San Francisco, 1979—; speechwriter various army gens. Served to capt. U.S. Army, 1966-70. Named to Duquesne U. Hall of Fame, recipient Meritorious Civilian Service award 6th U.S. Army, 1981; Univ. scholar Duquesne U., 1957-66. Mem. Pub. Relations Soc. Am., Bay Area Publicity Club, U.S. Army. Club: Presidio Officers. Office: Office Pub Affairs Sixth US Army San Francisco CA 94129

PETRIE, ALLAN KENDRICK, insurance company executive; b. Buffalo, Mar. 14, 1928; s. William Alexander and Hazel Victoria (Ball) P.; student U. Idaho, 1948-50; M.S. in Program Mgmt., West Coast U., 1978. Vice pres. Western Internat. Ins. Brokers, Newport Beach, Calif., 1979—; dir. Broco, Inc. Served to capt. U.S. Army, 1945-48. Mem. Am. Soc. Safety Engrs., Wine and Food Soc. So. Calif., Lambda Chi Alpha. Contbr. articles to mags. and newspapers. Home: 413 Ave F Redondo Beach CA 90277 Office: 901 Dove St Newport Beach CA 92660

PETRILLA, KENNETH JOSEPH, finance company executive; b. Warren, Ohio, July 17, 1946; s. Joseph George and Jenny (Lachendro) P.; m. Sarah Pennington, Aug. 24, 1974; children—Jennifer Cox, Emily Pennington. B.S., Bowling Green State U., 1968; M.P.A., Golden Gate U., 1973. With Wells Fargo Bank, 1970-81, v.p., mgr. internat. trade fin., San Francisco and Los Angeles, 1978-81; v.p. Phila. Overseas Fin. Co., San Francisco, 1981—; v.p., gen. mgr. First Chgo. Internat.; instr., U. Redlands. Asst. to No. Calif. campaign mgr. for Election of Pete Wilson to U.S. Senate from Calif.; bd. dirs. Cath. Social Services of Marin (Calif.). Mem. Export Mgrs. Assn., World Trade Inst. Republican. Roman Catholic. Clubs: Olympic, Commonwealth. Office: 555 California St San Francisco CA 94104

PETRIS, NICHOLAS C., state senator, lawyer; A.B., U. Calif.-Berkeley; LL.B., Stanford U.; m. Anna S. Vlahos. Mem. Calif. Assembly, 1958-66, Calif. Senate, 1966—. Pres. Redevel. Agy. Oakland, Calif., 1957-58; mem. San Francisco Bay Conservation Study Commn.; mem. Alameda County Council on Social Planning; vice chmn. Calif. Democratic Council, 1955-57; dir. YMCA Youth Legislature; chmn. Oakland Citizens Adv. Com. on Housing; bd. dirs. Jr. Statesman Found.; trustee Patten Bible Coll., Oakland; trustee Anatolia Coll., Thessaloniki, Greece; past pres. Greek Orthodox Ch. of Oakland. Served with U.S. Army, World War II. Decorated comdr. Order of Phoenix (Greece); archon of the Patriarchate, Greek Orthodox Ch., 1982. Democrat. Clubs: Turtles, Masons. Office: 1111 Jackson St Rm 7016 Oakland CA 94607

PETRISH, MARIA, dance instructor; b. Vela Luka, Croatia, Yugoslavia, Aug. 14, 1940; d. Juraj and Marija (Damjanovich) Franulovich; m. Nicholas James Petrish, Oct. 14, 1961; children—Nicholas James III, Michael John. Student U. Wash., 1959-60. Dancer, specializing Croatian dance, 1946—; dir. 2d congl. dist. office State of Wash., 1974-79; founder, dir. Vela Luka Croatian Dance Ensemble, Anacortes, Wash., 1975—; exec. dir. Anacortes C. of C., 1979-82. Founder Wash. Regional Arts Festivals, 1961; founder Anacortes Arts Found., 1967, pres. 1978-81; bd. dirs. Region IV Tourism Bd., bd. Wash. State Alliance Arts, Anacortes Arts/Crafts Found.; candidate for Wash. Ho. of Reps., 1974. Mem. Wash. Assn. C. of C. Execs. Democrat. Roman Catholic. Club: Croatian Fraternal Union Lodge 1121 (pres.). Office: 1319 Commercial Ave Anacortes WA 98221

PETROV, FERDINAND, fine art restorer, art conservation cons.; b. Tapiosuly, Hungary, July 16, 1930; came to Can., 1965, naturalized, 1976; s. Ferdinand and Maria (Dvorak) P.; student interior design U. of Fine Arts, Hungary, 1951-52, U. Winnipeg, Man., Can., 1969-71; Arts D. in Art Restoration History, Acad. of Sci. of Man, Eng., 1978; m. Szilvia Szody, July 4, 1969; children—Ferdinand, Aniko, Zsuzsi. Apprentice cabinet maker, Hungary, 1945-49; various positions in fine furniture mfg., Budapest, Hungary, 1949-52; asst. interior designer Hungarian Govt., 1952-55; draftsman, cabinet maker and free lance restorer, Switzerland, 1957-65; chief conservator restoration dept. Winnipeg (Man.) Art Gallery, Can., 1966-71; free lance restorer dept. public works Province of Man., 1971-73, Winnipeg, 1971-74, Montreal, Que., Can., 1974-75, Ottawa, Ont., Can., 1976-79; fine and decorative arts conservator Canadian Conservation Inst., Ottawa, 1975-76; pres. Petrov Restoration Gallery Ltd., Vancouver, B.C., Can., 1979—; restored numerous murals and panel paintings; guest lectr. on restoration techniques Chem. Inst. Can., 1973, U. Man., 1973, Winnipeg Art Gallery. Mem. Internat. Inst. Conservation, Can. Assn. Profl. Art Conservators, Arbeitsgemeinschaft des Technischen Museumpersonals. Designer, developer various tools and techniques for art restoration; contbr. articles to profl. jours. Home: 2909 Marine Dr West Vancouver BC V7V 1M3 Canada Office: 2448 Marine Dr W Vancouver BC Canada

PETTERSON, LEROY M., dentist; b. Rugby, N.D., Nov. 10, 1931; s. Henry and Elizebeth (Ehnert) P.; m. Janet Kragness, Sept. 13, 1958; children—Tanya, Lisa, Kray. B.A., Augsburg Coll.; D.D.S., U. Minn.; postgrad. Pankey Inst., 1976-80. Gen. practice dentistry, Havre, Mont., 1958—. Mem. ADA, Mont. Dental Assn. Soc. Dentistry for Children. Address: POC Havre MT 59501

PETTIS, SHIRLEY NEIL, former congresswoman; b. Mountain View, Calif.; d. Harold Oliver and Dorothy Susan (O'Neil) McCumber; student Andrews U., 1942, U. Calif., 1943-44; m. 2d, Jerry L. Pettis, Mar. 2, 1947 (dec. Feb. 1975); children—Peter Dwight, Deborah Neil. Mgr., Magnetic Tape Duplicator, Hollywood, Calif., 1953-67, Audio-Digest Found., Los Angeles, 1951-55; sec.-treas. Pettis, Inc., Hollywood, 1958-64; mgr. citrus and avocado ranch, Pauma Valley, Calif., 1950-80; mem. 94th-95th Congresses from 37th Calif. Dist., mem. Internat. Relations Com., Com. on Edn. and Labor; dir. 6 cos. of Kemper Group. Mem. Pres.'s Commn. on Arms Control and Disarmament. Republican. Clubs: Capitol Hill (Washington); Pauma Valley Country.

PETTIT, HENRY JEWETT, JR., editor; b. Olean, N.Y., Dec. 8, 1906; s. Henry Jewett and Anne Benson (Edwards) P.; student Bucknell U., 1924-25; B.A., Cornell U., 1932, Ph.D., 1938; M.A., U. Oreg., 1934; m. Mary Madelyn Mack, July 18, 1927 (dec.); 1 dau., Judith Walsh; m. 2d, Gertrude Stockton Evans, Apr. 9, 1977. Instr. English, U. Tulsa, 1934-36, Cornell U., Ithaca, N.Y., 1936-38, Yale, 1938-39; asst. prof. English, Beloit (Wis.) Coll., 1939-40; asso. prof. English, U. Colo., Boulder, 1940-72, prof. emeritus, 1972—, hon. keeper of rare books Norlim Library, 1950-62; vis. prof. U. Vt., summer 1958. Served with USNR, 1942-45. Recipient U. Colo. Faculty fellowships, 1948, 54, 60, 66, 69; Am. Philos. Soc. grantee, 1960, 66, 69; Am. Council Learned Socs. grantee, 1963. Mem. Modern Humanities Research Assn. (nat. sec. 1958-63), MLA (exec. sec. Rocky Mountain chpt. 1966-70), AAAS, Am. Assn. Advancement of Humanities, Naval Res. Assn., Nat. Ret. Tchrs. Assn. Democrat. Clubs: Town and Gown (Boulder); Univ. (Denver). Author: A Bibliography of Young's Night-Thoughts, 1954; A Collection of English Prose, 1660-1800, 1962; The Correspondence of Edward Young 1683-1765, 1971; Annual Bibliography of English Language and Literature, 1942-52; A Dictionary of Literary Terms, 1951; The Authentic Mother Goose, 1960. Editorial bd. Western Humanities Rev., 1950—, Colo. Quar., 1957-77; English Language Notes, 1963-74. Home: 1333 King Ave Boulder CO 80302

PETTIT, MARGARET ESTA, broadcasting exec.; b. Provo, Utah, July 22, 1926; d. Howard Hammil and Edith Susan (Cummins) Cain; student public schs.; m. Claud Martin Pettit, July 30, 1948; children—Ruth Elaine, Paul Martin. Co-owner, office supr. Sta. KEOS, Flagstaff, Ariz., 1960-61; co-owner, bookkeeper Sta. KWIV, Douglas, Wyo., 1965-74; co-owner, bookkeeper, program dir., office supr. Sta. KCMP, Brush Colo., 1976-81; co-owner Custom Broadcast Service, 1981—; sec.-treas., dir. Ranchland Broadcasting Co., 1975-81; dir., v.p. Better Day, Inc., 1982—. Mem. Model T Ford Club. Baptist. Home and Office: 8320 W 66th Ave Arvada CO 80003

PETTIT, RICHARD GEORGE, computer specialist; b. Tulare, Calif., May 14, 1940; s. Herbert Glen and Ruth Edna (Janes) P.; m. Rosa Maria Perez-Gil, Oct. 10, 1981; children by previous marriage—Jennefer Anne, Jonathan Richard. B.S. in Math., Elec. Engring. and Computer Sci., U. N.Mex., 1971. Asst. dir. computing ops. U. N.Mex., 1971-75; supr. interactive systems programming N.Mex. ADP Div., Santa Fe, 1975-78; mem. systems programming staff Los Alamos Sci. Lab., 1978-80; mem. staff Data Processing and Data Communication Planning Council, Santa Fe, 1980-82; staff programmer IBM, San Jose, Calif., 1982—; cons. in field. Sec. bd. dirs. Unitarian-Universalist Ch. of Santa Fe; bd. dirs., sec./treas. N.Mex. Motorcross Club. Mem. Internat. Word Processing Assn., Data Processing Mgmt. Assn. (dir.), ACM. Republican. Home: PO Box 23876 San Jose CA 95153 Office: 5600 Cottle Rd San Jose CA 95193

PETTIT, THOMAS GUY, marketing company executive; b. Bartlesville, Okla., Aug. 24, 1933; s. Franklin William and Lillian Elizabeth (Guy) P.; m. Lynn Springer, June 27, 1958; children—Sloan Lenox, Jessica Guy. B.A., U. Kans., 1958. Brand mktg. mgr. Proctor & Gamble Co., Cin., 1958-65; dir. advt. pub. relations, licensing Mattel Corp., Hawthorne, Calif., 1969-75; sr. v.p., gen. mgr. SDI Promotion Group, Palm Springs, Calif., 1979—; judge 44th Annual Internat. Broadcasting Award, 1972; cons., lectr. Gifted and Talented Edn. Program, Palm Springs Unified Sch. Dist. Active Am. Youth Soccer Orgn. Served with USN, 1954-56. Mem. Promotion Mktg. Assn. Am., Catalina Island Conservancy, Sigma Chi. Republican. Club: Los Caballeros. Home: 1103 Marion Way Palm Springs CA 92262 Office: SDI Promotion Group 420 S Palm Canyon Suite 205 Palm Springs CA 92262

PETTITE, WILLIAM CLINTON, pub. affairs cons.; b. Reno, Nev.; s. Sidney Clinton and Wilma (Stibal) P.; m. Charlotte Denise Fryer; children—Patrick Keane, William Ellis, Joseph Clinton. Owner, Market Lake Citizen & County Enterprise Newspapers, Roberts, Idaho, 1959-70, pub., 1959-61; publicity dir. Golden Days World Boxing Champs, Reno, 1970; public affairs cons., Fair Oaks, Calif., 1966—. County probate judge, Dubois, Idaho, 1959-61; acting county coroner, Dubois, 1960-61; sec., trustee Fair Oaks Cemetery Dist., 1963-72; dir. Fair Oaks Irrigation Dist., 1964-72, v.p., 1967-68, pres., 1968-70; dir., v.p. San Juan Community Services Dist., 1962-66, 68-72; exec. sec. Calif. Bd. Landscape Architects, 1976-77. Cons. Senate-Assembly Joint Audit Com. Calif. Legislature, 1971-73; exec. officer Occupational Safety and Health Appeals Bd., 1981-82; mem. regulatory rev. commn. Calif. FabricCare Bd., 1981-82; mem. Sacramento County Grand Jury, 1981-82. Election campaign coordinator for E.S. Wright, majority leader Idaho Senate, 1960, Henry Dworshak, U.S. Senator, 1960, Hamer Budge, U.S. Rep., 1960, Charles C. Gossett, former Gov. Idaho, 1959-74; asst. sgt. at arms Rep. Nat. Conv., 1956; chmn. Rep. County Central Com., 1959-61; del. Rep. State Conv., 1960. Chmn. Idaho County Centennial Commn., 1959-61. Recipient Idaho Centennial award, 1968, 69. Mem. Assn. Sacramento County Water Dists. (dir. 1967-72, pres. 1970-72), Nat. Council Juvenile Ct. Judges (com. 1959-61). Author: Memories of Market Lake, Vol. I, 1965; A History of Southeastern Idaho, Vol. II, 1977, Vol. III, 1983; contbr. articles to newspapers, profl. jours. Home: PO Box 2127 Fair Oaks CA 95628 Office: 2631 K St Sacramento CA 95816

PETTY, CLAYTON, anesthesiologist; b. Cedar City, Utah, Aug. 8, 1938; s. Bryant and Estella Petty; M.D., U. Utah, 1965; m. Zoe Leone Palmer, Sept. 5, 1961; children—Mason, Yvonne, Kendall, Valerie, Craig, Ember, Laura. Intern, Tripler Army Hosp., Honolulu; resident in anesthesiology Brooke Army Med. Center, San Antonio, 1966-69; asst. prof. anesthesiology U. Ariz. Med. Sch., Tucson, 1973-75; chief anesthesiologist Dixie Med. Center, St. George, Utah, 1975-81; prof. U. Utah, 1981—. Served with U.S. Army, 1965-73. Diplomate Am. Bd. Anesthesiology. Mem. Am. Soc. Anesthesiologists, AMA, Utah Med. Soc., Utah Soc. Anesthesiologists, Am. Coll. Anesthesiologists. Mormon. Contbr. research articles to med. jours. Home: 2838 Lancaster Dr Salt Lake City UT 84108 Office: Dept Anesthesiology U Utah Sch Medicine Salt Lake City UT 84112

PETTY, MATTIE LOIS, cosmetic company executive; b. Parrish, Ala., Aug. 18, 1947; d. John H. and Mattie W. (McGowan) P. B.A. in English, Clark Coll., 1970; postgrad. U. San Francisco, 1982—. Mktg. mgr., buyer Sears, Roebuck & Co. Chgo., 1970-79; div. sales mgr. Avon Products, Inc., Pasadena, Calif., 1979—. Recipient achievement awards Women in Mgmt. Chgo. chpt. YWCA, 1978, Los Angeles chpt., 1980; achievement award Nat. Assn. for Equal Opportunity in Higher Edn., 1983. Mem. Black Women's Forum, Orgn. Devel. Network. Office: Avon Products Inc 2940 E Foothill Blvd Pasadena CA 91121

PETTY, PATRICIA CURTIS, magazine editor; b. Pueblo, Colo., Sept. 1, 1927; d. Carlton Deloyd and Grace Estelle (Jackisch) Curtis; B.A. in English summa cum laude, Carroll Coll., Helena, Mont., 1975; postgrad. Colo. Sch. Mines, Golden; m. Jack Stanley Petty, Nov. 22, 1962; children—M. Sherrill, Susan P., Curtis R., Craig R. With advt. dept. Helena Ind. Record, 1970-73; advt. dir. McPherson Real Estate, Helena, 1973-75; placement dir. Colo. Sch. Mines Alumni Assn., 1975-77, editor Mines mag., 1977—; leader workshops, cons. in field. Republican precinct committeewoman, 1977-80. Mem. Women in Mining (pres. 1980-81), AIME (Women's aux.), Colo. Mining Assn., Denver Coal Club (bd. dirs. 1980—, chmn. bd. dirs. 1983—), Clear Creek County Metal Miners Assn., Colo. Press Women, Colo. Women Forward. Editor: Metals, 1980; Water in the West, 1981. Home: 559 S Xenon Ct Lakewood CO 80228 Office: Chauvenet Hall Colo Sch Mines Golden CO 80401

PETTY, SHARON ELAINE, accountant, hotel/casino executive; Wichita, Kans., Nov. 13, 1943; d. Eldo Beard and Darleen Fay (Reed) Jardon; m. Douglas LaVell Petty, May 27, 1960; children—Scott, Eric. Student U. Nev.-Las Vegas, 1972. Chief acct. Community Chevrolet, Las Vegas, 1962-64; corp. acct. auto sales and leasing firms, Las Vegas, 1964-73; controller Aladdin Hotel Corp., Las Vegas, 1973-80, Maxim Hotel & Casino, Las Vegas, 1980—; guest lectr., tchr. hotel adminstrn. U. Nev.-Las Vegas; substitute tchr. Golden Gate U., Nellis AFB, Nev. Mem. 2d Amendment Found.; treas., vestry mem. Christ Episcopal Ch., Las Vegas. Recipient Cert. of Achievement, Chrysler Inst., 1969; acctg. honor award, Chrysler Leasing System, 1970, 71, 72. Mem. Internat. Assn. Hospitality Accts. (pres. 1980) Nat. Assn. Female Execs., Nat. Com. on Gaming, Data Processing Mgrs. Assn. Republican. Home: 4725 S Pearl St Las Vegas NV 89121 Office: Maxim Hotel & Casino 160 E Flamingo Rd Las Vegas NV 89109

PETZEL, FLORENCE ELOISE, educator; b. Crosbyton, Tex., Apr. 1, 1911; d. William D. and A. Eloise (Punchard) P.; Ph.B., U. Chgo., 1931, A.M., 1934; Ph.D., U. Minn., 1954. Instr., Judson Coll., 1936-38; vis. instr. Tex. State Coll. for Women, 1937; asst. prof. textiles Ohio State U., 1938-48; asso. prof. U. Ala., 1950-54; prof. Oreg. State U., 1954-61, 67-75, 77, prof. emeritus, 1975—, dept. head. 1954-61, 67-75; prof., div. head U. Tex., 1961-63; prof. Tex. Tech. U., 1963-67; vis. prof. Wash. State U., 1967. Effie I. Raitt fellow, 1949-50. Mem. Sigma Xi, Phi Kappa Phi, Omicron Nu, Iota Sigma Pi, Sigma Delta Epsilon, Am. Assn. Ret. Persons. Author articles in field. Home: 730 NW 35th St Corvallis OR 97330

PEVAR, ALAN MARK, counselor, psychotherapist, educator, consultant; b. Bklyn., Nov. 1, 1950; s. Irving and Florence (Roff) P.; m. Cindy, Jan. 17, 1976. B.A. in Psychology, Richmond Coll., CUNY, 1975; M.A. in Psychology, New Sch. Social Research, 1977. Lic. marriage, family and child counselor; registered hypnotherapist. Counselor, Transitional Services N.Y., Inc., Queens Village, 1977-79; team supr. Builders for Family and Youth, Community Support System, Rockaway, N.Y., 1979-80; client program coordinator, counselor Kern Regional Ctr., Bakersfield, Calif., 1980—; practice marriage, family and child counseling and therapy, Bakersfield, 1981—; instr. psychology Bakersfield Coll., 1981—; cons. and therapist Arthritis Assn. Kern County; expert examiner Bd. Behavioral Sci. Examiners. Mem. Calif. Assn. Marriage and Family Therapists, Am. Personnel and Guidance Assn. Contbr. articles to profl. jours. Home: 3904 Casey Ct Bakersfield CA 93309 Office: 501 40th St Bakersfield CA 93301

PEVERLY, LUCILLE CARLEENE, home economist; b. Joplin, Mo., Jan. 18, 1934; s. James Madison and Dorothy Elizabeth (Mddleton) Harbin; m. William Everette Peverley, Aug. 10, 1951; children—Mark D., Rebecca Owens, Timothy, Elizabeth Huckabone. Student U. Redlands, 1969-70; B.A., San Diego State U., 1979. Tchr., nursery sch. Central Elem. Sch., Imperial Beach, Calif., 1962-66, mgr. sch. cafeteria, 1963-77; instr. recreation Chula Vista (Calif.) Schs., 1971-75; instr. home econs. Montgomery Adult Sch., San Diego, 1974—, Southwestern Jr. Coll., Chula Vista, Calif., 1978—. Mem. Sweetwater Tchrs. Assn., San Diego Food Service Assn., Calif. Sch. Employees Assn. Central PTA (hon.; life). Republican. Baptist. Author: Let's Have A Party, 1979. Home: 972 Harwood St San Diego CA 92154 Office: 3240 Palm Ave San Diego CA 92154

PEW, LAFAYETTE GLEN, electronics company executive, engineer; b. Mesa, Ariz., May 24, 1924; s. Lafayette and Emma Myrle (Horne) P.; B.S., Ariz. State U., 1950; m. Ella Louise Alexander, Jan. 11, 1945; children—Chearn, Kathleen, Bonnie, Stephen, Patricia, John. Owner-mgr., Hobby Shop, Santa Ana, Calif., 1946-47; engr., announcer KARV Radio Broadcasting System, Mesa, 1947-48; lab. instr. dept. engring. Ariz. State U., Tempe, 1948; engr. Sta. KPHO-TV, Phoenix, 1948-50; studio engr. KPIX-TV, San Francisco, 1950-57; designer constructed spl. equipment, 1952-54, studio engr. supr., maintenance engr., 1957; video service engr. Ampex Corp., Redwood City, Calif., 1957, instr., 1957-59, video field engr. (overseas), 1959, video service engr. mgr., Ampex Internat. Ops. (overseas), 1959-61, dept. mgr., Redwood City, 1961-62, coordinator worldwide Ampex depots and inventories, 1962-63; property mgr. Electro Acoustic Co., San Carlos, Calif., property mgr., 1952-70, pres., 1970-83; designed and constructed 1st comml. TV film recorder in San Francisco for Diner Films; spl. equipment VA Hosp., U. Calif. Med. Center, Stanford U.; cons. San Francisco Hearing and Speech Center, 1965—, instr. Stanford U., 1963-67, pres. Hyrum William Pew Family Orgn., 1967-80, Med. Measurements Inc., 1970-71. Mem. Soc. Motion Picture and TV Engrs., Blue Key. Mormon (bishop's counselor 1962-64, 73-80, Stake High Council 1964-73, ordained bishop 1980). Contbr. articles to profl. jours. Home: 1900 Eucalyptus Ave San Carlos CA 94070 Office: 5779 A-2 Winfield Blvd San Jose CA 95123

PFEFFER, J. ALAN, educator; b. Bklyn., June 26, 1907; s. Isaac and Henny (Halpern) P.; A.B. magna cum laude, U. Buffalo, 1935, M.A., 1936; Ph.D., Columbia, 1946; m. Bertha Manoff, Feb. 27, 1938; children—Robert I., JoAnne. Grad. asst. U. Buffalo, 1935-36, instr. German, 1939-46, asst. prof., 1946-48, asso. prof., 1948-49, prof., 1949-62, exec. officer German sect. modern lang. dept., 1952-62; prof. chmn. dept. Germanic langs., lit. U. Pitts., 1962-72, chmn. humanities council, 1968-69, dir. Inst. Basic German, 1960—; instr. German, Buffalo Collegiate Center, 1936-37, Columbia extension div., 1937-39; cons. prof. Stanford U., 1976—; cons. N.D. Lang. Insts.; lectr. various European univs. Recipient Gold medal Goethe Inst. Germany, 1972. Mem. AAUP (local pres.), N.Y. State Conf. U. Profs. (councilor), Am. Assn. Tchrs. German (pres. Western zone), Modern Lang. Assn. (adv. com. Publ. German Tchrs. Guides), N.Y. Fedn. Fgn. Lang. Tchrs. (pres.), Nat. Fedn. Modern Lang. Tchrs. Assn. (chmn. state survey acad. preparation tchrs. modern lang., exec. council, pres.), Delta Phi Alpha (nat. 1st v.p.), Phi Beta Kappa (local pres.). Author, editor: Civil and Military German, 1943; German-English and English-German Dictionary of Everyday Usage, 1947; The Proverb in Goethe, 1948; Essays on German Language and Literature in Honor of Theodore B. Hewitt 1952; Modern German-Civilization, Composition and Conversation, 1953; German Review Grammar, rev. edit., 1969; Basic Spoken German Series: vol. I, Word List, Level I, 1964, vol. II, Index of English Equivalents, Level I, 1965, vol. III, Idiom List, Level I, 1968, vol. IV, Dictionary of Basic (Spoken) German, 1970, vol. V, Word List, Level II, vol. VI, German-English Glossary of 2000 Utility Words, 1974; Basic Spoken German Grammar, 1974; Grunddeutsch: Erabeitung und Wertung dreier deutscher Korpora, 1975; Kontexte, 1976; Probleme der deskriptiven deutschen Grammatik, 1982; Studies in Descriptive German Grammar, 1983. Asst. editor Modern Lang. Jour., 1954-59, mng. editor, 1959-62; asso. editor German Quar., 1958-62; editorial bd. Zielsprache Deutsch, 1970-72. Contbr. articles, revs. to profl. publs. Home: 685 Cowles Rd Santa Barbara CA 93108

PFEIFFER, ROBERT JOHN, business exec.; b. Suva, Fiji Islands, Mar. 7, 1920; s. William Albert and Nina (MacDonald) P.; came to U.S., 1921, naturalized, 1927; grad. high sch., Honolulu, 1937; m. Mary Elizabeth Worts, Nov. 29, 1945; children—Elizabeth Pfeiffer Tumbas, Margaret Pfeiffer Colbrandt, George, Kathleen. With Inter-Island Steam Navigation Co., Ltd., Honolulu (re-organized to Overseas Terminal Ltd. 1950, merged into Oahu Ry. & Land Co. 1954), 1937-55, v.p., gen. mgr., 1950-54, mgr. ship agy. dept. 1954-55; v.p., gen. mgr. Pacific Cut Stone & Granite Co., Inc., Alhambra, Calif., 1955-56; v.p., gen. mgr. Matcinal Corp., Alameda, Calif., 1956-58; mgr. div. Pacific Far East Line, Inc., San Francisco, 1958-60; with Matson Nav. Co., San Francisco, 1960—, v.p., 1966-70, sr. v.p., 1970-71, exec. v.p., 1971-73, pres., 1973-79, chmn. bd., chief exec. officer, 1979—; v.p. The Matson Co., San Francisco, 1968-70, pres., 1970—; v.p., gen. mgr. Matson Terminals, Inc., San Francisco, 1960-62, pres., 1962-70, chmn. bd., 1970-79; chmn. bd.

Matson Services Co., 1973-79, Matson Agys., Inc., 1973-78; sr. v.p. Alexander & Baldwin, Inc., Honolulu, 1973-77, exec. v.p., 1977-79, pres., 1979-80, chmn., pres., chief exec. officer, 1980—, also dir.; dir. Matson Nav. Co., Inc., A&B Properties, Inc., Alexander & Baldwin (Far East) Ltd., Wailea Realty Corp., First Hawaiian, Inc., Hawaiian Western Steel Ltd., A&B Devel. Co., Princess Orchards, Inc., Wailea Land Corp., First Hawaiian Bank, Pacific Resources, Inc., Calif. and Hawaiian Sugar Co., McBryde Sugar Co., others. Past chmn. maritime transp. research bd. Nat. Acad. Sci.; former mem. select com. Am. Mcht. Marine Seamanship Trophy Award; former mem. commn. sociotech. systems NRC; mem. adv. com. Joint Maritime Congress; trustee Bishop Mus., U. Hawaii Found.; mem. adv. bd. Sch. Travel Industry Mgmt. U. Hawaii; bd. dirs. Oahu Devel. Conf.; mem. Army Civilian Adv. Group, Hawaii Stadium Authority, Hawaii Bus. Roundtable, Japan-Hawaii Econ. Council, 200 Club, Hawaii Imin Centennial Corp. Served to lt. USNR, World War II; comdr. Res. ret. Mem. Nat. Assn. Stevedores (past pres.), Internat. Cargo Handling Coordination Assn. (past pres. U.S. nat. com.), Propeller Club U.S. (past pres. Honolulu), Nat. Def. Transp. Assn. (life), Long Beach, Portland, Oakland, Richmond (Calif.), Seattle, Kauai, Los Angeles, San Francisco, Hawaii Island, Hawaii, Maui chambers commerce, Am. Bur. Shipping (bd. mgrs.), Aircraft Owners and Pilots Assn. Republican. Mason (32 deg., Shriner). Clubs: Pacific, Outrigger, Oahu Country (Honolulu); Maui (Hawaii) Country; Pacific Union, Bohemian, World Trade (San Francisco). Home: 535 Miner Rd Orinda CA 94563 Office: 822 Bishop St Honolulu HI 96813

PFISTER, JUDITH IRENE, nurse consultant, operating room nurse; b. Aurora, Ill., May 4, 1940; d. Ralph Edward and Irene P. Diploma, Copley Meml. Hosp., Aurora, 1961; B.S., Aurora Coll., 1971. Lic. R.N., Ill., Calif., Tex., Colo. Staff nurse operating room Copley Meml. Hosp., 1961-63, Hoag Presbyn. Hosp., Newport Beach, Calif., 1962-63; staff nurse, asst. dir. operating room Meth. Hosp., Houston, 1964-79; asst. exec. dir. Assn. Operating Room Nurses, Denver, 1979-80, cons., 1979-80; pres., dir. Edn. Design, Inc., Denver, 1981—; mem. adj. faculty Houston Community Coll., 1974-75. Editor: Laser Newsletter, Laser Network, 1983—; chmn. bd. mem. developer cert. process for operating room nurses, 1978-81. Active Denver Mus. Natural History. Mem. Assn. Operating Room Nurses (local chmn. 1973-78, nat. chmn. 1977-80), Am. Nurses Assn., Colo. Nurses Assn., Sigma Theta Tau. Republican. Contbg. author: Perioperative Nursing, 1983. Office: Education Design Inc 2150 S Belleaire Denver CO 80222

PFLUEGER, JOHN MILTON, architect; b. San Francisco, Aug. 23, 1937; s. Milton Theodore and Genevive (Wendgard) P.; B.S., Stanford, 1959, B.Arch., 1960; m. Lynne Williams, Jan. 23, 1963; children—Peter, John Thomas, Christopher Timothy. Partner-in-charge Pflueger Architects, San Francisco, 1976—; lectr. Urban Life Inst., U. San Francisco, U. Colo., 1978—; campus architect U. San Francisco, Coll. of Holy Names, City Coll. San Francisco. Mem. planning com. San Francisco Downtown Assn., 1971—. Lic. architect, Calif., Nev. Mem. AIA (pub. edn. com. No. Calif. chpt. 1970-79), Constrn. Specifications Inst., Soc. Coll. and Univ. Planning, San Francisco Planning and Urban Renewal, Sierra Club, U.S. C. of C., Audubon Soc., Smithsonian Instn., Calif. Acad. Scis., Soc. Am. Mil. Engrs., Delta Tau Delta. Clubs: Olympic (bldg. com. 1973-78, properties commn. 1979-81), Family (San Francisco). Major works include: Cowell Hall, Calif. Acad. Scis. (Prestress Concrete Inst. award 1969), Creative Arts Extension, City Coll. San Francisco, 1974 (AIA design excellence award 1974), Fish Roundabout, Calif. Acad. Scis., 1976, Natural Energy Office Bldg., 1977 (Honor award State of Calif.), Batmale Hall, City Coll. San Francisco, 1978, Calif. Farm Bur. Fedn., Sacramento, 1980 (Owens Corning and ASHRAE awards), San Jose State U. Library, 1982, Nev. Nat. Bank Hdqrs., Reno, 1982 (ASHRAE award), Performing Arts Ctr. and Fine Arts Mus., Sierra Arts Found., Reno; 8 major bldgs. at Stanford U., including Environ. Safety Facility, 1983; co-generation facility U. San Francisco, 1983; rehabilitator Santa Rosa Ferry Boat and James Licks Bathhouse, 1981; major hosps. include Shriners Hosp. for Crippled Children, Walter Reed Army Med. Ctr. (Pre-Stressed Concrete Inst., Dept. Energy, Dept. Def. design awards 1980). Home: 29 Redwood Dr Ross CA 94957 Office: 165 10th St San Francisco CA 94103

PFNISTER, ALLAN OREL, educator; b. Mason, Ill., July 23, 1925; s. Ardon Orel and Rose Margaret (Sandtner) R.; A.B., Augustana (Ill.) Coll., 1945; M.Div., Augustana Theol. Sem., 1949; M.A., U. Chgo., 1951, Ph.D., 1955; LL.D., U. Denver, 1978; m. Helen Edith Klobes, Dec. 18, 1948; children—Alicia Ann, Jonathan Karl, Susan Elaine. Instr., Augustana Coll., 1943-45, 46-47; instr. philosophy and German, Luther Coll., Nebr., 1949-52; research asst. U. Chgo., 1952-53; dean, prof. Luther Coll., 1953-54; asst. prof. U. Chgo., 1954-58; dir. research Lutheran Ch., Phila., 1958-59; asso. prof. U. Mich., 1959-63; prof. philosophy Wittenberg (Ohio) U., 1963-67, dean, 1963-67; provost, 1967-69, acting pres., 1968-69; prof. higher edn. U. Denver, 1969—, exec. vice chancellor, 1977-78, acting chancellor, 1977-78. Mem. AAAS, Am. Acad. Polit. and Social Sci., Am. Studies Assn., Comparative and Internat. Edn. Soc., Assn. Study of Higher Edn., Am. Assn. Higher Edn., Phi Delta Kappa, Phi Beta Kappa. Democrat. Author: Teaching Adults, 1967; Trends in Higher Education, 1975; Planning for Higher Education, 1975; contbr. chpts. to books, articles to profl. jours. Home: 7231 W Linvale Pl Denver CO 80227 Office: University of Denver Denver CO 80208

PFORZHEIMER, HARRY, III, public financial, government relations consultant; b. Cleve., June 6, 1954; s. Harry and Jean (Barnard) P.; m. Barbara Jean Flaig, June 7, 1975; 1 son, Harry IV. B.S., St. Johns U., 1973. Vice-pres. corp./pub. affairs and adminstrn. Paraho Devel. Corp., Denver, 1977-82; cons. pub., fin. and govt. relations, Denver, 1982—. Mem. Pub. Relations Soc. Am., Colo. Mining Assn., Downtown Devel. Assn. (dir.), Rocky Mountain Oil and Gas Assn., Grand Junction Petroleum Club (dir.). Republican. Roman Catholic. Home and Office: 6220 Hollowview Ct Parker CO 80134

PFORZHEIMER, HARRY, JR., oil co. exec.; b. Manila, Nov. 19, 1915; s. Harry and Mary Ann (Horan) P.; B.S. in Chem. Engring., Purdue U., 1938; postgrad. Case Inst. Tech., Law Sch., George Washington U., Case Western Res. U.; m. Jean Lois Barnard, June 2, 1945; children—Harry, Thomas. With Standard Oil Co. (Ohio), various locations, 1938—, v.p. Sohio Natural Resources Co., 1971—, program dir. paraho oil shale demonstration, Grand Junction, 1974—; pres., chmn. bd., chief exec. officer Paraho Devel. Corp., 1980—; dir. U.S. Bank Grand Junction. Mem. planning adv. bd. St. Mary's Hosp. and Med. Ctr.; bd. dirs. Colo. Sch. Mines Research Inst. Mem. Am. Inst. Chem. Engrs. (chmn. Cleve. 1955), Am. Petroleum Inst., Am. Mining Congress, Colo. Mining Assn., Rocky Mountain Oil and Gas Assn., Denver Petroleum Club, Purdue Alumni Assn., Sigma Alpha Epsilon. Clubs: Army and Navy (Washington); Bookcliff Country. Contbr. articles to tech. and trade jours. Home: 2700 G Rd Grand Junction CO 81501 Office: 300 Enterprise Bldg Grand Junction CO 81501

PFUND, EDWARD THEODORE, JR., electronics co. exec.; b. Methuen, Mass., Dec. 10, 1923; s. Edwrd Theodore and Mary Elizabeth (Banning) P.; B.S. magna cum laude, Tufts Coll., 1950; postgrad U. So. Calif., 1950, Columbia U., 1953, U. Calif., Los Angeles, 1956, 58; m. Marga Emmi Andre, Nov. 10, 1954; children—Angela M., Gloria I., Edward Theodore III. Radio engr., WLAW, Lawrence-Boston, 1942-50; fgn. service staff officer Voice of Am., Tangier, Munich, 1950-54; project. engr. Crusade for Freedom, Munich, Ger., 1955; project mgr., materials specialist United Electrodynamics Inc., Pasadena, Calif., 1956-59; cons. H.I. Thompson Fiber Glass Co., Los Angeles, Andrew Corp., Chgo., 1959, Satellite Broadcast Assocs., Encino, Calif., 1982; teaching staff Pasadena City Coll. (Calif.), 1959; dir. engring., chief engr. Electronics Specialty Co., Los Angeles and Thomaston, Conn., 1959-61; with Hughes Aircraft Co., various locations, 1955, 61—, mgr. Middle East programs, also Latin Am. and African market devel., Los Angeles, 1971—. Served with AUS, 1942-46. Mem. Phi Beta Kappa, Am. Inst. Aeros. and Astronautics, Sigma Pi Sigma. Contbr. articles to profl. jours. Home: 25 Silver Saddle Ln Rolling Hills Estates CA 90274 Office: PO Box 92919 Airport Station Los Angeles CA 90009

PHANDINH, RAPHAEL PAUL, educator, consultant; b. Khanh-Hoa, Vietnam, Apr. 13, 1926; s. Kim Phan and Bup Thi Nguyen. Baccalaureat, Dalat (Vietnam), 1955; Licence-es-Lettres, U. Saigon (Vietnam), 1968; Zeugnis, Goethe-Institut, Saigon, 1974; M.A., Portland State U., 1978, 80; postgrad. U. San Francisco, 1982—. Joined DeLaSalle Christian Bros., Roman Catholic Ch., 1946; tchr. high schs., Vietnam, 1951-55, Cambodia, 1956-59, Mauritius, 1960-63; researcher, Eng. and France, 1964-65; tchr. pvt. high schs., Vietnam, 1965-75; tchr. pvt. high sch., Oreg., 1975-78; tchr. ESL, Portland Community Coll., 1981; adj. faculty San Francisco Theol. Sem., 1981; tchr. communications, reading coordinator Sacred Heart High Sch., San Francisco, 1981—; cons. in field. Mem. N.W. Adult Edn. Assn., Assn. Supervision and Curriculum Devel., Nat. Cath. Edn. Assn.

PHELPS, HARVEY WILLIAM, physician, state senator; b. Pueblo, Colo., June 27, 1922; s. Harvey Jay and Honor Twinet (Wright) P.; B.S., Idaho State Coll., 1946; M.D., St. Louis U., 1949; m. Adah Lucile Godbold, Sept. 1, 1948; children—Castle Wright, Stuart Harvey, Martha Gail. Intern, Brooke Gen. Hosp., Fort Sam Houston, Tex., 1949-50; resident in internal medicine Fitzsimmons Gen. Hosp., Denver, 1951-54; practice medicine specializing in internal medicine, 1954—; commd. 1st lt. U.S. Army, 1949, advanced through grades to lt. col., 1961; chief med. service U.S. Army Hosp., Ft. MacArthur, Calif., 1955-57; asst. chief pulmonary disease service Fitzsimmons Gen. Hosp., Denver, 1958-59; chief dept. medicine U.S. Army Med. Center, Japan, 1959-62; cons. internal medicine to Surgeon, U.S. Army, Japan, 1959-62; cons. pulmonary disease Tri-Service, Japan, 1959-62; chief dept. medicine DeWitt Army Hosp., Fort Belvoir, Va., 1963-65; chief pulmonary disease service Valley Forge Gen. Hosp., Phoenixville, Pa., 1965-66, ret., 1966; dir. inhalation therapy St. Mary-Corwin Hosp. and Parkview Episcopal Hosp., Pueblo, Colo., 1966-78; Pueblo County coroner, 1967-76; cons. disease of the chest Colo. State Hosp., 1966-76; dir. So. Colo. State Coll. asso. degree program in respiratory therapy, 1971—; mem. Colo. State Senate, 1976—. Mem. Colo. State Air Pollution Variance Bd., 1967-76. Recipient James J. Waring award Am. Lung Assn., 1972. Fellow ACP, Am. Coll. Chest Physicians; mem. Colo. State Med. Soc. (del. 1970—, Community Service award 1980), Pueblo County Med. Soc., AMA. Democrat. Methodist. Clubs: Masons, Shriners, Vintage Motor of Am. Contbr. articles on respiratory disease to profl. jours. Home: 2424 N Greenwood St Pueblo CO 81003 Office: Senate Chambers Capitol Bldg Denver CO 80203

PHELPS, WILLIAM CLARENCE, airline sch. pres.; b. Denver, Apr. 19, 1928; s. Clarence Burgess and Altha Mae (Allen) P.; student public schs., Denver; m. Lillie Fern Everly, Nov. 4, 1961; children—Richard William, Janet Lynn Phelps Pettigrew, William Clarence. Pres., founder, pilot instr. Airline Ground Schs., Ltd., Rancho Cordova, Calif., 1967—. Served with USN, 1945-46, USAF, 1950-55. Mem. Nat. Aero. Assn., Aircraft Owners and Pilots Assn., Pilots Internat. Assn. Republican. Mormon. Home: 5721 Jasper Ct Diamond Springs CA 95619 Office: Airline Ground Schools Ltd 11050 Coloma Rd Suite U Rancho Cordova CA 95670

PHILBRICK, RALPH N(OWELL), botanist; b. San Francisco, Jan. 1, 1934; s. Howard R. and Elizabeth (Jauckens) P.; B.A., Pomona Coll., 1956; M.A., UCLA, 1958; Ph.D., Cornell U., 1963; children—Lauren E., Winston H., Edward W. Asso. botany U. Calif., Santa Barbara, 1963-64; biosystematist Santa Barbara Bot. Garden, 1964-73, dir., 1974—, curator herbarium, 1965—; research asso. U. Calif., Santa Barbara, 1964—. Mem. Goleta Valley Gen. Plan Adv. Com., 1972-80, Santa Barbara County Planning Commn., 1981—. Mem. Phi Kappa Phi, Sigma Xi. Office: 1212 Mission Canyon Rd Santa Barbara CA 93105

PHILIPPI, DIETER RUDOLPH, univ. ofcl.; b. Frankfurt, Germany, July 26, 1929; came to U.S., 1956, naturalized, 1961; s. Alfred and Ellen Marguerite (Glatzel) P.; B.B.A., Johann Wolfgang Goethe U., 1952; postgrad. Sorbonne, summers 1951, 52, U. Omaha, U. Tex.; M.B.A., Canadian Inst. Banking, 1953-55; children—Bianca Maria, Christopher Thomas; m. 2d, Helga Abram-Philippi, May 29, 1982; children—Stephan Andreas, Michael Joachim. With Toronto-Dominion Bank, Calgary, Edmonton, Alta., Can., 1953-56; chief accountant Baylor U. Coll. Medicine, Houston, 1956-63; controller Wittenberg U., Springfield, Ohio, 1963-68; bus. mgr. Park Coll., Kansas City, Mo., 1968-70; bus. mgr., treas. Lone Mountain Coll., San Francisco, 1970-75; v.p. bus. affairs Findlay (Ohio) Coll., 1975-76; bus. mgr. Bologna (Italy) Ctr., Johns Hopkins U., 1976-78; dir. bus. and fin. Mt. St. Mary's Coll., Los Angeles, 1978-81; asst. to v.p. overseas programs Boston U., Schwetzingen, W. Ger., 1981—; Lectr., Laurence U., Santa Barbara, Calif., 1973—; fin. cons. various charitable orgns. Pres., German Sch. of East Bay, 1970—; campaign coordinator United Appeals Fund, 1968, recipient Disting. Service award, 1970; active Boy Scouts, Germany, 1948-52, Can., 1952-56, U.S., 1956—, exec. bd. Tecumseh council, 1967—, recipient Silver Beaver award, Wood badge, 1968. Bd. dirs. Bellaire Gen. Hosp., Greenland Hills Sch. Mem. Am. Acctg. Assn., Am., Eastern fin. assns., Am. Mgmt. Assn., Am. Assn. Univ. Adminstrs., Nat., Western assns. coll. and univ. bus. officers, Nat. Assn. Accts., Am. Assn. Higher Edn., Coll. and Univ. Personnel Assn., San Francisco Consortium, Alpha Phi Omega. Clubs: Commonwealth of California (San Francisco); Harbor Heights Country (Punta Gorda, Fla.); Univ. (Kansas City). Office: Boston U Overseas Programs Tompkins Barracks APO New York NY 09081

PHILIPS, DAVID NEWMAN, city official; b. Iowa City, Feb. 4, 1946; s. Everett Allen and Mary Alice (Dorr) P.; m. Susan Carol Miller, Oct. 11, 1945; children—Miriam Chavva, Deborah Birdsall. Student U. Calif.-Irvine, 1972-76. With Twisp (Wash.) Dept. Sewage Treatment, asst. mcpl. supt., 1979—. Sec., treas. Methow Valley Theatre, 1981-82. Served with USMCR, 1966-68. Mem. Am. Water Works Assn., Water Pollution Control Fedn., Pacific N.W. Pollution Control Assn. (sec.-treas. Columbia Basin sect. 1981, pres. 1982). Democrat. Mem. Soc. of Friends. Home: 412 Burgar St Twisp WA 98856 Office: Box 278 Twisp WA 98856

PHILLIPS, ADRAN ABNER, oil company executive, geologist; b. Sugden, Okla., Feb. 6, 1924; s. James M. and Jennie Elizabeth (Norman) P.; m. Carmel Darlene Pesterfield, Aug. 20, 1949; 1 son, John David. B.S. in Geology, U. Okla., 1949. With Exxon Corp. and affiliates, 1949-76, dist. geologist, Chico, Calif., 1959-64, ops. geologist, Sydney, Australia, 1964-67, exploration coordinator North Slope Alaska, Houston, 1968-70, div. geologist, Denver, 1970-71, exploration mgr. P.T. Inc., Stanvac, Jakarta, Indonesia, 1971-73, exploration mgr. ESSO exploration, Singapore, 1973-76; div. mgr. Exxon U.S.A., Denver, 1976-79; v.p. Coors Energy div., Golden, Colo., 1979-80, pres., 1980—. Mem. Am. Assn. Petroleum Geologists, Ind. Petroleum Assn. Mountain States, Ind. Petroleum Assn. Am. (dir.). Office: Coors Energy Co Golden CO 30401

PHILLIPS, ARLENE MARIE, educator; b. Lindsborg, Kans., May 14, 1936; d. Herbert Jeremiah and Florence Eleanor (Swenson) Watts; m. Merle Dena Rolfs, Mar. 25, 1956, (div. 1977); children—Kirk, Scott; m. 2d Jerry Lee Phillips, July 29, 1977. B.S., McPherson Coll., 1959; postgrad. Colo. State U., 1966-67. Tchr. home econs. Alexander ((Kans.) High Sch., 1959-61; adult edn. tchr., Oberlin, Kans., 1964-65; tchr. home econs. Lincoln Jr. High Sch., Ft. Collins, Colo., 1967-68, Blevins Jr. High Sch., Ft. Collins, 1968—; cons. color analysis. Mem. Poudre Edn. Assn., Colo. Edn. Assn., NEA, Alpha Delta Kappa. Baptist. Home: 1933 Oakwood Dr Fort Collins CO 80521 Office: 2101 S Taft Hill Fort Collins CO 80521

PHILLIPS, BARBARA FLORENCE, real estate broker, educator; b. Santa Monica, Calif., Aug. 12, 1921; d. Hans Terkel and Eleanor Margurite (Stratton) Hansen; m. James L. Phillips, Aug. 27, 1949 (dec. June 1958); 1 son by previous marriage, Carl Anthony Smith; 1 dau., Andrea Ynez. Student Pasadena Jr. Coll., 1938-39; tchr. tng. course UCLA; grad. Realtors Inst., 1974. Real estate broker, Temple City, Calif., 1962-64, Incline Village, Nev., 1964-75; real estate broker, co. trainer Baldwin Realty, Arcadia, Calif., 1975-83; sales mgr. Sunset Realtors, Inc., Santa Maria, Calif., 1983—; tchr. real estate Pasadena City Coll., Rio Hondo Coll. Vol. Pasadena Hospice; mem. adv. com. Pasadena City Coll., 1976—, pres., 1981. Named Real Estate Tchr. of Yr., 1981. Mem. Calif. Assn. Realtors, Nat. Assn. Realtors, Real Estate Educators Assn., Calif. Assn. Real Estate Tchrs. (trustee). Republican. Contbr. to Handbook of Real Estate, to be pub. Office: 1660 B S Broadway Santa Maria CA 93454

PHILLIPS, BEVERLY REDDEN, educator; b. Loma Linda, Calif., Oct. 32, 1932; d. Lee Roy and Vera M. (Bruner) Redden; B.A., Pacific Union Coll., 1954; postgrad. U. Alta., (Can.), Edmonton, 1960, 62; M.A., U. Pacific, 1972, Ed.D., 1980; m. Eugene Henry Phillips, Jan. 10, 1957; children—Cheryl, Tom. Tchr. public schs., Edmonton, 1960-61, 62-63; tchr. public schs., Stockton, Calif., 1965-68, 69-80. math/curriculum specialist, 1980—; speaker ednl. confs., seminars. Bd. dirs. Stockton Seventh-day Adventist Elem. Sch., 1969-72; trustee Lodi (Calif.) Acad., 1979—. Mem. Assn. Supervision and Curriculum Devel., Calif. Ednl. Research Assn., Phi Delta Kappa. Home: 320 Los Felis Stockton CA 95210 Office: 1838 W Rose Stockton CA 95204

PHILLIPS, CECIL LARRY, accountant; b. Waco, Tex., June 20, 1947; s. Cecil A. and Wilma L. (McCollum) P.; m. Mary Lynn Zigel, Nov. 13, 1971; children—Gretchyn J., Robert Scott. Student U. Okla.-Norman, 1970-71; B.B.A., Baylor U., 1972. C.P.A., Tex., N.Mex., Ariz. Tax specialist Peat Marwick Mitchell & Co., Albuquerque, 1972-74; controller Invesco, El Paso, Tex., 1975-78; mgr. Moody, Kubiak & Nation, Albuquerque, 1979, ptnr., San Diego, 1980-82, mng. ptnr., Phoenix, 1982—. Mem. Grand Canyon Nat. Park Airport Devel. Selection Com. Served with U.S. Army, 1968-70. Decorated Purple Heart. Mem. Am. Inst. C.P.A.s, Tex. Soc. C.P.A.s, N.Mex. Soc. C.P.A.s, Calif. Soc. C.P.A.s, Ariz. Tax Inst., Ariz. Estate Planning Council, Phoenix Met. C. of C. Republican. Baptist. Lodge: Kiwanis. Office: 4041 N Central St Suite 645 Phoenix AZ 85012

PHILLIPS, D. HOWARD, research electronics electrical engineer; b. Paris, Tex., Sept. 9, 1940; s. Howard and Bess (Touchstone) P.; B.S. in Elec. Engring., Okla. State U., 1963; M.Nuclear Engring., U. Okla., 1966; Ph.D. in Elec. Engring. with honors, U. Mex., 1972. Radio announcer Sta. KOSU-FM, 1962-63; instr. radioisotopes tech. U. Okla., 1962-63; sr. research engr. Rockwell Internat., Anaheim, Calif., 1962-69, cons. resident engring. rep., Kirtland AFB, 1969-72, engring. cons., Albuquerque, 1969-72, mem. sr. tech. staff Electronics Research div., Anaheim, 1972-73, program mgr., 1973-75; communications cons. Sta. KSPI, 1962; tech. cons. components group Texas Instruments, Inc., Dallas, 1970; radiation effects tech. cons. Physics Internat. Co., S.W. Region Office, Albuquerque, 1970, San Leandro, Calif., 1971; cons. to Dept. Def., Air Force Weapons Lab., Kirtland AFB, 1971-72; mgr. research Lockheed Microelectronics Center, Sunnyvale, Calif., 1977-80; dir. electronics research Aerospace Corp., Los Angeles, 1980—; instr. Sch. Police Sci., John F. Kennedy U., 1974. Registered profl. engr., Okla., N.Mex., Calif. Mem. IEEE (tech. symposium chmn. 1979, 80, 81), Electrochem. Soc., Am. Nuclear Soc. (v.p. 1962-63), Nat. Soc. Profl. Engrs., Calif. Soc. Profl. Engrs., Okla. Soc. Profl. Engrs., Am. Radio Relay League, Nat. Mgmt. Assn., Phi Kappa Phi, Sigma Tau. Club: Engineers. Mem. editorial bd. Mil. Electronics, 1979-83, Microwave Systems News, 1982—; tech. editor Def. Systems Rev.; contbr. numerous articles on microelectronic tech. and engring. to profl. jours.; research in gallium arsenide and silicon devices. Office: Electronics Research Lab Bldg A6-1489 M2 238 Aerospace Corp PO Box 92957 Los Angeles CA 90009

PHILLIPS, DAVID POKRAS, sociologist, educator; b. Capetown, South Africa, Aug. 14, 1943; s. Harry Tarley and Eva Juliet (Salber) P.; children—Rachel, Miranda. B.A., Harvard U., 1964; Ph.D., Princeton U., 1970. Asst. prof. Sociology SUNY-Stony Brook, 1970-74; mem. faculty U. Calif.-San Diego, 1974—, assoc. prof. sociology, 1975—; cons. in field. Mem. Am. Assn. Suicidology (Shneidman award 1983), Population Assn. Am., Am. Sociol. Assn. Office: Univ Calif San Diego Sociology Dept La Jolla CA 92093

PHILLIPS, DEBORAH LEE, nurse; b. East Liverpool, Ohio, June 10, 1950; d. Thomas Eugene and Phyllis (Bair) P.; R.N., Presbyterian U. Hosp. Sch. Nursing, Pitts., 1971; cardiovascular nurse specialist cert. Tex. Heart Inst., 1976. Public health nurse trainee Allegheny County (Pa.) Health Dept., 1972; staff nurse coronary care unit U. Calif. at San Diego Hosp., 1972-73; staff nurse intensive care unit Stanford U. Hosp., Palo Alto, Calif., 1973-76; clin. supr. critical care St. Luke's Hosp., San Francisco, 1976-79, cardiovascular nurse cons., 1979—, instr. continuing edn. in nursing, 1976—; nurse Valley Meml. Hosp., Livermore, Calif., 1982—; rehab. nurse Berkeley Cardiac Rehab. Program, 1980—. Cert. Nat. Bd. Critical Care. Mem. Nat. Critical Care Inst., Am. Heart Assn., Am. Assn. Critical Care Nurses, Calif. Soc. Cardiac Rehab. Democrat. Club: Job's Daus. Home: 4095 Suffolk Way Pleasanton CA 94566 Office: 1111 E Stanley Blvd Livermore CA 94550

PHILLIPS, ELBERT LEE, personnel administrator; b. San Diego, May 11, 1938; s. Aaron Elbert and Winona Catherine (Ward) P.; m. Charlotte Katherine Currierr, Feb. 20, 1962 (dec.); m. 2d Rose Marie Martain, July 3, 1967; children—Michael Joseph, Shannon Sue. B.A. in Psychology, San Diego State Coll., 1961. Asst. personnel mgr. State Farm Ins., Santa Ana, Calif., 1965-72; personnel rep. Royal Industries, Santa Ana, 1972-77; dir. personnel Altec Corp., Anaheim, Calif., 1977-81; mgr. personnel adminstrn. Del Mar Avionics, Irving, Calif., 1981—. Served with U.S. Army, 1961-64. Mem. Am. Soc. Personnel Adminstrn. Republican. Episcopalian. Office: 1601 Alton Ave Irvine CA 92714

PHILLIPS, JAMES HUBER, airline pilot; b. Portland, Oreg., Oct. 28, 1938; s. Huber W. and Olive Letha (Updike) P.; B.S., Oreg. State U., 1960; children—Ronald Trevor, Michael John. Pilot, Continental Airlines, Los Angeles, 1970—; pres. E&J Corp., Stateline, Nev., 1979—. Served with USAF, 1960-69; lt. col. Calif. Air N.G., 1970—. Decorated D.F.C., Air medals. Mem. Airline Pilots Assn., N.G. Assn. U.S. Home: 241 Rees St Playa del Ray CA 90291

PHILLIPS, JOHN P(AUL), physician; b. Danville, Ark., Oct. 14, 1932; s. Brewer William Ashley and Wave Audrey (Page) P.; A.B. cum laude, Hendrix Coll., 1953; M.D., U. Tenn., 1956; m. June Helen Dunbar, Dec. 14, 1963; children—Todd Eustace, Timothy John Colin, Tyler William Ashley. Intern, Charity Hosp. La., New Orleans, 1957; resident in surgery U. Tenn. Hosps., 1958; resident in neurol. surgery U. Tenn. Med. Units, 1958-62; practice medicine, specializing in neurol. surgery, Salinas, Calif., 1962—; chief of staff Salinas Valley Meml. Hosp.; mem. staffs Community Hosp. Monterey Peninsula, U. Calif. Hosp., San Francisco; asst. clin. prof. U. Calif., 1962—. Commd. Ky. col. Diplomate Am. Bd. Neurol. Surgeons. Mem. ACS, Internat. Coll. Surgery, Harvey Cushing Soc., Congress Neurol. Surgery, Western Neurosurg. Assn., AMA, San Francisco Neurol. Soc., Pan Pacific Surg. Assn., Alpha Omega Alpha, Phi Chi, Alpha Chi. Home: 6 Mesa del Sol Salinas CA 93901 Office: 220 San Jose St Salinas CA 93901

PHILLIPS, KAY RANDELLE, association executive; b. St. Louis, Nov. 13, 1947; d. Clyde Randol and Esther (Moore) P.; m. Murvel D. Pretorius, Aug. 17, 1968; 1 dau., Jennifer Marie; m. 2d, A. Fred Timmerman, Apr. 1, 1980. Student Knox Coll., 1966-68; B.A. in Sociology, U. Ill., 1971; M.A. in Pub. Adminstrn., Sangamon State U., 1978. Juvenile probation officer, program coordinator DRI-Roads Program, Peoria County (Ill.), 1971-76; sales rep. Xerox Corp., Peoria, 1976; personnel coordinator, staff devel. and tng. mgr. Methodist Med. Ctr., Peoria, 1977; adminstrv. asst. Lutheran Med. Ctr., Wheat Ridge, Colo., 1978; assoc. dir. planning Swedish Med. Ctr., Englewood, Colo., 1979; v.p. planning, mktg. and pub. affairs Colo. Hosp. Assn., Denver, 1980—; cons. in field. Bd. dirs. Parent Tchr. League, University Hills Luth. Sch., 1982-83; fund raiser United Way; Mem. Am. Coll. Hosp. Adminstrs., Colo. Code of Cooperation (sec.), Pub. Relations Soc. Am., Am. Soc. Hosp. Pub. Relations, Colo. Soc. Hosp. Pub. Relations, Soc. for Hosp. Planning. Republican. Presbyterian. Office: 2140 S Holly Denver CO 80222

PHILLIPS, LOIS GAIL, exotic bird breeder; b. Detroit, June 21, 1939; d. John Patrick and Leona Victoria (Wagner) P.; B.S. in Chemistry, Fresno (Calif.) State Coll., 1962. Radiol. chemist Nat. Canners Assn., Berkeley, Calif., 1963-64; tchr. Progress Sch., Long Beach, Calif., 1966-67; vol. Peace Corps tchr., Nepal, 1967-69; univ. extension tchr. Nepal tng. programs, Davis, Calif., 1969-71; nursery employee Valley Gardens, Woodland, Calif., 1971-74, Farrell's Garden Center, Sonoma, Calif., 1974-75; mgr. 7-Eleven Store, Petaluma, Calif., 1977—; owner Bodega Birds. Bd. dirs. Sonoma County People Econ. Opportunity, 1978—, sec. to bd., 1978-79. Mem. ACLU, Am. Fedn. Aviculture, Nat. Audubon Soc., Sierra Club. Home: 1821 Lakeville St Apt 2 Petaluma CA 94952 Office: 860 Perry Ln Petaluma CA 94952

PHILLIPS, MIMI KOUMRIAN, public relations consultant, freelance writer; b. Los Angeles, Apr. 28, 1918; d. Harold H. and Grace (Irwin) Koumrian; m. Donald Eugene Phillips, May 27, 1950; 1 dau., Donna Kathleen. B.A., UCLA, 1939. Writer, account exec. direct mail advtg. Burroughs, Inc., Los Angeles, 1946-50; self-employed freelance writer, pub. relations cons., Santa Monica, Calif., 1950—. Bd. dirs. Children's Village USA, 1969-70. Served to lt. USNR, 1944-53. Mem. Women in Communications, Direct Mktg. Club So. Calif., Am. Soc. Interior Designers (press assoc.), Internat. Assn. Interior Designers (press Assoc.), UCLA Alumni Assn. (editor UCLA mag.). Democrat. Club: South Coast Corinthian Yacht (Marina del Rey); UCLA Gold Shield (past pres.). Contbr. articles to gen. mags. and trade jours. Office: 1535 6th St Suite 209 Santa Monica CA 90401

PHILLIPS, ROSEMARY, retail merchant; b. Montevallo, Ala., Dec. 7, 1946; d. Paul Haywood and Helen N. (Davis) Wooley; m. C.J. Phillips, Apr. 15, 1972. B.S., U. Montevallo, 1962; M.S., N.Mex. State U., 1969. VISTA vol. Elim, Alaska, 1968; counselor William E. Beltz Dormitory, Nome, Alaska, 1970-73; owner retail businesses, fisheries, Nome, 1972—; adv. bd. Alaska Airlines, Alaska Nat. Bank. Apptd. mem. Iditarod Trail Mgmt. Bd., Coastal Zone Mgmt. Bd.; mem. Nome City Council, 1978-82; chmn. Month Iditarod, 1973-82; bd. dirs. Alaska Visitors Assn., 1977-82; exec. bd. Iditarod Sled-Dog Race. Mem. Nome Bar Owners Assn. (past pres.), Nome C. of C. (bd. dirs. 1979-81, pres. 1977-82). Clubs: Pioneers of Alaska, Nome Kennel (past pres.), Igloo No. 1. Home and Office: PO Box 370 Nome Alaska 99762 also Pouch X Wasilla AK 99687

PHILLIPS, TED RAY, advertising agency executive; b. American Falls, Idaho, Oct. 27, 1948; s. Virn E. and Jessie N. (Aldous) P.; m. Dianne Jacqulynne Walker, May 28, 1971; children—Scott, Russell, Stephen. B.A., Brigham Young U., 1972, M.A., 1974. Account exec. David W. Evans, Inc., Salt Lake City, 1972-75; dir. advt. Div. Continuing Edn., U. Salt Lake City, 1975-78; sr. v.p. Evans/Lowe & Stevens, Inc., Atlanta, 1978, exec. v.p., 1979; pres., chief exec. officer David W. Evans/Atlanta, Inc., 1979-80; dir. advt. O.C. Tanner Co., Salt Lake City, 1980-82; pres. Thomas/Phillips/Clawson, Inc., Salt Lake City, 1982—; advt. instr. div. continuing edn. Brigham Young U., 1983. Dir. publicity, promotion Western States Republican Con., 1976. Mem. Am. Advt. Fedn. (7 Best-in-the-West awards, 2 nat. Addy awards), Utah Advt. Fedn. (v.p., pres. elect). Mormon. Home: 1094 E Gravel Hills Dr Sandy UT 84070 Office: Thomas/Phillips/Clawson Inc 375 W 200 S Suite 200 Salt Lake City UT 84101

PHILLIPS, TEDDY STEVE, conductor, saxaphone player, prodn. co. exec.; b. Chgo., June 15, 1917; s. Steve and Kaliope P.; student U. Ill., 1935-39; children—Jody, Teddy. Saxaphone player with big bands, across country, 1940-45; staff musician Radio Sta. CBS, Chgo., 1944-45; condr. Teddy Phillips Orch., across country, 1945-55, 1957-62; prin. Teddy Phillips Show, Sta. WBKB-TV-ABC, Chgo., 1956-57; condr. Tedd Phillips and Orch., Ambassador Hotel, Los Angeles and Flamingo Hotel, Las Vegas, Nev., 1962-80, Statler Hotels, Aragon Ballroom, Chgo., Hilton Hotels, Chgo.; dir. Guy Lombardo Orch. and Royal Conadians, 1980—; pres. P&M Prodns., Woodland Hills, Calif., 1976—; TV producer Great Concert in the Sky; record producer; writer Do the Camel Hump?, Wishin, Do the Camel Hump. Served with U.S. Army, 1940-41. Mem. Musicians Union. Greek Orthodox. Club: Masons. Rec. artist. Home and Office: 6252 1/2 Nita Ave Woodland Hills CA 91367

PHILLIPS, TERRY OKEN, business counselor; b. Portland, Oreg., Feb. 25, 1948; s. Ray I. and Dorothy Louise (Hurst) P.; A.A., Portland Community Coll., 1972; B.A., Portland State U., 1975; m. Becky Anne Connors, Dec. 21, 1979; children—Mike, Kim, Kate, Ryan. Grad. teaching asst. communications dept. Portland State U., 1975-76; dir. property mgmt. LanduraCorp., Woodburn, Oreg., 1976-79; property mgr. Property Mgmt. Services, Inc., Vancouver, Wash., 1979-80; dir. comml. dept. Property Mgmt. Services Comml., Vancouver, 1980-82; prin. Hart, Schaeffer & Phillips, 1982—; tchr. property mgmt. seminars Served with U.S. Army, 1967-70; Vietnam. Decorated Bronze Star with oak leaf cluster. Cert. mgr. Nat. Center Housing Mgmt.; cert. bus. counselor; cert. bus. appraiser. Mem. Vancouver C. of C., Inst. Real Estate Mgmt., Nat. Assn. Realtors. Author: Property Management Policies, 1980 (Inst. Real Estate Mgmt. 1st Pl. Nat. award). Home: 208 Tucson Way Vancouver WA 98661 Office: 500 Main St Vancouver WA 98660

PHILLIPS, WILLIAM AMBROSE, financial consulting company executive; b. Indpls., July 24, 1933; s. Earl Edward and Grace Lucile (Burgett) P.; B.S., Ball State U., 1957; M.A., Ind. State U., 1969; Ed.D., Oreg. State U., 1973; m. Janet E. Quade, Sept. 2, 1977; children by previous marriage—Kathryn L., William Ambrose, Michael E.; 1 adopted son, Reynaldo. Salesman B/L div. Prentice-Hall, Inc., 1957-58; asst. buyer L.S. Ayres & Co., Indpls., 1958-60; store mgr. Top Value Enterprises, Inc., 1960-62; store supr. E.F. MacDonald Stamp Co., Chgo., 1962-63; dist. sales mgr. Investors Diversified, Ft. Wayne, Ind., 1963-66; mut. fund mgr. Patterson Securities, Ft. Wayne, 1966-67; distributive edn. tchr., coordinator, Ft. Wayne, 1967-70; asst. prin., instrn. Career Opportunities Center, Saginaw, Mich., 1973-75; cons. ednl. adminstrn. and vocat. edn. seminars, dir. mgmt. devel. Coll. Bus. Adminstrn., No. Ariz. U., Flagstaff, 1975-81; now pres. Phillips, Prickett, Quadz, Inc. dba Bus. Data Solutions. No. Ariz. chmn. Coconino County Career and Vocat. Edn. Adv. Council, 1978—; mem. Indsl. Devel. Adv. Council of Flagstaff, 1980—, now v.p. Served with AUS, 1951-53. EPDA-Office of Edn. grantee, 1970. Mem. Ariz. Adult Vocat. Assn. (pres. 1980-81), Am. Soc. Tng. and Devel. (pres. Ariz. chpt. 1982—), Am. Mgmt. Assn., Am. Entrepreneur Assn., Am. Vocat. Assn., Flagstaff C. of C. (bd. dirs. 1982—), Phi Delta Kappa. Author: (with others) Orientation to Supervisory Roles and Responsibilities. Home: 801 W University Heights Dr S Flagstaff AZ 86001 Office: Ariz Bank Bldg Suite 201 Flagstaff AZ 86001

PHILLIPS, WILLIAM HIGBIE, management consultant; b. Newark, Nov. 3, 1936; s. William Lewis and Mary (Higbie) P.; grad. Hotchkiss Sch., 1955, B.A., Haverford Coll., 1963; Ph.D., LaJolla U., 1981; m. Susan Coejmans Hindle, Dec. 27, 1957 (div. 1979); children—Laura Phillips, Katharine Phillips; m. 2d Karen Glansberg, Sept. 12, 1982. Dir. sci. Shady Hill Sch., Cambridge, Mass., 1964-69; founder dir. Habitat Sch., Belmont, Mass., 1969-74; assoc. Liberty St. Assocs., Danvers, 1974-75; assoc. dir. New Eng. La Ger-Mgmt. Ctr., Boston, 1976-78; v.p., sr. assoc., dir. World-Wide cert. tng. for Adizes method Adizes Inst., San Diego, 1979—; chief instr. Northeast Outward Bound Sch., 1967; co-leader, various mountaineering expdns., N.Am. Andean Relief Expdn., Peru, 1971, others. Served with AUS, 1957-60. Recipient 1st hon. degree Nat. Outdoor Leadership Sch., 1968. Mem. Am. Alpine Club, Sierra Club. Author: Guide to Outdoor Education in New England, 1976. Office: 2001 Wilshire Blvd Santa Monica CA

PHILLIPS, WILMA FRANCES, sch. psychologist; b. St. Louis, May 2, 1927; d. Albert James and Anna Viola (Worstell) Fox; B.S. with highest honors, U. So. Miss., 1963; M.A.E., Ball State U., Muncie, Ind., 1972, Ed.D. (doctoral fellow), 1975; postdoctoral student U. Calif., Irvine and Loma Linda U., Riverside, Calif.; m. Doyle C. Phillips, Feb. 11, 1946; children—Lyndon C., Devaron Phillips Otis, Clayton C. Classroom tchr. Richmond (Ind.) Community Schs., 1969-73; asso. prof. curriculum instrn. Loma Linda U., 1975-80; sch. psychologist Moreno Valley Sch. Dist., Sunnymead, Calif., 1980—; chmn. liaison com. early childhood edn. Calif. Articulation Conf.; rep. task force on spl. edn. Gen. Conf. Seventh-day Adventist Pvt. Sch. System; chmn. early childhood edn. nat. com. Gen. Conf. Seventh-day Adventists. Cert. tchr., adminstr., spl. edn. tchr., reading specialist, early childhood edn. specialist, pupil personnel services, sch. psychologist, Calif. Mem. Council Exceptional Children, Internat. Reading Soc., Nat. Assn. Edn. of Young Children, Calif. Profs. Early Childhood Edn., Orgn. Mondiale pour l'Education, Prescolaire World Orgn. for Early Childhood Edn., Pi Lambda Theta, Phi Delta Kappa, Kappa Delta Phi. Republican. Cons. The Ladder of Life: Early Childhood Edn. Series, 1977—. Home: 5440 College Ave Riverside CA 92505 Office: 13911 Perris Blvd Sunnymead CA 92388

PHILLIPS-JONES, LINDA, research scientist; b. South Bend, Ind., Mar. 3, 1943; d. Robert M. and Priscilla A. (Tancy) Phillips; m. G. Brian Jones, Feb. 16, 1980; stepchildren—Laurie, Tracy. B.S., U. Nev., 1964; M.A., Stanford U., 1965; Ph.D., UCLA, 1977. Tng. Cons. Internat. Tng. Cons. and Edn. Cons., Saigon, Vietnam, 1966-71; research scientist Am. Inst. Research, Palo Alto, Calif., 1979—; mgmt./career devel. cons. Los Angeles and Los Gatos, Calif. Bd. dirs. Indochinese Resettlement Cultural Ctr., San Jose, Calif.; mem. Nat. Speakers Team, Palo Alto. Decorated Vietnam Civilian Labor medal; UCLA Leadership Devel. fellow, 1972-74. Mem. Am. Psychol. Assn., Am. Personnel and Guidance Assn., Am. Soc. Tng. and Devel., Nat. Vocat. Guidance Assn. Author: Mentors and Proteges, 1982. Office: PO Box 1113 Palo Alto CA 91303

PHIPPS, PAUL D. M., II, sports management executive; b. Lynwood, Calif., Jan. 6, 1947; s. Paul D. H. and Betty Alexandra (Rolfe) P.; m. Kathleen Louise, Aug. 6, 1966; children—Michele, Josel, Danielle, Jonathan. Student, Calif. Luth. Coll., 1964-66, Calif. State U.-Los Angeles, 1966-68, U. So. Calif., 1972. Managerial policy inst. cert., 1972. Fin. mgr. Coca Cola, Los Angeles, 1970-75; gen. mgr. beverage bus., 1975-76; gen. mgr. Athletes in Action Basketball, TV and radio, 1977-79; v.p. bus. ops. Dallas Mavericks, 1980-82; exec. v.p., gen. mgr. San Diego Clippers, 1982—. Bd. dirs. San Diego council Boy Scouts Am., Greater San Diego Sports Assn. Republican. Baptist. Office: 3500 Sports Arena Blvd San Diego CA 92110

PHITAKSPHRAIWAN, PHUANGNOI, child neurologist; b. Trang, Thailand, Sept. 19, 1927; d. Phra and Amphorn P.; came to U.S., 1962; M.D., Siriraj Med. Sch., Bangkok, Thailand, 1951; m. Wisutr Yontwises, Dec. 27, 1966. Intern, Siriraj Hosp., Bangkok, 1951-52; resident in pediatrics St. Louis Children's Hosp., 1955-56, Driscoll Found. Children's Hosp., Corpus Christi, Tex., 1962-63; mem. pediatric staff Children's Hosp., Bangkok, Thailand, 1956-62; fellow in neonatology Baylor U. Med. Coll., Houston, 1963-64, in pediatric neurology U. Okla. Med. Center, Oklahoma City, 1964-65; resident in neurology U. Miss. Med. Center, Jackson, 1967-68; staff physician, cons. neurologist Denton (Tex.) State Sch., 1969-74; instr. pediatrics U. Tex. Health Scis. Center, Dallas, 1975-76, asst. prof., 1976-80 pediatric dir. univ. affiliated facility, 1976-80; staff Lanterman State Hosp., Pomona, Calif., 1980—, cons. pediatric neurology, 1981—; cons. pediatric neurologist Ft. Worth State Sch., 1978-79. Fulbright scholar, 1954-55. Mem. Am. Acad. Neurology (asso.), Am. Assn. Mental Deficiency. Home: 23819 Country View Dr Diamond Bar CA 91765 Office: 3530 W Pomona Blvd Pomona CA 91786

PIAGET, GERALD WARREN, psychologist; b. Paterson, N.J., Nov. 10, 1942; s. Warren Edward and Grace Fitzgerald P.: B.S., Lehigh U., 1964; Ph.D., U. Mass., 1968. Staff psychologist Santa Clara County (Calif.) Mental Health Services, 1968-78; exec. dir. Inst. Advancement Human Behavior, Inc., Portola Valley, Calif., 1977—; clin. asst. prof. Stanford U. Sch. Medicine, Palo Alto, Calif., 1975—; practice medicine specializing in psychology, Portola Valley, 1970—. Mem. Am. Psychol. Assn., Am. Orthopsychiat. Assn., Assn. Advancement Behavior Therapy. Home: 430 Minoca St Portola Valley CA 94025 Office: 4370 Alpine Rd 205 Portola Valley CA 94025

PIANTADOSI, JEANETTE KEMCHICK, educational consultant; b. Point Pleasant, N.J., Sept. 2, 1954; d. Patrick John and Gloria E. (Stensland) Kemchick; m. Roger Anthony Piantadosi, Aug. 4, 1975; m. William J. Collard, Mar. 12, 1982. B.A. in Sociology magna cum laude, Am. U., 1977, M.Ed. in Student Devel., 1979; postgrad. Va. Poly. Inst. and State U., 1980, George Washington U., 1981, computer tng. courses UCLA Extension, 1983. Dir. fin. aid Am. U., Washington, 1977-81; legis. aide to Rep. Patricia Schroeder, Charles Revson fellow, Washington, 1981-82; dir. fed. and state relations Systems Research Inc., Washington, 1981—; v.p. mktg. Sigma Systems Inc., Los Angeles, 1982—; lectr., cons. various colls. and univs.; campus coordinator Project CHOICE. Gen. univ. scholar, 1975-76; Mathas scholar, 1975-76; recipient Meritorious Service award Am. U., 1977, 80. Mem. Del., D.C., Md. Assn. Student Fin. Aid Adminstrs. (sec. 1981-82), N.E. Assn. Student Employment Adminstrs. (D.C. rep. to exec. bd. 1978-81, pres. 1980-81), Eastern Assn. Student Fin. Aid Adminstrs. (ex-officio exec. council 1980-81), Nat. Assn. Women Deans, Adminstrs. and Counselors, Liaison for Fedn. of Orgns. of Profl. Women, AAUW, NOW, Phi Theta Kappa, Phi Kappa Phi. Democrat. Roman Catholic. Office: 1508 Cotner Ave Los Angeles CA 90025

PIATKOWSKI, FRANK JULIAN, architect; b. Flint, Mich., June 27, 1944; s. Stephan Leonard and Felice Marie P.; B.Arch., U. Mich., 1969, M.Arch., 1970; m. Eliza I. Wojtaszek, Nov. 27, 1969. Intern architect Architonics, Jackson, Mich., 1970-74; architect Kramer Chin & Mayo, Inc., Seattle, 1975-79; mgr. Alaska ops., Anchorage, 1979—. Bd. dirs. Skid Road Theater, 1978-79. Mem. AIA, Constrn. Specification Inst., Alaska State C. of C., Anchorage C. of C., Juneau C. of C., Alaska Mcpl. League, Nat. Trust Hist. Preservation. Home: 1016 Potlatch Circle Anchorage AK 99503 Office: 1113 W Fireweed Ln #101 Anchorage AK 99503

PIATT, LARRY LEON, genealogist, genealogy company executive; b. Oklahoma City, May 5, 1938; s. Leon Lafayette and Hazel Frances (Hile) P.; B.S., Okla. U., 1960, M.S., 1962; postgrad. 1963-64; postgrad. Ind. U., 1962-63; B.S., Brigham Young U., 1973; m. Dolly Sue (Worthington) Yorgason, June 6, 1980; 1 dau., Emily Dawn; stepchildren—John Gary Yorgason, Shauna Marie Yorgason, Justin Dale Yorgason. Geologist, Texaco Inc., Oklahoma City, 1964-68, Tulsa, 1968-71; genealogist Inst. Family Research, Inc., Salt Lake City, 1973-82, sec., treas. 1975-78, gen. mgr., 1979—, pres., 1980-81, also dir.; trustee Who Am I Library. Mem. Nat. Geneal. Soc. (life), Utah Geneal. Assn., Assn. Profl. Genealogists, New Eng. Hist. Geneal. Soc., Va. Hist. Soc., U. Okla. Assn. (life), Sigma Xi, Sigma Gamma Epsilon, Utah Soc. SAR (sec.-treas. 1976-80, 2d v.p. 1980, 1st v.p. 1981, pres. 1982, nat. trustee 1983), Salt Lake Chpt. SAR (sec.-treas. 1977-78, pres. 1978-79). Republican. Mormon. Home: 5539 Capitol Reef Dr Salt Lake City UT 84118

PICARD, JEAN-JACQUES, banker; b. France; m. Marie-Therese Cazenave; children—Anne, Emmanuel, Etienne. M.Econs., U. Paris I, 1969; grad. Inst. Polit. Scis., Paris, 1970. With Banque Nationale de Paris, 1972—, various managerial positions, Paris, 1972-79, dep. gen. mgr. B.N.P. (Suisse) SA, Basel, Switzerland, 1979-82, sr. v.p., gen. mgr., B.N.P., San Francisco, 1982—; dir. Bank of the West. Mem. French-Am. C. of C. (dir.), Assn. Corp. Growth, Calif. Bankers Assn., Calif. Council Internat. Trade, Alliance Française, World Affairs Council. Club: Cercle de l'Union. Home: 930 Vista Rd Hillsborough CA 94010 Office: 180 Montgomery St San Francisco CA 94104

PICK, JAMES BLOCK, research statistician; b. Chgo., July 29, 1943; s. Grant Julius and Helen (Block) P.; B.A., Northwestern U., 1966; M.S. in Edn., No. Ill. U., 1969; Ph.D., U. Calif., Irvine, 1974, C.D.P., 1980. Asst. research statistician, lectr. Grad. Sch. Mgmt. U. Calif., Riverside, 1975—; lectr. program in social ecology U. Calif., Irvine, 1976, 77; lectr. dept. sociology U. Calif.-Riverside, 1979, 80; cons. U.S. Census Bur. Internat. Div., 1978. Trustee Newport Harbor Art Mus., 1980—, treas. acquisitions council, 1979-81, chmn., 1982-83. Mem. Assn. Computing Machinery, Assn. Systems Mgmt. (profl., pres. Orange County chpt. 1978-79, sec.-treas. Div. 22 regional council 1979-80, vice chmn. 1980-81, chmn. 1981-82), AAAS, Am. Statis. Assn., Population Assn. Am., Internat. Union for Sci. Study of Population, History of Sci. Soc., Am. Inst. Biol. Sci. Clubs: Balboa Bay (Newport Beach); Standard (Chgo.). Author: (with Edgar W. Butler) Geothermal Energy Development: Problems and Prospects in the Imperial Valley, California, 1981, 82; condr. research in computer simulation and graphics, natural resource studies, population analysis; contbr. sci. articles to publs. in field. Home: 321 Poinsettia Ave Corona del Mar CA 92625 Office: Grad Sch Mgmt U Calif Riverside CA 92521

PICK, JANE, psychologist; b. Los Angeles, July 21, 1951; d. Patrick Thomas and Agnes Lucille (Riley) P., Ph.D., U.S. Internat. U., San Diego, 1979; m. Richard Alan Resnick, June 9, 1973. Pvt. practice psychology Thatcher Med. Ctr., Pasadena, Calif., 1979-82, Brentwood Med. Plaza, West Los Angeles, Calif., 1980—. Mem. Am. Psychol. Assn. Home: 1044 10th St Santa Monica CA 90403 Office: Brentwood Med Plaza 11900 San Vicente St West Los Angeles CA 90049

PICKARD, BRIAN ALAN, lawyer; b. London, Ont., Can., June 10, 1952; came to U.S., 1975; s. Harold Alan and Pearl Victoria (Pudney) P.; B.A., U. Western Ont., 1974; M.A.M., Embry-Riddle Aero. U., 1977; J.D., Western State U., 1980. Bar: Calif. 1981. With Pearpic Mgmt. Corp., London, Ont., 1973-75; pvt. practice law, Fullerton, Calif., 1981—; mgmt. cons. Pearpic Mgmt. Corp., 1977—. Recipient Nat. Pilots Assn. Flight award, 1979; Am. Jurisprudence award, 1979; award for best advocate in trial practice West Pub. Co., 1980. Mem. Calif. Trial Lawyers Assn., Orange County Trial Lawyers Assn., Assn. Trial Lawyers Am., Internat. Platform Assn., Alpha Eta Rho (v.p.). Republican. Club: Aviation Facilities Flying. Contbr. articles to profl. jours. Home: 1907 Deer Park Dr Fullerton CA 92631 Office: 17291 Irvine Blvd Suite 252 Tustin CA 92680

PICKARD, DAVID JANARD, endowment fund exec.; b. Colorado Springs, Colo., Nov. 23, 1933; s. Kenneth Leonard and Ann Ruth (Wemyss) P.; A.B., U. Nebr., 1956; student Berkeley Div. Sch., Yale, 1956-58; children—Laurel Jane, John Mark. Exec. v.p. Tri State Supply, Inc., Scottsbluff, Nebr., 1958-73, Tri State Supply of Sidney, Inc. (Nebr.), 1959-73, v.p. Tri State of Alliance, Inc. (Nebr.), 1965-73, pres. Tri State of Wyoming, Inc., Torrington, 1967-73, exec. v.p. Tri State Warehousing, Inc., Scottsbluff, 1965-73; commr., asst. treas. Kappa Sigma Endowment Fund, Denver, 1973—, also dir. devel. Named Adm., Nebr. State Navy. Mem. SAR, Colo. Yale Assn. Republican. Episcopalian. Clubs: Univ. (Lincoln, Nebr.); Masons. Home: 2035 Oriole Ave Colorado Springs CO 80909 Office: PO Box 7715 Colorado Springs CO 80933

PICKENS, ALEXANDER LEGRAND, art educator; b. Waco, Tex., Aug. 31, 1921; s. Alex LeGrand and Elma L. (Johnson) P.; m. Frances M. Jenkins, Aug. 20, 1955. B.A., So. Meth. U., 1950; M.A., N. Tex. State U., 1952; Ed.D., Columbia U., 1959. Tchr. art Dallas Pub. Schs., 1950-53, Elizabeth, N.J., 1953-54; faculty art dept. U. Mich. Coll. Architecture and Design, Ann Arbor, 1954-59; asso. prof. dept. art U. Ga., Athens, 1959-62; asso. prof. U. Hawaii Coll. Edn., Honolulu, 1962-68, prof. edn., 1968—; dir. children's classes Ft. Worth Children's Mus., 1951-53; head art Nat. Music Camp, Interlochen, Mich., summers 1957-58, Portland (Oreg.) State Coll., summers 1959-60, 62; cons. United World Films, Honolulu Paper Co.; ednl. cons. Kamehamcha Schs. Research Inst.; exhibited ceramics at Wichita Internat. Exhbn., Syracuse Nat. Exhbn., St. Louis Mus., Dallas Mus., San Antonio Mus., Detroit Inst. Art, others. Mem. adult com. Dallas County chpt. Jr. ARC, 1951-53; mem. exec. com. Dallas Crafts Guild, 1950-53; v.p., publicity chmn. Univ. Community Concert Assn., 1960-62; adviser Foremost Dairies Youth Art Activities, 1964—. Served with USAAF, 1942-44. Recipient award of merit Tex. State Fair, 1957. Mem. Internat. Soc. for Edn. through Art, Nat. Com. on Art Edn., NEA, Nat. Art Edn. Assn. (past mem. publs. com.), AAUP, Phi Delta Kappa, Kappa Delta Pi. Editorial bd. Arts and Activities Mag., 1955-81; editor U. Hawaii Ednl. Perspectives, 1964—. Contbr. articles to profl. publs. Home: 1471 Kalaepohaku St Honolulu HI 96816

PICKENS, ALLEN ARTHUR, accountant; b. Des Moines, Iowa, Nov. 29, 1940; s. Leo Arthur and Odessa Leona (Sly) P.; m. Dianne Patricia

Guelff, Feb. 15, 1969; children—Shawn, Courtney, Megan. B.S. in Bus. Adminstrn., Drake U., 1965. C.P.A., Hawaii, Guam. Acct. Peat, Marwick, Internat., Agana, Guam, 1965—, ptnr. in charge Guam office, Agana, 1975—; instr. U. Guam, Am. Inst. Banking. Chmn. Territorial Bd. Pub. Accountancy, 1970-78; pres. Guam Growth Council, 1978-83; pres. USO, 1976-77; pres. Guam Soc. Cultural Exchange, 1979-80. Served with USAF, 1958-62. Named Guam Person of Yr. 1979, Rotary Club of Tumon Bay. Mem. Am. Inst. C.P.A.s, Guam Soc. C.P.A.s (founder, pres. 1973-75), Assn. Govt. Accts., Am. Acctg. Assn., Navy League U.S. (pres. Guam 1978-79), Air Force Assn. (pres. Guam chpt. 1982-83), Guam C. of C. (chmn. 1982-83). Roman Catholic. Clubs: Rotary (Guam) (pres. 1975-76, 80-81).

PICKENS, ROBERT LEE, insurance company executive; b. Casper, Wyo., May 25, 1938; s. William Lee and Mary Eileen P.; B.A., U. Calif., Santa Barbara, 1966; M.B.A., U. Calif., Berkeley, 1972; m. Arlene C. Acuna, Dec. 10, 1977; children—Daniel Lee, Derek Lee, Carol Eileen. Agt., Met. Life Ins. Co., Fullerton, Calif., 1973-74, sales mgr., San Bernardino, Calif., 1975-77; advanced life cons. Gallop & Price, Inc., Los Angeles, 1977; dir. advanced life mktg. Cal-Farm Life Ins. Co., Sacramento, 1978-83; dir. mktg. services Phila. Life Ins. Co., San Francisco, 1983—. Served with USAF, 1957-62. C.L.U.; chartered fin. cons. Mem. Gen. Agts. and Mgrs. Assn., Am. Soc. C.L.U.s, Nat. Assn. Life Underwriters, Sacramento Assn. Life Underwriters (dir.). Author articles in field. Office: 1700 Montgomery St San Francisco CA 94111

PICKETT, MARGARET ANNE, educational adminstrator; b. Banning, Calif., May 9, 1924; d. Charles Sheldon and Mary Edith (Mack) H.; m. Ralph D. Pickett, Dec. 25, 1952; children—Mary Anne, Margaret E. B.A., U. Redlands, 1947, M.A., 1969. Dir. Head Start, Banning, Calif., 1966-68; tchr. kindergarten Beaumont (Calif.) Unified Sch. Dist., 1968-70, dir. spl. projects/elem. prin., 1973-80, dir. spl. projects, curriculum, spl. edn., 1980—; adviser Beaumont Presch., Am. Field Service, 1978—. Mem. Assn. Supervision and Curriculum Devel., Assn. Woman Mgrs., Nat. Assn. Adminstrs. State and Federally Funded Edn. Programs, Assn. Calif. Sch. Adminstrs., Delta Kappa Gamma. Republican. Religious Scientist. Office: PO Box 187 Beaumont CA 92223

PICKETT, RICHARD PHILLIP, technical support official; b. Tonawanda, N.Y., Aug. 8, 1949; s. Frank B. and Helen M. P.; B.B.A. in Mktg. and Speech, Central State U. Okla., 1973, M.Ed. in Bus., 1978; m. Cheryl K. Oliver, Jan. 14, 1976; 1 dau., Charlotte. Prodn. asst. Custom Wood of Oklahoma City, 1975-77, Woodworker of Denver, 1977-78; tech. supr. seven state Rocky Mountain Region, Haworth Mountain West Inc., Denver, 1978—; instr. mktg. jr. coll., 1977-78; cons. to non-profit orgns. Tech. Assistance Ctr.; guest lectr. bus. ethics. Active Ellis PTA and Phillips PTA. Served with USMC, 1967-69. Mem. Am. Mgmt. Assn., Kappa Delta Phi. Republican. Home: 1859 Niagra Denver CO 80220 Office: 5350 S Roslyn St Englewood CO 80111

PICKRELL, JACK EVON, acct.; b. Ottumwa, Iowa, Apr. 15, 1933; s. Robert Lee, Jr., and Emily Margaret (Merrill) P.; student Georgetown U., 1955-56, State U. Iowa, 1956, U. Md., 1957-58; B.S. in Acctg., Met. State Coll., Denver, 1980; m. Reiko Washizu, Feb. 6, 1959; 1 dau., Linda Reiko. Enlisted in U.S. Navy, 1950; served with USN, 1950-54, USAR, 1954-56, USNR, 1956-57, USAF, 1957-73, master sgt., 1968-73; ret., 1973; ops. mgr. Diamond Gas & Fuel Co., Englewood, Colo., 1973-76; office mgr. Alpine Pipe & Supply Co., Denver, also self-employed public acct., Denver, 1977—. Decorated Bronze Star, Air Force Commendation medal with three oak leaf clusters. Mem. U.S. Naval Cryptologic Vets. Assn. (treas.), Nat. Soc. Public Accts., Public Accts. Soc. Colo., Better Bus. Bur. Greater Denver, Colo. Geneal. Soc. (publs. dir.). Republican. Home: 3065 Olive St Denver CO 80207 Office: 4876 Leaf Ct Denver CO 80216

PICUS, GERALD SHERMAN, physicist; b. Madison, Wis., Jan. 9, 1926; s. Max and Mildred P.; B.S., U. Chgo., 1947, M.S., 1949, Ph.D., 1954; m. Joy Newberger, Mar. 9, 1952; children—Larry, Mark, Emily. With Hughes Aircraft Co., 1960—, mgr. chem. physics dept., research labs., Malibu, Calif., 1968-82, dir. tech. edn. ctr., 1982—; with U.S. Naval Research Lab., 1954-59; vis. prof. Calif. Inst. Tech., 1976-77. Served with USN, 1944-46. Mem. Am. Phys. Soc., IEEE, AAAS. Home: 22545 Marylee St Woodland Hills CA 91367 Office: 3011 Malibu Canyon Rd Malibu CA 90265

PIECZENTKOWSKI, HERMAN ARNOLD, ret. naval officer, engring. and constrn. co. exec.; b. Auburn, R.I., May 28, 1907; s. Albert George and Hulda (Sealander) P.; B.S., U.S. Naval Acad., 1930; M.S., MIT, 1940; postgrad. U.S. Naval War Coll., 1949-50; m. Helen Van Horn Herron, June 2, 1934; children—Peter Arnold, Marshall Albert. Commd. ensign USN, 1930, advanced through grades to rear adm., 1957; dir. torpedo research U.S. Naval Torpedo Sta., Newport, R.I., 1943-45; head ordnance dept. Naval Postgrad. Sch., 1950-52; comdg. officer USS Sturgeon, comdr. Sub Div. 72, Submarine Squadron 5; comdg. officer USS Hamul, comdr. Destroyer Squadron II, 1955-57, ret., 1957; staff asst. to v.p., mgr. bus. devel. Bechtel Power Corp., San Francisco, 1957-75; bus. cons., 1975-79. Decorated Silver Star, Bronze Star. Mem. U.S. Naval Acad., Mass. Inst. Tech. alumni assns., Submarine Vets World War II. Home: 716 Jacinto Pl Coronado CA 92118

PIEKARZ, ROBERT WALTER, minerals and environmental engineer; b. Chicopee, Mass., Mar. 30, 1935; s. Walter Robert and Adele Sophie (Szczur) P.; student Colo. Sch. Mines, 1952-54; B.S. in Mining Engring., Mo. Sch. Mines and Metallurgy, 1961, M.S., 1962; m. Dorothy J. McGlamery, June 6, 1961; children—Michael, Robert, Christopher. Asso. mining engr., mining engr. Armour Agrl. Chem. Co., Bartow, Fla., 1962-64; project engr., plant engr., mine mgr., chief engr., mgr. engring. and environ. affairs, v.p. engring. Eagle-Picher Industries, Reno, 1964—; guest lectr. U. Nev., Reno; cons. in field. Mem. Washoe County Water Well Hearing Bd. Served with USN; Korea. Registered profl. engr., Ill., Kans., Mo., Nev., Okla., Wis., Oreg., Calif. Mem. Nat. Soc. Profl. Engrs., Nev. Soc. Profl. Engrs., Soc. Mining Engrs. of AIME (indsl. minerals div.), Nev. Mining Assn. (chmn. environ. com., ad hoc com. on health and environ.), Am. Mining Congress, Nat. Council Engring. Examiners (profl. engrs. adv. com.), Sigma Xi, Sigma Gamma Epsilon. Republican. Roman Catholic. Home: 1425 Joshua Dr Reno NV 89509 Office: Suite 155 1755 E Plumb Ln Reno NV 89510

PIEPER, ORVILLE ELDEN, agri-business coordinator, farmer; b. Yuma, Colo., July 12, 1930; s. Ervin William and May Caroline (Imhof) P.; m. Bernice Ethel Bryant, July 24, 1955; children—Kathleen Kim Pieper Trum, Todd Bryant. B.S., U. Denver, 1959, M.A., 1963. Cert. in vocat. agr. State Bd. Community Colls. and Occupational Edn. Wheat, millet farmer, 1948-51, 54—; ins. agt. Farmers Union, 1954-63; tchr. bus. edn. Englewood (Colo.) High Sch., 1959-61; instr. bus. Northeastern Jr. Coll., Sterling, Colo., 1963-66; agri-bus. coordinator, 1966—. Served with U.S. Army, 1952-53. Mem. Colo. Vocat. Agr. Tchrs. Assn., Nat. Vocat. Agr. Tchrs. Assn., Colo. Vocat. Assn., Nat. Vocat. Assn., Colo. Edn. Assn., NEA, Nat. Assn. Colls. and Tchrs. Agr. Lutheran (Laymen's League). Contbr. articles to profl. jours. Home: Route 4 Sterling CO 80751 Office: Northeastern Jr College Sterling CO 80751

PIERCE, ANNE-MARIE BERNHEIM, educational administrator; b. Grenoble, France, Sept. 9, 1943; d. Joseph and Andree Georgette (Haguenauer) Bernheim; B.A., U. Calif.-Berkeley, 1965; M.A., Calif. State U.-Hayward 1973; m. Robert L. Pierce, Mar. 21, 1964; 1 son, Eric David. Tchr., head fgn. lang. dept. Head-Royce Schs., Oakland, Calif., 1965-75; tchr. San Francisco U. High Sch., 1975-80, dir. activities and public events, 1979-80; dir. Ecole Bilingue: East Bay French-Am. Sch., Berkeley, Calif. Mem. Assn. Supervision and Curriculum Devel., Am. Assn. Tchrs. French, Am. Council Fgn. Lang. Tchrs., Nat. Assn. Female Execs., Council for Women in Ind. Schs., French and Bilingual Schs. Assn. Democrat. Jewish. Office: 1009 Heinz St Berkeley CA 94710

PIERCE, DENNIS JAMES, marketing company executive; b. Reno, Mar. 3, 1941; s. Charles Victor and Juanita Alice (Miller) P.; m. Gay Marie Nikkenen, June 28, 1961 (div. 1976); children—Daniel James, David John; m. 2d. Marian Pauline Johnson, July 10, 1976. Account exec. Fall & Assoc., San Diego, 1966-69; owner, pres. Imperial Advt. Co., San Diego, 1969-72; pres., owner Old Del Mar Emporium, Spring Valley, Calif., 1975—. Served with USAFR, 1960-66. Mem. Splty. Equipment Mfrs. Assn. Republican. Club: Southwestern Yacht (San Diego). Contbr. numerous articles to automotive accessory jours. Office: Old Del Mar Emporium 10018 Dolores St Spring Valley CA 92077

PIERCE, FRANK LAWLER, real estate broker, developer; b. Oakland, Calif., May 11, 1933; s. James Clayton and Edith Helen (Lawler) P.; student Diablo Valley Coll., 1959-61; grad. Real Estate Inst.; m. Claudia Joan Grasse, June 7, 1951; children—Laura Pierce Holt, Carolanne Pierce Simkins, Jennifer Pierce Larson, Nancy Pierce Gubler. Salesman, gen. mgr. J.C. Pierce Desoto-Plymouth Co., Concord, Calif., 1951-60; realtor, Walnut Creek, Calif., 1960-70, St. George, Utah, 1970—; bd. dirs. Contra Costa (Calif.) Bd. Realtors, 1969-70; pres. Wash. County (Utah) Bd. Realtors, 1973-74. Mem. planning commn. City of St. George, 1970-73; mem. Cherokee Nation of Okla.; adv. to Indian students Dixie Coll., St. George. Named Outstanding Young Man of Year Walnut Creek Jaycees, 1968. Mem. Nat. Rifle Assn. (life), Clubs: Masons (32 deg.), Shriners, K.T., Elks; Lions (past pres. Ygnacio Valley (Calif.) and Bloomington (Utah)); Bloomington Country. Home: 3244 Three Bars Rd Bloomington UT 84770 Office: 720 E St George Blvd St George UT 84770

PIERCE, JAMES FRANKLIN, data systems consultant; b. Seaford, N.Y., Aug. 24, 1950; s. James Franklin and Marion April (Augustine) P.; m. Kit Lan Lee, July 4, 1980; 1 son, James Franklin. A.A.S., Olympic Coll., 1970. Cons. GTE-Informatics Co., N.Y.C., 1974-75, Frito-Lay Co., Dallas, 1976-77, Occidental Petroleum Co., Houston, 1977-78, Lockheed Missiles & Space Co., Sunnyvale, Calif., 1978-79; cons., owner Intel Corp., San Jose, Calif., 1979—. Mem. Republican Task Force. Served to maj. U.S. Army, 1970-74. Decorated Silver Star; Cross of Gallantry (Vietnam). Mem. Assn. Systems Mgmt., ACM. Home: 2707 Valley Heights Dr San Jose CA 95133 Office: 2707 Valley Heights Dr San Jose CA 95133

PIERCE, SAM, aerospace scientist; b. Los Angeles, 1943; s. William J. and Josephine R. P.; children—Robert M., Steven M. B.S., UCLA, 1965, M.S., 1967, Ph.D., 1970. Cert. tchr., Calif. Tchr. various univs., Los Angeles, 1965-70; sr. cons. to corps., Santa Monica, Calif., 1965-70; asst. prof. Calif. State U.-Fullerton, 1970-75; sr. staff mem. Aerospace Corp., El Segundo, Calif., 1975-78; sr. staff cognizant engr. Jet Propulsion Lab., Pasadena, Calif., 1978-81; sr. scientist lab. staff Hughes Aircraft, El Segundo, 1981—; chmn. computer sci. com., dir. computer sci. internship and grad. program Calif. State U. Research grant prin. investigator NASA, NSF; postgrad. researcher UCLA; NDEA fellow, 1965-68; faculty fellow UCLA, also study grantee; Calif. state scholar. Mem. N.Y. Acad. Scis., Am. Astron. Soc., Am. Inst. Physics, AIAA, AAAS, Soc. Indsl. and Applied Math., Assn. Computing Machinery, Numerical Analysis Interest Group (chmn.), Los Angeles First Mars Landing Soc., Mensa, Sigma Chi, Pi Mu Epsilon. Contbr. articles to profl. jours.

PIERCE, SHANCY, casting director; b. Los Angeles, Sept. 30, 1942; d. Warren Alfred and Loraine Rice (Potter) P. A.A., Valley Jr. Coll., 1973; B.A. in Anthropology, Calif. State U.-Northridge, 1979. Animation cameraperson Walt Disney Studios, Burbank, Calif., 1961-63; prodn. asst. Dick Clark Prodns., Los Angeles, 1972-73; talent coordinator Solowitz Orgn., Hollywood, Calif., 1975-77; casting dir. Spungbuggy Works Inc., Los Angeles, 1977—; owner, operator Slate Please, Los Angeles, 1983—. Pres., Van Nuys (Calif.) chpt. Young Republicans, 1974. Recipient CLIO award, 1980. Christian Scientist. Office: 8506 Sunset Blvd Los Angeles CA 90069

PIERCY, GORDON CLAYTON, banker; b. Tacoma Park, Md., Nov. 23, 1944; s. Gordon Clayton and Dorothy Florence (Brummer) P.; B.S., Syracuse U., 1966; M.B.A., Pace U., 1973; children—Elizabeth Anne, Kenneth Charles. Mktg. planning asso. Chem. Bank, N.Y.C., 1966-70; sr. market devel. officer Seattle-First Nat. Bank, 1970-74; product expansion adminstr., mktg. planning mgr. Nat. BankAmericard, Inc., San Francisco, 1974-76; v.p., dir. mktg. Wash. Mut. Savs. Bank, Seattle, 1976-82; v.p., mktg. and planning adminstr. 1st Interstate Bank of Wash. N.A., 1983—. Mem. Am. Mktg. Assn. (dir.), Bank Mktg. Assn. (state rep.), Mktg. Communications Execs. Internat. (dir.), Seattle Advt. Fedn., Sigma Nu, Alpha Kappa Psi, Delta Mu Delta. Episcopalian. Home: 6355 137th Ave NE Suite 302 Redmond WA 98052 Office: PO Box 160 Seattle WA 98111

PIERNO, ANTHONY ROBERT, lawyer; b. Uniontown, Pa., Apr. 28, 1932; s. Anthony Michael and Mary Jane (Saporita) P.; B.A. summa cum laude, Whittier (Calif.) Coll., 1954; J.D., Stanford U., 1959; m. Beverly Jean Kohn, June 20, 1954; children—Kathryn Ann, Robert Lawrence, Linda Jean, Diane Marie. Admitted to Calif. bar, 1960; pvt. practice, Los Angeles, 1960-67; chief dep. commr. corps. State of Calif., 1967-69, commr., 1969-71; pvt. practice, Los Angeles, 1971—; sr. partner firm Memel, Jacobs, Pierno & Gersh, 1976—; founder, dir. Exec. Savs. & Loan Assn., Century City, Calif., 1974-76; legal adv. bd. N.Y. Inst. Finance, 1971—; adv. bd. Legal Edn. Inst., 1975—; dir. ICAN Assos.; founding dir. Palos Verdes Nat. Bank, 1980—. Mem. Gov. Calif.'s Council, 1969-71, Gov. Calif.'s Task Force Higher Edn., 1970-71, Atty. Gen. Calif.'s Vol. Adv. Com., 1971-78; bd. advisers Whittier Coll. Law Sch., 1975—, trustee coll., 1977—; trustee Marymount Palos Verdes Coll., 1976—. Served with AUS, 1954-56. Recipient Outstanding Alumni award Whittier Coll., 1970. Mem. Am. Bar Assn., State Bar Calif. (chmn. com. corps. 1971-75, exec. com. bus. law sect. 1977-80), N.Am. Securities Adminstrs. Assn. (exec. com. 1969-71), Delta Theta Phi. Republican. Roman Catholic. Clubs: Peninsula Racquet, Palos Verdes Breakfast. Home: 2901 Via Anacapa Palos Verdes Estates CA 2901 Office: 1801 Century Park East 25th Floor Los Angeles CA 90067

PIERSON, DAVID GILBERT, marketing company executive; b. Los Angeles, May 10, 1933; s. Wilbur A. and Helen E. P.; m. Sue C. Mc Intyre, Oct. 25, 1966; 1 son, Greg. A.A., Calif. State U.-Fullerton, 1952; B.A., Woodbury Coll., 1955. With sales dept. Remington Rand Co., Los Angeles, 1958-60, Steelcase Inc., Los Angeles, 1960-62; v.p. sales Durochrome Products Co., Los Angeles, 1962-82; pres. Royal Screen Print Co., Los Angeles, 1983—. Served with USN, 1956-58. Recipient Salesman of Yr. award Sales and Mktg. Exec. Club, 1969. Clubs: San Gabriel Country, Indian Wells Racket. Address: 26700 Honey Creek Rd Rancho Palos Verdes CA 90274

PIES, RONALD E., city official; b. Rochester, N.Y., Mar. 21, 1940; s. Herman S. and Sylvia P.; m. Bernita Orloff, Aug. 27, 1964; children—Cara Jean, David Paul; B.S., Ariz. State U., 1963; Recreation leader City of Phoenix, Ariz., 1962-64; head recreation div. City of Scottsdale (Ariz.) Parks and Recreation Dept., 1964-69; dir. parks and recreation, City of Tempe, Ariz., 1969—; guest lectr. Ariz. State U. Mem., pres. Kyrene Sch. Dist. Governing Bd., 1979-82. Named Outstanding Young Man, Jaycees. Mem. Tempe C. of C., Ariz. Parks and Recreation Assn., (pres. adminstrs.), Nat. Recreation and Parks Assn. Club: Tempe Diablos.

PIGNATARO, AUGUSTUS, optical physicist; b. Bronx, N.Y., Aug. 12, 1943; s. Frank and Amelia (Tenneriello) P.; B.S. in Physics, Calif. State U., Los Angeles, 1965; M.B.A., Calif. Lutheran Coll., Thousand Oaks, 1975; m. Lynn Marie Kline, Oct. 16, 1965; children—Lisa Marie, Julie Marie, Jeffrey David. Engr., Atlantic Research Corp., Costa Mesa, Calif., 1965-67; optical physicist Navy Pacific Missile Test Center, Point Mugu, Calif., 1967—. Recipient various letters of commendation. Mem. Infrared Info. Symposium. Republican. Roman Catholic. Author papers, reports in field. Developer test and evaluation of infrared sensors and guidance systems, infrared countermeasures systems, infrared sources and ultraviolet sensors. Home: 1094 Harris Ave Camarillo CA 93010 Office: Code 1233 Pacific Missile Test Center Point Mugu CA 93042

PIGOTT, CHARLES MCGEE, transp. mfg. equipment company; b. Seattle, Apr. 21, 1929; s. Paul and Theiline (McGee) P.; B.S., Stanford U., 1951; m. Yvonne Flood, Apr. 18, 1953. With PACCAR Inc., Seattle, 1959—, exec. v.p., 1962-65, pres., 1965—, also dir.; dir. Boeing Co., Citibank, Citicorp, Standard Oil Calif. Bd. dirs. United Good Neighbors, Seattle, SRI Internat. Mem. Bus. Council. Office: Paccar Inc 777 106th Ave NE Bellevue WA 98004*

PIIRTO, DOUGLAS DONALD, forester; b. Reno, Nev., Sept. 25, 1948; s. Rueben Arvid and Martha Hilma (Giebel) P.; B.S., U. Nev., 1970; M.S., Colo. State U., 1971; Ph.D., U. Calif. at Berkeley, 1977; m. Mary Louise Cruz, Oct. 28, 1978. Research asst. Colo. State U., 1970-71, U. Calif. at Berkeley, 1972-77; forester, silviculturist U.S. Dept. Agr., Forest Service, Sierra Nat. Forest, Trimmer and Shaver Lake, Calif., 1977—; instr. evenings Kings River Community Coll., Reedley, Calif. Mem. Soc. Am. Foresters, Am. Forestry Assn., Forest Products Research Soc., Soc. Wood Sci. and Tech., Alpha Zeta, Xi Sigma Pi, Sigma Xi, Beta Beta Beta, Phi Sigma Kappa. Lutheran. Contbr. articles to sci. and forestry jours. Home: 3032 E Paul Ave Fresno CA 93710 Office: US Dept Agr Forest Service PO Box 300 Shaver Lake CA 93664

PIMENTEL, DAVID DELBERT, metalsmith, educator; b. Plymouth, Mass., June 29, 1943; s. Arthur Joseph and Catherine Frances (Griffin) P.; B.S. in Art Edn., Mass. Coll. Art, Boston, 1965; M.F.A., Sch. Am. Craftsmen, Rochester (N.Y.) Inst. Tech., 1972; m. Judith Carol Jones, June 28, 1969; 1 dau., Liesl Kalani. Art tchr. Port Pyron (N.Y.) Central Sch., 1965-67, Lincoln-Sudbery (Mass.) Regional High Sch., 1967-69, Kamehameha Schs., Honolulu, 1972-73; assoc. prof. Sch. Art, Ariz. State U.; lectr., tchr. workshops on metalsmithing; works include: mace and presdl. chain of office Hayden Library, Ariz. State U., 1982; 3 sculptures Hawaii State Found. on Culture and the Arts, 1975. Hawaii State Found. on the Culture and the Arts grantee, 1973. Mem. Soc. N.Am. Goldsmiths, Am. Crafts Council, Ariz. Artists Blacksmiths Assn. Republican. Unitarian. Office: Sch Art Ariz State U Tempe AZ 85281

PINAR, ELIZABETH SMITH, nutrition educator, dietitian; b. Mt. Vernon, Ohio, Mar. 13, 1918; d. Wiley and Susan Ada (McCormick) Smith; m. Robert E. Pinar, Aug. 17, 1946 (div.); children—Robert W., John F., Jeffrey K. B.S., Ohio State U., 1940, B.A., 1941, M.S., 1948; postgrad. Colo. State U., 1972—. Tchr. home econs. and English, LaGrange and Shelby, Ohio, 1941-43; asst., then head dietitian Marshall Coll., Huntington, W.Va., 1943-44, 45-46; asst. mgr. Pomerene Refectory, Ohio State U., Columbus, 1946-48, 61-62, lab. instr. quantity foods Pomerene Refectory, 1961-62; head dietitian Otterbein Coll., Westerville, Ohio, 1950-52; tchr. Tecumseh High Sch., New Carlisle, Ohio, 1963-70; clin. dietitian Porter Meml. Hosp., Denver, 1971-75; instr. nutrition, program dir. dietetic tech. Front Range Community Coll., Westminster, Colo., 1971—. Active numerous civic and ch. groups. Mem. Am. Dietetic Assn. (registered dietitian), Colo. Dietetic Assn., Denver Dietetic Assn., Nutrition Today Soc. (charter). Home: 5721 W 92d Ave Apt 80 Westminster CO 80030 Office: Front Range Community Coll Science and Health 3645 W 112th Ave Westminster CO 80030

PINCKNEY, NEAL T(HEODORE), psychologist, educator; b. N.Y.C., July 26, 1935; s. Leo Allen and Fran C. (Riggan) P.; cert. in polit., social and hist. issues Kings Coll., U. Durham (Eng.), 1957; A.B., U. So. Calif., 1958, postgrad., 1958-61; Ph.D., Oxford U., 1966; postgrad. U. Vienna, U. Hiroshima, Stanford U.; children—Andrew Allen, Jennifer Elizabeth, Matthew Ian. Intern, Los Angeles Police Dept., 1957-58, Pub. Welfare Commn. Los Angeles County, 1958-60; tchr. Pub. Schs. Los Angeles, 1960-61; tchr., counsellor, Las Vegas, 1961-62; adminstr.-therapist, psychiat. clinic, Las Vegas, 1962-63; educator, dir. guidance service Dept. Def. Overseas Dependent Schs., Eng. and Japan, 1963-67; lectr. Calif. State U., Sacramento, 1967-68, asst. prof., 1968-71, asso. prof., 1971-77, prof. psychology and edn., 1977—, chmn. dept. behavioral scis., 1980-81, prof. counseling psychology, coordinator grad. studies, counseling, adminstrn. and policy studies, 1981—; instr. enforcement psychology and human relations Calif. Hwy. Patrol Acad., psychologist Calif. Hwy. Patrol, 1967-80; tech. cons., adviser Ministry Edn. and Culture, Govt. Brazil, Brasilia, 1974-76; cons. psychologist to various law enforcement agys. Served to 3d Armored Div., U.S. Army, 1954-55. Queen's scholar in Eng., 1956-57; Dept. State Fgn. Service Inst. scholar, 1964; Ford Found. fellow, 1960-61. Mem. Am. Psychol. Assn., Brit. Psychol. Assn., Japanese Psychol. Assn., Brazilian Psychol. Assn., Am. Ednl. Research Assn., Am. Personnel and Guidance Assn., Phi Delta Kappa, Delta Phi Epsilon. Clubs: Commonwealth (San Francisco); Oxonian (Tokyo); Toastmasters (area gov. 1962-63), Masons. Office: Calif State U 6000 Jay St Sacramento CA 95819

PINCZKOWSKI, RAYMOND ERBIN, JR., actuary, consultant; b. Milw., July 6, 1941; s. Raymond E. and Maurita Marie (McCoy) P.; m. Cindy Newman, June 19, 1965 (div.); children—Matthew, Sara; m. 2d Jean Gallagher, Oct. 2, 1982. B.A. in Econs., Cornell U., 1963; M.S., U. Wis., 1965. Cons. actuary Milliman & Robertson, Inc., Milw., 1965-74, Denver, 1976—; actuary Internat. Harvester Co., Chgo., 1974-76. Fellow Soc. Actuaries (edn. and exam. com.), Conf. Actuaries in Pub. Practice; mem. Am. Acad. Actuaries, Denver Actuarial Club, Western Pension Conf., Internat. Found. Employee Benefit Plans, Assn. Pvt. Pension and Welfare Plans. Club: Downtown Denver Lions (bd. dirs.). Home: 2625 S Vaughn Way Aurora CO 80014 Office: 1580 Lincoln St Suite 560 Denver CO 80203

PINE, CHARLES JOSEPH, clinical psychologist, health services administrator; b. Excelsior Springs, Mo., July 13, 1951; s. Charles E. and LaVern (Upton) P.; m. Mary Day, Dec. 30, 1979; children—Charles Andrew, Joseph Scott. B.A. in Psychology, U. Redlands, 1973; M.A., Calif. State U.-Los Angeles, 1975; Ph.D., U. Wash., 1979; postdoctoral UCLA, 1980-81. Lic. psychologist, Calif. Psychology technician Seattle Indian Health Bd., USPHS Hosp., 1977-78; psychology intern VA Outpatient Clinic, Los Angeles, 1978-79; instr. psychology Okla. State U., 1979-80, asst. prof., 1980; asst. prof. psychology and native Am. studies program Wash. State U., 1981-82; dir. behavioral health services Riverside-San Bernardino County Indian Health Inc., Banning, Calif., 1982—; cons. Dept. Health and Human Services, USPHS, NIMH, 1980. Vol. worker Variety Boys Clubs Am., 1973-75; coach Rialto Jr. All-Am. Football League, 1974. U. Wash. Inst. Indian Studies grantee, 1975-76,

UCLA Inst. Am. Cultures grantee, 1981-82. Mem. Am. Psychol. Assn., Nat. Indian Counselors Assn., Soc. Indian Psychologists (pres. 1981—), Western Psychol. Assn., Sigma Alpha Epsilon. Republican. Baptist. Contbr. psychol. articles to profl. lit. Home: 365 W Grove Rialto CA 92376

PING, CHIEN-LU, soil scientist; b. Henan Province, China, Mar. 24, 1941; came to U.S., 1969; s. Chia-Yeh and Shu-Chun (Chao) P.; Ph.D., Wash. State U., 1976; m. Wu Shan, July 20, 1969; children—Andrew, Dennis. Forest soil specialist Wash. Dept. Natural Resources, Olympia, 1976-77, forest soil survey project leader, 1977—; natural resources scientist Wash. State Govt., Okanogan, 1980—; asst. prof. U. Alaska-Palmer, 1982—. Mem. Am. Soc. Soil Sci., Wash. Soc. Profl. Soil Scientists, Am. Register Cert. Profls. in Agronomy, Crops and Soils. Home: PO Box 2885 Palmer AK 99645

PINKEL, SHEILA MAE, artist, photographer, educator; b. Newport News, Va., Aug. 21, 1941; d. Benjamin and Anne (Abel) P. B.A. in Art and Art History, U. Calif.-Berkeley, 1963; M.F.A. in Photography, UCLA, 1977. Instr. photography and silkscreen, UCLA Extension, 1976—; instr. photography Otis Art Inst., Los Angeles, 1980—, Calif. Poly. Inst., Pomona, 1980-81; instr. silkscreen Santa Monica (Calif.) Coll., 1980—; instr. photography Sch. of Art Inst. Chgo., 1983; project dir. Multicultural Focus, Los Angeles, 1981, Los Angeles Portrait: Eleven Views, LACE Gallery, 1982, Bay Area Slide Library, Santa Monica Library, 1982. Coordinator Artists Against Proposition 13, City Hall and Los Angeles Mcpl. Gallery, 1978. NEA artist grantee in photography, 1979, 82. Mem. Soc. for Photog. Edn., Los Angeles Center for Photog. Studies. Contbr. to Park La Brea Towers Mural Instllation, Los Angeles, 1976, books including: The Print (Time-Life Series) 1981, 1980 Time-Life Photo Annual, Innovative Printmaking, 1978, Darkroom Art, 1981.

PINKUS, FRANK HARRY, electronics company executive; b. Pitts., Sept. 6, 1938; s. Ernst and Hilde (Frankel) P.; B.B.A. cum laude, U. Pitts., 1960; M.B.A., U. Pa., 1961; m. Roslyn Popick, June 10, 1962; children—Gary Stuart, Mark Norman, Lynn Rebecca. Divisional merchandise mgr. Kauffmann's, Pitts., 1967-73; v.p., gen. merchandise mgr. Ohrbachs, Los Angeles, 1973-76; exec. v.p. N'est-ce Pas?, Los Angeles, 1976-79; pres. Fashion Power, Los Angeles, 1979-80; chmn. bd. Pistache Inc., Los Angeles, 1981-82; pres. Pycon Computers, Tarzane, Calif., 1981—. Active City of Hope, 1975—, Save a Life, 1977—. Served with N.G., 1957-63. Club: Braemar Racquet (treas. 1978). Home: 18912 La Amistad Pl Tarzana CA 91356 Office: Pycon Computers 6000 Reseda Blvd Unit F Tarzana CA 91356

PINNEY, JAMES KENT, marketing educator, consultant; b. Salt Lake City, Oct. 29, 1934; s. James Granville and Nellie Elizabeth (Heil) P.; m. Beryl Bates, Dec. 18, 1960; children—Elizabeth, Corale Cynthia. B.A. in Econs., U. Utah, 1962; M.B.A. in Internat. Bus. Adminstrn., Ind. U., 1964, D.B.A. in Internat. Bus. Adminstrn., 1968. Research asst. Divs. Foreign Trade and Research, State of Ind., Indpls., 1964-68; asst. prof. internat. bus. adminstrn. Brigham Young U., Provo, Utah, 1967-72; assoc. prof. mktg. U. Nev., Las Vegas, 1973—, chmn. dept. mktg. Coll. Bus. and Econs., 1980—; mktg. cons. to small bus. Precinct capt., county del., Republican Party, 1974—; vol. social worker, Las Vegas. Served with U.S. Army, 1954-56. Ford Found. scholar, 1964-67. Mem. Greater Las Vegas Advt. Fedn., Acad. Mktg. Sci., Western Mktg. Educators Assn., Western Econs. Assn. Mormon. Author papers in field. Home: 2953 Peridot St Las Vegas NV 89121 Office: FDH 405 4450 S Maryland Pkwy Las Vegas NV 89154

PINNOCK, ROGER BODEN, accountant; b. Salt Lake City, Jan. 28, 1942; s. Lawrence S. and Florence (Boden) P.; m. Kathleen Cannon, Aug. 26, 1965; children—Roger, Kristina, Katherine. B.S., U. Utah, 1967. C.P.A., Utah. Ptnr. Pinnock, Robbins & Co., and predecessor cos., Salt Lake City, 1973—, mng. ptnr., Salt Lake City, 1978—, pres., 1978—; instr. tax seminars; mem. various bds. Mem. deferred gifts com. Primary Childrens Med. Ctr., 1979-81. Served with U.S. Army, 1961-62. Mem. Am. Inst. C.P.A.s, Utah Assn. C.P.A.s, Sigma Chi. Republican. Mormon. Home: 1878 Laurelwood Circle Salt Lake City UT 84121 Office: 275 E South Temple Suite 101 Salt Lake City UT 84111

PINSON, JOHN CARVER, electrical engineer; b. Lubbock, Tex., July 8, 1931; s. H. Bert and Vera N. (Carver) P.; m. Mary Ruth Sims, July 5, 1952; 1 son, J. Stephen. B.S., Tex. Tech. U., 1952; S.M., MIT, 1954, Sc.D. in Elec. Engring., 1957. Registered profl. engr., Calif. Sr. research engr. Rockwell Internat., Anaheim, Calif., 1957-58, research specialist, 1958-59, supr. systems engring., 1959-60, group chief, 1960-62, sect. mgr., 1962-63, asst. chief engr., 1963-65, chief scientist, autonetics strategic systems div., 1965—. Home: 5069 Crescent Dr Anaheim CA 92807 Office: Rockwell International 3370 Miraloma Ave Anaheim CA 92803

PINTA, WANDA BOHAN (MRS. R. JACK PINTA), home economist; b. Greenfield, Ia., Sept. 11, 1918; d. Edward Philip and Stella (Plymesser) Bohan; B.S., Ia. State U., 1943; postgrad. Los Angeles State Coll., 1956-59; m. R. Jack Pinta, Apr. 17, 1948. Tech. writer, editor Gen. Motors Corp., Milford, Mich., 1943-45; sr. home economist Los Angeles Dept. Water and Power, 1956-61, dir. home econs., 1961—, dir. ednl. services, 1981—. Sec. Assn. for UN, Des Moines, 1953-55. Mem. mayor's Community Adv. Com. Recipient Laura McCall Home Service Achievement award, 1960; acceptor Aham's Alma award, 1970-72. Mem. Am. (consumer interests com. 1968-70), Cal. (exec. council, pres. Los Angeles dist. 1966-67) home econs. assns., Los Angeles Home Economists in Bus., Elec. Women's Round Table (dir. 1974, nat. pres. 1978-80), Soc. Consumer Affairs Profls. in Bus. (sec. So. Calif. chpt. 1978-79), Los Angeles City/County Energy Edn. Council (communications chmn. 1981-83), LWV (exec. bd. Des Moines 1953-55), Los Angeles World Affairs Council, Town Hall, Ia. State U. Alumni Assn. Episcopalian. Mem. Order Eastern Star. Club: Pilot (pres. Van Nuys 1962-63). Home: 5744 Vantage Av North Hollywood CA 91607 Office: 111 N Hope St Los Angeles CA 90012 also PO Box 111 Los Angeles CA 90051

PINTO, JOHN, state senator, Indian community leader; b. Lupton, Ariz., Dec. 15, 1924; s. Jim and Ellen (Goodluck) P.; m. Joann Dennison, 1953; children—Flora Jean Footracer, Cecil B., Galen D., Karen. B.S., U. N.Mex., 1964, M.A., 1970. Chmn. Eastern Navajo Agy. road com. N.Mex., 1970-75; vice chmn. Gallup Inter-Agy. Alcoholism, 1973-76; treas. McKinley Area Govt. Council, 1973-76; chmn. Gallup Indian Community Cr., 1973—; mem. Tohatchi Planning Commn., 1975—; mem. N.Mex. State Senate, 1977—. Sec.-treas. Red Rock chpt. Dist. 16 Democratic Party, 1970—; mem. McKinley County Bd. Commrs., 1973-74, chmn., 1975-76; mem. Nat. Transp. Com., Washington, 1975-76; mem. Nat. Assn. Regional Councils, Washington, 1975-76. Served with USMC, 1945-46. Democrat. Roman Catholic. Home: 509 W Morgan Ave Gallup NM 87301 Office: New Mexico State Senate Santa Fe NM 87503

PIPES, KENNETH WAYNE, human resources administrator, former marine corps officer; b. Bakersfield, Calif., Oct. 19, 1937; s. Roy Jackson and Neva Opel (Wilcher) P.; m. Sharon Lee Hussey, Dec. 9, 1961; children—Daniel Grady, Timothy Shannon. A.A., Fresno City Coll., 1958, B.A., Fresno State Coll., 1961; M.A., U. Va., 1976; grad. Marine Corps Amphibious Warfare Sch., 1976, Marine Corps Command and Staff Coll., 1972. Commd. 2d lt., U.S. Marine Corps, 1961, advanced through grades to lt. col., 1977—, dep. asst. chief of staff, personnel services, Marine Corps Base, Camp Pendelton, Calif., 1981-82; instr. Marine Corps Amphibious Warfare Sch., 1972-76; inspector/instr. Marine Corps Res., 1968-71, recuriting officer, 1977-79, ret., 1982; human resource adminstr. security div. San Onofre Nuclear Generating Sta., San Clemente, Calif., 1982— Bd. dirs. Oxnard Salvation Army, 1968-71, Oceanside (Calif.) YMCA, 1981-82. Decorated Silver Star, Bronze Star medals, Meritorious Service medal; Vietnam Cross of Gallantry with Bronze and Silver Star, Purple Heart; recipient U.S. Navy League Disting. Service award, 1971; Salvation Army Service award, 1971; cert. of appreciation Combined Fed. Campaign, 1981, 82; cert. of commendation Boy Scouts Am., 1982. others; McMahan's scholar, 1959-60. Mem. Marine Corps Assn., Navy League, Sigma Alpha Epsilon. Republican. Baptist. Club: Rotary.

PIPKIN, DOLORES LOUISE, accountant; b. Granite City, Ill., May 19, 1933; d. George Edward and Maude Leona (Lewis) Robinson; m. James Lewis Pipkin, Aug. 16, 1957 (div.); children—Sandra Louise, Cynthia LaDele. A.A. in Edn., A.S. in Acctg., A.S. in Bus. Mgmt., Napa Coll., 1978. Bookkeeper Nesco, Ill., telephone co., Seattle, 1951-54; sales mgr. Avon products, Stanley Home products Dutchmaid clothing, 1956-66; interior decorater Macy's Co., Concord, Calif., 1966-69; office mgr. Spanish Flat Resort, Lake Berreyessa, Calif., 1969-75; acct. Appco Mfg. Co., Chula Vista, Calif., 1975-77; staff acct. John Fulkerson, C.P.A., Napa, Calif., 1977-78; pres. DLS Systems, Inc., Napa, 1978—. Mem. adv. com. Napa Coll., 1980-81. Mem. Nat. Assn. Accts. Mem. Assemblies of God Ch. Office: DLS Systems Inc 301 River St Napa CA 94558

PISCATELLA, JEAN MARIE, aluminum company manager; b. Torrance, Calif. Nov. 2, 1949; d. Hubert Charles and June Beth (Koehr) Stanwood; m. Steven Piscatella, Apr. 15, 1968; 1 son, Mathew Steven. Cert. sales tng. Loyola Marymount Coll., 1977, mgmt. skills Riverside City Coll., 1973. Clk. Riverside County (Calif.) Tax Collector's Office, Riverside, 1966-67; credit collector Sears Roebuck & Co., Riverside, 1967-69; sr. records officer Riverside County Probation Dept., 1969-74; sec. then inside sales area mgr. Alumax Mill Products, Riverside, 1974-76; extrusion inside salesperson Martin Marietta Aluminum Co., Torrance, Calif., 1976-78; inside sales mgr., asst. gen. mgr. Calif. Custom Shapes div. IMCOA, Garden Grove, Calif., 1978-81, gen. mgr., 1981—. Mem. Aluminum Extruders Council, Aluminum Window Assn. Office: 12360 Edison Way Garden Grove CA 92641

PITKIN, SANDY SANDERSON, real estate broker; b. Los Angeles, Nov. 28, 1944; d. Carl Foree and Mildred Anna (Bailey) Sanderson; m. Willis Lloyd Pitkin, Jr., June 9, 1965 (div.); children—Joseph Reeves, Sara Love, Mary Faith. B.A., Whittier Coll., 1966, M.A.T., 1967. Lic. real estate broker, Utah, Idaho. Sales assoc., assoc. broker Aloma Real Estate, Logan, Utah, 1979-82; founder, ptnr. Gold Key Realty, 1982-83; mgr. Wardly Corp.-Better Homes and Gardens, Salt Lake City, 1983—. Democratic precinct chmn., 1982; sponsor Logan Swim Team. Mem. Cert. Residential Specialists, Logan Women's Council Realtors (pres., founder), Internat. Fedn. Realtors, Utah State Farm and Land Inst. (sec.-treas.), Nat. Mktg. Inst., Logan Bd. Realtors (Sales Assoc. of Yr. 1981, Sales Achievement awards, 1980-83), Utah Assn. Realtors, Nat. Assn. Realtors, Nat. Assn. Women at Large. Contbr. to Utah State Assn. Realtors publ. Home: 329 Park Ave Condos UT 84068 Office: 2219 S 700 East Salt Lake City UT 84106

PITT, CARL ALLEN, educator; b. Three Forks, Mont., Sept. 6, 1911; s. John Marshall and Clara Rebecca (Biggs) P.; B.A., Intermountain Union Coll., 1933; M.A., Wash. State Coll., 1946; summer postgrad. U. Iowa, 1947, U. Mich., 1949; Ph.D., Purdue U., 1952; m. Olive Marguerite MacGillivray, June 29, 1935 (dec. Feb. 1963). Salesman, Nat. Biscuit Co., Butte, Mont., 1933-40; dir. forensics Highline High Sch., Seattle, 1942-46; dir. resources discussion U. Wash., 1946-48; faculty speech U. Ill., Chgo., 1950-73, prof., 1967-73, ret. Lectr. on communication problems to coll. and civic groups. Air Age fellow, 1946. Mem. Speech Communication Assn. Am., Central States Speech Assn., Western Speech Communication Assn., Am. Forensic Assn., Internat. Communication Assn., Am. Assn. Higher Edn., Am. Inst. Parliamentarians, Phi Delta Kappa, Pi Kappa Delta. Mason (Shriner). Editor. Chgo. Circle Studies, 1964-68. Former mem. editorial staff Parliamentary Jour., Central States Speech Jour.; contbr. articles to profl. jours. Home: 6326 37th Ave SW Seattle WA 98126

PITT, HARRIETT MAEOLA, nurse epidemiologist; b. Newport News, Va., June 13, 1938; d. David Mack and Iola Mae (Crayton) Crockett; children—Duane David, Darlyne Michele. B.S., Loma Linda U., 1960; postgrad. Calif. State U., 1969-71, 80—. Instr. Loma Linda U., 1961-63; staff nurse Los Angeles County Med. Ctr., 1963-65; staff nurse Dept. Health County of Los Angeles, 1965-66; dir., instr. Sch. Vocat. Nursing White Meml. Med. Ctr., Los Angeles, 1966-71, adminstrv. nursing supr., 1971-74, nurse epidemiologist, 1974—, asst. dir. nursing 1978. Mem. Assn. Practitioners in Infection Control (pres. 1982—). Republican. Adventist. Editor: Western Jour. Infection Control 1979-80. Office: 1720 Brooklyn Ave Los Angeles CA 90033

PITT, MARY ORA, dietitian; b. Savannah, Ga., Dec. 24, 1925; d. George Lee and Ora Elva (Leggett) P.; B.S., Fla. State U., 1947; postgrad. in public hosp. adminstrn. U. So. Calif. With VA, 1947-81, intern and dietitian, Memphis, 1947-49, Bklyn., 1950-52, Dublin, Ga., 1952-54, N.Y.C., 1954-58; chief dietetic service, Montrose, N.Y., 1958-60, area chief dietetic service, Atlanta, 1961-64, chief dietetic service, Asheville, N.C., 1964-65, VA Med. Center, Long Beach, Calif., 1965-81; cons. dietetic tng. programs Calif. State U. (Long Beach and Los Angeles). Recipient performance awards VA; registered dietitian. Mem. Am. Dietetic Assn., Calif. Dietetic Assn. (pres. 1980-81), Fla. State U. Alumni Assn. (life). Republican. Baptist. Home: 1140 Coastline Dr Seal Beach CA 90740

PITTENGER, RICHARD MADDEN, association executive; b. Pitts., Sept. 18, 1924; s. William Henry and Natalie (Madden) P; m. Ann Harriet Salter, Oct. 2, 1949; children—Sandra Carvell, Richard W., James L. M.B.A., U. Nebr., 1971; Ph.D., Western States U., 1983. Lic. profl. safety engr. Calif. Commd. officer U.S. Air Force, 1943; advanced through grades to lt. col.; pilot, navigator, 1943-74; dir. missle and nuclear safety SAC, Offutt AFB, Nebr., 1968-71; dir. safety, base comdr. Alaska Air Command, Elmendorf AFB, 1971-74, ret. 1974; exec. asst. Alaska chpt. Associated Gen. Contractors Am., Anchorage, 1974-80, mgr., 1980—; lectr. bus. courses Alaska Meth. U., 1972-76. Chmn. Citizens Mgmt. Alaskan Lands, Anchorage Safety Council, 1977-78, Alaska Safety Adv. Com., 1978-79. Decorated Air medal with 5 oak leaf clusters, Meritorious Service medal with 2 oak leaf cluster. Mem. Am. Soc. Safety Engrs., Am. Arbitration Assn., Nat. Safety Mgmt. Soc., Am. Soc. Assn. Execs., Alaska C. of C., Anchorage C. of C. Republican. Roman Catholic. Clubs: USAF Officers, Tower (Anchorage); Bahia de Santiago Country (Manzanillo, Mex.). Contbr. articles to nuclear safety and constrn. trade jours. Office: 3201 Spenard Rd Anchorage AK 99503

PITTMAN, JAMES EUGENE, JR., vermiculturist; b. Long Beach, Calif., May 28, 1948; s. James E. and Lenora Fern (Hunsaker) P.; student in vermiculture and soil husbandry; m. Brenda June Petker, Nov. 12, 1977; children—Kerri Lynn, Michelle N., Olivia Marie. Earthworm grower, owner Templeton (Calif.) Worm Ranch, 1975—; mktg. dir. Invivo Inc., Iowa City, 1977—, Bio-Eco-Systems Inc., Indpls., 1976—; pres. Am. Eco Systems Inc., Oceanside, Calif., 1977—; mktg. dir. other corps; mem. Calif. Farm Bur., 1975—. Recipient award of appreciation Rotary Internat., 1977, Kiwanis, 1977, Lions, 1976, C. of C. of Atascadero, Calif., 1976, Calif. U.-Calif. Poly. Inst., 1976, Madera Unified Sch. Dist., 1977; cert. Los Angeles County Health Dept. Mem. Vermiculturists Trade Assn., Western Organic Growers Assn., Calif. Water Pollution Control Assn. (San Diego sect.), Nat. Fedn. Ind. Bus., Nat. SBA. Clubs: Elks, Masons, Rotary (dir. local club 1977-78, chmn. world community services local club 1978-79). Home: 155 Madison St Oceanside CA 92054 Office: 368 E Broadway Vista CA 92083

PITTS, CELESTE IYONNE, insurance company executive; b. Charlotte, N.C., Oct. 26, 1949; d. Woodrow Judson and Amy Leigh (Freeman) Campbell; children by previous marriage; Scott Fowler, Terra Pitts. Student Jacksonville State U., 1967-69; B.S., Fla. Tech. Coll., 1970. Quality control analyst Blue Cross Fla., Jacksonville, 1968-71; supr. tng. Aetna Life Ins., Portland, Oreg., 1978, claim rep., 1979, tng. coordinator, Phoenix, 1980—. Mem. Am. Soc. Tng. and Devel., Claims Assn., Women's Network. Democrat. Home: 17249 N 7th St Apt 2144 Phoenix AZ 85022 Office: 3225 N Central St Suite 815 Phoenix AZ 85012

PITTS, THOMAS ROSS, orthodontist; b. Ely, Nev., Feb. 28, 1940; s. Arnold Deloss and Isabell (Smith) P.; B.S., U. Nev., Reno, 1961; D.D.S., U. Pacific, 1965; M.S. in Dentistry, U. Wash., 1970; m. Catherine Jean Oppio, Dec. 23, 1962; children—Arnold Charles, Thomas R.; m. 2d, Ouida Jean Hayden, June 1977. Dental lab technician, San Francisco, 1961-65; gen. practice dentistry, Reno, 1965, South San Francisco, Calif., 1968, Seattle, 1968-70; practice dentistry specializing in orthodontics, Reno, 1970—; instr. orthodontics U. Pacific, San Francisco, 1970-71; clin. instr. Western Nev. Community Coll., Reno, 1973—. Served with Dental Corps, U.S. Army, 1966-68. Mem. Soc. Preventive Dentistry, Am. Soc. Dentistry of Children, Nev. State Orthodontic Soc. (pres. 1976-77), Pacific Coast Soc. Orthodontists (bd. dirs.), Acad. Gen. Dentistry, Pierre Fauchard Acad., Am. Dental Assn., Internat. Gnathology Soc., Am. Assn. Orthodontists, Nev. State Dental Assn., Sierra Gnathological Study Club, Found. Orthodontic Research, No. Nev. Dental Soc. (pres. 1976—). Home: 1185 W Peckham Ln Reno NV 89509 Office: 3605 Grant Dr Reno NV 89509

PIZZATO, GENE F(RANK), foods corporation executive; b. Highland Park, Ill., July 15, 1934; s. Albert and Angelina (Busseto) P.; m. Geraldine R. Colton, Aug. 7, 1936; children—Tonia Lee, Andria Jene B.S., U. Ill., 1956. Exec. trainee Jewel Food Stores, Chgo., 1954-57; various sales and new product devel. positions Pillsbury, Mpls., 1957-64; regional sales ofcl. Western U.S., Premium Corp. Am., 1965-67; sales ofcl. Luncheon Is Served, Inc., Broomfield, Colo., 1968—, now v.p. sales. Active charities and Roman Catholic Ch. Served with U.S. Army, 1957-59. Recipient various sales awards Pillsbury and Luncheon Is Served. Mem. Am. Mgmt. Assn., Sales Mgmt. Lodge: KC. Address: 20095 Weld County Rd 3 Berthoud CO 80513

PLAKOSH, PAUL, JR., psychologist; b. Pitts., May 17, 1949; s. Paul and Leonora (Durso) P.; B.S. summa cum laude, U. Pitts., 1973; M.A., U. Iowa, 1976; Ph.D., Palo Alto Sch. Profl. Psychology, 1978. Research psychologist Langley Porter Inst., U. Calif., San Francisco, 1978-81; exec. dir. Franklin Clinic, San Francisco, 1981—. Mem. Am. Psychol. Assn., Internat. Neuropsychol. Soc., AAAS. Address: 291 Broderick St San Francisco CA 94117

PLANAS, RODOLFO E., planning consultant; b. Bremen, Germany, Apr. 1, 1915; s. Juan J.J. and Elsa H.C. (Koechert) Planas y Calvet, m. Herta Boeninger-Armstrong; m. 2d, Marian Traber. B.A., U. Barcelona (Spain); B.Sc. equivalent, Fed. Inst. Tech., Zurich; Ph.D. in Econs., U. Zurich. Jr. exec. Hoffmann-La Roche, Inc., Nutley, N.J., 1942-46; dir. internat. ops Forstner, Inc., Irvington, N.J., 1946-61, cons. internat. ops., East Orange, N.J., 1961-64; pres. Quickbonner Team, Inc., planning cons., Millburn, N.J., 1965-76; cons., lectr. on office facilities planning, 1976—, mem. speakers panel bi-ann. Office Landscape Symposium. Mem. adv. council to F.E. Seidman Coll. Bus. Adminstrn., Grand Valley State U., Allendale, Mich. Mem. Am. Soc. Interior Designers (hon.), Orgn. Facility Mgrs. and Planners (hon.). Introduced office landscape planning concept and methods, U.S and Can. Address: Apt 316 1640 Ufton Ct Kelowna BC V1Y 8L5 Canada

PLANT, KENNETH CECIL, personnel executive; b. Chgo., Feb. 21, 1952; s. Walter Cecil and Marjorie Elizabeth (Nordlie) P.; m. Catherine Lyn Starkey, Aug. 26, 1975; children—Kenneth Aaron, Eden Elizabeth. B.A., Brigham Young U., 1976, M.P.A., 1978. Ombudsman Brigham Young U., Provo, Utah, 1976-77; adminstrv. asst. personnel Utah State Tng. Sch., American Fork, 1977, asst. program dir., 1977-80, asst. dir. personnel, 1980-82; dir. human resources Murdock Internat., Provo, 1982—; mgmt. cons. Mem. Am. Soc. Personnel Adminstrn., Am. Compensation Assn., Am. Soc. Tng. and Devel., Personnel Assn. Central Utah (treas.). Mormon. Editorial reviewer Personnel Adminstrator. Home: 972 E Maple Dr Provo UT 84660 Office: PO Box 799 Provo UT 84603

PLANTE, GEORGE, systems analyst; b. San Pedro, Calif., Apr. 18, 1939; s. Joseph Henry and Elaine Hattie (Wilson) P.; B.A. in Fin., Columbia Coll., 1976; 1 son, Christopher Michael. Owner, George Plante Ins. Agy., Los Angeles, 1963-72; pres. U.S. Systems Devel. and Investments, San Diego, 1972—. Served to lt. USCGR, 1976—. Mem. Res. Officers Assn., U.S. Naval Inst. Republican. Home: 13850 Chaparral Terr Valley Center CA 92082 Office: PO Box 28759 San Diego CA 92128

PLATE, WILLIAM CARL, graphics company executive; b. Jennings, La., Dec. 14, 1946; s. Carl Ferdinand and Sara Evelyn (Noland) P.; A.A., Los Angeles Pierce Coll., 1970; B.S., San Jose State U., 1974; M.B.A., Pepperdine U., 1983; m. Nancy Lee Noddings, May 24, 1975 (div. May 1980); 1 dau., Eleanor Lindsey; m. 2d, Deborah Lynn Wilmot, 1982. Founder, pres. Arrow Graphics, San Jose, Woodland Hills, Sacramento and Tustin, Calif., also Phoenix, Dallas, and Houston, 1971—. Pres., Naglee Park Homeowners Assn., 1975-77; mem. San Jose Parking Adv. Bd., 1975-77. Mem. Sales and Mktg. Council, Bldg. Industry Assn. Democrat. Home: 1160 Britton Ave San Jose CA 95125 Office: 417 Lano St San Jose CA 95125

PLATT, LAWRENCE BRADLEY, furniture manufacturing company executive; b. Los Angeles, Aug. 9, 1952; s. Arthur and Barbara P.; m. Karen Kay, Mar. 1980. B.A., U. So. Calif., 1974, J.D., 1977. Bar: Calif. 1977. Vice pres. prodn. and overseas ops. Cal-Marble Furniture Mfg. Corp., Los Angeles, 1977—. Vice pres. Pacific Southwestern div. Am. Jewish Congress, 1978—, mem. nat. governing council, 1978-80, nat. exec. council, 1980—, nat. trustee, 1981—. Mem. ABA, Calif. Bar Assn., Am. Importers Assn., Calif. Furniture Mfg. Assn. (bd. dirs. 1983—), Skull and Dagger Soc., Order of the Palm, Phi Beta Kappa, Phi Kappa Phi. Office: 1630 Trinity St Los Angeles CA 90015

PLAUDIS, MICHELE DIANE, air force officer; b. Salem, Oreg., Sept. 19, 1943; d. Edward Neal and Marian (Gray) Snyder. B.S., Oreg. Coll. Edn., 1967. Commd. 2d lt., U.S. Air Force, 1967, advanced through grades to lt. col., 1983, info. officer 9th Weather Reconnaissance Wing, McClellan AFB, Calif., 1967-71, asst. info. officer 51st Air Base Wing, Osan, Korea, 1972, chief profl. pubs. Community Coll. of the Air Force, Randolph AFB, 1973-77, chief protocol Air Tng. Command, 1977-78, chief advt. and publicity 3568th USAF Recruiting Sqdn., Ft. Douglas, Utah, 1978-80, 3506th USAF Recruiting Group, Mather AFB, Calif.,

1980-81, comdr. 3563d USAF Recruiting Squadron, 1981—. Chmn., Bob Hope Christmas Show, Osan AB, Korea, 1972. Recipient Non-commd. Officers Assn. Achievement award, 1973; Air Force Sgts. Assn. Hon. Membership award, 1976. Mem. Air Force Assn., Am. Acad. Arts and Scis., Kappa Pi. Contbr. articles to profl. jours.

PLEMING, LAURA CHALKER, educator; b. Sheridan, Wyo., May 25, 1913; d. Sidney Thomas and Florence Theresa (Woodbury) Chalker; B.A., Long Beach State Coll. (now Calif. State U., Long Beach), 1953, M.A. in Speech and Drama, 1954; postgrad. U. So. Calif., 1960-63; Rel.D., Sch. Theology, Claremont, Calif., 1968; m. Edward Kibbler Pleming, Aug. 25, 1938; children—Edward Kibbler, Rowena Pleming Chamberlin, Sidney Thomas. Profl. Bible tchr., 1953—; lectr. Calif. State U., Long Beach, 1960-66, U. So. Calif., 1963-65; Bible scholar for teaching Scriptures Program, First Ch. of Christ Scientist, Boston, 1970-75; free-lance Bible lectr., tchr., resource person for adult seminars, 1954—; active in summer teaching for young people, 1963-68; tchr. adult edn. Principia Coll., summers 1969-71; tour lectr. to Middle East, yearly, 1974—; mem. archaeol. team, Negev, Israel. Mem. Am. Acad. Religion, AAUP, Soc. Biblical Lit. and Exegesis, Am. Schs. Oriental Research, Inst. Mediterranean Studies, Religious Edn. Assn., Internat. Congress Septuagint and Cognate Studies, Phi Beta, Zeta Tau Alpha, Gamma Theta Upsilon. Republican. Christian Scientist. Author: Triumph of Job, 1979; editor Bibleletter, 1968, 76, 81, 82, 83. Home: 2999 E Ocean Blvd Apt 2020 Long Beach CA 90803

PLENK, AGNES MERO, psychologist; b. Budapest, Hungary, Jan. 28, 1917; d. Julian and Rose (Szesci) Mero; m. Henry P. Plenk, June 17, 1938; children—Bruce, Penny Plenk Dalrymple, Timothy. B.A., Northwestern U., 1945, M.A., 1947; Ph.D., U. Utah, 1967. Lic. psychologist, Utah. Sr. psychologist dept. Psychiatry Med. Sch., U. Utah, 1947-50, instr. ednl. psychology, 1972—; pvt. practice, Salt Lake City, 1950-62; founder, dir., Holladay Community Nursery Sch., Salt Lake City, 1953-62; founder, The Children's Ctr., Salt Lake City, 1962, exec. dir., 1962—. Bd. dirs. Utah Assn. Mental Health. Recipient Jane Adams award, 1968. Mem. Am. Psychol. Assn., Utah Psychol. Assn. (pres. 1976), Am. Orthopsychiat. Assn., Am. Assn. Psychiat. Services for Children. Congregationalist. Clubs: Cottonwood, Salt Lake City Tennis, Bonneville Knife and Fork (dir.). Contbr. articles to profl. jours. Home: 865 S Monument Park Circle Salt Lake City UT 84108 Office: 1855 Medical Circle Salt Lake City UT 84112

PLENK, HENRY P., radiation oncologist; b. Vienna, May 19, 1917; came to U.S., 1938; s. Otto and Edith P.; cand.med., U. Vienna, 1935-38; B.M., Northwestern U., 1941, M.D., 1942, M.S. in Pathology, 1946; m. Agnes Mero, June 17, 1938; children—Bruce, Penny, Jane, Timothy Peter. Intern Evanston (Ill.) Hosp., 1942; resident in radiology Evanston Hosp.-Northwestern U., 1942-43, 46-47; asst. in gastroenterology U. Chgo. Clinics, 1943-44; chief dept. radiology Salt Lake Gen. Hosp. and U. Utah Med. Sch., 1947-52; dir. dept. radiology St. Mark's Hosp., Salt Lake City, 1952-69, dir. tumor inst., 1960-69; pres. Radiation Center Oncologists, LDS Hosp., Salt Lake City, 1969—; clin. prof. radiation oncology U. Utah. Served to capt. M.C., AUS, 1944-46. Diplomate Am. Bd. Radiology. Fellow Am. Coll. Radiology; mem. AMA, Utah Med. Soc., Utah Radiol. Soc., Radiol. Soc. N. Am., Am. Soc. Therapeutic Radiology, Brit. Inst. Radiology, Soc. Chmn. Acad. Radiation Oncology, Am. Assn. Cancer Research, Radiotherapy Oncology Group, Sigma Xi. Mem. United Ch. of Christ. Home: 835 Monument Park Circle Salt Lake City UT 84108 Office: 325 8th Ave Salt Lake City UT 84143

PLESSNER, GERALD MAURICE, fund raising management executive; b. St. Louis, Oct. 10, 1934; s. Herman and Ida Rose (Goldstein) P.; m. Carole Renee Spirtas, May 25, 1959; children—Mitchell Scott, Janice Aurelia, Ellen Beth. B.A. in Human Relations, Mo. Valley Coll., 1957. Cert. fund raising exec. Exec. Boy Scouts of Am., St. Joseph, Mo., St. Louis, Pitts., Miami, Fla., Chgo. and Pasadena, Calif., 1957-75; mng. editor Consumer Newsletter, Los Angeles, 1975-76; pres. Fund Raisers, Inc., Arcadia Calif., 1976—; adj. faculty U. So. Calif. Served as sgt. CIC, U.S. Army, 1959-62. Recipient Disting. Alumni award Mo Valley Coll. 1979; named Pro of Yr., 1983. Mem. Nat. Soc. Fund Raising Execs. (pres.' award 1982), San Fernando Valley Pub. Relations Round Table (exec. bd.). Clubs: Publicity of Los Angeles, Am. Humanics (Kansas City). Republican. Jewish. Author: Charity Auction Management Manual, 1980; Golf Tournament Management Manual, 1981; Testimonial Dinner and Luncheon Management Manual, 1981. Contbr. articles to profl. jours. Office: 59 W La Sierra Dr Arcadia CA 91006

PLIMPTON, JONATHAN FRED, airline mgr.; b. Beirut, July 2, 1948 (parents Am. citizens); s. Fred and Joanna P.; B.A., Case Western Res. U., 1970; M.B.A., U. Chgo., 1973; m. Anne Carmona, Aug. 19, 1978. Mgmt. tng. program, reservations agt. Pan Am. Airlines, Washington, 1970-71; group and conv. sales mgr. Braniff Internat. Airlines, Chgo., 1971-73; regional mgr. Mexicana Airlines, St. Louis, 1973-74, San Francisco, 1974-77, sales mgr. U.S. and Can., Los Angeles, 1977-81; owner Travel Industry Mktg., Inc., San Francisco, 1981—. Fellow Inst. Cert. Travel Agts., Assn. Cert. Travel Agts., Sales Mgmt. Execs.; mem. Am. Soc. Travel Agts., Pacific Area Travel Assn., Am. Soc. Assn. Execs., U.S.-Mexico C. of C. Republican. Office: 222 Agriculture Bldg Embarcadero San Francisco CA 94105

PLOTKIN, HARRIS M., management consultant, investor; b. Bklyn., Nov. 29, 1935; s. Benjamin and Celia (Poretzky) P.; m. Ruth Lois Wedeen, Aug. 24, 1958; children—James, Ellen, Deborah. B.S.E.E., Lehigh U., 1957; postgrad. UCLA, U. So. Calif. Design and project engr. Gen. Dynamics-Astronautics, 1957-60; asst. program dir. TRW Systems, 1960-66; dir. mktg. Heliodyne Corp., 1966-68; pres. Plotkin & Assocs., San Bernardino, Calif., 1968—. Bd. dirs. San Bernardino Community Arts Prodns., San Bernardino Tournament of Roses Assn. Mem. Am. Personnel and Guidance Assn., Am. Soc. Tng. and Devel., Mensa, San Bernardino C. of C., San Bernardino Execs. Assn. Republican. Jewish. Club: San Bernardino Rotary. Contbr. articles to profl. jours. Office: 1255 E Highland Ave Suite 209 San Bernardino CA 92404

PLUMB, PHILLIP LEE, farmer; b. Flagler, Colo., Dec. 8, 1931; s. Loren Wilber and Mabel Glendora (Roseberry) P.; m. Rosalynn McCue, Aug. 20, 1953; children—Loren, Rosalee, G. Dawn, RoxAnn. Grad. Flagler High Sch., 1949. Mechanic Ford Co., Flagler, 1949-52; farmer, Lakin, Kans., 1954-59; co-owner, mng. ptnr. Plumb & Mc Cue Co., 1959—. Mem. Arriba (Colo.) sch. bd., 1973-77. Served with U.S. Army, 1952-54. Mem. Am. Legion. Republican. Lutheran.

PLUMB, ROBERT GORDON, education educator, consultant; b. Boise, Idaho, Nov. 26, 1940; s. Hylon Theron and Geraldine (Holladay) P.; m. Cheryl Yvonne Johnson, Nov. 10, 1968 (div.); 1 son, Hylon Theron IV. B.S.Ed., U. Idaho, 1963, Ph.D., 1982; M.S.Ed., South Oreg. State Coll., 1967; M.Ed., Coll. Idaho, 1978. Cert. secondary tchr., Idaho. Tchr. Highlands High Sch., Sacramento, 1964-66; asst. prof. English and Speech Coll. South Idaho, 1966-70; dir. theatre activities, asst. prof. York Coll. (Pa.), 1973-77; asst. cons. Idaho Dept. Edn., Boise, 1977-78; assoc. prof., chmn. dept. edn., dir. Omak campus Heritage Coll., 1981—; cons. grants, evaluation. Chmn. Yakima (Wash.) Pub. Access TV Adv. Council. Mem. Wash. Council Deans and Dirs. Edn. (chmn.), Assn. Supervision and Curriculum Devel., Am. Ednl. Research Assn., Phi Delta Kappa. Author: Plumb's Poems by Bob, 1974; Idaho State Plan for Career Education, 1978; The Cognitive Effect on Cross-Age Tutors of Mathematics, 1982. Home: 111 N 22 S Ave Yakima WA 98902 Office: Heritage Coll Route 3 Box 3540 Toppenish WA 98948

PLUMMER, LEAVELLE, correctional educator; b. Sulligent, Ala., Sept. 5, 1941; d. Marvin G. and Azelle (Weaver) Duncan; m. John R. Plummer, June 14, 1959; children—Vicki Sue, Karen Kay Plummer. B.S., U. So. Colo., 1971; postgrad. U. No. Colo., Adams State Coll., Colo. State U. Teaching cert., Colo. Legal sec. J. Harrison Hawthorne, Canon City, Colo., 1965-67; adult edn. instr. Colo. State Penitentiary, Canon City, 1971-82; vocat. educator Pueblo Community Coll., Canon City, 1983—; presentor in English adult basic edn. div. State of Colo. Dept. Edn. Nominated Outstanding Correctional Educator, Colo., 1982. Mem. AAUW, Correctional Edn. Assn., Colo. Correctional Assn., Nat. Correctional Assn., Am. Vocat. Assn., Colo. Vocat. Assn., Colo. Edn. for and about Bus. Republican. Methodist. Club: Rebakah's Foresters. Home: 1015 Short St Canon City CO 81212 Office: PO Box 500 Canon City CO 81212

PLUMMER, RAYMOND EUGENE, U.S. judge; b. Harlan, Iowa, Mar. 27, 1913; s. Joseph Carl and Stella Mae (Keldgord) P.; A.B., U. Nebr., 1937, LL.B., 1939; m. Mary Marjorie Provost, Dec. 28, 1941; children—Raymond E., Marjorie Jane. Admitted to Nebr. bar, 1939; practiced in Lincoln, 1941-44; asst. U.S. atty., Anchorage, 1944-46, U.S. atty., 1946-49; pvt. practice, 1949-61; U.S. judge Dist. Ct. Alaska, 1961-74, sr. judge, 1974—. Former mem. Ty. Bd. Bar Examiners, Past pres. Boys' Club of Alaska, Inc. Former mem. Democratic Nat. Com.; Mem. Territorial Legislature, 1955. Mem. ABA, Fed. Bar Assn., Alaska Bar Assn., Nebr. Bar Assn., Am. Jud. Soc., Phi Alpha Delta. Roman Catholic. Home: 1729 W 11th Ave Anchorage AK 99501 Office: PO Box 1080 US District Ct Anchorage AK 99501

PLUTCHAK, NOEL BERNARD, oceanographer; b. Green Bay, Wis., Dec. 14, 1932; s. Bernard Edward and Violet Marie (Sherman) P.; B.S., U. Wis., 1960; M.S., Fla. State U., 1963; postgrad. Oreg. State U., 1969-71; m. Sandra Jean Kolvig, June 20, 1964 (div. 1976); 1 dau., Channin Paige. Research asst. Lamont Obs., Columbia U., 1963-66; head phys. oceanography Bendix Marine Advisers, Inc., LaJolla, Calif., 1966-69; mgr. TOTEM project Oreg. State U., Corvallis, 1971-73; sr. scientist environ. geology U. So. Calif., Los Angeles, 1973-76; chief scientist environ. engring. div. Interstate Electronics Corp., Anaheim, Calif., 1976—. Served with USAF, 1952-56. Mem. Am. Geophys. Union, Marine Tech. Soc., Oceanographic Found., Am. Mgmt. Soc., Town Hall, Sigma Xi. Contbr. articles to profl. jours. Patentee in field. Office: Interstate Electronics Corp Div 8000 707 E Vermont Ave Box 3117 Anaheim CA 92803

POAGE, THOMAS FRANSEN, civil engring. firm exec.; b. Torrington, Wyo., Sept. 21, 1940; s. Lucian Paul and Hilda Marie (Fransen) P.; student U. Oreg., 1959-60; B.S., Oreg. State U., 1964; m. Ginger Rae Gallatin, Mar. 16, 1963; children—Laura, Carol, Susan, Ellen. Oreg. State hwy. engr., 1964-67; asst. city engr. City of Eugene (Oreg.), 1967-73; partner Brown & Poage Cons. Engrs., Eugene, 1974-78; pres. Tom Poage Engring. & Surveying, Inc., Eugene, 1978—, Engring. Tech. Corp., Eugene, 1979—. Mem. Lane Utilities Coordinating Council, 1970—, bd. dirs., 1971-80; mem. City of Eugene Bike Com., 1971-79, City of Eugene Budget Com., 1974-76. Registered profl. engr. and land surveyor, Oreg. Mem. ASCE, Am. Water Works Assn., Homebuilders Assn., Profl. Land Surveyors Oreg., Nat. Fedn. Ind. Bus., Eugene Council of Engrs. (pres.). Republican. Club: Town of Eugene. . Home: 4325 Catalina St Eugene OR 97402 Office: Tom Poage Engring & Surveying Inc Suite 2-E 401 E 10th Ave Eugene OR 97401

PODBOY, JOHN WATTS, clinical psychologist; b. York, Pa., Sept. 27, 1943; s. August John and Harriett Virginia (Watts) P.; m. Carolyn Sue Baughman, Feb. 6, 1972; 1 son, Matthew John. B.A., Dickinson Coll., 1966; M.S., San Diego State Coll., 1971; Ph.D., U. Ariz., 1973. Dir., Vets. Counseling Center, U. Ariz., Tucson, 1972-73; project dir. San Mateo County (Calif.) Human Relations Dept., Redwood City, 1974; staff psychologist Sonoma State Hosp., Eldridge, Calif., 1975-81; cons. clin. psychologist Comprehensive Care Corp., Newport Beach, Calif., 1974-75, Sonoma County (Calif.) Probation Dept., 1976—; asst. prof. Sonoma State U., 1977-81; dir. Sonoma Diagnostic and Remedial Center, 1979-82. Chmn. San Mateo County Diabetes Assn., 1975. Served to lt. USNR, 1966-69. Mem. Am. Psychol. Assn., Western Psychol. Assn., Redwood Psychol. Assn. (pres. 1983), Nat. Council Alcoholism, Nat. Rehab. Assn. Home: PO Box 488 Kenwood CA 95452

PODEST, MABEL FRANCES, employment counselor; b. Monticello, N.Y., Jan. 16, 1952; d. Rudolph Frank and Mabel Veronica Podest. B.A. in Social Welfare, N.Mex. State U., 1974; M.S.W., Ariz. State U., 1976. Student social worker Ariz. Dept. Econ. Security, Coolidge, 1974-75, student social worker div. mental retardation, 1975-76; student govt. intern N.Mex. Div. Vocat. Rehab., Las Cruces, 1975; migrant outreach worker N.Mex. Employment Security Commn., Deming, 1976-77, employment counselor, 1977-81; dir., instr. Luna County Work Activity Ctr., Southwestern N.Mex. Services to Handicapped Children and Adults, Deming, 1981—. Bd. dirs. Luna County Assn. Retarded Citizens; active Nat. Assn. Retarded Citizens, Deming Community Band. Mem. Am. Personnel and Guidance Assn., N.Mex. Personnel and Guidance Assn., Am. Rehab. Counselors Assn., Nat. Employment Counselors. Assn. Office: 112 S Gold St Deming NM 88030

PODGUR, HAROLD, hospital executive; b. N.Y.C., Nov. 29, 1931; s. Max and Mollie (Lewis) P.; children—Marcie, Leslie. Student CCNY, 1949-51; B.B.A. in Acctg., U. Miami, 1957. Acct., Arthur Andersen & Co., C.P.A.s, 1957-60; asst. comptroller Lenox Hill Hosp., N.Y.C., 1960-63, comptroller, 1963-70; dir. fiscal services St. Mary's Hosp. and Med. Ctr., San Francisco, 1970-76; v.p. fin. Mt. Zion Hosp. and Med. Ctr., San Francisco, 1976—; mem. faculty M.B.A. program in health services mgmt. Golden Gate U., 1975-77, professorial lectr., 1977;. mem. spl. com. West Bay Hosp. Conf., 1978; mem. fin. com. San Francisco Peer Rev. Orgn., 1979—; mem. loan ins. com. Calif. Dept. Health, 1974—. Mem. budget and fin. com. Sta. KQED-TV, 1977—. Served with USAF, 1951-55. Fellow Hosp. Fin. Mgmt. Assn. (dir. No. Calif. chpt. 1973, v.p. 1974, pres.-elect 1975, Follmer award 1970, Reeves award 1976, Outstanding Mem. award 1975), Hosp. Council No. Calif. (rev. com. Commn. for Adminstrv. Services in Hosps. 1980). Club: Commonwealth (San Francisco). Office: Mt Zion Hosp and Med Center PO Box 7921 San Francisco CA 94120

POEDY, JAMES FREDERICK, newspaper editor, public relations executive; b. Montebello, Calif., May 31, 1951; s. Gaston Joseph and Marion Elizabeth (Reig) P.; m. Maree E. Church, Dec. 16, 1947; 1 son, Brian Daniel Alexander. Student Rio Hondo Coll., 1974-78. Staff reporter Los Angeles Citizen, 1978-79, assoc. editor, 1979-81, editor, 1981—; pub. relations dir. Los Angeles County Fedn. Labor. Mem. Los Angeles City Council Pres.'s Ballot Reform com., 1979; pub. info. com. Los Angeles County Region 5 United Way. Democrat. Lutheran. Office: 2130 W 9th St Los Angeles CA 90006

POESCHEL, ROBERT LESLIE, electrical engineer; b. Aurora, Ill., Oct. 11, 1932; s. Leslie Rudolf and Elsie Mae (Weddige) P.; m. Geraldine Helen Esch, Oct. 1, 1965; children—Anne-Marie, Jennifer. B.S., U. Ill., 1959, M.S. in Elec. Engring., 1961; Ph.D. in Elec. Engring., Calif. Inst. Tech., 1967. With Hughes Research Labs., Malibu, Calif., 1967—, sect. head, program mgr., asst. dept. mgr., mgr. projects, 1971—, asst. mgr. plasma physics dept., 1980—. Served with U.S. Army, 1953-56. Mem. Am. Phys. Soc., IEEE, AIAA (elec. propulsion tech. com.), Tau Beta Pi, Phi Kappa Phi, Eta Kappa Nu. Republican. Mem. United Church of Christ. Contbr. numerous articles to tech. jours. Home: 935 Calle Collado Thousand Oaks CA 91360 Office: 3011 Malibu Canyon Rd Malibu CA 90265

POLAHA, JEROME MICHAEL, lawyer; b. Allentown, Pa., Feb. 21, 1940; s. Andrew Stephen and Justine Rita (Lanshe) P.; m. Esther Eben, Dec. 27, 1975; children—Erik, Jon, Michael, Kristofer. A.A., Syracuse U., 1957; B.A., U. Nev., 1965; J.D., George Washington U., 1968. Bar: Nev. 1968. Assoc. Breen, Young, Whitehead & Hoy, Reno, Nev., 1968-69; trial dep. Washoe County Pub. Defender, 1969-72; ptnr. Grellman & Polaha, Reno, 1972-75, Grellman, Polaha & Coffin, Reno, 1975, Polaha, Conner, Semenza & Lutfy, 1975-82, Polaha & Conner, Reno, 1982—; adj. prof. criminal law Old Coll. Law, Reno, pro tem mcpl. judge Sparks, Nev., 1971—. Career adv. Boy Scouts Am.-Explorer Scouts, Post 415. Served with USAF, 1957-60. Recipient Achievement award for young lawyers ABA, 1973-74. Mem. Nev. Bar Assn., ABA, Nev. Trial Lawyers Assn. (dir.), Barrister Club Nev. (pres. 1974-76), Nat. Assn. Criminal Def. Lawyers, Calif. Trial Lawyers Assn., Assn. Trial Lawyers Am., Am. Bd. Criminal Lawyers (fellow, treas., dir.). Democrat. Clubs: Internat. Serra, Aquarian Toastmasters (Reno); Elks. Home: 115 Greenridge Dr Reno NV Office: 310 S Arlington Ave Reno NV 89505

POLAKOFF, KEITH IAN, historian; b. N.Y.C., Dec. 12, 1941; s. Irwin L. and Edna (Sopkin) P.; B.A. magna cum laude, Clark U., 1963; M.A., Northwestern U., 1966, Ph.D., 1968; m. Carol J. Gershuny, June 21, 1964; children—Amy Ellen, Adam Matthew. Lectr., Herbert H. Lehman Coll., CUNY, 1967-69; asst. prof. history Calif. State U., Long Beach, 1969-73, assoc. prof. 1973-78, prof., 1978—; editor The History Tchr., 1972-77, prodn. mgr., 1977-80; acting assoc. dean instrnl. support Sch. Social and Behavioral Scis., Calif. State U., Long Beach, 1980-81, assoc. dean ednl. policy, 1981—; mem. council Pacific Coast Athletic Assn., 1982—, Western Collegiate Athletic Assn., 1982—. Mem., clk. bd. trustees Los Alamitos Sch. Dist., 80; pres. Long Beach Grand Opera Assn. Mem. Orgn. Am. Historians (exec. bd. 1977-80), So. Hist. Assn., Phi Beta Kappa. Democrat. Jewish. Author: The Politics of Inertia, 1973; (with others) Generations of Americans, 1976; Political Parties in American History, 1981. Home: 2971 Druid Ln Los Alamitos CA 90720 Office: Calif State U Long Beach CA 90840

POLANSKY, GERALDINE FRANCES, public relations, mktg. and income diversification co. exec.; b. Kaska, Pa., Nov. 27, 1944; d. Michael and Wanda Frances (Garbish) P.; B.A., Kutztown State Coll., 1966; m. Leo Howard Cairns, May 19, 1974; 1 dau., Nicole. Computer programmer, analyst Air Products & Chemicals Inc., Pa., 1966-68; data processing cons. Booz, Allen & Hamilton, Inc., Chgo., Raleigh, N.C., San Juan, P.R., Los Angeles, Detroit, Mexico City, 1968-70; programming mgr. Fed. Res. Bank, Chgo., Detroit, 1970-72; mortgage project mgr. Del. Trust Co., Wilmington, 1972-74; info. analyst E.I. duPont de Nemours, Wilmington, 1974-75; internat. banking specialist, project mgr. Western Bancorp Data Processing Co., Los Angeles, London and N.Y.C., 1975-79; asst. v.p. new product devel. United Calif. Bank, Los Angeles, 1979; owner, mgr. G.F. Polansky, automation adv. and cons., Los Angeles, 1980—; sr. partner C/P Industries, Los Angeles, 1981—. Mem. AAUW, Nat. Assn. Female Execs. Club: Sunset Hills Country (Thousand Oaks, Calif.). Home: 683 Whispering Oaks Pl Thousand Oaks CA 91320

POLICH, KAREN JUNE SAFER, art and archtl. historian, archtl. photographer; b. Los Angeles, Feb. 2, 1951; d. Henry Edward and Gladys (Mooradian) Safer; B.A. cum laude, UCLA, 1974; M.A. with honors Calif. State U.-Long Beach, 1981; m. Frank Alin Polich, Dec. 29, 1979. Research asst., editor Art Dept., Calif. State U., Long Beach, 1975-76, 78-81, teaching asst., instr., 1981—; photographer ERA, Los Angeles, 1980; researcher, editor Los Angeles Artists Index; art and archtl. researcher, photographer, Los Angeles and Long Beach, 1974—; guest lectr., curator in field. Active Los Angeles Conservancy, Los Angeles County Mus. Art, Long Beach Mus., Smithsonian Instn. Mem. So. Calif. Hist. Soc. (Los Angeles), Los Angeles Architects, Theatre Hist. Soc., Soc. Archtl. Historians. Author: Functions of Decoration in the American Movie Palace, 1981; Los Angeles Architects Index 1900-80, 1982; contbr. Wayne Thiebaud Exhbn. Catalogue, 1976. Home and Office: 1136 E 3d St Apt 8 Long Beach CA 90802

POLIS, JOAN FRANCES, elementary school teacher; b. East Chicago, Ind., Dec. 29, 1933; d. John and Joan Bonefacich; m. John M. Polis, June 8, 1957; children—Annemarie, Thomas, James, Michael, Kathryn. B.A. in Edn., Marycrest Coll., 1956; M.S. in Edn., Purdue U., 1970. Cert. tchr., Calif. Tchr. elem. schs., East Chicago, 1956-58, 65, 69, Modesto, Calif., 1970—. Mem. Calif. Tchrs. Assn., Children's Home Soc. Roman Catholic. Home: 3916 Fieldcrest Ct Modesto CA 95355 Office: 800 Woodrow Ave Modesto CA 95355

POLITOVICH, JOHN JUNIOR, logistician; b. Centerville, Iowa, July 26, 1929; s. John Frank and Leola Grace (Farris) P.; B.S. in Physics, Western Ill. U., 1953; M.S. in Systems Mgmt., U. So. Calif., 1974; m. Nancy Abbott, Aug. 8, 1953; children—Marcia Kay, Karen Louise. Successively chief instr., ops. staff mem. v.p. field engring. and quality assurance, personnel dir., systems test supr. ITT-Gilfillan, Los Angeles, 1953-67; project staff engr., project logistician for advanced projects and developing programs Gen. Dynamics, Pomona, Calif., 1967—; night instr. electronics Chaffey Coll., 1967—. Served with USAF, 1946-51. Mem. Soc. Logistics Engrs. (internat. pres., dir. at large). Republican. Methodist. Home: 930 W E St Ontario CA 91762 Office: General Dynamics MZ 401-6 PO Box 2507 Pomona CA 91769

POLKINGHORN, BETTE ANN, economist, educator; b. Sacramento, Mar. 16, 1937; d. Tom and Lucille Elizabeth (Bander) Hall; m. R. Stephen Polkinghorn (div.); m. 2d, Paul Hatcher (div.); 1 son, Gordon P. Hatcher. B.A., Stanford U., 1960; M.A., Calif. State U.-Sacramento, 1971; Ph.D., U. Calif.-Davis, 1972. Mem. faculty U. Calif.-Davis, 1969, Calif. State U.-Hayward, 1970; faculty Calif. State U.-Sacramento, 1971-76, prof. econs., 1977—; vis. faculty U. of Cape Coast (Ghana), 1976. Mem. Am. Econ. Assn., History of Econs. Soc., Western Econ. Assn., Atlantic Econ. Assn. Democrat. Contbr. articles to profl. jours. Home: 1120B 24th St Sacramento CA 95816 Office: Calif State U 6000 J St Sacramento CA 95819

POLLACK, ELLIOT DAVID, banker; b. N.Y.C., June 3, 1945; s. Irving and Nettie (Cooper) P.; m. Cathy Pratt, July 11, 1980. B.S. in Bus. Adminstrn., Boston U., 1967; M.B.A., U. So. Calif., 1968. Securities analyst, portfolio mgr. Valley Nat. Bank Ariz., Phoenix, 1969-72; dir. research, 1972-75, v.p., mgr. econ. planning div., 1975—; instr. Glendale (Ariz.) Community Coll., Phoenix Coll. Bd. dirs. Camelback (Ariz.) Mental Health Found., active Valley Big Bros., Phoenix Urban League, Vis. Nurse Service, Valley Leadership. Mem. Nat. Assn. Bus. Economists, Phoenix Soc. Chartered Fin. Analysts, Inst. Chartered Fin. Analysts (cert.). Editor bank newsletters; contbr. articles in field to profl. jours. Home: 7609 Via del Reposo Scottsdale AZ 85258 Office: Valley Nat Bank Ariz PO Box 29514 Phoenix AZ 85038

POLLACK, MORTON JUDAH, television executive; b. Bklyn., Feb. 4, 1938; s. Nathan S. and Shirley (Goldstein) P.; children—Jill Feldman, Jonathan; m. Sharon A. Ripley, Nov. 29, 1973; m. Janice E. Levine, Nov. 27, 1980 (div.). Promotion mgr. Parents Mag., N.Y.C.; advt. mgr. Am.

Dairy Assn., Chgo.; promotion dir. Playboy, Chgo., Washington Post; v.p. advt. and promotion CBS, Los Angeles. Served with U.S. Navy. Recipient numerous maj. advt. awards including Addys and Clios. Mem. Hollywood Radio and TV Soc., Acad. TV Arts and Scis., Advt. Club Los Angeles, Jewish. Home: 3630 Barham Blvd Los Angeles CA 90068 Office: CBS 7800 Beverly Blvd Los Angeles CA 90036

POLLAK, MICHAEL, physics educator; b. Ostrava, Czechoslovakia, Sept. 1, 1926; s. Leo and Elsa (Winterstein) P.; m. Rosemarie Winterstein, June 13, 1964; children—Michelle, Tania. Student Tech. U. Prague, 1947-49; B.Sc.E.E., Israel Inst. Tech., 1953; M.S. in Physics, U. Pitts., 1956, Ph.D. in Physics, 1959. Jr. scientist Westinghouse Research Labs., Pitts., 1956-59; mem. tech. staff Bell Telephone Labs., Murray Hill, N.J., 1959-60; sr. scientist Westinghouse Research Labs., 1960-66; assoc. prof. physics U. Calif.-Riverside, 1966-69, prof., 1969—; cons. Jet Propulsion Labs.; vis. prof. U. Coll., Cardiff, Wales, 1972, Israel Inst. Tech., 1970, 77, U. Cambridge, 1977, UCLA, 1975. Served with Israeli Army, 1950-51. Sci. Research Council sr. fellow, 1972, 77; research grantee NSF. Mem. AAAS, Amnesty Internat. Editor: (with others) Low Mobility Materials, 1971; editorial bd. Jour. Biol. Physics, 1981—; contbr. articles to sci. jours. Home: 3051 Mountainview St Laguna Beach CA 92651

POLLAK, NORMAN LEE, accountant; b. Chgo., Aug. 16, 1931; s. Emery and Helen (Solomon) P.; diploma in commerce Northwestern U., 1955; postgrad. Pierce Coll., also U. Calif. at Westwood, 1960-63; m. Hilda Brower, June 16, 1980; children—Martin Joel, Elise Susan, Rhonda Louise. Jr., sr. acct. David Himmelblau & Co., Chgo., 1952-56, Barrios, Hilliard, Sain & Co., Beverly Hills, Calif., 1957-58; pvt. practice acctg., Encino and Van Nuys, Calif., 1958-62, Sherman Oaks, Calif., 1962—, Westlake Village, Calif., 1971—; pres. Norman L. Pollak Accountancy Corp.; guest lectr. U. Calif. at Westwood, also Los Angeles, 1962, Solar Energy Community Fair, Westlake Village, 1979, family law sect. Ventura County Bar Assn. Mem. Valley Estate Planning Council, sec., 1962-63, v.p., 1963-64, pres., 1964-65; v.p. Ventura County Estate Planning Council, 1973-74, pres., 1978-79. C.P.A., Calif. Mem. Am. Inst. C.P.A.s, Calif. Soc. C.P.A.s (com. cooperation credit grantors, securities industry com., chmn. San Fernando Valley tech. discussions group 1960-61), Am. Acctg. Assn., Nat. Assn. Accts., Delta Mu Delta, Northwestern Alumni Club, Sherman Oaks C. of C. (dir.), Westlake Village C. of C. Jewish (fin. sec. temple). Club: B'nai B'rith (treas.). Home: 31731 Foxfield Dr Westlake CA 91361 Office: Union Bank Plaza 15233 Ventura Blvd Sherman Oaks CA 91403 also Westlake Village 32107 Lindero Canyon Rd Westlake Village CA 91361

POLLARD, FRANK BOWLES, aeronautical engineering consultant; b. Hempstead, N.Y., Dec. 5, 1922; s. Frank J. and Christine A. (Bowles) P.; m. Catherine Mary, Feb. 22, 1945. B.S. in Aero. Engring., NYU, 1948. Registered profl. engr., Calif. Pres. Aircraft and Missile Cons., Hollister, Calif., 1957-63, 69-76; chief advanced program support Northrop Space Labs., Hawthorne, Calif., 1963-66; exec. adviser Douglas Missiles and Space Div., Huntington Beach, Calif., 1967-68; dir. advanced programs, Teledyne McCormick, Hollister, Calif., 1976-79; asst. to pres., dir. mktg. and contracts, Holex, Inc., Hollister, 1979-80; cons. in aerospace ordnance and microprocessors, 1980—. Served to capt. USAF, 1942-45. Assoc. fellow AIAA; mem. Aviation/Space Writers Assn., Golf Writers Assn. of Am., Calif. Golf Writers, San Benito County C. of C. (bd. dirs. 1977-80). Club: Ridgemark Golf and Country (Hollister, Calif.). Author Coll. textbook, golf book. Contbr. numerous articles to profl. jours. Office: 95 Caryl Ct Hollister CA 95023

POLLARD, LOUISE, systems librarian; b. Ft. Worth, Oct. 26, 1937; d. Sam Albert and Annie Bill (Prestridge) Kelley; m. Melvin E. Pollard, Apr. 2, 1961; children—Kelley Jean, Raymond Douglas. B.A. in English, N. Tex. State Coll., Denton, 1959; M.L.S., U. Md.-College Park, 1977. Interlibrary loan specialist Morgan, Lewis & Bockius, Washington, 1977-78; librarian U.S. Ct. Customs & Patent Apls., Washington, 1978-79; librarian Kennecott Minerals Co., Salt Lake City, 1979-82; systems librarian Consumer Fin. Services Am. Express Co., Salt Lake City, 1982—. Mem. Utah Library Assn., Spl. Libraries Assn., Assn. Info. Mgrs., Beta Phi Mu. Presbyterian. Office: 4315 S 2700 W Salt Lake City UT 84184

POLLCHIK, ALLAN LEE, psychologist; b. Denver, Sept. 18, 1949; s. Morris and Helen Ruth (Perlmutter) P.; B.A., UCLA, 1971; M.A., Vanderbilt U., 1973, Ph.D., 1975; m. Linda Lee Brown, Oct. 31, 1970. Intern, Langley Porter Neuropsychiat. Inst., U. Calif. Med. Sch., San Francisco, 1975-76; instr. San Diego State U., 1977—; clin., cons. psychologist El Camino Psychology Center, Oceanside, Calif., 1976-78; pres. Allan L. Pollchik, Ph.D., P.C., Oceanside, 1978—. Pres., Seawind/Oceanside Homeowners Assn., 1980. Nat. Merit scholar, 1967-71; NSF fellow, 1972-73; NIMH fellow, 1973-75. Mem. North County Psychol. Assn. (pres. 1980-81). Mem. Am. Psychol. Assn., Calif. Psychol. Assn., Interam. Soc. Psychology, Soc. Psychol. Study Social Issues, Zeta Beta Tau. Club: Oceanside Health. Home: 1973 Bluewater Way Oceanside CA 92054 Office: 2101 El Camino Real Suite 203A Oceanside CA 92054

POLLOCK, JOHN PHLEGER, lawyer; b. Sacramento, April 28, 1920; s. George Gordon and Irma (Phleger) P.; A.B., Stanford U., 1942; J.D., Harvard U., 1948; m. Juanita Irene Gossman, Oct. 26, 1945; children—Linda Pollock Fellows, Madeline Pollock Chiotti, John Phleger Jr., Gordon. Admitted to Calif. bar, 1949, U.S. Supreme Ct. bar, 1954; practice in Los Angeles, 1949—; partner firm Musick, Peeler & Garrett, 1953-60; mem. firm Rodi, Pollock, Pettker, Galbraith & Phillips. Pres., Los Angeles Area council Boy Scouts Am., 1970-71; former trustee Pitzer Coll., Claremont; trustee, pres. Jones Found., Los Angeles; trustee Good Hope Med. Found. Served with AUS, 1942-45. Fellow Am. Coll. Trial Lawyers; mem. Los Angeles County Bar Assn. (former trustee). Home: 30602 Paseo del Valle Laguna Niguel CA 92677 Office: 611 W 6th St Los Angeles CA 90017

POLLOCK, RICHARD EDWIN, former county adminstr.; b. Phila., Aug. 27, 1928; s. Ernest Edwin and Evelyn Marie (Scarlett) P.; student Armstrong Coll., 1947, U. Calif., Berkeley, 1949-51, 55; B.A. in Recreation, San Jose State U., 1961; postgrad. San Fernando Valley State U., 1969-70, U. Calif., Davis, 1963-77, UCLA, 1964, U. Calif., Santa Barbara, 1970, U. Redlands, 1979; m. Yvonne May Graves, Oct. 11, 1952; children—Colleen May, Karen Marie, Richard Irvin, Annette Yvonne, Mary Ann. Swim pool mgr. and instr. Berkley Tennis Club, 1955-56; police officer City of Berkeley, 1956; recreation and aquatic supr. Pleasant Hill (Calif.) Recreation and Park Dist., 1956-62; gen. mgr. Pleasant Valley Recreation and Park Dist., Camarillo, Calif., 1962-68; bldg. insp. Ventura County (Calif.), 1969-71; adminstr. Sacramento County-Carmichael Recreation and Park Dist., 1971-73; dir. parks and recreation Imperial County (Calif.), 1973-81; ret., 1981; mem. faculty Imperial Valley Jr. Coll., 1974-83, others; aquatic cons., 1957—; chmn. San Francisco Bay Area Conf. for Cooperation in Aquatics, 1958-59. Adviser/scoutmaster Desert Trails council Boy Scouts Am.; bd. dirs., instr. ARC; work with devel. disabled and handicapped children and adults. Served to 1st lt. U.S. Army, 1953-54; Korea. Recipient recognition for 41 years vol. service ARC, 1978; registered recreator and park mgr.; cert. elem., secondary and community coll. tchr., Calif. Mem. Nat. Recreation and Park Assn., AAHPER, Calif. Park and Recreation Soc., Calif. County Dirs. Parks and Recreation Assn., Calif. Boating Safety Officers Assn., Aircraft Owners and Pilots Assn., Nat. Assn. Emergency Med. Technicians. Democrat. Mormon. Author: Bibliography: A Pool of Aquatic Sources, 1960. Home: 1706 Lenrey Ave El Centro CA 92243

POLLOCK, WILLIAM EDWARD, sales engineer; b. Pedricktown, N.J., Apr. 29, 1941; s. William James and Elizabeth Blair (Carter) P.; B.S., U. S.C., 1969; B.S. in Fin., Calif. State U., 1975, M.B.A., 1977; postgrad. U. So. Calif., 1980—; m. Helga Franzizka Matejowics, Feb. 22, 1973; children—William Stephan, Erik Leopold. With Bank of Am., San Francisco, 1975-76, Detroit Diesel Allison, Berkeley, Calif., 1977-79; sales engr. Pfizer Inc., San Francisco, 1977-79; regional sales engr. So. Calif., Rogers Corp., Granada Hills, 1979—. Active PTA, Big Bros., Reagan election campaign. Served as lt. comdr. USN, 1959-63, 70-75. Mem. Navy League, Naval Res. Assn., Am. Mgmt. Assn., Am. Mktg. Assn., Res. Officers Assn., Delta Sigma Pi, Pi Kappa Alpha. Republican. Roman Catholic. Clubs: W. La Trojan, San Fernando Trojan. Address: 12266 Louise Ave Granada Hills CA 91344

POLLY, ZENA DENISE, clinical psychologist, therapist; b. Alhambra, Calif., Dec. 19, 1951; d. Paul Woodrow and Ruby Foy (Moore) P.; B.A., UCLA, 1973; M.S., Calif. State U.-Long Beach, 1975; Ph.D., Ariz. State U., 1977; m. Kim C. M. Sloat, June 27, 1981; stepchildren—Austin, Tyler, Kalani Sloat. Staff psychologist Columbia County Family Counseling Ctr., St. Helens, Oreg., 1978-80; dir. Diamond Head Mental Health Children's Team, Honolulu, 1980-82; pvt. practice clin. psychology, Honolulu, 1981—; mem. clin. faculty dept. psychiatry John Burns Sch. Medicine, U. Hawaii, Honolulu, 1981—; coordinator Divorce Experience Program, Family Ct., State Hawaii, Honolulu, 1982—. Mem. Am. Psychol. Assn., Am. Orthopsychiat. Assn., Assn. Family Conciliation Cts., Western Psychol. Assn., Hawaii Psychol. Assn. Office: 850 W Hind Dr Suite 224 Honolulu HI 96821

POLONSKY, DIMITRI, psychologist; b. Los Angeles, July 6, 1925; s. Joseph Boris and Olga (Skolnick) P.; A.B., U. Calif. at Los Angeles, 1950, 51, M.A., 1956; Ph.D., Claremont Grad. Sch., 1968; m. Manya Schaff, June 27, 1971. Supervising psychologist Calif. Dept. Mental Hygiene, Pomona, 1956-62; pvt. practice psychol. counseling, Beverly Hills, Calif., 1960—; courtesy med. staff Sierra Royale Hosp., Azusa, Calif., 1979—. Instr. psychology Mt. San Antonio Coll., Pomona, 1957-61; chief psychologist Calif. Youth Authority, Norwalk, 1962-66; research dir. OEO Vocat. Rehab. Adminstrn. spl. project, Calif. Dept. Rehab., Los Angeles, 1967-68; asst. prof. U. So. Calif. Med. Sch., Los Angeles, 1968-69; cons. Hathaway Home for Children, Highland Park, Calif., 1970—, Park Century Sch., Santa Monica, Calif., 1969—, Calif. Sch. Profl. Psychology, 1975—, Options House for Runaway Youths, 1982—; psychology examining com., oral exam. commr. Bd. Med. Quality Assurance, Sacramento, 1978; mem. governing bd. Thalians Community Mental Health Center, Los Angeles, 1979—. Served with AUS, 1944-46. Research grantee Calif. Dept. Mental Hygiene, Calif. Youth Authority, Rosenberg Found., OEO, Calif. Dept. Rehab. Fellow Am. Assn. Mental Deficiency, Am. Orthopsychiat. Assn.; mem. Am., Calif. psychol. assns., AAAS, Am. Acad. Psychotherapists. Contbr. articles to profl. jours. Office: 9720 Wilshire Blvd Beverly Hills CA 90212

POLSKY, RICHARD HENRY, applied clinical psychologist, researcher; b. Phila., July 9, 1947; s. Israel and Betty (Cohen) P. B.Sc., Ohio State U., 1970; Ph.D., U. Leicester (Eng.), 1974. Research ethologist U. Birmingham (Eng.), 1974-76; research psychologist UCLA, 1976-83, postdoctoral trainee, 1976-78; research psychologist Sepulveda (Calif.) VA Hosp., 1979—; pvt. practice animal clin. psychology, Santa Monica, Calif., 1981—; lectr., tchr. animal behavior. Mem. Am. Psychol. Assn., Animal Behavior Soc. Contbr. numerous articles on animal and human behavior to psychol., psychiat. jours. Home: 3833 Huron Ave Culver City CA 90230 Office: 309 Santa Monica Blvd Suite 214 Santa Monica CA 90401

POLSON, DONALD ALLAN, surgeon; b. Gallup, N.Mex., May 12, 1911; s. Thomas Cress and Carrie Fern (Cantrall) P.; B.M., Northwestern U., 1935, M.D., 1936, M.Sc., 1947; m. Cecily, Lady Avebury, Nov. 9, 1946; 1 dau., Carolyn Kathleen. Intern, then resident in surgery St. Luke's Hosp., Chgo., 1936-38; practice medicine specializing in gen. surgery, Phoenix, 1947—; chmn. Drs. Polson, Dorcus & Petelin, Ltd., chief staff Maricopa County Hosp., 1952-53, St. Joseph's Hosp., 1961; bd. dirs. Ariz. Blue Shield, 1950-55, pres., 1956. Served as col. M.C., AUS, World War II. Diplomate Am. Bd. Surgery. Mem. AMA, A.C.S., Ariz. Med. Assn. (dir. 1955-60), Maricopa County Med. Soc. (pres. 1954), Phoenix Surg. Soc. (pres. 1959). Republican. Episcopalian. Clubs: Paradise Valley Country, White Mountain Country. Home: 7619 N Tatum Blvd Paradise Valley AZ 85253 Office: 550 W Thomas Rd Phoenix AZ 85013

POLZIN, PAUL ELMER, economist, educator, consultant; b. Detroit, June 7, 1943; s. Elmer Otto and Elsie Caroline (Braun) P.; m. Catherine Louise Mackenzie, May 27, 1967; children—Thomas, Lindsay. B.A., U. Mich, 1964; M.A., Ph.D., Mich. State U., 1968. Faculty U. Mont., Missoula, 1968—, now research assoc., prof. bus. and econ. research; econ. cons. to bus. and govt. Contbr. articles to profl. jours. Office: Bur Bus and Econ Research U Mont Missoula MT 59801

POMER, MARSHALL IRA, socio-economist, educator; b. Hartford, Conn., July 6, 1944; s. Sydney and Francis P. m. Susan Gail Ruby, Nov. 1, 1969 (div.); children—Joshua, Jeremy. B.A., Yale U., 1967; Ph.D., Harvard U., 1976. Asst. prof. sociology and econs. U. Calif.-Santa Cruz, 1977—. Author: Intergenerational Occupational Mobility in the United States, 1981. Office: Dept Econs Merrill Coll U Calif Santa Cruz CA 95064

POMERANCE, JEFFREY JOSEPH, physician; b. Bklyn., May 13, 1942; s. William and Marjorie (Joseph) P.; m. Linda Jayne Chilton, Mar. 5, 1969; children—Elise Beth, Michel Paige. B.S. in Psychology, Bklyn. Coll., 1962; M.D., U. Vt., 1966; M.P.H., U. Calif., Berkeley, 1972. Pediatric intern Children's Hosp. of Buffalo, 1966-67, pediatric asst. chief resident, 1967-68; pediatric sr. resident Columbia-Presbyn. Med. Center, N.Y.C., 1968-69; perinatal research fellow U. Calif., San Diego, 1972-74; practice medicine specializing in neonatology, Los Angeles, 1974—; mem. cons. staff pediatrics Sacred Heart Hosp., Pensacola, Fla., 1970-71; assoc. physician perinatal medicine U. Hosp., U. Calif., San Diego, 1973-74; dir. neonatology Cedars-Sinai Med. Center, Los Angeles, 1974—; asst. prof. pediatrics UCLA Sch. Medicine, 1974-80, adj. assoc. prof., 1980—; pres. Perinatal Adv. Council of Los Angeles Communities, 1982-83. Served to lt. comdr. M.C., USN, 1969-71. Diplomate Am. Bd. Pediatrics. Fellow Am. Acad. Pediatrics; mem. Calif. Perinatal Assn. (pres. 1983-84), Soc. Pediatric Research, Western Soc. Pediatric Research, Los Angeles Pediatric Soc. Contbr. articles on pediatrics to profl. jours.; editor Jour. Calif. Perinatal Assn. Home: 2501 Nottingham Ave Los Angeles CA 90027 Office: 8700 Beverly Blvd Los Angeles CA 90048

POMERANZ, WILLIAM HERSCH, aircraft corporation executive; b. Cleve., Aug. 7, 1938; s. Aaron and Beatrice Edith (Kline) P.; B.S., UCLA, 1960, cert. indsl. relations, 1961; m. Barbara Walden, Jan. 9, 1971; children—Alex, Keli. With Douglas Aircraft Corp., 1960-61, Litton Industries, 1961-62, 3M Co., Camarillo, Calif., 1963-65; ops. mgr. comml. systems div. Hughes Aircraft Co., El Segundo, Calif., 1965—; sr. lectr. West Coast U., Grad. Sch. Bus., 1976—. Served with U.S. Army Res., 1961-66. Republican. Jewish. Club: Windjammers Yacht (staff commodore; founder Marina del Rey to San Diego race) (Marina del Rey, Calif.). Home: 55 Encanto Dr Rolling Hills Estates CA 90274 Office: PO Box 92919 Mail Sta S41/B329 Los Angeles CA 90009

POMEROY, STEVEN HAMBLIN, public accounting executive; b. Phoenix, Aug. 27, 1949; s. Benjamin Kent and Laverne (Hamblin) P; m. Patricia Ann Daily, Dec. 27, 1972; children—Elizabeth Ann, Amanda Suzanne, Rebecca Loree, Joseph Steven. B.S. in Acctg., Brigham Young U., 1973; M.S. in Acctg., Ariz. State U., 1975. C.P.A. Various positions with Pomeroy & Co., Phoenix, 1973—, sec., dir., 1975-79, pres., bd. chmn. 1979—. Scoutmaster, troop com. chmn, Explorer advisor Boy Scouts Am., 1973-80. Recipient Boy Scouts Duty to God award, 1967. Mem. Am. Inst. C.P.A.s, Ariz. Soc. C.P.A.s (treas. central chpt.). Republican. Mormon. Club: Sunrise Toastmasters (Phoenix). Home: 2942 E Laurel Ln Phoenix AZ 85028 Office: Pomeroy & Co 3003 N Central Ave Suite 2001 Phoenix AZ 85012

PON, WING YOU, software and systems engr.; b. China, Jan. 15, 1939; came to U.S., naturalized, 1947; s. Chuck Shew and Gim (Won) P.; B.A., San Francisco State U., 1964; M.S., Stanford U., 1968; postgrad. U. Santa Clara (Calif.); m. June L. Lui, June 30, 1968; children—Cynthia T., Daniel R. Vice pres. Data Dynamics, Inc., Mountain View, Calif., 1966-80; pres. Dialectic Systems Corp., Mountain View, 1980—; asst. prof. Calif. Inst. Asian Studies, 1979—; asso. prof. San Francisco State U., 1968-69; spl. adviser U.S. Congl. Adv. Bd. Served with USNR, 1964-65. Mem. Tech. Mktg. Soc. Am., Am. Def. Preparedness Assn., Air Force Assn., Armed Forces Communications and Electronics Assn., Stanford U. Alumni Assn. Author: Mathematical Theory for the Advanced Orbit Determination and Ephemeris Generation System, 1973, An East-West View of Reality: Integration of Eastern Philosophy and Western Science, 8 vols., 1981—. Office: 444 Castro St Suite 308 Mountain View CA 94043

POND, BARBARA WELLER, educator; b. Balt.,; d. Louis Christian, Jr., and Marie (Mesenbrink) Weller; B.A., Towson State U., 1970; M.A., U. Md., 1973; M.A. in Gifted and Talented Edn., U. Denver, 1981; m. Daniel C. Pond, Nov. 17, 1973; children—Jennifer Katherine, Christopher Kenneth. Instr. math., resource tchr., instr. inservice courses, writer curriculum Montgomery County, Md., 1974-78; instr. math. Douglas County, Colo., 1978—; guest cons. on gifted math. programs Denver U.; curriculum writer Douglas County, Colo. Named Best Tchr., Belt Jr. High Sch., 1977. Mem. NEA, Nat. Council Tchrs. Math., Assn. Curriculum and Supervision, Council Gifted Edn., Phi Delta Kappa. Lutheran. Research on motivating students in math. through small group learning, use of computers in classroom, devel. of computer curriculum, gifted math. curriculum, interdisciplinary 7th grade program with block time. Home: 7437 S Albion St Littleton CO 80122 Office: 6651 Pine Lane Ave Parker CO 80134

POND, SAMUEL AMES, publisher; b. San Francisco, Jan. 15, 1914; s. Samuel and Dorothy (Ames) P.; m. Dorothy Linke, June 2, 1951; children—Katharine A., Samuel F., Elizabeth B. B.S., Yale U., 1936; M.B.A., Stanford U., 1939. Labor relations supt. Pan Am. Airways, San Francisco and N.Y.C., 1946-50; dir. indsl. relations FMC Corp., N.Y.C., 1950-58; dir. personnel Chemetron Corp., Chgo., 1958-61; assoc. dean Bus. Sch. Stanford U. (Calif.), 1961-81; editor, pub., Brickers Internat. Directory, Woodside, Calif., 1981—; dir. Castle and Cooke, Inc., Am. Mut. Fund, Bonner Packing Co. Trustee Thacher Sch. Served to comdr. USN, 1942-46. Democrat. Club: Family (San Francisco).

PONDER, CATHERINE, clergywoman; b. Hartsville, S.C., Feb. 14, 1927; d. Roy Charles and Kathleen (Parrish) Cook; student U. N.C. Extension, 1946, Worth Bus. Coll., 1948; B.S. in Edn., Unity Ministerial Sch., 1956; m. Robert Stearns, June 19, 1970; 1 son by previous marriage, Richard. Ordained to ministry, Unity Sch. Christianity, 1958; minister Unity Ch., Birmingham, Ala., 1956-61; founder, minister Unity Ch., Austin, Tex., 1961-69, San Antonio, 1969-73, Palm Desert, Calif., 1973—. Mem. Assn. Unity Chs., Inc. (hon. D.D. 1976), Internat. New Thought Alliance, Internat. Platform Assn. Clubs: Bermuda Dunes Country, Racquet (Palm Springs, Calif.); Los Angeles. Author: The Dynamic Laws of Prosperity, 1962; The Prosperity Secret of the Ages, 1964; The Dynamic Laws of Healing, 1966; The Healing Secret of the Ages, 1967; Pray and Grow Rich, 1968; The Millionaires of Genesis, 1976; The Millionaire Moses, 1977; The Millionaire Joshua, 1978; The Millionaire from Nazareth, 1979; The Secret of Unlimited Prosperity, 1981; Open Your Mind to Receive, 1983; Dare to Prosper!; The Prospering Power of Prayer, 1983. Office: 73-669 Hwy 11 Palm Desert CA 92260

PONG, RAYMOND S., urol. surgeon; b. Hong Kong, Nov. 21, 1937 (Am. citizen); s. David C. and Saufong W. P.; A.B., Dartmouth Coll., 1960; M.S., M.I.T., 1966, Ph.D., 1970, M.D., Case Western Res. U., 1975. Postdoctoral research fellow Case Western Res. U., Cleve., 1971-73, resident in gen. surgery, 1975-77, fellow in surgery, 1976-77; resident in urology Mass. Gen. Hosp., Boston, 1977-80, chief resident in urology, 1980; fellow in surgery Harvard U. Med. Sch., Boston, 1979-80; sr. surgeon City of Hope Nat. Med. Center, Duarte, Calif., 1980-83; asst. clin. prof. U. So. Calif., 1980—; assoc. clin. prof. U. Calif.-Irvine, 1982—. Diplomate Am. Bd. Urology. Mem. N.Y. Acad. Scis., AAAS, Am. Soc. Cell. Biology, Sigma Xi. Contbr. articles to jours. Office: 11411 Brookshire Ave Suite 402 Downey CA 90241

POOLE, PATRICK HENRY, psychologist, educator; b. Columbus, Kans., Oct. 18, 1932; s. William Harvey and Dorothy Ann (Hicks) P.; student U. Kans.; A.B., U. Tulsa, 1955; M.S., Pittsburg (Kans.) State U., 1962; postgrad. San Francisco State U., 1964, San Jose State U., 1964, Stanford U., 1965, UCLA, 1966; Ph.D., U. So. Calif., 1976. Floor mgr. J.C. Penney Co., Tulsa, 1954-55; with Eagle-Picher Co., various locations, 1955-60, instr. spl. edn. elem. sch., Derby, Kans., 1962-63; instr. Wyandotte High Sch., Kansas City, Kans., 1963-64, Kansas City (Kans.) Jr. Coll., 1963-64; test officer Monterey (Calif.) Peninsula Coll., 1964-66; asst. prof. edn. Calif. State U., Fresno, 1966-68, student affairs officer, coordinator group counseling program, 1968—; mem. faculty Calif. Sch. Profl. Psychology, Fresno, 1978—; pvt. practice as marriage, family and child counselor; cons. A. & D. Life Edn. Center, Denver, 1976—; founder, owner, mng. dir. The Harbor Far from the Sea, 1971—, The Harbor Far from the Sea Co., 1980—, The Harbor Mus. Art, 1980—, The Harbor Midyear Cultural and Performing Arts Festival, 1980—; asst. to dean men Pittsburg (Kans.) State U., 1960, asst. instr. psychology, 1961; founder Psychotherapy Research Com. of Fresno, 1976—. Bd. dirs. Fresno Dance Repertory Assn., pres., 1972-73; bd. dirs., baritone soloist Fresno Community Chorus. Lic. counseling psychologist, S.C. Mem. Monterey Peninsula Counseling and Guidance Assn. (v.p. 1964-66), Am., Calif. personnel and guidance assns., AAUP, San Joaquin Psychol. Assn., Am. Cultural Soc. (founder, exec. dir. 1971—), Internat. Platform Assn., SAR (chpt. sec. 1973-75), County and City of Fresno C. of C. (cultural arts com.), Magna Charta Barons, Psi Chi, Phi Delta Kappa, Phi Mu Alpha, Pi Delta Epsilon, Delta Epsilon, Sigma Chi (founder Zeta Iota chpt.). Composer Missa Brevis performed by Monterey Peninsula Coll. Chorus, 1965. Extensive travel throughout C.Am., S.Am., Europe, Eng., N.Am., Middle East and Asia, 1955—. Harbor Far from the Sea Co., 1980—, The Harbor Mus. Art, 1980—, The Harbor Midyear Cultural and Performing Arts Festival, 1980—; asst. to dean men Pittsburg (Kans.) State U., 1960, asst. instr. psychology, 1961; founder Psychotherapy Research Com. of Fresno, 1976—. Bd. dirs. Fresno Dance Repertory Assn., pres., 1972-73; bd. dirs., baritone soloist Fresno Community Chorus. Lic. counseling psychologist, S.C. Mem. Monterey Peninsula Counseling and Guidance

Assn. (v.p. 1964-66), Am., Calif. personnel and guidance assns., AAUP, San Joaquin Psychol. Assn., Am. Cultural Soc. (founder, exec. dir. 1971—), Internat. Platform Assn., SAR (chpt. sec. 1973-75), County and City of Fresno C. of C. (cultural arts com.), Magna Charta Barons, Psi Chi, Phi Delta Kappa, Phi Mu Alpha, Pi Delta Epsilon, Delta Epsilon, Sigma Chi (founder Zeta Iota chpt.). Composer Missa Brevis performed by Monterey Peninsula Coll. Chorus, 1965. Extensive travel throughout C.Am., S.Am., Europe, Eng., N.Am., Middle East and Asia, 1955—. Home: 4718 N Bonadelle St Fresno CA 93726 Office: Counseling Center Calif State U Fresno CA 93720

POON, RICHARD, dermatologist; b. Hong Kong, Mar. 24, 1949; s. Felix Wing Hong and Christina Wai Yin (Ko) P.; came to U.S., 1956, naturalized, 1964; B.A. (Univ. scholar, Calif. State scholar), Stanford U., 1971; M.D., U. Calif., San Francisco, 1974. Intern in pathology Presbyn. Hosp. of Pacific Med. Center, San Francisco, 1975-76; resident in dermatology N.Y. Hosp.-Cornell Med. Center, 1976-79, chief resident, 1979; practice medicine specializing in dermatology, San Francisco, 1979—. Organist, St. Mary's Chinese Mission, San Francisco, 1960-76. Diplomate Am. Bd. Dermatology, Nat. Bd. Med. Examiners. Fellow Am. Acad. Dermatology; mem. AMA (Physicians Recognition award 1978—), Calif. Med. Assn. (cert. continuing med. edn. 1979—), San Francisco Med. Soc., U. Calif. San Francisco Med. Sch. Alumni Assn., Stanford U. Alumni Assn. (life), Calif. Scholarship Fedn. (life; past chpt. pres.). Office: 929 Clay St Suite 302 San Francisco CA 94108

POOR, CLARENCE ALEXANDER, physician; b. Ashland, Oreg., Oct. 29, 1911; s. Lester Clarence and Matilda Ellen (Doty) P.; A.B., Willamette U., 1932; M.D., U. Oreg., 1936. Intern, U. Wis., Madison, 1936-37, resident in internal medicine, 1937-40, instr. dept. pathology Med. Sch., 1940-41, clin. instr., clin. asst. dept. internal medicine, 1942-44; practice medicine specializing in internal medicine, Oakland, Calif., 1944—; mem. attending staff Highland Alameda County Hosp., Oakland, 1949—; mem. staff Providence Hosp., Oakland, 1947—, pres. staff, 1968-69; assoc. staff mem. Samuel Meritt Hosp., Oakland, 1958—, also Peralta Hosp., 1968—. Mem. Nat. Council on Alcoholism, 1974—, bd. dirs. Bay Area, 1977—. Diplomate Am. Bd. Internal Medicine. Mem. Am., Calif., Alameda-Contra Costa med. assns., Pacific Coast Fertility Soc., Alameda County Heart Assn. (trustee 1955-62, 72-82, pres. 1960-61), Calif. Heart Assn. (dir. 1962-72), Soc. for Clin. and Exptl. Hypnosis, Am. Soc. Clin. Hypnosis, San Francisco Acad. Hypnosis (dir. 1966—, pres. 1973). Home: 1241 West View Dr Berkeley CA 94705 Office: 400 29th St Oakland CA 94609

POPE, HENRY ORSON, museum director; b. St. Louis, Sept. 3, 1914; s. Joseph Frances and Anna Mae (Davidson) P.; student pub. schs., Canon City, Colo.; m. Evelyn Victoria Parker, Sept. 1, 1939; children—Henry Orson II, Larry Alan. Truck driver, buyer John Jacobs Co., Canon City, 1933; salesman Nash Finch Co., Cedar Rapids, Iowa, 1934-38, Great Falls, Mont., 1939-44; owner, operator Loma Mercantile Co. (Mont.), 1944-76; owner, operator Earth Sci. Mus., Loma, 1976—. Recipient Disting. Service awards U.S. Dept. Commerce Bur. Census, 1957, 58, 59, 60, 61, 62. Mem. N.W. Fedn. Mineral. Socs. (pres. 1966), Mont. Council Rock and Mineral Clubs (pres. 1963-64), Mus. Assn. Mont. (v.p. 1981-82), Whoop-Up Trail Rockhounds Club. Home: 108 Main St Loma MT 59460 Office: 106 Main St Loma MT 59460

POPE, KENNETH SAYLE, clinical psychologist, educator; b. Austin, Tex., Feb. 28, 1947; s. W. Kenneth and Kate (Sayle) P. B.A., So. Meth. U., 1969; M.A. in English, Harvard U., 1972; Ph.D. in Psychology, Yale U., 1977. Lic. psychologist, Calif. Intern. Langley Porter Inst., San Francisco, 1976-77; clin. psychologist Brentwood VA Med. Ctr., Los Angeles, 1978-79; psychology dir. Gateways Hosp. and Mental Health Ctr., Los Angeles, 1979-81; clin. dir. San Fernando Valley Community Mental Health Ctr., 1981; pvt. practice therapy; cons.; clin. faculty UCLA, 1982—. Mem. self help task force White House Conf. on Families, 1980. Recipient Belle Mayer Bromberg award for literature, 1969, Frances Mosseker award for fiction, 1969; Woodrow Wilson fellow Harvard U., 1971-72; NIMH trainee Yale U., 1973-76. Mem. Am. Psychol. Assn., Calif. Psychol. Assn. Author: On Love and Loving, 1980; co-author (with J. L. Singer) The Stream of Consciousness, 1978; The Power of Human Imagination: New Methods of Psychotherapy, 1978. Office: 11747 Sunset Blvd Los Angeles CA 90049

POPE, MAX LYNDELL, city ofcl.; b. Clinton, N.C., Nov. 5, 1932; s. William Walter and Maggie (Honeycutt) P.; B.A., Idaho State Coll., 1962; grad. U.S. Army Command and Gen. Staff Coll., 1977, Security Manpower Program, Indsl. Coll. Armed Forces, 1980; m. Sarah Jane Norris, Dec. 10, 1954. City mgr. City of Rangely (Colo.), 1963-66, City of Seaside (Oreg.), 1966-69, City of Pasco (Wash.), 1969-70; city adminstr. City of Coeur d'Alene (Idaho), 1971-72; planner State of Idaho, Boise, 1972-75; city adminstr. City of Woodburn (Oreg.), 1975—. Ordained elder Presbyn. Ch., 1958, elder, Woodburn, 1976—. Served with U.S. Army, 1953-56, 70-71. Recipient Distinguished Service award Rangely Jaycees, 1964. Mem. Internat. City Mgmt. Assn., Am. Soc. Public Adminstrn., Am. Public Works Assn., Internat. Union Local Authorities, Civil Affairs Assn., Res. Officers Assn., Woodburn C. of C. Clubs: Rotary, Gowen Field Officers, Elks. Home: 421 Hermanson St Woodburn OR 97071 Office: City Hall Woodburn OR 97071

POPE, PETER T., forest products company executive; b. 1934; married. B.A., Stanford U., 1957, M.B.A., 1959. With Pope & Talbot Inc., Portland, Oreg., 1960—, asst. sec., 1964-68, v.p., 1968-69, v.p., gen. mgr., 1969-71, chmn. bd., chief exec. officer, 1971—, also dir. Served with USAF, 1957-58. Office: Pope & Talbot Inc 1500 SW 1st Ave PO Box 8171 Portland OR 97207*

POPICK, LISA WENDY, banker; b. Balt., Aug. 15, 1955; d. Bernard and Harlee S. (Senzer) Popick. A.B., Radcliffe Coll., 1977. Asst. treas. Chase Manhattan Bank, N.Y.C., 1979-81, credit analyst, 1977-79; asst. v.p. Wells Fargo Bank, Corp. Banking Group, San Francisco, 1981—. Club: Radcliffe (San Francisco). Office: 420 Montgomery St 9th Floor San Francisco CA 94613

POPKA, AYLENE WAGGONER, counselor, consultant, lecturer; b. Long Beach, Calif., July 8, 1949; d. Byron Hartzel and Rose Ella (Pierce) Waggoner; m. Dennis George Popka, July 28, 1973; 1 son, John Byron. B.A., U. Calif.-Riverside, 1971, M.A. in Spl. Edn., 1975, Ph.D., 1981. Cert. tchr., learning handicapped specialist, adminstr., counselor, Calif. Elem. tchr. Alvord Unified Sch. Dist., Riverside, 1971-77, elem. counselor, 1977—; assoc. in edn. U. Calif.-Riverside, 1978-80; lectr. U. Calif. Extension, 1980-81, Calif. State U.-Fullerton, 1980; cons. in field; supervisory tchr./counselor field tng. Recipient Outstanding Employee award Alvord Unified Sch. Dist., 1980, 82. Mem. Assn. for Supervision and Curriculum Devel., Alvord Tchrs. Assn., Nat. Tchrs. Assn., Calif. Tchrs. Assn., Calif. Assn. for Gifted, Phi Beta Kappa, Phi Delta Kappa. Democrat. Home: 2855 Fenwick Pl Riverside CA 92504 Office: Alvord Unified Sch Dist 5891 Rutland Ave Riverside CA 92503

POPOV, DAN, psychologist, consultant; b. Butte, Mont., Sept. 27, 1945; s. Frederick Michael and Patricia (Tauson) P.; m. Carol Ruth Lark, May 22, 1973; m. 2d Linda Kavelin, July 24, 1981. B.S., U.S. Mil. Acad., 1968; M.S., U. Colo., Boulder, 1971, Ph.D., 1974. Lic. psychologist, Calif. Chief behavioral sci. consultation service Letterman Med. Ctr., 1974-76; pvt. practice psychology, Monterey, Calif., 1976-80; pres. Systems Effectiveness Assocs., Inc., Boulder, 1980—; v.p. research and devel. Info. Access Systems, Inc., Boulder, 1980—, Advanced Info. Designs, Inc., Portland, Oreg.; cons. organizational devel. to govt., industry; examiner in clin. and organizational psychology State of Calif.; mem. profl. staff Community Hosp. Monterey Peninsula, 1979-80. Served with U.S. Army, 1968-78. Decorated Meritorious Service medal. Mem. AAAS, Am. Psychol. Assn., Am. Soc. Tng. and Devel., Calif. Psychol. Assn. Baha'i. Club: Army Navy Country (Washington). Author Software Programs: Descriptive Model of Organizations, 1980; Personal Management Profile, 1982; Systematic Organizational Assessment Procedure, 1982. Office: 1520 Grove St Boulder CO 80302

POPOVICI, PETRU, clergyman; b. Harrisburg, Pa., Sept. 12, 1918; s. Simeon and Zana (Jurji) P.; grad. Baptist Theol. Sem., Bucharest, Romania, 1940; m. Hortensia Cristea, Oct. 24, 1945; children—Iedidia, Angela, Agnia. Ordained to ministry ARAD, Romania, 1945; pastor Bapt. Ch., Arad-Parneava, 1945-53; pres. Sunday Sch. Orgn., Romania, 1946-49; pastor First Bapt. Ch., Timisoara, Romania, 1953-67; co-pastor Romanian Bapt. Ch., Chgo., 1967-71; pastor Romanian Bapt. Ch., Los Angeles, 1971—; radio pastor Romania thru Trans World Radio, 1969—; pres. Romanian Bapt. Assn. U.S. and Can., 1981-83. Author: The Meeting with God, 1970, The Bible is True, 1972, The Promises of God, 1973, The Voice of Prophecies, 1976, The Voice of Martyre, 1975, Are you Sure?, 1974, Can I Believe in Jesus, 1977, Life of D.L. Moody, 1979, Lights over the Ages, 1981, Corner of Paradise, There is Life after Death, Winning of the Souls, 1983; translator: The Bible for Today's World, 1968, Did Man Just Happen?, 1969, The Country I Love Best, 1969, Precious Sermons, 1970, All of Grace, 1971. Home: 6902 Georgia Ave Bell CA 90201 Office: 9438 Alondra Blvd Bellflower CA 90706

POPPERWELL, GERALD FREDRICK, educator; b. Alhambra, Calif., Oct. 7, 1940; married, 4 children. A.A. in Humanities, Pasadena City Coll., Calif., 1960; B.A. in Edn., Calif. State U., Los Angeles, 1963, M.A. in Elementary Edn., 1967. Co-ordinator mentally gifted minors program Walnut Valley Unified Sch. Dist., Calif., 1969-72; lectr. Calif. State Poly. Coll., Pomona, Calif. 1973-77, Pepperdine U. Extension, Los Angeles, 1974-76; ednl. specialist Palos Verdes Peninsula Unified Sch. Dist., Rolling Hills, Calif., 1972-76, tchr., 1976—; tchr. Calif. Mus. Sci. and Industry, Los Angeles, 1976—; adminstr. ednl. affairs, sci. workshops Calif. Mus. Found., Los Angeles, 1983—; cons. dept. engrng. UCLA, 1976—. Ruling elder Westminster Presbyterian Ch., Pasadena, Calif. Mem. Computer Using Educators, Palos Verdes Adminstrs. Assn., Calif. Assn. Sch. Adminstrs. Profl. Advocates Gifted Edn., Calif. Assn. Gifted Children. Author: Simulation Games, Handbook for Educators of Mentally Gifted. Home: 1038 Alta Pine Dr Altadena CA 91001 Office: Calif Museum Found 700 State Dr Los Angeles CA 90037

POPYACK, JEFFREY LEE, mathematics and computer science educator; b. Alexandria, Va., Mar. 16, 1955; s. John James and Jeanne Marie (Neiswender) P.; B.S., George Mason U., 1976; M.S., U. Va., 1978, Ph.D., 1982. Grad. research asst. U. Va., Charlottesville, 1977-79, 81, instr., 1979-80; postdoctoral teaching assoc. math. Wash. State U., Pullman, 1981-82, pres. applied math/computer sci. grad. student group, 1978-79; asst. prof. applied math. and computer scis. Drexel U., Phila., 1983—. Umpire, Woodbridge Little League, 1974; coach Charlottesville Farm League, 1981. U. Va. fellow, 1976-77. Mem. Soc. Indsl. and Applied Math., Math. Assn. Am., Assn. Computing Machinery, Am. Cryptogram Assn. Tau Beta Pi. Home: 1708 Azalea Ln Woodbridge VA 22191

PORCELLA, DONALD BURKE, scientist; b. Modesto, Calif., Oct. 2, 1937; s. Stephen L. and Eileen Mary (Marchington) P.; A.B., U. Calif., Berkeley, 1959, M.A., 1961, Ph.D., 1967; m. Ann H. Greenwood, June 17, 1961; children—John, Mary, Amy. Sr. asst. USPHS, Cin., 1961-63; asst. research zoologist U. Calif., Berkeley, 1968-70; prof. Utah State U., Logan, 1970-79; prin. scientist Tetra Tech., Inc., Lafayette, Calif., 1979—; cons. in field. Fulbright postdoctoral fellow U. Oslo, Norway, 1967-68; named Outstanding researcher, Coll. of Engring., Utah State U., 1973. Mem. Am. Soc. Limnology and Oceanography, Internat. Assn. Water Pollution Research, Water Pollution Control Fedn., N.Am. Lake Mgmt. Soc. (bd. dirs.), Sigma Xi. Roman Catholic. Vice chmn. joint editorial bd. Standard Methods. Contbr. articles to profl. jours. Office: 3746 Mount Diablo Blvd Suite 300 Lafayette CA 94549

PORTER, ALBERT WRIGHT, artist, educator; b. Bklyn., Nov. 25, 1923; s. Arthur and Gertrude (Wright) P.; m. Shirley Alberta Owens, Feb. 2, 1946; children—Kim, Todd. Student Chouinard Art. Inst., 1946-47, Ecole des Beaux-Arts, Paris, France, 1947-48; B.A., UCLA, 1950; M.A., Calif. State U.-Los Angeles, 1957; postgrad. Otis Art Inst., 1968. Cert. tchr., Calif. High sch. tchr., Los Angeles, 1950-58; supr. art Los Angeles city schs., 1958-71; artist, 1960—; art prof. Calif. State U.-Fullerton, 1971—, exhibited 12 one man shows, numerous juried shows. Served to capt. USAF. Decorated D.F.C., Air medals, 5 battle stars. Mem. Nat. Art Edn. Assn., Calif. Art Educators Assn., Nat. Watercolor Soc. (1st v.p. 1977, award for Del Mar Coll. exhbn. 1972), Watercolor West. Author: Shape and Form: Design Elements, 1974; Pattern: A Design Principle, 1975; The Art of Sketching, 1977; Expressive Watercolor Techniques, 1982; co-author: Exploring Visual Design, 1978. Home: 8554 Day St Sunland CA 91040 Office: 800 N State Coll Blvd Fullerton CA 92634

PORTER, BRIAN STANLEY, police chief; b. Seattle, May 2, 1938; s. Jack D. and Margaret I. (Tuter) P.; grad. U. Alaska, 1970, Northwestern U. Traffic Inst., 1970-71, FBI Nat. Exec. Inst., 1981; m. Bette K. Schakohl, Apr. 26, 1958; children—Kelle, Kerry, Kory. With Anchorage Police Dept., 1960—, chief of police, 1980—; chmn. Alaska Police Standards Council, 1978-80. Served with U.S. Army, 1957-58. Office: Municipality of Anchorage Police Hdqrs Anchorage AK 99501

PORTER, DIXIE LEE, consultant; b. Bountiful, Utah, June 7, 1931; d. John Lloyd and Ida May (Robinson) Mathis. B.S., U. Calif. at Berkeley, 1956, M.B.A., 1957. Personnel aide City of Berkeley (Calif.), 1957-59; employment supr. Kaiser Health Found., Los Angeles, 1959-60; personnel analyst U. Calif. at Los Angeles, 1961-63; personnel mgr. Reuben H. Donnelley, Santa Monica, Calif., 1963-64; personnel officer Good Samaritan Hosp., San Jose, Calif., 1965-67; fgn. service officer AID, Saigon, Vietnam, 1967-71; gen. agt. Charter Life Ins. Co., Los Angeles, 1972-77; gen. agt. Kennesaw Life Ins. Co., Atlanta, from 1978; gen. agt. Phila. Life Ins. Co., San Francisco, from 1978; now pres. Women's Ins. Enterprises, Ltd.; cons. in field. Co-chairperson Comprehensive Health Planning Commn. Santa Clara County, Calif., 1973-76; bd. dirs. Family Care, 1978-80, Aegis Health Corp., 1977—, U. Calif. Sch. Bus. Adminstrn., Berkeley, 1974-76; mem. task force on equal access to econ. power U.S. Nat. Women's Agenda, 1977—. Served with USMC, 1950-52. C.L.U. Mem. C.L.U. Soc., U. Calif. Alumni Assn., U. Calif. Sch. Bus. Adminstrn. Alumni Assn., AAUW, Bus. and Profl. Women, Prytanean Alumni, Beta Gamma Sigma, Phi Chi Theta. Republican. Episcopalian. Home and Office: PO Box 64 Los Gatos CA 95031

PORTER, JACK WILLIAM, engineering recruitment company executive; b. Belvidere, Ill., July 23, 1937; s. William R. and Edna M. (Carpenter) P. m. Beverly J. Siverson, June 2, 1962; children—Keith, Joan, Jacquelyn, Robert, Steven. B.B.A., U. Wis., 1959. With Am. Can Co., 1959-79, salesman, Dallas, 1976-78, sales mgr., San Francisco, 1978-79; pres. Headhunters Nat. Agy. of Seattle, Inc., 1979—. Coach Little League Baseball, 1962-78; active Boy Scouts Am., 1964-78; organizer Spl. Olympics, 1979. Mem. Am. Soc. for Personnel Adminstrn., Nat. Assn. Personnel Cons., Nat. Fedn. Ind. Businessmen, Pacific N.W. Personnel Mgrs. Assn., Seattle C. of C., Issaquah C. of C. (chmn. Salmon Days parade 1980—), Delta Tau Delta, Phi Mu Alpha. Republican. Lutheran. Lodges: Issaquah Valley Kiwanis (v.p. 1980), Elks. Home: 24119 SW 18th Pl Issaquah WA 98027 Office: Headhunters Nat Agy of Seattle Inc 385 Front St N Issaquah WA 98027

PORTER, JAMES T., parks and recreation official; b. San Diego, Jan. 13, 1944; s. James T. and Bette (Sargent) P.; m. Maria Theresa Quiroz, Apr. 15, 1970; children—Lisa, Jennifer, Miranda. A.A., Rio Hondo Community Coll., 1968; B.A., Calif. State U.-Long Beach, 1970. Recreation leader City of Santa Fe Springs (Calif.), 1968-70; recreation supr. City of Montebello (Calif.), 1970-71, City of Imperial Beach (Calif.), 1971-72, City of Pico Rivera (Calif.), 1973, City of Alhambra (Calif.), 1973-77; dir. parks and recreation City of Vista (Calif.), 1977—. Served with USAF, 1963-66. Mem. Calif. Park and Recreation Soc. (past dist. pres.), So. Calif. Mcpl. Athletic Assn. Office: City Hall Vista CA 92083

PORTER, ROGER PETER, architect; b. Wheeling, W.Va., Oct. 18, 1931; s. Peter and Cecilia (Rogers) P.; student Ohio State U., 1950-51, 59; A.A., Long Beach City Coll., 1961; m. Helen Marie Maas, Dec. 25, 1975; children—Jolaine Dawn, Brian. Civil engr. Wheel Steel Corp.; archtl. designer, Long Beach, 1961-72; practice architecture, Long Beach, 1972—; pres. Roger Peter Porter, Inc., Architects and Planners, Porter Constrn., Inc., 1977—. Served with U.S. Army, 1952-54. Lic. architect, Calif., Ariz., Nev. Office: 3837 E 7th St Long Beach CA 90804

PORTER, WALTER THOMAS, JR., accountant; b. Corning, N.Y., Jan. 8, 1934; s. Walter Thomas and Mary Rebecca (Brookes) P.; m. Dixie Jo Thompson, Apr. 3, 1959; children—Kimberlee Paige, Douglas Thompson, Jane-Amy Elizabeth. B.S., Rutgers U., 1954; M.B.A., U. Wash., 1959; Ph.D., Columbia U., 1964. C.P.A., Wash., N.Y. Staff cons. Touche Ross & Co., Seattle, 1959-61; NDEA fellow Columbia U., 1961-64; dir. edn. Touche Ross & Co., N.Y.C., 1964-66; assoc. prof. U. Wash., 1966-70, prof., 1970-74; vis. prof. N. European Mgmt. Inst., Oslo, Norway, 1974-75; nat. dir. planning Touche Ross & Co., Seattle, 1975-78, dir. exec. fin. counseling, 1978—; vis. lectr. taxation U. Wash., 1978—. Mem. Seattle adv. bd. Salvation Army, 1975-83; trustee Ryther Child Ctr., 1975—, pres., 1979-81; trustee Lakeside Sch., 1977—, treas., 1970-81, 1st v.p. 1982-84; trustee Virginia Mason Research Ctr., 1982—; trustee Mus. History and Industry, 1982—. Served with U.S. Army, 1955-57. Mem. Am. Inst. C.P.A.s. Congregationalist. Club: Wash. Athletic. Author: Auditing Electronic System, 1966; (with William Perry) EDP: Controls and Auditing, 1970, 4th edit., 1984; (with John Burton) Auditing A Conceptual Approach, 1974; (with D. Alkire) Wealth: How to Achieve It, 1976. Office: Touche Ross & Co 1111 3d Ave Seattle WA 98101

PORTER, WILLIAM ALBRIGHT, architect; b. Memphis, Nov. 11, 1946; s.William Tandy and Marie (Powell) P.; B.Arch., Auburn U., 1970; M.Arch. (fellow), Rice U., 1976; M.P.H., U. Tex., 1977. Project designer Morris-Aubry Assos., Houston, 1973; urban designer David A. Crane Partnership, Houston, 1973-74; med. planner Med. Planning Assn., Malibu, Calif., 1976-78; project designer Falick/Klein Parthership, Houston, 1978-80; sr. project architect Kaplan/McLaughlin/Diaz, San Francisco, 1980—; one-man shows watercolors Fine Arts Mus. of South, Ala.; speaker. Served with U.S. Navy, 1971-73. Recipient 1st pl. award Watercolor Art Soc. Houston. Mem. AIA, Am. Public Health Assn., Am. Assn. Hosp. Planners, Am. Hosp. Assn. Democrat. Episcopalian. Home: 600 Fairhaven Way Novato CA 94947 Office: 222 Vallejo St San Francisco CA 94111

PORTER, WINSTON SEYMOUR, realty co. exec.; b. Port Maitland, N.S., Can., Sept. 17, 1909; s. Lyndon E. and Lillian D. (Sanders) P.; came to U.S., 1926, naturalized, 1935; student Northwestern U., 1936-38; m. Ruth Lyon, Sept. 29, 1934; children—Robert G., Lynne S. With Estate of Marshall Field, 1934-43, asst. regional rent dir. OPA, Chgo., 1944-46; v.p. Oliver S. Turner & Co. (now Turner, Bailey & Zoll, Inc.), Chgo., 1946-67; v.p. Arthur Rubloff & Co., 1967-78. Trustee Deerfield, Ill., 1959-63; chmn. finance com. Deerfield, 1959-63, chmn. Deerfield Plan Commn., 1954-59, N.W. Suburban Planning Commn., 1958; active Boy Scouts Am. Mem. Field Mus. Natural History (asso. life), Art Inst. Chgo., Nat. Assn. Bldg. Mgrs., Chgo. Real Estate Bd., Ill. C. of C., Order of Arrow, Smithsonian Assns., Lambda Alpha (chpt. pres. 1940). Presbyn. Clubs: Builders, Canadian (Chgo.); Northbrook (Ill.) Gun. Home: 24001 Muirlands Blvd Greenbriar 281 El Toro CA 92630

PORTWOOD, CHARLES STERLING, III, computing co. exec., research methods cons., educator; b. Memphis, Feb. 18, 1942; s. Charles S. and Mary Ruth (Cochran) P. B.S. in Chem. Engring., U. Kans., 1964; M.S. in Nuclear Engring., U. Calif., Berkeley, 1969; Ph.D. in Bus. Adminstrn., 1972. Teaching asst. nuclear physics and thermodynamics U. Calif., Berkeley, 1964-65; computer cons. radiation hazard Manned Spacecraft Center, Houston, summer, 1966; physicist Lawrence Radiation Lab., Berkeley, 1965-67; systems analyst Office Sec. Def., Pentagon, Washington, summer 1967; computer and statis. analysis dept. city and regional planning U. Calif., Berkeley, 1968-69; systems designer Space Scis. Lab., Berkeley, 1967-70; asst. prof. bus. econs. and stats. Coll. Bus. Adminstrn., U. Hawaii, Honolulu, 1970-71, vis. asst. prof. sociology, 1972-73, cons. program in futures research, 1972-74, asst. prof. edn. Coll. Edn., 1972-78, dir. evaluation curriculum research group, 1972-74, asst. prof. public health Sch. Public Health, 1977-78; pres. A Alpha Data Systems, Pan Pacific Computing Co., 1978; cons. in stats., econ., research methodology, ednl. evaluation, 1970—; dir. Research Cons., Inc., Honolulu, 1970—, now pres.; chmn. bd. Pacific Research Inst.; mem. tutorial faculty Internat. Coll., Los Angeles, 1973—; futures research cons. Hawaii State Legislature, 1973-74; mgmt. cons.; guest lectr. Thai Ministry of Edn., 1976, various ednl. instns., 1974—; expert witness on stats., econs., bus., computers, fin. analysis; mem. faculty Japan-Am. Inst. Mgmt. Scis., Bus. Tng. Inst., Hyderbad, India, Chulalongkorn U., Central Mich. U., Embry Riddle U., U. Calif.-Berkeley. NSF research grantee, 1974-75, U. Hawaii grantee, 1970-71; Charles A. Haskins scholar, 1963-64. Mem. Assn. Computing Machinery, Am. Inst. Decision Scis., Am. Ednl. Research Assn. (spl. interest group on regression analysis). Contbr. articles on stats. and math. analysis to profl. jours. Office: 2600 S King St Ste 207 Honolulu HI 96826

POSEDLY, THOMAS JOSEPH, architect; b. Cleve., Feb. 11, 1941; s. Joseph Thomas and Mary Rita (Marusa) P.; B.Arch., U. Ariz., Tucson, 1965, B.A. in Studio Art, 1966; m. Jane Penelope Hamilton, July 1, 1964. Propr., prin. Thomas J. Posedly A.I.A. Architect, 1971-80; partner The Posedly Partnership, Tucson, 1980—; lectr. U. Ariz., 1972; one-man exhbn. Tom Posedly 10-Year Retrospective Exhibit, U. Ariz., 1972. Chair person, Mayor's Com. Employment of Handicapped, 1981, Ariz. Council for Deaf, 1978—; mem. Tucson City Commn. on Handicapped, 1980—; vice chmn. Internat. Deaf Arts Center, Houston, 1980—. Recipient cert. of appreciation Ariz. Assn. of Deaf, 1978, Community Outreach Program for Deaf, 1978, archl. awards U. Ariz., 1960-65. Mem. AIA. Club: Tucson Racquet. Office: 2555 E 1st St Suite 111 Tucson AZ 85716

POSIN, MELVIN, computer co. exec.; b. N.Y.C., Apr. 1, 1925; s. Samuel B. and Nina P.; B.E.E., MIT, 1948; M.S., Poly. Inst. Bklyn., 1951; m. Alfreda Rosow, Sept. 14, 1947; children—Peter E., Cathy A. Western regional mgr. RCA, Los Angeles, 1959-70; v.p. Caelus Memories Inc., San Jose, Calif., 1970-71; asst. gen. mgr. Lockheed

Electronics Co., Los Angeles, 1971-74; sr. v.p. Printronix, Inc., Irvine, Calif., 1974—, also dir.; dir. Digidyne Inc., Rosscomp Inc. cons., speaker in field. Pres. Cherry Hill Civic Assn., 1965-66, Parkcrest Community Assn., 1977-78. Served with AUS, 1943-45; ETO. Decorated Purple Heart. Registered profl. engr., N.Y. Mem. Sigma Xi, Tau Beta Pi. Club: Masons. Author, patentee in field; contbg. author: McGraw Hill Handbook of Business Administration. Home: 22 Valley View Irvine CA 92715

POSNER, BARRY ZANE, management specialist, educator; b. Hollywood, Calif., Mar. 11, 1949; s. Henry and Delores Ann (Ginsberg) P.; m. Jacqueline Schmidt, July 23, 1972; 1 dau., Amanda Delores. B.A. with honors, U. Calif., 1970; M.A., Ohio State U., 1972; Ph.D., U. Mass., 1976. Regional dir. Sigma Phi Epsilon frat., Richmond, Va., 1970-71; teaching assoc. U. Mass., 1972-76; assoc. prof. organizational behavior and theory U. Santa Clara, 1976—. Named to Outstanding Young Men in Am., U.S. Jaycees, 1981; recipient Pres.'s Disting. Faculty award U. Santa Clara, 1981. Mem. Acad. Mgmt., Am. Psychol. Assn., Am. Inst. Decision Scis., Organizational Behavior Teaching Soc. (dir. 1982-85), Beta Gamma Sigma, Sigma Phi Epsilon (nat. bd. dirs. 1971-81). Democrat. Jewish. Author: Management Values & Expectations, 1982; Managerial Values in Perspective, 1983. Contbr. numerous articles to profl. jours. Office: Dept Mgmt U Santa Clara Santa Clara CA 95053

POSNICK, MARK KENNETH, mortgage banking executive; b. Bklyn., June 26, 1939; s. Harry and Pearl (Kastin) P.; m. Frances Sheridan, July 21, 1962; children—Jill Ellen, David Franklin. B.S. in Econs., U. Pa., Phila., 1961; postgrad. NYU Sch. Bus., 1964-65, Sch. Mortgage Banking, 1978. Pres., Interior Enterprises, Inc., N.Y.C., 1966-73; vice chmn., chief operating officer Margaretten & Co., Inc. div. Berg Enterprises, Inc., Perth Amboy, N.J.; 1974-82; pres. and chief exec. officer Criterion Fin. Corp., City Investing Cos., Dallas, 1982—; faculty mem. Inst. Real Estate Mgmt. div. Nat. Assn. Realtors, Sch. Mortgage Banking; dir. Pub. Securities Assn., Self Regulation Inc. Active Children's Psychiat. Ctr. Served to lt. (j.g.) USN, 1962-65. Willis Bryant scholar, 1978. Mem. Mortgage Bankers Assn. Am. (cert.; bd. govs.). Home: 3831 Turtle Creek Blvd Dallas TX 75219 Office: Criterion Fin Corp PO Box 802044 Dallas TX 75380

POST, ALAN, economist, artist; b. Alhambra, Calif., Sept. 17, 1914; s. Edwin R. and Edna (Stickney) P.; m. Helen E. Wills, Nov. 21, 1940; 1 son, David Wills. A.B., Occidental Coll., 1938; student Chouinard Inst. Art, 1938; M.A., Princeton, 1940; LL.D., Golden Gate U., 1972, Occidental Coll., 1974, Claremont Grad. Sch., 1978. In banking bus., 1933-36; instr. econs. Occidental Coll., 1940-42; asst. prof. Am. U., 1943; economist Dept. State, 1944-45; research dir. Utah Found., 1945-46; chief economist, adminstrv. analyst State of Calif., 1946-50, state legis. analyst, 1950-77; cons. to commn. studying higher edn. Wells Commn., N.Y.; cons. Milton Eisenhower Com. Higher Edn. and State, 1964; mem. Nat. Com. Support of Public Schs., 1967; mem. nat. adv. panel Nat. Center Higher Edn. Mgmt. Systems, 1971-72; chmn. Calif. Gov.'s Commn. on Govt. Reform, 1978—; mem. faculty U. So. Calif. Grad. Sch. Public Adminstrn., 1978—; Regents' prof. U. Calif., Davis, 1983; spl. cons. Touche Ross and Co., 1977—; mem. mgmt. adv. council Inst. Mgmt. Cons. Inc.; exhibited paintings numerous nat. shows and one-man shows; dir. Crocker Art Gallery Assn., pres., 1966-67; dir. IMMUDX Inc. Bd. dirs. People to People Council; mem. adv. com. on future ops. Council State Govts., 1965; bd. mgrs., pres. YMCA; chmn. art evaluation com. Sacramento Redevel. Agy; bd. dirs. Sacramento Civic Ballet Assn.; trustee Calif. Coll. Arts and Crafts, 1982—, Calif. State Task Force on Water Future, 1981-82, Sacramento Regional Found.; bd. dirs. Calif. Mus., pres., 1976-77. Served with USNR, 1943-44. Mem. Nat. Tax Assn., Western Govtl. Research Assn., Am. Soc. Public Adminstrn. (adv. com. legis. services program 1967—), Council State Govts. (research adv. com. 1966—), Nat. Legis. Service Conf. (exec. com. 1956-57), Nat. Acad. Public Adminstrn., Phi Beta Kappa, Kappa Sigma. Home: 1900 Rockwood Dr Sacramento CA 95825

POST, HOMER VINCENT, JR., govt. agy. ofcl., educator; b. Los Angeles, Nov. 2, 1948; s. Homer Lee and Eva Post; B.A. in Mass Communication, Calif. State U., Long Beach, 1971; cert. profl. bus. developer Ariz. State U., 1976; M.A. in Public Adminstrn., Calif. Poly. Inst., Pomona, 1979; m. Helen Fay Gray, Jan. 10, 1968; children—Rachel Sidney, Eva Kathleen Angela. Program mgr. Nat. Youth Sports Program, Los Angeles S.W. Community Coll., 1977-79, prof. bus., 1977—; program officer Dept. Commerce, Los Angeles, 1973-79; minority small bus. specialist SBA, Los Angeles, 1979—, asso. dir. minority small bus. and capital ownership devel. program 1980—; co-chmn. econ. devel. com. Los Angeles Fed. Exec. bd., 1979. Recipient various govt. certs. Mem. Tech. Transfer Soc., Nat. Assn. Community Developers, Nat. Assn. Public Adminstrs., So. Calif. Export Mgrs. Assn., So. Calif. Football Ofcls. Assn., Los Angeles Fed. Exec. Bd. Assos. Republican. Club: Masons. Editor SBA newsletter. Office: 350 S Figueroa St Suite 600 Los Angeles CA 90071

POST, RICHARD FREEMAN, physicist; b. Pomona, Calif., Nov. 14, 1918; s. Freeman and Miriam Jocelyn (Colcord) P.; B.A., Pomona Coll., 1940; D.Sc. (hon.), 1959; Ph.D., Stanford U., 1950; m. Marylee Armstrong, Aug. 7, 1946; children—Stephen, Marjorie, Rodney. Grad. asst. Pomona Coll., 1940-41, instr. physics, 1941-42; physicist Naval Research Lab., Washington, 1942-46; research asso. Stanford U., 1947-50; research group leader controlled thermonuclear research U. Calif. Lawrence Livermore Lab., 1951-74, dep. asso. dir. for magnetic fusion energy, 1974—; prof.-in-residence U. Calif., Davis/Livermore, 1963—. Recipient Outstanding Achievement award controlled nuclear fusion div. Am. Nuclear Soc., 1978; James Clerk Maxwell prize award Am. Phys. Soc., 1978; distinguished asso. award U.S. Dept. Energy, 1977. Fellow Am. Phys. Soc. (chmn. plasma physics div.), Am. Nuclear Soc. Congregationalist. Contbr. chpts. to books. Asso. editor Phys. Rev. Letters, 1978—; mem. bd. editors Nuclear Fusion, 1976—. Patentee in field. Home: 1630 Orchard Ln Walnut Creek CA 94595 Office: PO Box 808 Livermore CA 94550

POST, ROBIN DEE, clinical psychologist; b. Bronx, N.Y., Feb. 25, 1946; d. Herman D. and Blanche (Simon) P.; m. James Watson Tait, Oct. 3, 1981. B.A., Brandeis U. 1966; Ph.D., (univ. fellow), Syracuse U., 1973. Lic. psychologist, Colo. Assoc. psychiatry dept. U. Wash. Med. Ctr., 1970-72; asst. prof. psychology dept. Wash. State U., 1973-75; asst. prof. psychiatry dept. U. Colo. Sch. of Medicine, 1975-82, assoc. prof., 1982—. U. Colo. Sch. Medicine research grantee, 1977-1978, 83. Mem. Am. Psychol. Assn. (council reps.), Colo. Psychol. Assn. (bd. dirs. 1978-84), bd. dirs. polit. action com. 1982-85, peer reviewer 1983—), Colo. Women Psychologists (treas. 1977-79, pres. 1979-81). Editorial cons. Psychotherapy, Theory, Research and Practice, 1981—, contbr. articles to profl. jours. Office: C-258 U Colo Sch of Med 4200 E 9th St Denver CO 80262

POSTEL, MITCHELL PAUL, museum exec.; b. Chgo., May 27, 1952; s. Bernard and Rosalin P.; B.A., U. Calif.-Berkeley, 1974; M.A., U. Calif.-Santa Barbara, 1977; m. Kristie McCune, Mar. 29, 1981. Devel. officer San Mateo County Hist. Mus., San Mateo, Calif., 1977-81; exec. dir. Fort Point and Army Mus. Assn., San Francisco, 1981—; historian San Francisco Rotary Club. Bd. dirs. Ano Nuevo Interpretive Assn., 1981—. Mem. Calif. Hist. Soc., San Mateo County Hist. Assn., Alumni Assn. U. Calif.-Berkeley. Democrat. Jewish. Author: History of the Burlingame Country Club, 1982. Home: 350 Arballo Dr Apt 10M San Francisco CA 94132 Office: PO Box 29163 Presidio San Francisco CA 94129

POSTLER, PAUL ROBERT, JR., educator; b. San Francisco, Nov. 30, 1921; s. Paul Robert and Charlotte (Kane) P.; student City Coll. San Francisco, 1940-41; A.B., Fresno State Coll., 1954; m. Mildred Katheryn Upshaw, June 6, 1948; children—Paul Albert, Katheryn Ruth, Suzanne Marie, Lawrence Gerard, Marcella Jan, Keith David, Robert Paul. Employed as asst. purchasing agt. vessel materials Western Pipe & Steel Co. of Calif., 1941-44; dist. adminstrv. prin. Fort Washington-Lincoln Sch. Dist., Fresno County, Calif., 1947-59; adminstrv. dist. prin. Figarden Elem. Sch. Dist., Fresno, 1959-63; social sci. instr., student adviser, now ednl. guidance cons. Washington U. High Sch., Fresno; past prin. Washington Union Continuation High Sch.; instr. adult edn. evening high sch., Fresno; pupil personnel student welfare and attendance dean, dir. evening adult high sch., Easton, Calif.; evening lectr./instr. psychology West Hills Coll. Adult extension div., Coalinga, Calif., 1972-82; dist. cons. State Center Regional Adult and Vocat. Ednl. Council. Dist. commr. No. Fresno dist. Boy Scouts Am.; adv. CAP San Joaquin Valley. Served from pvt. to sgt. maj. U.S. Army, 1944-46. Mem. Calif. Tchrs. Assn. (pres. Clovis, 1955-57, local pres. 1966-67), Internat. Assn. Pupil Personnel Adminstrs., Calif. Sch. Adminstrs. Assn., Assn. Calif. Sch. Adminstrs., NEA (life), Am. Legion (adj. officer 1948), Calif. Council Adult Edn., Am. Edn. Research Assn., Calif. Guidance and Counseling Assn. (charter), DAV (life), Non-Commd. Officers Assn., Fresno State U. Bulldog Found., Fresno State U. Alumni Assn., Phi Delta Kappa (chpt. pres.), Delta Xi, Epsilon Delta Chi. Democrat. Roman Catholic. Clubs: Commercial, Commonwealth of Calif. (San Francisco); Lions, Y Men's (Fresno); Elks. Address: 5531 Columbia Dr N Fresno CA 93727

POSTON, KENNETH RONALD, telephone co. exec.; b. Inkster, Mich., Dec. 12, 1946; s. John Stoney and Colonia Athalee (Golding) P.; B.S., N.C. A&T State U., 1973. With Addressograph Multigraph Corp., 1973-78, mgr. distbn. center, Seattle, 1976-78; installment supt., then assignment supr. Pacific N.W. Bell Telephone Co., Seattle, 1978-79, staff specialist, 1979-81, bus. office supt., 1981-82, asst. mgr., 1982—. Served with USNR, 1966-70; Vietnam. Mem. So. Polit. Sci. Assn., Am. Mgmt. Assn., Seattle Multi-Greek Council, N.C. A&T State U. Alumni Assn., Alpha Phi Alpha (chpt. pres. 1980-81).

POSTON, WILLIAM KENNETH, JR., superintendent schools; b. Sioux City, Iowa, Nov. 11, 1938; s. William Kenneth and Wilma Beatrice (Schultz) P.; m. Marcia Sue Bottorff, Aug. 19, 1961; children—Heather Mikaleen, Holly Janelle. B.A., Iowa State Tchrs. Coll., 1961; Ed.S., Ariz. State U.-Tempe, 1966, Ed.D., 1969. Tchr. sci.-math., San Bernardino, Calif., 1961-63; tchr. sci. Tempe (Ariz.) High Sch., 1963-64; research asst. Ariz. State U., Tempe, 1964-65; research coordinator, asst. prin., prin. Jr.-Sr. High Sch., asst. supt. ednl. services Mesa (Ariz.) Pub. Schs., 1965-74; supt. Flowing Wells Schs., Tucson, 1974-83, Billings (Mont.) Pub. Schs., 1983—. Tucson chmn. United Way, 1982; mem. adv. panel Gallup Edn. Poll; active YMCA, Freedoms Found., Community Effort Council, Tucson. Served to capt. USMCR, 1958-61. Recipient Disting. Service award Ariz. State U., 1978; award Young Ednl. Leaders Am., 1980; Alumni Achievement award U. No. Iowa, 1981, award citation Freedoms Found., 1983. Mem. Am. Assn. Sch. Adminstrs., Assn. Supervision and Curriculum Devel., Assn. Sch. Bus. Ofcls., Phi Delta Kappa (past internat. pres.), Sierra Club, Sigma Phi Epsilon. Democrat. Presbyterian. Clubs: Rotary, Masons. Contbr. articles to profl. jours.

POSZ, JOSEPH DANIEL, educator; b. Roswell, N.Mex., Sept. 18, 1933; s. Joseph and Ruby Jeanette (Moen) P.; B.S., N.Mex. Mil. Inst., 1955; M.Criminal Justice, Am. Tech. U., 1975; m. Nancy Avis Thomas, June 16, 1957; children—Joseph Thomas, Julie Anne, John Franklin. Commd. 2d lt. U.S. Army, 1955, advanced through grades to lt. col., ret., 1976; dep. comdt. N.Mex. Mil. Inst., Roswell, 1976-77, instr. law enforcement and mil. history Jr. Coll. Div., 1977-80, asst. prof. social sci., 1980—. Co-chmn. U.S. Army Retiree Subcouncil, 1978—. Decorated Bronze Star, Meritorious Service Medal, Commendation medal, with oak leaf cluster, recipient Gold Medal award Freedoms Found., 1969, 70, 71, 72. Mem. Am. Criminal Justice Assn., Ret. Officers Assn., Am. Security Council (nat. adv. bd.), Mil. Order World Wars, Res. Officers Assn. Republican. Methodist. Contbr. articles to profl. jours. Home: 803 Pearson Dr Roswell NM 88201 Office: NMex Mil Inst Roswell NM 88210

POTASH, STEPHEN JON, international public relations counselor; b. Houston, Feb. 25, 1945; s. Melvin L. and Petrice (Edelstein) P.; m. Jeremy Warner, Oct. 19, 1969; 1 son, Aaron Warner. B.A., Pomona Coll., 1967. Account exec. Charles von Loewenfeldt, Inc., San Francisco, 1969-74, v.p., 1974-80; founder, pres. Potash & Co., Pub. Relations, Oakland, Calif., 1980—; cons. Am. Pres. Lines, 1979—; chief exec. officer Calif. Council Internat. Trade, 1970—. Mem. Pub. Relations Soc. Am. (counselors acad.), Japanese C. of C. Bd. dirs. Temple Sinai, Oakland, 1979-81. Columnist, Pacific Shipper, 1982—; editor newsletter Calif. Council Internat. Trade, 1969—. Office: 77 Jack London Sq Oakland CA 94607

POTT, RONALD WAYNE, manufacturing executive; b. Denver, June 6, 1926; s. Wayne Bailey and Hazel Francis (Harlan) P.; m. Mary True (Richards), June 1, 1947; children—Kathy, Steve, Becky, Rick, Terri, Brad, Dan, Shane. B.S. Denver U. Mgr. millwork dept. Carney Lumber Co., Denver, 1950-56; mgr. Curtis dept. Hallack & Howard, Denver, 1956-60; mgr. wholesale dept. U. Park Lumber Co., Denver, 1960-65; ptnr., pres. RW Specialties Inc., Denver, 1965—, also Western Turnings, Tacoma, Wash.; instr. in field. Served with USN. Mem. Denver Met. Home Builders Assn. (assoc.). Republican. Roman Catholic. Patentee convertible moulding, wonderail, newel attaching hardware. Home: 730 Crescent Ln Lakewood CO 80215 Office: 5301 Vasquez Blvd Commerce City CO 80022

POTTER, CHARLES ARTHUR, JR., trust company executive; b. St. Charles, Ill., July 25, 1925; s. Charles Arthur and Althea Mae (Whitney) P.; student Western Mich. Coll., 1943, Officers Candidate Sch., U.S. Marine Corps, Quantico, Va., 1945; B.S., U. Ill., 1948, J.D., 1949; student Northwestern U., 1956; m. Joan Patricia Johnson, June 12, 1948; 1 son, Charles Arthur. Admitted to Ill. bar, 1949; mem. law firm Gately & Burns, Chgo., 1949-50; spl. agt. FBI, Washington, Boston, N.Y.C., Chgo., 1951-54; asst. trust officer Elmhurst Nat. Bank, Elmhurst, Ill., 1955-59; asst. trust officer United California Bank, Los Angeles, 1959-61; vice-pres., trust officer First Am. Title Ins. Co., Santa Ana, Calif., 1961-68; pres. First Am. Trust Co., Santa Ana, Calif., 1968—; dir. First Am. Title Ins. Co., Santa Ana, Calif., Eldorado Bank, Tustin, Calif., First Am. Title Co. of Nev. Dir., Def. Orientation Conf. Assn., Washington, 1975—; dir. Orange County Sports Celebrities, 1971-80; dir. Orange County Estate Planning Council, 1966-69. Bd. dirs. Providence Speech and Hearing Center, Orange County (Calif.) chpt. Multiple Sclerosis Soc., 1978, Children's Hosp. Orange County Found., 1980—; adv. bd. Salvation Army, Santa Ana, 1980—. Served with USMC, 1943-45. Recipient County of Los Angeles Certificate of Commendation for pub. service, 1975. Mem. Soc. Former Spl. Agts. FBI (Western regional v.p. 1976-77), Calif. Bankers Assn. (chmn. trust div. 1982-83 dir. 1982-83), So. Calif. Trust Officers Assn. (pres. 1973-74), ABA, Ill. Bar Assn., Orange County bar assns., Def. Orientation Conf. Assn. (pres. 1982-84), Phi Delta Phi, Alpha Delta Phi. Clubs: Big Canyon Country (Newport Beach, Calif.); Indian Wells (Calif.) Country. Home: 47 Pinewood Irvine CA 92714 Office: 421 Main St Santa Ana CA 92701

POTTER, LYNNE A., law librarian; b. Pasadena, Calif., Sept. 20, 1955. B.A., San Diego State U., 1976; M.A., U. Denver, 1978; postgrad., Nat. U. Sch. of Law. Librarian, Ripey Car Mus., Denver, 1978; catalog librarian Western State Coll. Law, San Diego, 1978-79; law librarian Nat. U. Sch. Law, San Diego, 1979—; instr. legal research. Mem. ALA, Am. Assn. of Law Librarians, So. Calif. Assn. of Law Librarians. Office: Nat U Sch Law Library 3580 Aero Ct San Diego CA 92123

POTTER, MARY JOAN, management consultant; b. Indpls., July 23, 1947; d. Donald A. and Marian H. (Loughery) P.; B.A. in Sociology, Siena Heights Coll., Adrian, Mich., 1971; M.A. in Personnel and Counseling, Northwestern U., 1973. Vice pres. store ops. Betty's, Winnetka, Ill., 1972-74; dir. product mktg. Tratec Inc., Los Angeles, 1974-78; co-founder, 1979, since sr. partner Occidental Cons. Group Inc., Lafayette, Calif.; dir. McCord Group. Inc., Casper Mktg. Inc. Ill. State scholar, 1965. Mem. Sales and Mktg. Execs., Personnel Testing Council. Jr. League San Francisco. Republican. Roman Catholic. Club: San Francisco Tennis. Home: 9 Hawks Hill Ct Oakland CA 94618 Office: 3685 Mt Diablo Blvd Suite 291 Lafayette CA 94549

POTTER, NATHANIEL RESTCOME, JR., cement company marketing executive; b. Rochester, N.Y., Aug. 27, 1924; s. Nathaniel Restcome and Fannie (Furman) P.; m. Gail Caricof, Sept. 11, 1948; children—Charles B., C. Abigail, Jonathan M. B.A., Amherst Coll., 1948. Asst. buyer McCucoy & Co., Rochester, N.Y., 1948-50; v.p. Am. Tile Co., Honolulu, 1950-56; dept. mgr. Grace Bros., Honolulu, 1956-60; sales mgr., sec. treas. Hawaiian Cement Co., Honolulu, 1960-70; v.p. mktg. Cyprus Hawaiian Cement Corp., Honolulu, 1970—; dir. Cement and Concrete Products Industry. Served to 2d lt. USAAC, 1943-45. Republican. Episcopalian (sr. warden). Clubs: Pacific (past pres.). Home: 3710 Tantalos Dr Honolulu HI 96822 Office: 700 Bishop St Suite 610 Honolulu HI 96813

POTTS, LLOYD LEE, JR., pharm. co. sales mgr.; b. Wichita Falls, Tex., Sept. 23, 1951; s. Lloyd Lee and Billie Jean (Hamilton) P.; student San Jose City Coll., 1970-72, Calif. State U., Chico, 1972-74; m. Barbara Susan Talpas, May 29, 1976; children—Kelli Susan, Lloyd Lee III. Sales rep. Dome Labs., San Jose, Calif., 1975-78; sales mgr. Miles Pharms., San Francisco, 1978-82; with CIGNA/ESIS, 1982—. Mem. Sales and Mktg. Execs. Internat., Sales and Mktg. Execs. San Francisco. Address: 166 Sun Blossom Dr San Jose CA 95123

POTTS, ROY EARL, lawyer; b. Vincennes, Inc., Dec. 24, 1918; s. Roy F. and Elizabeth (Klein) P.; B.S. in Mech. Engring., Purdue U., 1940; Ll.B., Yale, 1951; m. Dorthy Birdeen Ragle, Aug. 16, 1940. Mgmt. trainee Santa Fe R.R., Albuquerque, 1940-42; instr. mech. engring. U. Tex., Austin, 1946-47; engr. Standard Oil Co. Inc., Whiting, Ind., 1947-49; admitted to Calif. bar, 1952; atty. O'Melveny & Myers, Los Angeles, 1951-62; atty. Kindel & Anderson, Los Angeles, 1962, ptnr., 1963-82; ptnr. firm Lyman & Prince, Los Angeles, 1982—. Mem. Town Hall, Los Angeles. Served to maj. AUS, 1942-46. Mem. Los Angeles County Bar Assn., Mchts. and Mfrs. Assn. Republican. Conglist. Clubs: Jonathan, Wilshire Country, Mens Garden (Los Angeles). Home: 645 Landor Ln Pasadena CA 91106 Office: 550 Flower St Los Angeles CA 90071

POULOS, CLARA JEAN, nutritionist, biologist; b. Los Angeles, Jan. 1, 1941; d. James P. and Clara Georgie (Creighton) Hill; Ph.D. in Biology, Fla. State Christian U., 1974; Ph.D. in Nutrition, Donsbach U., 1979; m. Themis Poulos, Jan. 31, 1960. Dir. research Leapou Lab., Aptos, Calif., 1973-76, Monterey Bay Research Inst., Santa Cruz, Calif., 1976—; nutrition specialist, Santa Cruz, 1975—; instr. Santa Cruz Extention U. Calif. and Stoddard Assos. Seminars; cons. Biol-Med. Lab., Chgo., Nutra Med Research Corp., N.Y., Akorn Miller Pharmacal, Chgo., Monterey Bay Aquaculture Farms. Recipient Najulander Internat. Research award, 1971, Wainwright Found. award., 1979, various state and local awards. Fellow Internat. Coll. Applied Nutrition, Am. Nutritionist Assn., Internat. Acad. Nutritional Consultants; mem. Am. Diabetes Assn. (profl.), AAAS, Internat. Platform Soc., Am. Public Health Assn., Calif. Acad. Sci., Internat. Fishery Assn. (health asct.), Club: Toastmistress. Author: Alcoholism—Stress - Hypoglycemia, 1976; The Relationship of Stress to Alcoholism and Hypoglycemia, 1979; contbr. articles to profl. jours. nutritionist, biologist; b. Los Angeles, Jan. 1, 1941; d. James P. and Clara Georgie (Creighton) Hill; Ph.D. in Biology, Fla. State Christian U., 1974; Ph.D. in Nutrition, Donsbach U., 1979; m. Themis Poulos, Jan. 31, 1960. Dir. research Leapou Lab., Aptos, Calif., 1973-76, Monterey Bay Research Inst., Santa Cruz, Calif., 1976—; nutrition specialist, Santa Cruz, 1975—; instr. Santa Cruz Extention U. Calif. and Stoddard Assos. Seminars; cons. Biol-Med. Lab., Chgo., Nutra-Med Research Corp., N.Y., Akorn-Miller Pharmacal, Chgo., Monterey Bay Aquaculture Farms. Recipient Najulander Internat. Research award, 1971, Wainwright Found. award., 1979, various state and local awards. Fellow Internat. Coll. Applied Nutrition, Am. Nutritionist Assn., Internat. Acad. Nutritional Consultants; mem. Am. Diabetes Assn. (profl.), AAAS, Internat. Platform Soc., Am. Public Health Assn., Calif. Acad. Sci., Internat. Fishery Assn. (health asct.), Club: Toastmistress. Author: Alcoholism—Stress - Hypoglycemia, 1976; The Relationship of Stress to Alcoholism and Hypoglycemia, 1979; contbr. articles to profl. jours. Office: 1595 Soquel Dr Suite 222 Santa Cruz CA 95065

POVALSKI, JAMES ALBERT, financial executive; b. Menominee, Mich., Apr. 21, 1920; s. Leo A. and Adeline M. (Valliere) P.; m. Irene M. Mathson, May 8, 1943; children—Nikki Lu, Marybeth Rae, Renee Jo, Helen Claire, Amy Suzanne. B.S., Mich. Tech. U., 1943; M.S., Purdue U., 1947. With Prescott Co., Menominee, Mich., 1941-42; commd. 2d lt., U.S. Air Force, 1944, advanced through grades to lt. col., 1963, ret., 1963; mgr. space systems planning, assoc. exploratory and advanced tech. activities Space Systems div. Air Force Systems Command, Los Angeles, 1959-63; with Douglas Aircraft Co., Huntington Beach, Calif., 1963-75; owner James A. Povalski & Assocs., Hawthorne, Calif., 1981—. Roman Catholic. Home: 900 Vai Del Monte Palos Verdes Estates CA 90274 Office: 13773 Hawthorne Blvd Hawthorne CA 90250

POWDRELL, DAVID DRANE, real estate broker; b. Reno, Dec. 18, 1954; s. Earle Carlisle and Frances (Drane) P.; B.A., U. Colo., 1976; m. Valerie Anna Lauria, June 28, 1981. Ops. officer Calif. Fed. Savs., Los Angeles, 1976-79; v.p. Molton/Cooper Mortgage Investors, Inc., Los Angeles, 1979-80; pres. Powdrell Fin. Co., Los Angeles, 1980-81; mgr. Century 21 Investment div. Bob Bree Realty, Inc., Santa Barbara, Calif., 1981—. Mem. Palos Verdes Investment Group (pres.), Investment Soc., Santa Barbara Bd. Realtors, Nat. Assn. Realtors. Home: 1222 E Mason St Santa Barbara CA 93103 Office: 2950 State St Santa Barbara CA 93105

POWELL, AMARYLLIS LILLES, music educator; b. Portland, Oreg., Nov. 12, 1931; d. Thomas Peter and Mary Jean (Manos) Lilles; m. George Chris Drougas, Jan. 1, 1956; m. 2d, Richard Lee Powell, June 7, 1962; children—Leslie, Christian, Donald, David, Mary. B.M.E., Willamette U., 1953, M.M.E., 1966. Mem. Honolulu Symphony, 1954-55; tchr. vocal/band Iolani Episcopal Sch. for Boys, Honolulu, 1954-55; tchr. vocal music Beaverton (Oreg.) Schs., 1962-63, 63-64; tchr. elem./jr. high band, elem. music coordinator Tigard (Oreg.) Schs., 1976—, mem. talented and gifted com., 1977—; mem. music textbook com. State Oreg. Dept. Edn., 1980—. Mem. alumni bd. Willamette U.; mem. troop com. Century Club, Boy Scouts Am.; active Oreg. Episcopal Schs. Rodney Soc., also alumni bd.; active Portland Rose Festival, Interlochen Nat. Music Camp. Mem. Music Educator's Nat. Conf. (life), NEA, Assn. Supervision and Curriculum Devel., Assn. Sch. Suprs., N.W. Women in Ednl. Adminstrn., Oreg. Advocates for the Arts, Oreg. Assn. Sch. Suprs. (profl. growth com.), Oreg. Edn. Assn., Conf. Oreg. Sch. Adminstrs., Oreg. Alliance for the Arts, Mid-Willamette Valley Music Suprs. (chmn.), Pi Beta Phi, Mu Phi Epsilon. Republican. Episcopalian. Club: West Hills Raquet (Portland, Oreg.). Home: 7455 SW Newton Pl Portland OR 97225 Office: 14650 SW 97th St Twality Jr High Sch Tigard OR 97223

POWELL, DEL OWEN, political organization official; b. Pasadena, Calif., June 6, 1958; s. Raymond Owen and Patricia Ann (Winchell) P. B.A., U. Calif.-San Diego, 1980; M.S. (Earle C. Anthony fellow), Calif. Inst. Tech., 1982. Research asst. U. Calif.-San Diego, 1978-80; research asst. Calif. Inst. Tech., Pasadena, 1981-82; mem. sr. canvass staff Citizens Action League, Sacramento, 1982, office mgr., 1982—. Mem. Am. Polit. Sci. Assn., Am. Econ. Assn., Midwest Polit. Sci. Assn., So. Polit. Sci. Assn., Pub. Choice Soc., Common Cause, ACLU. Democrat. Christian Scientist. Office: 1409 28th St Sacramento CA 95816

POWELL, DONALD ALLAN, advertising executive; b. Edmonton, Alberta (Canada), May 8, 1935; s. Harry Leonard and Joan Myrna (Smith) P.; m. Peggy Jean LaViolette, Sept. 14, 1957; children—Anthony, Alison. B.A. in Journalism, U. Calif.-Berkeley, 1957. Internat. creative dir. MacManus, John & Adams, London, 1967-72; dir. advt. The Irvine Co. (Calif.), 1972-75; pres. Don Powell Advt., Irvine, 1976—. Recipient 1st prize award Columbus Film Festival, 1962; Best Read Ad By Men award Gallup-Robinson London, 1969. Unitarian. Club: Racquet (Irvine). Home: 4971 Paseo de Vega Irvine CA 92715 Office: 2182 Dupont Dr Suite 207 Irvine CA 92715

POWELL, EARL ALEXANDER, III, museum director; b. Spartanburg, S.C., Oct. 24, 1943; s. Earl A. and Elizabeth (Duckworth) P.; A.B. with honors, Williams Coll., 1966; A.M., Harvard U., 1970, Ph.D., 1974; m. Nancy Landry Powell, July 17, 1971; children—Cortney, Channing. Teaching fellow fine arts Harvard U., 1970-74; curator Michener Collection, asst. prof. art history U. Tex., Austin, 1974-76; mus. curator, sr. staff asst. Nat. Gallery Art, Washington, 1976-79, exec. curator, 1979-80; dir. Los Angeles County Mus. Art, 1980—. Served with USN, 1966-69. Recipient King Olav medal King Olav V Norway, 1979; Harvard U. traveling fellow, 1973-74. Mem. Walpole Soc., Am. Assn. Museums, Am. Assn. Mus. Dirs., Archives Am. Art (So. Calif. adv. council). Club: Newport Reading Room. Contbr. articles to profl. jours. Office: 5905 Wilshire Blvd Los Angeles CA 90036

POWELL, FORBES RUSSELL, aerospace mfg. corp. exec.; b. Kansas City, Mo., Mar. 5, 1932; s. Russell Lee and Helen (Forbes) P.; B.S., Purdue U., 1954, Advanced Mgmt. Program, Harvard U., 1975; children—Constance Jane, Stephen Forbes. With Fisher Body div. Gen. Motors Corp., 1954-55, Del Mar Engring. Labs., 1957-61; with TRW Corp., 1961—, asst. mgr. Washington ops., 1973-76, mgr. electronic systems projects, Redondo Beach, Calif., 1976-81, v.p. electronic systems group, 1981—, instr. project mgmt., 1976—; dir. Bay Cities Nat. Bank. Chmn., City of Redondo Beach Public Improvements Commn., 1980—; bd. dirs. Redondo Beach Improvement Corp.; adv. Redondo Beach Coordinating Council; mem. exec. bd. Redondo Beach Round Table; mem. adv. bd. Salvation Army, Redondo Beach, 1980—, chmn. property com., 1981—; patron Los Angeles County Mus., 1979—. Served to capt. USAF, 1957. Registered profl. engr., Calif. Mem. Nat. Security Indsl. Assn. (exec. com., task group chmn.), Armed Forces Communications and Electronics Assn. (nat. dir.), AIAA, IEEE, Redondo Beach C. of C., So. Pacific Assn. AAU (chmn. diving 1970-71), Los Angeles World Affairs Council. Clubs: King Harbor Yacht, Annapolis Yacht, Los Angeles Wheelmen. Patentee aero. tng. system. Home: PO Box 3087 Redondo Beach CA 90277 Office: TRW 1 Space Park Redondo Beach CA 90278

POWELL, GENE A., lawyer; b. Falls City, Neb., Jan. 10, 1932; s. James B. and Venus C. (Martin) P.; m. Betty L. Brown, Oct. 28, 1955 (div.); children—Lynda, Steve, Robin; m. 2d Virginia M. Paron, July 1, 1972. B.B.A., J.D., Wahburn U., 1955. Bar: Calif. Asst. counsel Union Bank, Los Angeles, 1961-62; asst. counsel Douglas Aircraft and McDonnell Douglas Corp., 1962-67, sr. counsel, 1967-69; asst. v.p. Continental Airlines, 1969-81, asst. gen. counsel, 1981—. Served to lt. col. USAF. Mem. ABA, Calif. Bar Assn., Kans. Bar Assn. Presbyterian. Contbr. articles to profl. jours. Office: 7300 World Way West Los Angeles CA 90009

POWELL, JACK ROY, ins. co. exec.; b. Ann Arbor, Mich., June 27, 1933; s. Ray W. and Garnett J. (Beanblossom) P.; B.A., Whittier Coll., 1955; m. Katherine Ruth Pullan, Feb. 19, 1969; children—Shannon Ruth, Damon Ray. Claims mgr. Liberty Mut. Ins. Co., San Francisco, 1959-75; exec. v.p. claims Employee Benefits Ins. Co., San Jose, Calif., 1976—; pres. EBI Services, Inc., 1982—. Served with USCG, 1955-59. Mem. Fedn. Ins. Counsel, Pacific Claims Execs. Assn., Calif. Self/Insurers Assn. Republican. Home: 120 Starview Pl Danville CA 94526 Office: 66 E Rosemary St San Jose CA 95112

POWELL, JERRY ALAN, entomology educator; b. Glendale, Calif., May 23, 1933; s. Percy C. and Florence M. (Martin) P.; m. Frances L. Crisp, Sept. 15, 1956; children—Carolyn, David, Julia; m. Elizabeth M. Randal, July 9, 1977; B.S., U. Calif.-Berkeley, 1955, Ph.D., 1961. Asst. entomologist U. Calif.-Berkeley, 1962-67, assoc. entomologist, 1967-73, assoc. prof., 1969-73, curator Entomol. Mus., 1963-82, prof. entomology, entomologist Agrl. Expt. Sta., 1973—. Calif. Acad. Scis. fellow, 1971. Mem. Entomol. Soc. Am., Soc. Systematic Zoology, Lepidopterists Soc. (Karl Jordan medal 1982). Office: 201 Wellman Hall U Calif Berkeley CA 94720

POWELL, LAURA JEAN, chem. co. ofcl.; b. Evanston, Wyo., Apr. 18, 1929; d. Wallace and Marjory Marie (Godfrey) Bond; student U. Wyo., 1948-49; m. Gilbert Burgess Taylor, Mar. 5, 1948; children—Ginger, Jolynne, Gay, Melanie, Kimberly, Darin; m. Richard Evan Powell, Dec. 24, 1973. Accountant, Allied Chem. Co., Green River, Wyo., 1972-73; exec. sec. Texasgulf Inc., Granger, Wyo., 1974-79, scheduling coordinator asst., 1980, head scheduling dept., 1980-81, traffic coordinator, 1981—; owner, mgr. JRD Ct & Sta., Granger, 1975—; owner, mgr. ranch, Uinta County, Wyo., 1972—. Leader, Youth Fellowship, 1955-59; committeewoman Uinta County Republican party, 1963-64; leader Cub Scouts, 1975-76. Mem. Bus. Women, Mountain View Alumni Assn. (pres. 1953). Republican. Presbyterian. Club: Zonta. Home: Little America WY 82929 Office: PO Box 100 Granger WY 82934

POWELL, LENORA ELEVINE, public transportation administrator; b. San Diego, Apr. 12, 1940; d. William Robert Salle and Daisy Rosella (Dawson) S.; m. William Clifford Elkins, June 27, 1957; children—Debra Louise, Laurie Faye, William Clifford Jr., Richard Roy; m. 2, Michael Stanley Powell, Dec. 26, 1978. Student Grossmont Jr. Coll., 1972-74; San Diego State U., 1975-76. Basic edn. instr. San Diego County Assn. Retarded Citizens, 1966-72; gen. mgr. Ted's Bus Service, El Cajon, Calif., 1972-78; location supr. Community Transit Services, Inc., Chula Vista, Calif., 1979-81, gen. mgr., Santee, Calif., 1981—; defensive driving instr. Nat. Safety Council; sign lang. instr.; swim cons. spl. olympics. bd. dirs. San Diego County chpt. ARC, 1969-73. Named PTA Calif. Women of Yr. 1972; recipient numerous awards from mayors of San Diego and El Cajon for outstanding contbns. to children. Mem. Nat. Assn. Female Execs., Am. Legion, Transp. Profls. San Diego County, Santee C. of C., Poway (Calif.) C. of C., VFW Aux. (El Cajon). Republican. Club: Elks (El Centro, Calif.). Office: Community Transit Service 8656 Cuyamaca St Suite M Santee CA 92071

POWELL, LEROY EARLE, JR., municipal official; b. Washington, Sept. 5, 1949; s. Leroy Earle and Carroll (March) P.; m. Candace Ellen Sebring, Aug. 10, 1974; 1 son, Matthew Reid. B.A., Grinnell Coll., 1972; M.P.A., Lyndon B. Johnson Sch. Pub. Affairs, U. Tex.-Austin, 1975. Fin. dir. City of Cypress (Calif.), 1976—. Recipient Lyndon Baines Johnson Fellowship award, 1973-75. Mem. Mcpl. Fin. Officers Assn., Calif. Mcpl. Fin. Officers Assn. Office: 5275 Orange Ave Cypress CA 90630

POWELL, LEWIS NEWELL, municipal official; b. State College, Pa., Apr. 28, 1938; s. Albert Perry and Margaret Hope (Newell) P.; m. Nancy Louise Nicholson, June 11, 1964; children—Mary, Heather, Alan, Alice. B.M.E., Lafayette Coll., 1960. Registered profl. engr., Oreg., Wash. Results engr. Pa. Power & Light Co., Sunbury, Pa., 1961-68; camp ranger, maintenance supt. Crystal Lake Camps, Hughesville, Pa., 1968-69; v.p. Robert E. Meyer Engrs., Beaverton and Redmond, Oreg., 1969-78; pub. works dir. City of Medford (Oreg.), 1978—. Pres., Chehalen Sch. PTA, 1976-77; chmn. camp com. Winema council Girl Scouts U.S., 1982. Served with AUS, 1961-63. Mem. Am. Pub. Works Assn., Nat. Soc. Profl. Engrs., Water Pollution Control Fedn., Pacific NW Pollution Control Assn. Republican. Christian Scientist. Club: Kiwanis (pres. 1975). Office: 411 W 8th St Room 204 Medford OR 97501

POWELSON, JOHN PALEN, economist; b. N.Y.C., Sept. 3, 1920; s. John Abrum and Mary Elizabeth Rennie (Stephen) P.; grad. Phillips Acad., 1937; A.B., Harvard U., 1941, A.M., 1947, Ph.D., 1950; M.B.A., U. Pa., 1942; m. Alice Williams Roberts, May 31, 1953; children—Cynthia, Judith, Kenneth, Carolyn, Lawrence. Acct., Haskins & Sells, C.P.A.'s, N.Y.C., 1942-44; instr. acctg. U. Pa., 1944-45; teaching fellow econs. Harvard U., 1946-48; sr. acct. Price, Waterhouse & Co., C.P.A.'s, Paris, 1948-49; asst. prof. acctg. U. Buffalo, 1949-50; economist Internat. Monetary Fund, 1950-54, asst. chief tng., 1954-58; prof. econs. Sch. Advanced Internat. Studies Johns Hopkins U., 1958-64; prof. econ. devel. U. Pitts., 1964-66; prof. econs. U. Colo., 1966—; chmn. econs. dept. Inter-Am. U. Air, 1966-67; dir. tng. programs nat. accts. Centro de Estudios Monetarios Latinamericanos, Mexico City, 1963-64; econ. adviser Govt. Bolivia, 1960; vis. prof. econs. U. San Andres, La Paz, Bolivia, 1960; vis. scholar Harvard U., 1981-82; cons. Inter-Am. Devel. Bank, Washington, 1967-68; econ. adviser Ministry of Fin. and Planning, Kenya, 1972-74. Treas. Internat. Student House, Washington, 1952-59; C.P.A., N.Y. Mem. Am. Econ. Assn., Soc. Internat. Devel. Author: Economic Accounting 1955; National Income and Flow-of-Funds Analysis, 1960; Latin America-Today's Economic and Social Revolution, 1964; Institutions of Economic Growth, 1972; A Select Bibliography on Economic Development, 1979; co-author: The Economics of Development and Distribution, 1981; Threat to Development: Pitfalls of the NIEO, 1983; co-editor: Economic Development, Poverty and Income Distribution, 1977. Home: 45 Bellevue Dr Boulder CO 80302

POWER, CORNELIUS MICHAEL, archbishop; b. Seattle, Dec. 18, 1913; s. William and Kate (Dougherty) P.; student St. Patrick Sem., Menlo Park, Calif., 1933-35, St. Edward Sem., Kenmore, Wash., 1935-39; J.C.D., Cath. U. Am., 1943. Ordained priest Roman Catholic Ch., 1939; asst. pastor St. James Cathedral, Seattle, 1939-40; resident chaplain Holy Names Acad., Seattle, 1943-52; adminstr. Parish of Our Lady of Lake, Seattle, 1955-56, pastor, 1956-69; vice chancellor Archdiocese of Seattle, 1943-51, chancellor, 1951-69; apptd. domestic prelate, 1963; 2d bishop of Yakima, 1969; bishop of Yakima, 1969-74; archbishop of Portland (Oreg.), 1974—. Office: Archdiocese of Portland PO Box 351 Portland OR 97207

POWER, DENNIS MICHAEL, museum director; b. Pasadena, Calif., Feb. 18, 1941; s. John Dennis and Ruth Augusta (Mott) P.; B.A., Occidental Coll., 1962, M.A., 1964; Ph.D., U. Kans., 1967; m. Kristine Moneva Fisher, Feb. 14, 1965; children—Michael Lawrence, Matthew David. Asso. curator birds Royal Ont. Mus., Toronto, 1967-72; dir. Santa Barbara (Calif.) Mus. Natural History, 1972—; biol. researcher, writer, tchr., cons. Recipient numerous grants Am. Mus. Natural History, NSF, Province of Ont., Bur. Land Mgmt., others. Fellow Am. Ornithologists Union (sec. 1981—); mem. AAAS, Am. Assn. Museums (council 1980-83, dir. Western regional conf., v.p. 1979-81), Assn. Sci. Mus. Dirs., Calif. Assn. Mus. (steering com. 1979, dir. 1980), Cooper Ornithol. Soc. (dir. 1976-79, pres. 1979-81), Ecol. Soc. Am., Soc. Study Evolution, Soc. Systematic Zoology, Sigma Xi. Editor: The California Islands: Proceedings of a Multidisciplinary Symposium, 1980; contbr. articles to profl. jours. Office: 2559 Puesta del Sol Santa Barbara CA 93105

POWERS, EDWIN MALVIN, consulting engineer; b. Denver, July 20, 1915; s. Emmett and Bertha Malvina (Guido) P.; m. Dorothy Lavane Debler, Jan. 18, 1941; children—Dennis M., Kenneth E., James M., Steven R. B.S. in Chem. Engring., U. Denver, 1939, M.S., 1940. Registered profl. engr., N.J., Colo. Prodn. supr. Nat. Aniline Div., Buffalo, 1940-45; engr., project supr. Merck & Co., Rahway, N.J., 1945-72, purchasing engr., 1972-82; ret., 1982; cons. engr., Conifer, Colo., 1982—. Mem. Am. Chem. Soc., Nat. Soc. Profl. Engrs., Am. Inst. Chem. Engrs. (treas. N.J. 1960, exec. com. 1961-63). Home and office: 26106 Amy Circle Dr Conifer CO 80433

POWERS, KENNETH LAWRENCE, civil engr., assn. exec.; b. Kalispell, Mont., July 30, 1912; s. William Allan and Anna Dorcus (Harrington) P.; B.S., U. Puget Sound, 1935; postgrad. U. Wash., 1937; m. Gladys Marie Neff, June 5, 1940 (dec. July 1969); 1 dau., Sharron Marie (Mrs. Joseph Dennis Delaney); m. Catherine Elaine Coconougher, Dec. 26, 1970. Assayer, Alaska div. Kennecott Copper Corp., 1935-38; insp. gen. constrn. Grand Coulee, Altus project U.S. Bur. Reclamation, Altus, Okla., 1938-41, engr. Altus project, Denver, 1942-48, field engr. Bonny Dam, Republican River Valley, Sargent project, Farwell project, St. Paul, Nebr., 1948-61, constr. engr., 1961-65, chief constrn. coordination and estimates br., region 7, Denver, 1965-67, regional engr., region 4, Salt Lake City, 1967-73; cons. engr., Denver, 1973-74; exec. sec. Profl. Engrs. of Colo., 1974-81; ret., 1981. Registered profl. engr., Colo. Fellow ASCE, Nat. Soc. Profl. Engrs. (chpt. v.p. 1972-73), U.S. Com. on Large Dams, U.S. Com. on Irrigation and Flood Control. K.C. (4 deg.), Elk, Lion (dist. govt. 1964-65). Address: 12938 W Virginia Ave Lakewood CO 80228

POWERS, MARCUS E., lawyer; b. Cedarville, Ohio, Apr. 7, 1929; s. Frederick Armajo and Elizabeth Isabel (Rumbaugh) P.; B.A., Ohio Wesleyan U., 1951; J.D., N.Y. U., 1954, LL.M., 1958; m. Doris Mae Campbell, July 28, 1955; children—Douglas Keith, David Anthony, James Allen, Laura Ann, Bradley Clark. Admitted to Ohio bar, 1954, N.Y. State bar, 1959, Calif. bar, 1964; asst. prof. law N.Y. U. Sch. Law, 1956-60; atty. Am. Brake Shoe Co., N.Y.C., 1959-63; asst. gen. counsel Dart Industries Inc., Los Angeles, 1963-81; sr. v.p., gen. counsel, sec. Nat. Med. Enterprises, Inc., Los Angeles, 1981—. Served with U.S. Army, 1954-56. Mem. Los Angeles County Bar Assn. (chmn. corp. law depts. sect.), Inst. Corp. Counsel (bd. govs.), Am. Bar Assn., Assn. Bar City N.Y., Phi Beta Kappa, Omicron Delta Kappa, Phi Delta Theta, Kappa Sigma, Pi Sigma Alpha, Theta Alpha Phi. Office: 11620 Wilshire Blvd Los Angeles CA 90025

POWERS, RAY LLOYD, state senator, dairy farmer, rancher; b. Colorado Springs, Colo., June 27, 1929; s. Guy and Cora (Hill) P.; student public schs.; m. Dorothy Parrish, Dec. 14, 1975; 1 dau., Janet. Dairy farmer, Colorado Springs, 1947—; mem. Colo. Ho. of Reps., 1978-80; mem. Colo. Senate, 1981—. Bd. dirs. Mountain Empire Dairyments Coop., Denver, 1967-81; mem. Fed. Land Bank Bd., Colorado Springs, 1976-83. Clubs: Republican Men's; Lions. Home: 5 Markshefel Rd Colorado Springs CO 80909

POWERS, STEPHEN, educational researcher, consultant; b. Bakersfield, Calif., June 10, 1936; s. Robert Boyd and Mildred (Irwin) P.; m. Gail Marguerite Allen, Dec. 28, 1968; children—Rick, Joseph, Rebecca. B.S in Edn., No. Ariz. U., 1959; M.A., U. Ariz., Tucson, 1970, M.Ed., 1972, Ph.D., 1978. Cert. tchr., Calif.; cert. tchr., adminstr., jr. coll. tchr., Ariz. Policeman, City of Bakersfield, 1967-69; tchr. Marana (Ariz.) Pub. Schs., 1969-72; dir. Am. Sch. Belo Horizonte, Brazil, 1972-73; tchr. Nogales (Ariz.) Pub. Schs., 1973-75; research specialist Tucson Unified Sch. Dist., 1975—; cons. Pima Coll.; adj. prof. ednl. psychology, U. Ariz.; assoc. faculty mem. in computer sci. Pima Coll. Nat. Inst. Edn. grantee, 1980; Ariz. State Reading Council, 1982. Mem. Am. Ednl. Research Assn., Psychometric Soc., Assn. Supervision and Curriculum Devel. Bahai. Contbr. articles to profl. jours. Office: 1010 E 10th St Tucson AZ 85719

POYNTER, DANIEL FRANK, author, publisher; b. N.Y.C., Sept. 17, 1938; s. William Frank and Josephine E. (Thompson) P.; B.A., U. Calif., Chico, 1960; postgrad. San Francisco Law Sch., 1962. Gen. mgr. Tri-State Parachute Co., Flemington, N.J., 1963-64; sales mgr. Parachutes Inc., Orange, Mass., 1964-65; mktg. mgr. Strong Enterprises, North Quincy, Mass., 1966-74; author, pub. Para Pub., Santa Barbara, Calif., 1974—. Bd. dirs. Mus. of Parachuting and Air Safety, Washington, 1974-78. Served with USAR, 1957-66. Recipient Diplome d Honneur, Fedn. Aeronautique Internationale, 1979; Meritorious Achievement award, Central Atlantic Sport Parachute Assn., 1972; Achievement award U.S. Parachute Assn., 1980. Mem. U.S. Parachute Assn., Internat. Assn. Ind. Pubs. (dir. 1979-81), U.S. Hang Gliding Assn. (dir. 1975-76), Commission Internationale de Vol Libre (pres. 1976-77), Com. Small Mag. Editors and Pubs. Contbr. numerous articles to profl. jours.; patentee in field; author: Parachuting, The Skydivers Handbook, 4th edit., 1983; The Parachute Manual, 2d edit. 1978; Parachute Rigging Course, 2d edit. 1980; Parachuting Manual with Log, 7th edit. 1983; Word Processors and Information Processing, 2d edit. 1982; Publishing Short Run Books, 3d edit. 1982; also books on hang gliding and kiting, pub., bus. letters, others. Home: Route 1 Box P Goleta CA 93117 Office: PO Box 4232 Santa Barbara CA 93103

POYOUROW, ROCHELLE, educator; b. N.Y.C., Apr. 23, 1936; d. Gerald G. and Hortense (Philips) Bernheimer; children—Mitchell, Jill, David. A.A.S., Fashion Inst. Tech., 1955; student Hunter Coll., CCNY, Pace U.; B.P.S., 1974; M.Ed., Temple U., 1977. Cert. tchr. of handicapped, Pa.; cert. prin., sch. supt., Wyo. Fashion designer Skampalon, Inc., N.Y.C., 1955-60; tchr. fashion design Pleasantville (N.Y.) Cottage Sch., 1969-74; spl. edn. tchr. Horsham Clinic, Ambler, Pa., Phila., 1974-78; fed. project dir. Montgomery County Intermediate Unit, Norristown, Pa., 1978-80; exec. dir. Northeast Wyo. Bd. Coop. Ednl. Services, Gillette, 1980—. Pres., Yorktown (N.Y.) Community Relations Council, 1967-70; mem. adv. bd. Sheridan (Wyo.) Coll. Pace U. Trustee scholar, 1973; named Woman of Yr., Beta Sigma Phi, 1982. Mem. Council for Exceptional Children, Am. Assn. Sch. Adminstrs., Assn. Supervision and Curriculum Develop. Assn. Retarded Citizens, Assn. Serverely Handicapped, LWV, Beta Sigma Phi. Contbr. article to profl. jour. Office: 410 N Miller Ave Gillette WY 82716

POZA, HUGO BERNARDO, elec. engr., aerospace co. exec.; b. Havana, Cuba, Mar. 12, 1945; s. Hugo Ernesto and Carmen (Valle) P.; B.S.E.E., U. Dayton, 1966; M.S.E.E., Purdue U., 1967, Ph.D., 1971; m. Mary Karen Connors, Jan. 21, 1967; children—Hugh Thomas, Sean Christopher, Vanessa Kristi. Mem. tech. staff TRW Systems Group, Redondo Beach, Calif., 1971-73, dept. staff engr., 1973-75, sr. staff engr., 1975-77, asst. program mgr., 1977-80; mgr. mil. systems ops. TRW Def. and Space Systems Group, Redondo Beach, 1981—; mem. tech. adv. bd. Quest Tech. mag. Bd. dirs. Am. Martyrs Youth Group, 1975-78, Manhattan Beach Single Young Adults, 1979—; mem. Christian Family Movement, 1979—. Mem. IEEE, AIAA, World Affairs Council Los Angeles, Tau Beta Pi. Roman Catholic. Club: Las Canchas Tennis. Contbr. articles to profl. jours.; patentee in field. Home: 15245 Midland Rd Poway CA 92064 Office: TRW Def and Space Systems Group SD-8 1 Space Park Dr Redondo Beach CA 90278

POZZI, CAROLE ANN, foundation project coordinator; b. San Francisco, Feb. 26, 1949; d. Julian Felix and Rosamond Cyrena (Beltz) Pozzi; m. John Lee Carrico, Feb. 14, 1981 (div.). B.A. in Polit. Sci., U. Nev.-Reno, 1972, M.A. in Communications, 1980. Cert. substance abuse counselor, Nev. Project coordinator Reno Internat. Jazz Festival, Youth Music Found., Ltd., Reno, 1974—; counselor in pvt. practice, Reno., 1981—; exec. dir. Lake Tahoe Cultural Arts Alliance, 1983—; instr. U. Nev. Mem. Nat. Assn. Female Execs., AAUW. Democrat. Home: 119 Rissone Ln Reno NV 89503 Office: PO Box 6585 Reno NV 89513

PRACHT, PEGGY SUE, sci. lab. adminstr.; b. Oakland, Calif., Dec. 23, 1947; d. Loren Eugene and Frankie Ethelene (Dupree) P.; B.A. in Music, Calif. State U., Hayward, 1970, student in Bus. Adminstrn.; 1 son, John Thomas Yeandle. Computer operator Haskins & Sells, C.P.A.s, San Francisco, 1974-75; staff asst. to dir. Lawrence Berkeley Lab., 1976—. Mem. Nat. Notary Assn., Nat. Assn. Female Execs. Home: 15267 Central Ave San Leandro CA 94578 Office: Lawrence Berkeley Lab Calif 1 Cyclotron Rd Berkeley CA 94720

PRAEGER, DIRCK KENDALL, marine officer; b. Great Bend, Kans., Mar. 18, 1939; s. Walter Grizzell and Mary Edith (Kendall) P.; m. Anna Linda Hale, Aug. 31, 1963 (div.); m. 2d, Marcia Ann Kubik, May 12, 1972; children—Kendall Ann, Donald Carson Hale, Erin Brooke, Michael John. B.S., U.S. Naval Acad., 1963. Comd. 2d lt. U.S. Marine Corps., 1963; advanced through grades to maj., 1973; served with Basic Sch., Quantico, Va., 1963, 3d bn. 6th Marines, 2d Marine Div., Camp Lejeune, N.C., 1964-65, Marine Corp recruit depot Parris Island, S.C., 1965-66, marine detachment USS Ranger, 1966-67, 2d bn. 1st Marines, 1st Marine Div., 1967-68; marine corps recruiting sta. Des Moines, Iowa, 1968-70, 3d bn. 8th Marines, 2d Marine Div., Camp Lejeune, N.C., 1970-73, 1st Amphibian Tractor Bn., 3d Marine Div., Okinawa, Japan, 1973-74; advanced communication officer's sch. Devel. Ctr. Quantico, Va., 1974-76, USS Blue Ridge, San Diego, 1976-78; landing force tng. command Pacific, San Diego, 1978—, electronic warfare officer. Mem. Marine Corps Assn., Old Crows Assn. Republican. Roman Catholic.

PRATT, CHARLES DUDLEY, JR., utility exec.; b. Honolulu, Sept. 30, 1927; s. Charles Dudley and Dora (Broadbent) P.; B.C.E. with honors, Yale U., 1950, M.Structural Engring., 1951; M.B.A., U. Hawaii, 1971; m. Dale Logan, July 2, 1978; children by previous marriage—Charles Dudley, Timothy G., Sarah E., Melinda L. With Hawaiian Electric Co., Inc., 1953—, v.p. planning, 1971, then exec. v.p., 1980, pres., 1981—, also dir., chief exec. officer; dir. Maui Electric Co., Ltd., Hawaii Electric Light Co., Inc. Bd. dirs. Aloha United Way; v.p. Aloha council Boy Scouts Am. Served with AUS, 1946-48, 51-53. Registered profl. engr., Hawaii. Mem. ASCE (past pres. Hawaii sect.), Hawaii Soc. Corp. Planners, Hawaii C. of C. (dir.), U. Hawaii M.B.A. Alumni Group, USCG Aux., Beta Gamma Sigma, Tau Beta Pi. Clubs: Pacific, Kaneohe Yacht. Office: Hawaiian Eectric Co Inc 900 Richards St Honolulu HI 96813*

PRATT, CURGIE WINCHESTER, real estate developer; b. N.Y.C., June 15, 1933; s. Herbert Lee and Hope Gordon (Winchester) P.; m. Ann Violet Stauffer, Nov. 5, 1955; children—Catherine Pratt Peagler, Carolyn, m. 2d, Mary Ann Hewitt Mitchell, Nov. 11, 1968; children—Jennifer, Hewitt. B.A., Claremont McKenna Coll., 1958; B.A., Am. Grad. Sch. Internat. Mgmt., 1959. Asst. gen. mgr. Elizabeth Arden, N.Y.C. and Rio de Janeiro, 1959-61; Ariz. sales rep. James W. Newman & Assocs., Los Angeles, 1961-65; pres. Maricopa County Broadcasters, Mesa, Ariz., 1965-71; field rep. Rural Met. Fire Dept., Scottsdale, Ariz., 1971-74; pres. Page, Inc., Phoenix, 1974—; prof. broadcasting Maricopa County Community Coll., 1971; dir. Good Hope Corp., 1976-81. Publicity chmn. Mesa C. of C., 1968-70; pres. Pratt Found., Phoenix, 1974—; trustee Webb Sch. Calif., 1977—; mem. Luke's Men of St. Luke's Hosp., Phoenix, 1977—, bd. dirs., 1979-82. Mem. Met. Phoenix Broadcasters (dir. 1968-70). Republican. Episcopalian. Home: 4815 E Exeter Blvd Phoenix AZ 85018 Office: 7111 N 7th St Suite C Phoenix AZ 85020

PRATT, GEORGE JANES, JR., psychologist; b. Mpls., May 3, 1948; s. George Janes and Sally Elvina (Hanson) P.; B.A. cum laude, U. Minn., 1970, M.A., 1973; Ph.D. with spl. commendation for overall excellence, Calif. Sch. Profl. Psychology, San Diego, 1976; m. Christine Clinton, Dec. 17, 1977; 1 dau., Whitney Beth. Psychology trainee Center for Behavior Modification, Mpls., 1971-72, U. Minn. Student Counseling Bur., 1972-73; predoctoral clin. psychology intern San Bernardino County (Calif.) Mental Health Services, 1973-74, San Diego County Mental Health Services, 1974-76; affiliate staff San Luis Rey Hosp., 1977-78; postdoctoral clin. psychology intern Mesa Vista Hosp., San Diego, Calif., 1976; clin. psychologist, dir. Psychology and Cons. Assos. of San Diego, 1976—; pres. George Pratt Ph.D., Psychol. Corp., 1979—; founder LaJolla Profl. Workshops, 1977; clin. psychologist El Camino Psychology Center, San Clemente, Calif., 1977-78; grad. teaching asst. U. Minn. Psychology and Family Studies div., 1971; teaching asso. U. Minn. Psychology and Family Studies div., Mpls., 1972-73; instr. U. Minn. Extension div., Mpls., 1971-73; faculty Calif. Sch. Profl. Psychology, 1974—, San Diego Evening Coll., 1975-77, Nat. U., 1978-79, Chapman Coll., 1978, San Diego State U., 1979-80; vis. prof. Pepperdine U., Los Angeles, 1976-80; cons. U. Calif. at San Diego Med. Sch., 1976—, also instr. univ., 1978—, psychology chmn. Workshops in Clin. Hypnosis, 1980—; cons. Calif. Health Dept., 1974, Naval Regional Med. Center, 1978—, ABC-TV; also speaker. Mem. South Bay Youth Services Com., San Diego, 1976—. Served with USAR, 1970-76. Licensed psychologist, Calif. Fellow Am. Soc. Clin. Hypnosis; mem. Am. Psychol. Assn., Calif. Psychol. Assn., Internat. Soc. Hypnosis, San Diego Psychology Law Soc. (exec. com.), Am. Assn. Marriage and Family Therapists, Am. Assn. Sex Educators, Counselors and Therapists (cert.), San Diego Soc. Sex Therapy and Edn. (pres.), San Diego Soc. Clin. Hypnosis (pres.), Acad. San Diego Psychologists, Soc. Clin. and Exptl. Hypnosis., U. Minn. Alumni Assn., Beta Theta Pi. Republican. Lutheran. Cons. editor Psychology, Cons. Assos. Press, 1977—; author: A Clinical Hypnosis Primer; Sensory/Progressive Relaxation and Effective Stress Management; Clinical Hypnosis: Techniques and Applications. Office: LaJolla Med Psychol Ctr 6523 LaJolla Blvd La Jolla CA 92037

PRATT, HARVEY ARTHUR, cons. pharmacist; b. Syracuse, N.Y., Mar. 6, 1939; s. James Arthur and Lavina Charlotte (Harvey) P.; B.S. in Pharmacy, U. Pitts., 1960; m. Ann Louise Rogers, July 31, 1974; children—Linda, Leann, Michelle, Jennine, Arriana. Store mgr., various stores Walgreen Co., Chgo., Gary, Ind., Houston, Baton Rouge and Denver, 1960-67; buyer May D&F, Denver, 1967-69; pres. Drug Fair, Inc., Englewood, Colo., 1969-79; cons., prin. Pratt and Assos., Englewood, 1979—; small bus. rep. Health Care Fin. Adminstrn., adv. to adminstr. and assoc. adminstr. external affairs, 1980—; mem. pharmacy faculty U. Colo., 1977-80; bd. dirs., sec. Colo. Found. Med. Care, 1975-80, chmn. 20th Western States Pharmacy Conf. Chmn., Englewood Holiday Parade, 1976—; item writer Nat. Bds. Pharmacy Licensure Exam. Vice chmn. Englewood Bd. Adjustments and Appeals. Named Pharmacist of Distinction, 1974; recipient Outstanding Service award Englewood C. of C., 1976. Mem. Colo. Pharmacal Assn. (Elizabeth Taft Meml. award 1980), Am. Mgmt. Assn., Nat Assn. Retail Druggists, Am. Pharm. Assn. Denver Area Pharmacy Assn., Colo. Retail Liquor Dealers, Englewood United Suburban C. of C. (pres.-elect, Outstanding Service and Achievement award), Nat. Speakers' Assn. Republican. Lutheran. Club: Arapahoe County Republican Men's. Contbr. articles to profl. jours. Office: PO Box B Englewood CO 80150

PRATT, RICHARD HENRY, psychologist; b. Yreka, Calif., Mar. 24, 1941; s. William Andrews and Marie Helena (Van Vliet) P.; m. Saundra Lou Lansaw, May 23, 1964; children—Shawn, Ryan, Erin. B.A. in Psychology, Calif. State U.-Sacramento, 1970, M.A. in Social and Exptl. Psychology, 1975; Ph.D. in Ednl. Psychology, U. Tex., 1979. Instr. human relations Tarrant County Jr. Coll., Ft. Worth, 1975-76; assoc. software engr. Softech Inc., Waltham, Mass., 1976; social sci. researcher III U. Tex., Austin, 1976-79; clin. psychologist Valley Psychol. Services, Porterville, Calif., 1980; clin. psychologist IV rural clinics, State of Nev., Winnemucca Mental Health Ctr., 1980-82; instr. No. Nev. Community Coll., 1980—. Vice pres. Winnemucca Parks and Recreation Commn.; judo, self-def. instr. County Probation Dept. Served with USAF, 1963-68. Mem. Am. Psychol. Assn., Western Psychol. Assn., Mensa, Psi Chi. Contbr. articles to profl. jours. Home: 4961 Meadowspring Dr Reno NV 89509

PRATT, ROSALIE REBOLLO, harpist, educator; b. N.Y.C., Dec. 4, 1933; d. Antonio Ernesto and Eleanor Gertrude (Gibney) Rebollo; Mus.B., Manhattanville Coll., 1954; Mus.M., Pius XII Inst. Fine Arts, Florence, Italy, 1955; Ed.D., Columbia U., 1976; m. Samuel Orson Pratt, Aug. 11, 1964; children—Francesca Christina Pratt Ferguson, Alessandra Maria Pratt Jones. Prin. harpist N.J. Symphony Orch., 1963-65; soloist Mozart Haydn Festival, Avery Fisher Hall, N.Y.C., 1968; tchr. music public schs., Bloomfield and Montclair, N.J., 1962-73; mem. faculty Montclair State Coll., 1973-79; assoc. prof. Brigham Young U., Provo, Utah, 1979—. Fulbright grantee, 1979; Myron Taylor scholar, 1954. Mem. Am. Harp Soc. (Outstanding Service award 1973), AAUP (co-chmn. legis. relations com. N.J. 1978-79), Music Edn. for Handicapped (co-founder, co-chmn., project dir.), Coll. Music Soc., Music Educators Nat. Conf., Phi Kappa Phi, Sigma Alpha Iota. Co-author: Elementary Music for All Learners, 1980; contbr. articles to Music Educators Jour., Am. Harp Jour., others. Editor procs. 2d Internat. Symposium, Music Edn. for Handicapped, 1982. Office: Harris Fine Arts Center Brigham Young U Provo UT 84602

PRAY, RALPH EMERSON, metallurgical engineer; b. Troy, N.Y., May 12, 1926; s. George Emerson and Jansje Cornelius (Owejan) P.; student N.Mex. Inst. of Mining and Tech., 1953-56, U. N.Mex., 1956; B.S. in Metall. Engring., U. Alaska, 1961; D.Sc. in Metall. Engring. (Ideal Cement fellowship, Research grant), Colo. Sch. of Mines, 1966; m. Beverley Margaret Ramsey, May 10, 1959; children—Maxwell, Ross, Leslie, Marlene. Engr.-in-charge Dept. Mines and Minerals, Ketchikan, Alaska, 1957-61; asst. mgr. mfg. research Universal Atlas Cement div. U.S. Steel Corp., Gary, Ind., 1965-66; research metallurgist Inland Steel Co., Hammond, Ind., 1966-67; owner, dir. Mineral Research Lab., Monrovia, Calif., 1968—; pres., Keystone Canyon Mining Co., Inc., Pasadena, Calif., 1972-79, U.S. Western Mines, 1973—, Silveroil Research Inc., 1980—; v.p. Mineral Drill Inc., 1981—; owner Precision Plastics, 1973-82; ptnr. Mineral Research and Devel. Co., 1981—; lectr., Purdue U., Hammond, Ind., 1966-67; lectr. Nat. Mining Seminar, Barstow (Calif.) Coll., 1969-70; v.p., dir. Wilbur Foote Plastics, Pasadena, 1968-72; guest lectr. Calif. State Poly. U., 1977-81, also Greater Los Angeles area service orgns., 1979-81; strategic minerals del. People to People, Republic of S. Africa, 1983. Served with U.S. Army, 1950-52. Fellow Geol. Mining and Metall. Soc. India (life), Am. Inst. Chemists; mem. Soc. Mining Engrs., Am. Chem. Soc., Am. Inst. Mining, Metall. and Petroleum Engrs., Nat. Soc. Profl. Engrs., Can. Inst. Mining and Metallurgy, Sigma Xi, Sigma Mu. Contbr. articles to sci. jours.; guest editor Calif. Mining Jour., 1978—; patentee chem. processing and steel manufacture. Home: 212 W Sierra Madre Blvd Arcadia CA 91006 Office: 805 S Shamrock Ave Monrovia CA 91016

PRAZAK, PAUL RONALD, electronic engineer, consultant; b. Richmond, Calif., Feb. 11, 1949; s. Waldemar J. and Bernardine Rose (Beck) P.; m. Eva Linda Oliveira, Apr. 3, 971. A.S. in Electronics, Contra Costa Coll., 1968; B.S. in Elec. Engring., Calif. State U.-Sacramento, 1971; M.S. in Elec. Engring., U. Ariz., 1973. Electronic design engr. Burr-Brown Research Corp., Tucson, 1973-78, group leader, 1978-80, mgr. high-resolution data conversion, data acquisition design, 1980-82, product design mgr., 1982-83, mgr. data conversion product design, 1983—; cons. active filter design. Active Special Olympics. Mem. IEEE (sr.), Internat. Soc. Hybrid Microelectronics, Nat. Soc. Profl. Engrs., So. Ariz. Roadrunning Club, Clique Camera Club. Patentee digital-to-analog, analog-to-digital conversion methods; contbr. numerous articles to profl. jours. Home: 502 N Chalet Ave Tucson AZ 85710 Office: Burr-Brown Research Corp 6730 S Tucson Blvd Tucson AZ 85734

PREGERSON, HARRY, federal judge; b. Los Angeles, Oct. 13, 1923; s. Abraham and Bessie (Rubin) P.; B.A., UCLA, 1947, LL.B., Boalt Hall, Berkeley, 1950; m. Bernardine Seyma Chapkis, June 28, 1947; children—Dean Douglas, Kathryn Ann. Admitted to Calif. bar, 1951; partner William M. Costley, Van Nuys, 1953-65; judge Los Angeles Muncipal Ct., 1965-66, Los Angeles Superior Ct., 1966-67; judge U.S. Dist. Ct. Central Dist. Calif., 1967-79, U.S. Ct. Appeals for 9th Circuit, 1979—; faculty mem., seminar for newly appointed distr. Judges Fed. Jud. Center, Washington, 1970-72; mem. faculty Am. Soc. Pub. Adminstrn., Inst. for Ct. Mgmt., Denver, 1973—. Served to 1st lt. USMCR, 1944-46. Decorated Purple Heart. Mem. Am. (vice-chmn., com. on fed. rules of criminal procedure and evidence sect. of criminal law, 1972—), Los Angeles County, San Fernando Valley bar assns., State Bar Calif., Marines Corps Res. Officers Assn. (pres. San Fernando Valley 1966-78). Office: US Ct Appeals US Courthouse 312 N Spring St Los Angeles CA 90012*

PREIS, MICHAEL W., business executive; b. N.Y.C., Oct. 4, 1944; s. William J. and Elinor B. Preis. B.M.E., Ohio State U., 1969; M.B.A., Harvard U., 1972. Vice pres. Wometco-Lathrop Co., Anchorage, 1975-78; cons. Peat, Marwick, Mitchell & Co., Anchorage, 1978-82; pres., chmn. bd. Reynolds Equipment Co. Inc., Anchorage, 1982—. Contbr. articles to profl. publs. Club: Rotary (past sec.) (Anchorage). Home: PO Box 616 Anchorage AK 99510 Office: 1537 E 5th Ave Anchorage AK 99501

PREISSER, RODNEY JAMES, water company executive; b. Garden City, Kans., Nov. 29, 1946; s. James G. and Adarrine (Schanel) P.; m. Diane Herin, Aug. 27, 1967; children—Jason R., Cory S., Amy K. B.S., Colo. State U., 1968. Pres., Pikes Peak Water Co., Colorado Springs, Colo., 1973—; rancher. Mem. Am. Water Works Assn., Colo. Water Congress. Republican. Roman Catholic. Office: 4463 Whispering Circle Colorado Springs CO 80917

PRENDERGAST, BRIAN, international loan consultant, venture capital advisor; b. Denver, July 26, 1948; s. Edmund T. and Yvonne S. (Saliba) P.; B.S., U.S. Air Force Acad., 1970; M.A., Central Mich. U., 1972; m. Alice Sawaya, Dec. 26, 1970; children—Amy L., Christina M. Ins. agt. United Fidelity Life, 1976-78; partner, registered prin. Consol. Investment Services, Inc., Denver, 1979—; owner Prendergast & Assocs., Denver, 1979—; lectr. Sunset Life's Agt. Conf., 1980. Roman Catholic. Clubs: Cedars of Lebanon (pres. 1979-80), Denver Athletic. Author: (with Douglas Nutt) Property Profile, 1978. Home: 11890 E Louisiana Ave Aurora CO 80012 Office: 5777 S Rapp St Littleton CO 80120

PRENTICE, SARTELL, JR., counselor profit sharing; b. Newark, Dec. 28, 1903; s. Sartell and Lydia Beekman (Vanderpoel) P.; grad. Taft Sch., 1920; student Yale U., 1921-23; B.A., Stanford U., 1925; M.B.A., Harvard U., 1927; student Freedom Sch., Colorado Springs, summer 1958, Free Enterprise Inst., Los Angeles, 1962—; m. Marjorie Phelps Koop, Apr. 28, 1930 (div. 1938); m. 2d, Agnes L. Papekas, June 24, 1939 (div. 1956); 1 son, Peter Sartell; m. 3d, Elinor L. Haight Buck, Aug. 27, 1956 (dec. Aug. 1977); m. 4th, Geraldine Eleanor Hoyt, Nov. 24, 1978 (charter), Internat. Platform Assn., Sept. 1980). Security salesman, br. mgr. Nat. Cash Credit Assn., 1928-31; tng. for fgn. service Socony Vacuum Oil Co., N.Y.C., 1931, exec. asst. to pres. Vacuum Oil Co., S.A.I., Genoa, Italy, 1931-35, mktg. asst. fgn. dept. Socony Vacuum Oil Co., Inc., N.Y.C., 1935; research, script writer, publicity man March of Time Movie and Radio, Time, Inc., N.Y.C., 1935-37; actor summer stock Barter Theatre, Abingdon, Va., summer 1938; salesman Automatic Canteen Co., N.Y.C., 1940-41; pub. relations, advt. rep. N.Y., Boston, Time, Inc., 1941-46; adminstrv. sec. Commn. Chs. on Internat. Affairs, N.Y.C., 1947-48; field sec. N.E. chpt. Council of Profit Sharing Industries, 1950-54; mgmt. cons., counselor on profit sharing, 1954—; lectr. econs., 1956—; lectr. Assoc. Clubs U.S.A., 1956-58. N.Y. state chmn. Nat. Com. for Econ. Freedom, 1960; dir. Am. Waldensian Aid Soc., 1944-61. Recipient Liberty award Congress of Freedom, Inc., 1967, 73, 74, 75, 76, 77. Mem. Am. Graphol. Soc., Soc. Profl. Mgmt. Cons. (charter), Internat. Platform Assn., Town Hall Calif., Western Pension Conf. Clubs: Toastmasters Internat., Yale, Stanford, Harvard, Harvard Bus. Sch. (all So. Calif.). Congregationalist. Contbr. articles to various mags. and jours. Address: 1404 Chamberlain Rd Pasadena CA 91103

PRENTISS, CHARLES GARY, museum curator; b. Astoria, Oreg., June 29, 1942; s. Donald Crane and Marian Caroline (Gary) P.; m. Dianne Barrett Ritner, June 18, 1966; children—Carlos, Katherine; m. 2d Nikki Christine Silva, July 3, 1982. B.S., U. Calif.-Riverside, 1966. Curator Santa Cruz (Calif.) Mus. Served with USAR, 1963-69. Office: 1305 East Cliff Dr Santa Cruz CA 95062

PRESCOTT, HAROLD STURTEVANT, JR., civil engineering consultant; b. Providence, Nov. 25, 1931; s. Harold Sturtevant and Anna May (Knights) P.; m. Corrine Ann Rose, Aug. 10, 1951; children—Alan, Scott, Steven, Mark. B.A., Brown U., 1953; B.S., U. Calif.-Berkeley, 1962. Registered profl. engr., Calif., Nev., Hawaii, Wash. Civil engr. Cal-Pacific Resources Inc., 1962-69, v.p., chief engring., 1969-73; owner, mgr. Prescott Engring., Placerville, Calif., 1973—; dir. Western Sierra Nat. Bank, El Dorado County, Calif. Bd. dirs. Tahoe Paradise Resort Improvement Dist. Recipient Service cert. El Dorado County Bd. Suprs., 1976. Mem. ASCE, Nat. Soc. Profl. Engrs., Am. Water Works Assn., Water Pollution Control Fedn. Republican. Methodist. Clubs: Placerville Rotary, Masons, Shriners. Office: Prescott Engring 531 Main St Placerville CA 95667

PRESCOTT, LAWRENCE MALCOLM, health consultant, writer; b. Boston, July 31, 1934; s. Benjamin and Lillian (Stein) P.; B.A., Harvard U., 1957; M.Sc., George Washington U., 1959, Ph.D., 1966; m. Ellen Gay Kober, Feb. 19, 1961 (dec. Sept. 1981); children—Jennifer Maya, Adam Barrett; m. 2d, Sharon Lynn Kirshen, May 16, 1981; children—Gary Leon Kirshen, Marc Paul Kirshen. Nat. Acad. Scis. postdoctoral fellow U.S. Army Research, Ft. Detrick, Md., 1965-66; microbiologist/scientist WHO, India, 1967-70, Indonesia, 1970-72, Thailand, 1972-78; cons. health to internat. orgns., San Diego, 1978—; author mans. and contbr. articles in diarrheal diseases and lab. scis. to profl. jours., 1965-81; contbr. numerous articles, stories, poems to mags., newspapers, including Living in Thailand, Jack and Jill, Strawberry, Bangkok Times, Sprint, 1977-81; mng. editor Caduceus, 1981-82; med. writer Med. Post, Health, Health and Care, Genetic Engring. News, Diagnostic Imaging, Med. Tribune, Internal Medicine News, others, 1982—; pub./editor Teenage Scene, 1982-83; pres. Prescott Pub. Co., 1982-83. Home and Office: 11307 Florida Rd San Diego CA 92127

PRESLEY, ROBERT BUEL, state senator; b. Tahlequah, Okla., Dec. 4, 1924; s. Doyle and Annie (Townsend) P.; grad. FBI Nat. Acad., Washington, 1962; student Riverside City Coll., 1960; A.A., UCLA, m. Ahni Ratliff, Aug. 20, 1944; children—Donna Thurber, Marilyn Raphael, Robert Buel. Various positions Riverside County Sheriff's Dept. (Calif.), 1950-62, undersheriff, 1962-74; mem. Calif. Senate, 34th Dist., 1974—; lectr. ethics. Served with U.S. Army, 1943-46. Decorated Bronze Star. Mem. FBI Nat. Acad. Assn. (pres. Calif. chpt. 1974). Baptist. Clubs: Lions, Elks, Am. Legion, V.F.W., Moose, Riverside County Democratic Century (pres. 1972-73). Home: 5508 Grassy Trail Dr Riverside CA 92504 Office: 3600 Lime St Suite 111 Riverside CA 92501

PRESS, LEO COSMOS, elec. engr.; b. Los Angeles, July 24, 1922; s. Abraham E. and Bella R. Press; B.S. in Elec. Engring., UCLA; m. Ella-Rhe Ely, Apr. 12, 1947; children—Priscilla Diane Press Bean, Linda Francis Press Foy. Elec. engr. Kistner, Wright & Wright, Los Angeles, 1948-63; elec. engr., chmn. bd. Sampson, Randall & Press, Inc., Los Angeles, 1963—; mem. adv. bd. to Office of State Architect, Calif., 1968-79. Served to capt. USAAF, 1941-45. Decorated Air medal with 4 oak leaf clusters; registered profl. engr., Calif., Ariz., Nev. Fellow Inst. Advancement of Engring. (dir. 1980-83); mem. Assn. Cons. Elec. Engrs. (pres. Los Angeles chpt. 1976-77), Mech. Elec. Cons. Engrs. Council (chmn. 1975-76), Assn. Cons. Engrs. Calif. (dir. 1968-70, dir. Ins. Trust). Republican. Presbyterian. Office: 7470 N Figueroa St Los Angeles CA 90041

PRESSBURGER, THOMAS THEO, computer scientist; b. Los Angeles, Jan. 20, 1955; s. Michael and Bertha (Lefkowitz) P.; B.S. in Math., Calif. Inst. Tech., 1976; M.S. in Computer Sci., Stanford U., 1979. Research asst. Stanford U., 1976-78; computer scientist Kestrel Inst., Palo Alto, Calif., 1979—. Mem. Assn. Computing Machinery, Am. Assn. for Artificial Intelligence. Contbr. articles to profl. jours. Office: Kestrel Inst 1801 Page Mill Rd Palo Alto CA 94304

PRESSER, LEON, computer software executive; b. Matanzas, Cuba, Jan. 23, 1940; came to U.S., 1957, naturalized, 1969; s. Nuna and Raquel (Katz) P.; m. Blanca Engler, June 29, 1969; children—Liza, Anita. B.S. in Elec. Engring., U. Ill., 1961; M.S. in Elec. Engring., U. So. Calif., 1964; Ph.D. in Computer Sci., UCLA, 1968. Mem. staff and faculty UCLA, 1964-68; mem. faculty U. Calif.-Santa Barbara, 1968-76; founder, pres. Softool Corp., Goleta, Calif., 1976—. Mem. IEEE, Assn. Computing Machinery. Contbr. tech. articles and papers to publs. Office: 340 S Kellogg Ave Goleta CA 93117

PRESSLEY, JAMES RAY, elec. engr.; b. Ft. Worth, July 14, 1946; s. Loy Dale and Dorothy Helen (Foust) P.; B.S.E.E., U. Tex., Arlington, 1970; m. Barbara Kay McMillin, Oct.9, 1968; children—James Foust, Kreg Milam. Designer/draftsman Romine & Slaughter, Ft. Worth, 1967-71; engr. Crews MacInnes & Hoffman, Anchorage, 1971-73, O'Kelly & Schoenlank, Anchorage, 1973-75, Theodore G. Creedon, Anchorage, 1975-77; v.p. Fryer, Pressley Elliott, Anchorage, 1977-80, Fryer/Pressley Engring., 1980—; mem. elec. constrn. and maintenance industry evaluation panel, 1982-83. Registered profl. engr., Alaska, Hawaii, Oreg. Office: 1709 S Bragaw St Suite F Anchorage AK 99504

PRESTON, JOHN DAVID, clinical psychologist; b. Midland, Tex., July 13, 1950; s. Conrad Smith and Betty Jeanne (Stark) P.; m. Bonnie Lynn Johnson, Aug. 19, 1978; children—Matthew, David. B.A., Southwestern U., Georgetown, Tex., 1972; M.S., Trinity U., San Antonio, 1973; PsychologyD., Baylor U., 1979. Lic. psychologist, Calif. Program dir. outpatient clinic Nueces County Mental Health Ctr., Corpus Christi, 1979-80, dir. adult mental health services, 1980-81; clin. psychologist, psychiatry dept. Permanente Med. Group, Sacramento, 1981—; pvt. practice neuropsychology, 1981—; faculty Profl. Sch. for Psychol. Studies, Sacramento, 1981—. Mem. Am. Psychol. Assn. Author profl. cassette tape series: Differential Diagnosis of Psychoses, 1979, How to Conduct a Neuropsychological Examination, 1981, Neuropsychological Screening Examination, 1982; Medication Consult: Psychopharmacology, 1983; contbr. articles to profl. jours. Office: Psychiatry Dept Permanente Med Group 2025 Morse Ave Sacramento CA 95825

PRICE, ANNE HAYNES, psychotherapist, educator; b. Martinsville, Va., May 31, 1936; d. G. Nash and Mildred (Moran) Haynes; m. Stanley R. Price, June 29, 1962; children—Doug, Mike. B.A., Bridgewater Coll., 1957; M.S., Calif. State U.-Long Beach, 1974; Ph.D., U. Calif.-Irvine, 1976. Lic. marriage and family therapist, Calif. Dean of Women U. LaVerne (Calif.), 1966-69; dean of Students, dir. student activities McPherson (Kans.) Coll., 1969-71; therapist care unit alcohol treatment South Laguna, Calif., 1975-79; mem. staff Mission Community Hosp., South Coast Med. Ctr., 1978—; dir. psychol. services Saddleback Pediatric Med. Group, Mission Viejo, Calif., 1974—; pvt. practice psychotherapy, Mission Viejo, 1974—; prof. grad. program in psychology U. LaVerne, 1982—; bd. dirs. Family Intervention Ctr. Mem. Am. Psychol. Assn., Calif. Assn. Marriage and Family Therapists, Soc. Psychologists in Substance Abuse. Mem. Ch. of Brethren. Office: 27862 Puerta Real Suite 109 Mission Viejo CA 92691

PRICE, DAVID MICHAEL, librarian; b. Corpus Christi, Tex., Feb. 4, 1943; s. David Vernon and Martha (Tucker) P.; B.A., Tex. A & I U., 1966; postgrad. Southwestern Bapt. Theol. Sem., 1969; M.P.A., North Tex. State U., 1970, M.L.S., 1971; m. Sherry LaNette Crawley, Aug. 28, 1965. Asst. grocery mgr. Handy Andy, Inc., Corpus Christi, 1965-66; mcpl. reference librarian City of Ft. Worth, 1966-69; research budget analyst, asst. to city mgr. City of Ft. Worth, 1969-71; asst. dir. libraries Austin Pub. Library (Tex.), 1971-77; dir. libraries and TV services, City of Aurora (Colo.), 1977—. Mem. Colo. Library Assn. (pres. 1980-81), ALA, Mt. Plains Library Assn. Baptist. Club: Rotary. Home: 4602 S Lewiston Way Aurora CO 80015 Office: 14949 E Alameda Dr Aurora CO 80012

PRICE, EARL LAWRENCE, brokerage exec.; b. Laramie, Wyo., Feb. 25, 1946; s. Earl Raymond and Bella (Williams) P.; student U. Wyo., 1963-67; m. Elaine Duncan, Sept. 30, 1978; 1 dau., Julia Elizabeth. Pres., Price Motors, Laramie, 1968-70, Real Estate Investment Corp., Laramie, 1970-72; internat. fin. cons., Zurich, Switzerland, 1972-74; prin. Lawrence Price & Assos., 1974-76; mng. partner Price & Co., Chgo., 1976—, Newcomb Securities Co., N.Y.C.; chmn. bd. Newcomb Fin.

Group; dir. Imprint Editions, London, Altback, Price Entertainment, Inc., Los Angeles. Bd. dirs. Ft. Collins Symphony, Am. Symphony Orch. League. Mem. Internat. Assn. Fin. Planners, Chgo. Assn. Commerce and Industry. Episcopalian. Home: 2115 W Mulberry Fort Collins CO 80524 Office: 767 5th Ave 34th Floor New York NY 10153

PRICE, EDWARD DEAN, judge; b. Sanger, Calif., Feb. 12, 1919; s. Earl T. and Daisy Biggs (Shaw) P.; m. Katherine M. Merritt, July 18, 1943; children—Katherine Price O'Brien, Edward M., Jane E. A.B., U. Calif.-Berkeley, 1947, LL.B., 1949. Bar: Calif., U.S. Dist. Ct. (no. dist. Calif.), U.S. Dist. Ct. (ea. dist. Calif.), U.S. Ct. Appeals (9th cir.). Sole practice law, 1949-79; U.S. dist. judge U.S. Dist. Ct. (ea. dist.), Calif., Fresno, 1979—. Served with U.S. Army, 1943-46. Mem. ABA, State Bar Calif. Democrat. Methodist. Clubs: Rotary, Elks.

PRICE, GERALDINE MCCRABB, communications consultant; b. Stockton, Calif., May 7, 1940; s. Howard James and Edna (Eisle) McCrabb; A.A., Stockton Coll., 1958; B.S., U. Utah, 1965, M.S., 1972. Cert. tchr. of handicapped, Calif. Elem. sch. tchr. Granite Sch. Dist., Salt Lake City, 1961-70, spl. edn. cons. learning-handicapped children, 1972-74; dir. reading programs in Calif., Reading Devel. Inst., Salt Lake City, 1975-76; owner, dir. Price Assocs., communications cons., Stockton 1977—; guest lectr. various groups. Mem. Nat. Tchrs. Assn., Spl. Educators. Assn., Nat. Reading Assn., Am. Soc. Tng. Dirs., Utah Tchrs. Assn., Granite Tchrs. Assn. Office: Price Assocs PO Box 307 Sacramento CA 95802

PRICE, JAY BERRY, city ofcl.; b. Los Angeles, Mar. 9, 1915; s. John Berry and Nancy Alice (Gipson) P.; A.A., Compton Coll., 1957; m. Gertrude Margaret Lydon, Apr. 19, 1941; children—William Berry, John Jay, Nancy Alice. Insp., U.S. Internal Revenue Service, Los Angeles, 1939-76. Mayor, councilman, Bell, Calif., 1958—; dist. dir. So. Calif. Rapid Transit Dist., Los Angeles, 1971—. Dir. Los Angeles County Sanitation Dists. 1 and 2; mem. revenue and taxation com. Los Angeles County div., also mem. state revenue and taxation com. League Calif. Cities; trustee, pres. S.E. Mosquito-Abatement Dist., South Gate; alt. trustee rep. So. Calif. to trustee corporate bd. Calif. Mosquito Control Assn.; mem. adv. council 4th West County region Los Angeles County Library; City of Bell rep. of gen. assembly So. Calif. Assn. Govts. Mem. Christian Ch. (deacon, trustee, treas.). Home: 6900 Crafton Ave Bell CA 90201 Office: 6330 Pine Ave Bell CA 90201

PRICE, JEANNINE ALLEENICA, clinical psychologist; b. Cleve., Oct. 29, 1949; d. Q. Q. and Lisa Denise (Wilson) Ewing; m. T. R. Price, Sept. 2, 1976. B.S., Western Res. U., 1969; M.S., Vanderbilt U., 1974. Cert. alcoholism counselor, Calif. Health Service coordinator Am. Profile, Nashville, 1970-72; exec. dir. Awareness Concept, San Jose, Calif., 1977-80; mgr. employee assistance program Nat. Semiconductor, Santa Clara, Calif., 1980-81; mgmt. cons. employee assistant programs. Mem. Gov.'s Adv. Council Child Devel. Programs. Mem. Am. Bus. Women's Assn., Nat. Assn. Female Execs., AAUW, Coalition Labor Women, Calif. Assn. Alcohol counselors, Almaca. Author: Smile a Little, Cry a Lot; Gifts of Love. Office: 728 N 1st St San Jose CA 95112

PRICE, JONATHAN REEVE, author; b. Boston, Oct. 19, 1941; s. Robert DeMille and Newell (Potter) P.; A.B. cum laude, Harvard U., 1963; D.F.A., Yale U., 1968; m. Elizabeth Deuchar, Feb. 15, 1981; 1 son, Benjamin. Asst. prof. English, NYU, 1968-70, U. Bridgeport (Conn.), 1974-78; head Shakespeare Inst., Am. Shakespeare Theater, 1974-78; asst. prof. English, Rutgers U., 1978-79, U. Calif.-Berkeley extension, 1981-83; artist Westbroadway Galley, N.Y.C., 1974-78; video art exhbns. Kitchen, Anthology Film Archives, also cable TV stas.; co-founder, coordinator Assn. Artist Run Galleries, 1973-79; writer Apple Computer, 1982—; author: Critics on Robert Lowell, 1972; Life Show Anthology, 1974; Alphabet in the Spectrum of the Rainbow, 1974; Video Visions, 1977; The Best thing on TV, 1978; Classic Scenes, 1979; Three By Ben Jonson, 1980; Thirty Days to More Powerful Writing, 1981; How to Find Work, 1983; co-author: Life Show, 1973; The Definitive Word Processing Book, 1983. Woodrow Wilson fellow, 1963-68. Mem. MLA, Am. Soc. Tng. and Devel., Elizabethan Club. Address: 858 Neilson St Berkeley CA 94707

PRICE, LAWRENCE OZEL, electronics company executive; b. Bassett, Va., Aug. 10, 1940; s. Dan S. and Eva M. (Pilson) P.; m. Shirley Copening, Aug. 10, 1963; children—Cheryl D., Paula A., Tina Y. Student N.C. A&T State U., 1959-64; B.S. in Bus. Adminstrn., Regis Coll., 1982. With Boy Scouts of Am., Washington, 1965-71, personnel exec., nat. staff, North Brunswick, N.J., 1971-72, asst. regional personnel exec., nat. staff, Kansas City, Mo., 1972-76, asst. council exec., Denver, 1976-79; with Test Instruments div. Honeywell Inc., Denver, 1979—, mgr. human resources, 1981—. Mem. adv. council U. Denver; bus. adv. com. Regis Coll.; mem. tri-campus coop. edn. adv. com. Community Coll. of Denver; mem. mgmt. adv. com., chmn. electronic assembly adv. com. Arapahoe Community Coll.; mem. electronic assembly adv. com. Emily Griffin Opportunity Sch. Mem. Am. Soc. Tng. and Devel. Democrat. Club: Masons. Office: Test Instruments Div Honeywell Inc 4800 E Dry Creek Rd PO Box 5227 Denver CO 80217

PRICE, LAWRENCE THOMAS, engr., land surveyor; b. Newcastle, Wyo., Mar. 31, 1933; s. William Thomas and Ora Maude (Larson) P.; student Graceland Coll., 1952-53, U. Wyo., 1953-54; B.S. in Civil Engring., Ind. Inst. Tech., 1959; m. Patricia Joyce Patterson, June 1, 1954; children—Lawrence William, Lori Ardith Price Brown. Design engr. Fletcher-Robinson Engring., Newcastle, 1959-63; co-owner, cons. engr. Tri-State Co., Newcastle, 1963-70; sec.-treas., pres., cons. engr. Plains Engring., Inc., Newcastle, 1970-76; pres. Plains Engring. div. Hoskins-Western-Sonderegger, Newcastle, 1976—; v.p. Hosking-Western-Sonderegger; co-owner Castle Motors, Fletcher-Price Leasing Co., L & A Enterprises, Wyo Sur, Inc. Served with U.S. Army, 1954-56. Lic. profl. engr. and land surveyor, Wyo., Mont., S.D., Nebr. Mem. Wyo. Assn. Cons. Engrs. and Land Surveyors (pres. 1975), Am. Cons. Engrs. Council, Mont. Assn. Registered Land Surveyors. Republican. Mem. Reorganized Ch. Jesus Christ of Latter-day Saints (ordained elder). Club: Newcastle Jaycees (pres. 1967-69). Home: 239 S Spokane Newcastle WY 82701 Office: 24 4th Ave Newcastle WY 82701

PRICE, MARY MORTIMER, interior designer, lecturer; b. Evanston, Ill, Jan. 3, 1933; d. James Mortimer Price and Mary Triplett (Lilleston) P. Student Bard Coll., 1950-51. Interior designer Lammert Furniture Co., St. Louis, 1962-67; freelance interior designer, St. Louis, 1968-71; sr. interior designer Aloe Med., Health and Sci. div. Brunswick Corp., St. Louis, 1971-76; pres. designer Mary Price Hereford & Assocs., Inc., St. Louis, 1976-81; design dir. Borg-Warner Health Products, St. Louis, 1981—; dir. interior design Arthur Shuster, Inc., Mpls. and Santa Ana, Calif., 1981—. Mem. Am. Soc. Interior Designers (cert., Presdl. Citation awardee, 1978). Republican. Episcopalian. Contbr. articles to publs. Home: 627 Baywood Dr Newport CA 92660 Office: 1820 E Garry Ave Suite 105 Santa Ana CA 92705

PRICE, PAUL BUFORD, physicist, educator; b. Memphis, Nov. 8, 1932; s. Paul Buford and Eva (Dupuy) P.; B.S. summa cum laude, Davidson Coll., 1954, D.Sc., 1973; M.S., U. Va., 1956, Ph.D., 1958; m. JoAnn Margaret Baum, June 28, 1958; children—Paul Buford III, Heather Alynn, Pamela Margaret, Alison Gaynor. Fulbright scholar U. (Eng.) Bristol, 1958-59; NSF postdoctoral fellow Cambridge (Eng.) U., 1959-60; physicist Gen. Elec. Research & Devel. Center, Schenectady, 1960-69; vis. prof. Tata Inst. Fundamental Research, Bombay, India, 1965-66; adj. prof. physics Rensselaer Poly. Inst., 1967-68; prof. physics U. Calif. at Berkeley, 1969—, dir. Space Scis. Lab., 1979—, asso. dir. Calif. Space Inst., 1981—; cons. NASA on Lunar Sample Analysis Planning Team; mem. space sci. bd. Nat. Acad. Scis. Recipient Distinguished Service award Am. Nuclear Soc., 1964, Indsl. Research awards, 1964, 65, E.O. Lawrence Meml. award AEC, 1971, medal exceptional sci. achievement NASA, 1973. John Simon Guggenheim fellow, 1976-77. Fellow Am. Phys. Soc., Am. Geophys. Union; mem. Nat. Acad. Scis., Am. Astron. Soc. Author: (with others) Nuclear Tracks in Solids. Contbr. articles to profl. jours. Patentee in field; research on space and astrophysics, nuclear physics, particularly devel. solid state track detectors and their applications to geophysics, space and nuclear physics problems; discovery of fossil particle tracks and fission track method of dating; discovery of ultra-heavy cosmic rays. Home: 1056 Overlook Rd Berkeley CA 94708

PRICE, RAYMOND F., industrial engineer, manufacturing engineer; b. San Diego, Feb. 8, 1937; s. Earl Willard and Neoma Luella (Burke) P.; m. Joan Karlyn Lawson, Apr. 23, 1954 (div. 1961); children—Guy Warren, Ray Steven; m. 2d, Polly Louise Metts, Nov. 6, 1961; children—Thomas Howard, Kirsten Alys, Audra Paget. Tech. cert. indsl. engring. East Central Jr. Coll., Decatur, Miss., 1970; cert. mgmt. theory Brown U., 1972. Warehouseman Gen. Mills., San Diego, 1955-56, asst. foreman, 1956-64; erection supr. Taylor Machine Works, Louisville, Miss., 1964-69; indsl. engr., machining gen. foreman, 1969-71; indsl. mfg. engr. Allis Chalmers, Boston, 1972-73, mfg. engr., Jackson, Miss., 1973-75, assembly supr., 1975; sr. project mgr. computer aided mfg. systems Mgmt. Sci. Inc., Carson City, Nev., 1975—. Served to sgt. Army N.G., 1954-63. Mem. Soc. Mfg. Engrs. Republican. Baptist. Author manuals. Home: 2575 S Lompa Ln Carson City NV 89701 Office: 400 Hot Springs Rd Suite 7 Carson City NV 89701

PRICE, REGINALD LEE, educator; b. Jacksonville, Ill., Jan. 21, 1942; s. Glendyn Lee and Sylva Dee (Beck) P.; B.S., MacMurray Coll., 1964; M.A., Ohio State U., 1967; D.Ed., Okla. State U., 1973; m. Katherine Stout, June 12, 1964; children—Wendy Lynn, Christine Ann. Tchr., coach Ohio State Sch. for Blind, Columbus, 1964-66; asst. prof., coach Hiram (Ohio) Coll., 1967-70; asst. prof., chmn. dept. phys. edn. MacMurray Coll., Jacksonville, Ill., 1972-78; prof. Calif. State Coll., San Bernardino, 1978—, chmn. dept. phys. edn. and recreation, 1978—. Mcpl. trustee City of South Jacksonville (Ill.), 1977-78; dir., cons. for track and field Spl. Olympics Program. Mem. AAHPER and Dance, Calif. Assn. for Health, Phys. Edn., Recreation and Dance, Nat. Assn. for Phys. Edn. in Higher Edn., Calif. Assn. for Health, Phys. Edn. and Recreation, Am. Profl. Racquetball Orgn. (cert. racquetball instr.), AAUP (regional resource person sect. 504). Office: 5500 State College Pkwy San Bernardino CA 92407

PRICE, STEPHEN RODGERS, naval officer; b. Ft. Monroe, Va., Sept. 16, 1954; s. Robert Herald and Ruth Marie (Rodgers) P.; student N.Mex. Inst. Mining and Tech., 1972-74; B.S.C.E., U. N.Mex., 1977; grad. Nuclear Power Sch., Orlando, Fla., 1977. Commd. ensign U.S. Navy, 1977, advanced through grades to lt., 1980; communicator and elec. div. officer, 1978-80; reactor controls div. officer, engring. dept., nuclear powered submarine, 1980-82, asst. material officer Submarine Refit and Tng. Group, LaMaddalena, Sardinia, 1982—. Registered profl. engr., Wash. Mem. Am. Def. Preparedness Assn., Tau Beta Pi, Chi Epsilon. Republican. Baptist. Home: 12417 Placid Ave Albuquerque NM 87112 Office: COMSUBREFITRAGRU La Maddalena FPO New York NY 09501

PRICE, VINCENT CHARLES, accountant; b. Los Angeles, July 30, 1956; s. Charles Owen and Kazmere Marie (Zuanich) P.; m. Debbie Kay Morris, May 17, 1980. Student Los Angeles Harbor Community Coll., 1976-77; B.S. in Bus. Adminstrn. with honors, Calif. State U.-Long Beach, 1979. C.P.A., Calif. Sr. acct. Peat, Marwick & Mitchell & Co., C.P.A.s, Los Angeles 1980—. Usher, mem. fin. com. Gardena 1st So. Baptist Ch., 1980—. Mem. Phi Kappa Phi, Beta Gamma Sigma. Democrat. Home: 18328 Glenburn Ave Torrance CA 90504 Office: 555 S Flower St Los Angeles CA 90071

PRICE, WILLIAM LECESTRE, publisher; b. Detroit, Sept. 13, 1926; s. Jacob Ervin and Nona D. (Grimm) P.; B.Th., Life Coll., 1947; m. Doris Mae Levine, Nov. 6, 1943; children—William C., Haeja Diane, John B. Founder/pres. Christian Pilots, Inc., Fullerton, Calif., 1945-48; exec. dir. Greater Los Angeles Youth for Christ Internat., 1950-56; asst. to pres. World Vision, Inc., Monrovia, Calif., 1956-64; pres. Internat. Pictorial Publs., Orange, Calif., 1974—; pres. World Trade & Mktg. Cons., Inc., Orange, 1974—, Price Ednl. Products, 1978—; v.p. William Price Agy., Sierra Madre, Calif., 1968—; advtg. cons. Kings Travel, Pasadena, Akerman Nuclear, Inc., Glendale, Calif., Builders Fence Co., San Fernando, Calif. Recipient Silver Strobenar award Honeywell/Pentax, 1976. Mem. Pub. Relations Soc. Am., Am. Booksellers Assn. Republican. Author: Pictorial Images of Mexico Today, 1976. Home: 1045 Sierra Madre Villa Pasadena CA 91107 Office: 19 Suffolk Sierra Madre CA 91024

PRICE, ZANE HERBERT, biologist; b. Dunbar, Nebr., June 17, 1922; s. Frank Robert and Carrie Helen (Benner) P.; B.A., Walla Walla Coll., 1950; postgrad. UCLA, 1951-54; m. Maxine May Fitzgerald, Sept. 26, 1943; 1 dau., Peggy May. News photographer Downey Allen Photo Syndicate, 1941; owner, mgr. photog. studio, 1945-47; research asst. UCLA, 1950-53, grad. research microbiologist, 1953-56, jr. research microbiologist, 1956-59, asst. research microbiologist, 1959-62, assoc. specialist, 1962-67, specialist, 1967—, dir. Nina Anderton Lab. for Electron Microscopy, Med. Sch., 1957-60; vis. scientist Instituto Politécnico National, Méx., 1967-70. Served with USMC, 1942-45. Los Angeles County Heart Assn. fellow, 1956-57; recipient Electronic Eye award Biol. Photog. Assn. So. Calif., 1959; Alumnus of Yr. award Walla Walla Coll., 1981. Fellow Royal Micros. Soc.; mem. AAAS, Electron Microscope Soc. Am., Royal Micros. Soc., So. Calif. Soc. Electron Microscopy, Soc. Am. Microbiologists, Tissue Culture Assn., N.Y. Acad. Scis. Contbr. articles to profl. jours. Office: Dept Microbiology and Immunology Med Center U Calif Los Angeles CA 90024

PRICKETT, DAVID CLINTON, physician; b. Fairmont, W.Va., Nov. 26, 1918; s. Clinton Evert and Mary Anna (Gottschalk) P.; m. Mary Ellen Holt, June 29, 1940; children—David C., Rebecca Ellen, William Radcliffe, Mary Anne, James Thomas, Sara Elizabeth. A.B., W.Va. U., 1944; M.D., U. Louisville, 1946; M.P.H., U. Pitts., 1955. Intern, Louisville Gen. Hosp., 1947; surg. resident St. Joseph's Hosp., Parkersburg, W.Va., 1948-49; gen. practice, 1949-50, 55-61; physician USAF, N.Mex., 1961-62, U.S. Army, Calif., 1963-64, San Luis Obispo County Hosp., 1965-66, So. Calif. Edison Co., 1981—; assoc. physician indsl. and gen. practice Los Angeles County, Calif., 1967—; med. dir. S. Gate plant Gen. Motors Corp., 1969-71; physician staff City of Los Angeles, 1971-76. Med. officer USPHS, 1953-55, surgeon, res. officer, 1957-59; pres. W.Va. Pub. Health Assn., 1951-52; sec. indsl. and pub. health sect. W.Va. Med. Assn., 1956. Served to 2d lt. AUS, 1943-46. Mem. Am., Western occupational med. assns., Am., Calif., Los Angeles County med. assns., Phi Chi. Contbr. articles to profl. jours. Address: PO Box 4032 Whittier CA 90607

PRICKETT, MICHAEL J., electrical engineer; b. Santa Monica, Calif., Sept. 4, 1944; s. James Monroe and Afton (Leavitt) P.; m. M. Kathryn Ingrum, Sept. 5, 1965; children—Jennifer, Jeremy, Stephen; B.E.E., Calif. State Poly. U., 1966; M.E.E., San Diego State U., 1969; M.S., U. So. Calif., 1974. Registered profl. engr., Calif. Product design engr. Convair div. Gen. Dynamics, San Diego, 1966-68; with Naval Ocean Systems Center, San Diego, 1968—, microwave systems design engr. satellite communications, 1968-79, program mgr. radar devel., 1979—; adj. prof. elec. and computer engring. San Diego State U., 1980—; cons. engring. mem. adv. com. San Diego Unified Sch. Dist., 1978-79. Recipient Superior Achievement award Naval Electronics Lab., 1975; Outstanding Engring. award Naval Ocean Systems Center, 1979. Assoc. fellow AIAA; mem. IEEE (sr.). Republican. Contbr. articles to sci. and engring. jours. Patentee radar, electronic control, signal processing.

PRIEST, JOHN, mfg. co. exec.; b. Pocatello, Idaho, Oct. 5, 1920; s. Elias Lafayette and Jennie Claflin (Buckland) P.; B.S. with highest honors, UCLA, 1948; m. Emily Alice Richards, May 20, 1949; children—Wendy, Linda. Lead design engr. Boeing Aircraft Co., Seattle, 1941-46; dist. mgr. Jacobs Mfg. Co., Calabasas, Calif., 1948-61, regional mgr., 1961-63, Western mgr., 1963—; trustee U. Wash. Motor Vehicle Conf., 1971—. Councilman, City of Hidden Hills (Calif.), 1970-74, mayor, 1972-74; pres. Hidden Hills Community Assn., 1968-70. Served with CAP, 1941-45, USAF, 1946. Mem. Am. Mgmt. Assn., Am. Soc. Mfg. Engrs., Soc. Automotive Engrs., Western Hwy. Inst. (mem. com.), Calif. Trucking Assn., Beta Gamma Sigma. Republican. Lutheran. Home: 4718 Park Olivo Calabasas Park CA 91302 Office: E Dudley Town Rd Bloomfield CT 06002

PRIGMORE, ALMA LOUISE, real estate broker; b. Ft. Worth, Apr. 17, 1921; d. Arthur Cornelius and Helen (Dwiggins) Bjork; m. James S. Prigmore, Jan. 28, 1944. Student pub. schs., Ft. Worth. Adminstrv. sec. Farmers Ins. Group, Los Angeles, 1952-76; realtor assoc. Ken Fujiyama Realty Inc., Hilo, Hawaii, 1976-79, broker, 1979-82; prin. broker Tapa Realty, Hilo, 1982—; owner, dir. Hilo br. Pacific Diamond Exchange, 1982—, Hilo br. Arista Corp., 1982—. Named Realtor of Yr., Hawaii Island Bd. Realtors, 1980. Mem. Hawaii Exchangors (pres.), Hawaii Realtors Credit Union (chairperson), Nat. Million Dollar Real Estate Club, Nat. Council Exchangors (nat. dir.), Acad. Real Estate of Sarasota, Tigr Real Estate Exchange Club, Nat. Real Estate Bd., Hawaii Real Estate Bd., Hilo Real Estate Bd., Hilo C. of C. Baptist. Clubs: Hilo Women's, Paradise Hui Hanalike. Office: PO Box 4656 Hilo HI 96720

PRIME, EUGENIE ELSA, librarian; b. Trinidad, W.Indies; came to U.S., 1972; d. Harold John and Millicent L. Prime; B.A. with honors, U. W.Indies, 1966; M.A. in History, Andrews U., Berrien Springs, Mich., 1974; M.S. in L.S., Drexel U., Phila., 1976; M.B.A., UCLA, 1982. Postgrad. research fellow history U. W.Indies, 1966-69; head dept. history Naparima Girls High Sch., Trinidad, 1969-72; psychiat. social worker N.Y. State Dept. Mental Hygiene, 1974; exec. editor Cumulative Index to Nursing Lit., also med. librarian Glendale (Calif.) Adventist Med. Center, 1976—; pres. CINAHL Corp., 1981—. Mem. Med. Library Assn., Am. Soc. Indexers, Assn. Seventh-day Adventist Librarians, Assn. Info. Mgrs., Med. Library Group So. Calif. and Ariz. Seventh-day Adventist. Home: 1727 Holly Dr Apt 305 Glendale CA 91206 Office: 1509 E Wilson Terr Glendale CA 91206

PRINCE, BARBARA ANN HOFREITER, truck repair co. exec.; b. Pekin, Ill., July 16, 1943; d. Robert Christian Hofreiter and Frances (Rebufoni) Hofreiter Burke; jr. acctg. degree Midstate Coll. of Commerce, 1963; student U. Ariz., 1968, supervisory devel. certificate, 1970; m. Albert William Prince III, Mar. 14, 1970; 1 dau., Roberta Christiana. Bookkeeper, South Side Bank, Peoria, Ill., 1962-63, Pyrofax Gas, Pekin, 1963-64, Farmers Automobile Ins. Assn., Pekin, 1964-65, WEEK-TV, Peoria, 1965-66; bookkeeper Hamilton Equipment Co., Inc., Tucson, 1966-68, sec.-treas., 1968-71; partner, sec.-treas., dir. Pyramid Truck Repair, Silverton, Oreg., 1975—. Water safety instr. ARC. Mem. Oreg. Retriever Trial Club (dir.), Salem Retriever Trial Club (treas.), Common Cause. Home: 5365 Lancers Ct NE Salem OR 97303 Office: Pyramid Truck Repair 827 Rail Way NE Silverton OR 97381

PRINCE, FLOYD JEROME, JR., plastics company and coatings company executive; b. San Diego, Mar. 10, 1921; s. Floyd Jerome and Alice Ann (Wilcoxen) P.; m. Monsita Ramos, June 4, 1966; children—Kathleen, Glen, Blair. Student UCLA, 1939-40, Chounard Art Inst., 1947; B.A., Pepperdine U., 1950. Cert. tchr., sch. psychologist Calif.; cert. vocat. tchr., Calif. Pres., F. J. Prince Co., Inc., Torrance, Calif., 1947—, Liquid Plastics Co. of Calif., Torrance, 1952—; pres. F. J. Prince Co., Inc., Honolulu, 1969—; instr. on estimating Trade Tech. Jr. Coll., 1956-62; cons. coatings, 1975—. Bd. dirs. Children's Baptist Home, Inglewood, Calif., 1967—, chmn. bd., 1977-79. Served with USAAF, 1944-45. Recipient Merit cert. Coordinating Council Painting Industry, Los Angeles County, 1967. Mem. Assoc. Builders and Contractors, Painters and Decorators Council. Home: 5 Outrider Rd Rolling Hills CA 90274 Office: 22521 S Normandie Ave Torrance CA 90501

PRINCE, RICHARD EDMUND, educator, artist; b. Comox, B.C., Can., Apr. 6, 1949; s. Charles Robert and Patricia Rosaleen (Stubbs) P.; m. Kathryn Diane Beaulieu, Sept. 5, 1970. B.A., U. B.C., 1971. Instr. sculpture Vancouver (B.C.) Community Coll., 1974-75; instr. U. B.C., Vancouver, 1975-77, vis. lectr., 1977-78, asst. prof., 1978-83, assoc. prof., 1983—; one-man shows N.S. Coll. Art and Design, 1974, Issacs Gallery, Toronto, Ont., Can., 1976, 78, 82, Equinox Gallery, Vancouver, 1977, 82, Burnaby (B.C.) Art Gallery, 1979; exhibited in group shows Vancouver Art Gallery, 1977, 83, Harbour Front Art Gallery, Toronto, 1978, 80, U. Regina (Sask.), 1978, Alta. Coll. Art Gallery, 1980, Robson Sq. Centre, Vancouver, 1980, U. Man., 1982, others; represented in permanent collections Burnaby Art Gallery, City of Vancouver Art Collection, Govt. of B.C. Heritage Collection, Nat. Gallery of Can., Vancouver Art Gallery, Can. Council Art Bank, Kalico Devel. Co., Vancouver, B.C. Central Credit Union, Thorne, Riddell and Co., Vancouver, Shell Oil Co., Art Gallery of Brant (Ont.), Can. Paraplegic Assn., Toronto, Can. Council Arts grantee, 1973, 74, 77; Humanities and Social Sci. research grantee, 1979, 80, 81, 83. Mem. Royal Can. Acad., Univ. Arts Assn. Can. (Western rep.). Office: Dept Fine Arts Univ British Columbia Vancouver BC V6T 1W5 Canada

PRINCI, CARL VICTOR, broadcasting exec.; b. Boston, Sept. 27, 1920; s. Joseph Mario and Teresa Marguerite (Strati) P.; student Boston U., 1938-41; m. Althea Doris Giordano, Jan. 20, 1946; children—Elaine Althea, Valerie May, Carla Victoria. Announcer, newscaster sta. WESX, Salem, Mass., 1940-42; chief announcer, newscaster, then program dir. sta. WCHA, Chambersburg, Pa., 1946-48; program dir., newscaster sta. WLEA, Hornell, N.Y., 1948-49; gen. mgr. sta. WKMO, Kokomo, Ind., 1949-50; staff announcer sta. KEIV, 1950, sta. KMGM, 1950-51, sta. KWKW, 1952-53; opera host, commentator sta. KFAC, Los Angeles, 1953-72, v.p. in charge programs and community involvement, 1972—; narrator, actor films for theatre and TV, lectr., narrator classical record albums; mem. exec. bd. Music Center Opera Assn. Served with AUS, 1942-46; ETO. Recipient Man of Year award Miracle Mile Lions Club, 1975, spl. award Young Audiences, Johann award Viennese Cultural Soc.; also various citations. Mem. ANTA. Roman Catholic. Club: K.C. Office: 6735 Yucca St Hollywood CA 90028

PRINDLE, ROBERT WILLIAM, geotech. engr.; b. Los Angeles, Nov. 19, 1950; s. Robert Edward and Margaret Elizabeth (Johnson) P.; student St. John's Coll., Camarillo, Calif., 1968-70; B.S.C.E. summa cum laude, Loyola U., Los Angeles, 1974; M.S., Calif. Inst. Tech., 1975. Engring. aide Los Angeles County Sanitation Dists., 1973-74; student engr. Los Angeles Dept. Water and Power, 1974, 75; staff engr. Fugro, Inc., Long Beach, Calif., 1976-78; sr. staff engr. Woodward-Clyde

Consultants, Orange, Calif., 1978-79; mem. tech. staff Sandia Nat. Labs., Albuquerque, 1980—. Mem. N. Mex. Symphony Orch. Chorus, 1981—. Registered profl. civil engr., Calif.; Calif. State Grad. fellow, 1974-75, Calif. Inst. Tech. Inst. fellow, 1974-75. Mem. ASCE, Nat. Soc. Profl. Engrs., Internat. Soc. for Soil Mechanics and Found. Engring., Tau Beta Pi. Republican. Roman Catholic. Contbr. articles to profl. jours. Office: Sandia Nat Labs Div 6252 Albuquerque NM 87185

PRINTUP, ROBERT HALE, environmental services executive, consultant; b. Lincoln, Nebr., June 9, 1929; s. John Monroe and Grace A. (Ganschow) P.; m. Lanore Jean Coppens, Oct. 22, 1967; children—Robert H. Jr., Greggory, John, Tresa. Student, Tex. Christian U., 1948-50, U. Calif.-Riverside, 1971-72. Owner, operator Miracle Maintenance, Baldwin Park, Calif., 1957-64; pres. Miracle Investments, Baldwin Park, 1960-64; exec. housekeeper, dir. environ. services Pomona (Calif.) Valley Community Hosp., 1965-75, U. Chgo. Hosps., 1975-80, Brotman Med. Ctr., Culver City, Calif., 1980-81, St. John's Hosp. & Health Ctr., Santa Monica, Calif., 1981-83; tchr., lectr., cons. in ednl. instns. Pres. Baldwin Park Service Council, 1962; active REACT Radio Club. Served with USAF, 1947-50. Recipient Merit award Los Angeles County, 1960; Grand award Nat. Soap and Detergent Assn., 1971. Mem. Nat. Exec. Housekeepers Assn. (numerous offices, awards), Assn. Practitioners Infection Control, Aircraft Owners and Pilots Assn., Baldwin Park Democratic Club, Western Hosps. Assn. (past chmn. housekeeping div.), Opportunity Investments Inc. Lutheran. Clubs: Rotary Internat, Optimists (Baldwin Park). Author: Housekeeping Management for Health Care Units, 1970; contbr. Management Handbook for Plant Engineers, 1980; mem. tech. adv. com. Executive Housekeeper Today mag.; contbr. articles to profl. jours.

PRITCHARD, JOEL M., congressman; b. Seattle, May 5, 1925; student Marietta Coll., 1946-48; children—Peggy, Frank, Anne, Jean. Pres. Griffin Envelope Co., Seattle, 1948-72; mem. 93d-98th congresses from 1st Dist. Wash., mem. fgn. affairs com., com. on mcht. marine and fisheries; chmn. House Wednesday Group; mem. Rep. Com. on Coms.; congl. adviser Internat. Law of Sea Conf. Mem. Wash. Ho. of Reps., 1958-66, Wash. Senate, 1966-70. Mem. Wash. State Constl. Adv. Commn., Wash. State Women's Rights Council, 1971, Met. Planning Council. Served with AUS, 1944-46. Republican. Office: 2268 Rayburn House Office Bldg Washington DC 20515

PRITCHARD, PAUL DAVID, educator, consultant; b. Seattle, Mar. 9, 1948; s. Elgin Elmer and Louise Lynette (Juzeler) P.; m. Kayleen Rae Scott, Aug. 24, 1968; children—Nathan, Nolle. B.A. in Edn., Western Wash. State Coll., 1970, M.Ed., 1973. Cert. tchr., prin., Wash. Tchr. social studies, curriculum specialist, sch. counselor Pub. Schs. Everett (Wash.), 1970—, tchr. social studies N Middle Sch., 1980—; speaker local and regional history. Vice pres. Port Gardner Assn., 1981-82; mem. hist. adv. com. City of Everett, 1983—. Recipient Letter of Commendation, Everett Pub. Library, 1982. Mem. NEA, Wash. Edn. Assn. Home: 1101 Grandview St Everett WA 98203 Office: N Middle Sch Everett WA 98201

PRITCHARD, ROSS JOSEPH, univ. chancellor; b. Paterson, N.J., Sept. 3, 1924; s. Ross W. and Camille (Beltramo) P.; B.A. in History and Polit. Sci., U. Ark., 1951, M.A., 1951; M.A., Fletcher Sch. Law and Diplomacy, 1952, Ph.D., 1954; m. Emily Gregg, June 2, 1948; children—Michael, Russell, Irene, Vol Walker, Ross Joseph, Mehran, Feresteh. Asst. prof. Tufts U., 1954; asst. prof. internat. studies Southwestern Coll. at Memphis, 1955-57, asso. prof., chmn. dept. 1957-60, prof., chmn. dept., 1960-62; spl. asst. Peace Corps, 1962, dep. sec. gen. internat. secretariat, 1963, dir. for Turkey, 1963-65; regional dir. for East Asia and Pacific, 1965-68; v.p., project mgr. Devel. & Resources Corp., N.Y.C., 1968-71; pres. Internat. House, Phila., 1972; pres. Hood Coll., Frederick, Md., 1972-75, Ark. State U., 1975-78; chancellor U. Denver, 1978—. Dem. candidate for Congress, 1960. Served with USN, 1941-46. Recipient Silver Anniversary award Nat. Collegiate Athletic Assn., 1976. Office: U Denver Denver CO 80210

PRITCHETT, BETTY JENSEN, coll. dean; b. Omaha, Sept. 14, 1924; d. Lars Peter and Ruth (Norby) Jensen; B.S., Portland State U., 1965; M.B.A., U. Oreg., 1966; Ed.D., Oreg. State U., 1973 (dec. 1982); m. Morgan S. Pritchett, June 27, 1944; children—Randall Wayne, Robin Kay Pritchett Vukovic, Royce Marie Pritchett Creech. Buyer, Rodgers Stores, Inc., Portland, Oreg., 1947-62; chmn. bus. div. Mt. Hood Community Coll., Gresham, Oreg., 1966-70, dir. evening coll., 1970-71, asso. dean instruction, 1972-77, dean humanities and behavioral scis., 1977-79, dean planning and spl. projects, 1979—; mem. state com. for articulation between community colls. and higher edn., 1976-78; mem. Gov.'s Council Career and Vocat. Edn., 1977—, chmn., 1980-82. Mem. Gresham City Council, 1983—. Mem. Oreg. Bus. Edn. Assn., Am. Assn. Higher Edn., Nat. Assn. Staff and Orgnl. Devel., Oreg. Women's Polit. Caucus, Am., Oreg. vocat. assns. Club: Soroptimist (pres. Portland-East 1974-75, 80-81, pres. East Multnomah County 1981-82). Author: Values and Perceptions of Community College Professional Staff in Oregon, 1973; contbg. author: Case Study in Retail Management Cases, 1969; The Pritchett Study in Retailing, An Economic View, 1969. Home: 1635 NE Country Club Ave Gresham OR 97030 Office: Mount Hood Community Coll 26000 SE Stark St Gresham OR 97030

PRITT, ALFRED TENNYSON, chemist; b. Parsons, W.Va., Mar. 26, 1941; s. Alfred T. and Anna R. (DeVilder) P.; B.S. in Chem. Engring., U. N.Mex., 1964; Ph.D. in Chemistry, UCLA, 1976; m. Lenore Theuns, Nov. 10, 1973; 1 dau., Julia. Teaching fellow UCLA, 1968-74; mem. tech. staff Rockwell Internat., Thousand Oaks, Calif., 1974—. Bd. dirs. Bay Cities Jewish Community Ctr., 1983—. Served with USAF, 1964-68. Mem. Am. Phys. Soc., AAAS, Sigma Xi. Democrat. Presbyterian. Contbr. articles on chem. lasers to sci. jours. Home: 3553 Corinth Ave Los Angeles CA 90066 Office: 1049 Camino Dos Rios Thousand Oaks CA 91360

PROFFIT, HIGHT MOORE, state senator; b. Goshen, N.C., July 17, 1911; s. Robert Lee and Martha A. (McNeil) P.; m. Dorothy Ardell Marsh, 1938; children—Larry Mac, Donald Hight, Lola Emma Baldwin, Dorothy Deanne Richins. Student Appalachian State Tchrs. Coll. Mem. Wyo. Ho. of Reps., 1975-77, Wyo. State Senate, 1977—. Mem. Uinta County Commn., 1951-75; mem. Sulpher Creek Reservoir Bd. from 1954; mem. adult edn. adv. bd. U. Wyo., from 1968; mem. Land Use Adv. Council, from 1975. Named Outstanding County Ofcl., Wyo. County Officers, 1966; recipient Outstanding Community Service award Evanston C. of C.; exec. bd. Wyuta dist. Boy Scouts Am., 1965—. Mem. Wyo. Farm Bur. Democrat. Mormon. Home: Route 1 Box 23 Evanston WY 82903 Office: Wyoming State Senate Cheyenne WY 82002*

PROFIO, A(MADEUS) EDWARD, engineering educator, researcher; b. New Castle, Pa., Apr. 18, 1931; s. Amedeus Edward and Helen Agnes (Pearce) P.; m. J Janet Lee Lazaran, Sept. 29, 1954; children—Christopher, Claudia, Susan. S.B. in Physics, M.I.T., 1953, Ph.D. in Nuclear Engring., 1963. Scientist, Westinghouse Bettis Atomic Power Labs., West Mifflin, Pa., 1953-55; research assoc., asst. prof. M.I.T., Cambridge, 1957-64; scientist Gen. Atomic Co., La Jolla, Calif., 1964-69; prof. nuclear engring. U. Calif., Santa Barbara, 1969—. Served to lt. C.E., U.S. Army, 1955-57. Mem. Am. Nuclear Soc. (outstanding tech. achievement award 1977), Sigma Xi, Tau Beta Pi, AAAS. Author: Experimental Reactor Physics, 1976; Radiation Shielding and Dosimetry, 1979; contbr. sci. papers to publs. Office: Dept Chem and Nuclear Engring Univ Calif Santa Barbara 93106

PROLO, DONALD JAMES, neurol. surgeon; b. San Jose, Calif., Apr. 30, 1936; s. James Robert and Marie (Cantu) P.; B.A., Stanford U., 1957, M.D., 1961; m. Joanne M. Hickey, Sept. 1, 1979; 1 dau., Laura Marie. Intern, Johns Hopkins Hosp., 1961-62; resident in neurol. surgery Stanford U. Hosp., 1962-70; mem. faculty Stanford U. Med. Sch., 1969—, clin. assoc. prof., 1975—; practice medicine specializing in neurosurgery, San Jose, 1971—; mem. staff Good Samaritan Hosp., O'Connor Hosp.; dir. neuroskeletal transplantation lab. Inst. Med. Research, San Jose, 1972—; cons. VA Hosp., Oakland Naval Hosp. Bd. dirs. Hope for Mentally Retarded. Mem. ACS, Am. Assn. Neurol. Surgeons, Congress Neurol. Surgeons, Western Neurosurg. Soc., San Francisco Neurol. Soc., Stanford U. Med. Alumni Assn. (pres. 1983-84), Stanford Assocs. Republican. Roman Catholic. Contbr. articles med. jours. Office: 203 Disalvo Ave San Jose CA 95128

PROUT, CARL WESLEY, history educator; b. Bakersfield, Calif., Apr. 19, 1941; s. George Hecla and Ruth (King) P. B.A., U. Calif., Santa Barbara, 1964, M.A., 1965; postgrad. U. Tenn., Knoxville, 1968-71, Am. U. Cairo (Egypt), 1974, U. So. Calif., 1981, Ain Shams U., Cairo, 1981. Instr. history Santa Barbara Coll., 1965-66, U. Tenn., Knoxville, 1968-71; instr. history Orange Coast Coll., Costa Mesa, 1966-68, asst. prof., 1971-73, asso. prof., 1973-75, prof., 1975—; treas., dir. Willmore Corp., 1980-81. Mem. Long Beach Beautification Assn.; pres., chmn. bd. Alamitos Heights Improvement Assn., 1979-80, bd. dirs., 1980-82; co-chmn. Ban Ugly Light Bulbs, 1978; mem. East Long Beach Joint Council, 1979-80, Local Coastal Planning Adv. Com., 1979-80. Recipient Salgo outstanding tchr. award, 1974, 75, 76. Mem. Am. Hist. Assn. Brit. Hist. Soc., Sigma Nu. Research and publs. in field. Office: Orange Coast Coll 2701 Fairview Rd Costa Mesa CA 92626

PROUT, RALPH EUGENE, physician; b. Los Angeles, Feb. 27, 1933; s. Ralph Byron and Fern Leslie (Taylor) P.; B.A., Loma Linda U., 1953, M.D., 1957; m. Joanne L. Morris, Sept. 17, 1980; children—Michael, Michelle. Intern, Los Angeles County Hosp., 1957-58; resident in internal medicine White Meml. Hosp., Los Angeles, 1958-60; resident in psychiatry Harding Hosp., Worthington, Ohio, 1960-61; practice medicine specializing in internal medicine, Napa, Calif., 1961-63; physician and surgeon Calif. Med. Facility, Vacaville, 1963-68, chief med. officer, 1968—; clin. instr. Sch. Medicine, U. Calif., Davis, 1978—; cons. Calif. Dept. Corrections, 1978—, chief med. Services, 1983—; bd. dirs. Home Care Service, Inter-Community Hosp., Fairfield, Calif., 1978-80. Active Rep. Central Com. Solano County, 1974-78; treas. Vacaville Rep. Assembly, 1972-74. Mem. Am. Correctional Health Services Assn., Calif. Soc. Internal Medicine, Am. Soc. Internal Medicine, Calif. State Employed Physicians Assn. (pres. 1976-77), Union Am. Physicians, Air Force Assn., Vacaville C. of C. (dir., 1975-78). Clubs: Commonwealth of Calif., Native Sons of the Golden West. Home: 831 Linwood St Vacaville CA 95688 Office: 1600 California Dr Vacaville CA 95696

PROVENZANO, ANTHONY, artist; b. Tampa, Fla., May 19, 1921; s. Victor and Annie P.; student Chouinard Art Inst., 1949, Tampa U., Jepson Art Sch.; m. Alice Gonzalez, Dec. 2, 1950; children—Debbie Provenzano McClary, Lori. Tech. illustrator Tech. Products Co., 1954-55, Lockheed Missile Systems div., 1955-57, Bendix Electrodynamics Co., North Hollywood, Calif., 1957-69; mag. and tech. illustrator, 1959—; exhbns.: Calif. Art Club, 1946, Los Angeles County Mus., 1946, Burbank Central Library, 1975, Pasadena Library, 1972, Glendale Fed. Savs., 1972, Calif. Fed. Savs., 1974, Alhambra (Calif.) City Hall, 1971, Naval and Marine Research Center, Encino, Calif., 1973; represented in permanent collection Los Angeles County Mus.; numerdus pvt. collections; painted many Navy ships of World War II; tchr. art classes in oil, 1970—. Served with AUS, 1942-45. Decorated Bronze Star (2). Mem. Valley Artists Guild (bd. dirs. house com.), West Valley Art Guild, San Fernando Valley Art Club. Studio: 11577 Gilmore St North Hollywood CA 91606

PROVENZANO, DENIA, educator, contractor; b. Los Angeles, Sept. 27, 1935; children—Cory, Charles, Douglas. B.Ed., U. Miami, Coral Gables, Fla., 1961; M.A., U. Nev., 1971. Tchr. history, psychology, home econs., assertive tng. lectr. Clark County Sch. Dist., Las Vegas, 1963—, also drug intervention counselor; sec.-treas. Parkchester Estates; pres. Earth Movers Corp., lectr. Sertoma Club. Dir., Paul Laxalt for Senator campaign, 1981; vol. Sunrise Hosp., 1977—; Hope chaplain So. Nev. Hosp., 1975. Office: Earth Movers Corp 1600 Yellow Rose St Las Vegas NV 89106

PROVOST, DONALD EDGAR, engring. and constrn. co. exec.; b. Denver, Aug. 26, 1912; s. Charles Edgar and Beda Amanda (Rapp) P.; student U. Colo., 1932-33; m. Eldyne Herbst, Dec. 15, 1938; 1 dau., Sheila Kay Provost Meredith. With Stearns-Roger Corp., Denver, 1937—, mgr. power div., 1955-59, v.p., 1959-63, pres., 1963-83, chmn. bd., 1968-83; pres., chmn. Bd. Stearns-Roger Inc., Stearns-Roger Architects, Ltd., Stearns-Roger Equipment Co., Stearns-Roger Export, Ltd., Stearns-Roger Elec. Contractors Inc., Stearns-Roger Fabricators, Inc., Stearns-Roger Engring Co., Stearns-Roger Services, Inc., Stearns-Roger Engring Corp.; dir. Stearns-Roger Can. Ltd., Rio Grande Industries, Inc., Denver and Rio Grande Western R.R., 1st Nat. Bancorp., 1st National Bank of Denver, Mountain Bell Co., Gen. Iron Works Co.; dir., past pres. Rocky Mountain Elec. League. Bd. dirs. Lutheran Med. Center, 1968—; trustee U. Denver. Registered profl. engr., Colo. Republican. Congregationalist. Clubs: Cherry Hills Country, Denver Country. Office: 4500 Cherry Creek Dr Denver CO 80222*

PROWELL, ROY WALTERS, JR., orthodontist; b. Pitts., Oct. 6, 1945; s. Roy Walters and Dorothy Jane (Forney) P.; student U. Calif., Davis, 1963-65, D.D.S. in Orthodontics (Regents scholar), U. Calif., San Francisco, 1969; m. Evelyn Joyce Morgan, Aug. 1, 1971; children—Roy Walters III, Ian Morgan. Asso., Gordon Osser, D.D.S., Castro Valley, Calif., 1970-71, Willard Collins, D.D.S., Stockton, Calif., 1971-72; practice dentistry specializing in orthodontics, Pittsburg and Antioch, Calif., 1969-76; pres. R. Walt Prowell, D.D.S., Inc., Pittsburg and Antioch, 1976—; mem. staff Mt. Diablo Rehab. Center, Pleasant Hill, Calif.; mem. E. Bay (Calif.) Cleft Palate Panel. Pres., U. Calif. Orthodontic Alumni Found., 1978-81, treas., 1981—. Republican. Presbyterian. Club: Masons. Office: 3107 Lone Tree Way Suite D Antioch CA 94509 also 3715 Railroad Ave Suite D Pittsburg CA 94565

PRUDHOMME, HARRY P., utility exec.; b. San Jose, Calif., Feb. 11, 1924; s. George A. and Margaret C. (Del Ponte) P.; B.E.E., U. Santa Clara (Calif.), 1948; m. Virginia Myer, Dec. 27, 1947; children—Paul, James, Marilyn, Thomas, Karen, Jeffrey, Janice, Stephen. With Pacific Gas & Electric Co., 1954-78, mgr. pipeline ops., also mgr. Standard Pacific Gasline, Inc., 1968-78; pres., dir. Pacific Gas Transmission Co., San Francisco, 1978—, Pacific Transmission Supply Co., San Francisco, 1979—; dir. Angus Chem. Co., Northbrook, Ill., Angus Petrotech Corp., Golden, Colo. Served to 1st lt. C.E., AUS, 1943-45. Mem. Am. Gas Assn., Gas Research Inst., Interstate Natural Gas Assn. Am. (dir.), Pacific Coast Gas Assn. (Leadership award 1977), Can. Am. Soc. San Francisco, World Affairs Council No. Calif., Tau Beta Pi. Roman Catholic. Clubs: Commonwealth, Electric Engineers, World Trade (San Francisco). Home: 75 Lynwood Pl Moraga CA 94556 Office: Pacific Gas Transmission Co 245 Market St San Francisco CA 94105

PRUSSIA, LELAND SPENCER, bank executive; b. San Jose, Calif., Feb. 13, 1929; s. Leland Spencer and Doris E. (Fowler); m. Vivian Blom; children—Leslie, Alan L., Gregory. B.A., Stanford U., 1951, M.A., 1956; grad. advanced mgmt. program Harvard U., 1970. With Bank Am., San Francisco, 1956—, former vice chmn., now chmn. bd. Mem. adv. bd. Kellogg Grad. Sch. Mgmt., Northwestern U., Author: The Changing World of Banking—Bank Investment Portfolio Management. Office: Bank Am Ctr 555 California St San Francisco CA 94104*

PRYBUTOK, BENN, insurance company executive; b. Phila., June 12, 1947; s. Leonard and Shirley (Sagle) P.; m. Marsha R. Raske, Aug. 10, 1969; children—Mark David, Shara Jill. B.A., Temple U., 1970, M.A., 1972; postgrad. Columbia U. Spl. asst. to ins. commr. Pa. Dept. Ins., 1974-78; asst. dir. workers' compensation dept. Alliance Am. Insurers, Los Angeles, 1979; v.p. corp. planning and dir. govt. relations Allianz Ins. Co., Allianz Underwriters, Inc., Allianz Syndicate, Inc., Allianz Intermediaries Surplus Line Brokers, Inc., Los Angeles, 1979—; instr. poli. sci. Community Coll. Phila. and Fed. Employees On-Site Edn. Program, 1970-74. Mem. Democratic Com. and Exec. Com. Cheltenham Twp., Montgomery County, Pa., 3d ward leader, 1974-78; founding mem. Hi Point Neighbors Assn., Los Angeles, 1980; mem. pub. affairs com. and instr. civics and English, Westside Jewish Ctr., Los Angeles; coach Am. Youth Soccer Orgn., Beverly Hills Little League. Recipient Econ. Devel. award Westmoreland County (Pa.), 1976; Civic Achievement award Montgomery County (Pa.), 1977; I Day Featured Speaker's award Northwestern Pa. Ins. Assn., 1977, 78. Mem. Half Ax Soc. Contbr. articles to profl. jours. Home: 1172 Hi Point St Los Angeles CA 90035 Office: 6435 Wilshire Blvd Los Angeles CA 90048

PRYOR, HUBERT, mag. editor; b. Buenos Aires, Argentina, Mar. 18, 1916; s. John W. and Hilda A. (Cowes) P.; came to U.S., 1940, derivative citizenship; grad. St. George's Coll., Argentina, 1932; student U. London (Eng.), 1934-36; m. Ellen M. Ach, Sept. 25, 1940; children—Alan, Gerald, David; m. 2d, Roberta J. Baughman, Apr. 11, 1959; m. 3d, Luanne W. Van Norden, Oct. 31, 1967 (div. 1982). Corr. in S.Am. for United Press, 1937-39; pub. relations rep. Pan Am. Airways in Buenos Aires, 1939-40; reporter N.Y. Herald Tribune, 1940-41; writer, dir. short-wave newsroom CBS, 1941-46; asst. mng. editor Knickerbocker Weekly, 1946-47; sr. editor Look mag., 1947-62; creative supr. Wilson, Haight & Welch, advt., 1962-63; editor Science Digest, 1963-67; mng. editor Med. World News, 1967; editor Modern Maturity, NRTA Jour., 1967-82; editorial dir. Dynamic Years, 1977-82, pub. coordinator, 1982—. Served to lt. USNR, 1943-46. Mem. Am. Soc. Mag. Editors. Home: 1900 E Ocean Blvd Long Beach CA 90802 Office: 215 Long Beach Blvd Long Beach CA 90802

PUCKETT, RICHARD EDWARD, arts and craft exec.; b. Klamath Falls, Oreg., Sept. 9, 1932; s. Vernon Elijah and Leona Belle (Clevenger) P.; m. Velma Faye Hamrick, Apr. 14, 1957; children—Katherine Michelle Briggs, Deborah Alison Bolinger, Susan Lin, Gregory Richard. Student So. Oreg. Coll. Edn., 1951-56, Lake Forest Coll., 1957-58; Hartnell Jr. Coll., 1960-70; B.A., U. San Francisco, 1978. Asst. arts and crafts dir., Fort Leonard Wood, Mo., 1956-57; arts and crafts dir., asst. spl. services officer, mus. dir., Fort Sheridan, Ill., 1957-59; arts and crafts dir., Fort Irwin, Calif., 1959-60, Fort Ord, Calif., 1960—; dir. Art Gallery, Arts and Crafts Center Materials Sales Store, 1960. Recipient First Place, Dept. Army and U.S. Army Forces Command awards for programming and publicity, 1979, 80, 81, 1st and 3d place awards Monterey County Fair Fine Arts Exhibit, 1979. Mem. Am. Park and Recreation Soc., Am. Craftsman Assn., Glass Arts Soc., Monterey Peninsula Art Assn., Salinas Fine Arts Assn. One-man shows: Seaside City Hall, 1975, Fort Ord Arts and Crafts Center Gallery, 1967, 73, 79, 81, Presidio of Monterey Art Gallery, 1979; Glass on Holiday, 1981; also pvt. collections. Home: 1152 Jean Ave Salinas CA 93905 Office: Arts and Crafts Center Morale Support Activities Bldg 2250 2d Ave Fort Ord CA 92941

PUDNEY, GARY LAURENCE, television executive; b. Mpls., July 20, 1934; s. Lawrence D. and Agnes (Hansen) P.; B.A., UCLA, 1956. Vice-pres., ABC, Inc., N.Y.C., 1968—, v.p. spl. projects, sr. exec. in charge of talent ABC Entertainment, 1979—. Served to capt. USAF, 1957-60. Bd. dirs. Nat. Cerebral Palsy Found. Mem. Hollywood Radio and TV Soc., Acad. TV Arts and Scis. Democrat. Lutheran. Office: ABC Entertainment 2040 Ave of the Stars Century City CA 90067

PUENTE, JOSE GARZA, safety coordinator; b. Cuero, Tex., Mar. 19, 1949; s. Roque Leos and Juanita Vela (Garza) P.; m. Francisca Rodriguez Estrada, Sept. 7, 1969; 1 son, Anthony Burk. B.A., W. Tex. State U., Canyon, 1972; postgrad. U. Ariz.-Tucson, 1980; grad. U.S. Army transp. courses, 1972, 78; student U.S. Army Command and Gen. Staff Coll., 1981—. Cert. U.S. Council Accreditation in Occupational Hearing; cert. Audiometric Technicians of Am. Indsl. Hygiene Assn. Asst. gen. mgr. Am. Transit Corp., Tucson, 1972-75; pub. transp. supt. City of Tucson, 1975-77; asst. safety coordinator, Tucson, 1977-81; safety coordinator Mesa, Ariz., 1981—; owner La Paz Gospel Supplies & Gift shop, Tucson, 1979-80. Mem. Tucson Child Care Assn., 1973-74; mem. Citizen Task Force, Sunnyside sch. bd., 1977; co-founder Ray Morales Aid Fund, 1980. LaPaz Served to capt. USAR, 1971—. Fellow advanced mgmt. seminar Urban Mass Transp. Adminstrn., Northeastern U., Boston, 1976-77. Mem. Am. Soc. Safety Engrs., Mexican Am. Govtl. Employees (charter). Democrat. Baptist. Clubs: Internat. Order DeMolay, Dobson Ranch Lions, Mesa Bowling League. Home: 2341 W Del Campo Mesa AZ 85201 Office: 648 N Mesa Dr Mesa AZ 85201

PUFFER, PAUL JAMES, dentist; b. Beaver, Utah, Jan. 29, 1935; s. Ephraim LeRoy and Burdetta (Thrope) P.; student Utah State U., 1953-59; D.M.D., U. Oreg., 1963; m. Carma Rae Swalberg, Dec. 28, 1959; children—Kim, Sue, Jim, Jill, Shauna, Lance, Alicia, Benjamin, Richard, Marile, Stephen Frederick. Practice dentistry, Molalla, Oreg., 1963—; clin. asso. Sch. Dentistry, U. Oreg., 1976-77, mem. dean's ednl. council, 1980-81. Mem. Molalla Grad. Sch. Bd., 1971-74; bishop Ch. of Jesus Christ of Latter-day Saints, 1972-76; scout master Boy Scouts Am., 1976-80. Fellow Acad. Gen. Dentistry (clin. scholar); mem. Oreg. Acad. Gen. Dentistry (pres.-elect 1982-83), N.W. Dental Diagnostic Research Soc. (pres. 1979-80), Am. Soc. Dentistry for Children, Am. Orthodontic Soc. (Western dir. 1983—), ADA, Oreg. Acad. Cranio-Mandibular Disorders, Oreg. Masters Study Club (sec. 1982-83). Republican. Club: Molalla Rotary (past pres.). Contbg. author The Wisdom Tooth. Editor, producer Teeth Talk. Home: 623 Main St Molalla OR 97038 Office: 116 E 2d St Molalla OR 97038

PUGEL, ROBERT JOSEPH, publisher, educator; b. Pueblo, Colo., Aug. 15, 1941; s. Joseph E. and Margaret E. (Jachetta) P.; A.A., U. So. Colo., 1959; B.A., Western State Coll. Colo., 1961, M.A., 1965; postgrad. (Univ. internat. fellow) U. London, 1968, U. Denver, 1967-69; m. E. Elke Williamson, June 29, 1968. Asst prof. English, U. So. Colo., 1965-67; teaching fellow U. Denver, 1967-69; prof. English, Met. State Coll., 1969—; founder, pub. Scribes mag., Denver, 1975—; poetry judge; Can./U.S.A. grantee McMaster U., Hamilton, Ont., Can., 1975; Rocky Mountain advisor Brit. Univs., 1970—. Mem. Colo. Dem. Central Com., 1970-81; chmn. Colo. Dem. House Dist. 39, 1974-80; del. Colo. Gov.'s Conf. on Aging, 1980. Recipient award for outstanding community service Public Relations Soc. Am., 1978; named Outstanding Contbr. to Colo. Sr. Community, 1978, 79, 80. Mem. Nat. Council Tchrs. English, Internat. Assn. Bus. Communicators, Pub. Relations Soc. Am., Congress Colo. Communicators, Am. Poetry Soc., NEA, AAUP, English-Speaking Union (internat. bd. govs. 1970-81, v.p. 1974—, chmn. scholarship com. 1975—, organizer, condr. Conoco (Colo.) speech forum), Nat. Writers Club (featured poet 1978 Conf.), St. Andrew's Soc., Denver Zoo, Denver Art Mus., Denver Mus. Natural History, PEN, Colo. Poetry Soc., Poetry Soc. Am., Inst. Internat. Edn., Greenpeace,

Sierra Club, Nat. Wildlife Fedn., Fund for Animals. Roman Catholic. Club: Racquet World. Editor, pub. lit. mags. Paradigm Shift, Reality and Other Illusions, Turquoise Windows. Contbr. fiction, articles and poetry to various nat., region and local mags. and newspapers. Home: 7239 E Euclid Dr Englewood CO 80111 Office: Dept English Met State Coll Denver CO 80204

PUGH, DEBORAH ANN, nursing educator, health consultant; b. El Dorado, Ark., Jan. 1, 1952; d. Benjamin Frederick and Charlotte Yvonne (Everett) Kracht; m. Wayne Malone Pugh, June 17, 1973; children—Gregory Wayne, Britt Everett. B.S., cum laude (Ryerson Inland Found. Scholar), UCLA, 1973; M.S. in Nursing, Calif. State U.-Los Angeles, 1976. R.N., Calif., 1973. Staff nurse UCLA Med. Ctr., 1973-74, Brotman Med. Ctr., Culver City, Calif., 1974-76; nurse cons. Edwards Labs., Santa Ana, Calif., 1978; critical care educator St. Joseph Hosp., Orange, Calif., 1976-81, dir. nursing edn., 1981-82, dir. clin. edn., 1982—; adviser to nursing depts. Calif. State U.-Fullerton, Saddleback Coll., Santa Ana Coll.; instr. U. Calif.-Irvine. Active Orange County chpt. Am. Heart Assn.; elder-elect Presbyn. Ch., 1983-86. Named Outstanding Grad. Student in Nursing, Calif. State U.-Los Angeles, 1976. Mem. Am. Assn. Critical Care Nurses (cert.), Orange County/Long Beach Nursing Consortium (sec. 1982-83), Orange County Nursing Inservice Educators Council (v.p. continuing edn. 1981-82), Delta Gamma. Cons. editor: Critical Care Update, 1981. Mosby's Comprehensive Rev. of Critical Care, 1980. Home: 13522 Sussex Pl Santa Ana CA 92705 Office: 1100 Stewart Dr Orange CA 92667

PUGH, HELEN PEDERSEN, realtor; b. San Francisco, Feb. 17, 1934; d. Christian Edward and Gladys Phoebe Zumwalt Pedersen; m. Howard Brooks Pugh, Sr., Oct. 11, 1974; children—Catherine Collier, Stephen Leach, Matthew Leach, Virginia Leach. A.A., U. Calif.-Berkeley, 1955. Pvt. sec. to exec. dir. Republican party, Phoenix, 1972, Henderson Realty, Phoenix, 1973; sta. mgr. Mobil Oil Co., Phoenix, 1973-74; realtor, Bud Melcher & Associates, Scottsdale, Ariz., 1978—. Vol. coordinator William Baker for Congress, Phoenix, 1972; vol. Phoenix Meml. Hosp., Scottsdale Hosp. North Devel. Com.; master tchr. Presbyterian Ch., youth leader; troop leader Cactus-Pine council Girl Scouts U.S.A., 1960-74; v.p. Planned Parenthood Aux., Family Service Agy. Aux.; youth leader Toastmasters Internat.; vol. Phoenix Symphony Guild, Phoenix Art Mus.; deacon Presbyterian Ch. Mem. Scottsdale Bd. Realtors, Scottsdale Comml. Bd., Phoenix Comml. Bd. (Multiple Listing Service Forms Com. award 1981), Internat. Real Estate Orgn., Farm and Land Inst., Valley of Sun Real Estate Exchangers, LWV, Scottsdale C. of C. (ambassador), Scottsdale Republican Forum, Cactus Wren Rep. Women, Palo Verde Rep. Women, Paradise Rep. Women, Delta Zeta. Clubs: Toastmasters (past pres., youth leader), Soroptomists, Camelback. Home: 6929 E Chaparral St Scottsdale AZ 85253 Office: 7320 E Shoeman Ln Scottsdale AZ 85251

PUGH, WARREN EDWARD, state senator, business executive; b. Salt Lake City, Dec. 21, 1909; s. William E. and Eva (Murphy) P.; m. Leta Curtis, 1933; children—Carol Matheson, Lorin K., Donald E. Owner, mgr. Cummins Diesel Sales Co.; pres. Indsl. Devel. and Sales Corp., Cummins Intermountain Idaho Inc.; mem. Utah Ho. of Reps., 1959-60, chmn. transp. and pub. safety standing com., 1967-68, 71-72; mem. Utah State Senate, 1967—, maj. leader, 1969-70, pres., from 1973, chmn. edn. subcom. joint appropriations 1971-72, mem. Legis. Council higher edn. com., 1971-72, Legis. Council exec. com., 1973—. Recipient Edn. Service award Granite Edn. Assn., 1973. Republican. Mormon. Clubs: Alta, Hidden Valley Country. Home: 5124 Cottonwood Ln Salt Lake City UT 84117 Office: Utah State Senate Salt Lake City UT 84114

PUGH, WILLIAM OWEN, museum director; b. Terry, Mont., Feb. 7, 1918; s. Arthur Job and Opal Kerns P.; A.B., Whitman Coll., 1939; M.A., U. Pacific, 1947; postgrad. U. Iowa, 1939, 40; m. Sydney Houtz, Sept. 12, 1943; children—Michael W., Randall K., Christopher L. Instr., then asst. prof. Whitman Coll., 1946-49; vice-chmn. English dept. Am. U., Beirut, Lebanon, 1949-52; exec. Yakima (Wash.) C. of C., 1953-56; personnel and community services mgr. Republic Pub. Co., Yakima, 1957-58; regional blood services adminstr. Columbia River Region, Yakima, 1958-76; dir. Yakima Valley Mus. and Hist. Assn., Yakima, 1976—. Mem. Wash. State Adv. Council on Archaeol. and Historic Preservation. Served to maj. Adj. Gen. Corps, AUS, 1941-46. Lanham scholar Z.A. Lanham Found., 1936-40. Mem. Am. Assn. State and Local History, Res. Officers Assn., Wash. Museums Assn. (v.p.), Wash. Congress Parents and Tchrs. (life). Republican. Methodist. Clubs: Ice Skating, Lions, Elks (Yakima, Wash.).

PUGNETTI, DONALD ANTON, newspaper editor; b. Carbonado, Wash., Apr. 18, 1917; s. Anton Joseph and Mary (Rosatti) P.; B.A. in Journalism, U. Wash., 1941; m. Frances Willa Taylor, Aug. 11, 1946; children—Brian Taylor, Donald A., Eugene Francis, Mary Dawn, Lester Richard. Mgr., Athletic News Service, U. Wash., 1941; reporter Tacoma News Tribune, 1945-46; publicity dir. Seattle C. of C., 1946-47; mng. editor Tri-City Herald, 1947-69, editor, 1969-73; editor Tacoma News Tribune, 1973—; v.p. Scott Pub. Co., Inc., 1959-73; dir. Tribune Pub. Co., 1974—. Mem. Disciplinary Bd., Wash. State Bar Assn., 1978-81; dir. Tri-Cities and Tacoma Goodwill Assn., 1957-83, chmn., 1963-64. Served with U.S. Army, 1942-45. Recipient Thomas L. Stokes award, 1963; Stewart Holbrook award, 1978. Mem. Am. Soc. Newspaper Editors, AP Mng. Editors, Wash. Bench-Bar-Press Com., Wash. State Rds. and Transp. Assn. (exec. bd. 1967—), Assn. U.S. Army (exec. bd. 1976—), Wash. State Hist. Soc. (exec. bd. 1982—), Keep Wash. Green Assn. (exec. bd. 1970—), Sigma Delta Chi, Pi Sigma Alpha. Lutheran. Clubs: Rotary, Elks. Office: PO Box 11000 Tacoma WA 98411

PULITZER, MICHAEL EDGAR, newspaper editor; b. St. Louis, Feb. 23, 1930; s. Joseph and Elizabeth (Edgar) P.; grad. St. Mark's Sch., Southborough, Mass., 1947; A.B., Harvard, 1951, LL.B., 1954; m. Cecille Stell Eisenbeis, Apr. 28, 1970; children—Michael Edgar, Elizabeth E., Robert S., Frederick D., Catherine D. Eisenbeis, Christina H. Eisenbeis, Mark C. Eisenbeis, William H. Eisenbeis. Admitted to Mass. bar, 1954; asso. firm Warner, Stackpole, Stetson & Bradlee, Boston, 1954-56; reporter Louisville Courier Jour., 1956-60; reporter, news editor, asst. mng. editor St. Louis Post-Dispatch, 1960-71, asso. editor, 1978—; editor, pub. Ariz. Daily Star, Tucson, 1971—; pres., chief operating officer Pulitzer Pub. Co. and subs., 1979—, also dir. Mem. Nat. News Council, 1976—; bd. dirs. St. Louis Post-Dispatch Found. Clubs: St. Louis Country; Mountain Oyster (Tucson); Balboa (Mazatlan, Mexico). Home: 50 Portland Pl Saint Louis MO 63108 Office: 900 N Tucker Blvd Saint Louis MO 63101

PULLEN-SEYFERT, BEVERLY ANADEAN, educator; b. Clovis, N.Mex., July 25, 1949; d. Jimmie Junior and Rosa Aldean (Bohannan) Pullen; m. Dennis Ralph Seyfert, Apr. 25, 1972; children—Stepheny Denise, Kimberly Dawn. Student, Bethany Nazarene Coll., 1967-69; B.S., Eastern N.Mex. U., 1971; M.A., Western N.Mex. U., 1975. Tchr., Newcomb Elem. Sch., 1972-73, Newcomb Jr. High Sch., 1973-76; tchr. home econs. Kirtland (N.Mex.) Central High Sch., 1976—. Democrat. Methodist. Office: Box 96 Kirtland NM 87417

PULLIAM, JAMES TOWNSEND, college administrator; b. Pomona, Calif., Aug. 14, 1940; s. Floyd Townsend and Eleanor Jannet P.; B.A., U. Redlands, 1962; M.A., Calif. State U., Chico, 1966; M.A., Chapman Coll., 1971; postgrad. U. LaVerne, 1978-83; m. Jacqueline Marian Pulliam, June 16, 1962; children—Kevin Townsend, Jami Lynne, Jana Marie, Kenneth James. Tchr., Tustin (Calif.) Union High Sch. Dist., 1967-69; account exec. Mitchum, Jones & Templeton, Riverside, Calif., 1969-70; dean ednl. services Coll. of the Desert, Palm Desert, Calif., 1970—; instr. Pepperdine U.; cons. Tex. Instruments Corp. Bd. dirs. United Way, 1977-80; v.p. Calif. Dirs. Vocat. Edn., 1976-77; mem. adv. com. Morongo Unified Sch. Dist., 1976-77. NDEA fellow, 1967; Experienced Tchr. fellow, 1967-68. Mem. Assn. Calif. Community Coll. Adminstrs., Calif. Appliance Service Council (dir.). Home: 58290 Lisbon Dr Yucca Valley CA 92284 Office: 6785 Sage Ave Twentynine Palms CA 92277

PULLIAM, PAUL EDISON, electrical engineer; b. Nickerson, Kans., June 6, 1912; s. George Washington and Hattie Lucy (Vandeventer) P.; B.S. in E.E., U. Mo., 1951; m. Ila M. Catrett, Feb. 3, 1945; children—Carol Ann Pulliam Rolls, Paula Ann Pulliam Bermingham. Elec. engr. Ozark Dam Constructors, Powerhouse, Bull Shoals Dam, Baxter County, Ark., 1951-52; commd. 2d lt. U.S. Army Res., 1937, advanced through grades to maj., 1961; field engr. RCA, Fighter Wing Tactical Air Command, 1952-53; elec. engr. Goodyear Atomic Corp., 1957-60; missiles engr. Chrysler Corp., Redstone Arsenal, Ala., 1957-60; constrn. insp. Sacramento County Dept. Pub. Works, Sacramento, Calif., 1977—. Lt. col. Calif. Mil. Res. Registered profl. engr., Mo., Nev., Calif. Mem. Nat. Soc. Profl. Engrs., Calif. Soc. Profl. Engrs. (treas. Sacramento Valley chpt. 1977), Soc. Am. Mil. Engrs., IEEE (life), Res. Officers Assn., Electric Auto Assn. (pres. Santa Clara chpt. 1971). Democrat. Baptist. Club: Toastmasters. Home: 7916 Grandstaff Dr Sacramento CA 95823 Office: Capitol Telephone Co Inc 2700 Fruitridge Rd Sacramento CA 95820

PULLING, RICHARD KEILER, SR., manufacturing company executive; b. Erie, Pa., Sept. 19, 1928; s. Clairence Keiler and Ruth (McLeod) P.; m. Doris Coutier, May 15, 1954; children—Lori, Richard, Keith, Tracy. B.C.E., Pa. State U., 1951; M.B.A., U. Detroit, 1960; grad. advanced mgmt. program, Harvard U., 1970. Registered profl. engr. Ill., 1961. Engr., Dravo Corp., Pitts., 1954-55; successively engr., sales mgr., gen. mgr. Lock Joint Pipe Co., Chgo., 1955-62; various positions to div. pres., Interpace Corp., Parsippany, N.J., 1962-79; pres. R & G Sloane Mfg. Co., Inc., Sun Valley, Calif., 1979—; dir. R & G. Sloane, Canplas (Can.), Piezas Plasticas (Dominican Republic), Accesorios para Construcion (Costa Rica), 1979—. Mem. Dist. council, Cub Scouts, Boy Scouts Am., 1962-65; chmn. zoning bd., Kinnelon, N.Y., 1964-67; councilman City of Kinnelon, 1967-70; chmn. planning bd., Allamuchy, N.Y., 1971-79; founder Republican club, Allamucht, 1978. Served to lt. USN, 1951-54. Mem. Am. Soc. Mil. Engrs. (Gold medal 1951). Episcopalian. Clubs: Panther Valley Golf and Country (v.p., dir. 1975-79); Westlake Yacht. Office: 7660 N Clybourn Ave Sun Valley CA 91352

PUMERANTZ, PHILIP, coll. pres.; b. New London, Conn., Nov. 3, 1932; s. Harry and Pauline (Weiss) P.; B.A., U. Conn., 1959, M.A., 1961, Ph.D., 1967; L.H.D. (hon.), Coll. Osteo. Medicine of the Pacific, 1979; m. Harriet Krinsky, Aug. 21, 1960; children—Andrew, Beth, Richard. Tchr. history Waterford (Conn.) High Sch., 1959-63; adminstr. Tomlinson Jr. High Sch., Fairfield, Conn., 1963-66; asst. prof. edn. U. Bridgeport, 1967-71, asso. prof., 1971-74, dir. continuing edn., 1972-74; prin. P. Pumerantz Assos., Fairfield, 1974-75; dir. edn. Am. Osteo. Assn., Chgo., 1975-77; pres. Coll. Osteo. Medicine of the Pacific, Pomona, Calif., 1977—. Bd. govs. Fairfield Unquowa Sch.; bd. dirs. Park Ave. Hosp., Hollywood Community Hosp., Pomona chpt. ARC, Mt. Baldy council Boy Scouts Am. Served with U.S. Army, 1953-55. Recipient proclamation for devel. of med. coll. City of Pomona, 1978; Wesleyan U. grantee, 1961. Mem. Am. Assn. Colls. Osteo. Medicine (gov., chmn. accreditation com.), Phi Delta Kappa, Phi Alpha Theta, Kappa Delta Pi. Clubs: Univ. Claremont, Rotary. Author textbooks; adv. editor Osteo. Physicians Jour., 1978—. Office: College Plaza Pomona CA 91766

PUNNETT, AUDREY FRANCES, psychologist; b. Bremerton, Wash., Oct. 25, 1947; d. Louis and Marjorie Velma (Gibson) P.; A.A., Victor Valley Coll., 1967; B.S., U. Utah, 1971, M.S., 1975; Ph.D., Calif. Sch. Profl. Psychology, 1981. Psychologist Utah State Dept. Health, Salt Lake City, 1970-71, 73-74; proctor supr. testing div. counseling psychol. services U. Utah, Salt Lake City, 1974; psychometrist Wash. U. Med. Sch. Psychology Lab. St. Louis Children's Hosp., 1975-76; psychol. examiner spl. sch. dist., St. Louis County, 1976-78; psychol. asst. clin. psychologist Fresno Community Hosp. (Calif.); Membership drive com. psychol. asst. Fresno Psychol. Group. Mental Health Assn. Fresno, 1982. Mem. Am. Psychol. Assn., Calif. State Psychol. Assn., San Joaquin Psychol. Assn. (membership chmn. 1983), Fresno Jr. League (edn. chmn. 1982-83). Episcopalian. Office: 5100 N 6th St Suite 135 Fresno CA 93710

PURDIE, ROGER KENT, fire chief; b. San Diego, July 31, 1942; s. Alden A. and Elsie (Brizendine) P.; children—Roger, Christa. A.S., Chaffey Coll., 1968. B.S., Calif. State U., 1980; With City of Rialto (Calif.) Fire Dept., 1964—, battalion chief, 1974-77, fire chief, 1977—; fire sci. instr. San Bernardino Valley Coll., 1973-77, Crafton Hills Coll., 1981—. Field service rep. Rialto Salvation Army; mem. Am. Heart Assn. Bd. dirs., pres. Lung Assn. San Bernardino County, Inyo-Mono Counties. Mem. Rialto Firemen's Benefit Assn., Rialto Fire Police Protective League (past pres.), San Bernardino County Tng. Officers Assn. (v.p. San Bernardino County), San Bernardino County Fire Prevention Officers, Calif. Fire Chief-Fire Prevention Officers Assn., San Bernardino County Fire Chiefs Assn. (pres. 1979), Calif. Fire Chief Assn. (rescue and paramedic com. chmn. 1978, 79), Citrus Belt Fire Chief Assn. (pres. 1980). Republican. Lutheran (v.p. council). Home: PO Box 1104 Rialto CA 92376 Office: 131 S Willow Ave Rialto CA 92376

PURDOM, PAUL WAKEFIELD, public relations company executive; b. Williams, Ariz., Nov. 9, 1928; s. Paul and Mary L. (Doran) Wallace; B.A. in Polit. Sci., U. Calif., Berkeley, 1950; m. Elizabeth Jane Chapman, Apr. 9, 1955; children—Edward, Charles. Founder, pres. Paul Purdom & Co., San Francisco, 1960—. Served with U.S. Army, 1954-56. Mem. Public Relations Soc. Am., Nat. Investors Relations Inst. Club: Bankers. Office: 1845 Magnolia Ave Burlingame CA 94010

PURI, ANIL K., economist, educator, consultant; b. India, Dec 12, 1948; s. Gopal and Ram (Piari) P.; m. Sharon L. Puri, March 18, 1978. M.A. in Econs., U. Minn., also Ph.D. Asst. prof. Calif. State U.-Fullerton, 1977-81, assoc. prof., 1981—. Mem. Am. Econ. Assn., Western Econ. Assn., Statis Assn. Contbr. articles and book revs. to profl. jours. Office: Dept Econs Calif State U Fullerton CA 92634

PURI, YESH PAUL, agronomist; b. Sangrur, Punjab, India, Sept. 20, 1929; came to U.S., 1955, naturalized, 1965; s. Jawahar Lal and Satya Davi (Kaushal) P.; B.Sc., Punjab U., India, 1949; B.Sc., Benares Hindu U., India, 1954; M.S., Oreg. State U., 1958, Ph.D., 1960; m. Catherine M. Stewart, Apr. 3, 1971; children—Leila D., Jay Paul, Paul Nathan. Jr. agronomist Oreg. State U., Corvallis, 1959-61; asst. prof. U. Bagdad (Iraq), 1961; sr. research technician Imperial Valley, Field Sta., U. Calif.-El Centro, 1962-65, supt. specialist Tulelake Field Sta., 1965-83; specialist, supt. research facilities, dept. agronomy U. Calif.-Davis, 1983—. Cert. profl. agronomist; cert. profl. crop scientist. Mem. Am. Soc. Agronomy, Crop Sci. Soc. Am., Soil Sci. Soc. Am., Western Soc. Crop Sci., Council Agrl. Sci. and Tech., Am. Genetic Assn., N.Y. Acad. Sci., AAAS. Clubs: Kiwanis, Rotary. Home: 1720 Arlington Dr Klamath Falls OR 97601 Office: Hunt Hall Dept Agronomy and Range Science U Calif Davis CA 95616

PURNELL, CAROLYN JEAN, lawyer; b. Memphis, Aug. 16, 1939; d. James Clarence and Mardine (Taylor) P.; B.A., U. Wash., Seattle, 1961, J.D., 1971; divorced; children—Mardine Garbutt, Monica Garbutt. Admitted to Wash. bar, 1972; dep. pros. atty. King County, Seattle, 1972-74; legal counsel to mayor of Seattle, 1974-77; atty. Weyerhaeuser Co., Tacoma, Wash., 1977—, dir. purchasing, 1981-82, dir. corporate materials mgmt., 1982—; legal officer Weyerhaeuser Found.; del. Am. Assembly Law, Palo Alto, Calif., 1981. Vice pres. Housing Devel. Corp., 1977—. Mem. Wash. Bar Assn., Seattle-King County Bar Assn., Delta Sigma Theta. Office: Weyerhaeuser Co Tacoma WA 98477

PURSEL, HAROLD MAX, mining engr.; b. Fruita, Colo., Sept. 15, 1921; s. Harold Maurice and Viola Pearl (Wagner) P.; B.S. in Civil Engring., U. Wyo., 1950; m. Virginia Anna Brady, May 6, 1950; children—Harold Max, Leo William, Dawn Allen, Helen Virginia, Viola Ruth. Asst. univ. architect U. Wyo., 1948-50; with Sharrock & Pursel, Contractors, 1951-55; owner Max Pursel, Earthwork Constrn., 1955-59; project engr. Farson (Wyo.) Irrigation Project, 1960-61; owner Wyo. Builders Service, Casper, 1962-66; head dept. home improvement Gamble Stores, Rawlins, Wyo., 1967; resident work instr. Casper (Wyo.) Job Corps Conservation Center, 1968; P.M. coordinator Lucky Mc Uranium Mine, Riverton, Wyo., 1969-80. Served with U.S. Army, 1942-45. Mem. Nat. Rifle Assn., Mensa. Clubs: Eagles, Masons, Shriners. Exptl. research with log, timber and frame constrn. in conjunction with residential applications. Home: PO Box 572 Riverton WY 82501

PURSER, LEE WASHBURN, psychologist, educator, author; b. N.Y.C., Dec. 7, 1945; d. Carr Robinson and Grace (Pelzer) P.; m. Russell Lawrence Nichols, Oct. 1976 (div.); 1 dau., Sky. Student Vassar Coll., 1963-66, Inst. Des Professeurs de Francais a L'Etrange, 1967; B.A., U. N.C., 1969; Ph.D. in Philosophy, Internat. Coll., 1978. Asst. editor Macmillan Pubs., N.Y.C., 1968-69; editor Med. Aspects of Human Sexuality, N.Y.C., 1969-70; chmn. French dept., student counselor Barlow Sch., Amenia, N.Y., 1970-72; cons., tchr. San Diego Inst. Transactional Analysis, 1978-82; pvt. practice psychology, La Jolla, Calif., 1974—; nat. seminar leader, 1974-83; bus. cons.; media personality; guest lectr. Brandeis U., U. San Diego, Internat. Coll., others; speaker to Beyond Divorce, Denver, 1974-77, Women in Mgmt., 1983, others. Mastery Course scholar, 1982; named Outstanding Young Woman of Am. Fuller & Dees, Washington, 1975. Mem. Internat. Transactional Analysis Assn. (clin. mem.). Clubs: Winners' Circle Breakfast, City (San Diego). Author: Help Yourself, 1982; producer mini series People Talk for Sta. FM 89, San Diego, 1983; leader seminar series Good Life, San Diego, 1981-83. Office: PO Box 3252 La Jolla CA 92038

PURSINGER, MARVIN GAVIN, technology consultant; b. Terre Haute, Ind., Dec. 23, 1923; s. Walter E. and Nellie V. (Coleman) Persinger; A.B., Bowling Green State U., 1946, M.A., 1947; Ph.D., U. So. Calif., 1961; m. Elizabeth Jane Pursinger, Dec. 24, 1950; children—Gavin, Karen, Kristen, Beth, Bradley, Susannah. Prof., Calif. State U., Northridge, 1957-60; staff Surgeon Gen. of U.S., Washington, 1961-62; prof. U. Minn., Mpls., 1962-63; pres. Gavin Internat. Corp., Morris, Minn., 1963-68, T. L. Lords Internat. Corp., Mpls., 1968-70; pres., owner Pursinger Co., Portland, 1970-82; strategic planning cons., Portland, 1982—. Mem. White House Conf. on Edn., 1957. Served to capt. USMC, 1942-51. Ford Found. fellow, 1956-57. Republican. Episcopalian. Office: PO Box 8459 Portland OR 97207

PURVES, CECIL JOHN, city official; b. Edmonton, Alta., Can., Oct. 18, 1933; s. Cecil S. and Elsie Jean (Meakins) P.; m. Clare Heller, Dec. 19, 1956; children—Cindy, Corinne, Caroline, Catherine. Student pub. schs. Former gen. mgr. Apex Auto Upholstery Co., Edmonton, Alta.; alderman City of Edmonton, 1966-74, mayor, 1977—. Bishop Mormon Ch., 1974-77; mem. Edmonton Exhbn. Assn.; bd. mgmt. St. Joseph's Hosp.; pres. Fedn. Can. Municipalities, 1979-80. Mem. Edmonton C. of C., Can. Progress Club. Office: Office Mayor City Hall Edmonton AB T5J 2R7 Canada

PUSKAR, JAMES STEPHEN, fin. exec.; b. Pitts., July 17, 1946; s. Andrew Bernard and Irene (Bobick) P. B.B.A., Duquesne U., 1968. Contract analyst U.S. Defense Contract Audit Agy., Palo Alto, Calif., 1970-73; systems analyst, ops. auditor Rucker Co., Oakland, Calif., 1973-79; sr. systems analyst Hills Bros. Coffee, Inc., San Francisco, 1979-80; mgr. fin. systems Kaiser Cement Co., Oakland, 1980—. Docent Canton-Stanford House Preservation Assn.; mem. Oakland Mus. Assn. Served to lt. USN supply corps, 1968-70. Mem. Assn. Systems Mgmt., Assn. Human Resource Profls. Clubs: Oakland Athletic, Lake Merritt Rowing (Pres.) (Oakland). Home: 758 Mandana Blvd Oakland CA 94610 Office: 300 Lakeside Dr Oakland CA 94612

PUTNAM, PALMER COSSLETT, energy cons.; b. Canandaigua, N.Y., July 13, 1900; s. George Haven and Emily James (Smith) P.; B.Sc., M.I.T., 1923, M.Sc., 1924; postgrad. Yale U., 1926; m. Elizabeth Boyce Henley, July 13, 1962. Engring. geologist L'Union Miniére du Haut Katanga, Belgian Congo, 1925-26; pres. G.P. Putnam's Sons, Pubs., N.Y.C., 1928-32; project mgr. Smith-Putnam Wind Turbine, Rutland, Vt., 1935-39; spl. asst. dir. O.S.R.D., Office of Pres., Washington, 1940-46; cons. AEC, 1948-50; asst. dir. Psychol. Strategy Bd., Office of Pres., Washington, 1950-52; pres. Avicola de Cuernavaca, Cuernavaca, Mex., 1952-62; sr. cons. on large-scale wind turbines, 1980—. Served with Royal Flying Corps, World War I, to equivalent rank of maj. gen., World War II. Recipient Medal for Merit, Pres. U.S., 1945; spl. award NASA/DOE, 1981; award created in his honor ASME, 1982. Mem. Sigma Xi. Author: Power From The Wind, 1948, Energy in the Future, 1952; Chemical Relationships in the Mineral Kingdom, 1928; developed strategies, tactics and mil. weapons, including the DUKW and the WEASEL. Home and office: 5210 Capistrano Atascadero CA 93422

PUZON, JULY DIAZ, retail exec.; b. Manila, Philippines, July 17, 1947; s. Galacio Perez and Rosario Banzon (Diaz) P.; came to U.S., 1977; B.S., U. of East, Manila, 1967; M. Bus. Mgmt., Asian Inst. Mgmt., Makati, 1972; m. Virgina Nery, Feb. 14, 1970; children—Geraldine, JanPaul. Revenue acct. Japan Air Lines Ltd., Manila, 1967-70; prof. mgmt. acctg. MaryKnoll Coll., Quezon City, Philippines, 1970-72; asst. v.p. sales Philippine Carpets Co., Makati, Philippines, 1972-76; v.p. sales Terry York Group of Car Cos., Encino, Calif., 1981—; owner, pres. Old Fashioned Cookie Co., Santa Monica, Calif. Pres., Philippine Am. Community San Fernando Valley, 1980-81. Mem. Soc. Sales Execs. Am., Confedn. Philippine U.S. Orgns. Home: 17454 Collins St Encino CA 91316 Office: 16747 Ventura Blvd Encino CA 91436

PYBRUM, STEVEN MARK, tax accountant; b. Santa Cruz, Calif., Mar. 12, 1951; B.S. in Acctg., Calif. Poly. U., 1973; M.B.A. in Taxation, Golden Gate U., 1978. Cost acct. William Wrigley Jr. Co., Santa Cruz, 1974-75; with Ackerman Strauhal & Co., C.P.A.s, Santa Cruz, 1975-77; controller J.J. Crosetti Cos., Watsonville, Calif., 1977-78; owner, founder Steven M. Pybrum & Assocs., San Luis Obispo, Calif., 1978—, Exec. Mgmt. Services, San Luis Obispo, 1978—; profl. lectr. taxation; prof. taxation Calif. Poly. U., 1978—. C.P.A., Calif. Mem. Western Growers Assn., Calif. Bar Assn., Calif. Cattleman's Assn., Soc. Calif. Accts., Am. Inst. C.P.A.s. Clubs: Elks, Controllers Roundtable of San Luis Obispo County (founder). Syndicated columnist, Agribus. Tax Tips, 1980—, Business Cents, 1980—; producer, host radio show Tax Tips, 1980—. Address: PO Box 4360 San Luis Obispo CA 93403

PYE, DAVID THOMAS, life sciences company executive; b. Darby, Pa., June 12, 1942; s. David and Grace Marie (Dale) P. B.S., Widener U., 1964. C.P.A., Pa., Calif. Tax cons. Price Waterhouse & Co., Phila., 1964-70; dir. taxes AID, Inc., Phila., 1970-75; dir. tax adminstrn. Syntex Corp., Palo Alto, Calif., 1975—. Mem. Am. Inst. C.P.A.s, Calif. C.P.A. Soc., Pa. Inst. C.P.A.s, Tax Execs. Inst. Home: 9 Crags Ct San Francisco CA 94131 Office: Syntex Corp 3401 Hillview Ave Palo Alto CA 94304

PYE, DORI, association executive; b. Atlanta; d. Irving Joseph and Grayce Edna (Dobbins) Nowak; div.; children—Joshua, Kenneth. M.A., Columbia U. Sch. Journalism, 1948; postgrad. advanced acad. program mgmt. Notre Dame U., 1978, program exec. mgmt. UCLA, 1981. Cert. C. of C. exec., Calif. Motion picture, TV actress, 1950-60; pres., chief exec. officer Western Los Angeles Regional C. of C., 1969—; apptd. mem. Calif. Conf. Small Bus., 1980, 82; founder-organizer, chmn. bd. Westwood Thrift & Loan Assn., 1982—. Bd. dirs. Century City Hosp., 1982; mem. adv. bd. Western Los Angeles YWCA. Recipient Outstanding Community Service award Western Los Angeles Lions Club, 1975, Westwood Village Kiwanis Club, 1975. Mem. Nat. Assn. C. of C. Execs. (bd. dirs. 1978-81), So. Calif. Assn. C. of C. Execs. (pres. 1977), Am. Assn. C. of C. Execs., Calif. Assn. C. of C. Execs., Westwood-Brentwood Symphony Assn. Club: Regency. Columnist Westbrook/Brentwood Ind., Los Angeles News West. Office: 10880 Wilshire Blvd Suite 1103 Los Angeles CA 90024

PYKE, RONALD, mathematics educator; b. Hamilton, Ont., Can., Nov. 24, 1931; s. Harold and Grace Carter (Digby) P.; m. Gladys Mary Davey, Dec. 19, 1953; children—Darlene, Brian, Ronald, Gordon. B.A. (hon.), McMaster U., 1953; M.S. U. Wash., 1955, Ph.D., 1956. Asst. prof. Stanford (Calif.) U., 1956-58, prof. Columbia U., N.Y.C., 1958-60; prof. math. U. Wash., Seattle, 1960—; vis. prof. U. Cambridge (Eng.), 1964-65, Imperial Coll., London, 1970-71; cons. Boeing Co. NSF grantee, 1961—. Fellow Internat. Statis. Inst., Am. Statis. Assn., Inst. Math. Stats.; mem. Am. Math. Soc., Math. Assn. Am. Fundamentalist. Editor Ann Prob, 1972-75; contbr. articles to profl. jours. Office: Dept Math U Wash Seattle WA 98195

PYLE, DAVID BURTON, govt. ofcl.; b. San Francisco, July 26, 1942; s. Bennie B. and Gertrude E.Pyle; A.A., Napa Valley Coll., 1964; B.S., So. Ill. U., 1975; postgrad. Golden Gate U., 1980—; m. Linda Marie Bright, June 7, 1969; children—Dion, Daniel. Civilian naval architecture technician U.S. Navy Mare Island Shipyard, Vallejo, Calif., 1967-73; real property specialist USAF, Travis AFB, Calif., 1973-76; realty specialist GSA, San Francisco, 1976; property specialist Forest Service, U.S. Dept. Agr., San Francisco, 1976-80; mgmt. analyst U.S. Navy, Mare Island Naval Shipyard, Vallejo, Calif., 1980—; cons. local 11 Internat. Fedn. Profl. Tech. Engrs. Union, 1980-81. Mem. Napa Valley Comprehensive Health Planning Council, 1974-76; mem. O'Brian Park Planning Com., City of Napa, 1981-82. Served with USAF, 1963-64. Recipient various govt. service awards. Mem. Am. Soc. Public Adminstrs., Am. Mgmt. Assn. Clubs: Internat. Bonsia, Golden State Bonsia, N. Bay Bonsia, Napa Valley Bonsia. Home: 748 Jacob Ct Napa CA 94558

PYUN, JUNGJO, nuclear scientist; b. Seoul, Korea, Oct. 12, 1942; s. Muhrim and Bocksoon (Ham) P.; came to U.S., 1968, naturalized, 1976; B.S., Seoul Nat. U., 1965; M.S., SUNY, 1970; Ph.D., U. Mich., 1973; m. Saelan Park, Dec. 18, 1971; children—Jennifer Insook, Evelyn Inhae. Prin. investigator Combustion Engring., Inc., Windsor, Conn., 1973-76; assoc. nuclear engr. Brookhaven Nat. Lab., Upton, N.Y., 1976-77; staff mem. Los Alamos Sci. Lab., 1977—. Recipient Disting. Service award Brookhaven Nat. Lab., 1977. Mem. Am. Nuclear Soc., Sigma Xi. Home: 232 Canada Way White Rock NM 87544 Office: PO Box 1663 MS625 X7 Los Alamos Scientific Lab Los Alamos NM 87545

QUAAS, LEROY M., city engineer; b. Maple Plain, Minn., Feb. 24, 1942; s. Carl F. and Dorothy (Leiter) Q.; m. Patricia De La Cruz, Apr. 10, 1965; children—Thad, Theron, Tara, Travis; B.C.E., Valparaiso U., 1964; student U. So. Calif., 1965 66, Ariz. State U., 1975. Registered Profl. Engr., Calif., Ariz. Asst. bridge engr., resident engr. State of Calif., 1964-70; asst. county engr. Imperial County (Calif.), 1970-72; asst. city engr. City of Tempe (Ariz.), 1972-78, city engr., 1978—. Mem. Am. Pub. Works Assn., Tau Beta Pi. Office: 31 E 5th St Tempe AZ 85281

QUACKENBUSH, JUSTIN LOWE, U.S. dist. judge; b. Spokane, Wash., Oct. 3, 1929; s. Carl Clifford and Marian Huldah (Lowe) Q.; B.A., U. Idaho, 1951; LL.B., Gonzaga U., Spokane, 1957; m. Ollie M. Packenham, Sept. 12, 1952; children—Karl Justin, Kathleen Marie, Robert Craig. Admitted to Wash. bar, 1957; dep. pros. atty. Spokane County, 1957-59; partner firm Quackenbush & Dean, Spokane, 1959-80; U.S. dist. judge Eastern Dist. Wash., Spokane, 1980—; part-time instr. Gonzaga U. Law Sch., 1960-67. Chmn. Spokane County Planning Commn., 1969-73. Served with USN, 1951-54. Mem. Am. Bar Assn., Wash. Bar Assn., Spokane County Bar Assn. (trustee 1976-78), Internat. Footprint Assn. (nat. pres. 1967), Spokane C. of C. (trustee, exec. com. 1978-79). Episcopalian. Clubs: Spokane Country, Shriners. Home: 1103 Westover Rd Spokane WA 99218 Office: PO Box 1432 Spokane WA 99201

QUACKENBUSH, RITA JEAN, software and service firm exec.; b. Edinburg, Tex., Feb. 13, 1947; d. Chalmers Stanford and Deliah May (Mugrdechian) Stromberg; student New Coll., 1964-66, U. Minn., 1966, N.Y. Inst. Fin., 1968; m. Charles W. Quackenbush II, Dec. 16, 1978; 1 dau., Carrey Colleen. Profl. water skier Tommy Bartlett Water Ski Shows, Wis. Dells, 1964; ins. cons. Met. Life Ins. Co., Winter Park, Fla., 1969-70; sales rep. Norrell Temporary Services, Orlando, Fla., 1970-71; br. mgr. Staff Builders Internat., Miami and Orlando, 1971-74; sales rep. Bishop's Office Equipment Co., Orlando, 1975, Ivan Allen Co., Atlanta, 1976; area mgr. CDI Temporary Services, Atlanta, 1976-79, cons., 1979; cons. P.Q.A. Sykes Inc., Charlotte, N.C., 1979; with CDI Corp., Santa Clara, Calif., 1979; owner, founder, pres. Q Services/Q Tech., Santa Clara, 1979—; pres., chmn. bd. 2 Bit, 1983—. Participant Am. Electronics Assn. capitol caucus to present legislators with various needs, 1981; mem. United Republican Fin. Com., 1980—; assoc. mem. Calif. Rep. Central Com., 1981-82; mem. fin. com. Ed Zschau for Congress, 1981-82. Address: PO Box 4773 Santa Clara CA 95054

QUALE, MARK CHRISTOPHER, sales and marketing executive; b. Boston, Oct. 14, 1948; s. Andrew Christopher and Luella (Meland) Q.; m. Linda Johnson, Aug. 29, 1969; 1 son, Matthew. B.A., Princeton U., 1970; M.B.A., Harvard U., 1975. Asst. product mgr. Vick Internat., N.Y.C., 1970-72, sr. product mgr., 1972; asst. product mgr. Armour-Dial, Phoenix, 1975-76, product mgr., 1976-78, group product mgr., 1978-81; v.p. sales and mktg. Thompson Industries, Phoenix, 1982—; asst. prof. Ariz. State U., 1977-78. Dist. coordinator Sahauro Conservation Dist., 1981—. Clubs: Ariz. Biltmore (Phoenix); Harvard Bus. Sch., Princeton U. Home: 9444 N 38th St Phoenix AZ 85028 Office: 2501 E Magnolia Phoenix AZ 85036

QUALMANN, WALTER J., lighting designer; b. Detroit, July 15, 1949; s. Walter C. and Arleta L. (Kirlin) Q.; grad. Sch. Mktg./Bus., Fla. State U., 1971; m. Patricia C. Robble, Mar. 25, 1973; children—Zachary Ian, Naomi Joy. Owner, mgr. The Light Source, mfr.'s rep. for lighting products, Portland, Oreg., 1973-78; pres., lighting designer Illume, Inc., Gainesville, Fla., 1979—; condr. street lighting workshops for Oreg. Gov.'s Energy Office, Oreg. Atty. Gen.'s Office. Mem. Illuminating Engring. Soc., Internat. Assn. Lighting Designers, Am. Power Boat Assn. Contbr. articles on lighting to engring. publs. Office: Illume Lighting Design 213 SW Ash St Suite 209 Portland OR 97204

QUALTERS, Q. MICHAEL, advertising executive; b. Los Angeles, Aug. 19, 1936; s. Michael J. and Cecelia E. (Mathera) Q.; m. Evelyn M. Kuhenhust, June 1, 1958; children—Kathy, Kimary. A.A., Pasadena City Coll., 1965; B. Profl. Arts, ArtCenter Coll. of Design, 1963. With Carson/Roberts Advt. Agy., Los Angeles, 1965-66; packaging art dir. Dart Industries, Los Angeles, 1966-69; dir. sales promotion Max Factor & Co., Los Angeles, 1969-75; v.p., creative dir. Crocker Nat. Bank, San Francisco, 1975—. Served with USN. Club: San Francisco Advt. Lutheran.

QUAMME, HARVEY ALLEN, agricultural research scientist; b. Central Butte, Sask., Can., Apr. 23, 1940; s. Arthur Henry and Renee Rebecca Q.; m. Sonya Lynn McKenzie, Feb. 18, 1963; children—Darcie Lynn, Heather Ann. B.S. in Agr., U. Sask., Saskatoon, 1962, M.Sc., 1964; Ph.D., U. Minn., 1981. With Dept. Agr. Govt. of Can., 1963—, pomologist, Harrow, Ont., 1971-81, Summerland Research Sta., 1981—. Recipient Joseph Harvey Gourley award for research in pomology, 1973; Carroll R. Miller award, 1979. Mem. Am. Soc. Hort. Sci., Can. Soc. Hort. Sci., Am. Pomological Soc., Can. Inst. Agrologists. Mem. United Ch. Can. Contbr. numerous articles in field to profl. jours. Office: Research Station Summerland BC V0H 1Z0 Canada

QUAN, VICTOR HUNG-FONG, mech. engr.; b. Kow Kong, China, May 24, 1938; came to U.S., 1951; s. Thomas Lun-Hong and Joanne Bo-Yook (Gee) Q.; B.S., U. So. Calif., 1960, Ph.D. (Garrett Corp. fellow, Univ. fellow, NASA trainee), 1964; M.S., U. Calif., Berkeley, 1961; m. Vera Lee-Chen Liu, Mar. 14, 1970; children—Lisa, Janet. Staff engr. TRW Systems, Redondo Beach, Calif., 1962-71; prin. engr. KVB Inc., Tustin, Calif., 1971-75; mech. engr. Brookhaven Nat. Lab., Upton, N.Y., 1975-77; mem. tech. staff Rocketdyne div. Rockwell Internat., Canoga Park, Calif., 1977—; lectr. U. So. Calif., 1963-65. Recipient Achievement award Machinery mag., 1959; Innovation award NASA, 1969; lic. profl. engr., Calif. Mem. AIAA, ASME, Combustion Inst., Sigma Xi, Phi Eta Sigma, Pi Tau Sigma, Tau Beta Pi. Contbr. numerous articles to profl. jours. Home: 3203 N Allegheny Ct Westlake Village CA 91361 Office: 6633 Canoga Ave Canoga Park CA 91304

QUANDT, ELIZABETH, artist, educator; b. Oxford, Eng., July 13, 1922; d. James Herbert and Gwendoline (Hillman) Gunn; m. Roger T. Barr; children by previous marriage—William, Antoinette, Ward, Kristina, Jonathan. B.F.A., San Francisco Art Inst., M.F.A., 1969. Tchr. art Ursuline High Sch., Santa Rosa, 1962-64; instr. art Santa Rosa Jr. Coll., 1970—. One-woman show: Bruton Gallery, Somerset, Eng., 1982; group shows: San Francisco Mus. Art, 1971, 77, U. Mass., Amherst, 1974, Van Straaten Gallery, Chgo., 1975, Nat. Acad. Design, N.Y.C., 1976, 77, Mus. Contemporary Crafts, N.Y.C., 1978, Phila. Print Club, 1980, Pratt Inst., N.Y.C., 1980, others; works represented in permanent collections: N.Y. Pub. Library, Achenbach Found. for Graphic Arts, San Francisco, Library of Congress, Washington, Stanford U. Art Mus., City of San Francisco, Bibliotheque Nationale, Paris, France, City of Santa Rosa, others; illustrator work of Francis Ponge. Mem. Calif. Soc. Printmakers, World Print Council. Democrat. Home: 920 McDonald Ave Santa Rosa CA 95404 Office: Santa Rosa Jr Coll 1501 Mendocino Ave Santa Rosa CA 95401

QUARLES, JACK LYLE, rehab. orgn. exec.; b. Kansas City, Mo., June 21, 1916; s. William Montgomery and Octavia Leroy (Fowler) Q.; B.A., Armstrong Coll., 1950, M.B.A., 1952, m. Rosemary King, Sept. 5, 1937, children—Rosalene, Brian. Controller, Pacific Chem. Co., Berkeley, 1950-58, Rand-Fletcher Constrn. Co., 1958-63; with Goodwill Industries Am., 1963-78, exec., Santa Cruz, Calif., 1976-78; auditor County of Santa Cruz (Calif.), 1978-81; bus. adminstr. Redwood Christian Park, Boulder Creek, Calif., 1981—; cons. sheltered workshops. Served with USNR, 1943-46. Named Exec. of Year in Sacramento, 1974. Mem. Nat. Tehab. Assn., Soc. Calif. Accountants, Execs. Dirs. Goodwill Industries, Calif. Rehab. Assn., Sierra Club. Republican. Baptist. Clubs: Sertoma (Service award Tenn. 1968), Rotary, Lions, Civitan. Office: 1500 Two Bar Rd Boulder Creek CA 95006

QUEEN, PHILLIS AULD, real estate broker; b. Pasadena, Calif., Dec. 23, 1928; d. Samuel Hayward and Wilda Ballou (Jackson) Auld; grad. Pasadena Coll., 1946. U. Calif., Berkeley, 1947; m. James Michael Queen, May 11, 1947 (div. 1974); children—James Michael, John Gregory. Salesperson, Alps Realty, Huntington Station, N.Y., 1968-69; broker Babicz Realty, East Islip, N.Y., 1969-72, Quality Real Estate, East Islip, 1972-73; partner-owner Sure Enterprises, Inc., Fire House Five Car Wash; broker Carll S. Burr Real Estate, Sayville, N.Y., 1979—; antique dealer DBA Antiques Internat., doing bus. with Christies, Park Bernet Galleries, 1977-79; interior designer Jeri's Interiors, Chico, Calif., 1980—. Pres., PTA, 1958. Mem. L.I. Bd. Realtors (asso.). Episcopal Protestant. Club: Ind. Order Foresters.

QUICK, ELLEN KAUFMAN, clinical psychologist; b. Pitts., Dec. 11, 1949; d. A. Daniel and Mildred Helen (Colker) Kaufman; m. R. Frank Quick, Jr., Aug. 15, 1971. B.A. in Psychology (Durant Scholar), Wellesley Coll., 1970; M.S. in Clin. Psychology, U. Pitts., 1972, Ph.D., 1974. Lic. psychologist, Pa., 1976, Calif., 1980. Intern, U. Rochester Med. Center, 1973-74; psychologist Mayview State Hosp., Bridgeville Pa., 1974-76; base service unit dir. SW Pitts. Mental Health/Mental Retardation Center, 1976-77; clin. psychologist Staunton Clinic, Sewickley Valley Hosp. Pa., 1977-80, Sharp Rehab. Center, San Diego, 1980-81; clin. psychologist, program developer Adult Direct Services Kaiser-Permanente, San Diego, 1981—; pvt. practice clin. psychology, Pitts., 1977-80, San Diego, 1980—. Mem. Torrey Pines Docent Soc., Del Mar, Calif., 1981—. Mem. Am. Psychol. Assn., Nat. Register Health Service Providers in Psychology, Phi Beta Kappa. Contbr. articles in field to profl. jours. Office: 328 Maple St San Diego CA 92103

QUIGLEY, JOHN MICHAEL, economist; b. N.Y.C., Feb. 12, 1942; s. Joseph J. and Jane M. (Duffy) Q.; m. Mary E. Curran, Jan. 21, 1978; children—Johanna, Benjamin, Oliver Sam. Part-time lectr. George Washington U., Washington, 1967-68; lectr. U.S. Dept. Agr. Grad. Sch., 1966-68; teaching fellow in econs. Harvard U., 1969-71; asst. prof. econs. Yale U., 1972-74, assoc. prof., 1974-80; vis. prof. econs. and stats. U. Gothenberg (Sweden), 1978; prof. pub. policy U. Calif.-Berkeley, 1979—, prof. econs., 1981—; econometrician U.S. Air Force, Pentagon, 1965-68; research assoc. Nat. Bur. Econ. Research, N.Y.C., 1968-78; cons. in field. Served to capt. with USAF, 1960-68. Decorated Air Force Commendation medal. Fulbright scholar, 1964-65; NSF fellow, 1968-69; Woodrow Wilson fellow, 1968-71; Harvard U. fellow, 1969-71; NDEA fellow, 1969-71; Thord-Gray fellow, Am. Scandinavian Found., 1971-72; Fgn. Area fellow, 1971-72; Outstanding Dissertation award, Regional Sci. Assn., 1972. Contbr. articles to profl. jours.; editorial bd. Land Econs., 1974-81, Regional Sci. & Urban Econs., 1978—, Jour. Urban Econs., 1978—, Council on Pub. Policy and Mgmt., 1979—; gen. editor pub. fin. JAI Press, 1980—. Address: Univ Calif 2607 Hearst Berkeley CA 94720

QUIMBY, GEORGE IRVING, anthropologist, educator, mus. dir.; b. Grand Rapids, Mich., May 4, 1913; s. George Irving and Ethelwyn (Sweet) Q.; B.A., U. Mich., 1936, M.A., 1937, grad. fellow, 1937-38; postgrad. U. Chgo., 1938-39; m. Helen M. Ziehm, Oct. 13, 1940; children—Sedna H., G. Edward, John E., Robert W. State supr. Fed. Archaeol. Project in La., 1939-41; dir. Muskegon (Mich.) Mus., 1941-42; asst. curator N.Am. archaeology and ethnology Field Mus. Natural History, 1942-43, curator exhibits, anthropology, 1943-54, curator N.Am. archeology and ethnology, 1954-65, research asso. in N.Am. archaeology and ethnology, 1965—; curator anthropology Thomas Burke Meml. Wash. State Mus., prof. anthropology U. Wash., 1965—, mus. dir., 1968—; lectr. U. Chgo., 1947-65, Northwestern U., 1949-53; Fulbright vis. prof. U. Oslo, Norway, 1952; archaeol. expdns. and field work, Mich., 1935, 37, 42, 56-63. Wis., 1936, Hudson's Bay, 1939, La., 1940-41, N.Mex., 1947, Lake Superior, 1956-61. Fellow AAAS, Am. Anthrop. Assn.; mem. Soc. Am. Archaeology (pres. 1958), Am. Soc. Ethnohistory, Wis. Archeol. Soc., Soc. Historical Archeology (council 1971-74, 75-78), Assn. Sci. Mus. Dirs. (pres. 1973—), Norwegian Totemic Soc., Arctic Inst. N.Am., Am. Assn. Mus. (council 1971-74), Sigma Xi, Phi Sigma, Chi Gamma Phi, Zeta Psi. Author: The Goodall Focus, 1941, Aleutian Islanders, 1944; (with J. A. Ford) The Tchefuncte Culture, an Early Occupation of the Lower Mississippi Valley, 1945; (with P. S. Martin, D. Collier) Indians Before Columbus, 1947; Indian Life in the Upper Great Lakes, 1960; Indian Culture and European Grade Goods, 1966. Editor: (with others) 1914 documentary film In the Land of the War Canoes, 1973; co-editor Maritime Adaptations of The Pacific, 1975; (with Bill Holm) Edward S. Curtis in the Land of the War Canoes, 1980. Contbr. articles to profl. jours. Home: 6001 52d Ave NE Seattle WA 98115 Office: Thomas Burke Meml Wash State Museum U Wash Seattle WA 98195*

QUIMBY, SALLY CROSBY, nurse adminstr.; b. Washington, Nov. 19, 1946; d. Lowell Horace and Millicent Winn (Childs) Quimby. B.S. in Nursing, La. State U., 1975; M.S. in Nursing, Med. Coll. of Ga., 1980; R.N., Calif., La. Asst. head nurse E. Jefferson Hosp., Metairie, La., 1976; head CCU St. Joseph Hosp., Savannah, Ga., 1977-78, asst. supr. CCU, 1978-80, supr., 1980; head nurse ICU El Camino Hosp., Mountain View, Calif., 1980—; planner CCU for computer monitoring system, 1978-79; instr. CPR, 1978-80. Task force organizer Save Our Satellite, 1977. Named Outstanding Graduating Nursing Student, La. State U., 1975. Mem. Am. Nurses Assn., Calif. Nurses Assn. (dir. region 10 1981-82), Am. Assn. Critical Care Nurses, Calif. Soc. Nursing Service Adminstrs., Sigma Theta Tau. Democrat. Methodist. Home: 1315 Miravalle Los Altos CA 94022 Office: 2500 Grant Rd Mountain View CA 94042

QUINN, A. THOMAS, news service executive; b. Los Angeles, Mar. 14, 1944, s. Joseph Martin and Grace (Cooper) Q., B.S., Northwestern U., 1965. Reporter, newswriter ABC Radio, Chgo., Los Angeles, 1965-66; pres. Radio News West, Inc., Los Angeles, 1966-70; dep. sec. state Calif., Sacramento, 1971-73; mgr. campaign Jerry Brown for Gov., 1974; chmn. Calif. Air Resources Bd., Sacramento, 1975-80; chmn. City News Service Los Angeles, 1980—; dir. Parallel Communications; chmn. KBCR, Inc.; dir. presdl. primaries Jerry Brown, 1976; mem. Gov.'s Cabinet, Sacramento, 1975-80. Pres., Dec. Group, Lake Tahoe, Calif., 1982—. Democrat. Office: 304 S Broadway Suite 520 Los Angeles CA 90013

QUINN, DAVID HAROLD, JR., airline pilot; b. Evanston, Ill., July 1, 1931; s. David Harold and Hope Duncan (Naylor) Q.; A.B., Stanford U., 1953; m. Jo Ann Elizabeth Gregory, Aug. 20, 1955; children—Laura Elizabeth (Mrs. B. Bueermann), Paul Gregory. With Pan Am. World Airways, 1956—, 1st officer, 1966-76, capt. Boeing 707, 1976-77, check capt. 707, 1977-80, capt. Boeing 747, San Francisco, 1980—. Served to lt. col. U.S. Air Force Res. Decorated Air Force Commendation medal. Mem. Air Line Pilots Assn., Res. Officers Assn., Sigma Nu. Republican. Mormon. Clubs: Olympic (San Francisco); Outrigger Canoe (Honolulu). Home: 112 Lyford Dr Tiburon CA 94920 Office: San Francisco Internat Airport San Francisco CA

QUINN, FRANCIS A., bishop; b. Los Angeles, Sept. 11, 1921; ed. St. Joseph's Coll., Mountain View, Calif., St. Patrick's Sem., Menlo Park, Calif., Cath. U., Washington, U. Calif., Berkeley. Ordained priest, Roman Cath. Ch., 1946; ordained titular bishop of Numana and aux. bishop of San Francisco, 1978; apptd. bishop of Sacramento, 1979. Office: 1119 K St PO Box 1706 Sacramento CA 95808*

QUINN, JAMES ROWLAND, management consultant; b. Los Angeles, June 18, 1923; s. Harry Borden and Margaret (McCool) Q.; m. Betty June Elliott, Aug. 21, 1945; children—Karen Bess, Annette, Nancy Capra, Janet, Mary Ann Archuleta, James Edward. B.S., U. Denver, 1947, M.A., 1959, Ph.D., 1983. Exec. dir. Denver and Colo. Life Underwriters, 1957-60; dir. planning and research Jefferson County (Colo.) pub. schs., 1960-66; adminstrv. asst. HEW Region VIII, 1966-67; v.p. Fedn. Rocky Mountain States, 1967-69; exec. dir. Colo. Urban Drainage Dist., 1969-73; self-employed mgmt. cons., Denver, 1973-78; regional mgr. EDS Corp., Golden, Colo., 1978—. Chmn. Jefferson county bldg. adv. com., 1957, 58; mem. organizing com. Wheat Ridge-Lakewood, (Colo.), 1965. Served to 2d lt. AUS, 1945-47, 1st lt. Colo. N.G., 1947-49, capt. AUSR, 1949-55. Recipient Rock Doctor press award Colo. Sch. Mines, 1957. Mem. Am. Soc. Profl. Cons., Am. Assn. Cons. and Devel., Colo. Schoolmasters, Phi Delta Kappa. Club: Rolling Hills Country. Editor econ. sect. Colorado Golden West, 1959; contbr. articles to tourist mags. and profl. jours. Home: 10785 W 35th Pl Wheat Ridge CO 80033 Office: 1320 Simms Suite 1 Golden CO 80401

QUINN, JOHN R., archbishop; b. Riverside, Calif., Mar. 28, 1929; s. Ralph J. and Elizabeth (Carroll) Q.; Ph.B., Gregorian U., Rome, 1950, S.T.B., 1952, S.T.L., 1954. Ordained priest Roman Cath. Ch., 1953; asst. priest St. George Ch., Ontario, Cal., 1954-55; prof. theology Immaculate Heart Sem., San Diego, 1955-62, vice rector, 1960-62; rector St. Francis Coll. Sem., El Cajon, Calif., 1962-64, Immaculate Heart Sem., 1964-68; aux. bishop, vicar gen., San Diego, 1967-72; bishop of Oklahoma City, 1972-73, archbishop, 1973-77; archbishop of San Francisco, 1977—; provost U. San Diego, 1968-72. Mem. Cath. Theol. Soc. Am., Canon Law Soc. Am., Nat. Conf. Cath. Bishops (pres. 1977-80), Am. Cath. Hist. Soc. Address: 445 Church St San Francisco CA 94114*

QUINN, JOSEPH R., justice Colorado Supreme Court; b. Elizabeth, N.J., Nov. 18, 1932; s. Patrick F. and Claire E. Q.; A.B., St. Peter's Coll., 1957; LL.B., Rutgers U., 1961; m. Olga B. Taylor, July 28, 1962; children—Theresa, Lisa, Rita, James, Maria. Bar: Colo. 1962. Judge, Colo. Dist. Ct., from 1973; now justice Colo. Supreme Ct., Denver; instr. U. Denver Coll. Law, 1977. Served with USMC, 1951-53. Mem. ABA, Colo. Bar Assn., Denver Bar Assn. Contbr. articles to profl. jours. Office: Judicial Bldg 2 E 14th Ave Denver CO 80203*

QUINN, TOM, communications executive; b. Los Angeles, Mar. 14, 1944; s. Joseph Martin and Grace (Cooper) Q.; m. Amy Lynn Friedman, Nov. 24, 1982; children—Douglas, Lori. B.S., Northwestern U., 1965. Reporter, newswriter ABC Radio, Chgo. and Los Angeles, 1965; reporter, producer Sta. KXTV, Sacramento, 1966; day editor City News Service, Los Angeles, 1966-68, chmn., 1980—; pres. Radio News West, Los Angeles, 1968-70; campaign mgr. Jerry Brown for Sec. State, Los Angeles, 1970; dep. sec. state Calif., Sacramento, 1971-74; campaign mgr. Brown for Gov., Los Angeles, 1974; sec. Calif. Dept. Environ. Affairs, Sacramento, 1975-79; chmn. bd. Sta. KBCR, Inc.; pres. Dec. Group; pres. K-HITS Radio; dir. Parallel Communications Co. Recipient Headliner of Yr. award Greater Los Angeles Press Club, 1978; Environ. Protection award Calif. Trial Lawyers Assn., 1979. Democrat. Office: 304 S Broadway Suite 520 Los Angeles CA 90013

QUINNELLY, JAMES LESLIE, quality engineer; b. Meridian, Miss., June 16, 1920; s. James Basil and Maude (Stroud) Q.; m. Dolores Cecelia Brinkmann, May 16, 1946; children—Jane Quinnelly Orbison, Fred.

B.S., Miss. State U., 1941; M.S. in Engring., U. Mich., 1948. Registered profl. engr., Calif. Commd. 2d. lt., U.S. Army, 1942, advanced through grades to lt. col., 1959; with Office Research and Devel., Army Gen. Staff, 1963-66; ret., 1966; ops. analyst Aerojet-Gen. Corp., Downey, Calif., 1966-70; cons. mil. research and devel., Anaheim, Calif., 1970-74; quality engr. Bechtel Power Corp., Los Angeles, 1974—. Decorated Legion of Merit. Mem. Soc. Automotive Engrs., Nat. Soc. Profl. Engrs., ASME, Am. Nuclear Soc., Am. Soc. for Quality Control. Club: Masons. Home: 319 W Alberta St Anaheim CA 92805 Office: Bechtel Power Corp PO Box 60860 Los Angeles CA 90060

QUINTANA, JESSIE MARIE, registered nurse; b. San Felipe Angeles Zacatecas, Mexico, Nov. 5, 1943; came to U.S., 1946, naturalized, 1963; d. Thomas and Antonia (Salas) Aquilera; cert. practical nursing Pueblo Jr. Coll., 1963; A.A. in Nursing, So. Colo. State Coll., 1974; B.S.N., U. So. Colo., 1977; m. Robert James Quintana, Oct. 30, 1965; children—Christine Marie, Robert James. Staff nurse St. Mary Corwin, Pueblo, Colo., 1971-78, head nurse, 1978-79; instr. practical nursing Pueblo Vocat. Community Coll., 1979—; clin. instr. U. So. Colo., 1976-78. Mem. Am. Nurses Assn., Colo. Nurses Assn. Democrat. Roman Catholic. Club: So. Colo. Runners. Address: 900 W Orman Ave Pueblo CO 81004

QUIROLLO, EDNA STARR, medical technologist; b. Ft. Benning, Ga., Aug. 9, 1946; d. Ernest Edward and Dorothy Lula (Pittman) Starr; m. Lawrence Forrest Quirollo, Aug. 9, 1968; 1 son, Troy Alan. Student, U. Hawaii, 1965; B.S. in Med. Tech., Incarnate Word Coll., San Antonio, 1968. Lic. med. technologist, Calif. Lab. asst. Santa Rose Med. Ctr., San Antonio, 1967-68; staff technologist Gen. Hosp., Eureka, Calif., 1969—, evening supr., 1977-81, asst. dir. lab. services, 1981—. Mem. Am. Soc. Clin. Pathologists (lic. 1968), Am. Soc. Med. Technologists, Calif. Assn. Med. Lab. Technologists. Democrat. Methodist. Home: 1745 East Ave Eureka CA 95501

QUIST, PAUL STEVEN, horticulturist; b. Salt Lake City, Aug. 14, 1933; s. Niels Joseph and Sigrid Julia (Gustavsson) Q.; student U. Utah, 1950-51, Utah State U., 1951-52, 56-57; B.S., Brigham Young U., 1960, postgrad., 1961-62; m. Yvonne Arvilla Wahlen, Apr. 1, 1931; children—Susan Yvonne, Kerstin Lavern, Paul Jospeh, Elizabeth Sigrid, Robert Wahlen, Katherne Emma. Vice pres. Forest Hills Nursery Inc., Salt Lake City, 1956-79, pres., 1979—; pres. Forest Hills Turf Farm Inc., Riverton, Utah, 1973—; hort. judge Utah State Fair, 1972-74; cons. adv. hort. dept. Utah State U. Judge, Days of 47 Parade, Salt Lake City, 1971-72; Explorer Scout leader Salt Lake council Boy Scouts Am., 1961-63, 77-78. Cert. nurseryman, Utah. Mem. Utah Assn. Nurserymen (pres. 1962), Am. Assn. Nurserymen (gov. for Utah 1957-58, 76—), Am. Sod Producers Assn. Republican. Mormon. Club: Rotary (dir. club 1973-74). Home: 3814 W 13800 S Riverton UT 84065 Office: 4001 W 13400 S Riverton UT 84065

QUITTEL, FRANCES RITA, venture capitalist; b. Mt. Vernon, N.Y., Apr. 17, 1945; d. Morton and Pauline Q.; B.A., Hunter Coll., 1965; M.A., U. Ill., 1966; M.Phil., Yale U., 1969; cert. in internat. mktg., 1978. Instr., Spanish, Mills Coll., Oakland, Calif., 1970-73; dir. Latino mktg. Shaklee Corp., Emeryville, Calif., 1973-75; dir. Bus. Women's Week, Emeryville, 1977—; sr. cons. Corp. Services Group, 1981-83; pvt. practice mgmt. cons., 1977—. Mem. community adv. bd. KQED; bd. dirs. Tech. Tng. for Tchrs. Project. Mem. Women in Computing (chmn. spl. events). San Francisco Yale U. Alumni Assn. (bd. govs.). Office: 500 Sutter St Suite 901 San Francisco CA 94102

QUITUGUA, JUSTO SONGAO, educator; b. Rota Mariana Islands, Feb. 19, 1950; s. Grabiel Rios Quituqua and Vicenta De Leon Guerrero Songao; student Community Coll. of Micronesia, 1971-72; B.A., magna cum laude, U. Guam, 1976; M.Ed., U. Hawaii, Manoa, 1980; m. Judymae Mendiola Damian, July 25, 1978. Elementary sch. tchr., Saipan, 1969-71; sci. tchr. Hopwood Jr. High Sch., Saipan, 1972-74; math. tchr., 1976; remedial reading tchr., Santa Rita, Guam, 1980-81, lang. arts and math. resource tchr., 1981—; U.S. history mentor adult basic edn., 1976; social studies mentor Marianas Sr. High Sch., Saipan, 1980; asst. prof. U. Guam off-campus summer extension, 1980; condr. parent workshop in reading. East-West Center grantee, 1978-80; certified tchr., Guam. Mem. Internat Reading Assn., Guam Dist.-Wide Title I Parent Adv. Council, Guam Fedn. Teachers, U. Guam Scholastic Honorary Soc. Roman Catholic. Home: PO Box 10055 Sinajana GU 96910 Office: CL Taitano Elementary School Sinajana GU 96910

QURAISHI, MARGHOOB AHMED, mgmt. cons.; b. Jaipur, India, July 15, 1931; s. Nazeer Ahmed and Khudaija (Begum) Q.; B.Com., U. Karachi, 1955; postgrad. in Bus. Mgmt., McGill U., 1958; M.B.A., Stanford U., 1960; m. Iffat B., June 15, 1961; children—Asifa, Haleema, Amira, Kaleem. Auditor, Webb & Webb, C.P.A.s, San Francisco, 1961-63; controller, asst. to pres. CAPCOM, Oakland, Calif., 1963-64; v.p. CPM Internat., Cupertino, Calif., 1964-66; pres. Associated Mgmt. Systems, Inc., Palo Alto, Calif., 1966—; guest speaker civic orgns. and univs. in U.S., Can., Eng., S.Africa; pres., chief exec. officer Image Systems, Inc., Culver City, Calif., 1981—. Mem. planning com. Hoover Sch.; mem. site disposition com. Palo Alto Sch. Dist. Asia Found. scholar, 1959-60. Mem. Inst. Mgmt. Cons.'s.

RAAB, FREDRIK HOLGER, science writer, editor, private investigator; b. Burlington, Vt., Mar. 29, 1940; s. Wilhelm and Olga Elizabeth (Palmborg) R. B.A., U. Vt., 1962; student Princeton U., 1962-64. Phys. chemist, AeroChem Research Labs, Inc., Princeton, N.J., 1964-71; editor W. H. Freeman and Co., San Francisco, 1973-78; freelance tech. translator, San Francisco, 1971-73; freelance pvt. investigator, San Francisco, San Francisco, 1972—; freelance sci. writer, 1978—; cons. Lawrence Berkeley Lab. Bd. dirs. Friends of Mill Valley Library, Marin United Taxpayers Assn. Recipient Distinction award No. Calif. Soc. Tech. Communication, 1982; Achievement award, Internat. Soc. Tech. Communication, 1982. Fellow AIAA; AAAS, mem. Am. Chem. Soc., Am. Phys. Soc., Council Biology Editors, No. Calif., Sci. Writers Assn., Sigma Xi. Club: Sierra, San Francisco. Home and office: 14 Brooke Circle Mill Valley CA 94941

RABAGO, STEVEN ROBERT, investment banker; b. Los Angeles, Sept. 11, 1955; B.S., Calif. State U., Long Beach, 1978. Bus. devel./comml. lending officer Bank Am., Long Beach/Orange County, Calif., 1974-79; asst. v.p., sr. loan officer Am. City Bank, Costa Mesa, Calif., 1979-82; v.p. Pacific Nat. Bank, Newport Beach, Calif., 1982-83; pres., chief exec. officer Nat. Corp. Fin., Inc.; exec. Blood-Stock Agy., Inc., Laguna Niguel, Calif., 1983, Signal Hill (Calif.) Co., 1983; cons. Am. Fabricators, Glendale, Calif., 1979—, Barto Oil Co., Costa Mesa, Calif., 1980—, Psi Tech, Irvine, Calif., 1983. Chmn. celebrity roast Hoag Meml. Hosp. Presbyn., 1980—. Mem. Newport Harbor Area C. of C. (chmn. small bus. com. 1979-81, bd. dirs. 1979—), Kappa Sigma. Home: 357 Promontory Dr W Newport Beach CA 92660 Office: 1400 Quail St Suite 175 Newport Beach CA 92660

RABBANI, BOUCHAIB, educator; b. Kenitra, Morocco, Mar. 12, 1944; s. Ahmed and Itto (Bent Mohamed) R.; B.S., Universite Mohamed V, (Morocco), 1969; M.A. in Physics, Calif. State U., Long Beach, 1971, Ph.D. in Radiol. Scis., U. Calif., Irvine, 1976. Tchr. physics and chemistry Lycee Abdelmalek-as-Saadi, Kenitra, 1964-69; teaching asst. Calif. State U., Long Beach, 1970-71; research asst. U. Calif., Irvine, 1971-76, clin. instr., 1976-78, asst. prof., 1978—, radiation physicist, 1976—; cons. in field. Cert. radiol. physics Am. Bd. Radiology. Mem. Am. Assn. Physicists in Medicine, Am. Public Health Assn., AAAS. Contbr. articles to profl. jours. Office: U Calif Irvine Med Center 101 City Dr S Orange CA 92668

RABENOLD, KATHRYN TUTTLE, missionary, pianist, public accountant; b. Burlington Boro, Pa., Apr. 21, 1907; d. Clay F. and Mae Elsie (Beach) Tuttle; student public schs., Sayre, Pa., courses Internat. Accts. Soc., Pa. State U.; m. LeRoy M. Cook, Dec. 26, 1929 (dec. June 1953); children—Doris Anne (Mrs. Thomas P. Knapp), William LeRoy; m. 2d, Clarence R. Rabenold, Sept. 19, 1959 (dec. June 1971). Bookkeeper, Merritt Plumbing Shop, Waverly, N.Y., 1923-26; clk.-stenographer Ingersoll-Rand Co., Athens, Pa., 1926-29; payroll clk. Perfection Laundry, Sayre, 1930; partner with husband in acctg. office, Athens, 1937-53; owner, operator Cook Acctg. Service, Athens, 1953-69; public acct. with H. E. Weller, Athens, 1969-77; pianist with Patsy Prescott, gospel singer, 1977—. Telephone counselor Trinity Broadcasting Assn., Phoenix; mem. Glendale Women Aglow Fellowship, Enrolled to practice before IRS. Mem. Nat., Pa. socs. public accts., Nat. Soc. Tax Cons. (life). Mem. Assembly of God Ch. Home: 6500 W Glendale Ave Sp 49 Glendale AZ 85301

RABINOWITZ, JAY A., justice Alaska Supreme Court; b. Phila., Feb. 25, 1927; s. Milton and Rose (Rittenberg) R.; B.A., Syracuse U., 1949; LL.B., Harvard U., 1952; m. Anne Marie Nesbit, June 14, 1957; 4 children. Bar: N.Y. 1952, Alaska 1958. Practiced law, N.Y.C., 1952-57; law clk. U.S. Dist. Ct. judge, Fairbanks, Alaska, 1957-58; asst. U.S. atty., Fairbanks, 1958-59; dep. atty. gen., chief civil div. State of Alaska, 1959-60; judge Superior Ct., Alaska, 1960-65; justice Alaska Supreme Ct., 1965-73, chief justice, 1973-83, justice, 1983—; lectr. U. Alaska, 1965—. Served with U.S. Army, 1945-46. Mem. N.Y., Alaska bar assns. Club: Harvard (N.Y.C.). Office: Supreme Ct Alaska Juneau AK 99801*

RABORG, FREDERICK ASHTON, JR., journalist, author; b. Richmond, Va., Apr. 10, 1934; s. Frederick Ashton and Marguerette (Smith) R.; A.A., Bakersfield Coll., 1970; B.A. in English Lit., Calif. State Coll., Bakersfield, 1973, postgrad., 1973-75; m. Eileen Mary Bradshaw, Oct. 19, 1957; children—Frederick Ashton, Donald Wayne, Marguerette Jeannette, Wayne Patrick, Jayne Alyson, Kevin Douglas. Freelance writer, 1956—; columnist Bakersfield News Bull., 1972-74; editor Oildale News, 1968-70; drama and book reviewer Bakersfield Californian, 1974—; editor Amelia, lit. mag., 1983—; instr. journalism Bakersfield Coll., 1970-75; nat. judge Nat. League Am. Pen Women poetry contest, Phoenix br.; nat. judge Kans. Poetry Contest; sponsor Richard Hugo award for Poetry Soc. Tex. ann. contest; sponsor for Amelia awards in Poetry, 1983—; local judge Kern County Drama Festival, Kern County Shakespearean Festival; mem. PACT local drama prodn. co.; active Bakersfield Community Theatre. Writer med. needs progress reports for Kern Health Manpower Consortium; instr. creative writing for out-patients Kern View Hosp. Served to sgt. maj., F.A., U.S. Army, 1952-55. Decorated Am. Spirit Honor medal for leadership Citizens Com. of Army, Navy and Air Force, 1953, certificate of achievement Maj. Gen. Leslie D. Carter, comdr. 25th Inf. Div. in Korea, 1954; recipient 1st prizes Class Internat. Intercollegiate Creative Writing Competition, 1969-70, Guideposts mag. Writing Workshop Competition, 1973, Writers Digest Non-Fiction award, 1972, East Side Herald award in poetry New York Poetry Forum, 1974, Netherlands-U.S.A. 200 Found. award, 1982, various other poetry awards. Mem. Authors League Am., Authors Guild, Dramatists Guild, Poetry Soc. Am., Acad. Am. Poets, Modern Poetry Assn., Internat. Platform Assn. Democrat. Roman Catholic. Author 17 novels; poetry vol. Why Should the Devil Have All the Good Tunes, 1972; (plays) The Other Side of the Island, 1972; Making It!, 1973; Ramon and the Artist, 1974. Contbr. short stories, articles and poetry to mags. and ednl. jours. Home: 329 E St Bakersfield CA 93304 Office: PO Box 2385 Bakersfield CA 93303

RACHEL, STEVEN LOEDER, oil service company official, carpenter; b. Hobbs, N. Mex., Oct. 22, 1954; s. John Everet and Florence Carol (Williams) R. A.A., N.Mex. Jr. Coll., 1974; B.B.A. in Acctg., N. Tex. State U., 1976. Saleman, Zales, Hobbs, N.Mex., 1976; gen. acct. Texaco, Hobbs, Midland, Tex., 1976-79; asst. mgr. fin acctg. Llano, Hobbs, 1979-81; free-lance carpenter, Glendive, Mont. and Hobbs, N. Mex., 1981-82; office mgr., acct. D.C. Well Service, Denver City, Tex., 1982—. Scoutmaster Conquistador council Boy Scouts. Am., Hobbs, 1977-78. Republican. Methodist. Home: 121 Robert Ln Hobbs NM 88240 Office: D C Well Service Box 1449 Denver City TX 79323

RACHFORD, JAMES MICHAEL, optometrist; b. Long Beach, Calif., Nov. 19, 1944; s. Godfrey Avon and Laura Virginia (Zinn) R.; m. Hilda Maria Bruse, Aug. 28, 1964; 1 son, Michael James. A.A., San Bernardino Valley Coll., 1973; B.S., U. Calif.-Riverside, 1975, M.S., 1976; O.D., So. Calif. Coll. Optometry, 1980. Private practice optometry, Yucca Valley, Calif., 1980—. Served with U.S. Army, 1962-71. Mem. Calif. Optometric Assn., Am. Optometric Assn. Club: Lions.

RACINA, THOM (RAUCINA, THOMAS FRANK), writer, editor; b. Kenosha, Wis., June 4, 1946; s. Frank G. and Esther May (Benko) Raucina; B.F.A., Goodman Sch. Drama, Art Inst., Chgo., 1970, M.F.A. in Theatre Arts and Directing with honors, 1971. TV writer Hanna-Barbera Co., Hollywood, Calif., 1973-74, MTM Enterprises, Inc., Hollywood, 1974-76, ABC-TV, Hollywood, 1978-80; assoc. head writer Gen. Hosp. daytime series ABC-TV,1981—; novels: Lifeguard, 1976, The Great Los Angeles Blizzard, 1977, Quincy, M.E., 2 vols., 1977, Kojak in San Francisco, 1977, FM, 1978, Sweet Revenge, 1978, The Gannon Girls, 1979, Nine to Five, 1980, Tomcat, 1981; Secret Sex: Male Erotic Fantasies (as Tom Anicar), 1976; Magda (as Lisa Wells), 1981; ghost writer non-fiction: The Happy Hustler (Grant Tracy Saxon), 1976, Marilyn Chambers: My Story (Marilyn Chambers), 1976, Making Love (Grant Tracy Saxon), 1977, Xaviera Meets Marilyn Chambers (Xaviera Hollander and Marilyn Chambers), 1977; musical plays: A Midsummer Night's Dream, music and lyrics, 1968, Allison Wonderland, music and lyrics, 1970, The Marvelous Misadventure of Sherlock Holmes, book, music and lyrics, 1971; TV scripts: Sleeping Over segment of Family, ABC, 1978, Russian Pianist segment of Family, ABC, 1979, Child of the Owl, NBC After-sch. Spl., 1979; contbr. articles to Playboy, Cosmopolitan, Penthouse, Oui, Los Angeles, Gentlemen's Quar., Westways; West Coast editor Grosset & Dunlap, Inc., N.Y.C., 1978—; theatre dir.; pianist; organist; composer. U.S. Nat. Student Assn. grantee, 1965. Mem. Authors Guild Am., Writers Guild Am.—West. Democrat. Roman Catholic. Home and Office: 3449 Waverly Dr Los Angeles CA 90027

RADA, ALEXANDER, university official; b. Kvasy, Czechoslovakia, Mar. 28, 1923; s. Frantisek and Anna (Tonnkova) R.; came to U.S., 1954, naturalized, 1959; M.S., U. Tech. Coll. of Prague, 1948; postgrad. Va. Poly. Inst., 1956-59, St. Clara U., 1966-67; Ed.D., U. Pacific, 1975; m. Ingeborg Solveig Blakstad, Aug. 8, 1953; children—Alexander Sverre, Frank Thore, David Harald. Head prodn. planning dept. Mine & Iron Corp., Kolin, Czechoslovakia, 1941-42; mgr. experimenting and testing dept. Avia Aircraft, Prague, 1943-45; sec.-gen. Central Bldg. Office, Prague, 1948; head metal courses dept. Internat. Tech. Sch. of UN, Grafenaschau, W.Ger., 1949-50; works mgr. Igref A/S, Oslo, 1950-51; cons. engr., chief sect. machines Steel Products Ltd., Oslo, 1951-54; chief engr., plant supr. Nelson J. Pepin & Co., Lowell, Mass., 1954-55; sr. project engr., mfg. supt. Celanese Corp. Am., Narrows, Va., 1955-60; mgr. mfg., facilities and maint. FMC Corp., San Jose, Calif., 1960-62; mgr. adminstrn. Sylvania Electronic Systems, Santa Cruz, Calif., 1962-72; asst. to pres., devel. officer Napa (Calif.) Coll., 1972—; instr. indsl. mgmt. Cabrillo Coll., Aptos, Calif., 1963-72; mgmt. and engring. cons., 1972—. Pres. ARC, Santa Cruz, 1965-72, bd. dirs., pres., Napa, 1977—; mem. Nat. Def. Exec. Res., U.S. Dept. Commerce, Washington, 1966—, chmn. No. Calif. region 9, 1981—; mem. President's Export Council-DEC, San Francisco, 1982—. Recipient Meritorious Service citation ARC, 1972; registered profl. engr., Calif. Mem. Nat., Calif. socs. profl. engrs., Am. Def. Preparedness Assn., Assn. Calif. Community Coll. Adminstrs., Phi Delta Kappa. Editor-in-chief Our Youth, 1945-48; co-editor (with P. Boulden) Innovative Management Concepts, 1967. Home: 1019 Ross Circle Napa CA 94558 Office: 2277 Napa Vallejo Hwy Napa CA 94558

RADCLIFFE, DOROTHY JANE, educational consultant; b. Freeport, Ill., July 6, 1942; d. Elmer Buchen and Glenaire Alphia (Hilton) R.; m. William Justus Pritchard, Feb. 21, 1967 (div.). B.S., Bob Jones U., 1964; M.S., Calif. State U.-Hayward, 1969; Ed.D., U. San Francisco, 1982. Cert. elem. and secondary tchr., Calif. Elem. sch. tchr., counselor San Leandro (Calif.) Unified Sch. Dist., 1964-72; secondary counselor Fremont (Calif.) Unified Sch. Dist., 1972-79; ednl. adminstr., cons. Santa Clara County Office of Edn., San Jose, Calif., 1979-82. Recipient Outstanding Ednl. Leadership award Fremont Counseling and Guidance Assn., 1980; U. of Calif.-Berkeley grantee, 1963. Mem. Calif. Counseling and Guidance Assn., Assn. Calif. Sch. Adminstrs., Assn. Supervision and Curriculum Devel. Club: Toastmasters. Author: Learning Mastery Teaching, 1979.

RADCLIFFE, EVELYN W., journalist; b. Independence, Kans.; d. Thomas Milton and Kathleen (Williams) Winder; m. William Hickman Radcliffe, Jr., June 7, 1944; 1 son, William Hickman, III. Student U. Calif.-Berkeley. Asst. head foll. Shop John Wanamaker, Phila., 1939; personnel interviewer Q.M.C., U.S. Army, Oakland, Calif., 1942-45; employee counselor U.S. Naval Air Sta., Alameda, Calif., 1945-46; fashion editor, columnist, fashion photographer, Palo Alto, Calif., 1956-69; feature writer Christian Sci. Monitor, San Francisco, from 1958; book reviewer Peninsula Newspapers, Inc., Palo Alto, 1968—; fashion tour Condr. to Haute Couture, Paris, Rome, London, Madrid, 1964. Mem. Nat. League Am. Pen Women, Calif. Writers Club, Author's League, Author's Guild, Fashion Group, Inc., Twelve Acres Aux. (founder, 1st pres.). Club: Palo Alto Hills Golf and Country (Palo Alto). Author: The Lifetime Cookbook, 1979. Editor: Ghirardelli Chocolate Cookbook, 1977. Address: 2930 Alexis Dr Palo Alto CA 94304

RADER, DOUGLAS ALLAN, accountant; b. Coronado, Calif., Nov. 6, 1957; s. Edwin Alfred and Verna Pauline (Bosworth) R.; m. Karen Cecilia Daniel, Jan. 3, 1982. A.A., Scottsdale Coll., 1977; B.S. in Acctg., Ariz. State U., 1979; postgrad. Golden Gate U., Phoenix, 1982. C.P.A., Ariz. Acct. Sentry Ins., Scottsdale, Ariz., 1979-80; staff acct. Mackey, Shaphren & Tull, Phoenix, 1980-82; ptnr. Montgomery & Rader, C.P.A.s, Phoenix, 1982—. Mem. Am. Inst. C.P.A.s, Ariz. Soc. C.P.A.s, Nat. Assn. Accts. (v.p. Scottsdale Area chpt. 1983—, active Big Brother Program 1982—). Home: 8528 N 52d Ave Glendale AZ 85302 Office: 2226 W Northern Ave Suite C-109 Phoenix AZ 85021

RADER, MILDRED BELLE, auto co. exec.; b. Burkburnette, Tex., July 20, 1921; d. Charles Edward and Ida Esther Mills; student public schs., Lancaster, Calif.; m. Charles Pearce Rader, Nov. 30, 1941; children—Charles David, Mark Randall. Bus. mgr. Pioneer Lincoln Mercury, Lancaster, Calif., 1957—, sec. to corp., 1968—. Recipient Bus. Mgmt. award Ford Motor Co., 1958-79. Mem. Credit Women Internat. (pres. 1969, Cert. of Achievement 1958-80), Motor Car Dealers Assn., Bus. Mgrs. Assn. Democrat. Home: 2333 W Ave K Lancaster CA 93534 Office: 45005 N Sierra Hwy Lancaster CA 93534

RADER, RALPH WILSON, educator; b. Muskegon, Mich., May 18, 1930; s. Ralph McCoy and Nelle Emily (Fargo) R.; B.S., Purdue U., 1952; Ph.D., Ind. U., 1958; m. June Willadean Warring, Sept. 3, 1950; children—Lois Jean, Eric Conrad, Michael William, Nancy Anne, Emily Rose. Instr. dept. English, U. Calif., Berkeley, 1956-58, asst. prof., 1958-63, asso. prof., 1963-67, prof., 1967—, chmn. dept., 1976-80; F.I. Carpenter vis. prof. English, U. Chgo., 1970; dir. seminar Nat. Endowment for Humanities, summer 1975, 83; editorial com. U. Calif. Press, 1963-72, co-chmn., 1968-72; mem. exec. com. Assn. Depts. English, 1978-80. Am. Council Learned Socs. grantee, 1959; Guggenheim fellow, 1972-73; recipient Disting. Teaching award U. Calif., Berkeley, 1975-76. Mem. MLA, Phi Beta Kappa. Democrat. Author: Tennyson's Maud; The Biographical Genesis, 1963, reprinted, 1978: The Biographical Genesis, 1963. Co-author: Essays in Eighteenth Century Biography, 1968; New Approaches to Eighteenth Century Literature, 1974. Editor: (with Sheldon Sacks) Essays: An Analytic Reader, 1964; adv. bd. Yale edit. Private Papers of James Boswell; editorial bd. Critical Inquiry; The 18th Century: Theory and Interpretation; Prose Studies. Home: 465 Vassar Ave Berkeley CA 94708

RADFORD, LINDA ROBERTSON, management consultant, research scientist; b. Winnipeg, Manitoba, Canada, Nov. 6, 1944; d. William Robertson and Edith Aileen (Wheatley) R.; 1 son, Drew. B.A. in English, Seattle Pacific U., 1969; M. Ed. in Counseling Psychology, U. Wash., 1972, Ph.D. in Counseling Psychology, 1980. Cons. Bremerton Public Sch./Seattle Pub. Schs., Wash., 1972-73, 77; Clin. fellow and adminstrv. intern fellow Highline-West Seattle Mental Health Center, Wash., 1972-74, dir. support services, 1974-75; research asst. fellow U. Wash. Med. Sch. and Battelle Human Affairs Research Centers, Seattle, 1976-80; cons./sr. assoc. Martin Simonds Assos., Inc., Seattle, 1980-82; cons. Kirkland, Wash., 1982—; vis. scientist Battelle Labs., Seattle; mem. Manpower Planning Task Force Nat. Council Community Mental Health Centers, 1972. Mem. Am. Psychol. Assn. Contbr. articles to profl. jours. Office: 12012 101st NE H-1 Kirkland WA 98033 and Battelle 4000 NE 41st Seattle WA 98105

RADIN, JOHN WILLIAM, plant physiologist; b. N.Y.C., Jan. 8, 1944; s. Allan and Magdalene Marie (Lakatos) R.; m. Tari Guckes, Dec. 19, 1965; children—Katharine C., Andrew M. Student Calif. Inst. Tech., 1961-64; B.S. in Chemistry, U. Calif.-Davis, 1965, Ph.D., in Plant Physiology, 1970. Plant physiologist USDA, Western Cotton Research Lab., Phoenix, 1971—; adj. prof. dept. botany-microbiology Ariz. State U., 1978—. Mem. Am. Soc. Agronomy, Am. Soc. Plant Physiologists, Scandinavian Soc. for Plant Physiology, Am. Assn. Advancement Sci. Contbr. numerous papers to Sci. jours. Office: 4135 E Broadway Rd Phoenix AZ 85040

RAE, MATTHEW SANDERSON, JR., lawyer; b. Pitts., Sept. 12, 1922; s. Matthew Sanderson and Olive (Waite) R.; A.B., Duke U., 1946, LL.B., 1947; postgrad. Stanford U., 1951; m. Janet Hettman, May 2, 1953; children—Mary-Anna, Margaret, Janet. Began as asst. to dean Duke Sch. Law, Durham, N.C., 1947-48; bar: Md. 1948, Calif. 1951; assoc. Karl F. Steinmann, Balt., 1948-49, Guthrie, Darling & Shattuck, Los Angeles, 1953-54; nat. field rep. Phi Alpha Delta Frat., Los Angeles, 1949-51; research atty. Calif. Supreme Ct., San Francisco, 1951-52; ptnr. Darling, Hall & Rae and predecessor firms, Los Angeles, 1955—; mem. probate law cons. group. Calif. Bd. Legal Specialization, 1977—. Vice pres. Los Angeles County Republican Assembly, 1959-64; mem. Los Angeles County Rep. Central Com., 1960-64, 77—, vice chmn. 17th Congressional Dist., 1960-62, 28th Congressional Dist., 1962-64; chmn. 27th Senatorial Dist., 1977—; chmn. 46th Assembly District, 1962-64, mem. exec. com., 1977—; mem. Rep. State Central Com. Calif., 1966—, mem. exec. com., 1966-67; pres. Calif. Rep. League, 1966-67; trustee Rep. Assos., 1979—, pres., 1983—. Served to 2d lt., USAAF, World

War II Fellow Am. Coll. Probate Counsel; academician Internat. Acad. Estate and Trust Law (exec. council 1974-78); mem. ABA, Los Angeles County Bar Assn. (chmn. probate and trust law com. 1964-66 chmn. legis. com. 1980-81, 82—, chmn. program com. 1981-82, chmn. mem. retention com. 1982-83, trustee 1983—), South Bay Bar Assn., State Bar Calif. (chmn. state bar jour. com. 1970-71, chmn. probate com. 1974-75, exec. com. estate planning trust probate law sect. 1977-83), Lawyers Club Los Angeles (bd. govs. 1981—, 1st v.p. 1982-83), Am. Legion (comdr. Allied post 1969-70), Legion Lex (dir. 1964—, pres. 1969-71), Los Angeles Com. Fgn. Relations, Air Force Assn., Aircraft Owners and Pilots Assn., Town Hall (gov. 1970-78, pres. 1975), World Affairs Council, Internat. Platform Assn., Phi Beta Kappa, Omicron Delta Kappa, Phi Alpha Delta (supreme justice 1972-74, Disting. Service chpt. 1978), Sigma Nu. Presbyn. Clubs: Stock Exchange, Commonwealth, Rotary, Chancery. Home: 600 John St Manhattan Beach CA 90266 Office: 523 W 6th St Suite 400 Los Angeles CA 90014

RAEBER, JOHN ARTHUR, architect; b. St. Louis, Nov. 24, 1947; s. Arthur William and Marie T.; A.A., Jefferson Coll., Hillsboro, Mo., 1968; A.B., Washington U., 1970, M.Arch., 1973; m. Sandi Lee Hartupee, Aug. 16, 1969. Specifications writer Hellmuth, Obata & Kassabaum, St. Louis, 1973-78, constrn. adminstrn., 1978-79; mgr. specifications and materials research Gensler & Assocs., San Francisco, 1979-80, mgr. tech. services, 1980-82; ind. specifications cons., 1982—; cons. Calif. State Bldg. Standards Commn., 1981. Mem. AIA, Constrn. Specifications Inst., Nat. Council Archtl. Registration Bds., ASTM. Contbg. editor Building Code Bull.; author manual on Calif. archtl. barriers laws. Home and Office: 428 43d Ave San Francisco CA 94121

RAEL, HENRY SYLVESTER, foundation administrator; b. Pueblo, Colo., Oct. 2, 1928; s. Daniel and Grace (Abyeta) R.; A.B., U. So. Colo., 1955; B.A. in Bus Adminstrn., U. Denver, 1957, M.B.A., 1958; m. Helen Warner Loring Brace, June 30, 1956 (dec. Aug. 1980); children—Henry Sylvester, Loring Victoria. Sr. boys counselor Denver Juvenile Hall, 1955-58; adminstrv. asst. to pres. Stanley Aviation Corp., Denver, 1958-61; Titan III budget and fin. control supr. Martin Marietta Corp., Denver, 1961-65; mgmt. adv. services officer U. Colo. Med. Center, Denver, 1965-72; v.p. fin., treas. Loretto Heights Coll., Denver, 1972-73; dir. fin. and adminstrn. Colo. Found. for Med. Care, 1973—; instr. fin. mgmt., mem. fin. com. Am. Assn. Profl. Standards Rev. Orgn., 1980—; speaker systems devel., design assns., univs., 1967-71. Mem. budget lay adv. com. Park Hill Elem. Sch., Denver, 1967-68, chmn., 1968-69; vol. worker Boy and Girl Scouts, 1967-73; bd. dirs. Community Arts Symphony, 1981-83; controller St. John's Episcopal Cathedral, 1982-83; charter mem. Pueblo (Colo.) Coll. Young Democrats, 1954-55; block worker Republican party, Denver, 1965-68, precinct committeeman, 1978—; trustee Van Nattan Scholarship Fund, 1974—; bd. dirs. Vis. Nurse Assn., 1977—, treas., 1982—. Served with USAF, 1947-53. Recipient Disting. Service award Denver Astron. Soc., 1968; Stanley Aviation masters scholar, 1957; Ballard scholar, 1956. Mem. Assn. Systems Mgmt. (pres. 1971-72), Hosp. Systems Mgmt. Soc., Budget Execs Inst. (v.p. chpt. 1964-65, sec. 1963-64), Denver Astron. Soc. (pres. 1965-66), Am. Assn. Founds. for Med. Care (fin. com. 1981-82), Nat. Astronomers Assn. (exec. bd. 1965—). Epsilon Xi, Delta Psi Omega. Episcopalian. Home: 70 S Albion Denver CO 80222

RAETZ, KENNETH CARLTON, advertising executive, marketing consultant; b. Evanston, Ill., Apr. 4, 1922; s. Clarence Edward and Laura Anne (Neugebauer) R.; m. Elizabeth Jane Mackenzie, June 10, 1950; 1 dau., Elizabeth; m. 2d, Patricia Anne Taylor, May 15, 1970; children—Jane, Constance, Lora, Elizabeth. B.A., Northwestern U., Evanston, 1942. Meteorologist, Water Resources Devel. Corp., Denver, 1948-51; public relations chief Irving P. Krick, Palm Springs, Calif., 1951-60; chmn. bd. Raetz & Raetz Advt., Los Angeles, 1960—; tchr. advt. UCLA. Served with USNR, 1942-45. Mem. Am. Meteorol. Soc., Western Advt. Group (chmn.), Calif. State Water Resources Bd. Clubs: Jonathan, Los Angeles; Woodland Hills Country; Elks (Appleton, Wis.). Author: Making It Easy, 1956.

RAFFEL, BURTON NATHAN, English language and classics educator, lawyer; b. N.Y.C., Apr. 27, 1928; married; 4 children. B.A. cum laude, Bklyn. Coll., 1948; M.A., Ohio State U., 1949; J.D., Yale U., 1958. Bar: N.Y. 1960. Grad. teaching asst. English dept. Ohio State U., Columbus, 1948-49, grad. sch. fellow, 1952-53; lectr. English dept. Bklyn. Coll., 1950-51; instr. Ford Found. English Lang. Tchr. Tng. Program, Makassar, Indonesia, 1953-55; assoc. Milbank, Tweed, Hadley & McCloy, N.Y.C., 1958-60; instr. English SUNY-Stony Brook, 1964-65, asst. prof., 1965-66; assoc. prof. English SUNY-Buffalo, 1966-68; vis. prof. English, Haifa (Israel) U., 1968-69, U. Tex.-Austin, 1969-70, prof., 1970-71; dean Ont. Coll. Arts, Toronto, 1971-72; vis. prof. humanities York U., Toronto, 1972-75; vis. prof. English, Emory U., Atlanta, 1974; prof. English, U. Denver, 1975—; freelance screenwriter and editor; lectr. in field. Trustee, founder Theatre in the Street, N.Y.C. Recipient Frances Steloff prize, 1978; Citizens Chair U. Hawaii, 1978-79; Am. Philos. Soc. grantee, 1962-63; Research Found. N.Y. State grantee, 1966-68; NEH grantee, 1976; Nat. Endowment Arts grantee, 1982. Mem. Nat. Humanities Faculty, Order of Coif. Author: (with others) Short Story 3, 1960; The Development of Modern Indonesian Poetry, 1967; Mia Poems, 1968; The Forked Tongue: A Study of the Translation Process, 1971; Introduction to Poetry, 1971; Poems, 1971; Why Re-create?, 1973; Guide to Paperback Translations in the Humanities: A Teacher's Handbook, 1976; Four Humours, 1979; The Legend of Alfred Packer (film), 1979; Robert Lowell, 1981; T.S. Eliot, 1982; Lyrics from the Old English (recording), 1964; translator: Beowulf, 1963; Russian Poetry Under the Tsars, 1971; Lyrics for the Greek, 1978; The Essential Horace, 1983, numerous others; mem. editorial bd. Literature East and West, 1967-70. contbr. articles to profl. jours.; editor Found. News, 1960-63, Denver Quar., 1976-77; adv. editor Tri-Quar., 1974. Home: 765 Harrison St Denver CO 80206 Office: Dept English U Denver Denver CO 80208

RAGAN, RICHARD RYAN, management consultant, author; b. Cleve., Oct. 27, 1936; s. Fred Hathaway and Julia (Ryan) R.; m. Jeanne Remington, Sept. 3, 1958 (div.); children—Timothy Ryan, Corey Christina; m. 2d, Elna Herring, Dec. 28, 1978. B.B.A., U. Hawaii, 1961; M.S., U. Colo., 1963. Cert. coll. instr., Calif. Asst. mgr. Waikikian Hotel, Honolulu, 1958-62; mgr. corp. tng. Wells Fargo Bank, San Francisco, 1963-76; prin. RRR & Assocs., Concord, Calif., 1976—; cons., lectr. Served with USAFR, 1958-64. Mem. Am. Soc. Tng. and Devel. (Torch award 1974), Golden Gate Assocs. Republican. Methodist. Contbr. articles to profl. jours.

RAGGIO, WILLIAM JOHN, lawyer, state senator; b. Reno, Oct. 30, 1926; s. William John and Clara M. (Cardelli) R.; student La. Poly. Inst., 1944-45, U. Okla., 1945-46; B.A., U. Nev., 1948; J.D., U. Cal. at Hastings, 1951; m. Dorothy Brigman, August 15, 1948; children—Leslie Ann, Tracy Lynn, Mark William. Admitted to Nev. bar, 1951, U.S. Supreme Ct. bar, 1959; since practiced in Reno and Las Vegas; asst. dist. atty. Washoe County, Nev., 1952-58, dist. atty., 1958-71; partner firm Wiener, Goldwater, Galatz & Raggio, Ltd., 1971-72, Raggio, Walker & Wooster Reno and Las Vegas, 1974-78, Raggio, Wooster, Clontz & Lindell, 1978—; mem. Nev. Senate, 1973—, minority floor leader, 1977-81, 82—; mem. legis. commn., vice chmn. criminal law and adminstrn. com. Council State Govts., 1972-75. Bd. dirs. Am. Savs. & Loan Assn., 1967-70. Adv. bd. Salvation Army, Reno; mem. Nev. Am. Revolutionary Bicentennial Commn., 1975—; mem. Republican State Central Com. Bd. dirs. YMCA, Reno chpt. NCCJ, Salvation Army; trustee Nat. Dist. Attys. Found. (vice chmn. 1962-65); trustee Community Action Program Washoe County. Republican candidate for U.S. Senate, 1970. Served with USNR, 1944-46; to 2d lt. USMCR, 1946-47. Named Young Man of Yr., Reno-Sparks Jr. C. of C., 1959; recipient Disting. Nevadan award, 1968. Fellow Am. Bd. Criminal Lawyers (v.p. 1978—); mem. ABA (state chmn. jr. bar conf. 1957-60, ho. dels.) Am. Judicature Soc., Navy League, Air Force Assn., Nat. (nat. pres. 1967-68; named Outstanding Prosecutor 1965), Nev. State (sec. 1959, pres. 1960-63) dist. attys. assns., NCCJ (Brotherhood award 1965), Nev. Peace Officers Assn., Internat. Assn. Chiefs Police, Am. Legion, Alpha Tau Omega, Phi Alpha Delta. Republican. Roman Catholic. Elk. Lion. Club: Prospectors. Office: Box 3137 Reno NV 89505

RAGLAND, JACK WHITNEY, artist; b. El Monte, Calif., Feb. 25, 1938; s. Jack Rider and Dorsey (Whitney) R.; B.A., Ariz. State U., 1960, M.A., 1964; postgrad. U. Calif. at Los Angeles, 1961-64; m. Marilee J. Weaver, July 31, 1969; children—Roxanne, Natasha. Grad. asst. tchr. Ariz. State U., 1960-61; grad. teaching asst. UCLA, 1961-64; head art dept. Simpson Coll., Indianola, Iowa, 1964-76; one-man shows Kleine Gallery, Vienna, Austria, Billy Son Gallery, Coralville, Iowa, Tamarack Gallery, Stillwater, Minn., Percival Galleries, Des Moines, Simpson Coll., Art and Design Shop, Bonsall, Calif.; Lakes Art Center, Okaboji, Iowa, Mary Knowles Gallery, LaJolla, Calif.; exhibited in group shows Lyn Kottler Gallery, N.Y.C., Phoenix Art Mus., Tucson Festival Art, Talisman Gallery, Bartlesville, Okla., Exhibiting Artists Fedn., Poultney, Vt., Des Moines Art Center, Mary Knowles Gallery, Poulson Galleries, Pasadena, Calif., Joslyn Mus. Art, Omaha, Haymarket Gallery, Lincoln, Nebr., So. Calif. Exhbn., Del Mar; represented in permanent collections Albertina Museum, Vienna, Kunsthaus, Basel, Switzerland, Los Angeles County Mus., Simpson Coll., Phoenix Art Mus., Ariz. State collection, Graphische Bundes Versuchsanstalt, Vienna, Austria, Bibliothéque National, Paris, also pvt. collections; works include stained glass windows Meth. Ch., Perry, Iowa. Mem. Rainbow Community Plan Com. Recipient grand purchase prize Ariz. Ann. Art Show, 1961; 1st prize Iowa State Fair, 1974, others. Works reproduced Applause mag., 1971, New Woman mag., 1974. Home: 5490 Rainbow Heights Rd Fallbrook CA 92028

RAGLAND, KATHRYN MARIE, dancer, educator; b. Lakewood, Ohio, Nov. 22, 1948; d. Earl Albert and Alice Maxine (Outzs) R.; m. Donald Glen Rubright, Sept. 1, 1973 (div. 1977); m. Jack Victor Rutberg, Mar. 9, 1980; 1 dau., Jessica Erin. A.A., Los Angeles Valley Coll., 1971; B.F.A. cum laude, U. Utah, 1973, M.F.A. in Dance, 1975. With Momentum Dance Co., Los Angeles, 1975-77; dance specialist pub. schs., Los Angeles, 1975-76; instr. Scripps Coll., Claremont, Calif., 1976-77; dir. of dance Cypress (Calif.) Coll., 1978—; choreography work includes Man of La Mancha, 1976-80, Pippia, 1981, Fiddler on the Roof, 1982, Music Man, 1983; mem. arts assistance team of Los Angeles supt. schs. Mem. Calif. Dance Educators Assn. (v.p. 1980-82, legis. rep. 1982—), Calif. Music Educators (legis. com. 1982—), Los Angeles Area Dance Alliance, Faculty Assn. of Community Colls., Calif. Assn. Health, Phys. Edn., Recreation and Dance, AAHPERD, Calif. Ednl. Theatre Assn., ACLU, Calif. Confedn. of Arts. Democrat.

RAGLAND, SAMUEL CONNELLY, industrial engineer; b. Nashville, July 12, 1946; s. Julian Potter and Stella (Thompson) R.; m. Marilyn Margaret Oppelt, July 15, 1967; children—Sherry Anne, David Michael. B.S. in Bus. Adminstrn., Ariz. State U., 1974. Indsl. engr. First Interstate Bank, Phoenix, 1966-76, Beckman Instruments, Scottsdale, Ariz., 1976-78; mgmt. analyst Ariz. Legislative Budget Com., Phoenix, 1978; indsl. engr. mgmt. systems ITT Courier Terminal Systems, Tempe, Ariz., 1978-80; project control adminstr. Gen. Host Corp., Phoenix, 1980-81; sr. cons. Arthur Young & Co., Phoenix, 1981-82; ops. analyst City of Phoenix, 1982—; dir. Mary Moppets of Highland Inc., 1977-81. Mem. Inst. Indsl. Engrs., Assn. Systems Mgmt., Phoenix Philitelic Assn. Contbr. articles to profl. publs. Address: 2801 N 71st St Scottsdale AZ 85257

RAGLIANO, ALDO THOMAS, advertising and public relations executive; b. Tuckahoe, N.Y., Mar. 7, 1925; s. Alfred and Maria Nancy (Morrone) R.; m. Bettie Eleanor Fehrs, June 13, 1948; children—Susan, Betsy, Guy, Barbara, Robert. Student Syracuse U., 1946-49. Sports editor Port Chester (N.Y.) Daily Item, 1943-45; promotion dir. Fawcett Publs., Greenwich, Conn., 1949-54, 57-68, MacFadden Publs., N.Y.C., 1954-57, Dell Pub., N.Y.C., 1968-71; v.p. promotions Bartell Media, N.Y.C., 1971-73; promotion dir. Internat. Circulation Distbrs., N.Y.C., 1973-76, Kable News Co., N.Y.C., 1976-78; v.p. Pubs. Distbg. Corp., N.Y.C., 1978-80; dir. advt. Flynt Distbg. Co. Inc., Los Angeles, 1980-83; pres. PR Plus, 1983—. Served to sgt. USMC, 1942-45. Decorated Purple Heart; recipient Public Relations News Gold Key award, 1971. Republican. Roman Catholic. Home: 145 S Maple Dr Beverly Hills CA 90212

RAHE, TERRANCE MARSHALL, soil scientist, consultant; b. Chappell, Nebr., June 26, 1946; s. Emil Fred and Nell Susan Marshall R.; m. Patricia Ann Sparlin, Sept. 3, 1968; children—Shelly Ann, Nieka Christine. B.S. in Biology, So. Oreg. State Coll., 1968; M.S. in Soils, Oreg. State U., 1978. Registered sanitarian, cert. profl. soil scientist. Supervising sanitarian Columbia County (Oreg.) Health Dept., St. Helens, Oreg., 1971-75; prin., cons. sanitarian and soil scientist Cascade Earth Scis. Ltd., Albany, Oreg., 1975—. Served to 1st lt., U.S. Army, 1969-71. Mem. Am. Soc. Soil Sci., Internat. Soc. Soil Sci., Nat. Environ. Health Assn., Nat. Council Internat. Health. Lutheran. Home: 40544 McDowell Creek Rd Lebanon OR 97355 Office: 3425 Spicer Dr Albany OR 97321

RAHIMTOOLA, SHAHBUDIN HOOSEINALLY, cardiologist, educator; b. Pakistan, Oct. 17, 1931; s. Hooseinally M. and Kulsum R.; came to U.S., 1969; M.B.B.S., U. Karachi (Pakistan), 1954; M.B.B.S., Dow Med. Coll., Karachi, 1954; m. Shameem Virji, July 2, 1966; children—Aly, Nadia, Yasmin. Intern, Civil Hosp. and Jinnah Central Hosp., Karachi, 1954-56; sr. house officer Barrowmore Chest Hosp., Chester, Eng., 1956-57; sr. house officer Whittington Hosp., London, 1958-59, locum med. registrar, 1960; house physician cardiac unit London Chest Hosp., 1959-60; registrar to cardiac unit Wessex Regional Hosp. Bd., Chest Hosp., Southampton, Eng., 1960-63; Fulbright scholar, Mayo fellow in physiology, cardiovascular lab. St. Mary's Hosp., Rochester, Minn., 1963-64; Minn. Heart Assn. research fellow, research asst. cardiac lab. Mayo Clinic and Mayo Grad. Sch. Medicine, 1964-65, co-dir. cardiac lab., 1965-66; sr. registrar cardiopulmonary diseases dept. medicine Queen Elizabeth Hosp., Birmingham, Eng., research fellow dept. medicine U. Birmingham, 1966-67; research asst., hon. sr. registrar dept. medicine Royal Postgrad. Med. Sch. and Hammersmith Hosp., London, 1967-68, sr. registrar, 1969; asso. prof. medicine Abraham Lincoln Sch. Medicine U. Ill., Chgo., 1969-72; prof. medicine U. Oreg. Med. Sch., Portland, 1972-80, dir. research div. cardiology, dir. cardiac catheterization labs., 1973-80; co-dir. dept. adult cardiology Cook County Hosp., Chgo., 1969-70, dir., 1970-72; cons. in field; mem. panel circulatory system devices FDA, 1976-80, chmn., 1977-80, Cons., 1980—; mem. study sect., research manpower rev. com. NIH, 1979—; vis. scientist Cardiovascular Research Inst., vis. prof. medicine U. Calif., San Francisco; prof. medicine, chief sect. cardiology U. So. Calif., 1980—. NIH grantee, 1965-66, 71-72, 72-77, 78-80; Twyford Labs. grantee, 1968; Hektoen Inst. grantee, 1971; Chgo. Heart Assn. grantee, 1971-73; Oreg. Heart Assn. grantee, 1973-74, 74-75, 75, 75-76, 76—; Med. Research Found. Oreg. grantee, 1973-75, 76-77; recipient citation FDA, 1980. Fellow Am. Coll. Cardiology (trustee 1978-79, asst. sec. 1978-79), A.C.P., Council Clin. Cardiology (exec. com. 1977—, vice chmn. 1980—, editor newsletter 1979—, Oreg. rep. 1975-78), Am. Coll. Chest Physicians, Royal Soc. Medicine (London); mem. Central, Western socs. clin. research, Brit. Cardiac Soc., Am. Fedn. Clin. Research, Council Basic Sci., Council Circulation, Brit., Pakistan med. assns., Am. Heart Assn. (publs. com. 1980—, citation for internat. service 1980), AAAS, Western Assn. Physicians, Assn. Univ. Cardiologists, Western Assn. Physicians, Oreg. Soc. Internal Medicine. Author: Shock in Myocardial Infarction, 1974; Coronary Bypass Surgery, 1977; Infective Endocarditis, 1978; editorial bd. Circulation, Am. Jour. Cardiology, and Chest; contbr. numerous articles to profl. publs. Home: 1333 Via Gabriel Palos Verdes Estates CA 90274 Office: U So Calif 2025 Zonal Ave Los Angeles CA 90033

RAI, KAMTA, statistics educator; b. Azamgarh, India, Oct. 28, 1944; s. Ram Surat and Patti Devi (Patti) R.; came to U.S., 1973, naturalized, 1980; m. Tara, May 11, 1967; children—Neeraj, Shashank. B.Sc., U. Lucknow (India), 1963, M.Sc. Math. Stats., 1965; M.Sc. in Stats., McMaster U., 1973; Ph.D. in Stats., U. Wis., 1978. Asst. prof. math. Banaras Hindu U., India, 1965-72; asst. prof. dept. math. Calif. State Poly. U., Pomona, 1978-81, assoc. prof., 1981—; vis. statistician Brookhaven Nat. Lab., Long Island, N.Y., 1981-82. Nat. Inst. Environ. Health Scis. grantee, 1981. Mem. Am. Statis. Assn., Biometric Soc. Hindu. Developed computer program for low-dose extrapolation, statis. method of toxic chem. risk assessment. Contbr. articles to profl. jours. Home: 20122 E Padrino Ave Walnut CA 91789 Office: Calif State Poly Univ 3801 W Temple Ave Pomona CA 91768

RAINS, BILLIE JO, social work adminstr.; b. Shreveport, La., Oct. 11, 1927; d. Joe Jackson and Willie Mae (Bowman) R. A.B., Centenary Coll., 1948; postgrad. Columbia U., 1950-51, 52-53; M.S.W., U. Calif., 1955; postgrad. U. London, 1956-57. Lic. clin. social worker Calif. Psychiat. social worker Central Islip State Hosp., Long Island, N.Y., 1949-51, 52-53; social worker Childrens Home Soc., Oakland, Calif., 1954, psychiat. dept. U.S. Naval Hosp., Oakland, 1954-56; sr. social worker Los Guilucos Sch. Girls Calif. Youth Authority, Santa Rosa, Calif., 1958-62; dir. group services to youth YWCA, Oakland, 1962-67; asst. dir. counseling Nat. Bd. YWCA-Job Corps Program, 1967-68; supr. vol. services Dept. Social Service, San Francisco, 1968-69; field work instr., lectr. U. Calif., 1969-72; dir. social service Kaiser Hosp., Vallejo, Calif., 1973; med. social work supr. San Francisco Gen. Hosp. 1973-75, 81-83, chief psychiat. social worker, 1975-77, acting chief, 1977-81, pvt. practice clin. social work, 1983—. Fulbright scholar, 1956. Mem. Acad. Cert. Social Workers, Nat. Assn. Social Workers, Inst. Cert. Fin. Planners, Am. Assn. Individual Investors, Internat. Conf. Social Welfare, Nat. Conf. Social Welfare. Clubs: Galileo Gem and Mineral Soc., Sierra, Cortex (San Francisco); British Am. (San Jose, Calif.).

RAINS, CAROLYN MARIE, emergency medical technician; b. Denver, Jan. 27, 1939; d. Joseph Webber and Catharine Elizabeth (Feuerstein) Beidler; m. Maurice Wayne Rains, Feb. 8, 1958 (div.); children—Richard Allan, Mark Edward, Jeffrey Joseph, A. Delores. A.A. in Emergency Med. Tech., Pikes Peak Community Coll., 1979; student Pueblo Community Coll., 1952-56. Lic. practical nurse Colo.; cert. emergency medical technician, Colo. Nurse's aide Meml. Hosp. and Garden of the Gods Nursing Home, Colorado Springs, Colo., 1960-66; lic. practical nurse Norton's Nursing Home, Cheyenne, Colo., 1968-70; emergency med. technician U.S. Civil Service, Fort Carson, Colo., 1970-76, emergency medical technician motor vehicle operator, 1976—; sec., trustee, exec. v.p. Am. Fedn. Govt. Employees Local 1345, 1971-78, pres., 1978—, gen. editor monthly publ., 1982—; v.p. Colo. Springs Area Labor Council, 1981—, instr. emergency medicine Pikes Peak Community Coll., 1978-79; instr. Utah State Fed. Woman's Program Conf., 1980; asst. instr. 13th. dist. tng. seminars, 1979-82. Served with USN, 1956-57. Mem. Federally Employed Women, Coalition Labor Union Women, NOW. Democrat. Episcopalian. Home: 7479 Fortman St Fountain CO 80817

RAISBECK, JAMES DAVID, aircraft design executive; b. Milw., Sept. 29, 1936; s. Clifford Clinton and Minnie (Hommersand) R.; B.S., Purdue U., M.S. in Aero. Engring., 1961; 1 dau., Jennifer Lee Raisbeck Hunter. Aero. research engr. Boeing Co., Seattle, 1961-63, liaison to U.S. Air Force, 1966-68, program mgr. comml. STOL programs, 1968-69; chmn. bd., chief exec. officer Robertson Aircraft Corp., Renton, Wash., 1969-73; v.p. tech. Am. Jet Industries, Los Angeles, 1973-74; chmn. bd., chief exec. officer, founder Raisbeck Group, Los Angeles, 1974-80; founder, chmn. bd., chief exec. officer Raisbeck Engring., 1981—, dir. Raisbeck-Western Joint Venture, 1982—; cons. Served with SAC, USAF, 1955-58. Recipient Disting. Engring. Alumnus in Aeronautics, Purdue U., 1979. Mem. Soc. Automotive Engrs., AIAA, Tau Beta Pi, Sigma Gamma Tau, Phi Eta Sigma. Patentee in field of wing design. Address: 7536 Seward Park Ave S Seattle WA 98118

RAISTERS, ALFRED, aerospace engineer, consultant; b. Riga, Latvia, Apr. 30, 1921, came to U.S. 1950. s. Rudolph and Elizabeth (Vershinin) R.; m. Ludmila E. Novickis, 1947; children—Silvia I, Eric H. P.E., U. Riga, 1944; E.E., Tech. U., Stuttgart (Ger.), 1949; MBA, Pepperdine U., 1973. Chief, IRO Trade Tng. Sch., Ludwigsburg, Ger., 1949-50; radio engr. Radio Telephone Service Corp., Seattle, 1951-55; research engr. Boeing Aircraft Co., Seattle, 1955-60; group engr. Vanderberg AFB, Calif., 1960-64; sr. staff engr. Hughes Aircraft Co., El Segundo, Calif., 1964—; owner Mgmt. and Tech. Cons., El Segundo, Calif., 1975—; instr. UCLA, U. So. Calif., Calif. State U., Northridge; guest lectr. Canada, Ger., Sweden, Belgium, Australia. Founder, charter assoc. World Space Found. Fellow AIAA (assoc., bd. dirs.), Nat. Contract Mgmt. Assn. (bd. dirs.), World Space Found.; mem. IEEE, Inst. for Advancement of Engring., Hughes Mgmt. Club. Republican. Lutheran. Club: Athletic. Contbr. articles to profl. jours. Home: 3013 Palos Verdes Dr W Palos Verdes Estates CA 90374 Office: PO Box 902 E-1/A119 El Segundo CA 90245

RAITER, GEORGE LEWIS, aluminum company executive; city official; b. Susanville, Calif. July 2, 1942; s. Lloyd and Beulah Catherine (Leavitt) R.; m. Judith Ann Bartholomew, Aug. 21, 1965; children—Brian, Teddy. B.S. in Chemistry, Calif. State U., Chico, 1965; registered quality engr., Calif. Mgmt. trainee, control metallurgist, U.S. Steel, Pittsburg, Calif., 1965-67; product engr., engring. mgr., Gen. Cable Corp., Hot Springs, Ark., 1967-72; quality control mgr., Reynolds Aluminum Co., Longview, Wash., 1972—. Mayor of Longview, 1982—, mem. Longview City Council, 1977-81; pres. sta. KLTV, Community Access Television, 1975-77; youth soccer coach, 1977-80. Recipient outstanding members award Toastmasters, 1973, 74, 79. Mem. Quality Quality Control Soc., Assn. Wash. Cities, Northwest Electric Lighting and Power Assn., Longview C. of C. (v.p. 1979—). Republican. Presbyterian. Home: 1148 23 Ave Longview WA 98632 Office: City Hall 15th and Broadway Longview WA 98632

RAKOCZI, LASZLO LESLIE, computer co. exec.; b. Budapest, Hungary, Aug. 10, 1933; s. Jeno and Maria (Begidsan) R.; came to U.S., 1957, naturalized, 1961; postgrad. U. Pa., 1959-60; m. Katalin Fekete, Dec. 19, 1956; 1 dau., Kathleen. Mgr. advanced computers Gen. Electric Co., Phoenix, 1960-64; founder, dir., exec. v.p. Standard Computers, Santa Ana, Calif., 1965-73; group v.p. Technology Bus. group Tymshare Inc., Cupertino, Calif., 1974—; chmn. bd., dir. Am. Bus. Info., Inc., Debc Inc., Silrar-Lisco Inc., Sof Tyme Inc.; partner Hi-Tech Inventions. Mem. Assn. Data Processing Orgns. Club: Palo Alto Hills Country. Patentee micro programming networks and other computer and communication related processes; contbr. papers to publs. Home: 27815 Altamont Circle Los Altos Hills CA 94022 Office: 10340 Bubb Rd Cupertino CA 95014

RALEY, DAVID EARL, self-insurance company executive, ret. air force officer; b. Middletown, N.Y., Jan. 17, 1934; s. Foster Edward and Mary Lucille (Hatcher) R.; m. Diane Knowles, Sept. 3, 1956; children—Margaret Ann Raley Motamed, Mark David, Michael Charles. B.S., U. Md., 1965; M.B.A., Ariz. State U., 1973. Enlisted U.S. Air Force, 1954, advanced through grades to col., 1980; dir. safety Alaskan Air Command, 1972-75; chief ground safety dir. Air Force Inspection and Safety Ctr., Norton AFB, Calif., ret., 1980; v.p. Bierly & Assocs. of South Pasadena, Calif., 1980—; lectr. U. Redlands (Calif.), 1981-83, U. So. Calif., Norton AFB, Calif., 1980-83. Bd. dirs. Calif. Credit Union League, Pomona, 1981-83; pres. Norton Credit Union, 1980-83. Decorated Legion of Merit, D.F.C. with cluster, Bronze Star, Air medal with 10 oakleaf clusters. Mem. Am. Soc. Safety Engrs. (admission and fiscal affairs coms.), Order Daedalions. Republican. Episcopalian. Home: 1350 E Highland Ave Redlands CA 92373 Office: 1400 E 4th St Santa Ana CA 92701

RALPH, CHARLES LELAND, zoologist, educator; b. Flint, Mich., Aug. 16, 1929; s. John Leland and Ruby Martha (Proffer) R.; B.S., S.E. Mo. State Coll., 1952; M.S., Northwestern U., 1953, Ph.D., 1955; m. Reta Wick, Aug. 30, 1980; children by previous marriage—Alisa A., Paula E. Physiologist, U.S. Dept. Agr., Beltsville, Md., 1957-59; faculty U. Pitts., 1959-74; prof., chmn. dept. zoology and entomology Colo. State U., Ft. Collins, 1974—. Served with Chem. Corps, U.S. Army, 1955-57. Fellow AAAS; mem. Am. Assn. Anatomists, Am. Soc. Zoologists, Am. Physiol. Soc., Sigma Xi. Author: Introduction to Animal Physiology, 1978. Office: Colo State U Dept Zoology Fort Collins CO 80523*

RALSTON, ANNE STOMMES, utility co. executive; b. Sauk Centre, Minn., Oct. 12, 1950; d. Joseph and Dorothy Agnes (Shadeg) Stommes; m. Robert Orville Ralston II, Apr. 5, 1975. B.A., Coll. St. Benedict, 1971; M.A., U. Nebr., Lincoln, 1975, Ph.D., 1981. Research assoc. Bur. Bus. Research, Coll. Bus. Adminstrn., U. Nebr., Lincoln, 1979-81; with Pacific Tel. & Tel., San Francisco, 1981—, asst. staff mgr., residence market analyst, 1981-82, market mgr., 1982-83, mktg. planner direct mail response center, 1983—. Catholic Aid Assn. scholar, 1968-69, 69-70. Mem. Am. Mktg. Assn., Soc. Research in Child Devel., Population Assn. Am., Beta Gamma Sigma. Contbr. articles to profl. jours. Home: 2836 Judah St San Francisco CA 94122 Office: 1 Montgomery West Tower Suite 540 San Francisco CA 94104

RALSTON, EDWARD LINDSAY, JR., electrical engineer; b. Butte, Mont., Nov. 13, 1910; s. Edward Lindsay and Helen West (Pyle) R.; B.S., Ore. State U., 1932; m. Dorothea Johnstone Saunders, Apr. 5, 1941; children—Sara (Mrs. Laurence G. Bagg), Edward Lindsay III, Margaret (Mrs. Carlos de Giraldo), Caroline (Mrs. Todd Brethauer). Applications engr. Westinghouse Electric Corp., San Francisco and Honolulu, 1937-47; comml. engr. Hawaiian Electric Co., Honolulu, 1947-73, staff engr., 1973-75. Pres., Aloha Week Hawaii Inc., 1963; mem. adv. bd. Salvation Army, Honolulu. Campaign mgr. Republican part Hawaii, 1948, 52. Mem. Internat. Assn. Elec. Insps., IEEE, Illuminating Engring. Soc. Club: Lanikai Canoe (pres. 1972) (Kailua). Home: 1408 Mokolea Dr Kailua HI 96734

RALSTON, GILBERT ALEXANDER, author; b. Los Angeles, Jan. 5, 1912; s. Alexander Gilbert and Jeanette (Johnston) R.; grad. Pasadena Coll., 1929-32; grad. Am. Acad. Dramatic Arts, 1935; B.C.A., Sierra Nev. Coll., 1972; postgrad. doctoral program Fielding Inst., 1977; m. Mary K. Hart, Dec. 20, 1938; children—Michael, David. Actor, stage mgr. theatre prodns. N.Y.C., 1931-35; writer, dir. radio shows NBC, N.Y.C., 1936-38; prodn. supr. Compton Advt., Inc., N.Y.C., West Coast, 1939-42; organizer, mgr. radio dept. Proctor & Gamble, Cin., 1943-47, exec. producer inc. TV div., 1947-50; free lance producer TV films, 1950-55; exec. producer in charge TV drama CBS, 1955, dir. network programs originating in N.Y.C., 1956; producer High Adventure documentaries with Lowell Thomas, 1957; chmn. sch. communication arts Tahoe (Cal.) Paradise Coll., 1968; dean sch. communicative arts Sierra Nevada Coll., Incline Village, Nev., 1960-73, pres., 1973—; pres. Ralston Sch. Communicative Arts, Genoa, Nev., 1971—; v.p. Rule of Three Prodns., Los Angeles, 1973—; lectr. Fordham U., City Coll. City U. N.Y., Loyola U. of Los Angeles, St. Mary's Coll. of Calif. Mem. Authors Guild, ASCAP, Western Writers Am., Writers Guild Am., Am. Massage and Therapy Assn. Author: Ben, 1972; (with Richard Newhafer) The Frightful Sin of Cisco Newman, 1972; Dakota Warpath, 1973; Dakota: Red Revenge, 1973; Dakota Cat Trap, 1974; Dakota Murder's Money, 1974; Dakota: Chain Reaction, The Deadly Art, 1975, The Third Circle, 1976, The Tao of Touch, 1983, others. Author screenplays: No Strings Attached, 1962; A Gallery of Six, 1963; A Feast of Jackals, 1963; Cockatrice, 1965; Kona Coast, 1967; Night of the Locust, 1969; Ben, 1971, Third Circle, 1975, Sure, 1975. Author screen adaptations: Willard (by Stephen Gilbert), 1970; Bluebonnet (by Boris Sobelman and Jack H. Robinson), 1971. Author scripts for TV sometime under pseudonym Gil Alexander: High Adventure, Naked City, Route 66, Follow the Sun, Bus Stop, The Untouchables, Alcoa Theatre, Ben Casey, Richard Boone Show, 12 O'Clock High, The Name of the Game, Daktari, Laredo, Combat, Big Valley, Gunsmoke, Amos Burke, Slattery's People, Alfred Hitchcock, Star Trek, It Takes a Thief, O'Hara, Cannon, numerous others. Address: PO Box 350 Genoa NV 89411

RAM, SAMUEL BUCK, composer, record producer, song publisher, group musical director; b. Chgo., Nov. 21, 1908; s. Phillip R.; m. Lucille; children—Lynn Ram Paul, Melody. Law degree. Saxophonist Benny Goodman's band, Gene Krupa's band; musical arranger for big bands, including Duke Ellington, Glenn Miller, Count Basie, Dorsey Bros., and Cab Calloway; composer for motion pictures; rock composer, creator, musical dir. The Platters, 1954—; co-owner, co-mgr. Personality Prodns., Inc.; composer numerous songs, including: Only You, You've Got The Magic Touch, The Great Pretender, I'll Be Home For Christmas, You'll Never Never Know, One In A Million, I'm Sorry, I Wish, Twilight time, Where, Adorable, Remember When, Afterglow, Fool That I Am; discovered The Three Suns, 1940s, The Union Gap, 1960s. Winner 16 gold records Nat. Music Pubs.'s Assn., platinum record for The Great Pretender, 1982; songs recorded by various artists including Bing Crosby, Three Suns, Mario Lanza, Glenn Miller, Mahalia Jackson, The Inkspots, B.B. King, Frank Sinatra, Ella Fitzgeral, and numerous recs. by The Platters. Office: PO Box 39 Las Vegas NV 89125

RAMAGE, ROBERT THOMAS, research geneticist, plant science educator; b. New Braunfels, Tex., Aug. 15, 1928; s. Robert Thomas and Lola Adelle (Cobb) R.; m. Barbara Jean Wold, Dec. 20, 1952; children—Robert Thomas, Margaret Lynn, Elizabeth Lee, Timothy Allan. B.S., Tex. Technol. Coll., 1951; Ph.D., U. Minn., 1955. Geneticist U.S. Dept. Agr., Davis, Calif., 1955-58, Tucson, 1958-61, research geneticist, 1961—, research leader, 1974—; prof. plant sci. dept. U. Ariz., Tucson, 1959—. Served with U.S. Army, 1946-47. Recipient Superior Service award U.S. Dept. Agr., 1974; Nat. Council Comml. Plant Breeders award, 1973. Fellow Am. Soc. Agronomy, AAAS; mem. Am. Barley Workers Group, Am. Genetics Assn., Crop Sci. Soc., Genetics Soc. Can., Internat. Barley Genetics Group, Western Soc. Crop Sci. Democrat. Lutheran. Contbr. numerous articles and reports to profl. jours. Office: Plant Scis Dept U Ariz Tucson AZ 85721

RAMBERG, BENNETT, foreign policy research analyst, management consultant; b. Los Angeles, Oct. 25, 1946; s. Isaac and Rebecca (Malier) R. A.B., U. So. Calif., 1968; M.A., John Hopkins U., 1970, Ph.D. in Internat. Relations, 1976. Research fellow Arms Control Program, Stanford U., Palo Alto, Calif., 1975, Ctr. Internat. Studies, Princeton U., 1976-77; research assoc. Ctr. Internat. and Strategic Affairs, UCLA, 1977—, lectr. dept. polit. sci., UCLA, 1980-82; cons. congl. fgn. policy, 1970, 72-73; cons. Fed. Emergency Mgmt. Agency, 1980; media cons. pub. TV, 1982. Mem. Am. Polit. Sci. Assn., Internat. Studies Assn. Author: The Seabed Arms Control Negotiation: A Study of Multilateral Arms Control Conference Diplomacy, 1978; Destruction of Nuclear Energy Facilities in War: The Problem and the Implication, 1980; editor: (with Ray Maghroori) Globalism vs. Realism: International Relations Third Debate, 1982. Home: 9548 Sawyer St Los Angeles CA 90035 Office: Ctr Internat and Strategic Affairs UCLA Los Angeles CA 90024

RAMBERG, WOLFGANG PETER, banker; b. Copenhagen, May 10, 1921; came to U.S., 1928, naturalized, 1940; s. Karl Peter Hansen-Ramberg and Elfriede Antonie (Milbitz) Hansen-Ramberg; B.S., Drexel U., 1949; postgrad. Pacific Coast Banking Sch., U. Wash., 1954-56; m. Joan Morgan Young, Dec. 27, 1973; children—Marilyn Esther Ramberg Yildiz, Elizabeth Anne, Gregory Jon Murphy, Russell Maynard Murphy. Asst. treas. Chase Manhattan Bank, N.Y.C., 1949-57; sr. v.p. First Interstate Bank of Calif., Los Angeles, 1957-76; sr. v.p., dir. The Hibernia Bank, San Francisco, 1976-80; vice chmn. bd., pres., chief exec. officer Alaska Nat. Bank of the North, Fairbanks, 1980—, also dir., 1980—. Trustee Sitka Summer Music Festival Found., 1982—, Monroe Found., 1982—. Served with U.S. Army, 1940-45. Mem. Am. Bankers Assn. (community banking adv. bd. 1981—), Alaska Bankers Assn. (pres. 1982—), Robert Morris Assocs., Phi Kappa Phi. Clubs: University (San Francisco); Fairbanks Rotary. Home: S R 30320-Q Fairbanks AK 99701 Office: PO Box 60730 794 University Ave Fairbanks AK 99706

RAMEY, CHERI DOLORES, advt. agy. exec.; b. Montreal, Que., Can., Apr. 17, 1944; d. Harold Edward and Bette Evlyn (Cameron) R.; came to U.S., 1951, naturalized, 1961; grad. Sch. Visual Arts, N.Y.C., 1961-64. Asst. art dir./designer Composing Room, N.Y.C., 1964-65, Katz Jacobs & Zlotnick, N.Y.C., 1965-66; art dir. Young & Rubicam, N.Y.C., 1966-69, sr. art dir., Los Angeles, 1969-71; creative dir. Ramey Communications Co., Los Angeles, 1971—, now pres., creative dir. Adv. bd. Los Angeles Trade Tech. Recipient awards Cannes Film Festival, 1969, N.Y. Art Dirs. Club, 1966, 68, 73, 76; Best in West award, 1980, others. Mem. Western States Advt. Agys. Assn. (dir.), Los Angeles Creative Club (dir.), Am. Assn. Advt. Agys. Democrat. Home: 2482 Micheltorena St Los Angeles CA 90039 Office: 3008 Wilshire Blvd Los Angeles CA 90010

RAMIG, ROBERT ERNEST, research soil scientist; b. McGrew, Nebr., June 22, 1922; s. Carl James and Lydia (Hardt) R.; m. Lois F. Franklin, Nov. 28, 1943; children—Robert Franklin, Mary Kathleen, John Carl. B.S., U. Nebr., 1943, Ph.D., 1960; M.S., Wash. State U., 1948. Asst. agronomist U. Nebr., North Platte, 1948-51; soil scientist agrl. research service U.S. Dept. Agr., North Platte, 1951-61; research soil scientist, Pendleton, Oreg., 1961-71, ctr. dir., 1971-81, supervising research soil scientist, 1981—. Mem. Sch. Dist. Facilities Study Group, Pendleton, 1973-74, Sch. Dist. 16R Budget Com., 1972-77; mem. budget com. City of Pendleton, 1972—, councilman, 1973—, chmn. Mayor's Downtown Study Group, 1980. Served to lt. USNR, 1943-46. Sears, Roebuck & Co. fellow, 1939-40; recipient cert. of merit U.S. Dept. Agr., 1960; named First Citizen, Pendleton C. of C., 1980. Mem. AAAS, Am. Soc. Agronomy, Soil Sci. Soc. Am., Western Soil Sci. Soc., Soil Conservation Soc. Am., Sigma Xi. Democrat. Lutheran. Club: Rotary (Pendleton). Home: 1208 NW Johns Ave Pendleton OR 97801 Office: Agrl Research Service US Dept Agr PO Box 370 Pendleton OR 97801

RAMIREZ, DIANE NORTHROP, educational administrator, consultant; b. Columbus, Ohio, Dec. 22, 1945; d. James Abraham and Sharma Ann (Swank) Chamberlin; m. Richard Moreno Ramirez, Feb. 10, 1973; children—Ronan Northrop, Roderic Northrop. B.F.A., Ohio State U., 1967; student Columbus Coll. Art & Design, 1964-65; M. in Spl. Edn., Calif. State Coll.-Los Angeles, 1971; postgrad. U. So. Calif., 1977—. Cert. elem., secondary tchr., community coll. instr., adminstr., Calif. Tchr. arts, crafts Recreation Dept., Columbus, Ohio, 1966-67; cons. Family Effectiveness, Coachella Valley, Calif., 1968-79; cons. trainable mentally retarded, Riverside County, Calif., 1968-70; tchr. secondary trainable mentally retarded Riverside County (Calif.) Supt. Schs., 1968-69, tchr. elem. trainable mentally retarded, 1969-70; tchr. bilingual lang. devel. Desert Sands Unified Sch. Dist., Indio, Calif., 1970; tchr. secondary remedial reading Coachella Valley High Sch., Thermal, Calif., 1971-72, tchr., developer secondary educationally handicapped, 1972-74; counselor, instr. for handicapped, Coll. of the Desert, Palm Desert, Calif., 1974-75; dir. handicapped programs and services, assoc. prof. spl. edn., 1975—; facilitator Region 9/Calif. Community Colls. Handicap Programs & Services, 1980—; field reader Disadvantaged Programs, HEW, 1979. Named Outstanding Tchr., Found. Exceptional Children, 1968-69. Mem. NEA, Calif. Tchrs. Assn., Educare Profl. Edn. Found., Assn. Supervision and Curriculum Devel., Calif. Personnel and Guidance Assn., Phi Delta Kappa. Republican. Author: Guide: Education of Handicapped Adults, 1978; developer curriculum guides for trainable mentally retarded. Home: 75-289 Desert Park Dr Indian Wells CA 92260 Office: 43-500 Monterey Ave Palm Desert CA 92260

RAMIREZ, MARTHA, computer firm executive, consultant; b. Washington, Mar. 26, 1942; d. Gilberto Velasco and Louise (Franklin) R.; m. Arthur W. Luehrmann, Sept. 15, 1961; children—Mia Kerstin, Nils Gordon. Student Smith Coll., 1959-60, George Washington U., 1960-61; B.S., Ill. Inst. Tech., 1965; M.B.A., Amos Tuck Sch. Bus. Adminstrn., Dartmouth Coll., 1977. Asst. to pres. The Zischke Orgn., San Francisco, 1977-80; mgr. adminstrv. group The Wyatt Co., San Francisco, 1980-81; pres. Computer Literacy, Berkeley, Calif., 1981—. Bd. dirs. Berkeley Symphony Orch.; mem. Council on Ednl. Tech., State Bd. Edn., Calif. Recipient Lebovitz Prize, Amos Tuck Sch. Bus. Adminstrn., 1976; Amos Tuck scholar, 1977. Mem. Tuck Alumni Assn. No. Calif. (officer). Office: 1466 Grizzly Peak Blvd Berkeley CA 94708

RAMIREZ, RAUL ANTHONY, U.S. dist. judge; b. Los Angeles, Mar. 8, 1944; s. Joseph M. and Jessie A. Ramirez; B.A., Los Angeles State Coll., 1967; LL.B., J.D. (Am. Jurisprudence award criminal law 1970), U. Pacific, 1970; m. Sharon Anne Bush, May 26, 1979; children—John, Suzanne, Joseph. Admitted to Calif. bar, 1971; law clk. to presiding judge Sacramento Superior Ct., 1970; asso. firm Clarence S. Brown, Sacramento, 1971-74; individual practice, Sacramento, 1974-77; judge Sacramento Municipal Ct., 1977-80; U.S. dist. judge Eastern Dist. Calif., Sacramento, 1980—. Recipient various service awards, certs. commendation. Mem. Calif. Judges Assn. Address: 650 Capitol Mall Room 2042 Sacramento CA 95814

RAMO, SIMON, engineering executive; b. Salt Lake City, May 7, 1913; s. Benjamin and Clara (Trestman) R.; m. Virginia May Smith, July 25, 1937; children—James Brian, Alan Martin. B.S., U. Utah, 1933, D.Sc. (hon.), 1961; Ph.D., Calif. Inst. Tech. (teaching fellow), 1936; D.Engring. (hon.), Case Inst. Tech., 1960, U. Mich., 1966, Poly. Inst. N.Y., 1971; D.Sc. (hon.), Union Coll., 1963, Worcester Poly. Inst., 1968, U. Akron, 1969, Cleve. State U., 1976; LL.D. (hon.), Carnegie Mellon U., 1970, U. So. Calif., 1972, Gonzaga U., 1983; With Gen. Electric Co., 1936-46; v.p., dir. ops. Hughes Aircraft Co., 1946-53, Ramo-Wooldridge Corp., 1953-58; sci. dir. U.S. intercontinental guided missile program, 1954-58; pres. Bunker-Ramo Corp., 1964-66; dir. TRW Inc., 1954—, vice chmn. bd., 1961-78, chmn. exec. com., 1969-78; chmn. bd. TRW-Fujitsu Co., 1980-83; vis. prof. mgmt. sci. Calif. Inst. Tech., 1978—; regents' lectr. UCLA, 1981-82, U. Calif. at Santa Cruz, 1978-79; chmn. Center for Study Am. Experience, U. So. Calif., 1978-80; dir. Union Bank, Times Mirror Co., 1968-83. Chmn., Pres.'s Com. Sci. and Tech., 1976-77; co-chmn. Transition Task Force on Sci. and Tech. for Pres.-elect Reagan; mem. advisory council Sec. of Commerce, 1976-77; Roster of Consultants to Adminstr., ERDA, 1976-77; mem. White House Energy Research and Devel. Adv. Council, 1973-75, adv. com. sci. and fgn. affairs Sec. State, 1973-75; bd. advisors for sci. and tech. Republic of China, 1981—; fellow of faculty John F. Kennedy Sch. Govt., Harvard U. Bd. visitors UCLA Sch. Medicine; trustee Calif. Inst. Tech., Nat. Symphony Orch. Assn.; trustee emeritus Calif. State Univs.; bd. dirs. Los Angeles Music Center Found., Los Angeles Philharmonic Assn., Los Angeles World Affairs Council, W.M. Keck Found., 1983—. Recipient awards I.R.E., Eta Kappa Nu, Turnbull award IAS, 1956, Steinmetz award AIEE, 1959; award Arnold Air Soc., 1960; citation Air Force Assn., 1964; award Am. Iron and Steel Inst., 1968; WEMA medal of achievement, 1970; Disting. Service gold medal AFCEA, 1970; Outstanding Achievement award U. So. Calif., 1971, 79; Kayan medal Columbia U., 1972; award merit Am. Cons. Engrs. Council, 1974; IEEE/WEMA Golden Omega award, 1975; medal Franklin Inst., 1978; Bus. Statesman award Harvard Bus. Sch. Assn., 1979; Nat. Medal of Sci., 1979; Disting. Alumnus, U. Utah, 1981; UCLA medal, 1982; Presdl. Medal Freedom, 1983. others. Fellow IEEE (Founders medal 1980), AIAA (hon.), Am. Acad. Arts and Scis., Am. Phys. Soc., AAAS, Inst. Advancement of Engring.; founding mem. Nat. Acad. Engring.; mem. Am. Philos. Soc., Nat. Acad. Scis., Internat. Acad. Astronautics. Author sci., engring. and mgmt. books. Office: 1 Space Park Redondo Beach CA 90278

RAMOS, ALBERT A., elec. engr.; b. Los Angeles, Feb. 28, 1927; s. Jesus D. and Carmen F. (Fontes) R.; B.S. in Elec. Engring., U. So. Calif., 1950, M.S. in Systems Mgmt., 1972; Ph.D., U.S. Internat. U., 1975; m. Joan C. Pailing, Sept. 23, 1950; children—Albert A., Richard R., James J., Katherine. With guided missile test group Hughes Aircraft Co., 1950-60; with TRW Systems Co., 1960—, mgr. ballistic missile test Norton AFB, San Bernardino, Calif., 1969—. Served with USNR, 1945-46. Registered profl. engr., Calif. Mem. IEEE, Nat. Soc. Profl. Engrs., Air Force Assn., Mexican-Am. Engring. Soc., Mexican Am. Personnel and Manpower Assn. (mem. adminstering commn. dept. community services), Sigma Phi Delta, Eta Kappa Nu, Tau Beta Pi. Home: 1457 W Cypress Ave Redlands CA 92373 Office: PO Box 1310 San Bernardino CA 92402

RAMOS, JACK MARKUS, dentist; b. Fresno, Cal., June 15, 1925; s. Joseph Markus and Gladys (Leonardo) R.; A.B., Fresno State U., 1950; D.D.S., U. Pacific, 1954; postgrad. in Edn., U. Calif.-San Francisco, 1958; m. Marie J. Rojas, June 11, 1950; children—Loretta Marie, Laura Ann. Gen practice dentistry, Fresno, 1954—. Mem. planning com. Adult Activity Center for Mentally Retarded, 1969-71; mem. mental retardation com. Fresno Community Council, 1965-67; mem. exec. com. Central Calif. Regional Center for Retarded, 1971-72; mem. nominating com. Calif. Assn. for Retarded, 1972-73, vice pres., 1973-76, chmn. fiscal affairs com., 1976-79, pres., 1977-79; mem. Atty. Gen.'s Vol. Adv. Council, 1972-78; chmn. adv. bd. Porterville State Hosp., also Fresno County Mental Health Adv. Bd., 1973—; active PTA; pres. Fresno Assn. Mentally Retarded, recipient Ann. Golden Circle award, 1975, 82; mem. Parents of Gifted, Fresno County Coordinating Council Developmentally Disabled; mem. long-range planning com. Valley Med. Center, 1980-83; pres. Valley Dental Care 1980-83. Found., 1980-83. Bd. dirs. Fresno Found. Mental Retardation; mem. Central Valley citizen adv. council U. Calif. Served with USNR, 1943-46; PTO. Mem. Am. Dental Assn., Federation Dentaire Internationale, Acad. Gen. Dentistry; AAAS, V.F.W. (life), Fresno-Madera Dental Soc. (treas. 1976-77, sec., 1977-78, pres. 1980-82, chmn. legis. com., chmn. ins. com.), Acad. Dentistry for Handicapped, Calif. Dental Assn. (by-laws reference com. 1980-81), Am. Soc. Preventative Dentistry, Pub. Health League, Xi Psi Phi. Democrat. Roman Catholic. Clubs: Cabrillo, Rotary (vocat. services chmn., dir.). Home: 1163 W Morris Ave Fresno CA 93705 Office: 946 N Van Ness Ave Fresno CA 93728

RAMOS-WRIGHT, JILL, recreation specialist, educator, consultant; b. Indpls., June 21, 1942; d. William Robert and Harriett Vivian (Howell) W.; m. Ronald Jordan Ramos, Aug. 20, 1966 (div. 1982); children—Matthew William, Ryan Jordan; m. 2d, Steven Richard Wright, Dec. 2, 1983. B.S. in Edn., Ind. U., 1964, M.S. in Recreation Adminstrn., 1966. Nat. field counselor Alpha Xi Delta Soc., Indpls., 1965-66; dir. recreational therapy Mesa Vista Psychiat. Hosp., San Diego, 1966-68; pres. Recreation Assocs., La Jolla, Calif., 1968-70; cons. recreation, San Diego, 1973-74; asst. prof. recreational therapy San Diego State U., 1974-80; v.p. Wright & Assocs., bus. systems, San Diego, 1983—. Bd. dirs. PTA, Painted Rock Sch., Poway, Calif., 1976-79; mem. gifted and talented edn. steering com. Twin Peaks Sch., Poway, Calif., 1981—; mem. Marion Ross drama scholarship steering com. San Diego State U., 1982-83. Jill Ramos Scholarship established at San Diego State U., 1979. Mem. Calif. Park and Recreation Soc. (cert. supervision 1968, cert. achievement 1980, coll. rep. Dist. XII 1975-76, v.p. dist. XII 1977-78), Los Amados Childrens Home Soc. Republican. Methodist. Club: Home of Guiding Hands Aux. (San Diego). Home: 13233 Valle Verde Terr Poway CA 92064

RAMSAY, JOHN T., professional basketball coach; b. Phila., Feb. 21, 1925; m. Jean. Basketball coach St. Joseph's U., Phila., 1955-66; profl. basketball coach Phila. Flyers, 1968-72, Buffalo Braves, 1972-76, Portland Trailblazers, 1976—. Coach, Nat. Basketball Assn. Championship Team, 1977. Served with USN, 1943-46. Office: Portland Trailblazers 700 NE Multnomah Lloyd Bldg Suite 950 Portland OR 97232*

RAMSEY, CLAUDE, found. exec.; b. Ramsey, W.Va., May 25, 1918; s. Melvin G. and Maude (Hawkins) R.; B.S., Morris Harvey Coll., 1938; B.J., U. Mo., 1939; m. Lilien Ernst, June 9, 1945; children—Patrick (dec.), Terry, Perry. Writer, United Press, Kansas City and Denver, 1940-42, bur. chief Houston and Lower Rio Grande Valley, 1945-52; pub. relations counsellor Kostka & Assos., Denver, 1953-55; founder, pres. Pub. Relations Inc., Denver, 1956-64; exec. dir. Morris Animal Found., Denver, 1964—; guest lectr. pub. relations Colo. State U., 1972-79. Mem. City Council, City of Greenwood Village (Colo.), 1973-75; mem. Arapahoe County Republican Exec. Com., 1976-80; chmn. Rep. 6th Congl. Dist., 1982-83; chmn. Colo. div. Am. Cancer Soc., 1979-81. Served to capt. Signal Corps, U.S. Army, 1941-45. Decorated Bronze Star; recipient award of Excellence, Colo. div. Am. Cancer Soc., 1976. Mem. Pub. Relations Soc. Am. (past pres. Colo. chpt., mem. nat. bd. 1962-63, Silver Anvil award 1959), Council on Founds., Sigma Delta Chi. Lutheran. Club: Denver Press. Home: 5690 S Locust St Englewood CO 80111 Office: 45 Inverness Dr E Englewood CO 80112

RAMSEY, JAMES LEE, training and development director, educator, clergyman; b. Bell, Calif., May 4, 1938; s. George Ernest and Edna Lucille (Saywell) R.; m. Rita Jo Cunningham, May 14, 1959; m. 2d, Katherine Louise Slemsick, June 26, 1977. B.A. in Social Sci., Calif. State U.-Fullerton, 1964; M.Div., Garrett Theol. Sem., 1972. Ordained to ministry United Methodist Ch.; cert. in community coll. teaching, Calif. Dep. probation officer Sonoma County (Calif.), 1964-66; minister of edn. United Meth. Ch., So. Calif., 1972-81; dir. mgmt. devel. and tng.

Fluor Engring. and Constructors, Irvine, Calif., 1981—. Supervision edn. adv. com. Saddleback Coll., mgmt. inst. adv. com. Coastline Coll. Served with USN, 1957-60. Mem. Am. Soc. Tng. and Devel. (program dir. Orange County chpt.), Personnel and Indsl. Relations Assn. Democrat. Author: Who Am I Now That I Am Alone?, 1977; contbr. article to publ. Home: 12052 Brookhaven Garden Grove CA 92640 Office: 3333 Michelson Ave Irvine CA 92730

RANA, CHARUMATI, physician; b. Hazaribagh Bihar, India, Jan. 26, 1926; came to U.S., 1951, naturalized, 1963; d. Budhan Prasad and Bhuneshwari (Devi) Rana; L.M.P., Darbhunga Med. Coll., Darbhunga Bihar, India, 1946; M.B. B.S., Prince of Wales Med. Coll., Patna, Bihar, 1948; spl. certificate in obstetrics and gynecology U. Pa., 1952; m. Krishna V.S. Rao, Oct. 13, 1950; children—Subha Lakshmi, K. Krishna Narayan. Intern, Prince of Wales Hosp., Patna Bihar, 1949, resident, 1950-51; resident Chestnut Hill Hosp., Phila., 1953-54, also Nazareth Hosp., Rolling Hills Hosp., Woman's Hosp. (all Phila.); practice medicine, specializing in obstetrics and gynecology, Seattle, 1961-64, Glendive, Mont., 1965-66, Tacoma, 1967-68, Auburn, Wash., 1968-72, Kent, Wash., 1972-78, Mililani Town, Hawaii, 1978-82, Thousand Oaks, Calif., 1982—; past mem. staff St. Francis Cabrini, Providence, Seattle Gen., Doctors, Stimson-Cobb hosps. (all Seattle), Lakewood Gen. Hosp., Tacoma; founder B. Devi Med. Center, Kent, 1972-78, B. Devi Total Health Care Center, Mililani Town, Hawaii, 1978-82; instr. Prince of Wales Med. Coll. and Hosp., Patna, 1950-51; formerly med. officer U.S. Army Hosp., Honshu, Japan. Bd. dirs. Mililani Town Honpa Hongwanji Buddhist Sanga; charter mem., 2d v.p. Mililani Buddhist Ch. Mem. Am. Med. Women's Assn., Med. Assn. Fgn. Med. Grads., AAUW, India Abroad Found. (charter), Bus. and Profl. Women's Club, UN Assn. U.S. Office: 2318 Thousand Oaks Blvd Thousand Oaks CA 91360

RANA, DUANE LEE, optometrist; b. Redlands, Calif., Mar. 2, 1949; s. George Washington and Juanita Ina (Wagner) R.; m. Charlotte Ann Swift, Sept. 7, 1967; children—Alyssa Lynette, Andrea Elaine. B.S. in Psychology, Pacific U., 1974, O.D., 1976. Pvt. practice optometry, Bishop, Calif., 1976-77, Fontana, Calif., 1977-78; Brewster, Wash., 1978—; vision cons. to Grand Coulee Dam, Chief Joseph Dam. Served with U.S. Army, 1969-71. Decorated Bronze Star. Mem. Am. Optometric Assn., Wash. Optometric Assn., Optometric Extension Program. Adventist. Club: Brewster Lions (pres.).

RAND, JUDITH SEESE, interior designer; b. Milwaukee, Mar. 18, 1937; d. Austin Harland and Mildred Evelyn (Silliman) Seese; m. Douglas Harris Rand, Aug. 29, 1959; children—David Douglas, Lynda Lee. Student Ind. U.; cert. design degree Orange Coast Coll., 1983. Office mgr. Miller & Miller, Tustin, Calif., 1969-72; interior designer W. Lee & Assocs., Tustin, 1972-75; owner Judith Rand Interiors, Santa Ana, Calif., 1975—; instr. interior design internship program. Co-chmn. Docent Scholarship Comm.; fundraiser WMed. Center; designer Tujunga Open Bible Church (Beautification award), 1982. Mem. Internat. Soc. Interior Designers, Am. Soc. Interior Designers (assoc.), Pi Beta Omega. Republican. Protestant. Club: P.E.D.O. Address: 13831 Winthrope Santa Ana CA 92705

RAND, RICHARD MALCOLM, lawyer; b. Bellingham, Wash., May 20, 1930; s. Loren B. and Thurza D. (Warren) R.; student Seattle U., 1948-50; B.A., U. Wash., 1951, LL.B., 1958; m. Elise A. Planchard, July 26, 1952; children—Jeffry, Gregory, Eileen. Admitted to Wash. bar, 1958, Calif. bar, 1959; pvt. practice, San Diego, 1960—. Served to comdr. USNR, 1951-55. Cert. specialist in taxation law. Mem. Am. Calif., Wash. bar assns., San Diego Estate Planning Council. Home: 6730 Muirlands Dr La Jolla CA 92037 Office: 2120 4th Ave San Diggo CA 92101

RANDALL, LOIS CANNAVINA, biologist; b. Whitefish, Mont., Aug. 22, 1946; d. Anthony David and Grace Herrietta (Rickard) Cannavina; B.S., Whitworth Coll., 1968; postgrad. U. Calif., Irvine, 1968-72, U. Mont. Biol. Sta., 1974; m. Byron Cormack Randall, Feb. 2, 1974. Tchr., high sch., Almira, Wash., 1968; tchr. biology Villa Park (Calif.) High Sch., 1968-72; substitute tchr. Kalispell (Mont.) Sch. Dist., 1972; clk. Sportsman & Ski Haus, Kalispell, 1972-74; fishery mgmt. biologist, asst. project leader U.S. Fish and Wildlife Service, Kalispell, 1973—. Mem. Kalispell City-County Planning Bd., 1972-74. Mem. Am. Fishery Soc., Nat. Wildlife Fedn. Clubs: Flathead Wildlife. Author: Aquatic History of Red Rock Lakes National Wildlife Refuge, 1977; Glacier National Park Angler Use During 1979 and 1980, 1981, During 1981, 1982. Home: 788 Creston Hatchery Rd Kalispell MT 59901

RANDLETT, MARY WILLIS, photographer; b. Seattle, May 5, 1924; d. Cecil Durand and Elizabeth (Bayley) Willis; m. Herbert B. Randlett, Oct. 19, 1950 (div.); children—Robert, Mary Ann, Peter, Susan. B.A., Whitman Coll., Walla Walla, Wash., 1947. Free lance photographer, 1949—; one-woman shows: Seattle Sci. Center, 1971, Western Wash. State U., 1971, Seattle Art Mus., 1971, Art Gallery of Greater Victoria, 1972, Alaska State Mus., 1972, others; group shows: Am. Soc. Mag. Photographers, 1970, Whatcom Mus., Bellingham, Wash., Henry Gallery, Seattle, 1971, 74, Royal Photographic Soc., 1979, Heard Mus., Phoenix, 1979, others; works represented in permanent collections Met. Mus., Nat. Collection of Fine Arts, Nat. Portrait Gallery, Washington State Library, Manuscript div. U. Wash., Pacific Northwest Bell, Seattle, Swedish Med. Center, Seattle; works appeared in books: The Master and His Fish (Roderick Haig-Brown), 1982; Theodore Roethke: The Journey to I and Otherwide (Neal Bowers), 1982; Mountain in the Clouds (Bruce Bown), 1982; Masonry in Architecture (Louis Redstone), 1982; Writings and Reflections from the World of Roderick Haig-Brown, 1982; Pike Place Market (Alice Shorett and Murray Morgan), 1982; The Dancing Blanket, (Cheryl Samuel), 1982, others; works also appeared in newspapers and mags. Nat. Endowment for Arts grantee, 1976. Mem. Am. Soc. Mag. Photographers, Royal Photog. Soc. Gt. Britian, AAUW. Home: Box 10536 Bainbridge Island WA 98110

RANDOLPH, THOMAS FREDERICK, advertising executive; b. Milw., Sept. 23, 1930; s. Samuel William Randolph and Madeleine (Haugan) Zentner; m. Mary Katherine Preuss, June 29, 1952; children—Nancy Brandon, Katherine Cook, Thomas. B.A. in Econs., Stanford U., 1952. Account mgr. Foote, Cone & Belding/Honig, Los Angeles, 1955-68; gen. mgr. San Francisco, 1968-80, pres., 1980—; dir. Foote, Cone & Belding Communications Inc., 1980—. Served with USN, 1952-55. Mem. Am. Assn. Advt. Agys. (past dir.). Republican. Clubs: Bankers (San Francisco); Sharon Hts. Golf and Country (Menlo Park). Home: 1020 Whitney Dr Menlo Park CA 94025 Office: 55 Francisco St San Francisco CA 94133

RANDOLPH, VICKI LEAH, sales director; b. Los Angeles, Dec. 24, 1956; d. Edward W. and Frieda K. (Kinnory) R. B.S. in Bus., U. Colo., 1978. Sales dir. Carnival Cruise Lines, Miami, 1978—; lectr. Named Rookie of Yr., Carnival Cruise Line, 1979. Mem. Traffic and Transp. Research Assn., Travelarians, Cruise Mgr. Assn. Republican. Jewish. Office: Carnival Cruise Lines 3915 Biscayne Blvd Miami FL 33137

RANFTL, ROBERT MATTHEW, aerospace company executive; b. Milw., May 31, 1925; s. Joseph Sebastian and Leona Elaine (Goetz) R.; m. Marion Smith Goodman, Oct. 12, 1946. B.S. in Elec. Engring., U. Mich., 1946; postgrad. UCLA, 1953-55. Product engr. Russell Electric Co., Chgo., 1946-47; head engring. dept. Radio Inst. Chgo., 1947-50; sr. project engr. Webster Chgo. Corp., 1950-51, product design engr., 1951-53, head equipment design group, 1953-54, head electronic equipment sect., 1954-55, mgr. product engring. dept., 1955-58, mgr. reliability and quality control, 1958-59, mgr. adminstrn. 1959-61, mgr. product effectiveness lab., 1961-74; corp. dir. engring./design mgmt., Hughes Aircraft Co., El Segundo, Calif., 1974—; pres. Ranftl Enterprises Inc., Mgmt. Cons., Los Angeles, 1981—; guest lectr. Cornell U., Grad. Sch. Mgmt., U. Calif.-Irvine; mem. White House Conf. on Productivity, 1983. Mem. AAAS, AIAA, Am. Soc. Engring. Edn., Am. Soc. Tng. and Devel., IEEE, Inst. Mgmt. Scis., Internat. Platform Assn., N.Y. Acad. Scis., U. Mich. Alumni Assn., UCLA Alumni Assn. Author: R&D Productivity, 1974, 78; (with others) Productivity: Prospects for Growth, 1981; contbr. articles to profl. jours. Home: PO Box 49892 Los Angeles CA 90049 Office: PO Box 902 El Segundo CA 90245

RANGE, JOSEPH ANTHONY, JR., automobile and recreational vehicle dealer; b. Omaha, Dec. 20, 1937; s. Joseph Anthony and Rosalie (Caruso) R.; student pub. schs.; m. Charlene Alyce Nitz, July 5, 1957; children—Terri, Doug, Patti. With IBM Corp., 1960-71, instr., mgr. new products computer and tape systems, 1971; pres., owner Range Vehicle Center Inc., Fort Collins, Colo., 1971—; new automobile dealer, 1980—. Served with USNR, 1956-60. Lic. pvt. pilot. Mem. Nat. Ind. Automobile Assn., Recreational Vehicle Dealers Am. (nat. dir.), Am. Mgmt. Assn., Ft. Collins C. of C., Colo. Recreational Vehicle Assn. (pres.), Ft. Collins Automobile New Car Dealers (pres.), Nat. Auto Dealers Assn. Republican. Home: 4801 Chippendale Dr Fort Collins CO 80526 Office: 1429 E Mulberry St Fort Collins CO 80524

RANGILA, NANCY ARNEVNA, savings and loan executive, investment consultant; b. Petrozavodsk, Russia, Mar. 23, 1936; (mother Am. citizen); d. Henry Hjalmar and Myrtle Marie (Jacobson) Rangila. B.A. in Am. History, U. S.C., 1958, M.A. in Am. History, 1964; M.B.A. in Finance, U. So. Calif., 1973. Chartered fin. analyst; cert. employee benefit specialist. Fin. analyst Capital Research Co., Los Angeles, 1964-73; portfolio mgr., fin. analyst Capital Cons., Inc., Portland, Oreg., 1973-82; v.p., mgr. Franklin Securities, Inc. (subs. Benjamin Franklin Fed. Savings & Loan Assn.), Portland, 1982—; lectr. investments, retirement plans. Chmn. City of Portland Hosp. Facilities Authority. Mem. Portland Soc. Fin. Analysts, Fin. Analysts Fedn., Los Angeles Soc. Fin. Analysts, Western Pension Conf. (Portland chpt.). Republican. Clubs: City, Multnomah Athletic (Portland). Home: 2221 SW 1st Ave Apt 1625 Portland OR 97201 Office: Franklin Securities Inc 1 SW Columbia St Suite 1414 Portland OR 97201

RANKAITIS, SUSAN ANNE, artist; b. Cambridge, Mass., Sept. 10, 1949; d. Alfred Edward and Isabel (Shimkus) Rankaitis; m. Robbert Flick, June 5, 1976. B.F.A. in Painting, U. Ill., 1971; M.F.A. in Visual Arts, U. So. Calif., 1977. One-person shows: Los Angeles County Mus. Art, 1983, Internat. Mus. Photography, George Eastman House, 1983; represented in permanent collections: U. Ill., Santa Monica Coll., Ctr. for Creative Photography, UCLA, Mus. Modern Art, Santa Barbara Mus. Art, Los Angeles County Mus. Art, Mpls. Inst. Arts, San Francisco Mus. Modern Art, Security Pacific Bank, Mus. Modern Art, Lodz, Poland; adj. prof. art Chapman Coll. Overview panelist visual arts Nat. Endowment for Arts, 1983; mem. steering com. U. So. Calif. Friends of Fine Arts. Nat. Endowment for Arts fellow, 1980. Mem. Los Angeles Ctr. for Photographic Studies, Soc. for Photographic Edn., Los Angeles Inst. Contemporary Art, Los Angeles County Mus. Art, Friends of Photography, Center for Creative Photography. Studio: 707 Hyde Park Blvd Inglewood CA 90302

RANKIN, KELLY DAVID, physical education educator, consultant; b. Clinton, Okla., Mar. 9, 1940; m. Janice Lynn Cook, Sept. 3, 1961; children—John, Rachael, Jennifer. Student Kans. State U., 1958-62; B.S. in Elem. Edn., Kans. U., 1962, Ed.D. in Phys. Edn. (Elem. Adminstrn.), 1975; M.A. in Adminstrn., Washburn U., 1965; Ed.S. in Elem. Edn., Kans. State Tchrs. Coll., 1970. Tchr. elem. schs., Topeka, 1962-67, prin. Quincy Elem. Sch., Topeka, 1967; coordinator elem. phys. edn. Topeka Pub. Schs., 1967-69; head gymnastic coach, asst. track coach Topeka High Sch., 1968-69, phys. edn. supr. Butcher Children's Sch., Kans. State Tchrs. Coll., Emporia, 1969-71, Butcher-Roosevelt Middle Sch., 1971-72; instr. phys. edn. U. Kans., Lawrence, 1972-75; asst. prof. phys. edn. U. Oreg., Eugene, 1975-80, coordinator phys. edn. and athletics Vancouver (Wash.) Sch. Dist. 7, 1980—; judge gymnastic events; cons. in field. Deacon 1st Presbyn. Ch., Emporia, 1970-71; ruling elder Central Presbyn. Ch., Eugene, Oreg., 1977-80; pres. Kans. Assn. Health Phys. Edn. and Recreation, 1973. Named Coach Yr. Kans. Gymnastic Assn., 1968, Kans. Judge of Yr., 1972, 73. Mem. AAHPER, Phys. Educator, Nat. High Sch. Athletic Dirs. Assn., Scholastic Coach, Wash. Assn. Health, Phys. Edn. and Recreation. Contbr. chpts. to books, articles in field to profl. jours. Office: Vancouver Sch Dist 37 605 N Devine Rd Vancouver WA 98661

RANKIN, WILLIAM LEE, research psychologist; b. Marshalltown, Iowa, June 15, 1947; s. Howard Lee and Mary Jane (Baron) R.; m. Lynn Conner, Aug. 4, 1970; m. 2d Kathie Gail Larsen, June 25, 1976. B.A., Central Coll., Pella, Iowa, 1969; M.S. Psychology, Wash. State U., Pullman, 1975, Ph.D. Psychology, 1977. Research scientist II, Battelle Human Affairs Research Centers, Seattle, 1976—. Pres. Wash. State Council on Alcoholism. NSF fellow, 1973-74; Nat. Inst. Alcohol Abuse and Alcoholism fellow Wash. State U., 1975-76; NASA fellow, U. Nev., Reno, 1969-70. Mem. AAAS, Am. Psychol. Assn., Human Factors Soc. Contbr. articles to profl. jours. Office: 4000 NE 41st St Seattle WA 98105

RANKIN, WILLIAM PARKMAN, educator, former publishing company executive, consultant; b. Boston, Feb. 6, 1917; s. George William and Bertha W. (Clowe) R.; m. Ruth E. Gerard, Sept. 12, 1942; children—Douglas W., Joan W. B.S., Syracuse U., 1941; M.B.A., NYU, 1949, Ph.D., 1979. Sales exec. Redbook mag., N.Y.C., 1945-49; sales exec. This Week mag., N.Y.C., 1949-55, adminstrv. exec., 1955-60, v.p., 1957-60, v.p., dir. advt. sales, sales devel. dir., 1960-63, exec. v.p., 1963-69; gen. exec. newspaper div. Time Inc., N.Y.C., 1969-70; gen. mgr. feature service Newsweek, Inc., N.Y.C., 1970-74, fin. and ins. advt. mgr., 1974-81; assoc. prof. dept. journalism Ariz. State U., Tempe, 1981—; lectr. Syracuse U., NYU, Berkeley Sch.; mem. adv. council Sch. Journalism, Syracuse U. Mem. Soc. Profl. Journalists/Sigma Delta Chi, Alpha Delta Sigma. Clubs: N.Y. Dutch Treat, Met. Adv. Golf Assn.; Mesa Country. Author: Selling Retail Advertising, 1944; The Technique of Selling Magazine Advertising, 1949; Business Management of Consumer Magazines, 1980. Home: 1220 E Krista Way Tempe AZ 85284 also Bridge Rd Bomoseen VT 05732 Office: Dept Journalism Ariz State U Tempe AZ 85287

RANNEY, HELEN MARGARET, physician, educator; b. Summer Hill, N.Y., Apr. 12, 1920; d. Arthur C. and Alesia (Toolan) Ranney; A.B., Barnard Coll., 1941; M.D., Columbia, 1947; Sc.D., U. S.C., 1979. Intern Presbyn. Hosp., N.Y.C., 1947-48, resident, 1948-50; practice medicine specializing in internal medicine, hematology, N.Y.C., 1954-70; asst. physician Presbyn. Hosp., 1954-60; instr. Coll. Phys. and Surg. Columbia, 1954-60; asso. prof. medicine Albert Einstein Coll. Medicine, 1960-64, prof. medicine, 1965-70; prof. medicine State U. N.Y. at Buffalo, 1970-73; prof. medicine, chmn. dept. medicine U. Calif. at San Diego, 1973—. Diplomate Am. Bd. Internal Medicine. Fellow AAAS, A.C.P.; mem. Am. Soc. for Clin. Investigation, Am. Soc. Hematology, Harvey Soc., Am. Assn. Physicians, Nat. Acad. Sci., Inst. Medicine, Am. Acad. Arts and Scis., Phi Beta Kappa, Sigma Xi, Alpha Omega Alpha. Office: Dept Medicine U Calif-San Diego Sch Medicine La Jolla CA 92093*

RANSOM, GRAYCE ANNABLE, emeritus educator; b. La Porte, Ind.; d. Irving H. and Louisa Sabra (Sawin) Annable; B.R.E., McCormick Theol. Sem., 1937; M.A., Lewis and Clark Coll., 1954; B.A., Kalamazoo Coll., 1965; Ph.D., U. So. Calif., 1967; m. John T. Seeley, Mar. 20, 1970; children—Judith Ransom Burney, Kenneth C., Janet. Asst. camp dir., Portland, Oreg., 1947-55; tchr. religious edn., tchr. tng. Portland Council of Chs., 1949-54; tchr. elementary sch., Portland, Los Angeles, 1955-62; asst. prof. Calif. State U., Long Beach, 1963-65; faculty U. So. Calif., Los Angeles, from 1965, prof. curriculum and reading instrn., from 1974, now emeritus, chmn. dept. curriculum and instruction, dir. Campus and NCL Reading Centers, 1967—; cons. Calif. State Dept. Edn., 1966—, various sch. dists. in Calif., 1965—; reading test cons. Ednl. Testing Service, Princeton, N.J., 1971-72. Bd. dirs. Footlighters Child Guidance Clinic. Recipient Merit award Calif. State Bd. Edn., 1981. Mem. Internat. (dir.), Calif. (pres. 1976-77, Marcus Foster award for outstanding contbns. to reading 1979), Los Angeles (pres. 1973-74) reading assns., AAUP, Am. Ednl. Research Assn., NEA, Nat. Council Tchrs. English, LWV (pres. Portland 1947-48), Pi Lambda Theta, Phi Delta Kappa (award for research 1982). Presbyterian (elder 1971—). Author: Crackerjacks, 1969; Evaluating Teacher Education Programs in Reading, 1972; Teacher's Guide for Electronic Card-Reading Machines, 1974; The Ransom Reading Program, 1974; Multi Media Kits-Reading, Researching, Reporting in Social Studies, 1975, Science, 1977, Health, 1977; Preparing to Teach Reading, 1978; California Framework for Reading, 1980. Research in computers in early childhood edn. Home: 3436 NW Ashland Dr Beaverton OR 97005 Office: Early Childhood Edn Ctr 14485 NW W Union Rd Portland OR 97229

RANSOM, ROBERT LAUREN, corporate executive; b. Portland, Oreg., Nov. 14, 1940; s. Lauren Melvin and Hazel (Mason) R.; A.A., Multnomah Coll., 1960; B.S. in Psychology, Portland State U., 1963, M.S. in Ednl. Psychology, 1969; M.P.A., U. Puget Sound, 1979; postgrad. Union for Experimenting Colls. and Univs., 1977—; m. Georgene Sharon Van Cleave, Sept. 12, 1965; children—Tamara G., David L., Kimberly S., Jeanne L., Patricia R. Personnel examiner/analysts Portland Civil Service Bd., 1966-70; employment supr. King County (Wash.) Personnel Div., 1970-72, sr. personnel analyst, 1972-74, personnel psychologist, 1974-79; personnel dir. City of Everett (Wash.), 1979-82; mng. dir. Ransom Enterprises, 1982—; corporate 1st v.p. Northwest Multi-Service Council, 1981—; mem. Snohomish County Employment and Tng. Adv. Council, 1980-82, also past chmn.; personnel cons. to local govts., 1969-79. Mem. Republican Precinct Com., Portland, 1970; bd. dirs. Mental Health Services of Snohomish County, 1981-82. Lic. psychol. affiliate, Wash. Mem. Internat. Personnel Mgmt. Assn., Am. Soc. Personnel Adminstrs., Oreg. Psychol. Assn., Am. Psychol. Assn. Baptist. Prepared numerous defenses for ct., state human rights and EEO employment cases. Home: 16745 Burke Ave N Seattle WA 98133 Office: 3002 Wetmore St Everett WA 98201

RAO, MOCHERLA BHASKARA, insurance company executive; b. Eluru, India, Aug. 25, 1935; s. Viyyanna and Ramayamma (Vadrevu) R.; m. Vijaya Lakshmi, Feb. 9, 1969; children—Santi, Jyoti. B.S., Andhra U., 1954; B. Laws, Madras U., 1957; M.B.A., U. Calif.-Berkeley, 1964. Atty., Hyderbad, India, 1957-58; with Indian Audit and Accounts Dept., Calcutta, 1958-61; mgmt. trainee J.C. Penny & Co., Berkeley, 1964; with Firemans Fund Am. Ins. Co., San Francisco, 1965—, asst. dir. mktg. research, 1971-76, asst. sec., 1973, sec., 1974—, asst. v.p., 1975—, dir. mktg. research, 1976-82, head bus. research services, 1982—. Mem. Am. Mktg. Assn., Nat. Assn. Bus. Economists, Inst. Mgmt. Scis., Am. Risk and Ins. Assn., U. Calif. Alumni Assn. (life), Clubs: Commonwealth of Calif., Toastmasters (dist. lt. gov. 1969-70). Contbr. articles to ins. trade jours., also Indian lang. jours. Home: Prasanti 99 Van Buren Ct Novato CA 94947 Office: 777 San Marin Dr Novato CA 94998

RAO, PRABHAKARA POOVANDUR, aerospace engr.; b. Kay, India, Sept. 23, 1941; came to U.S., 1967, naturalized, 1979; s. Babu Poovandur and Leelavathi Poovandur R.; B.S., U. Mysore (India), 1963; M.Sc., Indian Inst. Sci., Bangalore, 1965; M.S., U. Minn., 1969, Ph.D., 1971; m. Revathi Poovandur Rao, May 15, 1972; children—Jyothi P., Arathi P., Ravikanth P. Aero. engr. Hindustan Aeros., Ltd., Bangalore, 1965-67; research fellow U. Minn., Mpls., 1967-71; sr. engr. Martin Marietta Aerospace, Denver, 1972-78, staff engr., 1978—. Treas., India Assn. Denver, 1980. Mem. AIAA. Hindu. Club: Toastmasters Denver (past v.p.). Contbr. articles to profl. jours. Home: 6752 S Lamar St Littleton CO 80123 Office: PO Box 179 Mail Stop G5440 Martin Marietta Aerospace Denver CO 80201

RAPAPORT, MARK SAMUEL, lawyer; b. N.Y.C., July 31, 1947; s. Joseph and Sadie (Schwartz) R.; m. Jennifer Munnell, Nov. 22, 1971. B.A. cum laude, U. Wis., 1968, J.D. cum laude, 1973. Bar: Wis. 1973, N.Y. 1974, Calif. 1981. Assoc. Dewey, Ballantine, Bushby, Palmer & Wood, N.Y.C., 1973-80; assoc. Hahn and Cazier, Los Angeles, 1980-82, ptnr. 1982—. Mem. donor fin. planning com. Greater Los Angeles affiliate Heart Fund, 1981—. Mem. State Bar Calif. (vice chmn. trust adminstrn. subcom.), ABA (investments by fiduciaries com.), N.Y. State Bar Assn., Stte Bar of Wis. Jewish. Note and comment editor Wis. Law Rev., 1972-73. Home: 5751 Stansbury Ave Van Nuys CA 91401 Office: Hahn and Cazier 42d floor 555 S Flower St Los Angeles CA 90071

RAPER, JOHN F., JR., state supreme court justice; b. Mapleton, Iowa, June 13, 1913; s. John F. and Anna S. (Peterson) R.; student Drake U., Des Moines, 1934-35; LL.B., U. Wyo., 1936; m. Nell M. Chesler, Aug. 4, 1939; children—Thomas J., Larry Harlan, Robert Bruce, Charles Ross. Bar: Wyo. 1936. Practiced in Sheridan, 1936-40, 45-50, 51-53; city atty., Sheridan, 1949-50, 51-53; U.S. atty., 1953-61; mem. law firm Hickey, Raper, Rooney and Walton, Cheyenne, Wyo., 1961-63; atty. gen. of Wyo., 1963-66; dist. judge First Jud. Dist. of Wyo., 1966-74; justice Wyo. Supreme Ct., 1974-83, chief justice, 1979-80. Served with AUS, 1941-45, 50-51; colonel, Wyo. N.G., now ret. Decorated Disting. Unit Citation, Silver Star; named Disting. Alumnus, U. Wyo., 1983. Mem. Am. Legion, VFW, Sigma Nu. Mason (Shriner). Rotarian. Home: 3733 Dover Rd Cheyenne WY 82001 Office: Supreme Ct Bldg Cheyenne WY 82001

RAPER, MARGARET ELAINE LEWIS, biologist; b. Arvida, Que., Can., Aug. 7, 1949; came to U.S., 1957, naturalized, 1971; d. Ronald Wilfred James and Helen Bernice (Johnston) Lewis; B.A. in Zoology, UCLA, 1972; M.S. in Zoology, U. Wyo., 1976; m. Robert B. Raper, Aug. 18, 1972. Biologist aid Wyo. Dept. Game and Fish, 1976, wildlife biologist, 1976-82, wildlife mgmt. coordinator, 1982—. Mem. Wildlife Soc. (dir. Wyo. chpt. 1978), Sigma Xi, Phi Kappa Phi, Nat. Audubon Soc., Nat. Wildlife Fedn., Soc. Range Mgmt. Home: 1635 E Teton St Green River WY 82935 Office: 351 Astle St Green River WY 82935

RAPP, MEIKLE DEAN, advertising executive; b. Idaho Falls, Idaho, Feb. 6, 1949; s. Bobby Dean and Iretta (Harding) R.; m. Ginger (Clement) R.; Dec. 6, 1947; children—Derek Scott, Meigin Lee, Dax Dean, Darci Dawn. Sales service rep. Associated Food Stores Inc., Salt Lake City, 1973-78, advt. coordinator Foodtown stores div., 1978. Recipient Excellence in Color Advt. award Coop. Food Distbrs. Am., 1981. Mormon. Office: 1377 S Redwood Rd Salt Lake City UT 84104

RAPP, ROGER GRIMM, petroleum products company sales engineer; b. Kenosha, Wis.; s. Erwin Harold and Janet Velma R.; m. Carolyn Ann, May 29, 1963; children—Valerie, Wayne. B.S. in Animal Husbandry, Calif. Poly. Inst., 1956. Chemist, Sinton & Brown Co., Betaravia, Calif., 1956-58; sr. lab. technician Richfield Oil Co./Atlantic Richfield Co., Anaheim, Calif., 1958-69; comml. and dist. br. salesman Atlantic Richfield Co., Los Angeles, 1969-70, contracted and leased dealer salesman, San Bernardino, Calif., 1970-75; lubricant sales engr. ARCO Petroleum Products Co., Glendale, Calif., 1975—; Bd. dirs. Irvine (Calif.) Harvest Festival; treas. South Coast Republican Forum, Irvine, 1979, pres., 1981. Served with USAR, 1958. Mem. Am. Soc. Lubricant Engrs. Republican. Episcopalian. Home: 15201 Chalon Circle Irvine CA 92714 Office: 300 W Glenoaks Blvd Glendale CA 91202

RAPPAPORT, LAWRENCE, horticulture and plant physiology educator, academic administrator; b. N.Y.C., May 28, 1928; s. Aaron and Elsie (Siegel) R.; m. Norma B. Horwitz, 1953; children—Meryl, Debra, Craig. B.S in Horticulture, U. Idaho-Moscow, 1950; M.S., Mich. State U., 1950, Ph.D. in Horticulture, 1956. Jr. olericulturist U. Calif.-Davis, asst. prof. vegetable crops, assoc. prof., prof., olericulturist, chmn. dept. vegetable crops., adminstrv. dir. Plant Growth Lab., 1973-77, acting dir. lab., 1977-78; co-dir. hort. subproject ADS-Egypt, dept. agronomy U. Tokyo, 1963; Hebrew U., Jerusalem, 1963-64; dept. organic chemistry U. Bristol (Eng.), 1970-71; U. Calif.-San Diego, La Jolla, 1977-78; cons. to pvt. firms. Served to sgt. maj. inf. U.S. Army, 1952-53. Decorated Bronze Star; NIH grantee, 1960-73, spl. fellow, 1970-71; Fulbright fellow, 1963-64; Guggenheim fellow, 1963-64; grantee NSF, 1971—, NATO, 1971—. Mem. Am. Soc. Plant Physiology, Scandinavian Soc. Plant Physiology, Japan Soc. Plant Physiology, Am. Soc. Hort. Sci., AAAS, Tissue Culture Assn., Am. Inst. Biol. Scis., Jewish Fellowship of Davis. Democrat. Contbr. numerous articles to profl. jours., chpts. to books. Office: Dept Vegetable Crops/Plant Growth Lab U Calif Davis CA 95616

RASBAND, JUDITH ANN, home economist, educator, columnist, lecturer; b. Longview, Wash., Oct. 7, 1942; d. Archie Lisle and Maxine E. (Klingaman) Packard; m. Shirley Neil Rasband, Sept. 12, 1963; children—Nanette, Matthew, Daniel. B.S., U. Utah, 1964; M.S., Brigham Young U., 1978. Home econs. tchr. secondary schs. Salt Lake City, 1965-68; instr. U. Utah, 1969; adult edn. instr., N.J., La., Utah, 1969-70; instr. Brigham Young U., Provo, Utah, 1973-82; home economist in bus., Provo, 1980—; cons. wardrobe and personal appearance, 1976—; contbr. weekly newspaper column: Let's Face It, 1980—; lectr., condr. workshops, seminars in field. Bd. dirs. Utah Valley Symphony Guild. Recipient Leah D. Widstoe award as outstanding home economist; named Utah's Outstanding Young Home Economist, 1983. Mem. Am. Home Econs. Assn., Utah Home Econs. Assn., Home Economists in Bus., Assn. Coll. Profs. of Textiles and Clothing, AAUW, Omicron Nu, Phi Kappa Phi. Republican. Mormon. Clubs: Brigham Young U. Women. Author: Alternative Methods of Pattern Alteration, 1978, How to Clothe Your Family, 1981; contbr. articles to profl. and popular mags. Office: PO Box 7052 University Station Provo UT 84602

RASIWALA, ABDULLA FAKHRUDDIN, accountant; b. Ahmedabad, India, Oct. 7, 1945; came to U.S., 1971, naturalized, 1980; s. Fakhruddin Mohamedali and Jenab Mohamedali (Dairywala) R.; m. Yolanda Yali, Sept. 25, 1976; children—Shabir, Husseni. B.S. in Acctg., H.A. Coll. Commerce, India, 1965; Chartered Acct., Inst. Chartered Accts. India, 1970. C.P.A., Alaska. Acct., Emar Separators Co., Inc., N.Y.C., 1971-74, Constrn. Products, Inc., Brookfield, Conn., 1974-75; controller Chugach Natives, Inc., Anchorage, 1975-76; pvt. practice acctg., Anchorage, 1976—. Mem. Am. Inst. C.P.A.s, Alaska Soc. C.P.A.s, Inst. Chartered Accts. India. Republican. Islam. Office: 5134 Sillary Circle Anchorage AK 99504

RASKOB, PATRICIA FARROW, religious association administrator; b. Leavenworth, Kans., May 30, 1937; d. Curt Ernest and Pam B. (Jeffries) Farrow; children by previous marriage—John, Katherine, Peter, Patricia, Pamela. B.S., Kans. State U., 1959; postgrad. U. Ariz. Dir. advt. Diocese of Tucson, 1978-83, exec. dir. Catholic Found., 1983—. Bd. dirs. Kino Learning Ctr., St. Mary's Hosp. and Health Ctr. Hospice; active Leadership Tucson Alumni, Mem. Innkeepers Assoc., Tucson Met. C. of C. Republican. Roman Catholic. Club: Skyline Country (Tucson). Office: 192 S Stone St Tucson AZ 85701

RASKOWITZ, ROBERT PHILIP, marketing executive; b. Bklyn., May 19, 1936; s. Harry and Betty (Horowitz) R.; B.S.E.E., Bridgeport Engring. Inst., 1966; M.S., U. Bridgeport, 1972; m. Hazel Myra Friedlander, June 16, 1963; children—Sheri Elena, Debra Helene. Project engr. Kollsman Instrument Corp., Elmhurst, N.Y., 1960-62, Perkin Elmer Corp., Wilton, Conn., 1962-63; sr. engr. Remington Office Machines div. Sperry Rand Corp., Norwalk, Conn., 1963-66; group leader Norden div. United Technologies, Norwalk, 1966-73; sales mgr. Panasonic Co., Div. Matsushita, Secaucus, N.J., 1973-77; dir. market and devel. Microelectronics Tech. Corp., Palo Alto, Calif., 1977—; instr., vis. lectr. U. New Haven, 1973, U. Bridgeport (Conn.), 1973, Rutgers U., New Brunswick, N.J., 1976. Mem. IEEE, Soc. Automotive Engrs., Soc. Photog. Scientists and Engrs., Internat. Soc. Hybrid Microelectronics. Jewish. Contbr. articles to profl. jours.; editor: ZNR Manuel, 1979. Home: 12642 Fredericksburg Dr Saratoga CA 95070 Office: 1072 East Meadow Circle Palo Alto CA 94303

RASMUSON, ELMER EDWIN, banker; b. Yakutat, Alaska, Feb. 15, 1909; s. Edward Anton and Jenny (Olson) R.; B.S. magna cum laude, Harvard, 1930, A.M., 1935; student U. Grenoble, 1930; LL.D., U. Alaska, 1970; m. Lile Vivian Benard, Oct. 27, 1939 (dec. 1960); children—Edward Bernard, Lile Muchmore (Mrs. John Gibbons, Jr.), Judy Ann; m. 2d, Col. Mary Louise Milligan, Nov. 4, 1961. Chief accountant Nat. Investors Corp., N.Y.C., 1933-35; prin. Arthur Andersen & Co., N.Y.C., 1935-43; pres. Nat. Bank of Alaska, 1943-65, chmn. bd., 1965-74, chmn. exec. com., 1975—; mayor, Anchorage, 1964-67. Civilian aide from Alaska to sec. Army, 1959-67; Swedish consul for Alaska, 1955-77; U.S. commr. Internat. N. Pacific Fisheries Commn., 1969—; mem. Nat. Marine Fisheries Adv. Com., 1974-77; mem. North Pacific Fishery Mgmt. Council, 1976-77; trustee Alaska Permanent Fund, 1980-82. Chmn. Rasmuson Found. Mem. city council, Anchorage, 1945, chmn. city planning commn., 1950-53; sponsor Atlantic Council U.S.; state sec. Rhodes Scholar Com., 1960-66; mem. Def. Orientation Conference Assn.; pres. Alaska council Boy Scouts Am., 1953; mem. nat. adv. bd. Girl Scouts U.S.A.; sec.-treas. Lousac Found.; regent U. Alaska, 1950-69; trustee King's Lake Camp. C.P.A., N.Y., Tex., Alaska. Decorated knight first class Order of Vasa, comdr. Order No. Star (Sweden); recipient Outstanding Civilian Service Medal; Alaskan of Yr. award, 1976. Mem. Pioneers Alaska, Alaska Bankers Assn. (past pres.), Phi Beta Kappa. Republican. Presbyn. Clubs: Masons, Elks; Anchorage Rotary (past pres.); Harvard (N.Y.C.; Boston); Washington Athletic, Rainier (Seattle); Explorers, Seattle Yacht; Thunderbird (Palm Desert); Bohemian (San Francisco). Office: Box 600 Anchorage AK 99510

RASMUSSEN, DENNIS LOY, personnel executive; b. Green Bay, Wis., Oct. 12, 1940; s. Maurice G. and Irene Rose (Heitzke) R.; m. Janet A. Meyer, Aug. 21, 1959; m. 2d., Jo Anne M. Lucero, June 15, 1981; 1 dau., Anne E. B.A. cum laude, St. Norbert Coll., 1966. Sales promotion mgr. Tape Inc., Green Bay, Wis., 1966-69; product sales mgr. Xerox Corp., Jacksonville, Fla., 1969-78; regional v.p. Foremost Guaranty Corp., Clearwater, Fla., 1978-82; dir. tng. and communications Gates Rubber Co., Denver, 1982—. Mem. Linn County Iowa personnel com., 1972. Served with AUS, 1959-61. Mem. Am. Soc. Tng. and Devel. Republican. Mormon. Mailing Address: 2685 S Dayton Way Apt 91 Denver CO 80231 Office: 999 S Broadway PO Box 5887 Denver CO 80217

RASMUSSEN, DONALD LINDEN, geologist; b. Lewistown, Mont., Apr. 13, 1941; s. Edward Linden and Francis Marie (Collins) R.; B.A. in Geology, U. Mont., 1963, M.A. in Geology, 1969; Ph.D., U. Kans., 1977; m. Geraldine Jule Dougherty, June 14, 1961; children—Stanley Linden, Dalton Lawrence. Geologist, Pan Am. Petroleum Corp., New Orleans, 1966-70, Amoco Prodn. Co., Denver, 1974-79, Davis Oil Co., Denver, 1979—. Mem. Rocky Mountain Assn. Geologists, Geol. Soc. Am., Mont. Geol. Soc., Soc. Vertebrate Paleontology, Tabacco Root Geol. Soc. Methodist. Contbr. articles to profl. jours. Office: Suite 1400 410 17th St Denver CO 80202

RASMUSSEN, EDWARD FREDERICK, airline co. exec.; b. Mpls., June 5, 1940; s. Hans Edward and Lois Ruth (Welch) R.; student pub. schs., Hopkins, Minn.; m. Lena K. Clement, Feb. 1981; stepchildren—Greg Carvalho, Heather Carvalho; 1 son by previous marriage, John Edward. Served as enlisted man U.S. Navy, 1959-67, with Western Air Lines, Los Angeles, 1967—, avionics line service foreman, Los Angeles, 1975-83, sr. avionics engr., 1983—. Mem. Internat. Platform Assn. Republican. Home: 10488 Apache River Ave Fountain Valley CA 92708 Office: PO Box 92005 World Way Center Los Angeles CA 90009

RASMUSSEN, JOHN EDWARD, research inst. exec.; b. Denver, May 28, 1925; s. Harry Edward and Louise Marie (Cunningham) R.; B.S., Northwestern U., 1947, M.A., 1949; Ph.D., Am. U., 1961; m. Dorothy Jean Eggeling, Mar. 22, 1949; children—Anne Louise, James Edward. Served as enlisted man U.S. Navy, 1943-44, commd. ensign, 1945, advanced through grades to capt. Med. Service Corps., 1966; head clin. psychology sect. Bur. Medicine, Navy Dept., Washington, 1956-58; dir. dept. behavioral sci. Naval Med. Research Inst., Bethesda, Md., 1959-64; liaison psychology Office of Naval Research, London, 1964-67; asst. for med. and allied scis. Chief Naval Devel., Navy Dept., Washington, 1967-69; ret., 1969; cons. to dir. Battelle-N.W., Richland, Wash., 1969-71, dir. Battelle Human Affairs Research Centers, Seattle, 1971-81, Virginia Mason Research Ctr., Seattle, 1982—. Bd. dirs. Seattle Urban League, 1974-80, Pvt. Sector Initiatives, Seattle, 1976-81; trustee Virginia Mason Research and Edn. Center, Seattle, 1979-82. Decorated Meritorious Service medal; recipient John Shaw Billings award Assn. Mil. Surgeons U.S., 1962; VA fellow, 1948-50. Fellow Am. Psychol. Assn., AAAS, Royal Soc. Medicine. Republican. Clubs: Army and Navy (Washington); Seattle Yacht (trustee 1979-82). Editor: (with Frederick O'R. Hayes) Centers for Innovation in the Cities and States, 1973; editor, contbg. author: Human Behavior in Isolation and Confinement, 1973. Home: 71 Cascade Key Bellevue WA 98006 Office: 1000 Seneca St Seattle WA 98101

RASMUSSEN, LUTHER ERLENN, accountant; b. Watertown, S.D., Dec. 5, 1950; s. Erlenn E. and Marion E. (Hemingson) R.; m. Roberta Rae Cavanaugh, Sept. 18, 1970; children—Kristina, Angela. B.S., No. State Coll., 1973. C.P.A., S.D., Colo. Sr. acct. Harlan W. Peterson & Co., Aberdeen, S.D., 1973-79; ptnr. Anderson-Rasmussen, C.P.A.s, Longmont, Colo., 1979—. Mem. Am. Inst. C.P.A.s, Colo. Soc. C.P.A.s, Longmont C. of C. Republican. Lutheran. Clubs: Optimists, Ambassador. Home: 42 Empire Pl Longmont CO 80501 Office: 16 Mountain View Ave Longmont CO 80501

RASMUSSEN, LYMAN MERRILL, petroleum company executive; b. Cardston, Alta., Can., Apr. 17, 1920; s. Lyman Merrill and Annie (Woolf) R.; attended Mt. Royal Coll.; B.Sc. in Petroleum Engring., U. Okla.; m. Enid Atkins, June 3, 1943; children—Ronald, Karen. With Gulf Oil Corp. and British American Oil Co., 1949-59; mgr. production Pacific Petroleums Ltd., 1959-64, v.p. exploration and production, 1964-67, sr. v.p., 1967-69, exec. v.p., 1969-70, pres., from 1970, chief exec. officer, 1974-79; pres., chief exec. officer Husky Oil Co., Cody, Wyo., 1979—; dir. Husky Oil Ltd., Husky Oil Operations Ltd., Westcoast Transmission Co. Ltd., Foothills Pipe Lines (Yukon) Ltd., Energy Equipment & Systems, Inc., Royal Bank Can., Grove Valve & Regulator Co., Oakland, Wagi Internat., Rome. Bd. dirs. Am. Petroleum Inst. Served to lt., Royal Can. Army, 1942-46. Mem. Assn. Profl. Engrs. Alta., Canadian Gas Assn. (past chmn.; dir.), Canadian Petroleum Assn. (past chmn. bd. govs.). Clubs: Calgary Petroleum, Glencoe, Calgary Golf and Country, Ranchmen's, Desert Island Country (Rancho Mirage, Calif.); Olive-Glenn Country (Cody), Eldorado (Calif.), Alta (Salt Lake City), Denver Petroleum. Office: Husky Oil Co PO Box 380 Cody WY 82414

RASMUSSEN, NEVA JANE, corporate safety administrator; b. Springdale, Ark., June 21, 1936; d. Charley Edward Rayfield and Ora Mae (Wallar) Rayfield; m. Lee S. Sayre, Nov. 22, 1962 (dec.); m. 2d, Loren L. Rasmussen, Apr. 12, 1974; children—Joseph F., Susan S. R.N., O'Connor Hospital, 1957; Student, U. Ill., 1959. Head nurse Santa Rosa Meml. Hosp., Calif., 1963-68; supr. Barton Hosp., South Lake Tahoe, Calif., 1971-75; nurse cons. SAIF Corp., Salem, Oreg., 1975-80; corp. safety and tng. adminstr. Agripac Inc., Salem, 1980—. Served as 1st lt., USAF, 1958-61. Mem. Am. Soc. Safety Engrs. Republican. Club: Altrusa (v.p.). Office: 325 Patterson NW Salem OR 97304

RASMUSSEN, RICHARD FRANK, construction equipment company sales executive; b. Salt Lake City, June 21, 1935; s. Frank Richard and Dorothy (Couch) R.; m. Jan Jones, Nov. 6, 1959; children—Jody, David, Julie, Rich. Student, U. Utah, 1954-56, Owner, mgr. Rasmussen Equipment Co., Salt Lake City, 1955—, pres. 1972—. Served Utah Air N.G., 1953-61. Mem. Assoc. Equipment Distbrs., Assoc. Iron and Steel Engrs., Assoc. Gen. Contractors, C. of C. Republican. Club: Salt Lake Country. Home: 2880 Kentucky Ave Salt Lake City UT 84117 Office: 3333 West 2100 South Salt Lake City UT 84119

RASMUSSEN, SHANNON ADELE DRISCOLL, educator; b. Murray, Utah, Apr. 15, 1952; d. Allen Andrew and Ardyth Adele (Jones) Driscoll; m. Craig Rasmussen, Jan. 11, 1975; children—Ryan Craig, Lacee. Student U. Utah, 1970-73; B.S., Utah State U., 1975. Nutritionist head start program, Logan, Utah, 1975; tchr. home econs. Logan Sr. High Sch., 1975-79; tchr. home econs., head dept. Logan Jr. High Sch., 1979—. Mem. NEA, Utah Edn. Assn., Logan Edn. Assn., Delta Delta Delta, Beta Sigma Phi. Democrat. Mormon. Office: 875 N 200 E Logan UT 84321

RASMUSSEN, STUART RICARD, newspaper librarian; b. San Francisco, Nov. 7, 1906; s. Emil Jorgen and Christine (Johnsen) R.; student U. Calif. Extension; m. Nairn Margaret Abbott, June 1, 1940; children—Nairn Christine, Mark Abbott. In library San Francisco Examiner, 1929-37; head librarian San Francisco Call Bull., 1937-59, San Francisco News Call Bulletin, 1959-66; library staff San Francisco Examiner, 1966—, asst. head librarian, 1966-75, acting head librarian, 1975-78; engaged in spl. research for Metro-Goldwyn-Mayer movies, San Francisco Bay area, 1935—; actor Maxwell Burke Stock Co., Oakland and Berkeley, Calif., 1927-28, Blake, Turner Stock Co., San Francisco area, 1928; dir. children and adult plays San Geronimo Valley Community Centers; sometimes dir. Ross Valley Players Barn Theatre. Pres. Lagunitas Dist. Sch. Bd., 1955-58, San Geronimo Valley Little League, 1961. Mem. Spl. Libraries Assn., Am. Newspaper Guild (charter mem. San Francisco/Oakland chpt.). Democrat. Club: San Francisco Press (life mem.). Author drama revs. for The Peninsulan, 1936; several plays for children, 1955-60. Home: Alta Rd Lagunitas CA 94938 Office: 110 5th St San Francisco CA 94118

RASMUSSEN, VICTOR PHILIP, JR., soil science educator, computer scientist, consultant; b. Logan, Utah, Apr. 3, 1950; s. Victor Philip and Mary Velda (Peterson) R.; m. Linda Kay Schamber, Sept. 6, 1973; children—Angela Kay, Bryan Philip, Jenniffer Lynn, Neal Robert. B.S., Utah State U., 1974, M.S., 1976; Ph.D., Kans. State U., 1979. Research technician 411 modelling group Agrl. Expt. Sta., Utah State U., 1974-76, asst. prof. soil sci. and biometeorology, state soils/computer extension specialist, 1981—; research assoc. NASA Wheat Modelling Group, Evapotranspiration Lab., Kans. State U., Manhattan, 1976-78; dir. microcomputer agrl. mgmt. lab., div. agr. Ricks Coll., Rexburg, Idaho, 1979-81; cons. agrl. microcomputer applications; mem., Utah State U. rep. Utah State Soil Conservation Commn., Utah Dept. Agr., Salt Lake City, 1981—; mem. Kellogg Found. Extension Computer Feasability Task Force for 13 Western States, 1982-83; apptd. to regional com. in charge of monitoring salinity control projects on Colo. River, 1982—; lead speaker Nat. Farm Computer Conf., Mpls., 1983. Mem. Am. Soc. Agronomy, Soil Sci. Soc. Am., Western Soil Sci. Soc., Internat. Soil Sci. Soc., Soil Conservation Soc. Am., N.W. Plant Food Assn. (sec. to Utah soil improvement com. 1981-83), Sigma Xi, Alpha Zeta, Phi Kappa Phi. Author Utah State U. Extension publs.; contbr. articles to profl. publs.

RASMUSSON, RICHARD ALLEN, pub. co. exec.; b. Mpls., July 31, 1931; s. Leonard Bennett and Ellen June (Rosendahl) R.; m. Mary Ann Wakeley, June 12, 1954; children—Susan Ellen Rasmusson Mowrey, Eric Dana, Margaret Mary, David William. Student journalism U. Minn., 1949-55. City editor Daily Dispatch, Brainerd, Minn., 1955-57; corr. Associated Press, Fargo, N.D., 1957-63; reporter Record, Stockton, Calif., 1963-69, city editor, 1969-79, news editor, 1979-80; owner, pub. City Escort Mag., Stockton, Calif., 1980-82; editor, pub. Morgan Hill (Calif.) Times and San Martin News, 1982—. Bd. dirs. Live Oak Found., Morgan Hill, Calif., 1982—. Served with U.S. Army, 1951-53. Mem. Nat. Newspaper Assn., Calif. Newspaper Pubs. Assn., Am. Press Inst., Morgan Hill C. of C. (dir. 1983—), Sigma Delta Chi. Democrat. Lutheran. Club: Rotary. Home: 51 Creekside Dr Morgan Hill CA 95037 Office: Morgan Hill Times and San Martin News 30 E 3d St Morgan Hill CA 95037

RASOR, LESLIE WILSON, vocational educator; b. Portland, Oreg., Jan. 7, 1944; d. Arthur W. and Helen B. (Ladd) Wilson; m. John F. Rasor, June 18, 1962 (div.); children—Crista, Michael. B.A., Evergreen State Coll., 1975; M.S., U. Oreg., 1978. Coordinator indsl. orientation Lane Community Coll., Eugene, Oreg., 1977-80, assoc. dept. head classroom tng. program, 1980—; cons. non-traditional occupations for women. Past chmn. Apprenticeship Info. Ctr. Adv. Com., 1977-83. Oreg. Dept. Edn. grantee, 1978—. Mem. Am. Vocat. Assn., Am. Assn. Women in Community and Jr. Colls., Oreg. Council Career and Vocat. Adminstrs. Republican. Episcopalian. Author: Industrial Orientation, 1980. Office: Lane Community Coll 4000 E 30th Ave Eugene OR 97405

RASPONE, FAYE JUANITA, city official; b. Whitman County, Wash., Sept. 1, 1929; d. Fred Garfield and Iona (Nation) Heaton; m. John Alfred P. Prahinski, Apr. 15, 1949; 1 son, Stephen Kip; m. 2d, Raymond Aue, Nov. 1, 1957; m. 3d, Paul John Raspone, Aug. 5, 1972. Student pub. schs., Pullman. Telephone operator Gen. Telephone, Pullman, Wash., 1955-57; staff toll billing sect. Gen. Telephone, Spokane, 1957-58; telephone operator Wash. State U., Pullman, 1962-63; police dispatcher City of Pullman, 1963-68, chief dispatcher, 1968-73, supr. support services Dept. Pub. Safety, 1973—; pub. speaker. Mem. Assn. Pub. Communications Officers. Office: NE 205 Kamiaken St Pullman WA 99163

RASSI, RANDY LEE, city official; b. Lynwood, Calif., Apr. 24, 1943; s. Harold E. and Dorthy M. (Conley) R.; m. Margarette L. Shaffer, Sept. 11, 1968 (div.); m. Maria M. Rodriguez, Aug. 16, 1979; children—Gina, Nicole. B.S. in Acctg., Calif. State U.-Long Beach, 1968. Asst. city controller Compton (Calif.), 1973-75; asst. fin. dir. Montebello (Calif.), 1975-78; auditor Long Beach (Calif.), 1978-80; city treas., fin. dir. Pico Rivera (Calif.), 1980—. Served with USMCR, 1968. Mem. Calif. Mcpl. Treas. Assn., Mcpl. Fin. Officers Assn., Calif. Soc. Mcpl. Fin. Officers. Office: 6615 Passons Blvd Pico Rivera CA 90660

RATCLIFF, BRUCE E., manufacturing company executive; b. Canton, Ill., Oct. 3, 1941; s. Ralph A. and Margaret H. Ratcliff. Student Coll. of San Mateo, 1960-62, U. Ariz., 1962, U. Calif.-Santa Barbara, 1965; B.A. in Econs., San Francisco State U., 1967. Vice pres. sales Ratcliff Hoist Co., San Carlos, Calif., 1967-69, exec. v.p., 1969-75, pres., 1975—. Office: 1655 Old County Rd San Carlos CA 94070

RATHANA-NAKINTARA, THAWORN, physician; b. Nakornstrithamaraj, Thailand, June 5, 1933; came to U.S., 1959, naturalized, 1975; s. Tawan and Joan (Leelabandhu) Rathana-N. M.D., Chulalongkorn U., 1957; M.S.P., UCLA, 1971; postgrad. U. Mich., 1962-63. Resident in psychiatry Henry Ford Hosp., Detroit, 1960-61; med. dir. Mohave Mental Health Clinic, Inc., Kingman, Ariz., 1971-72; regional dir. psychiat. services, Sask., Can., 1967-68; dep. chief services Bklyn. State Hosp., 1972-74; acting dist. dir. North County Mental Health, Los Angeles, 1980-81; exec. dir. Internat. Inst. Preventive Psychiatry, Studio City, Calif., 1981—; pres. Center for the Advancement of Ability to Love, North Hollywood, Calif., 19—. Served to capt. Royal Thai Army, 1957-59. NIMH fellow, 1969-71. Mem. AMA, Am. Psychiat. Assn., World Med. Assn. Author: An Introduction to Priciples of True Love, 1976; Understanding love: The Key to Growth and Fulfillment, 1981. Home: 11445 Dona Dolores St Studio City CA 91604 Office: 8240 Coldwater Canyon Ave North Hollywood CA 91605

RATHBUN, LARRY PETER, university dean, agricultural consultant; b. Modesto, Calif., July 15, 1941; s. Carl and Nellie Marie (Fenno) R.; children—Peter, Mark, Joyce, Chris, Cathy, Alan. Student Modesto Jr. Coll., 1959-62; B.S., Calif. Poly. State U., 1964, M.A., 1967; Ph.D. in Agrl. Edn. (EPDA fellow), Ohio State U., 1974. Tchr. Rio Vista (Calif.) High Sch., 1965-67, Los Banos (Calif.) High Sch., 1967-70; prof. tchr. edn. Sch. Agr., Calif. Poly. State U., San Luis Obispo, 1970-76, head dept. agrl. edn., 1976-82, assoc. dean Sch. Agr., 1982—; cons. Ministry Edn., Mexico, Pakistan; cons. in field. Mem. Calif. State Employees Assn., Calif. Agrl. Tchrs. Assn., Am. Vocat. Assn., Phi Delta Kappa. Republican. Office: Sch Agr Calif Polytechnic State U San Luis Obispo CA 93407

RATHCKE, DOROTHY ANNE, nursing adminstr., consultant; b. Napa, Calif., Mar. 19, 1922; d. Clifford Clark Harris and Florence Emily (Baldwin) Goodman; B.S. in Nursing, U. Calif., Berkeley, 1944; m. George L. Rathcke, Nov. 12, 1955; children—Karen Anne Boren, Clark Harold Kujawka, Karl Lewis. Staff nurse Napa State Hosp., Imola, Calif., 1951-52, psychiat. nursing edn., 1952-63, supt. nursing, 1963-71, nursing cons. office of program rev., 1971-77, coordinator nursing services, 1977-83; mem. task force to develop staffing standards for state hosps. Calif. Dept. Health, 1972-74. Mem. adv. bd. psychiat. technician and asso. degree nursing programs, Napa Coll.; mem. adv. bd. Regional Occupational Program, Napa Unified Sch. Dist.; mem. Com. on Continuing Edn. for Health Occupations, Napa County, 1975-83; bd. dirs. Napa chpt. Am. Heart Assn., 1975-81, v.p., 1976; mem. manpower adv. panel Dept. Mental Health State of Calif., 1981-83. NIMH grantee, 1964-72. Mem. Nat. League Nursing, Calif. League Nursing-Adminstrn., Napa County Mental Health Assn. Democrat. Office: 1912 Sierra Ave Imola CA 94558

RATIGAN, THOMAS MICHAEL, computer co. exec.; b. South Gate, Calif., Oct. 15, 1934; s. Thomas Michael and Betty (Clarke) R.; B.S. in Fgn. Trade, U. So. Calif., 1956; m. Marilyn Martha Busch, June 21, 1958; children—Thomas Michael, Kelli Marie, Theresia Margarethe. Sales rep., nat. account mgr., industry mktg. rep., program admnstr., industry mktg. mgr. IBM Corp., Los Angeles and Chgo., 1960-69; v.p. Cambridge Computer Corp., Los Angeles, 1970-71; br. mgr. Memorex Corp., Los Angeles, 1971-72; sales mgr. Singer Bus. Machines, Los Angeles, 1972-75; v.p. mktg. Logicon-Intercomp, Los Angeles, 1975-77; pres. Alpha Energy Systems, Inc., 1977-78; br. mgr. Documation Inc., Long Beach, Calif., 1978-79, regional mgr., Irvine, Calif., 1979-81; rep. ICOT Corp., 1981-82; regional mgr. Computer Consoles, Inc., Long Beach, 1982—. regional mgr. Computer Consoles, Inc., Long Beach, 1982—. Chmn. bd. trustees Marymount Schs., Palos Verdes, Calif. Served to lt. USNR, 1956-59. Club: Sacramento Host Breakfast. Contbr. articles to trade mags. Home: 22 Cresta Verde Dr Rolling Hills Estates CA 90274 Office: 4401 Atlantic Ave Suite 200-19 Long Beach CA 90807

RATWAY, JOSEPH CONLEY, training and development company executive; b. Mericaibo, Venezuela, Feb. 3, 1945 (parents Am. citizens); s. Joseph Gerald and Catherine Jane (Conley) R.; student Oklahoma City U., 1963-65; B.S. B.A., Central State U., 1969; M.S.A. in Indsl. Personnel Mgmt., George Washington U., 1974; m. Joy Louise Basham, June 20, 1970; children—Hilary Kathleen, Allison Noele. Mgmt. auditor GAO, Washington, 1969-72, staff mgr. tng. dept., 1972-76; dir. tng. Tracom Corp., Denver, 1976-79, dir. market devel., 1979-83, bus. mgr., 1983—; adj. prof. Regis Coll. Pres., Fox Ridge Homeowners Assn., Englewood, Colo., 1980; precinct capt. Democratic Party, Arapahoe County, Colo., 1980—; del. Colo. Dem. Conv., 1980. Served with USAFR, 1966. Recipient Meritorious Service award Comptroller Gen. U.S., 1975. Mem. Am. Mgmt. Assn., Am. Soc. Personnel Adminstrs., Am. Soc. Tng. and Devel. Roman Catholic. Home: 7796 S Poplar Way Englewood CO 80112 Office: 200 Fillmore St Denver CO 80206

RAU, CHARLES ALFRED, JR., metall. engr.; b. Phila., Jan. 28, 1942; s. Charles Alfred and Marjorie (Doyle) R.; B.S. in Metall. Engring. cum laude (coll. scholar 1959-63, Outstanding Metall. Engring. Grad. award 1963), Lafayette Coll., Easton, Pa., 1963; M.S. (univ. fellow 1963), Stanford U., 1965, Ph.D., 1967; m. Marion Gerda Cranz, Mar. 17, 1972; children—Scott Charles, Curtis Andrew, Monica Ellen. Project engr. wrought alloys group stellite div. Union Carbide Co., 1963; research asst. Stanford U., 1964-67; lectr. U. Conn., 1967-68; with Pratt & Whitney Aircraft Co., 1967-74, supr. lifetime prediction methods group, materials engring. and research lab., 1971-74; gen. mgr. Failure Analysis Assos., Palo Alto, Calif., 1974-76, exec. v.p., prin. engr., 1976—, also dir.; lectr. continuing edn. courses UCLA. Registered profl. engr., Calif. Mem. Am. Soc. Metals, AIME, ASTM, Soc. Exptl. Stress Analysis, Am. Nuclear Soc., ASME, Phi Beta Kappa, Tau Beta Pi, Alpha Sigma Nu, Delta Tau Delta. Club: Bayside Racquet. Author papers in field. Office: 2225 E Bayshore Rd Palo Alto CA 94303

RAUBENOLT, ALVIN L., savs. and loan assn. exec.; s. Lloyd L. and Ferne D. (Rice) R.; B.S., U. Ariz., 1966; m. Sarah M. Bush, June 30, 1962; children Vanessa, Kevin. Asst. treas., then asst. v.p. Tucson Fed. Savs. & Loan Assn., 1962-71; adminstrv. v.p. Home Fed. Savs. & Loan Assn., Tucson, 1971-75; chmn. bd., pres. First State Service Corp., Tucson, 1975-81; pres. Tierra Verde Devel. Corp., Tucson, 1981—. Mem. Fin. Mgrs. Assn., U.S. League Savs. Assns., Savs. and Loan League Ariz. (pres. 1974-75), Tucson C. of C. (chmn. govt. programs com. 1976-77), So. Ariz. Home Builders Assn. Republican. Roman Catholic. Club: Downtown Tucson Exchange. Home: 2550 Calle Los Altos Tucson AZ 85718 Office: 2550 Calle Los Altos Tucson AZ 85718

RAUCH, HERBERT EMIL, electrical engineer; b. St. Louis, Oct. 6, 1935; s. Herbert Leopold and Vera Hilda (Sieloff) R.; m. Marjorie Ann Beyer, June 18, 1961; children Marta, Erik, Evan, Loren. B.S. in Elec. Engring., Calif. Inst. Tech., 1957; M.S.E.E., Stanford U., 1958, Ph.D., 1962. Mem. tech. staff Hughes Space Sustems Div., Los Angeles, 1957-62; mem. tech. staff Lockheed Palo Alto Research Lab. (Calif.), 1962—; gen. co-chmn. Astrodynamics Conf. co-sponsored Am. Astron. Soc. and AIAA, 1975; tech. program chmn. Asilomar Conf. Circuits, Systems, and Computers, 1982; gen. chmn. Am. Control Conf., 1984, parttime tchr. San Jose State U., 1968-70. Mem. Peninsula Sch. Bd. Menlo Park, Calif., 1973-82, Selective Service Bd. Santa Clara Country, 1972-75; trustee Los Altos Sch. Dist., 1974-75; chmn. People for Los Altos Now (PLAN), 1974-75. Fellow Am. Astronautical Soc. (v.p. publs., 1980-82; v.p. tech. 1982—; mem. IEEE (sr. mem., community service award region 6, 1977, chmn. San Francisco chpt. Control Systems Soc. 1976-77, 1980-82), AIAA, Soc. Indsl. and Applied Mechanics, Internat. Fedn. Automatic Control (mem. math. control com., organizing chmn. working group control applications nonlinear programming, 1978—). Author and editor of articles in field; editor-in-chief Jour. Astron. Scis., 1980—. Office: Lockheed 5256/205 3251 Hanover St Palo Alto CA 94304

RAUGHTON, JIMMIE LEONARD, urban planner, ednl. adminstr.; b. Knoxville, Tenn., Oct. 9, 1943; s. George L. and Ann (Simotes) R.; B.A. in Urban and Regional Planning, U. No. Colo., 1974, M.A., 1976. Mgr., Flexitran div. Gathers, De Vilbliss Architects and Planners, Denver, 1966-68; asst. dir. planning City of Aurora, Colo., 1970-71, asst. dir., operational planner, 1973-74; planner City of Lakewood, Colo., 1971-73; planner City of Boulder, Colo., 1973-74, acting asst. dir. community devel., 1973-74; instr. urban planning Community Coll. of Denver, 1974-76, div. dir. Human Resources and Services, 1976-81, div. dir. sci. and tech., 1981—; coordinator Community Coll. devel. Rocky Mountain Energy and Environ. Tech. Center, 1980. cons. Denver Regional Council of Govts. for Model Sign Code, 1973, City of Boulder Transp. Dept., 1975—; chmn. profl. advisory com. to Colo. Gov.'s Land Use Adviser, 1973; also public speaker. Mem. exec. bd. Civic Center Assn., Denver, 1973-75; Democratic candidate for Denver City Council, 1975; bd. dirs. Plan Metro Denver, 1975-76. Recipient Citizen Award of Honor, Assn. of Beautiful Colo. Roads, 1972. Mem. Am. Inst. of Planners (mem. exec. bd. Colo. 1970-75, treas. 1972-73), Colo. City Mgrs. Assn., Am. Soc. Planning Ofcls., Am. Vocat. Assn., Am. Soc. for Tng. and Devel. Methodist. Contbr. articles to local newspapers. Home: 2501 High St Denver CO 80205 Office: 1111 W Colfax Ave Denver CO 80204

RAUH, ROBERT BRUCE, advt. exec.; b. San Francisco, July 24, 1942; s. Rudoulph L. and Virginia I. (Vincelli) R.; m. Darlene A. Colose, Apr. 3, 1971; children—Joshua Edward, Joanna Teresa. B.A., San Jose State U., 1964. Prodn. mgr., asst. account exec., market research analyist Allen & Dorward Advt., San Francisco, 1963-66; account supr. ATD Advt., Palo Alto, Calif., 1966-68; v.p., creative dir. Markman Inc., Los Gatos, Calif., 1968-69; owner Robert B. Rauh Advt., San Jose, Calif., 1969-74; founder, pres. Rauh, Good & Darlo Advt. Assocs. Inc., Los Gatos, 1974—; adj. prof. advt. San Jose State U. Served with USN, A.C., 1964-70. Mem. Am. Advt. Fedn. award 1982, Best in West award 1982), Am. Assn. Advt. Agys., San Jose Advt. Club (bd. dirs., past pres., Silver medal 1982), Monterey Advt. Club, Santa Clara Valley Advt. Agys. Assn. (co-founder, past pres.), Promotion Mgrs. No. Calif. Democrat. Roman Catholic. Club: Democratic Century of Santa Clara County. Office: 142 S Santa Cruz Ave Los Gatos CA 95030

RAUS, RICHARD ALLEN, advertising executive; b. Garfield Heights, Ohio, July 18, 1955; s. Richard Allen and Maxine Eleanore (Kuczkowski) R.; m. Vicki Lynn Liquori, Aug. 29, 1981. B.A. in Telecommunications, Pub. Relations, Calif. State U.-Fullerton, 1978. Pub. relations rep., Irvine Co., Newport Beach, Calif., 1978-79; acct. exec., Rubin Advt., Fullerton, 1979-80; v.p. mktg. Wizard Publs., Torrance, Calif., 1980-81; v.p. mktg. Barnett and Assocs., 1981-82; exec. v.p. Barnett and Raus Advt., 1982—. Republican. Roman Catholic. Clubs: Advt. of Los Angeles, Orange County Advt. Home: 6323 Rocking Horse Ridge Orange CA 92669 Office: Barnett and Raus Advertising 730 E 3d St Suite 100 Long Beach CA 90802

RAUSCHENBACH, HANS SIEGFRIED, electrical engineer; b. Leipzig, Ger., Apr. 21, 1929; s. Erich R. and Gertraud (Surkow) R.; m. Marianne Giesche, Dec. 3, 1966; children—Christian, Isabella, Angelina, David. Student Pasadena City Coll.; 1960-62; B.S.E.E., U. Calif.-Berkeley, 1964. Supr., spl. measurements unit, Hoffman Electronics Corp., El Monte, Calif., 1959-61; supr. in electronics metrology dept. Heliotek, Sylmar, Calif., 1962-65; supr., solar array design engring. TRW, Redondo Beach, Calif., 1969-80; sr. staff engr., spl. asst. advanced solar tech., 1980—; Com. chmn. Boy Scouts Am., 1970; treas., Orange-South Los Angeles U.S. Air Force Acad. Parents Assn., 1982. Recipient NASA New Tech. awards, 1977, Best Tech. Book award Profl. and Scholarly Pub. Div., Assn Am. Pubs., 1980. Mem. IEEE (program com. 16th Photovoltaic Splty. Conf.), AIAA. Eta Kappa Nu, Tau Beta Pi. Developer precision color temperature meter, 1958; 1st practical precision artificial simulator for solar cell testing, 1960; author: Solar Array Design Handbook, 1980; assoc. editor Trans. of ASME Jour. Solar Energy; contbr. articles to profl. jours. Office: 1 Space Pk R4/1130 Redondo Beach CA 90278

RAUSSER, GORDON CLYDE, agricultural and resource economics educator, consultant; b. Lodi, Calif., July 21, 1943; s. Elmer A. and Doyve Ester (Meyers) R.; m. Patricia J. Sandborn, June 20, 1964; m. 2d, Laura H. Hall, Dec. 30, 1979; children—Sloan, Stephanie, Paige. B.S. summa cum laude, U. Calif.-Davis, 1965, M.S. with highest honors, 1968, Ph.D. with highest honors, 1971. Asst. prof. econs. and agrl. econs. U. Calif., Davis, 1969-71, assoc. prof., 1971-74; prof. econs. and stats. Iowa State U., 1974-75; prof. bus. adminstrn. and econs. Harvard U., 1975-78; prof. agrl. and resource econs., chmn. dept. agrl. and resource econs. U. Calif., Berkeley, 1979—; pres. Agripac, Inc.; gen. ptnr. Creston Commodity Fund; dir. Geneva Group; mem. Arab-Am. Council for Cultural and Econ. Exchange, 1979-81; mem. exec. com. Giannini Found., 1979—; mem. coordinating com. Dept. Agr. Western Nutrition Ctr., 1980-83; chmn. Western Agrl. Research Council, 1981-82; speaker numerous profl. meetings. Recipient Outstanding Teaching award Harvard U., 1978; USDA grantee, 1975; NSF grantee, 1976-82; World Bank grantee, 1979-81; Chgo. Merc. Exchange grantee, 1980-81; U.S. Bur. Mines grantee, 1972-75. Mem. Am. Econ. Assn., Am. Acad. Polit. and Social Sci., Am. Agrl. Econ. Assn. (award for best pub. research 1976, 80, award for best jour. article 1982), Am. Stats. Assn., Econometric Soc., Math. Assn. Am., Ops. Research Soc., Western Agrl. Econs. Assn. (award for best pub. research 1978), Blue Key, Phi Beta Kappa, Alpha Gamma Rho, Alpha Zeta. Democrat. Methodist. Author: Dynamics of Agricultural Systems: Economic Prediction and Control, 1979; New Directions in Econometric Modeling and Forecasting in U.S. Agriculture, 1982; contbr. numerous articles to profl. publs.; editor: Decision-Making in Business and Economics, 1977-79; assoc. editor Jour. Am. Stats. Assn., 1973-77; assoc. editor Jour. Econ. Dynamics and Control, 1978-82; editor Am. Jour. Agrl. Econs., 1983-86.

RAUTERKUS, PETER ANTHONY, machine tool educator; b. Compton, Calif., Aug., 22, 1941; s. Alphons Joseph and Justine Ann R.; m. Linda Margaret LaCabe; children—Sharon Tami, Michael Anthony. A.A., Los Angeles Trade Tech. Coll., 1961; B.A., Calif. State U.-Los Angeles, 1963; M.A., Calif. State U.-Long Beach, 1978. Service rep. Brandt Machines Co., Irvine, Calif., 1960-66; with Cannon Electric Co. subs. ITT, Santa Ana, Calif., 1966-73; instr., adminstr. Los Angeles Trade Tech. Coll., 1973—, assoc. prof. machine tech.; cons., instr. Hitco, Gardena, Calif., 1974; instr. El Camino Coll., Torrance, Calif., 1974-76, Santa Ana Coll., 1975; bd. govs. Teaching Resources Ctr., Los Angeles Trade Tech. Coll. Recipient Cert. of Appreciation Los Angeles Trade Tech. Coll., 1979. Mem. Am. Tech. Edn. Assn. (rep. Pacific region), Am. Vocat. Assn., Soc. Mfg. Engrs. Democrat. Roman Catholic. Office: Los Angeles Trade Tech Coll 400 W Washington St Los Angeles CA 90015

RAVELING, DENNIS GRAFF, biology educator; b. Devil's Lake, N.D., Feb. 28, 1939; s. Ralph Gordon and Martha Irene (Graff) R.; m. Olga Catherine Masnyk, Mar. 3, 1962. B.A., So. Ill. U., 1960, Ph.D., 1967; M.A., U. Minn., 1963. Research scientist Can. Wildlife Service, Winnipeg, Man., 1967-71; asst. prof. dept. wildlife-fisheries biology U. Calif., Davis, 1971-74, assoc. prof., 1974-80, prof., 1980—. NSF grantee, 1963, 73, 75, 76, 77, 78. Fellow AAAS; mem. Am. Ornithologists Union (elective mem.), Am. Soc. Naturalists, Brit. Ornithologists Union, Cooper Ornithol. Soc., Wildlife Soc., Wilson Ornithol. Soc., Calif. Wetlands Fedn. (trustee), Sigma Xi. Contbr. articles to profl. jours. Office: Div Wildlife and Fisheries Biology Univ Calif Davis CA 95616

RAVEN, PENNY (PATRICIA ELAINE), real estate broker, fuel alcohol distillery exec.; b. Oakland, Calif., Apr. 27, 1943; d. Allen James and Patricia Elaine (McClure) Nichelini; student U. So. Calif., 1961-62, U. Calif., Fresno, 1963, Fresno City Coll., 1973; m. Larry Joseph Raven, June 15, 1963; children—Laurence Tagge Allen, Corbyn Lance. Model, 1960—; owner, operator Del Mar Motel, also apts. in Fresno, 1963-64; owner R Pantry Markets, Holy Cow Meat Market, Fresno, Hanford and Sanger, Calif., 1965-72; real estate salesman, developer, Fresno, 1973; real estate broker, owner The Raven Co., Fresno, 1974—; columnist Fresno Bee "Party Line", 1978—; owner Raven Alcohol Distillery, Selma, Calif., 1979—; pres. Am. Gasohol, Inc., Fresno, 1980—; v.p. Raven Devel., Inc., Fresno, 1980—; v.p. R Pantry Markets, Inc., Fresno, 1968-72. Pres., Fresno Cancer League, 1972-73; bd. dirs. Women's Symphony League, 1973-74; alt. Fresno County Democratic Central Com., 1977; Dem. candidate for lt. gov. Calif., 1978; pres. Jackson Sch. PTA, Fresno, 1980-82. Named Nat. Betty Crocker Homemaker of Tomorrow, 1961; recipient Fresno Mayor's award, 1976; Appreciation award Jackson Sch. PTA, 1982, United Cerebral Palsy Assn., 1982, Solid Waste Mgmt. Bd., 1982, Fresno Zool. Soc., 1982. Democrat. Roman Catholic. Author: (with husband) National Handbook on Toll Roads, 1977. Home: 3504 E Huntington Blvd Fresno CA 93702

RAVENBERG, DENNIS HENRY, transp. equipment mfg. co. exec.; b. Bingham Lake, Minn., Feb. 24, 1932; s. Henry Oliver and Leona May (Barklow) R.; B.A., Augustana Coll., 1954; m. Lois Ann McDonald, June 26, 1954; children—Gary, Lary, Kathy. Office and credit mgr. Firestone Tire & Rubber Co., Huron, S.D., 1954-55, Olson Bros. Firestone, Howard, S.D., 1955-56; acct. Fruehauf Corp., Sioux Falls, S.D., 1956-65, asst. office mgr., Sioux City, Iowa, 1966, office mgr., Billings, Mont., 1966-72, office mgr., controller, Salt Lake City, 1972-81, br. mgr., Boise, Idaho, 1981—; bd. dirs. Valley Fed. Credit Union, 1970-72. Actor community theatre groups, summer stock prodns.; pres. Ponderosa Sch. PTA, 1966-69; Webelo leader Boy Scouts Am., 1969-70. Mem. Utah Motor Transport Assn. (credit union Supervisory Com. 1980-81). Office: 770 W Amity Rd Boise ID 83705

RAWAL, KANTI MAFATLAL, plant breeder; b. Karachi, Pakistan, Sept. 25, 1940; came to U.S., 1965, naturalized, 1980; s. Mafatlal D. and Santosh Devi (Dave) R.; Ph.D., U. Ill., 1970; m. Jeya Srinivasan, June 22, 1972; children—Sanjay, Sampath. Research scientist Internat. Inst. Tropical Agr., Ibadan, Nigeria, 1970-75; chief scientist, info. sci./gen. resources Coll. Bus., U. Colo., Boulder, 1975-78; chief scientist, lab. for info. sci. agr. Colo. State U., Ft. Collins, 1978-80; plant breeder Del Monte Corp., San Leandro, Calif., 1980—. Mem. Am. Soc. Agronomy, Am. Genetic Assn., Crop Sci. Soc. Am., Soc. Econ. Botany. Contbr. articles in field to profl. jours. Office: Del Monte Corp 850 Thornton St San Leandro CA 94577

RAWLINGS, LAMAR ALMA, accounting firm exec., real estate consultant; b. Provo Utah, June 27, 1930; s. Alma C. and Neva (Hunter) R.; m. Kathryn Melville, Apr. 20, 1953; children—Patty, Susan, Nancy. B.S., Brigham Young U., 1953. C.P.A., Utah. Staff Haskins & Sells, 1953-62; ptnr. Laver, Mellor & Rawlings, Salt Lake City, 1962-70, Laver & Rawlings, 1970-76; sr. ptnr. Arthur Young & Co., Salt Lake City, 1976—; Salt Lake County auditor, 1966-67. Republican gubernatorial candidate, 1967. Recipient Ted Anderson Memorial award Salt Lake Jaycees, 1963. Mem. Am. Inst. C.P.A.s, Utah Assn. C.P.A.s, Utah Jaycees (pres. 1963-67), U.S. Jaycees (nat. dir. 1962-63, nat. fin. com. 1962-63), Thunderbird Investment Group. Clubs: Alta, Country, Rotary, Sentinel, Bloomington (Salt Lake City).

RAWLINGS, ROBERT HOAG, newspaper exec.; b. Pueblo, Colo., Aug. 3, 1924; s. John W. and Dorothy (Hoag) R.; student Colo. U., 1944-45; B.A., Colo. Coll., 1947; m. Mary Alexandra Graham, Oct. 18, 1947; children—Jane Louise, John Graham, Carolyn Anne, Robert Hoag II. With Pueblo (Colo.) Chieftain and Pueblo Star-Jour. 1947—, reporter, 1947-51, advt. rep. 1951-62, gen. mgr., 1962-79, pub. and editor, 1980—; sec. Star-Jour. Pub. Corp., 1962—; dir. Colo. Nat. Bank-Pueblo. Served with USNR, 1942-46. Mem. Colo. Press Assn. (dir. 1981—), Rocky Mountain Ad Mgrs. (past pres.), Colo. A.P. (past pres.). Presbyn. Elk, Rotarian. Home: 3100 Country Club Dr Pueblo CO 81008 Office: 825 W 6th St Pueblo CO 81003 also PO Box 36 Pueblo CO 81002

RAWSON, CAROL MARIE, realtor; b. Dayton, Ohio, May 22, 1949; d. Richard L and Dorothy M. (Coen) Buxton. B.A., Maryville Coll., 1971. Cert. tchr., Tenn., Ga.; realtor's license, Alaska, 1981. Tchr. Marietta (Ga.) Middle Sch., 1971-74; bookkeeper and office mgr. Northland Hub Wholesale Grocery, Fairbanks, Alaska, 1976-78; purchaser, office mgr. Fairbanks Machine and Steel, 1978-80, property mgr. several firms, Fairbanks, 1974-82; realtor, Fairbanks, 1983—; landlord-tenant mediator. Mem. Nat. Assn. Realtors Fairbanks Assn. Realtors. Methodist. Home and office: Box 1945 Fairbanks AK 99707

RAWSON, KAY THOMPSON, vocational education administrator; b. Ogden, Utah, July 20, 1939; d. Horman M. and Wanda (Knight) Thompson; m. Roger F. Rawson, Oct. 6, 1961; children—RaDene, Tana, Kamie, LaDawn, David, Rochelle. B.S. in Home Econs. Edn., Brigham Young U., 1961; M. Edn., Weber State Coll., 1980. Tchr. home econs. Wellsville Jr. High Sch., Logan, Utah, 1961-62; vocat. coordinator child and family studies Weber (Utah) State Coll., 1981—; pres. Luxury Living Co., 1970—; advisor Weber Community Schs., 1973-82; chmn. Families Alive Conf.; mem. White House Conf. on Families, 1980. Pres., Relief Soc. Ch. of Jesus Christ of Latter Day Saints; active PTA (hon. life mem.); del. Nat. Democratic Convention, 1980; mem. Dem. Central Com. Recipient Friend of Edn. award Utah Edn. Assn., 1979. Mem. Am. Home Econs. Assn., Nat. Council Family Relations, Women's Legis. Council, Phi Kappa Phi. Club: Hooper Women's. Home: 5151 W 4000 S Hooper UT 84315 Office: C&FS 1301 Weber State Coll Ogden UT 84408

RAWSON, RAYMOND D., dentist; b. Sandy, Utah, Nov. 2, 1940; s. James D. and Mable (Beckstead) R.; B.S., U. Nev. at Las Vegas, 1964; D.D.S., Loma Linda U., 1968, M.A., U. Nev., 1970, m. Linda Downey, July 23, 1959; children—Raymond Blaine, Mark Daniel, Pamela Ann, David James, Kristi Lynn, Kenneth Glenn, Richard Allen. Practice dentistry, Las Vegas, 1968—; instr. dental hygiene Clark County Community Coll., 1977—, dep. coroner, dental examiner, 1977—; adj. asso. prof. U. Nev., 1977—. Active Boy Scouts Am., 1968—; bishop Ch. Jesus Christ Latter-day Saints, 1978—. Diplomate Am. Bd. Forensic Odontology. Mem. Am. Acad. Forensic Scis., Inst. Forensic Dentistry (dir.), ADA, Federation Dentaire International, Omicron Kappa Upsilon. Republican. Mem. editorial bd. Am. Jour. Forensic Medicine and Pathology; contbr. articles to profl. jours. Office: 4121 Sahara Ave W Las Vegas NV 89102

RAY, BILL, state senator; b. Anaconda, Mont., Apr. 6, 1922; m. Jeanne Ray; 2 children. Student pub. schs. Ret. fisherman, laborer, cold storage worker; mem. Alaska Ho. of Reps., 1964-70, Alaska State Senate, 1970—. Chmn. Alcoholic Beverage Control Bd., 1959-64. Served with USNR, 1942-46. Democrat. Office: Alaska State Senate Juneau AK 99811*

RAY, BURKE FRENCH, ret. paper co. exec.; b. Yakima, Wash., Feb. 19, 1928; s. Irven E. and Esther F. Ray; B.B.A., U. Wash., Seattle, 1949; Ph.D. (hon.), Sunshine U., Pinella, Fla., 1980; m. Nov. 10, 1951 (div. 1979); children—David, Robin, Brian. Sales rep. Zellerbach Paper Co., Seattle, 1950-60; salesman, sales mgr. Fibreboard Corp., Seattle, Portland, Oreg. and Los Angeles, 1960-69; sales mgr. Boise Cascade Corp., Los Angeles, 1969-71; pres. Key Container Co., Los Angeles, 1971-82. Served as officer USNR, 1945-67. Mem. Fibre Box Assn. (dir.).

RAY, CHARLES KENDALL, univ. dean; b. Boise City, Okla., Mar. 15, 1928; s. Volney Holt and Mamie (Burton) R.; B.A., U. Colo., 1951; M.A., Columbia, 1955, Ed.D., 1959; m. Doris Derby, Aug. 26, 1951. Teaching prin. Bur. Indian Affairs, Savoonga, Alaska, 1951-54; mem. faculty U. Alaska, 1957—, prof. edn., 1960—, dean Sch. Edn., 1961—; dir. N.W. Regional Research Lab.; chmn. Gov.'s Task Force on Rural Edn. Served in U.S. Army, 1946-47. Recipient Travel award Ford Found., 1968-69. Mem. N.E.A., Am. Assn. Sch. Adminstrs., AAUP, Am. Assn. Colls. Tchr. Edn. (state liaison officer). Phi Delta Kappa. Author: A Program of Education for Alaska Natives; Alaskan Native Secondary School Dropouts; also articles. Home: 1209 10th Ave Fairbanks AK 99701 Office: U Alaska Fairbanks AK 99701

RAY, HOWARD EUGENE, agronomist; b. Iola, Kans., Aug. 15, 1926; s. Beatty Allen and Laura Leona (Kester) R.; B.S., Kans. State U., 1949, M.S., 1950; Ph.D., U. Minn., 1956; m. Dorothy Jane Sheppard, June 28, 1946; children—Nancy Jane, Susan Ann, Robert Wilson. Instr. soils Kans. State U., Manhattan, 1949-50; instr. vets. on-farm tng. program Kans., 1951; extension soils specialist U. Ariz., Tucson, 1951-54; research asst. U. Minn., St. Paul, 1954-56; asst. soil chemist, sect. leader Everglades Expt. Sta., Fla., 1956-58; extension specialist U. Ariz., 1958-63, 66; adv. soils and extension edn. U. Ceara, Fortaleza, Brazil, 1964-66; project adv., dep. team leader Ford Found., New Delhi, 1967-72; field team leader Basic Village Edn. Project, Acad. Ednl. Devel., Guatemala City, 1973-76; dir. Asian programs, Washington,

1977-79; chief party Agrl. Edn. Devel. Project, Sri Lanka, 1979-82; sr. program officer Acad. for Ednl. Devel., 1983—. Chmn. community adv. com. Am. Internat. Sch., New Delhi, 1971. Served with USNR, 1944-46. Mem. Am. Soc. Agronomy, Soil Sci. Soc. Am., Internat. Soc. Soil Sci., Indian Soc. Soil Sci., Soil Sci. Soc. Sri Lanka, Indian Soc. Extension Edn., Soc. Internat. Devel., Phi Kappa Phi, Gamma Sigma Delta, Sigma Xi. Republican. Presbyterian. Contbr. articles to profl. jours. Home: 2526 E Blanton Dr Tucson AZ 85716 Office: 1414 22d St NW Washington DC 20037

RAY, LEO ELDON, fish prodn. and mktg. co. exec.; b. Logan County, Okla., Dec. 9, 1937; s. Wilbur Houston and Florence Ivy (Doggett) R.; B.S. in Zoology, U. Okla., 1963; m. Judith Kay Croddy, Aug. 29, 1959; children—Tana Kim, Tod Kent, Kacy Kay. Research asst. U. Okla., 1961-63; tchr. public schs., Dumas, Tex., 1963-64, Grants, N.Mex., 1964-65, Anaheim, Calif., 1965-69; co-owner Fish Breeders, Niland, Calif., 1969—; pres. Fish Breeders of Idaho, Inc., Buhl, 1971—; pres. Big Bend Trout, Inc., 1977—. Served with U.S. Army, 1957-60. Mem. Calif. Catfish Farmers Am. (past pres.), Catfish Farmers Am. (past pres., dir.), U.S. Trout Farmers Assn. (past pres., dir.). Address: Route 3 Box 193 Buhl ID 83316

RAY, LEOPOLD AUGUSTUS, architect; b. Port Antonio, Jamaica, Oct. 30, 1951; came to U.S., 1959, naturalized, 1961; s. Robert, Jr. and Doris Beatrice (Byrd) R.; B.Arch. (AIA scholar Ariz. chpt. 1971, Sun Angel Found. archtl. scholar 1974, Dubois Found. scholar 1975, Dougherty scholar 1975), Ariz. State U., 1976; M.A. in Urban Planning (grad. fellow 1979), UCLA, 1980. Architect-in-tng. firms in Las Vegas, Nev., 1976-78; asst. economist Los Angeles Office Econ. Devel., 1980; assoc. A.K. Ngai & Assocs., architects/planners, Los Angeles, 1980-82; urban design cons. Vitalize Van Nuys, Inc., 1980; coordinator Sat. scholar program UCLA, 1979-80; architect/rehab. specialist Mark Briggs & Assocs., 1982; prin. works include DeMille Dr. Residence, Spreading Oak Residence (both Los Angeles), others. Mem. AIA, Am. Inst. Cert. Planners. Democrat. Roman Catholic. Co-author: Earth-Integrated Architecture, 1975. Office: 5800 S Eastern Ave Suite 340 Los Angeles CA 90040

RAY, ROBERT GLENN, advertising agency executive; b. Santa Monica, Calif., Jan. 13, 1950; s. Ben Gorchakoff and Kathryn (Coger) R.; m. Elizabeth Mary Adler, Jan. 12, 1971; 1 dau., Kelly Anne; m. 2d, Christine May Cheney, Apr. 30, 1976. A.A. in Telecommunications, Los Angeles City Coll., 1969; student U. So. Calif., UCLA, Occidental U., Calif. State U.-Los Angeles. TV producer Dating Game, 1966; nat. radio program dir., 1970-71; pres., owner Bob Ray Creative Services, Inc., Saratoga, Calif., 1975—; radio personality, 1967-79; host, producer TV show; syndicated voice radio sta. chains; radio/TV voice-over talent; guest lectr. advt. and telecommunications industry San Jose Unified Sch. Dist., San Jose State U. Grand Marshall Diabetes, Mar., 1977, San Jose March of Dimes, 1979, 80. Recipient 1st place Best Radio Comml. Cable Car Competition, 1980; Murphy Advt. awards in radio and TV, 1980-83. Mem. AFTRA, Internat. Brotherhood Elec. Workers, San Jose Ad Club, San Jose Women in Advt. Home: Saratoga CA 95070 Office: Bob Ray Creative Services Inc PO Box 691 Saratoga CA 97051

RAYMOND, EUGENE THOMAS, aircraft engineer; b. Seattle, Apr. 17, 1923; s. Evan James and Katheryn Dorothy (Kranick) R.; m. Bette Mae Bergeson, Mar. 1, 1948; children—Joan Kay, Patricia Lynn, Robin Louise. B.S.M.E., U. Wash., 1944; postgrad., 1953-55; registered profl. engr., Tex. Research engr. The Boeing Co., Seattle, 1946-59, sr. group engr., 1959-63, 66-71, sr. specialist engr., 1971-81, prin. engr. flight control tech., 1982—; project design engr. Gen. Dynamics, Ft. Worth, 1963-66. Served to lt., USNR, 1943-46, 49-52; PTO. Recipient prize Hydraulics and Pneumatics mag., 1958. Mem. Soc. Automotive Engrs. (cert. of appreciation), Fluid Power Soc., Puget Sound Fluid Power Assn., AIAA, Beta Theta Pi. Lutheran. Clubs: Meridian Valley Country, Masons, Shriners. Aircraft editorial adv. bd. Hydraulics and Pneumatics mag., 1960-70; contbr. articles profl. jours. Patentee in field. Home: 25301 144 Ave SE Kent WA 98031 Office: PO Box 3707 Seattle WA 98124

RAYMOND, GENE, actor, producer, director, composer; b. N.Y.C., Aug. 13, 1908; s. LeRoy D. and Mary (Smith) Guion; m. Jeanette Mac Donald, June 16, 1937 (dec. Jan. 14, 1965); m. Nel Bentley Hees, Sept. 7, 1974. Student Profl. Children's Sch., N.Y.C. Broadway debut in The Piper, 1920; other Broadway appearances include: Eyvind of the Hills, 1921, Why Not?, 1922, The Potters, 1923, Cradle Snatchers, 1925, Take My Advice, 1927, Mirrors, 1928, Sherlock Holmes, 1928, The War Song, 1928, Jonesy, 1929, Young Sinners, 1929, A Shadow of My Enemy, 1957; other theatre appearances include: The Man in Possession, 1946, The Guardsman, 1951, The Voice of the Turtle, 1952, Angel Street, 1952, Petrified Forest, 1952, Call Me Madam, 1952, Private Lives, 1953, The Moon Is Blue, 1953, Be Quiet, My Love, 1953, Detective Story, 1954, The Devil's Disciples, 1954, The Fifth Season, 1955, Will Success Spoil Rock Hunter, 1956, Romeo and Juliet (as Mercutio), 1956, Seven Year Itch, 1958, Holiday for Lovers, 1959, Nat. touring co. of The Best Man, 1960, Candida, 1961, Majority of One, Mr. Roberts, Kiss Me Kate, 1962, The Moon is Blue, 1963, Madly in Love, 1963; film appearances include: Personal Maid, 1931, If I Had A Million, The Night of June 13th, Ladies of The Big House, Forgotten Commandments, 1932, Red Dust, 1932, Ex-Lady, 1933, The House on 56th St., 1933, Zoo in Budapest, 1933, Brief Moment, 1933, Ann Carver's Profession, 1933, Flying Down To Rio, 1933, Sadie Mc Kee, 1934, I Am Suzanne, 1934, Coming Out Party, (Fox), 1934, Trans-Atlantic Merry-Go-Round, 1934, Behold My Wife 1935, The Woman in Red, 1935, Seven Keys to Baldpate, 1935, Hooray for Love, 1935, Walking on Air, 1936, The Bride Walks Out, 1936, The Smartest Girl in Town, 1936, Transient Lady, 1936, There Goes My Girl, 1937, Life of the Party, 1937, Cross Country Romance, 1938, Smilin' Thru, 1940, Mr. and Mrs. Smith, 1941, The Locket 1946, Assigned to Danger, 1948, Million Dollar Week-End, 1948, Sofia, Hit The Deck, 1955, Plunder Road, 1957, The Best Man, 1964, I'd Rather Be Rich, 1964; TV apperances include: Ed Sullivan's Toast of the Town, Ken Murray Show, Robert Montgomery Presents, Tales of Tomorrow, Lux Video Theatre, Pulitzer Prize Theatre, Broadway TV Theatre, Schlitz Theatre, Fireside Theatre (as host), Reader's Digest (as host), Barbara Stanwick Show, Sam Benedict, United States Steel Hour, Adamsburg, U.S.A., The Defenders, Outer Limits, Channing, The Loretta Young Show, Matinee Theatre, Playhouse 90, Climax, Johnny Ringo, Ethel Barrymore Theatre, F.B.I., Ironside, Apple's Way, Judd for the Defense, Bold Ones, The Interns, Mannix, and many others. Past v.p. and campaign chmn. Arthritis Found., So. Calif. chpt.; past pres. So. Calif. chpt. Air Force Assn.; pres. Motion Picture and TV Fund, 1980-82. Served with USAAF, 1942-45; ETO; served to col. USAFR, 1945-68. Decorated Legion of Merit; recipient Disting. Service award Arthritis Found., Humanitarian award Air Force Assn., Better World award VFW, Bronze Halo award So. Calif. Motion Picture Council. Mem. Screen Actor's Guild (former dir.), Actors Equity, AFTRA. Clubs: The Players, N.Y. Athletic (N.Y.C.); Army and Navy (Washington); Bel-Air Country (Los Angeles); Order Daedalians. Author teleplay: Prima Donna, 1951; composer songs: Will You?, 1939, Let Me Always Sing, 1940, Release, 1941. Address: 9570 Wilshire Blvd Beverly Blvd Beverly Hills CA 90212

RAYMOND, ROY BURDETTE, rancher; b. Fort Collins, Colo., Feb. 28, 1919; s. Burdette Augustus and Mabel Agnes (Beeson) R.; m. Mary Katherine Trussell, Oct. 30, 1949; children—Jnell Lorraine, Robert Warren. B.S. in Animal Husbandry, Colo. State U., 1942. Owner, operator, Ferris Mountain Ranch, Rawlins, Wyo., 1949—; vice chmn. adv. bd. First Wyo. Bank 1979-80. Vice pres. Dist. #1 Sch. Dist. (Wyo.), 1980-81. Served to chief petty officer USN, 1942-45. Recipient J. C. Penny 4-H leadership award, 1962; Wyo. Extension service rancher of the year award, 1982. Mem. Carbon County Stockgrowers Assn., Wyo. Stockgrowers Assn., Am. Nat. Cattleman's Assn., Wyo. Farm Bur. Republican. Home and office: Ferris Mountain Ranch Lander Rt Rawlins WY 82301

RAZRAN, GILBERT BRUCE, research co. exec., indsl. engr.; b. Walsenburg, Colo., Sept. 25, 1926; s. Bernard A. and Carolina I. (De Mallieu) R.; A.B., U. Miami (Fla.), 1949, M.S., 1950; Ph.D. in Indsl. Bioengring., Purdue U., 1953; m. Charlotte D. Bellant, Nov. 8, 1969; children—Rita Lynn, Steven Barry. Project engr. Gen. Electric Co., Ithaca, N.Y., 1953-59; systems analyst Burroughs Corp. Research Center, Paoli, Pa., 1959-63; dir. ops. research office Command & Control Systems, Washington, 1963-65; pres. Sci. Operational Systems, San Diego, 1965—; chmn. ILR Med. Clinics, Ltd., 1982—; prof. Grad. Sch., U.S. Internat. U., Calif., 1969-73; mem. U.S. Sci. Study Rev. Group, UN, Geneva, 1971. Mem. Library Bd., Upper Merion Twp., Pa., 1960-63. Bd. dirs. SOS-Disc, Inc., Las Vegas, Nev., chmn., 1972-75. Served with USNR, 1944-46; PTO; to capt. USAF, 1950-52. Recipient Inventor of Yr. award Patent Law Assn., 1980; registered profl. engr., N.Y., Pa., Calif. Mem. Nat. Security Indsl. Assn., Assn. for Advancement Med. Instrumentation, Mil. Ops. Research Soc., Am. Psychol. Assn., IEEE, Psi Chi, Sigma Xi. Author: Programmed Instruction Book in Electronics, 1966; CAI in Vocational Training, 1967. Contbr. articles to sci. jours. Inventor of oculometer. Office: SOS Inc 4380 Viewridge Rd San Diego CA 92123 also ILR Med Clinics Ltd 9 Tooting High St London SW17 England

RE, ANTON JOSEPH, pub. co. exec.; b. Bessemer, Mich., July 30, 1916; s. Battista and Mary Re; grad. U.S. Maritime Officer Candidate Sch., 1943; cert. Lewis and Clark Coll., 1949, Portland Extension Center, 1946, Los Angeles State Coll., 1962, UCLA, 1963; m. Angeline Cecelia Rucci, Aug. 30, 1941; 1 dau., Marion E. Traffic rep. Garrett Freightlines, Inc., Portland, Oreg., also Los Angeles, 1949-53; sr. rate clk. Loretz & Co., Los Angeles, 1953; So. Calif. dist. mgr. Albrechts Routing Guide, Los Angeles, 1953-64; with G.R. Leonard & Co., Los Angeles, 1964—, West Coast mgr. So. Calif. sales and servicing, Pasadena, Calif., 1981—; community coll. instr., adult edn. tchr. Chmn. safety services program Los Angeles chpt. ARC, 1968-69; ships mate, skipper Sea Scouts, Boy Scouts Am., 1957-59. Served with USN, 1934-40, U.S. Mcht. Marine, 1942-46; lt. comdr. U.S. Maritime Service ret. Recipient Merit award U.S. Power Squadron, 1958. Mem. Nat. Def. Transp. Assn., Am. Soc. Traffic and Transp., Nat. Council of Phys. Distbn. Mgmt., Calif. Trucking Assn., U.S. Coast Guard Aux. (life), Delta Nu Alpha. Democrat. Roman Catholic. Clubs: K.C., Lions, Elks. Home: 7520 3d St Downey CA 90241 Office: G R Leonard & Co 1072 N Allen Ave Pasadena CA 91104

READ, ELEANOR MAY, financial analyst; b. Arcadia, N.Y., July 4, 1942; d. Henry and Lena May (Fagner) Van Koevering; 1 dau., Robin Jo. Typist, clk., sec., credit corr. Sarah Coventry, Inc., Newark, N.Y., 1957-61; exec. sec. Mobil Chem. Co., Macedon, N.Y., 1961-68; bus. mgr. Henry's Hardware, Newark, 1968-72; with Xerox Corp., Hayward, Calif., 1973—, internat. clk. analyst, personnel adminstrv. asst., employment coordinator, exec. sec., cycle count analyst. Mem. Xerox/Diablo Mgmt. Assn., Am. Mgmt. Assn., Profl. Businesswomen's Assn. Office: 47600 Kato Rd FM-239 Fremont CA 94538

READ, JEREMY GRANGER, newspaper advertising executive; b. London, Mar. 31, 1951; came to U.S., 1951, naturalized, 1959; s. Raymond Charles and Lillian June (Gostick) R.; m. Catherine Clapp, Oct. 16, 1982. B.A. in Psychology, Westminster Coll., Fulton, Mo., 1973. Advt. salesman, classified ads Town & Country Rev., Boulder, Colo., 1974; sales rep. retail ads Aurora (Colo.) Sun, 1975, Telluride (Colo.) Times, 1975, Colo. Tri-Cities Weeklies, Broomfield, Colo., 1975, Longmont Daily Times-Call, Longmont, Colo., 1975-78; advt. mgr. Loveland (Colo.) Daily Reporter-Herald, 1978-81; advt. mgr. Daily Times-Call, Lehman Newspapers, Longmont, 1982—. Bd. dirs. Jr. Achievement, Loveland City and Boulder County (Colo.), 1979—. Mem. Mountain Advt. Mgrs. Assn., Sigma Chi Alumni Assn. Democrat. Club: Sertoma (Loveland). Office: 717 4th Ave Longmont CO 80501

READE, ROBERT MELLOR, advertising executive; b. Elmhurst, Ill., Jan. 9, 1940; s. M.G. and Virginia A. (Mellor) R.; m. Carol Jean Coon, May 26, 1962; children—Christopher, Gregory. B.A. in Liberal Arts, U. Ariz., 1962. Charting mgr. Eller Outdoor Advt., Phoenix, 1964-69; sales mgr. Mullins Neon, Denver, 1969-70; pres. Gannett Outdoor Co. Ariz., Phoenix, 1970—. Chmn. Phoenix chpt. Am. Humanics, 1983, Valley Youth Coalition, 1981; active Thunderbirds, 1978-83, Theodore council Boy Scouts Am., Community Council, Phoenix United Way, Camelback Mental Health Found. Served with USAR, 1963-69. Recipient U. Ariz. Alumni Appreciation award, 1975, 77, Slouaker award, 1977; Anti Defamation League Torch of Liberty award, 1981. Mem. Ariz. Safety Assn. (pres. 1981), Young Pres. Orgn., Outdoor Assn. Am., Inst. Outdoor Advt., Phoenix Advt. Club (pres. 1974). Club: Rotary (pres. 1982). Office: PO Box 934 Phoenix AZ 85001

REAGAN, GARY DON, lawyer; b. Amarillo, Tex., Aug. 23, 1941; s. Hester and Lois Irene (Marcum) R.; m. Nedra Ann Nash, Sept. 12, 1964; children—Marcum, Kristen, Karyn, Brenton. A.B., Stanford U., 1963, J.D., 1965. Bar: N.Mex. 1965. Atty. Smith, Ransom, Deaton & Reagan, Albuquerque, 1965-68; atty. Williams, Johnson, Houston & Reagan, Hobbs, N.Mex., 1968-69; ptnr. Williams, Johnson, Reagan, Porter & Love, 1969-82; sole practice, Hobbs, 1982—; tchr. real estate, oil and gas, banking law N.Mex. Jr. Coll., Hobbs, 1978-81; trustee Landsun Homes, Inc., pres., 1981—; trustee Lydia Patterson, Inc. Commr., City of Hobbs, 1970-78, mayor, 1972-73, 76-77; pres. Jr. Achievement, 1978. Mem. ABA, N.Mex. Bar Assn., Lea County Bar Assn. (pres. 1976-77). Democrat. Methodist. Clubs: Rotary, Hobbs Tennis (pres. 1974-75). Home: 200 Eagle Dr Hobbs NM 88240 Office: Law Offices of Gary Don Reagan PO Box 780 215W Broadway Suite 11 Hobbs NM 88241

REAGAN, JANET THOMPSON, psychologist, educator; b. Monticello, Ken., Sept. 15, 1945; d. Virgil Joe and Carrie Mae (Alexander) Thompson; m. Robert Barry Reagan, Jr., Aug. 7, 1977; children—Natalia Alexandria, Robert Barry. B.A. in Psychology, Berea Coll., 1967; Ph.D. in Psychology, Vanderbilt U., 1972. Mgr. research and eval. Nashville Mental Health Center, 1971-72; mgr. eval. Family Health Found., New Orleans, 1973-74; asst. prof. dept. health systems mgmt. Tulane U., New Orleans, 1974-77; dir. eval. Project Heavy West, Los Angeles, 1977-78; lectr. dept. pub. adminstrn. U. So. Calif., 1979-82; asst. prof. health adminstrn. Calif. State U.-Northridge, 1978—; cons. in field. Mem. ACLU. Mem. Am. Pub. Health Assn., Am. Psychol. Assn., Western Psychol. Assn., Eval. Research Soc., Psi Chi, Phi Kappa Phi. Contbr. articles to profl. jours. Home: 10881 White Oak Granada Hills CA 91344 Office: Dept Health Science Calif State U Northridge CA 91330

REAL, JACK GARRET, helicopter company executive; b. Baraga, Mich., May 31, 1916; s. Edward I. and Elizabeth Irene (Leary) R.; m. Janeth Paden, Nov. 20, 1941; children—Daniel, Patricia. B.S.M.E., Mich. Tech. U., 1937, D.Engring. (hon.), 1968. Registered profl. engr., Calif. With Lockheed Aircraft, 1939-71, chief engr. flight test, chief devel. engr., 1962-65, v.p., gen. mgr. Rotary Wing div., 1965-71; v.p. aviation Hughes Tool Co., 1971-74, sr. v.p. aviation, 1977-79; pres., chief exec. officer Hughes Helicopters, Culver City, Calif., 1979—; dir. Hughes Airwest Airline. Bd. dirs. Boy Scouts Am., 1965—; bd. overseers U. Pa. Coll. Engring. and Applied Sci., 1974-81. Mem. AIAA, Am. Helicopter Soc., Am. Army Aviation Assn. Roman Catholic. Contbr. articles to profl. jours. Office: Hughes Helicopters Centinela and Teale Sts Culver City CA 90230

REAL, MANUEL LAWRENCE, U.S. dist. judge; b. San Pedro, Calif., Jan. 27, 1924; s. Francisco Jose and Maria (Mansano) R.; B.S., U. So. Calif., 1944, student fgn. trade, 1946-48; LL.B., Loyola Sch. Law, Los Angeles, 1951; m. Stella Emilia Michalik, Oct. 15, 1955; children—Michael, Melanie Marie, Timothy, John Robert. Admitted to Calif. bar, 1952; asst. U.S. Atty.'s Office, Los Angeles, 1952-55; pvt. practice law, San Pedro, Calif., 1955-64; U.S. atty. So. Dist. Calif., 1964-66; U.S. dist. judge, from 1966, now chief judge. Served to ensign USNR, 1943-46. Mem. Am., Fed., Los Angeles County bar assns., State Bar Calif., Am. Judicature Soc., Chief Spl. Agts. Assn., Phi Delta Phi, Sigma Chi. Democrat. Roman Catholic. Club: Anchor (Los Angeles). Office: 312 N Spring St Los Angeles CA 90012*

REAMS, LEE THOMAS, business executive, tax accountant, mechanical engineer; b. El Centro, Calif., Sept. 11, 1934; s. Lee B. and Sarah E. R.; m. Anne M. Morton, Sept. 18, 1965; children—Cheryll, Susan, Lee, Robert. B.S. in Mech. Engring., Calif. State U.-San Luis Obispo, 1957. Enrolled agt. IRS. Mech. engr. Rocketdyne div. Rockwell Internat., Canoga Park, Calif., 1957-75; pvt. practice tax acctg., Woodland Hills, Calif., 1972—; founder, pres. Ind. Preparer Services, Inc., Glendale, Calif., 1977—; gen. ptnr. Accts. Realty Fund, Los Angeles, 1981—; lectr. tax law. Served with USN, 1952-60. Republican. Presbyterian. Author: Tax Implications of Divorce, 1981; Tax Implications of Real Estate Transactions, 1980, Tax Implications of Rental Property, 1981; Building A Successful Tax Practice, 1980. Office: Ind Preparer Services Inc 3441 Ocean View Blvd Glendale CA 91208

REAMS, LEROY MORRIS, superintendent schools; consultant; b. North Platte, Nebr., Oct. 6, 1923; s. Charley F. and Frances Elizabeth (Banta) R.; m. Charlotte Yvonne Zimmer, Feb. 26, 1950; children—Deborah Frances, Jerelynn Susan Reams Shields, David Craig. B.S., U. Colo., 1970, M.S., 1972, Edn. Specialist, 1978. Cert. type D tchr., secondary edn. adminstrn., K-12 adminstrn., Colo. Enlisted U.S. Army, 1943, advanced through grades to master sgt., 1967; ret., 1968; tchr. pub. schs., Aurora, Colo., 1970-72; prin. Arickaree Sch. Dist., Anton, Colo., 1972-75; vice prin. Delta (Colo.) High Sch., 1975-76; supt. schs. Otis (Colo.) Sch. Dist., 1976-78, Powhattan (Kans.) No. 510, 1979-80, Elbert (Colo.) Sch. Dist. No. 200, 1980—; cons. 4-day sch. week. Sustaining mem. Republican Nat. Com., 1978—. Mem. Assn. Supervision and Curriculum Devel., Colo. Assn. Sch. Execs., Am. Assn. Sch. Adminstrs., Phi Delta Kappa. Noncommd. Officers Assn., Ret. Enlisted Assn. Theta Xi. Methodist. Clubs: Elks (Aurora); Masons (Aurora, Denver); Order of Eastern Star (Kiowa, Colo).

REARWIN, KENNETH R(AY), foundation administrator; b. Salina, Kan., July 19, 1913; s. Ray A. and Leila W. (Sudendorf) R.; m. Suzanne Bickell, Sept. 1, 1934; children—Stephen D., David R., Penelope S., Amy Beth; m. Julianne McCall, Mar. 23, 1972. B.S. in Commerce magna cum laude, Northwestern U., 1935. Ptnr., Rearwin Airplanes, Kansas City, Kans., 1935-39; sec.-treas. Rearwin Aircraft & Engines, Inc., Kansas City, 1939-43; asst. treas. TWA, Kansas City, Mo., 1943-44; mgr. Merrill Lynch, LaJolla, Calif., 1949-58, mgr., v.p., San Francisco, 1958-64, San Diego, 1964-73; pres. The Parker Found., LaJolla, 1977—. Vice pres., treas. Putnam Found., San Diego, 1978-82; treas. Centre City Devel. Corp., San Diego, 1976-80; bd. dirs. Art Ctr. LaJolla, 1948-58, pres., 1953-54, 55-56; mem., trustee San Diego Bd. Edn., 1951-58, pres., 1955-56; bd. govs. Pacific Coast Stock Exchange, 1962-63; mem. San Diego County Planning Commn., 1966-67, San Diego City Retirement Bd., 1970-71; mem. San Diego County Air Pollution Hearing Bd., 1973-77, pres., 1974; mem. Calif. State Coordinating Council Higher Edn., 1967-74, pres., 1970-71. Served to lt. USNR, 1944-46. Recipient Silver Beaver award Boy Scouts Am., 1980. Mem. Fin. Analysts Soc. Clubs: LaJolla Beach and Tennis, Rotary. Home: 1410 Park Row LaJolla CA 92037 Office: PO Box 1355 LaJolla CA 92038

REASONER, ROBERT WILLIAM, school administrator; b. Berkeley, Calif., Apr. 16, 1928; s. William Henry and Helen Louise (Fox) R.; m. Joan Huggard, Sept. 1, 1950; children—Kathryn, David, Bruce; m. 2d, Nancy Lee Williams, Sept. 7, 1974; children—Sharon, Wendy, Ann. A.A., U. Calif., 1948, B.A., 1950, M.A., 1956. Tchr. Martinez (Calif.) Elem. Sch., 1950-53, tchr. Mt. Diablo Unified Sch., Concord, Calif., 1953-56, prin., 1956-62, 64-73; supervising prin. USAF Dependents Sch., Ramstein AFB, Germany, 1962-64; prin. Bancroft Elem. Sch., Walnut Creek, Calif., 1962-73; asst. supt. Los Altos (Calif.) Sch. Dist., 1973-79; supt. Moreland Sch. Dist., San Jose, Calif., 1979—; pres. Individual Instrn. Assn. Active YMCA. Served with U.S. Army, 1950-52. Calif. Drug. Commn. grantee, 1958; Packard Found. grantee, 1982-85. Mem. NEA, Calif. Tchrs. Assn., Assn. Calif. Sch. Adminstrs., Assn. Children with Learning Disabilities, Assn. Supervision and Curriculum Devel.

RECKER, KENNETH PAUL, interior designer; b. Toledo, Ohio, July 6, 1938; s. Stephen and Marjorie Stella Recker; m. Janice Lee Neeh, Dec. 1, 1971; m. 2d, Linda Ann Marcenaro, June 30, 1982; 1 dau., Rhonda Kay. Student Coumbia Basin Jr. Coll., 1961-62, U. Wash., 1962-63. Mgr., Habers Home Furnishings, Santa Cruz, Calif., 1965-79; owner, pres. Kenneth Becker Assos., Inc., Capitola, Calif., 1980—; adviser Showplace Sq., San Francisco. Mem. bd. dirs. Miss Calif. Pagent. Served with USN, 1957-61. Recipient Santa Cruz Scope award for hist. preservation, 1982. Mem. Am. Soc. Interior Designers (past chpt. pres., nat. dir.), AIA (affiliate). Democrat. Roman Catholic. Designs featured in numerous design publs. Office: 716 Capitola Ave Capitola CA 95010

RECKINGER, NANCY ROBINSON, professor education, child development; b. Detroit, Feb. 27, 1931; d. Rufo Gilbert and Ruth Alexandra (Morehouse) Robinson; m. James O. Reckinger. B.A., Wayne State U., 1952, M.A., Mich. State U., 1957; Ed.D., Wayne State U., 1970. Cert. teaching, counseling, adminstr. tchr., Royal Oak (Mich.) Schs., 1955-58, Air Force Overseas Dependents Schs., Tokyo and Madrid, 1958-60, Detroit Pub. Schs, 1960-72; prof. edn. and child devel. Calif. State U.-Fullerton, 1972—; chair Learning Alternative Resources Network; cons. Calif. State Dept. Edn. Mem. Calif. Alternative Edn. Assn. Author: Parents' Record of Educational Progress: How to Insure Your Child's Success in School, 1982. Office: EC 379 Calif State U Fullerton CA 92634

RECKO, BARBARA MARIA, television researcher, translator; b. Olsztyn, Poland, Sept. 14, 1947; d. Edward and Lucyna Leonia (Oleszczuk) R.; 1 son, Andrew John. B.A. in English and Drama, Incarnate Word Coll., San Antonio, 1969. Researcher, Sta. KTLA, Los Angeles, Viacom, N.Y.C., Petry TV, N.Y.C., 1972-75; research dir. Sta. KCOP, Los Angeles, 1975-76; asst. dir. research Sta. KGO, San Francisco, 1979-80; dir. research Sta. KTTV, Los Angeles, 1980—; guest lectr. extension media courses UCLA; Polish translator. Loan officer Polish Credit Union, 1976-77; pres. Our Own Sch., 1982-83. Mem. Am. Women in Radio and TV. Roman Catholic. Contbr. articles to publs. Home: 4216 Edenhurst Ave Los Angeles CA 90039 Office: 5746 Sunset Blvd Los Angeles CA 90028

RECTOR, PHILIP GRAHAM, facilities administrator; b. South Bend, Ind., Feb. 13, 1933; s. Paul Wasson and B. Marguerite (Holland) R.; m. Winifred Lee Rector, July 12, 1958; children—Paul, Bradley, Jill, Janis, Joy. B.M.E., Ga. Inst. Tech., 1955. Registered profl. engr., Ga. Mech. engr. So. Ry. Systems, Washington 1955-58; dir. phys. plant Ga. Tech. U. 1965-70; dir. phys. plant Calif. Inst. Tech. 1970-78; dir. facilities Stanford U. Med. Center 1979—. Served to capt. USAFR 1955-58. Mem. Assn. Phys. Plant Adminstrs. (meritorious service award 1975), ASME. Home: 820 Laverne Way Los Alto CA 94022 Office: Facilities Department Stanford Barn Stanford CA 94305

RECTOR, WILLIAM GORDON, state senator, businessman; b. Des Moines, July 22, 1922; s. Jesse and Viola (O'Connor) R.; m. Norma Louise Watkins, 1950; children—William Gordon, Christine Louise. B.S., Kearney State Coll., 1943. Owner, restaurant and drive-in; dir. 1st Cheyenne State Bank from 1971; mem. Wyo. Ho. of Reps., 1959-65, Wyo. State Senate, 1967—. Served with USMC, 6 yrs. Mem. Am. Legion, VFW. Democrat. Roman Catholic. Clubs: Elks, Exec., Optimists. Home: 301 W 5th Ave Cheyenne WY 82001 Office: Wyoming State Senate Cheyenne WY 82002*

REDDEN, JAMES ANTHONY, judge; b. Springfield, Mass., Mar. 13, 1929; s. James A. and Alma (Cheek) R.; student Boston U., 1951; LL.B., Boston Coll., 1954; m. Joan Ida Johnson, July 13, 1950; children—James A., William F. Admitted to Oreg. bar, 1955, dist. judge pro-tem, 1958; treas. State of Oreg., 1973-77, state atty. gen., 1977-80; fed. dist. judge, Portland, 1980—. Mem. Gov.'s Youth Commn., 1968-70; chmn. Gov.'s Task Force on Collective Bargaining in Pub. Sector; mem. Adv. Council to Ins. Commn., 1970. Mem. Oreg. Ho. of Reps., 1963-69, Oreg. Pub. Employe Relations Bd., 1969-72. Served with AUS, 1946-48. Mem. ABA, Mass. Bar Assn., Oreg. State Bar (gov.), Fed. Bar, Jackson County C. of C. (dir.). Democrat. K.C. Home: Portland OR Office: 608 US Court House 620 SW Main Portland OR 97205

REDDINGTON, DOUGLAS WILLIAM, architect; b. Richmond, Ind., Oct. 23, 1954; s. Willard Thomas and Norma Joanne (Nusbaum) R.; B.Arch., B.Environ. Design, Ball State U., 1978; m. Nancy Ann Marsio, Aug. 27, 1977; 1 son, Aaron Michael. Draftsman, Charles Gathers & Assos., Denver, 1978-79, archtl. designer, 1979-81, project mgr., 1981—. Republican. Quaker. Club: Sigma Chi. Home: 1440 S Jasmine Way Denver CO 80224 Office: 1825 Lawrence Denver CO 80202

REDENBAUGH, MARK KEITH, research scientist; b. Indpls., July 6, 1951; s. Robert Leroy and Mary Ruth (Caress) R.; m. Janet Marie Weichert, Dec. 29, 1950; 1 dau. Susan Jeanne. B.A. with honors, U. Calif.-Santa Cruz, 1975; Ph.D. (W. Alton Jones Cell Sci. Center Scholar, 1977, Anna E. Schoen-Rene Scholar, 1977, Coll. award, 1977 Grad. Fellow, 1977-79), SUNY Coll. Environ. Sci. and Forestry, 1979. Grad. asst. SUNY-Syracuse, 1975-76; research assoc. U. Calif.-Berkeley, 1980-81; research scientist Plant Genetics, Inc., Davis, Calif., 1982—. R. P. White Research grantee, 1978. Mem. Tissue Culture Assn. (plant program com. 1980-83), Internat. Assn. Plant Tissue Culture, Am. Inst. Biol. Scis., AAAS, Soc. Am. Foresters, Soc. Analytical Cytometry, Plant Molecular Biology Assn. Contbr. articles in field to profl. jours. Office: 1930 5th St Davis CA 95616

REDFEARN, MAXWELL SCOTT, veterinarian, microbiologist, univ. adminstr.; b. Exeter, Devonshire, U.K., Feb. 25, 1928, came to U.S., 1960, naturalized, 1966; s. Edward Scott and Dorothy Ada (Dark) R.; M.R.C.V.S., Royal Vet. Coll., U. London, 1948, M.S., U. Wis., Madison, 1953, Ph.D., 1960; m. Germaine Angele Palombieri, Oct. 23, 1958; children—Martine Noelle, Maxine Joelle. Staff, Can. Dept. Agr., 1950-51; research asst. vet. sci. U. Wis., Madison, 1953-54, project asst., 1954-56, instr., 1959-60; FAO tech. expert Institut Pasteur, Tunis, Tunisia, 1957-58; research biologist U. Calif., Berkeley, 1960-65, campus veterinarian, 1965—, dir. div. animal resources, 1973—; lectr., cons. in field; mem. adv. cons. use, care of animals and animal importation, Calif. Dept. Health. NIH grantee, 1969-72, 73-74. Fellow Royal Soc. Health; mem. AAAS, Am. Vet. Med. Assn., Am. Animal Hosps. Assn., Am. Assn. Lab. Animal Sci., Brit. Vet. Assn. Mem. Ch. of Eng. Author: Meliodosis and Glanders, Diseases of Animals Transmitted to Man (with N.J. Palleroni), 1975; Melioidosis and Glanders, An Update on the Zoonoses, 1980; contbr. chpts. to textbooks, articles to profl. jours. Office: Div Animal Resources U Calif 800 Hearst St Berkeley CA 94710

REDFIELD, ELAINE M., writer, critic, interior designer; b. N.Y.C., Dec. 9, 1917; d. Oscar L. and Gertrude (Hauser) Graf; student Wellesley Coll., 1934-37; A.B., U. Calif. at Los Angeles, 1943; m. Edward Mittelman, Apr. 11, 1943 (dec. Oct. 1960); m. 2d, William D. Redfield, Dec. 28, 1967. Book reviewer San Francisco Chronicle, 1943-45; sales asst. Asso. Am. Artists, Beverly Hills, Calif., 1947-48; free-lance editorial asst. W.H. Freeman Co., San Francisco, 1953-54; publicity dir. Orange County Philharmonic Soc., 1954-57, dir., 1957-70, adv. bd., 1970 ; interior design Elaine Mittelman Interiors, 1960—. Mem. Fullerton Cultural and Fine Arts Commn., 1965-77. Bd. dirs. Friends of Library of U. Calif. at Irvine, 1964-71; exec. bd. Friends of Calif. State U., Fullerton, 1968-70; bd. dirs. Music Assos. Calif. State U., Fullerton, pres., 1970-73; mem. pres.'s council Chapman Coll.; trustee South Coast Repertory, 1976—; mem. pres.'s assos. Calif. State U., Fullerton; bd. dirs. Fullerton Civic Light Opera, 1979-83, Pacific Symphony Orch., 1979—; bd. dirs. Orange County Performing Arts Ctr., 1974—, pres., 1979-80, chmn. bd., 1980-81; mem. Disneyland Community Service awards com., 1978—. Recipient Woman of Achievement award Fullerton Bus. and Profl. Women's Club, 1966; Woman of Yr. award Fullerton C. of C., 1971; 1st Patron of Arts award Orange County, 1979; Vol. Activist award Broadway Dept. Stores and Germaine Monteil, 1980; Today's Woman award Bullock's, 1980; silver medallion award YWCA, 1981; award for vol. service to arts City of Newport Beach Arts Commn., 1982; named Orange County Hon. Angel, Saddleback Found., 1981. Mem. Am. Soc. Interior Designers (comml. design award Orange County chpt. 1976, Community Service award 1980), AAUW, LWV. Clubs: Pacific, South Coast Wellesley (pres. 1962-64). Home: 1403 Sunny Crest Dr Fullerton CA 92635

REDMAN, PEGGY KENNA, management consultant; b. Billings, Mont., Sept. 21, 1930; d. Jewell W. and Irene (Alpaugh) Trower; m. Howard F. Kenna, Apr. 14, 1951; children—Julie Killorn, Mary Pat Bakley, Teresa K. Hinton; m. 2d, John F. Redman, Jan. 3, 1981. B.A. in Speech Communication, U. Mont., 1958, M.A. in Speech Pathology/Audiology, 1960; postgrad. Mont. State U., 1973-75. Dir. exec. search Women's Inc., Chgo., 1979; mgr. Western Personnel, Phoenix, 1980-81; ptnr. Career Services Unlimited, Phoenix, 1981—; career cons., active youth substance abuse program. Author publs. in field. Home: 723 W Curry Chandler AZ 85224

REDMAN, WILLIAM JOHN, educational administrator, consultant; b. San Francisco, July 25, 1946; s. William Carl and Blanca Christina (Zelaya) R.; m. Pamela Ann Metsker, June 8, 1968; children—Laura Ann and Michele Lynn (twins). B.A. in Sociology, San Francisco State U., 1969, M.A. in Ednl. Adminstrn., 1975. Calif. teaching credential K-9; Calif. standard supervision credential K-9; Calif. adminstrv. services credential K-12. Tchr., San Francisco Unified Sch. Dist., 1971; tchr. San Leandro (Calif.) Unified Sch. Dist., 1972-75, prin., 1975-82, dir. elem. edn., 1982—; needs assessment cons. Mem. Assn. Calif. Sch. Adminstrs., Assn. for Supervision and Curriculum Devel., Nat. Assn. Elem. Sch. Prins. Democrat. Roman Catholic. Home: 1662 Morgan Ave San Leandro CA 94577 Office: 14735 Juniper St San Leandro CA 94579

REDMON, EDWARD JOHN, aerospace co. exec.; b. Freeport, Ill., Sept. 25, 1914; s. Alexander E. and Mary Mabel (Hines) R.; A.B., UCLA, 1937; M.A., U. So. Calif., 1939; m. Helen Louise Brown, June 1, 1944. Sr. job analyst Lockheed Aircraft, Burbank, Calif., 1940-51, wage and salary adminstr., Marietta, Calif., 1951-53, with Missile Systems Div., 1953-57, mgr. wage and salary adminstrn., head mgmt. compensation, Sunnyvale, Calif., 1957-80; dir. spl. compensation projects Lockheed Corp., 1982—; cons. and lectr. in field. Mem. Western Mgmt. Assn., Calif. Personnel Assn., Electronics Salary and Wage Assn., Electronics Industries Assn., Calif. Salary Adminstrs. Assn., Am. Mgmt. Assn. Republican. Methodist. Contbr. articles in field to profl. jours. Home: 12190 Fallen Leaf Ln Los Altos CA 94022 Office: 1111 Lockheed Way Sunnyvale CA 94086

REDMOND, DOROTHY MAE, hospital administrator; b. Pineville, La., June 18, 1951; d. Oscar Charles and Exie (Peoples) R. B.A. in Polit. Sci., UCLA, 1973; M.A. in Human Relations, San Francisco State U., 1977. Cert. tchr., Calif. Admitting interviewer Mt. Zion Hosp., San Francisco, 1973-75; community coordinator tchr. corps Jefferson Elem. Sch. Dist., Daly City, Calif., 1975-77; adminstrv. asst. Mission Neighborhood Health Ctr., San Francisco, 1977-79; staffing coordinator Kaiser Hosp., San Francisco, 1980—; pub. speaker; theatrical cons. Bank of Am. scholar, 1969. Mem. Black Women Organized for Action (life), NOW (life), Alpha Lambda Delta. Democrat. Baptist. Home: 1475 Oakdale Ave San Francisco CA 94124 Office: 2425 Geary Blvd Suite 290 San Francisco CA 94118

REED, DAVID PETER, hospital executive; b. Belleville, Ill., Aug. 14, 1940; s. Clement Peter and Olivia Bernadette (Hoeffken) R.; m. Rita Marianne Keiser, Nov. 5, 1966; children—Laura, David, Tricia, Douglas, Daniel. B.S. in Mgmt., So. Ill. U., 1965; M.H.A., St. Louis U., 1969. Asst. adminstr. Creighton Meml. St. Joseph Hosp., Omaha, 1969-71, assoc. adminstr., 1972-75; asst. adminstr. St. Joseph Hosp., Denver, 1975-80, exec. v.p., 1980—; trustee Hall of Life, Inc., Denver. Mem. Am. Coll. Hosp. Adminstrn. Roman Catholic. Office: 1835 Franklin St Denver CO 80218

REED, CHARLES RUFUS, lawyer; b. Garden City, Kans., Aug. 16, 1948; s. Ambers, Jr., and Estelle (Robinson) R.; m. Paula Marie Weeg, June 6, 1970; 1 dau., Kim Nicole. B.S., U.S. Air Force Acad., 1970; M.P.A., Princeton U., 1972; J.D., Stanford U., 1978. Bar: Calif. 1978. Assoc. Campbell, Warburton, Britton, Fitzsimmons & Smith, San Jose, Calif., 1978-80; mem. Glaspy, Elliott, Creech, McMahon, Roth & Reed, San Jose, 1981—. Bd. dirs., bd. counsel San Jose Repertory Co., 1981-83; mem. Human Relations Task Force, Berryessa Sch. Dist., 1980-82; mem. San Jose Planning Commn., San Jose Horizon 2000 Task Force. Served to capt. USAF, 1970-75. Mem. ABA, Calif. Bar Assn., Santa Clara County Bar Assn., San Jose C. of C. (chmn. high tech. com.). Democrat. Home: 1735 Septembersong Ct San Jose CA 95131 Office: 1999 S Bascom Ave Suite 1020 Box 5812 San Jose CA 95150

REED, CLAIRE HARRISON, public relations and advt. exec.; b. N.Y.C., Apr. 18, 1934; d. Jack Carl and Arion (Nadler) Levine, B.A., Conn. Coll., 1955, postgrad. in Internat. Relations, U. Calif., Berkeley, 1956, in Clin. Psychology, Calif. State U., San Francisco, 1963; m. Edward G. Reed, Mar. 2, 1969; children by previous marriage—Stephen James Harrison, Martha Harrison Shocron. Exec. sec. San Francisco Jr. C. of C., 1955-56; exec. dir. No. Calif. div. UNA, San Francisco, 1959-61; asst. in research Langley Porter Neuropsychiat. Inst., U. Calif., San Francisco, 1963-64; chief, pub. relations and advt. San Francisco Theatre Div. United Artists, 1965-67; founder CHA/Claire Harrison Assos., San Francisco, 1967-70, pres. Claire Harrison Assos., Inc., 1970—; vis. lectr., speaker profl. groups, univs. Mem. Internat. Assn. Bus. Communicators, Public Relations Soc. Am. (Silver Anvil award for best community relations program 1980), San Francisco Chamber Music Soc. (dir.). Clubs: Metropolitan, Commonwealth. Office: 54 Mint St San Francisco CA 94103

REED, DALE FRANK, wildlife biologist; b. York, Nebr., Sept. 11, 1936; s. Curtis Seneca and Elizabeth (Williams) R.; m. Melinda Hill, June 13, 1964; 1 dau., Margaret Hall. B.S., U. Nebr., 1959, M.A., 1963; postgrad. U. Colo., 1964-66, Colo. State U., 1967-68. Cert. wildlife biologist. Biology instr. Wheat Ridge (Colo.) Sr. High Sch., 1962-68; wildlife researcher Colo. Div. Wildlife, Wheat Ridge, 1968—. Sponsor spl. fund Rocky Mountain Planned Parenthood, Denver, 1978—. Served with USN., 1959-61, capt. Res. Mem. Am. Inst. Biol. Sci., Wildlife Soc., Colo. Open Space Council, Nature Conservancy (life), Nat. Parks and Conservation Assn., Wilderness Soc., Population Inst., Negative Population Growth, Zero Population Growth, No Name Water Assn. (v.p. 1979—). Club: Masons. Co-patentee one-way deer gate; contbr. book chpt., wildlife articles to profl. pubs. Home and Office: 3671 Ward Rd Wheat Ridge CO 80033

REED, ELIZABETH ANN, registered nurse; b. Phila., July 14, 1943; d. Thomas B. and Ann B. (Kuzmann) Reed. Diploma, Thomas Jefferson U. Hosp. Sch. Nursing, Phila., 1961-64; student Temple U., 1964-68. Various nursing positions Thomas Jefferson U. Hosp., Phila., 1964-68, head nurse cardiac surgery, 1972; head nurse cardiovascular surgery Cooper Hosp., Camden, N.J., 1968-72, clin. coordinator cardiac surgery, 1972-75; head nurse clin. perfusion U. Calif.-San Francisco, 1975-76, quality assurance coordinator, 1976-78, adminstrv. nurse IV, 1978—; speaker numerous profl. meetings. Mem. Am. Nurses Assn., Calif. Nurses Assn., Assn. Operating Room Nurses (dir. 1977-81, dir. San Francisco chpt. 1980—), Nurse's Alumnae Assn. Thomas Jefferson U. Hosp. Sch. Nursing, Assn. Advancement Med. Instrumentation (dir. 1981—). Contbg. author Alexander's Care of the Patient in Surgery, 6th edit., 1983; contbr. articles to profl. jours. Home: 252B Esperanza St Tiburon CA 94920 Office: U Calif San Francisco Suite M423 3d & Parnassus Sts San Francisco CA 94143

REED, FRANK FREMONT, II, lawyer; b. Chgo., June 15, 1928; s. Allen Martin and Frances (Faurot) R.; student Chgo. Latin Sch.; grad. St. Paul's Sch., 1946; A.B., U. Mich., 1952, J.D., 1957; m. Jaquelin Silverthorne Cox, April 27, 1963; children—Elizabeth Matthiessen, Laurie Matthiessen, Mark Matthiessen, Jeffrey, Nancy, Sarah. Admitted to Ill. bar, 1958; asso. Byron, Hume, Groen & Clement, 1958-61, Marks & Clerk, 1961-63; individual practice, Chgo., 1963—; dir. Western Acadia (Western Felt Works), 1960-75, chmn. exec. com., 1969-71. Cubmaster, Cub Scout Pack 3014, Chgo. Area council Boy Scouts America, 1964-70; Republican precinct capt. 1972-78; candidate for 43d ward alderman, 1975; bd. dirs., sec. Chgo. Found. Theater Arts, 1959-64; vestryman St. Chrysostom's Ch., 1975-79, mem. ushers guild, 1964-79, chmn., 1976-78; bd. dirs. North State, Astor, Lake Shore Dr. Assn., 1975-78, pres. 1977-78; sustaining fellow Art Inst. Chgo., 1978—. Served to cpl. AUS, 1952-54. Mem. ABA, Ill., Chgo. bar assns., Am. Judicature Soc., Phi Alpha Delta. Republican. Episcopalian. Clubs: Racquet, Wausaukee (sec., dir. 1968-71, chmn. sailing com. 1962-70, 72-79) (Chgo.); Birnam Wood Golf (Santa Barbara, Calif.). Contbr. articles to The Am. Genealogist, 1972-73, 76-77; historian for the Faurot and Silverthorn families. Home: 1944 E Valley Rd Santa Barbara CA 93108 Office: 135 S LaSalle St Suite 4005 Chicago IL 60603

REED, FRANK METCALF, banker; b. Seattle, Dec. 22, 1912; s. Frank Ivan and Pauline B. (Hovey) R.; student U. Alaska, 1931-32; B.A., U. Wash., 1937; m. Maxine Vivian McGary, June 11, 1937; children—Pauline Jarnette (Mrs. Donald Scott Mackay), Frank Metcalf II. Vice pres. Anchorage Light & Power Co., 1937-42; pres. Alaska Electric & Equipment Co., Anchorage, 1946-50; sec., mgr. Turnagain, Inc., Anchorage, 1950-56; mgr. Gen. Credit Corp., Anchorage, 1957; br. mgr. Alaska SBA, Anchorage, 1958-60; sr. v.p. Alaska Bank of Commerce, Anchorage, 1960—, also dir.; pres., dir. Anchorage Broadcasters, Inc.; chmn. bd., pres. Microfast Software Corp.; ptnr. R.M.R. Co.; dir. Anchorage Light & Power Co., Turnagain, Inc., Alaska Fish and Farm, Inc., Life Ins. Co. Alaska, Alaska Hotel Properties, Spa Inc. Pres., Anchorage Federated Charities, Inc., 1953-54; mem. advisory bd. Salvation Army, 1948-58; mem. City of Anchorage Planning Commn., 1956; mem. City of Anchorage Council, 1956-57; police commr. Ter. of Alaska, 1957-58; chmn. City Charter Commn., 1958; mem. exec. com. Greater Anchorage, Inc., 1955-65; pres. Sch. Bd., 1961-64; mem. Gov.'s Investment adv. com., 1970-72; mem. Alaska State Bd. Edn.; mem. citizens adv. com. Alaska Meth. U.; chmn. Anchorage Charter Commn., 1975; chmn. bldg. fund dr. Community YMCA, 1976—; bd. dirs., mem. exec. com. Arts Alaska, 1976-78; sec.-treas. Breakthrough, 1976-78; bd. dirs. Anchorage Civic Opera, 1978, Alaska Treatment Ctr., Rural Venture Alaska, Inc.; trustee Marston Found., Inc. Served as lt. USNR, 1942-46. Elected to Hall Fame, Alaska Press Club, 1969; named Outstanding Alaskan of Year Alaska C. of C., 1976; recipient Community Service award YMCA, 1975-78. Mem. Am. Inst. Banking, Am. (exec. council 1971-72) Alaska (pres. 1970-71) bankers assns., Nat. Assn. State Bds. Edn. (sec.-treas. 1969-70), C. of C. U.S. (Western region legislative com.), Anchorage C. of C. (pres. 1966-67, dir.), Pioneers of Alaska, Navy League (pres. Anchorage council 1961-62). Clubs. Lion (sec. Anchorage, 1953-54, pres., 1962-63), Elks, Tower (life), Wash. Athletic. Home: 1361 W 12th Ave Anchorage AK 99501

REED, FRED WARREN, sociology educator, communication consultant; b. Sidney, Mont., Sept. 30, 1939; s. Fred Ward and Norda (Williams) R.; m. Susan Friedman, 1967; children—Benjamin, Ward, Reed. B.A. in Sociology, U. Mont., 1965; M.A. in Sociology, U. N.C., 1970, Ph.D. in Sociology, 1972. Asst. prof. U. Chgo., 1972-75; cons. UNICEF, Ethiopia, 1975-76; assoc. prof. sociology U. Mont., Missoula, 1976—; cons. in communication for social devel. UNICEF, AID, UNFPA, Korea, Nepal, Guyana, Kenya; devel. communication for population control, Indonesia, 1980-82. Mem. Missoula City Council, 1979-80. Served with U.S. Army, 1959-62. NSF research fellow, 1967-70. Mem. Am. Sociol. Assn., Population Assn. Am. Author: Pre-Testing Communications: A Manual of Procedures, 1974; (with Bjorn Berndtson) Rejuvenating the Moribund Clinic: An Experiment in Communication, 1974; contbr. articles to profl. jours. Office: Dept of Sociology University of Montana Missoula MT 59812

REED, GEORGE FORD, JR., automobile club exec.; b. Hollywood, Calif., Dec. 26, 1946; s. George Ford and Mary Anita Reed; B.A. in Econs. with honors, U. So. Calif., 1969, M.A., 1971; m. Kathryn Nixon, 1981. Analyst planning and research Larwin Group, Beverly Hills, Calif., 1971-72; with Automobile Club So. Calif., Los Angeles, 1972—, supr. mgmt. info., research and devel., 1973-74, mgr. fin. and market analysis, 1975-81, group mgr. fin. analysis and forecasting, 1981—; instr. bus. and econs. Los Angeles Community Coll. Mem. population task force Los Angeles C. of C., 1974—; mem. Gov. Calif. Statewide Econ. Summit Conf., 1974. Served with U.S. Army, 1969. Mem. Assn. Corp. Real Estate Execs., Nat. Assn. Bus. Economists, Western Regional Sci. Assn., Am. Mgmt. Assn., Am. Fin. Assn., So. Calif. Planners Assn., Omicron Delta Epsilon. Home: 1001 S Westgate Ave Los Angeles CA 90049 Office: 2601 S Figueroa St Los Angeles CA 90007

REED, GLORIA NORWOOD, marketing specialist; b. Tucson, Feb. 17, 1956; d. Nathaniel and Loraine (Joe) Norwood; m. Frank Eric Reed, Feb. 18, 1983. B.A. in Bus. Pub. Adminstrn., U. Ariz., Tucson, 1979. Loan officer Valley Nat. Bank, Tucson, 1974-80; loan officer Am. City Bank, Los Angeles, 1980-81; product specialist Banking Data Services, Los Angeles, 1981—. Mem. Nat. Assn. Female Execs., Delta Sigma Theta. Office: Banking Data Services 8616 Latijera Blvd Suite 212 Los Angeles CA 90045

REED, GORDON W., real estate broker; b. Boulder, Colo., Sept. 19, 1945; d. Wallace K. and Barbara J. (McKee) R.; student U. Wyo., Grad. Realtors Inst., 1976; m. Penny J. Bergman, Sept. 9, 1967; children—Stewart, Stephanie. With Am. Nat. Bank, Cheyenne, Wyo., 1967-69; owner Scottis Drive Inns, Scotts Bluff and Grand Island, Nebr., 1969-72; broker Atlas Realty Inc., Cheyenne, 1972-81, Wallick & Voik, Inc., Cheyenne, 1981—. Mem. Cheyenne Bd. Adjustments, 1981—. Cert. resdl. broker; cert. resdl. specialist. Served with Air N.G., 1967-73. Mem. Wyo. Assn. Realtors (dir.), Nat. Assn. Realtors, Nat. Assn. Home Builders, Cheyenne Assn. Home Builders, Wyo. Assn. Home Builders, Airplane Owners and Pilots Assn., Cheyenne Bd. Realtors (dir.), Cheyenne C. of C. Republican. Presbyterian. Club: Kiwanis. Home: 5150 McCue Dr Cheyenne WY 82009 Office: PO Box 685 Cheyenne WY 82003

REED, JOHN MURRY, airline co. exec.; b. Ancon, Panama Canal Zone, Feb. 3, 1944; s. John Walter and Leathea (Zoe) Yon; A.A., U. Nev., 1967, Western Nev. Community Coll., 1977. Sta. agent Bonanza Air Lines, Las Vegas, 1966-67; sta. agent Pacific Airlines, San Francisco, 1967; customer sr. mgr. Air Calif., San Francisco, 1968-70; sta. agent Hughes Airwest, Lake Tahoe, Calif., 1972-74; pres., gen. mgr. Ponderosa Airlines, Lake Tahoe, 1974-79; pres., chief exec. officer Tahoe Pacific Airlines, Sparks, Nev., 1980—; v.p., gen. mgr. Gt. Am. Airways, Inc., 1981-82; advisor El Dorado Airports, 1974-75. Sr. scoutmaster Nev. area Boy Scouts Am., Minden, 1963. Served with U.S. Navy, 1963-64. Mem. Nat. Geog. Soc., Oceanic Soc., Inter Am. Soc. Home: PO Box 20996 Reno NV 89515 Office: Cannon Internat Airport PO Box 10165 Reno NV 89510

REED, JULIE JIREL, home economics educator; b. Albany, Oreg., Sept. 8, 1941; d. William Jack and Gloria Marie (Jacobson) Jirel; m. Steven Leonard Reed. B.S., Oreg. State U., 1963, M.S., 1975. Exec. trainee Emporium-Capwell, San Francisco, 1963; tchr. Corvallis (Oreg.) Sch. System, 1964—, head tchr. home econs. dept. Highland View Sch., 1971—. Dir. Macedonean dance ensemble Ansambe Staro Srebro, 1963—. Mem. Tchrs. Home Econs. Oreg. Republican. Presbyterian. Club: Oreg. State U. Folk Dance. Office: Home Econs Dept Highland View Sch 1920 Highland Dr Corvallis OR 97330

REED, MARION GUY, research chemist; b. Osceola, Iowa, June 26, 1931; s. Guy Madison and Mamie Fayteen (Henrich) R.; m. Betty Pauline Patterson, Feb. 11, 1951; children—Karen, Janet. B.S., Iowa State U., 1957, Ph.D. in Soil Chemistry, 1963. Research assoc. in soils Iowa State U., Ames, 1957-62; research chemist Chevron Research Co., LaHabra, Calif., 1962-69, sr. research chemist Chevron Oil Field Research Co., 1969-73, sr. research assoc., 1973—. Author numerous tech. papers for profl. jours.; patentee in field. Served with AUS, 1952-54. Recipient Standard Oil Co. Calif. Mgmt. Incentive award, 1974, Mem. Am. Chem. Soc., Am. Soc. Agronomy, Soil Sci. Soc. Am., Clay Minerals Soc. (pres. 1985), Soc. Petroleum Engrs. Republican. Club: Skylarks So. Calif. Home: 15115 Los Altos Dr Hacienda Heights CA 91745 Office: 3282 Beach Blvd La Habra CA 90631

REED, MARY LOUISE, social worker; b. San Diego, Nov. 29, 1938; d. William M. and Veronica Josephine R.; A.B., Memphis State U., 1962; M.A., Columbia U., N.Y.C., 1966; M.S.W., UCLA, 1981. Med. technologist Bapt. Meml. Hosp., Memphis, 1960-62; tchr. Peace Corps, Nigeria, 1962-64; asst. to exec. dir. Youth Guidance Commn., Memphis, 1965-66; tchr. Tchr. Tng. Inst., Debre, Berhan, Ethiopia, 1966-67; social worker Dept. Public Social Service, County of Los Angeles, 1967—; med. social work intern Martin Luther King Jr. Hosp., 1979-80; social work intern in child psychiatry HGH/UCLA Med. Center, 1980-81. Registered med. technologist. Mem. Nat. Assn. Social Workers, Soc. Clin. Social Work, Los Angeles Mental Health Assn. Office: Long Beach CA

REED, NANCY, business communicator; b. Denver, Jan. 6, 1954; d. Jerry Edward and Betty Jayne (Vaughan) R. B.A. in English and German summa cum laude, U. Denver, 1975, M.A. in Info. Scis., 1977. Accredited bus. communicator. Communication specialist, tng. rep. Coors Porcelain Co., Golden, Colo., 1977-79, communication supr., 1979-82, employee communication and pub. relations supr., 1982—; speaker, cons. pub. relations U. Denver, 1978-79; cons. radiation/oncology dept., Presbyn. Hosp., Denver, 1980-81; task force mem. Futurism in Communications Conf., 1982. Vol. editor local publs. Am. Cancer Soc.; del. Pres.'s White House Conf. on Youth, 1971; girl pres. ARC Youth All-City Council, Denver, 1970-71. Lucille R. Brown Found. scholar, 1973-77; Harriet E. Howe Alumni scholar, 1976-77; Fulbright-Hayes scholar U. Heidelberg (Ger.), 1976; recipient Bronze Quill award YWCA Met. Denver Women in Achievement award, 1982. Mem. Internat. Assn. Bus. Communicators, Pub. Relations Soc. Am., Fulbright Alumni Assn., ALA (David H. Clift scholar 1976-77), Phi Beta Kappa, Alpha Lambda Delta (Disting. scholar 1972-73). Republican. Presbyterian. Office: 600 9th St Golden CO 80401

REED, SHARON RAE, psychotherapist, clinical consultant; b. Wichita, Kans., Jan. 5, 1939; d. Paul Stewart and Margaret Frances (Wachtel) R. B.A., U. Calif.-Santa Barbara, 1961; M.A., Peabody Coll., 1966, postgrad. in psychology, 1966-67; postgrad., U. Calif., 1971-72. Tchr. Riverside (Calif.) Unified Sch. Dist., 1961-62, Garden Grove (Calif.) Unified Sch. Dist., 1963-65; counselor/cons. Fulton County Sch. Dist., Atlanta, 1968-69, Alvord Unified Sch. Dist., Riverside, Calif., 1970-73, Burlington-Edison Sch. Dist., Burlington, Wash., 1973-75; family and child therapist Skagit Counseling and Psychiat. Services, Mt. Vernon, Wash., 1975-79; prochotherapist-cons., co-owner Dayspring Assocs., Inc., Seattle, 1979—; faculty Child Sexual Abuse Treatment-Tng. Inst., U. Wash.; clin. cons. to Valley Cities Mental Health, Children's Day Treatment Program, Sexual Assault Ctr., Harborview Med. Ctr., Seattle; supr. student interns, guest lectr. psychology dept. Western Wash. U., 1975-78; active Wash. State Coalition for Prevention of Child Abuse and Neglect, 1976-79, bd. dirs., 1979; mem. planning com. for Wash. State Gov.'s Conf. on Child Abuse and Neglect, 1977-78; founder, chmn. Skagit Council for Child Advocacy, 1976-79; trainer Bur. Alcohol and Substance Abuse, Dept. Social and Health Services, 1980. NIMH grad. fellow, 1965. Mem. Am. Personnel and Guidance Assn., Am. Women in Psychology. Speaker profl. confs.; author: Common Travellers: The Commitment of the Child Therapist, 1981. Office: 311 W McGraw St Seattle WA 98119

REED, SUSAN L., laboratory administrator, computer researcher, translator; b. San Rafael, Calif., May 10, 1959; d. Ronald J. and Anne P. (Brown) Scinski. B.A. in Russian, San Diego State U., 1981. Computer student Dr. Ludek Kozlik, San Diego, 1977-78; sch. adminstr. Congregation Beth Tefilah, San Diego, 1979-80; co-owner, mgr. S & S Stereos, San Diego, 1980-81; lab. adminstr. Helicon Found., San Diego, 1982, Syntro Corp., San Diego, 1982—; Russian translator. Recipient Appreciation award organizational activities Alpha Phi Omega, 1980. Mem. So. Calif. Council Soviet Jews. Mem. Dobro Slovo Honor Soc. (life), Alpha Phi Omega. Democrat. Jewish. Club: Circle K. Office: Syntro Corp 11095 Torreyana Rd Suite 103 San Diego CA 92122

REEDER, JIM, agronomist; b. Kearney, Nebr., Feb. 27, 1948; s. Ralph and Marie R.; m. Jean, May 25, 1973; 1 son, Brett. B.S. in Vocat. Agr. Edn. and Agronomy, U. Nebr., 1973. Tchr. agr. Windsor (Colo.) High Sch., 1973-76; purification mgr. N.Am. Plant Breeders, Berthoud, Colo., 1973—. Mem. Am. Soc. Agronomy. Home: 300 Leeward Ct Fort Collins CO 80525 Office: N Am Plant Breeders PO Box 30 Berthoud CO 80513

REEDER, SAMUEL KENNETH, food co. lab. mgr.; b. Vinita, Okla., July 25, 1938; s. Dwight Cecil and Melba Mae (Mattox) R.; B.A., LaSierra Coll., Loma Linda U., 1960; Ph.D. (NDEA fellow), Mont. State U., 1971; m. Camille Augusta Goepfert, Aug. 17, 1959; children—Jerold Kenneth, Jeanne Mae, Jodi Camille. Educator, Seventh-day Adventist Schs., Oreg. and Calif., 1961-66; chemist to chief scientist, Sunkist Growers, Inc., research and devel., Ontario, Calif., 1971-79; lab. mgr. Hunt-Wesson Foods research and devel., Fullerton, Calif., 1979—. Trustee, Ontario City Library, 1976-80, pres. bd. trustees, 1978-80. Recipient Bank of Am. award, 1956. Mem. Am. Chem. Soc., Inst. Food Technologists, Assn. Ofcl. Analytical Chemists (assoc.). Seventh-day Adventist. Contbr. sci. papers to profl. jours. Home: 11428 Gedney Way Riverside CA 92505 Office: 1645 W Valencia Dr Fullerton CA 92634

REES, FRANCES IRENE, computer company executive, educator; b. Douglas, Ariz., Oct. 11, 1942; d. Hugh Eldred and Carmen Emily (Kennedy) Mayfield; m. David Evans Rees, Aug. 29, 1980. B.A., UCLA, 1964; Mus. M., U. Ariz., 1975, M.B.A., 1980. Tchr. Washington and Smedeley Jr. High Schs., Long Beach and Santa Ana, Calif., 1964-68; tchr. Rabat (Morocco) Am. Sch., 1971-72; pvt. tchr. music, Simi Valley, Calif., 1968-71; office mgr. U. Ariz. Sch. Music, Tucson, 1973-75, dir. admissions, 1975-79; sr. planner Digital Equipment Corp., Phoenix, 1980-82, sr. edn. specialist, 1982-83, tng. and devel. cons., 1983—. Recipient Achievement award Bank Am., 1959; award Merit in Bus., Underwood, 1959; 1st pl. Talent award Calif. Businessmen's Assn., 1959. Mem. Am. Soc. Tng. and Devel. (chmn. Orgn. Devel. Support Group, Phoenix), Am. Prodn. and Inventory Control Soc. (cert.), Nat. Assn. Female Execs. Co-designer five-day tng. program for industry. Office: Digital Equipment Corp 2500 W Union Hills Dr Phoenix AZ 85027

REES, MARIAN JANET, librarian; b. Oak Park, Ill., July 3, 1934; s. Ewald and Gertrude Dorothy (Hilbert) Heimert; B.A., Ind. U., 1956; M.A., Calif. State U., San Jose, 1973; m. John Robert Rees, Jan. 28, 1956; children—Carol Ellen, John Alton. Mem. acad. staff Inst. Energy Studies, Stanford U., 1974—, head librarian, dir. info. center, 1974—; cons. in field. Chmn. fgn. langs. in elementary schs., Wheaton, Md., 1967-69. Mem. Spl. Libraries Assn., AAAS, Western Info. Network Energy (vice chmn. 1980-81), Calif. Library Assn., Stanford U. Library Assn., Internat. Assn. Energy Economists, Energy Librarians Bay Area (chmn. 1979-80). Democrat. Author: Energy Modeling: A Selected Bibliography, 1977; editor Energy Info. Center Selected Acquisitions List, 1975—. Home: 1340 Sunrise Ct Los Altos CA 94022 Office: Stanford Univ Bldg 500 Stanford CA 94305

REESE, ALBERT MOORE, JR., public relations executive; b. Morgantown, W.Va., Apr. 5, 1933; s. Albert Moore and Nelle (Summers) R.; m. Susan Holt. A.B., W.Va. U., 1954; M.S., Boston U., 1959. Dir. pub. relations United Community Services Met. Boston, 1963-68, United Way of San Diego County (Calif.), 1968-74; dir. pub. affairs San Diego Conv. and Visitors Bur., 1975—. Bd. dirs. San Diego chpt. Am. Cancer Soc. Served to capt. USAF, 1954-56. Mem. Pub. Relations Soc. Am. Democrat. Episcopalian.

REESE, ANDREW JOEL, lawyer; b. Los Angeles, May 5, 1945; s. John Henry and Margaret (Smith) R.; student U. So. Calif., 1963-64; B.S. with honors in Econs., Calif. State Poly. U., 1972; J.D., Harvard U., 1975; A.A. in Bus. and Real Estate, Mendocino Coll., 1979; m. Karon K. Wolf, Sept. 1, 1967 (div. 1981); 1 dau., Elisabeth K.; m. Beatriz P. Coleman, 1981. Admitted to Calif. bar, 1975; asso. firm Pacht, Ross, Warne, Bernhard & Sears, Inc., Los Angeles, 1975-76; dep. dist. atty. Mendocino County Dist. Atty.'s Office, Ukiah, Calif., 1976-79; partner firm Adams, Henderson & Reese, Ukiah, 1980; sole practitioner Law Office of Andrew J. Reese, Ukiah, 1979, 81—; contract public defender, Mendocino County, 1979-82; instr. law and real estate Mendocino Coll., Ukiah, 1978-80. Sec.-treas., dir. Mendocino County Employees Credit Union, 1979. Pres., Alcohol Rehab. Corp., 1980—; chmn. interim policy adv. council Mendocino Alcohol Project, 1980. Served with USAF, 1964-68. Mem. Am. Bar Assn., Calif. Bar Assn. Republican. Club: 20-30 Internat. (Ukiah). Home: 178 Jack London Dr Santa Rosa CA 95405 Office: 249-K W Gobbi St Ukiah CA 95482

REESE, GILBERT, cellist; b. Long Beach, Calif., May 26, 1925; s. Robert and Mae (Gilbert) R.; m. Marianne Marshall, Apr. 11, 1964. Lic. Ecole Normale Musique, Paris, 1951; pvt. studies with Pablo Casals, France, 1949-52; B.A. in French Lit., Calif. State U.-Long Beach, 1968. Prin. cellist Indpls. Symphony, 1952-63; cellist Jordan String Quartet, 1954-63; founder, participant Spring Chamber Music Festival, Indpls., 1957-63; dir. SYMF, Los Angeles, 1968-77; concert cellist, soloist with maj. orchs., recitalist throughout Europe and Asia, 1950—; recs. include: Musique de l'Amerique, 1972; Sonata by Grieg and Fantasy Pieces by Schumann, 1974; Scandinavian Cello Music, 1976; French Scenarios, 1980. Served with USAAF, 1943-45. Mem. Am. String Tchrs. Assn. (dir. 1970-73), Chamber Music Am., Am. Fedn. Musicians (life). Home: 34 66th Pl Long Beach CA 90803

REESE, JOHN MELVIN, lawyer; b. Spokane, June 16, 1931; s. William Bryan and Carmen Ardis (Batie) R.; m. Mary Elaine Land, Dec. 28, 1954; children—Daniel, Scott, William, Mary. B.S., Wash. State U., 1953; J.D., U. Idaho, 1956. Bar: Wash. 1956. Practice law, Walla Walla, Wash., 1958—; pres. Reese, Baffney, Schrag & Siegel, P.S., 1976—; city atty. Walla Walla, 1960-65. Mem. Republican State Com., 1966-70; pres. Walla Walla Family YMCA, 1981—. Served to 1st lt. JAGC, USAF, 1956-58. Mem. Walla Walla C. of C. (pres. 1974), Wash. Bar Assn., Walla Walla County Bar Assn., ABA. Presbyterian. Clubs: Walla Walla Country (pres. 1968), Exchange (pres. 1965), Elks, Masons. Home: 1121 Alvarado St Walla Walla WA 99362 Office: 707 Baker Bldg Walla Walla WA 99362

REESE, KAY THOMAS, dentist; b. Bloomington, Idaho, Apr. 20, 1935; s. Merrill J. and Stella (Giles) R.; student (Ford Found. scholar) U. Utah, 1952-55; D.D.S., Northwestern U., 1959; m. Bette Josephine Johns, Sept. 18, 1959; children—Bryan K., Gwendolyn Jeanette, Paula Helen, David Owen. Gen. practice dentistry, pres. corp. K.T. Reese, D.D.S., Tooele, Utah. Vice chmn. Deseret Peak dist. Gt. Salt Lake council Boy Scouts Am., staff mem. Woodbadge Troop, 1983. Served to lt. comdr. USN, 1959-66. Mem. ADA, Lic. Calif. Dentists Assn., Utah Dental Assn., Nat. Endodontic Soc., Brigham Young U. Acad. Dentists, Soc. Occlusal Studies, Am. Equilibration Soc., Acad. Gen. Dentists, Tooele County C. of C. Mormon. Home: 170 E Second S Tooele UT 84074

REESE, L. JOE, sporting goods cons. co. exec.; b. Hutchinson, Minn., June 28, 1942; s. Albert Clarence and Lilyan Emily R.; B.S., Gustavus Adolphus Coll., 1964; M.S., Ind. U., 1965; m. Patricia Lou Belgum, June 3, 1960; children—Cal Anthony, Tracy Lynn. Head football coach St. James (Minn.) High Sch., 1967-69; asst. football coach Hastings (Nebr.) Coll., 1969; salesman Arch Billmire Co., San Francisco, 1970-72, regional sales mgr., Kansas City, 1972-76, nat. sales mgr., San Francisco, 1976-77, gen. mgr., 1978-80; pres. Western Athletic Cons., 1980—. Mem. Nat. Sporting Goods Assn. Methodist. Home: 424 St Joseph Half Moon Bay CA 94019 Office: 2650 3d St San Francisco CA 94117

REESE, MICHAEL HENRY, govt. ofcl.; b. Rock Springs, Wyo., Jan. 5, 1949; s. Arthur Donald and Grace (Haggerty) R.; B.A., U. Wyo., 1971; J.D., 1974; m. Melanie Beck, Aug. 7, 1971; children—Jason, Libby, Megan. Admitted to Wyo. bar, 1974; legal analyst Legis. Service Office, Cheyenne, Wyo., 1974-75; dir. community assistance Wyo. Dept. Econ. Planning and Devel., Cheyenne, 1975-77, chief state planning, 1977-80; dir. Wyo. Water Devel. Commn., 1980—. Coach, youth soccer. Mem. Wyo. Bar Assn., Laramie County Bar Assn., Wyo. Planning Assn., Wyo. Water Devel. Assn. Democrat. Roman Catholic. Office: Wyo Water Devel Commn Barrett Bldg Cheyenne WY 82002

REESE, SUSAN HOLT, educational administrator and consultant; b. Muleshoe, Tex., Oct. 3, 1942; d. Arthur Wheeler and Margaret Frances (Guinn) Holt; m. Albert Moore Reese, Jr., Apr. 3, 1971. B.B.A. in Bus. Edn., Baylor U., 1964; M.A. in Edn. and Human Behavior, U.S. Internat. U., 1978. Life teaching credential, Calif., Tex.; adminstrv. services credential, Calif. Classroom tchr. San Diego City Schs., 1964-76, bus. edn. resource tchr., 1976-79, curriculum specialist, bus. edn., 1979—; cons. Calif. State Dept. Edn., Pacific SW Airlines, San Diego State U.; speaker bus. edn. and computer confs. Active San Diego Opera Assn., 1975—. Mem. Am. Vocat. Assn., Calif. Assn. Vocat. Educators, Nat. Assn. Supervisors of Bus. Edn., Nat. Bus. Edn. Assn., Western Bus. Edn. Assn., Calif. Bus. Edn. Assn., San Diego Computer Using Educators, Theta Alpha Delta, Delta Kappa Gamma. Democrat. Episcopalian. Author: (with Marilyn Runyan) Strategies for Student Recruitment and Program Promition, 1983; contbr. articles to profl. publs. and mags. Office: 4100 Normal St Room 2034 San Diego CA 92103

REESE, WADE MICHAEL, EDP systems consultant, information systems auditor; b. Upland, Calif., Sept. 4, 1956; s. Lester Leland and Joann (Petersen) R.; m. Vickie Ellen Olive, Nov. 28, 1980; 1 dau., Michelle Leigh. A.A. in Bus. Adminstrn., Chaffey Community Coll., 1977; B.S. in Mgmt. Sci. and Bus. Law, Calif. Poly. U., 1979, postgrad. in Bus. Adminstrn., 1982—. Cert. info. systems auditor; cert. data processor. EDP coordinator Kemper Mfg., Inc., Chino, Calif., 1973-79; mgmt. cons. Ernst & Whinney, Los Angeles, 1979-81; internal EDP cons. The Irvine Co., Newport Beach, Calif., 1981—; microprocessor cons., programmer. Bd. dirs. Bouquet Estates. Mem. EDP Auditor Assn., Assn. Systems Mgmt. Republican. Home: 1385 B Bouquet Dr Upland CA 91786 Office: Irvine Co 550 Newport Center Dr Newport Beach CA 92660

REEVE, CONNIE ETZEL, home economist; b. Price, Utah, Apr. 11, 1947; d. Remo P. and Shirlee (Robertson) Etzel; m. Doyle E. Reeve; 1 dau., LaRisse. A.A., Coll. Eastern Utah, 1967; B.S. in Home Econs. Edn., Brigham Young U., 1969; student Culminary Arts Inst. Chgo., 1979. Home economist Mountain Fuel Supply Co., Salt Lake City, 1969-79, sr. home economist, 1979-83; coordinator home econs. program, 1983—; corp. sec. Reeve Bros., Inc., 1980—. Active United Way, 1982—. Named Young Career Woman, Bus. and Profl. Women, 1970. Mem. Home Economists in Bus., Am. Home Econs. Assn., Utah Home Econs. Assn. (pres. 1983). Mormon. Office: Mountain Fuel Supply Co 180 E 1st S Salt Lake City UT 84139

REEVE, LYDIA RYDHOLM, advertising media specialist; b. Cleveland Heights, Ohio, Jan. 3, 1925; d. Carl Oscar and Marion Louise (Hager) Rydholm; m. Donald Burkett Reeve, Nov., 1956 (div.). B.S., NYU, 1948. Media clk. Alfred J. Silberstein, Bert Goldsmith, Inc., N.Y.C., 1948; media asst. Foote, Cone & Belding, Los Angeles, 1949-50, time buyer, 1951-56, media supr., 1957-63, assoc. media dir., 1964-67, media dir., v.p., 1968; v.p., media dir., Honig, Cooper & Harrington (name changed to Foote, Cone & Belding/Honig 1975), Los Angeles, 1969-70, assoc. media dir., 1980—. Vice chmn. communications com. Arthritis Found. of So. Calif.; mem. profl. women's com. So. Calif. Symphony/Hollywood Bowl Assn. Mem. Am. Advt. Fedn. (chmn. western region 1976-77, nat. dir. 1969-77, nat. sec. treas. 1977-79), Los Angeles Advt. Women (past pres.), Hollywood Radio and TV Soc. (past sec., v.p.), Pacific Broadcast Pioneers, Los Angeles Area C. of C. (women's council). Office: Foote Cone Belding/Honig 2727 W 6th St PO Box 60209 Los Angeles CA 90060

REEVES, BILLY D., obstetrician and gynecologist; b. Franklin Park, Ill., Jan. 17, 1927; s. William Barney and Martha Dorcas (Benbrook) R.; B.A., Elmhurst (Ill.) Coll., 1953; M.D., U. Ill., 1960; endocrine research Karolinska Inst., Stockholm, 1968-69; m. Phyllis Joan Faber, Aug. 25, 1951; children—Philip, Pamela, Tina, Brian, Timothy. Intern, Evanston (Ill.) Hosp., 1960-61, resident ob-gyn, 1961-64; practice medicine specializing in ob-gyn, 1964—, also gynecol. endocrinology, 1964-72; practice in Las Cruces, N.Mex., 1972-77; cons. staff Meml. Gen. Hosp., 1972—, chmn. dept. ob-gyn, 1974-75, chmn. infection control com., 1974-76; clin. asso. ob-gyn U. N.Mex. Sch. Medicine, 1972-77, U. Ariz. Sch. Medicine, 1975-78; prof., asso. chmn. ob-gyn Tex. Tech U Sch. Medicine Regional Acad. Health Center, El Paso, 1977-83; clin. dir. dept. ob-gyn R.E. Thomason Gen. Hosp., El Paso, also med. dir. Family Planning Service, 1977-83. Mem. sub-area council VII, N.Mex. Health Systems Agy., 1975-80. Served with U.S. Mcht. Marine, 1945-46, AUS, 1946-47, comdr. M.C., USNR, 1982—. Diplomate Am. Bd. Ob-Gyn. Mem. Am. Coll. Ob-Gyn, Am. Fertility Soc., ACS, Inst. Medicine Chgo., Central Assn. Obstetricians and Gynecologists, Endocrine Soc., AAAS. Contbr. articles to med. jours. Home: 1620 Altura Las Cruces NM 88001 Office: 4800 Alberta St El Paso TX 79905

REEVES, DANIEL EDWARD, professional football coach; b. Rome, Ga., Jan. 19, 1944; m. Pam; children—Dana, Laura, Lee. Student U. S.C. Player, Dallas Cowboys, NFL, 1965-72, player-coach, 1970-71, asst. coach, 1972, 74-80; head coach Denver Broncos, NFL, 1981—. Player, NFL Championship Game, 1966, 67, 70, 71; inducted in S.C. Hall of Fame, 1977. Office: Denver Broncos 5700 Logan St Denver CO 80216*

REEVES, DAVID EDMUND, employee health clinic executive; b. Norfolk, Va., Sept. 20, 1932; s. James Edmund and Marguerite Kimberlin (Lowe) R.; m. Lela May Barlow, June 21, 1958. A.B., U. Calif.-Berkeley, 1954; M.B.A., Stanford U., 1959. Spl. asst. dir. purchasing and materials mgmt. Stanford U., 1960-66; mgr. materials, facilities and planning RCA Corp., Palo Alto, Calif., 1966-68; v.p. Saga Instl. Services Menlo Park, Calif., 1968-70; supt. schs., Woodland, Calif., 1970-73; v.p. Tentagel, Inc., Redwood City, Calif., 1973-78; cons., investor, San Francisco and Honolulu, 1978-81; exec. dir. San Francisco Clinic, 1981—; cons. Synfuel Genesis, Inc.; Internat. Securities Corp.; dir. Copico, Scotch Mist Charters. Mem. Gov.'s Com. Polit. Reform. Served with U.S. Army, 1954-56. Recipient Judge's award English Shetland Sheepdog Club, 1977. Mem. Eureka Valley Mchts. Assn., Art-In-The-Park (budget dir.), Am. Kennel Club (judge), San Francisco Visitors and Conv. Bur. Episcopalian. Clubs: Lahaina Yacht (Maui), Masons. Co-author: Instructor's Guide for Purchasing and Materials Management, 1966. Office: Suite 1822 San Francisco Clinic 450 Sutter St San Francisco CA 94108

REEVES, DONALD JOSEPH, architect; b. Evansville, Ind., Oct. 20, 1936; s. Edward C. and Eula Goldsmith (Farrar) R.; B.F.A., U. Utah, 1958; children—Kathryn, Christopher, Timothy. Architect intern with William Stimmel, Architect, La Jolla, Calif., 1963-64, Livingstone & Brown Co., San Diego, 1964-66; job capt. Dale Naegle & Assos., La Jolla, 1966-67; project architect Mosher, Drew, Watson Assos., La Jolla, 1967-72, Frank L. Hope & Assos., San Diego, 1972-73; partner Munroe & Reeves, Architects, San Diego, 1973-77; prin. Donald J. Reeves & Assos., San Diego, 1977—; guest lectr. architecture and interior planning San Diego State U., 1970-79. Coach, University City Little League, 1973-75; mem. University Community Forum, 1973—; mem. hist. sites bd. City of San Diego, 1975-80, chmn., 1979-80; bd. dirs. Clairemont Community Hosp., San Diego, 1974-75; mem. bd. appeals City of Barstow (Calif.), 1977—. Served as officer USN, 1958-63; capt. USNR. Lic. architect, Calif. Mem. AIA (dir. 1973-75), Soc. Am. Mil. Engrs. (chmn. publicity com. 1981), Am. Arbitration Assn., Navy League U.S., Naval Res. Assn. (v.p. San Diego chpt. 1973-77, v.p. legis. 11th naval dist. 1979-80), Nat. Trust for Hist. Preservation, Zool. Soc. San Diego, San Diego Hist. Soc., Aircraft Owners and Pilots Assn., Res. Officers Assn. U.S., Forum of Arts (dir. 1978—). Republican. Roman Catholic. Clubs: Rotary, Armed Forces Aero. Home: 6180 Agee St Apt 170 San Diego CA 92122 Office: 835 5th Ave San Diego CA 92101

REEVES, JERRY DALE, pediatric hematologist; b. Port Arthur, Tex., Jan. 28, 1945; s. Murphy Orval and Dorcas (Carleton) R.; B.A., Baylor U., 1967, M.D., 1971; m. Alice Elaine Williams, June 8, 1968; children—Robin Renee, Natalie Ann. Commd. 2d lt. M.C., U.S. Air Force, 1968, advanced through grades to lt. col., 1979; intern David Grant Med. Center, Travis AFB, Calif., 1971, resident in pediatrics, 1971-74, dir. pediatric hematology-oncology, 1976—, program dir. transitional yr. residency, 1982—, dir. profl. edn., 1983; mil. cons. in pediatrics and hematology to surgeon gen.; fellow in pediatric hematology U. Colo. Med. Center, 1974-76; asst. clin. prof. U. Calif. Med. Sch., Davis, U. Calif.-San Francisco; affiliated asst. prof. pediatrics Uniformed Services U. Health Scis. Recipient Ogden C. Brutun award Uniformed Services Pediatric Seminar, 1977; Andrew Margileth award Uniformed Services Pediatric Seminar, 1980; Community Service award Air Force Assn., 1983, diplomate Am. Bd. Pediatrics, Sub.-Bd. Pediatric Hematology-Oncology. Mem. Am. Acad. Pediatrics (chmn. com. on 3d party payments Uniformed Service chpt. West) AMA, Western Soc. Pediatric Research, AAAS, Alliance for Continuing Med. Edn., Am. Soc. Hematology, Am. Soc. Pediatric Hematology and Oncology, Assn. Mil. Surgeons U.S., Am. Council on Sci. and Health, Parents for Heroes (founding mem., exec. com.). Author papers in field. Home: 1170 Kikenny Rd Vacaville CA 95688 Office: Pediatrics (SGHC) David Grant Med Center Travis AFB CA 94535

REEVES, JOHN FREDERICK, career consultant, educator, writer; b. Morristown, N.J., June 11, 1954; s. John F. and Harriet P. Reeves; student U. Alaska, 1973-74, 80-83; M.A. in Human Resource Devel., Norwich U., 1984. Dir., career devel. trainer Adult Learning Programs of Alaska, CETA Tng., Tech. Assistance Project, Fairbanks, Alaska, 1977-80; dir., founder, career cons. Alaska Life/Work Planning Ctr., Fairbanks, 1980—. Pres. adv. bd. North Star Borough Sch. Dist. Community Edn., Fairbanks, 1982—. Mem. Am. Soc. Tng. and Devel. (bd. dirs., communications chmn. Fairbanks chpt. 1982—), Nat. Career Devel. Project, Profl. Devel. League, Internat. Meditation Soc. Author: Integrating Career Development with Human Resource Information Systems, 1983. Home: PO Box 40 Ester AK 99725 Office: Alaska Life/Work Planning Ctr 600 University Ave Suite 100 E Fairbanks AK 99701

REEVES, LEEANN MOORE, educator, publisher; b. Colorado City, Tex., Mar. 27, 1947; d. Tom Clinton and Minnie L. (Hood) Moore; m. James Ray Reeves, Dec. 27, 1966; children—Brian, Shannon. Student Baylor U., 1965; B.S. in Child Devel., Tex. Tech. U., 1968; M.Ed., U. Utah, 1972, postgrad., 1974-75; postgrad. Whitworth Coll., 1981. Cert. tchr., Tex., 1968, Wash., 1975. Tchr. Ralls (Tex.) Elem. Sch., 1968-70, Granite Sch. Dist., Salt Lake City, 1972-74, Spokane (Wash.) Pub. Schs., 1981—; lectr. U. Utah, Salt Lake City, 1972; instr. Tex. Tech. U., Lubbock, 1970; lectr. Whitworth Coll., Spokane, 1977-82, adj. instr., 1982—; owner, pub. Word Works Pub. Co., Spokane, 1979—; cons. on children's books, Wash.; chmn. bd. Whitworth Early Learning Ctr. Mem. Wash. State steering com. White House Conf. on Children and Families, 1980; mem. steering com. Spokane Consortium for Internat. Studies, 1981-82; mem. Mead Sch. Dist. Gifted Edn. Com., 1979-81. Mem. AAUW (past officer, recipient 5-star award 1981), Assn. Supervision and Curriculum Devel., NEA, Assn. for Childhood Edn. Internat., Northwest Gifted Child Assn., Am. Home Econs. Assn. Presbyterian. Club: Women's Aux. Am. Inst. Mining Engrs. (Spokane). Author: Children's Guide to Spokane, 1982. Home: E1212 Glencrest Dr Spokane WA 99208

REEVES, PATRICIA, engineering and commercial writer; b. Seattle, Jan. 15, 1926; d. Thurlow Johnson and Dorothy (Todd) R.; m. Daniel Pershing Yates, 1944 (div. 1967). Student Los Angeles State U., 1949-53, Johns Hopkins U., 1966-67, UCLA, 1981-83, Institut de France Allience Francaise, Paris, 1971-72. Free-lance cons./writer tech. publs., 1950—; co-owner, dir. Falcon Press, La Jolla, Calif. and Beverly Hills, Calif., 1978—; prin. Reeves Assocs., Publs. Cons. Mem. MENSA, Nat. Acad. TV Arts and Scis., Am. Mgmt. Assn., Soc. Tech. Communication (sr.), ACLU. Republican. Author numerous tech. publs.; clients include: Bechtel Corp., Westinghouse, Lockheed, Philco-Ford, Martin-Marietta, Northrop Aircraft, Litton Data Systems, Lear-Siegler, N.V. Philips Telecommunicatie Industrie, Philips Centre Technique et Industriel, Messerschmitt-Bolkow-Blohm, Societa Italiana Avionica. Home: 8401 W 4th St Los Angeles CA 90048 Office: 8306 Wilshire Blvd Suite 142 Beverly Hills CA 90211

REFAI, GULAMMOHAMMED ZAINULABEDIN, historian; b. Baroda, India, Dec. 17, 1936; s. Zainulabedin Badruddin and Afzal Begum (Meer) R.; B.A. magna cum laude, Baroda U., 1959; M.A. summa cum laude, 1962; Ph.D. (Bombay Cambridge Soc. scholar, Lady Edwina Mountbatton scholar), U. Cambridge, 1968; m. Shama Banu Nagamian, May 19, 1963; children—Irfan, Saba, Farah. Vis. lectr. UCLA, 1969-70, U. Calif. at Berkeley, 1971; asst. prof. history Central Wash. U., Ellensburg, 1971-77, assoc. prof., 1977—; Smithsonian Instn. fellow, India, 1980-81. Contbr. articles to profl. jours. Home: Rt 1 286 Camas Dr Ellensburg WA 98926

REGAN, BRIAN JOSEPH, real estate executive; b. Seattle, Oct. 20, 1950; s. Joseph Earl and Kathryn Dee (King) R.; B.A. in Acctg., U. Wash., Seattle, 1975. C.P.A.; lic. real estate broker, security salesperson. Acct., Los Angeles and Seattle, 1976-78; broker William A. Bain Assos., realtors, Seattle, 1978-80; treas. Security Pacific Devel., Inc., Seattle, 1980—; pres. Urban Investments Corp., Urban Ventures Corp., 1982—. C.P.A., Wash. Mem. Wash. Soc. C.P.A.s, Beta Gamma Sigma, Beta Alpha Psi. Home: 3617 Bagley St N Seattle WA 98103 Office: 2030 1st Ave Seattle WA 98121

REGAN, GLEN BARRIE, metall. engr., semiconductor equipment mfg. co. exec.; b. Vancouver, B.C., Can., Oct. 28, 1946; s. Barrie Ford and Ada Valencia (Trevisan) R.; came to U.S., 1953, naturalized, 1968; A.A., Coll. of San Mateo, 1966; Met.E., Calif. State U., San Luis Obispo, 1971; m. Kay Jennison Heaton, June 9, 1973 (dec. 1980); children—Christopher Glen (dec.), Erik Brent (dec.), Elyse Valencia. Vice pres. Dynatex Corp., Redwood City, Calif., 1966—; pres. Dystatic Corp., Redwood City, 1971—, dir., 1973—; cons. Whittaker Corp., Los Angeles, 1968-70, Superstill Tech., Inc., Redwood City, Calif., Morgan Petroleum, Inc., Monterey, Calif. Bd. dirs. Skyline County Water Dist., Patrons of the Arts Vatican Mus.; bd. govs. Mills Meml. Hosp., San Mateo, Calif., adv. bd. St. Jude Children's Research Hosp., Memphis. Recipient Energy Conservation award Finishing Highlites Mag., 1975. Mem. Am. Soc. Metals. Republican. Roman Catholic. Patentee in field. Home: 17370 Skyline Blvd Woodside CA 94062 Office: 727 Shasta St Redwood City CA 94063

REGAN, MICHAEL JOHN, JR., educator; b. Pueblo, Colo., Mar. 27, 1933; s. Michael John and Catherine Genevieve (Marriman) R.; m. Rose Marie A. Clemens, June 19, 1953; children—Michael J. III, Robert A. A.A., Community Coll. Denver, 1978; B.Ed., Colo. State U., 1979; postgrad. U. So. Colo. Electronics journeyman, supr., civilian adviser to mil. groups, Taiwan, Japan, Korea, Germany, 1956-75; tng. specialist Lowry AFB, Denver, 1975-76, tng. officer, 1976-77, tng. specialist, 1977-80; instr., electronics program mgr. Pueblo (Colo.) Community Coll., 1980—. Mem. Colo. State Electronics Adv. Com., Colo. Computer High Tech. Com. Served with USAF, 1952-56. Mem. Colo. Vocat. Assn., Am. Vocat. Assn., Pueblo Community Coll. Faculty Assn. Club: So. Colo. Computer. Home: 2105 Sherwood Ln Pueblo CO 81005 Office: Pueblo Community Coll 900 W Orman Ave Pueblo CO

REGANOLD, JOHN PATRICK, environmental engineer, soil scientist; b. San Bernardino, Calif., Mar. 31, 1949; s. John Everistus and Veronica (Stromer) R. B.A. in German, U. Calif.-Berkeley, 1971, M.S. in Soil Sci., 1974; Ph.D. in Soil Sci., U. Calif.-Davis, 1980. Cert. profl. soil scientist, soil classifier. Research asst. U. Calif.-Berkeley, 1971-74; instr. Cabrillo Coll., Aptos, Calif., 1975; instr. U. Calif.-Davis, 1977-78, 80; soil scientist U.S. Dept. Agr. Soil Conservation Service, Santa Cruz, San Luis Obispo and Davis, Calif., 1974-80; environ. engr. Utah Internat. Inc., San Francisco, 1980—; cons. Redwood Meadows Ranch, Bonny Doon, Calif.; cons. Calif. Dept. Parks and Recreation, 1975. Author numerous articles for sci. jours. Recipient numerous ribbons and awards for swimming and running AAU. Mem. Soil Sci. Soc. Am., Am. Soc. Agronomy, Soil Conservation Soc. Am., Reclamation Research Council. Democrat. Club: Davis Aquatic Masters. Office: 550 California St San Francisco CA 94104

REHAK-ORTEGA, MARYANN, lawyer; b. Alamogordo, N.Mex., Mar. 12, 1946; d. Albert D. and Myra (Utter) O.; B.Bus., U. N.Mex., 1976, J.D. (Dean's award), 1979; m. Robert L. Rehak; children—Robert Gregory, Christopher Drue. Legal intern IRS, Dallas, summer 1978; legal clk. Sutin, Thayer & Browne, Albuquerque, 1978; legal asst. Horton & Assos., Albuquerque, 1978; pvt. practice law, Albuquerque, 1979—; dir. J&E Mgmt., Watkins Distbg. S.W. (both Albuquerque). Bd. dirs. Foothills Child Devel. Center, Albuquerque, 1979—. Served with USAF, 1966-67. Mem. Am. Bar Assn., Delta Theta Phi. Republican. Roman Catholic. Home: 9125 Copper NE Albuquerque NM 87123 Office: 3419 Silver St SE Albuquerque NM 87106

REHBERG, JEROME ALEXANDER, petroleum company executive; b. Bennington, Kans., Oct. 14, 1920; s. Alexander Cleveland and Arena Beatrice (Hooser) R.; m. Wanda Lynne Williams, Oct. 29, 1944; children—Kay, Susan Rehberg Tomayko, Lise. Student Kans. State U., 1938-40; B.S., U.S. Naval Acad., 1943; M.S., U. Pitts., 1956. Commd. ensign U.S. Navy, 1943, advanced through grades to capt., 1964; repair and gunnery officer, 1943-47; officer-in-charge Fuel and Ammunition Facility, San Diego, 1948-50; supply officer USS Skagit, 1950-52; staff Supply Corps Sch., 1952-54; logistics officer Mil. Assistance and Adv. Group Norway, 1954-55; planning officer U.S. Naval Fuel Supply Office, 1957-60; fuels officer Pacific Fleet, 1960-64; fuel adviser to chief naval ops., 1964-67; dir. supply ops. Def. Gen. Supply Ctr., 1967-69; chief petroleum team Joint Logistics Rev. Bd., 1969-70; dep. dir. Def. Fuel Supply Ctr., 1970-71, ret., 1971; asst. to pres. Hawaiian Ind. Refinery, Inc., Honolulu, 1971, v.p., 1972, exec. v.p., 1972—; sr. v.p. Pacific Resources, Inc., Honolulu, 1974—; pres. Pri Internat., Inc., Honolulu, 1979-82, chmn. bd., 1982—; dir. Brewer Pacific Agronomics, Inc., Honolulu. Hon. consul Republic of Indonesia, 1980—. Mem. Am. Petroleum Inst., Nat. Petroleum Refiners Assn. (bd. dirs.), Navy League. Clubs: Oahu Country, Pacific, Plaza, Outrigger Canoe, Rotary (Honolulu). Office: PO Box 3379 Honolulu HI 96842

REHM, SUSAN JANE, social work administrator; b. Yorktown, Va., May 17, 1945; d. Gilbert F. and Jeradean Dolly (Field) Rehm. B.A., U. Redlands, 1967; M.S.W., San Diego State U., 1969; lic. clin. social worker, Calif. Dir. social services Home of Guiding Hands, Lakeside, Calif., 1969-71; sr. social work counselor Regional Center for Devel. Disabled, San Diego, 1971-75; lectr. Sch. of Social Work San Diego State U., 1975-79; dir. social work services Mercy Hosp. and Med. Center, San Diego, 1979-80; assoc. dir. dept. clin. social work UCLA Med. Center, 1981-82, dir., 1982—; cons. in field. Mem. Nat. Assn. Social Workers, Am. Hosp. Assn., Am. Pub. Health Assn., Soc. for Hosp. Social Work Dirs., Nat. Assn. for Retarded Citizens. Office: 10838 Le Conte Los Angeles CA 90024

REIBER, ROBERT JOSEPH, air-conditioning co. exec.; b. N.Y.C., July 10, 1933; s. Raymond and Elsie R.; student CCNY, 1954-56; m. Patricia Farrell, Nov. 22, 1952; children—Bonnie Jean, Doreen, Robert Joseph, Kathleen, Patricia, Colleen. Employed with various banks, 1954-63; programmer Central Bank & Trust Co., Denver, 1963-64; br. systems mgr. Burroughs Corp., 1964-77; dir. data processing Goettl Air Conditioning Co., Phoenix, 1977—; lectr. various ednl. instns. Adviser Jr. Achievement, 1961, 67, 78, 79; bd. dirs. Little League Assn., 1967-68. Served with U.S. Army, 1952-54. Mem. Assn. for Systems Mgmt. (dir. 1980-81), Data Processing Mgmt. Assn. (dir. 1980-81, cert. data processor), Am. Mgmt. Assn. Club: Scottsdale Sportsmen. Home: 8555 E Orange Blossom Ln Scottsdale AZ 85253

REICH, MICHAEL, economist, educator; b. Poland, Oct. 18, 1945; s. Melvin and Betty (Mandelbaum) R.; m. Nancy Chadorow, June 19, 1977; children—Rachel, Gabriel. B.A., Swarthmore Coll., 1966; Ph.D., Harvard U., 1974. Asst. prof. Boston U., 1971-74; asst. prof. U. Calif.-Berkeley, 1974-81, acting assoc. prof., 1981-82, assoc. prof. econs., 1982—. Author: Segmented Work, Divided Workers, 1982; Racial Inequality, 1981; The Capitalist System, 1978. Office: Dept Econs Univ Calif Berkeley CA 94720

REICH, SHELDON, art history educator; b. Bklyn., Sept. 5, 1931; s. Hyman D. and Molly (Gubman) R.; m. Shirley Gish, Nov. 2, 1980; children by previous marriage—Robin, Jonathan, Adam. A.B., U. Miami (Fla.), 1954; M.A., NYU, 1957; Ph.D., U. Iowa, 1966. Asst. prof. art history Okla. State U., Stillwater, 1957-60; prof. art history U. Ariz., Tucson, 1960-68, 72—; chmn. dept. art history U. Cin., 1968-72; corr. Art News mag. Served with USAF, 1951-52. Grantee Archives Am. Art, 1963; sr. fellow Nat. Mus. Am. Art, 1971-72. Mem. Coll. Art Assn., AAUP. Democrat. Jewish. Author: John Marin: A Stylistic Analysis and Catalogue Raisonné, 2 vols., 1970; A.H. Maurer, 1973; Isable Bishop, 1974; Graphic Styles of the American Eight, 1976; Francisco Zuñiga, Sculptor, 1980; Contbr. numerous articles to profl. jours. Office: Art History Dept U Arizona Tucson AZ 85721

REICHARDT, CARL E., banker; b. 1931. A.B. in Econs., U. So. Calif., 1956; postgrad. Stanford U., Northwestern U. Grad. Sch. Mortgage Banking, So. Meth. U., Southwestern Grad. Sch. Banking. Program mgr. ops. and lending Citizens Nat. Bank, 1955-59; sr. statis. analyst N.Am. Aircraft Co., 1959-60; area exec. v.p. Union Bank, 1960-70; with Wells Fargo Realty Advisors, 1970—; exec. v.p. Wells Fargo Bank, N.A., San Francisco, 1975, corp. pres., 1978—, chief operating officer, dir., 1981—; with Wells Fargo & Co., 1973—, exec. v.p. real estate industries group, 1975, pres., chief operating officer, 1979—, dir., now also chmn., chief exec. officer, 1983—. Office: Wells Fargo & Co Inc 420 Montgomery St San Francisco CA 94104*

REICHE, MARVIN GARY, restaurant executive; b. Sacramento, Sept. 2, 1949; s. Robert A. and Kate Kathleen (Groo) R.; m. Kathleen Louise Price, Feb. 10, 1968; children—Bradford, Renee, Darren, Michelle, Ryan, Brandon. With Harman Mgmt. Corp., 1967-79, cook and pie shell operator, Lodi, Calif., 1967, cook, Carmichael, Calif., 1967-68, store mgr., Sacramento, 1968-72, Fair Oaks, Calif., 1972-77, dist. mgr. Central Sacramento, 1977-79; owner, investor Kentucky Fried Chicken, Covina, West Covina, Long Beach, Lakewood, Bellflower, Los Angeles County, Garden Grove and Anaheim, Calif., 1979—; sole owner Kasmar Enterprises; dir. So. Calif. Kentucky Fried Chicken Advt. Assn. Active local Cub Scouts Weblos; judge Bank Am. Achievement Awards Program, 1983. Republican. Mormon.

REICHEK, JESSE, artist; b. Bklyn., Aug. 16, 1916; s. Morris and Celia (Bernstein) R.; student Inst. Design, Chgo., 1941-42; diploma, Academie Julian, Paris, 1951; m. Laure Guyot, May 16, 1950; children—Jonathan, Joshua. Exhibited one man shows at Galerie Cahiers d'Art, Paris, 1951, 59, 67, Betty Parsons Gallery, N.Y.C., 1958, 59, 63, 65, 67, 69, Molton Gallery, London, 1962, Am. Cultura Center, Florence, 1962; exhibited in group shows at Bklyn. Mus., 1959, Mus. Modern Art, N.Y.C., 1962, 65, Knox-Albright Art Gallery, 1962, Art Inst. Chgo., 1963, Cin. Art Mus., 1966, Balt. Art Mus., 1966, Yale U. Art Gallery, 1967, U. Kans. Mus., 1969, Los Angeles County Mus. Art, 1971, Mus. Modern Art, Paris, 1971; others; rep. permanent collections at Mus. Modern Art, Art Inst. Chgo., Bibliotheque Nationale, Paris, Victoria & Albert Mus., London, Los Angeles County Art Mus., Grunwald Graphic Arts Found. U. Calif. Los Angeles, San Diego Mus. Art, Amon Carter Mus., Ft. Worth; instr. dept. architecture U. Mich., 1946-47; prof. Inst. Design Ill. Inst. Tech., 1951-53; asso. prof. dept. architecture U. Calif. at Berkeley, 1953-60, prof., 1960—; cons. Nat. Design Inst. Ford Found. Project, Ahmedabad, India, 1963, San Francisco Redevel. Agy. Embarcadero Center, 1966—; Can. Council, 1972—; lectr. Nat. Inst. Architects Rome, 1960, U. Florence, 1960, U. Naples, 1960, Israel Inst. Tech., 1960, Greek Architects Soc., Athens, 1960, U. Belgrade, 1960, Mass. Inst. Tech., 1965, U.N.M., 1964, Am. Cultural Center, Paris, 1960, 64, Gusarat Inst. Engrs. and Architects, 1963, U. Colo., 1961, Harvard, 1962. U. Minn., 1962, U. Coll. London, 1967, Inst. Contemporary Arts, London, 1967. Ecole Nationale des Beaux-Arts, 1967. Artist in residence Tamarind Lithography Workshop 1966; research prof. Creative Arts Inst. U. Calif., 1966-67; artist/architect-in-residence Am. Acad. in Rome, 1971-72. Served to capt., C.E., AUS, 1942-46. Author: Jesse Reichek-Dessins, 1960; La Monte de La Nuit, 1961; Fontis, 1961; Etcerta, 1965. Home: 5925 Red Hill Rd Petaluma CA 94952

REICHERT, NORMAN VERNON, business executive; b. Berwyn, Ill., Apr. 17, 1921; s. John G. and Valeria (Hoffman) R.; m. Wilma Eleanor Catey, Feb. 5, 1944; children—Susan, Norman V. B.S. in Bus. Adminstrn., Northwestern U., 1943; postgrad. Harvard U., 1943-44. C.P.A., Ill. Acct. Arthur Young & Co., Chgo., 1946-50; mem. central fin. staff, controller styling div. Ford Motor Co., Dearborn, Mich., 1950-61; asst. treas. Philco Ford Corp., Phila., 1961-69; asst. treas. United Air Lines, Inc., 1969-72; v.p. fin., treas. Trailer Train Co., Chgo., 1972-83, Railbox Co., Chgo., 1974-83; v.p. fin., treas., dir. Railgon Co., Chgo., 1979-83; v.p. fin., treas. U.S. Wind Power, Inc., San Francisco, 1983—. Served to lt. USNR, 1943-46. Mem. Am. Inst. C.P.A.s, Fin. Execs. Inst., Newcomen Soc., Beta Alpha Psi, Sigma Alpha Epsilon. Clubs: Union League, Knollwood, Executives. Home: 440 Davis Ct Apt 1310 San Francisco CA 94111 Office: 500 Sansome St Suite 205 San Francisco CA 94111

REID, ALBERT RAYMOND, public administrator, mechanical engineer; b. Braddock, Pa., Feb. 28, 1939; s. Albert John and Barbara Elizabeth (Rudy) R. m. Kathleen Louise Mauk, Nov. 9, 1963; children—David Albert, Anne Kathleen, Amy Louise, Daniel Raymond. B.S.M.E., Carnegie Inst. Tech., 1961; postgrad. U. So. Calif., 1962, U. Santa Clara, 1966. Systems analyst Lockheed Propulsion Co., Redlands, Calif., 1967-73; sr. adminstrv. services officer, spl. dists. coordinator County of San Bernardino (Calif.), 1974; asst. exec. officer Local Agy. Formation Commn., San Bernardino, 1974; dir. spl. dists., 1974-80; asst. county adminstr. County of San Bernardino, 1980—; lectr., speaker local univs., community groups. Cubmaster Grayback dist. council Boy Scouts Am., 1974-76, dist. vice chmn., 1981, chmn., 1981-82, exec. bd. dirs. Inland Empire Council, 1975-80, v.p., 1983; mem. parish council Sacred Heart Ch., 1977; mem. community diabetes council San Bernardino County Diabetes Demonstration Project, 1983; bd. dirs. Arrowhead United Way, 1983-84. Served to capt. USAF, 1962-67. Recipient Achievement award Nat. Assn. Counties, 1982. Mem. Am. Soc. Pub. Adminstrs., ASME. Republican.

REID, BILL, poet, psychotherapist, educator; b. Joplin, Mo., Mar. 8, 1936; s. James L. and Josephine (Kelley) R.; Ph.D., Brantridge Forest Sch., 1972; Litt.D. (hon.), U. Ryukyus, 1962; M.D., Ont. Med. Centre, 1978; m. Gwen Lewis; children—Cathy, James, Naida, Johanna, Elizabeth. Pvt. practice psychotherapy, Louisville, Ky., Jeffersonville, Ind., Reseda and Whittier, Calif., 1974—; nat. tech. tng. mgr. Epson Am., Inc., Torrance, Calif., 1983—; data processing educator Cert. Grocers of Calif., Ltd., 1981—1981-82; tchr. Spencerian Coll., Louisville, 1969-77, Van Nuys Coll. Bus., 1979-81; editor, pub. Internat. Violin and Guitar Makers jour., 1967—; v.p. Spectro-Chem., Inc., 1970-77. Diplomate Am. Bd. Examiners in Psychotherapy, Am. Bd. Cert. Psychoanalysts. Mem. Internat. Transactional Analysis Assn., Interam. Soc. Psychology, AAAS, AAUP, Nat. Assn. Sch. Psychologists, Internat. Rorshach Soc., Data Processing Mgmt. Assn., Assn. Humanistic Psychologists. Buddhist. Author: Just A Girl and A Night, 1969; Calling All Really Obscure Lovers, 1976; Do What Works, 1977; Thence A River, 1978; Who Was When, 1979; originator Causative Agency method of psychotherapy. poet, psychotherapist, educator; b. Joplin, Mo., Mar. 8, 1936; s. James L. and Josephine (Kelley) R.; Ph.D., Brantridge Forest Sch., 1972; Litt.D. (hon.), U. Ryukyus, 1962; M.D., Ont. Med. Centre, 1978; m. Gwen Lewis; children—Cathy, James, Naida, Johanna, Elizabeth. Pvt. practice psychotherapy, Louisville, Ky., Jeffersonville, Ind., Reseda and Whittier, Calif., 1974—; nat. tech. tng. mgr. Epson Am., Inc., Torrance, Calif., 1983—; data processing educator Cert. Grocers of Calif., Ltd., 1981—1981-82; tchr. Spencerian Coll., Louisville, 1969-77, Van Nuys Coll. Bus., 1979-81; editor, pub. Internat. Violin and Guitar Makers jour., 1967—; v.p. Spectro-Chem., Inc., 1970-77. Diplomate Am. Bd. Examiners in Psychotherapy, Am. Bd. Cert. Psychoanalysts. Mem. Internat. Transactional Analysis Assn., Interam. Soc. Psychology, AAAS, AAUP, Nat. Assn. Sch. Psychologists, Internat. Rorshach Soc., Data Processing Mgmt. Assn., Assn. Humanistic Psychologists. Buddhist. Author: Just A Girl and A Night, 1969; Calling All Really Obscure Lovers, 1976; Do What Works, 1977; Thence A River, 1978; Who Was When, 1979; originator Causative Agency method of psychotherapy. Home and Office: 8126 Flallon Ave Whittier CA 90606

REID, DAVID COLLINSON, surgeon; b. Hove, Sussex, Eng., Aug. 5, 1942; came to Can., 1965; s. Robert C. and Florence Edith (Pook) R.; diploma with distinction, U. Toronto (Can.), 1968; M.D. with distinction, U. Alta. (Can.), 1974; m. Kaye Erigunde Wieman, Feb. 17, 1979; children—Tim Leslie, Lauretta Suzanne. Intern, Royal Alexandra Hosp., Edmonton, Alta., 1974-75; resident U. Alta. Hosp. and Calgary Children's Hosp., 1975-79; practice medicine specializing in surgery, Oxford, Eng., 1979-80, Edmonton, 1980—; mem. staff U. Alta. Hosp., Glenrose Provincial Hosp.; prof. faculty rehab. medicine U. Alta., 1980—, dir. clin. research, 1977-80, also mem. faculty phys. edn., 1975—; cons. sports medicine, 1980—; cons. Edmonton Fitness Centre, 1979-81. Recipient Silver Jubilee medal, 1980; Lord Nuffield scholar, 1979-80. Fellow Royal Soc. Medicine, Royal Coll. Surgeons Can. Author: Functional Anatomy and Joint Mobilization, 1975. Office: Dept Surgery Faculty of Medicine 11-119 Clin Scis Bldg U Alberta Edmonton AB T6G 2G3 Canada

REID, FLOYD STUART, financial exec.; b. Detroit, May 17, 1933; s. William and Irma (Magaffin) R.; B.B.A., U. Mich., 1954, M.B.A., 1955; m. Gurnilla Ruth Larkins, June 7, 1958; children—Ruth Ann, Robert Stuart, William Scott Larkins, Susan Elizabeth. With Arthur Young & Co., C.P.A.'s, Los Angeles, 1955-57, Lybrand, Ross Bros. & Montgomery, C.P.A.s, Detroit, 1957-58; sr. accountant Edward G. Stotsenberg, C.P.A., Beverly Hills, Calif., 1958-62; Western regional controller Alloys Unltd., Chatsworth, Calif., 1962-64; vice pres. finance Basin Builders Corp., Venice, 1964-66; controller Newton Insert Co. (merged into Tridair Industries 1967), Los Angeles, 1967, corp. controller Tridair Industries, Redondo Beach, Calif., 1968-69; treas., controller Computer Automation, Inc., Irvine, Calif., 1969-73, sec., 1971-73; controller CFI Memories, Anaheim, Calif., 1973-74; v.p. Babcock Electronics Corp., Costa Mesa, Calif., 1974-75; dir., v.p., treas. LCS Homes (formerly Levitt Homes), Fountain Valley, Calif., 1975-78; v.p. fin. Griswold Industries, Costa Mesa, 1978-79; dir., v.p. fin. Symcon Marine Corp., Long Beach, Calif., 1980-82. Vice pres. expansion, bd. dirs. Los Angeles County Christian Endeavor Union, 1959-60, treas., 1957-59. Bd. mgrs. Saddleback Valley YMCA, 1975-78, treas. bd., 1976-78. Organizing dir., elder, treas. Grace Community Ch. Saddleback Valley, 1975—, dir. Synod So. Calif., United Presbyn. Ch. of U.S., 1969. C.P.A., Calif. Mem. Am. Inst. C.P.A.s, Calif. Soc. C.P.A.s, Nat. Assn. Accts., Tau Kappa Epsilon. Mason. Home: 22736 Islamare Lane El Toro CA 92630 Office: 17291 Irvine Blvd Suite 100 Tustin CA 92680

REID, HARRY, Congressman; b. Searchlight, Nev., Dec. 2, 1939; m. Landra Gould, 1959; children—Lana, Rory, Lief, Josh, Key. A.A. in Sci., So. Utah State Coll., 1959; B.S., U. Utah, 1961; J.D., George Washington U., 1946. Bar: Nev. 1963. City atty., Henderson, Nev., 1964-66; bd. trustees So. Nev. Meml. Hosp., 1967-69, chmn., 1968-69; mem. Nev. Assembly, 1969-70; lt. gov. of Nev., 1970-74, mem. exec. com. Nat. Conf. Lt. Govs.; chmn. Nev. Gaming Commn., 1977-81; mem. 98th Congress from 1st Nev. Dist.; mem. Com. Fgn. Affairs, Com. on Sci. and Tech., Select Com. on Aging; mem. steering com. U.S. Congl. Travel and Tourism Caucus. Judge, Nev. State Athletic Commn.; past bds. dirs. Am. Cancer Soc., Legal Aid Soc., YMCA, Operation Life; past pres. PTA; mem. exec. res. U.S. Office Emergency Planning. Named Man of Year, City of Hope, 1977. Mem. ABA, Nev. State Bar Assn.,

Clark County Bar Assn., Am. Bd. Trial Advos., Phi Kappa Phi. Office: US House of Reps Washington DC 20515

REID, ROGER HUFFMAN, consultant, psychologist; b. Carthage, Mo., Feb. 10, 1926; s. Thomas Simeon and Goldie Ellen (Huffman) R.; m. Dolores Margaret Boughner, Sept. 15, 1950; children—Norma, Christian, Gregory. A.B., U. Mo., 1948, M.A., 1950; postgrad. U. Denver, 1962. Intern, USPHS, Louisville, 1950, VA, Denver, 1951; asst. dir. Wallace Sch., 1952-54; chief psychologist Children's Hosp., Denver, 1954-63; psychologist Cerebral Palsy Assn., Denver, 1954-56; prin. Reid, Merrill, Brunson & Assocs., Denver, 1964-80; gen. mgr. TRACOM Corp., Denver, 1981—; cons. Served with USAAF, 1944-46. Mem. Am. Psychol. Assn., Colo. Psychol. Assn., Colo. Soc. Psychologists in Pvt. Practice (past pres.). Author: (with David W. Merrill) Personal Style and Effective Performance, 1981. Home: 9295 W 38th Ave Wheat Ridge CO 80033 Office: 200 Fillmore St Denver CO 80206

REID, SUSAN ELIZABETH, home economist; b. Fargo, N.D., Mar. 19, 1947; d. Tom Frederick and Dorothea Elizabeth (Golliet) R.; m. Frank Dean Paxton (div.). B.S. in Home Econs. Edn., N.D. State U.-Fargo, 1969, M.S. in Home Econs. Edn., 1976. Tchr., Benson, Minn., 1969-72; home econs. extension agt. McLean County (N.D.), 1976-78, Campbell County (Wyo.), Gillette, 1978—. Recipient Disting. Service award Jaycettes, 1981. Mem. Wyo. Assn. Extension Home Economists, Nat. Assn. Extension Home Economists, AAUW. Democrat. Presbyterian. Club: Thunder Basin Toastmistress.

REID, VIRGINIA ANNE (GINNY), health agency executive; b. Niagara Falls, N.Y., Aug. 29, 1936; d. William Russell and Virginia Elizabeth (Hunter) Kennedy; children—Jim, Steve, Scott; m. 2d, Harry R. Reid, Dec. 15, 1970. Student Santa Ana Coll., 1954-55, 1982; Orange Coast Coll., 1966. Assoc. dir. devel. Easter Seal Rehab. Inst. Orange County, Orange, Calif., 1966-76; dir. fund raising Am. Heart Assn. of Orange County, Santa Ana, Calif., 1976-79; exec. dir. Okla. chpt. Leukemia Soc. Am., Inc., Oklahoma City, 1980, Tri-County chpt. (Calif.), Garden Grove, 1981—. Loaned exec. to United Way of Orange County, 1976. Recipient citation for excellence Tension Envelope Corp., Los Angeles, 1978. Mem. Pub. Relations Soc. Am., Nat. Soc. Fund Raising Execs., Sales and Mktg. Execs. Assn., Combined Health Agys., Combined Fed. Campaign Coms.

REIDY, THOMAS JOSEPH, JR., psychologist; b. Worcester, Mass., Mar. 11, 1947; s. Thomas Joseph and Eunice Gladys (Lamlein) R. B.S. in Biology, Fairfield (Conn.) U., 1968; M.A. in Clin. Psychology, DePaul U., 1973, Ph.D., 1976. Lic. psychologist, Calif. Psychologist, Rehab. Inst. of Chgo., 1975-77; psychologist Community Hosp. of Monterey (Calif.) Peninsula, 1977-80; pvt. practice psychology, Salinas, Calif., 1980—; trustee, med. adv. Multiple Sclerosis Soc.; cons. and lectr. in field. Bd. dirs. Am. Diabetes Assn. Served to ensign, USN, 1968-69. DePaul Mental health trainee, 1971-74; Conn. Heart Assn. trainee, 1967. Mem. Am. Psychol. Assn., Assn. for Advancement of Behavior Therapy, Calif. Psychol. Assn. Democrat. Contbr. chpts. to books and articles in field to profl. jours. Home: 706 19th St Pacific Grove CA 93950 Office: 154 Central Ave Salinas CA 93901

REIFF, GLENN AUSTIN, electrical engineer, educator; b. Newton, Kans., Nov. 18, 1923; s. Tilman Erb and Ione Vera (Austin) R.; m. Amy Erl Little, Apr. 2, 1947; children—Glenn Austin II, Martha Jann. B.S., U.S. Naval Acad., 1945; B.S., U.S. Naval Postgrad. Sch., 1952, M.S., 1953. Registered profl. engr., Colo. Commd. ensign U.S. Navy, 1945, advanced through grades to capt., 1967, transferred to Res., 1961; systems analyst Sanders Assocs., Nashua, N.H., 1961-62; program engr. and mgr. NASA, Washington, 1962-70; sr. project engr. High Speed Ground Test Center, Dept. Transp., Pueblo, Colo., 1970-72, acting dir., 1972-74, chief tech. services, 1974-78; prof. U. So. Colo., Pueblo, 1978—; cons., 1977—. Recipient awards NASA. Mem. IEEE (sr.), Data Processing Mgmt. Assn. (internat. dir.), Pueblo C. of C. (dir., Disting. Service award 1974). Methodist. Club: Masons. Home: 59 Villa Dr Pueblo CO 81001 Office: U So Colo 2200 N Bonforte Blvd Pueblo CO 81001

REILLY, JAMES EDWARD, mining company executive; b. Salt Lake City, Mar. 16, 1941; s. James Maurice and Dorothy (Sheldon) R.; m. Sharon Diane Sadler, Apr. 12, 1967; children—Erie, Vaughn, Annette, Nancy, Aaron, Mark, Debi, Shawna. Student Latter Day Saints Bus. Coll., Salt Lake City, 1962-63. Acctg. supr. Wells Rural Electric (Nev.), 1963-65; bus. mgr. Sawyer Chevrolet, Elko, Nev., 1965-70, Elko Gen. Hosp., 1970-72, Sam Flood Chevrolet, Lovell, Wyo., 1972-74; self-employed, 1974-75; with Wyo-Ben, Inc., Greybull, Wyo., 1975—, health and safety dir., 1976—. Bd. dirs. South Big Horn County Hosp.; mem. town council Town of Deaver (Wyo.). Served with USAF, 1959-62. Mem. Am. Soc. Safety Engrs., Jaycees Internat., Lambda Delta Sigma. Club: Lions. Republican. Mormon. Home: 262 2d Ave Deaver WY 82421 Office: Box 1072 Greybull WY 82426

REILLY, MARY LOU, teacher educator; b. Hays, Kans., Aug. 1, 1942; d. Alois and Tillie Befort (Domitilla) Pfannenstiel; m. Edward Joseph Reilly, Apr. 27, 1974. B.S. in History & Edn., Marymount Coll., 1967; M.S. Edn., Kansas State U., 1970; Ph.D. Curriculum an Instrn. in Elem. Edn., Kans. State U., 1972. Elem. and jr. high sch. tchr. various schs. in Mich., Chgo., Kans., 1963-70; teaching asst. Kans. State U., Manhattan, 1970-72; asst. prof. Creighton U., Omaha, 1972-76; asst. prof. edn. Pacific Union Coll., Angwin, Calif., 1976-77; assoc. prof., 1977—; reading cons. mem. adv. bd. Cervantes Bilingual Sch. Recipient Edn. Inf. Cons. Seminar award, 1972. Mem. AAUP, Internat. Reading Assn., Assn. Supervision & Curriculum Devel., Assn. Tchr. Edn., Council for Basic Edn., Assn. Childhood Edn. Internat., AAUW, Internat., Platform Assn., Phi Delta Gamma. Democrat. Home: 5381 Eagan Ct Rohnert Park CA 94928 Office: Dept Edn Pacific Union Coll Angwin CA 94508

REILLY, PATRICK JOHN, engrng.-constrn. co. exec.; b. Nutley, N.J., Oct. 10, 1925; s. Philip and Anna (Cox) O'Reilly; B.S.C.E., N.Y. U., 1950; cert. practical constrn. law U. Santa Clara Sch. Law, 1977; m. Maria Garcia Vazquez, July 27, 1957; children—Anne Maria, Patrick John, Thomas J., Frank P. Shaft engr. Lincoln Tunnel third tube Walsh Constrn. Co., N.Y.C., 1950-54; asst. equipment mgr. Brown-Raymond-Walsh, Madrid, 1954-55, project engr., 1955-57; v.p., project mgr. wastewater treatment plants Shanley Constrn. Co., San Francisco, 1957-65; constrn. mgr. W.W. Kinnins & Sons, Buffalo, 1965-70, gen. supt. hwy, utilities and undergound constrn., 1970; dir. mcpl. waste projects, constrn. mgr. Monsanto Environ. Chem. Co., Chgo., 1970-74; v.p., project mgr., dir. constrn. and regional constrn. mgr. solid waste facilities BSP div. Envirotech, Belmont, Calif., 1974—. Served with USAAF, 1943-45. Decorated D.F.C., Air medal with 5 oak leaf clusters. Roman Catholic. Home: 20719 Woodward Ct Saratoga CA 95070 Office: 3000 Sand Hill Rd Menlo Park CA 94025

REILLY, RONALD WAYNE, advertising agency executive; b. N.Y.C., July 21, 1947; s. William John and Elsie (Hettler) R.; m. Solveiga Helena Vilkins, June 10, 1972 (div.); 1 dau., Liana Gillain. Student Hofstra U., 1966-71. With Ogilvy & Mather, 1972—, v.p., Houston, 1978-80, sr. v.p., 1980-82, sr. v.p., media dir., Los Angeles, 1982—. Chmn. media relations com. Houston ARC, 1981-82. Mem. Los Angeles Media Dirs. Council. Office: 5900 Wilshire Blvd Los Angeles CA 90036

REIMER, EILEEN FRIESEN, career counselor; b. Jadcherla, Andra Pradesh, India, Feb. 24, 1956 (parents Am. citizens); d. Jacob H. and Ruth S. (Berg) Friesen; m. Paul Nicholas Reimer, Nov. 27, 1982. B.A. magna cum laude in Social Sci., Tabor Coll., 1978; M.S. in Post-secondary Counseling, U. Kans., 1981. Career resource specialist U. Kans., Lawrence, 1979-80; dir. career devel. Tabor Coll., Hillsboro, Kans., 1980-81; assoc. dir. admissions Fresno Pacific Coll., Fresno, Calif., 1981-82; dir. career devel. and vocat. guidance Columbia Bible Inst., Abbotsford, B.C., Can., 1982—; workshop leader Columbia Bible Inst. Mem. Am. Personnel and Guidance Assn., Am. Coll. Personnel Assn. Liberal Republican. Mennonite. Office: Columbia Bible Inst Box 146 Sumas WA 98295

REIMER, ROBERT TIMOTHY, psychologist; b. Omaha, Aug. 9, 1949; s. Edward Barkman and Aganetha Cornelius (Stoesz) R.; m. Karen Elaine Duerksen, Sept. 18, 1971; children—Aaron D., Corrie D. B.A., Grace Coll. of Bible, 1971; B.A., Calif. State U., Fresno, 1972; M.A., Fuller Theol. Sem., 1975; Ph.D., U. Minn., 1979. Lic. psychologist, Calif. McKnight Found. grantee, child custody researcher, research assoc. Hennepin County (Minn.), 1977-78; dir. counseling Walnut Creek (Calif.) Presbyterian Ch., 1979—; cons. psychology. Mem. Nat. Republican Com. Agrl. Research Found. of U. Minn. research grantee, 1975-77. Mem. Am. Psychol. Assn., Calif. State Psychol. Assn., Christian Assn. Psychol. Studies, Psychologists Interested in Religious Issues. Club: Walnut Creek Racquetball. Author research monograph. Home: 2344 Mallard Dr Walnut Creek CA 94596 Office: 1720 Oakland Blvd PO Box 5606 Walnut Creek CA 94596

REIN, ROBERT STEVEN, lawyer; b. N.Y.C., Apr. 16, 1944; s. Martin Louis Rein and Helen Florence (Arkin) Marcus; B.A. cum laude, Brandeis U., 1966; J.D. cum laude, Harvard U., 1969; m. RaeLynne P. Rein, July 17, 1976; children—Rachel Lindsey, Adam Scott. Admitted to N.J. bar, 1970, Calif. bar, 1971; asso. firm McKenna & Fitting, Los Angeles, 1970-74; partner firm Saphier and Rein, Los Angeles, 1974—; clk. appellate div. N.J. Superior Ct., 1969-70. Mem. Los Angeles County Bar Assn. Office: 1801 Century Park E Suite 1720 Los Angeles CA 90067

REINCKENS, BERNARD JOSEPH, educational administrator, educator; b. N.Y.C., Apr. 11, 1939; s. Bernard Joseph and Catherine Elizabeth (Brown) R. B.A., Iona Coll., 1960; M.A., U. Notre Dame, 1969. Joined Christian Bros. Roman Catholic Ch., 1956; vice prin. Palma High Sch., Salinas, Calif., 1969-70; prin., 1970-75; dean discipline St. Laurence High Sch., Burbank, Ill., 1975-77, athletic dir., 1978-80; prin. Cantwell High Sch., Montebello, Calif., 1980—, also chmn. dept. fgn. langs., dir. audio-visual. Mem. Nat. Cath. Ednl. Assn., Nat. Assn. Secondary Sch. Prins. Republican. Club: K.C. (Chgo.). Home and Office: 329 N Garfield Ave Montebellow CA 90640

REINECKE, JEAN OTIS, industrial designer; b. Ft. Scott, Kans., July 9, 1909; s. Henry Hammon and Mary Estella (Knight) R.; student Kans. State Tchrs. Coll., Pittsburg, 1923-26; m. Esther Brabec (div.); 1 dau., Barbra Jean. Ptnr. Gen. Exhibits, Chgo., 1933-35, Barnes & Reinecke, 1935-48; pres. Reinecke Assoc., Flintridge, Calif., 1948—; cons. 3M Co., Caterpillar Tractor Co., Amana, McGraw-Edison, Union Oil, Motorola, Zenith Corp., M.I.T.I. Japan, Ency. Brit. Mem. Indsl. Designers Soc. Am. (pres., chmn. bd. dirs.). Office: 3780 Berwick Dr Flintridge CA 91011

REINER, ERIC ALAN, business consultant, author, lecturer, medical instrument company executive; b. N.Y.C., Feb. 3, 1944; s. Maury and Alice Jan (Berman) R. B.A. magna cum laude, Amherst Coll., 1966; postgrad. Oxford U., 1966-68, Grad. Inst. Film and TV, N.Y.U., 1969-70. Asst. buyer Gimbel Bros., 1966; asst. to pres. Fremantle Internat., 1968; free-lance motion picture cameraman, 1968-74; exec. dir. Celebrity Centre, N.Y.C., 1970-71, Narconon, N.Y.C., 1974-75; founder, pres. Eric Reiner Co., mgmt. cons., Los Angeles, 1974—; pres. Surg. Systems, Inc., Los Angeles, 1980—; lectr. on personal fin., inter-personal relationships, mgmt. skills. Bd. dirs. Hollywood Chorale; bd. dirs. Union Pacific Credit Union, 1979-80, Pres., 1980-81. Mem. Nat. Assn. Broadcast Engrs. in TV, Am. Arbitration Assn. (mem. bd. arbitrators), Concerned Businessmen's Assn. Am. (v.p.), Phi Beta Kappa. Republican. Scientologist. Editor-in-chief: (poetry anthology) Golden Horses, 1975. Office: PO Box 27714 Los Angeles CA 90027

REINERT, ROBERT ELLIOTT, chamber of commerce executive; b. Pitts.; s. Lawrence Edward and Wanda (Bucziniski) R.; m. Nancy Hormel, Mar. 6, 1976. B.A., SUNY-Buffalo, 1969. Tchr. music, drama, math. Buffalo pub. schs. 1969-71; film editor, TV prodn. asst. Videorecord Corp. Am., Westport, Conn., 1971-72; advt. services supr. Christian Sci. Monitor, Boston, 1972-77; pvt. study Ashland, Oreg., 1977-79; exec. dir. Ashland C. of C., 1979—. Regional adv. bd. So. Oreg. State Coll.; mem. Jackson County Econ. Devel. Commn. Mem. Oreg. C. of C. Execs. (bd. of dirs.), Pacific Northwest Travel Assn. (bd. dirs.). Office: Ashland Chamber of Commerce Box 606 Ashland OR 97520

REINES, FREDERICK, physicist, educator; b. Paterson, N.J., Mar. 16, 1918; s. Israel and Gussie (Cohen) R.; M.E., Stevens Inst. Tech., 1939, M.S., 1941; Ph.D., N.Y. U., 1944; D.Sc. (hon.), U. Witwatersrand, 1966; m. Sylvia Samuels, Aug. 30, 1940; children—Robert G., Alisa K. Mem. staff Los Alamos Sci. Lab., 1944-59, group leader Theorectical div., 1945-59; dir. AEC expts. on Eniwetok Atoll, 1951; prof. physics, head dept. Case Inst. Tech., 1959-66; prof. physics U. Calif.-Irvine, 1966—, also dean phys. scis., 1966-74. Mem. Cleve. Symphony Chorus, 1959-62. Recipient J. Robert Oppenheimer meml. prize, 1981; Guggenheim fellow, 1958-59; Sloan fellow, 1959-63. Fellow Am. Phys. Soc., AAAS; mem. Am. Assn. Physics Tchrs., Argonne U. Assn. (trustee 1965-66), Am. Acad. Arts and Scis., Nat. Acad. Sci., Phi Beta Kappa, Sigma Xi, Tau Beta Pi. Contbr. numerous articles to profl. jours. Contbg. author Effects of Atomic Weapons, 1950; Methods of Experimental Physics, 1961. Co-discoverer elementary nuclear particle, free antineutrino, 1956. Office: U Calif at Irvine Irvine CA 92717

REINHARDT, CARL ERNST, cons. engr.; b. Fürstenberg/Havel, Ger., Jan. 24, 1926; s. Carl Moritz and Maria Melitta (Ortman) R.; came to U.S., 1957, naturalized, 1962; ed. in Germany; m. Josephine V. Christ, Dec. 11, 1976; 1 dau., Elizabeth Ann. Various positions in Germany, 1950-52; archtl. and reinforced concrete steel detailer, draftsman Westeel, Winnipeg, Man., Can., 1952-54; project engr., asst. office mgr. cons. engring. UMA Group, Calgary, Alta., Can., 1954-57; project engr. Austin & Towill, and Austin Smith & Assos., Honolulu, 1958-62; cons. engr., pres. C.E. Reinhardt & Assocs. Inc., cons. engrs. and contractors, Honolulu, 1962—. Served with German Air Force, 1943-45. Recipient various engring. and constrn. industry awards. Mem. ASCE (past sec.-treas.), Engring. Assn. Hawaii, Bldg. Industries Assn. Hawaii (past pres., Hawaii Builder of Yr. 1982), Honolulu Exec. Assn., Am. Soc. Mil. Engrs., Nat. Assn. Homebuilders. Clubs: Toastmasters, Elks. Home: 1456 Ihiloa Loop Honolulu HI 96821 Office: 1517 Kapiolani Blvd Honolulu HI 96814

REINHARDT, JOHN OTTO, accountant; b. Clatskanie, Oreg., July 28, 1943; s. Arthur Benjamin and Albert C. (LaLande) R.; B.S. in Acctg., Golden Gate U., 1965; s. Lucille I. Paschke, Aug. 26, 1965 (div. 1980); children—Julie, Robert. Mgr., Moss, Adams & Co., Portland, Oreg., 1967-77; mng. ptnr. Reinhardt, Lackman & Co., Portland, 1978-80; pres. John O. Reinhardt, P.C., Beaverton, Oreg., 1981—. Co-founder Meml. Cremation Soc. Recipient Nat. Honor award Boy Scouts Am. C.P.A., Oreg. Mem. Soc. C.P.A.s (chmn. acctg. and auditing com.), Am. Inst. C.P.A.s (mem. acctg. standards exec. com.). Home: 4150 SW 55th Dr Portland OR 97221 Office: 4150 SW 110th Ave Beaverton OR 97005

REINHARDT, STEPHEN ROY, judge; b. N.Y.C., Mar. 27, 1921; s. Gottfried and Silvia (Hanlon) R.; children—Mark, Justin, Dana. B.A. cum laude, Pomona Coll., 1951; LL.B., Yale U., 1954. Bar: Calif. 1958. Law clk. to judge U.S. Dist. Ct., Washington, 1955-57; assoc. O'Melveny & Myers, Los Angeles, 1957-59; assoc. Fogel, Julber, Reinhardt, Rothschild & Feldman, Los Angeles, 1959-64, ptnr., 1964-80; judge 9th Cir. Ct. Appeals, Los Angeles, 1980—. Mem. exec. com. Democratic Nat. Com., 1969-72, nat. committeeman from Calif., 1976-80; mem. Los Angeles Police Commn., 1975-78, pres., 1978-80; sec., mem. exec. com. Los Angeles Olympic Organizing Com., 1980—. Served to 1st lt. USAF, 1954-56. Mem. ABA (labor law council 1975-77). Office: US Courthouse 312 N Spring St Los Angeles CA 90012

REINHART, ARTHUR SULLIVAN, consultant; b. Sabinal, Tex., Dec. 1, 1919; s. A.F. and Pocahontas E. (Sullivan) R.; B.S., Tex. Tech. U., 1941; postgrad., Air War Coll., 1961, Air Force Inst. Tech., 1962; M. Internat. Affairs, George Washington U., 1966; B.B.A., Boise State U., 1977; m. Hilma H. Ruuttila, Feb. 22, 1947; children—Arthur K., LauriAnne, Robin M., Brian M. Engr., U.S. Bur. Reclamation, Denver, 1946-51; commd. 2 lt. C.E., 1941, transferred to U.S. Air Force, advanced through grades to col., 1969; engaged in personnel, planning, ops.; dir. plans, comptroller Air Res. Personnel Center, Denver, 1969-74; ret., 1974; pvt. practice cons., Boise, Idaho, 1974—. Community adv. Downtown Boise Urban Renewal Traffic Com.; chmn. Ada County Citizens Adv. Com. Served with USAAF, 1941-46; USAF Res. ret. Decorated Legion of Merit. Mem. Ret. Officers Assn., Air Force Assn., Acad. Polit. Sci., Boise Com. on Fgn. Relations (chmn.), Tex. Tech U. Dad's Assn. (trustee). Episcopalian. Clubs: Masons, Elks. consultant; b. Sabinal, Tex., Dec. 1, 1919; s. A.F. and Pocahontas E. (Sullivan) R.; B.S., Tex. Tech. U., 1941; postgrad., Air War Coll., 1961, Air Force Inst. Tech., 1962; M. Internat. Affairs, George Washington U., 1966; B.B.A., Boise State U., 1977; m. Hilma H. Ruuttila, Feb. 22, 1947; children—Arthur K., LauriAnne, Robin M., Brian M. Engr., U.S. Bur. Reclamation, Denver, 1946-51; commd. 2 lt. C.E., 1941, transferred to U.S. Air Force, advanced through grades to col., 1969; engaged in personnel, planning, ops.; dir. plans, comptroller Air Res. Personnel Center, Denver, 1969-74; ret., 1974; pvt. practice cons., Boise, Idaho, 1974—. Community adv. Downtown Boise Urban Renewal Traffic Com.; chmn. Ada County Citizens Adv. Com. Served with USAAF, 1941-46; USAF Res. ret. Decorated Legion of Merit. Mem. Ret. Officers Assn., Air Force Assn., Acad. Polit. Sci., Boise Com. on Fgn. Relations (chmn.), Tex. Tech U. Dad's Assn. (trustee). Episcopalian. Clubs: Masons, Elks. Home and office: 4933 Sunderland Dr Boise ID 83704

REINHART, FRANK J., engineering executive; b. Alhambra, Calif., Sept. 8, 1934; s. Frank F. and Theresa R. (Shultz) R.; m. Thea Woodfin, May 3, 1935; children—Michael, Kirsten, Robert, Rex. B.S., UCLA, 1963, also postgrad. Engring. mgr. CALCOMP Corp., Anaheim, Calif., 1963-75; develop. engring. mgr., TRW, Hawthorne, Calif., 1974-78; v.p. engring. Microdata Corp., Irvine, Calif., 1978—. Served with USAF, 1953-57. Mem. IEEE, Am. Mgmt. Assn., Tau Beta Pi. Republican. Home: 24 Sycamore Creek Irvine CA 92715 Office: 1562 Reynolds Irvine CA 92715

REINING, BETH LAVERNE (BETTY), public relations cons., journalist; b. Fargo, N.D.; d. George and Grace (Twiford) Reimche; student N.D. State Coll., U. Minn., Glendale Community Coll., Calif. State Coll., Carson; 1 dau., Carolyn Ray Toohey Hiett; m. Jack Warren Reining, Oct. 3, 1976; stepchildren—Joan and Amy Reining. Originated self-worth seminars in Phoenix, 1970-76; owner Janzik Pub. Relations, 1971-76; talk show reporter-hostess What's Happening in Ariz., Sta. KPAZ-TV, 1970-73; writer syndicated column People Want to Know, Today newspaper, Phoenix, 1973; owner JB Communications, Phoenix, 1976—; freelance writer; tchr. How to Weigh Your Self-Worth courses Phoenix Coll., Rio Solado Community Coll., Phoenix, 1976—; muralist, works include 25 figures in med. office. Founder Ariz. Call-A-Teen Youth Resources, Inc., pres., 1975-76, v.p., 1976-77, now bd. dirs. Recipient awards including 1st pl. in TV writing Nat. Fedn. Press Women, 1971, numerous state awards in journalism Ariz. Press Women, 1971-76, Good Citizen award Builders of Greater Ariz., 1961. Mem. Ariz. Press Women, No. Ariz. Press Women (pres. 1982), Nat. Fedn. Am. Press Women, Public Relations Soc. Am., Phoenix Pub. Relations Soc., Nat. Acad. TV Arts and Scis., Phoenix Press Club. Inventor stocking-tension twist footlet, 1962. Office: 314 W Orangewood Ave Phoenix AZ 85021

REINING, HENRY, JR., polit. scientist, former univ. dean; b. Akron, Sept. 15, 1907; s. Henry and Elisabeth (Schilling) R.; m. Janet Bolton, June 27, 1934 (dec. 1948); children—William Henry, Judith Ellen; m. 2d, Darline Dickmann, June 11, 1950; children—Susan, Barbara (dec.), Richard. A.B., U. Akron, 1929, LL.D., 1963; A.M., Princeton U., 1929, Ph.D., 1932; Doc. hon. causa, Brazilian Sch. Public Adminstrn., Rio de Janeiro, 1964, U. Bahia, Salvador, Brazil, 1964. Instr., asst. prof. govt. U. So. Calif., 1932-34, prof. public adminstrn., 1947—, dean Sch. Public Adminstrn., 1953-67, dean Von Klein Smid Center Internat. and Public Affairs, 1967-73; resident mgr. Iran Pub. Sector Program, Tehran, 1975-78; mem. adv. bd. So. Calif. Earth Quake Safety Policy, 1980—; instr., politics, research assoc. Princeton local govt. surveys Princeton U., 1934-36; ednl. dir. Nat. Inst. Public Affairs, Washington, 1935-45; adj. prof. Am. U., 1936-42; professorial lectr. George Washington U., 1940-42; mgmt. cons. Rogers & Slade, N.Y.C., 1945-46; asst. to exec. dir. Port of N.Y. Authority, 1946-47; cons. various local, nat., internat. govtl. agys.; mem. regional loyalty bd. 12th Civil Service Region, 1949-51, U.S. Loyalty Rev. Bd., 1951-53; mem. safety adv. panel NASA, 1968-75; chmn. Los Angeles City Charter Commn., 1966-70. Bd. regents Calif. Lutheran Coll., 1958-75; trustee Boys Republic, 1973—. Served with USAR, 1930-35. Mem. Fed. Coll. Council So. Calif. (hon. life), Am. Soc. Pub. Adminstrn. (past pres.), Nat. Civil Service League (past nat. council mem.), Soc. Personnel Adminstrn., Am. Polit. Sci. Assn., Civil Service League So. Calif. (past pres.). Lutheran. Author: (with George A. Graham) Regulatory Administration, 1944; (with others) Elements of Public Administration, 1960, Cases of Public Personnel Administration, 1949. Democrat. Home: 5918 Condon Ave Los Angeles CA 90056 Office: Sch Public Affairs Univ So Calif Los Angeles CA 90089

REINOLD, CHRISTY DIANE, guidance counselor, consultant; b. Neodasha, Kans., July 21, 1942; d. Ernest Sherman and Etta Faye (Herbert) Wild; m. William Owen Reinold, Dec. 20, 1964; children—Elizabeth, Rebecca. B.A., Fresno State U., 1964, M.A., 1966; postgrad. U. Hawaii, U. No. Tex., U. No. Fla., U. Pacific. Cert. tchr., Calif.; guidance and counseling and mental health counselor, Fla. Tchr., Calif., 1964-67, Institut Internat. Chateaubriand, Cannes, France, 1967-68; vice prin., tchr. Malta Internat. Sch., Sliema, 1968-70; elem. sch. guidance counselor Duval County Schs., Jacksonville, Fla., 1977-81; chmn. elem. sch. counselors Lodi (Calif.) Unified Sch. Dist., 1982—; cons. parent workshops San Joaquin County, Calif., Dallas Assn. Parent Edn., 1971-75. Chmn., bd. dirs. Oak Crest Child Care Ctr., 1979-81; chmn. Work Area Edn. Oak Crest United Meth. Ch., 1976-78. Mem. Am. Personnel and Guidance Assn., Fla. Personnel and Guidance Assn., Calif. Personnel and Guidance Assn., AAUW (3d v.p. Tex. br., legis. chmn. Fla. br. 1981), Am. Sch. Counselor Assn., Fla. Sch. Counselor Assn., Calif. Sch. Counselor Assn., Kappa Delta Pi. Republican.

Author: Thinking, Learning, Caring, 1980. Home: 1180 Northwood Dr Lodi CA 95240 Office: Lodi Unified Sch Dist Lodi CA 95240

REINSTEIN, TODD RUSSELL, lawyer, educator; b. Chgo., July 30, 1937; s. Paul A. and Estelle R. (Goodkin) R.; 1 son, Leif W. B.S. in Acctg., UCLA, 1959, J.D., 1962; postgrad. U. So. Calif., 1962-63. Bar: Calif. 1963, U.S. Tax Ct. 1963, U.S. Ct. Claims 1969, U.S. Dist. Ct. (so. dist.) Calif. 1963, U.S. Ct. Appeals (9th Cir.) 1973, U.S. Supreme Ct. 1975; C.P.A., Calif. Prin., partner Todd Russell Reinstein, A Profl. Law Corp., Los Angeles, 1975—; prof. acctg., co-dir. M.S. degree program in taxation Grad. Sch. Bus. Adminstrn., Calif. State U.-Northridge, 1982—. Mem. ABA, Calif. Bar Assn. (cert. specialist in taxation law Calif. Bd. Legal Specialization), Los Angeles County Bar Assn., Beverly Hills Bar Assn., Beta Gamma Sigma. Office: 1880 Century Park E Suite 615 Los Angeles CA 90067

REISERT, THOMAS DONALD, aerospace engineer; b. East Greenwich, R.I., Apr. 29, 1921; s. John William and Catherine Theresa (Neilan) R., m. Margaret Edith Hamilton, June 14, 1947; children—Jean Reisert Gloff, Roger. B.S. in Mech. Engring., U. R.I., 1942. Aero. research scientist NASA, Langley Field, Va., 1942-55; test engr. Martin Marietta, Balt., 1955-68, Orlando, Fla., 1968-70, Denver, 1970-81, mgr. bus. devel., Denver, 1981—. Mem. AIAA, ASME. Republican. Home: 5255 W Portland Dr Littleton CO 80123 Office: Mail Number 1130 PO Box 179 Denver CO 80201

REISINGER, CURTIS WILLIAM, clinical psychologist, neuropsychologist; b. Middle Village Queens, N.Y., July 3, 1951; s. Curtis Herbert and Mary Mamie (Leniger) R.; m. Mercedes Chagoyen, July 22, 1975; children—Peter, Joey, Anna. B.A. summa cum laude in Psychology, Hunter Coll., CUNY, 1974, M.A. in Gen. and Exptl. Psychology, 1975; Ph.D. in Clin. Psychology, Brigham Young U., 1979. Cert. psychologist, Utah. Intern clin. psychology Timpanogos Mental Health Center, Provo, Utah, 1978-79; resident in clinic psychology, Rocky Mountain Family Inst., Salt Lake City, 1979-80; dir. clin. services Rocky Mountain Counseling Center, Salt Lake City, 1980-81; clin. child psychologist Primary Children's Med. Center, Salt Lake City, 1980-82, chief psychology, 1982—; private practice in clin., cons. psychology, assoc. Paul L. Whitehead, M.D. and Assocs., Salt Lake City, 1981—; clin. staff div. psychiatry Holy Cross Hosp., Salt Lake City, 1982—; clin. faculty dept. psychiatry div. child psychiatry U. Utah, 1982; adj. asst. prof. Brigham Young U. Recipient Original Research awards, 1st, 2d Ann. City U. New York Psychology Convs., 1973, 1974; Nat. Student Service award Psi Chi, 1974 (pres. 1973-74), Gertrude B. Wertenbaker scholar, Hunter Coll., 1974. Mem. Am. Psychol. Assn., Utah Psychol. Assn., Utah Psychologists in Public Service (bd. mem.), Utah Assn. Children with Learning Disabilities, Council Advancement Psychol. Professions, Scis., Phi Beta Kappa. Roman Catholic. Created automated revision Halstead Reitan Category Test, 1979, smile/frown classroom behavior modification work clock, 1976; contr. articles to profl. jours. Office: 1580 E 3900 S Suite 200 Salt Lake City UT 84117

REISINGER, GEORGE LAMBERT, mgmt. cons.; b. Pitts., Aug. 28, 1930; s. Eugene Merle and Pauline Jane (Lambert) R.; B.S. in Bus. Adminstrn., Central Coll., 1953; postgrad. Cleveland-Marshall Law Sch., 1962-67; m. Judith Ann Brush, Nov. 24, 1967; children—Douglas Lambert, Christine Elizabeth. Asst. personnel mgr. Continental Can Co., Houston, 1958-60; mgr. labor relations The Glidden Co., Cleve., 1960-67; dir. employee relations Mobil Oil Corp., N.Y.C., Caracas, Venezuela, Dallas, Denver, 1967-78; sr. v.p. Minton & Assocs., Denver, 1978-82; v.p., ptnr. Korn/Ferry Internat., Denver, 1982—. Bd. dirs. Ponderosa Hills Civic Assn., 1977-80; Republican campaign dir. for county commr., 1978. Served with USAF, 1953-58. Mem. Am. Soc. Personnel Adminstrs., N.Y. Personnel Mgmt. Soc., Colo. Soc. Personnel Adminstrn., Am. Soc. Profl. Consultants. Republican. Methodist. Clubs: Denver Petroleum, Denver Athletic, Pinery Country, Republican 1200. Home: 7924 Deertrail Dr Parker CO 80134 Office: 7800 E Union Ave Suite 740 Denver CO 80237

REISTRUP, JOHN VALDEMAR, journalist; b. Sioux City, Iowa, Apr. 10, 1936; s. James Andreas and Laura Fay (Moss) R.; m. Nancy Joan Cangelosi, Dec. 20, 1958; children—James, Christine, Olaf; m. 2d, Catherine Gloria Wolhowe, June 21, 1975. B.A., Brown U., 1960. Reporter, asst. state desk editor Worcester (Mass.) Evening Gazette, 1960-61; reporter, asst. nat. editor, asst. —Outlook— editor Washington Post, 1962-75; features editor, Saturday editor Toronto (Ont., Can.) Star, 1975-77; asst. mng. editor N.Y. Post, 1977; consumer affairs dir. U.S. Dept. Transp., 1977-79; exec. editor Seattle Post-Intelligencer, 1979—; editor-in-chief Calgary Albertan, 1979-80; instr. journalism Am. U., Washington, 1974-75. Scoutmaster, Boy Scouts Am., McLean, Va., 1978-79. Served with USMC, 1956-58. Named Guildsman of Yr. Washington-Balt. Newspaper Guild, 1970. Mem. Am. Soc. Newspaper Editors, Sigma Delta Chi. Lutheran. Home: 9429 45th Ave NE Seattle WA 98115 Office: 521 Wall St Seattle WA 98121

REITAN, HAROLD THEODORE, health services exec.; b. Max, N.D., Nov. 3, 1928; s. Walter Rudolph and Anna Helga (Glesne) R.; m. Margaret Lucille Bonsac, Dec. 29, 1954; children—Eric, Karen, Chris, Jon. B.A., St. Olaf Coll., 1950; M.A. in Social Psychology, U. Fla., 1962, Ph.D., 1967. Commd. officer U.S. Air Force, 1951, advanced through grades to col.; comdr., U.S. Air Force Spl. Treatment Ctr., Lackland, Tex., 1971-74, U.S. Air Force Corrections and Rehab. Group, Lowry, Colo., 1974-76, Tech. Tng. Wing, 1976-78, ret., 1978; mgr. health services Coors Industries, Golden, Colo., 1978—. Decorated Legion of Merit with oak leaf cluster, D.F.C. with oak leaf cluster, Bronze Star, Meritorious Service medal, Air medal with four oak leaf clusters. Mem. Am. Psychol. Assn. Republican. Lutheran. Contbr. articles to profl. jours.

REITEMEIER, TIMOTHY GEORGE, chamber of commerce executive; b. Pueblo, Colo., Jan. 17, 1931; s. Paul John and Ethel Regina (McCarthy) R.; m. JoAnn Lillian Perkins, May 19, 1952 (dec.); children—Michael Douglas, Ann Ellen. A.A.S. in Bus., So. Colo. State Coll., 1951. Cert. C. of C. exec., 1967. Mgr., Florence (Colo.) C. of C., 1952-53; sec. Cheyenne Frontier Days Rodeo, 1953; mgr. Longmont (Colo.) C. of C., 1953-55; dist. mgr. SW div. U.S. C. of C., 1955-57; mgr. Canon City (Colo.) C. of C., 1957-59; mgr. Casper (Wyo.) C. of C., 1959-64; v.p. Niagara Falls (N.Y.) C. of C., 1965-70; pres., gen. mgr. Spokane (Wash.) Area C. of C., 1970—. Served with USAF, 1949-50. Mem. Am. C. of C. Execs., Wash. C. of C. Execs. Roman Catholic. Home: 4717 South Pittsburg St Spokane WA 99210 Office: 1020 W Riverside St Spokane WA 99201

REITER, ROBERT LYLE, civil engineer; b. Redlands, Calif., Sept. 15, 1946; s. Richard Lyle and Ruberta Grace (Skells) R.; m. Jerry Lynn Cash, Jan. 19, 1974; children—Ryan Lyle, Richard James. B.S. in Engring. Sci., U. Redlands, 1968, M. Engring., 1975. Registered civil, control system engr., Calif., 1977. Computer operator, programmer, Calif., 1966; engring. aide San Bernardino (Calif.) Valley Mcpl. Water Dist., 1966-68, dir. computer ops., project engr., 1968-71, ops. engr., 1971-80, sr. engr., 1980-81, asst. chief engr., 1981—; dir. West Riverside 350 Water Co., Canal Co.; trustee employees' pension trust deferred compensation plan. Mem. devel. and bldg. com. Redlands YMCA, 1980—, past bd. dirs., treas.; trustee Redlands Calvary Baptist Ch., 1980—, fin. sec., 1981—. Mem. Am. Water Works Assn., ASCE. Republican. Club: Electric Vehicle Assn. (Fontana, Calif.). Home: 522 Alvarado St Redlands CA 92373 Office: San Bernardino Valley Mcpl Water Dist 1350 South E St PO Box 5906 San Bernardino CA 92412

REITHEL, ROBERT JAMES, physics and mathematics educator; b. Rosiclare, Ill., Oct. 15, 1917; s. Fred Arthur and Ruth Jane R.; B.S., Western Ky. U., 1939; M.S., U. Ky., 1953; m. Ada Louise Emmick, July 15, 1939; children—Mary Elaine, Theresa Louise, Robert Julian, Catherine June, James Fredrick, Brian Joseph. Grad. asst. dept. physics U. Ky., 1939-40; tchr. math. and sci., Henderson County, Ky., 1947-51; instr. dept. physics U. Ky., Lexington, 1951-53; physicist, staff mem. U. Calif., Los Alamos Sci. Lab., 1953-69; tchr. math. Clovis (N.Mex.) Mcpl. Schs., 1969-81; dir. SW Capital Corp., Albuquerque. Democratic chmn., Precinct 31, Curry County, N.Mex.; Scoutmaster Boy Scouts Am., 1958-61, 74-77, 80-82, dist. commr. Los Alamos dist., 1961-65, v.p. Kit Carson council, 1965; chmn. Los Alamos United Fund, 1966-67; chmn. Los Alamos City-wide PTA, 1962. Served with U.S. Army, 1940-47, lt. col. Res. ret. Decorated Bronze Star medal with V, Purple Heart. Mem. AAAS, Am. Assn. Physics Tchrs., Am. Phys. Soc., NEA, Ret. Officers Assn., Air Force Assn., Clovis Edn. Assn., Sigma Xi. Democrat. Methodist. Club: El Desayuno Kiwanis (pres.). Home: 1004 W Christopher Dr Clovis NM 88101

REITHMAIER, LAWRENCE (LARRY) WILLIAM, author; b. Chgo., May 28, 1921; s. Paul and Frieda R.; B.S. in M.E., U. Ill., 1944; children—Karl Dewees, Mark Lawrence, Barbara Anne. Engr. mil. aircraft McDonnell Aircraft Corp., St. Louis, 1947-60; mgr. Dewees Aviation Flight Sch., Jackson, Miss., 1960-62; project engr. Apollo and Skylab N. Am. Rockwell (now Rockwell Internat.), Downey, Calif., 1962-70; v.p. Aero Pubs., Inc., Fallbrook, Calif., 1970-75; pres. Omni Pubs., Escondido, Calif., 1975-78; author: Pilot's Handbook of Instrument Flying, 1969; Private Pilot's Guide, 1972; Aviation and Space Dictionary, 1974; Instrument Pilot's Guide, 1975; Aircraft Mechanic's Shop Manual, 1979; Aviation and Space Dictionary, 1980; contbr. numerous articles to aviation mags. Cert. comml. and instrument pilot, FAA. Recipient Apollo Achievement award, 1969. Mem. Aviation and Space Writers Assn. (Earl D. Osborn award 1973). Home: 38703 20th St E Palmdale CA 93550 Office: PO Box 445 Palmdale CA 93550

REMAKLUS, DONALD ROY, safety engr.; b. Maud, Okla., Nov. 21, 1928; s. Sylvester Joseph and Martha Margaret (Uleman) R.; B.A., Southeastern Okla. State U., 1958; postgrad. U. So. Calif., 1968; M.S., Calif. Western U., 1979; m. M. Margaret Wakefield, Oct. 25, 1952; children—Donald Roy, Susan Margaret. Commd. USAF, 1952, advanced through grades to maj., 1972; U.S. liaison Internat. Civil Aviation Orgn., Europe, 1960-63; dir. safety USAF, U.S., Asia, Europe, 1958-72; dir. health and safety Nat. Safety Council, Sacramento, 1972; tech. rep., dept. coordinator, sr. loss control rep. Ins. Co. N. Am., Sacramento, 1972—; asst. prof. air sci. So. Ill. U., Carbondale, 1958-60. Chmn., Combined Fed. Campaign, 1967; chmn. nat. conv. Order Daedalians, 1968. Served as staff sgt. Aus, 1945-46. Decorated D.F.C. Soldier's Medal, Air Medal; Legion d'Honneur, Croix de Guerre (France), others. Registered profl. engr., Calif. Mem. Am. Soc. Safety Engrs. (past pres.), Nat. Fire Protection Assn., Engring. Council Sacramento Valley, Order of Daedalians (past flight capt.), USCG Aux., Exptl. Aircraft Assn., Soaring Soc. Am., Tau Kappa Epsilon. Roman Catholic. Clubs: Quiet Birdmen, Elks, K.C. (4 deg.). Author: The Effect of the Occupational Health and Safety Act on Industry, 1979.

REMICK, DOUGLAS BERNARD, banker, realtor, executive; b. Red Lake Falls, Minn., Dec. 2, 1941; s. Bernard J. and Madeline J. (Amiot) R.; m. Sandra Schuman, May 15, 1978; m. 2d, Dianne Ott, July 4, 1980; children—Renee, Scott, Ryan, Kyle. Student Bemidji State Coll., 1959, 60; grad. U.S. Army Advance Sch., 1976, Command and Gen. Staff Coll., 1980. Asst. cashier No. State Bank, Thief River Falls, Minn., 1961-65; v.p. Valley bank of Kalispell, (Mont.), 1965-75; pres., chmn. bd. Glacier Nat. Bank, Columbia Falls, Mont., 1975—; pres. G.N.B., Inc. Chmn., City and County Planning Bd., 1980—. Serving as maj. Army N.G., 1962—. Mem. Ind. Bankers Assn. Am., Mont. N.G. Officers Assn. (v.p.), C. of C. (past pres., dir.). Clubs: Elks, Knights Columbus, Eagles (past pres.). Home: 560 Meadowlake Dr Columbia Falls MT Office: Glacier Nat Bank PO Box 190 Columbia Falls MT 59912

REMINICK, CORINNE AMALIA, cable television marketing director; b. Cleve., May 1, 1951; d. Joseph Lawrence and Dolores Ruby (DiLillo) Reminick; m. Robert Scott McCoy, July 27, 1980. B.A. in Math., Cleve. State U., 1973. Cert. secondary tchr., Ohio. Mng. editor Los Angeles Free Press, 1973-76; pub., editor, owner Good Evening, Los Angeles, 1976; editorial dir. Speciality Pub., Los Angeles, 1976-77; mng. editor East/West Network, Inc., Los Angeles, 1977-81; dir. mktg. services Spotlight, Los Angeles, 1982—. Mem. Women in Cable (v.p. Los Angeles chpt.). Office: 2951 28th St 2000 Santa Monica CA 90405

REMS, JACOB F., land surveying, planning and engring. company executive; b. Whiteville, N.C., July 22, 1950; student Joliet Jr. Coll., 1968-70, Santa Ana Coll., 1972-76, U. N.Mex. Extension, 1979-80. Pres., J.F. Rems Assocs., Newport Beach, Calif. 1977—. Mem. tech. adv. com. Santa Ana Coll., 1979-80. Mem. Internat. Right of Way Assn., Nat. Assn. Home Builders, Am. Planning Assn., Am. Congress on Surveying and Mapping, Calif. Land Surveyors Assn. (dir. 1979-80), Soc. Am. Mil. Engrs., Calif. Council Civil Engrs. and Land Surveyors (dir., sec. Orange County chpt. 1980—), Bldg. Industry Assn. So. Calif., Nat. Soc. Profl. Surveyors, Ill. Registered Land Surveyors Assn., Am. Soc. Photogrammetry. Office: 5100 Campus Dr Suite 100 Newport Beach CA 92660

REMY, IRMA MARJORIE, vocational educator; b. Maywood, Calif., Oct. 16, 1925; d. Charles Henry and Irma (Page) Bowers; m. Edward Earl Remy, Oct. 3, 1946; children—Christine Ann, Shelly Katherine. Student U. Redlands, 1943, Long Beach City Coll., 1959-60, Pepperdine U., 1974; B.A., Calif. State U.-Long Beach, 1963; M.A., 1966. Cert. secondary tchr., adminstr. Calif. Tchr. home econs. Westminster High Sch., Huntington Beach (Calif.) Union High Sch. Dist., 1963-72, dept. chmn., 1967-72, dist. dept. chmn., 1970-72; coordinator home econs., women's occupations Orange County Dept. Edn., Santa Ana, Calif., 1972-73; regional supr. home econs. vocat. cons. Specialist Regional Occupational Ctrs./Programs, State of Calif. Dept. Edn., Los Angeles, 1973-82, regional coordinator (so. region) vocat. edn., 1982—. Mem. Am. Vocat. Assn., Calif. Assn. Vocat. Adminstrs., Calif. Assn. Regional Occupational Programs/Ctrs., So. Calif. Council Vocat. Edn. Adminstrs., Calif. Assn. Vocat. Educators, Home Econs. Tchrs. Assn. Calif. Democrat. Mem. Ch. Jesus Christ of Latter-day Saints. Office: 601 W 5th St Suite 1010 Los Angeles CA 90017

RENCK, RICHARD TROY, marketing research company executive; b. Rock Island, Ill., Aug. 26, 1925; s. Troy Walker and Doreene Frances (Welch) R. Ph.B., U. Chgo., 1948, M.A., 1953, Ph.D., 1965. Dir. measurement research Indsl. Relations Ctr., U. Chgo., 1950-65; v.p. Social Research Inc., Chgo., 1965-74; v.p. KPR Assocs., Inc. Scottsdale, Ariz., 1974-80, pres., 1980—; sr. cons. Greenleigh Assocs., Inc., N.Y.C., 1960-64. Active Art Inst. of Chgo., Field Mus. Natural History, Heard Mus. (Phoenix), Scottsdale Ctr. for the Arts. Served with USNR, 1943-46. Decorated Presdl. citation. Mem. Am. Sociol. Assn., Am. Mktg. Assn. Office: IPR Assoc PO Box 1831 Scottsdale AZ 85252

RENCKEN, ROBERT HENRY, mental health counselor, school psychologist; b. Jersey City, N.J., Jan. 7, 1945; m. Susan H. Rencken, Oct. 5, 1968 (div.); children—David, Kristin. B.A., Rutgers U., 1966; M.Ed., U. Ariz., 1972, M.S., 1974. Cert. clin. mental health counselor. Asst. program dir. Tucson Child Guidance Ctr., 1974-79; lead sch. psychologist Sunnyside (Ariz.) Unified Sch. Dist., 1979—; dir. Family Devel. Ctr., Tucson. Bd. dirs. Family Life Council of Tucson, 1980-81; Southwest Inst. Sexuality, 1981. Served to capt. USAF, 1966-71. Decorated Air medal with 3 oak leaf clusters, Service medal (Vietnam); recipient Profl. Achievement award Am. Mental Health Counselors Assn., 1981, 82, 83. Mem. Am. Personnel and Guidance Assn. (jour. bd. cons. editors), Am. Mental Health Counselors Assn. (Southwest coordinator), Ariz. Counselors Assn. (pres.). Lutheran. Office: Family Devel Ctr 1160 N Craycroft Rd Tucson AZ 85712

RENDERS, JOSEPH ALFRED, JR., journalist, state ofcl.; b. Gilroy, Calif., Apr. 1, 1928; s. Joseph Alfred and Margaret (Gallagher) R.; B.A., U. Mont., 1950; m. Tempie Lou Daigle, July 6, 1948 (div. 1973); children—Arlana, Marsha, Robin, Cheryl, Jeff; m. 2d, Shirley Alling Grigsby, Oct. 22, 1976. News editor Dawson County Rev., Glendive, Mont., 1950; reporter Billings (Mont.) Gazette, 1950-51; mng. editor Miles City (Mont.) Star, 1951; telegraph editor, chief copy desk Great Falls (Mont.), Tribune, 1951-60; co-owner, partner Pub. Relations Assos., Great Falls, 1960-74; adminstrv. asst. to pres. Mont. Farmers Union, 1975-77, Mont. Livestock Coop., 1977-80; chief Moblzn. of Resources Bur., Community Services div. Dept. of Community Affairs, State of Mont., Helena, 1980-81, info. officer Dept. Health and Environ. Scis., 1981—. Vice chmn. Great Falls Fire Commn., 1967-69; pub. info. chmn. Great Falls Citizens Participation Com., 1968-69; mem. Forward Great Falls, 1969, Great Falls Traffic Commn., 1969-73; mem., chmn. Mont. Adv. Council Vocat. Edn., 1971-79; v.p. Mont. Legal Services Assn., 1966-72; pres. Cascade County Legal Services Bd., 1966-72; mem. Mont. citizens Com. on State Legislature, 1966-80; Mont. state chmn. McGovern for Pres., 1972; mem. Mont. Jud. Nominating Commn., 1973-80; mem. adminstrv. com. Mont. Community Action Bur., 1974; bd. mem., pres. Opportunities, Inc., 1965-72. Served with USNR, 1945-46. Mem. Am. Mensa Soc., Wilderness Soc., Ams. for Dem. Action, ACLU, Sigma Delta Chi. Democrat. Unitarian. Home: 479 S Park Helena MT 59601 Office: PO Box 1243 Helena MT 59624

RENETZKY, ALVIN, pub. co. exec.; b. Bklyn., Aug. 2, 1940; s. Sam and Anna Renetzky; m. Cheryl R. Linden, Oct. 9, 1981; 1 son, Davida P. Ph.D., U. So. Calif., 1966. Pub. Academic Media, Los Angeles, 1966-70, Ready Reference Press, Santa Monica, Calif., 1975—.

RENFREE, ELIZABETH MCQUILLAN, accountant; b. New Bedford, Mass., Mar. 14, 1949; d. Edwin Joseph and Mary Jane (Palmer) McQuillan; m. Peter Rodman Renfree, July 11, 1970 (div.); children—Joshua Rodman, Adam Palmer. B.S. in Biology, Southeastern Mass. U., 1970; M.B.A., Nat. U., 1981. Fin. analyst Foodmaker Inc., San Diego, 1977-79; fin. reporting acct. Security Pacific Fin. Corp., San Diego, 1979-80; asst. controller Zoological Soc. of San Diego, 1980-82, controller, 1982—; acctg. instr. Nat. U. Mem. Nat. Assn. Accts., Inst. Mgmt. Accts. Club: Soroptimists (San Diego). Office: PO Box 551 San Diego CA 92112

RENFRO, DONALD WILLIAM, architect; b. Bakersfield, Calif., Nov. 13, 1931; s. Donald Francis and Lennie Lorraine (Despain) R.; student Bakersfield Coll., 1949-51; children—Dayna, Trisha, Donna. Staff designer Whitney Biggar, Architect, 1955-61; asso. Eddy & Paynter Assos., Bakersfield, Calif., 1961-70; prin. Eddy Paynter Renfro & Assos., Bakersfield, 1970-78; pres. Donald Renfro & Assos., Bakersfield, 1978—; pres., dir. Design Research Assos., Inc. Mem. Bakersfield Coll. Archtl. Adv. Com.; mem. Bakersfield Design Rev. Bd. Served with U.S. Army, 1952-54. Mem. AIA (past pres. Golden Empire chpt.) past dir. So. Calif. chpt.). Republican. Club: Kiwanis (past dir.). Office: 4800 Stockdale Hwy Suite 304 Bakersfield CA 93309

RENFRO, EVELYN BIERNER, municipal official; b. Truth or Consequences, N.Mex., Jan. 11, 1942; d. Frank and Mary (Hovey) Bierner; m. Roy Calvin Renfro, Feb. 13, 1972; children—Shawnee Marie, Sonya Darlene. Student Truth or Consequences pub. schs. Waitress, 1960-62, sec. City of Truth or Consequences, 1962-65, city clk., treas., 1965-69, 71—; legal sec. to Raymond Keithly, 1969-71. Recipient cert. of appreciation Boy Scouts Am., 1982, Moose Lodge, 1982. Mem. Internat. Inst. Mcpl. Clks. Republican. Roman Catholic. Home: 824 Charles St Truth or Consequences NM 87901 Office: 605 Sims St Truth or Consequences NM 87901

RENHOWE, JOHN PAUL, architect; b. Fargo, N.D., May 2, 1945; s. Ingvald and Esther (Skavlan) R.; m. Nancy Carol Giffey, May 31, 1969; children—Lisa, Kathryn, Steven. B.Arch., N.D. State U., 1969. Registered architect, Nat. Council Archtl. Registration Bds., 1973. Draftsman, Seifert & Staszko Assocs., Fargo, N.D., 1969-72; designer Seifert & Staszko Assocs., Fargo, 1972-74; designer/job capt. Koehnlein Lightowler Johnson, Inc., Fargo, 1974-76, project architect, 1976-80, sr. architect, 1980-82; project architect Banner Assocs., Laramie, Wyo., 1982-83; project architect Gefroth Assocs., Inc., Ft. Collins, Colo., 1983—. Mem. F-M Architects, 1980-81. Named Draftsman of the Yr., N.D. chpt. AIA, 1970. Mem. AIA. Lutheran. Office: 555 S Howes Suite 100 Fort Collins CO

RENIGER, HENRY AUSTIN, III, sales manager; b. Lansing, Mich., June 21, 1952; s. Henry Austin and Shirley Ann (Cummings) R.; m. Carol Davis, Aug. 3, 1975; 1 son, Peter Austin. Student U. Salzburg, 1969; B.S. in Mass Communications, U. Utah, 1979; Print/graphic specialist U. Utah, Salt Lake City, 1973-77; advt. mgr. Oscar E. Chytraus Co., Salt Lake City, 1977-79; store mgr. H. J. Davis Co., Van Nuys, Calif., 1979-81; key accounts mgr. Allegretti & Co., Chatsworth, Calif., 1981-82, regional mgr., 1982—. Mem. Sigma Nu. Office: 9200 Mason Ave Chatsworth CA 91311

RENK, RUSSELL RICHARD, environmental engineer; b. Boise, Idaho, Mar. 17, 1947; s. Richard Conrad and Lila May (Benedict) R.; m. Lura Jean Morgan, Sept. 13, 1980; 1 son, Travis James. B.S. in Chemistry, Boise State U., 1969; M.S. in Phys. Chemistry, U. Fla., 1970; Ph.D. in Civil and Environ. Engring., Utah State U., 1976. Registered profl. engr. Teaching and research asst. U. Fla., Gainesville, 1969-70; phys. sci. research asst. U.S. Army Bioengring. Med. Research Devel. Lab., Walter Reed Hosp., Washington, 1971-73; research asst. Utah State U., Logan, 1973-76; vis. asst. prof. U. Ariz., Tucson, 1976-78; environ. engr. State of Idaho, Twin Falls, 1980—; cons. educator. Served with U.S. Army, 1971-73. Mem. ASCE, Internat. Graphoanalysis Soc., NOW. Club: Men's Municipal Golf Assn. Home: 833 Greenwood Dr Twin Falls ID 83301 Office: 963 Blue Lakes Blvd 3 Twin Falls ID 83301

RENNEBOHM, ANITA CAROL, secretarial service and construction company executive; b. Omak, Wash., Aug. 7, 1943; d. Lester and Ida Ellen (Moomaw) Waggoner; m. Dwayne McClellan, Feb. 15, 1960; children—Pamelia Carol McClellan, Lisa Lynn McClellan; m. 2d, Ronald Albert Rennebohm, May 28, 1982. Grad. CTC Bus. Edn. Systems, 1970. Bus. fin. mgr. automobile dealership, 1970-72; legal asst. to Harry B. Platis, Atty., Lynnwood, Wash., 1972-82; owner, operator ACR Enterprises, Inc., Lynnwood 1982-83; co-owner, gen. mgr. R & A Homes, Lynnwood, 19—. Mem. Snohomish County Women Bus. Owners Assn., South Snohomish County C. of C. Legal Secs. Assn., Secretarial Services Assn. Democrat. Methodist. Clubs: Elks.

RENNER, TOMMIE FRANKLIN, educator; b. Industry, Ill., June 14, 1929; s. Charles Oscar and Eva Helen (Adkisson) R.; B.S., Dakota State

Coll., 1969; M.S., Black Hills State Coll., 1974; m. Arliss Rae Rinegar, Aug. 22, 1953; children—Darla Ann, Russell Eugene, Tommie Franklin II, Trisha Rae. Heavy equipment operator Asbell Bros., Casper, Wyo., 1947-61; gen. mgr. Weiss Hardware & Lumber, Pukwana, S.D., 1961-64; elem. tchr. Weston County Sch. Dist. No. 7, Upton, Wyo., 1969-74; elem. prin. Shannon County Sch. Dist. No. 1, Batesland, S.D., 1975; internal project evaluator, curriculum cons. S.D. State Dept. Edn. and Cultural Affairs, Pierre, 1976; coordinating instr. Casper Coll., 1976—; Weston County Portal Sch. coordinator, instr. Math. and Sci. Teaching Center, U. Wyo., 1972-74. Defensive driving course instr. Wyo. Safety Council, 1977—; clk. bd. edn. Pukwana (S.D.) Public Sch.; organizer, leader Pukwana Cub Scouts; sec.-treas. Weston County Weed and Pest Control Bd. Recipient NACD Allis Chalmers Environ. Conservation Edn. award, 1974. Mem. Am. Soc. Safety Engrs., Wyo. Safety Council. Democrat. Methodist. Clubs: Dakota State Indsl. Arts, Masons, Elks. Home: 865 Horseshoe Rd Casper WY 82601 Office: 125 College Dr Casper WY 82601

RENNICK, ROBERT DEXTER, chemist; b. North Platte, Nebr., May 2, 1941; s. Robert Meredith and Eleanor Louise (Collier) R.; student U. Nebr., 1959-60; B.S., U. Wyo., 1964, M.S., 1965; postgrad. UCLA, 1966-67; m. Dianne Mary Puffer, Aug. 5, 1961 (dec.); children—Meridith, Laurie, Terri. Radiochemist, Tracelab., Richmond, Calif., 1961-62; mem. tech. staff Aerospace Corp., El Segundo, Calif., 1965-66; sr. chemist Kerr McGee Corp., Trona, Calif., 1967-69, Oklahoma City, 1969-72; sr. staff chemist Rockwell Internat., Canoga Park, Calif., 1972—. Bd. dirs., treas. Oklahoma County Assn. Retarded, 1970-72. Fellow Chem. Soc. London; mem. Sigma Xi. Patentee chem. process systems. Home: 229 Siesta Ave Thousand Oaks CA 91360 Office: 8900 Desoto Ave Canoga Park CA 91304

RENNIE, GLORIA TUCKER COKELY, broadcast company official; b. Oklahoma City, Mar. 17; d. Henry Vee and Norma (Redwine) Tucker; m. Brian Anthony Cokely, June 23, 1973 (div. 1978); 1 son, Edward Tucker; m. 2d, Raymond Morgan Rennie, May 15, 1982. Account supr. Bernard Schank Advt. Agy., Sunnyvale, Calif., 1978-80; br. mgr. Ogilvy & Mather Recruitment Advt., San Jose, Calif., 1980-82; mktg. and promotions dir. Davis Weaver Broadcasting, San Jose, 1982—.

RENSCH, JOSEPH ROMAINE, pub. utility holding co. exec.; b. San Bernardino, Calif., Jan. 1, 1923; s. Joseph R. and Lucille (Ham) R.; B.S., Stanford, 1947; J.D., Golden Gate U., 1955; m. June Elizabeth Burley, Mar. 25, 1946; children—Steven R., Jeffrey P. Admitted to Calif. bar; successively sales engr., regional gas engr., asst. regional gas supt., asst. mgr. gas supply and control Coast Counties Gas & Electric Co., San Francisco, 1947-54; sr. pipeline operations engr. Pacific Gas & Electric Co., 1954-56; prodn. control supt. Western div. Dow Chem. Co., Pittsburg, Calif., 1956; asst. counsel So. Counties Gas Co. of Calif., Los Angeles, 1957-58; asst. v.p., spl. counsel Pacific Lighting Gas Supply Co., Los Angeles, 1958-61, v.p., dir., 1962-65; sr. v.p. Pacific Lighting Service Co., 1965-67, exec. v.p., 1967-69, pres., 1969-71, chmn. bd., 1971-73; exec. v.p., dir. Pacific Lighting Corp., Los Angeles, 1968-72, pres., 1972—; dir. Union Bank, Kaiser Steel Corp., Foremost McKesson Inc., Olga Co., Lockheed Corp., Pacific Mut. Life Ins. Co. Trustee Occidental Coll. Served with USNR, 1942-46. Registered profl. engr., Calif. Mem. Pacific Coast Gas Assn. (pres. 1966-67), Fed. Power, Am. bar assns., Am. Gas Assn. (dir.), Tau Beta Pi, Alpha Tau Omega. Office: Pacific Lighting Corp 810 S Flower St Los Angeles CA 90017

RENSELAER, DIRK JOHANNES, aerodynamics engineer; b. Amsterdam, Netherlands, Feb. 8, 1920; s. Wilhelmus Johannes and Margaretha Hermanna (Kolenbrander) Reuselaars; Diploma in Engring., Tech. U. Delft (Netherlands), 1947; Ph.D. in Aeronautical Engring., Kensington U., Glendale, Calif., 1979. Aerodynamist, Fokker Aircraft Co., Amsterdam, 1947-52, Lockheed Aircraft Co., Burbank, Calif., 1952-55; aerodynamics specialist Douglas Aircraft Inc., Santa Monica, Calif., 1955-60, Northrop Aircraft Corp., Hawthorne, Calif., 1960-63; project aerodynamicist Rockwell Internat., NAAD, El Segundo, Calif., 1963—. Mem. AIAA. Developer new aerodynamic test prins. for vertical takeoff aircraft models. Home: PO Box 3001 Lennox CA 90304 Office: Mail Code GB15 Rockwell Internat Los Angeles Div PO Box 92098 Los Angeles CA 90009

RENTERIA, ESTHER G., coll. public relations adminstr.; b. East Los Angeles, Calif., May 1, 1939; d. Oliver Jay and Violet Gatfield; A.A., East Los Angeles Coll., 1958; B.A., Calif. State U., Los Angeles, 1974; m. Martin Renteria, Feb. 13, 1971; children—Christopher, David. Reporter, Alhambra (Calif.) Post Advocate, 1959-61; reporter, soc. editor East Los Angeles Tribune & Gazette, 1962-68; desk editor, newswriter Sta. KNX, Los Angeles, 1968; asso. producer, hostess-moderator Ahora! TV Series, Public Broadcasting Sta. KCET, 1969-70; public info. dir. East Los Angeles Coll., 1970—; producer Sta. KNXT TV Series: Bienvenidos and The Siesta is Over, 1970-74, ednl. cons. bilingual edn. series Juntos, 1979-82; sec., dir. Future Broadcasting Corp., 1980—; Bd. dirs. Plaza de la Raza Cultural Center; mem. East Los Angeles Service Center Adv. Council; bd. dirs. Bilingual Found. of the Arts, Cleland Ho. of Neighborly Service; bd. dirs. East Los Angeles Regional Occupational Center Adv. Bd.; public relations dir. Los Angeles Street Scene Festival, 1978—. Mem. Calif. Community and Jr. Coll. assn. Public Info. Dirs. Democrat. Roman Catholic. Club: Job's Daus. Home: 301 Dochan Circle Montebello CA 90640 Office: East Los Angeles Coll 1301 Brooklyn Ave Monterey Park CA 91754

RENTSCHLER, FREDERICK BRANT, consumer product co. exec.; b. N.Y.C., Aug. 12, 1939; s. George Adam and Rita (Mitchell) R.; B.A., Vanderbilt U., 1961; M.B.A., Harvard U., 1968; m. Marguerite Elizabeth Shaughnessy, Nov. 20, 1971. Dir. mktg. Armour Dial Inc., Phoenix, 1973, v.p. toiletries div., 1974, v.p. new bus. devel., 1975-76; pres. Armour Internat. Co., Phoenix, 1977, Armour-Dial Corp., Phoenix, 1978-80; pres., chief exec. officer Hunt-Wesson Foods Inc., 1980—; dir. Charleston Corp. Dep. dir. White House Fellows, 1971, 72; bd. dirs. Scottsdale Center for the Arts, 1974, 76; bd. dirs. Heard Mens Council-Heard Mus., 1975, 76, United Way Ariz., 1978—; trustee Heard Mus., 1978—. Served to capt. USMC, 1961-65. Mem. Young Pres. Orgn. Republican. Roman Catholic. Clubs: Links (N.Y.C.); Racquet (Chgo.); Paradise Valley Country (Scottsdale); Ariz. (Phoenix). Office: Hunt-Wesson Foods Inc 1645 W Valencia Dr Fullerton CA 92634

RENYER, GERALD BERNARD, lawyer, consultant; b. Topeka, Oct. 29, 1938; s. Laurence J. and Elizabeth M. (Michaelis) R.; m. Sue Myers, June 22, 1963; children—Jacqueline, Mark, Sara. B.A., U. Kans., 1963; J.D., U. Mo., 1967. Bar: Mo. 1967, Kans. 1969, N.Y. 1976. Sole practice, Kansas City, Mo., 1967-74; tax. cons. N.Y. Life Ins. Co., N.Y., 1974-78, Los Angeles Regional Hdqrs., 1978-83, sr. advanced underwriting cons., 1981—; lectr. bar assns., life ins. industry seminars. Scoutmaster Kaw council Boy Scouts Am.; Indian princess tribal chief YMCA; vestryman Christ Episc. Ch. Mo. State Bar scholar, 1966. Mem. Kans. Bar Assn., Mo. Bar Assn., N.Y. Bar Assn., Am. CLU Soc., Delta Theta Phi. Episcopalian. Contbr. articles to profl. jours. Office: NY Life Ins Co 2801 W 6th St Los Angeles CA 90057

REPIC, EDWARD MICHAEL, aerospace executive, consultant; b. Cleve., June 7, 1935; s. Michael and Ann Mary (Purkeli) R.; m. Patricia Rae Deblass, June 30, 1956; children—Terri Lynn, Raymond Anthony, Toni D'Ann, Edward Michael. B.S. in Aero. Engring., Ohio State U., 1962; M.S. in Aerospace Engring., U. So. Calif., 1964; M.B.A., Pepperdine U., 1975. Cert. profl. mgr. Engr., Rockwell Internat., Anaheim, Calif., 1962-68, mgr., 1968-81, dir. shuttle processing, 1981-82; pres. Effective Mgmt. Resources Corp., 1979—; prof. West Coast U.; dir. Key to Travel, Inc. Mem. ASME, AIAA, Am. Inst. Indsl. Engrs., Internat. Soc. Philos. Inquiry, Mensa. Club: Diogenes (Anaheim). Author: Managing Engineers, 1981; Project Management for Engineers, 1981; Improving Engineering Productivity, 1982; Business Development, Planning and Capture, 1983.

RESNICK, PAUL MARTIN, distbg. co. exec.; b. Boston, Feb. 20, 1936; s. Louis and Rose (Freedman) R.; children—Kerri, Julie, Jackie, Jessica, Jennifer. Salesman, Duddy's Inc., Boston, 1958-62; gen. mgr. Minn. Tires, Mpls., 1962-66; pres. Javelin Corp., Burlingame, Calif., 1967—. Republican. Jewish. Club: Masons. Office: 652 Bair Island Rd Redwood City CA 94063

RESNIKOFF, ARTHUR, psychologist, educator; b. Brooklyn, March 11, 1942; s. Israel and Berte (Eisenstat) R.; m. Jacqueline I. Levy, June 6, 1966; children—Ivan Reese, Rachel B.; A.B., Cornell U., Ithaca, N.Y., 1963; M.S., SUNY, Buffalo, 1965; Ph.D., Mich. State U., East Lansing, 1968. Lic. psychologist, Calif., Mo.; oral examiner, Psychology Examing Com., Calif. Assoc. prof. Washington U., St. Louis, also dir. counseling psychology program Grad. Inst. Edn., counseling psychologist in counseling center, 1968-78; counseling psychologist, dir. counseling center, U. Calif.-Irvine, 1978-81, clin. services dir., 1981—; pvt. practice, 1981—; condr. psychotheraphy, psychol. workshops, instr. soc. sci., soc. ecology. Mem. Am. Psychol. Assn. (treas. div. counseling psychology). Mgn. editor, The Counseling Psychologist; series editor, Brooks/Cole Series in Counseling Psychology; contbr. articles to profl. jours. Home: 2212 Margaret Dr Newport Beach CA 92663 Office: U Calif Counseling Center Irvine CA 92717

RESTIVO, RICHARD RENE, transportation company executive; b. Winnipeg, Man., Can., May 30, 1944; s. Sam and Theresa R.; B.A., Calif. State U.-Fullerton, 1968. Acct., Shell Oil Co., Los Angeles and Houston, 1971-72; various positions in moving and storage industry, Los Angeles, 1972-76; v.p. relocation systems, gen. mgr. Lido Van & Storage Co., Carson, Calif., 1974-75, v.p. relocation systems, after 1976; now pres. Relocation Systems of Tex., Inc., Houston. Served with AUS, 1968-70. Decorated Silver Star medal, Bronze Star medal, Air medal, Purple Heart, Combat Infantryman Badge. Club: Valley Transportation (pres. 1978). Home: 3107 Wagon Trail Dr Sugarland TX 77479 Office: 5707 Chimney Rock Rd Houston TX 77081

RETHORST, SCOTT CARSON, sci. co. exec.; b. Douglas, Ariz., Oct. 18, 1914; s. Otto William and Mary (Carson) R.; B.S., M.I.T., 1936; M.S., Calif. Inst. Tech., 1950, Ph.D., 1956; children—John Carter, Susan. Dir. research Vultee Aircraft Corp., 1938-39; gen. mgr. bonding div. Goodyear Aircraft Corp., 1940-44; scientist U.S. Air Force, 1945-53; sr. scientist Lockheed Aircraft Corp., 1955; cons. Douglas Aircraft Corp., 1957; pres. Vehicle Research Corp., Pasadena, Calif., 1957—; dir. strategic planning Westinghouse Electric Corp., 1958-59; teaching asst. Calif. Inst. Tech., 1954-56. Mem. AIAA, Air Force Assn., Sigma Xi. Clubs: Portage Country (Akron, Ohio), Kenwood Country (Washington); The Beach (Santa Monica, Calif.); Berkeley (Calif.) Tennis; Calif. Tennis, Olympic (San Francisco). Developer aerodynamic lift air cushion vehicle, 1962, aircraft induced drag reduction system, 1966, high speed ocean surfing ship, 1967, spinning tubular projectile, 1972, shock free supersonic aircraft, 1978, aircraft laminar flow system, 1979. Office: 650 Sierra Madre Villa Ave Pasadena CA 91107

RETTENMAYER, CLAUDIA DENKER, accounting executive; b. Detroit, June 21, 1953; d. Milton Henry and Irene Virginia (LeVeck) Denker; m. John William Rettenmayer, May 26, 1977; 1 son, Justin Cody. B.A. in Mgmt., U. Mont., 1975, M.B.A., 1976. Teaching asst. U. Mont. Sch. Bus., 1975-76; staff auditor Mont. Office Legis. Auditor, Helena, 1976-77; ops. research analyst U.S. GAO, Washington, 1977-79; co-owner Micro Bus. Assocs., Billings and Missoula, Mont., 1980—. Mem. Missoula City Zoning Commn., 1980-82. Home: 4119 Corbin Dr Billings MT 59106 Office: PO Box 21459 Billings MT 59104

RETTERER, RONALD J., mgmt. cons., engr., author; b. Chgo., July 24, 1940; s. Russell M. and Marietta T. Retterer; B.S., Ill. Inst. Tech., 1963; m. Karen E. Berg, Oct. 5, 1963; children—Kathryn, Anne, Laura, Dan. With Booz-Allen & Hamilton, Chgo., 1965-66; pres. Bus. Growth Services, Sacramento; coll. instr. Mem. Am. Mktg. Club, Calif. Inventors Council (state bd.), Am. Assn. Small Research Cos., Clubs: Comstock, Rollingwood. Office: 7996 California Ave Suite C Fair Oaks CA 95628

RETTS, WILLIAM LEE, psychologist; b. Long Beach, Calif., Jan. 20, 1945; s. William Morse and Virginia Marie (Snively) R.; m. Laurie Sue Ptak, Dec. 19, 1969; children—Aaron William, Ashley Suzanne. B.A., Wheaton (Ill.) Coll., 1966; M.A., Ariz. State U., 1967, Ph.D., 1973. Cert. psychologist, Ariz. Staff psychologist Univ. Counseling Service, Ariz. State U., 1970-71; research/tng. cons. Hueristic Systems, Inc., Tempe, Ariz., 1972-73; assoc. faculty, 1975-76, staff psychologist, 1972; pvt. cons. western region Dept. Labor, 1973-74; pvt. practice counseling psychologist Psychol. Counseling Services, Ltd., Scottsdale, Ariz., 1975—; workshop leader Stress Mgmt. and Biofeedback Mesa Elem. Sch. System, 1976; affiliate staff Fuller Theol. Sem., 1978—. Chmn. Phoenix Metro com. Young Life, 1982; bd. dirs. Christian Family Care Agy., Scottsdale, 1982—. Mem. Am. Psychol. Assn., Ariz. Psychol. Assn., Am. Assn. Marriage and Family Therapist, Western Assn. for Christians In Psychol. Studies, Ariz. Biofeedback Soc., Am. Personnel and Guidance Assn. Baptist. Contbr. articles to profl. jours.

REUBENSTEIN, STANLEY, mfrs. rep.; b. Los Angeles, Apr. 20, 1946; s. Robert and Esther (Kapshut) R.; student Calif. State U., Los Angeles, 1963-65, B.A., Northridge, 1967; m. Loretta Gayle Masucci, Mar. 1, 1977; 1 son, Benjamin Daniel. With, Photo-voltaics Engring. Lab., Jet Propulsion Lab., Calif. Inst. Tech., Pasadena, 1967-68; nat. sales mgr. Standard Communications Corp., Los Angeles, 1970-73, mktg. mgr., 1975-77; nat. sales mgr. TPL Communications, Gardena, Calif., 1973-75; founder, owner Aurora Mktg. Co., Denver, 1977—. Committeeman, Denver County Democratic party, 1979—, del. conv., 1980, 82. Served with M.C., U.S. Army, 1968-70. Mem. Assoc. Public Safety Communications Officers, Communications Mktg. Assn. (pres. 1979-81, dir. 1981-83), Radio Club Am., Aircraft Owners and Pilots Assn., Alpha Phi Omega. Jewish. Club: Optimist. Home: 1323 Monaco Pkwy Denver CO 80220 Office: Aurora Marketing Co 2020 S Oneida St Denver CO 80224

REUTTER, JOHN, III, computer co. exec.; b. Danville, Ill., Jan. 4, 1943; s. John and Gladys (McDonald) R.; student Pomona Coll., 1961-63; B.S., Calif. Poly. U., 1965; M.S. in Computer Scis., Rutgers U., 1970; postgrad. info. scis. Ga. Inst. Tech., 1970-71; m. Julia Castanieto, July 15, 1966; children—Paul Derek, Michael John, Steven Cosme. Sr. systems analyst Bell Telephone Labs., San Francisco, 1967-70; cons., programmer analyst ISA, Atlanta, 1971-73; owner, founder DR Assos., Inc., Altanta, 1973-74; mgr. systems devel. Pacific Telephone Co., San Francisco, 1974-78; v.p. systems VISA Inc., San Mateo, Calif., 1974-78; founder, owner Megasoft Computer Systems Inc., San Mateo, 1980—; v.p. software Dynabyte Inc., Menlo Park, Calif., 1980-81; pres. J. Reutter, Inc., San Jose, Calif., 1981—, Megasoft Computer Corp., San Jose, 1981—; instr. Skyline Coll., 1975-81, Golden Gate U., 1978-81. Mem. IEEE, Assn. Computer Machinery, Data Processing Mgmt. Assn. Author: Data Processing: Systems and Concepts, 1982. Home: 1115 Brandybuck Way San Jose CA 95121 Office: 115 Independence Dr Menlo Park CA 94025

REVEL, JOHN CHASE, syndicated columnist, author; b. Portland, Tenn., Dec. 25, 1936; s. Ricaro Michael and Ruby Jewel (Short) R.; B.A., Independence Coll., 1965; 1 son, Shah Kieran. Chmn. bd. Chase Revel, Inc., Los Angeles, 1973—, Entrepreneur Mag., Los Angeles, 1973—, Comprise, Inc., 1975-79; Pinnacle Prodns., Inc., Los Angeles, 1977—, Revelco Inc., Los Angeles, 1979—, Chase Resources, Inc., Los Angeles, 1979—; dir. Comprise Amusements Devices, 1971-73; syndicated bus. columnist Times Mirror Syndicate and Revel Syndications; lectr. in field. Chmn. bd. Internat. Entrepreneurs Assn., 1977-79; chmn. Movie Industry Devel. Bd., Los Angeles, 1980—; del., Pres. Carter's Conf. on Small Bus., 1980. Mem. Fedn. Ind. Businessmen, Small Bus. Assn., Assn. Am. Pubs. Republican. Clubs: Jockey, Tiffanys, Elysian, Elan. Author: Hottest Business Ideas, 1978; Who's Making a Bundle, 1979; Most Unique Ways People are Making Money, vol. I, 1979, vol. II, 1980; 184 Businesses You Can Start, 1981; Businesses Ideal for Women, 1983. Office: 2311 Pontius Ave Los Angeles CA 90064

REVELL, JOHN HAROLD, dentist; b. Lead, S.D., Dec. 12, 1906; s. Aris LeRoy and Margaret (O'Donnell) R.; A.B. in Engring., Stanford, 1930; postgrad. McGill Med. Sch., 1930; D.D.S. summa cum laude, U. So. Calif., 1941; postgrad. in Maxillo Facial and Plastic Surgery, Mayo Found., U. Minn., 1944; m. Catherine Cecelia Gerrard, Sept. 14, 1936; children—Mary Margaret (Mrs. Irwin Goodwin), Kathleen Dianne Hendrix, Timothy John, Maureen Frances Brown, Dennis Cormac. Engaged as instr. U. So. Calif. Dental Coll., Los Angeles, 1941-42; practice oral surgery, maxillo facial-plastic surgery, Shafter, Calif., 1946—; mem. staff Mercy Hosp., Bakersfield, Calif., 1948—, chmn. dental sect., 1955-60, 70-71; mem. surg. staff San Joaquin Hosp., Bakersfield; lectr. on applied nutrition; internat. pioneer lectr. surg. orthodontics. Served with AUS, 1932-37, 42-46; now maj. ret. Recipient of Special Clinic award Am. Soc. Dentistry for Children, 1964; Rotary Internat. Presdl. citation, 1982. Diplomate Internat. Bd. Applied Nutrition. Fellow Internat. Coll. Applied Nutrition; mem. ADA (life), Calif. Dental Assn. (life), Ventura Dental Soc. (life), So. Calif., Kern County (dir.), Los Angeles County (award 1941), Santa Barbara-Ventura County dental assns., Am. Acad. Dental Medicine, Am. Acad. Applied Nutrition, Am. Soc. Dentistry for Children (life), Pierre Fauchard Acad., Shafter C. of C. (dir. 1948-50), Alpha Tau Epsilon, Omicron Kappa Upsilon, Phi Kappa Phi, Theta Xi. Democrat. Roman Catholic. Rotarian (pres. Shafter 1950-51, dir. 1951-52). Patentee precisioner. Research on maxillary dental papilloma, rotation unerupted impacted teeth, channeling for extensive movement of teeth; also clin. research in cleft palate surgery; inventor rapid fabrication device for infant feeding; pioneer in pre-fab. bldgs. and homes while constrn. officer U.S. Army, 1932; developer prototype WW-2 Jeep machine gun mount. Author publs. in field; all research data presented to and housed at La. State U. Dental Coll., New Orleans. Home: 5173 Aurora Dr Ventura CA 93003

REVELLE, KEITH, librarian; b. Woodland, Calif., Dec. 20, 1942; s. Robert Keith and Cleo Imogene (Adams) R.; B.A. in History, U. Calif., Berkeley, 1964; M.S. in Librarianship, Simmons Coll., Boston, 1967. Jr. librarian Latin Am. Library of Oakland (Calif.) Public Library, 1967, sr. librarian, 1968-70, dir., 1970-74; asst. librarian Anchorage Mcpl. Libraries, 1974-76, mcpl. librarian, 1977—; dir. Plaza Nine, Inc., Jayell Enterprises, Inc. Mem. Mcpl. Art. Selection Adv. Com.; mem. art in public places jury Mcpl. Hdqrs. Library; bd. dirs. Anchorage Concert Assn., Basically Bach Festival, Anchorage Library Found., Inc.; mem. artistic adv. com. Anchorage Civic Opera. Mem. ALA, Alaska Library Assn. Office: 524 W 6th Ave Anchorage AK 99501

REVIER, CHARLES FRANKLIN, economist, educator; b. Lubbock, Tex., Sept. 1, 1944; s. Frank Fancher and Dorothy Charlene (Lawson) R.; m. Susan Ann Nethaway, Aug. 7, 1971; 1 dau., Emily Ann. B.A. cum laude in Physics, U. Colo., Boulder, 1966, M.A., 1968; Ph.D., MIT, 1978. Summer intern Council of Econs. Advisers, Washington, 1970; intern Adv. Commn. Intergovtl. Relations, Washington, 1971-72; teaching asst. dept. econs., M.I.T., 1972-73; Research asst. Nat. Bur. Econ. Research, Cambridge, Mass., 1972-73; instr. econs. Colo. State U., Fort Collins, 1974-78, asst. prof. 1978—. U. of Colo. Grad. fellow, 1967-68; NSF fellow, 1968-71; Charles Abrams fellow, 1973-74; recipient 1st place award doctoral dissertation in govt. fin. and taxation Nat. Tax Assn.-Tax Inst. of Am., 1978. Mem. Am. Econs. Assn. Democrat. Methodist. Contbr. articles to profl. jours. Office: Dept of Econs Colo State U Fort Collins CO 80523

REX, ROBERT WALTER, geothermal executive; b. N.Y.C., June 5, 1929. B.A. in Geology, Harvard U., 1951; M.S. in Mineral Sci., Stanford U., 1953; Ph.D. in Oceanography, Scripps Inst., U. Calif., 1958. Geologist, U.S. Geol. Survey, Idaho, 1951-53, U.S. Naval Electronics Lab., San Diego, 1953; sr. research geologist Chevron Oil Co., La Habra, Calif., 1958-68; research assoc. Hawaii Inst. Geophysics, U. Hawaii, 1967-79; prof. geol. scis. U. Calif., Riverside, 1968-72; asst. dir. Inst. Geophys. and Planetary Physics, UCLA, 1969-72; v.p. exploration Pacific Energy Corp., Marina Del Rey, Calif., 1972-73; pres., chief exec. officer Republic Geothermal, Inc., Santa Fe Springs, Calif., 1973-82, chmn., chief exec. officer, 1982—; cons. lectr. in field; adv. state and fed. legis. in field of geothermal energy. Chmn. Calif. Geothermal adv. bd., 1970-72; energy adv. panel Office Sci. and Tech., Exec. Office Pres., 1971-73; panel chmn. NSF Geothermal Resources Research Conf., 1972; mem. Hawaii Geothermal Project, 1973; ad hoc panel Alt. Energy Sources Developing Countries, 1974-76, Geothermal adv. com. U.S. Dept. Energy, Houston, 1979; chmn. subpanel high temperature resources devel. Energy Resources adv. bd., 1979-80. Mem. Geol. Soc. Am., Am. Geophys. Union, AAAS, Geochem. Soc. Geothermal Resources Council (bd. dirs., chmn. standing com., 1980), Sci. Research Soc. N.Am., Arctic Inst. N.Am., Sigma Xi. Corr., Nat. Acad. Scis. U.S. Geodynamics com. project; editorial bd. Journal Energy Sources; contbr. numerous articles to tech. jours. Office: 11823 E Slauson Ave Santa Fe Springs CA 90670

REXING, DAVID JOSEPH, water system executive; b. Evansville, Ind., Sept. 21, 1950; s. Joseph Henry and Anita Marie (Baehl) R.; m. Mariann McDuffee, Aug. 23, 1976; children—Patrick Joseph, Colleen Marie. A.B., U. Evansville, 1972; postgrad. U. Ariz., 1972-75; M.B.A., U. Nev., 1981. Lab. supt. Evansville (Ind.) Waterworks, 1970-72; research asst. U. Ariz., Tucson, 1972-75; div. mgr. labs. So. Nev. Water System, Boulder City, 1975—; prin. Desert Products, 1983—. Fellow Am. Inst. Chemists; mem. Am. Water Works Assn. (Grade IV water quality analyst, water treatment operator; joint editorial bd. Standard Methods), Water Pollution Control Fedn., Am. Pub. Health Assn., Am. Chem. Soc. Contbr. articles to profl. jours. Home: 619 Mosswood Dr Henderson NV 89015 Office: Nev Water System 243 Lakeshore Rd Boulder City NV 89015

REYES, LINDA RAGASA REALON, educator; b. San Vicente, Ilosos Sur, Philippines, Aug. 30, 1946; came to U.S., 1969, naturalized, 1974; d. Paul Rutab and Isidra Riberal (Ragasa) Realon; m. Jimmy Munsod Reyes, Dec. 18, 1977; children—Katherine Marie, Jamie Lynn. B.S. in Edn., Phillippine Normal Coll., Manila, 1967; postgrad. Calif. State U.-Fresno, 1969-74, M.A., 1982. Cert. elem. tchr., Calif. Tchr., Muntinglupa Sch. Dist., Manila, 1967-69; tchr. Raisin City (calif.) Sch. Dist., 1970-74; resource tchr., tchr. 3d grade Cutler (Calif.) Sch., 1974-79; region II Imigrant resource tchr. Madera (Calif.) Unified Sch. Dist.,

1979-80, Title VII instructional advisor, 1980-81; resource tchr. Richgrove (Calif.) Sch. Dist., 1981—; tchr. summer sch. Westside Sch. Dist., Five Points, Calif., 1972-81. Mem. Orgn. Filipino-Am. Educators, Assn. Calif. Sch. Adminstrs., Assn. Supervision and Curriculum Devel., Calif. Tchrs. Assn., Nat. Tchrs. Assn., IRA, Calif. Reading Assn., Bus & Profl. Women's Club (chmn. legis. com. 1976-77, chmn. Internat. Women of Yr. 1975-76, chmn. world awareness com. 1974-75). Democrat. Roman Catholic. Clubs: Filipino-Am. Women's (pres. 1975-77, sec. 1970-75), Filipino-Am. Community of Fresno & Vicinity (chmn. fund raising 1979-82).

REYNDERS, MICHEL ALBERT JOSEPH P., pathologist; b. Brussels, Belgium, June 29, 1931; came to U.S., 1961, naturalized, 1966; s. Joseph Henri J. and Ludwine Ida (Viscountess de Preud'homme d'Hailly de Nieuport) R.; m. Colette De Peet; children—Jean-Noel, Dominique. M.D., U. of Louvain, (Belgium), 1959. Freelance journalist, Belgium, 1952-59; intern and surg. resident U. Louvain Med. Center, Belgium, 1958-61; resident U. Colo. Med. Center, Denver, 1961-66; practice medicine specializing in pathology; asso. pathologist Bergen Pines Hosp., Paramus, N.J., 1967; pathologist Porter Meml. Hosp., Denver, 1967—; asst. clin. prof. pathology Sch. Medicine, U. Colo., 1967—. Diplomate Am. Bd. Pathology. Fellow Coll. Am. Pathologists, Internat. Soc. Hematology, Am. Soc. Coagulationists (founding); mem. AMA, Colo., Denver med. socs., Am. Soc. Cytology, Alliance Française de Denver (dir., editor newsletter), Chevaliers du Tastevin. Roman Catholic. Home: 131 S Birch St Denver CO 80222 Office: 2525 S Downing St Denver CO 80210

REYNERSON, DONALD MARTIN, electrical engineer; b. Kansas City, Mo., Nov. 21, 1941; s. Donald Theopolis and Martha Nell (Nash) R.; B.S. in Elec. Engring., N.C. State U., 1968, M.E.E., 1968; M.Mech.Engring., M.I.T., 1975, Naval Architect, 1975; m. Zilca Luana Thornton, Mar. 26, 1983; children—Kimberly Elizabeth, Charles Martin. Enlisted U.S. Navy, 1960; service in Vietnam; submarine officer Mare Island Naval Shipyard, Vallejo, Calif., 1979-80; ret., 1980; group leader mgmt. systems mirror fusion test facility Lawrence Livermore (Calif.) Nat. Lab., 1980—. Mem. Am. Soc. Naval Engrs., Soc. Naval Architects and Marine Engrs., Eta Kappa Nu, Tau Beta Pi. Mem. Christian Ch. (Disciples of Christ). Club: M.I.T. No. Calif. (v.p. (1980-83). Office: Lawrence Livermore Nat Lab Bldg 543 L-636 Livermore CA 94550

REYNOLDS, BARBARA JEAN, church office manager; b. Ridgefield, Wash., Mar. 16, 1931; d. James Howard and Kate Elizabeth (Homar) Alexander; m. John Whitcomb Reynolds; children—Kate Elizabeth, Thomas John, Nannette Louise. B.A. in Edn., Central Wash. U., 1953; postgrad. Portland State U., summers 1953, 54, winter 1972. Tchr. pub. schs., Vancouver, Wash., 1953-58; substitute tchr. pub. schs., Olympia, Wash., 1972-75; dir. Ret. Sr. Vol. Program Thurston-Mason Counties, Olympia, 1975-79, office mgr. 1st Christian Ch., Olympia, 1979—, also ch. program and planning cons.

REYNOLDS, CARL LESLIE, vocational agriculture educator; b. Vandalia, Ill., May 28, 1945; s. Archie Leslie and Lucille Annabelle (Doyle) R.; m. Christine Diane Kiersch, Feb. 1, 1969; children—Catherine Elizabeth, Richard Gregory. B.S., U. Ill., 1967, M.Ed., 1975, Ed.D., 1976. Tchr. vocat. agr., public schs., Warren, Ill., 1967-73; researcher, adminstrv. asst. U. Ill., Urbana, 1973-76; assoc. prof. vocat. edn. U. Wyo., Laramie, 1976—. Mem. Am. Soc. Agrl. Engrs., Am. Assn. Tchr. Educators in Agr., Am. Vocat. Assn., Nat. Vocat. Agr. Tchrs. Assn., Republican. Episcopalian. Club: Lions (pres. elect). Contbr. articles to Agrl. Edn. Mag.. Office: 03 Education Dept Univ Wyo Laramie WY 82071

REYNOLDS, EARL CHILDERS, JR., engineering consultant; executive; b. LaGrande, Oreg., Jan. 27, 1923; s. Earl C. and Frances Willard (Smith) R.; m. Harriet Ann Andrew, Apr. 10, 1950; children—James W., Andrew E., Joseph G. B.S.C.E. with honors, Oreg. State U., Corvallis, 1947; M.Engring. with honors, Yale U., 1948. Registered profl. engr., Idaho, Oreg., Utah, Nev., Wyo., Colo., Mont. Stakeman, chairman Oeg. Hwy. Dept., 1941; computer, topographer Corps of Engrs., 1942; student instr. engring. mechanics Oreg. State U., 1947; design engr. CH2M Hill, Corvallis, 1947-50, mgr. Boise office, 1950-80, v.p., 1966-80, Central Dist. mgr., 1977-80, chmn. bd., Boise, 1980-83; dir. N.W. Savs. & Loan Assn. Engring. adv. bd. U. Idaho; bd. dirs. St. Luke's Regional Med. Center; mem. Boise City Planning and Zoning Commn., 1960-76, chmn., 1962-66; mem. Boise City Bd. Adjustment, 1964-71, chmn., 1970; mem. Regional Planning Commn., Ada Council of Govts., 1971-76, chmn., 1974-75. Served with USNR, 1943-46. Named Disting. Citizen, Idaho Statesman, 1967, Boss of Yr., Capital Jaycees, 1970. Fellow ASCE (Outstanding civil Engr. So. Idaho sect. 1982); mem. Idaho Soc. Profl. Engrs., Nat. Soc. Profl. Engrs., Am. Water Works Assn. (Fuller award 1980), Am. Cons. Engrs. Council, Water Pollution Control Fedn., Am. Pub. Works Assn., AAAS, Boise C. of C., Am. Arbitration Assn., Cons. Engrs. Idaho, Sigma Xi, Phi Kappa Phi, Tau Beta Pi, Phi Delta Theta. Episcopalian. Clubs: Capital City Kiwanis, Arid (Boise). Home: 2848 Starlington Dr Boise ID 83702 Office: 700 Clearwater Ln Boise ID 83707

REYNOLDS, GARDNER MEAD, civil engineer; b. Ithaca, N.Y., Oct. 29, 1918; s. Minos Mead and Ruth Louise (Gardner) R.; m. Kathleen Kane, July 31, 1945; children—Marcia, Stephen, Timothy, Richard. B.S.C.E., Cornell U., 1948. Registered profl. engr., Del., N.J., N.Y., Mass., Pa., R.I, Va. Job engr. Dames & Moore, San Francisco, 1948-59, field cons. refinery project, N.Y.C., 1949-50, asst. to resident ptnr., 1950-54, ptnr., 1954—, mng. ptnr. cons. div., 1960-74, sr. ptnr., chmn. exec. com., 1974-80, sr. ptnr., 1980—; dir. Chiyoda/Dames & Moore; ptnr. Dames & Moore, U.K., Dames & Moore Australia. Mem. Wyckoff (N.J.) Planning Bd., 1965-68; mem. Los Angeles Olympic Citizens sdv. Commn., The Beavers; trustee Deep Founds. Inst. Served with USAAF, 1942-46. Decorated Purple Heart. Mem. ASCE (bd. dirs. 1965-68), Assn. Soil and Found. Engrs. (pres. 1978-79), Am. Inst. Cons. Engrs. (mem. council 1968-70), Am. Arbitration Assn. Clubs: Palos Verdes Breakfast, Palos Verdes Golf. Home: 2740 Via Campesina Palos Verdes Estates CA 90274 Office: 445 S Figueroa St Los Angeles CA 90071

REYNOLDS, HUGH MCGINNIS, mechanical engineer; b. Long Beach, Calif., July 13, 1946; s. Hugh Middleton and Marguerite Elaine Snow (McGinnis) R.; m. Mary Margaret Peart, June 19, 1971; children—Joanna Peart, Jennifer Mary; A.A., El Camino Coll., 1967; B.S., U. Calif.-Davis, 1969, M.S., 1970. Cert. community coll. tchr. Sr. design engr., project engr. chem. systems div. United Technols. Corp., Sunnyvale, Calif., 1972—. Recipient award United Technols., 1979. Mem. AIAA, AAAS, Sigma Xi, Tau Beta Pi, Phi Kappa Phi. Patentee in field. Office: 1050 E Argues St Sunnyvale CA 94086

REYNOLDS, JOYCE WHITAKER, ring manufacturing company executive; b. Nashville, July 20, 1949; d. James Carruth and June Betha (Chesney) Whitaker; m. David Reynolds, Aug. 14, 1971 (div.). B.S. in Commerce, Bus. Adminstrn., U. Ala., 1971; postgrad. U. Calif.-San Diego, 1978. Acct. various CPA firms, 1971-73; acct., then corp. fin. analyst Foodmaker, Inc. div. Ralston Purina Co., San Diego, 1973-78; sales rep. Art Carved Class Rings, Inc., San Diego, 1978-80, area mgr., 1980-81, dist. sales mgr., 1981—; tchr. profl. selling skills to sales reps. Mem. Christian Children's Fund, 1981—. Winner nat. sales contest Art Carved Class Rings, Inc., 1979, other sales contests, 1982, named charter mem. Pres.'s Club, 1981, spl. recognition, 1982, recipient Award of Excellence, 1982. Mem. Calif. Assn. Coll. Stores, Western Coll. Bookstore Assn., Nat. Assn. Coll. Stores, U. Ala. Alumni Assn., Alpha Delta Pi. Club: Women in Sales (San Diego). Home: 1807 Missouri St Apt #5 San Diego CA 92109 Office: Art Carved Class Rings, Inc 1964 1/2 Garnet Ave Suite B-1 San Diego CA 92109

REYNOLDS, MARCIA, hospital audio-visual specialist, consultant, educator; b. Phoenix, July 24, 1955; d. Samuel and Selma (Eil) Charns. B.S. in Mass Communications summa cum laude, Ariz. State U., 1979, postgrad. in counseling edn., 1982—; M.A. in Broadcast Communication Arts, San Francisco State U., 1982. Tng. coordinator Central Bag and Supply, Phoenix, 1976-79; audio-visual coordinator Camelback Hosps., Scottsdale, Ariz., 1982—; assoc. in telecommunications Ariz. State U., 1983—. Mem. Health-Sci. Communication Assn., Am. Soc. Tng. and Devel., Indsl. TV Assn., Phi Beta Kappa.

REYNOLDS, MARY LOUISE, nursing administrator; b. Miles City, Mont., Nov. 4, 1932; d. Clyde Lee and Mary Rebecca (Wilson) Hopper; student U. Calif., Berkeley, 1950-51; B.S. with honors, U. Calif., San Francisco, 1955; m. James Minor Reynolds, June 8, 1962; children—Linda, Laurie. Staff and head nurse Brookside Hosp., San Pablo, Calif., 1955-56, 57-58; staff nurse Babies Hosp., Columbia-Presbyn. Hosp., N.Y.C., 1956-57; public health staff and supr. Los Angeles County Health Dept., 1958-64; staff nurse ICU, supr., inservice dir. Albany (Oreg.) Gen. Hosp., 1969-75, dir. nursing service, 1975—; instr. coronary care course Community Coll., 1974-75; adv. com. asso. degree nursing program Linn Benton Community Coll. Active Campfire Girls, Willamette Council Girl Scouts U.S.A. Bank of Am. scholar, 1950-51. Mem. Nat. League for Nurses, Nat. Forum Adminstrs. of Nursing Services, Am. Assn. Critical Care Nurses, Am. Soc. Nursing Service Adminstrs., Oreg. Soc. Nursing Adminstrs. (past pres.), Albany C. of C. Republican. Methodist. Contbr. to Supr. Nurse. Home: 1030 NW Green Acres Rd Albany OR 97321 Office: 1046 W 6th Ave Albany OR 97321

REYNOLDS, PEGGY, newspaper executive; b. Takoma Park, Md.; d. Lewis H. and Minna (Abramson) Weiss; m. George Richard Reynolds, July 31, 1954; 1 son, Michael Alan. B.A. in Polit. Sci., U. Mich. Mgr., Aero Ins. Agy., Washington, 1947-55; reporter Washington Post, 1955-57; editor Mercer Island (Wash.) Reporter, 1967, pub., 1968—. Recipient Wash. Press Assn. Disting. Service award, 1975; John Fournier Meml. Award for Community Service, 1979. Mem. Soc. Profl. Journalists, Wash. Newspaper Pubs. Assn. Democrat. Home: 7727 SE 58th St Mercer Island WA 98040 Office: 21737 77th Ave SE PO Box 38 Mercer Island WA 98040

REYNOLDS, PETER JAMES, physicist; b. N.Y.C., Nov. 19, 1949; s. Rudolph and Lydia Mary (Schanzer) R.; m. Louise Perini, Aug. 7, 1982. A.B. in Physics, U. Calif.-Berkeley, 1971; Ph.D., MIT, 1979. Research assoc. and lectr. Boston U., 1979, asst. research prof., 1979—; mem. sci. staff Nat. Resource for Computation in Chemistry, Lawrence Berkeley Lab., U. Calif., 1980-81, mem. sci. staff materials and molecular research div., 1981—; lectr. in field. NSF fellow, 1971-74; IBM fellow, 1975; Lawrence Berkeley Lab. grantee, 1982-83 Mem. AAAS, Am. Phys. Soc., N.Y. Acad. Scis., Phi Beta Kappa, Sigma Xi. Lutheran. Contbr. chpts. to books and articles in field to profl. jours. Home: 127 Corbett Ave San Francisco CA 94114 Office: 1 Cyclotron Rd Lawrence Berkeley Lab U Calif Bldg 50D Berkeley CA 94720

REYNOLDS, RALPH ELVIN, psychology educator; b. Madison, Wis., Nov. 12, 1948; s. Elvin Walter and Elaine Mavis (Brager) R. B.A., U. Wis., 1971; M.A., Ariz. State U., 1975; Ph.D., U. Ill., 1979. Research assoc. U. Ill., Champaign, 1979-80; prof. ednl. studies and ednl. psychology U. Utah, Salt Lake City, 1980—. Served with USAF, 1971-75. Mem. Am. Ednl. Research Assn., Am. Psychol. Assn., Nat. Reading Conf. Presbyterian. Contbr. articles on psychology to profl. jours. Office: University of Utah 130 MBH Salt Lake City UT 84112

REYNOLDS, RAY THOMAS, planetary scientist; b. Lexington, Ky., Sept. 2, 1933; s. Oscar Ray and Margaret Louise (Gudgel) R.; m. Yolanda Maria de la Luz Gallegos, Oct. 15, 1962; children—Mark Andrew, Daniel Alan. B.S. in Chemistry, U. Ky., 1954, M.S. in Physics, 1960. Research scientist Am. Geog. Soc., Thule, Greenland, 1960-61, U. Calif., Los Alamos, N.Mex., 1961; chief theoretical students br. NASA Ames Research Ctr., Moffett Field, Ca., 1969-78, research scientist, 1962-69, 78—. Recipient Exceptional Sci. Achievement award NASA, 1980. Mem. Am. Geophys. Union, Am. Astron. Soc., Meteorol. Soc., AAAS (Newcombe prozo 1979), AIAA. Contbr. numerous sci. reports, abstracts, articles to profl. publs. Home: 1650 Shasta Ave San Jose CA 95128 Office: NASA Ames Research Theoretical Studies Br Moffett Field CA 94035

REYNOLDS, RICHARD D., medical center official; b. Miami, Okla., July 29, 1934; s. Charles Edward and Jennie Elenore (Pratt) R.; m. Carolyn Wilbanks, June 21, 1957; children—Michael, Steven, Marc; m. 2d, Kathryn I. Ellis, June 17, 1967. Student Denver U., 1963, Weber State U., 1970. With Swedish Med Center, Englewood, Colo., 1960—, dir. housekeeping, 1962—. Served with USAF, 1951-60; Korea. Recipient Outstanding Employee award Swedish Med. Center, 1970. Mem. Nat. Exec. Housekeepers Assn. Democrat. Home: 1021 W Stanford Pl Englewood CO 80110 Office: 501 E Hampden Ave Englewood CO 80110

REYNOLDS, RICHARD HENRY, art educator; b. N.Y.C., May 16, 1913; s. Raymond R. and Sarah Alice (Weeks) R.; m. Marjorie Merrihew Sharrer, Aug. 10, 1939; 1 dau., Barbara Gwynne Nagata. A.B., U. Calif., 1936; student U. Calif., Los Angeles, 1939, Mills Coll., 1940; M.A., Coll. Pacific, 1942; postgrad. Oreg. State U., 1962; D.F.A., Morningside Coll., Sioux City, Iowa, 1976. Window display artist Emporium, San Francisco, 1936-37. Foreman-Clark, 1937, Hastings Clothing Co., 1937-38; asst. chmn. div. arts and letters Stockton Jr. Coll., 1939-43; prof. art, chmn. dept. U. of the Pacific, 1948-73, sr. prof., 1973-80, prof. emeritus, 1980, faculty research lectr., 1960, chairman academic council (senate), 1967-68, chmn. president's task force on acad. programs, 1980; mem. Stockton Arts Commn., 1980-81; guest lectr. Alaska Meth. U., Liberal Arts Inst., Anchorage, 1962; lectr. in field; judge numerous competitive art exhbns.; judge art sect. Ariz. State Fair, 1971; one-man show (sculpture) John Muir Gallery, Modesto, Calif., 1956, (painting) Lanai Gallery, Sacramento, 1956, (polychromed wood-reliefs) Stockton Fine Arts Gallery, 1972, 74, U. Pacific Alumni House Gallery, 1972; mem. show, Five Artists, invited E. B. Crocker Gallery, Sacramento, 1956; sculpture accepted for national exhbn. 10th Ann. New Eng. Exhbn., New Canaan, Conn., 1958; invited exhibit sculpture Eric Locke Gallery, San Francisco, 3d Ann. West Coast Sculptors, 1960; exhibited painting Purdue U., 1966; 2-man show (with wife) Stockton Savs. Loan Bank Invitational, 1968; exhibited paintings at No. Calif. Arts Exhbn., Sacramento, 1970; exhibited selected paintings Mother Lode Art Assn. Annual Show, Sonora, Calif., 1968; commd. sculptures buildings and campus U. of the Pacific, 1958, 60, 62, 63, bronze relief Swenson Golf Course, Stockton, 1968, metal falcon sculpture Atwater (Calif.) High Sch., 4 foot bronze relief for Stockton Record Bldg., bronze plaque Quemado (N.Mex.) Library, 1973; TV and radio lectr., 1955—; pvt. architectural sculpture commns., 1956—; exhibited Da Vinci Internat. Exhbn., N.Y.C., 1970, U. Pacific, 1973, Modesto Jr. Coll., 1973, Unitarian Arts Festival, Stockton, 1976, Ann. Delta Art Assn. show, Pittsburgh, Calif., 1976, Stockton Art League Show, annually, 1976-80; judge Merced Art Assn., 1976. Bd. dirs. Stockton Art League, 1978-79 hon. bd. dirs. Stockton Symphony Ballet Assn., 1978—, San Joaquin Concert Ballet Assn.; mem. Stockton Arts Commn., 1980. Served as lt. (j.g.), U.S. Naval Res., active duty, 1943-46. Awarded prize in oils Spring Art Festival, Stockton Art League, 1951; Bronze medal sculpture, Oakland Art Gallery's Oil Painting-Sculpture Ann. Exhbn., 1952; Kingsley award for sculpture Crocker Art Gallery, Sacramento, 1952, 53, 79; San Joaquin Pioneer Museum, 1953; 2d prize, Nat. Mag. Cover Contest, 1957; sculpture prizes Unitarian Arts Festival, Stockton, 1959, 61; jurors mention Nat. Exhbn. Small Paintings, Tour Gallery Assos., 1962; hon. mention Stockton Art League, 1964, 68; Best of Show award, 2d prize (painting), honorable mentions in Calif. exhibitions, 1966; Transparent Painting award No. Calif. Spring Art Festival, 1968; Acrylic Painting award Unitarian Arts Festival, Stockton, 1968; purchase prize, painting Lodi Art Ann., Acampo, 1971, 79; 2d prize, painting San Joaquin County Fair and Expn., 1972, drawing and painting awards, 1974, 3d award, mixed media, 1981; 3 painting awards Stockton Art League Ann., 1974, purchase award, 1975; 1st prize sculpture San Joaquin County Fair and Expn. Art Show, 1976, 82; spl. award Crocker Kingsley Exhbn., 1982. 2d prize and hon. mention Bank of Stockton, 1976; 2d prize, other media San Joaquin County Fair, 1978; 2d award Lodi Spring Wine Show, 1982, 3d award, 1983; hon. mention Lodi Grape Festival and Nat. Wine Show, 1982; 2d award Unitarian Arts Festival, Stockton, 1982; hon. mention No. Calif. Arts, Inc. Exhbn., Sacramento, 1982; 2d award San Joaquin County Fair, also hon. mention, 1983; Order of Pacific award U. of Pacific, 1980, numerous others. Shell grantee, 1960. Life fellow International Inst. Arts and Letters, 1960. Mem. Coll. Art Assn. of Am., Pacific Arts Assn. (editor Journalette 1951-52; pres. No. Cal. sect. 1951-52), Stockton Art League (pres. 1952-53, 80-82), Nat. Art Edn. Assn. (nat. chmn. membership com. 1952-53), AAUP (v.p. local chpt. 1958-59), Nat. Soc. Lit. and Arts (charter), Navy League U.S. (dir. Stockton br. 1981-83), Phi Kappa Phi (pres.-elect 1980-81), Delta Epsilon, Phi Sigma Kappa, Phi Delta Kappa (emeritus). Episcopalian. Contbr. articles to art publs. Exhibitor paintings, sculptures. Home: 1656 W Longview Ave Stockton CA 95207

REYNOLDS, ROBERT HARRISON, export co. exec.; b. Mpls., Sept. 6, 1913; s. Clarence H. and Helen (Doyle) R.; student pub. schs., Vinton, Iowa; m. Gladys Marie Gaster, Apr. 7, 1934; 1 dau., Shirley Anne (Mrs. Frank S. Potestio); m. 2d, Viola E. Shimel, June 26, 1982. Export sales mgr., rolled products sales mgr. Colo. Fuel & Iron Corp., Denver, 1938-46; pres. Rocky Mountain Export Co., Inc., Denver, 1941—; pres. Projects Gen. Am., Inc., Denver, 1967—; dir. Electromedics, Inc. Club: Denver. Home: 580 S Clinton St Denver CO 80231 Office: 11100 Mississippi Ave Aurora CO 80012

REYNOLDS, THOMAS GEORGE, exec. and cons. engr.; b. Kalamazoo, Apr. 9, 1906; s. Henry Tinch and Katharine (Jirsa) R.; B.S. in Civil Engring., U. Ill., 1928; M.S. in Chem. Engring., Columbia, 1942; postgrad. N.Y. U., 1941-42; m. Edith B. Pillatt, Aug. 23, 1928; children—Thomas Gordon, Barbara Ann Reynolds Barney, Katharine Sylvia, Nancy Edith Reynolds Bartlit, Cynthia Rose Reynolds Seifert, Susan Victoria Reynolds Lister; m. 2d, Jannetje de Otter, Feb. 13, 1965. Design engr. Engring. Service Co., Aurora, Ill., 1928-29, Standard Oil Co. Ind., Whiting, 1929-32; asst. constrn. supt., constrn. engr. M. W. Kellogg Co., N.Y.C., 1932-34; asst. resident engr. Continental Oil Co., Ponca City, Okla., 1934-36, resident engr., Balt., 1936-37; sr. project and process engr. Foster Wheeler Corp., N.Y.C., 1937-42; research engr. Columbia U., 1942-43; sr. project and process engr. Kellex Corp., 1943-45; chief engr. J. F. Pritchard & Co., Kansas City, Mo., 1945-47, Universal Engring Co., Kansas City, Mo., 1947-48; chem. process engr. Research and Engring. div. Pitts. Consolidation Coal Co., 1947; sr. chem. process engr. United Engrs. & Constructors, Inc., 1948-51; exec. engr. Catalytic Inc., 1951-56; pres., cons. engr. Reynolds-Bohna & Co., Inc., Phila., 1956-60; project mgr. SunOlin Chem. Co., 1960-61; mgr. indsl. process div. Thatcher & Patient, Clayton, Mo., 1961-62; project mgr. Badger Co., 1962-64; project mgr. Arthur G. McKee & Co., Cleve., 1964-67; ind. cons. engr., 1964—. Fellow Am. Soc. C.E. (life); mem. Am. Inst. Chem. Engrs., Am. Chem. Soc., AAAS, Fedn. Am. Scientists, N.Y. Acad. Scis., Phi Lambda Upsilon, Tau Kappa Epsilon. Patentee in chem. engring. Home: 830 23d St Golden CO 80401

RHETT, WILLIAM MEANS SMITH, marketing executive, consultant; b. Miami Beach, Fla., Jan. 25, 1930; s. Haskell Smith and Eunice (Emery) R.; m. Ethelyn Eddy, May 29, 1965; children—Ian Christopher, Allison Wingate; m. Mary Frances Amill, Jan. 1, 1980. A.B., Hamilton Coll., 1952; M.B.A., Harvard U., 1957. Account group exec. McCann-Erickson Internat., N.Y.C., 1957-60; dir., chief client services Colón S.A., Madrid, 1960-61; mgr. market devel. and advt. Motorola Overseas Corp., Chgo., 1962-66; account mgr. Marsteller Internat., N.Y.C., 1966-67; area dir. Latin Am. Wells, Rich, Greene Internat., Lima, Peru, 1968-69, account supr., N.Y.C., 1968-70; v.p. Mktg. Control Inc., N.Y.C., 1971-73, cons., 1971-73; internat. mktg. mgr. Consumer Products div. Nat. Semicondr. Corp., Sunnyvale, Calif., 1974-75; mng. dir. Intermarkets Ltd., Orinda, Calif., 1975—; exec. v.p. CSA Inc., San Mateo, Calif., 1982-83; dir.-at-large Internat. Advt. Assocs., 1966-68; founder Midwest Internat. Mktg. Caucus, 1965. Pres. alumni No. Calif. Hamilton Coll., 1983, pres. midwest alumni, 1964-66, mem. alumni career counseling com., 1976-82. Served to comdr. USNR, 1954-78; Korea. Mem. San Francisco Advt. Club, Internat. Advt. Assn., U.S. Naval Inst. Republican. Episcopalian. Clubs: Harvard U. Bus. Sch. No. Calif.; Am. of Madrid, Hamilton of N.Y., Lawn Tennis (Lima and Stamford, Conn.), Yacht, Marines Meml. (San Francisco), Contbr. articles to profl. jours. Office: PO Box 141 Moraga CA 94556

RHEW, KI-WON, information processing systems executive; b. Kyunggi-Do, Korea, June 16, 1939; s. Cheol-Seop and Sang-Soon (Nahm) R.; came to U.S., 1967; B.S. in Physics, Yonsei U., Seoul, 1963; M.S., U. Oreg., 1972; m. Young-Keun Song, Feb. 17, 1968; children—Miriam M., Isaac C. Jr. Engr. El-Jay, Inc., Eugene, Oreg., 1972, systems analyst/programmer, 1973—, data processing project leader, 1977-78, supr. data processing, 1978-79, mgr. info. processing systems, 1979-80; instr. Korean lang. Lane Community Coll., Eugene, 1976-77, instr. prodn. and inventory control mgmt., 1980—; mng. partner Pacific Info. Processors of Oreg., Eugene, 1981-82, pres., 1982—. Served as officer Korean Army, 1963-65. Mem. Am. Phys. Soc., Data Processing Mgmt. Assn., Digital Equipment Computer Users Soc., Am. Prodn. and Inventory Control Soc. (cert. in prodn. and inventory mgmt.), Assn. for Computing Machinery. Presbyterian. Home: 1661 Stoney Ridge Rd Eugene OR 97405 Office: 2468 W 11th St Suite 7 Eugene OR 97402

RHINEHART, DERRELL LEE, optometrist; b. Belen, N.Mex., July 29, 1935; s. James Bonar and Dolores (Gilbertson) R.; m. Charlene Lenore Jones; children—Sandra Rhinehart Trevison, Linda Rhinehart Riner, James, Charles. B.A., U. Kans., 1959; B.S., U. Calif., 1962, O.D., 1964. Pvt. practice optometry, Escondido, Calif., 1964—; instr. pub. health Community Coll. Calif., 1976—; cons. optometry Project Concern Hosp., Tijuana, Mex.; sight conservation chmn. Lions Club, 1972. Mem. Am. Optometric Assn., Calif. Optometric Assn., Sports Vision Inc., Coll. Optometry in Vision Devel., San Diego County Optometric Soc. (dir. 1972-77, pres. 1977). Bd. dirs. Valley Center (Calif.) Community Ch. Office: 1299 E Pennsylvania St Escondido CA 92027

RHOADES, GEORGE FRANKLIN, JR., counselor, educator; b. Parsons, W.Va., July 26, 1956; s. George Franklin and Hazel Carrie (Maxwell) R.; m. Adela Baniaga, Dec. 19, 1976; children—Christopher, Shannon M. B.A. in liberal Arts, Hawaii Pacific Coll., 1977; M.A. in Clin. Counseling Psychology, Western Conservative Baptist Sem., 1981, Ph.D. in Clin. Counseling Psychology, 1983. Effectiveness evaluator and researcher Honolulu Community Coll., 1977; counselor Son Village, Wemme, Oreg., 1979; practicum counselor Psychol. and Counseling Services Ctr., Portland, Oreg., 1979-81; doctoral intern in psychology Oreg. State Hosp., Salem, 1981-82; doctoral intern in clin. psychology Ctr. Student Devel., U. Hawaii, Honolulu, 1982-83; instr. in psychology Internat. Coll., Honolulu; pvt. practice in marital and family counseling Wahiawa, Hawaii; counselor Oreg. Bapt. Retirement Home, Portland, 1979-80, Faith Bapt. Counseling Services, Portland, 1980-81. Atherton Family Found. grantee, 1979-81; Chung Kun Ai Found. scholar, 1981-83. Mem. Am. Personnel and Guidance Assn., Christian Assn. Psychol. Studies, Hawaii Psychol. Assn., Luria Study Group, Oreg. Neuropsychol. Study Group. Republican. Home: 95-155 Waimakua Pl Wahiawa HI 96786 Office: 302 California Ave Suite 211 Wahiawa HI 96786 also 803 Kamehameha Hwy Suite 411 Pearl City HI 96782

RHOADES, HAROLD EMERSON, exec. recruiter; b. Los Angeles, Aug. 9, 1912; s. George William and Elizabeth Florence (Heed) R.; student U. So. Calif., 1935-42; m. Marvel T. Smith, July 6, 1950; children—Linda Lee, Richard Alan. Dist. mgr. Nat. Cylinder Gas Co., San Francisco, 1936-56; sales mgr. F. Somers Peterson Co., 1956-58; v.p. Cepco, Inc., San Francisco, 1959-68; owner Calif. Galleries, Bolinas, 1968-72; account exec. Mgmt. Recruiters, San Francisco, 1972-75; v.p., sec.-treas., dir. Hughes Rhoades, Inc., San Francisco, 1975—. Bd. dirs. Great Western U., San Francisco, 1975—. Served with USCGR, 1943-45; mem. USCG Aux., 1956—. Mem. San Francisco Underwriters Forum, San Francisco Inland Marine Forum. Republican. Club: Bohemian (San Francisco). Home: 23350 Fuller Ave Hayward CA 94541 Office: 649 Mission St San Francisco CA 94105

RHOADS, CHERYL M. (SHERRY), public relations and advt. cons.; b. Bklyn., Oct. 28, 1947; d. Alton Norman Greenblatt and Isabel (Leeman) Marcus; student U. Nevada, 1964-67, U. Alaska, 1978-81; m. James Lane Rhoads, Oct. 29, 1965; children—Cedric, Michelle, Matthew. Sec., receptionist Hughes-Nevada Ops., Las Vegas, 1968-69; sec. Samaritan Health Service, Phoenix, 1969-72; info. specialist Trans Alaska Pipeline, Anchorage, 1972-78; account exec. Studio 8 Advt., Anchorage, 1978-79; v.p. mktg. Delta Cos., Anchorage, 1979; owner Serendipity Advt., Serendipity Gifts, Anchorage; ptnr. Kyle-Rhoads Pub. Relations, Anchorage; exec. dir. The New Anchorage Network. Mem. Women in Bus., Anchorage C. of C., Alaska Press Club, Alaska Press Women (regional dir. 1980-81; 1st place award TV advt. 1981), Public Relations Soc. Am., Nat. Fedn. Press Women (3d place award in advt. 1981), Advt. Fedn. Alaska. Jewish. Club: Anchorage Woman's. Home: SRA Box 2040-C Anchorage AK 95507 Office: Serendipity Services 2600 Denali St Denali Towers S Suite 102 Anchorage AK 99503 also Serendipity Services Inc 2958 Johnson St NE Suite 3 Minneapolis MN 55418 also Kyle-Rhoads Pub Relations 810 W 2d Ave Anchorage AK 99501

RHOADS, HOWARD, consulting agronomist, educator; b. Carterville, Mont., Mar. 20, 1926; s. Solomon Edgar and Sarah Maystella R.; B.S. in Agronomy, Mont. State U., Bozeman, 1951, M.S., 1952; m. Evelyn Jean Gee, July 2, 1948; children—Michael H., Kathryn Jean. Fieldman, Gt. Western Sugar Co., Billings, Mont., 1952-53; instr. Mont. State U., Bozeman, 1953-56; intermediate instr. crop sci. Calif. Poly. State U., San Luis Obispo, 1956, prof. crop sci., 1970-83, chmn. acad. senate, 1971-72; ret., 1983; acad. cons. Calif. State Employees Assn., 1968-69.; bd. dirs., 1974-77. Served with USNR, 1943-46. Recipient various grants including Assn. on Gasohol, 1980—; lic. pest control advisor, Calif. Mem. Am. Soc. Agronomy, Crop Sci. Soc. Am., Weed Sci. Soc. Am., Calif. Agrl Tchrs., Calif. Weed Conf. (pres., 1972), Western Soc. Weed Sci., AAUP, AAAS, Congress of Faculty Assos., Sigma Xi, Phi Kappa Phi. Republican. Clubs: Elks (San Luis Obispo), Toastmasters (pres. San Luis Obispo 1964-65, asst. area gov., 1965-66). Reviewer, Agronomy Jour., 1974; author various lab. manuals in crops sci. and weed sci.; songwriter country-western music. Office: Crop Science Dept California Poly State U San Luis Obispo CA 93407

RHODE, JANICE SUZANNE, campgrounds executive; b. Kansas City, Mo., Apr. 14, 1931; d. Marlin Eugene and Margaret Adeline (Weddle) Arrasmith; m. Harold Thomas Rhode, Jr., Mar. 25, 1951; children—Debra Ann Rhode Combs, Kevin Michael. Student William Woods Coll., 1949; A.A., Graceland Coll., 1950; student LaSalle Extension U., 1981. Sec., Am. Polled Hereford Assn., Kansas City, Mo., 1961-75; asst. librarian govt. documents div. Graceland Coll., Lamoni, Iowa, 1969-71; coordinator KOA-U of Kampgrounds of Am. Inc., 1975-80, dir. corp. offices, 1980—. Mem. Am. Soc. Tng. Devel. Republican. Mormon. Office: Kampgrounds of Am Inc PO Box 30558 Billings MT 59114

RHODES, ANNE LOU, social service adminstr., mgmt. analyst; b. Richmond, Ind., Oct. 9, 1935; d. George E. and Margaret (Jones) R.; B.A., Whittier Coll., 1957; M.S.W., Fresno State Coll. Sch. Social Work, 1968. Social worker San Bernardino (Calif.) County Welfare Dept., 1959-62, social work supr.I, 1962-63, social work supr.II, 1963-68, social service supr. III, 1968—. Instr. social welfare U. Calif. at Riverside, 1969; cons. headstart program Riverside County Econ. Opportunity Bd., 1970, Delman Heights Welfare Rights Orgn., 1968-71; participant German profl. minority exchange program, 1979, Statehouse Conf. on Children and Youth, 1979; mem. Calif. Com. on Credentials, 1980. Bd. dirs. Inland Area Adolescent Clinic, 1970—; mem. task force YWCA, 1976; bd. dirs. Inland Area Urban League, 1970-71, v.p. leadership devel., 1970-71; bd. dirs. Arrowhead United Way, 1980. Mem. NAACP (pres. 1960-61), Acad. Certified Social Workers, LWV of San Bernardino (pres. 1981-82), Nat. Urban League (mem. com. 1970-71), Friends Welfare Rights Orgn., League of Women Voters of San Bernardino (2d v.p. 1976-77), Nat. Council Negro Women, Alpha Tau Chi (dir. 1979-80). Home: 5710 Belvedere Ave Highland CA 92346 Office: City Hall San Bernardino CA 92418

RHODES, CECIL GLENN, metallurgist; b. Leesville, Ohio, Oct. 17, 1933; s. Lloyd Howard and Sibyl Imogene (Price) R.; B.S. in Math., Calif. State U., Northridge, 1968; m. Lois Irene Spellman, Jan. 1, 1953; children—Pamela Kay, Diane Christine. Metallographer, Battelle Meml. Inst., Columbus, Ohio, 1953-56, Gen. Electric Co., Cin., 1956-59; mem. tech. staff Rockwell Internat. Co., Thousand Oaks, Calif., 1959—. Mem. AIME (publns. com. Metall. Soc.), Electron Microscopy Soc. Am., So. Calif. Electron Microscopy Soc. Author papers in field. Office: PO Box 1085 Rockwell Internat Co Thousand Oaks CA 91360

RHODES, FEN, academic administrator, industrial psychologist; b. Jackson, Miss., Oct. 18, 1935; s. Fentress and Irene Gray (Kyser) R.; m. Mary Chilton McNeil, Feb. 21, 1961 (div.); children—Neil, Carolyn, Richard; m. 2d, Nancy Hawkins Corby, Nov. 26, 1977. B.S., Ga. Inst. Tech., 1956; M.S., George Washington U., 1961; Ph.D., Ohio State U., 1964. Research psychologist Aerospace Med. Research Labs., Wright-Patterson AFB, Dayton, Ohio, 1963-64; engring. psychologist Hughes Aircraft Co., Culver City and Fullerton, Calif., 1964-67; asst. prof. to prof. psychology Calif. State U.-Long Beach, 1964—, assoc. dean Sch. Social and Behavioral Scis., 1977—; mgmt. cons. Taco Bell, Torrance, Calif., 1967-69; field supr. Psychol. Corp., N.Y.C., 1971-73, 76-77. Mem. Am. Psychol. Assn. Contbr. articles profl. jours. Office: Calif State U Long Beach CA 90840

RHODES, GEORGE FORREST, JR., economics educator; b. Ogden, Utah, Aug. 3, 1947; s. George Forest and Barbara Joan (Miller) R.; m. Joan Ann Maddox, June 2, 1969; children—Heather, Natalie, Matthew, Adam. B.S. cum laude, Brigham Young U., 1971; M.S., Tex. A&M U., 1973, Ph.D., 1974. Asst. prof. econs. Ohio State U., 1974-78; assoc. prof. Colo. State U., 1978-82, prof., 1982—; cons. in field; lectr. in field. Grantee in field. Mem. Am. Econs. Assn., Am. Statis. Assn., Sigma Xi, Phi Kappa Phi. Mormon. Contbr. articles in field to profl. jours. Office: B-308 Clark Bldg Colorado State University Fort Collins CO 80523

RHODES, THOM, advertising agency executive; b. Coronado, Calif., Mar. 17, 1936; s. Herbert Cecil and Olga (Olsen) R. B.A. in Theatre Arts, Carnegie-Mellon U., 1956. Acct. dir. Skyline Advt. Ltd.-Afmal Ltd. Nairobi, Kenya, 1959-60, London, 1960-62; assoc. media dir. J. Walter Thompson, San Francisco, 1965-68; supr. broadcast activity Ketchum, MacLeod & Grove, Inc., Pitts., 1968-69; media cons., N.Y.C., 1969-71; v.p., dir. media ops. Spitzer, Mills & Bates, Ltd., Toronto, Ont., Can., 1972-74; v.p., media dir. Wilson, Haight & Welch, Inc., Hartford, Conn., 1974-78; v.p., assoc. media dir. D'Arcy-MacManus & Masius, Inc., St. Louis, 1978-79, v.p., mgr. corporate media planning, Chgo., 1979-80; v.p., acct. supr. Needham, Harper & Steers, Inc., Los Angeles, 1981-82; v.p. media Earle Palmer Brown, Bethesda, Md., 1982-83; sr v.p., dir. media Eisaman, Johns & Laws, Inc., Los Angeles, 1983—; guest lectr. UCLA, San Francisco City Coll., U. Toronto, U. Hartford, others. Mem. Internat. Radio and TV Soc., Nat. Acad. TV Arts and Scis., Internat. Platform Assn., Can. Media Dirs. Council, Sigma Nu. Office: 6255 Sunset Blvd Los Angeles CA 90028

RHODES, WAYNE LEON, service company administrator; b. Lamar, Mo., Aug. 1, 1922; s. John Elmer and Ellen (Thomas) R.; m. Colleen Joy Ready, Oct. 5, 1968; children—Terry, Janice, Richard, Joseph, Mark. Student UCLA, 1970. Salesman, Sears, Kansas City, Mo., 1941-46; engr. clk. Frank Horton Cons. Engrs., Lamar, Mo., 1946-47; assembler Douglas Co., Long Beach, Mo., 1947-49; refinery operator Union Oil, Wilmington, Calif., 1949-54; ins. salesman Farmers Ins. Group, Los Angeles, 1954-57, div. agy. mgr., 1957-63; owner, operator Badillo Arcade, Covina, Calif., 1963-68; personnel counselor Pro-Teen Agy., Temple City, Calif., 1968-69; laundry mgr. Inter-Community, Covina, Calif., 1969-71; linen services mgr. Beverly Hosp., Montebello, Calif., 1971—. Served with U.S. Army, 1943-45. Mem. Nat. Assn. Instl. Laundry Mgrs., So. Calif. Instl. Laundry Mgrs. Assn., Western Hosp. Assn. Democrat. Roman Catholic. Home: 514 N Sunset Ave West Covina CA 91790 Office: Beverly Hosp 309 W Beverly Blvd Montebello CA 90640

RHODEWALT, FREDERICK THOMAS, psychologist, educator, researcher; b. Upper Darby, Pa., Mar. 23, 1949; s. Thomas Walter and Loretta (Bahler) R.; m. Elaine Sue Soliwoda, May 17, 1975; 1 son, Stefan Thomas. B.A. in Psychology magna cum laude with honors, Lincoln U., 1975; M.A. in Social Psychology, Princeton U., 1977, Ph.D., 1979. Lectr., research assoc. Princeton U., 1979-80; asst. prof. psychology U. Utah, 1980—. NIH Biomed. Research Support grantee, 1981-82, 82-83; Utah Heart Assn. grantee, 1982-83. Mem. Am. Psychol. Assn., Soc. Advancement Social Psychology. Contbr. articles to profl. jours.; issue cons. Jour. Personality and Social Psychology, Psychol. Bull. Home: 5364 S Baldwin Park Murray UT 84107 Office: Dept Psychology U Utah Salt Lake City UT 84112

RHODY, RONALD E., public relations executive; b. Frankfort, Ky., Jan. 27, 1932; m. Patricia Ann Schupp; 4 children. Student Georgetown Coll., 1950-52, U. Ky., 1953-55. City editor Frankfort State Jour., 1952-54; news dir. Sta. WFKY, 1954-55; dir. pub. relations dept. Commonwealth of Ky., 1955-59; mgr. pub. relations Kaiser Aluminum & Chem. Corp., N.Y., 1959-67, mgr. corp. communications, Oakland, Calif., 1967-72, dir. pub. affairs and pub. relations, 1972, corp. v.p. domestic and internat. pub. relations and advt., 1976-83; sr. v.p. Corp. Communications div. Bank of Am., San Francisco, 1983—; adv. U. Calif. Grad. Sch. Bus. Vice pres. Cory Brythoniaid of Blaenau Ffestiniog, Wales; bd. dirs. Oakland Ballet Co. Named Pub. Relations Profl. of Yr., Pub. Relations News, 1981. Mem. Media Inst. (bd. trustees), Aluminum Assn. (chmn. communications policy com.), Advt. Council (bd. dirs. Western region), Internat. Pub. Relations Inst. (council), Pub. Relations Roundtable (San Francisco), Pub. Relations Soc. Am. Advisor Pub. Relations News. Office: Corp Communications Bank of Am Suite 3400 San Francisco CA 94137

RHOLL, KEITH NORRIS, marriage and family therapist, psychology educator; b. Lake Mills, Iowa, July 20, 1917; s. Clarence Gustav and Vera (Howes) R.; m. Estelle Ruth Peterson, Dec. 28, 1944; children—Carolyn, Kenneth. B.A., Hamline U., St. Paul, 1947; S.T.B., Boston U., 1951; Ph.D., U. So. Calif., 1968. Lic. marriage, family, and child counselor, Calif. Asst. dir. counseling Am. Inst. Family Relations, Los Angeles, 1958-65; asst. prof. social psychology Whittier (Calif.) Coll., 1965—; sr. cons. Peterson-Guedel Family Counseling and Research Ctr., Beverly Hills, Calif., 1968-82; pvt. practice marriage and family therapy, Whittier, Calif., 1958—. Chmn. bd. dirs. Project Info., Whittier; chmn. San Gabriel (Calif.) Liaison Com. for Mental Health; chmn. Whittier Dist. Citizens Adv. Com. for Mental Health. Fellow Calif. Assn. Marriage and Family Therapists (Clark Vincent award 1980); mem. So. Calif. Assn. Marriage and Family Therapists (bd. dirs.), Am. Assn. Marriage and Family Therapy, Calif. Assn. Marriage and Family Therapists, Am. Sociol. Assn., Pacific Sociol. Assn., Nat. Council Family Relations. Mem. United Ch. of Christ. Club: Lions (Whittier). Editor, Marriage and Family Counselors Quar., 1972-79. Office: 15844 E Russell St Whittier CA 90603

RIACH, DOUGLAS ALEXANDER, sales exec.; b. Victoria, B.C., Can., Oct. 8, 1919; s. Alex and Gladys (Provis) R.; came to U.S., 1925, naturalized, 1942; student U. Calif. at Los Angeles, 1937-38, Fenn Coll., 1959, Grad. Sch. Sales Mgmt. and Mktg., 1960, U.S. Army Command and Gen. Staff Coll., 1966, Armed Forces Staff Coll., 1968; m. Eleanor Montague, Mar. 28, 1942; 1 dau., Sandra Jean. Field rep. Gen. Motors Acceptance Corp., 1940-41, 46-47; with Ridings Motors, 1947-48; with Gen. Foods Corp., 1948-80, ter. sales mgr., San Francisco, 1962-80; with Mel-Williams Co., 1980—. Asst. scoutmaster Boy Scouts Am., Los Angeles, 1936-39, asst. dist. commr., 1940-41; co-chmn. Long Beach Tournament Roses, 1947. Served to capt. AUS, 1941-46; ret. col. Res. Decorated Bronze Star with V and cluster, Legion of Merit, Purple Heart, Combat Infantryman's badge; Medaille de la France Liberee (France); Commemorative War Cross (Yugoslavia); knight Order of the Compassionate Heart (Russia); knight Sovereign Mil. Order, Temple of Jerusalem; named to U.S. Army Inf. Hall of Fame, 1982. Mem. Long Beach Food Sales Assn. (pres. 1950), Asso. Grocers Mfrs. Reps. (dir. 1955), Am. Security Council (nat. adv. bd. 1975—), Res. Officers Assn. (San Francisco presidio pres. 1974-76, v.p. 1977-82, v.p. dept. Calif. 1979, exec. v.p. 1980, pres. 1981, nat. councilman 1981-82), Assn. U.S. Army (gov. East Bay chpt. 1974—), Jr. C. of C. Republican. Presbyterian. Clubs: Elks, Exchange (v.p. Long Beach 1955); Merchandising Execs. (dir. 1970-75, sec. 1976-77, v.p. 1978-79, pres. 1980) (San Francisco), Commonwealth of Calif. (nat. def. sect. vice chmn. 1964-66, chmn. 1967-72). Home: 2609 Trousdale Dr Burlingame CA 94010 Office: 2406 Merced St San Leandro CA 94577

RIBBLE, JAMES M(ERRITT), clergyman, educational administrator; b. Duluth, Minn., Mar. 11, 1932; s. Christian Merritt and Eva Agnes (Rivers) R.; B.A., Carroll Coll., 1953; M.A., U. Minn., 1959; M.Ed., Gonzaga U., 1962; Ed.D., Northwestern U., 1964; Ph.D., Wash. State U., 1976. Ordained priest Roman Catholic Ch., 1957; vocation dir. Diocese of Spokane (Wash.), 1957-68; rector Mater Clari Sem., 1960-68; pres. De Sales Prep. Sch., Walla Walla, 1968-70; mem. faculty Wash. State U., 1970-76; pres.-rector Mt. Angel Sem., 1976-82; rector Our Lady of Lourdes Cathedral, Spokane, 1982—; mem. Wash. Gov.'s Com. Higher Edn., Wash. Gov.'s Commn. on Cultural Affairs; pres. Diocese of Spokane Priests Senate; bd. dirs. Nat. Fedn. Priests Councils; chmn. bd. Mater Dei Inst. Mem. Phi Beta Kappa (Spl. award 1975). Clubs: K.C., Foresters, Elks. Author: Teacher-Student Interaction from Developmental Perspective, 1976. Office: Our Lady of Lourdes Cathedral West Riverside Spokane WA 99204

RIBBLE, PETER S., photographer, fireman; b. Palo Alto, Calif., Dec. 1, 1951; s. Marion C. and Doris L. (Goodman) R.; m. Debra K. Schell, Nov. 9, 1974; children—Justin, Aaron; student microbiology Oreg. State U., 1970-73. Cert. emergency med. technician Oreg. Fire lt. City of Bend (Oreg.), 1973—; owner, photographer, Backcountry Photography (name changed to Mirror Pond Photographics 1980), 1976—; instr. beginning and advanced photography. Mem. Profl. Photographers Am. (1979—), Profl. Photographers Oreg. (1978—). Republican. Lutheran. Home: 424 NW Riverside Bend OR 97701 Office: 1019 NW Brooks Bend OR 97701

RICARDI, LEON JOSEPH, electrical engineer, educator; b. Brockton, Mass., Mar. 21, 1924; s. Philip Julius and Eva Isabel (DuBois) R.; m. Angelena M. Giorgio, Jan. 19, 1947; children—Eva Marie Ricardi Mauer, John Philip, Richard Christopher. B.S.E.E., Northeastern U., 1949, M.S.E.E., 1952, Ph.D. in Elec. Engring., 1969. Registered profl. engr., Mass. Project engr. Andrew Alford Cons. Engr., Boston, 1949-51; sr. engr. Gabriel Labs., Needham, Mass., 1951; group leader Lincoln Lab., MIT, Lexington, Mass., 1951-82, head tech. adv. office, Los Angeles, 1982—; mem. faculty Northeastern U. Served with USAAF, 1943-45. Fellow IEEE; mem. Tau Beta Pi, Eta Kappa Nu. Roman Catholic. Home: 750 W Sycamore Ave El Segundo CA 90244 Office: MIT Lincoln Lab Los Angeles Air Force Sta Los Angeles CA 90009

RICARDO-CAMPBELL, RITA, economist, educator; b. Boston, Mar. 26, 1920; d. David and Elizabeth (Jones) Ricardo; B.S., Simmons Coll., 1941; M.A., Radcliffe Coll., 1945, Ph.D., 1946; m. Wesley Glenn Campbell, Sept. 15, 1946; children—Barbara Lee, Diane Rita, Nancy Elizabeth. Instr., Harvard U., Cambridge, 1946-48; asst. prof. Tufts U., Medford, Mass., 1948-51; labor economist U.S. Wage Stabilization Bd., 1951-53; economist ways and means com. U.S. Ho. of Reps., 1953; cons. economist, 1957-60; vis. prof. San Jose State Coll., 1960-61; sr. fellow Hoover Instn. on War Revolution and Peace, Stanford, 1968—; lectr. Health Service Adminstrn., Stanford Med. Sch., 1973-78; dir. Watkins-Johnson Co., Palo Alto, Calif., Gillette Co., Boston. Commr. Western Interstate Commn. for Higher Edn. Calif., 1967-75, chmn. 1970-71; mem. Pres. Nixon's Adv. Council on Status Women, 1969-76; mem. task force on taxation Pres. Council on Environ. Quality, 1970-72; mem. Pres. Com. Health Services Industry, 1971-73, FDA Nat. Adv. Drug Com., 1972-75; mem. Pres. Reagan's Econ. Policy Adv. Bd., 1981—. Bd. dirs. Ind. Colls. No. Calif., 1971—; mem. com. assessment of safety, benefits, risks Citizens Commn. Sci., Law and Food Supply, Rockefeller U., 1973-75; mem. adv. com. Ctr. Health Policy Research, Am. Enterprise Inst. Pub. Policy Research, Washington, 1974-80; mem. adv. council on social security Social Security Adminstrn., 1974-75; bd. dirs. Simmons Coll. Corp., Boston, 1975-80; mem. adv. council bd. assocs. Stanford Libraries, 1975-78; mem. council SRI Internat., Menlo Park, Calif., 1977—. Mem. Am. Econ. Assn., Nat. Council on Humanities, Mont Pelerin Soc., Phi Beta Kappa. Author: Voluntary Health Ins. in the United States, 1960; Economics of Health and Public Policy, 1971; Food Safety Regulation: Use and Limitations of Cost-Benefit Analysis, 1974; Drug Lag: Federal Government Decision Making, 1976; Social Security: Promise and Reality, 1977; The Economics and Politics of Health, 1982; contbr. articles to profl. jours. Home: 26915 Alejandro Dr Los Altos Hills CA 94022 Office: Hoover Instn Stanford CA 94305

RICCA, ANTONIO DOMENCIO, commercial photographer; b. Escondido, Calif., Mar. 10, 1919; s. Guiseppe S. and Emilia (Caesare) R.; m. Dorothy R. Norlin, July 27, 1960. Student N.Y. Inst. Photography, Mortensen's Sch. Photography, 1940-41, Winona Sch. Profl. Photography, 1958, 60; M. Photography, Profl. Photographers Am., 1965. Freelance photographer San Diego area, 1936-41; owner photog. studio Escondido, Calif., 1941-43, 45—, Hollywood, Calif., 1944; ofcl. photographer San Diego County Fair, 1956-58; adult edn. tchr. photography Escondido High Sch., 1952-54; judge Internat. Photography Exhibit, Los Angeles County Fair, 1961-62. Pres. Escondido Grape Day Assn., 1947. Named Photographic Craftsman, 1968. Mem. Profl. Photographers Am. (25 year club 1973, Nat. Dirs. award 1977, life mem.) Profl. Photographers Assn. San Diego County (pres. 1957, life mem.). Roman Catholic. Contbr. photography articles to nat. mags.

RICE, BARBARA POLLAK, advt. and mktg. co. exec.; b. Ft. Scott, Kans., Nov. 11, 1937; d. Olin N. and Jeanette E. (Essen) Brigman; student N. Central Coll., 1955, Elmhurst Coll., 1956; B.A. in Communications, Calif. State U., Fullerton, 1982; m. Stanley Rice, Apr. 28, 1978; 1 dau., Beverly Johnson. Art dir. Gonterman & Assos., St. Louis, 1968-71; advt. mgr. Passpoint Corp., St. Louis, 1971-73; advt., pub. relations mgr. Permaneer Corp., St. Louis, 1973-74; advt. cons., advt. mgr. Hydro-Air Engring., Inc., St. Louis, 1974-76; mgr. mktg. services Hollytex Carpet Mills subs. U.S. Gypsum Co., City of Industry, Calif., 1976-79; pres. B.P. Rice & Co., Downey, Calif., 1979—. Recipient Designer Best Exhibit award Nat. Farm Builders Trade Show. Mem. Am. Advt. Fedn., Los Angeles Advt. Women (pres., dir.), Bus. Profl. Advt. Assn., Beta Sigma Phi (past pres., outstanding mem.). Author: Truss Construction Manual, 1975. Home: 8178 Havasu Circle Buena Park CA 90621 Office: 8321 3d Ave Suite D Downey CA 90241

RICE, CLEVE ARCHIBALD, rancher, former airline pilot; b. St. Anthony, Idaho, Mar. 25, 1936; s. Rawleigh Cleveland and Eva (Archibald) R.; B.S. in Agrl. Econs., Utah State U., 1959; student Ricks Coll., 1954-55; m. Peggy Jean Dowdle, May 11, 1956 (div. 1973); children—Mikel Gail, Julee Ann, Mindy Sue, Angelee, David; m. 2d Marcella Rose Usselman, June 24, 1974. Pilot, United Airlines, 1964, 2nd officer, 1965-67, 1st officer, 1968-79, capt. B-727's, Chgo., 1979-81, medically ret., 1981; farmer, rancher, 1981—; dir. Farmers Friend Canal Co., 1980—, pres., 1981—. Served with USAF, 1959-64. Mem. Air Line Pilots Assn., Idaho Farm Bur. Republican. Mormon. Address: RFD 1 PO Box 22 Saint Anthony ID 83445

RICE, CONDOLEEZZA, political science educator; b. Birmingham, Ala., Nov. 14, 1954; d. John Wesley and Angelena (Ray) R. B.A. cum laude, U. Denver, 1974, Ph.D. (Nat. Fellowship Fund fellow, Ford Found. fellow), 1981; M.A., Notre Dame U., 1975. Intern U.S. Dept. State, 1977; intern Rand Corp., Santa Monica, Calif., 1980, cons., 1980—; cons. Sci. Applications Inc., Denver, 1980—; asst. prof. polit. sci. Stanford U. (Calif.), 1981—, asst. dir. arms control program, 1981—; speaker arms control, internat. relations. Mem. Am. Polit. Sci. Assn., Internat. Polit. Sci Assn. (del. World Congress, Moscow 1979), All-Univ. Seminar Armed Forces and Soc., Phi Beta Kappa, Alpha Chi Omega. Presbyterian. Author: The Politics of Client Command: Party-Military Relations in the Soviet Bloc, 1983. Office: Dept Polit Sci Bldg 160 Stanford U Stanford CA 94305

RICE, DOROTHY PECHMAN, medical economist, statistician; b. Bklyn., June 11, 1922; d. Gershon and Lena (Schiff) Pechman; m. John D. Rice, Apr. 3, 1943; children—Kenneth D., Donald B., Thomas H. Student Bklyn. Coll., 1938-39; B.A., U. Wis., 1941; Sc.D. (hon.), Coll. Medicine and Dentistry N.J., 1979. Statis. clk. Dept. Labor, Washington, 1941-42; economist War Prodn. Bd., Washington, 1942-44; labor economist War Labor Bd., Washington, 1945-47; health economist USPHS, Washington, 1947-49; analyst, chief health ins. research br. Social Security Adminstrn., Washington, 1960-65, dep. asst. commr. for research and stats., 1965-72; dir. Nat. Ctr. for Health Stats., Hyattsville, Md., 1976-82; Regent's lectr., dept. social and behavioral scis. Sch. of Nursing, U. Calif.-San Francisco, 1982—. Recipient Jack C. Massey award, 1978; Federally Employed Women Disting. Service award, 1982; Asst. Sec. for Health Spl. Recognition award, 1982; Presdl. Sr. Exec. Meritorious award, 1982. Fellow Am. Statis. Assn., Inst. of Medicine of Nat. Acad. Scis.; mem. Am. Econ. Assn., Am. Pub. Health Assn. (Democratic award for excellence 1978), AAUW, LWV. Democrat. Jewish. Contbr. articles in field to profl. jours. Home: 1055 Amito Ave Berkeley CA 94705 Office: School of Nursing N631 University of California San Francisco CA 94143

RICE, EDWARD WILLIAM, med. mgmt. cons.; b. Great Falls, Mont., July 24, 1911; s. Robert William and Laura (Martin) R.; B.A. in Econs., U. Kans., 1935, LL.B., 1938, J.D., 1968; m. Patricia Murray Arnold, July 20, 1940; children—Barbara Beth, Cathy Marie. Admitted to Kans. bar, 1938; with credit dept. Internat. Harvester Co., Chgo., 1938-42; sr. price adminstr. Idaho State Office OPA, 1942-43; med. mgmt. cons., Boise, Idaho, 1947—; pres. Doctors Bus. Bur., Profl. Adjustment Co. Mem. Boise Civil Service Commn., 1948-50, 61-63; city councilman, Boise, Idaho, 1963-68, pres. council, 1967-68; mem. Idaho Ho. of Reps., 1969-76. Trustee Med.-Dental Hosp. Burs. Am., 1959-63, pres., 1962. Served from lt. (j.g.) to comdr. USNR, 1943-46; PTO. Mem. Am. Bar Assn., Rocky Mountain (pres. 1955), Idaho (pres. 1957) assn. collectors, Am. Collectors Assn. (dir. 1955-57, 76—), Navy League, Res. Officers Assn., Ret. Officers Assn., Mil. Order World Wars, C. of C., Sigma Chi, Phi Delta Phi. Republican. Mason, Kiwanian. Home: 1214 Johnson St Boise ID 83705 Office: Box 1097 Boise ID 83701

RICE, ELMER HAROLD, biochemist; b. Alhambra, Calif., Feb. 1, 1923; s. William and Tena A. (Johnson) R.; A.A., Pasadena Jr. Coll., 1940; A.B., Whittier Coll., 1948; Ph.D., U. So. Calif., 1958; m. Leslie Irene Fulmer, June 30, 1947; children—Carolyn, Daniel. Research biochemist U. Calif., 1957-59; asst. prof. chemistry Calif. State Poly. Coll., Pomona, 1959-62, asso. prof., 1962-69, prof., 1969—. Mem. San Bernardino County Democratic Central Com., 1968-69. Served with AUS, 1942-45. Mem. AAAS, Am. Chem. Soc., Am. Oil Chemists Soc. Contbr. articles to profl. jours. Home: 1280 Loma Vista Pomona CA 91768 Office: 3801 W Temple Ave Pomona CA 91768

RICE, HUGH L., III, management consultant; b. Florence, Ala., Mar. 7, 1947; s. Hugh L. and Eleanor Virginia (Cliff) R.; B.S.E.E., Ga. Inst. Tech., 1969; M.B.A., U. N.C., 1972; m. Penny McKie, Aug. 19, 1971; children—John McKie, Jennifer Diann. With Fails Mgmt. Inst., Inc., Raleigh, N.C., 1971-79, Denver, 1979—, cons., 1971-74, sr. cons., 1974-76, assoc., 1976-79, v.p., ptnr., western regional mgr., 1979—, also dir.; dir. Concord Mgmt. Systems, Beltsville, Md. Mem. Inst. Mgmt. Cons., Profls. for Constrn. Contractors Council (pres. 1980-81), Inst. Bus. Appraisers, Assn. Corporate Growth, World Future Soc., Beta Gamma Sigma. Republican. Methodist. Club: Denver. Home: 140 Dahlia St Denver CO 80220 Office: 455 Shermon St Suite 400 Denver CO 80203

RICE, JAMES HOWARD, construction and mining machinery executive; b. Oswego, Ill., Jan. 11, 1926; s. Lawrence W. and Darle D. (Breedlove) R.; m. Margaret E. Simpson, Sept. 9, 1950; children—James C., Thomas Sullivan, Timothy W. B.S.E. in Mech. Engring., U. Mich., 1950; M.S. in Bus. Adminstrn. (Fin.), No. Ill. U., 1972. Sales mgr. Barber-Greene Can. Ltd. div. Barber-Greene Co., 1956-60, mktg. coordinator, 1961-66, product mgr. Barber-Greene Co., Aurora, Colo., 1967-72, v.p. planning and devel., 1972-76, v.p., 1976—, gen. mgr. Mine & Smelter Div., Denver, 1976—; dir. Card Drill Steel Corp.; dir. Am. Gold Minerals Corp. Served to 1st lt. U.S. Army, 1944-46. Douglas Aircraft scholar, 1949-50. Mem. Am. Soc. Metall. Engrs., Am. Fin. Assn., Colo. Mining Assn. (chmn.-elect, bd. dirs.). Republican. Methodist. Clubs: Denver Petroleum, Denver Rotary, Rotary Internat. Office: Mine & Smelter Corp 3800 Race St PO Box 16067 Denver CO 80216

RICE, JOHN REYNOLDS, investing corporation executive; b. N.Y.C., June 26, 1946; s. Anton Henry and Lydia (Sands) R.; B.A. cum laude, Harvard U., 1968; m. Deborah Ann Chadsey, Sept. 11, 1971. Vice pres. overseas ops. Mohawk Recreation Products, Ramsey, N.J.; chmn., pres., chief exec. officer Crestek, Trenton, N.J.; now pres., chief exec. officer Assoc. S.W. Investors, Inc., Albuquerque. Vol., High Commn. for Refugees. Mem. Hispano C. of C. (population action council), Albuquerque C. of C. Presbyterian. Home: 422 Hermosa St SE Albuquerque NM 87108 Office: Assoc SW Investors Inc 2425 Alamo St SE Albuquerque NM 87106

RICE, JONATHAN C., ednl. television exec.; b. St. Louis, Feb. 19, 1916; s. Charles M. and May (Goldman) R.; A.B., Stanford, 1938; m. Kathleen Feibleman, Aug. 6, 1946 (dec. June 1964); children—Jefferson Charles, Kathy May, May Nannette. Picture editor Look Mag. Book Dept., N.Y.C., 1946-47; news, spl. events dir. KTLA Paramount Pictures TV Sta., Los Angeles, 1947-52; program mgr., operations mgr. KQED Bay Area Ednl. TV Assn., San Francisco, 1953-67, dir. program operations, 1967-70, asst. gen. mgr. programming, 1970—; sta. mgr. KQED-TV, 1972, asst. to pres. KQED, Inc.: lectr. Stanford Radio TV Film Inst., 1958—; cons. various ednl. tv. stas., Dept. Justice and Nat. Acad. TV Arts and Scis. Served to maj. USMCR, 1942-46. Recipient nat. and regional awards for programs produced at KTLA and KQED, including Edison Found. award, Peabody award, Lowell award Corp. for Pub. Broadcasting, 1972, Gov's. award No. Calif. Acad. TV Arts and Scis., 1973. Mem. San Francisco Acad. TV Arts and Sci., Sigma Chi, Sierra Club. Editor: Look at America; The South, 1947, Official Picture Story of the FBI, 1947. Home: 1 Russian Hill Pl San Francisco CA 94133 Office: 500 8th St San Francisco CA 94103

RICE, JULIAN CASAVANT, lawyer; b. Miami, Fla., Jan. 1, 1924; s. Sylvan J. and Maybelle (Casavant) R.; student U. San Francisco, 1941-43; J.D. cum laude, Gonzaga U., 1950; m. Dorothy Mae Haynes, Feb. 14, 1958; children—Scott B., Craig M. (dec.), Julianne C., Linda D., Janette M. Admitted to Wash. bar, 1950, Alaska bar, 1959; practiced in Spokane, 1950-56, Fairbanks, Alaska, 1959—; mem. firm Rice Hoppner Brown & Brunner and predecessor, 1966—; dir. Alaska Pacific Bank, Anchorage; dir., mem. exec. com. Alaska Pac Bancorp., Anchorage; mayor Fairbanks, 1970-72; founder, gen. counsel Mt. McKinley Mut. Savs. Bank, Fairbanks, 1965—, chmn. bd., 1979-80; v.p., dir., gen. counsel Skimmers, Inc., Anchorage, 1966-67; gen. counsel Alaska Carriers Assn., Anchorage, 1960-71, Alaska Transp. Conf., 1960-67. Served from pvt. to 1st lt., AUS, 1943-46. Decorated Bronze Star. Fellow Am. Bar Found.; mem. Am., Wash., Alaska bar assns., Am. Judicature Soc., ICC Practitioners Assn., Motor Carrier Lawyers Assn. Office: Parkview Bldg 330 Wendell St Fairbanks AK 99701

RICE, KINGSLEY L(ORING) (JIM), JR., advertising agency executive, consultant; b. Evanston, Ill., Apr. 26, 1931; s. Kingsley Loring and Mary Jane (Judson) R.; m. Ann Roesing, June 20, 1953; children—Douglas K., Philip R., Jaine E., Charles J. B.A. in English, Williams Coll., 1952. Media buyer Leo Burnett Co., Inc., Chgo., 1956-59, account exec., 1959-62; advt. mgr. Hills Bros. Coffee, Inc., San Francisco, 1962-64, dir. advtg., 1964-68; v.p., dir. account mgmt. Hoefer Dieterich & Brown, Inc., San Francisco, 1968-74, pres., chief operating officer, 1974-76, also dir.; pres. San Francisco office D'Arcy-MacManus & Masius, 1977-80, chmn. West Coast, 1980-81, also dir.; pres., founder Rice & Assocs., Inc., San Francisco, 1981—. Trustee, Reed Union Sch. dist., Tiburon, Calif., 1964-69, chmn., 1968-69; mem. profl. adv. com. Am. Assn. Advt. Agys.; bd. dirs. Tiburon Peninsula Found., 1976—. Served to lt. USN, 1952-56. Recipient Advt. Club Pres. of Yr. award Am. Advt. Fedn., 1970, Silver medal, 1974. Mem. Am. Mktg. Assn., San Francisco Advt. Club (pres. 1969-70), Direct Mail/Mktg. Assn., World Affairs Council, San Francisco C. of C. (v.p., dir.). Republican. Congregationalist. Clubs: Family (San Francisco); Tiburon Peninsula. Writer songs.

RICE, MARIAN JOSEPHINE, software engineer; d. William Cyrus and Marian Louise (Terry) Wingblade; children—Jonathan, James, Eric. Grad. Phoenix Art Inst., 1948, Computer Tng. Inst., Phoenix, 1966; student Phoenix Coll., 1974, Ariz. State U., 1978. Computer programmer Gen. Electric Co., Phoenix, 1966-75; software engr. Honeywell Co. Process Mgmt. Systems Div., Phoenix, 1975—. Mem. Assn. Computing Machinery, Nat. Assn. Female Execs. Mem. United Ch. of Religious Sci. Office: Honeywell Process Mgmt Systems Div 16404 N Black Canyon Hwy Phoenix AZ 85023

RICE, PATRICIA ANN, computer company executive; b. Aldrich, Mo., Aug. 24, 1946; d. William Wayne and Wilda Mae (Lowery) R.; A.A., S.W. Baptist Coll., Bolivar, Mo., 1966; B.A., S.W. Mo. State U., 1967; postgrad. Calif. State U., Fullerton; m. Anthony Avila III; children—Jessica Jean Rice, Clifford Wayne Rice, Jacqueline Marie Avila. Office mgr. Patscheck-Veiga Constrn. Co., Tustin, Calif., 1972-75; asst. to controller Richards West Co., Newport Beach, Calif., 1976-78; acctg. supr. Warner Lambert Co., Anaheim, Calif., 1978-80, supr. fin. analysis and planning, 1980; mgr. fin. control Pepsi Cola, Torrance, Calif., 1980-82; sr. fin. planning mgr. Microdata Corp., Newport Beach, Calif., 1982—. Mem. Am. Mgmt. Assn., Nat. Assn. Female Execs., Am. Prodn. and Inventory Control Soc., Nat. Notary Assn., NOW (chpt. program chmn. 1977), LaLeche League (chpt. publicity chmn. 1972-73). Democrat. Roman Catholic. Home: 24525 Kings Rd Laguna Niguel CA 92677 Office: Microdata Corp 4000 MacArthur Blvd Newport Beach CA 92660

RICE, PAUL ROGER, optometrist, educator; b. Honolulu, Jan. 27, 1924; s. Harry H. and Mary E. (Runyon) R.; m. Loretta Lillian Canter, Sept. 5, 1950; children—Paul, Mary, Laura. B.S., Pacific U., 1950, O.D., 1952. Lic. optometrist, Calif. Practice optometry, Mill Valley, Calif., 1953—; clin. instr. U. Calif. Sch. Optometry, 1980—. Served with AC, U.S. Army, 1943-45. Decorated Air medal with 5 oak leaf clusters, Battle Star (5). Mem. Am. Optometric Assn. (award for 25 yrs. continuous membership 1978), Calif. Optometric Assn. Republican. Club: Sausalito (Calif.) Cruising (staff commodore). Inventor contact lens measure. Home: 165 Stanford Ave Mill Valley CA 94941 Office: 25 Evergreen Ave Mill Valley CA 94941

RICE, ROGER EUGENE, engineering executive; b. Maywood, Calif., Jan. 25, 1943; s. Robert William and LaVerne Louise (Elsasser) R.; A.S., Los Angeles Pierce Coll., 1968; B.S., Calif. State U., Long Beach, 1971; M.S., U. So. Calif., 1973; m. Judy Eileen Tice, May 31, 1980; children—Adam Eugene Tice, Rachael Elizabeth Tice. Data analyst, inertial guidance systems Litton Guidance Systems, Los Angeles, 1966-68; programmer Tech. Media Systems, Los Angeles, 1970-71; systems analyst Aerospace Corp., Los Angeles, 1968-75, 77-81, Washington, 1975-77, info. systems specialist, Los Angeles, 1978-80, mgr., 1980—. Served with USNR, 1960-63. Mem. IEEE, Assn. Computing Machinery, Data Processing Mgmt. Assn., Assn. Old Crows, Armed Forces Communications and Electronics Assn., Internat. Oceanographic Found., AIAA, AAAS, U.S. Naval Inst. Democrat. Lutheran. Home: 1013 Nonchalant Dr Simi Valley CA 93065 Office: Aerospace Corp PO Box 92957 Los Angeles CA 90009

RICE, WALTER BONHAM, former sales exec.; b. Miles City, Mont., Dec. 21, 1933; s. Robert E. and Grace N. (Bonham) R.; A.B., Marion Coll., 1956; postgrad. U. No. Iowa, 1960, Syracuse U., 1975; m. Beverly Iliff, July 23, 1954; children—Michael J., Mark A. Chief engr. Northwestern Coll. Radio, Waterloo, Iowa, 1961-66; chief engr. ops. Albany Radio Corp. (Oreg.), 1967-69; mem. mktg. staff Broadcast div. Harris Corp., 1969-83, nat. sales mgr., 1974-79. Served with USNG, 1951-52. Mem. Am. Mgmt. Assn., Sales Mktg. Execs., Inc. Republican. Baptist. Club: Computer.

RICE-HAUENSTEIN, BARBARA, hotel/casino executive; educator; b. Buffalo, May 8, 1952; d. John J. and Joan M. (Reilly) Rice. Letter of Assignment, U. Nev., Las Vegas, 1982. Dir. sales and mktg. E.G.H., Inc./Las Vegas Club, Hotel & Casino, 1981—; tchr. hotel adminstrn. div. U. Nev., Las Vegas. Mem. Hotel Sales Mgmt. Assn., Food Service Execs. Assn. Home: 2349 Cardiff Ln Las Vegas NV 89108 Office: 18 E Fremont St Las Vegas NV 89108

RICERETO, JAMES, III, engineering executive; b. Jersey City, Jan. 14, 1947; s. James and Helen (Mastropolo) R. B.S., Rutgers U., 1968; M.S.E., U. Pa., 1969; cert. in city planning U. Calif., Berkeley, 1975. Structural engr. Port Authority of N.Y. and N.J., N.Y.C., 1969; civil/structural engr. Modjeski & Masters, Phila., 1970; project mgr. Tudor Engring. Co., San Francisco, 1972-78; dep. mgr. bus. devel. Parsons Brinckerhoff Quade & Douglas, N.Y.C., 1978-79; mgr. project devel. Tudor Engring. Co., San Francisco, 1979-81; prin. J.R. Mktg. Assocs., 1981; dir. engring. Daniel, Mann, Johnson & Mendenhall, San Francisco, 1982—. Served as lt. U.S. Army, 1970-72. Decorated Bronze Star, Army Commendation medal; Ford Found. fellow, 1968-69; registered profl. engr., Calif., N.J., N.Y. Mem. Soc. Am. Mil. Engrs. (post dir. 1975-76, 80-81, nat. com. on new initiatives 1976-78, nat. dir. 1981—, recipient Service awards San Francisco post 1976, 77), ASCE (acting sect. sec. 1976, sect. newsletter editor 1976-78), San Francisco Bay Area Engring. Council (career guidance com. 1974-75, scholarship com. 1978, public relations com. 1980), Am. Inst. Cert. Planners, Am. Planning Assn., Nat. Soc. Profl. Engrs., Soc. for Mktg. Profl. Services (pres. San Francisco Bay Area chpt. 1983-84). Club: Engrs. of San Francisco. Co-author: The A/E Marketing Handbook: A User's Manual. Home: 20 San Antonio Pl San Francisco CA 94133 Office: 170 Maiden Ln Suite 500 San Francisco CA 94108

RICH, JOHN CHARLES, air force officer; b. Wichita, Kans., Oct. 12, 1937; s. Hubert E. and Alma Lorene (Sadler) R.; m. Kathleen Susan Hall, June 14, 1693; children—Susan, John N., Daniel. A.B in Applied Physics, Harvard U., 1959, A.M. in Applied Physics, 1960, Ph.D. in Astrophysics, 1967. Commd. 2d lt. U.S. Air Force, 1960, advanced through grades to col., 1975; physicist Spl. Weapons Ctr., 1960-63; physicist, br. chief Tech. Applications Ctr., 1966-70; div. chief Weapons Lab., 1970-75; comdr. Avionics Lab., 1976-77 Weapons Lab., 1977-78; dir. advanced radiation tech. Weapons Lab., Kirtland AFB, N.Mex., 1978—. Decorated Legion of Merit. Mem. Am. Astron. Soc., AIAA, Am. Geophys. Union, Air Force Assn., Sigma Xi. Episcopalian. Club: Harvard of N.Mex. Contbr. articles to profl. jours. Home: 701 Sagebrush Trail SE Albuquerque NM 87123

RICH, ROBERT STEPHEN, lawyer; b. N.Y.C., Apr. 30, 1938; s. Maurice H. and Natalie (Priess) R.; A.B., Cornell U., 1959; LL.B., J.D., Yale U., 1963; m. Myra N. Lakoff, May 31, 1964; children—David, Rebecca, Sarah. Admitted to N.Y. State bar, 1964, Colo. bar, 1973; individual practice law, 1963—; assoc. Shearman & Sterling, N.Y.C. and Paris, 1963-72; ptnr. Davis, Graham & Stubbs, Denver, 1973—; dir. several corps.; mem. adj. faculty Denver U.; U.S. del. to Internat. Fiscal Assn. Congress, 1978. Bd. dirs. Alliance Francaise of Denver, 1979-81, Denver Internat. Film Festival, 1979, Denver Art Mus., 1982—. Served to capt., AUS, 1959-60. Mem. ABA, Colo. Bar Assn., N.Y.C. Bar Assn. Clubs: Denver, Denver Tennis, Yale. Author: (with others) Taxation of Extractive Industries, 1978, International Business Transactions, 1981; contbr. articles law jours. Home: 458 Grape St Denver CO 80220 Office: 950 17th St Denver CO 80202

RICHARD, JOSEPH ERNEST, executive compensation consultant; b. Moncton, N.B., Can., Sept. 12, 1944; came to U.S., 1945, naturalized, 1955; s. Joseph Ernest and Aline Marie (Robichaud) R.; m. Coreen Evelyn LeBlanc, Apr. 16, 1966; m. 2d, Anita Louise Isaacson, May 16, 1981; children—Christine, Chad. B.B.A. in Mgmt., Western Mich. U., 1968; M. Labor and Indsl. Relations, Mich. State U., 1970. Sr. cons. Coopers & Lybrand, Boston, 1974-77; dir. personnel Fox & Jacobs, Dallas, 1977-79; mgr. Arthur Young & Co., Los Angeles, 1979-80; sr. v.p. Olanie, Hurst & Hemrich, San Francisco, 1980-82; dir. exec. compensation services Hay Assocs., San Francisco, 1982—; lectr. in field. Recipient research publ. prize Indsl. Relations Research Assn., 1969. Mem. Am. Compensation Assn., Am. Mgmt. Assn., Conf. Bd. Clubs: Los Angeles Athletic; Decathalon (Santa Clara, Calif.). Home: 483 Sausalito Blvd Sausalito CA 94962 Office: Hay Associates One Maritime Plaza Suite 1230 San Francisco CA 94111

RICHARD, PAUL STUART, financial counselor, corporation executive, writer; b. Endicott, N.Y., Oct. 29, 1945; s. Lisle Francis and Bertha Marie (Allard) R. Student Atlanta Bapt. Coll., 1970-71. Vice-pres. mktg. W. Hobbs Ltd., Atlanta, 1974-78; gen. mgr. Imperial Bronzelite Corp., Los Angeles, 1978-79; sr. v.p., gen. mgr. Brawn of Calif., Inc., San Diego, 1979-80; dir. Western Mktg. Assocs., Ltd., San Diego, 1980-81, also pres. Bullion Res. N.Am., Los Angeles, 1980-81; pres., founder Dollarplan Strategy Seminars, San Diego, 1981—, also chmn., founder Christian Fin. Enrichment Seminars, Las Vegas, 1982—; mem. faculty San Diego State U. Extension, 1982; workshop leader. Chmn. fin. com. 1st So. Baptist Ch.; hon. mem. O.L. Davis Fire Co. of Endwell (N.Y.) Fire Dept., served as capt., 1965-70; vice chmn. Christian Businessmen's Com., San Diego, 1982. Recipient Outstanding award for achievement Dale Carnegie & Assocs., 1972. Republican. Author: Dollarplan Strategy, 1981; The Gospel of Christian Personomics, 1983; Adventures in Personomics, 1983; contbr. articles to profl. jours. Home: 4801 Spencer Suite 210 Las Vegas NV 89109 Office: PO Box 3762 San Diego CA 92103

RICHARD, ROBERT CARTER, psychologist; b. Waterloo, Iowa, Apr. 4, 1938; s. Quentin Leroy and Adeline Pauline (Halverson) R.; student Pomona Coll., 1956-57, Westmont Coll., 1957; B.A., Wheaton (Ill.) Coll., 1960; B.D., Fuller Theol. Sem., 1963, Ph.D., 1973; S.T.M., Andover Newton Theol. Sch., 1964; m. Shirley Ruth Jones, Aug. 25, 1962; children—David, John. Ordained to ministry Am. Bapt. Conv., 1963; pastor Peninsula Bapt. Ch., Gig Harbor, Wash., 1965-68; marriage and family counselor Glendale (Calif.) Family Service, 1970-71; psychol. asst., Oakland and Pleasant Hill, Calif., 1972-74; clin. psychologist Rafa Counseling Assos., Pleasant Hill, 1974—; mem. faculty John F. Kennedy U., Orinda, Calif., 1975-78; affiliate staff Walnut Creek (Calif.) Psychiat. Hosp., 1978—. Co-founder, bd. dirs. New Directions Counseling Center, 1974-81. Recipient Integration of Psychology and Theology award, 1973; lic. psychologist, marriage, family and child counselor, Calif. Mem. Am., Calif., Contra Costa County (past pres.) psychol. assns., Christian Assn. Psychol. Studies. Republican. Presbyterian. Contbr. articles to profl. publs. Researcher assertiveness tng., stress mgmt., changes in counseling effectiveness and personality variables in adult lay counselor trainees. Office: 3490A Buskirk Ave Pleasant Hill CA 94523

RICHARD, ROBERT JOHN, library administrator; b. Oakland, Calif., Sept. 20, 1947; s. John Argyle and Vern Elizabeth (Bauer) R.; m. Anne Elizabeth Terrell, June 8, 1968 (div.); children—Kennifer Lynn, Laura Ellen, Constance Anne, Andrea Lee. Student Fullerton Coll., 1965-67; B.A. in Biology, Chapman Coll., 1972; M.S. in L.S., Calif. State U., 1973. Audiovisual specialist Fullerton (Calif.) Pub. Library, 1969-72, asst. to city librarian, 1972-73, librarian II, 1973-76, br. librarian Orange County Pub. Library, 1976-78, regional adminstr., 1978-80; assoc. dir. Long Beach (Calif.) Pub. Library, 1980-81; dir. Sacramento Pub. Library, 1981—; chmn. Mountain Valley Library System. Mem. Calif. Library Assn., Library Adminstrs. No. Calif., ALA, Library Adminstrn. and Mgmt. Assn., Library Info. and Tech. Assn., Pub. Library Assn. Office: 7000 Franklin Suite 540 Sacramento CA 95823

RICHARDS, FRANCES GRAY (PEGGY), Indian tribal development specialist; b. Chgo., May 25, 1920; d. John and Jessie Marion (Brown) Gray; m. Paul Baker Richards, June 20, 1939; children—Nathan B., Peter G., Alison M., Jonathan T., Joel D. Student Colo. Coll., 1938-39. Chief judge Jicarilla Apache Tribe, Dulce, N.Mex., 1960-66; judge Archuleta County, Pagosa Springs, Colo., 1960-66; exec. dir. So. Ute Community Action, Ignacio, Colo., 1966-70, dir. So. Ute Econ. Devel. Dept., 1972-77; self-employed Peggy Richards & Assocs., Durango, Colo., 1977-80; grants mgmt. analyst City of Durango, 1980-81; housing mgmt. officer Indian div. HUD, 1981-82; self-employed cons. various orgns., agys., local govt., Durango, Colo., 1982—. Pres., Four Corners Sheltered Workshop, 1970-72; mem. Durango Housing Rehab. Com., 1983; mem. finance com. San Juan Hospice, 1983. Mem. Nat. Assn. Female Execs., United Indian Planners Assn., Nat. Congress Community Economic Devel., Kappa Kappa Gamma. Episcopalian. Address: 703 5th Ave Durango CO 81301

RICHARDS, JOHN SAMUEL, real estate executive; b. Farnam, Nebr., Oct. 27, 1911; s. Herman and Effie C. (Ainlay) R.; student B.A., U. Colo., 1933; M.A., Tufts U., 1935; m. Leontine M. Subatch, June 4, 1935; children—Ellen K., John Samuel, Suzanne, Anthony J. With fgn. funds control div. U.S. Treasury, Washington, 1942-47, mng. dir., 1946-48; fin. mgr., dir. Ford Co., Brazil, W.Ger., 1948-56; v.p., staff exec. Chrysler Corp., 1957-58; pres. RCA Brazil, Sao Paulo, 1958-63; staff v.p. Olin Corp., Stamford, Conn., 1964-65; mgmt. cons., Brazil, 1966-70; pres. Triangle Devel., Inc., San Francisco, 1970—; Braker teaching fellow econs. Tufts U., 1933-35; internat. exec. Exec. Service Corp., N.Y.C. and Rio de Janeiro, Brazil, 1966. Mem. Am. C. of C. for Sao Paulo and Rio de Janeiro, U.S. Navy League, Phi Beta Kappa, Pi Gamma Mu. Republican. Home: 1916 Lyon St San Francisco CA 94115 Office: Triangle Devel Inc 807 Montgomery Ave San Francisco CA 94133

RICHARDS, LAWRENCE EDWIN, data processing corp. exec.; b. Chgo., July 22, 1941; s. George Edwin and Grace Minerva (Buckle) R.; student Parsons Coll., 1958-62; B.A. in Mgmt. Info. Systems, Eastern Wash. U., 1973. Systems analyst Nat. Cash Register Corp., Spokane, Wash., 1974-76, Computer Knowledge Corp., Spokane, 1976-78; owner, pres. Computer Profls. Inc., Spokane, 1978—; vis. asst. prof. Eastern Wash. U. Served with USAF, 1964-68. Cert. data processor. Mem. Data Processing Mgmt. Assn., Assn. Systems Mgmt. Unitarian. Home: 937 E 32nd St Spokane WA 99203 Office: PO Box 2501 Spokane WA 99220

RICHARDS, PAUL AUGUSTINE, lawyer; b. Oakland, Calif., May 27, 1927; s. Donnell C. and Theresa (Pasquale) R.; B.A., U. Pacific, 1950; J.D., U. San Francisco, 1953; m. Ann Morgans, Mar. 20, 1948; 1 son, Paul Morgans. Admitted to Nev. bar, 1953; law practice, Reno, 1953—; dir., dir. numerous small corps.; prof. environment law Sierra Nev. Coll.

Mem. Nev. Com. on Fed. Land Laws, 1973-79. Mem. Washoe Democratic Central Com., 1959-74, chmn., 1964-66; vice chmn. Nev. Central Dem. Com., 1966-68. Bd. dirs. Reno Rodeo Assn., 1969—, pres., 1978-79; dir. Internat. Rodeo Mgmt., 1976—; nat. trustee from Nev., Ducks, Unltd., 1964-72; trustee Sierra Nev. Coll., Sierra Nev. Research Inst., 1970-82. Served with USNR, 1945-46. Mem. Am., Nev., Washoe County bar assn., Nev. Orgn. Wildlife (dir. 1970-78). Roman Catholic. Elk. Club: Reno Press (dir. 1972—, pres. 1977-78). Home: 1230 Autumn Hills Dr Reno NV 89511 Office: 248 S Sierra St Richards Bldg Suite 1 Reno NV 89501

RICHARDS, REX ALTON, engr.; b. Ogden City, Utah, Sept. 15, 1941; s. Alton Franklin and Phyllis (Krogue) R.; A.S., Weber State Coll., 1964, B.S., 1965; M.S. (William C. Claypool fellow), Utah State U., 1967, Ph.D. (NDEA Title IV fellow), 1973; postgrad. Brigham Young U., Community Coll. of Am. Samoa; m. Fernalice Smith, Sept. 12, 1969; children—Douglas, Heather, Marne, Steven, Daniel, Rachel. Instr., Utah State U., 1968-72; tchr. Latter-day Saints Ch. Ednl. System, Am. Samoa, 1972-74; chemist, project engr. Thiokol Corp., 1974-80, standard missile project engr., Brigham City, Utah, 1980—; dir. sci. fair. Mayor Town of Mapusaga, 1973-74; acting chmn. Brigham City Democratic Party; del. county and state convs. Mem. AAAS, Weber Scholastic Soc., N.Y. Acad. Scis., Planetary Soc., Sigma Xi, Phi Kappa Phi, Delta Phi Kappa. Club: Japanese. Contbr. articles on solid propellant research to profl. jours. Research on plant sterols and plant enzymes. Home: 204 E 3d S Brigham City UT 84302 Office: Box 524 MS 266 Brigham City UT 84302

RICHARDS, ROBERT CHARLES (BOB), mgmt. cons.; b. Portland, Oreg., Jan. 18, 1939; s. Charles Robert and Mildred Marie (Merrill) R.; B.A., Lewis and Clark Coll., 1961; m. Marilyn Cornelia Poole, Sept. 1, 1961 (div.); children—Kristin Elizabeth, Jeffrey Robert. Tng. officer, mgr. edn. dept. U.S. Bancorp, Portland, Oreg., 1965-74; mgr. orgn. devel. Coors Container Co., Golden, Colo., 1974-77; mgmt. cons., mgt. western office Consulting Assocs., Inc., Lakewood, Colo., 1977—; instr. Portland State U., 1972-73, U. Oreg., Portland Extension, 1973-74, Portland Community Coll., 1971-74; mgmt. cons.; seminar leader; dir., sec. Sr. Mgmt. Programs, Inc., 1971-73, pres., 1973-74. Mem. adv. com. Community Coll. of Denver, scholarship and employment com. Portland State U. Found.; adj. faculty USMC Service Support Schs., Camp Lejeune, N.C. Served with USMCR, 1961-64; lt. col. Res., 1966—. Mem. Am. Soc. Tng. and Devel. (dir. chpt. 1976, v.p. 1977, dir. Oreg. chpt. 1972, pres. 1971, dir. Western region 1971-72), World Futures Soc., Planning Execs. Inst., Rocky Mountain Orgn. Devel. Network. Author tng. materials; contbr. articles to profl. publs. Home: 13362 W Montana Ave Lakewood CO 80228 Office: 21333 Haggerty Rd Suite 311 Novi MI 48050

RICHARDS, RONALD EDWARD, air force officer; b. Easton, Pa., Apr. 12, 1950; s. Edward Earl and Elvera Vivian (Wagner) R.; m. Diana Jo Leavitt, June 15, 1974; children—Kristi Lynn, Kari Leigh, Katie Loren. B.S. in Econs. with distinction, U.S. Air Force Acad., 1972; M.S., U. Pitts., 1973. Commd. 2d lt. U.S. Air Force, 1972, advanced through grades to maj., 1983, pilot, instr. pilot Zweibrucken (W.Ger.) Air Base, 1975-79, T-41 flight instr., 1979-83, tng. program mgr. U.S. Air Force Acad., Colo., 1979-81, comdr. cadet Squadron 27, 1981-83; counselor, instr. Air Command and Staff Course, 1980-81. Active Little League Baseball, football; adult Sun. sch. instr. Immanuel Luth. Ch., 1979-83. Decorated Air Force Commendation medal with oak leaf cluster; named Outstanding Classroom instr. Air Force Acad., 1979-80, Outstanding T-41 Instr., 1982; named Jr. Officer of Yr., 1982-83. Mem. Assn. Grads. U.S. Air Force Acad., Air Force Assn., U.S. Air Force Athletic Assn. Club: USAF Acad. Officers. Home: Quarters 4403G USAF Academy CO 80840 Office: Cadet Squadron 27 USAF Academy CO 80841

RICHARDS, THOMAS NEWTON, machinery company executive; b. Sioux Falls, S.D., Mar. 30, 1923; s. Raymond Duane and Gladys Marie (Murray) R.; B.S. in Bus. Adminstrn. summa cum laude, U. S.D., 1948; m. Darlene Marie Hanson, Apr. 7, 1946; children—Thomas J., Scott W., Greg M. Public acct., 1946-51; comptroller, then gen. sales mgr. Foster-Bell Co., Sioux Falls, 1951-70; founder, gen. mgr. ICM div. Wheeler Machinery Co., Salt Lake City, 1970-74, corp. dir. sales, 1974-81; gen. mgr. Western States Equipment Co., Spokane, 1981-83; pres., gen. mgr., treas. Ziegler Co., Inc., La Crosse, Wis., 1983—. Bd. dirs. S.D. Young Republicans, 1954-58; Rep. voting dist. chmn., Salt Lake City, 1976-80; chmn. bd. Boys Clubs Salt Lake, 1976—, asso. chmn. bldg. fund drive, 1979-80. Served with USNR, 1942-45. Mem. Sales and Mktg. Execs., No. Plains Caterpillar Dealers Sales Mgrs. Assn. (past pres., dir. 1966—), Pacific S.W. Caterpillar Dealers Sales Mgrs. Assn. (sec. 1981). Lutheran. Club: Sugar House Kiwanis (dir.). Home: W 514 Hastings Rd Spokane WA 99218 Office: PO Box 69 Onalaska WI 54650

RICHARDS, VINCENT PHILIP, librarian; b. Sutton Bonington, Nottinghamshire, Eng., Aug. 1, 1933; s. Philip Haslewood and Alice Hilda (Moore) R.; B. Liberal Studies with distinction, U. Okla., 1966; m. Ann Beardshall, Apr. 3, 1961; children—Mark, Christopher, Erika. Library asst. Brentford and Chiswick Pub. Library, London, Eng., 1949-51, 53-54, asst. reference librarian, 1955-56; cataloguer Manresa Coll. Library, London, 1954-55; asst. br. librarian Peace River br. B.C. Pub. Library Commn., Dawson Creek, B.C., Can., 1956-57; asst. dir. Fraser Valley Regional Library, Abbotsford, B.C., 1958-67; chief librarian Red Deer (Alta., Can.) Coll., 1967-77; dir. libraries Edmonton Pub. Library, 1977—. Cons. Manresa Coll. Library, 1955-56, St. Augustine's Abbey, Ramsgate, Kent, Eng., 1955-56, Westminster Abbey Library, Mission, B.C., 1958-67. Faculty rep., bd. govs. Red Deer Coll., 1972-73; bd. dirs. Alta Council, Camps Farthest Out, 1972-73, Red Deer Ednl. TV Assn., 1975-77; bd. dirs. Jeunesses Musicales, Red Deer, 1969, v.p., 1970; pres. Faculty Assn. Red Deer Coll., 1971-72; dir. Canadian Assn. Coll. and Univ. Libraries, 1972-74, chmn. community colls. sect. 1972-73. Served with Royal Army Edn. Corps, 1951-53. Mem. Library Assn. U.K., Library Assn. Alta., Can. Library Assn., Pacific N.W. Library Assn., Third Order Mt. Carmel. Roman Catholic. Club: Rotary. Contbr. articles to profl. jours. Home: 5103 109th Ave Edmonton AB T6A 1R9 Canada Office: 7 Sir Winston Churchill Sq Edmonton AB T5J 2V4 Canada

RICHARDSON, A(RTHUR) LESLIE, med. group cons.; b. Ramsgate, Kent, Eng., Feb. 21, 1910; s. John William and Emily Lilian (Wilkins) R.; came to U.S., 1930, naturalized, 1937; student spl. courses U. So. Calif., 1933-35; m. B. Kathleen Sargent, Oct. 15, 1937. Mgr., Tower Theater, Los Angeles, 1931-33; accountant Felix-Krueper Co., Los Angeles, 1933-35; indsl. engr. Pettengill, Inc., Los Angeles, 1935-37; purchasing agt. Gen. Petroleum Corp. Los Angeles, 1937-46; adminstr. Beaver Med. Clinic, Redlands, Calif., 1946-72, exec. cons. 1972-75; sec.-treas. Fern Properties, Inc., Redlands, 1955-75, Redelco, Inc., Redlands, 1960-67; pres. Buinco, Inc., Redlands, 1956-65; vice chmn. Redlands adv. bd. Bank of Am., 1973-80. Exec. cons. Med. Adminstrs. Calif., 1975-83. Pres., Redlands Area Community Chest, 1953; volunteer exec. Internat. Exec. Service Corps; mem. San Bernardino County (Calif.) Grand Jury, 1952-53. Bd. dirs. Beaver Med. Clinic Found., Redlands, 1961—, sec.-treas., 1961-74, pres., 1974-75. Served to lt. Med. Adminstrv. Corps., AUS, 1942-45. Recipient Redlands Civic award Elks, 1953. Fellow Am. Coll. Med Group Adminstrs. (life, disting. fellow 1980, pres. 1965-66, dir.); mem. Med. Group Mgmt. Assn. (hon. life; mem. nat. long range planning com. 1963-68, pres. western sect. 1960). Episcopalian. Mason, Kiwanian (pres. 1951). Clubs: Commonwealth (San Francisco). Home: 1 Verlie Dr Redlands CA 92373 Office: 2 W Fern Ave Redlands CA 92373

RICHARDSON, DONALD LEROY, vocational education educator/administrator; b. Morrill, Nebr., Dec. 23, 1939; s. George Lee and Ruby Inez (Varvel) R.; m. Marilyn Jean Henke, Sept. 6, 1959; children—Rebecca, Timothy, Donald, Amy. B.S. in Bus. Adminstrn., Colo. State U., 1962, M.Ed. in Vocat. Edn., 1971; Ed.D. in Higher Edn. Adminstrn., U. Colo., 1981. Mgmt. trainee Phillips Petroleum Co., Denver, 1962-63; mgr. Hughes Men's Wear, Ft. Collins, Colo., 1963-69; tchr.-coordinator St. Vrain Valley Schs., Longmont, Colo. 1969-74; asst. prof. dept. vocat. edn. Colo. State U., Ft. Collins, 1974-82, acting dept. head, 1982—. Mem. Am. Vocat. Assn., Colo. Vocat. Assn. (past pres.), Mktg. and Distributive Edn. Assn., Vocat. Adminstrs. Assn., Omicron Tau Theta (nat. exec. sec. past nat pres.), Phi Delta Kappa, Iota Lamda Sigma. Republican. Methodist. Home: 2700 Brookwood Ct Ft Collins CO 80525 Office: Dept Vocat Edn Colo State U Ft Collins CO 80523

RICHARDSON, DOROTHY VIRGINIA, acct.; b. Bennington, Okla., Sept. 26, 1937; d. William Lycurgus and Mittie Mae (Richardson) Ray; student Eastern Okla. A&M, 1955-56; B.B.A., U. Alaska, 1974; m. Charles Howard Richardson, Dec. 28, 1958; children—Charles Timothy, Michael Todd. Asst. accountant Peat, Marwick, Mitchell & Co., Omaha, 1975-76; gen. accountant U. Alaska Statewide System, Fairbanks, 1976; asst. bus. mgr. Geophys. Inst., Fairbanks, 1976-77; dir. grant and contract services U. Alaska, Fairbanks, 1977-80; controller Alaska Legal Services Corp., Anchorage, 1980-81; bus. mgr. div. community colls., rural edn. and extension U. Alaska, 1981—. Active Cub Scouts, Mothers March of Dimes, PTA. Served with USAF, 1957-59. Mem. Am. Soc. Women Accts., Am. Woman's Soc. C.P.A.s, Alaska State Soc. C.P.A.s, Am. Inst. C.P.A.s (dir.), Soc. Research Adminstrs. Club: Soroptimist. Office: 3605 Arctic #420 Anchorage AK 99503

RICHARDSON, DOUGLAS LEE, vocational educator; b. Elida, N. Mex., Aug. 5, 1943; s. Henry Lee and Iola Elizabeth (Cryer) R.; m. Patricia Rosetta Ridley; children—Kendall Lee, Neil Ross. B.S. in Indsl. Edn., Eastern N. Mex., 1966, M.Ed., in Vocat. Edn., 1969. Tchr. vocat. auto mechanics, Carlsbad, N. Mex., 1966-73; asst. supr. trade-indsl.-tech. edn., N. Mex. Dept. Edn., Santa Fe, 1973-74, supr. trade-indsl.-tech. edn., 1974—. Mem. Am. Vocat. Assn. (life mem.), N. Mex. Vocat. Assn., Nat. Assn. State Suprs. Trade-Indsl. Edn., Vocat. Instructional Materials Assn. Democrat. Club: Santa Fe Vintage Auto. Office: State Edn Bldg Santa Fe NM 87501

RICHARDSON, EVERETT VERN, hydraulic engineer, educator, adminstrator; b. Scottsbluff, Nebr., Jan. 5, 1924; s. Thomas Otis and Jean Marie (Everett) R.; m. Billie Ann Kleckner, June 23, 1948; children—Gail Lee, Thomas Everett, Jerry Ray. B.S., Colo. State U., 1949, M.S., 1960, Ph.D., 1965. Registered profl. engr., Colo. Hydraulic engr., U.S. Geol. Survey, Wyo., 1949-52, Iowa, 1953-66, research hydraulic engr., Ft. Collins, Colo., 1956-63, project chief, 1963-68; prof. civil engring., adminstr. Engring. Research Center, Colo. State U., Ft. Collins, 1968—, project dir. Egypt Water Use Project; cons. in field. Mem. Ft. Collins Water Bd. Served with AUS, 1943-45. Decorated Bronze Star, Purple Heart; U.S. Govt. fellow MIT, 1962-63. Fellow ASCE (J.C. Stevens award 1961); mem. Internat. Congress for Irrigation and Drainage, AAAS, Sigma Xi, Chi Epsilon, Sigma Tau. Editor: Highways in the River Environment, U.S. Bur. Pub. Rds., 1975; contbr. chpts. to books in field and articles to profl. jours. Home: 824 Gregory Rd Ft Collins CO 80524 Office: Engineering Research Center Colo State U Ft Collins CO 80523

RICHARDSON, FRANK KELLOGG, state supreme ct. justice; b. St. Helena, Calif., Feb. 13, 1914; s. Channing Alonzo and Jessie May (Kellogg) R.; student U. Pa., 1931-32; A.B., with distinction, Stanford U., 1935, LL.B., 1938; LL.D. (hon.), Western State U., San Diego, 1976, Mid-Valley Coll. Law, Los Angeles, 1977; m. Elizabeth Kingdon, Jan. 23. 1943; children—Stuart Channing, Paul Kellogg, Eric Kingdon, David Huntington. Admitted to: Calif bar, 1938; individual practice law, Oroville, Calif., 1939-42, Sacramento, Calif., 1946-71; presiding justice Calif. Ct. of Appeal, 3d Dist., 1971-74; assoc. justice Calif. Supreme Ct., Sacramento, 1974—; prof. law Mc George Sch. Law, 1946-51, 59-61, mem. adv. bd., 1959—; trustee McGeorge Sch. Law, 1959—; bd. visitors, mem. exec. com. law sch. Stanford (Calif.) U., 1966-69; mem. adv. bd. Nat. Inst. Justice. Pres., Meth. Hosp. Sacramento, 1965-71, Sacramento Community Welfare Council, 1956-57, Sacramento YMCA, World Affairs Council Sacramento, 1970-71; bd. regents U. Pacific, 1975—. Served with USAAF, 1942-43, U.S. Army, 1943-45. Fellow Am. Coll. Probate Counsel; Mem. Calif. Judges Assn., State Bar Calif. (mem. exec. com. 1965-69), Presiding Justices Cts. Appeal (chmn. 1972-73), Sacramento County Bar Assn. (pres. 1962-63), Order of Coif, Phi Beta Kappa. Methodist. Clubs: Commonwealth, Sutter (hon.), Del Paso Country (hon.). Home: 4140 Elderberry Ln Sacramento CA 95825 Office: 350 McAllister St San Francisco CA 94102*

RICHARDSON, GERALD CLEMEN, clergyman, former city ofcl.; b. Glendale, Calif., Jan. 8, 1937; s. Gerald O. and Kathleen E. (Bobier) R.; student U. Calif.-Berkeley, 1957, Calif. State U., Northridge, 1959; B.A. in Bible Ministries, Los Angeles Bapt. Coll., 1979; M.A., Calif. Grad. Sch. Theology, 1981; M.A., Azusa Pacific U., 1982; m. Jo Ann Cox, Sept. 21, 1963; children—JoAnn, Gerald, Charles, John. Coordinator youth employment service Calif. Dept. Employment, 1956-59; pastor Foothill Bapt. Ch., Sylmar, Calif.; mem. city council Manhattan Beach, 1970-74, mayor, 1972-73. Mem. exec. bd. So. Calif. Assn. Govts., 1971-73; mem. exec. bd. Los Angeles div. Calif. League Cities, 1971-73; parlimentarian Bapt. Gen. Conf. Conv., 1982; mem. bus. affairs bd. S.W. Bapt. Conf., 1981-82; chmn. bd. North Valley Christian Counseling Center; bd. dirs. Shepherd's House, Inc.; chmn. deacons Christian Ch., 1969, chmn. elders, 1973—. Mem. San Fernando-Sylmar Ministerial Assn. (pres. 1980-81). Republican. Clubs: Lions (pres. Manhattan Beach 1966-67, internat. zone chmn. 1967-68), Rotary (treas. San Fernando 1981-82).

RICHARDSON, H(AROLD) LEONARD, educator; b. Corning, N.Y., Aug. 15, 1927; s. Harold Leonard and Kathryn Virginia (Botti) R.; grad. Phillips Acad., Andover, Mass., 1945; B.A., Yale, 1949; M.A., U. Pa., 1952; postgrad. U. Toledo, 1954-56, Yale, 1955; m. Virginia Marie Giesen, Aug. 20, 1949; children—Harold Leonard III, John Holland, Victoria Susan. Instr. English, Peddie Sch., Hightstown, N.J., 1949-53; chmn. English dept., asst. headmaster Maumee Valley (Ohio) Country Day Sch., 1953-59; headmaster Scarborough Sch., Scarborough-on-Hudson, N.Y., 1959-66; headmaster The Katharine Branson/Mt. Tamalpais Schs., Ross, Calif., 1966-82; pres. Educators' Collaborative, Calif., 1971—. Trustee Edgewood Children's Home, San Francisco. Mem. Nat. Assn. Coll. Admissions Counsellors, Cum Laude Soc., Headmasters Assn., Nat. Assn. Prins. Schs. for Girls, Country Day Sch. Headmasters Assn., Screen Actors Guild, AFTRA, Phi Gamma Delta. Presbyn. Clubs: Bohemian, Commonwealth, ECV Yerba Buena (San Francisco); Inverness Yacht (Calif.); Tile (Toledo); Yale (N.Y.C.). Contbr. articles to ednl. jours. Home: 1869 California St #2 San Francisco CA 94109

RICHARDSON, H. L., state senator; b. Terre Haute, Ind., 1927; m. Barbara Budrow; children—Laurie, Carrie, Doug. Student Olympic Coll.; advt. degree, Cornish Conservatory, Seattle. Former owner graphic arts and advt. bus.; mem. Calif. State Assembly, mem. Calif. State Senate, 1966—, minority caucus, chmn., vice chmn. elec. and reapportionment com., mem. judiciary, natural resources and wildlife, revenue and taxation coms. Mem. Republican State Central Com. Served with U.S. Navy, 1946. Recipient Outstanding Legislator award Calif. Rep. Assembly, 1968, 70, 72, 75, 76, Calif. Dist. Attys. Assn., Calif. Correctional Officers Assn., Calif. So. Council of Conservation Clubs, George Washington award Freedom Found., Valley Forge. Mem. Nat. Rifle Assn. (dir.), Gun Owners Am. (founder, chmn.), Gun Owners Calif., Law and Order Campaign Com. (founder). Club: Safari. Home: 735 W Duarte Rd Apt 20 Arcadia CA 91006 Office: California State Senate Sacramento CA 95814*

RICHARDSON, JAMES ANDREW, optometrist; b. Oklahoma City, June 25, 1946; s. Darwin Lloyd and Andina (Martz) R.; m. Willetta Ohlwiler, Aug. 17, 1968; children—James Anthony, Julie Ann, Jynnae Alyse, Jeffery Allen. B.S. in Zoology, No. Ariz. U., 1968; O.D., Pacific U., 1972. Pvt. practice optometry, owner Colorado River Eye Care Center, Riviera, Ariz., 1974—. Asst. dir., adminstr., treas., past pres. Little League, Bullhead City, Ariz.; instr. firearm safety Ariz. Game and Fish. Served as capt. U.S. Army, 1972-74. Recipient Outstanding Service award Bullhead City Lions Club, 1979. Mem. Am. Optometric Assn., Ariz. Optometric Assn., Nat. Eye Research Found., Better Vision Inst. Republican. Mormon. Clubs: Rotary (Bullhead City); Elks, Moose. Home: 2324 Roadrunner Rd Riviera AZ 86442 Office: 1465 Hwy 95 Riviera AZ 86442

RICHARDSON, JAMES T., sociology educator; b. Charleston, S.C., Aug. 25, 1941; s. Lyle V. and Vera (King) R.; m. Cynthia M. Brown, Sept. 2, 1966; 1 dau., Tamatha Lea. B.A. in Sociology, Tex. Tech U., 1964, M.A., 1965; Ph.D., Wash. State U., 1968; postgrad. Old Coll. Law Sch., 1981—. Prof. sociology U. Nev.-Reno, 1968—; dept. visitor London Sch. Econs., 1974-75. Chmn. Washoe County (Nev.) Dem. Party, 1978-80. NEH grantee, 1978; Fulbright fellow, 1981. Mem. Am. Sociol. Assn., Internat. Conf. for Sociology of Religion, Assn. for Sociology of Religion, Soc. for Sci. Study Religion, Reno C. of C. Author: (with A. Brady) Programmed Learning Aid, 1974; co-author: Organized Miracles, 1979; editor: Conversion Careers, 1978; editor: (with D. Bromley) The Brainwashing Deprogramming Controversy, 1983; contbr. articles to profl. jours.

RICHARDSON, JEAN DODSON, computer co. advt. exec.; b. Kellyville, Okla., July 12, 1936; d. Guy Victor and Pearl Mae (Brumley) Dodson; student West Valley Coll., 1972-74; m. John Richardson, Apr. 15, 1966; children—Caryl, Connie, Christy, Greg. Dir. advt. and promotion Apple Computer, Inc., Cupertino, Calif., 1978—. Mem. Peninsula Mktg. Assn. Home: 47 Alpine St Los Gatos CA 95030 Office: 10260 Bandley Dr Cupertino CA 95014

RICHARDSON, JEFFERY HOWARD, chemist; b. Oakland, Calif., Nov. 23, 1948; s. Richard Bruce and Irmgard (Bishop) R.; B.S., Calif. Inst. Tech., 1970; Ph.D., Stanford U., 1974; m. Karen Elizabeth Cassell, Mar. 25, 1978. Chemist, Lawrence Livermore Lab., U. Calif., 1974—, group leader laser group, 1978-80, group leader spl. polymer projects, 1981—; cons. laser immunofluorescence assay, Mallinckrodt, 1978-79. NSF predoctoral fellow, 1970-74. Mem. Am. Chem. Soc., AAAS, Sigma Xi, Tau Beta Pi. Republican. Presbyterian. Research in laser photoelectrochemistry, laser analytical chemistry, oil shale recovery, polymers. Office: Lawrence Livermore Lab 1-325 Livermore CA 94550

RICHARDSON, JOAN FRANCES, educator; b. Springfield, Mass., Mar. 14, 1936; d. Ralph and Elizabeth (Young) Hamm; stepdau. Perley Joseph Wells; m. Carl A. Richardson, June 21, 1958; children—Paul, Scott, Pamela. B.S. in Home Econs. Edn., U. Mass.-Amherst, 1958; M.S. in Home Econs. Edn., Ariz. State U., 1977. Cert. vocat. home econs., vocat.-related occupation coordinator, secondary teaching. Tchr., Birthland Park Sch., East Longmeadow, Mass., 1958-60, Laveen (Ariz.)/Cash Schs., 1972-74, Black Mountain Sch. and Cactus Shadows High Sch., Cave Creek, Ariz., 1974—; adj. instr. energy and econs. Ariz. State U., 1982; community tchr. building solar ovens; active nat. field testing on solar energy N.Y. State Dept. Edn., 1981-82; promoter, speaker energy conservation. Dep. registrar Maricopa County Republican Com., 1974—; elder, deacon Desert Hills Presbyn. Ch. Recipient 1st prize cook-off category Nat. Solar Cook-Off, 1981. Mem. Am. Edn. Assn., Ariz. Edn. Assn., Cave Creek Tchrs. Assn., Am. Home Econs. Assn., Ariz. Home Econs. Assn., Ariz. Vocat. Assn., Ariz. Assn. Vocat. Home Econs. Educators, Ariz. Solar Energy Assn., Maricopa County Home Econs. Tchrs. (coordinating bd. with Ariz. State U. and Ariz. Dept. Edn.). Club: Rebekah. Home: PO Box 622 Cave Creek AZ 85331 Office: PO Box 426 Cave Creek AZ 85331

RICHARDSON, JOHN EASTBURN, II, air force officer, editor, educator; b. Abington, Pa., Nov. 28, 1942; s. Philip Briggs and Jane Graham (Cobb) R.; m. Jessica Frances Cleveland, Aug. 7, 1965; 1 son, Christopher. B.A., Trinity Coll., Hartford, Conn., 1965; M.B.A., So. Ill. U., Edwardsville, 1976. Commd. 2d lt. U.S. Air Force, 1965, advanced through grades to maj.; B-52 pilot, 1966-68; forward air controller, Vietnam 1969-70; instr. pilot, 1970-72; flight safety officer 1972-74; editor USAF Safety Jour., 1974-78; chief safety programs Hdqrs. U.S. Air Forces Europe, 1978-81; editor USAF Flying Safety Mag., 1981—. Decorated D.F.C., Meritorious Service medal, Air medal with 13 oak leaf clusters. Mem. Am. Soc. Safety Engrs., Order of Dadaelians. Republican. Episcopalian. Clubs: Masons. Contbr. articles to profl. jours.

RICHARDSON, JOHN VINSON, JR., library science educator; b. Columbus, Ohio, Dec. 27, 1949; s. John Vinson and Hope Irene (Smith) R.; m. Nancy Lee Brown, Aug. 22, 1971. B.A., Ohio State U., 1971; M.L.S., Vanderbilt U., 1972; Ph.D., Ind. U., 1978. Documents librarian U. Ky., Lexington, 1972-73, reference librarian, 1973-75, instr., summer 1974; assoc. instr. Ind. U., Bloomington, 1975-76; asst. prof. Grad. Sch. Library and Info. Sci., UCLA, 1978—. Bd. dirs. Wesley Found. Serving UCLA, 1980—, v.p., 1981—. Served alt. mil. service, 1973-75. Named Outstanding Young Man, U.S. Jaycees, 1979; UCLA Acad. Senate faculty research grantee, 1979, 81, 82; Newberry Library summer fellow, 1982. Mem. ALA, Am. Statis. Assn. Democrat. Methodist. Author: (with P. Hernon and others) Municipal Government Reference Sources, 1978; (with J. Davis) Calligraphy: A Sourcebook, 1982; The Spirit of Inquiry, 1982; contbr. articles to profl. jours. Office: Graduate School of Library and Information Science University of California Los Angeles CA 90024

RICHARDSON, KATHLEEN HARRIS, lawyer; b. Louisville, Apr. 13, 1948; d. John Manville and Roberta Jane (Burgess) Harris; m. Bruce Warren Richardson, June 17, 1972; 1 dau., Suzanne Elizabeth. B.A., U. Wash., 1972; J.D., Creighton U., 1977. Bar: Mont. 1977. Assoc. Morrison, Ettien & Barron, Havre, Mont., 1977-79; dep. atty. Hill County, Havre, 1979-82; sole practice, Havre, 1979—; instr. bus. law Northern Mont. Coll., Havre, 1980. Dir. Human Resources Devel. Council, Havre, 1978-80, chmn., 1979, 80; dir. Children's House, Havre, 1981-82, sec., 1981-82. Named Woman of Year, Beta Sigma Phi, 1981. Mem. ABA, Mont. Bar Assn., 12th Jud. Dist. Bar Assn. (v.p. 1983, treas. 1982). Republican. Club: Alpha Xi Delta. Office: 214 College Park Plaza Havre MT 59501

RICHARDSON, ROBERT DALE, JR., educator; b. Milw., June 14, 1934; s. Robert Dale and Lucy Baldwin (Marsh) R.; A.B. magna cum laude in English, Harvard U., 1956, Ph.D. in Lit., 1961; m. Elizabeth Hall, Nov. 7, 1959; children—Elizabeth, Anne. Instr. English, Harvard

U., 1961-63; asst. prof., U. Denver, 1963-68, asso. prof., 1968-72, prof., 1972—, chmn. dept., 1968-73, pres. Univ. senate, 1972-73, asso. dean grad. studies, 1975-76, Lawrence C. Phipps prof. Humanities, 1979-82; vis. prof. Harvard U. Summer Sch., 1976, City U. N.Y., 1978, Sichuan U., 1983; vis. fellow Huntington Library, 1973-74; dir. David R. Godine Pub. Trustee, Meadville-Lombard Theol. Sch. Mem. MLA, Rocky Mountain Modern Lang. Assn., Am. Studies Assn., Soc. Eighteenth Century Studies, Melville Soc., Thoreau Soc., Hawthorne Soc., Poe Soc. Democrat. Unitarian. Author: Literature and Film, 1969; (with Burton Feldman) The Rise of Modern Mythology 1680-1860, 1972; Myth and Literature in the American Renaissance, 1978. Office: English Department University of Denver Denver CO 80210

RICHARDSON, RUDYARD OMAR, real estate counselor; b. Salida, Colo., Feb. 24, 1952; s. Deal Weldon and Anna Lilac (Carpenter) R.; B.A., Western State Coll. Colo., 1974, M.A., 1975; m. Anne Michele Lampert, Aug. 5, 1975; children—Naomi, Nathaniel. Systems analyst Bus. and Office Systems, Grand Junction, Colo., 1975-76; br mgr. BOSS, Durango, Colo., 1976-79; mgr. Realty World San Juan Ltd., Durango, Colo., 1981-82; pres. PMS, Inc., Durango, 1979—; instr. mktg. and distributive edn. Jones Real Estate Coll., Durango, 1981—. Coordinator C. of C. Trade Show, 1979-81; mem. La Plata County Republican Central Com., 1981—. Mem. Inst. Creative Mktg. (S.W. regional dir.), La Plata County Bd. Realtors (pres.-elect), Full Gospel Businessman's Fellowship Internat. (v.p.), Hosanna Ministries, Inc. (pres.) (Durango, Colo.). Republican.

RICHARDSON, SHIRLEY ARLENE, career planning consultant, educator; b. Abilene, Kans., Jan. 25, 1927; d. Lawrence E. and Iva B. (Smith) Dial; m. Harold A. Kendall, July 20, 1946; m. 2d, Albert E. Richardson, May 9, 1959; children—Corinne, Elisabeth, David, Margaret, Anne, Stephen, John (dec.). Student Whitman Coll., 1944-45, Mont. State U., 1945-46; B.A., Northland Coll., M.A., N.Mex. State U., 1975, Ed.D., 1982. Music supr., Shell Lake, Wis., 1951-53; choral condr. pub. schs. David City, Nebr., 1954-57; choral condr. pub. schs. Las Cruces, N.Mex., 1957-64; in real estate sales, Las Cruces, 1975-79; dir. student retention program, career planning instr. N.Mex. State U., Las Cruces, 1979—. Active N.Mex. State U. Crisis Intervention Team, NOW. Mem. N.Mex. Mental Health Counselors Assn. (editor Interaction, dir., pub. relations chmn.), N.Mex. Personnel Guidance Assn., Nat. Assn. Mental Health Counselors, Western Coll. Reading Assn., Career Planning and Adult Devel. Network, Nat. Assn. Specialists in Group Work, Am. Soc. Tng. & Devel. Democrat. Episcopalian. Author: A Guide to Career and Life Planning (Workbook) 1983. Home: 2085 Thomas Dr Las Cruces NM 88001 Office: Room 140 Breland Hall Box 3335 N Mex State U Las Cruces NM 88003

RICHARDSON, WILLIAM BLAINE, congressman; b. Pasadena, Calif., Nov. 15, 1947; m. Barbara Flavin, 1972. B.A., Tufts U., 1970, M.A., 1971. Staff mem. U.S. Ho. of Reps., 1971-72, Dept. of State, 1973-75, U.S. Senate Fgn. Relations Com., 1975-78; exec. dir. N.Mex. Democratic Party and Bernalillo County Dem. Party, 1978; businessman, 1978-82; mem. 98th Congress from N.Mex. Active Big Bros./Big Sisters of Santa Fe. Mem. Santa Fe Hispanic C. of C., Santa Fe C. of C., Hispanic Council Fgn. Affairs, Santa Fe Jaycees, Am. GI Forum. Democrat. Office: 1610 Longworth House Office Bldg Washington DC 20515*

RICHARDSON, WILLIAM SHAW, chief justice Hawaii Supreme Court; b. Honolulu, Dec. 22, 1919; s. Wilfred and Amy (Wung) R.; A.B., U. Hawaii, 1941; J.D., U. Cin., 1943; m. Amy Ching, June 21, 1947; children—Corinne, Barbara, William. Bar: Hawaii 1946. Practiced in Honolulu; lt. gov. State of Hawaii, 1962-66; chief justice Supreme Ct. Hawaii, 1966—. Chmn. Conf. Chief Justices, 1972-73; dir. Nat. Center State Cts. Chmn. Democratic Central Com. Hawaii, 1956-62; bd. dirs. Episcopal Diocese Honolulu. Named Judge of Yr., Am. Trial Judges Assn., 1975. Served with AUS, 1943-46. Mem. Bar Assn. Hawaii (pres. 1961), Res. Officers Assn. (pres. Honolulu 1950), ADA (ho. dels. 1961). Episcopalian (sr. warden). Lodge: Masons. Club: Hawaiian Civic (dir.) (Honolulu). Office: Supreme Ct Bldg Honolulu HI 96813*

RICHEY, MARY ANNE REIMANN, judge; b. Shelbyville, Ind., Oct. 24, 1917; d. H. Wallace and Emma (Nading) Reimann; student Purdue U., 1937-40; J.D., U. Ariz., 1951; m. William K. Richey, Oct. 8, 1959; 1 dau., Anne Marie Richey. Admitted to Ariz. bar, 1951; dep. county atty. Pima County (Ariz.), 1952-54; asst. U.S. atty. Dist. Ariz., Tucson, 1954-59, U.S. atty., 1960; judge Superior Ct. Pima County, 1964-76, asso. presiding judge, 1972-76; U.S. dist. judge for Dist. Ariz., 1976—; mem. exec. com. 9th Circuit, 1978-81. Mem. Jud. Qualification Commn., 1970-76, Criminal Code Revision Commn., 1973-76, Gov.'s Commn. on Status of Women, 1971-73; co-chmn. Supreme Ct. Com. to Revise Civil Jury Instrns., 1971-73. Mem. adv. bd. Salvation Army, 1968—; pres. bd. dirs. YWCA, Tucson, 1968-69. Served with WASP, 1944-45. Mem. ABA, Pima County Bar Assn., State Bar Ariz., U.S. Jud. Conf. (chmn. fed.-state relations subcom. ct. adminstrn. com.). Office: US Dist Ct Room 301 US Courthouse 55 E Broadway Tucson AZ 85701

RICHMAN, ANTHONY E., uniform and towel rental service co. exec.; b. Los Angeles, Dec. 13, 1941; s. Irving M. and Helen V. (Muchnic) R.; B.S., U. So. Calif., 1964; m. Judy Harriet Richman, Dec. 19, 1964; children—Lisa Michele, Jennifer Beth. With Renta Uniform & Towel Supply Co., Los Angeles, 1964—, service mgr., 1969, sales and service mgr., 1970-73, plant mgr., 1973-75, gen. mgr., dir., 1975-78, chief exec. officer, 1978-82, v.p., sec.-treas., 1975-82, exec. v.p., chief exec. officer, 1982—. Bd. dirs. Guild for Children, 1979—, Valley Guild for Cystic Fibrosis, 1974—; Founding mem. Patrons for Cystic Fibrosis, 1983—. Recipient cert. of achievement Linen Supply Assn. Am., 1979. Mem. Textile Rental Services Assn. Am. (past dir.). Office: Renta Uniform & Towel Supply Co 3200 N Figueroa St Los Angeles CA 90065

RICHMAN, LARRY LEON, translator, publishing company executive; b. Brigham City, Utah, July 10, 1955; s. Lynn Thomas and Katheryn Joyce (Seely) R.; m. Teri Jackman, July 9, 1982. B.A. in Spanish and Linguistics, Brigham Young U., 1979, transl. cert. in Spanish/Cakchiquel/English, 1979, M.S. in Instructional Sci., 1981. Lang. specialist David O. McKay Inst.; text writer, test developer Brigham Young U., 1976-79, dir. recs. Brigham Young U. Sound Services, Guatemala, 1978; linguistic cons. New World Langs., Provo, Utah, 1978-80; translator Ch. of Jesus Christ of Latter-day Saints, Salt Lake City, 1977-80, prodn. coordinator, 1978-80, mgr. publs. project, 1980-82, supr. transl., 1982—; pres. Richman Communications, Provo, Utah, 1981—, Richman Pub., Provo, 1981—; cons. on Meso-Am. langs. and cultures. Recipient Eagle Scout award Boy Scouts Am., 1968. Mem. Am. Translators Assn., Deseret Lang. and Linguistics Soc. (sec./treas. 1980), Delta Sigma Pi. Republican. Mormon. Author: Culture for Missionaries: Guatemalan Indian, 1980; Diccionario Espanol-Cakchiquel-Ingles, 1981; contbr. articles on linguistics to Jour. Mayan Linguistics, Notes on Trans.; editor: Prominent Men and Women of Provo. Office: PO Box 11307 Salt Lake City UT 84147

RICHMAN, MARVIN JORDAN, real estate developer; b. N.Y.C., July 13, 1939; s. Morris and Minnie (Graubart) R.; m. Amy Paula Rubin, July 31, 1966; children—Mark Jason, Keith Hayden, Susanne Elizabeth, Jessica Paige. B.Arch., MIT, 1962; M.Urban Planning, N.Y. U., 1966, postgrad., 1967-69; M.B.A., U. Chgo., 1977; U.S. Dept. State fellow U. Chile, 1960. Architect, planner Skidmore, Owings & Merrill, N.Y.C., 1964, Conklin & Rossant, N.Y.C., 1965-67; ptnr. Jonas Vizbaras & Assos., N.Y.C., 1968-69; v.p. Urban Investment & Devel. Co., Chgo., 1969-79, sr. v.p., 1979; pres. First City Devels. Corp., Beverly Hills, Calif., 1979-80, Olympia & York Calif. Equities Corp., Los Angeles, 1981—; lectr. N.Y. U., 1967-69, Nat. Humanities Inst., other univs. Served with USAF, 1963-64. Registered architect, lic. real estate broker. Mem. AIA, Am Planning Assn., Am. Arbitration Assn., Central City Assn. Los Angeles (dir.). Internat. Council Shopping Centers, Chgo. Real Estate Bd., Lambda Alpha. Office: 400 S Hope St Los Angeles CA 90071

RICHMAN, PETER MARK, actor, painter, writer; b. Phila., Apr. 16, 1927; s. Benjamin and Yetta Dora (Peck) R.; B.S. in Pharmacy, Phila. Coll. Pharmacy and Sci., 1951; student Lee Strasberg, N.Y.C., 1952-54; m. Theodora Helen Landess, May 10, 1953; children—Howard Bennett, Kelly Allyn, Lucas Dion, Orien, Roger Lloyd. Appeared in little theater, Phila., 1946-51, on radio and in live TV, Phila., N.Y.C. and Los Angeles, 1948-62, Grove Theater, Nuangola, Pa., 1952, Westchester Playhouse, 1953; appeared in Broadway plays: End As A Man, 1953, Hatful of Rain, 1956-57, Masquerade, 1959; off-Broadway: End As A Man, 1953, The Dybbuk, 1954, The Zoo Story, 1960-61; numerous other theater appearances, including starring roles in stock; The Rainmaker, Funny Girl, The Deputy, Hold Me, Night of Iguana, Equus, Blithe Spirit, others; motion pictures: Friendly Persuasion, 1955, The Strange One, 1956, Black Orchid, 1958, The Dark Intruder, 1965, Agent for HARM, 1965, For Singles Only, 1967; appeared on TV series as Nick Cain in Cain's Hundred, 1961-62, as David in David Chapter III for CBC, 1966, as Duke Page in series Longstreet, 1971-72, as Andrew Laird in series Dynasty, 1981-83; guest star appearances on numerous TV shows, including: Playhouse 90, Marcus Welby, Bonanza, Twilight Zone, Mannix, The FBI, Vegas, Dallas, Three's Company, Hart to Hart, Glactica, Charlie's Angels, Fantasy Island, The Fall Guy; starred in TV movies: House on Greenapple Road, 1968, McCloud, 1969, Yuma, 1970, Wide World of Entertainment-Nightmare at 43 Hillcrest, 1974, Mallory, 1975, The Islander, 1978, Greatest Heroes of the Bible, 1979, Blind Ambition, 1979, The Psi Factor, 1981, Dynasty, 1981, The Jack Dempsey Story, 1983; one-man shows of paintings: Am. Masters Gallery, 1967, Orlando Gallery, 1966, McKenzie Gallery, 1969, 73, Hopkins Gallery, 1971, Goldfield Gallery, 1979 (all Los Angeles), Crocker Mus., others; group shows include: Adele Bednarz Gallery, Los Angeles, 1968, Dohan Gallery, Los Angeles, 1966, Celebrity Art Exhibits, 55-city tour, 1964-65; represented in permanent collections: Crocker Museum, Sacramento, SUNY, Albany, also numerous pvt. collections in U.S. and abroad; playwright: Heavy Heavy What Hangs Over?, 1971; mem. Actors Studio, 1954—; dir. plays: Apple of His Eye, 1954, Glass Menagerie, 1954. Mem. adv. bd. Valley Youth Orch. Assn.; trustee Motion Picture and TV Fund. Served with USN, 1945-46. Registered pharmacist, Pa., N.Y. mem. Screen Actors Guild, Actors Equity Assn., AFTRA, Assn. Can. TV and Radio Artists, Acad. Motion Picture Arts and Scis. Office: care David Shapira 15301 Ventura Blvd Suite 345 Sherman Oaks CA 91405

RICHMOND, CLAUDE HENRY, provincial government official; b. Blue, River, B.C., Can., Aug. 3, 1935; s. Francis Joseph and Olive Evelyn (Sloan) R.; m. Dorothy Patricia Simpson, Feb. 28, 1958; children—Bradley Craig, Valerie Dianne, Jeffrey Scott. With 'NL Broadcasting, 1970-78, gen. mgr., 1978-82; mem. Legis. Assembly, Province of B.C., 1981—, minister of tourism, 1982—, minister responsible for Expo 86. Alderman, City of Kamloops, 1975-78. Served with UCAF, 1952-55. Mem. Social Credit Party. Club: Kamloops Flying Home: 1051 Ollek St Kamloops BC V2B 5B1 Canada Office: 113 Parliament Bldgs Victoria BC V8V 1X4 Canada

RICHMOND, JOHN, lawyer; b. Oakland, Calif., Dec. 10, 1907; s. Samuel and Sarah (Stein) R.; B.S., U. Calif. at Berkeley, 1928, M.S., 1934; LL.B., Oakland Coll. Law, 1942; Ph.D. (hon.), Hamilton State U.; Pres., Richmond Enterprises, Berkeley, 1928—; admitted to Calif. bar, 1946 since practiced in Berkeley. Served with USAAF, 1942-45. Gen. chmn. Berkeley Meml. Services, 1963. Fellow Intercontinental Biog. Assn. (Eng.); mem. Am., Fed., Alameda County, Berkeley-Albany bar assns., AAAS, Internat. Platform Assn., State Bar Calif., Pan Xenia, Supreme Ct. Hist. Soc. (founding), U. Calif. Alumni Assn., VFW, Izaak Walton League Am., Internat. Oceanographic Found. Mason (Shriner). Club: Nat. Lawyers. Address: 1611 Bonita Ave Berkeley CA 94709

RICHMOND, JOHN WALKER, JR., library mgr.; b. Los Angeles, Oct. 3, 1920; s. John Walker and Mary Eugenia (Ransom) R.; m. Lois Marie Roquet, July 25, 1943; children—Susan Marie, John Walker III, David Arthur. B.A., UCLA, 1943; postgrad. Am. U., 1958-59; grad. Army Command and Staff Coll., 1963; M.L.S., U. Calif.-Berkeley, 1973. Commd. ensign U.S. Navy, 1943, advanced through grades to comdr., 1963; comdg. officer USS Interpreter (AGR 14), 1961-62, USS Donner (LSD 20), 1967-69; ops. officer Amphibious Squadron One, 1963-65; dir. evaluation U.S. Naval Amphibious Sch., Coronado, Calif., 1965-67; U.S. naval attache, Malta, 1969-70; exec. officer U.S. Naval Sta., Bklyn., 1970-72; ret., 1972; mgr. North Bay Coop. Library System Service Ctr., Santa Rosa, Calif., 1973-82; tech. services adminstr. Phoenix Pub. Library, 1982—. Active various community orgns. including Little League, PTA. Decorated 3 Commendation medals with 2 combat Vs. Mem. U.S. Naval Inst., Am. Mgmt. Assn., ALA, Calif. Library Assn., Spl. Library Assn., No. Calif. Tech. Processing Group. Democrat. Methodist. Club: Kiwanis. Home: 217 W Frier Dr Phoenix AZ 85021 Office: 12 E McDowell St Phoenix AZ 85004

RICHMOND, MARBETH, sales director; b. Fort Bragg, N.C., Nov. 6, 1943; s. Homer and Louise (Hale) R. B.A., San Francisco State U. Research dir. Sta. KCBS, San Francisco, 1969-70; dir. advt. and promotion Sta. KSFX-ABC-FM, San Francisco, 1971-73; div. mgr. ABC-FM Spot Sales, San Francisco, 1973-75; gen. sales mgr. Sta. KSFX-ABC-FM, San Francisco, 1975-80, dir. sales NBC Network Radio, West Coast, Burbank, Calif., 1981—. Recipient awards in field. Mem. So. Calif. Broadcasting Assn., Am. Women in Radio & TV, NOW, Photographer. Office: 3000 W Alameda Ave Burbank CA 91523

RICHMOND, ROSALIND, social worker; b. Boston, May 18, 1938; d. Leonard Julius and Esther Freda (Greenberg) R.; B.S., Simmons Coll., 1960, M.S., 1962. Clin. social worker, oncology service, handicapped children Mass. Eye and Ear Infirmary, Boston, 1962-65; clin. social worker med.-surg. services VA Med. Center, San Francisco, 1965-75, adminstr. psychiat. outpatient clinic, 1975—; tchr. seminars. Recipient Superior Performance award VA Med. Ctr., 1983. Lic. clin. social worker. Mem. Nat. Assn. Social Workers, Acad. Cert. Social Workers. Home: 2201 Laguna St San Francisco CA 94115 Office: 4150 Clement St San Francisco CA 94121

RICHMOND, SCOTT DAVID, lawyer; b. Orange, Calif., Dec. 30, 1938. S. Gordon X. and Ruth Ruggles (Miller) R.; m. Nancy Jill Smith, Sept. 26, 1964; children—Colleen Suzanne, Megan Ann. B.A., Stanford U., 1960; LL.B., U. Calif., San Francisco, 1964. Bar: Calif. 1965. Assoc. firm Richmond & Richmond, Laguna Hills, Calif., 1965—; seminar moderator Continuing Edn. of Bar. Extraordinary minister of eucharist La Purisima Ch., Orange, Calif., 1977—, mem. parish council, 1978-80; ski leader Orange-Villa Buckeroos 4-H Club; mem. adv. bds. Orange Nat. Bank, Orange Rotary Club, Orange Sr. Citizens Adv. Council; trustee Wilson Family Living, Inc., Rehab. Inst. So. Calif. Found. Mem. ABA, State Bar Calif., Orange County Bar Assn., Stanford Assocs. Served with U.S. Army, 1957. Republican. Roman Catholic. Clubs: Coto de Caza (Trabucco Canyon), Ridgeline Country (Orange). Home: 7825 Santiago Canyon Rd Orange CA 92669 Office: Richmond & Richmond Taj Mahal Suite 312 23521 Paseo de Valencia Laguna Hills CA 92653

RICHMOND, WILLIAM ADDISON, tax accountant, retired marine; b. Seymour, Ind., Jan. 12, 1935; s. William Lynn and Lucille Roberta (Clapesattle) R.; m. Dorothy J. Rogers, Feb. 16, 1956 (div. 1982); children—Mark Richmond, Joy Correia. B.A. in Acctg., Calif. State U.-Fresno, 1977. Enlisted man U.S. Marine Corps, 1953-74; ret., 1974; self-employed tax acct., Tulare, Calif., 1974—. Decorate Air Force Commendation medal. Republican. Episcopalian. Club: Kiwanis (pres. 1982) (Tulare); Masons, Elks. Office: 219 North M St Suite 105 Tulare CA 93274

RICHTER, BURTON, physicist, educator; b. N.Y.C., Mar. 22, 1931; s. Abraham and Fanny (Pollack) R.; B.S., MIT, 1952, Ph.D., 1956; m. Laurose Becker, July 1, 1960; children—Elizabeth, Matthew. Research asso. Stanford U., 1956-60, asst. prof. physics, 1960-63, asso. prof., 1963-67, prof., 1967—, Paul Piggot prof., 1980—, tech. dir. Linear Accelerator Ctr., 1982—; cons. NSF, AEC, Dept. Energy. Recipient Nobel Prize in physics, 1976, E.O. Lawrence medal, 1976. Fellow Am. Phys. Soc., Nat. Acad. Sci. Research elem. particle physics. Contbr. articles to profl. jours. Office: SLAC Stanford U Stanford CA 94305

RICHTER, JO LYNNE, educator; b. Clovis, N.Mex., Oct. 25, 1952; d. Douglas Eugene and Norma Jeanne (Wilhelm) Gill; m. William Edwin Richter, May 31, 1974; 1 son, Eric Eugene. Student U. No. Colo., Greeley, 1970-71, summers, 1979-80; B.A. in Edn., Colo. State U., 1974; postgrad. Western State Coll. Colo., summers 1979-82. Various clerical positions Montgomery Ward, 1971-74, Lakeside Nat. Bank (Colo.), 1973; tchr. Poudre Sch. Dist., Ft. Collis, Colo., 1974, Thompson Sch. Dist., Berthoud, Colo., 1974, Jefferson County Sch. Dist., 1974-75; tchr. communication arts Delta Sch. Dist., 1975-80, Delta-Montrose Voc.-Tech. Sch., 1979-80, Cripple Creek (Colo.) Victor Sch., 1980—. Trustee FFML Library, also v.p.; mem. accountability com. Arvada Hist. Soc. Mem. Nat. Council Tchrs. English, Colo. Lang. Arts Soc., Assn. Supervision and Curriculum Devel., Bus. and Profl. Women's Club. Club: Order Eastern Star. Contbr. articles to various periodicals. Office: PO Box 86 Cripple Creek CO 80813

RICHTER, ROBERT ALAN, weaponscraft innovator, safety profl.; b. Milw., Dec. 20, 1944; s. George G. and Pearl A. Richter; student Northrop U., 1963-67; A.A., Riverside City Coll., 1976; B.A. in Psychology, Calif. State Coll., San Bernardino, 1975-76; postgrad. Calif. State U., Fullerton, 1977-81. Police officer, Riverside, Calif., 1971-74; pistolsmith, Riverside, 1974-78; safety engr. Aetna Ins., San Bernardino, Calif., 1979-80; weaponscraft innovator, Riverside, 1974—; officer Indsl. Security, Los Angeles; cons. engr.; safety profl. Served in U.S. Army, 1967-69. Calif. State scholar, 1963-66; cert. peace officers standards of tng. Mem. Am. Soc. Safety Engrs. Innovator Richter Mini-.45 conversion, 1974; author: Two Kill, 1967; Correlation Factor, 1977; Cognitive Differences Between the Sexes, 1978. Office: 5792 Vista De Oro Riverside CA 92509

RICHTER, ROBERT EDWARD, advertising executive; b. New Prague, Minn., Oct. 12, 1947; s. Lloyd Edward and Helen Genevieve (Meinke) R.; m. Carolyn Jody Fancher, July 6, 1969; children—Jennifer Christine, Cara Jeanne. Student Marquette U., 1965-66; B.S. U. Oreg., Portland, 1969. Staff, then v.p. McCann Erickson, Inc., Portland, 1972-78; dir. mkgt. Grantee Corp.; pres. Multiform Enterprises, 1978-83; pres. Smart Solutions, Inc., 1983—; faculty, Marylhurst Coll., Portland. Served to 1st lt. U.S. Army, 1969-71. Decorated Bronze Star. Mem. Am. Mktg. Assn. Republican. Roman Catholic. Home: 8585 West Stark Portland OR 97229 Office: Grantee Corp PO Box 3210 Portland OR 97208

RICKART, KATHERINE MARY, home economist, administrator; b. Windsor, Colo., Nov. 11, 1943; d. Robert David and Mary Magdalina (Lind) Tigges; m. Curtis LeRoy Rickart, June 20, 1965; children—Russell David, Kimberlee Dawn, Garry Brian. B.S. in Home Econs., Colo. State U., 1965; M.A. in Psychology, U. No. Colo., 1979. Elbert County home econ. extension agt., Simla, Colo., 1965-66, 68-72, extension dir., 1973—; art instr. Big Sandy Sch., Simla, 1967-68; tchr. stress Workshops. Advisor Elbert County Fair bd.; vol. leader local 4-H club. Mem. Colo. Assn. County Agrl. Agts. (Search for Excellance Adminstrv. Mgmt. award 1978), Nat. Assn. County Agrl. Agts. (Search for Excellence award 1978), Nat. Assn. Extension 4-H Agts. (Disting. Service award 1981), Colo. Assn. Extension 4-H Agts., Epsilon Sigma Phi. Democrat. Lutheran. Editor News and Views newsletter. Office: PO Box 128 Simla CO 80835

RICKETTS, RICHARD DOUGLAS, editor, computer specialist; b. Aberdeen, Wash., Apr. 22, 1937; s. Clell Arthur and Elsie Mildred (Sherman) R.; m. Phyllis Mae Rowland, Nov. 25, 1966; children—David Clell, Darren Robert. M.A. in Secondary Edn., San Francisco State Coll., 1974. Instructional computing specialist, Lane E.S.D., Eugene, Oreg., 1976-78; computer edn. specialist Multnomah E.S.D., Portland, Oreg., 1978-81; mng. editor Internat. Council for Computers in Edn., Eugene, 1981—. Participant Oreg. Ednl. Computing Consortium, 1981. Served with U.S. Army, 1958-61. Mem. Northwest Council Computer Edn. Democrat. Baptist. Home: 1250 E 29th Pl Eugene OR 97403 Office: The Computing Tchr U Oreg 135 Education St Eugene OR 97403

RICKS, ROSEMARIE CARMICHAEL, educator, reading specialist, consultant; b. Birmingham, Ala., July 9, 1947; d. Johnny Harry and Rutha Mae (Washington) Carmichael; m. William Aaron Ricks, Aug. 21, 1971 (div.); children—Karen Michelle, Kathleen Delores. B.S., Hampton Inst., 1969; M.A., U. Wis.-Madison, 1970; M.A., Calif. State U.-Los Angeles, 1976. Cert. tchr., Calif. Reading specialist Jefferson High Sch., Portland (Oreg.) Pub. Schs., 1970-72; instr. history U. Portland, 1972; reading specialist Duarte (Calif.) High Sch., 1972-76; tchr. history, reading specialist Sweetwater Union High Sch. Dist., Chula Vista, Calif., 1977—; cons. black history, culture Los Angeles Pub. Schs., Sweetwater Union High Sch. Dist., Vice Pres. San Diego chpt. Chilren Homes Soc., 1980—. Danforth fellow, 1967-69; Mem. Am. Hist. Soc., AAUW, Calif. Reading Assn., Nat. Tchrs. English, Smithsonian Assocs., Calif. Tchrs. Assn., Nat. Urban League, NOW Quill and Scroll, Alpha Kappa Mu, Pi Lambda Theta. Democrat. United Methodist. Clubs: New Beginnings (San Diego), Evening Star (Arlington, Va.). Home: 11058 Westonhill Dr San Diego CA 92126 Office: Sweetwater Union High Sch 415 5th Ave Chula Vista CA 92101

RICO, LILLIAN KATHLEEN, industrial engineer; b. Yuma, Ariz., Apr. 8, 1953; d. Don and Lillian Abert; children—Donald, Mark, Brandy. Cert. in Indsl. Engring., Technology, Southwestern Coll., 1982. Indsl. engr. Wooltex, Internat., Chula Vista, Calif., 1980—. Active San Diego Zoo Vols. Mem. Am. Assn. Female Execs.; Am. Inst. Indsl. Engrs. Home: 2768 Casey St San Diego CA 92139 Office: Wooltex Internat 767 Anita St East Chula Vista CA 92011

RIDDER, DANIEL HICKEY, newspaper pub.; b. N.Y.C., May 3, 1922; s. Bernard Herman and Nell (Hickey) R.; A.B., Princeton U., 1943; m. Frani Cooper Ackerman, Oct. 13, 1971; children—Daniel H., Randy Helen, Richard J. With N.Y. Jour. Commerce, 1946-47, Grand Forks Herald, 1947-48; pub. St. Paul Dispatch and Pioneer-Press, 1952-58; co-pub. Long Beach (Calif.) Ind., Press-Telegram, 1958-69, pub., 1969—; v.p., mem. operating com. Knight-Ridder Newspapers, Inc.; pres. Twin Coast Newspapers, Inc.; dir. Associated Press. Dir., trustee St. Mary's Med. Center; mem. gen. bd. United Way, Inc.; dir. Los Angeles County Mus. Art; dir. Partnership for the Arts in Calif.; chmn., bd. trustees Calif. State U. and Colls., 1969-70. Served with U.S. Navy, 1942-46. Clubs: Virginia Country (Long, Beach, Calif.); El Dorado Country (Palm Springs, Calif.); Los Angeles Country; Cypress Point (Pebble Beach, Calif.). Office: 604 Pine Ave Long Beach CA 90844

RIDDER, PAUL ANTHONY, newspaper publisher; b. Duluth, Minn., Sept. 22, 1940; s. Bernard H. and Jane (Delano) R.; B.A. in Econs., U. Mich., 1962; m. Constance Louise Meach, Nov. 6, 1960; children—Katherine Lee, Linda Jane, Susan Delano, Paul Anthony. With Aberdeen (S.D.) Am. News, 1962-63, Pasadena (Calif.) Star News, 1963-64; with San Jose (Calif.) Mercury News, 1964—, bus. mgr., 1968-75, gen. mgr., 1975-77, pub., 1977—, pres., 1979—; pres. Indsl. Relations Bur., 1981-82. Pres. Santa Clara County United Way, 1979—; bd. regents Santa Clara U.; pres. adv. bd. San Jose State U.; mem. adv. bd. Ctr. for Econ. Policy Research, Stanford U. Recipient 2d ann. Disting. Citizen award Santa Clara County council Boy Scouts Am., 1976; Community Service award NCCJ, 1979; named San Jose Outstanding Young Man of Yr., San Jose Jr. C. of C., 1970. Mem. Santa Clara County Mfrs. Group (bd. dirs. 1979), San Jose C. of C. (chmn. bd. dirs. 1975), Young Presidents Orgn. Clubs: Rotary; Sainte Claire; La Rinconada Country (Los Gatos, Calif.); Cypress Point (Pebble Beach, Calif.). Home: 14751 Quito Rd Saratoga CA 95070 Office: 750 Ridder Park Dr San Jose CA 95190

RIDEOUT, MACK HALLMAN, ins. agt.; b. Salt Lake City, Jan. 16, 1942; s. Mack Sherman and Afton Jo (Hallman) R.; student U. Utah, 1959-61, 63-64; m. Susan Standing, Aug. 23, 1963; children—Rebecca, Nicole, Nathan. Salesman, Conn. Mut. Life Ins. Co., Salt Lake City, 1965—, asst. to gen. agt., 1974-76; mem. Ins. Commrs. Replacement Com., 1978. Missionary to Australia, Ch. of Jesus Christ of Latter-day Saints, 1961-63, bishop, 1974-77; dist. chmn. Republican Party, 1969, 80, 81, del. to state and county convs., 1967, 69, 71, 73, 75, 78, 79, 80; dist. rep. United Fund, 1970; mem. Medic Alert Fund-Raising Com., 1971. Recipient Nat. Quality awards, 1971—, Nat. Sales Achievement awards, 1971—; named life mem. Million Dollar Round Table, knight Million Dollar Round Table Found.; C.L.U. Mem. Nat. Assn. Life Underwriters, Salt Lake Valley Assn. Life Underwriters (pres. 1982-83, nat. committee-man 1983-84), Utah Assn. C.L.U.s (bd. dirs. 1983-84), Nat. Assn. Security Dealers, Salt Lake C. of C. Conn. Mut. Leaders Club. Home: 3634 Capstone Ave Salt Lake City UT 84121 Office: 139 E South Temple Suite 5000 Salt Lake City UT 84111

RIDGWAY, BRYANT, ednl. adminstr.; b. Safford, Ariz., May 16, 1945; s. George Richard and Velmat (Bryant) R.; m. Marsha Gene Gardner, June 10, 1967; children—Marcus Bryant, Brenton G., Melinda Briana. B.A., U. Ariz. 1967; M.A., Ariz. State U., 1972. Cert. tchr., Ariz. Tchr., Alhambra Sch. Dist., 1967-77; prin. Kayenta Sch. Dist., 1977-81, asst. supt., 1981-82; supt. schs., Duncan, Ariz., 1983—. Mem. Ariz. Edn. Assn., NEA, Am. Assn. Sch. Adminstrs. Assn. Supervision and Curriculum Devel. Republican. Mormon. Office: PO Box 866 Duncan AZ 85534

RIDGWAY, DAVID WENZEL, ednl. film producer-dir.; b. Los Angeles, Dec. 12, 1904; s. David Nelson and Marie (Wenzel) R.; A.B., U. Calif. at Los Angeles, 1926; M.B.A., Harvard, 1928; m. Rochelle Devine, June 22, 1955. With RKO Studios, Hollywood, Calif., 1930-42; motion picture specialist WPB, Washington, 1942-43; prodn. mgr., producer Ency. Brit. Films, Wilmette, Ill., 1946-60; dir. film activities, exec. dir. Chem. Edn. Material Study, U. Calif. at Berkeley, 1960—; cons. Mech. Universe project Cal Tech TV, also Am. Inst. Biol. Scis. Served to lt. comdr. USNR, 1943-46. Recipient Chris award for prodn. CHEM Study Ednl. Films in Chemistry, Film Council Greater Columbus, 1962-63; Bronze medal, Padua, Italy, 1963; CINE Golden Eagle awards, 1962-64, 73; Gold Camera award for film Wondering About Things, U.S. Indsl. Film Festival, 1971; diploma of honour Internat. Sci. Film Assn. Festival, Cairo, 1st prize Am. Biol. Photog. Assn. for film MARS: Chemistry Looks for Life, 1978. Mem. Soc. Motion Pictures and Television Engrs. (chmn. San Francisco sect. 1970-72), Am. Sci. Film Assn. (trustee 1974—), Delta Upsilon, Alpha Kappa Psi. Clubs: Faculty (U. Calif.), Bohemian (San Francisco). Author: (with Richard J. Merrill) The CHEM Study Story, 1969; also articles in ednl. jours. Home: 1735 Highland Pl Berkeley CA 94709 Office: Lawrence Hall of Science U of Calif Berkeley CA 94720

RIDLEY-THORNBURY, LANI SUE, sales exec.; b. Altadena, Calif., Mar. 21, 1948; d. Mahuel Joseph and Vera Jean (Van Steenwyk) Pedrini; m. Thomas R. Thornbury, Nov. 6, 1982; children—Jason Michael Ridley, Shane Thornbury, Todd Thornbury. B.A. magna cum laude, UCLA, 1971; M.Bus., U. So. Calif., 1973. Free lance graphic designer/comml. artist, 1966-77; prodn. mgr., comml. artist Lloyd's Fashion Advt., Los Angeles, 1972-73; advt. prodn. mgr. McMahan's Furniture Co., Santa Monica, Calif., 1973-75; media dir./prodn. mgr. Walgers & Assos. Advt., Inc., Hollywood, Calif., 1975-77; account exec./media dir./prodn. mgr. Darryl Lloyd Advt., Inc., Encino, Calif., 1977-78; mktg. rep. Memorex Corp., W. Los Angeles, 1978-79; sales mgr. Prime Computer Inc., Culver City, Calif., 1980—; pres. LRS, Inc.; condr. seminars in field. Recipient Quota Club-Prime Computer Million Club Award, 1980, 81; Rookie of Yr. award Prime Computer Inc., 1980, Top Producer in Western Region award, 1981, Field File award, 1982; Exec. Participation award Research Inst. Am., 1979, Sales Profl. award, 1979. Mem. Nat. Assn. Female Execs., Am. Soc. Profl. and Exec. Women, Working Women Soc., Data Processing Mgmt. Assn., Research Inst. Am., Assn. Women in Computing, U.S. Consumers Assn., Bankcard Holders Am., Am. Film Inst., Am. Rose Soc., Career Guild, Alpha Phi. Clubs: Data Processing, Personal Profit. Office: 6089 Bristol Pkwy Culver City CA 90230

RIEDER, KATHERINE MARIE, psychotherapist; b. Los Angeles, Feb. 26, 1937; d. Maurice D. and Julia C. (Ehrlich) Snipper; m. Howard E. Rieder, Aug. 10, 1957; children—Dee Anna, Leslie Ann, Linda Carol. B.A., San Fernando Valley State Coll., 1970; M.A., Calif. State U.-Northridge, 1974. Lic. therapist, Calif. Pvt. practice in psychotherapy, 1976-77; psychotherapist Valley Counseling Clinic, Sherman Oaks, Calif., 1978—. Mem. Am. Psychol. Assn., Am. Assn. Marriage and Family Therapists, Am. Personnel and Guidance Assn. Office: 14429 Ventura Blvd Sherman Oaks CA 91423

RIEDER, RONALD FREDERICK, public relations consultant; b. Oshawa, Ont., Can., Nov. 10, 1932; s. Joseph Samuel and Minnie R.; m. Pauline Feldman, Sept. 22, 1957; children—Mitchell William, Stephen Walter, Robert Warren. B.A., Concordia U., 1955; B. Journalism, Carleton U., 1956. Reporter Montreal (Que.) Star, 1956-58; city editor Valley News, Van Nuys, Calif., 1958-65; v.p. Hal Phillips and Assocs., Beverly Hills, Calif., 1965-69; dir. communications Daylin, Inc., Beverly Hills, 1969-76; ptnr. The Phillips Group div. Phillips/Rieder, Inc., Beverly Hills, 1976—. Mem. Pub. Relations Soc. Am., Valley Press Club (past pres.), Sigma Delta Chi. Home: 7240 Ranchito Ave Van Nuys CA 91405 Office: Phillips Group 280 S Beverly Dr Suite 500 Beverly Hills CA 90210

RIEDESEL, E. DUANE, mental health therapist and executive; b. Yakima, Wash., Mar. 26, 1944; s. Everett Lloyd and Lois Maude (Curtis) R.; m. Sandra Lee Perryman, June 20, 1969; 1 dau., Meliass Marie; m. 2d, Deborah Evelyn Cowan, Apr. 7, 1974; children—Sarah Catherine, Greta Valentine. B.S. in Psychology, U. Wash., 1978; M.Counseling, Seattle U., 1980. Cert. counselor. Advt. salesman Seattle Times, 1964-66; asst. pub. relations dir. Wendell West Corp., Seattle, 1966-67; asst. dir. advt. Sick's Ranier Brewing Co., Seattle, 1967-69; asst. media dir., account exec. McCann-Erickson Advt. Agy., Seattle, 1969-72; owner Interactions Communications, Seattle, 1971—; co-owner Compu/Systems Type and Art, Seattle, 1979—; mental health therapist in pvt. practice Stevens Meml. Hosp., Edmonds, Wash., 1980—; teaching asst. Seattle U. Grad. Sch., 1980, 81, 83; cons. Hoke Film Prodns., Wash. State Traffic Safety Commn. Served with USMC, 1963-69. Recipient award for Creative Excellence, Wash. Transit Advt., 1971, 1972; Internat. Broadcasting award for Creative Excellence in Radio, 1973; Spl. Service award Wash. Mental Health Counselors Assn., 1982. Mem. Wash. Mental Health Counselors Assn. (pres.-elect, govtl. relations/pub. relations chmn. 1980-83, licensure com. 1980-83), Am. Mental Health Counselors Assn., Am. Assn. Group Counselors. Democrat. Office: 1205 1st Ave S Seattle WA 98134

RIEDINGER, ALAN BLAIR, chem. engr.; b. Maquoketa, Iowa, Oct. 27, 1926; s. Clem A. and Opal (Griffin) R.; B.S., Iowa State U., 1948; M.S., Union Coll., 1958; m. Arlene Janet Swiedom, Aug. 1, 1953; children—Jodi, Bruce. Engr., Gen. Electric Co., Schenectady, 1948-54; engr. Knolls Atomic Power Lab., Schenectady, 1954-58; research staff mem. Gen. Atomic div. Gen. Dynamics Corp., San Diego, 1958-67, Gulf Gen. Atomic Co., San Diego, 1967-74; sr. staff engr. Fluid Systems div. UOP, Inc., San Diego, 1974—. Mem. Am. Inst. Chemists, Sigma Xi, Alpha Chi Sigma, Tau Beta Pi. Lutheran. Contbr. articles to profl. publs.; patentee method and apparatus for conditioning demineralized water. Home: 5925 Sagebrush Rd La Jolla CA 92037 Office: 10124 Old Grove Rd San Diego CA 92131

RIEGEL, BYRON WILLIAM, ophthalmologist, educator; b. Evanston, Ill., Jan. 19, 1938; s. Byron and Belle Mae (Huot) R.; B.S., Stanford U., 1960; M.D., Cornell U., 1964; m. Marilyn Hills, May 18, 1968; children—Marc William, Ryan Marie, Andrea Elizabeth. Intern, King County Hosp., Seattle, 1964-65; asst. resident in surgery U. Wash., Seattle, 1965; resident in ophthalmology U. Fla., 1968-71; pvt. practice medicine specializing in ophthalmology, Visalia, Calif., 1972—; mem. staff Kaweah Delta Dist. Hosp., chief of staff, 1978-79; mem. staff Visalia Community Hosp.; med. staff ophthalmology Valley Med. Center-Univ. Calif. Fresno Med. Edn. Program, 1972—; asst. clin. prof. ophthalmology U. Calif., San Francisco, 1981—. Bd. dirs. Kaweah Delta Dist. Hosp., 1983—. Served as flight surgeon USN, 1966-68. Co-recipient Fight-for-Sight citation for research in retinal dystrophy, 1970. Diplomate Am. Bd. Ophthalmology, Nat. Bd. Med. Examiners. Fellow A.C.S., Am. Acad. Ophthalmology; mem. AMA, Calif. (del. 1978-79), Tulare County med. assns., Calif., Am. assns. ophthalmology, Assn. Research in Vision and Ophthalmology, Contact Lens Assn. Ophthalmology, Am. Intra-Ocular Implant Soc., Internat. Phacoemulsification and Cataract Methodology Soc. Roman Catholic. Club: Rotary (Visalia). Home: 1101 W Whitendale St Visalia CA 93277 Office: 2830 W Main St Visalia CA 93291

RIEK, ROBERT JAMES, laser company executive; b. Johnson City, N.Y., Aug. 15, 1942; s. Carl Arthur and Margaret R.; m. Margaret Ann Goodwin, Sept. 12, 1964; children—Robert, John, Stephen. B.E.E., Cleve. State U., 1966; M.B.A., Memphis State U., 1971. With mfg. mgmt. program Gen. Electric Co., 1966-69, sr. quality engr., 1969-72, mgr. shop ops., 1972-76, mgr. quality control, 1976-79; exec. v.p. Lincoln Laser Co., Phoenix, 1979—. Mem. Delta Mu Delta, Beta Gamma Sigma. Republican. Roman Catholic. Office: 234 E Mohave Phoenix AZ 85004

RIEKE, PAUL VICTOR, lawyer; b. Seattle, Apr. 1, 1949; s. Luvern Victor and Anna Jane (Bierstedt) R.; m. Judy Vivian Farr, Jan. 24, 1974; children—Anna Katharina. B.A. in Chemistry, Oberlin Coll., 1971; student U. Wash.-Seattle, 1971, Shoreline Community Coll., 1972-73; J.D., Case Western Reserve U., 1976. Bar: Wash. 1976, U.S. Dist. Ct. (we. dist.) Wash. 1976, U.S. Tax Ct. 1978. Assoc. Quigley, Hatch, Loveridge & Leslie, Seattle, 1976-82, ptnr., 1982—. Mem. Dist. Council N. Pacific Dist. Am. Lutheran Ch., 1979—, exec. com., 1981—, chmn., 1982—, mem. ch. council Faith Luth. Ch., Seattle, 1978—. Mem. Wash. State Bar Assn., King County Bar Assn., ABA, Order of Coif. Home: 321 NE 161st St Seattle WA 98155 Office: Quigley Hatch et al 2920 Seattle First Nat Bank Bldg Seattle WA 98154

RIEKE, REGINA MILLER, stock broker; b. Duquoin, Ill., Dec. 8, 1938; d. Anthony J. and IdaMae (Schneider) Miller; m. Richard Davis Rieke, June 14, 1958 (div.); children—Linda Rieke Wilkinson, Alan Douglas, Brian David. Student So. Ill. U., 1956-58, Ohio State U., 1958-60; B.S., U. Utah, 1974. Nat. Assn. Security Dealers lic., Utah, Calif., Oreg., Idaho, Nev., Va., Wyo., N.Mex., Ill. Mem. adminstrv. staff Utah Ho. Reps., 1975-76; pres. LWV Utah, 1975-78; employee relations rep. Utah Public Employees Assn., 1978-79; account exec. Merrill Lynch, Pierce Fenner & Smith, Salt Lake City, 1979-83, Prudential-Bache Securities, Salt Lake City, 1983—. Mem. Salt Lake C. of C., LWV, Merrill Lynch Execs. Club, Phi Kappa Phi. Democrat. Methodist. Clubs: The New Yorkers, Snowbird. Home: 2998 Kohala Dr Salt Lake City UT 84117 Office: Prudential-Bache Securities Valley Tower 50 W Broadway Salt Lake City UT 84101

RIEKEN, WILLIAM M., JR., computer systems consultant, educator; b. Vallejo, Calif., Sept. 12, 1947; s. William M. and Billiemarie (Hall) R.; A.B. in Math., U. Calif.-Berkeley, 1971; M.S. in Math., U. Nev.-Reno, 1975; postgrad. in Computer Sci., Stanford U., 1978. Instr. computer sci., faculty asst. U. Wis.-Oshkosh, 1973-76; instr. computer sci. So. Ill. U., Carbondale and software cons. Modern Urban Systems Tech., St. Louis, 1976-77; sr. programmer Bendix Field Engring. Corp., Sunnyvale, Calif., 1977-78; software instr. Amdahl Corp., Sunnyvale, 1978-79; mgr. mktg. software support, software product mgr., program mgr. micrographic systems div. NCR, Mountain View, Calif., 1979-80; pvt. practice cons. in field, San Mateo, Calif., 1980—. Mem. Assn. Computing Edn. (founder), ACM (pres. Golden Gate Chpt. 1981-82, seminar chmn. 1982, disting. Service award 1981), IEEE-Computer Soc., Assn. Systems Mgmt., Ind. Computer Cons. Assn. (com. chmn.). Democrat. Baptist. Home and Office: 3956 O'Neill Dr San Mateo CA 94403

RIESEN, AUSTIN HERBERT, psychologist, educator; b. Newton, Kans., July 1, 1913; s. Emil Richert and Rachel Rebecca (Penner) R.; B.A., U. Ariz., 1935, D.Sc. (hon.), 1981; Ph.D., Yale U., 1939; m. Helen Haglin, July 29, 1939; children—Carol, Kent. Asst. in psychobiology Yale U., 1935-39, research asso., asst. prof., 1939-49; staff Yerkes Lab. Primate Biology, 1939-56; asso. prof. U. Chgo., 1949-56, prof., 1956-62; prof. psychology U. Calif., Riverside, 1962—, prof. emeritus, 1980—, chmn. dept. psychology, 1962-68, faculty research lectr., 1974; vis. research prof. U. Rochester (N.Y.), 1951-53; cons. in field. Served to capt. USAAF, 1943-46. Office of Naval Research grantee, 1950-55; USPHS grantee, 1955—. Fellow AAAS, Am. Psychol. Assn.; mem. Internat. Soc. for Devel. Psychobiology, Internat. Brain Research Orgn., Assn. for Research in Vision and Ophthalmology,. Soc. for Neurosci., Sigma Xi, Phi Beta Kappa, Phi Kappa Phi. Congregationalist. Condr. research on brain devel., primate behavior, vision; author: Postural Development of Infant Chimpanzees, 1952; editor: Advances in Psychobiology, 1972-76; editor, co-author: The Developmental Neuropsychology of Sensory Deprivation, 1975; contbr. chpts. to books, articles to profl. jours. Office: Dept Psychology U California Riverside CA 92521

RIETZ, KENNETH CHARLES, advertising executive, political consultant; b. Appleton, Wis., May 3, 1941; s. Howard K. and Catherine (Abbey) R.; m. Donna A. Armon, June 30, 1982; children—Matthew, Charlene, Kenneth Charles. Grad. George Washington U., 1973. Dep. chmn. Republican Nat. Com., 1973; v.p. MGM Records, 1974, Los Angeles and San Diego, Mike Curb Products, 1974-76; pres. Ken Rietz, & Co., Los Angeles and San Diego, 1976—. Mem. Am. Assn. Polit. Cons., Am. Council Young Polit. Leaders, Rep. Eagles. Presbyterian. Home: PO Box 99 Rancho Santa Fe CA 92067 Office: 9191 Towne Center Div San Diego CA 92122

RIFKIN, SANDRA ANDERSON, interior designer; b. Bismarck, N.D., May 22, 1938; d. Ervin William and Marguerite C. Anderson; student St. Mary's Hall, Faribault, Minn., 1957, Bergman Art Inst., Denver, 1959; m. Robert C. Rifkin, Oct. 24, 1971; 1 dau., Terri Lin. Owner, Design Studio, Denver, 1967-71, Design Assos., Denver, 1971—. Designs include Turn of the Century Restaurant, The Lady and the Dove Restaurant, Lyle Alzado's Restaurant, Juliano's Restaurant, Reflections Disco, Miss Rosy Bottoms Disco and Restaurant, The Parlour Disco, The Charley Horse Saloon, The Proof of the Pudding, also various pvt. residences. Office: 7300 E Hampden St Denver CO 80237

RIGG, JOHN BROWNLEE, oil company executive, lawyer; b. Lincoln, Nebr., May 31, 1947; s. John B. and Shirley A. (Tomlinson) R.; m. Mary Elizabeth Eaton, July 4, 1974 (div.); children—John III, Eaton James, Michael Torian. B.A., George Washington U., 1969; J.D., U. Denver, 1973. Staff, U.S. Senator Gordon Allott of Colo., Washington and Denver, 1967-73; adminstr. City of Idaho Springs (Colo.), 1973-75; regional rep. Motor Vehicle Mfrs. Assn., Denver, 1975-80; govt. affairs rep., Standard Oil Co. of Ind., Denver, 1980—. Chmn. Colo. Republican 1st. Cong. dist. Mem. Rocky Mountain Oil and Gas Assn. (govt. affairs com.), Denver C. of C. (govt. affairs com.), Hwy. Users Fedn. (govt. affairs com.). Episcopalian. Office: Standard Oil Co 1670 Broadway Suite 1984 PO Box 800 Denver CO 80202

RIGGENBACH, JUDY ANN, communications firm executive, educator, consultant, writer; b. Pueblo, Colo., Oct. 17, 1946; d. Simon F. and Ruth R. (Bezensky) Elliot. B.A., U. No. Colo., 1968; postgrad. U. Oslo (Norway), 1966-67. Tchr., Jefferson County Schs., Wheat Ridge, Colo., 1968-71; sales agt. Ten Eyck Realtors, Lakewood, Colo., 1971-75; tng. dir. Realty World, Denver, 1975-78; dir. edn. Perry & Butler Realty, Denver, 1978-79; pres., owner Communication Dynamics, Wheat Ridge, Colo., 1979—; instr. continuing edn. U. Colo.; cons. to attys., hosps. Named Disting. Instr., U. Colo., 1981; recipient Nat. Tng. award Realty World Internat., 1978; Rotary Internat. scholar, 1966-67. Mem. Am. Soc. Tng. and Devel., Nat. Assn. Realtors, Colo. Assn. Realtors. Author: Up Your Effectiveness, 1982. Office: PO Box 1461 Wheat Ridge CO 80034

RIGGS, KATHLEEN, extension home economist; b. Panguitch, Utah, Sept. 13, 1956; d. Jay Angus and Myrtle (Gardiner) Riggs. B.S., Brigham Young U., 1978. Missionary, Ch. of Jesus Christ of Latter-day Saints, Mex., 1978-80; instr. Spanish, Missionary Tng. Ctr., Provo, Utah, 1980; instr. household equipment lab. Brigham Young U., Provo, 1980—; 4-H agt. Utah State U. Extension Service; tchr. home econs. adult programs. Mem. Nat. Assn. Extension Home Economists, Utah Assn. Extension Home Economists. Republican. Office: Utah State U Extension 160 N Main Nephi UT 84648

RIGGS, RICHARD M., journalist; b. Chgo., Dec. 5, 1944; s. William Robert and Elizabeth (McDougall) R.; m. Diane Lee Terril, July 30, 1971; 1 son, Justin Michael. B.J., U. Mo., 1969. Reporter, Stevens Point (Wis.) Daily Jour., 1969-72; reporter The Daily Rev., Hayward, Calif., 1972—; freelance writer mags. Recipient Calif. AP award, 1980, 83. Mem. Investigative Reporters and Editors. Democrat. Club: East Bay Press. Office: 116 W Winton Ave Hayward CA 94544

RIGGS, RODSON LEE, newspaper editor; b. Aurora, Ill., Jan. 9, 1930; s. Leo Watson and Gwen (Boulden) R.; m. Marcia Lee Pratt, Apr. 14, 1951 (div. 1975); children—Andrew (dec.), Theodore, Thomas; m. Mary Kathryn Gunther, July 31, 1975. Student Drake U., 1947-48; B.A., U. Nebr., 1951; grad. Am. Press Inst., Columbia U., 1961; postgrad. Wilton Park, Oxford (Eng.) U., 1973. Reporter Lincoln (Nebr.) Star, 1949-51; advt. mgr. Dawson County Herald, Lexington, Nebr., 1953; city editor Kearney (Nebr.) Daily Hub, 1953-57; mgr. LaCrosse (Kans.) Rush County News, 1957; editor Ames (Iowa) Daily Tribune, 1957-75; dir. energy policy council State of Iowa, 1975-78; advt. mgr. San Diego Daily Transcript, 1978-81, editor, 1981—. Mem. Iowa adv. council SBA, 1967-69; bd. dirs. Nebr. Mid-State Pub. Power and Irrigation Dist., 1957-66; Iowa Republican del., 1958-78; mem. Iowa Rep. State Central Com., 1970-72. Served with AUS, 1951-53. Mem. San Diego C. of C. (dir.), Am. Legion, Sigma Delta Chi, Alpha Tau Omega. Methodist. Club: San Diego City. Lodge: Rotary. Office: 861 6th Ave San Diego CA 92138

RIGGS, STEVEN KENNETH, architect, city planning commissioner; b. Mt. Vernon, Wash., Apr. 8, 1949; s. Denny Kenneth and Alma June (Mitchell) R.; B.Arch., U. Wash., Seattle, 1972; 1 son, Matthew Steven. Owner, Steven Riggs & Assos., Seattle, 1970-74, The Clockworks, Inc., Kirkland, Wash., 1972-76; project architect MAC Devel. Corp., Redmond, Wash., 1975-77, Richard Dodd & Assocs., Newport Beach, Calif., 1977-78; owner Steven Riggs Architecture, Laguna Beach, Calif., 1978—; chmn. design rev. bd. City of Laguna Beach, 1977-80, chmn. planning commn., 1980—; prin. works include: Laguna Beach Community Center, numerous residences. Mem. Associated Architects Laguna Beach (founder, v.p. 1980), Nat. Assn. Watch and Clock Collectors (pres. Orange County chpt. 1979-81), Kirkland C. of C. (dir.). Republican. Mem. Christian Ch. Club: Laguna Beach Exchange. Office: 630 S Glassell St Orange CA 92666

RIGNEY, ROBERT BUFORD, county ofcl.; b. Long Beach, Calif., May 1, 1926; s. Harold Nevins and Nelly Amanda (Buford) R.; A.B., Stanford U., 1950; postgrad. Mexico City Coll., 1951, U. Redlands, Claremont, 1956, U. So. Calif., 1972; m. Lowenda May Morris, Dec. 21, 1952; children—Michael Owen, Jeffrey Owen. Sr. adminstrv. analyst, coordinator spl. dist. County of San Bernardino (Calif.), 1960-66, asst. county adminstrv. officer, 1966-73, 80, county adminstrv. officer, 1980—, adminstr., exec. officer Environ. Improvement Agy., 1973—; mem. Calif. Seismic Safety Com., chmn., 1977-78; exec. officer Blue Ribbon County Charter Rev. Com.; chmn. People's Republic of China/U.S. Constrn. Specialists Exchange Tour, 1978, 80; chmn. Western States Seismic Policy Council; mem. Earthquake Engring. Research Inst.; mem. Solar Energy Project Policy Adv. Bd.; mem. affirmative action adv. com. San Bernardino County, 1980—; del. to Commn. of Californias, 1981—. Bd. dirs. Calif. Inland Empire council Boy Scouts Am., 1974-79, pres., 1983—; bd. dirs. Inland Empire Cultural Found., 1980—, Kimberly Shirk Found. Recipient Achievement awards Nat. Assn. Counties, 1975-76, Silver Beaver award Boy Scouts Am., 1977, Community award Lighthouse for Blind, 1977. Mem. Assn. Environ. Profls. (dir.), County Adminstrv. Officers Assn. of Calif., Nat. Assn. County Ofcls., City Mgrs. Assn., Am. Soc. Pub. Adminstrn., League of Calif. Cities., Native Sons of Golden West. Democrat. Author publs. in field. Home: 1101 Cajon St Redlands CA 92373

RILES, WILSON CAMANZA, ednl. adminstr.; b. Alexandria, La., June 27, 1917; B.A., No. Ariz. U., 1940, M.A., 1947; hon. degrees: LL.D., Pepperdine Coll., 1965, Claremont Grad. Schs., 1972, U. So.

Calif., 1975, No. Ariz. U., 1976, U. Akron, 1976, Golden Gate U., 1981; L.H.D., St. Mary's Coll., 1971, U. Pacific, 1971, U. Judaism, 1972; m. Mary Louise Phillips; 3 sons, 1 dau. Tchr. elementary schs., adminstr. pub. schs., Ariz., 1940-54; exec. sec. Pacific Coast region Fellowship of Reconciliation, Los Angeles, 1954-58; with Calif. Dept. Edn., 1958-82, dep. supt. pub. instrn., 1965-70, supt. pub. instrn., 1971-82; dir. Wells Fargo Bank, Wells Fargo Co., Pacific Gas & Electric Co. Bd. regents U. Calif., 1971-82; trustee Calif. State Colls., 1971-82. Address: 4246 Warren Ave Sacramento CA 95822

RILEY, BRIAN ALBERT, police chief; b. Eugene, Oreg., June 6, 1942; s. Gerald Whitcomb and Ethel Mary (Spencer) R.; m. Susanne Marianne Friedemann, Jan. 10, 1970; children—Kelly, Paula, Cynthia, Dawn, Aric. Student U. Oreg., 1960-62; grad. FBI Nat. Acad., 1976. With City of Springfield Police Dept., 1964—, capt., 1971-74, chief of police, 1974—; instr. criminal justice mgmt. Lane Community Coll. Mem. Internat. Assn. Chiefs of Police, Oreg. Assn. Chiefs of Police. Republican. Methodist. Club: Springfield Lions. Office: 344 N A St Springfield OR 97477

RILEY, COLLEEN MARIE, oil co. sales rep.; b. Seattle, Oct. 6, 1950; d. William Lloyd and Eleanor (Schade) R.; student U. Wash., 1968-70, 74, N. Seattle Community Coll., 1975; B.A. in Bus., Central Wash. U., 1976. Receptionist Group Health Hosp., Seattle, 1971-73; with Shell Oil Co., Seattle, 1977—, ter. sales rep. in mgmt. tng., 1979—. Automotive adv. com. Seattle Public Schs. Roman Catholic. Club: Women's Univ. Office: 400 108th NE Bellevue WA 98004

RILEY, GRESHAM, university president, educator; b. Jackson, Miss., June 27, 1938; married 1959; 2 children. B.A., Baylor U., 1960; M.A., Yale U., 1963, Ph.D. in Philosophy, 1965. Asst. instr. philosophy Yale U., 1963-64; asst. prof. to assoc. prof. New Coll., 1965-67, acting provost to provost, 1972-75; prof. philosophy, dean Faculty Arts and Sci., U. Richmond, from 1976; Younger scholar fellow Nat. Found. Arts and Humanities, vis. scholar Ctr. Advanced Studies Behavioral Sci., Stanford U., 1968-69; cons. Nat. Endowment Humanities, 1971—; mem. Va. Found. Humanities and Pub. Policy, 1976; mem. adv. bd. Project Gen. Edn., 1978-82; pres. Colo. Coll., Colorado Springs, Colo., 1981—. Mem. Am. Philos. Assn., C.S. Pierce Soc., Soc. Values Higher Edn., Am. Conf. Acad. Deans, Am. Assn. Higher Edn. Contbr. articles to profl. jours., chpts. to books. Office: Colorado College Office of the President Colorado Springs CO 80903*

RILEY, JAMES REED, advt. exec.; b. Sundance, Wyo., Oct. 27, 1928; s. Rube and Lucy (Dennis) R.; student U. Wash., 1945-46, Wash. Bus. Coll., Yakima, 1950. Acct., Yakima Fruit & Cold Storage, 1951; sales mgr. Pacific Fruit & Cold Storage, Tacoma, 1952-56; account exec. McCann Erickson, Inc., San Francisco, 1956-65, Honolulu, 1966-68, traffic mgr., account supr. San Francisco, from 1969, now v.p. Campaign mgr. Walter Dods for constl. conv. rep., Hawaii, 1968. Served with USAF, 1947-50. Recipient several 1st pl. advt. awards Honolulu Advt. Clubs: Masons, Shriners. Office: McCann Erickson Inc 6420 Wilshire Blvd Los Angeles CA 90048

RILEY, MARGRETTE HOLMES, educator; b. Greenville, Miss., Aug. 10, 1944; d. Kye and Sarah (Banks) Holmes; children—Michael D., Reginald H. A.A., Contra Costa Coll., 1971; B.S., Calif. State U., 1972; M.A., Westminster Coll., 1974; tchr. edn. credential U. San Francisco, 1974. Lab. asst. U. Calif.-Berkeley, 1959-62, lab. technician Chevron Research Co., Richmond, Calif., 1965-66; counselor, dean Richmond (Calif.) Unified Sch. Dist., 1972—; profl. singer. Named Outstanding Black Woman, Nat. Council Black Women, 1974; recipient Rotary Golden Ruler award, 1975. Mem. Assn. Curriculum Devel., Phi Delta Kappa. Office: 1121 Allview St El Sobrante CA 94801

RILEY, OLIVE MURLE, oil well servicing executive; b. Crosbyton, Tex., Dec. 1, 1932; d. Olive Wildman and Nanny Pauline (Easter) R.; m. Donna Arline Root, Feb. 5, 1956; children—Murle Franklin, Ronald Ray, Gary Lee. B.A., Eastern N.Mex. U., 1960. Jr. acct. Renker & Rudolph, C.P.A.s, Hobbs, N.Mex., 1960-64, with D A & S Oil Well Servicing, Inc., Hobbs, 1964—, sec.-treas., 1971—. Exec. dir. Miss N.Mex. Pageant, 1965; mem. lay adv. bd. Secretaria Sci., N.Mex. Jr. Coll.; mem. acad. adv. bd. Hobbs Mcpl. Schs.; bd. dirs. Hobbs Jr. Achievement. Served with USN, 1951-55. Mem. Assn. Oil Well Servicers, Hobbs Jaycees (past pres.). Republican. Baptist. Club: Hobbs Downtown Lions (past pres.). Office: D A & S Oil Well Servicing Inc PO Box 2545 Hobbs NM 88240

RILEY, PATRICK JAMES, professional basketball coach; b. Rome, N.Y., Mar. 20, 1945; m. Chris. Student U. Ky. Basketball player San Diego Rockets, 1967-70, Los Angeles Lakers, 1970-76; broadcaster with Chuck Hearn, 1979; asst. coach Los Angeles Lakers, 1979-80, coach, 1981—, coach Nat. Basketball Assn. championship team, 1982. Office: Los Angeles Lakers PO Box 10 Inglewood CA 90306*

RILEY, ROBERT LEE, water desalination company executive; b. Iola, Kans., Jan. 8, 1935; s. William James and Frances Elizabeth (Nieman) R.; m. Zada Frances Schwartzman, May 30, 1958; 1 dau., Bridget Ann. B.S. in Chemistry, Regis Coll., 1956. Chemist, Convair div. Gen. Dynamics Corp., Ft. Worth, 1957-59; sr. chemist Gen. Dynamics Sci. Research Lab., San Diego, 1959-62; staff scientist Gen. Atomic Co., San Diego, 1962-74; dir. research Fluid Systems div. UOP Inc., San Diego, 1974—. Recipient Indsl. Research 100 award Indsl. Research Inc., 1972. Mem. Am. Chem. Soc., AAAS. Republican. Roman Catholic. Contbr. chpts. to books, articles to profl. jours.

RIME, DANIEL KEITH, marketing executive; b. Hermosa Beach, Calif., Sept. 12, 1945; s. Edward W. and Eunice M. (Broberg) R.; m. Dianne L. Scoville, Aug. 2, 1968; children—Kimberly, Shelly, Jaron, Helen Nicole. B.A., Brigham Young U., 1969; postgrad. U. So. Calif., 1970; M.A., Brigham Young U., 1982. Cert. bus. communicator. Account exec. Talo Assocs. Advt., Huntington Beach, Calif., 1968; advt. mgr. Vector Electronic Co., Sylmar, Calif., 1969-71; mktg. communication mgr. Beckman Instruments, Fullerton, Calif., 1971-81; mktg. communication mgr. Rockwell Internat., Newport Beach, Calif., 1981-83; mgr. sales promotion and advt., 1983—; cons. communications, market research. Mem. dist. commn. Boy Scouts Am. Recipient Silver Pyramid award Specialty Advt. Assn. Internat., 1980. Mem. Bus./Profl. Advt. Assn. (award of excellence), Am. Soc. Tng. and Devel. Republican. Office: PO Box C Newport Beach CA 82660

RINEHARD, PAULA, nursing educator, administrator, consultant; b. Soda Springs, Idaho, May 29, 1927; d. Delbert John and Madge (Butler) Panting; m. Jerry Longeway Cummings, Sept. 22, 1951; children—Mark G., Clifford S., Steven D.; m. 2d, Donald R. Rinehart, July 9, 1982. Diploma Mont. State Coll. Sch. Nursing; B.S. in Nursing, Mont. State U., 1970, M.S. in Nursing, 1971, postgrad. adult and higher edn., 1974—; R.N., Oreg. Supr. emergency room and outpatient dept. Billings Deaconess Hosp., Billings, Mont., 1947-49, supr. operating room, 1950-51, head med. services, 1966-69; operating room nurse Magic Valley Meml. Hosp., Twin Falls, Idaho, 1949-50; head nurse, nursery St. Anthony Hosp., Pocatello, Idaho, 1951-52; part-time and relief positions, 1952-63; night nurse Westminster, (Colo.) Convalescent Center, 1962-63; night supr. Valley View Hosp. Thornton, Colo., 1963-65; asst. prof. Boise (Idaho) Coll., 1972-73, dir. continuing edn. Sch. Health Scis., 1974-77; instr., part-time, dept. nursing Mont. State U., Bozeman, 1974; adj. assoc. prof. continuing edn. Oreg. Health Scis. U., Portland, 1979-80; clin. instr. (adj.) Oreg. Inst. Tech., Klamath Falls, 1979-80; asst. prof. Portland State U. div. continuing edn., 1977-80; dir., coordinator Oreg. Statewide Continuing Edn. Project for Nurses, Salem, 1977-80; coordinator staff devel. Salem Hosp., 1980—; cons. Closed Circuit TV Ednl. Program for Hosp. Personnel; developer self learning modules for critical care nursing; cons., liaison Salem Hosp., Chemeketa Community Coll., Clin. Experience for Health Care Personnel. Resource person Oreg. Legislators on nursing related issues, 1977—. HEW grantee, 1977-80; recipient continuing edn. grants. Mem. Nat. League for Nurses, Oreg. League for Nurses (pres. 1983-84, dir. 1981—, program chmn. 1981—), Am. Soc. for Healthcare Edn. and Tng. (pres. 1982), Am. Hosp. Am., Oreg. Continuing Nursing Edn. Network (pres. 1982), Am. Hosp. Assn., Willamette Continuing Nursing Edn. Coordinators (chairperson 1981), Phi Kappa Phi, Alpha Tau Delta. Republican. Lodge: PEO. Home: 3837 Meadowlawn Loop SE Apt 10 Salem OR 97301 Office: 665 Winter St SE Salem OR 97301

RINGER, BARBARA ANN, giftware importer and manufacturer; b. Los Angeles, Oct. 17, 1934; d. John Howard and Margaret (Jemison) Lucas; m. Warren George Ringer, Feb. 24, 1955 (div.); children—John D., Brian K., Julie D. Student U. So. Calif., 1953-55. Ptnr. Prisms Unlimited, Los Angeles, 1974-76; pres., owner Heirloom Editions Ltd. Rolling Hills, Calif., 1976—. Republican. Episcopalian.

RINGERT, WILLIAM FREDERICK, lawyer, state senator; b. Castleford, Idaho, June 1, 1932; s. Frederick William and Elizabeth (Knypstra) R.; m. Lynne Bing Kutchback, Mar. 20, 1959; children—John Franklin, Beth Anne. B.S. in Agronomy, U. Idaho, 1953; postgrad. San Angelo (Tex.) Coll., 1955; LL.B., So. Meth. U., Dallas, 1962. Bar: Idaho 1962, U.S. Dist. Ct. Idaho, 1962, U.S. Ct. Appeals (9th cir.) 1978, U.S. Supreme Ct. 1979. Flight engr. Braniff Internat. Airways, Dallas, 1956-62; ptnr. Anderson, Kaufman, Ringert & Clark, Boise, 1962—; sec., dir. Farm Devel. Corp., Boise, 1964—, Grindstone Butte Mut. Canal Co., Boise, 1972—; pres., dir. B & B Farms, Inc., Boise, 1973—; mem. Idaho Senate, 1982—. Served to 1st lt. USAF, 1953-56. Mem. ABA (vice chmn. agrl. law com. gen. practice sect. 1979—), Idaho Bar Assn., Delta Theta Phi. Republican. Methodist. Club: Crane Creek Country (Boise). Lodge: Elks. Office: 599 W Bannock St Boise ID 83702

RINNANDER, JON ALFRED, educational administrator; b. Chgo., Mar. 23, 1942; s. Adolph Julius and Marian (Grimes) R.; m. Elizabeth Hayward, July 12, 1969 (div.); 1 son, Erik Studley. B.A., U. Pa., 1962; M.A. in Romance Langs., Princeton U., 1966; M.A. in European History, U. Calif.-San Diego, 1983. Asst. prof. Spanish, Amherst Coll., 1966-69; asst. prof. SUNY-Old Westbury, 1969-71; mem. faculty Harvard Sch., North Hollywood, Calif., 1971-74; dir. coll. placement Crossroads Schs., Santa Monica, Calif., 1974-77; dir. coll. placement Bishop's Schs., La Jolla, Calif., 1977-82, dir. studies, 1982—; teaching asst. humanities U. Calif.-San Diego, 1983—. Chmn. commn. Hispanic ministry Episcopal Diocese San Diego, 1983; chmn. La Jolla Crop Walk, 1982. Fulbright grantee, 1962-63. Mem. MLA, Am. Personnel and Guidance Assn., Nat. Assn. Coll. Admissions Counselors, Western Assn. Coll. Admissions Counselors, Phi Beta Kappa. Episcopalian. Office: Bishop's Schs 7607 La Jolla Blvd La Jolla CA 92037

RINTOUL, BEECHER, indsl. engr., pub. relations cons.; b. Taft, Calif., Nov. 3, 1917; s. Beecher and Deane (O'Conner) R.; B.S., U. Calif., 1939, M.S., 1941; m. Mary Margaret Brown, May 21, 1946;children—Beecher III, Laurie Deane. Asst. engr. So. Pacific Co., 1938—; indsl. and pub. relations cons., 1938—; gen. chmn. Assn. R.R. Maintenance of Way Supervisors, Assn. Ry. Tech. Employes, 1944—. Registered profl. mech. engr., Calif. Mem. Sigma Xi, Tau Beta Pi. Democrat. Presbyn. Home: 614 Creston Rd Berkeley CA 94708 Office: 65 Market St San Francisco CA 94105

RIORDAN, WILLIAM F., state ofcl.; b. Wichita, Kans., Mar. 26, 1941; s. Robert Bernard and Helen Delores (Rapala) R.; B.B.A., U. N.Mex., 1965, J.D., 1968. Admitted to N.Mex. bar, 1968, U.S. Dist. Ct. bar, 1968, U.S. Supreme Ct. bar, 1971; atty. Legal Aid Soc. Albuquerque, 1968, asst. atty. gen. State of N.Mex., 1969, asst. dist. atty. County of Bernalillo (N.Mex.), 1969-72; judge. 2d Jud. Dist., State of N.Mex., 1972-80, justice Supreme Ct., 1981—. Office: PO Box 848 Santa Fe NM 87503

RIPLEY, RONALD STEWART, lawyer; b. Tacoma, Wash., Feb. 29, 1944; s. Robert Holmes and Maxine Alice (Eldridge) R.; m. Barbara Jean Hearing, Jan. 28, 1967; children—Kenneth, James. B.A. in Bus., U. Wash., 1966; J.D., U. Puget Sound, 1978. Bar: Wash. 1978. With Safeco Ins. Co., Seattle, 1970-75; mem. Pendergrass & Kaukl, P.S., Puyallup, Wash., 1978-81; sole practice, Tacoma, 1981—. Chmn. com., scoutmaster Cub Scouts, Boy Scouts Am. Served to capt. U.S. Army, 1967-70. Decorated Bronze Star. Mem. Wash. State Bar Assn., Tacoma-Pierce County Bar Assn. Clubs: Kiwanis (past pres.) (Puyallup); Elks. Office: Suite 351 Tacoma Mall Office Bldg Tacoma WA 98409

RIPLEY, STUART MCKINNON, real estate cons.; b. St. Louis, July 28, 1930; s. Rob Roy and Nina Pearl (Young) R.; B.A., U. Redlands, 1952; M.B.A., U. Calif., Berkeley, 1959; m. Marilyn Haerr MacDiarmid, Dec. 28, 1964; children—Jill, Bruce, Kent. Vice pres., dir. J.H. Hedrick & Co., Santa Barbara and San Diego, 1958-63; v.p. mktg. Cavanaugh Devel. Co., San Gabriel, Calif., 1963-65; v.p. mktg. dir. Calabasas Park, Bechtel Corp., Calabasas, Calif., 1967-69; v.p. mktg. Avco Community Developers, Inc., La Jolla, Calif., 1969-74; mktg. dir. U.S. Home Corp., Fla. Div., Clearwater, 1974-75; pres., dir. Howard's Camper Country, Inc., National City, Calif., 1975-77; v.p., mktg. dir. Valcas Internat. Corp., San Diego, 1976-77, pres., 1977-79; pres. Stuart M. Ripley, Inc., 1977—, Sunview Realty, Inc., a Watt Industries Co., Santa Monica, Calif., 1979-80; co-owner Everett Stunz Co., La Jolla, 1981—; avacado rancher, Fallbrook, Calif., 1978—; lectr. U. Calif. at Los Angeles, 1961. Served with USN, 1952-55. U. Redlands fellow, 1960—. Mem. Nat. Assn. Homebuilders, Sales and Mktg. Council, Sales and Mktg. Execs., Pi Chi. Republican. Episcopalian. Club: Elks. Home: 13180 Portofino Dr Del Mar CA 92014 Office: 2716 Ocean Park Blvd Santa Monica CA 90406

RIPLEY, THERESA MARGARET, counselor, educator; b. Pontiac, Ill., Sept. 24, 1944; d. William Raymond and Blanche Margaret (Phillips) R. B.S. with honors, Ill. State U., 1966; M.S. in Edn., Ind. U., 1968; Ph.D. in Counseling Psychology, U. Oreg., 1971. Asst. head counselor Ind. U., 1966-68; program coordinator U. Portland, Oreg., 1968-69; prof., counselor U. Oreg., Eugene, 1971—; prin. New Directions cons. firm, Eugene, 1979—; tchr., cons. South Africa, summer 1982. U. Oreg. NDEA fellow, 1971; Fulbright grantee to Sweden, 1979. Mem. Am. Personnel and Guidance Assn. Democrat. Contbr. articles to profl. publs.; co-author five books in field. Home: 1000 W 28th Eugene OR 97405 Office: U Oregon Eugene OR 97403

RIPPEL, MORRIS CONRAD, artist; b. Albuquerque, Jan. 23, 1930; s. Charles Willard and Thelma Mary (Baumgartner) R.; B.S. in Archtl. Engring., U. N.Mex., 1958; m. Betty Mae Drake, Dec. 16, 1961; children—Cherie, Gregory; children by previous marriage—Cheryl, Rebecca. Steel quantities estimator Albuquerque Steel Fabricators, 1949-54; architect various archtl. firms, Albuquerque, 1954-64; design architect Chambers & Campbell Architects, Albuquerque, 1964-67; egg-tempera and watercolor artist, Albuquerque, 1967—; one-man show: Nita Steward Haley Library, Midland, Tex., 1979; group shows include: Nat. Acad. Western Art, Oklahoma City, Western Heritage Sale, Houston, Artists of Am. Exhbn., Denver; egg-tempera paintings include Bluebirds (Prix de West award, 1979); pres., chmn. bd. M. Rippel, Inc. Served with U.S. Army, 1951-52. Recipient 5 Gold medals Nat. Acad. Western Art, 1976-79. Mem. Nat. Acad. Western Art, Am. Assn. Variable Star Observers, Aircraft Owners and Pilots Assn. Registered profl. architect, N.Mex. Republican. Roman Catholic. Design architect Fine Arts Center, Western N.Mex. U. Home: 1317 Florida N E Albuquerque NM 87110

RISCH, JAMES E., state senator; b. Milw., May 3, 1943; s. Elroy A. and Helen B. (Levi) R.; B.S., U. Idaho, 1965, J.D., 1968; m. Vicki L. Choborda, June 8, 1968; children—James E., Jason S., Jordan D. Admitted to Idaho bar; dep. pros. atty. Ada County (Idaho), Boise, 1968-69, chief dep. pros. atty., 1969-72, pros. atty., 1972-74; state senator Idaho from 18th Dist., 1974—, Senate majority leader, 1977-83, Senate pres. pro tem, 1983—. Tchr. criminal law Boise State Coll. Mem. Am. Bar Assns., Idaho State Bar, Nat. Dist. Attys. Assn. (dir.), Phi Delta Theta, Xi Sigma Pi. Home: 5400 S Cole Rd Boise ID 83709 Office: 407 W Jefferson St Boise ID 83702

RISCH, THEODORE DONALD, educator; b. New London, Conn., Nov. 7, 1930; s. Theodore A. and Elanor Rachel (Pierson) R.; B.A., U. Conn., 1952; M.A., Lehigh U., 1965; m. Barbara Lee Thompson, Oct. 1, 1955; children—Catherine Eleanor, Theodore William, Timothy Alan. Commd. 2d lt. U.S. Army, 1952, advanced through grades to lt. col., 1967; tng. and ops. adv. Republic of Bolivia, 1965-67; chief curriculum, dept. dir., dir. instrn. U.S. Army Sch. of Americas, 1970-73, U.S. Army Combat Surveillance Electronic Warfare Sch., 1973; author, instr. Army Command and Gen. Staff Coll., 1973-77; ret., 1977; dir., owner Southwest Inst. Life Mgmt., Tucson, 1978—. Decorated Legion of Merit (2), Meritorious Service medal, Air medal, also fgn. decorations. Mem. Am. Soc. Tng. and Devel., Ret. Officers Assn., Greater Tucson C. of C., Roman Catholic. Home: 11122 E Gunshot Circle Tucson AZ 85749 Office: Suite 120 2500 N Pantano Rd Tucson AZ 85715

RISEMBERG, LEON A(BRAHAM), cons. structural engr.; b. Cordoba, Argentina, Jan. 15, 1931; s. Isidoro and Yaneta Ana (Imas) R.; M.Sc. cum laude in Civil Engring., Nat. U. Cordoba, 1953; came to U.S., 1955, naturalized, 1960; m. Rosa C. Pozzo, Mar. 1, 1952 (div. 1968); children—Richard, Erik; m. 2d, Judi P. Samjohn, July 14, 1970 (div. 1976); children—Adam, Erin. Civil engr. Cordoba Dept. Pub. Works, 1954; structural designer Stiles and Robert Clements, Los Angeles, 1955, H. Whittlesey, Los Angeles, 1957, Ken Iwata, Los Angeles, 1958; job capt. E. Pankhurst, Los Angeles, 1958; project engr. Stacy and Skinner, Los Angeles, 1960-64; chief engr. John B. Parkin, Los Angeles, 1972-73; prin. Leon A. Risemberg, Cons. Structural Engr., Los Angeles, 1964—; instr. Calif. Community Colls.; instr. engring. Los Angeles Pierce Coll.; fallout shelter analyst Dept. Def.; lectr. on human sexuality; leader Sexuality Myth-Info. Workshops. Co-founder Arete, Bisexual Center of So. Calif.; founder, dir. Bi-Social Center, Los Angeles; founder, dir. Bisocial Network. Recipient Nat. U. Cordoba Univ. award, 1953; first award for Design of Welded Structures, James F. Lincoln Found., 1976. Mem. Fellows of Masters and Johnson Inst. Columnist: Bi-Line; Contbr. articles to tech. jours. Office: 7136 Matilija Ave Van Nuys Los Angeles CA 91405

RISER, GAIL VICKIE, packaging engineer; b. Detroit, Mar. 11, 1955; d. Herbert and Charlotte (Gould) Spiwak Gobel, stepdau. Frank E. Gobel; m. Richard James Riser, Nov. 26, 1978. B.S., Mich. State U., 1978. Packaging engr. Md. Cup Corp., Balt., 1978-79; sr. packaging scientist in charge internat. and pet food packaging Carnation Co., Van Nuys, 1979—. Mem. Packaging Inst. (v.p. 1983), Nat. Assn. Female Execs. (dir. local network 1984). Office: 8015 Van Nuys Blvd Van Nuys CA 91412

RISH, DAVID CHARLES, dermatologist; b. Chgo., June 4, 1944; s. Emmanuel M. and Dorothy (Spiegel) R.; A.A., Santa Monica City Coll., 1963; B.S., U. Ariz., 1966; postgrad. Med. Sch. U. N.S.W., 1969-71; M.D., U. So. Calif., 1973; m. Meredith Ann Wallace, Sept. 27, 1967; children—Devra Melanie, Marc Alan. Intern, Cedars Sinai Med. Ctr., Los Angeles, 1973-74; resident in dermatology Wadsworth VA Hosp./UCLA, 1974-77; practice medicine specializing in dermatology, Los Angeles, 1977—; mem. staff Midway Hosp., Wadsworth VA Hosp. Ctr., Cedars Sinai Med. Ctr. (all Los Angeles); asst. clin. prof. dermatology UCLA, 1978—. Diplomate Am. Bd. Dermatology. Mem. AMA, Calif. Med. Assn., Los Angeles County Med. Assn., Pacific Dermtol. Assn., Am. Acad. Dermatology, Internat. Soc. Tropical Dermatology, Los Angeles Dermatol. Soc., Met. Dermatol. Soc., Dermatology Found., Soc. Preservation Variety Arts, Acad. Magical Arts. Office: 435 N Roxbury Dr Suite 204 Beverly Hills CA 90210

RISHEL, HOWARD LEIGHTON, economist; b. Long Beach, Calif., Nov. 20, 1945; s. Dwight F. and Mary E. (Sturdy) R.; m. Diana J. Rishel, July 19, 1969; children—Branden S., Amanda B. B.A. in Econs., Parsons Coll. 1969, M.S. in Econs., U. Oreg. 1974. Chief underwriter State Farm Ins. 1969-72; staff economist Olson Labs., Anaheim, Calif., 1974-76; staff economist SCS Engrs., Long Beach, Calif., 1976-77, chief economist, 1977-81; life cycle cost analyst Rockwell Internat., El Segundo, Calif., 1982—. Mem. Am. Econ. Assn., Western Econ. Assn., Atlantic Econ. Soc., Model A Ford Club of Am. Home: 5322 Yale Ave Westminster CA 92683

RISKAS, HARRY JAMES, constrn. co. exec.; b. Shelton, Wis., Mar. 27, 1920; s. James and Anna (Pappeoanou) R.; student St. Mary's Naval Coll., 1941-43; m. Joan Evelyn Clark, Aug. 1, 1964; children—Lawrence, Douglas, Kimberly. Pres., Pacific Western Contractors, Inc., Millbrae, Cal., from 1951; pres., dir. Riskas Baker Riskas Devel. Corp., San Luis Properties, Inc.; pres., chmn. bd. Pacific Western Contractors, Inc., Sanfo-Bay Corp., H.J.R. Developers, Inc., Windrock Corp. Dir., Am. Pro- perties, & Investment Fund, 1970. Served to lt. comdr. USNR, 1942-46. Mem. Young Pres.'s Orgn. Clubs: Bankers, K.C. (San Francisco). Home: 2020 Fairmont Dr San Mateo CA 94402 Office: 1103 Juanita Suite B Burlingame CA 94010

RISTOW, BRUNO VON BUETTNER, plastic surgeon; b. Brusque, Brazil, Oct. 18, 1940; came to U.S., 1967, naturalized, 1981; s. Arno and Ally Odette (von Buettner) R.; student Coll. Sinodal, Brazil, 1956-57, Coll. Julio de Castilhos, Brazil, 1957-58; M.D. magna cum laude, U. Brazil, 1966; m. Urania Carrasquilla Gutierrez, Nov. 10, 1979; children by previous marriage—Christian Kilian, Trevor Roland. Intern in surgery Hosp. dos Estrangeiros, Rio de Janeiro, Brazil, 1965, Hospital Estadual Miguel Couto, Brazil, 1965-66, Instituto Aposentadoria Pensão Comerciarios Hosp. for Gen. Surgery, 1966; resident in plastic and reconstructive surgery, Dr. Ivo Pitanguy Hosp. Santa Casa de Misericordia, Rio de Janeiro, 1967; fellow Inst. of Reconstructive Plastic Surgery, N.Y. U. Med. Center, N.Y.C., 1967-68, jr. resident, 1971-72, sr. and chief resident, 1972-73; practice medicine specializing in plastic surgery, Rio de Janeiro, 1967, N.Y.C., 1968-73, San Francisco, 1973—; asst. surgeon N.Y. Hosp., Cornell Med. Center, N.Y.C., 1968-71; clin. instr. surgery N.Y. U. Sch. of Medicine, 1972-73; chmn. plastic and reconstructive surgery div. Presbyn. Hosp., Pacific Med. Center, San Francisco, 1974—. Served with M.C., Brazilian Army Res., 1959-60. Decorated knight Venerable Order of St. Hubertus; Knight Order St. John of Jerusalem; fellow in surgery Cornell Med. Sch., 1968-71; diplomate Am. Bd. Plastic and Reconstructive Surgery. Fellow A.C.S., Internat. Coll. Surgeons; mem. Am. Soc. Aesthetic Plastic Surgery, Am. Soc. Plastic and Reconstructive Surgeons, Internat. Soc. Aesthetic

Plastic Surgeons, Calif. Soc. Plastic Surgeons, AMA (Physician's Recognition award 1971-83), Calif. Med. Assn., San Francisco Med. Assn. Republican. Mem. Evang. Lutheran Ch. Clubs: San Francisco Olympic, Sprigateal Duck. Contbg. author: Cancer of the Hand, 1975; contbr. articles on plastic surgery to profl. publs. Office: 2351 Clay St Suite 308 San Francisco CA 94115

RISTOW, LESTER WAYNE, psychologist, educator; b. Belgrade, Mont., May 31, 1911; s. August A. and Lu Mary (Robison) R.; A.A., Sacramento Jr. Coll., 1934; tchr. cert. Eastern Mont. State Teachers Coll., 1935; B.A., U. Wash., 1939; M.S., U. So. Calif., 1948, Ed.D., 1951, postgrad., 1952-54; cert. in system analysis Chapman Coll., 1967; m. Clara Elizabeth Chancellor, Feb. 15, 1941; children—Celesta Ann Ristow Deter, Russell Wayne, Robert Michael. Tchr. schs., Fallon County, Mont., 1935-36, Sacramento, 1939-40; elem. sch. prin. Junction City, Calif., 1940-41; tchr., Avenal, Calif., 1941-42; tchr. high sch. and jr. coll., Compton, Calif., 1947-53; high sch. counselor, Compton, 1953-54; cons. research and guidance Los Angeles County Schs., 1954-64, asst. dir. div. research and guidance, 1964-73, acting dir., 1968-69; asst. prof. psychology Humbolt State U., summer 1958; pvt. practice psychology, Lower Lake, Calif.; part-time asst. prof. ednl. psychology U. So. Calif., 1958-66; part-time instr. psychology UCLA, 1962; part-time asst. prof. psychology Los Angeles State U., 1964-66; part-time asso. prof. ednl. psychology Pepperdine U., 1972-75; part-time instr. psychology Yuba Coll., 1975—; evaluator ESEA Title III projects, Rialto, Calif., 1967, Fresno, Calif., 1968-69; reviewer project proposals State Dept. Edn., Minn., 1968-77. Served to capt. U.S. Army, 1942-46. Cert. psychologist, Calif.; lic. psychologist, Calif.; life diplomas teaching, sch. adminstrn., sch. psychology. Mem. Am. Psychol. Assn., Am. Ednl. Research Assn., Calif. Teacher's Assn., Calif. Assn. Sch. Psychologists and Psychometrists, Calif. Counseling and Guidance Assn., Calif. State Psychol. Assn., Phi Delta Kappa. Author: Using Tests in the Schools, 1962; contbr. articles to profl. jours.; editorial bd. California Jour. Ednl. Research, 1968-73. Home: PO Box 756 Lower Lake CA 95457 Office: 16343 Riata Rd Lower Lake CA 95457

RITCHEY, SAMUEL DONLEY, JR., retail store exec.; b. Derry Twp., Pa., July 16, 1933; s. Samuel Donley and Florence Catherine (Litsch) R.; B.S., San Diego State U., 1955, M.S., 1963; postgrad. (Sloan Found. fellow), Stanford, 1964; m. Sharon Marie Anderson, Apr. 6, 1956; children—Michael Donley, Tamara Louise, Shawn Christopher. Store mgr. supermarkets Lucky Stores Inc., San Diego and Phoenix, 1957-61, store supr. Gemco div., 1965-66, dist. mgr. Gemco, 1966-68, nonfood mdse, mgr. parent co., 1968-69, div. mgr. Gemco, v.p. parent co., 1969-72, sr. v.p. Lucky Stores, Inc., Dublin, Calif., 1972-75, exec. v.p., 1975-78, pres., chief operating officer, 1978-80, pres., chief exec. officer, 1980-81, chmn., chief exec. officer, 1981—, also dir.; dir. Crocker Nat. Corp. and subs. Crocker Nat. Bank; grad. mgr. San Diego State U., 1961-63; lectr. in field. Bd. dir. Sloan Alumni Adv. Bd., Stanford U., Bay Area Council. Mem. Western Assn. Food Chains (dir.), Food Mktg. Inst. (dir.). Office: Lucky Stores Inc 6300 Clark Ave Dublin CA 94568

RITCHEY, WENDY LEA, psychologist; b. Seattle, Mar. 3, 1947; d. Curtis and Marion J. (Bailey) Sykes; m. James M. Ritchey, Dec. 27, 1969. B.A., U. Redlands, 1969; M.A., John F. Kennedy U., 1977; Ph.D., W.Va. U., 1981. Tchr., Juan Cabrillo Elem. Sch., Seaside, Calif., 1969-70, Wilmot Elem. Sch., Deerfield, Ill., 1970-74; counselor, dir. pub. relations Narconon, Berkeley, Calif., 1974-75; asst. to membership chmn. Calif. State Psychol. Assn., Walnut Creek, 1976-77; curriculum coordinator W. Va. System, Morgantown, 1977-78; instr. John F. Kennedy U., Orinda, Calif., 1981; sr. program assoc. Child Devel. Project, San Ramon, Calif., 1981—; pvt. practice psychology, stress control assoc., Walnut Creek, Calif., 1982—; instr. Calif. Sch. Profl. Psychology, Berkeley, 1982—. NIMH fellow, 1978-79. Mem. Am. Psychol. Assn., Assn. for Advancement Behavior Therapy, Internat. Assn. for Study of Coop. in Edn., Phi Kappa Phi. Contbr. articles to profl. jours. Home: 1732 Dover Pl Hayward CA 94545 Office: 130 Ryan Ct Suite 210 San Ramon CA 94583

RITCHIE, FRAN A., interior designer; b. Seminole, Tex., Nov. 23, 1940; d. Homer C. and Margret A. (Simmons) Kyle; m. Byron D. Ritchie, Dec. 23, 1959. Grad. Seminole High School; interior design student LaSalle Extension U., Chgo., 1967. Designer and sales staff Miller-Waldrop Furniture, Hobbs, N.Mex., 1967—, mgr., buyer, 1976—; buyer, part-owner Eileen's Bed, Bath, and Kitchen, Hobbs, 1976—; part-owner, buyer, Miller-Waldrop Furniture, Odessa, Tex., 1979-81; leader seminars and high school programs on design. Recipient Woman of Yr. award Am. Bus. Women's Assn., 1970. Mem. Am. Soc. Interior Design (assoc.), Am. Bus. Women's Assn., Beta Sigma Phi. Home: 620 Luna St Hobbs NM 88240 Office: 100 W Bender St Hobbs NM 88240

RITCHIE, JOE H., police officer; b. Logan, Utah, Apr. 16, 1937; s. Joseph H. and Eliza (Weston) R.; m. Jean Draper, Sept. 8, 1956; children—Jay, Jon, Jeffrey, Joy Lyn. Student Utah State U., 1955-56, Weber State Coll., 1962-64, U. Utah, 1964-65, U. Va., 1976, FBI Nat. Acad., 1976. Cert. police officer, Utah. With Golden West Markets, Ogden, Utah, 1956-60; investment counselor Prudential Ins. Co., Ogden, 1960-62; with Ogden City Police Dept., 1962—, chief of police, 1975—; bd. dirs. Utah Narcotics Info. Network, Community Correction Ctr., Utah Parole Bd.; mem. community relations council U.S. Dept. Interior Job Corps; bd. dirs. Community Youth Corrections Ctr. Served with AUS. Mem. Internat. Chiefs of Police Assn., Utah State Chiefs of Police Assn., FBI Nat. Acad. Assocs. Morman. Rotarian. Home: 5969 S 3850 W Roy UT 84067 Office: PO Box 9699 Ogden UT 84409

RITTER, LUCY ELIZABETH, retired insurance exec.; b. Shanghai, China, Sept. 10, 1910; d. Ovid Herbert and Lucy (Corker) Ritter; A.B., Stanford, 1930, M.A., 1931. Research sec. Calif. Taxpayers Assn., 1931-34; security analyst Calif.-Western States Life Ins. Co., 1935-43, asst. treas., 1943-54, 2d v.p. and asst. treas., 1954-68, v.p. securities, 1968-75. Past dir. Sacramento Community Chest; dir., past pres. Sacramento Children's Home; alt. del. Democratic Nat. Conv., 1956, 64; woman's chmn. Citizens for Kennedy, 3d Congl. dist., 1960; bd. adminstrn. Calif. State Retirement Fund, 1961-69; trustee Sacramento Symphony Found., Mercy Hosp. Found. Bd.; bd. regents U. Pacific, Stockton, Calif.; governing bd. Crocker Art Gallery, Sacramento, 1974-83; mem. vis. libraries com. Stanford U., 1976-82. Mem. Security Analysts San Francisco, Chartered Fin. Analysts, Stanford Alumni Assn. (past pres. Sacramento chpt., dir., past mem. nat. exec. bd.). Clubs: Metropolitan (San Francisco); Del Paso Country. Author: Lucy's Twentieth Century, 1974; An Ode to Common Sense, 1978, others; contbr. articles to profl. jours. Home: Capitol Towers 7th & O Sts Sacramento CA 95814

RITTER, MARY L., interior decorator; b. Wilmette, Ill.; children—Caroline Victoria, Mark Henry. B.A., Stanford U.; cert. N.Y. Sch. Interior Design. Interior decorator, N.Y.C., 1951-56; editorial scout various mags., N.Y.C. area, 1951-56, San Francisco area, 1956-63; interior decorator, San Francisco, 1956—; model home decorator Joseph Eichler Corp., San Francisco, 1958; cons. Earl W. Smith Devel. Corp., 1958-60, Draper Shopping Ctrs., Inc., 1959-61; instr. interior design adult edn. div. Redwood City Dept. Recreation (Calif.), 1968, West Valley Community Coll., 1976-78, Can. Coll., 1977; rep. sculptor Richard Lippold, 1983—. Bd. dirs. Children's Home Soc. Calif., 1966, sec. bd. dirs., 1968; chmn. internat. social services spl. event WAIF, 1976, v.p. spl. events, 1969; chmn. benefit March of Dimes, 1979; bd. dirs. San Francisco Host Com., 1979; chmn. dinner honoring mayor and consuls gen., 1979. Named as model room designer Children's Home Soc. Decorator Showhouse, 1968, San Mateo County Jr. Mus. Aux. Decorator Showcase, 1972. Mem. Nat. Home Fashion League, Internat. Platform Assn., Stanford U. Alumni Assn., Calif. Palace Legion of Honor, San Francisco Mus. Art, English Speaking Union, San Francisco Ballet Guild, Am. Soc. Interior Designers (bd. dirs. 1983-85). Clubs: Far West Ski, Far World Ski, Menlo Park Tennis. Contbr. articles to profl. mags. Home and Office: 349 Selby Ln Atherton CA 94025

RITTER, RUSSELL JOSEPH, mayor college administrator; b. Helena, Mont., July 22, 1932; s. Walter A. and Sally C. (Mellen) R.; m. Linaire Wells, Aug. 4, 1956; children—Michael, Leslie, Teresa, Gregory, Daniel. Student Carroll Coll., Helena, 1950-53; A.B. in History, U. Mont.-Missoula, 1957, M.A. in History and Polit. Sci., 1962, Ph.D. in History, 1963. Salesman, Capital Ford, 1953-54, 56-57; tchr., coach Billings (Mont.) Central High Sch., 1957-58, Loyola High Sch., Missoula, 1958-62, Flathead High Sch., Kalispell, Mont., 1962-69; dir. devel. and community relations Carroll Coll., Helena, 1969-76, v.p. for coll. relations, 1976—; commr. City of Helena, 1977-80, mayor pro-tem, 1980, mayor, 1981—; exec. sec.-treas. Carroll Coll. Found., Inc.; owner Danny's Drive In, Kalispell, 1965-69; ptnr. R-B Enterprises, Inc., Kalispell, 1967-71; bd. dirs. Brubaker & Assos., Inc., Kalispell, 1971-74; v.p. Capital Investment, Inc. (KMTX Radio), Helena, 1973-80; pres. Swinging Door Art Gallery, Inc., Helena, 1973—. Bd. dirs. All Am. Indian Hall of Fame, 1972-78, Jr. Achievement, 1975-79; mem. Citizen's Adv. Council, 1975-76; chmn. City-County Bldg., Inc., 1978; mem. Mont. Friendship Force. Served with USMC, 1953-56. Mem. Helena C. of C. (dir. 1972-75, v.p. 1973, pres. 1974, Ambassador's Club 1976—, chmn. 1978), Mont. C. of C. (dir. 1980—, exec. com. 1982—), Mont. Ofcls. Assn. Club: Montana. Lodge: K.C. (4th degree). Office: Carroll Coll Room 258 Helena MT 59601

RITTER, THOMAS NEAL, psychologist, univ. exec.; b. Newport, Ark., Sept. 23, 1948; s. Thomas Albert and Sammie Elizabeth (Bowie) R.; B.A., Hendrix Coll., 1970; M.A., U. Ark., 1974, Ph.D., 1978. Regional dir. Polk and Scott counties Western Ark. Counseling and Guidance Center, 1976-78; practice clin. psychology, Phoenix, 1978-79; clin. dir. Potential Research Found., Phoenix, 1979-80; pres. Profl. Studies Inst., Phoenix, 1980—; cons. in field. Mem. Am. Psychol. Assn., Ariz. Psychol. Assn. Home: 2615 N 36th St Apt Y103 Phoenix AZ 85008 Office: 3627 E Indian School Penthouse Suite Phoenix AZ 85018

RIVERA, ORLANDO ARTHUR, university administrator; b. La Jara, Colo., Nov. 11, 1930; s. Stella (Abeyta) R.; m. Irene M. Martinez, Aug. 16, 1957; children—Art, Patti, George, Selena. Ph.D., U. Utah, 1974. Cert. rehab. counselor, psychologist, marriage and family counselor. Asst. prof., U. Utah, Salt Lake City, 1974-83, assoc. v.p. acad. affairs, 1983—; assoc. dir. Utah State Div. Rehab. Services, Salt Lake City, 1965-70, rehab. counselor, 1959-65. Served with U.S. Army, 1955-57. Scholar, Adams State Coll., 1949-55, U. Utah, 1959-74. Mem. Nat. Rehab. Assn., Am. Personnel and Guidance Assn. Mormon. Author: Chicanos in Utah, 1974; Rehabilitation of Handicapped Migrant and Seasonal Farmworkers, 1981; La Familia, 1981. Office: 208 Park Bldg Salt Lake City UT 84112

RIVERA, TOMÁS, univ. chancellor; b. Crystal City, Tex., Dec. 22, 1935; s. Florencio and Josefa (Hernandez) R.; A.A. in English, SW Tex. Jr. Coll., 1956, B.S. in Edn., 1958, M.Ed., 1964; student NDEA Spanish Inst., 1962, 63; M.A. in Spanish Lit., U. Okla., 1969, Ph.D. in Romance Langs. and Lit., 1969; Ph.D. (hon.), Santa Clara U., 1980; L.H.D. (hon.), Western N.Mex. U., 1982; m. Concepción Garza, Nov. 27, 1958; children—Ileana Imelda, Irasema, Florencio Javier. Migrant worker until 1957; tchr. public secondary schs., Tex., 1957-65; instr. and chmn. dept. fgn. langs. SW Tex. Jr. Coll., 1965-66; teaching asst. dept. modern langs. U. Okla., 1966-68, instr., dir. lang. labs., 1968-69, asst. dir. Spanish studies program in Madrid, summer 1969; assoc. prof. Spanish, San Houston State U., Tex., 1969-71; prof. Spanish lit., dir. div. fgn. langs., lit. and linguistics U. Tex., San Antonio, 1971-73, prof. Spanish, assoc. dean Coll. Multidisciplinary Studies, 1973-76, v.p. for adminstrn., 1976-78; exec. v.p., acting v.p. acad. affairs U. Tex., El Paso, 1978-79; chancellor U. Calif.-Riverside, 1979—; lit. judge; speaker; cons. in field; chmn. bd., mem. exec. com. Nat. Council Chicanos in Higher Edn., 1976—, v.p., 1978; mem. task force on Hispanic arts Nat. Endowment Arts, 1977-79; trustee Carnegie Found. Advancement of Teaching, 1976-80; memb. bd. fgn. scholarships Dept. State, 1978—; mem. adv. com. Allied Health Professions, coordinating bd. state univ. and coll. system, Tex., 1979—; bd. dirs. Hubert H. Humphrey Inst. Public Affairs, U. Minn., 1979—, Tex. Commn. on Humanities, 1979—, Nat. Center Higher Edn. Mgmt. Systems, 1979—. Bd. dirs. Inman Christian Center, San Antonio, 1972-77, Commn. for Mexican-Am. Affairs, Archdiocese of San Antonio, 1972-77, Am. Issues Forum, San Antonio, 1975-76, Assn. Advancement Mexican Ams., Houston, 1977-79. Recipient Premio Quinto Sol., 1970-71; Project Milestone Recognition award Assn. Supervision and Curriculum Devel., 1977; Danforth Found. asso., 1971. Mem. Sigma Delta Pi (pres. U. Okla. chpt. 1968) Democrat. Roman Catholic. Clubs: Kiwanis (hon.), Sembradores de Amistad (hon.; Sembrador of Yr. 1974), Con Safo Artists San Antonio (hon.). Author books, the most recent being: Always and Other Poems, 1973; (with others) A Public Trust, 1979; contbr. articles, fiction to profl. publs.; subject of profl. publs. Office: Office of Chancellor U Calif Riverside CA 92507

RIVIERA, DANIEL JOHN, lawyer; b. N.Y.C., May 28, 1927; s. Charles Adrian and Ruth Blanche (Sinclair) R.; B.A. cum laude, Syracuse U., 1950; LL.B., Georgetown U., 1953; m. Charlotte E. Stevens, July 24, 1971; children—Daniel C., Sara J., Jodi, Jeffrey, Gloria, Spencer. Bar: Wash. 1953, D.C. 1980. Practiced in Seattle, 1953—; mem. firm Foster, Pepper & Riviera, Seattle, 1953—, ptnr., 1968—. Instr. bus. law U. Wash., 1957-59, Journalism law Seattle U., 1965-67, 75—; mem. Statute Law Com., 1963-72; mem. Bench, Bar, Press Com., 1964-72. Mem. Mercer Island City Council, 1961-68; bd. visitors J. Reuben Clark Law Sch., Brigham Young U., Provo, Utah, 1978-80. Served with AUS, 1946-47. Mem. ABA (vice-chmn. projects com. jr. bar conf. 1959-60), Wash. State Bar Assn. (mem. subcom. of local adminstrv. com. 1967-70), Seattle-King County Bar Assn. (labor law com. 1967—). Clubs: Bellevue (Wash.) Athletic. Home: 9031 NE 40th Pl Bellevue WA 98004 Office: 1111 3d Ave Bldg 34th Floor Seattle WA 98101

RIZK, FAHD MOHAMMED, state official; b. Bethlehem, Palestine, Dec. 18, 1942; came to U.S., 1970, naturalized, 1976; s. Mohammed Dib and Khadra (Abdel-Nabi) R.; m. Ikhlas Abdel-Muti Iktaishat, Nov. 30, 1967; children—Fabiola, Nancy, Fabius. B.S., Am. U.-Beirut, Lebanon, 1964; M.S., Calif. State U.-Long Beach, 1975. Tchr. chemistry Al-Hashimeyah Sch., Ramallah, Jordan, 1964-65; tchr. chemistry, sci. Am. Arabian Oil Co., Dhahran, Saudi Arabia, 1965-70; chem. lab. technician Productol Chem. Co. and W.R. Grace Corp., Los Angeles, 1970-74; surveyor Los Angeles Sanitation Dists., part-time 1974-75; san. engr. Calif. State Dept. Health Services, Los Angeles, 1977—. Scholar, Am. U., 1961-64. Mem. Am. Water Works Assn. Home: 8352 Birchcrest Rd Downey CA 90240 Office: Calif State Dept Health Services 1449 W Temple St Los Angeles CA 90026

RIZZA, JOSEPH PADULA, maritime academy president; b. Johnstown, Pa., Jan. 30, 1915; s. Paul and Concetta (Padula) R.; grad. Pa. Maritime Acad., 1936; B.A., U. Wash., 1951; M.A., Boston U., 1958; m. Marie Antoinette Follin, Aug. 30, 1947; 1 dau., Barbara Curwood Schwaner. Served as officer U.S. Mcht. Marine, 1936-42; commd. officer U.S. Navy, 1942, advanced through grades to capt.; ret., 1972; rear adm. U.S. Maritime Service, 1972—; pres. Calif. Maritime Acad., Vallejo, 1972—. Vice pres. Silverado council Boy Scouts Am. Decorated Legion of Merit (2), Joint Service Commendation medal, Navy Commendation medal; lic. master mariner unltd. tonnage. Mem. Am. Soc. Internat. Law, Council Am. Master Mariners, San Francisco Navy League (dir.) Nat. Assn. Indsl. Tech., Vallejo C. of C. (dir. 1979-82), Phi Beta Kappa. Presbyterian. Clubs: Masons, Rotary (pres. 1981-82) (Vallejo). Home and Office: California Maritime Academy PO Box 1392 Vallejo CA 94590

RIZZOLO, RALPH, orch. mgr.; b. Newark, Nov. 13, 1931; s. Silvio James and Gertrude Ann (Naiman) R.; A.B., Montclair (N.J.) State Coll., 1953; M.A., Columbia U., 1969; Ed.D., Ariz. State U., 1969; m. Joyce Ruth Lipson, July 2, 1959; children—Jayme I., Lisa. Public sch. tchr., N.J., Ariz., 1953-66; exec. dir. Ariz. Commn. Arts and Humanities, Phoenix, 1966-69; dir. research and devel. Am. Symphony Orch. League, Vienna, Va., 1969-71; asst. dir. music program Nat. Endowment Arts, Washington, 1971-76; exec. v.p., mng. dir. Phoenix Symphony Assn./Orch., 1976-83; tchr./performer clarinet, saxophone, 1947-69; tchr. music, Rockaway Borough, N.J., 1953-55, Berkeley Heights, N.J., Chatham, N.J., 1955-59, Parker, Ariz., 1959-60, Scottsdale, Ariz., 1960-66. U.S. Office Edn. fellow, 1967. Mem. Am. Symphony Orch. League (dir.), Regional Orch. Mgrs. Assn. (past vice-chmn.). Office: 6328 N 7th St Phoenix AZ 85014

RIZZUTO, CARMELA RITA, nursing educator, continuing professional education consultant; b. Waterbury, Conn., Aug. 26, 1942; d. Joseph Anthony and Carmela Rose R.; m. Thomas Lee Chernesky, Aug. 28, 1982. B.S., St. Joseph Coll., 1965; M.S., Boston Coll., 1971; postgrad. Sch. Edn., UCLA, 1979—. R.N., Calif. Staff nurse, asst. head nurse, head nurse St. Mary's Hosp., Rochester, N.Y., 1965-68; nursing instr. Samaritan Hosp. Sch. Nursing, Troy, N.Y., 1969; med. nursing coordinator, clin. specialist Harvard Community Health Plan, Boston, 1971-72; instr. inservice edn. Tufts-New Eng. Med. Center, Boston, 1972-73; pvt. duty nurse, Boston, 1974; instr. inservice edn. St. John's Hosp. and Health Center, Santa Monica, Calif., 1974-76; asst. clin. prof. Sch. Nursing, UCLA, 1976-79; educator, continuing edn. for nurses, Calif. State U., Los Angeles, 1979-80, U. Calif., Santa Barbara, 1981—; assoc. dir. nursing edn. St. Francis Hosp. of Santa Barbara, 1981—; cons. continuing profl. edn. health scis., 1981—. USPHS coronary care nurse trainee, 1968; USPHS nurse trainee, 1969-71; recipient Chancellor's Patent Fund, UCLA, 1972-73. Mem. Am. Assn. Critical Care Nurses. Contbr. articles to profl. publs. Home: 7614 Pine Tree Pl Goleta CA 93117 Office: St Francis Hosp 601 E Micheltorena St Santa Barbara CA 93103

RIZZUTO, JAMES T., state senator, business executive; b. LaJunta, Colo., Oct. 3, 1945; s. James and Donna (Znidarsich) R.; m. Margaret Nancy Stafford, 1969; children—Benjamin, Kate. A.A., Otero Jr. Coll., 1965; B.S., U. Colo., 1968; M.B.A./M.I.M., Am. Grad. Sch. Mgmt., 1973. Mgr. and v.p. R.N. Mason and Sons, LaJunta, Colo.; part-time instr. Otero Jr. Coll.; mem. Colo. State Senate, 1982—. Chmn. Otero County Democratic party, 1975—. Served with U.S. Army, 1970-71. Recipient Colo. Bus. Person of Yr. award, 1982; Annual Pres.'s award for service to community LaJunta C. of C., 1979, 81; LaJunta Jaycees Outstanding Young Citizen award, 1977. Mem. Colo. Tobacco Assn. (dir.), Phi Beta Lambda. Roman Catholic. Office: State Capitol Denver CO 80203*

ROACH, BARRY LEE, publishing company executive; b. Spokane, Wash., Aug. 23, 1949; s. Frank Vincent and Lois Jean (Cunningham) R.; m. Helene Rose Hink, Aug. 23, 1975. B.A. in Communications, Wash. State U., 1971. Advt. rep. Spokesman-Rev. and Spokane (Wash.) Daily Chronicle, 1971-73; advt. rep. N.W. Unit Farm Mags., Spokane, 1973-79, advt. mgr., 1979—; sec., bd. dirs. Spokane Agrl. Exposition. Mem. allocation bd. United Way, Spokane. Mem. Nat. Agrl. Mktg. Assn., Spokane C. of C. (agrl. bur.). Office: NW Unit Farm Mags Chronicle Bldg 2d Floor Spokane WA 99210

ROACH, ROGER DEAN, business exec.; b. Rutledge, Tenn., Mar. 15, 1937; s. Lester and Wave B. (Barnard) R.; B.S., Met. State Coll., 1977; m. Helen Vargas, June 27, 1954; 1 son, Richard L. Sr. computer systems designer Martin Marietta Corp., Denver, 1960-77, project mgr. spl. purpose computer lab. devel., 1977-79; project mgr., corp. bus. investments analyst Storage Tech. Corp., Louisville, Colo., 1979; exec. v.p., dir., incorporator Interactive Systems Corp., Littleton, Colo., 1979-81, pres., 1981-82; pres., dir., incorporator XYZTEK Corp., Englewood, Colo., 1982—. Served with USAF, 1955-58. Mem. Am. Soc. for Tng. and Devel., Am. Mgmt. Assn. Republican. Baptist. Club: Toastmasters. Home: 2664 S Balsam St Lakewood CO 80227 Office: 5500 S Sycamore St Littleton CO 80120

ROAKE, WILLIAM EARL, engineering company executive, chemist; b. Oregon City, Oreg., Sept. 30, 1919; s. Leslie Verne and Edith Marie (Hutchinson) R.; m. Betty Jean Bolton, May 31, 1942; children—Nancy Lee Roake Tecumseh, James William. B.S., Oreg. State U., 1941, M.S., 1942; Ph.D., Northwestern U., 1949. Chemist, Charlton Lab., Portland, Oreg., 1941; chemist Nat. Def. Research Com. Central Lab., Evanston, Ill. and Pasadena, Calif., 1942-45; chemist, tech. mgr. Gen. Electric Co., Richland, Wash., 1948-65; mgr. research devel. Pacific N.W. Lab., Battelle Meml. Inst., Richland, 1965-70; with Westinghouse Hanford Co., Richland, 1970—, asst. mgr. applied systems devel. dept., 1980—. Mem. U.S. del. to 4th UN Conf. on Peaceful Use of Atomic Energy, 1971. Br. bd. dirs. Children's Home Soc. of Wash., 1969-75, state adv. com., 1975-78; bd. dirs. Benton Franklin County Humane Soc. 1961-71; dist. officer Boy Scouts Am., 1970-72, council rep., 1972-75. Weston fellow, 1942; Charles A. Coffin fellow, 1946-47. Fellow Am. Nuclear Soc. (chmn. Richland sect. 1981-82); mem. Am. Chem. Soc., AIAA, Sigma Xi, Alpha Chi Sigma. Patentee U.S. and abroad; contbr. articles to profl. jours. Home: 2336 Harris Ave Richland WA 99352 Office: PO Box 1970 Richland WA 99352

ROARK, ROBERT CAMERON, insurance agency executive; b. San Diego, Jan. 11, 1931; s. Alfred T. and Virginia J. Roark; A.B. in Journalism, San Diego State U., 1954; m. Lois Joan Maynard, Aug. 19, 1952; children—Cynthia, Susan, Kellie, Robert. Agt., Mass. Mut. Life Ins. Co., San Diego, 1955-57; agy. supr. John Hancock Mut. Co., San Diego, 1957-59; gen. agt. Am. Mut. Life Ins. Co., San Diego, 1959-64; Southwestern regional v.p. Northwestern Life Ins. of Seattle, 1965-68; owner Roark Ins. Co., Laguna Niguel, Calif., 1968—. Pres., bd. dirs. Mission Hills Homeowners Assn., San Juan Capistrano, Calif., 1972-73, Marinita Homeowners Assn., Dana Point, Calif., 1981-82; regional treas., bd. dirs. Orange County chpt. Am. Youth Soccer, 1977-80. Republican. Club: Lions (pres., dir. Capitstrano 1970-71, zone chmn. South Orange County 1971-72).

ROBACK, ROSEMARY EVE, nurse, educator; b. Chgo., Mar. 28, 1931; d. Michael and Edith Lisetta (Mullen) Hunter; m. George Stanley Roback, Aug. 1, 1955; children—Diane, David, Steven. R.N., U. Ill., 1952; B.A., Pepperdine U., 1976; M.S., M.B.A., U. LaVerne, 1983. Nurse, Cook County Hosp., Chgo., 1952-54; staff nurse VA Hosp., Los Angeles, 1954-56, Beverly Hills (Calif.) Clinic, 1956-57; nurse various pvt. med. clinics, Los Angeles, 1960-70; surg. out-patient coordinator UCLA Med. Center, Los Angeles, 1974-75; dir. edn. and tng. Brotman Med. Center, Culver City, Calif., 1975—. Mem. Nat. League Nursing, Am. Soc. Health Edn. and Tng., Am. Soc. Tng. and Devel., Calif. Bus.

Profl. Women. Republican. Office: 3828 Delmas Terr Culver City CA 90230

ROBARDS, DONALD ALBERT, containerized transportation company executive; b. Red Bank, N.J., May 24, 1942; s. Chester O'Neil and Winifred Julia (Decatur) R. B.A., Miami U., Oxford, Ohio, 1964; postgrad. Howard U., 1964-67. With Prudential Ins. Co. Am., Newark, N.J. and Ft. Washington, Pa., 1967-72, assoc. mgr. tng., until 1972; area sales rep. Xerox Corp., Arlington, Va., 1972; personnel rep. Curtiss-Wright Corp., Woodridge, N.J., 1972-74; mgr. personnel, petroleum and chem. group Arthur G. McKee Co., Berkeley Heights, N.J., 1974-75; with Sea-Land Service, Inc., Oakland, Calif., 1975—, now mgr. personnel N.Am.-Pacific div.; lectr. careers in transp. industry; adviser network job tng. program; mentor Oakland pvt. sector program. Recipient Recognition award Assn. Calif. and Nev. Vol. Ctrs., 1983; Howard U. Trustees fellow, 1965-67. Mem. Am. Soc. Tng. and Devel., Am. Soc. for Personnel Adminstrn., No. Calif. Indsl. Relations Council, Assn. Personnel Profls. of Oakland, Alpha Phi Alpha. Episcopalian. Club: Propeller.

ROBB, HAROLD BUCHANAN, III, psychologist, educator, cons.; b. Dallas, Nov. 26, 1945; s. Harold Buchanan and Gloria Ann (Saal) R. m. Carolyn Atlee, Oct. 4, 1968; 1 dau., Katherine Atlee. B.A. Westminister Coll., 1968; M.A., U. Nebr., 1973, Ph.D., 1978. Lic. psychologist, Idaho; cert. therapist Inst. Rational-Emotive Therapy. Psychol. intern VA Hosp., Palo Alto, Calif., 1976-77; vis. asst. prof. dept. ednl. psychology and measurement U. Nebr., Lincoln, 1977-78; asst. prof. psychology, counseling psychologist Lewis-Clark State Coll., Lewiston, Idaho, 1978-81, assoc. prof., 1981-82, dir. counseling, 1982—. Served with USN, 1968-72. Decorated Nat. Def. medal. Mem. ACLU, Am. Humanist Assn., Am. Psychol. Assn., Western Psychol. Assn., Idaho Psychol Assn. (pres. 1981-83, editor newsletter, 1979-80), Am. Edn. Research Assn., Am. Personnel and Guidance Assn., State Line Guidance Assn. (pres. 1980-81), Fedn. Am. Scientists, Phi Delta Kappa. Contbr. articles to profl. jours. Office: Student Develop Lewis-Clark State Coll Lewiston ID 83501

ROBB, J(ACK) GARY, accountant; b. Seattle, Dec. 14, 1944; s. Jack P. and Alva Hazel (Bemer), R.; m. M. Jeanne Boyd, Sept. 5, 1964 (div.); children—Jeff, Kristi. B.A. in Bus. Adminstrn., U. Wash., 1967. C.P.A., Wash. Acct., Moss Adams, Tacoma, 1968—, mng. ptnr. Tacoma office, 1978—, chmn. bd. Pacific Luth. U. Acctg. Bd. Past bd. dirs., v.p. Bldg. Scholastic Heritage; project mgr. for rehab. of cert. hist. bldg., Tacoma. Served with USN, 1967-68. Mem. Am. Inst. C.P.A.s (minority bus. devel. com.), Wash. Soc. C.P.A.s (pres. Tacoma chpt.), various indl. assns. Lutheran. Club: Tacoma. Home: 2614 Deidra Circle Tacoma WA 98407 Office: Moss Adams Co 1702 Broadway Tacoma WA 98402

ROBB, JANANN HAZEL, engineering corporation executive; b. Seattle, Sept. 11, 1946; d. Jack Pershing and Alva Hazel (Bemer) R.; m. Joseph C. Hansen, June 16, 1980 (div.). Student U. Wash., 1964-65, Olympic Coll., 1965-66, Peterson Sch. Bus., 1964-66, City U., 1982-83. With DLI Engring. Corp., Bainbridge Island, Wash., 1966—, corp. sec.-treas., 1980—; pres. SunnyDay Enterprises, Inc., Bainbridge, 1977—; corp. sec.-treas. Secteur Corp., Bainbridge, 1980-82; owner, mgr. JR Leasing Co., Bainbridge, 1981-82; bus. and fin. cons. Active Girl Scouts U.S.A. Mem. Nat. Assn. Female Execs. Mem. Unity Ch. of Truth. Club: Sons of Norway, Bremerton Bus. and Profl. Author: The Enterprise Cookbook, 1981. Office: DLI Engring Corp 261 Madison Ave S Bainbridge Island WA 98110

ROBBINS, ALAN, state senator; b. Phila., Feb. 5, 1943; s. Martin and Gladys (Kessler) R.; B.A., UCLA, 1963, J.D., 1966; m. Miriam Elbaum, Sept. 27, 1967 (div. 1980), children—Jacob Harold, Leah Susan. Bar: Calif. 1966. Practice law, San Fernando Valley, Calif., 1966—; mem. Calif. Senate from 20th Dist., 1973—, chmn. com. on ins. and indemnity. Democrat. Author: Robbins Rape Evidence Law, 1974. Office: 6320 Van Nuys Blvd #404 Van Nuys CA 91401*

ROBBINS, PATTI CAMPBELL, hair styling salons corp. ofcl.; b. Indpls., Feb. 14, 1932; d. Leroy and Dorothy Turner (Vincent) Campbell; M.A. in Arts, U. Mex., 1957; 1 dau., Tracy Mallozzi. Nat. coordinator John Robert Powers Sch., 1964-72; account exec. Seligman & Latz, 1972-79; regional dir. Regis Corp., Los Angeles, 1979—; v.p. Inter-COsmetic Trading, Inc., N.Y.C. and Los Angeles. Bd. dirs. Los Angeles Soc. Easter Seals; pres. Easter Seal 500 for Los Angeles. Democrat. Roman Catholic. Home: 10960 Roebling Ave Los Angeles CA 90024 Office: 5000 Normandale Rd Minneapolis MN 55436

ROBBINS, RONALD DALE, accountant; b. Ogden, Utah, Oct. 31, 1945; s. Dale F. and Fern (Larson) R.; m. Gerrie Hadley, Sept. 6, 1967; children—Michelle, Jeffrey, Jason, Brian. B.A., Weber State Coll., 1970. C.P.A., Utah. Vice-pres. Pinnock, Robbins & Co., C.P.A.s, Salt Lake City, 1977—. Mem., Centerville (Utah) City Fin. Com., 1982-83; mem. troop com. Bonneville council Boy Scouts Am., 1978-83. Served to capt. U.S. Army, 1970-72. Decorated Bronze Star. Mem. Am. Inst. C.P.A.s, Utah Assn. C.P.A.s. Republican. Mormon. Home: 556 E 550 S Centerville UT 84014 Office: 275 East South Temple St Salt Lake City UT 84111

ROBBINS, THOMAS NELSON, public relations executive; b. Princeton, N.J., July 18, 1948; s. William Randolph and Sarah Craig (Wright) R.; m. Elizabeth Custis, May 25, 1974. B.S., Boston U., 1971. Pres., TNR & Assocs., N.Y.C., 1971-74; pub. info. officer U.S. Dept. Energy, Washington, 1974-80; v.p., dir. pub. relations J. Walter Thompson Co., Washington, 1980-81, San Francisco, 1981—. Active Cystic Fibrosis Found., O'Hara Handicapped Awareness Found. Mem. Nat. Acad. TV Arts and Scis., San Francisco Advt. Club. Home: 1922 Jackson St San Francisco CA 94109 Office: J Walter Thompson Co 4 Embarcadero Center 9th Floor San Francisco CA 94111

ROBERSON, BEVERLY BUD, physician; b. Lemoore, Calif., Apr. 29, 1922; s. Alexander Grace and Flossie Mae (Gregory) R.; B.A., Pacific Union Coll., 1942; M.D., Loma Linda U., 1945; m. Eleanor June Gourly, June 26, 1949 (div. 1974); children—Donald Edward, Cheryl Diane. Intern Glendale Sanitarium and Hosp., Glendale, Calif., 1945-46; practice medicine specializing in gen. practice, Clearlake Highlands, Calif., 1950-70; resident in anesthesiology White Meml. Med. Center, Los Angeles, 1970-72, instr., 1972-74, dir. anesthesiology, 1980—; asst. prof. anesthesiology Loma Linda (Calif.) U., 1974—; practice anesthesiology, Los Angeles, 1972-74, Loma Linda, 1974-80, Los Angeles, 1980—; pres. Lakeshore Investment Corp., 1963-77. Bd. dirs. Lakeshore Fire Protection Dist., 1968-70, Redbud Hosp., 1968-70; comdr. med. emergency team Los Angeles County Sheriff's Dept., 1979—. Served with U.S. Army, 1946-48. Diplomate Am. Bd. Anesthesiology. Fellow Am. Coll. Anesthesiologists; mem. Calif., Am. socs. anesthesiologists, Calif., Los Angeles County med. assns., AMA. Republican. Home: 3805 Karen Lynn St Glendale CA 91206 Office: White Meml Med Center 1720 Brooklyn Ave Los Angeles CA 91206

ROBERT, CAVETT MCNEILL, JR., surgeon; b. Douglas, Ariz., Jan. 16, 1940; s. Cavett and Gertrude (Buist) R. B.A., U. Pa., 1962, M.D., 1966. Intern surgery UCLA, 1966-67, resident surgery, 1967-68, resident neurosurgery, 1968-73; practice medicine specializing in neurosurgery, Concord, Calif., Walnut Creek, Calif., 1973—; mem. staff Mt. Diablo Hosp., Concord, Calif., John Muir Meml. Hosp., Walnut Creek, Calif., Delta Meml. Hosp., Antioch, Calif., Children's Hosp. No. Calif., Oakland, Contra Costa County Hosp., Martinez, Calif.; mem. clin. faculty U. Calif., San Francisco, 1976—, U. Calif., Davis, 1976—; house officer neurology Nat. Hosp., London, 1970-71. Diplomate Am. Bd. Neurol. Surgery. Fellow ACS; mem. Calif. Assn. Neurol. Surgeons, Am. Assn. Neurol. Surgeons, Congress Neurol. Surgeons, San Francisco Neurol. Soc., AMA, Calif. Med. Assn., Almeda-Contra Costa County Med. Assn. Contbr. articles on neurol. surgery to med. jours. Completed Ironman World Triathlon, 1982, Western States 100 mile endurance race, 1982. Home: 3959 Canyon St Lafayette CA 94549 Office: 2485 High School Ave Suite 309 Concord CA 94520

ROBERTI, DAVID A., state senator; b. Los Angeles, May 4, 1939; s. Emil and Elvira (Ligrano) R.; m. June Joyce, 1968. B.A., Loyola U., Los Angeles, 1961; J.D., U. So. Calif., 1964. Mem. Calif. State Assembly from 48th Dist., 1957-71, Calif. State Senate, 1971—, chmn. maj. caucus and select coms. on small bus. enterprises, chmn. joint com. revision of penal code, 1975, maj. leader, 1975—; dep. atty. gen. State of Calif., 1965-66. Mem. Calif. Democratic Council; chmn. Los Angeles County Young Dems., 1965; del. Dem. Nat. Conv., 1976, 80. Roman Catholic. Home: 6640 Sunset Blvd Apt 202 Hollywood CA 90028 Office: California State Senate Sacramento CA 95814*

ROBERTI, MARIO ANDREW, energy company executive, lawyer; b. Denver, May 12, 1935; s. Emil and Elvira (Ligrano) R.; m. Patricia Ann Ludwig, Apr. 27, 1963; children—Andrea Louise, Paul Richard, Robert Raymond. B.S., Loyola U.-Los Angeles (now Loyola Marymount U.), 1957, J.D., 1960. Bar: Calif. 1961, Hawaii 1977. Dep. atty. gen. State of Calif., Los Angeles, 1961-69; atty. Pacific Lighting Corp., Los Angeles, 1969-71; asst. gen. counsel, asst. sec. McCulloch Oil Corp., Los Angeles, 1971-76; v.p., gen. counsel Pacific Resources, Inc., Honolulu, 1976—; mem. adv. bd. Internat. Oil & Gas Ednl. Ctr.; mem. legal adv. com. Pacific Coast Gas Assn. Trustee Hawaii Sch. for Girls; bd. regents Loyola Marymount U., Los Angeles, Chaminade U., Honolulu; mem. adv. bd. Southwestern Legal Found. Served to capt. JAGC, USAR, 1966-70. Mem. Hawaii Bar Assn., Calif. Bar Assn., ABA, Fed. Energy Bar Assn., Phi Alpha Delta, Phi Kappa Theta. Roman Catholic. Clubs: Pacific, Outrigger Canoe (Honolulu). Office: Pacific Resources Inc 733 Bishop St Honolulu HI 96813 also PO Box 3379 Honolulu HI 96842

ROBERTS, ALAN SILVERMAN, physician; b. N.Y.C., Apr. 20, 1939; s. Joseph William and Fannie (Margolies) S.; B.A., Conn. Wesleyan U., 1960; M.D., Jefferson Med. Coll., 1966; children—Michael Eric, Daniel Ian. Rotating intern, Lankenau Hosp., Phila., 1966-67; resident orthopaedics Tulane U. Med. Coll., 1967-71; pvt. practice medicine, specializing in orthopedics and hand surgery, Los Angeles, 1971—; mem. clin. faculty UCLA Med. Coll., 1971-76; mem. staff Santa Monica (Calif.) Hosp., Brotman Meml. Hosp., Culver City, Calif. Served with AUS, 1961. Recipient Riordan Hand fellowship, 1969; Boyes Hand fellowship, 1971. Mem. Riordan Hand Soc., Western Orthopaedic Assn., A.C.S., AMA, Calif., Los Angeles County med. assns. Republican. Jewish. Contbr. articles to profl. jours.

ROBERTS, ARCHIBALD EDWARD, ret. army officer, author; b. Cheboygan, Mich., Mar. 21, 1915; s. Archibald Lancaster and Madeline Ruth (Smith) R.; grad. Command and Gen. Staff Coll., 1952; student U.S. Armed Forces Inst., 1953, U. Md., 1958; m. Florence Snure, Sept. 25, 1940 (div. Feb. 1950); children—Michael James, John Douglas; m. 2d, Doris Elfriede White, June 23, 1951; children—Guy Archer, Charles Lancaster, Christopher Corwin. Enlisted U.S. Army, 1939, advanced through grades to lt. col., 1960; served in Far East Command, 1942, 1953-55, ETO, 1943-45, 57-60; tech. info. officer Office Surgeon Gen., Dept. Army, Washington, 1950, Ft. Campbell, Ky., 1952-53, info. officer, Camp Chicamauga, Japan, Ft. Bragg, N.C., Ft. Campbell, Ky., 1953-56, Ft. Campbell, 1956-57, Ft. Benning, Ga., Wurzburg, Germany, 1957 58, spl. projects officer Augsburg, Germany, 1959-60, U.S. Army Info. Office, N.Y.C., 1960-61; writer program precipitating Senate Armed Services Hearings, 1962; ret., 1965; mgr., salesman Nu-Enamel Stores, Ashville, N.C., 1937-38; co-owner, dir. Roberts & Roberts Advt. Agy., Denver, 1946-49; pres. Found. for Edn., Scholarship, Patriotism and Americanism, Inc.; nat. bd. dirs. Com. to Restore Constn., Inc. Recipient award of merit Am. Acad. Pub. Affairs, 1967; Good Citizenship medal SAR, 1968; Liberty award Congress of Freedom, 1969; Man of Yr. awards Women for Constl. Govt., 1970, Wis. Legislative and Research Com., 1971; medal of merit Am. Legion, 1972; Speaker of Year award We, The People, 1973. Mem. Res. Officers Assn., Airborne Assn., SAR, Sons Am. Colonists. Author: Rakkasan, 1955; Screaming Eagles, 1956; The Marne Division, 1957; Victory Denied, 1966; Peace: By the Wonderful People Who Brought You Korea and Viet Nam, 1972; The Republic: Decline and Future Promise, 1975; Emerging Struggle for State Sovereignty, 1979; also numerous pamphlets and articles. Home: 2218 W Prospect PO Box 986 Fort Collins CO 80522

ROBERTS, CAROL MARIE, educational adminstrator; b. Los Angeles, Nov. 7, 1939; d. Earl Hugene and Marie Alberta (Royle) Peltier; m. Edward Earl Roberts, July 2, 1964; stepchildren—Linda Pezzopane, Dennis, Mark, Scott. B.A.Ed., Calif. State U.-Long Beach, 1965; M.S.Ed., Calif. State U.-Fullerton, 1977, M.S. Sch. Adminstrn., 1978; postgrad. U. So. Calif., 1980—. Tchr., Tustin (Calif.) Unified Sch. Dist., 1965-80; tchr. reading and writing U. Calif.-Irvine, 1977; tchr. reading Saddleback Coll., Mission Viejo, Calif., 1977-80; asst. prin. Greenville Fundamental Sch., Santa Ana, Calif., 1980-82; prin. MacArthur Fundamental Intermediate Sch., Santa Ana, 1982—; tchr.-trainer, staff devel. workshops presenter Orange County Conf. Gifted and Talented, 1980-81. Mem. Assn. Supervision and Curriculum Devel., Internat. Reading Assn., Assn. Calif. Sch. Adminstrs., Calif. Scholarship Fedn. (life), So. Counties Women Mgrs. in Edn. Presbyterian. Home: 1681 Cameo Dr Santa Ana CA 92705 Office: 600 W Alton Ave Santa Ana CA 92707

ROBERTS, CHARLES MORGAN, optometrist, educator, researcher; b. Roswell, N.Mex., June 13, 1932; s. Clarence Arthur and Annie Lorene (Perkins) R.; m. Gloria Vivian Lasagna, Feb. 24, 1962; children—Mike, Janis. A.A., Mt. San Antonio Coll., 1959; B.S., U. La Verne, 1961, M.A., 1965; B.S., So. Calif. Coll. Optometry, 1972, O.D., 1974. Diplomate Acad. in Contact Lenses; cert. contact lenses Nat. Eye Research Found. Design engr. Aetron, Aerojet Gen., Azusa, Calif., 1955-65; research chemist Sunkist OPD, Ontario, Calif., 1965-70; asst. prof. optometry So. Calif. Coll. Optometry, Fullerton, 1974—; pvt. practice optometry, San Juan Capistrano, Calif., 1975—; cons. Allergan Co., other contact lens mfrs.; researcher areas of contact lenses, solutions. Mem. San Juan Hist. Soc. With USN, 1950-55. Recipient Outstanding Achievement award Bausch & Lomb Soflens, 1974; named Instr. of Yr., So. Calif. Coll. Optometry, 1975; Bausch & Lomb Soflens fellow, 1974. Mem. Am. Acad. Optometry; Am. Optometric Assn., Calif. Optometric Assn., Orange County Optometric Assn., Nat. Eye Research Found., Calif. Profl. Hypnosis Assn., San Juan Capistrano C. of C., Omega Delta. Democrat. Lutheran. Clubs: Rotary Internat. (pres., named Rotarian of Yr. 1978), Elks. Contbr. numerous tech. papers to profl. jours. Office: 32282 Camino Capistrano Suite B San Juan Capistrano CA 92675

ROBERTS, DAVID LANCE, financial services marketing executive; b. Detroit, June 11, 1943; s. John Alvis and Gertrude Alma (Mays) R.; m. Emilie Mulloy, May 8, 1970; children—Julie Sarah, Nicole Marie. B.A. in Advt., Mich. State U., 1967. Media asst. D'Arcy-McManus-Masius Co., Bloomfield Hills, Mich., 1967-68; media planner Grey Advt. Co., Detroit, 1968-73; media supr. McCann-Erickson Advt. Co., San Francisco, Detroit, 1973-77; media mgr. Visa USA, Inc., San Francisco, 1977—. Republican. Presbyterian. Club: P.C.C. Tennis (Redwood City, Calif.). Home: 902 Emerald Hill Redwood City CA 94061 Office: PO Box 8999 San Francisco CA 94128

ROBERTS, DEAN L., JR., environmental engineer; b. Caliente, Nev., Oct. 18, 1946; s. Dean and Wilma (Lovell) R.; m. Linda Elizabeth Rogers, June 27, 1968; children—Kristin, Travis, Amy, Preston, Heather. B.S., Utah State U., Logan, 1973, M.S., 1977. Agrl. extension agt. Utah State U., Logan, 1975-78; asst. environ. engr. Atlas Minerals Corp., Moab, Utah, 1978, safety and environ. engr. Nuclear energy fuels. Blanding, Utah, 1978-80; chief environ. engr. Anaconda Minerals Co., Grants, N.Mex., 1981—. Mem. task force on acad. honors program, San Juan sch. dist., Blanding, Utah; pres. Bluewater (N.Mex.) PTA. Served with Utah N.G., 1968-80. Mem. Am. Soc. Safety Engrs., Am. Indsl. Hygiene Assn., Soc. Range Mgmt., Sigma Xi. Republican. Mormon. Contbr. articles to profl. jours. Home: Box A-44 Grants NM 87020 Office: Box 638 Grants NM 87020

ROBERTS, DENNIS WILLIAM, association executive; b. Chgo., Jan. 7, 1943; s. William Owen and Florence Harriet (Denman) R.; B.A., U. N.Mex., 1968; M.A., Antioch U., 1982. Gen. assignment reporter Albuquerque Pub. Co., 1964, sports writer, 1960-64, advt. and display salesman, 1967-68; dir. info. N.Mex. bldg. br. Asso. Gen. Contractors Am., Albuquerque, 1968-79, asst. exec. dir., 1979-82, dir., 1982—. Active United Way, Albuquerque, 1969-78; chmn. Albuquerque Crime Prevention Council, 1982. Recipient Pub. Relations Achievement award Assoc. Gen. Contractors Am., 1978. Mem. N.Mex. Pub. Relations Conf. (chmn. 1975, 82-83), Pub. Relations Soc. Am. (accredited, pres. N.Mex. chpt. 1981), Am. Soc. Assn. Execs., Contrn. Specifications Inst. (Outstanding Industry Mem. 1974, Outstanding Com. Chmn. 1978), Sigma Delta Chi (pres. N.Mex. chpt. 1969). Republican. Lutheran. Clubs: Toastmasters (dist. gov. 1977-78, Disting. Dist. award 1978, Toastmaster of Year 1979-80), Masons, Shriners, Elks. Home: 1709 Hiawatha NE Albuquerque NM 87112 Office: 1615 University Blvd NE Albuquerque NM 87102

ROBERTS, DONALD JOHN, economics educator; b. Winnipeg, Man., Can. Feb. 11, 1945; came to U.S., 1967; s. Donald Victor and Margaret Mabel (Riddell) R.; m. Kathleen Eleanor Roberts Taylor, Aug. 26, 1967. B.A. with honors, U. Man., 1967; Ph.D., U. Minn., 1972. Instr. dept. managerial econs. and decision scis. J.L. Kellogg Grad. Sch. Mgmt., Northwestern U., Evanston, Ill., 1971-72, asst. prof., 1972-74, assoc. prof., 1974-77, prof., 1977-80; research fellow Ctr. for Ops. Research and Econometrics, Leuven, Belgium, 1974-75; Jonathan B. Lovelace prof. econs. Grad. Sch. Bus., Stanford (Calif.) U., 1980—; cons. in field. Woodrow Wilson fellow, 1967-68; Can. Council fellow, 1968-71; CORE Research fellow, 1974-75; NSF grantee, 1974-82. Fellow Econometric Soc.; mem. Am. Econ. Assn. Assoc. editor Jour. Econ. Theory, 1977—. Contbr. articles to profl. jour. Office: Grad Sch Bus Stanford Univ Stanford CA 94305

ROBERTS, DWIGHT LOREN, historian/novelist; b. San Diego, June 3, 1949; s. James Albert and Cleva Lorraine (Conn) R.; B.A., U. San Diego, 1976, M.A., 1979; m. Phyllis Ann Adair, Mar. 29, 1969; children—Aimee Renee, Michael Loren, Daniel Alexandr. Engring. aide Benton Engring. Inc., San Diego, 1968-73; pres. Robert's Tech. Research Co., also subs. Marine Technique Ltd., San Diego, 1973-76; pres. Research Technique Internat., 1978—; freelance writer, 1979—. Served with U.S. Army, 1969-71. Mem. ASTM, AAAS, Nat. Inst. Sci., N.Y. Acad. Scis., NOW, Phi Alpha Theta. Baptist. Author: Geological Exploration of Alaska, 1898-1924; contbr. articles to profl. jours. Office: 3111 Victoria Dr Alpine CA 92001

ROBERTS, EARLE G., fire chief; b. Phoenix, Nov. 19, 1930; s. Snowden Tillman and Annie Gertrude (Johnson) R.; B.A. in Public Mgmt., St. Mary's Coll. Calif., 1977, student Phoenix Coll., 1960-73, m. Charlene Gietz, May 15, 1953; children—Karen Ann, Geary Earle, Randel Jeffery, Holly Rene. Asst. fire chief, architect paramedic program Phoenix Fire Dept., 1954-79; fire chief San Diego City, 1979—; guest lectr. various fire dept. confs. Mem. Calif. 42d Congressional Dist. Adv. Council Jobs/Economy; bd. dirs. San Diego chpt. ARC. Served with U.S. Navy, 1949-52. Mem. Calif. Fire Chiefs Assn. (mem. com.), Western Fire Chiefs Assn. (2d v.p.), Calif. Metro Fire Chiefs Assn. (vice-chmn.), Nat. Fire Protection Assn. (chmn. com.). Republican. Mormon. Club: Rotary. Office: 1222 1st Ave San Diego CA 92101

ROBERTS, EVELYN FREEMAN, composer, conductor, musician; b. Cleve., Feb. 13, 1919; d. Ernest A. and Gertrude (Richardson) Freeman; B.Mus., Cleve. Inst. Music, 1941; grad. student Calif. State U., Los Angeles, 1964-66, UCLA, U. So. Calif., 1967-70; m. Thomas S. Roberts; children—Anita, Ernest, Claire, Lisa. Tchr. music Karamu Ho., Cleve., 1937-40; performed Cafe Soc., N.Y.C., Town and Country, Club Elegante, Bklyn., Dunes Hotel, Las Vegas, Desert Inn Hotel Hilton, Las Vegas, Harrah's, Reno, Sahara-Tahoe; appeared in movies, including Toys in The Attic, A Clash of Cymbals; TV appearances include Jonathan Winters, Ed Sullivan shows, Andy Griffith Spl., Profiles in Courage, numerous local shows, spls.; staff arranger Leslie Uggams Show; spl. performance at White House, 1970; recorded albums; arranger for numerous rec. stars; co-founder, dir., program coordinator Young Saints Acad. Performing Arts and Skills, Los Angeles, 1971—. Recipient numerous commendations, citations, awards from civic orgns. Mem. ASCAP, Am. Guild Composers and Songwriters, Musicians Union (life), Calif. Confedn. Arts. Methodist. Home: 2000 Wellington Rd Los Angeles CA 90016 Office: 2000 Wellington Rd Los Angeles CA 90003

ROBERTS, FRANK LIVERZEY, state senator, educator; b. Boise, Idaho, Dec. 28, 1915; s. Walter Scott and Mary Elizabeth (Livezey) R.; m. Barbara K. Sanders; children—Mary Linda, Leslie. B.A., Pacific U., Forest Grove, Oreg., 1938; Ph.M., U. Wis., 1943; Ph.D., Stanford U., 1954. Prof. speech Portland State U., 1946—, dean undergrad. studies, assoc. dean faculty, 1963-66; mem. Oreg. Ho. of Reps. from 6th Dist., 1967-72, Oreg. State Senate, 1975—. Chmn. Multnomah County Democratic Central Com., 1960-63; mem. Portland Met. Study Commn., 1964-72; dir. Mt. Hood Community Coll., 1965-74; permanent chmn. Oreg. Dem. State Conv., 1966; del. Dem. Nat. Conv., 1968; mem. City-County Consol. Commn., 1974, Tri County Local Govt. Commn., 1976-77. Served with U.S. Army, 1943-46; ETO. Author: Basic Parliamentary Procedure, 1966. Home: 11609 NE Klickitat Portland OR 97220 Office: Oregon State Senate Salem OR 97310

ROBERTS, GEORGE ADAM, metallurgist; b. Uniontown, Pa., Feb. 18, 1919; s. Jacob Earle and Mary M. (Bower) R.; student U.S. Naval Acad., 1935-37; B.Sc., Carnegie Tech., 1939, M.Sc., 1941, D.Sc., 1942; m. Betty E. Matthewson, May 31, 1941; children—George Thomas, William John, Mary Ellen; m. 2d, Jeanne Marie Polk. Technician Bell Telephone Labs., N.Y.C., 1938; research dir. Vasco Metals Corp. (formerly Vanadium Alloys Steel Co.), Latrobe, Pa., 1940-45, chief metallurgist, 1945-53, v.p., 1953-61, pres., 1961-66; pres., dir. Teledyne,

Inc. (merger with Vasco Metals Corp.), Los Angeles, 1966—; hon. lectr. Societe Francaise de Metallurgie, 1960. Mem. Greater Latrobe Sch. Bd., 1959-64. Recipient silver medal from Paris, 1955. Fellow Metall. Soc. Am. Inst. Mining, Metall. and Petroleum Engrs., Am. Soc. for Metals (chmn. Pitts. chpt. 1949-50, internat. pres. 1954-55, trustee Found. Edn. and Research 1954-59, 63-64, pres. Found. 1955-56; Gold medal 1977); mem. Nat. Acad. Engring., Metal Powder Industries Fedn. (dir. 1952-55, pres. 1957-61), Am. Soc. Metals, Am. Iron and Steel Inst., Soc. Mfg. Engrs., Tau Beta Pi, hon. life mem. several fgn. socs. Methodist. Author: Tool Steels, 1944, 62. Contbr. articles trade jours. Office: Teledyne Inc 1901 Ave of the Stars Suite 1800 Los Angeles CA 90067

ROBERTS, GEORGE CHRISTOPHER, mfg. exec.; b. Ridley Park, Pa., May 27, 1936; s. George H. and Marion C. (Smullen) R.; m. Adriana Toribio, July 19, 1966; children—Tupac A., Capac Y. Sr. engr. ITT, Paramus, N.J., 1960-65; program mgr. Arde Research, Mawah, N.J., 1965-67; Space-Life Sci. program mgr., research div. GATX, 1967-69; dir. research and devel. Monogram Industries, Los Angeles, 1969-71; pres. Environ. Protection Center, Inc., Los Angeles, 1970-76; pres. INCA-One Corp, Los Angeles, 1972—, INCA-Two Corp., 1977—, INCA-Three Corp., 1978—; v.p. Chimu Assos. Advt. Agency, 1977—. Bd. dirs., trustee Fairborn Obs.; mem., dir., v.p. Peruvian Found. Mem. Am. Astron. Soc., Astron. Soc. Pacific. Patentee advanced waste treatment systems, automotive safety systems. Office: 3463 S La Cienga Blvd Los Angeles CA 90016

ROBERTS, HOWARD A., association executive; b. Dexter, Maine, Aug. 16, 1926; s. Mark S. and Helen A. Roberts; B.S., U. Maine, 1951; m. Bettie Lee Summers, Nov. 8, 1952; children—Christine, Patricia, Mark. Forester, Bur. Entomology and Plant Quarantine, Dept. Agr., Oreg. and Calif., 1951-52, U.S. Forest Service and Dept. Agr., San Francisco, 1953; forester, sec. Western Wood Products Assn., Portland, Oreg., 1954-72, exec. v.p., chief exec. officer, 1972—; mem. Am. Lumber Standards Com., Nat. Lumber Grading Com.; chmn. Japan/Am. Lumber Trade Promotion Com.; adv. to U.S. govt. on trade matters, to U. Idaho Sch. Forestry; del. leader European Softwood Conf. Served with USNR, 1944-46; PTO. Mem. Am. Wood Council (bd. dirs.), Nat. Forest Products Assn. (bd. dirs.), Soc. Am. Foresters, Am. Soc. Assn. Execs., Xi Sigma Pi. Republican. Clubs: Toastmasters, Hoo Hoo, Riverside Golf and Country, Multnomah Athletic. Office: 1500 Yeon Bldg Portland OR 97204

ROBERTS, JAMES GARFIELD, II, cost engineer; b. Tacoma Park, Md., June 13, 1952; s. James Garfield and Mary Louise (Markle) R.; m. Germaine Eleanor Dall-Winther, Sept. 25, 1982. B.S. in Mech. Engring., U. Colo., 1974. Cert. engr.-in-tng., Colo. Design engr. Gt. Western Sugar Co., Ft. Morgan, Colo., 1975-76; field engr. Colo. Interstate Gas Co., Denver, 1976-77, cost engr., Colorado Springs, 1977-79, sr. cost engr., 1979—. Mem. ASME, Am. Assn. Cost Engrs., Nat. Soc. Profl. Engrs. (Outstanding Service award 1982). Methodist. Club: Sno Jet Ski. Home: PO Box 2286 Colorado Springs CO 80901 Office: PO Box 1087 Colorado Springs CO 80944

ROBERTS, JAMES MCGREGOR, profl. acad. exec.; b. Moncton, N.B., Can., Nov. 24, 1923; s. Roland M. and Edith M. (Shields) R.; came to U.S., 1949, naturalized, 1956; B.Commerce, U. Toronto (Ont., Can.), 1949; m. Thelma E. Williams, May 6, 1944; 1 dau., Jana M. Auditor, Citizens Bank, Los Angeles, 1949-54; auditor Acad. Motion Picture Arts and Scis., Hollywood, Calif., 1954—, controller, 1956-71, exec. dir., 1971—, exec. sec. acad. found., 1971—. Served as pilot Royal Can. Air Force, World War II. Mem. Beverly Hills (Calif.) C. of C. Home: 450 S Maple Dr Beverly Hills CA 90212 Office: 8949 Wilshire Blvd Beverly Hills CA 90211

ROBERTS, JOHN ARTHUR, analytical chemist, translator; b. Oceanside, Calif., June 4, 1954; s. Arthur Renfrew and Mary Nell (Boone) R. B.S., U. Calif-Berkeley, 1976; postgrad. U. So. Calif., 1978-81, Kokusai Kiristokyo U., Tokyo, 1981. Engring. technician Geo Ekta Labs, Fullerton, Calif., 1976-77; tech. English instr., translator Japan Atomic Energy Research Inst., Tokai-mura, 1977-78; analytical chemist Associated Labs., Orange, Calif., 1978—. Mem. Soil Conservation Soc. Am., Am. Agronomy Soc., Calif. Profl. Soil Scientists Assn. Episcopalian. Club: Brotherhood of St. Andrew. Translator tech. and sales lit. Office: Associated Labs 806 N Batavia St Orange CA 92668

ROBERTS, JOHN DEWAR, pub. relations director; b. San Jose, Calif., Oct. 21, 1929; s. E. Dewar and Helen M. (Pors) R.; m. Barbara M. Lund, Aug. 21, 1955; children—Teresa, David, Jennifer. A.B. in Bus. Adminstn., San Jose State U., 1951; M.B.A., Stanford U., 1955. With Pacific Tel. & Tel., San Jose, 1955—, pub. relations dir. central area San Jose, 1981—. Bd. mgrs. Santa Clara Valley YMCA; active United Way of Santa Clara County. Recipient Arthur Page Pub. Relations Performance award AT&T, 1979. Mem. Pub. Relations Soc. Am., Peninsula Grantmakers (steering com.), Bay Area Pub. Affairs Council. Republican. Methodist. Clubs: Athletic (San Jose), Commonwealth (San Francisco), Masons.

ROBERTS, L. SCOTT, accountant, management consultant; b. Portland, Oreg., Dec. 21, 1940; s. Ellsworth Vance and Helen M. (Fisher) R.; B.S. in Bus. Adminstrn., So. Oreg. State Coll., 1979; m. Cherie R. Ford, Mar. 16, 1969. Controller, Sierra Cascade Communications, Grants Pass, Oreg., 1980, owner, sr. mgmt. cons., 1980-82. Chmn. bd. dirs. Applegate Parochial Sch., 1974—; pres. So. Oreg. Job Fair, 1977-80. Served with USNR, 1962-71. Mem. Nat. Assn. Accts., Am. Mgmt. Assn. Seventh-day Adventist. Home: 9844 N Applegate Rd Grants Pass OR 97526

ROBERTS, LORIN WATSON, botany educator; b. Clarksdale, Mo., June 28, 1923; s. Lorin Cornelius and Irene (Watson) R.; m. Forence Ruth Greathouse, July 10, 1967; children—Michael, Hamlin, Daniel Hamlin, Margaret Susan Roberts. A.B., U. Mo., 1948, A.M., 1950, Ph.D., 1952; vis. prof. botany Emory U., Atlanta, 1952-55; asst. prof. Agnes Scott College, Decatur, Ga., 1952-56, assoc. prof., 1956-57; asst. prof. U. Idaho, Moscow, 1957-62, assoc. prof., 1962-67, prof., 1967—; vis. prof. Bot. Inst., U. Bari (Italy), 1968; Fulbright vis. lectr. North-Eastern Hill U., Shillong, Meghalaya, India. Served with (France); USAAF, 1943-46. Decorated chevalier de L'Ordre de Merite Agricole Fulbright scholar, Kyoto U., Japan, 1967-68; Maria Moors Cabot fellow, Harvard U., 1974; Fulbright sr. scholar, vis. fellow, Australian Nat. U., 1980; recipient disting. faculty award U. Idaho, 1981. Fellow AAAS; mem. Am. Inst. Biol. Scis., Am. Soc. Plant Physiols., Internat. Assoc. Plant Tissue Culture, Internat. Soc. Plant Morphologists, Sigma Xi, Phi Kappa Phi, Phi Sigma. Author: Cytodifferentiation in Plants, Xylogenesis as a Model System, 1976; (with J.H. Dodds) Experiments in Plant Tissue Culture, 1982. Home: 920 Mabelle Ave Moscow ID 83843 Office: Dept Biological Sciences U Idaho Moscow ID 83843

ROBERTS, MALCOLM BLAIR, government and community relations consulting company executive; b. Hollywood, Calif., Nov. 25, 1936; s. Charles Erling and Muriel (Beaufoy) R.; m. Cynthia Ann Graham, Nov. 28, 1970; children—Cheyenne, Bret McKinley, Alexis Michelle. B.A. in History, Princeton U., 1958. Asst. mng. editor Pace Mag., Los Angeles, 1966-69; spl. asst. to U.S. Sec. Interior, 1970; adminstrv. asst. to Gov. Walter J. Hickel, State of Alaska, 1971-74; pres. Malcolm B. Roberts & Assocs., Anchorage, 1974-79, 82—; exec. dir. Commonwealth North, Inc., Anchorage, 1979-82; dir. Peninsula Savs. and Loan Assn. Mem. Alaska State Central Com. of Republican Party, 1974—; Republican candidate for lt. gov. of Alaska, 1982; mem. Alaska State Bd. Edn., 1976-77; mem. Alaska adv. bd. U.S. Civil Rights Commn., 1977. Recipient Emilio Zarco award Mexican Govt., 1968. Clubs: Commonwealth North, World Affairs Council, Alaska Press. Editor: Does One Way Of Life Have To Die So Another Can Live?, 1975; Solutions to the National Energy Crisis: Why Not Alaska?, 1979. Office: 3620 Clay Products Anchorage AK 99503

ROBERTS, PAMELA LANE, education specialist; b. Chgo., Apr. 8, 1949; d. James Norman and Mary Catherine Lane; m. Howard Thomas Roberts, Jr., June 3, 1972. B.A. in Elem. Edn., U. Ariz., 1971, M.Ed. in Spl. Edn., 1972, M.Ed. in Ednl. Adminstrn., 1982. Cert. tchr., adminstr., Ariz. Tchr. Sunnyside Sch. Dist., Tucson, 1972-73; tchr. emotionally handicapped Tempe (Ariz.) Unified Sch. Dist., 1973-76; adaptive edn. resource tchr. Tucson Unified Sch. Dist., 1976-80, adaptive edn. rep., 1980—. SELECT course instr. Ariz. State Dept. Edn., 1982—. Chmn. Pima County Foster Care Rev. Bd.; zone chmn. crusade com. Am. Cancer Soc. U.S. Dept. Edn. Bur. of Handicapped fellow, 1971; Kappa Kappa Gamma rehab. grad. studies scholar, 1971. Mem. NEA, Ariz. Edn. Assn., Tucson Edn. Assn., Assn. Supervision and Curriculum Devel., Council for Exceptional Children, Assn. for Children with Learning Disabilities, Delta Kappa Gamma, Kappa Kappa Gamma. Republican. Club: Old Pueblo (Tucson).

ROBERTS, PAUL ROBERT, health care mgmt. executive; b. Chgo., Apr. 11, 1943; s. Albert A. and Marion (Smith) R. A.A. in Microbiology, Fullerton Jr. Coll., 1967; B.A. in Philosophy, U. Calif., Berkeley, 1970; M.P.H., U. Mich., 1974. Med. lab. X-ray EKG technician, Bellflower, Calif., 1965-67; microbiology and blood bank technician VA Hosp., Long Beach, Calif., 1967; research technician Sch. Medicine U. So. Calif., Los Angeles, 1967-68; program adminstr. Marion County Health and Hosp. Corp., Indpls., 1970-71; prin. planner City of Indpls., 1971; adminstr. exptl. group practice project, Indpls., 1971-73; program devel. specialist Phila. Health Mgmt. Corp., 1973-74; health maintenance orgn. cons. USPHS, San Francisco, 1974-78; gen. partner, prin. Pro-Care Planning, Mill Valley, Calif., 1978-80; health maintenance orgn. cons. USPHS, San Francisco, 1980; pres., chief exec. officer Ventura County Health Maintenance Orgn., Inc., Oxnard, Calif., 1980—; part time lectr. Ind. U., 1970-73, Med. Coll. Pa., 1974, Golden Gate U., 1976; planner Med. Services Program First Internat. NATO Conf. on Cities, 1971; coordinator Gov.'s Conf. on Aging, Pa., 1974. Served with USAF, 1961-65. Recipient certificates, letters of appreciation and recognition, regional dir. HEW, 1976, Gov. Pa., 1974, City of Indpls., 1973, 71. Cert. sr. level mgmt. positions, U.S. Civil Service Commn. Mem. Am. Public Health Assn., Am. Assn. of Founds for Med. Care, Am. Planning Assn., Group Health Assn. Am. Author: Air Force Manual for TB Laboratories for USAF in Europe, 1965. Office: PO Box 832 Oxnard CA 93032

ROBERTS, PHILLIP ANTHONY, environ. and marine engr.; b. Norfolk, Va., Mar. 30, 1946; s. Gerald Lewis and Shirlee Curtis (Smith) R.; B.S. in Marine Engring., Calif. Maritime Acad., 1968; M.S. in Environ. Engring., Ill. Inst. Tech., 1975; m. Nanci Ann Nowicki, Aug. 28, 1976. Marine engring. officer U.S. Mcht. Marine, S. Am. and Orient, 1968-71; instr. Calif. Maritime Acad., Vallejo, 1971-72; head dept. marine engring. Clatsop Coll., Astoria, Oreg., 1972-73; project mgr., engr. ETA Engrs., Oak Brook, Ill., 1974-77; sr. engr. Woodward Clyde Consultants, San Francisco, 1977-80; sr. project engr. Four Corners Pipe Line Co. (ARCO), Long Beach, Calif., 1980-81, dist. engr., 1981—. Served to lt. (j.g.) USN, 1968-72. EPA grad. scholar, 1973-75. Lic. mcht. marine officer. Mem. Am. Petroleum Inst., Soc. Naval Architects and Marine Engrs., Alpha Gamma Sigma (life). Contbr. articles on oil spills, energy and environ. issues to publs. Home: 2123 E Ocean Blvd Long Beach CA 90802 Office: 5900 Cherry Ave Long Beach CA 90805

ROBERTS, RITA, educator, adminstrator; b. Chgo., Mar. 7, 1939; d. Elvin W. and June (Purcell) Fuesling; m. Charles McCammon Schlaudt, Apr. 14, 1957; children—Kay Schlaudt Jones, Carl; m. 2d, Robert Marcus Roberts, Nov. 24, 1974. B.A., U. Calif.-Berkeley, 1967; M.A., U. San Francisco, 1979. Cert. elem. tchr., secondary tchr., adminstr., Calif. Tchr. pub. schs., San Rafael, Calif., 1968-79, asst. instrn. and curriculum, 1979-81; supr. curriculum pub. schs., Modesto, Calif., 1981-83, supr. curriculum K-12, 1983—; cons. Bay Area Writing Project, U. Calif.-Berkeley, 1977-80; Curriculum in Writing Com., mem. Calif. State Dept. Edn. Chmn. drama com. 1st Unitarian Ch., Berkeley; dir. Squirrel Hill Theatre, Berkeley; bd. dirs. Children's Theatre and Lit. Prodn., Marin County. Mem. Dixie Tchrs. Assn., Marin County Sch. Adminstrs., Curriculum Dirs., Assn. Supervision and Curriculum Devel., Phi Beta Kappa, Phi Delta Kappa. Author: Dixie Delicacies: Successful Strategies for Teaching Composition, 1978; A Handbook: How to Use Group Process in Teaching Composition, 1979. Home: 41 Discovery Bay Blvd Byron CA 94514 Office: 426 Locust St Modesto CA 95351

ROBERTS, ROBERT CANTWELL, educational administrator; b. Butte, Mont., Aug. 28, 1935; s. Ellis Vaughn and Alice Marie (Cantwell) R.; m. Sheila Clare Hanley, Sept. 30, 1954; children—Evan, Deborah, Katherine, Elizabeth. B.S., Western Mont. Coll., 1957, M.S., 1962; Ed.D., U. Mont., 1970. Tchr. cert., vocat. dir. cert., supt. cert., Wash. Tchr., counselor Butte (Mont.) Sch. Dist., 1957-65; ednl. research coordinator Mont. Dept. Public Instrn., 1965-67; adminstrv. asst. Missoula (Mont.) County High Schs, 1967-71; asst. supt. K-12, Renton (Wash.) Sch. Dist., 1971—; dir. Renton Vocat. Tech. Inst., 1971—; tchr. trainer Wash. Dept. Public Instrn., 1975—; mem. evaluation teams N.W. Assn. Sch. and Colls.; mem. Wash. State Adv. Council Vocat. Edn., Wash. Dept. Public Instrn. Profl. Adv. Com. Mem. Seattle-King County Pvt. Industry Council. State of Mont. scholar, 1955-56, Elk's Found. scholar, 1953-54; Rotary fellow, 1957-58, NDEA fellow, 1963, 64, 67. Mem. Am. Vocat. Assn., Wash. Vocat. Assn., Internat. Soc. for Gen. Semantics, N.W. Adult Edn. Assn., Wash. Assn. Sch. Bus. Ofcls., Wash. Assn. Sch. Adminstrs., Wash. Council Vocat. Tech. Insts., Phi Delta Kappa. Home: 20466 SE 159th St Renton WA 98056 Office: 3000 NE 4th St Renton WA 98056

ROBERTS, TERESA LYNN, computer scientist; b. Cleve., Nov. 4, 1951; d. Donald Richard and Jean Bell (Pugh) R. B.S. in Computer Sci., Mich. State U., 1973; M.S. (NSF fellow), Stanford U., 1974, Ph.D. (IBM fellow), 1980. Systems programmer Lawrence Livermore Labs. (Calif.), summer 1972; applications programmer Esso Prodn. Research Co., Houston, summer 1973; systems programmer Control Data Corp., Sunnyvale, Calif., summer 1974; software devel. engr. Intel Corp., Santa Clara, Calif., summer 1975; instr., teaching asst. Stanford (Calif.) U. 1974, 76; prin. mem. sci. staff Xerox Corp., Palo Alto, Calif., 1977—. Mem. Foothill Evening Chorale, Los Altos, Calif. Mem. ACM, Human Factors Soc., Computer Profls. for Social Responsibility. Office: 3333 Coyote Hill Rd Palo Alto CA 94304

ROBERTS, TERRY G., country music promoter; b. Vernal, Utah, Mar. 9, 1954; d. Burnett and Reva Alberta (Dean) R. Fast food mgr. Burger Pit, Roosevelt, Utah, 1972-76; forestry technician, Ashley Nat. Forest, Roosevelt, Utah, 1976-79; gen. maintance person Plateau Refinery, Roosevelt, Utah, 1979—; country music promoter. Sec., treas. Oil, Chem., Atomic Workers Internat. Union Local 2-941, 1979—. Mem. Country Music Assn. Baptist. Home: 168 N State St Roosevelt UT 84066

ROBERTS, W(ILBUR) EUGENE, dentist; b. Lubbock, Tex., Nov. 16, 1942; s. Wilbur Eugene and Elva Etna (Chance) R.; student U. Denver, 1961-63; D.D.S., Creighton U., 1967; Ph.D. in Anatomy, U. Utah, 1969; cert. in orthodontics, U. Conn., 1974; m. Cheryl Ann Jones, June 6, 1967; children—Jeffery Alan, Carrie Jean. Resident in acad. orthodontics U. Conn., 1971-74; asst. prof. U. Pacific, San Francisco, 1974-77, assoc. prof. orthodontics, 1977-81, prof., 1981—; bd. dirs. Pacific Dental Research Found., pres., 1978-82. Mem. adminstrv. bd. San Ramon Valley United Methodist Ch., ch. sch. supt., 1979—. Served with Dental Corps, USNR, 1969-71; Viet Nam. Decorated Navy Commendation Medal; NIH research grantee, 1975—; NASA research grantee, 1980—. Fellow Internat. Coll. Dentists; mem. Am. Assn. Orthodontists, Am. Assn. Anatomists, Internat. Assn. Dental Research, Medico-Dental Study Guild of Calif. (pres. 1982), Delta Sigma Delta (pres. alumni chpt. 1983), Omicron Kappa Upsilon, Lambda Chi Alpha. Republican. Research and publs. on bone cell biology orthodontics and implantology. Home: 75 Saint Timothy Ct Danville CA 94526 Office: 2155 Webster St San Francisco CA 94115

ROBERTS, WILLIAM BYRON, research engineer; b. Bklyn., Feb. 22, 1944; s. William Byron and Regina Maria (Beardsworth) R.; B.M.E., Santa Clara U., 1966; M.S., N.Y.U., 1968; Dp.Turbomachinery, von Karman Inst., 1970; Dr.Applied Sci., U. Brussels, 1973; m. Alison Jane Raymond, Dec. 27, 1969; children—Elizabeth Frances, Annemarie Regina, Candace Alexandra, William Bryon. Research assoc. Von Karman Inst., 1970-73; sr. engr. Westinghouse Electric Corp., 1973-75; asst. prof. U. Notre Dame, 1976-78; project mgr. Nielsen Engring. and Research, Mountain View, Calif., 1978-80; dir., sr. assoc. Flow Application Research, Fremont, Calif., 1980—; cons. in field. NASA scholar, 1965; USAF fellow, 1969-70; ASEE, NASA fellow, 1976-77; NASA grantee, 1976—. Mem. ASME, AIAA, Sigma Xi. Contbr. 38 articles to profl. jours. Office: 1543 Vernal Ave Fremont CA 94538

ROBERTSON, CLYDE LAVERNE, school administrator; b. Sidney, Nebr., Mar. 20, 1935; s. Clyde Leroy and Leota Carmelita (Crosby) R.; m. Karen Kaye Kinner, Dec. 29, 1937; children—Shelly, Stuart. B.S. in Edn., Kearney State Coll., 1957; M.S. in Edn., U. N. Mex., 1966; Ed.S. in Edn. Adminstrn., U. Nebr., 1968. Cert. ednl. specialist. Tchr. pub. schs., Grant, Nebr., 1957-63; tchr., prin. pub. schs., Sutherland, Nebr., 1966-69; supt. schs., Julesburg, Colo., 1969-78, Salida, Colo., 1978—. NSF grantee, 1963. Mem. Colo. Assn. Sch. Execs., Am. Assn. Sch. Adminstrs. Club: Masons. Home: 1331 E St Salida CO 81201 Office: Salida Sch Dist 310 E 9th St Salida CO 81201

ROBERTSON, DOUGLAS GREY, physical scientist, land co. exec.; b. Madison, S.D., Feb. 4, 1933; s. Ralph Thomas and Elsie Mildred (Ennis) R.; m. Mercedes Funderburk, May 5, 1970 (div.); m. 2d, Carmencita Buenaventura Vite, Jan. 6, 1979 (dec.). Grad. DeVry Tech. Inst., 1954; B.S., U. Minn., 1957; M.A., Northwestern U., 1962. Acoustical research audiologist West Side VA Hosp., Chgo., 1960; cons. audiologist Otolaryngology Profl. Assos., St. Paul, 1962-66; ind. investigator St. Joseph's Hosp. Research Lab., St. Paul, 1962-66; clin. instr. otolaryngology U. Minn. Med. Sch., Mpls., 1963-66; research audiologist Naval Missile Center, Point Mugu, Calif., 1966-75; research audiologist Pacific Missile Test Center, Point Mugu, 1975-78, phys. scientist, tech. head, crew systems br. Flight Test div., 1978-82, phys. scientist engring. br. Pate div., 1982—; pres. Channel Islands Beach Co., Inc., 1983—. mem. com. on hearing, bioacoustics and biomechanics NRC. Pres. bd. dirs. Channel Islands Beach Community Services Dist., 1982—. Served with USNR, 1950-59. Louis and Maud Hill Family Found. research grantee, 1963-65. Mem. Am. Speech, Lang. and Hearing Assn., SAFE Assn., Acoustical Soc. Am., Inst. Noise Control Engring. (assoc.), Astron. Soc. Pacific, Aircraft Owners and Pilots Assn., Channel Islands Safety Council, Channel Islands Beach Community Council (vice chmn. 1981-82), Channel Islands C. of C., Sigma Alpha Eta. Republican. Lutheran. Club: Alfa Romeo Owners of Santa Barbara. Contbr. articles to profl. jours. Patentee in field. Home: 4045 Sunset Ln Channel Islands Beach CA 93030 Office: Pacific Missile Test Center (1031) Point Mugu CA 93042

ROBERTSON, ERNEST ARTHUR, engineering executive; b. Grosse Pointe, Mich., Dec. 13, 1940; s. Carl Arthur and Jenny Kristina (Janson) R.; m. Betty JoAnne Arnone, Sept. 30, 1967; children—Kevin, Christopher. B.S.E.E., MIT, 1963, M.S.E.E., 1965. Mem. tech. staff Bell Telephone Labs., Whippany, N.J., 1965-69, Comsat Labs., Clarksburg, Md., 1969-73; dep. dir. Comsat World Systems, Palo Alto, Calif., 1973-82, dir., El Segundo, Calif., 1982—. Mem. AIAA. Office: 999 N Sepulueda El Segundo CA 90245

ROBERTSON, GEORGE EDWARD, architect, design consultant; b. Seattle, Oct. 31, 1945; s. Thurman A. and Vera L. Robertson; B.Arch., U. Wash., 1971; m. Patricia J. Rachford, Sept. 6, 1970; 1 dau., Annett J. With Teufel Constrn., Seattle, 1969-71; designer, architect Denis Tusar & Assocs., Vancouver, B.C., Can., 1971-74; architect Hennquez & Todd, Vancouver, 1971-76; v.p., dir. architecture Whiteley Jacobson & Assocs., Seattle, 1976—; founder George E. Robertson, AIA, 1982. Mem. Land Use Adv. Task Force Citizens Com., Seattle, 1980-81; mem. Seattle Bicycle Adv. Bd., 1982; mem. urban design subcom. Downtown Seattle Devel. Assn., 1980-81. Mem. AIA (urban design subcom. Seattle chpt. 1982, met. and govt. affairs com. 1983), Archtl. Inst. B.C., Royal Archtl. Inst. Can.

ROBERTSON, HARRY LEROY, SR., manufacturing company executive; b. Glenns Perry, Idaho, May 10, 1921; s. William David and Lottie Bertha (Story) R.; student Citrus Coll., 1954-59; m. Barbara Jean Freitas, Feb. 22, 1948; children—Deborah, Michille, Paula, William, Monica, Harry Leroy. With Civilian Conservation Corps, 1936-38; rancher, 1938-41; fireman Union Pacific R.R., 1945-46; machinist Clary Corp., 1946-48; retail bus. automotive repairman, 1948-50; machinist, leadman, foreman drapery hardware co., 1950-54; technician, leadman, engring. technician, field service technician, adviser to pres., Hycon Inc., 1956-58; engring. prodn. mgr., plant mgr., chief engr., tech. adv. to sales staff, pres. trade shows Hymac Corp., Hycon Electronics, Molectronics, Inc., Pasadena, Calif., 1958-60; testing, supervising engr. Hycon & Molectronics, Inc., South El Monte, Calif., 1960-83; owner Robertson Instrument Co., Azusa, Calif., 1983—; pres., chief exec. officer Robertson-PAS Corp., Azusa, 1983—. Served with USMC, 1941-45. Decorated Purple Heart. Mem. VFW, DAV, Nat. Order Trench Rats. Patentee in field. Address: PO Box E Azusa CA 91702

ROBERTSON, JACQUELINE LEE, research entomologist, veterinary assistant; b. Petaluma, Calif., July 9, 1947; d. John Lyman and Nina Pauline (Klemenok) Schwartz; A.B. in Zoology, U. Calif.-Berkeley, 1969, Ph.D. in Entomology, 1973. Registered profl. entomologist. Supervisory research entomologist U.S. Dept. Agr. Forest Service, Pacific S.W. Forest and Range Expt. Sta., Berkeley, Calif., 1966—. Recipient Superior service award U.S. Dept. Agr., 1981. Mem. Entomol. Soc. Am., Entomol. Soc. Can., AAAS, Am. Inst. Biol. Scis., Am. Soc. Zoologists, N.Y. Acad. Scis. Contbr. articles to profl. jours. Editor Jour.

Econ. Entomology; patentee lab. pesticide spray chamber. Office: PO Box 245 Berkeley CA 94701

ROBERTSON, JAMES ALLEN, risk mgmt. cons.; b. Burlington, Iowa, Jan. 24, 1948; s. George Allen and Betty Irene (Beck) R.; student Knox Coll., 1965-66; B.A., U. Iowa, 1969; postgrad. San Francisco Theol. Sem./Grad. Theol. Union, 1969-70; M.S.A., Pepperdine U., 1976; m. Stephanie Peacock. Casualty underwriter Hartford Ins. Group, San Francisco, 1970-72, supervising underwriter, 1972-73, Los Angeles, 1973-74; asst. v.p. Tausch Ins. Brokers, Santa Ana, Calif., 1974-75; cons. Warren, McVeigh & Griffin, 1975-76; sr. v.p. Reed Risk Mgmt., San Francisco, 1976-78; pres. James A. Robertson & Assos., Inc., El Paso, Tex., 1978-79; prin. cons., v.p. Warren, McVeigh & Griffin, Newport Beach, Calif., 1979; asso. in risk mgmt. C.P.C.U. Mem. Soc. Chartered Property Casualty Underwriters, Omicron Delta Kappa. Republican. Author: The Umbrella Book, 1976, 2d edit., 1979. Office: 1420 Bristol St N Suite 220 Newport Beach CA 92660

ROBERTSON, JEANNE BENNETT, interior designer, artist; b. San Francisco, May 21, 1916; d. Willard Winslow Bennett and Mary Louise (Weymann) B; m. Charles Bennett Robertson, July 5, 1941; children—David Bennett, Philip Bennett, Anne Louise Thomas. A.B., U. Calif., Berkeley, 1938. Sales mgr. Furniture and Design Co., Mill Valley, Calif., 1966; owner, designer Jeanne Robertson Interiors Co., Belvedere, Calif., 1967-74, Honolulu, 1974—; pres. Clarke-Robertson, Ltd., 1974—; exhibited in one-woman and group shows; represented in permanent collection City Hall of Honolulu, also pvt. collections. coordinator artists workshops. Formerly active Girl Scouts U.S.A., Camp Fire Girls; past pres. local PTA. Served with Women's br. USAAF, 1943-44. Mem. Nat. Home Fashion League, Nat. League Am. Penwomen, Am. Soc. Interior Designers (assoc.), AAUW (1st v.p. Honolulu), Hawaii Watercolor Soc. (past pres.), Honolulu Artists (assoc.), Kalanianaole Art League. Republican. Presbyterian. Home: 1408 Kamole St Honolulu HI 96821 Office: 1365 Colburn St Honolulu HI 96817

ROBERTSON, MALCOLM RAY, educator; b. Stockton, Calif., Dec. 12, 1922; s. Malcolm C. and Selma C. (Halvorsen) R.; B.A., Pasadena Coll., 1948; Th.B., Pacific Bible Coll., 1950; M.A., Calif. State U., 1961; Ed.D., U. So. Calif., 1967; D. Hum. (hon.), Azusa Pacific Coll., 1973; m. Ruth Lois Smith, Oct. 15, 1944; children—Kenneth R., Kathleen J. Instr., Pacific Bible Coll., Azusa, Calif., 1948-50, registrar, instr., 1950-53, dean instrn., 1953-57; v.p., dean instrn. Azusa Coll., 1957-65; acad. v.p., dean instrn. Azusa Pacific Coll., 1965-72, acad. v.p., 1972-73, exec. v.p. acad. and instl. affairs, 1973-76, chmn. presdl. team, acting pres., 1975-76, v.p. planning, research and evaluation, 1976-77, prof. religion and psychology, 1977—; chair adminstrn. Calif. Bapt. Coll., Riverside, 1981—; adminstr. Thaddeus Found., 1979—. Served with U.S. Army, 1944-46. Recipient Spl. award Free Meth. Insts. of Higher Edn., 1974. Mem. Am. Assn. Higher Edn., Calif. Assn. Family Therapists, Calif. Tchrs. Assn., Phi Delta Kappa, Kappa Phi Kappa. Republican. Wesleyan Ch. (elder). Club: Kiwanis (pres. 1971-72). Asso. pub. Travelhost Mag., 1977-80. Home: 179 Oak Forest Circle Glendora CA 91740 Office: Hwy 66 at Citrus St Azusa CA 91702

ROBERTSON, MARILYN COOPER (MRS. ALFRED W. ROBERTSON), former television commentator; b. Victor, N.Y., July 12; d. Winfield Henry and Elzey (Carroll) Cooper; student Rollins Coll., 1921; m. William Layton Waterman, Feb. 14, 1925 (div. 1932); children—Douglas Arthur, Robert Hamilton; m. 2d, Alfred W. Robertson, Jan. 26, 1948 (dec. Jan. 1958). Soloist, Radio Sta. WGN, Chgo., 1931; staff soprano Saturday Night Nat. Barn Dance on Sta. WLS, NBC, Chgo., 1932-36, also soloist CBS; commentator CBS, N.Y.C., also Hollywood, Calif., 1938-40; originator news press show Hollywood News Club; capt. Hollywood Canteen Snack-Bar, 1942-45; commentator Channel 6, Meet Your Neighbor Pilot Show, Leisure World, Laguna Hills, Calif., 1970-74. Mem. DAR (life), Church Women United (pres. Saddleback unit area I 1973-77), Internat. Platform Assn. Clubs: Calif. (pres. 1976-77) (Laguna Hills); Saddle Club and Theatre Guild of Leisure World. Home: 2156-G Via Mariposa E Laguna Hills CA 92653 Office: Laguna Hills CA 92653

ROBERTSON, SAMUEL HARRY, III, research company executive, educator; b. Phoenix, Oct. 2, 1934; s. Samuel Harry and Doris Byrle (Duffield) R.; B.S., Ariz. State U., 1956; D.Aviation Tech. (hon.), Embry-Riddle Aero. U., 1972; m. Nancy Jean Bradford, Aug. 20, 1954; children—David Lyle, Pamela Louise. Head hazards div. Dynamic Sci., Phoenix, 1961-70; research prof., dir. Engring. Safety Center, Coll. Engring. Scis., Ariz. State U., Tempe, 1970-80; pres. Robertson Research Inc., Crash Research Inst., 1970—, Robertson Aviation, 1974—, Robertson Land & Cattle Co., 1975—; dir. Crash Survival Investigators Sch., 1970—, USAF Ground Safety Sch., 1976—, Vehicle Accident Investigations and Reconstrn. Sch., 1975—, Internat. Ctr. for Safety Edn., 1980—; cons. design and accident investigation of airplanes, 1961—; instr. Inst. Aerospace Safety, U. So. Calif., 1962-70, Armed Forces Inst. Pathology, 1970—, Dept. Transp. Safety Inst., 1970—. Served as pilot USAF, 1956-60, with N.G., 1961-75. Recipient Adm. Luis DeFlorez Internat. Flying Safety award, 1969, cert. of commendation Nat. Safety Council, 1969, CNA award for automotive racing safety, 1975, Chief Steward award for racing safety Speedway, 1980, Jerome Lederer award for aircraft accident investigations, 1981, Gen. William Spruance award for safety edn., 1982; registered profl. engr. Mem. Soc. Air Safety Investigators, Aerospace Med. Assn., AIAA, Soc. Automotive Engrs., Am. Helicopter Soc., Nat. Fire Protection Assn. (com. for aircraft rescue and fire fighting), Aircraft Owners and Pilots Assn., Soaring Soc. Am. Contbr. articles to profl. publs. Patentee on applying plastic to paper, safety valve components, crash resistant fuel system, safety aircraft seats, crashworthy aircraft control stick, movable wire markers for aircraft safety; designer, developer crash resistant fuel systems for aircraft and championship racing cars; mfr., seller fuel systems for helicopters and fixed-wing aircraft. Home: 2053 E Alameda Tempe AZ 85282 Office: 1024 E Vista del Cerro Tempe AZ 85281

ROBERTSON, STUART A., actuary, consultant; b. Montesano, Wash., Feb. 28, 1918; s. George Duncan and Anna (McLeod) R.; m. Marjory Belle Moch, Nov. 24, 1939; children—Richard S., Ann. Student U. Idaho, 1934-35, U. Wash., 1937. Vice pres. Gt. Northwest Life Ins. Co., Spokane, Wash., 1937-47; actuarial asst. No. Life Ins. Co., Seattle, 1947-49; actuary Northwestern Life Ins. Co., Seattle, 1949-50; cons. actuary, chmn. Milliman & Robertson, Inc., Seattle, 1950—; chmn. bd. M&R Services, Inc., Seattle, 1972—. Fellow Soc. Actuaries (bd. govs. 1972-75); mem. Seattle Actuarial Club (pres. 1958), Actuarial Club of Pacific States (pres. 1963), Conf. of Actuaries in Pub. Practice, Am. Acad. Actuaries. Clubs: Harbor (bd. dirs. 1980—), Wash. Athletic (Seattle), Wing Point Golf and Country (Bainbridge Island). Home: 14320 Sunrise Dr NE Bainbridge Island WA 98110 Office: 1301 5th Ave Suite 3600 Seattle WA 98101

ROBERTSON, WILLIAM ARCHIE, cons. engr.; b. Prescott, Ariz., Nov. 14, 1946; s. William David and Doris Eleanor (Thomas) R.; B.S. in Engring., Ariz. State U., 1972; M.S. in C.E., U. Alaska, 1976; m. Terry Lenore Judd, Sept. 11, 1971; children—William Abia, Scott Paul. Engr., surveyor U.S. Govt., Juneau, Alaska, 1967-69; engr., surveyor State of Alaska Div. Aviation, Anchorage, 1970-74; engr. KPFF Architects, Engrs., Planners, Anchorage, 1974-76; assoc., office mgr. R & M Cons., Anchorage, 1976-80; prin. Robertson & Assocs., Cons. Engrs. & Surveyors, Anchorage, 1980—. Registered profl. engr., Alaska; registered land surveyor, Alaska. Mem. ASCE (pres. Anchorage br. 1979-80, 2d v.p. Alaska sect. 1981-82, 1st v.p. 1982-83), Am. Congress on Surveying and Mapping, Constrn. Specifications Inst., Nat. Soc. Profl. Engrs. Contbr. articles to profl. jours. Office: 2820 C St Suite 2 Anchorage AK 99503

ROBERTSON, WILLIAM RAY, professional speaker, trainer, sales consultant; b. Covington, Ky., Jan. 4, 1945; s. William Rolf and Joan Wanda (Ward) R.; children—Merry, Scott, Steve. Owner Robertson Fin. Planning, 1974-76; exec. dir., seminar leader Network Enterprises, San Diego, 1983—; prin. Robertson Assocs. Mem. Nat. Speakers Assn., Jaycees (mentor Ohio chpt., pres. 1977-78). Home: 10239 Caminito Rio Branco San Diego CA 92131

ROBINETTE, HILLARY, JR., research lab. exec.; b. Wilmington, Del., Jan. 27, 1913; s. Hillary and Lillie Belle (Mitchell) R.; A.B., Temple U., 1934; m. Adele Jargowsky, Feb. 17, 1934; children—Hillary, Christine. Chemist, Rohm & Haas Co., 1933-39; pres. Jordan Chem. Co., 1939-40; market devel. exec. Comml. Solvents Corp., 1940-42; research exec. Publicker Industries, 1945-49; research dir. Amalgamated Chem. Corp., 1948-52; pres., chmn. bd. Robinette Research Labs., Inc., Berwyn, Pa., 1952-77, Youngstown, Ariz., 1977—; dir. Consultants Center, Inc., Berwyn. Served to capt. U.S. Army, 1942-46. Recipient award of merit Dept. Commerce U.S., 1976. Fellow Am. Inst. Chemists; mem. Am. Chem. Soc., Am. Assn. Textile Chemists and Colorists, Soc. Mil. Engrs., Soc. Chem. Industry, Societe de Chinie Industrielle (pres. Am. sect. 1967-71), Nat. Def. Exec. Res., Am. Council Ind. Labs. (hon.), S.A.R. Clubs: Chemists (N.Y.C.); Officers (Luke AFB); Rotary. Contbr. articles to profl. jours. U.S. and abroad; patentee U.S. and abroad. Home: 10333 Campana Dr Sun City AZ 85351 Office: PO Box 68 Youngstown AZ 85363

ROBINETTE, KAYE CHESTER, lawyer; b. Corvallis, Oreg., Jan. 29, 1936; s. Kelley Floyd and Itha Myrtle (Bowen) R.; m. Elna Mae Fitzhugh, Sept. 5, 1954; children—Daniel Cole, Katherine Ann. B.S., U. Oreg., 1958, LL.B., 1960. Bar: Oreg. 1960. Assoc., Koerner, Young, McColloch & Dezendorf, Portland, 1960-67; from assoc. to ptnr. Vonderheit, Hershner & Hunter, Eugene, 1967-75; ptnr. Robinette, Cleveland, Williams & Gebhardt, Eugene, 1975—; chmn. com. legal ethics and disciplinary rev. bd. Oreg. State Bar. Pres., Rubicon Soc., 1971, 79; chmn. Closure Task Force Eugene Sch. Dist., 1981, chmn. budget com. 1983. Mem. Oreg. State Bar Assn., Lane County Bar Assn. Republican. Office: 975 Oak St Suite 600 Eugene OR 97401

ROBINS, JUDY ROSELYN, interior designer; b. Cleve., Sept. 2, 1948; d. Stanley and Esther (Resnick) Waxman; m. Kenneth Michael Robins, Sept. 26, 1971. A.A.S., Fashion Inst. Tech.; B.S., N.Y.U., 1970, M.A., 1972. Fabric coordinator Celanese Corp., N.Y.C., 1970-71; merchandiser Bayly Corp., Denver, 1973-74; instr. Metro State Coll., Denver, 1977-81; self-employed interior designer, Denver, 1975—; mem. bd. Waxman Industries. Mem. Steering com. Alliance Contemporary Art, Denver Art Mus.; women's bd. Nat. Jewish Hosp., 1978-80; bd. mem., v.p. leadership Allied Jewish Fedn. recipient Young Leadership award, 1977; bd. dirs. congregation, Jewish Family and Children's Service Colo., 1975-83; founding mem. Young Women's Leadership Cabinet United Jewish Appeal, 1977-82. Address: 755 Lafayette St Denver CO 80218

ROBINS, MIRIAM CLAIR, ins. co. exec.; b. Denver, Sept. 19, 1935; d. H. Rupard and Mildred L. (Opie) R.; B.A., Colo. Coll., 1957; M.A., U. Denver, 1959. Instr. piano, organ, Denver, 1957-62; v.p., dir. Olinger Life Ins. Co., Denver, 1961-63, exec. v.p., dir., 1963-73, pres., dir., 1973-78, vice chmn. bd., 1978—. Tchr., music arranger for talent competition Miss America, 1958. Vice pres. Colo. Life Conv., Denver, 1966-67. Mem. Kappa Delta Pi, Mu Phi Epsilon, Kappa Alpha Theta. Republican. Clubs. Denver, Denver Athletic, Garden of the Gods, 1864 (U. Denver); Cutler (Colo. Coll.). Home: 5442 S Dayton Ct Englewood CO 80111 Office: Box 11128 Highlands Sta Denver CO 80211

ROBINSON, ARNOLD, aeronautical engineer, aviation company executive; b. N.Y.C., Oct. 27, 1929; s. Louis and Anna (Cohen) R.; m. Trudy Needleman, Nov. 14, 1954; children—Barry, Lisa, Sanford. B.S. in Aero. Engring., Poly. Inst. Bklyn., 1951; M.S., Drexel Inst. Tech., 1955. Registered profl. engr., Pa., N.Y., Fla. Aero. structures engr. U.S. Naval Air Devel. Ctr., Johnsville, Pa., 1951-55; asst. chief of structures Missiles div. Republic Aviation, Farmingdale, N.Y., 1955-57; chief of structures, asst. chief engr. Omega Aircraft Corp., New Bedford, Mass., 1957-59; chief engr., ptnr. DeVore Engring. Service, 1960-68; v.p., dir. DeVore Aviation Corp., Albuquerque, 1968—; cons. engr. aircraft design devel. and certification FAA; expert witness in aircraft accident investigations and testimony. Mem. AIAA, Am. Helicopter Soc., Internat. Assn. Air Safety Investigators, Albuquerque C. of C. (aviation sub com). Home: 1527 Wagontrain Dr SE Albuquerque NM 87163 Office: 6104-B Kircher Blvd NE Albuquerque NM 87109

ROBINSON, ARTHUR STEWARD, JR., lawyer; b. Washington, Dec. 21, 1948; s. Arthur Steward and Frances Davene (Clemons) R.; m. Cheryl Leigh Andrews, Apr. 6, 1968; m. 2d, Irene Jane Albayalde, Aug. 15, 1980; children—Sean, Aaron, Terry, Denise, Katy, Jackie, Tommy. B.A. in Polit. Sci., UCLA, 1973; J.D., 1973. Bar: Alaska 1974. Asst. dist. atty. Anchorage, 1974-75; dir. Cook Inlet Aquaculture Assn., Kenai, Alaska, 1979-82; sole practice, Soldotna, Alaska, 1976—; instr. bus. law Kenai Peninsula Community Coll. Mem. Alaska Bar Assn., ABA, Assn. Trial Lawyers Am. Bahai. Club: Rotary (charter mem. local chpt.). Address: PO Box 3519 Soldotna AK 99669

ROBINSON, BERNARD LEO, lawyer, communications company executive; b. Kalamazoo, Feb. 14, 1924; s. Louis Harvey and Sue Mary (Starr) R.; B.S., U. Ill., 1947, M.S., 1958, postgrad. in structural dynamics, 1959; J.D., U. N.Mex., 1973; m. Betsy Nadell, May 30, 1947; children—Robert Bruce, Patricia Anne, Jean Carol. Research engr. Assn. Am. Railroads, 1947-49; instr. architecture Rensselaer Poly. Inst., 1949-51; commd. 2d lt. Corps Engrs., U.S. Army, 1945, advanced through grades to lt. col., 1965, ret., 1968; engr. Nuclear Def. Research Corp., Albuquerque, 1968-69; admitted to N.Mex. bar, 1973, U.S. Supreme Ct. bar, 1976; practiced in Albuquerque, 1973—; sec., dir. Hi-Z Mining Corp.; sec., dir. Telstar Corp. Dist. commr. Boy Scouts Am., 1960-62. Vice chmn. Republican Dist. Com., 1968-70; bd. dirs. Bernalillo chpt. Am. Diabetes Assn. Decorated Air medal, Combat Infantryman's Badge, Joint Services Commendation medal. Mem. ASCE, Soc. Am. Mil. Engrs., Am., N.Mex., Albuquerque bar assns., Comml. Law League Am., Ret. Officers Assn., DAV, Assn. U.S. Army. Home: 4416 Glenwood Hills NE Albuquerque NM 87111 Office: 2901 Juan Tabo NE Suite 224 Albuquerque NM 87112

ROBINSON, CAROL SUSAN, advt. agy. exec.; b. Detroit, Oct. 28, 1938; d. Allen Lawrence and Sally (Cutler) R.; student Mich. State U., 1956-57; B.S., Boston U., 1960; student Soc. Arts and Crafts, Detroit, Calif. Coll. Arts and Crafts, Oakland, Otis Art Inst., Los Angeles; m. Richard Allen Clarke, Mar. 23, 1974; stepchildren—Richard, Janis Clarke Meldahl, William, Robert. Tchr. public schs., Sharon, Mass., 1960, Woodland Hills and Granda Hills, Calif., 1960-61; art buyer, exec. sec. Foote, Cone & Belding, Los Angeles, 1961-65; copy chief, continuity dir. KFOX, Long Beach, Calif., 1966-68; mgr. visual design Mattel, Inc., Los Angeles, 1968-75; pres. Seven Fleet St., Ltd., San Francisco, 1975-77; partner, v.p. King, Robinson & Clarke, San Francisco, 1978; pres., treas. bd. Robinson-Clarke, Inc., San Francisco, 1978—. Mem. Nat. Assn. Female Execs., NOW, San Francisco Art Commn., Los Angeles County Mus. Art, Oakland Art Mus., San Francisco Advt. Club. Office: 70 Gold St San Francisco CA 94133

ROBINSON, CAROLYN MAYE, elementary educator; b. Stephenville, Tex., Mar. 7, 1938; d. William Earl and Lula May (Pittman) Allen; m. William Lawrence Robinson, Aug. 5, 1956; children—Dale, Rhonda, Mike. B.S., Eastern N.Mex. U., 1959; M.A., U. N.Mex., 1973. Specialist reading and curriculum, N.Mex. Tchr., Eastern N.Mex. Presch., Portales, 1957-59; substitute tchr. Portales Jr. High Sch.-High Sch., 1959-60; tchr. Albuquerque Pub. Schs., 1970—; ednl. cons. Master Tchr., Albuquerque Pub. Schs., 1981-82. Mem. Internat. Reading Assn., Assn. Supervision and Curriculum Devel., N.Mex. Assn. Edn. of Young Children, Phi Delta Kappa. Republican. Mem. Ch. of Christ. Co-author slidetape; author activity booklets for Publ. Service Co. N.Mex. Home: 402 Fontana NE Albuquerque NM 87108 Office: 3311 Monte Vista NE Albuquerque NM 87106

ROBINSON, CHARLES GEORGE, safety engineer; b. San Francisco, Aug. 31, 1934; s. James Minor and Margaret Laverne (George) R.; m. Jo Ann Eads, May 25, 1958; children—Michael Charles, James George. A.A., Pasadena City Coll., 1956; B.A., Calif. State U., 1958; M.B.A., Calif. Coast U., 1983. Loss control mgr. State Compensation Fund, Santa Ana, Calif., 1963-74; environ. health and safety officer Calif. State U.-Fullerton, 1974—; instr. indsl. safety. Active Anaheim Jr. C. of C., 1963-70, City Orange Traffic Safety Com., 1967-80. Served to capt. USMC, 1957-65. Mem. Am. Soc. Safety Engrs. (past pres. local chpt.), Am. Indsl. Hygiene Assn., Nat. Safety Mgmt. Soc. Democrat. Presbyterian. Contbr. articles to profl. jours. Home: 424 Riverview Ave Orange CA 92665 Office: 800 N State College Blvd Fullerton CA 92634

ROBINSON, CLARK HOWARD, electrical contractor; b. Omaha, Mar. 6, 1942; s. William Andrew and Fern Viola (Feelhaver) R.; m. Carol Maxine Johnson, June 1, 1962; children—Kevin Scott, Stacy Kristine. With Electric Air, San Bernardino, Calif., 1961-70; estimator, designer, purchasing agt., supt. Magnolia Electric, Riverside, Calif., 1970-72; estimator, designer, purchasing agt., supt. Douglas Electric, Riverside, Calif., 1972-74; pres., treas., designer Streech Electric Co., Anaheim, Calif., 1974—, chmn. bd., 1979—. Mem. Nat. Elec. Contractors Assn., Associated Gen. Contractors. Mem. United Ch. Christ. Club: Elks. Office: 3870 E Eagle Dr Anaheim CA 92807

ROBINSON, CRAIG HIBBARD, psychologist; b. Port Huron, Mich., May 25, 1943; s. Don B. and Hazelbelle (Hibbard) R.; grad. Port Huron Jr. Coll., 1963; B.A., U. Hawaii, 1966, M.A., 1968, Ph.D., 1974; m. Patricia Ann Bankert, Aug. 15, 1970; children—Janna, Carey. Spl. edn. tchr. and tutor (part-time) Dept. Edn., State of Hawaii, 1966-68; sch. psychologist Clark AFB, 1968-69, Child Guidance Clinic, 1969-71; psychology intern Queen's Med. Center, Honolulu, 1971-72, Pacific Psychiatry and Psychology, Honolulu, 1972-73, clin. psychologist, 1973—; clin. research asso. Sexual Counseling Services, Kapiolani Hosp., Honolulu, 1973-74, asst. dir. clin. tng. and research, 1974-75; dir. edn. and tng. Enabling Systems, Inc., Honolulu, 1974-78; asst. clin. prof. dept. psychology U. Hawaii, 1978—; mem. adj. faculty Antioch U., San Francisco, 1978—; pvt. practice clin. psychology; psychol. cons. Disability Determination br., Social Security Adminstrn., Honolulu, 1975-80; cons. Sexual Counseling Service, U. Hawaii, 1974—. Mem. Am. Psychol. Assn., Western Psychol. Assn., Hawaii Psychol. Assn. (pres. 1977-78), Am. Coll. Sexologists, Assn. Advancement of Psychology, Am. Assn. Sex Educators and Counselors, Am. Assn. Marriage and Family Counselors, Acad. Psychologists in Marital and Family Therapy, Six Info. and Edn. Council of U.S., Soc. Clin. and Exptl. Hypnosis. Contbr. articles to jours. in psychology. Home: 6370 Hawaii Kai Dr Honolulu HI 96825 Office: 1380 Lusitana Honolulu HI 96813

ROBINSON, CURTIS JOHN, university administrator; b. N.Y.C., Dec. 13, 1951; s. Herschel Edward and Delores Viola (Westberg) R. B.A. with honors, U. Calif.-Davis, 1974, M.A., 1981. Editor in chief Calif. Aggie, U. Calif.-Davis, 1973-74, editor Univ. Extension, 1977-80, program promotion mgr., dir. pub. info. and data processing Extension, 1980—; teaching asst. geography dept. U. Tex., Austin, 1974-75; acct. ITT Arctic Services on Alaska Pipeline Fairbanks, 1975-76; student personnel asst. Consumnes River Coll., Sacramento, 1976-77; mktg. cons., 1976—; guest lectr., 1976—. Chmn. City of Davis Community Devel. Block Grant Adv. Com., 1979—; mem. Yolo County Housing and Community Devel. Coms., 1981-82. Leadership scholar Ankara (Turkey) Officers Wives, 1970. Republican. Home: 1913 Drexel Dr Davis CA 95616 Office: Univ Extension U Calif Davis CA 95616

ROBINSON, DAVID LEON, public relations executive, educator, writer; b. Los Angeles, May 16, 1948; s. Gilmer George and Jewell Rita (Starkweather) R.; m. Jacqueline McCurdy, Jan. 21, 1978. B.A. in English, San Diego State U., 1971, M.S. in Mass Communications, 1980. Promotion cons. Project Concern Internat., 1976; communications coordinator Home Fed. Savs. & Loan, San Diego, 1977-78; asst. pub. relations dir. Phillips-Ramsey Inc., San Diego, 1978-81; pub. relations mgr. Hewlett-Packard, San Diego Div., 1981-82; dir. pub. relations services Young & Rubicam, San Diego, (Young & Rubicam acquired by WFC 1982), v.p. WFC/Westcom, San Diego, 1982—; instr. pub. relations San Diego State U., 1982—. Co-author: The Basic Guide to Fly Fishing, 1979; The Far End of America, A Book About Ocean Beach, California, 1975, 76; contbr. articles to newspapers and mags. Bd. dirs. fundraising campaign Combined Health Agys. Drive, 1983; mem. Mex. and Am. Found. Com. Recipient news media award San Diego County Fire Chiefs, 1974. Mem. Pub. Relations Club San Diego (pres. 1982), Internat. Assn. Bus. Communicators (pres. 1981, communications awards 1977-82), Pub. Relations Soc. Am., San Diego Communications Council (co-founder). Presbyterian. Home: 7101 Boulevard Dr La Mesa CA 92041 Office: 6950 Friars Rd San Diego CA 92108

ROBINSON, DAVID PAUL, education educator; b. St. Louis, Aug. 27, 1943; s. Robert Roy and Eleanor (Opp) R.; B.A., Stanford U., 1965, M.A. in Edn., 1969, M.A. in History, 1973, Ph.D., 1977; m. Leslie Ann Soderquist, Mar. 4, 1967; children—Todd Kenneth, Keith Hulett, Shane Tyler. Social studies tchr. Monta Vista High Sch., Cupertino, Calif., 1969-71; teaching asst. Stanford U., 1971-74; asst. prof. secondary edn. and history U. Ark., Little Rock, 1975-80, acting chmn. dept. secondary edn., 1977-79; asst. prof. secondary edn. U. Ariz., Tucson, 1980—; Stanford-in-Washington intern Atlantic council, 1965; bd. dirs. Little Rock Vols. in Pub. Schs., 1975-78; course of study com. Ariz. State B. Social Studies Basic Goals, 1981. Served with U.S. Army, 1965-67. Donaghey Found. grantee, 1977. Mem. Nat. Council Social Studies (chmn. research com. 1980-81, chmn. founds. spl. interest group 1982-83), Coll. and Univ. Faculty Assembly (chmn. exec. com. 1979-80), Am. Ednl. Research Assn., History Edn. Soc., Soc. Study Curriculum History (award 1981), S.W. Ednl. Research Assn., Ariz. Council Social Studies (sec.-treas. 1980-82, v.p. 1982—), Kappa Delta Pi, Phi Delta Kappa. Democrat. Baptist. Mem. editorial bd. Theory and Research in Social Edn., 1978-81; mem. editorial rev. bd. Jour. Social Studies Research, 1980—. Home: 5325 E 7th St Tucson AZ 85711 Office: Dept Secondary Edn U Ariz Tucson AZ 85721

ROBINSON, ELIZABETH ANNE, psychologist, educator; b. N.Y.C., July 23, 1944; d. John M. and Mary Margaret R.; m. John Richard

Garner, Sept. 8, 1979. B.S., Cornell U., 1966; Ph.D., U. S.C., 1977. Lic. psychologist, Wash., 1980. Field adviser Green Valley council Girl Scouts U.S., 1966-67; tchr. Northridge High Sch., Dayton, Ohio, 1967-69; psychology asst. II Willard (N.Y.) State Hosp., 1969-72; psychology trainee VA, Richmond, Va., Cannadaigua, N.Y. and Columbia, S.C., 1973-74; research asst. U. S.C., 1974-75, instr. psychology, 1974-76; intern med. psychology U. Oreg. Health Scis. Ctr., Portland, 1976-77; vis. asst. prof. U. Oreg., Eugene, 1977-79; asst. prof. psychology U. Wash., Seattle, 1979—, prin. investigator Family Interaction Project, 1980—. NIMH grantee, 1980-83; Neidich fellow, 1975. Mem. Am. Psychol. Assn., Western Psychol. Assn., Wash. State Psychology Assn. Contbr. articles to profl. jours. Home: 4727 164th St SW Lynnwood WA 98036 Office: Dept Psychology U Wash Seattle WA 98195

ROBINSON, ELMER, research meteorologist, educator; b. Los Angeles, Oct. 3, 1924; s. Homer H. and Mary Luella (White) R.; m. Clara Elizabeth Wilkinson, June 29, 1947; children—Cynthia Claire, Douglas Barker, Scott Henry. B.A. in Meteorology, UCLA, 1947, M.A. in Meteorology, 1948. Cert. cons. meteorologist. Research meteorologist Stanford Research Inst., Menlo Park, Calif., 1948-57, mgr. environ. meteorology and chemistry program, 1960-72; head air analysis sect. Bay Area Air Pollution Control Dist., San Francisco, 1957-60; prof., research meteorologist and head air pollution research sect. Coll. Engring., Wash. State U., Pullman, 1972—; WHO cons. to govt. India, 1980. Served to 2d lt. USAAF, 1943-45. Fulbright lectr., India, 1978; NSF Antarctic research grantee U.S. Antarctic Research Program, 1977-83. Mem. Am. Meteorol. Soc., Air Pollution Control Assn., AAAS. Contbr. writings to tech. publs. in field. Office: Coll Engring Wash State U Pullman WA 99164

ROBINSON, FRANK, profl. baseball coach; b. Beaumont, Tex., Aug. 31, 1935; s. Frank and Ruth (Shaw) R.; student Xavier U., Cin.; m. Barbara Ann Cole, Oct. 28, 1961; children—Frank Kevin, Nichelle. Baseball player Cin. Reds, 1956-65, Balt. Orioles, 1966-71, Los Angeles Dodgers, 1972, Calif. Angels, 1973-74; player Cleve. Indians, 1974-76, mgr., 1975-77; coach Calif. Angels, 1977, Balt. Orioles, 1978-80; mgr. San Francisco Giants, 1981—. Named Rookie of Year, Nat. League, 1956, Most Valuable Player, Nat. League, 1961, Am. League, 1966; mem. Nat. League All-Star Team, 1956, 57, 59, 61, 62, Am. League All-Star Team, 1966, 67, 69-71, 74. Author: (with Al Silverman) My Life is Baseball, 1968. Address: care Candlestick Park San Francisco CA 94124*

ROBINSON, FRANK LAEDLEIN, investment management company executive; b. Upper Darby Twp., Pa., Aug. 4, 1934; m. Frank L. and Elizabeth (Stone) R.; m. Marsha Ann Healey, Mar. 29, 1961; children—Frances, Victoria. Grad. Sch. Bus. Adminstrn., U. Calif.-Berkeley, 1956. Vice pres., br. mgr. Moody's Investor Services, San Francisco, 1964; v.p., sr. investment counselor Lionel D. Edie and Co., San Francisco, 1969; pres. Fund Mgmt. Group, Inc., San Francisco, 1982, Wallstreet Software, Inc., San Francisco, Torani, Ltd. Hawaii. Served to lt., USN, 1958. Fellow Fin. Analysts Fedn.; mem. Security Analysts of San Francisco, Western Pension Conf. Republican. Episcopalian. Club: Olympic (San Francisco). Home: 4015 Tilden Ln PO Box 959 Lafayette CA 94549 Office: 44 Montgomery St San Francisco CA 94104

ROBINSON, GARY GARTH, clergyman; b. Grand Junction, Colo., Sept. 9, 1932; s. Clayton and Iola (Griffith) R.; B.Th., Life Bible Coll., 1954; A.A., Orange Coast Coll., 1966; B.A., Calif. State U., Long Beach, 1968, M.A., 1970; postgrad. Golden State U., 1980—; m. Gay Elizabeth Clara Guilmette, Feb. 3, 1952; children—Joy Leah, Clayton David. Ordained to ministry Internat. Ch. Foursquare Gospel, 1954; pastor churches Monrovia, Calif., 1954-55, Perris, Calif., 1955-58; Southwest dist. evangelist, 1958-60; pastor Ch. by the Sea, Huntington Beach, Calif., 1960—; missionary evangelist, 42 countries, 1965—; founder, dir. R&R Enterprises, Huntington Beach, 1976—; adv. Women's Aglow, Fountain Valley, Calif.; mem. internat. exec. council Internat. Ch. Foursquare Gospel, 1975—, internat. Christian edn. coordinator, 1975—, dist. coordinator, 1972—. Mem. Internat. Platform Assn., Breath of Life Fellowship (co-founder), Huntington Beach Ministers Assn. (sec. 1961), Life Alumni Assn., Phi Kappa Phi. Address: 715 Lake St Huntington Beach CA 92648

ROBINSON, GUNER SUZEK, electrical engineer; b. Nazilli, Turkey, Feb. 5, 1937; d. Ismail and Hatice (Baspinar) Susek; m. Prentiss Noble Robinson, June 18, 1966 (div.); children—John, Michael. M.S. in E.E., Istanbul Tech. U., Turkey, 1961; Ph.D in E.E. (grad. asst.). Poly. Inst. of Bklyn., 1966. Asst. prof. elec. engring. dept. Middle East Tech. U., Ankara, Turkey, 1966-68; mem. tech. staff Communications Satellite Corp., Clarksburg, Md., 1968-73; research scientist Image Processing Inst. UCLA, 1973-76; mgr. Signal Processing Lab Northrop Research & Tech. Ctr., Palos Verdes, Calif., 1977—; cons. UN Devel. Program in Turkey. Internat. Assn. Exchange of Students for Tech. Experience fellow, 1959; Fulbright Exchange fellow, 1962. Mem. IEEE, Soc. Photo Instrumentation Engrs., Robotics Internat. Soc. Mfg. Engrs. Contbr. articles to profl. jours. Patentee digital image processing. Office: Northrop Research and Tech Center One Research Park Palos Verdes Peninsula CA 90274

ROBINSON, GWYNN HERNDON, financial consultant; b. N.Y.C., Sept. 16, 1920; s. E. Gwynn and Corinne (Herndon) R.; m. Natalie Thompson Dec. 31, 1959; children—Kendall Fewel, Catherine Robinson Adamson, Gwynn M. Grad. Choate Sch., 1938; student MIT, 1938-41. Mgr. exports, Rochester Ropes, Inc., N.Y.C., 1946-48, Mathieson Chem. Corp., 1948-51; mng. ptnr. Feldt and Robinson, Colorado Springs, Colo., 1953-57; exec. Northrup Corp., 1958-67, v.p. mgr. European ops., 1965-67; pres. Diners Club Internat., sr. v.p. Diners Club, Los Angeles, 1967-71; v.p. Boyden Assocs. Inc., Los Angeles, 1972-77; sr. v.p. Eastman and Beaudine, Inc., Los Angeles, 1977-79; sr. v.p. THinc. Cons. Group Internat., 1979—. Served with USAFR, 1941-80 Decorated D.S.M., Legion of Merit, D.F.C., Air Medal with clusters. Office: THinc Internat 1900 Ave of the Stars Suite 709 Los Angeles CA 90067

ROBINSON, JAMES EDWARD, clinical psychologist; b. Montgomery, Ala., Nov. 10, 1934; s. James and Mamie Blance (Quimby) R.; m. Nancy Weston, Oct. 27, 1979; children—James E., Cynthia Robinson Born. Student Bradley U., 1955-57; B.A. in Mktg. Mgmt., San Francisco State Coll., 1959; M.S. in Adminstrn., George Wash. U., 1971; Ph.D. in Psychology, U.S. Internat. U., 1980. Lic. clinical psychologist, Calif. Intern psychologist, San Diego, 1980-82; pvt. practice psychotherapy, psychodiagnostics, San Diego, 1982—; cons., adj. asst. prof. Chapman Coll. Served with USN, 1950-53, 1959-76. Mem. Acad. San Diego Psychologists, Calif. State Psychol. Assn., Western State Psychol. Assn., Am. Psychol. Assn. Club: Toastmasters (chpt. pres.). Home: 9950 Ritter Ct San Diego CA 92131 Office: 2424 Congress St Suite D San Diego CA 92110

ROBINSON, JAMES WARREN, educational adminstrator; b. Vancouver, Wash., Mar. 12, 1948; s. James Walter and Emily Eve (Mickes) R.; m. Christine Mary Pemberton, Aug. 10, 1974; children—Mardy Emelja, Arianna Jaye. B.S., Lewis and Clark Coll., 1970; M.Ed., U. Oreg., 1975, Ph.D., 1980. Tchr. history, Sydney, Australia, 1972; reading specialist, Marcola, Oreg., 1975-77, Springfield, Oreg., 1977-79; curriculum specialist, Springfield, 1979-81; curriculum coordinator Park County Dist. 6, Cody, Wyo., 1981—; instr. dept. extended studies U. Wyo. Mem. Assn. Supervision and Curriculum Devel. Republican. Presbyterian. Club: Elks. Contbr. articles in field to profl. jours.

ROBINSON, JANET KAY, real estate executive; b. Borger, Tex., Aug., 19, 1943; d. Millard Jerome and Mamie Elizabeth (Miller) Newman; m. Eugene Edward Robinson, June 16, 1964 (div.); 1 dau., Alisa. B.A. in Bus. Adminstrn. with distinction, U. Redlands, 1982. Regional escrow mgr. Gulf Oil Corp., Los Angeles, 1962-64; asst. mgr. real estate dept. Mitsui Mfrs. Bank, Los Angeles, 1969-76; v.p., mgr. loan/equity adminstrn. Wells Fargo Realty Advisors, Marina del Rey, Calif., 1976-81, v.p. legal adminstrn., 1981—; dir. seminars for loan/equity officers; lectr. colls. and univs. Publicity chmn. Los Angeles Escrow Assn., 1975. Mem. Nat. Assn. Corp. Real Estate Execs. Republican. Author: A Short History of WFRA, 1983; The Advisor, 1983.

ROBINSON, JESSE LEE, personnel mgmt. cons.; b. Hattiesburg, Miss., Jan. 17, 1912; s. Jerry L. and Pearlie L. (Harrison) R.; m. Myrtle Elizabeth Comfort, Dec. 25, 1936; 1 dau., Pearl Elizabeth (Mrs. Dale Roussell). Tng. dir. Los Angeles P.O., 1955-67; prof. East Los Angeles City Coll., 1955-70; pres. Robinson's Research, Los Angeles, 1967—; chmn. bd. Enterprise Savs. & Loan, 1970-74; treas. Hi-Pro Foods, 1969-71; chmn. bd., comptroller Avalon Med. Mgmt. Inc. Co-chmn. Greater Los Angeles Urban Coalition, 1970—. Trustee Compton Union High Sch., 1963-69; bd. dirs. Los Angeles Heart Soc., Interracial Council Bus. Opportunity, Salvation Army; foreman Los Angeles County Grand Jury, 1974-75. Recipient Los Angeles County Suprs. award 1969, Disting. award of Yr., Interracial Council Bus. Opportunity, 1970. Mem. Am. Soc. Tng. and Devel., So. Pacific Assn.-Amateur Athletic Union (pres. 1973—), NAACP (pres. 1954-57). Rotarian. Address: 1702 N Wilmington Ave Compton CA 90222

ROBINSON, JOHN MINOR, ret. lawyer; b. Uniontown, Pa., Mar. 18, 1910; s. John M. and Martha (Downs) R.; A.B., Harvard, 1932, LL.B., 1935. Admitted to Calif. bar, 1936; assoc. Macdonald & Pettit, 1935-41; partner Musick, Peeler & Garrett, 1947-77; v.p., sec. Consol. Western Steel div. U.S. Steel Corp. and predecessors, 1941-57; dir. MAPCO, Inc., St. Trust Co. West. Clubs: Pacific Union (San Francisco); California (past pres.), Los Angeles Country (Los Angeles); Cypress Point (Pebble Beach); Old Capital (Monterey, Calif.); Royal and Ancient Golf of St. Andrews (Fife, Scotland). Home: 538 S Flower St Los Angeles CA 90071 also Oleada Rd Pebble Beach CA 93953 Office: One Wilshire Blvd Los Angeles CA 90017

ROBINSON, JOHN STEPHEN, air force officer, bioenvironmental engineer; b. Woonsocket, R.I., Feb. 15, 1943; s. Frank and Jean Alice (Wood) R.; m. Nancy Ai-Eng Wu, May 28, 1968; 1 dau., Caryn Lee. B.S.C.E., U. N.H., 1964; postgrad., U. N.C., 1969-71. Registered profl. engr. N.H. Commd. 2d lt. U.S. Air Force, 1964; advanced through grades to lt. col., 1980; bioenviron. engr. Lowry AFB, Colo., 1964-66, Ching Chuan Kang AFB, Taiwan, 1966-67, Homestead AFB, Fla., 1967-69, Hamilton AFB, Calif., 1971-73; staff bioenviron. engr. USAF Hdqrs. Europe, Ramstein AB, Germany, 1973-79, Air Force Inspection and Safety Ctr., Norton AFB, Calif., 1979-82; chief Bioenviron. Engring. Service, Kirtland AFB, N.Mex., 1982—. Decorated Meritorious Service medal. Mem. ASCE, Water Pollution Control Fedn., Am. Water Works Assn., Am. Conf. Govtl. Indsl. Hygienists. Republican. Home: 814 Suzanne Ln SE Albuquerque NM 87123 Office: USAF Hospital/SGPB Kirtland AFB NM 87117

ROBINSON, LAWRENCE BRANDON, lawyer; b. Omaha, Aug. 31, 1934; s. Lawrence I. and Gladys R.; B.A., Grinnell Coll., 1954; J.D., U. Colo., 1959; m. Ewa B. Andersson, Feb. 28, 1971; children—Patricia Ann, Lindsey Kathleen, Amanda Karen. Admitted to Colo. bar, 1959; chmn. bd. Chesapeake Bay Co., Boulder, Colo., 1966—; individual practice law, 1959—; asst. dist. atty. Boulder, 1960-64; town atty. Vail (Colo.), 1969-73; mem. draft bd. Boulder County, 1968-70; pres. Barclays, Ltd., Boulder, 1969—; municipal judge, Boulder, 1967-69. Bd. dirs. Jr. Achievement, Boulder, 1970-72. Clubs: Lions, Boulder Country, Denver Athletic, La Jolla Beach and Tennis. Home: 3850 Pinon Dr Boulder CO 80303 Office: Univ Plaza 777 29th St Boulder CO 80303

ROBINSON, LAWRENCE DANIEL, JR., physician, educator; b. Balt., Sept. 20, 1942; s. Lawrence D. and Elsie Lena (Brummel) R.; B.S., U. Pitts., 1964; M.D., Howard U., 1968; m. LeSans LaRue, Aug. 22, 1964; 1 son, Craig. Intern Johns Hopkins Hosp., Balt., 1968-69, resident, 1969-70; chief resident Sinai Hosp., Balt., 1970-71; fellow in allergy and immunology, Martin Luther King Jr. Gen. Hosp., Los Angeles, 1973-75; practice medicine specializing in pediatrics, allergy and immunology, Los Angeles, 1973—; assoc. prof. pediatrics Martin Luther King Jr. Gen. Hosp., Los Angeles, 1975—; dir. pediatric allergy and immunology Charles Drew Postgrad. Med. Sch., Los Angeles, 1975—; attending physician Children's Hosp. Los Angeles, Cedars Sinai Med. Center, Calif. Hosp. Med. Center, Fox Hills Community Hosp., Daniel Freeman Hosp.; columnist Essence Mag., 1971—; chief exec. officer Beak Billed Platypus Ltd. Mem. Air Resources Bd., State of Calif. Served to maj. M.C., U.S. Army, 1971-73. Diplomate Am. Bd. Pediatrics, Am. Bd. Allergy and Immunology. Fellow Am. Lung Assn. (dir. Los Angeles chpt.); mem. Am. Acad. Pediatrics, Los Angeles Soc. Allergy and Clin. Immunology (sec.-treas.), Nat. Med. Assn., Am. Thoracic Soc., Nat. Assn. Sickle Cell Disease (sci. advisory com. 1976—), Alpha Phi Alpha. Democrat. Contbr. articles in pediatrics and allergic diseases to med. jours. Home: 6517 Whitworth Dr Los Angeles CA 90035 Office: 5980 W Pico Blvd Los Angeles CA 90035

ROBINSON, LUCILE THURSTON, educational administrator; b. Stanford, Mont., June 13, 1916; d. H. Stanley and Alice (Carpenter) Thurston; m. Lindsay Peters, Feb. 12, 1942 (dec. 1944); 1 dau.; Susan Peters Couch; m. 2d, Roger T. Robinson, Feb. 1, 1952. B.A., Mont. State U., 1939, 1948; M.A., U. Redlands, 1956; Ph.D., Claremont Grad. Sch., 1970. Cert. tchr., adminstr., Calif. Social worker, San Bernardino County, Calif., 1948-50; tchr. San Bernardino County (Calif.) Schs., 1950-62, demonstration tchr., 1962-66; instr. U. Redlands, U. Calif.-Riverside, U. Calif.-Irvine, 1966-80; research cons. Title I Fed. Projects, Ont.-Montclair Sch. Dist., 1966-69, gen. cons., 1969-81, curriculum and instructional adminstr., 1981—. Mem. Internat. Reading Assn., Assn. Calif. Sch. Adminstrs., AAUW, Delta Kappa Gamma (chmn. Area XV legis. com. 1982—), Pi Lambda Theta, Phi Delta Kappa. Republican. Episcopalian. Club: Zonta (chmn. Dist. X Status of Women com. 1978-80). Home: 603 S Buena Vista St Redlands CA 92373 Office: Ontario-Montclair Sch Dist 950 W D St PO Box 313 Ontario CA 91761

ROBINSON, MICHAEL JAMES, accounting educator, consultant; b. Great Falls, Mont., Oct. 23, 1950; s. James Henry and Geraldine Ann (Sullivan) R.; m. Nancy Ann King, May 15, 1971. B.A. in Acctg., Carroll Coll., 1972; M.B.A., Wash. State U., 1974. C.P.A., Mont. Acct., Galusha, Higgins & Gallusha, Helena, Mont., 1974-78; acctg. educator Carroll Coll., Helena, 1978—, chmn. dept. bus. and econs., 1980—; cons. acctg., auditing and tax. Mem. Am. Inst. C.P.A.s, Am. Acctg. Assn., Mont. Soc. C.P.A.s. Roman Catholic. Club: Green Meadow Country (Helena). Home: 413 S California St Helena MT 59601 Office: Carroll College Helena MT 59625

ROBINSON, MICHAEL RICHARD, contracting executive; b. Los Angeles, Mar. 29, 1955; s. Willie Louis and Ruby Lee (Foster) R.; grad. U. So. Calif., 1978; 1 dau., Michele Antionette. Account specialist Robinsons Bldg. Maintenance, Los Angeles, 1974-77; mng. exec. Collins Foods Internat. Inc., Los Angeles, 1977-78; owner, pres. Nosnibor Services, Inc., Los Angeles, 1978—; dir. Ofavico, Inc., Compton, Calif. Recipient award of achievement City of Los Angeles. Mem. Bldg. Service Contractors Assn., Nat. Bartenders Assn., Am. Mgmt. Assn., Los Angeles Jaycees. Mem. Founders Ch. of Religious Science. Clubs: Marina Yacht, Masons. Patentee in field.

ROBINSON, NAOMI JEAN, training systems analyst; b. Storm Lake, Iowa, Oct. 10, 1951; d. Wendell and Norma (Wright) R.; B.A., Buena Vista Coll., 1973; M.A.Ed., George Washington U., 1978. Tchr., elem. schs., Storm Lake, Iowa, 1973-75; edn. specialist intern U.S. Army, Fort Monroe, Va., 1976-78, edn. specialist, Fort Eustis, Va., 1978-79, tng. systems analyst, White Sands Missile Range, N.Mex., 1979-82, TRADOC tng. effectiveness analysis study coordinator, 1982—. Vice pres., Young Republicans, 1972-73. Mem. Nat. Assn. Exec. Females, Federally Employed Women (1st v.p. chpt. 1982-83), Human Factors Soc., Iowa Edn. Assn. Republican. Presbyterian. Club: Bus. and Profl. Women. Author: Guidelines for Development of Skill Qualification Tests, 1977. Home: 2850 Fairway Dr Apt 4 Las Cruces NM 88001 Office: US Army TRASANA attn ATOR-TH White Sands Missile Range NM 88001

ROBINSON, PATRICK JOSEPH, safety engineer; b. Spokane, Wash., Mar. 3, 1935; s. James Newton and Elizabeth Marie (Llewellyn) R.; m. Barbara Jane Capshew, Dec. 15, 1956; children—Michael, Theresa Annette, Cynthia. Student Gonzaga U., 1958-59, Ariz. State U., 1962-64. Registered profl. safety engr., Calif. Safety engr. Convair Astronautics div. Atlas Missile, Spokane, Wash., Altus, Okla., 1960-62; safety engr. Motorola Semicondr., Phoenix, 1962-67, safety mgr., 1967-77, safety dir., various U.S. and internat. locations, 1977—. Adv. bd. Valle del Sol chpt. Occupational Nurses Assn., Served with USN, 1954-58. Mem. Am. Soc. Safety Engrs. (Ariz. chpt.), Semicondr. Safety Assn. (officer, co-founder, bd. dirs.), Semicondr. Industry Assn. Am. Indsl. Hygiene Assn. Republican. Roman Catholic. Contbr. articles to profl. jours. Office: PO Box 2953 Phoenix AZ 85062

ROBINSON, RANDALL, clinical psychologist; b. N.Y.C., Oct. 11, 1948; d. Richard Irwin and Edna (Randall) R.; m. Gregory Euless Pierce, Oct. 9, 1976; children—Casey, Whitney. B.S. with honors in Psychology, Conn. Coll., New London, 1970; M.S. in Clin. Psychology, Syracuse (N.Y.) U., 1974; Ph.D. in Clin. Psychology, Calif. Sch. Profl. Psychology, Fresno, 1976. Lic. clinical psychologist Calif. Staff psychologist Mental Health Dept., City of Madera (Calif.), 1977-79; pvt. practice, Fresno, 1979—; emergency room crisis coverage Valley Med. Ctr. Fresno, 1980-81. Mem. Am. Psychol. Assn., Calif. State Psychol. Assn., San Joaquin Psychol. Assn. Office: 5150 N 6th St Suite 177 Fresno CA 93710

ROBINSON, RICHARD ALLEN, JR., consultant, human resources development trainer; b. Ellensburg, Wash., Aug. 21, 1936; s. Richard Allen and Rosa Adele (Oswaldt) R.; m. R. Elaine Whitham, Sept. 8, 1956; children—Sharon E. Robinson Losey, Richard Allen, René L. B.A., U. Wash., 1958; postgrad. U.S. Army Command and Gen. Staff Coll., 1969-70; M.A., U. Mo., 1971. Commd. 2d lt. U.S. Army, 1958, advanced through grades to lt. col., 1972, various infantry assignments including command, 1958-72, research and devel. assignments including dep. dir. test of behavioral sci., dep. commandant U.S.A. Organizational Effectiveness, 1975-77, ret., 1979; chief human resource devel. Wash. Dept. Social and Health Services, Olympia, 1979—; pvt. practice orgn. and mgmt. devel. cons./trainer, 1979—. Decorated Legion of Merit with oak leaf cluster, Bronze Star. Mem. Am. Soc. Tng. and Devel., Organizational Devel. Network, Am. Hort. Soc., Mass. Hort. Soc. Contbg. author: Games Trainers Play, vol. II, 1983. Office: DSHS Mail 8315 W 27th St Tacoma WA 98466

ROBINSON, RICHARD GARY, management consultant; b. Oakland, Calif., Aug. 17, 1931; s. William Albert and Inez Wilhelmina (Zetterblad) R.; B.B.A., U. Minn., 1955; grad. Indsl. Coll. Armed Forces, 1972; M. Internat. Mgmt., Am. Grad. Sch. Internat. Mgmt., 1980; m. Lorraine Mary Deshaies, Nov. 13, 1965; children—Elisabeth Claudine (dec.), Christopher Paul. Commd. 2d lt. U.S. Air Force, 1956, advanced through grades to maj.; dir. radar ops. tactical air warfare, comdr. strategic missile operation and maintenance functions, project mgr., dir. mgmt. info. systems Dept. Def. activities, S.E. Asia; ret., 1976; mgmt. cons., Colorado Springs, Colo., 1976—; pres. Internat. Mgmt. Cons.; dir., chief fin. officer Unique Equipment Co. dir. Stage Engring. & Supply; mem. adj. faculty Embry Riddle Aero. U., Luke AFB, Ariz.; asst. prof. econs. and bus. Colorado Springs br. Regis Coll. Decorated Meritorious Service medal with oak leaf cluster, AF Commendation medal with 2 oak leaf clusters. Mem. Internat. Trade Assn. Colo. (v.p. communications), Am. Mktg. Assn., Armed Forces Communications and Electronics Assn., Am. Mgmt. Assn., Nat. Assn. Accts., Assn. Polit. Risk Analysts, N.Am. Soc. Corp. Planning. Lutheran. Home: 1610 McKay Way Colorado Springs CO 80915 Office: PO Box 2714 Colorado Springs CO 80901

ROBINSON, RICHARD HARDEN, judge; b. Carlsbad, N.Mex., Mar. 30, 1918; s. William Bata and Lillyan Exer (Green) R.; student George Washington U., 1935-39; LL.B., Am. U., 1948; m. Grace S. Henry, Mar. 16, 1980; children—Richard Harden, Patricia Ann, Pamela Elaine. Admitted to N.Mex. bar, 1948, Calif. bar, 1965; city judge, Carlsbad, 1949-50; atty. gen. N.Mex., Santa Fe, 1952-56; practice law, Palm Springs, 1971—; mem. firm Dillon, Boyd & Robinson, 1965-71; mcpl. judge, Palm Springs, 1971—; pres. Bodick, Inc., Palm Desert, Calif., 1962-65, R.H. Robinson & Assos., Inc., Albuquerque, G & R Llamas, Inc., Langlois, Oreg. Chmn. ad hoc com. Desert Sands Unified Sch. Dist. Calif., 1967; bd. dirs., v.p. Palm Springs Boys' Club. Served with USMCR, 1943-45. Mem. Am., N.Mex., Calif. bar assns., Nat. Arbitration Assn., Calif. Trial Lawyers Assn., Calif. Judges Assn. Clubs: Mission Hills Country (life) (Rancho Mirage, Calif.); Rotary. Home: PO Box 2538 Palm Springs CA 92263 Office: 3255 E Tahquitz-McCullum St Palm Springs CA 92262

ROBINSON, ROSEMARY MARGARET LEVONSKI, nursing administrator, army officer, educator; b. Little Falls, N.Y., Sept. 20, 1948; d. Leon Henry and Mary Elizabeth (Badgett) Levonski; m. LaRue F. Robinson, Oct. 31, 1969; children—Andrew C. F., Jessica A. B.S. in Nursing cum laude, U. Md., 1970; M.S. in Nursing, Cath. U. Am., 1975; postgrad. Acad. of Health Scis., Ft. Sam Houston, 1978. Commd. officer U.S. Army Nurse Corps, 1970, advanced through grades to maj., 1980; staff nurse, asst. head nurse Walter Reed Army Med. Ctr., Washington, 1970-72, asst. head urol. surgery, 1972-73; med.-surg. clin. nurse specialist 2d Gen. Army Hosp., Landstuhl, W.Ger., 1975-78; asst. dir. intensive care nursing course Fitzsimons Army Med. Ctr., Aurora, Colo., 1979-80, dir. intensive care nursing course (non-resident program of Acad. Health Scis., Ft. Sam Houston, Tex.), Fitzsimons Army Med. Ctr., 1980-82; nursing cons. to U.S. Army Surgeon Gen.; asst. chief nurse Munson Army Community Hosp., Ft. Leavenworth, Kans., 1982—. Mem. Am. Hosp. Assn., Am. Assn. Critical Care Nurses, Assn. Mil. Surgeons of U.S. (Soc. of Fed. Med. Agys.), Sigma Theta Tau (Pi chpt.). Democrat. Roman Catholic. Contbr. articles to profl. jours. Office: Dept Nursing Munson Army Community Hosp Ft Leavenworth KS 66027

ROBINSON, SERETA ANN, psychologist; b. Walla Walla, Wash., Oct. 10, 1936; d. Lewis James and Naomi Pauline (Pollard) Patton; student Wash. State U., 1954-56; B.S., U. Ariz., 1958, M.S., 1968, M.Ed., 1976, Ph.D., 1977; m. James L. Robinson, 1958 (div. 1970); children—Julie, Laurie, M'Liz; m. 2d, Robert R. Douglas, Sept. 30, 1977. Tchr. jr.

high sch., Tucson, 1959-61; lectr. U. Ariz., 1967-70, adj. asst. prof., 1977-79; pvt. practice psychol. counseling, 1977—; dir. Southwestern Inst. Human Devel., Inc., Tucson, 1980—. Mem. Am. Psychol. Assn., Ariz. Psychol. Assn., Ariz. Group Psychotherapy Soc. (pres. Tucson br. 1982-83), Nat., Tucson (past pres.) assns. edn. of young children, Phi Delta Kappa. Home: 4130 E River Rd Tucson AZ 85718 Office: 2415 E 6th St Tucson AZ 85719

ROBINSON, SHIRLEY JEAN, educational counselor; b. Gibsland, La., Feb. 19, 1941; d. George W. and Clara (Hewitt) Pearson; m. Cecil R. Robinson, July 31, 1939; 1 son, Taiye. B.A., San Francisco State Coll., 1968, M.A., 1972; postgrad. U. So. Calif., 1982—. Counselor, Calif. Blind Sch., Berkeley, 1965-68; counselor Peralta Community Coll. Dist., Coll. of Alameda (Calif.), 1968—. Recipient Outstanding Service award Coll. Alameda, 1982. Mem. Calif. Personnel and Guidance Assn., Am. Personnel and Guidance Assn., Am. Coll. Personnel Assn., Calif. Community Coll. Counselors Assn., East Bay Lit. Guild, Oakland Mus. Assn., Nat. Vocat. Assn., Delta Sigma Theta. Democrat. Office: 555 Atlantic Ave Alameda CA 94501

ROBINSON, WARREN ELMO, transportation company executive; b. Clarksburg, W.Va., Sept. 24, 1917; s. Warren E. and Mattie Lucinda (Rose) R.; diploma Heald's Bus. Coll., Oakland, Calif., 1938; diploma urban transp. Carnegie-Mellon U., 1973; m. Vera M. Eschenbach, Aug. 28, 1983; children—Vicki, Carol. Schedule clk. Key System Co., Oakland, Calif., 1936-62; supr. schedules, then acting dir. research and planning A.C. Transit Co., Oakland, 1962-67, transp. engr., mgr. schedules, 1967—; lectr. in field, 1970—; panelist Transp. Research Bd., NRC, 1979—. Treas., deacon Ch. of Brethren, Oakland, 1958—; personnel commr. San Lorenzo Sch. Dist., 1970-83. Served as pilot USAAF, 1942-45. Mem. San Leandro C. of C. Republican. Home: 16031 Gramercy Dr San Leandro CA 94578 Office: 508 16th St Oakland CA 94612

ROBINSON, WILLIAM PAUL, research organization executive, educator, consultant; b. Harrisonburg, Va., Apr. 14, 1953; s. Herbert Joshua and Florence Sue (Miller) R. B.A. in Tech. Assessment, Washington U., St. Louis, 1974; postgrad. in Architecture, U. N.Mex., 1977-83. Assoc. project engr. Ecosystems Internat., Gambrills, Md., 1975-76; research assoc. and project dir. Southwest Research and Info. Center, Albuquerque, 1976-80, exec. dir., 1980—; instr. environ. impact assessment, U. N.Mex., 1979—; cons. Atomic Indsl. Forum, Acoma Indian Pueblo, Zuni Legal Aid; defender Five Sandoval Indian Pueblos, Inc., Piedmont (Va.) Environ. Council. Council mem. SW Valley Area Council, Albuquerque, 1979-83; steering com. mem. Conservation Voters Alliance, Albuquerque, 1983; founder, bd. dirs. Coop. Fed. Credit Union, Albuquerque, 1977-83. Mem. N.Mex. Geol. Soc., Am. Water Pollution Control Fedn., Am. Pub. Health Assn. Jewish. Contbr. articles to profl. jours. Office: 105 Stanford SE Albuquerque NM 87106

ROBINSON, WILLIAM R., city mgr.; b. Chgo., June 2, 1935; s.-William E. and Eleanore M. (Hesley) R.; A.B.A., Muskegon (mich.) Community Coll., 1956; postgrad. U. Mich., 1957-58; M.P.A., U. Denver, 1980; m. Betty Jean Marton, July 28, 1956; children—Lori, Teri, Marty, Bill; m. 2d, Alice E. Smith, July 23, 1977. Village mgr. Spring Lake (Mich.), i966-72; project engr. Joiner Engring. Co., Spring Lake, Mich., 1972-76; city adminstr. Brush (Colo.), 1976-80; city mgr. Montrose (Colo.), 1980—; commr. Ottawa County (Mich.), 1969-71; mem. state bd. dirs. Grand River Watershed Authority, Lansing, Mich., 1967-72. Served with USAR, 1957-65. Mem. Internat. City Mgmt. Assn., Colo. City Mgmt. Assn., Colo. Mcpl. League, Montrose C. of C. Republican. Lutheran. Club: Rotary. Office: PO Box 790 Montrose CO 81401

ROBISON, DONALD GRAHAM, marine corps officer, shopping center executive; b. Hillsboro, Ill., Aug. 29, 1929; s. Marshall O. and Bess Lenora (Graham) R.; m. Elizabeth Ann Knisely, Sept. 7, 1951; children—William M., Melissa Lee, Kipling Bradley. B.S., Bradley U., 1951; postgrad. Command and Staff Coll., 1965, 66, Communications Officers Sch., 1954, 55; notary pub., Calif. Commd. officer U.S. Marine Corps, 1951—, advanced through grades to col., 1974; ret., 1979; ops. mgr. Edward J. DeBartolo Corp., Mission Viejo, Calif., 1979—. Mem. Nat. Planning Group for Bicentennial, 1975 76. Decorated Legion of Merit, Bronze Star medal, Joint Services medal; Korean Order Mil. Merit Mem. Marine Corps Assn., Marine Corps League. Republican. Episcopalian. Clubs: Nat. Capitol Mil. Collectors, S.A.R., Mil. Order World Wars, So. Calif. Model Soldier Soc. (pres.), Lambda Chi Alpha. Contbr. articles to profl. jours. author: Ground Reconnaisance in the Marine Division, 1966. Home: 24082 Ankara St Mission Viejo CA 92691 Office: 101 Mission Viejo Mall Mission Viejo CA 92691

ROBISON, WILLIAM H(ENRY), JR., school psychologist, educator; b. Providence, Dec. 1, 1947; s. William H. and Frances May (Lenderman) R.; m. Phyllis Marie Bailey, Dec. 17, 1977; 1 dau., Julie Noelle. B.S., U. Nev., 1972, M.A., 1977, M.Ed., ednl. specialist in sch. psychology, 1981. Cert. sch. psychologist, counselor, sch. adminstr., tchr., Nev. Tchr. 5th grade Gardnerville (Nev.) Elem. Sch., 1976-77, counselor kindergarten through 5th grades, 1977-80; sch. psychologist Douglas County (Nev.) Schs., 1980—; instr. in counseling and personnel services U. Nev. regional programs, continuing edn., 1979—. Mem. Douglas County Mental Health Adv. Bd., 1979-80, chmn., 1979-80; mem. Carson City (Nev.) Selective Service Bd., 1982—. Served with USN, 1967-69; Vietnam. U. Nev. grantee, 1971-77. Mem. Nat. Assn. Sch. Psychologists, Am. Personnel and Guidance Assn., Nev. Personnel and Guidance Assn. (life), Blue Key.

ROBLES, JULIAN J., painter, sculptor; b. N.Y.C., June 24, 1933; s. J.P. and Mary A. (Myles) R. Student Art Students League, 1963-64; Nat. Acad., Arts and Design, 1964-68; Freelance artist N.Y.C., 1950-55; tech. illustrator USAF, 1955-59; freelance portrait artist, Taos, N.Mex., 1959—. Served with USAF, 1955-59. Recipient Best in Show award Amarillo Legal Soc., 1963, Nell Boardman award, N.Y.C., 1963, Nat. Acad. Scholarship award, 1965, 1st pl. oils N.Mex. State Fair, 1971, 1st pl. pastels, 1972, Bronze award and Best in Show, 1981, Pastel award, Best in Show award; Pastel Soc. Am., 1981; Gold medal Nat. Western Artists Show, 1982; awarded Hildalgo Certificate for Devoted Services to State N.Mex., 1972. Mem. Pastel Soc. Am., Artists Equity, Western Artists Assn. (founder). Mem. Unity Ch. Work published in Southwest Art, 1975, Artist of the Rockies, 1982, Contemporary Artist of the West; 1982. Address: Box 1845 Taos NM 87571

ROCCA, JAMES VICTOR, political science educator; b. Spokane, Wash., Mar. 22, 1930; s. Victor Joseph and Pierina Balzargetti R.; m. Hilda Kalchhauser, Jan. 28, 1967. B.A. in Econs., Gonzaga U., 1952; postgrad. U. Vienna, 1962 (Absolutorium), Ph.D. in Polit. Sci., 1964. Trainee FRS, San Francisco, 1955-56; with Gen. Electric Supply Co., Emoryville, Calif., 1956-58; prof. polit. sci. N.Mex. Highlands U., Las Vegas, 1965—; small bus. counselor ACE, Santa Fe. Served to 1st lt. U.S. Army, 1952-55. Mem. Am. Polit. Sci. Assn., AAUP (pres. N.Mex. state chpt. 1968-69), Am. Soc. Internat. Law, Pi Gamma Mu, Phi Alpha Theta, Tau Kappa Epsilon. Democrat. Roman Catholic. Clubs: Elks, Eagles. Contbr. articles to profl. jours. Office: N Mex Highlands U Las Vegas NM 87701

ROCHETTE, EDWARD CHARLES, association executive; b. Worcester, Mass., Feb. 17, 1927; s. Edward Charles and Lilia (Viau) R.; student Washington U., St. Louis, Clark U., Worcester; m. Mary Ann Ruland, July 29, 1978; children by pervious marriage—Edward Charles, III, A. Paul, Philip. Exec. editor Krause Publns., Iola, Wis., 1960-66; acting exec. dir. Am. Numismatic Assn., Colorado Springs, Colo., 1967-68, editor The Numismatist, 1968-72, exec. v.p. assn., 1972—; bd. overseers Inst. Philatelic and Numismatic Studies, Adelphi U., Garden City, N.Y., 1979-81; chmn. medals com. Colo. Centennial-Bicentennial Commn., 1976; adv. panel Carson City Silver Dollar Program, GSA, 1979-80; mem. U.S. Assay Commn., 1965. Served with USN, 1944-46. Recipient Gold medal for syndicated column Numistic Lit. Guild, 1980. Life mem. Am. Numismatic Assn. (medal of merit 1972); mem. Am. Soc. Assn. Execs. Democrat. Roman Catholic. Club: Pikes Peak Kiwanis (dir. 1972). Co-author: World Book Ency. Money, 1979. Office: 818 N Cascade Ave Colorado Springs CO 80903

ROCK, PENELOPE LYNNE, nurse, consultant; b. Mpls., Dec. 16, 1945; d. Oscar and Hazel Elizabeth (Lemke) Trelstad; m. Michael William Rock, Nov. 10, 1973 (div.). R.N., Swedish Hosp. Sch. Nursing, 1966, Augsburg Coll., 1964; B.A., St. Mary's Coll., 1979; postgrad. U. Phoenix, 1984 . Asst. head nurse Army Nurse Corps, 1966-68, Walter Reed Hosp., Washington, 1966-67, Viet Nam, 1967-68, Palo Alto VA Hosp., 1968-70; head nurse San Jose Med. Clinic (Calif.), 1970-71; unit supr. mental health bur. Santa Clara County Health Dept. (Calif.), 1971-74, program mgr., 1974-80, program div. mgr. bur. drug abuse services, 1980—; pres mgmt. cons. co.; pub. speaker; tchr. seminars. Mem. Democratic Club. Mem. Am. Mgmt. Assn., Nat. Assn. Female Execs., Am. Soc. Trainers and Developers, Nat. Assn. Future Women, Network of Women Entrepreneurs, Women's Ednl. Service Assn. (area rep.), AAUW. Home: 870 Knollfield Way San Jose CA 95136 Office: Santa Clara County Health Dept PO Box 18725 San Jose CA 95158

ROCKEY, RUTH, fin. planner, investment adv.; b. N.Y.C., Mar. 5, 1929; d. Robert and Elizabeth (McFadden) Whiteman; student Bklyn. Coll., 1964-68; M.B.A., Pepperdine U., 1971; Coll. Fin. Planning, 1981; m. Edward H. Rockey, Oct. 23, 1948; children—John, Stephen, Paul. Dir. planning Pepperdine U. Sch. Bus. and Mgmt., Los Angeles, 1972-73, dir. program devel., 1973-74; v.p. mktg. Lawrence Co., Encino, Calif., 1975-76; pres. Ruth Rockey Investments, Inc., Encino, 1976-79; v.p. Fin. Planning Cons., Inc., Westlake Village, Calif., 1980; pres. Rockey Fin. Services Corp., Westlake Village, Calif., 1981—; dir. USLIFE Savs. and Loan Assn. Chmn. bd. trustees West Park Hosp. Lic. real estate broker. Mem. Nat. Assn. Securities Dealers (registered prin.), Internat. Assn. Fin. Planning, Nat. Assn. Realtors, Pepperdine Assocs., Women in Bus. Club: North Ranch Country, Westlake Yacht. Home: 1212 B Westlake Blvd Westlake Village CA 91361 Office: Rockey Fin Services Corp 2659 Townsgate Rd Suite 109 Westlake Village CA 91361

ROCKSTROM, ALBERT RAYMOND, former grocer; b. Spokane, Aug. 10, 1917; s. Claes Albert and Ruth Elizabeth (Jonsson) R.; B.S. in Chemistry and Biol. Scis., U. Oreg., 1947; m. Emma Alice Doran, Mar. 14, 1942; children—Thomas Albert, Ronald Charles, David Keith. Self-employed in grocery bus., 1948-75; maj. stockholder radio sta. KARY, Prosser, Wash., 1953-59, pres., 1957-58; engaged in real estate investing, 1950-75. Pres. Grandview (Wash.) Jr. C. of C., 1951-52, Grandview C. of C., 1977; mem. Grandview Kiwanis Club, 1971-78, pres., 1975-76; treas. Yakima (Wash.) chpt. S.P.E.B.S.Q.S.A., 1978-79, 83, sec. 1982-83, adminstrv. v.p. Grandview chpt., 1978-79, pres., 1981-82, Barbershopper of Yr., 1980, area counselor, 1982—; mem. Grandview Sch. Bd., 1956-69, chmn., 1968-69; mem. Citizens Adv. Com. Sch. Dist. Grandview, 1976 77; mem. KYVE-TV Bd., 1962-69. Named Distinguished Club Pres. in Kiwanis Pacific NW Dist., 1976, recipient new club bldg. award, 1977. Mem. Delta Tau Delta. Republican. Methodist. Club: Toastmasters (adminstrv. v.p. Grandview 1978), Yakima Kamiakin Kiwanis (lt. gov. Pacific N.W. dist. 1982-83). Address: 120 Terrace Park Dr Yakima WA 98901

ROCKWELL, BRUCE MCKEE, banker; b. Denver, Dec. 18, 1922; s. Robert B. and Florence (McKee) R.; B.A., Yale U., 1945; m. Virginia Packard, Apr. 22, 1950; children—David, Jane, Sarah. Exec. sec. to mayor of Denver, 1947-51; public relations and advt. account exec. William Kostka & Assos., 1952-53; with Colo. Nat. Bank, Denver, 1953 , pres., 1970-75, chmn., chief exec. officer, 1975—, also dir.; vice chmn. Colo. Nat. Bankshares, Inc., 1975-76, chmn., 1976—, also dir.; dir. Burlington No., Inc., mem. Colo. adv. bd. Mountain Bell Telephone Co.; pres., dir. Lenders Mortgage Corp., 1976-79; dir. VISA U.S.A. Inc. Vice-chmn., bd. dirs. The Denver Partnership, Inc.; bd. dirs. Downtown Denver Inc., 1977—, Kaiser Found.; chmn. Denver Urban Renewal Authority, 1958-68; mem. nat. council Salk Inst., 1978—; trustee Com. Econ. Devel., 1979—, Denver Symphony Orch., 1974-77, Denver Art Mus., 1965-72. Served to ensign USMC, 1945-46. Named Colo. Bus. Man of Yr., Colo. Bus. Mag., 1976. Mem. Assn. Res. City Bankers (dir. 1975—), Colo. Bankers Assn., Colo. Assn. Commerce and Industry (dir. 1977—, v.p. 1979-80), Denver C. of C. 1973-74). Clubs: Univ., Press, Tennis (Denver). Home: 815 Vine St Denver CO 80206 Office: Colo Nat Bank 17th and Champa Sts Denver CO 80202

ROCKWELL, JOHN ARTHUR, computer integrated manufacturing systems co. exec.; b. N.Y.C., Mar. 4, 1952; s. Douglas Cullins and Barbara Male (Rockwell) Sager; B.A. in Econs., Duke U., 1974; M.B.A., U. Va., 1980; m. Sarah Uihlein, Feb. 1, 1975; children—Page Cameron, Alexander. With Nat. Prodn. Systems Co., unit Nat. Supply Co., 1980-83, product supr. oilfield pumping units, Los Nietos, Calif., 1981-83; sr. sect. mgr. product mktg. Unigraphics CAD/CAM Systems, Cypress, Calif., 1983 . Served as officer USN, 1974-78. Mem. Am. Prodn. and Inventory Control Soc. Republican. Home: 1511 Miramar Dr Fullerton CA 92631 Office: McAuto K17-91 5552 Cerritos Ave Cypress CA 90630

ROCKWELL, MARTIN GUY, eletrical engineer; b. Seattle, Mar. 5, 1954; s. Robert E. and Anne M. (Frogue) R.; m. Laura Jeanne Stockton, Dec. 23, 1978 (div.). B.S.E.E., U. Wash., 1976, M.S.E.E., 1979. Devel. engr. MTS, Hewlett Packard Co., McMinnville, Oreg., 1979—; cons. in field. Mem. Planetary Soc. Contbr. articles to profl. jours. Office: 1700 S Baker St McMinnville OR 97128

RODDA, LYNN EDITH, pharmacist; b. Spokane, Wash., May 30, 1942; d. Robert Arthur and Lois Helen (Sylvester) Fisher; m. Thomas Cook Rodda, July 6, 1974; children—Paula Ruth, Kabrena Eileen. Student Whitman Coll., 1960-62; B.S., Portland State U., 1964; B.Pharmacy, Wash. State U., 1977. Lic. pharmacist, Wash., Idaho, Alaska. Tchr. jr. high sch. sci. and math., Beaverton, Oreg., 1964-65, St. Louis Park, Minn., 1965-66, Rochester, Minn., 1966-67; locum tenens pharmacist Pullman, Washington & Endicott, Washington, 1977; staff pharmacist Drug Fair Corp., Moscow, Idaho, 1976-78; staff pharmacist Pay'n Save Corp., Fairbanks, Alaska, 1978-80, head pharmacist, 1979-80; head pharmacist Teamster Health Care Corp., Anchorage, 1980, Pay'n Save Corp., 1980-81; staff pharmacist Providence Hosp. Pharmacy, Anchorage, 1981—, also acting interim asst. dir. pharmacy; pharmacy rep. pharmacy-nursing com. Anchorage Poison Ctr., Providence Hosp.; shared-services-locum tenens pharmacist Alaska Psychiat. Inst. Mem. Am. Soc. Hosp. Pharmacists, Alaska Pharm. Assn. Republican. Episcopalian (lic. lay reader). Office: Providence Hosp Pharmacy 3000 Providence Dr Anchorage AK 99504

RODE, EDDIE, real estate broker; b. North Chicago, Ill., Aug. 21, 1920; s. Jacob and Mary (Kosir) R.; m. Marguerite W. Wagner, Nov. 15, 1947; children—Susan, Mark, Joanne, Patricia. Student, U. Md., 1954-58; real estate broker, Calif. Commd. lt. col., U.S. Air Force, 1942, advanced through grades to lt. col., 1959, ret., 1963; mil. adviser, Yugoslavia, 1951-54; owner/broker Rode Realty, Santa Barbara, Calif., 1968—. Decorated Air Medal with 7 oak leaf clusters. Mem. Santa Barbara Bd. Realtors, Lompoc Bd. Realtors, Apt. Owners Assn., Channel City Air Force Assn., Ret. Officers Assn. Republican. Home: 3360 Braemer Dr Santa Barbara CA 93109 Office: 3114 State St Santa Barbara CA 93105

RODEN, JOHANNA WAHL, German educator; b. Kassel, Germany, Dec. 3, 1928; d. Johannes and Dina (Rode) Wahl; m. Hans Wilhelm Roden, July 28, 1962; 1 son, Martin Eric. B.A. in Sociology, Calif. State U.-Long Beach, 1961, M.A. in Social Sci., 1962; M.A. in German, U. So. Calif., 1966, Ph.D. in German, 1970. Field dir. Long Beach (Calif.) council Girl Scouts U.S.A., 1953-56; instr. Long Beach City Coll., 1961-62; prof. German, Calif. State U.-Long Beach, 1962—, chmn. dept. German, Russian and Classics, 1969—. Pres., United Ch. Retirement Home, 1978-80. Mem. UN Assn. (pres. Long Beach chpt. 1980-82), Am. Assn. Tchrs. German, Philol. Assn. Pacific Coast, Western Assn. German Studies. Contbr. articles on German exile writers in U.S. to profl. jours. Office: Calif State U Long Beach CA 90840

RODENBERGER, JEANNINE PAULINE, educator; b. Bellingham, Wash., May 21, 1934; d. Carl E. and Helen L. (Lewis) Lehmann; m. Robert F. Rodenberger, July 28, 1951; children—Bryan, Bradley. B.A., U. Wash., 1969; postgrad. Western Wash. State U., Oriel Coll., Oxford U. (Eng.), 1980. Cert. home economist, educator. Tchr., Olympic View/Mariner Sch., Mukilteo, Wash., 1969-71, Explorer Sch., Everett, Wash., 1973—, home econs., 1973-78, 6th grade 1978—; host fgn. students. Active Am. Heart Assn., Am. Cancer Soc., mem. bd. edn. First Bapt. Ch., Everett. Mem. Mukilteo Educators Assn., Wash. Edn. Assn., NEA, Club: Yacht (Orcas Island, Wash.). Designer home econs. dept. for schs., 1971, 73. Home: 11th St Mukilteo WA 98275 Office: 4900 Sharon Dr Everett WA 98204

RODERICK, WAYNE VERNON, horticulturist; b. Petaluma, Calif., Apr. 2, 1920; s. Frank S. and Martha C. (Albush) R. Student Santa Rosa Jr. Coll., 1941-42. With Roderick's Nursery, Petaluma, Calif., 1945-60; mus. scientist U. Calif-Berkeley, 1960-76; dir. Regional Parks, Bot. Garden, Berkeley, 1976-83; cons. Calif. Native Plant Soc. Served with U.S. Army, 1941-43. Recipient award Calif. Garden Club, 1977; named Man of Yr., U. Calif., 1974. Fellow Royal Hort. Soc.; mem. Alpine Garden Soc. of Eng., Am. Rock Garden Soc. (LePiniec award 1981), Am. Assn. Bot. Gardens and Arboreta, Heather Farm Soc., Calif. Hort. Soc. (Rixford award 1968, council), Calif. Native Plant Soc., San Francisco Businessmen's Garden Club. Discover species of plant life; contbr. chpt. to book, also articles to profl. jours. Home: 166 Canon Dr Orinda CA 94563 Office: Tilden Regional Park Berkeley CA 94708

RODEY, PATRICK MICHAEL, state senator; b. San Francisco, Jan. 22, 1943; s. James and Martha Leora (Phillips) R.; B.Ed., U. Alaska, 1966; J.D., U. Ariz., 1973; m. Barbara Jean Coffey, June 25, 1976. With Safeway Corp., 1963-66, U. Alaska, 1968-69, Peter Kiewits Sons, 1973; admitted to Alaska bar, 1973; asso. firm Abbott, Lynch & Farney, and predecessor firm, Anchorage, 1975—; mem. Alaska Senate, 1974—, chmn. statutory revision commn., 1976—, Senate majority leader, 1980-82. Researcher, Inst. Social, Econ. and Govt. Research U. Alaska, 1968-69. Mem. Am., Alaska bar assns., Phi Alpha Delta. Democrat. Episcopalian. Home: 2335 Lord Baranof Anchorage AK 99503 Office: 1200 Airport Hts Rd Suite 501 Anchorage AK 99504

RODGERS, AUDREY PENN, government official; b. Berkeley, Calif., Aug. 8, 1923; d. Lewis and Edith Penn; A.B., U. Calif., Berkeley, 1944, m. David Leigh Rodgers, June 13, 1943 (div. Mar. 1982); children—Timothy Leigh, Janice Leigh Rodgers Bracken. Research asst. U. Rochester (N.Y.) Sch. Medicine, 1943-46, 49-51, NIH, Bethesda, Md., 1948-49; design/cons. landscaping pvt. homes and gardens, 1960-69; pres. Campaign Data Service, Inc., San Francisco, 1970-80; public info. dir. East Bay Infiltration/Inflow Study, San Francisco, 1980 . Mem. San Francisco Charter Revision Com., 1968-70; chmn. design group Seward St. Park Task Force, Eureka Valley Promotion Assn., 1970-73; chmn. Dolores Hts. Spl. Use Dist. Com., 1978-80; bd. dirs. The Urban Sch., 1968-69, Dolores Hts. Improvement Club, 1962-64, San Francisco Planning and Urban Research Assn., 1968-78. Mem. Public Relations Soc. Am. (accredited), LWV (dir. San Francisco 1966-67), Acad. Polit. Sci., Orgn. Women in Landscape, Sierra Club, People for Open Space, Alpha Xi Delta. Democrat. Club: Met. Office: PO Box 489 San Francisco CA 94101

RODGERS, MARIE ALICE, personnel manager; b. Danville, Pa., May 29, 1953; d. William James and Margaret Marie (Zigray) Lamb; m. Vernon Gregory Rodgers, May 17, 1973. B.A. in Psychology, San Diego State U., 1976, M.S. in Indsl./Organizational Psychology, 1978. EEO coordinator Wavetek, Inc., San Diego, 1978-79; employee relations mgr. Bendix-Continental Controls Corp., San Diego, 1979-82; cons. compensation systems, 1982; personnel mgr. Coopervision Diagnostics, San Diego, 1982—; instr. fair employment hiring, 1981-82. Mem. Personnel Mgmt. Assn., Internat. Assn. Personnel Women (pres. San Diego 1982-83, newsletter editor 1980-81), Sigma Xi. Republican. Club: Cortez Racing Assn. Home: 9834 A Appletree Dr San Diego CA 92124 Office: 7356 Trade St San Diego CA 92121

RODGERS, NANCY LUCILLE, security co. exec.; b. Denver, Aug. 22, 1934; d. Francis Randolf and Irma Lucille (Budy) Baker; m. George J. Rodgers, Feb. 18, 1968 (dec. Dec. 1978); children—Kellie Rae, Joy Lynn, Timothy Francis, Thomas Francis. Pres., Western Telelarm, Inc., San Diego, 1973-75, pres., 1975—; pres. Rodgers Police Patrol, Inc., San Diego, 1973-83; br. mgr. Honeywell, Inc., San Diego, 1977-80; pres. Sabaens, Inc., Portland, Oreg., 1977—, Western Solar Specialties, 1979—, I.M.A.G.E. Inc., 1979—, Western Solar Spltys., 1979-80, IMAGE Travel Agy., Cairo, 1981—; cons., mem. speakers bur. MOVE, Profl. Women's Ctr. Ordained to ministry Catholic Ch. of Antioc, Malabar Rite, 1983. Named Woman of Accomplishment, San Diego, 1978. Mem. Am. Soc. Indsl. Security, Nat., Western burglar and fire alarm assns., Am. Bus. Womens Assn. (named Woman of Yr., Crown chpt. 1979), Calif. Assn. Lic. Investigators, Sales and Mktg. Execs. Internat., Apt. and Rental Owners Assn., Nat. Assn. Female Execs., Central City Assn. (dir.), Nat. Assn. for Holistic Health, Profl. Women's Assn., Nat. Assn. for Women Contractors. Republican. Clubs: Soroptimist Internat., San Diego Yacht.

RODGERS-BARSTACK, RENÉE ELIZABETH, educator; b. El Paso, Tex., Dec. 6, 1949; d. William Walter and Patricia Elizabeth (O'Brien) R.; B.S., Ind. U., 1971; M.A., Ariz. State U., 1972, Ed.D., 1980. Tchr. English, Sierra Vista (Ariz.) Public Schs., 1972-76; instr. English, Cochise Coll., 1975-76; instr. Dept. ArNy Edn. Center, Ft. Huachuca, Ariz., 1975, Glendale Community Coll., 1976-77; grad. assoc. Ariz. State U., 1977-80, faculty assoc. dept. edn., 1980-1981; coordinator career devel. and job placement Glendale (Ariz.) Community Coll., 1981—; cons. in field. Congressional intern U.S. Ho. of Reps., 1969-70; vol. Ariz. Kidney Assn. Recipient Excellence in Nat. Assn. Publs. award Assn. Trends Nat. Newsweekly, 1978; Edward A. Cummings Meml. scholar, 1979; Univ. scholar, 1976-80; Women's Equity grantee, 1980-81. Mem. AAUP, World Council Curriculum and Instrn., NEA, Assn. Supervision and Curriculum Devel. (yearbook editorial com. 1978), Assn. Tchr. Educators, Ariz. Edn. Assn., Ariz. Assn. Tchr. Educators (co-editor newsletter 1979), NOW, Phi Delta Kappa, Pi Lambda Theta, Delta Kappa Gamma. Democrat. Co-editor

Focusing on the Ariz. Ednl. Scene, 1978-80. Home: 8225 N Central Ave Phoenix AZ 85020 Office: Glendale Community Coll Glendale AZ 85302

RODIGER, GEORGIANA GLENN, psychotherapist; b. Cambridge, Mass., Feb. 11, 1931; d. Charles Leslie and Georgiana (Sibley) Glenn; children—Georgiana, William, James, John, Margaret. B.A., Pomona Coll., 1952; M.A., Fuller Theol. Sem., 1975; Ph.D. in Psychology, Fuller Grad. Sch., 1980. Field dir. Pasadena Area council Girl Scouts U.S.A., 1952-53; cons., trainer, research asst. Bur. Tng. and Manpower Devel., Calif. Dept Health, 1973-76; psychol. asst. Children's Hosp. Los Angeles, 1977-79, intern, 1978-80; exec. dir. Georgiana Rodiger Ctr., Pasadena, Calif., 1980—; faculty mem. Pacific Oaks Coll., 1980—, Fuller Grad. Sch. Psychology, 1980-81; spl. edn. cons. Pasadena Sch. Dist., 1979-81. Co-founder Hospice of Pasadena, Pasadena chpt. Candlelighters; adv. Women in the Middle, 1981; Anorexic Bulemic Group, 1981—; sr. high youth, All Saints Ch.; postulant for Holy Orders, Episcopal Ch. Recipient Newton D. Baker cert. of recognition, United Community Funds and Councils Am., 1968. Mem. Am. Physiol. Assn., Assn. Humanistic Psychology, Western Assn. Christians for Psychol. Studies, Am. Psychol. Assn., Jr. League Pasadena. Home: 1102 Arden Rd Pasadena CA 91106 Office: 54 N Oakland Ave Pasadena CA 91101

RODINO, ELAINE A(NN), psychologist; b. N.Y.C., Apr. 16, 1940; d. America J. and Rachel J. (Cafiero) Lamberti; m. Robert J. Rodino, July 3, 1965; 1 dau., Michelle Lyn. B.S. cum laude, C.S. Post Coll., L.I. U., 1961; M.A., Hofstra U., 1963; Ph.D., Calif. Sch. Profl. Psychology, 1978. Lic. clin. psychologist, Calif.; lic. sch. psychologist, N.Y. State, Calif. Sch. psychologist, pub. schs., Long Beach, N.Y., 1964-71, Roslyn (N.Y.) Sch. Dist., 1971-76, Gt. Neck (N.Y.) Sch. Dist., 1973-75; psychologist Suicide Prevention Ctr., Los Angeles, 1978—, dir. Life Clinic, 1982—; pvt. practice clin. psychology, Santa Monica, Calif., 1978—. Mem. Los Angeles County Psychol. Assn. (pres.-elect), Calif. State Psychol. Assn. (chpt. observer to bd.), Am. Psychol. Assn., Am. Assn. Suicidology. Office: 23 Wilshire Blvd Suite 910 Santa Monica CA 90401

RODMAN, GERALDINE ANNE, religious administrator; b. Can., Mar. 5, 1949; d. Walter J. and Irene (Dickson) R. B.A., U. Toronto, 1972; B. Phys. Health Edn., 1972; M.A., Wheaton Coll., 1979. Asst. dir. Community devel. City of Toronto, 1972, dir. community devel., 1973-75; dir. Med. Facilities for Olympiad, Toronto, 1975-76; dir. Campus Ministries in Bay Area, Berkeley, 1978—. Mem. Nat. Assn. Female Execs., Am. Mgmt. Assn. Presbyterian.

RODOLFA, EMIL RAYMOND, psychologist, educator; b. San Jose, Calif., Nov. 23, 1952; s. Joseph and Louise Alma (Cava) R.; m. Mary Jo Pyne, Jan. 6, 1979. B.A. in Psychology, San Jose State U., 1976; M.S. in Counseling, Calif. State U., 1977, M.S. in Edn., 1978; Ph.D. in Counseling Psychology, Tex. A&M U., 1981. Intern counselor child sexual abuse treatment program San Jose, Calif., 1976-78; jr. staff psychologist counseling service U. Iowa, Iowa City, 1980-81; staff psychologist counseling ctr. Humboldt State U., Arcata, Calif., 1981—. San Jose State U. Presl. scholar, 1975-76. Mem. Am. Psychol. Assn. (Div 30-Hypnosis), Am. Soc. Clin. Hypnosis, Assn. Calif. State U. Profs. Contbr. articles to profl. jours. Office: Counseling Center Humboldt State U Arcata CA 95521

RODRIGUES, ALFRED BENJAMIN KAMEEIAMOKU, telephone company executive; b. Honolulu, Jan. 23, 1947; s. Alfred Benjamin Kameeiamoku and Ruth Shiegeko (Kameda) R.; m. Gwendolyn Leiolani Kau, Aug. 8, 1981. B.S., U. San Francisco, 1969; postgrad. U. Wis., 1977. Pub. info. mgr. Hawaiian Telephone Co., Honolulu, 1979-80, pub. affairs program mgr., 1980—. Bd. dirs., pub. relations chmn. Am. Lung Assn. Hawaii, 1981—; trustee, pub. relations chmn. Hawaii Army Mus. Soc., 1982—. Served to capt. U.S. Army, 1969-79. Decorated Bronze Star, Army Commendation medal, Purple Heart with oak leaf cluster, Air medal. Mem. Am. Mktg. Assn., Am. Advt. Fedn., Pub. Relations Soc. Am., Res. Officers Assn., Honolulu Press Club. Republican. Roman Catholic.

RODRIGUEZ, EMILY GERTRUDE, agricultural products company executive, consultant; b. Schorndorf, Germany, Dec. 3, 1946; d. Michael and Valentine (Smolen) Gapa; came to U.S., 1951; m. Robert E. Rodriguez, Nov. 22, 1969 (div.); 1 son, Brian David. Student Elmhurst Coll., 1965-68, 69-71. With customer service dept. Hollister Inc., Chgo., 1969-71; asst. prodn. control mgr., 1971-72; with regional office, outside sales Brewer-Titchener Co., Cortland, N.Y., 1974-76; with Builder Marts, Elk Grove, Ill., 1976-78; mgr. food exports, rate negotiator Calif. Valley Exports, San Francisco, 1978-83; v.p. traffic and distbn. Boles Agricorp, San Francisco, 1983—; cons. fgn. label regulations; condr. export seminars. Mem. San Francisco Distbn. Assn., Marin County Distbn. Assn. Pullman Found. grantee, 1965. Mem. Oakland World Trade Assn., Nat. Assn. Female Execs., Nat. Freight Claims Council, Women in Transp., Pacific Traffic Assn. Club: We Runners (San Francisco). Office: Boles Agricorp 550 Kearny St Suite 310 San Francisco CA 94108

RODRIGUEZ, GERALD, social studies educator; b. Los Angeles, May 21, 1951; s. William and Lupe (Anguiano) R.; m. Mary Ann Zoria, Oct. 29, 1977; children—Roxanne Nicole, Veronica Ann. A.A., E. Los Angeles Coll., 1971; A.B., U. Calif.-Santa Cruz, 1973; M.A., U. San Francisco, 1978-82. Cert. tchr., adminstr., Calif. Tchr., Alum Rock Union Sch. Dist., San Jose, Calif., 1973-74; instr. Met. Adult Edn. Program, San Jose, 1975; tchr. Berryessa Union Sch. Dist., San Jose, 1975—; coordinator San Jose City Coll., 1981—. Mem. San Francisco Mus. Soc., Republican Nat. Com. Calif. Opportunity grantee, 1969-73. Mem. Assn. Supervision and Curriculum Devel., Calif. Tchrs. Assn., Nat. Assn. Christian Educators, Council Basic Edn., NEA, Nat. Middle Sch. Assn., Nat. Council Social Studies, Nat. Orgn. Legal Problems of Edn., Christian Legal Soc., Phi Delta Kappa, Pi Lambda Theta. Republican. Evang. Christian. Clubs Los Angeles Dodgers Booster, U. Calif.-Santa Cruz Alumni Assn., U. San Francisco Alumni Assn. Author: Mexican-American Selected Annotated Bibliography, 1970. Home: 152 Harriet Ave San Jose CA 95127 Office: 3155 Kimlee Dr San Jose CA 95132

RODRIGUEZ, JULIO ERNESTO, vocational counselor/educator; b. El Salvador, July 1, 1951; came to U.S., 1959; s. Victor Salvador and Maria Teresa (Lima) R.; m. Suzanne Carter, May 25, 1974; children—Julio Eduardo, Antonio Dante, Sara Maria. B.A. in Spanish, Weber State Coll., 1975. Asst. mgr. Housing Authority City of Los Angeles, 1975-79; vocat. counselor Career Guidance Ctr., Provo, Utah, 1979—; instr. Los Angeles S.W. Jr. Coll., 1979; speaker, instr. job seeking skills community orgns. Coach, team rep. Utah Soccer Assn., 1981—; sec. Nat. Intercollegiate Soccer Official's Assn., 1981-82. Mem. Am. Soc. Tng. Devel. Home: RD 3 Box 622-A Provo UT 84604 Office: Career Guidance Ctr 305 N 200 W Provo UT 84601

RODRIGUEZ, MARJORIE ANN KENWARD, food inspector; b. Fullerton, Calif., Jan. 25, 1951; d. Gordon Herbert and Edna Cleo (Hoffman) Kenward; m. Hector Mayagoitia Rodriguez, Sept. 10, 1977; children—Cristal Nikomi, Jessica Kathleen. B.S. in Animal Sci., Calif. State Poly. U., Pomona, 1973. Food insp. U.S. Dept. Agr., Vernon, Calif., 1974—. Treas., women's program mgr. Am. Fedn. Govt. Employees Local 0926. Home: 9608 Pinehurst Ave South Gate CA 90280 Office: US Dept Agr FSIS MPI 400 Oceangate Blvd Suite 220 Long Beach CA 90802

RODRIGUEZ, THOMAS EUGENE, accountant, tax consultant; b. Walsenburg, Colo., Aug. 28, 1944; s. Tom Enos and Mary Freda (Meader) R.; m. Marlene Louise Lake, Nov. 21, 1981. B.S., Colo. State U., 1967. C.P.A., Colo., N.D., Mont., Wyo. Jr. acct. Haskens & Sell, Denver and N.Y.C., 1967-68; sr. acct. Combellic-O'Connor & Co., Englewood, Colo., 1970-72; ptnr. Powers, Rodriguez & Assocs., Denver, 1972-75; owner, mgr. Thomas E. Rodriguez, C.P.A., Denver, 1975-78; prin. Rodriguez & Assoc., P.C., Denver, 1979-81, pres., gen. mgr. Rodriguez, Roach & Assoc., P.C., Denver, 1981—; lectr. bus. dept. Loretto Heights Coll.; contbr. La Voz newspaper; lectr. in field; dir. exec. com. Small Bus. Nat. Adv. Council, Washington, Treas. exec. com. Charro Com. Colo., 1981-83; active Voter Registration Drive Colo., 1981-84; mem. Mayor's Commn. Arts, Denver, 1982—; mem. appeals bd. SSS, 1982-83; mem. blue ribbon panel Govt. Awards Program, Colo. Hispanic Republican Com.; bd. dirs. Colo. Hist. Soc. Served to 1st lt. U.S. Army, 1968-70. Decorated Silver Star., Bronze Star, Air medal, Purple Heart; recipient cert. of Recognition, Nat. Rep. Congressional Com., 1983; award Fed. Exec. Bd., 1981; cert. Dept. Commerce, 1982; named Colo. Small Businessman of Yr., SBA, 1982; Colo. Acct. Adv. of Yr., SBA, 1983. Mem. Am. Inst. C.P.A.s, Colo. Soc. C.P.A.s (Pub. Service award 1983), Am. Hispanic C.P.A.s, Am. Assn. Spanish-Speaking C.P.A.s (chmn.), Assn. Govtl. Accts., Colo. Soc. Spanish Surnamed C.P.A.s (pres). Denver C. of C. (dir. 1982-85), Latin C. of C. (pres. 1981-83), Hispanic Rep. Assembly, Beta Epsilon, Roman Catholic. Contbr.: Colo History and the Minority Businessman, 1982. Office: Rodriguez Roach & Assoc PC 3515 S Tamarac St Suite 300 Denver CO 80237

RODRIGUEZ, WARD ARTHUR, psychology educator, statistical consultant; b. Oakland, Calif., Mar. 22, 1948; s. Arthur Fredrick and Florence Estelle (Mittnacht) R.; m. Marya Lee Hlebica, June 13, 1970; m. Clare Louise Wilson, Oct. 19, 1980. B.A., San Jose State U., 1970, M.A., 1973; doctoral candidate U. N.Mex. Instr., U. N.Mex., Albuquerque, summers 1974-75; prof. psychology N.Mex. Highlands U., Las Vegas, 1976—. Recipient Minority Biomed. Support award, 1978-80, Nat. Inst. Child Health and Human Devel. award, 1981-83. Mem. Am. Statis. Assn., AAAS, Sigma Xi. Roman Catholic. Contbg. author to publs. in field. Home: 619 Tecolote Las Vegas NM 87701 Office: Dept Psychology NMex Highlands U Las Vegas NM 87701

RODRIQUEZ, MARI, public relations consultant; b. Santurce, P.R., Feb. 12, 1957; d. Gilberto and Tete (Zayas) Rodriguez. A.A., Am. Coll., Leysin, Switzerland, 1976; B.A., Universidad de P.R., Mayaguez, 1978; M.A., Pepperdine U., 1982. Asst. dir. mktg., promotions Los Angeles Aztecs Soccer Club, 1980-81; pub. relations program cons. Am. Heart Assn., Los Angeles, 1981—. Recipient Cert. of Appreciation Am. Heart Assn., 1981; recipient Community Service award N.E. YMCA, Los Angeles, 1982. Mem. Pub. Relations Soc. Am., Publicity Club Los Angeles, Pub. Interest Radio and TV Ednl. Soc. Roman Catholic.

ROE, BENSON BERTHEAU, surgeon, educator; b. Los Angeles, July 7, 1918; s. Hall and Helene Louise (Bertheau) R.; A.B., U. Calif., 1939; M.D. cum laude, Harvard U., 1943; m. Jane Faulkner St. John, Jan. 20, 1945; children—David B., Virginia St. John. Postgrad. surg. tng. Mass. Gen. Hosp., Boston; Nat. Research fellow dept. physiology Harvard Med. Sch., 1947; Moseley Traveling fellow U. Edinburg (Scotland), 1951; instr. surgery Harvard Med. Sch., 1950; asst. clin. prof. surgery U. Calif. at San Francisco, 1951-58, chief cardiothoracic surgery, 1958—, prof. surgery, 1966—; practice medicine specializing in cardiothoracic surgery; chief thoracic surgery St. Luke's Hosp., 1953-58, St. Joseph's Hosp., San Francisco, 1952-58; cons. thoracic surgery VA Hosp., San Francisco, San Francisco Gen. Hosp., 1960—, Letterman Army Hosp.; cons. Baxter Labs., Ethicon, Inc. Bd. dirs. United Bay Area Crusade, 1958-70, exec. com., 1964-65; bd. dirs., chmn. exec. com. San Francisco chpt. Am. Cancer Soc.; bd. dirs. San Francisco Heart Assn., 1964-72, pres., 1964-65, chmn. research com., 1966-71; various coms. Am. Heart Assn., 1967—, mem. exec. com. Council Cardiovascular Surgery; pres., bd. dirs. Miranda Lux Found., Avery Fuller Found. Served with USNR, 1944-46. Diplomate Am. Bd. Surgery, Am. Bd. Thoracic Surgery (dir. 1971—, vice-chmn. 1979, chmn. 1981, chmn. programs com. 1975, exam. com. 1976, chmn. planning com. 1978). Fellow Am. Coll. Cardiology, ACS (chmn. adv. council thoracic surgery, mem. cardiovascular surgery com., SESAP exam. com., 2 ad hoc coms., past mem. Council No. Calif. chpt.); mem. Am. Assn. Thoracic Surgery (membership com. 1970—, chmn. 1975, 76, manpower com. 1970—, chmn. 1970), AMA (residency rev. com. thoracic surgery), Am., Pacific Coast surg. assns., Calif. Med. Assn. (com. cardiovascular diseases 1969-71, com. on relative value studies 1971-74), Howard C. Naffziger Surg. Soc., Internat. Cardiovascular Soc. (chmn. membership com. 1969-70), Mid Century Surgeons Club, San Francisco County Med. Soc., San Francisco Surg. Soc., Soc. Thoracic Surgeons (council 1971-77, pres. 1972, program com. 1970-72, chmn. standards and ethics com. 1975-78), Soc. Univ. Surgeons, Soc. Vascular Surgery (past v.p.), Western Soc. Clin. Research, Chilean Soc. Cardiology, Am. Soc. Artificial Internal Organs, Harvard Med. Alumni Assn. (pres. No. Calif. chpt. 1974). Author: (text) Perioperative Management in Thoracic Surgery. Mem. editorial bd. Annals of Thoracic Surgery, 1969—. Contbr. numerous articles to profl. pubs. Office: Dept Surgery U Calif San Francisco CA 94143

ROEHRKASSE, GLENN PAUL, statistics educator; b. Casper, Wyo., Apr. 13, 1925; s. Laurence Conrad and Ida Louise (Preis) R.; m. Marion Katherine Fichtner, Sept. 3, 1950; children—Russell L., Glenna K., Paula L. B.S., U. Wyo., 1951, M.S., 1953; Ph.D., Iowa State U., 1962. Instr. U. Wyo., 1953-57, asst. prof., 1957-62, assoc. prof., 1962-67, prof., 1968—, agrl. economist, 1953-62, agrl. expt. sta. statistician, 1962—. Served in USN, 1944-46. Mem. Am. Statis. Assn., Biometric Soc., Am. Legion (Sertoma), DAV, Alpha Zeta, Gamma Sigma Delta. Lutheran. Contbr. numerous articles to profl. jours. Home: 1428 Ashley Laramie WY 82070 Office: U Wyo PO Box 3354 Laramie WY 82071

ROELOFS, RICHARD VAN DER HART, engineering analyst; b. Los Angeles, Aug. 28, 1921; s. Richard Van Der Hart and Jennie Allison (Stokes) R.; student U. Calif., Berkeley, 1944-46, U. Calif. Extension, Los Angeles, 1959, 65-67; m. June Lorraine Paulson, Dec. 27, 1950; children—Leona Renay, Reigh Louis. Partner, Red Feather Candies Co., Los Angeles, 1946-47; electronics technician Western Electric Co., Los Angeles, 1947-50, 52-56, Lockheed-Missile Systems Div., Van Nuys, Calif., 1956-57; test engr. Westrex Corp., Hollywood, Calif., 1957-60; project engr. Mincom div. 3M Co., Los Angeles, 1960-62, Fairchild Winston Research Corp., Los Angeles, 1962-65; instr. electronics dept. Los Angeles Trade Tech. Coll., 1965-70, 72-78, sci. and math. dept., 1970-72, prof., 1975-78; tng. specialist IV, Gen. Telephone Co. Calif., Monrovia, 1978-82; SSOC support analyst, Mission Hills, Calif., 1982—; cons. engr. Beth Machine Tool & Devel. Co., Gardena, Calif., 1968-69, Vacuum Atmospheres Corp., North Hollywood, Calif., 1964-66. Served with USNR, 1942-46, 50-52. Mem. Calif. Vocat. Assn., Nat. Rifle Assn. Republican. Clubs: Silent Valley. Patentee magnetic recording system. Home: 36200 Paradise Ranch Rd Castaic CA 91310 Office: 11333 Sepulveda Blvd Mission Hills CA 91310

ROEPKE, DOLORES MAE, hospital volunteer services administrator; b. Hampton, Iowa, May 25, 1931; dau. Leslie Roy Krafft and Pearlina Ida Osterland; children—Deborah, Janine, Nancy; B.A. cum laude, Westmar Coll., Le Mars, Iowa, 1953; M.A. in Mgmt., U. Phoenix, 1982. Home econs. tchr. Mooseheart (Ill.) High School, 1953-55; music tchr. Bern (Kans.) High School, 1959-60; exec. sec. Willmar (Minn.) United Fund, 1966-70; spl. edn. teacher, Willmar High School, 1969-70; dir. vol. services, Willmar State Hosp., 1973-75; dir. vol. services Scottsdale Meml. Hosp., 1976—; dir. handicapped children's camp, 1966-68. Active AAUW, 1962-65, Common Cause, 1962-65. Mem. Dirs. Vol. Services, Ariz. Hosp. Assn. (pres. 1980), Dirs. of Vols. in Agys. Presbyterian. Office: 7400 East Osborn Rd Scottsdale AZ 85251

ROESCH, WARREN DALE, software co. exec.; b. Oakland, Calif., Aug. 8, 1945; s. George Oscar and Dorothy Wenifred (Smith) R.; A.A., Coll. of San Mateo, 1966; B.A., Calif. State U., 1968; m. Marguerite Mary Whitman, Aug. 1, 1970; 1 son, Warren Whitman. Programmer, operator Western Title Ins. Co., San Francisco, 1973-74, mgr. data processing, 1974; mgr. data processing E. Bay Regional Park Dist., Oakland, 1974-78, Jacuzzi Whirlpool Bath, Walnut Creek, Calif., 1978-82; sr. bus. programmer Bechtel Corp., San Francisco, 1978; cons. systems analyst Packaging div. Crown Zellerbach, San Francisco, 1979, project mgr. MIS installations, 1980; founder, chief exec. officer Total Resource Group, Inc., San Mateo, Calif., 1982—. Home: 333 Borica Dr Danville CA 94526 Office: 520 El Camino Real Suite 520 San Mateo CA 94402

ROESCHLAUB, JEAN (MARIAN) CLINTON, restaurant chain exec.; b. Berkeley, Calif., June 1, 1927; d. Clifford E. and Nelda M. (Patterson) Clinton; A.A., Stephens Coll., 1944; m. David J. Davis III, June 26, 1946 (dec. 1963); children—David J. Davis IV, Diane Davis Clardy, Bruce Clinton Davis; m. 2d, Ronald Curtis Roeschlaub, Jan. 9, 1965; 1 son, Ronald W. Civilian cons. on loan to Q.M. Gen., 1944-45; co-owner, dir. foods, v.p. Clinton's Restaurants, Inc., operators Clifton's Cafeterias, Los Angeles, 1944—; dir. Glendale Fed. Savs. and Loan Assn. Chmn. bd. curators Stephens Coll.; bd. dirs. Hollywood (Calif.) Presbyterian Med. Center, Los Angeles Orphanage Guild; bd. dirs., mem. exec. com. Assistance League of So. Calif.; mem. aux. bd. Braille Inst. Am., Los Angeles. Mem. Nat. Restaurant Assn., Calif. State Restaurant Assn. Republican. Presbyterian. Clubs: Los Angeles Country, Los Angeles Athletic. Home: 5005 Los Feliz Blvd Los Angeles CA 90027 Office: 515 W 7th St Los Angeles CA 90014

ROESELER, WILLIAM GENE, engineer; b. Rockford, Ill., Feb. 17, 1943; s. Ernest Frederick and Grace Belle (Cain) R.; m. Susan Dorothy Hoberman, Jan. 1, 1966; Charles Owen, Kristen Page, Corydon Cain; m. 2d, Marlene Brook Burnell, Dec. 31, 1978. B.S., MIT, 1965, M.S., 1966. Cert. profl. engr., Wash. Flight loads surveyor Boeing Comml. Airplane Co., Seattle, 1966-70, wing stress/supersonic transport engr., 1971, structural durability group engr., 1972, structural dynamics engr., 1973-74, hydrofoil struts and foils engr., 1975-76, composites engr., 1977—; chmn. 1981 Conf. AIAA Sailing Tech. Mem. AIAA. Republican. Author: The Sea Nymph and an Ancient Egyptian Yacht, 1977; patentee Hydrofoil Flap Hinge, 1979, patent pending Graphite Spring. Home: 3201 Evergreen Point Rd Bellevue WA 98004 Office: 44-56 Boeing Comml Airplane Co Renton WA

ROESGEN, WILLIAM NEWELL, editor; b. Williamsport, Pa., May 15, 1931; s. Jacob H. and Margaret (Sparks) R.; B.S. in Social Sci., Fordham U., 1953; m. Joan Danneker, July 23, 1954; children—Susan, Richard, Andrew, Theodore. Mng. editor S. Haven (Mich.) Daily Tribune, 1954-58, Burlington (Vt.) Daily News, 1958-60, Sandusky (Ohio) Register, 1960-64; group editor Sandusky-Kingsport Group, 1962-74; editor Kingsport (Tenn.) Time-News, 1964-74, Billings (Mont.) Gazette, 1974-80; pub. Helena (Mont.) Ind. Record, 1980—; asso. prof. journalism E. Tenn. State U., part-time 1966-74. Juror Pulitzer Prize, 1977-78; discussion leader Am. Press Inst. Mem. Am. Newspaper Pubs. Assn. Home: 1923 Lime Kiln St Helena MT 59604 Office: Ind Record Helena MT 59604

ROESIJADI, GURITNO, marine biologist; b. Tokyo, Apr. 4, 1948; came to U.S., 1966, naturalized, 1977; s. Roesijadi and Chizuko Kitamira; B.S., U. Wash., Seattle, 1970; M.S., Humboldt (Calif.) State U., 1973; Ph.D., Tex. A&M U., 1976; m. Pamela Kay Jaekel, June 6, 1970; children—Tanya, Dalen, Marissa. Research technician U. Wash. Med. Sch., 1970-71; research asst. Tex. A&M U., 1973-76; research scientist Battelle NW Labs., Sequim, Wash., 1976-80, sr. research scientist, 1980—; cons. in field, mem. govt. adv. panels. Mem. AAAS, Am. Soc. Zoologists, Western Soc. Naturalists, Pacific Estuarine Research Fedn., Sigma Xi. Author papers, revs. in field of marine biology; editor Marine Environ. Research, 1980—. Office: Battelle Marine Research Lab 439 W Sequim Bay Rd Sequim WA 98382

ROESSLER, CARL FRED, photographer, travel executive; b. New Haven, Sept. 1, 1933; s. Fred C. and Dorothy D. (Devlin) R.; B.S., Yale, 1955; m. Deborah Westfall, Sept. 1, 1975; children—Paul, Kira. Mgmt. trainee Gen. Electric Co., Schenectady and Lynn, Mass., 1955-59; sales rep. data processing IBM, New Haven, 1960-64; dir. computation Yale U., 1964-69; underwater photographer, 1969-72; pres. See & Sea Travel, San Francisco, 1972—; lectr. ecology and marine sci. Mem. Diving Equipment Mfrs. Assn. Republican. Clubs: Explorers, Adventurers (N.Y.C.). Author: The Underwater Wilderness, 1977; contbr. numerous articles to publs. U.S. and Europe. Office: See & Sea Travel 680 Beach St Suite 340 San Francisco CA 94109

ROGALSKI, ADRIENNE ALICE, biologist; b. Chgo., Aug. 2, 1953; d. Edward Joseph and Viola Veronica (Komen) R.; B.A., with spl. honors, U. Chgo., 1975; Ph.D., U. Ill., 1981. Sr. research technician U. Chgo., 1975-76; research asst., fellow U. Ill.-Chgo., 1976-81; postdoctoral fellow U. Calif.-San Diego, 1981—. Recipient Nat. Research Service award NIH, 1981-83; U. Ill. grad. fellow, 1979-80; Ill. State scholar, 1971-75. Mem. Am. Soc. Cell Biology, AAAS, Sigma Xi. Office: U Calif San Diego Dept Biology B-022 La Jolla CA 92093

ROGERS, CARL RANSOM, psychologist; b. Oak Park, Ill., Jan. 8, 1902; s. Walter A. and Julia (Cushing) R.; m. Helen Elliott, Aug. 28, 1924 (dec. 1979); children—David, Natalie. B.A., U. Wis., 1924; M.A., Columbia U., 1928, Ph.D., 1931; L.H.D. (hon.), Lawrence Coll., 1956, U. Santa Clara (Calif.), 1971; Litt.D. (hon.), Gonzaga U., 1968; D.Sc. (hon.), U. Cin., 1974; Ph.D. (hon.) U. Hamburg (Germany), 1975; Dr. Social Scis. (hon.), Leiden (Netherlands) U., 1975; Sc.D. (hon.), Northwestern U., 1978. Psychologist child study dept. Soc. Prevention Cruelty to Children, Rochester, N.Y., 1928-30, dir., 1930-39; dir. Rochester Guidance Ctr., 1939; prof. clin. psychology Ohio State U., 1940-45; dir. counseling services USO, 1944-45; prof. psychology, exec. sec. Counseling Ctr., U. Chgo., 1945-57; Knapp prof. U. Wis., 1957, prof. psychology and psychiatry, 1957-63; resident fellow Western Behavioral Scis. Inst., La Jolla, Calif., 1964-68, Ctr. Studies of the Person, La Jolla, 1968—; vis. prof. various times U. Rochester, Columbia U. Tchrs. Coll., UCLA, Harvard U., Occidental Coll., U. Calif.-Berkeley, Brandeis U. Recipient Disting. Sci. Contbn. award Am. Psychol. Assn., 1956; 1st Disting. Profl. Contbn. award, 1972; Nicholas Murray Butler medal Columbia U., 1955; Disting. Contbn. award Am. Pastoral Counselors Assn., 1967; Profl. award Am. Bd. Profl. Psychology, 1968; fellow Ctr. Advanced Study in Behavioral Scis., 1962-63; named Humanist of Yr., Am. Humanist Assn., 1964. Fellow Am. Acad. Arts and Scis.; mem. Am. Acad. Psychotherapists (pres. 1956-58), Am.

Orthopsychiat. Assn. (v.p. 1944-45), Am. Assn. Applied Psychology (pres. 1944-45), Am. Psychol. Assn. (pres. 1946-47), Phi Beta Kappa. Author: Measuring Personality Adjustment in Children, 1931; Clinical Treatment of the Problem Child, 1939; Counseling and Psychotherapy, 1942; (with J. Wallen) Counseling with Returned Servicement, 1946; Client-Centered Therapy, 1951; Psychotherapy and Personality Change (with others), 1954; On Becoming a Person, 1961; (with E.T. Gendlin, D.J. Kiesler, C.B. Truax) The Therapeutic Relationship and Its Impact: A Study of Psychotherapy with Schizophrenics, 1967; Freedom to Learn, 1969; Carl Rogers on Encounter Groups, 1970; Becoming Partners: Marriage and Its Alternatives, 1972; Carl Rogers on Personal Power, 1977; A Way of Being, 1980; Freedom to Learn for the 80s; contbr. numerous articles to profl. jours.

ROGERS, CHARLES STEPHEN, Canadian provincial government official; b. Vancouver, B.C., Can., Mar. 28, 1942; s. Forrest and Gwynneth (Thomas) R.; m. Margaret Wallace, Apr. 22, 1967; children—Mark Hayden, Ryan Wallace. Student Vancouver City Coll., Central Officers Sch. RCAF, Centralia, Ont., Can. Airline pilot. Mem. Legis. Assembly B.C. for Vancouver South, 1975—, dep. speaker, 1979, minister of environment, 1979—. Mem. Social Credit Party. Club: Vancouver. Office: Legis Bldgs Victoria BC V8V 1X4 Canada*

ROGERS, CHARLES THEODORE GRAHAM (TED ROGERS), metapsychologist; b. N.Y.C., Oct. 8, 1907; s. Charles T. and May (Church) G-R.; B.S., Wagner Coll., 1933; M.S., San Diego State U., 1962; certificate in counseling U. So. Calif., 1965; D.Sc., Miss. State Christian Coll., 1969; C.H., Dominion Coll., 1975; Ph.D., Newport U., 1977; Ph.D. in Metapsychology, U. Humanistics Studies, 1978; M.S.D., Inst. Metapsychology, 1980; m. Consuelo Yvonne d'Aguilar, March 11, 1933 (dec. July 1975); 1 dau., Patricia Suzanne. Dir. delinquency prevention N.Y.C. schs., 1934-39; assistant dir. personnel tng. Pub. Works Adminstrn., N.Y.C., 1940-41; mem. N.Y. State Div. Parole, 1941-46; chief probation officer San Diego County, San Diego, 1947-67; cons., researcher parapsychology, psychic phenomena, survival, metaphys. healing, 1967—; dir. Center for Edn. and Research, 1965-78; chmn. metapsychology U. Humanistic Studies, 1977-78, mem. psychology faculty, 1977—, dean Inst. Metapsychology, 1981—; guest lectr. San Diego State Coll., 1948; lectr. Calif. Western U., 1958-61; cons. Nat. Probation and Parole Assn., Ariz. Correctional Study, 1958; cons. Deliquency Control Inst., Ariz. State U., 1959-64; cons. Youth Studies Center U. So. Calif., 1963-65, youth problems Bishopric of Fiji, 1966; mem. County Parole Bd., 1961-67; mem. com. Probation Study, Dependent Child Study, State of Calif., 1963-67; mem. profl. advisory com. social work curriculum San Diego State Coll., 1959-61; probation adv. com. Calif. Youth Authority, 1958-67; v.p., chmn. research com. Parapsychology Found., lectr., 1962-67. Served to capt. USAAF, 1942-46; PTO. Recipient Legion of Honor, Order of DeMolay. Fellow Am. Soc. Psychial Research, Royal Soc. Health, Inst. Parapsychol. Research, Coll. Psychic Studies; mem. Soc. Psychical Research, Internat., Am. assns. social psychiatry, Acad. Parapsychology and Medicine, Soc. for Sci. Study of Religion, Acad. Religion and Psychical Research, Nat. Assn. Social Workers (charter), Acad. Religion and Mental Health, Internat. Assn. Metapsychology (pres. 1980—), So. Calif. Soc. Psychical Research, Cosmosophy Soc. (pres.), Am. Assn. Study Mental Imagery, Assn. Past-Life Research and Therapy, Assn. Transpersonal Psychology, Spiritual Frontiers Fellowship, Calif. Probation, Parole and Correctional Assn. (pres. 1961-62), Acad. Certified Social Workers, Church's Fellowship for Psychic Studies, Pi Sigma Alpha. Contbr. articles to various publs. Address: Box 666 Cardiff-by-the-Sea CA 92007

ROGERS, CONNIE MARIE, manufacturing company executive; b. McMinnville, Oreg., Feb. 28, 1948; d, Leon and Agnes (Thrasher) Harling; children—Chad Dixon, Lance Dixon. Student Bellevue Community Coll., 1969-70, Portland Community Coll., 1971-72. Office mgr. Acme Metal Inc., Portland, Oreg., 1971-80; pres., owner Roberts Equipment Inc., Portland, 1982—; bus. mgr. Sta. KKSN, Portland, 1981—; sec. Western Trail Builders Assn., Portland, 1982—. Mem. Nat. Assn. Credit Mgmt., Nat. Assn. Accts. Democrat. Episcopalian. Office: PO Box 20463 Portland OR 97220

ROGERS, DAVID EARL, accounting educator; b. Gallup, N.Mex., May 27, 1943; s. Earl James and Mabel Christell (Nelson) R.; m. Carol Jean Strong, Dec. 15, 1980; children—Christy, Loretta, Robert. B.A., U. N.Mex., 1966; M.B.A., Golden Gate U., 1972. C.P.A., Colo. C.P.A., Haskins & Sells, Denver, 1972-73, Lester Whitte & Co., Grand Junction, Colo., 1974; prof. acctg. Sch. Bus., Mesa Coll., Grand Junction, 1975—. Served to lt. USN, 1966-72. Decorated Vietnam Cross of Gallantry. Mem. Am. Inst. C.P.A.s, Colo. Soc. C.P.A.s. Republican. Baptist.

ROGERS, DOUGLAS GARY, advertising executive; b. Salt Lake City, Aug. 13, 1942; s. George Harold and Elizabeth Margaret (Williams) R.; m. Marjorie Jean Sharp, Dec. 10, 1974; children—Lisa Marie, David Mark. Student Brigham Young U., 1960-61. Sales mgr., salesman, Los Angeles, 1967-69; tng. mgr. Western region 3M Co., Los Angeles, 1969-76; nat. tng. dir. Pertec Computer Corp., Los Angeles, 1976-78; ind. tng. cons. Mattel Toys, Gen. Electric, Sears, Roebuck & Co., other cos., 1974-78; v.p. mktg. Common Carrier Advt., Los Angeles, 1978-81; exec. v.p., co-founder Mobile Billboard Advt., Inc., Midvale, Utah, 1981—, also dir. Served with USAF, 1964-70. Mem. Sales and Mktg. Execs. Assn., Am. Soc. Tng. and Devel. Republican. Mormon. Home: 2528 E Montebello Dr Sandy UT 84092 Office: Mobile Billboard Advt 942 E 7145 South Midvale UT 84047

ROGERS, DWANE LESLIE, management consultant; b. Maywood, Calif., Oct. 6, 1943; s. Lloyd Donald and Della (McAlister) R.; B.S., Ariz. State U., 1967; M.S., Bucknell U., 1968; m. Doris L. Fantel, Aug. 22, 1970; 1 dau., Valerie Lynn. Successively mktg. research coordinator, customer service analyst, merchandising mgr., product planning mgr., order processing mgr. Samsonite Corp., Denver, 1968-74; dir. adminstrn. WISCO Equipment Co., Inc., Phoenix, 1974-75; dir. discontinued ops. Bowmar Instrument Corp., Phoenix, 1975-77; mgmt. cons., dir. Ariz. ops. Mariscal & Co., Phoenix, 1977-80; mgmt. cons. Ariz. Small Bus. Devel. Center, 1980-81; dir. accounts payable, accounts receivable, crude and finished product acctg. Giant Industries, Phoenix, 1981—; instr. Maricopa County Community Coll., 1979—. Mem. Am. Mktg. Assn., Mass Retailing Inst. Republican. Episcopalian. Home: 1551 E Royal Palm Rd Phoenix AZ 85020 Office: 7245 N 16th St Phoenix AZ 85020

ROGERS, GERALDINE MARIE, association executive; b. St. Joseph, Mo., Dec. 31, 1924; d. Joseph Ross and Pauline (Harris) Lloyd; student U. Mo., 1947-49, U. Colo., 1958-69; m. John Lewis Rogers, Aug. 10, 1946; children—John Lewis, Valerie Marie. Clk., U.S. Dept. Agr., Washington, 1942-44; personnel clk. Farm Credit Adminstrn., Kansas City, Mo., 1944-46; asst. office mgr. Gates Credit Union, Denver, 1949-52; ch. adminstr. Burns Meth. Ch., Aurora, Colo., 1962-70; edn. loan officer Lowry Fed. Credit Union, Denver, 1971; exec. v.p., chief exec. officer Aurora Bd. Realtors, 1972—. Mem. Colo. Assn. Execs., Am. Soc. Assn. Execs., Nat. Assn. Realtors. Democrat. Methodist. Club: Civitan Internat. Home: 2913 S Scranton St Aurora CO 80014 Office: 14501 E Alameda Ave Suite 10 Aurora CO 80012

ROGERS, HELEN EVELYN WAHRGREN, newspaperwoman; b. Tacoma, Wash., Jan. 24, 1924; d. John Sigurd and Emma Elina (Carlson) Wahrgren; B.A., U. Wash., Seattle, 1946; m. Charles Dana Rogers, July 24, 1948. Mem. editorial staff Holiday mag., Phila., 1946; civilian public relations writer, Ft. Lewis, Wash., 1946-47; asst. society editor Tacoma News Tribune-Sunday Ledger, 1947-51, radio-TV editor-columnist, 1951—. Author: What's Your Line? vol. I: Delila Sprague Sherburne Harrington: Her Ancestors and Descendants. Mem. Newspaper Guild, Tacoma-Pierce County Geneal. Soc. Democrat. Lutheran. Home: 2906 N 24th St Tacoma WA 98406 Office: 1950 S State St Tacoma WA 98411

ROGERS, HOWARD H., chemist; b. N.Y.C., Dec. 26, 1926; s. Julian Herbert and Minnie (Jaffa) R.; B.S. in Chemistry, U. Ill., Urbana, 1949; Ph.D. in Inorganic Chemistry, M.I.T., 1952; m. Maureen Dohn Andersen, Dec. 28, 1978; children—Lynne Rogers Thomson, Mark David, Susan. Research group leader Allis-Chalmers Mfg. Co., West Allis, Wis., 1952-61; sr. tech. specialist Rocketdyne div. Rockwell, Canoga Park, Calif., 1961-70; chief research scientist Martek Instruments, Newport Beach, Calif., 1970-73; sr. scientist Hughes Aircraft Co., El Segundo, Calif., 1973—. Served with USN, 1944-46. Mem. Electrochem. Soc. (chmn. So. Calif./Nev. sect., 1976-78), Am. Chem. Soc., Sigma Xi. Developer nickel-hydrogen battery; patentee; contbr. sci. papers to profl. publs. in field. Home: 18361 Van Ness Ave Torrance CA 90504 Office: Hughes Aircraft Co S12/V330 PO Box 92919 Los Angeles CA 90009

ROGERS, JAMES BARRY, screenwriter, artist; b. Detroit, Apr. 24, 1933; s. Arthur T. and Shirley (Kahn) R.; m. Maxine Behrend, Aug. 31, 1953 (div. 1961); children—Andrew Marc, Wendy Lynn. Student U. Miami, 1952-53, Md. Inst. Art, 1953-55; B.F.A., U. Ill., 1952. Founder, pres. Rogers & Collins Advt. Agy., Balt., 1955-59; sr. v.p. Galbraith, Hoffman & Rogers Advt. Agy., N.Y.C., 1959-63; one-man shows include: Greenwich Gallery, N.Y.C., 1965, 67, 68, Bay Harbor Galleries, Miami, Fla., 1965, Chevy Chase Gallery, Washington, 1966, Calif. Fed. Bank, Los Angeles, 1968, McKenzie Gallery, Los Angeles, 1971; screenwriter, Los Angeles, 1975—, screenplays for TV shows include: All In the Family, 1975, Alice, 1976, The Jeffersons, 1977, 78, Three's Company, 1978, Trapper John, M.D., 1979, 81, Dukes of Hazzard, A Christmas for Boomer (spl.), 1981, Love Boat, 1982, Fantasy Island, 1982, Ladies' Night (movie), 1981. Mem. Writers Guild Am. West, Nat. Acad. TV Arts and Scis. Home: 9284 Flicker Pl Los Angeles CA 90069

ROGERS, JAMES GLADNEY, educator; b. Stamford, Conn., Nov. 20, 1927; s. James Thomas and Miriam Katherine (Pomeroy) R.; A.B., Yale U., 1949; M.S. in Engring., UCLA, 1963; M.A. in Psychology, 1970, Ph.D., 1974; m. Nancy Odelle Bejach, May 18, 1951; children—Deborah Anne, Rebecca Katherine. Optical engr., project engr. Technicolor Corp., Hollywood, Calif., 1950-56; with Hughes Aircraft Co., Fullerton, Calif., 1956-74, head human factors staff, 1965-70; mem. faculty Calif. State U.-Long Beach, 1972-73, Calif. State U.-Fullerton, 1973-74; assoc. prof. bus. adminstrn., Calif. State U.-San Bernardino, 1974-78, prof., 1978—; cons. Hughes Aircraft, E.G. Sloan Corp., others. Vice pres. North Orange County Community Concert Assn., 1966-68. Mem. Human Factors Soc. (pres. Los Angeles chpt.), AAAS, Am. Psychol. Assn., Calif. Psychol. Assn., Western Psychol. Assn., AAUP. Republican. Episcopalian. Club: Lions (treas.). Patentee computer circuitry, instrumentation and phys. optics; contbr. articles to profl. jours. Office: Calif State Coll Dept Bus San Bernardino CA 92407

ROGERS, JOSEPH WILSON, sociology educator; b. Pensacola, Fla., Oct. 13, 1925; s. Joseph Wilson and Florida Mary (Wallace) W.; m. Doris Gay Ellsworth, Sept. 26, 1953. A.B., San Diego State Coll., 1949; M.A., U. Wash., 1959, Ph.D., 1965. Acting instr. sociology U. Wash., Seattle, 1958-61; instr. sociology Wash. State U., Pullman, 1961-62; asst. prof. Kans. State U., Manhattan, 1962-68; prof. sociology N.Mex. State U., Las Cruces, 1968—, chmn. dept. sociology and anthropology, 1968-73. Bd. dirs. Girls' & Boys' Club Las Cruces; pres. bd. dirs. Children in Need of Supervision. Served in U.S. Army, 1943-46. Recipient Community Leadership award Dona Ana County Human Services Consortium, 1981; Outstanding Prof. award Coll. Arts and Scis., N.Mex. State U., 1982. Mem. Am. Sociol. Soc., Soc. Study of Social Problems, Am. Soc. Criminology, Acad. Criminal Justice Scis. Democrat. Author: Why Are You Not a Criminal?, 1977; contbr. articles, book revs. to profl. jours. Office: Dept Sociology Box 38V NMex State U Las Cruces NM 88003

ROGERS, JUDITH LYNN, public information coordinator, writer, editor; b. Chgo., May 27, 1946; d. Carl Edward and Shirley R. (Johnson) Rogers (Clarke); m. Daniel A. Dansak, May 9, 1981. B.A. in Journalism, U. N.Mex., 1968, M.A. in Ednl. Founds., 1976; postgrad., 1982—. Pub. relations asst. Doris Gregory Pub. Relations, Albuquerque, 1968-69; pub. info. officer, mktg. dir. Southwestern Ednl. Lab., Albuquerque, 1969-72; media writer, coordinator N.Mex. Regional Med. Program, Albuquerque, 1972-74; edn., publs. coordinator Cancer Research & Treatment Ctr., Albuquerque, 1974-76; dir. communications N.Mex. Cancer Control Program, Albuquerque, 1976-80; pub. info. coordinator, planner City of Albuquerque Employment Devel. Offices, 1980—; cons. communications; free-lance writer-editor. Mem. Pilot Club, 1981—. Mem. Pub. Relations Soc. Am., N.Mex. Press Women, Nat. Fedn. Press Women. Republican. Episcopalian. Contbr. articles to consumer and trade mags. Author, editor publs., manuals in edn. and health-related fields. Producer, scriptwriter videotape, film series on health edn. Office: City of Albuquerque Employment Devel Offices 1701 4th St SW Albuquerque NM 87107

ROGERS, JUDY KAY HAWKINS, educator; b. Madill, Okla., Sept. 22, 1946; d. Cliff Leon and Stella Aline (Teel) Hawkins; m. Robert A. Rogers, June 8, 1965 (div.); children—Robert Chad, Roc Ann. M.E., Okla. Southeastern State U., 1973; Edn. cert., Eastern N.Mex. U., 1979; postgrad. Amarillo Coll., 1981, U. Houston, 1981. Cert. tchr., Okla., Tex., N.Mex. Tchr. Dodge City (Kans.) Jr. Coll., 1968-69, Calera (Okla.) High Sch., 1969-73; adminstrv. sec. Grayson Coll., Denison, Tex., 1973-77; tchr. House (N.Mex.) High Sch., 1977-79, Ft. Sumner (N.Mex.) High Sch., 1980-81; tchr. 2d grade, Sunray, Tex., 1980-81; tchr. Tucumcari (N.Mex.) Area Vocat. Sch., 1981—; bus. instr. Amarillo (Tex.) Coll. Mem. NEA, Office Edn. Assn. N.Mex. Office Edn. Assn. (Outstanding Service award 1981), Vocat. Edn. Assn., Nat. Vocat. Edn., Tucumcari Area Vocat. Sch. Office Edn. Assn., Phi Omega Phi. Democrat. Methodist. Home: RD 1 PO Box 101 McAlister NM 88427 Office: Tucumcari Area Vocat Sch PO Box 1143 Tucumcari NM 88401

ROGERS, N. STEWART, wholesale executive; b. Seattle, Feb. 23, 1930; s. Nat S. and Marian W. (Wurzbacher) R.; m. Jane Steele, Mar. 15, 1952; children—Susan Cook, Mark S., Steven H. B.A., Stanford U., 1951. Asst. treas. Van Waters & Rogers, Inc., Seattle, 1954-56, treas., San Francisco, 1956-67; v.p. Univar Corp., Seattle, 1967-71, sr. v.p. fin., 1971—; dir. John Fluke Mfg. Inc., Everett, Wash., Penick & Ford, Ltd., Cedar Rapids, Iowa, Van Waters & Rogers Ltd., Vancouver, B.C.; pres., dir. Guardsman Ins. Co., Hamilton, Bermuda. Pres., The Arboretum Found., 1973-76; trustee United Way Seattle-King County, 1976-78, Nat. Opera Inst., 1981—. Republican. Clubs: Seattle Yacht, Rainier, Harbor (past pres.). Office: 1600 Norton Bldg Seattle WA 98104

ROGERS, NATHAN, oral and maxillofacial surgeon; b. San Francisco, Aug. 22, 1912; s. Dr. Nathan and Maria (de la Luz Urtuzuastegui) R.; A.B., Stanford U., 1937; B.S., U. Calif., 1943, D.D.S., 1943, postgrad., 1949, 55; postgrad. U.S. Nat. Naval Med. Center, 1944; m. Eleanor Marie Ludes, July 5, 1941; children—Ann Lenore, James William, Craig Edward, Glenn Joseph, Wayne Phillip. Grad. in oral and maxillofacial surgery Columbia-Presbyn. Med. Center, N.Y.C., 1947-48; resident oral and maxillofacial surgery Presbyn. Hosp., N.Y.C., 1948-49; pvt. practice oral and maxillofacial surgery, San Francisco, 1950-60; mem. exec. med. staff French Hosp., 1950-59, vis. oral and maxillofacial surgeon, 1950-60, lectr. in oral and maxillofacial surgery, 1955-60; vis. oral and maxillofacial surgeon St. Francis Meml. Hosp., 1951-61, cons. oral and maxillofacial surgery Cleft Palate Guidance Group Clinic, 1951-60; vis. oral and maxillofacial surgeon St. Mary's Hosp., 1951-60; oral and maxillofacial surgeon to Disaster Council and Corps, City and County of San Francisco, 1950— (all in San Francisco). Contributor U.S. Dept. Interior, Fish and Wildlife Service, 1961—. Instnl. rep. San Francisco council Boy Scouts Am., 1957-63, merit badge counselor, 1972—. Served as surgeon Dental Corps, USN, 1943-47. Mem. ADA, Calif. State, San Francisco dental assns., Internat. Assn. Anesthesiologists (charter mem.), Am. Dental Soc. Anesthesia, Pacific Marine Research Soc., No. Calif. Soc. Oral and Maxillofacial Surgeons (emeritus), Stanford (life), U. Calif. (life), Columbia Dental (life), Presbyn. Hosp. N.Y.C. alumni assns., San Francisco Opera Assn. (contbg.), San Francisco Symphony Assn. (contbg.), VFW (life), Ducks Unltd. (contbg.), Nat. Rifle Assn. Am. (life), Nat. Bench Rest Shooters' Assn., Alpha Sigma Phi (life, pres. San Francisco grad. chpt. 1953), Delta Sigma Delta (life mem., pres. San Francisco grad. council 1954). Republican. Episcopalian. Clubs: Chabot Gun; Associated Sportsmen of California; Refuge Gun 2 (pres. 1976-82). Home: 22 Lopez Ave San Francisco CA 94116

ROGERS, OTTO DONALD, artist, educator; b. Kerrobert, Sask., Can., Nov. 19, 1935. Cert., Sask. Tchr.'s Coll., 1953; B.S. in Art Edn., U. Wis., 1958, M.F.A., 1959. Group shows include Biennial, Nat. Gallery Can., 1966, Royal Can. Acad. Art Exhbn., 1970, Dirs. Choice Exhbn., 1968, Waddington Fine Arts Gallery, Montreal, 1969, Mendel Gallery, Saskatoon, 1972; represented in permanent collections at Nat. Gallery Can., Ottawa, Montreal Mus. Fine Arts, Nat. Mus. Iceland, Reykjavik, Fredericton (N.B., Can.) Art Gallery, Windsor (Ont.) Art Gallery; commns. include Prince Albert Regional Library, 1965; prof. painting U. Sask., 1959—, also head dept. art; mem. acquisitions com. Mendel Gallery, 1972-73. Recipient Sr. award for Study in Europe, 1967-68. Mem. Royal Can. Acad. Art. Office: Department Art University Saskatchewan Saskatoon SK S7N 0W0 Canada*

ROGERS, PATRICIA LOUISE, public health nurse; b. Ellensburg, Wash., June 17, 1926; d. Benjamin Bab and Ethel Mae (Cheney) Colwell; m. Clifford J. Rogers, Jr., Mar. 20, 1949. Diploma in nursing Swedish Hosp., Seattle, 1948; B.Sc. in Nursing, U. Wash., 1962. Staff nurse Swedish Hosp., Seattle, 1948-49, White Pass Hosp., Skagway, Alaska, 1949-51; physician's office nurse, Whitehorse, Y.T., Can., 1954-57; staff nurse, acting head nurse Doctor's Hosp., Seattle, 1960-61, pub. health nurse Seattle-King County Health Dept., 1962-64; staff and head nurse Fairbanks Clinic (Alaska), 1965-67; pub. health nurse Fairbanks Health Center, 1967-69, regional pub. health nursing supr. II, 1970-75, nursing mgr., 1975-81, regional nursing mgr., 1981—. Served with Cadet Nursing Corps, 1945-48. Mem. Am. Pub. Health Assn., Alaska Pub. Health Assn., Am. Nurses Assn., Alaska Nurses Assn., Fairbanks Rehab. Assn., Arctic Alliance for People, Fairbanks Community Health Assn. Episcopalian. Office: State of Alaska Dept Health and Social Services Div Pub Health Regional Nursing Office 1919 Lathrop St Drawer 34 Fairbanks AK 99701

ROGERS, PERCY GERALD, bus. exec.; b. Clear Lake, Wis., Jan. 21, 1938; s. Percy Gerald and Julia (Olson) R.; A.B. in Criminology, U. Calif., Berkeley, 1959; M.S. in Criminal Justice Adminstrn., Mich. State U., 1965; M.P.A., U. So. Calif., 1972, D.P.A., 1973; m. Patricia Parsons, Dec. 2, 1961; children—Ryan Todd, Brooke Mari, Erik Olson. Commd. 2d. lt. U.S. Air Force, 1960, advanced through grades to maj., 1969; spl. agt. Office Spl. Investigations, 1960-74, chmn. def. intelligence mgmt. course Def. Intelligence Agy., Washington, 1974-77, chief intelligence plans UN Command, Seoul, Korea, 1977-79, dir. intelligence, chief target processing March AFB, Calif., 1979-81, ret., 1981; pres. Global Risk Assessments, Inc., internat. bus. intelligence firm, Riverside, Calif., 1980—; lectr. criminal justice adminstrn. U. Md., College Park, 1973-77, lectr. bus. mgmt., 1978-79, lectr. systems mgmt. U. So. Calif., 1977-78, 82; assoc. prof. bus. Calif. Poly. U., Pomona, 1983—. Decorated Def. Meritorious Service medal, Meritorious Service medal, Joint Service Commendation medal, Air Force Commendation medal with two oak leaf clusters; recipient Order of the Arrow, Boy Scouts Am., 1978, Scouters tng. award, 1980. Mem. Am. Soc. Tng. and Devel., Am. Soc. Public Adminstrn. (vice chmn. membership and chpt. devel. com., adv. com., membership chmn. Washington chpt. 1974-76), World Future Soc., Orgn. Devel. Network, N. Am. Soc. Corp. Planning, So. Calif. Assn. Corp. Planners, Air Force Assn., Nat. Mil. Intelligence Assn. (pres. Korea chpt. 1979), Scapa Praetors U. So. Calif. (pres. Washington chpt., 1976-77), Phi Kappa Phi, Pi Alpha Alpha. Democrat. Methodist. Author: A Compendium of Analytical Book Reviews in Organizational Behavior, 1972; co-editor Juvenile Justice Management, 1973. Home: 2030 Madrid Ct Riverside CA 92506 Office: 3638 University Ave Suite 215 Riverside CA 92501

ROGERS, RICHARD HERMAN, industrial relations executive, consultant, educator; b. Oil City, Pa., Oct. 25, 1925; s. Herman and Floda Merle (McKissick) R.; m. Janis Brooks Esser, Mar. 18, 1951; children—Sharon Lee, Bruce Richard. Student, Edinburgh State Coll., 1947-48; B.A., Pa. State U., 1950; cert. exec. mgmt. UCLA, 1970. With numerous indsl. cos., Calif., 1954-72; dir. human resources South West Steel, Inc., Los Angeles, 1973-75, ASTECH Corp. div. T.R.E. Corp., Santa Ana, Calif., 1975-78; v.p. Am. Benefits Plan Adminstrs., Inc. div. AVCO, Los Angeles, 1979-81; personnel mgr. Baker Oil Tools Inc., Los Angeles, 1981-82; dir. personnel, compensation, benefits, human resources Singer-Librascope Corp., Glendale Calif., 1982—; instr. personnel mgmt., cons. Coastline Community Coll. Mgr., Brookhurst Little League, 1965-66, pres., recipient Disting. Service award, 1967-68; sr. v.p. Sr. Div. Baseball for Boys, Williamsport, Pa., 1969-71. Served to sgt. ETO, U.S. Army, 1944-46; to 1st lt. USAF, 1950-53. Mem. Personnel Indsl. Relations Assn. (dir. 1978-79, chmn. dist. 14 1978-79), Am. Soc. Personnel Adminstrn., Indsl. Relations Research Assn., Am. Soc. Tng. and Devel. Pa. State Alumnae Assn. Lutheran. Club: Elks. Home: 11281 Stratford Way Garden Grove CA 92640

ROGERS, RICHARD LEE, accountant; b. San Francisco, Jan. 1, 1938; s. Herman Lee and Elizabeth June (Quint) R.; m. Judith Ann, Aug. 27, 1955; 1 son, James William. B.S., Calif. State U.-Sacramento, 1967. C.P.A., Calif. With Ernst & Whinney, Sacramento, 1968-75, Tokyo, 1975-81, San Diego, 1981—, ptnr., 1978—. Chmn. acctg. adv. com. Am. River Coll.; bd. dirs. St. Peters Meml. Residence; treas. Big Bros. Sacramento, 1972-74, pres., 1975. Served with USAF, 1955-59. Mem. Am. Inst. C.P.A.s, Calif. Soc. C.P.A.s (chmn. healthcare com. Sacramento chpt.), Tokyo Am. Club (v.p., bd. govs. 1979-80), Healthcare Fin. Mgmt. Assn. Republican. Episcopalian. Club: Kiwanis (San Diego). Home: 2214 Del Mar Heights Rd Del Mar CA 92014 Office: Ernst & Whinney 110 W A St Suite 1000 San Diego CA 92101

ROGERS, RICHARD WARREN, insurance company executive; b. Washington, Aug. 19, 1931; s. Ulys Samuel and Helene Burland (L'Hommedieu) R.; B.S. in Bus. Adminstrn., St. Benedicts Coll., Atchison, Kans., 1969; B.S. in Accounting, Humphreys Coll., Stockton, Calif.,

1974; M.B.A., Pepperdine U., 1977; m. Mary Catherine Antonelli, May 1, 1954; children—Cynthia Jean, Victoria Lynn, Richard Warren, James Ulys. Commd. 2d lt. C.E., U.S. Army, 1953; advanced through grades to lt. col., 1967; dir. maintenance Sharpe Army Depot, Calif., 1971-72; ret., 1972; dep. dir. for adminstrn. San Joaquin County (Calif.) Dept. Pub. Assistance, Stockton, 1977-82; ret., 1982; dist. mgr. Equitable Life Assurance Soc., 1982—; tchr. San Joaquin Delta Coll., Humphreys Coll. Decorated D.F.C. Mem. Data Processing Mgmt. Assn., Calif. Assn. County Data Processors, County Welfare Dirs. Assn., Nat. Assn. Security Dealers, Nat. Assn. Life Underwriters, VFW, Am. Legion. Republican. Roman Catholic. Clubs: Elks, K.C. Home: 6863 Gettysburg Pl Stockton CA 95207 Office: 1212 Robinhood Dr Suite 3D Stockton CA 95207

ROGERS, ROBERT REED, mining and manufacturing company executive; b. Oak Park, Ill., Feb. 22, 1929; s. Glen Charles and Lucile (Reed) R.; m. Barbara June Fain, Feb. 22, 1951 (div.); children—Robin, Janeen, Kevin. B.S. in Chemistry, Berea Coll., 1951; M.B.A., Ill. Inst. Tech., 1958, postgrad., 1959-62. Asst. mgr. metallurgy research dept. Armour Research Found., Ill. Inst. Tech., 1955-56, mem. faculty, econs. dept., 1956-62; cons. McKinsey & Co., Inc., 1962-64; mgr. devel. planning, profl. group Litton Industries, Inc., 1964-67; pres. N.Am. subs. Muirhead & Co., Ltd., 1967-68; group v.p. Am. Electric Inc. subs. City Investing Co., 1968-70; pres. Cleartight Corp., 1971-73; pres. Newport Internat. Metals Corp., 1973-76; pres. Kensington Assocs., Inc., Newport Beach, Calif., 1976—; pres., chmn. bd. Proteus Group, Inc., Newport Beach, 1981—. Served as officer USN, 1951-55. Machinery and Allied Products Inst. fellow, 1956-62; Berea Coll. grantee, 1947-51. Mem. Navy League. Libertarian. Unitarian. Clubs: Lido Isle Yacht. Home: 819A W 15th St Newport Beach CA 92663 Office: 881 Dover Dr Suite 35 Newport Beach CA 92663

ROGERS, VERN CHILD, consulting engineering company executive; b. Salt Lake City, Aug. 28, 1941; s. Vern S. and Ruth (Child) R.; m. Patricia Powell, Dec. 14, 1962. B.S. in Physics, U. Utah, 1965, M.S. in Mech. Engring., 1965; Ph.D. in Nuclear Engring., MIT, 1969. Assoc. prof. Brigham Young U., Provo, Utah, 1969-73; vis. assoc. prof. Lowell (Mass.) Tech. Inst., 1970-1973; mgr. Intelcom Radiation Tech. Corp., San Diego, 1973-76; v.p. Ford, Bacon & Davis Utah, Inc., Salt Lake City, 1976-80; pres. Rogers and Assocs. Engring. Corp., Salt Lake City, 1980—; cons. in field. Mem. Health Physics Soc., Am. Soc. Profl. Engrs., Am. Nuclear Soc., Am. Phys. Soc., Am. Chem. Soc. Mormon. Contbr. sci. articles to profl. jours., chpts. to books. Office: Rogers and Assocs Engring Corp PO Box 330 Salt Lake City UT 84110

ROGERS, WELDON BRACY, III, communications company executive; b. Oxnard, Calif., July 19, 1947; s. Weldon Bracy and Eula (Moore) R.; m. Clarisse Azevedo, Feb. 19, 1970; children—Kellie Ann, Jamye Allison. B.A. in English/Comparative Lit., U. So. Calif., 1967, M.B.A. in Mktg., 1970; postgrad. spl. studies program Harvard U., 1968. Reporter, ABC News, Los Angeles, 1969; mktg. and communications dir. Dick Clark Prodns., Los Angeles and N.Y.C., 1969-75; dir. pub. relations Playboy Enterprises, Inc., Los Angeles, 1975—; instr. U. So. Calif., UCLA. Recipient Mktg. Success of Yr. award Los Angeles Advt. Club, 1979, 81. Mem. Pub. Relations Soc. Am. accredited; Prism award, 1981, Radio and TV News Assn. (dir.), Hollywood C. of C. (dir.), So. Calif. Broadcasters Assn., Am. Mktg. Assn., Advt. Club So. Calif., Los Angeles Filmex Soc., Publicity Club Los Angeles (Pro award), Phi Gamma Delta. Office: Playboy Enterprises Inc 8560 Sunset Blvd Los Angeles CA 90069

ROGGE, RICHARD DANIEL, former government executive, security consultant, investigator, private patrol operator; b. N.Y.C., July 5, 1926; s. Daniel Richard and Bertha (Sarner) R.; m. Josephine Mary Kowalewska, June 6, 1948; children—Veronica Leigh Rogge Erbeznik, Richard Daniel, Chrispopher Ames, Meredith Ann. B.S. in Bus. Adminstrn., N.Y.U., 1952. Cert. internat. investigator. Clerical worker FBI, N.Y.C., 1947-52, spl. agt., Phila., 1952-54, Washington, 1954-58, supr., 1958-65, asst. spl. agt. in charge, Richmond, Va., 1965-66, Phila., 1966-67, Los Angeles, 1967-69, inspector, 1969, spl. agt. in charge, Honolulu, 1969-72, Richmond, 1972-74, Buffalo, 1974-77, now security cons., investigator, patrol operator, Calif.; police tng. instr.; lectr. in field. Served with USMC, 1944-46; PTO. Mem. Am. Soc. Indsl. Security, Assn. Former Intelligence Officers, Calif. Assn. Lic. Investigators, Calif. Peace Officers Assn., Council Internat. Investigators, Internat. Assn. Chiefs of Police, Soc. Former Agts. FBI, Inc., World Assn. Detectives, Am. Legion. Republican. Roman Catholic. Club: K.C. Home and Office: 32010 Watergate Ct Westlake Village CA 91361

ROGOFF, ARNOLD M., book dealer, publisher, management consultant; b. Oak Park, Ill., Nov. 8, 1930; s. Julius J. and Lucile E. (Wingerhoff) R.; m. Janet E. Percy, July 16, 1968; children—Hilary, Peter. Student, U. Mo., 1948-49, Harvard U., 1951; B.S., Boston U., 1951. Pres., CGR Labs., Los Angeles, 1961-63; With McGraw-Hill Book Co., N.Y.C., 1963-77, sales mgr. Gregg div., 1974-75, dir. mktg. div., 1975-77; prin. ptnr. Arnold M. Rogoff & Assocs., Mill Valley, Calif., 1977—; pres. Ethnographic Arts Pubs., Mill Valley, 1978—. Home: 1040 Erica Rd Mill Valley CA 94941 Office: Ethnographic Arts Publs Industrial Center Bldg Gate 5 Rd Suite 108 Sausalito CA 94965

ROHDE, CHARLES RAYMOND, agronomist, wheat breeder; b. Glasgow, Mont., Sept. 3, 1922; s. Frank A. and Mabel (Peterson) R.; m. Edith B. Emmert, June 18, 1945; children—James, Charles, Linda Rohde Crocker, David, Beth. B.S., Mont. State Coll., 1947; Ph.D., U. Minn., 1953. Asst. prof. agronomy U. Wyo., Laramie, 1950-52; wheat breeder Pendleton Branch Exptl. Sta., Pendleton, Oreg., 1952-66, supt., 1966-75; wheat breeder Columbia Basin Agr. Research Ctr., Pendleton, 1975—. Bd. dirs. Intermediate Edn. Dist., Pendleton. Served to 1st lt. USAAF, 1943-45. Decorated Air medal. Mem. Am. Soc. Agronomy. Lutheran. Office: Columbia Basin Agr Research Ctr PO Box 370 Pendleton OR 97801

ROHDE, JAMES VINCENT, software systems company executive; b. O'Neill, Nebr., Jan. 25, 1939; s. Ambrose Vincent and Loretta Cecilia R.; B.C.S., Seattle U., 1962; children—Maria, Sonja, Daniele. Sales dir. GCE Telephone Co., Oakland, Calif., 1971-74; chmn. bd., pres., dir. Applied Telephone Tech., Oakland, 1974; v.p. sales and mktg. Automation Electornics Corp., Oakland, 1975-82; pres., chmn. bd. Am. Telecorp, Inc., 1982—. Republican. Roman Catholic. Office: 7700 Edgewater Dr N 360 Oakland CA 94621

ROHEN, WILLIAM THOMAS, computer programmer analyst; b. Portland, Oreg., June 15, 1956; s. Robert Clinton and Mitzi Guenieve (Murphy) R. B.S. in Bus. Adminstrn., Oreg. State U., 1978. Computer programmer analyst tech. devel. staff Boeing Computer Services, Richland, Wash., 1978—. Mem. Assn. Systems Mgmt. (profl.), Desert Ski Club, Delta Chi, Theta Delta Nu. Roman Catholic. Office: Boeing Computer Services Richland Fed Bldg Box 300 Richland WA 99352

ROHRBERG, RODERICK GEORGE, cons.; b. Minneola, Iowa, Sept. 26, 1925; s. Charles H. and Emma (Minsen) R.; B. Naval Sci., Marquette U., 1946; B.S., Iowa State U., 1949; m. Genevieve Mary Sogard, June 19, 1949; children—Karla (Mrs. George H. Witz, Jr.), Roderick K., Cheries, Timothy, Christopher. Bridge design engr. Alaska Rd. Commn., U.S. Dept. Interior, 1949-51; sr. tech. specialist North Am. Rockwell, research, Los Angeles, 1951-69; pres. Creative Pathways, Inc., advanced welding services, Torrance, Calif., 1969—; pvt. practice as cons. advanced welding process, equipment design and devel., Torrance, Calif., 1972—. Served with USNR, 1944-46. Recipient 1st nat. Airco Welding award, 1966, commendation NASA, 1965, Engring. Profl. Achievement citation Iowa State U., 1973, 3d pl. Von Karman Meml. Grand award, 1974. Registered profl. engr., Calif. Mem. Am. Welding Soc. Lutheran. Patentee in field. Address: 3121 Fujita St Torrance CA 90505

ROID, GALE HAROLD, research psychologist, educator, consultant; b. Bend, Oreg., June 28, 1943; s. Riedar Jon and Bernice Geolina (Eggen) R.; A.B. Harvard U., 1965; M.A., U. Oreg., 1967, Ph.D., 1969. Asst. prof. psychology McGill U., Montreal, Que., Can., 1969-72; research prof. teaching research div. Ore. State System Higher Edn., 1972-79; research psychologist, Oreg. State Mental Health Div., 1979-80; dir. research, Western Psychol. Services, Los Angeles, 1980—; vis. lectr. UCLA Grad Sch. Edn.; cons. U.S. Army Tng. Command. Councilman City of Monmouth (Oreg.), 1977-78, chmn. Water resources com., 1978. Elks scholar, 1961; Harvard Coll. scholar, 1961-65; Am. Fund Dental Health research grantee, 1976; Advanced Research Projects Agy. grantee, 1977-79; Nat. Inst. Edn. grantee, 1978-79. Mem. Am. Ednl. Research Assn., Am. Psychol. Assn., Nat. Council on Measurement in Edn. Republican. Mem. Missionary Ch. Author: (with T.M. Haladyna) A Technology for Tes-item Writing, 1982; Contbr. articles to profl. jours. Office: 12031 Wilshire Blvd Los Angeles CA 90025

ROIZ, MYRIAM, export import firm executive; b. Managua, Nicaragua, Jan. 21, 1938; came to U.S., 1949; d. Francisco Octavio and Maria Herminia (Briones) R.; m. Nicholas M. Orphanopoulos, Jan. 21, 1957 (div.); children—Jacqueline Elisa Orphanopoulos, Gene Eduardo Orphanopoulos, George Andres Orphanopoulos. B.A. cum laude in Interdisciplinary Social Sci., San Francisco U., 1980. Lic. ins. agt. Adminstr. asst. to curriculum dir., asst. supt. Hillsborough City Sch. Dist., 1968-74; asst. to v.p./gen. mgr. internat. mktg. Oxford-Lancers Labs., Foster City, Calif., 1974-77; sales rep. Met. Life Ins. Co., San Francisco, 1977-79; mktg. dir. Latin Am./Spain Allied Canners & Packers, Inc. div. Boles & Co., San Francisco, 1979—. Mem. Common Cause; coordinator Robert F. Kennedy Presdl. campaign, Millbrae, San Mateo County, local mayoral campaign, Millbrae, 1975; dir., organizer fund-raising campaign for earthquake-devastated Nicaragua. Named Outstanding Employee of Yr. Hillsborough City Sch. Dist., 1973; recipient Sales award Met. Life Ins. Co., 1977. Mem. Nat. Assn. Female Execs., AAUW, Venture Devel. Assn. (sec., treas.). Democrat. Roman Catholic. Club: Latino de Foster city. Office: Allied Canners & Packers Inc 550 Kearny St Suite 310 San Francisco CA 94108

ROIZEN, JO ANN HEIDI, software marketing executive; b. Palo Alto, Calif., Feb. 28, 1958; d. Joseph Roizen. B.A., Stanford U., 1980; postgrad Sch. Bus., 1983—. Mktg. analyst Tandem Computers Inc., Cupertino, Calif., 1981-83, mng. editor NonStop News, 1980-81; ptnr. mktgr. T/Maker Software, Palo Alto, 1980-82; co founder, ptnr. Draper-Roizen Prodns., Palo Alto, 1981—. Contbr. articles to profl. jours. Home: 528 Kendall St Apt 12 Palo Alto CA 94306

ROJAS, JOSEPH AUGUSTIN, obstetrician and gynecologist; b. Alexandria, La., Dec. 9, 1933; s. Joseph E. and Carol A. (Buhler) R.; student Loyola U., New Orleans, 1950-52; M.D., La. State U., 1957; m. Mona Robicheaux, Feb. 22, 1958; children—Joseph Augustin II, Mike, Tom, Lisa, Carol, John. Intern Charity Hosp., New Orleans, 1957-58; resident Tulane U. dept. ob-gyn Charity Hosp., 1958-61; pvt. practice ob-gyn, Las Vegas, 1963—; pres. J.A. Rojas, M.D. Ltd., 1970—; mem. staff Women's, So. Nev. Meml., Valley hosps. (all Las Vegas); chief gynecology Valley Hosp., 1973—; assoc. prof., vice chmn. dept. ob-gyn U. Nev. Med. Sch., Reno; assoc. clin. prof. Tulane Med. Sch. Served to capt. M.C., USAF, 1961-63. Diplomate Am. Bd. Obstetrics and Gynecology. Fellow ACS, Internat. Coll. Surgeons, Am. Sterility and Infertility Soc., Am. Coll. Obstetrics and Gynecology; mem. Nev., Clark County med. socs., Royal Coll. Medicine (asso.), AMA, Southwest, Conrad G. Collins, Clark County obstetrics/gynecology socs., Pan-Am. Cytology Soc. obstetrician and gynecologist; b. Alexandria, La., Dec. 9, 1933; s. Joseph E. and Carol A. (Buhler) R.; student Loyola U., New Orleans, 1950-52; M.D., La. State U., 1957; m. Mona Robicheaux, Feb. 22, 1958; children—Joseph Augustin II, Mike, Tom, Lisa, Carol, John. Intern Charity Hosp., New Orleans, 1957-58; resident Tulane U. dept. ob-gyn Charity Hosp., 1958-61; pvt. practice ob-gyn, Las Vegas, 1963—; pres. J.A. Rojas, M.D. Ltd., 1970—; mem. staff Women's, So. Nev. Meml., Valley hosps. (all Las Vegas); chief gynecology Valley Hosp., 1973—; assoc. prof., vice chmn. dept. ob-gyn U. Nev. Med. Sch., Reno; assoc. clin. prof. Tulane Med. Sch. Served to capt. M.C., USAF, 1961-63. Diplomate Am. Bd. Obstetrics and Gynecology. Fellow ACS, Internat. Coll. Surgeons, Am. Sterility and Infertility Soc., Am. Coll. Obstetrics and Gynecology; mem. Nev., Clark County med. socs., Royal Coll. Medicine (asso.), AMA, Southwest, Conrad G. Collins, Clark County obstetrics/gynecology socs., Pan-Am. Cytology Soc. Home: 3108 Sonia Dr Las Vegas NV 89107 Office: Suite 115 901 Rancho Lane Las Vegas NV 89106

ROLAND, HAROLD EUGENE, JR., safety engineering educator; b. Lincoln, Nebr., Aug. 10, 1924; s. Harold E. and Nell (Williamson) R.; m. Elayne M. Merriam, Aug. 5, 1947. B.S. in Aero. Engring., Naval Postgrad. Sch., 1956; M.S. in Aero. Engring., U. Minn., 1958; M.S. in Indsl. Engring., U. So. Calif., 1969; Ph.D., UCLA, 1974. Lic. profl. safety engr., Calif. Commd. USMC, 1943, advanced through grades to lt. col., 1963, ret., 1965; mem. faculty, safety dept. U. So. Calif., Los Angeles, 1965—; pres. Rolson & Co., Los Angeles. Decorated DFC (2), Air medal (5). Mem. AAUP, AIAA, System Safety Soc., Am. Soc. Safety Engr., Sigma Xi. Club: Rancho Verde Racquet. Author: System Safety Engineering and Management, 1983; contbr. numerous articles to profl. jours. Office: U So Calif University Park Los Angeles CA 90007

ROLL, RICHARD SHANNON, social services official; b. Mesa, Ariz., Oct. 29, 1949; s. Jack Pershing and Vernelle Harriett (May) R. B.A., U. Iowa, 1971; M.S.W., 1972. Social worker Monson State Hosp., Palmer, Mass., 1972; asst. adminstr./social worker Glenwood State Hosp. (Iowa), 1972-79; dir. community placement services Alpine Regional Ctr., Gaylord, Mich., 1979-81; dir. social services dept. Los Lunas Hosp. and Tng. Sch., N.Mex., 1981—. Mem. Soc. Hosp. Social Work Dirs., N.Mex. Soc. Hosp. Social Work Dirs., Am. Hosp. Assn. Democrat. Congregationalist. Co-developer new health facility program. Office: Los Lunas Hosp and Tng Sch PO Box 1269 Los Lunas NM 87031

ROLLIN, WILLIAM PAUL, computer ops. exec.; b. San Diego, Jan. 8, 1948; s. Paul Joseph and Esta Lee (Hill) R.; A.A., Grossmont Coll., 1971; A.S. in Computer Sci., Coleman Coll., 1971; m. Frances Fayette Marcks, Apr. 7, 1979. Computer ops. mgr. Univ. Hosp., U. Calif. Med. Ctr., San Diego, 1971—; pres. Alan-Paul, Inc. Mem. Assn. Computer Ops. Mgrs. Office: 225 Dickenson St San Diego CA 92103 also PO Box 188 El Cajon CA 92022

ROLLINS, DAVID THOMAS, rehab. cons.; b. N.D., Apr. 27, 1935; B.S., U. N.D., 1964; M.S., Canisius Coll., 1965; Ph.D., Med. Sch. U. Oreg., 1971; m. Eleanor Thorson, June 26, 1965; children—Lynn Rae, Jason David, Scott Jason, Amy Lynn. Spl. edn. therapist, N.D., 1953-57; rehab. specialist U. N.D., Grand Forks, 1961-64; rehab. specialist Canisius Coll. and St. Mary's Sch. for Deaf, Buffalo, 1964-65, U. Okla. Med. Center, Oklahoma City, 1965-66; rehab. coordinator Syracuse (N.Y.) U., 1966-68; rehab. clinician U. Oreg. Med. Sch., Portland, 1968-72; pres. Rehab. Cons. Services Corp., Portland, Ore., 1972-76, chief operating officer, 1976-77. Served with U.S. Army, 1957-60. N.Y. State Mental Hygiene scholar, 1966; HEW scholar, 1964; Vocat. Rehab. fellow, 1965; Neurol. and Sensory Diseases fellow, 1966-70. Mem. Nat. Rehab. Assn., Nat. Soc. of Disability Examiners, Am. Personnel and Guidance Assn., Am. Speech and Hearing Assn., Vocat. Evaluation and Work Adjustment Assn., Nat. Rehab. Counseling Assn., Am. Pub. Health Assn. Nat. panel advs. Forensics Services Directory. Home: 7112 SE 27th Ave Portland OR 97202 Office: 4936 SE Woodstock Blvd Portland OR 97206

ROLLINS, JOAN ELISE, personnel services corporation executive; b. Inglewood, Calif., Mar. 3, 1947; d. Richard H. and Irene C. (Morgan) McClellan; m. James Hood Rollins, Aug. 8, 1970. B.A. in Psychology, U. So. Calif., 1969; M.A. in Psychology, Calif. State U.-Long Beach, 1978. Registered employment cons., Calif. Employment Assn. Personnel counselor Nancy Nolan Agy., Los Angeles, 1969-70; reservation agt. Trans World Airlines, Los Angeles, 1970; personnel counselor, asst. mgr. A.E.A. Employment Agy., Long Beach, 1970-78; pres. Rollins & Assocs. Personnel Service, Inc., Long Beach, 1979—; guest lectr. classes and seminars in field; cons. ct. cases involving employment. Mem. Internat. Mktg. Assn. Orange County, Exec. Women Internat., Long Beach Area C. of C. (pres. Women's Council 1982-83, dir. 1982—), Commerce Assocs. U. So. Calif. Sch. Bus. Club: Harbor Transp. Office: 337 E San Antonio Dr #200 Long Beach CA 90807

ROLLS, JANA, garment manufacturing company executive, business consultant; b. Sarasota, Fla., May 7, 1950; d. Karl R., and Ruth C. Rolls; m. David J. Smith; children—Benjamin Ross, Kerstyn Smith. B.S. in Home Econs., B.S. in Secretarial Sci., So. Missionary Coll., 1971; M.A. in Intimate Apparel, Loma Linda U., 1972. Tchr. schs., Ventura, Calif., 1971-76; founder alterations and sewing bus., Napa. Calif., 1976, name now Jana's Mfg. Co., pres., owner, 1980—. Mem., participant Napa Women's Polit. Caucus. Mem. Nat. Assn. Female Execs., Bus-Minded Women's Network (founder), Am. Women's Econ. Devel. Corp. Home: 166 Homewood Napa CA 94558 Office: 1842 Jefferson St Napa CA 94558

ROMANO, JOSEPH, city official; b. Chgo., Sept. 22, 1947; s. Joseph I. and Wilhemenia (Dangel) R.; div.; 1 dau., Lisa Ann. A.A., Santa Rosa Jr. Coll., 1974; B.S., Calif. Western U., 1978, M.B.A., 1979; J.D., Empire Coll. Law, 1980. Dep. sheriff, Sonoma County, Calif., 1969-73; mgr. Graphics Inc., 1971-76; labor specialist Calif. Labor Dept., 1976-79; administrv. asst. City of Santa Rosa (Calif.), 1979, gen. mgr., water adminstr. 1980—; also cons. Served with USNR, 1964-68. Mem. Am. Water Works Assn., Am. Mgmt. Assn., VFW. Republican. Roman Catholic. Club: Masons. Office: 100 Santa Rosa Ave Room 6 Santa Rosa CA 95402

ROMBOUGH, BARTLETT B., petroleum company executive; b. Winnipeg, Man., Can., 1924. Pres., chief exec. officer, dir. Pan. Can. Petroleum Ltd., Calgary, Alta., Can.; dir. Panarctic Oils Ltd., Fording Coal Ltd., PanCan. Petroleum Ltd., Syncrude Can. Ltd., Rogers Cablesystems Inc. Office: Pan Canadian Petroleum Ltd 2000 One Palliser Sq Calgary AB T2P 2S5 Canada*

ROMBOUT, LUKE, art museum dir.; b. Amsterdam, Netherlands, May 4, 1933; s. Louis and Aleida (VanBuren) R.; came to Can., 1954, naturalized, 1959; B.F.A., Mt. Alison U., Sackville, N.B., Can., 1967. Acting curator Owens Art Gallery, Mt. Allison U., 1965-67, dir., 1968-71, curator, 1967-68; chmn., asst. prof., visual arts program Faculty of Fine Arts York U., Toronto, Ont., Can., 1972-74; mem. arts advisory panel Can. Council, Ottawa, Ont., 1969-70, dir. art bank, 1972-74, head, visual arts film sect., 1974-75; dir. Vancouver Art Gallery (B.C., Can.), 1975—; lectr. Canadian art history Mt. Alison U., 1968-71; lectr. art history N.S. (Can.) Coll. Art Design, 1970-72; lectr. Canadian art history U. Ottawa (Ont., Can.), 1974-75; asst. curator Beaverbrook Art Gallery, Fredericton, N.B., Can., 1960; chmn. art com. Com. Continuing Edn., St. John, N.B., 1960; mem. arts supervisory com. N.B. Mus., St. John, Can., 1967-68; organizer fine arts crafts exhibition, Atlantic pavilion, Expo '67, Montreal; mem. advisory com. art Canadian Dept. Pub. Works, 1973; mem. design advisory com. Can. Post, 1973; mem. fine arts com. Canadian Dept. External Affairs, 1973-75; mem. bd. Anna Wyman Dance Theatre, 1976—; mem. advisory com. art dept. Capilano Coll., 1976—; sec. Atlantic Provinces Art Circuit, 1964-67. Mem. Canadian Museums Assn. (v.p. 1970-71), Canadian Art Mus. Dirs. Orgn., Assn. Art Mus. Dirs., Assn. Am. Mus. Dirs., Canadian Assn. Mus. Dirs., Assn. Internat. Critiques d'Art. Maritime contbr. Vie des Arts, 1965; participant in films and radio programs. Address: Vancouver Art Gallery 750 Hornby St Vancouver BC V6E 3H2 Canada

ROMER, ROY R., state official; b. Garden City, Kans., Oct. 31, 1928; s. Irving Rudolph and Margaret Elizabeth (Snyder) R.; B.S. in Agrl. Econs., Colo. State U., 1950; LL.B., U. Colo., 1952; postgrad. Yale U.; m. Beatrice Miller, June 10, 1952; children—Paul, Mark, Mary, Christopher, Timothy, Thomas, Elizabeth. Engaged in farming in Colo., 1942-52; admitted to Colo. bar, 1952; ind. practice, Denver, 1955-66; mem. Colo. Ho. of Reps., Dist., 1958-62, Colo. Senate, 1962-66; owner, operator Arapahoe Aviation Co., Colo. Flying Acad., Geneva Basin Ski Area; engaged in home site devel.; owner chain farm implement and indsl. equipment stores in Colo.; commr. agr. State of Colo., 1975, state treas., 1977—; chief staff, exec. asst. to gov. Colo., 1975-77; chmn. Gov. Colo. Blue Ribbon Panel, Gov. Colo. Small Bus. Council; mem. agrl. adv. com. Colo. Bd. Agr. Past trustee Iliff Sch. Theology, Denver. Served with USAF, 1952-54. Mem. Colo. Bar Assn. (gov.), Order of Coif. Democrat. Presbyterian. Bd. editors Colo. U. Law Rev., 1960-62. Office: 140 State Capitol Bldg Denver CO 80203*

ROMIG, ALTON DALE, JR., metallurgist, educator; b. Bethlehem, Pa., Oct. 6, 1953; s. Alton Dale and Christine (Groh) R.; B.S., Lehigh U., 1975, M.S., 1977, Ph.D., 1979; m. Julie H. Romig. Metallurgist, mem. tech. staff Sandia Nat. Labs., Albuquerque, 1979—; adj. assoc. prof. N.Mex. Inst. Mining and Tech., Socorro, 1981—. Mem. Am. Soc. for Metals (various chpt. offices), AIME, Microbeam Analysis Soc., Meteoritical Soc., Sigma Xi, Tau Beta Pi. Republican. Mem. United Ch. of Christ. Mem. bd. rev. Metallurg. Transactions; contbr. articles to sci. jours. Home: 4923 Calle de Luna NE Albuquerque NM 87111 Office: Sandia Nat Labs Div 1832 Albuquerque NM 87185

ROMIG, THOMAS ALFRED, human resources administrator, educator; b. Chgo., June 12, 1943; s. Alfred F. and Geraldine L. (Charleston) R.; m. Carol Y. Speaks; children—Steve, Laurie. B.A., Allegheny Coll., 1965; M.A. in Personnel Adminstrn., U. Phoenix, 1981. Supr. personnel Westinghouse Electric Corp., 1967-71; mgr. employee relations Quaker Oats Co., 1971-72; div. mgr. Avon Products Inc., Wilmington, Del., 1973-77; mgr. employment, tng. and mgmt. devel. Am. Express Co., Phoenix, 1977-80; exec. dir. human resources devel. and staffing Greyhound Corp., Phoenix, 1980—; prof. personnel mgmt. U. Phoenix. Bd. dirs. Ariz. Alliance Businessman; bd. dirs. S.W. Projects for

Industry; mem. Mayor's Com. for the Handicapped. Served with USAF. Recipient Chgo. Tribute award for outstanding leadership. Mem. Am. Soc. Personnel Adminstrs., Human Resource Planning Soc., Am. Soc. Tng. and Devel., Employee Relocation Council, Phi Gamma Delta. Home: 9638 N 33d St Phoenix AZ 85028 Office: Greyhound Corp 111 W Clarendon Ave Phoenix AZ 85077

ROMINGER, RICHARD ELMER, farmer; b. Woodland, Calif., July 1, 1927; s. Albert H. and Anne (Ehrhardt) R.; B.S. in Plant Sci. summa cum laude, U. Calif., Davis, 1949; m. Mary Evelyne Rowe, Aug. 5, 1951; children—Richard S., Charles A., Ruth E., Bruce J. Mem. Calif. Bd. Food and Agr., Sacramento, 1975-77; dir. Calif. Dept. Food and Agr., 1977-82; mem. Calif. Gov.'s Cabinet, 1977-82; chmn. Yolo County Agrl. Round Table, 1973-75, Yolo County Water Resources Bd., 1971-77; v.p., founding dir. Western Grain Mktg., Inc., 1972-77; dir. Yolo County Farm Bur., 1953-77, pres., 1971-73; mem. U. Calif. Statewide Agrl. Adv. Council, 1970-73, chmn. com. agrl. prodn.; dir. Calif. Farm Bur. Fedn., 1954-55; chmn. Yolo County Agrl. Extension Service Adv. Com., 1973-75; pres. Western Assn. State Depts. Agr., 1981-82, Western U.S. Agrl. Trade Assn., 1982; bd. dirs. Nat. Assn. State Depts. Agr., 1981-82; chmn. Interstate Pest Control Compact, 1981-82, chmn. com. energy, transp., Weights and Measures, 1980-82. Founding bd. dirs. Calif. Farm. Bur. Scholarship Found., 1953-57; bd. dirs. U. Calif. Davis Alumni Assn., 1962-70, chmn. statewide scholarship com., 1965, Jerry Fielder Meml. award, 1978; Winters chpt. treas. Am. Field Service, 1974-77; com. Winters Unified Sch. Dist., 1970-74; trustee, pres. Winters High Sch. Dist., 1956-65; mem. Yolo County Grand Jury, 1955-57; bd. dirs. UN Assn., Davis, 1966-69. Served with USNR, 1945-46. Named Citizen of Yr., Winters Dist. C. of C., 1973; recipient service award U. Calif., Davis, 1972; named Conservation Farmer of Yr., Yolo County Assn. Resource Conservation Dists., 1972. Mem. Rice Growers Assn. Calif. (chmn. statewide adv. com. 1974-75), Westside Canal Assn. (v.p. 1973-77), Grain Growers Assn. Calif. (dir. 1967-77), San Joaquin Valley Hay Growers Assn., Calif. Bean Growers Assn., Calif. Beet Growers Assn., Calif. Ammonia Co., Western Grain Mktg. Assn., Alpha Zeta. Home: Route 1 Box 211B Winters CA 95694

ROMNEY, MARION GEORGE, religious official, lawyer; b. Colonia Juarez, Chihuahua, Mexico (parents Am. citizens), Sept. 19, 1897; s. George Samuel and Artemesia (Redd) R.; grad. Ricks Normal Jr. Coll., 1920; student Brigham Young U., 1924; B.S., U. Utah, 1926, J.D., 1932; m. Ida Olivia Jensen, Sept. 12, 1924; children—Richard J., Janet Ida (dec.), George J. Admitted to Utah bar, 1929; asst. atty. Salt Lake County, 1935; asst. dist. atty. 4th Jud. dist. State Utah, 1937-38; asst. atty. Salt Lake City, 1940; treas. Zions Securities Corp., 1947-59, chmn. exec. com. bd. dirs., 1961-82, dir., 1958-82, chmn. bd., 1975-82; chmn. bd. Beneficial Life Ins. Co., Beneficial Devel. Corp.; dir. Bonneville Internat. Corp., Deseret Mgmt. Missionary, Ch. Jesus Christ of Latter-day Saints, Australia, 1920-23, sec. Australian Mission, pres. New South Wales Conf., 1921-23, bishop 33d Ward, 1935-38, pres. Bonneville Stake, 1938-41, asst. to Council of Twelve Apostles, 1941-51, mem. Council, 1951-72, 2d counselor in 1st presidency, 1972-82, 1st counselor in 1st presidency, 1982—; mng. dir. Gen. Ch. Welfare Com., 1959, chmn., 1959-63, mem. com. on expenditures, 1963—, supr. Latin Am. mission, 1961-68, supr. Scandinavian, West European, South African missions, 1968-71, dir. Asian missions, 1971-72. Rep., Utah State Legislature, 1935-36; adv. welfare div. Utah State Civil Def. Council, 1950. Trustee Brigham Young U., Provo, Utah. Served as pvt. U.S. Army, 1918. Mem. ABA, Order of Coif, Phi Alpha Delta, Phi Kappa Phi. Office: 47 E South Temple St Salt Lake City UT 84111

RONA, JOHN MICHAEL, health care executive; b. Montreal, Que., Can., Dec. 9, 1951; came to U.S., 1953, naturalized, 1958; s. Thomas Paul and Monique Roberta (Noel) R.; B.A., Whitman Coll., 1973; M.H.A., U. Wash., 1977; m. Gail E. Wheeler, June 28, 1975. Asst. to adminstr. Harborview Med. Center, Univ. Wash. Hosps., 1976, asst. adminstr., 1978, asso. adminstr., 1981; asso. adminstr. Va. Mason Med. Center, The Mason Clinic, Seattle, 1981—; clin. asst. prof. U. Wash. Sch. Pub. Health, 19—; staff therapist Mental Health N., Seattle, 1974-75, Walla Walla Mental Health Center, 1973-74; computer operator, lab. asst. 1967-72. Mem. Seattle Area Hosp. Council Tech. Adv. Com. on Emergency Room, 1978, King County Emergency Med. Services Coordinating Council, 1978-79; mem. Seattle Area Hosp. Council Planning Com., 1978-80, rep., 1980-81, others. Recipient Time Mag. C. of C. One of 100 Newsmakers of Tomorrow, 1978. Mem. Am. Coll. Hosp. Adminstrs., Am. Hosp. Assn., Soc. Planners. Christian Ch. Home: 11320 23d St NE Seattle WA 98125 Office: 1100 9th Ave Seattle WA 98111

RONAN, JAMES DOUGLAS, JR., industrial counselor, writer; b. Oroville, Calif., Oct. 29, 1949; s. James Douglas and Dorothy Ben (Corry) R.; m. Penny Cathyren Wilkerson; m. 2d, Karen Lynn Cook; 1 dau., Terra Rhiannon. A.A., Butte Jr. Coll., 1973; B.A. in Psychology with honors, Sonoma State U., 1976, M.A. in Counseling, 1979. Lic. psychiat. technician. Psychiat. technician Sonoma State Hosp., Eldridge, Calif., 1976-79; counselor Sonoma County Office Edn., 1979; rehab. counselor VA, San Francisco, 1979-83; owner, operator FEDVETS, 1983—; coordinator Career Devel. Center, 1981-82; instr. guidance Santa Rosa Jr. Coll., 1979—; instr. San Francisco State U. Extension, 1982-83. Active ERA movement, environ. issues. Served to 1st lt. U.S. Army, 1968-71. Decorated Purple Heart, Bronze Star (2) with V device; recipient Pub. Service award VA Washington, 1983, Spl. Achievement award San Francisco VA, 1982; numerous awards for photography. Mem. Calif. Personnel and Guidance Assn., Am. Soc. Tng. and Devel., Am. Personnel and Guidance Assn. Contbr. articles in field to profl. jours.; photographs pub. various newspapers, mags. Home: 6333 Pacific Suite 111 Stockton CA 95207

RONDELL, THOMAS, executive search and marketing exec.; b. N.Y.C., Sept. 16, 1933; s. Lester and Florence (Robinson) R.; A.B., Bard Coll., 1958; m. Joan Carol Mesirov, Nov. 20, 1966; children—Alexis Sonya, Gabrielle Lee. Asst. dir. public relations Mut. Benefit Life Ins. Co., Newark, 1962-65; regional public relations coordinator J.C. Penney Co., San Francisco, 1965-69; eastern public relations mgr. Eaton Corp., N.Y.C., 1969; public relations dir. Computer Scis., Los Angeles, 1970-72; v.p. Booke and Co., Santa Monica, Calif., 1972-76; v.p. corp. communications Citizens Savs./United Fin. Corp., San Francisco, 1976-80; v.p. pub. relations Bozell & Jacobs, Palo Alto, 1981; pres. Thomas Rondell & Co., mktg. and fin. communications, Palo Alto, 1982—, Sequent Personnel Services, Mountain View, Calif., 1983—. Served with U.S. Army, 1954-56. Mem. Public Relations Soc. Am. (accredited), Nat. Investors Relations Inst. Club: Fremont Hills Country. Home: 253 Tennessee Ln Palo Alto CA 94306

RONDO, PHILLISTINE WARD, education administrator; b. Edmondson, Ark., Mar. 26, 1926; d. Granville William and Bertha Cleveland (Hicks) Ward. B.E. in Elem. Edn., Chgo. Tchrs. Coll., 1965; postgrad. U. Calif.-Riverside, 1965-71; M.S. in Edn., Sch. Adminstn., Calif. State U.-Fullerton, 1975. Cert. tchr., adminstr., Calif. Classroom tchr. Corona-Norco (Calif.) Unified Sch. Dist., 1965-72, prin. Title I summer sch., 1972; Title I resource tchr., 1972-76, Title I coordinator, 1976-77, coordinator elem. edn., 1977-78, elem. prin., 1978-80, adminstrv. asst. instructional services, 1980—; master tchr. edn. dept. Loma Linda U., 1965-72; dir. Corona-Norco Headstart/Presch. Program, 1978-80; speaker at profl. meetings. Past mem. adv. com. Riverside County Family and Children, Dept. Pub. Welfare, Riverside, Calif.; past mem. Calif. PTA; exec. sec. YMCA, Corona-Norco; mem. adv. com. Sch. of Adminstrn., Calif. State U.-Fullerton. Mem NEA, Calif. State U.-Fullerton Alumni Assn., Calif. Assn. for Compensatory Edn., Internat. Reading Assn., Calif. Reading Assn., Calif. Assn. for Tchrs. Other Langs., AAUW (past chmn. women in higher edn. com.), Corona-Norco Mgmt. Assn., Assn. for Supervision and Curriculum Devel., Assn. Calif. Sch. Adminstrs., Western Assn. Adminstrs. of State and Fed. Edn. Programs, Am. Assn. Sch. Adminstrs., Calif. Assn. Tchrs. of English to Speakers of Other Langs., Corona-Norco Tchrs. Assn. (past v.p.), Corona-Norco Edn. Assn. (past pres.), Western Assn. Schs. and Colls. (accreditation team), Western Catholic Edn. Assn. (accreditation team), Phi Kappa Phi, Kappa Delta Pi, Delta Kappa Gamma. Methodist. Club: Soroptimist Internat. (Corona). Author publs. for Corona-Norco Sch. Dist. Office: Corona-Norco Univied Sch Dist 300 Buena Vista Ave Corona CA 91720

RONDON, JOANNE DORIS, conservation consultant, writer, educator; b. Sacramento, June 30, 1943; d. Sam F. and Ruth R. (Moreno) Cemo; children—Kerin, Devin. A.A., Am. River Coll., 1963; student Colo. Women's Coll., 1979-80, Met. State Coll., 1980-81, U. Colo.-Denver, 1978-79. Planning asst. City of Aurora (Colo.), 1974-79; water conservation technician City of Aurora, 1979-81; owner, operator Water Conservation Concepts, Denver, 1981—; mktg. dir. Randall & Blake, Inc., Denver, 1981-83; mem. water workgroup Colo. Front Range Project, 1981, water conservation task force Denver Water Board, 1980-81; mem. faculty U. Colo.-Denver, Community Coll. Denver; speaker; cons. Mem. W. Washington Park Neighborhood Assn. Democrat. Mem. Ch. of Religious Sci. Author: Landscaping for Water Conservation in a Semiarid Environment, 1980; contbr. articles profl. jours.

RONEY, ALICE LORRAINE MANN, poet; b. Hartford, Mich., Dec. 6, 1926; d. Paul Douglass and Margaret Alice (Widener) Mann; A.A., Santa Monica Coll., 1946; B.A., UCLA, 1950; m. Robert Kenneth Roney, Oct. 6, 1951; children—Stephen Paul, Karen Margaret. Tech. writer Hughes Aircraft Co., Culver City, Calif., 1949-52; chmn. Ebell Jr. Blind Recording, Los Angeles, 1959-63; librarian St. Augustine-by-the-Sea Episcopal Day Sch., Santa Monica, Calif., 1961-68; author: Those Treasured Moments, 1972; The Seeds of Love, 1975; Psalms for My Lord, 1975; contbr. to anthologies, 1971—; contbr. poetry to mags., 1972—. Recipient Ebell Jr. Service award, 1959; hon. mentions Major Poets Poetry Contest, 1972. Fellow Internat. Acad. Poets; mem. Centro Studi e Scambi Internazionali, Academia Internazionale Leonardo da Vinci, World, Internat., Calif. State, Ky. State poetry socs., Nat. Fedn. State Poetry Socs., P.E.O., Calif. Fedn. Women's Clubs (creative writing awards poetry div. 1979-83, 1st pl. children's stories div. 1983). Episcopalian (mem. sch. bd. 1964-67, asst. dir. altar guild 1967-69, dir. altar guild 1969-71, treas. Diocese of Los Angeles Churchwomen 1970-73). Club: Santa Monica Bay Woman's (1st v.p. 1980-82, pres. 1982—). Home and Office: 1105 Georgina Ave Santa Monica CA 90402

RONEY, DON JAMES, ins. agy. exec.; b. Fairbury, Nebr., Aug. 13, 1936; s. Clyde H. and Helyn (Cox) R.; B.S. in Commerce, U. Notre Dame, 1958; m. Diane Badovinatz, Mar. 20, 1972; children—Mary Kathleen, Michael, Anne Marie. With Bayly, Martin and Fay-Continental, Salt Lake City, 1959—, spl. rep., 1959-66, v.p., 1966—, sales mgr., 1977—, exec. v.p., 1979—, also dir. Chmn. bd. Community Drug Crisis Center, Salt Lake City, 1970-72. Served to capt. Arty., USAR, 1958-66. Recipient Distinguished Mil. Grad. award U. Notre Dame, 1958, Ted Anerson Meml. award Salt Lake Jaycees, 1973. Mem. Salt Lake Jaycees (pres. 1963, Boss of Year award 1971), Salt Lake Ind. Agts. Assn. (pres. 1972), Utah Ind. Agts. Assn., Profl. Agts. Council Continental Nat. Am., Utah Mfrs. Assn. Roman Catholic. Club: Willow Creek Country. Home: 1817 Northwoodside St Salt Lake City UT 84117 Office: 320 E 400 S Salt Lake City UT 84111

RONEY, MARY CANDACE BELL, public relations executive; b. Evanston, Ill., Aug. 3, 1948; d. Jerome Bonaparte and Frances Frederica (Van Wart) Bell; m. Gerard Francis Roney, June 3, 1972. B.S. with distinction, San Jose State U., 1970, M.P.A., 1980. Asst. editor Calif. Sch. Employees Assn., San Jose, Calif., 1971-76; pub. relations mgr. San Jose Health Ctr., 1976—. Recipient David E. Olsson management excellence award San Jose Health Ctr., 1980. Mem. Women in Communications Inc., Internat. Assn. Bus. Communicators, Am. Hosp. Pub. Relations Assn. Office: 675 E Santa Clara St San Jose CA 95112

RONSMAN, WAYNE JOHN, ins. co. exec.; b. Milw., Jan. 21, 1938; s. Harry Martin and Martha Elizabeth (Popp) R.; student Marquette U., 1955-58, U. San Francisco, 1960-66; m. Joan P. Murphy-Mays, Nov. 30, 1974; children—Allison, Alanna; children by previous marriage—Rosemary, Harry, Martha. Accountant, Otis McAllister & Co., 1960-62; accountant, salesman of data processing Statis. Tabulation Corp., San Francisco, 1962-66; chief accountant, gen. mgr. Dillingham Bros. Ltd., Honolulu, 1966-67; ins. salesman Mut. Benefit Life Ins. Co., 1968-72; v.p. Brenno Assos., Honolulu, 1972—. Mem. Gov's Task Force to Program Correctional Facilities Land, 1970-72; mem. State Bd. Paroles and Pardons, 1972-75; treas. Spl. Edn. Center of Oahu, 1969-78. Served with USMCR, 1958-60. Mem. Nat. Assn. Accountants, Honolulu Assn. Life Underwriters (million dollar round table 1973—), Hawaii (state editor 1970-71, nat. dir. 1972-73), Kailua (pres. 1968-69) Jaycees, Honolulu Bd. Realtors, Anchorage C. of C., Small Bus. Mgmt. Assn., Nat. Assn. Securities Dealers, Kailua C. of C. (pres. 1977-78). Roman Catholic. Home: Eastwind Ct SRA Box 1902 A Anchorage AK 99507 Office: PO Box 336 900 Fort St Mall Suite 200 Honolulu HI 96809

ROOD, ERIC WESTBERG, county ofcl.; b. Chico, Calif., Apr. 23, 1921; s. Vernon Voorhees and Gudrun Elizabeth (Westberg) R.; m. Beatrice Gwendolyn Oates, Nov. 8, 1942; children—Cheryl Lynn, Linda Ann, Karen Suzanne. B.A., Sacramento State Coll., 1951; M.A., George Washington U., 1957; grad. Air Command Staff Coll., 1959, Air War Coll., 1964; postgrad. Harvard Bus. Sch., 1965. Joined U.S. Air Force, 1942, advanced through grades to col., 1964, ret., 1973; supr. Nevada County (Calif.), 1975—, chmn. bd. suprs., 1977-82. Pres. Sierra Econ. Devel. Dist.; chmn. Nevada County Local Agy. Formation Commn.; past pres. Regional Council Rural Counties. Mem. Calif. Assn. Local Agy. Formation Commns. (chmn.). Democrat. Methodist. Home: 10736 Holyrood Ln Grass Valley CA 95945 Office: Courthouse Nevada City CA 95959

ROOD, JOSEPH LLOYD, educator, physicist; b. Oak Park, Ill., May 2, 1922; s. William Lloyd and Helen Elizabeth (Boone) R.; A.B., U. Calif. at Berkeley, 1944, Ph.D., 1948; m. Elizabeth Card, June 11, 1949; children—John, Andrew, Stewart, Catharine. Asst. prof. physics, then asso. prof. U. San Francisco, 1948-56; sect. head research lab. Bausch & Lomb, Inc., Rochester, N.Y., 1956-67; mem. faculty U. Lethbridge, Alta., Can., 1967—, prof. physics, 1969—. Mem. Am. Phys. Soc., Optical Soc. Am. (pres. Rochester sect. 1962-63), Am. Assn. Physics Tchrs., Canadian Assn. Physics, Phi Beta Kappa. Author chpts. in books. Home: PO Box 1569 Fort Macleod AB T0L 0Z0 Canada

ROODMAN-HENRY, SHERRY LYNN, management corporation executive, consultant; b. St. Louis, Feb. 26, 1936; d. William and Opal Jane (Thomas) Harlow; m. Herman J. Roodman, Dec. 5, 1965; 1 dau., Diane Elizabeth; m. 2d, Michael M. Henry, Feb. 26, 1983. B.A., St. Louis U., 1956. Office mgr. Drs. Roodman & Yerger, Scottsdale, Ariz., 1969-73; dir. advt., pub. relations Prescott Valley, Inc., Phoenix, 1973-80; media dir., account exec. McGuinness-Brock Advt., Denver, 1980-81; dir. mktg. Fiesta Inn div. Interwestern Mgmt. Co., Tempe, Ariz., 1981—, asst. mgr., 1983—; cons. advt./pub. relations, 1973—, TV prodn., 1978—. Com. mem. Fiesta Bowl, 1972—, mem. parade steering com., 1972—, parade asst. chmn., 1983, mem. band pageant com., 1982—, children's parade com., 1981—; mem. Ariz. Spl. Olympics Com., 1982—, Phoenix Man and Woman of Year Com., 1983—, Friends of Channel 8, 1982-83. Mem. Ariz. Soc. Assn. Execs. Tempe C. of C. (chmn. tourism com. 1981—), Phoenix and Valley of Sun Conv. Bur. Clubs: Phoenix Ad, Ariz. Country (Phoenix). Home: 5517 E Avalon St Phoenix AZ 85018 Office: Fiesta Inn div Interwestern Mgmt Co 2100 S Priest Dr Tempe AZ 85282

ROONEY, JOHN J., chief justice Wyo. Supreme Ct.; b. 1915; B.A., L.L.B., U. Colo.. Admitted to bar, 1940; now chief justice Wyo. Supreme Ct., Cheyenne.

ROONEY, PAULA MICHELLE, educator; b. Boston, May 24, 1951; d. Paul Joseph and Irene Isabelle (Martin) R. B.A., Framingham State Coll., 1973; M.S., Ind. U., 1975, Ed.D., 1978. Asst. to dean univ. div. Ind. U., Bloomington, 1975-77; dean freshmen Colgate U., Hamilton, N.Y., 1978-81; v.p. student services Reed Coll., Portland, Oreg., 1981—; cons. organizational devel., mgmt. styles, leadership workshops. Bd. dirs. Eastmoreland Gen. Hosp., Portland, Oreg. Contemporary Theater, Portland. Mem. Nat. Assn. Student Personnel Adminstrs. (bd. dirs., dir. small coll. network, adv. bd. region V), Am. Coll. Personnel Assn. (exec. sec. commn. XIV). Office: Reed Coll 3203 SE Woodstock Portland OR 97202

ROONEY, WILLIAM BOYD, broadcasting executive, consultant; b. Martinsburg, W.Va., June 11, 1934; s. William Boyd and Grace Catherine (Wheeler) R.; m. Sandra J. Reimers; m. 2d Janice O. O'Dell. A.B., Shepherd Coll., 1955; M.A., U. Nebr., 1957. With Nebr. ETV Network, 1956-79; gen. mgr., dir. media and instructional services KUAT-AM-FM-TV, Tucson, 1979—; cons. on media to bus., industry. Served to 1st lt. Staff Spl. Corps, U.S. Army, 1957-62. Mem. Pacific Mountain Network (chmn. bd. govs.), Tucson Broadcasters Assn. (bd. dirs.). Producer and/or dir. numerous TV programs, 1956-70. Office: 225 Modern Langs Bldg U Ariz Tucson AZ 85721

ROOP, JOSEPH MCLEOD, economist; b. Montgomery, Ala., Sept. 29, 1941; s. Joseph Ezra and Mae Elizabeth (McLeod) R.; B.S., Central Mo. State U., Warrensburg, 1963; Ph.D., Wash. State U., Pullman, 1973; m. Betty Jane Reed, Sept. 4, 1963; 1 dau., Elizabeth Rachael. Economist, Econ. Research Service, U.S. Dept. Agr., Washington, 1975-79; sr. economist Evans Econs., Inc., Washington, 1979-81; sr. research economist Battelle Pacific N.W. Labs., Richland, Wash., 1981—; instr. dept. econs. Wash. State U., 1969-71. Served with U.S. Army, 1966-68. Dept. Agr. Coop. State Research Service research grantee, 1971-73. Mem. Am. Econ. Assn., Western Econ. Assn., Am. Assn. Agrl. Economists. Home: 715 S Taft St Kennewick WA 99336 Office: PO Box 999 Richland WA 99352

ROOS, ERIC EUGENE, plant physiologist; b. Lock Four, Pa., May 23, 1941; s. Carl F. and Isobel (McPherson) R.; m. Lois Bonita Bruno, Aug. 19, 1964; children—Michael Leslie, Erin Elizabeth. B.S., Waynesburg Coll., 1963; Ph.D., W.Va. U., 1967. Plant physiologist U.S. vegetable seed investigations Dept. Agr. Agrl. Research Service Ft. Collins, Colo., 1967-75, plant physiologist Nat. Seed Storage Lab., Colo. State U., Ft. Collins, 1975—. Mem. Am. Soc. Agronomy, Crop Sci. Soc. Am., Am. Soc. Hort. Sci., Sigma Xi, Gamma Sigma Delta. Office: US Dept Agr Agrl Research Service Nat Seed Storage Lab Fort Collins CO 80523

ROOT, CHARLES NORRIS, safety administrator; b. Corpus Christi, Tex., May 24, 1951; s. Chauncey Norris and Betty Lou (Cartwright) R.; m. Linda Kay Hampton, May 25, 1971. A.S. with distinction, N.Mex. Jr. Coll., 1978; B.B.A. summa cum laude, Coll. Southwest, 1982. Self-employed entertainer, 1969-75; laborer Unichem Internat., Hobbs, N.Mex., 1975-77, asst. plant mgr., 1977-78, safety dir., 1978—. Chmn. Lea County chpt. ARC, program dir. Jr. Achievement Hobbs Inc., 1981; active Students Free Enterprise. Mem. Am. Soc. Safety Engrs. (past pres., treas. SE N.Mex. sect., chmn. 1981), Baptist. Home: 914 W Coal Hobbs NM 88240 Office: 707 N Leech Hobbs NM 88240

ROPER, MORRIS FRANCIS, computer scientist, educator; b. Charleston, S.C., Dec. 10, 1928; s. Morris and Clara (Ellerbe) R.; B.S., W.Va. State Coll., 1952; M.A., Pasadena/Point Loma Coll., 1968; M.A., Claremont U., 1977, Ph.D., 1979; m. Birdie Alexander, Aug. 9, 1952; 1 dau., Andrée. Computing engr. N. Am. Rockwell, Downey, Calif., 1960-63; asst. prof. So. U., Baton Rouge, 1963-64; prof. computer sci. and data processing Pasadena (Calif.) City Coll., 1964—. Served with U.S. Army, 1952-53; Korea. Mem. NEA, AAUP, Calif. Tchrs. Assn., Assn. Computing Machinery, Phi Delta Kappa, Pi Lambda Theta. Roman Catholic. Office: Pasadena City College 1570 E Colorado Blvd Pasadena CA 91106

ROPER, WALTER WILLIAM, grain coop. exec.; b. American Falls, Idaho, Mar. 31, 1945; s. Allen Dwight and Evelyn Ruth (Schneider) R.; B.A. in Journalism, U. Idaho, 1968; m. Patrica Jo Morgan, June 20, 1970; children—Valorie Jo, Jason William, Alison Evon. Part time elevator operator, Power County Grain Growers, American Falls, summers 1963-68, bookkeeper, 1970, asst. mgr., 1971-76, mgr., sec., treas., 1976—; city, county news reporter, Moscow (Idaho) Daily Idahonian, 1968, Rexburg (Idaho) Standard and Jour., 1969, part time Power County Press, American Falls, 1970-71. Co-chmn. Concerned Citizens for Clean Growth, 1977. Mem. Grain Elevator and Processors Soc. (v.p. Intermountain chpt. 1982-83, pres. 1983—), Idaho Feed and Grain Assn. (bd. dirs. Eastern dist. 1982—), Farmers Grain Coop. Mgrs. Orgn. (sec., treas. 1976—). Democrat. Methodist. Clubs: American Falls Toastmasters (sec., treas. 1976-77), Tuesday Nighters Bowling League (pres. 1975-76, 76-77, sec., treas. 1977-78, 78-79). Home: PO Box 90 Sunbeam Rd American Falls ID 83211 Office: 138 Elevator Ave American Falls ID 83211

ROSANDER, ARLYN CUSTER, mathematical statistician, management consultant; b. Mason County, Mich., Oct. 7, 1903; s. John Carl and Nellie May (Palmer) R.; m. Beatrice White, Aug. 26, 1933 (div.); children—Nancy Rosander Peck, Robert Richard Roger (dec.); m. 2d, Margaret Ruth Guest, Aug. 15, 1964. B.S., U. Mich. 1925; M.A., U. Wis., 1928; Ph.D., U. Chgo., 1933; postgrad. Dept. Agr., 1937-39. Research asst. U. Chgo., 1933-34; research fellow Gen. Edn. Bd. Tech. dir. Am. Youth Commn., Balt. and Washington, 1935-37; chief statistician urban study U.S. Bur. Labor Stats., Washington, 1937-39; sect. and br. chief War Prodn. Bd., Washington, 1940-45; chief statistician IRS, Washington, 1945-61; chief math. and stats. sect. ICC, Washington, 1961-69; cons. Pres.'s Commn. on Fed. Stats., Washington, 1970-71; cons., Loveland, Colo.; lectr. stats. George Washington U., 1946-52. Recipient Civilian War Service award War Prodn. Bd., 1945; Spl. Performance award Dept. Treasury, 1961. Fellow AAAS, Am. Soc. Quality Control (25 yr. honor award 1980); mem. Am. Statis. Assn. Author: Elementary Principles of Statistics, 1951; Statistical Quality Control in Tax Operations, IRS, 1958. Home and Office: 4330 N Franklin Ave Loveland CO 80537

ROSASCHI, JAMES PRESCOTT CLEVENGER, librarian; b. Alma, Mich., Apr. 4, 1949; s. True Daniel and Mary Louise (Haas) R.; B.S., Brigham Young U., 1977, M.L.S., 1978; m. Gaylene Reynolds, Aug. 22, 1975; children—Nicole, Daniel, Michelle. Press photographer Petaluma Argus Courier, 1968-69; endl. courseware photographer Boise Interagy.

Fire Ctr., 1973-76; circulation/reference librarian Nampa (Idaho) Pub. Library, 1978-79, library dir., 1979-82; head librarian Petaluma Regional br. Sonoma County Library (Calif.), 1982—. Served with U.S. Army, 1969-72. Mem. ALA, Assn. Rec. Sound Collections, Calif. Library Assn., Pacific N.W. Library Assn. Republican. Mormon. Home: 310 Mountain View Ave Santa Rosa CA 95401 Office: Sonoma County Library 3d and E Sts Santa Rosa CA

ROSBERG, CARL GUSTAF, educator; b. Oakland, Calif., Feb. 28, 1923; s. Carl Gustaf and Ethel (Moore) R.; B.S., Georgetown U., 1948, M.S., 1950; D.Phil., Oxford U., 1954; m. Elizabeth Joanna Wilson, Oct. 23, 1954; children—James Howard, David Nils. Asst. prof., research asso. African Studies program Boston U., 1955-58; vis. asst. prof. U. Calif., Berkeley, 1958-59, asst. prof., 1959-63, asso. prof., 1963-67, prof., 1967—, chmn. dept. polit. sci., 1969-74, dir. Inst. Internat. Studies, 1973—; mem. field staff Rockefeller Found., head dept. polit. sci. U. Coll. Dar-es-Salaam, 1967-69; mem. Adv. Council on African Affairs U.S. Dept. State, 1962-67; cons. Rand Corp., 1964-67. Served with USAAF, 1943-45. Decorated Purple Heart, Air medal. Ford Found. fellow, 1954-55. Mem. Royal African Soc., African Studies Assn. (past pres.). Club: Commonwealth of Calif. Author: (with John Nottingham) The Myth of Mau Mau: Nationalist in Kenya, 1966; (with George Bennett) The Kenyatta Election, 1961; editor: (with James S. Coleman) Political Parties and National Integration in Tropical Africa, 1964; (with William H. Friedland) African Socialism, 1964; (with Thomas Callaghy) Socialism in Sub-Sahara Africa: A New Assessment, 1979; (with Robert M. Price) The Apartheid Regime: Polit. Power and Racial Domination, 1980. Home: 1015 Cragmont Ave Berkeley CA 94708 Office: Dept Polit Sci U Calif Berkeley CA 94720

ROSE, DAVID, printmaker, artist-reporter, educator; b. Malden, Mass., Mar. 10, 1910; s. Isaac and Dora (Susman) R.; m. Ida Claire Shapiro, July 13, 1945 (dec.); children—Marsha Annette, Lisa Joan. B.S. in Art Edn., Mass. Coll. Art, 1934; student Sch. of Mus. Fine Arts, Boston, 1932, Herman Struck, Haifa, 1933, Chouinard Art Inst., Los Angeles, 1938-40, Art. Ctr. Coll. of Design, 1940-42. Exhibited group shows Pa. Acad. Fine Arts, Bklyn. Mus., Los Angeles County Mus. Art, Calif. State Mus., Los Angeles; represented in permanent collections including Skirball Mus., Los Angeles, Israel Mus., Jerusalem, Mus. Modern Art, Haifa; layout artist Walt Disney Studios, 1936-40; art. dir. Erwin Wasey, advt. agy., Los Angeles, from 1945, then Mogge-Privett, advt. agy., Los Angeles, Cunningham & Walsh, advt. agy., Los Angeles, until 1957; art dir. film and TV, Warner Bros., Burbank, Calif., Universal Pictures, Burbank, KCEF Community TV; graphic designer, illustrator-court room sketch artist NBC, Burbank; ind. artist-reporter, court trials and news events for TV, newspapers and mags. including Cable Network News, ABC World News, NBC Nightly News, Newsweek, Los Angeles Herald Examiner, Palm Springs Desert Sun, Detroit News, Cleve. Press, Jerusalem Post; mem. faculty continuing edn. dept. Otis Art Inst., Parsons Sch. Design; lectr. various univs. and art socs. Mem. graphic arts council Los Angeles County Mus. Art; mem. art com. Jewish Fedn. Council, Los Angeles. Served with Signal Corps, U.S. Army, 1943-45. Recipient award Army Pictorial Service, 1945; 2 medals Art Dirs. Club, Los Angeles; others. Mem. Artists Equity Assn., Artists for Edn., Soc. Illustrators.

ROSE, DAVID WILLIAM, psychologist, researcher; b. Denver, Oct. 14, 1930; s. Clarence William and Marjorie (Skiff) R.; m. Ruth MacDonald, Dec. 27, 1957; m. 2d Loretta Espinoza, Oct. 5, 1973; children—Scott D., Fred W., Catharine J., Janet K. B.A., U. Colo., Boulder, 1953; M.S., U. Oreg., 1959, Ph.D., 1964. Lic. psychologist, Colo. With Colo. State Hosp., Pueblo, 1963—, program evaluator Colo. State Hosp., 1978-81, clin. psychologist Inst. Forensic Psychology, 1981—; cons. in field. Bd. dirs. Pueblo ACLU, Colo. ACLU. Served with U.S. Army, 1953-55. Mem. Am. Psychol. Assn., Am. Law-Psychology Soc., Nat. Council on Crime and Delinquency, Orgn. Program Evaluators in Colo., Rocky Mountain Psychol. Soc. Democrat. Author: (with other) CCAR Users Guide, 1980; (with Nancy Z. Wilson) Treatment and Security, 1981; evaluation research. Home: 627 Westacres St Pueblo CO 81005 Office: 1600 W 24th St Pueblo CO 81003

ROSE, DONALD STANLEY, safety and industrial hygiene analyst; b. Nyack, N.Y., Oct. 24, 1934; s. Arthur Ellis and Madeline Delaphine (Muise) R.; m. Mary Alice Bottini, July 17, 1955; children—Veronica Anne, Donna Marie, Dena Ellis; m. 2d, Patricia Ann Yurkovic, Sept. 2, 1978. Student NYU, 1957, Riverside City Coll., 1960, Los Angeles Valley Coll., 1961-64; B.S. in Pub. Adminstrn., St. Ambrose Coll., Davenport, Iowa, 1968; postgrad. Calif. State Poly. U., Pomona, 1974, U. So. Calif., 1974, Orange Coast Coll., 1979-82. Cert. occupational hearing conservationist. Trooper N.Y. State Police, 1954-60; sgt. Burbank Police Dept. (Calif.), 1960-68; chief of police City of Reedley (Calif.), 1968-74; safety adminstr. ITT Gilfillan, Van Nuys, Calif., 1975-79; safety and indsl. hygiene analyst, Santa Ana, Calif., 1979—. Mem. Am. Soc. Safety Engrs., Nat. Safety Mgmt. Soc., Pub. Agy. Safety Mgmt. Assn. Office: 20 Civic Ctr Plaza Santa Ana CA 92701

ROSE, ELAINE, psychotherapist, psychoanalyst; b. Milw., Apr. 14; d. Harry Carl and Sara Mendelsohn; B.A., Calif. State U., Northridge, 1968, M.S.W., U. So. Calif., 1970; children—Steven, Susan, Kenneth. Music tchr., music therapist, Sherman Oaks, Calif., 1963-68; social work intern VA Hosp., Sepulveda, Calif., 1969-70; clin. social worker Olive View Med. Center, Sylmar, Calif., 1970-74; crisis clin. coordinator Cedars-Sinai Med. Center, Thalians Community Mental Health Center, Los Angeles, 1974-76; pvt. practice specializing in psychotherapy, Sherman Oaks, 1972-80; cons. mental health Los Angeles County Probation Dept., 1974-75, Los Angeles City Schs., 1973—, Los Angeles County Regional Mental Health Services, 1974—; pvt. practice psychotherapy and psychoanalysis, Beverly Hills, Calif., 1979—; clin. supr. Cedars-Sinai Med. Center, Los Angeles, 1976—; Wright Inst., Los Angeles, 1979—. Mem. United Way Planning Council, 1974-76, S.Forum Task Force for Counseling and Community Coordinating Services, 1975-77. Lic. clin. social worker, Calif. Mem. Acad. Cert. Social Workers, Nat. Registry Health Care Providers, Nat. Assn. Social Workers, Calif. Soc. Clin. Social Work, Los Angeles Group Psychotherapy Soc., Los Angeles Inst. Psychoanalytic Studies. Author: Redefining and Preventing Mental Health Emergencies in the Schools., 1976; contbr. articles to profl. publs. Office: 360 N Bedford Dr Beverly Hills CA 90210

ROSE, KELLY ALLYN, accountant; b. San Jose, Calif. May 20, 1945; s. Leslie J. and Mary A. (Young) R.; m. Linda Jeanne Tuley, Nov. 28, 1975. Student U. B.C. (Can.), Vancouver, 1963-65, U. Nev.-Las Vegas, 1968; B.S. summa cum laude, Calif. State U.-Fresno, 1970; postgrad. Stanford U., 1970-71. C.P.A., Calif., Ohio, other states. Staff supr. Ernst & Whinney, San Jose, Calif., 1971-77, mgr. nat. hdqrs., Cleve., 1977-80, ptnr., regional dir. client services western hdqrs., Los Angeles, 1980—. Mem. fund raising com. San Jose Symphony, 1975-77; treas. San Jose Jaycees, 1976-77. Served with USAF, 1965-68; Vietnam. Decorated Bronze Star. Mem. Am. Inst. C.P.A.s, Calif. Soc. C.P.A.s, Ohio Soc. C.P.A.s, Am. Mktg. Assn. (publicity and program dir. 1979-80), Am. Mgmt. Assn., Planning Execs. Inst., Am. Legion, VFW (chpt. treas. 1968-69), Phi Beta Kappa, Beta Gamma Sigma, Beta Alpha Psi. Clubs: Jonathan, Cleve. Athletic. Home: 602 N Kenter Ave Los Angeles CA 90049 Office: 2700 Arco Tower 515 S Flower St Los Angeles CA 90071

ROSE, RICHARD ELGAR, control system engr.; b. Seattle, Apr. 14, 1936; s. John Ernest and Mildred Elgar (Crump) R.; B.S., Purdue U., 1958; M.S., U. Iowa, 1961, Ph.D., 1967; m. Anne Lydia Bratton, Aug. 26, 1961; children—Bruce Douglas, Thomas Richard. Instr., U. Iowa, 1961-63; with TRW Inc., Systems and Energy Group, Redondo Beach, Calif., 1963—, subsystem engr. for attitude control High Energy Astronomy Obs., 1974-77, attitude control subproject mgr. Internat. Solar Polar Mission, sr. staff, control and sensor systems lab. 1977—; lectr. on mechanics and dynamics U. So. Calif. Coach and referee Am. Youth Soccer Orgn. So. Calif.; asst. scoutmaster Troop 849, Los Angeles council Boy Scouts Am. Recipient Group Achievement award NASA, 1967, 79; NSF grantee, 1965-67; registered profl. engr., Calif. Mem. AIAA, Sigma Xi. Contbr. articles on optimal control and spacecraft control system design and performance to profl. jours. Office: TRW One Space Park Redondo Beach CA 90278

ROSE, ROBERT LEONARD, newspaperman; b. Detroit, Apr. 21, 1924; s. Leonard Cecil and Mildred Ernestine (Brothers) R.; student U. Colo., 1941-42, Drexel Inst. Tech., 1942-43, U. Del., 1943, U. Denver, 1947; m. Beverly Bain McKee, Aug. 1, 1947 (dec. Sept. 1978); 1 son, Michael; m. 2d, Lu Neill, Aug. 30, 1980. Reporter, Daily Plainsman, Huron, S.D., 1947-49; bur. mgr. U.P., St. Paul-Mpls., 1949-53, Des Moines, 1953-56; reporter-rewriteman, asst. city editor Chgo. Daily News, 1956-60, 1st asst. editor, 1961-63, city editor, 1964-66, West Coast bur. chief, 1966-78; polit. editor Spokane Spokesman-Rev., 1979-80, asso. editor, 1980, city editor, 1981-82, Wash. bur. chief, 1983—; bd. dirs. City News Bur., Chgo., Ill. Served with AUS, 1942-46. Mem. Sigma Chi. Episcopalian. Clubs: Masons, Shriners, Elks; Press, LaSalle St. Rod and Gun (Chgo.). Office: Spokesman-Review & Chronicle Spokane WA 99210

ROSE, ROBERT R., JR., justice Wyo. Supreme Ct.; b. Evanston, Ill., Nov. 1, 1915; s. Robert R. and Eleanor B. Rose; LL.B., Wyo. U., 1941; m. Kathryn W. Rose, June 14, 1948; children—Robert R. III, Cynthia Ann. Admitted to Wyo. bar, fed. ct. bars; sr. asso. firm Rose, Spence, Dobos and Duncan; with UNRRA; mem. Wyo. Ho. of Reps., 1949-51; mayor City of Casper (Wyo.), 1950-51; asst. sec. interior, 1951-52; legal counsel Casper Community Coll. Dist.; chmn. bd., pres. Title Guaranty Co. Wyo.; dir. Natrona County Abstract Co., Cheyenne (Wyo.) Abstract & Title Co., Hot Springs (Ark.) Abstract & Title Co., Shoshone Title Ins. Co.; dir. subs. corps. Title Guaranty Co. Wyo.; justice Supreme Ct. Wyo., 1975—, chief justice, 1981-82; mem. faculty Western Trial Advocacy Inst., U. Wyo. Chmn. Casper Community Chest Drive; Wyo. State Drive chmn. Am. Cancer Soc.; trustee, pres. bd. Casper Coll. Served with USAAF, World War II. Mem. Am. Law Inst., Nat. Coll. Criminal Def. Lawyers (faculty), Am. Judicature Soc., Am. Bar Assn., Wyo. State Bar, Casper C. of C. (past dir.). Episcopalian. Office: PO Box 1006 Cheyenne WY 82001

ROSE, SANFORD SAMUEL, equipment corp. exec.; b. Seattle, Feb. 10, 1938; s. Alec Julius and Brangie (Goodman) R.; B.A. in Mktg., U. Wash., 1960; m. Paula Jean Sussman, Nov. 19, 1963; children—Alisa, Michael, Megan. Salesman, Leed's, Seattle, 1957-58, Iden's Men's Store, Seattle, 1959-60; mgr. Roxbury Furniture, Seattle, 1961-67; pres. Equipment Importers, Inc., Tacoma, Wash., 1967—; dir. Gen. Metals of Tacoma. Bd. dirs., council of ops. Hertzl-Ner Tamid; pres. Sibleywood Assn., 1966. Served to lt. U.S. Army, 1960-61. Mem. Constrn. Industry Mfrs. Assn., Am. Rental Assn., Splty. Tools and Fasteners Distbrs. Assn., Nat. Tire Dealers Retreaders Assn., Asso. Equipment Distbrs., Material Handling Equipment Distbrs. Assn., World Trade Center, Am. Importers Assn., Motor and Equipment Mfrs. Assn., Seattle Symphony Assn., Seattle Art Mus., Bellevue Art Mus., Jewish Family Service. Jewish. Clubs: Central Park Tennis, Jewish Community Center Health. Office: Equipment Importers Inc 1901 Jefferson St Tacoma WA 98402

ROSEHNAL, MARY ANN, educational administrator; b. Bklyn., July 25, 1943; d. Frank Joseph and Mary Anna (Corso) R.; 1 son, Scott Stoddart. B.A. in Sociology, San Francisco State U., 1968; postgrad. Sch. Bus. Adminstrn., No. Ariz. U., 1975—. Lic. substitute tchr., Ariz.; lic. vocat. nurse, Calif. Deliquency counselor, Calif., 1969-73; office mgr. Nurses Central Registry, Sun City, Ariz., 1973-75; bus. mgr. Nadaburg sch. dist., Wittmann, Ariz., 1975-78, Morristown (Ariz.) sch. dist., 1978—; served on 1st Assessment Handbook editing task force, Fair Employment Practices Handbook task force, 1979-80. Clk. Morristown sch. bd., 1975-76; pres. Morristown PTA, 1977-78; sec. Wickenburg area bd., 1979; bd. dirs. Future Frontiers, 1979-81; rep. HUD block grant adv. com., 1979—. Mem. Ariz. Assn. Sch. Bus. Ofcls., Assn. Sch. Bus. Ofcls. U.S. and Can., Assn. Govt. Accts. Roman Catholic. Columnist Wickenburg Sun, 1975—. Office: PO Box 98 Morristown AZ 85342

ROSEN, ALVIN L., business executive; b. Bklyn., May 29, 1931; s. Charles and Elizabeth Rosen; m. Barbara Spector, Aug. 29, 1954 (div.); 1 dau., Norma Sue. B.B.A., CCNY Sch. Bus. and Civic Adminstrn., 1953. Personnel asst. Emerson Radio & Phonograph, Jersey City, 1953-54; asst. personnel mgr. Lightolier Inc., Elizabeth, N.J., 1954-56; prodn. control mgr. Marvin Electric, Los Angeles, 1956-59; prodn. mgr. Dorner Products, Los Angeles, 1959-61; propr. Rosen Lighting Co., 1961-63; pres., chmn. bd. Vanguard Pacific Inc., Santa Monica, Calif., 1962—; v.p., dir. Vanguard Pacific MetalBuilders Inc.; pres., dir. R.R. Distbrs. Inc. Democrat. Office: 1655 9th St Santa Monica CA 90404

ROSEN, BERNARD, engineering executive; b. Bklyn., Mar. 21, 1927; s. Hyman and F. (Kasofsky) R.; m. Janice Raskin, July 8, 1951; children—Steven, Stuart, Roberta-Sue. B.E.E., CCNY, 1951; M.E.E., Poly. Inst. N.Y., 1957. Registered profl. engr., N.Y. Gen. mgr. equipment dept. Polarad Electronics, N.Y.C., 1951-62; v.p. Probescope, Syosset, N.Y., 1962-64; mgr. Prodn. Systems div. Watkins-Joynson Co., Palo Alto, Calif., 1964-67, v.p., mgr. Recon div., San Jose, Calif., 1967—. Served with USNR, 1944-46. Mem. IEEE, Old Crows. Home: 1200 Patlen Dr Los Altos CA 94022 Office: 2525 N 1st St San Jose CA 94022

ROSEN, BERNARD, electronics company executive; b. N.Y.C., Mar. 2, 1927; s. H. and F. (Rosen) R.; m. Janice Raskin, Nov. 21, 1929; children—Steven, Stuart, Roberta. B.E.E., CCNY, 1950; M.E.E., Poly. Inst. N.Y., 1957. Registered profl. engr., N.Y. Gen. mgr. Polarad Electronics, N.Y.C., 1950-61; v.p. Probescope, Syosset, N.Y., 1961-63; v.p., mgr. Recon div. Watkins-Johnson Co., San Jose, Calif., 1964—. Mem. exec. bd. Santa Clara Jr. Achievement. Served with USN, 1945-46. Mem. IEEE, Tau Beta Pi, Etta Kappa Nu, Sigma Xi. Office: Recon Div Watkins Johnson Co 2525 N 1st St San Jose CA 95131

ROSEN, CATHERINE PICARD, lawyer; b. Manhattan, N.Y.C., Jan. 8, 1940; d. Jean Jacques and Maria (Roth) P.; m. Sanford Jay Rosen, June 22, 1958; children—Caren Emma, R. Durelle, Ian D., Melissa S. Student Vassar Coll., 1957-58, Cornell U., 1958-59; B.A., Conn. Coll., 1961; postgrad Yale Law Sch., 1961-62; J.D., U. Md., 1969. Bar: Tex. 1971, Calif. 1974. Assoc. Heller, Ehrman White & McAuliffe, San Francisco, 1975—. Mem. ABA, Calif. Women Lawyers, ACLU, San Francisco Bar Assn. Office: 44 Montgomery St San Francisco CA 94104

ROSEN, HERBERT IRVING, company executive; b. Seattle, Mar. 1, 1922; s. Albert and Bessie (Roffe) R.; m. Rita Ruth Feverberg, Feb. 8, 1947; children—Stanley Gene, Judith Patricia Rosen de Jonge. B.A., U. Wash., 1943. Sec., dir. Durabilt Luggage Mfg. Co., Seattle, 1946-58; pres., chmn. bd. Consol. Distbrs., Inc., Seattle, 1958-67; pres. and chmn. bd. Skipper's, Inc., Bellevue, Wash., 1969-72, chmn. bd., 1972—; dir. Manus Services. Pres. Jewish Community Ctr., 1971-72; pres. Jewish Fedn. Greater Seattle, 1974-75; bd. dirs., mem. exec. com. United Way King County, 1976-78, Wash., 1979—; mem. Gov.'s Adv. Bd., The Sounding Bd., 1982. Served to 1st lt. USCG, 1943-46. Republican. Jewish. Office: 14450 NE 29th Pl Bellevue WA 98007

ROSEN, MARTIN JACK, lawyer; b. Los Angeles, Sept. 9, 1931; s. Irving and Sylvia (Savad) R.; B.A., UCLA, 1953; J.D., U. Calif.-Berkeley, 1956; m. Joan D. Meyersieck, Oct. 22, 1954; children—Dirk Rosen, Marika. Bar: Calif. 1957. Sole practice, Merced, Calif., 1960-62, San Francisco, 1962-82; mem. Silver, Rosen, Fischer & Stecher, P.C., San Francisco, 1964—. Pres. Trust for Pub. Land, 1979—. Served with USAF, 1958-60. Fellow internat. legal studies U. Calif. Law Sch./Inst. Social Studies, The Hague, 1956-57. Mem. Motor Carrier Lawyers Assn. (trustee found.), Calif. Bar Assn., ABA, Assn. ICC, Conf. Calif. Pub. Utility Counsel.

ROSEN, STANLEY, political scientist, educator; b. Bklyn., June 15, 1942; s. Al and Frances (Manowitz) R. A.B., U. N.C., 1963; M.A., UCLA, 1970, Ph.D., 1979. Vis. lectr. dept. govt. and pub. adminstrn. United Coll., Chinese U. Hong Kong, 1971-73, 75-76; lectr. dept. polit. sci. U. Calif.-San Diego, 1978-79; asst. prof. dept. polit. sci. U. So. Calif., Los Angeles, 1979—. Contbr. articles to profl. publs. Mem. Am. Polit. Sci. Assn., Assn. Asian Studies. Home: 2174 Dudley St Pasadena CA 91104 Office: U So Calif Dept Polit Sci Los Angeles CA 90089

ROSENAU, JAMES NATHAN, political science educator; b. Phila., Nov. 25, 1924; s. Walter Nathan and Fanny Fox (Baum) R; m. Norah Rosenau, Aug. 5, 1955 (dec.); 1 dau., Heidi. A.B., Bard Coll., 1948; A.M., Johns Hopkins U., 1949; Ph.D., Princeton U., 1957. Instr. polit. sci. Douglass Coll., Rutgers U., New Brunswick, N.J., 1949-54, asst. prof., 1954-60, assoc. prof., 1960-62, prof., 1962-70, acting chmn. dept., 1963-64, chmn., 1968-70; prof. polit. sci. Ohio State U., Columbus, 1970-73; sr. fellow Ctr. Internat. and Strategic Affairs, UCLA, 1979—; prof. internat. relations and polit. sci., dir. inst. studies U. So. Calif., 1973—. Lectr., Internat. Communications Agy.; prin. investigator Fgn. Policy Leadership Project (NSF). Trustee, Bard Coll. Served in U.S. Army, 1943-46. Grantee NSF, of Edn., Kettering Found. Mem. Internat. Studies Assn. (pres.-elect 1983-84), Am. Polit. Sci. Assn., World Assn. Internat. Relations. Author: Public Opinion and Foreign Policy, 1961; National Leadership and Foreign Policy, 1963; The Adaptation of National Society, 1970; Citizenship Between Elections, 1974; The Dramas of Political Life, 1980; The Study of Global Interdependence, 1980; The Scientific Study of Foreign Policy, 1980; The Study of Political Adaptation, 1981; editor: International Aspects of Civil Strife, 1964; Domestic Sources of Foreign Policy, 1967; Linkage Politics, 1969; (with Klaus Knorr) Contending Approaches to International Politics, 1969; International Politics and Foreign Policy, 1969. Home: 1700 San Remo Dr Pacific Palisades CA 90272 Office: VKC 300 Univ So Calif Los Angeles CA 90089

ROSENBAUM, MORTIMER, retired engineer, lawyer; s. Samuel and Dora (Weisman) R.; m. Lorraine Schiller, Feb. 12, 1938; children—Janice Lee Dowling, Phillip Russell. B.S., MIT, 1935; J.D., U. San Diego, 1973. Bar: Calif. 1973. Engr. Consol. Vultee Aircraft Corp., San Diego, 1936-48; project engr. Gen. Dynamics-Convair, San Diego, 1948-58; v.p. Gen. Dynamics-Astronautics, San Diego, 1958-65; sole practice law, San Diego, 1974—. Commr. San Diego Pub. Library; pres. Jewish Family Service San Diego, Beth Israel Cemetery and Mausoleum Assn. Fellow AIAA. Clubs: Stardust, Space Pioneers. Home and Office: 2104 Willow St San Diego CA 92106

ROSENBERG, DAN YALE, plant pathologist; b. Stockton, Calif., Jan. 8, 1922; s. Meyer and Bertha (Naliboff) R.; A.A., Stockton Jr. Coll., 1942; A.B., Coll. Pacific, 1949; M.S., U. Calif. at Davis, 1952; m. Marilyn Kohn, Dec. 5, 1954; 1 son, Morton Karl. Jr. plant pathologist Calif. Dept. Agr., Riverside, 1952-55, asst. plant pathologist, 1955-59, asso. plant pathologist, 1959-60, pathologist IV, 1960-63, program supr., 1963-71, chief exclusion and detection, div. plant industry, 1971-76, spl. asst. div. plant industry, 1976—; pres. Health, Inc., 1972-73; cons. in field; dir. Health Inc., Sacramento, 1967, pres., 1971-72, 79-81, 81-83. Served with AUS, 1942-46; ETO. Mem. Am. Phytopath. Soc. (fgn. and regulatory com. 1975—, grape diseases sect. 1977-79, grape pests sect. 1979-82), Calif. State Employees Assn. (pres. 1967-69). Contbr. articles to profl. jours. Home: 2328 Swarthmore Dr Sacramento CA 95825 Office: 1220 N St Sacramento CA 95814

ROSENBERG, JEROME SAM, developer, gen. contractor; b. Los Angeles, Nov. 7, 1932; s. Max and Betty Rosenberg; m. Lynn Brown, Mar. 14, 1981; children by previous marriage—Steve, Debra. Pres., propr. Jero, Inc., Venice, Calif., 1977—; developer Aspen Hill, Denver. Mem. Nat. Assn. Home Builders (chmn. subcom.). Jewish. Office: Jero Inc 723 Ocean Front Walk Venice CA 90291

ROSENBERG, RICHARD MORRIS, banker; b. Fall River, Mass., Apr. 21, 1930; s. Charles and Betty (Peck) R.; m. Barbara K. Cohen, Oct. 21, 1956; children—Michael, Peter. B.S., Suffolk U., 1952; M.B.A., Golden Gate Coll., 1962, LL.B., 1962. Publicity asst. Crocker-Anglo Bank, San Francisco, 1959-62; banking services officer Wells Fargo Bank, N.A., San Francisco, 1962-65, asst. v.p., 1965-69, v.p. mktg. dept., 1968, v.p., dir. mktg., 1969, sr. v.p. mktg. and advt. div., 1970-75, exec. v.p., 1975-80, vice chmn. bd., 1980—; vice chmn. bd. Wells Fargo & Co.; dir. Saga Corp., Mastercard Internat., Inc., Sonoma Vineyards. Dir. Marin Ecumenical Assn. for Housing. Served to lt. USNR, 1953-59; comdr. Res. Mem. Western States Bankcard Assn. (dir.), Am. Bankers Assn. (dir.), Bank Mktg. Assn. (dir., pres. 1982-83), State Bar Calif. Jewish. Clubs: San Francisco Press, World Trade. Office: PO Box 54500 TA Los Angeles CA 90054

ROSENBERG, SANDERS DAVID, rocket propulsion scientist; b. N.Y.C., Dec. 21, 1926; s. Philip and Rose (Levine) R.; m. Rita Strauss, June 30, 1946; children—Nathan L., Robert B. A.B., Middlebury Coll., 19; Ph.D., Iowa State U., 1952. With Aerojet TechSystems Co., Sacramento, 1958—, chief scientist, 1982—. Served with USN, 1943-46. Mem. AIAA. Home: 628 Commons Dr Sacramento CA 95825

ROSENBERG, SYDNEY JULIAN, building maintenance company executive; b. San Francisco, Oct. 3, 1914; s. Morris and Gussie (Kaufman) R.; m. Jaclyn Barde, Mar. 22, 1968; children—Brad, Jill Hughes, Todd, Gregg Cobarr, Glenn Cobarr. B.A., Stanford U., 1936; M.B.A., Harvard U., 1938. Pres., chief exec. officer Am. Bldg. Maintenance Industries, Los Angeles, 1938—; dir. Craig Corp. Trustee, past pres. Jewish Big Bros. Assn., Los Angeles; benefactor Los Angeles Music Ctr. Mem. Chief Exec. Forum, Urban Land Inst., World Bus. Council. Republican. Jewish. Clubs: Hillcrest Country (Los Angeles), Big Canyon Country (Newport). Home: 1155 Shadow Hill Way Beverly Hills CA 90210 Office: Am Bldg Maintenance Industries 9831 W Pico Blvd Los Angeles CA 90035

ROSENBLATT, CAROLYN LOUISE, lawyer; b. Los Angeles, Feb. 15, 1948; B.S. in Nursing, U. San Francisco, 1971, J.D., 1978. Admitted to Calif. bar, 1978; community health researcher Vis. Nurse Assn. of San Francisco, 1974-76; public health nurse Health Conservation, San Francisco, 1976-79; asso. firm Sullivan, Graham and Camp, San Francisco, 1980-82, Marvin I. Barish, San Francisco, 1982—. Mem. San Francisco Big Sisters, 1974—. Mem. ABA, Calif. Bar Assn., San Francisco Bar Assn., San Francisco Trial Lawyers Assn., Sigma Theta Tau. Home: 65 Sonora Way Corte Madera CA 94925 Office: Four Embarcadero Center Suite 2410 San Francisco CA 94111

ROSENBLATT, MURRAY, mathematics educator; b. N.Y.C., Sept. 7, 1926; s. Hyman and Esther (Goldberg) R.; B.S., CCNY, 1946; M.S., Cornell U., 1947, Ph.D., 1949; m. Adylin Lipson: children—Karen, Daniel. Asst. prof. statistics U. Chgo., 1950-55; assoc. prof. math. Ind. U., 1956-59; prof. applied math. Brown U., 1959-64; prof. math. U. Calif.-San Diego, 1964—; vis. fellow Australian Nat. U., 1976, 79, Univ. and Imperials colls., 1972; overseas fellow Churchill Coll., 1979; Wald lectr., 1970. Guggenheim fellow, 1965-66, 71-72. Mem. Am. Math. Soc., Inst. Math. Stats., Soc. Indsl. and Applied Math. Editor: Studies in Probability Theory, 1978, Random Processes, 1974, Markov Processes, Structure and Asymptotic Behavior, 1971, Statistical Models and Turbulence, 1971, Time Series Analysis, 1963, Statistical Analysis of Stationary Time Series, 1957. Home: 7734 Esterel Dr La Jolla CA 92037 Office: Dept Math Univ Calif San Diego La Jolla CA 92092

ROSENBLATT, NED K., advertising executive, publisher; b. Salt Lake City, Mar. 29, 1917; s. Gurard B. and Elsie (Klein) R.; children—Marie Eloise, Suzanne, Carolyn, Robert G., Edwin J., Theodore. B.A. in Graphic Arts, Stanford U., 1935. Advt. mgr. Westinghouse Elec. Supply Co., Seattle, 1939-40, Brown-Bevis Equipment Co., Los Angeles, 1946-48; advt. and credit mgr. Shepherd Machinery Co., Los Angeles, 1948-54; owner Ned K. Rosenblatt Advt., pub. Aerial Applicator mag. and Engring. Contractors mag., 1954—. Served to maj. Adj. Gen. Dept., U.S. Army, 1941-45. Decorated Bronze Star. Republican. Office: 9836 Jersey Santa Fe Springs CA 90670

ROSENBLUM, DALE MARK, podiatrist; b. Akron, Ohio, Aug. 1, 1947; s. Irvin Robert and Frances (Taras) R.; student U. Akron, 1965-67; D.P.M., Ohio Coll. Podiatric Medicine, 1971; 2 daus., Rachel Jana, Reegen Narissa. Postgrad. tng. assoc. Calif. Coll. Podiatric Medicine, San Francisco, 1971-72; chief podiatry, mem. surg. com. Riverview Hosp., Santa Ana, Calif., 1977—; mem. credentials com., chmn. podiatric medicine div. med. staff, podiatric residency edn. com. Good Samaritan Hosp., Anaheim, Calif., 1977—; mem. attending staff So. Calif. Podiatric Med Center, Los Angeles, 1978—; mem. clin. staff Baja Foot Center, Mexacali, Mexico, 1978—. Mem. Pub. Edn. and Info. Com., 1979; chmn. Foot Health Week, 1978, 79; active March of Dimes Walkathon, Civic Foot Health Screenings. Fellow Am. Coll. Foot Orthopedists; mem. Am. Podiatry Assn., Am. Assn. Hosp. Podiatrists, Acad. Ambulatory Foot Surgery, Am. Coll. Foot Surgeons, Calif. Podiatry Assn., Orange County Podiatry Assn. Democrat. Jewish. Club: Toastmasters Internat. Office: 504 W Commonwealth St Fullerton CA 92632

ROSENBLUM, HERSCHEL HAROLD, podiatrist; b. Detroit, Mar. 13, 1936; s. Robert B. and Mary R.; B.S., Calif. Coll. Podiatric Medicine, 1959, D.P.M., 1962; m. Elisabeth Hermanson, Feb. 14, 1965; children—Wendy, Darren, Matthew. Practice podiatry, Los Angeles, 1962-65, Glendale, Calif., 1965—. Pres., Ben Schwartz chpt. City of Hope, 1970-71. Mem. Western Foot Surgery Assn. (pres. 1971-72), Am. Coll. Foot Orthopedists (pres. Western div. 1981—), Am. Podiatry Assn., Calif. Podiatry Assn., Los Angeles County Podiatric Assn. Home: 2655 Risa Dr Glendale CA 91208 Office: 535 N Brand Blvd Suite 406 Glendale CA 91203

ROSENBLUM, RICHARD MARK, engring. mgr.; b. N.Y.C., Apr. 28, 1950; s. Victor Sigmund and Julia (Kessler) R.; B.S., M.S., Rensselaer Poly. Inst., Troy, N.Y., 1972-73; m. Michele E. Cartier, Aug. 30, 1979; children—Gialisa, Jeremy Scott. Startup engr. Combustion Engring. Inc., Windsor, Conn., 1973-78; engr. So. Calif. Edison Co., Rosemead, 1978—, plant start-up supr. San Onofre Nuclear Generating Sta., 1978-82, project mgr., 1982-83, tech. mgr., 1983—. N.Y. State Regents scholar, 1968-73; registered profl. engr., Calif. Mem. Am. Nuclear Soc. (STD com.). Office: 2244 Walnut Grove Rosemead CA 91770

ROSENCRANZ, ARMIN DAVID, foundation director, lawyer; b. N.Y.C., Jan. 2, 1937; s. Oscar and Pauline (Brown) R.; m. Roberta Ann Engelmann, 1976; children—Jesse, Noel. A.B., Princeton U., 1958; J.D., Stanford U., 1962, M.A., 1963, Ph.D. in Polit. Sci., 1970. Bar: U.S. Supreme Ct. Assoc. Marshall Kaplan, Gans & Kahn, San Francisco, 1970-72; staff atty., social scientist Childhood and Govt. Project, U. Calif.-Berkeley Sch. Law, 1973-76; writer Holt Rinehart & Winston, N.Y.C., 1977-78; dir. German Marshall Fund Study Transboundary Air Pollution, Environ. Law Inst., Washington, 1979-80; exec. dir. Pioneer Fund, Inverness, Calif., 1980—. Trustee Stanford U., 1974-78. Congl. fellow, 1966; NEH fellow, 1974. Mem. Am. Polit. Sci. Assn. Democrat. Jewish. Author: Lawyers in the House of Commons, 1970; (with J. Kirby) Congress and the Public Trust, 1970; (with J. Chapin) American Government, 2d edit., 1982; (with G. Wetstone) Acid Rain in Europe and North America. Address: PO Box 33 Inverness CA 94937

ROSENCWAIG, ALLAN, physicist; b. Starachowitze, Poland, Jan. 1, 1941; came to U.S., 1969, naturalized, 1976; s. Samuel and Bina R.; B.A.Sc., U. Toronto, 1963, M.A., 1965, Ph.D., 1969; m. Joan L. Adams, June 4, 1974; children—Elaina, Amanda, David; children by previous marriage—Devra, Samantha. Research physicist Bell Labs., Murray Hill, N.J., 1969-76; sr. scientist Gilford Instrument Labs., Oberlin, Ohio, 1976-77; research physicist, group leader Lawrence Livermore Lab. (Calif.), 1977-81; pres. Therma-Wave, Inc., Fremont, Calif., 1982—. Mem. Am. Phys. Soc., Am. Chem. Soc., Optical Soc. Am., N.Y. Acad. Scis., Mensa, Gem Soc. Author: Photoacoustics and Photoacoustic Spectroscopy, 1980; editor Jour Photoacoustics, 1980—; developer photoacoustic spectroscopy of condensed matter, thermal wave imaging.

ROSENFELD, DANIEL ARTHUR, real estate exec.; b. Victorville, Calif., Nov. 17, 1952; s. Lloyd Bryand and Rosemarie (Frey) R.; B.A. in Architecture with distinction, B.S. in Gen. Engring. with distinction, Stanford U., 1975; postgrad. Yale U. Grad. Sch. Architecture, 1975-76; M.B.A. (Baker scholar), Harvard U., 1979. Asst. city engr. Town of Los Altos Hills (Calif.), 1973-74; structural designer firm Wolff, Zimmer, Gunsul, Frasca, Portland, Oreg., 1974; teaching asst. Stanford U., 1974-75; archtl. designer Fred Bassetti and Assos., Seattle, 1975; energy adv., asst. to dir. ops. Yale U., 1975-76; mem. energy task force Am. Council Edn., Washington, 1975-76; prodn. mgr. Welsbach Corp., New Haven, 1976-77; project mgr. Energy Resource Mgmt. Co., New Haven, 1976-78; summer assoc. McKinsey & Co., San Francisco, 1978; asst. to pres. Cadillac Fairview, U.S. Western region, Los Angeles, 1979-80, devel. exec. Cadillac Fairview/Calif., Inc., 1980-81, v.p., 1981—; mem. exec. com. dean's council UCLA Grad. Sch. Architecture. Nat. Merit scholar, 1970. Bd. dirs. Family Service of Santa Monica, Real Estate Council, Jewish Fedn. Council Los Angeles. Mem. Bldg. Industry Assn. Clubs: Harvard (Oreg. and So. Calif.); Stanford (Los Angeles). Office: 1800 Ave Stars Suite 730 Los Angeles CA 90067

ROSENFELD, GEORGE WALKER, clinical psychologist; b. N.Y.C., Oct. 10, 1945; s. George M. and Elise (Walker) R.; m. Jean Aaronson, July 24, 1967; children—Steff, Sunny. B.A. magna cum laude with distinction in Psychology, Boston U., 1967; Ph.D., U. Minn., 1976. Child care worker Walker Home, Needham, Mass., Boston Ctr. for Blind Children, 1965-67; psychodiagnostic clk. U. Minn., 1968-69, Anoka (Minn.) State Hosp.; tchr. Resurrection Sch., Mpls., 1969-71; intern Hennepin County Gen. Hosp. Mental Health Ctr., Mpls., 1971-72; instr. Inst. Child Devel., U. Minn., 1972-73; part time tchr., bd. dirs. Met. Open Sch., St. Louis Park, Minn., 1973-74; therapist Walk-In Counseling Ctr., Mpls., 1969-74; co-organizer, instr. tng. program for child-care workers and suprs. Sacramento County Dept. Mental Health, 1974-76; staff psychologist Sutter Diagnostic and Treatment Ctr., Sacramento, 1974—; clin. instr. Fuller Theol. Sem. Grad. Sch. Psychology, 1975; instr. tng. program Pediatric Nurses Assn. Calif., 1976, Calif. State U., Sacramento, 1981; pvt. practice clin. psychology, Sacramento, 1974—.

ROSENFELD, RALPH CHARLES, accountant; b. Cin., Aug. 14, 1949; s. Ralph C. and F. Dolores (Dunaway) R.; m. Nancy C. Perzel, Apr. 2, 1950; children—Jenni, Erik, Jill. B.B.A., U. Cin., 1972. C.P.A., Ohio. Ptnr. Peat Marwick Mitchell & Co., Cin., Ohio, 1972-81, Denver, 1981—. Bd dirs. Arapahoe Community Treatment Ctr., 1982—. Mem. Am. Inst. C.P.A.s, Ohio Soc. C.P.A.s, Colo. Soc. C.P.A.s, Fin. Mgrs. Soc. Republican. Roman Catholic. Club: Twenty-six. Home: 3249 E Otero Circle Littleton CO 80122 Office: Peat Marwick Mitchell & Co 707 17th St Suite 2300 Denver CO 80202

ROSENFELT, FRANK EDWARD, motion picture co. exec.; b. Peabody, Mass., Nov. 15, 1921; s. Samuel and Ethel (Litvack) R.; B.S., Cornell U., 1948, LL.B., 1950; m. Judith Roman, Nov. 1, 1943; children—Fred, Peter, Karen. Admitted to N.Y. and Mass. bars, 1950, Calif. bar, 1971; atty. RKO Radio Pictures, 1950-55; with Metro-Goldwyn-Mayer, Inc., 1955—, pres., chief exec. officer, dir., from 1973; chmn. bd., chief exec. officer Metro-Goldwyn-Mayer Film Co., 1980—. Served with inf. AUS, World War II. Decorated Purple Heart. Mem. Acad. Motion Picture Arts and Scis. (bd. govs. 1977—), Order of Coif. Bd. editors Cornell Law Quar., 1948-50. Office: MGM Film Co 10202 W Washington Blvd Culver City CA 90230*

ROSENHECK, HERBERT B., mgmt. cons.; b. Los Angeles, Aug. 31, 1929; s. David William and Anne (Rosler) R.; B.C.S., Southwestern U., 1953; m. Marcia Ann Levine, Dec. 24, 1950; children—Robin Lee Kale, Michael David. Dir. corp. systems and data processing Hoffman Electronics, El Monte, Calif., 1960-65; mgr. info. systems TRW Systems, El Segundo, Calif., 1965-69; exec. v.p. Data-Station, Culver City, Calif., 1969-70; v.p., gen. mgr. TRW Info. Services Div., Orange County, Calif., 1970-75; pres. HBR Assos., Mgmt. Cons., Northridge, Calif., 1975—. Served with U.S. Army, 1950-52. Republican. Club: Encino. Address: 18830 Los Alimos St Northridge CA 91326

ROSENSTEIN, ADAM MARK, mfg. co. exec.; b. Los Angeles, Mar. 26, 1957; s. Allen B. and Betty R. (Lebell) R. Dir. info. services Pioneer Magnetics, Santa Monica, Calif., 1978—. Mem. Am. Prodn. and Inventory Control Soc. Office: 1745 Berkeley St Santa Monica CA 90404

ROSENSTEIN, ALLEN BERTRAM, electrical engineer, educator; b. Balt., Aug. 25, 1920; s. Morton and Mary (Epstein) R.; B.S., U. Ariz., 1940; M.S., UCLA, 1950, Ph.D., 1958; m. Betty Lebell; children—Jerry Tyler, Lisa Nan, Adam Mark. Elec. engr. Consol. Vultee Aircraft, 1940-41; sr. elec. engr. Lockheed Aircraft Corp., 1941-42; chief plant engr. Utility Fan Corp., 1942-44; prof. engring. UCLA, 1946—; founder, chmn. bd. Inet, Inc., 1947-53, cons. engr., 1954—; chmn. bd. dirs. Pioneer Magnetics, Inc.; dir. Pioneer Research, Pioneer Internat., Internat. Transformer Co., Inc., Fgn. Resource Services; cons. ednl. planning UNESCO, Venezuela, 1974-76. Bd. dirs. Vista Hill Psychiat. Found. Served with USN, 1944-46. Fellow IEEE; mem. Am. Soc. Engring. Edn., AAAS, N.Y. Acad. Scis., Sigma Xi, Phi Kappa Phi, Delta Phi Sigma, Tau Beta Pi. Author: (with others) Engineering Communications, 1965; A Study of a Profession and Professional Education, 1968; contbr. articles to profl. jours.; patentee in field.

ROSENSTEIN, MELVYN, physician; b. Bklyn., Jan. 3, 1940; s. David and Rachael R.; B.S. magna cum laude, Tufts U., 1961; M.D., N.Y. U., 1965; m. Gitta Roslyn Rosensweig, Nov. 24, 1978; children by previous marriage—Michael, Peter, Joshua, Tracy. Intern, Bellevue Hosp., N.Y.C., 1965-66; resident in surgery Dallas and Univ. Hosp., 1966-67; resident inurology Bellevue, Univ. and Manhattan VA Hosp., 1967-71; practice medicine specializing in urology, Los Angeles, 1974—; pres. Multispeciality Med. Group, Inc., Los Angeles, 1978—; instr. Med. Sch. N.Y. U., 1966-68; chmn. infection control Los Angeles New Hosp., 1978-79; chief of urology, chief of surgery, bd. dirs. Brotman Med. Center, mem. staff Marina Mercy Hosp., Los Angeles New Hosp., Century City Hosp.; cons. in urology to chmn. research com. Family Plan of Greater Los Angeles; cons. urology Los Angeles Regional Family Planning Council, Hollywood Sunset Free Clinic mem. physician adv. com. Health Maintenance Network of So. Calif. Served with U.S. Army, 1969-75. Mem. Am. Fertility Soc., AMA. Office: 10001 Venice Blvd Los Angeles CA 90034

ROSENTHAL, HERSCHEL, state senator; b. St. Louis, Mar. 13, 1918; s. Saul Hyman and Minnie (Berkowitz) R.; m. Patricia P. Staman, 1946; children—Joel, Suzanne. Student UCLA, 1936-39. Ptnr., Adtype Service Co., 1946-74; former trustee, chmn. Employer-Union Pension Fund ITU 174; mem. Calif. State Assembly from 45th Dist., from 1974, now mem. Calif. State Senate. Chmn. Dollars for Democrats, Los Angeles, 1958, Los Angeles County, 1960; mem. Los Angeles County Dem. Central Com., 1960-70; del. Dem. Nat. Conv., 1972, 76, 80; commr. Los Angeles Community Redevel. Agy., 1973-74; western regional v.p. Nat. Assn. Jewish Legislators, 1980. Mem. Internat. Typographical Local 174, Trade Compositors and Typographers Group, Westside Jewish Community Ctr., ACLU, Am. Jewish Congress and Com. Served with U.S. Navy, 1944-46; PTO. Recipient Health award Los Angeles Met. Soc. Calif. Chiropractic Assn., Golden Ear award Hearing Aid Assn. Calif., 1980, Person of Yr. award Los Angeles County Council Nursing Home Assns., 1980; named Assemblyman of Yr., Los Angeles dist. Calif. Dietetic Assn., 1980. Office: California State Senate Sacramento CA 95814

ROSENTHAL, JACK, broadcasting exec.; b. Chgo., Aug. 7, 1930; s. Samuel J. and Celia (Weinberg) R.; B.A. in History, U. Wyo., 1952; m. Elaine Lois Brill, May 2, 1954; children—Michael Bruce, Robert Joseph, Richard Scott. Sec.-treas. Buffalo Theatre Corp., 1952-57, No. Wyo. Broadcasting Corp., 1957-64; v.p., gen. mgr. KTWO Radio and TV, Casper, Wyo., 1964-69; exec. v.p. Harriscope Broadcasting Corp., 1969-77, pres. broadcast div., Los Angeles, 1977—, also dir.; chmn. Wyo. industry adv. com. FCC; dir. Wyo. Nat. Bank, Wyo. Nat. Corp. Mem. Wyo. Travel Commn., 1969-71, Wyo. Land and Water Commn., 1965-66, Yellowstone Nat. Park Centennial Commn., 1972, Wyo. Council Arts, 1969, City of Casper Art Fund, 1979-80; bd. dirs. Milward Simpson Endowment, U. Wyo. Found., 1970—; adv. Nat. Park Service, Dept. Interior, 1974-76; mem. jud. planning com. Wyo. Supreme Ct., 1976-77. Served to 1st. lt. U.S. Army, 1952-54; Korea. Recipient Alfred I. DuPont Found. award broadcast journalism, 1965, U.S. Conf. Mayors award for outstanding community service, 1966; Disting. Alumnus award U. Wyo., 1982; Grover C. Cobb Meml. award Nat. Assn. Broadcasters, 1983. Mem. Nat. Assn. Broadcasters, Wyo. Assn. Broadcasters (pres. 1963), Fedn. Rocky Mountain States Ednl. TV Com. Republican. Jewish. Producer TV film Conrad Schwiering-Mountain Painter (Western Heritage award 1974). Home: 1200 S Mitchell St Casper WY 82601 Office: 4200 E 2d St Casper WY 82602

ROSENTHAL, JULIAN BERNARD, lawyer, assn. ofcl.; b. N.Y.C., July 4, 1908; s. Alex Sidney and Katherine (Goodman) R.; student Columbia U., 1925-26; LL.B., Fordham U., 1929; m. Frances Stone, Nov. 14, 1941; children—Brian, John L. Admitted to N.Y. bar, 1931, practiced in N.Y.C., 1931-72, Ga., 1972-78; mem. firm Javits & Javits, 1968-72, of counsel, 1972-74; mem. Air Force Assn., 1945—, life mem., 1946—, sec., 1946-59, chmn. bd. dirs., 1959-60, chmn. constn. com., 1946-71, chmn. resolutions com., 1946-61, permanent bd. dirs., 1960—; chmn. bd. dirs. Aerospace Edn. Council, N.Y.C., 1965-73; mem. Atlanta consumer adv. panel Gulf Oil Corp. Govt. appeal agent SSS, 1943-44. Chmn. steering com. com., Ga. joint legis. com. Am. Assn. Ret. Persons-Nat. Ret. Tchrs. Assn., 1975-78, mem. Ariz. joint state legis. com., 1978-80; mem. motion picture div. Democratic Nat. Com., 1940; past treas., dir. Lydia M. Morrison Found.; former sec. bd. dirs. Herbert I. and Shirley C. Rosenthal Found.; former v.p., treas., dir. Vanguard Found.; past trustee, sec. Aerospace Edn. Found.; former bd. dirs. Natser Found.; bd. dirs. Ariz. Recovery Centers Assn., 1978-82; bd. dirs. Walter Boswell Meml. Hosp. Aux., 1982-83. Served with USAAF, 1944-45. Recipient Man of Yr. award Air Force Assn., 1953. Mem. ABA. Address: 17631 Foothills Dr Sun City AZ 85373

ROSENTHAL, NEIL BRUCE, psychotherapist; b. Chgo., Oct. 7, 1947; s. Stanley and Florence (Podolsky) R. B.S., U. Colo., 1973; M.A. in Behavioral Sci., U. Houston, 1979. Colo. state pres. Council Internat. Relations and UN affairs, 1968-69; founder, coordinator, Denver Free U., 1969-70; project coordinator exptl. schs. program, Craig Sch. Dist., Alaska, 1973-75; adj. asst. prof. Okla. State U., 1979-80; instr. U. Colo., U. Denver, 1981—; dir. Assoc. Mgmt. Cons., 1980—; psychotherapist, pub. speaker. Mem. AAUP, Internat. Council Psychologists, Assn. Humanistic Psychology (pres. Colo. 1981-83). Contbr. articles to profl. jours. Home: PO Box 518 Pinecliffe CO 80471 Office: 3611 Osage St Denver CO 80211

ROSENTHAL, SOL ROY, physician; b. Tiktin, Russia; s. Hirsh and Sara Esther (Kahov) R.; m. Lucy Donna Lough, Dec. 23, 1972; children—Sara Lough, Sol Roy. M.S., M.D., Ph.D., U. Ill. Founder Instn. Tb Research-Biomed. Research, U. Ill., Chgo., dir. instn., from asst. prof. to prof. preventive medicine, now prof. preventive medicine emeritus; cons. USPHS, Chgo. Bd. Health. Founder-dir. Sol Roy Rosenthal Found., Challenge Exercise Group, People to People for Peace. Served to maj. M.C., U.S. Army. Jewish. Clubs: Chgo. Lit.; Santa Fe Hunt (Rancho Santa Fe, Calif.). Author monographs; contbr. articles to profl. jours.; patentee in field.

ROSENZWEIG, MARK RICHARD, psychologist; b. Rochester, N.Y., Sept. 12, 1922; s. Jacob Z. and Pearl (Grossman) R.; m. Janine S. A. Chappat, Aug. 1, 1947; children—Anne Janine, Suzanne Jacqueline, Philip Mark. B.A., U. Rochester, 1943, M.A., 1944; Ph.D., Harvard U., 1949; hon. doctorate U. René Descartes, Sorbonne, Paris, 1980. Postdoctoral research fellow Harvard U., 1949-51; asst. prof. U. Calif.-Berkeley, 1951-56, assoc. prof., 1956-60, prof. psychology, 1960—, assoc. research prof., 1958-59, research prof., 1965-66; vis. prof. biology Sorbonne, 1973-74; v.p. Internat. Union Psychol. Sci. Served with USN, 1944-46. Fulbright research fellow, 1960-61; Social Sci. Research Council faculty research fellow, 1960-61; NSF grantee, 1980-82; USPHS grantee, 1977-80, 82—; Easter Seal Found. grantee, 1977-79. Fellow Am. Psychol. Assn. (Disting. Sci. Contbn. award 1982), AAAS; mem. Nat. Acad. Sci., Am. Physiol. Soc., Internat. Brain Research Orgn., Soc. Exptl. Psychologists, Soc. Neurosci., Société Française de Psychologie, NAACP (life), Common Cause, Phi Beta Kappa, Sigma Xi. Author: Biologie de la Mémoire, 1976; (with A.L. Leiman) Physiological Psychology, 1982; editor: (with P. Mussen) Psychology: An Introduction, 1973, 2d edit., 1977; (with E.L. Bennett) Neural Mechanisms of Learning and Memory, 1976; editor Ann. Rev. Psychology, 1968—; contbr. articles to profl. jours. Office: Dept Psychology U Calif Berkeley CA 94720

ROSHKO, ANATOL, physics educator; b. Bellevue, Alta., Can., July 15, 1923; s. Peter and Helen (Macen) R.; m. Aydeth de Santa Ritta Seitz, Dec. 8, 1956; children—Peter, Tamara. B.S. in Engring. Physics, U. Alta., 1945; M.S., Calif. Inst. Tech., 1947, Ph.D. in Aeros. (research fellow), 1952. Engring. lectr. U. Alta., 1949-50, asst. prof., 1955, assoc. prof., 1958; prof. Calif. Inst. Tech., 1962; sci. liaison officer Office of Naval Research, London, 1961-62; U.S.-India exchange scientist, Bangalore, 1969; prof. aeros. Calif. Inst. Tech., 1962—. Served with Royal Can. Arty., 1945. Fellow Am. Acad. Arts and Scis., AIAA, Can. Aero. and Space Inst., Am. Phys. Soc.; mem. Nat. Acad. Engring., Arctic Inst. N.Am., AAUP, Sigma Xi. Co-author: Elements of Gasdynamics, 1957. Office: 1201 E Calif Blvd MC 105-50 Pasadena CA 91125

ROSICH, RAYNER KARL, physicist; b. Joliet, Ill., Aug. 28, 1940; s. Joseph F. and Gretchen (Cox) R.; B.S. cum laude in Physics, U. Mich., 1962, M.S., 1963; Ph.D., U. Colo., 1977; M.B.A., U. Denver, 1982; m. Judy Louise Jackson, Aug. 20, 1966; children—Heidi Ann, Kimberly Ann, Dawn Ann. Teaching fellow and research asst. U. Mich., Ann Arbor, 1962-67; staff, Argonne (Ill.) Nat. Lab. Applied Math. Div., summers 1961-63; physicist Inst. for Telecommunication Sci., U.S. Dept. Commerce, Boulder, Colo., 1967-80; sr. scientist and program mgr. Electro Magnetic Applications, Inc., Denver, 1980-82; applications mgr. Energy Systems Tech., Inc., Denver, 1982-83, mgr. R&D, 1983—. Vol. judo instr., county recreation dist., 1976-77. Recipient Spl. Achievement award U.S. Dept. Commerce, 1974, Outstanding Performance award, 1978, Sustained Superior Performance award, 1979; Libbey-Owens-Ford Glass Co./U. Mich Phoenix Meml. fellow, 1964-66; NSF Summer fellow, 1965. Mem. Am. Phys. Soc., AAAS, Assn. Computing Machinery, IEEE, Am. Mgmt. Assn., Sigma Xi, Phi Kappa Phi. Home: 7932 W Nichols Ave Littleton CO 80123 Office: 3669 S Huron St Suite 202 Englewood CO 80110

ROSINI, LARK ELLEN, sales exec.; b. Los Angeles, June 1, 1954; d. Nishon Archie and Neva Irene (Schroder) Karamardian; student Pepperdine U., 1972-74, B.S., U. Calif., Irvine, 1976; m. Zoran Rosini, June 13, 1980. With VAS Corp., Torrance, Calif., 1976—, Western regional sales mgr., 1978, nat. sales mgr., 1979, gen. sales mgr., 1980, dir. sales and mktg., 1980-81, v.p. sales and mktg., 1981—. Mem. Med. Mktg. Assn., S. Bay Internat. Trade Assn., Health Care Assn. Home: 28751 Enrose Ave San Pedro CA 90732 Office: 2525 Maricopa St Torrance CA 90503

ROSKY, BURTON SEYMOUR, lawyer; b. Chgo., May 28, 1927; s. David T. and Mary W. (Zeklin), R.; B.S., UCLA, 1948; J.D., Loyola U., Los Angeles, 1953; m. Leatrice J. Darrow, June 16, 1951; children—David Scott, Bruce Alan. Auditor, City Los Angeles, 1941-51; with firm Beidner, Temkin & Ziskinm C.P.A.'s, Los Angeles, 1951-52; supervising auditor Army Audit Agy., 1952-53; admitted to Calif. bar, 1954, also U.S. Supreme Ct., U.S. Tax Ct.; practice in Los Angeles and Beverly Hills, 1954—; partner firm Duskin & Rosky, 1972-82, Rosky, Landau & Fox, 1982—; judge pro tem Beverly Hills Mcpl. Ct., 1970; specialist in taxation law; lectr. in field. Mem. Mayor Los Angeles Community Advisory Council, 1971—; patron Los Angeles County Mus. Arts; asso. Smithsonian Instn., Am. Mus. Natural History; mem. exec. bd., pres. temple; pres. Jewish Brotherhood; mem. exec. bd. Nat. Fedn. Temple Brotherhoods, also exec. bd. So. Calif. council. Served with USNR, 1945-46. C.P.A., Calif. Fellow Jewish Chatauqa Soc. (life); mem. Am. (charter, pres. 1968), Calif. (charter, pres. 1963) assns. attys.-C.P.A.s, Calif. Soc. C.P.A.s, Calif., Los Angeles County, Beverly Hills, Century City bar assns., Am. Arbitration Assn. (nat. panel arbitrators), Am. Judicature Soc., Tau Delta Phi, Phi Alpha Delta. Mason; mem. B'nai B'rith. Contbr. articles to profl. jours. Office: 8383 Wilshire Blvd Beverly Hills CA 90211

ROSOW, IRVING, sociologist, educator, consultant; b. Cleve., Aug. 24, 1921; s. Eli and Mary (Chait) R.; m. Ursula Braatz, Sept. 17, 1949; children—Cordula, Ben; m. Corinne Nemetz Nydegger, Apr. 22, 1981. B.A., Wayne State U., 1943, M.A., 1948; Ph.D., Harvard U., 1955. Staff analyst Russian Research Ctr., Harvard U., Cambridge, Mass., 1951-54; sr. sociologist Nuffield Research, Belmont Hosp., Sutton, Eng., 1954-57; assoc. prof. sociology Purdue U., West Lafayette, Ind., 1957-58; prof., dir. Ford Found. Aging Study, Case Western Res. U., Cleve., 1958-69; prof. med. sociology Langley Porter Inst., U. Calif.-San Francisco, 1969—; cons. Nat. Inst. Aging, NIMH; spl. adv. White House Conf., 1980-81. Served in USAAF, 1943-45. Decorated Foragerre (Belgium); recipient San Francisco Sr. Citizens award, 1971; Prochovnik award Israel Gerontol. Soc., 1975. Mem. Am. Sociol. Assn. (Pitirim Sorokin award 1976), Internat. Sociol. Assn., Gerontol. Soc. (Kleemeier award 1979; v.p. 1979), Internat. Assn. Gerontology. Contbr. articles to profl. jours. Home: 81 Seal Rock San Francisco CA 94122 Office: Langley Porter Inst U Calif San Francisco CA 94143

ROSS, BETTY GRACE, medical distributing company executive; b. N.Y.C., July 14, 1931; d. Philip and Nancy Anna (Meredith) Boccella; R.N., Presbyn. Hosp., 1952; student Ariz. State U., 1960-62; m. Robert W. Ross, Mar. 1, 1968 (div. July 1976). Sr. operating rm. nurse Roosevelt Hosp., N.Y.C., 1953-58, pvt. surg. nurse, neurosurgery group, 1958-59, orthopedic surgery group, 1960-64; mem. sales staff Zimmer U.S.A., Phoenix, Ariz., 1964-71, owner, distbr. Zimmer Ross Assocs., Phoenix, 1971—, Zimmer-Ross Ltd., 1978—; instr. operating room nursing Englewood (N.J.) Hosp., 1960. Chmn. bd. dirs. Ctr. for Living; pres. bd. dirs. Gloria Dei Luth. Ch., Paradise Valley, Ariz. Mem. Assn. Operating Room Nurses Phoenix (charter mem.), Maricopa Mental Health Assn., Bloomfield Coll. Alumni Assn. Republican. Club: Century. Home: 5713 Cattletrack St N Scottsdale AZ 95253 Office: 1232 E Missouri St Phoenix AZ 95014

ROSS, CYNTHIA WILLIAMS, human services director, therapist; b. Kansas City, Mo., Sept. 6, 1937; d. Barnett Ray Williams and Mary Lucinda (Alexander) W.; m. Arthur L. Kelly, Oct. 27, 1956; children—Mary Lucinda, Thomas Lloyd, Alison Williams; m. 2d, David L. Ross, Aug. 22, 1982. Student Smith Coll., 1955-56, Yale U., 1956-57; B.S., Northwestern U., 1975; M.A., Lone Mountain Coll., 1977; Ph.D., Fielding Inst., 1984. Lic. marriage, family and child therapist, Calif. Counselor Extended Family Ctr., San Francisco, 1975-76; intern Human Sexuality Program, U. Calif.-San Francisco, dept. psychiatry, 1976-77; counselor Family, Youth and Children's Ctr., Berkeley, Calif., 1976, Adult Outpatient Clinic, Berkeley, 1976-79; asst. staff mem. U. Calif.-San Francisco, 1977-79; practice psychotherapy, San Francisco, 1977-81; dir. Counseling Ctr. Motivation Mgmt. Service, San Francisco, 1979-80; crisis counselor Napa County Mental Health Crisis Service, 1980-81; family cons. Travis AFB, Fairfield, Calif., 1980-81, dir. Family Support Ctr., 1981—. Bd. dirs. David Grant Med. Ctr., Travis; health consumers adv. bd. Child Advocacy Com., Travis. Mem. Am. Personnel and Guidance Assn., Assn. Humanistic Psychology, Calif. Assn., Marriage and Family therapists, Orgn. Devel. Network, Am. Assn. Marriage and Family Therapists, Nat. Council Family Relations, Nat. Assn. Women Execs. Republican. Clubs: Yale (San Francisco); Officers (Travis). Home: 1335 Grandview Dr Napa CA 94558 Office: 60 ABG/CFS Travis AFB Travis CA 94535

ROSS, DARRELL SCOTT, banker; b. Spokane, Wash., Dec. 30, 1953; s. Gerald Dwight and Diane Kay (Parmeter) R.; m. Bette Ann Gooding, Aug. 26, 1976 (div.). B.A. in Psychology, Eastern Wash. U., 1977, M.S. in Psychology, 1980. Cert. profl. tng. and devel., Eastern Wash. U. Affirmative action specialist Fidelity Mut. Savs. Bank, Spokane, Wash., 1978-80; dir. personnel Idaho Bank & Trust Co., Boise, Idaho, 1981-82, v.p., 1982—. Bd. dirs. Idaho Employers Council. Mem. Am. Soc. Personnel Adminstrn (dir. chpt.), Idaho Bankers Assn. (edn. com.), Nat. Assn. Bank Affirmative Action Dirs., Am. Soc. Tng. and Devel., Idaho Assn. Affirmative Action. Office: PO Box 2557 802 W Bannock Boise ID 83701

ROSS, GEORGE WEB, wood products company executive; b. Toledo, Oreg., Dec. 23, 1928; s. George W. and Nellie C. (Clark) R.; m. Ella Lee, Dec. 27, 1949; children—George, Thomas, Mary Ella. B.A., Oreg. State U., Corvallis, 1952. Salesman, Burroughs Corp., Portland, Oreg., 1952-55; purchasing agt. Scott Paper Co., Everett, Wash., 1956-63; mill mgr. Ga.-Pacific Corp., Crossett, Ark., 1963-74; mgr., ptnr. Hot Spring County Lumber Co., Malverne, Ark., 1974-76; v.p. timber and wood products Pubs. Paper Co., 1976—. Bd. dirs. Wash. Pulp and Paper Found., Christie Sch., 1981—. Served with USN 1946-48. Mem. TAPPI, Paper Industry Mgmt. Assn., N.W. Pulp and Paper Assn. (pres. bd. trustees). Republican. Presbyterian. Home: 2370 Palisades Crest Dr Lake Oswego OR 97034 Office: 4000 Kruse Way Place Lake Oswego OR 97034

ROSS, GLYNN WILLIAM, performing arts adminstr.; b. Omaha, Dec. 15, 1914; s. Herman Aus and Ida Carlson; ed. Powers Sch. Theater, Boston; m. Angelemaria Solimene, Nov. 15, 1946; children—Stephanie, Claudia, Melanie, Anthony. Stage dir. Teatro San Carlo, Naples, Italy, 1945-47, 60-63; participant Bayreuth Festival, Germany 1953, 54; stage producer San Francisco Opera, 1948, opera cos. Los Angeles, 1948-60, Fort Worth, 1948-56, New Orleans, 1949-62, Phila., 1960-62, Cosmopolitan Opera, San Francisco, 1950-60, Pacific N.W. Grand Opera, Seattle, 1953-55; gen. dir. Seattle Opera Assn., 1963—; cons. to Internat. Communications Agy., 1970—. Served with U.S. Army, 1942-47. Decorated knight Order of Star of Italian Republic, 1974; Service Cross 1st class Fed. Republic Germany, 1978; named Arts Adminstr. of Yr., N.Y. Bd. Trade, 1971, Man of Yr., Seattle Post Intelligencer, 1971; Outstanding Citizen of Omaha, 1976; recipient Cert. of Excellence, Wash. State Ho. of Reps., 1974; Cert. of Gratitude, City Council of Omaha, 1976. Mem. Opera Am. (founding 1970, dir.). Home: 4427 91st Ave NE Bellevue WA 98004 Office: 305 Harrison St PO Box 9248 Seattle WA 98109

ROSS, HOWARD, JR., philosophy and political science educator; b. Birmingham, Ala., July 30, 1946; s. Howard and Anita (Holley) R.; m. Brenda Ross, Feb. 15, 1975. B.A., Northwestern U., 1974, M.A., 1976, M.A. (fellow), 1980, Ph.D., 1980. Asst. prof. Eastern N.Mex. U., Portales, 1980-83, assoc. prof. philosophy and polit. sci., 1983—. Mem. Am. Philos. Assn., Am. Polit. Sci. Assn. Republican. Baptist. Club: Kiwanis. Office: Box 2235 Univ Sta Portales NM 88130

ROSS, J. PAUL, electrical engineer, computer programmer; b. Kelleyville, Okla., Oct. 5, 1913; s. John Haldren and Jeannette (Glenn) R.; grad. elec. engring. Internat. Corr. Schs., 1946; student UCLA, 1963-64, Calif. State U., Los Angeles, 1973—; m. Frances Lillian Jockisch, November 23, 1938; 1 dau., Paulette Elizabeth (Mrs. Michael D. Helland). With Pacific Tel. & Tel. Co., Los Angeles, 1940-75, staff supr., 1962-63, sr. engr., 1963-75, mem. task force long distance service. Mem. IEEE. Home: 6462 N Loma Ave Temple City CA 91780

ROSS, JANET NIELSEN, market researcher, writer; b. Oakland, Calif., Jan. 4, 1936; d. Gordon Andrew and Sarah Dorothy (Mason) Nielsen; B.A. in Comml. Art with honors, San Jose (Calif.) State U., 1957; m. Richard Ross, May 3, 1958 (div.); children—Lisa Janine, Peter Donovan. Tech. illustrator McClellan AFB, Calif., 1957; layout artist Weinstock-Lubin, Sacramento, 1957-58; substitute tchr., Ill. and Calif., 1970-73; library technician Sparks (Nev.) Br. Library, 1973-76; art dir. Dill & Assocs., Reno, 1976-77; media coordinator Capital Advt., Reno, 1977-79; office mgr. Mktg. Systems Internat., Reno, 1979, now v.p. adminstrn. assoc. editor Gambling Scene West, Mountain View, Calif., 1973—. Mem. Nat. Fedn. Press Women, Nev. Press Women (1st place award personal colums and feature articles 1975-79, sweepstakes award 1981, pres.-elect 1981), Reno Ad Club, Reno Women in Advt. (charter). Episcopalian. Club: Reno Ad. Office: 100 W Grove St Suite 475 Reno NV 89509

ROSS, JUDITH PARIS, life insurance executive; b. Boston, Dec. 23, 1939; d. Max and Ruth Paris; ed. Boston U., 1961, UCLA, 1978; grad. Life Underwriting Tng. Council, 1978; 1 son, Adam Stuart. Producer, co-host Checkpoint TV show, Washington, 1967-71; hostess Judi Says TV show, Washington, 1969; brokerage supr., specialist impaired risk underwriting Beneficial Nat. Life Ins. Co. (now Nat. Benefit Life), Beverly Hills, Calif., 1973-82, dir. Salary Savs. program for W. Coast, 1982—; mktg. dir. Brougher Agy. Spl. Ins. Services. Active local PTA, Boy Scouts Am.; mem. early childhood edn. adv. com. Beverly Hills Unified Sch. Dist., 1977. Mem. Nat. Assn. Life Underwriters, Calif. Assn. Life Underwriters (dir. W. Los Angeles 1980—, v.p. chpt. 1982—, chmn. public relations), W. Los Angeles Life Underwriters Assn. (v.p. fin. 1983-84). Office: 9100 Wilshire Blvd Suite 840 Beverly Hills CA 90212

ROSS, KENNETH MALCOLM, JR., banker; b. East Orange, N.J., Apr. 26, 1921; s. Kenneth Malcolm and Anna Helena (Millering) R.; B.A., Rutgers U., 1942; M.B.A., Harvard, 1952; m. Yvonne Violet Pelletier, Feb. 23, 1946; children—Kenneth Malcolm III, Carolyn, Mitchell, Scott, Laurie. Commd. ensign USN, 1943, advanced through grades to lt. comdr., 1952, ret., 1964; economist First Interstate Bank Ariz., Phoenix, 1964—; pres. Epi-Hab, Inc., 1972-73; faculty asso. Ariz. State U., 1974-77. Mem. Phoenix Commn. Housing, 1972-76; mem. Ariz. Treasurer's Econ. Adv. Com., 1972-74; mem. Ariz. Econ. Estimates Commn., 1978—; mem. adv. com. Joint Legislative Budget Com., 1971—. Mem. Ariz. Econ. Roundtable (pres. 1973), Nat. Assn. Bus. Economists, Am. Statistical Assn., Ariz. Harvard Bus. Sch. Club (chmn. 1973), Alpha Sigma Phi. Republican. Roman Catholic. Club: Arizona (Phoenix). Home: 1145 Concorda Dr Tempe AZ 85282 Office: First Interstate Bank Ariz Box 20551 Phoenix AZ 85036

ROSS, LANSON CLIFFORD, JR., religious executive, author, consultant; b. Killdeer, N.D., June 23, 1936; s. Lanson Charles and Mabel (Smith) R.; m. Mary Louise Freleigh, Dec. 20, 1957; children—David F., Lanson III. B.A. in Biblical Studies, Seattle Pacific U., 1960. Pres. Evangelistic Enterprises, Inc., Seattle, 1960-83; v.p. Christa Ministries, Seattle, 1972-75; pres. Ross Assocs., Inc., Seattle, 1977—; founder Planned Living Seminars, Seattle, 1978—. Precinct committeeman Republican Party. Mem. Evangelical Free Ch. Clubs: Seattle Yacht, Wash. Athletic. Author: Total Life Prosperity, 1983; producer film on proper learning environment, leader planned living seminars. Home: 13740 Riviera Pl NE Seattle WA 98125 Office: PO Box 8 Northgate Station Seattle WA 98125

ROSS, LEROY ELLSWORTH, JR., park ranger; b. Stoneham, Mass., Apr. 10, 1923; s. Leroy Ellsworth and Estelle March (Beckett) R.; m. Estelle Gemach, Mar. 21, 1946; children—Emmett Roger, Leroy E., Norman Douglass; m. 2d, Georgia Elaine Smith, Apr. 10, 1968. Student MIT, 1940-41, Mo. Sch. Mines, 1948-51; B.S. in Civil Engring., Boston U., 1954; M.A., Ohio State U., 1956. Registered profl. engr., Mo. Topographic engr., photogrammetric engr. U.S. Geol. Survey, 1946-51; commd. officer U.S. Air Force, 1951, advanced through grades to lt. col., 1968, ret., 1970; supervising ranger San Diego Coast Area, Calif. State Park System, 1970—. Served with U.S. Army, 1941-45. Mem. Am. Soc. Photogrammetry, Civil War Skirmish Assn., Co. Mil. Historians. Club: Masons. Contbr. articles to profl. jours.

ROSS, PHILIP NORMAN, JR., chem. engr.; b. Washington, Oct. 31, 1943; s. Philip Norman and Marian Genevive (Kah) R.; B.S., Yale U., 1965; M.S., U. Del., 1969; Ph.D., Yale U., 1972; m. Gillian Margaret Mailey, Oct. 1, 1966; 1 dau., Sara Ayesha. Process engr. Procter & Gamble, Cin., 1966-69; sr. research asso. United Technologies, Hartford, Conn., 1972-78; sr. staff scientist Lawrence Berkeley Lab., U. Calif., Berkeley, 1978—; cons. Tex. Instruments, Exxon, Lockheed Corp. Mem. Am. Chem. Soc., Am. Vacuum Soc., Electrochem. Soc. Episcopalian. Club: Golden Gate Fields Tennis. Author: Electrocatalysis, 1982. Contbr. articles to profl. jours. Patentee in field. Office: Lawrence Berkeley Lab Materials and Molecular Research Div Berkeley CA 94720

ROSS, RICHARD NORMAN, communications executive; b. Huntington Park, Calif., Sept. 20, 1930; s. Robert Norman and Elizabeth (Barrett) R.; m. Connie J. Brown; children—Ronald C., Nancy E., Andrew R. B.S., San Jose State Coll., 1953; Nat. events producer Boy Scouts Am., N.J., 1953-73; dir. entertainment Walt Disney Prodns., Orlando, Fla., 1973-78; creative v.p. Creative Service Group, Salt Lake City, 1978-82; pres. Communication Design Assocs., North Salt Lake, Utah, 1982—. Served with USNR, 1947-53. Mem. Meeting Planners Internat., Assn. Multi-Image (chpt. sec.-treas.), Am. Film Inst. Producer TV spls., including: Sing America, 1978; Wonderful World of the Waltz, 1980; Celebration, 1980; Maureen McGovern at Symphony Hall, 1981. Office: Communication Design Assocs Box 559 200 South Orchard St North Salt Lake UT 84054

ROSS, ROBERT DEAN, accountant; b. Albuquerque, Sept. 30, 1952; s. Carl Ellis and Shirley Jean (Brazeal) R.; m. Kary Lila Spencer, Nov. 23, 1973; children—Ryon Taylor, Spencer Dean. B.A., Eastern N.Mex. U., 1977. C.P.A., N.Mex. Asst. mgr. Hickory Acres, New Sharon, Iowa, 1974-75; staff acct. Fox & Co., Artesia, N.Mex., 1977-78; ptnr. Henry & Ross, C.P.A.s, Artesia, 1978—; instr. N.Mex. Mil. Inst., 1980—. Mem. city council, Artesia, 1980—, fin. chmn., 1980-84, personnel chmn., 1980-84; mem. legis. com. Nat. League Cities, 1981. Mem. N.Mex. Soc. C.P.A.s (legis. com.), Am. Inst. C.P.A.s, Artesia C. of C. (dir. 1981—). Republican. Clubs: Artesia Downtown Lions (dir., v.p.), Artesia Country (sec.-treas., dir.). Office: 512 W Texas St Artesia NM 88210

ROSS, TERENCE WILLIAM, architect; b. Saginaw, Mich., Sept. 27, 1935; s. Oran Lewis and Drucilla (Chadman) R.; B.Arch., U. Mich., 1958; m. Patricia Ann Marshall, Sept. 27, 1974; children by previous marriage—Deborah, David. Designer, Roger W. Peters Constrn. Co., Fond du Lac, Wis., 1958-62; draftsman Kenneth Clark, Architect, Santa Fe, N.Mex., 1962-63, Holien & Buckley, Architects, Santa Fe, 1963-64; office mgr. Philippe Register, Architect, Santa Fe, 1964-68; v.p. Register, Ross, & Brunet architects, engrs., Santa Fe, 1968-71; v.p. Luna-Ross & Asso., 1971-77; staff CNWC Architects, Tucson, to 1981, ADP Architects, 1981—. Vice chmn. N.Mex. R.R. Authority, 1969-74, sec., 1970-72. Bd. dirs. Colo.-N.Mex. Soc. Preservation of Narrow Gauge. Recipient award for hist. preservation N.Mex. Arts Commn., 1971, award for outstanding service to community Santa Fe Press Club, 1972; named col. aide-de-camp State of N.Mex., 1968, hon. mem. staff atty. gen. Mem. AIA (chpt. pres. 1970, dir.), Constrn. Specifications Inst., N.Mex. Soc. Architects (dir. 1972), Ariz. Soc. Architects, N.Mex. R.R. Authorities (chmn. joint exec. com. 1970-74). San Gabriel Hist. Soc. (hon.), Alpha Rho Chi. Clubs: Sashay Rounders Sq. Dance (pres. 1974), Diamond Squares Sq. Dance, Railroad (pres. N.Mex. 1969, 70, dir.). Author: Track of the Cats. Home and Office: 5050 N Avenida de La Colina Tucson AZ 85749

ROSS, WALTER LEE, management consultant; b. Balt., June 30, 1925; s. John Wesley and Florence Grace (Esposite) R.; m. Anita Agnes Brown, Sept. 15, 1946; children—Stephen P., Kristin, David M., Lisa M. B.S. in Mech. Engring., Duke U., 1946; Ph.D., Pa. State U., 1954. Asst. prof. mech. engring. Pa. State U., 1952-55; dir. research and devel. lab. Nat. U.S. Radiator Co., 1955-57; dir. new products AMF, Inc., 1957-60; v.p. corp. devel., v.p. product planning Mattel, Inc., 1960-72; mgmt. cons., Fallbrook, Calif., 1973—; dir. Hansen Foods, Inc., Hansen-Hill Natural Beverages, Inc., H&H Bottling, Inc., Mother Earth Enterprises, Inc.; past pres. Toy Mfrs. Am. Served with USNR, 1943-46. Mem. Phi Beta Kappa. Democrat. Roman Catholic. Clubs: San Luis Rey Country, Fallbrook Country. Address: 2127 Gird Rd Fallbrook CA 92028

ROSSE, WILLIAM, SR., tribal chairman; b. Round Mountain, Nev., Sept. 5, 1926; s. John and Rosie (Jack) R.; m. Virginia Raya, June 9, 1946; children—William Jr., Daniel, John, Raymond, Kathy, Barbara, Roger, Manuel, Jess. Various positions Banaza Farms, Bakersfield, Calif.; tribal chmn. Yomba Shoshone Tribe, 1981—. Served with USMC, 1944-45. Decorated Purple Heart. Mem. VFW. Democrat. Roman Catholic. Office: Route 1 Box 24-A Austin NV 89310

ROSSER, JAMES MILTON, university president; b. East St. Louis, Ill., Apr. 16, 1939; s. William M. and Mary E. (Bass) R.; B.A., So. Ill. U., 1962, M.A., 1963, Ph.D., 1969; m. Carmen Rosita Colby, Dec. 27, 1962; 1 son, Terrence. Diagnostic bacteriologist Holden Hosp., Carbondale, Ill., 1961-63; research bacteriologist Eli Lilly & Co., Indpls., 1963-66; coordinator Black Am. studies, instr. health edn., So. Ill. U., Carbondale, 1968-69, asst. prof., dir. Black Am. studies, 1969-70, asst. to chancellor, 1970; asso. vice chancellor for acad. affairs U. Kans., Lawrence, 1970-74, asso. prof. edn., toxicology and pharmacology, 1971-74; vice chancellor dept. higher edn. State of N.J., Trenton, 1974-79, acting chancellor, 1977; pres. Calif. State U., Los Angeles, 1979—, also prof. health care mgmt.; mem. tech. resource panel Center for Research and Devel. in Higher Edn., U. Calif., Berkeley, 1975-76; mem. health maintenance orgn. com. Health Planning Council, State of N.J., 1975-79; mem. standing com. on research and devel. bd. trustees Ednl. Testing Service, 1976-77; mem. steering com. and task force on retention of minorities in engring. Assembly of Engring., NRC, 1975-78; mem. Bd. Med. Examiners, State of N.J., 1978-79; vis. faculty mem. Inst. Mgmt. of Lifelong Edn., Grad. Sch. Edn., Harvard U., 1979; mem. Commn. on Acad. Affairs Am. Council Edn., 1979-81; bd. dirs., v.p. Life Found. Medicine and Law, 1980—. Mem. exec. bd., chmn. varsity scouting program Los Angeles Area council Boy Scouts Am., 1979—, local council rep. Nat. Council, 1980—; trustee Orthopedic Hosp., Los Angeles; bd. dirs. Hispanic Urban Center, Los Angeles, 1979—; mem. com. acad. affairs, com. on confidentiality Am. Council Edn., 1979-81; bd. dirs. Community TV of So. Calif., 1980—, v.p., 1980—; bd. dirs. United Way San Gabriel Valley, 1980; Vice-chmn. corp. adminstrn. and fin. com. United Way Greater Los Angeles, 1982—; bd. dirs. Los Angeles Urban League, 1982—, chmn. nominating com., 1983; mem. Los Angeles Council Internat. Visitors, 1982—. NSF fellow, 1961, NDEA fellow, 1967-68. Mem. Am. Assn. State Colls. and Univs. (mem. com. on urban affairs), Am. Ednl. Research Assn., Alhambra C. of C. (bd. dirs. 1979—), Am. Public Health Assn., Kappa Delta Pi, Phi Delta Kappa, Phi Kappa Phi, Kappa Alpha Psi. Roman Catholic. Author: An Analysis of Health Care Delivery, 1977. Home: 225 El Cielo Ln Bradbury CA 91010 Office: Calif State U 5151 State University Dr Los Angeles CA 90032

ROSSETTI, CARL JOSEPH, govt. transp. exec.; b. Hillsdale, Mich., Apr. 6, 1926; s. Carl M. and Genevieve Flora (Bonfiglio) R.; student Western Mich. U., 1943-45; B.S. in Mech. Engring., Columbia U., 1946; postgrad. U. Hawaii-Harvard U. Advanced Mgmt. Program, 1962, George Washington U., 1964; m. Margaret N. Mahi, June 5, 1946 (div. 1977); children—Farran F., Carlene A., Jacqueline L., Carl J. III; m. Gloria Aguilar, Dec. 30, 1977. Adminstrv. asst. transp. Pearl Harbor Hawaii Dist. Transp. Office, 1947-51, automotive transp. specialist, 1951-53; v.p. Rossetti Brothers Constrn. Co., Hillsdale, 1953-58; auto transp. specialist Dist. Pub. Works Office, Pearl Harbor, Hawaii, 1958-64; transp. specialist Naval Facilities Engring. Command, Pacific Div., San Francisco, 1964—, mgr. mgmt. br. Transp. Equipment Mgmt. Center, Pearl Harbor, 1965-77, dir., 1975—. Pres., Foster Village Community Assn., Honolulu, 1962, 64-65; pres. West Honolulu Little League, 1963-64. Bd. dirs. Aloha Week Hawaii, Inc., 1958—, pres. 1969. Served as ensign USNR, 1946; lt. (j.g.) Korean Emergency, 1950-52, lt. comdr. Res., ret. Named Fed. Employee of Year, 1964. Mem. Soc. Automotive Engrs. (chmn. Hawaii 1964-65), Am. Legion. Roman Catholic. Elk, Lion. Club: Toastmasters. Home: 1551 Haloa Dr Honolulu HI 96818 Office: Pacific Div Naval Facilities Engring Command FPO San Francisco CA 96610

ROSSFELD, JOHN EDWARD, hospital administrator; b. St. Louis, Oct. 19, 1948; s. Edward Clarence and Edna Helen (Lawson) R.; m. LaDonna Kay McClour, Sept. 6, 1975; children—John Paul, Robert, James, Kristopher. B.A., U. Mo., 1971; M.P.H. and M.H.A., UCLA, 1973. Asst. adminstr. Harbor Gen. Hosp., Los Angeles, 1972-76; asst. adminstr. Hosp. Good Samaritan, Los Angeles, 1976-79; asst. adminstr. St. Mary's Hosp., Reno, Nev. 1979—. Recipient W. Glenn Ebersole award Assn. Western Hosps., 1973. Mem. Am. Coll. Hosp. Adminstrs., Am. Hosp. Assn., Am. Mktg. Assn. Democrat. Roman Catholic. Club: Toastmasters. Contbr. articles to profl. jours. Office: 235 W 6th St Reno NV 89520

ROSSI, ARLINE MARTIN, psychotherapist; b. Escondido, Calif., Apr. 25, 1909; d. George Robb and Birdie Dora (Brady) Martin. B.A., San Diego State U., 1932; J.D., U. So. Calif., 1941; Ph.D., U.S. Internat. U., 1974. Lic. marriage and family therapist, Calif. Bar: Calif. 1942, U.S. Dist. Ct. Calif. 1942, U.S. Supreme Ct. 1965; enforcement atty. OPA, Los Angeles, 1942-45; asst. U.S. atty. Dept. Justice, Los Angeles, 1948-59; judge Bankruptcy Ct., San Diego, 1959-69; pvt. practice psychotherapy, Escondido, Calif., 1974—. Mem. San Diego County Bar Assn., Calif. State Bar Assn., Am. Psychol. Assn., Am. Assn. Marriage and Family Therapists, Assn. Humanistic Psychology, Calif. State Psychol. Assn. Democrat. Home: 13010 Paseo del Verano San Diego CA 92128 Office: 332 S Juniper St Suite 209 Escondido CA 92025

ROSSI, VERNON JOHN, retail merchandising co. exec.; b. Chgo., July 12, 1922; s. Frank Alexander and Mae Ross; student DePaul U., 1940-43; m. Patricia Corrine Rossi, Mar. 7, 1944; children—Carol LaVerne, Barbara Gay. Played guitar with various hotel orchs. in Midwest, 1946-51; gen. mdse. mgr. Kaufman's Dept. Stores, Colorado Springs, Colo., 1951-54; owner, pres. Casual Towne, Colorado Springs, 1954-56; pres., chmn. Retail Merchandising Service Automation, Riverside, Calif., 1956—. Served with U.S. Army, 1944-46. Author book; contbr. articles to trade publs. Office: 6600 Jurupa Ave Riverside CA 92506

ROSSMAN, BETTY BIRNEY, psychologist; b. Estherville, Iowa, Apr. 13, 1944; d. John W. and Constance O. (Peirce) Birney; m. Michael W. Rossman, June 16, 1966; 1 dau., Candace. B.A. in Gen. Psychology summa cum laude, U. Denver, 1966, M.A. in Exptl. Psychology (Ford Found. fellow), 1967, Ph.D. in Personality/Social Psychology (NASA fellow 1968, NIMH fellow 1969-70), 1970, postgrad. in child clin. psychology, 1975-78. Research assoc. dept. psychology U. Denver, 1970-74, 74-78, vis. asst. prof. psychology, 1977-78, research cons. Family Intervention Project, 1978-79, adj. asst. prof., 1978-80, sr. guest lectr., clin. assoc., 1980-81, 81—; research assoc., 1981—; research assoc. Mental Health Systems Evaluation Project, Denver Health and Hosps. Mental Health Ctr., 1974-76; clin. internship trainee Denver Health and Hosps. Mental Health Ctr. and Denver Gen. Hosp., 1978-80; research cons. Active Camp Fire Girls, Denver. NIMH research grantee, 1982-83. Mem. Am. Psychol. Assn., Rocky Mountain Psychol. Assn., Am.

Personnel and Guidance Assn., Phi Beta Kappa, Sigma Xi, Psi Chi. Contbr. chpt., articles to profl. publs.

ROSSMAN, MARTIN JAY, educator; b. Boston, June 6, 1940; s. Nathan and Dorothy Sylvia (Mascal) R.; B.S., Boston U., 1962, M.S., 1965; postgrad. U. N.H., U. Alaska, Boston Coll., Mass. State Coll., Alaska Methodist U. Tchr., Angoon, Alaska, 1965-67, Bethel, Alaska, 1967-72; tchr., prin., White Mountain, Alaska, 1972-74, 80—, Holy Cross, Alaska, 1974-78, Teller, Alaska, 1978-80; pres. Bethel Classroom Tchrs. Assn., 1969-71. 1978—; Active local Boy Scouts Am. Named Outstanding Elem. Tchr., Elem. Educators. U.S., 1972. Mem. NEA, Alaska Edn. Assn. Featured in films North to Teach and A Film Study of Classrooms in Western Alaska.

ROSSMAN, MAXINE ELLEN, educator, consultant; b. N.Y.C., Apr. 4, 1942; d. Sam and Shirley Irene (Sidrane) Chutick; m. Mark Henry Rossman, May 26, 1963; children—Kim Janet, Nicole Nayan. B.S., NYU, 1963; M.S., U. Bridgeport, 1970; C.A.G.S., U. Mass., 1974, Ed.D., 1977. Tchr. English, Stamford (Conn.) High Sch., 1963-66; employment counselor Mass. Div. Employment Security, Northampton, 1969-70; undergrad. adv. U. Mass., Amherst, 1970-72; counselor Springfield (Mass.) Tech. Community Coll., 1973-74; adj. faculty Phoenix Coll., 1975-78; faculty assoc. Ctr. Exec. Devel., Ariz. State U., Tempe, 1977-79; faculty Ottawa U., Phoenix, 1979—; cons. Unific Assocs., Phoenix. Bd. dirs. Work Life Options. Mem. Lyric Opera Theatre Guild; docent Phoenix Art Mus. Ottawa U. grantee, 1978. Mem. Am. Soc. Tng. and Devel., Mountain Plains Adult Edn. Assn., Ariz. Adult Edn. Assn., Council Advancement Exptl. Learning; Phi Delta Kappa. Baha'i. Contbr. articles to profl. jours. Office: 1777 W Camelback Rd Suite K 106 Phoenix AZ 85015

ROSTER, LAILA BERGS, museum, gallery director; b. Dresden, Germany, Dec. 12, 1944; d. Hugo Edgar and Valeska Milda (Koshkin) Bergs; m. Fred Howard Roster, Apr. 6, 1968; 1 son, Cade Nicholas; m. 2d, Thurston Twigg-Smith, Feb. 20, 1982. A.A., San Mateo Jr. Coll., 1964; B.A., San Jose State U., 1967. Free-lance model, San Francisco, 1957-62; customer service specialist Saks Fifth Ave, San Francisco and Palo Alto, Calif., 1962-63; asst. dir. Lytton Ctr. for the Visual Arts, Palo Alto, 1967-68, dir., Palo Alto and Oakland, Calif., 1968-69; tchr. Pacific Preparatory Acad., Honolulu, 1969-70; instr. Honolulu Acad. Arts, 1973-81; instr. continuing Coll. Edn., U. Hawaii, 1979; dir. Contemporary Arts Ctr., Honolulu, 1974—. Recipient Honolulu Printmakers award, 1975; State Found. on Culture and the Arts Purchase award, 1971, 75, grantee, 1978; Outstanding Achievement-Leader in the Arts award YWCA, 1979. Mem. Honolulu Acad. Arts, Hawaii Craftsmen, Honolulu Printmakers, Honolulu Art Educators Assn., Hawaii Artists League, Hawaii Mus. Assn., Pacific Regional Conservation Ctr., Pacific Inst. Environ. Art. Contbr. articles to profl. jours. Office: 605 Kapiolani Blvd Honolulu HI 96813

ROSTON, MARTIN FRANK, lawyer, educator; b. New Haven, Sept. 17, 1925; s. Harry and Lena (Mnushkin) R.; B.S. with high orations, Yale U., 1949; M.B.A., Harvard U., 1951; J.D., with distinction, U. Mich., 1956; m. Qudsia Rowe, Feb. 9, 1968; children—Rokeya, Rehanna, Rezia. Editor-analyst Value Line Investment Survey, N.Y.C., 1951-53; admitted to Mo. bar, 1956, Calif. bar, 1958; asso. firm Stinson, Mag, Thomson, McEvers & Fizzell, Kansas City, Mo., 1956-58; asst. studio counsel Columbia Pictures, Los Angeles, 1958-60; chief counsel Mirisch Pictures, Los Angeles, 1960-61; pvt. practice law, Orange County, Calif., 1961—; pres. Roston Inst., Inc., Anaheim, Calif., 1973—, Roston Montessori Schoolhouses, 1969—. Served with U.S. Army, 1944-46. Home: 12962 Villa Rose Ln Santa Ana CA 92705 Office: 1929 S Manchester Ave Anaheim CA 92802

ROSTVOLD, GERHARD NORMAN, economist; b. Nashwauk, Minn., Oct. 15, 1919; s. Arndt and Olive Mathilda (Ness) R.; m. Virginia Fay Faubion, Feb. 3, 1945; children—Roger Mark, Laura Ann, Christine Marie, Ellen Alicia. A.B. in Econs.-Accountancy with great distinction, Stanford U., 1948, M.A., 1949, Ph.D., 1955. Instr., Stanford U., 1949-51; price economist Office of Price Stabilization, 1951-52; Stedman-Sumner prof. Pomona Coll., 1952-66; economist Urbanomics Research Assocs. Laguna Hills, Calif., 1966—; vis. prof. Stanford U., summer 1974; lectr. Pepperdine U., 1972—; econs. commentator Sta. KHJ-TV, Los Angeles; econs. cons. to govt., industry. Trustee, PNB Mortgage and Realty Investors; nat. adv. bd. on Pub. Lands, 1960-77, chmn., 1974-77, also mem. Calif. Adv. Bd., 1962-75; trustee Econ. Literacy Council of Calif. Recipient Wig Disting. Professorship award Pomona Coll., 1962; Conservation award Dept. Interior, 1975. Served with USAAF, 1942-45. Mem. Am. Econ. Assn., Western Econ. Assn. (pres. 1966-67), Lambda Alpha. Author: The Southern California Metropolis, 1980; Financing California Government, 1967; The Economics of Energy, 1975; Economics and the Environment, 1975; The Economics of the Public Utility Enterprise, 1976; Understanding How the Economic System Works, 1976; Teacher's Instructional Program for Understanding How the Economic System Works, 1976; Charting Your Path to Economic and Financial Survival in the 1980s, 1979; How to Stretch Your Dollars to Cope with the Inflation of the 1980s, 1981; co-author: California Local Finance, 1960; Garcia-Rostvold Work Experience Education Series, 1974; social sci. editor Stone/Leswing Social Science series; contbr. articles to profl. jours. Home: 7 Wildbrook St Irvine CA 92714 Office: 23276 S Pointe Dr Suite 215 Laguna Hills CA 92653

ROSUL, LOUISE C(LARA), real estate broker; b. Rockville Centre, N.Y., Aug. 5, 1942; d. Henry and Rosanna (Musgnug) Dietershagen; m. Ronald C. Rosul, Apr. 8, 1962; children—Ronald C., Linda, Sean. Student Nassau Hosp. Sch. Radiology, 1962; grad. N.Mex. Real Estate Inst., 1980. Lic. real estate broker, N.Mex. Real estate sales Kennedy Realty, Los Lunas, N.Mex., 1979; v.p., assoc. broker Valencia Valley Real Estate, Los Lunas, 1980-82; assoc. broker Camco Realty, Los Lunas, 1982—; founder, broker Louise Rosul Real Estate Assocs., Inc., Los Lunas, 1983—; founder Gifts for You, 1983—. Sec., Los Alamos Republican Central Com., 1973; mem. Planning and Zoning Commn. Valencia County; bd. dirs. Greater Los Lunas Bus. Assn.; chmn. Valencia Crimestopper Program, 1980—. Recipient sales awards Valencia County Bd. Realtors, 1981. Mem. Nat. Assn. Realtors, Realtors Assn. N.Mex., Albuquerque Bd. Realtors, Valencia County Bd. Realtors, Profl. Salespersons Am. Roman Catholic. Home: Rt 4 Box 2991 Los Lunas NM 87031 Office: PO Box 1045 Los Lunas NM 87031

ROSZAK, BONNIE LOUISE, surgical nurse adminstrator, consultant; b. Langley, Va., Aug. 9, 1944; d. Cleo Mitchell and Annie Christine (Brown) Groves; m. Rudy Roszak, July 1, 1966; 1 son, Christopher Thomas. Diploma Gen. Hosp. Sch. Nursing, Nashville, 1965; B.S., Belmont Coll., 1969; postgrad. U. Colo., 1978. Cert. ARC nurse. Staff nurse Vanderbilt U. Hosp., Nashville, 1966; head nurse Bapt. Hosp., Nashville, 1966-72; physician asst. Anesthesiology Assocs., Nashville, 1972-73, Middle Tenn. Anesthesiology, P.C., Nashville, 1973-75; head nurse Rose Med. Ctr., Denver, 1975-76, asst. dir. surgery, 1976-77, dir. surgery, 1977-78; dir. surgeries Good Samaritan Hosp., Corvallis, Oreg., 1978-80; dir. surg. services Santa Monica (Calif.) Hosp. Med. Ctr., 1980—; operating room cons. Pacific Health Resources, Los Angeles. Mem. Assn. of Operating Room Nurses (Los Angeles chpt.). Office: 1225 15th St Santa Monica CA 90404

ROSZTOCZY, FERENC ERNO, business exec., scientist; b. Szeged, Hungary, Aug. 16, 1932; s. Ferenc Lipot and Edith Jolan (Kunzl) R.; M.S., U. Szeged, 1955; Ph.D., U. Calif. at Berkeley, 1961; m. Diane Elder, Dec. 21, 1963; children—Thomas Ferenc, Robert Anthony, Stephanie Elder, Edward Joseph. Came to U.S., 1957, naturalized, 1962. Phys. chemist Stanford Research Inst., Menlo Park, Calif., 1961-64; mem. tech. staff Bell Labs., Murray Hill, N.J., 1964-68; mgr. semicondr. materials Bell & Howell, Pasadena, Calif., 1968-69; mgr. semicondr. crystal growth and device engring. Varian Assos., Palo Alto, Calif., 1969-75; chmn. bd., pres. Ariz. Machinery Co., Phoenix, 1975—; dir. Ariz. Indsl. Machinery Co., 1975—. Cons. Siltec Corp., Menlo Park, Calif., 1971-72. Mem. Electrochem. Soc., Am. Inst. M.E. (electronic materials com.), Sigma Xi. Roman Catholic. Rotarian. Club: Goodyear Golf and Country. Contbr. articles to profl. jours. Patentee in field. Home: PO Box 1486 Litchfield Park AZ 85340 Office: Ariz Machinery Co 11111 W McDowell Rd Avondale AZ 85323

ROTBERG, ALBERT STARR, electronic engr.; b. Chgo., Apr. 30, 1923; s. Morris and Shirley (Hauser) R.; B.Sc.E.E., Pacific Internat. U., 1956; Sc.D.E.E., Universidad Nacional Autonoma de Mexico, 1958; m. Ana P. Kaminesky, May 6, 1952; children—Sheldon Jaime. Chief engr. Canoga Electronics, 1967-69; dir. engring. Data Products, 1970-73; dir. system effectiveness Systems Evaluation, Los Angeles, 1973-74; dir. engring. Besco Industries, Chatsworth, Calif., 1974-78; prin. engr., scientist Hughes Microwave Communications Products, Torrance, Calif., 1978—; pres. Technilog, Inc., Encino, Calif., 1966—. Recipient Letter of Commendation, USAF, 1975. Mem. IEEE. Patentee in field. Home and Office: 17084 Escalon Dr Encino CA 91436

ROTH, LESTER WILLIAM, presiding justice Calif. ct. appeals; b. N.Y.C., Apr. 5, 1895; s. Herman M. and Hannah (Kornfeld) R.; LL.B., U. So. Calif., 1916; m. Gertrude Frances Freedman, July 7, 1926; children—Harlan Charles (dec.), Eleanor Lois (Mrs. Hal Ross) (dec.). Admitted to Calif. bar, 1916; practiced in Los Angeles, 1916-18; Beverly Hills, 1952-63; partner firms Lissner, Roth & Gunter, Los Angeles, 1920-31, Mitchell Silberberg Roth & Knupp, Los Angeles, 1936-42, Roth Brannen, Los Angeles, 1942-47; judge Superior Ct., Los Angeles, 1931-36; justice pro tem Los Angeles Dist. Ct. Appeals, 1934-36; justice Calif. Dist. Ct. Appeals, 2d Appellate Dist., 1964, presiding justice, 1964—; dir. Guaranty Union Life Ins. Co., Beverly Hills, Calif., 1940-55; v.p. Columbia Pictures Corp., Hollywood, 1947-52. Bd. dirs. Los Angeles Legal Aid Found., Los Angeles Jewish Community Council, 1950-51; mem. nat. adv. com. Am. Jewish Com., 1952—. Trustee Cedars of Lebanon Hosp.; bd. dirs. Brandeis Inst. Served to 2d lt. USMCR, 1918-19. Mem. Beverly Hills (pres. 1959), Calif. State, Los Angeles County bar assns., Conf. Calif. Judges, Acad. Motion Picture Arts and Scis., Am. Coll. Trial Lawyers, Los Angeles Copyright Soc., Nat. Conf. Christians and Jews. Mem. B'nai B'rith. Clubs: Hillcrest County (pres., dir.) (Los Angeles); Tamarisk Country (dir.) (Palm Springs, Calif.). Home: 1201 Loma Vista Dr Beverly Hills CA 90210 Office: 3580 Wilshire Blvd Los Angeles CA 90010

ROTH, NORMAN RAPHAEL, social work educator; b. Rochester, N.Y., Dec. 18, 1921; s. Tobias and Carolyn (Myers) R.; m. Bettie Grace Garelick, May 30, 1946; children—Bruce Ivan, Marjorie Susan Roth Leon. B.A., Hobart Coll., 1942; M.A. in Sociology, U. Rochester, 1949; M.A. in Edn., Columbia U., 1950, Ph.D. in Sociology and Social Founds. of Edn., 1950. Asst. prof. dept. sociology U. Md., College Park, 1950-56; assoc. prof. Sch. Social Work, Syracuse (N.Y.) U., 1956-66; prof. social work Sch. Social Work, Calif. State U.-Sacramento, 1966—, v.p. acad. affairs, 1969-71; UN tech. assistance expert, Uganda, 1963-65; cons. numerous health, welfare, edn. agys. Bd. dirs. Community Child Care Programs, Inc., Sacramento, pres., 1973; bd. dirs. Albert Einstein Residence Ctr., Sacramento, 1979—; bd. dirs. Bur. Jewish Edn., 1982—. Served in USAAF, 1943-46. Mem. AAUP, Am. Sociol. Soc., Council Social Work Educ., Nat. Assn. Social Workers, Rural Sociol. Soc., Tau Kappa Alpha, Kappa Delta Pi, Phi Delta Kappa, Alpha Kappa Delta. Jewish. Contbr. numerous articles, monographs to profl. jours. Home: 5813 River Oak Way Carmichael CA 95608 Office: Div Social Work Calif State U 6000 J St Sacramento CA 95819

ROTH, SANFORD HAROLD, physician; b. Akron, Ohio, June 12, 1934; s. Charles S. and Rose Marie (Zelman) R.; B.Sc., Ohio State U., 1955, M.D., 1959; m. Margie Ann Solomon, June 8, 1957; children—Shana Beth, Sari Luanne. Intern, Mt. Carmel Hosp., Columbus, Ohio, 1959-60; fellow Mayo Grad. Sch. Medicine, Minn., 1962-65; practice medicine specializing in rheumatology, Phoenix, 1965—; co-dir. Am. Rheumatism Assn. Med. Info. System, 1977—; prin. investigator Phoenix Databank Network, 1977—; mem. staff Good Samaritan Teaching Hosp., 1968—, chmn. rheumatology sect. dept. medicine, 1974-76; med. dir. Arthritis Center Ltd., 1982—; med. research dir. Harrington Athritis Research Center, 1982—; dir. Arthritis Rehab. Program, St. Lukes's Hosp., 1983—; cons. rheumatology VA, Phoenix, 1970—, U.S. FTC, Boots Pharm. Co., FDA, Arthritis Adv. Com., 3M/Riker Pharm. Co.; guest lectr. various med. schs., 1965—; vis. scholar Beijing (China) Med. Coll., fall 1982. Chmn. doctors div. United Jewish Appeal, 1975-76, mem. council, 1975-79; mem. exec. bd. Ariz. chpt. Arthritis Found., 1967-74; bd. dirs. Jewish Fedn., 1974-79, chmn. Israel missions, 1974-75; bd. dirs. Temple Beth Israel, 1977-79, Phoenix Symphony Assn., 1981—. Served to capt. M.C., USAF, 1960-62. Fellow Am. Coll. Clin. Pharmacology, Am. Soc. Clin. Pharmacology and Therapeutics; mem. Am. Soc. Clin. Rheumatology (pres. 1970-74, exec. council 1974—), A.C.P., Am. Rheumatism Assn. (chmn. antiinflammatory drug study 1976-82, mem. therapeutic and drug com. 1979—, mem. glossary com. and uniform database computer com., co-dir. Med. Info. System), council on Arthritis in Ariz. (chmn. 1969-70), Soc. Internal Medicine, AMA, Mayo Clinic Alumni Assn. Republican. Jewish. Author: New Directions in Arthritis Therapy, 1980; co-author: Rehabilitation Management of Rheumatic Conditions, 1980; contbr. articles on rheumatic disease to med. jours.; mem. editorial bd. Drugs, 1977—; editor-in-chief Arthron, 1982—. Office: Arthritis Center Ltd 525 N 18th St Suite 906 Phoenix AZ 85006

ROTHBLATT, DONALD NOAH, educator, urban and regional planner; b. N.Y.C., Apr. 28, 1935; s. Harry and Sophie (Chernofsky) R.; B.C.E., City U. N.Y., 1957; M.S. in Urban Planning, Columbia U., 1963; Diploma in Comprehensive Planning (Traveling fellow), Inst. Social Studies, The Hague, 1964; Ph.D. in City and Regional Planning (research fellow), Harvard U., 1969; m. Ann S. Vogel, June 16, 1957; children—Joel Michael, Steven Saul. Planner, N.Y. City Planning Commn., 1961-62, N.Y. Housing and Redevel. Bd., 1963-66; research fellow Center for Environ. Design Studies, Harvard U., Cambridge, Mass., 1965-71; teaching fellow, instr. then asst. prof. city and regional planning Harvard U., 1967-71; prof. urban and regional planning, chmn. dept. San Jose (Calif.) State U., 1971—; Lady Davis vis. prof. urban and regional planning Hebrew U. Jerusalem, 1978; vis. scholar Indian Inst. Architects, 1979; cons. to pvt. industry and govt. agys. Mem. Citizens Community Improvement Com., San Jose, 1971-79; bd. dirs. Neighbors Abroad Program, Palo Alto, Calif. Served with C.E., U.S. Army, 1957-58. Research fellow John F. Kennedy Sch. Govt., Harvard U., 1967-69, William F. Milton Research fellow, 1970-71; NSF faculty research grantee, 1972-80; Calif. State U. Faculty grantee, 1980-83; recipient Innovative Teaching award Calif. State U. and Coll., 1975-79; co-recipient Best of West award Western Ednl. Soc. for Tele-communication, 1976; lic. profl. engr., N.Y. Mem. Assn. Collegiate Schs. of Planning (pres. 1975-76), Am. Inst. Planners, Planners for Equal Opportunity, Internat. Fedn. Housing and Planning, Am. Soc. Planning Ofcls., AAUP, Calif. Edn. Com. on Architecture and Landscape, Architecture, and Urban and Regional Planning (chmn. 1973-75). Author: Human Needs and Public Housing, 1964; Thailand's Northeast, 1967; Regional Planning; The Appalachian Experience, 1971; Allocation of Resources for Regional Planning, 1972; The Suburban Environment and Women, 1979; Regional-Local Development Policy Making: The Santa Clara Valley Corridor, 1981; Planning the Metropolis: The Multiple Advocacy Approach, 1982. editor: National Policy for Urban and Regional Development, 1974; Regional Advocacy Planning: Expanding Air Transport Facilities for the San Jose Metropolitan Area, 1975; Metropolitan-wide Advocacy Planning; Dispersion of Low and Moderate Cost Housing in the San Jose Metropolitan Area, 1976; Multiple Advocacy Planning: Public Surface Transportation in the San Jose Metropolitan Area, 1977; A Multiple Advocacy Approach to Regional Planning: Open Space and Recreational Facilities for the San Jose Metropolitan Area, 1978; Regional Transportation Planning for the San Jose Metropolitan Area, 1980; Planning Low and Moderate Cost Housing for the San Jose Metropolitan Area, 1981; contbr. articles to profl. jours.; dir. Pub. TV series, Sta. KTEH, 1976. Home: 4051 Scripps Ave Palo Alto CA 94306 Office: Urban and Regional Planning Dept San Jose State U San Jose CA 95192

ROTHE, ANDREW, paintings conservator; b. Bozano, Italy, Oct. 12, 1936; s. Hans Ludwig and Helen Hildegard (Falch) R.; m. Grazia de Santis, May 30, 1965; 1 dau., Elisabeth. Grad. high sch., New London, Conn.; restorer tng. Uffizi Labs., Florence, Italy, 1954-57, Bavarian State Galleries, Munich, Germany, 1957-58. Asst. to Oskar Kokoschka, Internat. Summer Acad. Fine Arts, Salzburg, Austria, 1955-63; pvt. cons. contractor various museums and chs., Florence, 1959-81; head of painting conservation lab. J. Paul Getty Mus., Malibu, Calif., 1981—. Mem. Internat. Inst. Conservation, Am. Inst. Conservation. Address: J Paul Getty Mus PO Box 2112 Santa Monica CA 90406

ROTHELL, GEORGE EDWIN, banker; b. Norfolk, Nebr., Dec. 17, 1930; s. Frank Stephen and Margaret Anna (Howorth) R.; m. Elaine Marie Jones; 1 dau., Leslie Elaine. B.S. in Bus. Adminstrn., U. Nebr., 1952. Vice pres. Bank of Am., Los Angeles, 1960-72; mng. dir. Western Am. Bank (Europe), Ltd., London, 1972-77; exec. v.p. 1st Interstate Bank of Calif., Los Angeles, 1977-78, pres., 1978-80; pres. 1st Interstate Bancorp, Los Angeles, 1980—; dir. 1st Interstate Banks of Idaho, Nev. and Wash. Trustee U. Nebr. Found.; founding bd. dirs. Hollywood Presbyn. Med. Ctr. Found.; bd. dirs. YMCA Met. Los Angeles; mem. Assocs. Calif. Inst. Tech. Mem. Assn. Res. City Bankers, Mchts. and Mfrs. Assn. (dir.). Office: 707 Wilshire Blvd Los Angeles CA 90017

ROTHENBERG, HARVEY DAVID, ednl. adminstr.; b. Fort Madison, Iowa, May 31, 1937; s. Max and Cecelia Rothenberg; A.A., Wentworth Mil. Acad., 1957; B.B.A., State U. Iowa, 1960; M.A., U. No. Colo., 1961; postgrad. Harris Tchrs. Coll., 1962-63, St. Louis U., 1962-63; Ph.D., Colo. State U., 1972; m. Audrey Darlynne Roseman, July 5, 1964; children—David Michael, Mark Daniel. Distributive edn. tchr. Roosevelt High Sch., St. Louis, 1961-63, Proviso West High Sch., Hillside, Ill., 1963-64, Longmont (Colo.) Sr. High Sch., 1964-69, 70-71; supr. research and spl. programs St. Vrain Valley Sch. Dist., Longmont, Colo., 1971-72; chmn. bus. div. Arapahoe Community Coll., Littleton, Colo., 1972-75; dir. vocat., career and adult edn. Arapahoe County Sch. Dist. 6, Littleton, 1975—; instr. Met. State Coll., Denver, part-time, 1975—, Arapahoe Community Coll., Littleton, 1975—, Regis Coll., 1979—; vis. prof. U. Ala., Tuscaloosa, summer 1972; dir. Chatfield Bank, Littleton, 1974-83, Yaak River Mines Ltd., Amusement Personified Inc.; pres. Kuytia Inc., Littleton, 1975—; co-owner Albuquerque Lasers, profl. volleyball team. Mem. City of Longmont Long-Range Planning Commn., 1971-72, pres. Homeowners Bd., 1978—. Recipient Outstanding Young Educator award St. Vrain Valley Sch. Dist., 1967. Mem. Am., Colo. (mem. exec. com. 1966-68, treas. 1972-73) vocat. assns., Littleton C. of C., Delta Sigma Pi, Delta Pi Epsilon, Nat. Assn. Local Sch. Adminstrs., Colo. Council Local Sch. Adminstrs. Clubs: Elks, Masons, Shriners. Home: 7461 S Sheridan Ct Littleton CO 80123 Office: 5833 S Prince St Littleton CO 80120

ROTHENBERG, SIMON JEREMY, environmental scientist; b. London, Apr. 27, 1940; came to U.S., 1976; s. Daniel and Hanna Miriam (Weinboum) R.; B.A. in Natural Sci., King's Coll., Cambridge (Eng.) U., 1962, Ph.D., 1968; m. Sheila Yolisa Cingo, July 16, 1970; children—Ronald, Ian, Michelle. Lectr. and tutor in chemistry Sch. Sci., U. Botswana, Lesotho, Swaziland, 1968-70; asso. prof. chemistry Abadan (Iran) Inst. Oil Tech., 1970-72; Med. Research Council fellow U. Essex (Eng.), 1973-75; asso. scientist in aerosol physics Inhalation Toxicology Research Inst., Albuquerque, 1976—; exhbn. at King's Coll., 1959-62. Mem. Am. Chem. Soc. (div. Fuel, Nuclear and Colloid Sci.), Am. Vacuum Soc. (award of excellence 1980), Am. Assn. for Aerosol Research, Cambridge Morris Men, King's Coll. Assn. Club: Sutton (Surrey, Eng.) Hard Courts Tennis, Cambridge Union Soc. Contbr. articles to profl. jours. Office: PO Box 5890 Albuquerque NM 87115

ROTHMAN, BARRY KENNETH, lawyer; b. N.Y.C., June 12, 1942; s. Abraham and Lillian R.; B.A., UCLA, 1965; J.D., Southwestern U., 1970; m. Joanne Ward, May 16, 1979; 1 son, Joshua. Admitted to Calif. bar, 1970; gen. counsel Warner Bros. Records, Burbank, Calif., 1968-73; pvt. practice law, Los Angeles, 1973—. Mem. Internat. Platform Assn., Am. Bar Assn. Office: 9200 Sunset Blvd Suite 509 Los Angeles CA 90069

ROTHMAN, DAVID, statistician; b. Bronx, N.Y., Aug. 9, 1935; s. Morris and Lena (Rothfeld) R.; m. Yolanda Sue Freilich, June 7, 1959 (div.); children—Mitchell Scott, Stuart Dean Nelson. B.A., U. Wis., 1954, M.A., 1955; postgrad. Harvard U., 1955-56, 62-63. With Rocketdyne, Canoga Park, Calif., 1956-61, 63-67; tech. staff Electronic Splty. Co., Los Angeles, 1961-62; research assoc. Bio-Sci. Labs., Van Nuys, Calif., 1972; tech. staff TRW Systems Group, Redondo Beach, Calif., 1973-74; statis. analyst Community Analysis Bur., Office of Mayor Los Angeles, 1975-77; sr. programmer Abacus Programming Corp., Los Angeles, 1977-78; sr. staff engr. Agbabian Assocs., El Segundo, Calif., 1978—. Exec. dir. Found. for Analysis of Competitions and Tournaments. Lectr. crime reduction. Mem. Am. Statis. Assn. (founder, co-chmn. ad hoc com. on stats. in sports and competition 1971-76), Mensa. Democrat. Home: 14125 Doty Ave Apt 23 Hawthorne CA 90250 Office: Agbabian Assocs 250 N Nash St El Segundo CA 90245

ROTHMAN, NATHAN FRANK, sailboat manufacturing company executive; b. N.Y.C., Mar. 26, 1945; s. Morris and Sylvia (Frank) R.; student Bradley U., 1962-64, Ill. Inst. of Tech., 1964-65, Northwestern U., 1965-67, Roosevelt U., 1967-69; m. Susan Barry Stevens, May 15, 1976. Salesman, Valspar Paint Co., Chgo., 1967; v.p., Count Down, Inc., Chgo., 1968; v.p., treas. The Garment Dist., Inc., Chgo., 1969; pres., Paralines, Chgo., 1969-71; sec.-treas., gen. mgr. Jay R. Benford & Assos., Inc. and asso. cos. (Bedford Boat Bldg., Bedford Pub.), Seattle, Wash., 1972-73, chief. exec. and sole proprieter Sea Life, Seattle, 1972—; pres. Valiant Yacht Corp., Seattle, 1974-80, Trade Interface Corp., 1982—; dir. world sales Valiant Yachts div. Unifute, Inc., 1981-82; treas., dir. Susan Barry, Inc. Recipient Offshore Cruiser of Decade award Sail mag. Club: Wash. State Athletic. Home: 2222 Sunset Ave SW Seattle WA 98116 Office: 2030 1st Ave Seattle WA 98121

ROTHMAN, STEWART NEIL, photographer; b. Rochester, N.Y., Dec. 27, 1930; s. Morris Zeus and Rose Mary (Cotler) R.; student Wayne State U., 1952-54; m. Shirley Mae Derry, Sept. 12, 1957; children—Leslie Paula, Karen Pat. Free-lance photographer, Detroit, 1952-57; photographer NASA, Gilmore Creek, Alaska, 1965-68; writer, photographer Jessen's Daily, Fairbanks, Alaska, 1968-69; propr. The Lens Unlimited,

Fairbanks, 1959—; pres., chmn. bd. Arctic Publs., 1968-72; pres. Public Relations Specialists Co., 1973—; editor Arctic Oil Jour., 1968-72, This Month in Fairbanks, 1974—. Publicity adviser to mayor of Fairbanks; pres. Tanana-Yukon Hist. Soc. Served with U.S. Army, 1948-52, USAF, 1957-65. Decorated Purple Heart with oak leaf cluster. Mem. Master Photographers Assn. Gt. Britain, European Council Photographers, Profl. Photographers Am., Fairbanks C. of C. Lion (dir.), Elk. Club: Farthest North Press. Author: Nudes of Sixteen Lands, 1971; Hobo and Dangerous Dan McGrew, 1975; The Lens is My Brush, 1977; China, The Opening Door, 1980; Pope John Paul II's First Visit to Alaska, 1981; Window on Life, 1982. Home and Office: 921 Woodway St Fairbanks AK 99701

ROTHSTEIN, BARBARA JACOBS, fed. judge; b. Bklyn., Feb. 3, 1939; d. Solomon and Pauline Jacobs; B.A., Cornell U., 1960; LL.B., Harvard U., 1966; m. Ted L. Rothstein, Dec. 28, 1968; 1 son, Daniel. Admitted to Mass. bar, 1966, Wash. bar, 1969; individual practice law, Boston, 1966-68; asst. atty. gen. State of Wash., 1968-77; judge Superior Ct., Seattle, 1977-80; judge Fed. Dist. Ct. Western Wash., Seattle, 1980—; faculty Law Sch. U. Wash., 1975-77, Hastings Inst. Trail Advocacy, 1977, N.W. Inst. Trial Advocacy, 1979—. Recipient Matrix Table Woman of Year award, 1980. Mem. Am. Judicature Soc., Am. Bar Assn. (judicial sect.), Phi Beta Kappa, Phi Kappa Phi. Jewish. Office: US Courthouse Seattle WA 98104*

ROTOLO, ELIO RICHARD, management consultant; b. Bklyn., Jan. 2, 1924; s. Rosario and Antoinette A. (Carbonaro) R.; B.S. in Indsl. Engring., Lehigh U., Bethlehem, Pa., 1949; children—Claudia Ann, Debra Carla. Mgr. indsl. engring. Dollin Corp., Irvington, N.J., 1952-60; prin. Arthur Young & Co., C.P.A.'s, N.Y.C., 1960-70; dir. mfg. engring. ITT Corp., N.Y.C., 1970-75; v.p. Security Pacific Nat. Bank, Los Angeles, 1975-82; pres. Rotolo & Whitney, Inc., Mgmt. Cons., 1982—; mem. productivity adv. council Bank Adminstrn. Inst., 1980—; mem. faculty Sch. for Bank Adminstrn., Madison, Wis., 1980, 81. Republican county commiteeman, Union, N.J., 1955-60; bd. dirs. Opera Guild of So. Calif.; bd. dirs. Productivity Council of S.W., 1980—; chmn. Los Angeles County Productivity Adv. Com., 1981-82. Served to 1st lt. AUS, 1942-45. Fellow Am. Inst. Indsl. Engrs. (pres. 1967-68, dir. San Fernando Valley chpt.), Engrs. Joint Council (dir.). Club: Lions. Contbr. articles to profl. jours. Home: 4369 LaBarca Dr Tarzana CA 91356 Office: 555 N El Molino Ave Pasadena CA 91101

ROTTAS, RAY, state treasurer; B.B.A. in Econs., Case Western Res. U., 1946; m. Barbara, Sept. 1956; children—Steven, Donna, Paul, Diane. Owner, pres. AMI Enterprises, Automotive Warehousing, Inc., Phoenix, 1956-83 M & L Auto Parts, Inc., Buckeye, Ariz., 1960—, Allied Auto Supply, Inc., Kingman, Ariz., 1962—; mem. Ariz. Senate, 1971-74, 77-82, chmn. fin. com., 1973-74, 79-82, co-chmn. joint select com. to study tax reform and sch. fin., 1979; state treas. State of Ariz., 1982—. Mem. Maricopa County (Ariz.) Rep. Com., Ariz. Rep. Com.; pres. Ariz. Methodist Ch. Extension Soc., 1959-69; mission trustee Ariz., So. Calif. and So. Nev. Meth. Conf., 1959-71, bd. dirs., 1963-71; bd. dirs. Jr. Achievement Phoenix, 1979—, pres., 1979-80; bd. dirs. Met. YMCA, Phoenix, 1971-77, 79—; mem. Ariz. Alcoholism Adv. Council, 1975-78; chmn. citizen adv. com. Ariz. Div. Motor Carriers, 1975-76. Served with U.S. Army, 1946-47, USAF, 1951-55. Mem. Phoenix Art Museum, Phoenix Fine Arts Assn., Heard Mus., Ariz. Acad., Air Force Assn. Clubs: Rotary (dir. 1977-80), Masons, Shriners, Elks, Ariz. (pres. 1977-78).

ROTTER, DORIS MIRIAM (MAURER), clinical psychologist, educator; b. Stuttgart, W.Ger., June 13, 1936; d. Christian and Maria Mina (Weiss) Maurer; m. Leo B. Rotter, June, 1964 (div. 1975); 1 son, Ronald Allan. B.A. with highest honors, Calif. State U.-Los Angeles, 1970; Ph.D. in Psychology, Claremont Grad. Sch., 1974. Lic. psychologist, Calif., Minn. Translator, NATO, France, 1961-64; asst. prof. behavioral scis., psychology, U. Minn., Duluth, 1975-77; mem. core faculty community psychol. and field placement Calif. Sch. Profl. Psychology, Berkeley, 1977-78; lectr. in psychiatry, U. Calif.-San Francisco, 1978; dir. A. Rotter Psychology Ctr., San Francisco and Berkeley, 1978—; mem. clin. pastoral edn. consultation com. St. Luke's Hosp., Duluth, Minn., 1975-77; mem. screening com. ARC Assn. Retarded Citizens, Alameda County, Calif., 1981—. U. Minn. research grantee, 1976; NSF trainee, NDEA fellow, Claremont, Calif., 1970-73. Mem. Am. Psychol. Assn., Calif. Psychol. Assn., Bay Area Psychol. Assn., Phi Kappa Phi, Tau Alpha Epsilon, Sigma Tau Sigma, Alpha Mu Gamma. Clubs: Sierra, Calif. Sailing, Claremont Pool and Tennis, Oakland. Contbr. articles to profl. jours., articles to profl. meetings. Office: 1365 Church St San Francisco CA 94114 also 555 Dwight Pl Berkeley CA 94114

ROUANZOIN, CURTIS CLAIR, clinical psychologist, psychology educator; b. Morgan County, Ohio, Mar. 12, 1952; s. Martin Clair and Mary Katherine (McElhiney) R.; m. Denne Jan Pierce, June 1, 1974; 1 son, Erick Curtis. B.A., Pacific Christian Coll., Fullerton, Calif., 1974; M.A., Pepperdine U., 1975; Ph.D., Brigham Young U., 1981. Lic. marriage, family and child counselor, clin. psychologist. Marriage, family and child counselor Pacific Counseling Ctr., Fullerton, Calif., 1976-77; marital and family therapist S.E. Christian Ch., Salt Lake City, 1977-80; clin. psychology intern and registered psychol. asst. Child Guidance Ctr., Fullerton, 1980-82; pvt. practice clin. psychology, Fullerton, 1982—; assoc. prof., chmn. depts. social sci. and psychology Pacific Christian Coll., Fullerton; lectr. profl. and religious meetings. Vice pres., bd. dirs. Western Family Inst., 1980—. Mem. Am. Assn. Marriage and Family Therapy, Am. Psychol. Assn., Orange County Soc. Clin. Hypnosis, Pi Beta Sigma, Delta Epsilon Chi. Democrat.

ROULAC, STEPHEN EARL, fin. cons. firm exec.; b. San Francisco, Aug. 15, 1945; s. Phil Williams and Elizabeth May (Young) R.; B.A., Pomona Coll., 1967: M.B.A., Harvard U., 1970; J.D., Boalt Hall Sch. Law, 1976; Ph.D., Stanford U., 1978; m. Holly Anne Gibson, Nov. 18, 1978; 1 son, Arthur Young. Constrn. supt. Roulac Constrn. Co., Pasadena, Calif., 1963-66; research asst. Econs. Research Assocs., Los Angeles, 1966-67; assoc. economist Urbanomics Research Assocs., Claremont, Calif., 1967; acquisition auditor Litton Industries, 1967-68; tax cons. Coopers and Lybrand, Los Angeles, 1968; planning cons. Owens-Corning Fiberglass Corp., Toledo, 1969-70; pres. Questor Assocs., San Francisco, 1972—; lectr. bus. adminstrn. Stanford Grad. Sch. Bus., 1970-79; lectr. bus. adminstrn. and architecture U. Calif., 1972-77; adj. prof. Hastings Coll. Law, San Francisco, 1977-78. Mem. real estate adv. com. Calif. Commr. of Corps., 1973; bd. govs. Am. Inst. Corp. Asset Mgmt. C.P.A., Hawaii. Mem. Am. Econs. Assn., Am. Fin. Assn., Am. Real Estate and Urban Econs. Assn. Clubs: Los Angeles Adventurers, Harvard (N.Y.C.). Author numerous books including: Modern Real Estate Investment, also articles; editor-in-chief, pub. Questor Real Estate Letter, 1979—, Questor Real Estate Investment Yearbook, 1980—. Office: 115 Sansome St San Francisco CA 94104

ROULSTON, LENA MAXINE, language therapist; b. Cisco, Tex., July 25, 1934; d. William Hudson and Maudie Mae (Green) Carlton; B.S., Coll. of Southwest, 1966; M.Ed., Eastern N.Mex. U., 1972, M.Ed. in Reading, 1977; m. Robert Roy Roulston, Jan. 2, 1951; 1 son, Gary. Elem. sch. tchr., Hobbs, N.Mex., 1966—, learning disabilities resource tchr., 1977—; off-campus instr. Eastern N.Mex. U., evenings 1977-79, mem. reading consortium, 1977-79. Mem. Internat. Reading Assn., NEA, N.Mex. Edn. Assn., Hobbs Edn. Assn., Hobbs Assn. Classroom Tchrs., Orton Soc., Delta Kappa Gamma, Phi Kappa Phi. Democrat. Baptist. Home: 608 Luna St Hobbs NM 88240 Office: 1520 Breckon Hobbs NM 88240

ROUMASSET, JAMES ALAN, ecomonist, educator; b. Berkeley, Calif., Oct. 14, 1943; s. Charles A. and Helen Louise (Nobles) R.; m. Elaine Akiko Higa, Dec. 26, 1970; children—Benton S., Brian J. B.A., U. Calif.-Berkeley, 1965; M.A., U. Hawaii, 1969; Ph.D., U. Wis.-Madison, 1973. Asst. prof. U. Calif.-Davis, 1972-76; prof. U. Hawaii, 1976—; Philippine rep. Agrl. Devel. Council, Inc., 1978-79; vis. prof. Australian Nat. U., Canberra, summer 1981. NSF grantee. Mem. Am. Econ. Assn., Am. Agrl. Econs. Assn. Author: Rice and Risk: Decision-Making among Low-Income Farmers in Theory and Practice, 1976; (with J. M. Boussard and I. Singh) Risk, Uncertainty and Agricultural Development, 1979; Contbr. articles to profl. jours. Home: 7248 Kipu Place Honolulu HI 96825 Office: Econs Dept U Hawaii Honolulu HI 96822

ROUNSAVILLE, HAYDEN DARRELL, soil scientist; b. Voca, Okla., May 20, 1942; s. Tom S. and Hazel D. (Payne) R.; A.S., Murray State Agrl. Coll., 1962; B.S., Okla. State U., 1964; postgrad. N.Mex. State U., 1969, Oreg. State U., 1971, Iowa State U., 1972, Colo. State U., 1974-75, Ariz. State U., 1975; m. Rose L. Stigers, Feb. 29, 1964; children—Sherry L., Janice L. Field reporter Agrl. Stblzn. Conservation Service, Atoka, Okla., 1958-62; soil lab. technician Okla. State U., Enid, 1962-64; soil scientist U.S. Dept. Agr., 1964-78, regional soil scientist, forest service, Rocky Mountain region, Lakewood, Colo., 1978—. Mem. Am. Soc. Agronomy, Soil Sci. Soc. Am., Am. Forestry Assn., Am. Rifle Assn., Western Sportman Assn. Republican. Methodist. Home: 8697 W 66th Pl Arvada CO 80004

ROUSE, LILLIAN MCPHERSON, publishing co. exec.; b. Santa Cruz, Calif., Nov. 23, 1908; d. Frederick Duncan and Matye Eliza (Patton) McPherson; student U. Calif., Berkeley, 1926-28; A.B., U. Wash., Seattle, 1930; postgrad. Stanford U., 1930, 31; tchr.'s cert. San Jose State U., 1931; m. Robert Parker Rouse, June 30, 1933; children—Mary Ellen, Robert McPherson, Ruth, James Charles. Tchr. public schs., Watsonville, Calif., 1931-34; partner Corner Drug Store, Watsonville, 1938-60, McPherson Land Co., Santa Cruz, Calif., 1960-82, Santa Cruz Sentinel News, 1941-60; v.p., dir. Santa Cruz Pubs., Inc., 1960-82. Mem. AAUW, Calif. Press Assn., Stanford U. Alumni Assn., PEO, hist. socs. Republican. Congregationalist. Club: Watsonville Woman's, also travel clubs. Home: 32 Gonzales St Watsonville CA 95077 Office: Santa Cruz Pubs Inc 207 Church St Santa Cruz CA 95060

ROUSELL, RALPH HENRY, pharmacologist, immunologist; b. Johannesburg, South Africa, Jan. 7, 1933; s. Reginald Henry John and Olive Agnes (Neilson) R.; came to U.S., 1979. M.B., B.Ch., Witwatersrand U., South Africa, 1958; M.Sc., U. London, 1976; diploma pharm. medicine Royal Colls. Physicians, Edinburgh, Glasgow and London, 1976. Intern medicine and surgery Johannesburg Gen. Hosp., 1959, resident surgery and anesthesiology, 1960-63; practice medicine specializing in anesthesiology London Teaching Hosps., 1963; fellow pharmacology St. Thomas's Hosp., London, 1964-65; med. dir. Pharmacia (Gt. Britain) Ltd., London, 1965-70; head med. services Hoechst U.K., London, 1970-79; dir. clin. research Cutter Biol. and Intravenous Nutritionals div. Miles Pharms., Berkeley, Calif., 1979—; mem. sci. council Am. Blood Resources Assn., 1980—. Mem. Brit. Med. Assn., Brit. Soc. Immunology, Royal Inst. Biology, Am. Soc. Clin. Pharmacology. Methodist. Clubs: Hammersmith Rugby (life), Brockley (London). Editor: Streptokinase in Clinical Practice, 1973; Antilymphocyte Globulin in Clinical Practice, 1976; Intravenous Immune Globulin: Its Use and Potential, 1981. Home: 5585 Cold Water Dr Castro Valley CA 94546 Office: 4th and Parker Sts Berkeley CA 94710

ROUSH, GARY MANIS, accountant; b. Casper, Wyo., Dec. 6, 1946; s. Manis Gustov and Mary Eudena (Humphreys) R.; m. Raule Gail Nemer, Dec. 28, 1969; div. B.S. in Bus. Adminstrn., U. Denver, 1970. C.P.A., Mont., Colo. Staff acct. Touche Ross & Co., Denver, 1972-78; mgr., 1978-81; ptnr. Hein & Assocs., Denver, 1981—. Pres., Am. Sighthound Field Assn. Mem. Am. Inst. C.P.A.s, Colo. Soc. C.P.A.s. Lutheran. Club: Denver Petroleum. Office: 717 17th St Suite 1600 Denver CO 80202

ROUSSELLE, WILLIAM A., hosp. engr.; b. Aurora, Ill., May 20, 1933; m., 5 children. Ins. broker, 1953-60; regional v.p. Springfield Fire and Marine Ins. Co., 1960-62; criminal investigator Yavapai County Sheriff Office, 1962-66; ins. broker, Prescott, Ariz., 1966-70; gen. contractor, Prescott, 1970-77; dept. head, chief engr., safety dir., chief security Yavapai Community Hosp., Prescott, 1977—. Chmn. bd. appeals Prescott Fire Dept.; pres. Prescott Little League, 1978-79; chmn. Yavapai Community Hosp.; mem. bd. appeals Prescott Bldg. Dept.; mem. Prescott Planning and Zoning Commn. Mem. Ariz. Soc. Hosp. Engrs., Nat. Fire Protection Assn., Am. Soc. Hosp. Engrs. Home: 1115 Middlebrook Prescott AZ 86301 Office: 1003 Willow Creek Rd Prescott AZ 86301

ROUTSON, RONALD CHESTER, soil scientist; b. Chewelah, Wash., Dec. 12, 1933; s. Chester A. and Lucille F. R.; Ph.D. in Soil Sci., Wash. State U., 1970; m. Mary Joan Boning, Dec. 26, 1958; 1 dau., Kelly L. Staff soil scientist Battelle Pacific N.W. Lab., 1967-78, Rockwell Hanford Ops., Richland, Wash., 1978—. Served with U.S. Army, 1958-62; mem. Res. NDEA fellow, 1964-68. Mem. Am. Soc. Agronomy, Soil Sci. Soc. Am., Am. Nuclear Soc., N.W. Sci. Assn., Western Soil Sci. Soc. and Geochem. Soc. Sci., Sigma Xi, Alpha Zeta. Republican. Roman Catholic. Home: Route 1 Box 1351 Benton City WA 99320 Office: M0-028 200 W Area PO Box 800 Richland WA 99352

ROVIRA, LUIS DARIO, justice Colo. Supreme Ct.; b. San Juan, P.R., Sept. 8, 1923; s. Peter S. and Mae (Morris) R.; B.A., U. Colo., 1948, LL.B., 1950; m. Lois Ann Thau, June 25, 1966; children—Douglas, Merilyn. Admitted to Colo. bar, 1950; now justice Colo. Supreme Ct. Mem. Pres.'s Com. on Mental Retardation, 1970-71; chmn. State Health Facilities Council, 1967-76; bd. dirs. YMCA, 1969-78; pres. Lowe Found. Served with AUS, 1943-46. Mem. Colo. Assn. Retarded Children (pres. 1968-70), ABA, Colo. Bar Assn., Denver Bar Assn. (pres. 1970-71), Alpha Tau Omega, Phi Alpha Delta. Clubs: Athletic, Country (Denver). Office: Colo Judicial Bldg 2 E 14th Ave Denver CO 80203

ROW, DENNIS GEORGE, engring. co. exec.; b. Lower Hutt, N.Z., Dec. 8, 1949; s. George Caird and Lola June (Leslie) R.; B.E. with honors, U. Canterbury (N.Z.), 1972, M.E. with distinction, 1973; Ph.D., U. Calif., Berkeley, 1978; m. Linda Janette Row, Feb. 28, 1978 (div.); 1 son, Dustin Cameron. Founder, pres. SSD, Inc., Berkeley, 1978—. Registered profl. engr., Calif. Mem. N.Z. Earthquake Engring. Soc. Club: Old Blues Rugby (sec.).

ROWAN, BRIAN PATRICK, sociologist, research scientist; b. Plainfield, N.J., May 6, 1950; s. Daniel A. and Phyllis (Bowman) R.; m. Yamina Sebihi, July 14, 1978; 1 son, Samir. B.A. with high honors, Rutgers U., 1972; Ph.D., Stanford U., 1978. Vis. lectr. dept. bus. adminstrn. U. Calif.-Berkeley, 1977-78; lectr. dept. sociology UCLA, 1978-79; asst. prof. sociology Tex. Christian U., Fort Worth, 1979-81; assoc. research scientist instrnl. mgmt. program Far West Lab. for Ednl. Research and Devel., San Francisco, 1981—. Stanford U. fellow, 1972-73; NIMH fellow, 1973-74, trainee, 1974-77. Mem. Am. Sociol. Assn., Am. Ednl. Research Assn., Phi Beta Kappa, Alpha Kappa Delta. Muslim. Contbr. articles to profl. jours.; reviewer Adminstrv. Sci. Quar., Rev. Ednl. Research. Office: 1855 Folsom St San Francisco CA 94103

ROWE, BRUCE WINDEN, manufacturing and distribution company executive; b. Everett, Wash., Dec. 19, 1928; s. Gordon and Doris (Winden) R.; m. Joan Mooney, Aug. 13, 1979; children from previous marriage—Bruce K., Andrew G., Julia W. B.S., U.S. Naval Acad., 1950; M.B.A., Harvard U., 1958. Pres., Van Daal Inc., Seattle, 1960—; chief exec. officer Cascade Pacific Internat. Inc., Seattle, 1977—, M-R Products Co., Seattle, 1963—, Bruce's Bldg. Matrials Inc., Seattle, 1975—, also chmn., dir. Served with USN, 1950-56; Korea. Mem. Am. Subcontractors Assn. (pres. Seattle 1976-77). Episcopalian. Office: 3700 W Valley Rd Renton WA 98057

ROWE, EDWARD THOMAS, international relations and political science educator, researcher; b. Plymouth, Mich., May 14, 1937; s. Milton Sterling and Ruth Elizabeth (Leonard) R.; m. Mary Jane Price, Sept. 15, 1955; children—Rebecca, Jennifer. B.A., U. Mich., 1959; M.A., U. Calif.-Berkeley, 1961, Ph.D., 1966. Teaching asst. U. Calif.-Berkeley, 1962-63; instr. U. Conn., Storrs, 1964-66, asst. prof., 1966-71; asst. prof. Va. Poly. and State U., Blacksburg, 1971-74; vis. assoc. prof. polit. sci. U. Colo., Boulder, 1983; assoc. prof. internat. relations Grad. Sch. Internat. Studies, U. Denver, 1974—, assoc. dean, 1979-81. Woodrow Wilson fellow 1959-60; U. Conn. summer fellow, 1967; Ford Found. Faculty Research fellow, 1970-71; Internat. Orgn. grantee, 1980; grantee U. Conn., U. Denver. Mem. Am. Polit. Sci. Assn., Internat. Polit. Sci. Assn., Midwest Polit. Sci. Assn., Internat. Studies Assn. (western sect. pres. 1983-85, pres. internat. orgn. sect. 1977-79), Consortium on Peace, Edn. and Devel. Author: Strengthening the UN, 1975; contbr. chpt. to book, articles to profl. jours. Home: 7148 N Village Rd Parker CO 80134 Office: U Denver Grad Sch Internat Studies Denver CO 80208

ROWE, JOHN BURK, microbiologist; b. Tucson, Sept. 28, 1937; s. Clyde F. and Catherine (Burk) R.; B.S., U. Ariz., 1960; postgrad Colo. State U., 1963-64, U. Utah, 1966-68; m. Carole I. Fairclough, Feb. 2, 1962; children—Kevin Scott, Brian Clark, Lisa Ann, Stacy Lynne, Cindy Leigh. Mgr. quality Meadow Gold Dairies, Salt Lake City, 1964-65; mgr. quality control and mfg. Deseret Med., Inc., Sandy, Utah, 1970-72, mgr. lab. services dept., 1972—; cons. microbiol. quality control and sterilization. Mem. Utah Ho. of Reps., 1979-80; chmn. Sandy City Elections Commn., 1981—. Served with U.S. Navy, 1963—. Mem. Parenteral Drug Assn., Am. Assn. Contamination Control, U.S. Naval Inst., Naval Res. Assn. Republican. Mormon. Home: 1125 E Fairoaks Way Sandy UT 84070 Office: 9450 S State St Sandy UT 84091

ROWE, ROBERT DAVID, economist, educator; b. Lakewood, Ohio, Jan. 2, 1949; s. Richard Thomas and Grace Martha (Wollenzien) R.; m. Nancy Lee Hehn, May 24, 1981. B.S. cum laude in Computer Sci., Mich. State U., 1971; Ph.D. in Econs., Tex. A&M U., 1975. Research asst. Tex. A&M U., 1972-73, teaching asst., 1971-74; instr. U. Wyo., 1974-75, asst. prof. 1975-80, research assoc. Resource and Environ. Econs. Lab, 1976-79; sr. economist, dep. area mgr. Abt Assocs., Inc., 1979-82; cons. Office Consummer Services, State of Colo., 1981, Clean Air Coalition, 1981; adj. prof. U. Denver, 1982; sr. economist, prin. Energy and Resource Cons., Inc., Boulder, Colo., 1982—; cons. Western Govs.' Policy Office. Mem. Assn. Environ. and Resource Economists, Am. Econ. Assn., So. Econ. Assn., Western Econ. Assn., Am. Statis. Assn., Phi Lambda Tau. Co-editor: Managing Air Quality and Scenic Resources in National Parks and Wilderness Areas, 1982; co-author: The Value of Visibility: Economic Theory and Practice for Air Pollution Control, 1983; contbr. articles to profl. jours. Home: 2680 S Jersey Denver CO 80222 Office: Energy and Resource Cons Inc 207 Canyon Blvd Suite 301A Boulder CO 80302

ROWEN, ELAINE, educational administrator; b. Bklyn., Feb. 24, 1934; d. Charles and Esther (Brand) Weiner; m. Nelson J. Rowen, Jan. 29, 1960; children—Dean, Hali. B.A., Bklyn. Coll., 1954; M.S., Calif. State U.-Fullerton, 1970; Ph.D., U.S. Internat. U., 1982. Tchr., 1954-64; psychologist Placentia (Calif.) Unified Sch. Dist., 1970-71; counselor Norwalk-La Mirada Sch. Dist., Norwalk, Calif., 1971-72; lectr. Calif. State U.-Fullerton, 1972-72; dir. ESEA Title III Project, Huntington Beach (Calif.) Union High Sch. Dist., 1972-75; research specialist Pomona (Calif.) Unified Sch. Dist., 1975-78; dir. spl. services Hemet (Calif.) Unified Sch. Dist., 1978—. Active ACLU, Common Cause, AAUW; mem. adv. com. Mt. San Jacinto Coll. Vocat. Edn. and Sch. of Handicapped. Mem. Assn. Calif. Sch. Adminstrs., Am. Ednl. Research Assn., Assn. Supervision and Curriculum Devel., Calif. Assn. Measurement and Evaluation in Guidance, Calif. Assn. Program Evaluation, Calif. Assn. Sch. Psychologists and Psychometrists, Council Exceptional Children, Calif. Personnel and Guidance Assn., So. Counties Women Mgrs. in Edn., Sierra Club. Democrat. Contr. papers to profl. jours. Office: 2350 W Latham Hemet CA 92343

ROWEN, MARSHALL, radiologist; b. Chgo.; s. Harry and Dorothy (Kasnow) R.; A.B. with highest honors in Chemistry (William Cook scholar), U. Ill., Urbana, 1951; M.D. with honors, U. Ill., Chgo., 1954, M.S. in Internal Medicine, 1954; m. Helen Lee Friedman, Apr. 5, 1952; children—Eric, Scott, Mark. Intern, Long Beach (Calif.) VA Hosp., 1955; resident in radiology Los Angeles VA Hosp., 1955-58; practice medicine specializing in radiology, Orange, -Calif., 1960—; chmn. bd. Moran, Rowen and Dorsey, Inc., Radiologists, 1969—; asst. radiologist Los Angeles Children's Hosp., 1958; asso. radiologist Valley Presbyn. Hosp., Van Nuys, Calif., 1960; co-dir. dept. radiology St. Joseph Hosp., Orange, 1961—, v.p. Staff, 1972; dir. dept. radiology Children's Hosp. Orange County, 1964—, chief of staff, 1977-78, now v.p.; asst. clin. prof. radiology U. Calif., Irvine, 1967-70, asso. clin. prof., 1970-72, clin. prof. radiology and pediatrics, 1976, pres. clin. faculty assn., 1980-81. Served to capt. M.C., U.S. Army, 1958-60. Recipient Rea sr. med. prize U. Ill., 1953; diplomate Am. Bd. Radiology. Fellow Am. Coll. Radiology; mem. AMA, Soc. Nuclear Medicine (trustee, 1961-62), Orange County Radiol. Soc. (pres., 1968-69), Calif. Radiol. Soc. (pres. 1978-79), Radiol. Soc. So. Calif. (pres. 1976), Pacific Coast Pediatric Radiologists Assn. (pres., 1971), Soc. Pediatric Radiology, Calif. Med. Assn. (chmn. sect. on radiology 1978-79), Orange County Med. Assn., So. Calif. Soc. Nuclear Medicine, So. Calif. Radiation Therapy Soc., Assn. Advancement Med. Instrumentation, Cardioradiology Soc. So. Calif., Radl. Soc. N. Am., Am. Roentgen Ray Soc., Phi Beta Kappa, Phi Eta Sigma, Omega Beta Phi, Alpha Omega Alpha. Mem. editorial bd. Western Jour. Medicine. contbr. articles to med. jours. Office: 1201 W La Veta Orange CA 92668

ROWERDINK, WILLIAM HENRY, financial executive; b. Rochester, N.Y., Aug. 19, 1919; s. Henry and Ethel (Wilcox) R.; m. Marion E. Shephard, Dec. 18, 1953; children—Jeffrey, Jay. B.S., Syracuse U., 1941. Commd. officer U.S. Air Force, 1941, advanced through grades to col., 1962, ret., 1962; dist. mgr. WestAm. Securities, Santa Ana, Calif.; mgr. M.H. Deckard & Co., Newport Beach, Calif.; mgr. Tital Capital Corp., Newport Beach. Decorated Air medal. Republican. Presbyterian. Clubs: Balboa Bay, Masons (Shriner), Elks. Home: 2607 Windover Dr Corona Del Mar CA 92625 Office: 3822 Campus Dr Suite 128 Newport Beach CA 92660

ROWLAND, EDWIN ROSS, architect, civil engr., govt. ofcl.; b. Logan, Utah, Aug. 18, 1923; s. Thomas Greaves and Zina (Hawkley) R.; B.S. in Civil Engring., U. Utah, 1950; m. Carolyn Shields, Oct. 30, 1948; children—Kathleen Rowland Kalvesmaki, James E., Patrice Lee Pearson. Pvt. practice engring. and gen. contracting, 1951-59; chief engr. fish and game dept. State of Utah, 1959-64; with HUD, Salt Lake City,

1964-67; asst. regional engr. Dept. Health and Human Services (formerly HEW), San Francisco, 1967-70, chief engr. facilities engring., 1970-79, dir. facilities engring. and constrn., San Francisco, 1979—. Scoutmaster, Boy Scouts Am., 1960-65; Sunday sch. tchr. 1st Bapt. Ch., Sunnyvale, Calif., 1967—; mem. exec. com. Am. Bapt. Ch., 1979—; bd. dirs. Am. Bapt. Homes of West, 1969-77. Served with USAAF, 1942-51. Decorated Air medal. Recipient Meritorious Service award State of Utah, 1964, Service award Sec. of HEW, 1972; award U. Wis., 1976; Asso. Gen. Contractors, 1977; registered profl. engr., Mass.; registered land surveyor, Utah. Mem. Nat. Soc. Profl. Engrs., Calif. Soc. Profl. Engrs. Co-author: Design of Timber Bridges, 1950; Construction Management Manual, 1973. Home: 1233 Windimer Dr Los Altos CA 94022 Office: 50 United Nations Plaza San Francisco CA 94102

ROWLANDS, STUART GRAHAM PHILLIP, communications executive, sportscaster; b. Newport Gwent, Wales, Oct. 11, 1942; came to U.S., 1968; s. John Leslie Phillips and Joan Phillips (Parlour) R. Student Monmouth Coll., 1960. Account exec. Vital Publicity, London, 1962-64; dir. pub. relations Ludgate Advt., 1964-68; v.p. Sheldon Saltman & Assocs., Los Angeles, 1968-72; prodn. exec. J.C. Creane Films, Hollywood, Calif., 1972-74; dir. internat. publicity T.W.I., Los Angeles, I.M.G., Cleve., 1974-77; pres. Stuart Rowlands & Assocs., Beverly Hills, Calif., 1977—; lectr. communications, television broadcasting. Mem. Young Conservatives, 1962-68. Mem. Brit. Am. C. of C. Clubs: Monmouthshire Croquet and Lawn Tennis, Monmouthshire Golf; ABC's The Club (Century City). Home: 906 N Doheny Los Angeles CA 90064 Office: 141 El Camino Dr 112 Beverly Hills CA 90212

ROWLEY, ALAN REID, physician; b. Salt Lake City, Aug. 7, 1945; s. Jack and Veda (Duste) Eden; stepson of Robert Norris Rowley; student Weber State Coll., 1964-66; B.S., U. Utah, 1972, M.D. (pediatric honors program), 1976; m. Kiyomi Yamada, Dec. 18, 1968; children—Daniel, Anthony, Monica. Enlisted USAF, 1966, served until 1970; commd. 2d lt. USAF, 1973, advanced through grades to maj., 1980; intern Naval Regional Med. Center, Camp Pendleton, Calif., resident in family practice, 1976-79; chief Family Practice Service, USAF Hosp., Misawa AFB, Japan, 1979-82; chief Family Medicine Clinic, March AFB, Calif., 1982-83; mem. Cassidy Med. Group., Oceanside, Calif. Active, Human Reliability Program, Alcohol and Drug Abuse Rehab. Program; mem. elders quorum presidency, young men's pres. Ch. of Jesus Christ of Latter-day Saints. Armed Forces Health Professions scholar, 1973-76; diplomate Am. Bd. Family Practice; lic. amateur radio operator. Fellow Am. Acad. Family Practice; mem. Nat. Assn. Residents and Interns. Contbr. articles in field to med. jours.; developer self-teaching aid on congestive heart failure in infancy.

ROWLEY, JOHN CHARLES, engr.; b. Grand Rapids, Mich., July 22, 1927; s. Lancelot Charles and Margaret Adell (Creswell) R.; B.Sc., U. Mich., 1945, M.Sc. in Physics, 1950, Ph.D. in Engring. Mechanics, 1957; m. Mary Livingstone McLean, June 18, 1950; children—Wendy Marie, Mikel Jon. Research supr. U. Mich., 1947-50, teaching fellow, 1953-56; with Los Alamos Nat. Lab., 1957—, engr. nuclear rocket propulsion div., 1957-71, advanced drilling research and devel. mgr. energy div., 1971-74, group leader, assoc. div. leader geosci. related research and devel., 1974-77, asst. group leader geothermal drilling tech., 1979—. Mem. Am. Nuclear Soc., AAAS, ASME, Am. Acad. Mechanics, Am. Geophys. Union, Geothermal Resources Council, Tech. Transfer Soc., Soc. Petroleum Engrs., Am. Mgmt. Assn., Sigma Xi. Contbr. articles to profl. jours. Office: PO Box 1663 MS 979 Los Alamos Nat Lab Los Alamos NM 87545

ROY, CHUNILAL, psychiatrist; b. Digboi, India, Jan. 1, 1935; s. Atikay Bandhu and Nirupama (Devi) R.; came to Can., 1967, naturalized, 1972; M.B., B.S., Calcutta (India) Med. Coll., 1959; diploma in psychol. medicine Kings Coll., Newcastle-upon-Tyne, Eng., 1963; m. Elizabeth Ainscow, Apr. 15, 1967; children—Nicholas, Phillip, Charles. Intern, Middlesborough (Eng.) Gen. Hosp., 1960-61; jr. hosp. officer St. Luke's Hosp., Middlesborough, 1961-64, sr. registrar, 1964; sr. hosp. med. officer Parkside Hosp., Macclesfield, Eng., 1964-66; sr. registrar Moorehaven Hosp., Ivybridge, Eng., 1966; reader, head dept. psychiatry Maulana Azad Med. Coll., New Delhi, India, 1966; sr. med. officer Republic of Ireland, County Louth, 1966; sr. psychiatrist Sask. (Can.) Dept. Psychiat. Services, 1967-68, regional dir., Swift Current, 1968-71; pvt. practice medicine, specializing in psychiatry, Regina, Sask., 1971-72; founding dir., med. dir. Regional Psychiat. Centre, Abbotsford, B.C., Can., 1972-82; cons. to prison adminstrs.; hon. lectr. psychology and clin. asst. prof. psychiatry U. B.C.; ex-officio mem. Nat. Adv. Com. on Health Care of Prisoners in Can.; cons. in field. Recipient Merit award Dept. Health, Republic of Ireland, 1966, Can. Penitentiary Service, 1974. Fellow Royal Coll. Psychiatry (Can.), Royal Coll. Psychiatry (Eng.), Royal Soc. Medicine (London) (asso.), Pacific Rim Coll. Psychiatrists (a founder); mem. World Psychiat. Assn., World Fedn. Mental Health, Internat. Council Prison Med. Services (founding sec.-gen. 1977), Can. Med. Assn., Can. Psychiat. Assn., Amnesty Internat., Internat. Acad. Legal Medicine and Social Medicine, Indian Psychiat. Assn. (life), Can. Assn. Profl. Treatment Offenders (founding; dir. 1975), Assn. Physicians and Surgeons who Work in Can. Prisons (founding pres. 1974), Internat. Found. for Tng. in Penitentiary Medicine and Forensic Psychiatry (founding pres. 1980), Australian Acad. Forensic Scis. (corr.). Author: (with D.J. West and F.L. Nichols) Understanding Sexual Attacks, 1978; contbr. articles to profl. jours.; mem. editorial rev. bd. Evaluation, 1977—; asso. editor Internat. Jour. Offender Therapy and Comparative Criminology, 1978—; bd. internat. editors Jour. Internat. Law and Medicine, 1979—. Office: 7778 227th St Langley BC V3A 4P9 Canada

ROY, ERROL GEORGE, rubber company executive; b. Portland, Maine, Dec. 24, 1937; s. George Edward and Vera Margarite (Fayle) R.; m. Doris Vivianne Harlin, Nov. 14, 1938; children—Anita, Monica, Brian. B.S. in Bus. Adminstr., Boston U., 1962; M.B.A. with high distinction, Babson Coll., 1972. Successively div. mgr., prodn. supt., and prodn. mgr., Goodyear Tire & Rubber Co., 1962-72; plant mgr. Bandag, Inc., Chino, Calif., 1973-76; v.p. mfg. Parco, Ontario, Calif., 1977-78; pres. Stillman Seal div. Sargent Industries, Carlsbad, Calif., 1978—. Bd. dirs. Carlsbad Boys and Girls Club, 1981—; mem. Carlsbad C. of C. Served with USNR, 1955-58. Mem. Soc. Mfg. Engrs. (sr.). Republican. Episcopalian. Home: 1734 Havens Point Pl Carlsbad CA 92008 Office: 6020 Avenida Encinas Carlsbad CA 92008

ROY, HAROLD EDWARD, research chemist; b. Stratford, Conn., June 2, 1921; s. Ludger Homer and Meta (Jepsen) R.; B.A., Duke U., 1950; m. Joyce E. Enslin, Oct. 9, 1946 (div. 1975); children—Glenn E., Barbara Anne, Suzanne Elizabeth. Chemist research div. Lockheed Propulsion Co., Redlands, Calif., 1957-61; sec., treas. The Halgene Corp., Riverside, Calif., 1961-63; self-employed chemist, Glendora, Calif., 1963-64; chief engr. propellant devel. Rocket Power, Inc., Mesa, Ariz., 1964-65; cons., Glendora, 1965-66; engring. specialist Northrop Corp., Anaheim, Calif., 1966-69; pres. Argus Tech., Beverly Hills, 1969-70, dir. Harold E. Roy & Assos., Glendora, 1969—. Served to lt. (j.g.) USNR, 1943-46. Mem. Exptl. Aircraft Assn., Am. Ordnance Assn., Am. Inst. Aeros. and Astronautics, Internat. Platform Assn., Acad. Parapsychology and Medicine, Calif. Profl. Hypnotists Assn., World Future Soc. Republican. Mormon. Home: 18853 E Sierra Madre Ave Glendora CA 91740

ROY, WILLIAM GLENN, sociologist, educator; b. Rochester, N.Y., Mar. 22, 1946; s. James Rider and Nona Alice (Monks) R.; m. Alice Madeleine Royer, Apr. 3, 1976; children—Margaret Alice, Joseph Edward. B.A., Emory U., 1968; Ph.D., U. Mich., 1976. Asst. prof. sociology UCLA, 1976—. Woodrow Wilson fellow, 1968; NSF grantee, 1973. Mem. Am. Sociol. Assn., Social Sci. History Assn., Pacific Sociol. Assn. Contbr. articles to profl. jours.

ROYBAL, EDWARD R., congressman; b. Albuquerque, Feb. 10, 1916; student UCLA, Southwestern U., Los Angeles; LL.D., Pacific State U., Claremont Coll. Grad. Sch.; m. Lucille Beserra, Sept. 27, 1940; children—Lucille (Olivarez), Lillian (Rose), Edward R. With Civilian Conservation Corps, 1934-35; social worker, pub. health educator Calif. Tb Assn., then dir. health edn. Los Angeles County Tb and Health Assn., 1942-49; mem. 88th-98th congresses from 25th Dist. Calif., mem. appropriations com., select com. on aging; chmn. subcom. on housing and consumer interests; sec.-treas. Congressional Hispanic Caucus. Mem. Los Angeles City Council, 1949-62, pres. pro tempore, 1961-62. Served with AUS, 1944-45. Recipient Excellence in Pub. Service award Am. Acad. Pediatrics, 1976; vis. Chubb fellow Yale. Mem. Nat. Assn. Latino Elected Ofcls. (pres.), Am. Legion. Democrat. Roman Catholic. Home: Los Angeles CA 90023 Office: Rayburn Office Bldg Washington DC 20515

ROYCE, REV. JAMES E., educator, priest, clinical psychologist; b. Spokane, Wash., Oct. 20, 1914; s. James E. and Lucie Frances (Reilly) R. B.A., Gonzaga U., 1940, M.A., 1941; Ph.D., Loyola U., Chgo., 1945; S.T.L., Alma Coll., Santa Clara U., 1948. Lic. psychologist, Wash. Instr., Gonzaga U., 1940-41; asst. prof. to prof. emeritus Seattle U., 1948—, dir. alcohol studies program, 1973—. Recipient Gov.'s Disting. Service award, 1965; Nat. Assn. Alcoholism Counselors award, 1981. Fellow Am. Psychol. Assn. (co-founder and 1st pres. elect div. on philos. psychology, charter mem. div. on religion and psychology. Roman Catholic. Author: Personality and Mental Health, 1954, rev., 1965; Man and His Nature, 1959; Man and Meaning, 1969; Alcohol Problems and Alcoholism, 1981. Office: Seattle U Seattle WA 98122

ROYCE, WILLIAM FRANCIS, fishery scientist, educator; b. DeBruce, N.Y., Jan. 5, 1916; s. James Seth and Mina (Winner) R.; m. Mary Savage, June 8, 1940; children—James Savage, William Francis III, Andrew Hertzel. B.S., Cornell U., 1937. Ph.D., 1943. Prof., dir. Fisheries Research Inst., U. Wash., Seattle, 1958-68, assoc. dean Coll. Fisheries, 1968-72, prof. Coll. Ocean and Fishery Scis., 1976—; assoc., dir. resource research U.S. Nat. Mar. Marine Fisheries Service, 1972-76; cons. fishery scientist, 1976—. Fellow AAAS, Am. Inst. Fishery Research Biologists, Internat. Acad. Fishery Scientists; mem. Am. Fisheries Soc. (cert.), Am. Inst. Limnology and Oceanography, Am. Inst. Biol. Scis. Clubs: Corinthian Yacht. Author: Introduction to the Fishery Sciences, 1972-75; contbr. articles to profl. jours. Home: 10012 Lake Shore Blvd NE Seattle WA 98125 Office: 10012 Lake Shore Blvd NE Seattle WA 98125

ROYER, CHARLES, mayor; b. Medford, Oreg., Aug. 22, 1939; s. Russell Theodore and Mildred Mae (Hampson) R.; B.A., U. Oreg., 1966; postgrad. Harvard U. and Mass. Inst. Tech., 1969-70; m. Rosanne Gostovich, Oct. 19, 1968; children—Jordan, Suzanne. Polit. reporter sta. KOIN-TV, Portland, Oreg., 1966-68; news analyst sta. KING-TV, Seattle, 1970-77; mayor City of Seattle, 1978—; pres. Nat. League Cities; bd. dirs. U.S. Conf. Mayors; mem. Nat. Conf. Dem. Mayors; del. Dem. Nat. Com.; pres. Japan-Am. Conf. Mayors and C. of C. Pres. Served with U.S. Army, 1961-63. Am. Polit. Sci. Assn. fellow, 1969-70; Washington Journalism Center fellow, 1968; Sigma Delta Chi award, 1976; Edward R. Murrow award, 1976. Democrat. Episcopalian. Office: Mayor's Office 1200 Municipal Bldg 600 4th Ave Seattle WA 98104

ROYLOA, FIRMAN BAREND, design engr.; b. Bandung, Indonesia, July 6, 1947; s. Loa Sooy Chien and Souw Giok Hwa; m. Hedy Cecilia Loa, Dec. 26, 1981. B. Marine Engring. Merchant Marine Acad., Jakarta, Indonesia, 1969; postgrad., Computer Learning Ctr., Los Angeles, 1979. Jr. engr. Nat. Bulk Carriers, N.Y.C., 1971-73, sales exec. power and generating Lindeteves, Indonesia, 1973-76; jr. engr. maintenance div. Alumtreat Inc., Monterey Park, Calif., 1976-79; design engr. research and devel. Peerless Pump, Montebello, Calif., 1979—. Mem. ASME, Computer and Automated Systems Assn. Mfg. Engrs., Pacific Energy Assn. Baptist. Home: 2713 Parco Ave Ontario CA 91761 Office: 1200 Sycamore St Montebello CA 90640

ROYSTON-JAKES, PENNY JANE, educator; b. Lewistown, Mont., Aug. 4, 1948; d. Keith Richard and Alice Jane (McCandless) Royston; student Eastern Mont. Coll., 1966-67; B.S., Mont. State U., 1970; M.Ed., U. Mont., 1981; m. David Earl Jakes, Mar. 15, 1970; children—Wendy Rebecca, Aimee Melissa. Sec., agt. Allstate Ins. Co., Missoula, Mont., 1971-73; tchr. adult edn. Missoula County High Schs., 1978—; tchr. vocat. bus. edn. and computer science Missoula Vocat. Tech. Ctr., 1973—. Mem. Am. Vocat. Assn., Nat. Bus. Edn. Assn., N.W. Adult Edn. Assn., Mont. Bus. Edn., Assn., Mont. Vocat. Assn., Western Bus. Edn. Assn., NEA, Mont. Edn. Assn., Missoula County Humane Soc., Tau Pi Phi, Pi Omega Pi. Republican. Methodist. Home: 3001 Mack Smith Ln Stevensville MT 59870 Office: 909 S Ave W Missoula MT 59801

ROZENDAAL, JAMES WILLARD, accountant; b. Lynnville, Iowa, Mar. 1, 1935; s. John B. and Jerena (Willensen) R.; m. Beverly A. Ford, June 30, 1967; children—Peggy A., Shari L. B.S., N.E. Mo. State U., 1961; M.B.A., U. Ark., 1970. C.P.A., Mo., Ark., Kans., Calif. Asst. prof. Washburn U., Topeka, 1970-72; 1st v.p. Capitol Fed. Savs. & Loan, Topeka, 1972-74; ptnr. Snyder & Rozendaal, C.P.A.s, Bishop, Calif., 1974-75; lectr., vis. assoc. prof. Calif. State U.-Chico, 1976-82; prin. James W. Rozendaal, C.P.A., Chico, 1976-82; mng. ptnr. Rozendaal & Marlais, C.P.A.s, Chico, 1982—. Served to cpl. U.S. Army. 1955-57. Mem. Am. Inst. C.P.A.s, Calif. Soc. C.P.A.s, Acctg. Research Assn., Butte Glenn Tech. Discussion Group. Republican. Club: Lions (Internat. Pres. award 1980, Dist. Gov. award 1980, 82) (Chico). Contbr. articles to profl. jours. Office: Rozendaal & Marlais 1074 East Ave Suite A Chico CA 95926

ROZETT, MARLENE CLAIRE, electronic co. exec.; b. San Francisco, July 20, 1945; d. Lawrence A. and Dorothy R. Harmon; student San Jose State U., 1976-82; m. Stephen M. Rozett, Apr. 7, 1979; 1 dau., Tara Lena. Materials mgr. Ramtex Corp., Sunnyvale, Calif., 1973-74; purchasing mgr. II Industries, Sunnyvale, 1974-75; materials mgr. Exidy, Inc., Mountain View, Calif., 1975-77; sales mgr. Solectron Corp., Sunnyvale, 1977-80; founder, pres., chief exec. officer Zyvex Corp., Santa Clara, Calif., 1980—. Mem. Am. Electronic Assn., Women in Electronics. Republican. Roman Catholic. Office: 2407 Qume Dr San Jose CA 95131

ROZIER, CLAIRE ANTOINE, educator, counselor; b. Tuolumne, Calif., Feb. 14, 1912; d. Alfred William and Mary Elizabeth (Hartman) R. B.S., Immaculate Heart Coll., Los Angeles, 1942; M.S., Creighton U., 1951. Life teaching credential, Calif. Joined Congregation Sisters of the Holy Cross, Roman Catholic Ch., 1930; tchr. Sacred Heart Acad., Ogden, Utah, 1933-34, St. Agnes High Sch., Los Angeles, 1934-35, Our Lady of Lourdes High Sch., Colusa, Calif., 195-38, St. Paul's Sch., Los Angeles, 1938-43; tchr., prin. Judge Meml. High Sch., Salt Lake City, 1943-55; prin. St. Joseph High Sch., Ogden, Utah, 1955-59; tchr., faculty rep. Bishop County High Sch., Los Angeles, 1959-63; tchr. Holy Cross High Sch., Mountain View, Calif., 1963-67; supr. sci. Teaching Sisters of the Holy Cross, 1967-68; tchr., counselor Cathedral High Sch. for Boys, Los Angeles, 1968-74; counselor, sci. tchr. Central Cath. High Sch., Modesto, Calif., 1974-79, dir. counseling, 1979—, counselor, 1979—; sci. tchr. summer schs. Calif. Mus. Sci. and Industry, St. Mary of the Wasatch Coll., Salt Lake City, 1950-63, St. Mary Coll., Notre Dame, Ind., 1963, Oak Ridge Inst. Nuclear Studies, 1961, Radiation Biology Inst., Boston Coll., 1968. Mem. Am. Personnel and Guidance Assn. Democrat.

RUBENSTEIN, LEONARD SAMUEL, creative consultant firm executive, ceramist, painter, sculptor, photographer; b. Rochester, N.Y., Sept. 22, 1918; s. Jacob S. and Zelda H. (Gordon) R.; widowed May 28, 1983; children—Carolinda, Eric, Harley. B.F.A. cum laude, Alfred U., 1939; student Western Reserve, 1938; postgrad. U. Rochester, 1940-41. Creative dir. Henry Hempstead Advt. Agy., Chgo., 1949-55; v.p., exec. art dir. Clinton E. Frank Advt. Agy., Chgo., 1955-63; v.p., nat. creative dir. Foster & Kleiser div. Metromedia, Inc., Los Angeles, 1967-73, v.p. corp. creative cons., Metromedia, Inc., Los Angeles, 1973—; guest lectr. U. Chgo.; instr. Columbia Coll., Chgo.; past. pres. Art Dirs. Club Chgo. (spl. citation); instr. Fashion Inst., Los Angeles; lectr. in field. Mem. Soc. Typographical Arts (past dir.), Am. Craft Council, Inst. Outdoor Advt. (past plans bd.), Los Angeles County Mus. Art, Palos Verdes (Calif.) Art Ctr., Phi Epsilon Pi. Club: Tennis (Palm Springs, Calif.). Lodge: B'nai B'rith. Author: (with Charles Hardison) Outdoor Advertising; contbr. articles in field to profl. publs. One-man show: Calif. Mus. Sci. and Industry, 1970; numerous juried nat. and regional group shows; creator concept for Smithsonian exhibition Images of China: East and West, 1982. Home: 30616 Ganado Dr Rancho Palos Verdes CA 90274 Office: 5746 Sunset Blvd Metromedia Square Los Angeles CA 90028

RUBEY, JOHN ALFRED, entertainment co. exec.; b. Evergreen Park, Ill., Oct. 5, 1951; s. Charles Andrew and Catherine Marie (Whalen) R.; B.S. in Acctg., Regis Coll., 1973; m. Donna M. Holton, Nov. 5, 1977; children—Andrew Joseph. Melissa Erin. Staff auditor Price Waterhouse & Co., Denver, 1973-74; with Feyline Presents, Inc., Englewood, Colo., 1974—, v.p., treas., 1976—. C.P.A., Colo. Mem. Colo. Soc. C.P.A.s, Am. Inst. C.P.A.s. Democrat. Roman Catholic. Home: 1966 S Locust St Denver CO 80224 Office: 2175 S Cherry St Denver CO 80222

RUBIN, GERALD K., social work educator; b. Devils Lake, N.D., Sept. 22, 1932; s. Louis and Ethel Rubin; divorced; children—Brenda, Lee. B.A., U. Minn., 1954; M.S.W., U. Denver, 1958, Ph.D., 1970. Social service investigator City of Mpls., 1954-56; psychiat. social worker Twin City Mental Health Clinic, Mpls., 1958-60; marriage and family counselor Family and Children's Service, Mpls., 1960-63; asst. prof. Jane Addams Grad. Sch. Social Work, U. Ill., 1964-68; chief social service Children's Hosp., Stanford, Calif., 1970-73; assoc. prof. Sch. Social Work, San Diego State U., 1973-76; assoc. prof. social work U. Nev.-Las Vegas, 1976—, also chmn. dept. social work; cons. on family therapy and social work in convalescent hosps. Mem. Nat. Assn. Social Workers, Council on Social Work Edn. Contbr. articles to profl. jours. Office: Dept Social Work Univ Nevada Las Vegas NV 89154

RUBIN, SHELDON, aerospace engineer; b. Chgo., July 19, 1932; s. George and Elsie (Braid) R.; m. Ann Lustgarten, July 3, 1955; children—Geoffrey, Kenneth, Beth. B.S., Calif. Inst. Tech., 1953, M.S., 1954, Ph.D., 1956. Registered profl. engr., Calif. Research engr., office of sound and vibration Lockheed Aircraft Co., Burbank, Calif., 1956-58; sect. head dept. electronic packaging Hughes Aircraft Co., Culver City, Calif., 1958-62; sr. project engr. div. vehicle engring. Aerospace Corp., El Segundo, Calif., 1962—; cons. in field. Recipient outstanding accomplishment award Aerospace Corp., 1979, disting. achievement award, 1981; shuttle flight cert. achievement award NASA, 1981. Mem. AIAA (assoc. fellow), Soc. Automotive Engrs., Am. Nat. Standards Inst. Jewish. Contbr. articles to profl. jours. Office: 2350 E El Segundo Blvd El Segundo CA 90245

RUBINSTEIN, MICHAEL A., physician, educator; b. Wilno, Poland, Nov. 28, 1915; s. Isaac I. and Esther C. (Flemsberg) R.; came to U.S., 1940, naturalized, 1946; Ph.D., U. Wilno, 1938, M.D., U. Wilno Sch. Medicine, 1939; m. Vera Freudmann, Mar. 31, 1948. Intern Maimonides Hosp., Bklyn., 1940-41; resident Columbia Univ., N.Y.C., 1941-42, mem. faculty, 1945-54; fellow in hematology Mt. Sinai Hosp., N.Y.C., 1942-46; hematologist Montefiore Hosp., N.Y.C., 1945-54; fellow Dazian Found. Med. Research, N.Y.C., 1942-46; asso. prof. medicine Loma Linda Univ., Los Angeles, 1954-64; attending physician, hematologist Cedar-Sinai Med. Center, Los Angeles, 1954—; mem. faculty UCLA, 1970—. Recipient sci. exhibits awards AMA, 1948, 64; diplomate Am. Bd. Internal Medicine. Fellow N.Y. Acad. Sci., N.Y. Acad. Medicine, AAAS, Internat. Soc. Hematology (award 1958), ACP; mem. AMA, Soc. Exptl. Biology and Medicine. Contbr. over 100 articles to med. publs.; research, developer techniques in bone marrow aspiration. Home: 803 N Bedford Dr Beverly Hills CA 90210 Office: 435 N Bedford Dr Beverly Hills CA 90210

RUBINSTEIN, SEYMOUR IVAN, software development company executive; b. Bklyn., Apr. 14, 1934; s. Max and Kate (Grenetz) R.; m. Phyllis E. Marmor, June 22, 1966. B.S., Bklyn. Coll., 1965. Cons. psychology, Bklyn., 1972-74; v.p. research and devel. Profata Internat. Corp., Rohnert Park, Calif., 1974-75; dir. comml. systems Varian Data Machines, San Francisco, 1975-77; dir. mktg. IMSAI Mfg. Corp., San Leandro, Calif., 1977-78; pres., founder, chief exec. officer Micropro Internat. Corp., San Rafael, Calif., 1978—. Dir. Osborne Computer Corp. Served with Signal Corps, U.S. Army, 1958-59. Mem. Assn. Data Processing Service Orgns. (dir. 19-). Office: Micropro Internat Corp 33 San Pablo St San Rafael CA 94903

RUBINSTEIN, SOL, statistician, computer scientist; b. N.Y.C., June 23, 1935; s. Hyman and Anna (Magidson) R.; m. Joan Susan Sindel (div.); m. 2d Paula S. Thomas, Aug. 27, 1981; children—Parker, Aaron Workman. B.S., CCNY, 1956; student Harvard U., 1956-57; M.A., Brandeis U., 1959; Ph.C., U. Wash., 1977. Vice-pres. entry level systems component Computer Resources Corp., Kennewick, Wash., 1983—; pres. CMS Services, Inc., Richland, Wash., 1983—; microcomputer cons. NSF fellow, 1956. Mem. Am. Statis. Assn., Inst. Math. Stats., Am. Math. Soc., Phi Beta Kappa. Home: 303 Gage Blvd Apt 311 Richland WA 99352 Office: 802 George Washington Way Richland WA 99352

RUBY, BERTHA M., rehab. services adminstr.; b. Ont., Can., July 9, 1937; d. Aaron and Laura (Schwartzentruber) R.; B.S. in Sociology, Ariz. State U., 1969; M.Rehab. Adminstrn., U. San Francisco, 1978. Correctional program officer Adobe Mountain Reform Sch., Phoenix, 1972-74; dir. adult services Glenhaven, Inc., Glendale, Ariz., 1974-77, adminstrv. asst., 1977-78; dir. program services United Cerebral Palsy Central Ariz., Phoenix, 1978-82. Mem. Nat. Rehab. Assn.

RUBY, CHARLES LEROY, lawyer, civic leader; b. Carthage, Ind., Dec. 28, 1900; s. Edgar Valentine and Mary Emma (Butler) R.; certificate Ball State U., 1921-22; A.B., Central Normal Coll., 1924, LL.B., 1926, B.S., 1931; M.A., Stanford, 1929; J.D., Pacific Coll. of Law, 1931; Ph.D., Olympic U., 1933; m. Rachael Elizabeth Martindale, Aug. 30, 1925; children—Phyllis Arline (Mrs. Norman Braskat), Charles L., Martin Dale. Prin., Pine Village (Ind.) High Sch., 1923-25; Glenwood (Ind.) Pub. Schs., 1925-26; tchr. El Centro (Calif.) Pub. Sch., 1926-27, Central (Calif.) Union High Sch., 1927-29; prof. law Fullerton Coll., 1929-66; prof. edn. Armstrong Coll., summer 1935, Central Normal Coll., summers 1929-33; admitted to Ind. bar, 1926, U.S. Supreme Ct. bar, 1970; pres. Ret. Service Vol. Program, North Orange County, Calif., 1973-76, 83-84; dir. North Orange County Vol. Bur., Fullerton Sr.

Citizens Task Force. Life trustee, Continuing Learning Experiences program Calif. State U., Fullerton, hon. chmn. fund com. Gerontology Bldg; founder, dir. Fullerton Public Forum, 1929-39; founder Elks Nat. Found.; pres. Fullerton Rotary, 1939-40, hon. mem., 1983—; mem. U.S. Assay Commn., 1968; mem. Orange County Democratic Central Com., 1962-78; bd. dirs. Fullerton Sr. Multi-purpose Ctr., 1981—; bd. dirs. Orange County Sr. Citizens Adv. Council. Recipient Medal of Merit, Am. Numis. Assn., 1954; Spl. Commendation, Calif. State Assembly, 1966, Calif. State Senate, 1978. Mem. Calif. (life, pres. So. sect. 1962-63, treas. 1964-65, dir. 1956-65), Orange County (pres. 1953-55) tchrs. assns., NEA (life), Ind. Bar Assn., Stanford U. Law Soc., Calif. State Council Edn., Am. Numismatic Assn. (gov. 1951-53, life adv. bd.), Ind. Bar Assn. (hon. life), Calif. Bus. Educators Assn. (hon. life), Calif. Assn. Univ. Profs., Pacific S.W. Bus. Law Assn. (pres. 1969-70, life), Numismatic Assn. So. Calif. (life, pres. 1961), Indpls. Coin Club (hon. life), Los Angeles Coin Club (hon. life), U.S. Supreme Ct. Hist. Soc., Calif. Town Hall, North Orange County Mus. Assn. (life, benefactor dir.), Stanford U. Alumni Assn., Old Timers Assay Commn. Methodist. Clubs: Elks, Fullerton Jr. Coll. Vets. (hon. life). Contbr. articles in field to profl. jours. Home: 308 N Marwood Ave Fullerton CA 92632

RUBY, ROBERT HOLMES, physician, surgeon; b. Mabton, Wash., Apr. 23, 1921; s. Henry Ward and Myrtle (Holmes) R.; m. Leila Jeanne Henderson, July 11, 1953; children—Edna, Henry, Robert, Mary. B.S., Whitworth Coll., 1943; M.D., Washington U., 1945. Diplomate Am. Bd. Abdominal Surgery. Intern, Woman's Hosp., Detroit, 1945-46; resident St. Louis County Hosp., 1949-53; chief med. service Pine Ridge (S.D.) Indian Agy., 1953-54; pvt. practice medicine specializing in surgery, Moses Lake, Wash., 1955—; mem. staff Samaritan Hosp., Moses Lake, 1956—, Ephrata (Wash.) Columbia Basin Hosp., 1962—, Big Bend Community Coll., 1984—. Chmn. bd. trustees Moses Lake Pub. Library, 1959-71; chmn. bd. dirs. Adam East Mus., Moses Lake, 1960-65; chmn. Wash. Gov.'s Conf. on Libraries, 1968; mem. adv. com. Upward Bound, Columbia Basin, 1968; mem. adv. com. State Library Commn. on Title III, Library Services and Constrn. Act., 1967-70; chmn. Wash. State Library Trustees Assn., 1967-69; mem. bd. dirs. Grant County Hist. Soc., 1962-72. Served with USAAF, 1946-47, with USPHS, 1953-54. Recipient Northwest Author award, 1966, Pacific Northwest Bookseller's award, 1966, Cert. of Recognition Gov.'s Festival of Arts, 1967, 71, 83, Disting. Author of History award, 1983. Fellow ACS; mem. AMA, Wash. State Med. Assn., Grant County Med. Assn. Author: The Oglala Sioux, 1955; Half Sun on the Columbia, 1963; The Spokane Indians, 1970; The Cayuse Indians, 1972; Ferryboats on the Columbia River, 1974; The Chinook Indians, 1975; Myron Ells and the Puget Sound Indians, 1975; Indians of the Pacific Northwest, 1981; A Guide to the Indian Tribes of the Pacific Northwest, 1984. Office: 1022 Ivy St Moses Lake WA 98837

RUCH, WILLIAM VAUGHN, editor; b. Allentown, Pa., Sept. 29, 1937; s. Weston H. and Dorothy D. (Daubert) R.; B.A., Moravian Coll., 1959; M.A. in Communication, Syracuse U., 1969; M.B.A., Fairleigh Dickinson U., 1972; Ph.D., Rensselaer Poly. Inst., 1980; J.D., Western State U., 1983. Reporter, Call-Chronicle Newspapers, Allentown, Pa., 1959-60; tchr. English conversation Jonan Sr. High Sch., Matsuyama, Japan, 1960-62; asst. editor Dixie News, Am. Can Co., Easton, Pa., 1964-65; fin. editor Pa. Power & Light Co., Allentown, 1967-69, sales promotion writer, 1965-66, advt. asst., 1966-67; tech. writer and editor Space Tech. Center, Gen. Electric Co., King of Prussia, Pa., 1969; asst. editor Bell System Tech. Jour., Bell Telephone Labs., Murray Hill, N.J., 1969-71; field rep. N.W. Ayers & Sons, Inc., N.Y.C., 1972-73; asst. prof. bus. communications Fairleigh Dickinson U., Madison, N.J., 1974-75, Bloomsburg (Pa.) State Coll., 1975-76; lectr. Sch. Bus. and Public Adminstrn., Calif. State U., Sacramento, 1977-79; assoc. prof. bus. writing Coll. Bus. Adminstrn., San Diego (Calif.) 1979-83; editor Small Bus. Report, Monterey, Calif., 1983—. State U., 1979—. Mem. Acad. Mgmt., Am. Bus. Communication Assn., Internat. Platform Assn., Internat. Assn. Bus. Communicators. Republican. Mem. United Ch. of Christ. Home: 661 Mc Clellan Ave Monterey CA 93940 Office: Small Business Report 497 Lighthouse Ave Monterey CA 93940

RUCKER, GEORGIA THOMAS, postmaster; b. Plum, Tex., Sept. 16, 1942; d. Curtis Douglas and Frankie Mae (Brown) Thomas; certificate indsl. mgmt. UCLA, 1972; M.B.A., Calif. State U., Dominguez Hills, 1978; m. Clarence Rucker, Apr. 19, 1965. With U.S. Postal Service, Los Angeles, 1962-77, dist. and hdqrs. assignments, 1977-79, postmaster, Lawndale, Calif., 1979—. Bd. dirs. A. M. Buktenica Ctr., Lloyd Tenn Mother Continuation High Sch.; com. chmn. Lawndale YMCA, 1982; 1st v.p. Sugar Ray Youth Found. Founders Guild, 1980-82. Recipient Suprs. award U.S. Postal Service, 1977, 78. Mem. Nat. Assn. Postmasters (U.S. nat. conv. entertainment chmn. 1980), Nat. Council Negro Women (Achiever 1979, 80), Federally Employed Women (pres. Los Angeles chpt. 1980-82), Nat. Fedn. Bus. and Profl. Women, (pres. Lawndale chpt. 1982), Los Angeles County Assn. Postmasters (1st v.p. Calif. chpt.), Los Angeles League Women Voters, Lawndale Bus. and Profl. Women's Club (Woman of Achievement 1981), Lawndale C. of C., UCLA Alumni Assn., Calif. State Dominguez Alumni Assn. Democrat. Club: Soroptimist (1st v.p. 1982) (Lawndale, Calif.). Office: 4320 W Compton Blvd Lawndale CA 90260

RUCKER, THOMAS DOUGLAS, purchasing exec.; b. Ottumwa, Iowa, Aug. 30, 1926; s. Everett Henry and Harriett Mary (Evans) R.; A.B., Loyola U., 1951; postgrad. St. Patrick's Coll., 1950-52; m. Rita Mary Rommelfanger, Apr. 18, 1953; children—David, Theresa, Martin, Paul. Asst. purchasing agt. Radio TV Supply, Los Angeles, 1952-53; buyer Consol. Western Steel div. U.S. Steel, Commerce, Calif., 1953-64, S.W. Welding & Mfg. Co., Alhambra, Calif., 1964-70; dir. purchasing Southwestern Engring., Commerce, Calif., 1970—. Served with USAAF, 1945-46. Home: 10642 Abisko Dr Whittier CA 90604 Office: 5701 S Eastern Ave Suite 300 Commerce CA 90040

RUCKER, WILLIAM WAYNE, county official; b. Maywood, Calif., Mar. 29, 1952; s. James Cunningham and Doris Virginia (Shreve) R.; m. Colleen Marilyn Patrick, May 25, 1974; children—Patrick James, Derek Wayne. A.A., Palomar Coll., 1973, cert. water tech., 1977, cert. mid-mgmt., 1979; B.B.A. summa cum laude, Nat. U., San Diego, 1980. Registered constrn. insp., cert. water treatment operator III, Calif. Custodian/groundsman Vista (Calif.) Unified Sch. Dist., 1969-73; engring. technician San Marcos County (Calif.) Water Dist., 1973-78, asst. mgr., 1982-83; gen. mgr. 29 Palms County (Calif.) Water Dist., 1983—; devel./engring. coordinator Rincon Del Diablo Mcpl. Water Dist., Escondidio, Calif., 1978-82; mem. water tech. adv. com. Palomar Coll., 1980-83. Pres. bd. dirs. San Marcos Cemetery Dist., 1978-83. Mem. Am. Water Works Assn. (cert. water distbn. operator III 1979), Calif. Spl. Dists. Assn., Assn. Calif. Water Agys. Republican. Club: Rotary (29 Palms). Home: 5580 Abronia Ave Twentynine Palms CA 92277 Office: 6544 Adobe Rd Twentynine Palms CA 92277

RUCKER, WINFRED RAY, educator; b. Stamford, Tex., Apr. 13, 1920; s. John L. and Lou Jean (Rea) R.; B.A., Tex. Christian U., 1946, M.A., 1947; Ed.D., Harvard U., 1952; m. Norma Ruth Johnston, Jan. 31, 1947. Instr. speech and edn. Tex. Christian U., 1946-47, coach varsity forensic squad, 1946-47; instr. Air U., Maxwell AFB, Ala., 1948-49; grad. asst. edn. Harvard U., 1949-50; supervising tchr. campus elem. sch. State U. Tchrs. Coll., Geneseo, N.Y., 1950-52; asst., asso. prof. edn. East Tex. State Coll., Commerce, 1952-56; chmn. div. elem. edn. U. Ariz.; dean Nat. Coll. Edn., Evanston, Ill., 1958-61, Sch. Edn., East Tex. State U., 1961-67; dean Sch. Human Behavior, U.S. Internat. U., San Diego, 1967-74, prof., 1967—. Served with U.S. Army, 1941-45. Mem. NEA, Calif. Tchrs. Assn. Author: Curriculum Development in the Elementary School, 1960; contbg. author: Human Values and Natural Science, 1970, The Human Values Series, 6 vols., 1967; (with V. Clyde Arnspiger and Arthur J. Brodbeck) Human Values in Education, 1969; Values and Human Behavior, 1978; contbr. articles on edn. to profl. jours. Home: 17863 Mirasol Dr San Diego CA 92128 Office: 10455 Pomerado Rd San Diego CA 92131

RUCKER-HUGES, WAUDIUR ELIZABETH, educator, administrator; b. Washington, July 30, 1947; d. Jeter and Jeannette Belle (Toomer) Rucker; B.S., D.C. Tchrs. Coll., 1969; M.A. in Edn., U. Redlands, 1974; 1 child, Teliece E.M. Tchr. history J.W. North High Sch., Riverside, Calif., 1969-76, dean students, 1976-79; lectr. Afro-Am. history Riverside City Coll., 1972-74; exec. dir. Inland Area Opportunities Industrialization Center, Riverside, 1979—; cons. in field. Commr. Community relations City of Riverside, 1972-76; sec. State Inter-Group Relations Educators, 1976-77; pres. Coalition of Urban Peoples, 1978-80; lay mem. Riverside County Jud. Selection Com., 1978—; Calif. State Bar ct. referee, 1979—. NSF fellow, 1970-71; Center for leadership Edn. grantee, 1978. Mem. Exec. Dirs. Assn. Opportunities Industrialization Ctrs. of Am. (nat. sec.), NAACP, Urban league, Riverside Women's Polit. Caucus, Nat. Women's Polit. Caucus, Exec. Dirs. Assn., Nat. Council Negro Women, Delta Kappa Gamma. Mem. C.M.E. Ch. Club: The Thurs. Group. Author: Canine Capers, 1976; A Book to Match our Diversity, 1980. Home: 8907 Delano Dr Riverside CA 92503 Office: 2222 Kansas Ave Riverside CA 92507

RUCKMAN, ROBERT LEONARD, chamber of commerce executive; b. Hollywood, Calif., Nov. 28, 1931; s. Leonard LeRoy and Carolyn Kathrine (Spraetz) R.; m. Doris Elizibeth Ferguson, June 24, 1953; children—Janice, Karen. Student Glendale (Calif.) Coll., 1950-52; UCLA Extension, 1957-58, Inst. Orgn. Mgmt., 1979—, San Jose State U. Field rep. Calif. State C. of C., 1961-67; mgr. Woodland Hills C. of C., 1967-70; circulation mgr. and sales Canoga Park Chronicle, 1970-73; mgr. So. Calif. Liquor Dealers Assn., 1973-80; exec. mgr. Canoga Park C. of C., 1980—. Served with AUS, 1952-55. Mem. Calif. Assn. C. of C. Execs. (planning com.). Methodist. Office: 6507 Fallbrook Ave Canoga Park CA 91307

RUDAVSKY, ALEXANDER BOHDAN, civil engineering educator; b. Poland, Jan. 17, 1925; came to U.S., 1949, naturalized, 1955; s. Leo and Zenovia (Orlov) R.; m. Juanita Jean Enga, Nov. 5, 1955; 1 dau., Natica. B.S., U. Minn., 1953, M.S., 1956; Dr. Ing., Franzius Inst. Hydraulic Lab., Hannover, Ger., 1966. Civil engr. Justin & Courtney, Phila., 1956-57, Iran, 1957-58; asst. prof. civil engring. San Jose (Calif.) State U., 1960-64, assoc. prof., 1964-75, prof., 1975—; pres., dir., owner Hydro Research Sci., Santa Clara, Calif., 1964—; cons., speaker in field. ASCE Freeman traveling scholar, Europe, 1959. Mem. U.S. Com. Large Dams, Internat. Assn. Hydraulic Research, ASCE. Author numerous model studies, reports, profl. papers. Office: 3334 Victor Ct Santa Clara CA 95050

RUDD, ELDON, congressman; b. Camp Verde, Ariz.; B.A., Ariz. State U.; J.D., U. Ariz.; m. Ann Merritt. Admitted to Ariz. bar, U.S. Supreme Ct. bar, 1953; spl. agt. FBI, 1950-70, diplomatic assignments in Mex., Central Am., Argentina; mem. 95th-97th Congresses from 4th Ariz. Dist., mem. House Com. on Appropriations; mem. Gov.'s Adv. Commn. on Intergovtl. Affairs, 1975-76. Mem. Maricopa County (Ariz.) Bd. Suprs., 1972-76; bd. dirs. Ariz.-Mex. Commn., 1972-76; mem. Scottsdale Sister City Commn., 1973-76. Served in USMC, 1942-46. Mem. Fed. Bar Assn. (pres. Ariz. chpt. 1976), Ariz. Bar Assn., Maricopa County Bar Assns. Republican. Home: Scottsdale AZ Office: 1110 Longworth House Office Bldg Washington DC 20515

RUDD, MERRILL W., accountant; b. Parker, Idaho, Sept. 8, 1935; s. Melvin John and Lila (Burr) R.; student Utah State U., 1953-54; Asso. Degree, Ricks Coll., 1959; B.A., Brigham Young U., 1960, postgrad., 1961-62; m. J'Lene Siepert, Dec. 19, 1958; children—Julie, Marlon, Mark, Melvin, Mitchell, Marshall. Staff acct. Peat Marwick Mitchell & Co., C.P.A.s, Provo, Utah, 1960-62, sr. acct., Salt Lake City, 1962-65; pvt. practice as Merrill W. Rudd, C.P.A., Rexburg, Idaho, 1965-75; ptnr. Rudd & DaBell, C.P.A.s, Rexburg, 1975-77, Rudd, DaBell & Hill, 1977-80, Rudd, DaBell, Hill & Call, 1981—; ptnr. Big Hole Investments, Nedrud Investments, Moirama Energy Resources, Inc., Ltd. Capital Investments; v.p. Rebco, Inc.; owner, operator Orange Julius Chain Stores; mem. faculty Brigham Young U. Ricks Coll. Eve. Sch., 1970—; bishop 24th ward Ricks Coll. C.P.A., Idaho. Mem. Am. Inst. C.P.A.s, Rexburg Estate Planning Council. Clubs: Pres.'s of Ricks Coll.; Rexburg Rotary (treas. 1977-79). Home: 209 Apache St Rexburg ID 83440 Office: 124 E Main St Rexburg ID 83440

RUDE, GARY GORDON, educational administrator; b. Seattle, Apr. 10, 1943; s. Gordon Ross and Marianne (Gleason) R.; m. Kathy Ann Baumunk, Mar. 29, 1980; children—Kristi, Scott, Heather, Charles. B.Ed., Seattle U., 1969; M.Ed., Western Wash. U., 1973; postgrad. in edn. Seattle U., 1983—. Cert. elem. and secondary tchr., elem. and secondary prin., Wash. Tchr., North Thurston Sch. Dist., Lacey, Wash., 1969-72, Lake Washington Sch. Dist., Kirkland, Wash., 1972-76, Aberdeen (Wash.) Sch. Dist., 1976-78; prin. Eatonville (Wash.) Sch. Dist., 1978-82, Lake Stevens (Wash.) Sch. Dist., 1982—, Mt. Pilchuck Elem. Sch., 1982—; condr. conduct effectiveness workshops for sch.-dist. personnel; dir. various ednl. coms.; co-chmn. devel. and implementation of cross-aged micro-computer program for disadvantaged kindergarten students, 1982-83. Active advocacy group for handicapped adults, Aberdeen, sch. levy election campaigns, drama groups. Served with U.S. Army, 1963-65. Fed. career edn. grantee, 1982. Mem. Nat. Assn. Supervision and Curriculum Devel., Wash. State Assn. Supervision and Curriculum Devel., Nat. Assn. Elem. Sch. Prins., Wash. State Assn. Elem. Sch. Prins., Phi Delta Kappa. Home: 2624 118th Dr NE Lake Stevens WA 98258 Office: 12806 20th St NE Lake Stevens WA 98258

RUDNICK, LINDA JANET, lawyer; b. Portland, Oreg., Dec. 15, 1950; d. William Joseph and Janet Clara (Huber) R.; m. Michael Royce Free, Jan. 1, 1982. B.S., Portland State U., 1974; J.D., Lewis and Clark Coll., 1977. Bar: Oreg. 1977. Sole practice, Portland, 1978—. Mem. Oreg. Bar Assn., Am. Trial Lawyers Assn., Oreg. Trial Lawyers Assn., Multnomah County Bar Assn. Office: 520 SW Yamhill Suite 1001 Portland OR 97204

RUDNIKOFF, ISADORE, b. Montreal, Can., Feb. 19, 1909; s. Max and Sophie (Izenson) R.; B.S., Coll. City N.Y., 1929, M.D., N.Y. U., 1933; m. Sarah Robowsky, Aug. 19, 1933; children—Carol Joan, Barbara, Robert William. Intern, Lebanon Hosp., N.Y.C., 1933-36; practice medicine, Yonkers, N.Y., 1936—; dir. medicine, pres. med. bd. chief internal medicine, attending cardiologist Yonkers Gen. Hosp.; attending physician Yonkers Profl. Hosp.; active staff Boswell Meml. Hosp., Sun City, Ariz.; dir. medicine Valley View Community Hosp., Youngstown, Ariz. Med. adv. com. to Mayor; med. adviser Selective Service System; awarded Presdl. medal for services. Diplomate Am. Bd. Internal Medicine. Fellow A.C.P., N.Y. Acad. Medicine, N.Y. Diabetes Assn., Am. Geriatrics Soc., Westchester Acad. Medicine; mem. Am. Soc. Internal Medicine, Internat. Soc. Internal Medicine, World Med. Assn. (founder), Yonkers Acad. Medicine (past pres.), Am. Heart Assn., Royal Soc. Medicine (affiliate), AAAS, Smithsonian Assos. (charter), Phi Beta Kappa. Mem. B'nai B'rith. Home: 6126 E Charter Oak Rd Scottsdale AZ 85254 Office: Maricopa County Gen Hosp Phoenix AZ 85008

RUDOFF, ALVIN, sociology educator; b. Bridgeport, Conn., Dec. 10, 1921; s. Isadore and Ralie (Beckman) R.; m. Belle Hellenberg, June 4, 1949. B.A., U. So. Calif., 1949, M.A., 1960; Ph.D., U. Calif.-Berkeley, 1964. Parole agt., counsellor, research coordinator Calif. Dept. Corrections, Los Angeles and Stockton, Calif., 1952-62; mem. faculty San Jose (Calif.) State. U., 1962—, prof. sociology, 1969—, chmn. sociology dept., 1970-74; vis. prof. Chinese U., Hong Kong, 1972-73; research assoc. Space Colonies and Search for Extraterrestrial Intelligence, NASA, 1976-78; lectr. U. Md., Asian div., Japan, 1981-82; cons. in field. Served with USMC, 1940-46, with USMCR, 1948-54. Recipient Outstanding Presentation award Police Community Relations Leadership Tng. Program, 1972; San Jose State Found. grantee, 1963-67, NIMH grantee, 1966-68. Mem. Am. Sociol. Assn., Pacific Sociol. Assn., Soc. for Study Social Problems, AAAS, Phi Kappa Phi, Alpha Kappa Delta. Author: The Spectrum of Criminology, 1983; Work Furlough and the County Jail, 1975; contbr. numerous articles to profl. publs. Office: San Jose State U Sociology Dept San Jose CA 95192

RUDOFF, CAROL DIANA, publisher, association executive; b. N.Y.C., Nov. 11, 1941; d. Benjamin and Esther (Krivoshey) Tenenbaum; m. Arnold G. Rudoff, Sept. 4, 1966; children—Neil, James. B.A., Stanford U., 1963; M.A., UCLA, 1966. Speech and hearing specialist Los Angeles City Schs., 1965-67; mgr. Spectrum Fin. Cos., 1976-79; owner, pub. Prologue Publs., 1976—; pres. Am. Allergy Assn., Menlo Park, Calif., 1978—. Author: Soundings, 1977; The Poetic Gourmet, 1977; Images, 1977; The Allergy Baker, 1980; The Allergy Gourmet, 1983. Office: PO Box 7273 Menlo Park CA 94025

RUDOLPH, ELAINE TAYLOR, executive search and financial placement executive; b. Milw., Nov. 25, 1926; d. Harry Arthur and Florence Ann (Randall) Taylor; m. Gordon Edmund Rudolph, Aug. 9, 1947; 1 dau., Nancy Jean Rudolph Wood. B.A., U. Wis., 1950; postgrad. U. So. Calif., 1961. Registered employment cons. Personnel dir. Knee Action div. A.O. Smith, Milw., polit. candidate cons., greater Los Angeles area, 1964-72; gen. mgr., v.p., Bookkeepers Unltd., Los Angeles, 1972-79; pres. Accts. Plus and Bookkeepers Plus Agy., Los Angeles, 1979—; profl. devel. dir. Los Angeles chpt. Nat. Assn. Accts.; vice chmn. exhibitor relations So. Calif. Bus. Show. Chmn. Crime Prevention Bd., Sierra Madra, Calif., 1982—; mayor, mem. city council, Sierra Madre, 1978-82; mem. pub. safety state com. League of Calif. Cities, 1978-82, Los Angeles County Sanitation Bd., 1981-82, del. So. Calif. Div. League of Calif. Cities, 1980-82; alt. del. San Gabriel Cities Assn., 1979-81; del. Ind. Cities, 1978-79; parks and recreation commr. Sierra Madre, 1977-78; del., alt., del. Republican State Central Com., 1956—, mem. 61st Rep. County Central Com., 1974-83, alt. mem. 42d Rep. County Central Com., 1983—; mem. adv. coms. for Assemblyman Richard Mountjoy, Congressman John Rousselot, Senator Bill Richardson; town chmn. Sierra Madre Republicans; bd. dirs. Sierra Madre Hosp. Mem. Nat. Assn. Accts., Century City C. of C. (speakers bur., membership com.), Western Los Angeles Regional C. of C. (fin. council), Town Hall, Nat. Assn. Female Execs. (network dir.), AAUW (pres. Arcadia br. 1971). Presbyterian. Author: So You Are Looking for a Job?, 1980, So You've Been Promoted?, 1981. Home: 1935 Liliano Dr Sierra Madre CA 91024 Office: 1100 Glendon #1417 Los Angeles CA 90024

RUDOLPH, HELEN PATRICIA, computer analyst; b. Tularosa, N.Mex., May 31, 1945; d. Frank Bill and Dosha Olive (Campbell) Sheehan; m. James A. Rudolph, Oct. 8, 1971. B.A., U. No. Colo., 1967; M.S., U. So. Calif., 1979. With Fed. Electric Corp./ITT, 1967—, data analyst, Vandenberg AFB, Calif., 1967-69, lead analyst, 1969-71, systems engr., 1971-73, tech. staff, metric integrated processing system, 1973-76, supr. software devel., 1976-79, mgr. software devel. projects, 1979—; instr. George Washington U.; employer-based counselor, pvt. sector involvement project. Treas., Rape Crisis Ctr. Lompoc, 1974-76. Recipient Fine Arts award Bank of Am., Lompoc, 1963; Community Career Devel. Council award, 1981. Mem. IEEE, ACM, Nat. Mgmt. Assn., Alpha Gamma Delta. Republican. Club: Soroptimist (pres. Lompoc 1979-81).

RUDOLPH, PHILIP MARTIN, educator, hypnotherapist; b. Seattle, May 14, 1926; s. Henry William and Obella Sophia (Lanier) R.; m. Pauline Lillian Cruickshank, June 6, 1950; children—Pamela K. Rudolph Bukowski, Pene J. Rudolph Baxter, Philip Martin, Patrick, Pegeen, Paula Rudolph Van Pelt. B.A. in Edn., Seattle U., 1950; M.A. in Psychology, Pepperdine U., 1980; M. Hypnosis, Calif. Coll. Hypnosis, 1981; postgrad. U. Calif.-Irvine, 1981—. Enlisted U.S. Marine Corps, 1944, advanced through grades to sgt. maj., 1967, lt., 1978; ret., 1978; instr. Santa Ana Coll., 1978-81; vice prin. tchr., counselor Barbara Sterling Sch. for Handicapped Child, Stanton, Calif., 1978—; cons. hypnotherapy; mem. Community Youth Council Crisis Intervention. Scoutmaster, com. chmn. Boy Scouts Am., 1957-60, 72-75; crisis counselor, 1978—; pres. Little League, 1966-69; mem. Presdl. Task Force, 1981-83, U.S. Senatorial Club, 1982-83. Decorated Air Medal, Purple Heart, Navy Commendation Medal; recipient Sikorsky Lifesaving award, 1970. Mem. Assn. Retarded Citizens (pres.), Council Exceptional Children, Orton Dyslexia Soc., Calif. Assn. Neurologically Handicapped, Tchrs. of English to Speakers Another Lang., Assn. Supervision and Curriculum Devel. Republican. Roman Catholic. Clubs: Ret. Officers, Fleet Res., Vets. for War. Contbr. articles to profl. jours. Home: 1722 Mitchell St Apt 109 Tustin CA 92680 Office: 7791 Cerritos Ave Stanton CA 90680

RUDY, RICHARD KENT, physician; b. Rochester, N.Y., Aug. 9, 1947; A.B., Georgetown U., 1969, M.D., 1974; M.P.H., U. Hawaii, 1981. Research asst. NIMH, 1970; intern USPHS Hosp., San Francisco, 1974; family practice clinician USPHS Clinic, Honolulu, 1975-78; clin. instr. family practice and community health John Burns Sch. Medicine, U. Hawaii, 1976—, clin. instr. Sch. Pub. Health, 1976-81; med. dir. life health program Rehab. Hosp. Pacific, 1977-78; dir. in-service programs USPHS Clinic, 1976-78. Diplomate Am. Bd. Family Practice. Fellow Royal Soc. Health; mem. Am. Pub. Health Assn., Am. Coll. Preventive Medicine, Assn. Mil. Surgeons U.S., Commd. Officers Assn. USPHS, Underseas Med. Soc., Aerospace Med. Soc., Coast Guard Officers Assn. (dir., exec. com. 1978), Hawaii Pacific Gerontol. Soc.

RUDZKI, GEORGE JERZY, consulting company executive, electrochemist; b. Cracow, Poland, Jan. 19, 1924; came to U.S., 1969, naturalized, 1974; s. Zygmunt and Ina (Rudzka) Bukowski. B.S. in Chemistry, Poly. Inst., Gliwice, Poland, 1950, M.S. in Electrochemistry, 1952. Mem. exec. com. for protection against corrosion Polish Acad. Sci., Warsaw, and ofcl. Polish State Com. Econ. Planning, Warsaw, 1958-68; research and devel. specialist, tech. dir. Polish metal-finishing industry, 1965-68; founder, pres. Internat. Forecasting Inst., San Diego, 1970—, Metal Finishing Systems, San Diego, 1971—; adj. prof. Sci. Research Inst. Precision Mechanics, Warsaw, Poland, 1962-65; mem. team of experts Polish Chief Tech. Orgn., 1957-68; mem. team for corrosion problems Polish Com. on Sci. and Techniques, 1958-68; lectr. U. Calif.-San Diego, U.S. Internat. U., San Diego State U., 1970-72. Served to capt. Polish Mil., World War II. Mem. Assn. Mechanic Engrs. and Technicians Chem. Industry. Republican. Author books, including: Surface Finishing Systems (Metal and Nonmetal Finishing Systems), 1983; contbr. numerous articles to profl. jours. Office: 1028 W Brookes Ave San Diego CA 92103

RUE, ARNOLD IRWIN, lawyer, mayor; b. Champion, Alta., Can., Apr. 24, 1911; s. Hans and Ella (Williams) R.; m. Eileen Faulconer, Feb. 14, 1937; children—Ethelyn Everhart, Ellen Scher. B.S., U. Calif.-

Berkeley, 1934; grad. Humphreys Coll. Law Sch., 1958. Bar: Calif. 1961; C.P.A., Calif. Acct., John F. Forbes & Co., C.P.A.s, San Francisco, 1934-42; ptnr. Rue, Hutchison, DeGregori, Gormsen & Co., Stockton, Calif., 1946-77; mayor City of Stockton, 1977-79, 81—, mem. City Council, 1962—. Served to lt. comdr. USN, 1942-46. Mem. Calif. Bar Assn., Calif. Assn. C.P.A.s. Democrat. Home: 1725 W Alpine St Stockton CA 95204 Office: 1401 N Hunter St Stockton CA 95202

RUEBUSH, BRITTON KENNETH, psychologist, educator, researcher; b. Deming, N.Mex. Jan. 30, 1929; s. Britton Norman and Bertie Vesta (Hamilton) R.; m. Avis LaNelle, Sept. 28, 1951; children—Kimberly Lynn, Susan Leslie, Britton Kenneth. B.A. in Psychology with great distinction, Stanford U., 1956; M.S. in Psychology, Yale U., 1957, Ph.D. in Clin. and Child Psychology, 1960. Cert. psychologist, N.Mex. Research asst. Yale U., 1956-58, USPHS trainee, clin. psychology intern Child Study Ctr., 1958-59, instr. in psychology, 1959-60; asst. prof. psychology and child devel. U. Minn., Mpls., 1960-63, assoc. prof., 1963-67, dir. Child Devel. Clinic, Inst. Child Devel., 1961-67; assoc. prof. psychiatry and psychology U. N.Mex., Albuquerque, 1967-74, prof., 1974—, exec. dir. Albuquerque Child Guidance Ctr. dept. psychiatry, 1967—; bd. dirs. Psychiat. Outpatient Centers Am. Served to staff sgt. USAF, 1951-54. Mem. Am. Psychol. Assn., Soc. Research in Child Devel., Am. Orthopsychiat. Assn. Author: (with others) Anxiety in Elementary School Children, 1960, German edit., 1971; contbr. articles to profl. publs.

RUETZ, JULIANNE MARGARET, journalism educator, consultant; b. Los Angeles, Apr. 6, 1929; d. Paul and Margaret Emma (Zinke) Brueggemann; m. Edward Joseph Ruetz, Sept. 30, 1950 (div.); children—Jeffrey Edward, Lynn Karen Ruetz Hertwig. M.A., U. Denver, 1969; Ph.B., Marquette U., 1950. Tchr. speech, English, Sch. Dist. 6, Littleton, Colo., 1961-71; instr. Arapahoe Community Coll., Littleton, 1971-74, adminstr., 1974-79; media services dir. corp. pub. relations dept. Mountain Bell Co., Denver, 1979-81; asst. prof. pub. relations dept. tech. journalism Colo. State U., Fort Collins, 1982—; cons., freelancer in field. Bd. dirs. Colo. Larimer County Unit, Am. Cancer Soc. Mem. Pub. Relations Soc. Am., Internat. Soc. Bus. Communicators, Assn. Edn. in Journalism and Mass Communication. Democrat. Unitarian. Home: 1705 Heatheridge Rd D 302 Fort Collins CO 80526 Office: Tech Journalism Dept C2299 Clark Colo State U Fort Collins CO 80523

RUFF, ANDREA LOUISE, dietitian, educator; b. Los Angeles, July 9, 1949; d. Orville Andrew and Kaye Louise Ruff. B.S. in Dietetics, Calif. State U.-Northridge, 1972; postgrad. U. Calif.-Berkeley, 1972-73; registered dietitian. Clin. dietitian, adminstrv. dietitian Hollywood Presbyterian Med. Ctr., Los Angeles, 1973-78, chief clin. dietitian, 1979—; instr. family and consumer studies; clin. instr. Calif. State U.-Los Angeles, 1974—. Mem. Soc. Nutrition Edn., Am. Dietetic Assn., Calif. Dietetic Assn. (speaker's burs., publs. adv. group), Los Angeles Dietetic Assn., Am. Hosp. Assn., Clin. Nutrition Mgmt. Interest Group. Author: A Guide to Protein Controlled Diets for Patients, 1977; A Guide to Protein Controlled Diets for Dietitians, 1977. Office: 1300 N Vermont Ave Los Angeles CA 90027

RUFF, GEORGE ROBERT, advertising agency executive; b. Salt Lake City, Nov. 5, 1918; s. George Alma and Mary (Jensen) R.; m. Betty Clark, Aug. 28, 1943; children—Alan Robert, Lynn William, Roger Joseph, Robin, Susan. A.B. magna cum laude, Brigham Young U., 1943; postgrad. U. Utah, 1946-50. Account exec. Stevens & Wallis Advt. Agy., Salt Lake City, 1941-42; account exec. David W. Evans & Assocs. Advt. Agy., Salt Lake City, 1943-53, v.p., 1953-65, sr. v.p., 1965-68, vice chmn. bd., 1968-72, exec. v.p., chmn. exec. com., 1972-74; corp. pres. David E. Evans, Inc., Salt Lake City, 1974—; v.p., dir. Evans Supply, Inc., 1953-73; dir. Evans/Lowe & Stevens, Inc., Atlanta; dir. Evans/Bartholomew, Inc., Denver; chmn. bd. Evans, Pacific, Inc., Seattle and Portland, Oreg.; dir. David W. Evans Calif., San Francisco, Evans/Weinberg, Inc., Los Angeles; dir. Mobile Billboards, Inc., 1981—; lectr. communications Brigham Young U., 1965-66; lectr. mktg. U. Utah, 1947-54, adj. prof. communications, 1980-82. Vice chmn. Red Butte dist. Boy Scouts Am., 1964-65; mem. exec. bd. Great Salt Lake council Boy Scouts Am., 1982—; chmn., exec. com. Friends of Brigham Young U. Library, 1963-67; pres. Brigham Young U. Alumni Assn., 1959-61; mem. nat. adv. council Brigham Young U., 1978—; trustee Ballet West, 1982—; bd. dirs. Hansen Planetarium; vice chmn. indsl. and econ. subcom. Salt Lake City C. of C., 1982—. Served with USAAF, 1942-45. Decorated Air medal with three oak leaf clusters; recipient Presdl. medal for extraordinary service Brigham Young U., 1969, Meritorious Service award in Mass Communications, 1977. Mem. Utah Advt. Fedn., Am. Mktg. Assn., Pub. Relations Soc. Am. (accredited; pres. chpt. 1970, chmn. N. Pacific dist. 1972-73, dist. bd. 1979, del. nat. assembly 1980-83), Utah Mfrs. Assn. Republican. Mormon. Clubs: University, Timpanogos, Kiwanis. Co-chmn. editorial com. Instr. mag., 1960-71, contbr. articles to profl. jours. Home: 658 17th Ave Salt Lake City UT 84105 Office: David W Evans Inc 110 Social Hall Ave Salt Lake City UT 84111

RUFF, RONALD MARK, neuropsychologist; b. San Jose, Calif., May 28, 1949; s. Richard Siegmund Willfried and Carola Paula (Lindross) R.; B.A., Calif. State U., Stanislaus, 1971; Lizentiat phil. I, U. Zurich (Switzerland), 1974, Dr. phil. I, 1978; postgrad. Oxford (Eng.) U.; m. Karen Catlin, Feb. 14, 1970; children—David, Saralyn. Clin. neuropsychologist Neurol. Univ. Clinic, Zurich, 1974-78; vis. scholar Stanford (Calif.) U., 1978-80; asst. prof. psychiatry U. Calif. Med. Sch., San Diego, 1980—, head neuropsychol. unit, 1980—, asst. prof. neurosurgery, 1982—, project dir. NIH funded research, 1980. Grantee, Swiss Nat. Sci. Found., 1978-80. Mem. Internat. Neuropsychology Soc., Am. Psychol. Assn., European Neurosci. Soc., Sigma Xi. Author research papers in field. Office: U Calif Gifford MHC 3427 4th Ave San Diego CA 92103

RUFOLO, ANTHONY MICHAEL, economist, educator; b. Newark, Aug. 9, 1948; s. Philip and Marie Antoinette (Petrillo) R.; m. Patricia Jeanne Lickorai, Aug. 29, 1970; children—Amy, Laura, Christine. B.S. in Econs, MIT, 1970; Ph.D., UCLA 1975. Economist, sr. economist Fed. Res. Bank, Phila., 1974-80; lectr. Temple U., Phila., 1976-79; lectr. U. Pa., Phila., 1978-80; assoc. prof. grad. program urban studies and planning Portland (Oreg.) State U., 1980—. Chmn. subcom Fin. Pub. Works Adv. Com., Washington County, 1981—; mem. organizing com. Econ. Devel. League, Oreg., 1982; mem. Oreg. Gov.'s Council Econ. Advs., 1983—. George T. Lees Meml. scholar City of Belleville (N.J.), 1966. Mem. Am. Econ. Assn. Contbr. articles to profl. jours. Home: 13255 SW Saratoga Ln Beaverton OR 97005 Office: PO Box 751 Grad Urban Studies Planning Portland State U Portland OR 97207

RUIZ, JOSE ALEJANDRO, constrn. co. exec.; b. Lima, Peru, Feb. 20, 1948; s. Pedro Alejandro and Estela Aida (Correa) R.; B. Mech. and Elec. Engring., Universidad Nacional de Ingenieria, Lima, Peru, 1968; B.S in E.E., Bucknell U., 1970; M.S. in E.E., Stanford U., 1974; m. Teresita Jesus Marquez, June 17, 1971; children—Noe Alfredo, Saul Efrain. Project engr. Amdhal Corp., Sunnyvale, Calif., 1972-74; owner, mgr. Reliable Packaging, San Jose, Calif., 1974-75; land officer Techo Inc., Watsonville, Calif., 1975-77, project devel. officer, 1977-78, chief exec. officer, 1978—; cons. Appropriate Tech. Internat. Cons., Capitola, Calif. Mem. adv. com. on tech. edn. U. Calif., Santa Cruz, 1978; bd. dirs. El Pajaro Community Devel. Corp., 1980—; bd. dirs., sec. Santa Cruz Community Credit Union, Inc., 1979—; bd. dirs., treas. South County Commn. on Alcoholism, 1979—; bd. dirs. Watsonville Area Devel. Corp., 1982—. Stanford U. fellow, 1970-74. Mem. IEEE, Nat. Soc. Profl. Engrs., Alexander Hamilton Inst., Soc. for Internat. Devel., Nat. Assn. Housing and Redevel. Ofcls., Calif. Coalition for Rural Housing, Internat. Assn. for Housing Sci. Home: PO Box 1133 Watsonville CA 95077 Office: 10 Alexander St Watsonville CA 95076

RUMBAUGH, MELVIN DALE, research geneticist, plant breeder, statistician; b. Pella, Iowa, Sept. 13, 1929; s. Herbert Robert and Lena (Schakel) R.; m. Annabelle Eis; children—Alan Lee, Rosemary Ann, Steven Thomas. B.S., Central Coll., 1951; M.S., U. Nebr., 1953, Ph.D., 1958. Asst. prof. agronomy Colo. State U., 1958-59; prof. plant sci. and stats S.D. State U., 1959-77; research geneticist Agrl. Research Service, U.S. Dept. Agr., Logan, Utah, 1977—; cons. plant breeding and range improvement. Served with U.S. Army, 1953-55. Mem. Crop Sci. Soc. Am., Am. Soc. Agronomy, Range Sci. Soc. Am. Republican. Contbr. numerous articles to profl. jours. Home: 1480 N 1525 E Logan UT 84321 Office: Utah State U Crops Research Lab UMC 63 Logan UT 84322

RUMGAY, JUDITH ANNE, educator, b. Oregon City, Oreg., July 14, 1941; d. Lewis Lamont and Ernestine (Anderson) R.; B.A. in Edn., Marylhurst Coll., 1963; postgrad. LaVerne U., 1977-80, Portland State U., 1981—. Tchr., Portland Public Schs., 1963-66, U.S. Dependent Schs., Germany, 1966-69; tchr. David Douglas Schs., Portland, 1969-71, coordinator elementary gifted edn., reading devel. specialist, 1977—; tchr. Oreg. Episcopal Sch., Portland, 1971-77. Mem. Internat. Reading Assn., Oreg. Reading Assn., Oreg. Assn. Talented and Gifted, Assn. Childhood Edn. Internat., Assn. Supervision and Curriculum Devel., Oreg. Council Tchrs. English, Oreg. Assn. Supervision and Curriculum Devel., Nat. Council Tchrs. English, Western Drafters (pres. 1981—, editor Wagon Master 1975—), Delta Kappa Gamma. Home: 13731 SE Stark St Portland OR 97233 Office: 145 SE 117th St Portland OR 97216

RUMMEL, ROBERT WILAND, aviation consultant; b. Dakota, Ill., Aug. 4, 1915; s. William Howard and Dora Elizabeth (Ely) R.; m. Marjorie B. Cox, Sept. 30, 1939; children—Linda, Sharon, Susan, Robert, Diana. Aero. Engr., Curtiss Wright Tech. Inst., 1934. With Hughes Aircraft Co., 1935, Lockheed Aircraft Corp. and Aero. Engring. Corp., 1936, Nat. Aircraft Co., 1937; chief engr. Rearwin Aircraft & Engines, Inc., 1937; successively chief engr., v.p. engring., v.p. planning and research, v.p. tech. devel. TWA, Inc., 1943-78; pres. Robert W. Rummel Assocs., Inc., Mesa, Ariz., 1978—; mem. aeros. adv. com. NASA, 1978-80, adv. council, 1981-82; mem. program evaluation and devel. com. White House, 1965-67; conf. speaker. Recipient Disting. Pub. Service medal NASA, 1979; cert. of merit FAA, 1982; Disting. Service cert. NRC, 1982. Fellow Soc. Automotive Engrs. (chmn. Kansas City sect. 1946), AIAA (treas. 1971-72); mem. Air Transport Assn., Internat. Air Transport Assn., Nat. Acad. Engring., NRC. Clubs: N.Y. Yacht, Saugatuck Harbor Yacht (Westport, Conn.), Masons, Shriners. Contbr. articles to tech. jours. Home and Office: PO Box 7330 Mesa AZ 85206

RUMMERFIELD, WALTER GLEN, clergyman; b. Protection, Kans., Nov. 14, 1911; s. Walter and Clara Zora (Bachman) R.; B.S., Cramwell Research Inst., 1956; Th.D., Toledo Bible Coll. and Sem., 1979; Ph.D., St. John's U., 1981; m. Grace King, July 12, 1936; children—Judith Ann, Michael Ray. Asst. supt. Am. Nat. Ins., Kansas City, Mo. and Peoria, Ill., 1937-38; agt. Nat. Life and Accident Ins. Co., Amarillo, Tex., 1941-46; gen. agt. Am. United, Amarillo, 1946-47; asst. mgr. Prudential Ins. Co., Amarillo, 1947-49, Sunday Sch. supt. Christian Ch., Amarillo, 1947-53; human relations cons., 1953-64; minister City Temple, Los Angeles, 1959-77, City Temple Christian Ch., Adelanto, Calif., 1977-81; archbishop, pres. Calif. Christian Univ., Los Angeles, 1971-77, Adelanto, 1977—; dir. City Ch. Univ. Truth, 1961-81. Mem. Mayor Yorty's Community Counsel, 1967-71. Served with USN, 1943-45. Decorated Purple Heart. Mem. V.F.W., Am. Legion. Republican. Clubs: Masons, Shriners. Author: Psychology of Religion Applied to Everday Living, 1960. Home: 17865 Adelanto Rd Adelanto CA 92301 Office: 18761 Bellflower St Adelanto CA 92301

RUNDELL, SHARON JEAN, educator, writer; b. Portland, Oreg., Jan. 16, 1946; d. William A. and Emma White; m. Dean Everett Rundell, Dec. 10, 1977; 1 son, Daniel Dale. B.A. in English, Portland State Coll., 1968; M.A.T. in English, Portland State U., 1973. Cert. lang. arts tchr., grades 5-12, Oreg. Tchr. English, Rainier (Oreg.) High Sch., 1968—, head dept. English, 1969-82, adv. yearbook, 1980—; mem. textbook adoption com. Oreg. Dept. Edn., 1981-82. Lectr., Grange, 1974-77. Recipient 1st place in instrumental music Oreg. Grange Conv., 1982. Mem. NEA, N.W. Oreg. Edn. Assn. (pres. area 1976-77), Rainier Edn. Assn. (pres. 1970, 77), Nat. Council Tchrs. English, Delta Kappa Gamma. Republican. Baptist. Contbr. short stories to lit. jours. Home: Route 3 Box 3351 Rainier OR 97048 Office: PO Box 498 Rainier OR 97048

RUNDQUIST, TIMOTHY LYNN, architect; b. Des Moines, Mar. 31, 1948; s. Delbert Harding and B. (Kachel) R.; B.Arch. (C. F. Bowers award), Iowa State U., 1971; m. Ann Christine Norgaard, July 1, 1972; children—Owen Wesley, Erin Rose. Sr. architect Bovay Engrs., Spokane, Wash., 1974-76; prin. Rundquist & Assos., Architects/Planners, Spokane, 1976-82; pres. Rundquist & Hard, P.C., Spokane, 1983—. Mem. Spokane Transit Commn., 1978-81, chmn. ops. com., 1979-81. Cert. Nat. Council Archtl. Registration Bds.; registered profl. architect, Wash., Wyo., Idaho, Mont. Mem. Soc. Am. Registered Architects, Constrn. Specifications Inst., Nat. Trust for Historic Preservation. Republican. Methodist. Club: Studebaker Drivers (chpt. pres. 1977-81). Home: W 608 19 Ave Spokane WA 99203 Office: N 10 Post St Spokane WA 99201

RUNGLIN, ARNOLD WALTER (ROGNLIEN), mfrs. rep.; b. Roland, Iowa, Sept. 19, 1912; s. Joseph B. and Walnette (Wierson) Rognlien; B.S., Iowa State Coll., 1935; m. Esther Lawrence, Nov. 2, 1942; children—Bruce, David, Julie. With Firestone Tire & Rubber Co., Akron, Ohio, 1935-42; founder A. Walt Runglin Co., Inc., Mfrs. Rep., Los Angeles, 1945, pres., 1945-76, chmn., 1977—; pres. Western Icee, Los Angeles, 1966-76, chmn. bd., 1977—; chmn. bd. Cardillo Travel Systems, Los Angeles, 1973—, pres., 1954-73. Mem. Republican Statesmen, Los Angeles, 1976—. Served to lt. (s.g.) USN, 1942-45. Mem. Affiliated Automotive Reps., Mfrs. Agts. Nat. Assn., Automotive Parts and Accessories Assn. Lutheran. Clubs: Bel Air Country, (Los Angeles); Springs Country (Rancho Mirage, Calif.); Los Angeles Athletic. Author: America's Newest Profession, 1976. Home: 515 Ocean Ave Santa Monica CA 90402 Office: 5710 Hannum Ave Culver City CA 90230

RUNNING RABBIT (KEVIN F. REDSTAR), painter, printmaker; b. Lodge Grass, Mont., Oct. 9, 1943. Student Inst. Am. Indian Art, 1962-65, San Francisco Art Inst., 1965-67, Mont. State U., 1968-69; B.A., Eastern Mont. Coll., 1972. Works exhibited in permanent collections: Heard Mus., Phoenix, No. Plains Mus., Browning, Mont., Inst. Am. Indian Art Mus., Santa Fe, Denver Art Mus., Chenyang Nat. Art Mus., Liaoning, China; commd. mural Crow Tribal Office, Crow Agy., Mont.; group shows: N. Mex. Mus. Fine Art, Santa Fe, 1965, Wheelwright Ceremonial Art Mus., Santa Fe, 1978, Okla. Mus. Art (author catalogue), 1978, Natural History Mus., Denver, Peking Exhibit of Am. Western Art (author catalogue), 1981; many others; chmn. Crow/No. Cheyenne Fine Arts Alliance, Ashland, Mont., 1974; art cons. Crow Tribe Central Edn. Crow Agy., 1974-75; instr. art, Lodge Grass, 1973-74, Am. Indian Art, Santa Fe, 1975-76. Recipient hon. mention Heard Mus. Ann. Indian Art Show, 1964; Gov.'s trophy Scottsdale Nat. Indian Art Exhibit, 1965; 1st place Central Wash. State Soll. Art Exhibit, Ellensberg, 1974. Office: Louis Newman Gallery 32 N Beverly Dr Beverly Hills CA 90210*

RUNYAN, S. H. (HAL), state senator; b. Clinton, Ind., Sept. 6, 1916; s. Samuel Edward and Mabel Esther (Hopkins) R.; student public schs., Clinton; m. Evelyn Margaret Hart, Dec. 30, 1946. Vocalist, 1932-41; commd. 2d lt. USAAF, 1941, advanced through grades to col., 1966; pilot, staff officer, comdr.; ret., 1969; mem. Ariz. Senate, 1970—, majority leader, 1979-80, chmn. appropriations com.; mem. Clearinghouse of Fed. Elections Commn., 1974—; chmn. ethics and elections com. Nat. Conf. State Legislatures. Bd. dirs. Westside United Fund. Decorated D.F.C. with 3 oak leaf clusters, Legion of Merit, Air medal with 6 oak leaf clusters, Commendation medal with oak leaf cluster. Mem. Am. Legion, VFW. Republican. Methodist. Clubs: Masons; Rotary. *

RUNYON, RICHARD PORTER, author, publisher; b. N.Y.C., June 1, 1925; s. Harold Remsen and Fleeta (Richardson) R.; A.B., Drew U., 1950; M.S., Yale U., 1952, Ph.D. (Sheffield sci. fellow, 1953), 1954; m. Lois Ann Lesinger, Sept. 28, 1947; children—Amy, Richard, Nancy, Thomas, Maribeth. Research asso. George Washington U., 1954; asst. prof. to prof. C.W. Post Coll., 1955-59, chmn. dept. psychology, 1955-67, dean of sci., 1970-72; pres. Osborne-Richardson Pub. Co., 1983—; author: (with L. Rocks) The Energy Crisis, 1972; Winning with Statistics, 1976; (with A. Haber) Fundamentals of Psychology, 3d edition, 1983, Fundamentals of Behavioral Statistics, 4th edition, 1980, How Numbers Lie, 1981. Energy advisor to Rep. Senatorial com., 1973; Served with U.S. Army, 1943-46. Recipient various research grants. Democrat. Home and Office: 11455 E Speedway Tucson AZ 85710

RUNYON, STEVEN CROWELL, univ. adminstr.; b. San Rafael, Calif., June 20, 1946; s. Charles A. and Katherine C. (Pease) R.; B.A. in Econs. (Calif. state scholar), U. San Francisco, 1971, postgrad., 1978—; Radio and TV, San Francisco State U., 1976; m. Lynna Lim, Mar. 9, 1974. Radio producer KGO, San Francisco, 1965-68; engr., announcer Sta. KSFR/KSAN, San Francisco, 1966-68; publicist Kolmar Assos./Chuck Barris Prodns., San Francisco, 1970; instructional media technician U. San Francisco, 1968-72; technician, archivist, mgr. Wurster, Bernardi & Emmons, San Francisco, 1972-73, projectionist So. Pacific R.R., San Francisco, 1974; broadcast ops. engr. KPEN/KIOI/KIQI, San Francisco, 1968-74, public and community affairs program producer, 1971-74, AM transmitter engr., 1974; lectr. communication arts, U. San Francisco, 1974—, gen. mgr. KUSF-FM, 1974—, dir. mass media studies program, 1975—, acting chmn. communication arts dept., 1976; TV historian; producer, engr., cons. radio and TV programs. Judge San Francisco Internat. Film Festival, 1976, 79, 80, 81, 82, 83, Calif. State High Sch. Speech Championships, 1976; public info. com. San Francisco Heart Assn., 1978—, Robert L. Biben award; project safe adv. bd. San Francisco Police Dept., 1979—; vol. reader Broadcast Services for Blind, 1981. Grantee Calif. Council Humanities in Public Policy, Rockefeller Found., Father Spieler Meml. Trust, NSF; recipient cert. of merit for documentary radio series Peninsula Press Club, 1979; Diploma of Honor, Internat. Robert Stolz Soc., 1981; lic. 1st class radiotelephone operator FCC. Mem. Soc. Broadcast Engrs., Broadcast Edn. Assn., Western Edn. Soc. Telecommunications, Assn. for Edn. in Journalism and Mass Communication, AAUP, Edn. and Tng. Panel Audio Inds. Assn. Recorded Sound Collections, Internat. Communication Assn., Com. Ethics in Public Affairs Broadcasting. Club: Press of San Francisco. Author: A Study of the Don Lee Broadcasting System's Television Activities, 1930-1941, 1976; Educational Broadcast Management Bibliography, 1974; contbr. articles to profl. jours. Office: 2130 Fulton St San Francisco CA 94117

RUOPP, FREDERICK JOHN, investment counselor; b. Chgo., Apr. 15, 1930; s. Frederick Otto and Evelyn Charlotte (Walker) R.; B.S. in Banking and Fin. with honors, U. Ill., 1952; M.B.A. in Fin., Northwestern U., 1957; m. Joyce Marie Bowker, Sept. 15, 1956; children—Frederick John, Christopher James. Trust officer First Nat. Bank Chgo., 1954-61; sr. security analyst Occidental Life Ins. Co., Los Angeles, 1961-69; mgr. family accounts Lehman Bros., N.Y.C., 1969-70; pres. Chelsea Mgmt. Co., Los Angeles, 1970—; mem. fin. com. Century Nat. Ins. Co. Bd. govs. Thomas Aquinas Coll. Served with arty. U.S. Army, 1952-54. Mem. N.Y. Soc. Security Analysts, Los Angeles Soc. Fin. Analysts, Inst. Chartered Fin. Analysts, Pepperdine Assos. Clubs: Calif.; Oak Tree Country. Office: 523 W Sixth St Los Angeles CA 90014

RUPERT, CAROLA G., museum director; b. Washington, Jan. 2, 1954; d. Jack Burns and Shirley Ann (Orcutt) Rupert. B.A. in history cum laude, Bryn Mawr Coll., 1976; M.A., U. Del., 1978, Cert. in Mus. Studies, 1978. Personnel mgmt. trainee Naval Material Command, Arlington, Va., 1972-76; teaching asst. dept. history, U. Del., Newark, 1976-77; asst. curator/exhibit specialist Hist. Soc. Del., Wilmington, 1977-78; dir. Macon County Mus. Complex, Decatur, Ill., 1978-81; dir. Kern County Mus., Bakersfield, Calif., 1981—; tchr. mus. studies course U. Calif.-Santa Barbara Extension, 1982; advisor Kern County Heritage Commn., Historic Records Commn. Mem. Arts Council of Kern and Cunningham Art Gallery; county co-chmn. United Way, 1981, 82; chmn. steering com. Calif. State Bakersfield Co-op Program, 1982-83; bd. dirs. Mgmt. Council, 1983-84. Hagley fellow Eleutherian Mills-Hagley Found., 1977-78; Bryn Mawr alumnae regional scholar, 1972-76. Mem. Nat. Trust for Hist. Preservation, Am. Assn. Mus., Am. Assn. for State and Local History. Unitarian Universalist. Home: 2517 Alturas Dr Bakersfield CA 93305 Office: 3801 Chester Ave Bakersfield CA 93301

RUPERT, PAUL RIDDER, systems engineer; b. Los Angeles, Oct. 30, 1939; s. Harold Monroe and Malinda Anna (Ridder) R.; B.S. in Aero. and Astronautical Engring., U. Okla., 1961; M.S. in Aeros., Calif. Inst. Tech., 1962; m. Viviane Claude Tatin, Apr. 17, 1962; children—Emily, Suzanne, Juliette. Field test engr. N. Am. Rockwell, Cape Kennedy, Fla., 1962-67, test condr. Apollo program, 1967-69; prin. investigator attitude reference systems Rockwell Internat., Downey, Calif., 1969-72, supr. shuttle systems integration, 1972-74; systems engr. Argus/Shiva Lasers, Lawrence Livermore (Calif.) Nat. Lab., 1978-81; engring. math. instr. Brevard Engring. Coll., 1963-65. Recipient Rockwell outstanding engr. award, 1973. Mem. AIAA, Tau Beta Pi, Sigma Tau. Republican. Presbyterian. Contbr. papers to profl. jours. and symposia. Home: 7900 Tesla Rd Livermore CA 94550 Office: PO Box 5508 Livermore CA 94550

RUPNICK, WALTER JOHN, hotel and motel exec.; b. Chgo., Nov. 30, 1921; s. John Harold and Florentine (Jercin) R.; student LaSalle Extension U., Fla. Profl. Hotel-Motel Acad.; children—Carol Dian, Walter John. Pres., chmn. bd. Rupnick's Inc., owners Wally's Imperial Inns, also hotels, motels, apts. and resorts, San Diego, 1972—. Served with USNR, 1942-45. Mem. San Diego C. of C. Roman Catholic. Clubs: Lions, Toastmasters. Address: 1775 Diamond St Suite 219 San Diego CA 92109

RUPP, SIGRID LORENZEN, architect; b. Bremerhaven, Ger., Jan. 3, 1943; came to U.S., 1953, naturalized, 1959; d. Harry Wilhelm and Mary Sophie (Gernert) Lorenzen; m. Steven Rupp, June 8, 1963 (div.). B.Arch., U. Calif.-Berkeley, 1966. Lic. architect, Calif., Tex., Utah,

Colo., Ariz. Assoc., Spencer Assocs., Palo Alto, Calif., 1971-76; founder, prin. Sigrid Lorenzen Rupp/Architects, Palo Alto, 1976-82; pres. SLR/Architects Inc., Palo Alto, Calif., 1982—; chairperson archtl. rev. bd. City of Palo Alto, 1975-77. Mem. AIA, Constrn. Specifications Inst. Office: 321 Lytton Ave Palo Alto CA 94301

RUSACK, ROBERT CLAFLIN, bishop; b. Worcester, Mass., June 16, 1926; s. Roy Leonard and Dorothy (Claflin) R.; B.A., Hobart Coll., 1946, D.D., 1970; priest-scholar, St. Augustine's Coll., Canterbury, Eng., 1957-58; S.T.D., Gen. Theol. Sem., 1965; m. Janice Morrison Overfield, June 26, 1951; children—Rebecca Morrison, Geoffrey Claflin. Ordained deacon, priest Episcopal Ch., 1951; vicar in Deer Lodge and Philipsburg, Mont., 1951-57; rector in Santa Monica, Calif., 1958-64; suffragan bishop Los Angeles, P.E. Ch., 1964-72, bishop coadjutor of Los Angeles, 1973-74, bishop of Los Angeles, 1974—. Pres., Los Angeles City Mission Soc., 1964—. Bd. dirs. Episcopal Home for Aged, Alhambra, Calif., 1964, Los Angeles World Affairs Council, 1974—, Neighborhood Youth Assn., 1965—, Seaman's Ch. Inst., San Pedro, Calif., 1964—; bd. dirs., pres. ex officio Gooden Home for Alcoholics; chmn. bd. trustees Bloy Episcopal Sch. Theology, Claremont, Calif.; hon. chmn. bd. Hosp. Good Samaritan, Los Angeles; chmn., trustee Harvard Sch., North Hollywood, Calif.; trustee Gen. Theol. Sem., Occidental Coll., Los Angeles; chmn. St. Paul's Cathedral Corp., Los Angeles, 1962—. Clubs: Los Angeles Country, California. Home: 13828 Sunset Blvd Pacific Palisades CA 90272 Office: PO Box 2164 Los Angeles CA 90051 also 1220 W 4th St Los Angeles CA 90051

RUSH, JEAN COCHRAN, painter, educator, researcher; b. Bloomington, Ill., Nov. 21, 1933; d. Gilbert E. and Florence M. (Scott) Cochran; m. Andrew W. Rush, Apr. 18, 1957 (div.); children—Benjamin E., Samuel C., Joseph H., Margaret R. B.F.A., Ill. Wesleyan U., 1955; M.F.A., U. Iowa, 1958; Ph.D., U. Ariz., 1974. Pvt. tchr. art, Tucson, 1958-70; ednl. researcher U. Ariz., 1970-71, lectr. in art, 1971-75, asst. prof. art, 1975-80, assoc. prof., 1980—, coordinator art edn. program, 1978—; one-woman shows include: Chuck Winter Gallery, Tucson, 1967; group shows include: Ariz. State Fair, Phoenix, 1960 (First prize in oil painting), S.W. Prints and Drawings, Mus. Fine Arts, Dallas, 1961, Ariz. Women's Caucus For Art, Phoenix, 1979; represented in permanent collections: Tucson Mus. Art, Mus. Fine Arts, Dallas; cons. art edn. Mem. Am. Ednl. Research Assn., Am. Psychol. Assn., Coll. Art Assn., Nat. Art Edn. Assn. (pacific regional v.p.'s award 1981), AAUP, Phi Kappa Phi. Contbr. articles to profl. jours.; co-editor Studies in Art Edn., 1981-83, sr. editor, 1983—; editorial cons. Rev. of Research in Visual Arts Edn., Jour. Aesthetic Edn. Office: Dept Art U Ariz Tucson AZ 85721

RUSH, STEVEN RAYMOND, business executive; b. Tacoma, Mar. 30, 1953; s. Raymond Samuel and Beverly (Warner) R. Student U. Colo., 1974-76, U. Miami (Fla.), 1976. Pres., Liberty Ambulance Service, Seattle, 1971-74; owner, mgr. At Home Auto Tune-Up, Whittier, Calif., 1977-80; pres. S.R. Rush Advt., San Diego, 1980-81; pres., chief exec. officer FirstWorld of San Francisco, Inc., 1981—; chmn. bd. Computer Brokers, Sausalito, Calif., 1983—; gen. ptnr. Franchise Connection, Sausalito; franchise devel. mgr. BYTE inds., Inc., lectr. computer system design, Marin County, Calif. Mem. Inst. Mgmt. Cons. Club: Cuyamaca (San Diego). Contbr. articles to profl. jours. Home: 12 Anchorage St Sausalito CA 94965 Office: FirstWorld of San Francisco Inc Schoonmaker Point Sausalito CA 94965

RUSHDOONY, HAIG ARA, educator; b. Kingsburg, Calif., May 22, 1925; s. Y.K. and Rose V. Rushdoony; m. Vula Pavlidou, Oct. 8, 1982; children—Jonathan H., James A.; stepchildren—Karen L. Krouscas, James A. Krouscas. A.B., U. San Francisco, 1949, M.A., 1953; Ed.D., U. Calif.-Berkeley, 1961. Tchr./adminstr. San Francisco Unified Sch. Dist., 1949-61; prof. edn. Calif. State Coll., Stanislaus, 1961—; cons. sch. dists., county offices, state dept. Pres. United Way Stanislaus Area, 1977-78; trustee United Way Calif., 1977-78. Served with U.S. Army, 1943-46. Tchr. Corps Fed. grantee 1978; Innovative program grantee 1971-72; recipient Disting. Leadership in Geographic Edn. award, 1975. Mem. AAUP, Internat. Platform Assn., Nat. Council. Geog. Edn., Nat. Council. Social Studies, Internat. Reading Assn. Republican. Methodist. Author: The Language of Maps, 1983; contbr. articles to profl. jours.

RUSHEN, RUTH L., corrections administrator; b. Laurel, Miss., Dec. 19, 1924; d. Samuel and Violet Harris; B.S. in Social Studies, Clark Coll., 1945; M.P.A., U. So. Calif., 1971; m. Allen R. Rushen, Feb. 7, 1953; children—Patrice, Angela. Dep. probation officer Los Angeles County Probation Dept., 1956-61, supervising dep. probation officer, k856-67, dir. I/Rodeo Project, 1967-70, probation dir. II, 1970-74, div. chief, 1974-75; mem. Calif. Parole Bd., 1975-77, vice-chmn., mem. Calif. Bd. Prison Terms, 1977-80; dir. Dept. Corrections, Sacramento, 1980—; instr. Sch. Pub. Adminstrn., U. So. Calif., Los Angeles, 1968-75; instr. sociology Compton Jr. Coll. (Calif.), 1968-69; cons. Calif. Dept. Human Resources and Devel., 1968-74; tng. cons. Calif. Youth Authority and Dept. Corrections, 1965-74; mem. adv. com. Criminal Justice Manpower Devel. for Project Safer Calif., 1974—; guest lectr. State Maine, Juvenile Justice Conf.; instr. Nat. Coll. State Calif. Probation Trial Judges, 1971—. Recipient Dean Joseph Lohman award Calif. Probation, Parole and Corrections Assn., 1969, Disting. Am. award KABC Radio, Los Angeles, 1971, John W. Donner Meml. Pub. award U. So. Calif. Sch. Pub. Adminstrn., 1971, John M. Pfiffner award Sch. Pub. Adminstrn., 1972, Trail Blazers award Nat. Assn. Negro Bus. and Profl. Women, 1975. Mem. NAACP, Calif. Probation, Parole and Correctional Assn., Black Probation Officers Assn., Calif. Black Corrections Coalition (bd. dirs.). Office: 630 K St Sacramento CA 95814

RUSMORE, JAY T., psychologist, educator. A.B., Fresno State Coll., 1938; M.A., Stanford U., 1940; Ph.D., U. Calif.-Berkeley, 1944. Lic. psychologist, Calif.; diplomate Am. Bd. of Profl. Psychology (indsl.). Chief testing sect. Pacific Div. U.S. Engrs., 1945; personnel dir. Hastings Clothing Co., San Francisco, 1946-47; cons. Pacific Telephone Co., San Francisco, 1948-59; prof. psychology San Jose State U., 1948—; pres. Calif.-Fresno Oil Co., 1950-78, mem. mgmt. bd., 1978—; dir. Adv. Human Systems Inst. San Jose State U., 1980—; cons. FMC, Lockheed Missiles and Space Co., City of San Jose. Served with USNR, 1942-44. Fellow Am. Psychol. Assn.; mem. Western Psychol. Assn. (past sec.), Calif. State Psychol. Assn. (past treas. div. indsl. and organizational psychology), AAAS. Author (with E. R. Hilgard) Instructor's Manual for Introduction to Psychology, 1954; A Casebook in Industrial and Personnel Psychology, 1958; contbr. Readings in Psychological Testing, 1963; contbr. articles to profl. jours. Office: Dept Psychology San Jose State U San Jose CA 95192

RUSSELL, CARL EDWIN, state ofcl.; b. Clinton, Ind., July 9, 1941; s. Carl William and Mable Elizabeth R.; A.A. in Bus. Adminstrn., Mesa Community Coll., 1970; B.S. in Criminal Justice, Ariz. State U., 1974, M.S. in Criminal Justice Edn., 1975; m. Bonita Jean Duff, Jan. 20, 1967; children—Courtney Carl, Bethany Alison. Police officer, Tempe, Ariz., 1971-74; dept. head justice adminstrn. Gila Pueblo Coll., Globe, Ariz., 1976-77; programs and projects coordinator Ariz. Dept. Public Safety, Phoenix, 1977-79, staff planner, 1979—; adj. faculty mem. Scottsdale (Ariz.) Community Coll., 1981—. Mem. justice adv. council South Mountain Community Coll. Served with USAF, 1959-63. Mem. State and Provincial Police Planners Assn., Ariz. Adminstrn. Justice Educators Assn., Lambda Alpha Epsilon. Home: 2048 E Ellis Dr Tempe AZ 85282 Office: 2310 N 20th Ave Phoenix AZ 85005

RUSSELL, DONALD GAMMELL, public relations official; b. Ogden, Utah, July 21, 1953; s. Donald Anderson and LaDona (Gammell) R.; m. Esther Blackham, Aug. 7, 1976; children—Rebecca, Brian, Michelle. B.A., Brigham Young U., 1977. Account exec. Gardiner Advt., Salt Lake City, 1977; asst. mgr. domestic ops. Latter-day Saints Public Communications, Salt Lake City, 1977—; publicity dir. Salt Lake Sister Cities; food writer Deseret News, Salt Lake City; stringer AP. Mem. Pub. Relations Soc. Am. Republican. Mormon. Club: Cougar (Salt Lake City). Home: 5455 Rockford St Salt Lake City UT 84118 Office: 50 E N Temple St Salt Lake City UT 84150

RUSSELL, JOHN KENNETH, psychologist, screenwriter, novelist, producer; b. Belfast, No. Ireland, Oct. 18, 1948; s. William Edward and Nancy R.; m. Denise Louise, June 6, 1981; children—James Allen, Christina Michelle. B.A., U. So. Calif., 1970; M.A., Pepperdine U., 1971; Ph.D., U.S. Internat. U., 1974. Lic. psychologist. Pvt. practice Affiliated Psychotherapy Assocs., Lakewood, Calif., 1974—; ptnr. Russell-McCartney Prodns., 1980—; novelist, screenwriter. Mem. Am. Psychol. Assn., Calif. State Psychol. Assn. Author numerous psychol. writings, screenplays, novels. Office: 5220 N Clark Ave Penthouse Suite Lakewood CA 90712

RUSSELL, MARY LOUISE, industrial counselor, consultant; b. Salem, Oreg., May 13, 1952; d. John Eric and Elsie Louise (Buldhaupt) Simila; m. Steven K. Russell, June 29, 1974. B.A., U. Wash., Seattle, 1974; M.S. in Counseling, San Francisco State U., 1979. Asst. advisor career planning and placement office U. Calif.-Berkeley, 1975-77; career counselor U. Calif.-San Francisco, 1978-79; career devel. specialist Lawrence Livermore Nat. Lab. (Calif.), 1980-81; personnel devel. specialist Lockheed Marine, Seattle, 1981—; cons. Ford Motor Co., 1982-83, City of Seattle; founder cons. groups (2). Vol. City Oakland Summer Jobs Program 1976, 77. Mem. Am. Soc. Tng. and Devel., Am. Personnel and Guidance Assn., McDaniel Found., Career Planning and Adult Devel. Network, Nat. Vocat. Guidance Assn., Assn. Labor, Mgmt. and Cons. on Alcoholism, Sierra Club. Contbr. articles to profl. jours.

RUSSIN, ROBERT ISAIAH, sculptor, educator; b. N.Y.C., Aug. 26, 1914; s. Uriel and Olga (Winnett) R.; B.A., CCNY, 1933, M.S., 1935; postgrad. (Inst. fellow) Beaux Arts Inst. Design, 1935-36; m. Adele Mutchnick, May 21, 1937; children—Joseph Mark, Lincoln David, Uriel Robin. One-man shows Tucson Fine Arts Center, 1966, Colorado Springs (Colo.) Fine Arts Center, 1967, Palm Springs (Calif.) Desert Mus., Chas. G. Bowers Meml. Mus., Judah L. Magnes Meml. Mus., Berkeley, Calif.; retrospective one-man exhbn. Nat. Gallery Modern Art, Santo Domingo, Dominican Republic, 1976; sculpture commns. include two 8-foot metal figures Evanston (Ill.) Post Office, 1939, three life-size carved figures Conshohocken (Pa.) Post Office, 1940, Benjamin Franklin Monument campus U. Wyo., 1957, Bust of Lincoln, Lincoln Mus., Washington, 1959 (now in Gettysburg Mus.), Lincoln Monument atop summit Lincoln Hwy. Wyo., 1959, Monumental bas-relief bronze Cheyenne (Wyo.) Fed. Bldg., 1966, two carved wood walls Denver Fed. Bldg., 1966, Monumental Fountain City of Hope Med. Center, Los Angeles, 1966-67, statue Brookhaven (N.Y.) Nat. Lab, 1968, life-size bronze sculpture fountain Pomona Coll., 1969, monumental bronze sculpture Prometheus Natrona County (Wyo.) Pub. Library, Casper, 1974, monumental bronze sculpture Man and Energy Casper (Wyo.) C. of C., 1974, 12-foot marble carving plaza of Menorah Med. Center, Kansas City, Mo., 1975, Einstein and Gershwin medals Magnes Meml. Mus., Berkeley, monumental sculpture and fountain Nat. Mus. Art, Santo Domingo, Dominican Republic, 1975, portrait head Charles Bluhdorn, chmn. Gulf & Western, 1975, portrait bust Pres. J. Balaguer of Dominican Republic, 1975, portrait head G. Wilson Knight, Shakespearean actor and scholar, 1975, 2 12-foot bronze figures The Greeting and the Gift for Bicentennial Commn., Cheyenne, Wyo., 1976, monumental marble head of Juan Pablo Duarte liberator Dominican Republic, Santo Domingo, 1976, monumental steel fountain sculpture Casper City Hall, 1980, Helios Dallas for Lincoln Ctr., Dallas, 1983, Wyo. U. Trio for U. Wyo., 1983, Isaac Basheirs Singer medal for Magnes Mus., 1983; tchr. sculpture Cooper Union Art Inst., N.Y.C., 1944-47; prof. art U. Wyo., Laramie, 1947—, prof., artist-in-residence, 1976—. Recipient awards sec. fine arts U.S. Treasury, 1939, 40, Lincoln medal U.S. Congress, 1959, Alfred G. B. Steel award Pa. Acad. Fine Arts, 1961; Medal of Order of Duarte, Sanchez y Mella (Dominican Republic). Ford Found. fellow, 1953. Mem. Nat. Sculpture Conf. (exec. bd.), Sculptors Guild, Nat. Sculpture Soc., AIA, AAUP, Coll. Art Internat. Inst. Arts and Letters, Phi Beta Kappa (hon.). Contbr. articles to profl. jours. Home: 716 Ivinson Ave Laramie WY 82070

RUSSOM, JERRY RAYMOND, public relations exec.; b. Clarendon, Tex., June 7, 1935; s. Raymond R. and Elsie L. (Eoff) R.; B.A. in English Lit., Long Beach (Calif.) State Coll., 1958; m. Margaret M. Jackson, June 18, 1966; children—Anne Leslie, Amy Lind. Vice pres. Lennen & Newell, Inc., San Francisco, 1964-71; exec. v.p. Russom & Leeper, San Francisco, 1971—. Trustee Dixie Dist. Bd. Edn., San Rafael, 1977-81; bd. dirs. Marin Symphony Assn., 1981—, Marin YMCA, 1982—, San Rafael Public Edn. Found., 1982—. Served with USCGR, 1958-61. Mem. Public Relations Soc. Am. Home: 97 Upper Oak Dr San Rafael CA 94903 Office: 350 Pacific St San Francisco CA 94111

RUST, CLINTON ALBERT, hospital administrator; b. Mangum, Okla., Aug. 5, 1934; s. William Albert and Velma Ella (Hill) R.; m. JoAnne Johnson, June 19, 1953 (div.); children—Robert Lindy, Gary Alan, Sally Anne. Student Los Angeles Valley Jr. Coll., 1954; B.S., U. So. Calif., 1956, M.P.A., 1976, cert. health services, 1976. Asst. personnel dir. Vegetable Oil Products Co., Wilmington, Calif., 1956-61, asst. v.p. sales, 1961-63, asst. to v.p., gen. mgr., 1963-66; personnel analyst, recruiter Calif. State Personnel Bd., Los Angeles and Sacramento, 1966-69; personnel analyst Calif. Dept. Mental Hygiene, Sacramento, 1969-70, personnel officer Napa State Hosp., 1970-73, asst. hosp. adminstr. Sonoma State Hosp., Calif. Dept. Health, Eldridge, 1973-74, adminstr. Atascadero State Hosp., 1974-76, exec. dir. dept. devel. services Camarillo State Hosp., 1976—; mem. psychiat. technician adv. com. Calif. Bd. Vocat. Nurse and Psychiat. Technician Examiners, 1974—; mem. registered nursing adv. bd. Ventura Community Coll., 1978—. State campaign chmn. United Way Ventura County, Calif., 1981-82, bd. dirs., 1980—. Recipient Cert. Appreciation ACTION Foster Grandparent Assn.; United Way Ventura County State Campaign Chmn. award 1981-82. Mem. Nat. Assn. Supts. Pub. Facilities for Mentally Retarded, U. So. Calif. Alumni Assn., Pub. Adminstr. Assn., Calif. Assn. Mgmt. Republican. Club: Masons. Office: PO Box A Camarillo CA 93011

RUST, MICHAEL KEITH, entomology educator; b. Akron, Aug. 26, 1948; s. Robert L. and Ardes D. (DeHaven) R.; m. Gayle D. Hughey, Apr. 4, 1970; children—Amy, Rachel. A.B., Hiram (Ohio) Coll., 1970; M.A., U. Kans., 1973, Ph.D., 1975. Assoc. prof. entomology U. Calif.-Riverside, 1975—, head div. econ. entomology, 1983—. Mem. AAAS, Am. Inst. Biol. Scis., Animal Behavior Soc., Entomol. Soc. Am., Sigma Xi, Gamma Sigma Delta. Office: Dept Entomology U Calif Riverside CA 92521

RUST, NICHOLAS CREGG, training executive, consultant; b. Idaho Falls, Idaho, May 31, 1946; s. Henry Dean and Marion (Maughan) R.; m. Pamela Westerberg, June 13, 1968; children—Cassandra Nichola, Nicholas Peter. Student Utah State U., 1964-65, 67-68; B.A., U. Pacific, 1970; M.A., U. Ariz., 1972, postgrad. 1972-73. Dir. Lodi Woodbridge Ctr. (Calif.), 1973-75; asst. tng. coordinator Longs Drug Store, Walnut Creek, Calif., 1975-78; tng. specialist Idaho First Nat. Bank, Boise, 1978-80; asst. v.p., mgr. tng. officer Bank of Idaho, First Interstate Bank, Boise, 1981-82; pres. Environ. Systems, Inc., Boise, 1982; tng. officer Bank of Stockton (Calif.), 1982—; cons., 1981-82. Mem. Am. Soc. Tng. and Devel. Republican. Mormon. Office: Bank of Stockton 301 E Miner Ave Stockton CA 95201

RUSTVOLD, CLARENCE ALFRED, JR., cons. co. exec.; b. Hibbing, Minn., Feb. 13, 1930; s. Clarence Alfred and Lilly Rosella (Ness) R.; A.A., Itasca Jr. Coll., 1950; B.S., Tex. A&M U., 1960; M.S., Rensselaer Poly. Inst., 1964; m. Donna Jean Riley, Aug. 28, 1954; children—Gordon, Jeralyn, Tamra, Linda, Alison, Karen. Commd. pilot U.S. Air Force, 1951, advanced through grades to lt. col., 1969, ret., 1971; v.p. ops. and adminstrn. Boyden Internat. Group, Inc., N.Y.C. and Los Angeles, 1971-74; v.p., exec. dir. Western region EEO Services, div. Jagerson Assoc., Inc., N.Y.C., 1974—; pres. R & R Aeros., Inc., Corona Del Mar, Calif., 1976-78, dir., 1976-78; ptnr. R/DD Assn., 1978—; dir. Career Devel. Systems, Inc., Santa Ana, Calif., 1978-79; dir. Executdex, Inc., San Francisco, 1975, Boyden Australia Pty., Ltd., 1972-74; cons. lectr. equal employment opportunity and exec. selection and evaluation. Mem. Newcomen Soc., Town Hall Calif., Air Force Assn., Combat Pilot's Assn., Aircraft Owners and Pilots Assn., Forward Air Controllers Assn., Am. Soc. Tng. and Devel., Internat. Platform Assn. Roman Catholic. Home: 18195 Santa Adela Circle Fountain Valley CA 92708

RUTAN, WILLIAM CARL, lawyer, real estate broker, tax consultant; b. Akron, Ohio, May 20, 1951; s. Curtis Merl and Cecelia Adelaide (Beaven) R.; m. Phyllis Marie Cook, June 9, 1973; children—Jennifer Sunshine. B.A., Akron U., 1973, A.A. in Real Estate, 1976; J.D., Ventura Coll., 1980. Bar: Calif. 1980; lic. real estate broker, Calif.; notary pub., Calif. Office mgr. Hal Watkins Chevrolet Inc., Oxnard, Calif., 1978-80; assoc. James Marsala & Assocs. Law Office, Ventura, 1980-81; sole practice, Ventura, 1981—; tax cons. Hal Watkins Chevrolet Inc. Baseball mgr. Ventura Sr. League, 1981-83. Mem. Calif. State Bar, Ventura County Bar Assn. Republican. Home: 10198 Mammoth Ventura CA 93004 Office: 5450 Telegraph Rd Suite 114 Ventura CA 93003

RUTHERFORD, MICHAEL AARON, water plant operator; b. Bremen, Ger., Dec. 24, 1951 (parents Am. citizens); s. Andrew Lewis and Annemarie G. (Kupsyck) R.; m. Rose M. Duny, June 21, 1948; children—David, Andrienne, Neil. A.A. in Natural Scis., U. Alaska, 1981. Cert. III level water operator, Alaska. Sr. operator Anchorage Water Plant, 1977—. Served in USAF, 1970-74. Mem. Am. Water Works Assn. Office: Anchorage Water Plant 3000 Artic Blvd Anchorage AK 99504

RUTHERFORD, REID, gemologist; b. Morristown, N.J., Dec. 30, 1952; s. Clinton Homer and Bonnie Beth (Bergner) R.; student Columbia U., 1971-72, Pepperdine U., 1973-75, Grad. Sch. Bus., Stanford U., 1979-81; grad. Gemol. Inst. Am. m. Beth Ann Husak, Apr. 3, 1977; 1 son, Ian Michael. Co-founder, exec. v.p. Analytics-Am. Gemol. Labs., N.Y.C., 1976-79; co-founder, prin. Bentley, Almond & Rutherford, Los Altos, Calif., 1980-81; pres. SoftLink, Santa Clara, Calif., 1981—. Mem. Ch. of Christ. Gem photographs in various publs.

RUTHERFORD, THOMAS TRUXTUN, II, former state senator, lawyer; b. Columbus, Ohio, Mar. 3, 1947; s. James William and Elizabeth Whiting (Colby) R.; B.B.A. (N.Mex. Broadcasters Assn. scholar), U. N.Mex., 1970, J.D., 1982; m. Linda Sue Rogers, Aug. 28, 1965; 1 son, Jeremy Todd. Page, reading clk. N.M. State Legislature, 1960-65; mem. N.Mex. Atty. Gen. Environ. Adv. Commn., 1972; radio broadcaster KOB Radio and TV, 1963-72; mem. N.Mex. Senate, Albuquerque, 1972—, majority whip; pres. Rutherford & Assos., public relations, Albuquerque, 1978-83; practice law, Albuquerque, 1983—. Mem. N.Mex. Gov.'s Commn. on Public Broadcasting; chmn. Albuquerque Cable TV Adv. Bd.; bd. dirs. Rocky Mountain Corp. for Public Broadcasting. Home and Office: 1133 Montclaire NE Albuquerque NM 87110

RUTKIN, STUART NEAL, mgmt. cons.; b. Los Angeles, July 2, 1947; s. Todd and Ruth (Orlijan) R.; B.A. in Polit. Sci., UCLA, 1969; M.A. in Community and Clin. Psychology, Pepperdine U., 1977; m. Randy Shapoff, Jan. 6, 1980. Program dir. YMCA Met. Los Angeles, Pacific Palisades, Calif., 1969-74; counselor, intake coordinator Santa Monica Bay Area Drug Abuse Council, 1976-77; mgmt. devel. coordinator May Co. Dept. Stores, Los Angeles, 1978-79; corp. tng. mgr. Allstate Savs. & Loan Assn., Los Angeles, 1979-80; cons. Stuart Rutkin & Assos., Pacific Palisades, 1980-81; asso. MRG Assos., Inc., Los Angeles, 1981—. Pres. Pacific Palisades Coordinating Council, 1974. Mem. Am. Soc. Tng. and Devel. (treas. Los Angeles chpt.). Jewish. Author: Camp Director's Manual, 1975. Home: 12537 Barbara Ave Mar Vista CA 90066 Office: 10801 National Blvd Suite 401 Los Angeles CA 90064

RUTKOWSKI, MICHAEL JOSEPH, aerospace engr., researcher; b. Buffalo, April 18, 1944; s. Joseph and Cecilia (Gollon) R.; m. Janet Sharp, Feb. 15, 1969; children—Michael Joseph Jr., Jonathan Sharp. B.S.E. in Physics, U. Mich., 1965, B.S.E. in Math., 1965, M.S.E. in Engring. Mechanics, 1967; Ph.D. in Aeros. and Astronautics, Stanford U., 1976. Aerospace engr. Manned Spacecraft Ctr., NASA, Houston, 1967-71, research assoc. Ames Research Ctr., Moffett Field, Calif., 1976-77, research scientist U.S. Army Aeromechanics Lab., 1978—. NASA trainee, 1971-73; NRC grantee, 1976-77. Mem. AIAA, Am. Helicopter Soc., Sci. Research Soc. N.Am. Contbr. articles to profl. publs. Home: 11348 Farndon Ave Los Altos CA 94022 Office: MS 215-1 Ames Research Ctr Moffett Field CA 94035

RUTLAND, ANDREW, obstetrician, gynecologist; b. Lake Alfred, Fla., May 30, 1943; s. James and Helen (Hayes) R.; B.S., Howard U., 1965, M.D., 1969; m. Sidney R., Jan. 19, 1970; children—Constanza, Andrea, Andrew and Anthony (twins). Commd. 2d lt. U.S. Air Force, 1965, advanced through grades to lt. col., 1977; intern David Grant Med. Center, Travis AFB, Calif., 1969-70; resident in ob-gyn U. So. Calif. Hosp., Los Angeles, 1973-76; chief infectious disease control Edwards USAF Hosp., Edwards AFB, Calif., 1977-81, chief ob-gyn dept., 1977-81; practice medicine specializing in ob-gyn, Los Angeles, 1981—; asst. clin. prof. UCLA, 1977—. Diplomate Am. Bd. Med. Examiners, Am. Bd. Ob-Gyn. Mem. Aerospace Med. Assn. Democrat. Home: 5101 Bedford Ave Los Angeles CA 90056 Office: 211 N Prairie Ave Inglewood CA 90301

RUTZEN, ARTHUR COOPER, JR., industrial chemical company executive; b. Chgo., Nov. 18, 1947; s. Arthur Cooper and Helen Doyle Rutzen; B.S. in Bus. & Econs., Lehigh U., 1970, M.B.A., 1972; Mktg. Mgmt. Program, Stanford U., 1982; m. Dolores Cornachia, May 26, 1973; children—Sandy, Arthur C., Judy. Account exec. Merrill Lynch Pierce Fenner & Smith, N.Y.C., 1971-75; mgr. bus. analysis and mktg. positions Union Carbide Corp., N.Y.C., N.Y., 1975-77; dir. nat.

accounts Liquid Air Corp., San Francisco, 1977—; participant nat. accounts mgmt. study Mktg. Sci. Inst., Sch. Bus., Harvard U., 1980-82. Head wrestling coach PAL, Nassau County, L.I., N.Y., 1974. Recipient Spl. Service award Union Carbide, 1976, Meritorious Achievement award, Union Carbide, 1977. Mem. Nat. Accounts Mktg. Assn. (bd. dirs., operating com. 1982), Merrill Lynch Exec. Club, Sales and Mktg. Execs. Assn. San Francisco (v.p., bd. dirs.). Protestant. Clubs: Golden Gateway Tennis, Lehigh U. Alumni. Home: 15 Whaleship Plaza San Francisco CA 94111 Office: One Embarcadero Center San Francisco CA 94111

RYAN, ARTHUR NORMAN, movie company executive; b. Gloucester, Mass., Dec. 22, 1938; s. Arthur Stanley and Mary (Ross) R.; B.S. in Polit. Sci., Suffolk U., Boston, 1962; children—Maya, Mark. Sr. acct. Price Waterhouse & Co., N.Y.C., 1962-66; asst. treas. Paramount Pictures, N.Y.C., 1966-67, dir. adminstrn. and bus. affairs, Los Angeles, 1967-70, v.p. prodn. adminstrn., 1970-75, sr. v.p. prodn. ops., 1975-76; pres., chief operating officer Technicolor, Inc., Los Angeles, 1976—. Dir. Hollywood Canteen Found., Permanent Charities Com. Entertainment Industry; bd. trustees Calif. Inst. Arts. Served with inf., U.S. Army, 1963. Mem. Acad. Motion Picture Arts and Scis., Acad. TV Arts and Scis. Office: Technicolor Inc 2049 Century Park E Suite 2400 Los Angeles CA 90067

RYAN, BOB, journalist, state senator; b. Bklyn., Oct. 17, 1947; s. Thomas Francis and Helen Louise (Schultz) R.; m. Victoria McNevin, Oct. 27, 1980; children—Anji, Rachael. B.S., Ithaca Coll., 1968. Various positions ABC, N.Y.C., 1969-78; spl. asst. to U.S. Senator Laxalt, Washington and Las Vegas, 1978-80; editorial writer Sta. KLAS-TV, Las Vegas, 1980—; mem. Nev. Senate, 1982—. Republican. Roman Catholic.

RYAN, CATHRINE SMITH, publisher; b. Calif., May 9, 1930; d. Owen W. and Margarette D. (Grimsley) Griffin; A.A., Bellevue Jr. Coll., Denver, 1948; grad. Barnes Sch. Commerce, Denver, 1950; student N.Y. Ballet Acad., 1954; m. Patrick J. Ryan, Apr. 28, 1972; children—Colleen, J. Michael, S. Alicen, Samantha L. Dir. Ballet Workshop, Enumclaw, Wash., 1958-64; dir. confs. and seminars San Francisco Theol. Sem., 1977-80; pres., dir. Cathi, Ltd., pub. and cons. office orgn. and mgmt., San Francisco, 1980—; freelance travel photographer, 1968-80; guest instr. in field. Active local PTA, March of Dimes, ARC. Recipient various certs. of recognition. Republican. Mormon. Author: Face Lifting Exercises, 1980; procedure and policy manuals. Office: PO Box 292 Kentfield CA 94904

RYAN, DIANE C., interior designer; b. Balt., Mar. 19, 1943; d. Bernhardt Emil and Clara Simon Pielke; m. Timothy J. Ryan, Jan. 6, 1968; children—Shannon Patricia, Brittany Michelle. Student Northwestern U., 1964-70, Fla. Tech. U., 1974-75, UCLA, 1979. Owner, mgr. Diane Ryan Designs Co., Sherman Oaks, Calif., 1977-80; sr. assoc., studio dir. Enrlich-Rominger Co., Palo Alto, Calif., 1980—. Mem. Am. Soc. Interior Designers (cert.), Inst. Bus. Designers (cert.). Office: 4800 El Camino Real Los Altos CA 94022

RYAN, EDWARD JOHN, JR., printing company executive; b. Warren, Ohio, May 25, 1936; s. Edward and Thelma (Veneman) R.; B.S. in Indsl. Relations, Northeastern U., 1963; m. Dorothy C. Ryan. Purchasing agt. Fenwal Co., Framingham, Mass., 1958-63; successively mfg. supr., reference supr., recruiting supr. Dupont Co., Wilmington, Del., 1963-70; corp. employment mgr. Appalachian Regional Hosps., 1970-72; v.p. profl. relations Hosp. Corp. Am., Nashville, 1972-77; dir. internat. recruiting Whittaker Corp., Los Angeles, 1977-79; sr. v.p. profl. relations Nat. Med. Enterprises, Los Angeles, 1979-81; pres. Ryan Devel. Co., 1981—, Bus. Cards, Inc., Chatsworth, Calif., 1981—, Eagle Thermographу Co., Chatsworth; cons. human resources and recruiting. Served with USAF, 1954-58. Mem. Internat. Personnel Assn., Am. Mgmt. Assn., Soc. for Advancement Mgmt., Am. Assn. Compensation Analysts, World Hosp. Assn., Am. Hosp. Assn., Internat. Thermographers Assn., Internat. Assn. Instant Printers. Club: Masons. Home: 1115 Evenstar Ave Westlake Village CA 91361 Office: Business Cards Inc 20428 Corisco St Chatsworth CA 91311

RYAN, JOHN A., geophysics educator, researcher; b. Pitts., Nov. 3, 1929; s. John A. and Crezentia Maria (Merk) R.; m. Margaret Ellen Eiseman, Sept. 4, 1955; children—Kelley Lynn, Douglas Allen. B.S. in Physics, Rice U., 1951; Ph.D. in Geophysics, Pa. State U., 1959. Chief lunar and planetary sci. sect., chief environ. scis. br. McDonnell Douglas Astronautics Co., Huntington Beach and Santa Monica, Calif., 1959-76; prof., chmn. earth sci. dept. Calif. State U.-Fullerton, 1976—; cons. engring. geology and geophysics. Served with USMC, 1952-54; served to capt. USMCR. Recipient spl. award Am. Meteorol. Soc., 1977. Mem. Am. Geophys. Union, AAAS (Newcombe-Cleveland award 1976). Contbr. articles to profl. publs. Office: Earth Sci Dept Calif State U Fullerton CA 92634

RYAN, LOYE MARIE JOHNSON, psychologist; b. Flandreau, S.D., Jan. 16, 1941; d. William F. and Catherine M. (Gage) Johnson; m. Robert A. Ryan, Dec. 15, 1973; children—Catherine, Carolyn, Robert, Jennifer. B.A., Moorhead (Minn.) State U., 1971, M.S., 1973; Ed.D., U. S.D., 1976. Counselor Moorhead State U., 1971-73; counselor U. S.D., 1975-76; research assoc. U. Wash., Seattle, 1976-77; scholar-in-residence White Cloud Ctr., Oreg. Health Scis. U., Portland, 1977-79; pvt. practice counseling psychology, Portland, 1978-80; mental health supr., therapist UIC Mental Health Clinic, Portland, 1980—. Pres. bd. dirs. Mental Health Services-West, Portland, 1982—. Ford Found. fellow, 1973-76. Mem. Am. Psychol. Assn., Mental Health Counselors Assn., Soc. Indian Psychologists, Soc. Individual Psychology. Home: 3365 SW Miles St Portland OR 97219 Office: 735 NW 21st St Portland OR 97218

RYAN, MICHAEL RUSSELL, clergyman; b. San Francisco, Dec. 25, 1950; s. Charles F. and Sue (Goade) R.; B.S., U. So. Calif., 1972; postgrad Talbot Sem. 1973-77; M.A., Grace Grad. Sch., 1979; m. Donna Sue Carter, June 17, 1972; children—Kasey Rene, Kelly Colleen. Ordained to ministry Grace Brethren Ch., 1978; field asso. Fellowship Christian Athletes, Los Angeles, 1972-73; football player So. Calif. Sun team, 1974-75, Sask. Roughriders, 1976; adminstr. Grace Brethren Ch., Seal Beach, Calif., 1975-79, sr. pastor, 1979-82; sr. pastor First Covenant Ch., San Francisco, 1983—; instr. Grace Grad. Sch. Theology, 1979—; mem. pres's adv. bd. Fellowship Christian Athletes, 1977—, state adv. bd., 1983—; v.p. Run the Race Ministries, 1982, pres., 1983; pres. So. Calif. Dist. Ministerium, 1980-81; dist. moderator Fellowship of Grace Brethren Chs., 1982-83. Mem. Community Restitution Bd. Orange County, 1979—. Named Outstanding Christian Athlete in Am., 1972, All Pro World Football League, 1975, Churchmen's Hall of Sports Fame. Mem. Nat. Assn. Ch. Bus. Adminstrs. Republican. Home: 9392 Souza St Garden Grove CA 92641 Office: 455 Dolores St San Francisco CA 94110

RYAN, PATRICK JAMES, international port executive; b. Oakland, Calif., Feb. 3, 1938; s. John J. and Mary E. (Connolly) R.; m. Cathi Smith, Apr. 28, 1972; children—Samantha, Alicen. B.S. in Econs. and Bus. Adminstrn., St. Mary's Coll., Moraga, Calif., 1959; M.B.A., Pepperdine U., 1978. Cert. profl. mgr.; cert. in port mgmt. With traffic and distbn. dept. Dow Chem. Co., Chgo., 1959-76; asst. to dep. exec. dir. Port of Oakland (Calif.), 1977—; lectr. in field. Mem. Soc. Logistics Engrs. (sr., cert. of appreciation), Pacific Traffic Assn., Chgo. Traffic Club, Mpls. Traffic Club, San Francisco Comml. Club, Oakland World Trade Assn. (pres. 1982-83, exec. com.), Oakland C. of C. (internat. affairs com.), Calif. Council Internat. Trade. Republican. Roman Catholic. Office: 66 Jack London Sq Oakland CA 94604

RYAN, PAUL BRENNAN, naval historian; b. Burlington, Vt., Apr. 19, 1913; s. Leo Thomas and Mary Elizabeth (Brennan) R.; B.S., U.S. Naval Acad., 1936; student U.S. Submarine Sch., 1941, Naval Lang. Sch., 1949; A.M. in Internat. Relations, Stanford U., 1964; M.A. in History, San Jose State U., 1965; m. Margaret Alice Hughes, Apr. 2, 1941; 1 dau., Holly Elizabeth Ryan Kaufman. Commd. ensign U.S. Navy, 1936, advanced through grades to capt., 1955; dep. dir. U.S. Naval Hist. Center, Dept. Navy, Washington, 1969-72; research fellow Hoover Instn. on War, Revolution and Peace, Stanford U., 1972—. Decorated Legion of Merit, Meritorious Service medal, Navy Commendation medal. Mem. Naval Hist. Found., U.S. Naval Inst., Am. Soc. Oceanic History, Navy League U.S. Author: (with T.A. Bailey) The Lusitania Disaster and Hitler vs. Roosevelt, The Undeclared Naval War; The Panama Canal Controversy; First Line of Defense: the U.S. Navy Since 1945; Disaster at Desert One: Why the Raid in Iran Failed, 1984; contbr. articles and revs. to profl. jours., newspapers. Home: PO Box 5628 Stanford CA 94305 Office: Hoover Instn Stanford U Stanford CA 94305

RYAN, RICHARD WALTER, insurance broker; b. N.Y.C., May 4, 1946; s. Walter Kevin and Jeanne (Sonner) R.; m. Constance Fine, June 13, 1969; children—Derek, Kyle. B. Marine Engring., SUNY, 1968. Instr., SUNY, Maritime Coll., 1970-71; boiler and machinery dept. mgr. Chubb & Sons, San Francisco, 1971-75; ins. broker Johnson & Higgins, San Francisco, 1975—. Past pres. Bay Area Boiler and Machinery Forum. Served to lt. USNR, 1968-72. Mem. ASME, Calif. Cert. Boiler Insps. Assn., Sports Car Club of Am. Contbr. articles to trade publs. Office: 601 California St San Francisco CA 94108

RYAN, SALLY (ANNE), public relations consultant; b. Van Nuys, Calif., Dec. 8, 1935; d. Walter Ralph and Nellie Lou (Ramsey) Smith; m. David Philip Ryan, Aug. 22, 1959 (dec.); 1 dau., Elizabeth Maria. B.A. in Speech and English, UCLA, 1958; postgrad. UCLA, 1959. Cert. gen. secondary sch. tchr. Social worker Los Angeles County Dept. Social Service, 1960-63; asst. regional mgr. corp. relations dept. ITT, Woodland Hills, Calif., 1965-81; owner, pub. relations cons. Ryan and Assocs., Granada Hills, Calif., 1981—. Bd. dirs. United Way Region I, Los Angeles County, 1979-81; bd. dirs. St. Mark's Parish Day Sch., Van Nuys, 1969-72, San Fernando Valley council Girl Scouts U.S.A., 1969-71, San Fernando Valley Pub. Relations Roundtable, 1970-76, 82—, San Fernando Valley Child Guidance Clinic, 1978-82; mem. Republican Central Com. 37th Assembly Dist., Los Angeles County, 1980-82, 39th Assembly Dist., 1982-84. Mem. Women in Communications (v.p., dir.), Valley Interchange Exec. Women (founding dir.), Nat. Assn. Female Execs., Granada Hills C. of C. (dir.), Valley Press Club (dir.). Mem. Ch. of Religious Science. Club: Northridge Rep. Women's. Columnist Herald Community Newspapers, 1982—. Office: Ryan and Assocs 17715 Chatsworth St Granada Hills CA 91344

RYAN, SHAWN, photographer, business executive; b. Portland, Oreg., Jan. 15, 1948; d. Frank Timothy and Marsha Gayle (Woodson) R.; m. June 14, 1973 (div.); 1 dau., Dawn. Diplome, Alliance Francaise, Nancy, 1968; Diploma Le Fleuron, Florence, Italy, 1969. Asst. heart and lung ops., Madrid, 1970; reporting photographer ABC, Hola Mags., Madrid, 1971; mng. dir. West Coast Image Bank Office, Los Angeles, 1979—. Recipient silver cup ABC Photog. Exhibit, 1971. Roman Catholic. Office: 6018 Wilshire Blvd Los Angeles CA 90036

RYAN, STEPHEN JOSEPH, JR., ophthalmologist, educator; b. Honolulu, Mar. 20, 1940; s. S.J. and Mildred Elizabeth (Farrer) R.; A.B., Providence Coll., 1961; M.D., John Hopkins U., 1965; m. Anne Christine Mullady, Sept. 25, 1965; 1 dau., Patricia Anne. Intern, Bellevue Hosp., N.Y.C., 1965-66; resident Wilmer Inst. Ophthalmology, Johns Hopkins Hosp., Balt., 1966-69, chief resident, 1969-70; fellow Armed Forces Inst. Pathology, Washington, 1970-71; instr. ophthalmology Johns Hopkins U., Balt., 1970-71, asst. prof., 1971-72, asso. prof., 1972-74; ophthalmologist USPHS Hosp., Balt., 1972-74, VA Hosp., Balt., 1973-74; prof., chmn. dept. ophthalmology Sch. Medicine, U. So. Calif., Los Angeles, 1974—; chief physician dept. ophthalmology Los Angeles County (Calif.) Gen. Hosp., 1974—, med. dir. Estelle Doheny Eye Found., Los Angeles, 1977—; advisory panel Calif. Med. Assn., 1974—; mem. Project Orbis, 1979—. Recipient Certificate of Merit, Am. Med. Assn., 1971; Louis B. Mayer Scholar award, Research To Prevent Blindness, 1973. Mem. Wilmer Ophthalmological Inst., Residents Assn., Calif. Assn. Ophthalmology (sci. adv. bd. 1976—), Am. Acad. Ophthalmology (award of Merit 1975), Pan-Am. Assn. Ophthalmology, Assn. Univ. Profs. Ophthalmology, Am. Ophthalmology Soc., Macula Soc., Retina Soc., Los Angeles County Soc. Ophthalmology, AMA, Calif., Los Angeles County med. assns., Pacific Coast Oto-Ophthalmological Soc. Editorial bd. Ophthalmic Surgery, 1975—, Jour. Ophthalmology, 1976—, Internat. Ophthalmology. Office: Estelle Doheny Eye Foundation Bldg 1355 San Pablo St Los Angeles CA 90033

RYDELL, RANDY JEROME, political scientist; b. Missoula, Mont., Sept. 29, 1952; s. Oscar Ferdinand and Jeanne Diane (Hutcheson) R.; B.A., U. Va., 1973; M.Sc. in Internat. Relations, London Sch. Econs., 1974; postgrad. U. Va., 1975-76; M.A. in Polit. Sci., Princeton U., 1977, Ph.D., 1980. Summer intern U.S. Dept. Def. (Pentagon), Washington, 1970-75; lectr. polit. sci. Princeton (N.J.) U. Grad. Sch., 1975-79; postdoctoral fellow, teaching asst. Harvard U., Cambridge, Mass., 1979-80; internat. polit. analyst Lawrence Livermore Lab., U. Calif., Livermore, 1980—. Mem. Am. Polit. Sci. Assn., Nat. Resources Def. Council, Phi Beta Kappa, Sierra Club. Democrat. Contbr. numerous publs. to profl. jours.

RYDELL, RICHARD LEWIS, hospital administrator, consultant; b. Harrison, N.Y., Feb. 23, 1940; s. Robert H. and Helen (Lewis) R.; m. Sandra Ford, May 1, 1961; children—Wendelin, Vicki, Elizabeth, Rodney, Jill. B.S. in Bus. Mgmt., Rensselaer Poly. Inst., 1961; M.B.A., San Jose State U., 1982. Registered profl. engr. Calif. Exec. dir. Western Heart Assn., San Jose; assoc. adminstr. Yakima (Wash.) Valley Meml. Hosp., 1977-78; exec. dir. Medishare Inc., San Jose, 1973-75, 78-80; dir. mgmt. systems Stanford (Calif.) U. Hosp., 1981—; dir. Medishare, Assn. Cardiovascular Nurses. Chmn. Planning Commn., City of Los Altos Hills; pres. Los Altos Hills Little League. Mem. Am. Coll. Hosp. Adminstrs., Inst. Indsl. Engrs. (sr. mem.), Hosp. Mgmt. Systems Soc. Club: Hills Athletic Team (pres.) (Los Altos Hills, Calif.). Contbr. articles to profl. jours. Home: 12220 Menalto Dr Los Altos Hills CA 94022 Office: Stanford U Hosp Stanford CA 94305

RYDER, SANDRA SMITH, communications specialist; b. Great Lakes, Ill., July 6, 1949; d. Dennis Murrey and Olga (Grosheff) Smith; B.S., Northwestern U., Evanston, Ill., 1971; postgrad. Calif. Luth. Coll. Editorial asst. The Broadcaster, Ventura County (Calif.) Farm Bur., 1978—; columnist, staff writer Camarillo (Calif.) Daily News, 1971-76, Sunday editor, 1979; editor Fillmore (Calif.) Herald, Inc., 1976-78; public info. officer Oxnard (Calif.) Union High Sch. Dist., 1980-82, Ventura (Calif.) Coll., 1982—. Recipient John Swett award Calif. Tchrs. Assn., 1975. Mem. Assn. Calif. Sch. Adminstrs., Sch. Public Relations Assn., Soc. Profl. Journalists (past pres. Los Padres chpt.), Women in Communications, Inc., Greater Los Angeles Press Club, Pub. Info. Communication Assn., Northwestern U. Alumni Assn., Republican. Home: 177 W Green Vale Dr Camarillo CA 93010 Office: 4667 Telegraph Rd Ventura CA 93003

RYDER, STEPHEN WILLIS, newspaper publisher; b. Kurume, Japan, May 10, 1923; s. Stephen Willis and Reba Catherine (Snapp) R.; m. Mary Irene Knappenberger, Dec. 7, 1946; 1 dau., Lynne Ryder Moke. B.A. in Journalism, Liberal Arts, Syracuse U., 1946. Sta. mgr. WENE, Endicott, N.Y., 1947-58; asst. to pub. News-Times, Danbury, Conn., 1958; pub. Press-Republican, Plattsburgh, N.Y., 1959-64; v.p., Ottaway Newspapers, Inc., Campbell Hall, N.Y., 1964—, dir., 1981-83; pub. Mail Tribune, Medford, Oreg., 1973-82, pres., 1982—. Bd. dirs. Rogue Valley Meml. Hosp., Medford, Oreg., 1975—; bd. dirs. Oreg. Shakespearean Festival Assn., 1975-83, pres., 1980-81; former dir. Endicott Girls Club, YMCA, Plattsburgh, Physicians Hosp. Champlain Med. Ctr., So. Oreg. State Coll. Found.; former chmn. Tri-Cities Aviation Council, Broome County, N.Y.; pres. Clinton County (N.Y.) Indsl. Devel. Commn.; bd. dirs. Oreg. Ind. Coll. Found., 1983—; officer Syracuse U. Sch. Journalism Adv. Council. Served with USAF, 1943-45. Recipient Man of Yr. Disting. Service award Endicott chpt. Jaycees, 1957; Ruhl fellow U. Oreg. Sch. Journalism, 1980. Mem. Oreg. Newspaper Pubs. Assn. (dir., pres. 1980-81), Am. Newspaper Pubs. Assn., Am. Press Inst. (chmn. western adv. bd.), Internat. Circulation Mgrs. Assn. Presbyterian (elder).

RYKER, NORMAN JENKINS, JR., aerospace company executive; b. Seattle, Dec. 25, 1927; s. Norman Jenkins and Adelia Gustine (Macombee) R.; m. Kathleen Marie Crawford (div.); children—Jeanne Ryker Flores, Christina, Vickie Ryker Risley, Norman Jenkins, Cathy. B.S., U. Calif., 1949, M.S., 1951; M.S., Harvard U., 1973. Registered profl. engr., Calif. With N. Am. Aviation, Downey, Calif., 1951-70, Apollo asst. chief engr., 1967-68, v.p. research and engring. space div., v.p. ops. newspaper press div., 1970-74, v.p., gen. mgr. Comml. Web div., 1974, v.p., gen. mgr. Transp. Equipment div., 1974, pres. Rocketdyne div., 1976—; mem. NASA Manned Spacecraft Ctr. team which evaluated and recommended the lunar orbit rendezvous concept for landing men on the moon. Recipient NASA award of merit, 1969, Disting. Pub. Service medal, 1981; Silver Knight award Nat. Mgmt. Assn., 1979; Indsl. Tech. Mgmt. award Calif. Soc. Profl. Engrs., 1979; Companion Instn. Prodn. Engrs. London, 1981; Engr. of Yr. award Inst. Advancement Engring. and Orange County Engring. Council, 1982. Fellow Inst. Advancement of Engring., AIAA; mem. ASCE, Am. Astron. Soc., AIAA, Nat. Mgmt. Assn., Sigma Xi, Phi Epsilon. Office: 6633 Canoga Ave Canoga Park CA 91304

RYLAND, JANE NORMAN, computer co. mgr.; b. Richmond, Va., Jan. 30, 1945; d. Guy Robert and Anne Thomas (Eubank) Norman; student Coll. William and Mary, 1962-64; B.A. in English, U. Richmond, 1966; M.P.A. in Mgmt. Systems, U. Colo., 1980. Systems engr. IBM Corp., Richmond, Va., 1966-70; systems devel. project mgr., data base adminstr. Va. Poly. Inst. and State U., Blacksburg, 1970-73; computer center dir., data base adminstr., Va. Community Coll. System, Richmond, 1973-76; dir. communication network State Higher Edn. Exec. Officers, Boulder, Colo., 1976-81; optical systems planning mgr. Storage Tech. Corp., Louisville, Colo., 1981-83; market support mgr. Reference Tech. Inc., Boulder, Colo., 1983— cons. higher edn. and data base systems; bd. dirs. Coll. and Univ. Systems Exchange, 1974-76. Mem. Assn. Instl. Research, Am. Soc. Public Adminstrn., Am. Assn. Higher Edn., Assn. Study of Higher Edn., Assn. Systems Mgmt. Club: Boulder Valley Racquet. Editor: Higher Education Information Systems: The Challenge of Change, 1975. Home: 84 Timber Ln Boulder CO 80302 Office: Reference Tech Inc 1832 N 55th St Boulder CO 80301

RYLAND, MERLE EDWARD, JR., electronics company executive; b. Key West, Fla., Oct. 11, 1944; s. Merle Edward and Maria R. (Rodrigues) R.; B.B.A., Nat. U., 1982; m. Michele Gordon Eddy, Mar. 21, 1978; 1 dau., Tahereh Marisa. Pres., Surfer Pub. Group-Products, Capistrano Beach, Calif., 1977-79; gen. mgr. Baha'i Pub. Trust, Wilmette, Ill., 1979-80; prof. bus. dept. Palomar Coll., San Marcos, Calif., 1981—; pres. Ryland Fin., San Marcos, 1981—; v.p. fin. Sullins Electronics, San Marcos, 1981—, also dir., gen. counsel Anisa, Inc., 1981-83; dir. Crutchfield Concessions. Served with USN, 1962-64. Mem. Nat. Assn. Accts. (past founding bd. dirs.), Nat. Mgmt. Assn., Am. Arbitration Assn. (panel of arbitrators). Baha'i. Pub./co-editor: Anisa Process Curriculum, 1981.

RYLAND, STEPHEN LANE, consulting geologist; b. Springfield, Mo., Sept. 27, 1949; s. Hollis Ivan and Juanita Elizabeth (Lane) R.; B.S., U. Mo., 1970, M.A. (Woodrow Wilson fellow), 1971; M.S. (NSF fellow), Calif. Inst. Tech., 1973; m. Rose Mary Eissler, June 26, 1971. Research asso., geology Calif. Inst. Tech., Pasadena, 1971-73; geophysicist Geophys. Systems, Pasadena, 1973; seismologist Dames and Moore, Los Angeles, 1973-76, spl. cons., Los Angeles, 1976—; dir. Seismosearch, Pasadena, 1976—; adj. instr. geology Calif. Poly. U., 1976—; partner Ryland, Cummings & Assos., 1979—; pres. Ryland Assocs., Inc., 1983—; dir. CalGold Mining. Mem. Phi Beta Kappa. Baptist. Home: 470 N Sunnyside Ave Sierra Madre CA 91024

RYLANDER, PATRICIA MARIE, educational administrator; b. Seattle, Aug. 12, 1945; d. James Edward and Luella Louise (Billiar) Arrants; m. Alan Edward Morneau, June 5, 1965; children—Eva Jane, Kerri Lynn; m. 2d, Richard Algot Rylander, Oct. 9, 1982. B.E., Seattle U.; M.Ed., Central Wash. U. Tchr., Central Kitsap Sch. Dist., 1967-70, South Kitsap Sch. Dist., 1971-77; vice-prin. East Port Orchard (Wash.) Elem. Sch., South Kitsap Sch. Dist., 1977-82; prin. Manchester Elem. Sch., South Kitsap Sch. Dist., Port Orchard, Wash., 1982—, dir. Project Life-gifted program, 1980-82. Mem. Nat. Assn. Elem. Sch. Prins., Wash. Assn. Elem. Sch. Prins., Peninsula Elem. Prins. Roman Catholic. Office: 1901 California Ave Port Orchard WA 98366

RYLES, NANCY, state senator; b. Portland, Oreg., Dec. 18, 1937; d. William Dunn and Madlyn (Hutting) Wyly; m. Vernon B. Ryles Jr., 1957; children—Scott, Ashley. Ed. Willamette U., 1955-56, Portland State U., 1969-72. Mem. Oreg. Ho. of Reps., 1979-83, Oreg. State Senate, 1983—. Mem. Beaverton Sch. Bd. Dist. 48, 1972-78, Gov.'s Commn. Status of Women, 1973-75; state adv. council career and vocat. edn., 1975-78; mem. Washington County Pub. Affairs Forum, Oreg. Women's Polit. Caucus. Recipient Human Rights award Oreg. Edn. Assn., 1974, Excellence in Action award Delta Kappa Gamma, 1976, 1st Citizen award, Beaverton, 1977, Disting. Service award Oreg. Vocat. Assn., 1978. Mem. Beaverton C. of C. Republican. Home: 8360 W Stark St Portland OR 97229 Office: Oregon State Senate Salem OR 97310

RYLEY-COBEAN, HELEN, educator, administrator, author; b. San Antonio, Oct. 20, 1940; d. William A. and Janet G. (Smith) King; m. Frederick G. Ryley, Apr. 21, 1962; children—Tami, Troy and Scott (twins), Christiania, Jay; m. 2d, Kelly J. Cobean, May 6, 1979. B.A. in Elem. Edn., Blackburn Coll., 1962; M.S. in Speech Pathology and Audiology, No. Ill. U., 1965. Tchr. elem. schs., Forest Park, Ill., 1962-63; tchr. deaf, hard hearing and drop-out prone pub. schs., Springfield, Ill., 1965-68; dir. Enrichment Ctr., Taipei, Taiwan, 1968-72; coordinator staff devel., material resources Boulder Valley Schs., Boulder, Colo., 1972-83; v.p., cons. Am. Tng. Ctr., Boulder, 1981—; adj. prof. U. No. Colo. Leader 4-H Club, Boulder, 1980—. Mem. Assn. Supervision and Curriculum Devel., Colo. Assn. Tchr. Educators, Boulder C. of C., Phi Delta Kappa. Author: Discipline With Love and Logic: A Guide for Teachers, 1981; editor: Who Says You're So Great, 1982; (audio tapes)

Discipline with Love and Logic for Parents, 1982. Office: Am Tng Forum 5735 Arapahoe St Boulder CO 80302

RYMES, CHARLES ARTHUR, housing executive; b. Kansas City, Mo., Dec. 21, 1929; s. Arthur James and Helen Mae (Stevenson) R.; m. Marguerite Joan Kidwell, June 21, 1952; children—Philip, Jeffrey, Arthur, Gretchen, Charles. A.B. in Econs., U. Mich., 1947, M.B.A. in Bus., 1952. Vice pres. Mid States Corp., Union City, Mich., 1957-61; v.p. Guerdon Industries, Southfield, Mich., 1961-68; pres. Central Home Inc., Greeley, Colo., 1968—; dir. Colo. Manufactured Housing, First Nat. Bank Greeley. Served with U.S. Army, 1952-54. Republican. Clubs: Greeley Country (pres.), Denver Country, Vail Racquet.

RYNEARSON, GARY MALIN, fin. exec.; b. Salt Lake City, Dec. 5, 1940; s. Thomas M. and Ethel Merle (Miller) R.; B.S. in Mgmt., U. Utah, 1968; postgrad. Pacific Coast Banking Sch., 1972-73, Am. Bankers Assn. Installment Credit Sch., 1970-71; m. Colleen Hinckley Sullivan, Mar. 23, 1962; children—John Sullivan, Michael Sullivan. Officer, Walker Bank & Trust Co., Salt Lake City, 1964-74; pres., gen. mgr. Allied Carriers Exchange, Inc. (name formerly Transport Clearings of Colo., Inc.), Denver, 1974—; guest lectr. U. Utah, 1970-74. Mem. Am. Transport Assn. (nat. acctg. and fin. council), Am. Mgmt. Assn., Denver C. of C., Salt Lake City Jaycees, Knights of Roundtable. Republican. Mormon. Home: 6554 S Sycamore St Littleton CO 80120 Office: 4242 Delaware St Denver CO 80216

RYNER, PAUL WARNER, mechanical engineer; b. Perry, Iowa, Nov. 27, 1934; s. Hal Jerome and Helen Onalee (Warner) R.; m. Frances Marie Bucelli, July 15, 1956 (div.); children—Lisa, Laura, Michael, David. B.S. in Math. and Electronics, City Coll. of San Francisco, 1954; postgrad. Coll. San Mateo, 1959, 78, Foothill Coll., 1967. Repair technician Kenney Bros., San Francisco, 1950-51; radio installation repairman Mobile Radio Technicians, San Francisco, 1952-55; draftsman time and motion study Link Belt Co., San Francisco, 1955-62; mech. engr. Lenkurt Electric Co., San Carlos, Calif., 1962-67; product dept. supr. Pacific Communications and Electronics, Palo Alto, Calif., 1967-68; engring. mgr. radio div. telecommunications products Granger Assocs., Santa Clara, Calif. 1968—. Mem. ASME. Patentee captive screw. Office: 3101 Scott Blvd Santa Clara CA 95051

RYNIKER, BRUCE WALTER DURLAND, industrial designer, manufacturing executive; b. Billings, Mont., Mar. 23, 1940; s. Walter Henry and Alice Margaret (Durland) R.; B. Profl. Arts in Transp. Design (Ford scholar), Art Ctr. Coll. Design, Los Angeles, 1963; grad. specialized tech. engring. program Gen. Motors Inst., 1964; m. Marilee Ann Vincent, July 8, 1961; children—Kevin Walter, Steven Durland. Automotive designer Gen. Motors Corp., Warren, Mich., 1963-66; mgmt. staff automotive designer Chrysler Corp., Highland Park, Mich., 1966-72; pres., dir. design Transform Corp., Birmingham, Mich., 1969-72; indsl. designer, art dir. James R. Powers and Assocs., Los Angeles, 1972-75; sr. indsl. designer Mattel Inc., Hawthorne, Calif., 1975—; dir. design and devel. Microword Industries, Inc., Los Angeles, 1977—, also dir.; exec. mem. Modern Plastics Adv. Council, 1976—; elegance judge LeCercle Concours D'Elegance, 1976-77; mem. nat. adv. bd. Am. Security Council, 1980; cons. automotive design, Toyota, Mazda, Datsun and Volvo, 1972—. Served with USMC, 1957-60. Mem. Soc. Art Ctr. Alumni (life), Mattel Mgmt. Assn., Second Amendment Found., Am. Def. Preparedness Assn., Nat. Rifle Assn. Designer numerous exptl. automobiles, electric powered vehicles, sports and racing cars, also med. equipment, electronic teaching machines, ride-on toys. Home: 21329 Marjorie Ave Torrance CA 90503 Office: 5150 Rosecrans Ave Mail Stop 11-337 Hawthorne CA 90250

RYSBERG, JANE ANN, educator, psychologist; b. Fort Lewis, Wash., Aug. 23, 1950; d. William Leonard and Phyllis Annette (Kranz) Rysberg; B.A. in Anthropology, U. Calif.-Davis, 1972; M.S. in Exptl. Psychology, Eastern Mich. U., 1974; Ph.D. in Ednl. Psychology, Ariz. State U., 1977. Asst. prof. psychology Ohio State U., 1977-81, Calif. State U.-Chico, 1982—; cons. local sch. dists. Mem. Am. Psychol. Assn., Soc. for Research in Child Devel., Western Psychol. Assn., Ohio State Psychol. Assn. Contbr. articles to profl. jours. Office: Dept Psychology Calif State U Chico CA 95929

SAATY, NABIL NAJIB, chemist; b. Mosul, Iraq, Oct. 15, 1933; s. Najib Jerjis and Vahanoush (Vartan) S.; B.S., Columbia Union Coll., Takoma Park, Md., 1956; M.S., Stanford U., 1958; m. Ella Jane Cluny, Dec. 15, 1956; children—Neil, Mark Nabil. instr. chemistry Iraqi Mil. Acad., 1959-60; lab. dir. Pattagansett Finishing Co., 1960-61; devel. chemist Chem. Products Corp., 1961-65; devel. chemist Donald S. Gilmore Labs., Upjohn Co., North Haven, Conn., 1965-68, head elastomer and micorcellular devel. CPR div., Torrance, Calif., 1968—; part-time faculty U. So. Calif., 1980—. Served to 2d lt. Iraqi Army, 1959-60. Recipient Sci. award Upjohn Co., 1980. Mem. Am. Chem. Soc. Patentee in field. Home: 1933 Mt Shasta Dr San Pedro CA 90732 Office: 555 Alaska Ave Torrance CA 90503

SAAVEDRA, LOUIS EMILIO, educational administrator; b. Socorro County, N.Mex., Mar. 18, 1933; s. Jose Ignacio and Nepumucena (Gabaldon) S.; m. Gail Griffith, Mar. 14, 1938; children—Ralph, Laura, Barbara. M.A., Eastern N.Mex. U., 1960. Chief exec. officer Albuquerque Tech.-Vocat. Inst., 1965—. Chmn. Albuquerque City Commn., 1973. Served with U.S. Army, 1954-56. Recipient Outstanding Alumni award Eastern N.Mex. U., 1968, Disting. Pub. Service award Gov. N.Mex., 1977.

SABA, ALEXANDRA A., psychologist; b. B.S. with honors, No. Ariz. U., 1970, M.A. in Psycholinguistics, 1972; M.C. Counseling Psychology, Ariz. State U., 1978; Ph.D., Psychol. Studies Inst., 1980. Linguist, Bur. of Indian Affairs, Kayenta, Ariz., 1969-70; chmn. English dept. Paradise Valley Sch. Dist., Ariz., 1971-78; sch. psychologist Phoenix South Mental Health Clinic, 1977-78; adolescent program supr. Ariz. State U., Tempe, 1976-78; instr. Maricopa County (Ariz.) Community Coll., 1975-78; vice pres. psychologist Drake-Beam-Morin, Inc., San Francisco, 1979-82; v.p., regional mgr. J.M. Boros & Assocs. Ltd., Los Angeles, 1982—; founder Mt. Bell Pioneer's Adult Edn. Fgn. Lang. Program, 1971. Mem. Republican Womens Caucus, 1976—; bd. dirs. Planned Parenthood, Tempe, Tempe Women's Center, South Mountain Free Clinic. Mem. Am. Psychol. Assn., Nat. Assn. Female Execs., Bay Area Exec. Women's Forum (edn. dir.), Am. Soc. Personnel Adminstrs., Am. Personnel and Guidance Assn., Am. Soc. Tng. and Devel., Human Resource Planning Soc., Bus. and Profl. Womens Club, San Francisco Symphony Guild, San Francisco Ballet, Phi Kappa Phi, Pi Beta Phi. Contbr. articles to profl. jours. Office: 700 S Flower St Suite 504 Los Angeles CA 90017

SABATELLE, ANTHONY JOSEPH, podiatrist; b. Dunmore, Pa., Jan. 27, 1927; s. Michael and Beatrice (Monaco) S.; student Johns Hopkins U., 1944, U. Scranton, 1948-50; D.P.M., Ohio Coll. Podiatric Medicine, 1954; m. Stella Yauorsky, May 12, 1956. Practice podiatry, Carbondale, Pa., 1955-62, Santa Clara, Calif., 1962—; mem. surg. staff O'Connor Hosp., San Jose, San Jose Hosp., Valley West Hosp., Los Gatos, Calif., VA Med. Center, Palo Alto, Calif. Served with USAF, 1944-48. Diplomate Am. Bd. Podiatric Surgery. Fellow Am. Coll. Foot Surgeons; mem. Am. Podiatry Assn. (past chmn. public edn. and info. com.), Calif. Podiatry Assn. (chmn. lose prevention and control com.), Am. Assn. History of Medicine, Internat. Soc. History of Medicine, Western History Assn., Hakluyt Soc. Republican. Roman Catholic. Club: Elks. Office: 1200 Scott Blvd Santa Clara CA 95050

SABBADINI, ALEX, fine arts appraiser; b. Rome, Italy, Oct. 26, 1916; s. Umberto and Silvia (Schunnach) S.; came to U.S., 1939, naturalized, 1942; student U. Rome, 1935-37; m. Elaine Judy Dreyfus, July 16, 1946 (dec.); children—Roger, Steven. Owner Alex Sabbadini, Sacramento; fine arts appraiser, 1952—; auctioneer, 1950—; lectr. in field. Active Boy Scouts Am., Am. Cancer Soc.; hon. life mem. PTA; bd. dirs. Am. Soc. Appraisers Edn. Found., 1972-78, Sacramento Symphony Assn., 1971-81. Served with AUS, 1942-45. Decorated Purple Heart. Fellow Inc. Soc. Valuers and Auctioneers, Am. Soc. Appraisers (internat. sr. v.p. 1976-77, pres. 1977-78); mem. Am. Arbitration Assn., Calif. Appraisers Council, V.F.W. Contbr. articles on tech. personal property valuation to profl. publs. Home: 2225 Woodside Ln #3 Sacramento CA 95825 Office: 601 University Ave Suite 150 Sacramento CA 95825

SABEL, ROBERT WALTER, security co. exec.; b. Chgo., Oct. 22, 1920; s. Walter Reuben and Ella Elizabeth (Andersson) S.; student Coe Coll., 1939-40, U. Md., 1948-49, El Camino Coll., 1980; m. Faith Carol Hammarlund, Dec. 9, 1950; children—Karen L., Ingrid M., James R., John G., Paul F., Kristin E. Mgr. nuclear research and devel. Cook Electric Co., Chgo., 1952-55; mem. tech. staff Ramo-Wooldridge Corp., Los Angeles, 1955-57; western regional mgr. Control Data Corp., Los Angeles, 1957-62; v.p. Electro Vision Industries, Los Angeles, 1962-65; owner Sabel Assos., Los Angeles, 1965-79; pres., dir. Zenith Internat. Protection, Inc., Redondo Beach, Calif., 1979—; lectr. Internat. Police Acad., 1969-72, U. So. Calif. Pres., chmn. Liaison League Rehab. Group, Inc. Served to lt. col. USAF, 1941-50. Decorated D.F.C. with 1 oak leaf cluster, Air medal with 3 oak leaf clusters; Croix de Guerre with Palm (France). Mem. Internat. Assn. Identification, Calif. Peace Officers Assn., Internat. Acad. Criminology, Calif. Assn. Lic. Investigators, Res. Officers Assn. U.S., Am. Law Enforcement Officers & Assn., VFW. Republican. Baptist. Clubs: Army-Navy (Washington); Elks, Masons. Home: 341 Paseo de Gracia Redondo Beach CA 90277 Office: 1303 1/2 Pacific Coast Hwy Redondo Beach CA 90277

SABEY, BURNS ROY, soil science educator, consultant; b. Magrath, Alberta, Can., May 17, 1928; s. Abel James and Genevieve (Toomer); m. Elaine Bingham, Nov. 10, 1948; children—Wendy J. Sabey Smith, Melvin, James, Karen Sabey La Couture, Mark, John. B.S., Brigham Young U., 1953; M.S., Iowa State U., 1954, Ph.D., 1958. Instr., Iowa State U., Ames, 1954-58; asst. prof. soil science U. Ill.-Urbana, 1958-64, assoc. prof., 1964-69, prof., 1969; prof. Colo. State U., Fort Collins, 1969—; researcher, tchr. mineland reclamation; cons. utilization of sewage sludge on land. NSF fellow, 1967-68; recipient Shephardson Teaching award Colo. State U., 1973. Fellow Soil Sci. Soc. Am., Am. Soc. Agronomy; mem. Sigma Xi, Gamma Sigma Delta. Republican. Mormon. Contbr. articles to profl. jours. Home: 3505 Canadian Pkwy Fort Collins CO 80524 Office: Dept Agronomy Colo State U Fort Collins CO 80523

SABHARWAL, RANJIT SINGH, mathematician, educator; b. Dhudial, India, Dec. 11, 1925; s. Krishan Chand and Devti (Anand) S.; came to U.S., 1958; naturalized, 1981; B.A. with honors, Punjab U., Pakistan, 1944; M.A., Punjab U., India, 1948; M.A., U. Calif. at Berkeley, 1962; Ph.D., Wash. State U., 1966; m. Pritam Kaur Chadha, Mar. 5, 1948; children—Rajinderpal, Amarjit, Jasbir. Lectr. math. Khalsa Coll., Bombay, India, 1951-58; teaching asst. U. Calif., 1958-62; instr. math. Portland (Oreg.) State U., 1962-63, Wash. State U., Pullman, 1963-66; asst. prof. math. Kans. State U., 1966-68; asso. prof. math. Calif. State U., Hayward, 1968-74, prof., 1974—. Mem. Am. Math. Soc., Math. Assn. Am., Sigma Xi. Author articles on non-Desarguesian planes. Research in geometries. Home: 27892 Adobe Ct Hayward CA 94542

SABIN, JACK CHARLES, engineering and construction firm executive; b. Phoenix, June 29, 1921; s. Jack Byron and Rena (Lewis) S.; B.S., U. Ariz., 1943; B.Chem.Engring., U. Minn., 1947; m. Frances Jane McIntyre, Mar. 27, 1950; children—Karen Lee, Robert William, Dorothy Ann, Tracy Ellen. With Standard Oil Co. of Calif., 1947-66, sr. engr., 1966—; pres., dir. Indsl. Control & Engring., Inc., Redondo Beach, Calif., 1966—; owner/mgr. Jack C. Sabin, Engr.-Contractor, Redondo Beach, 1968—; staff engr. Pacific Molasses Co., San Francisco, 1975-77; project mgr. E & L Assos., Long Beach, Calif., 1977-79; dir. Alaska Pacific Petroleum, Inc., 1968—, Marlex Petroleum, Inc., 1970, 71—, Served with U.S. Army, 1942-46; capt. Chem. Corps, Res., 1949-56. Registered profl. engr., Calif., Alaska; lic. gen. engring. contractor, Ariz., Calif. Mem. Nat. Soc. Profl. Engrs., Ind. Liquid Terminals Assn., Conservative Caucus, Calif. Tax Reduction Com., Tau Beta Pi, Phi Lambda Upsilon, Phi Sigma Kappa. Republican. Clubs: Elks; Town Hall of Calif. Address: 151 Camino de las Colinas Redondo Beach CA 90277

SABIN, MARC LESLIE, air force officer, engr.; b. Roswell, N.Mex., Mar. 25, 1944; s. Louis Simon and Sarah Francis (Levine) S.; m. Helen Marie Hill, June 30, 1974; children—Shanan, Ethan. B.S. in Engring. Sci., U.S. Air Force Acad., 1965; M.S. in Astronautics, Purdue U., 1966; Sc.D. in Instrumentation, MIT 1973. Cert. engr.-in-training, Colo. Commd. 2d lt. U.S. Air Force, 1965, advanced through grades to lt. col., 1981; missile test controller, Cape Kennedy, Fla., 1966-69; research assoc., dep. dir. aerospace mech. scis. F. J. Seiler Research Lab., U.S. Air Force Acad., 1973-76; lectr. dept. astronautics, computer sci., 1974; asst. chief, chief Reentry Tech. Div., Space, Missile Systems Orgn., Los Angeles, 1978-80; project mgr., Sec. Air Force Spl. Projects, 1980—; dep. dir. applied tech., 1982—; asst. instr. MIT, 1970. Decorated Meritorious Service medal, Joint Service Commendation medal. Recipient Outstanding and Significant Contbn. to U.S. Def. award Fla. chpt. Air Force Assn., 1967; Mem. AIAA, Sigma Xi. Jewish. Contbr. articles to profl. jours. Home: 24312 Hendricks Ave Lomita CA 90717

SABO, DAVID GEORGE, utility co. exec.; b. Albuquerque, Sept. 11, 1948; s. Dan and Elizabeth Jean (Beals) S.; B.S., U. N.Mex., 1974, M.S., 1977; m. Patti Ann Zuggman, June 17, 1982; 1 son, Daniel Joseph. Environ. cons. U.S. Fish & Wildlife Service, Albuquerque, U.S. Fish & Wildlife Service, 1977-82; environ. mgr. Nat. Demonstration Project, Dept. Energy, Baca Geothermal Demonstration Project, Albuquerque, 1978-81; environ. mgr. Coal-fired power plant N.Mex. Generating Sta., 1982—; mem. steering com. Geothermal Environ. Overview for N.Mex., 1978-80. Commr., Planning and Zoning Commn., Village of Corrales (N.Mex.), 1979-81, chmn. ordinance rev. com., 1979-80. Served with USN, 1967-70. U.S. Forest Service grantee, 1974. Mem. Am. Soc. Plant Physiologists, AAAS, Bio-Electro-Magnetic Soc., N.Mex. Native Plant Protection Adv. Bd., Sigma Xi. Club: Great Dane of N.Mex. (pres. 1975-76). Home: PO Box 276 Corrales NM 87048 Office: PO Box 2267 Albuquerque NM 87103

SACCO, GARY PATRICK, vocational consultant, business educator, entertainer; b. Ottawa, Ill., June 23, 1941; s. James and Ruth Emma (Nelson) Sacco. B. in Theatre Arts and Speech, San Jose State U., 1969; M. Edn., Stanislaus State Coll., 1976. Tchr., supr. day care ctr., 1966-69; day care supr., tutorial coordinator special programs Santa Clara (Calif.) Office Edn., 1966—, program supr., 1971-74; foster care cons. County of Stanislaus, Calif., 1977; group home dir. Boys on Probation, Gilroy, Calif., 1977-78; with Crawford Rehab. Services, Modesto and Sacramento, Calif., 1978-80; pvt. practice cons., Sacramento, 1980—; profl. dir., actor, composer, singer; active community theatre; pvt. counselor, leader communications workshops. Polit. campaign mgr., fund-raiser Caesar Chavez. Mem. Am. Personnel and Guidance Assn., Nat. Rehab. and Counseling Assn., Sacramento Rehab. Profls., Calif. Assn. Rehab. Profls., Nat. Fedn. Ind. Bus.

SACHS, ALVA J., psychologist; b. Detroit, June 11, 1933; d. Israel Ernest and Ann Rae (Fogelson) S.; children—Robert, Elise. Ph.D. in Psychology, UCLA, 1965. Lic. psychologist, Hawaii, Calif. Leadership trainer, Stanford and Palo Alto, Calif., 1961-62; mem. faculty dept. psychiatry U. Wis. Children's Hosp., Madison, 1965-70; pvt. practice, Southfield, Mich. 1978-80; psychologist W. Hawaii Mental Health Service, Kealakekua, 1980—; pvt. practice, Kailua-Kona, Hawaii, 1981—; cons. Mem. exec. bd. Kona Women's Ctr., 1980—, W. Hawaii Family Support Council, 1980—. Mem. Am. Psychol. Assn., Assn. Women in Psychology, NOW. Jewish. Office: W Hawaii Mental Health Service PO Box 228 Kealakekua HI 96750

SACHS, BERNARD ANATOLE, physician; b. Glendale, N.Y., Aug. 2, 1921; s. Samuel and Eva (Handelsman) S.; student Cornell U., 1938-41; M.D., State U. N.Y., 1944; m. Lillian Kornblum, Aug. 4, 1942; children—Jonathan, Robin, Althea, Gabriel. Intern, Montefiore Hosp., N.Y.C., 1944-45, resident, 1948-49; mem. staff Montefiore Hosp. and Med. Center, 1949-76, research asst., 1953-57, research asso., 1957-76, chief endocrine clinic, 1955-68, head Endocrine Service, 1960-68, sr. endocrinologist, 1968-76; fellow Johns Hopkins Hosp., Balt., 1948; resident L.I. Coll. Hosp., 1945-46; practice medicine specializing in endocrinology, N.Y.C., 1949-75, Long Beach, Calif., 1975—; cons. endocrinology Yonkers Gen. Hosp., 1972-76; asso. clin. prof. medicine Albert Einstein Coll., 1966-72, clin. prof. medicine, 1972-76; clin. prof. medicine U. Calif., Irvine, 1976—; endocrinologist Meml. Hosp. Med. Center, Long Beach, 1975—. Served from lt. to capt. M.C., AUS, 1946-48. Diplomate Am. Bd. Internal Medicine, Fellow A.C.P., Am. Coll. Nuclear Medicine; mem. Soc. for Exptl. Biology and Medicine, Am. Fedn. for Clin. Research Endocrine Soc., Am. Physiol. Soc., Am. Heart Assn. (arteriosclerosis council), Soc. Nuclear Medicine, N.Y. Acad. Scis., AMA. Contbr. 60 articles to profl. jours. Editor: The Brain and the Endocrine System, Medical Clinics of North America, 1978. Research in lipid metabolism and endocrinology. Office: 2840 Long Beach Blvd Long Beach CA 90806

SACHS, HUMBERTO WALDYR, engineering executive; b. Sao Angelo, Brazil, July 2, 1930; s. Heinz and Paulina (Bauer) S.; m. Maureen Patricia Hummel; children—Paulette, Andrew. B.A. in Bus., E.C.T. Sao Angelo, R.G. Sul, Brazil, 1952; B.S. in Aero. Engring., Northrop U., 1964; Lic. comml. pilot FAA. Various bus. positions, 1952-62; with Boeing Co., Seattle, 1964-71, program mgr. pilot advanced CAD/CAM system, 1978-82, mgr. 757 hydraulic and landing gear system, 1982—; pres. Revom, Inc., Kent, Wash., 1969-73; with aerospace cos. including Pratt & Witney, Northrop Corp., 1973-78; cons. in field. Mem. Republican Nat. Com. Served with Brazilian Army, 1949-51. Mem. AIAA, Boeing Mgmt. Assn., Nat. Computer Graphics Assn. Contbr. articles to profl. jours. Home: 1819 Anacortes Ave NE Renton WA 98056 Office: PO Box 3707 M/S OE-34 Seattle WA

SACKETT, HUGH F., financial services executive; b. Tulsa, Sept. 6, 1930; s. Hubert F. and Frances (Cozier) S.; B.S. in Bus. Adminstrn., Ind. U., 1955; m. Claudette Despres, Aug. 31, 1968; children—Michael Stanton, Deborah Faye, Stephanie Frances. Vice pres., gen. mgr. vender products group Cornelius Co., Anoka, Minn., 1969-72; group v.p. automotive Stellar Industries, Inc., Los Angeles, also pres. lawn care group, 1972-74; exec. v.p. Jefferson Mint, San Diego, 1974-79; pres. Graver Energy Systems, Inc., East Chicago, Ind., 1976-80, HFS, Inc., San Diego, 1979—, New H.S. Industries, Inc., 1980-82, Calif. Design Group, 1980-83, Am. Prins. Holdings, Inc., 1982—, also dir.; dir. Microbus. Applications Co., Pvt. Ledger Fin. Services, Inc., Am. Prins. Fin. Corp., Am. Prins. Pension Services, Inc., Am. Prins. Bank & Trust Co. Mem. chancellors council Purdue U., Calumet, Ind., 1977. Served with USNR, 1951-52. Mem. Conf. Bd., Am. Mgmt. Assn., Soc. Mayflower Desc., Alden Kindred Am., Ind. U. Alumni Assn. (life), Delta Tau Delta. Republican. Presbyterian. Clubs: Ruth Lake Country, Rancho Bernardo Swim and Tennis. Home: 17995 Bernardo Trails Pl San Diego CA 92128 Office: 2262 Carmel Valley Rd Del Mar CA 92014

SACKETT, JOHN C., state senator; b. Cutoff, Alaska, June 3, 1944; B.B.A., U. Alaska. Past pres., chmn. bd. Doyon, Ltd.; dir. Alaska Internat. Industries, Alaska Nat. Bank; mem. Alaska Ho. of Reps., 1966-72; mem. Alaska Senate, 1972—. Pres. Tanana Chiefs Conf., 1966-69; v.p. Fairbanks Native Assn.; mem. nat. adv. bd. Bur. Land Mgmt. Republican. *

SACKETT, ROBERT GEORGE, agronomist; b. Dodge County, Minn., June 29, 1920; s. Walter Orin and Louise Marie (Burzlaff) S.; B.S. with honors (Burpee scholar), U. Wyo., 1959, M.S., 1963; postgrad. Colo. State U., 1965-66; m. Emily M. Swanson, Sept. 14, 1943; children—Carol Marie Sackett Martensen, Richard Robert, Connie Ellen Sackett Fifer. Farmer, nr. Rochester, Minn., 1945-52; supply instr. U. Wyo., Laramie, 1959-67, instr., 1967-69; asso. agronomist U. Ariz., Tucson, 1969—; exec. sec. Ariz. Crop Improvement Assn., Tucson, 1969—; mem. Nat. Cert. Alfalfa Variety Rev. Bd., 1972-73, chmn., 1974-75; UN tchr., Aleppo, Syria, 1978. Lay leader, com. mem. Christ Ch. United Methodist, Tucson, 1979-80. Served with USCG, 1942-45. Recipient Little Internat. for Res. Champion in Agronomy trophy U. Wyo. 1957; Outstanding Seedsman plaque State Wyo., 1969. Mem. Crop Sci. Soc. Am., Am. Soc. Agronomy, Am. Seed Trade Assn., Western Seed Cert. Ofcls., Pacific Seedsmen Assn., Ariz. Cotton Planting Seed Assn., Pima County Farm Bur., Assn. Ofcl. Seed Cert. Agys. (pres. 1979-81), Sigma Xi, Gamma Sigma Delta, Alpha Zeta, Chi Gamma Iota. Clubs: Lions (dir. club 1974-75, chmn. club high sch. book scholarship com. 1976-80), Farm House (asso.). Author U. Ariz. Seed Industry Mgmt. Curriculum. Home: 6802 E Rosewood Circle Tucson AZ 85710 Office: Room 140 Coll Agr U Ariz Tucson AZ 85721

SACKLEY, GARY DAVID, sch. counselor; b. Tillamook, Oreg., May 6, 1950; s. Daniel David and Helyn Barbara (Klavin) S.; B.S. in Edn., Oreg. Coll. Edn., 1972, M.S., 1973. Sch. counselor North Clackamas Sch. Dist., Milwaukie, Oreg., 1974—. Democratic precinct committeeman, 1976—; chmn. Tillamook County Dem. Com., 1977-82; mem. Oreg. Dem. Exec. Com., 1978-82; Oreg. Dem. Central Com., 1978—; chmn. 1st Congl. Dist. Dem. Com., 1980-82; del. Dem. Nat. Conv., 1980; trustee Western Oreg. State Coll. Found. Recipient Outstanding Service award Oreg. Coll. Edn., 1969. Mem. NEA, Am. Personnel and Guidance Assn., Am. Sch. Counselors Assn., Oreg. Edn. Assn., Oreg. Assn. Sch. Counselors, Oreg. Personnel and Guidance Assn., North Clackamas Edn. Assn., Neskowin Community Assn. Roman Catholic. Home: PO Box 741 Neskowin OR 97149

SACKMAN, ROBERT, venture capital company executive; b. Bklyn., Mar. 5, 1918; s. David and Therese (Berkowitz) S.; m. Sylvia Koonin, Apr. 20, 1941; children—Barbara Ann, Ellen Therese. Student George Washington U., 1941-53. Registered profl. engr., D.C. With U.S. Patent Office, 1939-41; radio engr. Dept. Navy, 1941-44; chief recorder devel. br. Dept. Def., Washington, 1946-53; v.p., mgr. Instrumentation div. Ampex Corp., Redwood City, Calif., 1954-57, v.p., gen. mgr., exec. v.p. Ampex Corp., 1957-64; pres. Sackman Assos., 1964-66; chmn. bd. V.S.C. Corp., 1964-66; pres., chief exec. Time/Data Corp., Palo Alto, Calif., 1966-70; dir., cons. Vidar Corp., Mountain View, Calif., 1965-72; pres. Rodal Corp., Palo Alto, 1972-78; dir. Armstrong Med. Research Found., Menlo Park, Calif., 1968—; gen. ptnr. U.S. Venture Partners,

Menlo Park, 1981—; cons. Alza Corp. Served with USNR, 1944-46. Mem. IEEE (life), Instrument Soc. Am., Am. Mgmt. Assn., Sigma Tau. Home: 70 Stern Ln Atherton CA 94025 Office: 633 Menlo Ave Suite 250 Menlo Park CA 94025

SACKTON, FRANK JOSEPH, university administrator, retired army officer; b. Chgo., Aug. 11, 1912; student Northwestern U., 1936, Yale, 1946; student U. Md., 1951-52, B.S., 1970; grad. Army Inf. Sch., 1940, Command and Gen. Staff Coll., 1942, Armed Forces Staff Coll., 1949, Nat. War Coll., 1954; M.Pub. Adminstrn., Ariz. State U., 1976; m. June Dorothy Raymond, Sept. 21, 1940. Mem. 131st Inf. Regt., Ill. N.G., 1929-40; commd. 2d lt. U.S. Army, 1934, advanced through grades to lt. gen., 1967; brigade plans and ops. officer 33d Inf. Div., PTO, 1941, 33d Div., 1943-45; div. signal officer, 1942-43, div. intelligence officer, 1944, div. plans and ops. officer, 1945; sec. to gen. staff for Gen. MacArthur, Tokyo, 1947-48; bn. comdr. 30th Inf. Regt., 1949-50; mem. spl. staff Dept. Army, 1951; plans and ops. officer Joint Task Force 132, PTO, 1952; comdr. Joint Task Force 7, Marshall Islands, 1953; mem. gen. staff Dept. Army, 1954-55; with Office Sec. Def., 1956; comdr. 18th Inf. Regt., 1957-58; chief staff 1st Inf. Div., 1959; chief army Mil. Mission to Turkey, 1960-62; comdr. XIV Army Corps, 1963; dep. dir. plans Joint Chiefs Staff, 1964-66; army general staff mil. ops., 1966-67; comptroller of the army, 1967-70; ret., 1970; spl. asst. for fed./state relations Gov. Ariz., 1971-75; chmn. Ariz. Programming and Coordinating Com. for Fed. Programs, 1971-75; lectr. Am. Grad. Sch. Internat. Mgmt., 1973-77; vis. asst. prof., lectr. public affairs Ariz. State U., Tempe, 1976-78, dean Coll. Public Programs, 1979-80, prof. public affairs, 1980—, v.p. bus. affairs, 1981—. Mem. Ariz. Steering Com. for Restoration of the State Capitol, 1974-75, Ariz. State Personnel Bd., 1978-83, Ariz. State Regulatory Rev. Council, 1981—. Decorated D.S.M., Silver Star, also Legion of Merit with 4 oak leaf clusters, Bronze Star with 2 oak leaf clusters, Air medal, Army Commendation medal with 1 oak leaf cluster, Combat Inf. badge. Mem. Ariz. Acad. Public Adminstrn., Pi Alpha Alpha (pres. chpt. 1976-82). Clubs: Army-Navy (Washington); Arizona (Phoenix). Contbr. articles to public affairs and mil. jours. Home: 7814 E Northland Dr Scottsdale AZ 85251 Office: College Public Programs Ariz State U Tempe AZ 85287

SACMAN, ERNESTO IGLESIA, acct., tax cons., ins. agt.; b. Pangasinan, Philippines, May 5, 1939; came to U.S., 1967, naturalized, 1973; s. Federico Apostol and Maria Consolacion Gonzales (Iglesia) S.; B.S. in Commerce, Far Eastern U., Manila, 1959; m. Erlinda Q. Argao, June 22, 1963; children—Marcial Eugenio, Lino Eliseo, Gregoria Eileen, Angela Elizabeth. Acct., Aboitez Mfg. Corp., Manila, 1956-61; cost acct. Atlas Consol. Mining Corp., Cebu, Philippines, 1964-65; chief acct. Ammann & Whitney Internat. Ltd., Manila, 1965-67; br. acct. McKesson & Robbins, Inc., div. Foremost-McKesson, South San Francisco, Calif., 1967-70; acctg. supr. Santa Clara County Water Dist., San Jose, Calif., 1970-74; self-employed income tax practioner, Sunnyvale, Calif., 1969—, ins. agt., Sunnyvale, 1974—; bus. and mgmt. cons., 1971—. Pres., Filipino Social Circle; bd. dirs. Filipino Community Santa Clara County; mem. Better Bus. Bur. Santa Clara County, Philippine Cultural Cntr. Projects. Recipient Merit award Filipino Social Circle, 1975; C.P.A., Philippines. Mem. Philippine Bus. and Profl. Soc., Philippine Inst. C.P.A.s, Nat. Assn. Income Tax Practitioners, Am. Soc. Profl. Cons., Filipino Accts. Assn., Sunnyvale C. of C. Democrat. Roman Catholic. Club: Mabuhay Lions (San Jose). Home: 5836 Santa Teresa Blvd San Jose CA 95123 Office: 909 E Duane Ave Sunnyvale CA 94086

SADDLER, IVAN ROY, mfg. corp. ofcl.; b. Dallas, Oct. 31, 1918; s. Ray Elmer and Glendora (Hightower) S.; B.S.E.E., U. Tex., El Paso, 1950; postgrad. George Washington U., 1951; m. Helen Pauline Cox, Jan. 19, 1947; children—Robert Dean, Ellen Elizabeth, Kenneth Randolph. Engr., Sta. KEPO, El Paso, 1947-50; sales mgr., subcontract mgr. RCA, Washington, Camden and Somerville, N.J., 1951-62; v.p. Microlectron, Inc., Santa Monica, Calif., 1962-64; market devel. mgr., product mktg. mgr. Motorola Semiconductor Group, Phoenix, 1964, now patent tech. mgr., program mgr.; cons. U.S. Dept. Commerce, Inst. Def. Analyses, Los Alamos Sci. Lab.; mem. Dept. Def. Tech. Working Group. Served with U.S. Army, 1942-46, 50-52. Recipient cert. of appreciation U.S. Dept. Commerce, 1980. Republican. Clubs: Toastmasters Internat., Masons. Patentee in field. Home: 7229 E Vista Dr Scottsdale AZ 85253 Office: 5005 E McDowell Rd Phoenix AZ 85008

SADILEK, VLADIMIR, architect; b. Czechoslovakia, June 27, 1933; came to U.S., 1967, naturalized, 1973; s. Oldrich and Antoine (Zlamal) S.; Ph.D. summa cum laude in City Planning and Architecture, Tech. U. Prague, 1957; m. Jana Kadlec, Mar. 25, 1960; 1 son, Vladimir, Jr. Chief architect State Office for City Planning, Prague, 1958-67; architect, designer Bank Bldg. Corp., St. Louis, 1967-70, asso. architect, San Francisco, 1970-74; owner, chief exec. officer Bank Design Cons., San Mateo, Calif., 1974-81, West Coast Development Co., San Mateo, 1975—; pres., chief exec. officer Orbis Devel. Corp., San Mateo, 1981—. Served with Inf. of Czechoslovakia, 1958. Recipient awards of excellence from Bank Building Corp. and AIA for planning and design of fin. instns. in Hawaii, Calif. (1971), Ariz., N.Mex., Tex. (1972), Colo., Wyo. (1973), Idaho, Oreg., Washington (1974); lic. architect, 25 states. Republican. Roman Catholic. Home: 80 Orange Ct Hillsborough CA 94010 Office: 1777 Borel Pl San Mateo CA 94402

SADLER, BLAIR LEAMER, hosp. exec.; b. N.Y.C., Mar. 28, 1941; s. Alfred M. and Margaret S.; grad. Amherst Coll., 1962; J.D., U. Pa., 1965; m. Georgia Robins, Sept. 20, 1975; children—Noelle, Nicole. Med.-legal specialist NIH, Bethesda, Md., 1967-70; asst. prof. law, Yale U., New Haven, co-dir. Yale Trauma Program, 1970-73; asst. v.p. Robert Wood Johnston Found., Princeton, 1973-77; v.p. Scripps Clinic and Research Found., dir. Cecil H. and Ida M. Green Hosp. of Scripps Clinic, La Jolla, Calif., 1977-80; pres., chief exec. officer Children's Hosp. and Health Center, San Diego, 1980—; adj. clin. prof. Sch. Medicine, U. Calif., San Diego. Served to lt. comdr. USPHS, 1967-70. Mem. Hosp. Council of San Diego and Imperial Counties (pres. 1983), Calif. Assn. Children's Hosps. (pres. 1982), Calif. Hosp. Assn. Clubs: Univ. (Washington), Cuyamaca (San Diego). Co-author: The Physician's Assistant - Today and Tomorrow, 1972, 75, Emergency Medical Care: The Neglected Public Service, 1977; editor: The Robert Wood Johnson Foundation's First Five Years, 1976; contbr. writings to profl. publs. Office: 8001 Frost St San Diego CA 92123

SADLER, GREGORY JOHN, hotel company executive; b. Phila., Mar. 17, 1951; s. Harry and Virtelee (Cherry) S.; m. Nina Francine Ragland, Apr. 20, 1979. A.A., Peirce Jr. Coll., 1973; B.A. in Sociology, LaSalle Coll., 1975; postgrad. George Washington U., 1977-79. Supr. front office ops. Marriott Hotel, Phila., 1974-75; tchr. mgmt. edn. Marriott Corp., Washington, 1975-76, orgn. devel., mgmt. specialist, 1976-79; dir. tng. Bally's Park Pl. Casino & Hotel, Atlantic City, N.J., 1979-82; corp. mgr. tng. and devel. Westin Hotels, Seattle, 1982-83, dir. manpower planning and devel., 1983—. Bd. dirs. Rainier Vista Boys and Girls Clubs, Pvt. Industry Council Seattle/King County. Served with USMC, 1969-71. Mem. Am. Soc. Tng. and Devel., Human Resource Planning Soc. Office: Westin Hotels 2001 6th Ave Seattle WA 98121

SADLIER, JUDY HURST, financial management company executive; b. San Mateo, Calif., May 1, 1936; d. William Gainor and Helen Davis (Smith) Ebright; m. Ronald Hurst, Feb. 25, 1961; m. Timothy C. Sadlier, Sept. 29, 1972. B.S. in Bus. Adminstrn., U. Calif., 1957. Account exec. Reynolds & Co., 1966-77; br. mgr. Dean Witter Reynolds, Inc., Santa Cruz, Calif., 1977—, 1st v.p., 1983—. Mem. Charter Com. City of Santa Cruz, 1977; chmn. Offstreet Parking Commn., 1979, mem., 1980-83; bd. dirs. Santa Cruz Community Hosp. Named to pres.'s council Dean Witter Reynolds, Inc., 1976, recipient Pacesetters Mgmt. award, 1978, named Mgrs. Adv., 1982, Active Assets Mgmt. award, 1982, named to Tng. Faculty, 1983; recipient Mgmt. award Pub. Storage Inc., 1981, 1982, Fox & Carscadon, 1982, 83, Quinco Resources, Inc., 1983. Mem. Santa Cruz C. of C. (pres. 1975), Women's Network (founder; chmn. 1975-79). Club: Soroptimist (Woman of Achievement 1978). Home: 305 Arroyo Seco Santa Cruz CA 95060 Office: Dean Witter Reynolds Inc 111 Mission St Santa Cruz CA 95061

SADOWSKY, MEIER, electronics corp. exec.; b. San Antonio, May 16, 1915; s. Nathan and Judith (Freeman) S.; B.S., CCNY, 1936, M.S., 1939; Ph.D., Los Angeles U., 1976; m. Claire Mendelson, Dec. 19, 1942; children—Linda Gail, Steven Judd, Nina Ann. Instr., Essex Jr. Coll., Newark, 1940-42; engr. RCA, N.J., 1940-49; mgr. chem. engring. tube div. Philco Corp., Lansdale, Pa., 1949-59; pres. Continental Electronics, Vernon, Calif., 1959-63; v.p. Video Color Corp., El Segundo, Calif., 1963-70; pres. Spl. Purpose Tech. Corp., Van Nuys, Calif., 1970—; lectr. physics Calif. State U., Dominguez Hills, 1979. Fellow AAAS, Am. Inst. Chemists; mem. Soc. Info. Display, Sigma Xi. Home: 4131 Nagle Ave Sherman Oaks CA 91423 Office: 15818 Arminta St Van Nuys CA 91406

SAENZ, HULBERTO, chemical company executive, management consultant, educator; b. San Antonio, Aug. 8, 1934; s. Jesus G. and Maria M. (Mendiola) S.; m. Anita Grace Buckley, Nov. 15, 1969; children—Brett, Maria, Juliana, Angela; m. 2d, Marta Rosa Machicado, July 5, 1980; 1 son, Hulberto Javier. B.A., U. of Tex., 1963; M.A., Ball State U., 1972; B.S., Weber State Coll., 1978; doctoral candidate U. So. Calif., 1983—. Cert. tchr., adminstr., Utah, Tex. Commd. 2d lt. U.S. Air Force, 1959, advanced through grades to maj., 1969; various assignments air def. fighter squadrons, 1960-70; combat missions Vietnam, 1970-71; liaison to Spanish Air Force, 1973-77; ret., 1978; tchr. Franklin Elem. Sch., Salt Lake City, 1978-79, sch. adminstr. Salt Lake Dist., 1979-81; mgmt. trainer Hercules, Inc., Magna, Utah, 1981-82, sr. mgmt. devel. rep., 1983—; mem. Utah Tech. Coll. Adv. Bd., 1981-83. Mem. League United Latin Am. Citizens, 1980—; mem. Gov. Hispanic Adv. Council, 1981-84; pres. Latin Am. Edn. Found., 1982-83; state pres. Spanish Speaking Orgn. Community Integrity and Opportunity, 1982-84. Decorated D.F.C.; recipient cert. Appreciation Gov. Utah, 1982. Mem. Am. Mgmt. Assn., Am. Soc. Tng. and Devel., State of Utah Assn. Bilingual Edn. Roman Catholic. Clubs: Officer's (Hill AFB, Utah), Am. Mil. Scottish Rite Bodies. Home: 2713 Perez St San Antonio TX 78207

SAETA, JOANNE EDITH, educational administrator; b. Los Angeles, Aug. 15, 1931; d. Raymond Floyd and Ruth Leona (Gressley) Hixson; m. Philip Max Saeta, Aug. 28, 1954; children—David, Peter, Stephen, Sandra. B.A., Stanford U., 1953, M.A., 1954; M.A. in Ednl. Adminstrn., Calif. State U.-Los Angeles, 1983. Tchr. elem. sch., El Paso, 1954-55; master demonstration tchr. Stanford Elem. Sch., Palo Alto (Calif.) Unified Sch. Dist., 1955-57; tchr. Pasadena (Calif.) Unified Sch. Dist., 1958-59; with South Pasadena (Calif.) Unified Sch. Dist., 1974—, dist. office coordinator state and fed. projects, 1980-83, ednl. program asst. bilingual state and fed. projects, 1980—. Mem. formation bd. S. Pasadena Ednl. Found. Recipient San Gabriel Valley Adminstrs. Golden Apple award, 1979; Service award PTA, 1975, 77. Mem. Assn. Calif. Sch. Adminstrs., Stanford Profl. Women Los Angeles. Democrat. Home: 2036 Oak St South Pasadena CA 91030 Office: 1020 El Centro St South Pasadena CA 91030

SAFARJAN, WILLIAM ROBERT, psychologist; b. Visalia, Calif., Feb. 17, 1943; s. Robert and Alice Joy (Sharp) S.; m. Paula Tinder, May 26, 1978. B.A. in Internat. Relations, U. Calif.-Berkeley, 1966; A.B. in Psychology, San Diego State U., 1971, M.A., 1976; Ph.D. in Psychology, Rutgers U., 1980. Lic. psychologist, Calif. Research asst. San Diego State U., 1971, Naval Personnel Research and Devel. Ctr., San Diego, 1972-73, Bell Telephone Lab., Homdel, N.J., 1977; teaching asst., instr. Rutgers U., New Brunswick, N.J., 1974-78, research intern, 1978-80; staff psychologist Porterville (Calif.) State Hosp., 1980—. Served to lt. USN, 1966-69. Mem. Am. Psychol. Assn., AAAS, Assn. for Advancement of Psychology, Western Psychol. Assn., San Joaquin Psychol. Assn., Psi Chi, Delta Sigma Phi. Contbr. articles to profl. jours, chpts. to books. Office: PO Box 2000 Porterville CA 93258

SAFIR, PAULA BEATRIZ, psychiatric evaluation specialist; b. Santa Clara, Cuba, Feb. 20, 1954; came to U.S., 1962, naturalized, 1975; d. Enrique and Rosario (Lopez) Jimenez; m. Bernard Safir, July 14, 1978. B.A., Montclair State Coll., 1977; M.A. in Counseling, Hood Coll., 1982; postgrad. Calif. Sch. Profl. Psychology, 1982. Caseworker Mt. Carmel Guild-Community Mental Health Ctr., Union City, N.J., 1978-79; social worker N.J. Div. Youth and Family Services, Elizabeth, 1979; psychiatr. evaluation specialist Montgomery Gen. Hosp., Olney, Md., from 1981. Mem. Am. Personnel and Guidance Assn., Md. Personnel and Guidance Assn., Am. Psychol. Assn., Md. Mental Health Counselors Assn. Roman Catholic. Address: 4760 Conrad Ave No 137 San Diego CA 92117

SAFLEY, DOUGLAS ARTHUR, optometrist; b. Cut Bank, Mont., Apr. 29, 1952; s. Bruce Arthur and Margaret Ann (Cox) S.; m. Margie Joyce Stark, Jan. 10, 1976. Student, Mont. State U., 1970-72; B.S., Pacific U., 1975, O.D., 1976. Licensed optometrist, Mont., Idaho, Oreg. Head optometrist Mare Island Naval Shipyard, Vallejo, Calif., 1976-78; sr. ptnr. Havre (Mont.) Optometric Clinic, 1978—. Mem. Havre City-County Planning Bd., 1982—, chmn., 1983—. Served to lt., USNR, 1976-78. Named Mont. Optometric Assn. Young Optometrist of Yr., 1980; recipient Outstanding Service award, Oreg. Optometric Assn., 1976. Mem. Am. Optometric Assn., Mont. Optometric Assn. (Young Optometrist of Year, 1980), Optometric Extension Program, Am. Optometric Fund., Havre Area C. of C. (dir. 1979, v.p. 1981-82, pres. 1983). Republican. Methodist. Club: Havre Rotary, (pres. 1982-83). Home: 1315 Hoover Ave Havre MT 59501 Office: PO Box 551 416 3d Ave Havre MT 59501

SAFRAN, WILLIAM, political science educator; b. Dresden, Germany, July 8, 1930; s. Abraham Joshua and Golda (Chajes) S.; m. Marian Celia (Folk) S.; Mar. 25, 1961; children—Gabriella Sarah, Joshua Abraham. B.A., CUNY, 1953, M.A., 1955; Ph.D., Columbia U., 1964. Lectr., instr. Bklyn. Coll., CUNY, 1960-65, Hunter Coll., 1962; asst. prof. U. Colo., Boulder, 1965-68, assoc. prof., 1968-73, prof. polit. sci., 1973, assoc. chmn. polit. sci. dept., 1974-76, adminstr. internat. relations program, 1971-73, 79, 81; vis. prof., Jerusalem, Paris, Nice. Served with U.S. Army, 1955-57. Social Sci. Found. fellow, 1966; U. Colo. faculty research grantee, 1966, 69-70; Nat. Endowment Humanities grantee, 1980-81; recipient history honors award CUNY, 1953. Mem. Am. Polit. Sci. Assn., Internat. Studies Assn., Am. Acad. Polit. Sci., Western Polit. Sci. Assn., Assn. Française de Sci. Politique, Conf. Group French Politics and Soc., Conf. Group German Politics. Democrat. Jewish. Author: Veto-Group Politics, 1967; The French Polity, 1977, 79; Ideology and Politics: The Socialist Party of France, 1979; Comparative Politics, 1982; co-author: The Political Economy of Collectivized Agriculture, 1979; Global Human Rights, 1981; The Fifth Republic at Twenty, 1981; Constitutional Democracy: Essays in Comparative Politics, 1983. Office: Dept Polit Sci U Colo Boulder CO 80309

SAFRON, SUSAN LAURIE, instrument rental co. exec.; b. Bklyn., June 15, 1948; d. Martin and Phyllis Edith (Schwartz) Safron; student Coll. San Mateo, 1966-67; m. Mark A. Foote, Feb. 12, 1982; 1 son by previous marriage, Joshua M. Brzuchalski, Sec. fin. Phillips Petroleum Corp., San Mateo, Calif., 1971-74; sales sec. Calportland Cement Co., Redwood City, Calif., 1974-75; personnel asst. Free Flow Packaging Corp., Redwood City, 1976-78; mgr. personnel and adminstrv. services U.S. Instrument Rentals, Inc., San Mateo, Calif., 1978—; 1st vice chairperson San Mateo County Employers Adv. Council, State of Calif. Employment and Devel. Dept. Coordinator Bay Area Big Sisters Assn., 1973-74. Democrat. Office: 2988 Campus Dr San Mateo CA 94403

SAGAR, BOKKAPATNAM TIRUMALA ANANDA, cons. civil and mech. engr.; b. Guntur, India, Mar. 6, 1929; came to U.S., 1969, naturalized, 1970; s. Bukkapatnam T. Mohana and Bukkapatnam T. (Sakuntala) Raghavachari; B.E. with honors, U. Andhra, India, 1950; M.S. in Civil Engring. (AID fellow), U. Colo., 1959; Ph.D., Colo. State U., 1973; m. Yashoda, May 17, 1962; children—Mohan Raghava, Sangeetha. Asst. dir. Central Water and Power Commn., Govt. of India, 1950-58, dep. dir., 1958-69, dir., 1969-73; sr. mech. engr. PRC Engring. Cons.'s, Inc., Englewood, Colo., 1969-77, prin. engr., 1977-78, asst. chief mech. engring., 1978—; vis. faculty Water Resources Devel. Center, U. Roorkee (India), 1959-68; expert hydraulic gates and hydraulic machinery, 1970—; UN expert under Tokten Program, 1981-82. Founder mem. Swami Sivananda Inst., Delhi, India, 1965-69; bd. dirs. Andhra Edn. Trust, India, 1953-68; trustee Tirumala-Tirupati Devasthanam for Sri Venkateswara Coll., Delhi, 1966-68. NSF travel grantee, 1979. Mem. ASCE, Internat. Water Resources Assn., U.S. Com. on Large Dams, Sigma Xi. Club: Toastmasters. Contbr. articles on hydraulic research and high head gates to profl. publs. and confs. Home: 5727 S Lowell Blvd Littleton CO 80123 Office: PO Box 3006 Bldg 40W Denver Tech Tower Englewood CO 80155

SAGATUN, INGER JOHANNE, social psychologist; b. Kragero, Norway, Dec. 24, 1944; d. Jens and Ingeborg S.; m. Leonard Perry Edwards, Aug. 14, 1971; children—Erik, Gard. Ph.D., Stanford U., 1972. Asst. prof. sociology U. Calif.-Riverside, 1978—. Am. Field Service scholar, 1962-63; Ford Found. scholar, 1967-71; recipient Jr. Faculty Regents award, U. Calif., 1979. Mem. Am. Sociol. Assn., Am. Psychol. Assn., World Sociology Assn. Contbr. articles to profl. publs. including Scandinavian Jour. of Psychology, Jour. of Marriage and Family Therapy, Family and Juvenile Court Jour. Office: Sociology Dept U Calif Riverside Riverside CA 92521

SAGAWA, YONEO, horticulturist; b. Olaa, Hawaii, Oct. 11, 1926; s. Chikatada and Mume (Kuno) S.; A.B., Washington U., St. Louis, 1950, M.S., 1952; Ph.D., U. Conn., 1956; m. Masayo Yamamoto, May 24, 1962; children—Penelope Toshiko, Irene Teruko. Postdoctoral research asso. biology Brookhaven Nat. Lab., Upton, N.Y., 1955-57, guest in biology, summer 1958; asst. prof., then asso. prof. U. Fla., 1957-64; dir. undergrad. sci. edn. research participation program NSF, summer 1964; cons. biosatellite project NASA, 1966-67; research asso. botany U. Calif., Berkeley, 1970-71; cons. UN/FAO to Singapore, 1971; prof., horticulturist U. Hawaii, 1964-67, dir. Lyon Arboretum, prof., 1967—; fellow Agrl. U., Netherlands, ITAL, Netherlands, 1979-80; asso. dir. Hawaiian Sci. Fair, 1966-67, dir., 1967-68; mem. Internat. Orchid Commn. Classification, Nomenclature and Registration, 1968—; sci. adv. bd. Pacific Tropical Garden, 1975—; councillor Las Cruces Bot. Garden, Costa Rica, 1975—; hon. trustee Friends of Foster Garden, 1973—. Served with AUS, 1945-47. Recipient Disting. Service award S. Fla. Orchid Soc., 1968; grantee Am. Orchid Soc., AEC, NIH, IMS, Honolulu Orchid Soc., HEW, Stanley Smith Hort. Trust, 1958—. Hon. life mem. Am. Anthurium Soc., Am. Orchid Soc., Kaimuki Orchid Soc.; mem. Bot. Soc. Am., Am. Soc. Hort. Sci., AAAS, Assn. Bot. Gardens and Arboreta, Internat. Hort. Soc., Internat. Assn. Plant Tissue Culture, Palm Soc., Phi Kappa Phi (past chpt. pres.). Democrat. Clubs: Aloha Bonsai. Editor: Hawaii Orchid Jour., 1972—, Pacific Orchid Soc. Bull., 1966-71; editorial bd. Allertonia, 1976-79; contbr. numerous articles profl. jours. Office: 3860 Manoa Rd Honolulu HI 96822

SAGE, BILL BOWMAN, art educator; b. Rapid City, S.D., Oct. 3, 1929; s. William B. and Inez (Bowman) S.; m. Evelyn Ruzick, June 18, 1963; 1 son, Stirling W. B.S. Ed., Black Hills State Coll., 1951; M. Applied Arts, Mont. State U., 1959; M.F.A., Mills Coll., 1965. Tchr. art Jr. High Sch., Billings, Mont., 1956-58, Sr. High Sch., 1959-62; instr. Black Hills State Coll., Spearfish, S.D., part-time 1958, Eastern Mont. State U., 1960, U. Utah, 1965; mem. faculty Eastern Wash. U., Cheney, 1965—, assoc. prof. ceramics, jewelry, 1971-78, prof., 1978—; one-person shows: Gallery 81, Billings, 1962, 74, Ft. Wright Coll., Spokane, Wash., 1968, Bramante Gallery, 1981, All Clay Conf., Eastern Wash. U., 1982, others; exhibited in group shows: N.W. Craftsman Exhbns., Seattle, 1060, 61, 63, 67, 72, Spokane Ann. Art Exhbn., Cheney Cowles Art Mus., Seattle, 1969-72, 76, 77, 79, 80, N.W. Designer Craftsman, various galleries, 1968, 70, 75-83, Gov.'s Invitational, Olympia, Wash., 1967, 80, N.W. Craftsmen U.S.A., Portland, Oreg. and Mus. Polack Gallery, Mercer Island, Wash., 1966, Mus. Am. Crafts, N.Y.C., 1973, Utah State U., Logan, 1972-77, others; represented in permanent collections: Crocker Art Gallery, Sacramento, Mills Coll., Utah State Art Mus., Logan, U. Utah, others. Served with USAF, 1951-55. Mills Coll. scholar, 1963-65, Alumni grantee, 1965—. Mem. Nat. Council Edn. for Ceramic Arts, Northwest Designer Craftsmen, Archie Bray Found., Am. Crafts Council, Contemporary Crafts Assn. Home: Rt 2 Box 142 Cheney WA 99004 Office: Dept Art Eastern Wash U Cheney WA 99004

SAGE, DORIS LOUISE, university official; b. Tacoma, Apr. 3, 1927; d. Charles William and Anna Lois (Calvert) Stromberg; student public schs., Tacoma; m. Charles Eugene Sage, Oct. 19, 1946; children—Barbara Gene Sage Glenn, Christine Elizabeth Sage-Mullins. With U. Puget Sound, Tacoma, 1958—, bus. mgr. Law Sch., 1980—. Councilwoman Town of Ruston (Wash.), 1974-82. Mem. Nat. Assn. Ednl. Buyers. Methodist. Office: U Puget Sound Sch Law 950 Broadway Tacoma WA 98402

SAGE, WEBSTER LEGENE, JR., physician; b. St. Louis, Oct. 22, 1925; s. Webster LeGene and Alice Virginia (Gollehon) S.; B.S., U. Ariz., 1949; M.D., Baylor U., 1953; m. Marjorie Claudine New, May 20, 1952; children—Bryan LeGene, Evan Webster. Intern, Good Samaritan Hosp., Phoenix, 1953-54; resident White Meml. Hosp., Los Angeles, 1954-56; practice medicine, specializing in ophthalmology, Phoenix, 1956—; pres. Sage & Sage, P.A., Phoenix, 1971—; active teaching staff Good Samaritan Health Services, Phoenix, 1960—, chief ophthalmology, 1965—; active teaching staff St. Joseph's Med. Center, Phoenix, 1965—. Served to brig. gen. USAR, ret. Fellow A.C.S., Pan Am. Med. Assn., Internat. Coll. Surgeons, Am. Acad. Ophthalmology; mem. AMA, Ariz. Med. Assn., Maricopa County Med. Soc., Am. Intra-Ocular Implant Soc. (officer), Ariz. (pres. 1969-70), Phoenix (pres. 1968-69) opthal. socs., Alpha Omega Alpha. Episcopalian (mem. vestry). Mason, Kiwanian. Club: Phoenix Country. Home: 3109 W Manor Dr Phoenix AZ 85014 Office: 555 W Catalina Dr Suite 312 Phoenix AZ 85013

SAGUM, ROLAND DIAZ, state ofcl., investment co. exec.; b. Batangas, Phillippines, Jan. 1, 1912; s. Macario A. and Dionicia (Diaz) S.; came to U.S., 1912, naturalized, 1946; certificate Pub. Adminstrn., U. Hawaii, 1935; certificate Delinquency Control, U. So. Calif., 1958; m. Genevieve Anguay, Aug. 27, 1932; children—Roland Diaz, Ginger Vea, Marvin I., Nelson A., Catherine A. Hudson. With Honolulu Police, 1934-75, capt. of police, 1960-67, community relations coordinator, 1967-68, maj. in charge night ops., 1968-69, police commr., 1969, v.p., dir. pub. relations, 1969-75; chmn. bd. United Hawaiian Investment

Corp.; pres. Ambassador Travel Agy., Inc.; dir. United Hawaiian Acceptance, Inc., Paterrin Co., Nuuanu Meml. Park, Financial Security Ins. Co. Chmn. state bd. lay activities Meth. Ch., 1963-65, del. 1st world conf. Human Relations, 1958, del. 1st nat. conf. Christian Social Concerns, Washington, 1960, del. Jurisdictional Conf., World Meth. Conf. and World Meth. Conf. on Family Life, 1964. Mem. Gov.'s Com. on Sex Deviations, 1960-61, Com. on Alcholism, 1960-69, State Com. on Correction, 1968-69; commr. State Criminal Injuries Compensation, 1971-79; mem. Mayor's Com. on Children and Youth to study Drug Abuse, 1962-70, Citizens Com. on Municipal Auditorium, 1964-66; pres. Nat. Polio Found. Hawaii, Police Relief Assn.; pres. United Filipino Council, 1959-61, Hauola Club, 1950, pres. Honolulu Council Chs., Police Activities League; youth dir. Internat. Assn. Y's Men's Clubs; pres. Mental Health Assn. Hawaii, 1972-73, Palama Inter-Church Council, Filipino C. of C., 1979-82; treas. Internat. Christian Leadership, Hawaii Council on Crime and Delinquency, 1980; pres. Palama Settlement, 1970-72, Philippine Meml. Found., 1950; mem. Hawaii CD Adv. Council. Bd. dirs. Oahu Tb and Health Council, Nat. Assn. Mental Health, Liliuokalani Adv. Council, Child and Family Service, Pacific and Asian Affairs Council, Hawaiian Govt. Assn., Hawaii Cancer Soc., John Howard Assn., Nat. Soc. for Crippled Children and Adults, Honolulu Community Chest, Salvation Army Men's Social Service, Honolulu Met. YMCA, Nuuanu br. YMCA, Goodwill Industries, Recipient award U.S. Bur. Prisons, 1962; Nat. Lane Bryant award for civic acheivements, 1967; Outstanding Service to Youth award Pacific S.W. Area YMCA. 1964; certificate of appreciation Nat. Bd. YMCA, 1963; named Father of Year, Hawaii chpt. World Brotherhood, 1960; Am. of Week, Honolulu C. of C., 1950, Man of Week, 1952; Outstanding Citizen of Year, Hawaii Govt. Assn., 1964, Outstanding Community Worker, 1973. Mem. Internat. Assn. Chiefs of Police, Nat. Police Officers Assn., Am. Soc. Tng. Dirs., Am. Soc. Pub. Adminstrn. (dir.). Internat. Juvenile Officers Assn. (award merit 1966), Acad. Sci. Interrogation. Hawaii Assn. Parliamentarians, Am. Inst. Parliamentarians (cert.), Am. Correctional Assn. Methodist (del. numerous world confs.). Clubs: Masons, Knights of Rizal (comdr.). Home: 3008 Makini St Honolulu HI 96815 Office: Suite 407 33 S King St Honolulu HI 96813

SAHEKI, AKIRA, export company executive; b. Matsuyama, Japan, Sept. 6, 1924; s. Masataka Higashi and Shizuko Saheki; B.S., Matsuyama U. Commerce, 1944; m. Saeko Setsu, Apr. 28, 1952; children—Yoshiko, Hitomi, Ken. Came to U.S., 1956, naturalized, 1977. Portland (Oreg.) rep. F. Kanematsu & Co., Ltd., Japan, 1956-60; Portland rep. Kanematsu-Gosho (U.S.A.) Inc., N.Y.C., 1969-70, gen. mgr. Portland br. office, 1969-70; exec. v.p. Fibrex & Shipping Co., Inc., Portland, 1971-78, pres., 1979—. Active Portland Symphony Assn., Portland Opera Assn. Mem. Pacific Rim Trade Assn., Am. Pulpwood Assn., Nat. Forest Products Assn., Oreg. Trucking Assn., Portland C. of C., Assn. Oreg. Industries, Pacific Maritime Assn., U.S. C. of C., Japan Am. Soc. Oreg., Japanese Garden Soc. Oreg. Democrat. Buddhist. Clubs: Coos Bay Shipping, Down Town Rotary (Portland), Columbia Edgewater Country. Home: 2665 SW West Point Ave Portland OR 97225 Office: Fibrex & Shipping Co Inc 1420 Bank of Calif Tower 707 S W Washington St Portland OR 97205

SAHL, JEFFREY CLAUDE, psychologist; b. Pensacola, Fla., Apr. 18, 1953; s. Raleigh Olaf and Elaine Josephine (Dickman) S. B.A. cum laude, U. Colo., 1975; M.A., Ball State U., 1976; Ph.D., Calif. Sch. Profl. Psychol., 1981. Lic. psychologist, Calif. With St. Anthony's Hosp., Denver, 1976-78; with San Diego Dept. Edn., 1978-79; pre-doctoral intern Catholic Community Services, San Diego, 1979-81; psychologist Pacific Med. Ctr., San Francisco, 1981—; prin. Jeffrey Claude Sahl psychologist, 1983—. Mem. Coordinating Com. Lesbian and Gay for City & County of San Francisco. Mem. Am. Psychol. Assn. Office: 4326 18th St San Francisco CA 94114

SAHLSTROM, ELMER BERNARD, lawyer; b. Seattle, Feb. 25, 1918; s. August Walimer and Alma Carolyn (Ostrom) S.; B.S., U. Oreg., 1945, J.D., 1947; m. Phyllis May Horstman, June 18, 1946; children—Gary Bernard, Sherry Lynn (Mrs. Stephen Monohan), Gregory Lane. Acct., Haskins & Sells, N.Y.C., 1941-44; admitted to Oreg. bar, 1947, U.S. Supreme Ct. bar, 1977; mem. firms Thompson & Sahlstrom, Eugene, Oreg., 1947-57, Sahlstrom, Lombard, Starr & Vinson, and predecessor, Eugene, 1957—. Mem. bd. visitors U. Oreg. Law Sch., 1977-79. C.P.A. Oreg. Mem. Am. Judicature Soc., ABA, Internat. Bar Assn., Oreg. Bar Assn., Am. Trial Lawyers Assn. (pres. So. Oreg. chpt. 1973-75), Assn. Attys. and C.P.A.s Am. Inst. Accts., Oreg. Soc. C.P.A.s, Oreg. Law Sch. Alumni Assn. (pres. 1972-73), Beta Alpha Psi, Phi Alpha Delta. Elk. Clubs: Country, Town (dir. 1970-75, pres. 1978) (Eugene). Home: 715 Fair Oaks St Eugene OR 97401 Office: 915 Oak St Eugene OR 97401

SAIKI, LOREL KEIKO, art director, photographer; b. Chgo., May 8, 1954; d. Hiroshi and Jessie Keiko (Kawasuna) S. Student U. Colo.-Colorado Springs ext., 1972-73, Art Ctr. Coll. Design, Los Angeles, 1973-76. Art dir. Robertson Co., Los Angeles, 1975-76, Bozell & Jacobs, Inc., Los Angeles, 1976-82; sr. art dir. Evans/Weinberg Advt., Inc., Los Angeles, 1982—. Recipient award Art Dirs. Club Los Angeles Advt. Show, 1978, cert. of merit Am. Advt. Fedn. Show, 1978, Lulu awards Los Angeles Advt. Women, 1978, Gold medal Indsl. TV Assn., Los Angeles, 1982. Assoc. mem. Am. Soc. Mag. Photographers, Internat. Soc. Photography.

SAINI, RAM PERSHAD, plant manager; b. India, July 15, 1942; s. Punnu and Kauri S.; m. Swarana Devi, Feb. 19, 1956; children—Anita, Paul, Sunita. Student, Punjab Coll. Vet. Science; B.S. in Poultry Science, Calif. State U.-San Luis Obispo, 1971. Plant mgr. Rainbow Farms div. V.F.F. Inc., Turlock, Calif., 1971—, safety dir., 1974—. Mem. adv. bd. Citizen Planning Com. 1981—. Mem. Stanis Laus Safety Council (dir.), Am. Soc. Safety Engrs. Democrat. Hindu. Clubs: Lions (past v.p.).

ST. CLAIRE, SUE MARIE, interior designer; b. Hollywood, Calif., Jan. 3, 1938; d. Harold Pearce and Ora Mae (Smith) Valentine; student Mills Coll., 1956-57; B.A., Northwestern U., 1959; m. Donald A. Saint Claire, Dec. 20, 1959; children—Valeri Louise, Donald Anthony, Gregory Harold, Jeffrey Valentine. Designer, Mary C. Peck Interiors, Menlo Park, Calif., 1975-77; designer for Prince Mohammad, Royal Family of Saudi Arabia, Riyadn, 1977-78; owner, designer Valentine St. Claire Interior Design, Menlo Park, Calif., 1977—. Pres., Peninsula Aux. of Florence Crittenton Services, 1971; active Peninsula Vols. Inc., Stanford U. Com. for Art. Mem. Am. Soc. Interior Designers (assoc.), Internat. Soc. Interior Designers, Pi Beta Phi (pres. San Francisco alumni club). Roman Catholic. Clubs: San Francisco Bay, Commonwealth. Home: 150 Lombard St San Francisco CA 09411 Office: Valentine St Claire Interior Design Icehouse 151 Union St San Francisco CA 94111

ST. JOHN, JUANITA C., university administrator; b. South Bend, Ind., Nov. 5, 1931; d. William and Ethelwyn Ida Isabella (Ryan) Svenson; m. John Joseph St. John, June 8, 1956; children—Michael Bryan, Kathleen Ida Mae. B.A., St. Mary's Coll. for Women, 1952; Ph.C., U. Mich., 1955. Coordinator, Peace Corps Tng. for Africa, UCLA, 1964-68, asst. to dir. African Studies Ctr., 1968-78, asst. to vice chancellor, 1978—, dir. Mayor's Task Force for Africa/Los Angeles Relations, 1979—. Bd. dirs. Los Angeles Ethnic Arts Council, 1975-79, Friends of Cal-Tech Library, 1979-82; Fund African Students, Inc., 1980—, Mus. African-Am. Art, 1980—, Precision Planning, 1980—, Town Hall West, 1980—; sec. African Task Force; mem. exec. com. Los Angeles Sister Cities, 1980—; mem. Com. Fgn. Relations, 1979—; mem. citizens adv. commns. Los Angeles Olympic Organizing Com., 1982—. Democrat. Author: African Arts Study Kit for Elementary Schools, 1976. Office: UCLA Los Angeles CA 90024

ST. JOHN, RICHARD ARNOLD, accountant; b. Dayton, Ohio, Feb. 14, 1934; s. Marion W. and Helen M. (Wildman) St. J.; m. Marilyn K. Easton, Aug. 31, 1953; children—Scott, Joy, Jay, Kent. A.B. in Geol. Sci., Miami (Ohio) U., 1956; M.B.A., Xavier U., 1967. Technologist, mem. staff Nat. Lead Co., Cin., 1956-69; bus. mgr. mining and exploration dept. NL Industries, Inc., N.Y.C. and Golden, Colo., 1970-75; gen. mgr. retail ops. Colo. Geol. Industries, Denver and Ft. Collins, Colo., 1976; pres. Richard A. St. John Inc., Colorado Springs, Colo., 1977—. Mem. Am. Assn. Cost Engrs. (founding pres. S.W. Ohio chpt.) Office: 3520 Galley Rd Suite 201 Colorado Springs CO 80909

ST. JOHN, TERRY NOEL, museum curator, artist; b. Sacramento, Dec. 24, 1934; s. Walter Oliver and Marmina Rose (Skeahan) St. J.; m. Erika Eva Bock, July 9, 1964; children—Walter, Noel. B.A., U. Calif.-Berkeley, 1958; M.F.A., Calif. Coll. Arts and Crafts, Okland, 1966. Curator modern painting Oakland Mus., 1969—; instr. outdoor painter's project U. Calif.-Santa Cruz, 1979—; interviewer oral history Archives of Am. Art, San Francisco, 1980—; one man shows include: Brook House, Orinda, Calif., 1981, U. Calif.-Santa Cruz, 1978, Walnut Creek (Calif.) Art Ctr., 1976; lectr. on Calif. art; juror numerous county and city ann. art exhibits. Recipient James D. Phelan award Calif. Palace Legion of Honor, 1965; Regional 1st prize Contemporary So. Artists, 1966. Democrat. Author various exhbn. catalogues. Home: 2736 Shasta Rd Berkeley CA 94708 Office: 1000 Oak St Oakland CA 94607

SAITO, FRANK KIYOJI, import/export firm executive; b. Tokyo, Feb. 28, 1945; s. Kaoru and Chiyoko S.; LL.B., Kokugakuin U., 1967; m. Elaine Tamami Karasawa, Dec. 11, 1975; children—Roderic Kouki, Lorine Erika. With import dept. Trois Co. Ltd., Tokyo, Japan, 1967-68; founder import/export dept. Three Bond Co., Ltd., Tokyo, 1968-71; sales mgr. Kobe Mercantile, Inc., San Diego, 1971-76; pres. K & S Internat. Corp., San Diego, 1976—. Office: 7626 Miramar Rd Suite 3200 San Diego CA 92126

SAK, JAY BARRY, sales exec.; b. Los Angeles, Nov. 21, 1956; s. Maxwell Sak and Esther Sak Rand; B.S. in Bus. Adminstrn., Mktg., Calif. State U., Long Beach, 1977, B.S. in Bus. Adminstrn., Mgmt., 1977. Utility clk. Bank of Am., San Pedro, Calif., 1973-77; adminstrv. asst. Toyota Motor Dist., Toyota Co., Portland, Oreg., 1978; regional mktg. officer Bank of Am., Century City, Calif., 1978-79: ops. officer Bank of Am., Santa Monica, Calif., 1979-80; exec. v.p. Harvey Rand & Assocs., Inc., Torrance, Calif., 1980—. Home: 1711 Old Stone Ct San Pedro CA 90732 Office: 12444 Victory Blvd North Hollywood CA 91606

SAKAMOTO, MASATO, clin. bioanalyst; b. Berkeley, Calif., Oct. 28, 1932; s. Kakuichi and Setsu (Kawaoka) S.; B.A., Coll. of Pacific, 1953; LL.B., U. Calif., 1955, B.S., 1954, M.S., 1963; m. Jeni Kiyoko, Sept. 19, 1957; children—Yvonne H., Diana M., Tadd M., Anthony K. Clin. lab. technologist San Rafael (Calif.) Gen. Hosp., 1954-58; supr. clin. lab. technologist Permanente Med. Group, Oakland, Calif., 1958-74; clin. bioanalyst Meml. Hosp., Vesper Center, San Leandro, Calif., 1963-83; analytical cons. Sumar Corp., San Leandro, 1979—, Abington System Corp., 1982—. Mem. Forensic Sci. Soc. (London), Instrument Soc. Am. (sr.), Assn. Advancement Med. Instrumentation, Am. Chem. Soc., Soc. Applied Spectrography. Diplomate Am. Bd. Bioanalysis Dirs., N.Y. Acad. Sci. Republican. Methodist. Address: 2477 Lakeview Dr San Leandro CA 94577

SAKANIWA, YASUO, watch mfg. co. exec.; b. Tokyo, Sept. 29, 1925; came to U.S., 1952; s. Yoshio and Misao (Tsurumi) S.; m. Kayoko Ishibashi, Mar. 11, 1961; children—Hiroaki Robert, Hiromi Jane. B.A., Keio U., 1951; B.A., Tusculum Coll., 1953; M.B.A., Temple U., 1955; postgrad. U. Pa., 1959. With pub. relations dept. Hattori Trading Co., Ltd., Tokyo, 1959-61; mgr. Toyo Metall. & Chem. Co. Ltd., Seattle, 1961-70; pres. Seiko Instruments, Inc., Torrance, Calif., 1970—, Seiko Instruments U.S.A., Inc., Torrance, 1981—; dir. Micro Power Systems, Inc., Gato S.A. Brazil, Daini Seikosha Co., Ltd., Tokyo. Presbyterian. Clubs: Tokyo Lawn Tennis, Asahigaoka Golf; Rolling Hills Country. Home: 4 Silverbit Ln Rolling Hills Estates CA 90274 Office: 2990 W Lomita Blvd Torrance CA 90505

SAKOVER, RAYMOND PAUL, radiologist; b. Chgo., Oct. 8, 1944; s. Max and Lena (Berardi) S.; m. Patricia Ellyn Taylor, June 7, 1969; children—Shelley Lynn, David Evan, Michael Paul. B.S. (James scholar), U. Ill., 1965, M.D., 1969. Intern, St. Francis Hosp., Evanston, Ill., 1969-70, resident, 1970-73; practice medicine specializing in radiology, Riverside, Calif., 1975—; staff radiologist Riverside Community Hosp., 1975—; clin. instr. Loma Linda (Calif.) U. Med. Center, 1976—. Bd. dirs. Lung Assn. Riverside, 1978—, Riverside Humane Soc. Served with USNR, 1973-75. Diplomate Am. Bd. Radiology. Mem. Am. Coll. Radiology, Soc. Nuclear Medicine, AMA, Calif. Med. Soc., N.Am., Calif. radiol. socs. Roman Catholic. Club: Rotary. Contbr. articles to profl. jours. Office: 6941 Brockton Ave Riverside CA 92506

SAKS, LEANORE PATRICIA, investment co. exec.; b. N.Y.C., Nov. 6, 1929; d. Herman Alexander and Esther Marilyn (Lewis) Sacks; student UCLA, 1949-50, postgrad., 1973-75, U. Miami, 1970-71, Lumbleau Real Estate Sch., 1971, Anthony Schs., 1973, Gemol. Inst. Am., 1977; m. M. Stuart Liquorman, June 24, 1949 (div.); children—Wayne, Jan, Melinda. Founder, pres. Investments Ltd., Los Angeles, 1971—; officer Joseph Clapsaddle Presentations; dir. Westwood Bankcorp.; co-founder, chmn. bd. Gem Mchts. Ltd., 1981—; cons., public speaker, developer, syndicator. Mem. World Affairs Council, Western Los Angeles Regional C. of C., Women in Bus., Nat. Assn. Women Bus. Owners, UCLA Alumni Assn. Clubs: Rolls Royce Owners, Marina City (Los Angeles); Curzon House (London). Contbr. articles to newspapers and mags.; author: Out from Under: Strategies for Unloading Real Estate in a Down Market, 1982.

SAKURADA, MATTHEW S(HINJI), civil engineer; b. Scotts Bluff, Nebr., Apr. 2, 1952; s. Shoji and Phyllis Fusaye (Nukaya) S.; m. Susan Hays, Mar. 18, 1978. B.S. in Civil Engring. with high distinction, Colo. State U., 1974; M.Engring., U. Colo., 1979. Profl. engr., Colo. Engr., Stone & Webster Engring. Corp., Denver, 1974-78; civil engr. Colo. Westmoreland, Inc., Paonia, 1978-81, mgr. engring., 1981—. Mem. Delta County Planning Commn., Paonia Impact Team, 1980-81. Carl Rohwer Civil Engring. scholar, 1970; Japanese Am. Citizens League scholar, 1970; Rotary scholar, 1970. Mem. ASCE, Soc. Mining Engrs., Nat. Soc. Profl. Engrs. Democrat. Episcopalian. Home: 4036 Cedar Ln Paonia CO 81428 Office: Box E Paonia CO 81428

SALAHI, MOHAMAD, pharmacist, pharmacologist; b. Damascus, Syria, July 15, 1948; came to U.S., 1970, naturalized, 1980; s. Abdul Wahab and Wafika (Majdoub) S.; m. Raghda Shiekh Salem, May 12, 1976; children—Lynn, Reem. B.S., Damascus U., 1970; B.S. in Pharmacy, Auburn U., 1974, M.S. in Pharmacology, 1974. Research assoc. Auburn U., 1973-75; pharmacist intern Los Angeles County Gen. Hosp., 1975-76, pharmacist, 1976—; pharmacist cons. nursing homes; clin. instr. U. So. Calif. Mem. Rho Chi. Home: 25883 Galante Way Valencia CA 91355

SALAMEH, WALEED ANTHONY, clinical psychologist, consultant, author; b. Marmarita, Syria, Feb. 23, 1954; s. Anthony Joseph and Esperanza Moses (Catrib) S. B.A. magna cum laude, U. Mich.-Flint, 1976; M.A., Duquesne U., 1977; Ph.D. in Clin. Psychology, U. Montreal, 1981. Lic. psychologist, Calif., Que. Clin. psychology intern Queen Elizabeth Hosp., Montreal, 1977-78; doctoral intern Montreal Gen. Hosp., 1978-79; postgrad. tng. program Inst. Short-Term Dynamic Psychotherapy, McGill U., Montreal Gen. Hosp., 1979-80; pvt. practice clin. psychology, San Diego, 1982—; clin. psychologist Calif. Dept. Mental Health, Patton State Hosp., 1981—; instr. U. Montreal, 1977-80, Challenge Program of U. Mich., summers 1976-80; instr. Patton State Hosp., 1981—; faculty Calif. Sch. Profl. Psychology, San Diego, 1983—. Massabky grad. fellow, 1977-78; Birks Found. fellow, 1979; Sigma Xi grantee, 1980. Mem. Am. Psychol. Assn., Calif. Psychol. Assn., Western Psychol. Assn., Acad. San Diego Psychologists, Phi Kappa Phi, Psi Chi (cert. of recognition 1976). Editor: (with F.F. Fry, Jr.) Handbook of Humor and Therapy, 1983; contbr. articles profl. jours., chpts. in books. Office: 9636 Tierra Grande St Suite 206 San Diego CA 92126

SALAS, BENNIE, tribal governor; b. Santa Fe, Feb. 23, 1936; s. Remejio and Emma (Gallegos) S.; m. Pearl Mary Vallo, Apr. 23, 1939; children—Benjamin R., Ira V., Jerry P., Crystal I. B.S. in Bus. Adminstrn., U. Albuquerque, 1977. Edn. Coordinator All Indian Pueblo Council, Albuquerque, 1969-70; edn. technician Bur. Indian Affairs, 1970-74, realty officer, 1976—; aide to war chief Pueblo of Zia, 1961, 62, lt. gov., 1967, gov., 1972, 82-83. Served with USN, 1955-59. Ford Found. fellow, 1971. Democrat. Roman Catholic. Address: Zia Pueblo Route Box 1 San Ysidro NM 87053

SALE, LILLIAN, marketing and communications consultant; b. Los Angeles, Dec. 30, 1936; d. Leonard and Muriel (Stansfield) Weiss; student in bus. UCLA, 1954-58. Mgr. public relations non-profit found., Oakland, Calif., 1970-73; account exec. Ross Wurm & Assos., public relations agy., Modesto, Calif., 1974-76; prin., chief cons. Lillian Sale Communication Services (formerly Lillian Sale Public Relations), public relations, mktg., sales promotion, direct mail, advt., publs., audio-visual services, Los Angeles, 1976—. Mem. Public Relations Soc. Am. (accredited counselor, treas., bd. dirs. Los Angeles chpt.), Publicity Club Los Angeles (PRO awards 1980, 82), Nat. Direct Mktg., Assn., Direct Mktg. Club of So. Calif., Am. Mgmt. Assn. Author: How To Talk Banker-ese, 1979. Address: PO Box 48439 Los Angeles CA 90048

SALEM, SUSANNE FRANCES, consulting executive; b. San Francisco, Mar. 25, 1945; d. Edward L. and Mary F. (Adams) Ledinski; m. Lee C. Salem, July 14, 1979. B.S., Ariz. State U., 1979. Ins. agt. Atlantic Mut. Ins. Co. and Harris & Assocs., Los Angeles, 1964-73; ptnr. Acero Enterprises, Sierra Vista, Ariz., 1973-77; lease account mgr. Truck Leasing, Phoenix, 1979-80; sales and cons. Internat. Transp., Phoenix, 1980; owner Corp. Directions Cons. & Recruiting, Phoenix, 1980—; guest speaker. Bd. dirs. Southeastern Ariz. Drug Abuse Council, 1975-77. Am. Trucking Assns. scholar, 1977-79, outstanding transp. grad., 1979. Contbr. articles to profl. jours.

SALIBELLO, COSMO, optometrist, consultant, lecturer; b. N.Y.C., Sept. 21, 1943; s. Joseph and Maria (Patalano) S.; B.Mgmt.Engring., Rensselaer Poly. Inst., 1965; B.A. in Biology summa cum laude, Central Wash. U., 1979; D.D.Optometry, Pacific U., 1983. Diplomate Nat. Bd. Examiners in Optometry; cert. comml. pilot, FAA. Dep. aircrew tng. dir. Crumman Aerospace Corp., Tehran, Iran, 1974-76; practice optometry, Kirkland, Wash., 1983—; cons. to industry; lectr. edn. Mem. Ellensburg Community Choir, 1977-79; chmn. Laurel West Homeowners Assn., Forest Grove, Oreg., 1980-83. Served to lt. comdr. USN, 1966-74. Decorated Air medal; recipient Outstanding Student award Naval Schs. Command, 1966. Mem. Am. Optometric Assn., Wash. Optometric Assn., Oreg. Optometric Assn. Patentee design elbow rest, 1982. Office: Rowley Vision Clinic 10827 NE 68th St Kirkland WA 98033

SALIMENO, FRANK LOUIS, optometrist; b. Ogden, Utah, Aug. 31, 1943; s. Frank A. and Jolene (Ruger) S.; children—Nick Anthony, Kristin Lin. B.S., Weber State Coll., 1965; O.D., Pacific U. Coll. Optometry, 1969; cert. in gen. and ocular pharmacology U. Calif., 1977. Practice optometry, Ogden, 1972—. Vol. probation officer Utah Dept. Social Services, 1981-83; bd. dirs. St. Benedicts Hosp. Found., Ogden, 1982-83. Served to capt. MC., U.S. Army, 1970-72. Decorated Army Commendation medal. Fellow Am. Acad. Optometry; mem. Am. Optometric Assn., Utah Optometric Assn. (contbg. editor and author jour. 1976-79, Spl. award 1977, Optometrist of Yr. 1982), Beta Sigma Kappa. Club: Exchange (club Exchangite of Yr. 1982, pres. club 1982-83) Ogden. Home: 1830 E 5725 S Ogden UT 84403 Office: 5089 S Adams Ave Ogden UT 84403

SALING, LARRY DEAN, communications manager; b. Hailey, Idaho, Apr. 29, 1940; s. Wallace Marion and Verland (Penrod) S.; m. Oris Annette Wood, May 11, 1948; children—Cindy Ann, Larry, Christopher Don., Teresa Lyn. B.A. in Communications, Brigham Young U., 1968. Marketing mgr. F-B Truck Line, Salt Lake City, 1968-78; pub. info. officer Salt Lake County, Salt Lake City, 1978-79; pub. communications mgr. Emery Mining Corp., Huntington, Utah, 1979—. Bd. dirs., mem. allocations com. Southeastern Utah United Way, 1980-82. Served in USN, 1958-60. Mem. Pub. Relations Soc. Am., Internat. Assn. Bus. Communicators, Utah Mining Assn. (pub. relations com.), Nat. Assn. Govt. Communicators.

SALISBURY, BART R., political scientist; b. San Diego, Nov. 29, 1955; s. Albert M. and Elaine (Meier) S.; m. Gwen H.R. Roberts, Aug. 20, 1976. B.A., U. Wash., 1979, M.A., 1981, Ph.C., 1983. Research asst. Ctr. Law and Justice, Seattle, 1979-81; cons. Ctr. Social Sci. Computation and Research, Seattle, 1981-83; cons. Sch. Social Work, U. Wash., Behavioral Sci. Inst., Federal Way, Wash., Seattle-King County Jud. Evaluation Survey, others. Pres., Associated Students Edmonds Community Coll., 1975-76. Recipient Alfred A. Barron Citizenship award Gen. Telephone Co., 1973. Mem. Am. Polit. Sci. Assn., Western Polit. Sci. Assn., Phi Theta Kappa. Contbr. articles to profl. jours. Home: 11525 40th Ave NE Seattle WA 98125 Office: Dept Polit Sci U Wash Seattle WA 98195

SALK, JONAS EDWARD, physician, scientist; b. N.Y.C., Oct. 28, 1914; s. Daniel B. and Dora (Press) S.; B.S., Coll. City N.Y., 1934, LL.D., 1955; M.D. (fellow chemistry 1935-37, Christian A. Herter fellow chemistry 1936-37, exptl. surgery 1937-38, fellow bacteriology 1939-40), 1939, Sc.D., 1955; Sc.D., U. Mich., 1955; LL.D., U. Pitts., 1955; Ph.D., Hebrew U., 1959; LL.D., Roosevelt U., 1955; Sc.D., Turin U., 1957, U. Leeds, 1959, Hahneman Med. Coll., 1959, Franklin and Marshall Coll., 1960; D.H.L., Yeshiva U., 1959; Sc.D., Tuskegee Inst., 1964; m. Donna Lindsay, June 8, 1939 (div. 1968); children—Peter Lindsay, Darrell John, Jonathan Daniel; m. 2d, Francoise Gilot, June 1970. Intern, Mt. Sinai Hosp., N.Y.C., 1940-42; NCR fellow med. scis. Sch. Pub. Health, U. Mich., 1942-43, research fellow epidemiology, 1943-44, research asso., 1944-46, asst. prof. epidemiology, 1946-47; asso. research prof. bacteriology Sch. Medicine, U. Pitts., 1947-49, research prof. bacteriology, 1949-55, dir. virus research lab., 1947-63, Commonwealth prof. preventive medicine, 1955-57, Commonwealth prof. exptl. medicine, 1957-63; dir. Salk Inst. for Biol. Studies, San Diego, 1963-75, resident fellow, 1963—, founding dir., 1975—; adj. prof. health scis. U. Calif. at San Diego, 1970—; developed vaccine, preventive of poliomyelitis, 1955; cons. epidemic diseases Sec. War, 1944-47, Sec. Army 1947-54; mem. commn. on influenza Army Epidemiol. Bd., 1944-47, Army Forces Epidemiol. Bd., 1947-54; mem. expert adv. panel virus disease WHO, 1951—. Decorated chevalier, 1955, officer, 1976, Legion of Honor (France); Orden del Quetzal (Guatemala); Recipient Criss award, 1955,

Lasker award, 1956, Gold medal Congress and Presdl. citation, 1955, Pa. medal for meritorious service, 1955, Albert Gallatin award, 1957, Howard Taylor Ricketts award, 1957, Gold Medal award Nat. Inst. Social Scis., 1959, Koch medal, 1963, Truman Commendation award, 1966, Mellon Inst. award, 1969; Jawaharlal Nehru award for Internat. Understanding (India), 1976; Presdl. medal of freedom, 1977. Fellow AAAS, Am. Pub. Health Assn., Am. Acad. Arts and Scis., Am. Acad. Pediatrics (hon.), Royal Soc. Health (hon.); mem. Am. Coll. Preventive Medicine, Am. Assn. Immunologists, Assn. Am. Physicians (emeritus), Soc. Exptl. Biology and Medicine, Am. Soc. Clin. Investigation (emeritus), Am. Epidemiol. Soc. (emeritus), Phi Beta Kappa, Sigma Xi, Alpha Omega Alpha, Delta Omega. Author: Man Unfolding, 1972; The Survival of the Wisest, 1973; (with Jonathan Salk) World Population and Human Values, 1981; Anatomy of Reality; Merging of Intuition and Reason, 1983; contbr. sci. articles to profl. jours. Office: Salk Inst Biological Studies PO Box 85800 San Diego CA 92138

SALKIN, GERALDINE (JERI) FAUBION, dancer, dance therapist; b. Denver, Mar. 18, 1916; d. George Everett and Hanna Viola (Harvey) Faubion; student Lester Horton Dance Theater, Carmelita Maracci, Trudi Schoop, Los Angeles, 1937-47, Doris Humphrey, N.Y.C., 1952-53, Rudolf Von Laban, London, 1956-57, Hanna Fenichel, 1965-70, UCLA, 1959-60; Ph.D., Internat. U., Westwood, Calif., 1978; m. Leo Salkin, June 29, 1936; 1 dau., Lynn Salkin Sbiroli. Concert dancer Lester Horton Dance Group, Los Angeles, 1937-47, tchr. creative modern dance, 1939-47; tchr. creative modern dance Dance Assos., Hollywood, Calif., 1949-53, Am. Sch. of London (Eng.), 1956-57, Jeri Salkin Studio and Center for Child Study, Hollywood, 1968-73; developer body ego technique Camarillo (Calif.) State Hosp., 1957-64; movement specialist Nat. Endowment Arts grantee, 1973—; dir., body ego technique dept. Cedars-Sinai Thalians Community Mental Health Center, Los Angeles, 1965—; dance cons., tchr., Nat. Head Start Program, Calif., 1964; dir. workshops, mem. aux. faculty Goddard Coll., Antioch Coll., various hosps., and univs. Calif. Dept. Mental Hygiene grantee, 1960-63. Mem. Am. Dance Therapy Assn., AAHPER, Calif. Dance Educators Assn., Calif. Assn. Health Phys. Edn. and Recreation, Nat. Assn. Edn. Young Children, Com. Research in Dance. Democrat. Author: Body Ego Technique, an Educational and Therapeutic Approach to Body Image and Self-Identity, 1973; author choreographer film (with Leo Salkin and Trudi Schoop) Body Ego Technique, 1962 (U.S. Golden Eagle Council on Internat. Nontheatrical Events award 1963). Home: 3584 Multiview Dr Hollywood CA 90068 Office: 6305 Yucca St Suite 500 Hollywood CA 90028

SALLANDER, PAMELA K., publishing executive, lawyer; b. Hollywood, Calif., Aug. 15, 1947; d. Robert and Marjorie (Ripper) Sallander. B.A. in Math., UCLA, 1968; J.D., U. Calif.-San Francisco, 1971. Bar: Calif. 1972. With Matthew Bender & Co., San Francisco, 1971—, mng. editor, 1972-74, asst. editor-in-chief, 1974-79, sr. asst. editor-in-chief, 1980-81, dir. pub., 1981-83, exec. dir. pub. and adminstrn., 1983—. Mem. ABA, Calif. Trial Lawyers Assn. Contbg. editor The Hastings Law Jour., 1970-71; contbg. editor multi-vol. litigation guides. Office: Matthew Bender Co Inc 450 Sansome St San Francisco CA 94111

SALMON, CHARLES RAY, manufacturing company executive, professional engineer; b. Stockton, Mo., Oct. 18, 1927; s. John Ray and Eunice May (Jones) S.; m. Billie Jean Finnell, Sept. 5, 1950; children—Jon Wheaton, Steven Clay, Christopher Craig. B.A., Pomona Coll., 1950; postgrad. U. Wis., 1950-51, UCLA, 1951-52. Registered profl. engr., Calif. Pres. U.S. Motors Co., Oshkosh, Wis., 1969—, Buddy Bar Castings, South Gate, Calif., 1974—, Evans Industries West, Los Angeles, 1975—, Evans Import/Export Co., Los Angeles, 1979—; vice chmn. Ball Aluminum & Brass, Auburn, Ind., 1979—; dir. Evans Industries, Inc., Detroit; cons., dir. various corps. Mem. Am. Inst. Indsl. Engrs. (sr.), Phi Beta Kappa. Republican. Calvinist. Author: The Book of Purpose, 1974; Introduction to the Fourth Dimension, 1974.

SALMON, MERLYN LEIGH, lab. exec.; b. Macksville, Kans., June 24, 1924; s. Kenneth Elbert and Inez Melba (Prose) S.; student U. Kans., 1943-44; B.S., U. Denver, 1951, M.S., 1952; m. Flora Charlotte Sievers, Mar. 20, 1948; children—Charla Lee, Merlyn Leigh. Research engr. Denver Research Inst., U. Denver, 1951-56, owner-operator Fluo-X-Spec Lab., Denver, 1956—; cons. in field. Served with AUS, 1943-45, 45-47. Mem. Am. Chem. Soc., Soc. for Applied Spectroscopy (Outstanding Service award 1970), Am. Soc. Metals, Sigma Xi, Tau Beta Pi, Phi Lambda Upsilon. Omicron Delta Kappa. Democrat. Contbr. articles to profl. jours; editor column Applied Spectroscopy. Address: 718 Sherman St Denver CO 80203

SALOMAKI, DAVID CHARLES, elec. engr.; b. Shirley, Mass., Sept. 30, 1953; s. David William and Elma Miriam (Kangas) S.; B.S. in Elec. Engring., Worcester Poly. Inst., 1975; M.S. in Elec. Engring., Stanford U., 1977. U. Teaching asst. Stanford U., 1975-77; research engr. Stanford Research Inst., Menlo Park, Calif., 1976-78; devel. engr. data systems div. Hewlett Packard, 1977-79, project leader computer systems div., 1980-81, engring. project mgr., 1981—; cons. microprocessor applications, 1978—; part-time faculty San Jose State U., 1980—. Active Big Bros. Am. Mem. IEEE, Tau Beta Pi, Eta Kappa Nu, Pi Delta Epsilon, Phi Gamma Delta. Lutheran. Home: 2699 Forbes Ave Santa Clara CA 95051 Office: Hewlett Packard Computer Systems Div 19447 Pruneridge Ave Cupertino CA 95014

SALOMON, FELIX, clinical psychologist, consultant; b. Montevideo, Uruguay, July 24, 1943; came to U.S., 1947; s. Fred and Ettie S.; m. Sharon Bonita Matty, Sept. 1, 1967; children—Bianca L., Elise G. B.A., CUNY-Queens Coll., 1968; Ph.D., L.I. U., 1977. Cert. clin. psychologist, Ariz. Tchr. pub. schs., Bklyn., 1968-69; research asst. clin. psychology L.I. (N.Y.) U., 1969-71; clin. psychology clk. Payne Whitney Clinic, N.Y.C., 1971-72; clin. psychology intern Nassau County Med. Ctr., East Meadows, N.Y., 1972-73, staff psychologist, 1974-76, adminstrv. dir. Hempstead Community Mental Health Ctr. div., 1976-77; clin. psychologist Queens County Family Court, Jamaica, N.Y., 1973-74; staff psychologist Albert Einstein Coll. Medicine, N.Y.C., 1974; pvt. practice Phoenix Inst. Psychotherapy, Ltd., 1977—; cons. psychologist pvt. schs., Phoenix; 1977—; clin. psychologist Inst. Human Services, Inc., St. Lukes Hosp., Phoenix, 1977-78; tchr., lectr. L.I. U. teaching fellow, 1971-72. Mem. Am. Psychol. Assn., Ariz. Psychol. Assn., Maricopa Psychol. Soc. Office: Phoenix Inst Psychotherapy Ltd 6036 N 19th Ave Suite 309 Phoenix AZ 85015

SALRIN, ROBERT EUGENE, mfg. co. exec.; b. Elyria, Ohio, Nov. 16, 1927; s. Raymond Augustus and Helen Marie (Brucken) S.; student Fenn Coll., 1950; m. Mary Jean Kohl, Jan. 3, 1947; children—Robert Eugene, michael Thomas, Sheila Marie. Chief mfg. engr. Lear, Inc., Santa Monica, Calif. and Elyria, 1959; mfg. mgr. Litton Industries, Woodland Hills, Calif., 1959-62; dir. ops. Northrop Corp., Hawthorne, Calif., 1962-68; group v.p. internat. Rectifier Corp., El Segundo, Calif., 1968-70; v.p. A.C. & C., Inc., Torrance, Calif., 1970; pres. indsl. products group Aeronca, Inc., Montebello, Calif., 1971-73, corp. group v.p. environ. controls group, Charlotte, N.C., 1973-76; pres. Western Methods Corp., Gardena, Calif., 1976-77, dir., 1976-78; gen. mgr. So. Calif. Signal Industries, Carlsbad, 1976-77; staff v.p. mfg. Bourns, Inc., Riverside, Calif., 1977-78, pres. Bourns Instruments, Inc. subs. Bourns, Inc., 1978—, sr. v.p. tech. products group, 1980—. Registered profl. engr., Calif. Mem. Am. Prodn. and inventory Control Soc., Assn. Contamination Control Mfrs., Instrument Soc. Am., Soc. Mfg. Engrs. Republican. Roman Catholic. Clubs: Canyon Crest Country, Elks. Home: 6718 Rycroft Dr Riverside CA 92506 Office: 1200 Columbia Ave Riverside CA 92507

SALSBURY, BARBARA GRACE, consumer consultant, author, lecturer, enterprises executive; b. Toledo, Dec. 27, 1937; d. Vincent Joseph and Dorothy Minerva (Ramm) Thayer; m. Larry Philip Salsbury, Sept. 24, 1959; children—Erin Scott, Sandi Grace Salsbury Simmons. Student El Camino Coll., 1954-56; student in Resource Mgmt. and Hone Econs., Brigham Young U., 1975—. Spl. faculty mem. Brigham Young U., Provo, Utah, 1972—; guest lectr., condr. workshops and seminars on consumerism, emergency homepreparedness, practical home mgmt., supermarket survival, self improvement, various groups U.S., Can., 1961—. Leader, tchr. Women's Relief Soc. Orgn. Calif.-Wash., 1960—. Author: Just Add Water, 1972; Tasty Imitations, 1973; Just in Case, 1975; If You Must Work, 1976; Cut Your Grocery Bills in Half, 1982; booklets: The Lowly Little Lentil, 1971, Basic Home Drying of Fruits and Vegetables, 1975. Mem. Utah Authors League. Mormon. Office: PO Box 1305 Orem UT 84057

SALT, GEORGE WILLIAM, educator; b. Spokane, Wash., Oct. 9, 1919; s. George Frederick and Elsie Mary (Freakes) S.; m. Mary Katherine Pinder, July 30, 1942; children—Christopher Frederick, Jonathan Charles, Maryla Katherine. B.A., UCLA, 1942; M.A., U. Calif.-Berkeley, 1948, Ph.D., 1951. Mem. faculty dept. Zoology U. Calif.-Davis, 1951—, prof. zoology, 1968—; cons. Calif. Water Resources Control Bd., 1976—. Served with U.S. Army, 1943-46. NSF sr. postdoctoral fellow, 1959-60; Rockefeller Found. fellow, Universidad del Valle, Colombia, 1971-72. Mem. Am. Naturalists Soc., Ecol. Soc. Am., Brit. Ecol. Soc., Am. Ornithologists Union, Cooper Ornithol. Soc., Protozool. Soc., Sigma Xi. Episcopalian. Editor, The Am. Naturalist, 1979—. Office: Dept Zoology U Calif Davis CA 95616

SALTER, ROBERT MUNDHENK, JR., physicist; b. Morgantown, W.Va., Apr. 24, 1920; s. Robert Mundhenk and Sara Opal (Godfrey) S.; B.M.E., Ohio State U., 1941; M.A., UCLA, 1954, Ph.D., 1965; m. Darlene Jeanette Oliva, Jan. 21, 1977; children by previous marriage—Robert Mundhenk III, Wendy Lou Salter Reynolds, Gary Coddington. Research engr. Gen. Motors Research Labs., Detroit, 1941-42; research engr. Aerophysics Lab., N. Am. Aviation, Los Angeles, 1946-48; project dir. USAF satellite devel. Rand Corp., Santa Monica, Calif., 1948-54, phys. scientist, 1965-82; project dir. USAF satellite devel. Lockheed Aircraft, Palo Alto, Calif., 1954-59; pres. Quantatron, Inc., Santa Monica, 1960-62; sci. cons. to various industries, 1962—; pres. Spectravision, Inc., Santa Monica, 1973—. Served to lt. USN, 1942-46. Mem. Sigma Xi, Sigma Pi Sigma, Tau Beta Pi. Republican. Presbyterian. Club: Riviera Country. Home: 1514 Sorrento Dr Pacific Palisades CA 90272 Office: 360 N Crescent Dr Beverly Hills CA 90210

SALVERSON, CAROL ANN, religious orgn. adminstr.; b. Buffalo, June 30, 1944; d. Howard F. and Estella G. (Zehe) Heavener; B.A. in Philosophy, SUNY, Buffalo, 1966; M.S. in Library Sci., Syracuse U., 1968; grad. Sacred Coll. Jamilian Theology and Div. Sch., 1976. Library trainee and research asst. SUNY, Med. Center, Syracuse, 1966-67; asst. editor SUNY Union List of Serials, Syracuse, 1967-68; readers services librarian, asst. prof. Jefferson Community Coll., Watertown, N.Y., 1968-75; ordained to ministry Internat. Community of Christ Ch., 1974; adminstr. public services dept. Internat. Community of Christ, Chancellery, Reno, 1975—, also dir. theol. research library; mem. faculty Sacred Coll. Jamilian U. of the Ordained, Reno, 1979—, Jamilian Parochial Sch., Internat. Community of Christ, 1978—. Chmn. religious edn. com. All Souls Unitarian-Universalist Ch., Watertown, N.Y., 1970-71, treas. 1974-75; trustee North Country Reference and Research Resources Council, Canton, N.Y., 1974-75. Mem. ALA, Nev. Library Assn., Friends of Library Washoe County, Friends of Library U. Nev. Club: Coll. Women's. Contbr. articles on library sci. to profl. jours. Home: 2025 La Fond Dr Reno NV 89509 Office: Internat Community of Christ Chancellery 643 Ralston St Reno NV 89503

SALZMAN, DAVID ELLIOT, TV prodn. co. exec.; b. Bklyn., Dec. 1, 1943; s. Benjamin and Rose Harriet (Touby) S.; B.A., Bklyn. Coll., 1965; M.A., Wayne State U., 1967; m. Sonia Camelia Gonsalves, Oct. 19, 1968; children—Daniel Mark, Andrea Jessica, Adam Gabriel. Dir. TV ops. Wayne State U., 1966-67; producer Lou Gordon Program, 1967-70; program mgr. Sta. WKBD-TV, Detroit, 1970-71; program mgr. Sta. KDKA-TV, Pitts., 1971-72, gen. mgr., 1973-75; program mgr. Sta. KYW-TV, Phila., 1972-73; chmn. bd. Group W Prodns., N.Y.C. and Los Angeles, 1975-80; pres., founder. United Software Assocs., Los Angeles, 1980-81; pres., creator News Info. Weekly Service, Los Angeles, 1980-84; exec. v.p. Telepictures Corp., Los Angeles, 1980-83; creator Newscope-Nat. TV News Coop., 1983; guest lectr.; bd. govs. Films of Coll. and Univ. Students. Bd. dirs. Pitts. Civic Light Opera, Am. Blood Bank, Pitts., Hebrew Inst., Pitts., Jewish Community Ctr., Harrison, N.Y. Recipient Local Emmy award, 1972, award Golden Quill, 1971, Golden Gavel, 1971, AP, 1974, Detroit chpt. Am. Women in Radio and TV, 1969; Gold medal Broadcast Promotion Assn., 1983. Mem. Acad. TV Arts and Scis., Nat. Assn. TV Program Execs., Am. Mgmt. Assn., Am. Film Inst. Contbr. articles to N.Y. Times, Detroit Free Press, Playboy mag., Variety and communications trade publs. Office: 7800 Beverly Blvd Los Angeles CA 90036

SALZMAN, MARILYN B. WOLFSON, service company executive; b. Chgo., Dec. 25, 1943; d. Joseph and Sera (Krol) Wolfson; 1 son, Lawrence Todd. Student U. Ill., Barat Coll., Lake Forest, Ill., 1961-64. Adminstrv. project asst. Sci. Research Assocs., Chgo., 1964-70; reporter Suburban Trib of Chgo. Tribune, 1979-80; pres. MWS Assocs., Los Angeles and Fullerton, Calif., 1980—; exec. adminstrv. dir. Crystal Tips of No. Ill., Inc., 1980-83; dir. adminstrn. Ice Dispensers, Inc., 1981-83, Sani-Serv of Ill., Inc., 1981—; adminstrv. and orgnl. cons. 1140 Corp., 1980—; adminstrv. dir. Iceman's Ico Co., Inc., 1980—. Active Friends of Fullerton Library, Boy Scouts Am., Mid-West chpt. ARC. Mem. Mgmt. Forum, Women's Am. ORT. Contbr. articles to newspapers and indsl. jours. Home: 1112 N Ferndale Dr Fullerton CA 92631 Office: PO Box 3481 Fullerton CA 92634

SALZMAN, RICHARD WILLIAM, artist representative; b. Los Angeles, Nov. 22, 1958; s. Paul and Anne (Myersburg) S.; student public schs., Los Angeles. Stockboy, Marathon Clothing, Los Angeles, 1976-77, salesman, 1977, sales and mgmt. trainee, 1977-78, br. mgr., San Francisco, 1978-80, San Diego, 1980-82; artist rep., 1982—. Mem. adv. bd. Fashion Careers of Calif. Mem. Union of Concerned Scientists, Green Peace, Environ. Def. Fund, Coalition for Non-Nuclear World. ACLU. Democrat. Home: 12548 Everglade St Los Angeles CA 90066 Office: 1352 Hornblend St San Diego CA 92109

SAMARAS, MARY STENNING, educator; b. Detroit, June 19, 1928; d. Walter Jeffrey and Laura Eugenia (Karas) Stenning; B.A., Wayne State U., 1949, M.A., 1952; Ed.D., U. So. Calif., 1974; m. William T. Jones, 1949 (div. 1961); children—William T., Daniel Victor Jones; m. 2d, Thomas T. Samaras, June 23, 1962. Speech therapist, tchr., Mich. and Calif., 1951-70; dir. Claremont (Calif.) Speech and Reading Lab., 1965-70; learning disabilities specialist Southwestern Coll., Chula Vista, Calif., 1975—, instr. English as 2d lang., 1978—. Mem. Area Devel. Disabilities Bd.; bd. dirs. San Diego Soc. Autistic Children. Mem. Am. Assn. Mental Deficiency, Calif. Speech and Hearing Assn., Council for Exceptional Children, Nat. Soc. for Autistic Children. Research on cooperation among profoundly retarded children and adults. Address: 157 Theresa Way Chula Vista CA 92011 Office: Southwestern Coll 900 Otay Lakes Rd Chula Vista CA 92010

SAMEK, PAUL HERMAN, apparel manufacturing company exec.; b. New Rochelle, N.Y., May 28, 1923; s. Emil and Sophie (Rich) S.; student U. Wis., 1942; B.A., Dartmouth U., 1945; m. Sibella Oursler, Feb. 16, 1975 (div. 1978); 1 son, Benjamin George; m. Arlene Ellen Du Boff, Dec. 7, 1979; stepchildren—Mark Rosman, Rene Rosman. Actor, Barter Theatre, Abingdon, Va., 1939; radio announcer Sta. WDAE, Tampa, Fla., 1947; newspaper display salesman Tampa Daily Times, 1949; owner, operator women's specialty shop, Winston-Salem, N.C., 1950-57; territorial buyer Sears, Roebuck & Co., Alhambra, Calif., 1957-80; pres. Street Scene of Calif., Inc., Los Angeles, 1980—. Pres., founder Big Bros. Am., Jacksonville, Fla., 1961; v.p. apparel industry div. Save A Life, Los Angeles, 1970-79, pres., 1979-81. Served with USNR, 1942-44; PTO. Mem. Dartmouth Club Fla. (sec. 1960). Clubs: Masons, Shriners. Home: 4461 Van Noord Ave Studio City CA 91604 Office: 900 S Freemont Ave Alhambra CA 91802

SAMKO, MICHAEL RICHARD, clinical psychologist; b. Worcester, Mass., Mar. 1, 1950; s. Michael Charles and Jessie (Chlapowska) S.; m. Lisa Ross, Aug. 12, 1978. B.S., U. Mass., 1972; student Manchester (Eng.) U., 1970-71; M.S., Trinity U.-U. Tex. Med. Sch., San Antonio, 1973; Ph.D. in Clin. Psychology, Calif. Sch. Profl. Psychology, 1976. Lic. psychologist, Calif. Co-dir. alcoholism treatment program, San Diego, 1973-74; psychol. asst. El Camino Psychology Ctr., Oceanside, 1974-77; owner, dir., mgr. So. Calif. Psychotherapy Affiliates, Carlsbad, 1979—; prof. psychology, sociology Nat. U., San Diego, 1978—; v.p. Natana Corp. Los Angeles, 1982—; chairperson Com. Internat. Psychology Calif., 1980—. Mem. Am. Psychol. Assn., Internat. Council Psychologists (liaison officer 1981—), Am. Soc. Clin. Hypnosis, Calif.. State Psychol. Assn. (ethics com. Media Task Force 1982), Acad. San Diego Psychologists, Nat. Register Health Service Providers in Psychology. Producer, dir. documentary Films: Psychology in China, Milton Erickson, Egypt and Israel; contbr. articles to profl. jours. Office: 2885 Hope St Carsbad CA 92008

SAMMIS, THEODORE WALLACE, agricultural engineering educator; b. San Mateo, Calif., May 5, 1943; s. Arthur Maxwell and Eugenia Louise (Rutherford) S.; B.S., U. Calif., Davis, 1966; M.S., U. Ariz., 1972, Ph.D., 1974; m. Susan J. Krammes, Nov. 30, 1968; children—Matthew Arthur, Laura Frances. Land and water analyst Calif. Dept. Water Resources, Bakersfield, 1966-69; research asst. dept. hydrology and water resources U. Ariz., Tucson, 1969-74, research assoc., 1974-76; prof. dept. agrl. engring. N.Mex. State U., Las Cruces, 1976—. Mem. Am. Soc. Agrl. Engrs., Am. Geophys. Union, Ariz. Acad. Sci., Western Snow Conf., Sigma Xi. Methodist. Contbr. articles in field to profl. jours. Home: 4725 Northwind Rd Las Cruces NM 88005 Office: NMex State U PO Box 3268 Las Cruces NM 88003

SAMPATH, RAJAN KASTURI, agricultural economics educator; b. Madras, India, Dec. 11, 1948; s. Rajan and Sundaram (Soundarrajan) Kasturi; m. Vijaya Sampath, Mar. 30, 1977. B.A., Madras U., 1969, M.A., 1971; Ph.D., Indian Inst. Tech., 1975. Research assoc. Madras Inst. Devel. Studies, 1971-72; research fellow dept. humanities and social scis. Indian Inst. Tech., 1972-75; vis. fellow Harvard U., Cambridge, Mass., 1975-77; program officer/project specialist Ford Found., New Delhi, 1977-79; vis. assoc. prof. Colo. State U., 1979-80, assoc. prof., Ft. Collins, 1980—, co dir. Internat. Sch. Econ. Devel. Studies, 1980—. Mem. Am. Econ. Assn., Am. Agrl. Econ. Assn., Indian Econ. Assn., Indian Regional Sci. Assn., Indian Econometric Soc., Tamil Nadu Econ. Assn., Indian Agrl. Econs. Assn., Internat. Assn. Agrl. Economists. Contbr. articles to profl. jours. Home: 625 E Locust St Fort Collins CO 80523 Office: B339 Clark Bldg Dept Econs Fort Collins CO 80523

SAMPLES, WILLARD ENOCH, credit union exec.; b. Milnor, N.D., Mar. 9, 1927; s. William J. and Olive Alberta (Tanner) S.; student Pacific Coll., 1945-47, Retail Credit Mgmt. Sch., 1955-58, U. Alaska, 1974, U. Wis., 1975; m. V. Jeanette Ochampaugh, Apr. 17, 1949; 1 son, William J. Accountant, Chase Bag Co., Portland, Oreg., 1947-49; with Retail Credit Co., Inc., 1949-72, asst. mgr., Portland, 1959, mgr. Alaska, 1963-72; gen. mgr. Fed. Alaska Fed. Credit Union, Anchorage, 1972—. Pres., Western Alaska council Boy Scouts Am., 1976-78, nat. bd. rep., 1977—; sec. Charles W. Smith Meml., 1967; trustee First Christian (Disciples of Christ) Ch., Anchorage, 1967—, chmn. bd. elders, Anchorage, 1978—; chmn. Anchorage Mayor's Prayer Breakfast, 1965-66; coach Boys Club Alaska, 1965-72. Served with AUS, 1944-46. Decorated Merit award with oak leaf cluster; recipient Silver Beaver award Boy Scouts Am., 1970. Mem. Credit Union Execs. Soc., Credit Union Nat. Assn. (dir. 1974—), Alaska Credit Union League (dir. 1974-77, chmn. legis. affairs com. 1974-77), Anchorage C. of C. Republican. Clubs: Anchorage Rotary (sec. 1975-76, treas. 1977—), Civ Air (dir. 1974-76, 80—), Christian Businessmen's (dir. 1964—). Author articles in field; editor Thrifty Digest, 1972-79. Home: 2859 Knik Ave Anchorage AK 99503 Office: Pouch 7-505 731 I St Anchorage AK 99510

SAMPLINER, DONALD WALLACE, psychologist; b. Cleve., May 4, 1918; s. Jerome Mortimer and Charlotte J. Sampliner; B.A., UCLA, 1941, M.A., 1949; postgrad. Calif. State U., Los Angeles, 1952-53. Tchr., Los Angeles City Schs., 1948-75; lectr. psychology Los Angeles City Coll., 1952—; host radio program Sta. KPFK, 1971-74, Sta. KMAX-FM, 1973-78; prod., annotator phonograph records, 1982 . Coordinator, CanServ program Good Samaritan Hosp., 1975; pres. Canyon Dr. Hollywood Hills Improvement Assn., 1977-80. Mem. Am. Psychol. Assn., Am. Fedn. Tchrs. Coll. Guild, Theatre Hist. Soc., Am. Theatre Organ Soc. (chmn. Los Angeles chpt. 1961-62). Home: 2736 Hollyridge Dr Hollywood CA 90068

SAMPSON, CAROL ANN, interior design firm executive, writer; b. Wabash, Ind., Dec. 5, 1942; d. John Roland Bennett and Virginia Ann (Garthwait) Mulholland; student Bradley U., 1961-62; A.A., Riverside City Coll., 1971; B.S. cum laude, Woodbury U., 1975; children—Tracy Lee, John Russell IV (Arrison). Interior designer Imperial Co., Riverside, Calif., 1971-72; asso. interior designer Booth & Assos., Riverside, 1972-74; owner, prin., project designer Carol Sampson's Interior Designs, Riverside, 1974—; tchr. interior design bus. procedures San Bernardino Valley Coll., 1978—; house and home editor Inland Empire mag., 1978—; interior design staff writer Inland Empire Bus. Quar., 1978-81; interior design cons. radio program Sta. KPRO, Riverside, 1978-81. Recipient Gold Key award (2), Nat. Home Fashions League, 1975. Mem. Internat. Soc. Interior Designers (profl.). Episcopalian. Office: Carol Sampson's Interior Designs Inc 6876 Indiana Ave Riverside CA 92503

SAMPSON, J. FRANK, artist, educator; b. Edmore, N.D., Mar. 24, 1928; s. S. Abner and Mable Elizabeth (Trimble) S.; B.A., Concordia Coll., Moorhead, Minn., 1950; M.F.A., U. Iowa, 1952, postgrad., 1956-59. Asst. prof. fine arts U. Colo., Boulder, 1961-67, assoc. prof. fine arts, 1968-72, prof. fine arts, 1972—; one-man shows: Denver Art Mus., 1975; represented in permanent collections: Colorado Springs Fine Arts Ctr., Des Moines Art Ctr., Dulin Gallery of Art, Knoxville, Tenn., Joslyn Art Mus., Omaha, Library of Congress, Washington, Littleton (Colo.) Hist. Mus., Minn. Mus. Art, St. Paul, Mulvane Art Center, Washburn U., Topeka, Kans., Sheldon Meml. Art Ctr., U. Nebr., Lincoln, Springfield (Mo.) Art Mus., Walker Art Mus., Mpls., Boston Pub. Library, Nelson Gallery-Atkins Mus., Kansas City, Mo. Served with U.S. Army, 1954-56. Fulbright grantee, Brussels, Belgium, 1959-60. Address: 1912 Columbine Ave Boulder CO 80302

SAMPSON, JUNE ELISABETH, museum director; b. Phila., May 31, 1946; d. William Herbert and Helen Elizabeth (Whitall) Stafford; m. Earl Clinton Sampson, Jan. 22, 1972; stepchildren—Earl Brett, Daniel C., Shawn, Indira. B.A. in History, Earlham Coll., 1968; M.A. in History, SUNY-Oneonta, 1972. Mus. curator S.D. Hist. Soc., Pierre, 1969-72; asst. dir. W. H. Over Mus., U. S.D., Vermillion, 1972-73, dir., 1973-79, instr. dept. anthropology, 1973-79; dir. Western Heritage Ctr., Billings, Mont., 1980—. Mem. Landmarks, Inc., Billings, 1980—. Mem. Mountain Plains Mus. Assn., S.D. Mus. Assn. (pres., sec.), S.D. Archaeol. Soc. (charter), Mont. Archaeol. Soc., AAUW, Quaker. Office: 2822 Montana Ave Billings MT 59101

SAMPSON, ROY JOHNSON, economist, author; b. Elmwood, Tenn., Mar. 3, 1919; s. Bascom Virgle and Lizzie High (Farley) S.; m. Rosetta Lillian Pannier, May 30, 1942; children—Donald, Stuart, Carole, Linda. B.S., Tenn. Technol. U., 1946; M.B.A., U. Calif.-Berkeley, 1948, Ph.D. in Econs., 1951. Instr. U. Utah, 1950-51; dist. economist Office of Price Stabilization, U.S. Govt., 1951-53; asst. prof. Pacific U., 1953-55; asst. prof. Tex. Technol. U., 1955-59; mem. faculty U. Oreg., Eugene, 1959—, prof. transp., 1965-82, prof. emeritus, 1982—. Served with USN, 1942-45. Recipient Disting. Mem. award for outstanding contbns. to scholarship Transp. and Pub. Utilities Group, Am. Econ. Assn., 1980. Mem. Am. Econ. Assn., Western Econ. Assn., Am. Soc. Traffic and Transp., Pacific N.W. Shippers (adv. bd.). Author: American Economic Development, 1962; Domestic Transportation, 1966, 4th edit. 1979; Public Utilities, 1973; Economics, 1974; The American Economy, 1972, 3d edit., 1983, other books and monographs; contbr. more than 150 articles to profl. jours. Home: 38730 Dexter Rd Dexter OR 97431 Office: Coll Bus Adminstrn U Oreg Eugene OR 97403

SAMS, MARY ANN PACELLA, educational adminstr., corp. exec.; b. Chgo., Sept. 14, 1933; d. Carmen Harold and Helen Frances (Strauk) Pacella; A.B. cum laude, Mundelein Coll., 1958; M.Ed., U. Puget Sound, 1970; postgrad. U. San Francisco, 1977—; certificate San Francisco State U., 1973, Central Wash. State Coll., 1969, Am. Montessori Tchr. Tng. Inst., 1966, U. Kans., 1964, Chgo. Tchrs. Coll., 1960; m. Wendell M. Sams, Aug. 12, 1973; 1 son, Derek John. Spl. services tchr. Chgo. Pub. Schs., 1958-61; social and personal adjustment tchr. Vocat. Rehab. Div., Topeka, Kans., 1962-64; tchr. kindergarten, primary grades Chgo. Pub. Schs., 1964-66; master tchr., tchr.-trainer Park Ridge (Ill.) Montessori Sch., 1966-67, Spring Valley Montessori Sch., Federal Way, Wash., 1967-68; tchr. Annie Wright Sem., Tacoma, Wash., 1968-69; instr. U. Puget Sound, Tacoma, 1968-70; early childhood specialist Franklin Pierce Pub. Sch. Dist., Tacoma, 1969-70; project mgr. Project Learn, Behavioral Research Labs., Menlo Park, Calif., 1970-71; dir. Sullivan Presch. and Sullivan Sch. Redwood City, Calif., 1971, exec. dir. curriculum and personnel Sullivan Presch. and Sullivan Elem. Sch., Irving, Calif., 1971-73; coordinator reading and English as second lang. Dept. Def., Mil. Dependents Schs., Japan, 1973-74; program dir. Western Region, Mini-Skools Ltd., Irving, Calif., 1974-75; supr. personnel San Francisco Unified Sch. Dist., 1975-78, program mgr. Children's Centers Dept., 1978-79; dir. Children's Centers Dept., Oakland (Calif.) Unified Sch. Dist., 1979-80, adminstr. child devel. Piedmont Children's Center, 1981—; grad. instr. early childhood edn. U. San Francisco; cons. in field; lectr. in field. Recipient Cert. of Appreciation, San Francisco Unified Sch. Dist. Bd. Edn., 1978; Tribute, Oakland Unified Sch. Dist. Bd. Edn., 1980; Appreciation award Oakland Dept. Children's Centers, 1980. Mem. Calif. Child Devel. Adminstrs. Assn. (state exec. bd. 1979-81, Cert. of Excellence 1980, Keeper of Dream award 1981), United Adminstrs. of Oakland Schs., Nat. Assn. for Edn. of Young Children, Council for Exceptional Children, Am. Assn. Sch. Personnel Adminstrs., Am. Soc. for Personnel Adminstrs. Bay Area Sch. Personnel Assn., Am. Montessori Soc., Nat. Black Child Devel. Inst., Assn. Montessori Internationale, Assn. Calif. Sch. Adminstrs., Phi Delta Kappa. Roman Catholic. Contbr. articles in field to profl. jours. Office: 86 Echo Ave Oakland CA 94611

SAMSON, ROBERT FRED, soil scientist, researcher, soil classifier; b. Laramie, Wyo., Jan. 15, 1953; s. Robert Louis and Emma June (Ostertag) S.; m. Sandra Ann Mansfield, Oct. 4, 1974; children—Sheri Lynn Samson Winfield, Amy Marie. B.S., N.Mex. State U., 1977, M.S. in Agronomy, 1979. Cert. profl. soil scientist, 1983. Environ. engr. Utah Internat., Inc., Craig, Colo., 1979-81, San Juan Coal Co., Waterflow, N.Mex., 1981-83, Utah Internat., Inc., Fruitland, N.Mex., 1983—. Served with USN, 1972-75. Flight operations officer CAP, 1981—. Mem. Am. Soc. Agronomy, Soil Sci. Soc. Am. Republican. Lutheran.

SAMUELS, BETTY CHAMBERS, foundation president; b. N.Y.C., July 18, 1911; d. Bernard and Rosa A. (Baitler) Chambers; m. Arthur Dodd Fuller, June 26, 1939; m. 2d., Irving Samuels, Apr. 22, 1955. B.A., Barnard Coll., 1931. Founder, pres. Arthur Dodd Fuller Found. for Cardiovascular Research, Los Angeles, 1955—. Mem. Phi Beta Kappa. Home: 9255 Doheny Rd Los Angeles CA 90069 Office: Arthur Dodd Fuller Foundation 9255 Doheny Rd Los Angeles CA 90069

SANBORN, ALAN TILDEN, architect, real estate agt.; b. Hilo, Hawaii, Nov. 14, 1936; s. Jack William and Janet (Aitken) S.; grad. Punahou Sch., 1955; B.S. in Business, U. Colo., 1961; B.Arch., U. Wash., 1964; m. Patricia Kelley; children—Deborah, Kini, Elizabeth, Alan; adopted children—Donna, George, Anthony, Kelley. Draftsman, designer and asso. several archtl. firms, Seattle and Hawaii, 1964-67; project coordinator Oceanic Properties, Honolulu, 1967-68; pres., architect Anderson & Sanborn, Architects, Ltd., Honolulu, 1968-71; pres. Sanborn & Assos., Architects, Ltd., 1972-73, Sanborn, Cutting Assos., Ltd., 1973-76; archtl. cons., Honolulu, 1976-78, Kauai, Hawaii, 1978—; projects coordinator, v.p. Blackwell Builders, Inc., Lihue, Kauai, 1978—. Bd. dirs. Enchanted Lake Community Assn., Kailua, Hawaii, 1965-68, pres., 1966-67, 1st v.p., 1967-68; neighborhood commr. Boy Scouts Am., Honolulu, 1966-68, asst. dist. commr., 1968-69, cubmaster, 1975-76; bd. dirs., 1st v.p. Windward Citizens Planning Conf., Kailua, 1968-69, 71, part-time exec. sec., planning dir., 1970, treas., dir., 1972, sec., dir., 1973-76; mem. Oahu Devel. Conf., 1968-70, mem. comprehensive planning com., 1971; mem. citizens adv. com. Continuing Oahu Transp. Study, 1969-76; bd. dirs. Windward Dist. Community Action Program, 1969-71; treas., bd. dirs. Hawaii Community Design Center 1969-72, chmn. 1973, dir. 1974; chmn. Gov.'s Kahana Valley State Park Task Force, 1970-72; chmn. housing and relocation sub-com. Mayor's Workable Program Adv. Com., 1970, 71; mem. Gov.'s Youth Correctional Facilities Planning Task Force, 1970-72; mem. City and County of Honolulu Kailua Neighborhood Bd., 1976-78. Recipient Distinguished Service award Kaneohe Jr. C. of C., 1968; Hawaii State Jr. C. of C. Ten Outstanding Young Men award, 1969, 70. Mem. Constrn. Specifications Inst., Am. Arbitration Assn., AIA (pub. relations com. 1966-69, profl. practice com. 1973; archtl. design awards 1972, 76), Alpha Phi Omega. Home: PO Box 429 Hanalei HI 96714 Office: 3122 Kuhio Hwy Lihue Kauai HI 96766

SANBORN, DOROTHY CHAPPELL, librarian; b. Nashville, Apr. 26, 1920; d. William S. and Sammie Maude (Drake) Chappell; B.A., U. Tex., 1941; M.A., George Peabody Coll., 1947; M.P.A., Golden Gate U., 1982; m. Richard Donald Sanborn, Dec. 1, 1943; children—Richard Donald, William Chappell. Asst. cataloger El Paso (Tex.) Pub. Library, 1947-52, Library of Hawaii, Honolulu, 1953; cataloger Redwood (Calif.) City Pub. Library, 1954-55, 57-59, Stanford Research Inst., Menlo Park, Calif., 1955-57; librarian Auburn (Calif.) Pub. Library, 1959-62; cataloger Sierra Coll., Rocklin, Calif., 1962-64; reference librarian Sacramento City Library, 1964-66; county librarian Placer County (Calif.), Auburn, 1966—; chmn. Mountain Valley Library System, 1970-71, 75-76; cons. county librarian Alpine County Library, Markleeville, Calif., 1973-80. Served with WAVES, 1944-46. Mem. AAUW (pres. chpt. 1982-83), ALA, Calif. Library Assn. Democrat. Mem. United Ch. Christ. Club: Soroptimists. Home: 135 Midway St Auburn CA 95603 Office: Auburn-Placer County Library 350 Nevada St Auburn CA 95603

SANBORN, FRANK GEORGE, physiotherapist, acupuncturist; b. Grand Prairie, Alta., Can., Oct. 25, 1946; s. Frank and Violet (Billingsley) S.; student No. Coll. Phys. Therapies Life Scis. Inst., 1976; cert. Nat. Acad. Acupuncture, 1978; m. Nicolle Lubberts, Nov. 25, 1979; children—Michael, Tabitha. Physiotherapist, Vienna Clinics, until 1978; owner Stillpoint Clinics, Calgary, Alta., 1977-82; accupuncturist Royal Acupuncture Accupressure Assocs., 1980-81; nutritional cons. Can. Mt. Everest Expdn., 1982, Calgary rowing team, Can. full contact karate team; rep. Can. div. No. Coll. Phys. Therapies, Blackpool, Eng., 1976-79; dir. Northwestern Sch. Masseurs and Physars, 1980—; bd. dirs. Calgary Currie Progressive Conservative Assn. Alta., 1979—, Provincial United Found. Masseurs and Physars, 1980-81. Lic. physiotherapist. Mem. London and Counties Soc. Physiologists, Alta. Acupuncture Soc. Home: 39 Falsby Way Calgary AB Canada Office: Stillpoint Clinics Ltd 33 921 17th Ave SW Calgary AB T2T 0A4 Canada

SANBURN, ALLYSON ANNE, advertising agency executive; b. Fullerton, Calif., Mar. 21, 1953; d. Donald Duane and LaVerta Anne (Scott) Sanburn; m. Thomas A.E. Shumard, Nov. 11, 1970 (div.); 1 dau., Jennifer Anne. A.A. in Journalism, Fullerton Coll., 1976. Advt. asst. K. Esterley & Assoc., La Habra, Calif., 1977-78; advt. prodn. mgr. Technicolor Audio-Visual Co., Costa Mesa, Calif., 1978-79; graphic cons. Franciscan Graphics Co., Mountain View, Calif., 1979-81; account supr. Collateral Resources Unlimited, Mountain View, 1981-82; pres. Sanburn Godfrey Advt., Inc., Palo Alto, Calif., 1982—. Active Calif. Hist. Soc. Recipient Leif Johnson Meml. award Fullerton News Tribune, 1974; Alpha Gamma Eta Woman of Distinction award Associated Students Fullerton Coll., 1975; Mem. Peninsula Women in Advt., Bus. and Profl. Advt. Assn., Network Women Entrepreneurs San Jose, Women Entrepreneurs San Francisco, Nat. Assn. Women Execs.

SANCHEZ, DEIDRA KAY, interior designer, realtor; b. Phoenix, Mar. 22, 1951; d. Henri Bonafacio and Madeleine (Harkey) S. B.S. in Interior Design, No. Ariz. U., Flagstaff, 1973. Cert. interior designer Ariz. Bd. Realtors. Interior designer Lou Register's, 1973-74, Laura's, 1976-80; realtor Realty Execs., 1981—; pres. Redbird Oil Co., Scottsdale, Ariz., 1976—. Mem. Scottsdale Bd. Realtors, Am. Soc. Interior Designers. Home: 5731 E Edgemont Scottsdale AZ 85257 Office: 4110 N 70 St Scottsdale AZ 85251

SANCHEZ, DONNA BLAIR, interior designer; b. Columbus, Ohio, Apr. 23, 1947; d. William E. and Dorothy M. (Bazemore) Blair; m. David Julian Sanchez, Apr. 29, 1967 (div. 1978). Student Phoenix Coll., 1965-69, Minn. Sch. Art, 1961-65. Cert. interior designer, Calif. Preliminary draftsman Paddock Pools, Phoenix, 1968; visual merchandising designer Goldwaters Fashion Stores, Ariz. and N.Mex., 1970-75, Diamonds and Rhodes, Ariz., 1967-69; owner D.J. Sanchez Interiors, Phoenix, 1973—; mem. design staff Lou Regesters, Phoenix, 1983—. tchr. visual merchandising Phoenix Coll. and Mesa Community Coll. Mem. Nat. Home Fashions League, Internat. Soc. Interior Designers, Ariz. Design Council. Clubs: Jockey, Playboy. Office: 818 E Osborn St Suite 112 Phoenix AZ 85014

SANCHEZ, JOSEPH LUIS, JR., real estate and construction executive, consultant; b. N.Y.C., June 30, 1942; s. Joseph Luis and Frances (Picon) S.; m. Darya A. Terrill, Mar. 18, 1967 (div.); 1 son, Joey III; m. 2d Vonnie L. Spanswick, Feb. 22, 1974; children—Charity Raine, Christian Daniel Darin. B.C.E., Colo. U., 1965, B.S. in Bus., 1965, M.B.A. in Fin., 1967. Cons. engr. Sallada & Hanson, Denver, 1965-67; owner pres. JLS Enterprises, Inc., 1967—, chief exec. officer. Bd. dirs. San Juan Children's Learning Ctr., 1981—, pres., 1983. Mem. ASCE, Nat. Soc. Profl. Engr., Nat. Assn. Home Builders, Colo. Assn. Home Builders, Assn. Gen. Contractors, Nat. Assn. Indsl. Office Parks, Boulder C. of C. Clubs: Ritz Carlton (Chgo.); Jockey (Las Vegas).

SANCHEZ, PATRICIA COLLEEN, nurse, respiratory therapist; b. Cheyenne, Wyo., May 3, 1942; d. Harry Daniel and Lackawamma Colleen (Warren) Shea; m. Elmer Sanchez, Sept. 10, 1957; children—Douglas, Susan, Toby Lee. Student Laramie County Community Coll. Respiratory therapist DePaul Hosp., Cheyenne, 1969-74; staff nurse VA Hosp., Cheyenne, 1974—; pres. Am. Fedn. Govt. Employees, Local 1014, 1978—. Home: 707 Carlson St Cheyenne WY 82009 Office: 2360 E Pershing St Cheyenne WY 82001

SANCHEZ, RAYMOND G., state representative, lawyer; b. Albuquerque, Sept. 22, 1941; s. Gillie and Priscilla S.; m. Elizabeth Stanford, 1964; children—Raymond, Michael. B.A., U. N.Mex., 1964, J.D., 1967. Mem. N.Mex. Ho. of Reps., 1977—, house majority leader, now speaker of house; mem. com. on jud. selection and reform, law study com. N.Mex. Bar. Bd. dirs. Community Council of Albuquerque. Mem. U. N.Mex. Alumni Assn. (bd. dirs.), NCCJ, Sigma Xi. Democrat. Office: N Mex State House Santa Fe NM 87501*

SANCHEZ, ROBERT FORTUNE, archbishop; b. Socorro, N.Mex., Mar. 20, 1934; s. Julius C. and Priscilla (Fortune) S.; student Immaculate Heart of Mary Sem., Santa Fe, 1950-54, Gregorian U., Rome, 1954-60. Ordained priest Roman Catholic Ch., 1959, consecrated archbishop, 1974; tchr., asst. prin. St. Pius X High Sch., Albuquerque, 1960-68; pastor St. Joseph Parish, Mosquero, N.Mex., 1968-71, San Felipe Parish, Albuquerque, 1971-74; vicar gen. Archdiocese of Santa Fe, 1974, archbishop of Santa Fe, 1974—. Bd. dirs. Pontifical Coll. Josephinum, 1979; mem. USCC Commn. on Marriage and Family Life, 1979—. Mem. Am. Bd. Cath. Missions, U.S. Cath. Conf.; chmn. Ad Hoc Com. for Spanish Speaking; chmn. devel. com., bd. dirs. Mexican Am. Cultural Center, San Antonio; trustee Cath. U. Am.; del. of U.S. Cath. Conf. to Internat. World Synod of Bishops, 1980. Office: 202 Morningside Dr SE Albuquerque NM 87108

SANDBERG, JOHN SVEN, provincial government official; b. Leslie, Sask., Can., Aug. 10, 1938; s. Siegfred M. and Annie Martha (Eidem) S.; m. Delores Helen Funk, Dec. 27, 1969; children—Rachael, Heidi. Grad. Sask. Tchrs. Coll., Saskatoon, 1960. Tchr. pub. schs., Eston, Sask., 1960, Winnipeg, Man., Can., 1961-64; news and sports broadcaster, Winnipeg, Ft. Francis and Thunderbay, 1964-76; media mgr. Federated Coops. Ltd., Saskatoon, 1979-82; mem. Sask. Legis. Assembly, 1982—, minister consumer and comml. affairs, 1982-83, minister of cooperation and coop. devel., 1982—. Progressive Conservative. Club: Caledonia Curling (Regina). Office: Room 315 Legislative Bldg Regina SK S4S 0B3 Canada

SANDBERG, WILLIAM ALLEN, public relations administrator; b. Colfax, Wash., Oct. 20, 1947; s. Robert A. and Ruth M. (Cheatham) S.; m. Charlotte M. Marino, Aug. 4, 1973; 1 son, Matthew Allen. B.A. in Social Sci., Calif. State U., 1966. Program dir. Sacramento (Calif.) Assn. for the Retarded, 1970-72; dir. pub. relations and devel. Roseville (Calif.) Community Hosp., 1972-77; pres., dir. pub. relations Ballard Community Hosp. Found., Seattle, 1977-82; dir. pub. relations Group Health Coop. of Puget Sound, Seattle, 1982—. Mem. Pub. Relations Soc. Am. (accredited, past pres. Puget Sound chpt.), Nat. Assn. Hosp. Devel. Home: 22022 2d Pl W Bothell WA 98011 Office: Group Health Coop of Puget Sound 300 Elliott Ave W Seattle WA 98119

SANDEEN, RODERICK COX, newspaper editor; b. Mpls., Apr. 27, 1943; s. Clair William and Mary Ethel (Cox) S.; B.S. in Journalism, U. Colo., 1969; m. Patricia Anne McDermott, June 10, 1972; children—Peter, Mark. Reporter, The New Haven Post-Register, 1969-70; reporter Post-Register, Idaho Falls, Idaho, 1972-73; reporter, editor Idaho Statesman, Boise, 1973-78, mng. editor, 1978—. Office: Idaho Statesman 1200 N Curtis Rd PO Box 40 Boise ID 83707*

SANDER, STEVEN DAVID, advertising executive; b. N.Y.C. Nov. 3, 1953; s. Lothar Steven and Greta (Landwehr) S. B.S. cum laude in Journalism, U. Colo., 1974, B.A. in Urban Geography, 1974. Photographer, Boulder Daily Camera (Colo.), 1974-76; account exec. Schenkein and Assocs., Denver, 1976-78, sr. account exec., 1978-81; pres., founder, Sander Communications, Denver, 1981—. Bd. dirs. Big Bros. of Denver; mem. Gov.'s Council on Health Promotion and Phys. Fitness. Recipient award for Photojournalism excellence Colo. Press Assn., 1977-78. Mem. Denver Advt. Fedn. (career day seminar chmn., 1983), Pub. Relations Soc. Am., Nat. Press Photographers Am. Club: Cherry Creek Sporting (Colo.). Office: 1754 LaFayette St Denver CO 80218

SANDERLIN, OWENITA HARRAH, author, educator; b. Los Angeles, June 2, 1916; d. Owen Melville and Marigold (Whitford) Harrah; m. George William Sanderlin, May 30, 1936; children—Frea Elizabeth Sladek, Sheila Mary Buska, David George, John Owen. B.A. summa cum laude, Am. U., 1937; postgrad. U. Maine, 1939-40, U. Calif.-Santa Barbara, 1967, San Diego State U., 1969-70, U. Calif.-San Diego, 1974. Cert. Humanities, English, speech, drama tchr., Calif. Puppeteer, Theodore Tiller Marionettes, Washington, 1933-38; freelance writer, 1939—; head speech and drama dept. Our Lady Peace, San Diego, 1961-68; cons. gifted programs San Diego city schs., 1972-74, 80—; English instr. U. Maine, 1942, 46; creative writing instr. Maine Writers Conf., 1945. Poll insp. San Diego County, 1976-83. Recipient Double Ruby award Nat. Forensics League, 1966. Mem. Nat. Assn. Gifted Children, Assn. San Diego Educators Gifted. Democrat. Roman Catholic. Clubs: San Diego State U. Women, Singing Hills Tennis. Author: Jeanie O'Brien, 1965; Johnny, 1968; Creative Teaching, 1971; Teaching Gifted Children, 1973, Tennis Rebel, 1978; Match Point, 1979; (with Ruthe Lundy) Gifted Children How to Identify and Teach Them, 1979. Home and Office: 997 Vista Grande Rd El Cajon CA 92021

SANDERS, DANIEL SELVARAJAH, university dean; b. Sri Lanka, Sept. 18, 1928; came to U.S., 1965; s. David S. and Harriet C. (Handy) S.; B.A., U. Ceylon, 1953; diploma in social welfare U. Wales, 1958; M.S.W., U. Minn., 1967, Ph.D., 1971; m. Christobel C. Niles, Apr. 14, 1959. Asso. dir., lectr. Ceylon Inst. Social Work, 1955-61; exec. dir., research assoc. Inst. Social Study, Ceylon, 1961-65; spl. projects cons., adminstr. Minn. Dept. Public Welfare, 1967-69; assoc. prof. U. Hawaii, 1971-74, prof., dean, dir. internat. programs, 1974—, pres. Lutheran Campus Ministry, 1978-79; pres. Inter-Univ. Consortium for Internat. Social Devel., 1981—; bd. dirs. Council on Social Work Edn., 1983—. Brit. Council scholar, 1957-58; World Council Chs. Ecumenical scholar, 1965-66; Inst. Internat. Edn. Devel. fellow, 1966-67; NIMH doctoral fellow, 1969-71; NIMH cross-cultural tng. project dir. Sch. of S.W. of U. Hawaii, 1977-83 NIMH child welfare dir., 1979-82. Mem. Nat. Assn. Social Workers, Council Social Work Edn., Internat. Assn. Schs. Social Work, Internat. Soc. Community Devel., UN Assn. (pres. Hawaii div. 1982—), Internat. Conf. Social Welfare. Democrat. Author: Impact of Reform Movements on Social Policy Changes, 1972; (with Kurren and Fischer) Fundamentals of Social Work Practice, 1982; The Developmental Perspective in Social Work, 1982; Education for International Social Welfare, 1983; editorial adv. Internat. Social Work, 1978—, Law and Social Work, 1980—; Social Development Issues, 1982; founder, exec. editor Ceylon Jour. Social Work, 1955-60. Office: 2500 Campus Rd Honolulu HI 96822

SANDERS, GARY WAYNE, lawyer; b. Wilmington, Del., Dec. 29, 1949; s. Harland Wesley and Anna Marie (Herminau) S.; m. Cheryl Ann Clark, Aug. 22, 1980. B.S., Calif. Poly. Inst., 1972; J.D., Western State U., 1977. Bar: Calif. 1977. Corp. planner Cert. Grocers, Los Angeles, 1969-74; asst. character coordinator Walt Disney Prodns., Disneyland, Anaheim, Calif., 1968-78; sole practice, Seal Beach, Calif., 1978-79; gen. counsel Care Enterprises, Orange, Calif., 1979—, sec., 1983—. Mem. ABA, State Bar Calif., Orange County Bar Assn., Calif. Soc. Health Care Facilities, Calif. Hosp. Assn., Nat. Notary Assn., Nat. Health Lawyers Assn., Legal Task Force, Nat. Council Care Ctrs. Republican. Lutheran. Clubs: Elks, Masons.

SANDERS, JOHN R., professional football team manager; b. San Antonio, July 26, 1922; s. Ira William and Johnie Laurie (Manning) S.; B.A., Occidental Coll., 1949; m. Margaret Jean Werner, July 6, 1946; 2 children. Head football coach North Hollywood (Calif.) High Sch., 1952-58; dir. athletics, football coach U.S. Grant High Sch., Van Nuys, Calif., 1959-63; dir. player personnel Los Angeles Rams, 1964-75, asst. gen. mgr., 1967-75; asst. to pres. San Diego Chargers, 1975, gen. mgr., 1976—. Served with USN, 1943-46. Republican. Baptist. Office: PO Box 20666 San Diego CA 92120*

SANDERS, KATHRYN TERESA, public relations counsel; b. Vincennes, Ind., Mar. 18, 1950; d. William Robert and Olive Mae (Gouveneur) S.; Sanders; m. James Louis Kittle, Jr., Dec. 5, 1975 (div.). B.S. in Speech and Hearing Therapy, Spl. Edn. magna cum laude, Ind. State U., 1972; postgrad. San Francisco State U. Spl. educator Indpls. Pub. Schs., 1972-74, speech and hearing therapist, 1974-77; retail mgr., buyer Kittle's Other Side, Indpls., 1977-79; account exec. telecommunications dept. Ind. Bell Telephone, Indpls., 1980; account exec. Carl Byoir & Assocs., San Francisco, 1981-83, Carl Byoir, Arnold, Palmer & Noble, 1983—. Bd. dirs. Big Brothers San Francisco. Mem. Pub. Relations Soc. Am., Publicity Club San Francisco. Office: Carl Byoir Arnold Palmer & Noble 181 Fremont St San Francisco CA 94105

SANDERS, MICHELE GARSIDE HENSILL, school district administrator; b. Richmond, Calif., Nov. 10, 1942; d. John R. and Inez Sophia (Lonquist) Garside; B.A., Chico State U., 1964; M.A., San Francisco State U., 1973; Ph.D. candidate U. Calif., Berkeley; m. Steven Neil Sanders, Apr. 3, 1979. Tchr., Belmont and Richmond, Calif., 1964-76; adminstrv. asst. to supt. Belmont Sch. Dist., 1976-78, prin. Ralston Intermediate Sch., 1978-82; asst. supt. Portula Valley (Calif.) Sch. Dist., 1982—; instr. U. Calif., Berkeley Extension, U. San Francisco, Dominican Coll., 1974-80; cons. theatre arts, motivation, communications, mgmt. Performer, San Jose Civic Light Opera, San Francisco Lamplighters, Com. Workshop and Improvisation, Inc., San Francisco. Bd. mgrs. Carlmont YMCA, 1978-80; pres. bd. dirs. Homeowners Assn., 1977-78; auctioneer Sta. KQED, 1976-82; chmn. fin. Belmont Faculty Assn., 1975-76. Bank of Am. grantee, 1979. Mem. Assn. Calif. Sch. Adminstrs. (achievement award 1978), Assn. for Humanistic Psychology, Assn. Supervision and Curriculum Devel., Calif. Assn. for Gifted, PTA, Sierra Club, Alpha Delta Kappa, Phi Delta Kappa. Pub. Belmont Reports, 1976-78. Office: 200 Shawnee Pass Portula Valley CA 94025

SANDERSON, KENNETH CARLILE, aerospace cons.; b. Providence, Aug. 12, 1922; s. Cuthbert Stafford and Ada (Habershaw) S.; B.S.

in Engring. Physics, U. Tulsa, 1952; postgrad. Center Advanced Engring. Study, M.I.T., 1968; m. Margaret Alice Hoag, May 6, 1948; children—Hilary Surtees, Phoebe Sherman. With NASA Dryden, Edwards, Calif., 1950-80, dep. dir. data systems, 1960-80; aerospace cons., Lancaster, Calif., 1980—; mem. flight test instrumentation working grp., adv. group advanced research and devel. NATO, 1975-81. Served with RCAF, 1941-43, as pilot USAAF, 1943-46. Decorated Air medal, Purple Heart. Mem. Instrument Soc. Am., AIAA, Air Force Assn. Republican. Episcopalian. Author tech. papers in field; editor NATO AGARD Flight Test Instrumentation Series, 18 vols., 1975-81. Address: 43718 Gadsden Ave Lancaster CA 93534

SANDERSON, MILDRED ANN, home economics educator; b. Lyons, Kans., July 20, 1938; d. Harold Marvin and Lena M. (Heller) Heiken; m. James Richard Sanderson, June 12, 1960; children—Jane Dee, Michael Thomas. B.S. in Vocat. Home Econs., Kans. State U., 1960. Cert. tchr., Wis., Kans., Tex., Utah. Tchr. pub. schs., Kans., Wis., 1960-73; tchr. David Carter High Sch., Dallas, 1973-74, Osborne (Kans.) High Sch., 1974-76, Salt Lake Community High Sch., Utah, 1976-77; tchr., chmn. home econs. dept. Clayton Int., Salt Lake City, 1977—; sponsor various student clubs; chmn. positive discipline U.S. Office of Edn., Region Law Enforcement Agy., Trinity U. Tex.; supr. student tchrs. Tchr. Sunday sch., mem. council of ministry United Methodist Ch. Recipient Outstanding Service award Salt Lake Kiwanis, 1979. Mem. various state home econs. assns. Republican.

SANDERSON, ROGER SEWARD, surgeon; b. DeKalb, Ill., Jan. 19, 1930; s. Elmer Seward and Evelyn (Anderson) S.; B.A., U. Ill., 1950, B.S., 1951, M.D., Chgo., 1954. Intern VA Hosp., Long Beach, Calif., Los Angeles County Hosp., 1954-55; resident VA Hosp., Long Beach, Children's Hosp., Los Angeles, 1959-63; practice medicine, Long Beach, 1957-59, specializing in head and neck surgery, 1965—, mem. staff VA Hosp., Long Beach, Orange (Calif.) County Med. Center, Hoag Meml. Hosp., Newport Beach, Calif.; asst. clin. prof. surgery U. Calif., Irvine. Pres., chmn. bd., chief ops. officer Health Screening Orange County, 1974—, Research Surg. Systems Corp., 1974—, Vactron Plastic Co., R.S.S. Corp. Served with USNR, 1955-57. Fellow A.C.S.; mem. Am. Soc. Head and Neck Surgeons. Patentee various devices, including nose protector, mask, air filter, sterilization and vacuum packing process. Home: 24662 Santa Clara Ave Dana Point CA 92629 Office: 2645 Croddy Way Santa Ana CA 92704

SANDFORD, VIRGINIA ADELE, educator; b. Tacoma, Wash., Nov. 29, 1926; d. Fred John and Lucille Lillian (Skok) Wepfer; student U. Wash., 1946-49; m. Calvert H. Sandford, Sept. 16, 1949 (div. 1970); children—Susan L., Kaye E., James C. Tchr. stringed instruments dept. music Puyallup (Wash.) Sch. Dist., 1944-46; sec. Fife (Wash.) Sch. Dist., 1969-72; exec. sec. Tacoma (Wash.) Sch. Dist., 1972-75; tchr. cdnl. sec. program Clover Park Vocat. Tech. Inst., Tacoma, 1975-82; speaker, seminar producer Virginia Sandford & Assocs., 1982—. Violinist, Tacoma Symphony, 1972-75. Mem. Am. Vocat. Assn., Wash. Vocat. Assn., Wash. State Bus. Edn. Assn., Nat. Assn. Ednl. Office Personnel, Internat. Platform Assn., Nat. Speakers Assn., Alpha Chi Omega. Office: 811 Fife Heights NE Tacoma WA 98422

SANDHU, HARNEK SINGH, cytogeneticist, consultant; b. Sanehwal, Punjab, India; came to U.S., 1972, Naturalized 1978; s. Chanan Singh and Nihal (Kaur) S.; m. Sharanjit Kaur, Feb. 4, 1980. M.S., Punjab Agrl. U., Ladhiana Punjab, India, 1968; Ph.D., S.D. State U., 1978. Cert. profl. crop specialist. Agr. advisor, gen. mgr. DLF United Pvt Ltd. Connaugh Palace, New Delhi, 1969-72; incharge research and quality control Tracy Seed Corp., Janesville, Wis., 1972-74; incharge nat. sorghun and pearl millet improvement project USAID, Yemen Arab-Republic, 1979-81; agronomist/plant breeder dept. plant sci. U. Ariz., Tucson, 1981-82; research geneticist Agrl. Research Service, U.S. Dept. Agr., Utah State U., Logan, 1981—. Mem. Crop Sci. Soc. Am., Am. Soc. Agronomy, Am. Registry of Cert. Profls. in Agronomy, Crops and Soils, Alpha Gamma Rho, Gamma Sigma Delta. Club: Lace and Levi Square Dancing (Logan). Contbr. articles to profl. jours. Office: UMC-63 Crops Research Lab Utah State U Logan UT 84322

SANDLER, MARION OSHER, savings and loan executive; b. Biddeford, Maine, Oct. 17, 1930; d. Samuel and Leah (Lowe) Osher; m. Herbert M. Sandler, Mar. 26, 1961. B.A. in Econs., Wellesley Coll., 1952; postgrad. Harvard-Radcliffe program in Bus. Adminstrn., 1953; M.B.A. in Banking and Fin., NYU, 1958. Asst. buyer Bloomingdale's, N.Y.C., 1953-55; security analyst Dominick & Dominick, N.Y.C., 1955-61; sr. fin. analyst Oppenheimer and Co., N.Y.C., 1961-63; sr. v.p., co-mng. officer Golden West Fin. Corp. and World Savs. and Loan Assn., Oakland, Calif., 1963-75, vice chmn. bd., co-mng. officer, 1975-80, pres., chief exec. officer, 1980—, also dir.; dir. Macy's Calif., 1976-82; mem. Pres.'s Mgmt. Improvement Council, Washington, 1980; mem. Pres. Carter's Housing Task Force, 1980; mem. Capital Formation Task Force, White House Conf. Small Bus., 1979; mem. adv. council U. Calif., Sch. Bus. Adminstrn., 1977-79; mem. adv. council Fed. Nat. Mortgage Assn., 1983—. Mem. Phi Beta Kappa, Beta Gamma Sigma. Office: Golden West Fin Corp 1970 Broadway St Suite 1000 Oakland CA 94612

SANDLER, THOMAS R., accountant; b. Mt. Kisco, N.Y., Dec. 16, 1946; s. Louis and Susan (Rosen) S.; m. Alison G. Corneau, Aug. 26, 1972; children—Justin C., Shawn A. B.S. summa cum laude, Ithaca Coll., 1968; M.S., SUNY-Binghamton, 1972. C.P.A., N.Y., Colo. 1982. Asst. acct. Peat, Marwick, Mitchell, White Plains, N.Y., 1972, mgr., Phoenix, 1975, sr. mgr., N.Y.C., 1978, ptnr., Denver, 1981—. Bd. dirs. Found. Arts and Humanities, Colo.; committeeman Colo. Golf Assn. Served with USMC, 1968-70. Mem. Colo. Soc. C.P.A.s (chmn. govt. acctg. com.) Am. Inst. C.P.A.s. Clubs: Columbine Country (Littleton, Colo.); Whippoorwill Country (Armonk N.Y.). Contbr. articles to profl. jours. Home: 4 Spyglass Dr Littleton CO 80123 Office: Peat Marwick Mitchell 707 17th St Denver CO 80202

SANDLIN, GARRY M., interior designer; b. Clinton, Okla., Feb. 28; s. Bascomb P. and Gladys E. (Larkins) S. B.A. in Design (hon.), Brooks Coll. Design, 1981. Designer, Chandlers Furniture Co., Santa Ana, Calif., 1965-66; designer Davis Furniture Co., Long Beach, Calif., 1966-75; prin. Garry Sandlin Interior Designs, Inc., Long Beach, 1975—. Mem. Adv. Com. Brooks Coll., Long Beach, Calif.; mem. adv. bd. Calif. State U.-Long Beach, 1982-83; mem. Decor Council Pub. Corp. of the Arts, Design House, Long Beach. Mem. Nat. Bus. Honor Soc., Am. Soc. Interior Designers (pres. Los Angeles chpt. 1983), Industry Found. (chmn.), Alpha Beta Gamma. Republican. Mem. religious science, contbr. to Designers West, 1975, 1981. Office: Garry Sandlin Interior Designs 4144 Bus St Long Beach CA 90807

SANDOVAL, DONALD A., state senator, wholesale food distbr.; b. Denver, Jan. 30, 1935; student Regis Coll., U. Colo., 1957-61; m. Ruth Sandoval; children—Teresa, Diana, Ernie, Mathew. Former restaurant owner; now with wholesale distbg. co., Denver; mem. Colo. Senate, mem. bus affairs, labor and transp. coms. Vice-chmn. S.W. Community Complex; treas. Youth Employment Bd.; mem. Denver Democratic Central Com.; past pres. local union 1415 UAW; mem. State Personnel Bd. Mem. Am. Legion, Am. GI Forum. Democrat. Roman Catholic. Club: KC. Office: 823 Knox Ct Denver CO 80204*

SANDOVAL, JAMES PHILIP, concrete company executive; b. Trinidad, Colo., Jan. 14, 1929; s. Philip Joseph and Ermenia Minnie (Vigil) S.; student Idaho State U., 1951-52, Tex. Christian U., 1954-56, UCLA, 1960-61; m. Betty C. Loomis, Oct. 24, 1949; children—Patrick, Michael, Christopher, Sue Ann, Eugene, Catherine, Therese. With acctg. dept. Convair Corp., Ft. Worth, 1954-60; pvt. practice bookkeeping, Hacienda Heights, Calif., 1962-71; founder Blue Star Ready Mix Inc., Moorpark, Calif., 1976—; owner, gen. mgr. Blue Star Ready Mix Inc., 1976—. Served with AUS, 1948-51; Republican. Roman Catholic. Office: Blue Star Ready Mix Inc Box 696 Moorpark CA 93021

SANDOVAL, JULIAN, fin., estate and business cons.; b. Wichita, Kans., Feb. 16, 1924; s. Jose Hipolito and Felicitas (Frausto) S.; B.S. in Bus. Adminstrn., U. Wyo., 1953; m. Angelina Valdéz, Sept. 7, 1947; children—Rosalinda, Mary, Anthony. With Union Pacific R.R., 1942-67; pvt. practice acctg. and tax services, fin. cons., Laramie, Wyo., 1962-72; founder, pres. Mgmt. Cons., Inc., specializing in fin., estate, and bus. cons., Laramie, 1972—. Active local and state polit. campaigns, 1956-60. Served with USMC, 1942-46. Democrat. Roman Catholic. Home: 908 Mitchell St Laramie WY 82070 Office: 406 1/2 S 21st St Suite A Laramie WY 82070

SANDOVAL, ROBERT ANTHONY, accountant, consultant; b. Albuquerque, Feb. 9, 1950; s. Cornelio Savino and Trini G. (Giddings) S.; m. Robina Lynette Myers, Aug. 3, 1974; 1 dau., Aubrey. B.S. in Math., U. N.Mex., 1974, B.B.A. in Acctg., 1976. C.P.A., N.Mex. Staff acct. N.Mex. State Auditor, 1977-79; sr. acct. Gorden and Hale, P.C., 1979-80; sr. acct. Metler Gamlin Gaylord, C.P.A., 1980-82; ptnr. Gaylord Sandoval and Co., C.P.A.s, 1982-83, owner, 1983—. Mem. Am. Inst. C.P.A.s, N.Mex. Soc. C.P.A.s. Democrat. Roman Catholic. Club: Jaycees (Albuquerque). Home and Office: 4601 Rainbow NW Albuquerque NM 87114

SANDS, MAYNARD DALE, environ. cons.; b. Highland Park, Mich., Feb. 13, 1951; s. Maynard Duffy and Claire Tess S.; B.S., Central Mich. U., 1973; M.S., U. Mich., 1974; postgrad. Calif. State U.-Fullerton, 1978-81, Calif. State U.-Hayward, 1981—; m. Debra Jean Heath, Aug. 25, 1973; children—Hilaria Elizabeth, Trenton Dale, Kendrick Duffy. Research asst. U. Mich., Ann Arbor, 1973-74; lab. dir. oceanographic and environ. services Raytheon Co., Portsmouth, R.I., 1974-77; program mgr. ocean scis. dept. Interstate Electronics Corp., Anaheim, Calif., 1977-79, dept. dir., 1979-81; v.p. Marine Ecol. Cons.'s of So. Calif., Solana Beach, 1981; gen. mgr. McKesson Environ. Services, 1981—. Mem. Am. Chem. Soc., Marine Tech. Soc., Water Pollution Control Fedn. Episcopalian. Club: Amador Valley Athletic. Home: 4837 Muirwood Dr Pleasanton CA 94566 Office: 6363 Clark Ave Dublin CA 94568

SANDS, STEVEN PAUL, science/research company executive; b. Los Angeles, Sept. 8, 1944; s. Glenn Maurice and Henrietta (Castro) S.; m. Evelyn Lourett VanDerLee, Dec. 8, 1962; children—Steven Anthony, David Andrew. B.S. in Fin. and Acctg., UCLA, 1972. Purchasing agt. Wilkinson Co., Westlake Village, Calif., 1964-69; account mgr. Tech. Service Corp., Santa Monica, Calif., 1969-72; internal audit div. staff W.R. Grace & Co., N.Y.C., 1973; controller Tech. Service Corp., Santa Monica, Calif., 1974-77; v.p. fin. and bus. ops. Arete Assocs., Encino, Calif., 1977—, corp. pension adminstrn., 1982—; trustee Arete Assocs. Pension Trust, 1977-82. Treas. Venice (Calif.) Athletic Club, 1983—. Mem. Am. Mgmt. Assn., Nat. Assn. Accts. (dir. 1979-80). Republican. Office: 5445 Balboa Blvd PO Box 350 Encino CA 91316

SANDSTEDT, LYNN A., Spanish and foreign language educator, writer; b. Brush, Colo., Oct. 19, 1932; s. Reuben A. and Edna (Bartram) S.; m. Phyllis M. Troudt, June 24, 1961; children—Todd E., Scott David. Ph.D. in Spanish Lang. and Lit., U. Colo., 1972. Tchr., supr. fgn. langs. Dist. 6, Greeley, Colo., 1957-72; prof. Spanish, dept. hispanic studies U. No. Colo., Greeley, 1972—, cons., co-author coll. textbooks: Habla Espanol?-Conversacion y repaso, Puertas a la lengua espanola; Literature y arte, Puertas a la comunicacion; Civilizacion y cultura, Puertas al mundo hispanico. Served with U.S. Army, 1954-56. Fulbright grantee Spain; NEH grantee Fgn. Lang. Leadership Inst.; grantee NDEA Inst., U. Ariz., Guadalajara, Mex.; recipient various Outstanding Tchr. of Yr. awards. Mem. MLA, Am. Council on Teaching Fgn. Langs. (exec. council 1978-80), Am. Assn. Tchrs. Spanish and Portugese (pres. 1984), Colo. Congress of Fgn. Lang. Tchrs. Methodist.

SANDSTEDT, PATRICIA ANN, marketing executive; b. Denver, Nov. 11, 1932; d. Kenneth D. Smith and Lillian M. (Ramsour) Kirby; m. Earl C. Sandstedt, Aug. 12, 1953; children—Mark, D Cana, Lori. B.A. in Elem. Edn., U. No. Colo., 1954, Tchr., Denver Pub. Schs., 1955-57; regional mgr. Ency. Britannica Edn. Corp., Chgo., 1979-80; regional mgr. Learning Corp. Am., N.Y.C., 1981—. Bd. dirs. Harvey Park Improvement Assn. Mem. Am. Soc. Tng. and Devel. Lutheran. Home: 3740 W Eastman Ave Denver CO 80236 Office: Learning Corp America 1350 Ave of the Americas New York NY 10019

SANDUBRAE, ARNOLD ROBERT, designer, karate instructor; b. Detroit, Jan. 14, 1933; s. Morris and Nena (Sodos) S.; m. Joy F. Finsterwald, Nov. 21, 1953; children—Allen, Anna, Steven. Hon. degree in design, U. London, 1968. Designer, C.A. Finsterwald Co., Inc., Detroit, 1955-60; v.p. Co-Ordinated Interiors, Inc., Detroit, 1960-82, pres. 1982—; chmn. bd. Coordinated Electronic Research Corp., Inc., Lifelite Corp., A.R. Murray, Inc., A.R. West, Inc.; pres. Decorative Service Bur., Inc.; instr. Isshinryu karate. Served with U.S. Army, 1953-55. World Champion Isshinryu karate, 1977; Am. Okinawan Karate Assn. awardee. Fellow Inst. Profl. Designers (London); mem. Am. Soc. Interior Designers (cert.), Am. Designers Guild (cert.), Am. Okinawan Karate Assn., U.S. Karate Assn. Internat. Isshinryu Karate Assn. (cert.). Republican. Club: Masons. Patentee designs electronic devices, components. Home: 1655 E Palm Canyon Apt 708 Palm Springs CA 92262

SANDWEISS, HOWARD WAYNE, security service co. exec.; b. Los Angeles, May 26, 1940; s. Melvin and Charlotte (Leiman) S.; B.S., UCLA, 1969, M.S., 1971; M.B.A., Pepperdine U., 1978; m. Susan B. Levine, Dec. 5, 1980; children by previous marriage—Richard, Marni, Bryan; stepchildren—Hillary, Candice. With Los Angeles County Sheriffs Dept., 1965-71; sr. project engr. Canoga Electronics, Chatsworth, Calif., 1960-70; founder, pres., chief exec. officer Protectal Corp., Woodland Hills, Calif., 1970—; lectr. on electronics and security. Mem. Internat. Police Congress, Internat. Acad. for Criminology, Nat. Acad. for Criminology, Spl. Agents Assn., Chief of Police Assn., Am. Soc. Indsl. Security. Address: Protectal Corp 22130 Clarendon St Woodland Hills CA 91367

SANFORD, ALICE GOSNELL, financial consulting firm executive; b. N.Y.C., May 18, 1942; d. Charles Francis and Patricia (Aran) Gosnell; m. Donald Wilbur Smith, June 14, 1959; children—Richard D., James Michael; m. 2d, Clyde E. Sanford, Apr. 18, 1970; 1 dau., Ylisa I. B.S., U. Rochester, 1962. Lic. real estate agent, N.Y., Calif.; cert. equity sharing specialist Dept. Real Estate, 1980. Real estate assoc. Century 21 Rexford Realty Co., Rochester, N.Y., 1970-78; mgr. Vista Home Loans Co., Sebastopol, Calif., 1979-82; exec. dir. S & S Internat. Enterprises, Santa Rosa, Calif., 1982—; lectr. mgmt., mktg. motivation, real estate. Mem. Nat. Assn. Educators, Calif. Assn. Realtors, Internat. Execs. Assn.

SANFORD, DOROTHY ZERZAN, economics educator; b. Portland, Nov. 20, 1924; d. Charles J. and Margaret C. (Mahony) Zerzan; children—Mary Victoria, Veronica Maire, Virginia Marie, Thomas Joseph, Judith Ann, Theresa Rose, Timothy Michael, Julie Catharine. B.A., Willamette U., 1946; M.A., U. Oreg., 1948; Ph.D., U. St. Louis, 1950; postgrad. McGeorge Sch. Law, 1950-51. Prof. econs. Coll. Notre Dame, Belmont, Calif., 1954—, chmn. bus. adminstrn./econs., 1972-80; instr. econs. St. Louis U., 1947-50. Active Cath. Social Service, 1970-74. Mem. Am. Econ. Assn., Am. Mktg. Assn., Assn. of Social Econs. (dir.), Western Econ. Assn. Club: Democrat. Book reviewer in field. Home: 1222 Dore Ave San Mateo CA 94401 Office: 1500 Ralson St Coll of Notre Dame Belmont CA 94002

SANFORD, MARK, sociologist, researcher, consultant; b. Berkeley, Calif., Oct. 15, 1940; s. Robert Nevitt and Christine (Dickson) S.; m. Deborah Wilder, July 2, 1961; children—Craig, Colin, Nathan. B.A. cum laude, Stanford U., 1962; M.A., U. Calif.-Berkeley, 1966, Ph.D., 1970. Asst. prof. sociology U. Santa Clara (Calif.), 1969-71, Stockton State Coll., Pomona, N.J., 1971-76; asst. to pres. Wright Inst., Berkeley, 1976-79; pres. Montaigne, Inc., Orinda, Calif., 1979—; cons. research assessment AT&T; researcher experiential sociology. NIMH trainee, 1964-68; U. Calif.-Berkeley grad. research grantee, 1967-68; San Francisco Found. Research grantee, 1977-78. Mem. Am. Sociol. Assn., Action Methods Inst. Author: Making It in Graduate School, 1975. Home and Office: 99 El Toyonal St Orinda CA 94563

SANGSTER, JAMES BERNARD, vocational education administrator; b. Toronto, Ont., Can., June 16, 1929; s. James Frederick and Delia Irene (Mountenay) S.; m. Margaret Ann McKelvy, Sept. 15, 1955; children—Mary Kathryn, Patricia Ann; m. 2d, Sarah Evlyn Dorkings, Feb. 9, 1968; 1 stepson, Eric T. Hurford. B.Vocat.Edn., Calif. State U.-Los Angeles, 1973; M.S. in Edn., Calif. State U.-Fullerton, 1976. Cert. tchr., Ont., Calif. Service mgr. Wood Alexander Ltd. div. Gamble-Skogmo, Inc., Hamilton, Can., 1947-62; owner TV & Appliance Service, Toronto, 1962-63; adult edn. tchr. electronics Glendale High Sch., Hamilton, 1963-67; adult edn. tchr. electronics-refrigeration Downey (Calif.) Sr. High Sch., 1967-71; vocat. supr. S.E. Los Angeles Regional Occupational Program, Norwalk, Calif., 1971-72, supt., dir., 1972-76; coordinator Riverside County (Calif.) Supt. Schs. Regional Occupational Program, 1976—; cons. indsl. arts Calif. Dept. Edn., 1971, Cerritos Coll., 1976. Mem. vocat. edn. adv. com. Riverside Unified Sch. Dist., 1982. Mem. So. Calif. Council Vocat. Edn. Adminstrs., Calif. Assn. Vocat. Edn., Calif. Assn. Regional Occupational Coordinator Programs (dir. 1982—, chpt. pres. 1982—), Am. Vocat. Assn. Democrat. Home: 21443 Running River Ct Diamond Bar CA 91765 Office: Riverside County Supt Schs Regional Occupational Program 3939 13th St Riverside CA 92502

SANGUINETI, VITTORIO ENRICO, business executive; b. Sumi, Russia, Jan. 25, 1914; s. Felix and Marie (Vidovich) S.; m. Gilda de Sanctis, Feb. 4, 1914; children—Claudia Victoria, Carla Romana. Grad. Italian Lycée, Istanbul, 1931; Ph.D. in Econs., U. Rome, 1935. Mem. Italian Fgn. Trade Inst., 1937-79; sr. Italian comml. attaché, New Orleans and Houston, 1951-55, Detroit, 1970-71, Los Angeles, 1955-82; pres. Internat. Tech. Devel., Inc., Los Angeles, 1979—; dir. Indsl. Devel. Bd. Italian S.; banking cons. Internat. assoc. Stanford Research Inst.; instr. UCLA Grad. Sch. Mgmt., 1964-66. Served to lt. Italian Army, 1941-42. Decorated Mil. Cross Italy; knight comdr. Order of Merit (Italy); named Man of Yr. (Olafson award) Los Angeles C. of C., 1974. Mem. European Trade Promotional Orgns. (pres. 1969-70). Roman Catholic. Author: Poèmes Français de Poètes Etrangers (Académie française), 1933; The Industrial Development of Turkey Under Kamal Ataturk, 1936; contbr. articles to econ. revs. Home: 350 S Glenroy Ave Los Angeles CA 90049 Office: 1801 Century Park E Suite 1150 Los Angeles CA 90067

SANGUINETTI, EUGENE F., museum adminstr.; b. Yuma, Ariz., May 12, 1917; s. Eugene F. and Lilah B. (Balsz) S.; B.A., U. Santa Clara, 1939, postgrad. U. Ariz., 1960-62, children by previous marriage—Leslie, Gregory. Instr. art history U. Ariz., 1960-64; dir. Tucson Mus. and Art Center, 1964-67, Utah Mus. Fine Arts, Salt Lake City, 1967—; adj. prof. art history U. Utah, 1967—; chmn. adv. com. Salt Lake City Bicentennial Center for Arts; mem. Salt Lake City C. of C. Arts Council. Served with USAAF, 1942-44, M.I., U.S. Army, 1944-46. Mem. Am. Assn. Museums, Western Assn. Art Museums, Coll. Art Assn. Am., Am. Fedn. Arts. Contbr. articles to mus. exhbn. catalogs. Home: 851 E 5th St Salt Lake City UT 84102 Office: 101 AAC U Utah Salt Lake City UT 84112*

SANKS, ROBERT LELAND, environ. engr., educator; b. Pomona., Calif., Feb. 19, 1916; s. John B. and Nellie G. (Church) S.; B.S. in Civil Engring., U. Calif.-Berkeley, 1940, Ph.D. in San. Engring., 1965; M.S. in Structural Engring., Iowa State U., 1949; m. Mary Louise Clement, May 16, 1946; children—Margaret Nadine, John Clement. Draftsman, City of La Habra (Calif.), 1940; asst. engr. Alex Morrison, cons. engr., Fullerton, Calif., 1941; jr. engr. U.S. Army Engrs., Los Angeles, 1941-42; asst. research engr. dept. civil engring. U. Calif.-Berkeley, 1942-45, NSF fellow, 1961-63, assoc. specialist San. Engring. Research Lab., 1963-65, research engr., summer, 1966; structural engr. The Austin Co., Oakland, Calif., 1945-46; instr. dept. civil engring. U. Utah, Salt Lake City, 1946-49, asst. prof., 1949-55, assoc. prof., 1955-58; structural engr. The Lang Co., Salt Lake City, summer, 1950; instrument man Patti MacDonald Co., Anchorage, summer, 1951; checker Western Steel Co., Salt Lake City, summer 1952; structural engr. Moran, Proctor, Meuser and Rutledge, N.Y.C., summer 1953; structural engr. F.C. Torkelson Co., Salt Lake City, summer, 1955; soils engr. R.L. Sloane & Assocs., Salt Lake City, summer, 1956; prof., chmn. dept. civil engring. Gonzaga U., Spokane, Wash., 1958-61; prof. dept. civil engring./engring. mechanics Mont. State U., Bozeman, 1966-82, prof. emeritus, 1982—; vis. prof. U. Tex., Austin, 1974-75; part-time sr. engr. Christian, Spring, Sielbach & Assos., Billings, Mont., 1978—; part-time cons. engr., 1945—. Registered profl. engr., Mont.; diplomate Am. Acad. Environ. Engrs. Fellow ASCE (chmn. local qualifications com. intermountain sect. 1950-56, pres. intermountain sect. 1957-58); mem. Am. Water Works Assn. (George Warren Fuller award, 1976, pres. Mont. sect. 1981-82), Mont. Water Pollution Control Fedn., Sigma Xi, Chi Epsilon. Clubs: Elks, Rotary, Camera of Bozeman (pres. 1980-81). Author: Statically Indeterminate Structural Analysis, 1961; (with Takashi Asano) Land Treatment and Disposal of Municipal and Industrial Wastewaters, 1976; Water Treatment Plant Design for the Practicing Engineer, 1978; (with Carl W. Reh and A. Amirtharajah) Conf. Proc. Pumping Sta. Design for the Practicing Engr., 1981; contbr. articles on civil engring. to profl. publs. Home: 411 W Dickerson St Bozeman MT 59715 Office: Dept Civil Engring Montana State Univ MT 59717

SANNWALD, WILLIAM WALTER, librarian; b. Chgo., Sept. 12, 1940; s. William Frederick and Irene Virginia (Stanish) S.; B.A., Beloit Coll., 1963; M.A. in L.S., Rosary Coll., 1966; M.B.A., Loyola U., Chgo., 1974; m. Mary G. Blomberg, May 22, 1965; children—Sara Ann, William Howard. Mktg. mgr. Xerox Univ. Microfilms, Ann Arbor, Mich., 1972-75; asso. dir. Detroit Public Library, 1975-77; dir. Ventura County Library, Ventura, Calif., 1977-79, San Diego Public Library, 1979—; vis. instr. mktg. San Diego State U., 1979—, Nat. U., 1979—. H.W. Wilson fellow, 1965-66. Mem- ALA, Calif. Library Assn., Calif. Library Assn. for Systems and Services (pres. congress members 1980), UN Assn., Beta Phi Mu. Roman Catholic. Home: 3538 Paseo Salamoner La Mesa CA 92041 Office: City Adminstrn Bldg 202 C St Mail Sta 9B San Diego CA 92101

SANSONE, KATHLEEN OLDFIELD, home economics educator; b. Vancouver, B.C., Can., Apr. 9, 1949; came to U.S., 1949, naturalized, 1966; s. James Edmund and Mildred Evelyn (Atkinson) Oldfield; m. Stephen William Sansone, Aug. 11, 1973; children—Andrew, Brady. B.Home Econs. Edn., Oreg. State U., Corvallis, 1971, M.Home Econs., 1976. Cert. tchr., Oreg. Tchr. home econs. West Albany High Sch., Albany, Oreg., 1971-75, Whiteaker Jr. High Sch., Salem, Oreg., 1975, Sprague High Mch., Salem, 1975—; chmn. Child Care Adv. Council Salem Pub. Schs., 1982-83. Vol., Salem Childbirth Edn. Assn. Mem. Am. Home Econs. Assn., Oreg. Home Econs. Assn., Tchrs. Home Econs. Oreg., Home Econs. Edn. Assn., Phi Beta Phi. Democrat. Episcopalian. Office: 2373 Kubler Rd S Salem OR 97302

SANTLEY, THOMAS SAWYER, ins. co. exec.; b. Los Angeles, Sept. 4, 1935; s. Joseph Mansfield and Ivy Winifred (Sawyer) S.; B.A., U. So. Calif., 1957, M.B.A., 1966; m. Patricia Caughlan, Aug. 15, 1959; children—Michael, Susan. Mgmt. trainee Union Bank, Los Angeles, 1959-60, advt. and pub. relations mgr., 1960-62; asst. v.p. advt. and pub. relations Western Fed. Savs. & Loan Assn., Los Angeles, 1962-66; account exec. Bowes Co., advt. and public relations, Los Angeles, 1966-67; asst. v.p. communications Pacific Mut. Life Ins. Co., Newport Beach, Calif., 1967-76, asst. v.p. public relations, 1976-79, 2d v.p. public relations, 1979—; dir. Commuter Computer Inc., Orangewood. Chmn. public relations adv. council U. Calif., Irvine, 1978; pres. Friends of U. Calif., Irvine, 1980-83; pres. Newport Center Assn., 1977-78; vice chmn. council of support orgns. U. So. Calif., 1973-76, pres. Commerce Assos., 1972-73; mem. U. So. Calif. Assos.; chmn. communications div. United Way Orange County, 1973-75; pres. Orange County Community Relations Council, 1979; trustee Mardan Found. for Ednl. Therapy Inc.; mem. adv. council Orange County Transit Dist.; bd. dirs. Californians for Housing. Served to lt. USNR, 1957-59. Mem. Pub. Relations Soc. Am. (accredited, chpt. pres. 1981), U. So. Calif. Gen. Alumni Assn. (gov. 1972-75), Skull and Dagger, Kappa Alpha. Republican. Episcopalian. Clubs: San Marino City; Publicity (Los Angeles). Office: 700 Newport Center Dr Newport Beach CA 92660

SAPERSTEIN, DAVID DORN, physical chemist; b. N.Y.C., June 30, 1946; s. Charles Levy and Freda (Dornbush) S.; m. Bernelle Hope Welch, Feb. 28, 1976; 1 son, Robert Elliot. B.A. in Chemistry, Johns Hopkins U., 1967; Ph.D. in Phys. Chemistry, NYU, 1973. Sr. research chemist Merck, Sharp and Dohme Research Labs., Rahway, N.J., 1973-77, research fellow, 1977-81; applications scientist IBM Instruments, San Jose, Calif., 1981—. Mem. Am. Chem. Soc., AAAS, Western Spectroscopy Assn. (exec. com., sec.), Soc. for Applied Spectroscopy. Contbr. articles to profl. jours; patentee in field; developed concepts in spectroscopy. Home: 648 Matsonia Dr Foster City CA 94404 Office: 40 W Brokaw Rd San Jose CA 95110

SAPHIER, MICHAEL DONALD, lawyer; b. Los Angeles, Mar. 3, 1942; s. James L. and Arna (Finston) S.; m. Dona L. Heller, Jan. 30, 1981; children—Carol, Patricia. A.B., U., Calif.-Berkeley 1965; J.D., U. Mich., 1968; LL.M., UCLA 1970. Bar: D.C. 1968, Calif. 1970. Ptnr. Memel, Jacobs, Pierno & Gersh, Los Angeles, 1975—; lectr. in field. Bd. dirs. Los Angeles Coastal Cities unit Am. Cancer Soc., 1982—. Mem. Beverly Hills Bar Assn., Am. Soc. Hosp. Attys., Am. Soc. Law and Medicine, Calif. Soc. Healthcare Attys., ABA, Healthcare Fin. Mgmt. Assn., Nat. Health Lawyers Assn. Contbr. articles to profl. jours. Office: 1801 Century Park E Suite 2500 Los Angeles CA 90067

SAPIRO, DENIS, chemical security systems exec.; b. San Francisco, Jan. 17, 1949; s. Jerome and Mary Elizabeth (Calais) S.; B.S., St. Mary's Coll., Moraga, Calif., 1970, M.B.A., 1978; tchr. cert., U. San Francisco, 1971; marine fire fighting tng. Tex. A&M U., 1981. Chief chemist Michel & Pelton Co., Emeryville, Calif., 1968-74; sci. tchr. Livermore Valley (Calif.) Unified Sch. Dist., 1971-73; cons. Security Eye Patrol, Livermore, 1973-74; chemist Occidental Chem. Co., Lathrop, Calif., 1974-78; vessel safety engr. SeaLand Service Inc., Seattle, 1978-81; corp. safety mgr. Chem-Nuclear Systems Inc., 1981-82; site dir. Chem-Security Systems Inc., Arlington, Oreg., 1982-83, gen. mgr., 1983—. Scoutmaster local Boy Scouts Am., 1972, instl. rep., 1973-73, 78-79. Mem. Am. Chem. Soc., Am. Mgmt. Assn., Am. Soc. Safety Engrs. Republican. Roman Catholic. Club: Kiwanis (v.p., dir. Livermore chpt. 1973-74, v.p. W. Seattle chpt. 1979-80, pres. 1980-81, recipient Diamond Growth award). Editor safety manual; developer organic soap and lotion. PO Box 484 Arlington OR 97812 Office: CSSI Star Route Arlington OR 97812-9709

SARAF, DILIP GOVIND, electronics engineer; b. Belgaum, India, Nov. 10, 1942; s. Govind Vithal and Indira Laxman (Divekar) S.; m. Mary Lou Arnold, July 25, 1970; 1 son, Rajesh Dilip. B. Tech with honors, Indian Inst. Tech., Bombay, 1965; M.S.E.E., Stanford U., 1969. Sr. mgmt. trainee Delhi Cloth and Gen. Mills Co. (India), 1965-68; sr. research engr. SRI Internat., Menlo Park, Calif., 1969-78; project dir. Kaiser Electronics, San Jose, Calif., 1978—; cons. teaching U. Santa Clara (Calif.), 1972, 73. Mem. IEEE, Soc. Am. Inventors. Contbr. articles to profl jours. Patentee in field. Home: 98 Euclid Ave Atherton CA 94025 Office: 2701 Orchard Pkwy San Jose CA 94131

SARAFIAN, ARMEN, univ. pres.; b. Van Nuys, Calif., Mar. 5, 1920; s. Kevork A. and Lucy (Gazarian) S.; B.A. magna cum laude (Scholar) La Verne Coll., 1940, LL.D., 1967; M.A. (Scholar), Claremont Grad. U., 1947; Ph.D., U. So. Calif., 1964; children—Winston, Norman, Joy. Stockroom mgr. S.H. Kress Co., Pomona, Calif., 1940-42; tchr. elementary sch., Riverside and Kern County, Calif., 1940-43; tchr., chmn. English dept. Banning (Calif.) Union High Sch., 1945-47; tchr. Pasadena (Calif.) Jr. Coll. Dist., 1947-51; coordinator secondary and jr. coll. edn. Pasadena City Schs., 1951-59; adminstrv. dean for instrn. Pasadena City Coll., 1959-65; pres. Pasadena City Coll., also supt. Pasadena Area Community Coll. Dist., 1965-76; pres. emeritus Pasadena City Coll., 1976—; pres. La Verne (Calif.) Coll., also U. La Verne, 1976—; adj. prof. higher edn. adminstrn. U. So. Calif., 1967-78. Pres. Calif. Conservation Council, 1966-68; trustee La Verne Coll., 1969-76; mem. mgmt. team U. Alaska Statewide System, 1977-78; founder, adult adviser Pasadena Area Youth Council; founder Am. Armenian Internat. Coll. Bd., 1972. Recipient Conservation Merit award Calif. Conservation Council, 1964; Distinguished Service award Omicron Mu Delta, 1965; Service award U. So. Calif., 1972; Others award Salvation Army, 1975; Arthur Noble Gold Medal award Pasadena City Bd. Dirs., 1976. Mem. Pasadena Area Sch. Trustees Assn. (founder), La Verne C. of C. (pres. 1978), Pasadena C. of C. (v.p. 1972, hon. life mem.), Native Sons of Golden West, Pasadena Hist. Soc. Clubs: Kiwanis (v.p. 1971) (Pasadena); Oneonta, Univ. Home: 1912 1/2 Bluebird Rd Glendora CA 91740 Office: 1950 3d St La Verne CA 91750

SARAVO, ANNE COBBLE, psychologist, researcher; b. Atlanta, Feb. 23, 1938; d. William Edwin and Iris Benny (Norman) Cobble; m. James V. Saravo, June 13, 1958; children—Stacy Anne Saravo Karr, Lisa Ames. B.A., Tex. Technol. U., 1959; M.S., U. Mass., 1964, Ph.D., 1965. Lic. sch. psychologist, psychologist, Calif. USPHS postdoctoral fellow, research assoc. Fels Research Inst., Yellow Springs, Ohio, 1966-69; assoc. prof. Antioch Coll., 1967-69; mem. teaching faculty Antelope Valley Coll., 1969-70, psychologist, cons. Hosp. Med. Ctr., 1973-76; cons. Wessex Guidance, Winchester, Eng., 1971-73; psychologist S.E. Thames Regional Health Authority, London, 1977-80; psychologist Los Angeles County/U. So. Calif. Med. Ctr., 1980-81; clin. psychologist Superior Ct. Evaluation and Guidance Unit, Orange County, Calif., 1981—; pvt. practice clin. child psychology, Los Alamitos, Calif. Mem. AAUW, Rossmoor Homeowners Assn. Mem. Am. Psychol. Assn., Brit. Psychol. Soc., Calif. Psychol. Soc. Contbr. articles on children's learning to profl. jours., 1967-71; editorial cons. Jour. Exptl. Child Psychology, 1976. Office: 301 City Dr S Orange CA 92668

SARDINA, MARTA ISABEL, engineer; b. La Habana, Cuba, June 28, 1952; d. Alberto and Guadalupe (Zuniga) Sardina. B.A. in Math., UCLA, 1977; M.S. in Program Mgmt., West Coast U., Los Angeles, 1981. Sr. tracking system analyst Bendix Field Engring. Corp., Pasadena, Calif., 1978-81, project leader for performance analysis group spacecraft Doppler & Angle prediction project, 1981-82; sr. engr. Convair div. Gen. Dynamics, San Diego, 1982—. Mem. Nat. Assn. Female Execs., Inc.

SARGENT, DIANA RHEA, bookkeeper; b. Cheyenne, Wyo., Feb. 20, 1939; d. Clarence and Edith (de Castro) Hayes; grad. high sch.; m. Charles Sargent, Apr. 17, 1975; children—Rene A. Coburn, Rochelle A. Riddle, Weldy, Clayton R. Weldy, Christopher J.; stepchildren—Laurie E. Sargent, Leslie E. Sargent. IBM proof operator Bank Am., Stockton, Calif., 1956-58, gen. ledger bookkeeper, Modesto, Calif., 1963-66; office mgr., head bookkeeper Central Drug Store, Modesto, 1966-76; pres. Sargent & Sargent, Modesto, 1976—. Bd. dirs. Haven Stanislaus Women's Refuge Center; mem. Stanislaus County Commn. on Women, Stanislaus County Women's Resource Ctr. Mem. NOW, San Francisco Mus. Soc., Nat. Soc. Public Accts., Modesto C. of C., Merced Accts. Soc. Republican. Roman Catholic. Office: 1709 Tully Rd Modesto CA 95350

SARGENT, MCNEIL J. (JEAN BRALEY), printmaker, painter; b. Wilkesboro, N.C., Nov. 15, 1924; d. Sargent Duffield and Agnes (McNeil) Absher; m. Bill Braley, 1946 (div.); 1 dau., Robin Gomez. B.A., U. Calif.-San Diego, 1977, student Atalier 17, Paris, 1980-81, NYU, 1982. Comml. illustrator, N.Y.C., 1956-66, Washington, 1966-69; art instr. Corcoran Mus., Washington, 1970, Mira Costa Coll., Oceanside, Calif., 1979-81, Community Coll., San Diego, 1971—; one person shows: Yogesh Gallery, Bombay, India, 1982, Spectrum Gallery, San Diego, 1981, Foxhall Gallery, Washington, 1980, Prestige Gallery, Boston, 1979, Riverside (Calif.) Mus., 1976; group shows: Long Beach Mus., 1980, San Diego Mus., 1976, 77, 78, Palace of Fine Arts, Mexico City, 1977, Smithsonian Inst., Washington, 1969; represented in numerous corp. and pvt. collections including: Nat. Biblioteque, Paris, Nat. Archives, Washington, N.Z. Embassy, Washington. Bd. docents San Diego Mus., 1972-76; juror for prints, So. Calif. EXPO 1981; cons. Calif. Art Commn., 1975. Recipient numerous art awards. Mem. Atalier for Calif. Printmakers (bd. dirs. 1982), Calif. Printmakers (founder), Artists Equity Assn. San Diego (founder, 1st pres.). Works featured in popular mags. Home: 519 Stratford Ct Del Mar CA 92014 Office: PO Box 597 La Jolla CA 92038

SARGENT, WARREN NICHOLS, JR., consulting company executive; b. New London, Conn., Sept. 17, 1946; s. Warren Nichols and Janice Caroyln (Warner) S.; B.S.M.E., U. Conn., 1968, M.S., 1970, M.B.A., 1971; M.A., U. Tex., Dallas, 1980. Systems analyst, programmer U. Conn., 1965-71, City of Hartford (Conn.), 1968-71; instr. Univ. Computing Co., Arlington, Tex., 1973, cons., Nashville, 1973-74, mgr. bus. planning, Dallas, 1974-75, bus. devel., 1975-77; gen. mgr. Bonanza Internat., Houston, 1977, dir. franchising, Dallas, 1978; dir. computer services programs INPUT, Palo Alto, Calif., 1979-81; pres. The Strategist, Visalia, Calif., 1981—. Served to lt. USAF, 1971-73. Decorated D.S.M. Mem. Computer Industry Guide, Share, Adapso, Beta Gamma Sigma. Clubs: Sports, Internat. Mgmt. Address: PO Box 81 Visalia CA 93279

SARGENT, WAYNE CUMMINGS, newspaper editor; b. Bklyn., Feb. 7, 1925; student Stanford U., 1946-48; m. Marybeth Derham Street, Sept. 4, 1955. Polit. reporter United Press Internat., 1948-55, mgr. so. div., 1960-64, v.p. mktg., N.Y.C., 1964-72; pub. Nashville Banner, 1972-78; editor San Bernardino (Calif.) Sun, 1978—. Served with U.S. Air Force and U.S. Army. World War II. Office: Sun Co 399 D St San Bernardino CA 92401*

SARLAT, GLADYS, public relations company executive; b. Elizabeth, N.J., July 22, 1923; d. Max and Dora (Levin) S. B.S., U. Wash., 1946. Asst., Kay Sullivan Assn., N.Y.C., 1949-50; fashion dir. Warsaw & Co., N.Y.C., 1950-54; asst. fashion coordinator Emporium Dept. Store, San Francisco, 1955-56; asst. prodn. mgr. Cunningham & Walsh Advt., San Francisco, 1958-59; v.p., pub. relations dir. Harwood Advt. Inc., Tucson and Phoenix, 1959-68; v.p., dir. Waller & Sarlat Advt. Inc., Tucson, 1968-69; pres. Gladys Sarlat Pub. Relations, Inc., Tucson, 1970—. Active Tucson Tomorrow, 1980—; mem. adv. com. Downtown Devel. Corp., 1979—. Named Woman of Year for Bus., Ariz. Daily Star, 1963; recipient Lulu award Los Angeles Women in Advt., 1962. Mem. Pub. Relations Soc. Am. (past bd. mem., counselors acad.), Fashion Group, Tucson Met. C. of C. (v.p., dir. 1976—), Tucson Trade Bur. (dir. 1977-80). Republican. Jewish. Club: Old Pueblo (Tucson). Home: 5530 N Camino Arenosa Tucson AZ 85718 Office: 120 W Broadway Gladys Sarlat Pub Relations Inc Suite 411 Tucson AZ 85701

SARSFIELD, GEORGE P., lawyer; b. Vancouver, B.C., Can., Jan. 14, 1913 (parents Am. citizens); s. John M. and Margaret (LaValle) S.; B.A., J.D., U. Mont., 1950; m. Margeret Davis, May 23, 1942. Blk., laborer, miner, 1930-41; admitted to Mont. bar, 1950, since practiced in Butte. Past pres. Butte YMCA. Republican nominee Congress, 1st dist. Mont., 1960. Chmn. exec. bd. Mont. Coll. Mineral Sci. and Tech., 1968-71; chmn. bd. trustees U. Mont. Devel. Fund, 1967-70; adv. bd. Salvation Army, 1952—. Served from pvt. to capt. U.S. Army, 1941-46. Recipient Disting. Service award U. Mont., 1971, Pantzer award, 1975. Mem. Am., Mont. (past v.p.) bar assns., Am. Trial Lawyers Assn., U. Mont. Alumni Assn. (pres. 1964, chmn. bd. 1964-66), Mont. State Golf Assn. (past pres.), U.S. Golf Assn. (mem. sectional affairs com. 1968—), Phi Delta Phi, Alpha Kappa Psi, Phi Delta Theta. Clubs: Rotary (past local pres.; dist. gov. 1963-64, chmn. internat. constn. and by-laws com. 1969-70, internat. dir. 1973-75, internat. 1st v.p. 1974-75). Club: Butte Country (past pres.). Former Mont. open golf champion; Mont. amateur golf champion, 4 years. Home: 2700 Floral Blvd Butte MT 59701 Office: Mayer Bldg Butte MT 59701

SARTORI, JOHN ANTHONY, mfg. co. exec.; b. Los Angeles, Aug. 28, 1942; s. Attillo Joseph and Grace (Howard) S.; B.S.I.E., San Jose State Coll., 1964; M.S.I.E., B.S. in Math., U. So. Calif., 1968; m. Carol Lou Griffith, Mar. 28, 1975; children—Jon, Morgan. Chief indsl. engr. Hehr Mfg. Co., Los Angeles, 1964-67; project engr. Pharmaseal Labs., Irwindale, Calif., 1968; mfg. services mgr. Indsl. Electronic Engrs., Van Nuys, Calif., 1968-69; asst. dir. ops. Resdel Engring. Corp., Arcadia, Calif., 1969-71; dir. tech. products and mfg. services div. Ajax Hardware Corp., Industry, Calif., 1971-77; gen. mgr. Western Wheel Co., La Palma, Calif., 1977; plant mgr. Audio Magnetics Corp., Irvine, Calif., 1977-78; plant mgr. Kwikset Lock div. Emhart Corp., Anaheim, Calif., 1978-79; dir. ops. Elpower Corp. of Eldon, Ind., Santa Ana, Calif., 1979-81; pres. Sarco Internat., Newport Beach, Calif., 1981—. Registered profl. engr., Calif. Mem. Am. Inst. Indsl. Engrs., Am. Def. Preparedness Assn., Alpha Phi Mu. Home: 9482 Florence Circle Villa Park CA 92667

SARUK, SHELDON, psychologist; b. Chgo., Aug. 17, 1934; s. Abe and May (Thiess) S.; B.A. cum laude, Calif. State U., Northridge, 1971; M.A., Pepperdine U., 1972; Ph.D., U.S. Internat. U., 1974; children—Michael, Michele. Clin. psychology intern, VA Hosp., Sepulveda, Calif., 1973-74; clin. supr. North Hollywood (Calif.) Free Clinic, 1974-76; group therapist Olive View Med. Center/Calif. State U. Northridge child abuse program, Van Nuys, 1974-76; chief psychol. cons. Bay Harbor Rehab. Center chronic pain control program, 1977-78; clin. staff psychologist So. Recepition Center and Clinic, Norwalk, Calif., 1975-77; pvt. practice psychotherapy, Torrance, Calif., 1977—; cons. Calif. Youth Authority, 1977—, Torrance Meml. Hosp., 1979—, South Bay Human Resources Center, 1979—, Bay Harbor Hosp., 1977—; affiliate staff Del Amo Hosp.; instr. Los Angeles Pierce Coll., Woodland Hills, 1974-78, Los Angeles Valley Coll., Van Nuys, 1974-76. Mem. So. Calif. Psychology and Law Interest Group, Am. Psychol. Assn. Democrat. Jewish. Office: 3250 Lomita Blvd Torrance CA 90505

SARVER, MORTON DAVID, optometrist, consultant, educator; b. Oakland, Calif., May 9, 1922; s. Ysiel Dave and Eva (Ensler) S.; m. Anita Merle Donner, Aug. 7, 1943; children—Donald S., Howard D., Larry A. A.A., U. Calif., 1942, B.S. with honors, 1947, M.S. in Physiol. Optics, 1962. Dic. optometrist; cert. profl. engr., Ohio State U. Practice optometry, Oakland, 1947-60, part-time practice, 1960-72; ptnr. optometry practice, Oakland, 1972—; asst. clin. prof. optometry U. Calif.-Berkeley Sch. Optometry, 1962-68, assoc. clin. prof., 1968-72, clin. prof., 1972-74, prof., 1974—; adj. prof. ophthalmology dept. Pacific Med. Ctr., San Francisco, 1974—; cons. contact lenses, 1972—; contact lens design engr., 1978—. Served with U.S. Army, 1942-44; to 2d lt. C.E., U.S. Army. Named Alumnus of Yr., Optometry Alumni Assn. U. Calif., 1964; Optometrist of Yr., Alameda and Contra Costa County Optometric Soc., 1969; Bausch & Lomb Research grantee, 1976-83. Mem. Am. Optometric Assn., Am. Acad. Optometry, Internat. Soc. Contact Lens Research. Home: 272 Donald Dr Moraga CA 94618 Office: 5321 Coll Ave Oakland CA 94618

SARVER-SCHULTZ, SHARON MARIE, accountant; b. Wapato, Wash., May 17, 1942; d. Roy Clifton and Mila Ann (Logan) Sarver; m. Gerald E. Schultz, July 12, 1975; children—Jeffrey, Rebecca, Donald, Jerry. Student Edison Tech. Sch., 1960-63, Data Control Systems, 1964-65, Ventura Coll., 1966-67, Bellevue Community Coll., 1969-71, U. Wash., 1975; Emergency Med. Technician cert., 1974; Acct., Rochester Electronics, Redmond, Wash., 1972, Adby Industries, Seattle, 1973, Koenigsberg, Brown, Sin-Seimer, Stone & Meltzer, Seattle, 1975; bus. mgr. Community Psychiat. Centers, Kirkland, Wash., 1976; acct., owner Gen. Office Services, Redmond, and Woodinville, Wash., 1977—; owner, operator Shares' Constrn., gen. contractors, 1980—. Bd. dirs. Lower Snoqualmie Valley Sch. Bd., 1974-78, Redmond Miss Pageant, 1977-78. Mem. Nat. Assn. Accountants, Redmond C. of C. (dir.), U.S. C. of C., Nat. Fedn. Ind. Businesses, Assn. Wash. Bus. Home: Office: 15965 NE 85th St Suite 200 Redmond WA 98052 also 14245 Wood-Duvall Rd Woodinville WA

SASAKI, GORDON HIROSHI, plastic surgeon, educator; b. Honolulu, July 27, 1942; s. Tsutomu and Carla Harumi (Mirikitani) S.; m. Joanne I., Dec. 28, 1969; children—Lindsay Yukiko, Matthew Thomas Nobuo. B.A., Pomona Coll., 1964; M.D., Yale U., 1968. Diplomate Am. Bd. Surgery, Am. Bd. Plastic and Reconstructive Surgery. Intern U. Oreg. Med. Ctr., 1968-69, resident in surgery, 1968-69; resident in plastic surgery, instr. in surgery Yale U., 1977-79; asst. prof. plastic surgery U. Tex. Southwestern Med. Sch., 1979-82; asst. prof. U. So. Calif., 1982—, dir. plastic surgery labs., 1982—, chief plastic surgery hand and micro vascular service, 1982—. Served with M.C., U.S. Army, 1970-72. Mem. AAAS, Am. Assn. Hand Surgery, Am. Burn Assn., AMA, Assn. Acad. Surgery, Plastic Surgery Research Council, N.Y. Acad. Sci., Sigma Xi. Research in hemangiomas and steroid receptors, prostaglandins and microcirculation. Office: 1245 Wilshire Blvd Suite 403 Los Angeles CA 90017

SASAKI, Y(ASUNAGA) TITO, construction management company executive b. Tokyo, Feb. 6, 1938; s. Yoshinaga and Chiyoko S.; came to U.S., 1967, naturalized, 1983; B.S. in Mech. Engring., Chiba (Japan) U., 1959; Des RCA in Indsl. Design, Royal Coll. Art, London, 1961; M.S. in City Planning, Athens (Greece) Tech. Inst., 1964; m. Janet Louise Cline, June 27, 1963; 1 dau., Heather N. Chief designer Aires Camer Industry Co., Tokyo, 1958-59; tech. officer London County Council, 1961-62; researcher Athens Center Ekistics, 1964-66; sr. researcher Battelle Inst., Geneva, 1966-68; project engr. Marin County (Calif.) Transit Dist., 1968-69; chief planning and research Golden Gate Bridge Dist., San Francisco, 1969-74; pres. Visio Internat., Inc., San Francisco, 1974—; chmn. steering com. Kawada Industries, Inc., Tokyo, 1974-81; chief exec. officer, chief fin. officer Quantum Mechanics Corp., 1981—; mem. U.S. Senatorial Bus. Adv. Bd. Mem. Am. Inst. Cert. Planners, World Soc. Ekistics, Brit. Soc. Long-Range Planning, Am. Vacuum Soc., Aircraft Owners and Pilots Assn. Roman Catholic. Author: Theory of Transportation Hierarchy, 1964. Home: 66 Marina Court Dr San Rafael CA 94901 Office: 360 Post St San Francisco CA 94108

SASS, RICHARD GUY, mfg. co. exec.; b. Boston, Nov. 1, 1942; s. Clifton Hartman and Mildred Dora (Stewart) S.; B.A., Mich. State U., 1965; m. Jennifer Allen Bement, June 13, 1964; children—Gretchen Anne, Jeffrey Guy, Jason Stewart. Pres., The Mid-Central Co., Des Plaines, Ill., 1970-72; founder, partner Electric Cable Cons. & Design, Inc., Portland, Oreg., 1979—, Nat. Electric Gate Co., Elk Grove, Ill., 1974—, Nat. Electric Control Co., Elk Grove, 1972—; pres. Nat. Electric Cable, Portland, 1972—; dir. ITI, Portland. Mem. Am. Mgmt. Assn.—The Pres.'s Assn., Jaycees. Republican. Clubs: Multnomah Athletic, Ill. Athletic, Rotary. Home: 02000 SW Palatine Hill Rd Portland OR 97219 Office: 16566 SW 72nd St Portland OR 97223

SASSOON, VIDAL, hair stylist; b. London, Eng., Jan. 17, 1928; s. Nathan and Betty (Bellin) S.; ed. N.Y. U.; m. Beverly Adams, Feb. 16, 1967 (div. 1980); children—Catya, Elan, Eden, David. Founder, chmn. bd. Vidal Sassoon, Inc., beauty products and related mdse., beauty salons, N.Y.C., Beverly Hills, Chgo., San Francisco, Toronto, also schs. in London and Los Angeles; lectr. in field. Served with Palmach Israeli Army. Recipient award French Ministry of Culture; award for services rendered Harvard Bus. Sch.; Intercoiffure award Cartier, London, 1978; Hair Artists Internat. fellow. Clubs: Anabelle, Ambassadeurs, Claremont (London); Le Club (N.Y.C.). Author: Sorry I Kept You Waiting Madam (autobiography); A Year of Beauty and Health, 1976. Office: 2049 Century Park E Los Angeles CA 90067

SATHER, MARCUS JON, school counselor; b. Seattle, Oct. 13, 1950; s. Gilman Alexander and Anna Mae (Leikness) S. A.A., Skagit Valley Coll., 1970; B.S. in Psychology, U. Wash., 1973; M.Ed. in School Counseling, Western Wash. State Coll., 1977. Edn. Staff Assn. cert., 1977, 1979; Nat. Counselor cert., 1983. Asst. mgr. Southland Corp., Kansas City, Mo., 1974-75; tchr. Pre-Vocat. Tng. Ctr., Spokane, Wash., 1975-76; asst. tchr. Western Wash. State Coll., Bellingham, 1976-77; elem. sch. counselor, Quillayute Valley, S.D., 1978—, Forks, Wash., 1978—. Mem. Am. Personnel and Guidance Assn., Am. Sch. Counselors Assn., Wash. Counseling and Guidance Assn., Wash. Sch. Counselors Assn., (pres. 1982-83, govt. relations chmn. 1980-82, profl. standars, ethical practice com. 1980-82), Wash. Mental Health Counselors Assn., NEA, Wash. Edn. Assn., Alpha Tau Omega. Democrat. Office: Forks School District PO Box 60 Forks WA 98331

SATHRE, ROGER CURTIS, educational administrator; b. Rockford, Ill., June 23, 1930; s. H. Curtis and Florence R. Sathre; m. Juanita Wenstrom, Jan. 3, 1953; children—Connie, Judy, Nancy, Glenda, Roger. A.A., U. Minn., 1950, B.B.A., 1961, B.S., 1963; M.S., U. Idaho,

1972. Cert. secondary teaching. Salesman Eastman Kodak Stores, Mpls., 1950-62; instr. Lake Region Jr. Coll., Devils Lake, N.D., 1963-68; with Idaho Div. Vocat. Edn., Boise, 1968—, state supr. vocat. spl. needs programs, 1972—. Active Idaho Soap Box Derby Com., Boise Indian Guides. Served with U.S. Army, 1953-55. Edn. profession devel. grantee, U. Idaho, 1971; named Outstanding Local Pres., N.D. Jaycees, 1966. Mem. Am. Vocat. Assn., Idaho Vocat. Assn., Nat. Assn. Vocat. Edn. Spl. Needs Personnel (Disting. Service award 1981), Nat. Assn. Spl. Needs State Adminstrs. Contbr. chpt. to book. Home: 10680 Hollandale Dr Boise ID 83709 Office: 650 W State St LBJ Bldg Boise ID 83720

SATHRUM, CHARLES HERBERT, internat. energy cons. firm exec.; b. Louisville, Oct. 11, 1946; s. Eugene Henry and Dorothy MacElroy (Harrell) S.; B.S. in Physics, U. Minn., 1968; m. Cheryl Lee, Sept. 14, 1968. Tech. Russian translator dept. aero. engring. U. Minn., 1967-68; reactor physicist Prairie Island Nuclear Plant, No. States Power Co., Mpls., 1968-75; sr. engr. EDS Nuclear, Inc., san Francisco, 1975-77; project engr. Sargent & Lundy, Engrs., Chgo., 1977-79; Midwest regional mktg. mgr. Quadrex Corp., Campbell, Calif., 1979-81, acting mgr. computer engring. sales, 1981-82; v.p. mktg. and applications engring. INET Corp. Sunnyvale, Calif., 1982—. Registered profl. engr., Calif. Mem. Am. Nuclear Soc., Atomic Indsl. Forum, Am. inst. Physics, Inst. Nuclear Materials Mgmt., Am. Electric Assn. Office: INET Corp 536 Weddell Dr Sunnyvale CA 95086

SATO, AKIRA, architect; b. Nagoya, Japan, Nov. 16, 1933; s. Genhichiro and Kei S.; student Nagoya Poly. Inst., 1950-54; B.Arch., U. Oreg., 1968; m. Toshiko Matsunaga, Oct. 28, 1960; 1 child, Seiko. Project architect Nikken Setsukei, Architects and Engrs., Nagoya, Japan, 1954-62; asso. Robert Billsbrough Price, Fellow AIA, and Assos., Tacoma, 1968-73; partner in charge of design BJSS Architects and Planners, Olympia, Wash., 1973—. Winner prize internat. residential design competition, New Architecture mag., Japan, 1973; registered architect Wash., Oreg., Japan. Mem. AIA, Regional Urban Design Asst. Team (Com. of Olympia). Chief designer Thurston County Court House Complex, 1975, Olympia Tech. Community Coll., 1974, Clalam County Govtl. Complex, 1977, Virgil Adams Co. Office Bldg., Olympia, 1977 (letters of commendation from mayor and governor.). Home: 4128 Sunset Beach Dr Olympia WA 98502 Office: 320 W Bay Dr Olympia WA 98501

SATO, EUNICE NODA, mayor; b. Livingston, Calif., June 8, 1921; d. Bunsaku and Sawa (Maeda) Noda; m. Thomas T. Sato, Dec. 9, 1950; children—Charlotte P., Daniel R., Douglas R. A.A., Modesto Jr. Coll., 1941; B.A., Colo. State Coll. Edn., 1944; M.A., Columbia U., 1948. Tchr., Alpha, Mich., 1944-47; edn. missionary, Yokohama, Japan, 1948-51; mem. Long Beach (Calif.) City Council, 1975—, mayor, 1980—. Bd. dirs. Long Beach chpt. ARC, Goodwill Industries; trustee St. Mary's Hosp. Med. Center; adminstrv. bd. Silverado United Methodist Ch. Recipient Community Service award Long Beach Coordinating Council, 1969, Hon. Service award Calif. PTA, 1963; named Outstanding Laywoman of Yr., Long Beach Council Chs., 1976, Woman of Yr. Long Beach C. of C. State Women's Council, 1979, Mother of Yr., Silverado United Meth. Ch., 1973; hon. life mem. Nat. Congress PTAs, 1974. Mem. Calif. Elected Women for Edn. and Research, Calif. League Cities, U.S. Conf. of Mayors. Republican. Clubs: Virginia Country Internat. City (Long Beach.). Monthly contbr. to neighborhood publs. Office: 333 W Ocean Blvd Long Beach CA 90802

SATO, MILES MASAKAZE, technical service company engineering analyst; b. Honolulu, May 14, 1950; s. Seigi and Michi (Fujiwara) S., m. Miriam H. Nitta, Aug. 12, 1978; 1 son, Matthew T. A.B., Grinnell Coll., 1972; M.S. in Biostats., U. Hawaii, 1976, M.P.H., 1978. Research assoc. U. Hawaii Pacific Biomed. Research Ctr., Honolulu, 1973-75; data reduction analyst Kentron Internat., Inc., Honolulu, 1978—. Mem. Am. Statis. Assn., IEEE, IEEE Aerospace and Electronic Systems Soc., IEEE Computer Soc. Lutheran. Contbr. articles to profl. jours.

SATO, YOSH, electronic co. exec.; b. Newell, Calif., July 26, 1944; s. Jack Matsutaro and Yoshiko (Okamoto) S.; B.A. in Bus. and Industry, San Jose State U., 1968; m. Dorothy Kaku, Feb. 7, 1971; children Georgine, Cristine. Supr. prodn. control Peterbilt Motors Co., Newark, Calif., 1970-74; mgr. prodn. planning and control Quantor Corp., Mountain View, Calif., 1974-76; materials mgr. Applied Magnetics Co., Sunnyvale, Calif., 1976-77; material planning mgr. Datapoint Corp., Sunnyvale, 1977-78; material control mgr. Dysan Co., Santa Clara, Calif., 1978—. Served with U.S. Army, 1968-70. Mem. Am. Prodn. and Inventory Control Soc. (cert. in prodn. and inventory mgmt.). Democrat. Buddhist. Home: 2329 Oak Flat Rd San Jose CA 95131 Office: 5102 Patrick Henry Dr Santa Clara CA 95151

SATOH, YOSHIHARU, bank executive; b. Tokoyo, Nov. 18, 1928; s. Sotoji and Miyuki (Odake) S.; m. Ikuko, May 6, 1955; children—Kaoru, Keiichi. Law degree Tokoyo U., 1952. With Sumitomo Bank, Ltd., Japan, 1952; v.p., mgr. Sumitomo Bank of Calif., Sacramento, 1967-71, sr. v.p., mgr. San Francisco hdqrs. and internat. div., 1971-72; sr. v.p. Central Pacific Bank, Honolulu, 1972-74, exec. v.p., 1974-78, pres. chief exec. officer, 1978—. Active Japan-Am. Soc. Honolulu (trustee). Mem. Hawaii C. of C. (bd. dirs. 1980-83) Budhist. Clubs: Waialae Country, Honolulu Internat. Country, Pacific. Office: PO Box 3590 Honolulu HI 96811

SATRE, WENDELL JULIAN, utility exec.; b. Post Falls, Idaho, July 3, 1918; s. Julian J. and Myrtle A. (Clark) S.; B.E.E., U. Idaho, 1939, D.Sc. (hon.); m. Jessie E. Stewart, June 1, 1941; children—Janet Elizabeth, Clark Wendell, Jeanne Ellen Kanikeberg, Glen Walter. With Wash. Water Power Co., Spokane, 1939—, supt. prodn., maintenance and constrn., 1953-58, constrn. and maintenance mgr., 1958-63, exec. asst. to pres., 1963-64, asst. v.p., 1964-65, v.p., 1965, exec. v.p., 1965-71, pres., 1971-82, chmn. bd., 1975—, also dir.; pres., chmn. bd. Pacific NW Power Co.; pres., dir. Spokane Indsl. Park, Inc.; chmn. bd., chief exec. officer Wash. Irrigation & Devel. Co., Limestone Co., Inc., Devel. Assos., Inc., Water Power Improvement Co.; chmn. bd. NW Energy Services Co.; past trustee Fidelity Mut. Savs. Bank. Mem. adv. bd. to exec. council Inland Empire council Boy Scouts Am., 1965-82; bd. dirs. Inland Empire chpt. ARC, 1964-69, United Crusade Spokane County, 1965-67, Wash. State Council on Econ. Edn., 1973-80, 5th dist. United for Wash., 1977-80; bd. dirs., mem. exec. com. Spokane Unltd.; pres. Greater Spokane Music and Allied Arts Festival, 1967, Wash. Citizens Com. for Pub. Higher Edn., 1976—; past trustee Spokane Symphony Soc.; trustee Whitworth Coll., 1970-74; pres. WAMPUM, 1972-73, trustee, mem. exec. com., 1974—; mem. Spokane Little Hoover Commn., 1968-71; adv. bd. Wash. State U. Coll. Engring., 1972-80, U. Idaho Coll. Engring., 1972-82; mem. U. Idaho Found., 1976—, Greater Spokane Community Found., 1976—, Spokane Area Devel. Council, 1974-76; chmn. Gov.'s Adv. Council, 1974-80; mem. regional com. on banking policies and practices 13th Nat. Bank Region, 1975-76; past chmn. bd. dirs. Assn. Washington Bus.; mem. exec. com., former chmn. natural resources council; former co-chmn. Com. of 1000; mem. Wash. Gov.'s Council Econ. Advisors; mem. Wash. Energy Adv. Council. Served to lt. (j.g.) USNR, 1944-46. Named to U. Idaho Alumni Hall of Fame. Mem. Spokane C. of C. (trustee, v.p. 1972-74, exec. com. 1972-75, 78-80, chmn. 1981—), Am. (past dir., mem. exec. com.), Pacific Coast (past dir., past pres.) gas assns., NW Electric Light and Power Assn. (past pres., past dir.), Edison Electric Inst. (past dir.), Nat. Assn. Electric Cos. (past dir.) NAM (dir.), Assn. Wash. Gas Utilities (trustee, past pres.), Wash. Council for Internat. Trade (past v.p.), Western Environ. Trade Assn. Wash. (past dir., past 2d v.p.), Council for Washington's Future, Wash. State China Relations Council (past dir.), Navy League U.S., Sigma Tau. Presbyterian. Club: Rotary (Spokane). Home: West 39 33d Ave Spokane WA 99203 Office: East 1411 Mission Ave Spokane WA 99202

SATTIZAHN, SAHEDRAN, counseling psychologist, writer, educator; b. Petaluma, Calif., Oct. 17, 1951; d. Alexander Laurence and Eleanor Glades (Orr) Cunninghame. B.A. in Liberal Arts, San Jose State U., 1975; M.A. in Psychology, Sonoma State U., 1978; postgrad. Union Grad. Sch., 1980—. Research asst. Law Enforcement Tng., Research Assocs., Mountain View, Calif., 1974; paralegal research asst. Varian Assocs., Palo Alto, Calif., 1975; assoc. dir., tchr. Centre of Well-Being, Sebastopol, Calif., 1976; dir., writer Love Letter Press, Sebastopol, 1977—; counselor Pickett House, Santa Rosa, Calif., 1979-80; counseling intern Phobia Recovery Ctr., San Francisco, 1981; pvt. practice personalized tchr. psychology, women studies, Sebastopol, 1982—; acting v.p., sec. Inst. Clin. Philosophy, San Francisco, 1981—. Mem. Women for Nuclear Disarmament, 1982—; mem. Orgn. for Women, 1983—; mem. Nat. Coalition Democracy in Educ., 1982—; mem. United Neighbors in Action, 1982—; mem. Sonoma County Farmlands Group, 1981—. Named Outstanding Young Woman of Am., 1981. Mem. Assn. Transpersonal Psychology, Assn. Humanistic Psychology, Assn. for Advancement Clin. Philosophy, Nat. Council Geocosmic Research, Nat. Assn. Female Execs. Author: Love Letters: A Journal of Sharing (Vol. I-II), 1979; Journey within the One, 1975; in Search of God, 1975. Office: PO Box 996 Sebastopol CA 95472

SATTLER, JANIECE DONNA, sales executive; b. Avon, S.D., Jan. 28, 1932; d. Fred James and Fannie Grace (Burma) S.; student Colo. State U., 1965-66, City Coll., Seattle, 1979-80. Bookkeeper, King Lumber Co., Loveland, Colo., 1950-53; legal stenographer Seaman & Ball, Attys. at Law, Loveland, 1953-54; statis. clk. U.S. Bur. Reclamation, Loveland, 1955-64; sec. dept. radiology and radiation biology Colo. State U., Ft. Collins, 1964-67; asst. dir. Continuing Edn. Lab. Personnel, Wash./Alaxsa Regional Med. Program, Seattle, 1967-71; adminstrv. coordinator dept. pathology Providence Med. Center, Seattle, 1971-80, purchasing mgr., 1980-82; supr. sales Advanced Tech. Labs., Inc., Bellevue, Wash., 1983—. Mem. Nat. Writers Club. Republican. Author: A Practical Guide to Financial Management of the Clinical Laboratory, 1980; contbr. articles to various publs. Home: 1035 156th Ave NE #8 Bellevue WA 98007 Office: 14506 NE 20th Bellevue WA 98008

SAUER, HENRY JACK, educator; b. Portland, Oreg., Oct. 23, 1946; s. Henry Jack and Pauline Catherine (Rahn) S.; B.A., Wash. State U., 1970, M.Ed., 1981; m. Nancy Lee Lauber, July 25, 1970. Tchr., coach schs. in Wash., 1970—; learning mgr. experienced based career edn. Kennewick Sch. Dist., 1979-80, project mgr. CETA employer-edn. demonstration project, 1980-81, project dir. CETA employer-edn. project, 1981-82; asst. prin. Desert Hills Middle Sch., 1982—; cons. social studies. Active local United Way, Boy Scouts Am. Mem. Wash. Assn. Sch. Adminstrs., Assn. Supervision and Curriculum Devel., Phi Delta Kappa. Lutheran. Club: Kiwanis. Home: 2306 S Anderson Pl Kennewick WA 99336 Office: 6011 W 10th Pl Kennewick WA 99336

SAUGUES, EDMOND PIERRE, chemical company advertising executive, writer; b. N.Y.C., Apr. 11, 1934; s. Edmond Pierre and Andree (Moutier) S.; m. Sally Ann McManus, Apr. 20, 1963; 1 dau., Marcy M. B.A. in English, Northwestern U., 1956; postgrad. UCLA, 1965-68. Advt. mgr. br. store Barker Bros., Los Angeles, 1959-62; sales promotion specialist Gen. Electric, Los Angeles, 1963-64; advtg. mgr. Rexall Drug Co., Los Angeles, 1964-68; advt. mgr. Cooper's Lumber, Los Angeles, 1969-72; sales promotion mgr. Hyland Labs., Costa Mesa, Calif., 1973-78; advt. mgr. Am. Metal Products Co., Los Angeles, 1978-80; advt. mgr. Filon div. Sohio Chem. Co., Los Angeles, 1981—. League commr., coach, referee Am. Youth Soccer Orgn., Palos Verdes Estates, Calif. Served with U.S. Army, 1956-58. Republican. Roman Catholic. Contbr. articles to trade and consumer publs. Home: 28126 Peacock Ridge Dr Palos Verdes Peninsula CA 90274 Office: 12333 S Van Ness Hawthorne CA 90250

SAULS, FREDERICK INABINETTE, artist; b. Seattle, Mar. 22, 1934; s. Frederick Inabinette and Borghild Caroline (Zakarison) S., div., children—Karoline, Fritz. Student, Stanford U., 1951-57, also U. Paris, San Francisco Acad. Art, Calif. Coll. Arts and Crafts, Assoc. in art U. Calif.-Berkeley, 1960-65; vis. artist U. Ky., 1966-68; asst. prof. U. Minn., 1969-70, U. Calif.-Santa Cruz, 1972-73; one-man shows: U. Ky., 1968, La Tortue Gallery, Santa Monica, Calif., 1972; group shows: travelling exhibit internat. art UNESCO; works represented in permanent collections Skopje (Yugoslavia) Mus., Cornell U., U. Calif., U. Minn., others. Served with U.S. Army, 1952-54. Recipient Harry Lord Ford prize U. Calif.-Berkeley, 1962; grand prize for sculpture Paris Biennale, 1965. Mem. AAUP. Address: 1110 N Hudson Ave Studio C Los Angeles CA 90038

SAUNDERS, EARL RAY, building administrator; b. Mineapolis, Kans., May 22, 1938; s. Frank and Mary Jane S.; m. Ethel L. Saunders, Apr. 27, 1966; 1 son, Earl R. A.A.S. Colo. State Coll. 1958, postgrad. Kans. State Coll. 1959, Long Beach City Coll. 1969-73, B.S. Calif. State Coll. 1975. Refrigeration mechanic Kiesel Co., Salina, Kans. 1958-59, shop foreman 1959-60; refrigeration mechanic Holmes and Narver, Los Angeles 1964-65, foreman 1965-66; supr. refrigeration heating Pacific Architects, Los Angeles 1966-67, chief supr. 1967-68; refrigeration, air conditioning heating mechanic System Devel. Corp., Santa Monica, Calif. 1968; refrigeration mechanic Calif. Dept. Health Service, 1969-73, foreman 1973-77, bldg. crafts mgr. I, 1977-78, bldg. crafts mgr. III, 1978—. Served with USAF 1960-64. Mem. Am. Soc. Hosp. Engrs., Calif. Soc. Hosp. Engrs., Nat. Fire Protection Assn., Nat. Energy Conservation. Democrat. Baptist. Club: Mason. Office: 7601 E Imperial Hwy Downey CA 90242

SAUNDERS, JOHN RAMSEY, coin and bullion gallery exec.; b. Detroit, Aug. 16, 1949; s. Gordon Joseph and Ruth (Ramsey) S.; m. Masako Susukida, Feb. 2, 1979. children—Robert, Sakura, Michelle. B.S., Eckerd Coll., 1971; M.B.A., U. Pa., 1973. Asst. treas. fgn. exchange trading, medium term lending loan officer Euro-Dollar market Am. Express Internat. Banking Corp., London, 1971-73; pres. London Coin Galleries, Mission Viejo, Calif., 1973—. Mem. Am. Numis. Assn. (life), Brit. Numis. Trade Assn., Nat. Assn. Coin and Precious Metal Dealers, Space Studies Inst. Presbyterian. Contbr: Standard Catalogue of World Coins, 1981-83. Office: London Coin Galleries Suite 132 Mission Viejo Mall Mission Viejo CA 92691

SAUNDERS, SAM CUNDIFF, mathematics educator, consultant; b. Richland, Oreg., Feb. 24, 1931; s. Winston Elmer and Elizabeth Jane (Cundiff) S.; m. Ruth Ann Lake, Aug. 12, 1954; children—Winston A., Craig S., Susan L. B.S., U. Oreg., 1952, Ph.D., U. Wash., 1956. Research specialist Boeing Sci. Research Labs., Seattle, 1956-72; prof. pure and applied math. Wash. State U., Pullman, 1972—; prin. Math. Analysis Research Corp., 1974-82, prin. Sci. Cons. Services, Inc., Pullman, 1982—; cons. Adv. Com. Reactor Safeguards to NRC, Boeing Co., Battelle N.W. Labs., Nat. Bur. Standards. Am. Statis. Assn. fellow, 1968; grantee Air Force Office Sci. Research, Office Naval Research, NSF, Army Research Office. Mem. Am. Math. Assn. Am. Statis. Assn., Inst. Math. Stats. Democrat. Unitarian. Contbr. articles to sci. jours. Home: SE 615 High St Pullman WA 99163 Office: Dept Math Wash State U Pullman WA 99164

SAUNDERS, SUZANNE, lawyer; b. Okarche, Okla., June 27, 1948; d. Gordon Hubert and Annie Laurie (McGregor) S. B.A., Rice U., 1970; J.D., U. Houston, 1976. Bar: Tex. 1976, Colo. 1977. Law clk. Woodard, Hall & Primm, Houston, 1973-76; dep. state pub. defender, Golden, Colo. and Denver, 1977-81; asst. legal counsel Regional Transp. Dist., Denver, 1981-82; assoc. White and Steele, P.C., Denver, 1982—. Dist. co-capt. Denver Democratic party, 1978-79. Mem. Colo. Women's Bar Assn. (dir. 1979-81, 82-83, pres. 1983-84), Colo. Bar Assn., Denver Bar Assn., ABA, Order of Barons. Democrat. Office: White & Steele 1660 Lincoln St Suite 1660 Denver CO 80264

SAUNDERS, WARD BISHOP, JR., aluminum company executive; b. Gilroy, Calif., Nov. 26, 1919; s. Ward Bishop and Lamira A. (Doan) S.; m. Elaine McDermott, Oct. 11, 1942; children—Douglas L., Myra K., Leslie J. B.S.M.E., U. Calif.-Berkeley, 1942; J.D., Stanford U., 1948. Bar: Calif. 1948. Sole practice law, San Francisco and Palo Alto, Calif., 1948-51; with Kaiser Aluminum & Chem. Corp., Oakland, Calif., 1951—, v.p., 1971—; dir. Aluminum Bahrain, Hindustan Aluminum Co., Ltd., India; mng. dir. Volta Aluminum Co., Ltd., Ghana. Dir. Volta River Authority, Ghana. Served to lt. USNR, 1942-46. Mem. State Bar Calif. Republican. Unitarian. Club: Commonwealth (San Francisco). Home: 6123 Estates Dr Oakland CA 94611 Office: 300 Lakeside Dr Suite 2267 Oakland CA 94643

SAUTTER, EDWARD PETER, lawyer; b. San Francisco, Apr. 3, 1918; s. Albert D. and Bertha (Mathisen) S.; m. Letha A. Walker, Aug. 31, 1968. A.B., U. Calif., 1940, M.B.A., 1946; J.D., Stanford U., 1949. Bar: Calif. 1949; sole practice, Eureka, Calif., 1949—. Active Eureka Boys' Club, Big Brothers/Big Sisters. Served to lt. col. JAGC, USAR, 1950-73. Mem. Calif. Bar Assn. Republican. Lutheran. Clubs: Lions, Elks. (Eureka). Home: 4370 Campton Rd Eureka CA 95501 Office: 314 L St Eureka CA 95501

SAVAGE, HELEN ELIZABETH, insurance company executive; b. Pasadena, Calif., Oct. 23, 1934; d. Lucien Joseph and Genevieve Marie (Evers) Lanouette; m. Boyd Albert Savage, Oct. 3, 1953 (div. 1976); children—Pamela, Michael, Jane; m. 2d, Donald Joseph Voller, Oct. 6, 1980. Ins. broker, Calif. Corp. ins. mgr. Coldwell Banker & Co., Los Angeles, 1976-77; corp. ins. mgr. Aerojet-Gen. Corp., El Monte, Calif., 1977-78; ind. ins. broker, Los Angeles, 1978-79; asst. mgr. spl. risks Fremont Indemnity Co., Los Angeles, 1979-81; v.p. Mission Ins. Co., Los Angeles, 1981—. Author: Primer of Risk Financing Alternatives, 1982. Office: Mission Ins Co 2500 Wilshire Blvd Suite 746 Los Angeles CA 90057

SAVAGE, MICHAEL JOHN, oil company executive; b. Birmingham, Eng., Oct. 28, 1934; s. Leonard W. H. and Hilda C. (Fletcher) S.; came to U.S., 1962, naturalized, 1981; m. Elisabeth Karl, June 21, 1965 (dec.); m. 2d, Virginia Hooper, Aug. 31, 1978; 1 son, Matthew. M.A. in Econs. and Law, Cambridge U., 1958; postgrad. Manchester (Eng.) Bus. Sch., 1965, Middle East Centre Arab Studies, Shemlan, Lebanon, 1966-67. With Brit. Petroleum Co., 1958-82, various positions, Kuwait, Lebanon, Abu Dhabi, Alaska, Can., U.S., pres. BP Alaska, Inc., San Francisco, 1977, pres. Sohio Petroleum Co., San Francisco, 1978-82, internat. dir. Brit. Petroleum Ltd., London, 1982; pres. Merlin Petroleum Co., San Francisco, 1983—. Trustee Alaska Pacific U. Served to 2d lt. Royal Arty., Brit. Army, 1953-55. Office: Merlin Petroleum Co One Market Plaza San Francisco CA 94105

SAVAGE, RONALD WAYNE, marketing executive; b. Sioux City, Iowa, Aug. 8, 1943; s. Ronald Nathan and Bethel L. (Anderson) S.; m. Mary Lyn Kingsley, Sept. 19, 1964; children—Tod, Chad, Tonya. A.A. in Bus., Grossmont Coll., 1970. Mgr., Best Fire Equipment Co., 1964-65; mgr. G.S. Parsons Co., San Diego, Calif., 1965-74, div. v.p., 1974-83, corp. v.p. mktg., 1983—; instr. Nat. Safety Council. Mem. San Diego Police Res. Mem. Am. Soc. Safety Engrs., Nat. Fire Protection Assn., Nat. Assn. Fire Equipment Distbrs. (nat. dir.), Safety Equipment Distbrs. Assn., Welding Supply Assn., Am. Welding Soc. Club: Exchange. Office: 9010 Clairemont Mesa Blvd San Diego CA 92123

SAVEDRA, MANUEL ANGEL, dentist; b. Los Angeles, Oct. 22, 1943; s. Manuel Diaz and Evangeline (Vasquez) S.; m. Cheryl Dana Silver, Sept. 11, 1982. A.A., East Los Angeles Coll., 1967; B.A., UCLA, 1969, D.D.S., 1974; cert. Queens Med. Center, Honolulu, 1975. Lic. dentist, Calif., Hawaii. Dentist, Queens Med. Ctr., Honolulu, 1974-75; dentist, lectr. to asst. prof. UCLA, 1975-76; pvt. practice dentistry, Hawthorne and Los Angeles, Calif., 1976—; mem. med.-dental staff St. Joseph Med. Center, Burbank, Calif., 1976; mem. exam. com. Calif. Bd. Dental Examiners, 1981. Served with Dental Corps, U.S. Army, 1963-66. Named Outstanding Dental Resident, Queen's Med. Ctr., 1974-75. Mem. ADA, Calif. Dental Assn., Acad. Gen. Dentistry, Western Dental Soc., UCLA Dental Alumni Assn. (exec. com. 1978-83, v.p., pres.), Am. Legion, Omicron Kappa Upsilon, Alpha Gamma Sigma. Republican. Jewish. Home: 9645 Wendover Dr Beverly Hills CA 90210 Office: 4445 W Broadway Suite 201 Hawthorne CA 90250 also 11600 Wilshire Blvd Suite 312 Los Angeles CA 90025

SAVELY, CARL DAVID, geologist; b. Holbrook, Ariz., Oct. 29, 1953; s. Raymond Jason and Mary Melvina (Bedee) S.; B.A. in Geology, Adams State Coll., 1976; m. Jill Marie Tankersley, Dec. 30, 1978; children—Byron Cam Tankersley, Nadine Marie. Soils aide Rio Grande Nat. Forest, Monte Vista, Colo., 1975-76, consulting geologist, 1976-77; with Southway Constrn. Co., Alamosa, Colo., 1976-77; mine geologist Homestake Mining Co., Creede, Colo., 1977—. Chmn. Mineral County Republican Com., 1978-80; sec., treas. Ambulance Bd., Mineral County, 1979-83; mem. Greede Sch. Bd., 1983—. Mem. Am. Assn. Petroleum Geologists, Geol. Soc. Am., Colo. Mining Assn., Soc. Mining Engrs., AIME, Rocky Mountain Assn. Geologists, Soc. Econ. Geologists, Emergency Med. Technician Assn. Colo., Nat. Assn. Emergency Med. Technicians. Club: Elks. Home: PO Box 485 Creede CO 81130 Office: PO Box 100 Creede CO 81130

SAVIDGE, IRVIN RAY, ecologist; b. Hegins, Pa., Sept. 4, 1943; s. Norman E. and Twila M. (Artz) S. B.S., Pa. State U., 1965, M.S., 1967; Ph.D., Mich. State U., 1970; postgrad. N.C. State U., 1972-74. Sr. ecologist Tex. Instruments Inc., Buchanan, N.Y. and Richardson, Tex., 1974-77, program mgr. 1977-80; sr. ecologist Normandeau Assoc. Inc., Denver, 1981—. Served to capt. U.S. Army, 1970-71. Mem. AAAS, Am. Fisheries Soc., Am. Inst. Biol. Scis., Am. Soc. Mammalogists, Animal Behavior Soc., Ecol. Soc. Am., Soc. Population Ecology, Soc. for Study of Evolution. Contr. articles to profl. jours.

SAVINO, FRANK JOHN, JR., city official; b. Los Angeles, Mar. 24, 1947; s. Frank Joseph and Marian Delores (Enright) S.; m. Fleta Margaret Mullins, Sept. 27, 1975; children—Joshua Adam, Joseph Thomas, Amy Lyn and Bethany Dawn (Twins). Student Ariz. Western Coll., Yuma, 1965-67. Cert. water treatment operator, Ariz. Salesman, N.Y. Life Ins. Co., Yuma, Ariz., 1975-76; asst. park mgr. Ahvilla County Park, Parker, Ariz., Yuma County Parks, 1976-78; asst. park mgr., st. leadman Town of Parker, Ariz., 1978, asst. pub. works dir., 1978-79, acting pub. works dir., 1979-81, pub. works dir., 1981—, dir. emergency services, 1981—, bd. dirs. transp. com. Mem. Ariz. Parks and Recreation Assn., Nat. Safety Council, Nat. Environ. Tng. Assn., Nat. Water and Pollution Control Assn., Am. Water Works Assn., Am. Pub. Works Dirs. Assn., Ariz. Parks and Recreation Assn. (treas. Dist. I). Democrat. Mormon.

SAVONA, MICHAEL RICHARD, physician; b. N.Y.C., Oct. 21, 1947; s. Salvatore Joseph and Diana Grace (Menditto) S.; B.S. summa cum laude, Siena Coll., 1969; M.D., SUNY, Buffalo, 1973; m. Dorothy O'Neill, Oct. 18, 1975. Intern in internal medicine, Presbyn. Hosp., Columbia U., N.Y.C., 1973-74, resident in internal medicine, 1974-76, vis. fellow internal medicine Delafield Hosp./Columbia U. Coll. Physicians and Surgeons, 1974-76; practice medicine specializing in internal medicine, Maui Med. Group, Wailuku, Hawaii, 1976—; dir. ICU, Maui Meml. Hosp., also dir. respiratory therapy, CCU., chmn. dept. medicine, 1980—; clin. faculty John A. Burns Sch. Medicine, U. Hawaii. Bd. dirs. Maui Heart Assn.; dir. profl. edn. Maui chpt. Am. Cancer Soc.; mem. Maui County Hosp. Adv. Commn.; mem. council Community Cancer Program of Hawaii. Recipient James A. Gibson Wayne J. Atwell award, 1970, physiology award, 1970, Ernest Whitebsky award, 1971, Roche Lab. award, 1972, Pfiser Lab. award, 1973, Phillip Sang award, 1973, Hans Lowenstein M.D. Meml. award, 1973. Diplomate Am. Bd. Internal Medicine. Mem. AMA, Am. Thoracic Soc., Maui County Med. Assn. (pres.), Hawaii Med. Assn., Hawaii Oncology Group, A.C.P., SW Oncology Coop. Group, Alpha Omega Alpha, Delta Epsilon Sigma. Office: 2180 Main St Wailuku Maui HI 96793

SAWICK, KERRY ANN, data processor; b. N.Y.C., Nov. 4, 1946; d. Theodore and Katherine (Wood) Sawick; m. Michael W. Hager, Sept. 1, 1973. B.S. in Math., Coll. William and Mary. Programmer, IBM, Poughkeepsie, N.Y., 1968-71, assoc. systems engr. Boston, 1971-73, systems engr., 1973-76, adv. systems engr., 1976-78, sr. systems support rep., 1978-79, br. mgr., 1979-81; western region mgr. Nat. Advanced Systems, Long Beach, Calif., 1978—. Mem. Am. Mgmt. Assn., Nat. Assn. Women Computing, Nat. Assn. Female Execs. Republican. Roman Catholic. Home: 2377 Lyall Way Belmont CA 94402 Office: One Golden Shore Long Beach CA 90802

SAWIN, ENOCH IVOR, educator; b. Okobojo, S.D., Apr. 21, 1920; s. Charles Beman and Winnie (Moses) S.; student Huron Coll., 1938-39, Sioux Falls Coll., 1939-40; B.S. in Mathematics, U. Chgo., 1947, M.A. in Edn., 1948, Ph.D., 1951; m. Barbara Jackson, Aug. 23, 1943; children—Gregory Guy, David Marshall. Tchr., Brandt (S.D.) Ind. Sch., 1940-41; asst. prof. Syracuse (N.Y.) U., 1950-52; ednl. specialist Air Univ., Maxwell AFB, Ala., 1952-60; asso. prof. Sch. Edn., San Francisco State U., 1960-64, prof. edn., 1964—; cons. in field; cons., course writer Far West Lab. for Ednl. Research/Devel., San Francisco, summers 1970-74. Pres., Montgomery :Ala.) Mental Health Soc., 1958-59. Served with USN, 1941-45. Recipient Sustained Superior Performance award U.S. Civil Service, 1959. Mem. Am. Ednl. Research Assn., Assn. Supervision and Curriculum Devel., Calif. Assn. Program Evaluators. Author: Evaluation and the Work of the Teacher, 1969. Home: 800 N Delaware St Apt 309 San Mateo CA 94401 Office: Sch Edn San Francisco State Univ San Francisco CA 94132

SAWYER, CHARLES GARY, pet food company executive; b. Carrington, N.D., Oct. 7, 1935; s. Roy P. and Laura I. (Johnson) S.; m. Susan Virginia Studebaker, July 14, 1962; children—Michael, Virginia. B.S. in Bus. and Mktg., U. Wash., 1962. Div. mgr. Union Carbide Corp., Kansas City, Mo. and Los Angeles, 1971-75, brand mgr., N.Y.C., 1976-78; pres. Hervin Co., Tualatin, Oreg., 1981—. Served with U.S. Army, 1954-56. Mem. Portland (Oreg.) Execs., Assn. Oreg. Industries. Office: Hervin Co 8150 Nyberg Rd Tualatin OR 97062

SAWYER, DONALD D., marketing executive, consultant, lecturer; b. Bklyn., June 3, 1933; s. Murry S. and Bobbe Rose (Black) Schneiderman; m. Dolores Inez Geller, Sept. 24, 1953; m. 2d, Janice Elaine Thorsten, Apr. 16, 1974; children—Charles S., Robert A., Brett R., Kirsten M. B.A., U. Miami, 1956; postgrad. Cambridge U., 1956-57. Vice-pres., Young & Rubicam, Inc., N.Y.C., 1962-67; pres. Donald Sawyer Assocs., Inc., Beverly Hills, Calif., 1967-75, pres. The Original Cookie Company, Inc., Los Angeles, 1974-75; chmn. Whimsy, Inc. div. Rapid Am., Inc., Los Angeles, 1976-79; v.p. Mattel, Inc., Hawthorne, Calif., 1979-82; pres. People Protections Products Inc., Hawthorne, 1981-82; chmn. bd. Cookhouse, Inc., Sherman Oaks, Calif., 1983—; lectr. Sch. Bus., U. So. Calif.; dir. Atlanta Fin. Corp.; cons. ARCORP mgmt. Bd. dirs. Los Angeles Better Bus. Bur., L.I. Heart Inst., Inc. Served to lt. USAR, 1957-59.

SAWYER, ED CURTIS, state senator; b. Glasgow, Mont., Dec. 11, 1926; s. W.C. and Alleen (Robertson) S.; ed. Coyne Elec. Trade Sch.; m. Angie E. Cercone, June 14, 1947; children—Bette Sawyer Newman, Tom, Ed, Dennis, Greg. Owner, operator Cooper City Electric Co., Bisbee, Ariz., 1958-70, Indsl. Electric Service, Safford, Ariz., 1970—; mem. Ariz. Ho. of Reps., 1965-74; mem. Ariz. State Senate, 1974—, pres., 1977-78, chmn. rules com., legis. council. Served with USN, World War II. Mem. Elec. Apparatus Service Assn., Safford C. of C., Am. Legion. Democrat. Roman Catholic. Club: Elks. Office: 1274 Hopi St Safford AZ 85546

SAWYER, ERNEST WALKER, JR., petroleum, livestock and natural resources cos. exec.; b. Harrow-on-Hill, Hove, Eng.; s. Ernest Walker and Florence Virginia (Davies) S.; ed. Colo. Sch. Mines, Harvard U., grad. U. Calif., Berkeley, 1948; m. Miriam Camille Patty; children—Camille Agnes, Christian Emerson. Pres., Sawyer Petroleum Co., Los Angeles, 1955-69; dir. Sawyer Exploration Co.; pres. Oreg. Trail Land Cattle Co., Sawyer Cattle Co.; dir. U.S. Oil & Mineral Corp.; exec. Frawley Enterprises; chief exec. officer Royal Am. Petroleum Corp. Bd. dirs. Sawyer Found. Served to capt. C.E., U.S. Army. Mem. Am. Nuclear Soc., Am. Soc. Petroleum Geologists, AIME, Am. Inst. Profl. Geologists, Calif. Cattleman's Assn. Clubs: Alta (Salt Lake City); Bel-Air Bay. Address: 1801 Ave of Stars Suite 1025 Los Angeles CA 90067

SAWYER, JACK, social psychologist; b. Beatrice, Nebr., June 8, 1931; s. Proctor Herbert and Elisabeth Ann (Jack) S. B.S., Iowa State U., 1952; M.A., Ohio State U., 1953; Ph.D., Purdue U., 1955. Lic. psychologist, Calif. Personnel research psychologist Dept. of Army, Washington, 1955-58; mem. Chgo. Bd. Trade, 1962-64; fellow, lectr., asst. prof. U. Chgo., 1958-67; assoc. prof. Northwestern U., Evanston, Ill., 1967-72; vis. scholar Harvard U., 1970-72; vis. scholar U. Calif.-Berkeley, 1972-75; fellow Wright Inst., Berkeley, Calif., 1972-77; researcher and cons. social psychologist, Berkeley, Calif., 1972—; vice-chmn. EFT Mgmt. Systems Inc., San Diego, 1981—. Served with USNR, 1949-57. Rockefeller Found. fellow, 1958-59; NSF fellow, 1959-60; NIMH fellow, 1971-73. Mem. AAAS, Am. Psychol. Assn., Am. Sociol. Assn., Assn. Humanistic Psychology. Democrat. Author: (with Joseph Pleck) Men and Masculinity, 1974. Contbr. articles to profl. jours. Home: 3029 Benvenue Ave Berkeley CA 94705 Office: PO Box 5599 Berkeley CA 94705

SAWYER, KATHERINE H. (MRS. CHARLES BALDWIN SAWYER), librarian; b. Cleve., July 11, 1908; d. Willard and Martha (Beaumont) Hirsh; A.B., Smith Coll., 1930; M.S. in Library Sci., Western Res. U., 1956; m. Charles Baldwin Sawyer, Aug. 19, 1933; children—Samuel Prentiss, Charles Brush, William Beaumont. With Cleve. Pub. Library, prof. librarian hosps., instns. dept., 1956-61; med. librarian St. Luke's Hosp., Pittsfield, Mass., 1965-66; library cons. Ministry of Health, Guyana, S. Am., 1966-68; curator Sophia Smith Collection, Smith Coll. Library chmn. exec. com. Garden Center of Greater Cleve., 1959-65; chmn. Friends of Western Res. Hist. Library, 1973-78, trustee, 1980—. Bd. mgrs. Episcopal Ch. Home, 1954—, pres., 1961-64, trustee, 1965—; bd. govs. Western Res. U., 1957-66, bd. visitors Sch. Library Sci., 1958-68, 69—; trustee Friends of Cleve. Pub. Library, 1962-67, Christian Residences Found., 1976—; counselor Friends of Smith Coll. Library, 1962-68. Mem. ALA, Ohio Library Assn., Western Res. Hist. Soc., Archeol. Inst., Spl. Libraries Assn., Nat. League Am. Pen Women. Episcopalian (vestryman 1974-77). Clubs: Union, Kirtland Country; Intown. Co-author (talking books for blind) Gardening for Blind Persons, 1962; Beauty, Glamour and Style, 1963. Home: 525 Paseo del Oro Green Valley AZ 85614

SAWYER, THOMAS ARTHUR, data processing manager, consultant; b. Pocatello, Idaho, Apr. 26, 1946; s. Fred Ellis and Bertha Elizabeth (Adkins) S.; m. Cora Ada Davis, Sept. 4, 1969; children—Gaylan Thomas, Rebecca Lynn, Bradley Arthur, Mark Twain, Joseph Edward. Student Idaho State U., 1966-69; cert. data processing Boise State U., 1971, cert. inventory mgmt., 1980. Programmer, FMC Corp., Pocatello, 1967-70; mgr. systems and programming Ore Ida Foods, Inc., Boise, Idaho, 1970-77; mgr. base data systems devel. Tektronix, Inc., Beaverton, Oreg., 1977-83; dir. mgmt. info. systems Sidereal Corp., Portland, Oreg., 1983—; cons., instr. mfg. system principles. Served in USAF, 1966-73. Mem. Assn. Systems Mgmt., Am. Prodn. and Inventory Control Soc. Republican. Mormon. Home: 12295 SW Tippitt Pl Tigard OR 97223 Office: Sidereal Corp 9600 SW Barnes Rd Portland OR 97225

SAWYER, THOMAS EDGAR, management consultant; b. Homer, La., July 7, 1932; s. Sidney Edgar and Ruth (Bickham) S.; B.S., UCLA, 1959; M.A., Occidental Coll., 1969; m. Joyce Mezzanatto, Aug. 22, 1954; children—Jeffrey T., Scott A., Robert J., Julie Anne. Project engr. Garrett Corp., Los Angeles, 1954-60; mgr. devel. ops. TRW Systems, Redondo Beach, Calif., 1960-66; spl. asst. to gov. State of Calif., Sacramento, 1967-69; prin., gen. mgr. Planning Research Corp., McLean, Va., 1969-72; dep. dir. OEO, Washington, 1972-74; asso. prof. bus. mgmt. Brigham Young U., 1974-78; pres. Mesa Corp., Provo, 1978—, chmn. bd., 1978—; dir. Insul Chem. Corp., World Dairy and Food Research, Inc., Nooraid Chem. Corp., Nat. Applied Computer Tech., Inc., Indian Affiliates, Inc. Chmn. Nat. Adv. Council Indian Affairs; chmn. Utah State Bd. Indian Affairs; mem. Utah Dist. Export Council; mem. Utah dist. SBA Council; chmn. So. Paiute Restoration Com.; mem. adv. council Nat. Bus. Assn.; mem. Utah Job Tng. Coordinating Council. Served with USMC, 1950-53. Mem. Am. Mgmt. Assn., Am. Soc. Public Adminstrn., Utah Council Small Bus. (dir.). Republican. Mormon. Club: Masons. Author: Assimilation Versus Self-Indentity: A Modern Native American Perspective, 1976. Home: 548 W 630 S Orem UT 84057 Office: 1875 S State St Suite 3000 Orem UT 84057

SAX, JAY, software specialist; b. Newport, R.I., Oct. 17, 1955; s. Joe and Lee (Michael) S.; m. Nicole Annette Uzan, Mar. 7, 1981. B.A., U. Calif.-Riverside, 1978. Mem. tech. staff TRW DSSG, Redondo Beach, Calif., 1978-80; systems programmer Lockheed Calif. Corp., Burbank, 1980-82; software specialist Digital Equipment Corp., Culver City, Calif., 1982—; cons. in field. Home: 3843 Harriman Ave Los Angeles CA 90032 Office: 6101 W Centinela Culver City CA 90230

SAX, PAUL A., financial executive; b. Albany, N.Y., July 30, 1937; s. Louis T. and Rose S.; m. Peggy M. Sax, June 25, 1967; children—Michael, Jackie, Kent. B.B.A. in Acctg., U. Miami, 1965; Ph.D. in Econs., NYU, 1967. Founder, pres. Associated Tax Cons., 1967—; ptnr. Lord and Sax Fin. Services, Huntington Beach, Calif., 1982—. Served with AUS, 1959-62. Author: All You Need to Know about Foreclosures, 1982, All You Need to Know to Protect Your Home, 1982.

SAXE, LOUISE ELLEN, nurse educator; b. Blairsville, Pa., Mar. 17, 1930; d. Foster Charles and Mary Louise (Woods) Johnson; m. Charles L. Saxe, Jr., Dec. 22, 1951; 1 son, Karl. A.A., Ariz. Western Coll., 1972, B.S.N., Ariz. State U., 1974; M.A. in Health Edn., Sam Houston State U., 1976. Operating room nurse Washington County Hosp., Hagerstown, Md., 1950-51; pub. health nurse Yuma County Dept. Health, 1965-70, Ariz. Dept. Health, 1965-70; sch. nurse Kofa High Sch., Yuma, Ariz., 1970-74; staff nurse Huntsville (Tex.) Hosp., 1974-75; instr. U. Tex. Med. Br., Galveston, 1975-77; dir. nursing edn. Cochise Coll., Douglas, Ariz., 1977-81; dir. nursing edn. and health tech. Imperial Valley Coll., Imperial, Calif., 1981—. Mem. Am. Nurses Assn., Nat League for Nursing, Vocat. Edn. Assn., AAUW, Imperial County Council Nurses. Home: 564 Desert Gardens Dr El Centro CA 92243 Office: PO Box 158 Imperial CA 92243

SAXE-CLIFFORD, SUSAN JOY, psychologist, consultant; b. San Francisco; d. Julius S. and Mary S. Saxe; m. Francis G. Clifford, Aug. 27, 1976; children—Christopher, Brooke, Katherine. Ph.D., U. So. Calif., 1975. Staff psychologist Los Angeles Police Dept., 1970—; pvt. practice psychology, Sherman Oaks, Calif., 1975—; cons. psychology; stress mgmt. tng.; hostage negotiator. Mem. Am. Psychol. Assn., Calif. State Psychol. Assn. Club: Soroptimists. Contbr. articles to profl. jours. Office: 15300 Ventura Blvd Suite 425 Sherman Oaks CA 91403

SAXENA, ARJUN NATH, physicist; b. Lucknow, India, Apr. 1, 1932; s. Sheo and Mohan (Piyari) Shanker; came to U.S., 1956, naturalized, 1976; B.Sc., Lucknow U., 1950, M.Sc., 1952, profl. cert. in German, 1954; Post M.S. diploma, Inst. Nuclear Physics, Calcutta, India, 1955; Ph.D., Stanford U., 1963; m. Veera Saxena, Feb. 9, 1956; children—Rashmi, Amol, Varsha, Ashvin. Research asst. Stanford U., 1956-60; mem. tech. staff Fairchild Semicondr. Co., Palo Alto, Calif., 1960-65; dept. head Sprague Electric Co., North Adams, Mass., 1965-69; mem. tech. staff RCA Labs., Princeton, N.J., 1969-71; pres., chmn. bd. Astro-Optics, Phila., 1972; pres. Internat. Sci. Co., Princeton Junction, N.J., 1973-74; vis. scientist Centre de Récherches Nucléaires, Strasbourg, France, 1973, 77; sr. staff scientist, mgr. engring. Data Gen. Corp., Sunnyvale, Calif., 1975-80; mgr. process tech. Signetics Corp., Sunnyvale, 1980-81; dept. mgr. advanced process devel. and N-Channel tech. A.M.I., Santa Clara, Calif., 1981—. Treas. Pack 66, Boy Scouts Am., W. Windsor, N.J., 1970-74. Recipient Disting. Citizen award State of N.J., 1975. Mem. Am. Phys. Soc., IEEE, Electrochem. Soc., Stanford Alumni Assn. (life). Contbr. articles on semicondr. tech., optics, nuclear and high-energy physics to sci. jours., 1953—; patentee in field. Home: 4217 Pomona Ave Palo Alto CA 94306 Office: 3800 Homestead Rd Santa Clara CA 95051

SAY, WILLIAM MALCOLM, transp. co. exec.; b. Perry Twp., Pa., May 5, 1922; s. George Knox and Bertha Elizabeth (Holder) S.; student public schs., Karns City, Pa.; m. Shirley Anne Sweeney, May 15, 1948; children—Robert, Elizabeth, William H., Barbara, Richard, Paul. With Air Products and Chems., Inc., 1946-80, regional ops. mgr., Los Angeles, 1956-71, Western region distbn. mgr., Los Angeles, 1971-80; v.p. ops. Logistics Express, Inc. doing bus. as Logex, Inc., Anaheim, Calif., 1980—. Com. chmn. Stoneypoint council Boy Scouts Am. Served with USN, 1943-46. Recipient Apollo Achievement award NASA. Mem. Cryogenic Soc. Am., Am. Mgmt. Assn. Republican. Club: Masons, Kiwanis. Inventor cryogenic fill termination device. Home: 18735 Ludlow St Northridge CA 91326 Office: 1890 S Chris Ln Anaheim CA 92805

SAYANO, REIZO RAY, electrochem. engr.; b. Los Angeles, Dec. 15, 1937; s. George Keiichiro and Miyo (Nakao) S.; A.A., Los Angeles Community Coll., 1958; B.S., U. Calif. at Los Angeles, 1960, M.S., 1962, Ph.D., 1967; m. Tamiko Shintani, May 28, 1967; children—Kiyomi Coleen, Naomi Jennifer. Research asst. electrochem. and shock tube research, dept. engring. U. Calif. at Los Angeles, 1961-66; mem. staff TRW Systems, corrosion and advance battery research and devel., Redondo Beach, Calif., 1966-78; dir. engring. Intermedics Intraocular Inc., Pasadena, Calif., 1978-80, dir. research and devel., 1980-82, v.p. engring. devel. and research, 1982—. NASA predoctoral trainee, 1964-65. Mem. Electrochem. Soc., Nat. Assn. Corrosion Engrs., AAAS, Am. Mgmt. Assn., Sigma Xi. Home: 209 Casa Grande Ave Montebello CA 90640 Office: PO Box 70670 2650 E Foothill Blvd Pasadena CA 91107

SAYLES, ROBERT ARTHUR, mgmt. cons.; b. Stockton, Calif., Sept. 13, 1931; s. Arthur Leadbetter and Rena (Passovoy) S.; m. Judith Alles, June 29, 1952; children—Cathleen Carpenter, Kimberly O'Driscoll, Jeffrey, Nancy. B.B.A., U. Calif., Berkeley, 1952. With IBM, 1954-77, mgr. pub. sector industry mktg., 1973-77; pres. Robert A. Sayles Assocs., Inc., Sacramento, Calif., 1977—. Served with USMCR, 1952-54. Mem. Am. Mgmt. Assn. Republican. Office: 622 Lake Wilhaggin Dr Sacramento CA 95825

SAYLOR, RICHARD BENTON, corporation executive; b. Anchorage, Mar. 10, 1951; s. Richard George and Doris Annette (Gable) S.; m. Susan Jane Scarborough, 1982. Student N.Mex. Inst. Mining and Tech. Retailer, Albuquerque; investor in apts. and other real estate throughout N.Mex.; owner Trans Am. Audio, Albuquerque, 1982—; founder, co-owner Avnet Corp., Albuquerque. Mem. fin. com. to elect Gov. Bruce King, N.Mex., 1978; mem. campaign staff to elect Gov. Tony Anaya, N.Mex., 1982; contbr. The Storehouse Christian Mission, Sandia Prep. Sch. Recipient support award The Storehouse. Mem. N.Mex. Retail Liquor Dealer's Assn. Presbyterian. Club: Four Hills Country. Contbr. to retailer guide.

SAYRE, JAMES WILLIAM, statistician, educator, consultant; b. Los Angeles, Aug. 5, 1946; s. George William and Agnas Marie (Manger) S.; m. Monica Antonia Ruivenkamp, July 30, 1977; children—William Francis, Stephanie Marie. B.A. in Econs., U. Calif.-Los Angeles, 1969, M.S. in Biostats., 1974, Ph.D. in Biostats., 1977; M.S. in Ops. Research, Calif. State U., 1971. Community coll. instr. credentials, Calif. Instr. quantitative methods dept. Calif. State U.-Long Beach, 1972-73; asst. instr. Los Angeles County Assessor's Office, 1973; USPHS trainee, div. biostats. UCLA, 1972-75, asst. instr. div. epidemiology, 1975, sr. statistican, div. epidemiology, 1977-81, prin. statistician, 1981—, dir. data mgmt. and analysis lab., div. of epidemiology, 1979—, adj. asst. prof. biostats., 1981—; cons. Mem. Am. Statis. Assn., Biometric Soc., Soc. Epidemiologic Research, Internat. Epidemiologic Assn., Am. Coll. Epidemiology (assoc.). Democrat. Roman Catholic. Club: UCLA Football Alumni. Contbr. articles to profl. jours. Office: Division of Epidemiology School of Public Health University of California Los Angeles CA 90024

SAYRE, LANSING GLENN LYTLE, pub. accountant; b. Cin., July 24, 1901; s. Charles Lansing and Amanda Glenn (Lytle) S.; ed. pvt. tutors; m. Elizabeth Goble, Feb. 14, 1957. Pvt. practice pub. accounting, Los Angeles, 1943—. Mem. S.R. (past pres.), Soc. Colonial Wars (past governor), Order Founders and Patriots Am. (past gov. gen.), Mil. Order Loyal Legion, (past comdr.), Soc. War 1812, Huguenot Soc. (past v.p.) Calif., Mil. Order Crusades, Baronial Order Magna Charta (surety), Order Crown Charlemagne (past v.p. gen.), Nat. Soc. Public Accountants, Soc. Calif. Accountants, Nat. Gavel Club. Clubs: Masons (32 deg.), Shriners, Elks. Home: 901 Cumberland Rd Glendale CA 91202

SAYRE, STEVE ATHOL, education consultant; b. Boise, Idaho, Sept. 29, 1940; s. Athol Reed and Caroline V. (Henderson) S.; m. Elizabeth Ann Hall, Dec. 27, 1969; children—Kent S., Ryan R. B.S., Eastern Oreg., U., 1962; M.S., Oreg. State U., 1965; Ed.D., U. No. Colo., 1972. Sci. tchr. The Dalles, La Grande and Hillsboro, Oreg., 1962-69; instr. sci. U. No. Colo., 1971-72; chmn. dept. sci. edn. Wayne (Nebr.) State Coll., 1972-75; staff devel. cons. for educators, Hillsboro, 1976—; adj. prof. Oreg. State U., Portland State U.; dir. Sayre Assocs. Investments. Recipient DeShannon Forum award, 1967. Mem. Assn. for Curriculum Devel. and Supervision, Nat. Assn. Sci. Tchrs., AAUP. Republican. Contbr. articles to sci. teaching jours. Home: 4755 SW Stoddard St Aloha OR 97007 Office: Hillsboro Union High Sch Dist 625 NE Lincoln St Hillsboro OR 97007

SBORDONE, ROBERT JOSEPH, clinical neuropsychologist, educator; b. Boston, May 6, 1940; s. Sam and Phylliss (Dellaria) S.; m. Melinda Welles, June 30, 1972 (div.) A.B., U. So. Calif., 1967; M.A., Calif. State U.-Los Angeles, 1969; Ph.D., UCLA, 1976; postdoctoral trainee UCLA Neuropsychiat. Inst., 1976-77. Lic. psychologist, marriage, family and child counselor, Calif. Staff psychologist Neuropsychiat. Inst., UCLA, 1977-78, asst. research psychologist, 1978-80; pvt. practice clin. neuropsychology, Los Angeles, 1978—, Garden Grove, Calif., 1982—; chief psychol. services, adj. asst. prof. dept. phys. medicine and rehab. U. Calif.-Irvine, 1980-82, clin. asst. prof. depts. neurosurgery and phys. medicine and rehab., 1982—; bd. dirs. High Hopes Neurol. Recovery Group, Inc., 1981-83, So. Calif. Head Injury Found., 1982—. Exec. adv. bd. Mardan Sch., 1981—; U.S. Goodwill ambassador to Middle East, 1963. Served with USAF, 1962-66. Nat. Inst. Drug Abuse predoctoral fellow, 1973-75; NIMH postdoctoral fellow, 1976-77. Mem. Los Angeles County Psychol. Assn., Orange County Psychol. Assn., Calif. Psychol. Assn., Calif. Neuropsychology Soc., Computers in Psychology, Clinicians in Pvt. Practice, Western Psychol. Assn., Am. Psychol. Assn., Nat. Head Injury Found., N.Y. Acad. Scis., Am. Orthopsychiat. Soc., Behavioral Neuropsychology Spl. Interest Group, Am. Acad. Neuropsychology, AAAS, Am. Gerontol. Soc., Nat. Register Health Service Providers Psychology, Psychonomic Soc., Internat. Neuropsychol. Soc., Internat. Soc. Research in Aggression. Clin. editor Clin. Neuropsychology, 1979—; contbr. articles profl. jours. Office: 13412 Donegal Dr Garden Grove CA 92644

SBOROV, DAVID WILLIAM, farming company executive; b. Washington, Oct. 23, 1950; s. Victor Max and Carol (Reimers) S.; Student U. Denver, 1968-71; B.A., U. Calif.-Berkeley, 1972; m. Linda C. Smith, May 26, 1978. Gen. mgr. 1st Pacific Realty Corp., Palo Alto, Calif., 1972-73; owner, mgr. Sborov & Assocs., Palo Alto, 1973-74; mng. partner 1st Harvest, Palo Alto, 1974-76; pres. Golden West Farming Co., Inc., Palo Alto, 1976—, also dir.; dir. Gencor, Am. Harvesters Inc., Calif. Fruit Co. NSF grantee, 1969-70; Boetcher Found. fellow, 1970-71. Mem. Fin. Planning Forum, Calif. Pistachio Assn. Club: Commonwealth. Author: Migrant Community Studies Guide, 1971; Fine Art of Investing During Inflation, 1975. Office: Suite 603 2600 El Camino Real Palo Alto CA 94306

SCADDING, JOHN LESLIE, economist; b. Vancouver, B.C., July 11, 1940; s. Leslie Charles and Elizabeth Audrey (Baird) S. Student Victoria Coll., 1958-60; B. Comm., U. B.C., 1963; Ph.D., U. Chgo., 1974. Asst. to dir. econ. research Ont. Com. on Taxation, Toronto, 1963-64; staff economist Prices and Income Commn., Govt. of Can., Ottawa, Ont., 1970-71; asst. prof. Stanford U., 1968-75; sr. staff economist Council Econ. Advisers, Washington, 1975-76; assoc. prof. U. Toronto, 1976-79; economist, sr. economist, research officer Fed. Res. Bank San Francisco, 1979-83, dir. pub. info., 1983—; lectr. U. Calif.-Berkeley, Mills Coll., Woodrow Wilson fellow; Ford Found. fellow; Soc. Sci. Research Council grantee. Mem. Am. Econ. Assn. Contbr. articles to profl. jours. Office: 101 Market St San Francisco CA 94105

SCAFE, LINCOLN ROBERT, JR., air conditioning service co. pres.; b. Cleve., July 28, 1922; s. Lincoln Robert and Charlotte (Hawkins) S.;

student Cornell U., 1940-41; m. Mary Anne Wilkinson, Nov. 14, 1945; children—Amanda Katharine, Lincoln Robert III. Service mgr. Avery Engrng. Co., Cleve., 1946-51; nat. service mgr. Trane Co., LaCrosse, Wis., 1951-57; service and installation mgr. Mech. Equipment Supply Co., Honolulu, 1957-58; chief engr. Sam P. Wallace of Pacific, Honolulu, 1958-62; pres. Air Conditioning Service Co., Inc., Honolulu, 1962—. Served with USNR, 1942-45; PTO. Mem. ASHRAE, Alpha Delta Phi. Clubs: Cornell Hawaii (past pres.); Outrigger Canoe. Republican. Author tech. service lit. and parts manuals; contbr. articles to trade publs. Address: 314 Anolani St Honolulu HI 96821

SCAGLIONE, CECIL FRANK, airline mgr.; b. North Bay, Ont., Can., Dec. 2, 1934; came to U.S., 1967, naturalized, 1982; s. Frank and Rose (Aubin) S.; student North Bay Coll., 1947-52, Ryerson Tech. Inst., Toronto, Ont., 1955-56, San Diego State U. Inst. World Affairs, 1979; m. Mary Margaret Stewart, Nov. 11, 1954 (div.); children—Cris Ann, Michael Andrew, Patrick Andrew; m. 2d, Beverly Loise Rahn, Mar. 25, 1983. Fin. writer Toronto Telegram, 1955; reporter Sarnia (Ont.) Observer, 1956-57; reporter, editor Kitchener-Waterloo (Ont.) Record, 1957-61; reporter, editor, analyst Windsor (Ont.) Star, 1961-67; writer, editor, photo editor Detroit News, 1967-71; reporter, asso. bus. editor San Diego Union, 1971-80; mgr. corp. communications Pacific Southwest Airlines, San Diego, 1981—; v.p. Spl. Info. Services, Inc. Mem. adv. council SBA. Recipient award B.F. Goodrich Can., Ltd., 1962, 66, Spl. Achievement award Nat. Assn. Recycling Industries, 1978, award SBA, 1980; Herbert J. Davenport fellow, 1977; Canadian Centennial grantee, 1966. Mem. San Diego Press Club (hon. life; past pres.; awards 1978, 80), Airline Editors Forum (vice-chmn.; award 1982, 83), Pub. Relations Soc. Am. (dir.), Sigma Delta Chi. Roman Catholic. Founding editor-in-chief Aeromexico Mag., 1973; contbr. articles and photographs to various publs. Home: 3911 Kendall St San Diego CA 92109 Office: PSA Inc 3225 N Harbor Dr San Diego CA 92101

SCANDERBEG, DINO CASTRIOTA, aerospace controls tech. co. exec.; b. Asmara, Ethiopia, Dec. 17, 1938; came to U.S., 1959, naturalized, 1968; s. Anthony C. and Marie (Brisset) S.; B.S. in Aeros., Northrop Inst. Tech., 1962; postgrad. UCLA, 1965; m. Elizabeth Kiesewetter, Jan. 20, 1968; children—Donica, Danny. Project engr. Bendix Corp., North Hollywood, Calif., 1968-73; project engr. Hydraulic Research Textron, Valencia, Calif., 1973-74, engrng. mgr., 1974-75, operation mgr. European office, 1975-76, dir. engring., 1976-79, gen. mgr. systems engrng. group, 1979—. Recipient Group Achievement award NASA, 1977. Mem. Army Aviation Assn., Am. Helicopters Soc., Soc. Automotive Engrs., UCLA Sch. Mgmt. Alumni Assn. Roman Catholic. Home: 19116 Killoch Pl Northridge CA 91326 Office: 25200 W Rye Cny Rd Valencia CA 91355

SCANLAN, TRACY ALLEN, strategic management and aerospace systems consultant; b. Dallas, Feb. 28, 1934; s. James E. and Lila Inez (Miller) S.; M.S. in Aerospace Engrng., U. Tex., 1964; M.B.A.S., Anderson Schs. Bus., 1978; m. W. Elizabeth Minot, June 23, 1954; children—Kimberly Elizabeth Scanlan Lentz, Tracy Allen, Judy Kathleen Scanlan Casey. Commd. 2d lt. U.S. Air Force, 1954, advanced through grades to lt. col., 1973, pilot SAC, 1954-60, exptl. test pilot, 1965-68, sea combat tour, 1968-69, chief test planning B1 Systems Program Office, 1971, chief flight test Flight Dynamics Lab., 1971-73, Air Force Spl. Weapons Center, 1973-75, ret., 1975; cons. strategic risk mgmt. software devel. Mgmt. Scis., Inc., Albuquerque, 1975-80; prin. Tracy Scanlan Assocs., 1980—. Decorated D.F.C., Meritorious Service medal with oak leaf cluster, Air Medal with 5 oak leaf clusters, Purple Heart. Mem. Soc. Exptl. Test Pilots, Sigma Gamma Tau. Republican. Methodist. Condr. research, exptl. flight testing fly-by-wire flight control systems, 1967-73; developer software for personal and distbd. computer systems. Home and Office: 11 LaVillita Ct Albuquerque NM 87112

SCANLAND, THOMAS BOYD, marine ecologist, cons.; b. Honolulu, July 21, 1941; s. Francis Worth and Karina Marie (Erickson) S.; m. Teresa Kay Burns, Dec. 15, 1962, children—Teresa Erickson. B.S., San Diego State U., 1964; M.S., Fla. State U., 1966; Ph.D., Scripps Instn. Oceanography, 1971. Marine ecologist Marine Advisors, Inc., Del Mar, Calif., 1970-71, Marine Ecol. Cons., Solana, Beach, Calif., 1971-73; marine ecologist Dames & Moore, Los Angeles, 1973-75, prin., 1975-79, ptnr., 1979—, mgr. Tokyo office, 1975-77, New Orleans office, 1977-78; lectr. Calif. State U.-San Diego, 1971-72; mem. industry adv. bd. Calif. State U.-Long Beach, 1978—. Served with USN, 1959-61. U.S. Fish and Wildlife fellow, 1968-70. Mem. Ecol. Soc. Am., AAAS, Marine Biol. Assn. U.K., Biol. Soc. Washington, Scripps Alumni Assn. (pres. 1974-75). Office: Suite 1000 1100 Glendon Ave Los Angeles CA 90265

SCANLON, THOMAS JOSEPH, educator, consultant; b. Chgo., Sept. 11, 1946; s. Thomas P. and Marjorie B. (Mauer) S.; m. Mary Ann Trant, Dec. 28, 1968; children—Sean, Jennifer, Megan. A.B., Marquette U., 1968; M.A., Carnegie-Mellon U., 1969. Tchr. social studies Los Altos High Sch., Hacienda Heights, Calif., 1969-77, chmn. social studies dept., 1974-77; program coordinator K-12 social studies Hacienda La Puente (Calif.) Unified Sch. Dist., 1978—; cons. to sch. dists., profl. orgns.; mem. instructional materials evaluation panel Calif. Dept. Edn., 1983. Recipient Perryman Meml. award So. Calif. Social Studies Assn., 1979; NDEA fellow, 1968-69; Taft fellow, 1973. Mem. Assn. Supervision and Curriculum Devel., Nat. Council for Social Studies, Social Studies Supvrs. Assn., Calif. Council for Social Studies (dir. 1976), Phi Alpha Theta.

SCANLON, THOMAS SYLVESTER, III, anesthesiologist; b. Washington, Aug. 1, 1947; s. Thomas Sylvester and Dorothy Grace (Randolph) S.; m. Karen Lynn Wagner, May 20, 1973. B.S., Rockhurst Coll., 1969; postgrad. U. N.Mex., 1969-73, M.D., 1973. Diplomate Am. Bd. Anesthesia. Commd. officer U.S. Navy, 1972, advanced through grades to comdr., 1982; intern, Naval Regional Med. Ctr., San Diego, 1973-74, resident, 1974-77, staff anesthesiologist, 1977—; clin. instr. U. Calif.-San Diego, 1978—; obstetrical anesthesia staff Mercy Hosp. San Diego, 1980—. Fellow Am. Coll. Anesthesiologists; mem. Calif. Soc. Anesthesiologists, Am. Soc. Anesthesiologists. Office: Naval Regional Med Ctr San Diego CA 92134

SCANNELL, DANIEL ANDREW, found. exec.; b. San Francisco, Mar. 13, 1934; s. Andrew M. and Ann Elizabeth (White) S.; B.A., St. Marys Coll. Calif., 1957; postgrad. San Francisco State U., 1964; m. Maureen Anne O'Brien, Aug. 17, 1957; children—Sheila, Patrick, Sean, Colleen, Daniel J., Kathy. Publs. editor Kaiser Steel Corp., Oakland, Calif., 1957-64, mgr. communications, 1964-66, communication editor, 1966-68, dir. public affairs, Kaiser Found. Health Plan, 1969—. Mem. communications com. No. Calif. Cancer Program. Served with U.S. Army, 1953-55. Mem. Pub. Relations Soc. Am. (exec. com. health sect.), Am. Soc. Hosp. Pub. Relations, Am. Pub. Health Assn., Sci. Writers Am., Berkeley (Calif.) C. of C. (dir. 1980—). Home: 4333 Harbord Dr Oakland CA 94618 Office: Kaiser Foundation Health Plan 1924 Broadway Oakland CA 94612

SCARDACI, STEVEN CHARLES, agronomist; b. San Francisco, Aug. 25, 1954; s. Charles C. and Sarah E. (Cunningham) S.; m. Jeanette E. Wrysinski, Apr. 12, 1980. B.S. in Plant Sci., U. Calif.-Davis, 1976, M.S. in Plant Pathology, 1979. Nurseryman, Navlet's Nursery, Concord, Calif., 1972-75; lab. asst. U. Calif.-Davis, 1975-77, research asst., 1977-79, farm advisor, Colusa, 1979—. Mem. Am. Phytopath. Soc., Am. Agronomy Soc., Calif. Assn. Farm Advisors. Democrat. Presbyterian. Author: (with R.K. Webster) Common Root Rot of Cereals in California, 1982; (with R.K. White) Antagonism between the Cereal Root Rot Pathogens Fusarium graminearum and Bipolaris sorokiniana, 1983. Office: U Calif PO Box 180 Colusa CA 95932

SCHAAR, JACQUELINE KAY COUCH (MRS. ROBERT L. SCHAAR), public relations exec.; b. San Diego, Apr. 2, 1933; d. Edwin Newton and Nina Mae (Sweetwood) Couch; grad. pub. schs., 1951; m. Robert L. Schaar, May 11, 1962; children—Robert, Denise. Exec. sec. various firms, 1951-57; asst. to community relations dir. Convair-Astronautics, San Diego, 1957-59; advt., pub. relations exec. Frederick C. Whitney & Assos., San Diego, 1959-62, J. Jessop & Sons, 1962-64; regional dir. pub. relations United Way, Arcadia, Calif., 1964-73; dir. pub. relations Orange County United Way, 1973-77; asso. exec. dir. Orange County chpt. Bldg. Industry Assn. Calif., 1977-80; founder, pres., chief exec. officer Jacqueline Schaar Assos., 1980—. Vice pres. bd. dirs. Orange County council Girl Scouts U.S.A.; mem. adv. council Orange County Performing Arts Center, mem. public relations council U. Calif., Irvine. Mem. Pub. Relations Soc. Am. (accredited, past pres. Orange County chpt., nat. dir.), Charter 100, Orange County Press Club. Home: 23282 Morobe Circle Laguna Niguel CA 92677 Office: 1151 Dove St Suite 290 Newport Beach CA 92660

SCHABER, GORDON DUANE, law sch. dean; b. Ashley, N.D., Nov. 22, 1927; s. Ronald and Esther (Schatz) S.; A.B. with distinction, Sacramento State Coll., 1949; J.D. with honors, U. Calif. at San Francisco, 1952; LL.D., McGeorge Sch. Law, 1961. Admitted to Calif. bar, 1953; partner firm Schaber & Cecchettini, Sacramento, 1953-65; lectr. McGeorge Coll. of Law (now McGeorge Sch. of Law of U. Pacific), Sacramento, 1953-56, asst. dean., 1956, dean, prof. law, 1957—; presiding judge Sacramento County Superior Ct., 1965-69; dir. Air Calif., 1974—, Westgate Corp., 1979—, Sacramento Cablevision, 1980—; cons. establishment Sch. Law, U. Puget Sound, others. Mem. Calif. Bd. Control, 1962-64; chmn. Greater Sacramento Plan Commn., 1970; com. study jud. workload Jud. Council Calif., 1971-72; mem. Adv. Com. to Chief Justice Calif. on Superior Ct. Mgmt., 1971; cons. vehicle theft study Calif. Hwy. Patrol, 1972; panelist Sacramento Bee Crime Prevention Program, 1971—; mem. Commn. State Bar Calif. to Study Bar Exam. Processes, 1976—; vice chmn. Calif. Ednl. Facilities Authority, 1978—; mem. bd. advs. Coll. Public Interest Law, 1978—; mem. advisory com. Calif. OEO, Calif. Legal Services expt., 1972. Chmn., Sacramento City Planning Commn., 1957-64, Sacramento County Democratic Central Com., 1960-64; mem. Dem. State Central Com., 1960-64, 74—; chmn. Dem. Central Com. Sacramento, 1960, 62, 64; bd. dirs. Nat. Center Adminstrv. Justice, 1978, Stanford Homes Found., 1980—; mem. study com. bd. dirs. Sutter Hosps. of Sacramento, 1978. Named Sacramento County Young Man of Year, 1963; Trial Judge of Year, Calif. Trial Lawyers Assn., 1969. Fellow Am. Bar Assn. (chmn.-elect council of sect. legal edn. and admissions to bar 1973, adviser continuing legal edn. 1978); mem. Sacramento County Bar Assn. (v.p. 1970), State Bar Calif. (mem. com. legal edn. 1957—, chmn. 1974-75; mem. long range advisory planning com. 1972—), Am. Trial Lawyers Assn. (award 1965), Am. Judicature Soc., Order of Coif, Phi Delta Phi (hon.). Lutheran. Clubs: Commonwealth (San Francisco); Sutter, University (Sacramento); Comstock. Author: Contracts in a Nutshell, 1972. Contbr. articles to profl jours. Home: 937 Piedmont Dr Sacramento CA 95822 Office: McGeorge Sch Law 3200 5th Ave Sacramento CA 95817

SCHACHET, JOHN LARRY, optometrist; b. Denver, Sept. 21, 1946; s. Hyman and Esther (Sapper) S.; B.S., U. Colo., 1967; O.D., U. Houston, 1971; m. Nata Jean Strauss, Aug. 21, 1966; children—Ronald, Thomas, Jodi. Pvt. practice optometry specializing in contact lenses and corneal rehab., Denver, 1973—; asso. in practice, Arvada, Colo., 1974-78; cons. in field, 1973—. Past mem. advisory bd. B'Nai B'rith Youth Orgn., Denver; past pres. Park Vista Homeowners Assn., Denver. Served to capt. USAF, 1971-73. Recipient Neefe Optical award outstanding contact lens research, 1971, Harold Kohn Meml. Award Am. Optometric Found., 1971. Diplomate Nat. Bd. Examiners in Optometry. Mem. Am. Optometric Assn. (Colo. State polit. edn. coordinator 1982-83; communications div. exec. com. 1983-84), Nat. Eye Research Found. (fellow internat. orthokeratology sect.), Colo. Optometric Assn. (sec.-treas. 1978-79, pres.-elect 1979-80, pres. 1980-81, Young Optometrist of Year 1978), Beta Sigma Kappa. Democrat. Jewish. Club: Lions. Office: 3545 S Tamarac St Suite 170 Denver CO 80237

SCHACHT, PAUL G., grocery distribution company executive; b. Oakland, Calif., 1918. Grad. U. Calif.-Berkeley. Pres., chief exec. officer United Grocers, Ltd., Richmond, Calif. Office: United Grocers Ltd 1005 S 32d St Richmond CA 94804*

SCHACHT, WILLIAM EUGENE, accountant; b. Kokomo, Ind., Nov. 6, 1941; s. Francis Albert and Estella Lillian (Brockman) S.; m. Alma Lovely Megeath, Sept. 17, 1977; children—Julie Ann, Susan Ruth, Randolph Lee. B.S. in Acctg., Ball State U., 1970. C.P.A., Calif. Acct., Davidson, Dreyer & Hopkins, C.P.A.s, 1973-74, mgr., 1974-77; pvt. practice acctg., San Francisco, 1977—; chmn., treas. Unique Adventures Inc. Served with U.S. Army, 1959-62. Recipient Scholastic award Price-Waterhouse, 1968. Mem. Am. Inst. C.P.A.s, Calif. Soc. C.P.A.s, San Francisco C. of C. Republican. Office 140 2nd St 6th floor San Francisco CA 94105

SCHAEF, ANNE WILSON, psychotherapist; b. Silom Springs, Ark., Mar. 22, 1934; d. Virgil and Manilla Maude (Longin) Willey; children—Beth Wilson, Roddy Schaef. A.B., Washington U., St. Louis, 1956; postgrad. Union Theol. Sem., 1958-59, Columbia U. and Tchrs. Coll., 1958-59. Sch. psychologist White Plains (N.Y.) High Sch. and Elem. Sch., 1961-64; supervising psychologist youth ctr. St. Louis State Hosp., 1964-66; clin. dir. youth ctr. Alton (Ill.) State Hosp., 1966-68; community psychol. cons. community devel. and rural mental health Ill. Dept. Mental Health, Springfield, 1966-68; pvt. practice psychotherapy, Boulder, Colo., 1968—; cons. in field. Washington U. Nat. Honor fellow, 1952-56; Danforth grad. fellow, 1956; Danforth spl. fellow, 1957; NIMH fellow, 1957. Mem. Am. Psychol. Assn., Assn. Transpersonal Psychology, Assn. Humanistic Psychology, Psychosynthesis Research Found. Author: (with Patricia Kepler) Women and the New Creation, 1968; Women's Reality, 1981. Home and Office: Lee Hill Rd Boulder CO 80302

SCHAEFER, DANIEL L., state senator, public relations cons.; b. Gutenberg, Iowa, Jan. 25, 1936; B.A., Niagara U., 1961; postgrad. Potsdam State U.; m. Mary Schaefer; children— Darren, Danny, Joel, Jennifer. Pub. relations cons., Lakewood, Colo.; mem. Colo. Ho. of Reps., vice chmn. rules com.; mem. Colo. Senate, 1978—, asst. majority leader, mem. agr., natural resources and energy and state affairs coms. Past pres. bd. dirs. Foothills Park and Recreation Dist. Served with USMC, 1955-57. Mem. Lakewood C. of C., Jaycees. Republican. Roman Catholic. Office: 10755 W Iliff Ave Lakewood CO 80227*

SCHAEFER, DAVID HAROLD, advertising executive; b. San Francisco, Oct. 17, 1951; s. Klaus Herbert and Ann (Schuster) S.; m. Ellen Audrey Van Vliet, May 17, 1981. B.A. in Econs., U. Calif., 1973; M.B.A., Harvard U., 1975. Assoc. product mgr. Gen Foods Corp., White Plains, N.Y., 1975-78; product mgr. Crown Zellerbach, San Francisco, 1978; v.p., mgmt. supr. Foote Cone & Belding, San Francisco, 1978—. Club: Commonwealth (San Francisco). Office: 55 Francisco St San Francisco CA 94133

SCHAEFER, HALMUTH HANS, mgmt. cons.; b. Wiesbaden, Germany, May 16, 1928; came to U.S., 1952, naturalized, 1954; s. Ernst and Theresa (Fritz) S.; Ph.D., U. Chgo., 1958; m. Doris Marie Leininger, Sept., 1952; children—Shirley Gail, Christopher Garth. Asst. prof. psychology Loyola U., Chgo., 1958-60; asst. prof., asso. dir. behavior research lab. Pitts. U., 1960-61; project dir. Ency. Brit. Films Inc., Palo Alto, Calif., 1962-63; research specialist State of Calif., Atascadero, 1964—; research asso. Stanford U. Med. Center, 1962-63; asso. prof. psychology Claremont Grad. Sch., 1964-67; prof. clin. . psychiatry Loma Linda U., 1967-71; prof., mem. senate U. Auckland (N.Z.), 1971-77; cons. to govt. agys. Served with U.S. Army, 1952-54. Behavior Research Soc. fellow, 1971—; lic. psychologist, Calif. Mem. Am. Psychol. Assn., N.Y. Acad. Sci., Am. Mgmt. Assn., So. Calif. H-P Users Group, AAAS, N.Z. Assn. Behavior Therapy (hon.), Sigma Xi. Republican. Club: santa Lucia Sportmen's Assn. Author books, the most recent being: Learning and Programmed Instruction, 1965, German transl., 1971; Behavioral Therapy, 1969, rev. edit., 1975; contbr. numerous articles, chpts. to profl. publs. Home: 11950 Viejo Camino Atascadero CA 93422 Office: PO Drawer A Atascadero CA 93423

SCHAEFER, JOHN PAUL, foundation administrator; b. N.Y.C., Sept. 17, 1934; s. Conrad and Meta (Regelkamm) S.; B.S., Poly. Inst. Bklyn., 1955; Ph.D. in Chemistry, U. Ill., 1958; fellow Calif. Inst. Tech., 1958-59; m. Helen Marie Schwarz, May 18, 1958; children—Ann Marie, Susan Margaret. Asst. prof. U. Calif., Berkeley, 1959-60; mem. faculty U. Ariz., 1960—, prof. chemistry, head dept., 1968-70, dean Coll. Liberal Arts, 1970-71, pres., 1971-82; pres. Research Corp., N.Y.C. and Tucson, 1982—; dir. Home Fed. Savs., Olin Chem., TEC, Tucson Electric Power. Bd. dirs. Research Corp. Mem. Nat., Tucson (pres. 1961-65) Audubon socs., Nature Conservancy, Sigma Xi, Phi Lambda Upsilon. Democrat. Unitarian. Office: Research Corp 6840 E Broadway Tucson AZ 85710

SCHAEFFER, BENSON, clinical psychologist, educator; b. N.Y.C., Aug. 30, 1942; s. Charles and Gilda (Cwas) S.; m. Danna Wilner, Aug. 11, 1963; 1 dau., Rebecca. B.A., UCLA, 1959, M.A. in Psychology, 1962, Ph.D. in Psychology, 1967. Lic. clin. psychologist, Oreg. Asst. prof. dept. psychology U. Oreg., 1966-72, assoc. prof., 1972-82; research clin. psychologist Neurol. Sci. Ctr., Good Samaritan Hosp., Portland, Oreg., 1982—; pvt. practice clin. psychology, Portland. Mem. Am. Psychol. Assn., Oreg. Psychol. Assn., Oreg. Neuropsychiat. Soc., Assn. Severely Handicapped. Author: (with A. Musil, G. Kollinzas) Total Communication: A Signed Speech Program for Nonverbal Children, 1980. Office: 2330 NW Flanders St Suite 201 Portland OR 97210

SCHAFFER, JOHN DARRELL, educator; b. Dodge City, Kans., Dec. 3, 1937; s. Peter Paul and Gertrude May S.; B.S.B.A., Ft. Hays Kans. State U., 1959; M.S. in Bus. Edn., Okla. State U., 1966; Ed.S., U. No. Colo., 1974, Ed.D., 1979. Tchr. bus. edn. Arkansas City (Kans.) Sr. High Sch., 1959-62, Alameda Sr. High Sch., Lakewood, Colo., 1964-70; asso. prof. bus. edn. and communications Met. State Coll., Denver, 1970—. Served with U.S. Army, 1962-64. Recipient cert. of service Denver chpt. Nat. Secs. Assn. Internat., 1978. Mem. Am. Bus. Communications Assn., Nat. Bus. Edn. Assn., Mountain-Plains Bus. Edn. Assn., Colo. Educators for and About Bus., Profl. Secs. Internat. (asso.), Delta Pi Epsilon, Phi Delta Kappa. Democrat. Roman Catholic. Club: K.C. Home: 2067 S Vrain St Denver CO 80219 Office: 1006 11th St Denver CO 80204

SCHAFFLER, DIANE RUTH, direct marketing writer and consultant; b. Pitts., Feb. 18, 1945; d. Joseph and Sally (Antis) S. B.A. in English and Writing, U. Pitts., 1967. Editorial asst. Cook Newspapers, Pitts., 1967; pub. relations asst. to promotion mgr. Instrument Soc. Am., Pitts., 1968-74; sr. copywriter Direct Mktg. Corp. Am., Los Angeles, 1974-75; promotion writer Walt Disney Ednl. Media Co., Los Angeles, 1975-76; owner, pres. Direct Response Agy., Los Angeles, 1976—; cons. in field. Mem. Direct Mktg. Creative Guild-West Coast (past dir.), Direct Mktg. Club So. Calif., The Freelance Network. Office: 4549 Paulhan Ave Los Angeles CA 90041

SCHALLER, LEANDRA MARGARET, educator; b. St. Louis, Sept. 27, 1947; s. Charles Henry and Leona Frances (Lankau) Schaller. Student St. Louis U., 1966-67; B.A. in Biology, Fontbone Coll., St. Louis, 1970; M.S. in Biology, U. No. Ariz., Flagstaff, 1972; Ph.D. in Botany (E.J. Palmer fellow), U. Mo.-Columbia, 1977. Tchr. 7th and 8th grade sci. Desert Foothills Elem. Sch., Phoenix, 1972-74; joined Sisters of St. Francis of Penance and Christian Charity, 1977; prof. biology U. Mo.-St. Louis, 1977-78, Met. State Coll., Denver, 1979, Colo. Women's Coll., 1980; tchr. math. Holy Family High Sch., Denver, 1981-82; tchr. biology Regis Jesuit High Sch., Denver, 1982—; adj. prof. Regis Coll., 1981—, cons. Summer Health Inst. Mus. No. Ariz. research grantee, 1971; NSF grantee, 1973. Mem. Am. Inst. Biol. Scis., Mo. Acad. Sci., Colo. and Wyo. Acad. Sci. Contbr. articles to profl. jours.

SCHAMBER, ANITA LOUIS, high school counselor; b. Lincoln, Nebr., July 18, 1942; d. Henry Edward and Margaret May (Stewart) Rohn; m. Rex Odell Arney, Sept. 3, 1961; children—Dana Lynn Arney Barton, Jill, Michele, Ryan; m. 2d Karel Ray Schamber, June 19, 1982. Student U. Wyo., 1960-63; B.A., Augustana Coll., Rock Island, Ill., 1965; M.Ed., U. Ill., 1967; postgrad. U. Wyo.-Eastern Coll., 1981-83. Cert. tchr., Wyo. Tchr., Myna Thompson Sch., Rantoul, Ill., 1965-66; counselor Jefferson Jr. High Sch., Champaign, Ill., 1967-68, Sheridan (Wyo.) High Sch., 1979—; part-time instr. Sheridan Coll., 1971—. Co-chmn. Title XX Task Force Career Fair, Sheridan; chmn. Sheridan County Heart Assn.; organizer Divorce Recovery Group, Sheridan, 1981-82; ruling elder Presbyterian Ch., Sheridan, pres. United Presbyn. Women, 1981-82; bd. dirs. Civic Theatre Guild, 1969, Community Concert Assn., 1968—. Recipient Best Character Actress award Civic Theatre Guild, 1969; Emmy Mygatt scholar, 1982. Mem. Am. Personnel and Guidance Assn., Am. Sch. Counselors, Wyo. Personnel and Guidance Assn., Wyo. Sch. Counselors (pres. 1981—), Wyo. Council Children and Youth, Wyo. Writers (1st prize non-fiction div. 1982), Range Writers, Good Newscasters, U. Wyo. Alumni Assn. (life), Sheridan Hosp. Aux. (life), Friends of Library (life), AAUW, P.E.O. (past pres. chpt.) Republican Women (past sec.), Kappa Kappa Gamma, Kappa Delta Pi. Club: Dog Owners (Big Horn). Contbr. weekly articles to Country Jour., 1979-83. Home: Three Pine Ln Sheridan WY 82801 Office: Sheridan High Sch Adair and Lewis Sts Sheridan WY 82801

SCHANZ, GERI LYNN, communications specialist; b. Binghamton, N.Y., Dec. 27, 1955; d. George Charles and Jean Louis (Hastings) S. B.S., U. Colo., 1977. Pub. relations coordinator Sheraton Hotels, Aurora, Ohio, 1977-78; advt. coordinator Drawing Bd. Greeting Cards, Dallas, 1978-80; communications services specialist TRW Info. Services, Orange, Calif., 1980—. Mem. Internat. Assn. Bus. Communicators, Pub. Relations Soc. Am., Delta Gamma. Republican.

SCHAPIRA, MOREY RAEL, electronics sales mgr.; b. Chgo., Jan. 4, 1949; s. Julius and Rose (Schwartz) S.; B.S. with honors in Physics (Ill. State scholar 1966, Case scholar 1966-70), Case Western Res. U., 1970; M.B.A., Harvard U., 1977; m. Barbara Stein, May 29, 1977; children—Rachel, Deborah. Research scientist research div. Raytheon Co., Waltham, Mass., 1970-75; cons. scientist M.I.T. Lincoln Labs., Lexington, summer 1976; product mktg. engr. microwave semicondr. div. Hewlett Packard Co., San Jose, Calif., 1977-80, domestic sales mgr. optoelectronics div., Palo Alto, Calif., 1980-81, distbr. mktg. mgr. optoelectronics div., 1981—. Div. chmn. United Way Campaign., 1978; nat. v.p. Union of Councils for Soviet Jews, 1979—; pres. Bay Area

Council on Soviet Jewry, San Francisco, 1980—. Mem. Am. Mgmt. Assn., Tech. Mktg. Soc. Am., Am. Enterprise Inst. Assos., Am. Phys. Soc., Assn. Old Crows, World Affairs Council, Bus./Profl. Advt. Assn. Democrat. Editor-in-chief, then pub. A Guide to Jewish Boston, 1974-77; pub., editor-in-chief HarBus News, 1976-77. Home: 1154 Crespi Dr Sunnyvale CA 94086 Office: 640 Page Mill Rd Palo Alto CA 94304

SCHAREN, BRUCE ALLEN, corporate regional safety coordinator, consultant; b. Eugene, Oreg., Mar. 23, 1939; s. George Wilfred and Dorothy Angeline (Wells) S.; m. Sharon Marie Saal. B.S., U. Oreg., 1966. Personnel/safety mgr. Internat. Paper Co., Gardiner, Oreg., 1967-72, workers' compensation and safety mgr., Longview, Wash., 1972-77, corp. regional safety coordinator, Portland, Oreg., 1977—; safety cons. Served with USCGR, 1959—. Mem. Am. Soc. Safety Engrs., Oreg. Self Insurers Assn. (past pres.), Forest Products Safety Conf. (2d vice chmn.), Western Wood Products Assn. (safety chmn.), Res. Officers Assn. Republican. Home: 1129 SW Chastain Dr Gresham OR 97030 Office: PO Box 3860 Portland OR 97204

SCHARF, DIANA SUE, time management consultant; b. Huntington, W.Va., June 10, 1948; d. Otto Jerry and Geraldine Edna (Boster) Bostic; m. Donald T. Anderson, Nov. 6, 1970; m. Robert Evan Scharf, Oct. 24, 1979. A.A., Marshall U., 1968; B.S., Ohio State U., 1973; M.A., Ariz. State U., 1975, Ph.D., 1981. Parent advocate coordinator N.W. Colo. Child Study Ctr., Steamboat Springs, Colo., 1973; learning disabilities specialist Western Maricopa Spl. Services, Goodyear, Ariz., 1973-74; edn. dir. Upward Found. Ariz. Presch. for Retarded, Phoenix, 1974-78; dir. spl. edn. Laveen (Ariz.) Sch. Dist., 1978-79; pres. Timensions, Inc., Scottsdale, Ariz., 1981—. Mem. Nat. Assn. Tng. and Devel.

SCHARY, PHILIP B., marketing educator; b. Oakland, Calif., June 28, 1929; s. Harry Alexander and Helen Amy (Brandt) S.; m. Nancy Horne, July 23, 1955; children—Martha, Alison, Claire. B.S., St. Louis U., 1951; M.B.A., U. Calif.-Berkeley, 1955; Ph.D. in Bus. Econs., UCLA, 1966. Market analyst Douglas Aircraft Co., 1955-59, Lockheed Electronics Co., 1959-60, Flying Tiger Line, 1960-62; asst. prof. Oreg. State U., 1966-69, assoc. prof. Sch. Bus., 1969—; dir. Vineyard Mountain, Inc., Microcomp, Inc. Served with USAF, 1951-53. Mem. Am. Econ. Assn., Am. Mktg. Assn., Am. Soc. Traffic and Transp., Nat. Council of Phys. Distbrn. Democrat. Jewish. Author: (with M. Christopher and T. Skjott-Larsen) Customer Service and Distribution Strategy, 1979; contbr. articles to profl. jours.; Am. editor Internat. Jour. of Phys. Distbn. Office: Sch Bus Oreg State U Cornwallis OR 97381

SCHATTINGER, DALE SUSAN, advertising executive; b. Niagara Falls, Ont., Can., Dec. 2, 1956; d. Paul S. and Ramona (Jonusas) Pretkus; m. Jeffrey Charles Schattinger, Mar. 10, 1979. B.A. cum laude in Pub. Relations, U. So. Calif.-Los Angeles, 1978. Retail mgmt. The Broadway dept. stores, Los Angeles, 1973-78; pub. relations Basso & Assocs., Newport Beach, Calif., 1978-79; customer relations mgr., advt. supr. Bates File Co., Venice, Fla., 1979-80; pub. relations account exec. Bozell & Jacobs, Inc., Newport Beach, Calif., Omaha, Nebr., 1980-82; advt. account mgr. Gordon Bailey & Assocs., Food Fundamentals, Inc., Santa Ana, Calif., 1982—; freelance writer. Mem. Pub. Relations Soc. Am., Internat. Foodservice Mfrs. Assn. Roman Catholic. Office: 2107 N Broadway Suite 105 Santa Ana CA 92706

SCHAUBERT, LAUREL VIRGINIA, med. illustrator; b. Portland Oreg., Aug. 3, 1923; d. John and Mildred (Hall) Karg; student Reed Coll., 1940-43, U. Calif., 1947-49, Art League San Francisco, 1950-53, U. Calif. San Francisco Med. Center, 1953-55; m. Arvid D. Schaubert, Nov. 10, 1962; children—Gay Lee Schaubert Giannini, Leslie May (dec.). Med. illustrator Ft. Miley VA Hosp., 1955; sr. illustrator dept. surgery U. Calif., San Francisco, 1955-69; prin. illustrator Lange Med. Publs., Los Altos, Calif., 1961—; now also co-owner, pres. Biomed Arts Assocs., Inc., San Francisco; instr. U. Calif., 1959-61, 74-78. Recipient cert. of commendation Calif. Dist. Attys. Assn., 1977; Merit award Fedn. Biocommunication Socs., 1979. Mem. Assn. Med. Illustrators (Outstanding Service award 1972; chmn. bd. govs. 1971-72, v.p. 1975-76, pres. 1976-77), Graphic Artists Guild. Co-author: Scientific Illustration: Standards for Publication; contbr. articles to profl. jours. Office: 350 Parnassus Ave Suite 905 San Francisco CA 94117

SCHAUF, GEORGE EDWARD, physician, author; b. Los Angeles, Mar. 1, 1925; s. Henry George and Viola Lucille (Creason) S.; student Santa Clara U., 1946-49; B.E.E., A.B., San Jose State Coll., 1951, M.A. in Psychology, 1954; M.D., St. Louis U., 1957; m. Joanne Jenkins, Dec. 28, 1948 (div. 1981); children—Theresa, William Frederick, Caroline (dec.), Henry George II, Ralph Edward, Theodore Ignatius (dec.), Martha, George Edward (dec.), George Joseph, Joan, John Anthony. Intern, Mercy Hosp., Cedar Rapids, Iowa, 1957; staff physician Modesto State Hosp., 1958; practice gen. medicine, Riverbank, Calif., 1958—; mem. staffs Oak Valley Hosp., Oakdale, Calif., Dr.'s, City, Meml. North hosps., Modesto. Served with USAAF, 1943-46. Diplomate Am. Bd. Family Practice. Fellow Royal Soc. Health, Am. Acad. Family Practice; mem. Pan Am. Med. Assn., AMA, Calif. Med. Assn., Calif. Acad. Family Practice, Am. Soc. Clin. Hypnosis, Stanislaus County Med. Soc., Riverbank C. of C. (pres. 1963). Author: (with Jack LaLanne) The Power of Thinking Thin, 1968; Think, Eat and Lose Fat, 1970; The Etiology of Obesity, the QQF theory, 1973; Think Thin, 1976. Home: 2748 Topeka St Riverbank CA 95367 Office: 3443 Atchison St Riverbank CA 95367

SCHAUSS, ALEXANDER GEORGE, research criminologist; b. Hamburg, Germany, July 20, 1948; s. Frank W. A. and Anna (Demjanov) S.; came to U.S., 1953, naturalized, 1958; B.A., U. N.Mex., 1970, M.A., 1972; m. Sharon Lee Glinski, Dec. 24, 1971; 1 dau., Nova. Probation/parole officer 2d Dist. Ct. N.Mex., Albuquerque, 1969-73; criminal justice planner III, Albuquerque Metro Criminal Justice Coordinating Council, 1973-75; asst. state adminstr. S.D. Div. Corrections, Pierre, 1975-77; mem. profl. adv. council S.D. Dept. Social Services, 1975-77; dir. Pierce County (Wash.) Probation Dept., Tacoma, 1977-78; corrections tng. officer Wash. State Criminal Justice Tng. Commn., 1978-79; dir. Inst. for Biosocial Research, Grad. Sch., City U., Seattle, 1979-80; instr. Correctional Services Acad. Wash., 1977-79; dir. Am. Inst. Biosocial Research, 1980—; adj. faculty at 8 U.S. colls. and univs., 1978—; lectr. univs. in Can., U.K., Australia, N.Z., South Africa, 1980—; scholar Kans. Consortium of Colls., 1982. Recipient citation Mayor N.Y.C., 1966; award Nat. Am. Legion, 1966; numerous community service awards; Sid Morris YMCA scholar. 1966-70. Fellow Pub. Offender Counselor Assn. of Am. Personnel and Guidance Assn. (nat. region III coordinator 1975-77, Wash. state coordinator 1978), Am. Orthopsychiat. Assn., German Acad. Physiol. Psychology; mem. AAAS, Am. Pub. Health Assn., N.Y. Acad. Sci., Am. Soc. Criminology, Acad. Criminal Justice Scis., Am. Correctional Assn., Internat. Coll. Applied Nutrition, Am. Assn. Correctional Psychologists. Author: Orthomolecular Treatment of Criminal Offenders, 1978; Diet, Crime and Delinquency, 1980; Body Chemistry and Behavior, 1981; Effects of Nutrition on Behavior, 1984; editor Internat. Jour. Biosocial Research; contbr. articles to profl. jours. Directed first research effort in use of orthomolecular diagnosis, treatment and psychiat. treatment in rehab. of pub. offenders in U.S.; discovered hue that reduces violent behavior. Office: PO Box 1174 Tacoma WA 98401

SCHAWLOW, ARTHUR LEONARD, educator, physicist; b. Mt. Vernon, N.Y., May 5, 1921; s. Arthur and Helen (Mason) S.; B.A., U. Toronto (Ont., Can.), 1941, M.A., 1942, Ph.D., 1949, LL.D., 1970; D.Sc., U. Ghent (Belgium), 1968, Bradford (Eng.) U., 1970; m. Aurelia Keith Townes, May 19, 1951; children—Arthur Keith, Helen Aurelia, Edith Ellen. Postdoctoral fellow, research asso. Columbia U., 1949-51, vis. asso. prof., 1960; research physicist Bell Telephone Labs., 1951-61, cons., 1961-62; prof. physics Stanford U., 1961—, chmn. dept., 1966-70, acting chmn., 1973-74, J.G. Jackson-C.J. Wood prof. physics, 1978; AAAS Holiday Sci. lectr., Phila., 1965, Salt Lake City, 1966, Raleigh, 1967. Recipient Ballantine medal Franklin Inst., 1962, Thomas Young medal and prize Inst. Physics and Phys. Soc., London, 1963, named Calif. Scientist of Year, 1973; Nobel prize for physics, 1981; Marconi internat. fellow, 1977; Schawlow medal Laser Inst. Am., 1982. Fellow Am. Phys. Soc. (council 1966-69, pres. 1981), Optical Soc. Am. (dir.-at-large 1966-68, pres. 1975, Frederick Ives medal 1976), IEEE (Liebmann prize 1964), AAAS (chmn. physics sect. 1979), Am. Acad. Arts and Scis.; mem. Nat. Acad. Scis. Author: (with C. H. Townes) Microwave Spectroscopy, 1955. Editorial adv. bd. Phys. Review, 1963-65, Jour. Applied Physics, 1962-65, Laser Abstract, 1963-74. Inventor (with C. H. Townes) optical Maser or laser, 1958. Office: Dept Physics Stanford U Stanford CA 94305

SCHEAR, ROBERTA JANE, psychotherapist; b. Dayton, Ohio, Dec. 19, 1946; d. Irvin and Celia (Bearse) S.; m. Donald Martin Selcer, Dec. 22, 1968 (div.); 1 son, Perrin. B.A., U. Mich., 1969; M.A., Yeshiva U., N.Y.C., 1971, Ph.D., 1975. Lic. psychologist, Calif. Mem. staff Psychotherapy Inst., Berkeley, Calif., 1974-75; asst. prof. dept. ednl. psychology Calif. State U.-Hayward, 1975-76; mem. core faculty Calif. Sch. Profl. Psychology, San Francisco, 1974-75; supr. dept. health and med. scis. U. Calif.-Berkeley, 1976-78; mem. core faculty Antioch U., San Francisco, 1975-79; pvt. practice psychotherapy, Oakland, Calif., 1976—. Pres. bd. dirs. Park Day Sch., Oakland, 1979-81. Mem. Am. Psychol. Assn. Contbr. articles to profl. jours. Address: 5460 Carlton St Oakland CA 94618

SCHEER, CARL, professional basketball team manager; b. 1936; A.B., Middlebury Coll., 1958; LL.B., U. Miami, 1960; m. Marsha Scheer; children—Bobby, Lauren. Admitted to N.C. bar, 1962; practiced in Greensboro, 1960-69; asst. to commr. Nat. Basketball Assn., N.Y.C., 1969-71; gen. mgr. Buffalo Braves Nat. Basketball Assn., 1971; pres., gen. mgr. Carolina Cougars, Am. Basketball Assn., Greensboro, 1971-74, Denver Nuggets, Nat. Basketball Assn., 1974—; past announcer U. Miami, Guilford Coll. Office: Denver Nuggets McNichols Arena 1635 Clay St Denver CO 80204*

SCHEER, LAWRENCE EARNEST, aerospace engr.; b. Broken Arrow, Okla., Feb. 8, 1924; s. William Earnest and Geraldean (Meadows) S.; student Kans. State U., 1942-43, U. Ill., 1943-44, U. Mich., 1944-45, U. Notre Dame, 1945; B.S., Ariz. State U., 1968, M.S., 1974; m. Helen Erlene Hoppes, Dec. 20, 1945; children—Steven Lawrence, Lucinda Erlene, Mark Earnest, Carolyn Ruth. Aviator, U.S. Navy, 1942, advanced comdr., ret., 1968; with Garrett Corp., Phoenix, 1968—, advanced mfg. tech. engr., asst. project engr., 1981—; engring. cons., dir. Dyna-Waste Corp., Phoenix, 1970-78. Pres., Handicap Village of Ariz., Phoenix, 1980—; pres. Phoenix Area council Mo. Synod Luth. Ch., 1974-76; pres. council Christ Ch. Luth., Phoenix, 1976, dir. bd. deacons, 1973-82, sec. bd. missions and ch. extension English dist., 1980—, bd. dirs., 1983—; mem. Ariz. Mission Com., 1982—. Mem. Soc. Automotive Engrs. (vice chmn. student acitivities 1969-72, nat. del. 1979-80), Am. Inst. Indsl. Engrs. Democrat. Club: Caterpillar. Home: 5071 N 38th Pl Phoenix AZ 85018 Office: Garrett Pneumatic Systems Div 2801 E Washington St PO Box 5217 Phoenix AZ 85010

SCHEGLOFF, EMANUEL ABRAHAM, sociology educator, consultant; b. N.Y.C., July 24, 1937; s. Ber Mendelev and Helen (Faller) S.; m. Mysa Jill White, July 15, 1962; 1 dau., Naomi Eve. B.J.Ed. cum laude, Hebrew Tchrs. Coll., 1957; B.A. magna cum laude, Harvard U., 1958; M.A., U. Calif.-Berkeley, 1960, Ph.D., 1967. Research assoc. Ohio State U., Columbus, 1964-65; asst. prof. sociology Columbia U., N.Y.C., 1965-72; from asst. prof. to prof. sociology UCLA, 1972—, dept. chmn., 1980-82. Woodrow Wilson Nat. fellow, 1958; Netherlands Inst. Advanced Studies in Social Scis. and Humanities, 1978. Mem. Am. Sociol. Assn., Am. Anthrop. Assn., AAAS. Contbr. articles to profl. jours. Office: Dept Sociology UCLA Los Angeles CA 90024

SCHEIBLE, WILLIAM GUTHRIE, data communications cons.; b. Dayton, Ohio, Feb. 20, 1949; s. Wilbur Roy and Bernice (Myers) S.; B.B.A., Eastern N.Mex. U., 1973; m. Jill Mabe, Mar. 7, 1981; 1 dau., Carey Jeanne. Sr. analyst Tymshare, Inc., Cupertino, Calif., 1973-78; mgr. network operating systems Tymnet, Inc., Cupertino, 1979; sr. telecommunications cons. Bank of Am., San Francisco, 1979-80; mgr. telecommunications Tymshare Transaction Services, Fremont, Calif., 1980-82; mgr. projects and planning Tymnet, Inc., San Jose, Calif., 1982—, instr. Golden Gate U. Mem. Assn. Computing Machinery, Sports Car Club Am., Internat. Motor Sports Assn., Sigma Chi. Republican. Presbyterian. Home: 473 Donahe Pl Milpitas CA 95035 Office: 2710 Orchard Pkwy San Jose CA 95134

SCHEIDENHELM, RICHARD J., lawyer, legal historian; b. Erie, Pa., Sept. 13, 1942; s. Edward and Jean Thomas (Monrad) S.; m. Lynn Lettice Whitaker, Aug. 30, 1969; children—Colan, Galen. B.A., Kenyon Coll., Gambier, Ohio, 1964; M.A. in Am. History, U. Wis., 1966, Ph.D., 1970; J.D., U. Colo., 1976. Bar: Colo. 1977. Instr. Afro-Am. history Rockford Coll., 1969-70; editorial cons. Conn. Commn. on the Arts, 1972; asst. atty. City of Boulder (Colo.), 1977-80; sole practice, Boulder, 1980—; legal historian, Boulder, 1982—. Recipient Dalton prize Kenyon Coll., 1964; Am. Jurisprudence award in labor law U. Colo., 1976; Vilas fellow, 1966; Mem. Colo. Bar Assn., Boulder Bar Assn., Am. Hist. Assn., Boulder Interdisciplinary Com. on Child Custody (sec. treas. 1981-82). Democrat. Club: Boulder Tennis Assn. Author: The Response to John Brown, 1972; Artists in the Classroom, 1973.

SCHEIDING, DAVID OSCAR, air force officer, structural engr.; b. Marshalltown, Iowa, Nov. 14, 1942; s. Oscar E. and Jeanette (Welcome) S.; B.S. in Aerospace Engring., Iowa State U., 1964; M.S., U. Denver, 1973; M.B.A., U Utah, 1975; m. Janet Elizabeth Dearixon, Nov. 25, 1962; children—Douglas Scot, Randall Scott. Commd. 2d lt. U.S. Air Force, 1964, advanced through grades to lt. col., 1980; pilot trainee, Reese AFB, Tex., 1965; instr. pilot, Laughlin AFB, Tex., 1966-70; forward air controller, Vietnam, 1971-72; lead structural engr., C-5A-Kelly AFB, Tex., 1974-77; instr. pilot, Cannon AFB, N.Mex., 1978—; chief wing ops. and tng. div. 27th Tactical Fighter Wing, Cannon AFB, 1978-81, ops. officer, 1981-82, comdr., 1982—; project officer for Coronet Beacon, F-111D Deployment to Australia and Korea, 1979. Decorated D.F.C., Air medal with nine oak leaf clusters; Vietnam Cross of Gallantry with bronze star; registered profl. engr., Tex. Mem. Beta Gamma Sigma, Delta Tau Delta. Mem. Ch. of God. Home: 3501 Corlington Clovis NM 88101 Office: 27TFW/523 TFS/CC Cannon AFB NM 88101

SCHEIDING, JANET ELIZABETH, coll. adminstr.; b. California, Mo., Jan. 18, 1942; d. Herman U. and Mary Elizabeth (Reichel) Dearixon; m. David Oscar Scheiding, Nov. 25, 1962; children—Douglas Scot, Randall Scott. B.S., Iowa State U., Ames, 1964; M.Ed., Eastern N.Mex. U., Portales, 1980. Tchr. high sch. English, Del Rio (Tex.) Ind. Sch. Dist., 1966-67, 68-70, 71-72; tchr. high sch. English, biology and health Northside Ind. Sch. Dist., San Antonio, 1975-77; tchr. secondary English and speech St. James Sch., Montgomery, Ala., 1977-78; tchr. adult basic edn. Eastern N.Mex. U., Clovis, 1980-81, tchr. psychology, Portales, Clovis, 1980-82, acad. counselor, Clovis, 1981-82, dir. counseling, testing and advising, 1982—. Mem. Am. Personnel and Guidance Assn., Am. Psychol. Assn., N.Mex. Personnel and Guidance Assn., N.Mex. Sch. Counselor's Assn., N.Mex. Student Personnel Assn., N.Mex. Placement Council, Phi Delta Kappa, Phi Kappa Phi, Psi Chi, Kappa Delta. Baptist. Office: 417 Schepps Blvd Suite 136 Clovis NM 88101

SCHEIER, IVAN HENRY, consultant/trainer in citizen participation, publication company executive; b. Plattsburgh, N.Y., Jan. 7, 1926; s. Joel Henry and Melba (Gottlob) S. B.A. in Philosophy, Union Coll. N.Y., 1948; M.A., McGill U., Montreal, Que., Can., 1951, Ph.D. in Psychology, 1953. Research assoc. Human Resources Research Office, Washington, 1953-55; research assoc. in psychology U. Ill., 1955-58; test editor Inst. for Personality and Ability Testing, Champaign, Ill., 1958-62; dir. Boulder County (Colo.) Juvenile Delinquency Project, 1964-68; exec. dir. Nat. Info. Ctr. on Volunteerism, Boulder, Colo., 1969-77, pres., 1977-79; cons. to vol. programs and citizen participation efforts, 1967—; pres. Yellowfire Press, Boulder. Served with USNR, 1942-45. Recipient Nat. Meritorious Service award Nat. Council Juvenile Ct. Judges, 1971; Meritorious Service award Province Ont. (Can.), 1976; Leadership award Alliance for Volunteerism, Inc., 1976; Disting. Service award State Miss., 1982. Mem. Assn. for Vol. Adminstrn., Nat. Assn. on Vols. in Criminal Justice, Phi Beta Kappa, Sigma Xi. Jewish. Author books, including: The Meaning and Measurement of Neuroticism and Anxiety (with R. B. Cattell), 1961; Exploring Volunteer Space: The Recruiting of a Nation, 1980; (with Jorgensen and Fautsko) Solving Problems in Meetings, 1981; contbr. numerous articles, chpts. to various publs. Home and Office: Sugarloaf Star Route Boulder CO 80302

SCHEIFLY, JOHN EDWARD, lawyer; b. Mexico, Mo., Aug. 25, 1925; s. Luke Clauser and Isabella (Sprankle) S.; B.Sc., Brown U., 1945; J.D., Washington and Lee U., 1948; m. Patricia Ann Lenhart, Dec. 27, 1947; children—John Edward, Jan Ellen. Bar: W.Va. Assoc., Baker, Scheifly & Porter, Huntington, W.Va., 1949-53; ptnr. McClean, Salisbury, Petty & McClean, Los Angeles, 1953-57, Willis, Butler, Scheifly, Leydorf & Grant, Los Angeles, 1958-81, Bryan, Cave, McPheeters & McRoberts, Los Angeles, 1981—. Lectr., U. So. Calif. Tax Inst., 1960-74. Served with USNR, 1943-46, 51-53. Mem. Los Angeles County Bar Assn. (tax chmn. 1965-66), State Bar Calif., State Bar W.Va. Clubs: Hacienda Golf, Jonathan, Monterey Country. Home: 9441 Friendly Woods Ln Whittier CA 90605 Office: 333 S Grand Ave Suite 3100 Los Angeles CA 90071

SCHEINBERG, JERALD STANLEY, energy devel. co. exec.; b. Balt., Aug. 24, 1935; s. Moses Louis and Rena Ruth (Caplan) S.; A.B., U. Md., 1957; M.B.A., Pepperdine U., 1979; m. Carol Ann Grant, Feb. 26, 1961; children—Micah Grant, Anne Katherine, Matthew Loren. Mgmt. analyst Office Mgmt. Budget, Office of Pres. of U.S., Washington, 1968-72; asst. dir. fin. planning and devel. Health Care Fedn., San Francisco, 1972-74; mgr. commercialization Dept. Energy, 1974-80; v.p. corp. devel. Golden Gate Energy Center, Sausalito, Calif., 1980-81; pres. New Energy West, Inc., Sausalito, Calif., 1981—; dir. Trident Energy Systems, Davis, Calif.; asst. prof. econs. Pepperdine U. Bd. dirs. Area Devel. Disabilities Council, 1978—; bd. dirs. Marin Aid to Retarded Citizens, 1976-78. Mem. Internat. Assn. Energy Economists. Republican. Jewish. Home: 450 Wellesley Ave Mill Valley CA 94941 Office: 3020 Bridgeway Sausalito CA 94965

SCHEMINSKE, DENNIS LLOYD, corporate communications specialist; b. Spokane, Wash., Aug. 23, 1943; s. H. Richard and Leona Dell (Wycoff) S.; 1 son, Erick Robert. B.A. in Radio and TV, Eastern Wash. U., 1966. TV reporter, photographer Sta. WKY-TV, Oklahoma City, 1968-70, KOA-TV, Denver, 1970-80; TV specialist, corp. communications rep., corp. communications specialist Adolph Coors Co., Golden, Colo., 1980—. Vice pres. Denver Broncos Booster Club, 1981-84; active Univ. Club Denver. Served with USAR, 1966-72. Recipient Robert L. Perkin award for med. reporting, 1980. Mem. Nat. Press Photographers Assn., Internat. TV Assn., Radio and TV News Dirs. Assn., Pub. Relations Soc. Am., Sigma Delta Chi (award for Excellence in TV Photography 1981). Republican. Presbyterian. Patentee motion picture camera. Home: PO Box 357 Golden CO 80401

SCHEMNITZ, SANFORD DAVID, wildlife educator, researcher; b. Cleve., Mar. 10, 1930; s. David Arthur and Evelyn (Farber) S.; m. Mary Margaret Newby, July 8, 1958; children—Ellen Kay, Steven, Stuart. B.S. in Forestry (Wildlife), U. Mich., 1952; M.S. in Forestry (Wildlife), U. Fla., 1953; Ph.D. in Wildlife, Okla. State U., 1958. Cert. wildlife biologist. Cons. aide Upland Game and Waterfowl Studies, Mich. Dept. Conservation, 1951-52; research asst. N.Y. State Coll. of Forestry, 1952; with conservation Waterfowl Project, Wis. Conservation Dept., 1953; unit fellow Okla. Coop. Wildlife Research Unit, 1954-57; game research biologist deer and upland game birds Minn. Dept. Conservation, 1958-59; temporary asst. prof. wildlife resources, U. Maine, 1960, asst. prof. wildlife resources, 1963-66, assoc. prof., 1966-75, prof. wildlife resources, 1975; asst. prof. wildlife mgmt. Pa. State U., 1961; prof., chmn. dept. fishery and wildlife scis. N.Mex. State U., Las Cruces, 1976—. Mem. Wildlife Soc. (life), Ecol. Soc. Am., Am. Soc. Mammalogists, Wilson Ornithol. Soc., Nat. Wild Turkey Fedn., Nat. Audubon Soc., Nat. Wildlife Fedn., Desert and Bighorn Council, Sigma Xi. Editor: Wildlife Management Techniques Manual, 4th edit., 1980; contbr. articles to profl. publs. Office: Box 4901 Dept Fish and Wildlife Sci N Mex State U Las Cruces NM 88003

SCHENDEL, WINFRIED GEORGE, ins. co. exec.; b. Harpstedt, Germany, June 19, 1931; s. Willi Rudolf Max and Anna Margarete (Sassen) S.; came to U.S., 1952, naturalized, 1956; B.S. in Elect. and Indsl. Engring., Hannover-Stadthagen U., Hannover, W. Germany, 1952; m. Joanne Wiiest, Aug. 24, 1953; children—Victor Winfried, Bruce Lawrence, Rachelle Laureen. Elec. draftsman Houston Lighting & Power Co., 1954-57; elec. draftsman, corrosion technician Transcontinental Gas Pipeline Co., Houston, 1957-59; elec. engr. Ken R. White Cons. Engrs., Denver, 1959-61; sales engr. Weco div. Food Machinery & Chem. Corp., various locations, 1961-64; ins. field underwriter N.Y. Life Ins. Co., Denver, 1964-66, asst. mgr., 1966-70, mgmt. asst., 1970-71, gen. mgr., 1971-77, mgr., 1979—; ind. gen. agt., Denver, 1978-79. Instl. rep., advancement chmn. Denver Area council Boy Scouts Am., Lakewood, Colo., 1968-72; precinct chmn. Republican Party, Jefferson County, Colo., 1976, 78. Recipient Centurion award, 1966; Northwestern Region Leader Manpower Devel. award N.Y. Life Ins. Co., 1968, Salesman of Yr. award Jefferson County Salesman with a Purpose Club, 1983. Mem. Nat. Assn. Life Underwriters, Colo. Assn. Life Underwriters, Gen. Agents and Mgrs. Assn. (recipient Conf. Nat. Mgmt. award, 1975), Lakewood C. of C. (pres. people-to-people, Trailblazer of Yr. award 1982). Presbyterian (elder). Clubs: Lions, Edelweiss, Internat. Order Rocky Mountain Goats, N.Y. Life Star (leading asst. mgr. Continental region 1980), Masons, Shriners. Home: 13802 W 20th Pl Golden CO 80401 Office: 950 S Cherry St Suite 300 Denver CO 80222

SCHENK, KATHRYN LOUISE, computer scientist; b. New Orleans, Sept. 29, 1951; d. Theodore Michael and Shirley Victory (Begault) S.; B.A. in Math., U. New Orleans, 1973; M.S. in Computer Sci., U. Tenn., 1976; m. James Robert Pinkert, Dec. 19, 1974. Programmer Center for Bus. and Econ. Research U. New Orleans, 1972-73, U. Tenn., 1973-75; computer cons. Oak Ridge Nat. Labs., 1974; instr. Tech. Inst., Knoxville, Tenn., 1976-77; instr. Calif. State U., Chico, 1977-78, instructional cons., 1979—; programmer County of Butte, Calif.,

1978-79. Mem. Assn. Computing Machinery, Nat. Assn. Female Execs. Contbr. articles to profl. jours. Office: Computer Center California State U Chico CA 95929

SCHENK, LYNN ALICE, state official; b. N.Y.C., Jan. 5, 1945; d. Sidney and Elsa (Roth) S.; m. C. Hugh Friedman, Nov. 25, 1972. B.A., UCLA, 1967; J.D., U. San Diego, 1970; postgrad. London Sch. Econs., 1971. Bar: Calif. 1971, U.S. Supreme Ct. 1976, D.C. 1978. Dep. atty. gen. Criminal Div., Office Atty. Gen. State Calif., San Diego, 1971-72; adj. prof. law U. San Diego Law Sch., 1974-78; spl. asst. to Vice Pres. Rockefeller and Mondale, 1976-77; atty. San Diego Gas and Electric Co., 1972-77; dep. sec. Calif. Bus. and Transp. Agy., 1978-80; sec. Calif. Bus., Transp. and Housing Agy., Sacramento, 1980—; mem. State Atty. Gen. Consumer Protection Task Force, 1972-74; mem. San Diego Adv. Bd. on Status of Women, 1973-76; mem. State Atty. Gen. Women's Rights Task Force, 1975; ex officio mem. Calif. Coastal Commn., 1978; bd. dirs. Calif. Housing Fin. Agy., 1980; interim chmn., dir. State Calif. Safe-Bidco Bd. Dirs., 1981; chmn. State Calif. Small Bus. Adv. Bd., 1981; mem. State Calif. Commn. on Indsl. Innovation, 1981; mem. BiNat. Adv. Com. S.W. Border Regional Conf., 1982. Bd. visitors U. San Diego Law Sch., 1974—; bd. dirs., v.p. Equal Rights Advisors, Inc., 1973-75; Calif. del. Democratic Nat. Conv., 1976. Recipient Headliner of Yr. award San Diego Press Club, 1977; B'nai B'rith Women award, 1981; Achievement award Calif. Women in Govt., 1981; State of Israel Peace medal, 1981; named Outstanding Young Citizen of San Diego, 1975, Woman of Yr., San Diego, 1975, Disting. Alumni of Yr., U. San Diego Law Sch. Alumni Assn., 1979. Mem. ABA (coordinator placement assistance sect. on internat. law 1973-74), Calif. Women Lawyers (dist. gov., 1st v.p. 1975-76), San Diego County Bar Assn. (vice-chmn. land use planning com. 1977), Lawyers Club San Diego (pres. 1974-75). Office: 1120 N St Room 2101 Sacramento CA 95814

SCHENK, MARTIN L., tax executive; b. N.Y.C., Dec. 30, 1930; s. Emanuel and Evelyn (Jaller) S.; m. Joy Carol Barber, Sept. 1, 1957; children—Elisa, Jonathan, Rachel, Eve, David. B.S., NYU, 1953, LL.M., 1971; J.D., Bklyn. Law Sch., 1957. Bar: N.Y. 1958; C.P.A., N.Y. Pub. acct., N.Y.C., 1953-65; agt., conferee Manhattan dist. IRS, N.Y.C., 1964-69; tax editor Research Inst. Am., N.Y.C., 1969-72; sole practice, Monroe, N.Y., 1972-76; exec. dir. taxes Ramada Inns, Inc., Phoenix, 1977—; asst. prof. Orange County (N.Y.) Community Coll., 1964-69; instr. Golden Gate U. Mem. Tax Execs. Inst. (pres. Ariz. chpt. 1980-81). Club: Monroe Lions (pres. 1961 64). Editor Jour. Taxation, 1964 69. Home: 4251 N Miller Rd Scottsdale AZ 85251 Office: 3838 E Van Buren St Phoenix AZ 85008

SCHENK, RAY M(ERLIN), electronics co. exec.; b. Logan, Utah, Dec. 18, 1946; s. Merlin F. and Thelma E. (Birch) S.; B.S. in Acctg. magna cum laude, Utah State U., 1969. Staff acct. Haskins and Sells, Phoenix, 1969, Salt Lake City, 1969-71; controller Kimball Electronics, Salt Lake City, 1971—. Recipient Scholastic Achievement cert. Phi Kappa Phi, 1967, 68; 1st Security Found. scholar, 1968; Alpha Kappa Psi scholarship award, 1969; C.P.A., Utah. Mem. Nat. Assn. Accts., Am. Acctg. Assn., Utah Assn. C.P.A.s, Am. Inst. C.P.A.s. Home: 943 E 5290 S Salt Lake City UT 84117 Office: 350 Pierpont Ave Salt Lake City UT 84101

SCHENK, THEODORE ERNEST, financial counsultant, insurance agency executive; b. Gonzales, Calif., Aug. 11, 1922; s. Gottfried and Anna Marie Schenk; m. Joan Bickerton Whitehouse, July 13, 1943; children—Timothy Michael, Deborah Lynn Schenk Chretien. Agy. mgr. Calif. Western States Life Ins. Co., San Jose, 1953-69, New Eng. Mut. Life Ins. Co., San Jose, 1969-83; fin. cons., 1972—; pres. Schenk Ins. Agy., Inc., San Jose, 1978—, Pacific Retirement Cons., Inc., San Jose, 1981—. Mem. Los Gatos Planning Commn., 1972-78; past trustee, mem. adminstrv. bd. Los Gatos 1st United Methodist Ch.; mem. devel. bd. Good Samaritan Hosp. Annuities and Trust Com. Served with USNR, 1939-40, USN, 1940-47. Mem. San Jose Life Underwriters Assn. (dir. 1971-72), San Jose Gen. Agts. and Mgrs. Assn. (pres. 1967-68), Am. Soc. C.L.U.s (pres. San Jose chpt. 1974-75), Santa Clara County Estate Planning Council (pres. 1980-81), Million Dollar Round Table, New Eng. Life Leaders' Assn. Republican. Lodges: Rotary, Masons. Office: 1602 The Alameda 102 San Jose CA 95126

SCHEPIS, FRANK JOSEPH, III, library administrator; b. Weatherford, Tex., Aug. 27, 1943; s. Frank Joseph and Jackie Laverne (Swearingin) S.; m. Sharron Kaye Holt, May 5, 1979 (div.); 1 son, Ty Stephen. B.A. in History, U. Dallas, 1965; M.L.S., N. Tex. State U., Denton, 1970. Librarian, Hampton-Ill. br. Dallas Pub. Library, 1971, 1st asst. to br. mgr. Audelia Rd. br., 1972-76, br. mgr., 1976-77; asst. dir. Hurst (Tex.) Pub. Library, 1977-78; asst. dir. Springfield Greene County Library, Springfield, Mo., 1978-81; dir. Natrona County Pub. Library, Casper, Wyo., 1981—. Mem. ALA, Mountain Plains Library Assn., Wyo. Library Assn., Am. Soc. Personnel Adminstrs. Club: Rotary. Office: 307 E 2d St Casper WY 82601

SCHERER, WILLIAM THOMAS, management consultant; b. Ventura, Calif., June 9, 1931; s. George Frederick and Helen Jeanette (Hall) S.; B.A. in Polit. Sci., UCLA, 1954; m. Mary June Gusella, Dec. 28, 1954; children—Cynthia Anne Scherer Brossman, William Frederick. Mgmt. trainee to dist. mktg. mgr. Gen. Telephone and Electronics, 1957-61; mgmt. devel. specialist RCA, 1961-63; mgmt. tng. specialist N. Am. Aviation, Inc., 1963-64; mgr. corp.-wide mgmt. devel. and tng. Fluor Corp., Irvine, Calif., 1964-78; pres. Scherer Assocs., Inc., Lake Forest, Calif., 1978—; tech. adv. Roundtable Films, Inc., Beverly Hills, Calif. Fund raiser, mem. Hoag Hosp. 552 Club, Newport Beach, Calif. Served to capt. USAFR, 1954-57. Mem. Nat. Assn. Tng. and Devel., Am. Soc. Tng. and Devel., Newport Beach Area C. of C., UCLA Alumni Assn., Christian Businessmen's Assn., Kappa Sigma Alumni. Republican. Contbr. articles to profl. publs. Office: Lake Forest CA

SCHERICH, ERWIN THOMAS, civil and design engineer; b. Inland, Nebr., Dec. 6, 1918; s. Harry Erwin and Ella (Peterson) S.; student Hastings Coll., 1937-39, N.C. State Coll., 1943-44; B.S., U. Nebr., 1946-48; M.S., U. Colo., 1948-51; m. Jessie Mae Funk, Jan. 1, 1947; children—Janna Rae Scherich Thornton, Jerilyn Mae Scherich Dobson, Mark Thomas. Civil and design engr. U.S. Bur. Reclamation, Denver, 1948—, chief spillways and outlets sect., 1974-75, chief dams br., div. design, 1975-78, chief tech. rev. staff, 1978-79, chief div. tech. rev. Office of Asst. Commr. Engring. and Research Ctr., 1980—. Mem. U.S. Com. Internat. Commn. on Large Dams. Served with AUS, 1941-45. Registered profl. engr., Colo. Fellow ASCE (nat. dir.); mem. Nat. Soc. Profl. Engrs., Profl. Engrs. Colo. (past pres.), Wheat Ridge C. of C. Republican. Methodist. Home: 3915 Balsam St Wheat Ridge CO 80033 Office: Denver Federal Center Denver CO 80225

SCHERRER, DONALD GENE, accounting executive; b. Shawneetown, Ill., May 20, 1933; s. Daniel S. and Mayme S. (Stubbs) S.; m. Myrtle Lucille Coleman, Nov. 1, 1952; children—Michael C., Karen L., Mary C.; m. Ruth Emily Tartaglia, July 4, 1976; children—Daryl G., Donna G. B.S. in Acctg., So. Ill. U., 1958. Acct. Ill. Farm Supply, Chgo. and Bloomington, 1958-60; office mgr. McKean's Laundry & Dry Cleaning, Phoenix, 1960-63; supr. acct.'s pay Salt River Project, Tempe, Ariz., 1963-66, supr. gen. acctg., 1966-69, mgr. fin. acctg. div., 1969—, mem. polit. involvement com.; owner, mgr. Scherrer Acctg. & Tax Service. Mem. acctg. adv. com. Mesa Community Coll., S. Mountain Coll. Served with USN, 1952-56. Mem. Nat. Assn. Accts. (past pres., dir., mem. nat. com. chpt. operation, treas. Wild West council, treas. X club). Club: Rio Salado Optimists. Home: 3128 S Noche de Paz Mesa AZ 85202 Office: Salt River Project PO Box 1980 Phoenix AZ 85001

SCHERWITZ, LARRY WAYNE, medical researcher; b. Sweetwater, Tex., Oct. 28, 1946; s. Raymond Henry and Nora Lois (Staas) S.; m. Deborah Beth Kesten, Apr. 19, 1981. B.A. in Psychology, U. Tex., Austin, 1969, Ph.D. in Social Psychology, 1973; postgrad. Harvard Med. Sch., 1970, U. Wis.-Madison, 1973-76. Asst. prof. social psychology dept. community medicine Baylor Coll. Medicine, Houston, 1976—; research scientist Inst. Epidemiology and Behavioral Medicine, Pacific Med. Ctr., San Francisco, 1982—. NIH grantee. Mem. Soc. Behavioral Medicine, Am. Psychol. Assn., Soc. Psychophysiol. Research. Contbr. articles to profl. jours. Office: 2200 Webster Suite 308 San Francisco CA 94115

SCHERZER, ROBERTA WOLFF, interior designer; b. Portland, Oreg., Dec. 16, 1938; d. Frank Kales and Esther (Goldberg) K.; m. Arnold James Wolff, Nov. 29, 1959; children—Leslie Beth, Cynthia Joy; m. Louis Scherzer, Mar. 10, 1974. Student U. Wash., 1956-58; grad. N.Y. Sch. Interior Design, 1967. Design asst. Don Stevenson, Ltd., Portland, 1966-68; staff interior designer Meier & Frank Co., 1968-69, Lloyd's Interiors Co., 1971-73; owner, designer Roberta Wolff Co., 1975—. Active Contemporary Art Council, Portland Art Mus., Portland Art Assn., Portland Ctr. Visual Arts, Japanese Garden Soc.; trustee Oreg. Contemporary Theatre, March of Dimes; past bd. dirs. Camp Fire Girls. Mem. Am. Soc. Interior Designers cert.; dir. Portland chpt. 1975-77. Republican Jewish. Clubs: Multnomah Athletic, Mt. Park Racquet, University. Contbr. articles to profl. jours.; columnist local newspapers.

SCHERZINGER, DENNIS MARTIN, civil engineer; b. Bridgeport, Nebr., Feb. 24, 1936; s. Martin and Sylvia Pauline (Boodry) S.; m. Kay F. Ouelette, Aug. 16, 1958; children—Kurt Von, Kristi Lee. Student U.S. Naval Acad., 1953-55; B.S. in Civil Engring., U. Calif.-Berkeley, 1957. Registered profl. engr., Calif. Jr. civil engr. City of Vallajo (Calif.), 1957-58; asst. civil engr. San Mateo County, 1961-63; assoc. civil engr. Napa County (Calif.), 1963-68; sr. civil engr. Oakland (Calif.) Redevel. Agy., 1968-70; engr.-mgr. Vallejo (Calif.) Sanitation and Flood Control Dist., 1970-82. Napa (Calif.) Sanitation Dist., 1982—. Served with USN, 1958-61. Mem. Calif. Water Pollution Control. Assn. Club.: Vallejo Yacht. Home: 264 Parkview Terr Vallejo CA 94590 Office: 950 Imola Ave W Napa CA 94558

SCHEUER, ERNEST MARTIN, mathematics educator; b. Bad Nauheim, Germany, July 28, 1930; came to U.S., 1936; s. Sally and Hedwig (Rosenthal) S.; m. Sondra Lee Goldstein, Sept. 20, 1953; m. 2d, Mary Jean Aura, June 5, 1972; children—Susan Lynn, Michael Joseph. B.A. in Math., Reed Coll., Portland, Oreg., 1951; M.S. in Math. Stats., U. Wash., 1954; Ph.D. in Math., UCLA, 1960. Mathematician U.S. Naval Ordnance Test Sta., Pasadena, Calif., 1951-58; mathematician Space Tech. Labs, El Segundo, Calif., 1958-61; mathematician RAND Corp., Santa Monica, Calif., 1961-69; assoc. dir. C-E-I-R, Inc., Beverly Hills, Calif., 1969-70; prof. mgmt. sci., math. Calif. State U.-Northridge, 1970—. Fellow Am. Statis. Assn.; mem. Inst. Math. Stats., Internat. Statis. Inst., Inst. Mgmt. Sci., Math. Assn. Am., Sigma Xi. Jewish. Author: (with Richard Bellman and John Hogan) Programmed Statistics, 1970; (with Paul Baum) Statistics Made Relevant, 1972; contbr. articles to profl. jours. Office: Management Sci Dept Calif State U Northridge CA 91330

SCHICK, ROBERT BRYANT, geologist, oil and mining company executive; b. Salt Lake City, Oct. 3, 1922; s. Max F. and Minnie Ellilian (Kitchens) S.; B.S. in Bus. and Engring. Adminstrn. (Sigma fellow), M.I.T., 1947; M.S. in Geology, U. Utah, 1955; m. Gloria Love Thornley, Jan. 31, 1960; children—Robert Brighton, Holly Noel. Mgr., H.I. DeBar Orgn., 1947-49; mgr. exploration Utah So. Oil Co., 1949-54; oil and mining cons. Schick, Thayne & Assos. & Western Consulting Services, Salt Lake City, 1954-67, pres. Marine Oil Co. div., 1959-61, Western Consol. Oil Corp. div., 1959-61; dir. exploration Federal Resources Corp., Salt Lake City, 1967-73, v.p. exploration, 1973-81, cons. oil, gas and minerals, 1981—; pres. Utah Dynamics, 1981—; chmn. Mcpl. Pyrolysis, 1981—. Served to 2d lt. USAAF, 1942-45. Decorated Purple Heart. Registered profl. engr., Utah; registered geologist, Calif. Mem. AIME, Am. Assn. Petroleum Geologists, Wyo. Mining Assn., Idaho Mining Assn., Colo. Mining Assn., Am. Mining Congress. Roman Catholic. Contbr. articles and papers in field. Home: 241 N Vine St Apt 203W Salt Lake City UT 84103 Office: 310 S Main St Suite 1400 Salt Lake City UT 84101

SCHIEFER, GERALD ROBINSON, electronics engineer; b. Zion Nat. Park, Utah, Aug. 1, 1934; s. Arden Guy and Lucy (Crawford) Schiefer; B.S. in Elec. Engring., U. Utah, 1960; m. Loretta McArthur, Dec. 1, 1954; children—Heidi, Gerald Scott, Charles Sidney. Missile design engr. Naval Weapons Center, China Lake, Calif., 1960-70, tech. mgr. high speed anti-radiation missile harm, 1970-75, sci. advisor to comdr. operational test and eval. force, Norfolk, Va., 1975-77, head electronic warfare dept., 1977-81, head test and eval. directorate, 1981-82, dep. tech. dir., head lab. directorate, China Lake, 1982—. Chmn., Desert dist. South Sierra council Boy Scouts Am., also scoutmaster. Served with U.S. Army, 1955-56. Recipient Michelson Lab. award for engring. mgmt. Naval Weapons Center, 1974, L.T.E. Thompson award for mgmt., 1978. Mem. IEEE, AIAA. Mormon (bishop, stake pres.). Author tech. reports. Home: 615 Kevin Ct Ridgecrest CA 93555 Office: Code 01A Naval Weapons Center China Lake CA 93555

SCHIFFMAN, SONDRA HARRIET, interior designer; b. N.Y.C., Mar. 16, 1932; d. Samuel Robert and Esta (Redlich) Silberman; m. Gerald Jay Schiffman, July 4, 1955; children—Joel Aaron, Beth Susan. Student U. Fla., 1949-51, L.I. U., 1954, Queens Coll., 1955, UCLA, Westwood, 1975-77. Cert. profl. interior designer Calif. Interior designer, office mgr. Shirro Interiors, Northridge, Calif., 1967-70; owner, dir. interior design Interiors a La Mode, Encino, Calif., 1970-81, 82—, St. Cloud, France, 1982—; Western European mfrs. rep. DuRovan Rattan, S. Harris Fabrics, Vivid Acrylics; dir. interior design United Design Assocs., Inc., Los Angeles, 1981-82. Bd. dirs. People Helping People USA, Inc., Nat. Trust Hist. Preservation, Kidney Found. So. Calif. Mem. Am. Soc. Interior Designers, Internat. Soc. Interior Designers, Nat. Home Fashions League. Contbr. interior designs to design mags. Home: 2 Rue Josephine Saint Cloud 92210 France Office: PO Box 861 Tarzana CA 91356

SCHILL, ROBERT JAMES, architect; b. Chgo., Aug. 30, 1939; s. Edward John and Mabel Edna (Harroun) S.; B.Arch., U. Ill., 1962, M.Arch., 1963; m. Janice Elaine Dahlstrom, Dec. 21, 1963; children—Carla Grace, Craig Robert, Kelvin Edward. Designer, engr. Laz & Edwards, architects, Champaign, Ill., 1962-63, Jack C. Blackman, architect, Danville, Ill., 1963-64; asso. Richardson, Severns, Scheeler & Assos. Inc., Champaign, 1966-72, chief of prodn., 1968-72, also bd. mem.; project architect Metz, Train & Youngren, Inc., Chgo., 1972—, asso. partner, 1974-79, prin., 1979—; pres. Metz, Train & Youngren of Ariz., Inc., 1981—. Recipient citizenship award V.F.W., 1958. Mem. AIA (corporate; health facilities com. Chgo. chpt. 1974—), Central Ill. Constrn. Com., Am. Concrete Inst., Nat. Fire Protective Assn., Soc. Archtl. Historians, Nat. Trust for Historic Preservation. Mem. Evang. Free Ch. Prin works include Rush Med. Coll., Chgo., Indpls. Mus. Art Complex, Undergrad. Library, U. Ill., Urbana, Engring. Research Center, Ariz. State U., Tempe. Home: 5345 E Orchid Ln Paradise Valley AZ 85253 Office: 2721 N Central Ave Phoenix AZ 85004

SCHILLER, ANITA ROSENBAUM, librarian; b. N.Y.C., June 16, 1926; d. Aaron and Helen (Camnitz) Rosenbaum; B.A. in Econs., N.Y. U., 1949; M.L.S., Pratt Inst., 1959; m. Herbert I. Schiller, Nov. 5, 1946; children—Daniel T., P. Zachary. Reference librarian Nat. Indsl. Conf. Bd., 1960-61; instr. U. Ill. Grad. Sch. Bus. Adminstrn., 1961-62; reference librarian Pratt Inst., 1962-63; successively research asst., research asso., research asst. prof. U. Ill. Library Research Center, 1964-70; reference librarian, bibliographer U. Calif., San Diego, 1970—; Ralph R. Shaw vis. scholar Rutgers U., 1978. Fellow Council Library Resources, 1976-77. Mem. ALA (councillor 1972-76, sec.-treas. library research round table 1978-80, mem. council com. on status of women in librarianship 1980). Contbr. articles to profl. publs.; editor Aware column Am. Libraries, 1971-72; mem. editorial bds. profl. jours. Home: 7109 Monte Vista St La Jolla CA 92037 Office: Central U Library U Calif San Diego CA 92093

SCHILLER, BARRY MYRON, laywer; b. San Francisco, Jan. 28, 1944; s. Jerome L. and Terry (Wiseman) S.; m. Terry Solomon, Aug. 23, 1970. A.B., U. Calif.-Berkeley, 1965; M.A., Ohio State U., 1966; Ph.D., U. So. Calif., 1972; J.D., Southwestern U., 1976. Bar: Calif. Lectr. sociology and criminology U. So. Calif., 1968-70, Calif. State U., Long Beach, 1967-74, Northridge, 1970-72, Los Angeles, 1972-77; sole practice, Beverly Hills, Calif., 1977—. Mem. ABA, Calif. State Bar Assn., Los Angeles County Bar Assn., Beverly Hills Bar Assn., Los Angeles Trial Lawyers Assn., Calif. Trial Lawyers Assn., Assn. Am. Trial Lawyers, Law and Soc. Assn., Am. Sociol. Assn. Democrat. Jewish. Contbr. articles to profl. jours. and law revs. Home: 2814 Hutton Dr Beverly Hills CA 90210 Office: 8730 Wilshire Blvd Suite 206 Beverly Hills CA 90211

SCHILLER, ROBERT ACHILLE, television writer, producer; b. San Francisco, Nov. 8, 1918; s. Roland E. and Lucille (Block) S.; B.A., UCLA, 1939; m. Joyce Harris, July 20, 1947 (dec. 1965); children—Thomas, James; m. 2d, Sabrina Scharf, May 25, 1968; children—Abigail, Sarah. Writer radio shows including Duffy's Tavern, Jimmy Durante, Ozzie and Harriet, December Bride, 1946-50; writer TV shows, 1950—, including I Love Lucy, 1955-57, Lucille Ball-Desi Arnaz Hour, 1957-60, The Lucy Show, 1962-65, Red Skelton Hour, 1965-67, Carol Burnett, 1968, Flip Wilson Show, 1968-71, All in the Family, 1977-80; producer, writer The Good Guys, 1968, Maude, 1972-76; creator, writer, producer Ann Sothern Show, 1958, All's Fair, 1976-77. Served with U.S. Army, 1941-46. Recipient Emmy awards for Flip Wilson Show, 1971, All in the Family, 1978, Writer Guild awards for All in the Family, 1978, Maude, 1974, I Love Lucy, 1955. Mem. Writers Guild Am., AFTRA. Democrat. Club: Riviera Golf. Office: 20th Century Fox Studios Box 900 Beverly Hills CA 90213

SCHILLER, WILLIAM JOSEPH, development consultant; b. Pitts., June 25, 1946; s. William John and Irene (Molnor) S.; m. Lyn Grogan, Sept. 21, 1969; m. 2d, Lorraine Bash, Oct. 3, 1980. B.A. in Sociology, U. Miami, 1969; M.A. in Sociology, N.Mex. State U., 1973; Ed.D. in Counseling and Counselor Edn., Idaho State U., 1981. Nat. mgmt. trainee, mgr. Sears Roebuck & Co., Atlanta, 1969-71; counselor N. Eastern Ohio Council Drug Abuse, Warren, 1973-74; exec. dir., contact Ashtabula (Ohio) County, 1974-77; dir. family edn. ctr. Idaho State U., Pocatello, 1981-82; pres., co-adminstr. Consol. Counseling and Devel., Pocatello, 1981—; indsl. cons.; part-time faculty Idaho State U. Bd. dirs. Alfred Adler Inst. Mountain States, Pocatello. Mem. Am. Personnel and Guidance Assn., Am. Soc. Tng. and Devel. (Service award Pocatello chpt.), Phi Kappa Phi, Phi Gamma Mu, Kappa Sigma. Republican. Club: Rotary (Pocatello). Writer, producer radio spots relating to human problems and issues. Home and Office: PO Box 4301 Pocatello ID 83201

SCHINDLER-RAINMAN, EVA, organization and community resource consultant; b. Cologne, Germany, May 26, 1925; d. Hans and Alice (Goldstein) Schiff; 1 son, Peter Hans Schindler. B.A. in Social Welfare, U. Calif.-Berkeley 1945; M.S.W., U. So. Calif., Los Angeles, 1954, D.S.W., 1962. Pvt. practice cons., Los Angeles 1964—; disting. prof. behavioral sci. U. So. Calif. Sch. Pub. Adminstrn., Los Angeles, 1980—; vis. prof. U. Mich., U. Hawaii, UCLA, U. Victoria (B.C.). Nat. bd. dirs. Girl Scouts U.S.A., 1972-78, Future Homemakers Am., 1970—. Recipient Carnation Community Service award, 1978 and Outstaning Alumna award, 1981, U. So. Calif. Sch. Social Work; Outstanding Contbn. to Correctional Field award, Pepperdine Coll., 1963; Mem. Am. Soc. Tng. and Devel., Acad. Cert. Social Workers, Nat. Assn. Social Workers, Internat. Assn. Applied Social Scientists, Internat. Cons. Found., Women for Internat. Understanding, Adult Edn. Assn., Soc. Psychol. Study Social Issues, Assn. Vol. Action Scholars, Nat. Tng. Labs., Nat. Conf. on Social Welfare, Internat. Conf. Social Welfare, Internat. Assn. Vol. Effort, Los Angeles County Art Mus., Phi Kappa Phi. Author numerous books; contbr. chpts. to books; contbr. articles to profl. jours. Home and Office: 4267 San Rafael Ave Los Angeles CA 90042

SCHIPMAN, HENRY CHARLES, artist, cartoonist; b. Las Cruces, N.Mex., Oct. 11, 1924; s. Henry Charles and Rose Love (Johnson) S. Student N.Mex. State Coll., 1949-54. Photo retoucher local photographers, 1945-55; staff artist N.Mex. Farm and Livestock Bur., 1955-65; owner, curator Am. Cowboy Mus., Las Cruces, N.Mex., 1975—. Mem. Nat. Fedn. Ind. Bus., John Birch Soc., Spanish Mustang Registry, Am. Donkey and Mule Soc., Tex. Longhorn Breeders. Republican. Methodist. Club: Odd Fellows. Author: Different Types of Cowboys and Their Different Jobs, 1968; The Animal of Christmas and Easter, 1971; My Friends, The Cabdrivers, 1979; contbr., illustrator articles in Western Horseman, True West, Hoofs and Horns, Nat. Parks mags. Home: 644 W Court St Las Cruces NM 88005

SCHLANG, LAWRENCE HAROLD, aerospace and communications co. exec.; b. Bklyn., May 28, 1936; s. Aaron Arthur and Marion Lillian (Reiss) S.; B.S., U.S. Naval Acad., 1958; M.S. (N. Am. Aviation Sci. Engring. fellow), U. Nev., Reno, 1966; m. Shirley Ann Moritz, Oct. 26, 1962; children—Mark, David, Stephen. Enlisted in U.S. Navy, 1954, commd. ensign, 1958, aviator, 1958-64; test engr., asst. engring. group leader, sr. project engr. Rocketdyne div. N. Am. Aviation, Reno and Autonetics div., Los Angeles, 1964-66; capt. Continental Airlines, 1966-83; sr. engr., cons. Genge Industries, Oxnard, Calif., 1967-69; pres. Damark Engring. Assos., Oxnard, 1969-76; v.p. Teleshare, Inc., Cupertino, Calif., 1979-81, also dir.; pres., chief exec. officer Lear Fan Pacific, Reno, 1981—. State coordinator U.S. Naval Acad. Info. Program, 1976-78; v.p. Naval Air, Naval Res. Assn. Channel Island, 1973; ofcl. Little League, 1976, Pop Warner Football, 1980; bd. dirs. Reno Aquatic Club, 1980; comdg. officer Bonhomme Richard Div., U.S. Naval Sea Cadet Corps, Reno, 1978. Served to comdr. USNR, to 1978. Recipient J. Garrett Roach prize U.S. Naval Acad., 1958. Mem. Naval Inst. (life), Naval Res. Assn., Air Line Pilots Assn. (nat. spokesman 1981), Reno Bd. Realtors, Navy League, Ret. Officers Assn., Beta Gamma Sigma, Sigma Tau. Jewish. Club: Lehigh Country. Contbr. articles to profl. publs.; inventor burglar alarm devices. Office: 10090 N Blaney Suite 6 Cupertino CA 95014

SCHLEI, NORBERT ANTHONY, lawyer; b. Dayton, Ohio, June 14, 1929; s. William Frank and Norma (Lindsley) S.; B.A., Ohio State U., 1950; LL.B. magna cum laude, Yale U., 1956; children—Anne C. Schlei Buczynski, William K., Andrew M., Bradford L., Graham L., Norbert L., Norma Blake. Bar: Ohio 1956, Calif. 1958, D.C. 1963. Law clk. to Justice John M. Harlan, U.S. Supreme Ct., 1956-57; practice law with various firms, Los Angeles, 1957-62; 67—; asst. atty. gen. U.S.,

Washington, 1962-67; partner in charge firm Hughes Hubbard & Reed 1972—; dir. Carlsberg Corp., Pritchard Corp., Wedbush Corp.; Leatherbee lectr. Harvard Bus. Sch., 1962. Democratic nominee for Calif. Assembly 57th Dist., 1962, for Calif. Sec. State, 1966; chmn. Urban Child Center, 1968-72. Served to lt. (j.g.) USNR, 1950-53. Recipient Cardozo prize Yale U., 1954, Robinson prize, 1956; co-recipient Ann. Book award Am. Soc. Internat. Law, 1962. Mem. ABA, Fed. Bar Assn., Los Angeles Bar Assn., Am. Judicature Soc., Am. Soc. Internat. Law, Yale Law Sch. Assn., Phi Kappa Sigma, Phi Alpha Delta, Phi Eta Sigma. Club: Yale of So. Calif. Author: State Regulation of Corporate Financial Practices: The California Experience, 1962; (with McDougal and Assocs.) Studies in World Public Order, 1961. Office: 555 S Flower St Los Angeles CA 90071

SCHLEININGER, CHARLES, III, avionics representative; b. S.I., N.Y., Feb. 6, 1937; s. Charles, Jr., and Alice (Kashubeck) S.; m. Joyce Carol Jensen, Jan. 18, 1964; children—Monica Lynn, Kisten Aileen, Cynthia Dawn, Kurtis Addison; A.A., Coll. of Sequoias, 1974; B.A. in Liberal Arts, Consortium Calif. State Univ. and Colls., 1980. Avionics technician Grumman Aircraft Engring. Corp., Bethpage, N.Y., 1960-66; systems support engr. Raytheon Service Co., Boston, 1966-69; avionics rep. Vought Corp., Naval Air Sta., Lemoore, Calif., 1969—; advisor nav. and weapons delivery system A-7E light attach aircraft U.S. Navy. Com. mem. Cub Scouts; mgr. Little League. Served with USAF, 1954-57. Named Field Service Rep. of Month, Vought Corp., 1974; cert. sr. engring. technician Inst. Cert. Engring. Technicians. Mem. AIAA, IEEE, Assn. for Severely Handicapped, Navy League U.S., Assn. Naval Aviation, Inc. Author: A-7E Inertial Measurement System Maintenance Techniques, 1979; editor: A Pilot's Guide to the Use and Understanding of the A-7E Avionics System, 1973. Home: 2480 Chestnut St Hanford CA 93230 Office: PO Box 1206 Hanford CA 93230

SCHLESINGER, MYRON PHILLIP, rehab. counselor; b. Bronx, N.Y., Sept. 26, 1929; s. David and Rose (Hauptman) S.; B.S. cum laude, State U. N.Y., 1952; M.S. in Edn., Hofstra Coll., 1955; postgrad. Hofstra U., 1966-67; children by previous marriage—Edward B., Carole Carrie Barbara. Tchr., Common Branch Elementary, N.Y.C., N.Y., 1951-55, Wyandanch (N.Y.) Elementary Sch., 1957-58; instr. social scis. Harbor Country Day Sch., Smithtown, N.Y., 1958-61; instr. Summer Coll. of Guam, 1961—, Tumon Jr. High Sch., Agana, Guam, 1963; instr. sociology and reading Eastern Ariz. Jr. Coll., Thatcher, 1963-64, head dept. sociology and reading, 1963-64; sr. vocat. counselor N.Y.C. Human Resources Dept., 1964-66; vocat. rehab. counselor L.I. Jewish Hosp., Queens Center, N.Y., 1967-68; rehab. counselor Nassau County Med. Center, East Meadow, N.Y., 1968-69; vocat. rehab. counselor Tutoring Research Service, Hicksville, N.Y., 1970-72; community worker Dept. of Probation, Nassau County, N.Y., 1972-75; career counselor Employment Devel. Dept., Santa Barbara, Calif., 1976-78; dep. dir. Experience Unlimited, Calif. Employment Devel. Dept., 1978—; private practice, vocat. counseling, Goleta, Calif., 1978—. Certified rehab. counselor. Fellow AAAS; mem. Am., Nat. rehab. counseling assns., Nat. Vocat. Guidance Assn., Am. Coll. Personnel Assn., Nat. Employment Counseling Assn., Am. Sociol. Assn., Am. Econ. Assn., Soc. Bibl. Lit., Internat. Soc. Polit. Psychology, Human Factors Soc., Calif. Acad. Scis. Mem. Baha'i Faith. Club: Lions. Home: 5839 Encina Rd Apt 206 Goleta CA 93017

SCHLICK, ROBERT LEWIS, marketing executive; b. Bremerton, Wash., Feb. 26, 1941; s. Danual Franklin and Genevieve Josephine (Strutzel) S.; B.S., Hastings Coll., 1963; M.A.S., U. So. Calif., 1966; m. Ruth Ann Marcellin, July 17, 1965 (dec. Oct. 1975). Teledyne Systems cons. G.S. Rasmussen & Assos., 1964-70; project mgr., sales engr. Lockheed Aircraft Co., 1963-69; dir. marketing Univ. Computing Co., 1969-74; regional marketing dir. GTE Data Services, 1974-76; v.p., gen. mgr. Data Magnetics Corp., Torrance, Calif., 1976-78; v.p. mktg. and planning Gloria Marshall, Inc., Downey, Calif., 1978—; dir. CSMC Corp.; mgmt. cons.; lectr. U. So. Calif. Mem. Marina Property Bd. Recipient Scott Wilber award State of Nebr., 1962, Nat. Actuarial award, Nat. Actuarial Assn. Am., 1958, Lockheed Aircraft Pres.'s award, 1969. Mem. Am. Mgmt. Assn., Internat. Mktg. Assn., U. Nebr. Alumni Assn. Clubs: Marina City Yacht, Coral Tree Racket, Internat. Racket, Marina City. Contbr. articles tech. publs. Home: 7929 W 81st St Playa Del Rey CA 90291 Office: PO Box 10177 Marina Del Rey CA 90291

SCHLITT, ANNELIES JEANNE, software engr.; b. New Rochelle, N.Y., May 27, 1943; d. Matthew Marcellus and Aukje Hillegonde (Hoogeveen) Dorenbosch; B.S., Columbia U., 1967; m. Gerd Herbert Schlitt, Feb. 27, 1974; 1 son, Alexander Paul. Systems programmer Ciba-Geigy Corp., Ardsley, N.Y., 1968-70, Basel, Switzerland, 1970-71, Wehr, W.Ger., 1971-73; self-employed systems cons., Wehr, 1973-78; software engr. Intel Corp., Santa Clara, Calif., 1979—. Home: 22996 Standing Oak Ct Cupertino CA 95014 Office: 3065 Bowers Ave Santa Clara CA 95051

SCHLOMER, MARGARET JUDITH, public relations administrator; b. Colfax, Wash., Mar. 6, 1939; d. Herbert J. and Margaret T. (McGinn) Druffel; m. Harm Henry Schlomer, July 10, 1965; children—Erika, Harm Henry. B.A. in Sociology, Ft. Wright Coll., 1961. Social worker Wash. State Dept. Instns., Spokane, 1961-63; juvenile parole counselor Wash. Counties, 1963-66; dir. community relations Deaconess Hosp., Spokane, Wash., 1973—. Keyperson Spokane United Way Campaign, 1974, 76. Mem. Am. Soc. for Hosp. Pub. Relations (pres. Wash. chpt. 1981-82), Pub. Relations Soc. Am., Women in Communications, Spokane Area C. of C. (membership com.). Roman Catholic. Club: PEO. Contbr. articles on hosp. pub. relations to profl. jours. Home: 1212 E 56th Spokane WA 99203 Office: W 800 5th Ave Spokane WA 99210

SCHLOSS, HENRY H., educator; b. July 1, 1919. A.B., Nebr. Wesleyan U., 1946; M.B.A., Columbia U., 1948, Ph.D., 1953; postgrad. U. Leeds (Eng.), summer 1948, London Sch. Econs., summer 1952, U. Chgo., summer 1946. Fulbright prof. U. Dacca (East Pakistan), 1954-55, U. Bombay (India), 1959-60; advisor Inst. Bus. Adminstrn., Karachi, Pakistan, 1962-63; lab. asst. stats. Columbia U., N.Y.C., 1947-58; instr. econs. Rutgers U., 1948-49; asst. prof. internat. trade U. Tex.-Austin, 1949-51; instr. econs. Washington U., St. Louis, 1951-53, asst. prof., 1953-61; vis. assoc. prof. bus. econs. and internat. trade U. So. Calif., Los Angeles, 1961-63, assoc. prof., 1963-71, prof., 1971—; cons. in field. Columbia U. scholar, 1946-49; NYU fellow, 1966; Fulbright grantee, 1954-55; Smith-Mundt grantee, 1959-60; recipient Outstanding Alumni award Nebr. Wesleyan U., 1981. Mem. Am. Econ. Assn., Royal Econ. Soc. (U.K.), Pakistan Econ. Assn., AAUP, Soc. Internat. Devel. (chpt. past pres.), Acad. Internat. Bus. (exec. bd.), European Found. Mgmt. Devel., European Internat. Bus. Assn., European Fin. Assn., Western Econ. Assn., Pi Gamma Nu, Pi Kappa Delta. Omicron Delta Gamma, Beta Gamma Sigma. Editorial bd. Jour. Internat. Bus. Studies, 1975-78; contbr. articles to profl. jours. Address: Univ So Calif Sch Bus Los Angeles CA 90089

SCHLOSSER, ROBERT JULES, theatre administrator; b. Stockton, Calif., Jan. 9, 1935; s. Julius Christian and Wilma Marie (Walker) S.; m. Elizabeth Anne Freeman, Oct. 11, 1959; children—Brita Elizabeth, Christian Mark. B.S., U. San Francisco, 1956. Subscription mgr. San Francisco Actors' Workshop, 1962-65; audience devel. dir. Repertory Theatre, Lincoln Center, N.Y., 1965-73, Mark Taper Forum, Los Angeles, 1973—; founding dir. Theatre Audience Project, Los Angeles, 1979—. Founder, Project D.A.T.E. (Deaf Audience Theatre Experience), Los Angeles, 1978; mem. Greater Los Angeles Visitors and Conv. Bur., 1973—. Served with U.S. Army, 1958-60.

SCHMAL, WILLIAM G., dairy and agricultural products company executive; b. 1932. B.S., Ind. U., 1957, M.B.A., 1958. Products mgr. Colgate-Palmolive Co., 1958-64; v.p. Ogilvy & Mather, Inc., 1964-68; v.p. mktg., ptnr. King-Casey Inc., 1968-70; v.p. mktg. Carnation Internat., 1970-78; pres., chief operating officer Knudsen Corp., Los Angeles, 1978, pres., chief exec. officer, 1980, chmn., pres., chief exec. officer, 1981, chmn., chief exec. officer, 1982—, also dir. Office: Knudsen Corp 231 E 23d St PO Box 2335 Terminal Annex Los Angeles CA 90051*

SCHMALTZ, ROY EDGAR, JR., art educator, artist; b. Belfield, N.D., Feb. 23, 1937; s. Roy and Mercedes (Martin) S.; m. Julia Mabel Swan, Feb. 1, 1958; children—Liese Marlene, Jennifer Lynn, Gregory Jason. Student Otis Art Inst., Los Angeles, 1959-60, U. Wash., 1960-61, Akademie der Bildenden Kunste, Munich, W. Ger., 1965-66; B.F.A., San Francisco Art Inst., 1965. Lectr. art Coll. of Notre Dame, Belmont, Calif., 1968-70, M. H. De Young Meml. Art Mus., San Francisco, 1968-70; assoc. prof. art St. Mary's Coll. of Calif., Moraga, 1969—, chmn. dept. art; exhbns. include: Seattle Art Mus., 1959, M. H. De Young Meml. Art Mus., 1969, Frye Art Mus., Seattle, 1957, San Francisco Mus. Modern Art, 1971, U. Calif.-Santa Cruz, 1977, Fine Arts Mus. of San Francisco, 1978, Oakland Art Mus., 1979, Rutgers U., Camden, N.J., 1979, Springfield (Mo.) Art Mus., 1980, Butler Inst. Am. Art, Youngstown, Ohio, 1981, Huntsville (Ala.) Mus. Art, 1982, Haggin Mus., Stockton, Calif., 1982, U. Hawaii-Hilo, 1983, Alaska State Mus., Juneau, 1981, Tex. State U., San Marcos, 1980, Crocker Art Mus., Sacramento, 1982; represented in permanent collections: Frye Art Mus., San Francisco Art Inst., M. H. De Young Meml. Art Mus., Mills Coll., Oakland, Amerika-Haus, Munich, Contra Costa County Art Collection, Walnut Creek, Calif.; dir. Hearst Art Gallery, St. Mary's Coll.; vis. artist lectr. Academie Art Coll., San Francisco, 1971, grad. program Lone Mountain Coll., San Francisco, 1973-74. Coach Little League Baseball Team, Concord, Calif., 1982. Fulbright fellow, 1965-66; Frye Art Mus. traveling fellow, 1957; recipient Painting award All Calif. Ann., 1965; Nat. Watercolor award Chautauqua Inst., 1980; Seattle Art Assn. Painting award, 1957; San Francisco Art Inst. award, 1961; Otis Art Inst. award, 1959. Mem. Coll. Art Assn., Fine Arts Mus. of San Francisco, AAUP, San Francisco Art Inst. Alumni Assn. Home: 4267 Carter Ct Concord CA 94521 Office: Art Dept Saint Marys Coll Moraga CA 94575

SCHMEDINGHOFF, GERARD JOSEPH, human resources consultant educator; b. Chgo., Jan. 11, 1935; s. Alois John and Anna Marie (Buchholz) S.; m. Dorothy Sue Slaten, Nov. 23, 1973; children—Mark Gerard, Brian Joseph. B.A., St. Mary's U., San Antonio, 1955; S.T.L., U. Fribourg (Switzerland), 1966; M.A., Chapman Coll., 1973; Ph.D., Wash. State U., 1977. Tchr., McBride High Sch., St. Louis, 1955-58, Assumption High Sch., East St. Louis, Ill., 1958-61; chaplain Chaminade High Sch., Clayton, Mo., 1967-68; asst. dir. Marianist Apostolic Ctr., Glencoe, Mo., 1968-69; asst. prof. Eastern Oreg. State Coll., La Grande, 1976-81; v.p. Drake Beam Morin, Inc., San Francisco, 1981—. Served to capt. U.S. Army, 1969-72. Decorated Bronze Star (2). Mem. Am. Psychol. Assn., Am. Soc. Personnel Adminstrs. Contbr. articles to profl. jours. Home: 855 Belann Ct Concord CA 94518 Office: 417 Montgomery Suite 502 San Francisco CA 94104

SCHMID, ANNE MARIE, med. writer, editor; b. Columbus, Ohio, Aug. 10; d. Casimir J. and Petrona M. (Klimas) Mattsewecz; student U. San Francisco, 1932-35; m. Frank H. Schmid, Aug. 19, 1936; children—Frank R., Monica, Gregory, Elena. Editor, UN Charter, San Francisco, 1945; editor dept. pediatrics U. Calif. Sch. Medicine, San Francisco, 1949-77, prin. editor, 1971-78; freelance book editor, 1971—, thesis rewriter, 1973—; mng. editor Jour. Parenteral and Enteral Nutrition, 1977-81. Bd. dirs. San Francisco Chamber Music Soc., 1966-81, pres., 1980-82; bd. dirs. Calif. Christians for Israel; bd. dirs. Henry Harris Library Fund, 1975-81; mem. health clin. adv. com. Telegraph Hill Neighborhood Assn., 1962-66, Dist. V Health and Mental Health Services, 1981—; mem. child and adolescent health local adv. bd. San Francisco Dept. Pub. Health. Fellow Am. Med. Writers Assn. (past pres. No. Calif. chpt., nat. dir. 1975-76); mem. AAAS, MLA. Republican. Roman Catholic. Club: San Francisco Press. Home and Office: 1820 16th Ave San Francisco CA 94122

SCHMID, MAX OTTO, periodontist; b. Zurich, Switzerland, Sept. 13, 1941; came to U.S., 1969, naturalized, 1981; s. Max Julius and Elsa (Bolliger) S.; B.S., Gymnasium of Zurich, 1960; D.M.D., U. Zurich, 1967; m. Ursula Heer, Nov. 5, 1965; children—Daniel Max, Andreas Francis. Asst. prof. periodontology U. Zurich, 1965-69, asso. prof., 1972-76; lectr. periodontics Tufts U., 1969-71; asst. prof. periodontology U. Calif., San Francisco, 1971-72; asso. prof. UCLA, dir. undergrad. periodontics, 1976-81; attending dentist, med. staff UCLA Hosp. Bd. dirs. Palisades Village Sch., Pacific Palisades, Calif., 1980-81. Served to 1st lt. M.C., Swiss Armed Forces, 1960-69. Mem. ADA, Am. Acad. Periodontology, Calif. Dental Assn., Western Dental Assn., Western Soc. Periodontology, Calif. Soc. Periodontology, Swiss Soc. Dentistry, Swiss Soc. Periodontology, Flying Samaritans, Schlaraffia Frat., Sigma Xi. Research, publs. on oral hygiene and mucogingival surgery; contbg. editor Jour. Western Soc. Periodontology, 1976-81. Home: 809 Alma Real Dr Pacific Palisades CA 90272 Office: UCLA Sch Dentistry Los Angeles CA 90024

SCHMIDT, CAROL, communications consultant; b. Dearborn, Mich., Sept. 10, 1942; d. Emmett R. and Lorraine G. Schmidt; m. Michael J. Arnoldy, June 21, 1970 (div. June 28, 1977). B.A. magna cum laude, Marygrove Coll., 1964; postgrad. U. N.C., 1964-65, UCLA extension, U. Soc. Calif. City editor Mich. Chronicle Newspaper, Detroit, 1965-68; communications cons. Chrysler Corp., Detroit, 1968; edn. editor Macomb Daily Newspaper, Mt. Clemens, Mich., 1969-70; feature editor, sales promotion mgr. Brentwood Pub. Co., Los Angeles, 1971-78; communications dir. Research and Edn. Inst., Inc., Harbor-UCLA Med. Center, Torrance, Calif., 1978—; free-lance writer, polit. speech writer, cons.; part-time instr. Wayne County Community Coll., Detroit, 1969-70. Pub. relations dir. Sunset Junction Neighborhood Alliance and Street Fairs, Sunset Junction; state del. Mich. Democratic Conv., 1968-69; mem. Los Angeles Women's Community Chorus. Recipient 1st Prize Nat. Newspaper Pubs. Assn., 1969. Mem. Am. Soc. Assn. Execs., Am. Hosp. Assn. (communications sect.), Soc. for Hosp. Pub. Relations, Nat. Mgmt. Assn. (v.p. Harbor-UCLA chpt.), Women in Communications, Am. Med. Writers Assn., Feminist Women's Writers Guild, White Women Against Racism, CORE, NOW (pres. Beach Cities 1979-80, state bd. dirs. 1977-81). Office: 1124 W Carson St Torrance CA 90502

SCHMIDT, CHAUNCEY EVERETT, banker; b. Oxford, Iowa, June 7, 1931; s. Walter Frederick and Vilda (Saxton) S.; B.S., U.S. Naval Acad., 1953; M.B.A., Harvard U., 1959; m. Anne Garrett McWilliams, Mar. 3, 1954; children—Carla, Julia, Chauncey Everett. With First Nat. Bank Chgo., 1959-75, v.p., gen. mgr. br., London, 1965-68, v.p. for Europe, Middle East, Africa, 1968-69, sr. v.p., Chgo., 1969-72, exec. v.p., 1972, vice chmn. bd., 1973, pres., 1974-75; chmn. bd., pres., chief exec. officer Bank of Calif., N.A., San Francisco, 1976—, BanCal Tri-State Corp., 1976—; dir. Amfac, Inc., Calif. Bankers Clearing House Assn., mem. fed. adv. council FRS; mem. Adv. Council Japan-U.S. Econ. Relations. Exec. bd. San Francisco Bay Area council Boy Scouts Am.; bd. govs. San Francisco Symphony. Served with USAF, 1953-56. Mem. Am. Bankers Assn., Assn. Res. City Bankers, Bay Area Council (dir.), Calif. Roundtable (dir.), Internat. Monetary Conf., SRI Internat. Council. Clubs: Comml. of Chgo., Bohemian. Office: Bank of Calif 400 California St San Francisco CA 94104*

SCHMIDT, DONALD THOMAS, ch. librarian; b. Brighton, Ill., Sept. 13, 1919; s. Harvey and Helen (Jacoby) S.; B.A., U. Ia., 1947, M.A., 1949; M.A., U. Denver, 1964; m. Alice Mahany, June 7, 1947; children—Donald, Helen, Rebecca, David, Kenneth, Janet. Librarian, Brigham Young U., Provo, Utah, 1959-66, asst. dir. libraries, 1966-72; ch. librarian Ch. of Jesus Christ of Latter-day Saints, Salt Lake City, 1972-74, ch. librarian/archivist, 1974—. Active ARC, YMCA. Served with AUS, 1941-46; ETO. Mem. ALA, Spl. Libraries Assn., Mountain Plains Library Assn., Utah Library Assn., Soc. Am. Archivists. Home: 1882 N 1500 E Provo UT 84601 Office: 50 E North Temple Salt Lake City UT 84150

SCHMIDT, ECKART WALTER, chemist; b. Essen, Germany, Apr. 16, 1935; s. Wilhelm Heinrich and Margot Anna (Kmitta) S.; came to U.S., 1966, naturalized, 1974; m. Hildegard C. Breuninger, Sept. 22, 1962; children—Wolfram G., Andreas U. B.S., U. Marburg (Germany), 1958; M.S., U. Tuebingen (Germany), 1962, Ph.D., 1964. Research chemist Deutsche Versuchsanstalt fuer Luft-und Raumfahrt, Stuttgart, W. Ger., 1964-66; mgr. chem. research Rocket Research Co., Redmond, Wash., 1966-76, sr. staff scientist, 1976—. Assoc. fellow AIAA. Author: Raketentreibstoff (Rocket Propellants), 1968; Hydrazine and Its Derivatives, 1983; contbr. articles to profl. jours. Home: 55 151st Pl Bellevue WA 98007 Office: Rocket Research Co 11441 Willows Rd NE Redmond WA 98052

SCHMIDT, GAYLE VIRGINIA, health science services administrator, tax consultant; b. Cranston, R.I., Sept. 7, 1936; d. Edwin Edward and Virginia Louise (Walker) Whipple; m. Walter Henry Schmidt, May 30, 1962; children—Walter III, Stephen Stanley, Kymberlei Gayle. B.S. with honors in Health Sci. Adminstrn., U. Phoenix, 1981, M.B.A., 1983. Accredited record technician. Owner, tax preparer H&R Block Franchise, Benson, Ariz., 1973—; med. and nursing coordinator, Benson Hosp., Benson, Ariz., 1974-79; dir. med. records, 1979-82; supr. data collection Med. Info. Services Ariz. Health Sci. Ctr., Tucson, 1982—; tchr. tax preparation; researcher med. record studies. Recipient Extension award Lioness Internat., 1981. Mem. Am. Med. Record Assn. Republican. Episcopalian. Clubs: Sunset Belles Lioness (Huachuca City, Ariz.), Lioness (dist. program chmn.).

SCHMIDT, GLEN LEROY, aerospace corp. exec.; b. Bristol, S.D., Feb. 15, 1930; s. Frank and Veda Marie (Neal) S.; B.S./B.A. in Mech. Engring., Oreg. State U., 1957; M.Public Adminstrn., U. So. Calif., 1973, Ph.D., 1980; m. Elaine Evette Brethour, Dec. 24, 1976; children by previous marriage—David, Daniel, Damian, Dominic, Douglas, Darren, Dennis. Research engr. N. Am. Rockwell Corp., Canoga Park, Calif., 1957-58, nuclear reactor test engr., 1958-60, engring. supr., group leader, 1960-65, supt. mfg., 1966-68, engring. mgr., 1968-71; supr. Ventura County (Calif.), 1971-75; mem. tech. staff Rockwell Internat., Canoga Park, 1975-80, project engr. energy programs, 1980—; instr. Pasadena City Coll., 1959-60, Moorpark Community Coll., 1974-75. Personnel commr. Simi Valley Unified Sch. Dist., 1968-71; chmn. Simi Valley Incorp. Com., 1968-69. Served with USAF, 1948-52. Recipient Soldier's medal and Pres.'s medal U.S. Nat. Safety Council, 1951, Joint Resolution and Proclamation award Calif. State Senate and Assembly, 1974; registered profl. engr., Calif. Mem. Sigma Xi. Home: 4287 Tecolote Ct Box 461 Moorpark CA 93021 Office: Rockwell Internat 8900 DeSoto Ave Canoga Park CA 93104

SCHMIDT, HARVEY MARTIN, economic forecaster, consultant; b. Chgo., Sept. 15, 1925; s. Joseph David and Dorothy Schmidt; m. Barbara Bebe Bloom, Nov. 25, 1961; children—Ellen Louise, Jay Stephen, Gregg Arthur. Student U. So. Calif., 1943; B.A. magna cum laude, Woodbury U., 1947. Assoc. prof. bus. Woodbury U., 1947-48; pvt. practice acctg., Los Angeles, 1948-80; cons. mgmt., taxes and fins., Los Angeles, 1965-82; cons. fins. and econ. forecaster, Pacific Palisades, 1982—; exec. dir. Medic-Aid (of Calif.), Los Angeles, 1969-81, chmn., 1981—; pres. Med-Plan Operators, 1969—; lectr. in field. Served with USCG, 1943-44. Life Master, U.S. Contract Bridge League, 1960—. Mem. Calif. Bd. Accountancy. Clubs: Exchange (pres. local chpt. 1953-56); Sportsmen of South of UCLA. Contbr. articles to profl. jours. Office: 14201 Sunset Blvd Pacific Palisades CA 90272

SCHMIDT, HENRY LOUIS, III, package designer; b. Ann Arbor, Mich., Oct. 27, 1947; s. Henry Louis and Margaret Mary (Gauthier) S. Grad. Sch. Visual Arts, N.Y.C., 1969. Designer, Alan Berni Corp., Greenwich, Conn., 1972, DeMartin-Marona, Elnisford, N.Y., 1973-75, Glenn Monigle & Assocs., Denver, 1975; pres. Henry Schmidt Design, Boulder, Colo., 1976—. Recipient Zellerbach award, 1976, Mead Paper award, 1979, 80. Mem. Art Dirs. Club Denver (awards 1977, 78, 80). Republican. Office: 2885 E Aurora Suite 12 Boulder CO 80303

SCHMIDT, JAMES ROBERT, marketing manager; b. N.Y.C., May 10, 1946; s. John Adolph and Claire (Morrison) S.; m. Denise Ann Keane, Dec. 27, 1969; children—Pamela, Justin, Amanda. B.A., Rutgers U., 1968; M.B.A., Pacific Lutheran U., 1971. Lic. real estate broker, Calif. Sales mgr. Paper Products div. Procter & Gamble, Cranford, N.J., 1971-72; product mgr. Syrups Best Food div. CPC Internat., Englewood Cliffs, N.J., 1973-78; dir. mktg. dietary products Odgon Food Corp., Stockton, Calif., 1978-80; mktg. mgr. raisins and prunes Sun-Diamond Growers Calif., San Ramon, 1980—. Served to capt. USAF, 1968-71. Home: 3707 Hatchers Circle Stockton CA 95209 Office: Sun-Diamond Growers Calif 1320 El Capitan Dr San Ramon CA 94583

SCHMIDT, KLAUS DIETER, univ. adminstr., marketing and management educator; b. Eisenach, Germany, May 8, 1930; came to U.S., 1949, naturalized, 1952; s. Kurt Heinrich and Luise (Kruger) S.; B.A. in Econs., U. Calif., Berkeley, 1951; M.B.A., Stanford U., 1953; Ph.D. in Bus. Adminstrn., Golden Gate U., 1978; m. Lynda Hollister Wheelwright, June 29, 1950; children—Karen, Claudia. Buyer, jr. mdse. mgr. Broadway Hale, 1952-54; sales mgr. Ames Harris Neville Co., 1954-56, ops. mgr., 1956-57; gen. mgr. Boise Cascade Corp., 1957-60; pres., chmn. bd. Kimball-Schmidt Inc., San Rafael, Calif., 1960-73, chmn. subs. Kalwall Pacific, 1962-67, chmn. subs. AFGOA Corp., 1966-69; asst. prof. mgmt. and mktg. San Francisco State U., 1970-75, assoc. prof. mgmt., 1975-80, prof. mgmt. and mktg., 1980—, chmn. dept. mgmt. and mktg., 1970—, dir. Ctr. for World Bus., 1976—, dir. Inst. for U.S.-Japan Relations, 1981—, editor-in-chief Sch. Bus. Jours., 1981—; U.S. negotiator on Afghanistan issue, 1980; mem. Dept. Commerce Dist. Export Council, 1982; research cons. SRI Internat. Republican. Club: University (San Francisco). Author 16-booklet series Doing Business In ..., 1978-80. Office: 1600 Holloway San Francisco CA 94132

SCHMIDT, LOUIS BERNARD, JR., industrial distribution executive; b. Ames, Iowa, Sept. 19, 1922; s. Louis Bernard and Georgia Perle (Wilson) S.; m. Jeanette Hook, June 2, 1956. B.S., Iowa State U., 1944; post grad., 1948. Salesman, Agrl. Indsl., Pub. Works Distributive Co., Tucson, 1952-62, v.p. sales, Phoenix, 1962-72; mgr. engine, energy div. Ariz. Engine and Pump Co., div. I.S. Inds., Inc. Phoenix, 1972—. Active Phoenix Republican Forum. Mem. Am. Water Works Assn., Ariz. Water and Pollution Control Assn., Waukesha Dresser Western Distrs. (regional adv. council), Soc. Mayflower Descs. Ariz. (treas.), SAR, Ariz. Acad. Pub. Affairs; Gamma Sigma Delta Unitarian. Clubs: Sky Harbur

Kiwanis, Phoenix Press; Elks. Office: Arizona Engine and Pump Co 407 S 17th Ave Phoenix AZ 85007

SCHMIDT, MAARTEN, educator; b. Groningen, Netherlands, Dec. 28, 1929; s. Wilhelm and Antje Wilhelmina (Haringhuizen) S.; B.S., U. Groningen, 1949; Ph.D., U. Leiden, 1956; Sc.D. (hon.), Yale U., 1966, Wesleyan U., Middletown, Conn., 1982; m. Cornelia Johanna Tom, Sept. 16, 1955; children—Elizabeth Tjimkje, Maryke Antje, Anne Wilhelmina. Sci. officer U. Leiden, 1953-59; Carnegie fellow Mt. Wilson Obs., Pasadena, Calif., 1956-58; mem. faculty Calif. Inst. Tech., Pasadena, 1959—, prof. astronomy, 1964—. Recipient with J. Greenstein, Calif. Scientist of Year award Mus. Sci. and Industry, 1964; Rumford award Am. Acad. Arts and Scis., 1968; Russell Lecture award Am. Astron. Soc., 1978; Gold medal Royal Astron. Soc., 1980. Mem. Nat. Acad. Scis., Royal Astron. Soc. (asso.), Internat. Astron. Union, Am. Astron. Soc. Office: Calif Inst of Tech Pasadena CA 91125

SCHMIDT, ROBERT MILTON, physician, scientist; b. Milw., May 7, 1944; s. Milton W. and Edith J. (Martinek) S.; A.B., Northwestern U., 1966; M.D. (NSF and USPHS fellow, Mayo Found. trainee scholar, Virginia Kneeland Frantz scholar), Columbia U., 1970; M.P.H., Harvard U., 1975; Ph.D., Emory U., 1982; children—Eric Whitney, Edward Huntington. Med. intern Univ. Hosp., U. Calif., San Diego, 1970-71; commd. med. officer USPHS, 1971, advanced through grades to comdr., 1973, dir. hematology div. Nat. Center for Disease Control, Atlanta, 1971-78, spl. asst. to dir., 1978-79, ret., 1979; pres., med. dir. Internat. Health Resource Center of Hawaii, Lihue, Kanai, 1979-82; dir. Center Preventive Medicine and Health Research, Med. Research Inst. San Francisco, 1983—; sr. scientist Inst. Epidemiology and Behavioral Medicine, Inst. Cancer Research, 1983—; prof. clin. sci. San Francisco State U., 1983—; clin. asst. prof. Tufts U. Med. Sch., 1976—. Recipient Borden research award in medicine; pharmacology and Upjohn achievement awards, Columbia U., 1970; diplomate Am. Bd. Preventive Medicine. Fellow Am. Coll. Preventive Medicine, Am. Soc. Clin. Pathology, Internat. Soc. Hematology; mem. A.C.P., AAAS, Am. Public Health Assn., Internat. Commn. for Standardization in Hematology, Am. Soc. Hematology, Internat. Soc. on Thrombosis and Hemostasis, Acad. Clin. Lab. Physicians and Scientists, Assn. Tchrs. Preventive Medicine, AMA, Am. Soc. Microbiology. Club: Army and Navy (Washington). Mem. editorial bd. Am. Jour. Clin. Pathology, 1976—; author books and manuals, including Hematology Laboratory Handbook Series, 3 vols., 1979-81; contbr. articles to sci. jours. Home: 4339 Puaole St Lihue HI 96766 Office: 3420 Kuhio Highway Lihue HI 96766

SCHMIDT, ROBERT RUDOLF, chemical safety specialist; b. Binghamton, N.Y., Nov. 14, 1931; s. Wilhelm Rudolf and Harriet Arlene (Stone) S.; B.S. in Bus. Adminstrn. Ind. U., 1958; postgrad. in Safety and Health Adminstrn., W.Va. U., 1977-78; m. Joan Elaine Burdsall, June 6, 1958; children—William Robert and Kathryn Ann (twins), Linda Ann. Fire and safety engring. trainee, cons., asst. supr. Ind. Ins. Services, Indpls., 1958-68; safety dir. Meth. Hosp. of Ind., Indpls., 1968-72; internat. corp safety and health mgr. Senco Products, Inc., Newtown, Ohio, 1972-74; safety and loss prevention mgr. chems. mfg. Olin Corp., Brandenburg, Ky., 1974-76; safety engring. mgr. dept. energy liquefied coal devel. pilot mfg. operation, Cresap, W.Va., 1976-78; safety and risk mgr. Hooker Indsl. and Splty. Chems. Group, div. Occidental Chem. Corp., Tacoma, 1978—; chmn. health care sect. Nat. Safety Council, 1971-72, mem.-at-large indsl. conf. coms., 1972-76; sec., treas. So. Ohio Nat. Fire Protection Assn., Cin. chpt., 1973-74; active Nat. Fire Protection Assn., Cin.; co-chmn. Accident Prevention Clinic, Wash. Gov.'s 30th Ann. Safety Congress, 1981. Sec., treas. No. Ohio River Indsl. Mut. Aid Com., 1976-78; organizer, vice chmn. Tideflats Indsl. Mut. Aid Plan, Tacoma, 1980, chmn., 1982-83. Active fire protection sect. Cin. mayor's com. on community improvement, 1973-74; mem. Indpls. mayor's com. on shelters and evacuation plans, 1970-72; Sunday Sch. supt. and tchr. Northwood Christian Ch., Indpls., youth group leader, deacon, mem. ch. bd., 1960 72; elder, Sunday Sch. tchr., choir mem. First Christian Ch., Radcliff, Ky., 1974-76; deacon First Christian Ch., Wheeling, W.Va., head evangelism dept., 1977-78; deacon First Christian Ch., Tacoma. Recipient various awards in field. Mem. Am. Soc. Safety Engrs. (sec. Indpls. chpt., 1971-72, chmn. Puget Sound congress activities 1982, treas. Puget Sound chpt. 1983-84), Nat. Safety Mgmt. Soc., Vets. of Safety, Internat. Platform Assn. Republican. Club: Welcome Wagon Club of Gig Harbor, Wash. Contbr. articles to profl. jours.; active grant proposal, Indpls., 1972. Home: 3923 101st St Ct NW Gig Harbor WA 98335 Office: PO Box 2157 605 Alexander Ave Tacoma WA 98401

SCHMIDT, ROY HENRY, farmer; b. Stockton, Calif., Oct. 3, 1918; s. Henry Ludwig and Anna (Bock) S.; B.S. in Mech. Engring., U. Calif., Berkeley, 1941; M.S. in Agrl. Engring., U. Calif., Davis, 1961; m. Dorothy Elizabeth Meyn, July 30, 1955; children—Barbara Ann, Glenn George. Engring. designer N.Y.C. firms, 1947-57; research asst. U. Calif., Davis, 1958-60; owner-mgr. orchards farm, Modesto, Calif., 1960—; pres. Schmidt Orchards, Inc., 1980—. Mem. Democratic Central Com. Stanislaus County, 1972—. Served with AUS, 1943-46. Mem. Calif. Farm Bur., Sigma Xi. Address: 1737 Beverly Dr Modesto CA 95351

SCHMIDT, WARREN JAMES, electronic equipment designer; b. N.Y.C., Mar. 14, 1935; s. Otto August and Olga (Pierce) S.; m. Marie McCoy, Nov. 21, 1959; children—Greg Warren, Tynan Ray. B.S. in Physics, Carnegie Mellon U., 1957. Electronics cons NSA, Washington, 1957-60; electronic engr. Rabinow Engring. Co., Rockville, Md., 1960-64, FMC Corp., Santa Clara, Calif., 1964-71; v.p., engr. Data Recognition Corp., Palo Alto, Calif., 1971-73; owner, operator Impel Control Co., Cupertine, Calif., 1973—. Mem. IEEE, ACM. Patentee (2). Office: Impel Control Co Cupertino CA 95014

SCHMIDT, WAYNE WALTER, lawyer, assn. exec.; b. St. Louis, Feb. 8, 1941; s. Warren Walter and Geneva N. (Walker) S.; children—Nancy Karen, Andrew Martin. Dipl. English Law, City of London (Eng.) Coll., 1963; B.A., U. N.Mex., 1964; J.D., Okla. City U., 1966; LL.M., Northwestern U., 1974. Bar: N.Mex. 1966, Ill. 1968, D.C. 1970, N.Y. 1982. Dir. Police Legal Center, Internat. Assn. Chiefs of Police, Washington, 1970-73; dir. police legal adv. tng. program Northwestern U., 1968-70; exec. dir. Ams. for Effective Law Enforcement, Inc., after 1973. County constable, Albuquerque, 1962-66. Served with AUS, 1966-67. Ford Found. fellow, 1967. Mem. ABA, D.C., Ill., N.Mex., N.Y. bar assns. Author: Guidelines for Police Legal Units, 1971; Legal Aspects of Criminal Evidence, 1977; Introduction to Criminal Evidence, 1982. Legal editor The Nat. Sheriff, 1969-82; editor Fire and Police Personnel Reporter, 1974—. Office: 501 Grandview Dr Suite 209 PO Box 2105 South San Francisco CA 94080

SCHMIEDER, CARL, jeweler; b. Phoenix, Apr. 27, 1938; s. Otto and Ruby Mable (Harkey) S.; student Bradley Horological Sch., Peoria, Ill., 1959-61; B.A., Pomona Coll., 1961; m. Carole Ann Roberts, June 12, 1959; children—Gail, Susan, Nancy, Amy. Owner timepiece repair service, Peoria, 1959-61; clock repairman Otto Schmieder & Son, Phoenix, 1961-65, v.p., 1965-70, pres., 1970—, chief exec. officer, 1970—. Mem. subcom. Leap Commn., 1966; area rep. Pomona Coll., 1972-76. Cert. jeweler; cert. gemologist, gemologist appraiser; recipient Design award Diamonds Internat., 1965, Cultured Pearl Design award, 1967, 68, Diamonds for Christmas award, 1970; winner Am. Diamond Jewelry Competition, 1973; col. Confederate Air Force. Mem. Am. Gem. Soc. (dir. 1973—, nat. chmn. nomenclature com. 1975-77, chmn. membership com. 1977-81, officer 1981—), Ariz. Jewelers Assn. (Man of Yr. 1974), Jewelers Security Alliance (dir. 1974-78), 24 Karat Club So. Calif., Exptl. Aircraft Assn., Deer Valley (Ariz.) Airport Assn. (dir. 1980—). Republican. Methodist. Clubs: Valley of the Sun Kiwanis (pres. 1975-76); Friends of Iberia. Home: 537 W Kaler St Phoenix AZ 85021 Office: Park Central Phoenix AZ 85013

SCHMIEDER, JUNE HART, sch. adminstr.; b. Waterbury, Conn., Dec. 2, 1943; d. Eugene H. and Virginia (Collins) Hart; B.A., San Jose State U., 1963; M.A., Stanford U., 1975; Ph.D., 1981; 1 son, David. Tchr., Franklin McKinley Sch. Dist., San Jose, Calif., 1969-72; bus. mgr. San Joaquin (Calif.), Sch. Dist., 1975-77; dir. fiscal services Mt. Diablo Sch. Dist., Concord, Calif., 1977—. Mem. LWV, AAUW, Am. Assn. Sch. Adminstrs., Calif. Assn. Sch. Bus. Adminstrs., Pvt. Industry Council. Clubs: Toastmasters, Concord Century. Home: 1800 Camino Verde Walnut Creek CA 94596 Office: 1936 Carlotta Dr Concord CA 94519

SCHMIEDER, ROBERT WILLIAM, physicist, marine scientist; b. Phoenix, July 10, 1941; s. Otto and Ruby Maybel (Harkey) S.; children—Robyn, Russell Otto, Robert Randall. A.B., Occidental Coll., 1963; B.S., Calif. Inst. Tech., 1963; M.A., Columbia U., 1965; Ph.D. 1968. Physicist, Lawrence Berkeley Lab., 1969-72; instr. physics dept. U. Calif.-Berkeley, 1971-72; mem. tech. staff Sandia Nat. Labs., Livermore, Calif., 1972—; leader exploratory marine research Cordell Bank Expdns., 1977—. Grantee Nat. Geog. Soc., 1979, Explorers Club, 1980, San Francisco Found., 1981, NOAA, 1981-82. Mem. Am. Phys. Soc., Optical Soc. Am. Patentee in field; contbr. articles to profl. jours. Home: 4295 Walnut Blvd Walnut Creek CA 94596 Office: Sandia Nat Labs Livermore CA 94550

SCHMITT, ARDELL EDWARD, indsl. engr.; b. Epworth, Iowa, Oct. 13, 1924; s. Paul Cyril and Florence Mary (Nelson) S.; B.S., U. So. Calif., 1959, M.S., 1968; m. Dorothy Lee Yates, Mar. 5, 1947; children—Linda Mae, Debra Ann. Engring. asst. So. Calif. Gas Co., Los Angeles, 1955-59, constrn. planner, 1959-61, dist. engring. supr., 1961-68, adminstrv. aide, 1968-69; indsl. engr. Sunkist Growers, Inc., Ontario, Calif., 1969-72, indsl. engring. supr., 1972-78; plant indsl. engr. Glass Containers Corp., Los Angeles, 1978-79; indsl. engring. mgr. Lever Bros. Co., Los Angeles, 1979-81; indsl. engr. U.S. Dept. Def., Def. Logistics Agy., Fullerton, Calif., 1981-83; chief engring. resources mgmt. div. U.S. Army, Camp Darby, Italy, 1983—. Mem. Adv. com. Chino Basin Municipal Water Dist., 1975-78; dir. continuing edn. Productivity Council of Southwest, 1980—. Served to 1st lt., USAAF, 1943-46, USAF, 1951-53. Registered profl. engr., Calif. Mem. Am. Inst. Indsl. Engrs. (pres. 1974-75), Internat. Assn. Engrs. and Architects of Imperial/Mexicali Valleys (pres. 1968-69), Alpha Pi Mu. Republican. Methodist. Contbr. articles to profl. jours. Home: 2359 N 4th Ave Upland CA 91786 Office: PO Box 246 APO New York NY 09019

SCHMITT, CARVETH JOSEPH RODNEY, office supplies manufacturing official; b. Manitowoc, Wis., Sept. 10, 1934; s. Clarence C. and Thelma J. (White) S.; m. Carolyn Sue Jarrett, May 14, 1965. diploma in bus. adminstrn. and acctg. Skadron Coll. Bus., 1959; A.A., San Bernardino Valley Coll., 1962; B.S. in Bus. Adminstrn., U. Riverside-Calif., 1970; M.A. in Edn.-Manpower Adminstrn., U. Redlands, 1975; B.S. in Liberal Studies, SUNY-Albany, 1977; B.A. in Social Sci., Edison State Coll., 1978; postgrad. U. Calif. Extension, Riverside, 1976 80. Registered rep. Ernest F. Boruski, Jr., N.Y.C., 1956-61; acct. Barnum & Flagg Co., San Bernardino, Calif., 1959-70; registered rep., ins. agt. (part time) Inland Am. Securities, Inc., San Bernardino, 1966-70; registered rep. (part-time) Parker-Jackson & Co., San Bernardino, 1970-73, LeBarron Securities, Inc., 1973-74. credit mgr. Stationers Corp., San Bernardino, 1970-77, office mgr., credit mgr., 1977-83; internal auditor Stockwell & Binney Office Products Ctrs., San Bernardino, 1983—. Served with USAF, 1954-58. cert. tchr., community coll. counselor and personnel worker, Calif. Mem. Nat. Geog. Soc., Nat. Rifle Assn. (life), Nevada Mining Assn., Colo. Mining Assn., N.W. Mining Assn., Am. Philatelic Soc., Nat. Travel Club, Edison State Coll. Alumni Assn., U. Redlands Fellows, Friends of Library Assn. U. Redlands, Rex Alumni Assn., U. Redlands Alumni Assn., Friends of Library Assn. U. Redlands, Gold Prospectors Assn. Am. Republican. Clubs: Valley Prospectors, Fontana Tour, Hiking. Badminton, Bowling, Arrowhead Stamp, Masons. Home: 538 N Pampas Ave Rialto CA 92376 Office: 420 S E St PO Box 5129 San Bernardino CA 92412

SCHMITT, ROBERT CHARLES, statistician, state official; b. Cin., Jan. 25, 1922; s. William Michael and Ella Margaret (Graebe) S. B.A., U. Cin., 1944, M.A., 1947; postgrad. U. Mich., 1947. Statistician, urban planner with various firms, Cin., 1943-46, Honolulu, 1947-49, 52—, Seattle, 1949-52; state statistician Hawaii, Honolulu, 1963—, Hawaii Dept. Planning and Econ. Devel., 1958—; assoc. clin. prof. pub. health U. Hawaii, 1969—. Mem. Hawaii State Bd. Geog. Names, 1974—, chmn., 1979—; mem. research com. Hawaii Visitors Bur., 1958—; mem. Hawaii State Census Statis. Areas Com., 1948—, chmn., 1963—; mem. Commn. on Population and Hawaiian Future, 1974-80, Temp. Commn. Population Stblzn., 1970-72. Mem. Am. Statis. Assn. (pres. Hawaii 1963), Population Assn. Am., Hawaiian Hist. Soc. Author: Demographic Statistics of Hawaii, 1968; Historical Statistics of Hawaii, 1978; contbr. articles to tech. and profl. jours. Home: 1111 Wilder Ave Apt 16-A Honolulu HI 96822 Office: PO Box 2359 Honolulu HI 96804

SCHMITZ, DONALD WIENAND, engineering company executive; b. Brackenridge, Pa., Oct. 15, 1931; s. Wienand Gerard and Florence Marie (Grimm) S.; A.A., Phoenix Coll., 1951; student U. Colo., 1953; B.S.E.E., U. Ariz., 1958; grad. Grad. Exec. Program UCLA, 1978; postgrad. UCLA, 1968-72; m. Phyllis Ann Stevens, Sept. 15, 1960; children—Terry Lynn, Donald Wienand, Susan Stephanie. Instrumentation design engr. Gen. Dynamics Astronautics, San Diego, 1958-60; Mercury and Apollo program mgr. Bendix Pacific, Los Angeles, 1960-63, staff engr. Astral Electronics, Los Angeles, 1963-64, program mgr. Apollo program, dept. head telemetry products, dept. head design assurance, dept. head sonar products, project engr. CAPTOR program, 1972-77, chief engr. Electrodynamics div., North Hollywood, Calif., 1977-81, chief engr. oceanics div., 1981—; cons. engr. data handling and display systems, multiplex systems; v.p. Bendix Mgmt. Club, 1976, pres., 1979. Served with USAF, 1951-55. Mem. IEEE (sr.), Am. Soc. Automotive Engrs., Nat. Security Indsl. Assn., Am. Def. Preparedness Assn. Contbr. articles to tech. jours. Patentee in field. Home: 27061-1 Crossglade Ave Canyon Country CA 91351 Office: 15825 Roxford St Sylmar CA 91342

SCHMITZ, EUGENE GERARD, cons. engr.; b. Brackenridge, Pa., Sept. 17, 1929; s. Wienand Gerard and Florence Marie (Grimm) S.; student Phoenix Coll., 1946-47, Ariz. State U., 1959-61; m. Anna May Lee, May 3, 1952; children—Joyce Marie, Michael Paul, Carol Ann, John David, Eugene. Dist. mgr. Field Enterprise Ednl. Corp., Phoenix, 1955-59; designer, engr. Motorola Inc., Scottsdale, Ariz., 1961-67; project engr. space and re-entry systems div. Philco-Ford Co., Palo Alto, Calif., 1967-70; engring. program adminstr. Memorex Equipment Co., Santa Clara, Calif., 1970-71; plant mgr. Tijuana (Mex.) ops. Philco-Ford, 1971-72; engring. cons. FMC Corp., San Jose, Calif., 1972-75; staff cons. engr. Stetter Assocs., Inc., Palo Alto, 1975-80, Schmitz Engring. Assocs., 1980-82; project engr. FMC Corp., San Jose, 1982—; instr. electronic design Middlton Inst., Phoenix, 1965-66. Served with U.S. Army, 1948-55. Registered profl. engr., Calif. Mem. Soc. Mfg. Engrs. (cert.), Am. Inst. Indsl. Engrs. (sr.), Nat. Soc. Profl. Engrs., Profl. Engrs. in Pvt. Practice. Republican. Home: 3061 Vesuvius Ln San Jose CA 95132 Office: 3061 Vesuvius Ln San Jose CA 95132

SCHMITZ, STEVEN ALLEN, educator, consultant; b. Boise, Idaho, Oct. 20, 1947; s. Larry J. and Virginia M. (Talbott) S.; m. Judi Marie Kosterman, Feb. 20, 1982. B.S., Wash. State U., 1970, M.S., 1974, Ed.D., 1983. Lic. tchr. prin., supt., Wash. Tchr. and coach Alyers Jr. High Sch., Puyallup, Wash., 1970-71, Kamehameha Schs., Honolulu, 1971-73; lectr., intramural dir. Wash. State U., Pullman, 1974-76; asst. prin. Vancouver Sch. Dist. Vancouver, Wash., 1976-80; asst. supt. Kennewick (Wash.) Sch. Dist., 1981—; dir. intramural program, Wash. State U., 1980-81. Mem. Am. Assn. Sch. Adminstrs., Wash. Assn. Sch. Adminstrs., Nat. Pub. Relations Assn., Assn. Supervision Curriculum Devel. Democrat. Presbyterian. Club: Kiwanis Internat. Office: 200 S Dayton St Kennewick WA 99336

SCHMITZ-SMITH, KAREN LEE, communications company official; b. Warwick, N.Y., Dec. 6, 1946; d. Willard Franklin and May Bernyce (Maconeghy) Schmitz; B.S. magna cum laude, Western Carolina U., 1968; M.B.A. in Fin., U. Bridgeport, 1981; married. Gen. acct. Gen. Telephone Co. S.E., Durham, N.C., 1968, tax acct., 1968-69, revenue acctg. supr., 1969-70, internal auditor, 1970-71, disbursements supr., 1971-72, supr. div. revenue, 1972-73, mgr. revenues and earnings, 1973-77; adminstr. revenue requirements GTE Service Corp., Stamford, Conn., 1977-79, revenue planning mgr., 1979-81, dir. regulatory matters Gen. Telephone Co. Calif., Santa Monica, Calif., 1981—; lectr. in field. Named Career Woman, City Durham, 1974. Mem. Nat. Assn. Accts. (chpt. pres. 1972-73, nat. dir. 1975-76), Western Carolina U. Alumni Assn., Bus. and Profl. Women's Club, Beta Sigma Phi (v.p. chpt. 1972), Alpha Phi Sigma. Republican. Roman Catholic. Club: Toastmasters (pres. 1980). Office: Dept Regulatory Matters Gen Telephone Co 100 Wilshire Blvd PO Box 889 Santa Monica CA 90406

SCHNACK, HAROLD CLIFFORD, lawyer; b. Honolulu, Sept. 27, 1918; s. Ferdinand J. H. and Mary (Pearson) S.; B.A., Stanford, 1940, LL.B., 1947; m. Gayle Hemingway Jepson, Mar. 22, 1947; children—Jerrald Jay, Georgina Schnack Hankinson, Roberta Schnack Poulin, Michael Clifford. Admitted to Hawaii bar, 1947; dep. prosecutor City and County Honolulu, 1947-48; gen. practice with father F. Schnack, 1948-60; pvt. practice, Honolulu, 1960—; pres. Harcliff Corp., 1961—, Instant Printers, Inc., 1971-81, Koa Corp., 1964—, Nutmeg Corp., 1963—, Global Answer System, Inc., 1972-78. Pres. Goodwill Industries of Honolulu, 1971-72. Mem. Am., Hawaii bar assns., Phi Alpha Delta, Alpha Sigma Phi. Mason. Clubs: Outrigger Canoe, Pacific. Home: 4261 Panini Loop Honolulu HI 96816 also 1282 Riverside Dr Reno NV 89503 Office: PO Box 3077 Honolulu HI 96802

SCHNACKE, ROBERT HOWARD, judge; b. San Francisco, Oct. 8, 1913; s. Carl H. and Elfriede A. (Hanschen) S.; student U. Calif.-Berkeley, 1930-32; J.D., Hastings Coll. of Law, 1938; m. June Doris Borina, Sept. 7, 1956. Bar: Calif. 1938. Practiced in San Francisco 1938-42, 51-53, 59-68; dep. commr. div. corps. State Calif., San Francisco, 1947-51; chief criminal div. Office U.S. Atty., San Francisco, 1953-58; U.S. atty. No. Dist. Calif., San Francisco, 1958-59; judge Superior Ct., San Francisco, 1968-70; judge U.S. Dist. Ct., No. Dist. Calif., San Francisco, 1970—. Chmn. uniform rules of evidence com. 9th Circuit Jud. Conf., 1963-76. Pres. Guide Dogs for Blind, 1959-62. Bd. dirs. Fed. Jud. Center, 1975-79; mem. Jud. Panel on Multidist. Litigation, 1979—. Served with AUS, 1942-46. Mem. Calif. Hist. Soc., Fed., San Francisco bar assns., Am. Judicature Soc. Mason. Club: Burlingame Country. Home: Hillsborough CA 94010 Office: US Dist Ct No Dist Cal Box 36060 Fed Office Bldg San Francisco CA 94102

SCHNAKENBERG, RICHARD LEROY, fin. exec., cons.; b. Chgo., June 9, 1942; s. William Richard and Emily Louise (Rubbi) S.; B.S. in Mgmt., Ariz. State U., 1969; m. E. Loraine Johnson, May 4, 1969; children—Kelly Ann, Kerry Lynn, Brian John, Tammi J. Dist. mgr. Mountain Bell, Phoenix, 1963-69; mktg. dir. Honeywell, Phoenix and Oreg., 1969-78; pvt. practice Rells Investments, Phoenix, 1978-80; pres., chief exec. officer Appetito's, Inc., Phoenix, 1980—; sec./treas. Romanelli's Inc. gen. partner Triple S Properties; dir. Technology Bus. Assos., Inc. Recipient various mktg. awards including Sales and Mktg. Soc. of Phoenix, 1971. Mem. Am. Mgmt. Assn. Clubs: Plaza, Frontier, Hilton, Alumni Assn. Ariz. State U. Office: 8055 N 24th Ave Phoenix AZ 85021

SCHNEIDER, CALVIN, physician; b. N.Y.C., Oct. 23, 1924; s. Harry and Bertha (Green) S.; A.B., U. So. Calif., 1951, M.D., 1955; J.D., LaVerne (Calif.) Coll., 1973; m. Elizabeth Gayle Thomas, Dec. 27, 1967. Intern Los Angeles County Gen. Hosp., 1955-56, staff physician, 1956-57; practice medicine West Covina, Calif., 1957—; staff Inter Community Hosp., Covina, Calif. Cons. physician Charter Oak Found., Covina, 1960—. Served with USNR, 1943-47. Mem. AMA, Calif., Los Angeles County med. assns. Republican. Methodist. Home: West Covina CA also Laguna Beach CA Office: 475 W Badillo St Covina CA 91723

SCHNEIDER, CAROLYN BRAUCH, educator; b. N.Y.C., Dec. 15, 1946; d. Elliott David and Marie Alice (Giroux) Brauch; B.S., U. Bridgeport, 1968; m. Thomas J. Schneider, Aug. 3, 1978; 1 son, Logan Elliott. Tchr., Westview Elem. Sch., Northglenn, Colo., 1968-72, McElwain Elem. Sch., Thornton, Colo., 1972-75; with Northglenn Recreation Dept., part-time, 1969—; tchr. phys. edn. and health Northglenn Jr. High Sch., 1975—, cheerleading sponsor, coach gymnastics, volleyball, track. Mem. NEA, Colo. Edn. Assn., AAHPER. Home: 5316 E 113 Pl Northglenn CO 80233 Office: 1123 Muriel Dr Northglenn CO 80233

SCHNEIDER, DONALD BENJAMIN, electronics instrumentation company executive; b. Sorento, Ill., May 18, 1923; s. Benjamin F. and Edith M. (Barraclough) S.; m. Yolanda E. Pershing, Sept. 27, 1943. Student, Eastern Ill. State U., 1940-42; B.S.E.E., USAF Inst. Tech., 1951. Field engr. CEC/Bell & Howell, 1954-58; sales mgr. Neff Instruments, 1958-61; western mgr. Baldwin Lima Hamilton, 1961-64; dist. mgr. CEC, 1965-69; ops. mgr. Vibrometer Corp., Torrance, Calif., 1970-78; pres. Diagnostic Systems Corp., Torrance, 1978—. Served with USAF, 1942-54. Mem. Instrument Soc. Am., Am. Legion. Clubs: Masons, Elks. Home: 215 W Wistaria St Arcadia CA 91006 Office: 19148 Van Ness St Torrance CA 90508

SCHNEIDER, ELIZABETH KELLEY, law librarian; b. Bloomington, Ill., July 10, 1946; d. George R. and Lucille G. (Sutter) Kelley; m. John J. Schneider, Aug. 21, 1982. B.A. in History, Ill. Wesleyan U., 1968; M.A. in Library Sci., U. Minn., 1969; J.D., William Mitchell Coll., 1973. Cert. law librarian. Law librarian Ramsey County Law Library, St. Paul, 1971-73; asst. law librarian U. Akron Sch. Law, 1973-74; prof. law, librarian Hamline U. Sch. Law, St. Paul, 1974-81; dir. Maricopa County Law Library, Phoenix, 1981—; law library cons., lectr. legal bibliography; adv. bd. Mesa Community Coll. Library Technician program. Mem. ABA, Ariz. Women Lawyers, Am. Assn. Law Libraries, Phoenix Assn. Law Libraries, Southwestern Assn. Law Libraries, Alpha Gamma Delta. Contbr. to Law Books in Review. Office: 101 W Jefferson 2d Floor Phoenix AZ 85003

SCHNEIDER, FRANKLIN RICHARD, state official; b. Chelsea, Mich., May 9, 1935; s. Lewis William and Evelyn Bernice (Hall) S.; student Mich. State U., 1953-55; B.A., Linfield Coll., 1957; M.S.W., Fla. State U., 1960; Ph.D., Clayton U., 1976; m. Ruth Ann Eddy, Aug. 23,

1958; children—Daniel, Gary, Debra, Mark, Geoffrey, David. Dir., Housing Authority Yamhill County, Oreg., 1955-58; caseworker, dir. social services Winnebago Childrens Home, Neillsville, Wis., 1960-65; exec. dir. Buckhorn Childrens Center (Ky.), 1965-67; exec. dir. Spaulding for Children, Chelsea, 1967-68; dist. rep. Alaska Dept. Health and Welfare, Bethel, 1968-69; chief social worker Bur. Indian Affairs, Bethel, Alaska, 1969-73; dir. resident services rev. State of Oreg., Salem, 1976-79, dir. Clackamas region, 1979-80, program mgr., 1980-82, dir. Multnomah region, 1982—; cons. Bethel Social Services Inc., Wetangiwsch Corp.; dir. Sunrise New Life and Living, Inc., 1980—; pres. Schneider Acres, Inc.; mem. exec. com. Internat. Forum Clayton U., 1976—. NIMH grantee, 1958-60. Mem. Nat. Conf. Social Welfare, Internat. Conf. Social Work. Office: Public Service Bldg Salem OR 97310

SCHNEIDER, HAROLD, mathematician, industry tech. cons.; b. Cin., Apr. 8, 1930; s. Kalman and Ethyl Shneider; m. Joan Shirley Brown, July 3, 1960; children—Lynn, Steven Kalman. B.S. in Physics, U. Cin., 1951, M.S. in Applied Sci., 1954, Ph.D. in Physics, 1956. Aero. research scientist NASA Lewis Research Ctr., Cleve., 1951-62; staff mem. MIT Lincoln Lab., Lexington, Mass., 1962-72; prin. engring. mem. RCA Corp., Moorestown, N.J., 1978; staff engr. Lockheed Missiles & Space Co., Sunnyvale, Calif., 1978—; industry tech. cons. Mem. AIAA, Soc. Indsl. and Applied Math., Sigma Xi. Contbr. articles to profl. jours. Home: 855 Clara Dr Palo Alto CA 94303 Office: PO Box 504 Bldg 104 PLSS Sunnyvale CA 94086

SCHNEIDER, LAWRENCE PAUL, mayor; b. Regina, Sask., Can., Mar. 23, 1938; s. Paul Martin and Helen Caroline (Exner) S.; cert. in bus. adminstrn. U. Regina; m. Shirley Anne Wolfe, July 20, 1960; children—Janet, Joanne, Jon. Engring. technician U.S. Dept. Agr., 1957-69; mgmt. cons., 1970-79; now mayor City of Regina. Mem. Royal Lifesaving Soc. (award of Merit). Roman Catholic. Clubs: Optimist (pres. 1970), Rotary, Toastmasters (pres. 1972), Regina Flying (Regina). Office: Office of Mayor 2476 Victoria Ave Regina SK S4P 3C8 Canada

SCHNEIDER, LAWRENCE XAVIER, management consulting firm executive; b. Marion, Tex., May 29, 1934; s. Hugo and Leona E. Schneider; A.A., San Antonio Coll., 1954; student Tex. U., 1954-55; B.S., San Diego State Coll., 1961; m. Doris Janell Shelp, Aug. 27, 1960; 1 son, David Wayne. With Security Pacific Nat. Bank, 1961-69, mgr. exec. tng. program, 1968-69; owner Trend Fin., Vista, Calif., 1969-81; cons., pres. Trend Mgmt., Inc., Vista, 1981—; adv. to numerous corps., 1969—. Served with AC, USNR, 1955-60. Mem. Radiology Bus. Mgrs. Assn. Republican. Clubs: Rotary, Grange. Home: 1849 Alta Vista Dr Vista CA 92083 Office: Trend Mgmt Inc PO Box 2499 Vista CA 92083

SCHNEIDER, LOWELL JAMES, TV technician; b. Highland Park, Mich., Apr. 6, 1935; s. Andrew Joseph and Viola Mae (Henryes) S.; student in elec. engring. U. Wyo., 1954-57; student TV-Radio Repair Inst., Denver, 1957; A.A. in Engring. Tech., Foothill Coll., 1967; student in bus. San Jose State Coll., 1967-69; m. Mary Anne Anderson, Feb. 4, 1973; 1 son, Michael Andrew; 1 stepdau., Tamara Christine Anderson. Radar technician Philco Tech Div., 1959-60; service mgr. TV and organs, Schmoller & Mueller Piano Co., Scotts Bluff, Nebr., 1960-61; electronics technician Sylvania Electric Products, Mountain View, Calif., 1961-65; asst. engr. Fairchild Semiconductors, Mountain View, 1965-70; radio and electric mechanic United Airlines, San Francisco Airport, 1970; sr. technician Varadyne Semiconductors, Cupertino, Calif., 1970-71; test supr. DCA Reliability Lab., Mountain View, 1972-74; partner, mgr. TV Stereo Lab., Santa Clara, Calif., 1975-79, sole propr., 1979—; substitute tchr. TV audio class, San Jose Regional Vocat. Center, 1980. Served with Air N.G., 1957-61. Cert. electronic technician and service mgr.; lic. first class radio telephone operator with ships radar endorsement; vocat. tchr.'s cert., Calif. Mem. Nat. Electronic Service Dealers Assn., Nat. Assn. Retail Dealers Am., Nat. Assn. TV and Electronic Services Am., Calif. State Electronics Assn. (pres. Santa Clara chpt.), Internat. Soc. Cert. Electronic Technicians. Home: 2090 Treewood Ln San Jose CA 95132 Office: 294 N Capital Ave San Jose CA 95127

SCHNEIDERMAN, BARRY ALAN, lawyer; b. Seattle, June 28, 1933; s. Harry and Margaret S.; B.A., U. Wash., Seattle, 1955, J.D., 1957; m. Judith Arron, July 1, 1968; children—Paul L., Leah. Admitted to Wash. bar, 1957; dep. King County Pros. Atty.'s Office, Seattle, 1959-61; ptnr. firm Burns & Schneiderman, Seattle, 1961-67; pres. firm Burns, Schneiderman & Davis, P.S., Seattle, 1977—. Trustee Seattle chpt. Am. Jewish Com.; pres., bd. dirs. Caroline Kline Galland Home Aged, Seattle; trustee Temple DeHirsch Sinai, Seattle. Served as officer AUS, 1957-59; col. JAGC, Res. Decorated Army Commendation medal, Meritorious Service medal. Mem. ABA, Fed. Bar Assn., Wash. Bar Assn., Seattle-King County Bar Assn. Clubs: Wash. Athletic, College (Seattle), Shriners. Home: 5135 NE Latimer Pl Seattle WA 98105 Office: 2200 4th Ave Seattle WA 98121

SCHNEITER, GEORGE MALAN, golfer, devel. co. exec.; b. Ogden, Utah, Aug. 12, 1931; s. George Henery and Bernice Slade (Malan) S.; B.Banking and Fin., U. Utah, 1955; m. JoAnn Deakin, Jan. 19, 1954; children—George, Gary, Dan, Steve, Elizabeth Ann, Michael. Assoc. golf pro Hidden Valley Golf Club, Salt Lake City, 1957; golf pro Lake Hills Golf Club, Billings, Mont., 1957-61, sec., 1957-61, pres., 1964—; owner Schneiter Enterprises, Sandy, Utah, 1964—; player sr. golf tour PGA. Served with U.S. Army, 1956. Mem. Profl. Golfers Assn. Am. Mormon. Office: 8968 S 1300 E Sandy UT 84070

SCHNELLER, CHAD ANDREW, computer software company executive; b. Milw., Sept. 4, 1941; s. Alfred Rudolph and Rose Catherine (Mihalovic) S.; m. Linda Ann Biocini, Nov. 28, 1970; children—Stacey Lynn, Cas. B.S., San Jose State U., 1965, M.B.A. with honors, 1966. Mktg. rep. IBM, San Francisco, 1966-70, mktg. mgr., 1970, mktg. mgr., Washington, 1970-72; mgr. of edn. Service Bur. Co. div. of IBM, Washington, 1972-74; br. mgr. Service Bur. Co. div. of CDC, Phila., 1974-77; northeast area sales mgr. CDC Greenwich, Conn., 1978-81; v.p. mktg. and sales iconix Corp., Cupertino, Calif., 1981—; teaching asst. San Jose State U., Calif., 1965-66. Served with USCGR, 1966-72. Mem. Am. Mktg. Assn., Am. Electronics Assn., Am. Mgmt. Assn. Republican. Roman Catholic. Club: De Anza Racquet (Cupertino). Home: 232 Delphi Circle Los Altos CA 94022 Office: 10441 Bandley Dr Cupertino CA 95014

SCHNITZER, ARLENE DIRECTOR, art dealer; b. Salem, Oreg., Jan. 10, 1929; d. Simon M. and Helen (Holtzman) Director; m. Harold J. Schnitzer, Sept. 11, 1949; 1 son, Jordan. Student U. Wash., 1947-48. Founder, Fountain Gallery of Art, Portland, Oreg., 1961—; v.p. Harsh Investment Corp., 1951—. Bd. dirs. Oreg. Symphony Assn., mem. exec. com., bd. dirs. Artquake, Portland Ctr. for Visual Arts; trustee Reed Coll., Portland. Recipient Aubrey Watzek award Lewis and Clark Coll., 1981; honored by Portland Art Assn., 1979. Clubs: Univ., Multnomah Athletic (Portland). Office: 117 NW 21st Portland OR 97209

SCHNITZER, GARY ALLEN, steel co. exec.; b. Portland, Oreg., Jan. 29, 1942; s. Gilbert and Thelma Edith (Steinberg) S.; B.S., U. So. Calif., 1964; m. Wilhelmina Van Doorn, June 26, 1966; children—Andrea Beth, Gregory Nelson. With Schnitzer Steel Products, Oakland, Calif., 1965—, exec. v.p., 1975—; dir. Lasco Shipping Co., Island Equip. Co. Chmn., 1st ann. Oakland Marathon, 1979; mem. planning commn., Piedmont, Calif., 1975, commr., 1975, 76, Orinda, Calif., 1977, 78; mem. Alameda County Solid Waste Commn., 1975-76, Alameda Pretrail Adv. com., 1976; mem. vehicle theft legis. adv. com. Dept. Calif. Hwy. Patrol, 1975; vice chmn. fgn. trade com., Inst. Scrap Iron and Steel, 1974-77, pres. No. Calif. chpt., 1972-73, dir., 1972, 73, 77, nat. dir., West Coast rep., 1976; bd. dirs. Big Bros. Am., 1976, 77, 78, 79, B'nai B'rith Anti Defamation League, 1977; mem. Seven Hills Sch. Bd., 1982—. Mem. Oakland C. of C. dir. 1977-81. Republican. Jewish. Clubs: Lake Merritt Breakfast, Orinda and Silverado Country, Berkeley Tennis, Multnomah. Office: Schnitzer Steel Products Foot of Adeline St PO Box 747 Oakland CA 94604

SCHNITZER, LEONARD ELLIOTT, steel co. exec.; b. Portland, Oreg., 1924; s. Samuel and Rose Schnitzer; student Stanford U.; D.D.S., U. Oreg., 1946; m. Lois Shafer, Jan. 7, 1961; children—Rita Philip, Gayle Rosencrantz, Sandra, Mardi Lippman, Jill, Dina. With Schnitzer Steel Products Co., Portland, now pres.; pres. Yeon Shipping Corp., N.W. Shipping Corp.; dir. Am. Bur. Shipping. Vice chmn. Anti-Defamation League; trustee Reed Coll. Served with U.S. Army, 1943-45; with USN, 1952-54. Office: 3200 NW Yeon St Portland OR 97210*

SCHOBER, DOROTHY FLORENCE, consultant; b. Green Bay, Wis., Sept. 19, 1910; d. Max William and Addie (Stone) S.; B.A., U. Wis., 1932; M.P.H., Yale U., 1948; m. Ralph E. Hoffmeyer, Sept. 3, 1982. Visitor, dist. supr., dist. dir. Fla. Welfare Bd., Jacksonville, 1932-37; dir. Pub. Welfare Dept., Green Bay, Wis., 1937-42; cons. Div. Pub. Assistance, Wis. Dept. Pub. Welfare, Madison, 1942-44; counselor USPHS, 1944-45; health edn. cons. Council Social Agys., New Haven, 1946-49; heart work cons. State Com. on Tb and Pub. Health, N.Y., 1949-52; program cons., exec. asst. Am. Heart Assn., 1952-64, asst. dir. affiliate relations and services, 1964-65, asst. dir. dept. councils and internat. program, 1965-70, assoc. dir., 1970-73, assoc. dir. div. sci. affairs, chief sci. councils, 1973-75. Recipient Gold Heart Bracelet in appreciation 10 year service Staff Conf. Heart Assn., 1962. Fellow Am. Pub. Health Assn.; mem. Phi Kappa Phi, Alpha Kappa Delta. Home: 58-B Calle Cadiz Laguna Hills CA 92653 also 1114 11th Ave Albany GA 31707

SCHOCK, ROBERT NORMAN, geophysicist; b. Monticello, N.Y., May 25, 1939; s. Carl Louis and Norma Elizabeth (Greenfield) S.; B.S., Colo. Coll., 1961; M.S., Rensselaer Poly. Inst., 1963, Ph.D., 1966; postgrad. Northwestern U., 1963-64; m. Susan Esther Benton, Nov. 28, 1959; children—Pamela Ann, Patricia Elizabeth, Christina Benton. Jr. geophys. trainee Continental Oil Co., Sheridan, Wyo., 1960; jr. geologist Texaco Inc., Billings, Mont., 1961; teaching asst. Rensselaer Poly. Inst., Troy, N.Y., 1961-63, research asst., 1964-66; research asso. U. Chgo., 1966-68; sr. research scientist Lawrence Livermore (Calif.) Lab., U. Calif., 1968—, group leader high pressure physics, 1972-74, sect. leader geoscis. and engring., 1974-76, div. leader earth scis., 1976-81, head dept. earth sci., 1981—; cons. in field, 1969—; co-owner Pressure Systems Research; mem. faculty Chabot Coll., 1969-71. Fulbright sr. fellow U. Bonn (Germany), 1973; vis. research fellow Australian Nat. U., Canberra, 1980-81. Mem. AAAS, Am. Geophys. Union, Chem. Soc. (London), Sigma Xi. Mem. editorial bd. Rev. Sci. Instruments, 1975-77; asso. editor Jour. Geophys. Research, 1978-80; bd. asso. editors 11th Lunar and Planetary Sci. Conf., 1980; mem. adv. bd. Physics and Chemistry of Minerals, 1983. Research and publs. on high pressure physics, solid state physics, physics of earth interior, rock deformation; research on new window design for high pressure vessels, new deformation apparatus for study solids. Office: Lawrence Livermore Nat Lab PO Box 808 Livermore CA 94550

SCHOELLER, GUNTER HANS, health care exec.; b. Ger., 1939; came to U.S., 1956, naturalized, 1961; B.A., U. Calif., Berkeley, 1962; M.B.A., Calif. State U., Hayward, 1976; Ph.D., Golden Gate U., 1981. Operating mgr., then gen. mgr. Regal Apparel Inc., Oakland, Calif., 1970-75; chief engr., constrn. project dir. Mills Meml. Hosp., San Mateo, Calif., 1976-80; dir. planning, mktg. and govt. relations John Muir Meml. Hosp., Walnut Creek, Calif., 1980-81; assoc. adminstr. Eden Dist. Hosp., Castro Valley, Calif., 1981-83; dir. health services and ops. Herrick Alta Bates Service Co. Personal Care Physician Health Plan, Emeryville, Calif., 1983—; pvt. cons. internat. trade and health care mgmt., 1977—. Bd. dirs., chmn. import/export com. Oakland World Trade Assn., 1973-75, v.p., 1975. Served with AUS, 1957-60. Mem. Am. Soc. Hosp. Engrs., Calif. Soc. Hosp. Engrs., Am. Hosp. Assn. Soc. Hosp. Planning, Am. Mktg. Assn., Nat. Fire Protection Assn. Office: HEALS 5901 Christie Ave Emeryville CA 94608

SCHOEN, LINDA ALLEN, marketing director; b. Lynch, Ky., July 9, 1936; d. Wert Harvey and Mary Mabel (Ramsey) Allen; m. Stanly M. Schoen, Apr. 8, 1972. B.A., Northwestern U., 1958. Research technician G.D. Searle & Co., Chgo., 1958-60; research assoc., asst. sec. com. cutaneous health and cosmetics AMA, Chgo., 1960-75; dir. mktg. services Neutrogena Corp., Los Angeles, 1975—. Mem. AAAS, Soc. Cosmetic Chemists, The Fashion Group. Episcopalian. Club: Opera Assn. (Northwestern U. Alumni). Editor The Look You Like column Today's Health mag., 1962-74; The AMA Book of Skin and Hair Care, 1976; contbr. articles to Harper's Bazaar, Vogue, Redbook, Beauty Handbook. Home: 6505 Green Valley Circle Culver City CA 90230 Office: 5755 W 96th St Los Angeles CA 90045

SCHOENFELD, JOHN ALEXANDER, real estate/financial consultant, entrepreneur; b. Los Angeles, July 14, 1956; s. H. Kenneth and Barbara (Blumenthal) S. B.A. in Econs., UCLA, 1978; J.D., Southwestern U., 1981. Tax intern Kenneth Leventhal & Co., Los Angeles, summer 1980; sr. internat. tax specialist Peat, Marwick, Mitchell & Co., Los Angeles, 1980-83, real estate/fin. cons., 1983—. Youth services com. Los Angeles Olympic Organizing Commn.; grants, events and publicity coms. Concern II Found.; community services com. Jewish Fedn. Los Angeles; steering com. Young Execs. Group of United Jewish Welfare Fund. Mem. Blue Key. Jewish. Office: 555 S Flower St Los Angeles CA 90071

SCHOENHALS, PAUL JOHN, Canadian provincial cabinet minister, educator; b. Clinton, Ont., Can., Nov. 5, 1941; s. Stewart John and Phyllis Lillian (Elliott) S.; m. Dorenda Alene Stirton, June 21, 1969; children—Susan, Ryan, Karyn. B.Edn., U. Sask., 1964, postgrad. diploma, 1970. Tchr., Saskatoon Pub. Bd. Edn., Sask., Can., 1964-82; dept. coordinator Aden Bowman Collegiate, Saskatoon, 1981-82; cabinet minister, Govt. of Sask., 1982—; coach Saskatoon Hilltops, 1975-79. Coach of team Can. Jr. Football Champions, 1978. Mem. Progressive Conservative Party. Office: Room 302 Legislative Bldg Regina SK S4S 0B3 Canada

SCHOENWOLF, GARY CHARLES, embryologist, educator; b. Chgo., Nov. 22, 1949; s. Fred and Shirley Bertha (Dawrant) S.; m. Patricia Lee Wilke, Aug. 28, 1971; children—Jennifer Lee, Gregory Charles. B.A., Elmhurst Coll., 1971; M.S., U. Ill., 1973, Ph.D., 1976. Vis. lectr. dept. genetics and devel. U. Ill., Urbana, 1976-77; sr. research assoc. dept. anatomy U. N.Mex., Albuquerque, 1977-79; asst. prof., dept. anatomy U. Utah Sch. Medicine, Salt Lake City, 1979—. Deacon Mt. Olympus Presbyn. Ch., 1981-83. NIH fellow, 1978-79; NIH grantee, 1981-84, 82-85. Mem. AAAS, Am. Soc. Zoologists, Am. Assn. Anatomists, Soc. Devel. Biology, Electron Microscopy Am., Am. Soc. Cell Biology, Am. Inst. Biol. Scis. Co-author: Laboratory Studies of Chick, Pig, and Frog Embryos, 1979; assoc. editor The Anatomical Record 1981—; contbr. articles to profl. jours. Home: 2280 E 900 South Salt Lake City UT 84108 Office: Dept Anatomy U Utah Sch Med Salt Lake City Ut 84132

SCHOLDER, FRITZ, artist; b. Breckenridge, Minn., Oct. 6, 1937; s. Fritz William and Ella Mae (Haney) S.; student Wis. State Coll., 1956-57; A.A., Sacramento City Coll., 1958; B.A., Sacramento State Coll., 1960; M.F.A., U. Ariz.; m. Peggy Stephenson, June 28, 1958 (div. Mar. 1966); 1 son, Fritz VI; m. 2d, Romona Attenberger, July 30, 1966. Exhibited one-man shows: Crocker Art Gallery, Sacramento, 1959, Coll. Santa Fe, 1967, Roswell (N.Mex.) Art Center, 1969, Esther Baer Gallery, Santa Barbara, Calif., 1971, Tally Richards Gallery Contemporary Art, Taos, N.Mex., 1971, 73, 75, 78, 79, Elaine Horwitch Gallery, Scottsdale, Ariz., 1972-79, St. John's Coll., Santa Fe, 1972, Cordier & Ekstrom, N.Y.C., 1972, 74, 76, 78, Gimpel & Weitzenhoffer, N.Y.C., 1977, Graphics 1 and 2, Boston, 1977, Smith Andersen Gallery, Palo Alto, Calif., 1979, Plains Mus., Moorhead, Minn., 1980, Marilyn Butler Fine Art, Scottsdale, Ariz., 1981, Scottsdale Center for Arts, 1981, Tucson Mus. Art, 1981, Weintraub Gallery, N.Y.C., 1981, ACA Galleries. N.Y.C.; group shows: Carnegie Art Inst., Butler Inst. Am. Art, Calif. Palace of Legion of Honor, Houston Mus. Fine Arts, Dallas Mus. Fine Arts, San Francisco Mus. Art, Denver Art Mus., Ft. Worth Art Center, Basel Art 5, Linden Mus., Stuttgart, Philbrook Art Center, Oakland Art Mus., Tucson Art Center, N.Mex. Art Mus., Edinburgh Art Festival, Museo de Bellas Artes, Buenos Aires, Biblioteca Nacional, Santiago, Chile, Mus. voor Land-en-Volkenkunder, Rotterdam, Amerika Haus, Berlin Festival, Center for Arts of Indian Am., Washington, Yellowstone Art Center, Nat. Mus. Modern Art, Tokyo, Nat. Mus. Modern Art, Kyoto, Japan, also other fgn. and Am. shows; Smithsonian tour Bucharest, Berlin, London, Ankara, Madrid, Belgrade, Athens, 1972-73; represented in permanent collections: Mus. Modern Art, N.Y.C., Art Inst. Chgo., Center Culturel Americain, Paris, Art Gallery Toronto, NEA, Houston Mus. Fine Arts, Boston Fine Arts Mus., Milw. Art Mus., Portland (Oreg.) Art Mus., Dallas Mus. Fine Arts, Bur. Indian Affairs, Mus. N.Mex., Smithsonian Instn., Bklyn. Mus., Phoenix Art Mus., San Diego Fine Arts Gallery, Okla. Art Center, Brigham Young U., Heard Mus., Phoenix, Bibliotheque Nat., Paris, San Francisco Mus. Art, others; teaching asst. art Univ. Ariz. 1962-64; instr. art history, advanced painting Inst. Am. Indian Arts, 1964-69; artist in residence Dartmouth Coll., 1973. Recipient Ford Found. Purchase award, 1962; 1st prize W.Va. Centennial Exhibition, 1963; purchase prize 13th S.W. Print Drawing Show, 1963; John Hay Whitney fellow, 1962-63; Hallmark purchase award, 1965; 1st prize Scottsdale Indian Nat., 1966; Grand prize Washington Biennial Indian Show, 1967; Grand prize Scottsdale Indian Nat., 1969; jurors award S.W. Fine Arts Biennial, 1970, 71, 72; prize in painting Am. Acad. and Inst. Arts and Letters, 1977; Disting. Achievement award Ariz. State U., 1983; Gov.'s award N.Mex., 1983, others. Included in Politics in Art; American Indian Painters; Indian Voices; Indians Today, Indian Painters and White Patrons; The Vincent Price Treasury of American Art; Scholder/Indians; The World of the American Indian; Kein Platz fur Wilde Menschen, Art and Indian Individuals, Fritz Scholder Lithographs; Song from the Earth; Anpao; An American Indian Odyssey; Ency. of Artists of the American West; Many Smokes, Many Moons; Weg ohne Mokassins; Indian Kitsch: Photographs by Fritz Scholder; 20th Century Masters of Erotic Art; American Prints and Printmakers. Subject of PBS film Fritz Scholder, 1976. Home: Galisteo NM 87540 also: 118 Cattletrack Rd Scottsdale AZ 85251

SCHOLES, ROBERT THORNTON, physician, research adminstr.; b. Bushnell, Ill., June 24, 1919; s. Harlan Lawrence and Lura Zolene (Camp) S.; student Knox Coll., 1937-38; B.S., Mich. State U., 1941; M.D., U. Rochester, 1950; postgrad. U. London, 1951-52, U. Chgo., 1953; m. Kathryn Ada Tew, Sept. 3, 1948; 1 dau., Delia. Intern, Gorgas Hosp., Ancon, C.Z., 1950-51; lab. asst. dept. entomology Mich. State U., 1940-41; research asst. Roselake Wildlife Exptl. Sta., 1941; research assoc. Harvard U., 1953-57; served to med. dir. USPHS, 1954-71, med. officer, dep. chief health and sanitation div. U.S. Ops. Mission, Bolivia, 1954-57, chief health and sanitation div., Paraguay, 1957-60, internat. health rep. Office of Surgeon Gen., 1960-62; br. chief, research grants officer, acting assoc. dir. Nat. Inst. Allergy and Infectious Diseases, NIH, Bethesda, Md., 1962-71; pres. The Bioresearch Ranch, Inc., Rodeo, N.Mex., 1977—; cons. Peace Corps, 1961, Hidalgo County Med. Services, Inc., 1979—, N.Mex. Health Systems Agy., 1980—, N.Mex. Health Resources, Inc., 1981—. Served to capt. USAAF, 1942-45. Commonwealth Fund fellow, 1953. Mem. AAAS, Am. Soc. Tropical Medicine and Hygiene, N.Y. Acad. Sci., Am. Public Health Assn., Am. Ornithologists Union. Contbr. papers to profl. publs. Home and Office: PO Box 117 Rodeo NM 88056

SCHOLL, ALLAN HENRY, educator, consultant; b. Bklyn., May 6, 1935; s. Joseph Arnold and Edith (Epstein) S.; m. Marina Alexandra Mihailovich. B.A., UCLA, 1957; M.A., U. So. Calif., 1959, Ph.D. in History, 1973. Cert. tchr., adminstr. Tchr. jr., sr. high schs. Los Angeles Unified Sch. Dist., 1960-82, gifted, talented edn. coordinator Taft High Sch., 1980-82, social studies cons. sr. high sch. div., 1982—; instr. history Los Angeles City Coll., Cerritos Coll., Rio Hondo Coll.; cons. Coll. Bd. in Advanced Placement History. Bd. dirs. Pasadena Chamber Orch., 1978-79; mem. Nat. Found. Ileitis and Colitis. Served in U.S. Army, 1958-59. Chouinard Art Inst. scholar, 1952; NDEA grantee, 1962; U. So. Calif. fellow, 1968-69; Closeup Program fellow, 1983. Mem. Nat. Council Social Studies, Calif. Council Social Studies, So. Calif. Social Sci. Assn., Calif. Assn. for Gifted, Am. Hist. Assn., Assn. Supervision and Curriculum Devel., Phi Alpha Theta. Contbr. articles to profl. jours. Office: Sr High Sch Div Los Angeles Unified Sch Dist 644 West 17th St Los Angeles CA 90015

SCHOLL, DENNIS MICHAEL, clinical psychologist; b. Fairfield Calif., June 27, 1949; s. Frank N. and Margaret Genevieve (Archer) S.; m. Janice Sue Cooke, June 15, 1969; children—Genevieve Louise, Grace Audrey, Madeline Amber. B.A., St. Mary's Coll., Moraga, Calif., 1967-71; M.A., Notre Dame U., 1974, Ph.D. in Psychology, 1975. Lic. psychologist, Alaska. Commd. officer U.S. Air Force, 1975, advanced through grades to capt.; research psychologist USAF Sch. Aerospace Medicine, San Antonio, Tex., 1975-77; psychology intern Wilford Hall USAF Med. Ctr., San Antonio, 1977-78; staff psychologist USAF Hosp., Elmendorf Alaska, 1978-82; resigned, 1982; psychologist Seward Life Action Council, 1982—. Mem. Am. Psychol. Assn., Assn. Advancement Psychology, Alaska Psychol. Assn. (exec. officer 1980—). Contbr. articles to profl. jours. Home: PO Box 1251 Seward AK 99664 Office: PO Box 4-1885 Anchorage AK 99509

SCHONBRUN, MICHAEL K., hosp. adminstr.; b. N.Y.C., Jan. 26, 1948; s. Arnold L. and Madeline (Courland) S.; B.A., Yale U., 1969; J.D., U. Pa., 1973; m. Michelle I. Fredson, June 6, 1971. Admitted to Ohio bar, 1973, Colo. bar, 1976; gen. counsel Ohio Gov.'s Task Force on Health Care, 1973-74; research atty. Spectrum Research, Denver, 1974-75; asst. to gov. for health affairs, State of Colo., Denver, 1975-76; asst. dir. Colo. Dept. Health, 1976-78; exec. v.p. Nat. Jewish Hosp./Nat. Asthma Center, Denver, 1979-82, pres., 1982—. Chmn. staff com. on health info. systems Nat. Gov.'s Assn., 1977-78; adj. asst. prof. U. Colo. Health Sci. Center. VISTA fellow, 1971. Mem. Nat. Health Lawyers Assn. Office: 3800 E Colfax Ave Denver CO 80206

SCHOOLER, JO ANN, weight-control and smoking control center executive; b. Gloster, Miss., Oct. 30, 1931; d. Frank Walton and Grace (Hoff) S.; m. Harold Marcus Hilliard, Oct. 19, 1955 (div.). B.S., Centenary Coll., Shreveport, La., 1951; M.Ed., U. Tex.-Austin, 1953. Med. social worker M.D. Anderson Hosp. U. Tex., Houston, 1953-58; mgr. First Lady Health Spas, Houston, 1958-69; supr. Golden Venus Health Spas, San Francisco, 1969-74; divisional supr. Gloria Marshall

Figure Salons, Inc., Downey, Calif., 1974-82; exec. dir. tng. and devel. Schick Labs, Inc., Los Angeles, 1982—. Mem. Nat. Assn. Profl. Saleswomen, Nat. Assn. Female Execs. Republican. Episcopalian. Office: 1901 Ave of Stars Suite 1500 Los Angeles CA 90067

SCHOPPA, ELROY, accountant; b. Vernon, Tex., June 25, 1922; s. Eddie A. and Ida (Foerster) S.; m. Juanita C. Young, Aug. 11, 1956 (div.); children—Karen Marie, Vickie Sue. B.B.A., Tex. Tech U., 1943; postgrad. Law Sch., U. Tex., 1946-47; M.A., Mich. State U., 1950. C.P.A., Tex., Calif. Mem. faculty Tex. Tech U., Lubbock, 1943, U. Tex., Austin, 1946-47, Mich. State U., East Lansing, 1947-50; auditor Gen. Motors Corp., 1950-56; dir. systems and procedures Fansteel Metall. Corp., 1956-59; gen. auditor Consol. Dynamics Corp., 1959-60; auditor, sr. tax acct. Beckman Inst. Inc., Fullerton, Calif., 1960-70; pres. Elroy Schoppa Acctg. Corp., La Habra, Calif., 1960—; cons. to bus.; ins. agt., real estate broker. Treas. La Habra Devel. Corp. Served with USN, 1942-46. Mem. Alpha Phi Omega. Republican. Lutheran. Club: Phoenix (Anaheim, Calif.). Office: 801 E La Habra Blvd La Habra CA 90631

SCHORZMAN, MARK HEWIT, industrial hygienist; b. Spokane, Wash., Sept. 6, 1937; s. Lester Richard and Esther Ann (Cowen) S.; m. Judy Kennett Lavender, Aug. 22, 1959; children—Mark Hewit, Douglas Wheeler. B.S., U. Wash., 1961, M.S. in Pub. Health, 1975; grad. with honors, Army Command and Gen. Staff Coll., 1976; registered sanitarian, Wash.; diplomate Am. Acad. Sanitarians, Am. Acad. Indsl. Hygiene. Sanitarian, Thurston-Mason Health Dist., Wash., 1961-62; commd. 2d lt., U.S. Army, 1962, advanced through grades to maj., 1967, ret., 1982, chief environ. sanitation, N. Baveria Med. Dist., W. Germany, 1968-69, chief preventive medicine Madigan Gen. Hosp., Tacoma, Wash., 1970-74, preventive medicine cons. Comdr. U.S. Army Health Services Command, Ft. Sam Houston, Tex., 1975-77, chief environ. sci. Fitzsimons Army Med. Center, Denver, 1977-82; risk mgmt. officer Adams County, Colo., 1982—; instr. Nat. Inst. for Food Service Industry, 1980-83. Scouting chmn. Centennial dist. Boy Scouts Am., 1977-79, mem. tng. com., 1977-82. U.S. Army Med. Dept. scholar, 1974. Mem. Am. Indsl. Hygiene Assn., Nat. Environ. Health Assn., Automatic Merchandising Assn., Am. Conf. Govtl. Indsl. Hygienists, Royal Soc. Health U.K., Sigma Chi. Anglican. Contbr. articles to profl. jours. Home: 3419 S Nucla Way Aurora CO 80013 Office: 450 S 4th Ave Brighton CO 80601

SCHOTT, KIRK ROBERT, optometrist; b. Ft. Dodge, Iowa, Nov. 9, 1954; s. Robert Charles and Velda Kathleen (Jones) S.; m. Melissa Susan Thurow, Feb. 14, 1981; 1 son, Joshua Robert. B.S. in Zoology, Iowa State U., 1977; student Morningside Coll., 1977; O.D., Ill. Coll. Optometry, 1981. Sports dir. summer camp Prairie Gold Area Council, Boy Scouts Am., 1976, summer camp program dir., 1977; dir. summer camp scoutcraft Pike's Peak Council, Boy Scouts Am., Lake George, Colo., 1978, summer camp program dir., 1979-80; assoc. Gunnison (Colo.) Eye Clinic, 1982—; mem. Health Services Adv. Com. Gunnison Watershed Sch. Dist. Asst. scoutmaster Boy Scouts Am., 1981—. Recipient Vigil Honor Order of the Arrow, Vigil Honor Guide, Boy Scouts Am. Mem. Am. Optometric Assn., Colo. Optometric Assn., Optometric Extension Program, Gold Key Internat. Optometric Honor Soc. Lutheran. Club: Kiwanis (treas. 1982, v.p. 1982—). Home: 98 Farway Dr Gunnison CO 81230 Office: Gunnison Eye Clinic 420 N Main PO Box A Gunnison CO 81230

SCHOTZ, BARRY R., employee benefits cons.; b. Lorain, Ohio, May 4, 1951; s. Robert Edward and Ruby Katherine (Urquhart) S.; m. Kenalie Salters, Oct. 7, 1952. B.S., U. Kans., 1975, M.B.A., 1975. Pres., Creative Compensation, Inc., Lawrence, Kans., 1972-75, Lorain, Ohio, 1975-81, LaJolla, Calif., 1981—; mem. adv. bd., savs. and loan banks. Mem. Soc. Profl. Benefit Adminstrs., San Diego County Estate Planning Council, San Diego C. of C. Office: 9404 Genesee Ave Suite 300 LaJolla CA 92037

SCHRAM, JEAN ROSALER, investment co. exec.; b. N.Y.C., Oct. 22, 1948; d. Robert Carlton and Shirley (Sisenwein) Rosaler; B.A., Skidmore Coll., 1970; M.A., Stanford U., 1975, Ed.D., 1979; m. Richard Paul Schram, Jan. 20, 1980. Project coordinator in career edn. N.Y. State Dept. Edn., N.Y.C., 1972-74; cons. Calif. Dept. Edn., Sacramento, 1975-77; cons. edn., San Francisco, 1977-79; v.p. franchise div. Hdqrs., Investment Mortgage Internat., San Francisco, 1979-82, sr. v.p., dir. franchise div., 1982-83; cons., 1983—. Bd. dirs. Paul Scardina Dance Co., San Francisco, 1979-80, Jewish Vocation Service, 1983—; co-chmn. media communications div. Jewish Community Fedn., 1982—. Recipient Golden Reel of Merit award Internat. TV Assn., 1981; Edn. Professions Devel. Act scholar, 1974. Mem. Am. Soc. Tng. and Devel. Author: How to Make the Best School Site Council in the World: A Guidebook for School Improvement Councils and Other School Community Groups, 1979.

SCHREINER, ROBERT NICHOLAS, JR., systems engineer; b. Bronx, N.Y.C., Jan. 12, 1935; s. Robert Nicholas and Martha Louise (Picard) S.; B.S., Capital U., 1956; postgrad. U. So. Calif., 1956-58; m. Anne Louise Wendt, June 2, 1956; children—Sue Anne, Wendy Louise, Robert Edward, Kurt Nicholas, Martha Elizabeth, David Paul. Engr., Northrop Corp., Hawthorne, Calif., 1956-59; staff engr. research and tech. TRW Def. Systems Group of TRW Inc., Redondo Beach, Calif., 1959—, engring. and applied mechanics, 1959-65, interactive computer graphics advanced tech., 1965-68, indsl./ednl. coop. research and devel., 1968-72, real time computer application design and devel., 1972-78, hardware/software integration test and evaluation, 1978—; lectr. mech. engring. and advanced computer tech. to univs., indsl. firms. West Coast regional chmn. Centennial observance Capital U.'s Alumni Assn., 1967; chmn. Lutheran Ingathering for Edn., 1968, mem. ch. council, 1958-75, pres., 1965, 68, trustee, 1964-68, lay asst. pastor, 1972—. Mem. Luth. Brotherhood Frat. Soc. Republican. Contbr. articles on various specialties in mech. engring. and computer tech. Home: 30520 Via Rivera Rancho Palos Verdes CA 90274 Office: 1 Space Park Redondo Beach CA 90278

SCHRIVER, LAWRENCE ALPHONSE, occupational health specialist, consultant; b. Paris, Ark., Nov. 3, 1923; s. Thomas Alexander and Mathilda Catherine (Fredrich) S.; A.A., Little Rock Jr. Coll., 1949; student Rice Inst., 1949-50; B.A., LaVerne U., 1975; m. Lula J. Hitt, June 14, 1952; children—Terrence Walter, Lynne Allison. Engring. draftsman, Johns-Manville Corp., Lompoc, Calif., 1953-54, jr. mech. engr., 1954-55, mech. engr. 1960-67, area indsl. hygienist, 1967-75, indsl. hygiene supr., 1975-82; pvt. cons., Lompoc, 1983—; mech. engr. Kennecott Copper Corp., Chile, 1955-58; maintenance supt. Olin-Mathieson Corp., Beaumont, Tex., 1958-60. Served with USMC, 1946-48, USMCR, 1950-51. Mem. Am. Indsl. Hygiene Assn., DAV, Phi Theta Kappa. Republican. Roman Catholic. Clubs: Manville Quarter Century, KC, Elks. Home: 1117 N Orchid St Lompoc CA 93436

SCHROEDER, ARNOLD LEON, educator; b. Honolulu, May 27, 1935; s. Arnold Leon and Wynelle (Russell) S.; B.S. in Math., Oreg. State Coll., 1960, M.S. in Stats., 1962; NSF Insts. at UCLA, 1964, U. So. Calif., 1965; m. Maybelle Ruth Walker, Nov. 9, 1956; children—Steven, Michael, Wendy. Computer engr. Autonetics div. N.Am. Aviation Co., 1960-61; NSF fellow, research asst. State of Oreg., Corvallis, 1961; asso. prof. math. Long Beach (Calif.) Community Coll., 1962—; computer cons. McDonnell-Douglas Corp., 1966-74, statis. software specialist in biomed. and med. research, 1974-79, research statistician specialist in fin. strategies and tax reduction, 1979—; asso. prof. ops. research Calif. State U., Long Beach, 1965—; asso. prof. stats./math. Azusa Pacific Coll., 1967. Served with USAF, 1953-57. Mem. Faculty Assn. Calif. Community Colls., Calif. Teaching Assn., Nat. Bowlers Assn. (life). Evangelical Christian. Contbr. articles to profl. jours. Home: 5481 E Hill St Long Beach CA 90815 Office: 4901 E Carson St Long Beach CA 90808

SCHROEDER, EDWYNN EDGAR, orthodontist; b. Los Angeles, Dec. 2, 1930; s. Herbert Joseph and Faye (Dunham) S.; B.A., U. So. Calif., 1952, M.S., 1965, D.D.S., Coll. Physicians and Surgeons, 1959; m. Marla Stacy Berk, Dec. 30, 1975; children—Neil Nelson, Leslie Louise, Samuel George, Tarah Rose. Asso., Douglas F. Snow, North Hollywood, Calif., 1959-60; pvt. practice dentistry specializing in orthodontics, Northridge, Calif., 1960-65, Chatsworth, Calif., 1965—; staff Hollywood Presbyn. Hosp., 1962—, Los Angeles County Hosp., 1965—; clin. instr. Sch. Dentistry, U. So. Calif., 1971-75; treas. Orthodontic Assos., Inc., 1976-81; pres. Western Dental Plan Mgmt., Inc., 1978—; cons. Los Angeles City Sch. Dist., 1960-70; dental cons., dir. Dental Service Bur., 1968—; dental cons. Southwest Adminstrs., 1974—, Meat Cutters Trust, 1974—. Served with U.S. Army, 1952-54. Diplomate Am. Bd. Orthodontics. Mem. ADA, Am. Assn. Orthodontists, Fedn. Dentaire Internat., Coll. Physicians and Surgeons Alumni Assn., San Fernando Valley Dental Soc. (chmn. council on profl. services 1967), Pacific Coast Orthodontic Soc. (chmn. dental care com. 1972), Los Angeles City Schs. Physicians and Dentists Assn. (pres. 1963), Tau Kappa Omega, Psi Omega, Phi Kappa Tau. Contbr. articles to profl. jours. Office: 10234 Canoga Ave Chatsworth CA 91311 also 2241 Michael Dr Newbury Park CA 91320

SCHROEDER, ELROY DEAN, psychology educator; b. Grand Forks, N.D., Dec. 11, 1942; s. Elroy Herman and Donalda Lillian (MacDonald) S.; B.S., U. N.D., 1964, M.S., 1965; Ed.D., U. No. Colo., 1972. Psychology tchr. East High Sch., Cheyenne, Wyo., 1965-67; instr. psychology, counselor Luther Coll., Decorah, Iowa, 1967-69; dir. counseling services, asst. prof. psychology Wartburg Coll., Waverly, Iowa, 1969-73; clin. psychologist NE Colo. Mental Health Clinic, Sterling, 1973-75, SE Wyo. Mental Health Center, Cheyenne, 1975-77; sch. psychologist Laramie County Sch. Dist. 1, Cheyenne, 1977-80; prof. psychology Laramie County Community Coll., Cheyenne, 1977—; cons. Laramie County Sch. Dist. 1, 1980—. Mem. security com. Cheyenne Frontier Days, 1975—. N.D. State Bd. Higher Edn. scholar, 1964. Fellow Am. Orthopsychiat. Assn.; mem. Am. Psychol. Assn. Republican. Lutheran. Clubs: Quarterback (Cheyenne, Wyo.); Elks, Kiwanis. Home: 805 Cahill Dr Cheyenne WY 82001 Office: 1400 E College Dr Cheyenne WY 82001

SCHROEDER, HARVEY WILFRED, Canadian legislator; b. Main Centre, Sask., Can., June 16, 1933; married; children—Karen, Darrell, Duane. Grad. Can. Bible Coll., Sask., 1958. Cost acct. Can. Packers; retail merchandiser; founder, owner Palm Interior of Chillwack, 1954; active TV and stage prodn., pub. relations; mem. Legis. Assembly of B.C., from Chillwack Constituency, 1972—, dep. speaker, 1976, speaker assembly, 1978—, minister food and agr., 1982, 83—. Office: Province of BC Ministry Agr and Food Parliament Bldgs Victoria V8V 1X4 Canada

SCHROEDER, JANET GREGG WALLACE (MRS. HENRY A. SCHROEDER), sculptor; b. St. Louis, May 4, 1902; d. Cecil Dudley and Jessie Marian (Howard) Gregg; student Bryn Mawr Coll., 1920-21, Washington U. Sch. Art, 1929-30; m. Asa Brookings Wallace, 1922 (dec. 1942); children—Marian (Mrs. M. W. Ney), Janet, (Mrs. Andrew B. Jones), Eugenie (Mrs. Marius S. Darrow, Jr.); m. 2d, Henry Alfred Schroeder, May 20, 1949 (dec. Apr. 1975). Tchr. sculpture John Burroughs Sch., St. Louis, 1937-38, Hickory Ridge Sch., Putney, Vt., 1946-47; exhibited Feragils, Brit. Am. Gallery, St. Louis Art Mus., Julius Polk, Inc., St. Louis, Manchester (Vt.) Art Gallery, Book Cellar Gallery, Brattleboro, Vt., 1959, Black Starr, Gorham (N.Y.C.), 1948-49; portraits in bronze in permanent collections Robert S. Brookings, Dr. Arthur H. Compton, Rt. Rev. Father Alphonse Schwitalla, Rev. Mother Concordia, Pierre Laclede; exhibited permanent collections two portraits Nat. Portrait Gallery, Smithsonian Instn., Washington; portrait Marlboro (Vt.) Coll., works include bronze portrait Ambassador Ellsworth Bunker, 1974, Walter Muir Whitknell, 1977; represented by Jean Seth Gallery, Santa Fe, 1981—. Home: La Fonda Hotel Santa Fe NM 87501

SCHROEDER, MARY MURPHY, judge; b. Boulder, Colo., Dec. 4, 1940; d. Richard and Theresa (Kahn) Murphy; B.A., Swarthmore Coll., 1962; J.D., U. Chgo., 1965; m. Milton R. Schroeder, Oct. 15, 1965; children—Caroline Theresa, Katherine Emily. Admitted to Ill. bar, 1966, D.C. bar, 1966, Ariz. bar, 1970; trial atty. Dept. Justice, Washington, 1965-69; law clk. Hon. Jesse Udall, Ariz. Supreme Ct., 1970; mem. firm Lewis and Roca, Phoenix, 1971-75, partner, 1973-75; judge Ariz. Ct. Appeals, Phoenix, 1975-79; judge U.S. Ct. Appeals, 9th Circuits, Phoenix, 1979—; vis. instr. Ariz. State U. Coll. Law, 1976, 77, 78. Mem. Am. Bar Assn., Ariz. Bar Assn., Fed. Bar Assn., Am. Law Inst., Am. Judicature Soc. Democrat. Club: Soroptimists. Contbr. articles to profl. jours. Office: 6421 Federal Bldg 230 N 1st Ave Phoenix AZ 85025

SCHROEDER, PATRICIA SCOTT, congresswoman, educator, lawyer; b. Portland, Oreg., July 30, 1940; d. Lee Combs and Bernice (Scott) Scott; B.A. magna cum laude, U. Minn., 1961; J.D., Harvard, 1964; m. James White Schroeder, Aug. 18, 1962; children—Scott William, Jamie Christine. Admitted to Colo. bar, 1964; field atty. NLRB, Denver, 1964-66; pvt. practice law, Denver, 1966-72; hearing officer Colo. Dept. Personnel, 1971-72; faculty U. Colo., Denver, 1969-72, Community Coll., Denver, 1969-70, Regis Coll., Denver, 1970. Dir. Century Casualty Co., Denver. Bd. dirs. Jefferson County Human Relations Council, Denver Young Dems., Planned Parenthood of Colo. Mem. 93d-97th Congresses from 1st Dist. Colo., dep. regional whip; mem. Armed Services Com., P.O. and Civil Service Com., chmn. Com. on Civil Service, mem. Com. on Children, Youth and Families, co-chmn. Congl. Caucus on Women's Issues. Mem. Am. Bar Assn., LWV. Congregationalist. Office: 2410 Rayburn House Office Bldg Washington DC 20515

SCHROEDER, RITA MOLTHEN, chiropractor; b. Savanna, Ill., Oct. 25, 1922; d. Frank J. and Ruth J. (McKenzie) Molthen; m. Richard H. Schroeder, Apr. 23, 1948 (div.); children—Richard, Andrew, Barbara, Thomas, Paul, Madeline. Student, Chem. Engring., Immaculate Heart Coll., 1940-41, UCLA, 1941, Palmer Sch. of Chiropractic, 1947-49; D. Chiropractic, Cleve. Coll. of Chiropractic, 1961. Engring.-tooling design data coordinator Douglas Aircraft Co., El Segundo, Santa Monica and Long Beach, Calif., 1941-47; pres. Schroeder Chiropractic, Inc., 1982—; dir. Pacific States Chiropractic Coll., 1978-80, pres. 1980-81. Recipient Palmer Coll. Ambassador award, 1973. Parker Chiropractic Research Found. Ambassador award, 1976. Mem. Internat. Chiropractic Assn., Calif. Chiropractic Assn., Internat. Chiropractic Assn. Calif., Assn. Am. Chiropractic Coll. Presidents, Council Chiropractic Edn. (Pacific State Coll. rep.). Home: 9870 N Millbrook Ave Fresno CA 93710 Office: Schroeder Chiropractic Inc 2535 N Fresno Ave Fresno CA 93703

SCHROFF, ELLEN GAY, postal service executive; b. Caldwell, Idaho, June 19, 1944; d. Dell Wilson and Eleanor (Zoa) S. Student Boise State U. Comml. artist Caxton Printers Ltd., Caldwell, 1965-73; with U.S. Postal Service, 1973—, mail processing supr., 1978-79, dist. EEO specialist for Idaho, Mont., Utah and eastern Nev., 1979-81, mgr. employee relations, Salt Lake City, 1981-83, mgmt. sectional dir., employee and labor relations, Boise, 1983—. Mem. Fed. Personnel Mgmt. Council, Federally Employed Women, NOW, Nat. Assn. Female Execs., Nat. Mus. Natural History. Club: Sierra. Home: PO Box 8775 Boise ID 83707 Office: 770 S 13th St Boise ID 83708

SCHRUM, WILLIAM ROY, hosp. mgmt. cons.; b. Tacoma, Aug. 24, 1950; s. Roy Marshall and Agnes Elva (Pennant) S.; B.A., U. Colo., 1977; m. Valerie P. Sullivan, Apr. 28, 1973; 1 son, Jason. Owner, editor Lafayette (Colo.) Times, 1974-75; personnel dir. Internat. Hosp. Services, Denver, 1975-80, regional dir., 1980-83, v.p., 1983—. Mem. City Council Lafayette, 1975-76; mem. Lafayette Planning Commn., 1974-75, Lafayette Centennial Bicentennial Com., 1975-76. Served with USMC, 1968-71. Accredited, Personnel Accreditation Inst. Mem. Am. Mgmt. Assn., Am. Soc. Personnel Adminstrn., Internat. Platform Assn. Roman Catholic. Home: 1111 Pandora Ct Lafayette CO 80026 Office: 4200 W Conejos St #GL-2 Denver CO 80204

SCHUBACK, PAUL GUY, master violin maker; b. Barbados, W.I., Sept. 13, 1946; s. Herbert Wolf and Margaret Lucienne (Kirk) S.; m. Marie-Madeleine Girardin, July 29, 1967; children—Steven, Pascol. Grad. René Morizot Sch., Mirecourt, France, 1966. Apprentice in violin making, Mittenwald, W.Ger., 1966-67; apprentice in bow making, Mirecourt, 1967; violin maker, repairman Peter Prier Shop, Salt Lake City, 1968-71; prin. Schuback Violin Shop, Portland, Oreg., 1971—. Recipient gold medal Violin Soc. Am., 1976, 78, craftmanship award 1976, 78. Mem. Chamber Music Oreg. (pres.), Chamber Music N.W. (dir.), Entente Internationale des Maitres Luthiers et Archetiers d'Art, Am. Fedn. Violin and Bow Makers. Mem. Ch. of Jesus Christ of Latter-day Saints. Club: Rotary. Office: 3003 SE Milwaukie St Portland OR 97202

SCHUBERT, DONALD KEITH, clinical psychologist; b. Peoria, Ill., Feb. 24, 1951; s. Elliot N. and Eileen (Kranson) S.; B.A., U. Ill.-Urbana, 1972; M.A., U. Colo.-Boulder, 1977, Ph.D., 1979. Intern San Francisco VA Med. Ctr., 1978-79; staff psychologist St. Louis VA Med. Ctr., 1980-82; Long Beach (Calif.) VA Med. Ctr., 1982—; pvt. practice clin. supervision, psychotherapy. NIMH trainee, 1974-76; Univ. fellow, 1975-76. Mem. Long Beach Psychol. Assn. (info. and referral service 1982—), Western Psychol. Assn. Home: 215 Euclid Ave Apt 214 Long Beach CA 90803 Office: 5901 E 7th St Long Beach CA 90822

SCHUBERT, RUTH CAROL HICKOK, artist; b. Janesville, Wis., Dec. 24, 1927; d. Fay Andrew and Mildred Willimette (Street) Hickok; m. Robert Francis Schubert, Oct. 20, 1946; children—Stephen Robert, Michelle Carol Schubert Kump. Student DeAnza Coll., 1972-73; A.A., Monterey Peninsula Coll., 1974; B.A. with honors, Calif. State U.-San Jose, 1979. Owner, mgr. Casa De Artes Gallery, Monterey, Calif., 1977—; dir. Monterey Peninsula Mus. Art Council, 1975-76; one man shows: Aarhof Gallery, Aarau, Switzerland, 1977, Degli Agostiniani Recolletti, Rome, 1977, Wells Fargo Bank, Monterey, 1975, 78, 79, Seaside (Calif.) City Hall Gallery, 1979, Village Gallery, Lahaina, Hawaii, 1983; group shows include: Sierra Nev. Mus. Art, Reno, 1980, Bard Hall Gallery, San Diego, 1980, Rahr-West Mus., Manitowoc, Wis., 1980, Rosicrucian Mus., San Jose, 1981; represented in permanent collections: Monterey Calif. Peninsula Mus. Art, Nat. Biscuit Co. subs. Nabisco Brands, Inc., San Jose, Muscular Dystrophy Assn., San Francisco, also numerous pvt. collections. Recipient 1st prize Monterey County Artists, 1979; numerous other awards for watercolor paintings. Mem. Artists Equity Assn., Am. Watercolor Soc., Soc. Western Artists, Kona Art Assn., Santa Cruz Valley Art Assn., Monterey Peninsula Watercolor Soc., Monterey Contemporary Artists, Pacific Grove Art Ctr. Assn., Central Coast Art Assn. (1st, 2d, 3d prizes 1977, 1979, 1980), Nat. League Am. penwomen (pres. 1983), Art Alumni San Jose State U., Monterey Civic Club. Club: Eastern Star (Milw.). Author monographs on art and artists. Home: 134 Dunecrest Ave Monterey CA 93940

SCHUETTE, JOHN BUCHANAN, research co. exec.; b. Moscow, Idaho, Sept. 21, 1937; s. Sylvester S. S. and Lorna M. (Buchanan) S.; B.S. in Mech. Engring., U. Idaho, 1964; m. Patricia Ann Kelly, Aug. 20, 1960; children—John Kelly, Scott C., Monica R. Mech. engr. Rayonier, Inc., Hoquiam, Wash., 1964-67; project engr. Battelle Northwest, Richland, Wash., 1967-70, project mgr. Westinghouse Inc., Richland, 1970-73; mgr. Battelle Northwest Labs., Richland, 1973-78, mgr. project mgmt. dept., 1978-82, mgr. project mgmt. and engring. services dept., 1982—. Served with USMC, 1956-58. Registered profl. engr., Wash. Mem. Central United Ch. Clubs: Elks, Lynnwood Swim-Tennis (dir. 1978—). Home: 613 Lynnwood Ct Richland WA 99352 Office: PO Box 999 Richland WA 99352

SCHUETZ, CARY EDWARD, thermoscience engineer; b. San Diego, Dec. 6, 1953; s. Celestine Edward and Doris Marjorie (Berquist) S. B.S. in Mech. Engring., U. Calif.-Santa Barbara, 1978. Engr., U. Calif.-Santa Barbara, 1976-78; engr./scientist McDonnell Douglas Corp., Long Beach, Calif., 1978-81; engr. Northrop Corp., Los Angeles, 1981—. Mem. AIAA, Nat. Soc. Profl. Engrs., Calif. Soc. Profl. Engrs. Designed and built thermoelectric generator, 1978; developed advanced state of the art in aircraft ice-prevention technology, 1980; contbr. article on automatic computational methods for numerical heat transfer, 1982. Home: 10961 Roebling Ave Los Angeles CA 90024 Office: Northrop Corp 1 Northrop Ave 3818/85 Hawthorne CA 90250

SCHUG, JOHN EDWARD, media cons.; b. New Orleans, Oct. 24, 1945; s. Edward and Bertha A. (Brose) S.; B.S., Woodbury Coll., 1969; m. Patricia Sue Hart, June 6, 1970. Promotion coordinator Los Angeles Herald-Examiner, 1971-74; advt. dir. Crowley Foods, Inc., Binghamton, N.Y., 1974-75; mktg. dir. CBS Publs., Newport Beach, Calif., 1975-78; media cons. John Schug Media Mktg., Laguna Beach, Calif., 1978—. Home: Yacht Charisma Newport Beach CA Office: 580 Broadway #204 Laguna Beach CA 92651

SCHULER, BARRY GEORGE, community coll. pres.; b. Farmington, Minn., Apr. 5, 1932; s. George C. and Irene Marian (Stapf) S.; B.A., U. Minn., 1954, M.A. in Public Adminstrn., 1965; m. Ruth J. Bantau, Nov. 24, 1956; children—Heidi, Galen. With Minn. Civil Service Dept., 1957-58; instr. polit. sci., then asst. fellowship office U. Minn., 1960-62, admissions officer, 1964-65; sr. adminstrv. asst. Control Data Corp., 1962-64; dean of students and instrn. Mpls. Community Coll., 1966-68; pres. North Idaho Coll., Coeur d'Alene, 1968—. Pres., Kootenai Community Concerts Assn., Coeur d'Alene, 1969-70. Served with AUS, 1955-57. Mem. Acad. Polit. Sci., Am. Acad. Polit. and Social Sci., Mountain States Assn. Community Colls. (sec.-treas. 1974-80, pres. 1981-82), Assn. Humanities in Idaho (dir. 1975-80), Phi Beta Kappa, Psi Chi. Baptist. Club: Coeur d'Alene Rotary (pres. 1980-81). Office: 1000 W Garden St Coeur d'Alene ID 83814

SCHULTZ, DOROTHY CHRISTINE HANKINS, political science educator; b. Roswell, N.Mex., Nov. 17, 1940; d. Noble Arthur and Debbie Jane (Vineyard) Hankins; m. William Charles Schultz, Aug. 17, 1970; children—William Noble (dec.), Hazel Elizabeth Rose. B.A., Tex. Christian U., 1963, M.A., 1966; Ph.D., U. Ariz., 1978. Edn.-recreation dir. Lena Pope Home, Fort Worth, 1965-66; instr. govt. Tex. Christian U., Fort Worth, 1965-67; grad. asst. U. Ariz., Tucson, 1967-69; asst. prof. polit. sci. Western State Coll. Colo., Gunnison, 1969-71, Grambling (La.) State U., 1973-78; vis. prof. So. Ill. U., Carbondale, 1978-79, Eastern Ill. U., Charleston, 1979-80; asst. prof. polit. sci. N.Mex. Highlands U., Las Vegas, 1980—. Active Girl Scouts U.S.A.; bd. dirs. Las Vegas Campus Community Ministry; mem. various coms. N.Mex. Highlands U. Women's Ctr. Nat. Endowment Humanities grantee

Washington U., St. Louis, summer 1980. Mem. Am. Polit. Sci. Assn., Acad. Polit. Sci., Midwest Polit. Sci. Assn., Am. Judicature Soc., Ctr. Study of the Presidency, So. Polit. Sci. Assn., Am. Soc. Legal History, LWV, Pi Sigma Alpha, Pi Sigma Iota, Phi Alpha Theta, Alpha Chi, Las Vegas Women's Golf Assn. Democrat. Mem. Christian Ch. (Disciples of Christ). Contbr. articles to profl. jours.; speaker profl. meetings. Office: 127 Mortmer Hall NMex Highlands U Las Vegas NM 87701

SCHULTZ, DOUGLAS ALAN, architect, energy consultant; b. Upland, Calif., Nov. 15, 1951; s. David B. and H. Maxine (Kinnaman) S.; m. Linda L. Likta, Apr. 28, 1979; children—Rebecca Lynn, Heather Michelle. A.A., San Bernardino Valley Coll., 1973; B.A., Calif. Poly. Inst., 1976. Architect, Michael J. Murphy & Assocs., San Bernardino, Calif., 1972, 76—; pres. Archtl. Computer, San Bernardino, 1978—. Puppeteer.

SCHULTZ, EMMET LAVEL, oil company executive; b. Blackfoot, Idaho, Apr. 23, 1934; s. Emmet Franklin and Alba Elizabeth (Larsen) S.; m. Joan C. Kirby, Nov. 7, 1953; children—Joanne M., Jeanette G.; m. 2d Marilyn Barney, Aug. 4, 1978. Asst. to pres. Flying Diamond Corp., Salt Lake City, 1973-74; pres., dir. Shuhart Industries, Inc., Salt Lake City, 1974-75; v.p. Hunstman Chem. and Oil Corp., Salt Lake City, 1975-76; exec. v.p. Huntsman Coal Corp., Salt Lake City, 1975-76; pres., chmn. bd. Gulf Energy Corp., Salt Lake City, 1976—. Bd. dirs. Utah Symphony. Served with USN, 1952-56. Republican. Office: Gulf Energy Corp 505 E 200 S Salt Lake City UT 84102

SCHULTZ, SAMUEL, structural engineer; b. Chgo., May 9, 1918; s. Philip and Mollie Schultz; student UCLA, 1936-38; B.S. in Civil Engring., U. Calif., Berkeley, 1940; m. Carolyn Rose Merritt, May 25, 1941; children—Jeanne Gail, Donna Lynne. Jr. engr., Bethlehem Steel Co., Alameda, Calif., 1940-43; design engr. N.B. Green, Cons. Structural Engr., Los Angeles, 1946-47, Fluor Corp., Ltd., 1946-47; chief structural engr. Henry M. Layne, Los Angeles, 1947-48; prin. Samuel Schultz, Cons. Engr., Beverly Hills, Calif., 1948-55, Samuel Schultz, Cons. Structural Engrs., 1955-58, Samuel Schultz, Inc., 1958—; arbitrator Am. Arbitration Assn. Bd. dirs. Applied Tech. Council, 1979—, v.p., 1981, pres., 1982; mem. Town Hall Los Angeles. Served to lt. (j.g.) USNR, 1943-46. Registered profl. engr., Calif., N.Y., Pa., Ariz., Nev., Hawaii, Ky. Mem. Structural Engrs. Assn. So. Calif., Cons. Structural Engrs. Soc. Los Angeles, Guardians, Tau Beta Pi, Chi Epsilon. Office: 377 S Robertson Blvd Beverly Hills CA 90211

SCHULTZ, TARA, chemist; b. Balt., Aug. 29, 1950; d. Samuel Henry and Janice Lee (Ganz) Greenwood; m. Rodney Drew Schultz, Jan. 17, 1975. B.S. in Chemistry, Roanoke Coll., 1972. Cert. water IV, distbn. III, wastewater IV, collection III, Wyo. Dept. Environ. Quality; indsl. wastewater D, Ind. Pollution control technician Bethlehem Steel Corp., Burns Harbor Plant, Chesterton, Ind., 1973-74, sr. technician, 1974-75, environ. chemist, 1975-81; wastewater foreman City of Gillette (Wyo.), 1981—. Mem. Am. Chem. Soc., Am. Water Works Assn., Water Pollution Control Fedn. Home: 7890 Robin Drive Gillette WY 82716 Office: PO Box 3003 Gillette Way 82716

SCHULTZ, WILDERICH CORNELIUS, mech. design engr.; b. Munster, Germany, Nov. 10, 1920; came to U.S., 1959, naturalized, 1965; s. Cornelius C. and Huberta T. (Von Koslek) S.; student Tech. Coll., Dulman, Germany, 1936-38; student Air Force Tech. Coll., Germany, 1938-39, Handels Coll., Munster, 1950-52. Tech. supr. Brit. Corps. of Engrs., Egypt, Cyrenaica, Palestine and Ethiopia, 1948-50; partner and design engr. Schultz Engring. Co., Munster, Germany, 1950-52; field engr. tunnell constrn. Internat. Constrn. Co., Tasmania, Australia, 1952-53; field engr. New South Wales Mining Co., Australia, 1953-54; field engr. Greve Constrn. Co., Sydney, Australia, 1954-55; design engr. Thomas Anderson & Associates, Melbourne, Australia, 1955-57; machine design engr. Dunlop Rubber Co. of Australia, 1957-59; tech. illustrator Industrial Arts and Engring., San Diego, Calif., 1959; tech. writer and tech. illustrator Jules Fielding & Associates, San Diego, Calif., 1959; design engr., co-propr. Applied Science Labs., La Jolla, Calif. 1960-63; design engr. Carson Corp., Los Angeles, 1963-64, Rohr Corp., Riverside, Calif. also Chula Vista, Calif., 1964-71, San Diego Aircraft Engring., 1971, Material Systems Corp., Escondido, Calif., 1971-72; v.p. engring. San Diego Product Engring., Inc., Chula Vista, 1971-73; v.p. engring. and dir. invention developments Patent Engring., Inc., Chula Vista, 1973-78; sr. design engr. Rohr Industrial Systems, Inc., Chula Vista, Calif., 1978—; cons. patent causes, 1955—. Served with German Air Force, World War II. Decorated Iron Cross. Mem. Soc. Automotive Engrs., Am. Soc. Metals, Nat. Rifle Assn. Mem. Universal Life Ch. Patentee mech. engring. Home: PO Box 1182 449 D St Chula Vista CA 92010 Office: 310 Bay Blvd Chula Vista CA 92010

SCHULZ, MARIE BURNS, magazine editor, design coordinator; b. Evanston, Ill., Sept. 15, 1923; d. John A. and Esther A. (Hammar) Burns; children—Richard, Janet Schulz DeBard. Student Mich. State U., 1959-60; Northwestern U., 1965-66. Pub. relations rep. Whirlpool Corp., Benton Harbor, Mich., 1951-56; advt. rep. Heath Co., St. Joseph, Mich., 1956-61; pub. relations rep. Selvage & Lee, Chgo., 1961-63; communications coordinator Joanna Western Mills, Chgo., 1963-69; assoc. editor books Better Homes and Gardens, Des Moines, 1969-77; editor Home Beautiful Phoenix Mag., Phoenix, 1977—; coordinator Phoenix Design Plaza, 1980—. Mem. interior design adv. com. Scottsdale Community Coll.; Phoenix Coll.; design coordinator Home Hunter TV show. Mem. Phoenix Art Mus. Recipient Dorothy Daw award Am. Furniture Mart, Chgo., 1972. Mem. Am. Soc. Interior Designers, Inst. Bus. Designers, Ariz. Design Council (press mem.), Phoenix Press Club. Contbr. articles to profl. jours.

SCHULZ, RAINER WALTER, computer co. exec.; b. Berlin, Jan. 29, 1942; s. Horst and Marta S.; came to U.S., 1959, naturalized, 1964; B.A. summa cum laude in Math., San Jose State U., 1964; children—Heidi, Kenneth, Kirsten. System devel. asso. IBM, San Jose, Calif., 1964-65, SDS, Santa Monica, Calif., 1965-67, U. Calif., Berkeley, 1967-70; system mgmt. asso. Stanford (Calif.) U., 1970-77; v.p. Computer Curriculum Corp., Palo Alto, Calif., 1973-81, dir., sec., 1978-81; mgr. Tandem Computers Inc., Cupertino, Calif., 1981-83; dir. computing systems Teknowledge, Palo Alto, 1983—; cons. NSF., 1974-77. Mem. Am. Electronics Assn., Conf. Bd. Republican. Lutheran. Home: PO Box 50243 Palo Alto CA 94303 Office: 525 University Ave Palo Alto CA 94301

SCHULZ-OVERBY, TERESA JEAN, export and design-foodservice facilities company executive; b. St. Louis, Dec. 12, 1954; d. Arthur August and Norma Jean (Lyles) Schulz; m. Raymond Joseph Pokorny, Nov. 17, 1973 (div.); m. Richard Allen Overby, Nov. 6, 1982. Student (scholar) So. Ill. U.-Edwardsville, 1973-74. Draftsperson Bensinger's Inc., St. Louis, 1977-78; designer, project coordinator Anchor Inn Promotions Inc., various locations, 1978-80; designer, project coordinator Bolsa Restaurant Supply, Garden Grove, Calif., 1980-81; asst. projects dir., designer IMS Equipment Inc., Irvine, Calif., 1981—. Mem. Foodservice Cons. Soc. Internat., Nat. Assn. Female Execs. Home: 1855 E Rose Ave Apt 10B Orange CA 92667 Office: 2805 Barranca Rd Irvine CA 92714

SCHUMACHER, DAVID WILLIAM, financial corporation executive; b. Seattle, Jan. 7, 1948; s. Paul and Marian (La Fontaine) S.; m. Janet Stipp, July 29, 1972. B.A. in Econs. magna cum laude, U. Wash., 1972. With br. banking dept. Seattle First Nat. Bank, 1972, sr. trader investment div., 1973-76; v.p., mgr. bond trading Seattle N.W. Securities Corp., 1976—. Active Seattle Zool. Soc., 1981. Clubs: Seattle Tennis, Seattle Skeet and Trap. Home: 13246 8th Ave NW Seattle WA 98177 Office: Seattle NW Securities Corp Suite 3700 5th Ave Plaza Seattle WA 98101

SCHUMACHER, JOHN CHRISTIAN, semicondr. materials and equipment mfg. co. exec.; b. Spring Valley, Ill., Feb. 8, 1935; s. Joseph Charles and Theresa Isobel (Flynn) S.; B.S., Stanford U., 1956; M.S., M.I.T., 1958; Ph.D., Stanford U., 1973; 1 dau., Jennifer Lea. Research engr. Calif. Inst. Tech., 1958-60; research and teaching asst. M.I.T., 1960-62; dept. mgr. Lockheed Missile & Space Co., Sunnyvale, Calif., 1962-64, program mgr., Palo Alto, Calif., 1964-69; research asso., thesis dir. Stanford U., 1969-73; v.p. J. C. Schumacher Co., Oceanside, Calif., 1973-74, pres., 1974-76, pres., chief exec. officer, 1976—. Chmn. Oceanside New Bus. and Industry Commn., 1976-78. Mem. Oceanside C. of C. (dir. 1974-78), Electrochem. Soc., Newcomen Soc., IEEE, AAAS, Phys. Soc. Am., Am. Inst. Chem. Engrs. Republican. Club: La Jolla Country. Patentee improved semicondr. device processing materials and equipment; low cost silicon; energy efficient photovoltaic solar cell mfg. Home: 7204 Plaza de La Costa Carlsbad CA 92008 Office: 580 Airport Rd Oceanside CA 92054

SCHUMAN, KAY ELEANOR, mathematics consultant; b. Duluth, Minn., June 12, 1943; d. Earl Arnold and Clarissa Gyle (Hamilton) Ness; B.S., U. Minn., 1965; M.A., Calif. State U., Fresno, 1969; m. Gary Gene Schuman, Aug. 4, 1973; children—Melissa Joanne, Seth Michael, Kristin Michelle. Tchr., Vinland and Thomas elem. schs., Fresno, Calif., 1965-69; math. resource tchr. Calwa Elem. Sch., 1969-72, Columbia Elem. Sch., 1972-73, Mayfair Elem. Sch., 1973-79; curriculum specialist, lab. specialist math. and lang. arts Jefferson Elem. Sch., Fresno, 1979-81; western regional math. cons. Addison-Wesley Pub. Co., 1981—; cons.; condr. workshops; speaker math. confs.; part-time instr. U. Calif., Santa Cruz, Pacific Coll., Fresno. Cert. sch. reviewer Calif. Dept. Edn. Mem. NEA, Calif. Tchrs. Assn., Fresno Tchrs. Assn., Nat. Council Tchrs. of Math., Calif. Reading Council, Curriculum Leadership and Supervision Assn., Calif. Math. Council (public relations officer 1978-80, sec. 1980-81, conf. chmn. 1980-81), Assn. Supervision and Curriculum Devel., Calif. Assn. Compensatory Edn., Infant of Prague Children's Home Soc., Gamma Sigma Sigma. Author 36 tchr. resource books, 9 parents books; contbr. to Calif. Math. Council Newsletter. Home: 6614 N Locan St Clovis CA 93612 Office: Addison-Wesley Pub Co 2725 Sand Hill Rd Menlo Park CA 94025

SCHUMANN, VERNON KENNETH, indsl. investigator; b. Chgo., July 8; s. Edward Charles and Clara (Hansen) S.; B.S., Northwestern U., 1934, postgrad., 1935-36; m. Susan Nerney, Dec. 27, 1969. Copywriter, Lord & Thomas, Chgo., 1935-40; mgr. Sedgewick Advt., Chgo., 1940-42; dir. security U.S. AEC, Richland, Wash., 1946-52; mgr. Fed. Services, Inc., San Francisco, 1952-53; pres. Vernon K. Schumann Investigations, San Jose, Calif., 1953—; cons. AEC, Gen. Dynamics; exec. advisor Aetna Custodial. Served with AUS, 1942-46. Mem. Calif. Assn. Lic. Investigators, Nat. CIC Assn., Internat. Assn. Chiefs of Police, Soc. Am. Mil. Engrs., Mensa (ombudsman 1983—), Assocs. Stanford Libraries, Stanford Alumni Assn. Republican. Lutheran. Clubs: Elks, Kiwanis. Editor Mensa Research Jour., 1968-72. Home: 1042 Oakland Ave Menlo Park CA 94025 Office: PO Box 2283 Menlo Park CA 94025

SCHUPP, PRISCILLA LISTER, publishing company executive; b. La Jolla, Calif., Oct. 31, 1949; d. Keith F. and Margaret Jean (Boman) L.; m. Robert Olds Schupp, Nov. 18, 1982. B.A. in English, Northwestern U., 1971; student U. Wash., 1973-74, Western Wash. State U., 1974-75. Cert. secondary sch. tchr., Wash. Asst. account exec. Cole & Weber, Inc., Seattle, 1975-77; catalog copy chief Recreational Equipment, Inc., Seattle, 1978-80; editor La Mesa (Calif.) Courier, 1980—, pub., 1981—. Mem. Seattle Women in Advt. (co-founder, dir. 1976). Club: Soroptimist Internat. of La Mesa. Office: La Mesa Courier 8080 La Mesa Blvd La Mesa CA 92041

SCHUR, DONALD LEROY, JR., optometrist; b. Portland, Oreg., Apr. 19, 1944; s. Donald Leroy and Doris Ione (Boley) S.; m. Gwen L. Krebs, May 23, 1981; 1 son, Donald Aron. B.S., Pacific U., 1966, O.D., 1968. Practice optometry, Vancouver, Wash., 1970—, prin. Drs. Gilbert & Schur Optometrists Inc. P.S.; lectr. continuing edn. seminars. Pres. Vancouver Jaycees, Served with U.S. Army, 1968-70, to maj. Air N.G. Recipient Outstanding Project award U.S. Jaycees, 1975, Jaycee of Month, 1975. Mem. Am. Optometric Assn., Wash. Optometric Assn., S.W. Wash. Optometric Assn. (pres.), Phi Theta Upsilon. Clubs: Royal Oaks Country, Elks (Vancouver).

SCHUSSLER, SAMUEL, accountant; b. N.Y.C., Nov. 11, 1952; s. Benson and Dorothy (Miller) S. B.B.A. in Acctg. Practice, Pace U., 1974; M.B.A. in Fin., N.Y. U., 1977. C.P.A., N.Y., Ariz. Sr. acctg. analyst L.I. R.R. Co., Jamaica, N.Y., 1974-77; asst. acct. Deloitte Haskins & Sells, N.Y.C., 1977-78, sr. asst. acct., 1978-79, sr. acct., 1979-81, sr. acct., Phoenix, 1981-83, mgr., 1983—. C. Richard Pace Trustee scholar, 1970-74. Mem. Am. Inst. C.P.A.s, N.Y. State Soc. C.P.A.s., Assn. M.B.A. Execs., Jewish Community Center Phoenix. Home: 6201 N 16th St Apt 234 Phoenix AZ 85016 Office: First Interstate Bank Plaza Suite 1000 Phoenix AZ 85016

SCHUSTER, KIRK CHARLES, mortgage banker; b. Annapolis, Md., July 6, 1950; s. Charles and Evelyn Claire (Shea) S.; m. Judith Lynn Till, July 18, 1969; children—Erik Charles, Bryan Keith, Tamara Anne. B.A., Wash. State U., 1975. Area mgr. Pacific West Mortgage, Seattle, 1975-76, v.p. field ops., 1976-78, exec. v.p., 1978-81; pres., chief exec. officer N.W. Pension Investors, Inc., Seattle, 1981—; pres., chief exec. officer First N.W. Mortgage Corp., First N.W. Escrow Corp., N.W. Equities Ltd.; instr. Highline Community Coll., Wash. Grad. Realtor Inst., Boeing Aircraft and Aerospace Retirement Planning, Chief Sealth Community Sch., 1976—. Author: Creative Real Estate Finance for the 80s, 1980. Creator Mortgage Master, credit card to fin. home purchase. Home: 21930 34th Ave S Kent WA 98031 Office: 15215 52d St S Suite 15 Seattle WA 98188

SCHUSTER, RICHARD JAMES, retired newspaper pub., investment advisor; b. Dubuque, Iowa, Aug. 23, 1927; s. Lester James and Hilda Catherine (Summer) S.; m. Rae Ann Subcleff, Jan. 22, 1951; children—Patricia Ann Schuster Colon, David Lester, Jean M. Schuster Silvershield. B.Sc., U. Iowa, 1950; postgrad. Columbia U., seminars 1954, 60, 62. Pressman, printer, reporter and salesman Clinton (Iowa) Herald, 1942-63; promotion mgr. Gazette & Jour., Reno, 1963-66; pres., pub. Fremont (Nebr.) Tribune, 1966-68; pres., pub. Reno Evening Gazette-Nev. State Jour., 1969-76; printing cons., 1976-79; investment specialist, 1980—; lectr. U. Nev.-Reno. Active Nev. Area council Boy Scouts Am., v.p., 1974-76, 80, 81, pres., 1977-78; pres. United Way No. Nev., 1972; chmn. bd. trustees Channel 5 Pub. TV, 1983. Served with USN, 1945-46. Recipient Scouting award merit, 1968, Silver Beaver award, 1973. Mem. Reno C. of C. Republican. Roman Catholic. Clubs: Prospectors, Kiwanis, Elks. Contbr. articles to profl. jours. Home: 165 Village Blvd Incline Village NV 89450 Office: Suite 514 One E Liberty St Reno NV 89501

SCHUTZ, JOHN ADOLPH, historian, educator; b. Los Angeles, Apr. 10, 1919; s. Adolph J. and Augusta K. (Glicker) S.; A.A., Bakersfield Coll., 1940; B.A., UCLA, 1942, M.A., 1943, Ph.D., 1945. Asst. prof. history Calif. Inst. Tech., Pasadena, 1945-53; asso. prof. history Whittier (Calif.) Coll., 1953-56, prof., 1956-65; prof. history U. So. Calif., Los Angeles, 1965-74, prof., 1974—, chmn. dept. history, 1974-76, dean social scis. and communication, 1976-82; vis. prof. U. N.H., summer, 1967. Trustee Citizens Research Found. Nat. Endowment for Humanities grantee, 1971, Sr. Faculty grantee, 1971-74. Mem. Am. Hist. Assn. (pres. pacific coast br. 1972-73), Am. Studies Assn. (pres. 1974-75), Mass. Hist. Soc. (corr.), Colonial Soc. Mass. (corr.), New Eng. Hist. Geneal. Soc. (trustee 1979—). Author: William Shirley: King's Governor of Massachusetts, 1961; The Promise of America, 1970; Peter Oliver's Origin and Progress of the American Rebellion, 1967; The American Republic, 1978; Dawning of America, 1981; Spain in California, 1983. Home: 1100 White Knoll Los Angeles CA 90012 Office: U So Calif Los Angeles CA 90007

SCHWABE, PETER ALEXANDER, JR., judge; b. Portland, Oreg., July 23, 1935; s. Peter Alexander and Evelyn (Zingleman) S.; A.B., Stanford, 1958; J.D., Willamette U., 1960; m. Bonnie Jean LeBaron, June 21, 1958; children—Mark, Karen, Diane, Patricia, Kurt. Admitted to Oreg. bar, 1960; pvt. practice, Portland, 1960-76; fed. adminstrv. law judge, 1976—. Del. nat. policy council Office of Hearings and Appeals, Social Security Adminstrn., Dept. Health and Human Services, 1980—. Mem. Oreg. State, Am., Multnomah bar assns., Beta Theta Pi, Phi Delta Phi. Home: 4366 Dorking Ct Sacramento CA 95825 Office: 1029 J St Sacramento CA 95814

SCHWADERER, KENNETH NORMAN, optometrist; b. San Francisco, Dec. 22, 1945. B.S., U. Calif., 1967, O.D. with honors, 1971. Diplomate Nat. Bd. Examiners in Optometry; cert. pharmacologist. Ptnr. Mountain View (Calif.) Optometry and Contact Lens Clinic, 1971—; sr. clin. staff mem. Vision Rehab. Ctr. Santa Clara Valley, 1973—; co-founder, prin. Contact Lens Research Assocs., Inc., 1978—, Marriott Ctr. Health Group, 1982—; vision cons. NASA Ames Research Ctr., Mountain View, 1971—, Mountain View Sr. Citizens Ctr., 1981—; sch. screening cons. Santa Clara County Optometric Soc., 1972—; lectr. Mem. admissions com. U. Calif., 1976; past dist. chmn. Mountain View Council Boy Scouts Am., council mem. Stanford Area council; bd. dirs. Mountain View United Way Fund of Santa Clara County. Recipient Cert. of Merit, Optometric Extension Program, San Jose Vision Tng. Conf., 1975; Cert. of Honor for preventive health care research Assn. Nat. Health Research, 1975; named Calif. Young Optometrist of Yr., Calif. Optometric Assn., 1975. Fellow Am. Acad. Optometry; mem. Am. Optometric Assn. (founding mem. contact lens sect. and low vision sect.), Calif. Optometric Assn., Santa Clara County Optometric Soc. (past trustee, sec.), U. Calif. Optometry Alumni Assn. (trustee 1970-77, pres. 1974-76), Mountain View C. of C. (trustee, pres. 1983—), Beta Sigma Kappa. Club: Mountain View Rotary (pres. elect 1984). Contbr. articles to profl. jours. Office: Contact Lens Research Assocs Inc 495 Castro St Suite 103 Mountain View CA 94041

SCHWADERER, OWEN CLARK, real estate developer; b. Dearborn, Mich., Feb. 2, 1942; s. Clark James and Julia Margaret (Owen) S.; B.S. in Bus. Adminstrn., U. Fla., 1964; m. Melinda Jane Horner, Dec. 28, 1963; children—Kimberly Ann, Julia Alice, Katherine JoAnne. With Merrill Lynch Pierce Fenner & Smith, N.Y.C., 1964-65, Ft. Lauderdale, Fla., 1965-70; with Reynolds Securities, Ft. Lauderdale, 1970-72; founder, pres. Fla. Heritage Group, Inc., Ft. Lauderdale, 1972-74; pres. Blackhawk Corp., Danville, Calif., 1975-83. Mem. Urban Land Inst. (residential council 1979-81, new communities council 1982—), Bldg. Industry Assn. Democrat. Methodist. Clubs: Rotary, Blackhawk Country.

SCHWARTZ, BARBARA MARIE, educational consultant; b. Bklyn., Sept. 16, 1936; d. John and Stella (Radetsky) Farrett; m. George A. Schwartz, Jr., June 6, 1959; children—John D., Robert G., William G. B.S., Fordham U., 1957; M.A., Nat. Christian U. Mo., 1983. Tchr., N.Y.C. Pub. Schs., 1956-57, Englewood (Colo.) Pub. Schs., 1957-61, Denver Pub. Schs., 1961-78; cons. Assocs. in Awareness, Inc., Denver, 1978—; dir. nat. tng., nat. mktg. Personal Growth Found. Inc., 1982—; co-pres. Marriage Enrichment of Denver; Inc. Mem. Am. Soc. Trainers and Developers, Nat. Speaker's Assn., Am. Assn. Female Execs., Profl. Consultants Assn. Internat., Assn. Humanistic Psychology. Democrat. Roman Catholic. Address: 2425 S Steel St Denver CO 80210

SCHWARTZ, DOUGLAS WRIGHT, archaeologist, anthropologist; b. Erie, Pa., July 29, 1929; s. Harry and Vernon Kelsey (Schaaf) S.; B.A., U. Ky., 1950; Ph.D., Yale U., 1955; Litt.D., U. N.Mex., 1981; m. Rita Jaunita Hartley, Oct. 4, 1950; children—Steven, Susan, Kelsey. Pres., Sch. Am. Research, Santa Fe; dir. Am. Nat. Bank Santa Fe. Pres. Witter Bynner Found. for Poetry, Inc.; vice chmn. Harvard U. Overseers Com. on Peabody Mus.; trustee Jane Goodall African Wildlife Research Center; vice chmn. Archaeol. Conservancy; mem. council Nat. Park Service Adv. Bd. Mem. Soc. Am. Archaeology (past pres.). Clubs: Kiva, Harvard, Century Archeol. research No. Rio Grande area, N.Mex., Grand Canyon, Ariz., Ky., So. Italy. Author: Conceptions of Kentucky Prehistory; co-author: The Archaeology of the Grand Canyon: The Bright Angel Site, 1979; The Archaeology of the Grand Canyon: Unkar Delta, 1980; The Archaeology of the Grand Canyon: Walhalla Plateau, 1981. Office: PO Box 2188 Santa Fe NM 87501

SCHWARTZ, EDWARD J., judge; b. 1912; A.B., U. Calif.; LL.B., San Francisco Law Sch. Admitted to bar, 1940; judge Mcpl. Ct. and Superior Ct., San Diego; judge U.S. Dist. Ct., So. Dist. Calif., now sr. judge. Office: US District Court House Courtroom 1 940 Front St San Diego CA 92189*

SCHWARTZ, GEORGE ROBERT, physician; b. Caribou, Maine, Jan. 2, 1942; s. Milton and Beatrice Schwartz; B.A. with honors, Hobart Coll., 1963; M.D. magna cum laude, SUNY, Bklyn., 1967; children—Ruth, Rebekah, Rachel. Intern, King County Hosp., Seattle, 1967-68; resident in psychiatry Hillside Hosp., Glen Oaks, N.Y., 1968-69; resident in surgery Ind. U. Med. Center, Indpls., 1971-72; practice medicine specializing in emergency medicine, family practice, Pa. and N.J., 1972-76, Calif., 1976-78, Albuquerque, 1978—; dir. emergency services, instr. emergency medicine, asst. dir. emergency medicine program Med. Coll. of Pa., 1972-74, clin. asst. prof. emergency medicine, 1974; dir. emergency medicine West Jersey Hosp., 1974-76; dir. Camden (N.J.) County Poison Center, 1974-76; assoc. prof. dept. family, community and emergency medicine, dir. div. emergency medicine U. N.Mex. Sch. Medicine, Albuquerque, 1978-82; pvt. practice, 1983—; med. cons. N.Mex. Poison Center, 1979—; ednl. and fin. cons. to emergency medicine groups, 1974—; cons. in nutrition and food poisoning, 1974—; med.-legal cons., 1972—. Bd. dirs. Food Power Inst., 1982—. Served to capt., M.C., USAF, 1969-71. Diplomate Am. Bd. Family Practice. Mem. Am. Coll. Emergency Physicians, Am. Acad. Clin. Toxicology, Internat. Emergency Aid Assn., AMA, AAAS, Univ. Assn. for Emergency Med. Services, Healing Research Inst. Am. (v.p. 1977—). Author: Food Power: How Foods Can Change Your Mind, Your Personality, and Your Life, 1981; (with others) Emergency Medicine, 1981; contbr. numerous articles on emergency medicine to profl. jours.; editor: Principles and Practice of Emergency Medicine, Vols. I and II, 1978; editorial bd. Annals of Emergency Medicine, 1973-81, Emergency Med. Abstracts, 1978—, Resident and Staff Physician, 1978—. Address: PO Box 4189 115 Cornell SE Albuquerque NM 87106

SCHWARTZ, LAWRENCE, aeronautical engineer; b. N.Y.C., Nov. 30, 1935; s. Harry and Fanny (Steiner) S.; S.B. in Aero. Engring., M.I.T.,

1958, S.M. in Aero. Engring., 1958; postgrad. Ohio State U., 1960, U. Dayton, 1962-63; Ph.D. in Engring., UCLA, 1966; m. Cherie Anne Karo, Aug. 12, 1979; children—Ronda, Daran. Electronics design engr. M.I.T. Instrumentation Lab., Cambridge, 1959; aerospace engr., Wright-Patterson AFB, Ohio, 1962-63; mem. tech. staff Hughes Aircraft Co., Culver City, Calif., 1963-65, staff engr., 1965-67, sr. staff engr., 1967-72, sr. scientist, 1972-79, chief scientist lab., 1979—; cons. Served with USAF, 1959-62. Registered profl. engr., Colo., Calif. Mem. IEEE, AAAS, N.Y. Acad. Scis., Sigma Xi, Sigma Gamma Tau, Tau Beta Pi. Contbr. articles to profl. jours. Home: 10351 E Evans Ave 168 Denver CO 80231 Office: 6251 S Ulster St Englewood CO 80111

SCHWARTZ, MILTON LEWIS, fed. judge; b. Oakland, Calif., Jan. 20, 1920; s. Colman and Selma (Lavenson) S.; A.B., U. Calif. at Berkeley, 1941, J.D., 1948; m. Barbara Ann Moore, May 15, 1942; children—Dirk L., Tracy Ann, Damon M., Brooke. Admitted to Calif. bar, 1949; research asst. 3d Dist. Ct. Appeal, Sacramento, 1948; dep. dist. atty., 1949-51; practice in Sacramento, 1951-79; partner McDonough, Holland, Schwartz & Allen, 1953-79; U.S. dist. judge Eastern Dist. Calif., 1979—; prof. law McGeorge Coll. Law, Sacramento, 1952-55. Mem. Com. Bar Examiners Calif., 1971-75. Pres. Bd. Edn. Sacramento City Sch. Dist., 1961; v.p. Calif. Bd. Edn., 1967-68. Trustee Sutterville Heights Sch. Dist. Served to maj. 40th Inf. Div., AUS, 1942-46; PTO. Fellow Am. Coll. Trial Lawyers; mem. State Bar Calif., Am. Bar Assn., Am. Bd. Trial Advocates. Office: US Courthouse 650 Capitol Mall Sacramento CA 95814

SCHWARTZ, MORT, automotive distributor; b. Bklyn., Sept. 16, 1934; s. Harry and Helen (Rehr) S.; B.S. in Indsl. Engring., N.Y.U., 1956, M.S. in Indsl. Engring., 1961; m. Marilyn Carol Spill, Oct. 27, 1956; children—Jay, Richard, Andrew. With Westinghouse Electric Co., Pitts. Columbus, O., Metuchen, N.J., 1956-66, controller WASSCO div., Pitts., 1966-67, v.p. consumer service Westinghouse, Pitts., 1967-68; v.p. Maremont Corp., 1968-75; exec. v.p. Chanslor & Lyon, Chgo., 1968-69, pres., 1969-75, chmn. bd., pres., Brisbane, Calif. 1975—; faculty Rutgers U., 1959-61, Bd. dirs. Nat. Inst. Automotive Service Excellence, 1976-82. Pacific Auto Show, 1977; chmn. Calif. Automotive Task Force, 1978-80; trustee Nat. Automotive Technicians Edn. Found., 1982—. Served to capt. C.E., AUS, 1956-57. Mem. Automotive Warehouse Distbrs. Assn. (chmn. 1981-82, dir. 1975—), Calif. Automotive Wholesalers Assn. (dir. 1978—), Pacific Coast Wholesalers Assn. (dir., v.p. 1975), Automotive Parts and Accessories Assn. (dir. 1982—), Perstare Et Praestare, Zeta Beta Tau. Home: 2505 Rolling Hills Ct Alamo CA 94507 Office: 1500 Newell Ave Suite 702 Walnut Creek CA 94596

SCHWARTZ, PEPPER JUDITH, sociology educator; b. Chgo., May 11, 1945; d. Julius J. and Gertrude (Buris) S.; m. John A. Strait, June 19, 1971; m. 2d, Arthur M. Skolnik, Jan. 9, 1982. B.A., Washington U., St. Louis, 1968, M.A., 1970; M. in Philosophy, Yale U., 1972, Ph.D., 1974. Assoc. prof. sociology, adj. assoc. prof. psychiatry and behavioral sci. U. Wash., Seattle, 1972—. Chairperson, rev. com. NIMH; bd. dirs. Women's Research Ctr.; frequent quest and host local and network TV shows. Bd. dirs. Nat. Abortion Rights Action League; bd. dirs. Empty Space Theater, Seattle, pres., 1980; past mem. Gov.'s Commn. Venereal Disease; bd. dirs. ACLU; nat. bd. dirs. YWCA. Named Outstanding Young Woman of the Future, Time-Life mag., 1978; One of Most Powerful People of the 1980s, Next mag., 1981. Mem. Am. Sociol. Assn. (chairperson com. on coms.), Pacific Sociol. Assn., Nat. Conf. Family Relations, Groves Conf. Club: Yale (N.Y.C.). Author: Women at Yale, 1976; (with Judith Laws et al) Sexual Scripts, 1977; (with P. Blumstein) American Couples, 1983; co-author and editor. A Student's Guide to Sex on Campus, 1971, contbr. numerous articles to mags. and jours.; profiles in Cosmopolitan, N.Y. Times, others; articles on work in Time, Redbook, New West, others. Office: Dept Sociology DK-40 U Wash Seattle WA 98195

SCHWARTZBURD, LEONARD, clin. psychologist; b. Chgo., Jan. 23, 1939; s. Martin M. and Sandee S. (Wichman) S.; student U. Wis., 1958-61; B.A., Calif. State U., 1962; postgrad. U. Calif., 1962-63; M.S., U. Okla., 1968, Ph.D., 1971; children—Sabra Rahel, Micha Ben. Dep. probation officer Los Angeles County, 1964-65; coordinator Cleveland County Juvenile Services, Norman, Okla., 1970-71; dir. Austin Developmental Center, Chgo., 1971-74; pvt. practice clin. psychology, Berkeley, Calif., 1974—; clin. cons. Rockridge Med. Care Center; staff San Francisco Gen. Hosp.; teaching staff Psychotherapy Inst., treas., 1978. Mem. citizens adv. bd. on health edn. curriculum Albany (Calif.) Unified Sch. Dist. Recipient community service citation Juvenile Services, Norman, Okla., 1971; Ill. Dept. Mental Health grantee, 1969-70. Mem. Am. Psychol. Assn., Calif. State Psychol. Assn., Bay Area San Francisco Psychol. Assn., Israel Psychol. Assn., Psychotherapy Inst., Am. Acad. of Psychotherapists. Jewish. Author: The Timed Multiple Response Method, 1971; contbr. paper to profl. congress; inventor constant flow indoor drip irrigation. Home and Office: 860 The Alameda Berkeley CA 94707

SCHWARZ, MICHAEL HOWARD, lawyer; b. Brookline, Mass., Oct. 19, 1952; s. Jules Lewis and Estelle (Kosberg) S.; B.A. magna cum laude, U. No. Colo., 1975; postgrad. U. N.Mex., 1977, J.D., 1980; research reader in Negligence Law, Oxford U., summer 1978; diploma in Legal Studies, Cambridge U., 1981. VISTA vol., Albuquerque, 1975-77; research fellow N.Mex. Legal Support Project, Albuquerque, 1978-79; law clk. to field solicitor U.S. Dept. Interior, Santa Fe, summer 1979; admitted to N.Mex. bar, 1980, U.S. Dist. Ct. N.Mex. 1980, U.S. Ct. Appeals (10th cir.) 1982, U.S. Ct. Appeals (D.C. cir.) 1982, U.S. Ct. Internat. Trade, 1982, U.S. Tax Ct. 1982, U.S. Ct. Appeals (fed. cir.) 1982; supr. in law Cambridge (Eng.) U., 1980-81; law clk. to chief justice Supreme Ct. N.Mex., Santa Fe, 1981-82; sole practice, Santa Fe, 1982—. Vice dir. Colo. Pub. Interest Research Group, 1974; scoutmaster Great S.W. Area council Boy Scouts Am., 1977-79; mem. N.Mex. Acupuncture Licensing Bd. Recipient cert. of appreciation Cambridge U., 1981, Nathan Burkan Meml. award, 1980. Mem. ABA (scholar 1983), Fed. Bar Assn. (council on adminstrv. law), Assn. Trial Lawyers Am., State Bar N.Mex. Editorial adv. com. Social Security Reporting Service. Contbr. articles to profl. jours. Home and Office: PO Box 713 Santa Fe NM 87504

SCHWARZER, WILLIAM W., federal judge; b. Berlin, Apr. 30, 1925; s. John F. and Edith M. (Daniel) S.; came to U.S., 1938, naturalized, 1944; A.B. cum laude, U. So. Calif., 1948; LL.B. cum laude, Harvard U., 1951; m. Anne Halbersleben, Feb. 2, 1951; children—Jane Elizabeth, Andrew William. Admitted to Calif. bar, 1953, U.S. Supreme Ct. bar, 1967; teaching fellow Harvard U. Law Sch., 1951-52; asso. firm McCutchen, Doyle, Brown & Enersen, San Francisco, 1952-60, ptnr., 1960-76; U.S. dist. judge for No. Dist. Calif., San Francisco, 1976—; counsel Pres.'s Commn. in CIA Activities Within the U.S., 1975; mem. faculty Nat. Inst. Trial Advocacy, Fed. Jud. Center. Trustee, World Affairs Council No. Calif., 1961—; bd. dirs. William Babcock Meml. Endowment, San Rafael, Calif., 1962-78; pres. bd. trustees Marin Country Day Sch., 1963-66; chmn. Marin County Aviation Commn., 1969-76; mem. vis. com. Harvard Law Sch. Served with Intelligence, U.S. Army, 1943-46. Fellow Am. Coll. Trial Lawyers; mem. Am. Law Inst., Am., San Francisco bar assns., State Bar Calif. Contbr. articles to legal publs., aviation jours. Office: 450 Golden Gate Ave San Francisco CA 94102*

SCHWEICKART, KAY LORRAINE, hosp. adminstr.; b. Freeport, Ill., Apr. 12, 1946; d. Harold August and Mariella (Reed) Gutzmer; B.S.N., Capital U., Columbus, Ohio, 1968; postgrad. U. Mo., Columbia, 1973-74; M.S., U. Hawaii, Honolulu, 1976; 1 dau., Jamie. Staff nurse hosps., N.J., Ga., N.C. and Mo., 1968-69; dir. nursing Pulaski County Meml. Hosp., Waynesville, Mo., 1970-72; nursing coordinator U. Mo. Med. Center, Columbia, 1972-73; asst. dir. planning Mo. Regional Med. Care Program, instr. nursing U. Mo., 1973-74; clin. specialist Kaiser Found. Hosp., Honolulu, 1975-78; med. office adminstr. Kaiser Found., Oreg., 1978; assoc. adminstr. Bess Kaiser Med. Center, Portland, Oreg., 1978—; cons. Hawaii Dept. Health, 1975; mem. workshop faculties. Vol. Planned Parenthood, Waynesville, 1971; appointee Oreg. State Bd. Nursing, 1983-85. Mem. Am. Soc. Nursing Service Adminstrs., Am. Coll. Hosp. Adminstrs., Oreg. Soc. Nursing Home Adminstrs. (pres. 1983), Sigma Theta Tau. Lutheran. Home: 2555 SW Bertha Blvd Portland OR 97201 Office: 5055 N Greeley St Portland OR 97217

SCHWEICKART, RUSSELL L., astronaut, govt. ofcl.; b. Neptune, N.J., Oct. 25, 1935; s. George L. Schweickart; B.S. in Aero. Engring., M.I.T., 1956, M.S. in Aeros. and Astronautics, 1963; m. Clare Grantham Whitfield; children—Vicki Louise, Russell and Randolph (twins), Elin Ashley, Diana Croom. Former research scientist M.I.T. Exptl. Astronomy Lab.; astronaut NASA Johnson Space Ctr., Houston, lunar module pilot Apollo 9, 1969, dir. user affairs Office of Applications, NASA Hdqrs., Washington; formerly chmn. Calif. Energy Commn., now commr.; exec. interchange assignment as asst. for sci. and tech. to gov. State of Calif. Served as pilot USAF, 1956-60, 61; capt. Mass. Air N.G. Recipient Disting. Service medal NASA, 1970, De La Vaulx medal FAI, 1970, Spl. Trustees award Nat. Acad. TV Arts and Scis., 1969. Fellow Am. Astronautical Soc.; mem. Soc. Exptl. Test Pilots, AIAA, Sigma Xi. Club: Explorers. Office: 1516 9th St Sacramento CA 95814

SCHWEIKHER, PAUL, architect; b. Denver, July 28, 1903; s. Frederick and Elisabeth Ann (Williams) S.; student U. Colo., 1921-22; B.F.A. (fellow), Yale U., 1929, M.A. (hon.), 1953; m. Dorothy Miller, Dec. 17, 1923; 1 son, Paul. Practicing architect, 1933—; partner Schweikher & Elting, 1945-53; co-founder Chgo. Workshops, 1933-35; archtl. works exhibited Mus. Modern Art, N.Y.C., Renaissance Soc., U. Chgo., Carnegie Inst. Tech., Akron (Ohio) Art Inst., galleries U. Minn., U. Ill., U. Kans., Yale, Princeton, Ariz. State U., Carnegie Inst. Mus. Fine Arts; vis. critic architecture Yale, 1947, 50-53, chmn. architecture, 1953-56; head dept. architecture Carnegie-Mellon U., 1956-68, now prof. emeritus architecture; vis. prof. Princeton U., 1960-61; vis. critic architecture U. Kans., 1930, lectr. Syracuse U., 1951; 2 one-man exhbns. Harvard, 1968, Yale, 1968. Mem. U. Ill. Conf. Archtl. Edn., 1949; mem. panel Sch. Planning Conf., Nat. Art Edn. Assn., N.Y.C., 1951; mem. Conf. on Edn. in Architecture and the Fine Arts, Carnegie Inst. tech., 1953; mem. jury architecture Fulbright awards Inst. Internat. Edn., 1953-54, fellowships Am. Acad. Rome, 1955; mem. Pitts. Planning Commn., 1961-64. Mem. adv. council Sch. Architecture, Princeton, 1961-69. Served to lt. comdr. USNR, 1942-45. Registered Nat. Council Archtl. Registration Bds., also in 14 states. Recipient Ford Found. research grant in theater design, 1960-61. Mem. Art Inst. Chgo. (life), Chi Psi. Club: Arts (Chgo.). Contbr. articles to profl. publs. Address: 580 Skyline Dr High Tor Sedona AZ 86336

SCHWEITZER, FREDERICK VERNON, auditor, educator; b. Amarillo, Tex., May 19, 1907; s. Fred R. and Olive (Smith) S.; student Kans. Wesleyan U., 1924-26; A.B., U. So. Calif., 1928; postgrad. U. Berlin, 1933; M.A. in Pub. Adminstrn., Columbia U., 1943; m. Cora Henderson, 1928 (div. 1931); m. 2d, Ruth Twenhoefel, 1934 (div. 1940); m. 3d, Margaret Cunha, 1942 (div. 1948); m. 4th, Mary Ann Hiatt, 1948 (div. 1971); children by previous marriage—Gordon Merle, Fred Karl (dec.). Public acct. Arthur Anderson & Co., Los Angeles, 1927-30; vice consul Dept. State, Brisbane, Queensland, Australia, 1930-33; field auditor Dept. Agr., Washington, 1933-36; sr. public acct. Peat Marwick Mitchell & Co., San Francisco, 1936; chief div. research and statistics Calif. Dept. Social Welfare, Sacramento, 1936-37; chief acct. Marchant Calculators, Inc., Oakland, Calif., 1938-42; dep. dir. vets. preference div. War Assets Adminstrn., San Francisco, 1946-48, sr. adminstrv. analyst Calif. Joint Legis. Budget Com., Sacramento, 1949-53; S.W. div. dir. Olivett Corp. Am., Dallas, 1954-61; mgr. system sales Friden Inc., Sacramento, 1962-66; data processing systems analyst Calif. Water Resources Dept., Sacramento, 1966-72, internal auditor, 1972-75; instr. history dept. Sacramento City Coll., 1951-52; instr. Calif. State Internal Auditors Assn., 1973-75; instr. Dept. Fish and Game, 1973-75; pvt. practice pub. acctg., Sacramento, 1975—; owner, operator walnut orchard, Yuba City, Calif., 1966-79. Mem. Sacramento County Republican Central Com., 1966-70; chmn. data processing com. Calif. Rep. Central Com., 1968-70; pres. chpt. 165 Calif. State Employees Assn., 1964-66. Served to lt. comdr. USNR, 1942-47. Recipient letter of appreciation for services as instr. at Mgmt. Devel. Inst., Gov. Ronald Reagan, 1969. Mem. Nat. Assn. Accountants, Mgmt. Systems Assn., Western Govtl. Research Assn., S.R., VFW, Phi Mu Alpha. Presbyterian. Clubs: Shriners, Scottish Rite (Sacramento); Masons (Cambridge, Mass.). Author articles. Home: 3908 Heights Ct Cameron Park CA 95682 Office: Travelodge 43 902 Del Paso Blvd Sacramento CA 95815

SCHWENDIMANN, CAROL REICHELT, ednl. adminstr.; b. Jasper, Tex., Mar. 4, 1940; d. Masterson Paul and Vera (Foyil) Reichelt; B.S. Centenary Coll. La., 1962; M.Ed., So. Methodist U., 1968; postgrad. Tex. Women's U., U. New Orleans; m. Frederick William Schwendimann, July 21, 1962; children—Amy Carol, Paul Frederick. Tchr., Dallas Ind. Sch. Dist., 1962-63, Garland Ind. Sch. Dist., Garland, Tex., 1963-65, counselor, 1965-67; psychometrist Region X Ednl. Service Center, 1969; tchr. So. Methodist U. Reading Clinic; ednl. diagnostician Richardson Ind. Sch. Dist., Richardson, Tex., 1970-73; reading cons. Montgomery County Pub. Schs., Montgomery County, Md., 1973-74, instr. reading program for tchrs. Montgomery County, 1974; counselor Richardson (Tex.) Ind. Sch. Dist., 1974-77; dir. Crescent Acad., 1978-79; research asst. U. New Orleans, 1979-80; counselor Santa Fe Public Schs., 1981-82; guidance and counseling specialist N.Mex. Dept. Edn., 1983—; instr. Parent Effectiveness Training; drug abuse coordinator Liberty Jr. High Sch.; dir. St. Bede's Learning Ctr. Tchr. adult Sunday sch. 1st United Meth. Ch., Richardson; tchr. Munholland United Meth. Ch.; fin. chmn. LWV, 1969; precinct coordinator City Council Election, 1977; parent and family Life chmn. Heights PTA, 1977; legis. chmn. Richardson Assn. Gifted and Talented; bd. dirs. Com. for Orch. of Santa Fe. Cert. tchr., counselor, spl. edn., ednl. diagnostician, Tex., N.Mex.; reading specialist, Md. Mem. Am., Tex., N. Central Tex. (sec. 1967) personnel and guidance assns., Richardson Edn. Assn., Tex. Assn. Sch. Counselors, Richardson Assn. for Gifted and Talented, New Orleans Assn. for Children with Learning Disabilities, Crescent City Needlework Guild, AAUW (dir., pres. Santa Fe br.), Phi Delta Kappa, Chi Omega. Home: 1465 Seville Rd Santa Fe NM 87501 Office: Edn Bldg Santa Fe NM 87501

SCHWIERING, CONRAD, artist; b. Boulder, Colo., Aug. 8, 1916; s. Oscar C. and Willetta (Jamison) S.; m. Mary Ethel Smith, Sept. 1, 1939. B.A. in Commerce and Law, U. Wyo., 1938; postgrad. Art Students League, N.Y.C., 1939-41, Grand Central Sch. Art, N.Y.C., 1940-41. One-man show: Nat. Cowboy Hall of Fame, 1981; group shows: Nat. Acad. Western Artists, Oklahoma City, Artists of Am., Denver, Settlers West, Tucson, Corpus Christi (Tex.) Miniature Show; represented in permanent collections: Whitney Gallery Western Art, Cody, Wyo., Nat. Cowboy Hall of Fame, Oklahoma City, Wyo. State Mus., Cheyenne, U. Wyo., Laramie, Genesee County Mus., Rochester, N.Y.; instr. art U. Wyo., 1949, Teton Artists Associated, 1959-64. Active Grad Teton Natural History Assn., Jackson Hole Mus. Served to lt. col. C.E., AUS, 1941-46. Conrad Schwiering Day declared by Gov. Wyo., 1981; recipient Trustees Gold medal Nat. Cowboy Hall of Fam and Western Heritage Ctr., 1981; Disting. Alumni award U. Wyo., 1970. Mem. Nat. Acad. Western Art. Republican. Roman Catholic. Clubs: Salmagundi, Rotary. Subject of TV documentaries Harriscope Broadcasting Co., 1973, Pub. Broadcasting System, 1982; subject of books; Conrad Schwiering—Painting on the Square (Dean Krakel), 1981; Schwiering and the West (Robert Wakefield).

SCHWINDEN, TED, governor of Montana; b. Wolf Point, Mont., Aug. 31, 1925; s. Michael James and Mary (Preble) S.; student Mont. Sch. Mines, 1946-47; B.A., U. Mont., 1949, M.A., 1950; postgrad. U. Minn., 1950-54; m. B. Jean Christianson, Dec. 21, 1946; children—Mike, Chrys, Dore. Owner-operator grain farm, Roosevelt County, Mont., 1954—; land commr. State of Mont., 1969-76, lt. gov., 1977-80, gov., 1981—; mem. U.S. Wheat Trade Mission to Asia, 1968. Chmn., Mont. Bicentennial Adv. Council, 1973-76; mem. Mont. Ho. of Reps., 1959-61, Legis. Council, 1959-61, Wolf Point Sch. Bd., 1966-69, Pub. Employees Retirement System Bd., 1969-74. Served with inf., AUS, 1943-46. Decorated Combat Inf. Badge. Mem. Mont. Grain Growers (pres. 1965-67), Western Wheat Assos. (dir.), Nat. Govs. Assn. (chmn. com. on agr. 1983—), Western Govs. Assn. (vice chmn. 1982—). Democrat. Lutheran. Clubs: Masons, Elks. Office: State Capitol Helena MT 59620

SCHWINGER, JULIAN, physicist; b. N.Y.C., Feb. 12, 1918; s. Benjamin and Belle (Rosenfeld) S.; A.B., Columbia U., 1936, Ph.D., 1939, D.Sc., 1966; D.Sc. (hon.), Purdue U., 1961, Harvard U., 1962, Brandeis U., 1973, Gustavus Adolphus Coll., 1975; LL.D., City Coll. N.Y., 1972; m. Clarice Carrol, 1947. NRC fellow, 1939-40; research assoc. U. Calif. at Berkeley, 1940-41; instr. then asst. prof. Purdue U., 1941-43; staff mem. Radiation Lab., M.I.T., 1943-45; asso. prof. Harvard U., 1945-47, prof., 1947-72, Higgins prof. physics, 1966-72; prof. physics UCLA, 1972—, univ. prof., 1980—. Mem. bd. sponsors Bull. Atomic Sci.; sponsor Fedn. Am. Scientists; J.W. Gibbs hon. lectr. Am. Math. Soc., 1960. Recipient C.L. Mayer nature of light award, 1949, univ. medal Columbia U., 1951, 1st Einstein prize award, 1951; Nat. Medal of Sci. award for physics, 1964; Humboldt prize, 1981; co-recipient Nobel prize in Physics, 1965; Guggenheim fellow, 1970. Mem. Nat. Acad. Scis., Am. Acad. Arts and Scis., Am. Phys. Soc., Civil Liberties Union, AAAS, N.Y. Acad. Scis., Royal Instn. Gt. Britain. Author: Particles and Sources, 1969, (with D. Saxon) Discontinuities in Wave Guides, 1968; Particles, Sources and Fields, 1970, Vol. II, 1973; Quantum Kinematics and Dynamics, 1970. Editor: Quantum Electrodynamics, 1958. Office: Dept Physics U Calif 405 Hilgard Ave Los Angeles CA 90024

SCHYCKER, NANCY KINN, educational administrator, consultant, researcher; b. Chgo., Jan. 4, 1941; d. Fredrick Peter and Bette Lee (Riha) Kinn; m. Richard A. Schycker, Feb. 10, 1963 (div.); 1 son, Michael Vaughn. Student U. Ill., 1959; A.A., Pasadena City Coll., 1960; B.A., Calif. State U.-Los Angeles, 1962, M.A., 1972; Ph.D., Iowa State U., 1983. Life cert. elem., secondary teaching, gen. adminstrn., Calif. Tchr. Los Angeles Unified Sch. Dist., 1962-63; tchr. Covina (Calif.) Valley Unified Sch. Dist., 1964-67; tchr., master tchr. Garvey Sch. Dist., Rosemead, Calif., 1967-73, dir. Head Start State Pre-Sch. Program, 1973-80, prin., 1980-81, 83—; research assoc. Sch. Adminstrn. Iowa State U., Ames, 1981-82; adj. prof. Calif. State U., Los Angeles; cons. staff devel. pub., pvt. schs. Mem. adv. com. Pasadena Area Community Coll. Dist., 1974-75; chmn. Head Start State Pre Sch. Coordinators' Council, Los Angeles, 1979-80. Mem. Am. Assn. Sch. Adminstrs., Am. Soc. Tng. and Devel., Assn. Supervision and Curriculum Devel., NEA, Women in Ednl. Leadership, (charter), Phi Delta Kappa. Contbr. ednl. articles to various publs. Home: 14737 Calkin St Hacienda Heights CA 91745 Office: Garvey Sch Dist 2730 N Del Mar Ave Rosemead CA 91770

SCIBOR-MARCHOCKI, ROMUALD IRENEUS, research scientist; b. Highland Park, Mich., Dec. 29, 1926, s Sigismond August and Sophy L. (Scibor-Marchocka) S-M. B.S., Wayne State U., 1947, M.S., 1948; postgrad. Calif. Inst. Tech., U. So. Calif. Asst. physics Wayne State U., 1943-47, spl. instr., 1947-48; sr. engr. labs. div. Hoffman Radio Corp., 1949-59; design specialist Aerojet Gen. Corp. div. Gen. Tire & Rubber Co., 1959-62; sr. scientist Nortonics div. Northrop Corp., 1962-68; mem. tech. staff Jet Propulsion Lab., Pasadena, 1968-72, staff scientist, 1970-72; owner Mädchental Kennels, Baldwin Park, 1955—; with Wells Fargo Security Guard Services div. Baker Protective Services, 1973-81; tutor Mt. San Antonio Coll., 1978—, staff math. dept., 1979—; cons. in math. and computer sci., 1980—. Mem. Calavo Growers Assn., Acoustical Soc., Math. Assn., Am. Def. Preparedness Assn., Assn. Physics Tchrs., N.Y. Acad. Sci., AAAS, Nat. Rifle Assn., Free for All, Mensa, Naturist Soc., Nat. Free Lance Photographers Assn., Sigma Xi. Contbr. articles to profl. jours. Home: 15250 E Arrow Hwy Baldwin Park CA 91706

SCIORTINO, SANDY JAMES, human resources exec.; b. Cleve., Dec. 17, 1932; s. Stephen D. and Rose (Imperial) S.; student Miami U., Oxford, Ohio, 1951-52, John Carroll U., 1960-66; A.S., magna cum laude, Cuyahoga Community Coll., 1979; m. Rosemarie Miehs, Nov. 6, 1980; children—Michael, William, Steven; stepchildren—Donna, Carol, Phillip, Daniel, Mallory. Supr. employment Addressograph-Multigraph Co., Cleve., 1958-73; personnel mgr. Life Systems, Inc., Beachwood, Ohio, 1973-77; v.p., gen. mgr. Diagnostic Testing Lab., Mentor, Ohio, 1977-79; sr. employee relations rep. Picker Corp., Highland Heights, Ohio, 1979-80; mgr. staffing Solar Turbines Internat., San Diego, 1980-81; dir. human resources Med. Products div. Gould, Inc., Oxnard, Calif., 1981—; guest lectr. San Diego State U., Nat. U., 1960—; human resources cons. Mel Thompson and Assos., 1981—. Mem. San Diego EEO Council, Calif. Econ. Devel. Dept. Employer's Adv. Bd.; mem. adv. bd. Ventura County Community Coll.; mem. employer's adv. bd. Indsl. Relations Assn. Served with U.S. Army, 1952-54. Mem. Western States Coll. Placement Assn., Nat. Profl. and Corp. Recruiters Assn., Personnel Mgmt. Assn. (v.p. legis.), Phi Theta Kappa. Republican. Roman Catholic. Author: Handbook on Production of Plastic Credit Cards, 1961. Home: 790 N Valley Rd Westlake CA 91362 Office: 1900 Williams Dr Oxnard CA 93030

SCOLLIN, DAVID BROOKS, optometrist; b. Santa Barbara, Calif., Nov. 18, 1955; s. Harold Vincent and Ruth Potter (Brooks) S.; m. Christy Blanc, June 30, 1979. B.S. with honors in Biology, Calif. Poly. State U., 1977; O.D., U. Calif.-Berkeley, 1981. Gen. practice optometry, Ukiah, Calif., 1981—. Mem. Am. Optometric Assn., Calif. Optometric Assn., Redwood Empire Optometric Soc. Democrat. Presbyterian. Home: 350 Laughlin Way Redwood Valley CA 95470 Office: 555 S Dora St Ukiah CA 95482

SCOTT, CHARLES KENNARD, state senator, cattle rancher; b. Oreg., Aug. 19, 1945; s. Oliver Kennard and Deborah Ann (Hubbard) S.; m. Elaine Fenton, Dec. 20, 1975; children—Daniel, Abigail. A.B., Harvard Coll., 1967; M.B.A., Harvard U., 1969. Analyst, HEW and EPA, 1969-74; v.p., mgr. Bates Creek Cattle Co., Casper, Wyo., 1974—; mem. Wyo. Ho. of Reps., 1978-82; mem. Wyo. Senate, 1982—.

SCOTT, CLIFFORD RAY, minister, broadcasting station executive; b. Wilmington, N.C., June 15, 1930; s. DeWitt Talmadge and Ruth Elvera (Hufham) S.; student Reedley (Calif.) Coll., 1963-64, Internat. Coll., Honolulu, 1977-80; m. Billie Jean Gibson, Jan. 3, 1956; children—Clifford, Lisa, David, Rebecca. Ordained minister Bapt. Gen. Conf.

Announcer, Sta. WGBR, Goldsboro, N.C., 1956, Sta. WMFD, Wilmington, N.C., 1956-58, Sta. KBIS, Bakersfield, Calif., 1958; announcer, account exec. Sta. KRDU, Dinuba, Calif., 1958-67; asst. mgr. Sta. WFGW, Black Mountain, N.C., 1967-71; gen. mgr. Sta. KAIM, Honolulu, 1971—. Served with U.S. Army, 1949-52. Mem. Nat. Religious Broadcasters, Nat. Assn. Broadcasters. Republican. Baptist. Club: Kiwanis (past pres.). Office: KAIM 3555 Harding Ave PO Box 375 Honolulu HI 96816

SCOTT, CYNTHIA ANN, nurse anesthetist; b. Sioux City, Iowa, Oct. 7, 1953; d. Irwin Gerald and Catherine June (King) S.; m. John Mark Johnson, Aug. 24, 1974 (div.). R.N., Bishop Clarkson Meml. Hosp., 1974; anesthesia degree Creighton U., 1976. R.N., Nebr., S.D., Iowa, Mo., Hawaii; cert. registered nurse anesthetist. Nurse, St. Francis Hosp., Yankton, S.D., 1974-75; anesthetist Iowa Meth. Med. Ctr., Des Moines, 1976-78, St. Luke's Hosp., Kansas City, Mo., 1978-81, Bapt. Meml. Hosp., Kansas City, Mo., 1981-82, Straub Clinic and Hosp., Honolulu, 1982—. Mem. Am. Assn. Nurse Anesthetists, Hawaii Assn. Nurse Anesthetists. Republican. Mem. Reorganized Ch. Jesus Christ of Latter-day Saints. Club: South Seas Aquatics (Honolulu). Home: 3444 Maunaloa Ave Honolulu HI 96816 Office: Straub Clinic & Hosp 888 S King St Honolulu HI 96813

SCOTT, DONALD WAYNE, entomologist; b. Glendale, Calif., May 4, 1949; s. Charles F. and Minnie M. Scott; A.A.A., Green River Community Coll., 1969; A.A., 1971; B.S., (Julius Harold Bloedel forestry research scholar 1972), U. Wash., Seattle, 1973, M.S., 1974; Ph.D., Oreg. State U., Corvallis, 1978; m. Mary K. Henderson; children—Sarah K., Melissa D., Jeffrey B. Biol. lab. technician U.S. Dept. Agr.-Forest Service, Pacific NW Forest and Range Expt. Sta., Corvallis, Oreg., 1974-79, entomologist, 1979-80, supervisory entomologist Region 6 Forest Pest Mgmt. Staff, Portland, Oreg., 1980—, project mgr. Douglas-Fir Tussock Moth Baculovirus prodn. project, 1980—; grad. research asst. dept. entomology Oreg. State U., Corvallis, 1975-78. Served with Wash. Army N.G., 1970-74, USAR, 1974-76. Mem. Entomol. Soc. Am., Entomol. Soc. Can., Entomol. Soc. B.C., Pacific Coast Entomol. Soc., Sigma Xi, Xi Sigma Pi, Phi Sigma. Office: 3200 Jefferson Way Corvallis OR 97331

SCOTT, E. WALTER, corp. exec.; b. Chgo., Feb. 28, 1930; s. Ervin Walter and Louise Cleveland (Doss) S.; B.S., U. So. Calif., 1951, postgrad., 1952; postgrad. So. Meth. U., 1954, Harvard U., 1964; m. Gaynel Hirtensteiner, May 10, 1951; children—Steve Randall, Leslie Gaynel, Jeffrey Rawlins. Zone mgr. Time, Inc., Dallas, 1951-54; asst. to pres. Mecom Oil & Gas Co., Houston, 1954-55; promotion mgr. Disneyland, Anaheim, Calif., 1955-57; pres. Met. Realty Corp., Los Angeles, 1957-61, Orange Julius of Am., Los Angeles, 1961-69; chmn. bd., pres. Ranchaire Corp., 1969—; owner W.H. Spurgeon Bldg., Santa Ana, Calif.; pres. Community Hosp. Services Corp., Newport Beach, Calif., 1972-78, Centre Co. Inc., 1979—. Pres. bd. dirs. Hathaway Home for Children, Los Angeles, 1964-66; developer Colorado Springs Community Hosp., 1975. Served with USAF, 1950-51. Lic. real estate broker, Calif.; lic. airline transport pilot, amateur radio operator. Mem. Phi Kappa Psi. Presbyterian. Author: Poison and Burn Prevention Program for Young Children, 1976. Patentee metal panels lock system. Home: 615 Via Lido Soud Newport Beach CA 92663 Office: 206 W 4th St Suite 433 Santa Ana CA 92701

SCOTT, ELRETHA LAZELL, educational administrator; b. Homer, La., July 9, 1938; d. James Ardell and Carrie Lee (Norton) Turner; m. William McKinley Scott, Apr. 8, 1961; children—Sheelah, Kevin. B.A. in Edn. San Francisco State U., 1961; M.A. in Higher Edn., San Jose State U., 1982. Cert. tchr., adminstr. Probation officer Alameda County Probation Dept., 1963-71; tchr. Muriel Wright Sch., San Jose, Calif., 1972-79; adminstrv. intern Santa Clara County Office of Edn., 1979-82; prin. Lincoln Community Sch., San Jose, 1982—. Mem. Outreach Community Chorus. Mem. Assn. Supervision and Curriculum Devel., Safety Edn. Assn., Assn. Calif. Sch. Adminstrs., Women Leaders in Edn., Juvenile Ct. Sch. Adminstrs., Urban League, NAACP, Delta Sigma Theta. Democrat. Methodist. Club: Jack and Jill of Am. Home: 1828 Frobisher Way San Jose CA 95124 Office: 100 Skyport Dr San Jose 95110

SCOTT, FRANK NICHOLAS, venture capitalist; b. N.Y.C., Mar. 4, 1936; s. Frank Nicholas and Charlotte (Whiteside) S.; B.S., Calif. State U., 1961, M.S. with honors, 1962; postgrad. UCLA, 1963, Alexander Hamilton Inst., 1967; Ph.D., Union Grad. Sch., 1977; m. Joan Olsen, July 1, 1956; children—Nancy Ann, David Olsen. Dir. research center Calif. State U., Sacramento, 1968; exec. v.p. El Dorado Hills subs. John Hancock Ins. Corp., Sacramento, 1966; pres. Community Shelter Corp. subs. TRW, Inc., Sacramento, 1971; chmn. bd. 20 cos., including Frank Scott Enterprises, Info. Solutions, Inc., Ultramagnetics, Vocom, Frank Scott Securities, Red Carpet Corp. Am., Oakland Fin. Group, Vanguard. Office: 9057 Soquel Dr Bldg C PO Box 115 Aptos CA 95003

SCOTT, GEORGE WILLIAM, state senator, educator; b. Seattle, July 9, 1937; s. Arthur Pousette and Eleanor Irene (Bleasdale) S.; m. Carol Susan Rogel, 1965. B.A., Whitworth Coll., 1959; M.A., U. Wash., 1966, Ph.D., 1970. Mem. faculty Seattle Community Coll., 1969—; mem. Wash. Ho. of Reps. from 46th Dist., 1968-70, Wash. State Senate from 46th Dist., 1970—. Precinct committeeman 32d Dist., 1966-68. Served to capt., USMC, 1959-66; PTO; mem. Res., 1962-67. Mem. Seattle Mcpl. League, Am. Legion. Republican. Lodges: Lions, Rotary, Masons. Home: 8821 Paisley Dr NE Seattle WA 98115 Office: Washington State Senate Olympia WA 98504

SCOTT, HAROLD HUFFMAN, chem. engr.; b. Joseph, Oreg., May 8, 1920; s. David Anderson and Estella Mae (Huffman) S.; B.S. in Chem. Engring., Oreg. State U., 1943; postgrad. Harvard U., M.I.T. Grad. Sch. Naval Electronics Tng., 1943-44; M.S. in Chem. Engring., Oreg. State U., 1947; m. Kathleen Hayes, May 14, 1944; children—Martin David, Anne Marie, Michael Raymond. Engr. Aluminum Co. of Am., Vancouver, Wash., 1946; engr. Shell Oil Co., Martinez, Calif., 1947-54, mgr. engring. field, 1954-65, mgr. engring. services, 1965-75, sr. staff engr. in charge inspection, 1975-81, cons., 1981—; instr., comdg. officer Martinez Naval Res. Electronics Unit, 1950-54. Mem. Martinez Sch. Systems Adv. Com., 1958, 1964, Citizens Park Adv. Com., 1966, Martinez Human Resources Commn., 1967-69. Served to lt. USNR, 1943-46: PTO. Registered profl. corrosion and metall. engr., Calif. Mem. Am. Inst. Chem. Engrs., Nat. Assn. Corrosion Engrs., Am. Soc. Metals, Tau Beta Pi, Sigma Tau, Phi Lambda Upsilon, Phi Mu Epsilon. Republican. Roman Catholic. Home: 5404 Likins Ave Martinez CA 94553 Office: 5404 Likins Ave Martinez CA 94553

SCOTT, JUANITA FULLER, rehabilitation counselor; b. Sylacauga, Ala., Mar. 26, 1936; d. Allie B. and Mattie (Moon) Fuller; m. Arthur Bohannon, Mar. 17, 1956 (div.); children—Arthur Bohannon, Anthony Bohannon; m. 2d, Cornelius L. Scott. B.A., U. Colo., 1973; M.A., U. No. Colo., 1974. Instr. adj. faculty Met. State Coll., Denver, 1974-82, Community Coll. Denver, 1974-76, Arapahoe Community Coll., 1978-79; social worker Mile High Child Care Assn., Denver, 1974-76; rehab. counselor State of Colo., Denver, 1977; pvt. cons. marriages, substance abuse, 1974—. Bd. dirs. Lutheran Social Services. U. No. Colo. scholar, 1973-74. Mem. Internat. Assn. Black Women in Criminal Justice System, Colo. Juvenile Counselors, Colo. Coalition Black Social Workers, Kappa Delta Pi, Colo. Black Women for Polit. Action, Alpha Kappa Alpha, Black Psychologists of Denver. Democrat. Baptist. Home: 5303 Tucson Way Denver CO 80239 Office: 3520 W Oxford St Denver CO 80236

SCOTT, LARRY DONALD, physicist; b. Tucson, Mar. 25, 1935; s. Melvin Rufus and Bonnie Irene (Hawes) S.; B.S.E.E. with high distinction (Scholar 1964) U. Ariz., 1965; S.M., Harvard U., 1966, Ph.D., 1970; m. Enid Rollins Wylie, June 14, 1957; children—Yvette Patricia, Jean Diane, Brian William. Field engr. Bendix Field Engring. Corp., Keflavik, Iceland, 1960-62; mem. tech. staff Bell Telephone Labs., North Andover, Mass., 1965-66; research fellow, lectr. Harvard U., 1970-72; regional mgr. Mission Research Corp., Albuquerque, 1972—, also dir.; mem. exec. bd. Albuquerque joint chpt. Antennas and Propagation Soc., Soc. Microwave Theory and IEEE transactions group on electromagnetic compatability, 1977-79. Mem. ch. bd. Holiday Park Ch. of Nazarene, Albuquerque, 1978-82. Served with USAF, 1956-59. Recipient Best Paper of Yr. award IEEE and Antennas and Propagation Soc., 1970. Mem. Soc. Harvard Engrs. and Scientists, IEEE, Antennas and Propagation Soc., Soc. Electromagnetic Compatability, Sigma Xi, Tau Beta Phi. Republican. Home: 4605 Oahu Dr NE Albuquerque NM 87111 Office: 1720 Randolph Rd SE Albuquerque NM 87106

SCOTT, LEE MICHAEL (MELBOURNE SCOTHORN), mfg. co. mktg. exec.; b. Dodge City, Kans., May 7, 1941; s. Lee Roy and Charlotte L. G. (Jones) S.; B.S. in Bus. Adminstrn., U. Fla., 1961, M.S. in Oceanography, 1964; Ph.D. in Meteorology, U. Md., 1966; postgrad. U. Guam, 1966; m. Joy Cole-Harl, June 1, 1973; children—Hope, Kimberly, Michael, Bennett. Commd. E-1 U.S. Navy, 1958, advanced through grades to O-4, 1972; various assignments, Vietnam, 1964-72; ret., 1972; dist. mgr. Penn Central, Waco, Tex., 1972-73; regional mgr. City Investing, Longmont, Colo., 1973-76; mktg. dir. Eaton Corp., Hollywood, Calif., 1974—, regional mgr., 1979-80, Western regional mgr., Newbury Park, Calif., 1980—; mfrs. rep. for manufactured housing to State of Wyo., 1974-75. Mem. Agana (Guam) Sch. Bd., 1967-68; pres. Little League, Issaquah, Wash., 1980-81. Recipient awards, including: Mgr. of Yr., Penn. Central, 1972; Regional Mgr. of Yr., Eaton Corp., 1980. Mem. Nat. Officer Product Assn., Data Processing Assn., Nat. Office Machine Dealers Assn., Western Office Machine Dealers Assn., Internat. Word Processing Assn., Am. Mgmt. Assn. Republican. Mem. Christian Ch. (Disciples of Christ). Clubs: Lions (Citizen of Yr. 1972), Eagles. Home and Office: 220 Berthoud Way Golden CO 80401

SCOTT, MARGARET LOUISE, aerospace co. exec.; b. Santa Monica, Calif., June 21, 1925; d. Earl Joseph and Stella May (Miller) Scott; student Los Angeles City Coll., 1947-51, El Camino Coll., 1973. Flight test analyst N.Am. Aviation, Los Angeles, 1943-51; graphics artist N.Am. Rockwell, Los Angeles, 1951-74; illustrations project coordinator Rockwell Internat., Los Angeles, 1974-75, dept. head graphics art dept., Los Angeles div., El Segundo, Calif., 1975—. Mem. trade advisory com. El Camino Coll., Glendale Community Coll., West Los Angeles Coll., 1975—. Home: 1601 Sunset Plaza Dr Los Angeles CA 90069 Office: 815 Lapham St El Segundo CA 90245

SCOTT, PETER BRYAN, lawyer; b. St. Louis, Nov. 11, 1947; s. Gilbert Franklin and Besse Jean (Fudge) S.; m. Suzanne Rosalee Wallace, Oct. 19, 1974. A.B., Drury Coll., 1969; J.D., Washington U., St. Louis, 1972, LL.M., 1980. Bar: Mo. 1972, Colo. 1980; diplomate Ct. Practice Inst. Sole practice, St. Louis, 1972-80; assoc. firm McKie and Assocs., Denver, 1980-81; ptnr. firm Scott and Chesteen, P.C., Denver, 1981—; tchr. Denver Paralegal Inst. Vice pres. Jefferson Twp. Republican Club, St. Louis, 1979-80. Served to capt. USAR, 1971-79. Mem. ABA, Mo. Bar Assn., Colo. Bar Assn., Denver Bar Assn. Mem. United Church of Christ. Home: 26262 Wolverine Trail Evergreen CO 80439 Office: 6740 E Hampden Ave Suite 306 Denver CO 80224

SCOTT, ROLAND BURCKHALTER, JR., airline pilot; b. Dayton, Ohio, Nov. 18, 1944; s. Roland Burckhalter and Elizabeth (Lewis) S.; B.A. in Bus. Adminstrn., Coll. of Idaho, 1967; m. Judy Ann Baverstock, Nov. 13, 1971; children—Morgen Elizabeth, Regan Michell. Pilot, Western Airlines, 1973—; real estate asso. Coast Equities, Long Beach, Calif., 1975—; gen. partner, prodn. exec. for oil exploration Rolori Oil Group, 1980—, gen. partner San Felipe Group. Served as capt. USMC, 1968-72. Decorated D.F.C., Air medal (57); Vietnamese Cross of Gallantry; recipient Top Producer award Coast Equities. Mem. Airlines Pilots Assn., Aircraft Owners and Pilots Assn., Nat. Rifle Assn., Long Beach Bd. Realtors. Democrat. Episcopalian. Club: Century (Long Beach). Home: Long Beach CA Office: 6272 B E Pacific Coast Hwy Long Beach CA 90803

SCOTT, TONY (TONE), reviewer, critic, playwright, photographer; b. Redlands, Calif., Sept. 23, 1923; s. Herman Gross and Mary (Reilly) S.; B.A., Pomona Coll., 1947. Editor, Wilshire Press, Los Angeles, 1957-69; critic Daily Variety, Hollywood, Calif., 1969—; Gertrude Stein's Last G.I.; playwright, adapted Lysistrata (Aristophanes), 1956. Mem. Wilshire Beautiful Com., 1965; mem. pub. relations com., chmn. campaign promotion com. Los Angeles County Heart Assn., 1963-69. Bd. dirs. Hollywood-Wilshire Symphony Orch., Palomar Sch. Served with AUS, 1943-46. Recipient Apple of Gold, Internat. Sr. League, 1961, commendation USAF Recruiting Service, 1962, citation of merit Psychiat. Club of Am., 1962, Exceptional Service award Los Angeles County Heart Assn., 1965. Mem. Wilshire C. of C. (dir. 1964-65), Cath. Press Council (dir. 1973-74, membership chmn. 1972-74), Nat. Acad. TV Arts and Scis., Los Angeles Drama Critics Circle (founding mem.), Pacific Pioneer Broadcasters, Soc. Am. Theatre Critics Assn., St. John's Coll. Alumni Assn. (hon.), Preservation Variety Arts, Sigma Delta Chi, Nu Alpha Phi, Sierra Club. Clubs: Marines' Meml. (San Francisco); Authors. Home: 609 Prospect Ave South Pasadena CA 91030 Office: 1400 N Cahuenga Hollywood CA 90028

SCOTT, WILFRED ARMENDE, tribal government official; b. Lewiston, Idaho, Jan. 8, 1931; s. Lyman Antoine and Clara (Ramsey) S.; m. Bessie Greene, Mar. 25, 1952; children—Venita, Wilfred Armende, Jeffery, Dani, Lori. Student Lewis and Clark State Coll., Lewiston. Enlisted U.S. Navy, 1951, advanced through grades to chief petty officer; ret., 1972; mem. Nez Perce Tribal Council, 1972—, chmn., 1977-83, vice chmn., 1983—; chmn. Council Energy Resource Tribes, 1982—. Mem. VFW, Fleet Res. Assn. Lodge: Moose. Home: PO Box 131 Lapwai ID 83540

SCOULAR, ROBERT FRANK, lawyer; b. Del Norte, Colo., July 9, 1942; s. Duane William and Marie Josephine (Moloney) S.; student Carroll Coll., 1960-61; B.S. in Aero. Engring., St. Louis U., 1964, J.D., 1968; m. Donna Lee Votruba, June 3, 1967; children—Bryan Thomas, Sean Duane, Bradley Robert. Aerodynamics engr., contract adminstr. Emerson Electric Co., St. Louis, 1964-66; admitted to Mo., Colo., N.D., Calif. bars, U.S. Supreme Ct. bar; law clk. U.S. Ct. Appeals Eighth Circuit, St. Louis, 1968-69; partner firm Bryan, Cave, McPheeters & McRoberts, St. Louis, 1969-79, mng. partner, Los Angeles Office, 1979—; dir. Corley Printing Co., St. Louis. Bd. dirs. John Marshall Republican Club, 1974-76, Bar Assn. Met. St. Louis Found., 1975-76, 1979, Mo. Lawyers Credit Union, 1978-79, St. Louis U. Alumni Council, 1979-82. Recipient Outstanding Sr. award, St. Louis U., 1964; named Nat. Outstanding Civil Air Patrol Cadet, 1960. Mem. Am. (nat. dir. young lawyers sect. 1977-78, chmn. young lawyers corp. law com. 1973-74), Mo. (chmn. young lawyers sect. 1976-77, Disting. Service award 1978), Calif., Los Angeles County bar assns., Bar Assn. Met. St. Louis (chmn. young lawyers sect. 1975-76, exec. com. 1975-79, v.p. 1978-79), Am. Judicature Soc., Assn. Bus. Trial Lawyers, Los Angeles C. of C., Town Hall, AIAA, Engrs. Club St. Louis (chmn. public affairs com. 1972-73). Republican. Roman Catholic. Clubs: Mo. Athletic; University (Los Angeles). Contbr. articles to profl. jours. Home: 4 Horseshoe Ln Rolling Hills Estates CA 90274 Office: 3100 Crocker Center 333 S Grand Ave Los Angeles CA 90071

SCRIBNER, NANCY CAROLYN, holding co. exec.; b. Randleman, N.C., Aug. 10, 1937; d. Roy Leon and Maude Lee (Teasley) Whitson; ed. U. Md.; m. Thomas Scribner, Dec. 14, 1956. Asst. acctg. mgr. Pacific Architects and Engrs., Los Angeles, 1967-70; corp. sec. Exec. Mktg. Corp., Silver Spring, Md., 1971-74: corp. controller-sec. Chesapeake Industries Inc., Newport Beach, Calif., 1974—. Mem. Nat. Assn. Exec. Female. Democrat. Roman Catholic. Home: 21432 Dockside Circle Huntington Beach CA 92646 Office: 500 Newport Center Dr Suite 415 Newport Beach CA 92660

SCRITSMIER, JEROME LORENZO, lighting fixture mfg. co. exec.; b. Eau Claire, Wis., July 1, 1925; s. Fredrick Lorenzo and Alvera Mary (Schwab) S.; B.S., Northwestern U., 1950; m. Mildred Joan Lloyd, June 27, 1947; children—Dawn, Lloyd, Janet. Salesman, Sylvania Elec. Products, Los Angeles, 1951-69; owner, mgr. Real Properties, 1965—; pres. Environ. Lighting for Architecture Co., Los Angeles, 1973—; dir. Ind. Nat. Bank, Covina, Calif. Served with USAAF, 1943-46. Mem. Apt. Assn. (pres., dir. Los Angeles County). Republican. Club: Jonathan (Los Angeles). Home: 2454 N Cameron Ave Covina CA 91724 Office: 17891 Arenth St City of Industry CA 91748

SCRIVENER, LAWRENCE ALFRED, airline official; b. Memphis, Oct. 11, 1929; s. Charles Bailey and Alice Roberta (Parke) S.; student Tenn. Poly. Inst., 1947-48; B.E.E., U. Fla., 1956; m. Barbara Arnette Pankey, Sept. 7, 1951; children—Barry Alan, Laura Anne, Carol Arnette, Celia Alice. Elec. design engr. Pan Am. World Airways, Miami, 1956-58, DC-6 flight engr., N.Y.C., 1958-59; flight engr. Convair, San Diego, 1959-63; flight engr., co-pilot, capt. Pacific Southwest Airlines, San Diego, 1963—, dir. research and devel. flight ops., div. flight crew tng., 1979—. Elder, Presbyterian Ch., 1972—. Served with USAF, 1948-52. Mem. Southwest Flight Crew Assn. (officer 1967-74), United Presbyn. Mariner Club (skipper 1967, 83), San Diego Hist. Soc. Democrat. Home: 1655 Fuerte Hills Dr El Cajon CA 92020 Office: Crew Training Center 9850 Carroll Canyon Rd San Diego CA 92131

SCRIVER, ROBERT MACFIE, sculptor; b. Browning, Mont., Aug. 15, 1914; s. Thaddeus Emery and Ellison Westgarth (Macfie) S.; student Dickinson (N.D.) State Tchrs. Coll., 1933-34; B.A., Vandercook Coll. Music, 1936, M.A., 1941; postgrad. Northwestern U., U. Wash.; D.Art (hon.), Carrol Coll., Helena, Mont., 1976; m. Dorothy Lorraine Holdren; children by previous marriage—Margaret Alice Scriver DeSmet Paul (dec.), James Robert. Tchr. music, band leader, art supr. schs. in Browning and Matla, Mont., 1935-50; dir. All-Indian Band; lead cornetist Bob Lyon's Band; taxidermist, Browning; founder Scriver Mus. Mont. Wildlife, Browning, 1956; sculptor in bronze and clay, 1951—; one-man exhbn. in pvt. home, Northbridge, Calif., 1961, Gallery '85, Billings, Mont., 1968, Mont. Hist. Soc., 1968, 72, Buffalo Bill Meml. Center and Whitney Gallery Western Art, Cody, Wyo., 1969, Riveredge Found., Calgary, Can., 1973, Calgary Stampede, 1973. Served with USAAF, 1940-43. Recipient 1st place gold medal and purchase prize Cowboy Hall of Fame and Western Heritage Center, Oklahoma City, 1969, gold medal, 1970, 71, silver medal, 1972; Distinguished V.I.P. award radio sta. KSEN, Shelby, Mont., 1971; Gold medal CA Show, Phoenix, 1978; William F. Cody award Old West Trail Found., 1977; named One of 22 Outstanding Montanans, Mont. Arts Council; named One of three People in U.S. who contbd. most to promotion of Lewis and Clark Trail Heritage Found. commnd. by Hill County Mus., Havre, Mont., 1966, Cowboy Hall of Fame, 1973, Ft. Benton Community Improvement Assn., 1973, Mont. Bicentennial Project, 1976, Whitney Gallery Western Art, 1977, also by individuals. Mem. Soc. Animal Artists (charter), Internat. Art Guild, Nat. Sculpture Soc., Cowboy Artists Am. Club: Salmagundi (N.Y.C.). Mason. Home: Box 172 Browning MT 59417

SCRIVNER, GRETCHEN JULIE, oil co. mgr.; b. San Juan, P.R.; d. Carlos G. and Julie (Roman) Delucca; B.B.A. magna cum laude, U. P.R., 1967. Staff asst. U.S. Dept. State, Washington and Paris, 1967-70; legal asst. Anderson & Carey, Littleton, Colo., 1971-76; mgr. natural gas supply Husky Oil Co., Denver, 1977—. Mem. Rocky Mountain Gas Men's Assn. (dir. 1980-81), Rocky Mountain Oil and Gas Assn., Denver Art Mus. Republican. Episcopalian. Club: Denver Petroleum. Home: 6544 E Baker Pl Denver CO 80224 Office: 6060 S Willow Dr Englewood CO 80111

SCROGGIE, LOIS JEAN, educator, writer; b. Denver, Nov. 28, 1940; d. John and Ann Allison (Forsyth) Scroggie; B.A., U. Colo., 1964, M.A., 1966, postgrad., 1968, 73; m. Jan Whitinger, Dec. 25, 1975 (div.). Instr. English, Trinidad (Colo.) State Jr. Coll., 1966-82. Mem. Am. Film Inst., AAUP, MLA, Rocky Mountain Modern Lang. Assn., Women's Caucus for Modern Langs., Nat. Council Tchrs. English, English-Speaking Union, Nat. Writer's Club, Soc. Children's Book Writers, City News Service. Author articles, poems. Home and Office: 777 Monaco Pkwy Denver CO 80220

SCROGGS, MARIE FRAZIER, educator; b. Tonopah, Nev., June 21, 1923; d. Thomas Arthur and Rose (Craig) Frazier; B.A., UCLA, 1945; M.A., Calif. State U., Los Angeles, 1963; 1 dau., Linda. Tchr., Garfield Elem. Sch., Pasadena (Calif.) Unified Sch. Dist., 1950, tchr. Don Benito Elem. Sch., 1952-65, tchr.-cons. reading for dist., 1965-73, dist. reading cons., 1973-78; tchr. Linda Vista Primary Sch., 1978—. Mem. NEA, Calif. Tchrs. Assn., Los Angeles Reading Assn., Pasadena Edn. Assn., Delta Kappa Gamma. Republican. Episcopalian. Home: 316 W California Blvd Pasadena CA 91105 Office: Linda Vista Primary Sch 1259 Linda Vista Ave Pasadena CA 91103

SCRUGGS, LARRY GLEN, college administrator; b. White City, Oreg., Oct. 24, 1943; s. William Freeman and Claudia Rae (Constable) S.; m. Patricia Shafer, Sept. 16, 1967; children—Larry Glen, Laura Rae, William Price, Kerry Wright, Berry Monroe. B.S., So. Oreg. Coll., 1971, M.S., 1972; Ph.D., Portland State U. Security mgr. May Dept. Store, Portland, 1972-75; conf. dir. U. Portland, 1975—; cons. on conf. ops. Starlight Parade chmn. Portland Rose Festival Assn.; active Greater Portland Conv. and Visitors Assn. Served with USAF, 1961-65. Mem. Portland C. of C., Western Assn. Coll. Aux. Services (pres.), Nat. Assn. Coll. Aux. Services. Roman Catholic. Clubs: Pres.'s, City (Portland). Author: Conferences on Campus: Marketing and Managing, 1982; contbr. articles to profl. jours. Home: 6942 N Villard St Portland OR 97217 Office: Columbia 107 Univ of Portland Portland OR 97203

SCRYMGEOUR, JOHN A., petroleum company executive; b. Dartmouth, Can., 1921. Grad. Dalhousie Coll., 1943. Chmn., Westburne Industries, Ltd., Calgary, Alta., Can. Office: Westburne Internat Industries Ltd 535 7th Ave SW Calgary 2 AB T2P 0Y4 Canada*

SCULL, ANDREW, sociology educator; b. Edinburgh, Scotland, May 2, 1947; s. Allan Edward and Marjorie Therese S.; m. Nancy Principi, Aug. 16, 1970; children—Anna Theresa, Andrew Edward. B.A. with honors (Open scholar), Oxford (Eng.) U., 1969; M.A. (Nat. fellow), Princeton U., 1971, Ph.D., 1974. Asst. prof. sociology U. Pa., Phila., 1974-78; assoc. prof. U. Calif.-San Diego, 1978—. Am. Council Learned Socs. fellow, 1976-77; Davis Ctr. Hist. Studies fellow, 1978-79; Guggenheim fellow, 1981-82. Author: Decarceration, 1977; Museums of Madness, 1979; Die Anstalten Offnen, 1980; Madhouses, Mad-doctors, and Madmen, 1981; (with Steven Lukes) Durkheim and the Law, 1983; (with Stanley Cohen) Social Control and the Modern State, 1983; contbr. articles to profl. jours. Home: 2118 Belloc Ct Pacific Beach CA 92109 Office: Dept Sociology U Calif San Diego La Jolla CA 92093

SCULLY, GERALD DAVID, accountant, writer; b. Harrisburg, Pa., Apr. 27, 1944; s. Edwin James and Edith S.; m. Ing-Chu'n Tsun, Oct. 5, 1963 (dec. 1967); m. Gloriann Alexandria Caporusso, May 2, 1983. C.P.A., Calif.; enrolled agt. IRS. Various acctg. positions, Los Angeles, 1966-75; owner David Scully & Co., C.P.A.s, Van Nuys, Calif., 1975—. Served with USAF, 1963-66. Mem. Am. Inst. C.P.A.s, Calif. Soc. C.P.A.s, Better Bus. Bur., Marina del Rey C. of C., Van Nuys C. of C., Calif. Assn. Health Facilities (govt. relations com.). Home: 8462 Fulbright St Canoga Park CA 91306 Office: 14209 Burbank Blvd Van Nuys CA 91401

SCULLY, JAMES HENRY, JR., psychiatrist, educator; b. New Britain, Conn., Jan. 14, 1944; s. James Henry and Marietta (Maguire) S.; m. Mary Elizabeth Hailey, Sept. 6, 1969; children—Jennifer, Sarah. A.B., Georgetown U., 1965; M.D., Tulane U., 1969. Diplomate Am. Bd. Psychiatry and Neurology. Resident in psychiatry U. Colo., Denver, 1975-76, instr. psychiatry, 1976-78, dir. med. student edn. psychiatry, 1978—, asst. prof. psychiatry, 1978-82, assoc. prof., 1983—; chief cons. Denver VA, 1978—; dir. profl. edn. Colo. State Hosp., 1979—. Served to lt. comdr. USN, 1969-73. Recipient Kaiser Permanente teaching award Colo. U., 1982. Mem. Colo. Psychiat. Soc., Am. Psychiat. Assn., Assn. of Dirs. of Med. Student Edn. in Psychiatry, Assn. Acad. Psychiatry. Democrat. Club: Denver Barbarians Rugby Football. Contbr. chpts. to books. Office: 4200 E 9th Ave Denver CO 80262

SCZEKAN, MARJORIE EVELYN, nurse, sociologist, educator; b. Mountain View, Calif.; d. Donald Edward and Pearl Ivy (Hoyt) Davenport; m. Frank Sczekan, Dec. 3, 1950; children—Michael, Steven, Bernard. B.S., U. Colo., 1967, M.S., 1967; M.A., U. Tenn., 1971, Ph.D., 1976. Staff nurse miscellaneous agys., 1949-65; HEW long-term nurse trainee, 1965-67; asst. prof. nursing So. Missionary Coll., Collegedale, Tenn., 1967-68, part-time instr. sociology, 1970-72; chmn. dept. nursing Dalton (Ga.) Jr. Coll., 1971-75; prof., dean Sch. Nursing, U. Tenn.-Chattanooga, 1975-81; asst. dean for nursing U. So. Colo., Pueblo, 1981—, prof., 1981—; cons. in field. HEW fellow, 1969-71. Mem. Am. Nurses Assn., So. Sociol. Soc., Nat. League for Nursing. Office: Dept Nursing U So Colo 2200 N Bonforte Blvd Pueblo CO 81001

SEABORG, GLENN THEODORE, scientist, educator; b. Ishpeming, Mich., Apr. 19, 1912; s. H. Theodore and Selma (Erickson) S.; A.B., U. Calif. at Los Angeles, 1934; Ph.D., U. Calif. at Berkeley, 1937; LL.D., U. Mich., 1958, U. Mass., 1963, San Diego State Coll., Mich. State U., 1966, Miami U., Oxford, Ohio, 1969, Rutgers U., 1970, Duke U., 1978; D.Sc., U. Denver, 1951, Gustavus Adolphus Coll., Northwestern U., 1954, U. Notre Dame, Ohio State U., Fla. State U., U. Md., 1961, Temple U., Tulane U., Drexel Inst. Tech., Georgetown U., State U. N.Y., 1962, Mundelein Coll., Trinity Coll., 1963, U. Detroit, 1965, McGill U., Montreal, Que., Can., 1966, U. Miami, Wooster Coll., Widener Coll., Tristate Coll., U. Del., Lambuth Coll., 1967, John Carroll U., Duquesne U., 1968, Ind. State U., 1969, U. Utah, 1970, Rockford Coll., 1975, Kent State U., 1975, Uppsala (Sweden) U., 1977; L.H.D., No. Mich. Coll., 1962, Nebr. Wesleyan U., 1964, Carroll Coll., Waukesha, Wis., 1970; D.P.S., George Washington U., 1962; D.P.A., U. Puget Sound, 1963; Litt.D., Lafayette Coll., 1966; D.Eng., Mich. Technol. U., 1970; Sc.D., U. Bucharest, 1971; other hon. degrees; m. Helen Griggs, June 6, 1942; children—Peter, Lynne Seaborg Cobb, David, Stephen, John Eric, Dianne. Research chemist U. Calif. at Berkeley, 1937-39, instr. dept. chemistry, 1939-41, asst. prof., 1941-45, prof., 1945-71, univ. prof., 1971— (leave of absence 1942-46, 61-71), dir. nuclear chem. research, 1946-58, 72-75, assoc. dir. Lawrence Berkeley Lab., 1954-61, 71—, chancellor Univ., 1958-61; dir. Lawrence Hall of Sci.; sect. chief metall. lab. U. Chgo., 1942-46; chmn. AEC, 1961-71, gen. adv. com., 1946-50; research nuclear chemistry and physics, transuranium elements; co-discoverer elements 94-102 and 106: plutonium, 1940, americium, 1944-45, curium, 1944, berkelium, 1949, californium, 1950, einsteinium, 1952, fermium, 1953, mendelevium, 1955, nobelium, 1958, element 106, 1974; co-discoverer nuclear energy isotopes Pu-239, U-233, Np-237, other isotopes including I-131, Fe-59, Te-99m, Co-60; originator actinide concept for placing heaviest elements in periodic system; chmn. bd. Kevex Corp., Foster City, Calif., 1972—; dir. Geomet, Inc., 1972-80, Dreyfus 3d Century Fund, 1971-80; mem. Pres.'s Sci. Adv. Com., 1959-61, nat. sci. bd. NSF, 1960-61, Pres.'s Com. on Equal Employment Opportunity, 1961-65, Fed. Radiation Council, 1961-69, Nat. Aeros. and Space Council, 1961-71, Fed. Council Sci. and Tech., 1961-71, Nat. Com. Am.'s Goals and Resources, 1962-64, Pres.'s Com. on Manpower, 1964-69; mem. Nat. Council Marine Resources and Engring. Devel., 1966-71, electoral coll. Hall of Fame for Great Ams., 1969-77; chmn. Chem. Edn. Material Study, 1959-74; mem. Nat. Programming Council for Pub. TV, 1970-72; dir. Ednl. TV and Radio Center, Ann Arbor, Mich., 1958-64, 67-70; pres. 4th UN Internat. Conf. Peaceful Uses Atomic Energy, Geneva, 1971, also chmn. U.S. del., 1964, 71; U.S. rep. 5th-15th gen. confs. IAEA, 1961-71; chmn. U.S. del. to USSR for signing Memorandum Cooperation Field Utilization Atomic Energy Peaceful Purposes, 1963, U.S. del. for signing Limited Test Ban Treaty, 1963, commn. on humanities Am. Council Learned Socs., 1962-65, sci. adv. bd. Robert A. Welch Found., 1957—. Trustee Pacific Sci. Center Found., 1962-77; mem. Pacific Sci. Center, 1980—; trustee Sci. Service, 1965—, pres., 1966—; trustee Am.-Scandinavian Found., 1968—, Ednl. Broadcasting Corp., 1970-72; bd. dirs. World Future Soc., 1969—, Calif. Council for Environ. and Econ. Balance, 1974—, Am. Hiking Soc., 1980—; bd. govs. Am. Swedish Hist. Found., 1972-75, 78—, Named 1 of Am.'s 10 outstanding young men Jr. C. of C., 1947; recipient John Ericsson Gold medal Am. Soc. Swedish Engrs., 1948; Nobel Prize for Chemistry (with E. M. McMillan), 1951; John Scott award and medal City of Phila., 1953; Perkin medal Am. sect. Soc. Chem. Industry, 1957; U.S. AEC Enrico Fermi award, 1959; Joseph Priestley Meml. award Dickinson Coll., 1960; Sci. and Engring. award Fedn. Engring. Socs., Drexel Inst. Tech., Phila., 1962; named Swedish Am. of Year, Vasa Order of Am., 1962; Franklin medal Franklin Inst., 1963; 1st Spirit of St. Louis award, 1964; Leif Erikson Found. award, 1964; Washington award Western Soc. Engrs., 1965; Arches of Sci. award Pacific Sci. Center, 1968; Internat. Platform Assn. award, 1969; Prometheus award Nat. Elec. Mfrs. Assn., 1969; Nuclear Pioneer award Soc. Nuclear Medicine, 1971; Oliver Townsend award Atomic Indsl. Forum, 1971; Distinguished Honor, award U.S. Dept. State, 1971; Golden Plate award Am. Acad. Achievement, 1972; IPA Daniel Webster award, 1976; decorated officier Legion of Honor (France). Fellow Am. Phys. Soc., Am. Inst. Chemists (Pioneer award 1968, Gold medal award 1973), Chem. Soc. London (hon.), Royal Soc. Edinburgh (hon.), Am. Nuclear Soc. (Henry De Wolf-Smyth award), Swedish Council Am. (trustee 1976, pres. 1978), Internat. Platform Assn. (pres. 1968-69, v.p. 1970), Calif., N.Y., Washington acads. scis., AAAS (pres. 1972, dir. 1971-73, chmn. bd. 1973), Royal Soc. Arts (Eng.); mem. Am. Chem. Soc. (dir. 1975-77, pres. 1976, mem. joint bd. council internat. activities 1975, chmn. 1977-80; award in pure chemistry 1947, William H. Nichols medal N.Y. sect. 1948, Charles L. Parsons award 1964, Gibbs medal Chgo. sect. 1966, Madison Marshall award No. Ala. sect. 1972, Priestley medal 1979), Am. Philos. Soc., Royal Swedish Acad. Engring. Scis., Am. Nat., Argentine Nat., Bavarian, Polish, Royal Swedish, P.R., USSR acads. scis., Royal Acad. Exact, Phys. and Natural Scis. Spain (acad. fgn. corr.), Soc. Nuclear Medicine (hon.), Deutsche Akademie der Naturforscher Leopoldina (East Germany), Nat. Acad. Pub. Adminstrn., Phi Beta Kappa, Sigma Xi, Pi Mu Epsilon, Alpha Chi Sigma (John R. Kuebler award 1978), Phi Lambda Upsilon (hon.). Clubs: Bohemian (San Francisco); Chemists (N.Y.C.); Cosmos, Univ. (Washington); Faculty (Berkeley). Author: (with Joseph J. Katz) The Actinide Elements, 1954; (with Joseph J. Katz) The Chemistry of the Actinide Elements, 1957; The Transuranium Elements, 1958; (with E.G. Valens) Elements of the Universe (Thomas Alva Edison Found. award), 1958; Man-Made Transuranium Elements, 1963; (with D.M. Wilkes) Education and the Atom, 1964; (with E.K. Hyde, Perlman) Nuclear Properties of the Heavy Elements, 1964; (with others) Oppenheimer, 1969; (with W.R. Corliss) Man and Atom, 1971; Nuclear Milestones, 1972; editor: Transuranium Elements-Products of Modern Alchemy, 1978; Kennedy, Khrushchev and the Test Ban, 1981; editor: (with Walter Loveland) Nuclear Chemistry, 1982; assoc. editor Jour. Chem. Physics, 1948-50; editorial adv. bd. Jour. Inorganic and Nuclear Chemistry, 1954, Indsl. Research, Inc., 1967-75; adv. bd. Chem. and Engring. News, 1957-59; editorial bd. Jour. Am. Chem. Soc., 1950-59, Ency. Chem. Tech., 1975; mem. hon. editorial adv. bd. Internat. Ency. & Phys. Chemistry and Chem. Physics, 1957; mem. panel Golden Picture Ency. for Children, 1957-61; mem. cons. and adv. bd. Funk and Wagnells Universal Standard Ency., 1957-61; mem. Am. Heritage Dictionary panel Usage Cons., 1964; contbr. articles to profl. jours. Office: Lawrence Berkeley Lab U Calif Berkeley CA 94720

SEAL, GREGORY LOWE, lawyer; b. Murray, Utah, May 6, 1947; s. Frank Lowe and Carol Grace (Callicott) S.; B.S., U. Utah, 1971, J.D., 1973; m. Suzanne Seare, Mar. 19, 1969; children—Wendy, Amy, Steven, Angela. Field rep. Equifax, Salt Lake City, 1969-72; law clk. Richards, Bird & Kump, Salt Lake City, 1972-73; admitted to Utah bar, 1973; atty., officer, dir., shareholder Richards, Bird & Kump, Salt Lake City, 1973-78; practice law, Salt Lake City, 1978-80; founder, pres., dir., shareholder Seal & Kennedy, Salt Lake City, 1980-82; sr. ptnr. Seal, Kennedy & Frandsen, Salt Lake City, 1983—; corp. dir. Cottonwood Title, Salt Lake City, Am. Citigroup, Inc., Salt Lake City, Game Sta., Inc., Salt Lake City. Voting dist. chmn., 1970. Mem. ABA, Utah State Bar Assn., Salt Lake County Bar Assn. Republican. Mormon. Club: Kiwanis (pres. 1982-83). Home: 1903 Terrace Dr Sandy UT 84092 Office: 5200 S Highland Dr Salt Lake City UT 84117

SEALE, ROBERT MCMILLAN, office services co. exec.; b. Birmingham, Ala., Feb. 1, 1938; s. Robert McMillan and Margaret Sutherland (Miller) S.; B.A., Emory U., 1959. With N.Y. Life Ins. Co., San Francisco, 1960-67; with Dictaphone Office Services div. Dictaphone Corp., San Francisco, 1967-69; pres. Am. Profl. Service, Inc., Dictation West, Miss Jones' Word Processing, San Francisco, Pleasant Hill, South San Francisco, Calif., Los Angeles, Beverly Hills, Riverside, San Luis Obispo, Calif., and Denver, 1969—, Environments West, 1980—, Los Arcos Properties, 1980—; med. word processing cons. to hosps., health care insts., office equipment mfrs.; lectr. in field. Chmn. San Francisco Mayor's Com. for Employment of Handicapped, 1971-73; mem. Calif. Gov.'s Planning and Adv. Com. for Vocat. Rehab. Planning, 1968-69; pres. Calif. League for Handicapped, 1968-70, bd. dirs., 1966-73, adv. council, 1973-77; v.p. Stebbins Found., 1980—. Recipient Spoke and Spark award U.S. Jr. C. of C., 1967; KABL Outstanding Citizen's award, 1965, 71. Mem. Am. Med. Records Assn., Adminstrv. Mgmt. Soc., Sales and Mktg. Execs. Assn., Am. Assn. Med. Transcription, Emory U. Alumni Assn., Internat. Word Processing Inst., U.S. C. of C., Delta Tau Delta. Republican. Club: Olympic Athletic. Contbr. articles in field to profl. jours. Office: 1177 Mission Rd South San Francisco CA 94080

SEAMAN, NOEL WEBER, lawyer; b. Huntington, N.Y., Nov. 12, 1949; s. Gilbert Noah and Stella Virginia (DeSario) S.; A.B., Duke U., 1970; J.D., U. Fla. Law Sch., 1973; LL.M. London Sch. Econs., 1974. Admitted to Calif. bar, 1977; practice law, Atlanta, 1974-75, Los Angeles, 1976-78; fin. analyst, N.Y.C., 1975-76; mng. sr. counsel Calif. Assn. Realtors, Los Angeles, 1978-81; master instr. Profl. Advancement Inst., 1979-81; cons. Allstate Realtors, 1980-81; ednl. cons. Red Carpet Realty, 1980-81; faculty real estate broker preparation classes U. So. Calif., 1981—; adj. prof. U. San Francisco. Mem. Calif. Bar Assn., Fla. Bar Assn., Ga. Bar Assn., U.S. Dist. Ct., U.S. Tax Ct., U.S. Supreme Ct., Los Angeles County Bar Assn. Clubs: Calabasas Park Country; Jonathan (Los Angeles). Home: 1117 16th St Unit 3 Santa Monica CA 90403

SEAMANS, JAMES OTIS, aerospace company executive; b. Salem, Mass., Oct. 7, 1918; s. Richard Dodge and Nathalie Pearl (Gifford) S.; student Harvard Coll., 1936-38; B.S. with distinction, U.S. Naval Acad., 1941; m. Diana Fraser, Aug. 26, 1944; children—Richard Fraser, Jane Tyler. Sr. electronics engr. Western Electric Co., Winston-Salem, N.C., 1947-51; missile program mgr. Raytheon Co., Bedford, Mass., Mass., 1951-75, Motorola, Inc., Scottsdale, Ariz., 1975—; chmn. bd. Gen. Aircraft Corp., Bedford, Mass., 1974—. Served to lt. comdr. USN, 1941-47. Fellow AIAA (assoc.). mem. IEEE (sr. life). Republican. Episcopalian. Clubs: Concord Country, Nuttall Ornithol. Patentee in field. Home: 4136 E Solano Dr Phoenix AZ 85018 Office: 8201 E McDowell Rd Scottsdale AZ 85252

SEARIGHT, PATRICIA ADELAIDE, radio, TV cons.; b. Rochester, N.Y.; d. William Hammond and Irma (Winters) S. B.A., Ohio State U. Program dir. Radio Sta. WTOP, Washington, 1952-63, gen. mgr. info., 1964; radio and TV cons., 1964-84; ret., 1984; producer, dir. many radio and TV programs; spl. fgn. news corr. French Govt., 1956; v.p. Micro Beads, Inc., 1955-59; sec., dir. Dennis-Inches, Corp., 1955-59; exec. dir. Am. Women in Radio and TV, 1969-74. Mem. pres.'s council Toledo Mus. Art. Recipient Kappa Kappa Gamma Alumna achievement award. Mem. Am. Women in Radio and TV (program chmn.; corrs. sec.; dir. Washington chpt.; pres. 1958-60, nat. membership chmn. 1962-63, nat. chmn. Industry Info. Digest 1963-64, Mid-Eastern v.p. 1964-66), Soc. Am. Travel Writers (treas. 1957-58, v.p. 1958-59), Nat. Acad. TV Arts and Scis., Kappa Kappa Gamma. Episcopalian. Clubs: Soroptimist, Women's Advt. (2d v.p. Washington 1958-59, pres. 1959-60), Washington Press. Home: 7508 N San Manuel Rd Scottsdale AZ 85258 also 3610 W Bancroft St Toledo OH 43606

SEARLES, STEPHEN PROVOOST, water conditioning company owner; b. Evanston, Ill., Aug. 7, 1942; s. Charles Colden and Evelyn (Jacobson) S.; m. Connie Lee Miller, Aug. 6, 1966; B.A., Tulane U., 1966. Ops. mgr. Greyhound Computer Corp., Chgo., 1966-70; gen. mgr. Holton Inn, Jackson Hole, Wyo., 1970-74; owner Lindsay Water Conditioning and Solar Systems, Boise, Idaho, 1975—; dir. Jackson Hole Resort Assn., Teton Village, Wyo. Bd. dirs Better Bus. Bur., 1976-79, pres., 1978. Mem. Water Quality Assn., Idaho Water Conditioning Assn. (pres.), Homebuilders Assn. S.W. Idaho, C. of C. Republican. Episcopalian. Home: 3009 N Mountain Way Boise ID 83702 Office: 4724 Emerald St Boise ID 83706

SEARS, CHARLES RAYMOND, architect; b. Denver, Oct. 3, 1947; s. Charles Jefferson and Gertrude Ellen (Jones) S.; B.Arch., U. Colo., 1971; m. Leslie Hathaway Townsend, June 7, 1969; children—Tanner Rand, Brady Chase. Designer, Keith Ames, architect, Longmont, Colo., 1969-70; v.p., estimator Trautmann Millwork, Inc., Lafayette, Colo., 1971-81; gen. partner Trautmann Enterprises, investments, 1974-81, Kite Properties, 1981—, Seafare Properties, 1982—; pres. Chasm Ltd., 1982—. Lic. architect. Mem. Louisville (Colo.) C. of C. Republican. Presbyterian. Home: 409 Lois St Louisville CO 80027 Office: 409 Lois St Louisville CO 80027

SEARS, JAMES FRANCIS, physicist; b. Lapel, Ind., Jan. 13, 1912; s. Ira Virgil and Arta Marie (Badgley) S.; m. Anna Christina Fink, June 24, 1933; children—James A., Mary Ann Sears Thompson. B.S. in Physics with distinction, Purdue U., 1932, M.S., 1934. Instr. physics electronics U. Ill., Urbana, 1940-44; mem. faculty dept. physics and electronics U. Evansville (Ind.), 1946-58, assoc. prof., 1946-48, prof., 1948-58, head dept., 1946-58; mgr. projects, tech. mil. planning operation Gen. Electric Co., Santa Barbara, Calif., 1958-62; cons. U.S. Dept. Def., 1952—; cons. space programs div. Thompson Ramo Woolridge Co., Los Angeles, 1955-72, exptl. programs div. Lockheed Space & Missile Co., Sunnyvale, Calif., 1962-72, surface to air missile systems div. Hughes Aircraft Co., Los Angeles, 1969-74; cons. USAF, 1954—, U.S. Nat. Security Agy., Washington, 1958-62, U.S. State Dept., 1958-62, Internat. Culture Found., 1979—. Bd. dirs. Channel Cities Meml. Soc., Santa Barbara. Served to maj. USMCR, 1944-46. Fellow AIAA (assoc.); mem. IEEE (sr. mem., founding pres. Evansville chpt. 1949-51), Sigma Xi, Sigma Pi Sigma, Phi Beta Chi. Club: Kiwanis. Home and Office: 5548 Canalino Dr Carpinteria CA 93013

SEAWELL, DONALD RAY, lawyer, producer; b. Jonesboro, N.C., Aug. 1, 1912; s. A.A.F. and Bertha (Smith) S.; A.B., U. N.C., 1933, J.D., 1936, D.Litt., 1980; D.H.L., U. No. Colo., 1978; m. Eugenia Rawls, Apr. 5, 1941; children—Brook Seawell Speidel, Donald Brockman. Admitted to N.C. bar, 1936, N.Y. bar, 1947; with SEC, 1939-41, 45-47, Dept. Justice, 1942-43; chmn. bd., dir. Denver Post, until 1981, Gravure West, Los Angeles; partner firm Bernstein, Seawell, Kaplan & Block, N.Y.C., 1947-75; of counsel Bernstein, Seawell & Kove, N.Y.C., 1975-79, Bernstein, Seawell, Kove & Maltin, 1979—; dir. Swan Prodns., London; partner Bonfils-Seawell Enterprises, N.Y.C. Chmn. bd. ANTA, 1965—; dir. Met. Nat. Bank. Mem. theatre panel Nat. Council Arts, 1970-74; bd. dirs. Newspaper Advt. Bur.; mem. Bus. Com. for the Arts; trustee Am. Acad. Dramatic Arts, 1967—, Hofstra U., 1968-69, Central City Opera Assn., Denver Symphony; co-chmn. Mayor's Commn. on Arts; gov. Royal Shakespeare Theatre, London; bd. dirs. Air Force Acad. Found., Nat. Inst. Outdoor Drama, Walter Hampden Meml. Library, Hammond Mus.; pres. Helen G. Bonfils Found., Frederick G. Bonfils Found.; chmn. bd. Bonfils Theatre, Denver Center Performing Arts; pres. Denver Opera Found.; chmn., pres. Civilian Mil. Inst. Served with U.S. Army, World War II. Recipient 1st Am. Heritage award Anti Defamation League of B'nai B'rith, 1973; award of excellence Am. Coll. Theatre Festival, 1973; Disting. Eagle award Boy Scouts Am., 1976; Gold Plate award Am. Acad. Achievement, 1980. Clubs: Bucks (London); Players, Dutch Treat (N.Y.C.); Denver Country, Denver, Cherry Hills Country, Mile High (Denver); Garden of Gods (Colorado Springs, Colo.). Office: 225 Broadway New York NY 10007 also Denver Center for Performing Arts 1050 13th St Denver CO 80204 also Denver Center Theatre Co 1050 13th St Denver CO 80204

SECORD, TERRENCE CLYDE, mech. engr.; b. Hollywood, Calif., July 7, 1927; s. Roy Clyde and Una (Vacelle) S.; B.Engring., U. So. Calif., 1950; m. Mary Rose George, June 30, 1951; 1 dau., Debra Ann. Group engr. airconditioning, thermodynamics Douglas Aircraft, Long Beach, Calif., 1950-59, supr. advance projects and mech. systems, Douglas Missile Space Systems div., Santa Monica, 1969-64; br. chief Life support and power MSSD, Santa Monica, 1964-65, asst. chief engr. advance biotechnology dept. McDonnell Douglas Astronautics Co., Huntington Beach, 1966-72; prin. engr. life sci. payloads, 1973-82, program mgr. life sci. research facility, 1983—. Served with AUS, 1945-46. Past mem. Daniel Guggenheim and Elmer A. Sperry Medal Bd. Awards. Registered profl. engr., Calif. Fellow ASME (chmn. and mem. numerous coms.), Inst. Advancement Engring. Clubs. Archimedes Circle, (Los Angeles); Trojan (U. So. Calif.). Contbr. to numerous publs. in field. Office: 3301 Bolsa Ave Huntington Beach CA 92647

SECRIST, DOLLY ALVAREZ, translator; b. Bucaramanga, Columbia, June 24; d. Justo Jose and Elvira Maria (Rodriquez) Alvarez; grad. John Robert Powers, 1966; A.A., El Camino Coll., 1971; student UCLA, 1971-73, grad. Dale Carnegie Sch., 1976, B.S., U. Beverly Hills, 1982; postgrad. Golden Gate U., 1983; m. Harold B. Secrist, Aug. 30, 1975, Varitypist Biddle Publ. Co., Los Angeles, 1963-67, exec. sec. Alfred M. Lewis Co., Riverside, Calif., 1967-69; multilingual exec. sec. Gen. Electric TEMPO, Santa Barbara, Calif., 1969-71; multilingual exec. sec. UCLA, Westwood, Calif, 1971-73; adminstrv. asst., translator, expediter Bechtel Power Corp., Los Angeles, 1973—. Mem. Nat. Assn. Female Execs., Calif. Bus. Women's Network, Success Motivation Inst. Roman Catholic. Club: Toastmasters (officer). Home: 17341 Chicago Ave Yorba Linda CA 92686 Office: 12400 E Imperial Hwy Norwalk CA 90650

SEDMAK, ALLAN ANTHONY, mech. engr.; b. Cleve., Nov. 24, 1938; s. Tony and Francis (Kuznick) S.; B.B.A. in Indsl. Mgmt., Cleve. State U., 1969; M.B.A. in Indsl. Mgmt., Case Western Res. U., 1975; m. Dorothy Elaine Johnston, Nov. 22, 1958; children—Allan P., Russell A., Dianna D., Jason A. Shop mgr. Warner & Swasey, Solon, Ohio, 1969-71, mgr. mfg., 1971-72, mgr. mfg., Cleve., 1972-75; plant supt. Outboard Marine Corp., Galesburg, Ill., 1975-78; plant mgr. Sundstrand Aviation, Denver, 1978-82, dir. plant ops., Denver, York, Nebr. and Singapore, 1982—; bus. cons. SBA, Cleve., 1974-75. Mem. adv. bd. Salvation Army, 1973-75, Denver YMCA, 1980—; mem. Sundstrand Polit. Action Com., Denver, 1980—. Mem. Personnel Mgrs. Assn. (pres.), ASME, Denver C. of C. Republican. Presbyn. Clubs: Rolling Hills Country (Golden, Colo.); Pinehurst Country (Denver). Home: 14105 W Maple Ave Golden CO 80401 Office: 2480 W 70th Ave Denver CO 80221

SEDWAY, MARVIN MARK, optometrist, state legislator; b. Bklyn., July 24, 1928; s. Jack and Yetta Sedway; B.S., Pacific U., 1953, O.D., 1954; m. Rona Good; children—Roger, Stephanie, Michael. Pvt. practice optometry, Las Vegas, Nev., 1955—; cons. Nev. State Spl. Children's Clinic; mem. Nev. Legislature from 15th dist. Mem. Nev. State Health Coordinating Council, 1982—, Clark County Health Systems Agy.; chmn. Nev. Humphrey for Pres. Com., 1968. Mem. Nev. State Bd. Optometrists (sec.-treas. 1971-82), Am. Optometric Assn., Nev. Optometric Assn. Democrat. Jewish. Home: 3578 Tioga Way Las Vegas NV 89109 Office: 3101 Maryland Pkwy Las Vegas NV 89109

SEE, MALIN ELIOT, management consultant; b. Berkeley, Calif., Mar. 16, 1938; s. Walter C. and Madge B. (Hostetter) S.; m. Ruth Whitmore Parker, Aug. 26, 1960; children—Christopher, Jennifer. Student U. San Diego, 1957-58, Iowa State Coll., 1958-59, UCLA, 1964-65, Calif. State U.-Long Beach, 1966-67. Sr. data processing mgmt. cons. Stanford Research Inst., Menlo Park, Calif., 1973-76; cons. McSweeney & Assocs., Newport Beach, Calif., 1979-80; v.p. br. ops./mktg. Central Fed. Savs., San Diego, 1977-78; pvt. practice data processing mgmt. cons., San Diego, 1981—. Outdoor leader Girl Scouts U.S.A., 1980—; active Boy Scouts Am. Office: 11750 Sorrento Valley Rd Suite 119 San Diego CA 92121

SEEGALL, MANFRED ISMAR LUDWIG, physical science research consultant, educator; b. Berlin, Germany, Dec. 23, 1929; s. Leonhard and Vera Antonie (Vodackova) S.; came to U.S., 1952, naturalized, 1957; m. Alma R. Sterner Clarke; 2 stepchildren—James, Mark. B.S. magna cum laude, Loyola Coll., 1957; M.S., Brown U., 1960; postgrad. Stuttgart (Germany) Tech. U., 1962-65. Research engr. Autonetics Corp. div. N.Am. Aviation, Downey, Calif., 1959-61; physicist Astronautics div. Gen. Dynamics, Inc., San Diego, 1961-62; research scientist Max Planck Inst., Stuttgart, 1962-65; instr. stats. and algebra San Diego City Coll., 1966; sr. research engr. Solar div. Internat. Harvester Co., San Diego, 1967-73; research cons. in energy and pollution, San Diego, 1974—; part-time evening instr. Mesa Coll., San Diego, 1980-81; instr. Grossmont Coll., El Cajon, Calif., 1981; sr. scientist Evaluation Research Corp., San Diego, 1981-82, RCS analyst Teledyne Micronetics, San Diego, 1983—. Mem. Am. Phys. Soc., Internat. Platform Assn., Calif. Parapsychology Found. (sec. research com.), Cottage of Czechoslovakia of House of Pacific Relations, Rosicrucian Order, Loyola Coll., Brown U. alumni assns. Republican. Club: San Diego Lodge AMORC (historian). Contbr. articles on acoustics, pollution and temp. measurement methods to tech. jours.; patentee in field. Address: 8735 Blue Lake Dr San Diego CA 92119

SEELEY, BARBARA GAIL, human services exec.; b. Grand Forks, N.D., June 7, 1936; d. Alfred Thomas and Florence Micken S.; B.S., UCLA, 1957; M.S.W., U. So. Calif., 1970; children—John Mark Doss, Timothy Stephen Doss, Elizabeth Gail Doss. Psychiat. social worker State of Calif., Pomona and Santa Ana, 1970-73; sr. clin. social worker Orange County Mental Health Dept., 1973-79, dep. dir. mental health, 1979-80, dep. regional mgr. human services agy., 1980-82, program mgr. mental health dept. Health Care Agy., 1982—; field educator San Diego State U. Sch. Social Work. Lic. marriage, family and child counselor; lic. clin. social worker. Mem. Acad. Cert. Social Workers, Nat. Assn. Social Workers, DAR. Methodist. Home: 3310 Seashore Dr Newport Beach CA 92663 Office: 1617 Westcliff Dr Newport Beach CA 92660

SEELEY, FRANCIS JOSEPH, advertising executive, consultant; b. Hoboken, N.J., Feb. 12, 1917; s. John Guy and Celeste Maria (Giribaldi) S.; m. Marian Jane Morby, Jan. 12, 1945; children—Linda Joy, Carleton John, Christina Joanne. Student, CCNY, 1932-34, Coast Arty. Officer Candidate Sch., Ft. Monroe, Va., 1942, Washington and Lee U., 1943, UCLA, 1964-65, Grossmont Coll., 1968; B.S., San Diego State Coll., 1971; M.A., Calif. State U.-San Diego, 1973. With Walker Engraving Co., N.Y.C., 1934-36, J. Walter Thompson Co., N.Y.C., 1936-37; actor, asst. producer-dir. WNEW, N.Y.C., 1934-35; actor, producer-dir. Rainbow House, WOR-Mut., N.Y.C., 1935-36; asst. radio editor N.Y. Daily Mirror, N.Y.C., 1936-39; chief editorial sect., sr. producer-writer Armed Forces Radio Service, Hollywood, Calif., 1943-55; chief copywriter Ray Cormier Advt., Hollywood, 1955-56; sr. v.p., creative dir. Capener Co., La Jolla, Calif., 1979-81; pres. Frank Seeley Advt., El Cajon, Calif., 1956-81; vis. lectr. San Diego State U., 1982-83; mem. faculty communication dept. Brigham Young U., Provo, Utah, 1974-75; cons. mktg., advt., tchr. communications, Hollywood, San Diego, 1949—. Founder, pres. El Cajon Young Republicans, 1957-59; v.p. God Bless Am. Week, 1961-68; bd. dirs. Travelers Aid of San Diego, 1968-73; charter mem. bd. dirs., sec. Eastern San Diego County Jr. Fair, 1965-68. Served from pvt. to capt. U.S. Army, 1940-46. Mem. San Diego Assn. Advt. Agys. (pres. 1961-63), Latter-day Saints Bus. and Profl. Assn. San Diego, AFTRA, Pacific Pioneer Broadcasters, Broadcast Edn. Assn., San Diego C. of C. (state govt. com. 1956-58). Republican. Mormon. Club: Masquers. Contbr. numerous programs, commls. to radio, TV, articles to various newspapers. Address: 522 Claydelle Ave El Cajon CA 92020

SEEMAN, MELVIN, sociology educator; b. Balt. Feb. 5, 1918; s. Morris and Sophie (Kostman) S.; m. Alice Ruth Zerbola, June 30, 1944; children—Teresa Ellen, Paul Daniel. B.A., Johns Hopkins U., 1944; M.A., Ohio State U., 1946, Ph.D., 1947. Lectr. to assoc. prof. Ohio State U., 1946-59; assoc. prof. to prof. UCLA, 1959—. Mem. Am. Sociol. Assn. Home: 21532 Paseo Serra Malibu CA 90265 Office: Dept Sociology UCLA 405 Hilgard Ave Los Angeles CA 90024

SEEMANN, VIRGINIA HANKS, fin. exec.; b. Oak Park, Ill., June 4, 1944; d. John Ferguson and Fern Juanita (Tomlin) S.; B.S.J., Northwestern U., 1969. Life sci. editor World Book Ency., Chgo., 1966-69; v.p. Continental Bank, Chgo., 1969-79; pres. Knutsford Holdings, Inc., Beverly Hills, Calif., 1979—. Bd. govs. Chgo. Symphony Orch., 1977—; bd. dirs. Goodman Theater, Chgo., 1978—. Named an Outstanding Woman, Ladies Home Jour., 1978. Clubs: Racquet, Arts, Los Angeles Tennis, Jr. League of Chgo. Office: 1749 S La Cienega Blvd Los Angeles CA 90035

SEETHALER, ALBIN JAMES, broadcasting company executive; b. Provo, Utah, Aug. 26, 1941; s. Joseph Albin and Dora Irene (Kirk) S.; student Brigham Young U., 1959-60, 63-66; m. Jacqueline Jenkins, Oct. 8, 1965; children—Brian, Nicole. Route salesman Seethalers, Inc., Provo, 1959-61, mgr. sales, 1964-66, v.p., 1966-70; missionary, fin. sec., counselor to pres. Austrian Mission, Mormon Ch., Vienna, 1961-63; salesman KUTV, Inc., Salt Lake City, 1970-74, gen. sales mgr., 1974-80, v.p. sales, 1980-81, v.p. and sta. mgr., 1981-83, v.p., gen. mgr., 1983—. Mem. Utah Advt. Fedn. (dir. 1977-79, chmn. silver medal award com. 1978-79), Utah Broadcasters Assn. (dir. 1979-83, v.p. 1980-81, pres. 1981-82), Rocky Mountain Broadcasters Assn. (dir. 1981-82). Clubs: Rotary, Riverside Country. Home: 2617 Grandview Dr Sandy UT 84092 Office: 2185 S 3600 W Salt Lake City UT 84119

SEETHALER, WILLIAM CHARLES, internat. bus. exec., cons.; b. N.Y.C., Dec. 4, 1937; s. William Charles and Catherine Frances (Flaherty) S.; student Quinnipiac Coll., Conn., 1955-56; engring. student Ohio State U., 1956-58; B.S. in Bus. Adminstrn., U. San Francisco, 1977; M.B.A., Pepperdine U., 1980; m. Helen Margaret Betts, Oct. 7, 1966; 1 stepson, John Zorn. Asst. to v.p. sales T. Sendzimir, Inc., Waterbury, Conn. and Paris, 1960-66; mgr. internat. ops. Dempsey Indsl. Furnace Co., E. Longmeadow, Mass., 1966-67; mgr. internat. sales Yoder Co., Cleve., 1967-74; mng. dir., owner Seethaler & Assocs.; owner, chief exec. officer Seethaler Internat. Ltd., Palo Alto, Calif., 1974—; partner DFS Computer Assocs., San Jose, Calif., 1976—. Bd. dirs. Palo Alto Fund, 1979—. Mem. Menlo Park, Palo Alto (v.p. orgn. affairs 1976-77, pres. 1977-78, dir. 1975-79) chambers commerce, Assn. Iron and Steel Engrs., U. San Francisco Alumni Assn., Stanford U. Alumni Assn., Pepperdine U. Alumni Assn., Assn. M.B.A. Execs., Am. Mgmt. Assn. Clubs: Stanford Buck, Stanford Cardinal Cage, Stanford Diamond.

SEETO, DEWEY QUIN, economist; b. San Francisco, Apr. 12, 1945; s. Howard Quin and Kay (Woo) S.; m. Big-Qu Chin, Apr. 29, 1978; children—Conrad, Derrick, Margot. S.B., MIT, 1968; Ph.D., Columbia U., 1974. Asst. prof. econs. Columbia U., N.Y.C., 1973-74, Rutgers U., New Brunswick, N.J., 1974-78; economist Pacific Gas and Electric Co., San Francisco, 1978—. bd. dirs. Chinese-Am. Democratic Club, San Francisco, 1978—; chmn. Chinese Am. Voter Edn. Com., 1982. Served with USAR, 1968-74. Columbia U. Pres.'s fellow, 1970; Earhart fellow, 1971; Woodrow Wilson Dissertation fellow, 1972. Mem. Am. Econ. Assn., Nat. Assn. Bus. Economists, Western Econ. Assn., AAUP, Internat. Assn. Energy Economists. Congregationalist. Contbr. articles to profl. jours. Home: 2 Balceta Ave San Francisco CA 94127 Office: Rate Dept Pacific Gas and Electric Co San Francisco CA 94106

SEFTON, WILLIAM LEE, accountant; b. San Francisco, Dec. 7, 1943; s. Seibert Lee and Mimi (Stone) S.; B.A. in Econs., Willamette U., 1965; M.Acctg., U. So. Calif., 1966; m. Wilann Jean Schneider, Feb. 14, 1970; 1 child, Robin. Consolidations acct. Buttes Gas & Oil, Oakland, Calif., 1974-76; asst. controller Calif. Pacific Utilities, San Francisco, 1976-78; controller Dataquest, Inc., Cupertino, Calif., 1978-80; pvt. practice pub. acctg., San Ramon, Calif., 1980—. Served with USCG, 1977. C.P.A., Calif. Mem. Am. Inst. C.P.A.s, Calif. Soc. C.P.A.s, Nat. Speakers Assn. Republican. Mormon. Home: 2011 St George Rd San Ramon CA 94583 Office: 12901 Alcosta Blvd Suite A San Ramon CA 94583

SEGAL, D. ROBERT, pub. co. exec.; b. Oshkosh, Wis., Oct. 30, 1920; s. Morris Henry and Ida (Belond) S.; m. Kathryn McKenzie; children—Jonathan McKenzie, Janet Elizabeth. Currently pres., dir. Freedom Newspapers, Inc., Santa Ana, Calif.; pres. Freedom Communications, Inc.; pres. Kinston (N.C.) Free-Press, New Bern (N.C.) Sun Jour., Burlington (N.C.) Times-News, Jacksonville (N.C.) Daily News, Freedom Newspapers of N.Y., Huron (S.D.) Daily Plainsman, Greenville (Miss.) Delta Dem. Pub. Co., Dothian (Ala.) Progress, Fla. Freedom, Sta. WLNE-TV. Trustee, Children's Hosp of Orange County (Calif.). Served with USAAF, 1942-45. Office: 1055 N Main Suite 901 Santa Ana CA 92711

SEGAL, JACOB, investment cons.; b. Iasi, Romania, Aug. 11, 1946; s. Rubin and Tova S.; came to U.S., 1973, naturalized, 1977; B.A. in Econs. and Statistics, Hebrew U., 1972, postgrad., 1972-73; M.B.A., U. Calif., Los Angeles, 1976; m. Geri Slobin, Sept. 20, 1972. Computer operator Computer Center, Hebrew U. Jerusalem, 1969-72, programmer, 1972-73; research asst. dept. fin. UCLA, 1975, teaching asst., 1975; economist Home Savs. & Loan Assn., Los Angeles, 1976-78, sr. research analyst, from 1978, now v.p., mgr. real estate ops.; real estate cons. Wagner/Jacobson Co., 1978—; instr. econs. Inst. Fin. Edn., Los Angeles, 1977-78. Mem. Am. Mgmt. Assn., U. Calif. Los Angeles Alumni Assn. Home: 3318 Coolidge Ave Los Angeles CA 90066 Office: 1801 Century Park E Suite 2212 Los Angeles CA 90067

SEGAN, KENNETH AKIVA, artist; b. N.Y.C., 1950. B.A. in Art, So. Ill. U., 1977; M.F.A. in Printmaking and Drawing, U. Mo., 1980. One man shows: So. Ill. U., Vergette Gallery, Carbondale, 1976, U. Mo., Columbia, 1980, U. Ill., Illini Union Gallery, Urbana, 1980, 82, Donald Batman Gallery, Kansas City, Mo., 1980, Temple de Hirsch Sinai, Seattle, 1981, Seattle First Nat. Bank Bldg., 1981, Howell Street Gallery, Seattle, 1981, Arthead Gallery, Seattle, 1981, Polack Gallery, Jewish Community Ctr., Mercer Island, Wash., 1982, Springfield (Ohio) Art Mus., 1982, Mittleman Jewish Community Ctr., Portland, Oreg., 1982, AIA Gallery, Seattle, 1983; group shows include: Dakota Artists Guild Black Hills Regional, Rapid City, S.D., 1979, 9th Ann. Works on Paper Nat., Southwest Tex. State U., San Marcos, 1979, Paper Fiber III, Iowa City Arts Council, Iowa City, 1980, 12th Ann. Southeastern. Artist Exhbn., Civic Ctr., Pine Bluff, 1980, West '80-Art and the Law Nat. Exhbn., St. Paul, 1980, West '82, Fall Festival of Biblical Art and Jewish Themes, Seattle, 1981, Recent Acquisitions: Works on Paper, Portland (Oreg.) Art Mus., 1983, Pacific States Prints and Drawings, U. Hawaii at Hilo and Honolulu Art Galleries, 1983, Anacortes (Wash.) Arts and Crafts Printmaking Exhbn., 1983, September Competition, Alexandria (La.) Mus., Visual Arts Ctr., 1983, Soc. Am. Graphic Artists 60th Ann., C.W. Post Coll. Gallery, L.I. and F.I.T. Gallery, N.Y.C., 1983; represented in permanent collections: Ark. Arts Ctr., Little Rock, Dahl Fine Arts Ctr., Rapid City, S.D., DeCordova and Dana Mus., Lincoln, Mass., Judah L. Magnes Meml. Mus., Berkeley, Calif., MIT Mus., Minn. Mus. of Art, St. Paul, Musee des Beaux-Arts, Budapest, Hungary, Mus. Am. Jewish History, Phila., Mus. Art and Archaeology, U. Mo., Nat. Mus. Am. History, Smithsonian Instn., Washington, N.J. State Mus., Trenton, N.J., Portland (Oreg.) Art Mus., Skirball Mus. Hebrew Union Coll., Los Angeles, Tulane U. Art Collection, New Orleans, William Rockhill Nelson Gallery, Atkins Mus. Kansas City, Mo.; also represented in univ. and library collections instl. corp. collections. Office: Studio 701 909 4th Ave Seattle WA 98104

SEGGER, MARTIN JOSEPH, museum dir.; b. Ipswich, Eng., Nov. 22, 1946; immigrated to Can., 1957, naturalized, 1971; m. Gerald Joseph and Lillian Joan (Barker-Emery) S.; B.A., U. Victoria (B.C., Can.), 1969, diploma edn., 1970; M.Phil., Warburg Inst., U. London, 1973; m. Angele Denise Cordonier, Oct. 18, 1944; children—Cara-Michelle, Marie-Claire, Margaret Ellen. Lectr. Renaissance art U. Victoria, 1971, 73; dir. tng. B.C. Provincial Mus., Victoria, 1974-77; lectr., dir. Maltwood Art Mus. and Gallery, U. Victoria, 1978; bd. govs. Heritage Can. Found., 1979—; bd. dirs. B.C. Heritage Trust, 1978—, Soc. Architecture in Can., 1979; mem. B.C. Heritage Adv. Bd., 1978—. Recipient Heritage Can. Communications award, 1977; Commendation award Am. Assn. State and Local History, 1980. Fellow Royal Soc. Arts; mem. Internat. Council Museums (dir. Can.), Can. Museums Assn., Soc. Study Architecture in Can., Soc. Archtl. Historians, Assn. Cultural Adminstrs., Nat. Trust U.K. Roman Catholic. Author: Arts of the Forgotten Pioneers, 1971; Victoria-An Architectural History, 1979; City of Victoria Conservation Study, 1975; This Old House, 1980; British Columbia Parliament Buildings, 1980; Heritage Canada, 1980; editor papers series Soc. Study Architecture in Can., 3 vols., 1981—. Office: U Victoria Box 1700 Victoria BC V8W 2Y2 Canada

SEGIL, ANNETTE ROSELLE, industrial psychologist, retail consultant; b. Boksburg, S. Africa; d. Arnold and Miriam (Segal) S.; came to U.S., 1980; M.S.W., U. Witwaterstand, South Africa, 1966, Ph.D. in Indsl. Psychology, 1980. Cert. indsl. psychologist, social worker, South Africa. Mktg. services officer, sociologist Rand Mines, Johannesburg, South Africa, 1968-70; sr. profl. officer South Africa Council Child Welfare, Johannesburg, 1971-72; v.p. manpower planning, devel. Greatermans Stores Inc., Johannesburg, 1973-76; chief officer personnel research Council for Sci. and Indsl. Research, Johannesburg, 1977-79; group v.p. The Kenzer Group of Cos., Los Angeles, 1980—. Exec. v.p. South Africa Inst. Personnel Mgmt., 1978-80; founder Black Mgmt. Assn. South Africa, 1979; bd. dirs. U.S.-South Africa Leadership Program, 1977-80; founder Adv. Com. on Profl. Personnel Matters to South African Govt., 1978-80. Recipient South Africa Inst. Personnel Mgmt. Disting. Achievement award, 1979; Jaycees Pres.'s Honor award, 1978. Fellow Royal Soc. Encouragement Arts, Manufactures and Commerce; mem. Am. Soc. Tng. and Devel., Am. Soc. Personnel Adminstrs., Nat. Retail Mchts. Assn., Am. Mgmt. Assn., Internat. Assn. Personnel Women, Inst. Personnel Mgmt. South Africa, Witwaterstand Social Workers, South African Psychol. Assn. Transvaal. Developed and implemented first postgrad. program in social adminstrn. at U. Witwaterstand, 1979. Home: 13930 Northwest Passage Apt 301 Marina Del Rey CA 90291 Office: Kenzer Corp 6033 W Century Blvd Suite 990 Los Angeles CA 90045

SEGRÈ, EMILIO, physicist, educator; b. Tivoli, Rome, Feb. 1, 1905; s. Giuseppe and Amelia (Treves) S.; came to U.S., 1938, naturalized, 1944; Ph.D., U. Rome, 1928; Dr. honoris causa, U. Palermo (Italy), Gustavus Adolphus Coll., St. Peter, Minn., Tel Aviv U.; m. Elfriede Spiro, Feb. 2, 1936 (dec. Oct. 1970); children—Claudio, Amelia, Fausta; m. 2d, Rosa Mines, Feb. 12, 1972. Asst. prof. U. Rome, 1932-36; dir. physics lab. U. Palermo, 1936-38; research asso. U. Calif., Berkeley, 1938-43, prof. physics, 1945-72, prof. emeritus, 1972—, group leader Los Alamos Sci. Lab., 1943-46; hon. prof. St. Marcos U., Lima, Peru; vis. prof. U. Ill., Purdue U.; prof. physics U. Rome, 1974-80. Recipient Hofmann medal German Chem. Soc., Cannizzaro medal Accad. Lincei; Nobel prize in physics, 1959; decorated Great Cross Merit Republic of Italy; medal Benemeriti Cultura, Italy: Rockefeller Found. fellow, 1930-31; Guggenheim Found. fellow, 1958. Fellow Am. Phys. Soc.; mem. Nat. Acad. Scis., Am. Philos. Soc., Am. Acad. Arts and Scis., Heidelberg Akademie Wissenschaften, European Phys. Soc., Acad. Scis. Peru, Soc. Progress of Sci. (Uruguay), Società Italiana di fisica, Accad. Naz. Lincei (Italy), Accademia dei XL (Italy), Indian Acad. Scis. Bangalore, Phi Beta Kappa. Co-discoverer slow neutrons, elements technetium, astatine, plutonium and the antiproton. Home: 3802 Quail Ridge Rd Lafayette CA 94549 Office: Dept Physics U Calif Berkeley CA 94720

SEIBEL, STUART DALE, broadcasting exec.; b. Newton, Kans., Sept. 10, 1942; s. Arthur H. and Louise (Klassen) S.; student Bethany (Okla.) Coll., 1960-61, Wichita State U., 1961-63; m. Carol Nadine Helms, Aug. 24, 1963; children—Michael, Melinda, Stephani. Announcer, Sta. KCLO, Leavenworth, Kans., 1957-59, Sta. KBKC, Mission, Kans., 1959-60; engr. Sta. KMBC-TV, Kansas City, Mo., 1960; engr., announcer Sta. KOMA, Oklahoma City, 1960-61; announcer Sta. KLEO, Wichita, 1961-63, Sta. KIOA, Des Moines, 1963-65; co-owner Sta. KOLR, Sterling, Colo., 1965-66; studio mgr. Sta. KTVS-TV, Sterling, 1966-73; program and promotion mgr. Sta. KYCU-TV, Cheyenne, Wyo., 1973-81; program and promotion mgr. Cascade Broadcasting Co. (KIMA-TV), Yakima, Wash., 1981—. Mem. home health bd DePaul Hosp., Cheyenne, 1980-81; mem. Wyo. Gov.'s Commn. on Libraries and Info. Services. Mem. Radio TV News Dirs. Assn., Nat. Assn. TV Program Execs., Yakima C. of C. Lutheran. Club: Masons. N.E. Colo. corr. Denver Post, 1969-72. Office: 2801 Terrace Heights Rd Yakima WA 98907

SEIF, DEBRA LEE, controller, special events coordinator, caterer; b. Knoxville, Tenn., June 2, 1948; d. Morris S. and Ann K. Seif. Student Ind. U., 1967-68. Engaged in secretarial work Warner Bros. Film Distbn., Los Angeles, 1969, vocat. edn. dept. UCLA, 1970-74; sec., research asst. J.D. Power & Assocs., Los Angeles, 1974-76; exec. sec. Bernstein, Fox Accountancy Corp., Los Angeles, 1976-78; controller, spl. events coordinator KDC Distbg., Inc., Arcadia, Calif., 1978—; cons. bus. mgmt. Mem. nat. com. Republican party. Mem. Ch. of Nazarene.

SEIFERT, EMIL GEORGE, parks and recreation director; b. Sacramento, Nov. 20, 1918; s. Emil Richard and Rosalia (Hovath) S.; m. Melba Lorane Armstrong, Mar. 19, 1943; 1 son, Richard. B.A., St. Cloud U.; B.A., teaching cert. U. Pacific, 1948. Recreation supr. City of Stockton, Calif., 1948-54, supt. recreation, 1954-56, dir. parks and recreation, 1956—. Sec., Met. Parks and Recreation Commn.; pres. Stockton Jr. Coll. Hockey Club; past pres. Sr. Service Agy., mem.-at-large No. Calif. Jr. Hockey Assn. Served to capt. AUS, 1940-46. Mem. Calif. Park and Recreation Soc., Nat. Parks and Recreation Assn., Pub. Works Adminstrs. Assn., Am. Legion (2d v.p.). Republican. Roman Catholic. Clubs: San Joaquin Lions (past pres.), Moose, Eagles. Home: 2233 Manchester St Stockton CA 95204 Office: City Hall Room 301 Stockton CA 95202

SEIFERT, WOLFGANG KLAUS, chemist; b. Obernigk, Germany, Jan. 18, 1931; s. Franz and Gertrud Seifert; came to U.S., 1958; B.S. in Chemistry, Inst. Tech., Munich, Germany, 1952, M.S., 1956, Ph.D., 1958; M.S. in Bus. Adminstrn., U. Colo., 1960; m. Ingrid C. Hofmann, Aug. 29, 1959; children—Karin S., Birgit E. Postdoctoral fellow U. Colo., 1958-60; with Chevron Oil Field Research Co., Richmond, Calif., 1960—, sr. research asso., 1969—; tchr. petroleum chemistry U. Calif. at Berkeley Extension Div.; indsl. mem. del. U.S.-USSR Joint Working Group Oil Experts, USSR, 1978; vice-chmn. Gordon Research Conf. Organic Geochemistry, 1980, chmn., 1982—; invited lectr. internat. symposium, Munich, 1979, 10th World Petroleum Congress, Romania, 1979, 9th JPA meeting, Indonesia, 1980. Recipient Best Publ. award organic geochemistry div. Geochem. Soc., 1972, 78. Contbr. chpt. to Progress in the Chemistry of Organic Natural Products, vol. 32, 1975; also articles to profl. publs. Patentee in field. Home: 52 Katrina Ln San Anselmo CA 94960 Office: 576 Standard Ave Richmond CA 94802

SEIGLE, JOHN THOMAS, tax and business planning consulting company executive; b. Boulder, Colo., May 13, 1930; s. Everett Edward and Esther Elberta (Balis) S.; m. Dorlis Faith Sutton, Apr. 3, 1953; children—Sidney, Sharon, Jonathan, Amanda; m. 2d, Kathy Lynette Kaler, May 8, 1981. B.S., U. Utah, 1952; LL.D., Golden Gate U., 1962. Bar: Calif. 1963. Staff acct. John F. Forbes & Co., C.P.A.s, San Francisco, 1952-64, ptnr., 1964—. Served with USN, 1952-54. Mem. ABA, Calif. State Bar Assn., San Francisco Bar Assn., Am. Inst. C.P.A.s, Calif. Soc. C.P.A.s, San Francisco C. of C. (recipient U.S. Senator award 1967). Republican. Clubs: Villa Taverna, Stock Exchange, DeMolay (San Francisco). Office: Suite 300 4 Embarcadero Center San Francisco CA 94111

SEIM, EDWIN CHARLES, soil scientist, agronomist, educator, consultant; b. St. Louis, Oct. 9, 1932; s. Edwin Carl and Philipina (Reeg) S.; m. Livia Pellegrini, Jan. 3, 1959; children—Carla Philipina Seim Morey, Edwin Carlo. B.S. in Agr., U. Mo., 1954; M.S. in Soil Sci., U. Minn., 1966, Ph.D. in Soil Sci., 1970. Cert. profl. soil scientist and agronomist. Sales agronomist Allied Chem. Corp., N.W. Mo., 1956-58, So. Minn., 1958-60; agr. lab. technician Purity Oats, Gen. Mills, Mpls., 1960-62; research asst. dept. soil sci. U. Minn., St. Paul, 1962-68, teaching asst., 1968-70; postdoctoral fellow dept. agronomy, U. Nebr., Lincoln, 1970-72; sr. horticulturist, research and devel. Hunt Wesson Foods, Davis, Calif., 1972-74, group leader, 1974-77; agronomist, agrl. research Basic Vegetable, Inc., King City, Calif., 1977-78; asst. prof. dept. soil sci. Calif. Poly. State U., San Luis Obispo, 1978—; cons., researcher fertilizers, soil and water and plant relationships. Active Italian Cath. Fedn., Republican Party. Served to 1st lt. U.S. Army, 1954-56. Kroger scholar, 1950; Lange fellow, 1953, 54. Mem. AAAS, Council for Agrl. Sci. and Tech., Am. Soc. Agronomy, Soil Sci. Soc. Am., Soil Conservation Soc. Am., Internat. Soil Sci. Soc., Am. Inst. Biol. Sci., Alpha Zeta, Alpha Gamma Rho. Author research publs., abstracts. Home: 292 Charles Dr San Luis Obispo CA 93401 Office: Dept Soil Sci Calif Poly State Univ San Luis Obispo CA 93407

SEIMAS, JOHN STEPHEN (JACK), ground space environment engr.; b. San Jose, Calif., June 15, 1943; s. John Carlos and Viola Ramona (Garcia) S.; B.E.E., U. Santa Clara (Calif.), 1967, A.S. in Biology, West Valley Coll., 1971; B.A. in Biology, San Jose State U., 1976, M.A., 1979, postgrad. in chemistry, 1979—; m. Rosalie Annette Garcia, Aug. 1, 1965; children—John, Peter, James. Elec. engr. Dalmo Victor Co., Belmont, Calif., 1967, AmLabs, Sunnyvale, Calif., 1967-68, Air Force Satellite Test Center, Sunnyvale, 1968—. Served with USMCR, 1963-69. Recipient Apollo Achievement award NASA, 1969, Skylab Achievement award, 1974. Mem. Am. Radio Relay League (life), Am. Motorcyclist Assn. (charter life). Roman Catholic. Home: 1125 Archer Way Campbell CA 95008 Office: Sunnyvale Air Force Sta PO Box 430 Sunnyvale CA 94086

SEITZ, LAURA RUTH, graphic design company sales executive; b. Detroit, Nov. 29, 1951; d. John Calvin and Charlotte Mary (Collins) Seitz. Student Western Mich. U., 1969-72, Los Angeles Mcpl. Art Galleries, 1975-78, UCLA, 1978. Clothing designer, dressmaker Moonshadow Designs, Ann Arbor and Los Angeles, 1974-77; sales coordinator Edwards Bros. Inc., Ann Arbor, 1973-74; sec. Maher Elen Advt., Los Angeles, 1976-79; account exec., 1979-80, account supr., 1980-81; sales mgr. Sojourn Design Group, Pico Rivera, Calif., 1981-82; dir. sales and mktg. John Anselmo Design Assocs., Santa Monica, Calif., 1982—; cons., freelance copywriting, lectr. Mem. task force NOW, 1977; mem. Olympics Steering Com., Muscular Dystrophy Assn., 1979; mem. Superwalk Steering Com., March of Dimes, 1981. Mem. Los Angeles Ad Club, Nat. Assn. Female Execs., Internat. Assn. Bus. Communicators. Office: 233 Wilshire Blvd Suite 330 Santa Monica CA 90401

SEI WILSON, JEANNE, kitchen design consultant; b. Albuquerque, Sept. 23, 1949; d. Frank Joseph and Ida Rose (Monte) S.; B.S., U.

N.Mex., 1971. Home economist Public Service Co. N.Mex., Albuquerque, 1972-75, consumer info. specialist, 1975-77, edn. specialist, 1977-81; mem. consumer adv. council Albuquerque Public Schs., 1974; columnist, cons., 1975—; cons. The New Mexican, 1975—; cons. design custom kitchen, 1976—. Mem. nominating com. Sangre de Cristo council Girl Scouts U.S.A., 1981-83. Mem. Build Contractors Women's Aux. (social chmn. 1978), N.Mex. Home Econs. Assn. (chmn. public affairs 1978-80, pres. 1980-81, Home Economist of Yr. 1982), Illuminating Engring. Soc., Am. Home Econs. Assn., Home Economists in Bus. (past pres.). Democrat. Roman Catholic. Office: PO Box 2851 Santa Fe NM 87501

SEKI, AKIHIKO, wholesale company executive; b. Tokyo, Aug 18, 1939; s. Ayajiro and Michiko (Aoki) S.; B.A., Keio U., 1963; m. Asako Sato, May 5, 1965; children—Kaoruko, Akio. Aircraft mgr. C. Itoh & Co. Ltd., London, 1969-71, mgr. machinery dept., Nairobi, 1971-74, dep. mgr. indsl. electronics dept., Tokyo, 1974-79, v.p. C. Itoh Electronics, Los Angeles, 1979—. Clubs: Porter Valley Country, Marina City, Porter Valley Country. Home: 6650 El Rodeo Rd Rancho Palos Verdes CA 90274 Office: 5301 Beethoven St Los Angeles CA 90066

SELBY, ALYCE PATRICIA CORNYN, communications exec.; b. Wright-Patterson AFB, Ohio, Nov. 22, 1946; d. William B. and Alice Ruth (Kill) Sellers; B.A. in Communications and Mgmt., Marylhurst (Oreg.) Coll., 1980; 1 dau., Patricia Kathleen. Prodn. mgr. Instrumentalist Pub. Co., Evanston, Ill., 1971-72; design and reprographics mgr. Stevens, Thompson & Runyan Engrs./Planners Inc., Portland, Oreg., 1973-76; visual communications mgr. Port of Portland, 1976—; pres. Alyce Enterprises, Portland, 1979—; ptnr. Vintage Tin Prodns.; graphics cons. Oreg. Communicators Assn., 1979-80; instr. U. Hawaii, Honolulu, 1979-81, Portland Art Mus., 1979-81; chmn. graphics tech. adv. bd. Mt. Hood (Oreg.) Community Coll., 1975-77; Mem. Inst. Profl. and Managerial Women, Designers Roundtable, In-plant Printing Mgrs. Assn. Home: 1928 SE Ladd Ave Portland OR 97214 Office: 700 NE Multnomah Portland OR 97232

SELDITCH, ALAN DANIEL, environ. mgmt. engr.; b. Phila., Sept. 8, 1926; s. Jacob and Sarah Molly (Simons) S.; student St. Lawrence U., 1944-46; B.S., U. So. Calif., 1948; B.S. in Environ. Sci., Heed U., 1981, M.S., 1982, Ph.D., 1983; B.A. in Law, Thomas Jefferson U., 1982. postgrad. Los Angeles City Coll., LaSalle U.; children—Gretchen, Edward, Michael, Ronald, Kimberly. Chief projects and engring., pres. Sigma Assos., Los Angeles, 1950-57; chief indsl. and project engr. Semco, Sweet & Mayers, Los Angeles, 1957-61; mgr. indsl. engring. and plant maintenance Rexall Drug & Chem. Co., 1962-65; regional cons. mgr. H.B. Maynard & Co., Sherman Oaks, Calif., 1965-69; asst. to pres. P.O.P. Systems/ISI, Santa Ana, Calif., 1970-72; mgr. facilities and corp. planning Systems Resource Recovery/System Assos., Long Beach, Calif., 1972-75; gen. mgr. Flowtrace, Los Angeles, 1975-78; mgr. environ. affairs Signetics, Sunnyvale, Calif., 1978—; pres. A.D. Selditch & Assos., Newark, Calif., 1977—. Served with USNR, 1944-46. Registered profl. engr., Calif.; cert. profl. methods engr. Maynard Research Inst., 1969. Mem. AAAS, Am. Inst. Indsl. Engrs., Am. Pub. Works Assn., Am. Soc. Mgmt., ASME, Am. Soc. Metals, Am. Soc. Standards, Assn. Energy Engrs., Calif. Soc. Profl. Engrs., Govtl. Refuse Collection and Disposal Assn., Internat. Material Mgmt. Soc. (cert. in material mgmt. and handling), IEEE, Inst. Solid Wastes, Los Angeles Forum Solid Waste Mgmt., Mgmt. Inst. Los Angeles, Methods, Time-Measurement Assn. for Standards and Research (cert.), Nat. Assn. Solid Waste Mgmt., Nat. Soc. Profl. Engrs. Republican. Jewish. Contbr. articles to profl. jours. Home and Office: 6267 #E Joaquin Murieta Ave Newark CA 94560

SELENIUS, ONNI ERIC, engr.; b. Mass., July 21, 1933; s. Viljo and Mary (Jussilia) S., A.A., Victor Valley Coll., B.A., Calif. State Coll., San Bernardino; Ph.D.; D.D. Gen. mgr. Valley Avionics Corp., Calif., 1968-75; communications systems engr. Mobil Oil Corp., Torrance, Calif., 1975—; cons. U.S. Engring. Co., Calif., 1973-76; prof. graphic arts Van Nuys Coll., 1975; mem. aeros. adv. com. Victor Valley Coll., 1969-73; dir. Calif. State Civil Service Employment Commn., 1973-76; individual elec. contractor, Calif., 1977—. Chmn., County Mental Health Commn., 1972. Served with USN, 1952-60. Lic. elec. contractor, Calif. Mem. Nat., Calif. (sr.) socs. profl. engrs., IEEE (sr.), Armed Forces Communications and Electronics Assn. (life), Innovation Group for Tech. Communications (charter), Am. Radio Relay League, Am. Radio Club, Calif. State Coll. Alumni Assn., U.S. Power Squadron, Aircraft Owners and Pilots Assn., Am. Legion, VFW, Am. Hist. Assn., Nat. Hist. Soc., Internat. Platform Assn., Am. Mgmt. Assn., Am. Inst. Aeros. and Astronautics, AAAS, Soc. Broadcast Engrs., Marine Tech. Soc. Club: Eagles. Columnist, Calif. Vet. Lit. Rev., 1970—. Home: PO Box 909 Apple Valley CA 92307

SELF, EDWIN FORBES, editor, publisher; b. Dundee, Scotland, June 15, 1920; s. Robert Henry and Agnes (Dick) S.; A.B. magna cum laude with distinction in Polit. Sci., Dartmouth Coll., 1942; m. Dorothy McCloskey, Nov. 1, 1942; children—Joan, Robert; m. 2d, Gloria Eileen Winke Wade, Aug. 18, 1951; children—Winke, Carey. Advt. mgr. La Jolla (Calif.) Light, 1946; pub. North Shores Sentinel, Pacific Beach, Calif., 1947-48; bus. mgr. Frontier Mag., Los Angeles, 1949-55; editor, publisher San Diego Mag., 1948—; publisher cons. for San Francisco mag.; pub. cons. Washingtonian Mag. Mem. La Jolla Museum Art. Recipient Telesu award, Am. Inst. Planners, San Diego, 1963, Pub. Info. award Calif. A.I.A., 1970. Mem. San Diego C. of C., Phi Beta Kappa, Delta Tau Delta, Sigma Delta Chi. Clubs: La Jolla Country, Tennis. Home: La Jolla CA 92037 Office: 3254 Rosecrans St San Diego CA 92110

SELIG, JOHN MALCOLM, political science educator; consultant; b. San Francisco, Nov. 2, 1912; s. David and Matilda Florence (Doyle) S.; m. Elizabeth Ann McCrea, June 30, 1962. B.S., U. San Francisco, 1935; M.A., U. Calif.-Berkeley, 1938, Ph.D., 1953. Mem. faculty dept. polit. sci. City Coll. San Francisco, 1936-72, 1973-78, 82—, asst. to chancellor supt. San Francisco Community Coll. Dist., 1972-73; exec. dir. San Francisco Consortium, 1979-80, cons., 1981. Mem. Calif. Tchrs. Assn. (pres. San Francisco Higher Edn. Assn., (1971-74, WHO award 1972), No. Calif. Polit. Sci. Assn. (v.p. 1954, pres. 1955, sec.-treas. 1958-81; presl. citation award 1959, 82), Univ. San Francisco Edn. Club (pres. 1957-58), Am. Polit. Sci. Assn., Am. Soc. Pub. Adminstrn., Nat. Mcpl. League. Democrat. Club: University (San Francisco). Author: History of the San Francisco Consortium, 1981; contbg. editor: Dictionary of Political Science, 1981; contbr. articles to profl. jours. Home: 45 Fernwood Dr San Francisco CA 94127 Office: Dept Polit Sci City College San Francisco San Francisco CA 94112

SELL, JAMES DOYLE, geol. engr.; b. Casa Grande, Ariz., Apr. 25, 1930; s. William Henry and Ida May (Wegman) S.; Geol. Engr., Colo. Sch. Mines, Golden, 1955; M.S. in Geology, U. Ariz., Tucson, 1961; m. Margaret E. Smith, Dec. 27, 1956; children—Thomas A., Catherine M., Mark A. Sampler, drilling project U.S. Bur. Mines, Johnson Camp, Ariz., 1948; geologist Magma Copper Co., Superior, Ariz., 1955-61; geologist minerals div. Superior Oil Co., Denver, 1961-62, Tucson, 1962-63; geologist ASARCO, Tucson, 1963-82, mgr. S.W. expl., 1983—. Active Boy Scouts Am. Served to sgt., 45th inf. AUS, 1951-52; Korea. Mem. Ariz. Geol. Soc. (pres. 1973-74), Geol. Soc. Am. (meeting treas. 1968), Am. Inst. Profl. Geologists (nat. meeting planning com. 1975), Ariz. Acad. Sci. (life), Am. Inst. Mining Engrs., Soc. Econ. Geologists, Internal Assn. on Genesis Ore Deposits, Am. Quaternary Assn., Mining Club S.W. (charter; bd. govs. 1978-81). Home: 2762 W Holladay St Tucson AZ 85746 Office: PO Box 5747 Tucson AZ 85703

SELL, ROBERT EMERSON, elec. engr.; b. Freeport, Ill., Apr. 23, 1929; s. Cecil Leroy and Ona Arletta (Stevens) S.; B.S., U. Nebr., 1962; m. Ora Lucile Colton, Nov. 7, 1970. Chief draftsman Dempster Mill Mfg. Co., Beatrice, Nebr., 1949-53; designer-engr. U. Neb., Lincoln, 1955-65; elec. design engr. Kirkham, Michael & Assos., Omaha, 1965-67; elec. design engr. Leo A. Daly Co., Omaha, St. Louis, 1967-69; mech. design engr. Hellmuth, Obata, Kassabaum, St. Louis, 1969-70; chief elec. engr. Biagi-Hannan & Assos., Inc., Evansville, Ind., 1971-74; elec. project engr. H.L. Yoh Co., under contract to Monsanto Co., Creve Coeur, Mo., 1974-77; elec. project engr. Dhillon Engrs., Inc., Portland, Oreg., 1978—; instr. Basic Inst. Tech., St. Louis, 1971. Registered profl. engr., Nebr., Mo., Ill., Ind. O., W.Va., Ky., Ark., Tex., Oreg., Wash. Mem. ASHRAE, IEEE. Home: PO Box 02242 Portland OR 97202 Office: Suite 603 1600 SW 4th St Portland OR 97201

SELLERS, CAROL, lawyer; b. Durham, N.C., Mar. 2, 1943; d. George Grover and Mae (Savage) Sellers; m. James K. Herbert, Nov. 13, 1980; children—John, Kathie, Paul, Barry. B.A., Duke U., 1964; J.D. cum laude, Whittier Sch. Law, 1976. Bar: Calif. 1976. Tchr. high sch. English, Heber, Utah, 1964-67; founder, exec. dir. Fremont Scholastic Inst., Salt Lake City, 1967-71; adminstr. Office of Dean, Whittier Sch. Law, Los Angeles, 1973-76; assoc. Katz, Granof, Palarz, Beverly Hills, Calif., 1976-78; dir. Western div. Harcourt Brace Jovanovich Legal and Profl. Publs., 1977-81, pres., exec. dir. Harcourt Brace Jovanovich Multistate Workshop, 1981—; dean San Joaquin Coll. Law, 1982—; lectr. women in legal and bus. professions. Angier B. Duke scholar, 1961-64; Beverly Rubens Gordon scholar, 1972-76. Mem. Beverly Hills Bar Assn., Fresno County Bar Assn., Assn. Women and Law Com. (1st chmn. 1977), ABA. Home: 4412 N Wilson St Fresno CA 93704 Office: 11801 W Olympic St Suite 7 Los Angeles CA 93704

SELLS, THOMAS BARRY, accountant; b. Tulsa, Sept. 28, 1945; s. Halloway C. and Edna (Terrell) S.; B.S. in Acctg., U. So. Calif., 1972; m. Balorie Curry, Dec. 31, 1980. Media asst. Carson/Roberts/Inc., Advt., Los Angeles, 1969-71; supervising sr. acct. S.D. Leidosdorf & Co., Los Angeles, 1972-76; pres. TBS Associates, Inc., Los Angeles, 1977-78; instr. acctg. and econs. Los Angeles S.W. Coll. 1976—; prin. Thomas B. Sells, acct., Los Angeles, 1976—. Mem. ad hoc com. on revenue and taxation Los Angeles City Council, 1974-75; bd. dirs. Carter Agy., Los Angeles, 1976-78; bd. dirs. acctg. support group Sch. Acctg., U. So. Calif., 1980—. Served to sgt., inf., U.S. Army, 1964-68; Vietnam. Decorated Purple Heart, Bronze Star. Mem. Am. Inst. C.P.A.s, Calif. State Soc. C.P.A.s, Nat. Assn. Back Accts., Am. Arbitration Assn., U. So. Calif. Commerce Assos., Century City C. of C., Alpha Kappa Psi (s.w. regional dir. 1976-78, nat. v.p. alumni affairs 1979-81). Home: 22914 W Calvello Dr Valencia CA 91355 Office: 8665 Wilshire Blvd Suite 404 Beverly Hills CA 90211

SELMEIER, RICHARD JAMES, consumer financial services company executive; b. Grosse Pointe, Mich., Mar. 19, 1943; s. Henry Leroy and Richalou Mae (Hopson) S.; m. Lauren Kay Schueler, Jan. 2, 1983. B.B.A., U. Mich., 1965, M.B.A., 1966. With Procter & Gamble Brand Mgmt., Cin., 1966-76; with Foote, Cone & Belding Advt. Agy., San Francisco, 1976-79; pvt. practice mgmt. cons., San Francisco, 1979—; v.p. Am. Express, San Francisco, 1981—; cons. mktg., advt. Served to lt. USN, 1967-70. Mem. Commonwealth Club San Francisco, Am. Mgmt. Assn., U. Mich. Alumni Assn. (pres. 1973-75), Lambda Chi Alpha. Republican. Clubs: San Francisco Yacht, Tiburon Yacht. Home: 4670 Paradise Dr Tiburon CA 94920 Office: Am Express Co 601 Montgomery St Suite 725 San Francisco CA 94111

SELPH, ALBERT PIKE, III, geophysicist; b. New Orleans, Mar. 24, 1936; s. Albert P., Jr. and Edith A. (Breaux) S.; m. Sallye DeRussy, May 31, 1958; children—Albert IV, J. Scott, Stacy Lynn. B.S. in Geology, Tulane U., 1960, postgrad., 1960-62. Geophysicist, Mobil Oil, La., Tex., Fla., Colo., Calif., Alaska, 1962-68, 70-73, seismic party chief, 1968-70; geophysicist Union Oil (Alaska), Anchorage, 1973-77, dist. geophysicist, Anchorage, 1977—. Precinct chmn. Dist. 10 Republican party, 1973-75. Served with USN, 1954-56. Mem. Soc. Exploration Geophysics, Am. Assn. Petroleum Geologists, Alaska Geologic Soc., Alaska Geophys. Soc. Roman Catholic. Club: Anchorage Racquet. Office: Union Oil Co 909 W 9th St Anchorage AK 99501

SELZER, ARTHUR, cardiologist; b. Lwow, Poland, July 3, 1911; s. Martin and Janina (Lam) S.; came to U.S., 1938, naturalized, 1945; M.D., U. Cracow (Poland), 1936; postgrad. U. London (Eng.), 1936-38; m. Jadwiga Winkler, July 31, 1936; children—Martin Arthur, Peter Michael. Intern, Univ. Hosp., Lwow, 1935-36; vol. asst. Hammersmith Hosp., also Nat. Heart Hosp., London, 1936-38; practice medicine specializing in cardiology, San Francisco, 1941-59; cons. cardiology, San Francisco, 1959—; mem. faculty Sch. Medicine, Stanford U., 1941—, clin. prof. medicine, 1957-76, clin. prof. emeritus, 1976—; mem. faculty Sch. Medicine, U. Calif.-San Francisco, 1960—, clin. prof. medicine, 1960—; mem. staff Presbyn. Hosp., San Francisco, chief cardiology, 1959—. Chmn., Community Chest Health Council, 1953-55. Fellow ACP, Am. Coll. Cardiology; mem. Calif. Acad. Medicine (pres. 1972-73). Author: The Heart: Its Function in Health and Disease, 1966; Principles of Clinical Cardiology, 1975, 2d edit., 1983. Contbr. articles to profl. jours. and encys. Home: 5 Greenview Ln Hillsborough CA 94010 Office: Clay and Buchanan Sts San Francisco CA 94115

SELZNICK, STEPHEN ANDREW, computer software executive; b. N.Y.C.; s. Murray and Gertrude S.; children—Jonathan, Marc. B.S.E.E., U. Miami (Fla.), 1963. Programmer, Boeing Corp., Huntsville, Ala., 1963-64; systems analyst Gen. Dynamics, Pomona, Calif., 1964-66, Walter V. Sterling, Inc., Claremont, Calif., 1966-69; dir. data processing Genge, Inc. (Systems Planning Corp.), Los Angeles, 1970-77; pres. Professional Software Applications, Inc., Los Angeles, 1977—; instr. Calif. Poly. U., 1974-77. Office: 599 Barranca St Suite 555 Covina CA 91722

SEMEL, TERRY STEVEN, motion picture company executive; b. N.Y.C., Feb. 24, 1943; s. Ben and Mildred (Wenig) S.; B.S. in Acctg., L.I.U., 1964; postgrad. in market research CCNY, 1966-67; m. Jane Bovingdon, Aug. 24, 1977; 1 son, Eric Scott. Domestic sales mgr. C.B.S.-Cinema Center Films, Studio City, Calif., 1970-72; v.p., gen. mgr. Walt Disney's Buena Vista, Burbank, Calif., 1972-75; pres. W.B. Distbn. Corp., Burbank, 1975-78; exec. v.p., chief operating officer Warner Bros. Inc., Burbank, from 1979, now pres. Office: Warner Bros Inc 4000 Warner Blvd Burbank CA 91505

SEMENZA, LAWRENCE JOHN, lawyer; b. San Francisco, Nov. 1, 1942; s. Lawrence J. and Helen Maurine (Dearing) S.; m. Leanne Lowe, Sept. 10, 1966; 1 son, Lawrence J. III. Student Menlo Coll., 1960-62; A.B., U. Nev., Reno, 1965; J.D., U. Utah, 1968; postgrad Sch. Law N.Y. U., 1968-69; Bar: Nev. 1968, Calif. 1970, U.S. Dist. Ct. (no. dist.) Calif. 1970, U.S. Dist. Ct. (cer. dist.) Calif. 1979, U.S. Dist. Ct. (ea. dist.) Calif. 1982, U.S. Ct. Appeals (9th cir.) 1970; U.S. Ct. Appeals (10th cir.) 1979, U.S. Supreme Ct. 1981. Mem. firm Breen, Young, Whitehead & Hoy, Reno, 1969-70; asst. U.S. atty., Reno and Las Vegas, Nev., 1970-75; U.S. atty. Dist. Nev., 1975-77; ptnr. Semenza, Murphy & Pro, Reno, 1978-79, Belford & Semenza, 1979-80, Polaha Conner, Semenza & Luffy, Chartered, Reno, 1981-82, sr. ptnr., 1982; sr. ptnr. Semenza, Lufty & Griffin, Reno, 1983—. Sole practice, Reno, 1980-81. Mem. ABA, Nev. Bar Assn., Washoe County Bar Assn., Clark County Bar Assn., Calif. Bar Assn., San Francisco Bar Assn., Fed. Bar Assn., Nev. Trial Lawyers, Nat. Assn. Criminal Def. Lawyers, Nat. Assn. Former U.S. Attys. Office: 386 Holcomb Ave Suite 1 Reno NV 89506 also PO Box 11125 Reno NV 89510

SEMONES, JOANN, journalist, lecturer; b. Midland, Tex., Oct. 28, 1945; d. George William and Grace Marie (O'Neill) S. B.A., Calif. State U.-Northridge, 1968; postgrad. Am. U., Washington; M.P.A., Golden Gate U., 1978. Reporter, photographer San Fernando (Calif.) Valley Sun, 1969-70; press sec. Congressman James C. Corman, Washington, 1970-71; pub. info. specialist SBA, Washington, 1971-74; asst. regional dir. Pub. Affairs & Communications, San Francisco, 1975-80; press officer EPA, San Francisco, 1980—; lectr. seminars, confs., workshops for Stanford U., Calif. Press Women, San Francisco State U., Women in Communications and numerous others; Exec. bd. dirs. San Francisco Bay Area Fed. Pub. Affairs com. (outstanding Achievement award). Recipient numerous outstanding achievement awards by Valley Press Club, U.S. Navy Recruiting Service NYU div. of Bus. and Mgmt., Combined Fed. Campaign. Mem. Calif. Press Women (bd. dirs.), Nat. Assn. Govt. Communicators (dir. chpt.), Internat. Assn. Bus. Communicators, Am. Soc. Pub. Adminstrn., Internat. Communications Assn., Am. Mgmt. Assn., Women in Communications, San Francisco Press Club, Calif. Women in Govt. Author book; bus. columnist mags.; contbr. articles to mags. and profl. jours. Home: 313 Bluefish Ct Foster City CA 94404 Office: EPA 215 Fremont St San Francisco CA 94105

SENA, MARY LOUISE TAFOYA, educator; b. Belen, N.Mex., Apr. 24, 1947; d. Panfilo Avila and Clorinda (Jaramillo) Tafoya; B.S. in Edn., N.Mex. State U., 1970; M.A. in Ednl. Adminstrn., N.Mex. Highlands U., 1976; m. Gilbert L. Sena, May 7, 1983; 1 son, Richard Patrick. English tchr., Ocean Springs, Miss., 1970, Johnson High Sch., Austin, Tex., 1971-72; Upward Bound instr. English, reading, debate, dance Huston-Tillotson Coll., Austin, 1971-72, also Austin Civic Choir; tchr. Neighborhood Youth Corp., Raton, N.Mex., 1974-75, Raton Public Schs., 1974-82; tchr. remedial learners Raton Jr. High Sch., 1982—; tchr. gifted students Pecos Sch. System, spl. edn. coordinator participant profl. devel. workshops for teachers. Raton chmn. Sangre de Cristo council Girl Scouts U.S.A., 1973-74; active Raton Civic Chrous, 1976-78; chmn. Raton City Personnel Bd., 1979-82. Mem. NEA (chmn. instructional and profl. devel. commn. N.Mex., pres. NE Dist. 1979-80), Raton Classroom Tchrs. Assn. (sec. 1979-80), Delta Kappa Gamma, Epsilon Sigma Alpha, Women's Fedn. Raton (treas. 1977). Democrat. Methodist. Home: 1013 5th St Las Vegas NM 87701 Office: Pecos Ind Schs Pecos NM 87552

SENGA, ROBERT MANDU, chemist, microbiologist; b. Machakos, Kenya, East Africa, Oct. 16, 1947; s. Gedion M. Senga; m. Dorcas M. Mutuugi, July 7, 1979; children—Grace Wanza, Esther Nziloni B.S., Calif. Poly. U., Pomona, 1975; M.S., U. LaVerne, 1978; postgrad. Fullerton U., 1978—. Tech. dir., mgr. Electronic Reclamation Service, Anaheim, Calif., 1979; v.p. Reliable Recovery, Inc., Anaheim, 1980; environ. specialist Donald Bright & Assocs., Inc., Anaheim, 1981; prodn. chemist Armstrong Rubber, Inc., South Gate, Calif., 1982—; cons. environ. problems. Mem. AAAS, Am. Soc. for Indsl. Microbiology. Developer chem. method for precious metal refining, also non-chrominated aluminium cleaning compound.

SENNE, STEPHEN MICHAEL, fin. planner; b. Pasadena, Calif., July 5, 1944; s. Delmar Vincent and Penelope Ann (Hahn) S.; m. Ingrid Senne. A.A., Riverside City Coll., 1972; postgrad. U. Redlands, 1976-79. Asst. supr. SSP Products, Burbank, Calif., 1965-70; life field underwriter, supr., John Hancock Ins., Whittier, Calif., 1970-76; casualty field underwriter Sentry Ins., Ontario, Calif., 1976-79; pres., dir. Stephen Michael Senne, A. Fin. Planner, Inc., Ontario, 1977—; dir., treas. Karate Sch. of Oyama, Inc., Leopard Karate Sch., Inc. Chmn. nuclear radiol. health and safety course Am. Soc. Non-Destructive Testings, 1970—. Winner first place as editor of mgmt. newspaper nat. competition, 1969; named sportsman of month, Sportsman's Mag., Nov. 1970; winner numerous sales and karate awards; C.L.U. Republican. Lutheran. Clubs: Calif., Am. Sportsman, Glendale Elks. Full karate master (10th degree black belt). Author: The Jungle Detective, Your Financial Report Card, Get Billy Boy; The Joker Game. Address: PO Box 1665 Hesperia CA 92345

SEPPI, FRED LLOYD, phys. metallurgist; b. Ogden, Utah, Apr. 9, 1930; s. Fred and Mary (Maccani) S. B.S. in Physics, Northwestern U., 1951; M.S., U. Detroit, 1963; B.S. in Materials Engring., U. Utah, 1975, M.Engring. Adminstrn., 1981. Metallurgist, Lindberg Steel Co., Chgo., 1951-55, Detroit Arsenal, Warren, Mich., 1954-64, Ogden (Utah) Air Logistics Center, 1964-81, supr. Metall. Lab., 1981—. Mem. Am. Soc. Metals (chmn. Bonneville chpt. 1977-78), Soc. Materials Processing, Soc. Applied Spectroscopy, Am. Inst. Indsl. Engring. Roman Catholic. Researcher failure analysis, residual stress X-ray diffraction. Home: 3173 Tyler Ave Ogden UT 84403 Office: MAQM Ogden Air Logistics Center Hill AFB UT 84056

SERNATINGER, EDA MARGARET, clin. researcher; b. N.Y.C., May 28, 1943; d. Eugene M. and Margaret (Pudics) S.; B.S., SUNY, Albany, 1965; m. Robert P. Cook, II, Jan. 15, 1977. Asst. biochemist Burroughs-Wellcome & Co., Tuckahoe, N.Y., 1965-70; biochemist Hoffman LaRoche, Nutley, N.J., 1970-73, sr. research asso., 1973-77, San Francisco, 1977-80; mgr. clin. research, pharms. and oral health and dermatology worldwide Cooper Vision and Cooper Care divs. Cooper Labs, Inc., Cooper Research Center, Mountainview, Calif., 1980—; pres. ECR Collection, 1977—; v.p. Inst. Communications and Change, 1978—. Mem. N.Y. Acad. Scis., Am. Fedn. Clin. Research, AAAS, Sigma Xi. Roman Catholic. Home: 270 Vernal Ct Los Altos CA 94022 Office: 455 E Middlefield Rd Mountainview CA 94043

SERUTO, JOSEPH GEORGE, chem. mfg. cons. co. exec.; b. Tusa, Italy, Jan. 14, 1912; s. Rosario and Katherine (Grillo) S.; came to U.S., 1921, naturalized, 1941; A.B., Ohio State U., 1939; M.S., N.Y. U., 1942; m. Mary Elizabeth Reed, Jan. 30, 1940; children—Anna Dale, Katherine, Joseph Vincent, Barbara, Nancy. With research and devel. dept. Hoffman-LaRoche, Nutley, N.J., 1941-43; with Am. Cyanamid, Bound Brook, N.J., 1943-48; co-owner, gen. mgr. Western Organics, Inc., Santa Fe Springs, Calif., 1949-62; pres. Chem. Research & Devel. Co., 1962; owner, mgr. Specialty Organics, Inc., Irwindale, Calif., 1963—. Mem. Am. Chem. Soc., Am. Inst. Chem. Engrs., AAAS, Am. Inst. Chemists. Patentee in field. Office: 5263 N 4th St Irwindale CA 91706

SERVETNICK, RICHARD, financial company executive; b. Lynn, Mass., Jan. 24, 1943; student Brandeis U., 1960-61, U. Mass., 1961-62; B.A., Boston U., 1965; M.B.A., Pepperdine U., 1978; m. Marsha A. Blomquist, Apr. 24, 1976; children—Karen, Ryan, Scott. Salesman, Mobil Oil Corp., Boston, 1968-69; investment advisor Security Pacific Bank, Los Angeles, 1969; trader Shareholders Mgmt., Los Angeles, 1969-71; mgr. of trading Funds Inc., Houston, 1971-73, Am. Express Investment Mgmt. Co., San Francisco, 1973-75; v.p. instl. trading Shuman Agnew, San Francisco, 1975-77; v.p. instl. trading Morgan Stanley & Co. Inc., San Francisco, 1977-79, prin., 1977—. Served with Intelligence, U.S. Army, 1965-68. Mem. Nat. Securities Traders Assn., San Francisco Securities Traders Assn., Nat. Wildlife Fedn. (life), Calif. Hist. Soc. (sponsor). Episcopalian. Office: 595 Market St San Francisco CA 94105

SESAK, JOHN ROBERT, control engr.; b. Latrobe, Pa., Jan. 19, 1942; s. John and Margaret (Brillo) S.; student St. Vincent Coll., Latrobe, Pa., 1962; B.S.E.E., Pa. State U., 1965; M.S., U. Conn., Storrs, 1967; Ph.D., U. Wis., Madison, 1974. Sr. engring. specialist Gen. Dynamics, San Diego, 1976—; instr. extension courses U. Calif., San Diego. Bd. dirs. New Thought Episcopal Ch., 1978—. Named research engr. of year Gen. Dynamics Convair, 1978. Mem. Am. Soc. Engring. Edn., IEEE, AIAA (outstanding contbn. to aerospace engring. San Diego sect. 1979), Sigma Xi. Inventor new control method for flexible spacecraft; originator filter accommodated optimal control; contbr. articles to profl. publs. Office: General Dynamics Convair Div 5001 Kearny Villa Rd San Diego CA 92138

SESTINI, VIRGIL ANDREW, educator; b. Las Vegas, Nev., Nov. 24, 1936; s. Santi and Merceda Francesca (Borla) S. B.S. in Edn., U. Nev., 1959; postgrad., Oreg. State U., 1963-64; M.N.S., U. Idaho, 1965; postgrad., Ariz. State U., 1967, No. Ariz. U., 1969; cert. tchr., Nev. Tchr. biology Rancho High Sch., 1960-76; sci. chmn., tchr. biology Bonanza High Sch., Las Vegas, 1976—. Served with USAR, 1959-65. Recipient Rotary Internat. Honor Tchr. award, 1965, Region VIII Outstanding Biology Tchr. award, 1970, Nev. Outstanding Biology Tchr. award Nat. Assn. Biology Tchrs., 1970, Nat. Assn. Sci. Tchrs., Am. Gas Assn. Sci Teaching Achievement Recognition award, 1976, 1980, Gustov Ohaus award, 1980, Presdl. Honor Sci. Tchr. award, 1983. Mem. NEA, Nat. Sci. Tchrs. Assn., Nat. Assn. Biology Tchrs., Am. Soc. Microbiology, Nat. Audobon Assn., Nat. Sci. Suprs. Assn., Am. Inst. Biol. Scis. Roman Catholic. Office: Bonanza High Sch 6665 W Del Rey Ave Las Vegas NV 89102

SETCHKO, EDWARD STEPHEN, minister theological educator; b. Yonkers, N.Y., Apr. 27, 1926; s. Stephen John and Mary Elizabeth (Dulak) S.; m. Penelope Sayre, Nov. 18, 1950; children—Marc Edward, Kip Sherman, Robin Elizabeth, Jan Sayre, Dirk Stephen. B.S., Union Coll., 1948; M.Div. cum laude, Andover Newton Theol. Sch., 1953, S.T.M., 1954, Th.D., Pacific Sch. Religion, 1962. Ordained to ministry United Ch. of Christ, 1954; cert. profl. hosp. chaplain. Psychometrician, Union Coll. Character Research Project, Schenectady, N.Y., 1947-50; asst. pastor Eliot Ch., Newton, Mass., 1950-54; clin. tng. supr. Boston City Hosp., 1951-54; intern, chaplain Boston State Mental Hosp., 1953-54; univ. campus minister U. Wash., Seattle, 1954-58; Danforth grantee, 1958-59; grad. fellow in psychotherapy Pacific Sch. Religion, Berkeley, Calif., 1959-60, instr. dept. pastoral psychology, 1960-61, grad. fellow, lectr. theology and psychology, 1961-62, asst. prof. psychology and counseling, 1962-63, dir. continuing theol. edn., 1962-63; field research sec. laity div. United Ch. Christ, Berkeley, Calif. and N.Y.C., 1963-68; vis. prof. psychology Starr King Ctr. for Religious Leadership, Berkeley, 1967-69; assoc. prof. religion and soc. Starr King Ctr., Grad. Theol. Union, Berkeley, Calif., 1969-71, prof., 1971—; mem. faculty, chmn. curriculum and faculty com. Layman's Sch. Religion, Berkeley, 1960-67; cons. and lectr. in field. Mem. Peace Del., Mid-East, 1983; lectr. Internat. Conf. on the Holocaust and Genocide, 1982, Nuclear Disarmament Conf., W.Ger., 1980-83, Internat. Ctr. for Peace in the Middle East, Resource Ctr. for Non-Violence, Clergy & Laity Concerned, Ecumenical Peace Inst., Internat. Peace Acad.; World Policy Inst., Inst. Peace and World Order, Am. Friends Service Com., Ristad Found. Served as lt. (j.g.) USNR, 1944-46, WW II. Mem. Am. Psychol. Assn. (cert.), Calif. State Psychol. Assn., Assn. Clin. Pastoral Edn., World Future Soc., Soc. Sci. Study of Religion, Inst. Noetic Scis., Com. for Protection Human Subjects (U. Calif.). Democrat. Contbr. articles to profl. jours.; condr. seminars: Images of Women and Men; Changing Values in Roles Between the Sexes in a Technological Society; developer curriculum: Peace and Conflict Studies (U. Calif., Berkeley).

SETHALER, ALTA OPAL, electric supply co. exec.; b. Winside, Nebr., May 16, 1917; d. William and Sophia (Dreager) Petersen; student U. Denver, 1936-38, U. Colo., 1938-40; m. K.J. Sethaler, May 14, 1939 (dec.). Sec., bookkeeper Flex Tip Valve Co., Denver, 1936; cashier Comml. Savs. Bank, Sterling, Colo., 1937-40; enrolling clk. Colo. Legislature, 1940; acct. Parker Co., Denver, 1940-43; acctg. asst. Isadore Greenblatt Auditing Firm. Denver, 1943-45; with Central Electric Supply Co., Denver, 1945—, v.p., 1975-76, exec. asst. to chmn. bd., 1977—. Info. clk., asst. Human Services Travelers Aid, 1977-79; bd. dirs. Windsor Gardens Assn., 1980-83, v.p., 1982-83, pres, 1983—. Mem. Nat. Assn. Credit Mgmt. (dir. 1964-65, dir. adv. Rocky Mountain affiliate 1962-68, pres. Nat. Credit Women's Groups 1960-61), Credit Women's Group of Denver (dir. adv. 1962—, pres. 1951-52, Alta Sethaler Scholarship Fund established 1978, award 1979), Woman in Constrn. (charter. com. chmn. 1967-68). Democrat. Lutheran. Clubs: Women's Golf of Windsor Gardens (pres. 1980-81), Park Hill Golf. Home: 625 S Alton Way Denver CO 80231 Office: PO Box 267 500 Quivas St Denver CO 80201

SETTLE, ALLEN KINGSLEY, political science educator; b. Boston, Aug. 4, 1943; s. Philip O. and Eleanor (Stitt) S.; m. Kathleen L. Turner, July 10, 1971; children—Scott Kingsley, Matthew Turner. B.A., U. Calif., 1966, M.A., 1967, Ph.D., 1970. Mem. faculty polit. sci. dept. Calif. State U.-San Luis Obispo, 1971—. Mem. San Luis Obispo City Council, 1977—; polit. analyst Sta. KSBY-TV (NBC affiliate.) Pres., Channel Counties div. League Calif. Cities; pres. Area Council of Govts. Mem. Am. Polit. Sci. Assn. (grantee 1970), Am. Soc. Pub. Adminstrn., Western Polit. Sci. Assn. Democrat. Methodist. Author: American Public Administration: Concepts and Cases, 1975, 2d edit., 1980. Speaker profl. meetings. Home: 1244 Drake Circle San Luis Obispo CA 03401 Office: Polit Sci Dept Calif State U San Luis Obispo CA 93407

SETTLEMYER, KAREN MARIE, food service executive; b. Huntington, Ind., May 24, 1952; d. Lawrence Morris and Suzanna Jean Settlemyer. B.S., Purdue U., 1974, M.S., 1975. Registered dietitian. Mgr. Audrey's Sister's Buffet, Marriott Corp., Waukegon, Ill., 1974, mgr. food standards Marriott's Great Am., Gurnee, Ill., 1976, Gurnee and Santa Clara (Calif.), 1976-77; mgr. product research and devel. Sambo's Corp., Santa Barbara, Calif., 1977-80; dir. research and devel. Internat. House of Pancakes Corp., Hollywood, 1980, Straw Hat Restaurants, Dublin, Calif., 1980—; cons. menu design privately-owned restaurants. Mem. Home Economics in Bus., Am. Dietetic Assn., Am. Home Economics Assn., Calif. Home Economist Assn., Inst. Food Technologists (v.p. food service div.), Alpha Xi Delta. Methodist. Office: Straw Hat Restaurants 6400 Village Parkway Dublin CA 94568

SEUFERT, GORDON EDWARD, accountant, computer service bureau operator; b. Manhattan, N.Y.C., Jan. 27, 1953; s. George Edward and Janet S.; m. Mary Jo David, Oct. 17, 1980; children—Mark Andrew, Germaine Elysia. Student Met. State Coll., Denver, 1978—. Acct., Craftsmen Constrn., Inc., Denver, 1978-79; asst. controller Frank M. Hall & Co., Denver, 1979-81; controller Alvarado Constrn., Inc., Denver, 1981-82; ptnr. B&S Acctg.-Computer Service Bur., Denver, 1982—; dir. numerous corps.; ptnr. Favored Ventures. Office: 233 Bannock St Denver CO 80223

SEVCIK, JOHN JOSEPH, chem. engr.; b. Cleve., Feb. 1, 1952; s. John George and Lillian Jean (Hrabak) S.; B.S. in Engring. (John Huntington Fund scholar), Case Western Res. U., 1974. Engr. plastics div. Borg Warner Chems. Co., Parkersburg, W.Va., 1973; asso. engr. in mfg. research and devel. Boeing Comml. Airplane Co., Seattle, 1974; project engr. Structural Composites Industries Co., Azusa, Calif., 1975-77; project engr. McGaw Labs., Irvine, Calif., 1977-80; project engr. IVAC Corp., La Jolla, Calif., 1980-82, sr. project engr., 1982—. Mem. Soc. Plastics Engrs., Theta Tau (v.p. chpt., del. nat. conv.), U.S. Yacht Racing Union. Clubs: Orange County Cath. Alumni (Service award 1977, 79). Home: Apt B2 9685 Genesee St San Diego CA 92121 Office: 10300 Campus Point Dr San Diego CA 92121

SEVERAID, RONALD HAROLD, lawyer; b. Berkeley, Calif., July 13, 1951; s. Joye Harold and Irene Ann (Clark) S.; B.A., U. Calif.-Davis, 1973; J.D., Georgetown U., 1977. Assoc. firm Kindel & Anderson, Los Angeles, 1977-79; admitted to Calif. bar, 1977; exec. v.p., dir., gen. counsel Pacific Mktg./Devel., Inc., Sacramento, 1979-80, pres., 1980-81; pres. Ronald H. Severaid, P.C., Sacramento, 1979—; dir. Closson Market Research Group, 1979-81, chief fin. officer, 1980-81. Mem. ABA (chmn. internat. human rights com. 1979-81, assn. liaison com. on specialization 1981—, editor Internat. Ct. Justice-Opinion Briefs 1979), Calif. State Bar Assn. Republican. Office: Ronald H Severaid PC Suite 110 901 F St Sacramento CA 95814

SEVERSON, ELMER D., rancher, state senator; b. May 3, 1922; student pub. schs., Worden, Mont.; m. Bea Stevenson; 6 children. Rancher, Stevensville, Mont.; mem. Mont. Ho. of Reps., 1977; mem. Mont. Senate, 1979—. Served with USAF, World War II. Mem. Mont. Cattleman's Assn., Am. Legion, Grange. Republican. Club: Masons. Office: Route 1 Box 28 Stevensville MT 59870*

SEVERSON, HERBERT HENRY, psychologist; b. Madison, Wis., May 27, 1944; s. Clinton S. and Josephine (Kleinert) S.; m. Bonnie Kay McQueen, Dec. 30, 1975; 1 dau., Karyn. B.S., U. Wis.-Whitewater, 1966; M.S., U. Wis.-Madison, 1969, Ph.D. in Edn. Psychology, 1973. Research asst. U. Wis., Madison, 1968-69; tchr. Monona Pub. Schs., Madison, 1970, Madison Pub. Schs., 1971-72; prof. psychology U. No. Colo., Greeley, 1972-75; prof. ednl. psychology U. Oreg., Eugene, 1975—; dir. and research scientist Oreg. Research Inst., Eugene, 1979—, pres., 1980-82; cons. in field; chmn. bd. dirs. Drinking Decisions. Nat. Inst. Child Health and Human Devel. grantee. Mem. Am. Psychol. Assn., Oreg. Psychol. Assn., Nat. Assn. Sch. Psychologists, Oreg. Sch. Psychology Assn. Democrat. Editorial bd. School Psychology Digest, School Psychology Review, Psychology in the Schools; contbr. articles in field to profl. jours. Home: 2561 Chula Vista Eugene OR 97403 Office: 195 W 12th Eugene OR 97403

SEVILLE-JONES, CLIFFORD, physicist, manufacturing company executive; b. Flint, N. Wales, U.K., July 30, 1929; s. Albert Edward and Charlotte (Seville) Jones; came to U.S., 1962, naturalized, 1968; B.Sc., U. N. Wales, 1953, M.Sc. with honors in physics, 1954; M.S. in Bus. Administrn., Stevens Inst. Tech., 1965; m. Nesta Ann Roberton, Oct. 4, 1958; children—Sandra Ann, Peter Clifford, Dawn Elise, Dyan Nesta. Geo-physicist, Brit. Petroleum Corp., London, Kuwait and Libya, 1954-57; chief project engr. Gen. Electric Co., Hazel Grove, U.K., 1957-62; chief engr. Gen. Instrument Corp., Newark, 1962-65; prodn. mgr. Westinghouse Electric Corp., Elkridge, Md., 1965-68; mgr. ops. Transitron Corp., Wakefield, Mass., 1968-70, dir. ops., pres. subs. Electronic Memories Corp., Hawthorne, Calif., 1970-75; physical plant adminstr. U. Calif.-Santa Cruz, 1976-83; dir. ops. Beta Tech. Inc., Santa Cruz, Calif., 1983—; tech. adviser Calif. State Coll.-Long Beach, 1972-74. Recipient Service awards Hawthorne C. of C., 1974, Calif. State Coll.-Long Beach, 1972; lic. real estate broker, Calif. Mem. Am. Mgmt. Assn., Inst. Physics U.K., Arboretum Assocs. of U. Calif.-Santa Cruz. Home: 3600 N Park Ave Soquel CA 95073 Office: Beta Tech Inc 115 Harvey W Blvd Santa Cruz CA 95060

SEWELL, ROBERT HERBERT, advertising executive; b. Seattle, Sept. 4, 1927; s. Robert Herbert and Helen Louise (Servis) S.; m. Patricia Ann Corson, June 19, 1947; children—Sandra Ann, Robert L. Acct. exec. Budget Ln., Seattle, 1952-56; retail sales rep. Stokely Van Camp, Seattle, 1956-58; v.p., acct. exec. Graves Chambers, Seattle, 1958-67; Western Wash. mgr. Fenwick Pickett, 1967-68; food sales exec. Tacoma (Wash.) News Tribune, 1969—, gen. advt. mgr., 1980—. Served with USN, 1945-49. Mem. Mfrs. Rep. Club, The Illuminators Inc. Elks, Masons. Office: PO Box 11000 Tacoma WA 98411

SEXTON, WILLIAM PATRICK, hosp. adminstr., air force officer; b. Dallas, Feb. 22, 1948; s. Ralph Eugene and Bertha (Krallman) S.; B.S., So. Ill. U., 1970, M.B.A., 1976; M.H.A., U. Minn., 1977; m. Melyssa Jo Smith, Nov. 25, 1978. Commd. 2d lt. U.S. Air Force, 1970, advanced through grades to capt., 1976; asst. adminstr. med. logistics mgmt. USAF Hosp., Chanute AFB, Rantoul, Ill., 1972-73, asst. adminstr. personnel and adminstrv. services, 1973-74, asst. adminstr. patient affairs, 1974-75; adminstrv. resident Office Sec. Def., 1976-77; adminstr. USAF Clinic, Los Angeles, 1977-81, USAF Hosp. Hahn, W. Ger., 1982—; assoc. adminstr. USAF Hosp. Wiesbaden (W.Ger.), 1981-82; grad. instr., professorial lectr. Golden Gate U., Webster Coll.; clin. preceptor UCLA, Calif. State U., Dominguez Hills; keynote speaker community and civic groups. Decorated Air Force Commendation medal with oak leaf cluster, Def. Meritorious Service medal. Mem. Am. Coll. Hosp. Adminstrs. (cert.), Am. Hosp. Assn., Assn. Western Hosps., Assn. Mil. Surgeons U.S., Alumni Assn. Hosp. Adminstrn. U. Minn. Clubs: USAFE Hosp. Adminstrs. Jour. Home: USAF Hosp Hahn Box 1707 APO New York 09109

SEXTRO, ROBERT KEITH, chemist; b. Fairbury, Nebr., Dec. 12, 1948; s. George Henry and Ula (Jaedicke) S.; m. Andrea Rae Gladwin, Mar. 15, 1980. B.S. in Chemistry, Creighton U., 1970, M.S. in Chemistry, San Jose U., 1978. Cert. water treatment plant supr., Calif. Staff chemist Pacific Environ. Lab., San Francisco, 1970-72; lab. supr. Calif. Water Service Co., San Jose, 1972-79; lab. supr., chief analytical chemist BTC Labs. Inc., Ventura, Calif., 1980—; cons. Active ARC first aid and CPR program. Mem. Am. Water Works Assn., Am. Chem. Soc., Air Pollution Control Assn. Home: 1505 June Circle Ventura CA 93004 Office: 2978 Seaborg Ave Ventura CA 93003

SEYFERTH, HAROLD HOMER, real estate appraising company executive, educator; b. Stockton, Calif., Jan. 22, 1922; s. Lester L. and Bernice (Perkins) S.; m. Betty Jean Stanley, Mar. 2, 1943; children—Mary B., Laurence P. B.A., San Jose State U., 1948; M.B.A., Pacific Western U., 1981. Locomotive engr. Western Pacific R.R., 1939-50; asst. planner City of San Jose, 1950-54; mgr. City of Hollister (Calif.), 1959-63; property mgr. City of Salinas (Calif.), 1963-68; redevel. chief land officer City of Seaside (Calif.), 1968-69; pres. H. Seyferth Assocs., Monterey, Calif., 1969—; lectr. in field. Chmn., bd. dirs. Carmel Riviera Mut. Water Co.; bd. dirs. Boy's City Boy's Club, San Jose, Am. Cancer Soc., San Jose; trustee Enterprise Sch. Dist., Hollister, Calif. Served with USN, 1942-45. Coro fellow, 1950. Mem. Am. Assn. Cert. Appraisers (cert.), Am. Planning Assn., Calif. Assn. Real Estate Tchrs., Internat. Coll. Real Estate Cons. Profls., Internat. Inst. Valuers, Internat. Orgn. Real Estate Appraisers, Internat. Right of Way Assn., Nat. Assn. Cert. Real Property Appraisers, Nat. Assn. Rev. Appraisers, Real Estate Educators Assn., Urban Land Inst. Office: 1015 Cass St Monterey CA 93950

SEYMORE, WILLIAM ANDREWARTHA, finance co. exec.; b. Greensburg, Pa., Jan. 16, 1943; s. Francis Gerald and Rosehannah (Andrewartha) S.; student Duffs Bus. Sch., 1960-62, U. Hawaii, 1967-68, U. Calif. at Los Angeles, 1969-71; m. Elizabeth A. Waters, Feb. 20, 1971; children—Mary Elizabeth, David Matthew, Joshua William. Staff accountant Davies & Mulvihill, Pitts., 1962-65; mgr. Haskins & Sells, Honolulu, 1968-69, Los Angeles, 1969-74; exec. v.p. Calif. Life Corp., Los Angeles, 1974-79, also dir.; controller, treas. Allianz Ins. Co., Los Angeles, 1979—. Served with USNR, 1966-67. C.P.A., Pa. Mem. Am. Inst. C.P.A.'s. Republican. Episcopalian. Club: Jonathan (Los Angeles). Home: 2353 E Burnside St Simi CA 93065 Office: 3255 Wilshire Blvd Los Angeles CA 90010

SHACKELFORD, BARTON WARREN, utility executive; b. San Francisco, Oct. 12, 1920; s. Frank Harris and Amelia Louise (Schilling) S.; B.S. in Civil Engring., U. Calif., Berkeley, 1941; m. Charlaine Mae Livingston, July 24, 1949; children—Frank, Joan, Linda, Ann. Jr. engr. Todd-Calif. Shipbldg. Corp., 1941-44; with Pacific Gas & Electric Co., 1946—, sr. v.p., then exec. v.p., San Francisco, 1976-79, pres., 1979—, also dir. Address: 77 Beale St San Francisco CA 94106

SHACKELFORD, GORDON LEE, JR., educator; b. South Bend, Ind., Apr. 7, 1948; s. Gordon Lee and Leatha Mae (Andrews) S.; B.S. in Physics, San Diego State U., 1970, M.S. in Radiol. Physics, 1974; m. Janis Elizabeth Mead, Apr. 6, 1974. Electronic designer for physics dept. San Diego State U., 1969-70; electronic engr. Naval Electronics Lab., Point Loma, Calif., 1970; electronic engr. product design Info. Machine Corps., Santee, Calif., 1970-71; lectr. physics San Diego State U., 1971—, asst. dir. alumni and devel. Coll. of Scis., 1980-81, assoc. dean scis., external relations, 1981—; cons. power supply design, 1970—. Mem. Health Physics Soc. Author lab. manuals. Home: 9716 Red Pony Ln El Cajon CA 92021 Office: P 342 Physics Dept San Diego State Univ San Diego CA 92182

SHACKMAN, DANIEL ROBERT, psychiatrist; b. N.Y.C., Nov. 15, 1941; s. Nathan Howard and Dorothy (Kutler) S.; B.A., Columbia U., 1962, M.D., 1966. Intern, Mt. Sinai Hosp., N.Y.C., 1966-67, resident adult psychiatry, 1967-68, chief resident, 1968-69, fellow child psychiatry, 1969-70, asst. psychiatry Sch. Medicine, 1968-70; pvt. practice, Los Angeles, 1974—; attending psychiatrist Brentwood (Calif.) VA Hosp., 1972-79, asst. to chief psychiatry service, 1974-75, chief evaluation/admission service, 1976-79, dep. asso. chief staff ambulatory care, 1977-79; asst. prof. U. Calif. at Los Angeles Med. Sch., 1972-75, clin. asst. prof., 1975—; mem. attending staffs UCLA, St. John's, Westwood, Meml. hosps.; psychiat. cons. Calif. Dept. Rehab., 1975—. Bd. dirs. Spokane Family Counseling Service, 1971-72. Served as maj. M.C., USAF, 1970-72. Diplomate Am. Bd. Psychiatry and Neurology (invited examiner 1976, 78, 80). Mem. Am. Psychiat. Assn., So. Calif. Psychiat. Soc., Am., So. Calif. socs. adolescent psychiatry, N.Y. Council Child Psychiatry, Nat. Assn. VA Physicians (hosp. rep.). Contbr. to Am. Jour. Psychiatry. Home: 432 23d St Santa Monica CA 90402 Office: 1100 Glendon Ave Los Angeles CA 90024

SHACOCHIS, BARBARA ANN, retail store executive; b. Pittston, Pa., Sept. 3, 1953; d. John Paul and Helen Mary (Levenoskie) S.; B.A. with honors, Mich. State U., 1971; M.A., U. San Francisco, 1980; m. William H. Armstrong, June 20, 1980. Legal asst. coordinator McCutchen, Doyle, Brown & Enersen, San Francisco, 1976-79; mgmt. cons. Black, Borgman & Assos., Walnut Creek, Calif., 1979-80; dir. human resources Livingston Bros., Inc., San Francisco, 1980-83; regional personnel mgr. Mervyn's, Hayward, Calif., 1983—; seminar leader Council on Edn. in Mgmt., Walnut Creek, 1979-80; mem. faculty U. Calif., Berkeley and Santa Cruz, St. Mary's Coll., Moraga, Calif.; cons. to law firms, bus., 1977—. Mem. San Francisco Assn. Legal Assts. (dir. 1976-78), Calif. Alliance Paralegal Assns. (exec. dir. 1978-79), Am. Soc. Personnel Adminstrn. (accredited personnel specialist), Am. Compensation Assn., No. Calif. Indsl. Relations Council, Am. Soc. Tng. and Devel. Republican. Roman Catholic. Clubs: Commonwealth Calif., Golden Gate U. Assos. Office: 111 O'Farrell St San Francisco CA 94102

SHACTER, DAVID MERVYN, lawyer; b. Toronto, Ont., Can., Jan. 17, 1941; s. Nathan and Tillie Anne (Schwartz) S.; B.A., U. Toronto, 1963; J.D., Southwestern U., 1967. Bar: Calif. 1968, U.S. Supreme Ct. 1982. Law clk., staff atty. Legal Aid Found., Long Beach, Calif., 1967-70; asst. city atty. City of Beverly Hills (Calif.), 1970; ptnr. firm Shacter & Berg, Beverly Hills, Calif., 1971-83; del. State Bar Conf. Dels., 1976-82; lectr. Calif. Continuing Edn. of Bar, 1977, 82, 83; judge pro tem Los Angeles and Beverly Hills mcpl. cts., also Los Angeles Superior Ct.; mem. nat. panel arbitrators Am. Arbitration Assn. Bd. dirs., pres. Los Angeles Soc. Prevention Cruelty to Animals. Mem. Beverly Hills, Los Angeles County bar assns., Los Angeles, Calif. trial lawyers assns., City of Hope Med. Center Aux. Office: 3435 Wilshire Blvd Suite 1126 Los Angeles CA 90010

SHADE, VALERIA MAYANA KNOCK, educator; b. Davis, S.D., Sept. 8, 1919; d. Andy B. and Anna (Smith) Knock; m. Jerry M. Shade, Dec. 15, 1946; children—Kim M., Alan W. Tchr. home econs. pub. schs., Calumet, Iowa, 1942-43, Viborg, S.D., 1943-46, Centerville, S.D., 1946-47, Wellington, Colo., 1948-49, Pickstown, S.D., 1949-51, Irene, S.D., 1951-52, Brandon, S.D., 1954-56, Humboldt, S.D., 1956-57, Weber County Schs., Ogden, Utah, 1958—, head dept., 1982—. Mem. Weber Ednl. Assn., Utah Tchrs. Assn., Nat. Tchrs. Assn., AAUW. Presbyterian. Clubs: Order Eastern Star (past matron), Order White Shrine of Jerusalem (chaplain 1983). Home: 1335 E 2500 North Ogden UT 84404 Office: 165 W 5100 South Ogden UT 84403

SHAEVITZ, MORTON HERBERT, clin. psychologist; b. N.Y.C., June 23, 1935; s. Arthur and Dorothy (Spievak) S.; B.A., UCLA, 1957, M.A. (USPHS fellow), 1961, Ph.D., 1963; m. Marjorie E. Hansen, Mar. 11, 1972; children—Erica, Jonathon, Geoffrey, Marejka. Asst. prof. psychology U. Mich., Ann Arbor, 1963-69; dir. U. Calif. Counseling and Psychol. Services, San Diego, 1969-77; assoc. clin. prof. dept. psychiatry U. Calif. Med. Sch., San Diego, 1974—; clin. prof. Sch. Law U. San Diego, 1977-81; co-dir. Inst. Family and Work Relationships, LaJolla, Calif., 1977—; dir. Eating Disorders Clinic, Scripps Clinic Med. Group, LaJolla, 1978—; dir. M.H. Shaevitz, Ph.D. & Assocs., La Jolla, 1977—; co-pres. LaJolla Farms Assocs., 1977-78. Mem. Mental Health Assn. San Diego, 1972-74; chmn. Manpower Devel. and Inservice Tng. Task Force of Improving Mental Health Services, 1971-74. Served with AUS, 1959. Recipient grand OEO, 1967. Mem. Am. Psychol. Assn., Calif. Psychol. Assn., Western Psychol. Assn., Am. Orthopsychiat. Assn. Club: LaJolla Beach and Tennis. Author: (with D. Fader) Hooked on Books, 1966; (with M.H. Shaevitz) Making It Together As A Two-Career Couple, 1980; contbr. articles to profl. jours., mags., newspapers. Home: 2671 Greentree Ln LaJolla CA 92037 Office: 1020 Prospect St Suite 400 LaJolla CA 92037

SHAFER, JACOB ROBERT, safety engineer, industrial relations manager; b. Riegelsville, Pa., Feb. 26, 1937; s. Horace and Irene (Godown) S.; m. Mary Ellen Enos, Dec. 14, 1957; children—Robert, Patricia Ann. B.B.A., U. Nebr., 1969; M.S. in Systems Mgmt., U. So. Calif., 1973. Cert. hazard control mgr. Safety and quality control dept. mgr. Transp. Test Ctr., Pueblo, Colo., 1977-79; indsl. relations supt. Rockwool Industries, Inc., Pueblo, 1979-81; personnel and safety dept. mgr. Ideal Cement Co., Florence, Colo., 1981—. Pres. Pueblo Safety Council, 1980; chmn. Town Meeting Steering Com., Pueblo West, 1982. Served to maj., USAF, 1955-77. Named Safety Profl. of Yr., Pikes Peak region, 1982. Mem. Am. Soc. Safety Engrs., So. Colo. Indsl. Relations Mgrs. Club: Masons. Home: 1395 Ferncliff Ln Pueblo West CO 81007 Office: Box 349 Florence CO 81226

SHAFFER, ROBERT CLARENCE, aeros. materials co. exec.; b. Kalamazoo, Mich., Oct. 4, 1918; s. Clarence Daniel and Grace Virginia (Garlick) S.; B.A. in Chemistry, Western State Coll., 1939; postgrad. Wayne U., 1943-44; m. Delores Rita Burns, Nov. 22, 1943; children—

Rita Ann (Mrs. Ronald Joseph Bucholtz), Mary Kay (Mrs. Donald Earl Hackett, Jr.). Chemist, Ford Motor Research, Dearborn, Mich., 1940-42; head dept. chem. research Bendix Aviation Central Research, Detroit, 1942-49; supr. high polymer research lab. Ford Motor Sci. Center, Dearborn, 1949-53; research engr. North Am. Aviation, Los Angeles, 1953-56; dir. research Adhesive Engring., San Carlos, Calif., 1956-60; dir. research Westech Plastics, Menlo Park, Calif., 1960-65; mgr. materials research and devel. HITCO Materials Sci. Ctr., Gardena, Calif., 1965-72, staff asst. to v.p. research and engring. Hitco Def. products div., 1972-82, mgr. materials research and new material pilot plant ops. Hitco Fabricated Composites Div., 1982—. Cons. developed, planned and supervised research programs for def. contractors in fields of missile re-entry materials, 1960-65. Mem. Soc. Materials and Process Engrs. (treas. chpt. 1961-62). Patentee in field. Home: 8040 W 83d St Playa Del Rey CA 90291 Office: 1600 W 135th St Gardena CA 90249

SHAFIROFF, IRA LOUIS, lawyer; b. Bklyn., Dec. 29, 1951; s. Harry and Bella Shafiroff; B.A., Bklyn. Coll., 1973; J.D. magna cum laude, Southwestern U., 1979. Adminstrv. aide N.Y.C. Police Dept., 1974, tax auditor IRS, Los Angeles, 1974-80; admitted to Calif. bar, 1980, U.S. Tax Ct., 1981; practiced in Los Angeles, 1980—; assoc. prof. law, dir. continuing edn. Southwestern U., 1982—; instr. UCLA Extension; lectr. on taxes and IRS. Recipient Am. Jurisprudence awards, 1978; award West Pub. Co., 1978; award Wall St. Jour., 1980. Mem. Am. Bar Assn. (tax div.), Los Angeles County Bar Assn. Author: All You Need To Know about I.R.S. Audits. Office: 3325 Wilshire Blvd Suite 700 Los Angeles CA 90010

SHAH, GIRISH POPATLAL, data processing services company executive; b. Junagadh, India, Apr. 11, 1942; came to U.S., 1963, naturalized, 1972; s. Popatlal Gulabchand and Lalitaben Popatlal (Kamdar) S.; B. Tech., Indian Inst. Tech., Bombay, 1963; M.S., U. Calif.-Berkeley, 1965; m. Devmani Manilal Jhaveri, June 18, 1968; children—Nivisha, Munjal, Bhavin. Project analyst IBM, Palo Alto, Calif., 1965-67; v.p. Optimun Systems Inc., Palo Alto, 1967-72; pres. Banking Systems Internat. Corp., Jakarta, Indonesia & Campbell, Calif., 1972—; dir. software services Tymshare Transactions Services, San Francisco, 1980—. Adv. bd. Goodwill Industries San Francisco; bd. dirs. Gujarate Cultural Assn., 1982. J.N. Tata Trust nat. scholar, 1963. Mem. IEEE, Ops. Research Soc. Am., Assn. Indians in Am. (v.p. 1980). Democrat. Home: 4048 Twyla Ln Campbell CA 95008 Office: 39100 Liberty Ave Fremont CA 94538

SHAKARIAN, STEPHEN DEMOS, assn. exec.; b. Downey, Calif., July 12, 1947; s. Demos Dee and Rose S.; m. Debra G. Shakarian, Mar. 14, 1975; children—Stephanie Lynn, Stephen Demos. B.S.M., Pepperdine U., 1983; postgrad. in bus. adminstrn. UCLA, 1983—. Vice pres., Omega Advt., Los Angeles, 1973-74, exec. v.p., mgr., 1974-75, pres., 1975—; dir. ministries Full Gospel Bus. Men's Fellowship Internat., Irvine, Calif., 1978-80, dir. ministries and ops., 1980, chief operating officer, Costa Mesa, Calif., 1980—, also dir.; dir. Dee Rose Oil Co. Inc. Mem. Nat. Religious Broadcasters. Republican. Office: 3150 Bear St Costa Mesa CA 92626

SHAKED, MOSHE, mathematics educator, statistics researcher; b. Jerusalem, Feb. 21, 1945; s. Jacob and Anna (Berenson) Szek; came to U.S., 1971, permanent resident; m. Edith Haddad, June 15, 1977; children—Tal, Shanna, Lila. B.A. cum laude, Hebrew U., 1967, M.A. cum laude, 1971; M.A., U. Rochester, 1972, Ph.D., 1975. Prof. math. and stats. U. N.Mex., Albuquerque, 1975-78; prof. math. Ind. U., Bloomington, 1978-81; prof. U. Ariz., Tucson, 1981—. Sandia Labs. grantee, 1976-78; NSF grantee, 1979—. Mem. Inst. Math. Stats., Am. Statis. Assn. Contbr. numerous papers to profl. jours. Home: 3401 E Guthrie Mountain Pl Tucson AZ 85718 Office: Dept Math U Ariz Tucson AZ 85721

SHAKELY, JOHN (JACK) BOWER, found. exec.; b. Hays, Kans., Jan. 9, 1940; s. John B. and Martha Jean (Gaston) S.; B.A., U. Okla., 1962; 1 son, Benton. Vol., Peace Corps, Costa Rica, 1963-64; editor publs. Def. Dept., 1967-68; dir. devel. U. Okla., 1968-70, Westhaven Mental Health Center, Los Angeles, 1970-74; pres. Jack Shakely Assos., Los Angeles, 1974-75; sr. adv. Grantsmanship Center, Los Angeles, 1975-79, Council on Founds., Washington, 1979; exec. dir. Calif. Community Found., Los Angeles, 1980—. lectr. in field. Bd. dirs. Grantsmanship Center, 1972—, So. Calif. Assn. Philanthropy, 1980—, Involvement Corp., 1980—, Coro Found., 1982—. Served to 1st lt. U.S. Army, 1965-68. Decorated Army Commendation medal. Democrat. Home: 835 Hopkins Way Redondo Beach CA 90277 Office: 1151 W 6th St Los Angeles CA 90017

SHAKLEE, FORREST CLELL, business exec.; b. Carlisle, Iowa, Nov. 27; s. Robert Lenz and Martha Jane (Overton) S.; D.C., Palmer Coll., 1915; Ph.C., West Coast Chiropractic Coll., Oakland, Calif., 1932; N.D., Calif. Chiropractic Coll., 1933; D.D., Coll. Divine Metaphysics, Indpls., 1933; A.B., Neo-Sci. Soc. Am. Humanist Sch., 1949; Ph.D. in Psychology, Commonwealth U., Los Angeles, 1957; m. Ruth Alice Chapin (dec. 1941); m. 2d, Dorothy Eleanor Potter, Aug. 8, 1957; children—Forrest C., Raleigh L. Pvt. practice chiropractic medicine, Iowa, also Oakland, Calif., 1915-43; founder Shaklee Corp., Oakland, 1956, pres., chmn. bd., 1956-72, chmn. bd., 1972-75, chmn. emeritus, 1975; cons. human relations, Oakland, 1941-57. Ordained to ministry Ch. of Christ, 1929; pastor, Portland, Iowa, 1928-29. Recipient Outstanding Achievement award Standard Chiropractic Coll., San Jose, Calif., 1937, spl. recognition award Calif. Sec. State, 1968, Humanitarian award Nat. Health Fedn. Am., 1973, numerous others. Mem. Shaklee Found. Thoughtmanship (founder, pres. 1947), Hayward C. of C. (dir. 1965-66). Mason (Shriner). Author: Thoughtmanship Life's Questions and Answers, 1951; Thoughtmanship for Well Being, 1951; Thoughtmanship for the Salesman, 1951; Thoughtmanship in Love and Marriage, 1951; Thoughtmanship for the Bride, 1951; Shaklee Reference Treasure to Better Health Through Better Nutrition, 1960; Reflections on a Philosophy, 1973; When Nature Speaks: The Life of Forrest C. Shaklee Sr., 1977. Contbr. numerous articles to jours. and mags. Office: 444 Market St San Francisco CA 94111

SHALKOP, ROBERT L., museum dir.; b. Milford, Conn., July 30, 1922; s. Bertram L. and Dorothy (Boardman) S.; student Maryville Coll., 1941-42; M.A., U. Chgo., 1949, postgrad., 1950; postgrad. Sorbonne, Paris, 1951-52; m. Antoinette J. Benkowsky, Dec. 7, 1963; 1 son, Andrew Goforth. Dir., Rahr Civic Center, Manitowoc, Wis., 1953-56, Everhart Mus., Scranton, Pa., 1956-62, Brooks Meml. Art Gallery, Memphis, 1962-64; asst. dir. Colorado Springs Fine Arts Center, also curator Taylor Mus., Colorado Springs, Colo., 1964-71; dir. Anchorage Hist. and Fine Arts Mus., 1972—. Served with USAAF, 1942-45. Author: Wooden Saints: the Santos of New Mexico, 1967; Reflections of Spain, a Comparative View of Spanish Colonial Sculpture, 1968; A Comparative View of Spanish Colonial Painting, 1970; Arroyo Hondo: the Folk Art of a New Mexican Village, 1969; A Show of Color: 100 Years of Painting in the Pike's Peak Region, 1971; Russian Orthodox Art in Alaska, 1973; Sydney Laurence, an Alaskan Impressionist, 1975; Eustace Ziegler, 1977; Henry Wood Elliott, 1982. Editor: An Introduction to the Native Art of Alaska, 1972. Office: 121 W 7th Ave Anchorage AK 99501

SHANAHAN, EUGENE MILES, controls company executive; b. Great Falls, Mont., Sept. 18, 1946; s. Raymond Eugene and Helen Marjorie (Graham) S.; m. Beverly Ann Braaten, Sept. 18, 1967; children—Bret Allen, Shaun Eugene. B.S. in Mech. Engring., Mont. State U., 1968, M.S., 1969; M.B.A., Portland State U., 1976. Registerd profl. engr., Oreg. Mech. engr. Tektronix, Beaverton, Oreg., 1968-71, Shell Oil Co., Martinez, Calif., 1967; chief mech. project engr. Mears Controls, Beaverton, 1971-76, mktg. mgr., 1976-79; v.p., gen. mgr. Eaton Corp., Beaverton, 1979—; dir. Moderne Cabinet Shop, Great Falls. Bd. dirs., v.p. L.A. Water Coop., 1976-79. Served with N.G., 1969-75. NSF trainee, 1969. Mem. ASME, Tau Beta Pi, Phi Kappa Phi, Pi Tau Sigma. Home: Route 2 Box 654 Hillsboro OR 97123 Office: Eaton Corp 13725 S W Millikan Beaverton OR 97005

SHANAHAN, JACK SAMUEL, interior designer; b. Chgo., June 30, 1937; s. John J. and Marie M. (Lavezzi) S.; divorced; m. Sara Cantrell Zook, Jan. 15, 1983; children—Susan M., Michael J., Daniel J., Deborah L., Timothy P. Student DePaul U., Chgo., 1957; grad. Ray Vogue Coll. Interior Design, Chgo., 1958. Interior designer Arthur H. Lee & Sons, Chgo., 1958-62, Caledonian Inc., Winnetka, Ill., 1963-70; interior designer, prin. Devontry Design Cons., Winnetka, 1970-81, prin. Pouw & Assocs., Inc., Denver, 1982—. Served with USAFR, 1960-66. Mem. Am. Soc. Interior Designers (dir. nat. bd., past pres. Ill. charter, bd. dirs. Colo. chpt., recipient 50th anniversary award), Alpha Delta Gamma. Club: Toastmasters (Libertyville, Ill.). Contbr. interior designs to design and shelter mags. Home: 13424 Braun Rd Golden CO 80401 Office: 1660 17th St Suite 200 Denver CO 80202

SHANAHAN, LADY MABEL TERESA BALOCCHI, housing and marketing executive; b. Buenas Aires, Argentina, Sept. 15, 1936; came to U.S., 1955, naturalized, 1962; d. Joseph G. and Angela (Rebottaro) Balocchi; B.A., French Lycee, 1954; postgrad. Design Center, Calif., 1964, U. Calif.-Irvine, 19; m. Norman G. Shanahan, Dec. 7, 1967; children—Elizabeth Erin, Kathleen Olivia. Jewelry designer Tepper Enterprises, Santa Monica, Calif., 1956-65; asst. mgr. Toy Mart, Beverly Hills, Calif., 1961-67; fashion display coordinator Am. Fashion Products, Westwood, Calif., 1966-73; propr., dir. Terry's Antiques, Los Angeles, 1968-75; v.p. sales and mktg. Shanahan Homes, Inc., Palm Springs, Calif., 1974—; asst. mgr. adminstrn. Desert View Homes, Desert Hot Springs, Calif., 1975-76; land purchasing exec. Cahuilla, Inc., Palm Springs and Newport Beach, 1976—, now pres.; 1st v.p. Caligo, Inc., 1978-79; costume designer Palm Springs Dance Co., 1975-78. Founder, active Music Ctr. Los Angeles, 1960—; pres. Maarave Group of Hadassah, 1960, mem. adv. bd. Centro Pastoral Guadalupe, Santa Ana, Calif., 1977—. Recipient City of Hope award Mayor of Palermo (Sicility), 1964; Housing award Rural Council U.S., 1978-79. Mem. Calif. Escrow Assn., NOW, Los Angeles, C. of C., Sales-Mktg. Council Orange County, Japanese Pioneer Assn. Los Angeles, Palm Spring Hist. Soc., World Affairs Council of the Desert, Palm Springs Opera Guild, N.Y. Opera Guild, Nat. Notary Assn. Clubs: Palm Springs Tennis; Balboa Bay. Office: PO Box 2237 PO Box TT Newport Beach CA 92662

SHANAHAN, ROBERT H., newspaper publisher; b. Denver, Aug. 7, 1925; s. Harry B. and Ruth M. (Murphy) S.; student St. Thomas Coll., St. Paul; B.B.A., U. Denver, 1948; m. Patsy Glanville, Sept. 6, 1947; children—R. Kevin, Timothy D., Mary Pat, Brian. With Denver Post, Inc., 1948—, beginning as advt. salesman, successively personnel dir., retail advt. mgr., asst. bus. mgr., advt. dir., bus. mgr., gen. mgr., 1948-77, co-pub., from 1977, exec. v.p., dir., 1977—; vice chmn. bd. So. Prodn. Program, Inc., 1980—, pres., 1981, dir., 1970—. Bd. dirs. Mile High chpt. A.R.C., 1972-78, Colo. Soc. Prevention of Blindness, 1975-78, Colo. Safety Assn., 1976—, Denver C. of C., 1976-79, 80—, Mile High United Way, 1976—; bd. dirs. Denver Conv. and Visitors Bur., 1976—, exec. com., 1979—; chmn. bd. Jr. Achievement of Met. Denver, 1975-76, pres., 1974-75, hon. bd. dirs., 1980—; bd. dirs., exec. council St. Joseph Hosp., 1980—. Served with USNR, World War II; PTO. Mem. Colo. Press Assn. Clubs: Denver Athletic, Denver, Hundred of Denver, Denver Kiwanis (found. trustee 1976-78, dir. 1973-76); Cherry Hills Country (Englewood, Colo.); Garden of the Gods (Colorado Springs). Office: Denver Post 650 15th St Denver CO 80202*

SHANAMAN, JANE A., hospital official; b. Lewiston, Idaho, Dec. 7, 1940; d. John L. and Mary Jane (Pace) Aram; m. Frederick Charles Shanaman, July 7, 1962; children—Rick, Mara. B.A., Mills Coll., 1962; M.A., Pacific Luth. U., 1977. Columnist, reporter Suburban Times, Tacoma, 1962-65; dir. devel. Mental Health Ctr., Tacoma, 1969-71; pres. Future Publs., Tacoma, 1971-73; research assoc. dir. devel., asst. v.p. devel. Pacific Luth. U., Tacoma, 1973-78; v.p. planning and devel. Childrens Health Ctr., Tacoma, 1978-81; mktg. dir. Nalleys Fine Foods, Tacoma, 1981-83; v.p., corp. services Consol. Hosps., Tacoma, 1983—. Mem. Tacoma C. of C. (dir. 1979—). Republican. Episcopalian. Home: 11524 Clovercrest Dr SW Tacoma WA 98499 Office: Consolidated Hospitals 402 South J St Tacoma WA 98405

SHANDRICK, ALBERT JOSEPH, minister, physicist; b. Colorado Springs, Colo., Jan. 22, 1920; s. Michael and Susan (Haver) S.; B.A. cum laude, Colo. Coll., 1942; M.Th., Chgo. Sch. Theology, 1948; postgrad. U. Calif. at Berkeley, 1942-45, Iliff Sch. Theology, 1951-52, U. Mich., 1952; m. Wilma Elizabeth Huseman, June 12, 1948; 1 dau., Rebecca Lynn. Research physicist U.S. Naval Ordnance Lab., Berkeley, Calif., 1942-45; ordained to ministry Luth. Ch., 1948; minister Luth. Chs., San Francisco, 1948-52; faculty, registrar, librarian Luth. Theol. Sem., Chgo., 1952-61; minister Luth. Ch., Trinidad, Colo., 1961—. Stewardship rep. Colo. Council Chs., 1961-68, council rep., 1965; dist. sec. Rocky Mountain Synod Luth. Ch. Am., 1967—; condr. seminars, symposia on sci., theology various sci. fairs, 1963—. Model Cities evaluator, 1966-69; adviser San Rafael Hosp., Trinidad, Colo., 1963-71. Recipient citation U.S. Naval Ordnance Lab., 1944; other citations, awards. Mem. Assn. Am. Theol. Sems. (citation 1965). Rotarian (award 1967-68). Club: Knife and Fork. Contbr. articles on sci. and theology to various publs. Address: 613 Prospect St Trinidad CO 81082

SHANK, JOHN THOMAS, optometrist; b. Canton, Ohio, Jan. 13, 1944; s. Harold Arthur and Marjorie Ruth (Ault) S.; student Mt. Union Coll., 1962-65, Ohio State U., 1965-66; B.S., Pacific U., 1969, O.D., 1971; m. Virginia Elizabeth Ferber, May 17, 1968; children—Pamela, Kristin. Tchr., Willoughby East Lake Sch. Dist., Ohio, 1966-67; pvt. practice optometry, Kodiak, Alaska, 1974—; sec., treas. Kodiak Internat., Inc. Chmn. adv. bd. Kodiak Community Coll., 1978-79; mem. adv. bd. Alaska Community Coll., 1978-80. Served with U.S. Army, 1971-74. Fellow Am. Acad. Optometry; mem. Am. Optometric Assn., Armed Forces Optometric Soc., Better Vision Inst., Alaska Optometric Assn., Am. Public Health Assn., Alaska Bd. Optometry (adv. bd. 1978-80), Kodiak C. of C. (bd. dirs. 1977-79), Nat. Rifle Assn. Clubs: Kodiak Lions (pres., 1978-79), Elks. Home: 3855 Woodland Dr Kodiak AK 99615 Office: 202 Center St Kodiak AK 99615

SHANKS, MARIE JEANETTE, fin. exec.; b. Bloomington, Calif., Aug. 17, 1943; d. Marie Jeanette (Brodeur) Benedict; A.Acctg. & Bus. Mgmt., Central Ariz. Coll., 1972; m. Robert Shanks, Feb. 17, 1965; 1 son, Oscar Lee. Office mgr., med. asst. Dr. Linda Martin D.O., Apache Junction, Ariz., 1974-77; owner-operator Acctg. Dynamics, Tax Service, Apache Junction, 1975—; Cons. Ltd., fin. advising. Citizen response teaching coordinator Paramedics Unltd., Apache Junction, 1978—; emergency med. technician II, Ariz. Disaster Unit #1, 1978—; mem. Apache Junction City Council, 1978—; chmn. Human Resources Devel. Commn., 1979—; sr. health service coordinator, area chmn., 1979—; mem. Gov.'s Behavioral Health Adv. Council, 1980—; co-coordinator Vol. Income Tax Aide Service for Elderly; swim instr. ARC, 1978-79; charter mem., trustee Apache Junction Area Community Found., 1981—; mem. govtl. liaison com. Apache Junction Health Bd., 1982—. Recipient Vol. Service award Sr. Health Fair, 1979; Civic Service award Eagles, 1980, Jaycees, 1980; Appreciation plaque Apache Junction C. of C., 1981; Service award IRS, Nat. Assn. Ret. Persons/Nat. Assn. Ret. Tchrs., 1981; appreciation award Apache Junction Sch. Dist., 1982; Outstanding Community Works award Apache Junction Community Found., 1982. Mem. Nat. Assn. Female Execs., Ariz. Small Bus. Assn., League Ariz. Towns-Cities, Mcpl. Nat. League Towns-Cities, Am. Soc. Profl. and Exec. Women (area network coordinator), Superstition Mountain Horsemen's Assn., Am. Soc. Notaries. Democrat. Mem. Ch. of Jesus Christ of Latter-Day Saints. Clubs: Oddfellows, Rebekas, DAV Aux., Eagles, Ladies of Elks; Soroptomist (pres. Apache Junction 1981—). Address: 472 S Goldfield Rd Apache Junction AZ 85220

SHANNON, ALVIN RICHARD, telephone company manager, market researcher; b. Mountain View, Ark., Jan. 10, 1938; s. Arvil Richard and Versa Belle (Jenkins) S.; m. Edith Charity, June 24, 1958; children—Merry Edith, Mitzi Leanne. B.A. with highest honors in Econs., Wash. State U., 1963. Economist, Pacific Northwest Bell Telephone Co., Seattle, 1963-73, customer survey mgr., 1973—; research cons. Camp Fire Girls. Served with U.S. Army, 1956-57. Home: 5410 231st SE Issaquah WA 98027 Office: Pacific NW Bell Telephone Co 1600 Bell Plaza Room 2508 Seattle WA 98191

SHANNON, EDFRED L., JR., corp. exec.; b. 1926; B.S., U. Calif.-Berkeley, 1951; married. Petroleum engr. Union Oil Co. of Calif., 1951-53; with Santa Fe Internat. Corp., 1953—, v.p. Orange, Calif., 1960-63, chmn., chief exec. officer, 1963—, also dir. Office: Santa Fe Internat Corp 1000 S Fremont Ave Alhambra CA 91802*

SHANNON, MICHAEL CARLYLE, research geneticist; b. Clinton, Ind., Oct. 11, 1944; s. Charles Maxie and Edna Mae (Carlyle) S.; m. Deborah Jean Love, June 7, 1969; children—Michael Andrew, Tara Jeanine. Student Ind. U., 1965; B.S. in Biology, Tenn. Technol. U., 1966, M.S., 1971; Ph.D., U. Ariz., 1975. Research geneticist Salinity Lab., Agrl. Research Service, U.S. Dept. Agr., Riverside, Calif., 1974—. Served to 1st lt. U.S. Army, 1966-69. Mem. Am. Soc. Agronomy, Crop Sci Soc. Am., Am. Soc. Hort. Sci., Guayule Rubber Soc., Sigma Xi. Contbr. numerous articles to profl. jours. Home: 11425 Tiffany Ln Sunnymead CA 92388 Office: US Salinity Lab 4500 Glenwood Dr Riverside CA 92501

SHANSBY, J. GARY, corporation executive; b. Seattle, Aug. 25, 1937; s. John Jay and Jule E. (Boyer) S.; m. Barbara Anderson DeMeo, Jan. 1, 1983; children—Sheri Lee, Jay Thomas, Kimberly Ann. B.A. in Gen. Bus. and Mktg., U. Wash., 1959. Sr. mktg., sales positions Colgate Palmolive Co., N.Y.C., 1959-67; pres., gen. mgr. Household Research Inst. subs. Am. Home Products Corp., N.Y.C., 1968-72; v.p., gen. mgr. Clorox Co., Oakland, Calif., 1972-73; v.p., ptnr. Booz, Allen & Hamilton, Inc., San Francisco, 1973-75; chmn. bd., chief exec. officer Shaklee Corp., San Francisco, 1975—. Bd. dirs. Nat. Symphony Orch. Assn., Washington, Bay Area Council, U. Calif.-Berkeley Bus. Sch.; bd. govs. San Francisco Symphony, Calif. Roundtable, Ford's Theater Soc.; trustee U. San Francisco, Friends of Photography, Jr. Statesman Found.; bd. regents St. Mary's Coll.; bd. overseers U. Calif.-San Francisco; bd. dirs. San Francisco council Boy Scouts Am.; mem. adv. council Calif. State Parks Found.; mem. Mayor's Fin. Adv. Com., San Francisco; mem. Pres.'s Adv. Com. for Trade Negotiations, Pres.'s Com. for Internat. Youth Exchange; mem. Harold Brunn Soc. for Med. Research; mem. No. Calif. fin. com. United for Calif.; mem. collector's com. Nat. Gallery Art, Washington; mem. adv. group to State Senate Select com. govt. regulation. Mem. Newcomen Soc., Commonwealth Club San Francisco, Lincoln Club No. Calif. (chmn.), San Francisco C. of C. (past pres.). Clubs: Olympic, Villa Taverna (San Francisco); Silverado Country (Napa, Calif.); Pennask Fishing and Game (B.C.). Office: Shaklee Corp 444 Market St San Francisco CA 94111

SHANTZ, MICHAEL JOE, computer scientist; b. Alpena, Mich., June 19, 1944; s. Clifford Henry and Viola Louise (Stonebraker) S.; m. Vera Tesluk, Sept. 6, 1973; 1 dau., Kristin Rachel. B.A. Goshen Coll., 1966; M.S., Drexel U., 1971; Ph.D., Calif. Inst. Tech., 1976. Lectr. info. sci. Calif. Inst. Tech., Pasadena, 1976-77; image processing engr. Varian Assocs., Palo Alto, Calif., 1978; graphics image processing software engr. DeAnza Systems Inc., San Jose, Calif., 1979-82; mem. tech. staff Sun Microsystems Inc., Santa Clara, Calif., 1982—; cons. in field. Mem. Assn. Computing Machinery, AIAA. Mennonite. Contbr. articles to profl. jours. Office: 1023 Walsh Ave Santa Clara CA 95051

SHAPIRO, JACK, advertising and public relations executive; b. Salinas, Calif., Dec. 6, 1924; s. Morris and Rebecca (Kuperman) S.; m. Loretta Lowell, Oct. 11, 1946 (dec.); m. 2d, Jeannette Pearson, June 4, 1955; children—Karen Lynn Peterson, David Douglas, Victor Morris. Student, Hartnell Coll., 1946-47, Los Angeles City Coll., 1948-49; Dir., Sta. KFI-TV, Los Angeles, 1949-50; v.p. Inter-Mountain Network, Salt Lake City, 1956-59; mgr. Los Angeles office Forjoe Co., 1960-62; founder, pres. Shapiro Advt. and Public Relations, Salt Lake City, 1963—; lectr. Brigham Young U., 1979, U. Utah, 1981; chmn. 1st Ann. Intermountain Public Relations Seminar, 1980. Mem. Utah Republican Party Exec. Com., 1971-73, Central Com., 1971-73; chmn. Recreation Vehicle Adv. Council, 1973—; mem. Days of '47 Parade Com., 1965-67. Served with AUS, 1943-45, 50-51; PTO, Korea. Mem. Public Relations Soc. Am. (pres. local chpt. 1979), Utah Assn. Advt. Agys. (pres. local chpt. 1976-77). Jewish. Clubs: Ambassador Athletic, Utah Westerners, Masons, Shrine (editor Minaret 1977—). Office: 68 S Main St Suite 607 Salt Lake City UT 84101

SHAPIRO, RICHARD STANLEY, physician; b. Moline, Ill., June 11, 1925; s. Herbert and Esther Dian (Grant) S.; B.S., St. Ambrose Coll., 1947; B.S. in Pharmacy, U. Iowa, 1951, M.S. in Hygiene, 1951, M.D., 1957; m. Arlene Blum, June 12, 1949; children—Michele Pamela, Bruce Grant, Gary Lawrence; m. 2d, Merry Lou Cook, Oct. 11, 1971. Pharmacist, Rock Island, Ill., 1951-53; research asst. U. Iowa Coll. Medicine, Iowa City, 1950-51, 53-57; practice medicine specializing in allergy, Beverly Hills, Calif., 1958-62, Lynwood, Calif., 1962—; attending physician Good Hope Found. Allergy Clinic, Los Angeles, 1958-62, Cedars of Lebanon Hosp., Hollywood, Calif., 1959-68, U. So. Calif.-Los Angeles County Med. Center, 1962—; physician St. Francis Hosp., Lynwood, 1962—; asso. clin. prof. medicine U. So. Calif., 1978—. Bd. dirs. Westside Jewish Community Center, 1961-65, Camp JCA, 1964-65. Served with USNR, 1943-45; PTO. Diplomate Am. Bd. Allergy and Immunology. Fellow Am. Geriatric Soc., Am. Coll. Allergy, Am. Assn. Clin. Immunology and Allergy; mem. Am. Soc. Tropical Medicine and Hygiene, Am. Acad. Allergy, Los Angeles Allergy Soc., AMA, Calif., Los Angeles County med. assns., West Coast Allergy Soc., AAAS, Am., Calif. socs. internal medicine, Calif. Soc. Allergy, Am. Heart Assn., Sierra Club, Sigma Xi. Jewish. Mason; mem. B'nai B'rith. Contbr. articles to profl. jours. Office: 11411 Brookshire Ave Downey CA 90241

SHAPIRO, VICTOR LENARD, mathematician, educator; b. Chgo., Oct. 16, 1924; s. Joseph E. and Anna (Grossman) S.; B.S., U. Chgo., 1947, M.S., 1949, Ph.D., 1952; m. Florence Gilman, Mar. 21, 1948;

children—Pamela Sue Shapiro Baer, Laura Fern Shapiro Young, Charles R., Arthur G. Mem. faculty Rutgers U., New Brunswick, N.J., 1952-55, asso. prof., 1955-58, prof., 1959-60; mem. Inst. for Advanced Studies, Princeton, N.J., 1953-55, 58-59; prof. U. Oreg., Eugene, 1960-64; mem. faculty U. Calif., Riverside, 1964—, prof. math., 1959—, Faculty research lectr., 1978. Served with AUS, 1943-46. NSF postdoctoral fellow, 1954-55. Mem. Am. Math. Soc., Math. Assn. Am., Soc. Indsl. and Applied Math. Author: Topics in Fourier and Geometric Analysis, 1961. Contbr. articles to profl. jours. Home: 3224 Celeste Dr Riverside CA 92507

SHARBAUGH, W(ILLIAM) JAMES, plastics co. exec.; b. Pitts., Apr. 13, 1914; s. Oliver M. and Sadie (Wingenroth) S.; B.S., Carnegie Inst. Tech., 1935; m. Eileen Carey, May 14, 1938; children—William James, Eileen (Mrs. W. A. Pinkerton, Jr.), Susan (Mrs. Kenneth A. Cote). Plastics engr. Mil. Products div. Mine Safety Appliances Co., Pitts., 1935-48; pres. Enpro Plastics, St. Louis, 1948-58; mgr. plastics div. Vulcanized Rubber & Plastics Co., Morrisville, Pa., 1958-60; pres. Plastics Assos., consultants, Yardley, Pa., 1960-63; v.p. sales and engring. Robroy Plastics div., Robroy Industries, Morrisville, 1964-66; v.p. mfg. and engring. FESCO div. Cities Service Co., Pitts., 1966-69; exec. v.p. Alladin Plastics div. Lenox, Inc., Los Angeles, 1969-72; gen. mgr. Rigid Plastics div. Crown Zellerbach, Inc., San Francisco, 1972-78; dir. Plastx, Inc.; founder Isobet U.S.A., 1977, Computerized Mgmt. Systems, 1980; instr. plastics engring. Pa. State U., 1943-44. Mem. Soc. Plastics Industry, Am. Mgmt. Assn., Soc. Plastics Engrs. (1st pres. 1945-46), Soc. Plastics Industry, Plastics Pioneers, Am. Mgmt. Assn., Tau Beta Pi. Club: Newport Beach Tennis. Home: 1516 Seacrest Dr Corona Del Mar CA 92625 Office: Plastics Assos 110 Newport Center Dr Newport Beach CA 92660

SHARDA, BAM DEV, sociologist, educator; b. Lyallpur, Pakistan, Nov. 5, 1938; came to U.S., 1968; s. Parma Nand and Hira Devi (Sharma) S.; m. Chander Kanta, Mar. 4, 1960 ; children—Asutosh, Navneet, Gireesh. B.A., Panjab U., India, 1963, M.A. in Sociology, 1966; Ph.D., U. Wis., 1974. Lectr. sociology U. Wis.-Madison, 1972-73; asst. prof. sociology U. Utah, Salt Lake City, 1973-80, assoc. prof., 1980—. Research fellow U. Utah, 1976-77; Am. Inst. Indian Studies fellow, 1976-77; Am. Council Learned Socs./Social Sci. Research Council fellow, 1975, 76; David P. Gardner Faculty fellow, 1983. Mem. Am. Sociol. Assn. (grantee), Internat. Sociol. Assn., Pacific Sociol. Assn., Wis. Union (life). Hindu. Author: Status Attainment in Rural India, 1977; contbr. articles to profl. jours. Home: 8395 S 1575 E Sandy UT 84092 Office: Dept Sociology U Utah Salt Lake City 84112

SHAREEF, MAHMOOD, civil engr.; b. Hyderabad, India, July 17, 1938; came to U.S., 1976, naturalized, 1983; s. Kahder and Mahboob (Begum) S.; B.Sc. in Math., Osmania U. (India), 1957, B.S. in Civil Engring., 1961; diploma Surrey U. (Eng.), 1972; m. Mohammedi Alam Khan, Oct. 7, 1965; children—Javed, Farah. Asst. exec. engr. Govt. India, Calcutta, 1964-65; asst. engr., sr. engr. Brit. Ministry of Transport, U.K. firms, 1966-76; structural analyst B-1 div. Rockwell Internat., Los Angeles, 1976-78; sr. structures engr. ASTECH div. TRE Corp., Santa Ana, Calif., 1978-80; sr. structures analyst space div. Rockwell Internat., Downey, Calif., 1980—. Brit. Sci. Research Council fellow, 1971-72. Home: 2926 Silver Ln Newport Beach CA 92660 Office: 12214 Lakewood Blvd Downey CA 90241

SHARKEY, PAMELA CARROLL, architect; b. San Diego, June 12, 1954; d. William Thomas and Johanna Elizabeth (Remmey) Carroll; B.S. in Architecture, Calif. Poly. State U. Sch. Architecture, 1977. Lic. architect, Calif.; m. Thomas James Sharkey, Aug. 11, 1979. Design architect-in-tng. Simpson & Gerber, La Jolla, Calif., 1977; architect-in-tng. Howard Oxley Assocs., La Jolla, 1977-78, Ladd, Kesley, Woodward, Newport Beach, Calif., 1978-79; staff architect Daniel L. Dworsky, Architects & Assocs., Los Angeles, 1979-83, Leach & Kehoe, architecture and planning, 1983—. Mem. AIA. Republican. Presbyterian. Office: 400 Esplanade Dr Oxnard CA 93030

SHARMA, KISHANDUTT JAYDAYAL, management and research consulting company executive; b. Sabarmati, India, July 29, 1937, came to U.S. 1967; s. Jaydayal S. and Satyavati J. Sharma; m. Meera K. Dixit; 1 child, Seema. B.E. in Mech. Engring., Gujarat U., India, 1959, B.E. in Elec. Engr., 1960; M.S. in Elec. Engr., U. Ottawa, 1964; Ph.D. in Systems Sci., Portland State U., 1974. Sr. Scientist Sperry Rand Corp., Montreal, Que., Can., 1963-67; sr. engr. Bechtel Corp., San Francisco, 1974-77; sr. staff mem. SRI Internat. (formerly Stanford Research Inst.), Menlo Park, Calif., 1977-79; project mgr. Calif. Energy Commn., Sacramento, 1979; pres., chief ops. officer Nero & Assocs., Portland, Oreg., Inc., 1981—; cons. Recipient Nat. Research Council of Canada award for grad. edn., 1963. Mem. AAAS, Internat. Club, World Future Soc., Smithsonian Assocs., Portland C. of C. Hindu. Author, co-author numerous publs. Office: Nero & Assoc Inc 520 SW 6th Ave Suite 1120 Portland OR 97204

SHARON, J. HALL, firearms mfg. co. exec.; b. Falmouth, Ky., Sept. 27, 1922; s. William Hall and Mary Margaret (Cummins) S.; student pub. schs., Falmouth; m. Anna Elizabeth Hargett, June 28, 1947; children—Dennis Hall, Steven Carroll. Machinist, Allis Chalmers, Cin., 1940-42; coop. with Ohio Mech. Instn., 1946; with Cin. Milling Machine Co., 1947-53; machinist Hughes Aircraft, Culver City, Calif., 1953-60; owner, operator custom gun shop, part-time 1953-60; owner, operator Sharon Gun Shop, Kalispell, Mont., 1960—, Sharon Rifle Barrel Co., Kalispell, 1962-78, Sharon Wood Products, Kalispell, 1970-78; co-owner Sharon Gun Spltys., Sonora, Calif., 1979—. Served with USN, 1942-46. Mem. Christian Ch. Club: Rotary. Home and Office: 14587 Peaceful Valley Rd Sonora CA 95370

SHARON, TIMOTHY MICHAEL, physicist; b. Portsmouth, Va., Aug. 21, 1948; s. Lester Clark and Ruth May (Banister) S.; student Santa Ana Coll., 1966-68; B.A., U. Calif.-Irvine 1970, M.A., 1972, Ph.D., 1976; m. Carla Deon Colley, Dec. 17, 1977. Jr. specialist solid state theory U. Calif.-Irvine, 1976, research asst. radiation physics Med. Center and Sch. Medicine, 1976-77, cons. to attending staff Research and Edn. Found., 1976-77; mktg. physicist Varian Assos., Irvine, 1977-78; prin. engr., program mgr. Spectra Research Systems, Newport Beach, Calif., 1977-82; v.p. Brewer-Sharon Corp., Newport Beach, 1981—; adj. faculty physics and engring. Columbia Pacific U., San Rafael, Calif., 1981—; adj. asst. prof. radiol. scis. Sch. Medicine, U. Calif.-Irvine, 1982; dean Sch. Engring., Newport U., Newport Beach, Calif., 1983—; mem. adv. panel on pub. Am. Inst. Physics, 1974-75. Brython P. Davis univ. fellow, 1973-74. Mem. AAAS, Am. Phys. Soc., Brit. Interplanetary Soc. (asso. fellow), Am. Assn. Physicists in Medicine, Soc. Sci. Exploration, Smithsonian Instn., Am. Film Inst., Nat. Hist. Soc., Mensa, Intertel, Sigma Pi Sigma, Phi Theta Kappa, Alpha Gamma Sigma. Contbr. articles to profl. jours. Office: 3901 Westerly Pl Suite 205 Newport Beach CA 92660

SHARP, DAVID LEE, advertising executive, consultant; b. Chgo., Apr. 18, 1952; s. Homer Glenn and Jo Ann (Harbour) S.; m. Christine Rowe, Oct. 18, 1975; 1 dau., Tara Ann. B.S., Bradley U., 1974; M.S., U. Ill., 1975. Advt. exec. Caterpillar Tractor, Peoria, Ill., 1975-76; sales promotion supr. Armstrong Cork Co., Lancaster, Pa., 1976-78; sr. acct. exec. Kraft Smith Advt., Seattle, 1978-80; pres. Sharp, Hartwig Advt., Inc., Seattle, 1980—; chmn. Response Mktg., Inc., Seattle, 1982—; instr. Cornish Inst., 1980; cons. Simpson Timber Co., Seattle Opera. Trustee, Eastside Community Mental Health Center, 1983—. Bus. Profl. Advt. Assn. (v.p. 1982-83), Intermarket Assn. Advt. Agy., Am. Assn. Advt. Agy., Seattle Advt. Fedn. Republican. Methodist. Clubs: Wash. Athletic; Juanita Bay Athletic; Univ. Rotary (program chmn. 1982-83). Home: 10933 NE 160th Kirkland WA 98033 Office: 100 West Harrison Plaza North Tower Seattle WA 98119

SHARP, DOUGLAS RICE, clergyman; b. Monte Vista, Colo., Mar. 1, 1949; s. William Edward and Pauline Marie (Settle) S.; B.A., William Jewell Coll., 1971; M.Div., Am. Bapt. Sem. of West, 1975; Ph.D., Grad. Theol. Union, 1984; m. Linda K. Sharp; children—Michelle Lynn, Jason Douglas. Ordained to ministry Am. Baptist Ch., 1975; pastor Immanuel Chapel, South Fork, Colo., 1971; chaplain VA Hosp., La Jolla, Calif., 1972; asso. minister 1st Bapt. Ch., San Diego, 1973; adminstrv. asst. to v.p. Am. Bapt. Sem. of West, Berkeley, Calif., 1973-74, asso. dir. field edn., 1974-75, dir. field edn., 1975—, instr. theology, 1977—, registrar, 1977—; minister edn. Ch. of Valley, San Ramon, Calif., 1977-79. Recipient Clairborne M. Hill award Am. Bapt. Sem. of West, 1975; Pulliam scholar, 1975, 76; Order of Eastern Star grantee, 1975. Mem. Minister's Council Am. Bapt. Chs. U.S.A., Assn. for Theol. Field Edn., Assn. for Profl. Edn. for Ministry, Am. Soc. Ch. History. Democrat. Club: Masons. Research in 19th and 20th century reformed theology. Home: 377 Belmont Ave Oakland CA 94610 Office: Am Bapt Sem of West 2515 Hillegass Ave Berkeley CA 94704

SHARP, LINDA N., communications company executive; b. Clayton, N.Mex., Feb. 17, 1947; d. Frank and Ada Sharp. B.S., Oreg. State U., 1969. Correspondent, KOAT-TV, N.Mex. Tech. News Bur., 1966-67; sci. writer, news bur. Oreg. Stater Alumni Mag., 1966-67; pub. relations dir. St. Vincent Hosp. and Med. Center, 1969-71; mgr. in pub. relations dept. AT&T Long Lines, 1971-73; pres. Sharp Communications, Inc., San Mateo, Calif., 1974—. Mem. Internat. Assn. Bus. Communicators (founder, past pres. local chpt., awards San Francisco Peninsula chpt. 1973, 78), Women in Advt., Women in Communications, Soc. Profl. Mgmt. Cons., Pub. Relations Soc. Am. (award 1980), Ad Mark, Soc. Tech. Communications, Calif. Press Women (awards 1973, 78-82), No. Calif. Advt. Agys. Assn., San Francisco Publicity Club, Prodn. Women's. Clubs: Metropolitan, Commonwealth. Editor, pub.: Making Your Rome in the Bay Area, 1982. Office: 1650 Borel Pl Suite 234 San Mateo CA 94402

SHARP, VERNON EUEL, rancher; b. Perryton, Tex., Oct. 28, 1943; s. Clifton Perry and Juanita Winona (Morris) S.; student Tex. A&M U., 1962; student Otero Jr.Coll., 1963-65, A.A., 1969; m. Priscilla Kay Waddelow, Mar. 18, 1964; children—Billie Jo Irene, Bobbie Jo Kay, Vernon Lee. Mgr., Sharp Ranch, Lockwood, Colo., 1963-72, Wet Canyon, Colo., 1965-68, Branson, Colo., 1968—, v.p., 1973, sec., 1974—. Bd. dirs. Branson Community Ch., 1973—; del. Las Animas County Republican Conv., 1976, 78, 80, Colo. Conv.,1980; mem. parent adv. com. Branson Sch., 1976-80, chmn., 1979-80; mem. Sch. Improvement Com., 1979-82. Mem. Colo. Cattlemen's Assn., So. Colo. Livestock Assn. (exec. bd. 1981—), Am. Dairy Goat Assn., Colo. Dairy Goat Assn., Fur Taker of Am., Colo. Trappers Assn., NRA, Am. Def. Preparedness Assn., Nat. Right-to-Work Com., U.S. Chess Fedn. (tournament dir. 1981-84), Corr. Chess League Am. Address: Sharp Ranch Branson CO 81029

SHARROW, STEVEN HAROLD, range science educator, range ecologist, researcher; b. Kentfield, Calif., Jan. 29, 1949; s. Harold Howard and Joan (Loudon) S.; m. Margaret Ann (Ferguson, May 15, 1975. B.S. in Range Mgmt., U. Calif.-Davis, 1971; M.S., Tex. Tech. U., 1973, Ph.D. in Agr., 1975. Research asst. Tex. Tech. U., Lubbock, 1971-75; asst. prof. range sci. N.Mex. State U., Las Cruces, 1975-76; asst. prof. rangeland resources Oreg. State U., Corvallis, 1976-81, assoc. prof., 1981—. Recipient Outstanding Performance cert. U. Calif.-Davis, 1971; Outstanding Teachers Registry award Sch. Agr., Oreg. State U., 1982. Mem. Soc. Range Mgmt., Am. Soc. Animal Sci., Am. Soc. Agronomy, Oreg. Acad. Scis., Phi Kappa Phi, Alpha Zeta, Sigma Xi. Republican. Episcopalian. Assoc. editor: Jour. Range Mgmt., 1981—; contbr. articles to profl. jours. Office: Dept Rangeland Resources Oreg State U Corvallis OR 97331

SHARTS, CLAY MARCUS, chemist, educator; b. Long Beach, Calif., Feb. 9, 1931; s. Casper A. and Mary Ruth (Cowlishaw) S.; B.S., U. Calif., Berkeley, 1952; Ph.D., Calif. Inst. Tech., Pasadena, 1969; m. Jean Elizabeth Davis, Aug. 21, 1978; children—Christopher C., Melora Lee, Kimberly Ann, Vanessa Denise. Sr. research chemist explosives dept. E.I. du Pont de Nemours & Co. Inc., Wilmington, Del., 1958-62; summer research Naval Ordnance Lab., Corona, Calif., 1964, 65, 66; mem. faculty U. Calif., San Diego, summers 1974-76, 78-80; prof. chemistry San Diego State U., 1969—; cons. UNESCO, 1977-78; cons. in field. Served as lt. (j.g.), USNR, 1952-55; Korea; capt. Res. Recipient Disting. Teaching award Trustees Calif. State U. and Colls., 1967; NSF sci. faculty fellow U. Cologne, W. Ger., 1972-73. Mem. Am. Chem. Soc., AAAS, N.Y. Acad. Sci., U.S. Naval Inst., Naval Res. Assn., Sigma Xi. Author: (with W.A. Sheppard) Organic Fluorine Chemistry, 1969; contbg. author book, contbr. articles on organic chemistry to profl. jours.; patentee in field. Home: PO Box 15487 San Diego CA 92115 Office: Dept Chemistry San Diego State U San Diego CA 92182

SHAVEY, GARY LEE, architect; b. Enid, Okla., Aug. 20, 1933; s. Lee Orville and Sibyl Ione (Benson) S.; m. June Francis Brower, Sept. 1, 1960; children—Gregory, Geoffrey, Jason, Gary Lee. B.Arch., Okla. State U., 1956. Jr. ptnr. Ralf E. Decker, Architects, Seattle, 1956-66; ptnr. Shavey & Schmidt, Architects, Seattle, 1966-75, Shavey Schmidt Degrasse Shavey, Seattle, 1975-77; ptnr. Shavey-DeGrasse Shavey Ptnrs. in Architecture, Seattle, 1977—. Deacon, Mercer Island Presbyn. Ch., 1981—. Mem. AIA (1st v.p. Seattle chpt. 1982, pres. 1983), Seattle Execs. Assn. (pres. 1975), Soc. Mktg. Profl. Services. Republican. Club: Wash. Athletic. Home: 7900 Northbrook Ln Mercer Island WA 98040 Office: 1928 Pike Pl Seattle WA 98101

SHAW, AUDREY INA, contractor, construction manager; b. Los Angeles, Feb. 20, 1952; s. Sylvester Joseph and Florence Virginia (Steward) Ina; m. Anderson Fredrick Shaw, Jan. 1975; children—Anthony Michael, Audra Ina. Student UCLA, 1972-75. Lic. gen. contractor, constrn. mgr., Calif. Office mgr. Sylvester J. Ina & Co., Los Angeles, 1970-80; ptnr., v.p. SI Constrn. Mgmt., Inc., Los Angeles, 1981—; pres. Ina Constrn. Co., Inc., Los Angeles, 1980—. Mem. Wilshire Bus. Profl. Womens Club; Los Angeles Urban League. Democrat. Roman Catholic. Office: 5041 Venice Blvd Los Angeles CA 90018

SHAW, CHARLES BERGMAN, JR., physicist; b. Dallas, June 7, 1927; s. Charles Bergman and Estelle (Goldstein) S.; B.S., Calif. Inst. Tech., 1947; M.S., U. So. Calif., 1950, Ph.D., 1958; m. 2d, Luchia Evelyn Alcott Powers, June 6, 1966; children—David Elliot, Suzanne Roberta. Research asst. Los Alamos (N.Mex.) Sci. Lab., 1949; physicist Nat. Bur. Standards, Corona, Calif., 1951, Lockheed Missile Systems Div., Van Nuys, Calif., 1954-56, Hughes Research Labs., Malibu, Calif., 1956-64, Electro-Optical Systems, Pasadena, Calif., 1964-66; group scientist Autonetics div. N.Am. Rockwell Corp., Anaheim, Calif., 1966-70, scientist Rockwell Internat. Sci. Center, Thousand Oaks, Calif., 1970—, project mgr., 1971—. Lab. asso. physics U. So. Calif., 1947-49, lectr. math., 1951-54; vis. prof. physics Loyola U., Los Angeles, 1960; mem. U.S. del. Internat. Inst. Welding. Served with USNR, 1945. Mem. Am. Phys. Soc., Am. Math. Soc., Soc. for Indsl. and Applied Math., IEEE, Am. Welding Soc., Los Angeles World Affairs Council, Assocs. of Calif. Inst. Tech., Sigma Xi. Clubs: Town Hall, Athenaeum. Contbr. articles to profl. jours. Research in engring. physics and applied math. Home: 4524 Seven Oaks Ct Westlake Village CA 91361 Office: PO Box 1085 Thousand Oaks CA 91360

SHAW, EDDY LYNN, construction company executive; b. Ogden, Utah, Aug. 11, 1937; s. Lawrence Edmund and Elizabeth Marie (Lindsay) S.; m. Ilene Stark, Feb. 1, 1957; children—Sandra, Wade Lynn, Lisa. Student Weber State Coll., 1955-57. With Bouchard & Stark Constrn. Co., Ogden, 1957-67, foreman, 1958-67; owner, operator Eddy L. Shaw Constrn. Co. (inc. 1974), Layton, Utah, 1967-74, pres., 1974—. Merit badge counselor Booneville council Boy Scouts Am., 1958-75. Mem. U. S. C. of C., Associated Gen. Contractors. Club: Oakridge Country (Farmington, Utah). Office: 2788 E 200 N Layton UT 84041

SHAW, GEORGE WILLIAM, II, microsystems analyst; b. Castro Valley Calif., Oct. 13, 1959; s. George William and Julia Anna (Holmes) S. A.A. in Data Processing, Chabot Coll., 1981, A.A., in Bus. Adminstrn., 1982. Asst. mgr. Computer Systems Unlimited, San Lorenzo, Calif., 1976; mgr. Byte Shop, Haywood Calif., 1977, Mountain View, Calif., 1978; owner, mgr. Shaw Labs, 1978—. Mem. Forth Interest Group (charter com. mem., referee internat. standards team). Contbr. papers to profl. jours and confs. Office: Shaw Labs 24301 Southland Dr Suite 216 Haywood CA 94544

SHAW, GHITA MILGROM, educational administration consultant; b. N.Y.C., Dec. 25, 1929; d. Max and Getrude Etta (Lemberg) Milgrom; m. Arnold Shaw, May 18, 1959; 1 dau., Mindy Sura. B.S., U. Nev.-Las Vegas, 1971, M.Ed., 1974. Cert. spl. edn. tchr., sch. adminstr., Nev. Asst. to dir. N.Y. Herald Tribune Forum, N.Y. Herald Tribune, N.Y.C., 1950-52; asst. to dir. publicity Edward B. Marks Music Corp., N.Y.C., 1954-56; tchr. spl. edn. Clark County Sch. Dist., Las Vegas, Nev., 1972-75, coordinating cons., cons. in spl. edn., 1975—, site adminstr. elem. summer sch., 1983; guest lectr. U. Nev. Bd. dirs. Temple Beth Sholom Pre-Sch., Las Vegas, 1970-79; bd. dirs. Jewish Family Service Agy., 1982—. Mem. Assn. Supervision and Curriculum Devel., Council Exceptional Children Assn. Children with Learning Disabilities (mem. Nev. profl. adv. bd.), Phi Delta Kappa, Kappa Delta Pi. Author: Special Education Dictionary for Regular Classroom Teachers and Parents, 1981; (with Cansdale and Reid) Guidelines for Elementary Special Education, 1975, Developing Prerequisite Skills, 1980. Home: 2288 Gabriel Dr Las Vegas NV 89109 Office: Clark County Sch Dist 600 N Ninth St Las Vegas NV 89101

SHAW, IMARA, health care exec.; b. Glendale, Calif., Jan. 4, 1946; d. Clarence Gould and Mary Mahala Celeste (Cunningham) Leland; student Pasadena City Coll., 1965; m. Stephen Shaw, Dec. 19, 1971. Research dir. Hertz Lion, Beverly Hills, Calif., 1963-64; fashion model Nina Blanchard, Los Angeles, 1964-65, Model Service Agy., N.Y.C., 1965-67; dir. Shelton Health Club, Lexington, N.Y., 1967-68; communications officer Hubbard Research Found., Mediterranean, 1968-69; tech. cons. Beverly Hills Health Club for Women, 1969-70; mgr. Shaw Health Center, Reseda and West Los Angeles, Calif., 1970-76; chmn. bd. Shaw Mgmt. Corp., Los Angeles, 1976—. Bd. dirs. Thomas Paine Inst. for Human Action, 1982; spl. advisor U.S. Congl. Adv. Bd. Mem. Nat. Assn. Women Bus. Owners, Public Relations Soc. Am., Hollywood C. of C., Los Angeles Area C. of C., Book Publicists So. Calif., Women's Referral Services, Nat. Health Fedn., Nat. Women's Health Network, Delphian Found., Nat. Assn. Female Execs., So. Calif. Soc. Hosp. Pub. Relations, Producers and Assocs. Pub. Access, Direct Mktg. Creative Guild, Internat. Platform Orgn., Town Hall, others. Contbr. articles to profl. jours. Office: 5336 Fountain Ave Los Angeles CA 90029

SHAW, JOHN FIRTH, orchestra administrator; b. Chesterfield, U.K., June 28, 1948; s. Jack Firth and Mary Stuart (MacPherson) S.; m. Julia Valette Phillips, Dec. 29, 1973; children—Mary Valette, Mark Firth, Andrew Nicholas. Licentiate Royal Acad. Music, 1968; grad. Royal Schs. of Music, 1970. Freelance musician, 1966-70; prin. musician Calgary Phil. Orch., 1970-77, asst. mgr., 1977-78, asst. gen. mgr., 1978-79, gen. mgr., 1979—. Bd. dirs. Calgary Philharm. Soc., 1974-77, Calgary Centre for Performing Arts, 1980—. Mem. Assn. Can. Orchs. (dir. 1982—). Office: 505 5th St SW Suite 200 Calgary AB T2P 3J2 Canada

SHAW, JOHN SCRANTON, II, professional association executive; b. Atlanta, May 29, 1944; s. Philip M. and Ruth Jeanette (Pedersen) S.; m. Cornelia Stone Roberts, June 6, 1970; children—Jerol Stacy, Katharine Roberson, John Scranton. B.A., Wesleyan U., Conn., 1966; M.B.A., Fla. Atlantic U., 1977. Cert. assn. exec., Am. Soc. Assn. Execs. Gen. mgr. Screen Printing Assn. Internat., 1972-76; exec. dir. Associated Landscape Contractors Am., McLean, Va., 1976-81; exec. dir. Am. Soc. Plumbing Engrs., Sherman Oaks, Calif., 1982—. Served with U.S. Army, 1968-70. Mem. Am. Soc. Assn. Execs., Greater Washington Soc. Assn. Execs., So. Calif. Soc. Assn. Exec. Republican. Episcopalian. Office: 15233 Ventura Blvd #811 Sherman Oaks CA 91403

SHAW, MARC D., optometrist; b. Glendale, Calif., Nov. 10, 1951; s. H.R. and Dorothy Louise (Klimmer) S.; m. Cammie I. Hunt, Oct. 3, 1981. B.A. in Biology, U. Calif.-San Diego, 1973; O.D., U. Calif.-Berkeley, 1979. Lic. optometrist, Calif. Asst. clin. prof. Sch. Optometry, U. Houston, 1979-80; practice optometry, Ben Lomond, Calif., 1982—; dir. Doran Resource Ctr. for Blind. Recipient Bausch & Lomb award for excellence in contact lens fitting, 1979; Pres.'s Undergrad. fellow, 1972. Mem. Calif. Optometric Assn., U. Calif.-Berkeley Sch. Optometry Alumni Assn., Am. Optometric Assn., San Lorenzo Valley C. of C.. Office: Mark Shaw 7965 Hwy 9 Ben Lomond CA 95005

SHAW, RICHARD BLAKE, sculptor, educator; b. Hollywood, Calif., Sept. 12, 1941. Student Orange Coast Coll., 1961-63; B.F.A., San Francisco Art Inst., 1965; postgrad. Alfred U., 1965; M.A., U. Calif.-Davis, 1968. Works exhibited in permanent collections: Oakland (Calif.) Mus., San Francisco Mus., Nat. Mus. Art, Tokyo, Stdelijk Mus., Amsterdam, Holland, Whitney Mus. Am. Art., N.Y.C.; one-man shows: Dilexi Gallery, San Francisco, 1968, San Francisco Mus. Art, 1973, Braunstein Gallery, 1970, 71, 73, 76, 79, 81, Alan Frumkin Gallery, N.Y.C., 1980, Whitney Mus. Am. Art, 1970, 81, Contemporary Am. Ceramic Mus. Modern Art, Kyoto and Tokyo, 1971-72, Internat. Ceramics, 1972, Victoria & Albert Mus., London, 1972, Mus. Contemporary Art, Chgo., 1976, Renwick Gallery, Smithsonian Instn., Washington, 1976, 79, (painting and sculpture) Nat. Collection Fine Arts, Washington, 1977, Joslyn Art Mus., Omaha, 1977, San Jose Mus. Art, 1981, Boise Gallery Art, 1982, Mendel Art Gallery, 1982, Greenberg Gallery, Mo., 1982; chmn. ceramics dept. San Francisco Art Inst., 1965; mem. faculty U Wis.-Madison, summer 1971. Nat. Endowment Arts grantee, 1970, 74; U. Calif. faculty grantee, 1972; Agnus Brandenstein fellow, 1964-65. Office: San Francisco Art Inst 800 Chestnut St San Francisco CA 94133*

SHAW, RICHARD LOUIS, remote sensing cons.; b. Champaign, Ill., Apr. 27, 1924; s. Scott Neuton and Helen Elizabeth (Breen) S.; B.S. in Geology, Colo. Sch. Mines, 1949; m. Raquel Ferreira Sanchez, June 13,

1969; children—Kieran, Liam. Sr. resident engr. ITT, Can., Europe, 1961-67; cons. Louis Berger, Inc., 1968-73; pres., owner Am. Infrared & Ground Radar Cons., Inc., Beaverton, Oreg., 1973—. Served with U.S. Army, 1942-45. Roman Catholic. Club: Elks. Contbr. tech. papers to profl. jours.; pub. Remote Sensing News (newsletter). Home: PO Box 1103 Beaverton OR 97005 Office: 14755 SW Carolwood Dr Beaverton OR 97007

SHAW, ROBERT BARRY, landscape architect; b. Oakland, Calif., Aug. 16, 1937; s. Marshall Alexander and Nadene (Freitas) S.; B. Landscape Architecture, U. Calif. at Berkeley, 1962; m. Sandra O'Kelly, June 16, 1966 (div. 1974); children—Tambi, Kimberley; m. Libby Norman, Jan. 21, 1980. Lassen Forest landscape architect U.S. Forest Service, Susanville, Calif., 1962-66; landscape architect Bur. Indian Affairs, Denver, 1966-68; regional landscape architect HUD, Los Angeles, 1968—. Served with AUS, 1959-60. Mem. U. Calif. Alumni Assn., Am. Soc. Landscape Architects, Long Beach C. of C., Sierra Club, Aircraft Owners and Pilots Assn., Sigma Phi Epsilon. Home: 6226 Marina Pacifica Dr N Long Beach CA 90803 Office: 2500 Wilshire Blvd Los Angeles CA 90057

SHAW, STAFFORD EDGAR, railroad yardmaster; b. Adel, Ga., Apr. 16, 1934; s. Lacy Newton and Margaret (Sizemore) S.; m. Ann Marie Brozovich, June 30, 1956; children—Stafford Edgar, Jr., Lacie Ann, Erin Cristene Ward; m. 2d, Sharon Alma Webb, Nov. 27, 1972 (div.); m. 3d, Carolyn Sue Cox, May 27, 1983. Trainman N.P. Ry., Auburn, Wash., 1957-66; machinist A.C. Finishing Co., Tacoma, Wash., 1966-68; switchman, foreman, yardmaster Tacoma Belt Line, Tacoma, 1968—. Sec., treas. Union Local #1, Tacoma, 1980-82. Served with U.S. Army, 1952-56. Democrat. Baptist. Office: 2601 East West Rd Tacoma WA 98424

SHAW, STEPHEN KENT, political science educator; b. Shreveport, La., Aug. 19, 1952; s. Murph Douglas and Lucille (McNair) S.; m. Catherine Ann Henderson. B.A. in Polit. Sci., Bethany Nazarene Coll., 1974; M.A. in Polit. Sci., U. Okla., 1976, Ph.D. in Polit. Sci., 1983. Research, teaching asst. sci. and pub. policy program, U. Okla., Norman, 1976-78; prof. polit. sci. Bethany (Okla.) Nazarene Coll., 1977-79; prof.; polit. sci. N.W. Nazarene Coll., Nampa, Idaho, 1979—. Mem. Canyon County (Idaho) Democratic Central Com. Mem. Am. Polit. Sci. Assn., Idaho Polit. Sci. Assn., Pacific N.W. Polit. Sci. Assn., Western Polit. Sci. Assn., Ctr. Study of the Presidency Policy Studies Orgn. Home: 525 Burke Ln Nampa ID 83651 Office: NW Nazarene Coll Dewey and Holly Sts Nampa ID 83651

SHAW, VALERIE BRENDA, publisher; b. Los Angeles, Oct. 16, 1944; d. Bennie Bernard and Earline (Chase) Shaw; m. Matt Benson, Sept. 8, 1973 (div.). B.A., U. So. Calif., 1966, M.Publ. Relations, 1978. Ticket agt., community relations liaison Trans World Airlines, Los Angeles, 1965-71; mgr. dept. media research Carson/Roberts Advt., Inc., Los Angeles, 1971-72; ptnr., sales mgr. Profl. Promotions Disthg. Co., Los Angeles, 1972-75; mem. staff newsbur., broadcast specialist Lockheed Calif. Co., Los Angeles, 1976-78; film producer, writer FMS Prodns., Inc., Los Angeles, 1979; staff writer Los Angeles Times, 1980; pres., chief exec. officer L.A.-D.C. Connection, Inc., Los Angeles, 1980—; lectr. U. So. Calif. Sch. Journalism, 1980-81, Los Angeles Trade Tech. Coll., 1982. Recipient Drugs and Soc. award John Muir Med. Film Festival, 1980; Burson-Marsteller Communications grantee, 1979. mem. Black Journalists Assn. So. Calif. (co-founder), Pub. Relations Soc. Am., NOW, Black Women's Network, NAACP, Black Employees Assn. (co-editor jour. 1982-83, Sigma Delta Chi. Mem. Founders Ch. of Religious Sci. Club: Toastmasters. Author, publisher calendars, posters, sch. curricula Black Hollywood Yesterday; producer, writer film Women and Alcohol: Through the Drinking Glass, 1980, The Welfare Paradox: Cycles of Relief, 1979. Office: PO Box 38815 Los Angeles CA 90038

SHAWCROFT, ROY WAYNE, agronomist, soil scientist; b. LaJara, Colo., Aug. 17, 1938; s. John Howard and Marvelle (Reed) S.; m. Marian David, June 15, 1967; children—Julie, Steven. B.S., Colo. State U., 1961, M.S., 1965; Ph.D., Cornell U., 1970. Soil scientist U.S. Dept. Agr., Akron, 1961-65; soil scientist Agrl. Research Service, 1970-82; grad. research asst. Cornell U., 1965-70; irrigation extension specialist Colo. State U., 1982—. Mem. Am. Soc. Agronomy, Soil Sci. Soc. Am., Soc. Preservation and Encouragement of Barbershop Quartet Singing in Am. Mormon. Office: PO Box K Akron CO 80720

SHAWSTAD, RAYMOND VERNON, computer specialist; b. Brainerd, Minn., Mar. 17, 1931; stepson Klaas Ostendorf, s. Ruth Catherine Hammond; student W. Coast U., 1960-62; UCLA Extension, 1966-81, Liberal Inst. Natural Sci. and Tech., 1973—, Free Enterprise Inst., 1973—; m. Dora Arlene Campbell, Dec. 21, 1952; m. 2d, Winifred Ann Lory, Sept. 28, 1978. Salesman, Marshalltown, Iowa, 1952-53; asst. retail mgr. Gamble-Skogmo, Inc., Waverly, Iowa, 1953-54, retail mgr., Iowa Falls, 1954-57; sr. programmer County of San Bernardino (Calif.), 1958-64; info. systems cons. Sunkist Growers, Inc., Van Nuys, Calif., 1965-75, sr. systems programmer, 1975—; univ. extension instr. UCLA, 1980—; cons., tchr. in field, 1961-63. Mem. Assn. Computing Machinery, Bus. Data Processing and Software Engring., Assn. Systems Mgmt., Data Processing Mgmt. Assn. (cert.). Author numerous software programs. Home: PO Box 551 Van Nuys CA 91408 Office: PO Box 7888 Van Nuys CA 91409

SHAY, PETER YUNGCHING, investment company executive; b. Shanghai, China, July 17, 1934; came to U.S., 1974, naturalized, 1980; s. Chung Liu and Chi Chiou (Chen) S.; B.S., Cheng Kung U., 1958; M.S., Va. Poly. U., 1962; m. Jean Wu, Aug. 31, 1963; children—Shirley, Thomas, Dennis. Chief engr. Mayer Steel Pipe Mfg. Co., Tapei, Taiwan, 1963-65; v.p., plant mgr. Kuo Hwa Chem. Corp., Taiwan, 1965-77; pres. Golden Cosmos Investment Corp., Palos Verdes Estates, Calif., 1977—. Served to 2d lt. Engring. Corps., Republic of China, 1958-60. Office: 2340 W Sepulveda Blvd Suite J Torrance CA 90501

SHEA, JAMES GORMAN, educational administrator; b. Rochester, N.Y., Oct. 7, 1946; s. John Gill and Agnes (Jennings) S.; m. Margaret K. Owen, Feb. 8, 1969; children—Susan, Kathryn, Amy, Sarah. M.B.A., Utah State U., 1975. Br. mgr. Logan (Utah) Savs. and Loan, 1975-76; placement supr. Job Service, East Brigham City, Utah, 1976-80; dir. student services Bridgerland Area Vocat. Ctr., Logan, 1980—; cons. Career Dynamic, Inc., 1982. Served with USAF, 1968-72. Mem. Utah Personnel and Guidance Assn., Utah Employment Counselors Assn., Utah Pub. Employees Assn., Utah Assn. Fin. Aid Adminstrs., Nat. Employment and Tng. Assn., VFW (past comdr). Club: Lions. Office: UMC 10 Utah State U Logan UT 84322

SHEA, PHYLLIS N. T., accountant; b. Honolulu, Oct. 2, 1940; d. Edward S. and Dorothy L. (Ling) S.; B.S. in Bus. Adminstrn., Chaminade U. Honolulu, 1962. Staff acct. James W. Y. Wong, C.P.A., Honolulu, 1962-65; partner Wong & Shea, C.P.A.s, Honolulu, 1966-75; sole practitioner Phyllis N. T. Shea, C.P.A., Honolulu, 1975-79, pres., 1979—; dir. Imperial Assos., Ltd., Travel House, Inc., both Honolulu; mem. Hawaii State Bd. Accountancy, 1979—; trustee Lanakila Crafts, 1981—. Mem. Kaimuki Neighborhood Bd., 1979; treas. Chaminade U. Ednl. Found., 1980; regent Chaminade U.; mem. exec. bd. Community Scholarship Program, State of Hawaii, 1980. Mem. Am. Inst. C.P.A.s, Nat. Accts. Assn., Hawaii Soc. C.P.A.s, Am. Women Soc. C.P.A.s (pres. Ednl. Found. 1980-81). Roman Catholic. Office: 1575 S Beretania St Honolulu HI 96826

SHEA, TIMOTHY PETER, podiatrist; b. San Diego, July 11, 1947; s. Peter E. and Patricia M. (White) S.; B.S. in Biology, U. San Francisco, 1969; D. Podiatric Medicine, Calif. Coll. Podiatric Medicine, 1973; m. Angela Marie Neville, Sept. 4, 1971; 1 son, Matthew Taylor. Resident in surgery Calif. Coll. Podiatric Medicine, 1973-75; practice podiatric medicine, San Francisco, 1976-78, Concord, Calif., 1979—; assoc. prof. podiatric medicine Calif. Coll. Podiatric Medicine, San Francisco, 1975-79, prof. podiatric surgery, 1975—, prof. podiatric medicine and surgery 1979—, chief of staff, dir. clinics Podiatric Med. Center, 1975-78; mem. med.-surg. staff Calif. Podiatry Hosp., San Francisco, Mt. Diablo Hosp., Concord; mem. courtesy staff Port Hueneme Hosp., Ventura, Calif., John Muir Hosp., Walnut Creek, Calif.; mem. cons. staff Vallejo Gen. Hosp., Vallejo, Calif.; clin. instr. home care dept. U. Calif. Med. Center, San Francisco, 1974-78, guest lectr. podiatric medicine in primary care medicine, 1976—; podiatric cons. and guest speaker Over Easy, Sta. KQED-TV, 1977—; guest lectr. podiatric medicine local TV and radio programs, 1975—, Western Podiatry Congress, 1978-81; guest lectr. Am. Diabetes Assn., 1976, 77, 79, 81. Recipient Man of Yr. award Calif. Podiatry Student Assn., 1972; diplomate Am. Bd. Podiatric Surgery. Fellow Am. Foot Orthopedists, Am. Soc. Laser Medicine and Research; mem. Am. Public Health Assn., Am. Podiatry Assn. (lectr. convs. 1975, 81), Calif. Podiatry Assn., Am. Coll. Foot Surgeons (asso. mem.), Cousteau Soc., Condord C. of C., Alameda-Contra Costa Podiatry Soc., Calif. Coll. Podiatric Medicine Alumni Assn., Pi Omega Delta, Pi Delta, Omicron Theta Chi. Clubs: Kiwanis, Rotary. Home: 647 Augustine Ln Lafayette CA 94549 Office: Bacon-East Med Center 2425 East St Concord CA 94520

SHEARER, DAVID ROSS, behavioral medicine specialist, educator; b Houston, Mar. 2, 1950; s. Hutton A. and Francile (Thompson) S.; m. Penelope Lynn Potter, May 18, 1972 (div.). B.A. in Psychology and Biology, Tex. Christian U., 1972, M.A. in Clin. Psychology, 1977. Lic. marriage, family, child counselor, Calif.; cert. psychol. assoc. Tex. Supr. dept. respiratory therapy Smith Hosp., Ft. Worth, 1972-74; coordinator adolescent treatment Psychiat. Inst. Ft. Worth, 1974-75; psychol. assoc. Ft. Worth Psychol. Ctr., 1974-77; psychologist Tex. Dept. Mental Health, San Angelo Ctr., Carlsbad, Tex., 1977-78; flight service dir. Am. Airlines Inc., Los Angeles, 1979-81; behavioral med. specialist Healthing Ctr., Straub Clinic and Hosp., Honolulu, 1982—. Mem. adv. bd. Diamond Head Mental Health Ctr., chmn. children's team com. Mem. Am. Psychol. Assn., Hawaii Psychol. Assn., Am. Acad. Behavioral Medicine, Acad. Psychologists Marital Sex Family Therapy, Am. Orthopsychiat. Assn., Psy Chi, Alpha Phi Omega. Republican. Episcopalian. Clubs: Holland (Houston). Home: 2452 Tusitala St 710 Honolulu HI 96815 Office: Straub Clinic and Hosp 888 S King St Honolulu HI 96813

SHEARER, KENNETH EUGENE, telemarketing consultant; b. Cin., Apr. 23, 1931; s. Frank and Annabelle (Ervin) S.; student Ohio State U., 1949-51; B.S. in Sociology and Polit. Sci., Central State Coll., Wilberforce, Ohio, 1957; postgrad. Law Sch., Franklin U., Columbus, Ohio, 1957-60, Wharton Sch. Fin., U. Pa., 1971-74; M.A. in Community Orgn. and Urban Affairs, U. Pitts., 1964; div.; children—Kenneth Alexis, Elizabeth Anne. Adminstrv. asst. to welfare dir. State of Ohio, 1953-55; caseworker, br. office mgr. Newark and Zanesville, Cath. Welfare Bur., Columbus, 1957-62; dir. urban affairs Cath. Archdiocese, Omaha, 1964-66; exec. dir. Greater Omaha Community Action, 1966-70; v.p. Welcome Radio, Omaha, 1970-71; asst. dean med. and ednl. adminstrn. U. Nebr. Med. Center, Omaha, 1971-76; health mgmt. cons. Joint Commn. for Accreditation Hosps., Chgo., 1977—; staff mgr. bus. mktg. Direct Center, Mktg. Northwestern Bell Telephone Co., Omaha, 1977-79; telemktg. cons. Mountain Bell Telephone Co., Denver, 1979-81; telemktg. cons., 1979—; mem. faculty U. Nebr., Omaha, Creighton U., Peru State Coll., 1967-68; chmn. manpower com. Health Planning Council of Midlands, 1975-79; cons. adv. com. for neighborhood health centers NIH, 1968-70; mem. ambulatory care study com. Am. Assn. Med. Colls., 1973-75; regional rep. Nat. Parks and Recreation Commn., 1978-80; bd. dirs. Nebr. Regional Med. Program, 1968-70, Colo. Epilepsy Assns., Changing Scene Repertory Theater; mem. planning com. United Way, Omaha, 1966-68; pres. Omaha Parks and Recreation Adv. Bd., 1976-79; mem. parent adv. com. Creighton Prep. High Sch., 1977-79; bd. dirs. Council Bluffs Met. YMCA, Omaha, 1975-79. Served with U.S. Army, 1951-53. Recipient award Urban Soc., 1975, cert. of recognition OEO, 1970. Mem. Acad. Cert. Social Workers, Phi Alpha Theta, Alpha Kappa Mu. Democrat. Roman Catholic. Home: 1175 Emerson St Denver CO 80218

SHEARER, MARILYN JANE, property management executive; b. Gary, Ind., Aug. 26, 1936; d. Harold and Dorothy L. Oehmich; m. Angus T. Shearer, Jr., June 7, 1958; children—Mike A., David H. Student acctg. U. Utah, 1975-79; B.A., U. Tulsa, 1958. Treas., dir. Wallace Assocs., Salt Lake City, 1970—; pres., dir. W.A. Mgmt. Inc., Salt Lake City, 1971—; dir. Pioneer Thrift Co. Mem. Bldg. Owners and Mgrs. Assn. Office: 1518 Walker Bldg Salt Lake City UT 84111

SHEARER, WAYNE WILSON, JR., computer co. exec.; b. Columbia, Pa., July 31, 1947; s. Wayne Wilson and Janet May (Koller) S.; student Millersville (Pa.) State Coll., 1966; m. Carol F. Molyneaux, Aug. 31, 1968 (div. Aug. 1974); 1 dau., Stephanie Lynn. Field technician Itel Corp., 1970-72; sr. field engr. Compugraphic Corp., 1972-76; pres. Systems Control Corp., Denver, 1976—; sec., treas. Success Cycles, Inc.; dir. A.J. Rose Enterprises, Inc. Served with USAF, 1966-70. Mem. Assn. Field Service Mgrs. Democrat. Home: 17883 E Mississippi Pl Aurora CO 80017 Office: 1642 S Parker Rd Suite 97 Denver CO 80231

SHEAROUSE, HENRY GRADY, JR., librarian; b. Sardis, Ga., May 2, 1924; s. Henry Grady and Byrdice (Askew) S.; B.S., Ga. Tchrs. Coll., Statesboro, 1945; A.B., Emory U., 1947; M.S., U. Ill., 1949. Tchr., Swainsboro (Ga.) public schs., 1945-46; reference asst. Savannah (Ga.) Public Library, 1946-48; research asst. in testing U. Ill., 1948-49; head reference dept. Atlanta Public Library, 1949-53; dir./spl. asst. to dir. Ga. Public Library Service, 1953-55; dir. Regional Library Service, 1953-55; dir. Regional Library Service Center N.Y. State Library, Watertown, 1955-56, asso. supr. library extension div., 1957-63; asst. librarian, dir. public services Denver Public Library, 1963-69, city librarian, 1969—. Cons. Colo. State Library, 1959, Lower Merion Twp., Pa., 1960, Delaware County Commrs., Pa., 1963; bldg. cons. Longmont (Colo.) Public Library, 1970, Westchester Library System, Mt. Vernon, N.Y., 1966; mem. Internat. Assn. Met. City Libraries, 1969—; mem. Colo. Council for Library Devel., 1971-74, chmn., 1972-74; mem. exec. bd. Adult Edn. Council Met. Denver, 1969—, v.p., 1972-73, pres., 1974-76; mem. bd. Bibliog. Center for Research, Rocky Mountain Region, 1969-75. Bd. dirs. Greater Denver Council for Arts and Humanities, 1970-73, treas., 1970-72. Mem. ALA, Colo. Library Assn., Mountain Plains Library Assn. Office: 1357 Broadway Denver CO 80203

SHEATS, CHRISTOPHER CLAYBOURNE, JR., educator; b. Ute, Colo., Dec. 8, 1915; s. Christopher and Nell Irene (Hatchett) S.; B.E. in Chem. Engring., U. So. Calif., 1944; M.A.T., Adams State Coll., Colo., 1969; m. Hazel Alice Van Nest, Nov. 20, 1940; children—David, James. Chemist. U.S. Vanadium Corp., Uravan, Colo., 1934-36; asst. purchasing agt. sci. and engring. supplies U. So. Calif., Los Angeles, 1936-42; research chemist Swift & Co., Vernon, Calif., 1946-50; instr. sci. Aims Community Coll., Greeley, Colo., 1969—; chem. engring. cons., uranium and vanadium ore tech. Office Civil Def., 1950—, fallout shelter analyst, 1969—. Served to lt. col. USAF, 1942-46. Adams State Coll. fellow, 1968-69. Mem. Am. Inst. Chem. Engrs., Nat. Soc. Profl. Engrs., Am. Meteorl. Soc., Phi Delta Kappa. Republican. Baptist. Home: 3620 Yosemite Dr Greeley CO 80634 Office: 5401 W 20th St Greeley CO 80631

SHEEHAN, BRIAN TALBOT, chemical company executive; b. Melrose, Mass., July 20, 1937; s. John F. and Mildred S. B.S. in Chem. Engring., Cornell U., 1960, M.S., 1961; Ph.D., U. Wis., 1970. Bioengring. sect. head E. R. Squibb Co., New Brunswick, N.J., 1970-77; v.p. mfg. Genentech Inc., South San Francisco, Calif., 1977-80; pres. Armos Corp., South San Francisco, 1980—. Served with USNR, 1963-66. Office: 180 Kimball Way South San Francisco CA 94080

SHEEHY, JEROME JOSEPH, electronics engineer; b. Hartford, Conn., Dec. 3, 1935; s. Jeremiah Joseph and Anna (Foley) S.; B.S. in Elec. Engring., U. Conn., 1962, M.S., 1967; m. Eugenia Baldassari, Oct. 13, 1962; children—Caroline, Jerome, Daniel, Carlene. Elec. engr. U.S. Navy Underwater Sound Lab., New London, Conn., 1962-69; mem. tech. staff Rockwell Internat. Corp., Anaheim, Calif., 1969-74; staff engr. Hughes Aircraft Co., Fullerton, Calif., 1974-83; staff engr. Norden Systems, Santa Ana, Calif., 1983—. Served with USAF, 1954-57. Mem. Acoustical Soc. Am., IEEE. Democrat. Roman Catholic. Author tech. papers in field. Home: 22951 Belquest Dr El Toro CA 92630

SHEEHY, JOHN C., justice Montana Supreme Ccourt; b. 1918; student Mont. Coll. Mineral Sci. and Tech.; LL.B., Mont. State U. Admitted to Mont. bar, 1943; now justice Mont. Supreme Ct., Helena. Office: Supreme Ct State Capitol Helena MT 95620*

SHEFELMAN, HAROLD S., lawyer; b. N.Y.C., Apr. 15, 1898; s. Joseph and Henrietta (Lovett) S.; Ph.B., Brown U., 1920; LL.B., Yale, 1925; LL.D., Seattle Pacific Coll., Brown U.; m. Madolene Whitehead, 1924 (dec. June 22, 1955); children—Thomas Whitehead, June Henderson (Mrs. Jack Hensley); m. 2d, Sylvia Rogers, 1958 (div.); m. 3d, Nona Church, 1977. Admitted to Wash. bar, 1926, since practiced in Seattle; counsel firm Roberts & Shefelman; lectr. Sch. Law U. Wash., 1930-57. Mem. adv. council Bonneville Power Authority, 1940-45; mem. Seattle City Planning Commn., 1948-71, chmn., 1950-52; chmn. Wash. State Tax Adv. Council, 1957-59, Wash. Child Welfare Adv. Com., 1949-51, Wash. state del. to White House Conf. on Edn., 1955, Gov.'s Com. on Met. Problems, 1956-57; mem. Wash. State Bd. Edn., 1951-57; mem. Interim Com. for Nationwide Conf. on Met. Area Problems, East Lansing, Mich., 1957; dir. Nat. Met. Area Problems Conf., 1957—; chmn. Gov.'s Conf. on Ednl. Evaluation Com., 1956; chmn. Citizens Com. to Survey Wash. Pub. Welfare Problems, 1949-50; exec. com. Seattle Health and Welfare Council, 1950-52; dir. Nat. Civil Service League; chmn. Wash. State Com. on Govtl. Reorgn., 1951-55; participant 9th, 17th. Am. Assemblies on State Govt., Arden House, Harriman, N.Y., 1955. Mem. bd. regents U. Wash., 1957-75, former pres.; past trustee Brown U., Seattle World's Fair; former pres. Pacific Sci. Center Found.; chmn. Seattle Center Commn., 1956-71. Served as pvt. U.S. Army, World War I. Recipient Disting. Citizen award Nat. Mcpl. League, 1956; Citation Honor Wash. chpt. AIA, 1955; Distinguished Service award Wash. Bd. Edn., 1957; Alumnus citation Brown U., 1959; Outstanding Citizen award Seattle Municipal League, 1961; Others award Salvation Army, 1963, Outstanding Alumnus award Asso. Alumni Brown U., 1970; Bishop's Cross, Episcopal Diocese Olympia; Recognition award U. Wash., 1977, Law Sch. honoree, 1980; Seattle Center Medallion, 1981; Knight Order of Hospital of St. John of Jerusalem. Fellow Am. Bar Found.; mem. Yale Law Sch. Assn. (life mem.; exec. com.), Am. Soc. Planning Ofcls. (pres. 1959-61, dir.) Mcpl. League Seattle and King County (pres. 1956-58), Nat. Mcpl. League (former mem. council), ABA (ho. of dels., 1938-40, 54, 56, chmn. municipal law sect., 1952-54, council sect., 1948-61), Wash., Seattle (pres. 1937-38) bar assns., Am. Law Inst., Am. Judicature Soc. (dir.), Seattle C. of C., Municipal Forum N.Y., Am. Acad. Polit. and Social Sci., Acad. Polit. Sci., Phi Beta Kappa, Order of Coif. Episcopalian (chancellor Diocese of Olympia 1951-79, past vestryman). Clubs: College, Wash. Athletic (Seattle); Oval, Univ. of Wash. Masons, Shriners. Office: Roberts & Shefelman 4100 Seafirst 5th Ave Plaza 800 5th Ave Seattle WA 98104

SHEFFIELD, WILLIAM JENNINGS, gov. Alaska; b. Spokane, Wash., June 26, 1928; student De Forest Tng. Sch. Founder and chmn. Sheffield Enterprises, Inc.; gov. Alaska, 1982—. Pres. Alaska C. of C.; nat. dir. U.S. Jaycees; past mem. Anchorage City Planning Commn., Anchorage Charter Commn.; past pres. Alaska Visitors Assn. Served with USAAF, 1946-49. Democrat. Presbyterian. Office: Office of Governor State Capitol Pouch A Juneau AK 99811*

SHEINBAUM, STANLEY K., economist; b. N.Y.C., June 12, 1920; A.B. in Far East History summa cum laude, Stanford U., 1949, postgrad. in Econs., 1949-56; m. Betty Warner, May 29, 1964; 4 children. Mem. faculty dept. econs. Stanford U., 1950-53, Mich. State U., East Lansing, 1955-60, U. Calif., Santa Barbara, 1963; cons. in econs. Ency. Brit., 1961-64, Calif. State Commn. Manpower and Tech., 1963-65; campus dir. project U.S. Fgn. Aid Program, Mich. State U.,1955-59; cons. fiscal policy Govt. South Viet Nam, Saigon, 1957-59; cons. on Viet Nam, Spl. Ops. Research Office, Am. U., Washington, 1958-59; economist fellow Center for Study of Dem. Instns., Santa Barbara, 1960-70; econ. cons., Los Angeles, 1970—; v.p. Warner Ranch, Inc., Los Angeles, 1965-69, Warner Industries, Inc., Los Angeles, 1968-73. Dem. candidate for Congress from Santa Barbara, 1966, 68; bd. govs. Calif. Dem. Council, 1968-72; del. Dem. Nat. Conv., 1968, 72; so. Calif. fin. chmn. McGovern presdl. campaign, 1972; exec. dir. Com. to Improve Tchr. Edn., Calif. Citizens Lobbying Effort, 1961-62; bd. dirs. Scenic Shoreline Preservation Conf., Santa Barbara, 1967—, Council on Econ. Priorities, N.Y.C., 1970-75, Com. for Public Justice, 1972—, Bill of Rights Found., N.Y., 1973—, Center for Law in the Public Interest, Los Angeles, 1976—, Am. Jewish Com., Los Angeles, 1977—; organizer, coordinator legal def. team Pentagon Papers Trial, Los Angeles, 1971-73; mem. ACLU Nat. Adv. Council, N.Y.C., 1974—; chmn. bd. dirs. ACLU Found. So. Calif., Los Angeles, 1973—; founder, dir. Energy Action Com., Washington, 1975—; mem. ofcl. salaries authority City of Los Angeles, 1976-78; chmn. Clarence Darrow Found., 1977—; mem. Calif. Postsecondary Edn. Commn., 1978—; bd. dirs. Music Center Dance Assn., Los Angeles, 1978-79, chmn., 1979—; trustee Fedn. Am. Scientists Fund, Washington, 1979—; mem. adv. bd. Breast Center, Valley Med. Center, Van Nuys, Calif., 1979; bd. dirs. People for the Am. Way, Washington, 1980—; regent U. Calif., 1977—, now vice-chmn. Fellow Scientists Inst. for Public Info.; mem. Phi Beta Kappa, Phi Eta Sigma. Home: 345 N Rockingham Ave Los Angeles CA 90049

SHEINFELD, DAVID I(AN), lawyer; b. Atlantic City, June 2, 1954; s. Irving and Lorna (Wesler) S.; married. B.S., Am. U., 1976; J.D., Calif. Western Sch. Law, 1980; postgrad So. Meth. U., 1976-77. Admitted to Calif. bar, 1980; asst. to legal counsel Zale Corp., Dallas, 1977; law clk. firm Augustine & Delafield, San Diego, 1978-79; mem. firm Delafield & Gattis, 1979, Oliver, Sullivan & Cummins, 1980; ptnr. firm Lazarian, Sivas, Martinez, Vanian & Sheinfeld, San Diego, 1981—; pres. dir. Bake Shoppe Ltd., San Diego, 1982—; founder, dir. Syndicorp; dir. RTV

Video Network, Inc. Vol., Fedn. Jewish Agys., Mem. ABA, Calif. State Bar, San Diego County Bar Assn., San Diego Barristers. Author: The Insider's Guide to the Capitol, 1977; From Warsaw to Tenerife: Journal of Air Law and Commerce, 1980. Home: 8666-1 Villa La Jolla Dr La Jolla CA 92037 Office: 3430 Camino Del Rio N Suite 300 San Diego CA 92108

SHEINFELD, RICHARD BENNETT, plumbing mfr.; b. Boston, Jan. 5, 1936; s. Leonard and Sarah (Koffman) S.; B.S., Northeastern U., Boston, 1959; m. Leslie Felicia Fechtor, Nov. 5, 1955; children—William S.M., Terri Lynne. With Treasury Dept., Boston, 1959-60; exec. trainee L. Grossman & Sons, Boston, 1960-62; sales mgr. Glesby Bldg. Materials Co., Van Nuys, Calif., 1963-67; partner Cohart Products Co., mfrs. reps., 1968—, partner Western Am. Mfg. Inc., plumbing supplies, Valencia, Calif., 1974—, Pacific Am. Mfg. Inc., bath accessories, Valencia, 1981—, Hartco Indsl. Real Estate, 1970—. Served with Mass. N.G., 1954-62. Recipient various sales awards. Mem. Nat. Hardware Mfg. Assn., Am. Hardware Wholesales Assn., Calif. Retail Hardware Assn. (past v.p.), Nat. Hardware Assn. Republican. Jewish. Clubs: Mid Valley Racquetball and Athletic, Masons. Home: Encino CA Office: 25395 Rye Canyon Rd Valencia CA 91355

SHEINIUK, GENE, management consultant, consulting group executive; b. N.Y.C., Feb. 15, 1936; s. Jacob and Lilly (Zwick) S.; children—Robyn, Michael. B.S. in Factory Mgmt., NYU, 1957; M.B.A. in Indsl. Mgmt., U. So. Calif., 1965. Cert. data processor. Indsl. engr. Republic Aviation Corp., Farmingdale, N.Y., 1958-59, McCulloch Corp., Los Angeles, 1959-61; sr. systems analyst Tidewater Oil Co., Los Angeles, 1961-65; mgmt. cons. Ernst & Whinney, Los Angeles, 1965-66, Seattle, 1966-67; mgmt. cons., prin. J. Toellner & Assocs., Los Angeles, 1967-70; mgmt. cons., mgr. Main Hurdman, Los Angeles, 1970-74; v.p. data processing Imperial Bank, Los Angeles, 1974-75; sr. v.p. Gottfried Cons., Inc., Los Angeles, 1975-83; chmn. bd. Key Cons. Group, Los Angeles, 1983—; speaker to info. systems and civic groups. Served with U.S. Army, 1957. Mem. Assn. Systems Mgmt. (Achievement award 1975, pres. So. Calif. chpt. 1973-74, gen. chmn. Western Systems Conf. 1974), Mgmt. Info. Continuing Seminar (pres. West Coast chpt. 1977-78), Inst. Mgmt. Cons. (cert. mgmt. cons.). Clubs: Center Court (West Los Angeles, Calif.); Westside Tennis (Los Angeles). Contbr. articles on info. processing, mgmt. cons. and gen. bus. to various publs.

SHELBY, CHARLES S., vocational rehabilitation counselor, instructor; b. Phila., May 28, 1923; s. Joseph Maxwell and Sarah; m. Sondra Mae Smiley, Dec. 12, 1953; children—Matthew, Suanne, Donna. A.A., Los Angeles City Coll., 1947; B.S. in Psychology, Calif. State Coll.-Los Angeles, 1953, M.S. in Rehab. Counseling, 1969; postgrad. U. Ariz., 1972-82; certs. UCLA, 1972, U. Oreg., 1972, 75, U. San Francisco, 1979. Teaching certs. Lifetime adult, lifetime secondary, jr. coll., vocat. tech. and indsl., rehab. counseling, Calif. Major appliance service mgr. J.N. Ceaean Co. and Western Auto, Los Angeles, 1948-65; vocat. instr. Watts Skill Ctr. and Abraham Friedman Trade Sch., Los Angeles, 1966-70; mental retardation specialist Calif. Dept. Vocat. Rehab., Van Nuys, 1970-72; vocat. counselor specializing in developmental disabilities Ariz. Rehab. Services Adminstrn., Tucson, 1973—; chmn. adv. bd. U. Ariz. Tng. and Edn. Project, 1973-75, Beacon Tucson House for Retarded, 1979-80. Recipient Key and Gavel, Los Angeles City Coll., 1948, Hillel Found. award; various certs. of appreciation schs. and service orgns. Mem. Nat. Rehab. Assn., Ariz. Rehab. Assn., Nat. Rehab. Counselors Assn., Am. Vocat. Assn., Ariz. Vocat. Assn., Am. Assn. Ret. Persons. Democrat. Jewish. Clubs: Internat. Order Foresters, Masons. Home: 8440 E Pima Tucson AZ 85715

SHELDEN, RANDALL GEORGE, sociology educator, b. Glendale, Calif., Oct. 2, 1943; s. George R. and Myrna (May) S. B.A., Calif. State U.-Los Angeles, 1967; M.A., Memphis State U., 1972; Ph.D., So. Ill. U. 1976. Instr. sociology Memphis State U., 1972-73; asst. prof. sociology SUNY-Cortland, 1976-77; asst. prof. U. Nev.-Las Vegas, 1977-81, assoc. prof. dept. criminal justice, 1981—. Served USNR 1966-72. Mem. Am. Soc. Criminology, Western Soc. Criminology, Am. Sociol. Soc. Democrat. Author: Criminal Justice in America: A Sociological Approach, 1982. Home: 6116 Denver Circle Las Vegas NV 89107 Office: Dept Criminal Justice U NV Las Vegas NV 89154

SHELDON, NANCY WAY, management consultant; b. Bryn Mawr, Pa., Nov. 10, 1944; d. John Harold and Elizabeth Semple (Hoff) Way; B.A., Wellesley Coll., 1966; M.A. (faculty fellow 1966-68), Columbia U., 1968, M.Phil., 1972; m. Robert Charles Sheldon, June 15, 1968. Mgmt. cons. ABT Assocs., Cambridge, Mass., 1969-70; mgmt. cons. Harbridge House, Inc., 1970-79, Los Angeles, 1977-79, v.p., 1977-79; mgmt. cons., pres. Resource Assessment, Inc., 1979—; partner, real estate developer Resource Devel. Assocs., 1980—; partner Anubis Group, Ltd., 1980—. Recipient Nat. Achievement award Nat. Assn. Women Geographers, 1966; registered pvt. investigator, Calif. Mem. Am. Mining Congress, Am. Inst. Mining, Metall. and Petroleum Engrs., Fgn. Trade Assn. So. Calif., Grad. Faculties Alumni Assn. Columbia U. Clubs: Mt. Kenya Safari; Wellesley (Los Angeles). Author: Social and Economic Benefits of Public Transit, 1973. Contbr. articles to profl. jours. Office: 2261 Stradella Rd Bel Air CA 90077

SHELL, MARY KATHERINE JAYNES HOSKING (MRS. JOSEPH C. SHELL), mayor; b. Bakersfield, Calif., Feb. 9, 1927; d. Walter Charles and Mary Ellen (Young) Jaynes; student Bakersfield Coll., 1946-48; m. Richard Hosking, Aug. 21, 1948 (div. 1968); children—Geoffrey Richard, Timothy William (dec.), Meredith Katherine (dec.); m. 2d, Joseph C. Shell, Jan. 8, 1970. Mem. editorial staff Bakersfield Californian, 1944-45; mem. editorial staff Bakersfield News Bull., 1965-68, mng. editor, 1969; polit. columnist Bakersfield Californian, 1971-80; mayor City of Bakersfield, 1980—. Founding pres. Bakersfield Jr. Woman's Club, 1954-55. Mem. Kern County Republican Central Com., 1956-60; founder, state sec. United Reps. Calif., 1963; mem. Calif. delegation Rep. Nat. Conv., 1964. Clubs: Kern Press (founder 1967). Home: 2930 21st St Bakersfield CA 93301 Office: City Hall 1501 Truxtun Ave Bakersfield CA 93301

SHELTON, FRANK HARVEY, physicist; b. Flagstaff, Ariz., Oct. 5, 1924; s. Mark Harvey and Jessie Frankie (Foster) S.; B.S., Calif. Inst. Tech., 1949, M.S., 1950, Ph.D., 1953; m. Lorene Belle Gregory, Dec. 29, 1947; children—Jill Jeanette, Joyce Lynn, Gwen Elaine. Staff physicist Sandia Corp., Albuquerque, 1952-55; tech. dir. Armed Forces Weapons Project, Washington, 1955-59; v.p., chief scientist Kaman Sci. Corp., Colorado Springs, Colo., 1959—. Served to 2d lt. AUS, World War II. Fellow Am. Phys. Soc., Sigma Xi. Methodist. Club: Winter Night (Colorado Springs). Author papers, reports in field. Home: 215 W Columbia St Colorado Springs CO 80907 Office: 1500 Garden of Gods Rd Colorado Springs CO 80907

SHELTON, JOHN PERCIVAL, educator; b. Glendora, Calif., May 20, 1920; s. Leonard G. and Alice W. (Agee) S. A.B., Pomona Coll., 1941, M.B.A., Harvard U., 1949, Ph.D. in Bus. Econs., 1956. Editor, pub. Azusa (Calif.) Herald, 1946-47; research assoc. Harvard Bus. Sch., 1950-52; asst. prof. Grad. Sch. Indsl. Adminstrn., Carnegie-Mellon U., Pitts., 1952-56; assoc. prof. Claremont (Calif.) Grad. Sch., 1956-60; prof. Sch. Mgmt. UCLA, 1960—. Mem. alliance bd. Los Angeles Mus. Natural History. Co-author: California Local Finance; contbr. articles to profl. jours. Office: Graduate School Management University of California Los Angeles CA 90024

SHELTON, ROBERT CHARLES, electronics engr.; b. Los Angeles, July 31, 1934; s. Weir Mitchell and Martalena (Scavarda) S.; B.S. in Elec. Engring., Calif. State Poly. U., 1961; m. A. Corinne, May 28, 1962; 1 son, Kevin Lyle. Mgr. ops. Halcyon, Palo Alto, Calif., 1971-74; mgr. mfg. Programmed Power, Menlo Park, Calif., 1974-78; pres. Shelton Electronics, Menlo Park, 1976—. Bd. dirs. Herbert Hoover Boys Club, Menlo Park. Served with USN, 1952-56. Mem. IEEE, Profl. and Tech. Cons. Assn. Clubs: Elks (chmn. Palo Alto public relations); Rotary (bd. dirs., pres. 1981—) (Menlo Park). Research and publs. in telecommunications, short arc mercury lamps, frequency domain multiplexer, fixed head disc drive, disc. drive controller, digital Ion gauge controller, automatic call sequencer; patentee various crygenics and computer systems. Home: 94 Wilburn Ave Atherton CA 94025 Office: 2653 Spring St Redwood City CA 94063

SHENK, HOWARD FRED, executive recruiter; b. Greenville, S.C., Feb. 14, 1939; s. Donald Hugh and Ruth Aletha (Swartz) S.; B.S. in Bus. Adminstrn., U. Ala., 1961. Gen. mgr. H & R Block Co., Honolulu, 1967-71; v.p. ops. E. K. Fernandez Shows, Honolulu, 1971-75; pres. Micrographics Ltd., Honolulu, 1975-78; pres. Colo. Indsl. Communications, Denver, 1978-81; exec. recruiter Luther Moreau Ltd., 1981—; devel. and spl. events cons. Nat. Western Stock Show and Rodeo; dir. Fred Graham Communications Ltd., Frank C. Howard Holdings Ltd., Micrographics Ltd. Chmn. Hawaii State Fair, 1970; exec. dir. Colo. MetroFair. Served with USAF, 1962-67. Mem. Kings Alley Mchts. Assn. (pres. 1976—), SAR, Honolulu symphony Soc., Internat. Assn. Amusement Parks and Attractions, Opera Colo. (devel. council), Outdoor Amusement Bus. Assn., Smithsonian Assocs., N.Mex. Opera Assn. Republican. Presbyterian. Clubs: Royal Hawaiian Showmen, Kiwanis. Home: 471 Columbine St Denver CO 80206

SHENKER, MORRIS ABRAHAM, lawyer, hotel executive; b. Kalius, Russia, Jan. 10, 1907; s. Abraham and Tziporah (Meshurith) S.; A.B., St. Louis U., 1932; J.D., Washington U., St. Louis, 1932; m. Lillian Rose Koplar, Dec. 23, 1939; children—Morris Arthur, Patricia Ann. Admitted to Mo. bar, 1932, U.S. Dist. Ct. bar, 1936, U.S. Circuit Ct. Appeals bar, 1939, U.S. Supreme Ct. bar, 1940; practice law, Las Vegas; chmn. bd. Dunes Hotel, Las Vegas, 1975—, parent corp. M & R Investment Corp., 1975—, Vegas Village, Inc., 1975—, Sierra Charter Corp., Los Angeles; chmn. exec. com. M & R Investment Corp., 1975—; dir. Continental Connector Corp., 1975—, chmn. bd., 1977; pres., dir. I. J. K. Nev., Inc., v.p., dir. Citizens Bank of University City (Mo.), Nat. States Ins. Co., St. Louis; lectr. Washington U. Sch. Law, St. Louis U., Mo. U., Law Sci. Inst. of U. Tex.; mem. faculty Nat. Coll. Criminal Def. Lawyers and Public Defenders, 1972—; prof. charter session Nat. Coll., 1972. Pres., bd. dirs. Max and Thelma Manne Found., St. Louis, Morris and Lillian Shenker Found., St. Louis; sec., bd. dirs. Sam and Janet Koplar Found., St. Louis; bd. dirs. Israel Investors Corp., N.Y.C., Bd. Jewish Edn., 1954-64, Jewish Hosp. St. Louis, 1964-66, Am. Friends of Hebrew U., 1964—, Am. Friends of Tel Aviv U., 1965—, St. Louis Heart Assn., 1965-70, Council of Jewish Fedns. and Welfare Funds, Inc., 1969-73, Jewish Community Center Assn., 1970-75; hon. chmn. Nat. Meml. Day Observance for John F. Kennedy, Nov. 22, 1964; hon. bd. govs. Hebrew U. Jerusalem, 1973—; cons., adv. to Pres. John F. Kennedy, 1960, 62; Mo. coordinator Johnson-Humphrey campaign, 1964; former mem. Democratic Com. of Mo.; del. Dem. Nat. Conv., 1948, 52, 64, 68; former Democratic committeeman; mem. nat. exec. council Am. Jewish Com., bd. govs., 1970, mem. exec. com., 1963, 64; life mem. bd. dirs. Jewish Fedn. St. Louis, pres., 1966-68; chmn. St. Louis Commn. Crime and Law Enforcement, 1969-72; asso. chmn. bequest and legacy com. Nat. Jewish Hosp., 1964; mem. nat. cabinet United Jewish Appeal, 1970-73; del. 1st constituent assembly Jewish Agy. for Israel, 1971; mem. nat. steering com. Washington U., 1966-68; internat. bd. govs. Hebrew U., 1965-73; bd. govs. Devel. Corp. Israel, 1959—, Child Center of Our Lady of Grace, 1964-68, Technion, 1970—; trustee United Israel Appeal, Inc., 1966; mem. adv. bd. Am. Jewish Congress, 1964—; bd. overseers Jewish Theol. Sem. Am., 1964—; mem. cabinet Midwest Leadership Inst., United Jewish Appeal, 1969, mem. nat. cash com., 1971; mem. bd. nat. adv. council of Am. com. Weizmann Inst. Sci., 1967—; bd. regents Congregation of B'nai Amoona; mem. adv. bd. Am. Med. Center, 1953-66; mem. adv. com. United Way Las Vegas, 1976, chmn. corp. gifts, 1975. Recipient citation City of St. Louis March of Dimes Telethon, 1960; Merit award Cardinal Glennon Meml. Children's Hosp.; Louis Marshall award Jewish Theol. Sem. Am., 1963; Human Relations award St. Louis U., 1964; Disting. Service award Am. Jewish Com., 1965; Nat. award Sertoma; Merit award Louisville Bar Assn., 1965; Honor award Lawyers Assn. St. Louis, 1966; Disting. Alumni award Washington U., 1967; cert. of merit, Nat. Coll. Criminal Def. Lawyers and Public Defenders, 1974; Guardian of Menorah award B'nai B'rith Found. U.S., 1975; David Ben-Gurion award Israel Bonds, 1975; Humanitarian award Nat. Jewish Hosp. and Research Center, 1977; Keser Torah award St. Louis Rabbinical Coll., 1979; Human Relations award Inst. Human Relations of Am. Jewish Com., 1979; sect. of Little City dedicated in his honor, 1979; award Boys' Clubs Am., 1980. Fellow Nat. Coll. Criminal Def. Lawyers and Public Defenders; mem. Am. Bar Assn., Nat. Assn. Def. Lawyers in Criminal Cases (dir. 1961—, pres. 1968), Lawyers Assn. St. Louis (v.p. 1958, 59), Mo. Bar Assn., Bar Assn. St. Louis, Order of Coif, Alpha Kappa Psi. Contbr. articles to mags. and profl. jours. Office: Dunes Hotels & Casinos Inc 3650 Las Vegas Blvd S Las Vegas NV 89109

SHENKER, M(ORRIS) ARTHUR, JR., hotel exec.; b. St. Louis, June 24, 1947; s. Morris Arthur and Lillian R. (Koplar) S.; student Babson Inst.-Wellesley Coll., St. Louis U., U. Salford (Eng.); m. Deborah J. Hary, Dec. 27, 1970; 1 dau., Jennifer Ann. Account exec. I.M. Simon Co., St. Louis, 1970-73; exec. v.p. Murietta (Calif.) Hot Springs, 1973-75; v.p. Dunes Hotel and Casinos Inc., Las Vegas, 1975-80, pres., 1980—. Chmn. exec. com. Arthritis Found., 1979—; bd. dirs. Big Bros./Big Sisters, 1979, Boulder Dam Area council Boy Scouts Am., 1979—; mem. new leadership div. State of Israel Bonds, 1979; chmn. gifts com. for Nev., U. Judaism, 1980; fund raiser Variety Club. Served with USCG, 1969. Jewish. Club: Las Vegas Country. Office: 3650 Las Vegas Blvd S Las Vegas NV 89109*

SHEPARD, ALLAN GUY, justice Idaho Supreme Ct.; b. Gardner, Mass., Dec. 18, 1922; s. Guy H. and May (Kendall) S.; student Boston U., 1942-43; B.S., U. Wash., 1948, J.D., 1951; m. Donna K. Soderlund, Nov. 25, 1972; children—Lynn K., Paul V., Ann K. Admitted to Idaho bar, 1951; asst. atty. gen. State of Idaho, 1951-57; pvt. practice law, Boise, Idaho, 1957-63; atty. gen. State of Idaho, Boise, 1963-68; justice Idaho Supreme Ct., 1968—, chief justice, 1974—. Mem. Western States Hwy. Policy Com., 1959—; mem. Ida. Ho. of Reps., 1959-63, chmn. hwys. com., 1961-63. Mem. Am., Idaho, Boise bar assns., Western (chmn. 1965-66), Nat. (exec. com. 1964—, v.p. 1967-68, pres. 1968-69) assns. attys. gen. Republican. Episcopalian. Home: 4023 Delmonte Boise ID 83704 Office: Supreme Ct Bldg Boise ID 83701

SHEPARD, LEONARD GRIFFIN, computer company executive; b. Washington, July 2, 1953; s. David Hammond and Elaine (Raiss) S.; B.S., U. Calif.-Davis, 1975, M.S., 1977; m. Laura Jean Anders, July 17, 1976; 1 dau., Sara Elaine. Grad. student asst. Calif. Air Resources Bd., 1976-78; economist Devel. and Resources Corp., Sacramento, 1978-79; assoc. economist, chief fin. officer Auslam & Assocs., Inc., Sacramento, 1979-81; pres. Constrn. Scheduling, Sacramento, 1981—. Mem. Am. Agrl. Econs. Assn., Assn. Environ. and Resource Economists. Home: 202 Inca Pl Davis CA 95616 Office: 601 University Ave #241 Sacramento CA 95825

SHEPARD, VIOLET KATHERINE, home economist; b. Bend, Oreg., May 14, 1935; d. Peter Paul and Anna Rose (Bradetich) Klobas; B.S. in Home Econs. Edn., Oreg. State U., 1956, postgrad., 1959-65; m. Jerome Shepard, Nov. 26, 1958; children—Raymond, Philip. Tchr. home econs. Westfir (Oreg.) High Sch., 1956-57; tchr. home econs., social studies Salem (Oreg.) public schs., 1959-63; extension home economist Oreg. State U. Extension Service, 1958-59, 65-73; instr. Chemeketa Community Coll., 1963—; free-lance home economist in bus., Salem, 1973-78; home economist-cons. Oreg. Trawl Commn., Astoria, 1978-82; mem. Agri-Bus. Council. Vice pres. women's assn. First Presbyn. Ch., Salem, 1971; mem. ad-hoc adv. com. 4-H program, Salem; county and state judge, including 4-H and open class, 1965—. Mem. Oreg. Home Econs. Assn. (2d v.p. 1980-82), Am. Home Econs. Assn., Home Economists in Bus., Woman for Agr. (consumer adv. bd.), Internat. Farm Youth Assn., NEA, Oreg. Edn. Assn., Oreg. Nutrition Council, Pacific Fisheries Mgmt. Council, AAUW, Grad. Home Economists. Democrat. Club: Home Extension Homemakers. Author: Holiday Potpourri, 1978. Home: 1355 Mitzur St S Salem OR 97302 Office: 250-36th St Astoria OR 97103

SHEPHERD, ALICE ALLYNE, research and manufacturing company executive, communications specialist; b. Phoenixville, Pa., Oct. 27, 1931; d. Gustav Adolph and Celeste Lenore (Hoffman) Gertzen; m. Daryl Edwin Shepherd, Mar. 7, 1953 (div.); children—Alda Eugene, Roxanne. Student Met. Jr. Coll. Dist., Kansas City, Mo., 1972-73, Columbia Basin Coll., 1979-80. WAC/WAF recruiter, U.S. Air Force 1950-53; with U.S. Civil Service, U.S. and overseas, 1954-75, mgmt. asst. Hdgrs. Air Force Communications Service, Richards-Gebaur AFB, Mo., 1972-75; documentation auditor Burns & Roe, Richland, Wash. 1976-77; mgr. tech. editing Sigma Research, Inc., Richland, 1977-81, dir. corp. communications, 1981—. Active Nature Conservancy, 1981—. Recipient Zero Defects Program award Air Force Systems Command, Vandenberg, AFB, Calif., 1966-67; Superior Performance award Dept. Air Force 6200 Air Base Wing Clark Air Base, Philippines, 1968-69. Mem. Am. Advt. Fedn., Am. Mgmt. Assn., Nat. Assn. Female Execs., Tri-Cities C. of C., Am. Contract Bridge League (Unit 442). Republican. Author publs. in field. Office: Sigma Research Inc 3200 George Washington Way Richland WA 99352

SHEPHERD, MARVIN DALE, environ. health and safety technologist; b. Eureka, Calif., May 18, 1932; s. Charles Franklin and Melba Lily (Monck) S.; student Santa Rosa Jr. Coll., 1956, Coll. of Marin, 1964, Calif. State U., San Francisco, 1972; m. Patricia Ann James, Apr. 28, 1962; children—Sana, Dina. Jr. engr. Ampex, 1956-57; environ. health and safety technologist U. Calif. Med. Center, San Francisco, 1958—, supr. electroenvironmental safety, 1970—; safety cons. Calif. Dept. Health, 1972-74, 80-81, Hosp. Council No. Calif., 1973—; instr. indsl. safety Calif. Community Coll.; leader elec. safety, occupational residency program U. Calif.-San Francisco, 1981—; provider continuing edn. for R.N.'s; chmn. clin. engring. adv. com. Hosp. Council No. Calif., San Bruno, 1976-81; safety cons. Med-Equip, Inc., San Bruno, 1974—; tech. cons., mem. univ. coms.; speaker, panelist workshops and confs. in field. Served with USAF, 1950-54. Recipient paper of year award, Jour. Clin. Engineering, 1977; registered profl. safety engr. Mem. System Safety Soc., Am. Soc. Safety Engrs., Assn. for Advancement of Med. Instrumentation (com. elec. safety, 1971-73, 77—, com. edn. 1982—), IEEE, Am. Soc. Hosp. Engrs (codes/standards com., 1980—), Calif. Soc. Hosp. Engring. (ad hoc plant engring. com., 1979—), Calif. Hosp. Assn. (ad hoc com. code rev. 1976—). Editor: Device Techniques newsletter, 1980—; cons. editor for safety Med. Electronics, 1982—; contbr. papers to profl. publs. and confs. Home: 612 Wintergreen Ln Walnut Creek CA 94598 Office: U California 1344 3rd Ave San Francisco CA 94143

SHEPHERD, RONALD THOMAS, shopping mall executive; b. Bristol, Eng., Apr. 15, 1926; came to U.S., 1965, naturalized, 1978; s. Thomas Percy and Blanche Louise (Webber) S.; m. Joan Olive Reed, Mar. 26, 1964. Student, Orange Coast Coll., 1972-74. Casualty ins. broker cert. Mgr./buyer J.W. Robinson's Dept. Store, Beverly Hills, Calif., 1966-72; ins. broker, Fountain Valley, Calif., 1972-76; mktg. dir. La Mirada (Calif.) Mall, 1976-79, Montclair (Calif.) Plaza, 1979—. Bd. dirs. Montclair Plaza Mchts. Assn., 1979—. Served with U.S. Army, 1943-48. Recipient Merit cert. Travelers Ins., 1972, awards Am. Heart Assn., 1978, La Mirada Sch. Dist., 1978, NBC, 1978, Am. Children's Soc., 1978, Appreciation awards San Bernadino County, 1979-81, many others. Mem. Internat. Council Shopping Centers. Republican. Episcopalian. Club: British American (Fountain Valley). Home: 10245 Kingbird Ave Fountain Valley CA 92708 Office: Montclair Plaza 5060 Montclair Plaza Ln Montclair CA 91763

SHEPPARD, MARIAN LOUISE, counselor, educator; b. Santa Rosa, Calif., Jan. 3, 1946; s. Frederick Funston and Harriet Marian (Haas) S. A.B. with honors, U. of Pacific, 1967, M.Music Edn., 1972, M.Counseling Psychology, 1977. Lic. marriage, family and child counselor, cert. community coll. tchr./counselor, Calif. Tchr. Ripon (Calif.) Christian Schs., 1967-68; tchr. Lodi (Calif.) High Sch., 1968-72, counselor, 1972—; instr. San Joaquin Delta Coll. Extension, 1974, instr. in readiness psychology, summers 1976—; counselor Counseling Assocs., 1976—. Bd. dirs. Stockton (Calif.) Opera Assn., 1971-79, Lodi Community Concert, 1972-79, Lilliput Homes, 1983. Recipient cert. recognition and achievement in area of counseling adolescents Sacramento Area Inst. for Group Treatment, 1977. Mem. NEA, Calif. Tchrs. Assn., Lodi Edn. Assn., Am. Personnel and Guidance Assn., Calif. Personnel and Guidance Assn. (H.B. McDaniel award 1983), Internat. Transactional Analysis Assn., San Joaquin Psychol. Assn., Stockton People in Parenting, Calif. Assn. Marriage, Family and Child Therapists. Presbyterian. Clubs: Notre (Stockton); Lodi Democratic. Office: 3 S Pacific Ave Lodi CA 95240

SHEQUEN, WINSTON G., mfg. co. exec.; b. Los Angeles, Mar. 21, 1924; s. William G. and Nellie E. (Moore) S.; B.E., U. So. Calif., 1949; postgrad. UCLA, U. Calif.-Berkeley; m. Alice C. Ewing, Dec. 18, 1948; children—Katherine Louise, Daniel Brian. Sr. mech. engr. Hieatt Engring. Co., Burbank, Calif., 1949-52; dir. product planning, asst. to pres. Gen. Controls Co., Glendale, Calif., 1952-62; with Applied Research Labs., div. Bausch & Lomb, Sunland, Calif., 1962—, engring. mgr., 1966-76, field engring. mgr., 1976-80, mng. dir., Sydney, Australia, 1976-80, dir. tng., Sunland, 1980-82, mgr. mktg. adminstrn., 1982—. Served with U.S. Navy, 1943-46. Fellow Inst. Advancement of Engring.; mem. Am. Soc. Tng. and Devel., Instrument Soc. Am., Soc. Applied Spectroscopy, Sales and Mktg. Execs. Republican. Episcopalian. Home: 2416 Cinco Casitas Ln La Crescenta CA 91214 Office: 9545 Wentworth St Sunland CA 91040

SHERER, TIM JOHN, financial planner; b. Saratoga, Calif., Mar. 6, 1948; s. James E. and Reva A. Sherer; B.B.A. cum laude, Ohio U., 1970; M.B.A., U. Santa Clara, 1979; m. Theresa Marie, Apr. 6, 1974. Mgr. Provident Mut. Ins. Co., Santa Clara, Calif., 1979—; pres. Fin. Clinic, Inc. Bd. dirs. U. Santa Clara Grad. Sch., 1980-82. Mem. Nat. Assn. Life Underwriters, San Jose Assn. Life Underwriters, Nat. Assn. Securities Dealers, Million Dollar Round Table. Served as capt. USMC, 1970-76. Home: 15172 Peach Hill Rd Saratoga CA 95070 Office: Fin Clinic Inc 1333 Lawrence Expressway Suite 260 Santa Clara CA 95051

SHERIDAN, GEORGE EDWARD, manufacturing company executive; b. Emporia, Kans., July 4, 1915; s. George and Josephine Frances (Benson) S.; m. Edith Joye Card, July 4, 1940; 1 dau., Phyllis Lynne.

Liberal arts student Coll. of Emporia, 1934-36; engring. student Nat. Schs., 1936-37, Los Angeles City Jr. Coll., 1937-38. Cert. mfg. engr.; registered profl. engr., Calif. With Douglas Aircraft, Santa Monica, Calif., 1939-40, Northrop Aircraft, Hawthorn, Calif., 1940-45; pres. Sheridan Products, Inc., Inglewood, Calif., 1940—. Active, YMCA, Inglewood, 1960—. Mem. Soc. Mfg. Engrs. (life, award 1979-80, Industrialist of Yr. 1982 past chmn.), U.S. Power Squadron, Am. Ordnance Def. Preparedness Assn., Nat. Rifle Assn., Smithsonian Assos., Cutting Tool Mfg. Assn., Nat. Fedn. Ind. Bus. Republican. Quaker. Patentee double edge scraper. Home: 27692 Via Rodrigo Mission Viejo CA 92675 Office: 1054 E Hyde Park Blvd Inglewood CA 90302

SHERK, MARTHA JEAN, computer applications system designer; b. Indiana, Pa., Dec. 5, 1932; d. Joseph Alexander and Grace Margaret (Gaul) Kritzer; m. Warren Arthur Sherk, June 11, 1954; children—Elena E., Adra K., Lydian M., Warren M., Wilson E. B.S. in Edn., Indiana U. of Pa., 1954. Tchr. Greensburg (Pa.) High Sch., 1954, St. Peter's Sch. for Boys, Peekskill, N.Y., 1954; computer programmer UNIVAC, Phoenix, 1963-65; with Honeywell Info. Systems, Phoenix, 1966—, project leader, 1976-81, project mgr., 1981—. Mem. Nat. Assn. Female Execs., Am. Prodn. and Inventory Control Soc. Baptist. Clubs: Execs. Internat., Kiva (Phoenix). Office: PO Box 8000 MS K30 Phoenix AZ 85066

SHERK, WARREN ARTHUR, counselor, educator; b. Buffalo, July 12, 1916; s. Warren E. and Jennie (Taylor) S.; student Hiram Coll., 1934-35, U. Rangoon, Burma, 1938-39, Duke U., 1939-40; A.B., Allegheny Coll., 1938; B.D., Berkeley Bapt. Div. Sch., 1945, Th.M., 1952; S.T.D., Burton Sem., 1958; m. Martha Jean Kritzer, June 11, 1954; children—Elena E., Adra K., Lyndian M., Warren M., Wilson E. Minister, Meth. chs. in western N.Y., 1941-43; Protestant chaplain Ariz. State Prison, 1971-72; vis. prof. Iliff Sch. Theology, U. Denver, 1945-47; field sec. Pearl S. Buck, 1948-49; minister edn., Indiana, Pa., 1949-51; minister Waitsburg Meth. Ch., Washington, 1951-52, Community Ch., Watertown, Mass., 1955-58, Savanna, Ill., 1958-59, Nogales (Ariz.) United Ch., 1960-61; exec. Dynamics Found., Tuscon, 1962—; personal counseling service, 1962—; faculty Phoenix Coll., 1963-66, Mesa Community Coll., Eastern Ariz. Coll., Pima Coll. 1963-78; cons. spl. seminars Pepsi Cola Mgmt. Inst., 1967-68; lectr. U. Durham (Eng.), summer 1981, Iliff Sch. Theology, summer 1982, Elder Phostels, N.Y., summer 1983. Founder, exec. sec. Valley of Sun Forum, Phoenix, 1963-67; coordinator Asso. Bus. Execs. Phoenix, 1963-67. Chmn. spl. gifts div. Maricopa County Heart Fund. Mem. corp. Perkins Blind Sch.; bd. dirs. Boston World Affairs Council, N.E. Assn. UN. Fellow Am. Acad. Polit. Sci., Am. Geog. Soc.; hon. bd. govs. Pearl S. Buck Found.; mem. Thoreau Soc., Emerson Soc., Watertown, Pimeria Alta hist. socs., Maricopa Mental Health Assn., Execs. Internat. (founder, exec. dir. 1967—), Nat. Assn. Approved Morticians (exec. sec. 1967-69), Internat. Platform Assn., Tucson Com. Fgn. Relations NCCJ, AAUP, Theta Chi. Republican. Clubs: Ariz., Univ., Kiva. Author: Wider Horizons, 1941, Agnes Moorehead; A Biography, 1976. Contbr. to mags. Address: 8445 N 23d Ave Apt 245 Phoenix AZ 85021

SHERLOCK, EMMANELL PHILLIPS, educator, painter; b. Monroe, La., Oct. 27, 1914; d. Clarence Leroy and Amy Wallace (Holmes) Phillips; B.A. in Edn., Northwestern La. U., 1939; M.A. in Elem. Edn., Calif. State U., Long Beach, 1966; m. Frank J. Sherlock, Sept. 3, 1948 (div. Feb. 1973); children—Patricia, Michael (twins), Dan. Classroom tchr. St. Tammany and Calcasicu Parishes, La., 1934-41, Orange, Tex., 1941-42; elec. engring. draftsman Consol. Steel, Orange, 1942-43, H. Newton Whitlesey, Chgo., 1943-44, George G. Sharp, New Orleans, 1944-45; music tchr. Orange Public Schs., 1945-47; reading cons. Silver Burdett Publs., 1947-48; tchr., resource tchr. Cypress (Calif.) Elem. Sch. Dist., 1963-83. Cert. tchr., La., Tex., Calif.; cert. adminstr., supr., reading specialist, Calif. Mem. Calif. Tchrs. Assn., NEA, Calif. Reading Assn., Internat. Reading Assn., Orange County (Calif.) Reading Assn. (past exec. bd.), Assn. Supervision and Curriculum Devel. Home: 3701 Green Ave Apt D Los Alamitos CA 90720

SHERLOCK, GARY FULLER, newspaper publisher; b. Avalon, Catalina Island, Calif., May 3, 1945; s. Jay Robert and Dorothy Marilyn (Bryant) S.; m. D. Joyce Conrad, Aug. 24, 1966; children—Blake Edward, Regan Jay; m. 2d, Susan Paounoff, Jan. 2, 1982. B.S. in Bus. Adminstrn., U. Idaho, 1968. With Idaho Statesman, Boise, 1967—, advt. sales intern, 1968, retail advt. account exec., 1968-72, retail advt. mgr., 1972-76, advt. dir., 1976-81, pub., 1981—. Bd. dirs. YMCA, ARC, United Way; mem. adv. bd., exec. com. Salvation Army; past bd. dirs. Better Bus. Bur.; mem. exec. com. Boise Future Found.; mem. adv. council Jr. League of Boise. Recipient Best in the West award of merit Internat. Newspaper Promotion Assn., 1978, hon. mention Frank Tripp Meml. award, 1979; Silver Medal Am. Advt. Fedn., 1980. Mem. Sales and Mktg. Execs. (bd. dirs., Disting. Sales award 1969), Am. Mktg. Assn. (charter), Pacific Northwest Newspaper Advt. Execs. (v.p.), Idaho Advt. Fedn. (past chmn. and pres.), Internat. Newspaper Execs. Assn. (past state v.p.), Am. Advt. Fedn. (past state lt. gov.), Idaho Allied Dailies and Idaho Newspaper Assn., Allied Dailies, Idaho Council on Econ. Edn. (bd. dirs.), Greater Boise C. of C. (past bd. dirs.), Phi Delta Theta. Methodist. Clubs: Hillcrest Country, Crane Creek Country, Arid, Masons, Scottish Rite. Office: 1200 N Curtis Rd Boise ID 83706

SHERMAN, ANITA SUSAN, hair stylist; b. San Angelo, Tex., Aug. 17, 1950; d. John H. and Johnnye U. (Anderson) Routa. Grad. Colo. Barber Coll., 1969; student Community Coll. Denver, 1970-74, Canada Coll., Redwood City, Calif., 1980. Coll. San Mateo, 1980, U. San Francisco, 1982-83. Hair stylist, The Don, Cottage Barber Shop, Wheatridge, Colo., Danny's Hairstyling, Denver, 1969-74; RK dist. mgr. Redken Labs., Canoga Park, Calif., 1974-76; mgr., stylist Gentlemen's Choice, Ladies' Preference, San Mateo, Calif., 1976-77; guest artist Redken Labs., Canoga Park, Calif., 1978—; owner Hair Friends, San Carlos, Calif., 1978—. Mem. Nat. Assn. Female Execs., Profl. and Bus. Women's Forum, Calif. Cosmetologist Assn. (past bull. editor), San Carlos C. of C. (mem. steering com.). Office: 1750 Laurel St San Carlos CA 94070

SHERMAN, ERIC, filmmaker, writer, educator; b. Santa Monica, Calif., June 29, 1947; s. Vincent and Hedda (Comorau) S.; B.A. cum laude, Yale U., 1968; m. Eugenia Blackiston Dillard, Apr. 1, 1978; children—Cosimo, Rocky. Film producer, dir., writer, photographer and editor; films include: Charles Lloyd—Journey Within, 1968; Paul Weiss—a Philosopher in Process, 1972; Waltz, 1980; Inside Out, 1982; Measure of America, 1983; Michael Reagan's Assault on Great Lakes, 1983; represented in film festivals N.Y.C. Melbourne, Australia, Bilbao, Spain, others; books include: (with others) The Director's Event, 1970; Directing the Film, 1976; pres. Film Transform; film tchr. Art Center Coll. Design, Pepperdine U., UCLA; mem. FILMEX Program Com.; guest lectr. Yale, Calif. Inst. Tech., U. So. Calif.; Andrew Mellon lectr on arts Calif. Inst. Tech., 1977; contbr. numerous articles to film publs. and distbn. catalogues, book dedication; works include three oral histories for Am. Film Inst. under Louis B. Mayer Found. grant. Mem. Soc. Motion Picture and TV Engrs. (asso.), Assn. Ind. Video and Filmmakers, Los Angeles Internat. Film Exposition, Info. Film Producers Assn., Univ. Film Assn., Nat. Alliance Media Arts Centers. Home and Office: PO Box 845 Malibu CA 90265

SHERMAN, MARY KENNEDY, business exec.; b. Chgo., June 17, 1919; d. Robert Thomas and Mary Cecelia (Hammond) Kennedy; A.A., Los Angeles Valley Coll., 1966; B.S., Pepperdine U., 1973; M.B.A., 1974; m. Lloyd McBean Sherman, Dec. 1, 1967; children—Tom D. Akins, Mary Patricia Kraakevik. Indsl. relations supr. Douglas Aircraft Co., Inc., Santa Monica, Calif., 1942-61; dir. personnel Helene Curtis Industries, Studio Girl, Glendale, Calif., 1961-65; dir. personnel Semtech Corp., Newbury Park, Calif., 1965-73, v.p., 1973—; lectr., cons. in field. Accredited Personnel Accreditation Inst. Mem. Am. Mgmt. Assn., Internat. Assn. for Personnel Women, Am. Soc. for Personnel Adminstrn., Personnel and Indsl. Relations Assn., Am. Bus. Women's Assn., Personnel Women of Los Angeles. Republican. Roman Catholic. Club: Zonta Internat. Office: 652 Mitchell Rd Newbury Park CA 91320

SHERMAN, ROBERT (BERNARD), composer, lyricist, screenwriter; b. N.Y.C., Dec. 19, 1925; s. Al and Rosa (Dancis) S.; student UCLA, 1943; B.A., Bard Coll., 1949; m. Joyce Ruth Sasner, Sept. 27, 1953; children—Laurie Shane, Jeffrey Craig, Andrea Tracy, Robert Jason. Popular songwriter, 1950-60, including Tall Paul, Pineapple Princess, You're Sixteen (Gold Record); songwriter Walt Disney Prodns., Beverly Hills, Calif., 1960-68, for 29 films including The Parent Trap, 1961, Summer Magic, 1963, Mary Poppins, 1964, That Darn Cat, 1965, Winnie The Pooh, 1965, Jungle Book, 1967, Bedknobs and Broomsticks, 1971; co-composer song It's A Small World, theme of Disneyland and Walt Disney World, Fla.; composer, lyricist United Artists, Beverly Hills, 1969—, songs for film Chitty, Chitty, Bang, Bang, 1969, Snoopy, Come Home!, 1972; song score Charlotte's Web, 1972; composer for Walt Disney's Wonderful World of Color, TV, 1961—; co-producer NBC-TV spl. Goldilocks, 1970; v.p. Musi-Classics, Inc.; co-producer, composer, lyricist stage musical Victory Canteen, 1971; composer-lyricist Broadway show Over Here, 1975; screenplay and song score Tom Sawyer, United Artists, 1972, Huckleberry Finn, 1974, The Slipper and the Rose, 1977, The Magic of Lassie, 1978. Served with inf. AUS, 1943-45. Decorated Purple Heart, Combat Infantry badge with 3 battle stars; recipient 2 Acad. awards best score for Mary Poppins, 1964, best song for Chim Chim Cheree, 1965; Grammy award, 1965; Christopher medal, 1965, 74; nine Acad. award nominations; Acad. award nomination for song score Bedknobs and Broomsticks, 1971, for best song The Age of Not Believing, 1971, others; eleven golden, two platinum and one diamond record album, 1965-83; first prize best composer song score Tom Sawyer, Moscow Film Festival, 1973, B.M.I. Pioneer award, 1977. Mem. Acad. Motion Picture Arts and Scis. (exec. bd. music br. 12 yrs.), AFTRA, Nat. Acad. Rec. Arts and Scis., Composers and Lyricists Guild (exec. bd.), Writers Guild Am., Dramatists Guild, Authors League. Office: 1032 Hilldale Ave Los Angeles CA 90069 also care Mike Conner Office 1048 N Carol Dr Los Angeles CA 90069

SHERRATT, GERALD ROBERT, coll. pres.; b. Los Angeles, Nov. 6, 1931; s. Lowell Heyborne and Elva Genevieve (Lamb) S.; student So. Utah State Coll., 1949-52; B.S., Utah State U., 1953, M.S., 1954; Ph.D., Mich. State U., 1975. Program dir. Utah State U., Logan, 1957-59, dir. high sch. relations, 1962-64, asst. to pres., 1964-77, dir. devel., 1967-77, dir. alumni relations, 1967 79, dir. summer quarter, 1975 81, chmn. Festival of Am. West, 1972-81, v.p. for univ. relations, 1977-81; pres. So. Utah State Coll., Cedar City, 1982—; asst. exec. sec. Sigma Nu Nat. Fraternity, Lexington, Va., 1959-61; staff asso. U. Utah, 1961-62. Dir. Honeyville Grain Co. Sec. Utah State U. Devel. Fund; chmn. bd. trustees Utah Found. for Arts, 1980-81. Served with USAF, 1954-57. Recipient Robins award Utah State U., 1967, Disting. Alumnus award, 1974. Mem. Cedar City C. of C., Utah State U. Alumni Assn., Utah Hon. Col. Corps, Am. Assn. State Colls. and Univs., Sigma Nu (past regent), Phi Kappa Phi, Phi Delta Kappa. Clubs: Rotary, Utah State U. Old Main Soc. Author: The West: America's Odyssey, 1974. Editor: Delta Mag. (award Indsl. Editors Assn. 1962), 1960-63, 77-80; Utah State U. Mag. (award Time-Life mag.), 1965-68. Home: 331 West 200 South Cedar City UT 84720

SHERRILL, ANNE HUMMEL, history educator; b. Phoenix, Aug. 23, 1930; d. George William and Marcella Irene Sherrill; B.A. with honors, U. Ariz., 1952; M.A., U. Calif.-Berkeley, 1955, Ph.D., 1966; m. W. Paul Sherrill, Jr., Feb. 8, 1962. Instr., Am. River Jr. Coll., 1955-57; teaching asst. in history U. Calif., Berkeley, 1957-60, instr., 1959-65; asst. prof. history Mills Coll., Oakland, Calif., 1966-82, assoc. prof., 1982—; vis. lectr. Coll. Holy Names, 1967-68, San Francisco U., 1967-70; O'Connor chmn. in Am. Insts., Colgate U., 1977; cons. CCHPP NEH Bicentennial project, 1975-76, NEH selection com., 1980—. Mem. Potrero Hill Residents and Home Owners Council, 1962—. U. Calif., Berkeley research grantee, 1960; Mills Faculty research grantee, 1970, 72; Danforth fellow, 1975; NEH fellow, 1978; Mellon Found. fellow, 1982. Mem. Am. Hist. Assn., Orgn. Am. Historians, Am. Studies Assn., WCA Women Historians, Phi Alpha Theta. Democrat. Roman Catholic. Author: John Milton Hay: The Union of Poetry and Politics, 1977; contbr. articles and revs. to profl. jours. Home: 156 Texas St San Francisco CA 94107 Office: Mills Coll Oakland CA 94613

SHERRILL, VASHTI ELLEN, curriculum specialist; b. Hillsboro, Tex., Mar. 9, 1932; d. Charles Martin and Elizabeth Martha (Edwards) Moak; m. Virgil Eugene Sherill, Dec. 1, 1950; children—Ronald Eugene, Sandra Lynn. A.A., Bakersfield Community Coll., 1960; B.A., Calif. State Coll.-Bakersfield, 1970, M.A. in English, 1975, M.A. in Ednl. Adminstrn., 1980. Cert. tchr., adminstr., reading specialist. Tchr., Emerson Jr. High Sch., Bakersfield, 1971-77; tchr., Sierra Jr. High Sch., 1977—, also curriculum specialist; instr. Bakersfield Community Coll., summer 1980; mem. reading adv. com. Calif. State Coll.-Bakersfield. Mem. Calif. State Coll. Alumni Assn., Internat. Reading Assn., Calif. Tchrs. Assn. Home: 7608 Pack Saddle Ct Bakersfield CA 93309 Office: 3017 Center St Bakersfield CA 93306

SHERROW, RICHARD LEWIS, army officer; b. Douglas, Ariz., Mar. 31, 1946; s. Charles Henry and Myrtle Marie (LaFuze) S.; m. Dalene Lynell May, Feb. 18, 1979. Student U. Md., 1969, Jacksonville State U., 1972. Sgt., U.S. Army, 1963-83; instr. Chem. Biol. Explosive Ordnance Disposal Sch., Ft. McClellan, Ala., 1967-69; instr. Chem. Sch., Vilseck, Germany, 1964-66; staff instr. hazardous devices div., Redstone Arsenal, Ala., 1970-72, sr. explosive ordnance disposal supr., missile mishap officer White Sands Missile Range, N.Mex., 1976-83; explosive ordnance disposal supr. Presidio of San Francisco, 1983—. Mem. Internat. Assn. Bomb Technicians and Investigators, Nat. Rifle Assn. (life). Office: 87th Ordnance Detachment Presidio of San Francisco San Francisco CA 94129

SHERRY, MARGARET ANN JACKSON, curriculum specialist; b. Evanston, Ill., Sept. 9, 1921; d. John Lucas and Bernice Lilliam (Smith) Jackson; B.A., U. Oreg., 1942; M.A., Monterey Inst. Fgn. Studies, 1965; Ed.D., U. So. Calif., 1974; m. Joseph Edward Sherry, Feb. 8, 1947; s. Jo Ann Sherry Kluge, Laurel Margaret Sherry Armstrong, Mark, John Jackson. Tchr. USAF program, Ft. Ord, Calif., 1959-61; tchr. math. and social sci. Salinas City Sch. Dist., 1961-63; instr. French evening div. Monterey Peninsula Coll., 1969-70; tchr. French and math. Salinas (Calif.) Union High Sch. Dist., 1965-71, curriculum devel. specialist, 1971-75, evaluator bilingual edn. program, 1975-76, curriculum devel. specialist, 1975—, resource tchr., 1975—, editor spl. projects, 1975—; cons. Calif. Dept. Edn., 1977-78. Mem. Assn. Supervision and Curriculum Devel., Assn. Calif. Sch. Adminstrs., Phi Delta Kappa, Delta Kappa Gamma, Phi Beta AAUW. Republican. Presbyterian. Home: 179 Rio Verde Dr Salinas CA 93901 Office: Special Projects Office Alisal High School 777 Williams Rd Salinas CA 93905

SHERWOOD, ALLEN JOSEPH, lawyer; b. Salt Lake City, Sept. 26, 1909; s. Charles Samuel and Sarah (Abramson) Shapiro; student UCLA, 1927-30; A.B., U. So. Calif., 1933, LL.B., 1933, J.D., 1966; m. Edith Ziff, Jan. 19, 1941; children—Mary (Mrs. John Marshall), Arthur Lawrence. Bar: Calif. 1933, U.S. Supreme Ct. 1941. Practice, Los Angeles, 1933-54, Beverly Hills, 1954—; legal counsel Internat. Family Planning Research Assn., Inc., 1970-76; bd. dirs. Family Planning Centers Greater Los Angeles, Inc., 1968—, pres., 1973-76. Mem. Calif. Atty. Gen.'s Vol. Adv. Council, and its legis. subcom., 1972-78. Recipient alumni award U. So. Calif. Law Sch., 1933. Fellow Med.-Legal Soc. So. Calif. (bd. dirs. 1966-74); mem. Am., Los Angeles County, Beverly Hills bar assns., State Bar of Calif., Am. Arbitration Assn. (nat. panel arbitrators 1965—), Order of Coif, Tau Delta Phi. Mason. Club: Brentwood Country (Los Angeles). Mem. editorial bd. So. Calif. Law Review, 1932-33. Contbr. articles to profl. jours. Home: 575 Moreno Ave Los Angeles CA 90049 Office: 9033 Wilshire Blvd Penthouse Beverly Hills CA 90211

SHERWOOD, ERMA HELEN, retired educator; b. Corning, Kans., Mar. 27, 1918; d. Walter and Theda Pearl (Leach) Furnish; A.A., Coll. of Sequoias, 1962; B.A., Calif. State U., Fresno, 1965; M.A., Calif. State U., Bakersfield, 1976; m. Joseph Victor Sherwood, Apr. 8, 1939; children—Walter Joe, Robert Franklin, Charles Lawrence. Substitute tchr., 1962-63; tchr. elem. sch., public schs., Waukena, Calif., 1963-66, elem. and jr. high sch. tchr., 1969-70, primary tchr., 1972-73, coordinator-tchr. early childhood edn. program Waukena Union Elem. Sch., 1973-76, early childhood edn. tchr., 1976-77, unit leader, 1974-77; tchr. educationally handicapped Tulare County (Calif.) Dept. Edn., 1966-69, resource specialist for spl. edn. master plan, 1977-81; elem. reading specialist Corcoran (Calif.) Unified Schs., 1970-72. Recipient cert. for outstanding service Waukena Elem. Sch. Dist., 1973-76; subject of yearbook dedication Waukena Elem. Sch., 1977; life cert. elem. teaching, State of Calif. Mem. Calif. State Bakersfield Alumni Assn. (life), Nat. Ret. Tchrs. Assn., Calif. Tchrs. Assn., NEA, Council Exceptional Children, Assn. Supervision and Curriculum Devel., Waukena Elem. Sch. PTA, Calif. Congress Parents and Tchrs. (hon. life), Sequoia League (charter), Individualized Instrn. Assn. Clubs: Early Learning Book, Adminstrv. Educators Book. Home: 23778 5th Ave Corcoran CA 93212

SHIBLEY, WILLIAM HENRY, lawyer; b. Los Angeles, Feb. 27, 1946; s. George Edward and Eleanor (Scherr) S.; student Long Beach City Coll., 1964-65; B.S. in Chemistry (Calif. state scholar), Stanford U., 1969; J.D., U. Tex., Austin, 1972. Admitted to Calif. bar, 1973; assoc. firm George E. Shibley, Long Beach, Calif., 1973-77, Harold Q. Longenecker, Los Angeles, 1977-79, William H. Shibley, Long Beach, 1979—; mem. Conf. Dels. of Calif. State Bar, 1978; judge pro tem Long Beach Mcpl. Ct., 1975-78, Los Angeles Mcpl. Ct., 1982; arbitrator Los Angeles County Superior Ct., 1978—. Mem. Los Angeles County Democratic Central Com., 1977-78, Long Beach Central Neighborhood Facilities Center Adv. Com., 1975-80; bd. dirs. Long Beach Legal Aid Found., 1983—. Mem. Long Beach Barristers Club (pres. 1977), Long Beach Bar Assn. (gov. 1976-77, 83—), Calif. Young Lawyers Assn. (dir. 1979-82, sec. 1980-81), Los Angeles County Bar Assn., ABA. Mng. editor Am. Jour. Criminal Law, 1972; editor Opening a Law Office Handbook, 1983. Office: 19 Pine Ave Suite 200 Long Beach CA 90802

SHIELDS, JACK RICHARD, psychologist, educator; b. Chgo., Feb. 23, 1924; s. Forrest Randolph and Mildred Helen (Swingle) S.; m. Lillie Owease, Mar. 26, 1965. m. 2d, Carol Thompson, July 18, 1979. B.S., Stanford U., 1962; M.Ed., Northeastern U., 1968; Ph.D., U.S. Internat. U., 1978. Commd. officer U.S. Army Air Force, 1942, transferred to U.S. Army, 1962, advanced through grades to lt. col.; 1962 70, ret., 1970; psychologist Alaska Native Hosp., Anchorage, 1970-73, Alaska Psychiat. Inst., Anchorage, 1973-74, G. Pierce Wood Hosp., Arcadia, Fla., 1974-75; psychologist and adult supr. Anchorage Mental Health Clinic, 1975-79; psychologist Alaska Treatment Ctr. for Alcoholism, 1980; cons. Salvation Army, mcpl. agys.; assoc. prof., counselor Alaska Pacific U., Anchorage, 1980—. Mem. Am. Psychol. Assn., Am. Soc. Hypnosis, Soc. for Clinical and Exptl. Hypnosis, Alaska Psychol. Assn., Kappa Delta Pi. Clubs: Lomas Santa Fe Country (Solana Beach, Calif.), Masons. Contbr. articles to profl. publs. Home: PO Box 4-1443 Anchorage AK 99509

SHIELDS, LAURA AULL, public relations counselor; b. Taylorville, Ill., Oct. 24; d. Frank and Gladys (Montgomery) Aull; m. Roger V. Shields, Nov. 20, 1940 (div.); children—Deborah, Beth, Roger, Clark, Constance. Student Ill. State U., 1935-37. Feature writer San Gabriel Valley Tribune, Covina, Calif., 1960; Owner Shields Communications, Santa Monica, Calif., 1974—; speaker in field. Mem. Pub. Relations Soc. Am. and Counselors Acad., Women in Communications, Women in Bus., Santa Monica Bay Area C. of C. Home and Office: 159 Wadsworth Ave Santa Monica CA 90405

SHIFFER, H. ALFRED, food company executive; b. Providence Nov. 2, 1936; s. H. Alfred and Mary E. (O'Leary) S.; m. Brenda Ann McConaghy, Oct. 13, 1962. A.B., St. Anselm Coll., 1960. Div. sales mgr. C.F. Mueller Co., Phila., 1970-73, mktg. services mgr., Jersey City, 1973-77, dir. mktg., 1977-80; dir. sales Foremost McKessnon, Jersey City, 1980-82; exec. v.p. Familiar Foods, Inc., City of Industry, Calif., 1982—, also dir. Mem. Food Mktg. Inst., Nat. Assn. Food Brokers. Republican. Roman Catholic. Home: 2040 San Remo Laguna Beach CA 92651 Office: 14314 Lomitas Ave City of Industry CA 91744

SHIMER, R(OBERT) TIMOTHY, public relations director, photographer; b. Tiffin, Ohio, Dec. 28, 1953; s. Robert E. and Mary M. (Riggerio) S.; m. Linda Dawson, Aug. 25, 1953; children—Clifton, Jeffrey, Matthew. B.S. in Mass Communications, U. So. Colo., 1978; student N.Y. Inst. Photography, 1981. Pub. affairs officer Fairfax County (Va.), 1978-82; sr. account exec. Internat. Pub. Relations, Ltd., Honolulu, 1982; dir. pub. affairs Rehab. Hosp. of the Pacific, Honolulu, 1983—. Fund raiser, cons. Kapiolani dist. Boy Scouts Am.; active Va. Republican party, 1978-81, Hawaii Rep. party, 1982—, also spl. polit. cons. Served with U.S. Army, 1972-75. Faculty scholar U. So. Colo., 1977, dean's honor student, 1978; recipient Spl. award Kapiolani dist. Boy Scouts Am., 1983. Mem. Pub. Relations Soc. Am., Am. Mktg. Assn., Internat. Assn. Bus. Communicators, Hosps. Pub. Relations Assn. Hawaii. Methodist. Club: Honolulu Lions. Home: 3 Ilikupono St Kailua HI 96734 Office: 226 N Kuakini St Honolulu HI 96817

SHIMIZU, KAORU KARL, electronics engr.; b. Montebello, Calif., Mar. 19, 1917; s. Kitaro and Tose (Nishida) S.; B.E.E., Ind. Inst. Tech., 1949; certificate in math. U. Calif. at Los Angeles, 1961; M.E.E., Calif. State U., 1971; m. Toshiko Janie Wada, Oct. 1, 1955. Engr., Sherwin Williams Co., Chgo., 1949-50; design engr. Lockheed Aircraft Co., Burbank, Calif., 1951-55; mem. tech. staff Rockwell Internat., Los Angeles, Downey and Anaheim, Calif., 1955-70; electronics engr. Naval Weapon Center, China Lake, Calif., 1971—. Served with AUS, 1941-45. Recipient Tech. Dir. award Naval Weapon Center, 1973. Mem. IEEE, Am. Med. Technologists. Republican. Buddhist. Club: Shiga. Contbr. articles to profl. jours.; inventor in field. Home: 27610 Boston Dr Sun City CA 92381 Office: Code 3912 Naval Weapon Center China Lake CA 93555

SHINBORI, DENNIS DAIZO, dentist; b. San Francisco, Nov. 4, 1950; s. James Tatsuo and Mary Chima (Hirata) S.; A.A., San Francisco City Coll., 1970; B.A. magna cum laude, U. Pacific, 1972, D.D.S., 1975; m. Wendy Melani Drefke, Feb. 14, 1976. Pvt. practice dentistry, San Francisco, 1976—; instr. depts. fixed and removable prosthodontics U. Pacific Dental Sch., 1975-78, asst. prof., 1979—. Ch. elder, mem. ch. bd. Ch. interch. com. St. Johns Lutheran Ch., San Francisco, 1978, rep. to

Pacific regional conf., Denver, 1978. Recipient numerous awards for amateur ballroom dancing, 1966-74, N.Am. and Japanese amateur champion, 1969-71, 7th World amateur champion, 1969, Can. amateur champion, 1971-72, U.S. Amateur Champion, 1973-74; capt. World and Brit. Formation championship team, 1983. Mem. Am., Calif., San Francisco (chmn. dental health edn. com., dir.) dental assns., San Francisco Dental Care Found., U. of Pacific, Coll. Physicians and Surgeons alumni assns., Japanese Cultural and Community Center, (dir.), Nihonmachi Assn., Tau Kappa Omega. Office: 1788 Sutter St Suite 201 San Francisco CA 94115

SHINDLER, JOHN THOMAS, fin. co. exec., lawyer; b. St. Louis, Jan. 18, 1924; s. Harold Allen and Marie (McCawley) S.; A.B., Georgetown U., 1948; postgrad. Harvard Bus. Sch., 1945, U. Louvain (Belgium), 1949-51; LL.B., Ind. U., 1963, J.D., 1964. With Banque de Bruxelles, N.Y.C., 1951-53, Fidelity Bank and Trust Co., Indpls., 1954-58; admitted to Ind. bar, 1963, U.S. Dist. Ct. bar, 1963; asst. atty. gen. State of Ind., 1963-65; U.S. atty. Dept. Justice, Newburgh and Indpls. 1966-68; practice law, Evansville, Ind., 1968-75; v.p., gen. counsel The Thomas Co., Las Vegas, Nev., 1976—; dir. Nye Enterprises, Las Vegas, Francis Co., Pompano, Fla. Vice chmn. Ind. League Voters, 1954-64. Served as lt. (j.g.), USNR, 1942-52. Recipient Freedom Found. award, 1948. Mem. Theater Arts Soc. of Las Vegas, Georgetown Alumni Assn., YMCA. Democrat. Roman Catholic. Club: Theater Arts, Inc. (Las Vegas). Lectr. Office: 1111 Las Vegas Blvd S Suite 214 Las Vegas NV 89104

SHINDO, SHOJIRO, aerodynamicist, aeronautical engineer; b. Osaka, Japan, July 18, 1931; s. Mamoru and Ochie S.; m. Kazumi Hisada, Jan. 10, 1960; children—Kaori, Hiroyuki. B.S. in Aero. Engring., U. Wash., 1957. Project engr. Kawasaki Aircraft Co., Gifu, Japan, 1960-62; design engr. U. Wash. Aero. Lab., Seattle, 1958-60, 1963-67, aero. engr., 1967—; cons. in field. Recipient Japanese Govt. Research award Nat. Aerospace Lab., Tokyo, 1974. Mem. AIAA. Author papers and reports on low-speed wind tunnel testing; transl. (with Harold N. Wantiez): Eagles of Mitsubishi, The Story of the Zero Fighter (Jiro Horikoshi), 1981. Home: 20010 Burke Ave N Seattle WA 98133 Office: Dept Aero and Astro U Wash FS 10 Seattle WA 98195

SHINE, FRANK, ednl. adminstr.; b. Oliphant, Pa., Dec. 17, 1914; s. Paul and Frances (Knafelc) S.; B.A., U. W.Va., 1936; M.B.A., Stanford U., 1949; m., July 12, 1938; children—Frank, Peggy Shine Thurman, Robert. Commd. 2d lt. U.S. Marine Corps, 1936, advanced through grades to col., 1951; served as platoon leader to regimental comdr, S.Pacific combat, 1943-45, joint chiefs of staff, 1945-47, ret., 1962; dir. purchasing Chula Vista (Calif.) City Sch. Dist., 1963—. Decorated Bronze Star with oak leaf cluster. Cert. public purchasing officer, Calif. Mem. Nat. Assn. Purchasing Mgmt. (cert. purchasing mgr.), Calif. Assn. Public Purchasing Ofcls. (pres. San Diego 1972), Calif. Assn. Sch. Bus. Ofcls., Third Marine Div. Assn. Democrat. Episcopalian. Club: Chula Vista Kiwanis (pres. 1971-72). Home: 17 E Sierra Way Chula Vista CA 92011 Office: 84 E J St Chula Vista CA 92010

SHIPEK, FLORENCE MCKEEVER CONNOLLY, anthropology educator; b. North Adams, Mass., Dec. 11, 1918; d. Joseph and Florence (McKeever) Connolly; B.A. with distinction, U. Ariz., 1938, M.A. in Anthropology, 1940; Ph.D. in Anthropology, U. Hawaii, 1975; m. Carl Joseph Shipek, June 7, 1943; children—Carl Joseph, David Connolly. Grad. asst. Ariz. State Mus., U. Ariz., 1939-40; instr. dept. geology U. Wash., 1944-46; lectr. anthropology U. San Diego, 1967-68; teaching assoc. U. Calif., San Diego, 1968, lectr., 1969, 70; dir. program for community devel. edn. for So. Calif. Indian Reservations, dept. sociology U. San Diego, 1970-72; lectr. Calif. State U., Northridge, 1975-76; asst. prof. anthropology div. behavioral sci. U. Wis.-Parkside, 1977—; cons. in field. Fellow Am. Anthrop. Assn., Soc. Applied Anthropology; mem. Am. Ethnol. Soc., Am. Soc. Ethnohistory, Council on Anthropology and Edn., Southwestern Anthrop. Assn., Asociación Cultural de las Californias, Malki Mus. Assn., Soc. Econ. Anthropology, Phi Kappa Phi. Contbr. articles to profl. jours. Office: Div Behavioral Sci U Wis-Parkside Kenosha WI 53141

SHIPLEY, ARBIS DARRELL, airline exec.; b. McAlaster, Okla., May 4, 1927; s. Melvin Herbert and Goldie (Cockrum) S.; B.A., San Francisco State U., 1953; student U. Manila, 1969; m. Aileen Neal, June 17, 1945; children—Terry, Robin, Trenise, Kevin; m. 2d Yoshiko Nakasone, Dec. 23, 1976; children—Liza, Wanda, Allison. Gen. mgr. supermarket chain, San Francisco, 1946-55; tchr. San Mateo (Calif.) Jr. Coll., 1950-52; gen. mgr. J & G Co., Agana, Guam, 1955-58; producer, dir. TV shows, Guam, 1956-57; owner Silver Dollar Plaza, Lake County, Calif., 1958-66; pres. Internat. Dairies Japan, 1966-70, U.S.-Japan chamber, 1969-70; Olympic Prodn., 1970-73; chmn. Guam Telephone Authority, 1973-76; pres. Horizon Air Lines, Honolulu, 1976—. Pres. bd. trustees Windward Prep. Sch., 1979-81; v.p. Pacific Aerospace Mus., 1981-82; exec. vice-chmn. Honolulu Republican Com., 1980-81; candidate for U.S. Senate, 1982. Served with AUS, 1945-46. Mem. Commuter Airlines of Am., Am. Legion, VFW. Republican. Episcopalian. Clubs: Masons, Shriners, Lions. Home: 278 Kaha St Kailua HI 96734 Office: Box 29428 Honolulu HI 96820

SHIPMAN, GEORGE ANDERSON, equipment leasing company executive; b. Cortland, N.Y., Aug. 10, 1930; s. George Anderson and Laura Jennings (Smith) S.; m. Mary Jane Bartholmey, Mar. 20, 1953; children—Melisse, Steven, Neil. B.A., U. Wash., 1954; postgrad., 1966. Owner, operator Shipmans, Bellevue, Wash., 1954-63; gen. mgr. Olympic Radio & Television, Seattle, div. Lear-Siegler, Inc., 1963-66; founder, pres. Lease Assocs., Inc., Bellevue, Wash., 1966—; dir. Western Assn. Equipment Lessors. Bd. dirs. Family Services King County, United Way of King County; pres.-elect United Way of Washington. Served with USAF, 1950-51. Office: PO Box 412 Bellevue WA 98009

SHIPMAN, STEPHEN WARD, broadcasting co. exec.; b. San Francisco, Dec. 27, 1954; s. Emmett Ward and Marilyn June (Forde) S.; B.A., Georgetown U., 1977; m. Dolores Donovan Gavin, Aug. 18, 1979; 1 dau., Regan Donovan. Founder, dir., gen. mgr. Goleta (Calif.) Communications Corp., 1976—. Republican. Roman Catholic. Home: 4705-B 8th St Carpinteria CA 93013 Office: Goleta Communications Corp 354-C Fairview Ave Goleta CA 93117

SHIPPEN, DEAN ELDON, data processing co. exec.; b. Idaho Falls, Idaho, Aug. 23, 1937; s. Charles Westley and Ruth Mildred (Tomblinson) S.; B.S., U. Idaho, 1959; m. Susan Noel Sameth, Mar. 25, 1977; children—Misty, Sheri, Pam, Kristin, Leslie. Programmer, U. Calif. Livermore Lab., 1959-60; programmer Phillips Petroleum Co., Idaho Falls, Idaho, 1960-61; research specialist Lockheed Missiles and Space Co., Sunnyvale, Calif., 1961-69; pres. Aztec Computer Service, Santa Clara, Calif., 1970-79; pres. Computerac, Inc., Santa Clara, 1979—; dir., sec.-treas. SNS, Inc., San Jose, Calif. Mem. Data Processing Mgmt. Assn. Republican. Clubs: Sharon Heights Golf and Country, Elks. Home: 1045 Cascade Dr Menlo Park CA 94025 Office: 586 Weddell Dr 2 Sunnyvale CA 94086

SHIREY, MARK STEVEN, electronics company executive; b. Long Beach, Calif., Dec. 13, 1955; s. Kenneth Eugene and Marjorie Irene (Thorvick) S.; B.S. in Elec. Engring., U. Calif.-Irvine, 1977, M.S. in Adminstrn., 1980, M.Engring., Calif. Poly. State U., 1978. Lectr. engring. Calif. Poly. State U., San Luis Obispo, 1977-78; supr. adminstrv. services EECO, Inc., Santa Ana, Calif., 1979-83; research and devel. analyst So. Calif. Edison Co., Rosemead, 1983—; pres., chief exec. officer M.S.E., Irvine, Calif., 1977—. Mem. IEEE, Eta Kappa Nu. Episcopalian. Office: 2244 Walnut Grove Ave Rosemead CA 91770

SHIRLEY, DIANA ALICE DENOYELLES, library executive, writer, editor; b. Los Angeles, May 20, 1938; d. Gerhard A. and Hilda M. (Schmal) Nehus; m. Robert Edward McGowan, June 28, 1959 (div. 1969); 1 son, Barry James; m. 2d, Edward Harold DeNoyelles, Aug. 15, 1970 (div. 1972); m. 3d, Stephen Marlin Shirley, May 19, 1979. Student Mt. St. Mary's Coll., Los Angeles, 1956-58; B.A. in History, Calif. State Poly. U., 1970; postgrad. U. So. Calif. Sch. Library Sci., 1970-71; M.S. in Library Sci., Calif. State U.-Fullerton, 1976; postgrad., U. Iowa, 1978, Claremont Grad. Sch., 1981—. Librarian trainee Los Angeles Pub. Library, 1970-72; librarian Pomona (Calif.) Pub. Library, 1972-76; coordinator regional adult services Central Region, Los Angeles County Pub. Library, 1976-79, city librarian, La Canada Flintridge, 1979-80, sr. adminstrv. analyst, Chief Adminstrv. Office, Los Angeles County, 1980-81, spl. asst. to county librarian, 1981—; exec. dir. Los Angeles County Pub. Library Found., 1981—; mgmt. cons., Pomona, Calif. Mem. Los Angeles World Affairs Council, 1981—. Mem. ALA, Calif. Library Assn., Library and Info. Tech. Assn., Am. Soc. Info. Sci., Am. Soc. Pub. Adminstrn., NOW. Republican. Unitarian. Editor: Women in California: A Guide to Organizations and Resources, 1977. Home: 231 Vista Circle Dr Sierra Madre CA 91024 Office: Los Angeles County Pub Library 320 W Temple St Los Angeles CA 90012

SHIRLEY, JOSEPH FLOYD, metallurgical consultant; b. Cin., Jan. 28, 1932; s. Joseph Boomer and Luella May (Barnes) S.; B.S., U. Ariz., 1955, M.S., 1958, Ph.D., 1969; m. Nadine Rehm, June 26, 1954; children—Joseph Theodore, William Floyd. Research chemist Magma Copper Co., San Manuel, Ariz., 1960-64; ind. metall. cons., Tucson, 1964-73; metall. cons. Mountain States Research & Devel., Tucson, 1973-80, v.p. tech., 1980-82, sr. v.p., gen. mgr., 1982—. cons. in field. Served with USAF, 1955-57. Mem. AIME, Mining and Metall. Soc. Am. Republican. Presbyterian. Club: Masons. Patentee on flotation recovery of molybdenite, 1974; contbr. articles to profl. jours. Home: 5150 N Hidden Valley Rd Tucson AZ 85715 Office: PO Box 17960 Tucson AZ 85731

SHIRLEY, ROSEMARY HILL, investor; b. Kansas City, Mo., Aug. 15, 1926; d. James Henry and Ethel Briscoe (Hill) H.; student U. Calif., Berkeley; div.; children—Marvin E., Richard Dennis. Royalty holder Middle East Am. Oil Co., 1959—; pres. Gambit VII Investments, Vacaville, Calif., 1975—. Mem. Nat. Assn. Female Execs. (network dir.), Desert Hosp. Assn., St. Patricks Home Guild. Republican. Roman Catholic. Club: Canyon Country (Palm Springs, Calif.). Home: 309 Creekview Ct Vacaville CA 95688 Office: PO Box 4317 Palm Springs CA 92262 Office: PO Box 282 Vacaville CA 95696

SHIVELY, JOHN TERRY, holding company exec.; b. Middletown, N.Y., July 1, 1943; s. Marvin Rathfelder and Esther (Manning) Westerveet; adopted s. Harold Eugene Shively; B.A., U. N.C., 1965. Vol. worker VISTA, Behtel, Yakutat, and Fairbanks, Alaska, 1965-68; health planner Greater Anchorage Area Community Action Agy., 1968-69; health cons. Alaska Fedn. Natives, Anchorage, 1969; dep. dir. Rural Alaska Community Action Program, Anchorage, 1969-70, exec. dir., 1971-72; exec. v.p. Alaska Fedn. Natives, Anchorage, 1972-75; v.p. ops. NANA Regional Corp., Kotzebue, Alaska, 1975-77, NANA Devel. Corp., Anchorage, 1977-82, sr. v.p., 1982—; dir. Unicorp. Inc., United Bank of Alaska, NANA Oilfield Services. Mem. Greater Anchorage Area Comprehensive Health Plan Council, 1969-75, chmn., 1969-75; founding mem. bd. dirs. Alaska Pub. Interest Research Group, 1974-75; mem. Gov.'s Rural Affairs Council, 1971-76, Gov.'s Manpower Commn., 1971, Greater Anchorage Health Bd., 1969-75, Alaska Pipeline Edn. Com., 1973-74; bd. regents U. Alaska. Mem. Alaska Fedn. Natives. Democrat. Episcopalian. Home: PO Box 1758 Anchorage AK 99510 Office: PO Box 4-U Anchorage AK 99509

SHMERLER, STEVEN ALAN, marketing executive; b. White Plains, N.Y., Oct. 20, 1951; s. Walter and Hannah (Citron) S. Student, U. Denver, 1969-71, Berklee Coll. Mus., 1973-74, N.Y.U., 1979. Performed with several music groups, 1971-75; dir. mktg. Frank Kraus Co., New Rochelle, N.Y., 1975-77; mgr. rec. group, The Paul Winter Consort, N.Y.C., 1977-78; nat. product mgr. Associated Labels div. RCA Records N.Y.C., 1977-79; dir. product devel. Chrysalis Records, Los Angeles, 1979-80; mktg. exec. Chrysalis Records, Los Angeles, 1980-82; ind. mktg. cons., Los Angeles, 1982; v.p. mktg. Starcom Entertainment, Inc., 1982—. Democrat.

SHOCKLEY, WILLIAM (BRADFORD), physicist; b. London, Feb. 13, 1910 (parents Am. citizens); s. William Hillman and May (Bradford) S.; B.S., Calif. Inst. Tech., 1932; Ph.D., MIT, 1936; D.Sc. (hon.), U. Pa., 1955, Rutgers U., 1956, Gustavus Adolphus Coll., 1963; m. Jean Alberta Bailey, 1933; 2 sons, 1 dau.; m. 2d, Emmy I. Lanning, 1955. Teaching fellow MIT, 1932-36; mem. tech. staff Bell Telephone Labs., 1936-42, 45-54, dir. transistor physics dept., 1954-55, exec. cons., 1965-75; dep. dir. research Weapons System Evaluation Group, Dept. Def., 1954-55; dir. Shockley Semicondr. Lab., Beckman Instruments, Inc., Palo Alto, Calif., 1955-58; pres. Shockley Transistor Corp., 1958-60; dir. Shockley Transistor unit Clevite Transistor, 1960-63, cons., 1963-65; lectr. Stanford U., 1958-63, Alexander M. Poniatoff prof. engring. and applied sci., 1963-75, Alexander M. Poniatoff prof. engring. and applied sci., emeritus, 1975—; vis. lectr. Princeton U., 1946; vis. prof. Calif. Inst. Tech., 1954-55; dept. dir., dir. research weapons system evaluation Dept. Def., 1954-55; cons. Office Sec. War, 1944-45; mem. U.S. Army sci. adv. panel, 1951-63, 64, USAF sci. adv. bd., 1959-63, Nat. Acad. Sci., 1951; mem. Pres.'s Sci. Adv. Com. Panel on Sci. and Tech. Manpower, 1962; mem. tech. adv. com. NASA. Recipient Morris Liebmann prize IRE, 1951, Air Force citation of honor, 1951, O.E. Buckley prize Am. Phys. Soc., 1953, Wilhelm Exner medal Oesterreichischer Gewerberein, 1963, Holley medal ASME, 1963, Joint Nobel prize in physics, 1956, Calif. Inst. Tech. Alumni Disting. Service award, 1966, NASA cert. of appreciation, 1969, Pub. Service Group Achievement award NASA, 1969; named to Nat. Inventors Hall of Fame, 1974, Calif. Inventors Hall of Fame, 1983; fellowship fund established in his name with Bardeen and Brattain SEMI, 1977. Fellow IEEE (Gold medal 1972, medal of honor 1980), Am. Acad. Arts and Scis.; mem. Nat. Acad. Scis. (Comstock prize 1954), Am. Inst. Physics, Sigma Xi, Tau Beta Pi. Clubs: Cosmos, Univ. (Washington); Bohemian (San Francisco); Stanford Faculty; Palo Alto Yacht. Author: Electrons and Holes in Semiconductors, 1950; (with W.A. Gong) Mechanics, 1966; editor: Imperfections of Nearly Perfect Crystals, 1952; contbr. articles to profl. jours. Inventor junction transistor; research on energy bands of solids, Ferromagnetic domains, plastic properties of metals, theory of grain boundaries, order and disorder in alloys, semi-conductor theory applied to devices and device defects such as dislocations, electromagnetic theory, mental tools for scientific thinking, ops. research on human quality statistics. Home: 797 Esplanada Way Stanford CA 94305 Office: Stanford Electronics Labs McC 202 Stanford U Stanford CA 94305

SHOCKLEY-ZALABAK, PAMELA SUE, educator, consultant, author; b. Amarillo, Tex., May 25, 1944; d. James William and Leatha Pearl (Cartwright) Shockley; B.A. (Lew Wentz Tri Delt scholar 1961-65), Okla. State U., 1965, M.A., 1972; Ph.D., U. Colo., 1980; m. Charles Zalabak, Dec. 30, 1975. Account exec., v.p. Ross Cummings & Co., Oklahoma City, 1965-70; cons., pres. Communications Consultants of Okla., Inc., Colorado Springs, Colo., 1970—; asst. prof., program dir. U. Colo., Colorado Springs, 1980—. Mem. Speech Communication Assn., Internat. Communication Assn., Phi Kappa Phi. Democrat. Home: 5905 Ridge Brook Ln Colorado Springs CO 80907 Office: Univ Colorado Communication Dept Austin Bluffs Pkwy Colorado Springs CO 80907

SHOECRAFT, JOHN ALBERT, real estate developer, investment company executive; b. Indpls., Nov. 1, 1944; s. Willard Rendell and Billee (White) S.; m. Mari Helen Oaks, June 16, 1963; 1 dau., Jeanette Louise. B.S. with high distinction in Bus. Adminstrn., Ariz. State U., 1966. C.P.A., Ariz. Radio announcer, engr. Sta. KATO, Safford, Ariz., 1961-63; Stas. KIKO, KINO, KATO, Ariz., 1963-66; audit supr. Ernst & Ernst, Phoenix, 1966-70; pvt. practice acctg., Scottsdale, Ariz., 1970-72; chief exec. officer Enterprise Growth Group, Scottsdale, 1972—; pres. Equity Mgmt. Corp., SC Resources Corp., Shoecraft Contracting, Inc., Scottsdale, 1972—. Active Ariz. Boys Community, Phoenix, 1978—; donor Sojourner Ctr., Phoenix, 1979. Recipient Montgolfier award Fedn. Aeronautique Internationale, 1982. Mem. Am. Inst. C.P.A.s, Ariz. Soc. C.P.A.s, Nat. Aeronautics Assn. (cert.), Balloon Fedn. Am., Phi Kappa Phi, Beta Alpha Psi, Beta Gamma Sigma. Republican. Presbyterian. Clubs: Ariz. Balloon, Helium Heads Balloon, Elks. Completed 1st non-stop balloon flight across Am.

SHOEMAKER, GARY LYNN, psychologist; b. Wheatland, Wyo., Sept. 7, 1947; s. Cecil Dale and Marjorie June S.; B.A. cum laude, Calif. State U., San Francisco, 1969; Ph.D. in Clin. Psychology (Calif. state fellow, 1972), U.S. Internat. U., 1974. Counselor for Satori program, San Diego YMCA, 1971-72; intern in clin. psychology Counseling and Psychology Sers., U. Calif., San Diego, 1971-73; counseling psychologist U. Calif., Santa Cruz, 1973—; individual practice clin. psychology, 1977—. Lic. psychologist, Calif. Mem. Am. Psychol. Assn. Home: 125 Mattison Ln Aptos CA 95003 Office: 104 Cowell College Univ California Santa Cruz CA 95060

SHOEMAKER, HAROLD LLOYD, computer system developer; b. Danville, Ky., Jan. 3, 1923; s. Eugene Clay and Amy (Wilson) S.; A.B., Berea Coll., 1944; postgrad. State U. Ia., 1943-44, George Washington U., 1949-50, N.Y. U., 1950-52; m. Dorothy M. Maddox, May 11, 1947. Research physicist State U., Ia., 1944-45, Frankford Arsenal, Pa., 1945-47; research engr. N.Am. Aviation, Los Angeles, 1947-49, Jacobs Instrument Co., Bethesda, 1949-50; asso. head systems devel. group The Teleregister Corp., N.Y.C., 1950-53; mgr. electronic equipment devel. sect., head planning for indsl. systems div. Hughes Aircraft Co., Los Angeles, 1953-58; dir. command and control systems lab. Bunker-Ramo Corp., Los Angeles, 1958-68, v.p. Data Systems, 1968-69, corp. dir. data processing, 1969-75; tech. staff R & D Assos., Marina Del Rey, Calif., 1975—. Served with AUS, 1945-46. Mem. IEEE Patentee elec. digital computer. Home: PO Box 3385 Granada Hills CA 91344 Office: R & D Assos PO Box 9695 Marina Del Rey CA 90291

SHOEMAKER, STEVEN THOMAS, agrl. chems. corp. ofcl.; b. Fresno, Calif., Oct. 25, 1951; s. Dean Clinton and Edwinia Jean (Mercer) S.; student Fresno City Coll., 1969-72; B.A. in Biology, Calif. State U., Fresno, 1979; m. Susan Jean Jones, Feb. 23, 1974. Inventory coordinator Pure Gro Agrl. Chems., Stockton, Calif., 1979, wholesale rep. No. Calif., Stockton, 1979-81; comml. devel. rep. Calif., Nev. and Ariz., Am. Hoechst Corp., Galt, Calif., 1981—. Served with Army N.G., 1971-77, with USMC, 1979; 2d lt. Res. Mem. Am. Mgmt. Assn., Young Farmers and Ranchers, Farm Bur., Calif. Agrl. Prodn. Consultants Assn. Republican. Baptist. Office: 9845 Pringle Ave Galt CA 95632

SHOLL, JOHN GURNEY, III, physician; b. Phila., Mar. 6, 1915; s. John Gurney, Jr. and Helen (Hare) S.; B.S., Bucknell U., 1937; M.D., Harvard U., 1941; m. Marjorie Louise Hill, June 27, 1942; children—John Douglas, Debora Louise Sholl Humphreys, Robert Roy, David Gurney, Rebecca Ann Sholl Baer, Intern, Germantown Hosp., Phila., 1941-42; asst. resident in medicine Univ. Hosp., Cleve., 1942-43; assoc. prof. principles of medicine Dental Sch., Case Western Res. U., Cleve., 1955-76; asso. clin. prof. medicine, 1968-78; dir. med. edn. Univ. Suburban Health Center, Cleve., 1973-78; chmn. edn. com. Ohio Med. Assn., 1974-77; med. dir. E.F. Hutton Life Ins. Co., San Diego, 1978-81; clin. prof. medicine, dir. internal medicine group U. Calif., San Diego, 1978—. Served as officer M.C., U.S. Army, 1944-46. Diplomate Am. Bd. Internal Medicine, Nat. Bd. Med. Examiners. Fellow ACP; mem. AMA. Club: Rowfant (Cleve.). Home: 6546 Muirlands Dr La Jolla CA 92037 Office: U Calif Med Sch Mail Code M-019 La Jolla CA 92093

SHOMER, ROBERT BAKER, employee benefit cons.; b. Lakewood, Ohio, Aug. 26, 1943; s. John Edward and Margaret Jeannette (Yeager) S.; B.A. in Psychology, Central Wash. State U., 1966; m. Kristin Lee Langum, Dec. 30, 1977. Brokerage Supr. Aetna Life and Casualty Co., San Francisco, 1971-73; regional dir. Hartford Variable Annuity Co., 1973-75; dir. deferred compensation dept. Galbraith & Green, Inc., Tempe, Ariz., 1976-79, v.p., 1980-82; sr. v.p. Fred S. James, 1983—. Bd. dirs. So. Ariz. Health Alliance. Served as capt. USAF, 1967-71. Home: 4502 Heatherwood Pl Tucson AZ 85718 Office: 4911 E Broadway Suite 100 Tempe AZ 85711

SHONK, ALBERT DAVENPORT, JR., publishers rep.; b. Los Angeles, May 23, 1932; s. Albert Davenport and Jean Spence (Stannard) S.; B.S. in Bus. Adminstrn., U. So. Calif., 1954. Field rep. Los Angeles Examiner, 1954-55, asst. mgr. mktg. div. 1955-56, mgr., 1956-57; account exec. Hearst Advt. Service, Los Angeles, 1957-59; account exec., mgr. San Francisco area Keith H. Evans & Assos., 1959-65; owner, pres. Albert D. Shonk Co., Los Angeles, 1965—; pres., Signet Circle Corp., Inc., 1977-81, dir., 1962-81, hon. life dir., 1982—. Bd. dirs., sec., 1st v.p. Florence Crittenton Services of Los Angeles, exec. v.p., 1979-81, pres., 1981-83, chmn. bd., 1983—; founding chmn. Crittenton Assos. Recipient Medallion of Merit Phi Sigma Kappa, 1976, Founders award, 1961. Mem. Advt. Club Los Angeles, Bus. and Profl. Advt. Assn., Pubs. Rep. Assn. of So. Calif., Nat. Assn. Pubs. Reps. (v.p. West Coast), Jr. Advt. Club Los Angeles (hon. life; dir., treas., 1st v.p.), Trojan Club, Commerce Assos., Inter-Greek Soc. (co-founder, hon. life mem. and dir., v.p. 1976-79), Phi Sigma Kappa (dir. grand council 1962-70, 77-79, grand pres. 1979-83, chancellor 1983—, trustee, v.p. meml. found.), Alpha Kappa Psi. Home: 3460 W 7th St Los Angeles CA 90005 Office: 3156 Wilshire Blvd Los Angeles CA 90010

SHOOK, ROBERT MICHAEL, health care administrator; b. Yuma, Ariz., Mar. 5, 1943; s. William Arthur and Eleanor Eloise (Downey) S.; m. Jacqueline Palma Cetinich, July 5, 1970. B.S., No. Ariz. U., 1966. Program dir. Contra Costa Med. Services, Martinez, Calif., 1968-71; coordinator community mental retardation services, State of Oreg., 1971-74; exec. dir. Oreg. Devel. Disabilities Council, 1974-76; dir. child neurology clinic and comprehensive epilepsy program Good Samaritan Hosp. and Med. Ctr., Portland, Oreg., 1976-80, dir. planning and program devel., 1980—; past project dir. nat. model demonstration grants U.S. Dept. Edn.; lectr. on handicapped infants and children; del.

White House Conf. on Handicapped Individuals, 1977. Mem. Nat. Assn. Retarded Citizens, Nat. Epilepsy Found. Am., Hosp. Planning Soc., Am. Assn. Mental Deficiency (pres. Region I 1979), Assn. Severely Handicapped. Office: 1015 NW 22d Ave Portland OR 97210

SHORE, HERBERT CHIVAMBO, author, dramatist, educator; b. Phila., June 6, 1924; s. Meyer and Frances (Smiler) S.; B.A. (Mayor Phila. scholar), U. Pa., 1942; postgrad. Columbia U., 1946-48, Dramatic Workshop, New Sch., 1946-48; M.A., Stanford U., 1958; m. Yen Lu Wong, Dec. 23, 1977; children—Norman Jon, Pia Ilyen Wong, Maya Iming Wong. Author, dramatist, 1956—; provost Internat. Coll., 1983—; dir. Council Tech. and Cultural Transformation, 1974—; prof., U. So. Calif., 1979—; founding dir. TNR: The New Repertory, 1972—; dir. plays for theatre and TV, author plays, also cantata. Served with USMC, 1943-46. Ford Found. grantee, 1978-79; Rockefeller Found. grantee, 1966-67; grantee Nat. Endowment Humanities, 1979—, Helene Wurlitzer Found., 1958-60, Social Sci. Research Council, 1967-68, African and Am. Univs. Program, 1964-65, Kate Maremont Found., 1959-60, Centro Mexicano de Escritores, 1958, White-Williams Found., 1936-39, Am. Council Learned Socs., 1941-43; recipient Writers Digest prize fiction, 1963. Mem. MLA, Am. Theatre Assn., African Studies Assn. Author: Come Back Africa, 1970; Ashes Dark Antigone, 1972; ...toward the world of tomorrow, 1978; No Future Wrapped in Darkness, 1982; Cicada Images, Moulting, 1983, Seed of the Mango, 1983; also articles, short stories, poems. Office: International College 1019 Gayley Ave Los Angeles CA 90024

SHORE, KAREN FAY, chemist; b. St. Paul, Aug. 17, 1948; d. Hobart Paul and Irene Susan (Baierl) Kern; 1 dau., Kristen. B.S. in Chemistry, U. San Francisco, 1970, M.B.A., U. Santa Clara, 1983. Chemist, Sondell Sci. Inst., Palo Alto, Calif., 1970-71, SCM, Palo Alto, 1972-75, Diamond Shamrock, Redwood City, Calif., 1975-77; quality assurance chemist Beckman Inst., Palo Alto, 1977—, mgr., 1981—. Mem. Am. Soc. Quality Control, Am. Mgmt. Assn., Regulatory Affairs Profl. Soc. Democrat. Roman Catholic. Office: 1050 Page Mill Rd Palo Alto CA 94304

SHORR, MELVIN, aeronautical engineering executive, consultant; b. Cin., Apr. 3, 1915; s. Morris and Elsie (Piates) S.; m. Evelyn Blanche Gideon, Aug. 27, 1966; children—Howard L., Sandra R., Nancy J. B.Sc. in Aero. Engring., U. Cin., 1936, postgrad. in aero. engring., 1939. Registered profl. engr., Ohio. Aero. engr. U.S. Air Force, Wright-Patterson AFB, Ohio, successively chief stability and control, asst. chief aerodynamics, staff asst. aeromechanics div., finally, spl. advisor to chief Air Force Flight Dynamics Lab; asst. v.p. research and engring. N.Am. Aviation, 1966-68; asst. dir. advanced systems design Northrop Aircraft Corp., 1968-75; cons. aero. engring., solar heating, state-of-art control system for flying replica of 1903 Wright Flyer, USAF rep. various NASA coms., internat. coms. and sci. study groups; mem. Def. Research Exchange Com., Tokyo and Taipei, 1965. Decorated by Sec. U.S. Air Force for work as spl. advisor to chief Air Force Flight Dynamics Lab; Meritorious Civilian Service commendation (3) for developing spin test methods; recipient Zero-Defects Gold award, 1965; elected to Honor Roll of Inventors, Northrop Corp., 1965. Assoc. fellow AIAA; mem. Sigma Xi. Republican. Patentee auto film-jam shut off, cascade blown wing flaps; author of numerous flight test and stability reports on WW II combat aircraft. Home: 4776 La Villa Marina Apt D Marina Del Rey CA 90291 Died Jan. 2, 1983.

SHORT, ROBERT HENRY, utility co. exec.; b. Klamath Falls, Oreg., Oct. 15, 1924; s. Judge Haywood and Henrietta Luella (Lyon) S.; B.S. in Journalism, U. Oreg., 1950; m. Ruby Madalyn Rice, Aug. 1, 1946; children—Robert L., Victoria (Mrs. Gregory Baum), Casey. City editor Klamath Falls Herald and News, 1950-52; dir. pub. relations Water and Elec. Bd., Eugene, Oreg., 1952-55; mgr. pub. info. Portland Gen. Electric Co. (Oreg.), 1955-57, asst. to chmn., 1957-62, v.p., 1962-71, sr. v.p., 1971-73, exec. v.p., 1973-77, pres., from 1977, chmn. bd., chief exec. officer, 1980—, also dir.; dir. First Interstate Bank of Oreg. Bd. dirs. Edison Electric Inst., Oreg. Ind. Colls. Found., Oreg. United Way; trustee Oreg. Grad., Willamette U.; chmn. Oreg. Ind. Coll. Found.; bd. overseers Oreg. Health Scis. U. Served with USNR, 1942-45. Clubs: Congl. Country, Astoria (Oreg.) Country, Portland Golf, Arlington, University. Office: Portland Gen Electric Co 121 SW Salmon St Portland OR 97204

SHORTER, JOHN WILLIAM, manufacturing/research company executive; b. Staunton, Va., Mar. 7, 1931; s. Ardith Viviant and Louise Frances (Lynn) S.; m. Cynthia Ann Speck, June 5, 1954; 1 son, Jeffrey William. B.S., Va. Tech. & State U., 1954; M.S., U. So. Calif., 1978; postgrad. Air U., 1974, Air War Coll., Command Staff Coll., 1974. Commd. 2d lt., U.S. Air Force, 1955, advanced through grades to lt. col., 1971; ret., 1976; with McLaughlin Research Corp., Norco, Calif., 1980—, logistical engr., 1983—. Decorated Meritorious Service medal, Air Force Commendation medal; recipient plaque Air Force, as founder of Santas in Blue, Tucson, 1966; Silver Trophy, SAC combat crew, 1965. Mem. Soc. Logistical Engrs., Air Force Assn., Ret. Officers Assn., Arnold Air Soc., Scabbard and Blade, So. Calif. Hist. Soc., Va. Tech. Century, Air War Coll. Alumni Assn. Republican. Methodist. Club: Trojan. Lodges: K.T., Masons, Shriner, Order Eastern Star, Kiwanis (past pres.). Office: 2748 Hamner Ave Norco CA 91760

SHORTLE, PATRICK JOSEPH, training and management development consultant; b. Detroit, Nov. 16, 1951; s. Emmett Francis and Anne Mary (Mainville) S. B.A., U. Santa Clara, 1973. Cert. personnel mgmt. and employee relations U. Calif.-Irvine, 1979. Tng. and devel. officer United Calif. Bank, Los Angeles, 1978-81; tng. and devel. rep. First Interstate Bank, Los Angeles, 1981-82; tng. and devel. cons. Hosp. Council of So. Calif., Los Angeles, 1982—. Mem. Am. Soc. for Tng. and Devel., Hosp. Personnel Mgmt. Assn., Am. Soc. for Health Care Edn. and Tng. Office: Hosp Council of So Calif 6255 Sunset Blvd Suite 817 Los Angeles CA 90028

SHOUP, ALLAN EMERSON, elec. engr.; b. Coeur d'Alene, Idaho, June 12, 1921; s. Earl Ross and Iva Mildred (Hutchison) S.; B.S.E.E., Wash. State U., 1950; m. Evelyn Louise Coy, June 12, 1943; children—Julie Ann Shoup Martin, David Ross; m. 2d Margaret June Keating, Apr. 9, 1976; stepsons—John R., Randall G., Brian L. Hoffmann. Jr. engr., draftsman Bonneville Power Adminstrn., Portland, 1941-42; outfitting expeditor Willamette Iron & Steel Corp., Portland, 1942-45; field draftsman Bur. Public Rds., Portland, 1945; supr. elec. engring. Design Div., Planning Dept., Puget Sound Naval Shipyard, Bremerton, Wash., 1950—. Registered profl. engr., Wash. Mem. Wash. Soc. Profl. Engrs. (pres. chpt. 1974-75), Nat. Assn. Naval Tech. Suprs. (pres. Puget Sound chpt. 1979), Nat. Soc. Profl. Engrs. Republican. Methodist. Clubs: Elks, Bremerton Yacht, Bremerton Tennis and Swim. Home: 7052 Navajo Trail NE Bremerton WA 98310

SHOUSE, THELMA LOUISE, savs. and loan exec.; b. Owensboro, Ky., Oct. 1, 1944; d. James W. and Daisy P. (Anderson) W.; m. Charles Ray Shouse, Mar. 15, 1962; children—Kimberly Rhea Shouse DeMichele, Jeffrey Scott. Student, U. Wash., 1978-79. Loan service/foreclosure clk. Claremont (Calif.) Savs. & Loan, 1966-68; teller, new accounts clk. Pomona (Calif.) First Fed., 1970-71, savs. officer, 1971-73, ops. officer, 1973-75, computer liaison officer, 1973-75, asst. v.p., 1975-80, product mgr./savs., asst. v.p. Coast Fed. Savs. & Loan, Los Angeles, 1980—, mgr. systems and methods, 1981—. Office: Coast Federal Savings & Loan 855 S Hill St Los Angeles CA 90015

SHOWALTER, DIANE GAIL, educational administrator; b. Colville, Wash., Aug. 28, 1944; d. Dee L. and Ina I. (Koski) McKern; m. J. David Showalter, Aug. 28, 1965; children—Benjamin, Matthew. B.A. in Edn., Eastern Wash. U., 1966, B.A. in English, 1970, postgrad. 1979—. Cert. pub. sch. tchr., Wash. Tchr. Blair Elem. Sch., Fairchild AFB, Wash., 1966-69; pvt. tutor, 1975; freelance editor, cons., 1976; sec. phys. therapy program Eastern Wash. U., Cheney, 1977, sec. to provost, 1977-79, adminstrv. asst. to v.p. extended programs, 1979-82, coordinator alumni, community relations, asst. to v.p. extended programs (including alumni), 1982—; dir. Eastern Wash. U. Alumni Assn. Mem. adv. com. Cheney Sch. Dist., 1979—. Recipient Nat. Human Interest Story award Am. Nat. Cowbelles, 1974; Woman in Leadership award Spokane YWCA, 1982. Mem. AAUW, Nat. Assn. Female Execs., Wash. Edn. Assn. Clubs: Amber Grange, Am. Nat. Cowbelles (state sec. 1975). Contbr. articles to mags. Home: Route 1 Box 233 Cheney WA 99004 Office: Showalter 216 Eastern Wash U Cheney WA 99004

SHOWALTER, GLENN, aviation consultant; b. Staunton, Va., June 5, 1947; B.S. in Photog. Arts and Scis., Rochester Inst. Tech., 1969; M.S. in Edn.-Instrnl. Tech. summa cum laude, Syracuse U., 1976. Photojournalist, Gannett Rochester (N.Y.) Newspapers, 1967-69; advt. and illustration photographer; tech. rep. Photo Products div. DuPont Co., 1969-70; prof. Syracuse (N.Y.) U., 1972-74, Mont. State U., Bozeman, 1974-75, Ithaca (N.Y.) Coll., 1975-77; free lance journalist; aviation cons., Bozeman. Lic. comml. pilot instrument and multi-engine rated; cert. Scuba diver YMCA; lic. amateur radio operator. Contbr. articles to profl. jours.; numerous photog. exhbns. Address: PO Box 2038 Bozeman MT 59715

SHREEVE, JEAN'NE MARIE, chemist; b. Deer Lodge, Mont., July 2, 1933; d. Charles William and Maryfrances (Briggeman) S.; B.A., U. Mont., 1953, D.Sc. (hon.), 1982; M.S., U. Minn., 1956; Ph.D., U. Wash., 1961. Asst. prof. chemistry U. Idaho, 1961-65, asso. prof., 1965-67, prof., 1967—, head dept. chemistry, 1973—; NSF fellow, Cambridge, Eng., 1967-68; vis. prof. U. Bristol, 1977; Lucy W. Pickett lectr. Mt. Holyoke Coll., 1976. A.P. Sloan Found. fellow, 1970-72; recipient Alexander von Humboldt Found., U.S. sr. scientist award, 1978; Outstanding Achievement award U. Minn., 1975, award for creative work in fluorine chemistry, 1978, award for excellence in coll. teaching chem. Mfg. Chemists Assn., 1979. Mem. AAAS, AAUW, Am. Chem. Soc. (Garvan medal 1972), Am. Inst. Chemists, Assn. Women Chemists, Chem. Soc. (London), Idaho Acad. Sci., Phi Beta Kappa, Phi Kappa Phi, Iota Sigma Pi. Mem. editorial adv. bds. Jour. Fluorine Chemistry, Accounts of Chem. Research, Inorganic Syntheses. Contbr. articles to profl. jours. Office: Dept Chemistry Univ of Idaho Moscow ID 83843

SHROPSHIRE, CLAUDIUS NAPOLEON, JR., physician; b. Texarkana, Ark., Jan. 10, 1925; s. Claudius N. and Eulah M. (Brinker) S.; B.S. summa cum laude, Johnson C. Smith U., 1947; M.D., Meharry Med. Coll., 1951; m. Jane F. Moore, June 16, 1951; children—Claudius Napoleon III, Kenneth Leroy. Intern, Madigan Army Hosp., Tacoma, Wash., 1951-52; resident surgery Wadsworth Gen. Hosp., Los Angeles, 1953-57; practice medicine specializing in surgery, Los Angeles, 1957—; mem. attending staff Queen of Angels Hosp.; chief of staff Temple Hosp., 1977-81; asso. staff Marina Mercy Hosp., UCLA Med. Center Hosp.; asst. clin. prof. surgery UCLA Sch. Medicine, 1963—. Mem. bd. mgrs. Crenshaw YMCA, 1973-78; trustee Westminster Presbyn. Ch., 1970-72. Served to capt., M.C., USAF, 1951-57. Decorated Purple Heart, Bronze Star; diplomate Am. Bd. Surgery. Fellow A.C.S. (mem. bd. govs. So. Calif. chpt. 1977-79); mem. Am. Soc. of Abdominal Surgeons, Orange County Surg. Soc., Los Angeles Surg. Soc., Charles Drew Med. Soc. (pres. 1976-77), AMA, Calif. Med. Assn., Los Angeles Med. Assn., Am. Geriatrics Soc., Golden State Med. Soc., Am. Cancer Soc. (dir. Los Angeles chpt. 1969-73), NAACP, Urban League, Alpha Kappa Mu., Kappa Alpha Psi, Beta Kappa Chi. Home: 4134 Don Luis Dr Los Angeles CA 90008 Office: Suite 6 1828 S Western Ave Los Angeles CA 90006

SHROYER, SHERRY REICHARDT, interior designer, educator; b. Huron, S.D., Dec. 2, 1937; d. Floyd William and Gwenellen (Williams) Seemann; m. Jerry Edwin Reichardt, Oct. 29, 1960; m. 2d Eugene Milton Shroyer, July 2, 1976; children—James Jerald, Jennifer Jill. B.A., U. Iowa, 1960. Designer Twettens Furniture, Coralville, Iowa, 1961-64; designer, mgr. Gilpins Coordination Centre, Iowa City, 1964-66; designer Interiors by Freed, Coralville, 1966-69, Haafs Furniture, Phoenix, 1971; dir. interior design dept. Scottsdale Community Coll., 1971—. Mem. Am. Soc. Interior Designers (outstanding service award 1981, charter bd. dirs.), Nat. Home Fashions League (ednl. v.p.), Interior Design Educators Council. Republican. Episcopalian. Contbr. to publs. in field; frequent guest appearances on Rita Devenport's Open House, Channel 5. Home: 3503 Kachina Ln Scottsdale AZ 85251 Office: 9000 E Chapparral Scottsdale AZ 85253

SHRYOCK, CARL MICHAEL, clergyman; b. Newton, Ill., Aug. 29, 1952; s. Carl William and Anna Carolyn (Linz) S.; A.S., Olney Central Coll., 1972; B.A., Ky. Christian Coll., 1975, B.Th., 1977; M.Div., Lincoln Christian Sem., 1981. Youth minister Assumption (Ill.) Christian Ch., 1975-77; ordained to ministry Christian Ch., 1977; youth minister Clarks Hill (Ind.) Christian Ch., 1978-79; campus minister Christian Student Fellowship, U. Ky., Lexington, 1979-80; supply minister Galesburg (Ill.) Christian Ch., 1980-81; youth minister University Ave. Christian Ch., Bakersfield, Calif., 1981—; active New Eng. Fellowship, 1977-81. Vol., Day Care Center for Exceptional Children, Olney, Ill., 1971; mem. visitation group Fed. Correctional Center, Ashland, Ky., 1973-75; mem. Assumption Bicentennial Community Choir, 1976; active Big Brother program, Lexington, 1979-80, Boswell council Boy Scouts Am., 1977. Republican. Republican. Contbr. articles to profl. jours. Home: 1611 Howard St Bakersfield CA 93308 Office: 4201 University Ave Bakersfield CA 93306

SHULER, KURT EGON, chemistry educator; b. Nuremberg, Ger., July 10, 1922; s. Louis and Denise (Wald) S.; m. Beatrice Gwynne, Nov. 11, 1944. B.S., Ga. Inst. Tech., 1942; Ph.D. Cath. U. Am., 1949. Fellow John Hopkins U., Balt., 1949-51, sr. staff mem., 1951-55; sr. research fellow, asst. dir. Nat. Bur. Standards, Washington, 1955-68; prof. chemistry U. Calif.-San Diego, 1968—, chmn. dept., 1968-70; mem. Solvay Conf., 1962, 1978. Recipient Disting. Service award Nat. Bur. Standards, 1959; Gold medal U.S. Dept. Commerce, 1968; Solvay Found. fellow U. Brussels, 1975. Fellow Am. Phys. Soc., Am. Inst. Chemists; mem. Am. Chem. Soc. Club: Cosmos (Washington). Author four books and numerous papers on chem. physics; patentee carbon monoxide detection device. Office: Dept Chemistry U Calif-San Diego La Jolla CA 92093

SHULL, HARRISON, chemist, educator; b. Princeton, N.J., Aug. 17, 1923; s. George Harrison and Mary (Nicholl) S.; A.B., Princeton U., 1943; Ph.D., U. Calif. at Berkeley, 1948; m. Jeanne Louise Johnson, 1948 (div. 1962); children—James Robert, Kathy, George Harrison, Holly; m. 2d, Wil Joyce Bentley Long, 1962; children—Warren Michael Long, Jeffery Mark Long, Stanley Martin, Sarah Ellen. Asso. chemist U.S. Naval Research Lab., 1943-45; asst. prof. Iowa State U., 1949-54; mem. faculty Ind. U., 1955-79, research prof., 1961-79, dean Grad. Sch., 1965-72, vice chancellor for research and devel., 1972-76, dir. Research Computing Center, 1959-63, acting chmn. chemistry dept., 1965-66, acting dean arts and scis., 1969-70, acting dean faculties, 1974; mem. faculty, provost, v.p. acad. affairs Rensselaer Poly. Inst., 1979-82; chancellor U. Colo., Boulder, 1982—; asst. dir. research, quantum chemistry group Uppsala (Sweden) U., 1958-59; vis. prof. Washington U., St. Louis, 1960, U. Colo., 1963. Founder, supr. Quantum Chemistry Program Exchange, 1962—; chmn. subcom. molecular structure and spectroscopy NRC, 1958-63; chmn. Fullbright selection com. chemistry, 1963-67, mem. adv. com. Office Sci. Personnel, 1957-60; chmn. First Gordon Research Conf. Theoretical Chemistry, 1962; mem. com. survey chemistry Nat. Acad. Sci., 1964-65; mem. adv. panel chemistry NSF, 1964-67, mem. adv. panel Office Computer Activities, 1967-70, cons. chem. information program, 1965-71, mem. adv. com. for research 1974-76; mem. vis. com. chemistry Brookhaven Nat. Lab., 1967-70; mem. adv. com. Chem. Abstracts Service, 1971-74. Trustee Argonne U. Assn., 1970-75, Asso. Univs., Inc., 1973-76. Served as ensign USNR, 1945. NRC postdoctoral fellow phys. scis. U. Chgo., 1948-49; Guggenheim fellow U. Uppsala, 1954-55, NSF sr. postdoctoral fellow, 1968-69; Sloan research fellow, 1956-58. Fellow Am. Acad. Arts and Scis. (v.p. 1976-82, chmn. Midwest Center 1976-79), Am. Phys. Soc.; mem. Nat. Acad. Scis. (com. on sci. and public policy, 1969-72; council, exec. com., 1971-74, chmn. U.S.-USSR sci. policy subgroup for fundamental research 1973-81, naval studies bd. 1974-79, chmn. Commn. on Human Resources 1977-81, nominating com. 1978), Am. Chem. Soc., AAAS, Assn. Computing Machinery, Royal Swedish Acad. Scis. (fgn. mem.), Royal Acad. Arts and Scis. Uppsala (corr. mem.), Phi Beta Kappa, Sigma Xi, Phi Lambda Upsilon. Club: Cosmos (Washington). Asso. editor Jour. Chem. Physics, 1952-54; editorial adv. bd. Spectrochimica Acta, 1957-63, Internat. Jour. Quantum Chemistry, 1967—, Proc. Nat. Acad. Scis., 1976-80; cons. editor Allyn and Bacon. Contbr. articles to profl. jours. Office: Office of Chancellor U Colo Boulder CO 80309

SHULTZ, AL, advertising executive, poet; b. Port-of-Spain, Trinidad, West Indies, Sept. 2, 1943; s. Marshall Thomas and Marie Claire (Bossé) S.; m. Norma Pearl Shrum, Mar. 15, 1965; 1 son, Anthony Thomas; m. Diane Scherwood, Feb. 29, 1977. B.A. in English, Portland State U., 1966. Copywriter, Friden-Singer Bus. Machines, San Leandro, Calif., 1967-74, sales promotion mgr., 1974-76; advt. account mgr. Nat. Semiconductor, Santa Clara, Calif., 1976-80, account exec., copy chief Moorhead Mktg., San Francisco, 1980-81; account supr., copywriter Bozell & Jacobs, Palo Alto, Calif., 1981—. Vol. instr. sr. citizens writing workshops, San Jose, Calif.; bd. dirs. San Jose Poetry Ctr. Recipient 6th prize Bus. Week mag. Fabulous Ad Contest, 1982. Mem. Bus./Profl. Advt. Assn., Am. Assn. Advt. Agys., Phi Sigma Kappa. Democrat. Roman Catholic. Poems pub. in lit. jours. Office: Bozell & Jacobs 2440 Embarcadero Way Palo Alto CA 94303

SHUMAKER, EDWARD CHARLES, ins. corp. exec.; b. Jacksonville, Fla., Aug. 11, 1943; s. Allen and Maxine Ann (Chenoweth) S.; B.S. in Indsl. Tech., Calif. State U., Long Beach, 1968; m. Betty J. York, Mar. 28, 1979; children—Julie C., Jill S. Field engr. Factory Mut. Engring. Corp., Whittier, Calif., 1968-69; sales account rep. Protection Mut. Ins. Co., Pasadena, Calif., 1969-72; asst. property mgr. Frank B. Hall & Co., Los Angeles, 1972-74; pres. Bayly, Martin & Fay of Orange County, Inc., Newport Beach, Calif., 1974—. Served with USMCR, 1964-70. Mem. Sigma Chi. Republican. Lutheran. Clubs: Balboa Bay (Newport Beach); Santa Ana Country. Home: 9822 Raritan Ave Fountain Valley CA 92708 Office: 14 Corporate Plaza Dr Newport Beach CA 92660

SHUMAKER, MAURICE CALVIN, banker; b. Spokane, Wash., Jan. 13, 1921; s. John Calvin and Alice Mabel (Hendericksen) S.; B.A. in Fin., U. Wash., 1947; postgrad. Pacific Coast Banking Sch., 1961; cert. comml. lender U. Okla., 1974; postgrad. Exec. Mgmt. Acad., U. Mich., 1978; m. Beth Ramsey Harius, Apr. 29, 1944; children—Margaret Ann, John William, Mary Beth, David Calvin. With Rainier Bank, Spokane, 1946—, v.p., 1964-76, sr. v.p., mgr. Eastern region, office, 1976-79, sr v.p. Spokane main office, 1979-81, sr. v.p., mgr. Comml. Banking Ctr. Eastern Wash., Spokane, 1981—; mem. adv. bd. Small Bus. Devel. Ctr., Wash. State U. Pres., Twin Harbors council Boy Scouts Am., 1971-74, v.p. Inland Empire council, 1976-82, pres., 1983—, mem. internat. bd., 1980—; treas. U.S. Found. Internat. Scouting, 1982—; trustee St. George's Sch., 1983—. Served with USAAF, 1943-45; ETO. Decorated D.F.C., Air medal with 3 oak leaf clusters. Recipient Silver Beaver award Boy Scouts Am., 1970, Silver Antelope award, 1981, Disting. Eagle Scout award, 1982. Mem. Am. Inst. Banking, Wash. Bankers Assn., Robert Morris Assos. Presbyterian. Clubs: Manito Golf, Spokane City, Wash. Athletic (bd. govs. 1967-69), Elks. Home: E1503 Woodcliff Rd Spokane WA 99203 Office: PO Box 366 Spokane WA 99210

SHUMATE, CHARLES ALBERT, physician; b. San Francisco, Aug. 11, 1904; s. Thomas E. and Freda (Ortmann) S.; B.S., U. San Francisco, 1927, H.H.D., 1976; M.D., Creighton U., 1931. Pvt. practice dermatology, San Francisco, 1933-73, ret., 1973; asst. clin. prof. dermatology Stanford U., 1956-62; pres. E Clampus Vitus, Inc., 1963-64; hon. mem. staff St. Mary's Hosp. Mem. San Francisco Art Commn., 1964-67, Calif. Heritage Preservation Commn., 1963-67; regent Notre Dame Coll. at Belmont, 1965-78, trustee, 1977—; pres. Conf. Calif. Hist. Socs., 1967; mem. San Francisco Landmarks Preservation Bd., 1967-78, pres., 1967-69; trustee St. Patrick's Coll. and Sem., 1970—. Served as maj. USPHS, 1942-46. Decorated knight comdr. Order of Isabella (Spain); knight Order of the Holy Sepulchre, knight of St. Gregory, knight of Malta. Fellow Am. Acad. Dermatology; mem. U. San Francisco Alumni Assn. (pres. 1955), Calif. Book Club (pres. 1969-71), Calif. Hist. Soc. (trustee 1958-67, 68-78, pres. 1962-64), Soc. Calif. Pioneers (dir. 1979—). Clubs: Bohemian, Olympic, Roxburghe (pres. 1958-59) (San Francisco); Zamorano (Los Angeles). Author: Life of George Henry Goddard; The California of George Gordon, 1976, Francisco Pacheco of Pacheco Pass, 1977; Life of Mariano Malarin, 1980. Home: 1901 Scott St San Francisco CA 94115 Office: 490 Post St San Francisco CA 94102

SHUMWAY, FORREST NELSON, corporation executive lawyer; b. Skowhegan, Maine, Mar. 21, 1927; s. Sherman Nelson and Agnes Brooks (Mosher) S.; A.B., Stanford U., 1952; LL.D., U. So. Calif., 1974, Pepperdine U., 1978; m. Patricia Ann Kelly, Aug. 12, 1950; children—Sandra Brooks, Garrett Patrick. Admitted to Calif. bar, 1952; staff Office County Counsel, Los Angeles, 1953-57; sec. Signal Cos., Inc., Los Angeles, 1959-61, gen. counsel, 1961, group v.p. ops., 1963-64, pres., 1964-68, pres., dir., chief exec. officer The Signal Cos., 1968-80, chmn. bd., chief exec. officer, 1980—; dir. The Garrett Corp., UOP Inc., Ampex Corp., Transam. Corp., First Interstate Bancorp, Aluminum Co. Am. Adv. bd. Boy Scouts Am.; trustee U. So. Calif. Served to 1st lt. USMCR, 1945-46, 49-55. Mem. Am. Bar Assn., State Bar Calif., Phi Delta Theta. Clubs: Cypress Point (Pebble Beach, Calif.); Newport Harbor Yacht; Tuna (Catalina Island); La Jolla (Calif.) Country; Bohemian (San Francisco); Masons (Shriner). Office: 11255 N Torrey Pines Rd La Jolla CA

SHUMWAY, NORMAN DAVID, congressman; b. Phoenix, July 28, 1934; s. Wallace Loral and Zina (Owens) S.; B.S. in Polit. Sci., U. Utah, 1960; J.D., Hastings Coll. Law, 1963; m. Luana June Schow, June 30, 1960; children—Jennifer, Neal, Perry, Tyler, Stuart, Brenda. Admitted to Calif. bar, 1964; partner firm Cavalero, Bray, Shumway & Geiger,

Stockton, 1965-78; mem. San Joaquin County Bd. Suprs., 1974-78, vice chmn. bd., 1977, chmn., 1978; mem. 96th-98th Congresses from 14th Dist. Calif.; tchr. bus. law San Joaquin Delta Coll.; tchr. law Humphrey Coll., Stockton. Josephine Meade scholar U. Utah, 1958-59. Mem. Am. Bar Assn., Calif. Bar Assn. Republican. Mormon. Office: 1203 Longworth House Office Bldg Washington DC 20515*

SHUSHAN, ROBERT DANIEL, found. exec.; b. Bklyn., June 23, 1929; s. Max and Rose (Bellows) S.; A.B., U. Calif. at Los Angeles, 1951, M.Ed., 1953, Ed.D., 1974; m. Shirley Claire Bluestone, Dec. 26, 1948; children—Laurence Steven, Jeffrey Dean; m. 2d, Mary T. Maloney, Aug. 8, 1963; 1 dau., Debra Ellen. Tchr. delinquent adolescents Santa Fe High Sch., Los Angeles, 1952; tchr., asst. to vice prin. Huntington Park (Calif.) High Sch., 1952-56; tchr., counselor, dept. head, asst. to registrar Poly. High Sch., Los Angeles, 1956-58; exec. dir. Exceptional Children's Found., Los Angeles, 1959—, 1st v.p. Flame of Hope, Inc., Boston, 1972-73; chmn. exec. com. non-pub. sch. adv. bd. Los Angeles Unified Sch. Dist., 1967-71; prin. investigator, dir. demonstration project Social Rehab. Service, HEW, 1964-67; mem. Los Angeles Mayor's task force on establishing Adv. Council for Handicapped, 1974, mem. council and chmn. com. on intergovtl. relations, 1974—. Adv. bd. Lanterman State Hosp. and Developmental Ctr., 1977-78. Recipient Golden Rule award Calif. Assn. for Retarded, 1972; Spl. award Share, Inc., 1973. Fellow Am. Assn. Mental Deficiency (regional membership chmn. 1965-67); mem. Calif. (exec. com. 1960-63; a founder 1960), So. Calif. (sec., treas. 1960-61) assns. rehab. workshops, Calif. Assn. Residences for Retarded (1st pres. 1960-61), Nat. Rehab. Assn. (exec. com. 1963-65), Council for Exceptional Children, Phi Delta Kappa. Contbr. articles to profl. publs. Office: Exceptional Children's Found 3750 W Martin Luther King Blvd Los Angeles CA 90008

SHUTE, KIM MARGARET, real estate broker; b. Newark, Sept. 19, 1942; d. Robert Irving and Susan W. (Douglas) Horrocks; m. William J. Heronemus, Aug. 15, 1964 (div.); 1 son, Chad Douglas; m. 2d, Gary Gordon Shute, Nov. 2, 1972; children—Corynne Sue, Dawn Kristen. B.S. with honors, Cedar Crest Coll., Allentown, Pa., 1964; M.S. in Math., U. Minn., 1969. Tchr. high schs. Elkins, W.Va., 1964-67, Mpls., 1967-72, substitute tchr., San Jose, Calif., 1972-73; owner ins. brokerage, San Jose, 1973-76; real estate broker Century 21, Saratoga, Calif., 1982—; instr. West Valley Coll.; cons. Homepool. Active in Santa Clara County council Girl Scouts Am., YWCA. Home: 14200 Woodview Ln Saratoga CA 95070 Office: 14320 Saratoga-Sunnyvale Rd Saratoga CA 95070

SIBITZ, MICHAEL WILLIAM, assistant superintendent of schools; b. San Francisco, July 22, 1937; s. Michael Jacob and Erna Anna Elsa (Altendorf) S.; m. Marilyn Joyce Pricco, Nov. 19, 1966; children—Elizabeth, Ryan. B.A., San Francisco State U., 1959, M.A., 1964, Ed.D., U. San Francisco, 1980; postgrad. Notre Dame U. of Calif., Stanford U. Tchr., Pacifica, Calif., 1959-64, Dept. Def., 1964-65; tchr. Belmont, Calif., 1965-70, specialist, 1970-71, adminstr., 1971-80; asst. supt. Sylvan Union Sch. Dist., Modesto, Calif., 1980-83, asst. supt.-curriculum, 1983—; Supr. recreation City of Daly City (Calif.). Served to sgt. U.S. Army, 1960-66. Mem. Assn. Calif. Sch. Adminstrs. (charter), NEA, Assn. Supervision and Curriculum Devel., Phi Delta Kappa. Roman Catholic. Club: Kiwanis. Contbr. articles to profl. jours. Home: 6220 Olivetree Ln Riverbank CA 95367 Office: 605 Sylvan Ave Modesto CA 95350

SICILIANO, ROCCO CARMINE, financial company exec.; b. Salt Lake City, Mar. 4, 1922; s. Joseph Vincent and Mary (Arnone) S.; B.A. with honors, U. Utah, 1944; LL.B., Georgetown U., 1948; m. Marion Stiebel, Nov. 8, 1947; children—Loretta, A. Vincent, Fred R., John, Maria. Admitted to D.C. bar, 1949; legal asst. to bd. mem. NLRB, Washington, 1948-50; asst. sec.-treas. Procon Inc., Des Plaines, Ill., 1950-53; asst. sec. labor charge employment and manpower Dept. Labor, Washington, 1953-57; spl. asst. to Eisenhower for personnel mgmt., 1957-59; partner Wilkinson, Cragun & Barker, 1959-69; pres. Pacific Maritime Assn., San Francisco, 1965-69; under sec. of commerce, Washington, 1969-71; chmn. bd., chief exec. officer, Ticor, Los Angeles; dir. Pacific Lighting Corp., So. Pacific Co.; AMI, Penn Mut., J. Paul Getty Trust; mem. Fed. Pay Bd., 1971-73. Mem. nat. adv. council U. Utah; mem. vis. com. Grad. Sch. Mgmt., UCLA; chmn. Los Angeles Philharm. Assn.; mem. Calif. Roundtable; trustee Com. for Econ. Devel. bd. govs. Performing Arts Council; bd. dirs. Mus. Contemporary Art, New Community Devel. Corp., HUD. Served with AUS, 1943-46; 1st lt., 10th Mountain Div., Italy; personnel officer G-1, Hdqrs., U.S. Forces, Austria. Decorated Combat Infantryman Badge, Bronze Star, Army Commendation Ribbon (U.S.); Order Merit Italian Republic. Mem. Am. Bar Assn. Clubs: Met. (Washington); Family (San Francisco); Los Angeles. Office: Ticor 6300 Wilshire Blvd Los Angeles CA 90048

SIDDAYAO, CORAZON MORALES, economist, educator; b. Manila, July 26, 1932; came to U.S. 1968; d. Crispulo S. and Catalina T. (Morales) S. B.B.A., U. East, Manila 1962; cert. elem. teaching Philippine Normal Coll., 1951; M.A. in Econs., George Washington U., 1971, M.Phil., Ph.D., 1975. Tchr. pub. schs., Manila, 1951-53; asst. pensions officer IMF, Washington, 1968-71; cons. economist, Washington, 1971-75; research assoc. Policy Studies in Sci. and Tech., George Washington U., 1971-75, teaching fellow dept. econs., 1972-75; sr. research economist, assoc. prof. Inst. S.E.A. Studies, Singapore, 1975-78; sr. research fellow energy/economist East-West Ctr., 1978-81, acad. staff coordinator energy and industrialization, 1981—; prof. econs. U. Hawaii, 1979—; cons. Grantee in field. Mem. Am. Econ. Assn., Internat. Assn. Energy Economists, Soc. Policy Modelling, Southeast Asia Petroleum Exploration Soc., Philippine Econ. Soc. Roman Catholic. Clubs: Plaza, Pan Am. Clipper. Author: Increasing the Supply of Medical Personnel, 1973; The Offshore Petroleum Resources of Southeast Asia: Some Potential Conflicts and Related Economic Factors, 1978; Round Table Discussion on Asian and Multinational Corporations, 1978; The Supply of Petroleum Reserves in Southeast Asia: Economic Implications of Evolving Property Rights Arrangements, 1980; Critical Energy Issues in Asia and the Pacific: the Next Twenty Years, 1982; contbr. articles to profl. jours. Office: 1777 East-West Rd RSI Honolulu HI 96848

SIDEL, JOEL LEON, consumer products executive; b. Providence, Mar. 10, 1939; s. Philip Harold and Florence (Greenfield) S.; m. Carol Marie Casa, Apr. 25, 1964; children—Cheryl Lynne Mary, Marc David Anthony. A.B. in Psychology, Clark U., 1963; M.A. in Psychology, Northeastern U., 1967. Acting head acceptance lab. U.S. Army Natick Labs. (Mass.), 1966-69; head sensory evaluation lab. Hunt-Wesson Foods, Fullerton, Calif., 1969-71, Stanford Research Inst., Menlo Park, Calif., 1971-74; v.p., co-founder, dir. Tragon Corp., Palo Alto, Calif., 1974—. Reviewer Jour. Food Tech., 1982—; lectr. Mem. Inst. Food Sci. (chmn. sensory evaluation div. 1973-74), N.Y. Acad. Scis., ASTM. Club: Los Altos Athletic (Calif.). Contbr. articles to profl. jours. Home: 790 Vista Grande Ave Los Altos CA 94022 Office: Tragon Corp 750 Welch Rd Suite 210 Palo Alto CA 94304

SIDEROFF, STEPHEN IRWIN, psychologist; b. Mt. Vernon, N.Y., Mar. 17, 1947; s. Jerome L. and Ruth (Kessler) S.; B.A., SUNY, Binghamton, 1967; M.S., U. Miami, Coral Gables, Fla., 1970, Ph.D. (NDEA predoctoral fellow), 1971; m. Sharon Ashenfarb, June 26, 1969; children—Desirée, Alexandra. Physiologist, Perrine (Fla.) Primate Lab., 1970-71; NIMH postdoctoral fellow in psychobiology U. Calif., Irvine, 1971-72; asst. prof., profl. asso. psychology McGill U., Montreal, 1972-75; dir. Naltrexone Drug Program, VA Med. Center, Brentwood, Los Angeles, 1976-78; NIDA postdoctoral scholar psychiatry UCLA, 1976-79, asst. prof. dept. psychiatry, 1979—; psychologist VA Med. Center, Brentwood, Calif., 1978—; asso. trainer Gestalt Inst., Frankfurt, W. Ger., 1981—; lectr. Wright Inst., 1977; cons. Open Paths Community Counseling Center, Mar Vista, Calif., 1979—; pres., dir. Stress Mgmt. for Execs., 1980—; dir. psychol. services Health Integration Center, Santa Monica, Calif., 1981—; chmn. clinic com. Gestalt Inst. Los Angeles, 1977-79. McGill U. grantee, 1973-76; USPHS grantee, 1976-79, 78-79; Nat. Inst. Drug Abuse grantee, 1979—; lic. clin. psychologist, Calif. Mem. Am. Psychol. Assn., Soc. Neuroscis., Soc. Behavioral Medicine, Sigma Xi. Contbr. articles to profl. jours. Home: 26328 Ingleside Way Malibu CA 90265 Office: Dept Psychiatry U Calif Los Angeles CA 90024

SIDNEY, WILLIAM WRIGHT, aerospace co. exec.; b. Anaconda, Mont., Dec. 31, 1929; s. Paul and Lily Maud (Wright) S.; student U. Calif., Berkeley, 1953-56; div.; children—Kay Elise, Paul Daniel. Prodn. supr. Kaiser Aerospace, San Leandro, Calif., 1953-57, project engr., 1957-67, chief engr., 1967-69, gen. mgr., 1969-77; pres. Kaiser Aerotech, San Leandro, Calif., 1977—. Served with USN, 1948-52. Mem. Calif. Alumni Assn., Smithsonian Assos., Nat. Audubon Soc., Am. Mus. Natural History. Home: 18788 E Cavendish Dr Castro Valley CA 94546 Office: 880 Doolittle Dr San Leandro CA 94577

SIDORAK, STEPHEN JAMES, JR., clergyman; b. Cleve., Dec. 5, 1949; s. Stephen James and Anne (Hirus) S.; m. Alexis Carol Rascati, Dec. 18, 1976; children—Alissa Anne, Stephen Alexander, Kristin Carol. B.A., Baldwin Wallace Coll., 1971; M.Div., Yale U., S.T.M.; postgrad. San Francisco Theol. Sem. Ordained to ministry United Meth. Ch., 1975; assoc. minister 1st United Meth. Ch., Ft. Collins, Colo.; minister Centenary United Meth. Ch., Salt Lake City, 1st United Meth. Ch., Aurora, Colo.; exec. dir. Colo. Council Chs., Denver. Mem. steering com. Western Solidarity. Mem. Nat. Religious Pub. Relations Council. Contbr. articles to profl. jours. Office: 5209 Montview Blvd Denver CO 80207

SIDOW, JAMES ORVILLE, computer company executive; b. Olympia, Wash., May 3, 1949; s. Orville James and Esther Gertrude (Koehler) S.; m. Marie Leslie Castro, Nov. 16, 1970; 1 dau., SidneyAnn Marie. Student Ariz. State U., 1967-70; B.S. in Bus. Adminstrn., U. Phoenix, 1982; postgrad San Jose State U., 1983—. Enlisted U.S. Navy, 1970, served as electronic warfare technician, instr., 1970-79; tng. mgr. Cipher Data Products, San Diego, 1979-80; course developer ISS/Sperry-Univac, Santa Clara, Calif., 1980-81; sr. course developer Tandem Computers, Inc., Santa Clara, Calif., 1981—; bus. tng. cons. Named Master Tng. Specialist, USN, 1979. Mem. Am. Soc. Tng. Devel. Episcopalian. Club: Masons. Office: 2450 Walsh Ave Santa Clara CA 94050

SIEGEL, DORIS (MRS. WILLIAM E. SIEGEL), author; b. N.Y.C.; d. Russell E. and Cora G. (Davis) Taylor; B.A., U. Calif. at Los Angeles, m. William E. Siegel, Dec. 31, 1932; 1 son, Richard Taylor. Docent Los Angeles County Mus. Art; women's com. So. Calif. Symphony Assn.; costume council Los Angeles County Mus. Art. Mem. Colonial Order Crown, Nat. Soc. Magna Charta Dames, Colonial Dames 17th Century (past chpt. pres.; nat. chmn. def. programs 1969—), Los Angeles World Affairs Council, Friends Huntington Library, Soc. Fellows Huntington Library, Sovereign Colonial Soc. Ams. Royal Decent, Le Salon Francais, Calif. Writers Guild, Los Angeles County Mus. Alliance, Alumni Assn. U. Calif. Los Angeles, Friends Flintridge Library, Affiliates U. Calif. Los Angeles, Las Hermanas Guild Childrens Hosp. Soc., Pepperdine Assos., Asso. Women of Pepperdine, Chi Omega, Chi Delta Phi. Clubs: Founders (U. Calif. Los Angeles); Los Angeles Country. Author: (pen name Susan Wells) Murder is Not Enough, Footsteps in the Air, Death is My Name, The Witches Pond; (under own name) How Still My Love, 1957. Home: 1520 San Remo Dr Pacific Palisades CA 90272

SIEGEL, RICHARD LEWIS, political science educator; b. N.Y.C., Oct. 21, 1940; s. Samuel and Clara S.; m. Joan, June 30, 1963; children—Naomi, Daniel, Jordan. B.A., Brandeis U., 1961; Ph.D., Columbia U., 1967. Instr. polit. sci. U. Nev.-Reno, 1965-67, asst. prof. 1967-72, assoc. prof. 1972-78, prof., 1978—; asst. dir. Nev. Pub. Affairs Inst., U. Nev.-Reno, 1979—. Nat. bd. dirs. ACLU, 1975—; pres. ACLU Nev., 1981—; v.p. Jewish Community Council No. Nev., 1982—. Pres.'s fellow Columbia U., 1963-64; vis. fellow London Sch. Econs., 1974; residential fellow, Columbia U., 1983-84. Mem. Am. Polit. Sci. Assn., Internat. Studies Assn., Policy Studies Orgn. Author: Evaluating the Results of Foreign Policy, 1969; co-author: Comparing Public Policies: The United States, Soviet Union, and Europe, 1977; contbr. articles to profl. jours.; co-editor Nev. Pub. Affairs Rev., 1979—. Office: Nev Pub Affairs Inst U Nev Reno NV 89557

SIEMENS, WERNER HANS, engineering consultant; b. Berlin, Mar. 22, 1933; came to U.S., 1964, naturalized, 1973; s. Werner Detlef and Erna (Friedrich) S.; dipl., Mech. Trade Sch., Berlin, 1952; student Tech. U., Berlin, 1952-53; dipl. Internat. Corr. Sch., Montreal, Que., Can., 1960; m. Rosaline McKenna, Oct. 15, 1965; children—Brian Andrew, Bruce David, Kathleen Barbara, Kenneth Alexander. Sr. signal circuit designer Canadian Nat. Rwy., Edmonton, Alta., 1954-64; sr. signal application engr. Gen. Rwy. Signal Co., Rochester, N.Y., 1964-66; signals engr. Mass. Bay Transit Authority, Boston, 1966-71; mgr. electrification control systems Gen. Electric Co., Erie, Pa., 1971-74; chief engr. r.r. electrification Internat. Engring. Co., San Francisco, 1974-78; mgr. r.r. engring. Kaiser Engrs., Oakland, Calif., 1978-83; cons. Fed. R.R. Adminstrn. on design of EMC test facility at Dept. Transp. Test Center, Pueblo, Colo., 1980-81. Com. mem. Boy Scouts Am., Erie, Pa. and San Rafael, Calif., 1971-78. Registered profl. engr., Calif. Mem. Am. Assn. R.R.s, Am. Ry. Engring. Assn., Transp. Research Bd., U.S. Nat. Com. of Internat. Electrotech. Commn. Contbr. articles to profl. jours. Home: 102 Twelveoakhill Dr San Rafael CA 94903 Office: 300 Lakeside Dr PO Box 23210 Oakland CA 94623

SIGGSON, ALBERT NATHAN, aircraft company executive; b. Phila., Sept. 22, 1928; s. Nathan Harry and Grace Elizabeth (Fenester) S.; A.A., Long Beach City Coll., 1957; B.S., U. Phoenix, Irvine, Calif., 1983; m. Marjorie Jane Lindblom, July 17, 1966; children—Larry Jay, Randal Roy. Standards engr. Standards, Northrop, Nortronics, Hawthorne, Calif., 1966-67; sr. electronic engr. standards Hughes, Fullerton, Calif., 1967-68; lead engr. standards ITT/Gilfillan, Van Nuys, Calif., 1968-69; sr. standards engr. Northrop Aircraft, Hawthorne, Calif., 1969-82, Northrop Advanced Systems, Pico Rivera, Calif., 1982—; instr. blueprint reading evenings El Camino Coll., Torrance, Calif., 1980—. Served with USN, 1946-49. Registered profl. engr., Calif. Fellow Inst. Advancement Engring.; mem. Soc. Mfg. Engrs. (internat. award of merit and citation), Standards Engring. Soc., U.S. Metric Assn., Sigma Xi. Lutheran. Clubs: Civitan, Toastmasters. Contbr. articles to profl. jours. Office: 8900 E Washington Blvd Pico Rivera CA 90660

SIGLER, CARL OLIVER, pharmacist; b. Lancaster, Ohio, June 20, 1940; s. Paul Leo and Helen Ruth (Hibbs) S.; B.S. in Pharmacy, U. Toledo, 1963; m. Lili M. Terpening, Aug. 2, 1968; children—Melanie, Julie, Lori, Tammy, David, Jeff, Amy. Pharmacist, asst. mgr. Schuman Drugs, Inc., 1963-65; mgr. Groves-Kelco Inc., Kalamazoo, Mich., 1965-66; pharmacy specialist Meijer, Inc., 1966-68; supr. Lane Drug Corp., Toledo, Ohio, 1968-70; owner, mgr. Signet Enterprises, Inc., 1970-73; pres. Hunza Records, Inc., Toledo, 1970-72; pres., gen. mgr. Fate Inc., Fate Records, Toledo, 1972-75; physicians asst. Syl-Haven Clinic, Toledo, 1973-74; pharmacist Meml. Hosp., Monroe, Mich., 1974-75; dir. pharmacy Hillcrest Gen. Hosp., Silver City, N.Mex., 1975-81; owner C & L Enterprises, Silver City, 1977-78; owner, mgr. Profl. Assos., 1977—; tchr. Monroe County Schs., 1974-75; cons. in field. Mem. adv. com. local troop Boy Scouts Am., 1976-79; bd. dirs. Big Bros., 1970; 1st councilor to Sunday Sch., Ch. Jesus Christ of Latter Day Saints, 1977-80, pres. Sunday sch., 1980-82, exec. sec. to bishop, 1982—; mem. Mayor's Com. Beautification of City, 1979-81. Mem. Am., N.Mex. socs. hosp. pharmacists, N.Mex. Pharmacists, Aricraft Owners and Pilots Assn., Bedford Jaycees, Exptl. Aircraft Assn., SW N.Mex. Aviation Assn. (pres. 1979-81). Democrat. Clubs: Kiwanis (local pres. 1977-79, divisional lt. gov. elect 1979-80, lt. gov. 1980-81), Masons (local chaplain 1978; jr. steward 1979). Home and Office: PO Box 1244 Silver City NM 88062

SIGLER, WILLIAM FRANKLIN, natural resources adminstr.; b. LeRoy, Ill., Feb. 17, 1909; s. John Adam and Bettie (Homan) S.; B.S., Iowa State U., 1940, M.S., 1941, Ph.D., 1947; m. Margaret Brotherton, July 3, 1936; children—Elinor Jo, John William. Conservationist, Soil Conservation Service, U.S. Dept. Agr., LeRoy, Ill., 1935-37; cons. Central Engring. Co., Davenport, Iowa, 1940-41; research asso. Iowa State U., Ames, 1941-42, 45-47; asst. prof. wildlife sci. Utah State U., Logan, 1947-50, prof., head dept., 1950-74; pres., chmn. bd. W. F. Sigler & Assocs. Inc., Logan, 1974—; cons. U.S. Surgeon Gen., 1963-67, FAO, Argentina, 1968. Mem. Utah Water Pollution Control Bd., 1957-65, chmn., 1963-65. Served as lt. (j.g.) USNR, 1943-45. Named Wildlife Conservationist of Yr., Nat. Wildlife Fedn., 1970; Outstanding Educator of Yr., 1971; cert. of recognition Iowa Coop. Wildlife Research Unit, 1982. Fellow Internat. Acad. Fishery Scientists, AAAS; mem. Ecol. Soc. Am., Wildlife Soc. (hon.), Am. Fisheries Soc., AAUP, Outdoor Writers Am., Sigma Xi. Contbr. articles to profl. jours.; author: Theory and Method of Fish Life History Investigation, 1952; Wildlife Law Enforcement, 1956, 3d edit., 1980; Fishes of Utah, 1963. Home: 309 E 2d S Logan UT 84321 Office: PO Box 1350 Logan UT 84322

SIGURDSON, EDWIN DWAIN, accountant; b. Port Townsend, Wash., May 3, 1942; s. Clarence Edwin and Beverly S.; B.S., Oreg. State U., 1970; A.A., Clatsop Coll., 1967, A.S., 1968. Staff acct. Isler, Coling, McAdams, C.P.A.s, Portland, Oreg., 1970-71; controller Arcata Communications, Portland, 1972; staff acct. Edwin L. Luoma, C.P.A., Astoria, 1973-75; sr. utility auditor Public Utility Commn. Oreg., Salem, 1975—; individual practice acctg., mgmt. cons., 1975—; owner Formula I Computers, 1981—. Served with U.S. Army, 1964-66. C.P.A., Oreg. Mem. Am. Inst. C.P.A.s, Oreg. Soc. C.P.A.s, Nat. Soc. Public Accts., Salem Area Computer Club, Micro-Calc Bus. Users Group (founder, editor). Republican. Baptist. Office: PO Box 12039 Salem OR 97309

SIGWORTH, OLIVER FREDERIC, educator; b. Glendale, Ariz., July 31, 1921; s. Jay and Bjorg (Fredericksson) S.; student Phoenix Jr. Coll., 1940-42; U. So. Calif., 1942-43; B.A., U. Calif. at Berkeley, 1947, M.A., 1948, Ph.D., 1951; m. Alice V. Gibbs, Dec. 17, 1953 (dec. 1958); 1 son, George F.; m. 2d, Heather Brooks, Apr. 28, 1963; 1 stepdau., Rosalind. Instr. English, U. Nev., Reno, 1951-52; instr. English and humanities San Francisco State Coll., 1952-53; faculty U. Ariz., Tucson, 1953—, prof. English, 1967—, dir. grad. studies in English, 1968-77, chmn. univ. faculty, 1979-83; vis. lectr. U. B.C., 1964. Fund for Advancement Edn. fellow 1955-56. Mem. Am. Soc. Eighteenth Century Studies, Western Soc. Eighteenth Century Studies (treas. 1975-78, v.p. 1978-80, pres. 1980-82), MLA, Philol. Assn. Pacific Coast, Rocky Mountain Modern Lang. Assn., Rocky Mountain Coll. English Assn. (v.p. 1974-76). Author: Four Styles of a Decade, 1960; Nature's Sternest Painter, 1965; William Collins, 1965. Editor: Criticism and Aesthetics, 1660-1800, 1971. Contbr. articles to profl. jours. Home: 4241 N Camino Pintoresco Tucson AZ 85745

SIKULA, ANDREW FRANK, educational administrator; b. Akron, Ohio, Oct. 7, 1944; s. John and Anna Marie (Shimko) S.; m. Judith Lynn Roe, Dec. 30, 1981; children—Andrew Casey, Ana Celeste, Tyson Andrew Roe. B.A., Hiram (Ohio) Coll., 1966; M.B.A., Mich. State U., 1967, Ph.D., 1970. Instr., Grad. Sch. Bus. Adminstrn., Mich. State U., East Lansing, 1966-70; asst. prof. mgmt. Coll. Bus. Adminstrn., U. Ill., Chgo., 1970-73, assoc. prof. mgmt., 1973-76; prof. mgmt. Coll. Bus. and Pub. Affairs, Murray (Ky.) State U., 1976-77, assoc. dean, dir. grad. programs, 1976-77; prof. mgmt. Coll. Bus. and Adminstrn., Chgo. State U., 1978-80, dean, 1978-80; prof. bus. adminstrn. Sch. Bus., Calif. State U.-Chico, 1980—, dean, 1980—; pres., chief exec. officer Human Resource Mgmt., Inc., 1974-76. Bd. dirs. Butte County Pvt. Industry Council, Butte County Comprehensive Employment and Tng. Council, Woodoak Condominiums. Recipient Disting. Service award Am. Mgmt. Assn., 1975, Coll. Bus., Chgo. State U., 1980; Service award Midwest div. Acad. Mgmt., 1976, 77, 78. Mem. Acad. Mgmt. (pres. Midwest div. 1977-78, v.p., program chmn. 1975-76, sec.-treas. 1974-75, chmn. local arrangements 1972-73), Nat. Acad. Mgmt. (assoc. chmn. placement com. 1973-74), Am. Inst. Decision Scis. (chmn. mgmt. and behavorial sci. prof. Midwest div. 1978-79), Midwest Bus. Adminstrn. Assn. (chmn. mgmt. div. program 1976-77), Greater Chico C. of C. (dir.), Am. Assembly Collegiate Schs. Bus., Nat. Communications Forum. Author: Personnel Administration and Human Resources Management, 1976; Personnel Management, 1976; Administracion De Recursos Humanos En Empresas, 1979; Administracion De Personal, 1979; Personnel Administration: Text and Current Issues, 1983; others. Home: 555 Vallombrosa 48 Chico CA 95926 Office: Dean's Office Sch Business Calif State Univ Chico CA 95929

SILBAUGH, PRESTON NORWOOD, lawyer, savs. and loan assn. exec.; b. Stockton, Calif., Jan. 15, 1918; s. Herbert A. and Della Mae (Masten) S.; A.B. in Philosophy, U. Wash., 1940; J.D., Stanford U., 1953; m. Maria Sarah Arriola; children—Judith Ann Silbaugh Freed, Gloria Silbaugh Stypinski, Ximena Carey Silbaugh Braun, Carol Lee Silbaugh Morgan. Personnel asst., group head Lockheed Aircraft Corp., also Lockheed Overseas Corp., 1941-44; traffic rep. Naval Air Transport Service, Pam Am. World Airways, Inc., Honolulu, 1944; employee relations officer Hdqrs. Central Pacific Base Command, War Dept. Office Civilian Personnel, Honolulu, 1944-45; ins. and real estate broker, Palo Alto and Red Bluff, Calif., 1945-54; faculty Law Sch., Stanford U., 1954-59, assoc. prof. law, 1956-59, asst. dean, 1954-56, assoc. dean, 1956-59; chief dep. savs. and loan commr. State of Calif., Los Angeles, 1959-61; bus. and commerce adminstr., dir. investment, savs. and loan commr., 1961-63; dir. Chile California Aid Program, Sacramento and Santiago, Chile, 1963-65; chmn. bd. dirs., pres. Beverly Hills Fed. Savs. & Loan Assn. (Calif.), 1965-68, chmn. bd., 1968—; chmn. bd. Southland Co., Beverly Hills, Service Corp., Beverly Hills; dir. Cie. Europeenne de Reassurance Internationale, Belgium and U.K., Wickes Co. Inc.; admitted to Calif. bar; of counsel firm Miller, Boyko & Bell, San Diego. Mem. real estate adv. com. U. Calif.; bd. dirs., pres. Simon Bolivar Fund, Beverly Hills; bd. dirs. Beverly Hills YMCA, Calif. Good Citizenship Com.; mem. Calif. Gov.'s Cabinet. Served with USMCR, 1942-43. Mem. Soc. Internat. Devel., U.S., Nat., Calif. savs. and loan leagues, State Bar Calif., Am., Beverly Hills, San Diego County bar assns., U. Wash., Stanford alumni assns., Cal. Aggie Alumni Assn., Los Angeles World Affairs Council, Town Hall. Order Coif, Phi Alpha Delta. Democrat. Club: Commonwealth of Calif. (San Francisco). Office: 8813 Villa La Jolla Dr La Jolla CA 92037

SILL, ALEXIS MATTOS, data processing co. exec.; b. Rio de Janeiro, Brazil, Apr. 15, 1949; s. Bev Arthur and Gigi Lino (Mattos) S.; came to U.S., 1956, naturalized, 1960; student Golden Gate U., San Francisco; m. Sandra Sarah Ann Heaslip, Aug. 24, 1974; 1 dau., Courtney Jane. Sales mgr. United Calif. Bank, San Francisco, 1971-77; sales exec. Automatic Data Processing, Inc., San Francisco, 1977—. Served with USMCR, 1969-71. Republican. Home: 40 Hillside Ave San Rafael CA 94901 Office: 625 3d St San Francisco CA 94107

SILLEN, ROBERT, medical center administrator; b. N.Y.C., Dec. 8, 1942; s. Samuel and Janet (Feder) S.; m. Miriam Robinson, June 22, 1968; children—Shelby, Erik. B.A., U. Denver, 1965; M.P.H., Yale U. Dir. community and profl. relations UPSHS, 1965-68; adminstrv. asst. City Hosp. Ctr., Elmherst, 1968-70; asst. dir. Univ. Hosp., U. Calif. Med. Ctr., San Diego, 1972-76, assoc. dir., 1975-79; exec. dir. Santa Clara Valley Med. Ctr., San Jose, Calif., 1979—. Mem. Am. Hosp. Assn., Calif. Hosp. Assn., Am. Pub. Health Assn., Am. Soc. Pub. Adminstrn., Am. Mgmt. Assn., Hosp. Conf. Santa Clara County (exec. com.), Hosp. Conf. No. Calif. Office: 751 S Bascom Ave San Jose CA 95128

SILLEN, THOMAS, television broadcaster and producer; b. N.Y.C., May 9, 1940; s. Samuel and Janet Martha (Feder) S.; m. Connie Glenn, July 21, 1967. B.A., Ithaca Coll., 1964; postgrad. U. Ariz., 1964-65; cert. U. Buffalo, 1978. Asst. to pub. Fortune mag., N.Y.C., 1967-68; media dir., account supr. Mgmt. Communications Cons., 1969-71; Western advt. sales mgr. Redbook mag., Los Angeles, 1971-76; pres. Mgmt. Prospectives, 1977-78; San Francisco mgr. East/West Network, 1978-80; producer, host With Tom Sillen, Viacom TV 30 and 6, San Francisco, 1980—, also anchor, news dir. Sta. KTZO-TV, San Francisco, 1982—. Trustee Strong Ctr., Berkeley, Calif. Served with U.S. Army, 1966-68; Vietnam. Mem. Radio-TV News Dirs. Assn., World Affairs Council, UN Assn. U.S. Office: KTZO-TV 2500 Marin St San Francisco CA 94124

SILLS, DAVID GEORGE, lawyer; b. Peoria, Ill., Mar. 21, 1938; s. George Daniel and Mildred Mina (Luthy) S.; B.S., Bradley U., 1958; J.D., U. Ill., 1961; m. Susan Lee Cooey, July 26, 1968. Admitted to Calif. bar, 1965; counsel Ill. Nat. Bank & Trust Co., Rockford, Ill., 1961-62; pvt. practice in Orange, then Newport Beach, Calif., 1965—; mem. Irvine (Calif.) City Council, 1976—, mayor City of Irvine, 1976-77, 79-80, 82-83. Mem. Rep. State Central Com. Calif., 1965-68; chmn. Rep. Assocs., Orange County, Calif., 1968-69, bd. dirs. 1967-71. Served to capt. USMCR, 1962-65. Mem. State Bar of Calif., Phi Delta Phi, Pi Kappa Delta, Omicron Delta Kappa, Am. Legion. Home: 10 Ribera Irvine CA 92714 Office: 1201 Dove St Suite 600 Newport Beach CA 92660

SILLS, RONALD VERNON, general insurance agent; b. Yakima, Wash., Dec. 31, 1946; s. Vernon Forrest and Margarite Elizabeth S.; m. Leslie Howe, Sept. 2, 1970; children—Jason Durand, Adam Vernon, Catherine Anne. B.A. in Anthropology, U. Mont., 1972, B.S. in Fin., 1972. C.L.U. Dist. mgr. Mut. Benefit Life, Missoula, Mont., 1973-79, asst. gen. agt., Spokane, Wash., 1979-80; asst. supt. agys. Nat. Life of Vt., Montpelier, 1980-82, gen. agt., Denver, 1982—; fin. planner; tchr. in field; seminar recruiter and trainer. Served with USN, 1964-67; Vietnam. Mem. Am. Soc. C.L.Us., Denver Assn. Life Underwriters, Nat. Assn. Life Underwriters, Vt. Estate Planning Council, Gen. Agts. and Mgrs. Assn. (bd. dirs.). Episcopalian. Clubs: Masons (Whitefish, Mont.); Shriners (Spokane). Home: 6124 S Jackson St Littleton CO 80121 Office: 10200 E Girard Ave Bldg B Suite 234 Denver CO 80234

SILOS, LUZ JOVEN, coordinator community services and organization; b. Santa Lucia, Philippines, Apr. 2, 1920; came to U.S., 1972, naturalized, 1980; d. Venancio Hernandez and Marciala Luz (Aguilar) Joven; m. Roberto Jesus Silos, May 19, 1943; children—Roberto, Roberto III, Imelda Luz, Eduardo, Vincent. B.S. in Home Econs., Philippine Normal Coll., 1941; B.S. in Edn., Notre Dame Coll., 1963; postgrad. U. Philippines, 1972. Cert. tchr. Tchr. elementary sch. and high sch. on week-ends Bur. Pub. Schs., Manila, 1953-63, guidance coordinator, 1964-65, prin. elementary sch., 1966-74; learning lab. asst. Newark (Calif.) Unified Sch. Dist., 1975-78; corrections officer, Ft. Madison, Iowa, 1978; community reps. and community services coordinator Leisure Services Dept., Union City, Calif., 1979—. Dist. commr. Philippine Boy Scouts, 1966-74; vol. Nat. Center for Citizen Involvement; bd. dirs. Tri-Cities ARC, Tiburcio Vasquez Health Center; mem. adult info. and referral com. Union City Girl Scout Assn. Recipient Presdl. award for community services Philippines, 1973. Mem. Union City Friends of the Library, Philippine Pub. Sch. Tchrs. Assn., Assn. Vol. Adminstrn., Union City Filipino Sr. Citizens Assn., Union City Fil-Am. Council. Republican. Roman Catholic. Clubs: Union City Women's, United East Bay Catholics, Toastmasters (cdnl. v.p.). Office: Leisure Services Dept 34009 Alvarado-Niles Rd Union City CA 94587

SILVA, LOURDES ENID, educator; b. Santurce, P.R., Mar. 9, 1947; d. Dionisio and Maria Teresa (Lopez) Cancel; B.A., Loma Linda U., 1968, M.A., 1971, specialist in edn. cert. for ednl. adminstrn., 1981; m. Edwin Manuel Silva, Mar. 23, 1975. Temporary exec. sec., Los Angeles, 1966-69; tchr., chairperson bus. and fgn. lang. depts. San Gabriel Acad., San Gabriel, Calif., 1969-73; instr. secretarial sci. Antillian Coll., 1973-75; registrar, reading coordinator, instr. San Gabriel Acad., 1976-78; asst. prof. office mgmt. Loma Linda U., 1978-81, asso. prof., head dept., 1981—; founder, pres. cons. firm Success Through People; coordinator seminar series on profl. devel.; lectr., cons. office automation, office mgmt., human relations; condr. workshops, seminars for tchrs., secretarial and health care groups. Treas., Seventh-day Adventist Bus. Edn. Assn., Calif.-Pacific Union chpt., 1981. Named Outstanding Secondary Educator, 1973. Mem. Am. Bus. Communication Assn., Assn. Seventh-day Adventist Profl. Secs., Calif. Bus. Edn. Assn., Internat. Info./Word Processing (chpt. pres. 1982—), Nat. Bus. Edn., Western Bus. Edn. Assn., Loma Linda Alumni Assn. (treas. 1978—). Contbr. articles to profl. jours.; reviewer manuscripts for publ. Home: 11370 Gramercy Pl Riverside CA 92505 Office: Loma Linda U La Sierra Campus Riverside CA 92515

SILVER, BARNARD STEWART, mech. engr., energy cons.; b. Salt Lake City, Mar. 9, 1933; s. Harold Farnes and Madelyn Cannon (Stewart) S.; B.S. in Mech. Engring., MIT, 1957; M.S. in Engring. Mechanics, Stanford U., 1958; grad. Advanced Mgmt. Program, Harvard U., 1977; m. Cherry Bushman, Aug. 12, 1963; children—Madelyn Stewart, Cannon Farnes. Engr. aircraft nuclear propulsion div. Gen. Electric Co., Evandale, Ohio, 1957; engr. Silver Engring. Works, Denver, 1959-66, mgr. sales, 1966-71; chief engr. Union Sugar div. Consol. Foods Co., Santa Maria, Calif., 1971-74; directeur du complexe SODESUCRE, Abidjan, Ivory Coast, 1974-76; supt. engring. and maintenance U and I, Inc., Moses Lake, Wash., 1976-79; pres. Silver Enterprises, Moses Lake, 1971—, Silver Energy Systems Corp., Moses Lake, 1980—; pres., gen. mgr. Silver Chief Corp., 1983—; instr. engring. Big Bend Community Coll., 1980-81. Explorer adviser Boy Scouts Am., 1965-66, chmn. cub pack com., 1968-74, chmn. scout troop com., 1968-74; pres. Silver Found., 1971—; ednl. counselor MIT, 1971—; pres. Chief Moses Jr. High Sch. Parent Tchr. Student Assn., 1978-79; missionary Ch. of Jesus Christ of Latter-day Saints, Can., 1953-55; 2d counselor Moses Lake Stake Presidency, 1980—. Served with Ordnance Corps, U.S. Army, 1958-59. Decorated chevalier Ordre National (Republic of Ivory Coast); registered profl. engr., Colo. Mem. ASME, Assn. Energy Engrs., AAAS, Am. Soc. Sugar Beet Technologists, Internat. Soc. Sugar Cane Technologists, Am. Soc. Sugar Cane Technologists, Sugar Industry Technicians, Nat. Fedn. Ind. Bus.; Utah State Hist. Soc. (life), Mormon Hist. Assn., Western Hist. Assn., Univ. Archeol. Soc. (life), Sigma Xi (life), Pi Tau Sigma, Sigma Chi, Alpha Phi Omega. Republican. Mormon. Club: Kiwanis. Home: 1433 Skyline Dr Moses Lake WA 98837 Office: Silver Enterprises 1433 Skyline Dr Moses Lake WA 98837 also Silver Energy Systems Corp Moses Lake WA 98837

SILVER, JOHN RAY, psychoanalytic psychotherapist, counseling director; b. Los Angeles, July 15, 1948; s. Bud R. and Joy E. (Jacobson) S.; m. Leanne Haawkins, Sept. 6, 1981; 1 son, Matthew Ray. A.A. in Sociology, Pierce Coll., 1968; B.A. in Psychology, Calif. State U.-Northridge, 1977; Ph.D. in Psychology, Calif. Grad. Inst., 1982. Cert. sex counselor; lic. family and child counselor, Calif.; cert. Montessori tchr. Asst. behavioral sci. researcher Los Angeles County/U. So. Calif. Psychiat. Hosp., 1975-76; cons. Rand Corp., Santa Monica, Calif., 1976-78; sch. counselor, tchr., sex educator Santa Monica Montessori Sch., 1977-81; clin. dir. Counseling Ctr. of West Los Angeles (Calif.), 1979—; pvt. practice psychoanalytic psychotherapy, Los Angeles, 1979—; supr., trainer of psychotherapists. Active Klanwatch, Scientists for Social Concerns. Mem. Am. Psychol. Assn., Am. Personnel and Guidance Assn., Los Angeles County Psychol. Assn., Calif. Assn. Marriage and Family Therapists, Am. Mental Health Counselors Assn., Nat. Assn. for Advancement of Psychoanalysis. Office: 2100 Sawtelle Blvd Suite 206 Los Angeles CA 90025

SILVER, WILLIAM ROBERT, corporate finance executive; b. Oakland, Calif., Mar. 31, 1947; s. Vernon Lowell and Barbara Jean (Zaniboni) S.; m. Joan Ellen Pagani, July 29, 1973. B.S. in Elec. Engring., U. Calif.-Davis, 1970. With sales dept., then area sales mgr. Nuclear Energy div. Gen. Electric Co., San Jose, Calif., 1970-78; western regional mgr. Bankers Leasing & Fin. Corp. sub. So. Pacific Co., San Mateo, Calif., 1978-79, v.p. mktg., 1979-82, sr. v.p. fin., dir., 1982—. With Army N.G., 1970-76. Mem. Am. Assn. Equipment Lessors, Pacific Coast Elec. Assn., Mcpl. Fin. Officers Assn., Am. Gas Assn. Republican. Roman Catholic. Club: De Anza Racquet (Cupertino, Calif.). Office: Bankers Leasing & Fin Corp 2655 Campus Dr Suite 200 San Mateo CA 94403

SILVERBERG, STUART OWEN, physician; b. Denver, Oct. 14, 1931; s. Edward M. and Sara (Morris) S.; B.A., U. Colo., 1952, M.D., 1955; m. Joan E. Snyderman, June 19, 1954 (div. Apr. 1970); children—Debra Sue McBride, Eric Owen, Alan Kent; m. 2d, Kay Ellen Conklin, Oct. 18, 1970 (div. Apr. 1982); 1 son, Cris S.; m. 3d, Sandra Kay Miller, Jan., 1983. Intern Women's Hosp. Phila., 1955-56; resident Kings County Hosp., Bklyn., 1958-62; practice medicine specializing in obstetrics and gynecology, Denver, 1962—; mem. staff Luth. Hosp., Gen. Rose Hosp., Denver; mem. staff St. Anthony Hosp., chmn. dept. obstetrics and gynecology, 1976-77; clin. instr. U. Colo. Sch. Medicine, Denver, 1962-72, asst. clin. prof., 1972—; v.p. Productos Alimenticos, La Ponderosa, S.A.; dir., chmn. bd. Wicker Works Video Prodns., Inc.; cons. Ft. Logan Mental Health Center, Denver, 1964-70; mem. Gov.'s Panel Mental Retardation, 1966; med. adv. bd. Colo. Planned Parenthood, 1966—, Am. Med. Center, Spivak, Colo., 1967—. Mem. Colo. Emergency Resources Bd., Denver, 1965—. Served to maj. AUS, 1956-58; Germany. Diplomate Am. Bd. Obstetrics and Gynecology. Fellow Am. Coll. Obstetricians and Gynecologists, A.C.S.; mem. Am. Internat. fertility socs., Colo. Gynecologists and Obstetricians Soc., Hellman Obstet. and Gynecol. Soc., Colo. Med. Soc., Clear Creek Valley Med. Soc. (trustee 1978, 80), Phi Sigma Delta, AMA, Flying Physicians Assn., Aircraft Owners and Pilots Assn., Nu Sigma Nu, Alpha Epsilon Delta. Jewish. Mem. editorial rev. bd. Colo. Women's Mag. Office: 8407 Bryant St Westminster CO 80030

SILVERMAN, SIDNEY WILLIAM, electrical engineer; b. N.Y.C., Aug. 27, 1918; B.E.E., CCNY, 1947; M.S. in E.E., U. Mich., 1949; m. Charlotte Helen Kant, Sept. 7, 1947; children—Susan Marti, Barbara Ann. With Boeing Co., Seattle, 1949—, engr. elec. power systems, 1949-50, flight test instrumentation engr., 1950-56, elec. power systems supr., 1956—. Served with USAF, 1943-46. Mem. IEEE (sr., chmn. electric power systems com. 1976—), AIAA (chmn. elec. power systems com. 1975-76, mem. steering com. Intersoc. Energy Conversion Engring. Conf.), AAAS, Photog. Soc. Am., Am. Philatelic Soc. Home: 19670 Marine View Dr SW Seattle WA 98166 Office: PO Box 3707 Seattle WA 98124

SILVERN, LEONARD CHARLES, consultant; b. N.Y.C., May 20, 1919; s. Ralph and Augusta (Thaler) S.; m. Gloria Marantz, June 1948 (div. Jan. 1968); 1 son, Ronald; m. 2d, Elisabeth Beeny, Aug. 1969 (div. Oct. 1972). B.S. in Physics, L.I. U., 1946; M.A., Columbia U., 1948, Ed.D., 1952. Tng. supr. U.S. Dept. Navy, N.Y.C., 1939-49; tng. dir. exec. dept. N.Y. Div. Safety, Albany, 1949-55; resident engring. psychologist Lincoln Lab., M.I.T. for RAND Corp., Lexington, 1955-56; engr., dir. edn., tng., research labs. Hughes Aircraft Co., Culver City, Calif., 1956-62; dir. human performance engring. lab., cons. engring. psychologist to v.p. tech. Northrop Norair, Hawthorne, Calif., 1962-64; prin. scientist, v.p., pres. Edn. and Tng. Cons. Co., Los Angeles, 1964-80, Sedona, Ariz., 1980, pres. Systems Engring. Labs. div., 1980—; cons. hdqrs. Air Tng. Command USAF, Randolph AFB, Tex., 1964-68, Electronic Industries Assn., Washington, 1963-69, Edn. Research and Devel. Center, U. Hawaii, 1970-74, Center Vocat. and Tech. Edn., Ohio State U., 1972-73, Council for Exceptional Children, 1973-74, Canadore Coll. Applied Arts and Tech., Ont., Can., 1974-76, Centro Nacional de Productividad, Mexico City, 1973-75, N.S. Dept. Edn., Halifax, 1975-79, Aeronutronic Ford-Ford Motor Co., 1975-76, Nat. Tng. Systems Inc., 1976-81, Nfld. Public Service Commn., 1978, Legis. Affairs Office of U.S. Dept. Agr.; adj. prof. edn., public adminstrn. U. So. Calif. Grad. Sch., 1957-65; vis. prof. computer scis. U. Calif. Extension Div., Los Angeles, 1963-72. Dist. ops. officer, disaster communications service Los Angeles County Sheriff's Dept., 1973-75, dist. communications officer, 1975-76; bd. dirs. SEARCH, 1976—. Served with USNR, 1944-46. Registered profl. engr., Calif. Mem. IEEE (sr.), Radio Amateur Satellite Corp, Am. Psychol. Assn., Am. Radio Relay League (life), Friendship Vets. Fire Engine Co. (hon.), Soc. Wireless Pioneers (life), Quarter Century Wireless Assn. (life), Ariz. Archaeol. Soc., Verde Valley Archaeol. Soc., Sierra Club. Contbg. editor Ednl. Tech., 1968-73, 81—; reviewer Computing Revs., 1962—, Small Systems World. Contbr. numerous articles to profl. jours. Office: PO Box 2085 Sedona AZ 86336

SILVERSTON, RANDALL ABRAM, psychologist; b. Detroit, Apr. 6, 1947; s. Harold Morton and Sara (Medvedov) S.; B.A., U. Mich., 1970; M.Ed., Wayne State U., 1972; Ph.D., So. Ill. U., 1974; m. Bess Ellesberg, May 24, 1970. Asst. prof. U. Tex., Arlington, 1974-76; dir. Center for Skills and Assessment, Calif. State U., Dominguez Hills, 1976-79; dir. Psychol. Health Services, Downey, Calif., 1979—. Mem. So. Calif. Psychotherapy Affiliation (dir.), Calif. State Psychol. Assn., Am. Ednl. Research Assn., Am. Psychol. Assn., Kappa Delta Pi. Jewish. Office: 8320 E Florence Downey CA 90240

SILVIUS, DONALD JOE, educator, administrator; b. Kingsman, Kans., July 30, 1932; s. Henry Edgar and Gladys Mae (Beaty) S.; m. Jean Anne Able, Aug. 30, 1931; children—Laurie Dawn Silvius Gustin, Steven Craig, Jonathan Mark, Brian James. Student So. Calif. Coll., 1949-52; A.A., Bakersfield Coll., 1962; B.A., Fresno State Coll., 1963, M.A., 1968. Radio/TV announcer, musician, music arranger and copyist, life ins. underwriter, other positions, 1953-62; jr. high sch. English tchr., elem. jr. high counselor, child welfare, attendance and guidance supr., supr. spl. services Standard Sch. Dist., Oildale, Calif., 1963—; tchr. counseling/guidance and spl. edn. various colls. Mem. North of the River Assn., 7th Dist. Calif. Congress Parents-Tchrs., Kern Children's Service Ctr. Recipient Standard PTA-Hon. Service award, Bakersfield —Up With People— Appreciation award, Golden Apple Service award Standard Sch. Dist. Tchrs. Assn., Innovations award Calif. Tchrs. Assn., Hon. Service award Kern chpt. Calif. Assn. Sch. Psychologists, Outstanding Ednl. Leader award West Kern chpt. Assn. Calif. Sch. Adminstrs., 1977-78, 7th Dist. PTA-Silver Service award, Continuing Service award Highland-Wingland PTA, Outstanding Community Service for Developmentally Disabled award. Mem. NEA, Calif. Tchrs. Assn., Calif. Personnel and Guidance Assn., Calif. Assn. Supervision of Child Welfare and Attendance, Assn. Calif. Sch. Adminstrs., Am. Assn. Curriculum Devel., Phi Delta Kappa. Republican. Home: 611 Linda Vista Dr Oildale CA 93308 Office: Standard School District 1200 N Chester Ave Oildale CA 93308

SIMANTEL, GERALD MILO, plant breeder, agronomist, researcher; b. Huron, S.Dak., Oct. 12, 1934; s. Earl Edward and Esther Katrine (Wagner) S.; m. Joan Darlene Horning, Dec. 4, 1955; children—David, Daniel, Debra. B.S., Oreg. State U., 1960; Ph.D., S.Dak. State U., 1963. Asst. plant breeder Amalgamated Sugar Co., Nyssa, Oreg., 1963-68, chief plant breeder, 1968—. Served with U.S. Army, 1953-54. NDEA fellow, 1960-63. Mem. Am. Soc. Sugar Beet Technologists, Am. Soc. Agronomy, Crops Sci. Soc. Am., Alpha Zeta. Lutheran. Author numerous publs. Home: 530 Emison Ave Nyssa OR 97913 Office: The Amalgamated Sugar Co PO Box 1766 Nyssa OR 97913

SIMASKO, DONALD LEO, oil and gas exploration co. exec.; b. Milw., May 21, 1930; s. Leo Harry and Rose Marion (Szypulinski) S.; B.A., U. Denver, 1952; m. Lillian E. Jaeger, Sept. 15, 1952 (div. May 1980); children—Andrew Charles, Joel Loren, Steven Michael, James Robert; m. 2d, Barbara E. Kurz, Jan. 16, 1982. High sch. tchr., Casper, Wyo., 1952-54; land clk. Stanolind Oil & Gas Co., Casper, Wyo., 1955-58; landman Pan Am. Petroleum Corp., Salt Lake City and Farmington, N.Mex., 1956-59, mgr. land dept., Anchorage, 1959-63; land cons., Anchorage, 1963-65; ind. oil operator, pres. Petroleum Land Services, Inc., Anchorage, 1965-73; pres. Simasko Prodn. Co., Anchorage, 1974-80, chmn., Anchorage and Denver, 1980—; guest lectr. S.W. Legal Found., 1968, 69, 71. Bd. dirs. Bus.-Industry Polit. ActionCom., 1976—. Mem. Am. Assn. Petroleum Landmen (Disting. Service award 1972, past pres., dir.), U.S. C. of C. (public affairs task force), U.S. Indsl. Council, Soc. Petroleum Engrs., Aviation Hall of Fame, U.S. Ski Assn. (past dir.), Ind. Petroleum Assn. Am., Ind. Petroleum Assn. Mountain States (v.p. Colo.), Rocky Mountain Oil and Gas Assn., Alaska Assn. Petroleum Landmen (past pres., dir.), Alaska C. of C. (past dir.), Alaska Geol. Soc., Alaska Oil and Gas Assn., Denver Assn. Petroleum Landmen, Greater Anchorage C. of C. (past dir.), Petroleum Club Anchorage (past pres., dir.). Republican. Clubs: Alyeska Ski (past pres.), Tower (Anchorage). Office: PO Box 1515 Anchorage AK 99510 also 1380 Lawrence St Suite 1450 Denver CO 80204

SIMINI, JOSEPH PETER, accountant, financial consultant, author, former educator; b. Buffalo, Feb. 15, 1921; s. Paul and Ida (Moro) S.; B.S., St. Bonaventure U., 1940, B.B.A., 1949; M.B.A., U. Calif.-Berkeley, 1957; D.B.A., Western Colo. U., 1981; m. Marcelline McDermott, Oct. 4, 1968; 1 son, Paul. Insp. naval material Bur. Ordnance, Buffalo and Rochester, N.Y., 1941-44; mgr. Paul Simini Bakery, Buffalo, 1946-48; internal auditor DiGiorgio (Fruit) Corp., San Francisco, 1950-51; (past pres. accountant Price Waterhouse & Co., San Francisco, 1953; sr. accountant Richard L. Hanlin, C.P.A., San Francisco, 1953-54; prof. accounting U. San Francisco, 1954-79, emeritus prof., 1983—; mem. rev. bd. Calif. Bd. Accountancy, 1964-68. Mem. council com. Boy Scouts Am., Buffalo, San Francisco, 1942-65, Scouters Key, San Francisco council; bd. dirs. United Bay Area Fund Drive, U. San Francisco, 1960. Served to ensign USNR, 1944-46. Recipient Bacon-McLaughlin medal St. Bonaventure U., 1940, Laurel Key, 1940; Outstanding Tchr. award Coll. Bus. Adminstrn., U. San Francisco, 1973; Disting. Tchr. award U. San Francisco, 1975, Joseph Peter Simini award, 1977. Crown Zellerbach Found. fellow, 1968-69; decorated Knight Order of Merit, Republic of Italy, 1982. C.P.A., Calif. Mem. Am. Inst. C.P.A.s, Calif. Soc. C.P.A.s (past chmn. ednl. standards, student relations com. San Francisco chpt.), Nat. Assn. Accts. (past pres. San Francisco chpt.), Am. Acctg. Assn., Am. Mgmt. Assn. (lectr. 1968-78), Am. Arbitration Assn. (comml. arbitrator), Delta Sigma Pi (past pres. San Francisco alumni club), Beta Gamma Sigma. Roman Catholic. Clubs: K.C., Il Cenacolo (past pres.), Leonardo da Vinci Soc. (past dir.). Author: Accounting Made Simple, 1967; Cost Accounting Concepts for Nonfinancial Executives, 1976; Become Wealthy! Using Tax Savings and Real Estate Investments, 1982. Tech. editor, Accounting Essentials, 1972. Patentee Dial-A-Trig and Verbum Est card game. Home: 2 Mountain Springs Rd San Francisco CA 94114 Office: PO Box 31420 San Francisco CA 94131

SIMMONDS, KENNA MARRIOTT, organization development director; b. Pitts., Aug. 8, 1943; d. Regis Eugene and Grace M. (Blaugher) Marriott; m. J. Lee Simmonds, Nov. 7, 1967; children—Wayne Patrick, Jeannine Lea. B.S. in Journalism, Mt. Mercy Coll., 1964. Account rep. Xerox Corp., Washington, 1965-70; pres. Prospect Hall Coll., Ft. Lauderdale, Fla., 1970-73; v.p., co-owner Simmonds & Assocs., Ft. Lauderdale, 1973-78, Home Furnishings Mktg. Cons., Inc., Aiea, Hawaii, 1978—; dir. orgn. devel. Liberty House, Honolulu, 1982—; educator, cons. in field. Bd. dirs. Ft. Lauderdale C. of C., 1974-78, chmn. consumer affairs council, 1970-73; Ft. Lauderdale ambassador, 1970-75; mem. Energy and Conservation Commn., 1973-74. Named outstanding woman bus. leader in community Ft. Lauderdale, 1973, 75. Mem. Nat. Bus. Women's Assn., Am. Soc. Tng. and Devel., Sales and Mktg. Assn., Sales Mgmt. Assn. Author copyrighted manuals and tapes on tng.; author two books; lectr. in field.

SIMMONS, BOBBY GLEN, bank investigator; b. Hico, Tex., Mar. 29, 1951; s. Earl David and Juanita Rosa Simmons; A.A., Moorpark Jr. Coll., 1972; postgrad in bus. adminstrn. U. So. Calif. Internat. banking investigator Security Nat. Bank, Los Angeles, 1981—. Mem. Nat. Notary Assn. Home: 1519 Stow Ave Simi Valley CA 93063 Office: 333 S Hope St Los Angeles CA 90071

SIMMONS, CAROL HELEN, health administrator; b. Chgo., Aug. 16, 1932; d. Alphonse Emil and Esther Olga (Gierhahn) Adrian; m. Philip Kirby, Nov. 23, 1972; stepchildren—James, Michel, Sandra. B.A., Northwestern U., 1954. C.P.A., Ill. Bookkeeper, Vernon Fox Co., Chgo., 1950-58; office mgr. Continental Drill Corp., Chgo., 1958-59, asst. to pres., 1959-63; ptnr. CBS Acctg., Chgo., 1963-69; owner, mgr. CBS Acctg., Napa, Calif., 1970-79; adminstr. Lake County Health Dept., Lakeport, Calif., 1980—; tax cons., 1963—. Pres. A.W.A.R.E., 1982-83; mem. Hospice fin. com.; v.p. Riviera Heights Corp. Mem. County Health Care Adminstrs. Assn. (rep.). Lutheran. Office: 922 Bevins Ct Lakeport CA 95453

SIMMONS, JAMES BOYD, commodity broker-trader; b. Leavenworth, Kans., Oct. 2, 1944; s. James Louis and Louise (Boyd) S.; B.A. in Bus. and Polit. Sci., William Jewell Coll., 1966; m. Mary Susan Bauman, Oct. 4, 1969; children—Erin Michelle, James Bauman. Vice pres. Andco, Inc., Chgo., 1969-71 (merged with Heinold Commodities 1971); commodity broker and trader, mem. Chgo. Mercantile Exchange, 1971—; exec. v.p. First Fidelity Investments, Phoenix; pres. Simmons

Trading Co., Simmons-Rufenacht Securities Corp., RCS Fin. Services, Southwest Cattle Co.; v.p. RES Commodities; now mem. faculty Ariz. State U., Tempe; cons. Heinold Commodities; group leader Commodity Futures Polit. Fund. Pres. agrl. adv. council Ariz. State U. Republican. Mem. United Chs. of Christ. Club: Masons. Home: 4841 E Marston Dr Paradise Valley AZ 85253 Office: 6045 N Scottsdale Rd Scottsdale AZ 85254

SIMMONS, NOLA ANN, religious orgn. adminstr.; b. Knoxville, Iowa, Aug. 7, 1937; d. Harley Hanford and Edna Pearl (Wynn) Cox; student State U. Iowa, 1955-57; m. Jerry Laird Simmons, May 27, 1957; children—Christopher Laird, David Harley. Office mgr. Red Ball Engring. and Constrn. Co., Inc., Iowa City, 1957-61; owner, artist Fertile Earth Boutique, San Francisco, 1967-68; ordained to ministry Ch. of Scientology, San Francisco Acad., 1968; sec.-treas. Ch. of Scientology Mission of Davis (Calif.), 1969-71; co-dir. Ch. of Scientology Mission of South Bay, Redondo Beach, Calif., 1972—; pres. bd. dirs., exec. dir. Ch. of Scientology Mission of Long Beach (Calif.), 1974-82; hon. pub. relations officer for L. Ron Hubbard, founder Scientology; pastoral counsellor; chaplain; Hubbard profl. auditor. Mem. Citizen's Commn. for Human Rights, Los Angeles; mem. Nat. Commn. on Law Enforcement, Social Justice; mem. Ministry Pub. Relations, Los Angeles. Recipient Spl. Power award Office of Guardian, Tech. Upstat award Auditor's Assn., 1976, Triple Grades award Ch. of Scientology, San Francisco, 1969. Mem. Hubbard Assn. Scientologists Internat., Ch. of Scientology Mission Network Worldwide, Am. Citizens for Honesty in Govt., Am. Craft Council, Smithsonian Assocs., Craft and Folk Art Mus., Met. Museum Art (asso.), Auditors Assn., Abilities Research Assos. (asso.). Contbg. author: Glossary for Social Psychology: Sociological Approach, 1981. Co-editor Unicorn Hunter's Guidebook, 1982. Home and Office: 447 Camino De Las Colinas Redondo Beach CA 90277

SIMMONS, TED CONRAD, writer; b. Seattle, Sept. 1, 1916; s. Conrad and Clara Evelyn (Beaudry) S.; student U. Wash., 1938-41, UCLA and Los Angeles State U., 1952-54, Oxford (Eng.) U., 1980; m. Dorothy Pauline Maltese, June 1, 1942; children—Lynn, Juliet. Drama critic Seattle Daily Times, 1942; indsl. writer, editor Los Angeles Daily News, 1948-51; contbr. Steel, Western Metals, Western Industry, 1951—; now owner Ted Simmons & Assos.; poetry dir. Watts Writers Workshop; instr. Westside Poetry Center; asst. dir. Pacific Coast Writers Conf., Calif. State Coll. Los Angeles. Served with USAAF, 1942-46. Author: (poetry) Deadended, 1966; (novel) Middlearth, 1975; (drama) Greenhouse, 1977; Durable Chaucer, 1978; Rabelais and other plays, 1980, Dickeybird, 1981; Alice and Eve, 1983. short story, radio verse writer; contbr. poetry to The Am. Poet, Prairie Wings; Antioch Rev., Year Two Anthology; editor: Venice Poetry Company Presents, 1972. Address: PO Box 781 Redondo Beach CA 90277

SIMMONS, TROY WILLIAM, engring. co. exec.; b. Ft. Mill, S.C., Nov. 13, 1927; s. John Newman and Irish Jeannette (Beyers) S.; m. Pauline Mildred Wilson, Aug. 9, 1948; children—Troy William, Karen Anne, Robert Wayne, Ronald Gene. Student, Old Dominion U., 1962-63, Grossmont Coll., 1973-75, U.S. Navy Supply Sch., 1959, U.S. Navy Transp. and Traffic Mgmt. Sch., 1961. Enlisted in U.S. Navy, 1943, advanced through grades to lt. comdr., 1966, ret., 1969, dir. supply ops. U.S. Naval Shipyard, Long Beach, Calif., 1968-69; mgr. material control/traffic Vetco Off Shore Industries, Ventura, Calif., 1969-71; gen. supr. materials service Solar Turbines Internat., San Diego, 1971-74, 78-80; dir. ops. Aldila Inc., San Diego, 1975-78; pres. W. Coast Engring. Co., El Cajon, Calif., 1980—; mgmt. cons. Chmn., Combined Fed. Campaign Pearl Harbor, 1967; v.p., treas. Little League Assn., Pearl Harbor, 1966-68; neighborhood commr. Kamehameha dist. Aloha council Boy Scouts Am., 1966-68. Decorated Bronze Star (3). Mem. Ret. Officers Assn., Am. Prodn. and Inventory Control Soc. Republican. Mem. Assemblies of God Ch. Club: Masons. Contbr. articles to profl. jours. Address: 13574 Paseo Del Mar El Cajon CA 92021

SIMMONS, WILLIAM GUYTON, export mgmt. co. exec.; b. Gulfport, Miss., Apr. 11, 1945; s. George Lane and Sarah June (Clay) S.; B.A., U. Wash., 1968; M.B.A., So. Ill. U., 1976; m. Patricia Ann Vogel, Feb. 27, 1980; 1 son by previous marriage, Michael William. Commd. 2d lt. U.S. Air Force, 1968, advanced through grades to capt., 1971, discharged, 1977; assoc. Lincoln Nat. Life Ins. Co., Walnut Creek, Calif., 1977; dir. estate planning dept. United Fin. Planning, Inc., Oakland, Calif., 1978-80; mktg. dir. Indsl. Devel. Group, Inc., Palo Alto, Calif., 1980—. Dir., treas. Sea Ranch Assn., 1978-80. Decorated D.F.C., Air medal with 2 oak leaf clusters. Mem. Beta Gamma Sigma. Republican. Roman Catholic. Office: 411 Borel Ave Suite 340 San Mateo CA 94402

SIMOENS, ALVIN COSMAN, lawyer, business executive; b. Nucla, Colo., June 28, 1934; s. Constantine and Vessie Vera (Wilson) S.; B.S. in Elec. Engring., U. Colo., 1959, B.S. in Fin. magna cum laude, 1976, J.D., 1979; m. Earlene Joyce Herman, Feb. 14, 1956; 1 son, Alvin Cosman. Field rep. Philco Corp., Army Air Def. Sch., Ft. Bliss, Tex., 1959-61, New Boston Satellite Tracking Sta., New Boston, N.H., 1961-64; propr. Securities Tng. Inst., Denver, 1964-67; v.p., sec. Westam. Securities, Inc., Denver, 1967-73; v.p., gen. counsel J. Daniel Bell & Co., Inc., Denver, 1980-82; pres. Magnus, Ltd., Denver, 1982—. Served with AUS, 1956-58. Mem. ABA, Colo. Bar Assn., Denver Bar Assn., Assn. Trial Lawyers Am., Beta Gamma Sigma. Lion (dir. 1970). Editor The Westamerican and the Best of Westamerica, 1967, 68. Home: 7802 E Hampden Circle Denver CO 80237

SIMON, BRADLEY ALDEN, librarian; b. Meriden, Conn., Mar. 9, 1929; s. Walter Henry and Rachel (Wetherbee) S.; student Shenandoah Coll., 1947-48; B.S., So. Conn. State Coll., 1951; M.S., Fla. State U., 1955; postgrad. U. Miami (Fla.), 1956-57, Ariz. State U., Tempe, 1965-66. Extension librarian, Ft. Meade, Md., 1955-56; base librarian Homestead AFB, Fla., 1956-57; asst. dir. libraries Pub. Library Charlotte and Mecklenburg County (N.C.), 1957-61; dir. libraries Volusia County Pub. Libraries, Daytona Beach, Fla., 1961-64; library cons. M. Van Buren, Inc., Charlotte, N.C., 1964; head librarian Central Piedmont Community Coll., Charlotte, 1964-65; cons. Colo. State Library, 1965-66; coordinator Ariz. Library Survey, Ariz. State U., 1966; library dir. Scottsdale (Ariz.) Pub. Library, 1966-71; city librarian Pomona (Calif.) Pub. Library, 1971-77, Newport Beach (Calif.) Pub. Library, 1977-78, Chula Vista (Calif.) Public Library, 1978—; cons. on bldg. and adminstrn. various libraries, Calif., N.C., Fla., Colo., Ariz.; pres. Pub. Library Film Circuit. Mem. Scottsdale Fine Arts Commn., 1966-71; adminstrv. council Met. Coop. Library System, Los Angeles. Served in Intelligence, USAF, 1951-53. Recipient John Cotton Dana Library Pub. Relations award, 1974, 75, 76; Hometown Builder award, 1975. Mem. ALA (bd. dirs. Pub. Library Assn. 1975-79), Ariz. (pres. pub. libraries sect. 1969-70), Calif., Southwestern library assns., Pub. Library Execs. So. Calif. (pres. 1975-76), Library Automation, Research and Cons. Assn. (steering com. 1969-71), Royal Arcanum, Nat. Mgmt. Assn., Pomona Municipal Mgmt. Assn. (dir.), Newport Harbor Art Mus., Newport Harbor C. of C., Pomona Valley Hist. Soc., Kappa Delta Phi. Presbyterian. Club: Rotary. Contbr. articles to profl. jours. Home: PO Box 1843 Chula Vista CA 92012

SIMON, CHARLES KENNETH, corp. exec.; b. N.Y.C., Apr. 7, 1918; s. Herbert M. and Belle J. (Simon) S.; B.S., U. Pa., 1939; postgrad. N.Y. U., Pratt Inst.; m. Liane Nau, July 30, 1966; children—Charles Kenneth, Eric Nau, Lilia Nau. Exec., Brewster Aircraft, 1940-41, York Aircraft Co., 1941-43, Aerojet Gen. Corp., 1959-62; designer, creater Advanced Decision Data System, 1957—; mgmt. scientist, pres. Mgmt. Methods Corp., Sacramento and San Diego, 1962—; pres., mng. dir. Mgmt. Research Found., San Francisco and Coronado, Calif., 1975—; chmn. bd. dirs. Computer Mgmt. Corp., Salt Lake City, 1970—; bd. dirs. Automated Ct. Systems, San Diego, 1976—; pres., chmn. bd. Cal-Colombian Mines Ltd., Reo Magos Mining Co., Inc., Carson City, Nev. and North Key Largo, Fla., 1980—; pres. Compania Minera de Colombia y Texas, Houston, Bogota and Cali, Colombia, 1980—; cons. Dept. Def., aerospace industry, 1943—; mem. teaching staff U. Calif., 1960-62. Served with USNR, 1944-46. Decorated Bronze Star. Mem. Ops. Research Soc., Inst. Mgmt. Sci., Am. Ordnance Soc., Air Force Assn., Am. Mgmt. Assn. Home: 1720 Avenida Del Mundo Coronado Shores Coronado CA 92118 also 7 Harbour Island Dr North Key Largo FL 33037 Office: 44 Montgomery St Suite 500 San Francisco CA 94104 also 31 Ocean Reef Dr North Key Largo FL 33037

SIMON, DON VERNER, forest products co. exec.; b. Portland, Oreg., Apr. 12, 1932; s. John D. and Esther B. S.; B.S., U. Oreg., 1955; div.; children—Stephen, Janet, Gretchen. With Texaco, Inc., Portland, 1958-60; sales mgr. plywood Oreg. Pacific Industries, Portland, 1960-65, Continental Forest Products, Lake Oswego, Oreg., 1965-71, Willamette Industries, Albany, Oreg., 1971-74, Am. Internat. Forest Products, Beaverton, Oreg., 1974-76; pres. Simon, Crabtree & Ryan, Inc., Lake Grove, Oreg., 1976—. Served with USAF, 1955-57. Mem. Oreg. Assn. Credit Mgmt. Republican. Episcopalian. Club: Multnomah Athletic, Home: 4650 SW Murray Rd 74 Beaverton OR 97005 Office: 16325 SW Boones Ferry Rd Lake Grove OR 97034

SIMON, HERBERT GEORGE, JR., oil company executive; b. Chgo., Apr. 18, 1950; s. Herbert G. and Ruth F. (Fishman) S.; m. Kathleen M. Nielsen, Dec. 19, 1971; children—Julia, Laura, Jaclyn. B.A., Colo. State U. Lic. real estate broker Colo. Ind. petroleum landman, Denver, 1972-78; public info. coordinator U.S. Dept. Commerce, Washington, 1979-80; sr. landman Nielsen Resources Corp., Denver, 1980-81; land mgr. Orion Resources Inc., Englewood, Colo., 1981—; lectr. in field. Mem. Ft. Collins (Colo.) City Council, 1971-72; pres. Colo. Young Democrats, 1975-77, precinct committeeman, 1974, 76. Mem. Am. Assn. Petroleum Landmen, Rocky Mountain Assn. Mineral Landmen. Jewish. Home: 30103 Arena Dr Evergreen CO 80439 Office: 333 W Hampden Ave 10th Floor Englewood CO 80110

SIMON, JEFFREY DAVID, international relations analyst, researcher; b. Bklyn., Jan. 18, 1949; s. Julius and Mathilda (Greene) S. B.A., U. Calif.-Berkeley, 1971; M.A., Ind. U., 1973; Ph.D., U. So. Calif., 1978. Lectr., Sch. Continuing Edn., U. So. Calif. Los Angeles, 1977-78, prin. research assoc. Current World Stress Studies Project, 1978-79; pres. Polit. Risk Assessment Co., Santa Monica, Calif., 1980—; cons., instr. Mem. Am. Polit. Sci. Assn., AAAS. Contbr. articles to profl. jours. Home and Office: 612 Montana Ave Apt A Santa Monica CA 90403

SIMON, LEE WILL, astronomer; b. Evanston, Ill., Feb. 18, 1940; s. Clarence Turkle and Dorothy Elizabeth (Will) S.; B.A., Northwestern U., 1962, M.S., 1964, Ph.D. in Astronomy, 1972; m. Mary Jo Welsh, Feb. 19, 1966; children—John, Dan, Steve. Staff astronomer, program supr. Adler Planetarium, Chgo., 1969-77; dir. Morrison Planetarium, Calif. Acad. Scis., San Francisco, 1977—. Mem. AAAS, Am. Astron. Soc., Internat. Planetarium Soc., Sigma Xi. Presbyterian. Home: 245 San Marin Dr Novato CA 94947 Office: Morrison Planetarium Calif Acad Scis Golden Gate Park San Francisco CA 94118

SIMON, NORTON WINFRED, industrialist; b. Portland, Oreg., Feb. 5, 1907; s. Myer and Lillian (Glickman) S.; student U. Calif., Berkeley, 1923; m. Jennifer Jones, May 30, 1971; children by previous marriage—Donald Ellis, Robert Ellis (dec.). Founder, former chief exec. officer, now cons. Norton Simon Inc., N.Y.C.; founder, chief exec. officer 5 corp. and 1 family found., Los Angeles; former dir., chmn. fin. com. Burlington No., Inc. Mem. Courtauld Inst., London; former mem. Carnegie Commn. on Future of Higher Edn., Nat. Programming Council; mem. Nat. Com. on U.S.-China Relations, Founding Friends of Can.; chmn. bd. dirs. The Founders, Los Angeles Music Center; affiliated Calif. Sch. Profl. Psychology; bd. dirs., pres., trustee Norton Simon Mus., Pasadena, Calif.; trustee Inst. Advanced Study, Princeton, N.J.; formerly bd. dirs. Reed Coll., Inst. Internat. Edn., Los Angeles County Mus. Art; former regent U. Calif.; mem. advisory bd. Columbia U.-McGraw Hill Lectures; fellow Pierpont Morgan Library, N.Y.C.; mem., past chmn. Calif. State Transp. Commn. Office: care Norton Simon Museum Colorado and Orange Grove Blvds Pasadena CA 91105

SIMON, RUSSELL GENE, accountant; b. Kaplan, La., Nov. 9, 1948; s. John Rodney and Annie Mae (Landry) S.; B.S. in Math., U. Southwestern La., 1970; B.S.B.A. in Acctg., U. N.D., 1974; M.B.A., U. Santa Clara (Calif.), 1980. Cost acct. Hewlett-Packard, Santa Rosa, Calif., 1975-79; sr. cost acct. Amdahl Corp., Sunnyvale, Calif., 1979-80, cost acctg. supr., 1980-81; mgr. mfg. cost analysis Memorex Corp. div. Burroughs Co., Santa Clara, 1981-82, cost acctg. mgr., 1982, fin. planning and analysis mgr., 1983—. Served to capt. USAF, 1970-75. Mem. Nat. Acctg. Assn. Home: 2212 Calle De Primavera Santa Clara CA 95050

SIMON, SHELDON WEISS, political science educator; b. St. Paul, Jan. 31, 1937; s. Blair S. and Jennie M. (Dim) S.; m. Charlann Lilwin Scheid, Apr. 27, 1962; 1 son, Alex Russell. B.A., U. Minn., 1958, Ph.D., 1964; M.P.A. (Woodrow Wilson fellow), Princeton U., 1960; postgrad. U. Geneva, 1962-63. Asst. prof., then prof. U. Ky., 1966-75; prof. polit. sci. Ariz. State U., 1975—, chmn. dept., 1975-79, dir. Ctr. Asian Studies, 1980—; vis. prof. George Washington U., 1965, U. B.C. (Can.), 1972-73, 79-80, Carleton U., 1976; cons. USIA, Research Analysis Corp., Am. Enterprise Inst. Pub. Policy Research, Hoover Instn. Mem. Com. Fgn. Relations, Phoenix, 1976—; bd. dirs. Phoenix Little Theater, 1976-79. Am. Enterprise Inst. grantee, 1974; Earhart Found. grantee, 1979, 81, 82; Hoover Instn. grantee, 1980. Mem. Am. Polit. Sci. Assn., Assn. Asian Studies, AAUP, Internat. Studies Assn. Democrat. Jewish. Author: The Asian States and Regional Security, 1982; Asian Neutralism and U.S. Policy, 1975; editor: The Military and Security in the Third World, 1978; other books, numerous research articles; contbr. chpts. to books. Home: 5630 S Rocky Point Tempe AZ 85283 Office: Ctr for Asian Studies Ariz State U Tempe AZ 85287

SIMON, WILLIAM DIEN, video marketing company executive; b. Washington, Sept. 11, 1954; s. Jerome M. and Harriet (Dienstein) S. B.A., U. Calif.-Berkeley, 1976. Staff asst. to Congressman Thomas M. Rees, 1974-75; asst. to campaign dir. Carter-Mondale Campaign, 1976; dep. staff sec. White House, Washington, 1977-81; dir. Adler Video Mktg. Ltd., McLean, Va., 1981—. Democrat. Jewish.

SIMON, WILLIAM LEONARD, film writer; b. Washington, Dec. 3, 1930; s. Isaac B. and Marjorie (Felstiner) S.; B.E.E., Cornell U., 1954; M.A. in Ednl. Psychology, Golden State U., 1982, Ph.D. in Communications, 1983; m. Arynne Lucy Abeles, Sept. 18, 1966; 1 dau., Victoria Marie; 1 stepson, Sheldon M. Bermont. Writer features and TV movies, documentary and indsl. films, TV programs, 1958—; lectr. George Washington U., 1968-70. Pres. Foggy Bottom Citizens Assn., 1963-65, mem. exec. bd., 1965-69; v.p. Shakespeare Summer Festival, 1966-67, trustee, 1965-70. Served to lt. with USN, 1954-58. Recipient 8 Golden Eagle awards Cine Film Festival, gold medal N.Y. Internat. Festival, gold medal Freedoms Found., IFPA Gold Cindy, awards Berlin, Belgrade and Venice film festivals, numerous other awards. Mem. Nat. Acad. TV Arts and Scis. (gov. D.C. chpt. 1970-73), Writers Guild Am., Am. Film Inst., Eta Kappa Nu (chpt. pres. 1953-54), Tau Beta Pi. Writer over 500 produced works for motion pictures and TV, including screenplays Fair Woman Without Discretion, Majorca, Swindle. Home: PO Box 2048 Rancho Santa Fe CA 92067

SIMONDS, JOHN EDWARD, editor; b. Boston, July 4, 1935; s. Alvin Edward and Ruth Angeline (Rankin) S.; A.B., Bowdoin Coll., 1957; m. Rose Benjamin Muller, Nov. 16, 1968; children—Rachel, John B., Maximillian P., Malia G. Reporter, Seymour (Ind.) Daily Tribune, 1957-58; reporter UPI, Columbus, Ohio, 1958-60; reporter, asst. city editor Providence Journal-Bulletin, 1960-65; reporter, asst. city editor Washington Evening Star, 1965-66; Washington corr. Gannett News Service, 1966-75; mng. editor Honolulu Star-Bulletin, 1975-80, exec. editor, 1980—. Served with U.S. Army, 1958. Mem. Am. Soc. Newspaper Editors, Asso. Press Mng. Editors, Press Club Honolulu. Democrat. Home: 5316 Nehu Pl Honolulu HI 96821 Office: 605 Kapiolani Blvd Honolulu HI 96830

SIMONINI, RINALDO CHARLES, III, clinical psychologist; b. Greenville, N.C., Mar. 3, 1951; s. Rinaldo Charles, Jr. and Juanita (Thorne) (Evans) S.; B.A. in Psychology, Randolph-Macon Coll., 1973; postgrad., U. South Fla., 1973-74; Ph.D. in Profl. Psychology, U.S. Internat. U., 1977; m. Carol Ann Trope, Aug. 18, 1972. Clin. psychology intern Dept. Mental Health Orange County (Calif.), Santa Ana, 1976-77; commd. 2d lt. U.S. Air Force, 1973, advanced through grades to capt., 1977; staff psychologist, postdoctoral resident David Grant USAF Med. Center, Travis AFB, Calif., 1977-80, chief psychology service, 1980-81, resigned, 1981; adj. asst. prof. psychology dept. Chapman Coll.; staff affiliate Inst. Rational Living, San Francisco; cons. Napa County Mental Health Dept., 1981-82. Armed Forces health professions scholar, 1973-77; primary clin. cert. Inst. for Rational-Emotive Therapy, N.Y.C., 1980; lic. clin. psychologist, Calif. Mem. Am. Psychol. Assn., Calif. Psychol. Assn., Pi Gamma Mu. Contbr. articles to profl. publs. Home: 221 N Alamo Dr Vacaville CA 95688 Office: 3000 Alamo Dr Suite 200 Vacaville CA 95688

SIMON-MCWILLIAMS, ETHEL, research laboratory executive; b. Washington, May 25; d. Robert and Erma Katherine Simon; B.S., D.C. Tchrs. Coll., 1964; M.Ed., George Washington U., 1971; Ed.D., U. S.C., 1977; children—Cornell Christopher, Lisa Suzanne. Classroom tchr. D.C. Public Schs., 1964-69, 70-71, asst. prin. 1969-70; dir. Title I ESAA Reading and Math Programs, Chester (S.C.) Public Schs., 1971-75; program specialist S.C. Dept. Edn., Columbia, 1975; dir., asst. prof. U. S.C., Columbia, 1975-79; assoc. dir. N.W. Regional Ednl. Lab., Portland, Oreg., 1979—. Adv. bd. St. Vincent Hosp. and Med. Center, 1980—, chmn., 1983, mem. policy planning com., 1982—, active other coms.; mem. Portland Mayor's Com. Civil Service Reform, 1979—; adv. com. N.W. Area Found., 1980-82, mem. gifted/talented bd., 1982—; commr. Portland Cable Regulatory Commn., 1981—, Oreg. Commn. on Pub. Broadcasting, 1981—; mem. women's com. Reed Coll., 1983—. Recipient appreciation of contbns. to integration award Sch. Dists. S.C., 1978. Mem. Assn. Supervision and Curriculum Devel., Oreg. Assn. Supervision and Curriculum Devel., Alaska Assn. Sch. Adminstrs., Am. Assn. Sch. Adminstrs., Am. Mgmt. Assn. Clubs: Zonta Internat., Portland City. Author: Educational Uses of Technology, 1982; editor: Educational Telecommunications for Alaska: Public Project Report, 1979; contbr. chpts. to books. Home: 2218 SW Marigold St Portland OR 97219 Office: 300 SW 6th Ave Portland OR 97204

SIMONS, KENNETH K., statistician; b. Washta, Iowa, Sept. 18, 1937; s. Kenneth W. and Imogene D. (Koch) S.; m. Shirley Ann Clark, Aug. 28, 1960; children—Deborah, De Ann, Lorie. B.S. in Stats., Iowa State U., 1960, M.S. in Stats., 1962. Reliability engr. Martin Co., Denver, 1962-66; statistician math. modeling IBM, Boulder, Colo., 1966—. Mem. Am. Statis. Assn. Methodist. Clubs: Rocky Mountain Roadrunners, Elks (Denver). Contbr. paper to statis. conf. Office: PO Box 1900 Boulder CO 80302

SIMONS, LANGDON SAVAGE, JR, planning and development company executive; b. Portland, Maine, June 15, 1923; s. Langdon Savage and Carol Percy S.; m. Anne McBride, Oct. 15, 1951; children—Edith, Deborah, Melissa. A.B. in Engring. Scis., Harvard U., 1945. With Turner Constrn. Co., 1947-48; project mgr. Nowland & Co., 1948-57; v.p., dir. Laird Norton Co., 1957-80; pres. Hydro Drive Corp., Seattle, 1963-71; v.p. Expo '74 Corp., Spokane, Wash. 1973-74; pres. Langdon Simons Assocs., Inc., Seattle, 1974—, LSA Capital Corp., 1983—; dir. Potlatch Corp., Seattle Trust & Savs. Bank, Associated Vintners, Inc.; pres., trustee Northwest Seaport, Seattle. Trustee Virginia Mason Hosp., Seattle. Served with USAAF, 1942-45. Mem. Soc. Harvard Engrs. and Scientists, Soc. Naval Architects and Marine Engrs. Republican. Congregationalist. Clubs: Harvard (N.Y.C.); Old Capital (Monterey, Calif.); Rotary (Seattle); Carmel Valley Golf and Country, Seattle Yacht, Univ., Rainier. Office 1404 Norton Bldg Seattle WA 98104

SIMONS, LYNN OSBORN, state education official; b. Havre, Mont., June 1, 1934; d. Robert Blair and Dorothy (Briggs) Osborn; B.A., U. Colo., 1956; postgrad. U. Wyo., 1958-60; m. John Powell Simons, Jan. 19; children—Clayton Osborn, William Blair. Tchr., Midvale (Utah) Jr. High Sch., 1956-57, Sweetwater County Sch. Dist. 1, Rock Springs, Wyo., 1957-58, U. Wyo., Laramie, 1959-61, Natrona County Sch. Dist. 1, Casper, Wyo., 1963-64; credit mgr. Gallery 323, Casper, 1972-77; Wyo. state supt. public instrn., Cheyenne, 1979—; mem. State Bds. Charities and Reform, Land Commrs., Farm Loan, 1979—; mem. State Commns. Capitol Bldg., Liquor, 1979—; mem. Policy Com. Nat. Assessment Ednl. Progress, 1979-83. Ex-officio mem. bd. trustees U. Wyo.; ex-officio mem. Wyo. Community Coll. Commn.; adv. Nat. Trust Historic Preservation-State Bd. Edn., 1971-77, chmn., 1976-77. Mem. LWV (pres. 1970-71), Am. Assn. Sch. Adminstrs., Council Chief State Sch. Officers, Wyo. Assn. Sch. Adminstrs. Democrat. Episcopalian. Home: Box 185 Cheyenne WY 82002 Office: Hathaway Bldg Cheyenne WY 82001

SIMONS, STEVEN ROBERT, musician recording engr.; b. Long Beach, Calif., Mar. 27, 1956; s. Robert Duane and Patricia Ann (Donovan) S.; student Green River Coll., 1974-76, Golden West Coll., 1977-78, Orange Coast Coll., 1978. With Loren Scale, Inc., Long Beach, Calif., 1977—, pres., 1979—; pres. S&A Studios, 1978—. Mem. Long Beach C. of C. Patentee mus. instrument field. Home: 2223 Golden Circle Newport Beach CA 92660 Office: 315 N Pico Ave Long Beach CA 90802

SIMONSON, MICHAEL, lawyer; b. Franklin, N.J., Feb. 5, 1950; s. Robert and Eleanor (Weiss) S.; student NYU, 1968-70; B.A., U. Ariz., 1973; postgrad. S. Tex. Coll. Law, 1973-74; J.D., Southwestern U., 1976; LL.M. in Taxation, Washington U., St. Louis, 1978; admitted to Ariz. bar, 1977, U.S. Tax Ct. bar, 1978; cert. specialist tax law, 1981. Law clk. Maricopa County Superior Ct., Div. 2, Phoenix, 1976-77; individual practice law, Scottsdale, Ariz., 1978; chief counsel Group Legal Plan, Mesa, Ariz., 1979-81; chief counsel firm Simonson, Groh, and Lindteigen, Mesa, 1979-81; chief counsel Tax Info. Center, 1979-81. Mem. Democratic Precinct Com., Paradise Valley, Ariz., 1976-77; pres. Congregation Tiphereth Israel, Phoenix, 1980-81. mem. Maricopa County Foster Child Care Rev. Bd., 1978-81; pres. Camelback Mountainview Estates Homeowners Assn., Scottsdale, 1980-81. Mem. ABA (coms. on real property 1983—), Ariz. Bar Assn., Maricopa County Bar Assn., Scottsdale Bar Assn., Tri-Cities Bar Assn., Central Ariz. Estate

Planning Council. Office: 6925 5th Ave Suite B Scottsdale AZ 85251

SIMONSON, SIMON CHRISTIAN, III, nuclear engineering consultant; b. Fergus Falls, Minn., Dec. 20, 1938; s. Simon Christian and Flora Jane (Brown) S.; m. Jade Lin, Oct. 15, 1966; 1 son, Niko Christian; S.B., MIT, 1960; M.Sc., Ohio State U., 1965, Ph.D., 1967; M.Sc., U. Md., 1976. Sci. officer Leiden (Netherlands) Obs., 1967-69; asst. prof. astronomy U. Md., College Park, 1969-75; sr. project engr. Nuclear Assocs. Internat., Rockville, Md., 1976-78; sr. assoc. Utility Assocs. Internat., Sunnyvale, Calif., 1978—. Served to lt. (j.g.) USNR, 1960-63. Mem. Am. Nuclear Soc., ASME, Internat. Astron. Union, Internat. Union Radio Sci., Am. Astron. Soc., AAAS, Sigma Xi. Contbr. articles to profl. jours. Office: 215 Moffett Park Dr Sunnyvale CA 94089

SIMPSON, ALAN K., U.S. Senator; b. Denver, Sept. 2, 1931; s. Milward Lee and Lorna (Kooi) S.; B.S., U. Wyo., 1954, J.D., 1958; m. Ann Schroll, 1954; children—William Lloyd, Colin Mackenzie, Susan Lorna. Bar: Wyo. 1958, U.S. Supreme Ct. 1964. Former ptnr. Simpson, Kepler, Simpson & Cozzens, asst. atty. gen. Wyo., 1958-59; city atty. Cody (Wyo.) and U.S. commr., 1959-69; mem. Wyo. Ho. of Reps., 1964-77; mem. U.S. Senate from Wyo., 1979—, chmn. com. vets. affairs, chmn. judiciary com. subcom. immigration and refugee policy, chmn. environ. and pub. works com. subcom. nuclear regulation; mem. Rep. Senatorial Com. Former trustee N.W. Community Coll., Powell, Wyo., Buffalo Bill Hist. Center, Cody, Gottsche Found. Rehab. Center, Thermopolis, Wyo. Served with U.S. Army, 1954-56. Mem. U. Wyo. Alumni Assn. (pres. 1962-63), VFW (life), Am. Legion. Republican. Episcopalian. Clubs: Rotary (local pres. 1972-73), Eagles, Elks, Masons, Shriners (Cody). Office: US Senate Washington DC 20510

SIMPSON, ANDREA LYNN, energy company communications executive; b. Altadena, Calif., Feb. 10, 1948; d. Kenneth James and Barbara Faries Simpson; B.A., U. So. Calif., 1969, M.S., 1983; postgrad. U. Colo., Boulder, 1977. Asst. cashier United Calif. Bank, Los Angeles, 1969-73; asst. v.p. mktg. 1st Hawaiian Bank, Honolulu, 1973-78; v.p. corp. communications Pacific Resources, Inc., Honolulu, 1978—. Bd. dirs. Hawaii Heart Assn., Council of Pacific, Girl Scouts U.S.A., 1982—, 1977—, Arts Council Hawaii, 1978-81. Named Outstanding Young Person of Hawaii, Hawaii Jaycees, 1978; Panhellenic Woman of Yr., Hawaii, 1979; Outstanding Woman in Bus., Hawaii YWCA, 1980; Outstanding Young Woman of Hawaii, Hawaii Legislature, 1980. Mem. Am. Mktg. Assn., Pub. Relations Soc. Am., Pub. Utilities Communicators Assn., Honolulu Advt. Fedn., U. So. Calif. Alumni Assn. (bd. dirs. Hawaii 1981-83), Alpha Phi (dir. Hawaii). Clubs: Outrigger Canoe, Jr. League. Office: 733 Bishop St Suite 3100 Honolulu HI 96842

SIMPSON, CAROL ANN, psycholinguist; b. Norwalk, Conn., July 11, 1946; d. Roy Geary and Margaret Lucy (Benedict) S.; m. Douglas Hall Williams, Aug. 3, 1974. B.A. in Fgn. Langs., Antioch Coll., 1970; Ph.D. in Psycho-linguistics, U. Calif.-Berkeley, 1974. Research psycholinguist Smith-Kettlewell Inst. of Vision Sci., San Francisco, 1974; NRC fellow NASA Ames Research Ctr., Moffett Field, Calif., 1974-76; San Jose State U. research assoc., 1976-77; U. Utah research psycholinguist, 1977-78; co-owner Psycho-Linguistic Research Assocs., Menlo Park, Calif., 1976—. Mem. Acoustical Soc. Am., Linguistic Soc. Am., Human Factors Soc., Assn. Aviation Psychologists, Bay Area Nonoral Communication Group. Club: West Coast Cessna 120/140 (co-founder). Contbr. articles in field to profl. publs. Office: Psycho-Linguistic Research Assocs 2055 Sterling Ave Menlo Park CA 94025

SIMPSON, CAROLE JEAN, social worker; b. Portsmouth, Va., Nov. 3, 1934; d. Pretlow Green and Maybell (Burke) Green Melton; B.A., U. Mo., 1960, M.S.W., 1970; cert. youth counseling for U.S., U. Calif., Berkeley, 1964; children by previous marriage—Ansel Patillo, Gayle Yvonne, Jean Gina caSandra Patrice. Social work cons. Los Angeles County Dept. Public Social Services, 1966-81, vol. coordinator, 1981—; cons. to ct.-referred juveniles through Boone County Family Services, 1969; coordinator day care facilities for model neighborhood day-care program, Los Angeles County, 1971-73. Mem. adv. bd. Inglewood City Schs., 1977; mem. Crime Commn. for 4th Dist., City of Inglewood, 1981. Recipient awards for vol. services City of Inglewood (Calif.), 1977-79; named Woman of Yr., Psi Gamma Mu Sorority, 1982; cert. community coll. counselor, tchr., social workers for grades 1-12, Calif. Mem. Assn. Black Social Workers (life), Los Angeles Public Speakers Bur., PTA, ACLU, U. Calif. Alumnus, U. Mo. Alumnus, Democrat. Baptist (ch. choir, pres. missionary soc.). Club: Order Eastern Star. Author poem: A Black Man Sleeps (6th prize Clover Collection of Verse) pub. in anthology, 1974. Office: 1326 W Imperial Los Angeles CA 90044

SIMPSON, HOWARD DOUGLAS, research scientist; b. Carrizozo, N.Mex., May 30, 1937; s. Howard and Edna (Justiss) S.; B.S.Ch.E., U. N.Mex., 1959; M.S.Ch.E., U. Tex., Austin, 1965, Ph.D., 1969; m. Dianne Marcia Kennedy, Sept. 2, 1967; 1 son, Stephen Douglas. Maintenance engr. Standard Oil Co. Tex., El Paso, 1959-60, tech. service engr., 1962-63; with Union Oil Co. Calif., Brea, 1971—, sr. research engr., 1976-81, research asso., 1981—. Chmn. safety com. Culverdale Community Assn., Irvine, Calif., 1973-76. Served with Chem Corps, U.S. Army, 1960-62. Mem. Calif. Catalysis Soc. (sec.-treas., program chmn., pres.), Am. Chem. Soc., Materials Research Soc., Am. Crystallographic Assn., Sigma Xi. Democrat. Methodist. Patentee catalysis and petroleum processing. Contbr. articles to profl. jours. Office: 376 S Valencia Blvd Brea CA 92621

SIMPSON, JAMES LEE, interior designer; b. Beardstown, Ill., Oct. 11, 1924; s. Levis Leroy and Caroline (Post) S. B.A., Oberlin Coll., 1945; B.S., Juilliard Sch. Music; pvt. study, Paris, 1950-51. Mgr., owner Simpson's Furniture, Beardstown, Ill., 1952-55; salesman Bullocks Downtown, Los Angeles, 1955-56; designer Chandler Furniture, Santa Ana, Calif., 1956-58; mgr. Plummers Furniture, Santa Ana, 1958-59; designer Interior Design, Whittier, Calif., 1963-64; owner Outdoor Living, Orange, Calif., 1959-62; designer, owner Interiors Limited, Whittier, 1964-68; designer Vee Nisley Interiors, Rancho Mirage, Calif., 1968-70; designer, v.p. Noel Birns Interiors, Rancho Mirage, Calif., 1970-76; owner, mgr. J.L. Simpson, Interiors, Palm Desert, Calif., 1976—. Fellow Am. Soc. Interior Designers (pres. Palm Springs 1975, nat. dir. 1977-80, regional v.p. 1979, founding pres. Orange County chpt. 1965-68, Palm Springs 1971-73), Cal-Pro Legis. Assn. (v.p. So. Calif.). Served with USN, 1942-46. Clubs: Elks, Rotary. Designs in Perfect Home Mag., Christian Sci. Monitor, 1979. Home: 74339 Old Prospector Trail Palm Desert CA 92260 Office: Box 1821 Palm Desert CA 92261

SIMPSON, LEE WILLIAM, water association manager; b. Pueblo, Colo., June 6, 1931; s. William Isam and Anna Marie (Miller) S.; m. Kathryne Simpson, Aug. 6, 1952; children—Vicky Ann, William Lee, David Kevin, Thomas Clay. A.A., Pueblo Jr. Coll., 1961; cert. water treatment plant operator Colo.; lic. real estate sales, Colo. With elec. dept. Colo. Fuel and Iron Corp., Pueblo, 1949-50, 54-55; with Pueblo Army Depot (Colo.), 1955-64; gen. mgr. St. Charles Mesa Water Assn., Pueblo, Colo., 1964—, pres. bd. dirs., 1962-63, chmn. steering com., 1962-63; bd. dirs. Southeastern Colo. Water Conservancy Dist., 1981—; pres. bd. dirs. Colo. Rural Water Assn., 1980—; dir. from Colo. to bd. dirs. Nat. Rural Water Assn., 1980—; bd. dirs. Colo. Water Protective and Devel. Assn., 1977-79. Mem. Pueblo Regional Planning Comm., 1972; mem. Pueblo Area Council Govts., 1973-79, v.p., 1977, 78; active Pueblo 4-H, 1964-73, bd. dirs., 1964-73; pres. Pueblo County Extension Adv. Bd., 1970-73; sec. Pueblo County High Sch. Booster Club, 1972; foster parent; cubmaster Pack 57C, Pueblo, Colo.; bd. dirs. Pueblo County Sch. Dist. #70, 1973—, v.p., 1978-79, pres., 1980-81, 83—. Served in USAF, 1951-53; Korea. Mem. Colo. Water Congress. Democrat. Home: 26280 Williams Ln Pueblo CO 81006 Office: 1397 S Aspen St Pueblo CO 81006

SIMPSON, ROBERT EMMETT, JR., clin social worker; b. Bristol, Conn., Mar. 23, 1947; s. Robert E. and Helen V. (Burckess) S.; B.A. (John Woodruff Simpson scholar), Amherst Coll., 1969; M.S.W. (Shirley Wisenfeld scholar), Simmons Coll., 1975; M.P.H., Harvard U., 1979; D.S.W. (Marriner S. Eccles scholar), U. Utah, 1982; m. Genevieve Elizabeth Chandler, Aug. 2, 1975; children— Conor Chandler, Maura M. Asst. dean admissions, Mayo Smith fellow Amherst (Mass.) Coll., 1969-70; sr. mental health worker McLean Hosp., Belmont, Mass., 1971-73; intern trainee Trinity Mental Health Center, Framingham, Mass., 1973-74, Beth Israel Hosp., Boston, 1974-75; mem. adminstrv. staff, coordinator public relations Trinity Mental Health Center, Framingham, 1975-78; pvt. practice psychotherapy, Boston, 1976-79, Family and Group Therapy Inst., Salt Lake City, 1980-82; exec. dir. Salt Lake Child and Family Therapy Clinic, 1982—, clin. instr. Simmons Coll. of Social Work, Boston, 1977-78; cons. Harvard Community Health Plan, 1979; v.p. med. services Comprehensive Health Systems, Salt Lake City, 1979-80, sec.-treas., bd. dirs., 1980—; instr. U. Utah, 1981—; mem. social work peer rev. bd. Utah Dept. Bus. Regulation. AIESEC fellow U. Aarhus (Denmark), 1967; lic. clin social worker, Utah, Mass. Mem. Acad. of Cert. Social Workers, Nat. Assn. Social Workers, Nat. Register Clin. Social Workers. Home: 1080 3d Ave Salt Lake City UT 84103 Office: 515 S 700 E Suite 3D Salt Lake City UT 84102

SIMPSON, WILLIAM BRAND, economist, educator; b. Portland, Oreg., Nov. 30, 1919; s. John Alexander and Janet Christie (Brand) S.; m. Ruth Laura Decker, June 12, 1957. B.A., Reed Coll., 1942; M.A. in Stats., Columbia U., 1943; Ph.D. in Econs., Claremont Grad. Sch., 1971. Exec. dir. Cowles Commn. Research Econs., Chgo., 1948-53; co-founder, bd. dirs. Inst. Social and Personal Relations, Oakland, Calif., 1955-61; prof. econs. Calif. State U., Los Angeles, 1958—; econs. cons. higher edn. Served with CIC, U.S. Army, 1943-46. Fellow Nat. Social Sci. Research Council; mem. ACLU; Econometric Soc. (internat. sec. 1948-52); AAUP (state pres. 1975-76), nat. council 1978-81, com. govt. relations 1982-85), Am. Econs. Assn., Am. Assn. Higher Edn., Western Econ. Assn., Congress Faculty Assns., United Scottish Socs. So. Calif., Sierra Club (Los Angeles chpt.), Phi Beta Kappa. Democrat. Unitarian. Mng. editor, co-editor, Econometrica, 1948-53; contbr. articles to profl. jours. Home: PO Box 1456 South Pasadena CA 91030 Office: Calif State U Los Angeles CA 90032

SIMS, JOHN DAVID, aerospace co. exec.; b. Birmingham, Ala., Feb. 5, 1940; s. Joseph and Abeatrice Ruby (Love) S.; B.S. in Aero. Engring., U. Ala., 1961; postgrad. Pepperdine U. Sch. Bus. and Mgmt., 1975-76; m. Maria Jean Zimmerman, June 23, 1973; children—Jonathan Bradford, Kristin Laura, Amy Love. Successively aerospace engr., project engr., program mgr. Gen. Dynamics-Convair, San Diego, 1961-68, sr. customer engr. Lockheed-Calif. Co., Burbank, 1968-71; pres., chief exec. officer Am. Travelers, Inc., Van Nuys, Calif., 1971-73; programs/product mgr. Aerojet-Gen. Corp., Sacramento, 1973—; mktg. cons. to small bus. Mem. Tech. Mktg. Soc. Am., Air Force Assn. (life Patron), Assn. U.S. Army (patron). Republican. Baptist. Club: Fair Oaks Racquet. Home: 4512 Kewanee St Fair Oaks CA 95628 Office: PO Box 13222 Sacramento CA 95813

SIMS, LYDIA THERESA, city affirmative action exec.; b. Pennsgrove, N.J., Nov. 18, 1920; d. Clifton and Helen Elvira (Hoskins) Williams; student Wash. State U., 1971, Eastern Wash. State U., 1974-77; m. James M. Sims, Aug. 2, 1941; children—James M., Ronald C., Donald C. Stenographer, sec. YWCA, Spokane, Wash., 1951-63, Spokesman Rev., Spokane, 1964-66, Spokane Neighborhood Centers, 1966-68; dep. dir. Eastside Neighborhood Center, Spokane, 1968-70; manpower tng. specialist, personnel and affirmative action officer Community Action Council, Spokane, 1970-73; affirmative action dir. City of Spokane, 1975—. Precinct com. person Spokane County Central Democratic Com.; mem. Wash. state adv. com. U.S. Commn. Civil Rights; pres. NW Area Conf., NAACP, bd. dirs. N.W. Women's Law Center, YWCA, Spokane; chmn. Mut. World Services, Affirmative Action Com., Spokane County Democratic Central Com., minority task force of Eastern Wash. Area Agy. on Aging; vice-chmn. Interstate Task Force on Human Relations; mem. adv. com. Pine Lodge Correctional Center. Recipient Human Relations award Fairchild AFB, 1977, award of appreciation Kiwanis, 1979 Outstanding Community Service award Spokane County Black Students, 1982; East Central Community Ctr. Civic award, 1981. Mem. Am. Assn. Affirmative Action, Nat. Mgmt. Assn., Am. Soc. Personnel Adminstrn., Adminstrv. Mgmt. Soc., Northwest Women's Law Center. Baptist. Club: Links. Dir. research and devel. Black history slide show, 1979. Home: E 1218 5th Ave Spokane WA 99202 Office: N 221 Wall St Spokane WA 99201

SIMS, MARK LANDON, commercial pilot, aircraft mechanic, police officer; b. Glendale, Calif., June 12, 1952; s. Fred Landon and Naida Jean (Wirth) S.; m. Kathy Lynn Naifeh, June 3, 1980. Student U.S. Army UH-1 Helicopter Mechanic and Door Gunner Sch., 1970, Los Angeles Valley Coll., 1973-74, U.S. Air Force Air Traffic Controller Sch., 1975, Cessna Tng., 1978, Sawyer Sch. Aviation, 1978-79; A.A., Glendale Community Coll., 1976; comml./instrument/multi-engine airplane cert. Airline Ground Sch., 1980. Comml. pilot, aircraft mechanic Monument Valley Air Service, Navaho and Apache Indian Reservation, Ariz., 1979-80; police officer Globe (Ariz.) Police Dept. Res., 1980—; comml. pilot, helicopter and aircraft mechanic NHF Ltd., Houston, 1981—, pilot/mechanic, Malargüe, Argentina, 1981—; geophys. survey pilot Aero Service, comml. aviation co., 1981-83; sky diver, 1972-80; dir. ops. Air Ambulance; search pilot CAP, 1980—. Mem. Republican Nat. Com.; mem. Rep. Presdl. Task Force; mem. U.S. Senatorial Club. Served with U.S. Army, 1969-72, USAF, 1975-77. Decorated Air medal; recipient Don Flower Aviation Safety award World-Wide-Ins., 1979, Presdl. Achievement award; col. Confederate Air Force. Mem. Aircraft Owners and Pilots Assn. (charter mem. Ultralight div.), Nat. Rifle Assn., Cactus Combat League, Air Force Assn. PO Box 856 Litchfield Park AZ 85340 Office: PO Box 36798 Houston TX 77036

SIMS, WILBERT NORMAN, equipment manufacturing company executive; b. Bridgeville, Pa., Sept. 12, 1922; s. Wilbert Leroy and Margaret Belle (Gordon) S.; B.S. in Fuel Tech., Pa. State U., 1949; A.M.P., Harvard U., 1966; m. Martha Lois McClelland, Oct. 18, 1952; 1 son, Scott McClelland. Miner, Pitts. Coal Co., 1940-42; fuel engr. Phila. Coal & Iron Co., 1949-52; gen. purchasing agt. Am. Cyanamid Co., 1952-62; v.p., gen. mgr. indsl. chems. Kaiser Aluminium & Chem. Co., 1962-71; v.p., gen. mgr. Marconaflo Inc., 1971-78, Macronaflo div. McNally Group, Oakland, Calif., 1978-81, Salt Lake City, 1981—; chmn. High Techs. Inc., 1982—. Pres., East Bay Area Trails Council, 1978-79, San Ramon Valley Horsemen, 1970, 80; chmn. charitable trusts Calif. Horsemen's Assn., 1979-81; equine chmn. for Calif., Morris Animal Found., 1978-81; advisor Danville Jr. Horsemen, 1964-80. Served with USAAF, 1943-46. Mem. AIME, Slurry Transport Assn. (dir. 1981—), Newcomen Soc. N.Am., Phi Delta Theta. Republican. Methodist. Club: Stock Exchange. Author, patentee in field. Home: 10424 Dimple Dell Rd Sandy UT 84092 Office: PO Box 7660 Salt Lake City UT 84107

SIMTON, CHESTER, librarian, coach; b. Longstreet, La., Jan. 28, 1937; s. Jim Simton and Umie Lee (Crowell) Simon; m. Dorothy M. Powell, June 27, 1959 (div. 1977); 1 dau., Jessica; m. Peggy I. Neighbors, July 4, 1978; children—Jennifer, Annelle; 1 stepdau., Vonny Gonzalez. B.A., U. Calif.-Berkeley, 1974, M.L.S., 1976. Cert. librarian. Librarian, King Cove (Alaska) City Sch., 1977-80; librarian Nome Beltz High Sch., 1980—, jr. varsity basketball coach, 1980—. Mem. Alaska Library Assn., Alaska Librarians Assn., Nat. Tchrs. Assn. Democrat. Office: Nome Beltz High Sch PO Box 131 Nome AK 99762

SINASEK, BARBARA L., property manager; b. Mpls., Sept. 20, 1943; d. Leonard Maurice, Jr. and Barbara H. (Hagerman) Lilly; children—Haidee Lee Maxey, Tera Lynn Maxey. In entertainment field, 1965-70, constrn. field, 1970-76; property mgr. Koll Co., Newport Beach, Calif., 1977—. Bd. dirs. Braille Inst, Dolphins, Speak Up Newport, Sandpipers; mem. U.S. Olympic Pentathlon Com., Orange County Olympic Com. Mem. Bldg. Owners and Mgrs. Assn. (dir.), Newport Harbor Area C. of C. (citation; dir.). Office: Koll Co 4500 Campus Dr Suite 116 Newport Beach CA 92660

SINAY, HERSHEL DAVID, publisher; b. Chgo., Mar. 15, 1938; s. Irving P. and Gertrude (Drucker) S.; B.A., U. So. Calif., 1960; m. Florence Tsu, Nov. 6, 1970. With Carson Roberts Advt. Co., 1960-61; advt. sales rep. Wall St. Jour., 1961-64; account exec. R.J. Friedman Assos., 1964-66; dir. sales Performing Arts Mag., Los Angeles, 1966-72; v.p. publ. services, asso. pub. East/West Network, Los Angeles, 1972-79; pres., pub. Calif. Bus. Mag., Los Angeles, 1979—; dir. Calif. Bus. News, Inc. Recipient Maggie award Western Publs. Assn., 1980. Mem. Advt. Club Los Angeles, Mag. Pubs. Assn., Assn. Area Bus. Publs. (dir.). Office: 6420 Wilshire Blvd Suite 711 Los Angeles CA 90048

SINAY, RUTH DORIS, psychologist, educator; d. Maurice Howard and Marion Gertrude (Heller) Milman; B.A. cum laude, U. So. Calif., 1956, Ph.D. in Psychology, 1967; m. Joseph Sinay, Mar. 7, 1961; 1 son, Frederick Allen Schiff. Tchr. elementary schs. Wiseburn Sch. Dist., Hawthorne, Calif., 1957-58; fashion model and instr. Rita LaRoy Fashion Modeling Sch., Beverly Hills, Calif., 1958-61; instr. psychology U. So. Calif. Sch. Medicine, Los Angeles, 1967-71, asst. clin. prof. psychiatry, 1971-78, asso. clin. prof., 1978—; asso. clin. prof. psychology Fuller Theol. Sem., Pasadena, Calif., 1969-77; dir. child/adolescent psychol. tng. program Los Angeles County/U. So. Calif. Med. Center, 1969—, acting dir. child/adolescent psychol. services, 1969-71, dir., 1971—; oral examiner Calif. State Psychology Exam. Com., 1974—, written examiner, 1976-77; lectr. Calif. Sch. Profl. Psychology, Los Angeles, 1971; participant Nat. Conf. Postdoctoral Tng. in Psychology, 1973. Chmn. ways and means com. Los Angeles County Interagy. Task Force on Drug Abuse, 1972-74; alt. del. Democratic Nat. Conv., 1972; mem. Los Angeles Mayor's Com. on Youth and Aging, 1974-75. Recipient Judah Magnes award for humanitarianism Hebrew U., Jerusalem 1977; NIMH fellow, 1960-62. Mem. Am., Calif. (sec. 1975-77), Los Angeles County, Western psychol. assns., Psychologists in Pub. Service (sec. 1969-70). Club: Variety. Contbr. articles in field to profl. jours. Home: 1025 Carolyn Way Beverly Hills CA 90210 Office: 1934 Hospital Pl Los Angeles CA 90033

SINCLAIR, WILLIAM DONALD, ch. ofcl.; b. Los Angeles, Dec. 27, 1924; s. Arthur Livingston and Lillian May (Holt) S.; B.A. cum laude, St. Martin's Coll., Olympia, Wash., 1975; postgrad. Emory U., 1978-79; m. Barbara Jean Hughes, Aug. 9, 1952; children—Paul Scott, Victoria Sharon. Commd. 2d lt. USAAF, 1944, advanced through grades to col., USAF, 1970; service in Italy, Korea, Vietnam and Japan; ret., 1975; bus. adminstr. First United Methodist Ch., Colorado Springs, Colo., 1976—; mem. council fin. and adminstrn. Rocky Mountain conf. United Meth. Ch., U.S.A., 1979—. Bd. dirs. Chins-Up Colorado Springs, 1983—. Decorated Legion of Merit with oak leaf cluster, D.F.C. with oak leaf cluster, Air medal with 6 oak leaf cluster, Dept. Def. Meritorious Service medal. Fellow Nat. Assn. Ch. Bus. Adminstrs. (nat. dir., regional v.p.), v.p. 1983—; Ch. Bus. Educator of Yr. award 1983), Colo. Assn. Ch. Bus. Adminstrs. (past pres.), United Meth. Assn. Ch. Bus. Adminstrs. (nat. sec. 1978-81), Christian Ministries Mgmt. Assn. (dir. 1983—), USAF Acad. Athletic Assn. Club: Colorado Springs Country. Home: 3007 Chelton Dr Colorado Springs CO 80909 Office: 420 N Nevada Ave Colorado Springs CO 80903

SINDELAR, SCOTT JOHN, psychologist, educator; b. Oak Park, Ill., Oct. 9, 1951; s. Richard John and Marilyn Eraine (Fenske) S.; B.A., Rollins Coll., 1973; M.Ed., Ed.S., U. Fla., 1975; M.S., U. Ga., 1979, Ph.D., 1981; m. Susan Carroll Meade, June 8, 1974. Psychiat. counselor, Atlanta, 1975-76; alcoholism treatment counselor West Pacca Ferry Hosp., Atlanta, 1976-77; cons. psychologist N.E. Ga. Alcoholism and Drug Abuse Services, Athens, 1977-79; pub. relations officer Psychology Clinic, U. Ga., Athens, 1980-81; pvt. practice clin. psychology, Phoenix, 1981—; asst. dir. chem. dependency Camelback Hosps., Scottsdale, Ariz., 1982—; adj. asst. prof. dept. psychology Ariz. State U., Tempe, 1981—. Algernon Sidney Sullivan scholar; NSF research asst. grantee, 1972-73. Mem. Am. Psychol. Assn., Assn. Advancement Behavior Therapy, Soc. Behavioral Medicine. Libertarian. Club: Order DeMolay (past master councillor 1969). Editorial cons. Behavioral Assessment, 1979—. Home: 5338 N 77th St Scottsdale AZ 85253 Office: 4455 E Camelback Rd Phoenix AZ 85018

SINES, PAULINE LULU, nurse; b. Seattle, May 2, 1934; d. James Paul and Glow C. (Sackman) O'Connor; student San Diego Jr. Coll. 1952-53; B.S. in Nursing, San Diego State U., 1957; children—Shawn, Tim. Staff nurse County Hosp., San Diego, 1957-59; staff nurse Grossmont Hosp., LaMesa, Calif., 1962-70, supervising head nurse, 1970-78, unit mgr., 1978-83, clin splty. nurse, 1983—; organizer recovery room seminars U. Calif., LaJolla. Recipient cert. for recovery room seminars for U.S. nurses U. Calif., LaJolla, 1973; cert. advanced CPR, 1978. Mem. Am. Nurses Assn., Am. Hosp. Assn., Recovery Room Nurses, United Nurses Calif., Children's Hosp. Aux. San Diego. Republican. Baptist. Club: Duwamish Tribe. Home: 1292 Exeter St El Cajon CA 92021

SINES, RANDY DWAIN, corp. exec.; b. Spokane, Jan. 16, 1948; s. Myron Jones and Paula Inez (Walls) S.; student Wash. State U., 1966-67, U. Wash., 1968-69; m. Irene Cheng, Mar. 18, 1981. With Boeing Co., 1967; with Winchell's Donut House, Inc. (merged with Denny's Restaurants), Seattle, 1968-71; owner, mgr. bakeries, Wash. and Mont., 1972-78; owner, mgr. Sonsine Inc., Great Falls, Mont., 1976-79; pres. Gardian Port Corp., Oxnard, Calif., 1980—; exec. v.p., chmn. SNS Motor Imports, Inc., Oxnard. Recipient alumni grant Wash. State U., 1967; lic. water well contractor, Wash., Mont. Patentee automatic cue ball separating device and billiard game apparatus. Home: 463 Las Palomas Dr Port Hueneme CA 93041 Office: 500 Esplanade Dr Suite 1000 Oxnard CA 93030 also PO Box 759 Port Hueneme CA 93041

SING, RONALD LLOYD, school principal; b. Wailuku, Maui, Hawaii, Dec. 1, 1944; s. Lloyd Harold and Lucy Ah (Hee) S.; m. Wendy Joy Blevins, Aug. 30, 1969; children—Wendy Kuuipo, Asayo Uilani, Naomi Lucia, Kiyomi Iwalani. B.S., Brigham Young U.-Hawaii, 1969; M.S., Kans. State U., 1974; Ed.D., Brigham Young U., 1982. Cert. secondary adminstr., secondary indsl. edn. tchr., vocat. automechanics tchr., Utah. Mechanic, Phillips 66 Service, Laie, Hawaii, 1969-72; indsl. edn. tchr., dept. head Kailua High Sch., Kahuku High Sch., both Hawaii, 1969-76; instr., research asst., teaching asst. Brigham Young U., Provo, Utah, 1976-78; tchr., dept. head Alta High Sch., Sandy, Utah, 1978-79, vice prin., 1979—. Ednl. Profl. Devel. Act Vocat. fellow, 1973-74. Mem. Nat. Assn. Secondary Sch. Prins., Utah Assn. Secondary Sch. Prins., Am. Vocat. Assn., Utah Vocat. Assn., Nat. Inst. Automotive Service Excellence, Phi Kappa Phi. Mormon. Office: 11055 S 1000 E Sandy UT 84070

SINGER, GEORGE MILTON, clinical psychologist; b. Phila., Oct. 13, 1924; s. Benjamin and Bessie (Podlisker) S.; B.A., Temple U., 1950, A.M., 1952, Ph.D., 1958; m. Carol Ann Horton, June 15, 1977; children—Elizabeth Carol, Susan Theresa. Chief psychologist Phila. State Hosp., 1953-56; dir. psychol. services Pennhurst State Hosp., Spring City, Pa., 1958-61; clin. psychologist Kern County Mental Health Dept., Bakersfield, Calif., 1961-68; project dir., coordinator Kernview Community Mental Health Center, Bakersfield, 1968-70, now mem. affiliate med. staff health center and hosp.; individual practice clin. psychology, Bakersfield, 1953—; mem. affiliate med. staff Hoag Meml. Hosp., Newport Beach, Calif., 1972-73; cons. psychologist Pioneer Community Hosp., 1981—; mem. Kern County Mental Health Adv. Bd., 1976-83, adv. bd. Patton State Hosp., 1980—. Bd. dirs. Orange County Child Guidance Clinic, 1973-74. Served with USAAF, 1943-46; ETO, MTO. Recipient Service award Psi Chi, 1952; cert. of achievement S.E. Pa. Mental Health Assn., 1956. Mem. Am., Calif., Am. Soc. Clin. Hypnosis, So. Calif. Soc. Clin. Hypnosis, Kern County (pres. 1968-69) psychol. assns., Kern County Soc. Clin. Psychologists, AAAS. Club: Rotary (chpt. pres. 1960-61). Home: 1805 Ridgewood Dr Bakersfield CA 93306 Office: 1601 H St Suite 4 Bakersfield CA 93301

SINGER, JOEL, filmmaker, photographer; b. Montreal, Que., Can., Nov. 29, 1948. M.F.A., San Francisco Art Inst., 1976. Works exhibited in permanent collections: Mus. Modern Art, N.Y.C., San Francisco Art Inst.; exhibits: Mus. Modern Art, 1977, Cinematheque, San Francisco, 1977-81, Millennium Film Mus., N.Y.C., 1981, Pasadena (Calif.) Film Forum, 1981, Boston Film and Video Found., 1981, U. Colo., Boulder, 1981. Recipient 1st prize San Francisco Art Inst. Film Festival, 1977; 2d prize Bollevue Internat. Film Festival, 1978; award Ann Arbor Internat. Film Festival, 1981. *

SINGER, MICHAEL HOWARD, lawyer; b. N.Y.C., Nov. 22, 1941; s. Jack and Etta (Applebaum) S.; m. Saundra Jean Kupperman, June 1, 1962; children—Alison Jill, Pamela Faith. B.S. in Econs., U. Pa., 1962; J.D., NYU, 1965, LL.M. in Taxation, 1968. Bar: Nev. 1973, N.Y. 1965, U.S. Ct. Clms. 1968, U.S. Tax Ct. 1972, U.S. Supreme Ct. 1972, U.S. Dist. Ct. Nev. 1973, U.S. Ct. Appeals (6th cir.) 1970, U.S. Ct. Appeals (9th cir.) 1979. Law asst. N.Y. Appellate Term of Supreme Ct. N.Y., 1965-68; with tax div. U.S. Dept. Justice, Washington, 1968-72; assoc. Beckley, DeLanoy & Jemison, Las Vegas, 1972-74; sr. ptnr. Oshins, Brown, Singer & Wells, Las Vegas, 1974—. Pres., Nev. chpt. NCCJ, 1978-83. Mem. ABA, Nev. Bar Assn. Democrat. Clubs: Las Vegas Country, Cambridge Racquet. Home: 3730 Pama Ln Las Vegas NV 89120 Office: 520 S 1st St Las Vegas NV 89101

SINGER, SUSAN M., health education administrator, consultant; b. Passaic, N.J., Feb. 24, 1947; d. Norman J. and Ruth (Elfenbein) Dorff; m. A. Robert Singer, Mar. 2, 1969. B.A., George Washington U., 1968. Research asst. Nat. Council Crime and Delinquency, Washington, 1969-73; grants mgmt. specialist, correctional treatment specialist U.S. Dept. Justice, Washington and Burlingame, Calif., 1973-76; dep. exec. dir. Health Systems Mgmt. Corp., Oakland, Calif., 1976-78; v.p. for adminstrn. Nat. Ctr. Health Educ., San Francisco, 1978-83; mgmt. cons. nonprofit corps. Mem. San Francisco Symphony Vols., San Francisco Mus. Soc. Mem. Nat. Assn. Female Execs. Club: San Francisco Bay.

SINGER, TIMOTHY JAMES, aviation psychologist; b. Champaign, Ill., June 3, 1947; s. Robert Roy and Earline Elizabeth (Harris) S.; m. Ann Kathleen Widmer, Jan. 14, 1978; children—Rachael Linn, Lindsay Rose. B.A., Reed Coll., 1973; M.S., Yale U., 1975, M.Phil., 1976, Ph.D., 1977; Student Naval Postgrad. Sch., 1981. Flight surgeon training Naval Aerospace Med. Inst., Pensacola, Fla., 1980-81, spl. project officer, operation psychology, 1981; aviation med. safety officer COMNAVAIRPAC, San Diego, 1981—; cons. in organizational psychology; asst. prof. George Washington U., Med. Sch. Served to capt. USAF, 1976-80; lt. comdr. USNR, 1980—. NIH fellow, 1973-76. Mem. Am. Psychol. Assn., Aerospace Med. Assn., Assn. Aviation Psychologists, Human Factors Soc., Yale Sci. and Engring. Assn., Phi Beta Kappa. Contbr. articles to profl. jours. Home: 8939 Oviedo St San Diego CA 92129 Office: Aeromedical Safety Ops COMNAVAIRPAC Code 0143C NAS North Island San Diego CA 92135

SINGER, WILLIAM BERG, training consultant; b. Saginaw, Mich., July 16, 1943; s. Fred and Hannah Singer; m. Caroline Hale Yeager, July 8, 1978; 1 dau., Adina Atkinson. B.S. in Communication Arts, N.Y.U., 1965; M.A. in Ednl. Tech., Columbia U., 1972. Sr. tng. rep. Consol. Edison Co., N.Y.C., 1972-76; program mgr. TRATEC/McGraw Hill, Los Angeles, 1977-80; pres. Clarity Communications, Inc., Pasadena, Calif., 1980—. Served to 1st lt. AUS, 1965-67. Decorated Bronze Star. Mem. Nat. Soc. Performance and Instrn. (sec. chpt.), Nat. Assn. Soc. Profl. Cons. Author: The Fox with Cold Feet, 1980. Home and Office: 3520 Yorkshire Rd Pasadena CA 91107

SINGH, JOYCE HIDEKO, educator; b. Stockton, Calif., July 21, 1942; d. Ichiro and Mitsue (Nakai) Nakahara; B.A., San Jose State Coll., 1965, M.A., 1968; M.A., San Jose State U., 1976; m. Gurnam Singh, Aug. 22, 1970. Substitute tchr. Alumn Rock Sch. Dist., San Jose, Calif., 1965; tchr. Northwood Elem. Sch., Berryessa Union Sch. Dist., San Jose, 1965—; summer sch. tchr. Mem. Soc. Baptist Conv., 1960-67. Milpitas Metalcraft scholar, 1960; cert. kindergarten-primary tchr., cert. adminstr., Calif. Mem. Calif. Tchrs. Assn., NEA, Assn. Supervision and Curriculum Devel.

SINGHAL, AVINASH CHANDRA, educator; b. Aligarh, India, Nov. 4, 1941; came to U.S., 1960, naturalized, 1979; s. Shiam Sunder and Pushpa Lata (Jindal) S.; B.S., Agra U., India, 1957; B.S. in Engring., St. Andrews U., 1959, B.Sc. Engr. with honors, 1960; S.M., M.I.T., 1961, Civil Engr., 1962, Sc.D., 1964; cert. in bus. mgmt., UCLA, 1970; m. Uma Sharma, Sept. 5, 1967; children—Ritu, Anita. Research engr. Kaman Aircraft, Burlington, Mass., 1964-65; prof. Laval U., Quebec, Que., Can., 1965-69; asst. program mgr. TRW, Redondo Beach, Calif., 1969-71; mgr. systems engring. Gen. Electric Co., Phila., 1971-72; mgr. Engrs. India Ltd., New Delhi, 1972-74; cons. Weidlinger Assos., N.Y.C., 1974-77; asso. prof. civil engring. Ariz. State U., Tempe, 1977—. Pres., India Assn. Greater Boston, 1964-65; faculty adv. India Student Assn., Ariz. State U., 1977—. Dennison scholar, Instn. of Civil Engrs., London, 1959-60; Mclintock fellow, M.I.T., 1960-61; Carnegie scholar, 1960-63; Henry Adams awardee Structural Inst. London, 1972; grantee Engring. Found. N.Y., 1979-80; NSF grantee, 1981-83. Registered profl. engr., Ariz., N.Y. Mem. ASCE, Structural Engrs. Assn. Ariz., Earthquake Engring. Research Inst. Republican. Contbr. articles to profl. jours. Home: 2631 S El Marino Mesa AZ 85202 Office: Dept Civil Engring Ariz State U Tempe AZ 85287

SINGLEHURST, THOMAS WILLIAM GIBSON, retail executive; b. Honolulu, Nov. 14, 1899; s. William Gibson and Katie (Newcombe) S.; m. Carol Cochrane (dec.); children—Jean (Mrs. Carl Bruce Mason), Gay (Mrs. Roy E. Fraser); m. 2d, Dona Geisenheyner, May 16, 1959; 1 dau., Susanna. With Bank of Hawaii, 1918; with Hawaiian Trust Co., 1919-20; clk. Am. Exchange Nat. Bank, N.Y.C., 1920-22; with Bishop Trust Co., 1922-62, sr. v.p., 1959-62, dir., 1954-62; dir., part-owner Carol & Mary Ltd., Honolulu, 1937—, pres., gen. mgr., 1959—; past v.p., dir. Polynesian Food Spltys.; past v.p., treas., dir. Ross Sutherland Ltd.; past treas., dir. Ivy Shop; past pres., dir. August Ahrens Ltd., Wahiawa Transp. Service, Fed. Transp. Co., Indsl. Enterprises, Kailua Land Co.; past dir. Air Conditioning Co.; Bishop Ins. Agy.; Bishop Securities, Castle & Cooke, Hawaii Hotel & Restaurant Supply, Hawaiian Pineapple Co., Diamond Head Apts., Ewa Plant Co., Honolulu Rapid Transit Co., Helemano Co. Honolulu Ltd., Honouliuli Ltd., Pacific Ins. Co., Von Hamm-Young Co., San Carlos Milling Co., Waialua Agrl. Co., Served with AUS, 1918-19. Mem. adv. bd. Hawaii Com. on Alcoholism, 1956-60; past treas., bd. dirs. Hawaii chpt. Guide Dogs for the Blind; past treas., bd. dirs. Keys and Whistles; trustee Tax Found. of Hawaii, 1950-67; bd. dirs. Hawaii Found. for Am. Freedoms. Clubs: Pacific (past treas., dir.), Outrigger Canoe (past sec.-treas., dir.), Pearl Harbor Yacht (past sec.-treas., dir.), Beretania Tennis, Kauai Canoe and Racing, Mokuleia Polo. Republican. Episcopalian. Home: 67-290 Farrington Hwy Waialua Oahu HI 96791 Office: 1450 Ala Moana Blvd 2200 Ala Moana Center Honolulu HI 96814 also 1778 Ala Moana Blvd Honolulu HI 96815

SINGLETON, HAROLD COLLOM, consulting radio engineer; b. Golden, Colo., Feb. 7, 1904; s. Joseph Harrison and Martha Jane (Collom) S.; m. Estelle Fisher, Feb. 19, 1949; children—Richard, Dorothy, Kenneth, Marta. B.S. in Elec. Engring., U. Colo., 1925, E.E., 1939. With Gen. Electric Co., 1925-28, RCA, 1928-31, United Air Lines, 1931-33; chief engr. KGW, 1933-53, KWJJ, Portland, Oreg., 1953-71; mem. faculty electronics Reed Coll., Portland, Oreg., 1941-42, Oreg. State U., 1942-43; radar scientist OSRD-Harvard U., 1943-45; radio engr. Radio Liberty, CIA, Spain, 1958; instr., Multnomah Coll., Portland, 1945-47, head physics dept., 1948-52; cons. radio engr., 1933—, Lake Oswego, Oreg., 1973—. Active IRS VITA/TCE Income Tax Assistance program, 1978-83. Recipient commendation War Dept., 1945. Mem. AIEE, Acoustical Soc. Am., Geol. Soc. Oregon Country. Democrat. Unitarian. Clubs: Lake Oswego Adult Community Center; Portland Progressive Bus. Men's, Mazama, Masons, La Mesa Espánola (pres. 1977—), Optimist. Address: 2671 S W Glen Eagles Rd Lake Oswego OR 97034

SINGLETON, HENRY EARL, industrialist; b. Haslet, Tex., Nov. 27, 1916; s. John Bartholomew and Victoria (Flores) S.; S.B., S.M., Mass. Inst. Tech., 1940, Sc.D., 1950; m. Caroline A. Wood, Nov. 30, 1942; children—Christina, John, William, James, Diana. Vice pres. Litton Industries, Inc., Beverly Hills, Calif., 1954-60; chmn. bd., chief exec. officer Teledyne Inc., Los Angeles, 1960—. Office: Teledyne Inc 1901 Ave of the Stars Los Angeles CA 90067*

SINGLETON, JAMES ROBERT, mcpl. bldg. ofcl.; b. Mineral Wells, Tex., Dec. 21, 1931; s. Robert Floyd and Carrie Lou (Harvey) S.; student Tex. Tech. Coll., 1949-51; B.S.M.E., U. Wyo., 1963; m. Frances Earl Pruitt, June 6, 1953; children—Pamela Jane Singleton Stewart, Victoria Susan Singleton Topham. Commd. 2d lt., U.S. Air Force, 1951, advanced through grades to maj., 1966; served as radar observer, pilot, instr. pilot, devel. engr., combat pilot, comdr. Wing Command Center, 1951-71, ret., 1971; civil engr. City of Tucson, 1971-72, plans examiner, 1972-78, bldg. safety adminstr., 1978—. Decorated D.F.C., Air medal with 6 oak leaf clusters, Air Force Commendation medal; cert. bldg. ofcl. Mem. Internat. Conf. Bldg. Ofcls. (past pres. Ariz. chpt.), ASME (past pres. So. Ariz. sect.), Soc. Am. Mil. Engrs. (pres. Tucson post), Structural Engrs. Assn. Ariz., Air Force Inst. Tech. Assn. Grads., Air Force Assn. Democrat. Baptist. Research on concepts for recovery of radioactive debris using remotely controlled vehicles. Home: 8960 E Rosewood St Tucson AZ 85710 Office: PO Box 27110 Tucson AZ 85726

SINGLETON, KENT JOHN, property mgmt. and engring. co. exec., cons. engr.; b. South Ogden, Utah; s. Clarence Lyman and Lenna Estella (Read) S.; M.S. in Psychology, Utah State U., 1958, D.D. (hon.), 1961; M.S. in Chem.-Mech. Engring., U. Chgo., 1972; D.S., U. Du Bois, 1982; m. Joan Nielson, May 23, 1950; children—John, Saul, Kimla, Jenna, Jona, Portia. Refrigeration engr. Asael Farr & Sons Co., 1946-52, dist. mgr., 1952-56; dist. mgr., ednl. dir. Coop. Life Am., 1956-58; ednl. dir., asst. v.p. Ideal Nat. Ins. Co., 1958-60; dist. mgr. DuBois Chems., 1960-72; cons. engr. Dearborn Chems. subs. W.R. Grace & Co., 1972-75; gen. mgr. Gurries Mgmt., Carmel, Calif., 1974-82; prin. Singleton Consulting Services, Monterey Peninsula, Calif., 1974—; dir. Cal-Sin Assos., S. & G., Inc., MPDC, Bergie Mfg. and Fin., Big Valley News, Ideal Nat., Country Mut. Life, Mem. ASHRAE, Profl. Mgrs. Assn., Million Dollar Round Table, Profl. Cons. Assn., Am. Soc. Corrosian Engrs., Profl. Dialogue Engrs. Republican. Mormon. Clubs: Elks, Knife and Fork. Contbr. articles in field to profl. jours. and instructional manuals. Home: 31376 N Dome Dr Coarsegold CA 93614 Office: RB Box 2445 Coarsegold CA 93614

SINGLETON, LINDA MARIE, magazine editor; b. Shelton, Wash., Jan. 8, 1946; d. Chester Lyle and Gladys Martha (Wild) S. B.A. in Advt. and Home Econs., San Jose State U., 1969, postgrad., 1969; postgrad. U. Hawaii, 1964. Merchandising rep. Sunset mag., Menlo Park, Calif., 1969-73, editor, 1973—. Named to Writers Hall of Fame, So. Furniture Market, 1983. Mem. Nat. Home Fashions League, Nat. Assn. Female Execs. Office: Sunset Mag Co 80 Willow Rd Menlo Park CA 94025

SINKS, KENNETH DENZIL, JR., chem. engr., oil refinery exec.; b. St. Louis, Dec. 11, 1942; s. Kenneth Denzil and Thelma Elizabeth (Newbanks) S.; B.E.S. in Chem. Engring., Brigham Young U., 1970; m. Sandra Kay Nowland, Aug. 5, 1966; children—Wendy, Jeffrey Todd, Gregory Michael, Amy, Brent Justin. Jr. engr. Mobil Oil Corp., Torrance, Calif., 1970-71, engr., 1971-72, asst. sr. engr., 1972; supr. environ. surveillance Bridge River Ranch Co., Malta, Idaho, 1972-74, gen. mgr. farm and dairy replacement heifer op., 1974-75; mgr. ops. and maintenance Northland Oil & Refining Co., 1975-77; area supt. Coastal States Petrochem. Co., Corpus Christi, 1977-78; gen. mgr. Plateau Inc., Roosevelt Refinery, 1978-79, Bloomfield (N.Mex.) Refinery, 1979-82; exec. v.p. Tijan Energy Engring., Inc., 1982—; bd. dirs. Rocky Mountain Ethanol Systems. Chmn. Utah Pvt. Industry Council, 1979; unit commr. Anazaza Dist., Boy Scouts Am. Served with USAF, 1961-65. Registered profl. engr., N.D., W.Va., Tex., N.Mex. Mem. Am. Inst. Chem. Engrs. (profl. devel. recognition cert.), Nat. Soc. Profl. Engrs. Republican. Mormon. chem. engr., oil refinery exec.; b. St. Louis, Dec. 11, 1942; s. Kenneth Denzil and Thelma Elizabeth (Newbanks) S.; B.E.S. in Chem. Engring., Brigham Young U., 1970; m. Sandra Kay Nowland, Aug. 5, 1966; children—Wendy, Jeffrey Todd, Gregory Michael, Amy, Brent Justin. Jr. engr. Mobil Oil Corp., Torrance, Calif., 1970-71, engr., 1971-72, asst. sr. engr., 1972; supr. environ. surveillance Bridge River Ranch Co., Malta, Idaho, 1972-74, gen. mgr. farm and dairy replacement heifer op., 1974-75; mgr. ops. and maintenance Northland Oil & Refining Co., 1975-77; area supt. Coastal States Petrochem. Co., Corpus Christi, 1977-78; gen. mgr. Plateau Inc., Roosevelt Refinery, 1978-79, Bloomfield (N.Mex.) Refinery, 1979-82; exec. v.p. Tijan Energy Engring., Inc., 1982—; bd. dirs. Rocky Mountain Ethanol Systems. Chmn. Utah Pvt. Industry Council, 1979; unit commr. Anazaza Dist., Boy Scouts Am. Served with USAF, 1961-65. Registered profl. engr., N.D., W.Va., Tex., N.Mex. Mem. Am. Inst. Chem. Engrs. (profl. devel. recognition cert.), Nat. Soc. Profl. Engrs. Republican. Mormon. Home: 1606 Kenwood Circle Farmington NM 87401 Office: PO Box 159 Bloomfield NM 87413

SINTON, NELL W(ALTER), artist, educator; b. San Francisco, June 4, 1910; d. John I. and Florence (Schwartz) Walter; m. Stanley Henry Sinton, Jr., June 15, 1930 (div.); children—Margot Sinton Biestman, Joan Sinton Dodd, John W. Student San Francisco Art Inst., 1926-68, 38-40, Sonoma State Coll., 1971-72. Painter; solo shows include: San Francisco Mus. Modern Art, 1970, Oakland Mus., 1976, Mills Coll. 30 yr. retrospectivce, 1981; participant exhbns. mus. and galleries, N.Y.C., San Francisco, Boston, Los Angeles, 1948—; rep. Braunstein Gallery, San Francisco; guest artist, lectr. Smith Coll., U. Mass., 1975, U. Calif., Berkeley, 1973-75, La. State U., 1976, U. Ill., 1978, workshops in Hawaii, 1978, 82; instr. San Francisco Art Inst., 1970-72; instr. painting and drawing Coll. of Marin, Kentfield, Calif., 1981—; instr. painting, Inst. of Creative and Artistic Devel., Oakland, Calif.; painter mem. San Francisco City and County Art Commn., 1958-63. Mem. San Francisco Art Inst. (artist).

SIPE, GEORGE EMERY, IV, interior designer; b. Kansas City, Mo., Apr. 13, 1950; s. George Emery and Mary Patricia (Southwick) S. Student U. Ariz., 1968-70; B.A. with honors cum laude in English, Pa. State U., 1972; postgrad. U. Calif.-Berkeley, 1979-83. Adminstrv. asst. personnel dept. Hughes Aircraft, Tucson, 1974-76; asst. to pres. The Good Guys Stereo, San Francisco, 1976-78; acct., asst. mgr. Landsberg/Tarrant Inc., San Francisco, 1978-79; personnel adminstr. Davis, Skaggs & Co., San Francisco, 1979-80; showroom mgr. The Showcase Compendium, San Francisco, 1980—; intern Orsborn Pub. Relations Group, San Francisco, 1980. Pres., bd. dirs. Showplace Sq. Tenants Assn., San Francisco, 1982—; bd. dirs. Showplace Sq. Area Assn., 1982—. Mem. Golden Gate Bus. Assn., Nat. Hist. Preservation Soc. Republican. Episcopalian. Office: 195 Rhode Island San Francisco CA 94103

SIPES, DONALD, motion picture company executive; b. 1928; B.A, Ohio U., 1948; LL.B., Harvard U., 1951; married. Admitted to bar; asso. law firm, N.Y.C, 1953-57; atty., legal and bus. affairs NBC, 1957-61; agt. Frank Cooper Agy., 1961-63; v.p. bus. affairs and planning CBS, 1963-74; sr. exec. v.p. ICM, 1974-75; with MCA Inc., Universal City, Calif., 1975-81, v.p. Universal TV Co., 1975-76, sr. v.p., 1976-77, corp. v.p. and exec. v.p. Universal TV, 1977-78, pres. Universal TV, 1978-81, v.p. MCA Inc., 1981; pres., chief operating officer Metro-Goldwyn-Mayer Film Co., 1981—. Served with U.S. Army, 1951-53. Office: MGM Film Co 10202 W Washington Blvd Culver City CA 90230

SIRATOVICH, THOMAS A., association executive; b. Chgo., Jan. 24, 1940; s. Felix and Frances (Tauras) S.; m. Valerie E. Starke, Jan. 27, 1973; children—Alexandra, Paul. B.A., U. Colo., 1961; J.D., U. Wis., 1964. Bar: Wis. 1964. Spl. agt. FBI, 1964-67; with Mountain States Employers Council, Denver, 1967—, labor relations exec., 1967-81, dir. mgmt. devel., 1982—. Bd. dirs., sec. Big Bros., Inc. Denver. Mem. Am. Soc. Tng. and Devel., State Bar Wis. Home: 562 Gilpin St Denver CO 80218 Office: PO Box 539 Denver CO 80201

SIRIANNI, STEPHEN JOHN, lawyer; b. Rice Lake, Wis., May 26, 1950; s. Fred Anthony and Jean Marie Bergeron S.; m. Kathleen Donellan, June 6, 1973; children—Andrew Bergsron, Charles Donellan. A.B. cum laude, Georgetown U., 1972; J.D. cum laude, Harvard U., 1976. Bar: Wash. 1976. Instr. pub. speaking George Washington U., Washington, 1973; assoc. dir. debate Boston U., 1974-76; assoc. Bogle & Gates, Seattle, 1976-78; asst. prof. law Mercer Law Sch., Macon, Ga., 1978-80; ptnr. Murphy, Jerge & Sirianni, Seattle, 1981—. Mem. Am. Bar Assn., Wash. State Bar Assn. Home: 6020 86th Ave SE Mercer Island WA 98040 Office: Suite 1616 1111 3d Ave Bldg Seattle WA 98101

SISSON, JILL B(ARTLETT) W(OODMAN), lawyer; b. Waterville, N.Y., Nov. 24, 1967; d. Richard Sage and Mildren Louise (Bartlett) Woodman; m. Gary Reade Sisson, July 8, 1972. B.A., Middlebury Coll., 1969; J.D., U. Colo., 1974. Bar: Colo. 1974. Assoc., Hindry & Meyer, Denver, 1974, Roath & Brega, Denver, 1975-77, Atler, Zall & Haligman, P.C., Denver, 1977-80; prin. Constantine & Prochnow, P.C., Englewood, Colo., 1980—; speaker Women in Bus. Conf., 1979-80, Women's Sch. Network, Preretirement Inst. Bd. dirs. Denver Ear Inst.; active Soroptimist Internat. Mem. ABA (corp. banking, bus. law com.), Colo. Bar. Assn., Denver Bar Assn. (securities subcom.), Arapahoe County Bar Assn., Order of Coif. Editor Colo. Lawyer-Bus. Law Newsletter, 1980—.

SISTI, FRANK PHILLIP, mktg. co. exec.; b. Trenton, Feb. 1, 1935; s. Nicholas Francis and Alice Wood (Nichol) S.; B.A. in Edn., U. Calif., Santa Cruz, 1972; m. Antonia Verleye, Feb. 12, 1977; 1 son, Nicholas Francis. Sales exec. Blake, Moffitt & Towne, San Francisco, 1961; mktg. exec. Carpenter Offutt Inc., San Francisco, 1976-78; pres. Sandpiper Mktg. Corp., Redwood City, Calif., 1978—. Recipient Governors award Internat. Assn. Printing House Craftsmen, 1975. Mem. Nat. Assn. Corp. Dirs., Graphic Arts Tech. Found., Printing Industries No. Calif., Pacific Soc. Printing House Craftsmen. Republican. Author articles graphics and printing; contbg. editor Printing Jour., 1973—. Office: 2401 Charleston Rd Mountain View CA 94043

SIVEY, CHERYL COLVIN, communication company executive; b. Grand Island, Nebr., May 4, 1951; d. Lindsey B. and Margaret Jane (Maybury) Colvin; m. Michael E. Sivey, Mar. 6, 1977 (div.). B.S., U. Nebr., 1973; postgrad. Regis Coll., Denver, 1981—. Tchr. lang. arts and history Omaha Pub. Schs., 1973-76; asst. office mgr. Morton Meats, Inc., Omaha, 1976-77; mgmt. trainee Western Electric Co., Aurora, Colo., 1977-79, sect. chief drafting and reprodn. dept., 1979-83, sales account analyst, Englewood, Colo., 1983—. Bd. dirs. local units ARC, Am. Diabetes Assn.; chmn. Mile High Youth Services Com. Mem. Nat. Assn. Female Execs., Delta Delta Delta. Office: 7030 S Yosemite St Dept 705600 Englewood CO 80110

SKAGGS, L. S., supermarket chain executive; b. 1923; married. With Am. Stores Co., 1945—, pres. Skaggs Cos. Inc., subs., 1950-66, chmn. bd., chief exec. officer, then chmn. bd., pres., chief exec. officer, now chmn. bd., chief exec. officer Am. Stores Co., Salt Lake City, also dir. Office: Am Stores Co PO Box 27447 Salt Lake City UT 84127*

SKAGGS, SANFORD MERLE, lawyer; b. Berkeley, Calif., Oct. 24, 1939; s. Sherman G. and Barbara Jewel (Stinson) S.; B.A., U. Calif., Berkeley, 1961, J.D., 1964; m. Sharon Ann Barnes, Sept. 3, 1976; children—Stephen, Paula, Barbara, Darren. Admitted to Calif. bar, 1965; atty. Pacific Gas and Electric Co., San Francisco, 1964-73; gen. counsel Pacific Gas Transmission Co., San Francisco, 1973-75; partner law firm Van Voorhis & Skaggs, Walnut Creek, Calif., 1975—; dir. Security Nat. Bank, Walnut Creek, 1975-81. Bd. dirs. Alexander Lindsay Jr. Mus., 1972—, Diablo-Rossmoor Found., 1976—; councilman Walnut Creek, 1972-78, mayor, 1974-75, 1976-77; dir. East Bay Mcpl. Utility Dist., 1978—; trustee Alpha Delta Phi Meml. Found., 1974-80; exec. bd. Boy Scouts Am., Mt. Diablo Council, 1978-80. Mem. Calif. State Bar Assn., Contra Costa County Bar Assn., Fed. Energy Bar Assn., Calif. Trial Lawyers Assn., Alpha Delta Phi, Phi Delta Phi. Republican. Club: World Trade. Home: 2102 Wilmington Dr Walnut Creek CA 94596 Office: Van Voorhis & Skaggs 1855 Olympic Blvd Suite 111 Walnut Creek CA 94596

SKALAGARD, HANS MARTIN, artist; b. Skuo, Faroe Islands, Feb. 7, 1924; s. Ole Johannes and Hanna Elisa (Fredriksen) S.; came to U.S., 1942, naturalized, 1955; pupil Anton Otto Fisher, 1947; m. Mignon Diana Haack Haegland, Mar. 31, 1955; 1 dau., Karen Solveig Sikes. Joined U.S. Mcht. Marine, 1942, advanced through grades to chief mate, 1945, ret., 1965; owner, operator Skaalegaard Sq., Rigger Art Gallery, Carmel, 1966—; librarian Mayo Hays O'Donnel Library, Monterey, Calif., 1971-73; painter U.S. Naval Heritage series, 1973—; exhibited in numerous one-man shows including Palace Legion of Honor, San Francisco, 1960, J.F. Howland, 1963-65, Fairmont Hotel, San Francisco, 1963, Galerie de Tours, 1969, 72-73, Pebble Beach Gallery, 1968, Laguna Beach (Calif.) Gallery, 1969, Arden Gallery, Atlanta, 1970, Gilbert Gallery, San Francisco; group shows: Am. Artists, Eugene, Oreg., Robert Louis Stevenson Exhibit, Carmel Valley Gallery, Biarritz and Paris, France, David Findley Galleries, N.Y.C. and Faroe Island, Europe, numerous others; represented in permanent collections; Naval Post Grad. Sch. and Library, Allen Knight Maritime Mus., Salvation Army Bldg., Monterey, Calif., Robert Louis Stevenson Sch., Pebble Beach; lectr. Bd. dirs. Allen Knight Maritime Mus., 1973—, mem. adv. and acquisition coms., 1973-77. Recipient Silver medal Tommaso Campanella Internat. Acad. Arts, Letters and Scis., Rome, 1970, Gold medal, 1972; Gold medal and hon. life membership Academia Italia dell Arti e del Honoro, 1980; Gold medal for artistic merit Academia d'Italia. Mem. Navy League (dir. Monterey), Internat. Platform Assn., Sons of Norway (cultural dir. 1974-75, 76-77). Subject of cover and article Palette Talk, 1980, Compass mag., 1980. Home: 25197 Canyon Dr Carmel CA 93923 Office: PO Box 6611 Carmel CA 93921 also Dolores at 5th St Carmel CA 93921

SKALSKY, JUDITH A., communications executive; b. Cedar Rapids, Iowa, Jan. 31, 1943; d. Milton H. and Rose E. (Turecek) S. B.A., U. Iowa, 1965; M.A., Rutgers U., 1966. Press sec. to congressman, Washington; pub. affairs dir. Calif. Constn. Revision Commn., San Francisco; exec. asst. to chmn. Gt. Western United, Denver, N.Y.C.; spl. asst. to mayor N.Y.C.; mng. dir. Vignelli Assocs., N.Y.C.; corp. dir. pub. relations Bloomingdale's, N.Y.C., Robinson's, Los Angeles; v.p. corp. div. Mahoney/Wasserman, pub. relations, Los Angeles; pres. Scanlon, Skalsky & Menken. Vice pres. pub. relations architecture and design support group Mus. Contemporary Art, Los Angeles; bd. dirs. Innovative Design Fund; pub. speaker. Mem. Los Angeles Advt. Club, Pub. Relations Soc. Am. Office: Scanlon Skalsky & Menken 635 Westbourne Dr Los Angeles CA 90069

SKANNES, GEORGIA CAROL, public relations officer; b. Sitka, Alaska, May 20, 1950; d. George and Rose Mae (Daine) S.; m. Steven Lee Rhyner, Jan. 19, 1973 (div.); children—Richard Dapcevich, Steven Dapcevich, Nicole Rhyner. Student U. Alaska, 1975. Traffic mgr. Sitka Broadcasting, 1977; title III/fed. relations staff Sheldon Jackson Coll., Sitka, 1977-78; ptnr. Huckleberry House, Sitka, 1978-79; communications coordinator S.E. Alaska Regional Arts Council, Inc., Sitka, 1979-80; pub. relations officer Ketchikan (Alaska) Indian Corp., 1980—; coordinator S.E. Alaska Village Assn. of Presidents, 1981—; participant Alaska Native Leadership Project, 1982-83. Appointee, Sitka Community Action Group, Sitka Assembly, 1979. Named Woman of Yr., Bus. and Profl. Women, 1979. Mem. Pub. Relations Soc. Am., Nat. Congress Am. Indians, Ketchikan C. of C. Democrat. Club: Soroptomists (Ketchikan). Home: 3711 Baranof St Ketchikan AK 99901 Office: Ketchikan Indian Corp PO Box 6855 Ketchikan AK 99901

SKATOFF, ELIZABETH (BETTY) LORETTA, marketing communications manager; b. Los Angeles, Nov. 24, 1946; d. Walter and Edith Backer, Spatz; m. Michael W. Skatoff, June 21, 1970 (div.). B.A. in Psychology, UCLA, 1968; M.B.A., U. Colo., 1983. Researcher City of Los Angeles, 1968-70; dir. personnel Witkin Homes, Denver, 1972-73; mgr. mktg. services Lear Siegler, Denver, 1974-78; mgr. mktg. communications Auto-Trol Technology Corp., 1978—. Mem. MENSA, Phi Beta Kappa. Office: Auto-Trol Technology Corp 12500 N Washington Denver CO 80233

SKEEN, JOSEPH RICHARD, congressman; b. Roswell, N.Mex., June 30, 1927; s. Thomas Dudley and Ilah (Adamson) S.; B.S. in Agrl. Engring., Tex. A&M U., 1950; m. Mary Helen Jones, Nov. 17, 1945; children—Mary Elisa, Mikell Lee. Soil and water engr. Ramah Navajo and Zuni Indians, 1951; owner, operator Buckhorn Ranch, Picacho, N.Mex., 1951—; mem. N.Mex. State Senate, 1960-70; mem. 97th Congress from 2d N.Mex. Dist. Chmn., N.Mex. Republican party, 1963-66. Served with USN, 1945-46, USAFR, 1949-52. Mem. Nat. Cattle Growers Assn., Nat. Woolgrowers Assn., N.Mex. Woolgrowers Assn., N.Mex. Cattle Growers Assn., N.Mex. Farm and Livestock Bur. Republican. Roman Catholic. Clubs: Elks, Eagles. Home: PO Box 67 Picacho NM 88343 Office: 15 08 Longworth House Office Bldg Washington DC 20515

SKEWES-COX, BENNET, acct., educator; b. Valparaiso, Chile, Dec. 12, 1918; came to U.S., 1919, naturalized, 1943; s. Vernon and Edith Page (Smith) S.-C.; B.A., U. Calif., Berkeley, 1940; M.A., Georgetown U., 1947; B.B.A., Golden Gate Coll., 1953; m. Mary Osborne Craig, Aug. 31, 1946; children—Anita Page, Pamela Skewes-Cox Anderson, Amy Osborne. Asst. to press officer Am. Embassy, Santiago, Chile, 1941-43; state exec. dir. United World Federalists of Calif., 1948-50; pvt. practice acctg., San Francisco, 1953—; asst. prof. internat. relations San Francisco State U., 1960-62; grad. researcher Stanford (Calif.) U., 1962-63, Georgetown U., Washington, 1963-65; pres. Acad. World Studies, San Francisco, 1969—; sec. Alpha Delta Phi Bldg. Co., San Francisco, 1957—; lectr. in field. Mem. Democratic state central com. Calif., 1958-60, fgn. policy chmn. Calif. Dem. Council, 1959-61, treas. Marin County Dem. Central Com., 1956-62; founder, 1st. chmn. Calif. Council for UN Univ., 1976—; bd. dirs. Research on Abolition of War; treas. Marin Citizens for Energy Planning. Served as lt. (j.g.), USNR, 1943-46. Mem. Assn. for World Edn. (internat. council 1975—), Am. Soc. Internat. Law, Am. Polit. Sci. Assn., San Francisco Com. Fgn. Relations, Am. Acctg. Assn., Calif. State Univ. Profs., AAUP, Nat. Soc. Public Accts., Fedn. Am. Scientists, UN Assn., Internat. Polit. Sci. Assn. World Federalists Assn. (nat. bd. dirs.). Clubs: University, Commonwealth of Calif., Lagunitas Country. Author: The Manifold Meanings of Peace, 1964; The United Nations from League to Government, 1965; Peace, Truce or War, 1967. Home: Monte Alegre PO Box 1145 Ross CA 94957 Office: Acad World Studies 2820 Van Ness Ave San Francisco CA 94109

SKIDMORE, JOYCE FOX, public relations/communications firm executive; b. Murray, Utah, Dec. 30, 1926; d. Rolla Arden and Alice Luetta (Fox) Thorum; m. E. Douglas Jacobsen, Mar. 20, 1956 (dec.); 1 son, Kelly Douglas Jacobsen; m. 2d, Clarence E. Skidmore, Aug. 9, 1969. B.S., U. Utah, 1950, postgrad., 1953-55; postgrad. U. So. Calif., 1964, U. Calif.-Irvine, 1973-74. Sales and promotion devel. JBL Internat., Los Angeles, 1959-69. Adminstrv. asst. world hdqrs. Toastmasters Internat., Santa Ana, Calif., 1973; adj. prof. communications Pepperdine U., 1974, developer human resources, Oran, Algeria, 1975; promotions coordinator Utah Bicentennial Project, Salt Lake City, 1976; editor Saga Weekly Post, and editor Children's Page, Stavanger and Bergen, Norway, 1976-78; press. sec. Utah Auditor's Office, Salt Lake City, 1979-81; pres. Joyce Skidmore Cons./Snowflake Prodns., pub. relations, communications and devel. in arts, bus., edn. and govt., Sandy, Utah, 1980—; Utah dir. Nat. Health Screening Council for Vol. Orgns., 1982—; adj. prof. Westminster Coll., 1978-79, Brigham Young U., 1978-83; cons. pub. relations, health costs and tourism C. of C. of Salt Lake Area; guest dir. Westminster Theatre, 1974; guest dir./writer Cablevision, Newport Beach, Calif., 1975; organizer Stavanger Threatre Guild and Workshops, 1977; mem. steering com. for first nat. competition Utah Playwriting Conf., Sundance, 1979-80. Dist. pres. LWV, 1976; initiated invitation from Bergen Internat. Festival to Utah Symphony, 1981; campaign mgr. Mayor Lake Valley City (Utah), 1982; cons. Cottonwood Heights (Utah) Council, 1982-83; cons. to Utah pres. Instrumentation Soc. Am.; missionary leader Ch. of Jesus Christ of Latter-day Saints. Recipient 2 Top Editor's awards Calif. Press Women, 1977, 4 writing awards 1977-78; Internat. Yr. of Child award Family Acad., San Francisco and Stavanger, 1979; nat. Zeta Phi Eta scholar, 1948; U. Utah fellow, 1953-55; So. Calif. Credit Assn. scholar, 1964. Mem. Pub. Relations soc. Am. (student adv. 1980-82), Utah Press Women (6 writing awards 1979-81; 3d v.p. 1981-82), Instrument Soc. Am., Friendship Force Utah, MMB Reading Arts Soc. (v.p. devel.). Author: Happy Holidays, 1968; contbr. articles to Calif., Norwegian and Utah newspapers, 1973-83; newsletter editor Nat. Auditor's Assn., 1979-81, State Auditor's Assn., 1979-81, Utah Health Fairs, 1982-83; initiated use of old copper from Utah Capitol dome as collector's item, 1980. Home and Office: 2629 Oak Creek Dr Sandy UT 84092

SKIDMORE, MAX JOSEPH, political scientists, educational administrator, author, consultant; b. Springfield, Mo., Dec. 25, 1933; s. Joseph Franklin and Gladys Irene (Watt) S.; m. Charlene Alberta Hartman, June 20, 1976; children—Calvin Campbell, Max Joseph, Jr., Tricia Marie. B.S. in Music, B.S. in Edn., S.W. Mo. State U., 1956; M.Ed., U. Mo., 1956; Ph.D., U. Minn., 1964. Supt. schs., Climax Springs, Mo., 1956-57; mgmt. positions HEW, Washington, 1959-65; dir. Am. studies, assoc. prof. polit. sci. U. Ala., 1965-68; prof., dept. head S.W. Mo. State U., 1968-82; dir. Am. Studies Research Ctr., Hyderabad, India, 1978-79; dean Coll. Liberal Arts and Scis., Eastern N.Mex. U., Portales, 1982—; cons.; Fulbright lectr., India, 1978-79. Mem. Am. Polit. Sci. Assn., Am. Council Acad. Deans, Mid-Continent Am. Studies Assn. (pres. 1976-77), Western Polit. Sci. Assn., Pi Sigma Alpha, Phi Delta Kappa, Phi Kappa Phi. Democrat. Unitarian. Author: Medicare and the American Rhetoric of Reconciliation, 1970; Word Politics: Essays on Language and Politics, 1972; (with Marshall Carter Wanke) American Government, 1974, 77, 81; American Political Thought, 1978; (with J. Barnes and M. Carter) The World of Politics, 1980; mem. editorial bd. Am. Studies. Home: 516 S Ave B Portales NM 88130 Office: Coll Liberal Arts & Scis Eastern N Mex U Portales NM 88130

SKIFF, RUSSELL ALTON, plastic co. exec.; b. Waterford, Pa., Feb. 26, 1927; s. Albert Alton and Leah Gladys (Allen) S.; B.S., U. Pitts., 1950; m. Dolores Theresa Molnar, June 25, 1950; children—Russell James, Sandra Lee, Eric Alan, Rebecca Lynn. Metall. chemist Jones & Laughlin Steel Co., Alliquippa, Pa., 1950-51; research and devel. chemist Gen. Electric Co., Erie, Pa., 1951-57; mgr. tech. sales and plant operation Hysol Corp. of Calif., El Monte, 1957-60; sr. research engr. autonetics div. N.Am. Aviation, Downey, Calif., 1960-62; pres. Delta Plastics Co., Visalia, Calif., 1962—. Served with USAAF, 1944-46. Mem. Constrn. Specifications Inst. Republican. Presbyterian. Club: Lions (dir.). Contbr. articles to profl. jours. Home: 26525 Mulanax Dr Visalia CA 93277 Office: 7449 Ave 304 Visalia CA 93277

SKILLERN, GARY DEAN, national guard supervisor; b. Long Beach, Calif., Mar. 21, 1943; s. Robert Earl and Ruby (Page) S.; student Community Coll. Air Force, 1979—, Laramie County Community Coll., 1981—; m. Karen Renee Lahiff, July 2, 1962; children—Gardner Dean, Lisa Renee. Enlisted Wyo. Air Nat. Guard, 1960, advanced through grades to sr. master sgt., 1978, air ops. supr., Cheyenne, Wyo., 1961-63, aircraft loadmaster instr., 1963-72, aerial port loadmaster supt., 1972-80, aerial port supr., 1980—. Home: 342 Bocage Dr Cheyenne WY 82009 Office: PO Box 2268 Cheyenne WY 82003

SKILLICORN, BRIAN, elec. engr.; b. Liverpool, Eng., Feb. 22, 1931; came to U.S., 1959; s. Harold Herbert and Emma Lilian (Sayle) S.; B.Engring., U. Liverpool, 1952; m. Edna Muriel Howard, Sept. 4, 1958; children—Joan Louise, Margaret Ruth. Research engr. Met.-Vickers Elec. Co., Manchester, Eng., 1954-58; microwave tube engr. Canadian Marconi Co., Montreal, Que., 1958-59; project engr., dept. head High Voltage Engring. Corp., Burlington, Mass., 1959-69; founder, v.p. Deltaray Corp., Woburn, Mass., 1969-74; v.p., ops. mgr. Deltaray div. High Voltage Engring. Corp., 1974-78; head power conversion sect. Watkins-Johnson Co., Palo Alto, Calif., 1978-80; mgr. X-ray tube div. Kevex Corp., Scotts Valley, Calif., 1980—. Recipient I.R. 100 award, 1977. Patentee high voltage power supplies, high voltage shunt reactors and electron accelerators. Office: PO Box 66860 Scotts Valley CA 95066

SKINNER, DAVID LEE, astronautical engineer; b. Indpls., Dec. 12, 1953; s. Paul William and Dorothy Louise (Swain) S.; m. Deana Jo Brower, May 18, 1974 (div.); 1 dau., Heather Elaine. B.S., Purdue U., 1977; M.S., Calif. Inst. Tech., 1979. With NASA Jet Propulsion Lab., Pasadena, Calif., 1973—, astronautical engr., 1977—. Trustee World Space Found., South Pasadena, 1979—. Mem. AIAA, Soc. Allied Weight Engrs., Brit. Interplanetary Soc., Tau Beta Pi, Sigma Gamma Tau, Phi Kappa Phi. Contbr. sect. to Illus. Ency. Space Tech., 1981. Home: 7763 Day St Tujunga CA 91042 Office: 156-229 NASA Jet Propulsion Lab 4800 Oak Grove Dr Pasadena CA 91109

SKINNER, STANLEY THAYER, utility co. exec., lawyer; b. Fort Smith, Ark., Aug. 18, 1937; s. John Willard and Irma Lee (Peters) S.; B.A. with honors, San Diego State U., 1960; M.A., U. Calif.-Berkeley, 1961. J.D., 1964; m. Margaret Olsen, Aug. 16, 1957; children—Steven Kent, Ronald Kevin. Bar: Calif. 1965, U.S. Ct. Appeals (9th cir.) 1965, U.S. Ct. Appeals (10th cir.) 1966. Atty. Pacific Gas and Electric Co., San Francisco, 1964-73, sr. counsel, 1973, treas., 1974-76, v.p. fin., 1976, sr. v.p., 1977, exec. v.p., 1978—; dir. Pacific Gas Transmission Co., Nuclear Mut. Ltd., Natural Gas Corp. Calif., Calaska Energy Co., Eureka Energy Co., Alta. and So. Gas. Co. Ltd. Founding dir., pres. Friends of the Moraga Library, Inc., 1972; bd. dirs., trustee United Way of Bay Area; trustee Golden Gate U.; mem. exec. bd. San Francisco Bay Area council Boy Scouts Am. Mem. Calif. State Bar Assn., Fin. Officers No. Calif., Pacific Coast Elec. Assn., Pacific Coast Gas Assn. Republican. Presbyterian. Clubs: Bankers, Commonwealth. Office: 77 Beale St San Francisco CA 94106

SKIPP, BETTY ANN LINDBERG, geologist; b. Chgo., May 7, 1928; d. Hugo L. and Jacqueline Elizabeth (Orth) Lindberg; B.S., Northwestern U., 1949; M.A., U. Colo., 1956, postgrad., 1980—; m. James Merle Skipp, Sept. 15, 1951 (div. Feb. 1968); children—Gary Lindberg, Jacquelyn Ann. Tech. illustrator Northwestern U., Evanston, Ill., 1949-50; tech. asst. Pure Oil Co., Chgo., 1950-51; geol. field asst. U.S. Geol. Survey, Denver, 1952-54, geologist, Central Gen. Geology br., Denver, 1955—; guest lectr. in micropaleontoloy at univs., 1965-67. Bd. dirs. Boulder Philharm. Orch., 1963-65, mem., 1959—; mem. Westminster (Colo.) Woodwinds, 1967-71, Boulder Concert Band, 1977—; pres. Unitarian-Universalist Ch. Boulder, 1976-77. Served to 1st lt. USMC, 1949-58. Fellow Geol. Soc. Am.; mem. Soc. Econ. Paleontologists and Mineralogists (group chmn. 1980-81), Rocky Mountain Assn. Geologists, Colo. Sci. Soc., Paleontol. Research Assn., Phi Beta Kappa, Sigma Xi. Research in field, including geol. mapping. Contbr. articles to profl. jours. Home: 2035 Grape Ave Boulder CO 80302 Office: PO Box 25046 MS 913 Fed Center Denver CO 80225

SKIPPER, JAMES WILLIAM, contractor; b. Daingerfield, Tex., June 27, 1935; s. William Otis and Annie Fosque (Walters) S.; m. Norma Jean Niblett, Oct. 1, 1954; children—Dennis Paul, Diane Elaine. Projects mgr. Johnson Controls, Los Angeles, 1960-70; pres. Skipper & Co., Midway City, Calif., 1970—. Mem. Plumbing and Piping Industry Council. Baptist. Clubs: Masons, Shriners, Elks. Home: 5292 Vineland Dr Huntington Beach CA 92649 Office: 8271 Bolsa Ave Midway City CA 92655

SKOGEBO, PAUL RONALD, recreational vehicle co. exec.; b. Owatonna, Minn., Nov. 9, 1937; s. Elmer Leonard and Mabel Ophelia (Fossan) S.; student pub. schs., Albert Lea, Minn.; m. Janice Nora Joosten, Mar. 20, 1966; children—Julie, David. Mgr., R. Crist & Co., Mesa, Ariz., 1965-68, v.p., 1968-74, pres., chief exec. officer, 1974—, dir., 1968—. Mem. Recreational Vehicle Dealers Am., Holiday Rambler Dealer Adv. Bd. Republican. Lutheran. Clubs: Mesa Country, Elks. Home: 1727 Fairfield St Mesa AZ 85203 Office: 2025 E Main St Mesa AZ 85203

SKOOG, WILLIAM ARTHUR, oncologist; b. Culver City, Calif., Apr. 10, 1925; s. John Lundeen and Allis Rose (Gatz) S.; A.A., UCLA, 1944; B.A. with gt. distinction, Stanford U., 1946, M.D., 1949; m. Ann Douglas, Sept. 17, 1949; children—Karen, William Arthur, James Douglas, Allison. Intern medicine Stanford Hosp., San Francisco, 1948-49, asst. resident medicine, 1949-50; asst. resident medicine N.Y. Hosp., N.Y.C., 1950-51; sr. resident medicine Wadsworth VA Hosp., Los Angeles, 1951, attending specialist internal medicine, 1962-68; practice medicine specializing in internal medicine, Los Altos, Calif., 1959-61; pvt. practice hematology and oncology Calif. Oncologic and Surg. Med. Group, Inc., Santa Monica, Calif., 1971-72; pvt. practice med. oncology, San Bernardino, Calif., 1972—; assoc. staff Palo Alto-Stanford (Calif.) Hosp. Center, 1959-61, U. Calif. Med. Center, San Francisco, 1959-61; asso. attending physician U. Calif. at Los Angeles Hosp. and Clinics, 1961-78; vis. physician internal medicine Harbor Gen. Hosp., Torrance, Calif., 1962-65, attending physician, 1965-71; cons. chemistry Clin. Lab., UCLA Hosp., 1963-68; affiliate cons. staff St. John's Hosp., Santa Monica, Calif., 1967-71, courtesy staff, 1971-72; courtesy attending med. staff Santa Monica Hosp., 1967-72; staff physician St. Bernardino (Calif.) Hosp., 1972—, San Bernardino Community Hosp., 1972—; chief sect. oncology San Bernardino County Hosp., 1972-76; cons. staff Redlands (Calif.) Community Hosp., 1972—; asst. in medicine Cornell Med. Coll., N.Y.C., 1950-51; jr. research physician UCLA Atomic Energy Project, 1954-55; instr. medicine, asst. research physician dept. medicine UCLA Med. Center, 1955-56, asst. prof. medicine, asst. research physician, 1956-59; clin. asso. hematology VA Center, Los Angeles, 1956-59; co-dir. metabolic research unit UCLA Center for Health Scis., 1955-59, 61-65; co-dir. Health Scis. Clin. Research Center, 1965-68, dir., 1968-72; clin. instr. medicine Stanford, 1959-61; asst. clin. prof. medicine, assoc. research physician U. Calif. Med. Center, San Francisco, 1959-61; lectr. medicine UCLA Sch. Medicine, 1961-62, assoc. prof. medicine, 1962-73, assoc. clin. prof. medicine, 1973—. Served with USNR, 1943-46, to lt. M.C., 1951-53. Fellow ACP; mem. Am., Calif. med. assns., So. Calif. Acad. Clin. Oncology, Western Soc. Clin. Research, Am. Fedn. Clin. Research, Los Angeles Acad. Medicine, San Bernardino County Med. Soc., Am. Soc. Clin. Oncology, Am. Soc. Internal Medicine, Calif. Soc. Internal Medicine, Inland Soc. Internal Medicine, Phi Beta Kappa, Alpha Omega Alpha, Sigma Xi, Alpha Kappa Kappa. Episcopalian (vestryman 1965-70). Clubs: Redlands Country, Redlands Swim and Tennis. Contbr. articles to profl. jours. Home: 30831 Miradero Dr Redlands CA 92373 Office: 399 E Highland Ave Suite 201 San Bernardino CA 92404

SKOPIL, OTTO RICHARD, JR., judge; b. Portland, Oreg., June 3, 1919; s. Otto Richard and Freda Martha (Boetticher) S.; B.A. in Econs., Willamette U., 1941, LL.B., J.D., 1946; m. Janet Rae Lundy, July 27, 1956; children—Otto Richard III, Casey Robert, Shannon Ida, Mollie Jo. Bar: Oreg. 1946. Ptnr., Williams, Skopil, Miller, Beck & Wyllie, and predecessors, Salem, Oreg., 1946-72; judge U.S. Dist. Ct., Portland, 1972-79, U.S. Ct. Appeals 9th Circuit, 1979—; mem. Jud. Conf. com. on adminstrn. of magistrates system; bd. dirs. Fed. Jud. Center. Bd. elders Mt. Park Ch., 1979-80; mem. Citizens Adv. Com., City of Salem, 1970-71; master of ceremonies various state and city Prayer Breakfasts; trustee Willamette U., 1969-72; bd. dirs. Willamette Valley council Camp Fire Girls, 1946-56. Served with USN, 1942-45. Mem. ABA, Oreg. Bar Assn., Marion County Bar Assn., Internat. Soc. Barristers, Maritime Law Assn., Am. Bd. Trial Advs., Am. Judicature Soc. Republican. Baptist. Clubs: Salem Exchange (pres. 1947); Illahe Hills Country (pres., dir. 1964-67). Office: Pioneer Courthouse Portland OR 97204*

SKOUSEN, MARK ANDREW, econ. and fin. writer; b. San Diego, Oct. 19, 1947; s. Leroy B. and Helen L. (McCarty) S.; B.A., Brigham Young U., 1971, M.S., 1972; Ph.D. in Econs., George Washington U., 1977; m. Jo Ann Foster, Apr. 19, 1973; children—Valerie, Timothy, Leslie Ann. Economist, CIA, 1972-74; editor in chief Personal Fin., 1974-79; editor in chief Forecasts & Strategies, Washington, 1980—, also cons. editor Personal Fin. and Tax Angles, 1979—; fin. cons.; speaker fin. and econ. confs.; books include: Playing the Price Controls Game, 1977; The Insider's Banking and Credit Almanac, 1977-80; Mark Skousen's Complete Guide to Financial Privacy, 1979, 82; the 100% Gold Standard, 1978; New Profits from Your Insurance Policy, 1980; High Finance on a Low Budget, 1981; Tax Free, 1982; Never Say Budget, 1983. Mem. Am. Econ. Assn. Mormon. Office: PO Box 611 Merrifield CA 22116

SKOUSEN, W. CLEON, institute administrator; b. Raymond, Alta., Can., Jan. 20, 1913; s. Royal Pratt and Rita (Bentley) S.; m. Jewel Pitcher, Aug. 13, 1936; children—David, Eric, Julianne, Sharon, Harold, Kathleen, Paul, Brent. J.D., George Washington U., 1941. Bar: D.C., U.S. Supreme Ct. Agt. FBI; chief of police City of Salt Lake City; prof. Brigham Young U.; pres., founder Freemen Inst., Salt Lake City. Del. Republican Nat. Conv., 1960, 68, 72. Recipient Gold Medal Honor award Freedom, Found., 1982. Republican. Mormon. Author 7 books. Office: 3740 West 1987 South Salt Lake City UT 84104

SKOUZES, FOTIOS DEMOSTHENES, computer software company executive; b. Washington, Mar. 14, 1955; s. Demosthenes Fotios and Vasiliki (Dedousis) S.; Kimberly Raven, Dec. 2, 1979. Student George Washington U., 1973-74; B.S. in Computer Sci., Am. U., 1974-77. Applications cons. The Computer Co., Washington, 1977-78, Boeing Computer Services, McLean, Va., 1978-79; systems engr. Informatics, Inc., McLean, 1979-80; dir. data processing, researcher Fuel and Mineral Resources, Reston, Va., 1980-81; project leader Software AG N.Am., Lakewood, Colo., 1981—; coop. edn. advisor Community Coll., Denver, Mem. Assn. Systems Mgmt. Republican. Greek Orthodox. Club: The Point (Lakewood). Contbr. articles to profl. jours. Office: Software AG of NAm 300 Union Blvd 5th Floor Lakewood CO 80228

SKYLSTAD, WILLIAM STEPHEN, bishop; b. Omak, Wash., Mar. 2, 1934; s. Stephen Martin and Reneldes Elizabeth (Danzl) S.; B.A., Pontifical Coll. Josephinum, Worthington, Ohio, 1956, postgrad., 1956-60; postgrad. Wash. State U., 1960-61; M.Ed., Gonzaga U., 1968. Ordained priest Roman Catholic Ch., 1960; asst. pastor Sacred Heart Parish, Pullman, Wash., 1960-61; tchr. Mater Cleri Sem., 1961-74, rector, prin., 1968-74; pastor Assumption Parish, Spokane, Wash., 1974-76; chancellor Diocese of Spokane, 1976-77; bishop of Yakima, Wash., 1977—. Office: PO Box 505 222 Washington Mutual Bldg Yakima WA 98907*

SLADE, SANDRA LYNN, interior designer, educator, consultant; b. Seattle, April 22, 1946; d. Erwin R. Slade, M.D. and Leona Martha (Mears) S.; 1 son, David Slade Privette. B.F.A., U. Wash., 1969, M.F.A. in Interior Design, 1977. Draftsman, designer Western Service & Supply Co. (now Westin Hotels, Inc.), Seattle, 1969-70; interior designer William L. Davis, Sons, Inc., Seattle, 1970-71; owner-designer Image West Inc., Boise, Idaho, 1971-76; asst. prof. interior architecture, U.

Idaho, Moscow, 1977-81; asst. prof. interior design Wash. State U., Pullman, 1981—, cons. cafeteria remodeling, 1982; design cons. Latah County (Idaho) Library, 1980, U. Idaho. Active LWV, ERA. Recipient design award Institution Mag., 1980. Mem. Am. Soc. Interior Designers (cert. 1976), Interior Design Educators Council (NW regional dir.), Environ. Design Research Assn., Alpha Chi Omega. Republican. Episcopalian. Writer course materials. Home: 719 S Lynn St Moscow ID 83843 Office: Coll Home Econs Interior Design Program White Hall Wash State U Pullman WA 99164

SLADEK, LYLE VIRGIL, mathematician, educator; b. Pukwana, S.D., Oct. 13, 1923; s. Charles Frank and Emma Margaret (Swanson) S.; B.S., S.D. State U., 1948; M.A., U. S.D., 1949; Stanford U., 1963; Ph.D., UCLA, 1970; m. Patricia Knotts, Sept. 12, 1948; children—Susan, Ann, Laura, Karen. Tchr. high sch. Mitchell, S.D., 1950-56; asst. prof. math. Black Hills (S.D.) State Coll., 1957-62; prof. math. Calif. Lutheran Coll., Thousand Oaks, 1963—, chmn. dept., 1965-78; lectr. Pres. congregation Our Savior's Lutheran Ch., Spearfish, S.D., 1961. Served with U.S. Army, 1943-46; PTO, ETO. Shell Merit fellow, summer 1956, NSF fellow, 1956-57, sci. faculty fellow, 1962-63. Recipient Meritorious Achievement award edn. S.D. Sch. Mines and Tech., 1957; Fulbright-Hays lectr., Bahamas, 1980-81. Mem. Nat. Council Tchrs. Maths., Math. Assn. Am. Blue Key, Pi Kappa Delta, Phi Delta Kappa. Home: 3243 Pioneer Ave Thousand Oaks CA 91360

SLAKEY, PHILIP BERNARD, engineering executive; b. Oakland, Calif., Apr. 30, 1937; s. Louis T. and Vivian M. (Torrey) S.; m. Diana Perkes, June 4, 1960; children—Douglas, Karen, Sheryl. B.S.C.E., U. Calif.-Berkeley, 1959. Diplomate Assn. Environ. Engrs.; registered profl. engr., Calif., Miss., Mass., Ind. Design engr. Stoddard & Karrer, Fresno, Calif., 1959-63; v.p. Frederiksen Engring. Inc., Oakland, Calif., 1963-70; v.p., chief engr. Indsl. Clean Air Inc., Berkeley, Calif., 1970-77; v.p., gen. mgr. DB Gas Cleaning Corp., Pleasant Hill, Calif., 1977—; cons. in air pollution control systems. Bd. dirs. Orinda Assn., 1973-75. Mem. ASCE, Am. Water Works Assn., Air Pollution Control Assn. Republican. Roman Catholic. Patentee in field. Home: 11 Cedar Ln Orinda CA 94563 Office: 3470 Buskirk Ave Pleasant Hill CA 94523

SLATE, DANIEL MICHAEL, economies educator; b. Los Angeles, Feb. 6, 1930; s. Robin Hill and Madeline Carolyn (Burchard) S.; B.S. in Psychology, U. Wash., 1952, M.A. in Econ. Analysis, 1956, Ph.D. in Polit. Economy, 1961; m. Mary Lou Eagan, June 14, 1952; children—Gregory S., Laurie D., Mary C.; m. 2d Margie Ruth Earnest, June 6, 1969. Statis. clk. U.S. Rubber Co., Seattle, 1949; psychiat. aide, psychologist Pinel Psychiat. Hosp., 1951-52; asst. exec. sec., mgr. Distbrs. Assn. Seattle Inc., 1954-55, 55-56; labor and research economist Wash. Employers, Inc., Seattle, 1956-57; asst. prof. dept. econs. and bus. U. Hawaii, Honolulu, 1957-61, assoc. prof. Coll. Bus. Administrn., 1962-63, acting dir. Econ. Research Ctr., 1959-60, dir. Bur. Bus. Research, 1962-63; assoc. dir. exec. devel. programs in mass mktg. mgmt., asst. prof. Grad. Sch. Bus. Adminstrn., Mich. State U., East Lansing, 1961-63; assoc. researcher Bur. Econ. and Bus. Research, U. Ill., Urbana, 1963-64, assoc. prof. Grad. Sch. Bus. Adminstrn., 1963-67, acting dir., 1965-67, assoc. prof. mktg., head dept., 1964-67, acting head dept. indsl. adminstrn., 1966-67; prof., dir. Small Bus. Inst., Robert C. Anderson Grad. Mgmt., U. N.Mex., Albuquerque, 1967—; staff economist mgmt. scis. div. Arthur D. Little, Inc., Cambridge, Mass., 1969; cons. to various state agys., mfg. fin., profl. orgns., and research corps.; cons. Los Alamos Nat. Lab. Served to lt. (j.g.) USNR, 1952-54; Korea. Inst. Labor Econs. research fellow, 1955-56; Ford Found. fellow, 1960. Mem. Am. Econ. Assn., Pi Sigma Epsilon. Author: (with S.M. Mark) Economics in Action, 1959, 62; author various reports and articles in field. Home: 10011 Denali Rd NE Albuquerque NM 87111 Office: Grad Sch Bus Mgmt Univ NMex Albuquerque NM 87131

SLATER, JERRY GRANT, software corp. exec.; b. Cleve., July 22, 1946; s. Peter Allen and Jeanne J. (Richards) S.; B.S. in E.E., Calif. State Coll., 1969; m. Lillian Dodson, Dec. 9, 1980; 1 dau., Shayna Allene. Field engr. IBM Corp., Long Beach, Calif., 1965-69; mem. tech. staff elec. engrs. MTS programming Hughes Aircraft Co., Fullerton, Calif., 1969-72; tech. ops. specialist sr. Century Data Systems, Anaheim, Calif., 1972-73; systems programmer City of Long Beach (Calif.), 1973-75; pres., chmn. bd. Tone Software Corp., Anaheim, 1974—. Mem. Aircraft Owners and Pilots Assn. Office: 1735 S Brookhurst St Anaheim CA 92804

SLATER, WILLIAM THOMAS, university dean, communications researcher; b. Pitts., Oct. 31, 1942; s. William E. and Margaret Ruth (Briggs) S.; m. Deborah Lynn Folka, Aug. 12, 1978. B.A., Tufts U., 1971; A.M., Harvard U., 1972; M.A., Stanford U., 1973, Ph.D., 1977. Reporter, editor, Afro-Am. newspaper, 1959-61; reporter Newark News, 1961-62; news dir. Sta. WABQ, Cleve., 1962-64; reporter, anchor Sta. WBZ-TV-AM, Boston, 1964-69; asst. to Gov. of Mass., 1969-71; asst. prof. U. Wash., Seattle, 1973-75; asst. prof. U. So. Calif., Los Angeles, 1975-77; assoc. prof., head div. broadcasting U. Cin., 1977-79; prof., head dept. radio-TV, U. Ariz., Tucson, 1979-83; dean Sch. Fine Arts, Eastern Wash. U., Cheney, 1983—; cons. broadcasting and edn. planning. Mem. Phi Beta Kappa. Author: Aspen Handbook on Communication, 1972, 2d edit., 1975; contbr. articles to publs. in field.

SLATON, SHELL A., university administrator; b. Los Angeles, Dec. 16, 1953; d. William Henry and Nellie Frances (Becker) S.; B.A. cum laude in Journalism, Pepperdine U., 1976, M.S. (fellow), 1979. Free-lance writer Essence mag. and Encore Am., world-wide news mag., N.Y.C., 1975-76; asso. editor Right On mag., Los Angeles, 1976-83; editor Dazzle and Threads, 1980-83; news editor Eaton House Broadcasting, Los Angeles, 1981—; now pub. affairs coordinator Pepperdine U., Malibu, Calif., Mem. publicity bd. United Negro Coll. Fund telethon, 1980—. Recipient scholastic achievement awards in journalism, 1974-76, presdl. awards, 1974-76; winner first pl. award Sta. KDAY bicentennial essay contest, 1976; elected to Mademoiselle mag. coll. bd., 1976. Mem. Greater Los Angeles Press Club. Editor spl. issues for Laufer Co., 1976-80; co-author book on Martin Luther King, 1977; condr. research study on Saramaccanns, Surinam, 1977; elected Miss Greater Los Angeles Press Club, rep. on Rose Bowl Parade float, 1976. Office: Pepperdine U 24255 Pacific Coast Hwy Malibu CA 90265 Office: Public Information Pepperdine 9 Malibu CA 90265

SLATTERY, ALICE, art educator; b. Chico, Calif., Mar. 15, 1945; d. Charles William and Ruth Elizabeth (Dakin) Mauldin. A.A. in Art, Coll. San Mateo (Calif.), 1965; B.A., Chico State Coll., 1967, M.A., 1968; postgrad. Syracuse U., 1982—. Model, John Robert Powers Modeling Agy., Palo Alto, Calif., 1963-65; designer publs. office Chico State Coll., 1966-67; graphic artist Calif. State U., Chico, 1967-73; art instr. Live Oak (Calif.) High Sch., 1969; art instr. Sitka (Alaska) Community Coll., 1973-81; art instr. SARAC Fine Arts Camp, Sitka, 1974-75; art instr. Bur. Indian Affairs High Sch., Mt. Edgecumbe, Alaska, 1977; assoc. prof. art U. Alaska, Juneau, 1981—. Bd. dirs. Baranof Arts & Crafts Assn., chmn. ann. art show, 1976, v.p., exhibits chmn., 1977-81. Recipient numerous awards for artistry. Mem. Nat. Craft Council, Nat. League Am. Pen Women (v.p. 1980-81), Nat. Art Edn. Assn., Coll. Art Assn., Am. Crafts Council, AAUW, Graphic Communication Guild, Screen Printers Assn. Contbr. art exhibits to numerous art shows and museums. Home: 2961 Glacierwood Ct Juneau AK 99801 Office: Dept Fine Arts Univ Alaska 1120 Glacier Hwy Juneau AK 99801

SLAWSKI, CARL JAMES, sociology educator; b. Toledo, Aug. 25, 1938; s. Daniel Joseph and Genevieve Alice (Michalak) S. A.B. in Sociology, U. So. Calif., 1964; M.A., U. Calif.-Santa Barbara, 1966; Ph.D., U. Ill., 1969. Asst. prof. sociology Wayne State U., Detroit, 1968-70; mem. faculty dept. sociology Calif. State U., Long Beach, 1970—, assoc. prof., 1974—; universitats assistent U. Munich (W.Ger.), 1973-74; cons. Mem. Am. Sociol. Assn., Pacific Sociol. Assn., Midwest Sociol. Soc., Soc. for Study Symbolic Interaction, Soc. for Sci. Study Religion, AAAS, Soc. Gen. Systems Research, AAUP. Democrat. Roman Catholic. Club: Garden Grove Tennis. Author: Social Psychological Theories: A Comparative Handbook for Students, 1981; contbr. articles to profl. jours. Home: 6871 Stanford Ave Garden Grove CA 92645 Office: Dept Sociology Calif State U Long Beach CA 90840

SLIKER, TODD RICHARD, accountant, lawyer; b. Rochester, N.Y., Feb. 9, 1936; s. Harold Garland and Marion Ethel (Caps) S.; B.S. with honors (Ford Found. scholar), U. Wis., 1955; Ph.D., Cornell U., 1962; M.B.A., Harvard, 1970; J.D., U. Denver, 1982; m. Gretchen Paula Zeiter, Dec. 27, 1963; children—Cynthia Garland, Kathryn Clifton. Bar: Colo. 1983. With Clevite Corp., Cleve., 1962-68, head applied physics sect., 1965-68; asst. to pres. Granville-Phillips Co., Boulder, Colo., 1970; v.p., gen. mgr. McDowell Electronics, Inc., Metuchen, N.J., 1970-71; pres. C.A. Compton, Inc., mfrs. audio-visual equipment, Boulder, 1971-77; chief acct. C&S Inc., Englewood, Colo., 1977-80, v.p., 1980-82. Del., Colo. Republican Assembly, 1974, 76; Rep. dist. finance coordinator, 1974-75; precinct committeeman, 1974—; chmn. Boulder County Rep. 1200 Club, 1975-79; mem. Colo. Rep. State Central Com., 1977-81, asst. treas., 1979—; sect. corr. Harvard U., 1981—. Served to 1st lt. USAF, 1955-57. Recipient paper award vehicular communication group IEEE, 1966. Licensed real estate salesman, securities salesman; C.P.A., Colo. Mem. Colo. Soc. C.P.A.s (govt. relations task force 1983—), Colo. Bar Assn. (publs. com. 1982—), Am. Phys. Soc., Optical Soc. Am. (referee Jour.), Sigma Xi, Phi Kappa Phi, Theta Chi, Beta Alpha Psi. Club: Rotary. Contbr. articles to profl. jours. Patentee in field. Home: 1658 Bear Mountain Dr Boulder CO 80303

SLOAN, ROBERT FRANCIS, mgmt. cons.; b. Los Angeles, June 19, 1935; s. Lafayette F. and Frances (Walsh) S.; B.A. in Zoology, UCLA, 1957; Ph.D. in Oral Radiology, Osaka Dental U., 1977; m. Estela Alarid, June 8, 1961 (dec. May 1982); children—Patrick S., Cristina, Brett. Research asso. U. Calif. Med.-Dental Sch., Los Angeles, 1957-67; founding pres. Rocky Mountain Data Systems, 1967-70; founding exec. dir. Found. Orthodontic Research, 1968-70; exec. dir. InterAm. Orthodontic Seminar, 1964-70; mgmt. cons., Calif., 1978; prof. Grad. Sch. of Business, U.S. Internat. U., San Diego, 1977-79; producer documentary and tech. films. Served to capt. M.S.C., U.S. Army, 1957-69. Recipient Bronze N.Y. Film Festival award, 1973, 79, Chris award, 1965, 73, Cine awards, 1964, 65, 73, 74. Mem. Am. Speech and Hearing Assn., Am. Dental Assn., Brit. Inst. Radiology, AMA, Socieda de Brasileira de Foniatria (hon. mem.). Contbr. articles on radiol. studies to profl. jours. Home: 10342 Wilkins Ave Los Angeles CA 90024

SLOANE, BEVERLY LEBOV, writer; b. N.Y.C., May 26, 1936; d. Benjamin S. and Anne (Weinberg) LeBov; A.B., Vassar Coll., 1958; M.A., Claremont Grad. Sch., 1975, postgrad., 1975-76; grad. Exec. Program, UCLA Grad. Sch. Mgmt., 1982; grad. pub. course Stanford U., 1982; m. Robert Malcolm Sloane, Sept. 27, 1959; 1 dau., Alison Lori. Circulation librarian Harvard Med. Library, Boston, 1958-59; social worker Conn. State Welfare, New Haven, 1960-61; tchr. English, Hebrew Day Sch., New Haven, 1961-64; instr. creative writing and English lit. Monmouth Coll., West Long Branch, N.J., 1967-69; free lance writer, Arcadia, Calif., 1970—; adv. council for tech. and profl. writing Calif. State U., Long Beach, 1980-82. Chmn. Vassar Christmas Showcase, New Haven, 1966-67; mem. public relations bd. Monmouth County Mental Health Assn., 1968-69; mem. Town Hall of Calif., Los Angeles, 1976—; mem. women's campaign steering com. for dist. atty Los Angeles County, 1976; mem. League for Crippled Children, 1982—; v.p. Temple Beth David, 1983—; v.p. Council of Grad. Students, Claremont Grad. Sch., 1971-72; trustee Ctr. for Improvement Child Caring, 1981-83. Coro Found. fellow, 1979. Mem. Women in Communications (dir. 1980-82, v.p. community affairs 1981-82, chmn. Los Angeles chpt. 1st ann. Agnes Underwood Freedom of Info. Awards Banquet 1982, Recognition award 1983, N.E. area rep. 1980-81, nominating com. 1982, 83), Am. Assn. for Higher Edn., AAUW (legis. chmn. Arcadia br. 1976-77, books and plays chmn. Arcadia br. 1973-74, creative writing chmn. 1969-70, 1st v.p. 1975-76, networking chmn. 1981-82), Coll. English Assn., Am. Med. Writers Assn. (Pacific S.W. chpt. dir. 1980—, del. to nat. bd. 1980—, chmn. trade category com. nat. book awards nat. conv. 1983), Am. Pub. Health Assn., Calif. Press Women (dir. Los Angeles chpt. 1982—, v.p. program 1982—), AAUP, Town Hall of Calif. (vice chmn. community affairs sect. 1982—), Internat. Communication Assn., Soc. for Tech. Communication, Coro Assos. Clubs: Ex-Rotary of Duarte; Vassar of So. Calif. (co-chmn. book fair 1970-72), Calif. Inst. Tech. Women's. Author: (with R.M. Sloane) A Guide to Health Facilities-Personnel and Management, 1971, 2d edit., 1977; From Vassar to Kitchen, 1967. Adv. bd. Calif. Health Rev. Mag., 1982-83. Home: 1301 N Santa Anita Ave Arcadia CA 91006 Office: 1301 N Santa Anita Ave Arcadia CA 91006

SLOANE, HOWARD NORMAN, JR., psychology educator, consultant; b. N.Y.C., July 24, 1932; s. Howard N. and Lucille (Lipsett) S.; m. Davina N. Hecht, Aug. 15, 1954; m. 2d, Judith A. Crandall, Dec. 27, 1976; children—Gary Kenneth, Jeffrey Steven, Wendy Sarah. B.A., Dartmouth Coll., 1954; M.S., Pa. State U., 1955, Ph.D., 1959. Lic. psychologist, Utah. Psychology intern VA Hosp., Roanoke, Va., 1955-56; lectr. psychology dept. So. Ill. U., 1958-60; NIH postdoctoral fellow Water Reed Army Inst. Research, Washington, 1960-62; asst. prof. biochemistry Johns Hopkins Sch. Hygiene and Pub. Health, Balt., 1962-64; research asst. prof. psychology dept. U. Wash., Seattle, 1964-65, U. Ill., Urbana, 1965-66; assoc. prof. dept. ednl. psychology U. Utah, Salt Lake City, 1966-69, prof., 1966—; cons. local, state, fed. and fgn. agys., also corps. Mem. Ptnr. Appropriate Tech. for Handicapped Com., Utah/Bolivia Ptnrs., 1979—, chmn., 1975-79. USPHS fellow, 1956-58. Mem. Assn. for Behavior Analysis, Am. Psychol. Assn., Am. Ednl. Research Assn., Am. Soc. for Tng. and Devel., Assn. for Advancement of Behavior Therapy, Utah Psychol. Assn., Author: (with D. Buckholdt and others) Classroom and Instructional Management, 1974; (with D.A. Jackson) A Guide to Motivating Learners, 1974; (with D.A. Jackson and G.M. Della-Piano) How To Establish a Behavior Observation System, 1975; Classroom Management: Remediation and Prevention, 1976; (with others) Structured Teaching, 1979; The Good Kid Bood, 1979; editor: (with others) Behavior Analysis and Education, 1972; (with D.D. MacAulay) Operant Procedures in Remedial Speech and Language Training, 1982; bd. editors Behavioral Counseling Quar., 1979—, The Behavior Analyst, 1980-83, Jour. Applied Behavior Analysis, 1968-75; contbr. articles to profl. jours. Office: Ednl Psychology Dept U Utah Salt Lake City UT 84112

SLOANE, ROBERT MALCOLM, hosp. adminstr.; b. Boston, Feb. 11, 1933; s. Alvin and Florence (Goldberg) S.; A.B., Brown U., 1954; M.S., Columbia U., 1958; m. Beverly LeBov, Sept. 27, 1959; 1 dau., Alison. Adminstrv. resident Mt. Auburn Hosp., Cambridge, Mass., 1957-58; med. adminstr. AT&T, N.Y.C., 1959-60; asst. dir. Yale New Haven Hosp., 1961-67; asso. adminstr. Monmouth Med. Ctr., Long Branch, N.J., 1967-69; adminstr. City of Hope Nat. Med. Ctr., Duarte, Calif., 1969-80; pres. Orthopaedic Hosp. and Orthopaedic Found., Los Angeles, 1980—; mem. faculty Columbia U. Sch. Medicine, 1958-59, Yale U. Sch. Medicine, 1963-67, Quinnipiac Coll., 1963-67, Pasadena City Coll., 1972-73, Calif. Inst. Tech., 1973—, U. So. Calif., 1975-79; chmn. bd. dirs. Health Data Net, 1971-73; bd. dirs. Health Systems Agy. for Los Angeles County, 1977-78; dir. Calif. Hosp. Polit. Action Com., 1979—, vice chmn., 1981-82, chmn., 1983—; dir. Calif. Hosp. Assn. Ins. Service, 1981—. Served to lt. (j.g.) USNR, 1954-56. Fellow Am. Coll. Hosp. Adminstrs.; mem. Am. Pub. Health Assn., Am. Hosp. Assn., Hosp. Council So. Calif. (dir. 1978—, exec. com. 1982, sec. 1982, treas. 1983, chmn.-elect 1984). Author: (with B.L. Sloane) A Guide to Health Facilities: Personnel and Management, 1971, 2d edit., 1977; editorial and adv. bd. Health Devices, 1972—; contbr. articles to hosp. jours. Office: 2400 S Flower St Los Angeles CA 90007

SLOTKIN, ARTHUR LEWIS, computer co. exec.; b. Bklyn., May 8, 1946; s. Morris Jack and Ann S.; B.S., Auburn U., 1968; M.S. (USN fellow), Columbia U., 1969; postgrad. Harvard Bus. Sch., 1975; m. Marcella C. Hadarits, Dec. 31, 1966; children—Chandra, Jennifer. Project engr. U.S. Navy, Washington, 1969; dir. student programs, editor student jour. Am. Inst. Aeros. and Astronautics, N.Y.C., 1969-71; asst. to pres. System Devel. Corp., Santa Monica, Calif., 1971-73, mgr. compensation, 1974-75, v.p. Benefits Adminstrn. Services div., 1976-78, v.p., gen. mgr. SDC Corp. Services div., 1978-81; v.p., gen. mgr. Data Ctr. Services, 1982, asst. to chmn. bd., 1983—. Fellow Inst. for Advancement Engring.; asso. fellow AIAA; mem. Internat. Acad. Astronautics (co-sec. 1982—), Tau Beta Pi, Sigma Gamma Tau. Republican. Home: 2240 24th St Santa Monica CA 90405 Office: System Devel Corp 2500 Colorado Ave Santa Monica CA 90406

SLOVER, ARCHY F., chemist; b. Oshkosh, Wis., July 8, 1920; s. Archie F. and Josephine Petronella (Zindler); B.A., U. Calif., Los Angeles, 1947; m. Mary Beatrice Corkill, May 25, 1946; 1 dau., Mary Kay Slover Eckhardt. Devel. chemist Kelite Products Co., Los Angeles, 1946-49; v.p., gen. mgr. Delco Chems. Inc., Los Angeles, 1949-57; mgr. indsl. spltys. Pennwalt Corp., Los Angeles, 1957-74; chemist Custom Chem. Formulators Inc., Cudahy, Calif., 1974—; mgr. Cherokee Chem. Co., Inc., Compton, Calif., 1976—; cons. in field. Served to capt. U.S. Army, 1942-46. Fellow AAAS, Am. Inst. Chemists; mem. Nat. Assn. Corrosion Engrs., Am. Chem. Soc., Am. Electroplaters Soc., USAF Assn., Soc. Advancement Material Process Engrs., Res. Officers Assn., Sigma Alpha Epsilon. Club: Ky. Cols. Patentee in field. Address: 21 Hacienda Dr Arcadia CA 91006

SLUSSER, ROBERT WYMAN, aerospace co. exec.; b. Mineola, N.Y., May 10, 1938; s. John Leonard and Margaret McKenzie (Wyman) S.; B.S., Mass. Inst. Tech., 1960; M.B.A., Wharton Sch., 1962; m. Linda Killeas, Aug. 3, 1968; children—Jonathan, Adam, Robert, Patricia. Asso. adminstr.'s staff NASA Hdqrs., Washington, 1962-65; adminstr. mktg. and planning dept., space labs. Northrop Corp., Hawthorne, Calif., 1965-67, mgr. bus. and fin. Warnecke Electron Tubes Co. div., Chgo., 1968-71, controller Cobra Program Aircraft div., Hawthorne, 1971-72, mgr. bus. adminstrn. YF-17 Program, 1972-75, mgr. adminstrn. F-18/Cobra programs, also mgr. F-18 design to cost program, 1975-78, mgr. adminstrn. F-18L program, 1978-79, mgr. engring. adminstrn., 1980—, acting v.p. engring., 1982—. Grumman Aircraft Engring. scholar, 1956-60. Mem. AIAA. Home: 27604 Alvesta Pl San Pedro CA 90732 Office: One Northrop Ave Hawthorne CA 90250

SMALL, GENEVA LORENE, hosp. supr.; b. Lineville, Iowa, Jan. 27, 1927; d. Ross Dee and Margaret Francis (Waddle) Barker; student Broadlawns Gen. Hosp., Des Moines, 1945, UCLA, 1977-78; m. Thomas Woodrow Small, Dec. 2, 1945; children—Alice Lorene, Rhonda Louise, Brenda Lea, Tracie Lyn. Mem. adminstrv. staff Inter Community Hosp., Covina, Calif., 1956-73, asst. supr. central supply, 1970-73; supr. central supply Foothill Presbyn. Hosp., Glendora, Calif., 1973—; instr. Citrus Jr. Coll., Azusa, Calif. Mem. Internat. Assn. Hosp. Central Service Mgmt. Democrat. Mormon. Club: Frontier Squares Sq. Dance. Office: 250 S Grand Ave Glendora CA 91740

SMALL, HAROLD SHERWIN, lawyer; b. Chgo., Jan. 22, 1945; s. James Milman and Miriam Bernice (Elenbogen) S.; m. Susan Ilene Maltzman, June 22, 1969; children—Matthew Howard, Hillary Shayne, Allison Blythe. B.S., San Diego State U., 1967; J.D., U. Calif.-Hastings Coll. Law, 1970. Bar: Calif. 1971. Tax acct. Arthur Young & Co., 1970-71; ptnr. Borevitz & Malkus, San Diego, 1971-75; sole practice, San Diego, 1975-77, 82—; mng. ptnr. Roseman & Small, San Diego, 1978-82; instr. U. Calif.-San Diego, 1972—. Pres. Children's Mus. San Diego, 1982—. C.P.A., Calif. Mem. ABA, Am. Inst. C.P.A.s, State Bar Calif., Calif. Soc. C.P.A.s, San Diego County Bar Assn. (ins. com. 1977-78, law office econs. com. 1979, chmn. taxation sect. 1980), San Diego Soc. C.P.A.s, Estate Planning Council San Diego, Hastings Coll. Law Alumni Assn. (pres. 1975). Club: Tennis and Racquet (San Diego, Calif.). Office: 225 Broadway Suite 1313 San Diego CA 92101

SMALLEY, ISAAC MULFORD, state senator; b. Ewan, N.J., Sept. 10, 1904; s. Isaac Cannon and Lydia More (Davis) S.; B.S. in Econs., U. Pa., 1932; LL.B., So. Meth. U., 1942; m. Wandra Pollard, Apr. 9, 1936; 1 dau., Wandra S. Ward. Mayor, Deming, N.Mex., 1946-47; mem. N.Mex. Ho. of Reps., 1947-53; mem. N.Mex. Senate, 1957—, pres. pro tempore; admitted to N.Mex. bar; practiced in N.Mex., 1942—. Mem. Am. Bar Assn., N.Mex. Bar Assn. Democrat. Clubs: Rotary, Masons. Office: 101 S Copper St Deming NM 88030

SMARGON, ALAN PETER, YMCA executive, management consultant; b. N.Y.C., Dec. 15, 1944; s. Albert Jacob and Margareta Hedwig (Hausrath) S.; m. Janet Ruth Mellen, June 9, 1976; children—Elaine, Lori, Lynn, Adam, Alana. B.S., Springfield Coll., 1966, M.Ed., 1981. Cert. sr. dir. YMCA of U.S.A., 1969. World service worker YMCA, Bangkok, Thailand, 1966-68, various positions, N.Y.C., 1968-74, br. mgr. Twelve Towns YMCA, Bklyn., 1974-78, gen. dir. Cambridge (Mass.) YMCA, 1978-82, pres. Albuquerque YMCA, 1982—; dir. East N.Y.C. Devel. Corp., 1975-78. Vice pres. West Queen's Ind. Democratic Club, Bklyn., 1973-74. Recipient Service award YMCA Bangkok, 1968; Hurst-Williams award N.E. region Phys. Edn. Soc., 1971. Mem. Assn. Profl. Dirs. (pres. N.Y. chpt. 1972-74), Nat. Soc. Fund Raising Execs., Am. Mgmt. Assn., Am. Soc. Tng. and Devel., Springfield Coll. Alumni (pres. N.Y. chpt. 1976-78). Clubs: Kiwanis (pres. Highland Park, N.Y.

1974-76, pres. award 1976), Masons; Rotary (Albuquerque). Office: Albuquerque YMCA 301 Broadway St NE Albuquerque NM 87102

SMART, ANTHONY ERIC, physicist; b. Derbyshire, Eng., Nov. 1, 1942; s. Eric and Dorothy Elizabeth (Kind) S.; B.Sc., Imperial Coll. Sci. and Tech., London, 1965, Ph.D., 1968. Sr. scientist Rolls-Royce Ltd., Derby, Eng., 1961-77; sr. scientist, dir. electro-optical systems Spectron Devel. Labs., Inc., Costa Mesa, Calif., 1977—. Fellow Inst. Physics; mem. AIAA. Editor 1 book in field; contbr. articles to profl. jours. Patentee in field. Home: 1618 Corsica Pl Costa Mesa CA 92626 Office: 3303 Harbor Blvd Costa Mesa CA 92626

SMART, WILLIAM BUCKWALTER, editor; b. Provo, Utah, June 27, 1922; s. Thomas Lawrence and Nelle (Buckwalter) S.; student U. Wyo., 1943-44; B.A., Reed Coll., 1948; postgrad. U. Utah, 1949-51; m. Donna Toland, July 15, 1945; children—William Toland, Melinda, Kristen, Thomas Toland, Alfred Laurence. Reporter, Internat. News Service, Portland, Oreg., 1941-43; reporter The Oregonian, Portland, 1946-48; reporter The Deseret News-Salt Lake Telegram, Salt Lake City, 1948-52, chief editorial writer, editor, 1953-66, exec. editor, 1966-72, editor and gen. mgr., 1972—. Mem. nat. adv. bd. Am. Enterprise Inst., Snowbird Inst., Courses by Newspaper; mem. adv. com. Jud. Council, Utah Guidebook Found., Commn. on Colls., Northwest Assn. Schs. and Colls.; former mem. nat. council Boy Scouts Am., region 12 exec. bd.; v.p. Utah Heritage Found.; bd. dirs. Deseret Utah Arts Found., Pioneer State Theater Found., Internat. Visitors-Utah Found., Am. Council on Alcohol Problems, Utah Symphony, Provo-Jordan River Pkwy. Found., Utah Council Econ. Edn., Ft. Douglas Mus. Assn., Great Salt Lake council Boy Scouts Am. Served to 1st lt., inf., AUS, 1943-46; PTO. Recipient Meritorious Service award Brigham Young U., Dept. Communications; Service to Journalism citation U. Utah, Dept. Communications. Mem. Am. Soc. Newspaper Editors, Salt Lake City C. of C. (dir. Days of '47), Phi Beta Kappa, Sigma Delta Chi, Kappa Tau Alpha. Mem. Ch. of Jesus Christ of Latter-day Saints (bishop). Clubs: Bonneville Knife and Fork (pres., bd. dirs.), Timpanogos, Fort Douglas Country, Alta, Aztec, Salt Lake Exchange (past pres., nat. v.p. Rocky Mountain region, nat. dir.). Home: 55 Laurel St Salt Lake City UT 84103 Office: The Deseret News Box 1257 Salt Lake City UT 84110

SMEAD, BURTON ARMSTRONG, JR., lawyer, retired banker; b. Denver, July 29, 1913; s. Burton Armstrong and Lola (Lewis) S.; m. Josephine McKittrick, Mar. 27, 1943; children—Amanda Armstrong, Sydney Hall. B.A., U. Denver, 1934, J.D., 1950; grad. Pacific Sch. Banking Trust Sch., 1955. Bar: Colo., 1950. With United Bank of Denver (formerly Denver Nat. Bank), 1934-78, v.p., trust officer, 1948-78, also sec., dir.; sole practice, Englewood, Colo., 1978—; dir., trust counsel, Resources Trust Co., Englewood, Colo. Pres., trustee Stebbins Orphans Home Assn.; del. dir. Am. Cancer Soc., N.Y.C. Served to maj. U.S. Army, 1941-45; ETO. Decorated Bronze Star; Croix de Guerre (France). Mem. Denver Bar Assn., Colo. Bar Assn. Republican. Episcopalian. Club: University (Denver). Author: History of the Twelfth Field Artillery Battalion in the European Theater of Operations-1944-45, 1945. Home and office: 3130 Cherryridge Rd Englewood CO 80110

SMEDLEY, RONALD FRANK, human resources administrator, management consultant; b. Southgate, Calif., Mar. 30, 1955; s. Charles Allen and Theo (Freidman) S. B.A. in Psychology, Biola Coll., 1979; M.S.I. in Indsl. Psychology, Calif. State U.-Long Beach, 1981. Salesman Nordstrom Inc., 1975-81; asst. to chmn. counseling ctr. Biola Coll., La Mirada, Calif., 1978-79, instr. music, 1979-81, recruiter music dept., 1983—; dir. tng. and personnel KinderCare Learning Ctrs., Inc., Newport Beach, Calif., 1981-82; personnel mgr. Advance Paper Box Co., Los Angeles, 1982—; cons. Automobile Club So. Calif., 1982; trumpet player, tchr. Adult leader Awana, 1975-76; career class coordinator Whittier Area Baptist Fellowship, 1983—; mem. CAP, 1969-70. Mem. Am. Soc. Tng. and Devel., Personnel and Indsl. Relations Assn., Personnel Testing Council So. Calif., Am. Psychol. Assn., Soc. Indsl. Psychologists. Home: 13601 E Sunset Whittier CA 90602 Office: Advance Paper Box Co 6100 S Gramercy Pl Los Angeles CA 90047

SMELTZ, RAYMON TECUMSEH, accounting firm executive; b. Spokane, Wash., Jan. 2, 1911; s. Earl Tecumseh and Amanda Rebecca (Link) S.; B.A., Wash. State U., M.A., 1933; postgrad. U. Wash., 1933-34, Columbia U., 1934-35; m. Ruth Dorcas Lewis, June 29, 1934; 1 son, Eric T. Acct. LeMater & Daniels, C.P.A.s, 1942-53, Smeltz & Schoeff, C.P.A.s, 1953-64, Smeltz, C.P.A., Pullman, Wash., 1964-75; partner Smeltz & Lamb, C.P.A.s, Pullman, 1975—; lectr. Wash. State U., 1946-75. Councilman, City of Pullman, 1949-53. Served to 1st lt. U.S. Army, 1943-46. Mem. Am. Inst. C.P.A.s, Wash. State Soc. C.P.A.'s. Republican. Clubs: Rotary, Masons, Shriners. Office: Smeltz & Lamb CPA's 204 Old National Bank Bldg Pullman WA 99163

SMILLIE, WILLIAM STONE, county ofcl.; b. Monrovia, Calif., Mar. 22, 1948; s. Roy L. and Bettie L. S.; A.A. in Bus. Adminstrn., Victor Valley Jr. Coll., 1974; children—William Stone, Shelley Ann. Engring. With Desert Engring. Co., Apple Valley, Calif., 1966-72; maintenance supr. Boise Cascade Co., Apple Valley, 1972-74; water facilities mgr. County San Bernardino (Calif.), 1974—. Vice pres. Hesperia (Calif.) Mobile Estates, 1974, pres., mem. governing bd., 1976, men. governing com., 1978-79. Cert. water treatment operator, cert. waste water treatment operator, Calif. Mem. Am. Water Works Assn. (cert. water distbn. operator), Nat. Water Well Assn., Calif. Water Pollution Control Assn. (sect. sec. 1981), Nat. Rifle Assn. (life). Republican. Catholic. Lodge: Masons. Office: 13325 Spring Valley Pkwy Victorville CA 92392

SMIRNI, ALLAN DESMOND, lawyer, foundation executive; b. N.Y.C., Aug. 27, 1938; s. Donald William and Ruby M. (King) S.; m. Cherie F. Parham; 1 dau., Amie J. B.A., Bklyn. Coll., 1960; J.D., U. Calif.-Berkeley, 1971. Bar: Calif. 1972. Assoc., Brobeck, Phleger & Harrison, San Francisco, 1971-74; asst. gen. counsel, asst. sec. Envirotech Corp., Menlo Park, Calif., 1975-81; trustee Envirotech Found., Menlo Park, 1977-81; corp. csl., sec. TeleVideo Systems, Inc., Sunnyvale, Calif., 1982—; legal counselor small businesses. Adv. bd. Calif. Job Tng. and Devel., 1971-73. Served to capt. USAF, 1960-68. Mem. ABA, Am. Soc. Corp. Secs. Democrat. Episcopalian. Office: 1170 Morse Ave Sunnyvale CA 94086

SMIRNOFF, STEVE ROSS, telecommunications company official; b. Shanghai, China, Aug. 23, 1939; came to U.S., 1952; s. Vsevolod Nicolas Smirnoff; m. Cindy Cheney, Sept. 8, 1979. B.A. in Journalism, U. N.D., 1966; postgrad. U. Mont., 1968, U. Wis., 1969-70. Advt., sales specialist Gen. Electric Co., Chgo., 1966-68; dir. spl. communications U. Wis.-Oshkosh, 1970-71; dir. pub. relations Alaska Pacific U., Anchorage, 1971-74; sr. pub. affairs rep. Alascom, Inc., Anchorage, 1977—. Bd. dirs. Alaska Heart Assn. Mem. Pub. Relations Soc. Am. (cert.; dir. Alaka chpt.), Armed Forces Communications and Electronics Assn., Alaska Press Club, Alaska Advt. Fedn., Anchorage C. of C. Contbr. articles to trade publs. Home: 3581 Kachemak Circle Anchorage AK 99502 Office: Alascom Inc 949 E 36th Ave Anchorage AK 99502

SMITH, ALAN HUGGER, dentist; b. Evansville, Ind., Apr. 4, 1942; s. Claude Bryan and Marie (Hugger) S.; m. Bonita Elizabeth Peacock, Oct. 24, 1970; Student Ind. State U., 1960-62; D.D.S., Ind. U., 1966; postgrad. U. Nebr., 1966-68. Mem. staff Lincoln (Nebr.) Orthopedic Hosp., Lincoln State Hosp., 1967-68; pvt. practice dentistry, Vancouver, B.C., Can., 1968-71, Portland, Oreg., 1971—; mem. faculty U. Oreg. Dental Coll., part-time, 1973-78; vol. various local dental programs. Bd. dirs. Mt. Hood Kiwanis Camp for Handicapped Children. Mem. Am. Assn. for Advancement of Tension Control, ADA, Portland Acad. Hypnosis, Oreg. Dental Assn. (del.), Psi Omega. Clubs: East Portland TMJ Study, Kiwanis. Office: 16740 SE Stark St Portland OR 97233

SMITH, ALBERT CROMWELL, JR., investments consultant; b. Norfolk, Va., Dec. 6, 1925; s. Albert Cromwell and Georgie (Foreman) S.; B.S. in Civil Engring., Va. Mil. Inst., 1949; M.S. in Govtl. Adminstrn., George Washington U., 1965; M.B.A., Pepperdine U., 1975; m. Laura Thaxton, Oct. 25, 1952; children—Albert, Elizabeth, Laura. Enlisted USMC, 1944, commd. 2d lt., 1949, advanced through grades to col., 1970; comdr. inf. platoons, companies, landing force; variously assigned staffs U.K. Joint Forces, U.S. Sec. Navy, Brit. Staff Coll., Marine Staff Coll.; adviser, analyst amphibious systems; ret., 1974; pres. A. Cromwell-Smith, Ltd., Charlottesville, Va., 1973-77, head broker, cons. A. Cromwell Smith, Investments, La Jolla and Coronado, Calif., 1975—. Bd. dirs. Republicans of La Jolla, 1975-76; vestryman St. Martin's Episcopal Ch., 1971-73. Decorated Legion of Merit with oak leaf cluster, Bronze Star medal with oak leaf cluster, Air medal with 2 oak leaf clusters, Purple Heart. Mem. ASCE, Nat., Calif. assns. Realtors, San Diego, Coronado bds. Realtors, Stockbrokers Soc., So. Calif. Options Soc., Mil. Order Purple Heart. Club: Kona Kai. Author: The Individual Investor in Tomorrow's Stock Market, 1977; The Little Guy's Stock Market Survival Guide, 1979; Wake Up Detroit! The EVs Are Coming, 1982; contbr. articles to civilian and mil. publs. Office: 1001 B Ave Suite 319/320 PO Box 192 Coronado CA 92118

SMITH, ALLAN WISTER, retired navy officer, real estate broker; b. Media, Pa., May 14, 1921; s. Allan Meredith and Viola Minerva (Wister) S.; m. Modesta Maria Sousa, June 30, 1974; children—Thomas J., Elizabeth M., Tammy A. Student U. Pa., 1939-40, U. N.C., 1943, U.S. Naval War Coll., Skagitt Valley Coll., 1976-77. Registered rep. SEC; cert. real estate broker, Wyo. Commd. apprentice seaman U.S. Navy, 1941, advanced through grades to comdr., 1959, active duty, 1941-46, 51-67; patrol plane comdr., 1944-45; active NATO ops., Portugal and Greece, 1955-56; comdg. officer USNR Tng. Center, Cadillac, Mich., 1962-67; ret., 1967; pilot TWA, Kansas City, 1947-50; office mgr. Allstate Ins. Co., Sarasota, Fla., 1968-70; mgmt. cons. Snelling and Snelling, Alexandria, Va., 1970-71; real estate broker comml. dept. Mile High Realty, Cheyenne, Wyo., 1978-79, Rosenberg-Bennett, Cheyenne, 1979-80; owner, operator real estate co., 1981—; chmn., pres. Great Am. Properties, Ltd., Cheyenne, Wyo., 1981—. Active Republican Party. Decorated Air medal. Mem. Wyo. Assn. Realtors, Nat. Assn. Realtors, Cheyenne Bd. Realtors, Cheyenne C. of C. (Mayors bus. adv. com. 1982), Wyo. Ptnrs. of the Americas, Wyo. Archaeol. Soc. Home: 6305 Elk Ave Cheyenne WY 82009 Office: 1611 Morrie Ave Cheyenne WY 82001

SMITH, ANDREW VAUGHN, utility company executive; b. Roseburg, Oreg., July 17, 1924; s. Andrew Britt and Ella Mae (Vaughn) S.; m. Dorothy LaVonne Crabtree, Apr. 25, 1943; children—Janet L., James A. B.S.E.E., Oreg. State U., 1950. Registered profl. engr., Oreg. With Pacific Northwest Bell Telephone Co., 1959—, asst. v.p. ops. and gen. adminstrn., Seattle, 1965, v.p., gen. mgr. for Oreg., Portland, 1965-70, v.p. ops., Seattle, 1970-78, pres., 1978—; also dir.; dir. Airborne Freight Corp., Cascade Natural Gas Corp., Blue Cross of Wash. and Alaska, U.S. Bancorp. (Portland), U.S. Bank, Portland, Unigard Ins. Co., Unigard Mut. Ins. Co., Univar Corp.; com. and subcom. mem. Wash. Mut. Savs. Bank. Active United Way of King County (Wash.), 1974—, gen. campaign chmn., 1980-81, mem. spl. gifts div., 1981-82, bd. dirs., 1981-84; bd. dirs. Wash. State China Relations Council, Oreg. Shakespearean Festival Assn.; trustee Fifth Avenue Theatre Assn., Seattle Repertory Theatre, Wash. State Internat. Trade Fair; trustee Oreg. State U. Found., Corvallis; adv. bd. U. Wash. Grad. Sch. Bus. Adminstrn., Seattle; mem. Wash. State Council Internat. Trade; mem. capital fund adv. bd. Seattle YMCA; chmn. Chief Seattle council sports award breakfast Boy Scouts Am., 1982; mem. Nat. Corp. Theatre Fund Bd. Served with USN, 1943-46. Mem. Seattle C. of C. (exec. com.), World Affairs Council, Telephone Pioneers Am. Clubs: Seattle Yacht, Harbor, Rainier, Wash. Athletic (pres. 1982-83). Office: 1600 Bell Plaza Suite 3101 Seattle WA 98191

SMITH, ARMISTEAD BURWELL, JR., banker, former naval officer; b. Gastonia, N.C., Mar. 15, 1921; s. Armistead Burwell and Ruby Gardner (Spencer) S.; m. Margaret Madelene Pagliotti, Jan. 14, 1944; children—Sandra Smith Payne, Armistead Burwell, Michael Spencer. Student U. N.C., Chapel Hill, 1938-41, Naval Flight Tng., 1941, Naval Postgrad. Sch., Newport, R.I., 1946-47, Air War Coll., 1950-51, Naval War Coll., 1963-64. Commd. ensign U.S. Navy, 1941, advanced through grades to capt., 1961; comdr. fighter squadrons, carrier air wing U.S.S. Pine Island, Naval Air Sta. Miramar; held various sr. staff positions; comdr. fighter wings Pacific Fleet; ret., 1972; trust officer, sr. v.p., group head trust dept. Calif. 1st Bank, San Diego, 1972—. Chmn. bd. San Diego Aerospace Mus.; bd. dirs. San Diego Hall of Sci.; exec. com. Scripps Clinic; chancellors assoc. U. Calif., San Diego; pres. Am. Fighter Aces Assn. (pres. 1973); mem. Navy League, YMCA; trustee Powell Scholarship Fund, La Jolla Cancer Research Found. Decorated Silver Star, Legion of Merit with oak leaf cluster, DFC with 3 oak leaf clusters, Meritorious Service Medal, Air Medal with 7 oak leaf clusters, Navy Commendation Medal. Mem. Trust Officers Assn., Alpha Tau Omega. Methodist. Club: Lomas Santa Fe Country. Office: California 1st Bank 530 B St San Diego CA 92112

SMITH, AUDREY LISETTE, federal commission administrator, consultant; b. El Centro, Calif., Apr. 6, 1936; d. Edward and Charlesetta (Mason) Garmon; children—Deryl, Curve, Thomas. Student pub. schs., San Francisco. With Econ. Opportunity Comm.-Western Addition, 1965-68; founder Audrey L. Smith, Developmental Ctr., San Francisco, 1969-71; coordinator Infant Day Care Project, Mt. Zion Hosp., San Francisco, 1969-71; adminstrv. asst. Infant Day Care Project, Family Service Agy., San Francisco, 1971; asst. dir. Sacramento Neighborhood Health Service Corp., Sacramento, 1971-82; exec. dir. Econ. Opportunity Commn. of Yolo County (Calif.), 1982—; cons., trainer in filed, Sacramento, 1969—. Bd. dirs. Nat. Mental Health Assn., 1978-83, Mental Health Assn. Calif., 1971-79; mem. United Way citizen rev. com., 1980-83; Calif. Gov.'s Adv. Com. on Child Devel. Programs, 1976. Recipient Cert. of Honor, San Francisco Bd. Suprs., 1973, others. Mem. Nat. Com. Negro and Bus. and Profl. Workers, Nat. Assn. Female Execs., Cal-Nev. Exec. Dirs. Assn. Democrat. Baptist.

SMITH, BALLARD FLANDERS, JR., baseball club exec.; b. Indpls., June 20, 1946; s. Ballard Flanders and Mildred Smith; B.A. in Sociology, Carleton Coll., 1968; J.D., U. Minn., 1971; m. Linda Ardell Smith, Sept. 5, 1970; children—Allison, Amy, Amanda, Holly. Mem. firm Pepicelli & Pepicelli, Meadville, Pa., 1971-76; dist. atty., Crawford County, Pa., 1976; v.p., gen. mgr. San Diego Mariners Hockey Club, 1976-77; exec. v.p. San Diego Nat. League Baseball Club, Inc., San Diego Padres, 1977-79, pres., 1979—. Bd. dirs., Kroc Found., Santa Ynez Valley, Calif., San Diego County Boy Scouts Am., 1978—. Mem. Am. Bar Assn., Pa. Bar Assn., Am. Arbitration Assn., San Diego C. of C. (dir.). Episcopalian. Office: PO Box 2000 9449 Friars Rd San Diego CA 92120

SMITH, BARBARA GORDON, state ofcl.; b. Los Angeles, Oct. 13, 1927; d. Frank and Anna Louisa (Weidauer) Belcher; B.A., Occidental Coll., 1949; M.P.A., U. So. Calif., 1976; m. Kenneth H. Smith, Aug. 29, 1980 (dec.); children—Edward Kermit, Parker, Stephen Frank Parker. Tchr., Calif. Public Schs., 1949-72; adminstrv. intern Sacramento (Calif.) Superior Ct., 1975-77; legis. aide, sr. adminstr. Calif. Assembly, Office Speaker Pro Tempore, Sacramento, 1977-80; exec. dir. Calif. Health Facilities Authority, Sacramento, 1980—. Chmn., Contra Costa County Natural Resource Commn., 1965-68; bd. dirs. Pub. Service Skills, Inc., Council Hosp. Fin. Authorities. Named Citizen of Year, Orinda, Calif., 1968. Mem. Nature Conservancy, Audubon Soc. Office: 915 Capitol Mall Room 280 Sacramento CA 94814

SMITH, BERNALD STEPHEN, pilot, aviation consultant; b. Long Beach, Calif., Dec. 24, 1926; s. Donald Albert and Bernice Merrill (Stephens) S.; student in chem. engring. U. Calif., Berkeley, 1944-45, 50-51; m. Marilyn Mae Spence, July 22, 1949; children—Lorraine Ann Smith Foute, Evelyn Donice, Mark Stephen, Diane April (dec.). Capt., Transocean Airlines, Oakland, Calif., 1951-52, Tokyo, 1953, Hartford, Conn., 1954-55; first officer United Airlines, Seattle, 1955, San Francisco, 1956-68, flight instr., tng. capt., Denver and San Francisco, 1961-68, capt., San Francisco, 1968—; founder, v.p. AviAm., Palo Alto, Calif., 1970-72, Avia Internat., Palo Alto, 1972-74; cons. Caproni Vizzola, Milan, Italy, 1972—; instr. dept. aviation Ohlone Coll., 1976. Served with USN, 1944-49. Decorated Air medal, Humane Action medal. Mem. Calif. Alumni Assn. (life), AIAA (publs. bd.), Soc. Automotive Engring., Soaring Soc. Am. (dir. 1963—, pres. 1969-70, chmn. publs bd. 1971—, Exceptional Service award 1970, 1975, Warren Eaton Meml. trophy 1977), Nat. Soaring Mus. (pres. 1975-78, trustee 1975—), Nat. Aero. Assn. (cert. of appreciation 1971), Exptl. Aircraft Assn., Aircraft Owners and Pilots Assn., Airline Pilots Assn., Federation Aeronautique Internationale Commission de Vol a Voile (U.S. del. 1970-71, 78), Pacific Soaring Council (founder), Air Sailing Inc. (founder; trustee 1970—), Organisation Scientifique et Technique Internationale du Vol a Voile (U.S. del., dir. 1981—). Democrat. Methodist. Author books, including: American Soaring Handbook, 1975, 2d edit., 1980; contbr. articles to profl. publs.; contbg. designer for aircraft. Office: PO Box 3075 Fremont CA 94539

SMITH, BERNARD JOSEPH, cons. civil engr.; b. Liverpool, Eng., Aug. 29, 1900; s. Thomas J. and Sarah Anne (Crum) S.; came to U.S., 1912, naturalized, 1930; student St. Edward's Coll., Liverpool, 1914-20; ed. Oxford U., Eng., 1918; B.Engring. with honors, U. Liverpool, 1923, M.Engring., 1926; m. Julia Susan Connolly, June 4, 1929; children—Bernard, Sarah Anne Kathleen, Maureen, Una, Aislin, Malachy, Joan, John. Pvt. tutor in math. and physics, Liverpool, 1923-24; field engr. Underpinning & Found. Co., N.Y.C., 1924; underground conduit engr. N.Y. and N.J. Bell Telephone Co., 1924-25, Ohio Bell Telephone Co., Toledo, 1925-26; asst. engr. to Alexander Potter, cons. engr. on water and sewerage systems, N.Y. and N.J., 1926-30; design engr. Humble Oil & Refining Co., Baytown, Tex., 1930-32; city mgr. and engr. City of Baytown, 1932-33, cons. engr., 1930-34; engr. examiner Pub. Works Adminstrn., Ft. Worth, 1935-37; dir. research and personnel City of Ft. Worth, 1938-42; acting state dir. and state planning engr. Tex. Pub. Works Res., 1942; asst. regional dir. and regional economist Nat. Housing Agy., hdqrs. Dallas, 1942-46; cons. engr. on water systems and town planning, Dallas, 1946-65; cons. tides and water resources, San Francisco, 1965—, also Aptos, Calif.; water commr. Santa Cruz County, Calif.; planning engr. and chief San Francisco Bay sect. U.S. Corps of Engrs., 1957-65; lectr. urban devel. Tex. Christian U., Ft. Worth, 1939-43; guest lectr. on town devel. Ala. Poly. Inst., 1940; instr. econs. and engring. So. Meth. U., Dallas, 1943-53; guest panelist Ann. Radio Conf., U. Okla., Norman, 1946; speaker on econs. and town planning to various civic and bus. groups, 1939—; v.p. Southwestern States Water Co., 1949-51. Mem. bd. govs. Dallas Fed. Reference Exchange, 1943-46. Registered profl. engr., Calif., N.J., Tex.; registered pub. surveyor, Tex. Fellow ASCE (com. city planning tng. for civil engrs. 1942); mem. Am. Waterworks Assn., AAAS, Am., Western econ. assns., Assn. Evolutionary Econs., History of Econs. Soc., County Louth (Eire) Archeol. Soc., Irish Lit. and Hist. Soc. of San Francisco (pres. 1959-62), Serra Club. Club: Commonwealth of Calif. Contbr. articles and reports on water systems, flood control, urban devel. and pollution to profl. publs. Home: 1446 Day Valley Rd Aptos CA 95003 Office: PO Box 663 Aptos CA 95003

SMITH, BERNARD JOSEPH CONNOLLY, civil engineer; b. Elizabeth, N.J., Mar. 11, 1930; s. Bernard Joseph and Julia Susan (Connolly) S.; B.S., U. Notre Dame, 1951; B.S. in Civil Engring., Tex. A&M U., 1957; M.B.A. in Fin., U. Calif.-Berkeley, 1976; m. Josephine Kerley, Dec. 20, 1971; children—Julia Susan Alice, Teresa Mary Josephine, Anne Marie Kathleen. Asst. Bernard J. Smith, cons. engr. office, Dallas, 1947-57; hydraulic engr. C.E., U.S. Army, San Francisco, 1957-59, St. Paul dist., 1959-60, Kansas City (Mo.) dist., 1960-63, Sacramento dist., 1963-65; engr. Fed. Energy Regulatory Commn., San Francisco Regional Office, 1965—. Served with U.S. Army, 1952-54. Registered profl. engr., Calif., Mo.; lic. real estate broker, Calif. Mem. ASCE (sec. power div. San Francisco sect. 1969), Soc. Am. Mil. Engrs. (treas. Kansas City post 1962), Am. Econ. Assn., Nat. Soc. Profl. Engrs., U.S. Com. on Large Dams, Res. Officers Assn. (chpt. pres. 1973). Clubs: San Francisco Catholic Alumni (pres. 1968), Commonwealth of Calif. Home: 247 28th Ave San Francisco CA 94121 Office: Fed Energy Regulatory Commn 333 Market St San Francisco CA 94105

SMITH, BETTY DENNY, county ofcl., civic worker, fashion exec.; Centralia, Ill., Nov. 12, 1932; d. Otto and Ferne Elizabeth (Beier) Hasenfuss; student U. Ill., 1950-52, Los Angeles City Coll., 1953-57, UCLA, 1965; m. Peter S. Smith, Dec. 5, 1964; children—Carla Kip, Bruce Kimball. Free-lance fashion coordinator, Los Angeles and N.Y.C., 1953-58; instr. fashion Rita LeRoy Internat. Studios, 1959-60; mgr. Mo Nadler Fashions, Los Angeles, 1961-64; showroom dir. Jean of Calif. Fashions, Los Angeles, 1966—; staff writer Valley Citizen News, 1963; free-lance polit. book reviewer community newspapers, 1961-62. Bd. dirs. Pet Assistance Found., 1969-76; founder, pres., dir. Vol. Services to Animals of Los Angeles, 1972-76; mem. County Com. to Discuss Animals in Research, 1973-74; mem. blue ribbon com. on animal control Los Angeles County, 1973-74; dir. Los Angeles County Animal Care and Control, 1976-82, ind. legis. advocate for humane causes, 1969—; mem. State of Calif. Animal Health Technician Exam. Com., 1975—, chmn., 1979. Mem. exec. com. Republican State Central Com., 1971-72; mem. Calif. Rep. Central Com., 1964-72; mem. Rep. Los Angeles County Central Com., 1964-70, mem. exec. com., 1966-70; chmn. 29th Congl. Central Com., 1969-70; sec. 28th Senatorial Central Com., 1967-68, 45th Assembly Dist. Central Com., 1965-66; mem. speakers bur. George Murphy for U.S. Senate, 1970; campaign mgr. Los Angeles County for Spencer Williams for Atty. Gen., 1966. Mem. Lawyers Wives San Gabriel Valley (dir. 1971-74, pres. 1972-73), Mannequins Assn. (dir. 1967-68), Internat. Platform Assn., Delta Gamma, Pi Phi Theta. Clubs: Los Angeles Athletic, Town Hall. Home: 1766 Bluffhill Dr Monterey Park CA 91754

SMITH, BETTY LORETTA, art gallery ofcl.; b. Trinidad, Colo., Oct. 17, 1932; d. Howard Melvin and Anna Belle (Eastwood) Wade; student public schs.; m. Earl Gilbert Smith, Nov. 26, 1950; children—Wayne David, Christine Ella, Clifford Todd. Owner, operator Gilbert's Gallery and Frame Shop, Santa Rosa, Calif., 1964—; condr. seminars, cons., speaker in field. Former mem. Santa Rosa Civic Art Commn. Recipient Liberal Arts award Bank of Am., 1950. Mem. Profl. Picture Framers Assn. Republican. Presbyterian. Author papers, materials in field. Office: 865 3d St Santa Rosa CA 95404

SMITH, BOB GENE, biology educator, consultant; b. Floydada, Tex., Nov. 9, 1932; s. C. M. and Carrie A. Smith; m. Thralene Admirc, Dec. 26, 1953; children—Malcolm Shawn, Michael Brian. B.S., Tex. Tech U., 1958, M.S., 1961; credential in adminstrn. Calif. State U.-Los Angeles, 1963-64; M.S. in Biology U. Mont.-Missoula, 1966. Tchr. biology Colton (Calif.) High Sch., 1958-61; athletic dir., vice prin. pub. schs., Bloomington, Calif., 1963-66; asst. prof. biology San Bernardino Community Coll., 1966—, dean of men, 1968-70; cons. in herpetology, entomology, taxonomy San Bernardino County, Norton AFB. Served with USAF, 1951-53. Mem. Calif. Tchrs. Assn. Calif. Higher Edn. Assn. (state council 1973-74, NEA del. 1973-75), World Wildlife Fund. Democrat. Co-author numerous lab. manuals; designed lab. exercise on metric system; devised method of dating chaparral fires.

SMITH, BOB GENE, mech. designer; b. Larkesbourgh, Ark., Feb. 25, 1931; s. Haskell V. and Ethel Ione (Steen) S.; student Central State Coll., Okla., 1948-50; A.B., Okla. State U., 1957; m. Emma C. Felch, Mar. 2, 1952 (separated 1980); children—James William, Nancy Robertha. Designer, Sandia Corp., Albuquerque, 1957-60; supr. drafting Lytle Corp., Albuquerque, 1960-61; designer Thiokol Chem. Co., Brigham City, Utah, 1961-64, Vitro Engring. Co., Richland, Wash., 1964-67; sr. profl. designer Battelle Meml. Inst., Richland, 1967-70, Battelle Pacific NW Lab., Richland, 1981—; sr. designer Westinghouse Hanford Co., Richland, 1970-81; pres. Bow Trailer Sales, Inc., Kennewick, Wash., 1971-80; treas. Tri-City Ind. Auto Dealer Assn., 1974-77. Served with USAF, 1950-54. Recreational Vehicle Industry Assn., Tri-City Ind. Auto Dealer Assn., U.S. Ind. Auto Dealer Assn., Better Bus. Bur. Republican. Club: Tri-City Caravaners. Patentee high pressure quick release closure, other tech. innovations. Home: 3960 W Van Giesen Lot 18 West Richland WA 99352 Office: Room 117 OSB Bldg Battelle Blvd Richland WA 99352

SMITH, BRUCE AINSLIE, economist; b. Phila., Nov. 23, 1945; s. Theodore A. and Janice M. S.; children—Courtley L., Lindsay K. B.A. in Econs., Denison U., 1967; Ph.D. in Econs., Ind. U., 1972. With mgmt. info. systems group RCA Corp., 1967-68; industry economist Fed. Power Commn., Washington, 1972-74; program mgr. NSF, Washington, 1974-77; head econs. group Teknekron, Inc., Berkeley, Calif., 1977-78; prin. Econ. Resource Assocs., Berkeley, 1978—; v.p., sr. economist Minimax Research Corp., Berkeley, 1980—; lectr. Sch. Bus. Adminstrn., U. Calif.-Berkeley. Mem. Internat. Assn. Energy Economists, Am. Econs. Assn. Author: Technological Innovation in Electric Power Generation, 1950-70, 1977; contbr. articles to profl. jours. Office: Minimax Research Corp 2436 Durant Ave Berkeley CA 94704

SMITH, BRUCE LAZAR, clin. psychologist; b. San Francisco, Jan. 19, 1947; s. Irving and Dorothea Bernice (Spivak) S.; A.B., U. Calif., Berkeley, 1968; A.M., Harvard U., 1969, Ph.D. (NIMH research fellow), 1973; m. Nadine May-Ing Tang, July 28, 1979. Advanced fellow Austen Riggs Center, Stockbridge, Mass., 1973-77; dir. sociotherapy, dept. psychiatry Mt. Zion Hosp., San Francisco, 1977-79; pvt. practice psychotherapy, psychodiagnostics and orgnl. consultation, San Francisco, 1977—; asst. clin. prof. med. psychology U. Calif. (San Francisco); core faculty, dir. clin. tng. Grad. Sch. Psychology, Wright Inst., also dir. clinic; attending psychologist Mt. Zion Hosp. and Med. Center. Lic. psychologist, Mass., Calif.; cert. Nat. Register Health Service Providers in Psychology. Mem. Am. Psychol. Assn., Internat. Soc. Polit. Psychology, Soc. Psychol. Study of Social Issues, San Francisco Bay Area Psychol. Assn. (treas., dir.), Phi Beta Kappa. Research and publs. on psychotherapy and psychoanalytic process, group and systems theory and practice, psychol. interventions in phys. disease, inpatient treatment. Office: 2354 Post St San Francisco CA 94115

SMITH, CAREY BERNARD, real estate lending company executive; b. Los Angeles, Jan. 14, 1953; s. Floyd D. and Helen I. (Peterson) S.; m. Jacquelyn Louise Thomas, Dec. 7, 1974; children—Shelley Monique, Jamie Michele. Student Calif. State U., Los Angeles, 1971, Pasadena City Coll., 1981-83. With Haris Upham, Los Angeles, 1972-73; asst. mgr. Los Angeles Fed. Savs. and Loan Assn., 1974-77; asst. sec. Great Western Savs. and Loan Assn., Los Angeles, 1976-79; property rehab. specialist City of Pasadena (Calif.), 1981-83; exec. v.p. R.S. & Assocs., San Marino, Calif., 1983—; pres. Innovative Devel. & Community Services, Inc., Los Angeles, 1980—. Mem. Urban League of Pasadena, NAACP, Youth Motivation Task Force, Tournament of Roses Assn., City of Pasadena Tennis Tournament, San Marino C. of C., El Monte C. of C., Compton C. of C., Los Angeles C. of C. Clubs: Altadena Country, Rotary.

SMITH, CARTER BLAKEMORE, broadcaster; b. San Francisco, Jan. 1, 1937; s. Donald V. and Charlotte M. (Nichols) S.; A.A., City Coll. San Francisco, 1958; B.A., San Francisco State U., 1960; postgrad. N.Y. Inst. Finance, 1969-70, Coll. Fin. Planning, 1982; children—Carter Blakemore, Clayton M. Announcer, KBLF Radio, Red Bluff, Calif., 1954-56; personality KRE-KRE FM Radio, Berkeley, Calif., 1958-63, KSFO Radio, San Francisco, 1963-72, KNBR Radio, San Francisco, 1972—; faculty Radio-TV dept. San Francisco State U., 1960-61. Mem. adv. bd. Little Jim Club Children's Hosp., 1968-71. Bd. dirs. Marin County Humane Soc., 1968-73, San Francisco Zool. Soc., 1980—; trustee Family Service Agy. Marin, 1976-82. Recipient award San Francisco Press Club, 1965. Mem. Amateur Radio Relay League (life), Quarter Century Wireless Assn., Alpha Epsilon Rho. Club: Circumnavigators (N.Y.C.). Office: KNBR 1700 Montgomery St 4th Floor San Francisco CA 94111

SMITH, CATHERINE SHIRLEY, employment company executive; b. Malden, Mass., Apr. 10, 1930; d. Daniel John and Dolena (MacGinns) Mackenzie. Student Keene Tchrs. Coll., 1948-49, U. Fla., 1949-51; B.S. in Psychology, U. N.H., 1952. Dept. mgr. John Hancock Co., Boston, 1952-53; office mgr. Am. Standard Co., Denver, 1953-57; owner, pres. Mile-Hi Employment, Inc., Denver, 1958—. Mem. NOW, Nat. Assn. Female Execs., Am. Soc. Profl. Exec. Women, Smithsonian Assn., Denver Zool. Assn., Animal Protection Inst. Am., Audubon Soc., Am. Mus. Natural History, Nature Conservatory, Colo. Republican 250 Club. Office: Suite 120 1355 S Colorado Blvd Denver CO 80222

SMITH, CECIL ALDEN, sculptor, journalist; b. Salt Lake City, Feb. 12, 1910; s. Lafayette and Charlotte (Burdick) S.; m. Lucille Audrey Harkness, June 20, 1942 (div.); m. Marie Valma Weedon, May 28, 1952; children—Pauline, Gregory, Rockwell, Kent, Guy, Rinian, LaPriel, Stephen, Raychelle, Carey, Charlotta. Student U. Utah, 1929-30, Brigham Young U., 1932-33, U. Hawaii, 1944-45; pvt. art studies, 1928-42. Rancher, cowboy, 1920-60, painter known as Last of the Rare Breed; owner, operator BarBell Land & Cattle Co., 1925-60; fine artist, sculptor, journalist, 1928—; freelance illustrator, N.Y.C., 1942-43; art dir. Agnew Alvt. Agy., Lewiston, Idaho, 1959, Hwy. 95 Assn., Lewiston, 1962-66; asst. art. dir. Brigham Young Motion Picture Studio, Provo, Utah, 1966-69; muralist, Utah, 1966-69; freelance illustrator, Idaho and Utah, 1928-70, N.Y.C., 1970-71; fine arts artist, sculptor, journalist, Utah and Mont., 1969—; works exhibited: Grand Central Galleries, N.Y.C., 1976, Corcoran Gallery, Washington, 1937, Utah State Heritage Mus. Collection, Salt Lake City, 1937, Idaho State Bur. Mines, Boise, 1939, Cuban Mus. Art, Daytona, Fla., 1979, Jackie Fine Arts Collection, N.Y.C., 1980-82, Peggy and Harold Samuels Mus. Art, N.Mex., 1978, Reg Williams, Ltd., Adelaide, South Australia, 1950, W.J. Weedon, North Fremantle, West Australia, 1951, 80, Peter H. Dillingham, Scottsdale, Ariz. and Honolulu, 1981, 82; represented in permanent collection Brigham Young U., 1934; 30 murals commd. by Brigham Young U. Motion Picture Studio, 1966-69; only Western Am. artist exhibiting Paris Expn. Art Fair, Louvre, 1937. Vice pres. Blaine County Taxpayers League, 1952-54. Served with USNR, 1943-45. Recipient Silver medal Western Heritage Art Fair, Littleton, Colo., 1976, Gold medal, 1977, Gold medal Acad. Italy, 1979, others. Mem. N.W. Artists Group, Buckaroo Artists Am. (v.p.), Artists Fellowship, Inc., Accademia Italia delle Artie del Lavoro. Republican. Clubs: Salmagundi, Artists Fellowship. Home and Studio: 1485 Montana 82 Somers MT 59932

SMITH, CHARLES ANTHONY, state ofcl.; b. Santa Fe, Sept. 16, 1939; s. Frances (Mier) Smith; student adminstrv. and law courses; m. Paula Ann Thomas, June 26, 1965; 1 dau., Charlene Danielle. Circulation mgr. Daily Alaska Empire, 1960-63; agt. Mut. of N.Y. Life Ins. Co., Juneau, Alaska, 1964-65; mng. partner Future Investors in Alaska and Cinema Alaska, Juneau, 1961-62; SE Alaska rep. K & L Distbrs., 1966-68; mgr. Alaska Airlines Newspapers, SE Alaska, 1969; dep. Alaska Retirement System, Juneau, 1970-71; apptd. dir. hwy. safety, gov.'s hwy. safety rep., Juneau, 1971—. Alaska pres. Muscular Dystrophy Assn. Am.; pres. SE Alaska Emergency Med. Services Council, 1965-72. Served to capt. Army N.G., 1964—. Named Alaska Safety Man of Yr., 1977. Mem. Am. Assn. Motor Vehicle Adminstrs., Alaska Peace Officers Assn., Nat. Assn. Gov.s' Hwy. Safety Reps., N.G. Assn., Internat. Platform Assn. Roman Catholic. Club: Elks (Juneau). Author various hwy. safety manuals and plans, 1971—. Home: PO Box 493 Douglas AK 99824 Office: Pouch N Juneau AK 99811

SMITH, CHARLES CONARD, mfg. co. exec.; b. Mexico, Mo., Feb. 10, 1936; s. Charles Adelbert and Waldine Barnes S.; B.S.in Ceramic Engring., Iowa State U., 1958; M.B.A., Stanford U., 1962; m. Constance Eleanor Nagel, Oct. 6, 1962; children—Stewart Ashley, Graham Prior. Process engr. Kaiser Refractories, Moss Landing, Calif., 1962; materials mgr., Mexico, Mo., 1964-67, div. planning staff, Oakland, Calif., 1967-69, v.p., gen. mgr., Buenos Aires, Argentina, 1969-77, mktg. mgr., Oakland, Calif., 1977-80, gen. mgr. mfg., 1980-82, v.p., gen. mgr. refractories div., 1982—. Bd. dirs. Alameda County Easter Seal Soc., 1979—; chmn. bd. deacons Piedmont Community Ch., 1980. Served with USN, 1958-60. Mem. Am. Ceramic Soc. Republican. Patentee in field. Home: 63 Lincoln Ave Piedmont CA 94611 Office: 300 Lakeside Dr Oakland CA 94643

SMITH, CHARLES JENNINGS, electronics co. exec.; b. Los Angeles, July 15, 1927; s. George Roger and Caroline (Jennings) S.; student Calif. Inst. Tech., 1945, UCLA, 1949-52; M.B.A., Calif. State U., Dominguez Hills, 1976; m. Lillian Claire Fallon, June 16, 1972; children—Kathryn Edith, Michael Mackenzie. Acct., Westside Bldg. Material Corp., Culver City, Calif., 1953, credit mgr., 1954-58, br. mgr., 1958-60; owner, mgr. Smith Vending & Midway-Matic Wash, Escondido, Calif., 1961-65; spl. sales rep. U.S. Plywood Corp., Los Angeles, 1966-68; owner, mgr. Smith Investment & Adv. Co., Palos Verdes, Calif., 1968-74; controller, Craig Corp., Compton, Calif., 1974—; v.p. Dimension Splty. Co., 1981; sec., v.p. GRS Industries, 1979—, also dir.; cons., lectr. on stock market investments El Camino Coll. 1970-74. Troop leader Crescent Bay council Boy Scouts Am., 1944-45. Served with USN, 1945-48. Mem. Phi Kappa Sigma. Republican. Congregationalist. Club: Optimists. Home: 27928 Ridgebrook Ct Rancho Palos Verdes CA 90274 Office: 921 W Artesia Blvd Compton CA 90220

SMITH, CHARLES RICHTER, III, marine corps officer; b. Griffin, Ga., Apr. 9, 1943; s. Charles Richter and Peggy (Jones) S.; B.S. in Geology cum laude, U. Ga., 1971; postgrad. U. Utah, 1971-72; m. Janice Virginia Deas, Mar. 18, 1972. Pilot, EPPS Air Service, Chamblee, Ga., 1965-68; geol. asst. H.G. Schoenike, Inc., Houston, summers, 1969, 70; commd. 2d lt. USMC, 1972, advanced through grades to capt., 1981; fighter pilot Marine Corps Air Sta., Yuma, Ariz., 1972-81; exchange duty as fighter pilot Royal Australian Navy, Royal Australian Naval Air Sta., Nowra, New South Wales, 1981—. Decorated Nat. Def. medal, Overseas Service ribbon. Republican. Episcopalian. Office: c/o Royal Australian Navy NOWRA APO San Francisco CA 96209

SMITH, CHESTER, broadcasting executive; b. Wade, Okla., Mar. 29, 1930; s. Louis L. and Effie (Brown) S.; m. Naomi L. Crenshaw, July 19, 1959; children—Laurie, Lorna, Roxanne. Country western performer on Capitol records, TV and radio, 1947-61; owner, mgr. Sta. KLOC, Ceres-Modesto, Calif., 1953-81; owner, pres. Sta. KCSO, Modesto, 1966-83, Sta. KCBA-TV, Salinas-Monterey, 1981—, Sainte Broadcasting Corp., Salinas, 1966—. Mem. Calif. Broadcasters Assn. Republican. Mem. Christian Ch. Original rec. Wait A Little Longer Please Jesus, Country Music Hall of Fame, Nashville, 1955.

SMITH, CLIFFORD EDWARD, astronomer, educator; b. Olmstead County, Minn., July 30, 1901; s. Frank J. and Jessie May (Phillips) S.; A.B., Carleton Coll., 1923; M.A., Swarthmore Coll., 1926; Ph.D., U. Calif., Berkeley, 1936; m. Ruth Kinell, June 24, 1929; children—Helen Smith Stanley, Nelson Edward, Eric Thomas. Research asst. math. and astronomy Swarthmore Coll., 1924-26; instr. Carleton Coll., 1926-27; teaching fellow in astronomy U. Calif., Berkeley, 1927-28, 29-30; instr. Calif. State U., Fresno, 1928-29, asst. prof. astronomy, 1932-34; instr. Mills Coll., 1930-31; Lick fellow in astronomy Lick Obs., U. Calif., 1931-32, asst. computing, 1934-36; faculty San Diego State U., 1937—, prof. astronomy, 1946-69, prof. emeritus, 1969—; cons. Convair Astronautics, 1953-60; project dir. geodetic moon observing program San Diego State U. and U.S. Naval Obs., Internat. Geophys. Yr., 1957-61. Served with USNR, 1941-46; ret. as capt. USNR, 1961. Fellow AAAS; mem. Am. Astron. Soc., Astron. Soc. of Pacific, Sigma Xi, Sigma Pi Sigma. Condr. research stellar spectra, photographic photometry. Home: 707 Sacramento St Dutch Flat CA 95714

SMITH, CLIFFORD NEAL, business educator, writer; b. Wakita, Okla., May 30, 1923; s. Jesse Newton and Inez Lane (Jones) S.; B.S., Okla. State U., 1943; A.M., U. Chgo., 1948; postgrad. Columbia U., 1960; m. Anna Piszczan-Czaja, Sept. 3, 1951; children—Helen Inez Smith Barrette. Selector, U.S. Displaced Persons Commn., Washington and Munich, Germany, 1948-51; auditor Phillips Petroleum Co., Caracas, Venezuela, 1951-58; planning analyst Mobil Internat. Oil Co., N.Y.C., 1960, 65-66, Mobil Oil A.G., Deutschland, Hamburg, Germany, 1961-63; asst. to v.p. for Germany, Mobil Inner Europe, Inc., Geneva, 1963-65; asst. prof. No. Ill. U. Sch. Bus., DeKalb, 1966-69, prof. internat. bus., part-time 1970—; owner Westland Publs.; writer, lectr. Mem. at large exec. com. Friends Com. on Nat. Legis., 1968-75; mem. regional exec. com. Am. Friends Service Com., 1969-76; v.p. Riverside Democrats, N.Y.C., 1959-61. Recipient Distinguished Service medal Ill. Geneal. Soc., 1973, award for outstanding service to sci. genealogy Am. Soc. Genealogists, 1973. Mem. S.R., SAR, Soc. Descs. Colonial Clergy, Soc. Advancement Mgmt., Ill. Genealogic Soc. (dir. 1968-69), Phi Eta Sigma, Beta Alpha Psi, Sigma Iota Epsilon. Mem. Soc. of Friends. Club: American of Hamburg (v.p. 1962-63). Author: Federal Land Series, Vol. 1, 1972, Vol. 2, 1973, Vol. 3, 1980 Vol. 4, part 1, 1982; Ency. of German-American Geneal. Research, 1975; American Genealogical Resources in German Archives, 1977; numerous monographs in German-Am., Brit.-Am., French-Am. geneal. research series, German and Central European Emigration series; contbg. editor Nat. Geog. Soc. Quar., Geneal. Jour. (Utah); contbr. articles to profl. jours. Address: PO Box 117 McNeal AZ 85617

SMITH, CORTLAND BROSS, educational administrator, political science educator; b. Washington, May 28, 1944; s. Robert Lane and Carol (MacLean) S. B.A. with distinction, U. Calif.-Berkeley, 1968, M.A., 1969, Ph.D., 1975. Mem. faculty U. Pacific, Stockton, 1970—, dir. Taiwan Program, 1976-78, dir. Office of Internat. Programs, 1982—, prof. polit. sci., 1982—. Recipient Teaching Incentive award U. Pacific, 1976, 81; Spl. Career fellow, 1968-70. Mem. Am. Polit. Sci. Assn., Assn. for Asian Studies, African Studies Assn., Nat. Assn. Fgn. Student Advisors, Phi Beta Kappa, Pi Sigma Alpha. Office: Office of Internat Programs Bechtel Internat Ctr U Pacific Stockton CA 95211

SMITH, CYNTHIA JOY, computer analyst, programmer; b. Glen Ridge, N.J., Dec. 25, 1951; d. Herbert James and Frances Jane (Van Ness) S. B.A., Springfield Coll., 1973; M.S.W., U. Hawaii, 1976; M.B.A., Pepperdine U., 1982. Coordinator, Pacific Allied Health Project, Honolulu, 1977-78; programmer analyst Computab, Inc., Honolulu, 1980-82; exec. dir. Hale Ho'Ola Hou, Honolulu, 1977-81; med. cons. Microsystems U.S.A. Inc., Honolulu, 1982—; med. social worker Upjohn's Home Health Agy., Honolulu, 1976—; analyst, programmer The Queen's Med. Ctr., Honolulu, 1982—; instr. U. Hawaii Sch. Social Work, 1977-80. Mem. Women in Small Bus. Com., SBA, 1983; chmn. pub. affairs, bd. dirs. Hawaii Planned Parenthood Assn., 1981—. Mem. Assn. Women Entrepreneurs, Am. Bus. Women's Assn., Acad. Cert. Social Workers, Nat. Assn. Social Workers. Democrat. Home: 1802 Keeaumoku St Honolulu HI 96822 Office: 1301 Punchbowl St Room 217 Honolulu HI 96813

SMITH, CYRUS DONALD, III, accountant; b. Great Falls, Mont., Sept. 3, 1947; s. Cyrus Donald and Alice Kay (Newman) S.; m. Jane Carol James, Aug. 9, 1977. B.S., Calif. State U.-Hayward, 1971; M.B.A., Wash. State U., 1976. C.P.A., Wash., Calif., Alaska. Sr. auditor Peat, Marwick, Mitchell & Co., C.P.A.s, Oakland, Calif., 1971-73; sr. auditor TransAlaska Pipeline Project, 1974, procurement supr., 1975; asst. prof. acctg., taxation Central Wash. State U., 1976; mgmt. cons. Touche-Ross & Co., Seattle, 1977; pres. Smith-Feley & Co., P.S., C.P.A.s, Tacoma, Wash., 1978—. Chmn., Pierce County Planning Commn., 1982—. Served with AUS, 1966-69. Mem. Associated Gen. Contractors Tacoma, Utility Contractors Assn. Wash., Am. Inst. C.P.A.s, Wash. Soc. C.P.A.s. Roman Catholic. Clubs: Propeller, Optimist of West Tacoma, Elks. Home: 5310 66th Ave W Tacoma WA 98462 Office: 1102 Broadway Plaza Suite 401 Tacoma WA 98402

SMITH, DAVID BERYL DEAN, human factors educator; b. Willows, Calif., Apr. 13, 1933; s. Juddie Townsend and Glayds Mae (Clevenger) S.; m. Faith Victoria Smith, June 11, 1960; children—Deborah, Lawrence. B.A., UCLA, 1958, Ph.D., 1964. Research psychologist Ames Research Ctr., Moffett Field, Calif., 1964-69; asst. prof. dept. human factors U. So. Calif., 1970-76, assoc. prof., 1976—, chmn. dept., 1976—; research assoc. Andrus Gerontology Ctr., Los Angeles, 1976—. Mem. Am. Psychol. Assn., Soc. Psychophysiol. Research, Human Factors Soc., Internat. Ergonomics Soc., Sigma Xi. Democrat. Presbyterian. Author: Man-Environmental Factors in Systems Management, 1974. Home: 1311 S Brass Lantern Dr La Habra CA 90631 Office: U So Calif Los Angeles CA 90007

SMITH, DAVID EDWARD, vascular surgeon; b. Dothan, Ala., Oct. 24, 1944; s. Oliphant Samuel and Marian Palmer (Walker) S.; B.S., Davidson Coll., 1964; M.D., U. Pa., 1968; m. Cheryl Priscilla Grimes, July 29, 1967; children—Leigh Taliaferro, David Edward, Ashley May, Whitney Buchanan. Surg. intern U. Pa., 1968-69; resident in gen. surgery U.S. Naval Hosp., San Diego, 1969-73, staff surgeon trauma service, 1973-74, fellow peripheral vascular surgery, 1974-75, dir. surg. intensive care unit, 1975, dir. blood flow lab., 1976-78; dir. intensive care unit Good Samaritan Hosp., San Jose, Calif., 1978—; asst. clin. prof. surgery U. Calif., San Diego. Served to comdr. USN, 1969-78. Diplomate Nat. Bd. Med. Examiners. Fellow ACS, Southwestern Surg. Congress; mem. Am. Trauma Soc., Soc. Clin. Vascular Surgery, Assn. Acad. Surgery, Soc. Critical Care Medicine. Democrat. Episcopalian. Contbg. author: Vascular Surgery, 1977, 83; contbr. articles to profl. jours. Home: 116 Teresita Way Los Gatos CA 95030 Office: 2512 Samaritan Ct Suite M San Jose CA 95124

SMITH, DAVID ELVIN, physician; b. Bakersfield, Calif., Feb. 7, 1939; s. Elvin W. and Dorothy (McGinnis) S.; A.A., Bakersfield Coll., 1958; B.A., U. Calif. at Berkeley, 1960, M.D., U. Calif. at San Francisco, 1964, M.S. in Pharmacology, 1964; m. Millicent Buxton; children—Julia, Suzanne, Christopher Buxton. Christopher Buxton-Smith. Intern, San Francisco Gen. Hosp., 1965; fellow pharmacology and toxicology U. Calif. at San Francisco, 1965-67, assoc. clin. prof. toxicology dept. pharmacology Med. Ctr., 1967—, dir. psychopharmacology study group, 1966-70; practice medicine specializing in toxicology, drug abuse, alcoholism and sexology San Francisco, 1965—; physician Presbyn. Alcoholic Clinic, 1965-67, Contra Cost Alcoholic Clinic, 1965-67; dir. alcohol and drug abuse screening unit San Francisco Gen. Hosp., 1967-68; co-dir. Calif. drug abuse info. project U. Calif. Med. Ctr., 1967-72; founder, med. dir. Haight-Ashbury Free Med. Clinic, San Francisco, 1967—; chmn. Nat. Drug Abuse Conf., 1977; mem. Calif. Gov.'s Commn. on Narcotics and Drug Abuse, 1977—; nat. health adviser to Pres. Carter; dir. Benzodiazepine Research and Tng. Project, Amphetamine Edn. and Tng. Project, Substance Abuse and Sexual Concerns Project, PCP Research and Tng. Project; cons. numerous fed. drug abuse agys. Pres., Youth Projects, Inc.; founder, chm. bd., pres. Nat. Free Clin. Council, 1968-72. Recipient Research award Borden Found., 1964; AMA Research award, 1966; Community Service award

U. Calif. at San Francisco, 1974. Mem. San Francisco Med. Soc., Am. Pub. Health Assn., Calif. soc. Treatment of Alcohol and other Drug Dependencies (pres.), Phi Beta Kappa, Sigma Xi. Unitarian. Author: Love Needs Care, 1970; The New Social Drug: Cultural, Medical and Legal Perspectives on Marijuana, 1971; The Free Clinic: Community Approaches to Health Care and Drug Abuse, 1971; co-author: It's so Good, Don't Even Try it Once. Heroin in Perspective, 1972, Uppers and Downers, 1973, Drugs in the Classroom, 1973; Barbituate Use and Abuse, 1977; A Multicultural View of Drug Abuse, 1978; Amphetamine Use, Misuse and Abuse, 1979; co-author: PCP: Problems and Prevention, 1981; Sexological Aspects of Substance Use and Abuse; also drug edn. films. Founder, editor Jour. Psychedelic Drugs (now Jour Psychoactive Drugs), 1967—. Contbr. over 100 articles to profl. jours. Home: 80 Parnassus Ave San Francisco CA 94131 Office: 409 Clayton St San Francisco CA 94117

SMITH, DAVID EUGENE, educator; b. Boise, Idaho, Dec. 14, 1941; s. Roy Arthur and Anna Margaret (Fries) S.; B.S. in Applied Stats., San Francisco State Coll., 1964, M.S. in Mgmt. Sci., 1966; M.B.A., U. Santa Clara, 1969, Ph.D. in Bus. Adminstrn., 1969; m. Patricia Kay Stroy, Aug. 4, 1973; 1 son, Zachary Adam. Asst. to dir. The Mgmt. Center, Grad. Sch. Bus., U. Santa Clara (Calif.), 1966-69, lectr. in mktg., 1968; prof. bus. adminstrn., mktg. quantitative studies Sch. Bus., San Jose (Calif.) State U., 1976—, asst. prof., 1969-71, asso. prof., 1971-76. Mem. Inst. Mgmt. Sci., Ops. Research Soc. Am., Am. Inst. Decision Sci., Acad. of Mgmt., Am. Enterprise Inst. for Public Policy Research. Republican. Christian Ch. Author: Quantitative Business Analysis, 1977, internat. edit. 1979; contbr. articles to profl. jours. Home: 22448 Tim Tam Ct Los Gatos CA 95030 Office: Mktg Quantitative Studies San Jose State Univ San Jose CA 95192

SMITH, DENNY, congressman; b. Ontario, Oreg., Jan. 19, 1938; m. Kathleen Barrett, 1968; children—Maggie, Barrett, Ryan. B.A. in Polit. Sci., Willamette U., 1961. Chmn. Eagle Newspapers, Inc.; co-pilot/flight engr. Pan Am. World Airways, 1967-76; pvt. pilot; mem. U.S. Congress from 5th Congl. Dist. Oreg., 1980—. Exec. com. Nat. Republican Congl. Com. Served in Vietnam. Decorated Air Medal with 6 oak leaf clusters. Mem. Vietnam Vets. Caucus, Oreg. Newspaper Pubs. Assn., Nat. Newspaper Assn., Young Pres.'s Orgn., Assoc. Oreg. Industries, Aircraft Owners and Pilots Assn., Beta Theta Pi. Office: 1213 Longworth House Office Bldg Washington DC 20515*

SMITH, DONALD E., broadcast engr. and mgr.; b. Salt Lake City, Sept. 10, 1930; s. Thurman A. and Louise (Cardall) S.; B.A. Columbia Coll., Chgo., 1955; B.S.; U. Utah, 1970; postgrad. U. So. Calif., U. Utah; m. Helen B. Lacy, 1978. Engr., Iowa State U., (WOI-TV), 1955-56; asst. chief engr. KLRJ-TV, Las Vegas, 1956-60; studio field engr. ABC, Hollywood, Cal., 1960; chief engr. Teletape, Inc., Salt Lake City, 1961; engring. supr. KUER, U. Utah, Salt Lake City, 1962—, gen. mgr., 1975—. Free lance cinematography, 1950—; cons. engr. radio and TV prodns., 1965—. Mem. Soc. Motion Pictures and TV Engrs., Lambda Chi Alpha. Home: 963 Hollywood Ave Salt Lake City UT 84105

SMITH, DONALD EVANS, library cons.; b. Shenendoah, Iowa, Dec. 2, 1915; s. William Wesley and Bess Alice (Evans) S.; student Ricks Coll., 1939-40; B.A., Hastings Coll., 1946; M.L.S., U. Wash., 1964. Tchr. English, librarian Tenino (Wash.) High Sch., 1950-51, Rochester (Wash.) High Sch., 1954-59; librarian North Thurston High Sch., Lacey, Wash., 1959-67; head librarian, coordinator instructional materials Lakes High Sch., Lakewood Center, Wash., 1967-80; library cons., 1980—. Mem. awards com. Wash. Library Commn., 1964-66. Served with Signal Corps, AUS, 1942-45; to 1st lt., M.I., U.S. Army, 1951-54; to col. Wash. State Guard, 1971-80, now ret. Mem. Wash. Assn. Sch. Librarians (com. chmn.), Clover Park Edn. Assn. (com. chmn. 1970-71), Am. Legion, Phi Delta Kappa (del. nat. confs.). Home and Office: 4530 26th Loop SE Lacey WA 98503

SMITH, DONALD PEACOCKE, educator, administrator; b. Pasadena, Calif., Apr. 29, 1953; s. Richard Dillon and Marguerite Booth (Peacocke) S. B.A. in Counseling and Psychology, Antioch Coll., 1976; M.A. in Counseling, San Jose State U., 1983. Cert. pupil personnel services, Calif.; cert. adolescent devel. specialist Western Inst. for Study of Adolescence. Founder, dir. John Muir High Sch., Ojai, Calif., 1974—, assoc. dir., 1977—; cons. Challenge Edn./West, San Jose, Calif., 1978—, sr. cons., 1981—; pvt. practice counseling, Los Gatos, Calif., 1979-82; founder, dir. Almaden Valley Youth Counseling Service (Calif.), 1979; part-time faculty San Jose State U., 1981-82; program dir. St. Andrew's Residence for Boys, Cupertino, Calif., 1981—. Founder Ventura (Calif.) Community Outreach Programs, 1973-75; mem. adv. bd. Santa Clara County (Calif.) Children's Shelter, 1982—. State of Calif. youth authority grantee, 1975-76, youth services grantee, 1976. Mem. Am. Personnel and Guidance Assn., Phi Delta Kappa. Episcopalian. Author: The Self Directing Teenager, 1981. Home: PO Box 156 New Almaden CA 95042 Office: 21658 Almaden Rd New Almaden CA 95042

SMITH, DONALD SCHELLIN, advt. exec.; b. Chgo., June 19, 1924; s. Donald F. and Helen M. (Schellin) S.; Ph.B., U. Chgo., 1947, B.S., 1949; m. Virginia Lyons, Apr. 5, 1946; children—Allan, Rebecca, Philip, Pamela, Andrew, Marcella, Claudia. Sr. instr. Keesler AFB, Miss., 1949-53; communications mgr. Hughes Aircraft Co., Los Angeles, 1953-60; dir. communications American Systems, Hawthorne, Calif., 1960-62; pres. Donald S. Smith Assos., Anaheim, Calif., 1962—, Am. Portrait Films, Anaheim, Calif., instr. tech. writing Chapman Coll., Orange, Calif., 1965-66. Founder, pres. Crusade for Life, Inc.; mem. Christian Businessmen's Com. of Anaheim, chmn., 1970, 80; exec. dir. Calif. Pro Life Council, 1978-79. Served with USAF, 1942-45. Recipient Mike Blackshear award Calif. Pro Life Council, 1978, ad awards first place Orange County Advt. Fedn., 1972, cert. of excellence, ad awards, 1975. Mem. IEEE (sr.). Republican. Presbyterian. Tech. advisor on film: Assignment: Life, 1980. Home: 2511 Shady Valley Ln La Habra CA 90631 Office: 1695 W Crescent Suite 524 Anaheim CA 92801

SMITH, DONNA LILIAN, seminar co. exec.; b. Phila., Oct. 8, 1944; d. Joseph Patrick and Mary Elizabeth (Veronica) Burke; student Calif. State U., Northridge, 1962-64; Asso. degree, Fashion Inst. Calif., 1969. Fashion coordinator, 1963-68; dir. Fashion Mdsg. Inst., 1968-69; v.p. Fashion Inst. Design and Mdsg., 1969-78; pres., owner Seminars Internat., Los Angeles, 1979—; producer fashion shows, cons. in field; mem. costume council Los Angeles County Mus. Art. Mem. Costume Soc. Am., Fashion Group. Roman Catholic. Office: 15910 Ventura Blvd Suite 800 Encino CA 91436

SMITH, DORIS WILMA, mathematics educator; b. Greensboro, N.C., Aug. 21, 1933; d. David Harry and Wilma Gertrude (Kerns) Dunn; m. Ralph Ray Smith, June 1, 1957; children—August Glenn, Harriet Leigh, Marcus Ray. B.S., Flora Macdonald Coll., Red Springs, N.C., 1955; M.A.T. in Biol. Sci. and Math., U. Calif.-Irvine, 1973; Ph.D., U. Beverly Hills (Calif.), 1980. Cert. tchr., Calif. Tchr. sci. St. Paul's (N.C.) High Sch., 1955-57; tchr. math. Belmont (N.C.) City Schs., 1962-64, Charlotte-Mecklenburg Schs., N.C., 1964-65, Newport-Mesa Unified Sch. Dist., Newport Beach, Calif., 1965-67, Anaheim (Calif.) Union High Sch. Dist., 1967-81, Fontana (Calif.) Unified Sch. Dist., 1982—. Leader Open Adoption Records, N.C.; mem. Orange County (Calif.) Election Bd.; bd. dirs. Orange County Sci. and Engring. Fair. E.I. duPont de Nemours fellow, 1956. Mem. NEA, Calif. Tchrs. Assn., Fontana Tchrs. Assn. Democrat. Presbyterian. Club: Internat. Women's Writers Guild. Author: Science, Math and You, 1973; A Limb of Your Tree, 1983; poems: Thank You, Natural Mother, 1981, On Our Wedding Day, 1982. Home: 912 Hayward St Anaheim CA 92804 Office: 8425 Mango Ave Fontana CA 92335

SMITH, EDWARD BRUCE, state senator; b. Dagmar, Mont., May 7, 1920; s. Bruce Albert and Johanna (Grelong) S.; m. Juliet Elievold, 1945; children—Gary, Douglas, Bruce, Rodney. Mem. Mont. Ho. of Reps. from Sheridan County, 1967-73, Mont. State Senate, 1975—. Mem. County Fair Bd., 1960—; alt. del. Republican Nat. Conv., 1972; 4-H leader. Mem. Mont. Wool Growers (pres.), Sheridan County Grain Growers Assn. Republican. Lutheran. Clubs: Elks, Moose. Home: RR 1 Box 11 Dagmar MT 59219 Office: Montana State Senate Helena MT 59620

SMITH, ELIZABETH MARTINEZ, librarian; b. Upland, Calif., Apr. 14, 1943; d. Miguel S. and Venus E. (Espinoza) Martinez; m. Michael W. Smith, June 29, 1968; children—Nicolas, Maya. B.A., UCLA, 1965; M.S. in Library Sci., U. So. Calif., 1966. Children's librarian Los Angeles County Pub. Library, 1966-68, coordinator Spanish speaking services, 1968-72, regional adminstr., 1972-78, chief public services, 1978-79; county librarian Orange (Calif.) County, 1979—. Mem. bd. councillors Sch. Library and Info. Mgmt., U. So. Calif. Recipient George J. Sanchez award Nat. Assn. Spanish Speaking Librarians, 1976. Mem. Calif. Library Assn., ALA, Nat. Libraries Assn., New Majority Librarian Coalition, Women in Govt. Office: 431 City Dr S Orange CA 92668

SMITH, ERNEST KETCHAM, elec. engr.; b. Peking, China, May 31, 1922 (parents Am. citizens); s. Ernest Ketcham and Grace (Goodrich) S.; B.A. in Physics, Swarthmore Coll., 1944; M.Sc.E.E., Cornell U., 1951, Ph.D., 1956; m. Mary Louise Standish, June 23, 1950; children—Priscilla Smith Varland, Nancy Smith Glorvigen, Cynthia Smith Jackson. Chief plans and allocations engr. Mut. Broadcasting System, 1946-49; with Nat. Bur. Standards, 1951-65, chief ionosphere research sect., Boulder, Colo., 1957-60, div. chief, 1960-65; dir. aeronomy lab. Environ. Sci. Services Adminstrn., Boulder, 1965-67, dir. Inst. Telecommunication Scis., 1968, dir. Univ. relations, 1968-70; asso. dir. Inst. Telecommunication Scis., Office of Telecommunications, Boulder, 1970-72, cons., 1972-76; mem. tech. staff Jet Propulsion Lab., Calif. Inst. Tech., 1976—; vis. fellow Coop. Inst. Research on Environ. Scis., 1968; asso. Harvard U Coll. Obs., 1965-75; adj. prof. U. Colo., 1969-78; internat. vice-chmn. study group 6, Internat. Radio Consultative Com., 1958-70, chmn., 1970-76; mem. U.S. commn. Internat. Sci. Radio Union, Served with U.S. Army, 1944-45. Recipient Diploma d'honneur, Internat. Radio Consultative Com., Internat. Telecommunications Union, 1978. Fellow IEEE, AAAS; mem. Am. Geophys. Union. Mem. United Ch. of Christ. Clubs: Harvard Faculty, Univ. (Boulder), Athenaeum (Pasadena, Calif.); Flint Canyon Tennis (Pasadena). Author: Worldwide Occurrence of Sporadic E, 1957; (with S. Matsushita) Ionospheric Sporadic E, 1962; contbr. numerous articles to profl. jours.; editor: Electromagnetic Probing of the Upper Atmosphere, 1969. Home: 5019 Merita Pl La Canada CA 91011 Office: 161-228 Jet Propulsion Lab 4800 Oak Grove Dr Pasadena CA 91109

SMITH, FARROW JAMES, personal holding co. exec.; b. Ridgeland, S.C., Oct. 20, 1928; s. Farrow James and Claudia Anne (Brunson) S.; m. Grace Emily Hofmann, Apr. 7, 1951; children—Farrow J., Darrell F.H. Student Internat. Accts. Soc., 1960, U. S.C., 1965-66. Sec.-treas., dir. Blue Channel Corp., Port Royal, S.C., 1956-70; sec.-treas., dir. Alexander Dawson, Inc., Las Vegas, 1971-72, exec. v.p., dir., 1972-73, pres., treas., dir., 1973—; vice chmn. bd. dirs. Alexander Trust Co., Zurich, Switzerland, Blue Channel Corp., Port Royal; dir. ADI Communications, Inc., Dawson Oil Corp., Clearwater Communications Inc. Vice chmn. bd. trustees Alexander Dawson Found., Las Vegas. Mem. U.S. Power Squadrons. Republican. Lutheran. Club: Vet. Motor Car Am. Lodge: Masons. Home: 3551 Pueblo Way Las Vegas NV 89109 Office: Alexander Dawson Inc PO Box 19720 Las Vegas NV 89119

SMITH, FRAN KELLOGG, archtl. lighting designer; b. Chgo., Oct. 28, 1940; d. James Hull and Jean Mathieson (Defrees) Kellogg; B.A., Pomona Coll., 1966; postgrad. Claremont Grad. Sch., 1966-68; B.S. in Interior Design, Woodbury U., 1973; m. Frederick John Bertolone, July 3, 1976; children by previous marriages—Wayne E. McConnell III, Carol Jean McConnell, Scott Kellogg McConnell, Christina L. Smith. Partner, lighting designer Omnia, Los Angeles, 1970-71; staff lighting cons. Black, Swarens & Okada, Los Angeles, 1972-73; founder, owner, operator Luminae Lighting Cons., Los Angeles, 1973-76; chmn. bd. Luminae Inc., Los Angeles and San Francisco, 1976—; instr. interior design cert. program UCLA, 1980—; guest lectr. various seminars throughout U.S. Founder, charter pres. service sect. Faculty Wives Club, Calif. State U., Los Angeles, 1967, v.p., 1969; bd. dirs. Villa Esperanza Sch. for Retarded, Pasadena, Calif., 1969-72. Recipient 1st place award Los Angeles Art and Antiques Show, 1971, 2d place award for rendering Nat. Soc. Interior Designers, 1972, 1st pl. award for instns. Inst. Bus. Designers, 1974. Mem. Am. Soc. Interior Designers (2d pl. Halo award 1980, dir. No. Calif. 1980-81), AIA (chpt. affiliate), Designers Lighting Forum (founder, charter pres. Los Angeles chpt. 1972-74), Internat. Assn. Lighting Designers, Illumination Engring. Soc. (CASI award 1976). Republican. Episcopalian. Contbr. articles to Designers West, Miami Herald, Chgo. Tribune; designer low voltage luminaire (Pacifica cert. of merit 1980). Home: 315 Orange St San Gabriel CA 91776 Office: 3955 Washington St San Francisco CA 94118

SMITH, FRANK LEONARD, III, lawyer; b. Albuquerque, Oct. 16, 1946; s. Frank Leonard, Jr. and Mary Frances (Wilson) S.; LL.B., Armstrong Coll., Berkeley, Calif., 1973, M.B.A., 1977; m. Sandra Terepka. Admitted to Calif. bar, 1974; asso. firm Graves & Mallory, Oakland, Calif., 1973-74; ptnr. firm Bradley & Smith, Vallejo, Napa, Calif., 1974—. Pres., Vallejo Symphony, Marin County Commuters Assn., Calif. Young Republicans of Solano County; treas. San Francisco Annex; bd. dirs. Silverado council Boy Scouts Am., Solano County YMCA. Recipient Am. Jurisprudence award Armstrong Law Sch., 1973. Mem. Am. Bar Assn., Calif. Trial Lawyers Assn. Republican. Roman Catholic. Club: Silverado Country. Contbr. legal articles to Update Mag., 1978, 79. Home: 2060 Big Ranch Rd Napa CA 95688 Office: 521 Georgia St Vallejo CA 94590

SMITH, GAROLD DAVID, JR., architect-engineer; b. Colorado Springs, Colo., July 4, 1936; s. Garold David and Helen Louise (Sopko) S.; B.S., U. Colo. in Archtl. Engring., 1968; m. Mary Louise Mills, July 4, 1959; children—April Marie-Francine, Heather Anne-Elizabeth, Tiffanie Louise, Garold David III. Prin., Garold D. Smith Jr., Colorado Springs, 1970-73; project coordinator architect, asso. Page, Southerland & Page, med. cons., Austin, Tex., 1973-76; prin. Garold D. Smith Jr., AIA, Architect, Structural Engr., Passive Solar Cons., Colorado Springs, 1977—. Bd. dirs. Colorado Springs Regional Bldg. Dept. Plumbing Com., 1979—. Mem. Nat. Soc. Profl. Engrs., AIA (past pres. S. Colo. chpt., sec. Colo. Soc. Architects 1983), Internat. Solar Energy Soc., Constrn. Specifications Inst., Internat. Platform Assn. Republican. Roman Catholic. Clubs: Colorado Springs Rocky Mountain, Sertoma. Home: 1213 High Point Lane E Colorado Springs CO 80904 Office: 830 N Tejon St Suite 300B Colorado Springs CO 80903

SMITH, GENEVIEVE GRANT, elementary school principal; b. Meridian, Idaho, Dec. 3, 1922; d. Lawrence Jessie and Melitta Mae (Stiegelmeier) Grant; m. Jasper William Smith, Dec. 13, 1940; children—Lawrence Jasper, Lynda Jean, Eldon Howard, Stanley Dayle. A.A., Boise Jr. Coll., 1957, B.A., Northwest Nazarene Coll., 1964; M.Ed., Coll. Idaho, 1969. Classroom, vocal music tchr./coordinator Boise (Idaho) Ind. Sch. Dist., 1957-73, adminstrv. team leader Lowell Sch., 1973-76; asst. prin. Garfield Sch., 1976-78; prin. Whitney Sch., 1978—; workshop instr., active dist., state edn. coms. Mem. Vista Neighborhood Housing Services; active numerous fund-raising coms. Recipient Idaho Gem award Idaho Assn. Elem. Sch. Prins.; Life Merit award Idaho State PTA; Red Apple award Boise Sch. Dist.; grantee Title IV-C Match Program. Mem. Assn. Supervision and Curriculum Devel., Idaho Soc. Individual Psychology, Idaho Assn. Elem. Sch. Prins., Nat. Assn. Elem. Sch. Prins., Idaho Assn. Sch. Adminstrs., Boise Assn. Sch. Prins., Boise Edn. Assn., Idaho Edn. Assn., NEA, Northwest Women in Ednl. Adminstrn., Alumni Assn. Boise State U., Northwest Nazarene Coll. Assn., Yokefellows Assn., NOW, Phi Delta Kappa, Delta Kappa Gamma, Phi Delta Lambda. Republican. Contbr. articles to local newspapers. Home: 1825 S Pacific Boise ID 83705 Office: Whitney Elementary School 1609 S Owyhee Boise ID 83705

SMITH, GERALD ALVIN, data processing services co. exec.; b. Paso Robles, Calif., Mar. 31, 1939; s. Clark Murson and Eunice Deloris (Nicklas) S.; B.S. in Math., Calif. Poly. U., 1961; m. Patricia Fuhs, Jan. 26, 1963; children—Lisa Marie, Shauna Rae. Mgr. systems Saga Co., Menlo Park, Calif., 1964-66; v.p. Applied Cybernetics Corp., Sunnyvale, Calif., 1966-70; salesman Tenent Co., Sunnyvale, 1970-71; pres. G.A. Smith Co., Santa Clara, Calif., 1972—; founder, v.p. Applied Cybernetics Corp., Sunnyvale, 1965—. Mem. Data Processing Mgmt. Assn. Home: 14081 Sobey Meadows Ct Saratoga CA 95070 Office: 1075 Comstock St Santa Clara CA 95050

SMITH, GERALD ARTHUR, museum director; b. Gravette, Ark., June 5, 15; s. George A. and Mary Grace (Knox) S.; B.A., U. Redlands, 1937, M.A., 1939; Ed.D., U. So. Calif., 1953; m. June 17, 1938; children—Jerilynn, Geoffrey, Meredith, David. Tchr. jr. high sch., Bloomington, Calif., 1937-40; coach of freshmen U. Redlands (Calif.), 1937-38; tchr. adult edn. Colton (Calif.) High Sch., 1938-40; teaching prin. Warm Springs Elementary Sch., San Bernardino, Calif., 1940-41; dist. supt. Warm Springs Sch. Dist., San Bernardino, 1941-43; adviser Vet.'s Guidance Center, San Diego, 1945; coordinator Vet.'s Guidance Center, San Bernardino Valley Coll., San Bernardino, 1945-46; dist. supt. Bloomington (Calif.) Sch. Dist., 1954-56; assoc. supt. then dist. supt. Colton Joint Unified Sch. Dist., 1966-71; dir. San Bernardino County Museums, Redlands, 1971-83; vis. prof. edn. U. Calif.-Riverside, 1955. Bd. dirs., sec.-treas. Bloomington Park and Recreation Dist.; bd. dirs. Arrowhead Area council Boy Scouts Am., Arrowhead United Fund, ARC, Bloomington, YMCA, San Bernardino; coordinator San Bernardino County Info. Ctr., Calif. Archeol. Inventory; Served with USNR, 1943-45. Decorated Purple Heart; recipient Am. Educators medal Freedoms Found., 1963; spl. award Indian affairs Conf. of Calif. Hist. Socs., 1971. Mem. Soc. Calif. Archaeology, Calif. Conf. Hist. Socs. (pres.), Am. Assn. Museums, Calif. Assn. Museums (v.p.), Am. Assn. State and Local History, Pacific Coast Archaeol. Soc., NEA, Am. Assn. Sch. Adminstrs., Assn. Supervision and Curriculum Devel., Assn. Childhood Edn., Am. Legion (past comdr. Bloomington post), San Bernardino County Hist. Soc. (past pres.), San Bernardino County Mus. Assn. (exec. dir., past pres.), So. Calif. Archaeol. Survey Assn. (past pres.), Soc. Profl. Archaeology, Calif. Assn. Mus. (v.p). Author articles in history and anthropology to profl. jours.; project dir., mem. various archaeol. expdns., ethnol. studies. Office: San Bernardino County Museum Assn 2024 Orange Tree Ln Redlands CA 92373

SMITH, GLENN RICHARD, soil scientist; b. North Platte, Nebr., Sept. 2, 1922; s. Glenn William and Jennie Mae (Shields) S.; B.S. in Agr., U. Wyo., 1947; m. Clarice Olivia Jackson, Feb. 27, 1955; children—Elaine Marie, John Richard. Supervisory soil scientist Land Classification sect. Bur. of Reclamation, various locations, 1948-66; supervisory soil scientist Dept. Natural Resources and Conservation State of Mont., Helena, 1966-83; mem. Gov.'s Adv. Council, State Saline-Alkali Control Program, 1974-77; mem. urban and rural lands com. Pacific NW River Basins Commn., 1973-76, chmn., 1976. Mem. council St. John's Luth. Ch., Helena, 1972-73. Served with USAAF, 1943-45. Decorated 6 Air medals. Mem. Soil Sci. Soc. Am., Agronomy Soc. Am., U. Wyo. Alumni Assn., Soil Conservation Soc. Am., Alpha Zeta. Clubs: Mason, Shriner, Sons Norway. Developed irrigation suitability land classification State of Mont. Home: 1600 Cheryl St Albert Lea MN 56007

SMITH, GLORIA JEAN, actuary; b. Hollis, Okla., Feb. 27, 1929; d. Benjamin J. and Lena B. (Edwards) Roy; student City Coll. San Francisco, 1952, U. Calif., San Francisco, 1964, London Sch. Journalism, 1967-70; m. Wilbert Sims, Sr., Dec. 3, 1946; children—Wilbert, William David, Evelyn Jo Cheatham; m. Mayfield Wesley Smith, Sr., Dec. 12, 1956; 1 son, Mayfield Wesley. Ins. agt. Watchtower Life, Dallas, 1949-50; mgr. bus. office San Francisco Med. Assos., 1960-61; asst. bookkeeper I. Magnin & Co., San Francisco, 1961-65; asst. actuary Coates, Herfurth & England, San Francisco, 1967-70; asst. cons. actuary, San Francisco, 1970—. Active Opera, Symphony, ARC, Smithsonian Instn., San Francisco Womens Democratic Forum, St. Mary's Coll. Guild. Mem. Am. Mgmt. Assn., Nat. Writers Club, Research Inst. Am. Democrat. Baptist. Address: PO Box 15305 Sta A San Francisco CA 94115

SMITH, H. RUSSELL, mfg. co. exec.; b. Clark County, Ohio, Aug. 15, 1914; s. Lewis Hoskins and Eula (Elder) S.; A.B., Pomona Coll., 1936; m. Jeanne Rogers, June 27, 1942; children—Stewart Russell, Douglas Howard, Jeanne Ellen. Security analyst Kidder, Peabody & Co., N.Y.C., 1936-37; economist ILO, Geneva, 1937-40; asst. to pres. Blue Diamond Corp., Los Angeles, 1940-46; pres., dir. Avery Internat. Corp., San Marino, 1946-75, chmn. bd., 1975—; dir. So. Calif. Edison Co., Rosemead, Beckman Instruments, Inc., Fullerton, Security Pacific Corp., Security Pacific Nat. Bank, Los Angeles. Bd. dirs., past pres., chmn. Los Angeles Philharmonic Assn.; bd. fellows Claremont Univ. Center; chmn. bd. trustees Pomona Coll., Claremont, Calif., Children's Hosp. Los Angeles; past chmn. bd. Community TV of So. Calif. (Sta. KCET), Los Angeles. Served with USNR, 1943-46. Home: 1458 Hillcrest Ave Pasadena CA 91106 Office: 415 Huntington Dr San Marino CA 91108

SMITH, HAROLD DEAN, school administrator; b. St. Louis, May 18, 1946; s. Harold Dean and Betty Jo; m. E. Christie Norton, Dec. 18, 1973; 1 dau., Erin. B.A. in Speech and History, U. Wash., St. Louis, 1971; M.Ed. in Ednl. Adminstrn. and Bus., Seattle U., 1973; Ed.D. in Ednl. Adminstrn., 1982. Cert. tchr., prin., supt., Wash. Asst. prin./tchr. Issaquah (Wash.) Sch. Dist., 1971-73, asst. to supt., 1973-75; sch. bd. negotiator Wash. State Schs., 1975-78; dir. gen. adminstrn. South Kitsap Sch. Dist., Wash., 1978-80; supt. Finley Sch. Dist., Wash., 1980-82, Sedro-Wooley Sch. Dist., Wash., 1982—; cons. Lake Washington Sch.

Dist., 1980, Clover Park Vocat. Sch., 1980, all Wash. State govtl. Agys., 1977-78; instr. Central Wash. U., 1974-77, U. Denver, 1975-76; evaluator U. Oreg.; 1974-75, U. Hawaii, 1974-75. Served with U.S. Army, 1968-70. Decorated Silver Star, Bronze Star (2), D.F.C., Air Medals, Cross of Gallantry. Mem. Am. Assn. Sch. Adminstrs., Assn. Supervision and Curriculum Devel. Clubs: Rotary, Ranier, Glendale Country. Contbr. numerous papers and articles to profl. jours. Home: 806 Dana Dr Sedro-Wooley WA 98284 Office: 2079 Cook Rd Sedro-Wooley WA 98284

SMITH, HARRIET FULLEN, author, civic worker; b. Vincennes, Ind., Sept. 12, 1906; d. William Martin and Zola (Stewart) Fullen; m. Lewis Elden Smith, Aug. 12, 1934 (dec. 1964); children—Hannah Kully, Lewis, Deborah, Martin. B.A., U. So. Calif., 1926, M.A., 1927, postgrad., 1927-30, postgrad. in counseling, 1977-78; postgrad. Columbia U. Tchrs. Coll., summer 1929; postgrad. in poetry UCLA, 1960-65. Teaching asst., instr. U. So. Calif., Los Angeles, 1926-30; instr. in psychology, dean of women Compton (Calif.) Jr. Coll., 1930-36; textbook author Ginn and Co., Boston, 1943-76; free-lance writer, 1976—. Bd. dirs. Fullen-Smith Found., 1964—, Child Guidance Clinic, Los Angeles, 1964-71, Los Angeles chpt. ARC, 1965-66, Continuing Edn. Women, Claremont Coll., 1966-76, Internat. Assn. Vol. Edn., 1970—, Blaisdell Inst. Claremont Coll., 1971-83, Otis Art Inst., 1979-80; nat. bd. dirs. Exptl. Internat. Living, 1970-79. Recipient Appreciation award Goodwill Industries So. Calif. Mem. Town Hall Los Angeles, World Affairs Council, Women's Council Community TV of Los Angeles (hon. life), Trojan League, U. So. Calif. Assocs., Claremont Grad. Sch. Assocs., The Amazing Blue Ribbon (music ctr.), Phi Beta Kappa, Phi Kappa Phi, Pi Lambda Theta, Alpha Delta Pi. Democrat. Congregationalist. Author: (with Florence Means) Raphael and Consuelo, 1929; My Shadow Self, 1931; Your Life as a Citizen, 1952, rev. edits., 1961, 65, 67, 70, 76.

SMITH, HARRY LECATO, III, safety engr., mgmt. cons.; b. Charlottesville, Va., Apr. 4, 1944; s. Harry LeCato and Sarah Lotta (Bagwell) S.; m. Phyllis Anne Oberhofer, Aug. 4, 1968 (dec. 1970); m. 2d, Linda Kay Souza, Oct. 20, 1978. Served in U.S. Navy, 1963-72; safety cons. Hawaiian Ins. and Guaranty, Hawaii, 1976-78; loss control mgr. Fremont Indemnity Co., San Mateo Calif., 1978-82; dir. loss control Jardine Ins. Brokers, Inc., San Francisco, 1982—. Founding mem. Hawaii Safety and Health Council; trustee San Mateo Safety Council. Mem. Am. Soc. Safety Engrs. (pres. chpt., mem. region I operating com.). Home: 2170 Agnew Rd Santa Clara CA 95054 Office: 50 Francisco St San Francisco CA 94133

SMITH, JACK LEE, chemical engineer, business executive; b. Delta, Colo., Oct. 29, 1931; s. Joseph George and Violet Esther (Wilson) S.; m. Barbara H. Jackson, July 7, 1957; children—Beverly Ellen, Leland Andrew. B.S. in Chem. Engring., U. Utah, 1955; B.A. in Bus. Adminstrn. with high honors, Idaho State U., 1969, M.B.A., 1971. Registered profl. engr., Idaho. Dist. corrosion engr. Mountain Fuel Supply Co., Salt Lake City, 1954-56; instrumentation engr. Bechtel Corp., San Francisco, 1956-58; various engring. positions J.R. Simplot Co., Pocatello, Idaho, 1958-65; project engr. Hooker Chem. Co., Tacoma, 1965; various tech. and mgmt. positions Simplot Co., Pocatello, 1965-77, v.p. devel. and planning M & C div., 1977—. Mem. Pocatello Citizens Adv. Council, 1974-76, Pocatello Air Quality Com., 1975-80. Served with U.S. Army Res., 1950-60. Recipient project award N.W. Pollution Control Assn., 1981. Mem. Am. Inst. Chem. Engrs. (past chmn. Idaho sect.), Fertilizer Inst. (co. rep., past chmn. mfg. environ. com.), Am. Chem. Soc., Air Pollution Control Assn., Water Pollution Control Fedn., Am. Mgmt. Assns. Contbr. articles on fertilizer prodn. and environ. protection to tech. publs.; patentee in field. Office: 151 N 3d Ave Pocatello ID 83201

SMITH, JAMES CLOIS, JR., publishing, graphics and advt. co. exec.; b. Union, Miss., Mar. 18, 1935; s. James Clois and Nelie John (Wilson) S. B.S., Miss. Coll., 1955; postgrad. U. Miss., 1955-56, La. State U., 1956-57. Chemist, Grace Chem. Co., Baton Rouge, 1957-58; editor Chem. Week Mag., N.Y.C., 1958-61, Bell Telephone Labs, N.Y.C., 1961-63; supr. advt. N.Y. Telephone Co., N.Y.C., 1963-76; pres. Sunstone Corp., Santa Fe, 1976—, also dir. Mem. steering com. Greer Garson Theatre Coll. of Santa Fe; sec. bd. trustees Orch. of Santa Fe; bd. dirs. Santa Fe Council for Arts, Ballet del Monte Sol.; pres. Southwestern Choral Insts. Recipient Bausch & Lomb award, 1952, award United Fund, N.Y.C., 1975, Citizens Com. for Cleaner N.Y., 1974. Mem. Hist. Soc. N.Mex., Opera Guild of Santa Fe Opera, Smithsonian Assos., Sch. Am. Research, Old Santa Fe Hist. Soc. Christian Scientist. Club: Rotary. Contbr. articles, illustrations, and photographs to books, mags. and newspapers; pub. writings of southwestern authors. Office: PO Box 2321 Santa Fe NM 87501

SMITH, JAMES ELWOOD, management and executive search consultant; b. Frederick, Md., May 21, 1925; s. Lloyd Lowndes and Irene Elizabeth (Eyler) S.; m. Naomi Helen Nothstein, Sept. 18, 1948; children—Jeffrey Alan, Bruce Douglas, Brian David. A.B., Muhlenberg Coll., 1949; M.A., Lehigh U., 1950; Ph.D., Ohio State U., 1954. Lic. psychologist, Calif. Corp. psychologist, ptnr. Rohrer, Hibler & Replogle, Cleve., Phoenix and Los Angeles, 1954-71; dir. mgmt. devel. Kaufman & Brond, Los Angeles, 1971-72; assoc., v.p. Heidrick & Struggles, Los Angeles, 1972-80; owner, mgr. Smith, Goerss & Ferneborg, Los Angeles, 1980-82; pres. Smith & Assocs., Los Angeles, 1982—. Served to lt. USN, 1943-46. Mem. Am. Psychol. Assn., Calif. Exec. Recruiters Assn. Presbyterian. Clubs: Jonathan (Los Angeles); Palos Verdes Country (Palos Verdes Estates, Calif.). Home: 2929 Via Pacheco Palos Verdes Estates CA 90274 Office: 655 Deep Valley Dr Suite 303 Rolling Hills Estates CA 90274

SMITH, JAMES EMORY, fin. cons.; b. Fresno, Calif., Sept. 15, 1947; s. Arthur Ralph and Corda Avaleen (Foster) S.; B.A. in Econs., Stanford U., 1969; m. Kathryn E. St. George, Feb. 23, 1974; children—Jessica, Zachary. Acct., Gen. Electric Co., San Jose, Calif., 1969-73; mgr. strategic planning Gen. Electric Japan Ltd., Tokyo, 1974-77; asst. treas. Gen. Electric Tech. Services Co., N.Y.C., 1978-79; pres. Westpro Ltd., San Jose and Monterey, Calif., 1979—; pres. Thompson & Smith, Inc., securities brokers, San Jose and Los Angeles, 1980—. Mem. Nat. Assn. Security Dealers (registered prin.), Soc. Enrolled Agts. Am., San Jose C. of C. Democrat. Unitarian. Office: 151 Bernal Rd San Jose CA 95119

SMITH, JAMES PAYNE, JR., educator; b. Oklahoma City, Apr. 13, 1941; s. James Payne and Ara Bella (Poston) S.; B.S., U. Tulsa, 1963, B.A., 1963; Ph.D., Iowa State U., 1968. Teaching asst. U. Tulsa, 1962-63, Iowa State U., Ames, 1963-65; asst. prof. botany Humboldt State U., Arcata, Calif., 1969-72, assoc. prof., 1973-78, prof., 1978—, chmn. dept. biol. sci., 1979—. Mem. Am. Soc. Plant Taxonomists, Am. Soc. Pharmacognosy, AAAS, Internat. Assn. Plant Taxonomists, Bot. Soc. Am., Soc. Study Evolution, Soc. Econ. Botany, Calif. Bot. Soc., New Eng. Bot. Soc., Calif. Native Plant Soc. (bd. dirs. 1973—). Author: A Key to the Genera of Grasses of the U.S., 1975; Vascular Plant Families, 1977; Keys to the Families and Genera of Vascular Plants in Northwest California, 1978; Inventory of Rare and Endangered Vascular Plants of California, 1980, Supplements, 1981, 82. Home: 193 13th St Arcata CA 95521 Office: Humboldt State Univ Dept Biol Scis Arcata CA 95521

SMITH, JAMES WALKER, horticulturist, consultant, plant breeder; b. Glendale, Calif., Sept. 29, 1946; s. Dale Walker and Eleanor Grace (Hoven) S. Student Los Angeles Pierce Coll., 1964-66, Mira Costa Coll., 1971-72; B.S., Calif. Poly. State U., 1974. Nurseryman, Greenthumb Nursery, Newhall, Calif., 1970-71; instr. Calif. Poly. State U., San Luis Obispo, 1974; grower Pacifica Evergreen Nursery (Calif.), 1975; head estate gardener for pvt. estate, Woodside, Calif., 1975-78; ptnr. landscaping design firm, San Francisco, 1978-79; head estate gardener Whittell Estate Trust, Woodside, 1979-80; horticulturist, plant breeder Plant Smith, Jamestown, Calif., 1980—; hort. cons. Served with USAF, 1966-70. Decorated Bronze Star; commendation medal (Vietnam). Mem. Calif. Hort. Soc., Strybing Arboretum Soc., Calif. Native Plant Soc., Saratoga Hort. Found., Western Hort. Soc. Democrat. Roman Catholic. Home and office: 11560 La Grange Rd Jamestown CA 95327

SMITH, JAMES WEAVER, physician; b. Sheridan, Mont., Dec. 15, 1941; s. Delbert Weaver and Leah L. (Wade) S.; B.S., Coll. Idaho, 1964; M.D., George Washington U., 1968; m. Mary Barbara Vanek, June 23, 1973. Intern, UCLA Med. Center, med. chief resident, 1975-76; practice medicine, specializing in cardiology, Boise, Idaho, 1977—; asst. prof. medicine UCLA Med. Center, 1976-77; assoc. med. dir. UCLA Emergency Med. Center, 1976-77; clin. asst. prof. medicine U. Wash., 1977—. Served to lt. comdr. USN, 1970-72. Fellow Am. Coll. Cardiology (bd. govs. Idaho); mem. Ada County Med. Soc. (pres. elect), Alpha Omega Alpha. Home: 1024 Parkhill Dr Boise ID 83702 Office: 220 N 1st St Boise ID 83702

SMITH, JEAN ANTONETTE, interior design firm executive; b. Oklahoma City, Aug. 30, 1921; d. A. H. and Goldy K. (Engle) Hearn; m. W. D. Smith, Dec. 2, 1939; children—Kaye Smith Hunt, Sidney P. Student Chgo. Sch. Interior Design, 1970. Vice pres. Billco-Aladdin Wholesale, Albuquerque, 1950—. Pres. Albuquerque Opera, 1979-83; active Civic Chorus, Central Meth. Ch.; pres. Inez PTA, 1954-55, life mem.; hon. life mem. Albuquerque Little Theater. Republican. Clubs: Albuquerque County, Four Hills Country, Daus. of the Nile (soloist Yucca Tample). Home: 1009 Santa Ana SE Albuquerque NM 87123 Office: 7617 Menaul NE Albuquerque NM 87123

SMITH, JEAN VERNELLE, public relations consultant; b. Kansas City, Kans., Dec. 2, 1935; d. Jabors and Opal Roberta (Hayes) Welton; m. Hollis Thomas Smith, Dec. 31, 1960. Student, U. Kans., 1955-56, UCLA. Exec. asst. Contemporary Records, Los Angeles, 1957; adminstrv. asst. McFadden, Strauss & Irwin, Los Angeles, 1957-67, spl. projects coordinator, 1969-74; v.p. Clive Hoffman Assocs., Los Angeles, 1974—; Mem. adv. council Abram Friedman Occupational Ctr. Mem. Pub. Relations Soc. Am., Women in Communications, Los Angeles C. of C. (human resources com.). Exec. producer weekly TV pub. affairs programs Of Crisis and Concern, 1980-81, Family Focus, 1980-81. Home: 1163 S Highland Ave Los Angeles CA 90019 Office: Clive Hoffman Assocs 3348 Overland Ave Suite 102 Los Angeles CA 90034

SMITH, JERIANNE CATHERINE, speech and language pathologist, hearing impaired consultant; b. Hollywood, Calif., Feb. 17, 1954; d. Gerald Ashley and Anita Catherine (Clarke) S. B.A., N.Mex. State U., 1976, M.A., 1981. Cert. tchr., speech pathologist, Colo. Speech and lang. pathologist N.E. Colo. Bd. Coop. Ednl. Services, Haxtun, 1978—; hearing-impaired cons., parent trainer Colo. Dept. Health, Holyoke and Wray, 1982—; speech pathologist N.E. Colo. Services for Handicapped, Sterling, 1982—; deaf interpreter Haxtun Community Hosp., Melissa Meml. Hosp., Holyoke; speech, lang. and hearing cons. Phillips and Sedgwick Counties, Colo. N.E. Colo. Bd. Coop. Ednl. Services grantee, 1980. Mem. Am. Speech and Hearing Assn., Bus. and Profl. Women's Orgn. Democrat. Episcopalian. Home: 642 W Strohm St Haxtun CO 80731 Office: PO Box 98 Haxtun CO 80731

SMITH, JEROME BURTON, investment management company executive; b. Chgo., May 1930; s. Paul S. Smith and Della A. Smith Gross; B.S., Iowa State Coll., 1953; children—SaraLee Grace, Bradley Lawrence. Pres., Arboreal Tree Service, Park Ridge, Ill., 1947-52; visual info. supr. Weyerhaeuser Co., Tacoma, 1956-65; pres. Acad. Communicative Arts and Scis., Inc., Tacoma, 1962-69, Congress of Internat. Logging Championships, Inc., Tacoma, 1967-69; exec. v.p. Greenacres, Inc., Seattle, 1967-68; pres. Investors Inst. Inc., Tacoma, 1971-77, Inversionismo S.A., Mexico City, 1973-78, Transworld Trade Tech., Inc., Tacoma, 1976—; cons. to Govt. of Mex., 1973-78. Exec. mgr. United Citizens for Sound City Govt., Tacoma, 1958. Served to capt. USAF, 1955. Recipient Outstanding Service award Soc. Am. Foresters-Seattle World's Fair, 1963. Mem. Soc. Am. Foresters, Western Forestry and Conservation Assn., Order of Hoo Hoo, Izaak Walton League. Independent Republican. Presbyterian. Clubs: Tacoma Horse Polo; Mexico City Horse Polo; Woodbrook Hunt (dir.); Alpental Ski; Tacoma Businessmen's; Sunset Beach Boathouse, Univ. Pl. Boosters. Home: 285 Valley St Los Altos CA 94022

SMITH, JERRY EDWARD, automotive aftermarket exec.; b. Sturgis, Mich., Apr. 3, 1952; s. Robert Bennett and Leola Josephine Shinavar S.; B.A., U. Ariz., 1975; now postgrad. in bus. adminstrn. Calif. Coast U. Store mgr. Jay's 3, Tucson, 1975-77; warehouse mgr. United Warehouse Sales, Tucson, 1977-78; nat. sales mgr. TR-3 Chem. Corp., Orange, Calif., 1978-81, v.p. sales, 1981-82; mgr., sales dir. Jay's Da-Nite Auto Supply, Tucson, 1978-80; head instr. Counterman's Sch., 1980-81; sr. v.p. Sunshine Makers, Inc., 1982—. Charter mem. Republican Presdl. Task Force, Rep. Majority Fund. Recipient Presdl. Sports award, 1976; Bronze Laurel membership U.S. Olympic Soc., 1980; Disting. Automotive Aftermarket Sales Mgmt. award; Cert. of Merit for disting. achievement; named to Automotive Hall of Fame. Mem. Automotive Wholesalers Ariz. (pres.), Automotive Aftermarket Assn., Nat. Hot Rod Assn., Automotive Parts and Accessories Assn., Splty. Equipment Market Assn., Nat. Speakers Assn. (profl.), U.S. Senatorial Club, 500 Automotive Execs. Club, Salesman with a Purpose Club (bd. govs. 1982—). Home: 4791 Lago St #201 Huntington Beach CA 92649 Office: 16771 Pacific Coast Hwy Sunset Beach CA 90742

SMITH, JOEL PRITCHARD, univ. ofcl.; b. Toledo, June 30, 1933; s. Lavern Pritchard and Florence (Blish) S.; B.A. summa cum laude, Beloit (Wis.) Coll., 1955, LL.D., 1970; B.A., Oxford (Eng.) U., 1957; J.D., U. Wis., 1961; children—Rebecca, Jennifer. Admitted to Minn. bar, 1961; with firm Cant, Havenstock, Beardsley, Gray & Plant, Mpls., 1961-65; asso. dean of students Stanford U., 1965-67, asso. provost, dean of students, 1967-69, cons. Devel. Office, 1976-77, v.p.-devel., 1977-82, sec., trustee, 1982—; pres. Denison U., 1969-76. Mem. Great Lakes Colls. Assn. (chmn. 1972-74), Order of Coif, Phi Beta Kappa, Beta Theta Pi, Phi Delta Phi. Office: Bldg 10 Stanford U Stanford CA 94305

SMITH, JOHN KEVIN, accountant; b. Monroe, Oreg., Apr. 28, 1949; s. John and Vera Jane (Murray) S. Computer program certificate San Diego Coll. Bus., 1972; B.S., San Diego State U., 1978. Auditor, Atlas Corp., San Diego, 1976, Sheraton Corp., San Diego, 1976-77, Hyatt Corp., San Diego, 1977-78; acct. Hawthorne Machinery Co., San Diego, 1978-79; acct. Presto Foods, Inc., Los Angeles, 1979-81, also chief acct. subs. Jon Donaire Pastries, Inc. until 1981; sr. staff Van de Kamps, Los Angeles, 1981-82; owner, mgr. JKS Acctg. Service, Inc., Arcadia, Calif., 1982—. Served with U.S. Army, 1967-71; Vietnam. Mem. Nat. Assn. Accts. Am. Mgmt. Assn. Republican. Clubs: Masons, Rotary. Home and Office: PO Box 3395 Arcadia CA 91006

SMITH, JOHN WARD, chemist; b. Cedar City, Utah, May 28, 1923; s. John Henry and Agnes (Brown) S.; B.A. cum laude, U. Utah, 1946; m. 2d, Harriet Youtz; children by previous marriage—Debbie Jo Smith Schilz, Robin Sue. Research chemist Laramie Energy Research Center (Wyo.). U.S. Bur. Mines and Dept. Energy, 1947-60, project leader, 1960-73, research supr., 1973-76, div. mgr., 1976-80, cons., 1980—; dir. Colo. Synfuels. Served with AUS, 1943-45. Fellow Am. Inst. Chemists; mem. N. Am. Thermal Analysis Soc. (pres. 1974, exec. bd. 1970-75), Am. Chem. Soc., AAAS, Geochem. Soc., Internat. Confedn. Thermal Analysis (Plenary lectr. 1971), Am. Legion, Soc. Preservation Barbershop Quartet Singing in Am., Sigma Xi. Contbr. articles on oil shale and tar sands resources, geochemistry, composition, phys. properties, thermal properties, minerology, analysis, geology to profl. jours. Co-discoverer major dawsonite deposits, 1966. Home: 1722 Boswell Dr Laramie WY 82070 Office: 1472 N 5th St Laramie WY 82070

SMITH, JOSEPH WILLIAM, real estate development executive; b. Duquesne, Pa., Jan. 4, 1939; s. James T. and Mary A. (Garella) S.; B.A., Mich. State U., 1963; m. Cheri Lynn; children—Scott, Ashley. Sales rep., area mgr. Standard Oil (Ind.), Detroit and Flint, Mich., 1963-67; v.p. ops., sales and mktg. Lawrence Custom Homes, Flint, 1967-70; sales rep. Avco Community Developers, Laguna Niguel, Calif., 1971-73, sales mgr., 1973-74, gen. sales mgr., 1974-76, dir. sales and mktg., 1976—; speaker. Named Salesman of Yr., Nat. Assn. Homebuilders, 1974; MAME award (8) from sales and mktg. council So. Calif. Bldg. Industry Assn., 1976-79, also Max C. Tipton Meml. award, 1979; Gold Nugget award, Merit awards Pacific Coast Builders Conf., 1978. Mem. So. Calif. Bldg. Industry Assn. (pres. sales and mktg. council 1978), Mich. State U. Alumni Assn. Clubs: El Niguel Country; Roosters of Chanteclair (Newport Beach, Calif.).

SMITH, JULIA MARGARET, statistician, consultant, educator; b. Radford, Va., May 23, 1943; d. Larry Cooper and Ruby Evelyn (Sale) S.; children—Laura Elaine. B.A. in Math., Chemistry Radford U., 1965; M.S. in Stats., Va. Poly. Inst. and State U., Blacksburg, 1971. Mathematician, Shell Oil Co., Metarie, La., 1966; instr. chemistry Radford U., 1967-69; instr. math. Va. Poly. Inst. and State U., 1970-71; statistician AEC, Washington, 1971-72; statistician Nuclear Fuel dept., Gen. Electric, Wilmington, N.C., 1972-77; statistician Brookhaven Nat. Lab., Upton, N.Y., 1977-81; sr. statistician Rockwell Hanford Ops., Rockwell Internat., Richland, Wash., 1981—; cons. and lectr. in field. Mem. Inst. Nuclear Materials Mgmt., Nat. Mgmt. Assn., Am. Statis. Assn., Phi Kappa Phi., Va. Poly. Inst. and State U. Alumni Assn., Radford U. Alumni Assn. Club: Mensa. Contbr. in field. Office: Rockwell Hanford PO Box 800/200W/2704 S Richland WA 99352

SMITH, KAREN MARGARET, school counselor, counsultant; b. Salt Lake City, Apr. 7, 1944; d. Ray George and Margaret (Howell) S. B.S., Utah State U., 1966, M.Ed., U. Nev.-Reno, 1972, ednl. specialist, 1979. Cert. counselor, phys. edn. educator, sch. psychologist, Nev. Tchr. pub. schs., Huntsville, Utah, 1966-68, Ogden, Utah, 1968-69, Reno, 1969-71; counselor Fred W. Truner Middle Sch., Reno, 1971—; guest instr. U. Nev.-Reno, 1980—; cons. region 8, Calif. Dept. Edn., Pyramid House. Bd. dirs. People Inc. Mem. Washoe County Tchrs. Assn., Nev. Tchrs. Assn., NEA, No. Nev. Counselors Assn., Nev. Sch. Counselors Assn., Am. Sch. Counselors Assn., Am. Personnel and Guidance Assn. (past pres., senator western region).

SMITH, KATHRYN JOYCE, secretarial service executive; b. Maud, Okla., Nov. 29, 1930; d. Elisha Alvin and Doris Louise (Kirk) Dooley; m. Richard A. Smith, Aug. 11, 1950; children—Rick L., John A., Kathy Keele. Student pub. schs., Boise. Steno-clk. Dept. Pub. Assistance, Boise, Idaho, 1948-49; officer Salvation Army, 1949-52; mem. duplicating dept. Suburban Gas Co., Pomona, Calif., 1960-63; sec. to headmistress Girls' Collegiate Sch., Claremont, Calif., 1964-66; steno-clk. FAA, Ontario, Calif., 1968-70; sec. spl. programs office, U. Redlands (Calif.), 1972-73, sec. various offices, 1975-81; owner The Word Co., Redlands. Active Variety Club Telethon. Republican. Mem. Ch. of Christ. Office: 416 E State St Redlands CA 92373

SMITH, KATHY COLLINS, banking institute executive; b. Boulder, Colo., Sept. 16, 1949; d. Erwin F. and Patricia J. (Benson) Mantooth; student Met. State Coll., Denver, 1980-81; 1 son, Jeffrey. Phys. therapist Santa Barbara (Calif.) Cottage Hosp., 1969-73; sec. Adams County Sch. Dist. 12, Northglenn, Colo., 1973-76; asst. tng. dir. 1st Nat. Bank Denver, 1976-81; exec. dir., mgr., corp. sec. Denver chpt. Am. Inst. Banking, 1981—; dir. Bankers Video Service, Cedar Rapids, Iowa; speaker in field. Advisor Jr. Achievement, 1967-68; mem. panel Nat. Commn. on Excellence in Edn., 1982. Mem. Am. Inst. Banking (2d v.p. Denver chpt. 1980); Colo. Bankers Assn. (chmn. edn. com. 1980-81), Nat. Assn. Bank Women, Am. Soc. Tng. and Devel. (Colo. treas.), Nat. Soc. Performance and Instrn., Downtown Profl. Bus. Women. Roman Catholic. Office: Am Inst Banking 1554 California St Denver CO 80217

SMITH, KEITH LARUE, research co. exec.; b. Salida, Colo., Dec. 15, 1917; s. Leroy Holt and Verna Lea (Tunnell) S.; student Marion Coll., 1935-38; A.B. in Math., Ind. U., 1946; postgrad. DePauw U., 1946-47; M.A. in Internat. Affairs, Harvard U., 1955; M.P.A., Calif. State U.-Fullerton, 1979; m. Evelyn May De Bruler, Aug. 29, 1943; 1 son, Eric Douglas. Mil. intelligence research specialist Dept. of Army, Washington, 1951-60; staff engr. Librascope div. Gen. Precision, Inc., Glendale, Cal., 1960-61; sr. operations research analyst Space div. N.Am. Rockwell Corp., Downey, Cal., 1961-71; dir. research Am. Research Corp., Paramount, Calif., 1972—; instr. math. and polit. sci. DePauw U., 1946-47; cons. model bldg. and gaming techniques, 1960—; mgmt. cons., 1970—; instr. math. and sci. Verbum Dei High Sch., 1974—. Adult leader Boy Scouts Am., Long Beach, Calif., 1961-75. Treas., UN Council Harvard, 1947-49, Young Democratic Club, Arlington, Mass., 1949-50. Served to capt. USAAF, 1941-46; ETO. Recipient scholarship award Inst. World Affairs, 1947, Outstanding Efficiency award Dept. Army, 1960, Apollo 11 medallion NASA, 1970. Mem. Am. Phys. Soc., AAAS, Am. Mus. Natural History, Nat. Geog. Soc., Cal. Acad. Scis., Harvard Alumni Assn., Nat. Hist. Soc., Pi Sigma Alpha. Methodist. Mason. Research on lunar mission cartography, mil. operations research and war game model bldg. Home: 3451 Curry St Long Beach CA 90805

SMITH, KELLY LINCOLN, chemical engineer; b. Eugene, Oreg., Mar. 10, 1951; s. Roy L. and Louise (Rickabaugh) S.; B.S. in Chem. Engring., Stanford U., 1974, M.S. in Biomed. Engring., 1974; m. Sande Schmidt, June 15, 1974. Chem. engr. Alza Corp., Palo Alto, Calif., 1974-78; research engr., dir. controlled release div. Bend (Oreg.) Research, Inc., 1978—. Mem. Am. Inst. Chem. Engrs., Am. Chem. Soc., Controlled Release Soc. Contbr. articles to profl. jours.; patentee in field. Home: 19295 Dayton Rd Bend OR 97701 Office: 64550 Research Rd Bend OR 97701

SMITH, KENDRIC CHARLES, radiation biologist, photobiologist; b. Oakwood, Ill., Oct. 13, 1926; s. Russell Wilson and Virginia Frances (Mozley) S.; m. Marion Edmonds, Feb. 5, 1955; children—Nancy Carol, Martha Allen. B.S., Stanford U., 1947; Ph.D., U. Calif.-Berkeley, 1952. Research asst. dept. radiology Med. Sch. U. Calif.-San Francisco, 1954-56; research assoc. dept. radiology Med. Sch. Stanford (Calif.) U., 1956-62, asst. prof., 1962-65, assoc. prof., 1965-73, prof., 1973—; mem. U.S. Nat. Com. for Photobiology Nat. Acad. Sci./NRC (chmn. 1970-74), 1964-74, U.S. Nat. Com. Internat. Union Biol. Scis. (sec. 1971-73), 1967-73, Tech. Adv. Council GTE Labs., 1970-74. USPHS fellow, 1952-54. Recipient Research Career Devel. award USPHS, 1966-71. Mem. AAAS, Am. Soc. Photobiology (pres. 1972-74, Disting. Service award 1974), Am. Chem. Soc., Am. Soc. Biol. Chemists, Am. Soc. Microbiology, Am. Inst. Biol. Scis. (pres. 1982-83), Radiation

Research Soc., Sigma Xi. Author: (with P.C. Hanawalt) Molecular Photobiology, 1969; author, editor: Aging, Carcinogenesis and Radiation Biology, 1976; The Science of Photobiology, 1977; editor: Photochemical and Photobiological Reviews, 1976-83; mem. editorial bd. Carcinogenesis, 1979—. Home: 927 Mears Ct Stanford CA 94305 Office: Dept Radiology Sch Med Stanford U Stanford CA 94305

SMITH, KENNETH OWLER, journalism educator; b. San Jose, Calif., May 13, 1920; s. William Kenneth and Velma Erin (Owler) S.; m. Patricia Ann Nowack, May 23, 1980. A.B., Stanford U., 1941; M.S., UCLA, 1958; Ed.D., 1967. Editor various newspapers and mags., Calif., 1940-42, 46-49; pub. relations dir. Western Airlines Inc., Los Angeles, 1950-60; faculty UCLA, 1960-64, 67-70, adminstr., 1965-67; prof. Sch. Journalism U. So. Calif., Los Angeles, 1970—, dir. Sports Info. Program, 1979—; pub. relations/sports info. mgmt. cons. Served with U.S. Army, 1942-46. Recipient Outstanding Faculty award U. So. Calif. 1974-75; Chasqui award Internat. Pub. Relations Assn. 1977. Mem. Pub. Relations Soc. Am. (accredited, Silver Anvil award, 1969, pres. 1977, Educator of Yr. 1979), AAUP, U.S. Olympic Soc., Sigma Delta Chi, Kappa Tau Alpha, Phi Delta Kappa. Club: Univ. So. Calif. Faculty Ctr. Author: Professional Public Relations, 1968; The Practice of Public Relations, 1969; A Chronology of Sports, 1982; numerous jour. articles. Office: School of Journalism Univ So Calif Los Angeles CA 90089

SMITH, LAWRENCE MORTON, publishing and printing company executive; b. Red Cloud, Nebr., Jan. 23, 1921; s. Harrison Morton and Winifred (Norton) S.; m. Dorothy May Haugsten, May 8, 1943; children—Peter, Michael, Susan. Student U. Lebr., 1942. With Daily Jour. Commerce, Portland, Oreg., 1946—, now pres. Bd. dirs. Vis. Nurses Assn. Served with USAAF, from 1942; capt. Res. (ret.). Clubs: Waverly Country, Multnomah Athletic (Portland); Astoria (Oreg.) Golf and Country. Home: 6432 SW Loop Dr Portland OR 97221 Office: 2014 NW 24th Ave Portland OR 97210

SMITH, LE ROI MATTHEW-PIERRE, III, city official; b. Chgo., Jan. 11, 1946; s. Le Roy Matthew and Norma Buckner (McCamey) S.; m. Lois Divine, Jan. 30, 1969; 1 son, Le Roi Matthew Pierre. B.A. in Psychology, Idaho State U., 1969; Ph.D. in Psychology, Wash. State U., 1977. Instr. psychology Idaho State U., Pocatello, 1969-70, Wash. State U., Pullman, 1970-71; mem. faculty dept. psychology Evergreen State Coll., Olympia, 1971-81, equal opportunity officer Port of Seattle, 1981—; cons. in field. Bd. dirs. Thurston-Mason County Community Mental Health Ctr., Olympia; v.p., Idaho State Human Rights Commn., Bannock County, Idaho, 1968-70. Office Edn. fellow, 1969-70; U.S. Dept. Labor grantee, 1968; NSF grantee, 1972; Lilly Found. fellow, 1980. Mem. Am. Psychol. Assn., Am. Personnel and Guidance Assn., Wash. State Black Econs. and Edn. Conf., Assn. Black Psychologists, Am. Assn. of Affirmative Action Officers, Phi Delta Kappa. Democrat. Roman Catholic. Home: 761 S 45th St Tacoma WA 98408 Office: PO Box 1209 Seattle WA 98111

SMITH, LEILA RAE, business educator; b. Bklyn., May 7, 1928; d. Frank and Rose Simon; B.S., NYU; M.A., U. San Francisco; m. Seymour Smith, Sept. 5, 1954; children—Roberta Ellen, Eric Andrew. Instr., Bay Path Jr. Coll., Longmeadow, Mass., 1950-52; instr. secretarial sci. L.A. Pierce Coll., Woodland Hills, Calif., 1956-65; mem. faculty bus. div. L.A. Harbor Coll., Wilmington, Calif., 1965—, prof. office adminstrn., 1970—. Recipient Eugene Pimentel award for excellence in edn., 1982. Mem. Nat. Bus. Edn. Assn., Calif. Bus. Edn. Assn., Am. Bus. Communication Assn., Soc. Accelerative Learning and Teaching, Am. Soc. Tng. and Devel., Theta Alpha Delta, Pi Omega Pi. Author: English for Careers, 1977; English for Careers: Business, Professional, Technical, 1981; Personal Learning Guide for English for Careers, 1981; English for Careers (15 cassettes), 1981; Superlearning RSVP, 1982. Office: Los Angeles Harbor Coll 1111 Figueroa Pl Wilmington CA 90744

SMITH, LESLIE ANN, city official; b. Pasco, Wash., Apr. 17, 1945; s. Ralph E. and Melba (Simmonds) S.; div.; A.A., Columbia Basin Coll., 1971; student Wash. State U., 1964-65, Central Wash. State U., 1971-76. Admissions and registration sec. Columbia Basin Coll., 1966-70, scheduling coordinator, 1970-76; city clk. City of Richland, Wash., 1976—. Mem. LWV, Columbia Basin Chpt. Records Mgrs., Am. Assn. Records Mgrs. and Adminstrs., Wash. State Mcpl. Clks., Internat. Mcpl. Clks., Allied Arts Assn., PEO. Methodist. Home: 1850 Stevens St Apt 110 Richland WA 99352 Office: PO Box 190 Richland WA 99352

SMITH, LONNIE LOUIS, vocational eduator; b. Electra, Tex., Apr. 24, 1932; s. Robert Lee and Shirley Irene (Walraven) S.; m. O. Winell Towles, Jan. 25, 1957; children—Mark, Mike. A.S., Odessa Coll., 1956; B.S. in Indsl. Arts, North Tex. State U., 1958, M.Ed., 1961. Cert. tchr. Tex., Calif., N.Mex. Tchr. indsl. arts Dallas Ind. Sch. Dist., 1958-62; tchr. indsl. crafts, driver edn., Artesia (N.Mex.) Pub. Schs., 1962-65; tchr. indsl. arts Fremont (Calif.) Unified Schs., 1965-80; instr. mfg. processes Ohlone Coll., Fremont, 1977-80; instr. welding, N.Mex. Jr. Coll., Hobbs, 1980—; sponsor Vocat. Indsl. Clubs Am. Served with USN, 1950-54; Korea. Decorated Am. Spirit of Honor, UN Service medal with two stars; ARC Service award, 1982. Mem. Am. Welding Soc., N. Tex. chpt. Am. Welding Soc., Am. Vocat. Assn., N.Mex. Vocat. Assn., Phi Delta Kappa. Democrat. Baptist. Sculpture exhibited in private collections; contbr. articles to profl. jours. Office: NMex Jr College Lovington Hwy Hobbs NM 88240

SMITH, LOUISE KOHL, artist, lecturer; b. Jersey City, Sept. 5, 1922; d. Henry and Lavenia B. (Yale) Kohl; grad. Finch Jr. Coll., 1942; Ph.D. (hon.), Colo. Christian Coll., 1973; m. Arthur William Nelson, Aug. 26, 1944 (div. Aug. 1951) 1 dau., Lavenia Yale Nelson; m. 2d Lloyd Victor Smith, Feb. 14, 1953 (div. Dec. 1960); 1 dau., Lucinda Rockwood Smith Sharman One-man shows: Stead Air Force Library, Reno, 1963, Washoe Med. Center, 1963, 64, Colonial Title & Loan, Reno, 1964, Continental Restaurant, Reno, 1964-65, 68; exhibited in two-man show at Reno Art Gallery, 1963; group shows include: Dade County Ann. Jr. Art Show, West Palm Beach, Fla., 1937, Nev. Mus., Carson City, 1963, Chautauqua (N.Y.) Art Gallery, 1961, 62, 63, Sonora Regional Art Show, 1963, 20th Century Club, Reno, 1963, Scottsdale Artists League, 1979-83. Active Girl Scouts U.S.A., 1942-44, founder troops 13 and 131, 1962-64; Red Cross nurse's aide, 1941-48; active ARC, Cancer Fund, PTA, United Fund, St. Mary's Hosp. Guild; state dir. (Nev.) women's activities Civil Def., 1960-64; founder Washoe Med. Center Women's League Ann. Tombola, 1957, chmn., 1957-59, league pres., 1961-62; chmn. Reno Emblem Club Arabian Nights Fair, 1967; founder Henry Kohl Meml. Chapel Washoe Med. Center, Reno, 1964; Nev. state chmn. Nat. Cathedral Assn., 1971-73, Nat. Cathedral Sch. for Girls, 1972-73; Recipient 2d place award Dade County Ann. Jr. Art Show, 1937, 20th Century Club, 1963, 1st place award for state of Ariz., Nat. League Am. Pen Women. Mem. Nat. League Am. Pen Women (award of excellence for Ariz. 1982), Nat. Soc. Arts and Letters (life), Scottsdale Artists League, Scottsdale Women's Aglow, Pacific Internat. Trap Assn. (life), Nat. Skeet Shooting Assn. (life), Amateur Trapshooting Assn. (life). Republican. Address: 5115 N 78th Pl Scottsdale AZ 85253

SMITH, MAERICE OLIVIA, educator; b. Lawrence, Kans., Dec. 27, 1937; d. Robert James and Essie Beatrice (Lawson) Wood; m. Walter John Smith, Aug. 6, 1960 (dec.); 1 son, Leland Wayne. B.S. in Elem. Edn., Oreg. Coll., 1959; M.S. in Elem. Edn., Portland State U., 1975. Tchr., Portland, Oreg. 1959-68, San Bernardino, Calif., 1968-70; univ. supr. Portland (Oreg.) Pub. Schs., 1970-74; workshop coordinator curriculum dept., Portland, 1976—. Active NAACP. Mem. Am. Soc. Curriculum Devel., Alpha Kappa Alpha. Baptist. Home: 6726 E Burnside Portland OR 97215 Office: 501 N Dixon Portland OR 97227

SMITH, MALCOLM ANDREWS, lawyer; b. Scotland, Dec. 2, 1953 (parents Am. citizens); s. Ralph I and Todd C. Smith; B.A., U. Calif., San Diego, 1977; J.D., U. San Francisco, 1981. Bar: Calif. 1981. Ptnr., Sunrise Specialty Co., 1977-81; intern Calif. Ct. Appeals, San Francisco, 1981—. Mem. Am. Bar Assn. Address: 2054 University Ave Suite 501 Berkeley CA 94704

SMITH, MARK D., broadcasting co. exec.; b. Youngstown, Ohio; student U. Ohio; 6 children. Vice-pres., gen. mgr. Sta. KLAS-TV, Las Vegas, Nev., 1968—; mem. CBS TV Affiliated Adv. Bd. Named Conv. Man of Yr., Las Vegas chpt. Hotel-Sales Mgmt. Assn., 1972; Exec. of Yr., Oasis chpt. Profl. Secs. Assn., 1980. Mem. Nev. Broadcasters Assn. (past pres.), Nat. Assn. Broadcasters (past TV chmn.), Rocky Mountain Broadcasters Assn. (dir.), Greater Las Vegas C. of C. (past pres.). Office: PO Box 15047 Las Vegas NV 89114

SMITH, MELVIN T., historian, association director; b. Cowley, Wyo., June 15, 1928; s. Heman T. and Edetha (Thomas) S.; m. Marlene Threet, Dec. 30, 1952 (div.); children—Heman T., Dione, Lyn, Danet, Dirk, Keri, Tana, Renele, Keil. Student Northwest Community Coll. Jr. Coll., 1956-57; B.A. in Edn., U. Wyo., 1959, M.A., in Am. Studies, 1960; postgrad. Brigham Young U., 1963-65, Ph.D., 1972. Cert. tchr., Wyo. Instr. Northwest Community Coll., Powell, Wyo., 1960-63; grad. student instr. Brigham Young U., 1963-65; assoc. prof. history, dept. head Dixie Jr. Coll., St. George, Utah, 1965-69; historian Utah State Hist. Soc., Salt Lake City, 1969-71, dir., 1971—, Utah State Hist. Preservation Officer; mem. State Records Com., State Library Commn., Utah Endowment for Humanities, Nat. Conf. State Hist. Preservation, Mormon Pioneer Nat. Hist. Trail Adv. Council. Justice of Peace and city judge, Washington, Utah, 1967-69; active Democratic polit. campaigns. Served with USN, 1952-56. William R. Coe fellow U. Wyo. Mem. Am. Assn. State and Local History, Mormon Hist. Assn. (past pres.), Utah State Hist. Soc., Nat. Council on Pub. History (officer, bd. dirs.), Western History Assn. Mormon. Club: Nat. Pony Express Assn. Contbr. articles on Utah and Mormon history to profl. jours. Office: 300 Rio Grande Salt Lake City UT 84101

SMITH, MERIL RALPH, public school administrator; b. Oakland, Calif., Feb. 19, 1943; s. Ralph Virgil and Betty Mathilda (Sherman) S.; m. Barbara Sue Forkash, June 30, 1968; children—Rachel Esther, Leah Amy. B.A., San Jose (Calif.) State U., 1965, M.A., 1973. Tchr., Cambrian Sch. Dist., San Jose, 1970-72; with Oak Grove Sch. Dist., San Jose, 1972-82, dir. instrn., 1979-82; asst. supt. Berryessa Sch. Dist., San Jose, 1982—. Served to capt. USAF, 1966-70. Recipient Honor award Cambrian Dist. Tchrs. Assn., 1966, 71, 72. Mem. Assn. Calif. Sch. Adminstrs., Assn. Supervision and Curriculum Devel., Assn. Direct Instrn., Asia-Am. Educators Assn., South San Jose Fine Arts Assn. (founding mem. 1981), Phi Delta Kappa. Republican. Author: Sakamoto School Program Support System, 1974; Kid Country Spelling Program, 1978, Quick and Painless Curriculum Development Method, 1982. Home: 333 Viscaino Way San Jose CA 95119 Office: 1376 Piedmont Rd San Jose CA 95132

SMITH, PATRICIA ANN, public relations consulant, educator; b. Chgo., June 7, 1933; d. Clarence Richard and Ruth Margaret (Jacobson) Nowack; m. Kurt E. Ferber, Feb. 14, 1954; m. 2d, Robert K. Hunsicker, June 28, 1968; children—Gail, Deborah, Kurt, Lori, Nancy, Janna; m. 3d, Kenneth Owler Smith, May 23, 1980. Student Cornell U., 1951-52; B.A., Centenary Coll., Hackettstown, N.J., 1983. Prodn. asst. Your Hit Parade Batten, Barton, Durstine & Osborne, 1953-54; pvt. practice polit. cons., 1954-66; legal sec., asst. Atty. John C. Cushman, 1966-68; field dep. Los Angeles County Assessor, 1968-69, pub. info. officer Los Angeles County Probation Dept., 1969-73; dir. consumer relations Fireman's Fund, San Francisco, 1973-76; pvt. practice pub. relations cons., 1976-77; spl. projects officer Los Angeles County Transp. Commn., 1977-78; tchr. Calif. State U.-Dominguez Hills, 1979—; editor, writer Jet Propulsion Lab., 1979-80; pub. info. dir. Los Angeles Dept. Pub. Works, 1980-82; pub. info. cons. City of Pasadena, (Calif.), 1982—. Mem. First United Methodist Ch. Commn. on Missions and Social Concerns, 1983. Recipient Pro award Los Angeles Publicity Club, 1978, Outstanding Achievement award Soc. Consumer Affairs Profls. in Bus., 1976. Mem. Pub. Relations Soc. Am. (award for consumer program 1977), Nat. Press Women, Calif. Press Women (recipient awards 1974, 78, 83). Republican. Club: Pasadena Women's City. Contbr. articles to publications. Office: 100 N Garfield Ave Room 220 City Hall Pasadena CA 91109

SMITH, PATRICIA JEAN, public relations executive; b. Boston, Mar. 3, 1947; d. Franklin A. and Evelyn A. Hulland; m. Daniel L. Smith, June 14, 1969 (div.). B.A., U. Calif.-Santa Barbara, 1968; M.A. in Journalism, UCLA, 1973. Pub. relations dir. Occidental Life Ins. Co., Los Angeles, 1973-80, Calif. First Bank, San Francisco, 1980—. Chmn., San Francisco Symphony 500. Mem. Pub. Relations Soc. Am., Calif. Bankers' Assn. (pub. relations), Women in Communications Inc. (bd. dirs. 1979-80), Los Angeles Jr. C. of C. (v.p., dir. 1978-80), Sigma Delta Chi. Office: Calif First Bank 350 Calif St San Francisco CA 94104

SMITH, PAUL REED, office systems executive; b. Paducah, Ky., Mar. 9, 1953; s. J.C. and Peggy (Thomas) S.; B.A. with honors, U. Ky., 1975; student U. Heidelberg (Germany), 1975-76, U. Wash., 1976-77; m. Sally Ann Porter, Nov. 30, 1978. Account mgr. Benchmark Computer Systems, Inc., Seattle, 1977-79; mgr. Office Systems Services, U. Wash., 1979—. Fulbright scholar. Mem. Assn. Records Mgrs. and Adminstrs. (exec. v.p. Greater Seattle chpt.), Info. Processing Assn. (chmn. pub. relations), Nat. Office Machine Dealers Assn. Home: 2503 NW 65th St Seattle WA 98117 Office: U Wash HA-50 Seattle WA 98195

SMITH, RAYMOND EDWARD, health care administrator; b. Freeport, N.Y., June 17, 1932; s. Jerry Edward and Madelyn Holman (Jones) S.; B.S. in Edn., Temple U., 1953; M.H.A., Baylor U., 1966; children—Douglas, Ronald, Kevin, Doris Jean, Raymond. Commd. 2d lt. U.S. Army, 1953, advanced through grades to lt. col., 1973; helicopter ambulance pilot, 1953-63; various hosp. adminstrv. assignments, 1963-73; personnel dir. Valley Forge (Pa.) Gen. Hosp., 1966; adminstr. evacuation hosp., Vietnam, 1967; dep. insp. Walter Reed Gen. Hosp., Washington, 1970; dir. personnel div. Office of Army Surgeon Gen., Washington, 1971-73, ret., 1973; adminstr. Health Care Centers, Phila. Coll. Osteo. Medicine, 1974-76; dir. bur. hosps. Pa. Dept. Health, Harrisburg, 1976-79; contract mgr. Blue Cross of So. Calif., 1979—. Decorated Bronze Star, Legion of Merit. Mem. Am. Hosp. Assn., Am. Legion, Ret. Officers Assn., Kappa Alpha Psi. Episcopalian. Club: Masons. Home: 7630 Lake Adlon Dr San Diego CA 92119 Office: 3878 Old Town Ave San Diego CA 92110

SMITH, REUBEN WILLIAM, university dean; b. San Mateo, Calif., May 2, 1929; s. Reuben William and Hazel (Huber) S.; A.B., U. Calif., Berkeley, 1951, M.A., 1952; Ph.D. (univ. travelling fellow), Harvard U., 1963; m. Nelda Augustine Herby, Aug. 31, 1957; children—Walter H.F., Margaret C.A. Carnegie postdoctoral fellow U. Chgo., 1963, instr., then asst. prof. Islamic history 1964-72, dean students, social scis. div., 1970-72; provost Callison Coll., U. Pacific, Stockton, Calif., 1972-74, dean Grad. Sch., 1974—; cons. Ency. Brit., 1965-68. Bd. dirs. 57th St. Art Fair, Chgo., 1965-70, 49er council Boy Scouts Am., 1976-79. Served to 1st lt. AUS, 1952-54. Mem. Western Assn. Grad. Schs. (pres. 1981), Council Grad. Schs. U.S. (dir. 1983—), Am. Oriental Soc., Middle East Studies Assn., Nat. Council Univ. Research Adminstrs. Editor: Islamic Civilization Syllabus, 2d edit., 1967, (M.G.S. Hodgson) Venture of Islam, 3 vols., 1974; contbr. articles to Ency. Brit. Book of Year, 1965—. Office: 3601 Pacific Ave Stockton CA 95211

SMITH, RICHARD CLARK, city official; b. New Kinsington, Pa., Mar. 25, 1935; s. Ralph Burdette and Margaret Mary (Maracci) S.; A.S., El Paso Community Coll., 1971; m. Audrey Darlene Montgomery, Dec. 29, 1971; children—Richard Clark, Diane Kay, Gary Allen, David Mark, Carol Lynn. With Colorado Springs (Colo.) Fire Dept., 1962—, fire capt., 1969-77, bn. chief, 1977-78, div. chief, 1978-79, fire chief, 1979—; program dir. Fire Sci. Asso. Degree, El Paso Community Coll., 1969-72. Mem. Bd. Edn. El Paso County Sch. Dist. 2, 1973-79, treas., 1973-79. Mem. Internat. Assn. Fire Chiefs, Nat. Fire Protection Assn., Colo. Fire Chiefs Assn. Mem. Christian Ch. of Security. Club: Sertoma. Office: 31 S Weber St Colorado Springs CO 80903*

SMITH, RICHARD EDWIN, accountant; b. Topeka, June 8, 1938; s. Thomas G. and Madeline M. (McKinney) S.; m. Patricia Ann Smith, Aug. 2, 1969; children—Linda, Chris Wendell, Thomas Richard. B.B.A., Washburn U., Topeka, 1960, postgrad. Law Sch., 1960-62. Mem. staff Arthur Andersen & Co., Kansas City, 1962-65; controller, v.p. Berry World Travel, Inc., Kansas City, 1965-68; dir. internal audit Parkview-GEM, Kansas City, 1968-69; exec. v.p. Beltz Travel Service, Inc., San Francisco, 1969-73; C.P.A., San Rafael, Calif., 1973-80; ptnr. in charge Fox & Co., 1980—. Served with USAR, 1955-64. C.P.A., Kans., Calif. Mem. Am. Inst. C.P.A.s, Calif. Soc. C.P.A.s, Marin Estate Planning Council, Internat. Assn. Fin. Planners, Washburn U. Alumni (life), Sigma Phi Epsilon. Republican. Clubs: Elks, Masons, Marin Golf and Country (dir., treas., Mchts. Exchange, Commonwealth. Contbr. articles on fin. and acctg. in travel industry to periodicals.

SMITH, RICHARD HOWARD, banker; b. Tulare, Calif., Aug. 27, 1927; s. Howard Charles and Sue Elizabeth (Cheyne) S.; B.A., Principia Coll, 1958; LL.B., LaSalle U., 1975; postgrad. Sch. Banking U. Wash., 1970-72; m. Patricia Ann Howery, Mar. 12, 1950; children—Jeffrey Howard, Holly Lee, Gregory Scott, Deborah Elaine. Prin., Aurora Elementary Sch., Tulare, 1951-53; prin. Desert Sun Sch., Idyllwild, Calif., 1953-55; trust adminstr. trainee Bank of Am., San Diego, 1955-58, asst. trust officer, Ventura, Redlands, Riverside and Los Angeles, 1958-65; asst. trust officer Security Pacific Bank, Fresno, Calif., 1965-68; trust officer, 1968-72, v.p., mgr., 1972—; instr. San Bernardino Valley Coll., 1962—, Fresno City Coll., 1977. Served with USN, 1945-46. Mem. Fresno, Bakersfield, Merced estate planning councils. Club: Kiwanis. Home: 3222 W Dovewood St Fresno CA 93711 Office: PO Box 5026 Fresno CA 93755

SMITH, ROBERT FREEMAN, Congressman; b. Portland, Oreg., June 16, 1931; m. Kay Tomlinson, 1966; children—Christopher, Matthew, Tiffany. B.A., Willamette U., 1953. Rancher-owner, Oreg.; mem. Oreg. Ho. of Reps., 1960-72, majority leader and speaker pro-tem, 1964-66, speaker, 1968-72, chmn. Com. on State and Fed. Affairs, 1965-69; mem. Oreg. Senate, 1972-82, Republican leader, 1978-82; mem. 98th Congress from 2d Oreg. Dist. Trustee Willamette U.; bd. dirs. PACWEST. Mem. Harney County C. of C. Lodges: Masons, Elks. Office: US House of Reps Washington DC 20515

SMITH, ROBERT HAMIL, fund raiser; b. Oak Park, Ill., Nov. 8, 1927; s. Henry Garfield and Mary Ellen (Hamil) S.; student U. Denver, 1946-48, LL.B., 1953, J.D., 1960; m. Mary Helen Kingsley, Dec. 29, 1948; children—David H., Mark K., Steven H., Rebecca Ann Smith Quintana. Dep. clk. County Ct., City and County of Denver, 1948-53, with Colo. Ins. Group, 1953-59; mgr. claims dept. R.H. Smith & Assos., 1959-64; pres. Am. Bapt. Home Mission Soc., 1964-68; asso. dir. devel. Ill. Wesleyan U., 1968-69; asst. to chancellor U. Calif., San Diego, 1969-77; exec. dir. devel. Scripps Clinic and Research Found., La Jolla, Calif., 1977-82, v.p. devel., 1982—; fund raising cons. deferred giving. Served with USNR, 1945. Mem. Nat. Soc. Fund Raising Execs., Internat. Yachting Fellowship of Rotarians (San Diego fleet comdr. 1979-81). Republican. Baptist. Club: Oceanside Yacht. Author: Guide to Harbors, Anchorages and Marinas So. and No. California edits., 1983. Home: 12720 Via Felina Del Mar CA 92014 Office: Scripps Clinic and Research Foundation 10666 N Torrey Pines Rd LaJolla CA 92037

SMITH, ROBERT PRESS, mktg. exec.; b. Berkeley, Calif., Feb. 5, 1953; s. Temple and Anita June (Maher) S.; B.S.E.E., U. Calif., Davis, 1975; M.S.E.E., Stanford U., 1979. Mem. tech. staff Hewlett-Packard, Cupertino, Calif., 1975-79; mktg. mgr. Am. Microsystems, Inc., Santa Clara, Calif., 1979-80; v.p. mktg., engr. Synmos, Inc., Palo Alto, Calif., 1980—; ptnr. Sand Castles, Mountain View, Calif., 1982—. Mem. IEEE, Tau Beta Pi. Home: 3328 Kimberly Way San Mateo CA 94403

SMITH, RONALD EDWARD, ophthalmologist; b. Walkersville, Md., Oct. 7, 1942; B.A., Johns Hopkins U., 1964, M.D., 1967; m. Suzette Le Blanc, Oct. 7, 1980; children by previous marriage—Kelly, Matt. Intern, Johns Hopkins Hosp., Balt., 1967-68; resident in ophthalmology Wilmer Eye Inst., Johns Hopkins U., 1968-71, chief resident, instr., 1972-73; fellow Francis I. Proctor Found. for Research in Ophthalmology, San Francisco, 1971-72; practice medicine, specializing in ophthalmology, Los Angeles, 1975—; mem. staff Corneal and External Disease Consultation Service, Estelle Doheny Eye Found., Los Angeles, 1975—; asst. prof. dept. ophthalmology Los Angeles County/U. So. Calif. Med. Center, 1975-78, asso. prof., 1978-81, prof., 1981—; mem. sci. adv. panel Friends of Eye Research, Boston, 1979—. Served with USPHS, 1973-75. Diplomate Am. Bd. Ophthalmology. Fellow A.C.S.; mem. Am. Acad. Ophthamology (asso. sec. for continuing edn. 1981—), Am. Assn. Ophthalmology, Assn. for Research in Vision and Ophthalmology, Pan Am. Assn. Ophthalmology, Contact Lens Assn. Ophthalmology, Calif. Assn. Ophthalmology, Pan Pacific Surg. Assn., Ophthalmology Research Club Los Angeles, Calif. Cornea Club, Los Angeles Ophthal. Soc., Johns Hopkins Med. and Surg. Assn., Am. Uveitis Soc., Assn. Proctor Fellows, Pacific Coast Oto-Ophthal. Soc., Internat. Soc. Refractive Keratoplasty, Salerni Collegium, AMA, Calif. Med. Assn., Los Angeles County Med. Assn., Sigma Xi. Contbr. chpts. to med. books, articles to med. jours.; editorial bd. Retinal, 1980—. Office: Estelle Doheny Eye Foundation 1355 San Pablo St Los Angeles CA 90033

SMITH, SAM, city ofcl; b. Gibsland, La., July 21, 1922; s. Stephen Kelly and Berniece C. (Smith) S.; B.S.S., Seattle U., 1951; B.A., U. Wash., 1952; m. Marion King, Jan. 29, 1947; children—Amelia, Aldwin Carl, Anthony E., Donald C., Ronald C., Stephen. Fiscal accounts clk. U.S. Civil Service, 1947-51; expediter Boeing, 1951-67; mem. Wash. Ho. of Reps., 1959-67; city councilman Seattle, 1967—, pres. council, 1974-78. Past mem. nat. bd. ministries Am. Bapt. Chs. U.S.A.; chmn. Area-Wide Project Mainstay. Served with AUS, 1942-46. Recipient Legislator of Year award, 1967; Annual Urban League award, 1968; Community Service award, 1971; Disting. Alumnus award Seattle U., 1976, Disting. Service award Central Area Jaycees, 1974-75, Exemplary Leadership award Mt. Zion Bapt. Ch., 1973, Gold medal Prince Hall Scottish Rite, 1978, Medal of Honor, DAR, 1980, others. Mem. Am. Acad. Polit. and Social Scis., VFW (Meritorious and Disting. Service award), Phi Beta Sigma. Democrat. Mason (33 deg.). Home: 1814 31st Ave Seattle WA 98122 Office: New Municipal Bldg Seattle WA 98104

SMITH, SANDRA WOOD, home economist, educator; b. Cedar City, Utah, Jan. 6, 1939; d. Elmer Hunter and Melba (Hollingshead) Wood;

B.S., Utah State U., 1961, M.S., 1981; m. Gary Leonard Smith, June 5, 1961; children—G. Gregg, Steven W. Tchr. home econs. schs. in Utah, 1965-81; asst. prof. child devel., parenting, home econs. edn. and clothing So. Utah State Coll., Cedar City, 1981—; mem. Utah adv. bd. Future Homemakers Am., 1978-81; cons. in field. Utah Future Homemakers Am. scholar, 1957-58; recipient leadership stipend, 1973-74 Girls State, 1956. Mem. Utah Assn. Vocat. Home Econs. Tchrs. (editor Newsletter 1979-81, pres.-elect 1981-82, pres. 1982-83). Jordan Dist. Home Econs. Assn. (chmn. 1975-77), Granite Edn. Assn., Jordan Edn. Assn. (faculty rep. 1978-79), Utah Edn. Assn., NEA, Utah Vocat. Assn. (bd. dirs. 1981-83), Am. Vocat. Assn., Am. Home Econs. Assn., Utah Home Econs. Assn. (bd. dirs.), Delta Kappa Gamma. Mormon. Home: 151 W College Ave Cedar City UT 84720 Office: Sci Bldg 208 So Utah State Coll Cedar City UT 84720

SMITH, SELMA MOIDEL, lawyer, composer; b. Warren, Ohio, Apr. 3, 1919; d. Louis and Mary (Oyer) Moidel; student Los Angeles City Coll., 1936-37, U. Calif., 1937-39, U. So. Calif., 1939-41; J.D., Pacific Coast U., 1942; 1 son, Mark Lee. Bar: Calif. 1943, U.S. Dist. Ct. 1943, U.S. Supreme Ct. 1958. Gen. practice law; mem. firm Moidel, Moidel, Moidel & Smith. Field dir. civilian adv. com. WAC, 1943; mem. nat. bd. Med. Coll. Pa. (formerly Woman's Med. Coll. Pa.), 1953—, exec. bd., 1976-80, pres.-elect, 1980, pres., 1980-82. Decorated La Order del Merito Juan Pablo Duarte (Dominican Republic). Mem. ABA, Calif. Bar Assn. (servicemen's legal com.), Los Angeles Bar Assn. (psychopathic ct. com.), Los Angeles Lawyers Club (public defenders com.), Nat. Assn. Women Lawyers (chmn. com. unauthorized practice of law, social commn. UN, regional dir. western states, Hawaii 1949-50, mem. jud. adminstrn. com. 1960, nat. chmn. world peace through law com. 1966-67), League of Ams. (dir.), Inter-Am. Bar Assn., So. Calif. Women Lawyers Assn. (pres. 1947, 48), Women Lawyers Assn. (chmn. Law Day com. 1966), State Bar Conf. Com., Council Bar Assns. Los Angeles County (charter sec. 1950), Calif. Bus. Women's Council (dir. 1951), Los Angeles Bus. Women's Council (pres. 1952), Calif. Pres.'s Council (1st v.p.), Nat. Assn. Composers U.S.A. (dir. 1974-79, ann. luncheon chmn. 1975), Nat. Fedn. Music Clubs (nat. vice chmn. for Western region, 1973-78), Calif. Fedn. Music Clubs (state chmn. Am. Music 1971-75, state conv. chmn. 1972), Docents of Los Angeles Philharmonic (v.p. 1973—, chmn. Latin Am. community relations 1972-75, press and public relations 1972-75, cons. coordinator 1973-75), ASCAP, Euterpe Opera Club (v.p. 1974-75, chmn. auditions 1972, chmn. awards 1973-75), Plato Soc. of UCLA Iota Tau Tau (dean Los Angeles, supreme treas). Composer: Espressivo-Four Piano Pieces. Home: 5272 Lindley Ave Encino CA 91316

SMITH, STANFORD S., state official; b. Colo.; m. Harriet; 2 children. B.X., U.S. Naval Acad. Served with U.S. Navy, 11 yrs.; comdr. U.S.S. Mockingbird, Korea; instr. marine engring. U.S. Naval Acad.; ret.; owner, operator ranch, nr. Thermopolis, Wyo.; commr. Hot Springs County (Colo.), 8 yrs.; mem. Wyo. Senate, 4 yrs.; mem. Wyo. Ho. of Reps., two terms, until 1982, mem. mines, minerals, and indsl. devel. com., agr., pub. lands, and water com., mem. Wyo. Livestock Bd.; treas. State of Wyo., Cheyenne. Decorated Bronze Star. Mem. Wyo. Wool Growers (past pres.), Am. Murray Grey Cattle Assn. (past nat. dir.), Wyo. Prodn. Credit Assn. (past dir.). Office: Office State Treas State Capitol Bldg Cheyenne WY 82002*

SMITH, STEWART ERWIN, ins. service co. exec.; b. Long Beach, Calif., Feb. 20, 1932; s. George Stewart and Bessie Irene (Crum) S.; student Orange Coast Coll., 1949-50; A.A., Santa Ana Community Coll., 1957; m. Barbara Ann Morris, June 6, 1954; children—Lazette Marie, Suzette Cherrie. Teller, Bank of Am., 1954-55; field insp. Retail Credit Co., 1955-59; v.p., br. mgr., dir. Jensen & More, Inc., Mesa, Ariz., 1959—. Former elder Ch. of Redeemer; mem. Cornerstone Bible Fellowship. Served with USCG, 1950-53. Mem. Am. Soc. Safety Engrs., Ariz. Ins. Auditors Assn. (past pres.), Asso. Safety Engrs. Ariz. Republican. Office: PO Box 1179 Mesa AZ 85201

SMITH, STEWART RUSSELL, investment co. exec.; b. Los Angeles, Aug. 29, 1946; s. Howard Russell and Jeanne (Rogers) S.; B.A. magna cum laude, Pomona Coll., 1968; J.D. cum laude, Harvard U., 1971; m. Patricia Ann Heydt, Mar. 11, 1972; children—Cameron Stewart, Graham Russell, Logan Stewart. Admitted to Calif. bar, 1972; trial atty. antitrust div. U.S. Dept. Justice, Washington, 1971-73; asso. firm Paul, Hastings, Janofsky & Walker, Los Angeles, 1973-77; individual practice law, San Marino, Calif., 1977-79; pres., dir. Kinsmith Fin. Corp., San Marino, 1979—. Bd. dirs. Pomona Coll. Assos., 1980—, Kidspace, A Participatory Mus., 1982—; mem. Pasadena Tournament of Roses Assn., 1978—, Los Angeles Philharm. Men's Com., 1977—. Lic. real estate broker. Mem. ABA, Calif. State Bar, Los Angeles County Bar Assn., Phi Beta Kappa. Republican. Presbyterian. Clubs: Jonathan (Los Angeles); Annandale Golf (Pasadena). Office: 2600 Mission St Suite 201 San Marino CA 91108

SMITH, SUSAN AMNER, college administrator; b. Fayetteville, Ark., Aug. 4, 1950; d. Reh Lee and Barbara Berniece (Stark) S.; B.S., Okla. State U.-Stillwater, 1972; M.A., U. Tulsa, 1974. Credentials examiner U. Colo., Denver, 1974-78, instr. English, 1976-78; instr. English Met. State Coll., Denver, 1976-78; admissions counselor Ft. Lewis Coll., Durango, Colo., 1978-79, registrar, 1979—. Elder, 1st Presbyterian Ch., Durango. EPDA scholar, 1973-74. Mem. Am. Assn. Collegiate Registrars and Admissions Officers. Democrat.

SMITH, THERESA CATHERINE, ednl. adminstr.; b. San Louis Obispo, Calif., Sept. 9, 1924; d. Michael Mitchell and Lena Evelyn (Onetto) Sullivan; student Immaculate Heart Coll., 1942-44, St. Vincent Hosp. Sch. Nursing, 1944, Hunter Coll., 1944-45, U. Calif., Berkeley, 1947, Ariz. State U., 1947-49; B.S., U. Nev., 1971, M.Ed., 1973; Ph.D., Waldon U., 1982; m. Jack Riley Smith, July 17, 1948 (dec. 1972); children—Linda, David K., Patricia, Nancy. Coordinator spl. services Mohave Valley (Ariz.) Sch. Dist., 1966-72; cons. Diocesan Schs., Las Vegas, Nev., 1972-80; cons. Title VI-G Child Service Demonstration Centers, Nat. Learning Disabilities Assistance Project, Western States, 1976, Nev. Child Service Demonstration Center, Title VI, Clark County Sch. System, Las Vegas, 1974, Clark County Diagnostic-Prescriptive Center, Las Vegas, 1975; master tchr. U. Nev., Las Vegas, 1973—; instr. Clark County Community Coll., Las Vegas, part-time, 1974—; prin. Our Lady of Las Vegas Elem. Sch., 1974-76; dir. spl. services New Horizons Center for Learning, 1975-76; co-founder New Horizons Center for Learning, Las Vegas, 1974, exec. dir., 1976—; bd. dirs., 1973-80; cons. Structure of Intellect Inst., Las Vegas, 1979—; psychoednl. diagnostician, cons., Las Vegas. Bd. dirs. Mohave Mental Health Center, 1968-71; pres. confs. Nev. Assn. for Children with Learning Disabilities, 1970-80, pres., bd. dirs., 1973-79; mem. Nev. State Title I Adv. Bd., 1975. Served with U.S. Navy Women's Reserve, 1944-46. Roman Catholic. Home: 4034 S Great Plains Las Vegas NV 89121 Office: 401 Campbell Dr Las Vegas NV 89107

SMITH, THOMAS EDGAR, JR., environ. planner, cons.; b. Monrovia, Calif., Nov. 29, 1947; s. Thomas Edgar, Sr., and Jean Catherine (Blackburn) S.; m. Lorraine Cordaro, Sept. 23, 1972; children—Julia Renee, Anna Nicole. B.A. in Social Ecology cum laude (Irvine Co. scholar), U. Calif.-Irvine, 1974; M.A. in Urban Planning (Acad. Senate Research fellow), UCLA, 1976; cert. Am. Inst. Cert. Planners. Research asst. Ultrasystems, Inc., Newport Beach, Calif., 1974-76; environ. planner So. Calif. Assn. Govts., Los Angeles, 1976-79; assoc. Phillips, Brandt, Reddick, Irvine, 1979-82; exec. v.p. Michael Brandman & Assocs., Inc., 1982—. Mem. dean's council UCLA Sch. Architecture and Urban Planning, 1979-82; life mem. UCLA Alumni Assn. Served in USAF, 1967-71. Mem. Am. Planning Assn. (session moderator 1982), Am. Inst. Cert. Planners, Assn. Environ. Profls. (dir.), Orange County Water Assn., Water Supply Improvement Assn., Phi Beta Kappa. Contbr. articles profl. jours. Office: 18021 Sky Park Circle Suite E-2 Irvine CA 92714

SMITH, THOMAS JOSEPH, advertising executive; b. Bklyn., Sept. 7, 1949; s. Edward James, and Helen Marie (Kelly) S.; m. Donna E. Meisse, June 3, 1972; children—Kelly, Brian. B.A., Rutgers, 1971. Mgr., Corporate Fin. Advt., Washington Post Newspaper, 1971-79; advt. mgr. Seattle Post-Intelligencer, Seattle, 1979-80, advt. dir., 1980—. Mem. mgmt. com. Downtown Seattle Devel. Assn.; active Patrons of N.W. Civic, Cultural and Charitable Orgns. Mem. Internat. Newspaper Advt. and Mktg. Execs.; Seattle Advt. Fedn.; Seattle C. of C. Roman Catholic. Clubs: Washington Athletic, (Seattle), Mill Creek Country (Bothwell Wash.). Home: 14703 Fairway Dr Bothwell WA 98011 Office: Seattle Post-Intelligencer 521 Wall St Seattle WA 98121

SMITH, TOM LEO, psychologist, educator; b. Pendleton, Oreg., July 9, 1942; s. Leo Mansfield and Delma Irene (Miller) S.; B.A. summa cum laude, Whitman Coll., 1964; postgrad. U. Iowa, 1964, 65-67; M.A. in Chinese Studies, U. Oreg., 1973, M.A. with honors and distinction in Psychology, 1973, Ph.D., 1973. Clin. psychology trainee VA Hosp., Iowa City, 1965-67; research asst. Asian studies U. Oreg., Eugene, 1967-69, research, teaching asst., 1969-71, NIMH research fellow, 1971-73; research asst. Oreg. Research Inst., Eugene, 1970-71; asst. prof., head exptl.-social psychology dept. U. Denver, 1973-79, mem. spl. faculty Sch. Profl. Psychology, Inst. Gerontology, psychology dept., 1979—; dir. grad. psychology Antioch U. West-Denver, 1979—; co-dir. Oreg. Research and Edn. Inst. Denver, 1979—; gerontology trainee HEW, Eugene, 1969-70; cons. various instns., 1972—; cons. film making, 1969-80. Bd. dirs. Bapt. Nursing Home, 1975-77; mem. long term health care rev. bd. Colo. Found. for Med. Care, 1978-81; mem. spl. com. Colo. Endowment for Humanities, 1976-77; human rights worker Denver Commn. for Community Relations, 1979-81. Recipient Peabody award, 1977; Ford Found. research fellow Nat. Republic China, 1968-69; NIMH fellow, 1971-73; NSF fellow, 1963; HEW tng. grantee, 1967-68; U. Denver research grantee, 1974-77; Grant Found. grantee, 1975-77; NIMH grantee, 1977. Mem. Am. Psychol. Assn., Rocky Mountain Psychol. Assn., Colo. Psychol. Assn., Nat. Gerontology Soc., AAAS, AAUP, Phi Beta Kappa, Sigma Xi. Democrat. Developer technique for social interaction research, concept for understanding social psychology. Contbr. chpt. to Handbook of Social Psychology, 1981. Home: 1050 Lafayette St Apt 207 Denver CO 80218 Office: Antioch U West-Denver 875 Delaware St Denver CO 80204

SMITH, TURK, columnist; b. Detroit, June 24, 1917; s. Talbot Truxtun and Constance (Fitch) S.; student U. Ariz., 1935-38; m. Leslie Collie, Apr. 4, 1942 (dec. 1972); children—Talbot Truxtun III, Chopeta Constance. Reporter, feature writer Ariz. Republic, Phoenix, 1952—, automotive columnist, 1964—; corr. Newsweek, 1952-64, USIA, 1952-79. Contbr. articles to mags. Home: 4825 E Picadilly St Phoenix AZ 85018 Office: 120 E Van Buren St Phoenix AZ 85002

SMITH, WALDO GREGORIUS, former government official; b. Bklyn., July 29, 1911; s. John Henry and Margaret (Gregorius) S.; m. Mildred Pearl Prescott, July 30, 1935; 1 dau., Carole Elizabeth Smith Levin. Student CCNY, N.Y., 1928-29; B.S. in Forestry, Cornell U., 1933. Forester, Forest Service, U.S. Dept. Agr., Atlanta, 1933-41, Ala. Div. Forestry, Brewton, 1941-42; engr., civil engring. technician Geol. Survey, U.S. Dept. Interior, 1942-71, cartographic technician, 1972-75; chmn. Public Transp. Council, 1975—. Recipient 40 year Civil Service award pin and scroll; 42 Yr. Govt. Service award plaque. Registered profl. engr., Colo. Fellow Am. Congress Surveying and Mapping (life; sec.-treas. Colo. chpt. 1961, program chmn. 1962, reporter 1969, mem. nat. membership devel. com. 1973-74, rep. to Colo. Engring. Council 1976-77); mem. AAAS, Denver Fed. Center Profl. Engrs. Group (U.S. Geol. Survey rep. 1973-76, Engr. of Yr. award 1975), Nat. Soc. Profl. Engrs., Profl. Engrs. Colo. (chpt. scholarship chmn. 1979—, advt. corr., service award 1983), Cornell U. Alumni Assn. (alumni secondary schs. com.), Common Cause, Colo. Engring. Council (chmn. library com., spl. rep. Regional Transp. Dist., 1974-75; mem. sci. fair com. 1970-71; rep. ex officio Denver Pub. Library Found. Bd. Trustees 1975-80), Fedn. Am. Scientists, Am. Soc. Engring. Edn., People for Am. Way. Contbr. proposals to science-for-citizens program and research applied to nat. needs program NSF. Contbr. articles to profl. jours. Home: 3821 W 25th Ave Denver CO 80211

SMITH, WAYNE CALVIN, chemical engineer; b. Beaver, Okla., Mar. 19, 1935; s. Dean C. and Loraine (Tice) S. Student Tex. A&M U., 1953-54; B.S., U. Okla., 1958, M.S., 1964; postgrad. Tulsa U., 1967-69; Ph.D., U. Colo., 1974. Process engr. Shell Oil Co., Dear Park, Tex., 1958-59; sr. engr. Chemstrand Co., Pensacola, Fla., 1964-66; sr. engr. Phillips Petroleum Co., Bartlesville, Okla., 1967-69; dep. chief EPA, Denver, 1971-78; mgr. pollution control Dames & Moore, Golden, Colo., 1978-81; regional mgr. Hittman Assocs., Denver, 1981-82; pres. EnCon Environs Control Services, Inc., Golden, 1982-83; chief hazardous waste mgmt. Woodward-Clyde Cons., Englewood, Colo. Served with USMC, 1959-62. Mem. Am. Inst. Chem. Engrs., Soc. Plastics Engrs., Water Pollution Control Fedn., Sigma Xi. Contbr. articles to profl. jours. Office: Harlequin Plaza N 7600 E Orchard Rd Englewood CO 80111

SMITH, WILBER EUGENE, assn. exec.; b. Omaha, Oct. 22, 1919; s. Paul Edward and Beatrice (McClain) S.; B.S., U. Calif., Berkeley, 1941; M.Govtl. Adminstrn., U. Pa., 1949; m. Barbara Louise Conley, June 17, 1943; children—Paul M., Kevin C. Field rep. League Calif. Cities, Sacramento, 1949-53; city mgr. City of San Rafael (Calif.), 1953-57; asst. dir. Nat. League Cities, Washington, 1957-61; exec. dir. Assn. Bay Area Govts., Berkeley, Calif., 1961-64; asst. to pres. Automotive Safety Found., Washington, 1964-66; exec. dir. So. Calif. Assn. Govts., Los Angeles, 1966-69; pres. Wil Smith & Assos., Los Angeles, 1970-76; exec. dir. Assn. Monterey Bar Area Govts., Monterey, Calif., 1976—; instr. Golden Gate U., Monterey, 1977—. Served with U.S. Navy, 1942-49. Mem. Internat. City Mgmt. Assn., Am. Soc. Public Adminstrn., Western Govtl. Research Assn., Internat. Fraternity Lambda Alpha. Democrat. Methodist. Clubs: Rotary; Monterey Peninsula Country. Contbr. articles to profl. jours. Office: PO Box 190 Monterey CA 93940

SMITH, WILLARD GRANT, educational psychologist; b. Sidney, N.Y., June 29, 1934; s. Frank Charles and Myrtle Belle (Empet) S.; m. Ruth Ann Dissly, Sept. 14, 1957; children—Deborah Sue Henri, Cynthia Lynn Koster, Andrea Kay Richards, John Charles. B.S., U. Md., 1976; M.S., U. Utah, 1978, Ph.D., 1981. Cert. sch. psychologist, sch. adminstr., tchr., Utah. Research asst. Med. Ctr., U. Utah, 1977, teaching asst. dept. ednl. psychology, 1976-78, research cons. dept. edn., 1977; program evaluator Salt Lake City Sch. Dist.; program evaluator and auditor Utah State Bd. Edn., 1978; sch. psychologist Jordan Sch. Dist., Sandy, Utah, 1978-82, tchr., 1979-80; exec. dir. Utah Ind. Living Ctr., Salt Lake City, 1982—. Active Nat. Assn. Ind. Living, Nat. Council Ind. Living. Served to master sgt. USAF, 1953-76. Decorated Air Force Commendation medal with 2 clusters; recipient U. Md. scholastic achievement award, 1975. Mem. Am. Psychol. Assn., Nat. Assn. Sch. Psychologists, Nat. Rehab. Assn., Am. Ednl. Research Assn., Assn. Supervision and Curriculum Devel., Air Force Sgts. Assn., Ret. Enlisted Assn., Phi Kappa Phi, Alpha Sigma Lambda. Home: 6879 Maverick Circle Salt Lake City UT 84121 Office: 764 S 200 W Salt Lake City UT 84101

SMITH, WILLIAM, II, safety engineer; b. Bay City, Tex., Nov. 30, 1941; s. William and Willie Mae (Perry) S.; B.S., Tuskegee Inst., 1964; postgrad. Washington U., 1968-70; m. Sylvia Knight, Feb. 4, 1977; children—William III, Maurice. Equipment engr. Boeing Co., Huntsville, Ala., 1964-67; plant design engr. McDonnell Douglas Corp., St. Louis, 1967-69; project engr. St. Louis County Govt., 1969-72; div. engr. E.I. duPont de Nemours & Co., Inc., Wilmington, Del. and Victoria, Tex., 1972-74; engring. mgr. Westinghouse Corp., Millburn, N.J., 1974-76; bldg. safety engr. Denver Public Schs., 1976—, project adminstr., 1977—, energy conservationist, 1978—. Served with USNR, 1979—. Bd. dirs. Denver Opportunities Industrialization Center, 1979-80, Nat. Commn. on Future of Regis Coll.; mem. Mayor's Citizens Adv. Com. on Energy, 1980—. Recipient Pres.'s Nat. award for energy conservation, 1980. Mem. Am. Soc. Safety Engrs., Colo. Assn. Sch. Energy Coordinators, Am. Assn. Blacks in Energy, Denver Pub. Schs. Black Adminstrs. and Suprs. Assn. (treas.), Tuskegee Inst. Alumni Assn. Democrat. Home: 102 S Balsam St Denver CO 80226 Office: Denver Public Schs 900 Grant St Denver CO 80203

SMITH, WILLIAM R., elec. engr.; b. Denver, Nov. 10, 1938; s. William F. and Blanche E. (Rouse) S.; B.S.E.E., Colo. State U., 1960; M.S.E.E., Iowa State U., 1961, Ph.D., 1963; m. Lillie R. Smith, June 6, 1959; children—Jeffrey, Janet, Deborah. Project mgr. SYMBOL, Fairchild Semicondr. Research & Devel., Palo Alto, Calif., 1963-70; mgr. memory systems ops. Fairchild Systems Tech. div., San Jose, Calif., 1970-72, dir. research and devel. computer systems, 1973-75; v.p. systems engring. Caere Corp., Los Gatos, Calif., 1975-81; v.p. Multidata Corp., San Jose, 1982—. Recipient Outstanding Young Alumnus Recognition, Iowa State U., 1970; Nat. Def. fellow, 1960-63. Mem. IEEE, Phi Kappa Phi, Eta Kappa Nu, Sigma Tau, Kappa Mu Epsilon. Baptist. Contbr. articles to profl. jours.; patentee in field. Home: 1866 Golden Way Mountain View CA 94040 Office: 100 Cooper Ct Los Gatos CA 95030

SMITH, WILLIAM SPENCER, oil co. exec.; b. Eagle Grove, Iowa, Oct. 5, 1950; s. Spencer Barker and Gerene Ethel S.; B.A. in Bus., U. No. Iowa, 1973; m. Luann E. Peterson, July 29, 1977. Mktg. rep. IBM, Denver, 1973-76; v.p. ENI Corp., Denver, 1976-80; v.p. Knight Royalty Corp., Denver, 1980-83, pres., 1983—, also dir.; pres. Knight Securities Corp. Mem. youth activities bd. YMCA, 1978—; mem. Nat. Republican Senatorial Com., 1980—; trustee, chmn. Rockland Community Ch., 1978—. Republican. Mem. United Ch. of Christ. Club: U. No. Iowa Alumni Athletic. Home: 1506 Shooting Star Dr Golden CO 80401 Office: 1675 Broadway Suite 1910 Denver CO 80202

SMITH, WILLIAM WEBER, physician; b. San Diego, Aug. 16, 1914; s. Grover Eugene and Sophia Johanna S.; m. Gertrude Janeway, Feb. 25, 1941; children—Anthony, Gertrude, Gregory, Diana, Hillary, Mark. B.S., Stanford U., 1935, M.D., 1939; Intern, Los Angeles Gen. Hosp., 1938-39, resident, 1939-40; instr. U. So. Calif. Med. Sch., 1939-42, Good Samaritan Hosp., Los Angeles, 1944-49; practice medicine, specializing in internal medicine, Los Angeles, 1940-50, Beverly Hills, Calif., 1950—; mem. staff St. Johns Hosp., Santa Monica, Calif., Santa Monica Hosp. Trustee, St. Johns Hosp., 1974—, mem. exec. bd., 1980-83; trustee Los Angeles Heart Assn., 1944-47. Served to 1st lt. USNR, 1942-44. Recipient Disting. Service award Hathaway House, 1974; Beverly Hills C. of C., 1966. Mem. A.C.P., Los Angeles Acad. Medicine, AMA, Los Angeles Med. Assn., Calif. Med. Assn. Republican. Roman Catholic. Club: Los Angeles Country. Home: 334 Burlingame Los Angeles CA 90049 Office: 133 Lasky Dr Beverly Hills CA 90214

SMITHEY, DONNA LEE, insurance company supervisor; b. Beech Grove, Ind., Nov. 10, 1949; s. William K. and Deloris M. (Costelow) S. B.S. in Math., Ball State U., 1970; postgrad. Purdue U., 1970-71, Lewis and Clark Northwestern Sch. Law, 1980—; A.A. in Bus., LaSalle Extension Sch., 1979. With Unigard Ins. Co., 1971-75, 76—, dist. claims mgr., Portland, Oreg., 1976, br. supervising adjuster, 1976-82, reins. claims supr., Seattle, 1982—; freelance ins. adjuster, 1975; chmn. Portland Arbitration Com., 1981. Mem. Internat. Assn. Arson Investigators, Casualty Adjusters Assn., Delta Zeta. Presbyterian. Office: 1215 SW 4th Ave Seattle WA 98101

SMITH-RITCHIE, JERILYNN SUZANNE, educator; b. Loma Linda, Calif., Aug. 15, 1944; d. Gerald A. and Maxine (McGowan) Smith; m. Lynn A. Choate, May 8, 1971; 1 dau., Catherine Anne; m. 2d, C. Alen Ritchie, Feb. 17, 1981. B.A., U. Redlands (Calif.), 1966, M.A.T., 1968; M.A.Ed., Calif. State Coll., San Bernardino, 1980. Tchr. elem. sch. Redlands Unified Sch. Dist., 1966-69, tchr. eductionally handicapped, 1969-71, tchr. intermediate grades, 1971-74, tchr. bilingual edn., 1975-79, resource specialist, 1979—; supr. student tchrs. Calif. State Coll., 1975; lectr. in field. Bd. dirs. San Bernardino County Mus. Assn. Recipient Hon. Service award Lugonia PTA, 1982. Mem. Council for the Exceptional Child, Calif. Assn. Bilingual Edn., Nat. Assn. Bilingual Edn. Democrat. Office: 202 E Pennsylvania Ave Redlands CA 92373

SMOKE, RICHARD, social scientist; b. Huntington, Pa., Oct. 21, 1944; s. Kenneth Ludwig and Lillian (Harbaugh) S.; B.A., Harvard U., 1965; Ph.D., MIT, 1972. Asst. dean research, lectr. J.F. Kennedy Sch. Govt., Harvard U., 1971-73; postdoctoral fellow Inst. Personality Assessment and Research, U. Calif.-Berkeley, 1973-74; fellow Center for Advanced Study in Behavioral Scis., Palo Alto, Calif., 1974-75; research fellow and prof. Wright Inst., Berkeley, 1975-81, interim dean, 1981-82; co-founder, research dir. Peace and Common Security, Berkeley, 1982—; cons. Internat. Inst. Applied Systems Analysis, Orgn. for Econ. Cooperation and Devel., Com. on Econ. Devel., Woods Hole Oceanographic Instn., N.J. Neuropsychiat. Inst. Recipient (with Alexander George) Bancroft prize, Columbia U., 1974. Mem. Am. Polit. Sci. Assn. (Helen Dwight Reid award 1971-72), Am. Psychol. Assn., Internat. Soc. Polit. Psychology (governing council 1980-82). Author: War: Controlling Escalation, 1977, National Security and Nuclear Weapons: an Introduction to the American Experience, 1983; (with Alexander L. George) Deterrence in American Foreign Policy: Theory and Practice, 1974; assoc. editor: Polit. Psychology. Home: 1786 Spruce St Berkeley CA 94709

SMOLLAN, DAVID LESLIE, tax practitioner; b. Middlesbrough, Eng., June 22, 1928; came to U.S., 1948, naturalized, 1954; s. Philip and Sarah (Freedman) S.; B.B.A., Woodbury Coll., 1950; m. Sheila Joy Glassman, Aug. 5, 1956; children—Jeffrey, Debbie. Chief acct. Lucky Plastic Co., Inc., Los Angeles, 1951-64; self-employed tax practitioner, Encino, Calif, 1965—. Named Kiwanian of Yr., Pacoima Kiwanis Club, 1968; enrolled to practice before the IRS, 1967. Mem. Nat. Assn. Enrolled Fed. Tax Accts. (pres. 1969-70), Nat. Assn. Enrolled Agts. (pres. 1973-74), Calif. Soc. Enrolled Agts. Club: Kiwanis. Office: 18075 Ventura Blvd Suite 212 Encino CA 91316

SMYRL, WILLIAM HIRAM, chemist; b. Brownfield, Tex., Dec. 12, 1938; s. Garvin and Opal Faye (Coor) S.; B.S. in Chemistry, Tex. Tech. U., 1961; Ph.D. in Chemistry, U. Calif.-Berkeley, 1966; m. Donna Kay Clayton, Nov. 29, 1964; children—Eliot K., Clifford G. Asst. prof. Sch. Pharmacy U. Calif., San Francisco, 1966-69; mem. tech. staff Boeing Research Labs., Seattle, 1969-72; mem. tech. Staff Sandia Nat. Lab., Albuquerque, 1972—. Mem. Electrochemical Soc., Sigma Xi. Baptist. Mem. editorial bd. Journal of Electrochemical Soc.; contbr. articles in field to profl. jours. Office: Sandia National Laboratory Albuquerque NM 87185

SMYSER, CHARLES ARVIL (SKIP), state senator, lawyer; b. Caldwell, Idaho, Nov. 14, 1949; s. Samuel H. and Mildred A. S.; m. Melinda Sloviaczek, Aug. 22, 1981. B.A., Eastern Wash. U., 1972; J.D., Gonzaga U., 1977. Bar: Idaho 1977. Dep. pros. atty. Ada County, Idaho, Boise, 1977-79; dep. atty. gen. State of Idaho, 1979-80; ptnr. Connolly and Smyser, Chartered, Boise and Parma, Idaho, 1980—; mem. Idaho Ho. of Reps., 1980-82; mem. Idaho Senate from Dist. 11, 1982—. Served to 1st lt., U.S. Army, 1972-74. Mem. Idaho State Bar Assn., Idaho Trial Lawyers Assn., Order of Barristers, Lambda Chi Alpha. Republican. Presbyterian. Lodges: Lions, Masons. Office: 134 S 5th St Boise ID 83702 also PO Box 157 Parma ID 83660

SMYTH, C. EDWARD, educator; b. Marhsall, Mich., July 7, 1943; s. James and Mary Ann S.; B.A., Taylor U., 1968; M.Rel.Ed. magna cum laude, Gordon-Conwell Theol. Sem., 1972; Ed.D., Boston U., 1978; m. Ellen C. Ridley, Sept. 20, 1969, children—David Edward, Melanie Joy. Dir. edn. Pompano Beach (Fla.) United Meth. Ch., 1972-73; dir. ednl. ministries Park Temple United Meth. Ch., Ft. Lauderdale, Fla., 1973-75; prof. Christian edn. and religion Seattle-Pacific U., Seattle, 1975—, dir. grad. programs Sch. Religion, 1975—. Bd. dirs. Lake Somamish Bible Camp, 1982. Served with USNR Res., 1962. Mem. Assn. Researchers in Religious Edn., Religious Edn. Assn., Nat. Assn. Profs. Christian Edn. (pres. 1982—), Assn. Ednl. Tedh., Assn. Curriculum Supervision and Devel., United Meth. Assn. Profs. Christian Edn. Republican. Home: 845 NW 116th St Seattle WA 98177 Office: Seattle Pacific Univ Seattle WA 98119

SMYTH, DAVID SHANNON, real estate investor, land developer; b. Denver, May 13, 1943; s. William James and Constance Ruth (Sherman) S.; student Regis Coll., 1967-69, USAF Acad., 1961-65, U. No. Colo., 1965-67; m. Sharon Kaye Swiderski, Jan. 3, 1980; 1 dau., Julia Caitlin; 1 son by previous marriage, Shannon David. Accountant, Colo. Nat. Bank, 1966-69; bus. analyst Dun & Bradstreet, 1969-70; pres., dir. Georgetown Valley Water & Sanitation Dist., 1973-74, Realists, Inc., 1973-74, Silver Queen Constrn. Co., 1973-74; v.p., sec., dir. Georgetown Assos., Inc. (Colo.), 1970-74; pres., chief ops. officer Lincoln Cos., Denver, 1975-76; project mgr., sales mgr., prin. Brooks-Morris Homes, Fox Ridge, Colo., 1976-77; project mgr. U.S. West Homes, Denver, 1977-78; pres., dir. Denver Venture Capital, 1978-81; prin., dir., pres. Shelter Investment Co., 1982—; owner, dir., exec. v.p. Maple Leaf Realty Corp.; v.p., dir. Gibraltar Devel. Corp., Dominion Properties Ltd., 1978-82. Served with USAF, 1961-65. Lic. real estate broker. Home: 6093 E Briarwood Dr Englewood CO 80112 Office: 4880 Riverbend Rd Boulder CO 80301

SMYTH, DOROTHY LILLIAN, real estate agency executive, musician, florist; b. Albuquerque, July 4, 1934; d. Joseph Franklin and Grace Lillian (Ruppee) Johnson; m. Leo Ralph Smyth, Sept. 2, 1953; children—Robert Lee, Larry Alan, Kathleen Ann Smyth Walsh. Student music edn. U. N.Mex., 1952-54; B.A., U. Tex.-El Paso, 1968. Lic. real estate agt., N.Mex.; cert. floral art designer, Albuquerque. Tchr. pub. schs., Los Lunas, N.Mex., 1952, pvt. tchr. music, Los Lunas, 1953-57, La Cueva, N.Mex., 1957-60, Los Lunas, 1960-64; postmaster, La Cueva, 1958-60; tchr. music, kindergarten pub. schs., El Paso, 1964-69; real estate agent N.Mex. Farm Bur., 1973-75; real estate agt. Century 21, Robertson Realty, Inc., Albuquerque, 1975-83, co-owner, mgr., relocation dir., 1977—, also trainer; owner, mgr. Smyth Flower & Greenhouse, Albuquerque, 1980 . Active extension clubs N.Mex. Extension Service, 1960-64; pres. Mesa Vista PTA, El Paso, 1964-69; sec. Booster Club West Mesa, N.Mex., 1969-75; vol. 4-Seasons Nursing Home, Albuquerque; mem. choir, tchr. Sunday Sch. Fruit Avenue Bapt. Ch., Albuquerque. Recipient numerous certs. N.Mex. Extension Service; cert. Albuquerque Bd. Realtors. Mem. Nat. Realtor Assn., Albuquerque C. of C. Democrat. Home: 192 Willow Rd NW Albuquerque NM 87107 Office: 6360 2d St NW Albuquerque NM 87107

SMYTH, JACK BORDEN, computer software company executive; b. Cleve., Jan. 5, 1947; s. Clark Pidgeon and Gladys Marie (Cherna) S.; m. Linn Elizabeth Jensen, Aug. 23, 1969; children—Kristy Newett, Karen Elizabeth, Kim Mc Lean. B.S. in Indsl. Engring., Cornell U., 1969, M.B.A., Stanford U., 1975. Cert. welder, Ohio. Owner, operator Univ. Photo Service, Ithaca, N.Y., 1968-69; tech. rep. Lincoln Electric Co., Cleve. and Chgo., 1969-73; regional dir. Nat. Affiliation Concerned Bus. Students, San Francisco and Chgo., 1973-75; sales mgr. data processing products TAB Products Co., Palo Alto, Calif., 1975-77, nat. mktg. dir., 1977; nat. sales mgr. media products Electronic Memories and Magnetics, San Jose, Calif., 1977-78; product mgr. INMAC, Santa Clara, Calif., 1978-80; co-founder, exec. v.p. Challenge Computer Supplies, Palo Alto, 1980-81, dir., 1980-81; co-founder, pres. Learning Co., Menlo Park, Calif., 1981-82, dir., 1981-82; founder, pres., dir. Add-on Software Inc., Dublin, Calif., 1983—; dir. Childware Corp., Menlo Park, 1983—. Clarence J. Hicks meml. fellow, 1974. Mem. Stanford U. Bus. Sch. Alumni Assn. (dir. 1982—, Bay Area coordinator 1981-82, pres. Peninsula chpt. 1980-81, v.p. programs 1979-80, v.p. communications 1978-79), Peninsula Mktg. Assn. (dir. 1976-79, pres. 1977-78). Republican. Christian Scientist. Clubs: Stanford Golf, Alpine Hills Tennis. Author: (pamphlet) Marketing Research: A Tool for Strategic Planning, 1974. Home: 1899 White Oak Dr Menlo Park CA 94025 Office: 11879 Dublin Blvd Dublin CA 94568

SNAVELY, ODELL LEROY, businessman, clergyman; b. Lindsay, Okla., June 14, 1918; s. William Patrick and Cenith Dove (Cox) S.; m. Evelyn Marie McDonald, Mar. 27, 1946; children—Gary, Carol. Student Pacific Bible Sem., 1957; M.Th., Reed Coll. Religion, 1959. Salesman, 1950-61; ordained to ministry Christian Ch., 1961; pastor Buena Park, Calif., 1961-67; bus. license supr. City of South Gate (Calif.), 1967-77; owner Del's Gift Shop, South Gate, 1977—; mayor City of South Gate, 1980-81, 82-83. Served with USNR, 1943-46. Mem. South Gate C. of C. Democrat. Clubs: Kiwanis, Eagles. Home: 8992 Annetta Ave South Gate CA 90280 Office: 8650 California Ave South Gate CA 90280

SNEED, JOSEPH TYREE, judge; b. Calvert, Tex., July 21, 1920; s. Harold Marvin and Cara (Weber) S.; B.B.A., Southwestern U., 1941; LL.B., U. Tex., Austin, 1947; S.J.D., Harvard, 1958; m. Madelon Juergens, Mar. 15, 1944; children—Clara Hall, Cara Carleton, Joseph Tyree IV. Admitted to Tex. bar, 1948; instr. bus. law U. Tex., Austin, 1947, asst. prof. law, 1947-51, asso. prof., 1951-54, prof., 1954-57, asst. dean, 1949-50; counsel Graves, Dougherty & Greenhill, Austin, 1954-56; prof. law Cornell U., 1957-62; prof. law Stanford Law Sch., 1962-71; dean Duke Law Sch., 1971-73; dep. atty. gen. U.S. justice dept., 1973; judge U.S. Ct. Appeals, 9th Circuit, San Francisco, 1973—. Cons. estate and gift tax project Am. Law Inst., 1960-69. Served with USAAF, 1942-46. Mem. Am. Bar Assn., Stte Bar Tex., Am. Law Inst., Order of Coif. Author: The Configurations of Gross Income, 1967. Contbr. articles to profl. jours. Address: PO Box 547 San Francisco CA 94101

SNELL, FRANK LINN, lawyer; b. Kansas City, Mo., Dec. 23, 1899; s. Frank Linn and Marie Louise (Genult) S.; LL.B., Kans. U., 1924; m. Elizabeth S. Berlin, Aug. 3, 1927; children—Richard B., Kathryn L. Admitted to Ariz. bar, 1924; practiced in Phoenix, 1927—; sr. mem. firm Snell & Wilmer, 1934—; past dir., chmn. bd. Ariz. Pub. Service Co.; dir. Combined Communications Corp. Chmn. dedication Phoenix Civic Plaza, 1972; past chmn. Phoenix Civic Center Mgmt. Bd.; past chmn. bd., past dir. Am. Grad. Sch. Internat. Mgmt.; hon. bd. dirs. Samaritan Health Services. Recipient Distinguished Service award U. Kans., 1964, Distinguished Alumnus citation, 1973; Man of Year award Phoenix Advt. Club, 1966; Distinguished Achievement award Coll. Bus. Adminstrn., Ariz. State U., 1977. Mem. Phoenix C. of C. (pres. 1934), Ariz. Nat. Livestock Show Inc. (past pres.), Am., Ariz. bar assns., Internat. Solar Energy Soc. (hon. dir.), Phoenix Fine Arts Assn. (past pres.). Republican. Presbyterian. Clubs: Phoenix Kiwanis (past pres.); Paradise Valley Country (past pres.). Home: 5201 E Arroyo Rd Scottsdale AZ 85253 Office: 3100 Valley Center Phoenix AZ 85073

SNELL, RICHARD, hotel co. exec.; b. Phoenix, Nov. 26, 1930; s. Frank L. and Elizabeth (Berlin) S.; B.A., Stanford, 1952, J.D., 1954; m. Alice Cosette Wiley, Aug. 1, 1954; children—Karen, Marilyn, Sarah. Admitted to Ariz. bar; partner firm Snell & Wilmer, Phoenix, 1956-81; chmn., chief exec. officer Ramada Inns., Inc., Phoenix, 1981—; dir. Ariz. Public Service Co., Western Tech. Inc. Trustee Am. Grad. Sch. Internat. Mgmt., Phoenix; bd. dirs. Ariz. region NCCJ, 1978—; past pres. YMCA Met. Phoenix and Valley of Sun. Served with U.S. Army, 1954-56. Mem. Am., Ariz., Maricopa County bar assns. Republican. Lutheran. Clubs: Paradise Valley Country; John Gardiner's Tennis Ranch. Office: 3838 E Van Buren St Phoenix AZ 85008

SNELSON, WILLIAM MITCHELL, contractor; b. Asheville, N.C., July 18, 1926; s. Frank and Connie B. (Sluder) S.; m. Dolores M. Simaz, Nov. 25, 1949; children—Linda, Chris, Nancy, Susan, Julie, Mary, Barbara. Student pub. schs., Sedro Woolley, Wash. Pres., chmn. bd. Snelson Co., Inc., Sedro Woolley, 1957—; cons. Peter Kiewit & Sons, 1983—; pres., chmn. bd. Skagit Mining Ltd., 1983—. Served with USAAF, 1945-46. Mem. Pacific Energy Assn., Distbn. Contractors Assn. (pres. 1982, dir. 1976-83), Mech. Contractors Assn. (pres. 1966-70, dir. 1964-77), Pipeline Contractors Assn. Republican. Clubs: Fidalgo Yacht, Eagles, Elks. Home: 814 Garden of Eden Rd Sedro Woolley WA 98284 Office: 601 W State St Sedro Woolley WA 98284

SNIDER, DAVID PAUL, librarian; b. Highland Park, Mich., May 22, 1948; s. Paul Bernard and June P. (Milner) S.; student Kalamazoo Coll., 1966-68; B.A., Am. U. of Beirut, 1972; M.S. in L.S., Wayne State U., 1974; m. Marian K. Setterberg, Sept. 14, 1979. Library clk. Mesa (Ariz.) Public Library, 1973-74, ref. librarian, 1974-75, head public services, 1975-77; dir. library services Casa Grande (Ariz.) City Library, 1977—. Pres., Casa Grande Police Athletic League, 1978-80, bd. dirs., 1980-82. Mem. ALA (planning and budget assembly 1980-82, exec. bd. 1982—), Ariz. Library Assn. (chpt. councilor 76, 78-82, exec. bd. 1982—), Southwestern Library Assn. Home: 4418 W Keating Circle Glendale AZ 85308 Office: 405 E 6th St Casa Grande AZ 85222

SNIDER, GERI TEREZAS, health edn. cons. co. exec.; b. Canton, Ohio, Feb. 23, 1939; d. Sam and Mary M. (Kopp) Terezas; R.N. Aultman Hosp. Sch. Nursing, Canton, 1960; B.S. in Nursing, U. San Francisco, 1974; M.S. in Nursing Adminstrn., U. Calif., San Francisco, 1975; M.A. in Transpersonal Psychology, Calif. Inst. Transpersonal Psychology, 1982, now postgrad.; m. Delmar E. Snider, Dec. 24, 1970 (div. 1980). Staff nurse med. surg. unit Massillon (Ohio) City Hosp., 1960, Timken Mercy Hosp., Canton, Ohio, 1960-61; charge nurse Mt. Agustine Infirmary, West Richfield, Ohio, 1961-62; supr. intern St. Vincent Charity Hosp., Cleve., 1963-64; supr. pediatrics, med.-surg. unit, St. John's Hosp., Cleve., 1964-66; supr. intensive care and neurosurgery unit St. Vincent Charity Hosp., Cleve., 1966-67; asst. clin. instr. Aultman Hosp., Sch. Nursing, Canton, 1967-68) staff nurse U. Hosps., Cleve., 1968-69; head nurse post-anesthesia recovery room Stanford (Calif) U. Hosp., 1969-72; assoc. dir. nurses St. Mary's Hosp., Reno, Nev., 1975-77; founder, owner dir. Delphic Assocs., Carson City, Nev., now Carmel, Calif., 1978—; acupressure practitioner and tchr. Founder pres. Council of Post Anesthesia Nurses, 1973-77, chmn., 1973-77. Western Hosps. Assn. scholar, 1972. Mem. Nat. League for Nurses, Am. Assn. of Critical Care Nurses, Am., Nev. nurses assns., Internat. Flying Nurses Assn., Carson City Pilots Assn., Nat., Carson-Tahoe bds. realtors, U. San Francisco Alumni Assn. (dir. No. Nev.), Sigma Theta Tau. Contbr. articles on nursing edn. to profl. jours.; conf. organizer and leader. Address: PO Box 222397 Carmel CA 93922

SNOOK, QUINTON, constrn. co. exec.; b. Atlanta, July 15, 1925; s. John Wilson and Charlotte Louise (Clayson) S.; student U. Idaho, 1949-51; m. Lois Mullen, Jan. 19, 1947; children—Lois Ann Snook Matteson, Quinton A., Edward M., Clayson S., Charlotte T. Rancher, Lemhi Valley, Idaho, 1942—; owner, mgr. Snook Constrn., Salmon, Idaho, 1952—; owner Snook Trucking, 1967—, Lemhi Posts and Poles, 1980—. Mem. Lemhi County Commn., Dist. 2, 1980—. Mem. Am. Quarter Horse Assn., Farm Bur., Nat. Rifleman's Assn., Am. Hereford Assn., Idaho Cattlemen's Assn. Republican. Episcopalian. Club: Elks. Home: Route 1 Box 49 Salmon ID 83467

SNOTHERLY, EVERRETTE VERNE, JR., aerospace engr.; b. High Point, N.C.; s. Everett Verne and Ola Mae (Whitley) S.; B.A. in Physics, Duke U., 1961; M.S. in Physics, U.S. Naval Postgrad. Sch., 1969; grad. Def. Systems Mgmt. Sch., 1972; m. Barbara Rodgers, Aug. 26, 1963; 1 son, Everrette Verne III. Commd. ensign U.S. Navy, 1961; submarine office on U.S.S. Trigger, Charleston, S.C., 1962-63, U.S.S. Thomas Jefferson, New London, Conn., 1964-66; project officer Strategic Systems Project Office, Washington, 1969-72; head engring. div. Naval Plant Rep. Office, Sunnyvale, Calif., 1972-77; ordnance officer Naval Weapons Stas., Charleston, S.C., 1977-81; ret., 1981; sr. research scientist Sci. Applications, Inc., Colorado Springs, Colo., 1981—. Chmn., Berkeley County (S.C.) Planning Commn., 1979. Mem. Am. Forestry Assn., AAAS, Sigma Xi. Republican. Home: 1355 Winding Ridge Terr Colorado Springs CO 80907 Office: 2860 S Circle Dr Suite 2224 Colorado Springs CO 80906

SNOW, GEORGE EDWARD, biologist; b. Denver, Aug. 6, 1945; s. Wendell Aloysius and Verdie Cecilia (Sorg) S.; B.A., Rockhurst Coll., 1967; M.A., U. Colo., 1974, Ph.D., 1977; m. Lynn Frances Hurley, July 1, 1967 (dec.); children—Michelle Minette, Ryan Christopher. Teaching asst. U. Colo., 1971-76; instr. Community Coll. Denver, 1972, 74-77; asst. prof. Mt. St. Mary's Coll., Los Angeles, 1977—. Served with U.S. Army, 1968-70. Mem. AAAS, Nat. Assn. Biology Tchrs., Am. Soc. Zoologists, Sigma Xi. Office: 12001 Chalon Rd Los Angeles CA 90049

SNOW, KARL NELSON, JR., state senator, educator; b. St. George, Utah, July 1, 1930; s. Karl Nelson and Wanda (McGregor) S.; B.S., Brigham Young U., 1956; M.A., U. Minn., 1958; M.P.A. (Univ. scholar 1959-61), U. So. Calif., 1965, D.P.A., 1972; m. Donna Jean Dain, Jan. 29, 1960; children—Karl Nelson III, Melissa, Daniel D., Jeanmarie, Elisabeth, Howard H. Budget examiner Dept. of Adminstrn., State of Minn., St. Paul, 1956-59; staff asst., instr. Sch. Public Adminstrn., U. So. Cal., Los Angeles, 1959-62; asst. prof. Brigham Young U., Provo, Utah, 1962-66, dir. Inst. Govt. Sci., 1969-79, prof. public mgmt. Grad. Sch. Mgmt., 1979—; analyst Utah State Legislature, Salt Lake City, 1966-70; mem. Utah Senate, 1972—, majority leader, 1980—; cons. Inst. Public Adminstrn., N.Y.C., and Nat. Inst. Adminstrn., Saigon, South Vietnam, 1971. Mem. Utah State House Fellowship Commn., 1973-79; chmn. Utah Constl. Revision Commn.; bd. dirs. Legis. Leaders Found., 1981—. Mem. Am. Soc. for Public Adminstrn. (chpt. pres. 1968-69, dir. nat. council 1969-72), Sons of the Utah Pioneers, Mem. Ch. of Jesus Christ of Latter-day Saints (missionary) 1950-52; now mem. stake high council). Bd. editors Pub. Adminstrn. Rev., 1969-70; State and Local Govt. Rev., 1977—. Contbr. articles in field to profl. jours. Home: 1847 N Oak Lane Provo UT 84601 Office: 768 TNRB Brigham Young U Provo UT 84602

SNOW, REUBEN JOSEPH, university administrator, political science educator; b. Cedar City, Utah, Oct. 15, 1973; s. Glenn E. and Laura (Gardner) S.; m. Marilyn Melville, June 20, 1962; children—Gina Lynne, Laura Dawn, Scott Glenn, Sara Noelle. B.A., U. Utah, 1962, M.A., 1963; M.A., Northwestern U., 1965, Ph.D., 1966; postgrad. Harvard U., 1982. Social Sci. Research Council research tng. fellow Cook County, Ill., 1965-66; postdoctoral fellow in politics and edn. Ctr. Advanced Study Ednl. Adminstrn, U. Oreg., Eugene, 1966-67; asst. prof. polit. sci. U. Calif.-Santa Barbara, 1967-73; assoc. prof. U. Calif. Study Ctr., U. Bordeaux III (France), 1971-73; asst. to pres. U. Utah, Salt Lake City, 1973-75, v.p. univ. relations, 1975—, dir. Hinckley Inst. Politics, 1975—, assoc. prof. polit. sci., 1974—. Mem. Gov.'s Com. on Exec. Reorgn.; mem. adv. bd. Sta. KSL-TV and Radio, 1982—; bd. dirs. Utah Symphony, past v.p.; bd. dirs. Greater Salt Lake Area United Way, 1982—, campaign co-chmn., 1982-83. Recipient Utah Hist. Soc. award, 1962. Mem. Am. Soc. Pub. Adminstrn., Am. Polit. Sci. Assn., Council Advancement and Support of Edn., Nat. Collegiate Athletic Assn. (faculty rep.), Western Athletic Conf. (faculty rep.), Phi Kappa Phi, Phi Beta Kappa. Contbr. articles to profl. publs. Office: Univ Utah 206 Park Bldg Salt Lake City UT 84112

SNYDER, JAMES LEWIS, civil engr.; b. New Brunswick, N.J., July 25, 1945; s. Lewis F. and Margaret C. S. B.S., Rutgers U., 1967, M.S., 1969, Ph.D. in Civil and Environ. Engring., 1977. Environ. engr. U.S. Air Force, Panama City, Fla., 1975-76, N.J. Dept. Environ. Protection, 1977, U.S. Army, Schofield Barracks, Hawaii, 1978-81; civil engr. U.S. Navy, Barking Sands, Kauai, Hawaii, 1981-82, U.S. Navy Logistics Command, Pearl Harbor, 1982—. Served to lt. (j.g.) USNR, 1971-75. Recipient N.J. Prestressed Concrete Inst. award, 1967; Edward Fuller Brooks Meml. award, 1967; Louis Bevier fellow, 1976-77. Mem. ASCE, Engring. Assn. Hawaii, Sigma Xi, Tau Beta Pi. Home: 98-588 Holopuni St Aiea HI 96701

SNYDER, JOHN ARTHUR, warehouse distributor; b. Carthage, Mo., Jan. 20, 1922; s. John Charles and Elsie Mary (Klinefelder) S.; m. Donna Lee Bradley, July 29, 1945; children—Patricia Ann, John Whitney. Student pub. schs. Engaged in automobile repair bus., 1946-51; owner Synder Tool Supply Co., Sacramento, 1951-60; pres. John SnyderTool Inc., Portland, Oreg., 1965—; past pres. Oreg. Motor Credit Bus. Served with USN, 1940-46. Mem. Nat. Fedn. Ind. Bus., Automotive Warehouse Distbr. Assn., Oreg. Automotive Parts Assn., Portland Automotive Trades Assn., Portland C. of C., Better Bus. Bur. Portland. Republican. Baptist. Club: Masons. Home: 3715 Multnomah St Portland OR 97232 Office: 2416 N Ross St Portland OR 97227

SNYDER, JOYCE COMBS, human services agency administrator; b. Canton, Ohio, Oct. 19, 1927; d. Arthur Oliver and Corinne Louise (Dierker) Combs; m. Ellsworth Snyder, Feb. 18, 1950 (div.); children—Candace Ann, Bradley Andrew. B.A. cum laude, Gettysburg Coll., 1950; M.B.A., Nat. U., 1979. Govt. sales mgr. Gilpin Drug Co., Washington, 1950-52; exec. dir. Community Christian Service Agy. Inc., San Diego, 1973—; cons. North Park and Mid-City Christian Service Agys.; founder Clairemont Friendship Ctr., 1976. Mem. Psi Chi, Alpha Xi Delta. Republican. Lutheran. Home: 4973 Pacifica Dr San Diego CA 92109 Office: 4167 Rappahannock Ave San Diego CA 92117

SNYDER, PHILIP CONRAD, educational administrator; b. Boise, Idaho, Nov. 15, 1927; s. Wallace M. and Inez Bell (Knight) S.; children—John, Tom. B.S.G.S., Lewis and Clark Coll., 1951; M.S.Ed. Cert. elem. and secondary tchr., cert. in adminstrn., Calif. Indsl. engr. Boeing; tng. coordinator BICI; supt. prodn. and control AVCO/NADCO; tng. supr. Bell Helicopter; supt. Quincy Sch.; prin. Orient Sch. Served with USN, 1943-46. Mem. Am. Soc. Tng. and Devel. Home: 2139 Mount Diablo St Concord CA 94520

SNYDER, RUSSELL DEWEY, JR., neurologist, educator; b. Phila., Sept. 18, 1932; s. Russell Dewey and Alice Virginia (Kagey) S.; m. Alicia Allman, Sept. 9, 1960; children—Christine, Phillip. B.S., Swarthmore Coll., 1954; M.D., U. Pa., 1958. Diplomate Am. Bd. Pediatrics, Am. Bd. Psychiatry and Neurology (Child Neurology). Intern, Bryn Mawr (Pa.) Hosp., 1958-59; resident in pediatrics U. Colo. Med. Ctr., Denver, 1959-61, 63-64, fellow in child neurology, 1964-67; asst. prof. pediatrics and neurology U. N.Mex. Med. Ctr., Albuquerque, 1967-71, assoc. prof. neurology and pediatrics, 1971-76, prof., 1976—, dir. Muscular Dystrophy Clinic and div. pediatric neurology; cons. Crippled Children's Service, USPHS. Served with M.C., USAR, 1961-63. Mem. Am. Acad. Neurology, Child Neurology Soc., Profs. Child Neurology, Computer Applications in Neurology. Contbr. articles to profl. jours. Office: Dept Neurology New Mexico Med Ctr Albuquerque NM 87131

SNYDER, WILLIAM HENRI, lawyer; b. West Chester, Pa., Mar. 14, 1931; s. Robert Paul and Helen Louise (Bable) S.; 1 dau., Terri Elizabeth. B.S. in Econs., Franklin and Marshall Coll., 1953; J.D., UCLA, 1958. Bar: Calif. 1959. Ptnr., Collins & Snyder, Pacific Palisades, Calif., 1959-76; sole practice, Pacific Palisades, 1976-82; ptnr. Snyder & Polin, Pacific Palisades, 1982—; Bd. dirs. Palisades-Malibu YMCA, 1968-76; pres. bd. trustees Pacific Palisades Presbyterian Ch., 1972. Mem. ABA, Santa Monica Bar Assn. (pres. 1976-77), Los Angeles County Bar Assn., Calif. State Bar, Pacific Palisades C. of C. (bd. dirs. 1980-82). Republican. Club: Optimist (Pacific Palisades pres. 1965-66). Served to Lt. USNR, 1953-55. Office: Snyder & Polin 881 Alma Real Dr Suite 309 Pacific Palisades CA 90272

SOANES, DAVID LEE, architect, landscape architect, planner; b. Buffalo, July 18, 1950; s. Justus Arnold Thomas and Dorothy Ellen (Bonney) S.; B.Arch., U. Miami, 1973; M.L.A. (Univ. fellow), Cornell U., 1976; m. Jo Anne Moore, Dec. 24, 1975; 1 dau., Summer Leigh; stepchildren—Shannon, Brooke. Draftsman, Warshaw Assos., Miami, Fla., 1972, Drexler Assos., Miami, 1972-73; apprentice architect Wright Architect, Miami, 1973-74; apprentice architect, site planner Fred Thomas Assos., Ithaca, N.Y., 1974-76; cons. designer, Ithaca, 1976-77; architect/land planner PRC Toups, San Diego, 1977-80; pres., prin. architect, David Lee Soanes, Ltd., San Diego, 1980—; teaching asst. landscape architecture Cornell U., 1975-76. Registered architect, landscape architect, Calif. Mem. AIA, Am. Soc. Landscape Architects, Constrn. Specifications Inst., Nat. Trust Hist. Preservation, Tau Beta Pi. Baptist. Author: LaGrange Town Center, 1976; Bowdoin Park Study, 1976; designs include: master plan for Jamsil Center, Seoul, 1978, for MX weapons system community for SAC, 1980. Home: 9788 Canforero Terr San Diego CA 92124 Office: 8910 Clairemont Mesa Blvd San Diego CA 92123

SOARD, RAYMOND, telephone co. exec.; b. Lexington, Ky., Feb. 12, 1922; s. Raymond J. and Betty (Lowry) S.; student Bklyn. Poly. Inst., 1943-44; B.S. in Elec. Engring., U. Ky., 1949; postgrad. U. Ga., 1956, Harvard U., 1958, Mich. State U., 1959, U. Nev., 1963, 76-77, U. Kans., 1976; m. Faye LaVerne Jacobs, May 2, 1942; children—Jane Rae Soard Dionisio, Raymond Randolph, Suzanne Soard Curtin, William Thomas. Central office repairman Gen. Telephone Co. Ky., Lexington, 1946-49, plant foreman, 1949-52, gen. traffic engr., 1952-54, gen. traffic mgr., 1954-58, chief engr., 1958-62; engring. mgr. Central Telephone Co., Las Vegas, Nev., 1962-78, gen. mgr., 1978—. Vice chmn. Nev. State Industry Adv. Com., 1965; exec. com. Nev. Drug Abuse Council, 1976-78, pres., 1978—; mem. Las Vegas Bd. Elec. Examiners, 1965-77; committeeman

Boulder Dam council Boy Scouts Am., 1962-66; chmn. Clark County (Nev.) Utilities Com., 1970; mem. Emergency Resources Mgmt. Bd., CD, 1967. Served with Signal Corps, AUS, 1942-46; PTO. Decorated Bronze Star medal with 2 oak leaf clusters; registered profl. engr., Ky., Nev. Mem. Nat. Soc. Profl. Engrs. (award 1968), Telephone Pioneers Am., Ind. Telephone Pioneer Assn., Armed Forces Communications and Electronics Assn. (pres. 1959), Lexington Ky. Civic Club (pres. 1961), Las Vegas Exchange Club (dir. 1965-68, 77, v.p. 1979—, pres. 1980). Home: 2112 Burnham Ave Las Vegas NV 89104 Office: 330 S Valley View Blvd S Las Vegas NV 89152

SOARES, W. BUDDY, businessman, state senator; b. Honolulu, Sept. 4, 1929; student U. Hawaii; married, 4 children. Dir. community affairs Hawaiian Electric Co.; sales mgr. hotel and restaurant div. AMFAC, Inc.; dir. mktg. and sales Kaanapali Beach, AMFAC Properties, Inc.; account exec. Pan Am.; gen. sales mgr. Western Dairy Products; mem. Hawaii Ho. of Reps., 1967-75, house leader, 1969, minority floor leader; mem. Hawaii Senate, 1975—. Mem. Hawaii Kai Community Assn., St. Louis Alumni Assn., Hawaii C. of C. Office: 974 Pepeekeo St Honolulu HI 96825*

SOASH, RICHARD MORTON, state senoator, rancher; b. Steamboat Springs, Colo., Aug. 3, 1941; s. Irvin Elwood and Nellie (Gray) S.; B.A. in English, Colo. State U., 1964; m. Sharman Serene Ursich, Mar. 3, 1973; children—Curtis, William, Richard Morton, Stacey, Josephine, Douglas, Nicholas. Rancher, 1964—; mem. Colo. Senate, 1977—, chmn. interim com. hwy. legis. rev., mem. agr., bus. affairs and labor coms. Mem. Farmers Union. Democrat. Roman Catholic. Office: State Capitol Room 214 Denver CO 80203*

SOBEL, JOANNE WOLFE, advertising executive; b. Seattle, Mar. 31, 1929; d. George and Gertrude (Pearl) Wolfe; m. Earl L.C. Sobel, Nov. 24, 1956; children—David Samuel, Daniel George. Student U. Wash., 1946-49. With Koret of Calif., 1950-52, RL Sines Advt. Agy., 1952-54; assoc. Vernor Advt., San Francisco, 1955-64; pres. Sobel Advt. Inc., San Rafael, Calif., 1964-81, vice chmn., 1981—. Mem. No. Calif. Indsl. Relations Council, Audubon Soc., ACLU, Sierra Club, Pi Alpha Sigma, Alpha Epsilon Phi. Jewish. Clubs: Womens ORT. Home: 678 Barberry Ln San Rafael CA 94903 Office: PO Box 6068 San Rafael CA 94903

SOBOTKA, FRANCIS EUGENE, air force officer; b. New Kensington, Pa., May 15, 1943; s. Frank Anthony and Mary Jane (Wisnewski) S.; m. Carolyn Satomi, Nov. 24, 1967; children—Lisa Paige, Chad Anthony. M.A. in Psychology and Guidance Counseling, U. No. Colo., 1976. Enlisted in U.S. Air Force, 1965, advanced through grades to maj., 1978; mgr. tactical squadron aircraft maintenance, Ill., Ariz., S.C., Vietnam, 1965-71; detachment commdr. Strategic Aircraft Maintenance Tng., Wash., 1972-74; squadron supr. Aircraft Maintenance Ops., Tex., 1974-76; crew comdr. Strategic Missle Combat, 1976-78; chief Wing Strategic Missle Op. Simulators, Wyo., 1978-80; chief program mgmt. and evaluations SAC Hdqrs. Strategic Missile Op. Simulators, Vandenburg AFB, Calif., 1980—. Contbr. articles to mil. publs. Pres. La Honda PTO; dir. men's ministries Trinity Ch. Nazarene. Decorated: Air Force Meritorious Service, Air Force Commendation, Nat. Def. Service medals, Republic Vietnam Gallantry Cross. Mem. Air Force Assn., Am. Personnel and Guidance Assn., Assn. Counselor Edn. and Supervision. Office: 3901 SAC Missile Evaluation SQ/DOM Vandenberg AFB CA 93437

SODERLUND, DAVID CARL ERNEST, safety engr.; b. Clearfield, Pa., June 10, 1943; s. Carl August Victor and Elenor (Petersen) S.; student Pa. State U., 1961-63; B.S., San Diego State U., 1969; m. Carol Ann Murray, Dec. 27, 1969; 1 son, Eric. Student engr. Pa. Electric Co., Shawville Station, Pa., 1962; safety engr. Fireman's Fund Ins. Cos., San Diego and Los Angeles, 1969-71, loss control tech. advisor, Honolulu, 1972, Hilo, Hawaii, 1974—. Sec.-treas. Mauna Loa Sch. Assn., 1979; referee Am. Youth Soccer Orgn. and High Sch., 1981—; pres. Paradise Hui Hanalike, 1976, dir., 1974-77. Served with USN, 1963-67. Named Engr. of Yr., Am. Soc. Safety Engrs., Hawaii chpt., 1977; registered profl. engr., Calif.; cert. safety profl. Mem. Gen. Ins. Assn. Hawaii (pres. 1978), Nat. Soc. Profl. Engrs. (treas. Hawaii chpt.), Am. Soc. Safety Engrs. (sec.-treas. Big Island sect.), Am. Indsl. Hygiene Assn., Big Island Safety Assn. (dir. 1980-81). Clubs: Hawaii Yacht, Hilo Sailing (commodore 1979, sailing instr. 1981), Mission Bay Yacht, Elks. Editor, Soc. for Advancement of Mgmt., San Diego State U. Jour., 1967; contbr. articles to profl. jours. Home: 250 Paradise Dr Keaau HI 96749 Office: 120 Pauahi St Suite 210 Hilo HI 96720

SODHI, JAG, computer analyst; b. Lahore, India, Jan. 1, 1935; came to U.S., 1970, naturalized, 1977; s. Joginder Singh and Puran Devi S.; m. Lynda Jann Swanda; children—Rani, Sonia, Prince, Lynn, Anita. B.A. in Math. with honors, U. Delhi, 1955, M.Math., 1958. Programmer analyst Western Life Ins. Co., St. Paul, 1970-73; pres. J.S. Enterprises, Inc., St. Paul, 1973-79; programmer analyst Control Data Corp., Mpls., 1979-80; sr. programmer, analyst Hosp. Data Systems, Denver, 1980-81; prin., computer system designer Martin-Marietta Data Systems, Denver, 1981-83; with Devi Computers, Inc., Aurora, Colo., 1983—. Recipient Outstanding Service award. Govt. India, 1969. Mem. ACM, Assn. Systems Mgmt., Denver Mgmt. Assn. Club: Masons. Contbr. articles to profl. jours.; author: Computer Systems Development Techniques. Office: Devi Computers Buckingham Sq Shopping Ctr Aurora CO 80012

SOFTELAND, OISTEIN TORULF, export trade co. exec.; b. Bergen, Norway, Aug. 29, 1913; s. John Johnson and Nelly Malene (Nordbotten) S.; came to U.S., 1948, naturalized, 1949; grad. Bergens Fagskole (Tech. Sch.), Bergen, Norway, 1931; grad. Ant. Johannesens Coll. Bus., Bergen, 1936; m. Mary Ella Jordan, Dec. 6, 1949; 1 son, Oistein Jordan. Propr., mgr. retail and wholesale stores, Bergen, 1936-38; propr., mgr. farm Henne, Fana, Norway, 1938-40, farm Rossoy, Tjotta, Norway, 1940-46; cons. for disabled people at Sophus Minde, Oslo, 1946-48; various assignments in constrn. work Paul Paulsen Constrn. Co., Salt Lake City, 1948-51; mechanic for Hill Field AFB, Ogden, Utah, 1951-62; distbr. La Vone Cosmetics, Idaho and Utah, 1963-65; owner O. T. Softeland Export & Import, Salt Lake City, 1965—; pres. O.T. Softeland, Mortage and Bus. Loan Broker, 1973—, Great Salt Lake Enterprises, Inc., 1973-74, Troldhaugen Sr. Citizens Home, Centerville, Utah, 1977—, Internat. Land Mgmt., 1980—. Del. to county and state Democratic convs., Utah, 1962-83; election judge, Bountiful and Centerville, Utah, 1963-76; candidate for Utah State Seante, 1978; tchr. in elders quorum Ch. Jesus Christ of Latter Day Saints, Bountiful, 1974-77; mem. Utah State Coalition Sr. Citizens, 1976—. Mem. Utah Internat. Traders Assn., Sons of Norway (Pres. of Yr. award 1977, publicity dir. 1980—, dist. and internat. del. 1982). Instrumental in developing a home industry program for physically disabled.

SOIN, ROMESH CHANDER, materials engineer; b. Gujranwala, W. Punjab, India, Nov. 5, 1941; came to U.S., 1963, naturalized, 1974; s. Amar Chand and Tara Vanti S.; B.Sc., Punjab U., India, 1960; B.S., San Jose State U., 1967, M.S., 1972; M.B.A., U. Santa Clara, 1975; m. Alicia Sainz Figueroa, Nov. 1, 1969. Lectr. chemistry D.A.V. Coll., Jullundur, India, 1960-61; booking clk. Brit. Rys., Grays-Essex, Eng., 1962-63; jr. metall. engr. ITT Jennings, San Jose, Calif., 1966-68; sr. materials engr. Gen. Electric Co., San Jose, 1968—. Pres., Internat. Student Center, San Jose, 1967-68; treas. Robert Smith Cultural Found., San Jose, 1972-73. Mem. Am. Soc. Metals (treas. Santa Clara Valley chpt. 1977-78), Santa Clara County Beekeepers Assn. (treas. 1975). Club: San Jose Coin. Home: 4255 Rosenbaum Ave San Jose CA 95136 Office: Mail Code 777 175 Curtner Ave San Jose CA 95125

SOKOL, JEFFREY HOWARD, engr.; b. Bklyn., May 20, 1946; s. Abraham Issac and Libby (Salinger) S.; B.E.S., SUNY, Stony Brook, 1968; M.S. in Elec. Engring. (NDEA Title IV fellow), N.Y. U., 1972; Ph.D. (teaching fellow), Poly. Inst. N.Y., 1979. Engr., Grumman Aircraft, Bethpage, N.Y., 1967, 68; cons. Research Found. State of N.Y., 1979; mem. tech. staff Hughes Aircraft Co., El Segundo, Calif., 1979—. Served with U.S. Army, 1969-71. Mem. IEEE, AAAS, Sigma Xi. Contbr. articles to profl. jours. Office: Hughes Aircraft Co Bldg S-30 M/S P-313 PO Box 92919 Los Angeles CA 90009

SOKOLOW, MAURICE, medical educator; b. N.Y.C., May 19, 1911; s. Alexander and Anna (Spiegelman) S.; A.B. cum laude, U. Calif., Berkeley, 1932; M.D., U. Calif., San Francisco, 1936; m. Ethel Schwabacher, June 30, 1941 (dec. 1970); children—Gail Anne, Jane Carol (dec.), Anne May. Intern, San Francisco Gen. Hosp., 1935-36; resident U. Calif. at San Francisco, New Eng. Med. Center, Boston, Michael Reese Hosp., Chgo., 1936-40; pvt. practice medicine, San Francisco, 1946-62; mem. faculty cardiovascular div. dept. medicine Sch. Medicine, U. Calif., San Francisco, 1946—, asso. prof., 1952-58, prof. medicine, 1958-78, prof. emeritus, 1978—, also chief cardiovascular div., 1954-73, sr. mem. Cardiovascular Research Inst., 1957—; program dir., tng. program clin. cardiology USPHS, 1959-73; vis. lectr. U. Oxford (Eng.), 1973-74; cons. in field; mem. nat. adv. hypertension com. NIH, 1972-74. Bd. dirs. U. Calif. Art Mus. Council, Fromm Inst. Life Long Learning, U. San Francisco. Served to lt. comdr. M.C., USN, 1942-46. Recipient grants Nat. Heart Inst., NIH, 1950—. Mem. Am. Fedn. Clin. Research (v.p.), Am. Coll. Cardiology (hon. fellow), Assn. Univ. Cardiologists, Am. Soc. Clin. Investigation, Brit. Cardiac Soc. (corr. mem.), Am. Heart Assn., San Francisco Heart Assn. (pres.). Club: Menlo Circus. Contbr. articles to med. jours., texts; editorial bd. Western Jour. Medicine, 1946—, Cardiovascular Revs. and Reports, 1980—. Home: 3452 Jackson St San Francisco CA 94118 Office: Univ Calif San Francisco CA 94143

SOLDO, NICHOLAS JAMES, physician; b. East Palestine, Ohio, May 9, 1934; s. James and Teresa S.; B.S., Bethany (W.Va.) Coll., 1956; M.D., Ohio State U., 1960; m. Lizabeth F. Schiff, Apr. 26, 1980; children—Nicholas James, Anne T., Mark S., John G., Matthew P. Intern, Youngstown (Ohio) Hosp. Assn., 1960-61; gen. practice medicine, East Palestine, 1961-64; resident in anesthesiology UCLA Center Health Scis., 1964-66; anesthesiologist, Salem, Ohio, 1968-74; practice medicine specializing in anesthesiology, Phoenix, 1974—; mem. staff six hosps. Served to capt. M.C., USAF, 1966-68. Mem. AMA, Ariz. Med. Assn., Maricopa County Med. Soc., Am. Soc. Anesthesiology, Ariz. Soc. Anesthesiology, Maricopa County Soc. Anesthesiology, Internat. Anesthesia Research Soc., Pheonix Wine and Food Soc., Far Western Ski Assn. Home: 4436 E Camelback Rd #34 Phoenix AZ 85018 Office: 200 E Monterey Way Suite 2 Phoenix AZ 85012

SOLEM, JILL PRYOR, counselor; b. Ada, Okla., Aug. 26, 1946; d. Joseph Hoyt and Edwina Aurora (Jones) Pryor; m. Dana L. Solem, Apr. 11, 1980. Student Oklahoma City U., 1972-73, Central State U., Edmond, Okla., 1973-76; B.A., East Central Okla. State U., 1977, M.S., 1978. Sec., U.S. govt. agys., Ada, 1966-69, 76-77, Oklahoma City, 1971-76; staff psychologist Transitional Services, D. E. Burrell Community Mental Health Ctr., Springfield, Mo., 1978-79; pvt. practice counseling, including psychotherapy, cons., testing, Grants Pass, Oreg., 1979—; mem. Josephine County (Oreg.) Mental Health Task Force, 1981. Recipient Achievement in Research award State Colloquium of Research, 1977, Outstanding Achievement in Psychology award, 1977, 78. Mem. Am. Psychol. Assn. (assoc.), Oreg. Psychol. Assn., Western Psychol. Assn., Psi Chi. Office: 109 NE Manzanita Suite 4 Grants Pass OR 97526

SOLIMAN, KHAIRY M., agronomist; b. Egypt, Oct. 25, 1943; naturalized U.S. citizen, 1974; s. Mohamed Soliman and Khadra (Mohamed) S.; B.Sc., U. Cairo, 1965; M.S., U. Calif., Davis, 1972, Ph.D. (chancellor's fellow 1974), 1975; m. Abdehumid Ibrahiem, 1976; 1 dau., Sherry. Mem. research staff U. Calif., Davis, 1975—, D.J. Jones postdoctoral fellow, 1976, maize breeder, 1979-80. research asso. agronomy, 1980—; cons. in field. Mem. Am. Soc. Agronomy, Crop Sci. Soc. Am., Genetics Soc. Am., Sigma Xi. Republican. Moslem. Home: 3323 Cowell St Davis CA 95616 Office: Genetics Dept U Calif Davis CA 95616

SOLIS, CAROL JOSEPHINE, educator, consultant; b. Honolulu, Aug. 1, 1947; d. Joseph Asperas and Caroline (Balabala) S.; 1 son, David Alexander. B.A., Holy Names Coll., 1969; M.S., Calif. State U.-Hayward, 1980. Tchr. primary grades St. Mary Sch., Oakland, Calif., 1969-71; tchr. kindergarten and adult sch. Am. Sch., Guadalajara, Jalisco, Mex., 1971-72; tchr. grades K-6, Franklin-McKinley Sch. Dist., San Jose, Calif., 1973-76, project dir., 1976-77, vice-prin. intermediate sch., 1977-78, coordinator bilingual/crosscultural edn., 1978—. Mem. TESOL, Nat. Assn. Bilingual Edn., Assn. Calif. Sch. Adminstrs., Calif. Assn. TESOL, Calif. Assn. Bilingual Edn., Santa Clara County Reading Council. Republican. Office: 2072 Lucretia Ave San Jose CA 95122

SOLIS, MELCHIZEDEK MARAON, clergyman; b. Philippines, July 13, 1928; came to U.S., 1972, naturalized, 1980; s. Honorato Sumogat Solis and Magdalena Zuniga Maraon; B.A., Silliman U., Dumaquete City, Philippines, 1952; B.Div. cum laude, Union Theol. Sem., Manila, 1958; M. Communication Arts, Ateneo de Manila (Philippines) U., 1968; m. Mutya Lopez, Apr. 15, 1956; children—Sharon, Melanie, Lawrence, Reev. Ordained to ministry United Ch. of Christ in Philippines, 1958; dir. religious programming Sta.-DYSR. Dumaquete City, 1956-58; organizer, Pastor Visayan Congregation of Ellinwood-Malate Ch., Manila, 1958-59; missionary to Ch. of Christ, Thailand, 1959-64; mem. English faculty Silliman U., 1964-66; pastor Filipino Am. Ecumenical Ch., Chgo., 1972-76, St. Philip's United Presbyn. Ch., Salinas, Calif., 1976—; organizer, dir./coordinator Arts Research and Acculturation Workshop; chmn. racial ethnic ministries com., gen. council San Jose Presbytery; dir. Nat. Asian Presbyn. Council, United Presbyn. Ch. U.S.A. Charter mem. bd. dirs. Monterey County (Calif.) Community Devel. Credit Union. Named Most Outstanding Mem. of Filipino Community, 1978. Mem. World Assn. Christian Broadcasters, Inst. Cultural Affairs. Club: Lions (charter v.p. Salinas chpt.). Author: Handbook on Speech for Filipinos (Vowels), 1957; Handbook on Speech for Filipinos (Consonants), 1958; author poetry, hymns, plays. Home: 1647 Seville St Salinas CA 93906 Office: 615 Leslie Dr Salinas CA 93906

SOLOMON, DARWIN DALE, rural sociologist; b. Wyo., Aug. 11, 1919; s. Jerry P. and Ethel Belle (Reed) S.; m. Elizabeth Ann Farnham, June 3, 1950; children—Charles Reed, David Ray, Christopher. B.S. in Agronomy, U. Wyo., 1943; M.S. in Agr., Cornell U., 1950, Ph.D. in Rural Sociology, Econs. of Agr. and S.E. Asian Studies, 1956. Civilian pub. servant Intermountain Forest and Range Expt. Sta., U.S. Forest Service, 1943-46; vol. tractor trainer, operator Agrl. Industry Service, Un Relief and Rehab. Adminstrn., 1946-47, agrl. liaison officer, 1947-49; rice research asst., extension specialist U.S. Dept. State, Bangkok, Thailand, 1951-53; teaching and research asst. Cornell U., Ithaca, N.Y., 1953-54, extension instr., 1955-56; rural sociologist Coll. Agr. Agrl. Extension Service, U. Md., 1956-58; chief tng. officer Ctr. Community Studies, Saskatoon, Can., 1958-61, adminstrv. asst. program resources, 1961-62; officer tech. dept. FAO, UN, Rome, 1962-67, rural institutions officer social programmes, 1968-76, rural devel. officer, 1979, women's programme officer, 1978-79, sociologist rural orgns., 1979-81; self-employed cons. in rural devel. and applied social sci., Boulder, Colo., 1981—; extensive cons. assignments in Middle and Far East, Asia, Africa and Latin Am. throughout career. U. Wyo. high sch. honor scholar, 1937-42; Russel Sage fellow, 1950; social sci. research grantee U. Wis., 1954. Fellow Soc. Applied Anthropology; mem. Acad. Ind. Scholars, Am. Acad. Polit. and Social Sci., Am. Sociol. Assn., Soc. Study Social Problems, Soc. Internat. Devel., Wyo. U. Alumni Assn., Internat. Rural Sociology Assn., Rural Sociol. Soc. (past mem. devel. and membership coms.), European Rural Devel. Soc. (organizing com.), European Soc. Rural Sociology, Alpha Zeta. Author numerous papers and articles on rural devel., agr. and related topics. Office: 970 Aurora Campus Box 64 Boulder CO 80303

SOLOMON, JACK DAVID, corp. exec.; b. Detroit, July 27, 1930; s. Alex C. and Rosalie Z. S.; A.A., Los Angeles City Coll., 1954; B.A., Los Angeles State Coll., 1956; B.A., Calif. State U., Los Angeles, 1970; postgrad. U. Nev., Las Vegas, 1975; children—Jacqueline, David, Gregg, Diana. Vice pres. JSH Electronics, Inc., 1954-60; pres. Fed. Electronics, 1960-66; chmn. bd. Western Fed. Fin. Corp., 1964-66; chmn. bd., pres. Advanced Patent Tech., Inc., Las Vegas, 1968-80; pres. APT Games, Inc., 1978-80. Bd. dirs. Las Vegas Symphony Soc.; past pres. 25th Congressional Dist. Council; candidate Calif. Senate, 1966; nat. bd. dirs. Equal Opportunities Found., 1963-66. Served with USAF, 1948-52. Recipient medal for Humane Action Berlin Air Lift, 1950, Marshall medal, 1964, Carson White award, 1964; named So. Calif. Man of Year, 1963; hon. Ky. col., 1970. Mem. Nat. Aeros. Assn., Armed Forces Communications and Electronics Assn., Los Angeles C. of C., Town Hall, Las Vegas C. of C., World Affairs Council, Internat. Platform Assn. Jewish. Clubs: Masons, Shriners, B'nai B'rith (internat. overseer), L.M. Yacht (dir. 1970). Office: 512 S Tonopah Dr Las Vegas NV 89106

SOLOMON, JOSEPH MICHAEL, cosmetics and tolietries executive; b. Bklyn., May 3, 1946; s. Albert and Vivian Geraldine (Lautenberg) S.; student public schs.; m. Beatrice H. Ilumin, Nov. 6, 1968. Haridresser, Vidal Sassoon, Inc., N.Y.C., 1965-69, asst. mgr. Beverly Hills Salon (Calif.), 1969-71, mgr., 1971, gen. mgr., 1971-73, exec. v.p. ops., 1973-74, pres., chief exec. officer, Los Angeles, 1977—. Served with U.S. Army, 1967-68. Mam. Frat. of Friends for Los Angeles Music Center. Club: Riviera Country (Los Angeles). Office: Vidal Sassoon Inc 2049 Century Park E Los Angeles CA 90067*

SOLOMON, JULIUS OSCAR LEE, pharmacist; b. N.Y.C., Aug. 14, 1917; s. John and Jeannette (Krieger) S.; student Bklyn. Coll., 1935-36, Coll. City N.Y., 1936-37; B.S. in Pharmacy, U. So. Calif., 1949; postgrad. Long Beach State U., 1971-72; Southwestern Colls., 1979, 81-82; m. Sylvia Smith, June 26, 1941 (div. Jan. 1975); children—Gary Richard, Dennis Edward, Marc Irwin, Evan Scott, Jeri Lee; m. 2d, Ana Maria C. MacFarland, Apr. 5, 1975; children—George, Anamaria, Gabriella, Arthur. Dye maker Fred Fear & Co., Bklyn., 1935; apprentice interior decorator Dorothy Draper, 1936; various jobs, N.Y. State Police, 1940-45; research asst. Union Oil Co., 1945; lighting cons. Joe Rosenberg & Co., 1946-49; owner Banner Drug, Lomita, 1949-53, Redondo Beach, Calif., 1953-72, El Prado Pharmacy, Redondo Beach, 1961-65; pres. Banner Drug, Inc., Redondo Beach, 1953-72, Thrifty Drugs, 1972-74, also Guild Drug, Longs Drug, Drug King, 1976—; chmn. bd. Banner Drug Stores Inc. Charter commr., founder Redondo Beach Youth Baseball Council; sponsor Little League Baseball, basketball, football, bowling; pres. Redondo Beach Boys Club; v.p. South Bay Children's Health Center, 1974, Redondo Beach Coordinating Council, 1975; founder Redondo Beach Community Theater, 1975; active maj. gift drive YMCA, 1975; mem. SCAG Com. on Criminal Justice, 1974, League of Calif. Environ. Quality Com., 1975; pres. South Bay Democratic Club; mem. Dem. State Central Com., Los Angeles County Dem. Central Com.; del. Dem. Nat. Conv., 1972; chmn. Redondo Beach Recreation and Parks Commn.; mem. San Diego County Parks Adv. Commn., 1982; mem. human resource devel. com., pub. improvement com. Nat. League of Cities; v.p. Redondo Beach Coordinating Council; councilman, Redondo Beach, 1961-69, 73-77; treas. 46th Assembly Dist. Council; candidate 46 Assembly dist. 1966; nat. chmn. Pharmacists for Humphrey, 1968, 72; pres. bd. dirs. So. Bay Exceptional Childrens Soc., Chapel Theatre; bd. dirs. So. div. League Calif. Cities, U.S.-Mexico Sister Cities Assn., Boy's Club Found. of San Diego County, Autumn Hills Condominium Assn. (pres.), Calif. Employee Pharmacists Assn.; mem. South Bay Inter-City Hwy. Com., Redondo Beach Round Table, 1973-77; mem. State of Calif. Commn. of Californias (U.S.-Mexico), 1975-78; mem. Chula Vista Safety Commn., 1978, chmn., 1980-81; chmn. San Diego County Juvenile Camp Contract Com., 1982—; mem. San Diego County Juvenile Delinquency Prevention Commn., 1983—; spl. participant Calif. Crime and Violence Workshop. Served with USCGR, 1942-45. Recipient Pop Warner Youth award, 1960, 1962, award of merit Calif. Pharm. Assn., 1962. Diplomate Am. Bd. Diplomates Pharmacy Internat. Fellow Am. Coll. Pharmacists (pres.); mem. South Bay Pharm. Assn. (pres.), South Bay Councilmans Assn. (founder, pres.), Palos Verdes Peninsula Navy League (charter), Am. Legion, U. So. Calif. Alumni Assn. (life), Rho Pi Phi (pres. alumni). Elk (life). Mason (32 deg.; life), Lion (charter mem. North Redondo). Club: Trojan (life). Established Lee Solomon award for varsity athlete with highest scholastic average at 10 South Bay High Schs. Home and Office: 1640-57 Maple Dr Chula Vista CA 92011

SOLOMON, ROGER MORRIS, clin. psychologist; b. San Francisco, Oct. 13, 1951; s. Bertram Clifford and Sylvia Maureen (Rosekind) S.; B.A., U. Calif., Berkeley, 1972; M.A., U. Chgo., 1974; Ph.D., Auburn U., 1979. Postdoctoral intern Ariz. Dept. Public Safety, 1978-79; police psychologist Colorado Springs (Colo.) Police Dept., Pikes Peak Mental Health Center, 1979, 81—, Colo. Psychotherapy Center, 1980-81; part time pvt. practice, cons., teaching in field. Mem. Am. Psychol. Assn., El Paso County Psychol. Assn., Internat. Law Enforcement Stress Assn., Nat. Council on Alcoholism, Phi Beta Kappa. Republican. Jewish. Condr. research, co-author article in field. Home: 2629 Hearthwood Ln Colorado Springs CO 80917 Office: 1515 S Tejon Suite 101 Colorado Springs CO 80906

SONDGEROTH, LILLIAN JO, lawyer; b. Carroll, Iowa, Jan. 5, 1948; d. John Charles and Arlene Mary (Grossman) S.; B.A., U. Nev., 1969, M.A. in Psychology, 1971; J.D. (grantee), Calif. Western Sch. Law, 1976. Admitted to Nev. bar, 1976, D.C. bar, 1979; cert. intern San Diego County Dist. Atty., 1975-76; staff atty. Clark County Legal Services Program, Las Vegas, Nev., 1977; psychologist Clark County Sch. Dist., Las Vegas, 1972-73; instr. sociology, psychology Clark County Community Coll., Las Vegas, 1972-73; pvt. practice law, Las Vegas, 1977—; instr. continuing edn. U. Nev., Las Vegas, 1979—; atty. Community Action Against Rape; community lectr. on fed. and Nev. legis. affecting women, 1978—; commentator Las Vegas Women's Resource Network. Bd. dirs. March of Dimes, 1977-79; mem. panel Clark County Lawyer's Referral Services, 1978-80; del. Republican State Conv., 1978. Fed. Public Defenders intern, 1975; Daus. of Erin scholar, 1975-76. Mem. Am. Bar Assn., Nev. Bar Assn., Clark County Bar Assn., Nat. Assn. Women Attys., NOW, Am. Trial Lawyers Assn., Nev. Trial Lawyers Assn., Psi Chi (v.p.). Office: 1829 E Charleston Blvd Suite 106 Las Vegas NV 89104

SONNENSCHEIN, ABRAHAM HENRY, aircraft company executive; b. Vienna, Austria, June 21, 1926; s. Israel Markus and Martha

(Sigal) S.; came to U.S., 1941; m. Helene S. Fichtenbaum, Sept. 30, 1934; children—Marc, Jayne, Russell, Renee. B.E.E. cum laude, CCNY, 1948; M.E.E., Poly. Inst. N.Y., 1951; postgrad. Columbia U., 1964, UCLA Sch. Mgmt., 1970. Registered profl. engr., N.Y., Calif., Ariz. Mem. tech staff Polarad Electronics Corp., 1948-51, program mgr., dir. engring. ops., asst. to pres., 1951-60; v.p. Fed. Sci. Corp., N.Y.C., 1961-65; asst. to pres. Heliodyne Corp., Van Nuys, Calif., 1965-66; successively chief scientist, program mgr., dir. engring. Hughes Aircraft Co., Torrance, Calif., 1966—, now. mgr. Microwave Communications Products; cons. mgmt., engring. Served with Signal Corps, U.S. Army, World War II. Mem. IEEE, AIAA, Soc. Motion Picture and TV Engrs., Am. Mgmt. Assn., Navy League, Soc. Cable TV Engrs. (bd. dirs.), Nat. Cable TV Assn. (bd. dirs.), Tau Beta Pi, Sigma XI, Eta Kappa Nu. Holder numerous patents; contbr. numerous tech. papers to profl. jours. Home: 7030 N 3d St Phoenix AZ 85020 Office: Hughes Aircraft Co PO Box 2999 Torrance CA 90509

SOO HOO, PEGGY HOM, indsl. engr.; b. Tucson; d. Ray and Rose Hom; m. Randolph Eric Soo Hoo, Dec. 4, 1982. B.S. in Systems Engring., U. Ariz., 1974; M.S. in Ops. Research, Stanford U., 1975. With IBM, Tucson, 1976—, facilities, space and manpower planner, Tucson, 1980, indsl. engring. plan coordinator, 1980-81, tape product planner, 1981—. Mem. Soc. Women Engrs., Orgn. Chinese Americans, Phi Kappa Phi, Tau Beta Pi. Home: 1535 Entrada Segundo Tucson AZ 85718 Office: IBM Corp 63D/71-2 Tucson AZ 85744

SOPER, HENRY VICTOR, neuroscientist, neuropsychologist; b. Glen Ridge, N.J., Mar. 10, 1945; s. Kenneth L. and Sylvia (Caldwell) S.; B.A., Yale U., 1966; M.A., U. Conn., 1972, Ph.D., 1974. Neurophysiologist, Brain Research Inst., UCLA, 1974-76; NIH fellow dept. psychology, 1976-78; asst. prof. Calif./State U.-Northridge, 1978; research neuroanatomist, clin. psychologist U. Ill.-Chgo., 1978-82; clin. psychology intern Camarillo (Calif.) State Hosp., 1982-83, research scientist, neuropsychologist UCLA Neuropsychiat. Inst. Program, 1982—. Served to 1st lt. C.E., U.S. Army, 1966-68; Decorated Bronze Star; recipient Norman Hall award Yale U., 1965, Robert R. Chamberlain award, 1965; State of Conn. predoctoral fellow, 1972-74; NIH fellow, 1976-78. Mem. Am. Psychol. Assn., Soc. Neurosci., N.Y. Acad. Sci., Psychonomic Sci., Am. Assn. Primatologists, Internat. Primatol. Soc., AAAS, Sigma Xi. Club: Los Angeles Rugby. Author publs. in field; editorial cons. profl. jours. Office: UCLA-NPI Research Program Box/A Camarillo CA 93010

SOPER, JOHN DAVID, assn. exec.; b. Walla Walla, Wash., Dec. 9, 1938; s. John Keith and Dorothy Louise (Fox) S.; B.A., U. Idaho, 1965; postgrad. Gonzaga U., 1967-68; m. Jane Leland Byrne, Dec. 30, 1965; children—Jennifer Leland, John Stephen. Stock broker Blyth and Co., Inc., Spokane, 1966-72; mng. dir. Wampum Cattle Co., Inc., Spokane and Union, Oreg., 1973-75; dir. community relations and admissions Expo '74 World's Fair '74, Spokane; exec. dir. United Nursing Homes Assn., Seattle, 1976—. Mem. Wash. State Jud. Retirement Bd., 1972-78; vice chmn. Spokane United Way, 1972-74. Served with U.S. Army, 1958-62. Mem. Am. Soc. Assn. Execs., Wash. Soc. Assn. Execs., Internat. Assn. Bus. Communicators, Pacific N.W. Assn. Bus. Communicators. Club: Lake Washington Saddle (treas. 1980-82). Office: Suite 410 16400 South Center Pkwy Seattle WA 98188

SOPHY, MICHAEL MERRILL, lawyer; b. Rapid City, S.D., June 20, 1935; s. Merle Edward and Dorothy Lucile (Beith) S.; B.A. cum laude in Philosophy, U. Notre Dame, 1957; postgrad. (Patrick Lucey scholar 1957-58), Georgetown U. Law Center, 1957-58, M.A. in Philosophy, U. Notre Dame, 1959, postgrad., 1960-61; LL.B., U. Ariz., 1965; m. Sandra Beregovsky, Aug. 17, 1965; children—Daniel Merle, Theodore Joseph. Admitted to Ariz. bar, 1966; law clk. Ariz. Ct. Appeals, Tucson, 1965; asso. Whitehill, Feldman, Scott & Berger, Tucson, 1966-68; partner firm Goddard, Sophy, L'Ecuyer & Ahearn, Phoenix, 1969-75; pres. Campaign Assos. Inc. Dir. Culligan of Mankato, Inc. (Minn.). Teaching fellow dept. philosophy U. Notre Dame, 1960-61; tchr. St. John's Coll., Sekondi, Ghana, 1961-63. Co-chmn. So. Ariz. R.F. Kennedy for Pres., 1968; campaign coordinator Samuel P. Goddard for Gov., 1968; campaign dir. Carolyn Warner for U.S. Senate; polit. dir. Ariz. Dem. Legis. Trust Fund, 1969—; Ariz. coordinator Muskie for Pres., 1972; legal counsel Maricopa County Central Dem. Com., 1970-71; campaign mgr. Robert E.B. Allen for Nat. Young Dems. Pres., 1971; dir. Ariz. Grassroots for McGovern/Shriver, 1972; mem. Ariz. Dem. Exec. Com., 1973; campaign mgr. Bruce Babbitt for Atty. Gen., 1974, spl. asst. atty. gen., 1975-77; campaign cons. Bill Schulz for U.S. Senate, 1980; polit. cons. com. for Dist. Representation, 1982, Terry Goddard for Phoenix Mayor, 1983; mem. Phoenix Employment Relations Bd., 1982-83. Served with U.S. Army, 1959-60. Mem. State Bar Ariz. (bar counsel 1981—), Am. Arbitration Assn. (regional adv. counsel), Phoenix Fire Fighters Assn. (hon.), Phi Delta Phi. Clubs: Notre Dame (v.p. 1970-71) (Phoenix). Home: 5131 E Monterey Way Phoenix AZ 85018 Office: Suite 858 234 N Central Ave Phoenix AZ 85004

SOPP, TRUDY JANE, city official, consultant; b. Huntington Park, Calif., Aug. 13, 1951; d. Edwin John and Angela Rose (Pelzl) S.; m. Hayden Wayne Thomas, Dec. 4, 1982. B.A. in Sociology, San Diego State U., 1974; M.A. in Sociology in Edn. (Fellow), U. Toronto, 1976, Ph.D. in Sociology in Edn. (Fellow), 1982. Research and devel. officer Ontario (Can.) Inst. Studies in Edn., 1975-78; program evaluation and staff devel. cons. Grad. Sch. Urban Resources and Social Policy, San Diego, 1978-79; orgn. devel. specialist City of San Diego, 1979—; pvt. cons. Prrat & Assocs., 1982—; part-time instr. Nat. U., 1982—; lectr. productivity improvement, orgn. devel., power and politics. Bd. dirs. YWCA of Can., 1977-78; past dir. Laurel Springs Tng. Inst., San Diego, 1979-81; mem. Calif. State Democratic Central Com., 1979-81; spl. programs chmn. Calif. Women in Govt., 1982-83. Mem. Am. Soc. Tng. and Devel., Am. Sociol. Assn., OD Can. Network, OD San Diego Network. Contbr. articles to tech. jours., manual. Office: 202 C St MS 8a San Diego CA 92101

SORENSEN, JACKI FAYE, aerobic dance company executive, choreographer; b. Oakland, Calif., Dec. 10, 1942; d. Roy C. and Juanita F. (Bullon) Mills; m. Neil A. Sorensen, Jan. 3, 1965. B.A., U. Calif., 1964. Cert. tchr., Calif. Ptnr., Big Spring Sch. Dance, 1965; tchr. Pasadena Ave. Sch., Sacramento, 1968; founder, chmn. bd. dirs., choreographer Aerobic Dancing, Inc., Northridge, Calif., 1969—; cons., lectr. on phys. fitness. Trustee, mem. Spl. Olympics adv. bd. Women's Sports Found. Recipient Honor award Tex. Gov.'s Commn. Phys. Fitness, 1976; Diamond Pin award Am. Heart Assn., 1979; Individual Contbn. award Am. Assn. Fitness Dirs. in Bus. and Industry, 1981; Spl. Olympics Contbn. award, 1982; Contbn. to Women's Fitness award Pres.'s Council Phys. Fitness and Sports, 1982. Mem. Am. Coll. Sports Medicine, Alliance for Health, Phys. Exercise, Recreation and Dance, Nat. Intramural and Recreation Assn., Com. of 200, AFTRA. Author: Aerobic Dancing, 1979; The Jacki Sorensen Aerobic Lifestyle Book, 1983; creator numerous dance and exercise records, video cassette. Office: Aerobic Dancing Inc 18907 Nordhoff St Northridge CA 91324

SORENSON, DONNA RUTH, educator; b. Providence, Utah, Nov. 6, 1926; d. Ether Leslie and Constance Rose (Bullock) Nielsen; m. Hoyle L. Sorenson, Jan. 28, 1949; children—Craig H., Brian K., Scott M., Kevin L. Student Brigham Young U., 1945-46, U. Utah, 1949; B.S., Utah State U., 1949. Cert. profl. tchr. (elem., middle, secondary), vocat./consumer home econs., Utah. Tchr. pub. schs., Salt Lake City, 1951-52, Logan, Utah, 1952-53; tchr. English, phys. edn. Wayne (Utah) High Sch., 1957-58; tchr. homemaking, phys. edn., speech-drama, pep club, Daggett (Utah) Sch., Manila (Utah) High Sch., 1959-61; tchr. English Richfield (Utah) High Sch., 1961-67; tchr. home econs., speech/drama, Highland Jr. High Sch., Ogden Sch. Dist., 1968—; co-founder coop nursery sch., Richfield; leader Stake Relief Soc. sewing group. Mem. Vocat. Edn. Assn., Home Econs. Assn., NEA, Ogden Edn. Assn., Utah Edn. Assn., Daus. of Utah Pioneers, Art Internat. Assn. Republican. Mormon. Club: Federated Women's. Office: Highland High Sch 325 Gramercy St Ogden UT 84404

SOSA, DAN, JR., justice Supreme Court New Mexico; b. Las Cruces, N.Mex., Nov. 12, 1923; s. Dan and Margaret (Soto) S.; B.S. in Bus. Adminstrn., N.Mex. State U., 1947; J.D., U. N.Mex., 1951; m. Rita Ortiz, Aug. 31, 1950; 7 children. Bar: N.Mex. 1951. Tchr., coach, public schs., Mesilla, N.Mex., 1947-48; Cruces, 1952-75; judge Las Cruces City Ct., 1952-55; spl. agt. Office of Price Stblzn., 1951-52; asst. dist. atty., then dist. atty. N.Mex. 3d Jud. Dist., 1956-64; spl. asst. atty. gen. for prosecution capital criminal cases Dept. Justice, 1965-66; justice N.Mex. Supreme Ct., 1975—. Served to 1st lt. AC, U.S. Army, 1942-45. Democrat. Roman Catholic. Office: Supreme Ct N Mex 327 Don Gaspar Ave Santa Fe NM 87501*

SOSKEL, NORMAN TERRY, physician; b. Norfolk, Va., Sept. 1, 1948; s. Fred and Ruth (Chapel) S.; cert. piano teaching St. Louis Inst. Music, 1966; B.A., U. Va., 1970, M.D., 1974; m. Judith Anne Barrie, Apr. 9, 1980; 1 son, Daniel Aaron. Intern, Hosp. of St. Raphael-Yale U., New Haven, 1974-75; resident in internal medicine Salem (Va.) VA Hosp.-U. Va., 1975-77; pulmonary fellow U. Utah, Salt Lake City, 1980-82, instr. medicine and pathology, 1980-82, asst. prof. medicine, 1982—; cons. in field. Recipient Paderewski medal Nat. Guild Piano Tchrs., 1967; Am. Lung Assn. fellow, 1979-80; Utah Heart Assn. grantee, 1979—; Pulmonary Acad. award Nat. Heart-Lung-Blood Inst., 1980—. Mem. Am. Lung Assn., Nat. Speleological Soc., Western Connective Tissue Soc., N.Y. Acad. Sci., Am. Fedn. Clin. Research, Sigma Chi. Contbr. articles to profl. jours.; research in field of pulmonary connective tissues with respect to lung injury. Office: U Utah Med Center Pulmonary Div 50 N Medical Dr Salt Lake City UT 84132

SOTO, ROGELIO ROY, state personnel officer; b. Honokaa, Hawaii, Sept. 21, 1946; s. Esteban Ramelb and Josephine (Kelekolio) S.; m. Ellen Asako Uemura, Apr. 18, 1970; children—Stephanie K., Kelsey Ann Y. Higher acctg. cert. Cannon's Coll. Commerce, Honolulu, 1967. With Dept. Hawaiian Lands, Honolulu, 1967—, bookkeeper, acctg. clk., 1967-75, personnel technician, 1976; mem. Gov.'s Com. for Excluded Employees, 1982. Councilman, Democratic Party, Mililani Town, 1976—; pres. Dem. Precinct, Mililani Town, 1977-78; voter registrar, campaign mgr. Dem. campaign 39th Dist. Hawaii, 1982; bd. dirs. Mililani Town Assn., 1979—. Served with U.S. Army, 1967-69. Decorated medal for valor. Recipient Outstanding State Officer award Hawaii Jaycees, 1979; Outstanding Young Person award Hawaii Jaycees, 1980; Dept. Dirs. award Dept. Hawaiian Home Lands, 1980. Mem. Mililani Town Jaycees (bd. dirs. 1976-82, pres. 1976—), Jaycee of Yr. award 1976, 78), ARC, YMCA, Hawaii Claims Assn. Baptist. Home: 94 581 Holaniku St Mililani Town HI 96789

SOUDER-JAFFERY, LAURA, research cons.; b. Agana, Guam, Aug. 15, 1950; d. Paul B. and Mariquita (Torres) Souder; m. Syed Zaigham Shafiq Jaffery, Apr. 21, 1980. B.A., Emmanuel Coll., 1972; M.A., U. Hawaii, 1976, postgrad., 1979—. Adminstrv. asst. Guam Dept. Commerce, 1972-73, office adminstr., 1973-74; spl. asst. to gov. for cultural and pub. affairs, Office of the Gov., 1976-78; research cons. Guam History and Culture, 1979—; participant Culture Learning Inst., East-West Center, Honolulu, 1979—. Appointed Ambassador-at-Large, Gov. Guam, 1976; Gov.'s personal rep. Internat. Sister City Conv., 1976, 77; coordinator Guam's Participation in Pres. Carter's Inaugural Parade, 1976-77; Guam, del. to Japan, 1977; treas. Democratic Party of Guam, 1974, mem., 1972—; Guam del. White House Conf. on Libraries and Info. Services, 1977-80, others. East-West Center degree scholar grantee, 1974-76, 79-82. Mem. Chamorro Studies Assn., Insular Arts Council Guam, Smithsonian Assn., Oral History Assn., Nat. Geographic Soc., Am. Assn. Mus., Nat. Trust for Historic Preservation, Nat. Archives Trust Fund, Hawaii Am. Studies Assn., Am. Studies Assn. Democrat. Roman Catholic. Clubs: E-W Center Alumni Assn., Guam Beauty Assn., Others. Editor: Women of Guam, 1977; contbr. articles to profl. jours., mags., newspapers. Home: PO Box 1651 Agana GU 96910

SOULAKIS, GEORGE, mechanical engineer; b. Pasadena, Calif., Jan. 11, 1936; s. George Helius and Stella (Patestos) S.; B.S. in Mech. Engring., U. Calif., San Luis Obispo, 1964; m. Diana Bette Jane Davis, Jan. 28, 1968; children—Derek, Damon. Design engr. Spectrol Electrons, Industry, Calif., 1964-67; dir. engring. Mattel, Inc., Hawthorne, Calif., 1968-75; dir. engring. Eldon Industries, Hawthorne, 1975-81, v.p. engring., 1981—. Active Little League, Hermosa Beach; soccer coach Am. Youth Soccer Orgn., 1980, 81; active Torrance South Bay YMCA, 1978-83; mem. Hermosa Beach (Calif.) Planning Commn., 1983—. Served with USN, 1954-57. Mem. ASME, Soc. Plastic Engrs. Greek Orthodox. Patentee in field. Home: 2726 El Oeste Hermosa Beach CA 90254 Office: Eldon Industries 1130 E 230th St Carson CA 90745

SOULE, ROGER GILBERT, educator; b. Northport, N.Y., Feb. 21, 1935; s. Freeman Gilbert and Rosemond Merecedes (Shanks) S.; B.S., SUNY-Cortland, 1957; M.S., U. Ill., 1958; Ph.D., Wash. State U., 1967; m. Janet Carol, June 13, 1959; children—Steven Walker, Thomas Roger, Elizabeth Janet. Faculty, Dutchess Community Coll., Poughkeepsie, N.Y., 1960-64, Wash. State U., Pullman, 1964-67, Boston U., 1967-75, Liberty Bapt. Coll., Lynchburg, Va., 1976-77; chmn. dept. phys. edn. and athletics, Biola U., La Mirada, Calif., 1978—; research physiologist Natick Labs., summers 1968-74. Served with U.S. Army, 1958-60. Fellow Am. Coll. Sports Medicine; mem. Am. Physiol. Soc., Sigma Xi. Baptist. Contbr. articles to sci. jours. Home: 14203 Figueras Rd La Mirada CA 90638 Office: 13800 Biola Ave La Mirada CA 90639

SOULÉ, WILLIAM MARTIN, electrical engineer; b. Laramie, Wyo., March 2, 1927; s. Martin H. and Claire Grace (Sneller); m. Martha Florence Patrick, June 1, 1948; children—Laura Bowling, Thomas, Bruce. B.S.E.E., U. Wyo. Profl. engr., Calif., 1976. Ops. mgr. (engring. specialist) Martin Marietta, Balt., 1961-63; site rep. U.S. AEC, Hallam, Nebr. and Platteville, Colo., 1963-74; project engr. AEC/Dept. Energy/ERDA, Canoga Park, Calif., 1974-79, sr. project mgr. (acting dir.) ETEC/SITE office. Examiner, Calif. Bd. Registration for Profl. Engrs., 1977. Served in U.S. Navy, 1945-46. Recipient Spl. Achievement award ERDA, 1975; Mgr.'s Recognition award Dept. Energy, 1978, Superior Performance award, 1981. Mem. Nat. Soc. Profl. Engrs., AAAS, IEEE (sr.), Am. Nuclear Soc. (charter), Am. Legion, VFW. Republican. Presbyterian. Lodge: Masons. Home: 8321 Joan Ln Canoga Park CA 91304 Office: Box 1446 Canoga Park CA 91304

SOUTH, (RICHARD) KENT, city official; b. Salt Lake City, July 13, 1935; s. Richard Taylor and Alice Utahna (Ainsworth) S.; 1 dau., Shawna Joan; m. 2d, Ruth Anderson, July 31, 1964; children—Brooke Ann, Richard Whitney. B.S. in Bus. Adminstrn., Brigham Young U., 1956; M.B.A., UCLA, 1962. Acct., systems analyst Union Oil Co., Los Angeles, 1956-62; mgmt. and systems mgr. City of San Jose (Calif.), 1963-68, asst. dir. fin., 1968-75, dir. fin., 1975—. Cubmaster Boy Scouts Am., 1979—; mem. YMCA. Recipient Profl. Achievement recognition Mcpl. Fin. Officers Assn. U.S. and Can., 1981, 82. Mem. Mcpl. Fin. Officers Assn. U.S. and Can., Calif. Soc. Mcpl. Fin. Officers (pres.), Beta Gamma Sigma, Phi Kappa Phi. Republican. Mormon.

SOUTHERBY, NORM, television production executive, consultant; b. Windsor, Ont., Can., Mar. 28, 1935; s. John Henry and Doris May (Hughes) S.; m. Charmion Conn; children—Paul Dean, Sara Kim; m. 2d, Alexandra Beck, Apr. 6, 1973 (div.). B.S., Nyack (N.Y.) Coll., 1958; M.S., SUNY-Oneonta, 1960; M.A. Internat. Coll., Los Angeles, 1982. Lifetime cert. tchr., N.Y., Calif. Radio announcer, Niagara Falls, Ont., 1955; tchr. San Diego (Calif.) Unified Sch. Dist., 1960-65, Niagara Falls Unified Sch. Dist., 1958-60; owner Courtesy TV & Appliance, Canoga Park, Calif., 1965-70; tchr. Los Angeles Unified Sch. Dist., 1970-72; cons. to chief adminstrv. office HEW, Los Angeles, 1972-78; pres., chief exec. officer Southerby Prodns., Inc., Southerby & Assocs., Pub. Service Distbrs. and Southerby & Assocs., Long Beach, Calif., 1974—; guest speaker; host, producer 36 ednl. TV programs Sta. KNXT, Channel 2, Los Angeles, 1972-74. Coordinator Los Angeles and Fed. Govt. Alcohol Awareness Week; mem. Pres.'s Task Force on Creative Employment for Sr. Citizens. Recipient film awards Am. Film Festival, Internat. Film Producers Assn., other; award of excellence HEW, 1973; John Swet award for new perspectives on alcoholism edn. CBS TV Series, 1973. Mem. AFTRA. Author: (films) So Long Pal, 1973, The New Life of Sandra Blain, 1974, Alcohol and Nutrition, 1980, Sexuality, Alcohol and Drugs, 1982, Taking Charge, the Manager Film, 1982. Office: 5000 E Anaheim St Long Beach CA 90804

SOUTHERN, RONALD DONALD, b. Calgary, Alta., Can., July 25, 1930; s. Samuel Donald and Alexandra (Cuthill) S.; B.Sc., U. Alta., Edmonton, 1953; LL.D. (hon.), U. Calgary, 1976; m. Margaret Visser, July 30, 1954; children—Nancy, Linda. Pres., chief exec. officer dir. ATCO Ltd., Calgary, 1954—; mem. Calgary Exhbn. and Stampede Bd.; gov. Olympic Trust Can.; dir. Nova Alta. Corp., Can. Cement Lafarge Ltd., Canadian Pacific Enterprises Ltd., Crown Zellerbach Can. Ltd., Pacific Western Airlines Ltd., Royal Ins. Co. Ltd. Can. Utilities Ltd., Easton United, Securities Ltd. Mem. United Church of Can. Clubs: Calgary Petroleum, Earl Grey Golf, U. Calgary Chancellors. Home: 67 Massey Pl SW Calgary AB T2V 2G7 Canada Office: 1243 McKnight Blvd NE Calgary AB T2E 5T2 Canada

SOUTHWARD, WALTER WILLIAM, public relations co. exec.; b. Pitts., July 16, 1936; s. Walter William and Hilda (Geider) S.; student Marshall U., 1957-59; m. Leilani Akoni, Mar. 30, 1963. Reporter, Herald-Dispatch, Huntington, W.Va., 1957-59; reporter, Sunday editor Hilo Tribune-Herald, 1959-62; asst. Sunday editor Honolulu Advertiser, 1962-63, Big Island Bur. chief, Hilo, 1963-70; mgr. public affairs Waikoloa, Hilo, 1970-77; owner Walt Southward: Public Relations, Hilo, 1977—; various sportscasting and free lance writing assignments, 1957—. Pres., Hilo Nat. Little League, 1966-68, Big Island Women's Softball League, 1968-73, Waikoloa Village Assn., 1971-74; head coach Hilo Comets Women's Softball Team, 1970—, U. Hawaii at Hilo Athletic Boosters, 1976-77. Served with U.S. Army, 1954-57. Named Booster of Year, U. Hawaii at Hilo, 1974. Mem. Am. Numis. Assn. (life), Public Relations Soc. Am., Hawaii Island C. of C. (pres. 1982-83). Clubs: Big Island Coin (pres. 1964), Big Island Press, Honolulu Press, Big Island Golf Courses Assn. (pres. 1974-75), Lions. public relations co. exec.; b. Pitts., July 16, 1936; s. Walter William and Hilda (Geider) S.; student Marshall U., 1957-59; m. Leilani Akoni, Mar. 30, 1963. Reporter, Herald-Dispatch, Huntington, W.Va., 1957-59; reporter, Sunday editor Hilo Tribune-Herald, 1959-62; asst. Sunday editor Honolulu Advertiser, 1962-63, Big Island Bur. chief, Hilo, 1963-70; mgr. public affairs Waikoloa, Hilo, 1970-77; owner Walt Southward: Public Relations, Hilo, 1977—; various sportscasting and free lance writing assignments, 1957—. Pres., Hilo Nat. Little League, 1966-68, Big Island Women's Softball League, 1968-73, Waikoloa Village Assn., 1971-74; head coach Hilo Comets Women's Softball Team, 1970—, U. Hawaii at Hilo Athletic Boosters, 1976-77. Served with U.S. Army, 1954-57. Named Booster of Year, U. Hawaii at Hilo, 1974. Mem. Am. Numis. Assn. (life), Public Relations Soc. Am., Hawaii Island C. of C. (pres. 1982-83). Clubs: Big Island Coin (pres. 1964), Big Island Press, Honolulu Press, Big Island Golf Courses Assn. (pres. 1974-75), Lions. Home: 94 Pukalana St Hilo HI 96720 Office: PO Box 251 Hilo HI 96720

SOUTHWICK, CHARLES HENRY, biology educator; b. Wooster, Ohio, Aug. 28, 1928; s. Arthur F. and Faye (Motz) S.; m. Heather Milne Beck, July 12, 1952; children—Steven B., Karen L. B.A., Coll. Wooster, 1949; M.S., U. Wis., 1951, Ph.D., 1953; postdoctoral fellow Oxford U., 1954-55, Aligarh U., India, 1959-60. Research asst. Delta Waterfowl Research Sta., Man., 1950; research assoc. C.Z. Biol. Sta., 1951; asst. prof. biology Hamilton Coll., 1953-54; asst. to assoc. prof. zoology Ohio U., 1955-61; assoc. prof. to prof. Johns Hopkins U., Balt., 1961-79; prof. biology U. Colo., 1979—; chmn. dept. EPO biology 1979-82; editorial bd. Quar. Rev. Biology, Am. Jour. Primatology; cons. NIH, FDA, Merck Corp., Charles River Labs., NAS, NRC, Govt. India; mem. com. research and exploration Nat. Geog. Soc.; mem. Md. Gov.'s Sci. Adv. Bd. Fellow NIH, Nat. Geog. Soc., U.S. Ednl. Found., Md. Dept. Natural Resources, Wis. Alumni Research Found.; U.S. Fish and Wildlife Service grantee; recipient Mateer Biology prize, 1949. Fellow AAAS, Acad. Zoology, Am. Philos. Soc.; mem. Am. Soc. Zoologists, Am. Soc. Mammalogists, Ecol. Soc. Am., Am. Inst. Biol. Scis. (exec. com. 1981-83), Am. Soc. Primatologists, Internat. Primatol. Soc., Animal Behavior Soc., Internat. Soc. Research on Aggression. Phi Beta Kappa, Sigma Xi. Author: Primate Social Behavior, 1963; Aggressive Behavior, 1970; Ecology and the Quality of Our Environment, 1976; Primate Usage in Biomedical Research, 1975; contbr. numerous articles to profl. jours. Pioneered primate population studies in India, Nepal, Malaysia and Hong Kong New Ters. Office: Dept EPO Biology Box B-334 U Colo Boulder CO 80309

SOUTHWICK, EDWARD HALE, civil engineer, water resources executive; b. Washington, Apr. 7, 1929; s. Edward W. and Ellen Elaine (Christenson) S.; m. Althea Sylvester, Aug. 27, 1952; children—Edward, Meg, Elizabeth, James. B.S. in Civil Engring., U. Utah, 1955. Registered profl. engr. and land surveyor, Utah. Commr. Sevier River, 1955-57, Weber River, 1957-61; sec.-treas., gen. mgr. Pineview Water Systems, 1962—. Mem. Bd. Water Resources State of Utah, 1967-81, chmn., 1975-77; bd. dirs. Utah Water Users Assn., 1962—, pres., 1964-66. Served with U.S. Army, 1947-48. Mem. Nat. Water Resources Assn. (dir. 1966-82, pres. 1977). Mormon. Club: Rotary (Ogden). Home: 3443 Fowler Ave Ogden UT 84403 Office: Pineview Water Systems 1483 Wall Ave Ogden UT 84404

SOUTHWICK, JAMES HENRY, safety engineer; b. Idaho Falls, Mar. 9, 1935; s. Glen and Gladys (Porter) S.; m. Reula Arveta Mickelson, Sept. 27, 1955; children—Susan, Pamela, James L., Michael G., Eric W. Student Idaho State Coll., 1954-55; B.S., U. Idaho, 1958; M.Ed., Brigham Young U., 1972. R&D chemist Thiokol Wasatch Div., Brigham City, Utah, 1960; radio chemist Gen. Electric (Nuclear Aircraft), Idaho Falls, 1961; health physics engr. INEL, Idaho, 1961-75; sr. safety engr. EG&G Idaho Inc., INEL, Idaho Falls, 1975—. Vol. fireman, 1966—; mem. Ammon (Idaho) Planning and Zoning Commn., 1969—, Bonneville County Planning and Zoning Commn., 1980—. Served as capt. U.S. Army, 1958-60. Mem. Am. Soc. Safety Engrs., Health Physics Soc., Am. Nuclear Soc. Home: 3968 E 17th St Idaho Falls ID 84301 Office: PBF 601 PO Box 1625 Idaho Falls ID 83415

SOUTHWORTH, ASAHEL DIMMICK, librarian; b. Northfield, Minn., Jan. 19, 1938; s. Asahel Dimmick, II and Lois Vivian (Oslie) S.;

B.S., Mankato (Minn.) State U., 1962, M.S., 1979; m. Joan Ruth Wilson, Apr. 11, 1981; children by previous marriage—Ann Noel, Leah Susanne. Installer, Western Electric Co., 1956-57; librarian Cloquet (Minn.) Sch. Dist., 1973-76, Elk River (Minn.) Sch. Dist., 1976-77; dir. Mt. Vernon (Wash.) Pub. Library, 1977—. Violist, Skagit Valley Symphony, 1980—. Served as officer U.S. Navy, 1962-73; Korea, Vietnam. Mem. Exptl. Aircraft Assn. (dir. Fly-in Arlington 1981—; chpt. sec. 1979-82). Office: 315 Snoqualmie St Mount Vernon WA 98273

SOWARDS, GLADE M., state legislator; b. Vernal, Utah, Sept. 9, 1929; s. Harmon S. and Ida Rebecca (Jensen) S.; B.S. magna cum laude in Acctg., U. Utah, 1954; m. Rachel Elizabeth Farley, May 29, 1952; children—Rebecca Jane, Olivia, H. Scott, J. Farley, Paula, Allen H., Samuel L., G. Michael, Christen Ned; 1 foster dau., Trinidad Madge Ben. With H.S. Sowards & Sons, Inc.; mem. city council, Vernal, 1959-67; mem. Utah Ho. of Reps. from 61st Dist., 1969-79, speaker of house, 1977-79; mem. Utah Senate, 1979—; vice chmn. state fed. assembly Nat. Conf. State Legislatures, 1978, mem. energy com., 1982-83. Chmn. Utah State Air Travel Commn., 1980-82; chmn. Utah State Energy Conservation and Devel. Council, 1980-83. Mem. Vernal C. of C. (past pres.). Mormon. Club: Lions (past pres.). Office: Box 308 Vernal UT 84078

SOWERS, MIRIAM RUTH, painter; b. Bluffton, Ohio, Oct. 4, 1922; d. Paul S. and Edith E. (Triplehorn) Hochstettler; m. H. Frank Sowers, Apr. 15, 1944; children—Craig V., Keith A. Student Miami U., Oxford, Ohio, Art Inst. Chgo., U. N.Mex. One-woman shows: Winblad Galleries, San Francisco, L'Atelier Gallery, Cedar Falls, Iowa, Southwestern Galleries, Dallas; group shows: Am. Bicentennial, Dayton (Ohio) Art Inst., Butler Art Inst., Akron Art Inst., Massilon (Ohio) Art Inst., Toledo Mus. Art, Canton (Ohio) Art Inst., Roswell (N.Mex.) Mus. Recipient show awards. Christian Scientist. Author: Parables from Paradise, 1976, The Suns of Man, 1982; pub. art cards. Address: 3020 Glenwood Dr NW Albuquerque NM 87107

SOWERWINE, ELBERT ORLA, JR., cons. engring. planning and mgmt.; b. Tooele, Utah, Mar. 15, 1915; s. Elbert Orla and Margaret Alice (Evans) S.; B. Chemistry, Cornell U., 1937, Chem. Engr., 1938; m. Norma Borge; children—Sue-Ann Sowerwine Jacobson, Sandra Sowerwine Montgomery, Elbert Orla 3d, John Frederick, Avril Ruth, Albaro Francisco, Octavio Evans, Zaida Margaret. Analytical chemist Raritan Copper Works, Perth Amboy, N.J., summers 1936, 37; research chem. engr. Socony-Vacuum Oil Co., Paulsboro, N.J., 1938-43; prodn. supr. Merck & Co., Elkton, Va., 1943-45; asst. plant mgr. U.S. Indsl. Chems. Co., Newark, 1945-48; project engr. and research dir. Wigton-Abbott Corp., Newark, 1948-50, Cody, Wyo., 1950-55; cons. engring., planning, indsl. and community devel., resource evaluation and mgmt. Wapiti, Wyo., also C.Am., 1955—. Commr. N.J., Boy Scouts Am., 1938-43; mem. Wapiti and Park County (Wyo.) Sch. Bds., 1954-58; dir. Mont. State Planning Bd., 1959-61; exec. bd. Mo. Basin Research and Devel. Council, 1959-61. Fellow Am. Inst. Chemists; mem. Am. Inst. Chem. Engrs., Am. Planning Assn., Nicaraguan Assn. Engrs. and Architects. Libertarian. Mem. Christian Ch. Researcher desulfurization of petroleum products, process control; patentee in petroleum and chem. processes and equipment. Home: Broken H Ranch Wapiti WY 82450 Office: Sowerwine Cons Wapiti WY 82450

SPADA, JAMES, author, publisher; b. S.I., N.Y., Jan. 23, 1950; s. Joseph Vincent and Mary (Ruberto) S. Student, Wagner Coll., 1968-71, Calif. State U., 1979-80. Pres., Spada Pubs, Los Angeles (pub. Barbra Quar.), Los Angeles, 1980—. Mem. Authors Guild, ACLU. Democrat. Author: Katharine Hepburn: Her Life in Pictures, 1984; Judy and Liza, 1983; Monroe-Her Life in Pictures, 1982; Streisand-the Woman and the Legend, 1981; The Spada Report, 1979; The Films of Robert Redford, 1977; Barbra: The First Decade-The Films and Career of Barbra Streisand, 1974. Office: 7985 Santa Monica Blvd Suite 109 Los Angeles CA 90046

SPADOTTO, BEVERLY THERESE, editor; b. Syracuse, N.Y., July 11, 1951; d. Ted and Beverly Jean (Loughlin) S.; B.A. in Journalism, George Washington U., 1973; M.A., U. So. Calif., 1975. Dir. public relations D'Arcy-MacManus & Masius, advt., Los Angeles, 1976-78; editor Rangefinder mag., Santa Monica, Calif., 1978-81; communications editor INA and Ross Loos Healthplans, Glendale, Calif., 1982—; ptnr. Flash & Class, Los Angeles, 1982—. Mem. Western Publs. Assn., Sigma Delta Chi. Democrat. Roman Catholic. Home: 410 S Hobart Blvd Los Angeles CA 90020 Office: 700 N Brand Blvd Glendale CA 91203

SPALDING, PHILIP EDMUNDS, JR., land co. exec.; b. Honolulu, July 21, 1918; s. Philip Edmunds and Alice Cooke S.; student Princeton U., 1937-39; m. Mary Carver, July 18, 1980; children from previous marriage—Philip Edmunds III, Alfred Tozzer, Anne, Joan, Kit, Michael, Alana. Budget dir. Dole Pineapple Co., Honolulu, 1940-45; pres. Pacific Pineapple Co. Ltd., Honolulu, 1946-56, Hawaiian Western Steel Ltd., Honolulu, 1957-71, Molokai Ranch Ltd., Honolulu, 1973—. Trustee, Oahu Devel. Conf., Ocean Inst.; mem. Republican Nat. Com. Hawaii, 1968. Club: Plaza. Home: 700 Richards St Honolulu HI 96813 Office: PO Box 4039 Honolulu HI 96813

SPANGLE, CLARENCE WILBUR, lawyer, computer company executive; b. Wilkinsburg, Pa., Feb. 16, 1925; s. Carl C. and Blanche E. S.; B.S.M.E., Yale U., 1945; J.D., George Washington U., 1952; m. Virginia Galliher, Aug. 11, 1951; 1 son, Henry Bryan. With Honeywell Inc., Mpls., 1947—, sr. v.p., 1970-71, exec. v.p., 1971-74, pres. Honeywell Info. Systems, Inc., Mpls., 1974-80; pres. Memorex Corp., 1980, chmn. bd., chief exec. officer, 1980—, also dir.; admitted to Minn. bar, 1952; dir. Gelco Corp., 1st Bank System, Inc., Mpls. Served with USNR, 1942-46. Methodist. Home: 499 Walsh Rd Atherton CA 94025 Office: Memorex Corp San Tomas at Central Expressway Santa Clara CA 95052

SPANGLER, SCOTT MICHAEL, agribus. co. exec.; b. Toledo, Aug. 4, 1938; s. Walter J. and Martha Zoe (Hirscher) S.; B.M.E., U. Cin., 1961; M.B.A., Harvard U., 1963; m. Jean Galt Schmonsees, June 10, 1963; children—Karen Elizabeth, Scott Michael, Andrew Galt. Fellow (In Africa), research assoc. M.I.T., Boston, 1963-65; fin. exec. Cooper Industries, Inc., Mt. Vernon, Ohio, 1965-68; v.p. indsl. group White Motor Corp., Cleve., 1968-70; pres. Spangler and Co., Houston, 1970-73; pres. Procor, Inc., Phoenix, 1973-78; pres., chief exec. officer AZL Resources, Phoenix, 1978—, also dir.; dir. Mogas Machine Works, Houston, Alamosa Nat. Bank (Colo.), First So. Capital Corp., New Orleans, Internat. Energy Devel. Corp., Geneva, Switzerland; mem. Am. Agribus. Council, 1973—. Trustee Mt. Vernon YMCA, 1965-68, Amarillo YMCA, 1975-79, Phoenix YMCA, 1980—. Republican. Presbyterian. Clubs: Harvard (N.Y.C.), Paradise Valley Country. Home: 7837 N 54th St Paradise Valley AZ 85253 Office: 5025 E Washington St Phoenix AZ 85038

SPANN, AL EARL, rehabilitationist, therapist, consultant, researcher; b. Geneva, Ala., Mar. 7, 1945; s. Adril Foyette and Lola Vivian (Hoffman) S.; Student Troy (Ala.) State U., 1964; A.A., Coalinga Coll., 1965; B.A., Calif. State U.-Fresno, 1967, M.A., 1972; postgrad. UCLA Med. Sch., 1973; Ed.D. in Rehab., Brigham Young U., 1980. Cert. rehab. counselor, reality therapist, Calif. community coll. instr. and counselor and supr., cert. in standard services, all Calif. Indsl. psychology asst. Market Test Corp., Fresno, Calif., 1965-67; rehab. asst. Calif. State U., Fresno, 1967-68, instr., counselor, 1975-76; sch. counselor Merced (Calif.) High Sch. and Dept. Rehab., Merced, 1968-70; mental health counselor Fresno County Mental Health Dept. and Dept. Rehab., Fresno, 1970-73; rehab. cons. for So. Calif. counties including Los Angeles Children's Hosp., 1973-74; program supr. Dept. Rehab., Fresno, 1976-82; ednl. cons. and therapist Spann Enterprises, Fresno, 1978-82, also ednl. and therapy cons.; cons. Dept. Rehab., Newport Beach, Calif., 1983—; expert witness field of psychiat. rehab. Vol. counselor Fresno Youth, Inc., 1974; profl. vol. Help in Emotional Trouble Hotline, Fresno, 1975; civil mem. Human Services Coalition, 1983; rehab. counselor Cert. Establishment Bd., Fresno, 1974. Served with Army N.G., 1969-74. Recipient Cert. of Appreciation, Assn. for Mentally Handicapped of Madera County, 1979. Mem. Nat. Rehab. Assn., Am. Personnel and Guidance Assn., Calif. Personnel and Guidance Assn., Nat. Mental Health Counselor Assn., Phi Kappa Phi. Democrat. Baptist. Club: Lions. Contbr. articles to profl. publs. Office: 3822 Campus Dr Suite 100 Newport Beach CA 92660

SPANN, KATHARINE DOYLE, mktg. exec.; b. Holton, Kans.; d. Edward James and Josephine (Hurla) Doyle; B.S., Emporia State Coll.; m. Hugh J. Spann (div. Feb. 1952); 1 dau., Susan Katharine. Vice pres. Bozell & Jacobs Advt. (formerly L.C. Cole Co.), San Francisco, 1951-76; pres. Katharine Doyle Spann Assos., 1977—; propr. Kate's Vineyard, Napa Valley, Calif.; exec. producer TV shows Doctors News Conf., The Ben Alexander Show, Land of Jazz, 1956—; communications counsel to health professions, 1970—. Bd. dirs. San Francisco Heart Assn., Bay Area Health Mus., Caymus Found., Heritage Fund. Named Advt. Woman of Year, 1962; recipient El Capitan award Peninsula chpt. Pub. Relations Soc. Am., 1962, 66; Am. Silver Anvil award, Pub. Relations Soc. Am., 1962, 66; Best of Show award, award of excellence Publicity Club of Bay Area, 1966. Mem. AAUW, Acad. TV Arts and Scis. (dir.), Advt. Club San Francisco (bd. govs. 1966—), Am. Soc. Enology, Napa Valley Women in Wine, Delta Sigma Epsilon. Club: Met. (San Francisco). Home: 1447 S Whitehall Ln Saint Helena CA 94574

SPANSKI, GARY STEPHEN, stock broker; b. Bad Axe, Mich., July 26, 1953; s. Eugene Vincent and Doris Emilia Spanski; B.S., Mich. State U., 1975; M.B.A., Pepperdine U., 1981. Test engr. Gen. Motors Co., Lansing, Mich., 1975-78, lab. technician Farr Co., El Segundo, Calif., 1978-79; account exec. Dean Witter Reynolds Inc., Manhattan Beach, Calif., 1980-82; investment specialist Sutro & Co., Inc., Beverly Hills, Calif., 1982—. Mem. Am. Mktg. Assn., Intra-Sci. Research Found., Beverly Hills Bus. Forum (bd. dirs.), Nat. Ski Patrol Systems, Sierra Club, Republican. Roman Catholic. Clubs: Sea D Sea Dive, Southbay Ski, Beverly Hills Men's (bd. dirs.), Beverly Hills Kiwanis. Investment columnist, Healthcare Horizons. Home: 1902 Grant Ave Apt 1 Redondo Beach CA 90278 Office: 9696 Wilshire Blvd 2d Floor Beverly Hills CA 90212

SPARE, ANTHONY EDWARD, securities analyst; b. Chgo., Oct. 1, 1939; s. Alexander T. and Rita H. S.; m. Eleanor Doyle, July 14, 1962; children—Alexander, Samantha, James. B.A., Tufts U., 1961; M.B.A., Stanford U., 1963. With Bank of Calif., San Francisco, 1963—, analyst, 1965-74, dir. research, 1975—; guest instr. San Francisco State Coll. Active fund-raising various local and univ. groups. Chartered fin. analyst. Mem. Nat. Assn. Bus. Economists, Security Analysts San Francisco (past pres.), Fin. Analyst Fedn. Home: 119 Baywood Ave Hillsborough CA 94010 Office: Bank of California 400 California St San Francisco CA 94145

SPARKS, DAVID DEAN, cons. energy engr.; b. Loma Linda, Calif., June 25, 1955; s. Delmon D. and Geraldine Ruth (Baske) S.; B.S. in E.E., Calif. State Poly. U., 1976; postgrad. U. Calif., Riverside, 1980—. Engring. aide City of Riverside, 1976-77, energy info. coordinator, 1977-78, utilities conservation rep., 1977-81; energy conservation cons. to bus. and industry, 1977—. Recipient Achievement award Bank Am., 1972. Mem. IEEE, Assn. Energy Engrs., Nat. Soc. Profl. Engrs., Calif. Soc. Profl. Engrs., Cal-Poly Alumni Assn. (life). Republican. Office: 2680 Walnut Suite C Tustin CA 92680

SPARKS, GARY JOSEPH, educational administrator, editor; b. Toledo, Aug. 17, 1942; s. Charles Augustus and Mildred Eileen (Owens) S.; m. Geraldine Leona Welter, July 23, 1941; children—Joseph, Gregory, Eileen, Gwen. B.A., M.Ed., U. Toledo, Ed.D., 1981. Tchr. Toledo Pub. Schs., Catholic Schs., 1964-70; prin. Toledo Cath. Schs., 1970-75; prin. Ohio Pub. Schs., 1975-80; tchr. St. Francis High Sch., Toledo, 1980-81; dir. curriculum Archdiocese Portland (Oreg.), 1981-82; dir. schs., 1982—; editor Cath. Sch. Adminstr. Mem. Ecumenical Ministries Oreg.; active Boy Scouts Am. Mem. Chief Adminstrs. Cath. Edn., Nat. Cath. Edn. Assn.; Assn. Supervision and Curriculum Devel. Republican. Home: 2820 SW Labbe Portland OR 47226 Office: Archdiocese of Portland 2838 E Burnside Portland OR 97214

SPARKS, IRVING ALAN, Biblical scholar, educator; b. Ft. Wayne, Ind., June 15, 1933; s. James Edwin and Isabelle Mildred S.; A.B., Davidson (N.C.) Coll., 1954; B.D., Union Theol. Sem., Richmond, Va., 1959; S.T.M., Lancaster (Pa.) Theol. Sem., 1960; Ph.D., Claremont (Calif.) Grad. Sch., 1970; m. Helen Daniels, Sept. 3, 1954; children—Lydia Isabelle, Leslie Bishop, Robin Alan. Lectr. philosophy and religion LaVerne (Calif.) Coll., 1965-69; asst. prof. religion Claremont Grad. Sch., 1970-74, asso. dir. Inst. Antiquity and Christianity, 1971-74; mem. faculty San Diego State U., 1974—, prof. religious studies, 1980—, chmn. dept. religious studies, 1983—, asso. dean grad. div. and research, 1974-83; founder/dir. Inst. Bibl. Studies, 1981—; cons. photog. archival conservation of Dead Sea Scrolls in Jerusalem, 1980; adv. bd. Inst. Antiquity and Christianity, 1974—; Disting. Vis. scholar James Madison U., 1982. Trustee, Claremont Collegiate Sch., 1970-75, pres., 1972-74; trustee, mem. exec. com. Ancient Bible Manuscript Center, 1981—; Fellow Lilly Found., 1964-65, Layne Found., 1965-66. Mem. Am. Soc. Papyrologists, Soc. Bibl. Lit. Author: The Pastoral Epistles: Introduction and Commentary, 1981; editor Studies and Documents; contbr. articles on papyrology and Bibl. studies to scholarly jours. Office: San Diego State Univ San Diego CA 92182

SPARKS, MILDRED THOMAS, educator; b. Montgomery, Ala., Oct. 2, 1943; d. Leon and Annie Lee (Johnson) Thomas; m. John H. Sparks, Aug. 29, 1964; children—Melanie J., Jennifer L., Regina F. B.S., Ala. State U., 1964; M.S., Pepperdine U., 1978. Cert. reading specialist. Tchr., Dayton (Ohio) Schs., 1964-66; tchr. Oxon Hill (Md.) Schs., 1966-70; technician Reading Lab., Grambling (La.) State U., 1972; reading lab. aide California City (Calif.) Schs., 1975; reading instr. Cerro Coso So. Outreach, Edwards AFB, Calif., 1976-78; substitute tchr. San Bernardino City Schs., 1979, Aquinas High Sch., San Bernardino, 1978-79; reading lab. tchr. San Bernardino High Sch., 1979; instr. reading lab. San Bernardino Valley Coll., 1980-81, assoc. prof. reading, 1981—. Mem. Calif. Tchrs. Assn., Nat. Council Tchrs. English, Assn. Supervision and Curriculum Devel., Western Coll. Reading Assn., Bus. and Profl. Women's Club, Delta Kappa Gamma, Alpha Kappa Alpha. Democrat. Roman Catholic (Norton lay lector). Home: 3355 Mirada Rd Highland CA 92346 Office: 701 S Mount Vernon St San Bernardino CA 92410

SPATAFORA, RON JAMES, avionics specialist; b. Neu-Isenberg, W.Ger., Sept. 24, 1951; came to U.S., 1952; s. James Roger and Elfriede (Krueger) S.; m. Katherine Ann Molnar, Dec. 31, 1978. Student in Elec. Engring., So. Ill. U., 1970; B.S. in Aircraft Maintenance Engring., Parks Coll., 1974; aircraft maintenance officer course USAF; lic. pilot and mechanic, FAA. Chief engr. L-K Electronics, Cahokia, Ill., 1972-74; service mgr. Mt. Hawley Aviation, Peoria, Ill., 1976-77; chief insp. and avionics supr. Am. Jet Aviation, St. Louis, 1977-78; avionics engr. Gates Learjet Corp., Tucson, 1979; avionics specialist Electrospace Systems Inc., Richardson, Tex., 1980—. Served to 1st lt. USAF, 1974-76. Mem. Arnold Air Soc., Air Force Assn., VTI Electronics Assn., Aircraft Owners and Pilots Assn. (Air Safety Found.), Internat. Omega Assn., Aircraft Maintenance Found. Club: ESI TRS-80 Mod III User. Office: 1601 Plano Rd Richardson TX 75081

SPAULDING, JOHN PIERSON, public relations executive, marine consultant; b. N.Y.C., June 25, 1917; s. Forrest Brisbine and Genevieve Anderson (Pierson) S.; m. Eleanor Rita Bonner, Aug. 18, 1947; children—Anne Spaulding Balzhiser, John F., Mary T.; m. 2d, Donna Alene Abrescia, May 15, 1966. Student Iowa State Coll., 1935-36, Grinnell Coll., 1936-38, U. Chgo., 1938-39. Reporter, Chgo. City News Bur., U.P.I., 1939-40; editor Cedar Falls (Iowa) Daily Record, 1940-41; picture editor Des Moines Register & Tribune, 1941-42, 47-50; pub. relations dir. Motor Club Iowa, Davenport, 1950-51; commd. 2d. lt. USAF, 1942, advanced through grades to maj., 1947, recalled, 1951, advanced through grades to lt. col.; ret., 1968; v.p. Vacations Hawaii, Honolulu, 1969-70; dir. pub. relations, mgr. pub. relations services Alexander & Balwin, Inc., Honolulu, 1970-76; mgr. community relations Matson Navigation Co., Honolulu, 1976-81. Pres., Econ. Devel. Assn., Skagit County, Wash., 1983—; pres. Anacortes (Wash.) Sch. Bd., 1982—; mem. Gov.'s Tourism Devel. Council, 1983—; mem. adv. com. State Ferry System, 1982—. Decorated Air medal. Mem. Pub. Relations Soc. Am. (pres. Hawaii chpt. 1974), Hawaii Communicators (pres. 1973), Nat. Def. Transp. Assn. (pres. Aloha chpt. 1980-81, Disting. Service award 1978-79), Air Force Assn., Anacortes C. of C., Sigma Delta Chi (life). Clubs: Propeller (pres. Port of Honolulu 1979-80), Honolulu Press, Fidelgo Yacht, Hawaii Yacht, Royal Hawaiian 400 Yacht (comdr. 1977-81), Rotary. Home: 6002 Sands Way Anacortes WA 98221

SPAULDING, WALTER GEOFFREY, botany and paleoecology educator, researcher; b. Fort Leavenworth, Kans., Feb. 21, 1950; s. Walter Lincoln and Georgette Marie-Therese (Biscarat) S.; B.A. in Anthropology, U. Ariz., Tucson, 1972, M.S., 1974, Ph.D. in Geoscis., 1981; m. Susan Mary Brower, Dec. 21, 1969; children—Walter Lincoln and Robert Scott (twins). Grad. research asst. Lab. Paleoenviron. Studies, U. Ariz., Tucson, 1972-79; research assoc. Coll. Forest Resources, U. Wash., Seattle, 1979-82, research asst. prof. dept. botany and Quaternary Research Ctr., 1982—. NSF research grantee in paleoecology, 1977-79; U.S. Geol. Survey research grantee in climate reconstrn. and prediction, 1979-82. Mem. AAAS, Am. Quarternary Assn., Am. Inst. Biol. Scis., Ariz.-Nev. Acad. Scis. Club: U. Wash. Faculty. Contbr. numerous articles and papers to profl. jours. Office: Quarternary Research Center AK-60 Univ Wash Seattle WA 98195

SPAYD, SARA ELIZABETH, food technologist, educator; b. Burgaw, N.C., Sept. 24, 1952; d. George William and Joanne Louise (Auchy) S.; B.S., N.C. State U., 1974; M.S., U. Ark., 1977, Ph.D. in Food Sci., 1980. Grad. research asst. dept. hort. food sci. U. Ark., Fayetteville, 1975-80; asst. food scientist Wash. State U., Prosser, 1980—. Mem. Inst. Food Technologists, Am. Soc. Hort. Sci., Am. Soc. Enologists, Internat. Soc. Hort. Sci., AAAS. Methodist. Contbr. articles to profl. jours. Office: Box 30 Irrigated Agr Research and Extension Center Prosser WA 99350

SPAZIANO, ROBERT ANTHONY, hospital administrator; b. Providence, R.I., Oct. 4, 1937; s. Domenico and Marie Elena (Baldassarre) S.; m. Eleanor Louise McGinn, Oct. 12, 1959; children—Donna Jean, Lori Ann, Denise Marie. B.S. in Bus. Adminstrn., U. R.I., 1963; postgrad. in edn. UCLA, 1966. Cert. tchr., Calif. Mgr. data processing Culver City (Calif.) Unified Sch. Dist., 1965-67; mgr. ops., Pasadena (Calif.) Unified Sch. Dist., 1967-69; gen. mgr. The Data Corp., Los Angeles, 1969-71; with Huntington Mem. Hosp., Pasadena, 1971—, dir. systems services 1971—; adj. faculty hosp. info. systems Calif. State U., Los Angeles, 1977—. Mem. adv. council Calif. State U., Los Angeles, 1980-82. Mem. Hosp. Info. Systems Sharing Group, Data Processing Mgmt. Assn., Assn. Systems Mgmt., Hosp. Mgmt. and Systems Soc. Contbr. articles to profl. jours. Office: 100 Congress St Pasadena CA 91105

SPEAR, ARTHUR S., toy and game executive; b. 1920. B. in Archtl. Engring., MIT, 1941. Prodn. engr. Artisan Metal Products, 1943-44; prodn. mgr., gen. mgr. Sperry Mfg. Co., 1945-56; plant mgr., gen. mgr. mfg. and distbn. and corp. ops. coordinator Revlon Inc., 1956-64; dir. distbn. Mattel Inc., Hawthorne, Calif., 1964, v.p. ops., 1965, exec. v.p. ops., 1966, pres., 1973, chief exec. officer, 1974, chmn. bd., chief exec. officer, 1978—, also dir. Office: Mattel Inc 5150 Rosecrans Ave Hawthorne CA 90250*

SPEAR, PAUL STANLEY, psychologist; b. Minot, N.D., July 26, 1941; s. Paul Edwin and Anna Louise (Meier) S.; m. Sara Armstrong, Apr. 3, 1970; children—Kimiko Victoria Bostwick, Paul Armstrong. B.A. in Psychology, Taylor U., Upland, Ind., 1963; postgrad. U. Wash., 1963-64; M.A. in Psychology, U. Wyo., 1965; Ph.D., U. Denver, 1968. Lectr., U. Denver, 1966-67; asst. prof. psychology San Diego State U., 1968-70; prof. psychology Calif. State U.-Chico, 1970—, chair Faculty Senate, 1982—; dir. Calif. Profs. for Early Childhood Edn., 1973-74, 77-81; cons. Head Start, 1966. Mem. vestry St. John's Episcopal Ch., Chico; pres. adv. bd. Chico Symphony, 1980-83. Mem. Am. Psychol. Assn., Western Psychol. Assn., Soc. Research in Child Devel. Contbr. articles to profl. jours. Office: Dept Psychology Calif State U Chico CA 95929

SPEARK, CHARLES JUNIOR, manufacturing company executive; b. Columbia City, Ind., July 23, 1933. S. Charles Albertson and Mina Rebecca (Windle) S.; m. Lora Ann Rice, Nov. 22, 1952; children—Veronica Ann, Charles Gregory, Frederick Joseph. Student Gen. Elec. Apprentice Sch., Ft. Wayne, Ind., 1951-55, Lincoln Elec. Welding for Supervision, Cleve., 1979. Field engr. Lab. Equipment Corp., Mooresville, Ind., 1969-72; plant engr. Gen. Tire & Rubber, Wabash, Ind., 1972-79; plant mgr. Kennedy Tank & Mfg., Indpls., 1979-80, Evans Steel & Mfg., Gilbert, Ariz., 1980-81; facilities supr. Honeywell Process Mgmt. Systems Div., Phoenix, 1981—; cons. elec. design; instr. computer and fluid power. Served with U.S. Army, 1955-61. Mem. Am. Mgmt. Assn., Fluid Power Soc. Clubs: Moose, Masons. Home: 2166 W Farmdale Mesa AZ 85202

SPECHT, EDWARD JAMES, mechanical engineer, electric company executive; b. Bklyn., Dec. 12, 1919; s. Augustus R. and Grace D. (O'Malley) S.; B.S. in Mech. Engring., Rensselaer Poly. Inst., 1941; m. Marguerite L. Yglesias, Feb. 5, 1949; children—Edward James, Marguerite L. Specht Tischler, Mary Kristopher, Sally Ann. With Gen. Electric Co., 1941—, applications engr., 1942-46, mgr. advanced propulsion system Western region, Los Angeles, 1959-68, mgr. aerospace and engines Western region, 1968-75; mgr. aerospace Western region, 1975—. Chmn. Los Angeles Opportunities Industry Adv. Council; mem. pres. engring. adv. bd. Loyola Marymount U., 1982—. Fellow Los Angeles Coll. Engrs.; asso. fellow AIAA (sect. chmn. 1959-60); mem. ASME, Am. Def. Preparedness Assn. (chmn. Los Angeles chpt. 1983), Navy League, Assn. U.S. Army, Air Force Assn., Pi Kappa Alpha. Republican. Clubs: Lakeside Country, Jonathan, Marina City. Developer jet engine applications. Home: 3710 Newhaven Rd Pasadena CA 91107 Office: 6151 W Century Blvd Los Angeles CA 90045

SPECTOR, WILLIAM IRVING, ophthalmologist; b. West Chester, Pa., Dec. 31, 1938; s. Samuel Stanley and Patricia Rosella (Rosenberg) S.; B.S., Dickinson Coll., 1960; M.D., Temple U., 1964; m. Marion Grace Taylor, Sept. 6, 1970; children—Kimberly Lynn, William Samuel, Billie Eileen. Intern, Bryn Mawr Hosp., 1964-65; resident U. Pa. Hosp., 1967-70; practice medicine specializing in ophthalmology, Carson City, Nev., 1970—. Served with USAF, 1965-67; Vietnam. Decorated Air medal. Diplomate Am. Bd. Ophthalmology. Fellow Am. Acad. Ophthalmology and Otolaryngology, Internat. Coll. Surgeons, A.C.S.; mem. AMA, Am. Assn. Ophthalmology, Contact Lens Soc. Am., Pan Am. Assn. Ophthalmology, Nev. State, Lahotan med. socs. Home: 13 W Sunset Way Carson City NV 89701 Office: 1208 N Carson St Carson City NV 89701

SPEED, JOHN WILLIAM, city official; b. Fresno, Calif., July 8, 1935; s. John Moody and Dorothy Ann (Lucas) S.; student Diablo Valley Coll., 1963-64, Contra Costa Coll., 1965-67, Solano Community Coll., 1968; m. Virginia H. Polk, Oct. 8, 1958; children—Dorothy Sue, Valorie Lynn, Lorilee. With Vallejo (Calif.) Fire Dept., 1961-71, 73-76, fire chief, 1973-76; fire chief Tracy (Calif.) Fire Dept., 1971-73; fire chief Aurora (Colo.) Fire Dept., 1976—; instr. fire sci. Solano Coll., 1968-75. Mem. adv. bd. Salvation Army, Aurora, 1976—. Served with USAF, 1952-61. Mem. Nat. Fire Protection Assn., Internat. Fire Chiefs Assn., Colo. State Fire Chiefs Assn., Met. Fire Chiefs Assn. Democrat. Episcopalian. Clubs: Masons, Shriners. Office: 1470 S Havana St Aurora CO 80012*

SPEER, DANIAL WAYNE, air force officer; b. Texas City, Tex., Aug. 25, 1953; s. Robert Houston and Azelle (Gray) S.; m. Grace Brown, June 14, 1975; children—Lindsay Koren, Nathan Daniel. B.S., U.S. Air Force Acad., 1975; M.B.A., U. Utah, 1982. Commd. 2d lt. U.S. Air Force, 1975; advanced through grades to capt., 1979; student navigator Mather AFB, Calif., 1975-76; navigator Little Rock AFB, Ark., 1976-80; instr. standardization-evaluation navigator Elmendorf AFB, Alaska, 1980—. Decorated Air Force Commendation medal. Mem. Air Force Assn. Republican. Baptist. Home: 948 Norman St Anchorage AK 99504 Office: 616 Mil Airlift Group Elmendorf AFB AK 99506

SPEIRS, ALFRED CLEVENGER, plastic and reconstructive surgeon; b. Runnemede, N.J., Oct. 27, 1933; s. Harold B. and Ethel (Clevenger) S.; m. Kathleen Hansen, May 15, 1970; children—Kristen, Jan, Glenn, Mary. B.A., Houghton Coll., 1955; M.D., Jefferson Med. Coll., 1959. Intern, Mary Hitchcock Meml. Hosp., Hanover, N.H., 1959-60; resident Butterworth Hosp., Grand Rapids, Mich., 1960-63, Henry Ford Hosp., Detroit, 1963-65; pvt. practice plastic and reconstructive surgery, Colorado Springs, Colo., 1965—; clin. instr. surgery U. Colo. Med. Sch.; cons. Air Force Acad. and Hosp., Colo. State Penitentiary, Fitzsimmons Gen. Hosp. Bd. dirs. Am. Cancer Soc., 1977-79; med. advisor Nat. Found. March of Dimes, 1966-70; bd. dirs. Colorado Springs Symphony, Fine Arts Council; founder, bd. dirs. El Paso County Horseman's Council. Fellow ACS; mem. Am. Soc. Plastic and Reconstructive Surgery, Am. Soc. Aesthetic Plastic Surgery, AMA, Colo. Med. Soc., El Paso County Med. Soc., Rocky Mountain Traumatologic Soc., Rocky Mountain Assn. Plastic Surgeons, Am. Cleft Palate Assn., Denver Acad. Surgery. Clubs: Broadmoor Golf, Garden of the Gods, El Paso. Contbr. articles to profl. jours. Office: 430 N Tejon St Colorado Springs CO 80901

SPELLMAN, DOUGLAS TOBY, media cons.; b. Bronx, N.Y., May 12, 1942; s. Sydney M. and Leah B. (Rosenberg) S.; B.S., Fairleigh Dickinson U., 1964; m. Ronni I. Epstein, Jan. 16, 1966; children—Laurel Nicole, Daren Scott. Media buyer Doyle, Dane, Bernbach, Inc., N.Y.C., 1965-67; media supr. Ogilvy & Mather, Inc., N.Y.C., 1967-69, media dir., Los Angeles, 1969-75; pres., chmn. bd. Douglas T. Spellman, Inc., Los Angeles, 1976—; guest lectr. sch. bus. UCLA, 1975, U. So. Calif., 1976. Served with U.S. Army Res. N.G., 1964-69. Mem. Aircraft Owners and Pilots Assn. Jewish. Clubs: Rolls Royce Owners, Mercedes Benz Am.

SPELLMAN, JOHN, governor Washington; b. Seattle, Dec. 29, 1926; B.S. in Polit. Sci., Seattle U., 1949; J.D., Georgetown U., 1953; LL.D., 1981; m. Lois E. Murphy; children—Margo, Bart, David, Jeffrey, Teresa, Katherine. Bar: Wash. bar, 1954. Practiced law, Seattle, 1954-67; elected 1st King County exec., Seattle, 1969-81, commr. King County, 1967-69; gov. State of Wash., Olympia, 1981—; v.p. Seattle-King County Econ. Devel. Council, 1972-73; chmn. King-Snohomish Manpower Consortium; chmn. Statewide Citizens Com. for Revenue Sharing; vice chmn. U.S. Coastal Zone Mgmt. Adv. Com., 1973-77; pres. Puget Sound Council of Govts., 1974-75. Chmn., Seattle Civil Service Commn., 1962-67; chmn. King County Library Bd., 1961-67; dir. Ch. Council of Greater Seattle, 1969-75. Served with USN., World War II. Recipient First Citizen of Arts award, 1980. Mem. Wash. State Bar Assn., Nat. Assn. Counties (1st v.p. 1980-81, dir., past pres. council of elected county execs., past chmn. crime and public safety com.), Nat. Govs. Assn. (chmn. task force export fin.; vice-chmn. com. internat. trade and fgn. relations), Nat. Agrl. Lands Project Adv. Com. (chmn.), Am. Legion. Republican. Roman Catholic. Office: Office of Gov Legis Bldg Olympia WA 98504*

SPELLMAN, JOHN DAVID, engineer; b. Beaver Dam, Wis., July 27, 1935; s. John Joseph and Elsie Marguerite (Schultz) S.; B.S. in Elec. Engring., U. Wis., 1959; m. Kathleen Burns King, May 26, 1972; stepchildren—Kathleen Olivier, Karen Silva, Kimberly Olivier. Jr. engr., part time, Malleable Iron Range Co., Beaver Dam, 1952-59; mem. tech. staff Rockwell Internat., Anaheim, Calif., 1961—, lead engr., 1969-78, 81—; cons. Data Processing, Santa Maria, Calif., 1965. Served to 1st lt. Signal Corps, AUS, 1959-61. Recipient U.S. Army Accomodation award, 1961, USAF Outstanding Achievement award for Civilian Personnel. Mem. Assn. Computing Machinery, Air Force Assn., Res. Officers Assn. Clubs: Birnam Wood Golf (Montecito, Calif.); Santa Maria Country. Contbr. publs. on minutemen data systems, PCM Telemetry systems. Home: 666 Meadowbrook Santa Maria CA 93455 Office: PO Box 5181 Vandenberg AFB CA 93437

SPELTZ, LEONARD JAMES, aerospace engr.; b. New Hampton, Iowa, Apr. 16, 1936; s. Bernard Joseph and Marie Ann (Mersch) S.; B.S. in Physics, Loras Coll., 1958; postgrad. U. Minn., 1960, U. Iowa, 1961, UCLA, 1963; m. Corrine Gladys Eide, Aug. 19, 1961; children—John, Christine, Michael, Daniel. Engr., Collins Radio Co., Burbank, Calif., 1960-61; mem. tech. staff Hughes Aircraft Co., Culver City, Calif., 1961-64; chief requirements engr. Gen. Dynamics-Convair, 1964-66; mgr. program devel. Space Communications div. TRW, Redondo Beach, Calif., 1966—. Pres., Jr. All Am. Football Assn., 1974-75; bd. dirs. Rolling Hills High Sch. Boosters, 1976-82. Mem. AIAA, IEEE, Assn. Old Crows, Air Force Assn., Armed Forces Communications and Electronics Assn. Republican. Roman Catholic. Home: 27413 Warrior Dr Rancho Palos Verdes CA 90274 Office: 1 Space Park Redondo Beach CA 90278

SPENCER, BETTY GAISFORD, writer, public relations specialist; b. American Fork, Utah, July 12, 1925; d. Charles Joseph and Nellie La Rue (Spratley) Gaisford; student Brigham Young U., 1970-73, Utah Tech. Coll., 1972-73, U. Utah, 1973-74, Utah State U., 1975; m. Lawrence W. Hansen, June 7, 1943 (div. 1948); 1 son, Larry J.; m. 2d, Ralph H. Spencer, Dec. 9, 1949; children—Brent Guy, Alan Charles, Marsha. With gen. offices Columbia Steel, Hansen Bros., Dr. W.W. Ricks, 1943-51; reporter, photographer, columnist The Daily Herald, American Fork (Utah) Citizen, 1962, 71; info. and tng. officer Utah State Tng. Sch., American Fork, 1972-74, dir. info. services, 1974-77; columnist, editorial writer, free lance mag. writer, 1968-79; public relations dir. Utah Pageant of the Arts, 1972-80, script writer, 1972—; public relations cons., 1968-79; contbg. editor Mountainwest Mag., 1975-79; editor six publs. fields of mental retardation and communications; dir. workshops in fields. Utah del. Nat. Arts for Handicapped Com., 1975-78; bd. dirs. Alliance of Arts Edn., Utah, 1975-78; mem. Miss American Fork Scholarship Com., 1966-71, American Fork Library Com., 1967-68. Winner first prize hist. article writing contest, 1976, various prizes for exhibits Utah State Fair; recipient service award American Fork City, 1972, citation State Forester, 1965, journalism Beehive award, 1974, 76, 78, profl. service award Mental Retardation Assn. Utah, 1978, writing awards Utah State Inst. Fine Arts, 1970, 73, other awards. Mem. Nat. Fedn. Press Women (recipient 17 awards for excellence in journalism, historian 1979-80, 81—, hon. mem. chmn. 1977-78), Utah Press Women (state pres. 1975-76, Utah Woman of Achievement 1973), League of Utah Writers (recipient 2 Gold Quills, pres. 1970-71), Utah State Poetry Soc., Nat. Writers Club, League Am. Pen Women, Utah State Hist. Soc., Am. Assn. Mental Retardation. Republican. Mormon. Co-author, producer documentary film: That Faraway Prize (winner four nat. awards including Best TV Documentary, Nat. Fedn. Press Women 1975); poetry included in Utah Sings, 1964, 74; contbr. articles to mags., regional and nat. publs. Home: 180 South 500 East American Fork UT 84003

SPENCER, CAROLINE M., fashion designer; b. Dallas, Nov. 22, 1932; d. Harold Austin and Anna M. (Grube) Spencer. B.F.A., Mpls. Coll. Art and Design, 1955; Profl. designation in bus. mgmt. UCLA, 1982. Guest fashion editor Mademoiselle Mag., 1955; designer Wonderalls, Mpls., 1958-62; sportswear designer Jr. House of Milw., 1962-63; sr. fashion designer, clothes and accessories Barbie Doll, Mattel Toys, Hawthorne, Calif., 1963—. Recipient Best Toy award Mattel Toys, 1973, 77. Mem. Fashion Group, Inc., Costume Soc. Am., Women at Mattel, Mattel Mgmt. Assn., Nat. Assn. Female Execs. Democrat. Roman Catholic. Club: Marina City (Marina Del Ray, Calif.). Home: 10316 Wilkins Ave Los Angeles CA 90024 Office: Mattel Toys 5150 Rosecrans Ave Hawthorne CA 90250

SPENCER, DOUGLAS LLOYD, chemist, manufacturers' representative; b. Berkeley, Calif., July 19, 1952; s. Alma Glenn and Anna Lea (Lloyd) S.; A.A., Diablo Valley Coll., 1971; B.S., Brigham Young U., 1974; m. Connie Jeanette Whitesel, Aug. 23, 1974; children—Jeanette Dawn, Jared Douglas, Jilissa Annette, Janine Marie. Lab. instr. chemistry dept. Brigham Young U., 1973-74; lab. asst., computer cons. Hartley Internat., Provo, Utah, 1974; research chemist Dow Chem. Western div., Pittsburg, Calif., 1975-80; pres. Sunset Distbg., Inc., Brentwood, Calif., 1980-82; pres. Maier & Assocs., Inc., Brentwood, 1982-83; pres. Doug Spencer & Assocs., Inc., Brentwood, 1983—. Mem. Brentwood Planning Commn., 1980-81; missionary, dist. zone leader Eastern States Mission, 1971-73. Rossmoor residents scholar, 1969-71, Brigham Young U. scholar, 1973-74. Mem. Nat. Eagle Scout Assn., Alpha Gamma Sigma (Calif. state treas. 1970). Republican. Mormon. Club: Liahona. Home: PO Box 427 Brentwood CA 94513 Office: 1203 Hwy 4 #6 Brentwood CA 94513

SPENCER, GORDON HALL, computer scientist; b. Orlando, Fla., s. Porter Newton and Beatrice Augusta (Scovell) S.; B.S., U. Rochester, 1957; Ph.D., 1963; m. Joan Anna Barringer, Aug. 3, 1963; children—Keith, Stacey. Co-founder, Sci. Calculations, Inc., Rochester, 1963; founder, v.p. Western Tech. Center, Santa Cruz, Calif., 1977—, also dir.; founder Soquel Systems Corp., Santa Cruz, 1983. Fellow Optical Soc. Am. (Adolph Lomb medal 1964); mem. Sigma Xi. Republican. Congregationalist. Home: 4150 Old San Jose Rd Santa Cruz CA 95065 Office: 4243 Capitola Rd Capitola CA 95010

SPENCER, JANET LEE, financial planner, family therapist; b. Woodward, Iowa, Aug. 1, 1935; d. L. Marvin and Mabel Miller (Schaal) Sturgeon; m. Gerre L. Spencer, June 9, 1956 (dec.); children—Kristen Petersen, Kimberly Spencer, David Spencer. B.S., Iowa State U., 1956; student Lewis Clark State Coll., U. Idaho; M.A., Whitworth Coll., 1980. Cert. mental health profl., Wash. High sch. tchr., dir. homemaker tng., 1956-69; community orgn. specialist Community Action Agy., Hillsboro, Oreg., 1969-70; children's protective services worker Dept. Social Health Services, Clarkston, Wash., 1970-75; tchr. Walla Walla Community Coll., 1974-80; family therapist, cons. Asotin County Mental Health Clinic, 1974-80; mktg. mgr. K. Foster & Assoc., Bellevue, Wash., 1980-83, Spencer & Assocs., Bellevue, 1983—; agy. cons., trainer in family therapy, Seattle, 1980—. Chmn. Lewiston Arts Festival, 1967-68; bd. dirs., sec. Orchards Swimming Pool Assn., 1967-69; leader Diamond L Club, 1967-69. Named Jr. Women's Club outstanding mem. Eastern region, 1968. Mem. Am. Personnel and Guidance Assn. Home: 17133 NE 5th Pl Bellevue WA 98008 Office: Spencer Assocs ONB Plaza Suite 312 Bellevue WA 98004

SPENCER, JOHN M., safety engineer; b. New Martinville, W. Va., May 14, 1950; s. Harrison J. and Frances L. (Askew) S.; m. Kathleen Ann Lafferty, July 7, 1972; 1 dau., Jennifer Kathleen. A.B. in Ed., Fairmont State Coll., 1972; M.S. in Safety Mgmt., W.Va. U., 1974. Safety supr. Kaiser Aluminum and Chemical Corp., Ravenswood, W.Va., 1974-77; div. safety engr. Ford Motor Co., Dearborn, Mich., 1977-81; supt. safety protection services and ins. Kaiser Aluminum and Chem. Corp., Spokane, Wash., 1981—. Mem. Am. Soc. Safety Engrs., Nat. Safety Council (exec. safety com.). Home: N 5416 Northwood Dr Spokane WA 99212 Office: PO Box 6217 Spokane WA 99207

SPENCER, JOHN RICHARD, lawyer, govt. ofcl.; b. Kansas City, Mo., Apr. 11, 1940; s. Paul Ripley and Teressa (Wagner) S.; B.B.A., U. Tex., 1964, LL.B., 1965; m. Joyce Ann Rhodenbaugh, Dec. 19, 1961; children—Stephen Myles, Kelly Lynn. Admitted to Tex. bar, 1965, Alaska bar, 1971, U.S. Supreme Ct. bar; assoc. Jarrard Cammack & Assos., Pasadena, Tex., 1965-66; post judge adv. Ft. Richardson, Alaska, 1967-70; city atty. City of Anchorage, 1971-75, exec. mgr., chief exec. officer municipality utilities, 1977-81; regional adminstr. EPA, Seattle, 1981-83; sr. v.p. Riedel Internat., Portland, Oreg., 1983—; v.p., gen. counsel RCA Alascom, Anchorage, 1975-77; pres. Anchorage Tire Center; trustee Alaska Elec. Health and Welfare and Pension Trust; past chmn. fed. regional council Seattle Fed. Exec. Bd. Former vice pres. Anchorage Retarded Childrens Assn.; former pres. Rehab. Industries Anchorage; former mem. Anchorage Police and Fire Retirement Bd.; chmn. energy com. Alaska Mcpl. League; former treas. Susitna Power Now, Inc.; chmn. bd. Olympics '92, Inc.; former state chmn. U.S. Olympic Com. Served with AUS, 1966-67; maj. Res. Decorated Army Commendation medal, Legion of Merit. Mem. Fed. (pres. Alaska chpt.), Am., Alaska, Tex. bar assns., Republican. Presbyterian. Clubs: Rotary, Newport Yacht, Anchorage Racquet. Contbr. articles to profl. jours. Home: 2920 Bluegrass West Linn OR 97068 Office: PO Box 3320 Portland OR 97208

SPENCER, JOHN WILLIAM, clin. neuropsychologist; b. Chgo., Oct. 23, 1940; s. Daniel Y. and Jean M. (Miller) S.; m. Patricia Yee, June 12, 1982. B.A., Drake U., 1965; M.A., U. Nebr., 1969, Ph.D., U. Okla., 1974. Chief neurophysiology div. behavioral scis. Nat. Naval Med. Center, Bethesda, Md., 1974-77; dir. outpatient mental health Gallup (N.Mex.) Indian Med. Center, 1978—; tchr. U. Okla., 1976. Loyola Coll., 1977, Johns Hopkins U., 1978, U. N.Mex., 1979. Served with USNR, 1958-61, 74-77. NIH research grantee, 1970; NIMH research grantee, 1975-77; U.S. Navy grantee, 1974-77. Mem. Southwestern Psychol. Assn., Am. Psychol. Assn., Undersea Biomed. Assn., Soc. Neurosci., Nat. Acad. Neuropsychologists. Democrat. Baptist. Contbr. articles to profl. jours. Home: 114 Fairway St Gallup NM 87301 Office: Gallup Indian Medical Center Gallup NM 87301

SPENCER, LEWIS NEAL, constrn. co. exec.; b. Lander, Wyo., May 9, 1923; s. Clyde Hudson and Mary Neal (McCann) S.; B.S., Oreg. State Coll., 1947; m. Mary Lucille Ikard, Nov. 25, 1949; children—Melissa, Mark. Engring. aide C.E., U.S. Army, Bonneville (Oreg.) Dam, 1947-48; city engr., Ontario, Oreg., 1948; with Morrison-Knudsen Co., Inc., 1948—, v.p., 1968-73; mgr. No. Constrn. Co. div., 1968-71, v.p. charge Canadian and European ops. 1971-72, v.p. charge internat. ops., 1972-73, exec. v.p. internat., Boise, Idaho, 1973—, also dir. Served with C.E., U.S. Army, 1943-46, 51-52. Mem. Asso. Gen. Contractors Am., The Beavers. Clubs: Arid, Hillcrest Country (Boise); Capilano Golf and Country (Vancouver, B.C., Can.); Internat. (Washington); World Trade (San Francisco). Home: 4330 Hillcrest Dr Boise ID 83705 Office: 1 Morrison-Knudsen Plaza Boise ID 83729

SPENCER, OTIS LEE, hosp. adminstr.; b. Opelika, Ala., Dec. 5, 1937; s. James and Addie Lena (Hugley) S.; B.S. in B.A., Roosevelt U., 1971; M.B.A., San Francisco State U., 1974; m. Shirley Ann Hadwiger, Oct. 27, 1962; children—Otis Lee, Serena A. Asst. adminstr. Naval Dispensary, Treasure Island, San Francisco, 1971-74; commd., U.S. Navy, 1955, ret., 1974; dir. materials Presbyn. Hosp. of Pacific Med. Ctr., San Francisco, 1974-76; asst. adminstr. St. Vincent Med. Center, Los Angeles, 1976-78; chief exec. officer/adminstr. Viewpark Community Hosp., Los Angeles, 1978-80; adminstr. Los Angeles New Hosp., 1980-81; asst. clinics adminstr. Kaiser Permanente, Harbor City, Calif., 1981—. Planning commr., San Bruno, Calif., 1975-77, chmn. environ. com., 1975-76; mem. Community Manpower Commn., San Mateo, Calif., 1974-75. Decorated Navy Commendation medal. Registered nurse, med. technologist. Mem. Health Care Execs. So. Calif. (treas. 1976-81), Am. Coll. Hosp. Adminstrs. Democrat. Club: Kiwanis. Home: 2072 Kinneloa Canyon Rd Pasadena CA 91107 Office: 25825 S Vermont Ave Harbor City CA 90710

SPENCER, ROGER KEITH, lawyer; b. N.Y.C., July 2, 1946; s. Martin and Ruth Edith (Weiss) S.; m. Barbara Natalie Kipnis, Jan. 31, 1977; children—William Cary, Elizabeth Ann. B.S., U. Mich., 1968; J.D., Northwestern U., 1976. Bar: Ariz. 1976, U.S. Dist. Ct. Ariz. 1976, U.S. Ct. Appeals (9th cir.) 1976, U.S. Supreme Ct. 1983. Mem. Ryley, Carlock & Ralston, Phoenix, 1976-78, Snell & Wilmer, Phoenix, 1978—, lectr. real property law. Mem. Phoenix Men's Symphony Guild, 1977-78, Men's Arts Council Phoenix Art Mus., 1983—. Served to capt. USAF, 1968-73. Mem. State Bar Ariz., Maricopa County Bar Assn., ABA (sect. corp., banking and bus. law, sect. real property, probate and trust law), U. Mich. Alumni Assn., Northwestern U. Alumni Assn. Club: Phoenix Sunrise Rotary. Contbr. articles to legal jours.

SPENCER, STEPHEN GREENE, accountant, consultant; b. Salt Lake City, Aug. 25, 1947; s. Orson Daniel and Phyllis (Greene) S.; m. Jill Brasher, Jan. 27, 1972; children—Stuart, Melissa, Stephanie, Stacey. B.S. in Acctg. cum laude, U. Utah, 1972. C.P.A., Utah. Acct./auditor Price, Waterhouse & Co., Los Angeles, 1972-74; controller C.R. England & Sons, Inc., Salt Lake City, 1974-78, 81-82; pvt. practice acctg., Salt Lake City, 1978-81; dir. acctg. Salt Lake County Govt., Salt Lake City, 1982—; fin. cons., acct. interstate trucking cos., 1976-82. Mem. Utah State Local Govt. Adv. Com.; del. Utah State Republican Conv., 1976. Served to capt. JAGC, USAR, 1970-76. Commerce Clearing House Fin. scholar, 1970; William C. Browning Endowment scholar, 1965-67. Mem. Am. Inst. C.P.A.s, Utah Assn. C.P.A.s (chmn. local govt. com.). Mormon. Club: Sigma Chi Alumni Assn. Home: 3245 McNeill Circle Sandy UT 84092 Office: 72 E 400 S Suite 400 Salt Lake City UT 84111

SPERAW, OLIVER W., state senator; b. Mpls., Mar. 26, 1921; s. Lester H. and Ione (Wagner) S.; ed. Long Beach City Coll., Los Angeles Trade Tech. Sch.; m. Carolyn S. Manuel, Feb. 21, 1980; children—Dan, Roger, Mike, Todd, Stephanie, Chris, Keri. Painter, carpenter, 1939-42; gen. contractor, 1946-55; salesman, then sales mgr., 1955-64; with Z Office Real Estate Co., 1964-72, Century 21, from 1972; tchr. real estate, 1957-69; mem. Calif. Senate, 1979—. Served with USAAF, 1942-45. Named Outstanding Young Man, City of Long Beach, 1953. Mem. Sales and Mktg. Execs. (pres.), Long Beach Bd. Realtors, Nat. Assn. Realtors, C. of C. Republican. Clubs: Lions; Internat. City; Northridge Country; Elks. Office: Room 5052 State Capitol Sacramento CA 95814*

SPERBER, HENRY, mfg. co. exec.; b. Poland, Mar. 4, 1933; s. Philip and Halina S.; m. Hannah Sperber, Sept. 29, 1956; children—Pennie, Nance, Debbie. Owner, pres. Andrex, Inc., Inc., Detroit, 1965-77; pres. Ark-Seal, Inc., Denver, 1981—. Home: 8 Red Fox Ln Englewood CO 80111 Office: 2185 S Jason Denver CO 80223

SPERBER, ZANWIL, psychologist; b. N.Y.C., Feb. 3, 1926; s. Martin and Dina (Baron) S.; m. Evelyn Wagner, Apr. 3, 1955; m. 2d, Merilee Oakes, Mar. 16, 1975; children—Rachel Shelly, Wendy, Benjamin, Mikko, Tali, Bjorn. B.S., CCNY, 1949; M.A., U. Mich., 1951, Ph.D., 1956. Diplomate Am. Bd. Profl. Psychology. VA trainee U. Mich., 1949-51, research asst., 1952-54, research assoc., 1954-55; instr. UCLA, 1955-57, asst. prof., 1957-58; research coordinator Children's Hosp., Phila., 1958-61, cons. USPHS Nat. Inst. Neurol. Diseases, 1959-61; chief psychologist dept. child psychiatry Cedar-Sinai Med. Ctr., Los Angeles, 1961-75, chief psychologist dept. psychiatry, 1975—, dir. clin. psychol. tng., 1974—; lectr. dept. psychology UCLA, 1961-81, clin. prof. psychology, 1981—. Served with USNR, 1944-46. USPHS predoctoral fellow, 1951-52; Merrill-Palmer fellow, 1951-52; recipient CCNY Ward medal in psychology, 1949. Fellow Am. Psychol. Assn. (pres. sect. clin. child psychology, div. clin. psychology), Am. Orthopsychiat. Assn.; mem. Am. Bd. Profl. Psychology (dirs. western region). Contbr. articles to profl. jours. Office: Dept Psychiatry Cedar-Sinai Med Ctr 8730 Alden Dr Los Angeles CA 90048

SPERRY, MARK, health care adminstr.; b. Mt. Vernon, N.Y., June 26, 1945; A.B., Rutgers U., 1968; M.P.H., U. Hawaii, 1972; m. Mary Jane Anderson, Aug. 17, 1969; children—Malia Elyse, Megan Noelani. Asst. dir. Health and Community Services Council of Hawaii, Honolulu, 1972-74; coordinator Lucy Henriques Med. Center, Kamuela, Hawaii, 1974-76, adminstr., 1977—; mem. Hawaii Subarea Health Planning Council, 1977-81; chmn. Hawaii County Emergency Med. Services Council, 1978-80, Waimea Sch. Adv. Council, 1980-81. Bd. dirs. Mental Health Assn. Hawaii, 1980—, Hawaii United Way, 1978—, Kamuela Montessori Sch. Served with U.S. Army, 1968-70. Mem. Am., Hawaii public health assns., Hosp. Assn. Hawaii, Am. Acad. Health Care Adminstrn., Med. Group Mgrs. Assn. Clubs: Exchange (pres. 1983-84), Jaycees (pres. 1975-80), Waimea Gymnastics (pres. 1983-84). Home: Box 938 Kamuela HI 96743 Office: Box 1108 Kamuela HI 96743

SPERRY, ROGER WOLCOTT, neurobiologist; b. Hartford, Conn., Aug. 20, 1913; s. Francis B. and Florence (Kraemer) S.; B.A., Oberlin Coll., 1935, M.A., 1937, D.Sc. (hon.), 1982; Ph.D., U. Chgo., 1941, D.Sc. (hon.), 1977; D.Sc. (hon.), Cambridge U., 1972, Kenyon Coll., 1979, Rockefeller U., 1980; m. Norma G. Deupree, Dec. 28, 1949; children—Glenn Tad, Janeth Hope. Research fellow Harvard and Yerkes Labs., 1941-46; asst. prof. anatomy U. Chgo., 1946-52; sect. chief Nat. Inst. Neurol. Diseases of NIH, also assn. prof. psychology U. Chgo., 1952-53; Hixon prof. psychobiology Calif. Inst. Tech., 1954—; research brain orgn. and neural mechanism. Recipient Oberlin Coll. Alumni citation,

1954; Howard Crosby Warren medal Soc. Exptl. Psychologists, 1969; Calif. Scientist of Year award Calif. Mus. Sci. and Industry, 1972; award Passano Found., 1973; Albert Lasker Basic Med. Research award, 1979; co-recipient William Thomas Wakeman Research award Nat. Paraplegia Found., 1972, Claude Bernard sci. journalism award, 1975, Nobel prize in physiology, 1981. Fellow AAAS, Am. Acad. Arts and Scis., Am. Psychol. Assn. (recipient Disting. Sci. Contbn. award 1971); mem. Royal Acad. (fgn. mem.), Nat. Acad. Scis., Am. Physiol. Soc., Am. Assn. Anatomists, Internat. Brain Research Orgn., Soc. for Study of Devel. and Growth, Psychonomic Soc., Am. Soc. Naturalists, Am. Zool. Soc., Soc. Developmental Biology, Am. Philos. Soc. (Lashley prize 1976), Am. Neurol. Assn. (hon.), Soc. for Neurosci. (Ralph Gerard award 1979), Internat. Soc. Devel. Biologists, AAUP, Pontifical Acad. Scis., Sigma Xi. Author: Science and Moral Priority, 1983. Contbr. articles to profl. jours., chpts. to books. Editorial bd. Exptl. Neurology, Exptl. Brain Research, Neuropsychologia, Internat. Jour. Neurosci., Behavioral Biology. Home: 3625 Lombardy Rd Pasadena CA 91107 Office: Calif Inst Tech 1201 E California St Pasadena CA 91125

SPEYER, RONALD JEFFREY, merger/acquisitions specialist; b. N.Y.C., Aug. 30, 1945; s. Walter L. and Hilda (Cannstatt) S.; B.A., Syracuse U., 1967; M.A., Columbia U., 1968; Ph.D., St. John's U., 1974; m. Ellen D. Vigman, July 3, 1968; children—Joshua A., Gabriel D. Pres., The Nexus Corp., Newport Beach, Calif., 1973-74; market mgr. W. R. Grace & Co., N.Y.C., 1974-76; exec. v.p. August Group, Newport Beach, 1976; exec. v.p. Calif. Leisure Products, Newport Beach, 1976-78; dir. merger/acquisition group Peterson, Diehl Speyer & Brown, Newport Beach, 1978—. Mem. Assn. Corp. Growth, Corp. Acquisitions and Mergers Affiliates. Office: Peterson Diehl & Co 102 Dove St Suite 570 Newport Beach CA 92660

SPIDELL, ROBERT A., pub. co. exec.; b. Andover, Maine, Nov. 12, 1933; s. Avard F. and Rena A. S.; B.A. in Econs., Long Beach State Coll., 1965; m. Janet Ann Murphy, Dec. 28, 1963; children—Robert, Susan, Jennifer, James. Pres., Spidell Pub., Inc., Anaheim, Calif., 1978—. Served with USMC, 1953-56. Mem. Inland Soc. Tax Cons. (pres. 1975-76), Nat. Soc. Public Accts., Nat. Assn. Enrolled Agts., Calif. C. of C., Orange County C. of C., Orange County Indsl. League, Newsletter Assn. Am., Alpha Kappa Psi.

SPIEGEL, ARTHUR HENRY, investment counsellor; b. Chgo., Nov. 18, 1908; s. Arthur Henry and Mae Spiegel; B.A., Dartmouth Coll., 1931; m. Eleanor Friedman, Jan. 1, 1937 (dec. Feb. 1968); children—Arthur Henry, III, Margaret Collister, Joseph F.; m. 2d, Elisabeth Mayer, Jan. 17, 1970. Sec., Walter Field Co., Chgo., 1931-48; partner Arthur Stuart Co., Albuquerque, 1949-62; cons. Naess and Thomas Co., Albuquerque, 1963-76, Fiduciary Trust Co. N.Y.C., 1977—. Bd. dirs. N.Mex. Council Crime and Delinquency, 1962—, chmn., 1962-64; chmn. Gov. N.Mex. Organized Crime Prevention Commn., 1972-77; bd. dirs. Presbyn. Hosp., Albuquerque, 1956—, vice chmn. hosp. found., 1969-78; chmn. Marion K. Van Devanter Fund drive, 1978-79; pres. United Fund Albuquerque, 1963-64; chmn. exec. com. Albuquerque June Music Festival, 1969—, Gov. N.Mex. Prayer Breakfast, 1971—; treas. Nat. Ghost Ranch Found., 1973—. Recipient award NCCJ, 1978, N.Mex. Disting. Pub. Service award, 1979, Law Day Liberty Bell award, 1981, Jefferson Day award, 1980, Disting. Humanitarian award Nat. Jewish Hosp. and Research Ctr. Nat. Asthma Ctr., 1982. Address: Box 1042 Albuquerque NM 87103

SPIEGELBERG, EMMA JO, educator; b. Mt. View, Wyo., Nov. 22, 1936; d. Joseph Clyde and Dorcas (Reese) Hatch; B.A. with honors, U. Wyo., 1958, postgrad. 1958—; m. James Walter Spiegelberg, June 22, 1957; children—William L., Emory Walter, Joseph John. Tchr. bus. edn. Laramie (Wyo.) High Sch., 1960-61, 65—, chmn. Bus. Edn. Dept., mgr. computer system, 1974—; cons. for VEDS program State Dept. Edn., Wyo., 1980-81; guest lectr. U. Wyo., summer, 1979; chmn. Gov.'s and State Supt.'s Task Force on Vocat. Edn., 1982-83. Bd. dirs. Cathedral Home for Children, Laramie, 1967-70, 72-81; precinct committeewoman, 1964-72; pres. Beitel PTA, 1965-66; 4-H leader, 1969-75; bd. dirs. Laramie Plains Mus., 1970-79; mem. Wyo. Telephone Consumer Panel, 1982-83. Named Wyo. Bus. Tchr. of Yr., 1982. Mem. Am. Vocat. Assn., Wyo. Vocat. Assn. (exec. bd. 1978-80, pres. 1981-82, Outstanding Contbns. to Vocat. Edn. award 1983), Nat. Bus. Edn. Assn., Mt. Plains Bus. Edn. Assn. (Wyo. rep.), Wyo. Bus. Edn. Assn. (pres. 1979-80), NEA, Wyo. Edn. Assn., Albany County Edn. Assn. (sec. 1970-71), Phi Delta Kappa, Alpha Delta Kappa (state pres. 1978-82), Chi Omega. Mem. United Ch. of Christ. Clubs: Zonta, Laramie Jr. Women's (pres. 1962-63). educator; b. Mt. View, Wyo., Nov. 22, 1936; d. Joseph Clyde and Dorcas (Reese) Hatch; B.A. with honors, U. Wyo., 1958, postgrad. 1958—; m. James Walter Spiegelberg, June 22, 1957; children—William L., Emory Walter, Joseph John. Tchr. bus. edn. Laramie (Wyo.) High Sch., 1960-61, 65—, chmn. Bus. Edn. Dept., mgr. computer system, 1974—; cons. for VEDS program State Dept. Edn., Wyo., 1980-81; guest lectr. U. Wyo., summer, 1979; chmn. Gov.'s and State Supt.'s Task Force on Vocat. Edn., 1982-83. Bd. dirs. Cathedral Home for Children, Laramie, 1967-70, 72-81; precinct committeewoman, 1964-72; pres. Beitel PTA, 1965-66; 4-H leader, 1969-75; bd. dirs. Laramie Plains Mus., 1970-79; mem. Wyo. Telephone Consumer Panel, 1982-83. Named Wyo. Bus. Tchr. of Yr., 1982. Mem. Am. Vocat. Assn., Wyo. Vocat. Assn. (exec. bd. 1978-80, pres. 1981-82, Outstanding Contbns. to Vocat. Edn. award 1983), Nat. Bus. Edn. Assn., Mt. Plains Bus. Edn. Assn. (Wyo. rep.), Wyo. Bus. Edn. Assn. (pres. 1979-80), NEA, Wyo. Edn. Assn., Albany County Edn. Assn. (sec. 1970-71), Phi Delta Kappa, Alpha Delta Kappa (state pres. 1978-82), Chi Omega. Mem. United Ch. of Christ. Clubs: Zonta, Laramie Jr. Women's (pres. 1962-63). Home: 3301 Grays Gables Laramie WY 82070 Office: 1275 N 11th St Laramie WY 82070

SPIES, HAROLD GLEN, anatomy and physiology educator, researcher; b. Mt. View, Okla., Mar. 30, 1934; s. Chester Charles and Tessie Elizabeth (Hawkins) S.; div.; children—Russell Lee, Terry Wayne. B.S., Okla. State U., 1956; M.S., U. Wis., 1957, Ph.D., 1959; NIH spl. fellow UCLA, 1966-67. Research asst. animal genetics and physiology U. Wis.-Madison, 1956-59; asst. prof. animal physiology Kans. State U., Manhattan, 1959-64, assoc. prof., 1964-66; research assoc. dept. anatomy UCLA, 1967-68; research assoc. Delta Regional Primate Research Ctr., New Orleans, 1968-72; assoc. prof. dept. anatomy Tulane U., New Orleans, 1968-72; chmn. reprodn. physiology Oreg. Regional Primate Research Ctr., Beaverton, 1972-82, assoc. dir. research, 1983—; prof. dept. anatomy Oreg. Health Sci. U., Portland, 1973—. Mem. Am. Physiol Soc., Endocrine Soc., Soc. Study of Reprodn. (dir. 1978-79, v.p. 1979-80, pres. 1980-81), Neurosci. Soc., Internat. Neuroendocrine Soc. Am. Assn. Anatomy, Soc. Study Exptl. Biol. Medicine, Am. Soc. Animal Sci., Sigma Xi, Phi Kappa Phi, Phi Eta Sigma, Alpha Zeta, Gamma Sigma Delta. Contbr. numerous articles to profl. jours.; mem. editorial bd. Biology of Reprodn., 1974-78, Endrocrinology, 1975-79. Office: Oregon Regional Primate Research Center 505 NW 185th Ave Beaverton OR 97006

SPIGAI, FRANCES DANA GAGE, online publishing co. exec.; b. Salina, Kans., Sept. 29, 1938; d. Francis Dana and Mina Lola (Jackson) Gage; B.S., CCNY, 1960; m. Edwin B. Parker, Dec. 28, 1976. Librarian, Union Carbide Co., Oak Ridge, 1961-62, L.N. Amax, N.Y.C., 1963-64; systems analyst Control Data Corp., Bethesda, Md., 1965-66; info. analyst Oreg. State System Higher Edn., Corvallis and Ashland, 1967-70, 73, 74-75; editor Advanced Tech./Libraries, Becker & Hayes, Calif. and Md., 1971-72; mktg. dir. Dialog Info. Services, Inc., Palo Alto, Calif., 1976-79; pres. Database Services, Los Altos, Calif., 1980—; instr. computer appreciation Linn Benton Community Coll., Oreg., 1973; cons. Info. Analysis and Mgmt. Assn. Oreg., 1970. Recipient Disting. Service award Nat. Micrographics Assn., 1976. Mem. Am. Soc. Info. Sci. (Appreciation cert. 1975), Info. Industry Assn., Spl. Libraries Assn., ALA. Author: (with Peter Sommers) Electronic Publishing-Opportunities in Online and Videotext Services, 1982; Invisible Medium, 1973. Contbr. articles to profl. lit. Office: Database Services Suite H 885 N San Antonio Rd Los Altos CA 94022

SPIGELMAN, AURI, physician; b. N.Y.C., Feb. 26, 1941; s. William and Rivka S.; B.A., B.H.L., Yeshiva Coll., 1962; M.D., U. So. Calif., 1967; m. Deena Sigler, Nov. 28, 1963; children—David, Shari Anne, Loren. Intern, Cedars-Sinai Med. Center, Los Angeles, 1967-68; resident in surgery Wadsworth VA Hosp., Los Angeles, 1968-70, Kaiser Found. Hosp., Los Angeles, 1970-72; preceptorship in vascular surgery, Long Beach, Calif., 1972-73; practice medicine specializing in vascular surgery, Beverly Hills, Calif., 1973-79, Los Angeles, 1979—; asst. clin. prof. surgery U. So. Calif. Sch. Medicine; mem. staff Cedars-Sinai Med. Center. Diplomate Am. Bd. Surgery, Nat. Bd. Med. Examiners. Fellow A.C.S.; mem. AMA, Calif. Med. Assn., Los Angeles County Med. Assn., Los Angeles Surg. Soc., Soc. Clin. Vascular Surgery, Internat. Cardiovascular Soc. Republican. Jewish. Office: 8631 W 3d St Suite 925 E Los Angeles CA 90048

SPILDIE, DUANE EUGENE, photographer; b. Bozeman, Mont., Mar. 6, 1955; s. Eugene Neil and Shirley Mae (Wright) S.; m. Theresa Raye Lane, Jan. 7, 1978; children—Michelle Lynn, Melissa Raye; B.S. in Film and TV Prodn., Mont. State U., 1977. Photographer, Baumgartner Weller Studio, Billings, Mont., 1978-79, Qualitone Studio, Rapid City, S.D., 1979-80; owner, photographer Foote Photography, Casper, Wyo., 1980—. Mem. Profl. Photographers Am., Wyo. Profl. Photographers Assn., Soc. Preservation and Encouragement of Barbershop Quartet Singing in Am. (treas. Casper). Baptist. Office: 1747 E 2d St Casper WY 82601

SPILLAR, PAUL VICTOR, management consultant; b. Prague, Czechoslovakia, Jan. 30, 1932; came to U.S. 1941; s. Charles V. Spillar and Margaret (Mandler) S; children—Charles, Catherine. M.B.A., Wharton Sch., U. Pa., 1954. Advt. and pub. relations dir. Baldwin-Lima, Hamilton, N.Y., 1957-60; asst. to pres., v.p., creative group head Ted Bates, Doyle, Dane Bernbach, Cunningham & Walsh Advt., N.Y.C., 1960-70; co-founder Sharp Communications, San Francisco, 1970-78; mgmt. cons., 1978—. Served with U.S. Army, 1955-57. Mem. Soc. Profl. Mgmt. Cons., Am. Mktg. Assn. (bd. dirs.), Aviation-Space Writers Assn., Futurist Soc. Republican. Presbyterian. Clubs: Penn, Milw. Athletic, Wharton. N.Am. editor Analisis (Mexican monthly); editor Indsl. Equipment News.

SPILLMAN, NANCY ZOE, economics educator; b. Chgo.; d. Leo and Sarah S.; student Los Angeles City Coll., 1958-61; B.S., U. So. Calif., 1963, M.B.A. magna cum laude, 1965; postgrad. Claremont U., 1966-68, UCLA, 1969-73. Faculty, Los Angeles Trade Tech. Coll., 1968—, now prof. econs.; pres. Econ. Edn. Enterprises, cons. firm; mem. Calif. State Atty. Gen.'s Subcom. Consumer Edn.; mem. consumer adv. council Fed. Res. Bd.; expert witness House subcom. on Consumer Affairs and Coinage; condr. radio program Consumer Mailbag, Sta. KJOI, Los Angeles. Bd. dirs. Consumer Credit Counselors, Los Angeles; sec. tax and pub. fin. sect. Town Hall of Calif.; mem. State of Calif. Retail Credit Adv. Com.; public mem. Calif. Beef Council. Recipient Freedoms Found. award, 1981. Mem. Am. Economic Assn., U.S. Metric Assn. (past nat. sec.), Calif. Bus. Edn. Assn., Community Coll. Social Sci. Assn., Am. Council Consumer Interests (editor Consumer Edn. Forum), U. So. Calif. M.B.A. Alumni Assn. (former editor alumni bull.). Editor: Consumers: Personal Planning Reader; author: Bright Ideas for Consumer Educators; Personal Finance Study Guide; series of consumer articles Glendale Fed. mag.; contbr. articles to profl. jours. Office: Los Angeles Trade Technical College 400 W Washington Blvd Los Angeles CA 90015

SPIRO, HERBERT TSVI, economist, educator, cons.; b. Germany, Feb. 1, 1927; s. George Josef and Antonie (Kaufmann) S.; m. Helen Goldstein, Aug. 19, 1952; children—Valerie, Carolyn, Neal. B.S. in Indsl. Engring., U. Pitts., 1952; M.S. in Indsl. Adminstrn., Carnegie-Mellon U., 1953; Ph.D. in Mgmt., UCLA, 1972. Fin. analyst Ford Motor Co., Detroit, 1953-55; sr. analyst Tech. Ops., Inc., Fort Monroe, Va., 1957-58; mgr. systems econs., Planning Research Corp., Los Angeles, 1958-62; mgr. comml. environ. McDonnell Douglas Corp., Santa Monica, Calif., 1962-69; prof. fin. Calif. State U.-Northridge, 1969—. Served with U.S. Army, 1955-57. Mem. Am. Econ. Assn., Western Fin. Assn., Inst. Mgmt. Scis., Am. Soc. Appraisers (sr.). Co-author: Automation and the Library of Congress, 1963; author: Financial Planning for the Independent Professional, 1978; Finance for the Nonfinancial Manager, 1982. Office: 18111 Nordhoff Northridge CA 91330

SPITALERI, VERNON ROSARIO, newspaper publisher, manufacturing company executive; b. Pelham, N.Y., Aug. 2, 1922; s. Rosario S. and Martha (Landerer) S.; m. Marjorie A. Ferrar, Oct. 14, 1952; children—Marc, Eric, Kris, Lynn. B.S., Carnegie Inst. Tech., 1942. Mgr. mech. dept. Am. Newspaper Pubs. Assn., N.Y.C., 1946-53; research dir., gen. adminstr. Miami Herald and Knight Newspapers (Fla.), 1953-57; chmn. bd., pres. Sta-Hi Corp., Newport Beach, Calif., 1957-74; chmn. bd. Sta-Hi Color Service, Sta-Hi Europe, Brussels, Concrete Floats-Huntington Engring. Corp., Huntington Beach, Calif.; editor, pub. Laguna Beach (Calif.) News-Post; pres. Laguna Pub. Co.; dir. Suburban Newspapers Am.; pres. Nat. Newspaper Found. Pres., Boys Club, Laguna Beach; mem. citizens adv. com. Laguna Beach; pres. Laguna Beach Library Bd., Laguna Coordinating Council; bd. dirs. Sta-Hi Found. Served to lt. comdr. USNR, 1942-46. Decorated Purple Heart. Mem. Am. Mgmt. Assn., Nat. Newspaper Assn. (dir.), Calif. Newspaper Pubs. Assn. (dir.), Laguna Beach C. of C. (dir.), Alpha Tau Omega. Republican. Roman Catholic. Club: Balboa Bay. Office: 23011 Moulton Pkwy Laguna Hills CA 92653

SPITZER, ALLAN THOMAS, retail shoe co. exec.; b. Honolulu, Aug. 31, 1955; s. Arthur Hoerman and Blanche Helen (van Oort) S.; B.A., U. Portland, 1977. With Standard Shoe Store Ltd., Honolulu, 1971—, v.p., sec., gen. mgr., 1977—, also dir. Mem. U.S. C. of C., Hawaii C. of C., Nat. Fedn. Ind. Bus., Hawaii Visitors Bur., Hawaii Employers Council. Republican. Roman Catholic. Clubs: Outrigger Canoe, Red Carpet. Home: 1422 Nanaloko Pl Kailua HI 96734 Office: Standard Shoe Store Ltd 2213 Ala Moana Center Honolulu HI 96814

SPITZER, MATTHEW L., retail store exec.; b. Pitts., June 20, 1929; s. Martin and Ruth G. S.; student U. Buffalo, 1948-50; children—Mark, Edward, Eric, Joseph. Product line mgr. Gen. Dynamics, Rochester, N.Y., 1962-67; dir. contracts Friden div. Singer, San Leandro, Calif., 1968-69; asst. v.p. Talcott Computer Leasing, San Francisco, 1970-71; pres. Spitzer Music Co., Inc., Hayward, Calif., 1972—. Clubs: Masons, Mensa. Office: 943 B St Hayward CA 94541

SPIVAK, JACQUE R., bank executive; b. San Francisco, Nov. 5, 1929; d. Robert Morris and Sadonia Clardine Breitstein; m. Herbert Spivak, Aug. 26, 1960; children—Susan, Donald, Joel, Sheri. B.S., U. So. Calif., 1949, M.S., 1950, M.B.A., 1959. Mgr. Internat. Escrow, Inc., Los Angeles, 1960-65, Greater Los Angeles Investment Co., 1965-75; mgr. escrow Transam. Title Ins. Co., Los Angeles, 1975-78; mgr. escrow, asst. v.p. Wells Fargo Bank, Beverly Hills, Calif., 1979-80; adminstr. escrow, v.p. 1st Pacific Bank, Beverly Hills, 1980—. Recipient awards PTA, Girl Scouts U.S.A., Jewish Fedn. Los Angeles, Hadassah. Mem. Calif. Escrow Assn., Nat. Assn. Bank Women, Inst. Trustees Sales officers. Republican. Jewish. Office: 469 N Canon Dr Beverly Hills CA 90210

SPIVEY, BILL GENE, state government official; b. Dale County, Ala., Sept. 9, 1937; s. Hollie W. and Blanche P. (Brannon) S.; m. Joan M. Bahnsen, July 18, 1975; children—Brenda, Janet, Brett, Ferrin, Hillorie, Paul. B.A. in Pre-Law, Carroll Coll., 1963; M.S. in Social Service Adminstrn., Ariz. State U., 1967. Counselor, Lewis & Clark County, Helena, Mont., 1965-66; reservation worker Sacaton Indian Reservation, Phoenix, 1966-67; assoc. prof. Mont. State U., Bozeman, 1969-74; staff devel. specialist State of Mont. Helena, 1968-75, chief staff devel. officer, 1975—; prof. U. Mont., Missoula, 1976—. Bd. dirs. Child Welfare League Am. Served to staff sgt. USAF, 1956-60. Ariz. State U. Mont. grantee, 1966-68. Club: Masons. Author: Basic Interviewing Skills, 1974; Education in Isolated Populations, 1977; Competency-Based Methods for Teaching, 1978; The Career Advancement Program—A System for Education in Rural Areas, 1978. Home: 1811 Winne Helena MT 59601 Office: PO Box 4210 Helena MT 59601

SPIVEY, BRUCE ELDON, health care company executive, physician; b. Cedar Rapids, Iowa, Aug. 29, 1934; s. William L. and Grace L. (Barber) S.; m. Nancy Howe, Mar. 31, 1956 (div.); children—Lisa L., Eric W. B.A. cum laude, Coe Coll., 1956, D.Sc. (hon.), 1980; M.D., U. Iowa, 1959, M.S., 1964; M.Ed., U. Ill., 1969. Diplomate Am. Bd. Ophthalmology. Intern Highland-Alameda County Hosp., Oakland, Calif., 1959-60; resident in medicine U. Iowa Hosps., Iowa City, 1960-64, research assoc. dept. ophthalmology Coll. Medicine, 1963-64, asst. prof., 1966-69, assoc. prof., 1969-71; prof., chief dept. ophthalmology Pacific Med. Ctr., San Francisco, 1971—, dean Sch. Med. Scis., Pacific Med. Ctr., U. Pacific, Stockton, San Francisco, 1971-76; pres. bd. trustees, chief exec. officer Pacific Med. Ctr. Inc., San Francisco, 1976—. Pres. bd. trustees, chief exec. officer, mem. exec. com. Presbyn. Hosp. of Pacific Med. Ctr., 1976—; bd. dirs. Pacific Coast Eye Found., 1976—, Pacific Vision Found., 1977—, Found. for Systematic Teaching of Continuing Edn. in Ophthalmology, 1977—, U.S.-China Ednl. Inst., 1978—; mem. Calif. Grad. Med. Edn. Adv. Com., 1980—; bd. dirs. Am. Bd. Ophthalmology, 1975—; v.p. Am. Bd. Med. Spltys., 1978-80, pres., 1980-82. Served as capt. U.S. Army, 1964-67; Vietnam. Decorated Bronze Star; recipient Disting. Service award Am. Acad. Ophthalmology and Otolarynology, 1972; Emile Javal Gold medal Internat. Contact Lens Council of Ophthalmology, 1982. Fellow ACS, Am. Acad. Ophthalmology (exec. v.p. 1978—); mem. Council of Med. Splty. Socs., Coordinating Council on Med. Edn. (chmn. 1980), Council for Med. Affairs (chmn. 1980-81), ACS, San Francisco Med. Soc., Calif. Med. Assn., AMA, Assn. Am. Med. Colls., Assn. for Research in Vision and Ophthalmology, Am. Ednl. Research Assn., AAAS, N.Y. Acad. Scis., Calif. Acad. Medicine, Assn. Univ. Profs. of Ophthalmology, Pacific Coast Oto-Ophthalmological Soc., Pan-Am. Assn. Ophthalmology, Am. Ophthal. Soc., San Francisco Opthalmol. Round Table, Societe Francaise d'Ophthalmologie, Academia Ophthalmologica Internationalis, Sociedad Peruana de Oftalmologia (hon.), Sociedad Chilena de Oftalmologia (hon.), Royal Australian Coll. Ophthalmologists (hon.). Clubs: Pacific-Union (San Francisco), University. Author: Report on a New School of Health Professions, 1975; editor; Educational Objectives and Evaluation I, 1970, II, 1971; Ophthalmology Study Guide for Medical Students, 1975; Ophthalmology Study Guide for Medical Students, 3d edition, 1978; mem. editorial bd. Western Jour. Medicine, 1979—; contbr. chpts., book prefaces, forwards to books; contbr. articles, book revs., editorials to profl. jours.; contbr., editor profl. conf. proc., lectr. profl. confs. Home: 1142 Filbert St San Francisco CA 94109 Office: Pacific Med Ctr 2340 Clay St San Francisco CA 94115

SPIWAK, ALAN MICHAEL, clin. psychologist; b. Jacksonville, Fla., June 25, 1954; s. Abe and Myrna (Zoslow) S.; m. Sheila Baran, Aug. 17, 1980. B.S. with honors, Tulane U., 1976; M.A. in Clin. Psychology, Calif. Sch. Profl. Psychology, 1979, Ph.D. in Clin. Psychology, 1982. Intern, Children's Baptist Home, Inglewood, Calif., 1977-78, Orange County Dept. Mental Health, Santa Ana, Calif., 1978-79, Ctr. for Legal Psychiatry, Santa Monica, Calif., 1979-80; intern in pediatric psychology UCLA, 1980-81; psychologist New Sch. for Child Devel., Van Nuys, Calif., 1981-82; condr. workshops. Mem. Am. Psychol. Assn., Western Psychol. Assn., Calif. Psychol. Assn. Jewish.

SPOOR, JAMES EDWARD, oil co. exec.; b. Rockford, Ill., Feb. 19, 1936; s. Frank Kendall and Genevieve Eileen (Johnson) S.; B.S. in Psychology, U. Ill., 1958; m. Nancy E. Carlson, Sept. 8, 1962; children—Sybll K., Kendall P., Andrea K., Marcie K. Personnel mgr. Nat. Sugar Refining Co., N.Y.C., 1960-64, Pepsico, Inc., N.Y.C., Auburn, N.Y., 1964-67; mgr. internat. personnel Control Data Corp., Mpls., 1967-75; v.p. personnel and employee relations Vetco, Inc., Ventura, Calif., 1975-79; v.p. employee relations Hamilton Bros. Oil Co., Denver, 1979—; cons., speaker on human resources. Mem. adv. bd. Salvation Army, 1978-79; chmn. Spl. Commn. for Ventura County Bd. Suprs., 1978; mem. task force on human resources Colo. Sch. Mines, 1983. Served with U.S. Army, 1958-60. Mem. Am. Soc. Personnel Adminstrn. (contbg. author handbook), Colo. Soc. Personnel Adminstrn. Republican. Episcopalian. Clubs: Denver, Masons, Shriners, Lions. Contbg. author: Am. Soc. Personnel Adminstrn. Personnel and Indsl. Relations Handbook. Office: 1600 Broadway Denver CO 80202

SPORCK, CHARLES E., electronic products manufacturing company executive; b. 1928. B.S. in Mech. Engring., Cornell U. With semiconductor div. Fairchild Camera and Instrument Co., 1949-67; pres., chief exec. officer Nat. Semiconductor Corp., Santa Clara, Calif., 1967—, also dir. Office: Nat Semiconductor Corp 2900 Semiconductor Dr Santa Clara CA 95051*

SPOTTISWOOD, DAVID JAMES, mineral engineer; b. Melbourne, Australia, Aug. 28, 1944; came to U.S., 1968; s. David C. and Mary (Walker) S.; B.E. in Chem. Engring., U. Melbourne, 1965; Ph.D. in Metall. Engring., Colo. Sch. Mines, 1970; m. Irene Griscti, July 5, 1973; children—Robert Alexander, Steven Kenneth. Chem. engr. C.S. Labs., Melbourne, Australia, 1965-66; asst. prof. mining engring. Queen's U., Can., 1970-75; asso. prof. metall. engring. Mich. Tech. U., Houghton, 1975-79; prof. metall. engring. Colo. Sch. Mines, Golden, 1979—; dir. Engring. Systems Research, Inc., Colo., 1980—; cons. in mineral industry, U.S., Can., Australia, India, S.Am.; vis. prof., Australia, Chile. Registered profl. engr., Ont. Mem. AIME, Australasian Inst. Mining and Metallurgy, Can. Inst. Mining and Metallurgy, Instrument Soc. Am., Fine Particle Soc., Am. Inst. Chem. Engrs., Sigma Xi. Author: (with E.G. Kelly) Introduction to Mineral Processing, 1982; contbr. articles to profl. jours.

SPRAGUE, PETER JULIAN, business executive; b. Detroit, Apr. 29, 1939; s. Julian K. and Helene (Coughlin) S.; student Yale, 1961, Mass. Inst. Tech., 1961, Columbia, 1962-66; m. Tjasa Krofta, Dec. 19, 1959; children—Carl, Steven, Kevin, Michael. Chmn. bd. dirs. Nat. Semiconductor Corp., Santa Clara, Calif.; chmn. Aston Martin Lagonda, Inc., N.Y.C.; dir. Pizzatime Theatre, Inc. Bd. dirs. Police Athletic League, Center for Entrepreneurial Mgmt.; trustee Strang Clinic, Boston Symphony Orch., Lenox Library Assn.; asso. Lehman Inst. Clubs: Yale, Marks. Office: Nat Semiconductor Corp 2900 Semiconductor Dr Santa Clara CA 95051

SPRAGUE, PHILLIP ROGER, security and personnel consultant, voice stress analysis researcher; b. Dallas, Sept. 23, 1946; s. Maurice Beranard and Frances Marie (Gieber) S. Student Sam Houston State U., 1971-73, Abilene Christian Coll., 1971-73. Cert. voice stress analyst instr.; lic. Tex. Bd. Pvt. Investigators and Security Agts. Investigator, Dallas Police Dept., 1966-73; spl. criminal investigator Dallas County Dist. Attys. Office, 1973-77; legal researcher, staff investigator Thomas Clayton and Timothy Finnical Law Firm, Dallas, 1977-78; owner, security cons. Law Enforcement Assocs. Am., Dallas, 1978—; indsl. security and personnel cons. Los Control Assocs. Inc., San Diego, Calif., 1979-82; owner, operator Profiles, San Diego, Calif., 1982—; cons. to law enforcement on voice stress analysis; trainer use of voice analyzer, personnel and security depts. Served with USAR, 1967-73. Mem. Internat. Soc. Stress Analysts, Fla. Polygraph and Stress Evaluators, Tex. Soc. Profl. Investigative and Analytical Hypnotists, Tex. Assn. Stress Analysts, Calif. Assn. Stress Analysts (dir.). Club: Harbor Lions of San Diego (1st v.p.), Harbor. Contbr. articles to newspapers; inventor Interviewer System for employee screening and psychol. testing. Office: 8322 Clairemont Mesa Blvd Suite 202 San Diego CA 92111

SPRAGUE, RICHARD THOMAS, environmental scientist; b. Detroit, Dec. 12, 1945; s. Walter S. and Eleanor Gail (Childs) S.; m. Donna M. Ferber, Oct. 10, 1981; children—Aaron, Benjamin. B.S., U. Mich., 1968; M.S., Mich. State U., 1977. Cert. profl. soil scientist. Environ. engr. Mich. Dept. Natural Resources, Lansing, 1977-81; environ. scientist, project mgr. Post Buckley, Schuh & Jernigan, Columbia, S.C. and Boulder, Colo., 1981—. Served with USAF, 1969-73. Mem. Water Pollution Control Fedn., Soil Sci. Soc. Am., Am. Soc. Agronomy, Nat. Assn. Environ. Profls., Sigma Xi. Contbr. articles to profl. publs. Office: PO Box 3157 Boulder CO 80307

SPRAINGS, VIOLET EVELYN, psychologist; b. Omaha, Aug. 1, 1930; d. Henry Elbert and Straunella (Hunter) S.; A.B., U. Calif., Berkeley, 1948, M.A., 1951, postgrad., 1960-64; Ph.D., U. San Francisco, 1982. Tchr., Oakland (Calif.) Public Schs., 1951-58; psychologist Med. Edn. Diagnostic Center, San Francisco, 1959-62; dir. psychol. edn. and lang. services Calif. Dept. Edn., 1963-71; asst. prof. San Francisco State U., 1964-71; assoc. prof. ednl. psychology Calif. State U., Hayward, 1971-79: dir. Lang. Assocs., Orinda, Lafayette and Redwood City, 1971-79; psychologist in pvt. practice, 1962—; dir. Western Women's Bank; mem. adv. bd. Bay Area Health Systems Agy.; instr. U. Calif., Berkeley extension, 1964—; mem. oral bd. for Ednl. Psychologists, 1972—; mem. adv. com. Foothill Jr. Coll. Dist. Recipient Phoebe Apperson Heart award San Francisco Examiner, 1968. Mem. Am. Psychol. Assn., Internat. Neuropsychol. Assn. (charter), Calif. Psychol. Assn., Calif. Assn. Sch. Psychologists and Psychometrists, Western Psychol. Assn., Nat. Council Negro Women, AAUP, Delta Sigma Theta, Psi Chi, Pi Lambda Theta. Contbr. articles to profl. jours. Home: 170 Glorietta Blvd Orinda CA 94563 Office: 3408 Deer Hill Rd Lafayette CA 94549

SPRAY, JOSEPH LAURENCE, lawyer; b. Los Angeles, Nov. 22, 1927; s. Joseph A. and Jean (Paine) S.; m. Vibber Zahle, Sept. 26, 1953; children—Nina, Stefanie. Student Lake Forest Coll., 1945-46; J.D., U. Calif.-Berkeley, 1951. Bar: Calif. 1952. Assoc., also ptnr. Spray Gould & Bowers, Los Angeles, 1952-66; ptnr. Archbald & Spray, Santa Barbara, Calif., 1966—; lectr. Com. on Continuing Edn. State Bar, 1958, 76, 77. Served with USNR, 1945-46. Mem. Legion Lex of U. So. Calif., 1962—; fellow Calif. Luth. Coll., Thousand Oaks, 1969—. Diplomate Am. Bd. Trial Advocates (pres. 1960). Fellow Internat. Acad. Trial Lawyers, Am. Coll. Trial Lawyers; mem. State Bar Calif. (chmn. adminstrv. com. for Santa Barbara County 1971-75; mem. pro tem disciplinary bd. 1976-78, referee State Bar Ct. 1978—), Internat. Assn. Ins. Counsel. Episcopalian. Clubs: Jonathan (Los Angeles); Santa Barbara, Coral Casino Beach and Cabana, La Cumbre Golf and Country, Masons (Santa Barbara). Office: 3944 State St Santa Barbara CA 93105

SPREITER, JOHN ROBERT, engineering educator; b. Oak Park, Minn., Oct. 23, 1921; s. Walter F. and Agda E. (Hokanson) S.; m. Brenda Owens, Aug. 7, 1953; children—Terry A., Janet L. Spreiter Adler, Christine P., Hilary M. B. Aero. Engring., U. Minn., 1943, M.S., Stanford U., 1947, Ph.D., 1954. Research scientist NASA Ames Aero. Lab., Moffett Field, Calif., 1943-58; with NASA Ames Research Ctr., Moffett Field, 1958-69, chief theoretical studies br., 1962-69; lectr. Stanford U., 1951-68, prof. applied mechanics, aeros. and astronautics, 1968—; cons. Nielsen Engring. and Research Inc., others. Served with USN, 1944-46. Recipient Achievement award NASA, 1979. Fellow AIAA, Royal Astron. Soc.; mem. Internat. Assn. Geomagnetism and Aeronomy, Am. Geophys. Union, Am. Phys. Soc., AAAS, Sigma Xi, Tau Beta Pi. Clubs: Fremont Hills Country (Los Altos Hills, Calif.); Saratoga (Calif.) Tennis. Contbr. articles to sci. and tech. publs. Home: 1250 Sandalwood Ln Los Altos CA 94022 Office: Div Applied Mechanics Durand Bldg Stanford U Stanford CA 94305

SPRINGER, BERNARD GEORGE, physicist; b. N.Y.C., Feb. 26, 1935; s. Abraham Jacob and Sarah (Tannenbaum) S.; B.A., U. Chgo., 1954, M.S., 1957, Ph.D., 1964; children—Matthew, Jessica. Nat. Acad. Scis.-NRC postdoctoral fellow, 1964-65; asst. prof. dept. physics U. So. Calif., 1966-69; with Hughes Aircraft Co., Culver City, Calif., 1969-72; mem. sr. staff Rand Corp., Santa Monica, Calif., 1972-82; pres. Policy & Technology, Inc., Los Angeles, 1982—. Nat. Lead fellow, 1961-62. Mem. Am. Phys. Soc. Office: PO Box 4637 Panorama City CA 91412

SPRINGER, CHARLES EDWARD, state supreme court justice; b. Reno, Nev., Feb. 20, 1928; s. Edward and Rose Kelly (Firth) S.; LL.B., Georgetown U., 1953; B.A., U. Nev., 1950; m. Jacqueline Sirkegian Springer, Mar. 17, 1951; 1 dau., Kelli Ann. Admitted to Nev. bar, 1953; pvt. practice law, 1954-80; atty. gen. State of Nev., 1962; master Juvenile Ct., Reno, 1973-80; justice Supreme Ct. of State of Nev., Reno, 1981—; faculty Nat. Coll. Juvenile Justice, 1978—, McGeorge Sch. Law, 1982—; lectr. Nat. Judicial Colls., 1979; instr. U. Nev., 1968, Truckee Meadows Community Coll., 1980. Dem. Nat. committeeman, Nev., 1962; chmn. Nev. Dem. Central Com., 1960-62; vice chmn. Western States Dem. Conf., 1961-62. Served with U.S. Army, 1945-47. Recipient Nat. Outstanding Service to Youth of Am. award, 1980, Nat. Council Juvenile and Family Ct. Judges; Outstanding Young Dem. in U.S. award, 1961. Mem. Nat. Coll. Juvenile Ct. Judges Assn. (pres. 1976-78), Nat. Council Juvenile and Family Ct. Judges (trustee 1982—), Am. Judicature Soc., ABA, D.C. Bar Assn., Internat. Assn. Youth Magistrates, Nat. Acad. Law and Sci. Club: Boys of Am. Office: Supreme Ct Bldg Capitol Complex Carson City NV 89710

SPRINGER, DONALD CAMPBELL, geologist; b. Grants Pass, Oreg., Mar. 9, 1925; s. Donald Leland and Luella Campbell S.; B.S., N.D. State U., Fargo, 1950; m. Joan Susan Springer Duckworth, Feb. 10, 1952; children—Diana Lee, Patricia Ann, Katharine Lynn. Mine and field geologist ASARCO, Wallace, Idaho, 1952-61; mgr. geology div. Bunker Hill Co., Kellogg, Idaho, 1961-69, geologic cons., Osburn, Idaho, 1969—. Pres., Coeur d'Alene Mining Dist. Mus., 1970—; city councilman, Osburn, Idaho, 1960-72; commr. Shoshone County Planning and Zoning, Wallace, Idaho, 1967-82. Served with U.S. Army, 1943-45, 50-51; ETO. Mem. Soc. Econ. Geologists, AIME, Idaho Assn. Profl. Geologists, Idaho Bd. Profl. Geologists (chmn.). Republican. Club: Elks. Home and Office: 116 W Fir Ave Osburn ID 83849

SPRINGER, KIRK WILLIAM, dentist; b. Ottumwa, Iowa, July 17, 1922; s. James Madison and Lucile Evelyn (Kirkhart) S.; student U. Puget Sound, 1953-57; D.D.S., U. Wash., 1961; m. Alameda Verna Ayers, Aug. 25, 1944; children—Alvin Joseph, Pamela Joyce, Richard Lawrence. Practice dentistry, Edmonds, Wash., 1961—. Mem. Wash. Acad. Gen. Dentistry (recipient Outstanding Service award 1975-76, pres. 1980-81), Fedn. Dentaire Internationale, Am., Wash. dental assns., Am. Soc. Dentistry for Children, Wash. Soc. Dentistry for Children (pres. 1973, exec. sec. 1974—), Chgo. Dental Soc. Clubs: Lions, Elks, Edmonds Yacht, Mason. Editor Wash. Acad. Gen. Dentistry bull., 1970—.

SPRINGER, ROBERT JOHN, educator; b. Chgo., Oct. 21, 1931; s. John Francis and Helen Monica (Mlodzikowski) S.; student Christian Bros. Coll., Memphis, 1955-57; B.S. cum laude, St. Louis U., 1959; M.A. in Spl. Edn., Calif. State U., Los Angeles, 1964; M.A. in Adminstrn. and Supervision, Calif. State U., Northridge, 1967; m. Mary Patricia Ryan, July 1, 1961; children—Martin Bernard, Robert Thomas. Prof. div. continuing edn. Pasadena City Coll., 1970-75, Ambassador Coll., 1979—; tchr. deaf Pasadena Unified Sch. Dist., 1962-79, chmn. dept. deaf edn., 1964-79; lectr. Calif. State U., Los Angeles; tchr. sign lang. and lipreading Culver City (Calif.) Adult Sch., 1979—; instr. sign lang. Dominguez Valley Hosp., Compton, Calif., 1981—, Calif. State U., Dominguez Hills, 1980—; founder, pres. co. offering services to handicapped. Served with USN, 1951-55. Cert. Council on Edn. of Deaf, Conv. of Am. Instrs. of Deaf. Mem. Nat. Assn. of Deaf, Pasadena Edn. Assn., Calif. Tchrs. Assn., NEA, Registry Interpreters for Deaf, So. Calif. Registry Interpreters for Deaf, Calif. Assn. Tchrs. Deaf and Hard of Hearing Children, Center for Living Independently in Pasadena, Advocates of Quiet Minority, Internat. Assn. Parents of Deaf, Nat. Leadership Tng. Program Alumni Assn., Greater Los Angeles Area Council on Deafness, Psi Chi. Republican. Roman Catholic. Office: PO Box 1417 San Gabriel CA 91778

SPRINGMEYER, ROBERT LAWRENCE, JR., management consultant; b. Provo, Utah, July 1, 1943; s. Robert Lawrence and Venice Springmeyer; B.S. in Polit. Sci., U. Utah, 1966, cert. internat. relations, 1966, B.S. in Econs., 1967; m. Gwen Rowley, Oct. 18, 1978; children—Jonathan Lawrence, Robert Koller, William Rowley, Elizabeth Rowley. Project dir. S.U.A. div. Dillingham Corp., Beverly Hills, Calif., 1967-70; cons. Booz, Allen & Hamilton, San Francisco, 1970-71; dir. Region XII Law Enforcement Planning Agy., Salt Lake City, 1971-76; prin. Bonneville Research, Salt Lake City, 1976—, Springmeyer & Assos., Salt Lake City, 1976—. Mem. com. on emergency med. services Utah Med. Soc., 1973-76; mem. adv. bd. Salt Lake County Sheriff's Merit Commn., 1974-76; mem. Task Force on Shelter Care Standards, Salt Lake City, 1974; chmn. planning and evaluation com. Community Services Council, Salt Lake City, 1974; pres. Citizen's Com. for Utah Cts., 1975; chmn. Salt Lake County Commn. on Youth, 1975; mem. higher edn., govt., industry com. U. Utah; active Democratic Party of Utah, voting dist. chair-del., 1976-78; candidate Salt Lake County Commn., 1976; mem. Parley's Park Com., 1976—; bd. dirs. Utah chpt. Common Cause, 1981—; mem. public affairs bd. Utah Planned Parenthood; bd. dirs. Utah chpt. Internat. Visitors Council, 1981, v.p., 1982—; treas. Utah Health Care Cost Found., 1982—; chmn. Salt Lake Sister Cities Com., 1981—. Served with U.S. Army, 1968. Named to Outstanding Young Men in Am., U.S. Jaycees, 1978; named Chmn. of Yr. for Project of Yr., Salt Lake Jaycees, 1978; recipient Liberty Bell award Utah State Bar, 1980. Mem. Am. Soc. Public Adminstrn., Public Relations Soc. Am., Salt Lake Area C. of C., Tenn. Squires. Mormon. Clubs: Rotary, Alpenbock Mountain (v.p.). Home: 1289 4th Ave Salt Lake City UT 84103 Office: 50 S Main Salt Lake City UT 84101

SPRINKEL, WARREN REED, contractor; b. Los Angeles, June 30, 1922; s. Walter Reed and Florence (Werdin) S.; B.S., U. So. Calif., 1946; m. Rita Lorentze Indrebo, Aug. 12, 1978; children—Steven, Annette, Susan. Pres., Vernon Asphalt Constructors, Fontana, Calif., 1967-80; pres., chief exec. officer Fontana Paving, Inc., 1956—. Chmn. Contractors' Calif. State License Bd., 1973-74; del. Republican Nat. Conv., 1972, 76. Served with USAF, 1943-52. Decorated D.F.C. Mem. Asso. Gen. Contractors Calif., Am. Road and Transp. Builders Assn. Presbyterian. Clubs: Rotary, Lincoln. Home: 1026 Santiago Dr Newport Beach CA 92660 Office: PO Box 947 Fontana CA 92335

SPRINKLE, RONALD LEO, psychologist, educator; b. Rocky Ford, Colo., Aug. 31, 1930; s. Rex Houston and Annas Martha (Dodson) S.; m. Marilyn Joan Nelson, June 7, 1952; children—Nelson, Eric, Matthew, Kristen. B.A., U. Colo., 1952, M.Personnel Service, 1956; Ph.D., U. Mo., 1961. Lic. psychologist, Wyo. Instr., counselor, dir. Stephens Coll., Columbia, Mo., 1956-61; asst. prof. psychology U. N.D., Grand Forks, 1961-64, dir. counseling ctr., 1963-64; assoc. prof. guidance U. Wyo., Laramie, 1964-65, asst. prof. psychology, 1965-67, assoc. prof. psychology, 1967-70, dir. counseling and testing, 1970-82, psychologist, prof. counseling and testing, 1983—. Served with U.S. Army, 1952-54. Mem. AAAS, Am. Psychol. Assn. (former mem. edn. and tng. bd. Div. 30), Am. Soc. Clin. Hypnosis, Am. Soc. Psychical Research. Contbr. articles to profl. jours. Home: 1425 Steele St Laramie WY 82070 Office: Box 3708 U Wyo Laramie WY 82071

SPROGER, STEVEN ROBERT, social worker; b. Los Angeles, Nov. 8, 1941; s. Jack and Sydelle (Rosenthal) S.; A.A., Mt. San Antonio Coll., 1961; B.A., Calif. State Coll., Los Angeles, 1963; M.S.W., U. So. Calif., 1979; 1 dau., Miriam Ingrid. Supr. child welfare dept. social services County of Los Angeles, West Covina, Calif., 1963-64, 67-68, 69, 71-71; social worker Boys and Girls Aide Soc., Spring Valley, Calif., 1971-73; state hosp. liaison unit leader San Diego Regional Center, 1973-80, intake supr., 1980—. Served with U.S. Army, 1964-67. Lic. clin. social worker, Calif. Mem. Am. Assn. Mental Deficiency (regional treas.), ACLU. Author: Happiness is a Good Home, Guidelines for Community Care, Misunderstanding Deinstitutionalization; contbr. articles to profl. publs. Office: 4355 Ruffin Rd San Diego CA 92123

SPROUL, JOHN ALLAN, public utility executive; b. Oakland, Calif., Mar. 28, 1924; s. Robert Gordon and Ida Amelia (Wittschen) S.; A.B., U. Calif., Berkeley, 1947, LL.B., 1949; m. Marjorie Ann Hauck, June 20, 1945; children—John Allan, Malcolm J., Richard O., Catherine E. Admitted to Calif. bar, 1950; atty. Pacific Gas & Electric Co., San Francisco, 1949-52, 56-62, sr. atty., 1962-70, asst. gen. counsel, 1970-71, v.p. gas supply, 1971-76, sr. v.p., 1976-77, exec. v.p., 1977—; gen. counsel Pacific Gas Transmission Co., 1970-73, v.p., 1973-79, chmn. bd., 1979—, also chief exec. officer, dir.; atty. firm Johnson & Stanton, San Francisco, 1952-56; chmn. bd., dir. Natural Gas Corp. Calif.; dir. Alta. and So. Gas Co. Ltd.; Alta. Natural Gas Co. Ltd., Angus Chem. Co., Angus Petrotech Corp. Served to 1st lt. USAAF, 1943-46. Mem. Calif. Bar Assn., Am. Gas Assn., Pacific Coast Gas Assn. Clubs: Engineers, World Trade (San Francisco), Commonwealth, Bohemian, Pacific-Union, Orinda Country. Office: 77 Beale St San Francisco CA 94100

SPURGIN, ROBERT ANDREAS, hazardous material transport and disposal co. exec.; b. Santa Monica, Calif., Feb. 13, 1954; s. Herbert Andreas and Vivian Claire (Bradley) S.; B.B.A., Calif. Poly. State U., San Luis Obispo, 1976; M.B.A., Calif. State U., Fullerton, 1981; m. Nanci Ellen Myers, Aug. 20, 1976; 1 son, Christopher Charles. Loan counselor Glendale Fed. Savs. & Loan, Long Beach, Calif., 1976-77; asst. mgr. W. D. Bingham Inc., Huntington Beach, Calif., 1977, service mgr., 1977-78, v.p., 1980-82, exec. v.p., 1982—; cons. mktg., fin. Sustaining mem. Santa Monica Sister City Assn., 1968-76. Republican. Christian. Home: 36 Winterbranch St Irvine CA 92714 Office: 5140 Birch St Newport Beach CA 92660

SQUAIR, JEAN MARIE, ednl. adminstr.; b. Vancouver, B.C., Can., Jan. 19, 1925; came to U.S., 1943; d. Alfred Ernest and Bertha Edith (Bailey) Hall; student Stanford U., 1943-47, Boston U., 1964-65, U. Calif., Berkeley, 1965-68; m. Stuart Davidson Squair, Feb. 14, 1948; children—Roslyn Marie, Elizabeth Ann. Mgr., Oakland (Calif.) Symphony Chorus, 1963-70; dir. vol. services Goodwill Industries, Oakland, 1970-80; professorial lectr., dir. Grad. Sch. Arts Adminstrn., Golden Gate U., San Francisco, 1976—. Bd. govs. San Francisco Symphony, 1976-81; bd. dirs. San Francisco Opera Western Opera Theater, 1970-78; trustee Calif. Hist. Soc., 1970-76; co-chmn. Piedmont Arts Festival, 1970-78; pres. San Francisco Symphony League, 1973-76. Recipient Disting. Service award Oakland Symphony, 1966; award Nat. Aux. to Goodwill Industries, 1978. Mem. Assn. Arts Adminstrn. Educators (dir.), Assn. Calif. Symphony Orchs. (founding pres.), Am. Symphony Orch. League (mem. vol. council bd.). Home: 6001 Acacia Ave Oakland CA 94618 Office: 536 Mission St San Francisco CA 94105

SQUIBB, JOHN FRANKLIN, educator; b. Zanesville, Ohio, Feb. 21, 1931; s. Robert William and Clarice Berthel (Stiles) S.; m. Brenda Carol, Dec. 1981; 1 son, John Franklin; stepchildren—Calvin Russell, Kenneth Zane. Student Ariz. State U., 1950-52, B.A. in Edn. and Earth Sci., 1955, M.A., 1960; student Ohio U., 1952-54, U. N.Mex., 1954; postgrad. Mexicano-Norte Americano, 1960, U. Redlands, 1963, No. Ariz. U., 1965, 66, U. Nev., 1969, Ariz. State U., 1970, Pepperdine U., Brigham Young U., N.Mex. Mining Inst. With juvenile detail Maricopa County Juvenile Dept., Phoenix, 1952; tchr. Wilson Skiff Sch. Dist., Phoenix, 1956-59, Washington-Cortex high schs., Glendale, Ariz., 1959-61; tchr. Needles (Calif.) Sch., 1961—; also tchr. San Bernardino Valley Coll.; lectr. geology Mohave Community Coll., Lake Havasu, Bullhead City, Ariz.; dir. Environ. Sci. Research Center, Environ. Sci. Research Assos., Squibb Ecotopics; pres. Squibb Enterprises of Needles; reporter Colorado River News Bull., Mojave Valley, Ariz., 1963, Desert Star, 1964—. Cons., earth scientist on geography and geology of local region, geoenvironmental aspects Mohave Valley. Commr., Needles Park and Recreation Dept., 1966-68; commr. Needles Utility Bd., co-chmn., 1971-74, chmn., 1974-76; mem. Needles City Council, 1978-80; v.p. Needles chpt. ARC, 1966-68; explorer coordinator Boy Scouts Am., 1972-74. Bd. dirs. Needles chpt. San Bernardino County Mus. Assn. Recipient Thomas J. Croaff award Ariz. State U., 1952; NSF scholar, 1970. Mem. Nat., Calif. tchrs. assn., Nat. Assn. Geology Tchrs., Ariz. Acad. Sci. (charter), Archaeol. Soc. So. Calif., Sigma Phi Epsilon. Research, publs. on geology, geography; geology columnist Desert Star. Home: 2001 Flora Vista Needles CA 92363 Office: Needles CA 92363 also 2716 Martin Rd Zanesville OH 43701

SRIGLEY, CONNIE LEE, beverage co. mgr.; b. Lansing, Mich., Feb. 2, 1943; d. Theron Kingsley and Leolyn Lorena (Scheurer) Slade; B.A. in English Edn., Mich. State U., 1964; profl. designation in personnel mgmt. UCLA Extension, 1980; m. William Richard Srigley, Apr. 3, 1965; children—Karen Marie, Teresa Rochelle. Personnel asst. Coldwell, Banker & Co., Los Angeles, 1969-70; personnel interviewer City Nat. Bank, Beverly Hills, Calif., 1972-73; personnel asst. Products Research & Chem. Corp., Glendale, Calif., 1973-75; employment rep. Metro-Goldwyn-Mayer Inc., Culver City, Calif., 1975-80; employment mgr. Seven-Up Bottling Co. So. Calif., Vernon, 1980-81, employee relations mgr., 1981—. Mem. Personnel and Indsl. Relations Assn., NOW, AAUW. Office: 3220 E 26th St Vernon CA 90023

SRIGLEY, WILLIAM RICHARD, pharm. co. ofcl.; b. Grosse Pointe, Mich., Nov. 5, 1941; s. William Neil and Jeanne Claire (McCallum) S.; B.S. in Physiology, Mich. State U., 1963; postgrad. Wayne State U., 1964-65, U. So. Calif., 1969-71; m. Connie Lee Slade, Apr. 3, 1965; children—Karen, Rochelle. Biologist, prodn. supr. Parke Davis & Co., Detroit, 1965-68; filling supr. Hyland div. Travenol Labs., Los Angeles, 1968-70, packaging mgr., 1970-71, prodn. mgr., 1971-73, asst. plant mgr., 1973-75, quality assurance mgr., 1975-76, asst. to dir. regulatory affairs, 1976-78, asst. to pres., 1978-79, mgr. field ops., 1979-81, dir. quality control, 1982—. Mem. Pharm. Mfrs. Assn., Parenteral Drug Assn. Office: 4501 Colorado St Los Angeles CA 90039

SRIVASTAVA, JAYA NIDHI, educator; b. Lucknow, India, June 20, 1933; d. Mahabir Prasad and Madhuri (Devi) S.; M. Math. Stats., U. Lucknow, 1954; Statistician's diploma Indian Statis. Inst., Calcutta, 1958; Ph.D., U. N.C., 1961. Came to U.S., 1959, naturalized, 1966. Agrl. statistician in India, 1954-59; research asso. U. N.C., 1961-63; asso. prof. U. Nebr., 1963-66; prof. math. stats. Colo. State U., Ft. Collins, 1966—, chmn. Disting. Vis. Lectr.'s Program in Stats., U.S.A. and Can., 1973-75; organizer, dir. Internat. Symposium on Combinatorial Math., 1971, 78; organizer, dir. Internat. Symposium Statis. Design and Linear Models, 1973; vis. prof. many instns., worldwide. Fellow Am. Statis. Assn., Inst. Math. Stats. (mem. memls. com.); mem. Forum for Interdisciplinary Math. (v.p. 1975-79), Indian Soc. Agrl. and Biol. Stats. (pres. 1977, prize excellence in research 1960), Internat., Indian statis. insts., Biometric Soc., Bernoulli Soc. for Stats. and Probability, N.Y. Acad. Scis. Author: (with S.N. Roy and R. Gnanadesikan) Analysis and Design of Certain Quantitative Multiresponse Experiments, 1971. Co-editor: Survey of Combinatorial Theory, 1973; editor: Survey of Statistical Design and Linear Models, 1974. Mem. editorial bd. Advances in Mgmt. Sci., Jour. Organizational Behavior and Stats., Jour. Info., Combinatorics and Systems Sci., Communications in Stats., Jour. Indian Soc. Agrl. Stats., Jour. Multivariate Analysis, Jour. Combinatorics, Info. and Systems Sci.; chief editor Jour. Statis. Planning and Inference; I.M.S. Tables Com. Contbr. articles to profl. jours. Home: 1318 Hillside Dr Fort Collins CO 80521 Office: Dept Statistics Colo State U Fort Collins CO 80523

STAAB, JOSEPH RAYMOND, govt. ofcl.; b. Hays, Kans., Jan. 2, 1932; s. Joseph Leo and Esther Isea (Eaton) S.; B.S., Ft. Hays State U., 1958; postgrad., Kans. State U., 1958-59; m. Joan Annette Schumacher, Nov. 25, 1961; children—Gregory Joseph, William Eric. Regional audit mgr. GAO, FAA, USAF, OEO, Washington, Los Angeles, Chgo., 1959-67; account exec. Dean Witter & Co., Inc., Pasadena, Calif., 1967-69; financial planner Powell, Johnson, & Assos., Inc., Pasadena, 1969-70; sr. fin. analyst Standard & Poor's Corp., Los Angeles, 1970-71; mgmt. cons., Los Angeles, 1971-74; supervisory mgmt. analyst FAA, Seattle, 1974-76, Washington, 1977-80, staff asst. to dir., Seattle, 1980-82, mgr. tech. support group, 1982—; dir. Center for Small Bus., Urbana (Ohio) Coll., 1976-77. Served with USN, 1952-56. Mem. Assn. Govt. Accts., Am. Mgmt. Assn., Ellis County Hist. Soc., Ft. Hays State U. Alumni Assn., Sigma Tau Gamma. Home: 3703 SW 319th St Federal Way WA 98003 Office: FAA Pacific Hwy S Seattle WA 98188

STACK, GEOFFREY LAWRENCE, real estate exec.; b. Trinidad, Sept. 16, 1943; came to U.S., 1944; s. Gerald Francis and Virgilee Louise (Bell) S.; B.A., Georgetown U., 1965; M.B.A., U. Pa., 1972; m. Victoria Hammack, Aug. 8, 1970; 1 dau., Kathryn Anne. From asst. to fin. v.p. to dir. acquisitions J.H. Snyder Co., Los Angeles, 1972-75; project mgr., then exec. v.p. charge ops. Richards West Co., Newport Beach, Calif., 1975-77; founder, exec. v.p. Regis Homes, Inc., Newport Beach, 1977-78, pres., 1978—; dir. Arral & Partners Ltd.; bd. dirs. Nat. Multi-Housing Council. Trustee South Coast Repertory Theatre, Harbor Day Sch. Served with USMC, 1967-70; Vietnam. Decorated Bronze Star (2), Air medal (20), Purple Heart, Navy Commendation medal. Mem. YPO Community Assns. Inst., Californians for Environ. of Excellence, Full Employment and Strong Economy Through Planned

Devel. Roman Catholic. Clubs: Big Canyon Country, Balboa Bay, Pacific. Office: 5120 Campus Dr Newport Beach CA 92660

STACY, WILLIAM EARL, systems analyst; b. Cin., May 8, 1949; s. Robert A. and Delores Mae (Stewart) S.; B.S. in E.E. and Computer Sci., U. Ill., 1972; grad. Coleman Coll., 1980; m. Sharon Ann Pillote, June 29, 1974. Project engr. VSE Corp., Corona, Calif., 1979-80; scientific/systems analyst D2S Assocs., Escondido, Calif., 1980-83; v.p. Info. Evaluation Systems, Inc., Escondido, 1983—; air warfare cons. Readiness Estimation Systems, Inc., Escondido, 1980-83. Served with USN, 1972-79. Recipient Gen. Dynamics Outstanding Achievement award Naval ROTC, 1972. Mem. Automation One Assn. Author articles in field; developer microcomputer/graphics software for air combat tng. Home: 11464 Osoyoos Pl San Diego CA 92126 Office: PO Box 27920 Escondido CA 92027

STADDEN, CECINE B., artist; b. Springfield, Ill., May 23, 1924; d. Hermon Harrison and Kathrine (Stadden) Cole; student MacMurry Coll., 1942-44, U. Colo., 1945, U. Ill., 1946, Coll. San Mateo (Calif.), 1981-82; children—Siscine Burnes, Charles Bunn, Jr. Free-lance comml. artist Marshall Mitchell Art firm Reuben F. Donnelly Corp., Springfield, Ill., 1947-53; compiler art techniques books Los Altos (Calif.) Pub. Schs., 1967-68; demonstrator Hunt Vanguard Acrylics, 1970-71; designer, producer 25th Anniversary plates City of Los Alto, 1977—; one-woman shows Univ. Club, Palo Alto, Calif., 1967-68, Philco-Ford Western Devel. Lab. Div., Palo Alto, 1968, C Gallery, Los Altos, Calif., 1976-78, Triton Mus. Dirs. Choice Show, others; group shows include U.S. Fed. Bldg. in San Francisco, San Francisco Civic Center Festival, 1965, San Francisco Art Mus.-Civic Center, 1967, De Young Mus., 1969, 70, Hall of Flowers, Golden Gate Park, San Francisco, 1971-76, C. Lorillard Exhibit, 1980, Electric Research Inst., 1981, Jack London Sq., Oakland, Calif., Rosicrucian Mus., San Jose, Calif.; represented in permanent collections Hall of Justice, San Francisco, Menlo Park (Calif.) Civic Center. Triton Mus., Santa Clara, Calif., U. of Ark. Shelia Spencer Art Meml., Springfield (Ill.) Art Assn.; founder Viewpoints Arts Gallery, 1971; owner Viewpoint Fine Art Studio and Gallerie, Los Altos, 1969-81, Greenleaf Gallery, 1981, Saratoga Artique, Carmel, Calif., 1980-82. Mem. Soc. Western Artists (degree of honor award 1974), Penninsulia Outdoor Painters, Palo Alto Art Club (pub. service award 1971, v.p. 1971) P.E.O. Episcopalian. Author: Salt and Watercolor technique, 1976; illustrator: Painting Warps, 1974; also law manual, 1981; contbr. to Lively Arts Mag., 1980-81; inventor travel and protector bd. for etchers and pastelists, Protec-Tote. Address: 169 Giffin St Los Altos CA 94022

STADLEY, PAT ANNA MAY GOUGH (MRS. JAMES M. STADLEY), author; b. El Paso, Tex., Aug. 31, 1918; d. Thomas and Leona (Plitt) Gough; A.A., Chaffey Jr. Coll., 1936; m. James M. Stadley, Aug. 15, 1936; children—William T., Jerry M. Author books, anthologies, short stories published in over 15 fgn. langs., works include: The Black Leather Barbarians, 1960; Autumn of a Hunter (Edgar Allen Poe spl. award 1970, produced as The Deadly Hunt TV Friday Night Movie Week 1971), 1970; The Deadly Hunt; 1977; The Murder Hunt, 1977; also numerous short stories including The Doe and The Gantlet, 1957, The Waiting Game, 1961, Kurdistan Payload, 1962, Something for the Club, 1963, The Big Measure, 1976, The Tender Trap, 1977, The Stranger, 1980. Democrat. Mem. Christian Ch. Clubs: Calif. Writers (v.p. 1967) (Citrus Heights), Calif. Writers (v.p. 1967—), Mystery Writers Am. Home: 6439 Donegal Dr Apt 2 Citrus Heights CA 95610

STAEHS, JAMES PAUL, mechanical engineer and designer, researcher, company executive; b. Beatrice, Nebr., Jan. 19, 1933; s. Paul Otto and Elsie Margaret (Koenig) S.; m. Dorthy Maxine Sand, Aug. 23, 1953; children—Jerri Lynn Staehs Mills, Sandra, J. Matthew. B.S.C.E., Tex. A&M U., 1955. Hydraulic engr. Waterways Expt. Sta., Vicksburg, Miss., 1955; State of Calif., Sacramento, 1958-61; assoc. mgr., test engr. Aerojet Gen. Corp., Sacramento, 1961-65; v.p. SDS Enterprises, Inc., Dallas, 1965-68; supr. Lockheed Missiles & Space, Sunnyvale, Calif., 1968-73; pres. JASTA, San Jose, Calif., 1974—; bus. cons. Scoutmaster Santa Clara County council Boy Scouts Am., 1972-76, bd. dirs., 1975-81, v.p. council, 1976-80; pres. Almaden Boys Baseball, San Jose, 1975-76; pres. County Eagle Scout Assn., Santa Clara County, 1980-81. Served to capt. USAF, 1955-58. Recipient Dist. Award of Merit, Boy Scouts Am., 1975, Silver Beaver award, 1976. Mem. Robotics Internat., Soc. Mech. Engrs., U.S. C. of C. Republican. Club: Bible Study Fellowship (Los Altos, Calif.); patentee swimming pool equipment. Office: 2471B Autumnvale Dr San Jose CA 95131

STAFFORD, CHARLES F., state justice; b. June 24, 1918; m. Katherine Grimm (dec.); 1943; children—Mrs. John E. Schmidt, Mrs. David E. Halverstadt; m. 2d, Elizabeth Jane Greenwell, Aug. 18, 1981. B.A. with honors, Whitman Coll., LL.D., 1956; LL.B., Yale U.Admitted to Wash. State bar; practiced in Mt. Vernon, Wash., until 1952; judge Superior Ct. for Skagit County (Wash.), 1952-69, Wash. Ct. Appeals, 1969-70; justice Wash. State Supreme Ct., Olympia, 1970—, chief justice, 1975-76; an organizer Wash. Bench-Bar-Press Com.; State Jud. Council; mem. Govs. Council on Criminal Justice; former adviser, faculty mem. Nat. Coll. State Trial Judges, summer; tchr. jud. seminars. Past bd. dirs. YMCA, Mt. Vernon; past mem. bd. visitors U. Puget Sound Law Sch., Tacoma, 1976—; bd. overseers Whitman Coll., Walla Walla, Wash., 1976—; bd. visitors Willamette U., Salem, Oreg., 1980—; adminstrv. bd. First United Meth. Ch. of Olympia; past bd. dirs. Boy Scouts Am., Mt. Vernon. Served to 1st lt. AUS, 1942-46. Mem. State Capitol Hist. Assn. (trustee), Am. Law Inst., Am., Wash. bar assns., Am. Judicature Soc., Phi Beta Kappa. Club: Rotary (past pres. Mt. Vernon). Contbr. articles to legal jours. Home: 2016 Clairemont Circle Olympia WA 98502 Office: Supreme Court Temple of Justice Olympia WA 98504

STAFFORD, EDWARD GERALD, real estate executive; b. Bronxville, N.Y., Sept. 24, 1948; s. Gerald E. and Edith (Yule) S.; m. Frida Silvana Vaccari, July 7, 1983. B.A., Pace U., 1972. Lic. real estate salesperson, Calif. Asst. mgmt. analyst City of N.Y., 1972; sales rep. Merck Sharpe & Dohme, Can., 1972-74; with George Elkins Co., Beverly Hills, Calif., 1974-76; v.p. Ronald S. Kates & Co., Los Angeles, 1976—. Mem. Nat. Republican Congl. Com. Mem. Beverly Hills Realty Bd. Republican. Home: 13044 Mindanao Way Marina Del Rey CA 90291 Office: 8900 Beverly Blvd Los Angeles CA 90048

STAFFORD, HELEN ADELE, biology educator; b. Oct. 9, 1922; d. Morton O. and Ethel (Scherer) Stafford. B.A., Wellesley Coll., 1944; M.A., Conn. Coll., 1948; Ph.D., U. Pa., 1951. Research assoc., instr. dept. biochemistry, instr. dept. botany U. Chgo., 1951-54; asst. prof. biology Reed Coll., Portland, Oreg., 1954-58, assoc. prof., 1959-65, prof., 1965—. Guggenheim fellow, 1958-59; NSF fellow, 1963-64. Contbr. articles to profl. jours. Office: 4203 SE Woodstock Blvd Portland OR 97202

STAGG, R. TED, accountant; b. Salt Lake City, June 25, 1941; s. Ernest George and Madge Ione (Harper) S.; m. Patricia Ann Davies, Feb. 25, 1961; children—Julie, Susan, Scott, Daniel, Christopher. B.S., U. Utah, 1964. C.P.A., Calif., Utah. Acct. Cobun, Baldwin & Vilmure, C.P.A.s, Los Angeles, 1964-66, Hansen, Barnett & Maxwell, C.P.A.s, Salt Lake City, 1966-68, Blue Cross of Utah, Salt Lake City, 1968-70, Catten, Baldwin, Vilmure & Stagg, C.P.A.s, Salt Lake City, 1970-73; ptnr. Catten, Stagg, Pacheco & Stagg, C.P.A.s, Salt Lake City, 1973-76, Stagg, Rock & Assocs., C.P.A.s, Salt Lake City, 1976-79, Stagg, Cupit, Thomson & Assocs., C.P.A.s, Salt Lake City, 1979-82; mng. ptnr. Stagg, Thomson, Andersen & Assocs., Salt Lake City, 1982—. Bd. dirs. Utah chpt. Easter Seals Soc.; treas. Utah affiliate Am. Diabetes Assn. Mem. Am. Inst. C.P.A.s, Nat. Assn. Accts. (past pres. Utah chpt.), Utah Assn. C.P.A.s, Hosp. Fin. Mgmt. Assn. Republican. Mormon. Club: University of Salt Lake City.

STAHELI, HARVEY KENT, surgeon; b. Provo, Utah, May 21, 1929; s. Harvey Rulon and Letha (Taylor) S.; B.A., Brigham Young U., 1951; M.D., U. Utah, 1955; m. Lauralee Fawson, Dec. 30, 1958; children—Suzanne, Michael, John. Intern, Georgetown Service, D.C. Gen. Hosp., 1955-56; resident in surgery Highland Alameda Hosp., Oakland, Calif., 1958-62; practice medicine specializing in surgery, Pocatello, Idaho, 1962—. Served with M.C., U.S. Army, 1956-58. Fellow Southwestern Surg. Congress; mem. ACS (bd. govs. 1978—), Idaho Med. Assn. (pres. 1978-79), Am. Cancer Soc. (pres. Idaho div. 1970-72). Clubs: Pocatello Rotary; Pocatello Country. Home: 1330 Juniper Dr Pocatello ID 83201 Office: 246 N 18th Ave Suite A PO Box 4208 Pocatello ID 83201

STAHELI, LANA RIBBLE, psychology counselor, management consultant; b. Battle Creek, Mich., June 21, 1947; d. Vercil LeRoy and Mildred Irene (Sponseller) Ribble; m. Lynn Taylor Staheli, June 11, 1977; children—Linda, Diane, Todd. B.A. cum laude, U. Wash., 1974, M.Ed., 1976; Ph.D., Union Grad. Sch.-San Francisco, 1978. Chmn. bd. dirs. Human Alternatives, N.W., Seattle, 1973-74; adminstr. orthopedic med. office, Seattle, 1975-76; pres. Profl. Practice Cons., Seattle, 1974-79; pvt. practice psychol. counseling, Seattle, 1978—; pres. Staheli, Inc., 1979—; cons. orthopedic dept. Children's Orthopedic Hosp., 1974-76; adj. faculty Antioch Coll., 1974—. Bd. dirs. Univ. Tutoring Service, 1979-80; patron Seattle Art Mus. Mem. Am. Psychol. Assn., Wash. Psychol. Assn., Orthopsychiat. Assn. (pres. Psychology Forum 1981-82), NOW. Democrat. Club: U. Wash. President's. Home: 2301 Fairview E #404 Seattle WA 98102 Office: 2301 Fairview E #307 Seattle WA 98102

STAHL, JACK LELAND, real estate co. exec., state ofcl.; b. Lincoln, Ill., June 28, 1934; s. Edwin R. and Edna M. (Burns) S.; B.S. in Edn., U. N.Mex., 1957; m. Carol Anne Townsend, June 23, 1956; children—Cheryl, Nancy, Kellea. Tchr., Albuquerque Public Schs., 1956-59; pres. House Finders, Inc., Albuquerque, 1959-65; v.p. N.Mex. Savs. & Loan Assn., Albuquerque, 1965-67; chmn. bd. Hooten-Stahl, Inc., Albuquerque, 1967-77; pres. The Jack Stahl Co., Albuquerque, 1977—; mem. N.Mex. Ho. of Reps., 1969-70, mem. N.Mex. Senate, 1981—. Bd. dirs. Better Bus. of N.Mex., 1968-82, pres., 1975-76; trustee Univ. Heights Hosp., 1980—. Named Realtor of Yr., Albuquerque Bd. Realtors, 1972. Mem. Nat. Assn. Realtors, Nat. Homebuilders Assn. Republican. Methodist. Clubs: 20-30 (pres. 1963-64), Elks, Rotary. Office: 1911 Wyoming Blvd NE Albuquerque NM 87112

STAINTON, BRIAN JAMES, food products co. exec.; b. N.Y.C., June 29, 1942; s. Richard G. and Edna M. (Kane) S.; B.A., U. South Fla., 1966; M.B.A., U. N.C., 1972; m. Josephine Tooker, Dec. 8, 1963. Mgr. acctg. Continental Baking Co., Tampa, Fla., 1967-68; mgr. acctg. ITT, Tampa, 1968-71, comptroller, Raleigh, N.C., 1971-78; v.p. fin. Shrimp Peddler Cos., San Diego, 1978-83; comptroller ITT DiCarlo Baking Co., San Pedro, Calif., 1983—. Mem. Nat. Assn. Accts. Republican. Roman Catholic. Home: 27472 Esquina Mission Viejo CA 92691 Office: 1701 N Gaffey St San Pedro CA 90733

STAIR, ERNEST THOMAS, accountant; b. Bartley, W.Va., Oct. 26, 1938; s. Ernest Logan and Julia Oddessa (Beard) S.; A.A., American River Coll., 1963; B.S., Golden Gate U., 1968, postgrad., 1969-72; m. Sherry Allen, June 26, 1958; children—Christopher A., Craig S. Elec. technician Aerojet Gen., Sacramento, 1960-63; jr. accountant Costanzo & Greene, C.P.A.'s, 1963-64; accountant Carter & Schulte, C.P.A.'s, 1966-67, Soderblom & Co., C.P.A.'s, 1968-69; sr. accountant R.L. Bounre, P.A., San Rafael, Calif., 1969-70; partner R.L. Bourne-Bourne & Stair, San Rafael, 1970-73; pres. Stair Accountancy Corp., C.P.A.'s, San Rafael, 1974-78; pres. Stair, Pedersen & Williams Accountancy Corp., C.P.A.'s, San Rafael, 1978—; dir. various small businesses. Bd. dirs. San Rafael Little League, 1971-72, San Rafael council Boy Scouts Am., 1969-70. Served with USN, 1956-59. C.P.A., Calif. Mem. Am. Inst. C.P.A.'s, Calif. Soc. C.P.A.'s, Soc. Calif. Accountants (pres. Northbay chpt. 1978-79), Nat. Soc. Public Accountants Marin County Estate Planning Council, Marin County Motorcycle Assn. (pres. 1977-78), Sierra Old Timers Assn. Republican. Baptist. Club: Elks (San Rafael). Author: How To Buy, Sell, or Merge an Accounting Practice, 1978. Home: 11 Miraflores San Rafael CA 94901 Office: PO Box 1350 San Rafael CA 94915

STAIRES, EDWARD HARLIN, educator; b. Alton, Mo., Dec. 25, 1925; s. Ode Alvin and Eva Lee (Clay) S.; B.S. in Edn., U. Mo.-Columbia, 1949, M.Ed., 1951, Ed.D. (Phi Delta Kappa scholar), 1958; m. Mary K. Stoll, Apr. 15, 1947; children—Steven Lee, Deborah Sue, Phillip Dan. Classroom tchr. Riverview Gardens High Sch., St. Louis County, Mo., 1949-51; high sch. prin., Rogersville, Mo., 1951-53, El Dorado Springs, Mo., 1953-54, Grandview, Mo., 1954-60; supt. schs., Grandview, 1960-69; dean Sch. Edn., Central Mo. State U., Warrensburg, 1969-70; v.p. adminstrv. services No. Ariz. U., Flagstaff, 1970-80, prof. ednl. adminstrn., 1980—. Trustee Grand Canyon Coll., Phoenix, 1976-83; pres. Grand Canyon council Boy Scouts Am., 1974, Jackson County Community Welfare League, 1966. Served with USNR, 1943-46. Paul Harris fellow, 1978. Mem. Am. Assn. Sch. Adminstrs., Mo. Congress Parents and Tchrs. (life), Nat. Orgn. Legal Problems of Edn., NEA (life), Phi Delta Kappa. Democrat. Baptist. Club: Flagstaff East Rotary (pres. 1972). Home: 781 University Heights Dr S Flagstaff AZ 86001 Office: 222D Eastburn Edn No Ariz U Flagstaff AZ 86011

STALEY, ARMISTRE AMETJIAN, educator; consultant; b. Tulare, Calif., Apr. 21, 1925; d. Owagin and Eva (Onanian) A.; m. Hugh Edmund Staley, Sept. 14, 1968. A.B., U. Redlands, 1946; M.A. (Scholar), Stanford U., 1955, Ed.D., 1966. Social worker 1946-48; tchr. Tulare (Calif.) City Sch. Dist., 1948-54, supr. basic skills, 1955-58, dir. curriculum, instrn., 1958-63; instr. Fresno (Calif.) State U., U. Calif., Santa Cruz, U. Calif., Davis, 1963-65; cons. Calif. State Dept. Edn., 1970-72; prof. edn. San Jose (Calif.) State U., 1965—; cons. Head-start, Follow-through programs; cons. sch. dists. Calif. Mem. Assn. Supervision and Curriculum Devel., Am. Ednl. Research Assn., Assn. Childhood Edn. Internat., Assn. Calif. Sch. Adminstrs., Delta Kappa Gamma, Pi Lamda Theta. Contbr. edn. articles to profl. jours. Home: 503 St Andrews Dr Aptos CA 95003 Office: San Jose State U Washington Sq San Jose CA 95192

STAMBAUGH, EDWARD EUGENE, II, psychologist; b. York, Pa., Mar. 18, 1943; s. Edward Eugene and Mary Ernestine (Hawkins) S.; m. Elizabeth Louise Brown, Jan. 3, 1970; children—Edward Eugene III, James Conrad. Student Franklin and Marshall Coll., 1961-64; B.A., U. Utah, 1968; M.A., Pacific Sch. Religion, 1970, M.Div. cum laude, 1970; B.S. summa cum laude, Abilene Christian Coll., 1971; Ph.D., U. Tenn., Knoxville, 1974. Lic. psychologist, Ky., W.Va., Calif. Asst. prof. Eastern Mich. U., 1975-76; staff psychologist Mountain Comprehensive Care Ctr., Prestonsburg, Ky., 1976-77; dir. mental health Landsdowne Mental Health Ctr., Ashland, Ky., 1977-80; pvt. practice psychology, Pleasant Hill, Calif., 1981—; assoc. clin. prof. psychiatry Marshall U., 1978-80; clin. cons. in field. Mem. Am. Psychol. Assn., Am. Soc. Clin. Hypnosis, Internat. Neuropsychol. Soc., Nat. Acad. Neuropsychologists, Internat. Soc. Hypnosis, Calif. State Psychol. Assn., Soc. Pediatric Psychology, Christian Assn. Psychol. Studies, Am. Mensa Ltd., Intertel, Internat. Soc. Philos. Enquiry. Author: Ecological Assessment of Child Problem Behavior, 1976; contbr. articles to profl. jours. Office: 3490-A Buskirk Ave Pleasant Hill CA 94523

STAMER, HOWARD, lawyer, oil company executive; b. N.Y.C., May 4, 1929; s. George and Gertrude (Fidelman) S.; m. Kay B. Buchanan, 1962; children—George J., Judith, Elizabeth; m. Jennifer Mary Mullins, Mar. 19, 1975. B.S., L.I. U., 1950; LL.B. cum laude, Bklyn. Law Sch., 1953. Bar: N.Y. 1953, Oreg. 1975, U.S. Ct. Appeals (9th cir.) 1975, U.S. Supreme Ct. 1975. Atty., Port of N.Y. Authority, 1953-56; assoc. Aranow Brodsky Bohlinger Einhorn & Dann, 1956-59; with Stamer & Haft, and successors, 1959-74, Haessler, Stamler Offler, and successors, Oreg., 1975-79; chmn. bd. Agoil, Inc., Portland, 1979—; lectr. Mem. Conf. on State Def., 1953-56; del. Nat. Inst. Mcpl. Law Officers, 1956; dir. Ind. Petroleum Assn. Am., 1981—; bd. dirs. Oreg. Leukemia Found., 1979-81. Mem. N.Y. Bar Assn., N.Y.C. Bar Assn., N.Y. County Lawyers Assn., ABA, Oreg. Bar Assn., Ind. Petroleum Producers Assn. Am. Republican. Clubs: Washington Athletic; Astoria Country; Atrium; Les Ambassadeurs (London); Le Club (N.Y.C.). Address: 1800 SW 1st Ave Portland OR 97201

STAMES, WILLIAM ALEXANDER, realtor, cost mgmt. exec.; b. Douglas, Ariz., Mar. 26, 1917; s. Alex Basil and Teresa (Ruis) S.; A.A., Long Beach Coll., 1941; postgrad. U. Calif., Berkeley, 1962-64; cert. mgmt. practices Naval Officers CIC Sch., Glenview, Ill., 1955; m. Marguerite Winifred Nelson, June 11, 1943; 1 dau., Wynn Lorain. Owner, Stames Beverage Co., Brawley, Calif., 1945-50; liaison engr. Lockheed Missiles & Space Co., Sunnyvale, Calif., 1958-60, liaison engr. sr., 1960, adminstr., 1960-62, staff adminstr., 1962-63, liaison engr., sr., design engr. sr., 1965-76; owner, mgr. Cost Reduction Equipment Sales & Tech., Sunnyvale, 1967-76. Served to comdr. USNR, 1941-69, ret.; World War II, Korea, Vietnam. Decorated D.F.C., Air medal with two gold stars, Presdl. citation. Mem. Am. Mgmt. Assn., Mountain View Real Estate Bd. (pres.), Calif. Assn. Realtors (bd. dirs.), Tailhook Assn. Clubs: Commonwealth San Francisco, Ret. Officers (past pres. Peninsula chpt.), Lions. Author: Polaris Electrical Subsystems Design History, 1964; Poseidon Subsystem Invention, 1971. Home: 10640 Ainsworth Dr Los Altos CA 94022 Office: 341 Castro St Mountain View CA 94041

STAMPER, BOB, mfg. co. exec.; b. Dayton, Ohio, Apr. 19, 1951; s. Robert L. and Joan (Fickweiler) S.; student Loyola U., Los Angeles, 1969-71, B.A. in Edn., Ariz. State U., 1973. Tchr. spl. edn. Deveroux Day Sch., 1973-74; salesman Smithbaker Agy., Phoenix, 1974-78; salesman R.C. Lurie Co., Phoenix, 1978—, v.p. sales and mktg., 1980—, partner, 1981—; v.p. sales and mfg. Smith Craft Mfg. Co., 1982—. Pres., Scottsdale Young Republicans, 1975; mem. Ariz. Young Rep. Exec. Bd., 1973-75; mem. Airport Adv. Commn., 1979—; active local polit. campaigns; candidate for Scottsdale City Council, 1982. Recipient Outstanding Service award Republican State Com., 1972. Mem. Ariz. Electric League, Illuminating Engring. Soc. Scottsdale Jaycees (pres. 1979-80), Scottsdale C. of C. Roman Catholic. Clubs: U.S. Senatorial, Naupuj. Office: PO Box 2042 Scottsdale AZ 85252

STAMPER, MALCOLM THEODORE, aerospace co. exec.; b. Detroit, Apr. 4, 1925; s. Fred Theodore and Lucille (Cayce) S.; student U. Richmond (Va.), 1943-44; B.E.E., Ga. Inst. Tech., 1946; postgrad. Law Sch., U. Mich., 1946-49; m. Marion Philbin Guinan, Feb. 25, 1946; children—Geoffrey, Kevin, Jamie, David, Mary, Anne. With Gen. Motors Corp., 1949-62; with Boeing Co., Seattle, 1962—, asst. dir. ops., mgr. electronics ops., asst. to gen. mgr. aerospace group, v.p., gen. mgr. turbine div., 1964-66, v.p., gen. mgr. 747 airplane program, 1966-69, v.p., gen. mgr. comml. airplane group, 1969-71, corp. sr. v.p. ops., 1971-72, pres., 1972—, also dir.; dir. Nordstrom, Inc., Travelers Ins. Cos., Travelers Corp. Trustee, Seattle Art Mus., Seattle Repertory Theatre. Served to ensign USNR, 1943-46. Named Industrialist of Year, 1967; recipient Educator's Golden Key award, 1970. Mem. Phi Gamma Delta. Contbr. articles to profl. jours. Office: Boeing Co 7755 E Marginal Way Seattle WA 98124*

STANFILL, BERNICE HARRIETT, stock broker, investor relations administrator; b. Coalgate, Okla., Feb. 3, 1944; d. Harris Connor and Bernice Cleo (Willis) Shearer; m. Jack L. Stanfill, Nov. 24, 1962; children—William L., Theressa J., Michelle C., Jack A. Paralegal cert. Mesa Coll., 1972; student Palomar Coll., 1974-75; Registered securities prin., Fla., Ga., Washington, Calif., Mo., Ohio, N.Y., Kans. Dir. stockholder relations Sci. Applications, Inc., 1972—; v.p., dir., Bull, Inc. subs. Sci. Applications Internat. Corp., La Jolla, Calif., since 1972—. Team rep., mem. North County Women's Soccer Assn., 1981-85; team mem. North County Women's Softball Assn., 1982-83. Mem. Nat. Assn. Female Execs., Am. Assn. Individual Investors, Nat. Assn. Securities Dealers. Republican. Office: Suite 237 476 Prospect St La Jolla CA 92037

STANFILL, WILLIAM EVERETT, pub. relations counselor; b. El Dorado, Kans., Jan. 12, 1927; s. Albert Blaine and Anna Elizabeth (Peppers) S.; B.S., U. Kans., 1953; m. Beverly Teresa Staib, Dec. 26, 1949; children—Teresa Louise Stanfill Benns, Kathleen Marie Stanfill Garrison, Mark Stephen, Judith Ann Stanfill Chainhalt, Michael David. Reporter, Daily Tribune, Great Bend, Kans., 1953-55; reporter Reporter-News, Abilene, Tex., 1955-57; asst. news bur. mgr. Boeing Co., Wichita, Kans., 1957-61; dir. pub. relations and advtg. The Duo-Bed Corp., Wichita, Kans., 1961-65; pres. William E. Stanfill Assos., Denver, 1965-74; pres. Stanfill, Marcum & Spillane, Inc., Denver, 1974-76; pres. Stanfill & Assos., Inc., Denver, 1976—; dir., Mobile Alert, Inc., Denver, Solid State Instruments, Inc., Denver; dir., sec. Serpentix Conveyor Corp., Denver. Democratic precinct committeeman, 1965-67. Served with USN, 1944-47. Decorated Bronze Star medal, Purple Heart medal. Mem. Pub. Relations Soc. Am., Colo. Press Assn., Sigma Delta Chi. Democrat. Roman Catholic. Home: 2759 S Raleigh St Denver CO 80236 Office: Plaza Profl Bldg Suite 250 3375 S Bannock St Englewood CO 80110

STANILOFF, HOWARD MEDA, cardiologist, epidemiologist; b. Saskatoon, Sask., Can., Sept. 18, 1948; s. Sidney and Ethel (Epstein) S.; m. Robin Debra Dushey, June 27, 1981. B.Sc., U. B.C., 1970, M.D., 1973; M.P.H., UCLA, 1980. Intern, Toronto (Ont.) Gen. Hosp., 1973-74, resident, 1974-75, cardiology fellow, 1975-78; cardiology fellow Cedars-Sinai Med. Ctr., Los Angeles, 1978-80, mem. staff, 1980—, dir. outpatient cardiac rehab., 1981—; adj. asst. prof. medicine UCLA, 1980—, adj. asst. prof. pub. health, 1981—; vol. Greater Los Angeles affiliate Am. Heart Assn. NIH Research Career Devel. awardee, 1982. Fellow Am. Coll. Cardiology, Royal Coll. Physicians and Surgeons Can. Jewish. Home: 15825 Vose St Van Nuys CA 91406 Office: Cedars-Sinai Medical Center 8700 Beverly Blvd Los Angeles CA 90048

STANLEY, DARROL JAMES, investment banker; b. Berkeley, Calif., Dec. 26, 1944; s. Charles J. and Maxine (Phillips) S.; B.S., U. Calif., Berkeley, 1966; M.B.A., U. So. Calif., 1968, D.B.A., 1973; m. Carole Tait, Feb. 3, 1968. Lectr. fin. U. So. Calif., 1968-71; asst. prof. fin. Calif. State U., Northridge, 1971-73; asso. prof. fin. Pepperdine U., Los Angeles, 1973—; mgr. corp. fin. and research Wagenseller & Durst, Inc., Los Angeles, 1972-76; pres. D.J. Stanley & Co., Inc., Los Angeles, 1976—; chmn. Century Gen. Corp., 1973-79; mgr. corp. fin. Birr, Wilson & Co., Inc., 1980—; chmn. Plastronics Corp., 1981—. Mem. Am. Soc. Appraisers, Am. Econ. Assn., Am. Fin. Assn., Los Angeles World

Affairs Council. Republican. Presbyterian. Home: 10825 Savona Rd Los Angeles CA 90024

STANLEY, FORREST EDWIN, ednl. adminstr.; b. Bakersfield, Calif., Sept. 6, 1942; s. James Edwin and Lucile Haworth (Sloan) S.; student U. Calif., Los Angeles, 1960-63, M.S., 1970; B.S., Calif. State U., Northridge, 1969; m. Suzanne Roberts, June 15, 1968; children—John Forrest, Cheryl Suzanne. Sr. clk. So. Calif. Gas Co., 1963-65, programmer analyst, 1965-70; fin. analyst Continental Bldgs. Co., Burbank, Calif., 1970-72; fin. analyst McKinsey & Co., Inc., Los Angeles, 1972-74; analyst Unionamerica Advisors, Beverly Hills, Calif., asst. v.p., asst. treas., 1974-75; dir. alumni and devel. Grad. Sch. Mgmt., UCLA, 1976-80; dir. spl. campaigns U. Calif., Berkeley, 1980—. Mem. Los Angeles Jr. C. of C., Burbank Jaycees (treas. 1972), Assn. for Computing Machinery, Council for Advancement and Support of Edn., UCLA Mgmt. Alumni Assn. (v.p. 1974, pres. 1975-77), Sons Am. Colonists, Mensa, Lambda Chi Alpha (UCLA alumni charter pres. 1974-77, treas. 1977-80) Club: Crystalaire Country. Home: 649 Candleberry Rd Walnut Creek CA 94598 Office: Development Office University California Berkeley CA 94720

STANLEY, R. C., artist; b. Chgo., May 18, 1930; s. Adolph and Marie (Zdeborsky) Nosek; student San Diego State Coll., 1947-49; children—Robert Merrill, Eileen Cheryl, Scott Darryl. Ordained to non-denominational ministry, 1949; pastor churches, Pacific Palisades, Calif., 1949-59; one-man shows: Arco-Plaza, Los Angeles, 1973, House of Wimberly, Peyton, Ariz., 1973, Comstock Silversmiths, Carson City, Nev., 1973, Rembrandt Galleries, San Francisco, 1974, Lahaina Gallery, Moui, 1976-77, Woodsmoke Gallery, Chico, Calif., 1977; group shows include: Stock Gallery, Beverly Hills, Calif., 1976, Morseburg Galleries, Los Angeles, 1976, Laguna Originals, Laguna Beach, Calif., 1976-77, Biltmore Galleries, Los Angeles, 1980, Fisher Gallery, Palm Springs, 1980; represented in permanent collection Nev. State Mus., Museum Internat. Seamens Inst., Leningrad, USSR, Academie de Musique, Alexandria, Egypt; art adviser Pacific Far East Line, 1972—; dir. The Artisans, 1966-73; creator dir. Pacific Art 7 continuous art program at sea, Am. cruise ships, 1972—; instr. art, 1962—, now instr. Santa Monica (Calif.) Coll. Recipient 1st award Malibu Sealion Gallery Festival, 1960, Western Artist award, Festival of Creative Arts, Phoenix, 1972. Mem. Pacific Palisades Art Assn. (past dir.), Santa Monica Art Assn. (past dir.). Republican. Home and studio: 30355 Morning View Dr Malibu CA 90265

STANNARD, GEORGE PARKER, education consultant/therapist; b. Youngstown, Ohio, Dec. 9, 1925; s. George M. and Martha L. (Parker) S.; m. Dixie Lee, Oct. 15, 1961; 1 child: Kirby J.; m. Valene Davies, Apr. 11, 1967. B.A., U. Nev., 1960; M.S., Nova U., 1979. Tchr., Boulder City, Nev., 1963-67, Knudson High Sch., Las Vegas, Nev., 1967-83; ednl. cons./therapist, Las Vegas, 1981—; dir. Personal Instructional Therapy Assocs., ednl. cons., 1983—. Served with USN, 1942-46, USCG, 1961-63. Mem. Assn. Hypnotists of Am., Biofeedback Soc. Am., Am. Fedn. Astrologers, Am. Personnel and Guidance Assn. Democrat. Club: Subvets of Am. Office: 901 Rancho Ln Suite 216 Las Vegas NV 89106

STANTON, EDWARD JAMES, JR., aerospace company executive; b. Pitts., Sept. 10, 1951; s. Edward James and Joann (Weyels) S. B.A. in History, Gannon U., 1974; M.B.A. in Mgmt. and Internat. Bus., U. Notre Dame, 1976. Constrn. insp. engring. and constrn. div. U.S.-Turkey ops. dept. Koppers Co., Inc., Eregli, Turkey, 1975, econ. and resources planning advisor space div., space shuttle integration segment Rockwell Internat., Downey, Calif., 1979-81, mgr. bus. devel., space sta. program, shuttle integration and satellite systems div., 1981—. Advisor Erie Hist. Soc., 1973-74; mem. Republican Nat. Com., 1981—. Served to 1st lt. U.S. Army, 1976-79. Recipient U.S. and Can. Mil. Parachute awards, 1977, 78; Pres. award Rockwell Internat., 1983. Mem. AIAA, Nat. Mgmt. Assn., Assn. M.B.A. Execs., Planetary Soc., Smithsonian Assn., Ctr. for Archaeostronomy, Gannon U. Alumni Assn., U. Notre Dame Alumni Assn., Pi Gamma Mu. Roman Catholic. Club: Earthwatch (Belmont, Mass.). Home: 5941 E Pacific Coast Hwy 4 Long Beach CA 90803 Office: D/704 AC05 Shuttle Integration and Satellite Systems Div 12214 Lakewood Blvd Downey CA 90241

STANTON, GRACE PATRICIA, communications executive, consultant; b. Jersey City, Dec. 17, 1951; d. John Joseph and Marjorie Theresa (Nolan) S.; m. Mark Edward Rieger, July 11, 1976; 1 son, Brian Stanton. Student Wroxton Coll., Oxford U., 1972; B.A., Fairleigh Dickinson U., 1973; M.A., Seton Hall U., 1974; Ph.D., U. Denver, 1979. Reporter Jersey Jour., Jersey City, 1970-73; editorial asst. IBM, Franklin Lakes, N.J., 1973; pub. relations mgr. Fairleigh Dickinson U., 1973-75; editor Kraft, Chgo., 1976-77; mgr. pub. relations IHS, Denver, 1977-78; dir. communications CMC, Denver, 1978-80; v.p. Johnston Group, Denver, 1980-82; pres. Stanton & Assocs., Denver, 1982—. Mem. Leadership Denver Assn., Denver C. of C.; v.p., dir. Arapahoe Mental Health Ctr.; dir. Met. Denver Hospice. Mem. Colo. Press Women (dir., communications award), Internat. Assn. Bus. Communicators (award Chgo. chpt.), Pub. Relations Soc. Am., Speech Communication Assn., Counselor's Acad. Democrat. Roman Catholic. Home: 7985 S Field St Littleton CO 80123 Office: 1620 Market St Mezzanine Suite Denver CO 80202

STANTON, PETER HARRISON, electronics company executive; b. N.Y.C., June 21, 1922; s. Stanley and Margaret (Berndt) S.; B.E.E. cum laude, NYU, 1943; M.B.A. with high distinction, Harvard U., 1948; children—Carol, Peter. Vice pres. fin. and adminstrn. Topp Industries, Inc., Los Angeles, 1955-59; pres. Astro-Sci. Corp., Los Angeles, 1959-64, Infonics, Inc., Santa Monica, Calif., 1966-73, Electroscale Corp., Santa Rosa, Calif., 1974-82, Fluidyne/Electrodata, Inc., Santa Rosa, 1982—. Mem. exec. com. univ. devel. council Sonoma State U., 1982—; bd. dirs. United Way Sonoma County, 1981—. Served with USNR, 1945-46. Mem. Fin. Execs. Inst., Young Pres.' Orgn., Psi Chi, Eta Kappa Nu. Republican. Episcopalian. Clubs: Rotary, Harvard. Office: PO Box 11366 Santa Rosa CA 95406

STANTON, WILLIAM JOHN, JR., educator; b. Chgo., Dec. 15, 1919; s. William John and Winifred (McGann) S.; B.S., Ill. Inst. Tech., 1940; M.B.A., Northwestern U., 1941, Ph.D., 1948; m. Imma M. Mair, Sept. 14, 1978; children by previous marriage; Kathleen Louise, William John III. Mgmt. trainee Sears Roebuck Co., 1940-41; instr. U. Ala., Tuscaloosa, 1941-44; auditor Olan Mills Portrait Studios, Chattanooga, 1944-46; asst., assoc. prof. U. Wash., Seattle, 1948-55; prof. U. Colo., Boulder, 1955—, head mktg. dept., 1957-71, acting dean, 1963-64, assoc. dean Sch. Bus., 1964-67; vis. prof. U. Utah, summer 1946, 49, U. Calif., Berkeley, summer 1950, UCLA, summer 1957. Mktg. cons. various bus. firms, govtl. agys., 1950—. Mem. Am., So., Western, Southwest mktg. assns., Assn. Mktg. Educators, Beta Gamma Sigma. Roman Catholic. Author: Economic Aspects of Recreation in Alaska, 1953; (with Richard H. Buskirk) Management of the Sales Force, 6th edit., 1983, also Spanish transl.; Fundamentals of Marketing, 7th edit., 1984, also Spanish and Portuguese transl., (with Montrose Sommers and James Barnes) Can. 3d edit., 1982; (with others) Challenge of Business, 1975. Editorial bd. Jour. Mktg., 1963-69. Home: 1445 Sierra Dr Boulder CO 80302

STAPLES, RICHARD F., JR., marketing executive; b. Boston, Feb. 10, 1949; s. Richard F. and Mary K. (Kingsbury) S.; m. Randi C. Wood, Sept. 14, 1974; 1 son, Eric T. B.B.A., Colo. Coll., 1974. Personal banking and mktg. rep. United Bank of Skyline N.A., Denver, 1974-76; mktg. officer/asst. v.p. United Bank of Lakewood (Colo.), 1976-79; v.p. and dir. mktg. United Bank of Pueblo (Colo.), 1980-81; dir. mktg. and devel. St. Mary-Corwin Hosp. Regional Med. and Health Ctr., Pueblo, 1981—. Chmn. Fountain Creek Commn., 1982-83; bd. dirs., v.p. Pueblo Family YMCA, 1982-83; mem. adv. bd. Salvation Army; vice chmn. Leadership Pueblo '84; bd. dirs. Jr. Achievement of Pueblo. Mem. Am. Mktg. Assn., Am. Soc. Hosp. Pub. Relations. Clubs: Rotary #43 of Pueblo, 30 of Pueblo. Home: 2102 Elizabeth St Pueblo CO 81003 Office: 1008 Minnequa Ave Pueblo CO 81004

STAPRANS, RAIMONDS, artist, writer; b. Riga, Latvia, Oct. 13, 1926; s. Teodors and Elvira Leontine (Ulmanis) S.; m. Ilona Peics; children—Mareta, Alda. B.A., U. Wash., 1952; M.A., U. Calif.-Berkeley, 1954. Work exhibited in U.S., Can., USSR, Eng., France. Chmn. Z. Lazda Meml. Found. Recipient Merit award San Francisco Arts Festival, 1980; award Calif. Expo, 1958. Mem. Latvian Writers Union. Address: 2052 20th St San Francisco CA 94107

STARCHUK, TRICIA WILLAMINA, nurse; b. Drumbeller, Alta., Can., 1949; d. Frederick and Georgiana Evenly (Kempt) S. R.N., U. Alta., 1973, B.A., 1978, M.P.A., 1979, Ph.D., 1982; Ed.D., Pepperdine U., 1983. Cert. tchr. community coll., Calif., 1982. Charge nurse Edmonton U., Can., 1973-74; open heart specialist Cedar Sinai Med. Ctr., Los Angeles, 1977-79, psychiat. charge nurse, 1979-83; research asst. Shock Research Ctr., Los Angeles, 1975-76; critical care specialist Hollywood Prebyn. Med. Ctr., Los Angeles, 1976-77. Mem. Am. Heart Assn., Am. Assn. Emergency Room Nurses, Am. Assn. Critical Care Nurses, Can. Assn. Critical Care Nurses, Can. Assn. Psychiat. Nursing. Roman Catholic. Author: Curriculum Development in Nursing Arena, 1982; Effective Management Skills for Nurses Entering Management Arena; 1983; Nurses Entering Executive Management, 1983.

STARING, GRAYDON SHAW, lawyer; b. Deansboro, N.Y., Apr. 9, 1923; s. William Luther and Eleanor Mary (Shaw) S.; student Colgate U., 1943-44; A.B., Hamilton Coll., 1947; J.D., U. Calif. at Berkeley, 1951; m. Joyce Lydia Allum-Poon, Sept. 1, 1949; children—Diana Hilary (Mrs. Lawrence A. Hobel), Christopher Paul Norman. Admitted to Calif. bar, 1952, U.S. Supreme Ct.; atty. Office of Gen. Counsel, Navy Dept., San Francisco, 1952-53; atty. Admiralty and Shipping sect. U.S. Dept. Justice, San Francisco, 1953-60; asso. firm Lillick, McHose & Charles, San Francisco, 1960-64, partner, 1965—. Instr. speech Hamilton Coll., Clinton, N.Y., 1947-48; lectr. Calif. Continuing Edn. of Bar. Mem. San Francisco Lawyers Com. for Urban Affairs, 1972—. Served to lt. (j.g.) USNR, 1943-46. Fellow Am. Bar Found.; mem. Am. (chmn. maritime ins. com. 1975-77, mem. standing com. on admiralty and maritime law) Fed. (pres. San Francisco chpt. 1968), Calif. (chmn. fed. cts. com. 1975-76) bar assns., Bar Assn. San Francisco (dir. 1969-70, treas. 1973), Legal Aid Soc. San Francisco (dir. 1974, v.p. 1975-79, pres. 1980-82), Maritime Law Assn. of U.S. (chmn. practice and procedure com. 1976-80, exec. com. 1977-80, 2d v.p. 1980-82, 1st v.p. 1982—), Propeller Club of U.S., World Trade Club San Francisco, Marine Exchange of San Francisco (bd. dirs. 1983—), Lambda Chi Alpha, Phi Alpha Delta. Episcopalian (vestryman 1966-68, 77-79). Republican. Contbr. articles to profl. jours. Home: 195 San Anselmo Ave San Francisco CA 94127 Office: 2 Embarcadero Center San Francisco CA 94111

STARK, CARLYN KAISER, camp dir.; b. Washington, Oct. 24, 1933; d. Edgar Fosburgh and Sue (Mead) Kaiser; student Bryn Mawr Coll., 1952-54, m. Franklin Culver Stark, July 18, 1976, children by previous marriage—Kathy, David, Kim, Robin, Mead. Counselor Four Winds Camp, Deer Harbor, Wash., 1952-54, dir., 1968 , mem. found. bd., 1970—; dir. Four Winds-Westward Ho Camps, Deer Harbor, 1968—; exec. dir. Four Winds Found. Bd. dirs. Children's Hosp., East Bay, Calif., 1965-68, Calif. Nev. Meth. Homes, 1976—, Fred Finch Youth Ctr., 1976-82; trustee Totem Girl Scout Council, Seattle, 1970-78, Oakland (Calif.) Met. YMCA, 1976-78; bd. dirs. Oakland Symphony Assn., 1977—, UN Assn., 1980—. Mem. Am. Camping Assn., San Francisco Opera Assn. (dir. 1966-69). Clubs: Orcas Island Yacht, Oakland Women's Athletic, Lake Merritt Rowing. Home: 333 Wayne Ave Apt E Oakland CA 94606 Office: Box C Deer Harbor WA 98243

STARK, FORTNEY (PETE) HILLMAN, JR., congressman; b. Milw., Nov. 11, 1931; s. Fortney Hillman and Dorothy M. (Mueller) S.; B.S., MIT; M.B.A., U. Calif.; children—Jeffrey Peter, Beatrice Ann, Thekla Brumder, Sarah Gallun. Teaching asst. MIT, 1953-54; prin. Skaife & Co., Berkeley, Calif., 1957-61; founder Beacon Savs. & Loan Assn., Antioch, Calif., 1961; pres., founder Security Nat. Bank, Walnut Creek, Calif., 1963—; mem. 93d Congress from 8th Dist. Calif., 94th and 97th Congresses from 9th Dist. Calif. Bd. dirs. ACLU, 1971, Housing Devel. Corp.; adv. com. Contra Costa County Coalition; bd. dirs. Common Cause, 1971; bd. dirs. Starr King Sch. Served to capt. USAF, 1955-57. Mem. Delta Kappa Epsilon. Democrat. Club: University (San Francisco). Office: House of Reps Washington DC 20515

STARK, FRANKLIN CULVER, lawyer; b. Unityville, S.D., Apr. 16, 1915; s. Fred H. and Catherine (Culver) S.; J.D., Northwestern U., 1940; A.B., Dakota Wesleyan U., 1937, LL.D., 1959; m. Alice C. Churchill, Sept. 16, 1941 (dec. May 1975); children—Margaret C., Wallace C., Judith C., Franklin Culver; m. 2d, Carlyn Kaiser Saxton, July 18, 1976. Bar: Ill. 1940, Calif. 1946. Assoc. Sidley, McPherson, Austin & Burgess, Chgo., 1940-41, Fitzgerald, Abbott & Beardsley, Oakland, Calif., 1946-47; sr. mem. firm Stark, Stewart, Wells and Robinson and predecessor firms, Oakland, 1947—; lectr. comml. law U. Calif. Sch. Bus., 1946-66. Staff, Office Gen. Counsel, OPA, Washington, 1941-42. Bd. dirs. Merritt-Peralta Found., Alameda County chpt. UNA-USA, Claremont Sch. Theology, Dakota Wesleyan U., Fred Finch Youth Center, 1970-82, Calif.-Nev. United Meth. Found., 1974-80, Oakland Meth. Found, 1953-82; chmn. bd. trustees Calif.-Nev. Meth. Homes, 1966-73; pres. Oakland Council of Chs., 1954-56; nat. vice chmn. Campaign for UN Reform. Served with USNR, 1942-45; now comdr. Res. ret. Named Alumnus of Yr., Dakota Wesleyan U., 1966; certified taxation law specialist. Mem. Am., Calif., Alameda County bar assns., State Bar Calif., World Peace Through Law Center (charter), Oakland C. of C., Am. Legion, Phi Kappa Phi, Pi Kappa Delta, Phi Alpha Delta, Order Coif. Methodist. Mason (Shriner), Elk. Clubs: Athenian Nile (Oakland); Commonwealth (San Francisco). Editor Ill. Law Review, 1939-40. Home: 333 Wayne Ave Oakland CA 94606 Office: Citicore Savs Plaza 14th Floor Oakland CA 94612

STARK, JACK LEE, college president; b. Wabash, Ind., Sept. 26, 1934; s. Lynn C. and Helen L. (Haley) S.; m. Jill Harris, June 20; children—Janet, Jeff, Jennifer, Jonathan. B.A., Claremont (Calif.) McKenna Coll.; L.H.D. (hon.), U. Redlands. Dir. alumni affairs Claremont McKenna Coll., 1961-63, adminstrv. asst. to pres., 1963-70, acting pres., 1970-71, pres., 1971—; also trustee; dir. Angeles Corp. Trustee Foothill Country Day Sch., Claremont; bd. dirs. Pomona Valley Community Hosp., Los Angeles Region II United Way. Served to capt. USMCR, 1957-60. Mem. Young Pres. Orgn., Newcomen Soc. N.Am., Town Hall Los Angeles, World Affairs Council. Clubs: California, University (Los Angeles). Home: 1679 Tulane St Claremont CA 91711 Office: Bauer Center Claremont McKenna Coll Claremont CA 91711

STARK, PHILIP HERALD, petroleum executive; b. Iowa City, Mar. 2, 1936; s. Herald I. and Helen Annis (Ogilvie) S.; m. Marybelle Goode, Dec. 20, 1960; m. 2d, Christine Katherine Baumgartner, Aug. 21, 1981. B.S. in Geology, Okla. U., 1958; M.S. in Geology, U. Wis., 1960, Ph.D., 1962. Cert. profl. geologist, Am. Inst. Profl. Geologists, 1975. Exploration geologist Mobil Oil Corp., Wichita, Kans., 1962-65, data processing coordinator, Denver, 1965-69, tech. services mgr. petroleum info., 1969-74, dir. data applications 1974-78, v.p. internat. data applications, 1978-81, v.p. spl. projects, 1981-83, exec. v.p. sci. and tech. sect., 1983—; lectr. Del., Republican State Conv., 1972; mem. Leadership Denver Program, 1978. Recipient W.A. Tarr award in Geology, Okla. U., 1958. Mem. Am. Assn. Petroleum Geologists. Club: Denver Petroleum. Contbr. articles to profl. jours. Home: 2770 S Elmira #154 Denver CO 80231 Office: 4100 E Dry Creek Rd Littleton CO 80122

STARK, RAY, film producer; Student Rutgers U. Lit. agt. after World War II, writers included Costain, Marquand, Hecht; with Famous Artists Agy., until 1957, represented Marilyn Monroe, Kirk Douglas, Richard Burton; founder (with Elliot Hyman) Seven Arts Prodns., serving as exec. v.p., head prodn., 1957-66; producer numerous films including: Reflections in a Golden Eye, 1970, The Owl and The Pussycat, 1972, Fat City, 1973, The Way We Were, 1973, Funny Lady, 1975, The Sunshine Boys, 1975, Murder by Death, 1976, Smokey and the Bandit, 1977, the Goodybye Girl, 1978, The Cheap Detective, 1978, California Suite, 1978, Chapter Two, 1979, The Electric Horseman, 1979, The Hunter, 1980, Seems Like Old Times, 1980, Annie, 1981; chmn. Raster Films, Inc., Burbank Calif. Office: Rastar Films Inc 300 Colgems Sq Burbank CA 91505*

STARK, RON, artist; b. Sidney, N.Y., June 27, 1944. B.A., Ph.D., U. Denver. Work exhibited in permanent collections: Balt. Mus. Art.; Smithsonian Inst., Washington, Corcoran Gallery Art, Washington; exhibits: Internat. Art Fair, Paris, 1977, George Ponpidou Ctr., Paris, 1977, Corcoran Gallery Art, Washington, 1978; one-man shows: Richmond (Va.) U., 1979, Rudzinoff Galleries, Paris, 1980, Curtis Gallery, Mill Valley, Calif., 1980, others. Va. Mus. grantee, 1974; Internat. Inst. Edn. Travel grantee, 1974. Office: PO Box 641 Mendocino CA 95460*

STARKEY, HARRY CHARLES, geologist; b. Wheeling, W.Va., Dec. 10, 1925; s. Burtice Johannes and Mary Irene (Hilton) S.; B.S., W.Va. U., 1950; m. Ruth Woods, May 16, 1964. With U.S. Geol. Survey, 1955—, geologist specializing in clay mineralogy, Denver, 1958—. Served with inf. U.S. Army, 1944-46. Mem. Colo. Sci. Soc., Geol. Soc. Washington, Mineral. Soc. Am., Soil Sci. Soc. Am., Clay Minerals Soc., Mensa. Methodist. Research in clay mineralogy, ion-exchange in clay and zeolites, chem. reactions involving clays; contbr. articles to profl. jours. Home: 1636 S Yarrow Ct Lakewood CO 80226

STARR, BENJAMIN FREDRICK, III, systems engr.; b. Atlanta, June 27, 1947; s. Benjamin Frederick, Jr. and Virginia Anne (White) S.; B.S., USAF Acad., 1969; m. Maureen Kay Cziske, May 1, 1975; children—Rebecca Virginia, Jessica Kate. Specialist in info. sci. Seattle public schs., 1974-79; resource controller Boeing Co., Everett, Wash., 1979-80, systems engr., 1980—. Served as officer USAF, 1969-70. Mem. AIAA, AAAS, USAF Acad. Assn. Grads., Seattle Profl. Engring. Employees Assn., Mensa, Tau Beta Pi.

STARR, MELVIN LEE, counselor; b. N.Y.C., Mar. 17, 1922; s. Herman and Martha (Aberman) S.; m. Eileen Ferne Kagan, Sept. 7, 1947; children—Marianne, Lisa Caren. B.B.A., U. Miami, 1947; postgrad. Columbia U., 1949-53, U. Denver, 1955-56, Ariz. State U., 1956-57; M.A., U. Ariz., 1950; Ed.D., Western Colo. U., 1974. Faculty, adminstrn. Tucson Pub. Schs., 1950—; tchr. Doolen Jr. High Sch., 1951-53, counselor high sch., 1953-62, asst. prin. Alice Vail Jr. High Sch., 1962 64, Catalina High Sch., 1964 68; prin. Rincon High Sch., 1968-71, Tucson High Sch., 1971-74; asst. supt. Tucson Pub. Schs., 1974-78, assoc. supt., 1978-82; pvt. practice family counseling. Mem. Tucson Mayor's Com. on Human Relations, 1969—; mem. Ariz. state com. Anti Defamation League, 1971; Ariz. state adv. bd. Good Shepherd Sch. for Girls, 1971; mem. Central Com. Democratic party Pima City, Ariz., 1968—; bd. dirs. Amigos dos los Americanos, AnyTown, Ariz., Lighthouse YMCA, Beacon Found., Big Bros., NCCJ, Jr. Achievement, Tucson Community Center, Pacific Western region Anti-Defamation League, Handmaker Nursing Home Pima County, United Way, CODAC, Planned Parenthood, Girl Scouts Am., Ariz. Mobile Meals, Epilepsy Soc. So. Ariz., Drug Abuse and Alcohol Consortium; adv. bd. Tucson Free Med. Clinic; bd. dirs. Los Ninos Crisis Center. Mem. Ariz. Assn. Student Teaching (state treas.), NEA, Ariz. Interscholastic Assn. (pres. conf. 1971, legis. council), Ariz. Personnel and Guidance Assn., Nat. Assn. Secondary Sch. Prins., Am. Assn. Sch. Adminstrs., Assn. Supervision and Curriculum Devel., Ariz. Sch. Adminstrs., Phi Epsilon Pi, Phi Delta Kappa. Home: 6612 E Villa Dorado Dr Tucson AZ 85715 Office: 899 N Wilmot Rd Suite A-1 Wilmot Profl Plaza Tucson AZ 85711

STATLER, IRVING CARL, aero. engr.; b. Buffalo, Nov. 23, 1923; s. Samuel William and Sarah (Strauss) S.; B.S. in Aero. Engring., B.S. in Engring. Math., U. Mich., 1945; Ph.D., Cal. Inst. Tech., 1956; m. Renee Roll, Aug. 23, 1953; children—William Scott, Thomas Stuart. Research engr. flight research dept. Cornell Aero. Lab., Inc., Buffalo, 1946-53, prin. engr. flight research dept., 1956-57, asst. head aero-mechanics dept., 1957-63, head applied mechanics dept., 1963-70, sr. staff scientist aeroscis. div., 1970-71; research scientist U.S. Army Air Mobility Research and Devel. Lab., Moffett Field, Calif., 1971-73, dir. Aeromechanics Lab., 1973—; research scientist research analysis group Jet Propulsion Lab., Pasadena, Cal., 1953-55. Chmn. flight mechanics panel adv. group aerospace research and devel. NATO, 1974-76. Lectr., U. Buffalo, Millard-Fillmore Coll., Buffalo, 1957-58. Served with USAAF, 1945-46. Asso. fellow AIAA (chmn. atmospheric flight mechanics tech. com. 1970-73, coordinator mechanics and control flight tech. splty. group 1973-76); fellow Royal Aero. Soc.; mem. AAAS, Am. Helicopter Soc., Sigma Xi. Home: 781 Woodstock Ln Los Altos CA 94022 Office: Aeromechanics Lab US Army Aviation R & D Command Ames Research Center Moffett Field CA 94035

STAUDENMAYER, HERMAN, clinical psychologist, researcher; b. Munich, W.Ger., May 12, 1946; came to U.S., 1954, naturalized, 1964; s. Herman and Amalie (Dillmann) S.; m. Toni Pawlowsky, Aug. 14, 1982. B.A. in Psychology, UCLA, 1968; M.A. in Psychology, SUNY, Stony Brook, 1971; Ph.D. in Psychology, U. Colo., 1973; cert. psychologist, Colo. Asst. prof. psychology Grad. Faculty, New Sch. Social Research, 1974-77; asst. prof. clin. psychology U. Colo. Health Scis. Center, 1977-80; psychologist Nat. Jewish Hosp., Denver, 1977-80; dir. Behavioral Medicine and Biofeedback Clinic Denver, 1980—; pvt. practice psychotherapy and biofeedback for stress-related disorders and chronic diseases. Mem. Am. Psychol. Assn., Biofeedback Soc. Am. Research in chronic diseases, cognitive factors in stress mgmt., psychophysiol. stress profiling. Office: 5800 E Evans Ave Denver CO 80222

STAUDHAMMER, PETER, astronautical engineer; b. Budapest, Hungary, Mar. 4, 1934; s. John and Josephine (Decker) S.; m. June A. Fochler, June 28, 1958; children—Debra J., Julia D., Christina L. B.S., UCLA, 1955, M.S., 1956, Ph.D. in Engring., 1957. Sr. research engr. Jet Propulsion Lab., Pasadena, Calif., 1957-59; successively chief engr., Apollo lunar descent engine, engring. mgr. Viking Mars biology instrument, mgr. research labs., mgr. energy systems ops. TRW, Inc., Redondo Beach, Calif., 1959—; dir. Fusion Power Assocs., Washington. Bd. dirs. So. Calif. Repertoire Orch., Arrowbear Music Camp; bd. councilors South Coast Bot. Garden, Palos Verdes, Calif. Lockheed Engring. fellow, 1952; recipient Achievement award for Viking Mars biology instrument Inst. Advancement Engring., 1976, NASA Achievement award for Voyager Jupiter/Saturn ultraviolet spectrometer, 1981. Assoc. fellow AIAA; mem. Internat. Combustion Inst., AAAS, Sigma Xi. Roman Catholic. Contbr. articles profl. jours. Patentee automobile afterburners. Home: 5060 Rolling Meadows Rd Rolling Hills Estates CA 90274 Office: 1 Space Park Redondo Beach CA 90278

STEAD, REXFORD ARTHUR, mus. consultant, art historian; b. Recife, Pernambuco, Brazil, Jan. 24, 1923; s. Frank Arthur and Doris Margaret (Norrell) S.; came to U.S., 1929, naturalized, 1943; student Brown U., 1945-46; M.A. in Asian Art, Asia Inst., N.Y., 1949; m. Priscilla Alden Steers, Sept. 3, 1949 (div. 1967); children—Penelope Alden, Mark Alden. Lectr., exec. asst. to chancellor Asia Inst., 1947-50; chief Chinese div., internat. broadcasting div. State Dept., 1950-53; dir. Mus. Fine Arts, St. Petersburg, Fla., 1953-67; dep. dir. Los Angeles County Mus. Art, 1967-79; trustee Mus. Fine Arts, St. Petersburg, 1968—. Contbr. articles to profl. jours., exhbn. and collection catalogs. Home: 1688 Marmont Ave Los Angeles CA 90069

STEARNS, MARIAN SHERMAN, social science research group administrator, consultant; b. Washington, July 9, 1938; d. Allan Sherman and Isabel Bibb (Kimbrough) S.; m. Peter Rynders Stearns, July 26, 1970. A.B., Brown U., 1960; Ph.D., U. Calif.-Berkeley, 1966. Sr. research coordinator U.S. Office Edn., Washington, 1966-70; cons. Rand Corp., Santa Monica, Calif. and U.S. Office Child Devel., 1970-71; psychologist Stanford Research Inst., Menlo Park, Calif., 1972-78, sr. psychologist, SRI Internat., 1978-81, dir. Social Scis. Ctr., 1981—; cons. Active Common Cause, 1979—. Mem. AAAS, Am. Ednl. Research Assn., Evaluation Research Soc., Am. Vocat. Assn. Club: Brown U. of No. Calif. Author: Report on Preschool Programs, 1971; (with David Greene and Jane David) Local Implementation of Public Law 94-142, 1980; (with Michael Knapp and others) Cumulative Effects of Federal Education Policies on Schools and Districts, 1983. Office: SRI Internat 333 Ravenswood Ave Menlo Park CA 94025

STEARNS, STEWART WARREN, charitable assn. exec.; b. Denver, Apr. 8, 1947; s. Vinton H. and Marjorie L. (Tedro) S.; B.S., Eastern N.Mex. U., 1970; M.A., No. Ill. U., 1973; postgrad. SUNY, Albany, 1974—; m. Marjorie L. Fuller, Jan. 25, 1969; children—Theresa Lyn, Gregory Robert. Mng. editor Studies in Linguistics, DeKalb, Ill., 1972-73; instr. No. Ill. U., DeKalb, 1972-73; cons. AID, Guatemala, 1973-74; instr. Skidmore Coll., Saratoga Springs, N.Y., 1975; OAS fellow, Guatemala, 1976-77; asst. dir. Chaves County Community Action Program, Roswell, N.Mex., 1977-78; exec. dir. United Way Chaves County, Roswell, 1978-83, Eastern N.Mex. Med. Ctr. Found., Roswell, 1983—; bd. dirs. Eastern N. Mex. U.-Roswell, 1982; bd. mem. Chaves County Community Action Program, 1979; treas. Chaves County Interagy. Council, 1980. Mem. All-America City Task Force, Roswell, 1978-79. NDEA fellow, Dallas, 1970-71. Mem. Am. Anthrop. Assn., Latin Am. Antropology Group, Am. Soc. Applied Antropology, Sigma Xi. Presbyterian. Clubs: Rotary (com. chmn. 1979-80), Noonday Toastmasters (adminstrv. v.p. 1979-80) (Roswell). Home: 2302 Mills Roswell NM 88201 Office: 405 W Country Club Rd Roswell NM 88201

STECK, FERNE COLLEEN, state official, educator; b. Marceline, Mo., June 17, 1928; d. Lawrence Sandsberry and Ethel Lulu (Sportsman) Braley; m. Donley G. Steck, Oct. 11, 1948; children—Darla M. Steck Parker, Allen R., Jana L. Steck Paulauskis. B.A., San Diego U., 1964, M.S., 1969; Ed.D., Brigham Young U., 1979. Tchr., Pub. Schs. San Diego, 1963-74; in-service coordinator U. Calif.-Los Angeles, 1974-75; ednl. cons., 1975—; regional supr. Calif. Dept. Edn., Chico, 1975—. Mem. Am. Vocat. Assn., Am. Home Econs. Assn., Calif. Home Econs. Assn., Home Econs. Tchrs. Assn. Calif., Calif. Assn. Vocat. Educators, Kappa Delta Pi, Phi Upsilon Omicron. Democrat. Adventist.

STECKEL, BARBARA JEAN, city ofcl.; b. Los Angeles, Mar. 9, 1939; d. John Herschel and Bernice Evelyn (Selstad) Webb; B.A. in Acctg., U. Alaska, Anchorage, 1980; m. Dale R. Steckel, Mar. 16, 1962; children—Leanna Virginia, Debra Lynn, Richard Alan. Adminstrv. officer dept. public works Govt. Am. Samoa, Pago Pago, 1967-69; sec. to sch. bd. supt. Nome (Alaska) public schs., 1970-72; city clk.-treas. City of Kotzebue (Alaska), 1973-74, city mgr.-treas., 1974-76; grants adminstr. Municipality of Anchorage, 1976-79, controller, 1979-82, mcpl. mgr., 1982—; v.p. P.G. Hupperten & Assocs., Inc.; owner, mgr. Barb's Bus. Services, acctg., mgmt. services, 1976—; dir. Star Internat. Inc. Mem. Am. Soc. Women Accts., Am. Soc. Public Adminstrn., Mcpl. Fin. Officers Assn. (past pres. Alaska chpt.), Internat. City Mgmt. Assn., Alaska Mcpl. Mgrs. Assn., Nat. Council Govtl. Acctg. (bd. dirs. 1982—), Nat. Assn. Accts. Clubs: Soroptimists, Women of Moose. Office: 632 W 6th Pouch 6-650 Anchorage AK 99502

STEDMAN, JOHN MICHAEL, engineering research and development manager; b. San Francisco, Nov. 17, 1944; s. Milton Bertram and Joanna (Schelling) S.; m. Linda Carole Jones; children—Janet Lynn, Leslie Anne. B.E.E., Walla Walla (Wash.) Coll., 1966; M.E.E., Calif. State U.-San Jose, 1969. Research engr. Ames Research Ctr., NASA, Mountain View, Calif., 1967-69; devel. engr. Hewlett-Packard Co., Santa Clara, Calif., 1969-72, project/sect. mgr.-minicomputers, Cupertino, Calif., 1972-77, research and devel. mgr. computer peripherals, Boise, 1977—; lectr. computer architecture, Stanford U., 1976; campus recruiting mgr. for Hewlett-Packard, Stanford U., 1975-77, U. Utah, Utah State U., 1977—. Mem. IEEE. Contbr. articles in field to profl. jours. Home: 4834 Cresthaven Circle Boise ID 83704 Office: Hewlett-Packard Co PO Box 39 Boise ID 83707

STEED, GERALDINE ANN, ceramic tile company executive; b. Seattle, July 9, 1934; d. Edward Thomas and Helen Theresa (Flynn) Murphy; A.A., Los Angeles Valley Coll., 1954; C.T.C., Cermaic Tile Inst., 1976; m. Feb. 11, 1956; children—Edward Lee, Colleen Ann, William Lee, Heather Ann, Amanda Ann. Vice pres., fin. officer William L. Steed Tile, Inc., Ventura, Calif., 1970—; pres., fin. officer Buena Tile Supply, Inc., Ventura, 1978—; assoc. ceramic tile cons. program Ceramic Tile Inst., Los Angeles, 1976—. Treas., Y.L.I., Ventura, 1964-66, v.p., 1967-68, pres., 196-69, trustee, 1969-70; treas., fin. sec. Parent-Tchr. Guild, Our Lady of Assumption Sch., Ventura, 1972-74; mem. ways and means com. St. Bonaventure High Sch., Ventura, 1974-75. Mem. Ceramic Tile Inst. (Woman of Yr. award 1975), Ventura County Contractors Assn., Western States Ceramic Tile Contractors Assn., Tile Contractors Assn. Am., Tile Contractors Assn. So. Calif. Republican. Roman Catholic. Office: 11019 Nardo St PO Box 3259 Ventura CA 93006

STEELE, DONALD DICKINSON, public relations agency executive; b. Bozeman, Mont., Apr. 17, 1909; s. Fred M. and Cecille Roberta (Heywood) S.; student pub. and pvt. schs.; m. Evelyn Jane de Clairmont, May 8, 1932; 1 son, Donald de Clairmont. Founder, 1941, now chmn., pres. Steele Group, San Francisco; San Francisco pntr. IPR Group of Cos. Mem. Pub. Relations Soc. Am. (accredited), Pub. Relations Round Table. Republican. Clubs: Rotary, San Francisco Press, Olympic, Metropolitan, Shriners. Address: 703 Market St San Francisco CA 94103

STEELE, DONALD JOHN, JR., educational administrator; b. Saginaw, Mich.; s. Donald John and Maxine (Allison) S.; B.Sc., Central Mich. U., M.A. in Edn.; Ph.D., Ohio State U., 1973; m. Cheryl K. Lynes, Apr. 1, 1967; children—Mitchell, Kathryn. Successively, tchr., coach, prin., adminstr., supt. Saginaw (Mich.) Public Schs., 1965-78; supt. Toledo Public Schs., 1978-81; supt. Seattle Public Schs., 1981—; mem. faculty Ohio State U., Central Mich. U., U. Toledo. Mem. Sta. KCTS Ednl. TV Adv. Bd.; mem. exec. bd. Boy Scouts Am.; bd. dirs. Jr. Achievement. Recipient Educator of Year award Saginaw C. of C. Mem. Am. Assn. Sch. Adminstrs., Nat. Sch. Bds. Assn., Council of Great City Schs., Large-City Sch. Supts., Wash. Assn. Sch. Adminstrs., Wash. State Sch. Dirs. Assn., Supts. Ednl. TV Com., Seattle C. of C., World Futures Soc., Seattle Urban League. Club: Rotary (Seattle). Contbr. articles to profl. jours. Home: 4326 SW Donovan Seattle WA 98136 Office: 815 4th Ave N Seattle WA 98109

STEELE, ELLEN LIVELY, bus. devel. co. exec., pub. exec.; b. Fayette County, W.Va., Jan. 22, 1936; d. Alfred French and Sarah Ellen (Pritchard) L.; student N.Mex. State U., 1962-74; m. Henry Gilmer Steele, July 20, 1981; children—Gregory Benjamin Pake, Seana Ellen Pake. Civilian adminstrv. officer Dept. Army, White Sands Missile Range, N.Mex., 1962-67; mgr. Kelly Services Inc., Las Cruces, N.Mex., 1967—; pres. Lively Enterprises, Inc., Las Cruces, 1967-76; sec., treas. Adam II, Ltd., Las Cruces, 1973-77; pres. Dr. Romero's Symposium Internat. Inc., Las Cruces, 1977-78, Asset & Resource Mgmt. Corp., Las Cruces, 1978—; lit. agt., prin. Ellen Lively Steele & Assocs., 1979—; pres. AVVA III, 1981—; gen. dir. Gasco Internat., Inc., 1981-82; dir. Rosa Resources Corp. Served with USAF, 1954-57. Mem. Internat. Assn. Fin. Planners, Sales and Mktg. Execs. Internat., Internat. Alliance Sports Ofcls. (sec.-treas. 1982—), Am. Mgmt. Assn., D.A.R. Republican. Episcopalian. Club: Order Eastern Star; Assn. (Las Cruces). Home: Box 188 Organ NM 88052 Office: San Augustine Pass NM

STEELE, ELLEN LIVELY, management consultant; b. Long Branch, W.Va., Jan. 22, 1936; d. Alfred F. and Sarah Ellen (Pritchard) Lively; student N.Mex. State U.; children—Gregory Benjamin Pake, Seana Ellen Pake. With Dept. Army, White Sands Missile Range, N.Mex., 1962-68; pres. Lively Enterprises, Inc., Las Cruces, N.Mex., 1967-75; licensee Kelly Services, Inc., Las Cruces, 1967—; pres. Asset and Resource Mgmt. Corp., Washington and N.Mex., 1978—, Steele-Lively Industries, 1978—; owner Ellen Lively Steele & Assos., lit. agts., 1979—; pres. AVVA III, 1981-83; mng. dir. Savir, Inc., 1981—; adv. Dona Ana County Occupational Extension Program, N.Mex. State U., 1975-78; gen. ptnr. Internat. Alliance Sports Ofcls., 1981—. Mem. Task Force on Public Relations, N.Mex. Republican Party, 1977; vice chmn. Rep. Party of Dona Ana County, 1983; bd. dirs. Am. Cancer Soc., Dona Ana County chpt., 1970-71, fund drive chmn., 1970, v.p., 1970-71; bd. dirs. Planned Parenthood Assn. Dona Ana County, public affairs chmn., 1971-77. Served with USAF, 1954-57. Recipient Community Service Gold medal Kelly Services Inc., 1969-77. Mem. Internat. Assn. Fin. Planners, Am. Mgmt. Assn., DAR, Las Cruces C. of C. (mem. public relations com. 1968-73). Republican. Episcopalian. Clubs: Picacho Hills Country (chmn. bd. govs. 1981—), Order Eastern Star. Address: PO Box 188 Organ NM 88052

STEELE, JOHN ROY, real estate broker; b. Detroit, Feb. 16, 1945; s. Wallace Lee Roy and Kay F. (Fitzpatrick) S.; B.A., Alma Coll., 1967; M.B.A., Central Mich. U., 1968; m. Beverly Louise Rauh, June 3, 1972; children—Josh Oliver, Matt Edward, Anne Elizabeth. Owner/broker Century 21 Steele, Realtors, Jackson, Calif., 1981—; partner/broker Century 21, Lewis-Steele, Realtors, Inc., Jackson and Truckee, Calif., 1976-81; dir. Amador Title Co., 1978-83, pres., 1978-79. Bd. dirs. Trinity Episcopal Ch., Sutter Creek, Calif., 1978-79, 80-83, jr. warden, 1979; trustee Citizens for Progress, 1981—. Mem. Amador County Bd. Realtors (bd. dirs. 1974-82, pres. 1978), Calif. Assn. Realtors (dir. 1978). Club: Friends of the Library. Office: PO Box 210 Jackson CA 95642

STEELE, JUDI KANDEL, ednl. adminstr.; b. N.Y.C., Nov. 14, 1943; d. Robert and Evelyn (Golden) Abrams; B.A., Hunter Coll., 1965, postgrad., 1965-66; M.A., U. Nev., 1971, postgrad., 1972-77; m. Arthur Steele, Sept. 18, 1975; children—Elyse Kandel, Arthur Lewis. Elem. tchr. N.Y.C. Bd. Edn., 1965-67, Steward Sch., Providence, 1967-69; tchr. Clark County Sch. Dist., Las Vegas, 1969-70, 71-75, coordinator spl. student services, 1975-78, dir. spl. student services, 1978—; lectr. U. Nev., Las Vegas, 1970-71. Mem. Nat. Elem. Sch. Prin. Assn., Council for Exceptional Children, Clark County Assn. Sch. Adminstrs., Assn. Supervision and Curriculum Devel., Western Exchange for Gifted and Talented, Phi Delta Kappa. Office: Clark County School Dist 2832 E Flamingo Rd Las Vegas NV 89121

STEELE, KEVIN EDWARD, editor; b. Paterson, N.J., Sept. 4, 1954; s. Edward Peter and Helen Catherine (Konzelman) S.; B.A. in Journalism, San Diego State U., 1975; grad. Dale Carnegie Mgmt. Seminar, 1976. Media dir. Carelli, Glynn & Ward Advt., Butler, N.J., 1976-77; dir. public relations Thomas J. Collins & Assocs., Cerritos, Calif., 1977-82; asst. editorial dir., mng. editor Publs. Devel. Corp., San Diego, 1982—; mng. editor Survive Mag., Omega Group Ltd., Boulder, Colo.; firearms cons., writer. Mem. Nat. Rifle Assn. Republican. Roman Catholic. Contbr. articles to various publs. Home: 363 Dudes Dr Rollinsville CO 80474 Office: 5735 Arapahoe Ave Boulder CO 80303

STEELE, ROBERT NORMAN, university trust and investment officer; b. Salmon, Idaho, Aug. 10, 1940; s. Norman W. and Ruby F. (Jackson) S.; m. Pamela Rae Bunch, June 10, 1963; children—Robert Broc, Wendy Malia, Summer Rae. B.S. in Bus. Aminstrn., U. Idaho, 1963; cert. Coll. Bus. Mgmt. Inst., U. Nebr., Omaha, 1974, Bus. Mgmt. Inst., Stanford U., 1975. Staff auditor Haskins & Sells, Seattle, 1967-71; controller Wyckoff Co., Seattle, 1971-72; internal auditor U. Idaho, Moscow, 1973-74, asst. bus. mgr., 1974-75, trust and investment officer, 1975—; dir., treas. Idaho Research Found., Inc. Served with Signal Corps, U.S. Army, 1963-67. Decorated Nat. Def. medal; Commendation medal. Mem. Nat. Assn. Univ. and Coll. Bus. Officers, Idaho Ad Club (trustee meml. scholarship trust). Club: Rotary (pres. Moscow 1980-81). Home: 209 S Garfield Moscow ID 83843 Office: Office of Fin Affairs U Idaho Moscow ID 83843

STEELE, RODERICK M., lumber and paper company executive; b. 1925. B.A. in Bus., U. Wash., 1947. Sr. acct. Arthur Andersen & Co., 1947-51; contractor Twin Feather Mills Inc., 1951-53; treas. River Lumber Co., 1953-54, Pack River Co., 1943-63; div. contractor Potlatch Corp., San Francisco, 1963, gen. mgr. western ops. wood products group, 1967, v.p. western wood products group, 1968, corp. v.p., 1970, group v.p. wood products, 1972, exec. v.p. ops., 1974, pres., chief operating officer, 1977—; chmn. bd. govs. Nat. Council Paper Industry for Air and Steam Improvements Inc. Mem. Nat. Forest Products Assn. (bd. dirs.), Western Wood Product Assn., Am. Wood Council. Served with USN, 1943-46. Office: Potlatch Corp One Maritime Plaza PO Box 3591 San Francisco CA 94119*

STEELE, WILLIAM CLINTON, geologist, computer programmer; b. Kansas City, Mo., Sept. 1, 1950; s. William Herbert and Hilah May (Moss) S.; B.S., Ind. State U., 1972; Ph.D., Stanford U., 1979; m. Judith Ann Jordan, Sept. 1, 1971. Geologist, remote sensing analyst U.S. Geol. Survey, Menlo Park, Calif., 1975-79, analyst/computer programmer, 1979—. Recipient U.S. Geol. Survey Spl. Achievement award, 1977, 81; Alice C. Steel Meml. fellow, 1972-73; William W. Orcutt Meml. fellow, 1972-75; H.G. Schenek Meml. fellow, 1973-74; Robert H. Palmer Meml. fellow, 1974-75; Harvey S. Mudd Meml. fellow, 1975; Ernest Gale Martin Meml. fellow, 1975; Shell Cos. Found. grantee, 1973; Sigma Xi. research grantee, 1974. Mem. Geol. Soc. Am., Am. Soc. Photogrammetry, Sigma Xi, Sigma Zeta, Sigma Gamma Epsilon. Contbr. articles to profl. jours. Office: 345 Middlefield Rd Menlo Park CA 94025

STEELMAN, SUSAN JEAN, public relations executive; b. Los Angeles, Aug. 25, 1957; d. Claude and Leota (Chapman) S. B.A. in Journalism and Polit. Sci., Pepperdine U., 1980. Intern, Congl. Environ. Study Conf., Washington, 1978, White House Press Office, summer 1980; regional press coordinator Carter/Mondale Re-election Campaign, Washington, 1980; account exec. DJMC Advt., San Francisco, 1981; communications dir. Calif. Beef Council, Foster, City, 1982—. Leader 4-H Club; YMCA Youth and Govt. program advisor. Recipient Editorial Leadership award Pepperdine U., 1980, named best all-around journalist, 1979. Mem. Soc. Profl. Journalists (Outstanding Journalism grad. 1980), Pub. Relations Soc. Am., Women for Agriculture. Club: Commonwealth of Calif. Editor-in-chief coll. newspaper: Pepperdine Univ. of the Graphic, 1980, coll. mags.: Oasis, 1979, Impressions, 1978. Home: 920 Walnut St San Carlos CA 94070 Office: 551 Foster City Blvd Foster City CA 94404

STEEN, ATLE, ocean engineer; b. Hamar, Norway, July 12, 1946; came to U.S., 1966, naturalized, 1977; s. Odd and Rita Alice (Lövheim) S.; student U. Vt., 1966-68; B.S. in Architecture, M.I.T., 1970, M.S. in Naval Architecture, engr.'s degree Ocean Engring., 1974. Sr. ocean engr. Kennecott Exploration, Inc., San Diego, 1974-80; sr. staff engr. TRW, Redondo Beach, Calif., 1980—. Mem. Sigma Xi, Four Sigma. Co-author article in field. Home: 1396 Summit Ave Cardiff CA 92007 Office: S-2049 1 Space Park 1 Space Park Redondo Beach CA 90278

STEEN, PETER, copper company executive; b. Johannesburg, S. Africa, Dec. 8, 1930; s. Oscar Jul and Eleen Edward (Brock) S.; came to U.S., 1978; Asso., Camborne (Eng.) Sch. Mines, 1956; m. Norma Valerie Crawford, Feb. 16, 1956; children—Beverley Ann, Gregory Jul, Karen Louise, Michael Rodney. From ofcl. learner to mine supt. Anglo American, Zambia, 1956-68; mine supt. Rio Algom Mines, LaRonge, Sask., Can., 1968-70; gen. mgr. Whitehorse, Copper Mines, Yukon, Can., 1970-73; exec. v.p. Cassiar Asbestos Corp., Vancouver, B.C., Can., 1973-74, pres., chief exec. officer, 1974-78; pres., chief exec. officer Inspiration Consol. Copper Co., Phoenix, 1978—; dir. Apache Powder Co. Mem. Am. Inst. Mining Engrs., Mine Mgrs. Assn. S. Africa, Profl. Engrs. Assn. of Ont., Can. Inst. Mining and Metallurgy. Office: 100 W Washington St Phoenix AZ 85003

STEENBLOCK, DAVID ALAN, physician, research scientist; b. Buffalo Center, Iowa, Jan. 7, 1943; s. Raymond and Opal (Sterenberg) S.; m. Noyemy der Alexanian, June 30, 1979; 1 dau., Karen. B.S. in Zoology, Iowa State U., 1964; M.S. in Biochemistry, Coll. Osteo. Medicine, 1967, D.O., 1970. Diplomate Am. Bd. Family Practice. Pres. Steenblock Med. Clinic, El Toro, Calif., 1978—; pres. Aging Research Inst., El Toro, 1979—; asst. clin. prof. Mich. State U.; instr. Coll. Osteo. Medicine, Pomona, Calif. Mem. Ortho Molecular Med., Soc., Am. Holistic Med. Assn., N.Y. Acad. Scis., Internat. Acad. Nutritional Cons. Republican. Home: 22821 Lake Forest Dr #114 El Toro CA 92630

STEER, JERRY HARVEY, contractor real estate investor; b. Chgo., July 14, 1936; s. Theodore and Yetta (Sloan) S.; student public schs., Chgo.; m. Muritta Elverman, Apr. 19, 1969; children—Darci, Theodore, Shane. With various automobile franchises, Chgo., 1955-69; real estate developer, home builder, exec. v.p. Northwestern Ranches, Phoenix, 1974—, Valley Land Co., Chgo., 1970—, Scottsdale (Ariz.) Nat., Inc., 1973—, Steer West Enterprises Inc., J.R. Ventures Inc., 1982—. Active Boys Club, Girl Scouts U.S.A., Phoenix. Mem. Am. Land Developers Assn., Homebuilders Assn., Better Bus. Bur., Airline and Owners Pilots Assn. Jewish. Clubs: The Plaza, LaCosa Hotels and Spas, Chapparal Racquet. Home: Paradise Valley AZ 85253 Office: 4235 N 32d St Phoenix AZ 85018

STEERE, SUSAN HELENE BOYD, writer; b. Winona, Minn., Oct. 7, 1941; d. Fredrick E. and Dolores M. (Mohrbacher) Leicht; student Coll. St. Teresa, 1960-61; B.S. in Art Edn. with distinction, U. Minn., 1963; M.A. in Social Anthropology, U. Mont., 1975; m. Lance R. Boyd, Apr. 4, 1964 (div. 1978); m. Peter Lawson Steere, Dec. 29, 1979; children—Bretton Thomas, Megan Helene Boyd. Art educator Minn. schs., 1964-67, Northwest Mo. State U. Lab. Sch., Maryville, 1967, Mpls. Inst. Arts, summer 1966; research asso. Western Mont. Planning Area Guide Team, U.S. Forest Service, 1975; instr. dept. anthropology U. Mont., 1977; editorial asst. dept. social mgmt. of tech. U. Wash., Seattle, summer 1978; cons.-mgr. Mont. Human Resources Devel. Council Dirs. Assn., Helena, 1978-79, Mont. Land Reliance, Helena, 1979; free lance writer, 1980—; editor cultural resources div. Mineral Research Center, Butte, Mont., 1981; cons. Nat. Endowment for Arts, 1977-78. Recipient awards for playwriting. Fellow Assn. Anthrop. Study of Play; mem. Am. Anthrop. Assn., Am. Theater Assn., Soc. Am. Archaeology, Mont. Archaeol. Soc., Dramatists Guild, Pacific Northwest Writers Assn., Soc. Visual Edn., Am. Ethnol. Soc., Butte Hist. Soc., Butte Art Chateau, Sigma Xi, Sigma Delta Pi. Episcopalian. Author: (plays) Cockfight, St. Mael and the Maldunkian Penguins; contbr. articles to anthrop. jours. Home: 4912 Santa Maria St Amado AZ 85640 Office: PO Box 422 Amado AZ 85640

STEFFEN, THOMAS LEE, state supreme court justice; b. Tremonton, Utah, July 9, 1930; s. Conrad Richard and Jewel Prudence (McGuire) S.; student U. Utah, 1948-49, B.S. in Polit. Sci., 1957; postgrad. U. So. Calif., 1955-56; J.D. with honors, George Washington U., 1964; m. LaVona Ericksen, Mar. 20, 1953; children—Elizabeth, Catherine, Conrad, John, Jennifer. Bar: Nev. 1965, U.S. Dist. Ct. (no. dist.) Nev. 1965, U.S. Tax Ct. 1966, U.S. Ct. Appeals (9th cir.) 1967, U.S. Supreme Ct. 1977. Sr. ptnr. Steffen, Simmons & Vannah, Las Vegas, Nev., 1979-82; justice Supreme Ct. of Nev., Carson City, 1982—; former chmn. Medico-Legal Screening Panel, So. Nev. Dist.; former chmn. Eagle Character Bd. of Rev. Bd. dirs. NCCJ. Mem. Nev. Trial Lawyers Assn. (dir.), Nev. State Bar (chmn. Amicus com. 19). Mormon. Contbr. articles to legal publs. Home: 1204 Charmast Ln Las Vegas NV 89102 Office: Capitol Complex Carson City NV 89710

STEGALL, BENJAMIN IRVING, JR., investment company executive; b. Griffin, Ga., Oct. 1, 1933; s. Benjamin Irving and Hilda (Span) S.; m. Doris Ilene Schoenberg, Mar. 4, 1962; children—Wendy Lauren, Sheri Dawn. B.Indsl. Engring., Ga. Tech. U., 1954; postgrad. UCLA, 1958-61. Registered rep. N.Y. Stock Exchange, 1961. Engr., Douglas Aircraft, Santa Monica, Calif., 1956-60; account exec. Merrill Lynch Pierce Fenner & Smith, Inc., Los Angeles, Hollywood and Santa Monica, Calif., 1960—. Nation chief Indian Princess program Santa Monica YMCA, 1981-82; trustee Beth Sholom Temple, 1979-81. Served to 1st lt. U.S. Army, 1954-56. Jewish. Clubs: Wilshire West Optimist (sec. treas. 1963-66, pres. 1966-67), Crescent Bay Toastmasters (pres. 1965-66), Red Ribbon Squares (pres. 1980-81), (Santa Monica), Masons, Shriners. Home: 424 Euclid St Santa Monica CA 90402 Office: 1299 Ocean Ave Santa Monica CA 90001

STEIGER, KENNETH DAVID, symphony manager, musician, music contractor; b. Far Rockaway, N.Y., July 6, 1956; s. Aaron and Florence Betty (Cohen) S.; m. Kathryn Sue Berbos, June 10, 1983. B.A. in Music, SUNY-Binghamton, 1978, M.B.A., 1981. Mgmt. intern, asst. to mng. dir. Hartford (Conn.) Symphony Orch., 1981; gen. mgr. Casper (Wyo.) Symphony Orch., 1982—, ex-officio dir. orch.; music performer and contractor. Coach Casper Ice Hockey Assn., 1982-83; mem. Casper Mcpl. Band, 1982, 83. Regent's scholar, N.Y., 1974-78; fellow Sch. Mgmt., SUNY, Binghamton, 1980, intern scholar, 1981. Mem. Am. Council for Arts, Am. Symphony Orch. League (S.W. regional rep., mem. div. bd.), Am. Fedn. Musicians Local 381, Wyo. Arts Alliance,

Casper Area C. of C. (econ. and community devel. com. 1982—). Republican. Jewish. Club: Casper Lynx Men's Ice Hockey, Jaycees. Editor: Con Moto, News of the Casper Symphony Orchestra, 1983—. Office: 333 N Wolcott Casper WY 82601

STEIN, ARTHUR OSCAR, physician; b. Bklyn., Apr. 3, 1932; s. Irving I. and Sadie (Brander) S.; A.B., Harvard U., 1953; M.D., Tufts U., 1957; postgrad. U. Chgo., 1963-66; m. Judith Lenore Hurwitz, Aug. 27, 1955; children—Susan, Jeffrey, Benjamin. Intern U. Chgo. Hosps., 1957-58, resident, 1958-59; resident N.Y. Hosp.-Cornell U. Med. Center, 1959-61; practice medicine specializing in pediatrics, 1963—; instr. pediatrics U. Chgo., 1963-66, asst. prof. pediatrics, 1966-70; mem. Healthguard Med. Group, San Jose, Calif., 1970-72; mem. Permanente Med. Group, San Jose, 1972—; asst. chief pediatrics Santa Teresa Med. Center, 1979—; clin. instr. Santa Clara Valley Med. Center, Stanford U., 1970-72. Served to capt., M.C., AUS, 1961-63. USPHS Postdoctoral fellow, 1963-66. Fellow Am. Acad. Pediatrics. Jewish (v.p. congregation 1969-70, pres. 1972-73). Clubs: Light and Shadow Camera (pres. 1978-80) (San Jose); Central Coast Counties Camera (v.p. 1980-81, pres. 1981-82). Co-discoverer (with Glyn Dawson) genetic disease Lactosylceramidosis, 1969. Home: 956 Redmond Ave San Jose CA 95120 Office: Kaiser/Permanente Med Group 260 Internat Circle San Jose CA 95119

STEIN, BARRY MARK, psychologist; b. N.Y.C., Aug. 19, 1948; s. Sol George and Ruth (Edelsohn) S.; B.A., U. Louisville, 1970; M.A., Spalding Coll., 1971. Research assoc. Kemper & Assocs., Louisville, 1969-71; sr. psychometrist Neuropsychiat. Inst., UCLA, 1972-73; vocat. psychologist Calif. Depts. Corrections and Rehab., San Luis Obispo, 1973-76; vocat. psychologist, lead instr. Calif. Dept. Rehab., Los Angeles, 1976-82; instr. Rancho Los Amigos Hosp., 1978-79; adj. clin. faculty, supr. grad. students Calif. Sch. Profl. Psychology, Los Angeles, 1982—; supr. grad. students Loyola Marymount U., Calif. Grad. Inst., Calif. State U.; lectr., cons. in field. Mem. Western, San Luis Obispo psychol. assns., Epilepsy Found. Am. Am. Personnel and Guidance Assn., Am. Correctional Assn., Calif. Correctional Psychiatrists and Psychologists Assn., Soc. Am. Inventors, Zeta Beta Tau. Jewish. Patentee headrest. Home: 7742 Redlands St Box 3032 Playa Del Rey CA 90293 Office: 8929 S Sepulveda Blvd Suite 300 Los Angeles CA 90045

STEIN, DONALD EUGENE, manufacturing company executive; b. Upper Gwynedd, Pa., Mar. 31, 1932; s. Albert M. and Esther N. (Sweigert) S.; B.S. in Mech. Engring., U. Ariz., 1957; m. Germaine M. Krauss, Jan. 7, 1956; children—Jeffrey E., Wendelin A., Dorlissa J. Project mgr. Honeywell Co., Pottstown, Pa., 1958-62; mgr. engring. Compudyne Corp., Hatboro, Pa., 1962-65; pres. K-Tron Internat., Scottsdale, Ariz., 1965—. Nat. dir. Big Bros. and Big Sisters Am., Am. Humanics; chmn. bd. Mgmt. Inst., Glassboro State Coll., 1977-78. Mem. Assn. Corporate Growth (mem. pres.' assn.), Delta Sigma Phi. Republican. Club: Masons (Lansdale, Pa.). Patentee in field. Office: 7975 N Hayden Rd Scottsdale AZ 85258

STEIN, JUSTIN JOHN, physician, educator, b. Haskell, Tex., Oct. 18 1907; s. Justin John and Annie Minnie (Frederick) S.; M.D., Baylor U., 1933; m. Lillian May Kolar, Oct. 23, 1936; 1 dau. Justine Johanna. Intern, Cin. Gen. Hosp., 1934-35; spl. student Mayo Clinic and Found., 1933-34; tumor surgeon, radiotherapist Edward Hines Jr. VA Hosp., Hines, Ill., 1935-41; cons. Elmhurst (Ill.) Community, West-Lake hosps., Melrose Park, 1938-41; tumor surgeon, radiotherapist Los Angeles Tumor Inst., 1946-52; attending surgeon, mem. tumor bd., malignancy service Los Angeles County Hosp., 1948-59; cons. onocologost VA, West Los Angeles, 1948-75; attending surg. staff Calif. Hosp., Los Angeles, 1945-52; dir. Calif. Inst. Cancer Research, 1955-76, sec., 1966-75; prof. radiology U. Calif. Sch. Medicine, Los Angeles, 1952-75, prof. emeritus radiol. scis., 1975—, chief div. radiation therapy, dept. radiology, 1955-70, radiologic safety adv. com. (all campuses), 1955-60, acting chmn. dept. radiology, 1960, cancer coordinator, 1955-75, dir. Cancer Research Inst., 1956-70, cons. to lab. nuclear medicine and radiobiology, 1960-64, exec. coordinator for radiation therapy residency tng. program UCLA, 1970-75; clin. prof. radiol. scis. U. Calif., Irvine, 1976—; chief radiation therapy VA Hosp., Long Beach, Calif., 1975—, cons.-lectr. U.S. naval hosps., San Diego, Long Beach; exchange prof. Ministry Higher and Specialized Edn. USSR, 1963; chmn. Gov.'s Emergency Med Adv. Com., 1950-67, dir. Calif. div. Am. Cancer Soc., 1950-79, mem. exec. com., 1963-65, dir.-at-large, 1963-65, del. to nat. soc., 1966, pres. Los Angeles br., 1964-65, dir.-at- large, vice chmn. med. and sci. exec. com. N.Y. br., nat. dir.-at-large, 1968-74, chmn. nat. exec. com. of med. and sci. com., 1970-73, v.p., 1972-73, pres., 1973-74, nat. past officer dir., 1976-82, pres. Calif. div., 1977; cons. radiotherapy or radiology to various hosps. and health agys.; mem. Calif. Bd. Med. Examiners, 1952-70, v.p., 1955, pres., 1956; cancer rep. from Am. Coll. Radiology to ACS, 1960-68. Hon. life mem. state and nat. bd. dirs. Am. Cancer Soc. Served to lt comdr. M.C., USNR, 1941-46. Diplomate Am. Bd. Radiology (trustee, chmn. com. on recertification), Internat. Bd. Surgery. Fellow Am. Coll. Nuclear Medicine, ACS (exec. com care of patient with cancer 1967-70), Internat. Coll. Surgeons (pres. So. Calif. chpt. 1952, vice regent 1953-65), Royal Soc. Medicine (Eng); mem. Am. Radium Soc. (pres. 1965-66, mem. exec. com. 1962-69), Pan Pacific Surg. Assn., AAAS, Radiation Research Soc., Research Soc. Calif., Soc. Nuclear Medicine, Am. Soc. Therapeutic Radiologists, Radiol. Soc. So. Calif., Am. Roentgen Ray Soc. (2d v.p. 1965-66), Med.-Dental Vets. Assn. (pres. 1949), James Ewing Soc., Los Angeles Surg. Soc. (sr.), Calif., Los Angeles radiol. socs., Radiol. Soc. N.Am., Am., Los Angeles County (councillor 1950-53), Calif. (ho. of dels. 1950-54, 55-57, 61-63, chmn. com. sci. info. 1964-66) med. assns., Dallas So. Clin. Soc. (hon.), Peruvian Cancer Soc. (hon.), Am. Cancer Soc. (hon. life), Ky. Obstetrical and Gynecol. Soc. (hon.), Mil. Order World Wars (surgeon gen. 1954), Kappa Sigma, Phi Chi. Asso. editor Breast. Contbr. numerous sci. articles to med. jours. Home: 3526A Bahia Blanca W Laguna Hills CA 92653

STEIN, PAT, accountant, business appraiser; b. Galion, Ohio, Dec. 20, 1934; d. Howard G. and Margaret M. (Burns) Whitesell; m. Nathan Stein, Dec. 30, 1958; children—Andrea, Victoria, Barron. B.S. in Bus., Ohio State U., 1956; postgrad. in Acctg., UCLA, 1968-70; postgrad. in Econs., La Universidad de las Americas, 1956-57. C.P.A. Pres. Pat Stein Accountancy Corp., Torrance, Calif., 1978—, Business Valuations, Inc., Torrance, 1980—. Treas. Peninsula Symphony Assn.; active Palos Verdes Republican Women. Mem. Am. Women's Soc. C.P.A.s, Calif. Soc. C.P.A.s, Am. Inst. C.P.A.s, South Bay Estate Planning Council, Bus. and Profl. Women, Torrance C. of C. Club: Torrance Athletic. Office: 3828 W Carson 101 Torrance CA 90503

STEIN, RANDY, accountant; b. Detroit, June 23, 1953; s. Lester H. and Rosalyn (Binder) S. B.S. in Acctg., Fla. State U., 1975. C.P.A. Acct., Coopers & Lybrand, Denver, 1975-80, Petro-Lewis Corp., Denver, 1980—. Mem. Young Men's Active 20/30 Club. Mem. Oil Investment Inst. (chmn. tax com.), Ind. Petroleum Assn. Mountain States. Club: Internat. Athletic (Denver). Home: 8760D E Yale Ave Denver CO 80231 Office: Petro-Lewis Corp PO Box 2250 717 17th St Denver CO 80201

STEINBECK, JOHN WITHERUP, II, ednl. adminstr.; b. St. Louis, Feb. 14, 1931; s. John William and Fayne Harriet (Witherup) S.; B.A. magna cum laude, Westminster (Mo.) Coll., 1952; postgrad. law U. Mich., Ann Arbor, 1952-53; M.A., Ind. U., 1955, postgrad., 1960-61; Ph.D., La Jolla U., 1983; m. Jeanette Palmer Hubbard, June 16, 1957; children—Jeffrey Alan, John Witherup, Sarah Jane Bunker. Tchr., Judson Sch., Scottsdale, Ariz., 1954-55; research tchr., counselor Imperial Valley Coll., El Centro, Calif., 1955-56; tchr., chmn. dept. social studies Citrus Coll.; tchr. Azusa (Calif.) High Sch., 1957-60; master tchr. Morton Jr. Coll., Cicero, Ill., 1961-63; instr. Ind. U., Bloomington, 1960-61; founder, owner, dir., headmaster The Villa Sch., Casa Grande, Ariz., 1964—. Pres., The Villa Sch. Found. Edn., Inc., 1973—. Mem. S.A.R., Ariz., So. Ariz. assns. ind. acad. schs., Phi Gamma Delta, Phi Alpha Theta. Episcopalian. Mason. Club: Cholla Bay (Mexico) Sportsmen's. Home: 3640 N Toltec Rd Toltec AZ 85231 Office: The Villa-Oasis School PO Box 1218 Casa Grande AZ 85222

STEINBERG, GUNTHER, chemist, cons. and mfg. co. exec.; b. Cologne, Germany, Apr. 14, 1924; came to U.S., 1938, naturalized, 1943; s. Herbert H. and Hetty (Kohsen) S.; B.S., UCLA, 1948, M.S., 1950, Ph.D., 1956; m. Beatrice Rose, Aug. 20, 1949; children—Paul Gunther, Julia Claire. Chemist, Martinez Research Lab., Shell Oil Co., 1956-61, Shell Devel. Co., 1961-64, Stanford Research Inst., 1964-67; sr. chemist, mgr. research, mgr. advanced devel., sr. staff scientist Memorex Corp., Santa Clara, Calif., 1967-77; founder, pres., dir. Steinberg Assocs. (inc. 1980), Portola Valley, Calif., 1977—. Active home owners groups, Walnut Creek, Menlo Park, Portola Valley. Served with M.I., U.S. Army, 1943-45. Decorated Bronze Star, Purple Heart. Mem. Am. Chem. Soc., N.Am. Thermal Analysis Soc., Profl. and Tech. Cons. Assn., Internat. Assn. Colloid and Interface Scientists. Republican. Jewish. Contbr. articles on physiol. chemistry, surface chemistry and surface calorimetry to tech. publs. Home and Office: 95 Lerida Ct Portola Valley CA 94025

STEINBERG, HERMAN WILLIAM, JR., clinical psychologist; b. Passaic, N.J., Dec. 12, 1948; s. Herman William and Selma Moore S.; A.B., Duke U., 1969; M.A., U.Calif., Santa Barbara, 1971; M.A., Calif. Sch. Profl. Psychology, 1974, Ph.D., 1976. Psychol. intern C.G. Jung Inst. and Clinic, Los Angeles, 1974-76, Olive View Hosp. Community Mental Health Center, Los Angeles, 1975-76; exec. dir. Santa Barbara Night Counseling Center, 1977; staff psychologist Met. State Hosp., Norwalk, Calif., 1978-80; pvt. practice clin. psychology, Pasadena, Calif., 1978-80, Long Beach, Calif., 1980—; chief psychol. services St. Mary Med. Center, Long Beach, Calif., 1980—; clin. asst. prof. Grad. Sch. Psychology, Fuller Theol. Sem., 1980-82. Mem. Am. Psychol. Assn., Calif. Neuropsychol. Soc. Office: St Mary Med Center PO Box 887 Long Beach CA 90801

STEINBERG, JOAN EMILY, educator; b. San Francisco, Dec. 9, 1932; d. John Emil and Kathleen Helen (Montgomery) S.; B.A., U. Calif.-Berkeley, 1954; Ed.D., U. San Francisco, 1981. Tchr., Vallejo (Calif.) Unified Sch. Dist., 1959-61, San Francisco Unified Sch. Dist., 1961—, tchr. life and phys. sci. jr. high sch., 1978—. Fulbright scholar U. Sydney (Australia), 1955-56. Mem. Audubon Soc., Nat. Wildlife Fedn., Oceanic Soc., Nature Conservancy, Astron. Soc. Pacific, Am. Fedn. Tchrs., AAAS, Calif. Acad. Scis., Calif. Malacozool. Soc., Nat. Sci. Tchrs. Assn., Elem. Sch. Sci. Assn., Calif. Sci. Tchrs. Assn., Internat. Reading Assn., Sigma Xi. Democrat. Contbr. articles to profl. jours. Home: 424 43d Ave San Francisco CA 94121 Office: San Francisco Unified Sch Dist San Francisco CA 94102

STEINBERG, LAURENCE DAVID, psychologist, educator, cons.; b. Long Branch, N.J.; s. Irwin I. and Mollie S.; m. Wendy Brodhead, Aug. 27, 1982. A.B. in Psychology with honors with distinction, Vassar Coll., 1974; Ph.D. (Univ. fellow), Cornell U., 1977; lic. psychologist, Calif. Asst. prof. social ecology U. Calif.-Irvine, 1977-82, assoc. prof., 1982—; cons. in field. Mem. Am. Psychol. Assn., Soc. Research in Child Devel., Phi Beta Kappa. Author: The Life Cycle: Readings on Human Development, 1981; Adolescent Development in Context; contbr. articles to profl. jours.

STEINBERG, LEON HARRY, physician; b. Warsaw, Poland, Jan. 8, 1928; s. Morris Arron and Lena (Baum) S.; came to U.S., 1938, naturalized, 1944; B.S., U. Ill., 1950, M.D., 1954; m. Frieda Stendig, Aug. 28, 1954; children—David, Alan, Diane, Brian and Suzanne. Intern at VA Hosp., Long Beach, Calif., 1954-55; resident U. Ill. Research and Ednl. Hosp., Chgo., 1955-58, practice medicine specializing in radiology, Las Vegas, Nev., 1958—; chief radiology Sunrise Hosp., Las Vegas, 1958-71; mem. staff Valley Hosp., co-chmn. dept. radiology Valley Hosp., Las Vegas, 1977—; cons. radiology Nellis AFB, Las Vegas, Nev., Nev. Test Site Dispensary, Mercury, Nev.; dir. Nev. Nat. Bank. Served as cpl. USAAF, 1946-47. Mem. AMA, Am. Coll. Radiology, Radiol. Soc. N.A., Nev. Med. Soc., Phi Beta Kappa, Alpha Omega Alpha, Phi Kappa Phi, Phi Eta Sigma, Phi Delta Epsilon. Home: 1717 Chapman Dr Las Vegas NV 89104 Office: 2300 Rancho Dr Las Vegas NV 89102

STEINBERG, RICHARD DAVID, psychologist, educator; b. Chgo., Apr. 22, 1947; s. Martin and Betty (Soglin) S.; m. Nancy Elizabeth Johnson, June 27, 1980. B.A. with honors in Psychology, U. Calif.-Berkeley, 1968; M.A. in Clin. Psychology, York U., Toronto, Ont., Can., 1970, Ph.D. in Clin. Psychology, 1975. Lic. psychologist, Calif., B.C. Instr., U. Toronto, 1974; clin. psychologist dept. psychiatry Nanaimo (Can.) Regional Hosp., 1975-79; vis. faculty mem. U. B.C., Vancouver, Can., 1977; lectr. U. Victoria (B.C.), 1977; pvt. practice, Santa Barbara, Calif., 1979—; staff psychologist Camarillo (Calif.) State Hosp., 1979—; psychol. cons. Sansum Med. Clinic, Santa Barbara, 1981—; instr. U. Calif. Extension, Santa Barbara, 1981—. Can. Council doctoral fellow, 1971-73. Mem. Santa Barbara Assn. Clin. Psychologists (pres. 1982), Am. Psychol. Assn., Calif. State Psychol. Assn., Can. Psychol. Assn. B.C. Psychol. Assn., Western Psychol. Assn., Am. Personnel and Guidance Assn., Calif. Neuropsychology Soc., Assn. for Advancement Psychology. Democrat. Jewish. Home: 5058 Ella Ln Santa Barbara CA 93111 Office: 2417 Castillo St Santa Barbara CA 93105

STEINBERG, WARREN LINNINGTON, school principal; b. N.Y.C., Jan. 20, 1924; s. John M. and Gertrude (Vogel) S.; student U. So. Calif., 1943-44, U. Calif. at Los Angeles, 1942-43, 46-47, B.A., 1949, M.Ed., 1951, Ed.D., 1962; m. Beatrice Ruth Blass, June 29, 1947; children—Leigh William, James Robert, Donald Kenneth. Tchr., counselor, coach Jordan High Sch., Watts, Los Angeles, 1951-57; tchr. athletic coordinator Hamilton High Sch., Los Angeles, 1957-62; boys' vice prin. Univ. High Sch., Los Angeles, 1962-67, Crenshaw Hig Sch., Los Angeles, 1967-68; cons. Center for Planned Change, Los Angeles City Sch., 1968-69; instr. edn. UCLA, 1965-71; boys' vice prin. LeConte Jr. High Sch., Los Angeles, 1969-71, sch. prin., 1971-77; adminstrv. cons. integration, 1977-81; prin. Gage Jr. High Sch., 1982—. Pres. Athletic Coordinators Assn., Los Angeles City Schs., 1959-60; v.p. P-3 Enterprises, Inc., Port Washington, N.Y., 1967-77, Century City (Calif.) Enterprises, 1966—. Vice pres. B'nai B'rith Anti-Defamation League, 1968-70; mem. adv. com. Los Angeles City Commn. on Human Relations, 1966-71, 72—, commr., 1976—, also chmn. edn. com.; pres. Los Angeles City Human Relations Commn., 1978—; mem. del. assembly Community Relations Conf. of So. Assembly, 1975—; mem. citizens' adv. com. for student integration Los Angeles Unified Sch. Dist., 1976-79; chmn. So. Calif. Drug Abuse Edn. Month com., 1970. Bd. dirs. DAWN, an anti-narcotics youth group. Served with USMCR, 1943-46. Recipient Beverly Hills B'nai B'rith Presdl. award, 1965; commended Los Angeles City Council, 1968. Mem. West Los Angeles Coordinating Council (chmn. case conf., human relations). Lion (dir. 1960-62), Kiwanian. Contbr. articles on race relations, youth behavior to profl. jours. and newspapers. Home: 2737 Dunleer Pl Los Angeles CA 90064 Office: 450 N Grand Ave Los Angeles CA 90054

STEINBERGER, JEFFREY W(AYNE), lawyer; b. Bronx, N.Y., Nov. 27, 1947; s. Martin and Shirley (Blumen) S.; m. Marlene Zimmelman, Apr. 30, 1976; 1 son, Darren. B.S., Queens Coll., 1969; J.D., UCLA, 1976. Founder, owner, mgr. Jeridean Industries, Inc., Los Angeles, 1971—; founder, owner, mgr. Nat. Real Estate, specializing in real estate syndications, Los Angeles, Calif., 1974—; bar: Calif. 1979; with Dist. Atty.'s Office Calif., West Covina, 1976-77; prin. Jeffrey Steinberger Appraisals, specializing in litigation real estate appraisals, Los Angeles, 1978-81; theatrical agt. Clout Agy., Century City, Calif., 1979—; individual practice law, Los Angeles, 1979—; cons. San Fernando Valley chpt. City of Hope. Served with USAR, 1969. Lic. artist mgr., lic. real estate broker, Calif. Mem., Mensa, ABA, Los Angeles Bar Assn., Lawyers Club, Trial Lawyers Calif., Beverly Hills Bar Assn., Los Angeles Bd. Realtors, Beverly Hills Bd. Realtors. Democrat. Jewish. Editorial bd. UCLA Law Rev., 1978; developed, produced, hosted public TV program Jeff's Law, 1981—. Office: 2720 S La Cienega Blvd Los Angeles CA 90034

STEINBRENNER, EUGENE CLARENCE, research forester; b. St. Paul, Sept. 3, 1921; s. Clarence Christopher and Sophia Francis (Lesch) S.; m. Erlyse E. Champine, Feb. 12, 1944; children—Peter, David, Joseph, Judy. B.S. with distinction, U. Minn. 1949; M.S., U. Wis., 1951; Ph.D., U. Wash., 1954. Project leader Forest Soils, Weyerhauser Co., Centralia, Wash., 1951-82, unit mgr. soil research, 1951-77, dir. soil survey program, 1977-82; cons. in forest soil and forest mgmt., Centralia, 1982—; affiliate prof. U. Wash., 1973—. Mem. Centralia Planning Adv. Bd., 1982—. Served with USAAF, 1942-45. Weyerhauser fellow, 1951-52; Bullard fellow, 1968-69, others. Fellow Am. Soc. Agronomy; Soil Sci. Soc. Am.; mem. Soc. Am. Foresters, Forest Sci. Council. Republican. Episcopalian. Club: Grange (master). Contbr. articles to profl. jours. Address: 3315 Tiger Ln Centralia WA 98531

STEINER, JACQUE, state senator; b. Pasadena, Calif., Nov. 4, 1929; d. John C. and Claire C. (Howard) Yelland; B.A., Stanford U., 1951, M.A., 1952; m. Frederick Karl Steiner, Jr.; children—Frederick Karl, Katherine Claire, Ann Carole. Tchr. English West Phoenix High Sch., 1952-55, Phoenix Union High Sch., 1956; mem. Ariz. State Ho. of Reps., 1976-80; mem. Ariz. Senate, 1980—, chmn. joint juvenile justice com., 1978-81. Mem. Phoenix Civic Center Mgmt. Bd., Ariz. Criminal Justice Planning Supervisory Bd.; mem. Maricopa County Community Council; adv. bd. Ariz. Center for Law-Related Edn. Named Citizen of Yr., Phoenix Bd. Realtors, Inc., 1976. Mem. Nat. Council State Legislators (alt. mem. edn. com.). Republican. Lutheran. Office: Senate Wing Capitol Bldg Phoenix AZ 85007

STEINER, LOREN PARRY, state ofcl.; b. Molalla, Oreg., May 21, 1921; s. Philip and Sarah (Parry) S.; B.S., U. Oreg., 1952; postgrad. Portland State U., 1951-56, U. Wash., 1960, Whittier Coll., 1961; M.S., Oreg. Coll. Edn., 1956; m. Thelma Naomi Johnston, June 8, 1951; children—Donald L., Shari Lee. Tchr., Conklin Elem. Sch. and Ontario Jr. High Sch., Ontario, Oreg., 1941-42, Molalla (Oreg.) Elem. Sch., 1945-46, Toledo (Wash.) High Sch., 1946-47; dep. county clk. Clackamas County (Oreg.), 1947-50; tchr. Oak Grove (Oreg.) Elem. Sch., 1950-57, vice prin., 1953-57; prin. Harbor Lights Jr. High Sch., Bandon, Oreg., 1957-64; cons. elem. and gen. edn. Oreg. Dept. Edn., Salem, 1964-71, specialist in sch. standardization, 1971-77, coordinator sch. standardization program, 1977—; trustee Oreg. Coll. Edn. Devel. Found., 1968-80. Mem. Bandon City Planning Commn., 1961-63, chmn., 1961-62; bd. dirs. So. Coos Gen. Hosp. Dist., Bandon, 1962-63. Served with AC, U.S. Army, 1942-45. Cert. tchr., adminstr., Oreg. Mem. Oreg. Assn. Supervision and Curriculum Devel. (exec. sec. 1967-78), Assn. Supervision and Curriculum Devel., Oreg. Coll. Edn. Alumni Assn., Phi Delta Kappa. Contbr. articles to Oreg. Assn. Curriculum Devel. Bull., Oreg. Elem. Prin. Jour. Home: PO Box 365 Monmouth OR 97361 Office: 700 Pringle Pkwy SE Salem OR 97310

STEINHAUER, GENE DOUGLAS, educator; b. Fresno, Calif., Jan. 1, 1944, s. Wilbert Peter and Rosie Nielsen (Askov) S.; M.A., Calif. State U., Fresno, 1974; Ph.D., (NIMH predoctoral fellow 1975-77), U. Mont., 1977; children—Christopher William, Karlie Elizabeth. Asst. prof. SUNY Coll., Oswego, 1977-78; asst. prof. Calif. State U., Fresno, 1978—; prof. psychology Calif. Sch. Profl. Psychology, 1979—; research cons. Nat. Council on Children, Media, and Mdsg.; NSF grant reviewer, 1978—. Served with USAF, 1961-65. Mem. Am. Psychol. Assn., Sigma Xi. Author chpt. in The Best of the Computer Fairs, 1979; also articles. Office: Dept Psychology Calif State U Fresno CA 93710

STEINHAUS, LESLIE MARIE, educational administrator; b. Grand Rapids, Mich., Sept. 21, 1947; d. Willard Elton and Arlene Beatrice (Bohn) Lowing; m. James Eugene Yager, Jan. 27, 1968; m. 2d, Warren Duane Steinhaus, June 2, 1979; children—Karly, James, Kelly. B.A., Mich. State U., 1969; M.Ed., U. Wyo., 1978. Cert. edn. specialist. Tchr. jr. high social studies Meade Sch. Dist. #101, Sturgis, S.D., 1970-73, Campbell County Sch. Dist., Gillette, Wyo., 1975-77; prin. Carbon County Sch. Dist. #2, Saratoga, Wyo., 1978-82, dir. curriculum and instrn., 1982—. Named Adminstr. of Yr., Carbon County Sch. Dist. #2, 1982. Mem. Nat. Assn. Secondary Sch. Prins., Wyo. Assn. Secondary Sch. Prins. (pres. 1983), Delta Kappa Gamma (Alpha Xi chpt.), Beta Sigma Phi (Theta chpt. 1975-78). Democrat. Office: Carbon County Sch Dist #2 Box 160 Elk Mountain WY 82324

STEINHAUSER, JOHN WILLIAM, lawyer, energy exec.; b. Akron, Ohio, June 25, 1924; s. John Hugo and Francis Lillian (Pearson) S.; B.Sc. in Bus. Adminstrn., Ohio State U., 1949; J.D., U. Mich., 1950; m. Patricia E. Mooney, Dec. 1, 1956; children—John, Christian, Mark, Sharon. Bar: Colo. 1972, Mich. 1950. With Chrysler Corp., 1950—, beginning as atty., successively dir. Latin Am., dir. export sales, gen. mgr. Africa-Far East, dir. Chrysler Internat., Geneva, dir. Africa-Far East, 1950-71, corp. atty., Denver, 1971—; founder, pres. Pearson Energy Corp., 1977, Sharon Energy, Ltd., Denver, 1980, also dir., 1971—. Sponsor Platte Valley Pony Club, Denver Symphony; active Colo. Republican Party. Served with USNR, 1943-46. Mem. Colo. Bar Assn., Mich. Bar Assn., Am. Bar Assn., Soc. Internat. Law, Rocky Mountain Mineral Law Found. Club: Cherry Hills. Home: 4210 S Dahlia St Englewood CO 80110 Office: Suite 201 7100 E Belleview Ave Englewood CO 80111

STEINMANN, JOHN COLBURN, architect; b. Monroe, Wis., Oct. 24, 1941; s. John Wilbur and Irene Marie (Steil) S.; B.Arch., U. Ill., 1964; postgrad. Ill. Inst. Tech., 1970-71; m. Susan D. Koslosky, Aug. 12, 1978. Project designer C.F. Murphy Assos., Chgo., 1968-71, Steinmann Architects, Monticello, Wis., 1971-73; design chief, chief project architect State of Alaska, Juneau, 1973-78; project designer Mithun Assos., architects, Bellevue, Wash., 1978-80; owner, prin. John C. Steinmann Assos., Architect, Kirkland, Wash., 1980—; lectr. Ill. Inst. Tech., 1971-72; prin. works include: Grant Park Music Bowl, Chgo., 1971, Menomonee Falls (Wis.) Med. Clinic, 1972, Hidden Valley Office Bldg., Bellevue, 1978, Kezner Office Bldg., Bellevue, 1979, Sunriver Condominiums, Sun River, Oreg., 1980, 2d and Lenora highrise, Seattle, 1981, Bob Hope Cardiovascular Research Inst. lab. animal facility, Seattle, 1982, Wash. Ct., Bellevue, 1982, Anchorage Bus. Park, 1982, Garden Townhouses, Anchorage, 1983, Vacation Internationale, Ltd. corp. hdqrs., Bellevue, 1983, also pvt. residences. Served to 1st lt. C.E., USAR, 1964-66; Vietnam. Decorated Bronze Star. Registered architect, Wash., Oreg., Calif., N.Mex., Ariz., Utah, Alaska, Wis., Ill. Mem. Am. Mgmt. Assn., Nat. Council Archtl. Registration Bds., Alpha Rho Chi.

Republican. Roman Catholic. Club: U. Wash. Yacht. Address: 4316 106th Pl NE Kirkland WA 98033

STEINRUCK, JAMES MICHAEL, health care adminstr.; b. Seattle, Jan. 17, 1951; s. Robert Thomas and Mary Jean (Shaver) S.; m. Dawn Marie Gilbertson, Sept. 6, 1975; 1 dau., Brooke Noelle. B.A. in Pre-Phys. Therapy, Eastern Wash. State Coll., 1974; M.B.A., Golden Gate U., 1981. Adminstrv. asst. Providence Hosp., Everett, Wash., 1981-82; dir. profl. services St. Mary's Hosp., Reno, 1982—. Served to capt., Med. Service Corps, U.S. Army, 1974-81; mem. Res. Mem. Am. Hosp. Assn., Assn. Western Hosps., Wash. State Hosp. Assn., Am. Coll. Hosp. Adminstrs., Am. Rifle Assn. Home: 2645 Desert Flower Ct Sparks NV 89431 Office: St Mary's Hospital Reno NV 89520

STELLFLUG, JOHN NORMAN, physiologist; b. Glasgow, Mont., May 24, 1947; s. John L. and Thelma L. (Benda) S.; B.S. in Animal Sci., Mont. State U., 1969, M.S., 1972; Ph.D. in Dairy Sci., Mich. State U., 1976; m. Sheryl Kathyleen Thompson, Aug. 24, 1974; children—Caitlin Michelle, John Nicholas. Research asst. Mont. State U., 1970-72, Mich. State U., 1972-76; research physiologist U.S. Sheep Expt. Sta., Dept. Agr., Dubois, Idaho, 1976—. Mem. Clark County Sch. Bd., Idaho, 1979-82, chmn., 1980-82. Served with U.S. Army, 1970. Mem. Am. Soc. Animal Sci., Soc. Study of Reproduction, Sigma Xi. Lutheran. Clubs: Lions, Toastmasters. Contbr. articles to jours. in animal sci. Office: US Sheep Experiment Station Dubois ID 83423

STEMMER, AUGUST L., physician, data processing cons.; b. Harvey, Ill., Mar. 20, 1929; s. August and Marie Stemmer; student Miami U., Oxford, Ohio, 1948; D.M.D., Harvard U., 1953, M.D., 1955; children—Cynthia Denell, August Randall, Kimberly Jean, Michelle Marie, Valerie Susan. Intern, Boston City Hosp., 1955-56; resident Mass. Eye and Ear Infirmary, Boston, 1956-59; pres. Maxillofacial Research and Edn. Found., 1965-75, ProTran Inc., San Francisco, 1975—. Fellow ACS, Royal Soc. Medicine; mem. Am. Assn. Cosmetic Surgery, Am. Acad. Otolaryngology-Head and Neck Surgery, Am. Soc. Maxillofacial Surgeons, Nat. Food Brokers Assn., Soc. Computer Medicine, Sierra Club. Republican. Lutheran. Club: Aston Martin U.S.A. Contbr. papers on maxillofacial surgery and computers in medicine to profl. publs.; discover The Peak pure glacier water. Office: 921 Post St San Francisco CA 94109

STENBIT, JOHN PAUL, engineer, consultant; b. Oakland, Calif., June 1, 1940; s. Paul Charles and Antoinette (Inguglia) S.; m. Albertine Heederik, Aug. 19, 1966; children—Elisabeth Francesca, Antine Elaine. B.S., Calif. Inst. Tech., 1961, M.S., 1962; postgrad. Technische Hogeschool, Eindhoven, Netherlands, 1962-63, 1965-67. Staff, Aerospace Corp., El Segundo, Calif., 1962-68; with TRW Def. and Space Systems Group, Redondo Beach, Calif., 1968-73, v.p. Def. Systems Group, 1977—; staff Office Sec. of Def., 1973-77; cons. Def. Sci. Bd., Dept. Def.; mem. sci. adv. group Def. Communications Agy. Fulbright fellow, 1962-63; Aerospace Corp. fellow, 1965-67. Mem. AIAA, Armed Forces Communications and Electronics Assn. Republican. Home: 1108 Via Zumaya Palos Verdes Estates CA 90274 Office: 1 Space Park Redondo Beach CA 90278

STENINGER, ALVIN LEONARD, range mgmt. cons.; b. Elko, Nev., Jan. 16, 1937; s. Eber Barret and Violet (Phillips) S.; B.S., Colo. State U., 1959, M.S., 1962; postgrad. Oreg. State U., 1962. Range mgr. Bur. Land Mgmt., Lakeview, Oreg., 1962-68; owner, range and ranch mgmt. cons. Western Range Service, Elko, Nev., 1968—. Ranch broker and appraiser, Elko, 1971—. Mem. Am. Soc. Farm Manager and Rural Appraisers, Soc. Range Mgmt., Am. Soc. Agr. Cons., Sigma Chi. Office: PO Box 1328 Elko NV 89801

STEPHAN, COOKIE WHITE, social psychologist, educator; b. Oklahoma City, Aug. 28, 1942; d. Neil and Janie (Holt) White; m. Walter G. Stephan, June 16, 1967. B.A. in Psychology with honors, U. Okla., 1965, M.S., 1965; Ph.D., U. Minn., 1971. Asst. prof. psychology dept. S.W. Texas State U., 1971-72; asst. prof. sociology dept. U. Tex., Austin, 1972-78, asst. dean Coll. Social and Behavioral Scis., 1973-75; assoc. prof., head dept. sociology and anthropology N.Mex. State U., 1978—; action editor Jour. Personality and Social Psychology, 1978-79; assoc. editor Jour. Applied Behavioral Scis., 1979—; editorial bd. Soc. Sci. Quar., 1975—, ASA Newsletter, 1981—. Grantee NIMH, Hogg Found., Soc. Psychol. Study of Social Problems, U. Tex., N.Mex. State U. Mem. Am. Sociol. Assn., Am. Psychol. Assn., Soc. Exptl. Social Psychology, Southwestern Sociol. Assn., Southwestern Social Sci. Assn., Co-author: The Jigsaw Classroom, 1978; contbr. articles to profl. jours. Home: 3241 Jupiter Rd Las Cruces NM 88001 Office: Dept Sociology/Anthropology NMSU Las Cruces NM 88003

STEPHENS, KAY JEFFERS, accountant; b. Sheridan, Wyo., Jan. 21, 1950; d. Deyo Raymond and Vieva Claire (Paulus) Jeffers; m. Joseph Edward Hettle, Dec. 18, 1971; m. 2d, Kermit E. Stephens, Apr. 14, 1980. Student Eastern Mont. Coll., 1968-69; A.A., Sheridan Coll., 1970. Lic., Dept. Treasury, 1982. Bookkeeper, sec. Barker & Collins, Sheridan, 1969-70; sec. FBI, Washington, 1970-72; acct. Millard T. Charlton & Co., C.PAs, Washington, 1973-75; acct., bookkeeper Karen M. Moody, CPA, Sheridan, 1975-77; acct., controller Peter Widener Co., Sheridan, 1977-80; owner, mgr. Stephens Acctg. & Tax Service, Sheridan, Wyo., 1980—. Mem. Sheridan Centennial Com., 1981-82, chmn. Sheridan Centennial Birthday Cake. Mem. Am. Bus. Women Assn., Sheridan County C. of C., Nat. Assn. Female Execs., Nat. Soc. Pub. Accts., Beta Sigma Phi. Republican. Club: Does. Home: PO Box 327 Sheridan WY 82801 Office: 1335 N Main St Sheridan WY 82801

STEPHENS, MICHAEL GARY, microelectronics packaging engr.; b. Los Angeles, Dec. 12, 1947; s. Stanley Carmeron and Aline Mary (Tremblay) S.; A.A. in Engring., Math. and Sci., Cerritos Coll., 1973; m. Bobbie Jo Robertson, Nov. 30, 1974; 1 son, Samuel Cole. Designer, Pacific Sci. Co., Anaheim, Calif., 1966-71; microelectronics engr. Western Digital Corp., Newport Beach, Calif., 1973-75; mgr. microelectronics packaging engring. Xerox Corp., El Segundo, Calif., 1975-81; prin. engr. hermetic packaging Silicon Systems, Inc., 1981—. Mem. Semicondr. Equipment and Materials Inst. Republican. Roman Catholic. Patentee in field. Home: 1013 S Nicklett St Fullerton CA 92631 Office: 14351 Myfork Rd Tustin CA 92680

STEPHENS, STANLEY GRAHAM, state senator, communications company executive; b. Calgary, Alta., Can., Sept. 16, 1929; s. Joseph Stephens and Margaret (Farrelly) S.; m. Ann Hanson, 1954; children—Alan, Carol Ann. Student pub. schs., Calgary. Mem. Mont. State Senate, Helena, 1969-72, senate pres.; v.p., sec. Sta. KOJM, Havre, Mont., 1965—; pres. Big Sky TV Cable Inc., Sidney, 1968—; pres. Glasgow TV Cable Inc., 1968—; pres. Community TV Inc., Havre, 1968—. Del. Republican Nat. Conv., 1976. Served with U.S. Army, 1951-53; Korea. Named Outstanding Young Man of Havre, 1962; recipient Mont. Assn. Press Radio Edn. award, 1968-69. Mem. Am. Legion. Lutheran. Lodges: Masons, Shriners, Elks. Office: Office of Senate Pres State Capitol Helena MT 59601*

STEPHENS, WARREN CLAYTON, JR., fin. co. exec.; b. Mobile, Ala., Apr. 6, 1942; s. Warren Clayton and Ellen Story (Fretz) S.; B.A., Notre Dame U., 1964; M.B.A., Stanford U., 1966; m. Millicent A. Wynne, Dec. 28, 1963; children—Warren Clayton III, Brent Christopher, Craig Gordon, Keith Wynne. Second v.p. Chase Manhattan Bank, N.Y.C., 1966-69; corp. v.p., div. pres. Genway Corp., Chgo., 1969-72; v.p., treas. Wheelabrator Frye, Inc., Hampton, N.H., 1972—, also pres. subs. Trailmobile Fin. Co., San Francisco. Nat. alumni sec. U. Notre Dame, 1964-74. Mem. Bus. and Industry Assn. N.H. (chmn. taxation com. 1976-78, dir. 1977—), Notre Dame Alumni Assn., Stanford Bus. Sch. Assn. Roman Catholic. Contbr. articles to profl. jours. Home: 2704 Rollo Rd Santa Rosa CA 95404 Office: 640 Hegenberger Rd Oakland CA 94621

STEPHENSON, DEBRA ANN, health firm executive, consultant, educator; b. San Diego, Aug. 21, 1950; d. Roger Edward and Bonnie R. (Rule) Saum; m. Dennis Karas, Aug. 3, 1968 (div.); m. 2d, William W. Stephenson, Oct. 7, 1978. Student San Diego State U., 1968-69, Mira Mesa Jr. Coll., 1972-73, Grossmont Jr. Coll., 1972-73, Southwestern Jr. Coll., 1972-73. Instr. retarded adults San Diego Assn. Mentally Retarded Citizens, 1976-77; co-mgr. New Aeon Yoga Ctr., National City, Calif., 1976-77; instr. Hatha Yoga YWCA, Imperial Beach Recreation Ctr., San Diego, 1977, Carina Windsor Salons, La Jolla, Calif., 1977; program asst. Office Continuing Edn. in Health Scis., U. Calif.-San Diego Sch. Medicine, 1977-78; instr. fitness Golden Door Health Spa, San Marcos, Calif., 1979-81; instr. Hatha Yoga, 1981—; owner, prin. Naturally Fit, Escondido, Calif., 1981—; lectr. in field. Vol. tchr. retarded adults. Mem. Nat. Assn. Female Execs. Office: Naturally Fit PO Box 27046 Escondido CA 92027

STEPHENSON, HERMAN HOWARD, banker; b. Wichita, Kans., July 15, 1929; s. Herman Horace and Edith May (Wayland) S.; B.A., U. Mich., 1950; J.D., U. Mo. at Kansas City, 1958; m. Virginia Anne Ross, Dec. 24, 1950; children—Ross Wayland, Neal Bevan, Jann Edith. Bar: Kans. 1958. Mem. fgn. dept. City Nat. Bank, Kansas City, Mo., 1952-54; asst. sec. City Bond & Mortgage Co., Kansas City, Mo., 1954-59; with Bank of Hawaii, Honolulu, 1959—, asst. cashier, 1960-62, v.p., 1962-68, sr. v.p., 1968-72, exec. v.p., 1972-80, pres., dir., 1980—; v.p., dir. Bancorp Finance Hawaii, Inc.; chmn., dir. Bancorp Bus. Systems Hawaii, Inc.; vice-chmn., dir. Bankoh Adv. Corp.; chmn., trustee RAMPAC; exec. v.p., dir. Bankoh Corp.; pres., dir. Bank Hawaii Internat., Inc.; v.p., dir. Bankoh Fin., Inc.; vice-chmn., dir. Hawaii Fin. Corp. (Hong Kong) Ltd.; chmn., dir. Bancorp Ins. Agy. Hawaii, Inc., Bancorp Life Ins. Co. Hawaii, Inc.; dir. Investors Pacific Ltd. (Fiji), Banque de Nouvelle-Caledonie, Banque de Tahiti, Bank of Hawaii Internat. Corp., N.Y.C. Bd. dirs. Aloha United Way, Honolulu Symphony, Maunalani Hosp.; chmn. urban renewal com. Oahu Devel. Conf., 1966-68, mem. comprehensive planning com., 1970-71; trustee, past pres. Tax Found. Hawaii; former trustee Hawaii Conf. Found., United Ch. of Christ. Served with U.S. Army, 1950-52. Mem. Am. Bankers Assn. (past chmn. exec. com. housing and real estate fin. div., dir. 1976-77, governing council 1976-77), Mortgage Bankers Assn. Hawaii (past pres.), ABA, Kans. Bar Assn., Kappa Sigma, Pi Eta Sigma. Clubs: Rotary, Oahu Country, Pacific, Waialae. Office: PO Box 2900 Honolulu HI 96846

STEPHENSON, LARRY KIRK, health services planner, management and geography educator; b. Seattle, Sept. 22, 1944; s. Norman Eugene and Virginia Dare (Frost) S.; m. Tamara Leah Ladin, June 24, 1967; children—Mathew Alan, Leah Anela. B.S., Ariz. State U., 1966, M.A., 1971; Ph.D., U. Cin., 1973; Manpower research analyst Employment Security Commn. of Ariz., 1969-70; asst. prof. dept. geography U. Hawaii, Hilo, 1973-76, assoc. prof., 1976-78, chmn. dept., 1975-77; vis. lectr. dept. geography Ariz. State U., 1978, adj. assoc. prof., 1979—; planner Ariz. Dept. Health Services, Phoenix, 1978—; vis. assoc. prof. dept. geography, area devel. and urban planning U. Ariz., 1978; mem. faculty U. Phoenix, 1979—; lectr. Golden Gate U., 1981—; ptnr. Urban Research Assocs., Phoenix, 1981—; adj. prof. Coll. St. Francis, 1982—. Mem. Hawaii Island Health Planning Council, 1974-78. Served with U.S. Army, 1966-68. NDEA fellow, 1971-72. Mem. Am. Planning Assn., Assn. Am. Geographers, Assn. Pacific Coast Geographers, Am. Pub. Health Assn., Southwest Profl. Geog. Assn. Unitarian. Author books in field; contbr. chpts. to textbooks, articles to profl. jours. Mem. editorial advisory bd. Yearbook of Assn. of Pacific Coast Geographers. Home: 306 W Encanto Blvd Phoenix AZ 85003 Office: 1740 W Adams St Phoenix AZ 85007

STEPHENSON, TONI EDWARDS, investment mgmt. co. exec.; b. Bastrop, La., July 23, 1945; d. Sidney Crawford and Grace Erleene (Shipman) Little; B.S., La. State U., 1967; m. Arthur Emmet Stephenson, Jr., June 17, 1967; 1 dau., Tessa Lyn. Computer programmer Employers Group Ins., Boston, 1967-68; systems analyst Computer Tech., Inc., Cambridge, Mass., 1968-69; founding partner Stephenson & Co., Denver, 1971—; gen. partner Viking Fund; partner Stephenson Resources, Stephenson Properties, Stephenson Ventures, Stephenson Mgmt. Co., Stoneacre Co.; exec. v.p., dir. Gen. Communications, Inc., Globescope Corp.; underwriting mem. Lloyd's of London; dir. Stephenson Internat., Inc., Charter Bank & Trust. Bd. dirs., mem. exec. council St. Joseph Hosp.; bd. dirs., officer County Children's Hosp. Guild, Jr. League of Denver. Mem. Rocky Mountain Wang Computer Users Assn. (founding pres.), DAR, Children's Hosp. Aux. (dir.), Delta Gamma. Clubs: Annabel's of London, Petroleum. Home: 11102 E Harvard Dr Aurora CO 80014 Office: 899 Logan St Denver CO 80203

STEPHENSON, VIVIAN ARQUERO, travel agency executive; b. Paauilo, Hawaii, June 23, 1939; d. Liborio E. and Becky P. Borge Arquero; m. Richard H. Stephenson, June 17, 1961; children—Debra, Kimi. B.S., Drake U., 1961; postgrad. Iowa State U., 1962-63, U. Hawaii, 1965-67. Tchr. social scis. and history, Iowa, 1961-63, Hawaii, 1963-68, Colo., 1968-78; pres., owner Tiffany Travel Co., Denver, 1978—. Active Minority Enterprises. Mem. Women's Ednl. Service Assn. Republican. Congregationalist. Office: 7800 E Hampden Suite 48 Denver CO 80231

STEPOVICH, MICHAEL LEO, orthodontist; b. Fairbanks, Alaska, Nov. 17, 1929; s. Mike and Vuka (Radovich) S.; A.B., San Jose State Coll., 1956; D.D.S., Marquette U., 1961; M.S., St. Louis U., 1964; m. Arline Audry Gentry, June 10, 1956; children—Michael John, Matthew James, Dean Alexander, Lynn Diane. Intern, USPHS Hosp., Fort Worth, 1961-62; pvt. practice orthodontics, San Jose, Calif., 1964—; mem. staff Good Samaritan Hosp., San Jose. Pres., Orthodontic Edn. and Research Found., St. Louis, 1969; bd. dirs. Tweed Found. for Orthodontic Research, 1978—. Served with AUS, 1953-54; PTO. Diplomate Am. Bd. Orthodontists. Mem. Am., Calif., Santa Clara County dental assns., Am. Assn. Orthodontists, Pacific Coast Soc. Orthodontists (pres. Central sect. 1975), Angle Soc., DeMolay, Interfrat. Council San Jose State Coll. Alumni (chmn. 1966), Omicron Kappa Upsilon, Delta Upsilon. Contbr. articles to profl. jours. Home: 19557 Arden Ct Saratoga CA 95070 Office: 4110 Moorpark Ave San Jose CA 95117

STERBENZ, JOANNE RUTH, accountant; b. New Orleans, June 16, 1947; d. Joseph Roch and Merlin (Prieto) S.; B.S., U. Southwestern La., 1969; M.B.A., Tulane U., 1971. With Arthur Young & Co., Los Angeles, 1971—, prin. computer audits, 1976—, coordinator computer auditing, 1976-80, office dir. edn., 1979-80, office dir. mktg. resources, 1980—. C.P.A., Calif.; Tulane U. fellow, 1969-71. Mem. Am. Inst. C.P.A.'s, Nat. Assn. Female Execs., Am. Women's Soc. C.P.A.'s EDP Auditors Assn., NOW, Tulane Assn. Bus. Alumni, Greater Los Angeles Zoo Assn., Smithsonian Assos. Democrat. Roman Catholic. Club: Univ. Home: 222 7th St Apt 107 Santa Monica CA 90402 Office: Arthur Young Co 515 S Flower St Los Angeles CA 90071

STERLING, DONALD JUSTUS, JR., newspaper executive; b. Portland, Oreg., Sept. 27, 1927; s. Donald Justus and Adelaide (Armstrong) S.; A.B., Princeton U., 1948; postgrad. (Nieman fellow) Harvard U., 1955-56; m. Julie Ann Courteol, June 7, 1963; children—Sarah, William, John. Reporter, Denver Post, 1948-52; news staff mem. Oreg. Jour., Portland, 1952-82, editor, 1972-82; asst. to the pub. The Oregonian, Portland, 1982—. Pres., Tri-County Community Council, 1972-73; bd. dirs. Oreg. Hist. Soc., pres., 1977-79. Recipient Golden Beaver award Izaak Walton League, 1969; Edith Knight Hill award Women in Communications, 1978; Jessie Laird Brodie award Planned Parenthood Assn., 1982; English-Speaking Union traveling fellow, 1959. Mem. Soc. Nieman Fellows, Phi Beta Kappa, Sigma Delta Chi. Clubs: City (pres. 1973-74), Multnomah Athletic (Portland); Dial Lodge (Princeton). Home: 1718 SW Myrtle St Portland OR 97201 Office: 1320 SW Broadway Portland OR 97201

STERLING, JOHN EWART WALLACE, university chancellor; b. Linwood, Ont., Can., Aug. 6, 1906; s. William Sterling and Annie (Wallace) S.; came to U.S., naturalized, 1947; B.A., U. Toronto, 1927; M.A., U. Alta., 1930; Ph.D., Stanford U., 1938; LL.D., Pomona Coll., Occidental Coll., 1949, U. San Francisco, U. Toronto, 1950, U. B.C., Northwestern U., U. Calif., 1958, U. Denver, Loyola U., McGill U., 1961, Columbia U., 1962, McMaster U., 1966, Harvard U., 1968, U. Alta., 1970; D.C.L., Durham U., England, 1953; Litt.D., U. Caen (France), 1957, U. So. Calif., 1960; L.H.D., St. Mary's Coll., 1962, Santa Clara U., 1963, Mills Coll., 1967, U. Utah, 1968; m. Anna Marie Shaver, Aug. 7, 1930; children—William W., Susan Hardy (Mrs. Bernard Monjauze), Judith Robinson (Mrs. Frank Morse). Lectr. history Regina (Sask., Can.) Coll., 1927-28; asst. in history, dir. phys. edn. U. Alta., 1928-30; mem. research staff Hoover War Library, Stanford U., 1932-37, instr. history, 1935-37; asst. prof. history Calif. Inst. Tech., 1937-40, asso. prof., 1940-42, prof. history, 1942-45, Edward S. Harkness prof. of history and govt., exec. com., 1945-48, chmn. faculty, 1944-46; news analyst CBS, 1942-48; dir. Huntington Library, 1948-49; pres. Stanford U., 1949-68, lifetime chancellor, 1968; past dir. Fireman's Fund Am. Ins. Cos., Kaiser Aluminum & Chem. Corp., Shell Oil Co., Tridair Industries, Dean Witter & Co. Civilian faculty Nat. War Coll., 1947, bd. cons., 1948-52; bd. visitors U.S. Naval Acad., 1956-58, Tulane U., 1960-74; mem. nat. adv. council Health Research Facilities, HEW, 1956-57; chmn. Commn. Presdl. Scholars, 1965-68; adv. bd. Office Naval Research, 1953-56; chmn. Am. Revolution Bicentennial Commn., 1969-70; mem. Ford Internat. Fellowship Bd., 1960; mem. Can.-Am. Com., 1957-74; mem. Am. adv. com. Ditchley Found., Eng., 1962-76; mem. adv. com. fgn. relations U.S. Dept. State, 1965-68; bd. dirs. Council Fin. Aid to Edn., 1967-70; mem. Brit.-N.Am. Com., 1969-74. Decorated knight comdr. Order Brit. Empire, 1976; comdr.'s cross Order Merit Fed. Republic Germany; chevalier Legion d'Honneur (France); 2d degree Imperial Order Rising Sun (Japan), Grand Gold Badge of Honor for Merits (Republic of Austria); Herbert Hoover medal Stanford Alumni Assn., 1964; Clark Kerr award U. Calif., Berkeley, 1969; Uncommon Man award Stanford Assos., 1978; fellow Social Sci. Research Council, 1939-40. Fellow Am. Geog. Soc.; mem. Council on Fgn. Relations, Western Coll. Assn. (pres. 1953), Am., Pacific Coast hist. assns., Assn. Am. Univs. (pres. 1962-64). Clubs: Commonwealth, Bohemian, California, Burlingame Country, Family, Pacific-Union, University (hon.) (Palo Alto, San Francisco, N.Y.C., Los Angeles). Editor: (with H.H. Fisher, X.J. Eudin) Features and Figures of the Past (V.I. Gurko), 1939. Office: Office of Chancellor Stanford U Stanford CA 94305

STERLING, ROBERT FILLMORE, chem. engr.; b. Toledo, Aug. 19, 1919; s. Harry Phipps and Orra Louise (Barnaby) S.; student Marion (Ind.) Coll., 1938-40; B.S. in Chem. Engring., Carnegie Inst. Tech., 1942; cert. in Bus. Mgmt., U. Pitts., 1960; m. Margery E. Canedy, Sept. 21, 1947; children—Barbara C., William B. Research metallurgist Dow Chem. Co., Midland, Mich., 1943-44; research scientist Westinghouse Research Labs., Forest Hills, Pa., 1946-55, supr. and mgr. chemistry and ceramics sects. Atomic Power div., Pitts., 1955-62, fellow engr. Marine div. Westinghouse Electric Corp., Sunnyvale, Calif., 1962—. Chmn. Churchill (Pa.) Town Meeting, 1960-61; commr. Sunnyvale Public Library, 1978—. Served with USNR, 1944-46. Mem. Am. Chem. Soc. (chmn. polymer chemistry div. Pitts. sect. 1950-51). Republican. Patentee in field. Home: 1457 Hollenbeck Ave Sunnyvale CA 94087 Office: Westinghouse Electric Corporation Bldg 71-6 Hendy Ave Sunnyvale CA 94088

STERMER, DUGALD ROBERT, designer/illustrator, publisher, writer, cons.; b. Los Angeles, Dec. 17, 1936; s. Robert Newton and Mary (Blue) S.; B.A.; UCLA, 1960; children—Dugald II, Megan, Chris, Colin. Designer for 2 studios, Los Angeles, Houston, 1959-65; art dir., v.p. Ramparts mag., 1965-70; freelance designer, illustrator, writer, cons., 1970—; founder Public Interest Communications, San Francisco, 1974; cons. editor Communications Arts mag., Palo Alto, Calif., 1974—; designer Oceans mag., 1976-82; pres. Frisco Pub. Group, Ltd. Bd. dirs. Delancey St. Found., 1976—. Recipient various medals, awards for design and illustration, nat. and internat. design competitions. Mem. Soc. Publ. Designers, Am. Inst. Graphic Arts, San Francisco Soc. Communicating Arts. Editor: The Environment 1972, Vanishing Creatures 1980. Author: The Art of Revolution, 1970; Vanishing Creatures, 1980. Office: 1844 Union St San Francisco CA 94123

STERN, BART ROBERT, spice company executive; b. Czechoslovakia, Nov. 4, 1926; came to U.S., 1955, naturalized, 1960; s. Mor Moshe and Regina Rivka (Weiss) S.; m. Anne Catherine, May 3, 1942; children—Jonathan Barry, Nina Renee. B.A., Karl's U., Prague, Czechoslovakia, 1948; M.A., U. Bern (Switzerland), 1950; Ph.D., U. Geneva, 1953; Ph.D., London Sch. Econs., 1955. Pres., Bartley Trading Corp.; v.p. F.D. Lawrence & Co.; founding pres., chief exec. officer Spice King Corp., Culver City, Calif., 1958—; cons. to developing countries; mem. Israel Econ. Conf.; active Vols. Internat. Tech. Assistance. Mem. Bur. Jewish Edn. Bd., United Jewish Appeal, 1970—; founding mem. Holocaust Survivors Conf.; Olympic commr., 1984. Mem. Inst. Food Technologists (lectr.), Am. Spice Trade Assn., Herb Trade Assn., Greater Los Angeles Nutritional Council, YMHA, YMCA, U.S. Army-Navy League, Union of Orthodox Jews. Club: B'nai B'rith (mem. Anti-Defamation League). Author: Die Gemeinschaftsiedlung in Staate Israel, 1952; inventor banana chips, dehydrated pineapple and papya, many convenience foods. Office: 6009 Washington Blvd Culver City CA 90230

STERN, DANIEL DAVID, conductor; b. Locarno, Switzerland, July 28, 1943; came to U.S., 1949, naturalized, 1955; s. Frans Martin and Dorette (Tchenio) S.; Mus.B., Eastman Sch. Music, Rochester, N.Y., 1965; Mus.M. (NDEA fellow), U. Oreg., 1969. Mus.D. (NDEA fellow), 1973; children—Rebecca, Frances String specialist Salem (Oreg.) public schs., 1965-67; asst. condr. U. Oreg. Symphony Orch., 1968-71; asst. prof. music N.Mex. Highlands U., 1971-74; music dir. Boise (Idaho) Philharm., also Boise Civic Opera, 1974—; condr.-in-residence Boise State U., 1974-79; founder, 1975, since dir. Sun Valley, also Idaho music festivals; bd. dirs. Idaho Civic Ballet, 1977-79. Religious leader Beth Israel Congregation, Boise, 1981—. Recipient Performers cert. conducting U. Oreg., 1971. Mem. Am. Symphony Orch. League, Condrs. Guild. Club: Boise Rotary. Address: PO Box 2205 Boise ID 83701

STERN, EDGAR BLOOM, JR., corporate exec.; b. N.Y.C., Sept. 1, 1922; s. Edgar Bloom and Edith (Rosenwald) S.; m. Pauline Stewart, May 23, 1947; children—Sandra Stern MacIver, Eric, Monte, Lessing.

Grad. Hotchkiss Sch., 1940; B.S. cum laude, Harvard U., 1943. Chief engr. Offshore Navigation, Inc., radar surveyors, 1946-48; mng. partner WDSU Broadcasting Services, Inc., 1949-50; chmn., pres., dir. Royal St. Corp. (formerly WDSU Broadcasting Corp.), New Orleans, 1948—, Royal St. Investment Corp., Royal St. Louis, Inc., 1975-81, New Orleans; chmn. bd. Aspen Music Assos., Inc., 1971-81; dir. Sears, Roebuck & Co., Chgo.; chmn. bd. Royal St. of Utah. Dir. United Fund Greater New Orleans, 1951-57, treas., 1953, pres., 1954; chmn. pub. relations adv. com. United Community Funds and Councils Am., 1956-59, exec. com., dir., mem. United Fund adv. com., vice chmn. United Community campaigns, 1956-63, v.p., 1958-63; dir. Internat. Trade Mart, Council for A Better La., Internat House, New Orleans; past dir. Council Social Agencies. Trustee U. Chgo., 1972-82, Com. Econ. Devel., N.Y.C.; mem. univ. resources com. Harvard, 1963-73; mem. vis. com. Harvard Grad. Sch. Edn., 1963-69, 70-73; bd. adminstrs. Tulane U., 1959-77; bd. govs. Ochsner Found. Hosp., New Orleans, 1959-73. Served as 1st lt. Signal Corps, AUS, 1943-46, 50-52. Home: Box JJ Aspen CO 81612 Office: New Orleans LA 70139

STERN, JEAN, art gallery dir.; b. Casablanca, Morocco, Mar. 28, 1946; B.A. in History, Calif. State U.-Northridge, 1968; M.A. in Art History, Calif. State U.-San Diego, 1972; m. Carol Elizabeth Adams, June 2, 1970; 1 dau., Carrie Dona. Guest curator San Diego Mus. Art, 1973, 75, 76; instr. art history San Diego Mesa Coll., 1976-77; dir., curator Petersen Galleries, Beverly Hills, Calif., 1978—; lectr. Am. painting. Mem. Appraisers Assn. Am. Author: (with others) Pre-Hispanic Art: The Jules Berman Collection, 1973; editor: (with others) Pre-Hispanic Art History, 1977. Contbr. articles to art publs. Office: Petersen Galleries 270 N Rodeo Dr Beverly Hills CA 90210

STERN, LOUIS, art dealer; b. Casablanca, Morocco, Jan. 7, 1945; s. Frederic and Sultana (Ifergan) S.; B.A., Calif. State U.-Northridge, 1968; m. Karen Anne Honeman, Oct. 12, 1969; children—Deborah Beth, Daniel William. Dir., Stern Art Galleries, Los Angeles, 1971-75; chmn. bd., pres. Wally Findlay Galleries, Beverly Hills, Calif., 1975-82; pres. Louis Stern Galleries, Beverly Hills, 1982—. Active Los Angeles County Mus. Art. Served with U.S. Army, 1968-71. Mem. Am. Art Council. Home: 13206 Addison St Sherman Oaks CA 91423 Office: 9538 Brighton Way Beverly Hills CA 90210

STERN, SANDRA SILVERSTONE (MRS. ROBERT LOWELL STERN), television actress; b. London, Eng.; d. Arthur Joseph Silverstone and Pearl (Finkelstein) Newsom; A.B., Vassar Coll., 1955; m. Robert Lowell Stern, June 19, 1955; children—Antony Ian, Michael Keith, Wendy Joy, Peter Jonathan, Valery Jennifer. Summer stock actress, Ogunquit, Maine, 1954; apprentice actress, 1955-56; writer, performer children's TV program Jr. Clubhouse, Sta. CHCT-TV, Calgary, Alta., Can., 1957-59, Romper Room hostess, 1959-60, writer, producer, performer Teddy Bear Quiz and 12 and Under, 1960-61; writer, producer children's TV program TV Partytime, CFCN-TV, Calgary, 1962-65, writer, producer, hostess Rocket IV Club, 1965-67; pres. Exec. Suite Co. Ltd., Calgary, 1967—; co-owner Court Stars, tennis sportswear boutiques, West Vancouver and Vancouver, 1978—. Children's theatre chmn. Jr. League Calgary, 1970—; bd. dirs. Calgary Dance Theatre, Festival Calgary. Mem. Amnesty Internat. Club: W. Vancouver Newcomers (pres.), Jr. League of Vancouver, Variety, Can't Wait Tennis Assn. Author: (play for dance demonstration) The Absent-Minded Sorcer-Bird, 1974. Home: 889 Farmleigh Rd West Vancouver BC V7S 1Z8 Canada

STERNITZKE, VINCENT LEO, psychologist; b. Boonville, Mo., July 7, 1925; s. William Leo and Maurene A. (Knapp) S.; m. Mary Margaret Jones, July 8, 1947; children—David Leo, Carol Jane. B.S., Pittsburg (Kans.) State U., 1948, M.S., 1953; Ed.D., U. Kans., 1957. Lic. psychologist, lic. marriage, child and family counselor, Calif. Instr. in graphic arts No. Okla. Coll., 1949-55; asst. Reading Clinic, U. Kans., 1955-57, asst. prof. edn. Sam Houston State U., 1957-59, asso. prof., 1959-66; test officer Calif. State U., Chico, 1966-68; staff psychologist Fairview (Calif.) State Hosp., 1968-69, sr. psychologist, 1969-70, program dir., 1970-77; counseling psychologist VA, San Francisco, 1977-79; psychologist Napa State Hosp., Imola, Calif., 1979—; pvt. practice counseling psychology, Vallejo, Calif. Tng. officer Radio Emergency Affiliated Citizens Team, Vallejo, 1981—. Served with USNR, 1943-46; to lt. col. Calif. Mil. Res., 1981—. Mem. Am. Psychol. Assn., Calif. Psychol. Assn., Nat. Rehab. Assn., Nat. Rehab. Counselors Assn. Roman Catholic. Author: Percentile Rank Tables, 1960; Dictionary of Educational Psychology 1964; (filmstrip) Meeting Your Military Obligation, 1960, rev. as Choosing Your Military Service, 1966. Home: 1424 Granada St Vallejo CA 94591 Office: Program 1 Napa State Hosp Box A Imola CA 94558

STERNS, PATRICIA MARGARET, lawyer, cons.; b. Phoenix, Jan. 30, 1952; d. Lawrence Page and Mildred Dorothy (Barbaras) S. B.A., Ariz. State U., 1974; J.D., U. Ariz., 1977. Admitted to Ariz. bar, 1978, U.S. Dist. Ct. Ariz., 1978; Sterns and Tennen, Phoenix, Tucson, 1978—; cons. internat. law. Mem. Am. Dairy Goat Assn., Ariz. Dairy Goat Assn., Am. Soc. Internat. Law, AIAA, ABA, Maricopa County Bar Assn. (family law com.), Internat. Inst. Space Law, Aviation/Space Writers Assn. Contbr. articles to profl. publs.; mem. Ariz. Law Rev. Office: 11 W Jefferson Suite 519 Luhrs Bldg Phoenix AZ 85003

STERRITT, GRAHAM MINOR, psychologist, educator; b. Jamaica, N.Y., Dec. 28, 1927; s. Donald Blake and Elmira Cross (Polley) S.; B.A., Adelphi Coll., Garden City, N.Y., 1950; M.A., CCNY, 1951; Ph.D., U. Colo., Boudler, 1956; m. Sarah McCullough, Feb. 14, 1952; children—Phillip Graham, Michael Keith, Christopher Lindsey. Psychology intern Elgin (Ill.) State Hosp., 1952-53; postdoctoral research fellow Yale U., 1956-57; instr., then asso. prof. psychology U. Colo. Med. Center, 1957-73; dir. McClelland Learning Inst., Pueblo, Colo., 1969-73; prof. psychology, dir. grad. program in psychology U. Colo., Denver, 1973—. Served with AUS, 1946-47. Recipient Britt award Psi Chi, 1955. Mem. Am. Psychol. Assn., AAAS, Pediatric Psychology Assn., Colo. Psychology Assn., Colo. Assn. Profl. Psychology. Club: Internat. Windsurfing Assn. Co-editor: Exceptional Infant, vol. 3, 1975; contbr. articles to profl. jours; patentee teaching devices. Home: 560 S Corona St Denver CO 80209 Office: U Denver 1100 14th St Denver CO 80202

STESSEL, LARRY ROBERT, record company executive; b. N.Y.C., Dec. 27, 1953; s. Saul and Grace Stessel; B.S. in Mktg., U. Fla., 1975. Nat. mgr. coll. promotion CBS Records, 1975-77, prodn. mgr. E/C, 1977-78, dir. prodn. mgmt. East Coast, 1978-79, dir. mdsg. West Coast, 1979—. Address: 1801 Century Park West Los Angeles CA 90067

STETSON, ROBERT FRANCIS, atomic company technical specialist; b. N.Y.C., Oct. 20, 1928; s. Ralph Jerome and Margaret Mary (Feeley) S.; m. Rita Marie Jubach, Dec. 30, 1950; 1 dau., Barbara Ann. Cert. in metallurgy Pa. State U., 1955; cert. sr. engring. tech., Calif. Supr. insp. Babcock-Wilcox Co., Beaver Falls, Pa., 1950-58; tech. specialist GA Tech. Co., San Diego, 1958—. Served with USAF, 1945-47. Recipient Lincoln Arc Welding Found. award for outstanding achievement in welding design, engring. and fabrication, 1979. Fellow Am. Soc. Metals (nat. metal assos. award 1979, engring. assos. award San Diego chpt. 1975, past chmn. and mem. exec. com.); mem. San Diego Council Engring. Soc. (sec.). Roman Catholic. Contbr. articles to profl. jours. Patentee in field. Home: 6918 Tanglewood Rd San Diego CA 92111 Office: GA Tech Co PO Box 91608 San Diego CA 92138

STEUER, NEIL BURT, geologist, flight instructor; b. Cleveland Heights, Ohio, Jan. 2, 1924; s. Harry and Jeannette (Kanner) S.; m. Marjorie Macy, Jan. 17, 1962. B.A. in Geology, UCLA, 1950. Geologist Shell Oil Co., 1950-54; gen. mgr. CEM Tungsten Mine, Fresno, Calif., 1954-56; sr. geologist Sonoma Quicksilver Mine, Guerneville, Calif., 1956-58, Kaiser Aluminum Co., Hilo, Hawaii, 1956-58, Petrobras, Belem, Brazil, 1958-60; engring. geologist AEC, Nev., Miss., Panama, Brazil, Alaska, 1961-75; program mgr. NRC/state coop. regional geology seismology programs U.S. Nuclear Regulatory Commn., Washington, 1974—; cons. in field, 1942-45. Served with AUS. Recipient cert. for contbns. to Brazil expdn. NSF, 1966, cert. for contbr. to solar eclipse expdn. to Brazil, 1966; cert. for outstanding work in formulating and mng. nat. program in regional tectonics and seismicity Nuclear Regulatory Commn., 1980; cert. of appreciation for sci. benefits derived from state-fed. seismotectonic program Assn. Am. State Geologist, 1981; award for fostering geol. research in Kans., Kans. Geol. Soc., 1982. Fellow Explorers Club (sec. Washington group); mem. Am. Assn. Petroleum Geologists, Geol. Soc. Am., Am. Inst. Profl. Geol. Scientists, Am. Nuclear Soc. Aircraft Owners and Pilots Assn. Clubs: Quiet Birdmen; Westerners, Masons, FAA Flying (v.p., safety officer 1975-77) (Washington). Author: Journal of the First Official Reconnaissance for and Interoceanic Sea Level Canal, Panama, 1965; Journal of the Expedition Solar Eclipse, Brazil, 1966; contbr. articles to profl. jours. Home and office: 2284 N 13th St Redmond OR 97756

STEVANAK, THOMAS JOHN, JR., accountant; b. Cleve., Aug. 22, 1921; s. Thomas John and Susan (Sirak) S.; student Oberlin Coll., 1943-44; B.B.A. Case Western Res. U., 1947; m. Emily Jane Schwass, Sept. 7, 1946; children—Susan Emily, Dorothy Anne, Thomas Frederick. Accountant Price Waterhouse & Co., Cleve., 1947-50; accountant Peat, Marwick, Mitchell & Co., Denver, 1950-53; corporate tax mgr. CF & I Steel Corp., Denver, 1953-72; dir. acctg. C.A. Norgren Co., Littleton, Colo., 1972—. Served as lt. (j.g.) USN, 1944-46. C.P.A., Colo. Mem. Nat. Assn. Accountants (past pres. Denver chpt.), Am. Inst. C.P.A.'s. Republican. Lutheran. Home: 1830 Zinnia Ct Golden CO 80401 Office: 5400 S Delaware Littleton CO 80120

STEVENS, ALVA LEWIS, manufacturing management consultant; b. Traverse City, Mich., Oct. 15, 1938; s. Jack Jerome and Dorothy Rose (Hunter) S.; B.A., Golden Gate U., 1973; diploma smaller co. mgmt. program Harvard Grad. Sch. Bus., 1976; m. Anna Maria Montano, July 9, 1960; children—Donald, James, Thomas, Robert. Cost acctg. mgr. Optical Coating Lab., Santa Rosa, Calif., 1962-68; v.p., gen. mgr. T. & W. Mfg. Co., Santa Rosa, 1968-69; mgr. materials Prescolite, San Leandro, Calif., 1969-74; v.p. mfg. The North Face, Berkeley, Calif., 1974-77, pres. A.L. Stevens, Inc., Diablo, Calif. Served with USN, 1956-59. Mem. Am. Prodn. and Inventory Control Soc. (pres. Golden Gate chpt. 1975, regional v.p. 1976-77, Personal Achievement award 1976). Republican. Roman Catholic. Contbr. papers to profl. meetings. Home: PO Box 381 2552 Caballo Ranchero Dr Diablo CA 94528 Office: PO Box 381 Diablo CA 94528

STEVENS, CLARENCE CHARLES, JR., theatrical lighting designer, musician; b. Pueblo, Colo., Nov. 15, 1901; s. Clarence Charles and Josephine Abby (Shinn) S.; m. Margarita Espana, July 2, 1932; children—Charles S., Jose. Theatrical lighting expert to motion picture studios; owner, operator Los Angeles Stage Lighting Co., cons. in field. Designer lighting at San Diego, San Francisco and New York Expositions. Home: 1184 N Normandie Ave Hollywood CA 90029 Office: 1451 Venice Blvd Los Angeles CA 90026

STEVENS, DANNY ROSS, advertising executive; b. Tooele, Utah, Sept. 18, 1946; s. Darrel Lundquist and Ruth Bonita (Bailey) S.; m. Karen Annette Evans, April 19, 1967; children—Richmond, Rochelle, John, Alexandra, Joshua, Caroline. B.A. in Communications, Brigham Young U., 1969. Advt. salesman, Logansport (Ind.) Tribune and Press, 1969-71; advt. mgr., Powell (Wyo.) Tribune, 1971-74; acct. exec. Gardiner Advt. Agy., Salt Lake City, 1974-77; advt. dir., Collett's Furniture, Midvale, Utah, 1977-81, pres. Collett Agy., Midvale, 1981—; instr. U. Utah. Recipient numerous awards for creative advt. Mem. Assn. Latter-day Media Artists; Utah Advt. Fedn.; Jaycees. Mormon. Clubs. Exchange, (Logansport); Kiwanis (Powell Wyo). Author several works of fiction. Home: 905 Marion Village Rd Sandy UT 84070 Office: Collett Agy 77 E 7200 St So Midvale UT 84047

STEVENS, ELEANOR SANDRA, professional services executive; b. Okla. City, Nov. 1, 1932; d. Benjiman Franklin and Mary Lou (Smith) Williams; children—Fred W., Nathandra, Benjiman, Ola Enaid. A.S., Fresno State U., 1954; student Fresno Adult Edn., Los Angeles Trade Tech., 1972-73. Bookkeeper Los Angeles County Assessor, 1961-69; supervisor Holzman-Begue Real Estate Co., Los Angeles, 1969-73; dist. mgr. United Systems, Inc., Los Angeles, 1973-77; pub. relations cons. Harold G. Simon & Assoc., Vernon, Calif., 1977-81; pres. Stevens Personalized Services, Los Angeles, 1982—. Mem. Nat. Assn. Female Execs. Club: Order of Eastern Star. Office: 4614 S Western Ave Los Angeles CA 90062

STEVENS, GREG, provincial government official; b. Toronto, Ont., Can., Nov. 24, 1935; s. Greg and Gladys Stevens; m. Patricia Beeby; children—Laura, Tom, Linda. B.Sc. in Civil Engring., U. Man., 1958, M.Sc. in Community Planning, 1962. Planning officer City of Edmonton (Alta., Can.), 1962; planner City of Vancouver (B.C., Can.), 1962-65; asst. city planner City of New Westminster, 1965-67; city planner City of Kelowna, 1967-71; townsite mgr. Townsite of Banff, 1971-73; gen. mgr. Alta. Housing Corp., Ft. McMurray, 1975-76, v.p. so. region, 1977-78; mem. Legis. Assembly, 1979—, minister responsible for personnel adminstrn., 1979—. Chmn. Banff Provisional Adminstrn. Bd., 1975; coordinator Banff Townsire Options Rev. Com., 1974; chmn. Banff Social Planning Com., 1973; bd. dirs. Banff Hosp., 1971-74. Served with RCAF, 1958-61. Mem. Assn. Profl. Engrs., Geologists and Geophysicists Alta. Office: 222 Legislative Bldg Edmonton AB T5K 2B6 Canada

STEVENS, HELEN GROOM, victim prevention specialist; b. Whittier, Calif., Mar. 23, 1930; d. Homer Pearl and Stella Earl (Hibbs) Groom; m. James Henry Stevens, May 26, 1951; children—Mara, Jamie, Lisa, Kevin, Michael, Michele. Black belt Judo, Aikido. Instr. martial arts, 1947-81; co-founder Gihokan Judo Sch., San Diego, 1974-77; with U.S. Judo Assn., 1967-83; victim prevention specialist, 1974—; founder Women's Self Def. Council, 1977; performer, Bob Hope Mil. shows, 1944-47, Earl Carroll Theatre, 1947-49; also in movies, on stage and TV, 1947-51. Mem. Stamp Out Crime Council, Colo. Police Assn., SLAM. Author: The Privilege of Self-Defense: A Capsule View of the Law, 1975. Office: PO Box 5057 CO 80034

STEVENS, MARIO RUDOLPH, pharm. cons.; b. Hoboken, N.J., May 11, 1922; s. Julius and Louise S.; B.S., St. John's U., 1944; M.S., N.Y. U., 1947; m. Gloria Frances Moldt, May 7, 1944; children—Karen, Mark. Head advanced analytical lab. Jet Propulsion Lab., Pasadena, Calif., 1970-73; group leader Towne-Paulsen Co., Monrovia, Calif., 1973-77; chief chemist U.S.A. Petrochem. Corp., Ventura, Calif., 1977-80; cons., 1980—. Served with M.C., U.S. Army, 1944-46. Mem. Am. Chem. Soc., Soc. Applied Spectroscopy, Acad. Pharm. Scis., N.Y. Acad. Scis. Roman Catholic. Home: 256 Lynn Oaks Ave Thousand Oaks CA 91320

STEVENS, PHILLIP JOSEPH, engineering and construction co. exec.; b. Los Angeles, Jan. 17, 1929; s. Joseph A. and Mildred S.; B.S., UCLA, 1951, M.S., 1958; m. Joan Scudder, Dec. 6, 1952; children—Gregory, Kimberly, Sherry. Devel. engr. Hughes Aircraft Co., Culver City, Calif., 1951-57; dir. Minuteman III program TRW Systems, Inc., Redondo Beach, Calif., 1957-69; pres. Ultrasystems, Inc., Irvine, Calif., 1969—. Founding mem. Orange County Music Ctr. Assoc., fellow AIAA. Patentee advanced rocket propulsion systems. Office: 2400 Michelson Dr Irvine CA 92715

STEVENS, ROBERT WILLIAM, religious assn. fin. exec.; b. Coquille, Oreg., Mar. 23, 1936; s. Stanton Frank and Eva R. (Mossholder) S.; B.A., Williamette U., 1958; postgrad. U. Wash., 1958-59; m. Marilyn Ludlow, Sept. 10, 1957; children—Paul, Ruth. Acctg. supr. Boeing Co., Seattle, 1960-66; conf. treas. Pacific N.W. Ann. Conf., United Methodist Ch., Seattle, 1966—, mem. com. audit and rev. Gen. Council on Fin. and Adminstrn., United Meth. Ch., 1972—, mem. council, 1976—. Del. Western Jurisdictional Conf., United Meth. Ch., 1968, 72, 76, 80, 84, treas. Western Jurisdictional Conf., 1975—, del. Gen. Conf., 1976, 80, 84; trustee Seabeck (Wash.) Christian Conf. Camp, 1973—. Office: 2112 3d Ave Suite 300 Seattle WA 98121

STEVENS, STEPHEN EDWARD, psychiatrist; b. Phila.; s. Edward and Antonia S.; B.A. cum laude, LaSalle Coll., 1950; M.D., Temple U., Phila., 1954; LL.B., Blackstone Sch. Law, 1973; m. Isabelle Helen Gallacher, Dec. 27, 1953. Intern, Frankford Hosp., Phila., 1954-55; resident in psychiatry Phila. State Hosp., 1955-58; practice medicine specializing in psychiatry Woodland Hills, Calif., 1958-63, Santa Barbara, Calif., 1970-77; asst. supt. Camarillo (Calif.) State Hosp., 1963-70; cons. ct. psychiatrist Santa Barbara County, 1974-77; clin. dir. Kailua Mental Health Center, Oahu, Hawaii, 1977—. Served with M.C., USAAF. Diplomate Am. Bd. Psychiatry and Neurology. Fellow Am. Geriatrics Soc. (founding); mem. Am. Acad. Psychiatry and Law, AMA, Am. Psychiat. Assn., Am. Legion, DAV (Oahu chpt. 1), Caledonia Soc., Am. Hypnosis Soc., Am. Soc. Adolescent Psychiatry. Clubs: Hawaiian Canoe, Honolulu, Elks, Aloha String Band (founder and pres.). Home: PO Box 726 Kaneohe HI 96744 Office: 45-691 Keaahala Rd Kaneohe HI 96744

STEVENS, THEODORE FULTON, senator; b. Indpls., Nov. 18, 1923; s. George A. and Gertrude (Chancellor) S.; B.A., UCLA, 1947; LL.B., Harvard U., 1950; m. Ann Cherrington, Mar. 29, 1952 (dec. Dec. 1978); children—Susan, Beth, Walter, Theodore Fulton, Ben; m. 2d, Catherine Bittner Chandler, Dec. 30, 1980; 1 dau., Lily Irene. Bar: Calif. 1950, U.S. Supreme Ct., 1954, Alaska 1960. Practiced in Washington, 1950-52; Fairbanks, Alaska, 1953, Anchorage, 1961-68; U.S. atty., Fairbanks, 1953-56; legis. counsel Dept. Interior, Washington, 1956-58, asst. to sec. interior, 1958-60, solicitor, 1960-61; mem. Alaska Ho. of Reps., 1964-68, majority leader, speaker pro tem, 1967-68; mem. U.S. Senate from Alaska, 1968—, now asst. majority leader. Served as 1st lt. USAAF, 1943-46. Decorated D.F.C., Air medal (U.S.); Yuan Hai medal (Republic China). Mem. Fed., Alaska, Calif., D.C. bar assns., Am. Legion, VFW. Republican. Rotarian. Office: 145 Russell Senate Office Bldg Washington DC 20510*

STEVENSON, BETTY LEWIS, mgmt. cons.; b. Wenona, Ill., Oct. 22, 1915; d. George D. and Erma D. (Swartz) Butcher; student Pleasant View Luther Coll., 1933-35; A.A., N.Mex. State U., 1972; 1 son, Scott L. Dep. county clk. LaSalle County, Ottawa, Ill., 1937-46; asst. exec. dir. LaSalle Fed. Public Housing Authority, 1937-43; steno pool supr. Manhattan Project, Hanford Engr. Works, Richland, Wash., 1944; various secretarial positions, Chgo., 1945-48; sec. White Sands (N.Mex.) Missile Range, 1948-50; asst. adminstr. phys. sci. lab. N.Mex. State U., Las Cruces, 1951-59, adminstr. research center, 1959-69, adminstr., dir. Office of Grants and Contracts, 1969-79; pres. Lewis Ltd., Las Cruces, 1978—, Double L Constrn., 1979—. Mem. exec. bd. Las Cruces Girls and Boys Club, 1976—. Mem. Soc. Research Adminstrs. (bd. advs. 1977-80), Project Mgmt. Inst., The Assn., Las Cruces C. of C. (pres. women's div. 1980-82), Delta Zeta. Republican. Presbyterian. Club: Dona Ana County Rep. Women's 1982). (pres. 1982). Contbr. articles to profl. jours. Office: Lewis Ltd PO Box 3009 Las Cruces NM 88003

STEVENSON, DAVID JOHN, planetary science educator; b. Wellington, N.Z., Sept. 2, 1948; s. Ian McIvor and Gwenyth (Carroll) S. B.S. with honors, Victoria U. (Wellington), 1971, M.S., 1972; Ph.D., Cornell U., 1976. Research fellow Australian Nat. U., 1976-78; asst. prof. planetary physics UCLA, 1978-80; assoc. prof. planetary sci. Calif. Inst. Tech., Pasadena, 1980—; mem. coms. NASA. Fulbright grantee, 1972. Mem. Am. Astron. Soc., Am. Geophys. Union, AAAS, Sierra Club. Contbr. chpts. to books, articles to sci. publs. Office: Calif Inst Tech 170-25 Pasadena CA 91125

STEVENSON, JAMES RICHARD, radiologist; b. Ft. Dodge, Iowa, May 30, 1937; s. Lester Lawrence and Esther Irene (Johnson) S.; B.S., U. N.Mex., 1959; M.D., U. Colo., 1963; m. Sara Jean Hayman, Sept. 4, 1958; children—Bradford Allen, Tiffany Ann, Jill Renee, Trevor Ashley. Intern U.S. Gen. Hosp., Tripler, Honolulu, 1963-64; resident in radiology U.S. Gen. Hosp., Brook, San Antonio, Tex., 1964-67; radiologist, partner Van Atta Labs., Albuquerque, 1970—; adj. asst. prof. radiology U. N.Mex., 1970-71; pres. med. staff AT & SF Meml. Hosp., 1979-80, trustee, 1982—. Served with U.S. Army, 1963-70; Vietnam. Decorated Bronze Star Medal. Diplomate Am. Bd. Radiology, Am. Bd. Nuclear Medicine. Allergy fellow, 1960. Fellow Am. Coll. Radiology (councilor 1981—); mem. AMA (physicians recognition award 1969—), Am. Coll. Nuclear Medicine (charter), Am. Coll. Nuclear Physicians (charter), Soc. Nuclear Medicine (v.p. Rocky Mountain chpt. 1975-76), Am. Inst. Ultrasound in Medicine, N.Mex. (pres. 1978-79), N.Am. radiol. socs., N.Mex., Albuquerque-Bernalillo County (scholar 1959) med. socs., Sigma Chi. Republican. Presbyterian. Clubs: Elks, Albuquerque Country, Masons, Shriners. radiologist; b. Ft. Dodge, Iowa, May 30, 1937; s. Lester Lawrence and Esther Irene (Johnson) S.; B.S., U. N.Mex., 1959; M.D., U. Colo., 1963; m. Sara Jean Hayman, Sept. 4, 1958; children—Bradford Allen, Tiffany Ann, Jill Renee, Trevor Ashley. Intern U.S. Gen. Hosp., Tripler, Honolulu, 1963-64; resident in radiology U.S. Gen. Hosp., Brook, San Antonio, Tex., 1964-67; radiologist, partner Van Atta Labs., Albuquerque, 1970—; adj. asst. prof. radiology U. N.Mex., 1970-71; pres. med. staff AT & SF Meml. Hosp., 1979-80, trustee, 1982—. Served with U.S. Army, 1963-70; Vietnam. Decorated Bronze Star Medal. Diplomate Am. Bd. Radiology, Am. Bd. Nuclear Medicine. Allergy fellow, 1960. Fellow Am. Coll. Radiology (councilor 1981—); mem. AMA (physicians recognition award 1969—), Am. Coll. Nuclear Medicine (charter), Am. Coll. Nuclear Physicians (charter), Soc. Nuclear Medicine (v.p. Rocky Mountain chpt. 1975-76), Am. Inst. Ultrasound in Medicine, N.Mex. (pres. 1978-79), N.Am. radiol. socs., N.Mex., Albuquerque-Bernalillo County (scholar 1959) med. socs., Sigma Chi. Republican. Presbyterian. Clubs: Elks, Albuquerque Country, Masons, Shriners. Home: 3333 Santa Clara Dr SE Albuquerque NM 87106 Office: 8307 Constitution Dr NE Albuquerque NM 87110

STEVENSON, MICHAEL MCCLAIN, psychologist, sleep consultant; b. Los Angeles, Aug. 14, 1940; s. Alexander and Geraldine Evelyn (McClain) S.; m. Judith Ann Baumann, Aug. 8, 1964; 1 dau., Laurie Ann; m. 2d, Marsha Kay Weinstein, Sept. 20, 1981. A.A., Pasadena City Coll., 1960; B.A., Calif. State U-Los Angeles, 1962, M.A., 1965; Ph.D., Kans. State U., 1969. Lic. psychologist, Calif. Asst. prof. psychology Eckerd Coll., St. Petersburg, Fla., 1970-73; research anatomist UCLA,

1973-77, research psychologist, 1977-81; research psychologist neurophysiol. research VA Med. Ctr., Sepulveda, Calif., 1980-82; sleep psychologist Sleep Disorders Ctr., Holy Cross Hosp., Mission Hills, Calif., 1981—; pvt. practice psychology, Reseda, Calif., 1982—; counseling supr. Los Angeles Suicide Prevention Ctr. Mem. ACLU. Served in USMC, 1958-64. NASA predoctoral fellow, 1966-68, postdoctoral fellow, 1968-70. Mem. Am. Psychol. Assn., AAAS, Western Psychol. Assn., Sleep Research Soc., Sigma Xi, Sierra Club. Office: Holy Cross Hosp Sleep Disorders Ctr Mission Hills CA 91335

STEVENSON, ROBERT MURRELL, music educator; b. Melrose, N.Mex., July 3, 1916; s. Robert Emory and Ada (Ross) S.; A.B., U. Tex. at El Paso, 1936; grad. Juilliard Grad. Sch. Music, 1938; M.Mus., Yale 1939; Ph.D., U. Rochester, 1942; S.T.B., Harvard, 1943; B.Litt., Oxford (Eng.) U.; Th.M., Princeton. Instr. music U. Tex., 1941-43, 46; faculty Westminster Choir Coll., Princeton, N.Y., 1946-49; mem. faculty to prof. music UCLA, 1949—. Vis. asst. prof. Columbia, 1955-56; vis. prof. Ind. U., Bloomington, 1959-60, U. Chile, 1965-66; cons. UNESCO, 1977. Served with AUS, 1943-46. Decorated Army Commendation ribbon. Recipient Fulbright research awards, 1958-59, 64, 70-71, Carnegie Found. teaching award, 1955-56. Ford Found. fellow 1953-54, Carnegie Found. fellow 1955-56; Gulbenkian Found. fellow 1966, 81; Guggenheim fellow, 1962; Nat. Endowment for Humanities fellow, 1974; Del Amo Found. fellow, 1983. Author: Music in Mexico, 1952; Patterns of Protestant Church Music, 1953; La musica en la catedral de Sevilla, 1954; Music before the Classic Era, 1955; Shakespeare's Religious Frontier, 1958; The Music of Peru, 1959; Juan Bermudo, 1960; Spanish Music in the Age of Columbus, 1960; Spanish Cathedral Music in the Golden Age, 1961; La musica colonial en Colombia, 1964; Protestant Church Music in America, 1966; Music in Aztec and Inca Territory, 1968; Renaissance and Baroque Musical Sources in the Americas, 1970; Music in El Paso, 1970; Philosophies of American Music History, 1970; Written Sources For Indian Music Until 1882, 1973; Christmas Music from Baroque Mexico, 1974; Foundations of New World Opera, 1973; Seventeenth Century Villancicos, 1974; Latin American Colonial Music Anthology, 1975; Vilancicos Portugueses, 1976, Josquin in the Music of Spain and Portugal, 1977; American Musical Scholarship, Parker to Thayer, 1978; contbg. editor Handbook Latin Am. Studies, 1976—; editor Inter-Am. Music Rev., 1978—; contbr. to New Grove Dictionary of Music and Musicians Office: 405 Hilgard Ave Los Angeles CA 90024 American Achievements Are As Nothing Unless They Are Written About And Remembered. My Mission Has Been To Rescue The Musical Past Of The Americas. Present-day Composers Are Too Busy Making Their Own Music To Worry About Their Predecessors. As A Result, Every New Generation Of Composers Thinks That They Are The First Ones To Descry Mount Olympus. Not So. The Past Is A Succession Of Musical And Artistic Glories.

STEWARD, PATRICIA ANN RUPERT, financial consultant; b. Panama City, Panama, Apr. 20, 1945 (parents Am. citizens); d. Paul S. and Ernestina M. (Ward) Rupert; grad. Sch. of Mortgage Banking, Grad. Sch. of Mgmt., Northwestern U., 1979; m. Robert M. Levine, Oct. 28, 1978; children by previous marriage—Donald F. Steward, Christine Marie Steward. Vice pres. Asso. Mortgage & Investment Co., Phoenix, 1969-71; v.p., br. mgr. Sun Country Funding Corp., Phoenix, 1971-72, Freese Mortgage Co., Phoenix, 1972-74, Utah Mortgage Loan Corp., Phoenix, 1974-81; pres. Elles Corp., 1982—; condr. numerous seminars on mortgage fin. State chmn. Ariz. Leukemia Dr., 1977-78, mem. exec. com., 1979—; troop leader Cactus Pine council Girl Scouts U.S.A., 1979-80. Recipient cert. of appreciation Multiple Listing Service, Phoenix Bd. Realtors, 1975, Multiple Listing Service, Glendale Bd. Realtors, 1977. Mem. Mortgage Bankers Assn. Am., Ariz. Mortgage Bankers Assn. (dir. 1981-82, chmn. edn. com. 1981-82, founder continuing edn. seminar series 1981), Young Mortgage Bankers Assn. (chmn. exec. com. 1980-81), Phoenix C. of C., Phoenix Real Estate Bd., Glendale Real Estate Bd., Central Ariz. Homebuilders Assn., Scottsdale Real Estate Bd. Republican. Office: Elles Corp 4520 N Central Ave Phoenix AZ 85012

STEWART, AMY MARGARET, curriculum specialist; b. Long Beach, Calif., Dec. 1, 1950; d. Virgil Edmond and Lorena Beatrice (Curtis) Bradford; m. Dennis Lee Stewart, Apr. 21, 1973. B.S., Tex. Tech. U., 1972. Cert. secondary tchr. in phys. edn. and biology, learning handicapped, Calif. Tchr. Los Angeles Unified Sch. Dist., 1972-73; tchr. Marysville (Calif.) Unified Sch. Dist., 1977-80, curriculum specialist, 1980—. Bd. dirs., v.p. Arts Council Yuba County. Mem. Assn. Calif. Sch. Adminstrs., Assn. Supervision and Curriculum Devel., Golden Empire Reading Council, Calif. Reading Council, Nat. Assn. Female Execs., Phi Delta Kappa. Republican. Office: 1919 B St Marysville CA 95901

STEWART, B. CHARLENE, data processing manager; b. Bath, N.Y., July 27, 1934; d. Fay Henry and Norma Elizabeth (Gage) Stewart; m. W. B. Stewart, June 18, 1955; children—Jim, Debbie, Shirley. B.A. in Chemistry, Houghton (N.Y.) Coll., 1955. Cert. real estate salesman, Alaska. Tchr. high sch., Bradford, N.Y., 1955-56, Kenai, Alaska, 1956-57; acctg. clk. U.S. Army, Kenai, FHA, Anchorage, 1957-59; EDP prgrammer State of Alaska, Juneau, 1966-71, systems analyst, Anchorage, 1972-80; customer service mgr. Anchorage Data Ctr., 1980—; lectr. on data processing. Mem. Anchorage Republican Women, 1982—, LWV. Mem. Data Processing Mgmt. Assn., Am. Assn. Motor Vehicle Adminstrs. Republican. Methodist. Clubs: Juneau Sweet Adelines, Internat. Women's Barbershop. Designer, programmer state on-line system to issue motor vehicle registrations and titles. Home: PO Box 1007 Willow AK 99688 Office: 3300 Fairbanks St Anchorage AK 99503

STEWART, BARBARA JEAN, advertising executive; b. Chgo., Dec. 5, 1941; d. O.F. and Elinor Catherine (Dunn) Smith; divorced; 1 son, Marc M. Stewart. Student U. So. Calif., 1964-67. Asst. advt. mgr. Bekins Van and Storage, Los Angeles, 1964-69; v.p. Hubbert Advt., Costa Mesa, Calif., 1969-76; chief exec. officer B.J. Stewart, Advt. and Pub. Relations, 1976—; instr. Calif. State U.-Fullerton. Active Nat. Republican Congl. Com. Mem. Osage County Advt. Fedn. (Golden Orange award 1980), Los Angeles Advt. Club (Lulu award 1979), Bus. Profl. Advt. Assn. (Pro-Communications award 1982), Pub. Relations Soc. Am., Sales and Mktg. Council, Am. Assn. Advt. Agys. Office: BJ Stewart Advertising 3300 Irvine Ave Suite 125 Newport Beach CA 92660

STEWART, DARLA GRACE, business executive, writer, publisher; b. Little Rock, June 4, 1940; d. Leo A. and Lorraine M. Shanafelt; m. Byron Leigh Knerr, Jan. 27, 1962 (div. Apr. 1968); 1 son, Keith Steven; m. Richard David Stewart, Apr. 7, 1973; 1 dau., Serena Lalene. Student San Jose State Coll., 1957-58; grad. with honors, Vector Counseling Inst., 1971; student Aims Coll., 1979-81; M.A., U. N.C., 1983. Logic design asst. Computer div. Gen. Electric Co. 1958-60; flight test analyst Lockheed Missiles & Space Div., 1960-62; research asst. Rand Corp., 1966-68; counselor Vector Counseling Inst., Vector Ch., 1970-72; free-lance writer, 1971, 72-82; writer Brentwood Pub., 1972; pres. dg Enterprises, Greeley, Colo., 1983—; instr. Aims Coll., 1983—. Pub. relations facilitator Greeley Creative Arts Ctr., 1983. Mem. Internat. Assn. Bus. Communicators, Nat. Assn. Female Execs. Libertarian. Unitarian-Universalist. Contbr. articles, short stories and poetry to mags. Home: 3506 Audubon Ct Loveland CO 80537 Office: 3139 19th St Dr Greeley CO 80631

STEWART, DONALD BAILEY, JR., engineer; b. Galveston, Tex., Feb. 13, 1951; s. Donald Bailey and Margaret Jean (Stead) S.; m. Sally Jan O'Hair, June 9, 1973; 1 dau., Kristal Lyn. B.S., U.S. Air Force Acad., 1973. Devel. engr. Garrett Turbine Engine Co., Phoenix, 1980—. Served to capt. USAF, 1973-80. Mem. Air Force Assn., Thunderbird Model R.R. Club, Nat. Model R.R. Assn. (supt. Ariz. div. 1982—). Republican. Home: 4848 N 63d Dr Phoenix AZ 85033 Office: 111 S 34th St Suite 503 IE Phoenix AZ 85010

STEWART, DONALD MARTIN, plant pathologist; b. Rembrandt, Iowa, Jan. 20, 1908; s. Alexander Porter and Nellie Louise (Martin) S.; B.S., U. Minn., 1931; postgrad. U. Calif., Berkeley, 1938; Ph.D., U. Minn., 1953; m. Marion G. Christiansen, May 14, 1938; children—Margo Jeanne, Bonnie Ann. Dist. leader White Pine Blister Rust Control, U.S. Dept. Agr., Duluth, Minn., 1935-51, research plant pathologist U. Minn., St. Paul, 1951-70, liaison officer, project mgr. improvement field crops in Egypt, 1970-74, agronomist, nat. sorghum millet project Yemen Arab Republic, 1977-78; adj. prof., cons. for new crops, dept. plant scis. U. Ariz., Tucson, 1978—; pres. Minn. Archeol. Soc., 1965. Fulbright-Hays grantee, Romania, 1965; recipient cert. of appreciation U.S. Dept. Agr., 1974, Mpls. Public Schs., 1968-69; cert. of Merit award U.S. Dept. Agr., 1958. Mem. Am. Phytopath. Soc., Sigma Xi. Club: Mason. Contbr. articles to profl. jours. Home: 9476 E Shiloh St Tucson AZ 85710 Office: Univ Ariz Room 201 Dept Plant Sciences Tucson AZ 85721

STEWART, ELIZABETH BRYAN, psychologist, lawyer; b. Pocatello, Idaho, Jan. 14, 1931; d. Donald N. and Geraldine S. Bryan; m. I. Daniel Stewart, Jr., Sept. 10, 1959; children—Elizabeth Ann, Shannon. B.A. in Psychology, U. Utah, 1953, M.A. in Psychology, 1954, Ph.D. in Psychology, 1958, J.D., 1976. Diplomate Am. Bd. Profl. Psychology; bar: Utah 1976. Chief psychologist U. Utah Rehab. Ctr., Salt Lake City, 1958-62; postdoctoral resident St. Elizabeth's Hosp., Washington, 1962-64, staff psychologist, 1964-65; mem. faculty dept. psychology U. Utah, 1965-67, chief child psychologist, 1967-68; pvt. practice psychology, Salt Lake City, 1968—, specializing in forensic psychology, 1976—; mem. Utah Psychology Lic. Com., 1970-80; adv. bd. Women Lawyers in Utah, 1981—; seminar leader Postgrad. Inst. Psychology of Am. Bd. Profl. Psychology, 1982. Mem. Gov.'s Com. Employment of Handicapped, 1977-78; mem. Legal Aid Soc. Utah, 1981—. Mem. ABA, Utah Bar Assn., Salt Lake County Bar Assn., Am. Psychol. Assn., Utah Psychol. Assn. Contbr. articles profl. jours. Home: 2900 Millicent Dr Salt Lake City UT 84108 Office: 77 S 700 E Suite 250 Salt Lake City UT 84102

STEWART, GERALD DAVID, nurseryman; b. Antioch, Calif., Jan. 22, 1948; s. Francis Daniel and Ardis Mae (Molander) S. Student Calif. Poly. State U., 1968-72. Mgr. stock control Hines Wholesale Nurseries, San Ana, Calif., 1972-76; also asst. sales mgr., mgr. mktg. communications; sales and mktg. mgr. Calif. Western Vine Corp., Fallbrook, 1976-77; co-owner Bill Lindsey & Assocs., 1977-78; ptnr. New Leaf Wholesale Nurseries, Vista, Calif., 1977—. Mem. Mira Costa Coll. Agrl. Adv. Bd., 1981—, Vista High Sch. Agrl. Adv. Com., 1982—. Mem. Calif. Assn. Nurserymen (vice chmn. mgmt. tng. com. 1976-77, pres. Orange County chpt. 1975-76, pres. North San Diego chpt. 1979-80, state area gov. 1981-83), Alpha Zeta, Blue Key, Mensa. Republican. Roman Catholic. Home and Office: 2456 Foothill Dr Vista CA 92083

STEWART, ISAAC DANIEL, JR., state supreme court justice; b. Salt Lake City, Nov. 21, 1932; s. Isaac Daniel and Orabelle (Iverson) S.; B.A., U. Utah, 1959, J.D., 1962; m. Elizabeth Bryan Stewart, Sept. 10, 1959; children—Elizabeth Ann, Shannon. Atty., U.S. Dept. Justice, 1962-65; asst. prof. law Coll. Law, U. Utah, 1965-68, assoc. prof., 1968-70; ptnr. Jones, Waldo, Holbrook & McDonough, Salt Lake City, 1970-79; justice Utah Supreme Ct., 1979—; dir. Med. Devel. Corp. Mem. Utah Bd. Oil, Gas and Mining, 1976-78, chmn., 1977-78; Utah rep. to Interstate Oil Compact Commn., 1977-78; mem. exec. com. Interstate Oil Compact Commn., 1978; chmn. subcom. on legal rights and responsibilities of youth Gov.'s Com. on Youth, 1972. Mem. ABA, Utah Bar Assn., Salt Lake County Bar Assn., Am. Judicature Soc., Order of Coif, Phi Beta Kappa, Phi Kappa Phi, Sigma Chi. Mormon. Office: 332 State Capitol Bldg Salt Lake City UT 84114

STEWART, JOAN LORENE, newspaper editor; b. Ft. Benton, Mont., Oct. 5, 1947; d. Leland Wilson and Doris Elizabeth (Nelson) Overholser; m. John Robert Stewart, June 10, 1976; children—David, Wesley, Daniel. Student U. Mo., 1965, U. Mont., 1966. With Ft. Benton River Press, 1963—, editor, 1980—. Chmn. bd. Crimestoppers; CPR instr.; mem. Quick Response Unit, county jail com., county EMS council, Lewis and Clark Meml. Commn. Mem. Mont. Press Assn., Chouteau County Homemakers Council (pres.). Methodist. Club: Homemakers (Ft. Benton). Home: PO Box 696 Fort Benton MT 59442 Office: PO Box 69 Fort Benton MT 59442

STEWART, LARRY GENE, rehabilitation and counseling psychologist, consultant; b. San Angelo, Tex., Oct. 9, 1937; s. John Summers and Bertha Irene (Barnes) S.; m. Shirley Josephine Hanrahan, Dec. 30, 1958 (div.); children—Lamar Gregory, Lee Garrett. B.S., Gallaudet Coll., 1957; M.Ed., U. Mo., 1963; Ed.D., U. Ariz., 1970. Lic. psychologist, Calif., Tex., Ariz. Psychol. cons. Ariz. State Sch. for Deaf and Blind, Tucson, 1973-79; supt. Gulf Coast Regional Program for Deaf, Houston, 1976; pvt. practice psychology, Tucson, 1973-79; assoc. prof. U. Ariz.-Tucson, 1972-75, research specialist, 1976-79; exec. dir. Tex. Commn. for Deaf, 1979-80; pvt. practice psychology, Huntington Beach, Calif., 1979—; cons. in area of deafness including edn., rehab., forensic psychology, neuropsychol. evaluations. Active devel. support service programs for deaf, Kansas City, Mo., Tucson, State of Ariz. HEW grantee. Mem. Am. Psychol. Assn., Calif. Psychol. Assn. Contbr. chpts. to books, articles to newspapers, other publs. Office: 5200 Warner St Suite 109 Huntington Beach CA 92649

STEWART, LUCILLE MARIE, special education program specialist; b. Pittsburgh, Feb. 24; d. William H. and Edna (Hoffman) S. B.Ed. Duquesne U.; M.Ed., U. Pittsburgh; postgrad. courses Columbia U., U. Calif., Calif. State U. Cert. elem. and secondary tchr., spl. edn. tchr., supr., adminstr. Tchr. Lincoln (Ill). State Sch., 1953; group leader Retarded Education Alliance, N.Y.C., 1954-58; program dir. Pomona (N.Y.) Camp for Retarded, summers 1960-63; tchr. Stockton Sch., San Diego, 1964-65; tchr. Cathdral City (Calif.) Sch., 1967-78; prin. elem. summer schs. Palm Springs (Calif.) Unified Sch. Dist., 1971-72; prin.-tchr. Summer Extended Sch. for Spl. Students, 1979-82; ptnr. Computer World Learning Ctr., Cathedral City, Mem. NEA, Calif. Tchrs. Assn., Palm Springs Tchrs. Assn., Palm Springs Ednl. Leadership Assn., Calif. Assn. Program Specialists, AAUW, Assn. for Supervision and Curriculum Devel., Am. Assn. Childhood Edn. Alpha Kappa Alpha, Phi Delta Kappa. Clubs: Toastmistress, Cath. Daus. Office: 333 S Farrell Palm Springs CA 92262

STEWART, MEREDITH LEE, hosp. adminstr.; b. Kellogg, Idaho, Aug. 20, 1940; d. Norval Rupert and Dorothy Jean (Cameron) Jones; grad. high sch.; m. Donald Eugene Stewart, June 17, 1972; children—Jamie, Jennifer, Jeffery, Jean, Jason. Bookkeeper, Deaconess Hosp., Spokane, Wash., 1970-71, supr. accounts payable, 1971-73, echocardiographer and cardiovascular coordinator, 1973-79, mgr. central supply, 1979—; part time instr. Spokane Community Coll., 1977-79, pres. echocardiography com., 1979, adv. com. cardiopulmonary and echocardiography program, 1977-79; guest speaker, organizer seminars in field. Registered diagnostic med. sonographer. Mem. Echocardiography Soc., Am. Hosp. Assn. Home: Route 1 Box 282 A Colbert WA 99005 Office: W 800 5th Ave Spokane WA 99210

STEWART, RONALD K., state senator; b. Longmont, Colo., Aug. 16, 1948; s. William S. and Doris J. (Whitmer) S.; B.A. in Polit. Sci., U. Colo., 1974; m. Dottie Martin, Apr. 19, 1980. Lectr. Regis Coll., Denver, 1974-75; mem. Colo. Senate, 1976—, minority leader, 1982—. Chmn. Boulder County Democratic Com., 1970-75; exec. dir. Colo. Dem. Central Com., 1972-76; mem. Dem. Nat. Com., 1977-79; chmn. Boulder County Budget Adv. Com., 1976; chmn. Boulder County United Way Bd., 1976; mem. Colo. Gov.'s Commn. on Public Broadcasting, 1978; mem. Reapportionment Commn., 1981; mem. Boulder County Parks and Open Space Adv. Com., 1977-82; pres. resident council St. Vrain Service Center, 1968-69; mem. Colo. Gov.'s Commn. on Edn., 1983—. Home: Box 1442 Longmont CO 80501 Office: Room 214 State Capitol Denver CO 80203

STEWART, WILLIAM LEMLEY, weed scientist; b. Renton, Wash., Apr. 1, 1943; s. Frank Edwin Stewart and Audrey Jean (Lemley) Stewart May; A.A.S., Everett Community Coll., 1968; B.S. in Range Mgmt., Wash. State U., 1971, M.S. in Range Mgmt., 1973, Ph.D. in Agronomy, 1981; m. JoAnne Spencer, Sept. 2, 1966; children—Amy Diane, Nicholas William. Extension asst. Extension Service, Wash. State U., Pullman, 1972-73, 78-79; range conservationist Beaverhead Nat. Forest, U.S. Forest Service, Ennis, Mont., 1973-75, range scientist Intermountain Forest and Range Expt. Sta., Bozeman, Mont., 1975-77, regional pesticide specialist, Missoula, Mont., 1979-81; regional ecologist Dept. Agr. Forest Service, 1981—. Served with U.S. Army, 1965-67; Vietnam. Named Outstanding Range Mgmt. Sr., Wash. State U., 1971, Lion of Yr., Ennis Lions Club, 1975. Mem. Soc. Range Mgmt. (pres. chpt. 1970), Weed Sci. Soc. Am., Sigma Xi (asso.). Alpha Zeta, Xi Sigma Pi (v.p. chpt. 1971). Club: Lolo Lions (v.p.). Contbr. articles to profl publs. Home: 1200 Lakeside Dr Lolo MT 59729 Office: Fed Bldg Missoula MT 59801

STICKEL, FREDERICK A., publisher; b. Weehawken, N.J., Nov. 18, 1921; s. Fred and Eva (Madigan) S.; student Georgetown U., 1939-42; B.S., St. Peter's Coll., 1943; m. Margaret A. Dunne, Dec. 4, 1943; children—Fred A., Patrick F., Daisy E., Geoffrey M., James E., Bridget A. Advt. salesperson Jersey Observer daily, Hoboken, N.J., 1945-51; retail advt. salesperson Jersey Jour., Jersey City, 1951-55, advt. dir., 1955-66, pub., 1966-67; gen. mgr. Oregonian Pub. Co., Portland, Oreg., 1967-72, pres., 1972—, publisher, 1975—. Bd. regents U. Portland; bd. dirs. Portland Rose Festival Assn., United Way Oreg. Served to capt. USMC, 1942-45. Mem. Assn. for Portland Progress (dir.), Portland C. of C. (dir.), Oreg. Newspaper Publishers Assn. (past pres.), Pacific N.W. Newspaper Assn. (treas.), Am. Newspaper Publishers Assn. Clubs: Univ., Multnomah Athletic Waverley Country, Arlington, Rotary. Office: Oregonian Pub Co 1320 SW Broadway Portland OR 97201*

STICKLEY, THOMAS HENRY, safety specialist, consultant; b. Rennsselaer, N.Y., Aug. 22, 1921; s. Thomas Edwin and Henrietta May (Fowler) S.; m. Vera Robison, July 4, 1946; children—Daniel, Sharon, John, Tim. B.S. in Chem. Engring., Rennsselaer Poly. Inst., 1948. Cert. safety profl. Plant safety engr. Phillips Petroleum Co., Idaho Falls, 1954-66; safety dir. Idaho Nuclear Corp., Idaho Falls, 1966-69; OSHA coordinator Aerojet Nuclear Corp., Idaho Falls, 1971-72; mgr. PBF-CFA safety br. EG&G Idaho, Idaho Falls, 1972-76, safety engr. specialist, 1978—. Served with USNR, 1942-45. Mem. Am. Soc. Safety Engrs., Idaho Soc. Profl. Engrs., Nat. Soc. Profl. Engrs., ASME (chmn. com. cranes for nuclear facilites). Methodist. Home: 290 N Bellin Rd Idaho Falls ID 83402 Office: EG&G Idaho PO Box 1625 Idaho Falls ID 83415

STICKNEY, DOUGLAS HENRY, biostatistician; b. Little Rock, Feb., 21, 1956; s. Henry E. and Delphine D. (Perse). B.S. in Biology, Davidson (N.C.) Coll., 1977; M.S. in Biostats., UCLA, 1980. Statis. cons. Gateways Hyperkinetic Research Clinic, Los Angeles, 1979-81; health care analyst Systemetrics Inc., Santa Barbara, Calif., 1980-81; statis. cons. Ventura (Calif.) County Air Quality Mgmt. Bur., 1982—; biostatistician Am. Edwards Labs., Irvine, Calif., 1980—. Mem. Am. Statis. Assn. Episcopalian. Contbr. articles to profl. jours. Office: American Edwards Labs PO Box 11150 Santa Ana CA 92711

STICKNEY, SHARON ROGGY, hosp. planner; b. Bloomington, Ill, June 20, 1946; d. Paul and Hazel M. (Rice) Roggy; m. Benjamin D. Stickney, Jan. 6, 1967; children—Benjamin Paul, Stephanie Ann-Loria. B.A. magna cum laude in Psychology, U. Miami (Fla.), 1971; M.Ed. in Ednl. Research, U. Mass., 1976. Social service program evaluation worker, Mass., 1974-75; ednl. coordinator Sojourn, Inc., Northampton, Mass., 1976-77; dir. Domestic Violence Prevention Ctr., Colorado Springs, Colo., 1979-81; staff planner Penrose Hosps., Colorado Springs, 1981—. Bd. dirs. Domestic Violence Prevention Ctr. Named Outstanding Young Woman of Am., 1980. Mem. Soc. Hosp. Planning of Am. Hosp. Assn., Am. Assn. Hosp. Planning, Colo. Women's Forum Health Adminstrn. Home: 5025 Secota Ln Colorado Springs CO 80917 Office: Penrose Hosps PO Box 7021 Colorado Springs CO 80933

STIEGEMEYER, CONNI RUTHE, restaurant equipment dealer; b. London, Mar. 18, 1943; came to U.S., 1963; d. Frederick John and Kathleen Cordery (Percival) Trent; m. Byron George Stiegemeyer, Nov. 18, 1973; 1 dau., Jodi. Student Santa Monica (Calif.) City Coll., 1965, Valley Coll., San Fernando, Calif., 1973-74. Sec., Can. Gen. Elec., Toronto, 1960-63; various modeling and secretarial positions worldwide, 1963-66; office mgr. LongLok Corp., Los Angeles, 1967-69; with Uniworld Foods, Los Angeles, 1970-72, salesperson and restaurant equipment coordinator Elsters, Inc., Los Angeles, 1972-76, Foodservice Spltys., Irvine, Calif., 1977-79; owner Trent Group, Ltd., Laguna Hills, Calif., 1979—. Mem. Am. Youth Soccer Orgn., Am. Youth Soccer Orgn. Cultural Exchange. Club: Daus. of Brit. Empire (Mission Viejo, Calif.).

STIEGHORST, JUNANN JORDAN, seed co. exec.; b. Hydro, Okla., June 8, 1923; d. John Wallace and Myrtle Mae (Harrison) Jordan; student Southwestern Coll., Weatherford, Okla., 1940-41; B.A. in L.S., U. Okla., 1944, B.A. in English, 1947, postgrad., 1959-60; postgrad. So. Meth. U., 1945; m. Guenther Paul Stieghorst, Aug. 13, 1955; 1 son, Theodore Mark. Stewardess, Braniff Airways, 1944-45; advt. copywriter, model Neiman-Marcus, Dallas, Tex., 1945-46, dir. clientele and charge account promotion, 1947-55; advt. copywriter Wilhelm-Laughlin-Wilson, Dallas, 1946; dir. public relations and clientele Lichensteins, Corpus Christi, Tex., 1955-56; clientele dir. Joskes of Tex., San Antonio, 1957-58; children's librarian Jefferson County Public Library, Golden, Colo., 1967-69; co-owner Stieghorst Seed Co., Golden, 1973—. Recipient award for outstanding book U. Okla., 1966. Mem. AAUW, Colo. Archaeol. Soc., DAR (nat. chairman's award 1975, nat. chmn. western div., state chmn., chpt. regent), Alpha Chi Omega. Republican. Lutheran. Clubs: Soroptimist, Braniff Clipped B's. Author: Bay City and Matagorda County: A History, 1965; Colorado Historical Markers, 1978; History of Mount Lookout Chapter 1923-1960, 1983; contbr. articles on retail bus. to various mags. Home and Office: Golden CO 80401

STIEHLER, JEAN MARIE DINGEL, business analyst; b. Rice Lake, Wis., Oct. 8, 1946; d. Arthur Samuel and Dorothy Marie (Shafer) Quentmeyer; student Coll. San Mateo, 1973, U. Okla., 1977; m. Robert M. Stiehler, June 13, 1981; children by previous marriage—Dawn Marie Henderson, Melani Jean Dingel. Data base mgr. Morton Salt Co.,

Burlingame, Calif., 1970-74; data control mgr. Coen Co., Inc., Burlingame, 1974-79; mfg. systems analyst Zilog, Inc. div. Exxon Enterprises, Cupertino, Calif., 1979; mgr. mfg. systems edn. Exxon Enterprises, Inc., Cupertino, 1980-82; bus. systems analyst Atari, Inc., Sunnyvale, Calif., 1982—. Mem. Am. Prodn. and Inventory Control Soc. (dir. Silicon Valley chpt., dir. Region 10), Am. Soc. Tng. and Devel. Democrat. Roman Catholic. Home: 40335 Imperio Pl Fremont CA 94539 Office: 1265 Borregas Ave Sunnyvale CA 94086

STIERN, WALTER W., state senator, veterinarian; b. San Diego; D.V.M., Wash. State Coll.; m. Alysjune Dunning; children—Christina, Janet. Practice vet. medicine, Bakersfield, Calif.; mem. Calif. Senate, 1958—. Served with U.S. Army, World War II; to maj. USAF Res. Mem. AVMA, Calif. Vet. Med. Assn., Kern County Hist. Soc. Democrat. Clubs: Horseless Carriage, Rotary. Office: Calif State Senate Sacramento CA 95814*

STIGLICH, JACOB JOHN, JR., metallurgical engineer; b. Milw., Dec. 21, 1938; s. Jacob John and Augusta Prezel S.; B.S.M.E., Marquette U., 1961; Ph.D., Northwestern U., 1970; m. Kira Fay Kramer, Sept. 26, 1963; children—Mary, Cynthia. Chief engr. Boride Products, Traverse City, Mich., 1971-74; mgr. ceramic materials mfg. Valeron Corp., Detroit, 1974-76; asst. dir. Eagle Picher Research Lab., Miami, Okla., 1976-78; mgr. R&D, San Fernando Labs., Pacoima, Calif., 1978—. Served with U.S. Army, 1967-70. Mem. Am. Ceramic Soc., Am. Nuclear Soc., Am. Soc. Metals, AIME. Patentee in field. Office: 10258 Norris Ave Pacoima CA 91331

STILES, GERALD JOE, air force officer; b. Norman, Okla., Aug. 16, 1941; s. Charles James and Jewel Lena (Kuntz) S.; m. Anne M. Saccone, May 5, 1980; 1 son, Gerald. B.S. with honors in Elec. Engring., U.S. Naval Acad., 1963; M.S. in Aero. Engring., U. Ariz., 1971; M.S. in Mgmt. Engring., George Washington U., 1977. Commd. 2d lt. U.S. Air Force, 1963, advanced through grades to maj., 1983; weapons developer; instr. bus. and math. Embry-Riddle U. and Chapman Coll. First v.p. Greentree Neighborhood Assn. Decorated D.F.C. (2). Mem. Assn. Old Crows (Tng. award 1981), Air Force Assn. citation of Honor 1982). Republican. Baptist. Developed false alarm inhibitor. Home: 14483 Camrose Ct Victorville CA 92392

STILES, VICTORIA JANE, personnel manager; b. Ft. Worth, Aug. 24, 1937; d. Victor McCormick and Ruthie Mae (Smith) Smith; m. Dwight Dermott Stiles, July 19, 1955; 1 son, Greg Lyman; m. 2d, Orville Eugene Blatherwick, Jan. 9, 1982. B.A. in Mgmt., St. Mary's Coll. of Calif., Moraga, 1980. With Georgia-Pacific Corp., 1973—, personnel mgr., Tracy, Calif., 1978—. Mem. Am. Soc. Personnel Adminstrn., Am. Soc. Safety Engrs. Democrat. Methodist. Home: 430 S Central St Tracy CA 95376 Office: 75 W Valpico Rd PO Box 239 Tracy CA 95376

STILGENBAUER, ROBERT MELVIN, quality assurance engr.; b. Coshocton County, Ohio, Mar. 24, 1918; s. Jacob John and Clara Matilda (Hoffman) S.; student pub. schs.; m. Joan Marguerite Johnson, June 18, 1948; children—Gerald, Teresa, Emily, Ronald, Carolyn, John, Lorraine. Various positions in industry, 1936-50; tester, engr. Hughes Aircraft Co., Culver City and El Segundo, Calif., 1951—, quality assurance engr., 1967—. Served with AUS, 1942-45. Developed world's largest crossword puzzle, 1949, world's largest color crossword puzzles, 1963, 75, factors of odd numbers, 1979. Address: 1660 Edgecliffe Dr Los Angeles CA 90026

STILL, ROBERT MILTON, interior designer; b. Madison, Kans., Oct. 13, 1932; s. Orval Alexander and Esther Marie (Helmer) S.; m. Sally Rae Robbins, Apr. 7, 1962; children—Todd, Ross, Erik. A.A., Kansas City (Mo.) Jr. Coll., 1953; B.F.A., U. Wash., 1956. Employed in interior design studio Frederick & Nelson, Seattle, 1958-59, head home furnishings display dept., 1959-60; interior designer B.K. Alsin Imports, Seattle, 1960-70; owner Robert M. Still, interior designer, Mercer Island, Wash., 1970—; vis. team mem. Found. for Interior Design Edn. Research. Served with USNG, 1951-56, U.S. Army, 1956-58. Mem. Am. Soc. Interior Designers (past pres. Wash. chpt.), Tau Kappa Epsilon. Home and Office: 4518 W Mercer Way Mercer Island WA 98040

STILL, RONALD ROY, chief of police; b. Gresham, Oreg., May 24, 1932; s. Roy E. and Marie (Welsh) S.; m. Patricia R. Amos, Oct. 22, 1954; children—Darolyn, Ronald Roy Jr., Colleen. A.A. in Police Sci., Portland (Oreg.) Community Coll.; B.S. in Adminstrn. Criminal Justice, U. Portland, M.S. in Adminstrn. Criminal Justice; grad. FBI Nat. Acad. Patrol officer Portland Police Dept., 1954-61, detective, 1961-63, uniform sgt., 1963-64, detective sgt., 1964-68, uniform lt., 1968-70, detective lt., 1970-71, comdg. officer spl. investigations div., 1971-73, dir. regional narcotics control unit, 1971-73, capt. spl. investigations div., 1973, capt. central precinct, 1974, capt. East precinct, 1974, asst. dep. chief strike force ops., 1974, capt. central precinct, 1976, capt. detectives, 1977-81, capt. spl. investigations div., 1981, chief of police, 1981—. Served with USCG, 1951-54. Mem. Oreg. Narcotics Enforcement Assn., Internat. Assn. Chiefs of Police (Western rep.), Portland Police Assn., FBI Nat. Acad. Assocs. Episcopalian. Lodges: Elks, Rotary. Contbr. articles to various periodicals. Office: Portland Police Bur 222 SW Pine St Portland OR 97204

STILLMAN, ALFRED WILLIAM, JR., logistics support engr.; b. Biloxi, Miss., Sept. 11, 1942; s. Alfred William and Marie Ann (Hengen) S.; A.A., Am. River Coll., 1966; B.S. in Elec. Engring., Calif. Poly. State U., 1970, B.S. in Applied Math., 1970, M.S. in Applied Math., 1973; M.E. in Indsl. Engring., Tex. A. and M. U., 1976; postgrad. elec. engring. N.J. Inst. Tech., 1977; Ph.D. in Mgmt., Calif. Coast U., 1983; children—Shannon Lynn, Laura Marie. Cert. profl. logistician. Engring. intern U.S. Army Material Command, Texarkana, Tex., 1973-75, electronic systems staff maintenance engr., Ft. Monmouth, N.J., 1975-77, mil. tactical data system integrated logistics support mgr. Office of Project Mgr., ARTADS, Ft. Monmouth, 1977-78, tactical ADP ILS Mgr., ILS dir. CORADOM, Ft. Monmouth, 1978-79, engring. mgr. regional dist. office Office of Project Mgr., Firefinder, Hughes Aircraft Co., Fullerton, Calif., 1979-80; prof. systems acquisition mgmt. Dept. Def. Systems Mgmt. Coll., Ft. Belvoir, Va., 1980-82; integrated logistics support engring. specialist, advanced systems div. Northrop Corp., Pico Rivera, Calif., 1982-83; program mgmt. rep. space systems group Rockwell Internat., Downey, Calif., 1983—; pres. AWS Assocs., Inc., Woodbridge, Va., 1982—, AWS Assocs. Calif., Inc., Huntington Beach, 1983—; corp. v.p., div. pres. HOPE Assocs., Inc., Huntington Beach, 1983—; corp. v.p. Chgo. Motor Works, Inc., Huntington Beach, 1983—. Served with USAF, 1962-66. Mem. IEEE, Am. Mgmt. Assn., Am. Inst. Indsl. Engrs. (sr.) Soc. Logistics Engrs. (sr.), Am. Def. Preparedness Assn., Am. Security Council, Tau Beta Pi. Presbyterian. Club: Acacia. Home: 16211 Parkside Ln #177 Huntington Beach CA 92647 Office: 12214 Lakewood Blvd MS 041-777-36BA Downey CA 90241

STILLMAN, GEORGE, artist, educator; b. Laramie, Wyo., Feb. 25, 1921; s. Herman and Ester (Heimlich) S.; m. Lillian Blitz, Jan. 17; children—Paul, David, Anthony. D.A., Calif. Sch. Fine Arts, San Francisco, 1949; B.F.A., Ariz. State U., 1968, M.F.A., 1970. Chief U.S. Army Reprodn. br. Inter-Am. Geodetic Survey, Panama C.Z., 1952-59; communications resources officer AID, Brazil, 1959-63; chmn. dept. art Columbus (Ga.) Coll., 1970-72, Central Wash. U., Ellensburg, 1972—; cons. in field; commd. works: Wash. Arts Commn., 1977, Seattle Arts Commn., 1981, 82. Served with AUS. Recipient awards Tex. Fine Arts Commn., Seattle Arts Commn., Wash. Arts Commn., also others. Mem. Coll. Art Assn. Office: Central Wash Univ Ellensburg WA 98926

STILSON, WALTER LESLIE, educator, physician; b. Sioux Falls, S.D., Dec. 13, 1908; s. George W. and Elizabeth M. (Zager) S.; B.A., Columbia Union Coll., 1929; M.D., Loma Linda U., 1933; m. Grace Beall Bramble, Aug. 15, 1933; children—Carolyn Grace (Mrs. Richard Palmieri), Walter Edwin, Judith Arlene (Mrs. Paul Stirling). Intern, White Meml. Hosp., 1933-34; radiology resident Los Angeles County Gen. Hosp., 1934-36; instr. dept. radiology Loma Linda U., 1935-41, asst. prof., 1941-49, asso. prof., 1949-53, prof., 1953—, founder Sch. Radiologic Tech., 1941, chmn. dept. radiology, 1955-69, chmn. dept. radiologic tech. Sch. Allied Health Professions, 1966-75, med. dir. dept. radiologic tech., 1975—, chief radiology White Meml. Hosp., 1939-65; chief diagnostic radiology Loma Linda U. Med. Center, 1969-77; attending staff Riverside Gen. Hosp., 1966-76. Served with USPHS, 1943-48. Diplomate Nat. Bd. Med. Examiners, Am. Bd. Radiology. Fellow Am. Coll. Radiology; mem. Am., Calif., San Bernardino County med. assns., Los Angeles (sec. 1960-62, v.p. 1962-63, pres. 1963-64) Inland (pres. 1971) radiol. socs., Radiol. Soc. N.Am., N.Y. Acad. Sci., AAAS, Am. Roentgen Ray Soc., Alpha Omega Alpha (Disting. Univ. Service award Loma Linda U. 1978). Contbr. articles to profl. jours. Home: 25045 Crestview Dr Loma Linda CA 92354

STIMATZ, LAWRENCE G., lawyer, state senator; b. Walkerville, Mont., May 25, 1919; A.B., Gonzaga U.; A.B., LL.B., U. Mont.; m. Peggy Stimatz; 11 children. Bar: Mont. 1951. Asst. U.S. atty., 1961-65; county atty., 1971-74, dep. county atty., 1957-60; mem. Mont. Ho. of Reps., 1961-67, 69, Mont. Senate, 1979—. Served with Signal Corps, U.S. Army, World War II. Democrat. Office: 1615 C St Butte MT 59701*

STINI, WILLIAM ARTHUR, educator; b. Oshkosh, Wis., Oct. 9, 1930; s. Louis alois and Clara (Larsen) S.; B.B.A., U. Wis., 1960, M.S., 1967, Ph.D., 1969; m. Mary Ruth Kalous, Feb. 11, 1950; children—Patricia Lorraine, Paulette Ann, Suzanne Kay. Planner cost acct. Kimberly-Clark Corp., Niagara Falls, N.Y., 1960-62; asst. prof. Cornell U., Ithaca, N.Y., 1968-71, assoc. prof., 1971-73; assoc. prof. U. Kans., Lawrence, 1973-76; prof. anthropology U. Ariz., Tucson, 1976—, head dept. anthropology, 1980—; panelist anthropology program NSF, 1976-78; cons. NIH, 1974—. Mem. Gov.'s Adv. Council on Aging, State of Ariz., 1980-83. Nat. Inst. Dental Research tng. grantee, 1964-68; Clark Found. grantee, Cornell U., 1973. Fellow AAAS, Am. Anthrop. Assn., N.Y. Acad. Sci.; mem. Am. Assn. Phys. Anthropologists (exec. com. 1978-81), Soc. Study Human Biology, Human Biology Council (exec. com. 1978-81), Soc. Study Social Biology, Am. Inst. Nutrition, Western Gerontol. Soc., Sigma Xi. Author: Ecology and Human Adaptation, 1975; Nature, Culture and Human History - A Biocultural Introduction to Anthropology, (with Davydd J. Greenwood), 1977; Physiological and Morphological Adaptation and Evolution, 1979; editor-in-chief Am. Jour. Phys. Anthropology, 1983—; contbr. articles to profl. jours. Home: 6240 N Camino Miraval Tucson AZ 85718 Office: Dept Anthropology Univ of Ariz Tucson AZ 85721

STINSON, CAROLYN HOLLEY, research inst. adminstr.; b. Paris, Tex., Nov. 23, 1936; d. Wilbert Willis and Treva May (Young) Holley; student Los Angeles City Coll., 1954-55; m. Charles David Stinson, Nov. 11, 1966; 1 son, Eric Zsasha. Acctg. mgr. Amax Aluminum Co., Riverside, Calif., 1956-67; asst. treas. Archtl. Engring. Products Co., Inc., San Diego, 1967-68; asst. treas., asst. sec. Salk Inst., La Jolla, Calif., 1969—, dir. program analysis, 1978—. Served with USAF, 1955-56. Mem. Soc. Research Adminstrs., Nat. Assn. Coll. and Univ. Bus. Officers, Nat. Assn. Accts., Nat. Assn. Female Execs. Democrat. Home: 2118 Belloc Ct San Diego CA 92109 Office: PO Box 85800 San Diego CA 92138

STINSON, KARL BARRY, environmental engineer; b. Lindsay, Calif., July 14, 1949, s. E. Howard and R. Minalee (Woolsey) S. B.S. magna cum laude in Engring., UCLA, 1971; M.S. magna cum laude, U. So. Calif., 1975. Registered profl. engr., Calif. Asst. san. engr. City of Los Angeles, 1972-76, assoc. san. engr., 1976; assoc. environ. engr. East Bay Mcpl. Utility Dist., Oakland, Calif., 1976-81, sr. engr., 1981-83, mgr. treatment and distbn., 1983—. Bd. dirs. Utility Dist. Credit Union. Mem. ASCE, Am. Water Works Assn., Bay Area Water Works Assn. (dir.), Calif. Water Pollution Control Assn., Tau Beta Pi. Contbr. numerous articles to profl. jours. Office: East Bay Municipal Dist 2127 Adeline St Oakland CA 94623

STIRLING, STEPHANIE KAY FOX, historian; b. Seattle, Nov. 29, 1951; d. Franklin George and Rosemary (Knudtsen) F.; B.A. in Internat. Ethnic Relations (scholar 1973-74), Fairhaven Coll., Bellingham, Wash., 1974; postgrad. U. Wash., 1975-76, Union Grad. Sch., 1979—. Tchr., Chief Joseph Summer Seminars, Joseph, Oreg., summers 1971, 72; vol. VISTA, 1971-72; asst. archives and manuscript div. U. Wash., 1973-74; research asst. Inst. Devel. Indian Law, 1974-75; asst. PNW collection U. Wash. Library, 1975-76; research assoc. coop. parks study unit U. Alaska, Fairbanks, 1976-78, asst. to v.p. acad. affairs, 1978-80; historian office of history and archeology Alaska Div. Parks, Anchorage, 1980—. Social Sci. Found. scholar, 1974-75, Daus. of Pioneers scholar, 1976; Nat. Endowment for Humanities grantee, 1972-73. Mem. Am. Hist. Assn., Orgn. Am. Historians, Oral History Assn. Home: 3809 Barbara Dr Anchorage AK 99503 Office: Alaska Div Parks 619 Warehouse Ave Suite 210 Anchorage AK 99501

STIRN, REBECCA ATKINSON, optical co. exec.; b. Kansas City, Mo., Feb. 23, 1953; d. Russell Jay and Virginia (Cox) Atkinson; B.A., Smith Coll., 1975; M.B.A., Stanford U., 1978; m. Bradley Albert Stirn, Aug. 30, 1975. Asst. mgr. market devel. So. Pacific Transp. Co. San Francisco, 1978-79, fin. analyst, fin., adminstrn., 1979-80, asst. mgr. fin. adminstrn., 1980-81; mgr. market research Cooper Vision Optics div. Cooper Labs., Palo Alto, Calif., 1981-82, mgr. new products and planning, 1982-83, dir. profl. mktg., 1983, dir. mktg., 1983—; market researcher Saga Corp., Menlo Park, Calif., summer 1977; research asst. Fed. Res. Bank of San Francisco, 1975-76. Mem. devel. com. Nairobi Day Sch., 1978; bd. dirs. Wilmer Eye Inst. at Johns Hopkins Hosp., Peninsula Smith Coll. Club, 1977-80. Home: 590 Albion Ave Woodside CA 94062 Office: 2801 Orchard Pkwy San Jose CA 95134

STIVERS, THOMAS WALTER, state representative, securities company executive; b. Maroa, Ill., Sept. 6, 1918; s. Walter Daniel and Naomi (Potter) S.; m. Winifred Barton, 1940; children—Richard, Susan Stivers Waters. County clk., Twin Falls (Idaho) County, 1951-63; mem. Idaho Ho. of Reps., 1975—, speaker of house; owner, mgr. Boone Land Title Co., Twin Falls, 1963-69; pres. Sawtooth Title Co. Inc., Sun Valley, Idaho, 1965-76, Title Fact, Inc., Twin Falls, 1969, Western Title Co., Custer Co., 1968-78; v.p. Real Estate Securities Corp., Twin Falls, 1969; dir. Am. Bank of Commerce, Boise, 1976—. Del. Republican Nat. Conv., 1976, 80; dir., nat. sec. Am. Legis. Exchange Council. Served with USN, 1942-45; PTO. Mem. Idaho Land Title Assn., Twin Falls Bd. Realtors, Magic Valley Bldg Contractors Assn., Am. Legion, DAV. Office: Office of Speaker State Capitol Boise ID 83720*

STOCK, GREGG FRANCIS, association executive, former museum administrator; b. Kansas City, Mo., Jan. 30, 1926; s. Arthur Robert and Verna Marie (Prawitz) S.; m. Sarah Ellen Smart, Nov. 8, 1947; children—Gregg Francis, Hedi Frances, Peter Huston. Student Rockhurst Coll., 1942, Central Mo. State Coll., 1942-43; B.A. in Journalism, U. Kans., 1948, B.S. in Advt., 1948. Pres., Wayne-Fastock Equipment Co., Kansas City, 1953-65; nat. dir. employee relations Automatique, Inc., Kansas City, 1965-70; dir. Kansas City (Mo.) Mus. History and Sci., after 1971, now dir. emeritus; exec. dir. Better Bus. Bur. Santa Fe (N.Mex.); exec. dir. Old Santa Fe Assn. cons. in field. Mem. adv. bd. Hist. Kansas City Found.; bd. dirs. Native Sons of Greater Kansas City; mem. Kansas City Mayor's Corps of Progress. Served to lt. (j.g.) USNR, 1943-46; PTO. Fellow Explorers Club; mem. Mo. Mus. Assocs. (past pres.), Midwest Mus. Conf., Am. Assn. Museums (sr. examiner), Assn. Sci.-Tech. Centers, Assn. Sci. Mus. Dirs., Kansas City Archeology Soc. (J. Mett Shippee award 1976, past v.p.), Mo. Archeology Soc. (past v.p.). Clubs: Mercury, Wockholl, Rotary; Author: (film) Line Creek Man, 1976; Story Line for a Kansas City Regional History Museum, 1973; adv. bd. Explorer mag. Office: 127 E Palace Suite C Santa Fe NM 87501

STOCK, NANCY JEAN, educator; b. Bloomington, Ill., Mar. 11, 1929; d. William Dean and Sara Elizabeth (Stoddard) McCully; m. Richard Crow Livingston, June 20, 1948 (div.); children—Beth Christine Livingston Hakes, Mary Therese Livingston Carlson, Patrick Charles, Michael Neil, Will Richard; m. 2d, Ray Evans Stock, July 28, 1978 (div.). B.Ed., Ill. State U., 1966; M.A. in TESL, No. Ariz. U., 1972, postgrad., 1973—. Cert. elem. sch. tchr., supr., prin., Ariz. Tchr. elem. schs., Ill., 1954-66; tchr. elem. schs. Bur. Indian Affairs Navajo Area, Ariz. and N.Mex., 1967-69, edn. specialist Fort Defiance Agy., 1969-74, tchr.-supr. Kaibeto Boarding Sch. Western Navajo Agy., Ariz., 1974-79; tchr. English as a 2d lang., K-8 coordinator Tuba City (Ariz.) pub. sch., 1979—. Active Tuba City Pub. Sch. PTA. Mem. Teaching English to Speakers of Other Langs., Assn. for Supervision and Curriculum Devel., Sigma Alpha Iota. Republican. Methodist. Dir. tchr. devel. of English as a second lang. curriculum and testing program for Navajo and English speaking sch. children. Home: Box 794 Grandview St Apt 8 Tuba City AZ 86045

STOCKARD, WILLIAM HENRY, school administrator; b. Lewisville, Tex., May 8, 1926; s. J. Allie and Garnette Lillian (Womack) S.; m. Myra Reynolds, June 22, 1946; children—Kyle, Kraig. B.S. in Speech, N. Tex. State Coll., 1949, M.Ed. in Ednl. Adminstrn., 1951; Ed.D. in Elem. Edn., U. Fla., 1962. Sci. and social studies tchr., prin., Temple, Tex., 1949; tchr., Rhome, Tex., 1950-52; tchr./prin., Ozona, Tex., 1952-53, prin., 1953-55; asst. dir. curriculum, Corpus Christi, Tex., 1955-56; supr. tchr. interns U. Fla., Gainesville, 1956; elem. cons., Merced County (Calif.) Schs., 1958-62, dir. curriculum, 1962-63, asst. supt. schs., 1963-74, supt., 1975—; spl. assignments dir. Neighborhood Youth Corps, Merced; cons. State Dept. Edn., Sacramento. Active Merced County Human Relations Com., 1960-68, Merced County Democratic Central Com., 1961-64, Merced County Econ. Opportunity Com., 1965-66, Merced County United Way, 1982-83, Merced County Decathlon Com., 1981-83. Served with USN, 1944-46. Recipient Merced County NAACP Educator of Yr. award, 1978; Merced County Spl. Edn. Program award, 1979; Outstanding Club Pres. award, Kiwanis Club of Merced, 1980-81. Mem. Am. Assn. Sch. Adminstrs., Am. Assn. Supervision and Curriculum Devel., Assn. Calif. Sch. Adminstrs., Calif. Assn. County Sch. Supts., Calif. State Assn. Local Elected Ofcls. Democrat. Methodist. Clubs: Mercedes, Blue Devil Basketball Boosters, Los Banos Sportsmen's, Elks, Masons. Home: 2640 E Cardella Rd Merced CA 95340 Office: 632 W 13th St Merced CA 95340

STOCKDALE, WILLIAM KENNETH, civil engr.; b. Rock Island, Ill., Oct. 11, 1928; s. Robert Ferguson and Irene Mildred (Kail) S.; B.S., U.S. Mil. Acad., 1951; M.S., U. Ill., 1958, Ph.D., 1959; m. Alice Marie Carr, June 9, 1951; children—Mary, William, Jacqueline, Barbara, Theresa; adopted children—Sharon, David. Commd. 2d lt. C.E., U.S. Army, 1951, advanced through grades to col., 1972, from asst. prof. to prof. civil engring. U.S. Mil. Acad., West Point, 1967-78; ret., 1978; mgr. engring. services Wash. Public Power Supply System, Richland, Wash., 1978-81, lead civil/structural engr., tech. services coordinator, 1981—. Served with AUS, 1946-47. Registered profl. engr., Pa., Ill., Wash. Mem. Soc. Am. Mil. Engrs. (pres. West Point Stewart Post chpt. 1973-74), ASCE, Nat. Soc. Profl. Engrs., N.Y. Acad. Scis., Sigma Xi. Roman Catholic. Home: 1873 Marshall Ave Richland WA 99352 Office: 3000 George Washington Way Richland WA 99352

STOCKING, BEAU CAROL DIANE, optometrist; b. Arlington, Va., Feb. 28, 1949; d. John Howard and June Lillian (Mathurin) Stapf. m. Reginald Angus Stocking, Mar. 6, 1976. B.S., Whittier Coll., 1970; postgrad. U. So. Calif., 1970-72; O.D., So. Calif. Coll. Optometry, 1976. Lic. optometrist, Calif. Optometrist USAF, 1976-79; gen. practice optometry, Burbank, Calif., 1980—. Served to capt., USAF, 1976-79. Mem. Calif. Optometric Assn., Am. Optometric Assn. Republican. Episcopalian. Office: 933 N Hollywood Way Burbank CA 91505

STOCKMAN, LEO WARREN, consulting engineer; b. Hutchinson, Kans., Mar. 1, 1934; s. Leo Warren and Dorothy (Alene) (Randles) S.; m. Ruth Chaffee, June 23, 1956 (dec.); children—Gayle Norris, Karen Frye, John, Michael. B.S., U.S. Naval Acad., 1956; M.S. in Aeros. and Astronautics, MIT, 1962; Ph.D., U. Okla., 1967. Registered profl. engr., N. Mex., Okla. Commd. 2d lt. U.S. Air Force, 1956, advanced through grades to lt. col., 1973; prof. aeros. U.S. Air Force Acad., 1967-77, ret., 1977; v.p., chief scientist Scott Sci. and Tech., Albuquerque, 1978-83; prin. Stockman Assocs., Albuquerque, 1983—. Mem. AIAA, Am. Soc. for Non-destructive Testing. Republican. Address: 7708 Pickard Ave NE Albuquerque NM 87110

STOCKS, CHESTER LEE, JR., hospital administrator; b. Montgomery, Ala., Oct. 8, 1928; s. Chester Lee and Evelyn (Cooley) S.; B.S., Auburn U., 1949; M.H.A., Washington U., St. Louis, 1955; m. Mary Gwendoline Hase, June 5, 1954; children—Susan Bradley Hase, Charles Lee, Sally. Resident Baylor U. Med. Center, Dallas, 1954-55, adminstrv. asst., 1955-57, asst. adminstr., 1957-63; exec. v.p. Good Samaritan Hosp. and Med. Center, 1963, Portland, Oreg., 1963—. Preceptor grad. programs in hosp. adminstrn., U. Calif., U. Iowa, Washington U.; lectr., participant programs on health care; mem. exec. com. Oreg. Regional Med. Programs, 1966-74, v.p., 1969-76; mem. Oreg. Commn. on Nursing, 1969-75, Oreg. Health Manpower Commn., 1966-73, Comprehensive Health Planning Assn. Met. Portland, 1969-76, Oreg. Health Commn. Siting Com., 1974-77; dir. Oreg. Med. Polit. Action Com., 1974-77. Oreg. chmn. Wash. U. devel. program, 1967-70. Trustee Fred Hutchison Cancer Center, Seattle, 1972-79, Oreg. Comprehensive Cancer Center, 1973-75, Blue Cross Oreg., 1965—; pres. Oreg. Hosp. Found., 1979. Served to 1st lt. USAF, 1950-53. Fellow Am. Coll. Hosp. Adminstrs. (regent 1969-75, gov. 1975-78, chmn. 1979); mem. Assn. Western Hosps. (trustee, pres. 1973-74), Am. Hosp. Assn. (various coms. 1965—), Oreg. Assn. Hosps. (pres. 1967-68, trustee 1973-76), Portland Council of Hosps. (pres. 1966-67), NW Oreg. Council Hosps. (exec. com. 1980—), Portland C. of C. (bd. dirs. 1967-69), Nat. Assn. for Practical Nurse Edn. and Service (trustee 1960—), Protestant Hosp. Assn., Nat. League for Nursing, Pi Kappa Alpha. Episcopalian (dir. William Temple House 1965-70). Rotarian. Clubs: Multnomah Athletic, Arlington (Portland). Home: 282 NW Macleay Blvd Portland OR 97210 Office: 1015 NW 22 Ave Portland OR 97210

STOCKTON, ANDERSON B(ERRIAN), communications company engineering executive; b. Ga., Oct. 7, 1943; s. Berrian Henry and Mary Grace (Warbington) S.; m. Linda Arlene Milligan, June 9, 1963; 1 son, Christopher Lee. Supr., Western Union Telegraph Co., Atlanta, 1965-67; mgr. applications engring. RCA Service Co., Cherry Hill, N.J., 1967-69, mgr. service/sales, 1969-72; v.p. mktg. Universal Techs. Inc., Clifton, N.J., 1972-76; dir. engring. Siemens Corp., Anaheim, Calif., 1976-83;

v.p. engring., prin. Concorde Computer, Inc., 1983—. Served with USAF, 1961-65. Office: 23152 Verdugo Dr Laguna Hills CA 92630

STOCKTON, RUTH SMALL (MRS. TRUMAN ALEX STOCKTON, JR.), state senator; b. Ridgefield Park, N.J., June 6, 1916; d. Arthur Everett and Mary Rose (Hart) Small; ed. Vassar Coll., Columbia, Colo. U.; m. Truman Alex Stockton, Jr., Nov. 1, 1937; 1 dau., Alexe. Co-chmn. 11 Western States Council of Young Republicans, 1946-47; nat. co-chmn. Young Reps., 1947-49; Rep. nat. committeewoman, 1955-56; mem. Colo. Ho. of Reps., 1961-65; mem. Colo. Senate, 1965—, pres. pro tem, 1979-81, chmn. joint budget com., 1981-82, 83-84. Mem. Gov.'s Com. on Mental Health and Mental Retardation, 1966, Gov.'s Com. on Vocational Rehab., 1966, Gov.'s Council on Alcohol and Drug Abuse, 1971-78; adv. council Colo. Workman's Compensation Fund, 1971-79; mem. Nat. Hwy. Safety Adv. Commn., 1975-78; bd. dirs. Denver Goodwill Industries; trustee Mt. Airy Psychiat. Hosp. Named Woman of Yr., East Jefferson Sentinel, 1969; recipient Golden Bus. and Profl. Women's award, 1966; Top Hat award Colo. Bus. and Profl. Women's Assn., 1970; Florence Sabin award Colo. Pub. Health Assn., 1970; Colo. Community Mental Health Centers award, 1979. Methodist. Office: 1765 Glen Dale Dr Lakewood CO 80215

STODDARD, MARGERY MIESSNER, editor; b. St. Louis, May 26, 1929; d. George Emil and Myrtle Antoinette (Wolf) Miessner; A.A., Santa Monica Coll., 1948; student U. So. Calif., 1948-50; m. Scott Powell Stoddard, Nov. 5, 1955; children—Scott Wilcox, Janet Faye Stoddard Bouweraerts. Photo and fashion model (part-time) Caroline Leonetti Studios, Hollywood, Calif., 1948-51; tech. artist and scene coordinator Metro-Goldwyn-Mayer. Motion Picture Studios, Culver City, Calif. 1951-54; story editor Playhouse 90, CBS-Television City, Los Angeles, 1954-56, free-lance non-fiction and features writer various publs., 1956-78; mng. editor Plastics mag. (Western Plastics News, Inc.) Santa Monica. Calif., 1978—, public relations and press rep. Western Plastics Expns., Santa Monica. also creative advt. and graphics artist. Patron Santa Monica Coll. Mem. Soc. Plastics Engrs., Soc. Advancement of Material and Process Engring., Los Angeles Soc. Coatings Tech., Nat. Assn. Female Execs., AAUW (mem.-at-large). Republican. Presbyterian. Home: 502-26th St Santa Monica CA 90402 Office: 1704 Colorado Ave Santa Monica CA 90404

STODDARD, STEPHEN DAVIDSON, materials scientist; b. Everett, Wash., Feb. 8, 1925; s. Albert and Mary Louise (Billings) S.; student Conn. Coll., 1946; B.S., U. Ill., 1950; m. Joann Elizabeth Burt, June 18, 1949; children—Dorcas Ann, Stephanie Kay. Asst. ceramic engr., asst. prodn. supr. Coors Procelain Co., Golden, Colo., 1950-52; sect. leader ceramics poweder metallurgy Los Alamos Sci. Lab., 1952-80; pres., sec. Materials Tech. Assos., Inc., Los Alamos, 1980—; new bus. cons. Bank of Los Alamos, 1980—; dir. Bank of Los Alamos. Justice of peace, Los Alamos County, 1956-62; commr. County Los Alamos, 1966-68; municipal judge, 1975-76; mem. N.Mex. Senate, 1981—. Served with AUS, 1943-46: ETO. Decorated Bronze Star, Purple Heart, Combat Infantryman badge; registered profl. engr., N.Mex. Mem. Nat. Inst. Ceramic Engrs. (PACE award 1964), Am. Soc. Metals, Am. Ceramic Soc. (treas. 1974-76, v.p., then pres. 1976-77), DAV, VFW, Am. Legion, Keramos, Sigma Xi. Republican. Episcopalian. Clubs: Kiwanis (pres.), Elks (ruler, dist. dep. grand exalted ruler), Eagles, Eastern Star, Masons, Shriners. Patentee in field. Contbr. articles to profl. jours. Address: 326 Kimberly Lane Los Alamos NM 87544

STODDER, JOHN WESLEY, fin. co. exec.; b. N.Y.C., Mar. 15, 1923; s. John David and Helen Adele (Watson) S.; B.S., Holy Cross Coll., 1944; M.B.A. with distinction, Harvard U., 1950; m. Gay Bauman, July 7, 1950; children—John Wesley, David B., Mark W.C., Matthew T., Seth M.M. Salesman, Brailsford & Co., Chgo., 1946-48; with A.G. Becker & Co., Inc., Chgo., 1950-62, v.p. corp. fin., 1957-62; v.p., dir. Smith Barney & Co., Inc., N.Y.C., 1962-68; advisor, dir. exec. com., vice chmn. Josten's, Inc., Mpls., 1973—; dir., chmn. fin. com. Talley Industries, Phoenix, 1970—; dir. Palm Beach Co., N.Y.C. and Cin. Served with USN, 1941-46. Clubs: Los Angeles Yacht, St. Francis Yacht (San Francisco), Harvard (N.Y.C.), Palos Verdes Tennis. Home: 908 Via Rincon Palos Verdes Estates CA 90274 Office: Suite 301 2516 Via Tejon Palos Verdes Estates CA 90274

STOFFEL, CHARLES RANDALL, Realtor, developer, politician; b. Syracuse, N.Y., Dec. 9, 1947; s. Charles Howard and Alma Carolyn (Kreaser) S.; B.A., Syracuse U., 1970; postgrad. U. So. Calif., 1980-81, U. Calif.-Irvine, 1981-83 Staff asst. to Senator Charles E. Goodell, N.Y., 1969-70; asst. to police chief Syracuse Police Dept., 1970-71; press sec. Rep. William O. Mills of Md., 1971-72; legis. analyst Ho. of Reps. Republican Conf., Washington, 1972; exec. asst. to adminstr. OSHA/ Dept. Labor, Washington, 1972-73; staff asst. to asst. sec. for energy and minerals Dept. Interior, Washington, 1973; dep. dir. congl. affairs Fed. Energy Office, Exec. Office of Pres., Washington, 1973-74; partner Stoffel & Starek, 1974-77; v.p. corp. devel. Garrett/Simes Co., Hollywood, Calif., 1977-78; dir. mktg. and govt. affairs AT&T Rec., Inc., Hollywood, 1978-80; Realtor, mgr. Coldwell Banker, Huntington Beach, Calif., 1980-82; pres. Am. Redevel., Long Beach, Calif., 1982—; dir. Great Outdoors Travel, Inc.; cons. World Airways, 1980. Pres. Syracuse U. Young Reps., 1969-70; mem. Onondaga County (N.Y.) Rep. Adv. Council, 1969; regional coordinator Rep. Congl. Com., Washington, 1970; mem. Pres. Ford's Advance Team, 1976; adv. Rep. Congl. Com., 1976; mem. Los Angeles Olympic Organizing Adv. Com.; mem. nat. adv. bd. FAIR. Mem. Los Angeles Pub. Affairs Officers Assn., Syracuse U. Alumni Assn. Roman Catholic. Co-author: No U Turn: A Portrait of Charles Goodell, 1970; author: The Need for Local Governments to Have Personal Representation in Washington, 1976. Editor: Federal Energy Briefing Book, 1974. Office: 211 E Ocean Blvd Long Beach CA 90802

STOFFELS, FRANCIS GILBERT, govt. ofcl.; b. Roseville, Calif., July 2, 1921; s. John Mathias and Anna Margaret (Runckel) S.; A.B., San Jose (Calif.) State U., 1943; M.A., U. Calif., Berkeley, 1948; m. Elizabeth Jane Bishop, Sept. 9, 1953; children—Kathy Ann, Susan Claire. With Calif. Dept. Food and Agr., Sacramento, 1948—, deptl. personnel officer, 1969-77, dept. fiscal officer, 1977-78, spl. cons., 1978-79, exec. asst. Dir.'s Office, 1979—; adj. prof. pub. adminstrn. Golden Gate U., San Francisco, 1971—. Bd. dirs. Sierra Coll. Found., 1972-81, pres., 1974-75; chmn. Roseville Personnel Bd., 1966-74; mem. Charter Rev. Commn., City of Roseville, 1980. Served to 1st lt. USAF, 1951-53. Named Outstanding Instr. of Yr., Golden Gate U., 1978. Mem. Phi Delta Kappa. Methodist. Club: Masons. Home: 504 Vine Way Roseville CA 95678 Office: 1220 N St Sacramento CA 95814

STOFFEY, ROBERT EDWARD, career consultant; b. Coaldale, Pa., Dec. 27, 1934; s. John Joseph and Anna Mary (Gavalla) S.; m. Eleanor Rita Dedinsky, Nov. 24, 1960; children—Monica E., Robert D., Edward W. B.Engring., Pa. State U., 1955. Instruments design engr. Link Aviation, Binghampton, N.Y., 1955-56; mfg. engr. Air Products, Allentown, Pa., 1956-57; commd. 2d lt. U.S. Marine Corps, 1957, advanced through grades to lt. col., ret., 1979; account exec. petrochems. VIP Agy., San Diego, 1979-80; pres. Profl. Career Cons., Carlsbad, Calif., 1980—. Decorated D.F.C. (2), Bronze Star medal, Navy Marine Corps medal, Navy Commendation medal, Vietnemese Disting. Flying Cross, Cross of Gallantry. Mem. Am. Petroleum Inst. Club: Officers. Address: 1728 Havens Point Pl Carlsbad CA 92008

STOKES, BARBARA LYNN, dietetic service adminstr.; b. San Diego, Jan. 25, 1947; d. Charles Fowler and Marguerite (McPherson) McCabe; student San Diego State U., 1964-66; B.A., U. Calif., Santa Barbara, 1968; m. James A. Stokes, Apr. 3, 1971; children—, Daniel James, Bonnie Lynn. Intern, U. Calif., San Francisco, 1969-70; asst. dietitian Tri-City Hosp., Oceanside, Calif., 1970-71, dir. dietetics, 1971-80; relief dietitian Tri-City Hosp. West, 1981—. Mem. Am., Calif. (pres. San Diego dist.) dietetic assns., Am. Soc. Hosp. Food Service Adminstrs., San Diego County Assn. Food Service Adminstrs. in Health Care Facilities (pres.), Alpha Mu Gamma. Clubs: San Diego Highland Dancers Assn., Alpha Chi Omega Alumna, P.E.O. Home: 232 Turner Ave Encinitas CA 92024 Office: 1100 5th St Oceanside CA 92054

STOKES, DELORIS KATHERINE, educator; b. Bogalusa, La., Apr. 14, 1942; d. Luther Walter and Earnestine (Jackson) Mark; m. Larry Dillon, Sept. 8, 1968; 1 son, Larry Gerard; m. 2d, Roland Stokes, Oct. 19, 1974 (dec.). B.S., So. U. A&M Coll., 1965; postgrad. Pepperdine U., 1980-81. Tchr., Los Angeles Unified Schs. Dist., 1966-73; instructional aide Lynwood (Calif.) Unified Schs. Dist., 1975-78; tchr. English, Fred W. Hosler Jr. High Sch., Lynwood, 1978—, chmn. English dept., 1982—. Coe fellow Pepperdine U., 1968. Mem. NAACP, NEA, Nat. Council Tchrs. English, Assn. Supervision and Curriculum Devel., Calif. Tchrs. Assn., Calif. Alliance Black Sch. Educators, Lynwood Tchrs. Assn. Democrat. Baptist. Office: Fred W Hosler Jr High Sch 11300 Spruce St Lynwood CA 90262

STOKES, JAMES DIGBY, wildlife biologist, consultant; b. Mill Valley, Calif., Apr. 2, 1914; s. Charles J. and Annette J. (Jeffreys) S.; m. Blanche Hattie Evan, Mar. 13, 1946; children—James, Charles, John. Student Santa Rosa Jr. Coll., 1931-32, Merritt Coll., Oakland, Calif., 1933-35. With Calif. Dept. Fish and Game, 1936-70, regional mgr. No. Calif., 1952-64, chief planning, Sacramento, 1964-70; co-founder, v.p., treas. Jones & Stokes Assocs. Inc., wildlife and environ. investigations, Sacramento, 1970-76; cons. wildlife biology, environ. problems, 1976—; condr. wildlife planning seminars U.S. Fish and Wildlife Service, nationwide, 1965-70; wildlife biologist member Earthwatch, Chilean expdn. Search for the Huemul, 1981-82. Mem. adv. council Ukian Dist. (Calif.), U.S. Bur. Land Mgmt.; speaker, mem. adv. com. Vina Plains Preserve, Nature Conservancy, Chico, Calif. Served to 1st lt. inf. U.S. Army, 1942-45. Decorated Bronze Star, Purple Heart (U.S.); Order of Leopold (Belgium); Recipient Commr.'s award U.S. Fish and Wildlife Service, 1970; resolution of commendation Assembly Rules Com., Calif. Legislature, 1970. Mem. Wildlife Soc. (cert. wildlife biologist), Audubon Soc., Sierra Club. Republican. Episcopalian. Prin. author: Calif. Wildlife Resources Plan, 1965; Fish and Wildlife Planning Guide, 1969; Hawaii Fish and Wildlife Resources Plan, 1973. Home: 8758 Churn Creek Rd Redding CA 96002

STOKES, JAMES SHERWOOD, marine technologist; b. Los Angeles, Sept. 7, 1926; s. Marcus McKinley and Barbara Alice (Wright) S.; student Olympic Coll., 1945-64, Brigham Young U., 1959-60, U. Utah, 1959-60. Naval elec. apprentice, 1948; electronics engr. guided missiles, jet planes Boeing Airplane Co. and Rohr Aircraft Co., Seattle, 1948-80; marine technologist Tacoma (Wash.) Boat Co., 1980—. Mem. local Bd. of Equalization; advisor to Am. Security Council; candidate for county commr., 1973, for Wash. State Senate, 1978, for U.S. Senate, 1980, 82. Served with USN, World War II, Korean War. Mem. Am. Def. and Preparedness Assn., Air Force Assn. Democrat. Mormon. Club: Eagles. Pilot. Home: 2271 Beach Dr E Port Orchard WA 98366

STOKES, ROBB LYLE, psychologist; b. Albany, Ore., Aug. 13, 1949; s. Lyle Eldon and Ellenor Isabelle S.; m. Cleo Klemzak, Nov. 19, 1977. B.S., Portland (Oreg.) State U., 1972, M.S., 1976; Ph.D., Walden U., Naples, Fla., 1983. Lic. clin. psychol. assoc., Alaska. Counselor, Sheldon Jackson Coll., Sitka, Alaska, 1976-77; program dir. Mt. Edgecumbe Comprehensive Alcohol Program (Alaska), 1977-79; psychologist Norton Sound Health Corp., Nome, Alaska, 1980-83; psychologist, Petersburg, Alaska, 1983—. Mem. Western Psychol. Assn., Christian Assn. Psychol. Studies; assoc. mem. Am. Psychol. Assn., Alaska Psychol. Assn. Home and Office: Gen Delivery Petersburg AK 99833

STOKES, TERRY LYNN, bank exec.; b. Salt Lake City, May 13, 1946; s. Leslie Darrell and Grace (Kendrick) S.; B.A. in Econs. cum laude, Brigham Young U., 1970; M.A. in Econs. (Nat. Def. Fgn. Lang. fellow), Vanderbilt U., 1972. Ops. officer 1st Security Bank of Utah, Salt Lake City, 1972-75, statis, analysis and budget officer, 1975-77, asst. v.p., br. planning and profit planning supr., 1978-81, asst. v.p., cash mgmt. services supr., 1981—; instr. econs. and bus. Am. Inst. Banking. NDEA fellow, 1970. Mem. Am. Inst. Banking (gov. Salt Lake chpt. 1975-77, 1st v.p. 1978-79, pres. 1979-80), Bank Adminstrn. Inst., Salt Lake Bank Officers Assn. Mormon. Editor: Seagull Banker, 1975-77; mem. Salt Lake Mormon Tabernacle Choir, 1977—. Office: 79 S Main St Salt Lake City UT 84110

STOKKE, ROBERT J. (BOB), training adminstrator; b. Salt Lake City, Aug. 20, 1943; s. Otto John and Barbara (Parkison) S.; m. Margaret Louise Whitford, Apr. 23, 1976; children—John, Brian, Michele, Justin. B.A. in Social Scis., Eastern Wash. U., 1965; M.S. in Human Resources Mgmt., Gonzaga U., 1976; M.A. in Human Relations, Pacific Luth. U., 1977. With Skipper's Inc., Bellevue, Wash., 1976—, successivley mgmt. trainee, unit mgr., corp. tng. mgr., dist. mgr., corp. adminstr. tng., 1982—. Served to maj. U.S. Army, 1965-74, currently maj. USAR. Decorated Bronze Star, Meritorious Service medal. Mem. Am. Soc. Tng. and Devel., Res. Officers Assn. U.S. Club: Interflight Eagles (Everett, Wash.). Home: 1848 226th Pl NE Redwood WA 98052 Office: 14450 NE 29th Pl Suite 200 Bellevue WA 98007

STONE, ARLENE, poet; b. Phila.; d. Robert A. and Rae (Feinberg) Finke. B.F.A., Temple U.; M.Creative Writing, Boston U., 1974. Author (poetry): The Shule of Jehovah, 1976, The Image Maker, 1976, Through A Coal Cellar, Darkly, 1977, The Women's House, 1978, At the Gates of Hell: Poems to Survive by, 1982; plays include: A Ladies' Room, 1978; HAG, 1981. Macdowell Colony fellow, 1977; Helene Wurlitzer Found. fellow, 1978; Montalvo Centre for the Arts fellow, 1978. Mem. Poets and Writers. Address: PO Box 880203 San Francisco CA 94188

STONE, BRYSON WILLIAM, newspaper publisher; b. Edmonton, Alta., Can., Feb. 10, 1930; s. Cyril Dennis and Florence Isabel (Deyl) S.; m. Maureen Elizabeth Stone, May 27, 1953; children—Martin Harry, Darren Cyril, Robert Bryson. Student Banff Sch. Advanced Mgmt. With Southam Inc., Edmonton Jour., 1947-80, advt. dir., 1970-78, asst. pub., 1978-80; pub. Prince George (B.C., Can.) Citizen, 1980—. Mem. Can. Daily Newspaper Pubs. Assn., Can. Press (dir.). Baptist. Lodge: Rotary. Home: 3311 Riverview St Prince George BC V2N 2J2 Canada Office: 150 Brunswick St Prince George BC V2L 5K9 Canada

STONE, DAVID ULRIC, mgmt. exec., author; b. Santa Cruz, Calif., Feb. 4, 1927; s. Ernest Marshall and Grace (Stone) S.; student Theol. Ministry Sch., San Jose, Calif., 1945-48; grad. Real Estate Inst., Nat. Inst. Real Estate, 1964; m. Iva Dell Frazier, July 20, 1947; children—Katherine LaVerne, Russell Keith, Susan Marie. With E.M. Stone Realty, San Jose, 1945-48; mgr. Broadway-Hale Co., San Jose, 1948-52; sales mgr. William Perry Co., San Francisco, 1952-56; gen. mgr., ptnr. Stone & Schulte, Inc., San Jose, 1956-66; pres. Stone Inst. Mktg. Mgmt., Santa Cruz, St.Louis, Mpls., 1966—; dir. Realty Programming Corp. St. Louis. Mem. Nat. Inst. Real Estate Brokers (faculty mem. 1965—), Nat. Assn. Real Estate Bds. (chmn. joint task force 1966-68), Calif. Real Estate Assn. (dir.), Nat. Assn. Home Builders (award 1960, Sales Mgr. of Year 1960, chmn. joint task force 1966-68). Author: How to Operate a Real Estate Trade-In Program, 1962; Training Manual for Real Estate Salesmen, 1966; Guaranteed Sales Plan for Realtors and Builders, 1968 New Home Sales Training Course; The Professional Approach To Selling Real Estate; How To Communicate with Persuasive Power; How to Sell New Homes and Environmental Communities; How to Market and Sell Condominiums; How to Hire, Train and Motivate Real Estate Salespeople, How to Profitably Manage a Real Estate Office, 1977; The Road to Success in Real Estate, 1978; New Horizons in Real Estate, 1980; New Home Sales, 1982. Home: 236 Camino Del Cerro Los Gatos CA 95030

STONE, DEVON MERLIN, constrn. and engring. co. exec.; b. Preston, Idaho, Mar. 27, 1942; s. Merlin Porter and Leota (Corbridge) S.; B.S. in Engring., Brigham Young U., Provo, Utah, 1966; M.S. in Civil Engring., U. Santa Clara (Calif.), 1972; m. Linda Marie Brown, July 26, 1963; children—Robert, Sandra, Richard, Rodney, Annette, Aaron, Jessica, Jennifer. Project engr. Philco-Ford Corp., Palo Alto, Calif., 1966-72; chief structural engr. Food Industries Research & Engring., Inc., Yakima, Wash., 1972-76; supr., mgr. engring. Pullman Torkelson Co., Salt Lake City, 1976-79; pres. Devon M. Stone & Assocs., Midvale, Utah, 1979—, Sanders, Stone & Allred Inc., Salt Lake City, 1980-81, Stone & Assocs. Inc., Salt Lake City, 1981-82; spl. insp. Salt Lake County. Registered profl. engr., Calif., Utah, Idaho, Wash. Mem. ASCE, Am. Concrete Inst. Republican. Mormon. Home: 7847 Willowcrest Circle Salt Lake City UT 84121 Office: 6909 S State Midvale UT 84047

STONE, GLENN E., optometrist; b. Artesia, N. Mex., Oct. 28, 1914; s. Edward and Aluena T. (Moser) S.; m. Cathryn E., Jan. 28, 1939; children—Camille, Glenn E. Jr. B.S., Los Angeles Coll. Optometry, 1938. Pvt. practice optometry, Artesia, N. Mex., 1938—. Mem. Artesia Bd. Edn., 1965-77, Community Concert Assn., 1962—, Hist. Commn., 1959—; bd. dirs. Rio Grande Hist. Collections, 1980—. Served with MC, USAF. Recipient Silver Beaver award Boy Scouts Am., 1951, Community Leader Am. award, 1969, Jefferson award, 1978; named Artesia Man of Yr., 1967. Mem. Am. Optemetric Assn., N. Mex. Optometric Assn., Better Vision Inst., Optometric Extension Program, Am. Optometric Found., Tex. Optometric Assn. Democrat. Methodist. Clubs: Lions, Am. Legion, Cottonwood Gun (Artesia).

STONE, HERBERT, nutritionist; b. Washington, Sept. 14, 1934; s. Joseph and Marion (Solomon) S.; m. Marjorie Nelke Sterling, June 13, 1964; children—Joanna, Lisa. B.S., U. Mass., 1955, M.S., 1958; Ph.D. in Nutrition, U. Calif.-Davis, 1962. Specialist exptl. sta. U. Calif., Davis, 1961-62; food scientist Stanford Research Inst., 1962-67; dir. dept. food and plant sci., 1967-74; pres. Tragon Corp., Palo Alto, Calif., 1974—; cons. NSF, NIH; dir. Etel Inc., Palo Alto, 1978-80. Served with U.S. Army, 1955-57. D. Peebles fellow in nutrition, 1958-60; Campbell Soup fellow, 1960-61; NIH fellow, 1961-62. Mem. AAAS, Am. Soc. Enology, N.Y. Acad. Scis., Inst. Food Tech. (pres. sensory evaluation div., 1977-78), ASTM (com. E-18), European Chemoreception Orgn., Am. Chemosensory Soc. Sigma Xi. Club: Ladera Oaks Swim and Tennis. Assoc. editor Jour. Food Sci.; contbr. articles to profl. jours.; patentee in field. Home: 990 San Mateo Dr Menlo Park CA 94025 Office: 750 Welch Rd Suite 210 Palo Alto CA 94304

STONE, NORMAN CLEMENT, psychologist, found. exec.; b. Evanston, Ill., Apr. 28, 1939; s. W. Clement and Jessie Verna (Tarson) S.; m. Karen Louise Fernstrom, July 25, 1959 (div. 1976); children—Bryan C., Norman Clifford, Mark C., Amy M. A.B.A., Nichols Jr. Coll., 1959; B.A., Stanford U., 1962; doctoral candidate Wright Inst., 1977—. Pvt. investor, venture capitalist, 1964-76; gen. ptnr., founder San Francisco Venture Capital, 1970-76; trustee, founder Nueva Day Sch. and Learning Center, Hillsborough, Calif., 1967-76; psychotherapist Bay View Hunter's Point Community Mental Health Center, San Francisco, 1976—; v.p. W. Clement and Jessie V. Stone Found.; pres. Norman C. Stone Found.; chmn. bd. Golden West Sales. Democrat.

STONE, RONALD NORMAN, electronics company executive; b. N.Y.C., Feb. 6, 1944; s. Adolphus and Theresa (Kunze) S.; B.S., U. So. Calif., 1967; m. Lori Kahan, Sept. 13, 1967; children—Tiffany, Brian. Vice pres. fin. Norton Triump Corp., Duarte, Calif., 1973-75; div. controller Fleetwood Enterprises, Riverside, Calif., 1971-73; with Arthur Andersen & Co., Los Angeles, 1967-71; sr. v.p. fin. Pioneer Electronics (U.S.A.) Inc., Long Beach, Calif., 1975—. Served with U.S. Army, 1962-63. C.P.A., Calif. Mem. Assn. Electronic Importers (pres., treas., dir.), Sycamore Park Home Owners Assn. (dir., pres.), Sycamore Park Tennis Assn. (treas., dir.), Fin. Execs. Inst., Am. Inst. C.P.A.s, Nat. Assn. Accts. Office: 1925 E Dominguez St Long Beach CA 90810

STONE, SANFORD KENNETH, II, ednl. adminstr.; b. Denver, July 27, 1944; s. Sanford Kenneth and Thelma Ellen (Mann) S.; B.A., U. Colo., 1967; M.Ed., Northeastern U., 1973. VISTA trainer Northeastern U., Boston, 1968; new careers coordinator, Pine Ridge, S.D., 1969-71; adult edn. coordinator Northeastern U., Boston, 1971-74; dir. tng. Sir Casserole Restaurants, Denver, 1974-77; prin. Pine Hill (N.Mex.) Schs., 1977-81, Puerco Unified Sch. Dist., Sanders, Ariz., 1981—; tchr. Navajo Community Coll., 1979—; cons. Brandeis U., 1974, Colo. Migrant Council, 1971. Mem. Internat. Reading Assn., Assn. Supervision and Curriculum Devel., NEA (chpt. pres.). Home: Box 484 Sanders AZ 86512 Office: Puerco Unified Sch Dist Sanders AZ 86512

STONE, WILLARD JOHN, lawyer; b. Toledo, May 19, 1913; s. Willard John and Charlotte Hall (Walker) S.; student Stanford, 1930-31; A.B., U. Mich., 1936, J.D. cum laude, 1936; m. Mabel-June Lindauer, June 15, 1940 (div. Jan. 1952); 1 son, Arthur Walter; m. 2d, Juanita Marian Hammond, June 22, 1952 (dec. Apr. 1976); children—Willard Andrew, Stewart Hall, Marian Louise Stone Neuhouser; m. 3d, Charlotte Deane Haas, Jan. 2, 1977. Admitted to Calif. bar, 1937, Supreme Ct. U.S., 1942, practiced in Los Angeles, 1937-41, 45-51, Pasadena, Calif., 1951—; mem. firm Stone & Doyle and predecessor firms, 1975—; certified specialist in taxation law; atty. war div. Dept. Justice, 1941-43. Asst. prof. law Southwestern U., 1937-41. Bd. dirs. San Gabriel Valley council Boy Scouts Am. Served to lt. USNR, 1943-46. Decorated Bronze Star medal. Fellow Am. Coll. of Probate Counsel; mem. Am. Arbitration Assn. (mem. nat. panel arbitrators 1963—), Am. Judicature Soc., Am., Los Angeles County, Pasadena bar assns., State Bar Calif., Order of Coif. Republican. Episcopalian. Mason (32 deg., Shriner). Clubs: Fine Arts (pres. 1969-70), University, (Pasadena); Oneonta. Editorial bd. Mich. Law Rev., 1934-36. Contbr. articles to profl. jours. Home: Unit 134 700 S Lake Ave Pasadena CA 91106 Office: Suite 114 Oak Knoll Office Park 77 N Oak Knoll Ave Pasadena CA 91101

STONEBRIDGE, JERRY BERT, construction company executive, consultant; b. Issaquah, Wash., June 2, 1941; s. Harold William and Phoebe Kay (Hoye) S.; m. M. Suzanne Carlson, July 28, 1976; children—Jerry Edward, Jeffrey Scott. B.S. in Zoology and Chemistry, Wash. State U., 1963; postgrad. U. Wash., 1970-75. Research asst. rehab. medicine dept. U. Wash.-Seattle, 1964-72, research assoc., 1972-78; pres. Stonebridge Constrn. Co., Inc., Whidbey Island, Wash., 1978—; cons. on on-site sewage disposal systems and their mgmt., 1978—. Pres. Freeland Community Assn., 1980-82; trustee Saratoga Beach Community Assn., 1982—; mem. tech. rev. bd. Island County Health Dept., 1980-82. Bausch & Lomb grantee, 1959-60; Nellie Martin grantee, 1960; named Outstanding Freshman Student Wash. State U.,

1960; recipient 1st place prize for research exhibit Am. Phys. Therapy Assn., 1973; Silver medal Am. Congress Rehab. Medicine, 1974. Mem. Pi Ti Iota. Republican. Contbr. articles to profl. jours. Home and Office: 3329-S E Harbor Rd Langley WA 98260

STONEHAM, EDWARD BRYANT, physicist, electronics company executive; b. Coronado, Calif., Oct. 13, 1946; s. Samuel C. and Jennie L. (Reagor) S.; A.B. in Physics, U. Calif.-Berkeley, 1968; Ph.D. in Applied Physics, Stanford U., 1975; m. HaeSook Nam, July 4, 1972; 1 dau., Anita Lynn. Engr. research and devel. Hewlett-Packard Co., Palo Alto, Calif., 1971-75, project mgr., Santa Rosa, Calif., 1975—; partner Tamler-Stoneham Instruments, San Francisco, 1977—. Served with U.S. Army, 1969-71. Mem. Soaring Soc. Am., Sigma Xi, Phi Beta Kappa. Contbr. articles on process tech. and theory of semicondr. devices to profl. jours.; developer first ion implantation process utilized in production of gallium arsenide transistors; designer advanced instrument for testing dental pulp vitality. Office: 1412 Fountain Grove Pkwy Santa Rosa CA 95404

STONEHOUSE, JAMES ADAM, lawyer; b. Alameda, Calif., Nov. 10, 1937; s. Maurice Adam and Edna Sigrid (Thuesen) S.; A.B., U. Calif., Berkeley, 1961; J.D., Hastings Coll. Law, U. Calif., San Francisco, 1965; m. Marilyn Jean Kotkas, Aug. 6, 1966; children—Julie Aileen, Stephen Adam. Bar: Calif. 1966. Assoc. Hall, Henry, Oliver & McReavy, San Francisco, 1966-71; partner firm Whitney, Hanson & Stonehouse, Alameda, 1971-77; individual practice law, Alameda, 1977-79; partner firm Stonehouse & Silva, Alameda, 1979—; judge adv. Alameda council Navy League, 1978—. Founding dir. Alameda Clara Barton Found., 1977-80; mem. Oakland (Calif.) Marathon-Exec. Com., 1979; mem. exec. bd. Alameda council Boy Scouts Am., 1979—; bd. dirs. Lincoln Child Ctr. Found., 1981—, pres., 1983—. Named Boss of Yr. Alameda Jaycees, 1977; Coro Found. fellow in public affairs, 1961-62. Mem. Am. Bar Assn., State Bar Calif., Alameda County Bar (vice chmn. com. office econs., 1977-78). Republican. Roman Catholic. Clubs: Rotary (dir. club 1976-78), Elks (past exalted ruler, all state officer 1975-76, all dist. officer 1975-77, 78-79) (Alameda); Commonwealth. Home: 2990 Northwood Dr Alameda CA 94501 Office: 512 Westline Dr Suite 204 Alameda CA 94501

STONER, BARTINE ALBERT, JR., advertising executive; b. Trenton, N.J., Apr. 18, 1926; s. Bartine Albert and Estella (Hart) S.; m. Elizabth Ann Bond, Mar. 18, 1949 (div.); children—Bartine Albert III, Jonathan West; m. 2d, Madeleine Ruskin, 1973. B.S., Princeton U., 1948. With Westinghouse Electric Corp., Boston, Newark and Phila., 1948-56; account exec. N.W. Ayer & Son, Inc., Phila., 1956-65; v.p., dir. account service, 1965-67, dir., exec. v.p., gen. mgr. Phila. region, 1967-73, dir. internat. ops., N.Y.C., 1974-76; pres. Ayer Baker Advt. Seattle, 1974-75; mng. dir. Ayer Barker Hegemann Internat. B.V., London, 1976-79; pres., chief exec. officer Ayer, Jorgensen, Macdonald, Los Angeles, 1979-80; exec. v.p., dir. N.W. Ayer Inc., pres. Western div., 1981—; dir., pres. Settembrini and Tecchio ABH Internat., Milan, Italy, 1976-79; dir. Charles Barker, GmbH, Frankfurt, W. Ger., 1978-79, Moussault ABH Internat., Amsterdam and Antwerp, 1976-79. Bd. dirs. Greater Phila. Movement, 1973-74, Elwyn Inst.-Hosp., 1967-76; bd. pensions United Presbyn. Ch. U.S.A., 1971-76. Served to lt. (j.g.) USNR, 1944-46. Mem. Pa. Soc. Presbyterian (elder). Clubs: Phila. Racquet; Hurlingham (London); Princeton (N.Y.C.); Riviera Tennis, Rotary, Jonathan (Los Angeles). Home: 1050 Chantilly Rd Los Angeles CA 90077 Office: N W Ayer Inc 707 Wilshire Blvd Los Angeles CA 90017 also 1345 Ave of Americas New York City NY 10019

STONESIFER, SHANE GIL, army officer; b. Dixon, Ill., Oct. 21, 1953; s. Billy Frank and Anna Lorraine (Lehman) S.; B.S., U.S. Mil. Acad., 1976; m. Susan Marie Hisle, Feb. 3, 1979 (div.). Commd. 2d lt. U.S. Army, 1976, advanced through grades to capt., 1980; platoon leader 3/34th Field Arty. Bn., Ft. Lewis, Wash., 1976-77, communications and electronics officer, 1977-78, leader command ops. platoon 9th Signal Bn., 1978, exec. officer 9th Aviation Bn., 1980-81, dep. dir. Bn. Tng. Mgmt. System, 1981-82, ops. officer and intelligence officer 9th Signal Bn., 1982—; communication and electronics officer 2d Aviation Bn., Korea, 1979-80. Decorated Army Commendation medal (2). Mem. U.S. Cycling Fedn., U.S. Triathlon Assn. Republican. Home: 8409 Redtail Ct SE Olympia WA 98501 Office: HHC 9th Signal Bn Fort Lewis WA 98433

STONICK, VICTOR H., instructional technologist; b. Clairton, Pa., Feb. 25, 1930; s. Joseph John and Mary Agnes (Sprites) S.; B.A., UCLA, 1956, postgrad., 1964; postgrad. Calif. State U., Fullerton, 1972; m. Patricia Ann Sims, Mar. 25, 1967; children—Mark A., Cynthia L., Lyndell M., Timothy M., Christopher P., Amelia D., Jennelle D. Comml. TV dir., prodn. supr., Los Angeles, 1953-59; supr., coordinator Ednl. TV Broadcasting, Los Angeles, 1959-62; cons., dir. communications Loyola U., Los Angeles, 1962-65; dir. motion pictures, supr., writer, producer Gen. Dynamics, Pomona, Calif., 1965-67; motion picture producer, writer N.Am. Rockwell Autonetics, Anaheim, Calif., 1967-69; sr. multi media producer So. Calif. Regional Occupational Center, Torrance, 1969-74; dir. ops. and spl. projects Hoffman Occupational Learning Systems, El Monte, Calif., 1974-76; pres. Multi Communications div. Nat. Tech. Schs., Anaheim, 1976-81, group dir. WICAT Systems, Orem, Utah, 1981-82; with Trainex-Saudi Arabia Ltd., 1983—; cons. Stonick & Assos.; v.p. Varcon Industries Internat. Mktg. Group, 1977. Cub Scouts pack master, 1979-81. Served with USAF, 1948-52. Mem. Calif. Assn. Media and Ednl. Tech., Am. Soc. Tng. and Devel. Home: 616 E 445 S Orem UT 84057 Office: 1875 S State St Orem UT 84057

STORRO, LAWRENCE, bowling lanes owner; b. Lodi, Calif., June 4, 1920; s. John and Kristine (Korsedal) S.; m. Blanche Robles, Mar. 3, 1939; children—Jacquelyn, Judith. Student pub. schs., Lodi. Mgr. grocery wholesale Bert McDowell Co., Lodi and Oroville, Calif., 1935-48; with United Grocer Ltd., Sacramento, 1949-72, supr. computer operation, 1965-72; owner, operator Ponderosa Bowl, Portola, Calif., 1973—. Mem. Sacramento County Sheriff's Mounted Posse and Drill team, 1965-75. Home: 500 W Plumas Ave Portola CA 96122 Office: 265 Commercial St PO Box 489 Portola CA 96122

STORY, HARRY JOE, economics educator; b. Long Beach, Calif., July 16, 1937; s. Harry Ervin and Margaret Marietta (Herrick) S.; m. Barbara Elizabeth Sedgwick, Jan. 28, 1966; children—Elizabeth Ann, Bruce Robert. B.A., U. Calif.-Santa Barbara, 1959; M.A., Calif. State U., 1968; Ph.D., U. Oreg., 1975. Lic. real estate broker, Oreg. Faculty, Pacific U., Forest Grove, Oreg., 1968—, asso. prof. econs. and chmn. dept. bus. and econs., 1978—; cons. in field. Trustee, Pacific U., 1976-79; mem. Forest Grove Planning Commn., 1975-77. Served to lt. USN, 1959-62. U. Oreg. grad. fellow, 1970-72; Pacific U. research grantee, 1970-71; Danforth assoc., 1976-82; Dept. Energy grantee, summer 1978. Mem. Am. Econs. Assn., Western Econs. Assn., Danforth Assocs. Democrat. Contbr. articles to profl. jours.

STORY, PETER REINALD, state senator, rancher; b. Los Angeles, Dec. 19, 1932; s. Malcolm Chilton and Rose (Ashby) S.; B.S., Colo. U.; m. Eileen Cavanaugh, June 14, 1958; children—Robert, Michael, Nelson, Rose, Tom. Owner, operator Story Ranch, Emigrant, Mont., 1958—; mem. Mont. Senate, 1973—, chmn. state adminstrn. com., vice chmn. fin. and claims com. Served with USNR, 1955-58. Republican. Club: Elks. *

STOTHART, ROBERTA BATES, bookstore mgr.; b. Long Beach, Calif., Mar. 29, 1934; d. Morley DaCosta and Dorothy Clarice (Graham) Bates; student U. Ariz., 1952-53; children—Lisa, Camille, Anna, Elizabeth. Library asst. Am. Sch. Switzerland, Lugano, 1967-70; mus. bookstore mgr. J. Paul Getty Mus., Malibu, Calif., 1974—. Mem. Mus. Stores Assn. (dir.). Home: 22560 Carbon Mesa Rd Malibu CA 90265 Office: 17985 Pacific Coast Hwy Malibu CA 90265

STOTLAR, SUZANNE CORA, solid state physicist; b. Niagara Falls, N.Y., Aug. 27, 1947; d. Harvey Lewis and June Catherine (Mark) Wince; M. James Christopher Stotlar, June 10, 1972; children—Leslie Diane, James Harvey. B.S. with honors, Ohio U., 1969; postgrad. U. Calif.-Irvine, 1969-70. Mem. tech. staff Rockwell Internat., Anaheim, Calif., 1969-70; supr. infrared detectors group Harshaw Chem. Co., Solon, Ohio, 1970-76; staff psysicist Los Alamos Nat. Lab., 1976—; chmn. Los Alamos Conf. on Optics, 1979, 81. Co-chmn. 81 Expanding Your Horizons Conf. Mem. Optical Soc. Am., IEEE, Quantum Electronics and Applications Soc., IEEE (sr.), Soc. Photo-Optical Instrumentation Engrs., Los Alamos Optical Soc. (pres. 1978-82). Roman Catholic. Editor QEAS/IEEE Newsletter; contbr. articles profl. jours. Patentee in field. Home: 1618 Camino Uva Los Alamos NM 87544 Office: MS G770 Los Alamos Nat Lab Los Alamos NM 87545

STOTT, PETER WALTER, trucking co. exec.; b. Spokane, Wash., May 26, 1944; s. Walter Joseph and Rellalee (Gray) S.; student Portland State U., 1962-63, 65-68, Univ. Americas, Mexico City, 1964-65; m. Carole Ann Sizer, Aug. 20, 1972. Founder, chmn. bd., pres. Market Transport Ltd., Portland, Oreg., 1969—; dir., officer Market Industries, Ltd., United Express Ltd.; dir. United Bank Oreg.; dir., officer Portland Beavers Baseball Club. Bd. dirs. Sunshine div. Portland Police Bur. Served with USAR, 1966-72. Mem. Nat. Football Found. and Hall of Fame, Oreg. Trucking Assn., Western Hwy. Inst. Republican. Roman Catholic. Clubs: Mazamas, Multnomah Athletic. Office: 110 N Marine Dr Portland OR 97217

STOUT, BENJAMIN BOREMAN, forester, univ. dean; b. Parkersburg, W.Va., Mar. 2, 1924; s. Clarence Patterson and Laurane Dudley (Boreman) S.; m. Phyllis Marie Ingraham, Sept. 4, 1945; children—Susan L., David F., Bruce D. B.S.F., W.Va. U., Morgantown, 1947; M.F., Harvard U., 1950; Ph.D., Rutgers U., 1967. Forester Pond & Moyer Co., Ithaca, N.Y., 1947-48; supr. Harvard Black Rock Forest, Cornwall, N.Y., 1950-58; asst. prof. to assoc. prof. Rutgers U., 1959-78, chmn. dept. bio. scis., 1974-77, assoc. provost, 1977-78; dean Sch. Forestry, U. Mont., Missoula, 1978—. Mem. Friends of Mansfield Library, Friends of Ft. Missoula Mus. Mem. Am. Inst. Biol. Scis., Soc. Am. Foresters, AAAS, Am. Forestry Assn., Sigma Xi, Kappa Alpha Order, Xi Sigma Pi. Clubs: Missoula Country, Mont. State Sr. Golf Assn., U.S. Golf Assn., Century. Editor: Forests in the Here and Now (Hugh Miller Raup), 1981.

STOUT, CHARLES LOWELL, lawyer; b. Tamaha, Okla., July 23, 1928; s. Charlie Wilson and Rosetta (Easley) S.; student Northeastern State Coll. (Okla.), 1946-49, Okla. U., 1949-51; LL.B., U. N.Mex., 1952; m. Lucie Liliane Josue; children—Georgianna, Mark Lowell. Admitted to N.Mex. bar, 1952; practiced in Hobbs, N.Mex., 1952—; mem. firm Easley, Quinn & Stout, Hobbs, 1954-58, Girand & Stout, Hobbs, 1958-60, Lowell Stout, Hobbs, 1960-80, Stout & Stout, 1980—. Served with AUS, 1952-54. Fellow Am. Coll. Trial Lawyers; mem. Assn. Trial Lawyers Am., N.Mex. Trial Lawyers Assn., Def. Research Inst., Am., Lea County (pres. 1968) bar assns., State Bar N.Mex., N.Mex. Assn. Def. Counsel, Phi Delta Pi, Sigma Tau Gamma. Baptist. Club: Country (dir. 1970-72) (Hobbs). Home: 218 W Lea St Hobbs NM 88240

STOVALL, DORIS ELAINE, industrial training specialist; b. Rochester, N.Y., Oct. 4, 1934; d. Charles Henry and Pearl Ethel (Jackson) Coleman; m. Donovan Stovall, Sept. 21, 1952 (div.); children—Stanley Vincent, Darrell Jay. Student pub. schs. Rochester, N.Y. Cert. vocat./tech. instr., Ariz. Electronic assembler Gen. Electronic, Phoenix, 1963-70; electronic assembly instr. Teledyne Job Corps Ctr., Phoenix, 1970-78; sr. indsl. tng. instr. ITT Courier Terminals Systems, Inc., Phoenix, 1978-81; electronic instr., cons. Checkerboard Tutorial Service, Phoenix, 1981-82; indsl. tng. specialist Hughes Helicopter Co., Inc., Mesa, Ariz., 1982—; pvt. electronic cons.; part-time electronic assembly instr., lectr. community coll. vocat. programs; past ptnr., columnist Ariz. Informant newspaper. Vocat. advisor Phoenix Job Corps, Phoenix Coll. Electronics programs; advisor Job Corps Alumni Assn. Recipient Outstanding Black Woman of Phoenix award Greyhound Corp., Ariz. Informant, 1975; Mem. Nat. Assn. Female Execs. Republican. Methodist. Co-author: Checkerboard Textbook of Electronic Assembly.

STOVER, MILES RONALD, mfg. co. exec.; b. Glendale, Calif., Dec. 23, 1948; s. Robert Miles and Alberta Mae (Walker) S.; B.S., U. So. Calif., 1974, postgrad., 1976-80; M.B.A., Pepperdine U., 1980; m. Cynthia Ann McNeil, Jan. 25, 1975. Corp. account exec. Merrill Lynch, Pierce, Fenner & Smith, Inc., Santa Ana, Calif., 1974-76; fin. v.p. AMERDEC W., Inc., Santa Ana., 1976-78; v.p., chief fin. officer, dir. MIS Dept., corp. officer Asso. Piping & Engring. Corp., Norwalk, Calif., 1978—; dir. Neurol. Recovery Group, Inc., 1979-80. Bd. dirs. Big Bros. of Orange County, 1978-80; mem. Orange County Environ. Protection com., 1978-79. Served with USN, 1968-71. Mem. Am. Inst. Corp. Controllers, Nat. Assn. Accts., Am. Mgmt. Assn., U. So. Calif. Commerce Assocs., Fin. Execs. Inst., U.So. Calif. Alumni Assn., Inst. Mgmt. Accts. Republican. Congregationalist. Clubs: U. So. Calif., Acctg. Circle, Alpha Kappa Psi, Jonathan, Masons, Shriners, Jonathan Gourmet Soc., Hoag Hosp. 552. Home: 10575 Grove Oak Dr Cowan Heights CA 92705 Office: 14830 Carmineta Rd Norwalk CA 90584

STOWE, NOEL JAMES, history educator; b. Sacramento, Jan. 16, 1942; s. Harold James and R. Elaine (Hildreth) S.; A.A., Sacramento City Coll., 1961; B.A., U. So. Calif., 1963, Ph.D., 1970; m. Gwendolyn Joyce Lee, Nov. 6, 1965; 1 son, James Edward. Lectr., U. Nev., Las Vegas, 1967; asst. prof. Ariz. State U., Tempe, 1967-75, assoc. prof., 1975—. Mem. Nat. Council on Pub. History, Western Hist. Assn., Am. Hist. Assn., Orgn. Am. Historians, Am. Assn. for State and Local History, Latin Am. Studies Assn., Pacific Coast Council on Latin Am. Studies. Author: California Government: The Challenge of Change, 1975, 2nd edit. 1980; contbr. articles to profl. jours. Home: 953 E Driftwood Dr Tempe AZ 85283 Office: Dept History Ariz State Univ Tempe AZ 85287

STOWELL, DENNIS EARL, chem. engr.; b. Ogden, Utah, June 18, 1944; s. Verland Desmond and Grace Cecelia (Jensen) S.; B.S., Brigham Young U., 1972, M.S., 1973; m. Marilee Adams, Mar. 10, 1966; children—Kip Dennis, Kyle Adams, Cami Caseel, Caralee, Coy, Kelly Alexander. Process engr. Kennecott Copper Corp., Salt Lake City, 1970-72; research asst., chem. engring. dept. Brigham Young U., Provo, Utah, 1972-73; smelter process engr. Kennecott Copper Corp., McGill, Nev., 1973-74, project engr., 1974, reduction plant environ. engr., 1974-75, smelter plant engr., 1974-77; project engr. Martin Marietta Aluminum, The Dalles, Oreg., 1977-79, anode supt., 1979-80; pres., dir. Silica Sand Co., Inc., Parowan, Utah, 1980—, H A Farms, Inc., Parowan. Bishop, Ely 2d Ward, Ely (Nev.) Stake, Ch. Jesus Christ of Latter-day Saints, 1974-77. Served with U.S. Army, 1966-69. Mem. Am. Inst. Chem. Engrs., AIME. Republican. Home: 200 N 300 W Parowan UT 84761 Office: PO Box 796 Parowan UT 84761

STOWELL, KENT, ballet director; b. Rexburg, Idaho, Aug. 8, 1939; s. Harold B. and Maxine (Hudson) S.; ed. San Francisco Ballet Sch., Sch. Am. Ballet; m. Francia Russell, Nov. 19, 1965; children—Christopher, Darren, Ethan. Lead dancer San Francisco Ballet, 1957-62, N.Y.C. Ballet, 1962-68; ballet dir., ballet master Frankfurt Opera, 1973-77; artistic dir. Pacific N.W. Ballet, Seattle, 1977—; choreographer: Coppelia, Daphnis and Chloe, L'Heure Bleue, Over the Waves, Symphonic Impressions, Symphony No. 5, Swan Lake. Office: Pacific Northwest Ballet 4649 Sunnyside Ave N Seattle WA 98103

STRAHLER, EMILY DOROTHY, home economics educator; b. Kenosha, Wis., Feb. 4, 1926; d. Louis Frank and Pauline Josephine (Tudjan) Slamar; m. Regis Daniel Strahler, July 27, 1963; 1 dau., Barbara Ann. B.S., Stout State U., 1948; M. Ed., Colo. A&M U., 1953. Tchr., Sterling (Colo.) Jr. Coll., 1948-50, Benton Harbor (Mich.) Jr. High Sch., 1950-53, No. Mich. Coll., Marquette, 1953-57; tchr. jr. high schs., Tucson, 1957—, home arts tchr. Gridley Middle Sch., 1974—. Named Ariz. Tchr. of Yr., 1980. Mem. Am. Home Econs. Assn., Ariz. Home Econs. Assn. Democrat. Roman Catholic. Club: Desert Stitchers (Tucson). Author publs. in field. Home: 6811 E 3d St Tucson AZ 85710 Office: Gridley Middle School 350 S Harrison St Tucson AZ 85748

STRAIN, JOHN WILLARD, aerospace engineer, consultant; b. Ottumwa, Iowa, Dec. 31, 1929; s. John Wells and Agnes Gertrude (Kearns) S.; m. Elizabeth LaVonne Moment, Dec. 27, 1952 (dec.); children—James Anthony, Mary Therese, Michael Douglas, Meagan Kathaleen. Student Upper Iowa U., 1947-48; B.A., U. No. Iowa, 1952. Supr., aero. rocket power plant engr. White Sands Proving Ground, N.Mex., 1954-55; mgr. Santa Cruz test and Hunters Point, Missile Systems div. Lockheed Missiles & Space Co., Sunnyvale, Calif., 1960-63, mgr. Ea. Test Range support, 1966-73, chief test engr. Aquila RPV/STD Program, 1975-78, factory test mgr. Army RPV Program, 1979-82, qualification and test engring. div. mgr., chief test engr., 1982—; owner Indsl. Systems Co. Bd. dirs. San Jose Civic Light Opera, 1971-73; treas. Assn. Unmanned Vehicle Systems, 1982—. Served with AUS, 1952-54. Recipient Alumni Service award U. No. Iowa, 1981. Assoc. fellow AIAA; mem. Nat. Mgmt. Assn., AAAS, Inst. Environ. Scis. (sr.). Republican. Roman Catholic. Assoc. editor Missile Away mag. Am. Rocket Soc., 1954-55. Office: 1111 Lockheed Way Box 504 Sunnyvale CA 94086

STRAKA, GEORGE JOHN, police chief; b. Hazleton, Pa., Mar. 14, 1937; s. George and Mary (Orach) S.; m. Gloria Helen Newton, Feb. 18, 1956; children—Leslie Anne, Stephen John. A.A., Fullerton Jr. Coll., 1964; B.A. in Police Sci., John F. Kennedy U., 1972, M.A. in Pub. Adminstrn., 1975; grad. FBI Nat. Acad., 1980. Advanced cert. peace officer's standards and tng., Calif. Police officer, Fullerton, Calif., 1958-65; police officer, Concord, Calif., 1966-68, police sgt., 1968-71, police chief, 1981—; instr. No. Calif. Peace Officer's Acad., 1965-72. Mem. exec. bd. Mt. Diablo Council Boy Scouts Am., 1981—. Served with USMC, 1954-57. Mem. Internat. Assn. Chiefs Police, FBI N.Am. Assn., Calif. Police Chiefs Assn., Calif. Peace Officers Assn. Republican. Lutheran. Club. Century (exec. bd. 1981—) (Concord). Office. Concord Police Dept Willow Pass and Parkside Concord CA 94519

STRALING, PHILLIP F., bishop; b. San Bernardino, Calif., Apr. 25, 1933. Student Immaculate Heart Sem., St. Francis Sem., U. San Diego, San Diego State U. Ordained priest Roman Catholic Ch., 1959, ordained 1st bishop of San Bernardino, 1978. Office: Diocese of San Bernardino 1450 D St San Bernardino CA 92405

STRAND, MELFORD LIEN, physician; b. LaCrosse, Wis., Aug. 15, 1940; s. Clarence Melford and Eunice Rosalind (Lien) S.; B.S., U. Wis., 1963; M.D., U. Ia., 1967; m. Cynthia Ann Kuecker, Aug. 15, 1964; children—Susan, Kristin, Erin. Intern, Sacramento County Hosp., 1967-68; resident anesthesiology U. Colo., 1970-72; mem. anesthesiology staff Denver Gen. Hosp., 1972-76, asst. prof. anesthesiology U. Colo., 1972-76; mem. Staffs Denver, Aurora Presbyn. Hosps. Served to capt. M.C., AUS, 1968-70. Diplomate Am. Bd. Anesthesiology. Mem. Am., Colo. socs. anesthesiologists, Am., Denver, Colo. med. assns., Fellowship Christian Athletes, Presbyterian. Home: 10927 E Crestline Circle Englewood CO 80111 Office: 1834 Gilpin St Denver CO 80218

STRAND, TIMOTHY H., optometrist; b. Forest City, Iowa, Apr. 14, 1952; s. Alvin G. and Eunice M. (Erdal) S. A.A., Waldorf Coll., 1972; B.S., Pacific U., 1975, O.D., 1976. Clin. optometrist Indian Health Service, USPHS, Ft. Washakie, Wyo., 1976-81, acting area optometrist Billings (Mont.) area, 1979-81; mem. staff Cheyenne (Wyo.) Community Solar Greenhouse, VISTA, 1982; pvt. practice optometry, Cheyenne. Mem. Tri-State MX Coalition, 1982—, Western Solidarity Exec. Com., 1982—. Mem. Am. Optometric Assn.

STRAND, WALTER RICHARD, SPFTWARE; engr.; b. Spokane, Wash., Oct. 9, 1953; s. Richard L. and Ruth S.; B.S. in Math. with high honors, Portland State U., 1979, postgrad. in elec. engring and math., 1979—. Engring aide electronics design group Tektronix, Beaverton, Oreg., 1973-75, software engr., software design group, 1975-77, software evaluation group, 1977, computer aided design devel., 1977—; software cons. Periphicon, Beaverton. Mem. IEEE, Soc. Indsl. and Applied Math. Home: 4735 SW 200th Aloha OR 97007 Office: PO Box 500 Beaverton OR 97077

STRATTON, EASTER KEIKO, real estate broker; b. Los Angeles, June 13, 1953; d. Mitsuaki and Masako (Nakamura) Noda; B.A., U. So. Calif., 1976; m. Stanley Colburn Stratton, June 9, 1979. Flight attendant Trans World Airlines, N.Y.C., 1975-76; Playboy bunny Los Angeles Playboy Club, 1977-78; sales agt. Hoover Realty, 1979; adminstrv. asst. Century 21 Ascot II, 1979; dir. Am. Home Mortgage, 1979; adminstrv. exec. Weston & Assocs., 1980; real estate broker Stratton & Assocs. Property Mgmt., Los Angeles, 1981—. Republican. Mormon. Address: 930 N Martel Ave Apt 204 Los Angeles CA 90046

STRATTON, JAMES MALCOLM, JR., real estate co. exec.; b. San Francisco, Aug. 24, 1928; s. James Malcolm and Katherine Dey (Whitney) S.; student Coll. of Marin, 1949-50, U. Calif., Berkeley, 1950-51; 1 dau., Michelle Denise. Co-pilot, Pan American Airlines, N.Y.C. and San Francisco, 1956-60; pilot Overseas Nat. Airlines, 1960-61; pilot Japan Airlines, San Francisco and Tokyo, 1961-64; chief pilot, asst. to the pres. Roth Properties, San Francisco, 1964-71; chief pilot, real estate mgr. Reynold C. Johnson Co., Pleasanton, Calif., 1971-73; Western area real estate mgr. Vorelco, Inc., Pleasanton, 1973—. Bd. dirs. Planned Parenthood, San Francisco, 1980-83. Served with USNR, 1951-65; Korea. Decorated Air medal. Mem. Nat. Assn. Corp. Real Estate Execs., Aircraft Owners and Pilots Assn., San Francisco Air Sheriffs Assn. (past comdr.), Sierra Club, Pleasanton C. of C. Club: University (San Francisco). Office: Vorelco Inc 7106 Johnson Dr Suite A Pleasanton CA 94566

STRAUCH, CLAIRE MUNSON, household products manufacturing company staff; b. Hempstead, N.Y., Apr. 6, 1933; d. Alexander Lawrence and Bertha Louise (Geer) Munson; m. Harry Carter Strauch, Mar. 3, 1956; children—Diana Strauch Swenson, Cindy Louise, Harry Carter, Mark S. Student Smith Coll., 1951-53, Eastman Sch. Music, Rochester, N.Y., summer 1971. Vice-pres. adminstrn. Litton-Fuller Group, Walnut Creek, Calif., 1981-82; mem. staff community affairs dept. The Clorox Co., Oakland, Calif., 1982—. Pub. relations dir. Diablo Music Festival, 1978; cellist Diablo Symphony Orchestra, 1973-78; mem., bd. dirs. Symphony of the Mountain, 1978-80; bd. dirs. Oakland Youth Chorus; producer, dir. Noye's Fludde, 1977-78. Mem. Dramatists Guild, Authors League Am. Composer, arranger Dracula Baby, 1970;

Wind in the Willows, 1972; Gaslight Girl, 1973; arranger Beggars Opera, 1973; composer Song of Oakland for City of Oakland, 1983. Office: The Clorox Co 1221 Broadway Oakland CA 94612

STRAUCH, DONALD WILLIAM, JR., mayor; b. Clermont, Iowa, Apr. 8, 1926; s. Donald William and Mary Grace (Mulloy) S.; student Ariz. State U.; m. Lorna Marian Christian, July 26, 1950; children—Christina, Donald William. With Strauch's Stationers, Inc., Mesa, Ariz., from 1950; mem. Mesa City Council, 1972, vice mayor, 1974, mayor City of Mesa, 1980—. Served with U.S. Army, 1944-46. Republican. Episcopalian. Club: Rotary. Home: 453 W Hillview Mesa AZ 85201 Office: 55 N Center St Mesa AZ 85201

STRAUS, DAVID ARTHUR, architect; b. Medford, Oreg., Nov. 8, 1943; s. Arthur Lewis and Bertha Jane (Arnspiger) S.; m. Sherry Feenan, Aug. 14, 1973; children—Lara, Shaun. B.Arch., U. Oreg., 1967; lic. architect, Oreg. Architect, Patterson & Stewart, Architects and Planners, 1970-79; pvt. practice architecture, Medford, 1979-80; ptnr. Straus & Breeden, AIA, Medford, 1980—; designer Central Point (Oreg.) City Hall, fire stas., banks, office bldgs., custom residences. Bd. dirs. Medford YMCA, service award; bd. dirs. Rogue Valley art Assn., service award; bd. dirs. Arts Council So. Oreg. Served to lt., USNR, 1967-70. Decorated Navy Commendation Medals; recipient award for office bldg. design City of Medford, 1981. Mem. AIA (past pres. So. Oreg. chpt.), Oreg. Council Architects. Democrat. Club: Univ. (Medford). Office: 201 W Main St Suite 3C Medford OR 97501

STRAUSER, JEAN MARIE, accountant; b. Sheridan, Wyo., Jan. 25, 1949; d. Alfred Fredrick and Justine Aileen (Long) Germann; m. Robert Dee Strauser, Aug. 22, 1970; children—Kelly Dee, Dawn Marie. B.S., U. Wyo., 1971, M.S., 1972. C.P.A., Wyo. Bookkeeper, Skiles & Wickersham, Pub. Accts., Laramie, Wyo., 1971; staff acct. Jeffryes & Jeffryes, C.P.A.s, Laramie, 1972-74, Harris Huffsmith & Assocs. P.C., C.P.A.s, Casper, Wyo., 1975-78, Curtis W. Christensen, C.P.A., Sheridan, 1978-81, Mulholland & Strauser, C.P.A.s, Sheridan, 1981; ptnr. Strauser & Strauser, C.P.A.s, Sheridan, 1981—. Mem. Am. Inst. C.P.A.s, Wyo. Soc. C.P.A.s (v.p. Sheridan chpt. 1982-83, pres. 1983-84), Beta Alpha Psi, Beta Gamma Sigma, Phi Gamma Nu, Beta Sigma Phi (rec. sec. 1983-84). Home: PO Box 287 Ranchester WY 82839 Office: PO Box 4068 Sheridan WY 82801

STRAW, RICHARD MYRON, college administrator; b. St. Paul, July 25, 1926; s. Myron George and Emma Aglen (Hesli) S.; m. Dorothy Jane Johnson, Nov. 21, 1949; children—Richard, Michael, Martha, Maija. B.A. in Zoology, U. Minn., 1949; Ph.D. in Botany, Claremont (Calif.) Coll., 1955. Asst. prof. Deep Springs (Calif.) Coll., 1955-56; asst. prof. to prof. biology Calif. State U.-Los Angeles 1956-81, prof. emeritus, 1981—, assoc. dean Sch. Letters and Sci., 1970-75, assoc. dean acad. planning, 1975-78; mgr. acad. computing services So. Oreg. State Coll., Ashland, 1981—; cons. for sci. and math. edn. U.S. Peace Corps, Malaysia, 1966-68; Fulbright lectr., Peru, 1963-64. Served with AUS, 1944-46, 50-52. NSF grantee, 1953-55, 57-63. Mem. Data Processing Mgmt. Assn., Am. Soc. Naturalists, Soc. Study of Evolution, Phi Beta Kappa, Sigma Xi, Delta Phi Lambda. Democrat. Episcopalian. Contbr. articles on biology and computer applications to profl. jours. Office: So Oregon State Coll Ashland OR 97520

STRECKENBACH, JACK MONROE, retired aeronautical engineer; b. Seattle, Mar. 25, 1918; s. Roy Irving and Anna (Hansen) S.; student U. Wash., 1938-42; B.S. in Mech. Engring., U. Dayton (Ohio), 1953; m. Dorothy Ruth Bradley, May 30, 1942; children—David Roy, Ann Lee. With Boeing Co., Seattle, 1940-42, 53-81, aero. engring. mgr., 1956-81. Served with USAAF, 1941-46, USAF, 1951-53. Registered profl. engr., Wash., Ohio; lic. pilot. Assoc. fellow AIAA; mem. Am. Watchmakers Inst., Brit. Horological Inst. Methodist. Club: Masons. Authors papers in field. Home: 8203 Roosevelt Way NE Seattle WA 98115

STREED, JAMES GREGORY, city official; b. Whittier, Calif., Jan. 2, 1953; s. Henry Griffin and Rita Grace (Murdock) S.; m. Margaret Mary Tyskiewicz, June 11, 1977; 1 son, Adam Joseph. B.S. in Communication Arts-Pub. Relations, Calif. State Poly. U., 1978. Account exec. Murray, Bradley & Rockey Pub. Relations, Anchorage, 1978, Bruce Pozzi Pub. Relations, Anchorage, 1978-80; asst. press officer Municipality of Anchorage, 1980-83, utilities affairs specialist, 1983—. Chmn. pub. relations com. Salvation Army Booth Meml. Home. Recipient 3d place best annual report award Alaska Press Club, 1980; Leadership award Los Angeles area Boy Scouts Am., 1977. Mem. Pub. Relations Soc. Am. (sec. Alaska chpt.). Lutheran. Club: St. Anthony's Folk Group. Office: Pub Utilities Municipality of Anchorage 600 E 38th Ave Anchorage AK 99503

STREET, DAVID RUSSELL, JR., school psychologist; b. Baton Rouge, Nov. 6, 1955; s. David Russell and Betty Mae S.; m. Carol Suzane Felix, May 29, 1982. BS., Ariz. State U., 1977; M.A., No. Ariz. U., 1980, Ed.D., 1983. Cert. psychometrist, sch. psychologist, Ariz. Patient rep. Desert Samaritan Hosp., Tempe, Ariz., 1975-78; instr. No. Ariz. U., Flagstaff, 1979-81; ednl. diagnostician Spl. Edn. Diagnostic Services, Flagstaff, Ariz., 1980-81; sch. psychologist Verde Valley Community Guidance Clinic, Inc., Cottonwood, Ariz., 1982—; psychol. cons. Camp Verde (Ariz.) Pub. Schs., No. Ariz. Council Govts., Head Start Programs. Dougherty Found. scholar, 1975; Allen E. Dubois Found. scholar, 1980-82. Mem. Nat. Assn. Sch. Psychologists, Am. Psychol. Assn., Ariz. State U. Alumni Assn., No. Ariz. U. Alumni Assn., Psi Chi. Democrat. Roman Catholic. Club: Camp Verde Kiwanis. Home: PO Box 906 Camp Verde AZ 86322 Office: Verde Valley Community Guidance Clinic Inc PO Box 925 Cottonwood AZ 86326

STREETER, DONALD JAMES, chamber of commerce executive; b. Cody, Wyo., Feb. 19, 1945; s. Don J. and Priscilla M. (Jacobs) S.; children—Tarilee Ann, Mialee Jo. B.A., Chadron State Coll., Nebr., 1970; student Inst. for Orgn. Mgmt., U. Colo. Owner motel and cafe, 1967-73; exec. mgr. Powell Valley C. of C., 1973—. Served with U.S. Army, 1967-69. Decorated Bronze Star, Air medal; named Elk of the Yr., 1977-78. Mem. Am. C. of C. Execs., Wyo. C. of C. Execs. (past pres.), Mountain States Assn. (dir.), No. Wyo. Travel Assn. (dir.), Am. Legion, V.F.W. Republican. Roman Catholic. Clubs: Rotary, Elks, Eagles. Home. PO Box 401 Powell WY 82435 Office: PO Box 814 Powell WY 82435

STREETER, EARL LOUIS, lawyer, mgmt. cons. co. exec.; b. Chgo., July 1, 1935; s. Everett William and Grace Louise (Whitney) S.; B.A., Whittier Coll., 1957; M.B.A., UCLA, 1965, J.D. (dean's council), 1967; m. Patricia Ellen Hare, June 20, 1958; 1 dau., Michelle Lynn. Research and teaching asst. behavioral sci. UCLA Grad. Sch. Mgmt., 1962-65, adminstrv. analyst and counselor, 1967-69; admitted to Calif. bar, 1968; dir. personnel and mgmt. cons. K. Leventhal Co. C.P.A.s, Los Angeles, 1969-73; cons. mgmt. adv. services Haskins & Sells C.P.A.s, Los Angeles, Houston, 1973-75; ptnr., cons. mgmt. adv. services Streeter and Assocs., Los Angeles and N.Y.C., 1975—; mgmt. cons. Pacific Missile Range, USN, 1975. Cons., Republican Central Com. Los Angeles County, 1976. Served as naval flight officer USNR, 1957-61; lt. comdr. Naval Air Res. (ret.). Author: A Behavioral Analysis of Executive Recruiting, 1975; The Executive Search Process, 1976. Office: 3250 Wilshire Blvd Suite 900 Los Angeles CA 90010

STREETER, EUGENE CLARENCE, museum director, college administrator, educator; b. Fond du Lac, Wis., Apr. 14, 1924; s. Clarence L. and Lillian R.S. 1 adopted son, Vincent J. DeMarco. B.A., Brooks Inst. Photography, 1965. Civilian adv. U.S. Army, Fond du Lac, 1951-63; faculty Brooks Inst. Photography, Santa Barbara, Calif., 1965—, v.p. instl. affairs, 1970-72, 78—, pres. Brooks Photographic Research and Devel. Found., 1977—, prof. history of photography, 1982—; dir., curator Western States Mus Photography, Santa Barbara, 1977—. Served with U.S. Army, 1942-51, to maj. Res. ret., 1951-67. Decorated Bronze Star. Mem. Western Photog. Collectors Assn., Soc. Tchrs. Profl. Photography. Home: 1323 Rialto Ln Bel Air Knolls Santa Barbara CA 93105 Mailing Address: Brooks Inst Photography 2190 Alston Rd Santa Barbara CA 93108

STREHLAU, BETTY GENE, public relations executive; b. Seattle; d. John A. and Clara (Wabraushek) S. B.A., U. Wash., 1944, M.A., 1954. Asst. advt. and asst. sales promotion dir. The Bon Marche, Seattle; sales promotion dir. Western Hotels Internat., Seattle; propr., dir. Strehlau Publicity and Advt. Services, Seattle; co-pub. West Woodland-Fremont News, Seattle; prof. journalism and mass media Highline Coll., Midway, Wash., 1961—; pub. relations exec. Alaska N.W. Pub. Co., Edmonds, Wash. Mem. Wash. Press Women (Superior Performance award 1965, Torchbearer award 1979), Community Coll. Journalism Assn. (nat. pres. 1979—), Pacific N.W. Assn. Journalism Educators (regional pres. 1979-80), Am. Women in Radio and TV (Wash. State pres. 1979), Nat. Council Coll. Publ. Advisors (Nat. Disting. Advisor 1977), Nat. Press Women Assn., Women in Communications (Founders' award for leading communicator 1980), Pi Lambda Theta, Alpha Delta Pi. Club: Wash. Athletic. Office: Suite 835 Securities Bldg 1904 3d Ave Seattle WA 98101

STREIKER, CONNIE LORRAINE, exec. suites, secretarial services co. exec.; b. Redding, Calif., Apr. 23, 1940; d. Glen Dale and Betty (Aberg) Johnson; student Sacramento State Coll., 1958-59, Sacramento City Coll., 1959-60, 1973-74; m. Lowell Dean Streiker, Aug. 1, 1975; children—Todd Paul Blankenship, Matthew Dale Blankenship. Exec. dir. Mental Health Assn., Yolo County, Calif., 1972-74; crusade coordinator Am. Cancer Soc., Wilmington, Del., 1974-76; exec. sec. Am. Motel Brokers, Burlingame, Calif., 1976-77, owner, mgr. The Home Office, Burlingame, 1977—. Mem. Yolo County Mental Health Advisory Bd., 1973-74; v.p. Mental Health Assn., 1972; mem. allocation and orgns. com. United Way, 1972, town chmn. fund dr., 1973. Mem. Profl. Assn. Secretarial Services (No. Calif.), Women Entrepreneurs Fedn. of Women's Clubs (sec. Sutter dist. 1973, v.p. 1971, pres. 1972), Fedn. Women's Clubs (sec. dist. 1973). Office 1633 Old Bayshore Hwy Suite 265 Burlingame CA 94010

STREMBITSKY, MICHAEL ALEXANDER, school administrator; b. Smoky Lake, Alta., Can., Mar. 5, 1935; s. Alec and Rose (Fedoretz) S.; m. Victoria Seminiuk, Aug. 12, 1954; children—Michael, William John. B.A., U. Alta., 1955, B.Ed., 1958; M.A., Columbia U., 1968, M.Ed., 1972. With Edmonton (Alta.) pub. schs., now supt. of schs. Mem. Can. Coll. Tchrs., Can. Edn. Assn., Conf. Alta. Sch. Supts., Am. Assn. Sch. Adminstrs., Can. Soc. for Study Edn., Assn. Sch. Bus. Ofcls., Edmonton Edn. Soc., Assn. for Supervision and Curriculum, Can. Assn. Sch. Adminstrs., Nat. Assn. Ednl. Negotiators, Nat. Ukrainian Profl. and Bus. Club, Univ. Council for Ednl. Adminstrn., Edmonton C. of C., Phi Delta Kappa. Office: Edmonton Public Schools 10010 107 A Ave Edmonton AL T5H 0Z8 Canada

STRICKLAN, CHARLES LESLIE, JR., advertising executive; b. St. Louis, Apr. 5, 1950; s. Charles Leslie and Helen Marie (Williams) S.; m. Virginia Lea Stoner, Nov. 4, 1972; 1 son, Charles Leslie. A.A., Forest Park Community Coll., 1971; B.F.A., Washington U., St. Louis, 1973. Art dir. Sta. KPLR-TV, St. Louis, 1968-73; founder, pres., creative dir. Stricklan Studios, Stricklan Communications & Mktg., Phoenix, 1968—; lectr. in field. Advt., pub. relations chmn. Cen. Ariz. Home Builders Assn. multi-family housing council; bd. dirs. Scottsdale Girls Club, Scottsdale Ctr. Arts. Recipient Am. Mktg. Assn. Excellence Mktg. award, 1979. Mem. Scottsdale C. of C., Nat. Assn. Home Builders. Republican. Lutheran. Club: Rotary (pub. relations chmn.) (Scottsdale). Office: 6991 E Camelback Rd Suite A-320 Scottsdale AZ 85251

STRICKLAND, TED L., state senator; b. Austin, Tex., Sept. 17, 1932; student Okla. A&M U., U. Denver; m. LuAnne Strickland. Gen. mgr. Petroleum Info., Denver; mem. Colo. Ho. of Reps., 1966-68; mem. Colo. Senate, 1968—, chmn. joint budget, health, environ. welfare and instns; acting lt. gov., 1973-74, former asst. majority leader, pres. 54th Gen. Assembly. Served with U.S. Army, 1952-54. Mem. Rocky Mountain Assn. Geologists, Denver Landmen's Assn., Rocky Mountain Petroleum Pioneers, Adams County C. of C., Westminster C. of C. Republican. Baptist. Office: 9361 Knox Ct Westminster CO 80030*

STRICKLIN, MARY LOU, nurse; b. Holly Spring, Miss., May 21, 1929; d. Abeham and Minnie (Harris) Ivy; m. James Edward Hicks, June 7, 1947 (div.); children—Phenitta, James, Alton; m. 2d, James Stricklin, July 1, 1973. Lic. vocat. nurse East Los Angeles, 1959; A.A., Mt. San Antonia, 1978; R.N., Los Angeles County Sch. Nursing, 1982. Vocat. nurse Los Angeles County Gen. Hosp., 1960—. Democrat. Methodist. Home: 22637 Ironbark Dr Diamond Bar CA 91765 Office: 1200 N State St Los Angeles CA 91765

STRINGER, WILLIAM JEREMY, university admnistrator; b. Oakland, Calif., Nov. 8, 1944; s. William Duane and Mildred May (Andrus) S.; B.A. in English, So. Methodist U., 1966; M.A. in English, U. Wis., 1968, Ph.D. in Ednl. Adminstrn., 1973; m. Susan Lee Hildebrand; 1 dau., Shannon Lee. Dir. men's housing Southwestern U., Georgetown, Tex., 1968-69; asst. dir. housing U. Wis., Madison, 1969-73; dir. residential life, asso. dean student life, adj. prof. Pacific Lutheran U., Tacoma, Wash., 1973-78; dir. residential life U. So. Calif., 1978-79, asst. v.p., 1979—, asst. prof. higher and post-secondary edn., 1980—. Danforth Found. grantee, 1976-77. Mem. Northwest Assn. Coll. and Univ. Housing Officers (pres. elect), Am. Assn. Higher Edn., Nat. Assn. Student Personnel Adminstrs., Am. Personnel and Guidance Assn., Sierra Club, Phi Eta Sigma, Sigma Tau Delta, Phi Alpha Theta. Democrat. Lutheran. Author: How to Survive as a Single Student, 1972; The Role of the Assistant in Higher Education, 1973. Home: 3060 Oneida St Pasadena CA 91107 Office: U So Calif Los Angeles CA 90007

STROBER, MICHAEL ARTHUR, educator, psychologist; b. N.Y.C., Feb. 22, 1949; s. Emanuel and Joan (Kristal) S.; B.A. in Psychology, Queens Coll., City U. N.Y., 1971; M.S., U. Pitts., 1973, Ph.D. in Clin. Psychology, 1975; m. Sheila Lois Shapiro, Aug. 7, 1971. Asst. to assoc. prof. dept. psychiatry Neuropsychiat. Inst. UCLA Center for Health Scis., 1975—. Mem. Am. Psychol. Assn., Calif. Psychol. Assn., Am. Orthopsychiat. Assn., AAAS, N.Y. Acad. Scis., Phi Beta Kappa. Contbr. articles to profl. jours. Office: Neuropsychiat Inst U Calif 760 Westwood Pl Los Angeles CA 90024

STROBER, MYRA HOFFENBERG, educator, economist; b. N.Y.C., Mar. 28, 1941; d. Julius and Regina (Scharer) Hoffenberg; m. Samuel Strober, June 23, 1963; children—Jason, Elizabeth. B.S., Cornell U., 1962; M.A. in Econs., Tufts U., 1965; Ph.D., MIT, 1969. Lectr. dept. econs. U. Md., 1967-69, asst. prof., 1969-70; lectr. dept. econs. U. Calif.-Berkeley, 1970-72; asst. prof. Grad. Sch. Bus., Stanford U., 1972-79, assoc. prof., 1979—, assoc. prof. Sch. Edn., 1979—, dir. Ctr. for Research on Women; cons. in field. Stanford U. fellow, 1975-77. Mem. Am. Econ. Assn. (com. on status of women in econ. profession 1972-75). Assoc. editor Signs: Jour. of Women in Culture and Society, 1980—, bd. editors, 1975-80; contbr. articles to profl. jours. Office: Sch Edn Stanford U Stanford CA 94305

STROBL, DONALD LOUIS, psychiatrist; b. Cleve., May 18, 1947; s. Charles John and Rose Helen (Sourek) S.; B.S. in Mech. Engring., Cornell U., 1969; M.D., Ohio State U., 1973; m. Sally Joanne Derrick, June 27, 1970; children—Staci Elizabeth, Kerry Allison. Psychiat. intern Upstate Med. Center, Syracuse, N.Y., 1973-74, psychiat. resident, 1974-77; staff psychiatrist Tri-City Mental Health Center, Mesa, Ariz., 1977-80, interim dir., 1980-81; practice medicine specializing in psychiatry, Tempe, Ariz., 1981-82; mem. staff Grossmont Dist. Hosp., chmn. psychiatry dept., 1983-84; mem. staff Alvarado, Mesa Vista, Sharp, El Cajon Valley, College Park hosps. Diplomate Am. Bd. Psychiatry and Neurology. Clubs: Cornell Club (San Diego), Morgan Plus Four (San Diego). Home: 1673 Hillsmont Dr El Cajon CA 92020 Office: 5565 Grossmont Center Dr Suite 540 La Mesa CA 92041

STROCK, HERBERT LEONARD, motion picture producer, dir., editor, writer; b. Boston, Jan. 13, 1918; s. Maurice and Charlotte (Nesselroth) S.; B.A., U. So. Calif., 1941, M.A., 1942; m. Geraldine Polinger, Dec. 25, 1941; children—Leslie Carol, Gail Ellen, Candice Dell. Editorial dept. Metro-Goldwyn-Mayer, 1942-46; producer 13 TV films for CBS, Cases of Eddie Drake, 1948-50; asso. producer, film editor Storm over Tibet, 1951; dir., editor Dragnet, 1952; asso. producer, dir., film editor Magnetic Monster, 1952, Donovan's Brain, Riders to the Stars; dir. and editor Gog, 1953; producer, dir. I Led Three Lives, Mr. District Attorney, Favorite Story, Corliss Archer, Sci. Fiction Theatre, Hwy. Patrol, Dr. Christian, Man Called X, Harbor Command, 1954; dir. Battle Taxi; exec. producer, dir. Tom Swift Series; TV shows: Mann of Action; Red Light and Siren; Sky King; (for Warner Bros.); Maverick, Alaskans, Colt 45, Bronco, Cheyenne, 77 Sunset Strip; (for Paramount Studios) Bonanza, for NBC, Hans Brinker spl., Decisions-Decisions; feature pictures: Perfect World of Rodney Brewster, I Was a Teenage Frankenstein, Blood of Dracula, How to Make a Monster, Rider on a Dead Horse, Strike Me Deadly, Search the Wild Wind; editor, dir. The Crawling Hand, One Hour of Hell; editorial supr. Shark; writer, dir. Brother on the Run; editor So Evil My Sister, Chamber-Mades; co-producer Small Miracle on Hallmark Playhouse; editor, dir. They Search for Survival documentary, supervising film editor Hunger Telethon (both for World Vision, Internat.); editor The Making of America, 2-hour spl. for BBC and NBC; co-writer, film editor Hurray for Betty Boop; dir., chief prodn. coordinator for U.S., Miss World 1976, NBC; editor documentaries: UFO Journals, UFO Syndrome, Legends, all 1979; pres. Herbert L. Strock Prodns.; co-dir., film editor: Witches' Brew, 1979; pres., chmn. bd. Hollywood-World Films, Inc.; writer, film editor Flipper TV series, 1981; lectr. U. So. Calif. Mem. Acad. Motion Picture Arts and Scis., Dirs. Guild Am., Am. Cinema Editors (dir.), Motion Picture Editors Guild, Delta Kappa Alpha (pres.). Editor post prodn. services China-Mao to Now, Eucatastrophe, Tibet, El Papa. Office: 6500-6502 Barton Ave Hollywood CA 90038

STROESSNER, ROBERT JOSEPH, museum curator; b. Denver, Dec. 12, 1942. B.F.A., U. Denver, 1964; postgrad. U. Colo., 1970. Asst. curator Denver Art Mus., 1968-70, curator New World dept., 1970—; lectr.; tchr. symposia; organizer art exhibits. U. Denver scholar, 1960-64; grantee. Author: The New World Collections of the Denver Art Museum, 1981; author catalogs; contbr. articles to profl. jours., chpts. to books. Address: 811 Downing St Denver CO 80209

STROH, JAMES ROBERT, agronomist; b. San Francisco, May 12, 1934; s. Roy Leon and Helen Erdeen (Whitmore) S.; B.S., Wash. State U., 1958, M.S., 1965; m. Linda Ray Perrine, Apr. 11, 1959; children—Kathleen Lynore, Jeffrey Warren. Agronomist, Soil Conservation Service, U.S. Dept. Agr., Pullman, Wash., 1958-65, plant materials center mgr., Bridger, Mont., 1965-73, Palmer, Alaska, 1973-77, plant materials specialist, Anchorage, 1977-80, Spokane, Wash., 1980—. Mem. AAAS, Am. Soc. Agronomy, Crop Sci. Soc. Am., Western Soc. Crop Sci., Council Agrl. Sci. and Technology, Am. Rabbit Breeders Assn., Nat. Fedn. Flemish Giant Rabbit Breeders. Contbr. articles in field to profl. jours. Office: US Dept Agriculture 360 US Courthouse Spokane WA 99201

STROJAN, CARL LEE, ecologist; b. Greensburg, Pa., Oct. 9, 1943; s. Frank H. and Pauline C. (Dernoshek) S.; B.A. in Biology, Antioch Coll., 1966; Ph.D. in Ecology, Rutgers U., 1975; m. Linda Jewell, Apr. 10, 1976. Research ecologist UCLA, 1975-79; sr. environ. scientist Solar Energy Research Inst., Golden, Colo., 1979-81; cons., 1981—. Served with U.S. Army, 1967-69. Johnson & Johnson fellow, 1973-74; NSF research grantee, 1970-74. Mem. AAAS, Ecol. Soc. Am., Sigma Xi. Contbr. articles to profl. jours. Office: 11840 Swadley Dr Lakewood CO 80215

STROJNY, SALLY ANN, educator; b. Yonkers, N.Y., June 1, 1950; d. Edward and Margaret (Sinnott) Liberatore; m. Richard John Strojny, June 2, 1950. B.A., Ariz. State U., 1972, M.A., 1975; Ed.D., U. Colo., 1979. Cert. tchr., Colo. Tchr. spl. edn. Gilbert (Ariz.) Sch. Dist., 1973-76; teaching asst. U. Colo., Boulder, 1977-79; supr. day program Wallace Village for Children, Broomfield, Colo., 1979—; environ. edn. cons. N.Am. Wildlife Ctr. Mem. Colo. Assn. Supervision and Curriculum Devel., Am. Assn. Environ. Edn., Nat. Assn. Advancement Humane Edn. Office: PO Box 345 Broomfield CO 80020

STROMBERG, MARK ROBERT, ecologist, zoologist; b. Albuquerque, June 20, 1951; s. Robert P. and Patricia A. (Peterson) S.; m. Barbara Ann Beyers, June 3, 1979; 1 son, Brian Robert. B.S., Colo. State U., 1973; M.S. (grad. teaching fellow 1973-79, Davis fellow 1978), U. Wis., 1975, Ph.D., 1979. Program co-ordinator, zoologist The Nature Conservancy, Cheyenne, Wyo., 1979-82, Rocky Mt. land steward, Denver, 1982—. Nat. Geog. Soc. grantee, 1974. Mem. AAAS, Am. Ornithologists Union, Am. Soc. Mammalogists, Cooper Ornithol. Soc., Ecol. Soc. Am., Southwestern Assn. Naturalists, Phi Kappa Phi. Contbr. articles in field to wildlife mags. Office: 1244 Pine St Boulder CO 80302

STROMLEY, JAMES ARTHUR, engineer; b. Mason City, Iowa, Aug. 10, 1943; s. Orven Arthur and Maurine Luella (Young) S.; m. Ferrill Diane Shoup, June 6, 1964; children—Erin Lisa, Sara Katheryn. B.S.M.E., U. Iowa, 1967. Cert. profl. engr., Colo. Mech. engr. Tech. Center, Union Carbide Corp., Charleston, W. Va., 1967-72; sr. project engr. Fluid Handling div. Sundstrand Corp., Arvada, Colo., 1972-82. Mem. ASME. Republican.

STRONG, DON ROBERT, lawyer; b. Payson, Utah, Oct. 19, 1939; s. Ernest A. and Harriett (Miner) S.; B.S., Brigham Young U., 1964; J.D., Columbia U., 1967; m. Sydna Whiting, Sept. 28, 1962; children—Layton Robert, Stacy, Steven Whiting, Karen, Aileen. Admitted to Utah bar, 1967; atty. firm Clyde, Mecham & Pratt, Salt Lake City, 1967-69, 1969-71; asst. atty. gen. Utah, 1971-73; atty. firm Howard, Lewis & Peterson, Provo, Utah, 1971-72; atty. firm Strong & Mitchell, Springville, Utah, 1973—; mem. Utah Ho. of Reps., 1972, 76, 78, 80. Chmn. Transp. and Public Safety Appropriations Com. and Interim Com., 1978—. Served with Utah N.G., 1958-67. Mem. Springville C. of C., Utah County Bar Assn., Utah State Bar Assn., Am. Bar Assn., Nat. Conf. State Legislators, Utah Municipal Attys. Assn. Republican. Mormon. Club: Kiwanis. Home: 1205 Hillcrest Springville UT 84663 Office: 197 S Main St Springville UT 84663

STRONG, DORIS BAHM, medical services center executive; b. Cherokee, Okla., Dec. 21, 1927; d. Clinton John and Lillie (Resler) Bahm; m. Stanley Sterling Strong, May 25, 1947; children—Cynthia, Kris. B.A., Okla. U., 1950; M.A. Calif. State U.-Long Beach, 1967. Speech pathologist Cerebral Palsey Inst., Norman, Okla., 1949-51, supr. student tng. Braille Inst. Am., Los Angeles, 1972-77; exec. dir. Lions Blind Center, Oakland, Calif., 1977—. Recipient grants Dept. Rehab. Mem. Am. Assn. Workers for Blind (pres. No. Calif.), Nat. Council Pvt. Agencies Serving Blind (v.p.), Calif. Council Pvt. Agys. Serving Blind., No. Calif. Thoroughbred Assn., Desert Wind Arabians Assn. Republican. Lutheran. Home: 511 Waxlax Way Livermore CA 94550 Office: 3834 Opal St Oakland CA 94609

STRONG, GARY EUGENE, librarian; b. Moscow, Idaho, June 26, 1944; s. A. Dwight and Cleora Anna (Nirk) S.; B.S. in Edn., U. Idaho, 1966; M.A. in L.S. (Oreg. Library scholar), U. Mich., 1967; m. Carolyn Jean Roetker, Mar. 14, 1970; children—Christopher Eric, Jennifer Rebecca. Reference, adminstrv. asst. U. Idaho Library, 1963-66; extension librarian Latah County Free Library, Moscow, 1966; head librarian U. Mich. Markley Residence Library, 1966-67; library dir. Lake Oswego (Oreg.) Pub. Library, 1967-73, Everett (Wash.) Pub. Library, 1973-76; asso. dir. Wash. State Library, 1976-79, dep. state librarian, 1979-80; state librarian Calif. State Library, 1980—; chief exec. officer Calif. Library Services Bd., 1980—; v.p. bd. Calif. Coop. Library Agy. for Systems and Services, 1981—; founder, dir. Calif. State Library Found., 1982—; vis. lectr. Marylhurst (Oreg.) Coll., 1968; Oreg. Div. Continuing Edn., 1972; host weekly cable TV program, 1973-76. Bd. dirs. Oreg. Council Pub. Broadcasting, 1969-73, Sr. Service of Snohomish County, 1973-76, Pacific N.W. Bibliog. Center, 1977-80, No. Region Library Bd., 1983—; bd. dirs. Thurston-Mason County Medical Health Clinic, 1977-80, pres., 1979-80; mem. adv. bd. Calif. State PTA, 1981—, Ctr. for the Book, Library of Congress, 1983. ALA (commn. on freedom of access to info. 1983—, chmn. legis. com. 1983-84), Wash., Oreg. (hon. life) (pres. 1970-71), Pacific N.W. (hon. life, treas. 1974-77, pres. 1978-79) library assns., Library Adminstrn. and Mgmt. Assn. (dir., pres.-elect 1983), Everett Area C. of C. (dir.), Snohomish County Hist. Assn. (bd. govs. 1974-76). Clubs: Book of Calif. Comstock (Sacramento). Office: PO Box 2037 Sacramento CA 95809

STRONG, GAY, industrial relations executive; b. Santa Monica, Calif., Jan. 13, 1930; d. Claude Roderick and Katherine Anna (Brown) Riley; student UCLA, 1947-49; A.A., Pierce Coll., Los Angeles, 1969; B.A. in English, Calif. State U.-Northridge, 1973; m. Duane Gordon Strong, Aug. 20, 1949; children—Philip, Katherine, Patricia, Barbara. With credit office, store ops., then asst. personnel mgr. Builders Emporium, Van Nuys, Calif., 1969-74, personnel mgr., 1974-78; dir. indsl. relations GC Internat., Hawthorne, Calif., 1978-81; personnel mgr. Lok Products Co., Fullerton, Calif., 1981-82; chief exec. officer Asset Recovery, Santa Monica, Calif., 1982-83; personnel mgr. Targeted Coverage, Inc., Pomona, Calif., 1983—. Mem. Am. Mgmt. Assn., Am. Soc. Personnel Adminstrs., Personnel and Indsl. Relations Assn., Electronic Assn. Calif. Republican. Editor Builders Emporium house organ, 1972-78. Office: 4241 Redwood Ave Los Angeles CA 90066

STRONG, GEORGE GORDON, JR., lawyer, mgmt. cons., fin. exec.; b. Toledo, Apr. 19, 1947; s. George Gordon and Jean Boyd (McDougall) S.; B.A., Yale U., 1969; M.B.A., Harvard U., 1971; J.D., U. San Diego, 1974; m. Annsley Palmer Chapman, Nov. 30, 1974; children—George Gordon III, Courtney Chapman, Meredith Annsley, Alexis Palmer. Admitted to Calif. bar, 1974; controller, asst. to pres. Vitredent Corp., Beverly Hills, Calif., 1974-76; sr. mgr. mgmt. adv. services dept. Price Waterhouse & Co., Los Angeles, 1976-82; v.p. fin. Internat. Customs Services, Inc., Torrance, Calif., 1982—. C.P.A., Hawaii, Calif. Mem. Am. Inst. C.P.A.s, Calif. Soc. C.P.A.s, Am. Mgmt. Assn., State Bar Calif., Los Angeles County Bar Assn., Inst. Mgmt. Cons., ABA, Presbyterian. Clubs: Jonathan (Los Angeles); Olympic (San Francisco); Flint Canyon Tennis (Flintridge). Home: 4251 Woodleigh Ln La Canada CA 91011 Office: 2730 Monterey Blvd Torrance CA 90503

STRONG, JAMES BENTLEY, state ofcl.; b. N.Y.C., Nov. 30, 1920; s. Earl D. and Margaret (Bentley) S.; B.A., Grinnell Coll., 1942; LL.B., Yale, 1952; m. Sylvia Kolden, July 10, 1945; children—Stephen, Mary, Nancy, Sarah. Bus. analyst Office Alien Property, Dept. Justice, 1946; land field agt. Bur. Indian Affairs, Dept. Interior, Juneau, Alaska, 1946-49; admitted to Wash. bar, 1952; asso. Witherspoon, Witherspoon & Kelley, Spokane, 1952-54; pvt. practice, Moses Lake, Wash., 1954-68; municipal judge, Moses Lake, 1957-58, 61-68; appeal examiner Wash. Employment Security Dept., Olympia, 1968-70, chief appeal examiner, 1970-82, adminstrv. law judge Office Adminstrv. Hearings, 1982—. Served from pvt. to 1st lt. AUS, 1942-46. Decorated Purple Heart. Mem. Am., Wash., Grant County (pres. 1959-60) bar assns., Nat. Assn. Adminstrv. Hearing Officers (v.p. 1977-78), Am. Judicature Soc., Am. Arbitration Assn. (nat. panel), Phi Beta Kappa. Lutheran (ch. council 1955-56, 59-61 78-80). Home: 7344 Marvin Rd NE Olympia WA 98506 Office: 1025 E Union St ES-31 Olympia WA 98504

STRONG, MAURICE FREDERICK, resource co. exec., former UN ofcl.; b. Oak Lake, Man., Can., Apr. 29, 1929; s. Frederick Milton and Mary (Fyfe) S.; 23 hon. degrees from Can., U.S., Europe, including U. Toronto, 1972, Acad. U., 1972, LaSalle Coll., 1972, U. Alta., 1973, Brandon U., 1973, Springfield Coll., 1973, Yale U., 1973. m. Hanne Marstrand, 1981; children by previous marriage—Frederick Maurice, Maureen Louise, Mary Anne, Kenneth Martin; 1 foster dau., Alice Szojka. Fin. analyst James Richardson & Sons, Winnipeg, Man., and Calgary, 1948-51, asst. to pres., 1951-52; mktg. asst. Caltex (Africa) Ltd., Nairobi, Kenya, 1953-54; v.p., treas. Dome Petroleum Ltd., Calgary, 1955-59; pres., Can. Indsl. Gas Ltd., Calgary, 1959-64, Power Corp. Can., Montreal, 1962-66, Can. Internat. Devel. Agy. Ottawa, 1966-70; exec. dir. environment program UN, also sec.-gen. UN Conf. Human Environment; N.Y.C., 1971-75; chmn. bd. Petro-Can., 1975-78; chmn. Internat. Devel. Research Centre, 1977-78, Procor, Inc., 1978-83; chmn. AZL Resources Inc., Phoenix; former chmn. Internat. Union for Conservation of Nature and Natural Resources; chmn. Can. Devel. Investment Corp.; chmn. exec. com. Société Générale pour l'Energie et les Ressources; chmn. Internat. Energy Devel. Corp., Geneva; vice chmn. Can. Devel. Corp., also dir. Mem. adv. bd. York U., Toronto, 1969-70, vis. prof. govt. adminstrn., 1969; alt. gov IBRD, Asian Devel. Bank, 1968-70, Caribbean Devel. Bank, 1970; gov. Internat. Devel. research Centre, 1970-71, 77-78; bd. dirs. Centre D'Etudes Industrielles, Geneva, Switzerland, Aspen Inst. Humanistic Studies; trustee Rockefeller Found. Pres. Nat. Council YMCA's Can., 1967-68; chmn. com. extension and inter-movement aid World Alliance YMCA's, 1963-65; mem. joint com. soc. justice peace World Council Chs., Vatican, 1969-71; Montague Burton prof. internat. relations, U. Edinburgh, 1973; lectr. Rockefeller U., 1973-77; lectr. numerous other univs. Decorated officer Order of Can.; Henri Pittier Order (Venezuela); comdr. Order Golden Ark (Netherlands); recipient Tyler Ecology award, 1974, Nat. Audubon Soc. award, 1975, Mellon award, 1975, Freedom Festival award, 1975, 1st Internat. Pahlavi Environ. prize, 1976, Charles A. Lindbergh award, 1981, old Environ. Leadership Decade award UN Environ. Program, 1982; René Dubos Only One Earth award, 1983. Mem. Century Assn. Clubs: Mount Royal (Montreal); Rideau (Ottawa); Century, Yale, Metropolitan. Office: 355 Burrard St Suite 1031 Vancouver BC V6C 2G8 Canada

STRONG, MAYDA NEL, psychology educator; b. Albuquerque, May 6, 1942; d. Floyd Samuel and Wanda Christmas (Martin) S.; 1 son, Robert Allen Willingham. B.A. cum laude in Speech-Theatre, Tex. Western Coll., 1963; M. Ed. in Sch. Counseling, U. Tex., 1972, Ph.D. in Counseling Psychology, 1978. Cert. secondary instr. and sch. counselor, Tex. Tchr., Tornillo Ind. Sch. Dist. (Tex.), 1963-64; television personality Sta. KHFI-TV, Austin, Tex., 1964-65; tchr. Austin Ind. Sch. Dist., 1965-67, 70-71, Dallas Ind. Sch. Dist., 1967-68; dir. Frank Baird Youth Theatre, Waco, Tex., 1968-70; academic asst. to dir. counseling psychology, dept. counseling edn., U. Tex., Austin, 1973-75; instr. psychology Austin Community Coll., 1974-78; asst. instr. ednl. psychology U. Tex., Austin, 1974-78; dir. outpatient and emergency services Southeastern Colo. Family Guidance and Mental Health Center, La Junta, 1978-81; instr. psychology Otero Jr. Coll., La Junta, 1980—; pvt. practice psychology, Pueblo, Colo., 1981—; cons. in field. Active Picketwire Theatre, La Junta. Recipient Austin chpt. AAUW fellowship, 1976-78; named outstanding Theatre Major, Tex. Western Coll., 1963. Mem. Am. Psychol. Assn., Colo. Psychol. Assn., Bus. and Profl. Women (bd. dirs., legislative chmn.), Chenrizig, Alpha Psi Omega, Alpha Chi, Pi Lambda Theta, Kappa Delta Pi, Phi Kappa Phi. Contbr. articles to profl. jours. Home and Office: 910 San Juan Ave La Junta CO 81050

STRONG, ROBERT GEORGE, sales engr., mktg. cons.; b. Rochester, N.Y., Sept. 23, 1916; s. Robert H. and Sadie E. (McNeil) S.; M.E., Rochester Inst. Tech., 1936; grad. U. Rochester, 1938; m. Dorothy M. Reimer, Sept. 28, 1939; 1 dau., Susan Diane Evans. Govt. project supr. Stromberg Carlson Co., Rochester, 1937-41; pres. Strong Appliance Industries, Danbury, Conn., 1942-48; cons. to gen. mgr. Allan B. DuMont Labs., East Paterson, N.J., 1948-51; asst. chief engr. Bendix Aviation Corp., North Hollywood, Calif., 1951-55, sales mgr. F. Somers Paterson Co., Los Angeles, 1955-57; v.p., gen. mgr. Western div. Keco Industries, Santa Ana, Calif., 1957-71, mktg. cons., 1978—; pres. Strong Industries, San Juan Capistrano, Calif., 1971—, Honolulu, 1975—; cons., mktg. and acquisitions for environ. control industry, 1978—. Mem. Am. Soc. Refrigerating Engrs., Am. Ordnance Assn., Air Force Assn., Instrument Soc. Am., Am. Soc. Plastic Engrs., Internat. Platform Assn., Mfrs. Agents Nat. Assn. Designer, developer household and indsl. electric can opener. Address: 22882 Mariano Dr Laguna Niguel CA 92677

STRONG, WILLIAM JAMES, physicist; b. Idaho Falls, Idaho, Jan. 1, 1934; s. William A. and June (Engberson) S.; B.S., Brigham Young U., 1958, M.S., 1959; Ph.D., MIT, 1964; m. Charlene Fuhriman, June 8, 1959; children—William, Stephen, Kathleen, John, David, Richard. Mem. staff MIT Lincoln Labs., Lexington, Mass., 1960-61; mem. staff Air Force Cambridge Research Labs., Bedford, Mass., 1963-66; lectr. physics Holy Cross Coll., Worcester, Mass., 1963-64, Northeastern U., Boston, 1964-66; prof. physics Brigham Young U., Provo, Utah, 1967—; vis. scientist Gallaudet Coll., Washington, 1974; Fulbright sr. fellow U. New Eng., Australia, 1980. Served with USAF, 1964-67. Fellow Acoustical Soc. Am.; mem. IEEE, Sigma Xi. Mormon. Author: Music, Speech, and High Fidelity, 1977, 2d edit., 1983; patentee in field. Office: Dept Physics Brigham Young U Provo UT 84602

STRONG, WILLIAM LEE, former manufacturing company executive; b. Jacksonville, Fla., Sept. 17, 1919; s. William M. and Hedwig C. (Ulm) S.; m. Betty Jean Stream, Dec. 13, 1941; children—William Lee, Thomas B., Robin E. A.B. in Econs., Occidental Coll., 1942; M.B.A., Harvard U., 1947. Budget dir. Byron-Jackson div. Borg Warner Corp., Los Angeles, 1954-56, controller, 1956-57; budget dir. Consol. Freightways, Inc., Menlo Park, Calif., 1957-60, treas., chief fin. officer, 1960-62; v.p. fin., treas., dir. Packard-Bell Electronics Corp., Los Angeles, 1962-65; treas. Allis-Chalmers Mfg. Co., Milw., 1965-68; v.p., treas. Continental Can Co., Inc., 1968-75; sr. v.p., chief fin. officer Firestone Tire & Rubber Co., Akron, Ohio, 1976-77, exec. v.p., dir., 1973-81; dir. Transatlantic Fund, U.S. Life Corp.; mem. adv. bd. Lorimar, Inc., Equity Strategies Fund, Mfrs. Hanover Trust Co., N.Y.C.; guest lectr. various grad. bus. schs., other groups. Trustee Fin. Execs. Research Found. Served to lt. comdr. USN, 1942-54; PTO. Mem. Am. Mgmt. Assn. (fin. planning council), Treas. Club N.Y., Council Fin. Execs., Conf. Bd., Fin. Execs. Inst., Phi Gamma Delta. Club: Harvard Bus. Sch. (N.Y.C.). Home: 258 Calle Cuervo San Clemente CA 92672

STRONGE, WILLIAM JAMES, JR., mech. engr.; b. Chgo., Mar. 6, 1937; s. William James and Lillian Mae S.; B.S., Oreg. State U., 1960; M.S., UCLA, 1964; Ph.D. in Applied Mechanics, Stanford U., 1969; children—Brent R., Leslie Ann. Mech. engr. Naval Weapons Center, China Lake, Calif., 1960-81, head structural dynamics br., 1979-81; prof. dept. engring. Cambridge (Eng.) U., 1981—. Pres., China Lake Mountain Rescue, 1979-80. Mem. AIAA, Sigma Xi. Contbr. articles to profl. jours. Research on wave propagation, dynamic plasticity. Office: Dept Engring U Cambridge Cambridge England

STROOCK, THOMAS FRANK, state senator; b. N.Y.C., Oct. 10, 1925; s. Samuel and Dorothy (Frank) S.; B.A. in Econs., Yale U., 1948; m. Marta Freyre de Andrade, June 19, 1949; children—Margaret, Sandra, Elizabeth, Anne. Landman Stanolind Oil & Gas Co., Tulsa, 1948-52; pres. Stroock Leasing Corp., Casper, Wyo., 1952—, Colonel Petroleum Corp., Casper, 1980—; partner Stroock, Rogers & Dymond, Casper, 1960—; dir. Wyo. Bancorp., Cheyenne, First Wyo. Bank, Casper, Century Oil & Gas Corp., Denver; mem. Wyo. Senate, 1967-69, 71-75, 79—, chmn. appropriations com. 1983. Pres. Natrona County Sch. Bd., 1960-69; pres. Wyo. State Sch. Bds. Assn., 1965-66; chmn. Casper Community Recreation, 1955-60; chmn. Natrona County United Fund, 1963-64; chmn. Wyo. State Republican Com., 1975-78; chmn. Western States Rep. Chmn. Assn., 1977-78; chmn. Wyo. Higher Edn. Commn., 1969-71; mem. Nat. Petroleum Council, 1972-77. Served with USMC, 1943-46. Mem. Rocky Mountain Oil and Gas Assn., Petroleum Assn. Wyo. Republican. Unitarian. Clubs: Kiwanis; Casper Country; Casper Petroleum; Denver. Office: PO Box 2875 Casper WY 82602*

STROUM, SAMUEL N., automotive exec.; b. Waltham, Mass., Apr. 14, 1921; s. Nathan and Ethel (Onigman) S.; m. Althea Diesenhaus, Aug. 9, 1942; children—Marsha Lynn (Mrs. Stuart M. Sloan), Cynthia Stroum Meagher. Chmn. bd. Schuck's Auto Supply Inc., Seattle, 1967—; dir. Seafirst Corp., Seattle-First Nat. Bank, Seattle. Pres. Jewish Fedn. Greater Seattle, 1979-81, also chmn. endowment fund; gen. chmn. campaign United Way King County, 1981-82; chmn. U. Wash. Hosp., 1982-83; bd. govs. Hebrew U.; bd. dirs., past pres. A Contemporary Theatre, Seattle; chmn. pres.'s club U. Wash., 1980-82; v.p. Seattle Found.; bd. dirs. Damon Runyon-Walter Winchell Cancer Fund; trustee Jerusalem Inst. Mgmt.; mem. U.S. Commn. on Presdl. Scholars, Richard Tucker Music Found., N.Y.C. Served with USAAF, 1940-46. Mem. Nat. Electronic Distbrs. Assn. (past v.p. nat. bd.), Automotive Parts and Accessories Assn. (past dir.), Quarter Century Club Automotive Industry, Wash. State Bus. Roundtable. Jewish (past pres. temple 1973-74). Clubs: Wash. Athletic, Harbor, Rainier, Rotary, Masons, Shriners, B'nai B'rith (Seattle); Bellevue Athletic, Glendale Golf and Country (Bellevue, Wash.); Palm Springs (Calif.) Tennis, Tamarisk Country (Palm Springs). Home: 1301 Spring St Apt 32 Seattle WA 98104 Office: 3714 Seattle 1st Nat Bank Bldg Seattle WA 98154

STROZIER, WENDELL, nuclear medical technologist; b. St. Louis, Sept. 21, 1952; s. Harvey and Hattie Beatrice (Bell) S.; m. Juanita L. Watts, Sept. 1983. A.A., Los Angeles City Coll., 1977; B.S., Calif. State U., 1980; postgrad. U. Redlands, 1980-81; diploma Excel Security Acad., 1982. Distbr. Amway Products, Los Angeles, 1979—; radiol. technologist U.S. Air Force Res. North AFB, Calif., 1974-78; nuclear medicine staff technologist NuclearMedico Services, Van Nuys, Calif., 1977-81, nuclear medicine mgr., Los Angeles, 1981; staff technologist Kaiser Permanente of W. Los Angeles, 1982—; call technologist Meml. Hosp., Gardena, Calif., 1982—; lectr. in field. Vol., UCLA Med. Center, 1979-80; counselor Watts Labor Community Action Com., 1982. Served with USAF, 1972-73. Mem. Soc. Nuclear Medicine, Student Nat. Med. Assn., Am. Mgmt. Assn., Am. Legion. Home: PO Box 6340 Beverly Hills CA 90212 Office: 2310 La Cienaga Blvd Los Angeles CA 90019

STRUHL, STANLEY FREDERICK, real estate developer; b. Bklyn., Oct. 10, 1939; s. Isidore and Yvette (Miller) S.; B.S. with honors in Engring., UCLA, 1961, M.B.A. in Data Processing, 1963; m. Patricia Joyce Wald, Feb. 26, 1966; children—Marc Howard, Lisa Lynn. Mem. tech. staff Hughes Aircraft Co., Fullerton, Calif., 1963-65; sr. asso. Planning Research Corp., Los Angeles, 1965-70; mgr. corporate info. systems Logicon, Inc., Torrance, Calif., 1970-73; mgr. operations analysis System Devel. Corp., Santa Monica, Calif., 1973-77; gen. partner TST Developers, Canyon Country, Calif., 1977-81; pres. Struhl Enterprises, Inc., Northridge, Calif., 1977—; owner Struhl Properties, Northridge, 1979—. Lic. real estate broker, Calif. Mem. Assn. For Computing Machinery, San Fernando Valley Bd. Realtors, Tau Beta Pi, Beta Gamma Sigma, Alpha Phi Omega. Home: 17074 Knapp St Northridge CA 91325

STRUNKA, JOSEPH VINCENT, educator; b. Chgo., Apr. 24, 1937; s. Joseph and Rosemary (Foytik) S.; m. Elke Erika Langmann, July 26, 1942. B.S. in Edn., Western Ill. U., 1961; M.S., Eastern Ill. U., 1969; Ph.D., U. Nebr., 1979. Cert. tchr., adminstr., Alaska. Instr. secondary edn. U. Nebr., Licoln, 1973-74, asst. prof. Calif. State Coll.-Bakersfield, 1974-79; dir. staff devel., secondary curriculum and instrn. U. Alaska, Fairbanks, 1979-80, dir. staff devel. and research, 1980-81, dir. staff devel. and student activities, 1981-82; instr. social sci. Fairbanks (Alaska) North Star Borough Sch. Dist., 1982—, dir., 1979-82; behavioral and systems cons. Owner, Ivy Mining Co. Coordinator Polka Fest, Alaska Crippled Children and Adult Soc., 1982. Mem. Nat. Council Geog. Edn., Assn. Supervision and Curriculum Devel., Phi Delta Kappa (Kern chpt. Service Key award 1976). Republican. Author curriculum, instrnl. and tchr. evaluation materials; contbr. articles to profl. jours. Home: PO Box 550 Fairbanks AK 99707

STUART, BRUCE B., microcomputer industry exec.; b. Glendale, Calif., Feb. 21, 1942; s. John B. and Margaret E. (Rice) S. Student Glendale Coll., 1960-62; B.S. in Bus. Adminstr., Union Coll., 1965; postgrad. in law U. Nebr., 1966; M.B.A., Pepperdine U., 1980. Fin. analyst Hughes Aircraft Co., Canoga Park, Calif., 1967-68, asst. to controller, 1968-70; mgr. systems and audit Tridair Industries, Torrance, Calif., 1970, controller, 1971, plant mgr., 1972; mgr. fin. planning Basic Four Corp., Tustin, Calif., 1973-75; dir. fin. planning Am. Telecommunications, El Monte, Calif., 1976, dir. ops., gen. mgr., 1977, dir. corp. procurement, 1978-79; exec. v.p. Aqua Pet Industries, Los Angeles, 1979-80, pres., 1980—; chief exec. officer IJG, Inc., 1981—, also dir.; dir. LNW Research Inc. Bd. dirs. Calif. Condo Assn.: bd. dirs., past pres. 1849 Condo Assn., Mammoth Condominium Assn. Mem. Delta Theta Phi. Republican. Home: 8 Summerwalk Ct Newport Beach CA 92663

STUART, CHARLES EDWARD, economist, educator; b. Troy, N.Y., Jan. 5, 1950; s. George Wallace and Neda Lois (Samuels) S.; m. Lisbeth Ingeborg, July 16, 1971; 1 dau., Andrea Elisa. B.A., UCLA, 71, M.A., 72; Ph.D., U. Lund, Sweden, 1975. Research economist U. Lund, 1975—; asst. prof. U. Western Ont., Can., 1976-78; asst. prof. U. Calif., Santa Barbara, 1980—. Bank of Sweden Tercentenary Found. grantee, 1976-79, 1980—; Swedish Council for Research in Social Scis. and Humanities grantee, 1979. Mem. Am. Econ. Assn., Eastern Econ. Assn., Western Econ. Assn., Public Choice Soc. Contbr. articles to profl. jours. Office: Dept Econs U Calif Santa Barbara CA 93106

STUART, DAVID EDWARD, anthropologist; b. Calhoun County, Ala., Jan. 9, 1945; s. Edward George and Avis Elsie (Densmore) S.; B.A. (Wesleyan Merit scholar 1965-66), W.VA. Wesleyan Coll., 1967; M.A. in Anthropology, U. N.Mex., 1970, Ph.D., 1972, postdoctoral student, 1975-76; m. Cynthia K. Morgan, June 14, 1971. Research asso. Andean Center, Quito, Ecuador, 1970; continuing edn. instr. anthropology U. N.Mex., 1971, research archeologist Office Contract Archeology, 1974, research coordinator, 1974-77, asst. prof. anthropology, 1975-77; asst. prof. Eckerd Coll., St. Petersburg, Fla., 1972-74; cons. archeologist right-of-way div. Public Service Co. N.Mex., Albuquerque, 1977-78; cons. anthropologist Bur. Indian Affairs, Albuquerque, 1978, Historic Preservation Bur. N.Mex., Santa Fe, 1978-81, Nat. Park Service, 1980, Albuquerque Mus., 1981; sr. research asso. Human Systems Research, Inc., 1981-83; bd. dirs. Table Ind. Scholars, 1979—; adv. Human Systems Research, Inc., Tularosa, N.Mex., 1978—; mem. research and publ. coms. N.Mex. Archeol. Council, 1978-80. Grantee Eckerd Coll., 1973, Historic Preservation Bur., 1978-80. Mem. Am. Anthrop. Assn., Royal Anthrop. Inst. Gt. Britain, N.Mex. Archeol. Council, Albuquerque Archeol. Soc., Descs. Signers Declaration Independence, Sigma Xi, Phi Kappa Phi. Presbyterian. Co-author: Archeological Survey: 4 Corners to Ambrosia, N.Mex., 1976; A Proposed Project Design for the Timber Management Archeological Surveys, 1978; Prehistoric New Mexico, 1981; Ethnoarcheological Investigations of Shepherding in the Pueblo of Laguna, 1981; Author: Ancient New Mexico, 1983; others; editor: Archeological Reports, No. 1, 1975, No. 2, 1981. Address: 308 Girard St SE Albuquerque NM 87106

STUART, DWIGHT LYMAN, food products executive; b. Seattle, Sept. 27, 1924; s. Elbridge Hadley and Nan (Fullerton) S.; student U. Wash., 1947; children by former marriage—Dwight Lyman, William W., Bruce F.; m. 2d, Kathleen Gallant, Oct. 27, 1958; children—Douglas F., Gregory M. With Carnation Co., 1947-48, 50—, asst. v.p., 1957-64, v.p., after 1964, exec. v.p., until 1973, pres., 1973—, also dir.; mfrs. rep., 1948-50; dir. E. A. Stuart Co., Security Pacific Nat. Bank. Served to lt. (j.g.) USNR, 1943-46. Mem. Phi Delta Theta. Club: Los Angeles. Office: 5045 Wilshire Blvd Los Angeles CA 90036*

STUART, GERARD WILLIAM, JR., bus. exec.; b. Yuba City, Calif., July 28, 1939; s. Gerard William and Geneva Bernice (Stuke) S.; student Yuba Jr. Coll., 1957-59, Chico State Coll., 1959-60; A.B., U. Calif., Davis, 1962; M.L.S., U. Calif., Berkeley, 1963; m. Lenore Frances Loroña, 1981. Rare book librarian Cornell U., 1964-68; bibliographer of scholarly collections Huntington Library, San Marino, Calif., 1968-73, head acquisitions librarian, 1973-75; sec.-treas., dir. Ravenstree Corp., 1969-80, pres., chmn. bd., 1980—; pres., chmn. bd. William Penn Ltd., 1981—. Lilly fellow Ind. U., 1963-64. Mem. Bibliog. Soc. Am., Phi Beta Kappa, Alpha Gamma Sigma, Phi Kappa Phi. Clubs: Rolls-Royce

Owners; Grolier (N.Y.C.); Zamorano (Los Angeles). Home: 1472 Gateway Dr Yuma AZ 85364 Office: 350 S 3d Ave Yuma AZ 85364

STUART, JAMES RILEY, aerospace engineer, educator; b. Renton, Wash., Apr. 16, 1946; s. James Carroll and Rosemary Juanita (Aust) S.; m. Susan Frith Stutsman, Sept. 13, 1968 (div.). B.S. in Physics, U. Wash., 1968; M.S. in Elec. Engring., U. So. Calif., 1972, M.S. in Ops. Research, 1977, Ph.D. in Engring., 1979. Engr., Boeing Comml. Airplane Co., Seattle, 1968-69; engr., mgr. Jet Propulsion Lab., Calif. Inst. Tech., Pasadena, 1970-82, mgr. advanced planetary studies, 1982—; asst. dir. Lab. for Atmospheric and Space Physics, U. Colo., 1982—, prof. elec. engring., 1982—. Mem. AIAA. Contbr. numerous articles and papers to profl. jours. Home: 1300 Meadowbrook Rd Altadena CA 91001 Office: 4800 Oak Grove Ave Pasadena CA 91109

STUART, JOHN GOODSPEED, school administrator; b. Utica, N.Y., Sept. 28, 1926; s. Donald Cameron and Gertrude (Goodspeed) S.; m. Ann Mulroy, June 23, 1951; children—John, Mary, Rosemary, Elizabeth, William. B.A., Denver U., 1949; M.A., Columbia U., 1952, Ed.D., 1954. Prin., Jefferson (Colo.) Sr. High Sch., 1960-62; supt. schs. Gunnison (Colo.) Sch. Dist. Re-1J, 1962-65, Adams County Sch. Dist. 14, Commerce City, Colo., 1965-70; assoc. sec. Am. Assn. Sch. Adminstrs., Arlington, Va., 1970-74; supt. schs. Aurora (Colo.) Pub. Schs., 1974—. Mem. Nat. Assn. Sch. Security Dirs., NEA, Am. Assn. Sch. Adminstrs., Nat. Acad. Sch. Execs., Colo. Assn. Sch. Execs., Colo. Schoolmasters, Denver Sch. Supts. Council, Phi Delta Kappa. Episcopalian. Office: Aurora Public Schools 1085 Peoria St Aurora CO 80011

STUART, MICHAEL JOSEPH, association executive; b. Pasadena, Calif., Oct. 14, 1953; s. Donald Joseph and Elizabeth Ann (Wulfekuhl) S.; m. Karen Moffett, June 19, 1976; 1 son, Nicholas Paul. B.A. in Journalism, Calif. State U.-Long Beach, 1978. Asst. in corp. communications dept. Ralphs Grocery Co., Compton, Calif., 1978-79; pub. relations asst. Western Growers Assn., Irvine, Calif., 1979-80, dir. pub. relations, asst. pub., 1980-81, v.p. pub. relations, pub. Western Grower and Shipper Mag., 1981—; guest lectr. in pub. relations Calif. State U.-Long Beach. Mem. Pub. Relations Soc. Am., Sigma Alpha Epsilon Alumni.

STUART, PETER MARTIN, II, medical company executive; b. Los Angeles, Apr. 19, 1937; s. Peter M. and Lillian V. (Esquirel) S.; A.A., Valley Coll., 1957; B.A., UCLA, 1961; m. Lynda Krois, Mar. 3, 1980; children by previous marriage—Theresa Louise, Kimberly Anne, James Patrick. With West Chem. Products, Los Angeles, 1959-66, Nat. TV Services, Los Angeles, 1966-67; sales mgr. Rank Precision Industries, Los Angeles, 1967-72; exec. v.p. Fujinon Optical, Santa Clara, Calif., 1972-78; pres. Jet-Age Products, Inc., San Jose, Calif., Los Angeles, and Nassau, 1979-81; pres. Sun-Optics, Sunnyvale, Calif., 1981—; lectr. in field. Served with USN, 1956-58. Mem. Nat. Assn. Ednl. Broadcasters, Nat. Assn. Broadcasters, C. of C. (dir. 1975-79). Writer, Ins. News, 1977-78. Office: 1240 Birchwood Dr Sunnyvale CA 94086

STUART, RICHARD BERNARD, psychologist; b. Newark, Oct. 8, 1933; s. Charles Lewis and Frances (Diamond) S.; B.A., NYU, 1955; M.S., Columbia U., 1960, D.S.W., 1965; children—Jesse Reid, Toby Evan, Gregory Lyal. Mem. faculty U. Mich., 1965-73, U. B.C., 1974-76, SUNY-Stony Brook, 1976-77; pres. Behavior Change Systems, Salt Lake City, 1969; prof. family and community medicine U. Utah Med. Sch., 1977—; psychol. dir. Weight Watchers Internat., 1972; sr. ptnr. McLean, Wilson and Stuart, Vancouver, B.C., 1977—; exec. dir. One-to-One Weight Mgmt. System, Inc., 1981—. Served with U.S. Army, 1955-57. Fellow Am. Psychol. Assn.; mem. Assn. Advancement Behavior Therapy (past pres.), Soc. Behavioral Medicine (exec. com.). Author: Trick or Treatment, 1971, Slim Chance in a Fat World, rev. edit., 1978, Act Thin: Stay Thin, 1978, Helping Couples Change, 1980; also articles. Home: 4814 Quail Point Rd Salt Lake City UT 84117 Office: 1C-303 Medical Center Univ Utah Salt Lake City UT 84132

STUBBLEFIELD, THOMAS MASON, educator, agricultural economist; b. Taxhoma, Okla., Apr. 16, 1922; s. Temple Roscoe and Martha Lacy (Acree) S.; B.S., N.Mex., State U., 1948; M.S., A. and M. Coll. Tex., 1951, Ph.D., 1956; postgrad. U. Ariz., 1954; m. Martha Lee Miller, Mar. 7, 1943; children—Ellen (Mrs. Richard Damron), Paula (Mrs. James T. Culbertson), Thommye (Mrs. Gary D. Zingsheim). Specialist cotton mktg. N.Mex. State U., 1948; extension economist, then asst. agrl. economist U. Ariz., Tucson, 1951-58, assoc. prof., agrl. economist, from 1964, now prof., agrl. economist, acting asst. dir. agrl. expt. sta., 1966-68, asst. to dir. sta., 1973-74, chief party Brazil contract, 1968-70. Mem. Pima Council Aging, 1974-77; chmn. adv. com. Ret. Sr. Vol. Program, Pima County, 1974-77, 80-83. Chmn. bd. Saguaro Home Found. Served with AUS, 1942-45. Mem. Soc. Range Mgmt. Author bulls. Home: 810 Calle Milu Tucson AZ 85706

STUBBS, CAP, marketing executive; b. Los Angeles, Jan. 30, 1936; s. Milton A. and Lillian M. (Sutton) S.; B.S. in B.A., U. So. Calif., 1957; postgrad. U. Calif., 1960-62; m. Nancy Shirey, Jan. 31, 1958; children—Lea Anne, David Michael. Lic. pvt. pilot. With Air Supply Co. div. Garrett Corp., Beverly Hills, Calif., 1959-60; ptnr. Arielco, Beverly Hills, Calif., 1960-62; sales mgr. Eldema Corp., El Monte, Calif., 1962-63; distbn. sales mgr./advt. mgr. Master Spltys. Co., Los Angeles, 1963-64; Western regional engring. mgr., dist. sales mgr. wire & cable div. ITT, Los Angeles, 1964-67; corp. dir. mktg. Raychem Corp., Menlo Park, Calif., 1967—; guest lectr. UCLA Grad. Sch. Bus. and Exec. Mgmt., Ariz. State U. Served to lt. (j.g.) USN, 1957-59. Recipient Apollo Achievement award NASA, 1969. Mem. Delta Tau Delta, Commerce Assn. U. So. Calif. Office: 300 Constitution Dr Menlo Park CA 94025

STUBBS, DANIEL GAIE, consultant; b. Charleston, S.C., Nov. 13, 1940; s. Daniel Hamer and Esther Virginia (Garlow) S.; student U. Fla., 1959-60; B.A., W.Va. U., 1965; postgrad. Temple U., 1965-67. Tchr., Sch. Dist. of Phila., 1965-67; rep. Am. Fedn. Tchrs., Washington, 1967; exec. sec. Calif. State Coll. Council, Am. Fedn. Tchrs., AFL-CIO, Los Angeles, 1967-68; rep. Am. Fedn. Tchrs., AFL-CIO, Los Angeles, 1968-69, dir. orgn. Balt. Tchrs. Union, 1969-70; employee relations specialist Calif. Nurses Assn., Los Angeles, 1971-72; exec. dir. United Nurses Assn. Calif., Los Angeles, 1972-74; labor relations cons. Social Services Union, Service Employees Internat. Union, Local 535, AFL-CIO, Los Angeles, 1974-76; exec. dir. Met. Riverside UniServ Unit, Calif. Tchrs. Assn., 1976-79, exec. dir. San Bernardino/Colton Uniserv Unit, 1979-80; gen. services adminstr. Housing Authority, City of Los Angeles, 1980-82; cons. Blanning & Baker Assocs., Tujunga, Calif., 1983—; lectr. in field. Served with U.S. Army, 1961-62. Recipient W.Va. U. Waitman Barbe Prize for creative writing, 1965. Mem. So. Calif. Indsl. Relations Research Assn., Orange County Indsl. Relations Research Assn., Indsl. Relations Research Assn., Soc. of Profls. in Dispute Resolution. Democrat. Presbyterian. Club: Town Hall of Calif. Home: PO Box 9219 Glendale CA 91206 Office: 9945 Commerce Ave Tujunga CA 91042

STUCK, BYRON MICHAEL, hospital administrator; b. Detroit, Sept. 26, 1950; s. Martha (Polifko) S.; m. Doris Ann Laybourn, Mar. 4, 1978. B.S. in Indsl. Engring., U. Mich., 1972, M. in Health Services Adminstrn., 1978. Mgmt. cons. Hosp. Systems Improvement Program, Ann Arbor, Mich., 1972-75; mgmt. cons. Health Mgmt. Advs. Ann Arbor, 1976-78; sr. health care analyst Group Health Co-op. of Puget Sound, Seattle, 1979-81, asst. hosp. adminstr., 1982—; mem. bd. King County Health Planning Council. Mem. Am. Hosp. Assn., Hosp. Mgmt. Systems Soc., Am. Inst. Indsl. Engrs., Northwest Motorcycle Assn., Am. Motorcycle Assn. Office: 2700 152d St NE Redmond WA 98052

STUCKI, GRANT ALFRED, dentist; b. Delta, Utah, Oct. 2, 1928; s. Herman Wilford and Anna Elizabeth (Nelson) S.; student Brigham Young U., 1946-47, U. Utah, 1950-51; D.D.S., Northwestern U., 1954; student U. Louisville, 1954-55; m. Sharon Turner, Dec. 19, 1952; children—Sharee A., Grant Turner, Candice J., Randall M., Turner G., Taylor C. Attending dentist Ventura Correctional Sch. for Girls, Ventura, Calif., 1954-55; pvt. practice dentistry, Chgo., 1957-69, Torrance, Calif., 1972—; cons. dentist Ettie Lee Homes for Youth, 1975-80; cons. dentist Internat. Monetary Funders, 1978. Pres., Internat. Commerce Exchange, Success Market Unltd., Internat. Retirement Accounts, Coastal Leasing Services. Bd. dirs. Ettie Lee Homes for Youth; instr. on Constn., Freeman Inst. Served with USAF, 1955-57. Mem. Am. Endodontic Soc., Acad. Gen. Dentistry, Profl. Speakers Assn., Internat. Found. Profl. Excellence, Food for Millions Found., Donovan Acad. Orthodontics, Denticare Corp., Internat. Platform Assn. Republican. Mem. Ch. Jesus Christ of Latter-day Saints. Club: Toastmasters Internat. Office: 3318 E Anaheim St Long Beach CA 90804

STUDARUS, PHILIP GLENN, internat. fin. cons.; b. San Francisco, June 3, 1944; s. Glenn W. and Ruth E. (Robinson) S.; B.A., Am. U. Beirut, 1966; M.B.A., U. Oreg., 1970; m. Tahere Abharroudi, Feb. 8, 1969; children—John Philip, James Joseph. Sr. auditor Price Waterhouse & Co., San Jose, Calif., 1971-74; asst. controller Triad Holding Corp., Beirut, 1974-75; chief fin. officer Triad Internat. Mktg. Group, London and Paris, 1976-81; internat. fin. cons., San Francisco, 1981—; underwriting mem. Lloyds of London, 1981—. C.P.A., Calif. Mem. Am. Inst. C.P.A.s, Calif. Soc. C.P.A.s. Home: 25 Van Tassel Lane Orinda CA 94563

STUDDERT, STEPHEN MARK, special assistant to President of U.S.; b. Petaluma, Calif., Nov. 17, 1948; B.A., Brigham Young U., 1970; m. Bonnie Jane Beck, June 1, 1968; children—Mark Andrew, Christopher Wayne, Stephanie, David Jay, Allyson, Michael. With Idaho State Police, Boise, 1969-71; coordinator of police planning State of Utah, 1971-74; chief police, Brigham City, Utah, 1974-75; staff asst. to the Pres., White House, Washington, 1975-77; v.p., dir. Maple Hills, Inc., Bountiful, Utah, 1977-80; dep. press sec., dir. press advance Office of Ronald Reagan, Washington, 1980-81; spl. asst. to Pres., dir. Presdl. Advance, The White House, 1981—; dir. Gov.'s Police Standards Task Force, Utah, 1973; instr. Weber State Coll., 1973-75. Mem. City Council, Bountiful, 1979-80; mem. nat. adv. council Internat. Native Am. Devel. Found., 1974-76; mem. adv. com. N.G., 1975; mem. police sci. adv. com. Weber State Coll., 1974-76; chmn. Utah Public Safety Retirement Study Com., 1975; mem. Brigham City Airport Planning Com., 1974-75; active Boy Scouts Am.; polit. cons. U.S. Sen. Robert Dole, 1976, 78, Rep. James Hansen, 1980; bishopric Bountiful Utah East Stake, Ch. Jesus Christ of Latter-day Saints, 1977-80, dir. mission public communications, 1977. Republican. Clubs: Jaycees (pres.), Kiwanis. Home: 10204 Country View Ct Vienna VA 22180 also Bountiful UT

STUDENMUND, ARNOLD HARWOOD, economist, educator; b. Cooperstown, N.Y., Oct. 6, 1944; s. Walter Russell and Elizabeth Potter (Harwood) S.; m. Jaynie Kay Miller, July 12, 1980. A.B., Hamilton Coll., 1966; M.A., Cornell U., 1969, Ph.D., 1970. Asst. prof. econs. Occidental Coll., Los Angeles, 1970-74, asso. prof., 1975-82, Richard W. Millar prof. econs. and fin., 1983—, chmn. dept. econs., 1975-80; sr. economist Free Transit Expt., Transp. Systems Center, Cambridge, Mass., 1977-79; cons. in field; research coordinator So. Calif. Research Council, 1979—. NDEA fellow, 1967-69; Center Advanced Study of Behavioral Scis. fellow, summer 1977; Dept. Transp. grantee, 1979-80; Urban Mass Transp. Adminstrn. grantee, 1979-80. Mem. Am. Econ. Assn., Western Econ. Assn., So. Calif. Econs. Assn. (past pres.), Cornell Econs. Assn. (past pres.), Phi Beta Kappa. Author: (with James Gwartney and Richard Stroup) Coursebook for Economics, 3d edit., 1983; contbr. articles to profl. jours. Home: 823 Milmada Dr La Canada CA 91011 Office: 1600 Campus Rd Los Angeles CA 90041

STUDER, CONSTANCE ELAINE, nurse; b. Lodi, Ohio, Dec. 4, 1942; d. Lucien Kellogg and Evelyn Lois (Motter) Adams; m. Kenneth Eugene Studer, Aug. 17, 1963 (div.); 1 son: Christopher Eugene. R.N., Toledo Hosp. Sch. Nursing, 1963; B.A. in English Lit., Ill. Coll., Jacksonville, 1971; M.A. in English Lit., U. Colo., 1980. R.N., Colo. Nurse, Chestnut Hill Hosp., Phila., 1963-65, Luthersche Deakonessen Inrichting, Amsterdam, The Netherlands, 1967; nurse ICU-CCU Boulder (Colo.) Community Hosp., 1973—, p.m. clin. supr., 1980—; instr. creative writing Colo. U. Ctr. Life-Long Learning, Boulder, 1978-80; instr. creative writing YWCA, Boulder; owner Wing Communications, Boulder. Recipient Mary Wade Seybold prize in English Lit., Ill. Coll., 1970-71; 1st pl. winner Ann Woodbury Hafen Meml. Contest, Poetry Soc. Colo., 1977. Mem. Nat. Assn. Female Execs., Internat. Women's Writing Guild, Nat. Writers Club. Author, contbr. numerous poems to mags., books; translater Dutch to English; contbr. articles to profl. jours. Home: 4518 Aberdeen Pl Boulder CO 80301

STUDLEY, HELEN ORMSON, artist, poet, writer, designer; b. Elroy, Wis., Sept. 8, 1937; d. Clarence Ormson and Hilda (Johnson) O.; m. William Frank Studley, Aug. 1965 (div.); 1 son, William Harrison. Owner RJK Original Art, Sherman Oaks, Calif., 1979—; designer Aspen Series custom greeting cards and stationery notes, lithographs Love is All Colors, 1982; represented in numerous pub. and pvt. collections throughout U.S., Can., Norway, Sweden, Austria, Germany, Eng., France. Mem. Soc. Illustrators, Am. Watercolor Soc., Internat. Soc. Artists, Calif. Woman's Art Guild. Club: Sons of Norway. Office: RJK Original Art 5020 Hazeltine Ave Sherman Oaks CA 91423

STUDY, DONALD GEORGE, safety engineer; b. Walla Walla, Wash., Dec. 6, 1946; s. Fred Mason and Ethel (Thomas) S.; m. Betty Jane Thomas, July 31, 1971. Student in mktg./mgmt. Blue Mountain Community Coll., 1974; student in bus. adminstrn. U. Idaho, 1976. Cert. emergency med. technician. Owner, operator Chalet Inn bar and restaurant, 1980; field nurse Bechtel Power, Boardman (Oreg.) project, 1980; safety asst. Tonopah project, 1980; safety engr., Chino project, 1981-82, San Onofre Project, 1983—. Mem. Grant County Search and Rescue. Served with U.S. Army, 1963-71. Decorated Vietnamese Cross of Gallantry, Air medal with 9 clusters, Vietnam Service medal. Named to Warrant Officer Hall of Fame, Ft. Rucker, Ala., 1968. Mem. Am. Soc. Safety Engrs. Clubs: Elks. Office: PO Box 450 San Clemente CA 92672

STUECKLE, ARNOLD F., educator, consultant; b. Lacrosse, Wash., Feb. 22, 1933; s. Fred and Emma (Sauer) S.; m. Diane Lynn Marie Banks, children—Todd Alan, Matthew Scott, Kelli Lynn. B.A., Whitworth Coll., 1955, M.A., 1962; Ed.D., U. Idaho, 1968. Tchr., coach Moseslake, Wash., 1955-56, 57-59, tchr. and coach, 1959-60, Cle Elum, Wash., 1960-61; alumni dir., placement dir., assoc. dir. admissions Whitworth Coll., Spokane, Wash., 1962-66; prof. edn. Eastern Wash. U., Cheney, 1968—. Pres. Coll. Regional Ministries, 1973—; active Div. Higher Edn., N.W./Alaska Synod-Presbyn., 1978—. Served with USN, 1956-57. Mem. NEA, Wash. Edn. Assn., Assn. Tchr. Educators, Assn. Supervision and Curriculum Dirs., Nat. Assn. Sports Officiating, Phi Delta Kappa. Author: Conceptual Planning with Behavioral Objectives, 1969, 71; Planning for Creative Learning, 1976, 81, 83. Home: 3003 W 21st Spokane WA 99204 Office: Edn Dept Eastern Wash U Cheney WA 99004

STUECKLE, DONALD NORMAN, interior designer; b. Whitman County, Wash., Oct. 6, 1929; s. Arthur and Mary (Walters) S.; m. Wilma Merle Divine, Apr. 24, 1954; children—Shannon, Tamera, Megan. B.A., Wash. State U., 1952. Interior designer Barclay Brown Co., Spokane, Wash., 1952-55; ptnr. Larson & Assocs., Spokane, 1955-59; interior designer Paul Schatz Co., Portland, Oreg., 1959-63, Velte Home Furnishings Co., Vancouver, Wash., 1963-66; co-owner, mgr. Designed Interiors, Inc., Portland, 1966-82; ptnr. New Market South Partnership, 1982—; instr. Mt. Hood Community Coll., 1972-73. Arbitrator Am. Arbitration Assn., 1978, pres. Skidmore Fountain Village Assn., 1975; chmn. bd. Community Design Ctr., 1977; mem. Portland Hist. Landmark Commn., 1976-82; bd. dirs. Portland Beautification Assn., 1970-82. Named Disting. Alumnus, Wash. State U., 1978; recipient Urban Devel. Action Grant Excellence award, 1981. Mem. Am. Soc. Interior Designers (dir. Oreg. chpt. 1960-83, pres. chpt. 1962-63, 1978-79, v.p. No. Pacific region 1982-83, nat. bd. dirs. 1981-84), outstanding contbr. in community service award 1974, presdl. citation 1974), Council Continuing Edn. Republican. Office: 79 SW First St Portland OR 97204

STULP, PATTY SUE, marketing executive; b. Yuma, Colo., May 1, 1953; d. John Revelle and Nina Elaine (Dunafon) Stulp. Student Colo. State U., 1972-74. Farmer, rancher, Yuma, 1974-79; dir. Am. Agr. Found., Denver, 1979-82; mktg. dir. Ethanol Mktg. Co., Denver, 1982—. Mem. alcohol fuel adv. bd. U.S. Dept. Energy, 1981; mem. farm women group U.S. Dept. Agr., 1980; mem. research adv. bd. Colo. State U., 1982; spokesman Nat. Young Farmers Am., 1980, Colo. Young Farmers Assn., 1980. Mem. Colo. Alcohol Fuel Producers (sec.), Nat. Assn. Female Execs., Nat. Fedn. Republ. Women. Methodist. Developer fuel alcohol plant lab. manual. Office: 2044 Lake Ave Pueblo CO 81004

STUMP, BOB, congressman; b. Phoenix, Apr. 4, 1927; s. Jesse Patrick and Floy Bethany (Fields) S.; B.S. in Agronomy, Ariz. State U., 1951; children—Karen, Bob, Bruce. Cotton farmer; mem. Ariz. Ho. of Reps., 1959-67, mem. Ariz. Senate. 1967-76, pres. Ariz. Senate, 1975-76; mem. 95th-98th Congress from 3d Dist. Ariz. Served with USNR, 1943-46. Mem. Ariz. Farm Bur., Ariz. Legion. Republican. Seventh-Day Adventist. Office: 211 Cannon Office Bldg US House Representatives Washington DC 20515*

STUMP, WAYNE HOWARD, state senator, chiropractor; b. Elkhart, Ind., Dec. 28, 1935; s. Howard W. and Ethel M. (Keck) S.; m. Kathleen V. Hunter, June 10, 1959; children—Mark W., Beth K. D. of Chiropractic, Lincoln Chiropractic Coll., 1961. Pvt. practice chiropractor, Phoenix, 1962—; mem. Ariz. Senate, 1978-80, 82—. Served with USAF, 1954-57. Mem. World-Wide Christian Chiropractors Assn. Republican. Office: 5831 N 23d Ave Phoenix AZ 85015

STURDEVANT, BRUCE LAYTON, mech. engr.; b. What Cheer, Ia., Dec. 5, 1922; s. Louis A. and Ethel (Phillips) S.; B.S., U. Ia., 1948; m. Helen L. Clevenger, Apr. 17, 1943; children—Celeste, Christine, Constell. With Stanley Engring. Co., Muscatine, 1948-69, successively engr.-in-tng., design engr., asst. chief coordinating engr., chief coordinating engr., asst. chief mech. engr., head mech. dept., head power dept., head design group, head indsl. dept., 1948-65, head power and indsl. group, v.p., 1965-66, head power group, 1966-69; dir. Stanley Consultants, Inc., 1966-69; asst. mgr. Central Design Office, R.W. Beck & Assos., Denver, 1969-70, asso., asst. mgr., 1970-71, partner, asst. mgr., 1971-76, partner, mgr., 1976—, mem. exec. com., 1978—. Chmn. budget and admissions com. United Fund, 1963, 64, pres., 1966, 67, bd. dirs.; mem. adv. com. tech. curriculum devel. Muscatine Community Coll., 1962; v.p., dir. Ia. Children's and Family Services. Bd. dirs. Douglas County Sch. Dist., 1975, 78. Trustee Hillcrest Services to Children and Youth. Served from cadet to 2d lt. USAAC, 1943-46. Registered profl. engr., Colo. Mem. Nat. Rifle Assn. (life), Am. Mgmt. Assn., ASME, Nat. Soc. Profl. Engrs., ASTM, Iowa Engring. Soc. (chmn. constrn.-industry relations com. 1963, 64). Methodist (lay del. to ann. conf. 1956-69, chmn. adminstrv. bd. 1971, 73, chmn. pastor parish relations 1974, 75, chmn. fin. com. 1979, 80). Mason. Author articles in field. Home: 505 Wrangler Rd NEDC Castle Rock CO 80104 Office: RW Beck & Assos 660 Bannock Denver CO 80204

STURGULEWSKI, ARLISS, state senator; b. Blaine, Wash., Sept. 27, 1927; B.A., U. Wash. Mem. Assembly Municipality of Anchorage; vice chmn. New Capital Site Planning Commn., mem. Capital Site Selection Com.; chmn. Greater Anchorage Area Planning and Zoning Commn.; mem. Alaska State Senate, 1978—; dir. Denali Drilling, Inc., Alaska Pacific Bancorp. Mem. Alaska Mcpl. League (chmn. legis. com.). Home: Pouch V Juneau AK 99811

STUTTS, ELBERT HARRISON, financial consultant, educator; s. Royal Armstead and Sallie Ann (Buie) S.; m. Evelyn Ruth Bailey, Jan. 3, 1947; 1 dau., Sharon Kay Stutts Carlson. M.A. in Edn., St. Andrews Coll., 1968; M.A. in Fin. Devel., Am. Coll. Fin., Sunnyvale, Calif., 1982. Served in U.S. Navy, 1944-50, U.S. Army, 1950-55; dir. Army Armor Sch., Red Springs, N.C., 1950-57; with nat. council Boy Scouts Am., Dallas, 1972-77, dir. fin., Sunnyvale, Calif., 1978—; assoc. regional dir., pres. Am. Coll. Fin., Sunnyvale, 1981—; founder, dir. Western Fin. Inst. Mem. Am. Soc. Tng. and Devel., Nat. Soc. Fund Raising Execs., Pvt. Univ. and Coll. Adminstrs. Calif. Author: Approved Fin. Devel. Program for Non-Profit Orgns. Office: Boy Scouts America 185 N Wolfe Rd Sunnyvale CA 94088

STUTZMAN, THOMAS CHASE, lawyer; b. Portland, Oreg., Aug. 1, 1950; s. Leon H. and Mary L. (Chase) S.; B.S. with high honors, U. Calif., Santa Barbara, 1972; J.D. cum laude, Santa Clara U., 1975; m. Wendy Jeanne Craig, June 6, 1976; children: Sarah Ann, Thomas Chase. Bar: Calif. 1976; individual practice law, San Jose, Calif., 1976-79; pres., sec., chief fin. officer Thomas Chase Stutzman, P.C., San Jose, 1979—; legal counsel, asst. sec. Robt. A. Greenley, O.D. and Charles P. Wolf, O.D., Inc., 1978—, Leon H. Stutzman & Assos. Phys. Therapy, Inc., 1978—; legal counsel, asst. sec. Dandridge Constrn. Co., Eilmar Corp., CDM Systems, Inc., others. instr. San Jose State U., 1977-78. Bd. dirs. Santa Cruz Campfire, 1978-80, Happy Hollow Park, 1978-80, 83—. Mem. Calif. Bar Assn., Santa Clara County Bar Assn. (chmn. environ. law com. 1976-78), San Jose Jaycees (Dir. of the Year 1976-77), Phi Beta Kappa. Congregationalist. Clubs: Lions (dir. 1979-81, 2d v.p. 1982-83, 1st v.p. 1983-84), Masons, Scottish Rite. Office: 102 Park Center Plaza San Jose CA 95113

STYLES, MARVALENE HUGHES, univ. adminstr.; b. Eutaw, Ala.; d. Judge and Alberta (Hall) Hughes; student Columbia U., 1964-65; Ph.D., Fla. State U., 1969; postgrad. Harvard U., 1969, 79; m. David J. Brinks, Aug. 29, 1974; 1 son, Jan C. Counselor, prof. St. Petersburg Jr. Coll., 1962; dir. counseling 16th St. Sch., 1963-64; research asst. N.Y. Med. Coll., 1964-65; dir. edn. Job Corps Center for Women, 1965-67; residence hall dir./counselor Fla. State U., Tallahassee, 1967-69; vis. prof. Fla. A. and M. U., Tallahassee, 1968-69; dir. counseling and career devel. Eckerd Coll., St. Petersburg, Fla., 1970-72; prof., counselor San Diego State U., 1972-77, dir. counseling services, career devel., student employment and placement, 1977—; prof. Calif. Sch. Profl. Psychology, San Diego, 1974-77. Chmn. evaluation com. San Diego County Sch. Desegration Plan, 1980—; chmn. Pres. Affirmative Action Adv. Com., San Diego State U., 1975-80; mem. adv. com. Displaced Homemakers, 1979—; mem. adv. com. for mayor, St. Petersburg, Fla., 1970-71. Mem. Am. Coll. Personnel Assn. (senator, Outstanding Service award 1979), Am. Personnel and Guidance Assn. (senator), Calif. Coll. Personnel

Assn., Orgn. Counseling Center Dirs. in Higher Edn. (chairperson 1980-81), Western Coll. Placement Assn., Phi Kappa Phi, Delta Sigma Theta. Democrat. Home: 2111 Del Mar Heights Rd Del Mar CA 92014 Office: HA 860 San Diego State U San Diego CA 92182

STYPULA, EDWARD W., electronics company executive; b. Walla Walla, Wash., Jan. 3, 1948; s. William J. and Marie Alice (Wallace) S.; m. Patricia Jean Young, June 5, 1973; children—William J. II, Alice Marie. B.S. in Elec. Engring., U. Wash., 1972, M.S. in Elec. Engring., 1975. Elec. engr. Blankenshire Mfg. Co., Tacoma, 1975-76, Foster Engring. Co., Tacoma, 1976-78; head elec. engring. dept. Gordon's Best Products, Seattle, 1978-81; supr. elec. engring. dept. Werik Electronics Co., Spokane, Wash., 1981—. Troop leader Boy Scouts Am., Spokane. Served with USAF, 1972-73. Mem. IEEE, Am. Physics Assn., Electronics Mfrs. Assn. Wash., Beta Theta Pi. Republican. Lutheran. Club: Tacoma Luncheon. Lodges: Masons, Shriners, Rotary. Office: S 209 Washington St Spokane WA 99204

STYSKAL-O'KEEFE, LUKI, financial consulting firm executive; b. Los Angeles, June 7, 1937; d. Ladislav Jakup and Lucia Marie (Matulich) Styskal; children by previous marriage—Thomas Lad, Jerome David, Tricia Marie. B.S. in Mktg., Loyola-Marymount U., Los Angeles, 1959. Registered securities prin. Nat. Assn. Securities Dealers. Vice pres. mktg. Burlingame Mortgage Investors, Tustin, Calif., 1980-83; pres. Investors Equity Council, Inc., Tustin, 1983—; dir. San Clemente (Calif.) Sav. & Loan, 1978—. Pres. Children's Home Soc., San Clemente, 1972-74; chmn. Council Mem. Election Com., San Clemente, 1966-78; chmn. pro-tem Orange County Grand Jury, 1978-79. Mem. Western Pension Conf., Internat. Assn. Fin. Planners. Office: Investors Equity Council Inc 2600 Walnut Suite E Tustin CA 92680

SUAREZ, NICHOLAS GUNDRAN, architect, constrn. co. exec.; b. Solano, Nueva Vizcaya, Philippines, Dec. 6, 1937; came to U.S., 1968, naturalized, 1973; s. Edilberto Salamanca and Maxima Gundran S.; B.S. in Arch., U. Santo Tomas, 1960; m. Lilia Obon Crisologo, Jan. 28, 1961; children—Marites, Marilou, Nicholas, Edwin. Pvt. practice architecture, Manila, 1964-66; architect Govt. of Ghana, Accra, 1966-68; sr. designer Warnecke & Assos., San Francisco, 1968-75; sr. designer, project mgr. Ditz-Crane, Santa Clara, Calif., 1975-78; owner, mgr. Suarez & Sons Constrn. Co., San Jose, Calif., 1978—. Mem. AIA, Philippine Profl. and Bus. Soc. Santa Clara County, Philippine-Am. Soc. Architects and Engrs., Filipino Community of Santa Clara County (dir. 1978). Democrat. Filipino Cursillo. Lions. Home: 2874 Sweetleaf Ct San Jose CA 95148 Office: 2170 Scott St San Jose CA 95132

SUCHIN, MILTON BERNARD, producer, personal manager; b. Bklyn., Feb. 19, 1944; s. Martin and Gizela (Mermelstein) S.; m. Vicki L. Rosenberg, June 14, 1981. B.S., L.I. U., 1971. Pub. relations cons., N.Y.C., 1967-70; pres. The Moss and Suchin Corp., 1979-81; sr. talent agt. Internat. Creative Mgmt., N.Y.C. and Los Angeles; guest lectr. UCLA, Beverly Hills Law Symposium on Music and Entertainment Bus.; producer Gov. William Clement's fund raiser, Dallas, 1981, Most Watchable Man TV show for Metromedia TV, 1983; co-producer Calif. Celebrity 500 Auto Race, Labor Day weekend, 1979, Am. Cancer Research Ctr. show, 1981, Human Dolphin Found. show, San Francisco, 1981, An Evening with Sammy Davis, Jr. for Temple Emet, Los Angeles; talent cons. celebrity div. Cerebral Palsy Assn. Fund raiser Actor's Temple N.Y.C.; mem. entertainment com. 3d ann. Los Angeles Street Scene Festival, 1980; mem. allocations com. Permanent Charities Orgn. Served with USN, 1963-66. Recipient cert. of appreciation Mayor of Los Angeles. Mem. Conf. Personal Mgrs. (exec. com., legis. and grievance com.), Acad. TV Arts and Scis., Hon. Order Ky. Colonels. Club: Friars (N.Y.C.). Lodge: B'nai B'rith (v.p. performing Arts lodge N.Y.C., cert. of appreciation Dist. 1). Office: Milton B Suchin Co 9220 Sunset Blvd Suite 306 Los Angeles CA 90069

SUDLER, BARBARA WELCH, historical society executive; b. Honolulu, Apr. 20, 1925; d. Leo F. and Barbara (Petrikin) Welch; B.A., U. Colo., 1944; m. James Stewart Sudler, Dec. 30, 1950 (dec. 1982); children—Eleanor, James. Book critic The Denver Post, 1955-75; exec. adminstr. Historic Denver, 1971-79; asso. dir. Colo. Hist. Soc., Denver, 1979-81, pres., 1981—; coordinator Colo. Adv. Commn. for Nat. Hist. Publs. and Records. Dir., Women's Bank. Recipient Soroptimist Internat. award for contbns. to women; Big Sisters award, 1981. Mem. Denver Woman's Press, Women's Forum. Editor: Nothing is Long Ago, 1976. Office: 1300 Broadway Denver CO 80203

SUEOKA, SARAH SAKAE, school principal; b. Punaluu, Oahu, Hawaii, Mar. 3, 1925; d. Jinhichi and Aki (Tanimoto) Kaya; m. Ken K. Sueoka, Dec. 21, 1946 (div.); children—Steven K., Carlton S., Sandra J. B.A., U. Hawaii, 1950. Elem. tchr. Hawaii Dept. Edn., 1951-53, 57-65, supr. beginning tchrs., 1965-71, ednl. specialist Kamehameha Schs., 1971-79, prin. Kamehameha Early Edn. Program, 1979—. Mem. Assn. Supervision and Curriculum Devel., Internat. Reading Assn., Nat. Council Tchrs. Math., Delta Kappa Gamma Soc. Internat., Nat. Rifle Assn. Home: 3540 Nuuanu Pali Dr Honolulu HI 96817 Office: Kamehameha Schs 1850 Makuakane St Honolulu HI 96817

SUGARMAN, ALAN STEPHEN, psychologist, educator; b. Detroit, July 17, 1947; s. George Joseph and Esther (Golden) S.; m. Julie Diane Cooper, July 1, 1973; 1 son, Eli Cooper. Student U. Mich., 1965-67; B.A., Wayne State U., 1969; Ph.D., U. Tenn., 1974. Lic. psychologist Conn., Calif. Staff psychologist Yale Psychiat. Inst., 1976-77, acting dir. psychology, 1977-81; asst. prof. psychology Yale U., 1976-81; assoc. prof., dir. core curriculum Calif. Sch. Profl. Psychology, San Diego, 1981—; asst. clin. prof. psychiatry U. Calif., San Diego, 1981—. Menninger Found. postdoctoral fellow, 1974-76. Mem. Am. Psychol. Assn., Soc. Personality Assessment, Psychologists Interested in Study Psychoanalysis, Am. Psychoanalytic Assn., Phi Beta Kappa, Psi Chi. Jewish. Contbr. numerous articles to profl. jours. Home: 310 W Eastridge Ln Escondido CA 92026 Office: 737 Pearl St Suite 206 La Jolla CA 92037 also 925 E Pennsylvania St Suite 1A Escondido CA 92025

SUGERMAN, LEONARD RICHARD, university administrator; b. N.Y.C., June 24, 1920; s. Matthew and Gertrude Sugerman; m. Lois Irene Peterson, Nov. 12, 1940; 4 children. B.S., MIT, 1955; M.B.A., U. Chgo., 1960; postgrad. Indsl. Coll. Armed Forces, 1962, Air War Coll., 1966. Enlisted U.S. Air Force, 1942, commd. officer and advanced to col., 1968; supr. bomb-navigation br., dept. armament tng. Lowry AFB, Colo., 1950-53, air staff officer Office Dept. Chief Staff Devel., Hdqrs. USAF, Pentagon, Washington, 1955-59, research and devel. staff officer Hdqrs. Systems Command, Andrews AFB, 1960-62, hdqrs. research and tech. div., Bolling AFB, 1962-64, exec. officer central inertial guidance test facility, missile devel. center, Holloman AFB, 1964-68, chief Athena Test Field Office, Ballistic Reentry Systems Program, 1968-70, dep. to comdr. White Sands Missile Range, chief Air Force Range Ops. Office, 1970-72, dep. chief staff plans and requirements Air Force Spl. Weapons Center, Kirtland AFB, Albuquerque, 1972-75; ret., 1975; asst. to dir. resource mgmt. Phys. Sci. Lab., N.Mex. State U., Las Cruces, 1975—. Decorated Legion of Merit. Recipient Air Force Assn.-Air Force Systems Command Meritorious Mgmt. award, 1967. Mem. Am. Def. Preparedness Assn., Am. Inst. Navigation (pres. 1970-71, Norman P. Hays award 1972), AIAA. Home: 3025 Fairway Dr Las Cruces NM 88001 Office: PO Box 3548 Las Cruces NM 88003

SUGIKI, SHIGEMI, physician; b. Wailuku, Hawaii, May 12, 1936; s. Sentaro and Kameno (Matoba) S.; A.B., Washington U., St. Louis, 1957, M.D., 1961; m. Bernice T. Murakami, Dec. 28, 1958; children—Kevin S., Boyd R. Intern St. Luke's Hosp., St. Louis, 1961-62, resident ophthalmology, 1962-65; chmn. dept. ophthalmology Straub Clinic, Honolulu, 1965-70; chmn. dept. opthalmology Queen's Med. Center, Honolulu, 1970-73, 80-83; asso. clin. prof. ophthalmology Sch. Medicine, U. Hawaii, 1973—. Served to maj. M.C., AUS, 1968-70. Decorated Hawaiian NG Commendation medal, 1968. Fellow ACS; mem. Am., Hawaii med. assns., Honolulu County Med. Soc., Am. Acad. Ophthalmology, Soc. Mil. Opthalmologists, Contact Lens Assn. Opthalmologists, Soc. Eye Surgeons, Pacific Coast Oto-Ophthal. Soc., Am. Intra-Ocular Implant Soc., Pan-Pacific Surg. Assn., Am. Soc. Contemporary Ophthalmology, Washington U. Eye Alumni Assn., Hawaii Ophthal. Soc., Research To Prevent Blindness, Keratorefractive Soc. Home: 2398 Aina Lani Pl Honolulu HI 96822 Office: 1380 Lusitana St Suite 508 Honolulu HI 96813

SUINN, RICHARD M(ICHAEL), psychologist, educator; b. Honolulu, May 8, 1933; s. Maurice and Edith (Wong) S.; m. Grace D. Toy, July 26, 1958; children—Susan, Randall, Staci, Bradley. B.A. summa cum laude, Ohio State U., 1955; Ph.D., Stanford U., 1959. Lic. psychologist, Colo. Counselor, Stanford U. Counseling Center, 1958-59, research asso. Med. Sch., 1964-66; asst. prof. Whitman Coll., 1959-64; asso. prof. psychology U. Hawaii, 1966-68; prof. Colo. State U., 1968—, head dept. psychology, 1972—; cons. Olympic Games, 1976, 80, mem. sports adv. com. U.S. Olympic Com., 1982—. Mem. Colo. Gov.'s Mental Health Council, 1982; mem. city council City of Ft. Collins, 1975-79, mayor, 1978-79. Fellow Am. Psychol. Assn. (chmn. bd. ethnic minority affairs); mem. Assn. Advancement Psychology (trustee 1983—), Asian Am. Psychol. Assn. (dir. 1983—). Author 5 books, including: Fundamentals of Behavior Pathology; Psychology in Sports; contbr. numerous articles to profl. jours. Office: Dept Psychology Colo State U Fort Collins CO 80023

SUKONECK, HARRIET, psychologist, computer scientist; b. Newark, Jan. 30, 1945; d. Edward and Mae S.; B.A., Rutgers U., 1966; M.A., U. So. Calif., 1968, Ph.D. (NIMH fellow), 1971. NIMH clin. postdoctoral fellow, div. psychiatry Children's Hosp. of Los Angeles, 1971-73; lectr. Calif. State U., Los Angeles, 1971-76; core faculty research series Calif. Sch. Profl. Psychology, Los Angeles, 1973-78, clin. psychologist in pvt. practice, Santa Monica, Calif., 1973-78; vis. asst. prof. Loyola Marymount U., Los Angeles, 1976-78; research assoc. Neuropsychiat. Inst., UCLA, 1978-79, adminstrv. analyst office of vice chancellor UCLA, 1979; sr. mem. tech. staff, project leader Computer Scis. Corp., El Segundo, Calif., 1979-81; systems cons./project adminstr. First Interstate Services Co., El Segundo, Calif., 1981-83; dir. research and product planning Data Line Service Co., 1983—. Lic. psychologist, Calif. Mem. Assn. Computing Machinery, Am. Psychol. Assn., AAAS. Contbr. articles to profl. jours. Editor et. al, social sci. jour., 1971-76. Office: 885 S Village Oaks Dr Covina CA 91724

SUKUT, DARWIN LEE, city official, bridgetender; b. Fredonia, N.D., Oct. 25, 1941; s. Gustav and Pearl Emma (Templein) S.; m. Margie Lynn Dunn, Nov. 3, 1974; children—Gordon Lee, Sybil Anne, Margie Eileen. Student Shoreline Community Coll., 1966-69, U. Wash., 1969-76. Asst. dock agt. Matson Navigation Co., Seattle, 1963-64; sta. agt. W. Coast Airlines Co., Seattle, 1965; design, liaison engr. Boeing Co., Seattle, 1966-71; bridgetender city of Seattle, 1971—. Mayor City of Snoqualmie 1982—, councilman, 1978-82; mem. Puget Sound Council Govts., 1978—; chmn. SnoValley Juvenile Ct. Conf. Com., 1979—. Served with USMC, 1959-63. Mem. Bridgetenders Assn. (treas.). Clubs: Rotary, Snoqualmie. Home: Route 1 Box 46 Snoqualmie WA 98065 Office: PO Box 337 Snoqualmie WA 98065

SULLIVAN, DENNIS MICHAEL, lawyer; b. San Francisco, Jan. 6, 1945; s. Albert Gifford and Eileen Winona (Ganshirt) S.; B.S.C., U. Santa Clara, 1966; postgrad. Internat. Sch. Law, The Hague, Netherlands, 1967, J.D. (Dean Snodgrass scholar), Hastings Coll. Law, U. Calif., San Francisco, 1969; m. Evie Ellen Rankin, Oct. 26, 1971; children—Dennis, Ethan, Jennifer, Meghan, Patrick. Bar: Calif. 1970, U.S. Supreme Ct. 1978. Sr. acct. Boitano & Sargent, Santa Clara, Calif., 1963-66; dep. dist. atty. Alameda County (Calif.), 1971-74; ptnr. Sullivan Nakahara DuBois Hove, Oakland, Calif., 1974-80; individual practice law, Oakland, 1980—; gen. counsel, dir., chief fin. officer various closely-held corps.; spl. cons. to Consulate Gen., Fed. Republic Germany, San Francisco; spl. counsel to Consulate Gen. of Switzerland, San Francisco; judge pro tem Oakland-Piedmont Mcpl. Ct., 1978—; ct. commr. pro tem dist. cts. Fed. Republic Germany; referee Calif. State Bar Ct., 1982—; ct. arbitrator Alameda County Superior Ct., 1982—; comml. arbitration panelist Am. Arbitration Assn., 1982—. Served with U.S. Army, 1970-71. Decorated Army Commendation medal. Recipient Editorial award Hastings Law Jour., 1968. Mem. Alameda County Bar Assn., Am. Bar Assn. (vice chmn. continuing legal edn. sub com., sect. on taxation), Order of Coif. Democrat. Roman Catholic. Editorial bd. Hastings Law Jour., 1968-69. Home: 9 Seaview Ave Piedmont CA 94611 Office: One Kaiser Plaza Suite 1115 Oakland CA 94612 also 810 Mills Bldg 220 Montgomery St San Francisco CA 94104

SULLIVAN, EDWARD ROBERT, mag. exec.; b. Chgo., Mar. 23, 1923; s. Edward Francis and Marie Elizabeth S.; B.A., St. Thomas Coll., Oak Park, Ill., 1950; Ph.B., St. Rose Coll., Dubuque, Iowa, 1954; postgrad. DePaul U., Chgo., 1956-57; m. Patricia Ann O'Leary, Feb. 18, 1972. Tchr., Fenwich High Sch., Oak Park, 1954-57; prof. St. Teresa Coll., Winona, Minn., 1956-61; with the Boeing Co., Seattle and Renton, Wash., 1958-69; creative dir. Gorin & Holmes Advt. & Public Relations, Seattle, 1969-70; v.p., officer Trans-West Co., Seattle, 1970-71; mgr., editor Seattle Bus. Mag., 1971—; lectr. in field. Mem. Am. Soc. Bus. Press Editors. Office: 1 Union Sq Suite 1200 6th and University Sts Seattle WA 98101

SULLIVAN, GERALD JAMES, ins. co. exec.; b. Olympia, Wash., Sept. 30, 1937; s. John F. and Elizabeth J. (Yater) S.; B.B.A., U. Wash., 1959; M.B.A., Wharton Sch. U. Pa., 1966; m. Martha A. Kuehlthau, June 12, 1959; children—Gerald James, Thomas, Katheleen, Shannon. Security analyst Hartford Ins. Group (Conn.), 1966-67; chief dep. ins. commr. State of Wash., Olympia, 1967-68; sec. John F. Sullivan Co., Seattle, 1968-71; pres. Walker Sullivan Co., Los Angeles, 1971-80, chmn., 1979; chmn. bd., pres. Gerald J. Sullivan & Assocs., Inc., ins. brokers, 1980—; mem. exec. com., chmn. security com. Calif. Surplus Lines Assns., San Francisco, 1974-80; mem. NAIC Industry Adv. Com. on Surplus Lines Laws and Reins. Served to capt. USAF, 1959-64. C.P.C.U., C.L.U. Roman Catholic. Clubs: Wilshire Country, Pauma Valley Country, Jonathan, Calif., Stock Exchange, K.C. Author: Trends in International Reinsurance Affecting American Reinsurers, 1966. Office: 800 W 6th St Los Angeles CA 90017

SULLIVAN, JERRY VERN, lawyer; b. Nampa, Idaho, Feb. 24, 1940; s. Robert Leslie and Myra Emma (Tiffany) S.; m. Beverly Briggs, Aug. 16, 1965; children—Angie, Tiffany, Diana. B.A., Brigham Young U., 1971; J.D., Southwestern U., Los Angeles, 1975. Bar: Nev. 1980. Electrician, 1962-64; lineman Calif. Pacific Utilities, 1964-68; prin. Sullivan Roofing, Nampa, 1975-80; dep. dist. atty. Pershing County (Nev.), 1983—; city atty. City of Lovelock (Nev.), 1983—. Counsel Democratic Central Com., Lovelock. Served with USMC, 1958-62. Mem. Nev. Bar Assn., C. of C. Democrat. Mormon. Home: PO Box 1198 Lovelock NV 89419

SULLIVAN, JOANN MARIE, safety engineer; b. Oakland, Calif., June 10, 1951; d. Bennett William and Barbara Jean (Johnson) Brown; m. Thomas Leo Sullivan, Aug. 19, 1972; children—Benjiman, Natalie. B.A. in Indsl. Edn., Ariz. State U., 1974, M.Tech., 1980. Tchr. indsl. arts Lafayette Elem. Sch., Phoenix, 1974-75, Chualar Sch. (Calif.), 1975-76; chef, mgr. Steinbeck House, Salinas, Calif., 1977-78; grad. asst. safety office Ariz. State U., Tempe, 1979-80; sr. loss control rep. Transamerica Ins. Services, Phoenix, 1980—. Sec., del.-at-large Ariz. Young Republican League, 1980, 81-82; sec. Dist. 30 Rep. Com., 1982-83, precinct capt., 1981, 82, 83. Recipient Outstanding Sr. award Ariz. State U. Coll. Edn., 1974; cert. of merit Ariz. Indsl. Arts Assn., 1975; Service award Ariz. Young Rep. League, 1982. Mem. Am. Indsl. Arts Assn., Ariz. Indsl. Arts Assn., AAUW, Am. Soc. Safety Engrs. (chmn. edn. com. 1982-83, treas. 1983-84). Roman Catholic. Office: 2141 E Highland St Phoenix AZ 85016

SULLIVAN, JOANN MARIE, medical technologist; b. Butte, Mont., May 31, 1938; d. Joseph D. and Ann E. (Melvin) Bracco; m. Thomas Roy Sullivan, Jan. 25, 1964; children—Michelle Ann, Renee Marie. B.S., Carroll Coll., 1960; grad., internship for medical tech. Sacred Heart Hosp., Spokane, Wash., 1960. Lic. med. technologist, Calif. Med. technologist, hematology U. Wash. Hosp., Seattle, 1960-63, Stanford U. Hosp., Palo Alto Calif., 1963-64; med. technologist, hematology supr. Guam Meml. Hosp., Tamuning, 1964-65; med. technologist Seventh-Day Adventist Clinic, Agana Heights, Guam, 1965-67; co-owner, med. technologist, dir. Physicians Diagnostic Lab., Tamuning, 1972—; mem. adv. council for med. technologist program U. Guam, 1975. Bd. dirs. Am. Cancer Soc., 1971-78, P.E.A.C.E. Found., 1975—; mem. Comprehensive Health Planning Bd., 1973-75; pres. Blood Exchange Bd., 1977-79. Mem. Am. Soc. Clin. Pathologists (affiliate; med. technologist), Am. Soc. Med. Technologists, Beta Sigma Phi. Roman Catholic. Home: PO Box 7 Agana GU 96910 Office: PO Box 8115 Tamuning GU 96911

SULLIVAN, JOHN CHARLES, newspaper publisher and editor; b. Spokane, Wash., Feb. 25, 1946; s. Dalton B. and Helen L. (Schnitzler) S. A.B., Stanford U., 1968; postgrad. U. Denver. Reporter, Bend (Oreg.) Bull., 1970-71, Longmont (Colo.) Daily Times-Call, 1971; mng. editor Livingston (Mont.) Enterprise, 1972-73, editor, 1974, pub., editor, 1975—; pres. Yellowstone Newspaper Group. Mem. Mont. Highway Commn., 1980—; bd. dirs. Buffalo Bill Hist. Ctr., Cody, Wyo. Roman Catholic. Club: Elks. Office: Livingston Enterprise PO Box 665 Livingston MT 59047

SULLIVAN, JOHN L., JR., corp. exec.; b. Macon, Ga.; A.B. in Econs., Duke U., 1950; M.B.A., U. Pa., 1957; grad. Advanced Mgmt. Program, Harvard Bus. Sch., 1975. Br. mgr. IBM, Phila., mgr. edn., Endicott, N.Y., asst. to pres. data processing div., White Plains, N.Y., dist. mgr., Washington, 1957-69; eastern regional mgr. Memorex Corp., Santa Clara, Calif., 1970-71; v.p. mktg. Infonet div. Computer Scis. Corp., El Segundo, Calif., 1971-75; exec. v.p. Fin. Services div. Automatic Data Processing, Inc., Clifton, N.J., 1975-77; asso. Heidrick and Struggles, San Francisco, 1977-79, v.p., 1979-80, v.p., mgr., Los Angeles, 1980-81, sr. v.p., dir., 1981—. Served as lt. (j.g.) USN, 1950-53. Office: 445 Figueroa St Suite 2330 Los Angeles CA 90071

SULLIVAN, JOHN PATRICK, graphic design executive; b. Youngstown, Ohio, Mar. 9, 1945; s. Thomas L. and Anne G. (Shaffee) S.; m. Kathy M. Hanlon, Dec. 28, 1968; 1 son, Joey Patrick. B.S., Ariz. State U., 1970. Art dir. Robert A. Mullen, Phoenix, 1971-76, Young & Rubicam West Advt., Phoenix, 1976-78; ptnr. Whittington & Sullivan Design Firm, Phoenix, 1978-80; owner, mgr. Jack Sullivan Design Group, Phoenix, 1980—. Served with USAF, 1964-68. Mem. Phoenix Art Dirs. Club, Communication Art Group. Democrat. Roman Catholic. Home: 712 W Palm Ln Phoenix AZ 85007 Office: Jack Sullivan Design Group 1320 N 7th Ave Phoenix AZ 85007

SULLIVAN, JOSEPH WILLIAM, psychologist; b. Balt., May 11, 1947; s. Joseph Patrick and Virginia Catherine (Lynch) S.; married Kathleen McCarthy, Nov. 24, 1971; children—Seamus Padraic, Teige Michael. B.A., U. Fla., Gainesville, 1971; M.A., U. Colo., 1976; Ph.D., U. Kans., Lawrence, 1980. Asst. prof. dept. psychiatry U. Colo. Health Scis. Center, Denver, 1980—; chief of research John F. Kennedy Child Devel. Center. Mem. edn. commn. Good Shepherd Catholic Sch. Nat. Inst. Child Health and Human Devel. grantee, 1982-84. Mem. Am. Psychol. Assn., Soc. Research in Child Devel. Roman Catholic. Home: 925 Saint Paul St Denver CO 80206 Office: U Colo Med Sch Box C-234 Denver CO 80262

SULLIVAN, MARK JAYE, urologist; b. Casper, Wyo., Mar. 23, 1946; s. Jaye Michael and Virginia Sullivan; B.A. cum laude, U. Calif., Riverside, 1968; M.D., U. Calif., Irvine, 1972; 1 child. Resident in urology U. Oreg., Portland, 1972-77; practice medicine, specializing in urology, Laguna Hills, Calif., 1977—; mem. staff Mission Community Hosp., Mission Viejo, Calif., Saddleback Hosp., Laguna Hills. Mem. AMA, Calif. Med. Assn., Orange County Urol. Soc. Contbr. articles to profl. jours. Address: 24953 Paseo De Valencia Suite 8C Laguna Hills CA 92653

SULLIVAN, MICHAEL EVAN, investment and management company executive; b. Phila., Dec. 30, 1940; s. Albert and Ruth (Liebert) S.; B.S., N.Mex. State U., 1966, M.A. (Ednl. Research Tng. Program fellow), 1967; B.S., U. Tex., 1969; M.B.A., U. Houston, 1974; M.S., U. So. Calif., 1976, M.P.A., 1977, Ph.D. in Adminstrn., 1983; B.S. in Acctg., U. La Verne, 1981. Sr. adminstrv. and tech. analyst Houston Lighting & Power Co., 1969-74; electronics engr. U.S. Govt., Point Mugu, Calif., 1974-77; mem. tech. staff Hughes Aircraft Co., El Segundo, Calif., 1977-78; staff program adminstr. Ventura div. Northrop Corp., Newbury Park, Calif., 1978-79; div. head engring. div. Navastrogru, Point Mugu, 1979—; pres., chmn. bd. Diversified Mgmt. Systems, Inc., Camarillo, Calif., 1978—. Served with U.S. Army, 1958-62. Ednl. Research Info. Clearing House fellow, 1965-67. Mem. Am. Math. Soc., Math. Assn. Am., Am. Statis. Assn., Am. Soc. Pub. Adminstrn., Am. Personnel and Guidance Assn., Fed. Mgrs. Assn., Am. Assn. Individual Investors, Mcpl. Mgmt. Assts. So. Calif., Assn. M.B.A. Execs., Phi Kappa Phi, Pi Gamma Mu. Home: PO Box 273 Port Hueneme CA 93041 Office: Navastrogru Co Point Mugu CA 93042

SULLIVAN, MICHAEL VERNON, librarian; b. Houston, Aug. 11, 1939; s. Vernon Lillard and Mable Ruth (White) S.; B.A., U. Calif., Berkeley, 1964; M.L.S., 1973; Ph.D., Stanford U., 1971; m. Barbara Magana, Feb. 29, 1964. Reference librarian U. Wash. Health Sci. Library, 1975-77; reference librarian Lane Med. Library, Stanford U., Palo Alto, Calif., 1977-79, head librarian Falconer Biology Library, 1979-81, Engring. Library, 1981—. NIMH fellow, 1972. Mem. Spl. Libraries Assn., Med. Library Assn., AAAS, Sigma Xi. Home: 638 Hamilton Palo Alto CA 94301 Office: Engring Library Stanford Univ Stanford CA 94305

SULLIVAN, PETER WILLIAM, ins. sales rep.; b. Townsend, Mont., May 11, 1935; s. L. Dan and Marie E. S.; A.B. in Bus., Carroll Coll., 1957; cert. Am. Inst. Banking, 1961; C.L.U., Am. Coll. Life Underwriters, 1973; m. Sheila M. Sullivan, Nov. 28, 1959; children—James R., Margaret M., ReNell P., Peter D., Shawn P., Erin A. With installment loan office 1st Nat. Bank of Helena (Mont.), 1959-63; sales rep. Northwestern Nat. Life Ins. Co., Helena, 1963—; dir. 1st Nat. Bank of Helena. Mem. Community Concert Bd., 1976. Mem. Am. Soc. C.L.U.'s, Life Underwriters Polit. Action Com., Mont. Assn. Life Underwriters (past pres., Agt. of Yr. 1973), Helena Assn. Life Underwriters (past pres.), Helena C. of C. (pres. 1979). Republican. Roman Catholic. Clubs: Mont., Met. Dinner.

SULLIVAN, RICHARD FREDERICK, chemist; b. Olathe, Colo., Dec. 26, 1929; s. Fred Grant and Laura Helen (Wolf) S.; B.A., U. Colo., 1951, Ph.D., 1956; m. Judith Jones, Mar. 23, 1968; children—Erin Colleen, Amy Patricia. Research chemist Chevron Research Co., Richmond, Calif., 1955-68, sr. research chemist, 1968-78, sr. research asso., 1978—. E. I. duPont de Nemours & Co. fellow, 1954-55. Mem. Am. Chem. Soc., Calif. Catalysis Soc., Am. Inst. Chem. Engrs. Author numerous publs. on catalytic upgrading of shale oil, coal liquids and petroleum; patentee in field. Home: 23 Upper Oak Dr San Rafael CA 94903 Office: Chevron Research Co Richmond CA 94802

SULLIVAN, RICHARD MICHAEL, JR., systems engineer; b. Worcester, Mass., Jan. 9, 1933; s. Richard Michael and Mary Frances (Fleming) S.; student U. Mass., 1951-52; B.S. in Naval Sci., U.S. Naval Postgrad. Sch., 1964; M.S. in Systems Mgmt., U. So. Calif., 1979; m. Claire Louise Nadean, Sept. 4, 1955 (dec. 1982); children—Richard, Mark, Paul, Mary, Thomas. Commd. ensign U.S. Navy, 1955, advanced through grades to lt. comdr., 1964; aircraft squadrons, 1955-61; USS Forrestal, 1964-66; in Vietnam, 1970; ret., 1974; project mgr. Systems Assos., Inc., San Diego, 1974-78; systems engr. Rohr Marine, Inc., Chula Vista, Calif., 1978-80; asst. adminstr. ops. Cabrillo Med. Ctr. San Diego, 1980-82; program mgr. J. Allan Flora & Assocs. Inc., San Diego, 1982—. Mem. Am. Inst. Indsl. Engrs., Republican. Roman Catholic. Home: 3261 Casa Bonita Dr Bonita CA 92002 Office: 591 Camino de la Reina San Diego CA 92108

SULLIVAN, ROBERT LEWIS, manufacturer's representative; b. Girard, Ohio, Aug. 28, 1928; s. John Joseph and Mary Maud (Jones) S.; student Kent (Ohio) State U., 1949; m. Lois Urban, July 8, 1950; children—Robert, Susan. Profl. prize fighter, 1949-50; sales mgr. Yukon Radio Supply Co. (Alaska), 1953-54; v.p. Willamette Radio Supply Co. (Oreg.), 1955-62; field engr. Ron Merritt Co., Wash., 1962-66; pres. Fleehart & Sullivan, Inc., Bothel, Wash., 1966—. Served with USAF, 1950-54. Mem. Electronics Reps. Assn., Nat. Audio Visual Assn., Soc. Broadcast Engrs. Republican. Roman Catholic. Home: 19925 13th Pl Bothel WA 98011 Office: 10109 Aurora Ave N Seattle WA 98133

SULLIVAN, STEPHEN JEROME, psychologist; b. Wilmington, N.C., Apr. 13, 1943; s. Jerome John and Ann (Holmes) S.; m. Carol Fischer, May 22, 1982. B.A., St. John's U., 1965; Ph.D., Catholic U. Am., 1970. Lic. psychologist, Oreg. Dir. Dept. Psychology Fairview Hosp. and Tng. Ctr., Salem, Oreg., 1971-74; pvt. practice clin. psychology, Salem, 1974—. Mem. Salem Airport Adv. Bd. Fellow John's Hopkins U. Sch. Medicine, Baltimore, 1970-71. Mem. Am. Psychol. Assn., Oreg. Psychol. Assn., Salem Area C. of C., Oreg. Pilots Assn. Office: 635 Church St NE Salem OR 97301

SULLIVAN, TIMOTHY REESE, broadcasting executive; b. Los Angeles, June 15, 1938; s. Charles Gardner and Ann Beatrice (May) S.; B.S., U. Ariz., 1961; M.B.A., Pepperdine U., 1978; m. Nancy Lee Robbins, July 6, 1967; children—Kelly Ann, John Casey. Vice-pres., West Coast mgr. Metro Radio Sales, Los Angeles, 1968-71; gen. sales mgr. Sta. KIAC, Los Angeles, 1971-72; v.p., dir. sales Metromedia Radio West Coast, 1972-73; v.p., gen. mgr. Sta. KNJ, Los Angeles, 1973-79; gen. mgr. Sta. KHTZ, 1978-80; v.p., gen. mgr. Sta. KMGG, Los Angeles, 1980—. Mem. radio adv. com. U. So. Calif.; mem. exec. bd. Los Angeles March of Dimes, treas., 1977-79; mem. exec. bd. Pacific Palisades YMCA, 1978. Served with USMC, 1961-65. Mem. Nat. Assn. Broadcasters, Nat. Radio Broadcasters Assn., So. Calif. Broadcasters Assn. (chmn. 1980-81), Sigma Alpha Epsilon. Republican. Presbyterian. Club: Los Angeles Country, Beach. Office: 6430 Sunset Blvd Los Angeles CA 90028

SUMA, JOHN TRYGUE, lawyer, educator; b. Glen Ellyn, Ill., Feb. 5, 1948; s. John and Ruth L. (Grundahl) S. B.A. cum laude, Augustana Coll., Rock Island, Ill., 1979; J.D. and M.A. in Econs., U. Ill., Urbana, 1973, Ph.D. in Econs., 1975. Bar: Ill. 1973, D.C. bar 1976. Trial atty. Antitrust div., Dept. Justice, Washington, 1975-79; asst. prof. law U. Denver, 1979-82, assoc. prof. law, 1982—. Served to capt. JAG Corps, USAF, 1970—. Mem. Ill. Law Forum (bd. editors 1972-73), ABA, Fed. Bar Assn., Am. Econ. Assn, Res. Officers Assn. Author: The Computer Industry, 1976. Home: 721 Lafayette St Denver CO 80218 Office: U Denver Coll Law 200 W 14th Ave Denver CO 80204

SUMIDA, GERALD AQUINAS, lawyer; b. Hilo, Hawaii, June 19, 1944; s. Sadamu and Kimiyo (Miyahara) S.; A.B. summa cum laude, Princeton U., 1966; cert. Woodrow Wilson Sch. of Public and Internat. Affairs, 1966; J.D., Yale U., 1969; m. Sylvia Whitehead, June 23, 1970. Research asso. Center of Internat. Studies, Princeton (N.J.) U., 1969; admitted to Hawaii bar, 1970, U.S. Dist. Ct. bar, 1970, U.S. Ct. Appeals for 9th Circuit bar, 1970, U.S. Supreme Ct. bar, 1981; assoc. firm Carlsmith, Carlsmith, Wichman and Case, Honolulu, 1970-76, ptnr. firm, 1976—; mem. Study Group on the Law of Armed Conflict and the Law of the Sea, Comdr.-in-Chief Pacific, USN, 1979—; mem. Hawaii Adv. Group, Law of Sea Inst., 1977—. Chmn., Hawaii State Commn. on the Year 2000, 1975-79; bd. govs., exec. v.p. Pacific and Asian Affairs Council of Hawaii, 1978-82, pres., 1982—, treas., 1977—; mem. exec. com. Honolulu Community Media Council, 1976—; bd. dirs. Hawaii Inst. Continuing Legal Edn., 1979—, v.p., 1978, pres., 1979—; mem. sci. and statis. com. Western Pacific Fishery Mgmt. Council, 1979—; bd. dirs. Hawaii Council on Legal Edn. for Youth, 1980—, pres., 1980—; chmn. internat. com. Hawaii chpt. ARC, 1983—; bd. dirs. Hawaii Imin Centennial Corp., 1983—, Hawaii Pub. Radio, Inc., 1983—. Recipient Gov.'s Cert. of Appreciation, 1979, Paul S. Bachman award Pacific and Asian Affairs Council of Hawaii, 1978; Japan Found. grantee, 1979. Mem. ABA (mem. internat. law, antitrust law and bus. law sections), Hawaii State Bar Assn. (sec. 1975, pres. Young Lawyers sect. 1974, editor Hawaii Bar News 1972-73), AAAS, Am. Judicature Soc., Am. Soc. Internat. Law, Hawaii Ocean Law Assn. (dir. 1978—, pres. 1978—), Japan-Hawaii Lawyers' Assn., Phi Beta Kappa. Democrat. Clubs: Colonial, Princeton; Yale (N.Y.C.); Plaza (Honolulu). Home: 1130 Wilder Ave Honolulu HI 96822 Office: Pacific Trade Center 190 S King St Suite 2200 Honolulu HI 96809

SUMMERS, FRANCES PHAYE, vocational rehabilitation consultant; b. Klamath Falls, Oreg., Apr. 15, 1938; d. Phayo Grindol and Frances Ruth (Henry) Pfefferle; m. C. Oakley Summers, Jr., Apr. 25, 1953 (div.); children—Katherine Summers Tucker, Anne, Donald O., Wayne P. Grad. in Social Work, Salvation Army Officers Tng. Coll., 1957; postgrad. U. Oreg., 1980-84. Cert. rehab. counselor, Oreg. Exec. dir. Salvation Army, Oreg., Ariz. and Calif., 1957-69, exec. sec. Salvation Army Employment Div., Flagstaff, Ariz., 1969-72, Medford, Oreg., 1975-76; with Workers Compensation Dept., Oreg. Employment Div., 1976-80, area supr., acting regional mgr., 1978-80; vocat. rehab. cons., Eugene, Oreg., 1980; regional mgr. Siskiyou Rehab. Assocs. Inc., Springfield, Oreg., 1982—. Bd. dirs., publicity chmn. U. Oreg. Parents Assn., 1981-84. Mem. Am. Personnel and Guidance Assn., Am. Vocat. Assn., Oreg. Vocat. Assn., (conf. com. chmn. 1982), Oreg. Assn. Rehab. Profls. in Pvt. Sector, Alpha Lambda Delta, Phi Eta Sigma. Contbr. articles to profl. jours. Home: 2576 N 16th St Springfield OR 97477 Office: Siskiyou Rehab Assocs Inc PO Box 7426 Eugene OR 97401

SUMMERS, MARSHA JOY, educational administrator; b. San Francisco, Dec. 24, 1953; d. James Benton and Berniece Glendora (Bernard) Summers. B.A., San Francisco State U., 1976, M.A., 1984. Receptionist Mary's Help Hosp., Daly City, Calif., 1972-77; ECE instr. Jefferson Elem. Sch. Dist., Daly City, 1978; adminstrv. supr. San Francisco State U., 1979—; tchr. Recipient Achievement award Bank of Am., 1971; award Modern Music Masters, 1971. Mem. Assn. Supervision and Curriculum Devel., Basic Edn. Assn., Student Calif. Teachers Assn. (recipient awards 1979, 80), Phi Delta Kappa. Republican. Roman Catholic. Contbr. articles to profl. jours. Office: San Francisco State U 1600 Holloway Ave San Francisco CA 94132

SUMNER, ELAINE MARY GERHARD, educator; b. Pasadena, Calif.; d. C.F. and I.M. Gerhard; B.A., Calif. State Coll. at Los Angeles, 1962, M.A., 1968; postgrad. Whittier Coll., 1969, U. So. Calif., 1963, U. Calif. at Los Angeles, 1970; children—Valerie Elaine, Richard Joseph. Sec. Calif. Inst. Tech., 1951-52; elementary tchr. Los Angeles City Schs., 1962—. Brownie leader Pasadena council Girl Scouts U.S., 1960. Mem. Assn. for Childhood Edn. (v.p. 1963), Calif. Tchrs. Assn., Affiliated Tchrs. Los Angeles, Nat. Trust for Historic Preservation. Home: 8502 Los Olivos Dr San Gabriel CA 91775

SUMNER, HELEN MIRIAN, sporting goods store owner; b. Cheyenne, Wyo., Jan. 17, 1954; d. George S. and Roslyn W. (Wolf) Kaufman; m. Gary Lee Sumner, May 19, 1983. B.S. in Bus. Acctg., Colo. State U., 1979. Acct., Colo. State U., Ft. Collins, 1978-79, supervisory acct., 1979-81; co-owner, treas., buyer, fiscal officer Peoples Sporting Goods, Inc., Cheyenne, 1981—. Bd. dirs. Cheyenne Downtown Assn. Mem. Nat. Sporting Goods Assn., Wyo. Retail Mchts. Assn., Profl. Bus. women's Assn., C. of C. Office: Peoples Sporting Goods Inc 217 West 16th St Cheyenne WY 82001

SUMPTER, GLENN ROY, psychologist, educator; b. Seattle, May 27, 1941; s. G. Roy and Beth (McCrary) S.; M. Joan Marie Nelson, Feb. 1, 1964; children—Kristyn Marie, Erica Lynn. B.A., Bob Jones U., Greenville, S.C., 1963; M.S., Fla. State U., 1965, Ph.D., 1967; N.D., John Bastyr Coll. Naturopathic Medicine, 1982. Ordained minister. Asst. prof. Auburn (Ala.) U., 1967-68, Fla. State U., 1968-70; assoc. prof. Youngstown (Ohio) State U., 1970-75; pres. Inst. Human Devel., Seattle, 1975—. Law Enforcement Assistance Adminstrn. grantee, 1970-77. Mem. Am. Psychol. Assn., Evang. Theol. Soc., Nat. Acad. Research Biochemists. Contbr. articles to profl. jours. Home: 18911 33d Ave NE Seattle WA 98155

SUN, SAMUEL SAI-MING, plant biochemist; b. Canton, China, Sept. 15, 1942; s. Kuen and Siu-Ying (Wong) Sun; B.Sc. cum laude (Govt. Hong Kong scholar, New Asia Distinction scholar), Chinese U. Hong Kong, 1966; B.Sc. with special honors, U. Hong Kong, 1968, M.Sc., 1971; Ph.D., U. Wis.-Madison, 1974; m. Piera S. Sun, May 25, 1974; 1 son, Bryan K. Demonstrator, U. Hong Kong, 1968-71; research assoc. U. Wis.-Madison, 1971-74, postdoctoral research assoc., 1975-79, asst. scientist, 1979-80; sr. scientist Arco Plant Cell Research Inst., Dublin, Calif., 1980—. Mem. N.Y. Acad. Sci., Am. Soc. Plant Physiologists, Am. Inst. Biol. Scis., Sigma Xi. Contbr. articles to profl. jours., chpts. to books. Office: Arco Plant Cell Research Inst 6560 Trinity Ct Dublin CA 94568

SUND, JOHN LEONARD, lawyer, business executive; b. Ketchikan, Alaska, Feb. 14, 1949; s. Otto Arthur and Karen (Berre) S.; m. Kathleen A. MacKinnon, Aug. 7, 1971; children—Kevin, Theresa. B.A. in History, Polit. Sci. and Edn., Western Wash. U., 1971; J.D., Lewis and Clark Coll., 1974. Bar: Alaska 1974, U.S. Dist. Ct. Alaska 1975, U.S. Ct. Appeals (9th cir.) 1976. Ptnr., Ellis, Sund & Whittaker, Ketchikan, 1974-79; chief counsel to speaker Alaska Ho. of Reps., Juneau, 1979-81; pres. Waterfall Group Ltd., Ketchikan, 1981—; apptd. Gov.'s Com. for Study of Bodily Injury Reparations, 1978-79, Fisheries Ctr. Study Com., 1980-81. Chmn. Ketchikan Overall Econ. Study Com., 1977-79. Mem. ABA, Alaska Bar Assn., Am. Judicature Assn. Democrat. Club: Sons of Norway (Ketchikan). Office: PO Box 6440 Ketchikan AK 99901

SUNDARARAJAN, CHELLIAH, civil engr.; b. Trivandrum, India, Oct. 4, 1944; s. Sathyanathan Chelliah and Rose Sundaram. Ph.D. in Civil Engring., U. Waterloo, Ontario, Can., 1972. Engr. Lummus Co., Toronto, Can., 1974-75; sr. engr. Foster Wheeler Corp., Livingston, N.J., 1975-77; tech. specialist EDS Nuclear Inc., San Francisco, 1977—. Sr. research scholar, India, 1968-69. Mem. ASCE, ASME, Am. Nuclear Soc., Earthquake Engring. Research Inst. Editor-in-chief: Decade of Progress in Pressure Vessel Technology; contbr. articles to profl. jours. Home: 288 Whitmore St Apt 325 Oakland CA 94611

SUNDBERG, ROSE JOY, American Indian tribal chairperson; b. Ya-tur He-wan, Calif., Mar. 25, 1932; d. Edward Henry and Lila Elaine (Natt) Crutchfield; m. Fred G. Sundberg, Mar. 12, 1949 (div.); children—Fred, Dan, Marshall, Garth, Mark, Lisa. Student Coll. of Redwoods. Eminence credential in Indian issues. Owner restaurant and cocktail lounge, caterer; jewelry maker Aboriginals; tribal chairperson Trinidad (Calif.) Community Council; coordinator Indian programs six no. counties Calif.; dir. NW Indian Cemeteries Protective Assn.; lobbyist, advocate Indian and environ. issues. Past pres. PTA, Humboldt County Hist. Soc.; mem. Calif. State Hist. Resource Commn.; mem. Sch. Bd. Recipient Inter-Tribal Council Calif. award. Mem. maj. Indian orgns. (officer), Am. Indian Scholarship (pres.). Democrat. Mormon. Office: PO Drawer AA Trinidad CA 95570

SUNDBY, DIANNE YVONNE, clin. psychologist; b. Mpls., Nov. 2, 1942; d. Olaf E. and Mavis Elizabeth (Prichard) S.; B.S., U. Wis., Superior, 1964; M.S. (univ. fellow 1964-65), Purdue U., 1965, Ph.D. (NDEA fellow 1966-69), 1971; m. Michael J. Driver, May 29, 1976; children—Jennifer Suzanne, Steven Thor, Maia Perelandra. Girls counselor Lombard (Ill.) and Westlake jr. high schs., 1965-66; asst. prof. counselor edn. Calif. State U., Los Angeles, 1969-71, dir. guidance clinic, 1970-71; psychotherapist Los Angeles Psychosocial Center, 1971-72; lectr. U. So. Calif., 1972-78; psychotherapist Inst. Humanistic Psychology, Beverly Hills, Calif., 1972-74; postdoctoral intern Northridge (Calif.) Hosp. and Mental Health Center, 1973; pvt. practice clin. psychology, Los Angeles, 1974—; dir. Career Counseling and Assessment Assos., Los Angeles, 1976—; asso. dir. career and edn. research project, career research program U. So. Calif., 1975-79, dir. fin. analyst profile study, 1977-79; cons. in field. Mem. Am. Psychol. Assn., Calif. Psychol. Assn., Los Angeles County Psychol. Assn. Author papers in field, editor handbook. Office: 9229 W Sunset Blvd Suite 502 Los Angeles CA 90069

SUNDEM, GARY LEWIS, accounting educator; b. Montevideo, Minn., Nov. 8, 1944; s. Clifford Leroy and Sylvia Edna (Larson) S.; m. Jennifer McGilvray, Aug. 20, 1969; children—Garth Clifford, Jens Lewis. B.A., Carleton Coll., 1967; M.B.A., Stanford U., 1969, Ph.D., 1971. Asst. prof. U. Wash., Seattle, 1971-74, assoc. prof., 1974-80, prof., 1980—; vis. prof. Norwegian Sch. Econs., Bergen, 1974-75; vis. assoc. prof. Cornell U., Ithaca, N.Y., 1977-78; cons. in field; editor The Accting. Review, 1982—. Bd. trustees The Little Sch., 1978-82, also v.p. fin. Named Seattle Newsmaker of Tomorrow, 1979, Time Mag. and Seattle C. of C. Mem. Am. Acctg. Assn., Am. Fin. Assn., Fin. Execs. Inst., Nat. Assn. Accts., Fin. Mgmt. Assn., Inst. Mgmt. Sci., Am. Econ. Assn. Contbr. articles to profl. jours. Home: 307 36th Ave E Seattle WA 98112 Office: Sch Bus Adminstrn Univ Wash Seattle WA 98195

SUNDERLAND, DAVID KENDALL, real estate developer; b. Detroit, Mar. 25, 1930; s. Maurice Briggs and Helen (Bell) S.; B.A., Dartmouth Coll., 1952; postgrad. U. Mich. Sch. Bus. Adminstrn., 1956-58, Gen. Motors Inst., 1955-56; m. Brooke Williams, Sept. 13, 1975; children—Mark, Caryn, Matthew, Tracy. Fin. analyst Chevrolet div. Gen. Motors Corp., Detroit, 1955-58; budget mgr. Raytheon Co., Andover/Bedford, Mass., 1958-61, div. controller, Oxnard, Calif., 1961-64; v.p. Janss Corp., Los Angeles, 1964-68; pres. Gates Land Co., Colorado Springs, Colo., 1968—. Bd. regents U. Colo., 1978—; bd. dirs. St. Francis Hosp., Colorado Springs, 1973-78. Served in USN, 1952-55. Named Colorado Springs Builder of Yr., 1975; recipient Colo. Builders Disting. Service award, 1977. Mem. Colorado Springs C. of C. (dir. 1974-77), Nat. Assn. Home Builders, Colo. Home Builders Assn. (pres. 1979), Urban Land Inst. Republican. Club: Country of Colo. Office: 155 W Lake Ave Colorado Springs CO 80906

SUNLIGHT, CAROLE, psychologist; b. DuBois, Pa., Aug, 19; d. Andy and Mary Ann Gaborick; Med. Tech., Carnegie Coll., 1959; B.A. in Psychology, Cleve. State U., 1971; M.A. in Psychology (Univ. scholar), Pepperdine U., 1973; Ph.D. in Psychology, U.S. Internat. U., 1980. Med. technologist Doctors Piercy, Fertig, Schneider and Doran, Cleve., 1959-67; chief technologist med. dept. U.S. Steel Corp., Lorain, Ohio, 1967-69; office mgr. dept. philosophy and religious studies Cleve. State U., 1969-70; counselor Gardena Valley Counseling Service, Gardena, Calif., 1971-72; clin. intern Pepperdine U. psychology clinic, 1972-73; testing technician Norco-Corona (Calif.) Sch. Dist., 1973; dir. treatment services Unfinished Symphony Ranch, Inc., Agoura, Calif., 1973-77; pvt. practice, Westlake Village, Calif., 1977-78; staff Kaiser Permanente Mental Health Center, 1977—; pvt. practice, Torrance, Calif., 1980—; speaker in field. Bd. dirs. COMOSI Mental Health, Thousand Oaks, Calif., 1977-78. Registered med. technologist. Mem. Am. (sects on psychology of women, clin. neuropsychology, Calif., Los Angeles County (newsletter editor 1982—) psychol. assns., Am. Med. Technologists (Ohio State Soc. Publ. award 1972), Calif. Neuropsychol. Soc., Psychologists for Social Responsibility, NOW, Psi Chi. Office: 765 W College St Los Angeles CA 90012 also 3250 W Lomita Blvd Suite 305 Torrance CA 90505

SUOZZI, DANIEL PETER, elec. design engr.; b. Buffalo, N.Y., Sept. 11, 1951; s. Daniel M. and Jane P. (Pettite) S.; B.S. in Elec. Engring, Ariz. State U., 1974. Electronic technician Optical Electronics, Inc., Tucson, 1974, jr. engr., 1975-78, sr. design engr., 1978-80; dir. engring., 1980—. Mem. Internat. Soc. Hybrid Microelectronics, IEEE. Republican. Roman Catholic. Home: 8321 E 4th St Tucson AZ 85710 Office: 3150 E 46th St Tucson AZ 85713

SUPPES, PATRICK, social scientist; b. Tulsa, Mar. 17, 1922; s. George Biddle and Ann (Costello) S.; B.S., U. Chgo., 1943; Ph.D., Columbia U., 1950; hon. degree in social sciences, U. Nijmegan (Netherlands); Dr. h.c., Université René Descartes (France), 1982; m. Joan Farmer, Apr. 16, 1946 (div. 1970); children—Patricia, Deborah, John Biddle; m. 2d, Joan Sieber, Mar. 29, 1970 (div. 1973); m. 3d, Christine Johnson, May 26, 1979; 1 dau., Alexandra Christine. Mem. faculty Stanford U., 1950—, dir. Inst. Math. Studies in the Social Scis., 1959—; pres. Computer Curriculum Corp., Palo Alto, Calif., 1967—. Served with USAAF, 1942-46. Recipient Disting. Service medal Columbia U. Tchrs. Coll. Mem. Finnish Acad. Sci. and Letters, Nat. Acad. Edn., Am. Ednl. Research Assn., Am. Philos. Assn., Am. Psychol. Assn., Internat. Inst. Philosophy, Nat. Acad. Scis. Author: Probabilistic Metaphysics, 1974; A Probabilistic Theory of Causality, 1970; Studies in the Methodology and Foundation of Science: Selected Papers from 1951-69, 1979; Logique du Probable, 1981; Axiomatic Set Theory, 1960; Introduction to Logic, 1957. Home: 678 Mirada Ave Stanford CA 94305 Office: Ventura Hall Stanford University Stanford CA 94305

SURBEY, WILLIAM WADE, aircraft co. exec.; b. New Orleans, Aug. 4, 1939; s. Charles Wade and Elenor May (Chrissy) S.; B.S., U. Okla., 1962, postgrad., 1962-66; m. Joy Olsen, 1982; children—Christopher Wade, Kelley Lynn. Chief structural engr. Aero Comdr./Rockwell, Oklahoma City, 1961-68; project mgr. Citation, Cessna, Wichita, Kans., 1968-78; v.p. ops. Lear Avia, Reno, 1978-80; pres. Lear Fan Corp., Reno, 1980-82, also dir.; v.p. advanced programs Ventura div. Northrop Corp., Newbury Park, Calif., 1983—. Registered profl. engr., Okla. Republican. Methodist. Home: 2517 Pepperwood Camarillo CA 93010 Office: 1515 Rancho Conejo Blvd Newbury Park CA 91320

SURBROOK, DAVID BURCH, social services agy. adminstr.; b. DeTour, Mich., Nov. 11, 1942; s. Burch Harley and Zoe Linnea (Duncan) S.; A.A., Riverside City Coll., 1967; m. Patricia Lucille Deane, May 9, 1964; children—Jonathan, Jeremy. Painting contractor Surbrook & Son, Riverside, Calif., 1966-67; ter. mgr. Sherwin Williams Co., 1967-69; sales mgr. No. Calif. Meyercord Co., San Francisco, 1969-71; exec. v.p. Calif. Nat. Health Agys., San Mateo, 1971—; owner Chari-Tech., 1973—; owner Surbrook Sales; owner, dir. mktg. Am. Alumination, Inc., 1980—. Founder, pres. Marina Watch, 1979. Adv. Calif. Solid Waste Mgmt. Bd. Served with U.S. Navy, 1960-63. Mem. Nat. Soc. Fund-Raising Execs., Assn. Voluntary Action Scholars. Club: Met. Yacht (Oakland, Calif.). Office: 1308 Old Bayshore Suite 101 Burlingame CA 94010

SUSSMAN, MITCHELL REED, lawyer, real estate broker; b. Bklyn., Feb. 9, 1951; s. Sy and Pauline (Frank) S.; B.B.A., George Washington U., 1973; J.D., Pepperdine U., 1976. Admitted to Calif. bar, 1977; pres., founder Legal Research Assos., Newport Beach, Calif., 1975—; individual practice law, Newport Beach, 1977—; owner, operator New Horizon Realty & Investment Co., 1980—. Recipient Time-Life award, 1969; N.Y. Regents scholar, 1969. Mem. Am., Calif. (real estate sect.), Orange County (bankruptcy panel) bar assns., Comml. Law League. Jazz pianist. Asso. editor Pepperdine U. Advocate, 1975-76. Office: 3345 Newport Blvd Newport Beach CA 92663 also 9465 Wilshire Blvd Beverly Hills CA 90012

SUTCLIFFE, ERIC, lawyer; b. Calif., Jan. 10, 1909; s. Thomas and Annie (Beare) S.; A.B., U. Calif. at Berkeley, 1929, LL.B., 1932; m. Joan Basche, Aug. 7, 1937; children—Victoria, Marcia, Thomas; m. 2d, Marie C. Paige Nov. 1, 1975. Admitted to Calif. bar, 1932; mem. firm Orrick, Herrington & Sutcliffe, P.C., and predecessor firm, San Francisco, 1943—. Trustee San Francisco Law Library. Fellow Am. Bar Found.; mem. Am. (chmn. state regulation securities com. 1960-65), San Francisco (dir. 1952) bar assns., San Francisco C. of C. (treas. 1962-63, dir. 1968-70), State Bar of Calif., Phi Gamma Delta, Phi Delta Phi, Order of Coif. Clubs: Pacific Union, Bohemian, Commonwealth (San Francisco). Home: 260 King Ave Piedmont CA 94610 Office: 600 Montgomery St San Francisco CA 94111

SUTHERLAND, BRUCE, composer, pianist; pupil Halsey Stevens, Ellis Kohs, Ethel Leginska, Amparo Iturbi; b. Daytona Beach, Fla.; s. Kenneth Francis and Norma (Williams) S.; Mus.B., U. So. Calif., 1957, Mus.M., 1959. Harpsichord soloist with Telemann Trio in concert tour, 1969-70; tchr. master class for pianists U. Tex., Austin, 1971; dir. Bach festivals Music Tchrs. Assn. Calif., 1972-73; compositions performed in numerous contemporary music festivals in U.S., 1957—; piano faculty Calif. State U. at Northridge, 1977—; adjudicator music competitions and auditions Nat. Guild Piano Tchrs., others; dir. Brentwood-Westwood Symphony ann. competition for young artists, 1981-84; composer: Allegro Fanfara for Orch., world premiere conducted by José Iturbi with Bridgeport Symphony Orch., 1970; Saxophone Quartet,

1971; Quintet for Flute, Strings, Piano, 1972; Notturno for Flute and Guitar, 1973; also string trio, piano and vocal works. Recipient grand prize Internat. Competition Louis Moreau Gottschalk, 1970; Stairway of Stars award Music Arts Soc., Santa Monica, 1973; named one of Los Angeles' Finest Piano Tchrs., New West Mag., 1977. Mem. Nat. Assn. Am. Composers and Condrs., Pi Kappa Lambda.

SUTHERLAND, DOUG, mayor of Tacoma, business executive; b. Helena, Mont., May 2, 1937; s. Chris and Marie Sutherland, m. Patricia Sutherland, Dec. 15, 1957; children—Karen, Scott. B.A., Central Wash. U. With program mgmt. dept. Boeing Co., 1960-71; pres. Tacoma Tent and Awning Inc., 1971—; mayor City of Tacoma. Republican. Office: 740 St Helens Ave Suite 1220 Tacoma WA 98402

SUTHERLAND, LOWELL FRANCIS, lawyer; b. Lincoln, Nebr., Dec. 17, 1939; s. Lowell Williams and Doris Genevieve (Peterson) S.; A.B., San Diego State Coll., 1962; LL.B., Hastings Coll. Law, 1965; m. Sandra Gaylynne Stengel, June 12, 1965; children—Scott Thorpe, Mark James, Sandra Doris. With Cooper, White & Cooper, attys., San Francisco, 1963-66; admitted to Calif. bar, 1966; with Wien & Thorpe, attys., El Centro, 1966-67; ptnr. Wien, Thorpe & Sutherland, El Centro, 1967-74, Wien, Thorpe, Sutherland & Stamper, 1973-74, Sutherland, Stamper & Feingold, 1974-77, Sutherland & Gerber, 1977—; ptnr. Sutherland & Sutherland, investments; instr. bus. law Imperial Valley Coll., 1967. Pres. El Centro Active 20-30 Club, 1968-69; finance chmn. Salvation Army, 1972. Pres. bd. dirs. Boys Club of El Centro, 1969-71; bd. dirs. Imperial Gen. Hosp., 1971. Mem. Am., Calif., Imperial County bar assns., Am., Calif. (Recognition of Experience awards), San Diego (named outstanding trial lawyer April 1981, trial lawyer of yr. 1983), trial lawyers assns., Thurston Soc., Am. Bd. Trial Advocates (diplomate), Theta Chi. Mem. editorial staff Hastings Law Jour., 1964-65. Home: 1853 Sunset Dr El Centro CA 92243 Office: 300 S Imperial Ave 7 El Centro CA 92243

SUTHERLAND, ROBERT LOUIS, engineering company executive, educator; b. Fellsmere, Fla., May 15, 1916; s. John Alexander and Georgia Myrtle (Legg) S.; B.S., U. Ill., 1939, M.S., 1948; m. Mary Alice Reed, May 18, 1945; children—Robert Hynes, Wayne Muzzy, Connie Anne, Nancy Lee, John Gary. Devel. engr. Firestone Tire & Rubber Co., Akron, Ohio, 1939-41; research engr. Borg & Beck div. Borg-Warner Corp., Chgo., 1941; test engr. Buick Motor div. Gen. Motors Corp., Melrose Park, Ill., 1942-43; sr. engr. research dept. Aeronca Aircraft Corp., Middletown, Ohio, 1943-45; research assoc. Coll. Engring., U. Ill., 1945-48; asst., then assoc. prof. mech. engring. State U. Iowa, Iowa City, 1948-58; city engr., Coralville, Iowa, 1950-53; prof. mech. engring. U. Wyo., Laramie, 1958-79, head dept., 1960-70, prof. emeritus, 1979; pres. Skyline Engring. Co., Inc., Laramie, 1972—; cons. engr. Summit Engring. Inc., Laramie, 1980—. Co-recipient Richard L. Templin award ASTM, 1952; ASME legis. fellow to Nat. Conf. State Legislatures, 1982—. Registered profl. engr., Ill., Iowa, Wyo. Fellow ASME (regional v.p. 1965-67); mem. Soc. Automotive Engrs., Sigma Xi, Sigma Tau, Pi Tau Sigma, Tau Beta Pi. Methodist. Club: Kiwanis (lt. gov. 1970-71, life) (Laramie, Wyo.). Author: Engineering Systems Analysis, 1958; contbr. articles to profl. jours.

SUTRO, ROBERT, mortgage banker, retired accountant; b. St. Joseph, Mo., Feb. 21, 1909; s. Ralph C. and Ellabelle (Greensfelder) S.; A.B., Stanford, 1931; M.A. in Econs./Accountancy, 1932; LL.D. (hon.), Linfield Coll., 1980; m. Dora Edith McMullen, Apr. 25, 1946; children—James Bernard, Thomas Lionel, Victoria Belle, William Gower, Margaret Zoe. Teaching asst. Stanford, 1931-32, 34-35; pub. accountant Haskins & Sells, Oscar Moss & Co., R.W.E. Cole & Co., C.P.A.'s, Los Angeles, 1933-36; partner Ralph C. Sutro Co., mortgage bankers, Los Angeles, 1937-41, pres., 1946-68, chmn. bd., 1959-81, chief exec. officer, 1968-79, ret., 1981; chmn. bd. trustees Sutro Mortgage Investment Trust, 1963-79; dir. Investors Mortgage Ins. Co. Pres., Sutro Sch. Music, Dance, Drama. Chmn. So. Calif. Research Council, 1974-76; trustee Pomona Coll.; trustee Linfield Coll., Oreg., chmn., 1974-77; trustee Calif. State U., Northridge; past bd. dirs. Trinity Coll. Parents Assn., Hartford, Conn., 1974-76. Served to col. AUS, 1941-46; PTO, ETO. Recipient Humanitarian award real estate and constrn. industries div. NCCJ, 1976; C.P.A., Calif. Mem. Am. (past chmn. mortgage market, membership, investor liaison coms.; instr. Sch. Mortgage Banking, regional v.p., gov.-at-large, trustee research and ednl. trust fund, Disting. Service and Aubrey Costa awards 1967), So. Calif. (past dir.), Calif. mortgage bankers assns., Nat. Assn. Real Estate Investment Trusts (past gov.), Hancock Park Home Owners Assn. (dir., treas.), Apt. Assn. Los Angeles (past dir.), Am. Inst. C.P.A.'s, Calif. Soc. C.P.A.'s, Los Angeles, Wilshire (past dir., named Man of Yr. 1973) chambers commerce, Ret. Officers Assn., Nat. Assn. Realty Bds., Mil. Order World Wars, Res. Officers Assn., Lambda Alpha (chpt. pres. 1979-81, internat. v.p. 1981—). Clubs: Los Angeles (dir.), Univ. of Los Angeles, Miracle Mile Lions (Man of Yr. 1978). Home: 130 S McCadden Pl Los Angeles CA 90004

SUTTER, CAROLYN SUE, city official; b. Kalamazoo, Oct. 9, 1942; d. John Martin and Lorraine Eleanor (Kloosterman) Opthoff; B.S., Calvin Coll., 1964; M.S., Western Mich. U., 1970; M.P.A., Calif. State U., Long Beach, 1982; children—Chandra, Stephan. Dir., Library System of Southwestern Mich.; asso. dir. Long Beach (Calif.) Public Library; dir. library and mus. services City of Long Beach, also head telecommunications; gen. mgr. Tidelands Agy. Chairwoman, Mich. 4th Dist. Tricounty Women's Polit. Caucus, 1972-76. Mem. Long Beach C. of C. (dir. women's council), AMA, Urban Land Inst., Cal. Assn. for Local Econ. Devel. Office: Tidelands Agy City Hall 333 W Ocean Blvd Long Beach CA 90802

SUTTER, HARVEY MACK, cons. engr.; b. Jennings, La., Oct. 5, 1906; s. Josiah Harvey and Effie Relief (Murray) S.; A.B., U. Wichita, 1932; m. Julia Genevieve Wright, Sept. 19, 1936; children—James Houston, Robert Mack, Julia Ann (Mrs. Richard D. Boyd), John Norman. Design and prodn. engr. Boeing Aircraft, Wichita, Kans., 1936-38; supr. arts, crafts and coop. activities Bur. Indian Affairs, U.S. Dept. of Interior, 1938-42, chief procurement br. Bur. of Reclamation, Washington, 1946-54, chief div. procurement and property mgmt., 1954-58; asst. to adminstr. Bonneville Power Adminstrn., 1958-61, asst. to chief engr., 1962-66; cons. engr., 1967—; analyst, chief prodn. service WPB, Denver, 1942-44; chief div. supply C.E., Denver, 1944-46. Mem. exec. bd. Portland area Boy Scouts Am. Recipient Silver Beaver award. Presbyterian. Mem. Nat., Western woodcarvers assns., Internat. Wood Collectors Soc. Club: Electric of Oreg. Author or co-author books and articles on woodcarving. Home: 3803 SE Carlton Portland OR 97202

SUTTLE, CLYDE TRAVERS, JR., accountant; b. Lancaster, Wis., July 14, 1915; s. Clyde Travers and Ruth (Gerhardt) S.; A.A. cum laude, Los Angeles City Coll., 1956; B.S. with highest honors, UCLA, 1958, M.B.A., 1959; D.B.A., U. So. Calif., 1968; m. Teresa Agnes Giguere Collins, Aug. 11, 1956; children—Lynn, Diane, Roy. Enlisted in U.S. Marine Corps, 1932, commd., advanced through grades to maj., 1949; UN mil. observer, Palestine, 1948-49; ret., 1955; instr. Los Angeles Met. Coll. Bus., 1959-60; instr. acctg. Calif. State U., Long Beach, 1960-61, asst. prof., 1961-73, prof., 1973-82, prof. emeritus, 1982—; bus. cons., 1982—. Cert. mgmt. acct. Mem. Am. Acct. Assn., Nat. Assn. Accts. (pres. Long Beach chpt. 1971-72), Beta Gamma Sigma, Phi Kappa Phi, Beta Alpha Psi. Democrat. Roman Catholic. Clubs: So. Calif. Meccano (sec.), K.C. Home: 6062 Cerulean Ave Garden Grove CA 92645

SUTTON, BETTY JEAN RUCKER, psychologist; b. Dixon, Ill., Aug. 27, 1940; d. Roy D. and Florence L. (Brindle) Rucker; children—William, Mark. B.A., Knox Coll., 1962; M.T., St. Luke's Sch. Med. Tech., 1963; M.A., No. Ill. U., 1975, Ph.D., 1978. Lic. psychologist, Calif. Research asst. dept. pathology Presbyn.-St. Luke's Hosp., Chgo., 1963-67; research assoc. scientist Schering Labs., Bloomfield, N.J., 1971-72; grad. research ast. dept. psychology No. Ill. U., DeKalb, 1973-75, grad. instr., 1972-75, grad. student coordinator, 1975-76, intern, liberal arts/sci. counseling officer, 1976-77; clin. psychology intern Patton (Calif.) State Hosp., 1977-78, staff psychologist, 1978—. Ingersoll scholar, 1958-61. Mem. Am. Psychol. Assn., Western Psychol. Assn., Calif. Psychol. Assn., Inland So. Calif. Psychol. Assn., Nat. Register of Health Service Providers in Psychology. Contbr. articles to profl. jours. Address: 3102 E Highland Ave Patton CA 92369

SUTTON, FRANKIE LEE, hosp. adminstr.; b. Sayre, Okla., Oct. 30, 1948; s. Howard E. and Cleo Zuma (McMullan) S.; B.S., S.W. Okla. State U., 1971; m. Cathy Jane Cook, Nov. 3, 1967. Pharmacy intern Wayne's Pharmacy, Erick, Okla., 1968, Miller Drug, Weatherford, Okla., 1968-71; pharmacist St. Anthony Hosp., Oklahoma City, 1971; dep. chief pharmacist USPHS Alaska Native Hosp., Mt. Edgecumbe, Alaska, 1971-74, chief pharmacist, 1974-78, hosp. adminstr., 1978—; cons. pharmacist Alaska Pioneer Home, 1971-72; clin. instr. U. Wash., 1976—; adj. faculty Oreg. State U. Mem. Am., Alaska pharm. assns., Alaska, Am. socs. hosp. pharmacists, Am. Acad. Med. Adminstrs., Am. Coll. Hosp. Adminstrs., Am. Public Health Assn., Commd. Officers Assn. USPHS (commendation medal 1979), Assn. Mil. Surgeons U.S. Republican. Baptist. Club: Lions. Home: Box 4140 Mount Edgecumbe AK 99835 Office: PHS Alaska Native Hosp Mount Edgecumbe AK 99835

SUTTON, J. RUSSELL, human resources center exec.; b. Omaha, June 25, 1943; s. John A. and Irma K. (Rauh) S.; B.S., Ball State U., 1966; postgrad. Ind. U. Law Sch., 1966-69, Purdue U., 1969-70; m. Ann L. Peters, Aug. 27, 1966; children— Brittany Suzanne, John Barrett. Various positions in personnel RCA Consumer Electronics, Indpls., 1966-72, mgr. employment and devel., 1970-71, mgr. employment and personnel records, Bloomington, Ind., 1972-74; asst. v.p. Steak-n Shake, Inc., Indpls., 1974-76; dir. ops. and human resources Wienerschnitzel Internat., Inc., Newport Beach, Calif., 1976-79; v.p. human resources mgmt. VSI Aerospace div. Fairchild Industries, Culver City, Calif., 1979-80; pres. Center for Human Resources, Newport Beach, 1980—; chmn. bd. G.L.M. Mgmt. Co. (The Good Earth Restaurants of San Francisco, Contra Costa and Alameda Counties), 1979—; cons. human resources mgmt., 1978—; dir. Popcorn Palace, Inc., Irvine, Calif.; instr. Coastline Community Coll., Fountain Valley, Calif, 1979—, Ind. U.-Purdue Sch. Bus., 1976, Ind. Central Coll., Indpls., 1972-76. Named hon. Ky. Col., 1980. Mem. Am. Mgmt. Assn., Am. Assn. Personnel Adminstrs., Am. Soc. Tng. and Devel. (past chpt. pres.), Orange County C. of C. (edn. and legis. com. 1978-79), Council of Hotel and Restaurant Trainers, Sigma Phi Epsilon. Clubs: Fox Cliff Country, Athletic, Atheneum Turners, Riviera. Contbr. articles to profl. publs. Office: Center for Human Resources 3185 Airway Ave Suite J Costa Mesa CA 92626

SUTTON, JAMES PAUL, mgmt cons.; b. Excelsior, Minn., June 18, 1924; s. Luverne Lyman and Hazel Woods (Gilman) S.; B.Aero. Engring., U. Minn., 1947; m. Barbara Stanley, Oct. 13, 1971; children—Marquerite Marie, Maureen Diane, Kerry Diana. Pres., Daton Engring. Co., Los Angeles, 1966-74; v.p., gen. mgr. Ostgaard Industries, Inc., Gardena, Calif., 1974-76; exec. v.p. Corporate Group, Inc., Rolling Hills, Calif., 1976-78; pres. Gemini Mgmt. Resources, Inc., Los Angeles, 1978—. Del., Commn. of Californias, 1979. Served with USN, 1942-46. Mem. Am. Mgmt. Assn., Phi Kappa Psi. Republican. Episcopalian. Clubs: U. Minn. M, Big Ten, Riviera Tennis, Toastmasters, (lt. gov.). Home: 17158 Avenida de la Herradura Pacific Palisades CA 90272 Office: 11901 Sunset Blvd Suite 108 Los Angeles CA 90049

SUTTON, MARCELLA FRENCH, interior designer; b. Prague, Czechoslovakia, Sept. 4, 1946; came to U.S., 1952, naturalized, 1956; d. Eugen E. and Frances V. (Pruchovia) French; B.S. in Profl. Arts, Woodbury U., 1971; m. Michael D. Sutton, Feb. 11, 1978; 1 son, Kevin Christopher. Mgr. design dept. W. & J. Sloane, Beverly Hills, Calif., 1972-76; project dir. Milton I. Swimmer, Beverly Hills, 1977-78; owner, interior designer Marcella French Designs, Woodland Hills and La Crescenta, Calif., 1969—; property mgmt. coordinator, interior designer Home Savs. and Loan., State of Calif., Los Angeles, 1979-82; regional premises officer, asst. v.p. regional hdqrs. Bank of Am., Los Angeles, 1981—; cons. pvt. residences. Active Young Republicans. Recipient various scholarships. Mem. Moravian Brothers Ch. Office: Bank of Am 2049 Century Park E Los Angeles CA 90067

SUTTON, MILO WILTON, marketing executive; b. Hartford, Kans., Dec. 24, 1928; s. Joseph Bernard and Genevieve Loraine (Campbell) S.; m. Erna Doreen Clemmer, Dec. 18, 1946; children—Cynthia, Janet, Rita, Debbie, Wendy, Michael. Student Kans. State Tchrs. Coll., 1948-50, UCLA, 1969. Mem. Kans. Ho. of Reps., 1950-54; owner, pub. Salina (Kans.) Advertiser-Sun, 1954-59; with advt. and editorial depts. Los Angeles Mirror-News, 1959-60; promotion mgr. South Bay Daily Breeze, Torrance, Calif., 1960-74; dir. promotion and research Dallas Times Herald, 1974-77; dir. mktg. services, mem. operating com. Los Angeles Herald Examiner, 1977—. Served with USN, 1946-48. Mem. Internat. Newspaper Promotion Assn. (dir.), Am. Mktg. Inst., Los Angeles Advt. Club. Democrat. Lutheran. Author numerous trade mag. articles. Home: 415 2nd St Hermosa Beach CA 90254 Office: 1111 S Broadway Los Angeles CA 90015

SUTTON, PHILIP D(IETRICH), psychologist; b. Ridgewood, N.J., June 20, 1952; s. Clifton C. and Ida-Lois (Dietrich) S.; m. Kathleen E. Duffy, June 17, 1973; children—Heather, Shivonne. B.A., So. Ill. U., 1974; M.A., U. Chgo., 1975; Ph.D., U. Utah, 1979. Lic. psychologist, Colo. Psychologist VA Hosp., Salt Lake City, 1975-76; psychology intern Salt Lake Community Mental Health Ctr., Salt Lake City, 1976-78; counselor, instr. Counseling Ctr., U. Utah, Salt Lake City, 1976-78; counselor, acting dir. spl. services program Met. State Coll., Denver, 1978-80; staff psychologist Kaiser-Permanente Health Plan, Denver, 1980-83; adj. prof. U. Colo., 1979—; pvt. practice psychology, Boulder, Colo., 1981—; cons. spl. programs for disadvantaged students in higher edn. Mem. Am. Psychol. Assn. Home: Box 810 Nederland CO 80466 Office: Boulder Med Ctr 2750 Broadway Boulder CO 80302

SUTTON, RICHARD CARPENTER, businessman, former state legislator; b. Honolulu, Apr. 5, 1917; s. E. White and Alice (Carpenter) S.; A.B., Stanford, 1937, J.D., 1950; m. Anne Colgate, Feb. 28, 1942; children—Richard Carpenter, Linda Lee (Mrs. John C. Kemp), Beverly Warner Colgate. Admitted to Hawaii bar, 1951; practice law, Honolulu, 1951; real estate broker, 1951—; fed. judge Wake Island, 1971-74; mem. Hawaii Ho. of Reps., 1975-80. Dir., Pehang Rubber Co.; owner Malihini Hotel, Waikiki, Hawaii. Hawaiian del. 1968 Constl. Conv. Trustee Selema Dingdings. Served to lt. comdr., USNR, 1941-45. Decorated Purple Heart. Mem. Hawaii Bd. Realtors, Fed. (pres. Hawaii chpt. 1973), Am., Hawaii bar assns., Am. Legion (dept. comdr., judge adv.), Navy League. Republican. Episcopalian. Clubs: Hawaii Quarterback (dir.), Lion, Oahu Country, Hui Nalu Canoe (sec.). Home: 3539 Kahawalu Dr Honolulu HI 96817 Office: 217 Saratoga St Honolulu HI 96817

SUYENAGA, ELSIE SAKAE, educator; b. Honolulu, Dec. 19; d. Shigeji Jinbo-Shimizu and Misao Jinbo; B.A., Honolulu Christian Coll., 1962; A.B. (Fed. grantee, 1962), Pasadena Coll., 1963; postgrad. U. Hawaii, 1963-81; m. James Saburo Suyenaga; 1 son, Matthew Masao. Sec., Nuuanu Bapt. Ch., 1954-62; tchr. Ewa Beach Elem. Sch., Ewa Beach, Hawaii, 1964—; exchange tchr. Laurel Elem. Sch., Los Angeles Sch. Dist., 1968-69; advisor student council. Sec., Palisades Community Assn., 1977, news editor; active polit. campaigns, 1962, 78, 80, 82; treas. Neighborhood Bd. Pearl City, 1982. Recipient student council award for advisors, 1978, cert. of merit Community Assn., 1977. Mem. Hawaii State Techrs. Assn. (cert. of merit 1969, dir. 1981—, sec. fin. com. 1981, vice-chmn. 1982), Leeward Tchrs. Assn. (treas.), PTA (treas., dist. award 1976), Am. Mus. Natural History, DAV, Alpha Delta Kappa (treas. Lambda 1980-81). Democrat. Baptist. Home: 2381 Anihinihi St Pearl City HI 96782

SVERDSTEN, TERRY LEE, state senator; b. Cataldo, Idaho, Sept. 8, 1932; s. Edward William and Alida (Warner) S.; B.A. in Bus., Pacific Luth. U., 1957; m. Dee Ann Duea, Sept. 14, 1957; children—Lucia, David, Paul, Ronald. Pres., Sverdsten Logging Co., Inc., Cataldo, 1979-81, Triad Contractors, Inc., Cataldo, 1979-81; mem. Idaho Senate, 1980—. Trustee, Kootenai Sch. Dist., Harrison, Idaho, 1968-78. Served with U.S. Army, 1953-55. Mem. Pacific Logging Conf., Intermountain Logging Conf. Lutheran. Office: Box 51 Route 1 Cataldo ID 83810

SVOBODA, ROBERT ALLAN, bank exec.; b. Lewistown, Mont., May 12, 1926; s. Herman Joseph and Helen Ross (Allan) S.; B.A., U. Mont., 1949; postgrad. Harvard U. Advanced Mgmt. Program, 1973; m. Jean Kaiser, Sept. 11, 1949; children—Kathy, Thomas. Exec. v.p. Amfac Properties, 1961-65; pres. Realty Fund, 1965-72; chmn. bd. Calif. Thrift & Loan, Santa Barbara, Calif., 1972—. Bd. dirs. ARC, county disaster chmn., 1981. Served with USNR, 1943-45. Baptist. Clubs: University, Birnam Wood Golf, La Cumbre Country, Masons, Shriners. Home: PO Box 1477 Santa Barbara CA 93102 Office: Calif Thrift & Loan 25 E Anapamu St Santa Barbara CA 93101

SWACKHAMER, WILLIAM D., state official; Mem. Nev. Assembly, 1946-71, speaker, majority leader, chmn. ways and means com., taxation com., chmn. Cow County Caucus, mem. Legis. Commn.; sec. state Nev., 1973—. Democrat. Office: Office Sec State State Capitol Carson City NV 89710*

SWAGEL, DENNIS JAY, lawyer; b. N.Y.C., May 25, 1946; s. Harry R. and Sah Belle (Fisher) S.; student Harvard U., 1966; certificat de langue pratique U. Paris, 1967; A.B. (Dana scholar), Hamilton Coll., 1968; J.D., Fordham U., 1971; postgrad. U. So. Calif. Sch. Law, Los Angeles, 1976, 79. Admitted to N.Y. bar, 1972, Calif. bar, 1974; law clk. firm Lord, Day & Lord, N.Y.C., 1969; legal asst. (part-time) Legal Aid Soc., N.Y.C., 1969-70; law clk. (part-time) Greenbaum, Wolff & Ernst, N.Y.C., 1970-71; ptnr. Casa de Cynjaden Co., Cypress, Calif., 1972-73; assoc. firm William J. Bluestein, Beverly Hills, Calif., 1974; ptnr. firm Bluestein, Heimbach & Swagel, Beverly Hills, 1975; individual practice law, Los Angeles, 1975—. Mem. Am., Los Angeles County, Beverly Hills bar assns., Assn. Trial Lawyers Am., Calif. Trial Lawyers Assn., Los Angeles Trial Lawyers Assn., Lawyers Club Los Angeles, Fordham Law Alumni Assn., ASCAP, Am. Film Inst., U.S. Olympic Soc., ACLU, Los Angeles County Mus. Art, Town Hall, Internat. Platform Assn., Nat. Trust Hist. Preservation, Am. Guild Authors and Composers, Sierra Club. Democrat. Jewish. Clubs: Los Angeles Racquet. Home: 4329 Latona Ave Los Angeles CA 90031 Office: 350 S Figueroa St Suite 460 Los Angeles CA 90071

SWAN, HERBERT JUNIOR, Canadian legislator, farmer; b. Beechy, Sask., Can., Jan. 10, 1927; s. Herbert Frederick and Frieda Suzanna (Land) S.; m. Anita Poltava Syroishka, July 1, 1949; children—Karen, Bonnie, Kirk, Heather. Grad. Pub. Acct., Success Bus. Coll., 1945. With Can. Imperial Bank, Saskatoon, Sask., Can., 1946; acct. McDonald's Consol., Saskatoon, 1947, Hudson's Bay Co., Saskatoon, 1948-49; mgr. People's Credit Jewellers, Saskatoon, 1949-53, farmer, Beechy, Sask., 1953—; mem. Sask. Legis. Assembly for Rosetown-Elrose, 1978—, speaker Legis. Assembly of Sask., 1982—; dir. Northwest Food & Fuel. Mem. Outlook Sch. Bd., 1964-79; pres. Sask. Sch. Trustees Assn., 1975-78; bd. dirs. Can. Sch. Trustees Assn., 1973-78; active Gideons Internat. Mem. Commonwealth Parliamentary Assn. Progressive Conservative. Mennonite. Office: Room 129 Legislative Bldg Regina SK S4S 0B3 Canada

SWANER, BRAD LEE, lawyer; b. Ogden, Utah, Nov. 5, 1948; s. Clarence D. and Joan (Krumperman) S.; B.S., Weber State Coll., 1971; J.D. cum laude, Gonzaga U., 1975; m. Betty Jean Sirstins, July 8, 1981; children by previous marriage—Lora, Marie. Admitted to Utah bar, 1975; mem. firm Stewart & Swaner, Salt Lake City, 1975-77, Stewart, Swaner & Taylor, Salt Lake City, 1977-79; partner firm Swaner & Taylor, Salt Lake City, 1979—; judge pro tem small claims div. Salt Lake Circuit Cts., 5th Circuit, 1979-80. Mem. Utah State Bar Assn. (cts. and judges com. 1981—), Utah Trial Lawyers Assn., 10th Circuit Ct. of Appeals. Mormon. Editor: Gonzaga Law Rev., 1972-74. Office: 9 Exchange Pl Salt Lake City UT 84111

SWANSON, BARBARA JOAN, librarian; b. Starbuck, Minn., Aug. 5, 1939; d. Milton L. and Louise Elizabeth (Hume) S. B.A. in English, U. Minn., 1961, M.A. in Library Sci., 1968. Librarian Hennepin County Library, Mpls., 1962-68, book mobile and reference librarian; young adult librarian Los Angeles Pub. Library, Eagle Rock br., 1969-81, adult reference librarian, 1981—. Mem. ALA, Calif. Library Assn. Club: Soroptimists. Home: 132 Franklin Ct Glendale CA 91205

SWANSON, DAVID ARTHUR, demographer; b. Mpls., Feb. 28, 1946; s. David Leonard and Mary June (Peterson) S. B.S., Western Wash. U., 1972; diploma U. Stockholm, 1974; M.A., U. Hawaii, 1976, Ph.D., 1983. Programmer/analyst Hawaii Ctr. Environ. Edn., 1973; researcher East-West Population Inst., Honolulu, 1975-77; research investigator Office Fin. Mgmt., State of Wash., 1977-80; info. systems mgr. Wash. State Bd. Community Coll. Edn., 1980-81; adj. faculty Western Wash. U., Bellingham, 1980-81; state demographer Alaska Dept. Labor, Juneau, 1981—; Mem. Am. Statis. Assn., Pacific N.W. Assn. Instl. Research and Planning, Population Assn. Am. Club: Elks (Pasco, Wash.). Contbr. articles to sci. jours. Home: 326 4th Apt 1109 Juneau AK 99801 Office: Dept Labor State of Alaska PO Box 1149 Juneau AK 99811

SWANSON, EDWIN ARCHIE, educator; b. Boone County, Nebr., July 5, 1908; s. Andrew E. and Alma (Nordgren) S.; student George Washington U., 1933-34; B.S., Nebr. State Tchrs. Coll., Kearney, 1932; M.S., U. So. Calif., 1936, Ed.D., 1949; m. Fern E. Anderson, Aug. 25, 1933; children—Edwin Burton, John LeRoy. Elementary, high sch. tchr., Nebr., 1925-35; instr. Fullerton Jr. Coll., 1936-37, 38-39; teaching and research fellow in edn. U. So. Calif., 1935-36, instr. edn. and commerce, 1937-38; asso. prof., dept. head Ariz. State Coll., 1939-46; prof. bus. San Jose (Calif.) State U., 1946-79, emeritus prof. bus., 1979—, chmn. dept., 1957-68. Vis. faculty mem., summer sessions U. Tenn., Woman's Coll. U. N.C., Armstrong Coll., Colo. State Coll., U. So. Calif., U. Fla. Mem. AAUP, AAAS, Am. Mgmt. Assn., Nat. (pres. 1950-51, mem. and chmn. publs. com. and editorial bd. 1959-62, editor Yearbook 1965), Western (pres. 1954-55, gen. program chmn. conv. 1965), Cal. bus. edn. assns., NEA, Calif. Tchrs. Assn., Phi Delta Kappa (chpt. pres. 1945-46, 54-55, area coordinator 1955-66), Kappa Delta Pi,

Pi Omega Pi, Delta Pi Epsilon (mem. nat. commn. bus. and econ. edn. 1964-65, mem. bd. govs. for research and devel. in bus. edn. 1968-74), Gamma Rho Tau, Xi Phi, Phi Kappa Phi (chpt. pres. 1956-57). Presbyn. Club: Commonwealth (San Francisco). Contbr. publs. in field. Home: 2390 Mazzaglia Ave San Jose CA 95125

SWANSON, EVELYN DELL, sch. adminstr.; b. Ashdown, Ark., June 8, 1942; s. Henry Howard and Idell (Dickerson) Fenton; B.A., Calif. State U., Hayward, 1969, teaching credential, 1970; M.A., adminstrn. credential U. San Francisco, 1972; m. Richard Duane Swanson, Dec. 17, 1966; children—Jason Richard, Jennifer Eden. Clk., Met. Life Ins. Co., 1960-65, Fed. Res. Bank, 1965-70; prin. Patten Acad. Christian Edn., Oakland, Calif., 1970—, bd. dirs. Patten Coll., 1976—. Recipient cert. appreciation Soc. Disting. Am. High Sch. Students, 1976; founder, pres.'s award of commendation and appreciation Patten Acad. Christian Edn., 1980. Mem. Assn. for Supervision and Curriculum Devel., Am. Assn. Sch. Adminstrs., Calif. Elem. Edn. Assn., Assn. Christian Schs. Internat., Western Assn. Secondary Schs. and Colls. Office: Patten Acad Christian Edn 2433 Coolidge Ave Oakland CA 94601

SWANSON, GERALD CRAIG, management consultant; b. Portland, Oreg., Nov. 12, 1946; s. Norman Emil and Albertine Louise (Spaulding) S.; m. Teresa Anne Zappone, July 4, 1968; children—Craig Michael, Holly Marie. B.S. cum laude in Chemistry, Gonzaga U., Spokane, Wash., 1968; M.S. in Chemistry, U. N.Mex., Albuquerque, 1973, Ph.D., 1975; M.A. in Applied Behavioral Sci., Whitworth Coll., Spokane, 1980. Mem. staff Los Alamos Sci. Lab., 1968-75; sr. scientist Westinghouse Hanford Co., Richland, Wash., 1975-80; tng. dir. J.A. Jones Constrn. Services Co., Richland, 1980-81; quality circle facilitator Lockheed Shipbldg. and Constrn. Co., Seattle, 1981—; cons. in Applied Behavioral Sci., Whitworth Coll. Mem. Internat. Assn. Quality Circles (dir. Seattle Chpt. 1982), Am. Soc. Tng. and Devel. (v.p. Columbia Basin chpt. 1980-81). Contbr. articles to profl. jours. Office: 2929 16th Ave SW Seattle WA 98134

SWANSON, RICHARD WILLIAM, operations research analyst; b. Rockford, Ill., July 26, 1934; s. Richard and Erma Marie (Herman) S.; B.S., Iowa State U., 1958, M.S., 1964; m. Laura Yoko Arai, Dec. 30, 1970. Ops. analyst Stanford Research Inst., Monterey, Calif., 1958-62; statistician ARINC Research Corp., Washington, 1964-65; sr. scientist Booz-Allen Applied Research, Vietnam, 1965-67, Los Angeles, 1967-68; sr. ops. analyst Control Data Corp., Honolulu, 1968-70; mgmt. cons., Honolulu, 1970-73; exec. v.p. SEQUEL Corp., Honolulu, 1973-75; bus. cons. Hawaii Dept. Planning and Econ. Devel., Honolulu, 1975-77, tax research and planning officer Dept. Taxation, 1977-82; ops. research analyst U.S. Govt., 1982—. Served with AUS, 1954-56. Mem. Am. Statis. Assn., Sigma Xi. Home: 583 Kamoka St Apt 3505 Honolulu HI 96826 Office: HQ PACAF/OA Hickam AFB HI 96853

SWANSON, ROBERT KILLEN, business executive; b. Deadwood, S.D., Aug. 11, 1932; s. Robert Charles and Marie Elizabeth (Kersten) S.; B.A., U. S.D., 1954; postgrad. U. Melbourne, Australia, 1955; m. Nancy Anne Oyaas, July 19, 1958; children—Cathryn Lynn, Robert Stuart, Bart Killen. With Gen. Mills, Inc., Mpls., 1955-58, 71-79, v.p., 1971-73, group v.p., 1973-77, exec. v.p., 1977-79; with Marathon Oil Co., Findlay, Ohio, 1958-60; sr. v.p., dir. Needham, Harper & Steers, Inc., Chgo., 1961-69; joint mng. dir. S.H. Benson (Holdings) Ltd., Eng., 1969-71; pres., chief operating officer Greyhound Corp., Phoenix, 1980; pres., chief operating officer Del E. Webb Corp., Phoenix, 1981—; dir. Gunstream Industries, Inc., SFI, Inc. Bd. dirs. Ariz. Community Found., Ariz. Parklands Found., Compas IX, Harrington Arthritis Research Center, Phoenix Art Mus. Served to 2d lt. U.S. Army, 1955. Fellow U.S.D. Found.; Fulbright scholar, 1954-55; Woodrow Wilson scholar. Mem. U.S. Council Fgn. Relations, U.K. Dirs. Inst., U.S. Internat. Scholars Assn. Episcopalian. Clubs: Mansion, Masons; Phoenix Country, Plaza. Office: 3800 N Central Ave Phoenix AZ 85038

SWANSON, ROCHELLE ANITA, public relations program coordinator, lecturer; b. Kenmare, N.D., Apr. 16, 1949; d. Arthur Reuben and Verna Waneta (Nederbo) S. Student Phoenix Coll., 1968-69, Ariz. State U., 1966; B.S. in Pub. Adminstrn., U. Ariz., 1971; postgrad. U. So. Calif., 1973-75. Cert. recreation therapist. Recreation supr., Cypress, Calif., 1971; recreation specialist aide County of Los Angeles Dept. Parks and Recreation, 1972-74, recreation specialist, 1974-82; program coordinator Jesse Owens Games, Atlantic Richfield Co., Los Angeles, 1982—; cons. Fountain Val, 1980-82; lectr. U. Redlands, U. So. Calif., Calif. State U.-Northridge; cons. U. So. Calif., Energy Resource Edn. Program, various confs. Calif. Spl. Olympics Gymnastics chmn., 1972-83; dir. Orange County Spl. Olympics Track and Field Meet, 1983; Dist. IX bowling chmn. Mentally Retarded Citizens, 1974-83; chmn. bd. First Lutheran Day Sch., 1983; co-chmn. Community Hunger Appeal of Ch. World Service Walk, First Luth. Ch.; state bowling commn. handicapper Assn. Retarded Citizens. Recipient awards Los Angeles Basin Parks and Recreation Commn. and Bd., 1982; Am. Legion award, 1963. Mem. Calif. Park and Recreation Soc. (sec. dist. XIII, 1981), Sons of Norway, VASA, Chi Kappa Rho. Republican. Contbr. article to profl. jour. Home: 1756 N Verdugo Rd #22 Glendale CA 91208 Office: 515 S Flower St WIB 860 Los Angeles CA 90071

SWARTZ, ALLAN JOEL, pharmacist, hosp. adminstr.; b. Phila., July 2, 1935; s. Milton and Rosalie S.; A.B., Central High Sch., 1955; Pharm.D., U. So. Calif., 1958; postgrad. Loyola U. Sch. Law, Los Angeles, 1964-66; M.A. in Edn., Pepperdine U., 1976; m. Roslyn Thelma Holt, Jun 2, 1963. Asst. dir. pharmacy City of Hope Nat. Med. Center, Duarte, Calif. 1966-69; dir. pharm. services, 1969-78; dir. pharmacy services Encino (Calif.) Hosp., 1978—; asst. clin. prof. pharmacy U. So. Calif., 1971-82; asst. clin. prof. U. of Pacific, 1978-83; chmn. pharm. group purchasing com. Hosp. Council So. Calif., 1978-82; mem. profl. edn. com. Am. Cancer Soc., 1970-78. Bd. dirs. H.O.P.E. Unit Found., 1980-83; bd. dirs. Vis. Nurse Assn. Los Angeles, 1983—. Served with M.C., U.S. Army, 1958-59. Recipient Order of Golden Sword award Calif. div. Am. Cancer Soc., 1974, cert. merit, 1978. Mem. AAAS, Am. Med. Writers Assn., Am. Soc. Hosp. Pharmacists (commendation 1976), Calif. Soc. Hosp. Pharmacists (pres. 1976), QSAD Centurions, Rho Pi Phi. Feature editor for pharmaceutics Cancer Nursing, 1977-81; cons. editor Am. Jour. Hosp. Pharmacy, 1978-83. Home: 1353 Comstock Ave Los Angeles CA 90024 Office: 16237 Ventura Blvd Encino CA 91436

SWARTZ, BARBARA ANN, interior designer; b. Edmonton, Alta., Can., Aug. 20, 1930; d. Ian and Beatrice Kathleen (Lutz) Murray; m. Billie Waldo Nichols, July 10, 1949 (div.); m. 2d, John Cleland Swartz, Aug. 19, 1951; children—John Cleland, Keith Murray, Janet Elizabeth. Ed. pub. schs., various coll. courses. Cert. Nat. Council Interior Design Qualification. Interior designer, Pasadena, Calif., 1965-68, Westlake Village, Calif., 1968-72; owner, head designer Barbara Swartz Interiors, Westlake Village, 1972—; photographs of design pub. Designers West, 1980, 81, Conejo Mag., 1982, The Designer, 1983. Bd. dirs. Orange County Philharm. Soc., 1958; pres. Pasadena Guild of Rosemary Cottage, 1961; officer San Marino League, 1963; pres., founder Westlake Village Art Guild, 1972; pres. Westlake Village C. of C., 1979. Mem. Am. Soc. Interior Designers, Conejo Assn. Profl. Interior Designers (pres. 1982), Conejo Women in Bus. Republican. Presbyterian. Home: 3327 S Allegheny Ct Westlake Village CA 91361 Office: 960 2 Westlake Blvd Westlake Village CA 91361

SWARTZ, MELVIN JAY, lawyer, businessman, author; b. Boston, July 21, 1930; s. Jack M. and Rose (Rosenberg) S.; B.A., Syracuse U., 1953; LL.B., Boston U., 1957; m. Beth Ellen Ames, Dec. 27, 1959; children—Julianne, Jonathan Samuel. Admitted to N.Y. bar, 1959, Ariz. bar, 1961; sr. partner firm Swartz and Jeckel, P.C., Scottsdale and Sun City, Ariz., 1961—; pres. Melvin Jay Swartz Retirement Seminars, Inc., Scottsdale, 1979—; columnist Swartz on Aging, News-Sun, Sun City, 1978—; pres. Life Strategies Corp.; guest instr. Rio Salado, Community Coll., Maricopa County. Mem. ABA, Ariz. Bar Assn., State Bar N.Y., State Bar Ariz., Maricopa County Bar Assn., Scottsdale Bar Assn., Am. Judicature Soc., Central Ariz. Estate Planning Council. Jewish. Clubs: Masons, Shriners (Phoenix). Author: Don't Die Broke (A Guide to Secure Retirement), 1975, rev. edit., 1978. Office: 7100 E Lincoln Dr Suite D-227 Scottsdale AZ 85253

SWARTZ, RODERICK GARDNER, librarian; b. Fairbury, Nebr., May 25, 1939; s. E. Wayne and Dorine B. (Gardner) S.; B.A., U. Nebr., 1961, M.A., 1962; M.A., U. Chgo., 1963; m. Marianna Moore, Sept. 1, 1972. Asst. to exec. sec. library adminstrn. div. ALA, 1963-64; library cons. Mo. State Library, 1964-66; asst. and asso. dir. Tulsa City-County Library, 1966-72; dep. dir. Nat. Commn. Libraries and Info. Sci., 1972-74; Wash. State librarian, exec. officer Wash. Library Network, Olympia, 1975—; mem. faculty U. Okla., 1969-72, U. Denver, 1970, Cath. U. Am., 1972-74, Inst. Library and Info. Sci., Tampere, Finland, 1975, Sch. Librarianship, U. Wash., Seattle, 1980—; network cons. in N.Z., 1980; library cons., Philippines, 1983. Fulbright fellow, Finland, 1975; Council on Library Resources fellow, Germany, 1975. Mem. ALA, Pacific N.W. Library Assn., Wash. Library Assn. Contbr. articles to library publs. Office: Washington State Library AJ 11 Olympia WA 98504

SWATH, MARGARET MARY, dietitian, hosp. adminstr.; b. Parsons, Kans., Dec. 21, 1936; d. John Joseph and Margaret Mary (Conley) Flynn; B.S., U. Colo., 1958; m. Stephen Eugene Swath, July 18, 1959; children—Margaret Lynn, Patricia Louise. Dietetic intern Colo. State Hosp., 1958-59, staff dietitian, 1958-61; clin. dietitian St. Mary Corwin Hosp., 1961-62; dietitian part-time Parkview Episcopal Hosp., Pueblo, Colo., 1966-70, adminstrv. dietitian, 1970-74, asst. dir., 1974-77, dir. dietetics, 1978-82; dir. nutrition services Colo. State Hosp., 1982—. Mem. Pueblo Dietetic Assn. (pres.), Colo. Dietetic Assn. (dir.), Am. Dietetic Assn., Am. Soc. Hosp. Food Service Adminstrs. Republican. Roman Catholic. Home: 191 University Circle Pueblo CO 81005 Office: 400 W 16th Pueblo CO 81003 also 1600 W 24th St Pueblo CO 81003

SWEARINGEN, LOUISE ADELINE (POE), counselor, educator; b. Buhl, Idaho, Mar. 5, 1918; d. George Perry, Sr. and Louise Sophia (Larson) Poe; m. Gordon Clifford Swearingen, Dec. 26, 1939 (div.); children—Dona Louise Swearingen McLean, Ann Marie Swearingen DeFrance, James Gordon, Jean Leinani Swearingen Martin. Teaching cert. Albion (Idaho) State Normal Sch., 1938; B.A. in Psychology and Sociology, Adams State Coll., 1967, M.A. in Guidance and Counseling, 1968; postgrad. U. Iowa, 1974-75, Utah State U., summer 1983—, U. Nev.-Las Vegas, 1982-83, U. Nev.-Reno, 1969-70, Oreg. State U., 1973-74. Elem. tchr., Bliss, Idaho, 1938-40; social worker state depts. welfare Colo. and Mo., 1962-67; high sch. counselor, Ely, Nev., 1968-79, elem. counselor, Ely, 1979-83, jr. and sr. high sch. counselor, 1982—; part-time instr., counselor with parents No. Nev. Community Coll., 1981-83; condr. community classes in parenting; cons., speaker in field. Community counselor Mental Health Adv. Council Ely, 1975-83; Vocat. and Adult Edn. Adv. Council Ely, 1973-83. ESEA Title IV-C grantee, 1979-82. Mem. Am. Vocat. Assn., Nev. Vocat. Assn., Nev. Personnel and Guidance Assn., Sch. Counselors Assn., NEA, Nev. Edn. Assn. Republican. Mormon. Home: 558 Stevens Ave Ely NV 89301 Office: 844 Altman St Ely NV 89301

SWEENEY, JAMES LEE, engineering-economic systems educator, cons.; b. Waterbury, Conn., Mar. 22, 1944; s. James Wallace and Aletha B. Sweeney; M. Susan L. Van Every, Aug. 21, 1971; children—Erin, Ryan, Regan. S.B. in Electric Engring., M.I.T., 1966; Ph.D. in Engring.-Econ. Systems, Stanford U., 1971. Dir. office energy systems, modeling and forecasting U.S. Fed. Energy Adminstrn. Washington, 1974-76; with Stanford U. 1967—, prof. engring.-econ. systems, 1971—; dir. Energy Modeling Forum, 1978—, chmn. Inst. Energy Studies, 1981—, cons. faculty Sch. of Law, 1980-82, steering com. econ. policy research, 1982—. Recipient Disting. Service award Fed. Energy Adminstrn., 1975; grantee Electric Power Research Inst., U.S. Dept. Energy, Gas Research Inst., Exxon, NSF. Mem. Econometric Soc., Am. Econ. Assn., Internat. Assn. Energy Economists (v.p. for publs.), Eta Kappa Nu, Tau Beta Pi. Club: University (Palo Alto). Contbr. numerous publs. in field to profl. jours. Home: 1020 Continental Drive Menlo Park CA 94025 Office: Terman 406 Stanford U Stanford CA 94305

SWEENEY, R. CAROL, ednl. adminstr.; b. Bklyn.; d. Benjamin and Dorothy Helen (Leboe) Leinseider; B.S. cum laude, Pepperdine U., 1976, M.S., 1978; postgrad. Claremont Grad. Sch.; m. Neil Gordon Sweeney; children—Steven, Jeffrey, Russell. Sch. sec. Los Angeles Unified Sch. Dist., 1966, adminstrv. asst., 1971, classified tng. officer, 1977—; owner Strategies for Success and Success Image, Tng. and Cons. Firm, Chatsworth, 1977—; cons. in field; faculty Pepperdine U., 1978, U. Redlands, 1979, U. San Francisco, 1980, Calif. State U., Los Angeles. Mem. Commn. for Sex Equity Los Angeles City Schs. Named Nat. Ednl. Sec. of Yr., 1974; recipient resolution City Council Los Angeles; Woman of Yr., Sylmar Bus. and Profl. Women, 1974. Mem. Am. Soc. Tng. and Devel., Calif. Assn. Sch. Bus. Ofcls., Assn. Calif. Sch. Adminstrs., Calif. Assn. Ednl. Office Employees (pres. 1978), Nat. Assn. Female Execs., Phi Delta Kappa. Contbr. articles to profl. jours. Author: Transition: Secretary to Manager; (with Emery Stoops) Handbook for Educational Secretaries and Office Personnel. Home: 20248 Labrador St Chatsworth CA 91311 Office: 450 N Grand Ave Los Angeles CA 90012

SWEENEY, URBAN JOSEPH, librarian; b. St. John, N.B., Can., Jan. 18, 1922; came to U.S., 1927, naturalized, 1945; s. Urban James and Dorothy E. (Murray) S.; B.S., N.Y. U., 1956; M.S., Pratt Inst., 1957; m. Margaret Stretz, Jan. 12, 1952; children—Dennis, Steven, Edward, Mark, Barbara. Chief librarian Republic Aviation, Farmingdale, N.Y., 1958-66; chief librarian electronics div., Gen. Dynamics, Rochester, N.Y., 1966-71, Convair div., San Diego, 1971—; vis. instr. Sch. Library Sci., SUNY, Geneseo, 1967-70. Served with USAAF, 1941-45; ETO. Mem. Assn. Computing Machinery, Am. Soc. Info. Sci., Spl. Libraries Assn. (chmn. aerospace div. 1978-80, chpt. pres. 1973-74). Contbr. articles to profl. jours. Home: 7311 Borla Pl La Costa CA 92008 Office: PO Box 85386 San Diego CA 92138

SWEET, CAROL LYNN, compensation analyst; b. N.Y.C., Dec. 11, 1952; d. William John and Vera Edna (Gretschel) Sloan; m. Stanley Karl Sweet, June 16, 1974; 1 son, Kenneth Justin. A.A., Suffolk County Community Coll., 1973; B.S. in Bus. Adminstrn., SUNY-Buffalo, 1980. Internship affirmative action planning Carborundum Bonded Abrasives Co., Niagara Falls, N.Y., 1980; compensation analyst St. Luke's Med. Ctr., Phoenix, 1981—. Mem. Am. Soc. Personnel Adminstrs., Ariz. Hosp. Personnel Assn. Home: 3042 W Dailey St Phoenix AZ 85023 Office: St Lukes Medical Center 525 N 18th St Phoenix AZ 85006

SWEET, MALCOLM STUART, clergyman; b. Canandaigua, N.Y., Sept. 16, 1905; s. Louis Matthews and Margaret (Stuart) S.; A.B. summa cum laude, Hobart Coll., 1933; B.D., McCormick Theol. Sem., 1936, Bernadine Orme Smith fellow, 1936-37; m. Mildred Emily Wood, Sept. 6, 1934; children—Martha Lee, Bonnie Jean, Mildred Emily, Mary Margaret. Asso. Halsey, Stuart & Co., 1924-29; ordained Presbyn. minister, 1936; minister 1st Presbyn. Ch., Carbondale, Pa., 1949-53, No. Light Presbyn. Ch., Juneau, Alaska, 1953—; broadcaster Religion in the News program, Juneau, Alaska; dir. KSEW The Voice of Sheldon Jackson (Sitka, Alaska); chaplain of senate Alaska, 1955-63; pastor Shepherd of the Hills United Presbyn. Ch., Lakewood, Colo., 1963—. Organizing minister Bd. Nat. Missions, United Presbyn. Ch. U.S., Snyod Colo.; chmn. Dept. on Care of Candidates, Presbytery of Denver; chmn. adv. council Alaska Employment Security Commn. Mem. permanent commn. on inter-ch. relations Gen. Assembly Presbyn. Ch. U.S. Dir. Alaska Crippled Childrens Assn.; mem. Committee of 100 for Lackawanna Indsl. Fund Enterprise and co-chmn. Upper Lackawanna Valley; chmn. 1953 Community Chest Campaign and Permanent Com. on Planning. Mem. Mayor's Com. Indsl. Rehab.; adv. com. Sheldon Jackson Jr. Coll. Served as chaplain AUS, regimental chaplain 363d Regt., 91st Inf. Div., Rome-Arno-North Apennines campaigns, 1943-46. Mem. Presbytery of Alaska, moderator 1956, pres. trustees, chmn. stewardship and promotion com., mem. council; mem. stewardship and promotion com. Synod Wash.-Alaska. Scranton Ministerium; chmn. dept. communications Synod Colo., mem. gen. council; mem. communications commn. Colo. Council of Churches; chaplain Colo. Senate, 1969—. Mem. Am. Legion (local chaplain), Officers Res. Corps, Res. Officers Assn., Mil. Order World Wars, Juneau C. of C. (vice pres. 1961, dir.), Juneau Ministers Assn. (pres. 1958), Founders and Patriots Am., V.F.W., Mil. Chaplains Assn., Ill. Hist. Soc., Sons Union Vets. Civil War (chaplain Colo.), S.A.R. (chaplain Colo.), Sons Am. Colonists, Internat. Platform Assn., Phi Beta Kappa. Mason. Clubs: Rotary, Exchange. Author: The Pastoral Ministry in Our Time (with Louis Matthews Sweet), 1948; Unto Everlasting Life, 1954. Home: 7653 Lee Dr Arvada CO 80002 Office: 11500 W 20th Ave Lakewood CO 80215

SWENNES, THOMAS RICHARD, trucking co. exec.; b. Portland, Oreg., May 27, 1930; s. Alf and Ellen Taylor (Bennison) S.; B.B.A., U. Oreg., 1954; postgrad. transp. mgmt. program Stanford U., 1965; m. Joan Hodges Swennes, Oct. 8, 1955; children—Kimberly Ellen, Clerin Michelle, Thomas Richard II. With Convoy Co., various locations, 1955—, v.p. ops., Portland, 1974-78, exec. v.p., gen. mgr., Portland, Oreg., 1978, pres., gen. mgr., 1979—; past pres. Western Hwy. Inst.; chmn. motor carrier adv. com. U.S. Dept. Transp., 1982-83; trustee Episcopalian Diocese of Oreg., 1979-82. Served with Army NG, 1951-62. Mem. Am. Trucking Assn. (vice chmn.), Oreg. Trucking Assn. (past chmn.), Nat. Automobile Transporters Assn. (exec. com.), Wash. Trucking Assn. (dir.), Idaho Motor Transport Assn. (dir.), Nat. Def. Transp. Assn. (life), Pi Kappa Alpha, Delta Nu Alpha. Republican. Office: 3900 NW Yeon Ave Portland OR 97210

SWENSON, DENNIS MALCOLM, accountant; b. Denver, Apr. 7, 1935; s. Louis Edmond and Clarice Juanita (Stephens) S.; m. Constance Colleen Conroy, July 22, 1961; children—Kristin, Carla, Kathleen, Carolyn. B.S., Brigham Young U., 1958; M.B.A., U. Denver, 1960. C.P.A., Colo. Acct., Ernst & Whinney, Denver, 1960-73, ptnr., 1973—, ptnr.-in-charge privately owned bus. practice, 1982, chmn. nat. agr. com., 1979—. Mem. exec. com. Central YMCA, Denver, 1977—; v.p. Bow Mar South Homeowners Assn., Littleton, Colo., 1983. Named Layman of Yr., Central YMCA, 1975. Mem. Am. Inst. C.P.A.s (spl. agribus. com. 1977—), Colo. Soc. C.P.A.s, Nat. Soc. Accts. for Coops. (v.p. M.W. chpt. 1982-83, mem. nat. acctg. and auditing com.). Republican. Mormon. Clubs: Denver, Pinehurst Country (Denver). Home: 5831 S Laurel Pl Littleton CO 80123 Office: 633 17th St Suite 2400 Denver CO 80202

SWENSON, NORMAN PHILIP, economist; b. Van Nuys, Calif., Jan. 7, 1939; s. Carl August and Florence Osci (Beck) S.; children—Steven, Jon. B.A., N.Mex. State U., 1964; M.A., Washington U., St. Louis, 1966, Ph.D., 1970; M.P.A., Golden Gate U., 1975. Asst. prof. econs. W.Va. U., 1969-71; chief econs. sect. Memphis dist. U.S. Army C.E., 1971-73, economist, South Pacific div., San Francisco, 1973—. Served with USNR, 1956-61. Mem. Am. Econs. Assn., Atlantic Econ. Soc. Clubs: Sierra, Telegraph Hill. Home: 440 Davis Ct Apt 1708 San Francisco CA 94111 Office: 630 Sansome St Room 752 San Francisco CA 94111

SWERDA, PATRICIA FINE, artist, author, educator; b. Ft. Worth, Aug. 10; d. William Emerson and Margaret Ellen (Cull) Fine; B.S. cum laude, Tex. Woman's U., 1941; student Ikenobo U., Tokyo, 1965-66, Ikenobo Dojo, Kyoto, Japan, 1976, 77; m. John Swerda, July 7, 1941; children—John Patrick James, Susan Ann Mary Swerda Foss, Margaret Rose Swerda Yovino. Pres., Ikenobo Sch., Seattle, 1960—; exhibited ikebana in one-person shows including: Bon Marche, Tacoma, 1966, Seattle, 1967, Gallery Kokoro, Seattle, 1972-78; exhibited in group shows including: Takashimaya Dept. Store, 1965, Matsuzakaya Dept. Store, Tokyo, 1966, Ikenobo Center, Kyoto, 1966, Seattle Art Mus., 1974-80, Sangyo Kaikan, Kyoto, 1976, Ikenobo Center, Kyoto, 1977, Burke Mus., U. Wash., ann. Cherry Blossom Festival, Seattle; demonstrations in field for various groups. Master of Ikebana of Ikenobo Ikebana Soc., Kyoto. Mem. Ikenobo Ikebana Soc. (pres. Seattle-NW Sakura chpt. 1965—), Ikebana Internat., Bonsai Clubs Internat., Puget Sound Bonsai Assn., Japan-Am. Soc., Seattle-Kobe Affiliation, Seattle Rose Soc., Seattle Chrysanthemum Soc., Nat. Press Women, Bellevue-Yao Affiliation, AAUW, Good Shepherd Movement. Democrat. Roman Catholic. Author: Japanese Flower Arranging: Practical and Aesthetic Bases of Ikebana, 1969; Creating Japanese Shoka, 1979; contbr. articles to mags. in field; numerous radio and TV appearances. Home and Office: 23025 NE 8th St Redmond WA 98052

SWERDLOW, SKIP, food service exec.; b. Columbus, Ohio, Aug. 12, 1947; s. George and Dorothe (Holzberg) S.; B.S. summa cum laude, Ariz. State U., 1969, M.B.A. summa cum laude, 1970, D.B.A. summa cum laude, 1974. Western region supr. Western Big Wheel, Inc., San Diego, 1974-75; dir. mgmt. systems Bricklin Vehicle Corp., Scottsdale, Ariz., 1975; mgmt. cons., Tempe, Ariz., 1975-76; prof. Mesa (Calif.) Community Coll., 1976, Clark County Community Coll., Las Vegas, Nev., 1976-81; asst prof. fin. U. Nev., Las Vegas, 1981—; v.p. Triple S. of Las Vegas, Inc., Burger King franchisee for 6 restaurants, 1975—; spl. cons. Coll. Bus. Adminstrn., Ariz. State U., Tempe, 1970-71, mem. exec. council, 1967-68; owner Pecos Center, shopping center. Named Businessman of Year, Distributive Edn. Clubs Am., 1977. Mem. Nev. Restaurant Assn. (sec. exec. bd.), Mensa, Phi Kappa Phi, Sigma Iota Epsilon, Beta Gamma Sigma. Republican. Jewish. Home: 3839 S Edmond St Las Vegas NV 89103 Office: 3308 S Arville Suite F 102 Las Vegas NV 89102

SWETT, HERBERT EUGENE, newspaper publisher; b. Portland, Oreg., Sept. 8, 1943; s. Herbert Lazarus and Ellen (Schwartz) S. B.A., Lewis and Clark Coll., 1965; B.S. U. Oreg., 1969. Reporter, Tri-City Herald, Kennewick, Wash., 1969-70; news editor Hermiston (Oreg.) Herald, 1970-72; wire editor Ft. Dodge (Iowa) Messenger, 1972-74; copy editor Press-Courier, Oxnard, Calif., 1974-75; wire editor Observer, La Grande, Oreg., 1975-76; pub. Pacific Tribune, Ilwaco, Wash., 1976-78; pub. Union County Review-Recorder, La Grande, 1979-81; pub. Sun Enterprise, Monmouth-Independence (Oreg.), 1981—. Mem. Monmouth-Independence Devel. Corp., Independence Beautification Assn., Monmouth-Independence Community Arts Assn. Mem. Oreg. Newspaper Pubs. Assn., Nat. Newspaper Assn., Monmouth-Independence Area C. of C. Republican. Jewish. Clubs: Lions, Elks. Home: 506 S 13th St Independence OR 97351 Office: 1697 Monmouth St Suite 1 Independence OR 97351

SWICKARD, JACK MARJEAN, publishing company executive; b. Big Spring, Tex., Mar. 5, 1943; s. Jack David and Marjorie J. (Caldwell) S.; m. Renee Marie Edwards, Feb. 10, 1968; children—Derek, Meredith. Student Ohio State U., 1961-62, Ind. U., 1963-65, U. N.Mex., 1971-73. Reporter, Indpls. Times, 1963-65, Albuquerque Tribune, 1965; reporter, city editor, 1970-74; editor Roswell (N.Mex.) Daily Record, 1974—; mem. journalism adv. council N.Mex. State U. Bd. dirs., v.p. Eastern N.Mex. State Fair, Roswell; bd. dirs. Roswell Symphony Orch. Served to chief warrant officer U.S. Army, 1965-69. Decorated D.F.C. with oak leaf cluster, Bronze Star, Air medal; Cross of Gallantry (Vietnam). Mem. N.Mex. Press Assn. (former bd. dirs.). Club: Rotary (Roswell). Home: 912 Mason Dr Roswell NM 88201 Office: PO Box 1897 Roswell NM 88201

SWIFT, AL, congressman; b. Tacoma, Sept. 10, 1935; student Whitman Coll., 1953-55, Central Wash. U., 1956-57; m. Paula Jean Jackson, 1956; children—Amy, Lauri. Dir. public affairs KVOS-TV; adminstrv. asst. to Rep. Lloyd Meeds, 1965-69; mem. 96th-98th Congresses from 2d Dist. Wash. Active, Bellingham City Charter Revision, Bellingham Housing Authority; chmn. Bellingham Citizens Adv. Com. Democrat. Office: 1502 Longworth House Office Bldg Washington DC 20515

SWIGERT, JOHN LEONARD, Congressman, businessman; b. Denver, Aug. 30, 1931; s. John Leonard and Virginia Ann (Seep) S. B.S., U. Colo., 1953; M.S. in Aerospace Sci., Rensselaer Poly. Inst., 1965; M.B.A., U. Hartford, 1967; D.Sc. (hon.) Western Mich. U., 1970, Am. Internat. Coll., 1970; Litt.D. (hon.) Western State Coll., Gunnison, Colo., 1970. Test pilot Pratt & Whitney, 1957-65, N.Am. Aviation, 1965-66; astronaut NASA, 1966-73, mem. support crew Apollo 7 and 11, module pilot Apollo 13; exec. dir. Com. on Sci. and Tech., Washington, 1973-77; v.p. technol. devel. BDM Corp., Denver, 1979-81; v.p. adminstrn. and corp. affairs Internat. Gold & Minerals Ltd., Denver, 1981; mem. 98th Congress from dist. Colo.; U.S. rep. Coral Sea Commemoration, Australia and N.Z.; speaker Republican Nat. Com., Citizens for a New Beginning. Served to capt. USAF, 1953-56. Recipient Presdl. Medal for Freedom, 1970; NASA Disting. Service medal, 1970. Fellow Am. Astron. Soc. (Flight Achievement award 1970), Soc. Exptl. Test Pilots (assoc.), AIAA (assoc.); mem. Pi Tau Sigma, Sigma Tau, Phi Gamma Delta. Republican. Roman Catholic. Home: 6350 W Mansfield Ave Apt 55 Denver CO 80235 Died Dec. 27, 1982.

SWIHART, H. GREGG, real estate co. exec.; b. San Francisco, Sept. 25, 1938; s. Lawson Benjamin and Violet Mary (Watters) S.; B.A., U. Ariz., 1958; postgrad. U. Heidelberg (W.Ger.), 1958-59, Harvard U., 1959-60; M.A., Boston U., 1961; postgrad. U. Freiburg (West Germany), 1961-65; m. Ilse Paula Rambacher, Dec. 24, 1958; children—Tatjana Etta, Brett Marc, Natascha Theda. Stock broker Walston & Co., Tucson, 1966-71; with Solot Co., Tucson, 1971-74; pres. Cienega Properties, Inc., property mgmt. and investment, Tucson, 1975-77; pres. GT Realty Assocs., Ltd., Tucson, 1977—. Mem. Tucson Com. Fgn. Relations, 1973—; pres. Forum for Greater Outdoors, 1977-79; bd. dirs. Tucson Mus. Art, 1968-74, pres. 1969-70; pres. and trustee Canelo Hills Sch., 1977-79. Cert. property mgr. Mem. Tucson Bd. Realtors, Inst. Real Estate Mgmt. (pres. Tucson-So. Ariz. chpt. 1982), Realtors Nat. Mktg. Inst. Clubs: Harvard (pres. 1973-74), Active 20-30 (pres. 1969), Downtown Tucson. Home: PO Box 555 Tunnel Springs Ranch Sonoita AZ 85637 Office: 660 N Swan Tucson AZ 85711

SWIHART, JOHN MARION, aircraft manufacturing company executive; b. New Winchester, Ohio, Dec. 27, 1923; s. Harry Miron and Fay I. (Cress) S.; m. Gloria Ann Stocker, June 15, 1947; children—Vicki Ann, John Richard, Thomas Marion, Mark Andrew. B.S. in Physics, Bowling Green State U., 1947; B.S. in Aero. Engring., Ga. Inst. Tech., 1949, postgrad., 1951-53. Asst. group leader propulsion group NASA, 1956-58, group leader spl. projects, 1958-59, head advanced configurations group aircraft, 1959-62, chief large supersonic tunnels br., 1962; with Boeing Co., 1962—, dir. internat. sales for Far East, Boeing Comml. Airplane Co., Renton, Wash., 1971-74, v.p. Japan, Boeing Internat. Corp., Tokyo, 1973-74, dep. dir. internat. sales, Renton, 1974-75, 7x7 program mgr., Kent, Wash., 1975-76, dir. new airplane product devel., sales, mktg., Seattle, 1976-78, dir. product devel., sales, mktg., 1978-79, v.p. U.S., Can. sales, 1979-83, v.p. govt. tech. liaison, 1983—. Served to 1st lt. USAAF, 1943-45. Decorated D.F.C., Air medal with 3 oak leaf clusters. Fellow AIAA (chmn. aircraft design com. 1970-72, chmn. Pacific N.W. sect. 1969-70, gen. chmn. aircraft systems and design meeting 1977); mem. Am. Ordnance Assn., Japan-Am. Soc. (pres. 1978-79). Contbr. articles to profl. jours. Office: Boeing Commercial Airplane Co PO Box 3707 Seattle WA 98124

SWINDELLS, WILLIAM, JR., lumber and paper company executive; b. 1930. BS., Stanford U., 1953. With Willamette Industries Inc., Portland, Oreg., 1953—, sr. v.p. prodn. and mktg. bldg. materials, exec. v.p., pres. forest products div., pres., chief exec. officer, 1982—, also dir., chief operating officer; dir. Oreg. Bank, Portland Office: Willamette Industries Inc 1300 SW 5th Ave Portland OR 97201*

SWING, M(ARIE) JOAN, educational administrator, reading coordinator, consultant; b. Lansing, Mich., Nov. 24, 1930; d. Michael John and Marie Pauline (Nemeth) Hynes; m. Herbert Ralston Swing, Jr., June 7, 1952; children—Sandra Lynne, Michael Daniel. B.A. in Elem. Edn., Wittenburg U., 1966; M.A. in Reading, U. Md., 1970; Ed.D. in Reading, U. No. Colo., 1978. Cert. B-type teaching, Reading K-12; D-type adminstrv. Tchr. elem. schs., Ohio and Md., 1962-71; tchr. Air Acad. Jr. High Sch., Colorado Springs, Colo., 1971-74; reading coordinator Air Acad. Sch. Dist., Colorado Springs, 1974—, also chpt. I coordinator; cons., lectr. lang. arts K-12. Mem. Internat. Reading Assn., Phi Delta Kappa, Delta Kappa Gamma. Republican. Mem. Christian Ch. Author: The Family that Reads Together Succeeds Together, 1981; co-author: Grooving with Reading Games, 1976; What Do I Do Next Teacher?, 1978. Office: 8061 Horizon Dr Colorado Springs CO 80918

SWINK, RHONDA LYNN, data processing cons., software co. exec.; b. Ft. Dodge, Iowa, Mar. 15, 1954; d. Robert Leo and Donna Jean (Nordstrom) S.; student Calif. State U., Fresno, 1972-73, Rio Hondo Community Coll., 1973-77, IBM Learning Ctr., Norwalk, Calif.; cert. in programming Basic Four Corp., 1975. With Nev. Meats Inc., Las Vegas, 1973; computer operator, collections Monfort Food Distbg. Co., Long Beach, Calif., 1973-75; computer operator, programmer accounts receivable Rod's Food Products, Inc., Los Angeles, 1975-77; data processing mgr., statistician Wilcour Food Products, Inc., Los Angeles, 1977-80, systems analyst Monogram Aerospace Fasteners, City of Commerce, Calif., 1980; pres. owner Basic 4 Software and Ops. Cons., Hacienda Heights, Calif., 1980—; regional sr. systems analyst for new devel. CFS Continental, Vernon, Calif.; lectr. to fgn. students. Mem. Data Processing Mgmt. Assn., Nat. Assn. Female Execs., Am. Entrepreneurs Assn., Library Computer and Info. Scis., Am. Mgmt. Assn., Western Basic Four Users Group, Am. Assn. Aviculture, Am. Lovebird Soc., Am. Cockatiel Soc. Republican. Roman Catholic. Club: Orange County Bird Breeders. 2310 S Stimson St Hacienda Heights CA 91745 Office: 2300 E 57th St Vernon Los Angeles CA 90058 also 2310 S Stimson St Hacienda Heights CA 91745

SWISTOK, JOHN EDWARD, electrical engineer; b. Lordstown, Ohio, June 18, 1933; s. John and Matilda Margaret (Mathe) S.; A.A., Long Beach City Coll., 1959; B.S. in Elec. Engring., U. Calif., Berkeley, 1961; m. Nancy Ann Miloch, Mar. 29, 1955; children—John Robert, Paula Marie Swistok Elston, Roberta Paula, Diana Nannette, Nancy Ann, Robert John, Vetura Roberta. Research engr. Autonetics, Anaheim, Calif., 1961-62; engr. Nortronics, Anaheim, 1962-63; elec. engr. Gen. Dynamics, Pomona, Calif., 1963-64; sr. engr. Northrop Corp., Newbury Park, Calif., 1968-69, Hawthorne, Calif., 1969-74; sr. engr. Litton Industries, Woodland Hills, Calif., 1964-68; engring. specialist Litton Industries, 1974-76; reliability engring. specialist Northrop Corp., Hawthorne, Calif., 1977—. Tchr., Religious Sci. Jr. Ch., 1971—. Served with USN, 1952-56; Korea. Mem. IEEE, Northrop Mgmt. Club. Home: 2037 N Chouteau St Orange CA 92665 Office: One Northrop Ave Hawthorne CA 90250

SYERS, WILLIAM EDWARD, mfg. co. exec.; b. DeKoven, Ky., Feb. 26, 1926; s. John Benedict and Mary Helen (Watson) S.; student Lockyear's Bus. Coll., Evansville, Ind., 1950-52; m. Veda Marie Swisher, Dec. 23, 1950; children—David Bruce, Drew Edward. With Internat. Harvester Co., Evansville, Ind., 1946-52, IBM, 1952-68, subs. Service Bur. Corp., 1968-70; with Teledyne Econ. Devel. Co., Phoenix, 1970—, dir. adminstrv. services, 1979—. Served with Q.M.C., AUS, 1946-48. Mem. Adminstrv. Mgmt. Soc. (pres. Phoenix chpt. 1977-78, dir. 1978-79), Phoenix C. of C. Republican. Mem. Ch. of Christ. Office: Teledyne Econ Devel Co 518 S 3d St Phoenix AZ 85004

SYKES, BARBARA SUE SHOULTS, vocational coordinator/educator; b. Gallup, N.Mex., Jan. 12, 1939; d. Merle G. and Esther Radford (Shoults) Brown; m. Harley Ray, Sept. 26, 1959; children—Marvin Ray, Melinda Sue, Martin Farris, Marie Frances. B.A. in Psychology, Calif. State U.-Chico, 1972; M.S. in Occupational Edn., Central Wash. U., 1978; Ed.D., Seattle U., 1982. Prin., tchr., presch. dir., Calif., 1963-1972; dir./adminstr. Lake County Day Care, Lakeview, Oreg., 1972-73; tchr. Tacoma Day Nursery, (Wash.), 1975-76; day care coordinator/instr. home and family life dept. Clover Park Vocat.-Tech. Inst., Tacoma, 1976—; cons. child sexual abuse programs. Recipient Wash. State award Delta Kappa Gamma, 1980; Wash. State vocat. adminstrv. intern, 1981-82. Mem. Am. Vocat. Assn. (life), Wash. Vocat. Assn. (life; pres. chpt. 1980-81), Wash. Assn. Edn. Young Children, Tacoma Assn. Edn. Young Children, AAUW, N.W. Women in Ednl. Adminstrn., Nat. Assn. Vocat. Home Econs. Tchrs., Nat. Assn. Post-Secondary Adult Vocat. Home Econs., Phi Delta Kappa. Democrat. Roman Catholic. Author: The Kids Are Cooking, 1977; curriculum/manual on child sexual abuse. Home: 8105 52d Ct W Tacoma WA 98467 Office: Clover Park Vo-Tech Inst 4500 Steilacoom Blvd SW Tacoma WA 98499

SYKES, BOBBY WYATT, psychologist; b. Lineville, Ala., July 22, 1945; s. Wallace W. and Lola M. (Robertson) S.; A.A., Triton Jr. Coll., 1970; B.A., U. Ill., 1971; M.A., U. Kans., 1975, Ph.D., 1977; m. Judith Ann Atwell, Mar. 7, 1980. Dir. spl. tng. for exceptional people, Billings, Mont., 1976-77; supr. dept. spl. edn. Eastern Mont. Coll., Billings, 1977; pediatric psychologist No. N.Mex. Rehab. Center, Las Vegas, 1977-78; asst. prof. dept. psychology N.Mex. Highlands U., summer, 1978; cons. Albuquerque Public Schs., 1979-82, Los Lunas (N.Mex.) Hosp. and Tng. Sch., 1979-81, no. N.Mex. public schs., 1977—; clin. psychologist psychol. services unit, div. of vocat. rehab., Albuquerque, 1977—; pvt. practice clin. psychology, Rio Rancho, N.Mex., 1980—. Mem. Black Communication Forum, Albuquerque, 1980—; chmn. Concerned Black Citizens for Correctional Reform, 1980-82. Served with U.S. Army, 1963-66. Decorated Purple Heart. Mem. Nat. Rehab. Assn., Nat. Soc. Autistic Children, N.Mex. Rehab. Assn., Assn. Advancement of Behavior Therapy, Am. Psychol. Assn., N.Mex. Psychol. Assn., Biofeedback Soc. N.Mex., N.Mex. Psychol. Soc., Am. Assn. Mental Deficiency, Epilepsy Council Albuquerque, N.Mex. Psychologists in Public Service, Albuquerque Assn. Children with Learning Disabilities. Baptist. Contbr. articles to jours. in psychology. Home: 1735 Laird Ct Rio Rancho NM 87124 Office: 122 LaVeta NE Albuquerque NM 87108

SYLVESTER, RICHARD RUSSELL, fin. cons. co. exec.; b. Newton, Iowa, Jan. 10, 1938; s. Leslie Gardner and Effie (Williams) S.; B.A., UCLA, 1959, Ph.D., 1970; M.B.A., U. So. Calif., 1962; J.D., Loyola U., 1981; m. Irene Elizabeth Lehman, Apr. 17, 1976; children—Bonnie Ann, Vicky Ellis, Juliesta Elaine. Designer corp. offices Gen. Motors Corp., Warren, Mich., 1958; sr. analyst Lockheed Aircraft Corp., Burbank, Calif., 1962-66; sr. planner corporate offices Hughes Aircraft Co., Culver City, Calif., 1966-68; sr. staff economist, staff mgr. TRW, Inc., Redondo Beach, Calif., 1969-70; asst. prof. Calif. State U., 1970-73; mgr. corp. planning Brunswick/Defense/Celesco, Costa Mesa, Calif., 1973-75; mgmt. cons., engring. cons., Los Angeles, 1970—; owner, gen. mgr. Def. Research Co., Ph.D. Pub. Co., Sylvester Appraisal Co., 1975-81; staff specialist, strategic planning Gen. Dynamics Corp., 1981-83; sr. staff specialist strategic planning Northrop Corp., 1983—; lectr. Northrop U., U. Calif., U. So. Calif., Loyola U., 1961-76, La Verne U., 1976-79; asso. prof. Pepperdine U., 1975-76; co-founder Theta Cable TV, Los Angeles, 1966-67. Bd. dirs., deacon Westwood Hills Christian Ch. Gen. Motors Corp. scholar, 1953-57; Ford Found. grantee, 1965; U.S. Fed. Govt. research grantee, 1967-70; U. Calif. postdoctoral scholar in systems engring., 1970-73. Mem. Beta Gamma Sigma, Alpha Kappa Psi. Author: Management Decisions and Actions, 2d edit., 1982; Tax Planning, 4th edit., 1980; Investment Planning, 1982; contbr. tech. reports to profl. lit. Patentee in field. Home: 10860 Arizona Ave Culver City CA 90230

SYMMS, STEVEN DOUGLAS, senator; b. Nampa, Idaho, Apr. 23, 1938; s. Darwin and Irene (Knowlton) S.; B.S., U. Idaho, 1960; m. Frances E. Stockdale, 1959; children—Dan, Susan, Amy, Katy. Mem. 93th-96th Congresses from 1st Dist. Idaho; mem. U.S. Senate, from Idaho, 1980—, mem. Fin., Budget, Environment and Pub. Works coms. Office: Senate Office Bldg Washington DC 20510 also 304 N 8th St Boise ID 83701

SYMONS, ROBERT SPENCER, electronic engineer; b. San Francisco, July 3, 1925; s. Spencer W. and Avesia (Atkins) S.; B.S., Stanford U., 1946, M.S., 1948; m. Alice Faye Smith, Dec. 21, 1960; children—Julia Ann, Robert Spencer. Engr., Eitel-McCullough, Inc., San Bruno, Calif., 47, Heinz & Kaufman, South San Francisco, 1948, Pacific Electronics Co., Los Gatos, Calif., 1949; sr. engring. mgr. Varian Assocs., Palo Alto, Calif., 1950-83; product line mgr. Litton Industries, San Carlos, Calif., 1983—. Served to 1st lt. AUS, 1950-53. Fellow IEEE; mem. Phi Beta Kappa, Tau Beta Pi. Club: Commonwealth of Calif. Assoc. editor IEEE Transactions on Electron Devices, 1980-83. Patentee in field. Home: 290 Surrey Pl Los Altos CA 94022 Office: 960 Industrial Rd San Carlos CA 94070

SYPULT, ROBERT LYNN, utility ofcl.; b. Bloomington, Ill., Apr. 20, 1945; s. Francis Eugene and Dorothy Lucille (Freed) S.; B.S., U. Ariz., 1968; cert. FBI Acad., Quantico, Va., 1973; m. Nancy Sue Case, July 27, 1979. Investment counselor Warren Rustand & Assos., Tucson, 1970-71; prodn. control mgr. Griffiths Electronics, Tucson, 1971-72; subcontract adminstr. govt. div. Motorola, Scottsdale, Ariz., 1972-73; spl. agt. FBI, Washington, 1973-78; mgr. corporate security Salt River Project, Phoenix, 1978—; loss prevention cons. Mem. Mesa Crime Prevention Com., 1981-82. Served with U.S. Army, 1968-70. Decorated Bronze Star. Mem. Am. Soc. Indsl. Security (chmn. Phoenix; mem. nat. public utility com.), Soc. Former FBI Agts., Planning Execs. Inst. Republican. Home: 2564 Onza Ave W Mesa AZ 85202 Office: PO Box 1980 Phoenix AZ 85001

SYRING, WILLIAM RICHARD, hosp. cons.; b. Toledo, Mar. 31, 1942; s. Karl Michael and Carolyn Addison (D'Arneille) S. B.S., Fla. Atlantic U., 1969; M.B.A., U. San Francisco, 1974; Ph.D., Golden Gate U., 1978. Asst. v.p. Rothrock Internat., N.Y.C., 1970-71, v.p., San Francisco, 1971-76, exec. v.p., 1976—; founder, dir. Med. Mgmt. Services Am., Inc. Mem. Pan Am. Med. Assn., Acad. Polit. Sci., SCV. Republican. Episcopalian. Author: The Delivery of Health Care in the United States, 1950-1975, 1978. Office: 201 S Lake St Suite 500 Pasadena CA 91101

SYVERSON, LAVAND MERLYN, hosp. adminstr.; b. Willmar, Minn., Apr. 8, 1932; s. Reuben and Hattie (Anderson) S.; M.S. in Bus. Adminstrn., Columbia U., 1955, M.S. in Hosp. Adminstrn., 1957; m. Beverly Brush, June 14, 1954; children—Cheryl Anne, Carol Lynne, Cynthia Joy. Adminstrv. resident Barnert Meml. Hosp., Paterson, N.J., 1956-57; asso. dir. Am. U. Hosp., Beirut, also prof. program hosp. adminstrn., 1957-68; exec. dir. St. Paul Ramsey Med. Center, 1968-80; adminstr., v.p. Presbyn. Hosp. Center, Albuquerque, 1980—; cons. WHO, Am. U. Beirut Services Corp., govts. Bahrain and Saudi Arabia. Recipient citation 8th Army Command, 1958; Student award Wall St. Jour., 1954. Mem. Am. Coll. Hosp. Adminstrs. Baptist. Clubs: Albuquerque Rotary. Office: 1100 Central SE Albuquerque NM 87102

SYVERTSON, CLARENCE ALFRED, aeronautical engineer; b. Mpls., Jan. 12, 1926; s. Alfred and Esther Louise (Goertemiller) S.; m. Helen Hammon Connella, May 4, 1953 (dec.); 1 dau., Marguerite Louise; m. 2d, JoAnn Caruso Single, May 8, 1982. B. Aero. Engring., U. Minn., 1946, M.S., 1948; postgrad. Stanford U., 1950-57; grad. Advanced Mgmt. Program, Harvard U., 1977. Research scientist Ames Aero. Lab. NACA, Moffett Field, Calif., 1948-58; with Ames Research Ctr., NASA, Moffett Field, 1958—, exec. dir. Joint Dept. Transp./NASA Civil Aviation Research and Devel. Policy Study, 1970-71, dep. dir. Ames Research Ctr., 1969-78, dir., 1978—. mem. adv. bd. Coll. Engring., U. Calif.-Berkeley; mem. engring. adv. council San Jose State U.; mem. adv. council dept. aerospace engring. and mechanics U. Minn. Served with AC, U.S. Army, 1946-47. Recipient Invention and Contbn. award NASA, 1964, Exceptional Service medal, 1971. Fellow Am. Astronautical Soc., AIAA (Lawrence Sperry award 1957); mem. Nat. Acad. Engring., Am. Helicopter Soc., Air Force Assn. Club: Nat. Space (gov.). Home: 15725 Apollo Heights Ct Saratoga CA 95070 Office: NASA-Ames Research Ctr MS 200-1 Moffett Field CA 94035

SZALAI, KENNETH JOHN, engineering administrator; b. Milw., June 1, 1942; s. John and Elsie (Centgraf) S.; m. Mary Kathryn Surges, Mar. 21, 1942; children—Jeffrey, Christine, Terrill. B.S.E.E., U. Wis., 1964; M.S.M.E., U. So. Calif., 1970. Research engr. NASA, Dryden Flight Research Facility, Edwards AFB, Calif., 1964-71, principal investigator F-8 digital fly-by-wire program, 1971-79, chief, flight controls, 1979-81, chief, dynamics and controls, 1981-82, dir. engring., 1982—. Exceptional Service award NASA, 1978. Mem. AIAA, Eta Kappa Nu. Lutheran. Contbr. articles to profl. jours. Office: PO Box 273 Edwards CA 93523

SZARNICKI, ROBERT JOSEPH, pediatric/adult cardiovascular surgeon; b. Natrona Heights, Pa., Oct. 29, 1943; s. Frank John and Xaviera (Zolnowski) S.; A.B., Columbia Coll., 1965; M.D., Boston U., 1969; m. Mary; children—Robert Stuart, Lauren Kathleen. Gen. surg. intern Boston City Hosp., 1969-70; resident in surgery, Boston Univ. Hosp., 1971-74; exchange registrar U. Wales, 1972-73; surgery resident St. Luke's Hosp., N.Y.C., 1970-71; cardiac surgery resident Columbia U. and Harlem Hosp., N.Y.C., 1974-76; sr. registrar in pediatric cardiac surgery Hosp. for Sick Children, London, 1976-77; pediatric cardiovascular surgeon Children's Hosp. of San Francisco, 1980, asso. pediatric and adult cardiovascular surgeon Pacific Med. Center, San Francisco, 1977—, mem. critical care com. 1980—, joint clin. practice com., 1979-80. Diplomate Am. Bd. Surgery, Am. Bd. Thoracic Surgery. Fellow ACS, Am. Coll. Cardiology; mem. AMA, Calif. Med. Assn., San Francisco Med. Soc., Soc. Thoracic Surgeons, Soc. Thoracic and Cardiovascular Surgeons Gt. Britain and Ireland, Pan Pacific Surg. Assn., San Francisco Surg. Soc., Pediatric Cardiac Surg. Group. Clubs: San Francisco Bay, Guardsmen, Garfield Gentlemen's. Contbr. articles to profl. jours., invented exptl. extra cardiac bypass of obstructed mitral valve, 1979. Home: 140 Castenada St San Francisco CA 94116 Office: PO Box 7999 Clay and Buchanan Sts San Francisco CA 94120

SZIKLAI, GEORGE CLIFFORD, cons. scientist; b. Budapest, Hungary, July 9, 1909; came to U.S., 1930, naturalized, 1940; s. Eugene Clifford and Helen (Hajdu) S.; diploma in Chem. Engr., Munich Tech. Inst., Germany, 1928; absolutorium Pazmany U., Budapest, 1930; m. Violet Jambor, Jan. 12, 1934; 1 dau., Kate Violet Sziklai Alexander. Asst. chief engr. Aerovox Corp., 1930-31; chief engr. Polymet Mfg. Co., 1932-35; research engr. Micamold Radio Corp., 1935-39; physicist RCA Corp., 1939-56; dir. research Westinghouse Electric Corp., Pitts., 1956-67; sr. scientist Lockheed Missiles & Space Co., Palo Alto, Calif., 1967-75; pvt. practice cons. scientist, Los Altos Hills, Calif., 1976—; lectr. in field. Recipient David Sarnoff Research Lab. awards, 1947, 51, 52. Fellow IEEE; mem. N.Y. Acad. Scis., Optical Soc. Am., Sigma Xi. Republican. Presbyterian. Contbr. articles to profl. publs.; patentee in field. Address: 26900 St Francis Rd Los Altos Hills CA 94022

SZMUCH, OSCAR, language educator; b. USSR, July 2, 1943; came to U.S., 1966; s. Isaac and Genya (Fogel) S.; m. Eileen Robbins, Mar. 9, 1980; children— Genya, Orley Robbins. Exec. dir., owner Michel Thomas Lang. Ctr., Encino, Calif., 1975—; producer TV show R. Buckminster Fuller. Mem. adv. bd. Calif. State U.-Los Angeles; regional bd. dirs. Anti-Defamation League. Served with Israeli Def. Forces, 1963-66. Mem. Encino C. of C. (dir.). Home: 11254 Key West Northridge CA 91326 Office: 16133 Ventura Blvd Encino CA 91436

SZYNAKA, EDWARD M., library director, consultant; b. N.Y.C., Sept. 26, 1948; s. Edward J. and Catherine A. (Regan) S.; m. Diane Pickering; children—Edward, Andrew, Emily. B.A. in Polit. Sci., SUNY-Fredonia, 1972; M.L.A., Syracuse U., 1973. Dir. libraries, Massena, N.Y., 1972-75, Midland, Mich., 1975-80; dir. Pasadena (Calif.) Pub. Library, 1980—; mgmt. cons. Bd. dirs. ARC; active Big Bros. Served to lt. U.S. Army, 1966-68. Mem. ALA, Calif. Library Assn., Mich. Library Assn. Democrat. Roman Catholic. Club: Kiwanis.

TABACHNICK, KENNETH, clinic sch. adminstr.; b. Chgo., July 13, 1934; s. Louis A. and Bertha (Usprich) T.; B.A. in Psychology, U. Calif. at Los Angeles, 1956; M.S., Los Angeles State Coll., 1958; m. Barbara Joyce Gerson, Aug. 28, 1955. Ednl. therapist Marianne Frostig Center of Ednl. Therapy, Los Angeles, 1954-64; staff psychologist Los Angeles County Probation Dept., 1964-65; exec. dir. W. Valley Center for Ednl. Therapy, Canoga Park, Calif., 1965-72, Calif. Center for Ednl. Therapy, Woodland Hills, 1972—; past pres., co-founder Found. for Perceptual and Psycholinguistic Devel., Canoga Park, bd. dirs., 1965-72; pres., co-founder Calif. Found. to H.E.L.P., Woodland Hills, bd. dirs., 1972—; instr. spl. edn. Pepperdine U., Los Angeles; asst. prof. psychology Calif. State U.; guest lectr. various colleges; cons. in field; co-owner numis. firm Blu-Tab. USPHS fellow, 1961-62; honored by spl. resolution City Council of Los Angeles, 1971; licensed marriage, family and child counselor, Calif. Mem. Am., Western, Calif. State, Los Angeles County, San Fernando Valley psychol. assns., Calif. State Marriage Counseling Assn., Calif. Assn. for Neurologically Handicapped Children, Assn. for Children with Learning Disabilities. Contbr. articles to profl. and numis. jours. Office: 6016 Fallbrook Ave Suite 201 Woodland Hills CA 91367

TABER, ROBERT RUSSELL, advertising educator, counsultant; b. Richland, Wash., Aug. 4, 1949; s. Robert Russell and Catherine Cordelia

(Foote) T.; m. Karen Jean Chrisman, Jan. 23, 1970; 1 son, Benjamin Guy. B.A. in Journalism, U. Idaho, 1971; M.A. in Journalism, U. Oreg., 1973. Acct. exec. Dailey & Assocs. Advt. Agy., San Francisco, 1973-75; acct. supr. Ayer/Baker Advt. Agy., Seattle, 1975-78; v.p., acct. supr. N.W. Ayer Advt. Agy., N.Y.C., 1978-80; asst. prof. advt. U. Oreg., 1980—; cons. in field. Mem. Am. Advt. Fedn., Mid-Oreg. Advt. Club, Am. Acad. Advt., Kappa Tau Alpha, Phi Kappa Phi. Contbr. articles to profl. publs. Home: 2036 Olive St Eugene OR 97405 Office: School of Journalism University of Oregon Eugene OR 97403

TABOR, DORIS DEE, educator; b. Maryville, Mo., Sept. 17, 1918; d. Mark Rolla and Golda Mae (Roach) Hiles; B.S., N.W. Mo. State U., 1939; M.S., U. Nebr., 1958, Ed.D., 1967; m. John S. Tabor, June 28, 1942 (dec.); children—Teresa Ann Tabor Griffith, Patricia Annette Tabor Vallat. Tchr. public schs., Omaha, 1947-58; instr. U. Nebr., Omaha, 1958-59, asst. prof., 1959-61, asso. prof., 1961-63, prof., 1963-67; prof. edn. Calif. State U., Long Beach, 1967—, chairperson dept. tchr. edn., 1980—; faculty U. No. Iowa, summer 1967, UCLA extension, 1968, Pepperdine U. extension, 1968; cons. Calif. State Dept. Edn., 1968-70, Redondo Beach (Calif.) Public Schs., 1967-73; dir. field center ABC Sch. Dist., 1974—. Bd. dirs. Armed Services YMCA, Long Beach, 1974-76, Travelers Aid of Long Beach, 1974-76. Recipient Emily Gates Outstanding Alumnae Achievement award Sigma Sigma Sigma, 1970; Kappa Delta Pi Honor key, 1974. Mem. Nebr. Congress of Parents and Tchrs., Internat. Orgn. Tchr. Educators of Reading (pres. 1981-82), Calif. Profs. Reading (pres. 1974-76), Mid Cities Reading Council (pres. 1980-81), Orange County Reading Assn. (bd. dirs. 1975-79), Calif. Assn. Profs. of Elem. Edn. (pres. 1979-80), Kappa Delta Pi (nat. v.p. 1976-78), Sigma Sigma Sigma (nat. parliamentarian 1959-67). Democrat. Presbyterian. Clubs: Zonta, Women's Service Club for Exec. and Profl. Women (pres. 1969—), Job's Daus. Contbr. articles to profl. jours.; contbr.: An Annotated Bibliography: Selected Books on American Indians for Children and Young Adolescents, 1978. Home: 6000 Stearns St Long Beach CA 90815 Office: 1250 Bellflower Blvd Long Beach CA 90840

TABRISKY, JOSEPH, radiologist; b. Boston, June 23, 1931; s. Henry and Gertrude Tabrisky; B.A. cum laude, Harvard U., 1952; M.D. cum laude, Tufts U., 1956; m. Phyllis Eleanor Page, Apr. 23, 1955; children—Joseph Page, Elizabeth Ann, William Page. Flexible intern U. Ill. Hosp., 1956-57; resident in radiology Fitzsimons Army Hosp., 1958-60; instr. radiology Tufts U. Med. Sch., 1964-65; cons. radiologist Swedish Med. Center, Denver, 1966-68; chief radiologist Kaiser Found. Hosp., Harbor City, Calif., 1968-72; mem. faculty UCLA Med. Sch., 1972—, prof. radiol. scis., 1975—, vice chmn. dept., 1976—; chmn. radiology dept. Harbor-UCLA Med. Center, 1975—, pres. faculty soc., 1979-80; chmn. Los Angeles County Radiol. Standards Com., 1979. Mem. Harvard-Radcliffe Schs. Com.; bd. dirs., treas., Harbor-UCLA Med. Found.; mem. UCLA Council for Ednl. Planning. Served to maj. M.C., U.S. Army, 1957-63. Diplomate Am. Bd. Radiology. Fellow Am. Coll. Radiology; mem. Radiol. Soc. N. Am., Assn. U. Radiologists, Am. Heart Assn. (cardiovascular radiology council), Calif. Med. Assn., Calif. Radiol. Soc., So. Calif. Radiol. Soc., Los Angeles Med. Assn., Los Angeles Radiol. Soc., Alpha Omega Alpha. Contbr. articles to med. jours. Office: 1000 W Carson St Torrance CA 90509

TADA, MITSURU, architect; b. Fukuoka, Japan, Sept. 11, 1929; s. Hidegoro and Hisae (Takenaga) T.; came to U.S., 1949; B.Arch., U. Calif. at Berkeley, 1956; m. Fusako Atsuta, Dec. 15, 1956; 1 son, Izumi. Project architect firm Corwin Booth & Asso. Architects, San Francisco, 1967-69; practice architecture, San Francisco, 1969—; pres. Mitsuru Tada, AIA, Inc., architects and planners, San Francisco and Los Angeles; dir. Sumitomo Constrn. Am. Inc., San Francisco. Archtl. advisor Sumitomo Bank Calif., San Francisco, 1973—; cons. C. Itoh Co. Ltd., Tokyo, 1975-77; fallout shelter analyst. Mem. A.I.A., Japan Soc. San Francisco, Japanese Am. Assn. San Francisco Cultural Ctr., Japanese C. of C. Club: Mira Vista Golf and Country. Contbr. articles on arts, architecture to profl. jours. Exhibited sculpture metal abstract U. Cal. at Berkeley, Davis, Los Angeles, Riverside, Santa Barbara, 1956, metal abstract San Francisco Mus Art, 1956, metal abstract Forum Gallery, N.Y.C., 1956. Home: 911 and 927 San Benito Rd Berkeley CA 94707 Office: 305 Grant Ave San Francisco CA 94108 also 650 S Grand Ave Suite 814 Los Angeles CA 90017

TAFOYA, ARTHUR N., bishop; b. Alameda, N.Mex., Mar. 2, 1933; ed. St. Thomas Sem., Denver, Conception (Mo.) Sem. Ordained priest, Roman Cath. Ch., 1962; ordained bishop of Pueblo, Colo., 1980. Office: 1426 Grand Ave Pueblo CO 81003*

TAFT, PERRY HAZARD, lawyer; b. Los Angeles, Jan. 23, 1915; s. Milton T. and Sara Eleanor Taft; A.B., UCLA, 1936; LL.B., George Washington U., 1940; children—Stephen D., Sally L., Sheila R.; m. 2d, Callie S., Aug. 15, 1968. Admitted to Calif. bar, 1941; spl. atty. antitrust div. U.S. Dept. Justice, Los Angeles, 1941-42; dep. atty. gen. Calif., San Francisco, 1943-44; Western regional rep. Council State Govts., San Francisco, 1944-45; Western dir. govt. affairs TWA, Los Angeles, 1945-46; Pacific Coast mgr. Am. Ins. Assn., San Francisco, 1948-66; gen. counsel Assn. Calif. Ins. Cos., Sacramento, 1967-73; asst. city atty. Stockton, Calif., 1973-79; pres. Perry H. Taft, P.C., Stockton, 1979—; dir. Compair, Inc., Burlingame, Calif., Pacific Aerospace, Inc., Campbell, Calif.; arbitrator Surplus Line Assn. Calif., 1965—. Bd. dirs. Stockton-E. Water Dist., 1979—, pres., 1981—; mem. San Joaquin County Water Adv. Com. Mem. State Bar Calif., San Joaquin County Bar Assn., No. Calif. Soc. Assn. Execs. (pres. 1960-61), Nat. Aeros. Assn. (pres. San Francisco chpt. 1953-54). Democrat. Clubs: Elkhorn Country (sec. Men's Club 1976-82), Yosemite. Home: 8615 Stonewood Dr Stockton CA 95209 Office: Perry H Taft PC PO Box 7453 Stockton CA 95207

TAGALA, ISABEL MARTINEZ, lawyer, ins. exec.; b. Philippines, Oct. 12, 1930; naturalized, 1964; d. Gaspar P. and Vicenta (Martinez) T.; LL.B., Far Eastern U., 1956; postgrad. Law Sch., U. Calif., Berkeley, 1958; children by previous marriage—Wenceslao T. Vinzons, Gavino T. Vinzons, Alexander T. Vinzons. Admitted to Philippine bar, 1957; aide Hawaii Legislature, Honolulu, 1966-67; law clk. Hawaii Atty. Gen. Office, Honolulu, 1967-69; exec. sales staff Mfrs. Life Ins. Co., Honolulu, 1969—. C.L.U. Mem. Honolulu Commn. on Status of Women, 1975. Mem. Fil-Am. Assn. (pres.), Waikiki Bus. and Profl. Women (v.p. 1978), Philippine Bar Assn., Hawaii Bar Assn., Filipino Lawyers Assn. (v.p.), Honolulu C. of C., Million Dollar Round Table (life). Democrat. Roman Catholic. Office: 745 Fort St Suite 1600 Honolulu HI 96813

TAGERT, JOHN LINCOLN, city ofcl.; b. Colorado Springs, Colo., June 23, 1933; s. Charles Lincoln and Sarah Ruth (Jumper) T.; student Northrup U., 1960, Arapahoe Coll., 1967-68, U. So. Calif., 1968; B.A. in Sociology, U. Colo., 1970, M.P.A., 1976; postgrad. Colo. Coll., 1971, U. Va., 1975, 80; student Police Found. Exec. Tng. Program, 1975-77; grad. Nat. Exec. Inst., 1980; B.S. in Criminal Justice (hon.), Colo. Tech. Coll., 1977; m. Catherine Margaret Chavez, July 1, 1977; children—James Lincoln, Michael John. Exptl. designer Aircraft Mechanics, Inc., Colorado Springs, 1956-57; heavy equipment mgr. City of Colorado Springs, 1957-58, 60-62; with Colorado Springs Police Dept., 1962—, dep. chief, 1974-76, chief police, 1976—; cons. in field; mem. Colo. Gov.'s Bd. Crime and Delinquency Control, 1970-77; mem. criminal justice adv. com. Pikes Peak Area Council Govts., 1973-75, chmn. com., 1974-75, mem. council youth task force, 1974, mem. info. systems tech. com., 1975; mem. Colo. Gov.'s Planning Bd. on Crime and Delinquency Control, 1976—; bd. dirs. Criminal Justice Info. Center, 1978—; mem. adv. bd. Victim Witness Assistance Program, 1979—; mem. Colo. Council on Criminal Justice, 1979—; chmn. Colo. Jail Standards Commn. 1980-81. Mem. Colo. Juvenile Council, 1970-74; mem. Community Schs. Bd. Colorado Springs, 1972-74; v.p. services Boys' Club, Colorado Springs, 1972-76; 1st v.p. Pikes Peak Family Counseling and Mental Health Centers, 1972-77; mem. USO Council, El Paso County, 1975-76; pres. Mental Health Assn. of Pikes Peak Region, 1975; adviser U.S. Olympic Com. Sports Festival, 1981. Served with USAF, 1952-55. Decorated Purple Heart; recipient spl. citation of merit Colorado Springs Bd. Realtors, 1968, Outstanding Service award Boys' Club Colorado Springs, 1970, award of appreciation Def. Agy. El Paso County, 1972, spl. recognition citation Colo. Juvenile Council, 1972, Service to Mankind award (3) Sertoma Internat., 1976, award of appreciation Lambda Alpha Epsilon, 1977, cert. of merit Jobs for Progress-Minority Youth, 1978, Outstanding Citizen award award Colorado Springs Boosters-SAT-UP, 1978, Mayor's commendation City Colorado Springs, 1978, plaque of appreciation Dept. Army Criminal Investigation Command, 1979, award of appreciation 46th Security Police Squadron Peterson AFB, 1979, citation of honor for disting. service, Nat. Assn. Legions of Honor, 1980, cert. of appreciation Am. Criminal Justice Assn., 1980, resolution of commendation, Colorado Springs City Council, 1980. Mem. Internat. Assn. Chiefs Police, Colo. Assn. Chiefs Police, Colo. Assn. Law Enforcement Officers, Colo. Police Protective Assn., Police Exec. Research Forum, Univ. Research Corp., SEARCH Group, Wash. State Sheriff and Police Chief Assn., Phi Beta Kappa. Clubs: Masons, Shriners, Moose. Author profl. reports, including Colo. Jail Standards, 1980. Office: Office of Chief of Police Colorado Springs Police Dept Colorado Springs CO 80901*

TAGGART, CAL SNELL, former state senator; b. Cowley, Wyo., Feb. 6, 1924; s. Grant and Fern (Snell) T.; B.S., Brigham Young U., 1946; grad. Inst. Ins. Mktg., So. Methodist U., 1948; m. Norma Irene Dover, Oct. 17, 1945; children—Todd, Dana. Life ins. underwriter Taggart Agy., 1948-74; mem. Wyo. Senate, 1972-82, chmn. hwy. transp. Mem. Yellowstone Centennial Commn., 1972; chmn. Big Horn County (Wyo.) 75th Anniversary Commn., 1965; mem. Wyo. Adv. Council for Pub. Land Rev., 1966; original dir. Wyo. Indsl. Devel. Corp., 1965; mem. Old West Trail Found., 1971-73, pres., 1974. Mayor, Town of Lovell (Wyo.), 1962-68; pres. Wyo. Assn. Municipalities, 1967-68. Served with USNR, 1943-46. Recipient Outstanding Community Service award, 1965. Mem. Nat. (state chmn. polit. action com. 1970—), Wyo. (pres. 1972, legis. chmn. 1973—) assns. life underwriters, Lovell C. of C. (pres. 1953, past dir.), Bighorn Canyon Nat. History Assn. (pres.). Mem. Ch. of Jesus Christ of Latter Day Saints. Office: PO Box 445 Lovell WY 82431

TAGGART, SONDRA, fin. planner, investment advisor; b. N.Y.C., July 22, 1934; d. Louis and Rose (Birnbaum) Hamov; B.A., Hunter Coll., 1955; children—Eric, Karen. Founder, dir. Copyright Service Bur., Ltd., N.Y.C., 1957-69; dir., officer Maclen Music, Inc., N.Y.C., 1964-69; pres. Westshore, Inc., pub. internat. bus. materials, Mill Valley, Calif., 1965-80. Active, Diane Feinstein for Mayor Campaign, San Francisco, Ronald Reagan for Pres. Campaign. Mem. Internat. Assn. Fin. Planners, Advt. Club San Francisco, Women's Polit. Caucus, San Francisco Art Inst., Bus. and Profl. Women's Club. Republican. Clubs: Commonwealth, Bankers. Editor: The Red Tapes: Commentaries on Doing Business With The Russians and East Europeans, 1978. Home: 350 Spalding Dr #1 Beverly Hills CA 90212

TAGGART, WILLIAM AREND, public policy and administration educator; b. Thomas River, N.J., July 29, 1955; s. Robert and Martha T. B.A., Fla. Atlantic U., 1978, M.P.A. (Jessie Smith Noyes fellow), 1979; Ph.D., Fla. State U., 1982. Research asst. Joint Ctr. Environ. and Urban Problems, Fla. Atlantic U., Ft. Lauderdale, 1978-79; teaching and research asst. dept. polit. sci. Fla. State U., Tallahassee, 1979-81; research asst. policy scis. program, 1981-82; asst. prof. pub. policy dept. govt. N.Mex. State U., Las Cruces, 1982—. Grantee Inter-Univ. Consortium for Polit., Social Research U. Mich., 1979; N.Mex. State U. grantee, 1982. Mem. Am. Polit. Sci. Assn., Am. Soc. Pub. Adminstrn., Western Polit. Sci. Assn., Southwestern Social Sci. Assn., Policy Studies Orgn., Midwest Polit. Sci. Assn., So. Polit. Sci. Assn. Contbr. papers to profl. meetings. Office: Dept Govt Box 3BN N Mex State U Las Cruces NM 88003

TAI, HAROLD YUNHOW, dental products manufacturing company executive; b. Changhai, China, Oct. 25, 1936; came to U.S., 1962, naturalized, 1971; s. David C. L. and Mamie T.; B.S. in C.E., Nat. Taiwan U., 1960; M.S., U. Calif.-Berkeley, 1964; m. Joan S. C. Hau, Sept. 18, 1962; children—Betty, Raymond. Engr., AiResearch, Los Angeles, 1964-69; chief engr. Robin Tech, Inc., Binghamton, N.Y., 1969-72, regional mgr. Western region, 1972-75; v.p., gen. mgr. Flow Industries, Equipment div., Kent, Wash., 1975-77; v.p. Dynamics Tech. Inc., Torrance, Calif., 1977-78; pres. Royal Dental Mfg. Inc., Everett, Wash., 1978—; dir. Dynamics Technology, Inc., Torrance. Served with Chinese Air Force, 1960-62. Home: 13822 SE 43d St Bellevue WA 98006 Office: 12414 Hwy 99 Everett WA 98204

TAIMUTY, SAMUEL ISAAC, physicist; b. West Newton, Pa., Dec. 20, 1917; s. Elias and Samia (Hawatt) T.; B.S., Carnegie Mellon U., 1940; Ph.D., U. So. Calif., 1951; m. Betty Jo Travis, Sept. 12, 1953 (dec.); children—Matthew, Martha; m. 2d, Rosalie Richards, Apr. 3, 1976. Physicist, U.S. Naval Shipyard, Phila. and Long Beach, Calif., 1942-46; research asst. U. So. Calif., 1947-51; sr. physicist U.S. Naval Radiol. Def. Lab., 1950-52, SRI Internat., Menlo Park, Calif., 1952-72; sr. staff engr. Lockheed Missiles & Space Co., Sunnyvale, Calif., 1972—; cons. physicist, 1971—. Mem. Am. Phys. Soc., Sigma Xi. Episcopalian. Mason. Contbr. articles to sci. publs. Patentee in field. Home: 3346 Kenneth Dr Palo Alto CA 94303 Office: PO Box 504 Sunnyvale CA 94086

TAKAGI, PAUL TAKAO, educator, consultant; b. Auburn, Calif., May 3, 1923; s. Tomokichi and Yasu (Niimi) T.; m. Mary Anna Hiroko, Sept. 16, 1950; children—Tani H., Dana Y. A.B., U. Calif.-Berkeley, 1949; M.A., Stanford U., 1963, Ph.D., 1967. Correctional worker State of Calif., 1951-63; mem. faculty U. Calif.-Berkeley, 1965—, now prof. edn.; tech. cons. on criminal justice matters to cities, states, and fed. govt. Mem. Mayor's Blue Ribbon Crime Commn., Oakland, Calif., 1981-82. Served with U.S. Army, 1943-45. Mem. Nat. Council on Crime and Delinquency, Am. Sociol. Assn., Soc. for Study of Social Problems, Western Criminology Soc. (Tappan award 1981), Crime and Social Justice Assocs. Democrat. Author 3 books; contbr. articles to profl. jours. Home: 7028 Colton Blvd Oakland CA 94611 Office: Dept of Edn U Calif Berkeley CA 94720

TAKAMUNE, ROBERT KATSUTOSHI, life insurance agent; b. Paauilo, Hawaii, Nov. 20, 1929; s. Koichi and Edith Nobue (Nakashima) T.; student Hilo Comml. Coll., 1947-49; m. Janet Tsurue Kawahara, June 30, 1956; children—Audrey, Claire, Daniel, Joyce. Bookkeeper, Frank Huff Agy., Hilo, Hawaii, 1949-52, Yamada Ins. Agy., Ltd., Honolulu, 1952-63; div. mgr. Investors Equity Life Ins. Co. Hawaii, Ltd., Honolulu, 1963-70; spl. agt. Northwestern Mutual Life Ins. Co., Honolulu, 1970—. Treas., Life Underwriters Polit. Action Com., 1978-80; treas. Parents Scouters Guild, 1976-81, pres., 1981-82, committeeman, 1981—; past chmn. bd. trustees Harris United Meth. Ch., Honolulu. Recipient Diamond award Northwestern Mutual Life Ins. Co., 1977. Mem. Am. Soc. C.L.U.'s (C.L.U. Jour. discussion moderator Hawaii chpt. 1980-81, dir. Hawaii chpt. 1981—), Life Underwriting Tng. Council (advanced sales course moderator 1980-81), Nat. Assn. Life Underwriters, East Honolulu Assn. Life Underwriters (treas. 1982-83), Hawaii Estate Planning Council (life), Million Dollar Roundtable (life), Honolulu Assn. Life Underwriters (fin. chmn. 1980-81). Club: Lions. Home: 4747 Analii St Honolulu HI 96821 Office: 1000 Bishop St Honolulu HI 96813

TAKANO, THOMAS HARUO, purchasing manager; b. Hawi, Hawaii, Feb. 2, 1925; s. Kishichi and Sen (Goto) T.; m. June T. Kiyosaki, Aug. 4, 1951; children—Tracy Jay, Sara Alison. B.A., U. Hawaii, 1950, M.B.A., Pepperdine U., 1975, M.A.E., 1978. Cert. purchasing mgr., Hawaii. Commd. 2d lt. U.S. Army, 1951; advanced through grades to lt. col., 1965; served in various logistical and adminstrv. posts; gen. staff officer, 1951-69; ret., 1969; purchasing and contracting mgr. Hawaii Dept. Edn., Honolulu, 1969—; lectr. in field. Mem. Hawaii Fish and Wildlife Adv. Com., 1977-81. Decorated Bronze Star. Mem. Purchasing Mgmt. Assn. Hawaii. Democrat. Office: 1106 Koko Head Ave Honolulu HI 96816

TAKASUGI, NAO, mayor, business developer; b. Oxnard, Calif., Apr. 5, 1922; s. Shingoro and Yasuye (Hayashi) T.; m. Judith Shigeko Mayeda, Mar. 23, 1952; children—Scott, Russell, Ronald, Tricia, Lea. B.S., Temple U., 1945; M.B.A., U. Pa. Wharton Sch., 1946. Mem. city council City of Oxnard, 1976-82, mayor, 1982—; bus. developer, cons. Mem. Oxnard Planning Commn., 1974-76. Mem. Ventura County Japanese Am. Citizens League. Republican. Methodist. Club: Optimists (Oxnard). Home: 1221 El Portal Way Oxnard CA 93033 Office: 305 N Third St Oxnard CA 93030

TAKASUGI, ROBERT MITSUHIRO, judge; b. Tacoma, Sept. 12, 1930; s. Hidesaburo and Kayo (Otsuki) T.; B.S., UCLA, 1953; LL.B., J.D. (Harry J. Bauer scholar), U. So. Calif., 1959; m. Dorothy O. Takasugi; children—Jon Robert, Leslie Mari. Admitted to Calif. bar, 1960; practiced law, Los Angeles, 1960-73; judge East Los Angeles Municipal Ct., 1973-75, adminstrv. judge, 1974, presiding judge, 1975; judge Superior Ct., County of Los Angeles, 1975-76; U.S. dist. judge U.S. Dist. Ct. for Central Dist. Calif., 1976—; legal counsel Japanese-Am. Welfare Rights Orgn., Asian-Am. Soc. Blind; nat. legal counsel Japanese Am. Citizens League; guest lectr. law seminars, Harvard U. Law Sch. Careers Symposium; commencement speaker; mem. Criminal Justice Standards Rev. Com., Com. for Standards for Admission to Fed. Practice; bd. dirs. East Los Angeles Coll. Found.; mem. fed. indigent def. panel com., mem. exec. com. U.S. Dist. Ct., Central Dist. Calif.; mem. Legion Lex U. So. Calif. Law Center; mem. atty. liaison/lawyers reps. to Circuit Conf., other coms. Bd. dirs. East Los Angeles-Montebello YMCA; mem. Calif. adv. com. Western Regional Office, U.S. Commn. on Civil Rights. Served with U.S. Army, 1953-55. Recipient U.S. Mil. Man of Yr. award for Far East Theater, U.S. Army, 1954; certificate of merit Japanese-Am. Bar Assn., other awards. Mem. U. So. Calif. Law Alumni (dir.). Club: Optimists (hon. dir. local club) (Los Angeles). Mem. editorial bd. U. So. Calif. Law Rev.; contbr. articles to profl. jours. Office: US Dist Ct US Courthouse 312 N Spring St Los Angeles CA 90012

TAKATA, SAYOKO, educator; b. Los Angeles, July 12, 1937; d. Henry Takuji and Fujie (Udo) Nishi; m. Isao Jon Takata, Nov. 24, 1961; 1 son, Stephen Isamu. B.A. in Bus., U. No. Colo., 1959; M.Ed. in Vocat. Edn., Colo. State U., 1980. Life teaching cert., Colo. Tchr. home econs. Erie (Colo.) Jr. and Sr. High Sch., 1959-60; tchr. bus. and office edn. Manual High Sch., Denver, 1960-63, 68-78, chmn. dept., 1977-78; asst. bookkeeper Century Fixtures, Inc., Los Angeles, 1963-64; tchr. bus. and office edn. East High Sch., Denver, 1978-79; tchr. bus. and office edn. Met. Youth Edn. Ctr., Zuni Ctr., 1978-79; tchr. bus. and office edn. East extension, Denver, 1979—, chmn. dept., 1980—; mem. Colo. Spl. Needs Ad Hoc Com., 1980. Mem. Am. Vocat. Assn., Nat. Bus. Edn. Assn., NEA, Colo. Educators For/About Bus. (treas. 1981—), Colo. Vocat. Assn., Mountain Plains Bus. Edn. Assn., Denver Classroom Tchrs. Assn., Colo. Edn. Assn., Delta Pi Epsilon. Buddhist. Home: 561 W 87th Pl Denver CO 80221 Office: 3800 York St Bldg 1 Unit A Denver CO 80205

TAL, JACOB, civil engineer, educator; b. Tiberias, Israel, Nov. 29, 1940; came to U.S., 1966, naturalized, 1977; s. Refael and Seniora Tboul; B.S. with high distinction, Technion, Israel, 1966; M.S. in Elec. Engring. (William Seeger fellow, 1967), U. Minn., 1968, Ph.D., 1971; m. Rachel Alkony, Oct. 22, 1962; 1 child, Tomer. Research fellow U. Minn., Mpls., 1971; asst. prof. elec. engring. U. Utah, Salt Lake City, 1971-78, asso. prof., 1978-81; engr. Hewlett-Packard Labs., Palo Alto, Calif., 1978—; founder Motion Control Seminars, Engring. Edn. Inst., Motion Control Products; vis. sr. lectr. Ben Gurion U. Israel, 1974-76; cons. various cos. including Ford Motor Co., Control Data Corp., Burroughs, Electro-Craft Corp. Recipient Best Tchr. award, 1973. Mem. IEEE, Sigma Xi. Co-author: Incremental Motion Control, vol. I, 1978; patentee field of system control; contbr. articles to profl. jours. Home: 49 Showers Dr G442 Mountain View CA 94040

TALBOT, FRANK HAMILTON, marine ichthyologist, museum director; b. Pietermaritzburg, South Africa, Jan. 3, 1930; s. Ralph West and Willemina (Altmann) T.; m. Mabel Suzette Logeman, July 21, 1953; children—Helen Campbell, Richard Bill, Jonathan Charles, Neil Hamilton. B.S., U. Witwatersrand, 1949; M.S., U. Cape Town, 1951, Ph.D., 1959. Demonstrator, U. Durham (Eng.), 1952-53; research officer Brit. Colonial Service, Zanzibar, 1954-58; marine biologist South African Mus., Cape Town, 1959-60, dep. dir., 1960-64; curator of fishes Australian Mus., Sydney, 1964-65; dir., 1966-75; dir. Ctr. Environ. Studies, Macquarie U., Sydney, 1976-81; dir. Calif. Acad. Scis., San Francisco, 1982—. Fellow Linnean Soc. (London), Royal Zool. Soc. (New South Wales), Royal Soc. Arts (London); mem. Ichthyology and Herpetology Soc., Explorers Club. Clubs: Bohemian, St. Francis Yacht. Contbr. writings to sci. publs. Office: Calif Acad Scis Golden Gate Park San Francisco CA 94118

TALBOT, MATTHEW JOSEPH, oil company executive, rancher; b. Mt. Vernon, N.Y., Sept. 4, 1937; s. Matthew J. and Margaret A. (Green) T.; B.B.A., Iona Coll., 1963; m. Maureen Donlan, June 3, 1958; children—Maureen, Kathleen, Matthew. Accountant, S.D. Leidesdorf & Co., N.Y.C., 1961-67; sr. analyst Gen. Foods Corp., White Plains, N.Y., 1967-68; with Tosco (formerly Oil Shale Corp.), Los Angeles, 1968—, comptroller, 1970—, v.p., 1971-76, sr. v.p., 1976-78, exec. v.p., 1978-83, pres., 1983—, also dir.; pres. Talbot Ranch, 1979—. Trustee, Craft and Folk Art Mus. Los Angeles County, 1976; bd. dirs. Center Theatre Group of Los Angeles, 1980—. C.P.A., N.Y. Mem. Am. Inst. C.P.A.'s, N.Y. State Soc. C.P.A.'s, Nat. Assn. Accountants, Calif. Almond Growers Exchange, Sunkist Growers, Inc. Office: 10100 Santa Monica Blvd Los Angeles CA 90067

TALBOTT, GEORGE ROBERT, physicist, biophysicist, mathematician, educator; b. San Diego, Oct. 1, 1925; s. George Fletcher and Mary (Lanz) T.; B.A. with honors, UCLA, 1960; D.Sc., Ind. No. U., 1973. Physicist, mem. tech. staff Rockwell Internat. Co., Anaheim, Calif., 1960—; mem. faculty thermodynamics Pacific States U., 1971-77, prof., 1972-80, chmn. dept. math. studies, 1973-80; lectr. computer sci. Calif. State U., Fullerton, 1979—; cons. physics, computer sci.; disting. guest lectr. Brunel U., London, 1974, 76; spl. guest Forschungsbibliothek, Hannover, W. Ger., 1979; assoc. editor KRONOS jour., Glassboro (N.J.) U., 1978—. Served with M.C., U.S. Army, 1956. Recipient Vis. Scholar's award Western Mich. U., 1979. Mem. Am. Soc. Med.

Technologists, Am. Math. Soc., Math. Assn. Am., Am. Soc. Clin. Pathologists (lic. med. lab. technologist). Buddhist. Author: Electronic Thermodynamics, 1973; Philosophy and Unified Science, 1977; co-inventor burner. Home: 4031 Charter Oak Dr Orange CA 92669

TALLEY, CAROLYN SUE, business executive; b. Cin., Sept. 30, 1945; d. LeRoy Millard and Betty Jane (West) Hughes; student Secord's Bus. Coll., 1963-64; m. Jerry Dale Talley, May 17, 1967; stepchildren—Julie Ann, Jonie Gail, Jodie Ellen. With Shilliot's, Cin., 1964-65, R.L. Polk Co., Cin., 1965, Cin. and So. Bell Telephone Co., Cin., 1965-66; buyer Sterling Electric Motors, Los Angeles, 1966-67; credit union clk. Beckman Instruments, Fullerton, Calif., 1967-68; with Federated Dept. Stores, Cin., 1968-69, Macpro, Inc., Loveland, Ohio, 1969-71, Orange Coast Advt., Inc., Santa Ana, Calif., 1971-73; pvt. acct., Orange County, Calif., 1973-75; office mgr./acct. L. Blain Co., Paramount, Calif., 1975-77; controller Relkoff Constrn., Santa Ana, Calif., 1977; controller Framing Div., Warmington Devel., Irvine, Calif., 1977, Brattain Contractors, Inc., Santa Ana, 1977-78; v.p., controller L. Blain Co., Paramount, 1978—1978-82; C.T. Constrn., Inc., Paramount, 1977—; owner Fine Line Co., agt. Preston Trucking Co., Paramount, 1982—; notary pub., Calif. Licensed gen. contractor, Calif. Mem. Nat. Assn. Women in Constrn. (pres. chpt. 1979-81), Nat. Notary Assn., Nat. Rifle Assn., Silver Lakes Assn., Smithsonian Assn. Club: N. Am. Hunt (charter). Home: 616 S Walnut St Anaheim CA 92802 Office: 16247 Illinois Ave Paramount CA 90723

TALLEY, DON L., state senator; b. Tacoma, Wash., 1918; m. Dolores T. Talley; 4 children. Student pub. schs. Supr. Port of Longview, Wash.; now mem. Wash. State Senate. Served with U.S. Navy. Mem. Am. Legion. (Lodges): Masons, Elks, Moose, Eagles. Democrat. Home: 4460 Pleasant Hill Rd Kelso WA 98626 Office: Washington State Senate Olympia WA 98504*

TALLMAN, RICHARD JOHN, college administrator; b. N.Y.C., June 3, 1956; s. William Joseph and Marilyn Joan (Hansen) T. B.A. in Anthropology, SUNY-Geneseo, 1978; M.A. in Edn., Ohio State U., 1980. Asst. coordinator for Greek affairs Ohio State U., Columbus, 1978-79; resident counselor Ohio Wesleyan U., Delaware, 1979-80; asst. to dean Colo. Coll., Colorado Springs, 1980—. Mem. Colorado Springs Symphony Guild, 1982—; mem. exec. bd. Pikes Peak Council of Alcoholism, 1980-81. Mem. Nat. Assn. Student Personnel Adminstrs., Am. Coll. Personnel Assn., Am. Personnel and Guidance Assn., Assn. Fraternity Advisors. Office: Mathias Hall Colorado Coll Colorado Springs CO 80903

TALMADGE, CHARLES EUGENE, naval officer, consulting architect and urban designer; b. Norfolk, Va., Jan. 27, 1947; s. Charles Junior and Annabelle Emily (Rylander) T.; m. Janet Belle Baker, May 30, 1969; children—Danika Marie, Erik Forester. B.Arch., U. So. Calif., 1970; M. Urban Planning, U. Wash., 1983; Registered architect, Minn. Jr. designer various archtl. firms, 1967-70; commd. ensign C.E., U.S. Navy, 1970, advanced through grades to lt. comdr., 1979; served in facilities design, constrn. and maintenance in Nfld., 1970-72, Yuma, Ariz., 1972-74, Port Hueneme, Calif., 1974-76, Yokosuka, Japan, 1976-79, Trident Submarine Base, Bangor, Wash., 1979-81; cons. in urban design and pvt. residential work Kasprisin/Petinari Design, Seattle. Mem. Am. Planning Assn. Democrat. Address: 2890 Spartacus NE Bremerton WA 98310

TALMADGE, PHILIP ALBERT, state senator, lawyer; b. Seattle, Apr. 23, 1952; s. Judson H., Jr., and Jeanne C. T.; m. Darlene L. Nelson, Sept. 6, 1970; children—Adam, Matthew, Jessica. B.A. magna cum laude with honors in Polit. Sci., Yale U., 1973; J.D., U. Wash., 1976. Bar: Wash. 1976. Assoc. Karr, Tuttle, Koch, Campbell, Mawer & Morrow, Seattle, 1976—; mem. Wash. Senate, 1978—, chmn. judiciary com., vice chmn. parks and ecology, mem. senate ways and means com. Trustee, South Seattle Community Coll. Found.; bd. dirs. Genesee Hill Community Council, Seattle Consumer Credit Counseling Service; mem. Policy Bd. Southwest Youth Service Bur.; mem. Mcpl. League, 34th Dist. Democratic Club, Met. Dem. Club, South End Dem. Club, Young Men's Dem. Club. Mem. Wash. State Bar Assn., Seattle-King County Bar Assn. Author: The Nixon Doctrine and the Reaction of Three Asian Nationa, 1973; editor Law Rev., U. Wash., 1975-76; contbr. articles to legal publs.

TAMASHIRO, CYRUS KAORU, seafood co. exec.; b. Honolulu, July 22, 1953; s. Walter Hajime and Louise Yoneko (Yontanza) T.; B.B.A. in Mktg., U. Hawaii, Manoa, 1975, M.B.A., 1980. Office mgr. Tamashiro Market, Inc., Honolulu, 1974-80, dir., 1975—, v.p., adminstrv. mgr., 1980—. Treas. Hui Ma-Kaala, scholarship and service orgn., 1981-82, pres., 1983-84. Mem. Liliha-Palama Bus. Assn. (dir.), Hawaii Food Industry Assn. (dir.), Hawaii C. of C., Young Okinawans Hawaii (1st pres. 1981), United Okinawan Assn. Hawaii, Nago Cho Jin Kai. Home: 1717 Mott-Smith Dr Honolulu HI 96822 Office: 802 N King St Honolulu HI 96817

TAMASHIRO, THOMAS KOYEI, electrical engineer; b. Paia, Maui, Hawaii, Aug. 4, 1926; s. Kokichi and Mashi (Shinyashiki) T.; B.E.E., Tri-State U., Angola, Ind., 1951, E.E., 1964; m. Mary E. Oden; children—Cheryl M., Venita. Project engr. Jackson & Church Co., Saginaw, Mich., 1953-55; project mgr. Aerojet-Gen. Corp., Azusa, Calif., 1955-72; sr. staff engr. Aerojet Nuclear Corp., Idaho Falls, Idaho, 1972-75; project mgr. Allied Chem. Corp., Idaho Falls, 1976-79, Exxon Nuclear-Idaho, Idaho Falls, 1979—; lectr. in field. Mem. Instrument Soc. Am., Am. Nuclear Soc. Club: Shriners. Home: RFD 9 Box 176 Idaho Falls ID 83402 Office: 550 2d St Idaho Falls ID 83401

TAMBARA, TERRY GENE, cosmetic co. exec.; b. Hood River, Oreg., May 12, 1951; s. Yori and Kikue (Suzuki) T. Student, U. Oreg., 1970; A.A., Lane Community Coll., 1973; B.S., Portland State U., 1976; diploma of photography N.Y. Inst. Photography, 1977. Adminstrv. asst. Don Nunamaker Realtors, Hood River, Oreg., 1974; graphic designer, profl. photographer Terry Tambara Design, Portland, Oreg., 1976—; v.p., gen. mgr. Taischo Internat., Portland, 1981—; pres. Asobi Industries, Portland, 1982—; cosmetic exec. Kamo Internat., 1982—.

TAMBURINI, JOSEPH URBAN, engineer; b. New Brunswick, N.J., May 23, 1951; s. John Eugene and Barbara Elizabeth (Gunther) T.; m. Connie Lynn Murray, July 3, 1976; children—Joseph Ryan, Steven James. B.S.C.E., Bucknell U., 1973; M.S., U. Colo., 1977. Registered profl. engr. Colo., N.J. Project engr., br. office mgr. Van Cleef Engring., Clinton, N.J., 1973-76; research asst. U. Colo.-Boulder, 1976-77; project mgr. Wright-McLaughlin Engrs., Denver, 1977-80; sr. engr. Culp, Wesner, Culp, Denver, 1980—; cons. Blue Mountain Water Dist. Mem. Water Pollution Control Fedn., Am. Water Works Assn., Nat. Soc. Profl. Engrs. Roman Catholic. Home: 9223 Fern Way Golden CO 80403 Office: Suite 310 Culp Wesner Culp 1777 S Harrison St Denver CO 80210

TAMKIN, CURTIS SLOANE, real estate devel. co. exec.; b. Boston, Sept. 21, 1936; s. Hayward and Etta (Goldfarb) T.; B.A. in Econs., Stanford U., 1958; m. Priscilla Martin, Oct. 18, 1975; 1 son, Curtis Sloane. Vice pres., treas., dir. Hayward Tamkin & Co., Inc., mortgage bankers, Los Angeles, 1963-70; mng. ptnr. Property Devel. Co., Los Angeles, 1970-82; pres. The Tamkin Co., 1982—. Bd. govs. Music Center Los Angeles, 1974—; pres. Los Angeles Master Chorale Assn., 1974-78; mem. vis. com. Stanford U. Libraries, 1982—. Served to lt. (j.g.) USNR, 1960-63. Mem. Los Angeles Jr. C. of C. (dir. 1968-69). Republican. Clubs: Burlingame Country, Los Angeles, University. Office: 3600 Wilshire Blvd Los Angeles CA 90010

TAMMANY, ALBERT SQUIRE, III, savings and loan executive; b. Paget, Bermuda, Aug. 21, 1946; s. Albert Squire Jr. and Marion Genevieve (Galloway) T.; B.A., Stanford U., 1968; M.B.A. (Woodrow Wilson fellow), U. Pa., 1973; m. Teresa Reznor, Sept. 8, 1973. Budget and planning officer Tuskegee Inst., Ala., 1973-74; budget analyst controllers dept. Chase Manhattan Bank, N.Y.C., 1974-75; v.p., div. controller Wells Fargo Bank, San Francisco, 1975-78, v.p., retail group controller, 1978-79; v.p., controller Imperial Bank, Los Angeles, 1979-81, sr. v.p. fin., 1981-83; exec. v.p., Deauville Savs. & Loan Assn., Los Angeles, 1983—; cons. Inst. for Services to Edn., Inc., 1973-74. Served with USMC, 1968-71. Wharton Pub. Policy fellow, 1972. Mem. Am. Bankers Assn. (trust ops. com.). Episcopalian. Clubs: Wharton, Stanford. Office: 1880 Century Park E Suite 300 Los Angeles CA 90067

TAMSKY, LEONARD IRWIN, physician; b. St. Louis, Dec. 12, 1944; s. Abraham Michael and Charlotte (Goldberg) T.; m. Carolyn Ann Larabell, May 11, 1975. B.A. cum laude, Amherst Coll., 1966; M.D. U. Mo., 1970. Diplomate Am. Bd. Internal Medicine. Intern and resident in internal medicine USPHS Hosp., San Francisco, 1970-73; primary care physician, Maricopa Community Health Network, Phoenix, 1973-74; clinic dir., 1974; asst. dir. Emergency Med. Service, Maricopa County Gen. Hosp., Phoenix, 1974-75, dir., 1975-82, dir. med. edn., 1979—; cons. internal medicine Chem. and Dependency Unit, St. Luke's Hosp. and Med. Ctr., Phoenix. Served to lt. comdr. USPHS, 1970-73. Mem. ACP. Home: 749 E Circle Rd Phoenix AZ 85020 Office: 2601 E Roosevelt St Phoenix AZ 85008

TAN, KONG-MENG, radiologist; b. Malacca, Malaysia, Nov. 9, 1943; s. Hin Jin and May (Woon) T.; came to U.S., 1965; B.S., U. Ill., Chgo., 1967, M.D., 1971; m. May Chen; 1 dau., Jennifer Mei-Sim. Intern, Ill. Masonic Med. Center, Chgo., 1971-72; resident radiology, 1972-75; instr. radiology U. Ill. Coll. Medicine, Chgo., 1974-75; chief dept. radiology, dir. med. edn. Kaiser Permanente Med. Center, Richmond, Calif., 1976—; dir. Permanente Med. Group, Inc., 1982—; governing bd. Alameda Contra Costa Health Systems Agy., 1979-83, vice chmn., 1982. Mem. adv. council Bay Area Air Quality Mgmt. Dist., 1978—, chmn., 1982; bd. dirs. Oakland Chinese Community Council, 1981—, pres., 1983; chmn. Bay Area Health Alliance, 1980. Fgn. scholar U. Ill., 1966-67, Fgn. travel scholar, 1970. Mem. AMA (chmn. com. house staff affairs 1974-75, mem. adv. com. continuing med. edn. 1978—), Ill. State Med. Soc. (com. housestaff affairs 1973-75), Calif. Med. Assn. (cons. com. continuing med. edn. 1979—), Alameda Contra Costa Med. Assn., Phi Delta Epsilon, Omega Beta Pi. Contbr. articles to sci. jours. Home: 952 Sunnyhills Oakland CA 94610 Office: Kaiser Med Center 901 Nevin Ave Richmond CA 94801

TAN, LUCAS GO, anesthesiologist; b. Maasin, Leyte, Philippines, Oct. 18; came to U.S., 1962, naturalized, 1971; s. Yu Chin and Nga Sio G.; M.D., U. Santo Tomas, 1960; m. Victoria Abundo Ong, Oct. 18, 1967; children—Lowell, Vivian, Verna Lou, Veoleta. Intern, Mercy Hosp., Pitts., 1962-63; resident Bronx (N.Y.) Lebanon Hosp., 1963-67, Toronto (Ont., Can.) U. Hosps., 1969-70; practice medicine specializing in anesthesiology; mem. staff Alexian Bros. Hosp., San Jose, Calif., chief anesthesia dept., 1977-78, 81-83. Diplomate Am. Bd. Anesthesiology. Fellow Am. Coll. Anesthesiologists; mem. Internat. Anesthesia Research Soc., Union Am. Physicians and Dentists, Am. Soc. Anesthesiologists, Calif. Med. Assn., Calif. Soc. Anesthesiologists, Santa Clara County Med. Soc., Republican. Roman Catholic. Home: Route 2 Box 619-G Dougherty Ave Morgan Hill CA 95037

TANABE, HARUTO, accountant; b. Lahaina, Maui, Hawaii, Apr. 1, 1920; s. Tokuichi and Fusayo (Fukuba) T.; student U. Hawaii, 1948; m. Setsuko Tanaka, July 9, 1944; children—Andrew T., Timothy M., Alvin T. Pub. acct., Honolulu, 1945—; chief acct. Wahiawa (Hawaii) Gen. Hosp., 1947-52; comptroller Cyprus Hawaiian Cement Corp., Honolulu, 1960-79; dir., sec. Alii Plumbing, Inc., 1969-79; mem. Hawaii State Bd. Accountancy, 1981—. Treas., Pearl City (Hawaii) Community Assn., 1970-71. Dist. councilman Democratic party, 1968, 70, 74, 76, 78; trustee, sec.-treas. Pub. Employees Health Fund State of Hawaii, 1974-79; bd. dirs. Wahiawa Hongwanji Buddhist Mission, 1980—. Mem. Nat. Assn. Accts., Nat. Soc. Public Accts. (bd. govs.; gov. dist. 11, 1979—), Hawaii Assn. Public Accts. (v.p. 1972-74, pres. 1974-75), Inst. Corp. Controllers, Honolulu Japanese C. of C. Democrat. Clubs: Masons (32 deg.), Shriners, Rotary. Home: 1657 Paaaina Place Pearl City HI 96782 Office: 94-889 Waipahu St Room 202 Waipahu HI 96797

TANAKA, STANLEY KATSUKI, optometrist, consultant; b. Honolulu, Sept. 19, 1932; s. Tomikichi and Hatsue T.; m. Esther K. Kokubun, Oct. 31, 1959; children—Glen A., Fay M. Student U. Hawaii, 1950-52; B.S., U. Okla., 1952; O.D. magna cum laude (Jackson award), Ill. Coll. Optometry, 1956. Enlisted U.S. Army, 1957, advanced through grades to col. Res., 1981; optometrist Hawaii Permanente Med. Group, Honolulu, 1968—; cons. opthalmic firms. Mem. Am. Optometric Assn., Hawaii Optometric Assn., Armed Forces Optometric Soc., Contact Lens Soc., Am. Optometric Found., Better Vision Inst., Inc., Optometric Extension Program, Beta Sigma Kappa. Democrat. Club: Toastmasters. Home: 2645 Oahu Ave Honolulu HI 96822 Office: 1697 Ala Moana Blvd Honolulu HI 96815

TANAKA, TOGO W(ILLIAM), financial exec.; b. Portland, Oreg., Jan. 7, 1916; s. Masaharu and Katsu (Iwatate) T.; A.B. cum laude, U. Calif. at Los Angeles, 1936; m. Jean Miho Wada, Nov. 14, 1940; children—Jeannine, Christine, Wesley. Editor Los Angeles Japanese Daily News, 1936-41; documentary historian War Relocation Authority, 1942; staff mem. Am. Friends Service Com., Chgo., 1943-45; editor to head publs. div. Am. Tech. Soc., 1945-52; pub. Chgo. Pub. Corp., 1952-56; pub. School-Indsl. Press, Inc., Los Angeles, 1956-60; chmn. Gramercy Enterprises, Inc., Los Angeles; pres. Rossmore Mgmt. Co.; treas. T.W. Tanaka Co., Inc. dir. Los Angeles Wholesale Produce Market Devel. Corp., Fed. Res. Bank, San Francisco; mem. adv. bd. Calif. First Bank, Los Angeles, 1976-78. Mem. citizens mgmt. rev. com. Los Angeles Unified Sch. Dist., 1976-77; adv. council to assessor Los Angeles County; bd. govs. Goodwill Industries; trustee Wilshire United Methodist Ch., 1976-78, Calif. Acad. Decathlon; bd. dirs. Meth. Hosp. So. Calif., Crippled Children's Soc., Am. Heart Assn., Los Angeles chpt. Nat. Safety Council, Los Angeles Visitors and Conv. Bur., ARC, Met. YMCA, Boy Scouts Am.; city commr. Los Angeles Community Redevel. Agy., 1973-75; adv. council Calif. World Trade Commn.; chmn. Meth. Hosp. Found. So. Calif. Recipient merit award Soc. Advancement Mgmt., 1950, mag. award Inst. Graphic Arts, 1953, 1st award Internat. Council Indsl. Editors, 1955, UN literacy award, 1976. Mem. Los Angeles Area C. of C. (dir. 1974-76), Japan-Am. Soc. So. Calif. (council, 1957-82), Phi Beta Kappa, Pi Sigma Alpha, Pi Gamma Mu. Clubs: Masons, Shriners, Rotary (dir., pres. Los Angeles dist. 5), Stock Exchange. Author: (with Frank K. Levin) English Composition and Rhetoric, 1948; (with Dr. Jean Bordeaux) How to Talk More Effectively, 1948; (with Alma Meland) Easy Pathways in English, 1950. Home: 949 Malcolm Ave Los Angeles CA 90024 Office: 4500 Wilshire Blvd Los Angeles CA 90010

TANCREDI, CHERYL GRANT (SHERRY GRANT), television producer; b. Phoenix, Mar. 1, 1944; d. William Edward and Mary Louise (Weldon) Grant; m. Louis Tancredi, Nov. 27, 1976; children—John Francis, Jennifer Grant. B.A., Coll. Notre Dame, Md., 1965; Student U. Fribourg (Switzerland), 1963-64; M.S. in TV-Radio, Syracuse U., 1966. Pres., exec. producer Carter-Grant Prodns. Inc., Los Angeles, 1976—, Sherry Grant Enterprises Inc., Los Angeles, 1982—. Recipient Freedom Found. award, 1978, Gold award Internat. Film and TV Festival of N.Y., 1978, Golden Halo award Calif. Motion Picture Assn., 1982. Mem. Acad. TV Arts and Scis., Women in Bus., Women in Film, Am. Women in Radio and TV, AFTRA, Women in Cable. Roman Catholic. Producer and assoc. producer numerous local and nat. TV programs. Office: 17915 Ventura Blvd Encino CA 91316

TANENBAUM, BASIL SAMUEL, coll. dean; b. Providence, Dec. 1, 1934; s. Harry Milton and Rena Ada (Herr) T.; B.S. in Physics summa cum laude, Brown U., 1956; M.S. (NSF predoctoral fellow 1956-60, Woods Hole Oceanographic Inst. fellow 1959), Yale U., 1957, Ph.D., 1960; m. Carol Binder, Aug. 26, 1956; children—Laurie, Stephen, David. Staff physicist Raytheon Co., Waltham, Mass., 1960-63; prof. engring. Case Inst. Tech., 1963-75; vis. scientist Cornell U.-Arecibo (P.R.) Obs., 1968-69; vis. asso. prof. Northwestern U., 1970; dean faculty Harvey Mudd Coll., Claremont, Calif., 1975—; sci. adv. com. Nat. Astronomy and Inosphere Center, 1972-77; adv. com. Calif. State U., Fullerton, Calif. Poly. Inst., Pomona; cons. to govt. and industry. Bd. dirs. Univ. Circle, Inc., Minority Engrs. Indsl. Opportunity Program, 1973-75. Recipient Wittke Teaching award Case Inst. Tech., 1974. Mem. AAAS, AAUP, Am. Phys. Soc., Am. Soc. Engring. Edn., IEEE, Sigma Xi (Research award 1969). Author: Plasma Physics, 1967. Office: Harvey Mudd Coll Claremont CA 91711

TANG, EDWARD YIU-YAN, software mfg. co. exec.; b. Shanghai, China, Oct. 10, 1939; came to U.S., 1958, naturalized, 1971; s. William Sai-Tsien Tang and Ling-Van Chang; B.E.E., Cornell U., 1963; M.S., Columbia U., 1965; m. Florence Chen, Mar. 21, 1964. Sr. design engr. NCR, Dayton, Ohio, 1965-66; supr. metal oxide semicondr. circuit devel. Microelectronics div. Philco-Ford Co., Santa Clara, Calif., Blue Bell, Pa., 1966-69; dir. engring. Intersil Inc., Cupertino, Calif., 1969-71; v.p. engring., founder, dir. Eurosil GmbH, Munich, W. Ger., 1971-74; v.p. research and devel. Micro Power Systems Inc., Santa Clara, 1974-78; exec. v.p., chief operating officer Nitron Inc., Cupertino, 1979-82, also dir.; pres. Answer Software Corp., Cupertino, 1982—. Mem. IEEE, Am. Electronics Assn. Republican. Contbr. articles to mags.; patentee in field. Home: 1628 Belvoir Dr Los Altos CA 94022 Office: Answer Software Corp 20863 Stevens Creek Blvd Cupertino CA 95014

TANG, MARILYN MILLET, cons. co. exec.; b. Salt Lake City, Oct. 28, 1936; d. Orson Paul and Norma Rowena (Allan) Millet; grad. high sch.; m. Gary Bernard Tang, June 19, 1970; 1 son, Larry Curtis Ward; Drayage clk. Salt Lake Transfer, 1960-61; gen. acct. Alta Engring., Inc., Salt Lake City, 1961-63; office mgr. Scott & Stevens, Inc., Salt Lake City, 1967; pres., gen. mgr. Cert. Interior Systems, Salt Lake City, 1967—; partner Tang, Tang Schneiter Leasing. Mem. Salt Lake Council of Women; mem. Women's Info. Network of Salt Lake; mem. minority bd. Utah Supplier Devel. Council. Mem. Salt Lake C. of C., Material Handling Equipment Distbrs. Assn., Women's Legislature Council. Mem. Ch. Jesus Christ of Latter-day Saints. Club: Soroptimist Internat. (past pres., chmn. growth and devel. Rocky Mountain region) (Salt Lake City). Home: 3391 E Larchmont Dr Salt Lake City UT 84104

TANG, STEPHEN SHIEN-PU, aerospace engr., scientist; b. Hunan, China, Nov. 13, 1935; came to U.S., 1961, naturalized, 1969; s. Joh and Chang-I (Lee) T.; B.S., Nat. Taiwan U., 1959; M.S., U. Calif.-Berkeley, 1961; Ph.D., Princeton U., 1969; m. Tanya Tun-Fu Hu, Apr. 19, 1972; children—Bruce Yun-Biao, Judy Yun-San. Research asso. Yale Univ., New Haven, 1969-70; vis. asso. prof. Nat. Taiwan U., Taipei, 1971; vis. asso. prof., research scholar Technische Universitat, Hannover, W. Ger., 1971-73; research scientist TRW Def. and Space Systems Group, Redondo Beach, Calif., 1974-80; project engr./engr. specialist The Aerospace Corp., El Segundo, Calif., 1980—. U.S. Advanced Research Project Agy. research grantee, 1974-76; Chinese Nat. Sci. Found. grantee, 1970-71; Alexander von Humboldt Stiftung grantee, 1971-73. Mem. Am. Phys. Soc., AIAA, Sigma Xi. Contbr. numerous articles to tech. jours. Home: 1611 Toscanini Dr San Pedro CA 90732 Office: The Aerospace Corp PO Box 92957 Los Angeles CA 90009

TANG, THOMAS, judge; b. Phoenix, Jan. 11, 1922; B.S., U. Santa Clara, 1947, postgrad. law Sch., 1948-50; LL.B. with distinction, U. Ariz., 1950. Admitted to Ariz. bar, 1950, Calif. bar, 1951; dep. county atty. Maricopa County, Ariz., 1953-57; asst. atty. gen. State of Ariz., 1957-58; judge Ariz. Superior Ct., 1963-70; mem. firm Sullivan, Mahoney & Tang, Phoenix, 1971-77; councilman City of Phoenix, 1960-62, vice mayor, 1962; judge U.S. Ct. of Appeals 9th Circuit, Phoenix, 1977—. Mem. State Bar Ariz. (bd. govs. 1971-77, pres. 1977), State Bar Calif. Office: care US Court of Appeals Federal Bldg 230 N 1st Ave Phoenix AZ 85025

TANGEN, KENNETH L., company executive, counselor, researcher; b. Seattle, Mar. 7, 1949; s. Robert B. and Mildred E. Tangen; m. Rebecca Wood, Aug. 18, 1973; 1 dau., Katrina Rose. B.A., Seattle Pacific U., 1972; M.S., Central Wash. U., 1974; Ph.D., U. Wash., 1983. Dir. counseling and ednl. services 1st Assembly Ch., Anchorage, 1975-76, Spanaway (Wash.) Assembly, 1977-80; dir. edn. Bethany Temple, Everett, Wash., 1980-81; nat. coordinator services for blind Gen. Council Assemblies of God, Springfield, Mo., 1981; pres. Matrix Found., Everett, 1981—; family therapist Harborview Mental Health Ctr., Interpersonal Clinic, Seattle. Mem. Am. Personnel and Guidance Assn., Nat. Vocat. Guidance Assn., Assn. Religious and Value Issues in Counseling, Am. Psychol. Assn. Mem. Assemblies of God Ch. Author: Five Life-Changing Ideas, 1980; composer 16 songs; contbr. articles to jours. Office: Matrix Found 11020 27th Ave SE Everett WA 98204

TANGNEY, DEBBIE J., interior designer; b. Tacoma, Wash., Apr. 24, 1955; d. Alvin P. and Dolores J. (Wilson) Olson; m. James R. Tangney, Jan. 24, 1955. Student, Tacoma Community Coll., 1973-74, Clover Park Vocat. Tech. Sch., 1974-77, 81. Head design dept. Bargreen-Ellingson, Tacoma, 1977-81; ptnr., owner Tangney & Tangney, interior and graphic design, Tacoma, then Gig Harbor, Wash., 1981—. Mem. Am. Soc. Interior Designers (assoc.). Roman Catholic. Address: 5720 144th St NW Gig Harbor WA 98335

TANIGUCHI, RICHARD RYUZO, wholesale building supplies executive; b. Eleele, Hawaii, Oct. 21, 1913; s. Tokuichi and Sana (Omaye) T.; B.A., U. Hawaii, 1936; m. Sumako Matsui, July 22, 1939; children—Grace Fujiyoshi, Susan Penisten. Acctg. clk. Bank of Hawaii, 1935-36; treas., gen. mgr. Hawaii Planing Mill, 1944-54; pres., gen. mgr. Hawaii Hardware Co., Ltd., Hilo, 1954—; pres., dir. Enterprises Hilo; v.p., dir. Hawaii Funeral Home. Chmn. Hawaii County CSC, 1950-56; vice chmn.

Hawaii County Tidal Wave Adv. Com., 1961-68; vice chmn. Hawaii Council Tb and Health Assn., 1965; pres. Am. Cancer Soc., 1969-72, state bd. dirs., 1970-78; pres. Hilo Hongwanji Mission 1968-70, sr. adviser, 1972—; v.p. Hawaii State Hongwanji Mission, 1969—; mem. Hawaii Comprehensive Health Planning Com., 1970-72. Named Hawaii Vol. of Year, Am. Cancer Soc., 1973, recipient Nat. award Am. Cancer Soc., 1978. Mem. Am. Supply Assn., Nat. Plumbing Wholesalers Assn., Japanese C. of C. and Industry of Hawaii (pres. 1957), Hawaii (dir. 1958-59), Japanese (hon. dir.) chambers commerce, Phi Kappa Phi, Pi Gamme Mu. Office: 550 Kilauea Ave Hilo HI 96720

TANIGUCHI, TOKUSO, surgeon; b. Eleele, Kauai, Hawaii, June 26, 1915; s. Tokuichi and Sana (Omaye) T.; B.A., U. Hawaii, 1941; M.D., Tulane U., 1946; 1 son, Jan Tokuichi. Intern Knoxville (Tenn.) Gen. Hosp., 1946-47; resident in surgery St. Joseph Hosp., also Marquette Med. Sch., Milw., 1947-52; practice medicine, specializing in surgery, Hilo, Hawaii, 1955—; chief surgery Hilo Hosp.; teaching fellow Marquette Med. Sch., 1947-49; v.p., dir. Hawaii Hardware Co., Ltd. Served to capt. M.C., AUS, 1952-55. Diplomate Am. Bd. Surgery. Fellow Internat., Am. colls. surgeons; mem. Am., Hawaii med. assns., Hawaii County Med. Soc., Pan-Pacific Surg. Assn., Phi Kappa Phi. Contbr. articles in field to profl. jours. Patentee automated catheter. Home: 277 Kaiulani St Hilo HI 96720

TANIS, BEVERLY HOLLAND, public relations counselor; b. Sheboygan, Wis., May 10, 1952; d. Robert Clinton and Virginia Bell (DeGolier) H.; m. Richard Charles Tanis, Aug. 24, 1974. B.S., U. Ill.-Urbana, 1974, M.S. in Journalism, 1977. Records officer Coll. Liberal Arts and Scis., U. Ill.-Urbana, 1975-76; tchr. Homer (Ill.) Pub. Schs., spring 1976; nutrition edn. media asst. U. Ill. Sch. Basic Med. Scis., Urbana, 1976-77; nutrition communicator Gen. Mills, Inc., Mpls., 1977-79; pub. relations dir. Tacoma/Pierce County Family YMCA, Tacoma, 1979-80; pub. relations coordinator Am. Plywood Assn., Tacoma, 1980-82; account exec. foodservice pub. relations Evans/Pacific Inc., Advt., Seattle, 1982; owner, operator B.T. Communications, Tacoma, 1979—. Bd. dirs. Planned Parenthood Pierce County; mem. communications com. Pierce County United Way, 1983-84. Mem. Tacoma/Pierce County C. of C. (communications council), Better Bus. Bur., Pub. Relations Soc. Am., Am. Soc. Profl. Journalists, Women in Communications (chpt. sec. 1983-84). Office: 7011 S 19th St Suite 405 Tacoma WA 98466

TANJI, KENNETH KAZUO, chemist, educator; b. Honolulu, Jan. 13, 1932; s. Bunsaku and Shizue (Ichikawa) T.; B.A. in Chemistry, U. Hawaii, 1954; M.S. in Soil Sci., U. Calif., Davis, 1961; m. Flora N. Tanji, Mar. 24, 1952; children—Lydia H., Lorelei A., Kenneth K. Staff research asso. in water quality for agr. U. Calif., Davis, 1958-67, specialist in water quality and pollution, 1967-71, lectr. water sci., asso. water scientist, 1971-76, prof. water sci., water scientist, 1976—, dept. chmn., 1981—; cons. water and land problems. Served with U.S. Army, 1954-56. Fellow Am. Inst. Chemists, Am. Soc. Agronomy, Soil Sci. Soc. Am. (chmn. div. soil chemistry); mem. Am. Chem. Soc., Internat. Soil Sci. Soc., AAAS. Contbr. chpts. to books, articles to profl. jours. Home: 807 Malaga Ave Davis CA 95616 Office: Dept LAWR U Calif Davis CA 95616

TANKERSLEY, ROBERT KARL, theatre equipment co. exec.; b. Decatur, Ill., July 31, 1927; s. Allen W. and Dorothy (Reynolds) T.; student Internat. Corr. Schs., 1948-49, Dale Carnegie Inst., 1958; m. Susan Jane Whitfield, Nov. 10, 1946; children—Rodney A., Sandra Sue, Steven Mark, Anthony Karl. Salesman, Nat. Theatre Supply Co., Denver, 1947-59; pres., gen. mgr. Western Service & Supply Co., Denver, 1959—; pres. Theatre Operators, Inc., Bozeman, Mont. Served with USNR, 1945-46. Mem. Soc. Motion Picture and TV Engrs. (past bd. mgrs.), Rocky Mountain Motion Picture Assn. (past pres.), Theatre Equipment Assn. (pres. 1969-70, past dir.). Found. Motion Picture Pioneers, U.S. Ski Assn. Club: Sports Car Am. (dir. Colo. region). Home: 2538 S Dover Way Lakewood CO 80227 Office: 4081 S Eliot St Englewood CO 80110

TANNEHILL, VICTOR CARL, association executive; b. Fort Wayne, Ind., Jan. 21, 1933; s. Carl Louis and Charlotte Louise (Spice) T.; m. Patricia Jane Herr, Nov. 28, 1959; children—Kathleen S. Zickus, Elizabeth A., Kelly R. B.A., Wittenberg U., 1955. Div. personnel supr. Ind. & Mich. Electric Co., South Bend, Ind., 1964-66, pub. relations asst., Ft. Wayne, Ind., 1958-64; with EAGR, Inc., Grand Rapids, Mich., 1967-69; mgr. MEA, Inc., Racine, Wis., 1969-81; exec. dir. Am. Inst. Profl. Geologists, Arvada, Colo., 1981—; cons. in field. Served with U.S. Army, 1955-57. Recipient Freedom's Found. at Valley Forge George Washington medal, 1961; U.S. Presdl. Commendation, 1976. Mem. Am. Soc. Assn. Execs. Republican. Lutheran. Home: 6164 W 83d Way Arvada CO 80003 Office: 7828 Vance Dr Suite 103 Arvada CO 80003

TANNER, GARY ARLAN, oil and gas co. exec.; b. Santa Fe, July 7, 1943; s. Lewis Ray and Bettie Arlene (Marshall) T.; B.B.A. in Finance, U. N.Mex., 1971; m. Carol Ann Marohnich, Oct. 20, 1973; children—Kelly Lynn, Brandon Ray. Partner, Financial Services Corp., Denver, 1972-76; prin. Tanner & Assos., Denver, 1976—; regional v.p. Petro-Search, Inc., Denver, 1976-78; pres., chief exec. officer dir. TPEX Exploratin, Inc., Denver, 1978—. Served with USN, 1963-66. Decorated Disting. Service medal. Mem. Internat. Assn. Fin. and Bus. Cons., Presidents Club, Fin. Execs. Club. Republican. Baptist. Office: 1380 17th St Denver CO 80202

TANNER, HELEN BLANCHE, home economics educator, caterer, music educator; b. Malad, Idaho, Apr. 19, 1934; d. Morgan Wilford and Mary Ann (Deschamps) Harris; m. Glenn Myron Tanner, June 10, 1959; children—Stephen, Jon, Jedd, Aimee, Robert. B.S., Utah State U., 1956; postgrad. U. Utah, 1958, U. Colo., 1964, 74, 83, U. No. Colo., 1972-83; M.Ed., Colo. State U., 1978. Cert. secondary tchr., Colo., vocat. home econs. tchr., Colo., Utah. Tchr. home econs. Cedar City (Utah) High Sch., 1956-59; substitute tchr. home econs., Bountiful (Utah) High Sch., 1960-64, Boulder, Colo., 1965-69; tchr. home econs. Boulder High Sch., 1970-80, Centaurus High Sch., Boulder, 1980—; prin. Helen's Originals Catering, Boulder, 1975—; tchr. piano, Idaho, Utah, Colo., 1950—; dist. cons. State of Colo. Future Homemakers Am./Home Econs. Related Occupations; mem. Adv. Com. Home Econs.; dist. team curriculum writer Colo. Future Homemakers Am./Home Econs. Related Occupations Leadership Conf.; cons. in field. Vol. Community Hosp., Boulder, 1965-70. Mem. Colo. Home Econs. Assn., Boulder Valley Edn. Assn., NEA, Am. Home Econs. Assn., Knife and Fork Club, Phi Kappa Phi. Republican. Mormon. Home: 110 Cherokee Way Boulder CO 80303 Office: 10300 S Boulder Rd Lafayette CO 80026

TANNER, JON MOESE, financial advisor; b. Ogden, Utah, Apr. 1, 1952; s. John Woods and Anita (Galbraith) T.; m. Mira Kay Schoenbeck, Aug. 17, 1978; children—Dana, Tera. B.S. in Acctg., Weber State Coll., 1978. Budget analyst, estimator Williams Internat. Co., Ogden, 1977-80; sales mgr. M.B.C.H., Inc., Ogden, 1980-82; sec.-treas. fin. planning Concise Fin. Mgmt. Inc., 1982—; ptnr. Amtal Capital Fund, 1982—; bus. cons. Snarr & Assocs.; cons. Distbn. Data Co. Active Layton Improvement Dist., 1982. Served with USAFR, 1970-78. Mem. Utah Life Underwriters Assn., Million Dollar Roundtable. Republican. Mormon. Address: 468 W Phillips St Kaysville UT 84073

TANNER, WILLIAM, newspaper editor; b. Cleve., Feb. 22, 1925; s. Benjamin and Rae T.; B.A., Case Western Res. U., 1952; m. Doris (Rusty) Brown, Dec. 31, 1972; children by previous marriage—Douglas B., Claude W., Russell P. Reporter, Cleve. Press, 1943, 46-67, asst. city editor, 1963-68, city editor, 1968-77, exec. news editor, 1977-78, mng. editor, 1978-80; editor Albuquerque Tribune, 1980—, also v.p. Served with AUS, 1943-46. Office: NMex Tribune 717 Silver St SW Albuquerque NM 87102*

TANNER, WILLIAM WOODLAND, dentist; b. Salt Lake City, Feb. 18, 1936; s. Henry Bernard and Edna Bertha (Malan) T.; D.D.S., U. So. Calif., 1963; student U. Utah, 1954-56, 58-59; m. Elizabeth Findlay, Aug. 14, 1959; children—William Brent, Troy Findlay, Stephen Jay, Richard Woodland. Instr., U. So. Calif. Sch. Dentistry, Los Angeles, 1963-66; pvt. practice dentistry, Westwood, Calif., 1963-64, Beverly Hills, Calif., 1964—; examiner State of Calif. Bd. Dental Examiners, 1978; lectr. in field. Mem. exec. bd. Crescent Bay Area council Boy Scouts Am., 1970-72, Great Western council, 1972-73, Los Angeles Area council, 1973—, Hollywood-Wilshire Dist. chmn., 1975-76, 76-77, dist. chmn. explorer career div., 1977-78, vice chmn. Mormon relationships com., recipient award of merit, 1978, Silver Beaver award, 1979, Silver Bruin, 1973, William H. Spurgeon III award; mem. citizens adv. council Overland Ave. Sch., 1971-72; mem. PTA, 1965—; elder's quorum pres. Ch. of Jesus Christ of Latter Day Saints, 1960-63, high councilor, 1964-68, councilor in stake presidency, Los Angeles stake, 1968-77, regional exec. sec., 1977-78, stake pres., 1978—; priesthood adv. So. Calif. Mormon Choir; bd. dirs. Los Angeles Area Deseret Industries, 1973-78; mem. Los Angeles Area Employment Center com., 1973-78. Served with Utah Air N.G., USAFR, 1954-62. Mem. ADA (del. 1979—), Calif. Dental Assn. (del. 1976), Los Angeles Dental Soc. (v.p. 1981-82, 83-84, sec. 1982-83), U. So. Calif. Alumni Assn., Beverly Hills Acad. Dentistry (sec. 1980-81), Chgo. Dental Assn., Pierre Fouchard Acad., Alpha Tau Epsilon, Pi Kappa Alpha. Republican. Club: Western Study of Combined Therapy. Home: 10021 Cheviot Dr Los Angeles CA 90064 Office: 9100 Wilshire Blvd Beverly Hills CA 90024

TANQUARY, JANICE RAE, lawyer; b. Hinsdale, Ill., Feb. 27, 1946; d. Raymond H. and Mary Elizabeth (Hadley) Vavrinek; B.A., U. Denver, 1968, J.D., 1976, LL.M. in Taxation, 1977; 1 dau., Kimberly P. Tax auditor IRS, Detroit, 1969-71; research asst. U. Denver, 1975-76, asst. to dir. grad. tax program, 1977, adj. prof. law, 1979-80, lectr. program advanced devel., 1980; admitted to Colo. bar, 1977, U.S. Tax Ct., 1977; asso. firm Kutak Rock & Huie, Denver, 1977-80; individual practice law, Denver, 1980—. Mem. Am. Bar Assn., Colo. Bar Assn., Denver Bar Assn. Home: 13236 E Kansas Dr Aurora CO 80012 Office: 2121 S Oneida St Denver CO 80224

TANZI, VITO ANTHONY, management consultant; b. N.Y.C., Jan. 22, 1927; s. Guido and Sarina (DiGregorio) T.; m. Ella Tanzi, May 15, 1944; children—Robert, Richard; m. 2d, Shirley J. Eggard, Nov. 25, 1977. B.S. in Engring., Ohio Inst. Tech., 1948; D.Arts (hon.), Northwestern Coll. Allied Scis., 1981. Accredited Soc. Profl. Mgmt. Cons. Pres., Durable Plastics, Inc., 1955-62; founder Tanzi Orgn., San Diego, 1963, chief exec. officer, 1982—, sr. mng. dir., 1963-82; chmn. bd. Am. Inst. Merger and Acquisition Cons. Served to capt., USAAF, 1944-47. Decorated Air medal. Mem. Nat. Assn. Accts. (cert.). Republican. Roman Catholic. Author: A Management Audit-Capsule Picture, 1976. Office: Chamber Bldg Suite 1407 110 W C St San Diego CA 92101

TAPER, S. MARK, financial corp. exec.; b. 1901. Real estate agt., builder and developer, London, 1920-39; land developer, Calif., 1941-55; with First Charter Financial Corp., 1955—, chmn. bd., pres., chief exec. officer, 1956-62, 66-70, chmn. bd., 1962-66, chmn. bd., chief exec. officer, 1970—, now chmn., also dir.; pres., chmn., chief exec. officer Am. Savs. & Loan Assn. Office: 9465 Wilshire Blvd Beverly Hills CA 90212*

TAPP, RONALD GENE, ins. co. exec.; b. Bloomington, Ind., July 15, 1941; s. Wayne E. and Golda G. Tapp; student Ind. U., 1959-63; m. Helen L. Black, Sept. 24, 1977; children—Rhonda Jean, Randy G., Rita Jean. Printer, Phoenix Newspapers, Inc., 1972-76; ins. agt. Am. Republic Ins. Co., Phoenix, 1976-77; ins. agt. Minn. Protective Life Ins. Co., Phoenix, 1977-78, gen. agt., 1978-82, Southwestern regional mgr., 1978-82; sec.-treas. Internat. Benefit Cons., Ltd., 1981—; mktg. dir. Lincoln Benefit Life, 1982—; pres. Empire-Am. Ins. Cons., Ltd., 1982—. Republican precinct committeeman, also state committeeman for dist. 19. Served with U.S. Army, 1964-65. Recipient various profl. awards, 1977-81. Mem. Ariz. Public Employees Assn. (assoc.). Home: 18401 N 45th Dr Glendale AZ 85308 Office: 18401 N 45th Dr Glendale AZ 85308

TARANTO, IRWIN, computer systems consultant; b. N.Y.C., Aug. 21, 1935; s. Victor and Ann (Goldstein) T.; m. Arlene Harriet Schaffer, Oct. 16, 1956; children—Barry Keith, Marc Alan, Roger Eric. B.B.A., CUNY, 1951. Programmer Western Elec. Co., N.Y.C., 1957-60; sr. systems rep. R.C.A., San Francisco, 1960-65; mgr. Standata Computer Data Ctr., San Francisco, 1965-67; computer cons. Taranto & Assocs., Inc., San Rafael, Calif., 1967—. Commr. San Rafael Parks and Recreation commn., 1964-65; treas. Hashacha Youth Orgn., 1974-75. Mem. CUNY Alumni Assn. (pres. San Francisco chpt.). Clubs: KP, B'nai B'rith. Home: 144 Duran Dr San Rafael CA 94903 Office: 121 Paul Dr San Rafael CA 94903

TARBET, GLEN F., writer; b. Salt Lake City, Sept. 30, 1931; s. David E. and Carol (Cornia) Haskell; B.A., Brigham Young U., 1956; student Utah State U., 1949-50, U. Utah, 1970-79; B.S., Westminster Coll., 1982; m. Betty Bennion Brown, Oct. 26, 1966; children—Lauris, Linda, Alan, Jan, Scott, Jami, Carrie, David, Steven, Penny, Victor. Office mgr. Nu Day Elec. Corp., Provo, Utah, 1954-56; specification engr. Radioplane Co., Van Nuys, Calif., 1956-57; reports writer Marquardt Co., Ogden, Utah, 1957-58; asso. engr. Thiokol Corp., Brigham City, Utah, 1958-60; prin. publ. engr., publs. mgr. Sperry Univac, Salt Lake City, 1960-71; editor Brigham Young U. Press, 1972; tech. writing services editor Brigham Young U. Computer Services, Provo, 1973; tech. writing services editor U. Utah Computer Center, 1974-75; sr. tech. writer N.W. Pipeline Co. and N.W. Alaskan Pipeline Co., Salt Lake City, 1975—. Served with USN, 1950-54. Mem. Soc. Tech. Communications (sr.; past chmn. Intermountain chpt.). Republican. Mormon (high priest). Home: 1967 Lambourne Ave Salt Lake City UT 84106 Office: N W Pipeline Corp PO Box 1526 Salt Lake City UT 84110

TARLOW, ARTHUR LEE, lawyer; b. Portland, Oreg., Mar. 15, 1942; s. Elvin and Virginia (Fisher) T.; m. Judie Elyce Morris, Apr. 30, 1972; children—Damin, Griffin. Student Whitman Coll., 1960-62; B.S. in Law, U. Oreg., 1963, J.D., 1966; grad. career prosecutor course Nat. Coll. Dist. Attys., 1970; A.A.S., Portland Community Coll., 1973. Bar: Oreg. 1966, U.S. Dist. Ct. Oreg., 1970, U.S. Ct. Appeals (9th cir.), 1976, U.S. Supreme Ct., 1971, U.S. Ct. Claims, 1976. Dep. dist. atty. Multnomah County, Oreg., 1969-71; mem. firm Bolliger, Hampton & Tarlow, Portland, 1971—; dir. Oreg. Title Ins. Co.; instr. Portland Community Coll., 1971-73; mem. constrn. industry panel Am. Arbitration Assn. Pres. Washington County Pub. Affairs Forum; assoc. dir. Portland Rose Festival Assn. Served with M.I., U.S. Army, 1966-69. Mem. Oreg. Bar Assn., Assn. Gen. Contractors, Western Shipbuilders Assn., Am. Electronics Assn., Oreg. Remodelers Assn., Am. Coll. Constrn. Arbitrators, Beaverton Area C. of C. (pres.). Office: Suite 102 1600 SW Cedar Hills Blvd Portland OR 97225

TARLOW, GERALD, psychologist; b. Brookline, Mass., Jan. 8, 1949; s. Saul and Mildred (Alperin) T.; B.A., UCLA, 1970; M.A., Pepperdine U., 1971; Ph.D., U. Mont., 1974. Research psychologist Camarillo-UCLA Neuropsychiat. Inst., 1974-75; clin. psychologist Lake's Crossing Center, Reno, 1976-77; vis. asst. prof. Loyola Marymount U., Los Angeles, 1977-78; psychologist, asst. clin. prof. psychiatry UCLA, 1978—; pvt. practice, Los Angeles, 1978—. Mem. Am. Psychol. Assn., Assn. Advancement Behavior Therapy. Democrat. Jewish. Author: (with M.K. Holland) Using Psychology, 2d edit., 1980; contbr. articles to profl. jours. Home: 14507 Mulholland Dr Los Angeles CA 90077 Office: Dept Psychiatry UCLA Los Angeles CA 90024

TARNOFF, JOHN BROOKS, motion picture production executive; b. N.Y.C., Mar. 3, 1952; s. Norman and Dorothy (Brooks) T. B.A. magna cum laude, Amherst Coll., 1973. Field distbn. exec. Billy Jack Enterprises, 1974-75; lit. agt. Paul Kohner-Michael Levy Agy., Los Angeles, 1975-78, head TV dept., 1978; v.p. motion picture devel. M.G.M. Film Co., Culver City, Calif., 1979-81, sr. v.p. prodn., 1981-82; exec. v.p. Kings Road Prodns., Los Angeles, 1983—. Office: Kings Road Prodns 1901 Ave of Stars Suite 540 Los Angeles CA 90067

TARQUINIO, GARRY MICHAEL, construction company executive; b. McKees Rocks, Pa., Dec. 16, 1946; s. Armand John and Marabelle Theresa (Garofalo) T.; B.S. in Mgmt., Pepperdine U., 1980, M.B.A., 1981; m. Suzanne Staples, Apr. 4, 1970; 1 son, Garry Michael. With Mission Viejo Co. (Calif.), 1968—, project supt., 1973-76, gen. supt., 1976-78, constrn. mgr., 1978-80, dir. constrn., 1980—; instr. extension program U. Calif.-Irvine, 1983. Chmn. adv. council light constrn. and devel. mgmt. program U. Calif.-Irvine, 1982; mem. Barrymore chpt. Orange County Music Cntr. Served with U.S. Army, 1966-68; Vietnam. Decorated Vietnam Commendation medal; recipient Philip Morris Silver Ring Merit award for excellence in mgmt., 1981. Mem. Home Builders Council (dir.), Bldg. Industry Assn. So. Calif. (coll. programs adv.). Democrat. Roman Catholic. Home: 27352 Becedas Mission Viejo CA 92691 Office: 26137 La Paz Rd Mission Viejo CA 92691

TARR, WILLIAM WINSHIP, JR., photographer; b. Los Angeles, 1953; s. William Winship and Shirley (Wright) T.; B.A. in Biology, Calif. State U.-Northridge, 1983; postgrad. Mt. St. Mary's Coll., 1983-84. Cert. sci. and math. secondary tchr., Calif.; m. Catherine Ann Byrer, Oct. 28, 1978. Sales specialist J.C. Penney Corp., Canoga Park, Calif., 1973; customer service technician, tech. demonstrator Berkey Mktg. Corp., West Coast, 1974; show mgr. photo expn. Los Angeles Conv. Center, 1974, publicity and advt. mgr. Olympic Camera, 1975; owner, mgr. Winship Photo Studio, Canyon Country, Calif., 1973—; chmn. arts dept. Alemany High Sch., Mission Hills, Calif. Mem. Los Angeles Mus. Natural History Alliance, Sierra Club, CSUN Sailing Club (commodore 1976-77), Oceanic Soc., USCG Aux. (instr., vessel examiner). Republican. Office: PO Box 1895 Canyon Country CA 91351

TARRISH, JOSEPH CROMAN, investment bank exec.; b. New Haven, Jan. 1, 1917; s. Abraham and Sonia (Croman) T.; student U. So. Calif., 1935-36, Southwestern U., 1937; m. Pearl Richman, Jan. 31, 1944; children—Sonia, Barbara, Laura. Partner, Tarrish & Shapiro, 1940-46; owner J.C. Tarrish Co., 1947-51; partner Auster-Tarrish Co., 1951-55; owner Melrose Co., 1956-65; pres., chief stockholder J.C. Tarrish Co., Inc., Phoenix, 1967—. Served to adj. gen. Q.M.C. Corps, AUS, 1942-46. Mem. Assn. for Corp. Growth. Office: J C Tarrish Co Inc Suite 1000 3225 N Central Ave Phoenix AZ 85016

TARSON, HERBERT HARVEY, edn1. adminstr.; b. N.Y.C., Aug. 28, 1910; s. Harry and Elizabeth (Miller) T.; B.A., UCLA, 1949; Ph.D., U.S. Internat. U., 1972; m. Lynne Barnett, June 27, 1941; 1 son, Stephen. Entered U.S. Army as pvt., 1933, advanced through grades to maj., 1942; trans. to USAF, 1947, advanced through grades to lt. col. 1949; adj., exec. officer, Ft. Snelling, Minn., 1940-42, asst. adj. gen. 91st Inf. Div., 1942-43, chief of personnel, adv. sec. Comd. Zone, ETO, 1944-45; dir. personnel services 8th AF, 1946-47; dep. dir. dept. info. and edn. Armed Forces Info. Sch., 1949-51; dir. personnel services Japan Air Def. Force, 1951-53; dir. personnel services Continental Air Command, 1953-62; dir. adminstrv. services, spl. asst. to Comdr. 6th AF Res. Region, 1962-64; ret., 1964; asst. to chancellor L.I. U., Brookville, N.Y., 1964-69; dean of admissions Tex. State Tech. Inst., San Diego Indsl. Center, 1970-72; v.p. acad. affairs Nat. U., San Diego, 1972-75, sr. v.p., 1975—. Decorated Bronze Star with oak leaf cluster, Air Force Commendation medal with 2 oak leaf clusters. Fellow Bio-Med. Research Inst.; mem. Doctoral Soc. U.S. Internat. U., Air Force Assn., Navy League U.S., Ret. Officers Assn., World Affairs Council (life), Am. Soc. Tng. and Devel. Home: 4611 Denwood Rd La Mesa CA 92041 Office: 4141 Camino del Rio S San Diego CA 92108

TASAKA, MASAICHI, hospital executive; b. Hilo, Hawaii, Feb. 3, 1925; s. Sunao and Shizue (Katayama) T.; m. Toshiko Kohatsu, Aug. 30, 1952; children—Sharon Lei, Russell Ken. M.S. in Hosp. Adminstrn., Northwestern U., 1955. Bookkeeper, Francis Kiu & Co., 1948-50; bus. mgr. South Shore Hosp., 1950-53; asst. adminstr. Highland Park Hosp., 1955-64; asst. adminstr. Kuakini Med. Ctr., Honolulu, 1964-69, pres., 1969—; asst. prof. Sch. Pub. Health. Mem. Am. Hosp. Assn. (life), Am. Coll. Hosp. Adminstrs., C. of C. of Hawaii, Honolulu Japanese C. of C. Club: Lions. Office: 347 N Kuikini St Honolulu HI 96817

TASCHEK, CAROL JEAN, soil scientist; b. Los Alamos, Mar. 24, 1950; d. Richard F. and Inez M. (Milbauer) T. Student U. Calif.-Davis, 1968-70, N.Mex. State U., 1970-72; B.S., U. Calif.-Riverside, 1973; postgrad. Kansas State U., 1973-74, N.Mex. State U., 1976-80. Materials engring. technician Bur. Reclamation, Nambe, N.Mex., 1975-76; soil scientist Earth Environ. Consultants, Hanksville, Utah, 1979; soil scientist Soil Conservation Service, Chama, N.Mex., 1980—. Mem. NOW, ACLU, Nat. Abortion Rights Action League, Soil Conservation Soc. Am., Am. Soc. Agronomy, Soil Sci. Soc. Am., AAAS, Phi Kappa Phi. Recipient cert. of Merit, U.S. Dept. Agr., 1982; Performance award U.S. Bur. Reclamation, 1976. Home: Box 92 Chama NM 87520 Office: Box 25 Soil Conservation Service Chama NM 87520

TASHIMA, ATSUSHI WALLACE, U.S. dist. judge; b. Santa Maria, Calif., June 24, 1934; s. Yasutaro and Aya (Sasaki) T.; A.B. in Polit. Sci., UCLA, 1958; LL.B., Harvard U., 1961; m. Nora Kiyo Inadomi, Jan. 27, 1957; children—Catherine Y., Christopher I., Jonathan I. Admitted to Calif. bar, 1962; dep. atty. gen. State of Calif., 1962-67; atty. Spreckels Sugar div. Amstar Corp., 1968-72, v.p., gen. atty., 1972-77; ptnr. firm Morrison & Foerster, Los Angeles, 1977-80; U.S. dist. judge Central Dist. Calif., Los Angeles, 1980—; mem. Calif. Com. Bar Examiners, 1978-80. Served with USMC, 1953-55. Mem. ABA, State Bar Calif., Los Angeles County Bar Assn. Democrat. Office: US Courthouse Los Angeles CA 90012*

TASHJIAN, DAVID REITLER, aeronautical and electrical engineer; b. Kalamazoo, June 22, 1911; s. Haig and Janette (Reitler) T.; B.S. in Engring. Physics, U. Mich., 1932; M.S. in Physics, M.I.T., 1934; B.A.,

Western Mich. U., 1935, D.Sc. (hon.), 1959; m. Georgian Rawlinson, June 19, 1938; children—David, Robert, Mary, Allan. Research engr. Clarage Fan Co., Kalamazoo, 1935-40; design engr. Westinghouse Electric Corp., Balt., 1941-46, sect. mgr., 1946-53, engring. mgr., 1953-63; cons. engr. Lockheed Missiles & Space Co., Sunnyvale, Calif., 1963-76; cons. engring., Los Altos, Calif., 1976—. Mem. IEEE (sr.), AIAA. Author: English Writers—A Pocket Guidebook With Maps, 1977; editor: From Erzurum To Kalamazoo, 1978; patentee in field. Office: 177 Hemlock Ct Palo Alto CA 94306

TATA, GIOVANNI, museum curator; b. Taranto, Italy, Apr. 26, 1954; s. Vito and Angela (Colucci) T.; B.S. cum laude (scholar), Brigham Young U., 1977, M.A., 1980; grad. cert. area studies U. Utah, 1980; postgrad. U. Turin (Italy), 1980-81; came to U.S., 1974, naturalized, 1982; m. Brenda Susan Smith, Feb. 14, 1978. Archaeologist, Utah State Hist. Soc., Salt Lake City, 1979; teaching asst. dept. langs. U. Utah, Salt Lake City, 1979-80; Mediterranean specialist Soc. Early Hist. Archaeology, Provo, Utah, 1978—; mus. curator Pioneer Trail State Park, Salt Lake City, 1982—; instr. dept. art Brigham Young U., Provo, 1982—; research fellow Direzione Generale per la Cooperazione Scientifica Culturale e Technica, Rome, 1980-81. Republican. Mem. Ch. Jesus Christ of Latter-day Saints. Mem. Am. Assn. State and Local History, Western Interpreters Assn., Utah State Hist. Soc. Home: PO Box 8414 Salt Lake City UT 84108 Office: 2601 Sunnyside Ave Salt Lake City UT 84108

TATE, EVELYN RUTH, real estate broker; b. Ottumwa, Iowa, Sept. 21; d. Frank Edward and Ella Belle (Smith) Ross; student public schs., Huntington Park, Calif.; m. William Tate (dec.); 1 son, William. Owner, mgr. Evelyn R. Tate Realty Co., Sherman Oaks, Calif., 1943-53, Beverly Hills, Calif., 1976—; owner, mgr. Evelyn Tate Fine Arts, San Francisco, 1976—; mgr. Beverly Hills Galleries, Hyatt Regency Hotel, San Francisco, 1979—; mgr. art gallery Fairmont Hotel; owner, mgr. Tate Gallery, Buena Vista Winery, Sonoma, Calif., Cathedral Hill Hotel, San Francisco, Hyatt Regency Hotel, San Francisco. Mem. Nat. Assn. Female Execs., The Exec. Female. Home: 999 Green St Apt 1003 San Francisco CA 94133

TATE, WILLIAM JAMES, business counselor, tax adviser; b. Sarnia, Ont., Can., May 4, 1922; came to U.S., 1924, naturalized, 1940; s. Alfred Carlisle and Myrtle May (Hamilton) T.; m. Nancy Lou Arnold, Mar. 30, 1946; children—William James, Gary S., Cheryl A. Tate Pendergast, Franklin H. B.A., U. Mich., 1947. C.P.A., Mich.; enrolled agt. IRS. Auditor, Touche, Ross, C.P.A.s, Detroit, 1947-52; controller Grinnell Bros., Detroit, 1953-54; div. controller Chrysler Corp., Detroit, 1955-66, dir. and v.p. fin. and adminstrn. Chrysler U.K., London, 1967-70; v.p. fin. and adminstrn. Xerox Data Systems, also controller west region Xerox Corp., Los Angeles, 1970-75; sr. ptnr. Gen. Bus. Services, Oceanside, Calif., 1976—. Served to 1st lt. USAF, 1943-46, ETO. Mem. Nat. Assn. Enrolled Agts., Mich. Assn. C.P.A.s, Calif. Assn. Enrolled Agts., Oceanside C. of C. (ambassador). Club: Oceanside Rotary. Office: Gen Bus Services 1310 Union Plaza Ct Suite 206 Oceanside CA 92054

TATE-RAMIREZ, FRAN M., small business owner; b. Auburn, Wash., Oct. 5, 1929; dau. Frank Joseph and Theresa Mary (Bingesar) Pfulg; m. Rory Tate, Sept. 30, 1970 (div.); children—Michael C., Joseph M.; m. 2d, Juan Ramon Ramirez, Sept. 6, 1981. Student U. Wash. Gen. mgr., Sorensen Heating Co., Auburn, 1952-70; cons. Success Motivation Inst., Bellevue, Wash., 1970-72; field engr., draftsman, J. Dalton and Assocs., Point Barrow, Alaska, 1973-75; pres., owner Inupiat Water Delivery Co., Barrow, Alaska, 1977—; pres., owner Elephant Pot Sewage Haulers, Barrow, 1977—; owner, operator Pepe's Restaurant, Barrow, 1978—; disc jockey, Sta. KBRW, Barrow. Recipient Boss of Yr. award Credit Women Internat., 1969; Outstanding Service award Barrow PTA. Mem. Barrow C. of C., Nat. Geog. Soc., Smithsonian Instn., Jazz Heritage Found., Dallas Jazz Soc. Roman Catholic. Club: Las Vegas Jazz.

TATRO, RICHARD BRADY, advertising agency executive; b. South Fork, Pa., May 7, 1939; s. Willard Jasper and Violette Mae (Wood); m. Carrol Ann Hull, Dec. 19, 1964 (div.). B.A., UCLA, 1962. Asst. editor Hicks-Deal Newspapers, Los Angeles, 1965-66; editor employee communications ITT Gilfillan, Los Angeles, 1966-67; advt. mgr. Technicolor, Inc., Costa Mesa, Calif., 1968-73; corp. advt. dir. Technicolor, Inc., Hollywood, Calif., 1973-77; v.p. mktg. Bell Helmets, Inc., Norwalk, Calif., 1977-78; sr. account supr. Dailey & Assocs., Los Angeles, 1978-81; mgmt. supr. Cochrane Chase, Livingston, Inc., Irvine, Calif., 1981—. Served with U.S. Army, 1962-64. Contbg. editor mktg. Problem Solver, 1972. Office: 19600 Fairchild Suite 300 Irvine CA 92713

TAUB, ERIC, magazine editor, filmmaker, writer; b. N.Y.C., Apr. 9, 1948; s. Meyer Richard and Sonya (Epstein) T; m. Judith Nissman Taylor, Feb. 19, 1983. B.A. in Psychology, Queens Coll., 1968; student U. Birmingham, (Eng.), 1966-67; M.F.A. in Screenwriting, UCLA, 1976. Documentary filmmaker Camera News, N.Y.C., 1968-70; youth worker Soho Project, London, 1970-73; filmmaker InterAction Ltd., London, 1970-73; editor, Paul Kagan Assocs., Carmel, Calif., 1980-82; West Coast bur. chief CableVision Mag., Beverly Hills, Calif., 1982—; lectr., cons. on cable TV. Mem. Queens (N.Y.) Symphony, 1966-68, Penzance (Eng.) Symphony, 1970-72, Pride of Murray Bagpipe Band. Mem. Nat. Cable TV Assn., Psi Chi. Contbr. articles on entertainment industry to newspapers, mags. Office: CableVision Mag 101 N Robertson St Suite 206 Beverly Hills CA 90211

TAUBITZ, FREDRICKA, financial exec.; b. Los Angeles, Feb. 25, 1944; d. Ferdinand C. and Marie L. (Stewart) T.; A.A., Pasadena City Coll., 1963; B.S. in Bus. Adminstrn., U. Calif., Berkeley, 1965; M.S. in Bus. Adminstrn., UCLA, 1967; grad. Advanced Mgmt. Program, Harvard U., 1980. Acct., Coopers & Lybrand, Los Angeles, 1965-75, partner, 1976—; founding dir. First Women's Bank Calif., Los Angeles, 1974-76. Bd. dirs. Soroptimist Found. Los Angeles, 1978-79; bd. dirs. Girls' Club, Pasadena, Calif., 1973—, pres., 1981-83; mem. Calif. Mus. Found. Adv. Bd., 1978-81. Recipient Outstanding Young Bus. Leader award Los Angeles Jr. C. of C., 1978, Internat. Achievement award Soroptimist Internat., 1977. C.P.A., Calif. Mem. Am. Inst. C.P.A.s, Calif. Soc. C.P.A.s, Los Angeles C. of C. (dir. women's council 1978-81), Inst. Internal Auditors (chpt. dir.), Phi Beta Kappa. Office: 1000 W 6th St Los Angeles CA 90017

TAVEGGIA, THOMAS CHARLES, management consultant; b. Oak Lawn, Ill., June 15, 1943; s. Thomas Angelo and Eunice Louise (Harriss) T.; m. Brigitte I. Adams, Jan. 23, 1965; children—Michaela, Francesca. B.S., Ill. Inst. Tech., 1965; M.S., U. Oreg., 1968, Ph.D., 1971. Prof., U. Oreg., Eugene, 1970, U. B.C. (Can.), Vancouver, 1970-73, U. Calif.-Irvine, 1973-74, Ill. Inst. Tech., Chgo., 1974-77; mgmt. cons. Towers, Perrin, Forster & Crosby, Chgo., 1977-80; ptng. Manplan Cons., Chgo., 1980-81; dir. compensation cons. services Coopers & Lybrand, San Francisco, 1981—. NDEA Title IV fellow, 1967-71; U. B.C. faculty research grantee, 1970, 71, 72. Mem. Am. Compensation Assn., Am. Sociol. Assn., Human Resource Planning Soc. Presbyterian. Author: (with R. Dubin and R. Arends) From Family and School To Work, 1967; (with Dubin) The Teaching-Learning Paradox: A Comparative Analysis of College Teaching Methods, 1968; (with Dubin and R.A. Hedley) The Medium May Be Related to the Message: College Instruction by TV, 1969; contbr. numerous articles to profl. jours. Home: 188 Lariat Ln Walnut Creek CA 94596 Office: 333 Market St San Francisco CA 94596

TAVENNER, PATRICIA MAY, artist, photographer; processes; b. Doster, Mich., Mar. 22, 1941; d. Raymond Paul and Ruth Viola T. B.A., Mich. State U., M.F.A., Calif. Coll. Arts and Crafts. Solo show, Mills Coll., Oakland, Calif., 1974; participant exhbns. including Small Format, Los Angeles County Mus Art, 1969, Photo Media, Mus. Contemporary Crafts, N.Y.C., 1971, Books by Artists, More Coll. Phila., First Environ., Paris, 1974, Site Sculpture, Mills Coll.; comms. include facade Mus. Contemporary Crafts, N.Y.C., 1971, sect. of wall Can. Nat. Research Library, Ottawa, Ont., 1973; works represented San Francisco Mus Art, Oakland Mus Art, Mills Coll., Kansas City Art Ins., Mo.; art faculty U. Calif., Berkeley Extension, 1967—; asst. prof. art painting Calif. State U.-San Jose, 1972-73, Calif. Sate U.-San Francisco, 1972-73; lectr. in field. Mem. Women's Caucus for Art, Pro Arts, Internat. Sculpture Ctr. Contbr. to publs. including Art & Communication Marginale, 1974, Women See Women, 1975, Art: A Womans Sensibility, 1975, Rubber Stamp Art, 1978. California Artists Cook Book, Correspondence Art. Office: 55 Laguna St San Francisco CA 94102

TAVROW, RICHARD LAWRENCE, lawyer, shipping co. exec.; b. Syracuse, N.Y., Feb. 3, 1935; s. Harry and Ida Mary (Modess) T.; m. Barbara J. Silver, Mar. 22, 1972; children—Joshua Michael, Sara Hallie. A.B. magna cum laude, Harvard U., 1957, Ll.B., 1960, Ll.M., 1961; postgrad. U. Copenhagen, 1961-62, U. Luxembourg, 1962. Bar: N.Y. 1961, U.S. Supreme Ct. 1969, Calif. 1978. Atty. W.R. Grace & Co., N.Y.C., 1962-66; asst. chief counsel Gen. Dynamics Corp., N.Y.C., 1966-68; asst. chief counsel Office of Fgn. Direct Investments, U.S. Dept. Commerce, Washington, 1968-69, chief counsel, 1969-71; ptnr. Schaeffer, Dale, Vogel & Tavrow, N.Y.C., 1971-75; vp., sec., gen. counsel, dir. Prudential Lines, Inc., N.Y.C., 1975-78; v.p., sec., gen. counsel, dir. Am. Pres. Lines Ltd., Oakland, Calif., 1978-80, sr. v.p., sec., gen. counsel, dir., 1980-82, sr. v.p. legal and govt. affairs, sec., gen. counsel, dir., 1982—; gen. counsel Natomas Transp. Co.; instr. Harvard Coll., 1959-61; lectr. Am. Mgmt. Assn., Practising Law Inst. Recipient Silver Medal award Dept. Commerce, 1970; Fulbright scholar, 1961-62. Mem. Am. Steamship Owners Mut. Protection and Indemnity Assn. (dir.), Statewide Transp. Com. of Calif. C. of C., Pacific Mcht. Shipping Assn. (chmn. bd. dirs.), ABA, San Francisco Bar Assn., Internat. Bar Assn., Am. Soc. Internat. Law, Maritime Law Assn., Am. Corp. Counsel Assn., Harvard Law Sch. Assn. Democrat. Jewish. Clubs: Commonwealth of Calif., World Trade, Alpine Hills Swimming and Tennis, Palo Alto Tennis; Harvard (N.Y.C. and San Francisco). Contbg. author: Private Investors Abroad-Problems and Solutions in International Business, 1970. Home: 195 Harcross Rd Woodside CA 94062 Office: 1950 Franklin St Oakland CA 94612

TAWASHA, IBRAHIM Y., mgmt. cons.; b. Ramallah, Palestine, Dec. 13, 1924; s. Yacoub Ghnaim and Jaleeleh Saleeba (Rafeedy) T.; came to U.S., 1947, naturalized, 1954; student law Jerusalem, 1941-45; J.D., London U. Kings Coll., 1947; m. Leila T. Kashi-shou, Oct. 12, 1958; children—Carolyn, Jack, Joseph. Dir., League Arab States, Arab Info. Center, Western region, San Francisco, 1970-74; pres. Arab Am. Ventures, Inc., San Francisco, 1974—. Mem. parish council St. Nicholas Ch., past pres. Mens Fellowship; chmn. Arab Americans for Finch, 1976, for Corey, 1978. Ky. Col. Mem. Nat. Assn. Arab Americans (dir., exec. sec.), Assn. Arab Am. Univ. Grads (nat. v.p.), Western Fedn. Americans of Arabic Heritage (gov.), Arab Am. Anti Discrimination Com. (adv. bd.), World Affairs Council No. Calif., Vets. for Polit. Action No. Calif. (past exec. com.). Republican. Mem. adv. bd. Diplomacy Mag., 1976-79, Joint Mideast Am. Bus. Conf., 1977-80. Clubs: Commonwealth, Ramallah. Contbr. articles to profl. jours. Home: 1990 18th Ave San Francisco CA 94116 Office: 155 Montgomery St San Francisco CA 94104

TAXELIUS, THOMAS GRAHAM, energy cons. exec.; b. Spokane, Jan. 24, 1928; s. Claude William and Bess Maude (Graham) T.; B.S. in Mech. Engring., Wash. State U., 1949; m. Joanne Kelly Trimble, Apr. 18, 1954; children—Robert, Teri. Sr. engr. writer Westinghouse Bettis Atomic Power Lab., Pitts. and Idaho Falls, 1956-62; publications mgr. Kaman Nuclear Co., Colorado Springs, Colo., 1962-65; chief tech. publications Aerojet Nuclear Co., Idaho Falls, 1965-72; pres., chief exec. officer Stafco, Inc., Portland, 1972—; cons. in field. Mem. Am. Mgmt. Assn., Am. Nuclear Soc. Republican. Methodist. Clubs: Aero, Masons, Shriners. Home: 2030 SW Pheasant Dr Aloha OR 97006 Office: 621 SW Morrison St Portland OR 97205

TAYLOR, ALISON YARNOLD, counselor, mediator; b. Gary, Ind., Aug. 10, 1950; d. Tyler Richard and Mary Rosalie (Smith) Yarnold; m. Gerald Brian Taylor, Aug. 9, 1974; 1 son: Ian Birkin. B.A., Coe Coll., 1972; M.A. in Counseling and Personnel, Western Mich. U., 1979. Cert. mediator for spl. edn., Oreg. Supr., Found. II Crisis Ctr., Cedar Rapids, Iowa, 1972-74; adminstr. Autos House Group Home, Kalamazoo, 1975-77; counselor Reproductive Health Care Ctr., Kalamazoo, 1975-78; mediator Western Mich. U., Kalamazoo, 1978-79; adv. Oreg. Devel. Disabilities Advocacy Ctr., Portland, 1979-80; propr. Divorce and Custody Mediation Service, Hillsboro, Oreg., 1982—; mem. adj. faculty, instr. counseling Northwestern Sch. Law, Portland, 1979—. Chmn. Displaced Homemakers Services Coalition, Western Mich. U., 1979; chmn. Oreg. 4-H Outdoor Challenge Metro Devel. Com., 1982—. Johnson Found. Wingspread fellow, 1968-70; Rotary scholar Inst. for European Studies, Vienna, 1970-71. Mem. Am. Personnel and Guidance Assn., Assn. Family Conciliation Cts., Alpha Lambda Delta. Contbr. chpt. to Civil Litigation Manual (Oreg. State Bar), 1982; contbr. articles to profl. jours.

TAYLOR, BANNING VAIL, SR., tribal official, rancher; b. Warner Springs, Calif., Oct. 19, 1905; s. Samuel Brown and Mary Jane (Helm) T.; married, Apr. 4, 1930; children—Benning Vail, Earl Frank. Student Sherman Indian Sch., Riverside, Calif. Chmn. gen. council Los Coyotes Reservation, Warner Springs, Calif., 1947—; v.p. Indian Health Council, bd. dirs., 1979—. Active Indian politics. Served with USNG, 1975-83. Mem. Nat. Tribal Chmn. Assn. (sec. 1979-80, bd. dirs.), Calif. Tribal Chmn. Assn. (v.p. 1980-83, bd. dirs. 1983—), So. Calif. Tribal Chmn. Assn. (v.p. 1975-83, bd. dirs. 1983—). Roman Catholic.

TAYLOR, BETTIE GENA, educator; b. Sulpher Springs, Tex., Sept. 10, 1936; d. Morgan Reid and Mary Eleanor (Black) Estes; student Tarleton State U., 1966-68; B.S. in Edn., U. Tex., El Paso, 1970; M.A. in Edn., U. N.Mex., 1975; m. Gordon Wayne Taylor, Apr. 18, 1954; children—Paul Reid, Gordon Scott, Tracie Dianne. Tchr. reading Hagerman (N.Mex.) Mcpl. Sch. Dist., 1970-74, curriculum coordinator, 1974-76; Title I coordinator Aztec (N.Mex.) Mcpl. Sch. Dist., 1976-78, curriculum coordinator, 1978—; instr. N. Mex. State U., San Juan Coll., Farmington, N.Mex., 1977-82; grad. asst. Manzarita Center Reading Program, U. N.Mex., 1973-75; cons. on reading instrn. to public schs. Mem. Internat. Reading Assn. (treas. 1973-75, pres. Pecos Valley Council 1974, pres. San Juan Basin Council 1979, pres. N.Mex. Council 1982-83). Assn. Supervision and Curriculum Devel. Democrat. Presbyterian. Home: 1105 N McCoy St Aztec NM 87410 Office: care South Park Ave Sch Aztec NM 87410

TAYLOR, BRIAN MICHAEL, mfg. co. exec.; b. Moultrie, Ga., Jan. 11, 1943; s. William Lonnie and Laura Drucilla (Robbins) T.; student Norman Jr. Coll., 1961-62; B.S., Northrup U., 1965; postgrad. exec. program Carnegie-Mellon U., 1980; m. Carol Camilla Christel, June 28, 1969; children—Shannan Michelle, Tara Suzanne, Sean Fitzpatrick. Asso. engr., flight test analysis engr. Boeing Co., Seattle, 1966-69; sr. project engr., sales engr., account mgr. B.F. Goodrich, Troy, Ohio and San Mateo, Calif., 1969-77; with Kenworth Truck Co., Seattle, 1977-81, asst. plant mgr., 1980-81; product mgr. PACCAR, Inc., 1982—. Mem. Am. Mgmt. Assn., Soc. Automotive Engrs., Am. Prodn. and Inventory Control Soc. Republican. Presbyterian. Office: Bus Central Bldg 777 106th Ave NE Bellevue WA 98004

TAYLOR, CAROL CORNATZER, educational administrator; b. Vineland, N.J., Feb. 22, 1935; d. Warner Bogan and Ruth (Newcomb) C.; m. Duane Edwin Taylor, Aug. 15, 1958; children—Laura Taylor Van Luven, Douglas Edwin. B.S., N. Tex. State U., 1961; M.A., Ariz. State U., 1971. Tchr., Mesa (Ariz.) Pub. Schs., 1964-73, reading specialist, 1973-80, elem. prin., 1980—. Mem. Mesa Assn. Sch. Adminstrs., Ariz. Sch. Adminstrs. Assn., Assn. Supervision and Curriculum Devel., Nat. Assn. Elem. Sch. Prins., Phi Delta Kappa. Republican. Baptist. Home: 7918 S Juniper St Tempe AZ 85284 Office: 1435 E McLellan Rd Mesa AZ 85203

TAYLOR, DAVID MICHAEL, computer services cons.; b. Winnipeg, Man., Can., Aug. 8, 1953; came to U.S., 1964, naturalized, 1973; s. Albert George and Kathleen Rose (Westman) T.; A.S. in Bus., Southwestern Jr. Coll., 1974; B.S. in Bus. Info. Systems, San Diego State U., 1976; m. Buena Flo West, July 26, 1973; children—Eric David, Tanya Jennifer. Systems analyst San Diego County, Calif., 1973-76; chief bus. computer systems Pacific S.W. Airlines, San Diego, 1976-79; computer services cons., San Diego, 1979—. Mem. Data Processing Mgmt. Assn., U.S. Chess Fedn., Internat. Platform Assn., Baja Calif. and Imperial County Chess Confedn. (pres.). Home and Office: 4228 Seri St San Diego CA 92117

TAYLOR, DELORIS —LOIS—, oil company executive; b. Osceola, Ark., Dec. 25, 1931; d. Milo and Roetta (Grogan) Overstreet; m. Virgil N. Taylor, July 3, 1948. Student pub. schs., Conroe, Tex. With McClellan Oil Corp., Roswell, N.Mex., 1959—, head land dept., fin. dept., 1962-80, sec.-treas., head fin., 1972—, also dir.; dir. Sulimar Corp., Cortez Drilling Co., both Roswell; instr. Eastern N.Mex. U., Roswell campus, mem. adv. com. on support personnel program, 1982—. Ch. clk. Tabernacle Baptist Ch., Roswell, 1954—, in charge women's prayer group and mem. choir. Democrat. Club: Roswell Desk & Derrick (sponsor 1982, 83). Home: 1012 N Lea Ave Roswell NM 88201

TAYLOR, DONALD EDWARD, mech. engr.; b. Chgo., Jan. 24, 1928; s. James Edward and Agnes Thompson (Dewar) T., B.S. in M.E. with high honors, U. Ill., 1949, M.S. in M.E., 1952; m. Winifred A. Radde, June 16, 1951; children—Diane Lee, James William, Mark Edward, Barbara Joan. Research engr. Armour Research Found., Chgo., 1952-56; asst. dir. Lab. for Applied Sci., U. Chgo., 1956-62; mgr. engring. research dept. Lockheed Propulsion Co., Redlands, Calif., 1962-75; sr. engr. Pyronetics Devices, Inc., Cerritos, Calif., 1976-78; engring. specialist Gen. Dynamics, Pomona, Calif., 1978—. Registered profl. engr., Ill. Mem. ASME (sect. chmn.), AIAA, Pi Tau Sigma, Sigma Tau, Tau Beta Pi. Home: 218 Phlox St Redlands CA 92373 Office: Gen Dynamics Pomona Div PO Box 2507 Pomona CA 91766

TAYLOR, DONALD LEE, engr.; b. Fenn, Idaho, Aug. 1, 1931; s. Lester Benedict and Lucille (Chaney) T.; B.S. in Mech. Engring., U. Wash., 1961, M.S., 1963; m. LaVerne Norene Sorenson, June 16, 1951. Journeyman mechanic Pacific Car and Foundry Co., Renton, Wash., 1952-58; engr. Boeing Comml. Airplane Co., Renton, 1961-62, 63—, sr. engring. specialist, 1980-81, supr. engring. on automatic flight controls, 1981—; research asst. U. Wash., 1962; FAA designated engring. rep. Served with USAF, 1951-52. Mem. Aircraft Owners and Pilots Assn., Sigma Xi (asso.), Tau Beta Pi, Pi Mu Epsilon, Zeta Mu Tau. Amateur radio operator. Office: PO Box 3707 Seattle WA 98124

TAYLOR, DOUGLAS GRAHAM, Canadian provincial minister and member legislative assembly; b. Wolseley, Sask., Can., July 4, 1936; s. Robert Douglas and Isabella Roy (Graham) T.; m. Katherine Isabel Garden, Oct. 3, 1959; children—Robert Douglas, Katherine Isabel Marie, Susan Joan, Peter Samuel. B.Ed., U. Regina (Sask.), 1966, Diploma in Ednl. Adminstrn., 1972. Tchr. Kipling (Sask.) High Sch., 1962-64; prin. Wolseley High Sch., 1967-79; mem. Sask. Legis. Assembly for Indian Head-Wolseley, 1979—, minister of health, opposition house leader, 1979, opposition critic for edn. and continuing edn. Founder Qu'Appelle Valley Sci. Fair, Sask. Mem. Indian Head Superintendency Tchrs.' Assn., pres., Qu'Appelle Valley Prins.' Assn. Progressive Conservative. Mem. United Ch. of Canada. Club: Lions (Wolseley). Office: Legis Bldg Room 38 Regina SK S4S 0B3 Canada

TAYLOR, FLORENCE IRENE WAUL (FROSTY), editor; b. Montrose, S.D., Apr. 9, 1937; d. Emmett Alphonso and Rena Gerdena (Reeves) Waul; student Scottsdale Community Coll., 1972-73, Rio Salado Coll., 1979; m. Duane Mervin Taylor, Aug. 18, 1957; children—Kent Duane, Dana Sue. Telephone operator, Wiota, Iowa, 1953-55, Maryvale, Mo., 1957-59; bookkeeper Walnut Grove Products Co., Atlantic, Iowa, 1955-57; owner, operator portrait studio, Bellevue, Nebr., 1957-67, Phoenix, 1967-75; assoc. editor Paradise Valley News-Progress, Phoenix, 1970-81; editor Paradise Valley Press, 1982—, P.V. News, 1983—. Sec. Little League East, 1973, Paradise Valley Athletic Assn., 1974, Paradise Valley Community Edn. Adv. Council, 1978; mem. Paradise Valley Vocat. Edn. Adv. Council, 1978—. Recipient Outstanding Service award Little League, 1973; Community Service award Girl Scouts U.S., 1974, 80; Outstanding Community Service award Jaycees, 1977; Little Angel award Sr. Citizens, 1979; named Mrs. Nebr. Mrs. America Pageant, 1964. Mem. Nat. Photographers Assn., Copperstate Photographers Assn., Ariz. Press Women (writing award 1977, 78), Ariz. Press Club (writing award 1975), Paradise Valley C. of C., Am. Bus. Women's Assn. (charter), Sigma Delta Chi. Republican. Methodist. Clubs: Lioness (charter mem.), Paradise Valley Bus. and Profl. Woman's (charter mem.), Paradise Valley Woman's. Home: 3521 E Gold Dust St Phoenix AZ 85028 Office: 3521 E Gold Dust Phoenix AZ 85028

TAYLOR, FRED MONROE, U.S. dist. judge; b. Nampa, Idaho, Feb. 25, 1901; s. Robert F. and Pearl (Christine) T.; LL.B., U. Idaho, 1926; m. Gwen E. McLeod, Mar. 17, 1929; children—Jacquelyn Rae, Marta Kaye. Admitted to Idaho bar, 1926; practiced in Boise, 1938-54; pros. atty. Valley County, Idaho, 1927-33, 35-38; city atty. Boise, 1944-45; U.S. dist. judge, Boise, 1954—, now sr. judge. Mem. U.S. Jud. Conf., 1969-72. Mem. Idaho Senate, 1943-51. Mem. Idaho Bar Assn., Am. Judicature Soc., Phi Alpha Delta, Sigma Nu. Republican. Episcopalian. Mason (Shriner). Office: Fed Bldg Boise ID 83702*

TAYLOR, GAGE, artist; b. Ft. Worth, Jan. 20, 1942; s. Jack and Virginia Taylor; m. Aneicc, Dec. 28, 1962; children—Lincoln, Deva Rose. B.F.A., U. Tex.-Austin, 1965; M.F.A., Mich. State U., 1967. Instr., Mich. State U., 1967; San Francisco Acad. Art, 1969; Olivet Coll., workshop, Mich., 1971; San Francisco Inst., 1971. One-man shows: McBean Gallery, San Francisco Art Inst., 1970, Berkeley Gallery, San Francisco, 1970, Nat. Mus. Fine Art, Santiago, Chile, 1972; Am. Cultural Ctrs., Valparaiso, Chile, 1971, Lima, Peru, 1972, Cuzco, Peru,

1972; Zara Gallery, San Francisco, 1977, 79; group shows: San Francisco Art Inst., 1970, 71; Pioneer Mus., Stockton, Calif., 1971; U. So. Calif. Galleries, Los Angeles, 1971; Smithsonian Instn., Washington, 1973; Whitney Mus., N.Y.C., 1973; Mus. Modern Art, Paris, 1975; Mus. Contemporary Art, Chgo., 1976; Nat. Collection Fine Art, Washington, 1977; India Triennale, U.S.I.S., 1978. Author: Visions, 1977; contbr. articles to profl. jours. Home: Box 383 Woodacre CA 94973

TAYLOR, GEORGE EDWARD, training and employee relations executive; b. Ashdown, Ark., Apr. 26, 1936; s. Oscar and Sarah Lucille T.; m. Margaret Leonard, Aug. 18, 1962; m. 2d, Gwen Scott Miller, Apr. 30, 1972; children—Arthur, Sabrina, Rodney, Terrence. B.A. in Polit. and Phys. Sci., Pepperdine Coll., 1958; M.A. in Ednl. Adminstrn., Claremont Grad. Sch., 1974, Ph.D. in Bus. Adminstrn., 1975. Tchr., counselor Nightingale Jr. High Sch., Los Angeles, 1962-67, Jefferson Sr. High Sch., Los Angeles, 1967-69; adminstr. Locke High Sch., Los Angeles, 1969-71; manpower devel. specialist Urban League, Memphis, 1971-73; prodn. supr. Crown Zellerback Paper Co., City of Industry, Calif. 1973-75; adminstr. spl. edn. div. Los Angeles Unified Sch. Dist., 1975-77; mgr. profl. devel. and employee relations Jet Propulsion Lab., Pasadena, Calif., 1977—; cons. on profl. devel. and career opportunities in industry to educators. Served with U.S. Army, 1961-64. Mem. Am. Soc. for Tng. and Devel., Calif. Coop. Edn. Assn., Personnel and Indsl. Relations Assn., Omega Phi Psi. Democrat. Baptist.

TAYLOR, GUY, conductor; b. Anniston, Ala., Dec. 25, 1919; s. Stokely Brackston and Ola Mae (Shaw) T.; diploma Juilliard Sch. Music, 1948; student Mannes Sch. Music, N.Y.C., 1945-46, Birmingham Conservatory of Music, 1937-41; m. Renee Lifton, Oct. 19, 1947; children—Eric Anthony, Ellen Jane. Condr., mus. dir. Springfield (Ohio) Symphony Orch., 1948-51, Nashville Symphony Orch., 1951-59, Phoenix Symphony Orch., 1959-69, Fresno Philharm. Orch., 1969—; guest condr. in U.S., Gt. Brit., Can., Mex., Philippines and P.R. Served with AUS, 1942-45. Recipient Am. Symphony Orch. League Condr. Recognition award, 1960, Alice M. Ditson Orch. award, 1961; ASCAP award for adventuresome programming of contemporary music, 1977; Rockefeller Found. contemporary music grantee, 1966. Mem. Phi Mu Alpha. Contbr. mus. articles to Springfield News and Sun, 1948-51, Ariz. Republic, 1959-60, Fresno Bee, 1970-76. Home: 1300 W Calimyrna Ave Fresno CA 93711 Office: 1362 N Fresno St Fresno CA 93703

TAYLOR, HARRY GEORGE, printmaker, photographer; b. Detroit, Aug. 17, 1918; s. Donald Stinson and Ruth M. (Carlyn) T.; m. Alice Dean Boughton, Dec. 22, 1952; children—Paul, Deborah, Sally. M.F.A., Art Inst. Chgo., 1949. Instr. St. Bonaventure Coll., Olean, N.Y., 1947, Weber State Coll., Utah, 1959-79; art dir. Meridian Pub. Co., Ogden, Utah, 1960-83; exhibited in regional and nat. shows; represented in permanent collections of state of Utah, Union Pacific Co.; design cons. Served with inf. U.S. Army, 1940-44. Recipient numerous awards. Mem. Calif. Soc. Printmakers, Kimball Art Ctr., Salt Lake City Art Ctr., Eccles Art Ctr. Club: Ogden Palette. Woodcuts in (with poet Barbara Bernstein) Beasts, Bugs & Birds, 1982. Address: 905 Rancho Blvd Ogden UT 84404

TAYLOR, HELEN JEAN, health service adminstr.; b. Dixonville, Pa., May 14, 1927; d. Robert Clyde and Helen (Coalmer) Sickenberger, R.N., Jefferson Med. Coll., 1948; B.A. in Health Edn., Calif. State U., Northridge, 1971, M.S. in Health Sci., 1976; postgrad. UCLA, 1978 U. So. Calif., 1982—; 1 son, Brian Robert. Staff nurse Santa Monica (Calif.) Hosp., 1948-51; sch. nurse St. Martin's in the Fields, Canoga Park, Calif., 1963-65; sch. nurse, health educator, tchr., dist. health supr. William S. Hart Union High Sch. Dist., Newhall, Calif., 1971-79; adminstr. Mgmt. Health Services, Glendale (Calif.) Unified Sch. Dist., 1979—; cons. AIMS Cahill Films, Bur. Indsl. Edn., Calif. Dept. Edn.; vol. clinic nurse Intensive Vaccination Program, Los Angeles County Health Dept., 1961-63. Mem. community edn. task force United Way Planning Council of Los Angeles; mem. Glendale Community Coordinating Council, v.p., 1982-83; active ARC Disaster Nursing; mem. Am. Lung Assn.'s Children Health Com.; active Valley Symphony Guild, Tree People (Calif. Conservation project). Mem. Assn. of Calif. Sch. Adminstrs., Calif. Sch. Nurses Orgn., Los Angeles County Sch. Nurses Assn., Glendale Mgmt. Assn., Calif. State U., Northridge Alumni Assn., Jefferson Med. Coll. Nurses' Alumni Assn., Delta Kappa Gamma. Home: 7249 Quartz Ave Canoga Park CA 91306 Office 223 N Jackson St Glendale CA 91206

TAYLOR, HOWARD, self-adhesive labels, base material and labeling systems mfg. co. exec.; b. Thomasville, Ga., Feb. 21, 1943; s. Ceasar and Marie (Lewis) T.; student Howard U., 1961-62, Midwestern U., 1963-65, Pasadena City Coll., 1968-72; m. Virginia R. Owens, Oct. 1, 1966; children—Marina La Shunn, Yolanda Marie. Flight operator Bendix Engring., Pasadena, Calif., 1966-67; computer programmer Electro-Optical System Co., Pasadena, 1968-71; computer programmer/systems analyst Price Pfister Brass Co., Pacoima, Calif., 1971-74; dir. corp. data ctr. Avery Internat., Pasadena, Calif., 1974—. Served with USAF, 1962-66. Mem. Data Processing Mgmt. Assn. Mem. Ch. of Living God. Office: 150 N Orange Grove Blvd Pasadena CA 91103

TAYLOR, JAMES FISHER, psychologist; b. Mpls., Mar. 27, 1946; s. Henry L. and Catherine Morton (Elliott) T.; m. Geraldine Elizabeth Connel; 1 son, Keenan Connel. B.S., Bard Coll., 1970; M.A., New Sch. Social Research, 1973; Ph.D., U.S. Internat. U., 1976. Lic. psychologist, Calif. Postdoctoral internship Montreal (Que., Can.) Gen. Hosp., dept. psychiatry McGill U., 1976-77; psychologist Raleigh Hills Hosp., Redwood City, Calif., 1978-83; psychologist Stanford (Calif.) Alcohol Clinic dept. psychiatry Stanford U. Med. Sch., 1981—. Mem. San Mateo Psychol. Assn. (exec. com.). Home: 1067 Acacia St Montara CA 94037

TAYLOR, JANE CARVEY, marketing executive; b. Nashville, Apr. 15, 1927; d. Thomas B. and Florence E. (Haney) Carvey; m. Waller Taylor, II, Oct. 31, 1947 (div. 1972); children—Stephen, Grant, Waller. B.A., U. Puget Sound, 1977; postgrad. U. Alaska, 1977. Investor, real estate cons. Sun Valley, Idaho, 1970-80; exec. v.p. JDF Fin. Corp., Palm Springs, Calif., 1981-82; account exec. Heinold Commodities, Bellevue, Wash., 1982—. Active Las Madrinas Children's Hosp., 1959—; pres. Jr. League Pasadena, 1959-60; docent Council Los Angeles Mus. Art, 1963-66; bd. dirs. Otis Art Inst., 1967-70. Mem. Acad. Real Estate. Republican. Episcopalian. Office: 11201 SE 8th St Suite 270 Bellevue WA 98004

TAYLOR, JEAN, educator; b. Paintsville, Ky., July 13, 1950; d. John L. and Lillian (Steele) T.; B.A., Morehead U., 1974; M.P.A., Calif. State U., Sacramento, 1981. Adminstrv. asst. vets. program Sacramento City Coll., 1973-76; vets. officer Fed. Vets Cost of Instrn. Program, HEW, Marysville, Calif., 1976-77; instr. div. bus., math. and sci. Yuba Coll., Marysville, 1977—, lectr., organizer Yuba Coll. Women's Center, 1976-80; cons. women in mgmt. Procter & Gamble Paper Products Co., 1981. Mem. Am. Soc. Public Adminstrn., NOW, Am. Mgmt. Assn., Calif. Tchrs. Assn., Calif. Bus. Edn. Assn., Kappa Delta Pi, Kappa Delta. Episcopalian. Home: 2315 Edwards St Marysville CA 95901 Office: 2088 N Beale Rd Marysville CA 95901

TAYLOR, JOHN ASHBY, JR., air force officer; b. Atlanta, Oct. 8, 1948; s. John Ashby and Martha Boatwright) T.; B.S., U.S. Air Force Acad., 1970; M.S., Troy State U., 1979; m. Louise Alynne Taylor, May 8, 1976; children—Christopher Ashby, Andrew Rhodes. Commd. 2d lt. USAF, 1970, advanced through grades to maj., 1981; F4 pilot, Udorn Air Base, Thailand, 1972-73; instr. George AFB, Calif., 1973-76, Nellis AFB, Nev., 1976; mem. wing staff Hahn AB, Germany, 1977-80; test pilot, Edwards AFB, Calif., 1980—. Decorated D.F.C., Air medal (12). Republican. Episcopalian. Home: 6703 Doolittle Dr Edwards CA 93523 Office: 6513 Test Squadron Edwards CA 93523

TAYLOR, JOHN FREDERICK, psychologist; b. Akron, Ohio, Dec. 13, 1944; s. John Idris and Winnifred Jane (Fletcher) T.; student U. Akron, 1962-64; B.S., Ohio State U., 1966; M.A., Kent State U., 1969, Ph.D., 1970; m. Linda Jean Bolinger, Mar. 20, 1965; children—Tamara, Brian, Dana, Beth, Sharon, John. Psychologist, Chattanooga Psychiat. Clinic, 1970-71, Marion County (Oreg.) Community Mental Health Program, 1971-76; pvt. practice family psychology, Salem, Oreg., 1976—; instr. psychology U. Tenn., Chattanooga, 1971, Linn Benton (Oreg.) Community Coll., 1974-75, Chemeketa Community Coll., Salem, 1972-75. Chmn. Pacific N.W. Family Life Steering com. YMCA. Served with U.S. Army, 1970. Mem. N.W. Family Tng. Inst., Assn. Mormon Counselors and Psychotherapists, Am. Psychol. Assn., Oreg. Soc. Individual Psychology, N. Am. Soc. Adlerian Psychology, Oreg. Psychol. Assn. Republican. Mormon. Author: The Hyperactive Child and the Family, 1980; author columns: Psychology Works for You, Oreg. Statesman, 1972-76, Counselor's Survival Kit, Practical Ideas for Counselors, 1980—. psychologist; b. Akron, Ohio, Dec. 13, 1944; s. John Idris and Winnifred Jane (Fletcher) T.; student U. Akron, 1962-64; B.S., Ohio State U., 1966; M.A., Kent State U., 1969, Ph.D., 1970; m. Linda Jean Bolinger, Mar. 20, 1965; children—Tamara, Brian, Dana, Beth, Sharon, John. Psychologist, Chattanooga Psychiat. Clinic, 1970-71, Marion County (Oreg.) Community Mental Health Program, 1971-76; pvt. practice family psychology, Salem, Oreg., 1976—; instr. psychology U. Tenn., Chattanooga, 1971, Linn Benton (Oreg.) Community Coll., 1974-75, Chemeketa Community Coll., Salem, 1972-75. Chmn. Pacific N.W. Family Life Steering com. YMCA. Served with U.S. Army, 1970. Mem. N.W. Family Tng. Inst., Assn. Mormon Counselors and Psychotherapists, Am. Psychol. Assn., Oreg. Soc. Individual Psychology, N. Am. Soc. Adlerian Psychology, Oreg. Psychol. Assn. Republican. Mormon. Author: The Hyperactive Child and the Family, 1980; author columns: Psychology Works for You, Oreg. Statesman, 1972-76, Counselor's Survival Kit, Practical Ideas for Counselors, 1980—. Office: 1333 Edgewater St NW Salem OR 97304

TAYLOR, KENDRICK JAY, microbiologist; b. Manhattan, Mont., Mar. 17, 1914; s. William Henry and Rose (Carney) T.; B.S., Mont. State U., 1938; postgrad. (fellow) U. Wash., 1938-41, U. Calif. at Berkeley, 1952; m. Hazel Marguerite Griffith, July 28, 1945; children—Stanley, Paul, Richard. Research microbiologist Cutter Labs., Berkeley, Calif., 1945-74; microbiologist Berkeley Biologicals, 1975—. Committeeman Mount Diablo council Boy Scouts Am., 1955, dist. vice-chmn., 1960-61, dist. chmn., 1962-65, cubmaster, 1957, scoutmaster, 1966; active Contact Ministries, 1977-80; bd. dirs. Santa Clara Community Players, 1980—; vol. instr. English as a Second Lang., 1979-80. Served with AUS, 1941-46, lt. col. Res., ret. Recipient Scout's Wood badge Boy Scouts Am., 1962. Mem. Am. Soc. Microbiology (chmn. local com. 1953, v.p. No. Calif. br. 1963-65, pres. 1965-67), Sons and Daus. Mont. Pioneers. Presbyterian (trustee 1951-53, elder 1954—). Home: 550 S 13th St San Jose CA 95112 Office: 2d and Hearst Sts Berkeley CA 94710

TAYLOR, LEIGHTON ROBERT, JR., marine biologist; b. Glendale, Calif., Nov. 17, 1940; s. Leighton Robert and Mary A. (Highberger) T.; B.A., Occidental Coll., 1962; M.S., U. Hawaii, 1965; Ph.D., Scripps Instn. Oceanography, 1972; m. Linda Louise Puder, Feb. 2, 1963; children—Leighton, Maria Louise. Mus. curator Scripps Instn. Oceanography, 1971-72; mem. grad. faculty dept. zoology U. Hawaii, Honolulu, 1972—, dir. Waikiki Aquarium, 1975—; fishery biologist U.S. Fish and Wildlife Service, Honolulu, 1972-75; research asso. Calif. Acad. Scis. Bd. dirs. Lahaina Restoration Found., 1976—; pres. Phoenix Sci. Center. Fellow Am. Assn. Zool. Parks and Aquariums; mem. Bishop Mus. Assn., Hawaii Small Bus. Assn., Exploreres Club, Western Soc. Naturalists, Am. Miscellaneous Soc. Clubs: Bohemian, Outrigger Canoe. Contbr. articles to profl. jours. Office: 2777 Kalakaua Ave Honolulu HI 96815

TAYLOR, LENNY LEE, consultant, corporation executive, writer; b. Weston, W.Va., June 30, 1941; s. Clifford Albert and Monna Madeline (Bonnett) T.; m. Leticia Liwanag Suarez, Apr. 18, 1965; children—Jonathan Len, Timothy Lee, Matthew Paul. Student U. S.C., 1960-61, U. Md., 1965-66; A.B., U. Philippines, 1969; postgrad. U. Colo.-Denver, 1975-76. Ordained to ministry Evang. Ch. Alliance; mem. Bible Fellowship Ch.; lic. realtor, ins. broker. Speakers bur. rep., prodn. analyst, merchandising analyst Western Electric Co., Denver, 1970-75; dist./adminstrv. aide, rep. U.S. Congressman James P. Johnson, 4th Dist. Colo., 1975-81; pres., owner, prin. mgr. Taylor Internat. Services, Denver, also Len Taylor and Assocs. and Taylor Communications Group, 1981—; cons. to govs., nonprofit orgns., bus. and industry; tchr. seminars, lectures. Bd. dirs. Filipino-Am. Community of Colo., Inc., 1974-82; mem. Leadership Denver Assn; bd. dirs. Denver Christian Servicemen's Cen., Inc.; bd. dirs., co-founder Assocs. in Ministry, Inc., Ramona, Calif.; mem. Metro North Denver C. of C.; bd. dirs. Metro YMCA, 1981; bd. mgrs. Adams County YMCA, chmn., 1981, Vol. of Yr. award, 1981; chmn. State Senate Dist. 17 br. Republican Central Com., 1979-80; mem. U.S. Jaycees, 1973-75. Served with USAF, 1962-67; Vietnam. Mem. Assn. Profl. Cons. Internat., Am. Soc. Pub. Adminstrn., Am. Entrepreneurs Assn., Am. Soc. Tng. and Devel., Am. Soc. Profl. Cons. Club: Rotary. Editor News-Notes, 1974-75; contbr. articles to newspapers. Office: 13073 Dyanna Dr Suite 101 Denver CO 80241

TAYLOR, LINDA TRACEH, information systems executive; b. Cambridge, Mass., Apr. 16, 1942; d. Ferdinand and Hazel Irene (Towne) Karamanoukian; m. John Robert Taylor, Jan. 21, 1961; 1 son, John Robert; m. F. Jason Gaskell, Nov. 30, 1978. A.A. in Bus. Adminstrn., West Los Angeles Coll., 1976; B.S., West Coast U., 1978, M.S. in Bus. and Info. Scis., 1980. Corp. sec., gen. mgr. Seaboard Planning Corp., Boston, 1967-67, Los Angeles, 1969-72; prin. Tay-Kara Mgmt., Los Angeles, 1972-73; chief systems adminstrn. Comp-La, Los Angeles, 1973-74; mgr. systems analysis Trans Tech Inc., Los Angeles, 1974-77; mgr. software engring. and tech. audit depts. System Devel. Corp., Los Angeles, 1977-81; v.p. Gaskell & Taylor Engring., Inc., Los Angeles, 1981—; sr. lectr. West Coast U., Los Angeles, 1980—; vis. lectr. sr. seminar Calif. Poly. U., Pomona, 1978—. Chmn. bus. and profl. women's com. Calif. Republican Central Com., 1974; mem. White House Com. on Workers Compensation, 1976; mem. fiscal adv. com. Santa Monica Unified Sch. Bd. Edn., 1979-81. Recipient Pub. Service award West Los Angeles C. of C., 1974. Mem. Assn. Women in Computing (pres. 1980-84, v.p. Los Angeles chpt. 1979-80), Nat. Computer Conf. (vice chmn. 1980, mem. adv. com. 1983), Data Processing Mgmt. Assn. (v.p. local chpt. 1979-80), IEEE (software engring. terminology task force 1980), Assn. Systems Mgmt. (sec. local chpt. 1974-75), EDP Auditors Assn., Assn. for Computing Machinery. Office: Gaskell & Taylor Engring Inc 3572 Greenfield Ave Los Angeles CA 90034

TAYLOR, MALCOLM SCOTT, insurance executive; b. Bremerton, Wash., Jan. 16, 1943; s. Henry C. and Maxine C. (Scott) T.; m. Judith A. Stayer, Aug. 15, 1969; 1 dau., Serena K. B.A. in History, U. Wash., 1965, postgrad., 1966. With Safeco Life Ins. Co., Seattle, 1971—, underwriting mgr. group dept., 1976-79, asst. v.p., 1979-80, v.p. spl. markets, 1980-82, v.p. group dept., 1982—. Mem. adv. bd. KNOW. Served to capt. USAF, 1967-71. Mem. Health Ins. Assn. Am., Group Officers Round Table. Club: Glen Acres Golf and Country (Seattle). Office: Safeco Life Ins Co Seattle WA 98185

TAYLOR, MAX TOURNER, surgeon; b. Bloomington, Ind., Oct. 2, 1928; s. Forest E. and Bernice (Kern) T.; B.A. in Chemistry, Andrews U., 1950; M.D., Loma Linda U., 1955; m. Nina Elloway, Dec. 27, 1953; children—Denise, Larisa, Maxwell, Todd. Intern, Indpls. Gen. Hosp., 1955-56; resident Marion County Gen. Hosp., Indpls., 1955-60; surgeon, pres. Surg. Clinics of Ariz. Ltd., Phoenix, 1962—; pres. Double Circle Ranch Inc., Eagle Creek, Ariz., 1968—; partner Max Taylor & Co., Phoenix, 1978—, Taylor-Sherrow Devel. Co., Phoenix, 1975—; owner Kachina Travel, 1981—; dir. Camelhead Devel. Corp. Served with U.S. Army, 1960-62. Fellow A.C.S., Am. Coll. Chest Physicians; mem. Pan-Pacific Surg. Soc., Southwestern Surg. Soc., Phoenix Surg. Soc., Pan Am. Med. Soc., AMA, Ariz. Med. Soc. Republican. Contbr. articles to profl. jours. Home: 5725 E Camelback Rd Phoenix AZ 85018 Office: 525 N 18th St Phoenix AZ 85006

TAYLOR, PETER VAN VOORHEES, advt. and public relations cons.; b. Montclair, N.J., Aug. 25, 1934; s. John Coard and Mildred (McLaughlin) T.; B.A. in English, Duke U., 1956; m. Janet Kristine Kirkebo, Nov. 4, 1978; 1 son, John Coard III. Announcer, Sta. WQAM, Miami, 1956; announcer, program dir. Sta. KHVH, Honolulu, 1959-61; promotion mgr. Sta. KPEN, San Francisco, 1962; with Kaiser Broadcasting, 1962-74, Gen. Electric Broadcasting Co., 1974-78; program/ops. mgr. Sta. KFOG, San Francisco, 1962-66; mgr. Sta. WXHR AM/FM, Cambridge, Mass., 1966-67; gen. mgr. Sta. WJIB, Boston, 1967-70; mgr. FM div. Kaiser Broadcasting, 1969-72; v.p., gen. mgr. Sta. KFOG, San Francisco, 1970-78; pres. Taylor Communications, 1978—, No. Calif. Broadcasters Assn., 1975-77, Broadcast Skills Bank, 1975-77. Trustee, WDBS, Inc., Duke U., 1974-80; bd. dirs. San Francisco Better Bus. Bur., 1976-78. Served to lt. USCGR, 1957-63. Mem. Nat., Internat. radio clubs, Calif. Hist. Soc., Mus. Assn., Calif. Broadcasters Assn., San Francisco Symphony, N.Z. Radio Dx League, Worldwide TV/FM Dx Assn. Clubs: Advertising Tennis Assn. (pres. 1976-77), San Francisco Tennis, Marina Tennis, Thursday Night Tennis (treas. 1975-76, pres. 1976-77). Home: 2614 Jackson St San Francisco CA 94115 Office: World Trade Ctr San Francisco CA 94111

TAYLOR, PHYLLIS JOHNSTONE, clergywoman; b. Minnetonka, Minn., Apr. 20, 1933; d. William Wycoff and Arna Leona (Yahn) Johnstone, Jr.; m. Richard Bartlett Taylor, June 16, 1956; children—Beverly Taylor Sher, Richard, William and Virginia (twins), Peggy. B.A., U. Minn., 1956; M.Div., Iliff Sch. Theology, Denver, 1979; postgrad. Grad. Theol. Union, Berkeley, Calif., 1983—. Ordained to ministry Denver Assn. United Ch. of Christ, 1979. Interim assoc. minister Wheatridge Congregation of United Ch. of Christ, Denver, 1977; assoc. minister Applewood Valley United Meth. Ch., Denver 1977; assoc. pastor Lakewood United Ch., Denver, 1978-79; pastor 7th Avenue Congl. Ch., Denver, 1980—; chairperson adv. bd. Shalom House, Denver, 1982—; chaplain Denver chpt. Am. Guild Organists, 1980-82. Active Jefferson County (Colo.) Sch. Dist., 1977—, mem. adv. bd. Wheat Ridge area, 1977—. Mem. Metro Denver Assn. United Ch. Christ, Phi Beta Kappa, Sigma Alpha Iota. Republican.

TAYLOR, QUINTARD, JR., educator; b. Brownsville, Tenn., Dec. 11, 1948; s. Quintard and Grace (Brown) T.; B.A., St. Augustine's Coll., Raleigh, N.C., 1969; M.A., U. Minn., 1971, Ph.D., 1977; m. Carolyn Fain, Aug. 2, 1969; children—Quintard, Jamila, William. Instr., Gustavus Adolphus Coll., 1970, U. Minn., 1970; asst. prof. Wash. State U., 1971-74; asso. prof. Calif. Poly. State U., 1977—; asst. dir. documentary TV series South By Northwest, 1974-75; reviewer Nat. Endowment for Humanities; hist. cons. Gt. Plains Mus., Black Am. West Mus., Afro-Am. Cultural Arts Center, Spokane Centennial, 1981. Bush fellow, 1974-77, Kent fellow, 1974-77; recipient Carter G. Woodson award Assn. Study of Afro-Am. Life and History, 1980. Mem. Am. Hist. Assn., Assn. Study of Afro-Am. Life and History, Robert Maynard Hutchins Center for Study of Democratic Instns., Martin Luther King Found., NAACP, ACLU, So. Conf. Afro-Am. Studies, Wash. Hist. Soc., Western History Assn., Central Coast Cultural Assn., Alpha Phi Alpha. Democrat. Methodist. educator; b. Brownsville, Tenn., Dec. 11, 1948; s. Quintard and Grace (Brown) T.; B.A., St. Augustine's Coll., Raleigh, N.C., 1969; M.A., U. Minn., 1971, Ph.D., 1977; m. Carolyn Fain, Aug. 2, 1969; children—Quintard, Jamila, William. Instr., Gustavus Adolphus Coll., 1970, U. Minn., 1970; asst. prof. Wash. State U., 1971-74; asso. prof. Calif. Poly. State U., 1977—; asst. dir. documentary TV series South By Northwest, 1974-75; reviewer Nat. Endowment for Humanities; hist. cons. Gt. Plains Mus., Black Am. West Mus., Afro-Am. Cultural Arts Center, Spokane Centennial, 1981. Bush fellow, 1974-77, Kent fellow, 1974-77; recipient Carter G. Woodson award Assn. Study of Afro-Am. Life and History, 1980. Mem. Am. Hist. Assn., Assn. Study of Afro-Am. Life and History, Robert Maynard Hutchins Center for Study of Democratic Instns., Martin Luther King Found., NAACP, ACLU, So. Conf. Afro-Am. Studies, Wash. Hist. Soc., Western History Assn., Central Coast Cultural Assn., Alpha Phi Alpha. Democrat. Methodist. Office: Dept History Calif Poly State U San Luis Obispo CA 93407

TAYLOR, ROBERT CHARLES, JR., lawyer; b. Seattle, July 16, 1953; s. Robert Charles and Frances Fagan (Hogan) T.; m. Leslie Chapman, July 2, 1977. B.A. magna cum laude, Pomona Coll., 1975; J.D., UCLA, 1978. Bar: Calif. 1978. Ptnr. Segretti, Pitman & Erdbacher, Salinas, Calif., 1978—. Commr. Salinas City Traffic and Transp. Commn., 1982—; bd. dirs. Salinas Valley Vis. Nurses Assn., 1982—. Mem. State Bar Calif., Order of Coif. Republican. Roman Catholic. Club: Corral de Tierra Country (Salinas). Contbg. author profl. jour.; mem. UCLA Law Rev., 1976-78. Home: 207 Hawthorne St Salinas CA 93901 Office: Segretti Pitman & Erdbacher 21 W Alisal St Suite 119 Salinas CA 93901

TAYLOR, SAMUEL JOHN, editor, publisher; b. Moab, Utah, May 28, 1933; s. Loren L. and Pearl E. Taylor; m. Adrien Foote, Feb. 3, 1961; children—Thomas S., Sena Jane, Jerrold Loren, Zane William. B.S. in Journalism, U. Utah, 1959. Editor, pub. Moab Times-Independent, 1956—. Utah state senator, 1961-67; mem. Utah Air Travel Commn., 1967-68, Utah Com Exec. Reorgn., 1969-71; pres. bd. Grand Sch., 1970-76; mem. Utah Transp. Commn. Recipient Quintus C. Wilson journalism alumni award 1965 U. Utah, 1965; Outstanding Alumni award Utah State U., 1980. Mem. Utah Press Assn. (Master Pub. award 1967), Nat. Newspaper Assn., Soc. Profl. Journalists. Republican. Baptist. Mason. Office: 35 E Center St Moab UT 84532

TAYLOR, SHARON KAY, public relations officer; b. San Diego, July 6, 1945; d. Glenn L. and Marie G. (Turner) T. B.A. in Journalism, San Diego State U., 1968, M.S. in Mass Communications, 1977; B. Internat. Mgmt., Am. Grad. Sch., 1969. Tchr. pub. schs., Encinitas and Poway, Calif., 1970-76; adminstrv. asst. San Diego C. of C., 1977; mng. editor Arts & Activities, Pubs. Devel. Corp., San Diego, 1978-80; pub. communications officer San Diego Met. Transit Devel. Bd., 1980—. Recipient Outstanding Journalism Tchr. award N. Coast Pub. Assn., 1976. Mem. Pub. Relations Soc. Am., Internat. Assn. Bus. Communicators (Silver 6 award 1981, Merit award 1981), Pub. Relations Club San Diego, San Diego Press Club, Women in Communications, Inc. (Star award 1982). Home: 5033 Montessa St San Diego CA 92124 Office: San Diego Met Transit Devel Bd 620 C St Suite 400 San Diego CA 92101

TAYLOR, SHELLEY ELIZABETH, psychology educator; b. Mt. Kisco, N.Y., Sept. 10, 1946; d. Charles Fox and Pearl May (Harvey) T.;

m. Mervyn Frances Fernandes, May 1, 1972; 1 dau., Sara Fernandes Taylor. A.B. in Psychology, Conn. Coll., 1968; Ph.D. in Social Psychology, Yale U., 1972. Mem. vis. faculty Yale U., 1971-72; asst. prof. Harvard U., 1972-77, assoc. prof., 1977-79; assoc. prof. psychology UCLA, 1979-81, prof., 1981—; 10th Ann. Katz-Newcomb lectr. U. Mich., 1982; mem. adv. bd. UCLA-U. So. Calif. Cancer Info. Service, UCLA Ctr. for Health Enhancement, UCLA Epilepsy Ctr. Recipient Research Scientist Devel. award NIMH, 1981-86; NIMH grantee, 1974—; NSF grantee, 1976-79. Fellow Am. Psychol. Assn. (Disting. Sci. award 1980), Acad. Behavioral Medicine Research, Soc. for Psychol. Study Social Issues, Soc. Exptl. Social Psychology, Jonsson Cancer Ctr. Democrat. Author books, including: Social Cognition, 1983; Handbook of Health Psychology, 1983; contbr. 60 articles on social psychology, social cognition and health to profl. jours.; research on adjustment to chronic illnesses, particularly cancer and heart disease. Office: Dept Psychology UCLA Los Angeles CA 90024

TAYLOR, TAMARA ANN, editor, publisher; b. Los Angeles, July 18, 1958; d. Richard Blackburn and Charlene (Belknap) Taylor. Student Brigham Young-Hawaii, 1976-80, U. Hawaii 1980; B.S., Brigham Young U., 1981. Editor, owner, pub. Beehive newspaper, Las Vegas, 1981—. Mem. Youth for Responsible Govt., Citizens for Pvt. Enterprise. Mem. Nat. Assn. for Female Execs. Republican. Office: Beehive PO Box 26264 Las Vegas NV 89126

TAYLOR, TIMOTHY DAVIES, psychologist; b. Tacoma, Jan. 25, 1945; s. Thomas Gibson and Eleanor Jane (Davies) T.; B.A., Central Wash. U., 1968; M.A., U. Puget Sound, Tacoma, 1975; Ph.D., U.S. Internat. U., 1980. Tchr. schs. in Wash., 1968-72; v.p. Tom Taylor Ins. Brokers, Tacoma, 1972-81; pvt. practice psychology, Tacoma, 1981—. Vice chmn. Pierce County March of Dimes, 1977-78, chmn.-elect, 1979-80, chmn., 1980; active Tacoma-Pierce County YMCA; assoc. chmn. United Way Pierce County, 1981-82. Mem. Ind. Ins. Agts. and Brokers Am., Family Service Assn. Am., Profl. Ins. Agts. Wash., Am. Psychol. Assn., Am. Assn. Marriage and Family Therapy. Democrat. Clubs: W. Tacoma Optimist (pres. 1977, Optimist of Yr. award 1977), Elks. Home: 4416 N 27th St Tacoma WA 98407 Office: 915 1/2 Pacific Ave Tacoma WA 98402

TAYLOR, WALTER WALLACE, lawyer; b. Newton, Iowa, Sept. 18, 1925; s. Carrol W. and Eva (Greenly) T.; A.A., Yuba Coll., 1948, A.B., 1950; M.A., U. Calif., 1955, J.D., McGeorge Coll. Law, 1962; m. Mavis A. Harvey, Oct. 9, 1948; children—Joshua Michael (dec. 1980), Kevin Eileen, Kristin Lisa, Jeremy Walter, Margaret Jane, Melissa E., Amy M. Adminstrv. analyst USAF, Sacramento, 1951-53; personnel, research analyst Calif. Personnel Bd., Sacramento, 1954-56; civil service, personnel analyst, chief counsel, gen. mgr. Calif. Employees Assn., Sacramento, 1956-75; staff counsel, chief profl. standards Calif. Commn. Tchr. Credentialing; tchr. discipline civil service, personnel cons. Served USCGR, 1943-46. Mem. Calif. State Bar, Am., Sacramento County bar assns. Democrat. Author: Know Your Rights, 1963-64. Home: 4572 Fair Oaks Blvd Sacramento CA 95825 Office: 1020 O St Sacramento CA 95814

TAYLOR, WILLIAM JESSE, III, aircraft co. exec.; b. Wilson, N.C., Nov. 4, 1942; s. William Jesse and Eleanor Matilda (Townsend) T.; m. Linda Kay Baker, May 7, 1977. Student Garden City (Kans.) Jr. Coll., 1960-62; B.S. in Aero. Engring., Embry Riddle Aero. Inst., 1964. With Gov. Products div. Pratt & Whitney Aircraft, West Palm Beach, Fla., 1964—, Los Angeles rep., 1977—. Mem. AIAA, Exptl. Aircraft Assn., Am. Aviation Hist. Soc., Planetary Soc., Assn. Naval Aviation, Brit. Interplanetary Soc., Air Force Assn., U.S. Naval Inst. Home: 21216 New Hampshire Ave Torrance CA 90502 Office: 4818 Lincoln Blvd Suite 313 Marina Del Rey CA 90291

TAYLOR, WILLIAM ROBERT, cardiologist; b. Bklyn., Dec. 10, 1944; s. William R. and Gladys Marie Taylor; B.A., Ohio Wesleyan U., 1966; M.D. (Mosby scholar, Pfizer Med. scholar), U. Kans., 1970; m. Linda Ann Berta, Oct. 2, 1982; children—William, Richard, Linda. Internal medicine intern Cornell Cooperating Hosps., N.Y.C., 1970-71, resident in internal medicine, 1971-72; fellow in cardiology Cedars-Sinai Med. Center, Los Angeles, 1974-76; practice medicine, specializing in cardiology, Modesto, Calif., 1976 ; mem. staff Drs. Hosp., Meml. Hosp., City Hosp.; instr. med. program for interns and residents Scenic Gen. Hosp., Modesto, 1976—. Served to capt. M.C., USAF, 1972-74. Diplomate Am. Bd. Internal Medicine. Fellow Am. Coll. Cardiology; mem. ACP, AMA, Am. Heart Assn., Alpha Omega Alpha. Home: 212 King Arthur Way Modesto CA 95350 Office: 1540 Florida Ave Suite 100 Modesto CA 95350

TAYMAN, JEFFREY MICHAEL, demographer, statistician; b. Balt., Dec. 4, 1951; s. Bernard Oscar and Sheila Evelyn (Sandburg) T. B.A. in Anthropology, Fla. Atlantic U., 1974; M.S. in Demography, Fla. State U., 1976, Ph.D. in Demography, 1979. Research asst. Fla. State U., Tallahassee, 1976-78; cons. HUD, Washington, 1978-79; research analyst Fla. Dept. Health and Rehab. Services, 1978-79; research investigator State of Wash., Olympia, 1979-80, Office of Fin. Mgmt., 1980-81; research assoc. San Diego Assn. Govts., 1982—; cons. computer software and stats.; adj. coll. instr.; adv. council Pacific N.W. Regional Power Council, 1981, Oreg. and Idaho State Census Data Ctrs., 1980-81; chmn. Wash. State Census Data Network, 1980-81. Nat. Inst. Child and Human Devel. fellow, 1977-79; recipient Gov.'s Commendation State of Wash., 1982. Mem. Population Assn. Am., Am. Statis. Assn., Los Angeles Demographic Group. Contbr. articles to profl. jours. Home: 1488 Reed Ave Apt 16 San Diego CA 92109 Office: 1200 3d Ave Suite 524 San Diego CA 92101

TEAGUE, GARY ROLAND, marketing executive; b. Westboro, Mo., Sept. 21, 1937; s. Arthur Dale and Marie (Brugger) T.; m. Lois E. Percy, Mar. 15, 1960; m. 2d., Frances E. McGowan, June 2, 1970; children—Michele Marie, Christopher Dennis. A.A., El Segundo Coll., 1967. Analyst, Lockheed Missiles, Van Nuys, Calif., 1959-64; mgr. mktg. devel. Materials Research, Gardena, Calif., 1964-76; owner GRT Mktg. Assocs., Torrance, Calif., 1976—; cons. in field. Served with USAF, 1955-58. Mem. Mfrs. Agts. Nat. Assn., Nat. Council Salesmen Orgn. Inc., Soc. Safety Engrs. (asso.).

TEAGUE, LAVETTE COX, JR., archtl. cons., educator; b. Birmingham, Ala., Oct. 8, 1934; s. Lavette Cox and Caroline Green (Stokes) T.; student Auburn U., 1951-54; B.Arch., MIT, 1957, M.S.C.E., 1965, Ph.D., 1968; M.Div. with distinction, Ch. Div. Sch. Pacific, 1979. Archtl. designer Carroll C. Harmon, Birmingham, 1957, Fred Renneker, Jr., Birmingham, 1958-59; architect Rust Engring. Co., Birmingham, 1959-62, Synergetics, Inc., Raleigh, N.C., 1962-64, Rust Engring. Co., Birmingham, 1964-68; research asst., inst., research assoc. MIT, Cambridge, 1964-68; dir. computer services Skidmore, Owings & Merrill, San Francisco, Chgo., 1968-74; postdoctoral fellow UCLA, 1972; adj. assoc. prof. architecture and civil engring. Carnegie-Mellon U., Pitts., 1973-74; archtl. systems cons., Chgo., 1974-75, Berkeley, Calif., 1975-80, Pasadena, Calif., 1980-82, Altadena, Calif., 1982—; lectr. info. systems Calif. State Poly. U., Pomona, 1980-81, prof., 1981—. Recipient Tucker-Voss award M.I.T., 1967. Mem. AIA (Arnold W. Brunner scholar 1966), Assn. Computing Machinery, Sigma Xi, Phi Eta Sigma, Scarab, Scabbard and Blade, Tau Beta Pi, Chi Epsilon. Episcopalian. archtl. cons., educator; b. Birmingham, Ala., Oct. 8, 1934; s. Lavette Cox and Caroline Green (Stokes) T.; student Auburn U., 1951-54; B.Arch., MIT, 1957, M.S.C.E., 1965, Ph.D., 1968; M.Div. with distinction, Ch. Div. Sch. Pacific, 1979. Archtl. designer Carroll C. Harmon, Birmingham, 1957, Fred Renneker, Jr., Birmingham, 1958-59; architect Rust Engring. Co., Birmingham, 1959-62, Synergetics, Inc., Raleigh, N.C., 1962-64, Rust Engring. Co., Birmingham, 1964-68; research asst., inst., research assoc. MIT, Cambridge, 1964-68; dir. computer services Skidmore, Owings & Merrill, San Francisco, Chgo., 1968-74; postdoctoral fellow UCLA, 1972; adj. assoc. prof. architecture and civil engring. Carnegie-Mellon U., Pitts., 1973-74; archtl. systems cons., Chgo., 1974-75, Berkeley, Calif., 1975-80, Pasadena, Calif., 1980-82, Altadena, Calif., 1982—; lectr. info. systems Calif. State Poly. U., Pomona, 1980-81, prof., 1981—. Recipient Tucker-Voss award M.I.T., 1967. Mem. AIA (Arnold W. Brunner scholar 1966), Assn. Computing Machinery, Sigma Xi, Phi Eta Sigma, Scarab, Scabbard and Blade, Tau Beta Pi, Chi Epsilon. Episcopalian. Home: 1696 N Altadena Dr Altadena CA 91001 Office: 3801 W Temple Ave Pomona CA 91768

TEAGUE, RONALD WALLACE, clinical psychologist, educator; b. Hanford, Calif., Sept. 16, 1948; s. Roland Wallace and Maxine Maple (Dillon) T.; m. Elinor Marie Hewitson, Apr. 2, 1978. B.A., Sonoma State Coll., 1969, M.A., 1970; Ph.D., Calif. Sch. Profl. Psychology, San Francisco, 1973. Lic. psychologist, Calif. Staff psychologist Fresno Community Hosp., 1973-78, mgr. mental health dept., 1978-82, chief psychologist, 1978-82; assoc. prof. Calif. Sch. Prof. Psychology, 1974—; pvt. practice clin. psychology, 1982—; prof. clin. psychology U. Calif. Med. Sch., San Francisco, 1981-82; commr. Psychology Examining Commn. 1978—; commr., Central Calif. Criminal Justice Planning Commn., 1977-79. Awarded Mil. Hospitilar Order of St. John of Jeruselem, 1982. Mem. Am. Psychol. Assn., Calif. Psychol. Assn., Western Psychol. Assn., San Joaquin Psychol. Assn. Roman Catholic. Clubs: Octavian Soc., Augustan Soc. Author numerous papers in clin. psychology, psychiatry and psychohistory. Office: 1350 M St Fresno CA 93721

TEAL, MICHAEL LOUIE, city public services director; b. Inglewood, Calif., Jan. 16, 1944; s. Michael Stuart and Gladys Ethel Teal; m. Carmen García, Nov. 5, 1977; children—Anya, Michael. B.A., U. So. Calif., 1966; M.A., San Jose State U., 1971. Adminstrv. asst. City of Ontario (Calif.), 1971-78, sr. adminstrv. asst., 1978-80, pub. services dir., 1980—. Served with USAF, 1967-70. Mem. Am. Pub. Works Assn., Am. Water Works Assn. Office: 303 E B St Ontario CA 91764

TEARE, MARALYN LOIS, marriage, family, and child counselor; b. Montclair, N.J., Sept. 2, 1937; d. Malcolm and Dolores (Griffin) T.; B.S., Fla. State U., 1959, M.S., 1978; m. William E. Jacobs, Jan. 30, 1959 (div. 1974); children—Cheri Kay, Shanna Lynn. Intern, Parent Tng. Clinic, Neuropsychiat. Inst., UCLA, 1977-79; pvt. practice counseling specializing in treatment of anxiety and phobias, especially environ. phobias, Beverly Hills, Calif., 1980—; clin. instr. psychiatry and behavioral sci. U. So. Calif. Med. Sch.; lectr. to state, nat. orgns., TV. Mem. Mental Research Inst. Palo Alto, Phobia Soc. Am. (charter), Assn. Humanistic Psychology (clin.), Calif. Assn. Marriage and Family Therapists (clin.). Episcopalian. Office: 383 S Robertson Blvd Suite A Beverly Hills CA 90211

TEASDALE, CARRIE, physician; b. Chgo., Apr. 20, 1949; d. Robert Daniel and Audrey (Brinkerhoff) T.; B.S. in Humanistic Medicine (Regent's scholar), U. Calif.-Davis, 1975, M.D., 1976. Intern Kern Med. Ctr., 1976-77; pvt. practice medicine specializing in holistic medicine and health, Fullerton, Calif., lectr. on natural childbirth. Mem. AAUW, AMA, Calif. Med. Assn., Am. Acad. Family Practice.

TEBET, DAVID WILLIAM, TV exec.; b. Phila., Dec. 27, 1920; s. Joshua and Edith (Dechowits) T.; student Temple U., 1941. Public relations ofcl. legitimate theatre prodns. for John C. Wilson, Theatre Guild, others; pub. relations Max Leibman Prodns., 1950—; gen. program exec. NBC-TV, N.Y.C., 1950—; v.p. talent NBC-TV, 1959-79, sr. v.p. NBC, 1975-79; v.p. talent Marble Arch Prodns., Studio City, Calif., 1979—; exec. v.p. Johnny Carson Prodns., Los Angeles. Adv. bd. Stevens Coll. Named Man of Yr., Conf. Personal Mgrs. West, 1977. Club: Friars (bd. govs., chmn. spl. events com., exec. chmn. ann. testimonial dinners) (N.Y.C.). Home: Beverly Hills Hotel Beverly Hills CA 90210 also Dorset Hotel 30 W 54th St New York NY 10019 Office: Carson Prodns 4123 Radford Ave Studio City CA 91604

TEDFORD, CHARLES FRANKLIN, biophysicist; b. Lawton, Okla., June 26, 1928; s. Charles E. and Loula B. (Waters) T.; B.S. with distinction in Chemistry, S.W. Tex. State U., 1950, M.S., 1954; postgrad. in radiobiology Reed Coll., 1957, in biophysics U. Calif., Berkeley, 1961-63; m. Julie Reme Sauret, Sept. 15, 1951; children—Gary Franklin, Mark Charles, Philip John. Served as enlisted man U.S. Navy, 1945-47, Commd. ensign, 1950, advanced through grades to capt., 1968; biochemist U.S. Naval Hosp., San Diego, 1953-54, U.S. Naval Biol. Lab., Oakland, Calif., 1954-56; sr. instr., radiation safety officer Nuclear, Biol. and Chem. Warfare Def. Sch., Treasure Island, Calif., 1956-61; asst. chief nuclear medicine div. Navy Med. Sch., Bethesda, Md., 1963-66; adminstrv. program mgr. radiation safety br. Bur. Medicine and Surgery, Washington, 1966-72; dir. radiation safety and health physics program Navy Regional Med. Center, San Diego, 1972-74; mgr. Navy Regional Med. Clinic, Seattle, 1974-78, ret., 1978; dir. radiation health unit Ga. Dept. Human Resources, Atlanta, 1978-79; dir. Ariz. Radiation Regulatory Agy., Tempe, 1979—. Decorated Legion of Merit; recipient Meritorious Service award U.S. Navy, 1970. Mem. Health Physics Soc., Am. Nuclear Soc. Contbr. articles on radiation safety to profl. publs. Office: 925 S 52nd St Tempe AZ 85281

TEEL, HARRY CHANEY, engring. co. exec.; b. Portland, Oreg., Apr. 18, 1927; s. Harry C. and Winifred A. (Brooks) T.; student Oreg. State U., 1948-49, Pacific U., 1949-50; m. Delores Benge, Sept. 4, 1949; children—Bradford, Bruce, Susan, Brett, Shelley. Prin., H. C. Teel and Assos., constrn. co., Hillsboro, Oreg., 1950-55; archtl. coordinator CH2M Hill Inc., Corvallis, Oreg., 1955-70, ops. mgr., San Francisco, 1970-75, v.p. constrn. mgmt. and tech. services, Corvallis, 1975—; bd. dirs. Constrn. Edn. Found., Oreg. State U. Mem. Corvallis City Council, 1966-70; mem. Oreg. Gov.'s Com. on Devel. Willamette Valley, 1968-69; chmn. Oreg. Dist. 4 Council Govts., 1967-70; mem. Corvallis Budget Com., 1975-80, Benton County Consolidation Com., 1982; mem. bd. intercollegiate athletics Oreg. State U. Served with USMC, 1944-47. Mem. Am. Soc. Cert. Engring. Technicians (Oreg. chpt. Service award 1969, dir. 1968—), Project Mgmt. Inst., Constrn. Specification Inst., Associated Gen. Contractors, Inst. Cert. Engring. Technicians. Republican. Clubs: Oreg. State U., Beaver (pres.), Elks, Moose (club gov. 1953-54). Home: 3710 NW Witham Hill Dr Corvallis OR 97330 Office: 2300 Walnut Blvd Corvallis OR 97330

TEER, HAROLD BENTON, marketing educator, consultant; b. Eunice, La., June 12, 1945; s. Harold Benton and Kathryn (Weems) T.; m. Faye Peltier, Mar. 9, 1973. B.S. in Bus. Adminstrn., Northwestern State U., 1969; M.B.A., Miss. Coll., 1977; postgrad. La. Tech. U. Salesman patient care div. Johnson & Johnson, Jackson, Miss., 1973-77; instr. mktg. Hinds Jr. Coll., Raymond, Miss., 1978-79; instr. econs. La. Tech. U., Ruston, 1979-81; asst. prof. Ft. Lewis Coll., Durango, Colo., 1981—; cons. in field. Served to sgt. M.I., U.S. Army, 1969-71. Mem. Am. Mktg. Assn., Southwestern Mktg. Assn., So. Mktg. Assn., Mid-South Acad. Economists, Southwestern SBA. Home: 711 Clovis Dr Durango CO 81301 Office: Sch Bus Fort Lewis Coll Durango CO 81301

TEERLINK, J(OSEPH) LELAND, real estate developer; b. Salt Lake City, July 16, 1935; s. Nicholas John and Mary Luella (Love) T.; student U. Utah, 1953-55; m. Leslie Dowdle, Nov. 5, 1975; children—Steven, David, Andrew, Suzanne, Benjamin. Sales rep. Eastman Kodak Co., Salt Lake City, 1960-69; founder Graphic Systems, Inc., Salt Lake City, 1969-82, pres., 1969-79, chmn. bd., 1979-82; founder Graphic Ink Co., Salt Lake City, 1973, pres., 1975-79, chmn. bd., 1979-82; founder G.S.I. Leasing Co., Salt Lake City, 1975, pres., 1975-82; chmn. bd. Graphic Systems Holding Co., Inc., Salt Lake City, 1978-82; dir. leasing and acquisitions Terra Industries, Inc., real estate developers, 1982—. Bd. dirs. ARC, Salt Lake City, 1979-82; vice consulate of the Netherlands for Utah, 1977—; mem. active corps of execs., SBA, 1979-83. Named Small Businessman of the Yr. for Utah, SBA, 1978. Mem. Graphic Arts Equipment and Supply Dealers of Am. (dir. 1978-82), Printing Industry of Am., Nat. Assn. Indsl. and Office Parks, Nat. Fedn. Ind. Businessmen, Salt Lake City C. of C. Republican. Mormon. Clubs: Univ., Rotary. Home: 2984 Thackeray Pl Salt Lake City UT 84108 Office: 1225 E Ft Union Blvd Midvale UT 84047

TEETERS, CLARENCE, salt co. mgr.; b. Mt. Pleasant, Pa., Dec. 22, 1933; s. Clarence and Edna Marie (Grimm) T.; student U. Toledo, 1952-55, U. So. Calif., 1978; m. Sandra Jean Ulery, Aug. 2, 1958; children—Deanna Marie, Douglas James. Buyer, mgr. Tiedtkes, Toledo, 1955-60; sales rep. Morton Salt Co., 1960-69, dist. sales mgr., No. Calif., Nev., Hawaii, 1969-78; mgr. consumer products Leslie Salt Co., Newark, Calif., 1978—. Mem. The Illuminators. Republican. Presbyterian. Clubs: San Francisco Sales Mgrs., Masons. Address: 7200 Central Ave Newark CA 94560

TEETS, JOHN WILLIAM, food service executive; b. Elgin, Ill., Sept. 15, 1933; s. John William and Maudie T.; student U. Ill.; m. Nancy Kerchenfaut, June 25, 1965; children—Jerri, Valerie, Heide Jane, Suzanne. Pres., partner Winter Garden Restaurant, Inc., Carpenterville, Ill., 1957-63; v.p. Greyhound Food Mgmt. Co., also pres. Post Houses, Inc. and Horne's Enterprises, Chgo., 1964-68; pres., chief operating officer John R. Thompson Co., Chgo., 1968-71; pres., chief operating officer restaurant div., also corp. v.p. Canteen Corp., Chgo., 1971-74; exec. v.p., chief operating officer Bonanza Internat. Co., Dallas, 1974-76; chmn., chief exec. officer Greyhound Food Mgmt., Inc., Phoenix, 1976-80; group v.p. food service Greyhound Corp., 1976-80, group v.p. services group and corp. vice-chmn., 1980-82, chmn., 1982—, chief exec. officer, 1981—, chmn., chief exec. officer subs. Armour & Co.; chmn., pres. Post Houses, Inc., Prophet Foods Co.; vice-chmn. Pres.'s Conf. on Foodservice Industry. Adv. bd. Phoenix and Valley of Sun Conv. and Visitors Bur. Mem. Nat. Automatic Mdsg. Assn., Nat. Restaurant Assn., Am. Mgmt. Assn., Nat. Inst. Foodservice Industry (trustee), Christian Businessmen's Com. (chmn. steering com. 1977), Nat. Speakers Assn. Club: Arizona. Office: Greyhound Tower Station 3103 Phoenix AZ 85077

TEGTMEYER, JOHN LOUIS, architect; b. St. Louis, Nov. 1, 1950; s. Adolph H. and Elise (Desloge) T.; B.A., Wesleyan U., 1972; M.Arch., Calif. State Poly. U., 1977. Draftsman, H.K. Ferguson, San Francisco, 1973-74; designer Lewis Homes, Upland, Calif., 1976-77; architect, project mgr. Harrison, Beckhart E. Mill, Architects, Los Angeles, 1977—. Bd. dirs. San Gabriel Valley Fair Housing Council, 1979—, v.p., 1981-82, pres., 1982—. Mem. Calif. Poly. Alumni Assn. (v.p. environ. design 1977—), Pasadena Jr. C. of C. (dir. 1980—, v.p. 1981—), AIA, Beta Theta Pi. Democrat. Roman Catholic. Home: 1640 Raymond Hill Apt 2 South Pasadena CA 91030 Office: 930 Colorado Blvd Los Angeles CA 90047

TEICHMAN, SOL, store display mfg. co. exec.; b. Mukacevo, Czechoslovakia, May 9, 1929; s. Sam and Lujza (Friedman) T.; came to U.S., 1946, naturalized, 1954; m. Ruth Noe, Nov. 22, 1959; children—Bernard, Lisa, Alan. Salesman Pacific Fixture Co., Los Angeles, 1949-56; owner, sec.-treas. Teichman Enterprises (T & H Store Display), Los Angeles, 1956—. Chmn. bd., 1st v.p. Emek Hebrew Acad.; chmn. bd. Valley Torah Center, bd. dirs. Los Angeles Bur. Jewish Edn. and B'Nei Akiva (youth orgn.), Congregations Mishkan Israel and Shaarey Zedek, UOJCA. Served with AUS, 1951-53. Recipient award for efforts for Jewish community Los Angeles City Council, 1971; Man of Yr. award Emek Hebrew Acad., 1971; David Ben Gurion award Mizrachi Orgn. and State of Israel, 1975, others. Patentee in field. Home: 5323 Genesta Ave Encino CA 91316 Office: 2035 E 46th St Los Angeles CA 90058

TEITSWORTH, ROBERT ALLAN, petroleum co. exec.; B.S., Stanford, 1952, M.S. in Engring., 1953. Geologist, Amerada Petroleum Co., Los Angeles, 1953-59; with Occidental Petroleum Corp., Bakersfield, Calif., 1959—, exec. v.p., 1971-73, dir., 1979—; pres. Occidental Exploration and Prodn. Co., 1973-75, chmn., chief exec. officer, 1975-81, chmn., pres., 1981—; chmn., chief exec. officer Occidental Oil & Gas Corp., 1975—; dir. Can. Occidental Petroleum Ltd., Calgary, Can., 1964—, chmn., 1970-78, 81—; exec. v.p., chief exec. officer (oil & gas) Occidental Petroleum Corp., Los Angeles; dir. Varco Internat., Inc. Mem. Am. Assn. Petroleum Geologists, Am. Inst. Profl. Geologists, Am. Inst. Mining, Metall. and Petroleum Engrs., Western Oil and Gas Assn. (dir. 1973—). Office: Occidental Exploration & Prodn Co 5000 Stockdale Hwy Bakersfield CA 93309*

TELLER, EDWARD, physicist, author, educator; b. Budapest, Hungary, Jan. 15, 1908; came to U.S., 1935, naturalized, 1941; s. Max and Ilona (Deutch) T.; student Karlsruhe Tech. Inst. (Germany), 1926-28, U. Munich (Germany), 1928; Ph.D., U. Leipzig (Germany), 1930; Sc.D. (hon.), Yale U., 1954, U. Alaska, 1959, Fordham U., 1960, St. Louis U., 1960, U. So. Calif., 1960, George Washington U., 1960, Rochester Inst. Detroit, 1964, Clemson U., 1966, Clarkson Coll., 1969; LL.D., Boston Coll., 1961, Seattle U., 1961, U. Cin., 1962, U. Pitts., 1963, Pepperdine U., 1974, U. Md. in Heidelberg, 1977; Ph.D. (hon.), Tel Aviv (Israel) U., 1972; L.H.D. (hon.), Mt. Mary Coll., 1964; D. Natural Sci. (hon.), De La Salle U., 1981; m. Augusta Harkanyi, 1934; children—Paul, Susan Wendy. Research asso. U. Leipzig, 1929-31, U. Gottingen (Germany), 1931-33; Rockefeller fellow Inst. Theoretical Physics, Copenhagen, 1934; lectr. U. London, 1934-35; prof. physics George Washington U., 1934-41, Columbia U., 1941-42; physicist U. Chgo., 1942-43, Manhattan Engring. Dist., Chgo., 1942-46, Los Alamos (N.Mex.) Sci. Lab., 1943-46, asst. dir., 1949-52; prof. physics U. Chgo., 1946-52; cons. Livermore br. Radiation Lab., U. Calif., 1952-53; prof. physics U. Calif., Berkeley, 1953-60, prof. physics-at-large, 1960-70, dir. Lawrence Livermore Lab., 1958-60, asso. dir., 1960-75; chmn. dept. applied sci. U. Calif., Davis/Livermore, 1963-66, cons. Lawrence Livermore Nat. Lab., 1975—, asso. dir. emeritus, 1975—; univ. prof. emeritus U. Calif., 1975—; sr. research fellow Hoover Instn. on War, Revolution and Peace, Stanford U., 1975—; vis. prof. Arthur Spitzer chair energy mgmt. Pepperdine U., Calif., 1976-77. Mem. adv. bd. Americans for More Power Sources, 1979; mem. sci. adv. bd. USAF, 1951; mem. bd. govs. American Friends of Tel Aviv, 1973; mem. Coalition for Asian Peace and Security, Com. of Protectors of Andrei Sakharov, 1980—, Com. on the Present Danger; bd. dirs. ThermoElectron, Def. Intelligence Sch. Recipient numerous awards including: Harrison medal Am. Ordnance

Assn., 1955, Albert Einstein award, 1958, Gen. Donovan Meml. award, 1959, Enrico Fermi award, 1962, Robins award of Am., 1963, Leslie R. Groves Gold Medal award, 1974, Semmelweiss Medal award, 1977, Albert Einstein award Technion Inst. of Israel, 1977, Henry T. Heald award Ill. Inst. Tech., 1978, Gold Medal award Am. Coll. Nuclear Medicine, 1980; named Disting. Scientist, Nat. Sci. Devel. Bd., 1981. Fellow Am. Phys. Soc., Am. Nuclear Soc.; mem. Am. Acad. Arts and Scis., Am. Acad. of Achievement AAAS, Am. Geophys. Union, Am. Def. Preparedness Assn., Soc. of Engring. Scientists (A.C. Eringen award 1980), Internat. Acad. Quantum Molecular Sci., Nat. Acad. Scis., Scientists and Engrs. for Secure Energy, Internat. Platform Assn., Am. Ordnance Assn. Author: (with Francis Owen Rice) The Structure of Matter, 1949; (with Albert L. Latter) Our Nuclear Future, 1958; (with Allen Brown) The Legacy of Hiroshima, 1962; The Reluctant Revolutionary, 1964; (with others) The Constructive Uses of Nuclear Explosives, 1968, Great Men of Physics, 1969; The Miracle of Freedom, 1972; Energy: A Plan for Action, 1975; Nuclear Energy in the Developing World, 1977; Energy from Heaven and Earth, 1979; Pursuit of Simplicity, 1980; editor: Fusion, Vol. 1, Magnetic Confinement, 1981; pioneer in thermonuclear reaction studies; contbr. to spectroscopy of polyatomic molecules. Address: PO Box 808 Lawrence Livermore Laboratory Livermore CA 94550

TELLYER, HARRY B., constrn. co. exec.; b. Fort Worth, Mar. 15, 1928; s. Harry B. and Helen M. (Parish) T.; student U. N.Mex., 1946; m. Lila Mae Hubbell, June 4, 1949 (div. Dec. 1954); 1 dau., Donna Mae; m. 2d, Brigitta H. Ressel, Nov. 10, 1955. Plant mgr. Tellyer Pipe Co., 1946-50, v.p., 1950-56; dist. mgr. Am. Marietta Co., 1957-59; v.p. Tellyer Industries, 1956-62; pres. Dircks-Beath, Inc., 1957-62, Tellyer Mfg.-Constrn. Co., 1962—, Short & Tellyer, Inc., 1962-70, Tel Mac Telecasting Co., 1964-66, Tellbrook Assos. Developers, 1976—; agt. State Mut. Life Assurance Co. Mem. N.Mex. Ho. of Reps., 1962-64; chmn. Las Cruces City Indsl. Bd., 1963-67; mem. N.Mex. State Penitentiary Bd., 1967-69, N.Mex. Parole Bd., 1970-72, N.Mex. Corrections Commn., 1973-76; nat. bd. dirs. Camp Fire Girls, 1958. Mem. ASTM, N.Mex. Motor Carriers Assn. (pres. 1955), N.Mex. Soc. Profl. Engrs., NAM, C. of C., N.Mex. Life Underwriters. Mason. Home: PO Box 1318 Las Cruces NM 88004

TELNAES, INGE SIGURD, marketing director, consultant; b. Oslo, Mar. 19, 1930; came to U.S., 1961, naturalized, 1976; s. Audun H. and Ingrio B. (Michaelsen) T.; m. Gisela Bauer, Apr. 3, 1958; children—Ralph W. (dec.), Ann C. Diplom Ingenieur, Technische Hochschule Darmstadt (Germany), 1958. Project sect. mgr. Kongsberg Våpen Fabrikk, Norway, 1958-60; project engr. IBM Nordic Labs., Solna, Sweden, 1960-61; asst. to v.p. engring. IBM WTC, N.Y.C., 1961-62; project mgr. testing IBM Olympic System, Austria, 1964-66; mgr. product test IBM WTC, N.Y.C., mgr. hardware testing, Raleigh, N.C., 1966-67; product devel. mgr. Nordic Lab., Lidingö Sweden, 1967-70, asst. to exec. v.p., 1970-72; engr. mfg. and service IBM, 1970-72, mgr. scanner devel., Raleigh, N.C., 1972-74; dir. Nev. Research Ctr., Bally Mfg. Corp., Reno, 1974-79; cons., dir. new products and systems Summit Systems, Los Angeles, 1979—; dir. mktg. Playtime Distbg. Co., Las Vegas. Served with Royal Norwegian Air Force, 1949-52. Mem. Norwegian Engring. Assn., Norwegian Assn. Automatic Control. Republican. Lutheran. Home: 4435 Canyon Dr Reno NV 89509 Office: 3230 Polaris Ave Las Vegas NV 89102

TEMBY, FREDERICK ELROY, manager agricultural chemical research station, agronomist; b. Dodgeville, Wis., June 10, 1929; s. Luman James and Leona E. (Jewell) T.; m. Elise G. Wallenta, Feb. 27, 1965; children—Sharon, Mardelle, Angela. B.S., U. Wis., 1954, M.S., 1959. Tech. supr. Pennwalt Corp., Aurora, Ill., 1961-75, research sta. mgr., Fresno, Calif., 1975—; researcher mgmt., agrl. chem. field. Served with U.S. Army, 1954-56. Mem. Am. Soc. Agronomy, Western Soc. Weed Sci., San Joaquin Entomological Soc., Plant Growth Regulator Soc. Am.

TEMIANKA, HENRI, conductor, violinist, author; b. Greenock, Scotland, Nov. 19, 1906; s. Israel and Fanny (Hildebrand) T.; came to U.S., 1939, naturalized, 1945; student conservatory, Rotterdam, Netherlands, Nat. Conservatory, Berlin, Paris; grad. Curtis Inst., Phila., 1930; m. Emmy Cowden, Jan. 28, 1943; children—Daniel, David. Founder, dir., condr. Calif. Chamber Symphony, Los Angeles, 1960—; prof. Calif. State U., Long Beach, 1964-74, prof. emeritus, 1974—; vis. prof. U. Calif., Santa Barbara, U. Utah, U. Colo., Brigham Young U.; cons. Ford Found., Martha Baird Rockefeller Found. Decorated officier des Arts et Lettres (France). Author: Facing the Music, 1973. Recorded numerous albums. Home: 2915 Patricia Los Angeles CA 90064 Office: 2219 S Bentley Los Angeles CA 90064

TEMPEST, BRUCE DEAN, physician; b. Catasauqua, Pa., Nov. 3, 1935; s. Comley Quinton and Eleanor Dorthy (Wenner) T.; A.B., Lafayette Coll., 1957; M.D., U. Pa., 1961; m. Phyllis Rems, June 20, 1959; children—Peter, Rebekah, Andrew. Intern, Phila. Gen. Hosp., 1961-62, resident in internal medicine, 1962-65; fellow in immunology and allergy Hosp. U. Pa., 1965-67; med. dir. USPHS, HEW, 1967; chief medicine USPHS Hosp., Tuba City, Ariz., 1967-70; chief, dep. chief medicine Gallup (N.Mex.) Indian Med. Center, 1970—. Fellow A.C.P. Republican. Mem. Christian Reformed Ch. Contbr. articles to profl. jours.; research epidemiology of pneumonia. Home: 1603 Monterey Dr Gallup NM 87301 Office: Gallup Indian Med Center Gallup NM 87301

TEN EYCK, DAVID RODERICK, physician; b. Portland, Oreg., Oct. 24, 1929; s. Carrol F. and Marjory (Thompson) TenE.; A.B., Occidental Coll., 1951; M.D., U. So. Cal., 1955; M.P.H., Johns Hopkins U., 1968, Dr. P.H., 1973. Commd. lt. (j.g.) USN, 1955, advanced through grades to capt., 1970; resident internal medicine Naval Hosp., Oakland, Calif., 1958-61; chief, med. service Naval Sta. Hosp., DaNang, Viet Nam, 1965-66; research fellow Center for Research Johns Hopkins, Calcutta, India, 1968-69; dep. dir. Naval Med. Research Unit #3, Addis Ababa, Ethiopia, 1969-71; comdg. officer Naval Med. Research Unit #1, Berkeley, Calif., 1971-74, Naval Health Research Center, San Diego, 1974-75, ret., 1975; chief disease control San Bernardino County (Calif.) Health Dept., 1976-78; field rep. Joint Commn. on Accreditation of Hosps., Chgo., 1978-82; cons. Hosp. Quality Assurance, 1982—. Home: 17412 Hart St Van Nuys CA 91406 Office: 17409 Marlin Pl Van Nuys CA 91406

TENNANT, FOREST SEARLS, JR., physician; b. Dodge City, Kans., Jan. 23, 1941; s. Forest Searls and Vivian (White) T.; A.A., Hutchinson (Kans.) Jr. Coll., 1960; B.A., U. Mo., 1962; M.D., U. Kans., 1966; M.P.H., U. Calif., Los Angeles, 1973, D.P.H., 1974; m. Miriam Isaac, Sept. 17, 1966. Intern, U. Louisville, 1966-67; resident in internal medicine U. Tex. Med. Br., 1967-68; postdoctoral fellow USPHS, also resident in preventive medicine UCLA, 1972-74; exec. dir. Community Health Projects, Inc., West Covina, Calif., 1974—; asso. prof. dept. public health UCLA; cons. Calif. Dept. Justice. Bd. dirs. Am. Cancer Soc., 1976, Am. Lupus Soc., 1978, ARC, 1979; pres. West Covina Republican Club, 1976; mem. West Covina City Council, 1980—. Served to maj. M.C., AUS, 1968-72. Decorated Army Commendation medal, Meritorious Service medal. Diplomate Am. Bd. Family Practice, Am. Bd. Preventive Medicine, Nat. Bd. Med. Examiners. Fellow Am. Coll. Preventive Medicine; mem. Calif., Los Angeles County med. assns., So. Calif. Assn. Physicians in Drug Dependence (pres.), AMA, Calif. Soc. Treatment of Dependency Disorders, Am., Calif. pub. health assns., Assn. Tchrs. Preventive Medicine, Am. Geriatrics Soc., Am. Assn. Automotive Medicine, AAAS, Calif. Soc. Treatment of Alcoholism and Other Durg Dependencies (dir.). Methodist. Club: Rotary (dir. 1978). Contbr. articles to profl. jours. Home: 1744 Aspen Village Way West Covina CA 91791 Office: 336 1/2 S Glendora Ave West Covina CA 91790

TENNANT, FRANK ARTHUR, public relations educator; b. Los Angeles, May 25, 1928; s. Frank J. and Elsie (Leo) T. B.A., UCLA, 1950, M.S. in Journalism, 1953. Editor Monterey Park (Calif.) Californian, 1950; reporter Los Angeles Mirror, 1953; press relations dir. Title Ins. and Trust Co., Los Angeles, 1954-55; prof. communications arts Calif. State Poly. U., Pomona, 1955—. Served to sgt. U.S. Army, 1950-52. Mem. Am. Bus. Press Assn., Pub. Relations Soc. Am., Soc. Profl. Journalists, Assn. for Edn. in Journalism and Mass Communications, Greater Los Angeles Press Club. Republican. Roman Catholic. Home: 1779 N 2d Ave Upland CA 91786 Office: Communication Arts Dept Calif State Poly U 3801 West Temple Ave 1 310 Pomona CA 91768

TENNEN, LESLIE IRWIN, lawyer, cons.; b. Toronto, Ont., Can., Aug. 26, 1952; s. Edward and Elsie (Liberbaum) T. B.A. with distinction, U. Ariz., 1973; J.D., 1976. Admitted to Ariz. bar, 1977; U.S. Dist. Ct., 1979; individual practice law, Tucson, 1977-78; ptnr. firm Sterns and Tennen, Phoenix, Tucson, 1978—; cons. internat. law, outer space human activities. Writer, Ariz. Law Review, 1975-76. Mem. Internat. Inst. Space Law, AIAA, Aviation Space Writers Assn. Contbr. articles to profl. jours. Office: 932 N Swan Rd Tucson AZ 85711

TENNES, KATHERINE JOSEPHINE, psychology educator; b. Moline, Ill., Sept. 19, 1919; d. Joseph F. Hrusovar and Berta (Hornik) H.; m. Joseph A. Tennes, Sept. 22, 1942; 1 dau., Mary. B.A., State U. Iowa, 1942; M.A. in Psychology, U. Mich.-Ann Arbor, 1945. Cert. psychologist, Colo. Psychologist, Child Research Council, Denver, 1950-66; instr. U. Colo. Health Sci. Ctr., Denver, 1966—; research assoc., Nat. Jewish Hosp., Denver, 1974-75. Research grantee NIH, 1963-64, 1981-84; William T. Grant Found. grantee, 1981-83; MacArthur Found. grantee, 1982-84. Mem. Am. Psychol. Assn., Soc. Research in Child Devel., Assn. Psychosomatic Medicine; Soc. Psychoneuroendocrinology. Contbr. numerous articles to profl. jours. Office: 4200 E 9th Ave C-264 Denver CO 80262

TEPPER, ANDREW STEPHEN, software designer; b. Washington, July 22, 1949; s. Morris and Ruth Shirley (Klorman) T.; student U. Waterloo (Ont., Can.), 1972-78, M.Math., 1978; B.S.E.E., M.I.T., 1972; student Drexel U., 1967-70; m. Jeannie Hsu, July 31, 1981. Sr. tech. specialist Bank of Montreal, Toronto, Ont., 1973-80; software designer Cambridge Systems Group, Santa Clara, Calif., 1980-83; dir. ASTCO, Palo Alto; cons. in microcomputer systems. Mem. Am. Radio Relay League, Mensa, Sigma Xi, Eta Kappa Nu. Home: 926 Amarillo Ave Palo Alto CA 94301

TEPPER, NANCY BOXLEY, lawyer; b. Mar. 7, 1933, Va.; d. Joseph Harry and Mathilda (Appell) Boxley; children—Amanda, Nicholas, Eliza. B.A., Radcliffe Coll., 1953; LL.B., Harvard U., 1958. Bar: N.Y. 1959, Calif. 1969. Assoc. Simpson Thacher & Bartlett, N.Y.C., 1958-63; with Prentice Hall, Inc., Englewood, N.J., 1963-69; assoc. Robertson, Howser & Garland, Laguna Hills, Calif., 1969-70, Kindel & Anderson, Laguna Hills, 1970-77; sole practice, Laguna Hills, 1977—; instr. U. Calif.-Irvine, 1971-72. Mem. ABA, Calif. Bar Assn., Orange County Bar Assn., Orange County Estate Planning Council, Phi Beta Kappa. Club: Harvard Orange County (dir. 1970-72). Home: 331 Vista Suerte Newport Beach CA 92660 Office: 24031 El Toro Rd Suite 130 Laguna Hills CA 92653

TERADA, HARRY TAKASHI, optometrist; b. Haiku, Maui, Hawaii, Apr. 8, 1922; s. Takeo and Hatsuyo (Miura) T.; m. Alice M. Marutani, Aug. 28, 1951; children—Suzanne, Keith, Lance. B.S., U. Hawaii, 1949; O.D., So. Calif. Coll. Optometry, 1952. Diplomate Am. Acad. Optometry. Gen. practice optometry, Honolulu, 1953—; instr. gen. optometry U. Hawaii, Honolulu, 1954-64; staff optometrist Hawaii Vocat. Rehab. Div., Honolulu, 1964—; instr. Tripler U.S. Army Hosp., Honolulu, 1964-70; cons. State Low Vision Clinic. Served with U.S. Army, 1944-46. Mem. Am. Optometric Assn., Nat. Eye Found., Hawaii Optometric Assn., Omega Epsilon Phi. Episcopalian. Clubs: Honolulu, Kalia Lions, Honolulu Toastmasters. Office: 1109 12th Ave Honolulu HI 96816

TERENTJEV, KONSTANTIN PETER, aerospace and mechanical engineer; b. Caracas, Venezuela, Dec. 17, 1954; s. Peter Konstantin and Helen Mesalin. B.S. in Mech. Engring., Worcester Poly. Inst., 1977; M.S. in Aero. and Astronautics, U. Wash.-Seattle, 1980. Registered profl. engr., Wash. Engr., Boeing Co., Seattle, 1978-80, specialist engr. 1980—. Mem. AIAA. Club: Boeing Employees Soaring (Seattle). Contbr. articles to profl. jours. Home: 5119 S Hudson St Seattle WA 98118 Office: The Boeing Co PO Box 3707 Seattle WA 98124

TERMEER, HENRY ADRIANUS, medical supply company executive; b. Tilburg, Holland, Feb. 28, 1946; s. Jacques and Mary (Van Gorp) T.; came to U.S., 1971; m. Margaret Amy Davis-Riches, Oct. 8, 1971. B.A. in Econs., Ekonomisch Hogeschool, Rotterdam, Netherlands, 1969; M.B.A., U. Va., 1973. Mgr. mgmt. services Norvic Co., Norwich, England, 1969-71; mgr. internat. product planning Baxter Travenol, Inc., Deerfield, Ill., 1973-74, internat. mktg. mgr., 1975-76; gen. mgr. Travenol GMBH, Munich, W.Ger., 1976-79, v.p. Hyland Therapeutics div. Baxter Travenol, Glendale, Calif., 1979-81, exec. v.p., 1981—; cons. World Hemophilia Fedn., Montreal, Que., Can. Served to 1st lt. Netherlands Royal Air Force, 1966-67. Mem. World Hemophilia Fedn. Roman Catholic. Office: Hyland Therapeutics Div Baxter Travenol 444 W Glenoaks St Glendale CA 91212

TERPSTRA, DAVID ELWIN, management psychology educator; b. Bellingham, Wash., March 12, 1951; s. Wilburn Herman and Nelliw (Bosman) T.; m. Nancy Jean Christie, June 29, 1974, (div.). B.A. cum laude in Psychology, Western Wash. U., 1974; Ph.D. in Indsl./Organizational Psychology, U. Tenn., 1978. Grad. research asst. U. Tenn., 1974-76, grad. teaching asst., 1976-78; asst. prof. mgmt. U. Idaho, 1978-80; asst. prof. mgmt., Wash. State U., 1980—; cons. Dealer Info. Systems Corp., 1979-80. Ctr. Bus. Devel. and Research Faculty (U. Idaho) research awardee, 1978-80. Mem. Acad. Mgmt., Am. Psychol. Assn. Contbr. to profl. jours. Home: NW 1220 State #9 Pullman WA 99163 Office: Dept Mgmt Wash State U Pullman WA 99164

TERRELL, (NELSON) JAMES, (JR.), physicist; b. Houston, Aug. 15, 1923; s. Nelson James and Gladys Delphine (Stevens) T.; B.A., Rice U., 1944, M.A., 1947, Ph.D., 1950; m. Elizabeth Anne Pearson, June 9, 1945; children—Anne, Barbara, Jean. Research asst. Rice U., Houston, 1950; asst. prof. physics Western Res. U., Cleve., 1950-51; staff mem. Los Alamos Nat. Lab., U. Calif., 1951—. Served to 1st lt. AUS, 1944-46. Graham Baker scholar, 1943-44; Rice U. fellow, 1946-48, AEC fellow, 1948-50. Fellow Am. Phys. Soc., AAAS; mem. Am. Astron. Soc., Internat. Astron. Union, Phi Beta Kappa, Sigma Xi. Clubs: Los Alamos Ski, Los Alamos Choral Soc. Contbr. articles to profl. jours. Home: 85 Obsidian Loop Los Alamos NM 87544 Office: Mail Stop D436 Los Alamos Nat Lab Los Alamos NM 87545

TERRELL, WARNER LOUIS, III, banker; b. Boise, Idaho, Aug. 5, 1939; s. Warner Louis and Clara Mae (Stevens) T.; B.S., Coll. of Idaho, 1962; M.B.A., Boise State U., 1973; m. Grace Maurgerite Johnson, Nov. 24, 1974. Med. lab. technologist St. Alphonsus Hosp., Boise, 1962-73; exec. trainee Idaho First Nat. Bank, Boise, 1973-74, investment officer, 1974-78, asst. v.p. investments, 1978-79, v.p., mgr. investments, 1979—. Bd. dirs. Ada County Council on Alcoholism, 1980—; mem. Leadership Boise, 1979; bd. dirs. Leadership Boise Alumni, 1983; mem. Model Cities Citizens Adv. Bd., 1971-73. Mem. Adminstrv. Mgmt. Soc. (dir. 1982, 1st v.p. 1983—). Republican. Roman Catholic. Club: KC. Home: 1420 Shenandoah Dr Boise ID 83702 Office: PO Box 8247 Boise ID 83733

TERRIEN, FREDERIC WILLIAM, sociologist; b. East Lansing, Mich., Oct. 24, 1915; s. Frederic Francois and Sara (McEnery) T.; m. Margaret Geisenhoff Rink, Mar. 1, 1954; 1 dau., Sara Margaret; m. 2d, H. Joyce Ayrault, Feb. 23, 1963. A.B., Stanford U., 1937; M.A., Yale U., 1947, Ph.D., 1950. Research asst. Yale Lab. Mgmt. Ctr., 1946-47; acting instr. dept. sociology Conn. Coll., 1948; lectr. sociology, research asst. Inst. Labor and Indsl. Relations, U. Ill., Urbana, 1949-50; asst. prof. Stanford (Calif.) U., 1950-53; prof. sociology San Francisco State U., 1953—; cons. human relations, 1953—. Served to lt. USNR, 1942-46. Kellog Found. grantee, 1953-54; Office Naval Research grantee, 1962-67; NIMH grantee, 1962-64. Mem. Am. Sociol. Assn., Pacific Sociol. Assn. Democrat. Club: Presidio Golf (San Francisco). Contbr. articles to profl. jours. Home: 62 Morningson Ave Mill Valley CA 94941 Office: San Francisco State U San Francisco CA 94132

TERRILL, JERRY LEE, school administrator; b. Page, Nebr., July 1, 1936; s. Otto Lee and Susan Louise Terrill; m. Jeanne Shelley, July 20, 1957; children—Kimberly Sue, Kevin Lee. B.A., Marion Coll., 1957; M.A., U. Nebr., 1961; Ph.D., U. Colo., 1969. Tchr. Lincoln (Nebr.) Pub. Schs., 1958-62; counselor Littleton (Colo.) Pub. Schs., 1962-67, 69-72, 74-77; counseling intern U. Colo., 1968-69; guidance cons. Colo. Dept. Edn., 1972-74, 77-81; coordinator student guidance services Jefferson County Schs., Lakewood, Colo., 1981—; cons. in field. Mem. Am. Personnel and Guidance Assn., Colo. Sch. Counselor Assn., World Future Soc., Jefferson County Adminstrs. Assn., Jefferson County Counselor Assn., Assn. Counselor Edn. and Supervision, Colo. Assn. Counselor Edn. and Supervision. Republican. Mem. Wesleyan Ch. Office: 1209 Quail Lakewood CO 80215

TERRY, CHARLES JAMES, metallurgical engineer; b. Milw., Dec. 12, 1949; s. Norbert Matthew and Olive Louise (Runte) T.; m. Karen Barbara Macejkovic, June 9, 1973; children—Jeanine, Suzanne, Kristen. B.S. in Metall. Engring., U. Wis., 1972. Registered profl. engr., Wis. Preparation engr. Midland Coal Co. div. Asarco, Trivoli, Ill., 1972-73, metall. engr., El Paso, Tex., 1973-76; research engr. Allis Chalmers Corp., Milw., 1976-80; metallurgist Kennametal Inc., Fallon, Nev., 1981—. Active Republican Party. Mem. Metall. Soc. AIME. Roman Catholic. Contributed to development of proprietary crushing process.

TERRY, DAVID RAY, higher education administrator, medical microbiologist, educator; b. Idaho Falls, Idaho, June 28, 1935; s. Elvin Ray and Geraldine (Larsen) T.; m. Joyce Hansen, June 8, 1953; children—Aleesa Terry Solberg, David, Dru. Student George Washington U., 1954-55; B.S. in Zoology, Brigham Young U., 1958, M.S. in Microbiology, Biochemistry, 1962; Ph.D. in Vocational Edn., U. Ill., 1973. Dir. civilian research Germ Warfare, Dugway (Utah) Proving Ground, 1962-65; asst. prof. microbiology Weber State Coll., Ogden, Utah, 1965-68, chmn. dept. health facility occupations, 1968-70; researcher Bur. Ednl. Research, U. Ill., Urbana, 1970-73; dir. Sch. Allied Health Professions No. Ill. U., DeKalb, 1973-77; research dir. NSF grant Utah System Higher Edn., Salt Lake City, 1977-80, asst. commr. Vocational and Allied Health Programs, 1981—. Bd. dirs. South Ogden City (Utah) Neighborhood Community Council System, 1978—. Recipient 1st place award Nat. Com. Careers in Med. Tech., 1968-69; nominee Utah outstanding citizen South Ogden City, 1982. Mem. Am. Vocat. Assn., Am. Soc. Allied Health Professions, Am. Soc. Microbiology, Phi Delta Kappa. Mormon. Author vocat. edn. publs.; contbr. articles to profl. jours. Home: 5432 S 800 E South Ogden City UT 84403 Office: Utah System Higher Edn 807 E South Temple St Salt Lake City UT 84102

TERRY, HELEN, personnel executive; b. Redmesa, Calif., Jan. 10, 1937; d. Kenneth and Georgina (Burnham) Hunt; m. L.V. Terry, June 19, 1953 (div.); children—Craig, Kendle. B.A. in Human Services, Evergreen State Coll., 1978; postgrad. Lewis and Clark Coll., 1978-80. Personnel dir. Woodland Park Hosp., Portland, Oreg., 1973-74; dir. tng. McKay-Dee Hosp. System, Ogden, Utah, 1962-69; dir. personnel and civil service examiner, City of Vancouver (Wash.), 1975—. Mem. vocat. adv. com. Vancouver Sch. Bd. Mem. Personnel Assn. Clark County (steering com.), Internat. Personnel Mgrs. Assn. Office: Personnel Dept City of Vancouver PO Box 1995 Vancouver WA 98668

TERRY, LEE MARION, employment company executive; b. Tuatapere, N.Z., May 4, 1937; d. Andrew and Edna (Jordan) Mathieson; came to U.S., 1967; m. Richard Lee Terry, Oct. 26, 1967 (div.). A.A., Southland Coll., Invercargill, N.Z., 1953. Owner, pres. Personnel Concepts, Inc., San Mateo, Calif., 1978—; lectr. Mem. Calif. Assn. Personnel Cons. (pres.), Nat. Assn. Personnel Cons. (dir. 1981-83), Calif. Employment Assn. (J.R. Pierce award 1976, Jean Widdicombe award 1979), Nat. Assn. Female Execs., Am. Soc. Profl. and Exec. Women, Adv. Council Status of Women. Club: Pena Taurina Sol y Sombra (San Francisco). Office: Suite 300 2121 S El Camino San Mateo CA 94403

TERRY, MAURICE BROOKS, retail exec.; b. Maryville, Mo., June 29, 1938; s. Laurence Eugene and Edrie Pearl (Lowe) T.; B.B.A., U. Mo., Kansas City, 1961; m. Dorothy Ann Cottam; children—Jana, Laurence, Bill, Tina, Keith, Van. Acct., controller Dick Bruhn, Inc., Salinas, Calif., 1969-74; acctg. mgr. Univ. Bookstore, Salt Lake City, 1974-78, dir., 1978-80; controller Clarklift of Utah, Inc., Salt Lake City, 1980—. Capt. contbn. drive Community Chest; capt. advanced donation telethon Am. Cancer Soc. Mem. Salinas Jaycees (treas.). Mormon. Home: 1782 Holladay Blvd Salt Lake City UT 84117 Office: 2120 S 3600 W Salt Lake City UT 84125

TERRY, MILTON O., safety engineer; b. Oakland, Calif., Oct. 13, 1919; s. Milton J. and Nola W. (Galloway) T.; married; children—Patricia Terry Howard, Phillip, Paul. B.A., San Jose State U., 1953; cert. safety profl.; registered profl. engr., Calif. Safety insp. U.S. Naval Air Sta., Alameda, Calif., 1950-56; safety engr. State Calif., San Francisco, 1956-65, dist. engr., 1965-66, sr. safety engr., 1966-72, dist. mgr., 1972-75, prin. safety mgr., 1975-76, regional mgr., 1976-79, prin. safety engr. Div. Occupational Safety and Health, 1979—. Mem. Am. Soc. Safety Engrs., Veterans of Safety. Democrat. Presbyterian. Club: Masons.

TERRY, WILLIAM E., electronics company executive; b. San Jose, Calif., Apr. 11, 1933; s. Edward L. and Mary P. Terry; m. Janice Faye Arnold, Nov. 8, 1980; children—Catherine, Carol, Tom, Chris. Exec. v.p. Hewlett-Packard Co., Palo Alto, Calif.; dir. Applied Magnetics Corp., Goleta, Calif. Republican. Roman Catholic. Office: 3000 Hanover St Palo Alto CA 94304

TERVET, IAN GEORGE, electronic engineer; b. Lasswade, Scotland, Apr. 13, 1937; s.Ian W. and Margaret (Blair) T.; student Whitman Coll., Walla Walla, Wash., 1955-59; m. Pham Thi Cuc, Oct. 20, 1965; children—Kim Lynn, Ian P. Staff assoc. M.I.T. Lincoln Lab., Lexington, Mass., 1957-58; staff engr. Scantlin Electronics, Los Angeles, 1959; maintenance supr. Page Communications Engrs., Hawaii, Guam, Denmark, Labrador, Washington, 1959-64; mem. research and devel. staff Hoffman Electronics, Los Angeles, 1965; systems engr. Page Communications Engrs., Vietnam, 1965-71; telecom cons. U.S. Navy, Vietnam, 1971; telecomm mgr. Ratanake Ltd., Khmer Republic, 1972; transmission engr. ITT/FEC, Vietnam, 1972-73; radio sta. mgr. AFRTS, Dept. Def., Am. Embassy, Saigon, 1973-75; telephone engr. County Los Angeles, 1976; radio engr., fgn. service office Voice of America, various locations, 1976-82; sr. engr. Litton D.C.S., Agoura, Calif., 1982—; owner, partner Sea Ltd., Los Angeles, 1967—. Mem. IEEE (sr.), Am. Radio Relay League (life), Nat. Geog. Soc. (life), Amateur Satellite Corp. (life), Mensa, Delta Tau Delta, Pi Kappa Delta. Republican. electronic engineer; b. Lasswade, Scotland, Apr. 13, 1937; s.Ian W. and Margaret (Blair) T.; student Whitman Coll., Walla Walla, Wash., 1955-59; m. Pham Thi Cuc, Oct. 20, 1965; children—Kim Lynn, Ian P. Staff assoc. M.I.T. Lincoln Lab., Lexington, Mass., 1957-58; staff engr. Scantlin Electronics, Los Angeles, 1959; maintenance supr. Page Communications Engrs., Hawaii, Guam, Denmark, Labrador, Washington, 1959-64; mem. research and devel. staff Hoffman Electronics, Los Angeles, 1965; systems engr. Page Communications Engrs., Vietnam, 1965-71; telecom cons. U.S. Navy, Vietnam, 1971; telecomm mgr. Ratanake Ltd., Khmer Republic, 1972; transmission engr. ITT/FEC, Vietnam, 1972-73; radio sta. mgr. AFRTS, Dept. Def., Am. Embassy, Saigon, 1973-75; telephone engr. County Los Angeles, 1976; radio engr., fgn. service office Voice of America, various locations, 1976-82; sr. engr. Litton D.C.S., Agoura, Calif., 1982—; owner, partner Sea Ltd., Los Angeles, 1967—. Mem. IEEE (sr.), Am. Radio Relay League (life), Nat. Geog. Soc. (life), Amateur Satellite Corp. (life), Mensa, Delta Tau Delta, Pi Kappa Delta. Republican. Home: 9500 Penfield Ave Chatsworth Ca 91311 Office: Litton DCS Box 5000 Agoura CA 91301

TESCH, STEPHANIE THORPE, school administrator; b. Valley City, N.D., July 21, 1937; d. Rudolph A. and Edith E. (Estrem) Ofstedal; m. Kenneth Blaine Tesch, Dec. 21, 1959; children—Dawn, Dana, Nathan. B.A., Luther Coll., 1959; M.Ed., Wash. State U., 1977; postgrad. 1979-83. Tchr. elem. schs., Decorah, Iowa and Pasco, Wash., 1959-73; reading specialist, Capt. Gray Sch., Pasco, 1973-75, lang. arts coordinator Pasco Sch. Dist., 1975-77, curriculum coordinator, 1980-82; curriculum dir., 1982—. Bd. dirs. Wash. State Luth. Social Services. Mem. Assn. Supervision and Curriculum Devel., Wash. State Assn. Supervision and Curriculum Devel., Internat. Reading Assn., Wash. Orgn. Reading Devel., Wash. Assn. Sch. Adminstrs., S.E. Wash. Assn. Sch. Adminstrs., Phi Delta Kappa. Home: 2105 N 8th Ave Pasco WA 99301 Office: 1006 N 16th Ave Pasco WA 99301

TESCHER, ELWOOD CHARLES, urban designer/planner; b. Glendale, Calif., Dec. 22, 1943; s. Charles Bernard and Marian Ruth (Dinger) T.; B.Arch. cum laude, U. So. Calif., 1967; M.Arch., Urban Design, UCLA, 1969. Urban planner Quinton-Budlong, Los Angeles, 1969-72; dir. planning and urban design Quinton-Redgate, Quinton Assos., Long Beach, Calif., 1972-79; v.p. urban and regional planning Envicom Corp., Calabasas, Calif., 1979—; lectr. UCLA, U. So. Calif., Occidental Coll. Recipient award of Merit, Am. Inst. Planners, 1974; Honor award Calif. Office Planning and Research, 1978. Mem. Am. Planning Assn., Archtl. Guild. Democrat. Baptist. Home: 611 Hampshire Rd #517 Westlake Village CA 91361 Office: 4764 Park Granada St Calabasus CA 91302

TESTA, CLAUDIA JEAN, hosp. adminstr.; b. Bend, Oreg., May 13, 1943; d. John Lee and Hazel Bernice (Nelson) Hollenbeck; B.S. in Mktg., U. Oreg., 1965, B.B.A., 1965; m. June 30, 1970 (div.); 1 son, Fabio John. Retail purchasing mgmt. The Emporium, San Francisco, 1965-67; div. mgr. U.S. Army, Europe, 1969-72; owner The Sandwich Shoppe, Portland, Oreg., 1972-74; dir. materials mgmt. Albany (Oreg.) Gen. Hosp., 1974—; regional chairperson Intermountain Healthcare, Inc. Shared Services. Active United Way, Albany, 1978—. Mem. Am. Soc. Hosp. Purchasing Materials Mgmt., Western States Hosp. Purchasing Mgrs. Assn. (pres. 1980-81), Cascade Central Service Assn., Oreg. Hosps. Group Purchasing Coop. (dir. 1979-80). Club: Altrusa Internat. Home: 1223 12th Ave SW Albany OR 97321 Office: 1046 W 6th Ave Albany OR 97321

TESTER, JOHN LEE, air force officer; b. Hazel Green, Ky., Oct. 4, 1939; s. Oliver and Pansy (Madden) T.; m. Rachel Ellen Taulbee, Dec. 24, 1958; children—John, Shell, Robert, Cher. B.S. in Bus., Ohio State U., 1971; M.A. in Econs., U. Okla., 1978; M.S.T.M., Am. U., 1978. Commd. capt. U.S. Air Force, 1957; cryptologic research analyst, Zweibruchen, Germany, 1959-62; sr. cryptologic analyst Nat. Security Agy., Ft. Meade, Md., 1963-64; surveillance and warning supr., Darmstadt, Germany, 1966-69; project engr. over-horizon radar, RAF Bentwaters, Eng., 1971-73; spl. security officer Pentagon, Washington, 1974-78; chief intelligence software applications, Lowry AFB, Colo., 1979—. Vice pres. Jr. Officers Council, RAF Bentwaters, Eng., 1972-73; project leader March of Dimes, Lowry AFB, also Denver, 1982. Named Outstanding Officer Instr., Lowry AFB, 1979. Mem. Am. Mgmt. Assn., Assn. Systems Mgrs., Am. Econ. Assn., Soc. Govt. Economists. Mem. Ch. of Christ. Contbr. articles to profl. jours. Office: AFAITC/TTMNI Lowry AFB CO 80230

TESTERMAN, SYLVIA AMELIA, reading consultant; b. Tacoma, Wash., July 16, 1933; d. John Jacob and Hilma Kathleen (Hamileena) Johnson; m. William H. Testerman, July 27, 1956; children—Tamra, Sandra Testerman Hall, Brian. B.A., U. Wyo., 1970; M.A., Ed.S., U. N.Mex. Tchr. Sunset Mesa Schs., Albuquerque, 1973-78; grad. asst. U. N.Mex., Albuquerque, 1978-79; reading cons. Albuquerque Pub. Schs., 1979—. Mem. Assn. Supervision and Curriculum Devel., Phi Delta Kappa. Democrat. Unitarian. Club: Beta Sigma Phi (Albuquerque).

TETLOCK, PHILIP EYRIKSON, social psychology educator; b. Toronto, Ont., Can., Mar. 2, 1954; came to U.S., 1976; s. Harold O. and Avril (Eyrikson) T.; m. Terry L. Murray, May 23, 1977; 1 son, Paul Christopher. B.A., U. B.C. (Can.), Vancouver, 1975, M.A., 1976; Ph.D., Yale U., 1979. Asst. prof. psychology U. Calif.-Berkeley, 1979—, research psychologist Survey Research Ctr., 1980—. Mem. Am. Psychol. Assn., Internat. Soc. Polit. Psychology. Exptl. and archival research on judgment and decision making. Home: 2831 Nevin Ave Richmond CA 94804 Office: 3210 Tolman Hall Dept Psychology U Calif Berkeley CA 94720

TETSCHLAG, RICHARD ROBERT, electronics company executive; b. Sheboygan, Wis., June 12, 1947; s. Carl Leonard and Erna Malida (VanderVaart) T.; B.S., U. Wis., 1970; M.B.A., U. Santa Clara, 1973; m. Penelope A. Krueger, Aug. 31, 1968; children—Craig Richard, Cara Michelle. Quality control supr. Fairchild Semiconductor, Mountain View, Calif., 1970-72; quality control mgr., mfg. mgr., mng. dir., dir. reliability and quality control, product mktg. mgr. Litronix, Inc., Litronix Mauritius Ltd., Cupertino, Calif., 1972-77; ops. mgr., Tech. Glass Corp., Sunnyvale, Calif., 1977-78, exec. v.p., 1978-80, pres., 1980—, also dir., sec. Mem. Internat. Soc. Hybrid Mfrs., Semiconductor Equipment and Materials Inst. Democrat. Lutheran. Club: Decathlon (Santa Clara, Calif.). Home: 3757 Woodbark Ct San Jose CA 95117 Office: 390 Potrero Ave Sunnyvale CA 94086

THACHER, JAMES HOLLIS, engineering manager; b. Fitchburg, Mass., March 15, 1934; s. Hollis Perry and Susan Elizabeth (Tait) T.; m. Pauline Mae Griffith, Feb. 7, 1959; children—Thomas, Andrew, Daniel; B.S. in Chem. Engring., MIT, 1955, M.S. in Chem. Engring.; Dr. Engring., Cath. U., Washington. Supr. materials group Hercules, 1965-68, supr. structural analysis group, 1968-72, tech. supt., combustion and detonation group, 1972-80, engring. project mgr., Navy programs, 1980-81, mgr. engring. design and analysis, 1981—. Served to capt. USAR, 1956-64. Assoc. fellow AIAA. Baptist. Co-Author: Rheology, 1965; contbr. reports and articles to profl. jours. Home: 5666 Hunter Park Circle West Valley City UT 84120 Office: PO Box 98 Magna UT 84044

THACKER, HERBERT DICKEY, real estate exec.; b. Honolulu, Oct 5, 1929; s. Earl Maxwell and Dorothy Dimond (Dickey) T.; B.A., Stanford U., 1951; M.B.A., Harvard U., 1953; m. Susan; children by previous marriage—William Dickey, Peter Earl, Mark Allen (dec.). With Earl Thacker Ltd., Honolulu, 1956—, pres., 1958—. Chmn. Waikiki Beach Improvement Com., 1970-71. Served to lt. USNR, 1953-56; Korea. Named Hawaii Realtor of Yr., 1969; recipient Bus. Achievement award Hawaii C. of C., 1981. Mem. Nat. Assn. Realtors (dir. 1967-82), Nat. Inst. Farm and Land Brokers, Soc. Real Estate Appraisers (v.p. 1967), Hawaii Assn. Real Estate (pres. 1968-69), Honolulu Bd. Realtors (pres. 1968-69), Honolulu C. of C., Stanford U. Alumni Assn. Clubs: Harvard Bus. Sch., Outrigger Canoe, Pacific (Honolulu). Office: 2222 Kalakaua Ave Suite 1415 Honolulu HI 96815

THAL, BERNHARDT NEWMAN, optometrist; b. Toledo, Nov. 9, 1917; s. Fred S. and Gussie (Newman) T.; m. Betty Stamer, Sept. 27, 1942; 1 son, Lawrence Stamer. B.S., Colo. State U., 1939; B.S. in Optometry, U. Calif.-Berkeley, 1948. Lic. optometrist, Calif. Instrument designer, researcher Mann Instrument Co. and Solex Labs., 1948-52; pres. Instrument Co. Am., Berkeley, Calif., 1952-56; gen. practice optometry, Berkeley, 1952—; founding pres. Calif. Vision Services, 1954-60, dir., 1954-61, 63-70; lectr. U. Calif. Inst. Indsl. Relations, 1959-61, Sch. Optometry, 1970-72; mem. State of Calif. Bd. Optometry, 1970-77, pres., 1973-75; clin. investigator soft contact lenses, bifocal contact lenses Bausch & Lomb, Vistakon, OcuEase, HydraCurve. Mem. Kensington (Calif.) Improvement Bd., 1963-70; bd. dirs. Berkeley Vis. Nurses Assn., 1969-76; bd. dirs. Berkeley Non-Partisan Forum, 1980—; trustee advisor Alta Bates Hosp., 1982—. Served to capt. USAF, 1940-45. Decorated D.F.C., Air medal with seven oak leaf clusters; named O.D. Of Yr., Alameda and Contra Costa County Optometric Soc., 1968, 76. Fellow Am. Acad. Optometry; mem. Am. Optometric Assn., Calif. Optometric Assn. (O.D. of Yr. 1982), Berkeley C. of C. (dir. 1981—). Democrat. Clubs: Berkeley Commons, Rotary Internat. Office: 2150 Shattuck Ave Berkeley CA 94704

THAL, LAWRENCE STAMER, optometrist, educator; b. Oakland, Calif., Jan. 28, 1946; s. Bernhardt N. and Betty (Stamer) T.; m. Esther Gordon, Dec. 22, 1968. B.S. U.S. Air Force Acad., 1967; B.S., U. Calif.-Berkeley, 1973, O.D., 1975; M.B.A., Golden Gate U., 1978. Commd. 2d lt. U.S. Air Force, 1967, advanced through grades to maj., 1971, served in Vietnam, resigned, 1971; pvt. practice optometry, Kensington, Calif., 1975—; clin. instr. neurooptometry U. Calif. Sch. Optometry, Berkeley, 1978-79; clin. prof. gen. clinic, Berkeley, 1979—; professorial lectr. Grad. Sch. Banking and Fin. Golden Gate U., San Francisco, 1978—; pres. Farallon Devel. Corp., 1980-83; mem. Calif. State Bd. Optometry, 1981—. Bd. dirs. Kensington Community Service and Police Dist., 1980—, pres. 1981, 83. Kensington Improvement Club, 1979—; mem. Kensington City Council, 1982. Decorated Air medal with oak leaf cluster; Vietnamese Cross of Gallantry with palm. Mem. Am. Optometric Assn., Council on Sports Vision, Vision Conservation Inst., Calif. Optometric Assn. (Calif. Young Optometrist of Yr. 1981), Alameda-Contra Costa Counties Optometric Soc. (pres. 1982-83), Kensington Bus. and Profl. Assn. (pres. 1979-83), Beta Sigma Kappa. Republican. Club: Lions. Contbr. articles to profl. jours. Home: 216 Amherst Ave Kensington CA 94708 Office: 291 Arlington Ave Kensington CA 94707

THANANOPAVARN, CHALEMPHOL, physician; b. Bangkok, Thailand, June 10, 1946; came to U.S., 1971; s. Fad Yong and Luk (Liu) Ng.; M.D., Chulalonakorn U., 1979; postgrad. UCLA, 1972-77; m. Srisook Boonsue, July 15, 1974; children—Paul, Ann. Intern, Sinai Hosp. of Balt., 1971-72; resident in medicine Sepulveda VA-UCLA Sch. Medicine, 1972-74; fellow in hypertension research UCLA, San Fernando Valley Med. Program, 1974-77; asst. clin. prof. medicine UCLA, 1977-79, adj. asst. prof., 1979—; med. dir. Valley Hypertension Clinic, Sherman Oaks, Calif., 1981—. NIH grantee, 1977-80. Mem. Am. Fedn. Clin. Research, Am. Heart Assn., Am. Coll. Clin. Pharmacology, Am. Geriatric Soc. Republican. Buddhist. Contbr. articles to profl. jours. Home: 9689 Moorgate Rd Beverly Hills CA 90210 Office: 12926 Riverside Dr Sherman Oaks CA 91423

THAW, ARNOLD, clin. psychologist; b. Bklyn., Apr. 21, 1931; s. Max and Rose Leah T.; B.A., N.Y. U., 1952; M.Div., Starr King Sch. for Ministry, 1956; postgrad. York U., Toronto, Can., Gestalt Inst. Cleve., 1970-71; Ph.D., Calif. Sch. Profl. Psychology, 1974. Ordained to ministry Unitarian Universalist Ch., 1957; minister Unitarian Ch. of Natick, Mass., 1956-61, Unitarian Congregation of S. Peel, Mississauga, Can., 1961-69; pvt. practice marriage and family counselling, Mississauga, 1969-71; intern, staff psychologist Resthaven Psychiat. Hosp., Los Angeles, 1971-73; chief psychologist Coconino Community Guidance Center, Flagstaff, Ariz., 1975-77; cons. psychologist Ariz. Heart Inst., Phoenix, 1977-79; pvt. practice clin. psychology, Phoenix, 1977—; mem. tng. faculty Gestalt Inst. Phoenix, 1977—; affiliate mem. med. staff St. Luke's Hosp., Phoenix, 1979—; cons. psychologist Valley Nat. Bank, 1978-80. Vol. minister counselling First Unitarian Universalist Ch. of Phoenix, Paradise Valley, 1978-80; nat. bd. dirs. Unitarian Fellowship for Social Justice, 1958-61; mem. nat. adv. com. Can. Civil Liberties Assn., 1967-71. Mem. Am. Psychol. Assn., Rocky Mountain Psychol. Assn., Ariz. State Psychol. Assn., Maricopa Psychol. Soc., Unitarian Universalist Ministers Assn. Club: Mensa. Home: 4840 N 31st Pl Phoenix AZ 85016 Office: 4302 N 32d St Phoenix AZ 85018

THAXTON, THEODORE JAMES, JR., civil engr.; b. Chandler, Ariz., Sept. 6, 1937; s. Theodore James and Thelma Ann (Armstrong) T.; m. Edythe Lorraine Cracroft, June 21, 1961; children—Christopher, Robert, Julianne, Glen, Melissa, Amy, Susan. B.S.C.E., U. Utah, 1966; M.P.A., Brigham Young U., 1982. Registered profl. engr., Utah, profl. land surveyor, Utah. Engr., Utah Dept. Transp., 1963-79, resident engr. constrn., 1977-79; city engr. City of Orem, Utah, 1979—. Mem. ASCE. Mormon. Home: 1088 E 650 N Orem UT 84057 Office: 56 N State St Orem UT 84057

THAXTON, VERA, home economics educator; b. Wenatchee, Wash., Aug. 15, 1933; d. Charles Clay and Ruth Ellen (Parsons) T. A.A., Mt. San Antonio Coll., 1954; B.A., San Diego State U., 1956; M.S., U. Ill.-Urbana, 1958. Cert. secondary tchr., Calif. Child welfare worker I, Lucas County (Ohio) Child Welfare, Toledo, 1958-60; home econs. instr. Bridgewater (Va.) Coll., 1960-62; licensing caseworker I, Los Angeles County Dept. Charities, Bur. Licensing, 1962-63; home econs. tchr. Pomona (Calif.) Unified Sch. Dist., 1963-69, Sonora (Calif.) High Sch., 1969-71, Banning (Calif.) High Sch., 1971-73, Coachella High Sch., Thermal, Calif., 1974—. Sec., La Quinta Property Owners Assn., 1979-82. Mem. Assn. Supervision and Curriculum Devel., AAUW, Am. Home Econs. Assn., Calif. Home Econs. Assn. (dist. past pres., treas.), Nat. Assn. Edn. Young Children, Calif. Assn. Edn. Young Children, Future Homemakers Am. (sponsor). Republican. Presbyterian. Club: U. Ill. Alumni (past treas.). Home: PO Box 85 La Quinta CA 92253 Office: 83-800 Airport Blvd Thermal CA 92274

THAYER, EDNA ISABELLE, nurse; b. Manchester, N.H., July 25, 1923; d. Charles Everett and Maude Isabelle (Messenger) Trask; R.N., Elliott Community Hosp., 1944; B.S.N., UCLA, 1953; m. Charles Albert Thayer, Feb. 18, 1946; 1 dau., Linda Louise, Supr., Menden (Conn.) Hosp., 1950-53, Inst. Living, Hartford, Conn., 1954-59; vol. tchr. educationally handicapped Brockton Sch., West Los Angeles, 1972-78; dir. nurses Canoga Terr., Canoga Park, Calif., 1979-80; dir. nurses Corbin Convalescent Hosp., Reseda, Calif., 1981-82; dir. nurses Sun Air Convalescent Hosp., 1982—. Served with Nurse Corp, AUS, 1945-46. Recipient Golden Apple award Los Angeles Unified Sch. Dist. 1976. Mem. Am., Calif. nurses assns., Nat. League Nursing Edn., Calif. Congress Parents and Tchrs., Bus. and Profl. Womens Club, Am. Legion. Republican. Baptist. Club: Emblem. Home: 7819 Ponce Ave Canoga Park CA 91304 Office: 7120 Corbin Ave Reseda CA 91335

THAYER, HANFORD, cons. engr.; b. Maple Island, Minn., Sept. 12, 1909; s. Nap Bon and Ida May (Purchase) T.; B.S. in C.E., Iowa State U., 1935; m. Lois Mae Foster, June 12, 1934; children—Roger Hanford, Diane Mae (Mrs. Robert Anthony Hill), Alden Bon, Shirley Anne. Field engr. constrn. Stone & Webster Engring. Corp., Rock Island Dam, Wash., 1935-36; field engr. Bur. Fisheries, Seattle, 1936; jr. engr., asst. engr. design and constrn. Bur. Reclamation, Coulee Dam, Wash., 1936-39; regional supt. constrn. Fish and Wildlife Service, Seattle, 1939-41, regional engr., Portland, Oreg., 1941-42; asst. engr. Office of Div. Engr., C.E., U.S. Army, Portland, 1942, asst. engr., asso. engr. engr. and supervising civil engr., Seattle, 1942-62, flood plain planning engr., 1962, sr. Army project coordinator and chief architect engring. sect., 1963-67; dir. research and devel. Quinton-Budlong Engr. Corp., Seattle, 1967-69; asst. v.p., 1969-70; cons. engr., planner, mgr. Tudor Engring. Co., 1970-76; mgr. Thayer Studio, Seattle, 1972-76. Mem. Puget Sound Engring. Council, chmn., 1959; v.p. Nat. Advanced Tech. Mgmt. Conf., 1962-70. Fellow ASCE (life mem.; pres. Seattle 1956, named Engr. of Yr. 1960), Soc. Am. Mil. Engrs. (pres. Seattle 1950, nat. dir. 1952-67, named Engr. of Yr. 1959-60, regional v.p. 1967-76, life; highest nat. award gold medal 1974); mem. Seattle Municipal League, Newcomen Soc. N.Am., Nat. Rifle Assn., Nat. Soc. Profl. Engrs., Wash. Soc. Profl. Engrs. (dir. 1970-71), Allied Arts of Seattle, Metric Assn., Seattle Area Indsl. Council. Mem. Ch. of Christ. Clubs: Kiwanis, Seattle Engrs., Wenatchee Fencing (pres. 1937-39), Cascade Sportsmens Rifle (pres. 1951). Primary organizer of Radiation Biol. Lab., U. Wash., 1943-46; project liaison Manhattan Atomic Project, 1943-46; researcher Herbert Hoover Oral History Program, 1967-70. Home: 5647 S Mc Donald Dr Langley WA 98260

THAYNE, RICHARD GRANT, photographer, writer; b. Murray, Utah, May 29, 1930; s. Clifton Earl and Mirla (Greenwood) T.; m. Ann C. Nielsen, Apr. 2, 1959; children—Catherene, Kay, Laurie; B.S. in Photography, Brigham Young U., Provo, Utah, postgrad. in photography, still and motion picture, newswriting; cert. Nord Photo Engring., 1972, Photog. Tech., Brigham Young U., 1968. Pub. 1st picture in mag. at age 12; printed 8x10 brown tone prints for Brown Studio, 1947-48; began Creative Art Photography lab at age 18, 1948—; instr. photography Brigham Young U., 1970-75; instr./producer motion pictures and video; past pres. Thayne Family Orgn. Mem. Sons of Utah Pioneers (past pres.). Served in Army N.G., 1950-52. Mem. Profl. Photographers Am., Wedding Photographers Internat., Photog. Soc. Am., Fine Arts Club (Salt Lake City), Intermountain Profl. Photographers Assn. Mormon. Patentee in creative art photography. Author: Goodbye for Now (1981); contbr. articles to profl. jours. Home and Office: 992 E 3d N Provo UT 84601

THEAL, ALFRED ROBERT, civil engineer, public administrator; b. Pasadena Calif., Dec. 5, 1924; s. Alfred Thompson and Glendora Marie (Mellon) T.; m. Connie Saenz, May 23, 1953; children—Robert M., Susanne M. B.S., U. So. Calif., 1945, B. Engring., 1949 postgrad., 1979—. Registered profl. engr., Ariz., Calif., Oreg., Wash. Assoc. civil engr. City of Los Angeles, 1947-55; sr. civil engr. Orange County Flood Control Dist., Santa Ana, Calif., 1955-57; assoc. engr. So. Calif. Edison Co., Los Angeles, 1957; v.p. Waveguide Inc., Van Nuys, Calif., 1957-59; asst. city engr. City of Riverside (Calif.), 1959-66; pres. Airhardware Inc., Van Nuys, 1966-69; v.p. Koebig & Koebig Inc., Riverside, 1969-72; dir. pub. works City of Laguna Beach (Calif.), 1973-78, city mgr., 1973-78; city mgr. City of Buena Park (Calif.), 1978-81; dir. pub. works City of Everett (Wash.), 1981—. Served to lt. USN, 1942-46. Recipient Cert. of Appreciation, Buena Park C. of C., 1979, 80; honored for outstanding service Aliso Water Mgmt. Agy., Orange County, Calif., 1978. Mem. Am. Pub. Works Assn., Am. Water Works Assn., ASCE, Internat. City Mgrs. Assn. Club: Rotary (Everett). Condr. sewer and water studies for FHA, 1971, 1972. Home: 10510 34th Dr SE Everett WA 98204 Office: Dept Pub Works 32 Cedar St Everett WA 98201

THELEN, MAX, JR., foundation executive, lawyer; b. Berkeley, Calif., Aug. 18, 1919; s. Max and Ora Emily (Muir) T.; m. Phyllis J. Barnhill, Mar. 8, 1952; children—Nancy B., Jane M., Max, William B. A.B. with highest honors, U. Calif.-Berkeley, 1940; J.D. cum laude, Harvard U., 1946. Bar: Calif. 1946. Sole practice, San Francisco, 1946—; ptnr. Thelen, Marrin, Johnson & Bridges, 1957—; pres., trustee S.H. Cowell Found., 1970—; pres., dir. Oramax Fund; dir. Ind. Bankshares Corp., Kaiser Steel Corp. Pres., World Affairs Council. Served to lt. USNR, 1942-46. Mem. Am. Coll. Trial Lawyers, ABA, State Bar Calif., Bar Assn. San Francisco, Com. Fgn. Relations. Republican. Presbyterian. Clubs: Commonwealth (past gov.), World Trade, Marin Tennis, Marines Meml. Home: 199 Mountain View Ave San Rafael CA 94901 Office: 2 Embarcadero Center Suite 2200 San Francisco CA 94111

THEM, THEODORE FREDERICK, chemist, consulting company executive; b. Meshoppen, Pa., Oct. 16, 1951; s. Theodore Roland and Betty (Jackson) T.; m. Julie Ann Holland, June 30, 1979; 1 dau., Alexis Katherine. B.A., Gettysburg Coll., 1973; M.S., U. N.Mex., 1975, Ph.D., 1977. Co-founder, v.p., dir. analytical services and chem. cons. Ana-Chem, Inc., Albuquerque, 1977-81, mgr. br. office, Farmington, N.Mex., 1980-81, also dir. research and devel.; dir. Core Labs., Bell Petroleum Labs. div. Bell Petroleum Services, Inc., Midland, Tex., 1981-82, dir. labs. Rocky Mountain region, Casper, Wyo., 1982—; cons. chemico-legal cases, forensic analysis, art authentication; participant profl. seminars. Mem. Southwestern Assn. Forensic Scientists (assoc.), Am. Chem. Soc., Am. Spectroscopy Assn., Soc. Petroleum Engrs., Sigma Xi. Democrat. Methodist. Contbr. articles to profl. jours. Address: 3400 W Yellowstone Casper WY 82601

THEOBOLD, ERWIN, psychologist; b. Columbia, Ill., Nov. 12, 1913; s. George and Caroline (Danewitz) T.; student U. Houston, 1958-62, La. State U., 1960, (Oakley fellow 1966-68) U. So. Calif., 1964-74; M.A., Claremont Grad. Sch., 1966; Ph.D., Calif. Sch. Profl. Psychology, 1976; 1 dau., Eileen. Counselor, U. Houston, 1960-62; instr. logic and philosophy Calif. State U., Long Beach and Los Angeles, 1969-75, Los Angeles Community Colls., 1970-78; behavioral cons. Spastic Children's Found., Los Angeles, 1971-73; instr. logic, philosophy and psychology Pasadena City Coll., 1972-78; exec. dir. Clark Sch. of the Desert, Palm Desert, Calif., 1973-74; pvt. practice psychotherapy, Pasadena, 1976—;

psychotherapist for adults with developmental disabilities United Cerebral Palsy-Spastic Children's Found., Los Angeles, 1977—; cons. in field. Lic. psychologist, Calif., Ariz. Mem. AAAS, Am. Humanist Assn., Am. Psychol. Assn., Ariz. Psychol. Assn., Assn. Behavior Analysis, Pasadena Area Psychol. Assn., Calif. Psychol. Assn., Nat. Register Health Service Providers in Psychology. Home: 754 Ladera St Pasadena CA 91104 Office: 711 E Walnut St Pasadena CA 91101

THEROUX, DAVID JON, economist, educator, research exec.; b. Lansing, Mich., May 25, 1949; s. Paul Richard and Marjorie Erma (Withrow) T.; m. Elaine Laconia Shipp, Mar. 20, 1976; 1 son, Paul Jacques. A.B. in Applied Math., U. Calif.-Berkeley, 1973, B.S.M.E., 1973, M.S.M.E., 1974; M.B.A., U. Chgo., 1977. Research asst. Richmond Field Sta., U. Calif.-Berkeley, 1974; project engr. Exxon Co. U.S.A., 1975-76; research asst. U. Chgo., 1976, dir. vis. lecture program in econ. sci., 1977; v.p., dir. acad. affairs, dir. pub. policy studies Cato Inst., San Francisco, 1977-79; pres., dir. Pacific Inst. Pub. Policy Research, San Francisco, 1979—; mem. adv. bd. No. Calif. Econ. Seminars, 1981—. Trustee William Koch Found., 1978-79. Served with USAF, 1967-72. Mem. Am. Econ. Assn., Royal Econ. Soc., Western Econ. Assn., So. Econ. Assn., Nat. Assn. Bus. Economists, Pub. Choice Soc., Pi Tau Sigma, Omicron Delta Epsilon. Sr. editor: Policy Report, 1978-79; editor: Cato Papers, 1978-79; The Energy Crisis: Government Policy and the Economy, 1978; (with P. Truluck) Private Rights and Public Lands, 1983. Home: 6311 Girvin Dr Oakland CA 94611 Office: 635 Mason St San Francisco CA 94108

THERRIAN, MICKAELA, lawyer, educator; b. Rapid City, S.D., Oct. 30, 1952; d. Fergus Manfred and Pahla Yuvette (Marvin) Therrian. B.S. in Speech and Theatre, Lewis Clark State Coll., 1974. J.D., U. Idaho, 1977. Bar: Idaho 1978, U.S. Dist. Ct. Ariz. 1980, U.S. Ct. Appeals (9th cir.) 1983; cert. community coll. tchr., Ariz. Intern, State of Alaska Pub. Defender, Fairbanks, 1977; lawyer, chief staff Bur. Support Enforcement, Boise, Idaho, 1978-79; dep. county atty. Coconino County (Ariz.), Flagstaff, 1980—; prof. law Yavapai Community Coll. Bd. dirs. Theatrikos, Flagstaff; mem. Friends Coconino County/Flagstaff City Library, Flagstaff Vol. League, Friends of the River. Caroline Silverthorn scholar, 1972. Mem. Idaho Bar Assn., Ariz. Bar Assn., ABA, Ariz. Women Lawyers Assn., Am. Trial Lawyers Assn., N.Am. Basque Orgn. (pres. local chpt.). Republican. Christian Scientist. Office: Coconino County Courthouse Flagstaff AZ 86001

THETFORD, WILLIAM NEWTON, educator, psychologist; b. Chgo., Apr. 25, 1923; s. John Randolph and Edna Mabel (Klein) T.; A.B., DePauw U., 1944; Ph.D., U. Chgo., 1949; postgrad. Washington Sch. Psychiatry, 1951-54. Research psychologist Inst. Psychosomatic and Psychiat. Research and Tng., Michael Reese Hosp., Chgo., 1949-51; sr. psychologist U.S. Govt., Washington, 1951-54; cons. Fgn. Service Inst., Beirut, 1953; dir. div. clin. psychology Inst. of Living, Hartford, Conn., 1954-55; asst. prof. psychology, also chief psychologist human ecology study program Cornell U. Med. Coll., 1955-57; assoc. prof. med. psychology Columbia Coll. Physicians and Surgeons, 1958-71, prof., 1971—, asst. project dir. child devel. program, 1960-68; cons. div. human ecology dept. medicine Cornell U. Med. Coll., 1960; dir. div. clin. psychology Columbia-Presbyn. Med. Center, 1958-78; cons. NIH; prin. investigator learning behavior and personality traits Human Ecology Fund, 1960—. Fellow Am. Psychol. Assn., Soc. Projective Techniques, Am. Orthopsychiat. Assn., Internat. Council Psychologists; mem. Am. Psychosomatic Soc., Am. Fedn. Clin. Research, AAAS, World Fedn. Mental Health, Assn. Am. Med. Colls., N.Y. Soc. Projective Techniques (pres.), Com. on Orthopsychiatry in Pediatric Settings, N.Y. Acad. Scis., Internat. Congress of Psychology, Inter-Am. Psychol. Assn., Sigma Xi. Assoc. editor Jour. Abnormal Psychology. Home: 2030 Paradise Dr Tiburon CA 94920

THIE, JOHN FRANCIS, chiropractor; b. Detroit, Jan. 25, 1933; s. John C. and Mary (Butkevich) T.; A.A., Pasadena City Coll., 1952; B.S. in Fin., U. So. Calif., 1954; D.Chiropractic, Los Angeles Coll. Chiropractic, 1957; m. Carrie Pauline Wright, Dec. 27, 1952; children—John Francis, Luther, Matthew. Mem. faculty Los Angeles Coll. of Chiropractic, 1957-58, mem. vis. faculty, 1957-74; dir. Thie Chiropractic Corp., Pasadena, Calif., 1974—; lectr. Parker Chiropractic Research Found., Ft. Worth, 1967—; mem. faculty adult div. Alhambra Sch. Dist., Calif., 1971-72, Pepperdine U., Malibu, Calif., 1972—. Chmn. adult adv. bd. Pasadena Area Youth Council, 1960-64; chmn. bylaws com. Pasadena Commn. Human Needs and Opportunities, 1964-66; mem. health adv. bd. Calif. Dept. Rehab., 1977—; deacon Pasadena First Congregational Ch., 1966-71; trustee Malibu Meth. Ch., 1980—; founder, pres. Touch for Health Found., 1975—. Recipient Disting. Service award Parker Chiropractic Research Found., 1967, Disting. Service award Central Fla. Acad. Chiropractic Studies, 1972, Boss of Year award Am. Bus. Women's Assn., 1980. Mem. Calif. Chiropractic Assn. (Robert Botterman award 1977), Am. Chiropractic Assn., So. Calif. Chiropractic Soc. (pres. 1965-66), Internat. Coll. Applied Kinesiology (chmn. 1973-76), Los Angeles County Chiropractic Soc. (pres. 1963-64), San Gabriel Valley Chiropractic Soc. (Dr. of Year 1960, Disting. Service award 1961, pres. 1958-59), AAAS, Los Angeles Coll. Chiropractic Alumni Assn. (pres. 1958). Author: (with Mary Marks) Touch for Health, 1973, rev. edit., 1980; contbr. articles to profl. jours. and mags. Home: 6162 La Gloria Malibu CA 90265 Office: 1192 N Lake Pasadena CA 91104

THIEL, WARREN HARRY, tech. consultant; b. Grand Rapids, Mich., Jan. 12, 1919; s. Harry and Josephine Johanna (Timmers) T.; Asso. Sci., Grand Rapids Jr. Coll., 1938; B.S. in Chemistry, U. Mich., 1940, M.S. in Chemistry, 1942; grad. AEC Oak Ridge Sch. Reactor Tech., 1953; certificate in Contract Adminstrn., U. Cal., Los Angeles Ext., 1966; m. Vitalina Coello Laborde, June 8, 1957. Research engr. E.H. Sargent & Co., Chgo., 1943-45; project engr. Bell & Howell Co., Chgo., 1945-47; asso. chemist, engr. AEC Argonne Nat. Lab., Chgo., 1947-51; design specialist Convair div. Gen. Dynamics Corp., San Diego, 1951-61; sr. project engr. Aerojet-Gen. Corp., Downey, Cal., 1961-62; prin. engr., scientist Douglas Aircraft Co., Santa Monica, 1962-65; sr. project engr. Hughes Aircraft Co., Culver City and Canoga Park, Cal., 1965-70; ind. cons. in tech., 1968—. Tech. cons. to small bus. on new product ventures, 1968—. E.H. Sargent grantee, 1943. Registered profl. engr., Ill. Mem. Am. Rocket Soc. (pres. San Diego sect. 1960-61), Am. Security Council, Am. Def. Preparedness Assn., Nat. Rifle Assn., Am. Chem. Soc., IEEE, AIAA, Armed Forces Communications and Electronics Assn. Office: PO Box 92232 Long Beach CA 90809

THIELEN, LAWRENCE RAYMOND, electronics co. exec.; b. Huron, S.D., Jan. 12, 1927; s. Peter Joseph and Marie Anna (Hoffard) T.; B.S.E.E., S.D. State U., 1950; m. Jacqueline S. Srill, June 5, 1955; children—Laura, Mark, Edward, Peter, John, Sarah. With Ampex Corp., 1953-61; dir. mktg. Applied Tech., Inc., Itek Corp., 1961-65; founder, pres., chmn. bd. Avantek, Inc., Santa Clara, Calif., 1965—. Served with U.S. Army, 1945-47. Mem. Am. Electronics Assn. (dir.), Nat. Assn. Security Dealers (dir.). Roman Catholic. Office: 3175 Bowers Ave Santa Clara CA 95051

THIENE, PAUL GEORGE, applied physics consultant; b. Pasadena, Calif., Dec. 10, 1919; s. Paul G. and Lola (Stake) T.; m. Sonja Navall, Feb. 15, 1946; children—Pamela, Kristin, Maya. B.S., Calif. Inst. Tech., 1943, Ph.D. in Phys. Electronics, 1952. Asst. physicist Calif. Inst. Tech., 1943-45; research engr. Jet Propulsion Lab., 1946-47; dept. chief and research adminstr. Western Div., Office of Sci. Res., USAF 1952-55, cons. Air Tech. Intelligence Ctr., 1955-57; sr. physicist Giannini Plasmadyne Corp., Santa Ana, Calif., 1958-62; sr. staff scientist MHD Magneto hydrodynamics Research Inc., Newport Beach, Calif., 1962-66; supr. research lab. Optical Physics Sect., Aeronutronic Div. Philco-Ford Corp., Newport Beach, 1966—; cons. Litech, Inc., P.W. Webster Co., Surg. Mech. Research Inc. & Curt Deckert Assocs., 1973—. Mem. Am. Phys. Soc. Contbr. articles in field to profl. jours. Address: 401 Le Droit Ln Laguna Beach CA 92651

THIERIOT, RICHARD TOBIN, publisher; b. San Francisco, Jan. 18, 1942; s. Charles de Young and Barbara Mary (Tobin) T.; B.A., Yale U., 1963; M.B.A., Stanford U., 1969; m. Angelica Maria Reynal, Sept. 30, 1972; children—Charles de Young, II, Richard Reynal; stepchildren—Juan P. Withers, Simon Withers. Reporter, Camden (N.J.) Courier-Post, 1963-64; asso. editor San Francisco Chronicle, 1969-77, editor, pub., 1977—; treas. Chronicle Pub. Co., 1969-77, pres., 1977—. Served with USMCR, 1964-67. Mem. Am. Newspaper Pubs. Assn., A.P., Am. Soc. Newspaper Editors, Am. Press Inst., Calif. Press Assn., Calif. Newspaper Pubs. Assn., Sigma Delta Chi. Address: Chronicle Publishing Co 901 Mission St San Francisco CA 94103*

THIESSEN, JO CAULA, ednl. adminstr.; b. Covington, Ky., Jan. 19, 1931; d. Joe and Mildred (Payne) Gregg; B.S., Wheaton Coll., 1952; M.B.A., U. So. Calif., 1976; m. Jacob I. Thiessen, Apr. 23, 1954; children—Heather, Jacob. Med. technologist Los Angeles County/U. So. Calif. Med. Center, 1953-58; med. technologist supr. Thatcher Labs., Pasadena, Calif., 1959-65; chief technologist Meth. Hosp., So. Calif., Arcadia, 1965-74; adminstrv. chief technologist, program dir. sch. Med. Tech., Huntington Meml. Hosp., Pasadena, 1975—; career counselor. Clin. lab. scientist Nat. Cert. Agy.; lic. clin. lab. technologist, Calif. Mem. Am. Mgmt. Assn., Am. Soc. Med. Tech., U. So. Calif. M.B.A.'s, U. So. Calif. Alumni Assn., Beta Gamma Sigma, Huntington Meml. Fed. Credit Union. Home: 444 109 W Huntington Dr Arcadia CA 91006 Office: 100 Congress St Pasadena CA 91105

THIFFAULT, MARK, editor; b. Toronto, Ont., Can., Aug. 15, 1949; came to U.S., 1951, naturalized, 1963; s. Stanley Richard Thiffault and Grace Mary (Lamontagne) Calcagno; student Sacramento State Coll., 1967-68, Saddleback Coll., 1977-79, Calif. State U., Fullerton, 1979—; m. Robyn Ann Stewart, Oct. 9, 1971; children—Brett, Shane Stewart, Megan Kathleen. Reporter, Feather Pub. Co., Quincy, Calif., 1966-68; editor Charger Publs., Capistrano Beach, Calif., 1971-75, 76—, mng. editor Horse and Horseman, 1973-75, 76—; copy editor Sydney (Australia) Morning Herald, 1975-76; founder, pres. MT Enterprises, Laguna Hills, Calif.; cons. and lectr. in field. Served with USMC, 1968-71, officer Res., 1979—. Mem. U.S. Marine Corps Combat Corrs. Assn. Republican. Office: 34249 Camino Capistrano Capistrano Beach CA 92624

THILL, DONALD CECIL, weed scientist; b. Colfax, Wash., Aug. 30, 1950; s. Cecil Edward and Mildred Virginia (Dahmen) T.; m. Dorothy Elizabeth Drader, Aug. 28, 1971; children—Troy, Tracy, Tobias, Kathryn. B.S., Wash. State U., 1972, M.S. in Agronomy, 1976; Ph.D. in Crop Sci., Oreg. State U., 1979. Lic. pesticide cons., Wash., Idaho. Plant physiologist Agrl. Research Sta., U.S. Dept. Agr., Pullman, Wash., 1974-79; biochem. field specialist PPG Industries Inc., Pitts., 1979-80; asst. prof. weed sci. U. Idaho, Moscow, 1980—; cons. in field. Mem. Weed Sci. Soc. Am., Western Soc. Weed Sci., Idaho Weed Control Assn., Inland Empire Agrl. Chem. Assn., Sigma Xi, Alpha Zeta. Roman Catholic. Contbr. numerous articles to profl. jours.

THINH, NGO DINH, consultant, educator; b. Hue, Vietnam; came to U.S., 1956; B.Aero. Engring., U. Minn., 1964; M. Engring., Concordia U. (Can.), 1971, Ph.D., 1975; m. Thanh Van; children—Tan, Tu-Son. Mech. designer Mid America Engrs., Inc., Chgo., 1964-67; aerodynamicist Pratt & Whitney Aircraft Can., Longueuil, Que., 1967-78; engring. specialist Aerojet Liquid Rocket Co., Sacramento, 1978-80; assoc. prof. Sch. Engring. and Computer Sci., Calif. State U., Sacramento, 1979—; cons. Tantu Research, 1981—. Office: Calif State U Sch Engring and Computer Sci 6000 J St Sacramento CA 95819

THISIUS, JOAN LORETTA, educator; b. Easton, Minn., Aug. 19, 1930; d. Lawrence William and Theresa Margurite (McGoff) Ascheman; B.S., San Francisco State U., 1966, M.S., 1973; m. Orville Lawrence Thisius, Aug. 29, 1950; children—Ann Louise, Timothy Neil, Rebecca Gail, Maxine Therese, Edward John, Jennifer Kay. Sch. sec., 1951-54; public sch. tchr., 1959-63, 66-69; resource tchr., 1969-74; prin. Hidden Valley Elem. Sch., Concord, Calif., 1974-80, adminstr. Title IV project, 1980-81; staff devel. adminstr. library/media Mt Diablo (Calif.) Unifield Sch. Dist., 1981—; condr. leadership seminars. Pres. ch. aux., 1955-56. Mem. Assn. Calif. Sch. Adminstrs., Elem. Sch. Prins. Assn., Calif. Assn. Gifted, Diablo Assn. Calif. Sch. Adminstrs., VFW Aux. (pres. 1953-55), Sea Scout Aux. (pres. 1968), Delta Kappa Gamma (past pres.). Republican. Roman Catholic. Club: Jr. Women's. Author articles in field, also poetry. Home: 23 Kirkwood Ct Concord CA 94521 Office: 1936 Carlotta Dr Concord CA 94520

THOMAS, ALAN, candy co. exec.; b. Evansburg, Pa., Jan. 1, 1923; s. William Roberts and Letta (Garrett) T.; student Rutgers U., 1941-42, 46-47; B.S., Pa. State U., 1949; M.S., U. Minn., 1950, Ph.D., 1954; m. Marguerite Atria, July 1, 1972; children—Garrett Lee, Michael Alan, Randall Stephen, Brett Eliot. Instr., Temple U., Phila., 1950-51, U. Minn., St. Paul, 1951-54; research asst. Bowman Dairy Co., Chgo., 1954-56; research project mgr. M&M Candies div. Mars, Inc., Hackettstown, N.J., 1956-60, product devel. mgr., 1961-64, chocolate research dir. 1964; v.p. research and devel. Mars Candies, Chgo., 1964-67; v.p. research and devel. M&M/Mars Div., Hackettstown, 1967-77, v.p. sci. affairs, 1977-78; gen. mgr. Ethel M, Las Vegas, 1978—. Chmn. industry council of industry liaison panel Food and Nutrition Bd., Nat. Acad. Scis./NRC, 1972-73; adv. U.S. del. Codex Alimentarius Com. on Cocoa and Chocolate Products, 1967-78. Served to 1st lt. inf. AUS, 1942-46. Recipient research award Nat. Confectioners Assn. U.S., 1971. Mem. AAAS, Grocery Mfrs. Am. (chmn. tech. com. 1975-76), Chocolate Mfrs. Assn. (chmn. FDA liaison com. 1975-77), Inst. Food Technologists, N.Y. Acad. Sci., Am. Assn. Candy Technologists, Gamma Sigma Delta, Phi Kappa Phi. Home: 1625 Westwood Dr Las Vegas NV 89102 Office: Ethel M PO Box 18413 Las Vegas NV 89114

THOMAS, ARTHUR NEWTON, JR., aero. engr.; b. Duluth, Minn., Sept. 27, 1922; s. Arthur Newton and Ethel (Goering) T.; B.S. in Aero. Engring., U. Minn., 1948, M.S., 1949; m. Marjorie Schasch, Mar. 25, 1970; children—Steven, Colleen, Peter, David, Fredrick. Asst. gen. mgr., chief engr. Marquardt Co., Van Nuys, Calif., 1950-69, v.p. engring., 1978—; br. mgr., sr. project mgr. McDonnell Douglas, St. Louis, 1969-76; dep. for air and missile def. Office Asst. Sec. Army, 1976-78; lectr. engring. UCLA Extension. Served to capt. USMCR, 1941-45. Decorated Air medal. Assoc. fellow AIAA, Christian Bus. Men U.S.A. Contbr. articles to nat. publs.; patentee in field. Home: 19240 Ballinger St Northridge CA 91324 Office: 16555 Saticoy St Van Nuys CA 91409

THOMAS, BYRON EUGENE, optometrist; b. Colville, Wash., May 18, 1941; s. William Clarke and Mae Deen (Gafford) T.; children—Katherine Marie, Kenneth Clark. B.S., Pacific U., 1963, O.D., 1964. Pvt. practice optometry Ellensburg (Wash.) Vision Clinic, P.S., Inc., 1968—; lectr. Wash. Bd. Optometry, 1977; mem. Western Vision Service Bd., 1978-82; lectr. Pacific U. Student Assn., 1982. Pres. Ellensburg Sch. Bd., 1979-81, mem. bd., 1971—; campaign chmn. pres. United Way.; active Ft. Simco council Boy Scouts Am. Served to 1st lt. USAF, 1965-68. Recipient Silver Beaver award Boy Scouts Am., 1978. Mem. Am. Optometric Assn., Wash. Optometric Assn., Yakima Valley Optometric Soc., C. of C. Clubs: Lions, Elks, Moose. Office: 410 N Pine St Ellensburg WA 98926

THOMAS, BYRON RICHARD, soil scientist, educator; b. Filer, Idaho, Jan. 21, 1933; s. Raymond Henery and Dorothy (Brazie) T.; m. Sharon Darlene Pease, Sept. 6, 1957; children—Gerald, Katherine, Carol. B.S., U. Idaho, 1959, M.S., 1961; Ph.D., Oreg. State U., 1970. Soil scientist U.S. Forest Service, Mont., 1961-65, Oreg. State U., Corvallis, 1965-68, soil scientist Oreg. and Wash. Bur. Land Mgmt., Portland, Oreg., 1970—; affiliate prof. Coll. Forest Resources, U. Wash., 1973—. Served with U.S. Army, 1953-55. Mem. Am. Soc. Agronomy, Oreg. Soil Sci. Soc., N.W. Forest Soils Council, Sigma Xi. Club: Elks. Contbr. articles to profl. jours. Office: 825 NE Multnomah St PO Box 2965 Portland OR 97208

THOMAS, CHARLES WILLIAM, II, urban studies educator; b. Md., Apr. 26, 1926; s. Charles W. and Estella T.; m. Shirley Wade, Aug. 30, 1958; children—Charles W. III, Shawn. B.S., Morgan State Coll., 1951; M.A. (Jesse Smith Noyes fellow), John Carroll U., 1955; Ph.D. (Cleve. Found. fellow), Western Res. U., 1961. With Highland View Cuyahoga County Hosp., Cleve., 1955-63, acting dir. Sheltered Workshop Research Project, 1956-58, co-prin. investigator and dir. Aging Research Project, until 1963; asst. prof., dir. counseling services and personnel devel. Job Corps Ctr., U. Oreg. 1963-66; evaluation design analyst and dir. edn. and tng. South Central Multipurpose Health Service Ctr., U. So. Calif., 1966-69, assoc. prof. community medicine Sch. Medicine, 1966-69; prin., dir. Ctr. for Study Racial and Social Issues, Los Angeles, 1969-71; prof. urban studies and planning U. Calif. at San Diego Third Coll., La Jolla, 1977—, coordinator urban studies and planning, 1977-82, Danforth assoc., 1979; lectr. John Carroll U., 1961-63, Calif. State Coll., Los Angeles, 1967-68, Calif. State Coll., Dominguez Hills, 1970, Claremont Coll. Black Studies Ctr., 1970-71; vis. prof. counseling psychology Ariz. State U., 1970-71; vis. scholar Howard U. Inst. for Urban Affairs, 1979-80; vis. scientist Am. Psychol. Assn., 1969-70, Assn. Black Psychologists, 1969-70; mem. Calif. Psychology Examining Commn.; active Calif. Bd. Edn., 1975-79; facilitator, chmn. pro tem Nat. Ad Hoc Com. on Homicidal Violence Among Blacks; facilitator for devel. Nat. Black Mental Health Workers Assn.; founder, coordinator Ann. Conf. on Issues in Ethnicity and Mental Health, speaker, cons. in field. Served with AUS, 1944-46. Recipient Father of Black Psychology award Black Students' Psychol. Assn., 1970; cert. of recognition Nat. Assn. Sch. Psychologists, 1971; Outstanding Service award San Diego br. NAACP, 1976; commendation Mayor of San Diego, 1976; legis. commendation state of Ohio, 1979; Legal Aid Soc. San Diego award, 1979; Outstanding Contbn. award So. Regional Edn. Bd. Community Clin. Psychology Project, 1980; Christ Ch. of San Diego commendation, 1980; San Diego Black Achievement award in Sci., 1981, in Journalism, 1983; Charles W. Thomas psychology scholarship established in his honor at Morgan State U., 1976; named to Scroll of Honor for Ednl. Leadership, Omega Psi Phi, 1979. Fellow Am. Psychol. Assn. (chmn. edn. and tng. bd. 1971-72, chmn. task force on master's level edn. 1973); mem. Calif. State Psychol. Assn., Nat. Acad. TV Arts and Scis., AAAS (adv. bd.), Council for Advancement Psychol. Profession and Scis. (gov. 1969), Assn. Black Psychologists (founding chmn. 1968, hon. nat. chmn.), Black Action Council San Diego (hon.), NAACP (pres. San Diego chpt. 1977), Nat. Acad. Black Scientists (chmn.). Republican. Contbr. articles, chpts. tp profl. publs., popular mags. Home: 610 Bradford Rd El Cajon CA 92021 Office: Urban Studies and Planning D-009 Third Coll U Calif at San Diego La Jolla CA 92093

THOMAS, DAVID WALTER, JR., manufacturing executive; b. Asheville, N.C., May 19, 1938; s. David Walter and Frances (Warren) T.; children—David, Anne. B.S.M.E., N.C. State U., 1962; M.S. in Indsl. Mgmt., U. Tenn., 1974. With Huyck Corp., 1962-80, beginning as field service engr., successively sales engr., product mgr., product mgr., mgr. mfg. services, project mgr., constrn. mgr., start-up engr., plant mgr., mfg. mgr., v.p., div. gen. mgr., 1974-79, corp. dir. planning, Wake Forest, N.C., 1979-80; sr. v.p. corp. devel. Ameron, Inc., Monterey Park, Calif., 1981—. Dist. chmn. Boy Scouts Am., 1977-78, exec. com. East Tenn. council, 1976-78; budget com. Tenn. United Way, 1977-78; sect. leader Los Angeles United Way, 82-83. Served with AUS, 1960-61. Mem. Golden Chain, Blue Key, Thirty and Three, Beta Gamma Sigma. Clubs: Lions, Exchange. Contbr. articles to profl. jours. Home: 13910 Old Harbor Ln 303 Marina del Rey CA 90291 Office: Ameron Inc PO Box 3000 Monterey Park CA 91754

THOMAS, DELBERT DALE, engineering executive, consultant; b. Portland, Oreg., June 14, 1930; s. Theodore C. and Esther E. (Kemnitz) T.; m. Phyllis B. Bartlett, Jan. 8, 1949; children—James, Leonard, Stephen, Timothy, Susan. Student San Jose City Coll., Santa Rosa Community Coll., 1950-51. Lic. contractor, Calif., Ariz., Nev. Pres., Shale Devel. Corp. Redlands, Calif., 1976—; v.p. Energy '80 Scientific, Inc., Sepulveda, Calif., 1981—; chmn. bd. Impex, Inc., Redlands, 1982—; Solar Electric Engring., Inc.; dir. various cos.; developer indsl. projects Govt. of Pakistan. Awarded 3rd place Inventor of Yr., Inventors Workshop Internat., 1976. Mem. ASHRAE. Republican. Baptist. Patentee in field; mech. contractor on space shuttle assembly facility, Palmdale, Calif., 1973. Home: 1522 Cameo Dr Redlands CA 92373 Office: Impex Inc 313 High St Redlands CA 92373

THOMAS, DIAN, author, TV commentator; b. Moab, Utah, May 19, 1945; d. Julian Robert and Norene Clara (Richins) T. B.S., Brigham Young U., 1968, M.S., 1973. Tchr. home econs. jr. high sch., Orem, Utah, 1968-71; instr. Brigham Young U., Provo, Utah, 1973-75; author: Roughing It Easy, 1974, Roughing It Easy II, 1976, Backyard Roughing It Easy, 1980, Today's Tips for Easy Living, 1982; family life cons. NBC Today Show, 1980—. Recipient Outstanding Service award Forecast and Home Econs. Mag., 1975, Oustanding Home Economist award Utah Home Econs. Assn., 1981. Mem. Am. Home Econs. Assn., Am. Home Econs. in Bus., AFTRA. Republican. Mem. Ch. Jesus Christ Latter-day Saints. Contbr. articles to mags. Home: PO Box 7530 Provo UT 84602 Office: 1675 N 200 W Suite 9A-5 Provo UT 84604

THOMAS, FORREST LEE, chem. co. material handling specialist; b. Sutherland, Nebr., Feb. 12, 1931; s. James Madison and Ina Evelyn (Himmelright) T.; student Union Coll., Walla Walla Coll., 1948-51, Loma Linda U., 1954-55; m. Owena Lou Gibson, Apr. 15, 1951; children—James Owen (dec.), Lea Etta Thomas Eaton, JeNe Marie. With Dow Chem. Co., Torrance, Calif., 1956—, various positions, 1956-78, material handling specialist, 1978-82, safety coordinator, Los Angeles, 1982—, ind. distbr. Skaklee Products, Lomita, Calif., 1969—. Mem. agy. relations and budget com. Region 3, Los Angeles County United Way, 1976-81; mem. lay adv. bd. So. Calif. Conf. Seventh-day Adventist Ch., 1978-80. Served with M.C., U.S. Army, 1951-53; Korea. Decorated Bronze Star with 2 oak leaf clusters. Republican. Home: 2263 248th St Lomita CA 90717 Office: 305 Crenshaw Blvd Torrance CA 90503

THOMAS, FRANK JOSEPH, corporate executive, research engr.; b. Pocatello, Idaho, Apr. 15, 1930; s. Emil and Jennie (Jones) T.; m. Carol

Jones, Feb. 4, 1949; children—Dale, Wayne, Keith, Ralph. B.S. in Elec. Engring., U. Idaho, 1952; M.S.E., U. Calif.-Berkeley, 1957. Registered profl. engr., Calif. Staff, Sandia Corp., Albuquerque, 1952-56; mgr. engring. Aerojet Gen., San Ramon, Calif., 1957-64; asst. dir. research Office of Sec. of Def., Washington, D.C., 1964-67; sr. staff RAND Corp., Santa Monica, Calif., 1967-71; pres., dir. research, Pacific-Sierra Research Corp., Santa Monica, Calif., 1971—. Recipient Meritorious Civilian Service medal Sec. of Def., 1967; Master Design award Product Engring. Mag., 1963. Mem. AAAS, Sigma Xi. Author: Evasive Foreign Nuclear Testing, 1971. Contbr. articles to profl. jours. Office: 12340 Santa Monica Blvd Los Angeles CA 90025

THOMAS, FRED, III, marketing executive; b. Los Angeles, Jan. 27, 1952; s. Fred and Frances Marie (Elliott) T.; m. Judith C. Leslie, Mar. 15, 1976; children—Tanisha, Tiffany. A.A. in Bus. Adminstrn., Los Angeles Southwest Coll., 1979; B.S. in Mktg., U. Redlands, 1980. Sales rep. Union Fidelity Ins., Los Angeles, 1976-78, Investors Life Ins., W. Ger., 1978-79; project coordinator 1984 Olympic info. office Los Angeles Southwest Coll., 1979 ; mktg. coordinator Hollywood Park Race Track, Inglewood, Calif., 1980—. Mem. adv. com. Inglewood Adult Sch. Dist. Mem. Am. Mktg. Assn., Mktg. Dirs. So. Calif., Working Adults Athletic Assn. Democrat. Baptist. Home: 2635 S Harvard Blvd Los Angeles CA 90018 Office: 1150 Ave of Champions Inglewood CA 90301

THOMAS, GAIL SUSAN, bus. cons.; b. San Francisco, July 7, 1948; d. Samuel Benson and Evelyn Emelia (Sjogren) T.; A.A. with high honors, Long Beach City Coll., 1969; B.A. with honors, U. Calif., Riverside, 1971; M.S. in L.S., U. So. Calif., 1974. Pres., owner Ms. G.S. Thomas Corp., Long Beach, Calif., 1976—. Mem. Long Beach Area C. of C., Long Beach Dist. Bd. Realtors, Nat. Assn. Home Builders, Bldg. Industry Assn., AAUW, ALA, Spl. Libraries Assn., Calif. Library Assn., Phi Beta Kappa, Alpha Gamma Sigma, Alpha Mu Gamma, Beta Phi Gamma, Phi Delta Gamma. Republican. Mem. United Ch. of Christ. Office: PO Box 1269 Long Beach CA 90801

THOMAS, GEORGE EDWARD, museum director; b. São Paulo, Brazil, June 3, 1943; B.A., U. Calif.-Santa Barbara, 1966, M.F.A., 1968; m. Anara C. German, Apr. 28, 1962; children—George Clifford, Daniel Leigh. Teaching fellow art dept. U. Calif.-Santa Barbara, 1967-68; prodn. designer Ben Mayer Design, Inc., Los Angeles, 1968-70; mem. vis. faculty, dept. art Western Wash. U., 1969; curator Whatcom Mus. History and Art, Bellingham, Wash., 1970-77, dir., 1977—. Mem. Whatcom County Adv. Council Hist. Preservation; bd. dirs. Friends of Bellingham Maritime Heritage Ctr. Mem. Am. Assn. Museums, Allied Arts of Whatcom County (steering com. 1979), Wash. Mus. Assn. (bd. dirs.). Author intro. to exhibit catalog: Margaret Tomkins paintings and sculpture 1969-1978, 1978; editor: Beyond The Veil: The Etchings of Helen Loggie, 1979. Office: 121 Prospect St Bellingham WA 98225

THOMAS, GERALD WAYLETT, university president; b. Small, Idaho, July 3, 1919; s. Daniel Waylett and Mary (Evans) T.; student Pasadena Jr. Coll., 1936-38; B.S., U. Idaho, 1941; M.S., Tex. A & M Coll., 1951, Ph.D., 1954; m. Jean Ellis, June 2, 1945; children—David Gerald, Peggy Jeane, Marianne. With U.S. Forest Service in Idaho, 1938-40; range conservationist, work unit conservationist Soil Conservation Service, St. Anthony and Rexburg, Idaho, 1946-50; asst. and assoc. prof. dept. range and forestry Tex. A&M Coll., College Station, 1951-56; research coordinator Tex. Agrl. Expt. Sta., 1956-58; dean agr. Tex. Tech. U., 1958, exec. v.p., 1968; now pres. N.Mex. State U., Las Cruces; mem. Bd. for Internat. Food and Agrl. Devel.; mem. exec. bd. Assn. State Univs. and Land-Grant Colls., Associated Western Univs. Served to lt. USNR, 1942-45. Decorated D.F.C. (3), Air medal (2). Mem. Am. Soc. Range Mgmt. (bd. dirs., pres.), Soil Conservation Soc., AAAS, Sigma Xi, Phi Kappa Phi. Rotarian. Author: Progress and Change in the Agricultural Industry, Food and Fiber for a Changing World; also numerous publs. on ecology and agrl. subjects. Home: University Park Las Cruces NM 88003

THOMAS, GRACE FERN, psychiatrist; b. Gothenburg, Nebr., Sept. 23, 1897; d. George William and Martha C. (Johnson) T.; B.S., U. Nebr., 1924; M.A., Creighton U., 1926, M.D., U. So. Calif., 1935, postgrad. U. Colo., 1942-43, Inst. of Living, 1943, U. So. Calif., 1946, UCLA, 1947-50, Columbia U., 1953; M.A. in Religion, U. So. Calif., 1968. Ordained to ministry United Methodist Ch., 1963; instr. chemistry, biology Duchesne Coll., 1924-27; lab. technician various hosps., 1927-32; intern Los Angeles County Hosp., 1934-35; resident physician Riverside County Hosp., 1935-36; resident psychiatrist Los Angeles County Psychopathic Hosp., 1936-37; staff psychiatrist Calif. State Hosp. System, 1937-42, Glenside Sanitarium, 1943-44; pvt. practice neuropsychiatry, Long Beach, Calif., 1946-51; chief mental hygiene clinic VA, Albuquerque, 1951-54; dir. psychiat. edn. Miss. State Hosp., Jackson, 1955; dir. Stark County Guidance Ctr., Canton, Ohio, 1956-58, Huron County Guidance Ctr., Norwalk, Ohio, 1958-61, Arrowhead Mental Health Ctr., San Bernardino, Calif., 1962-64, Mendocino County Mental Health Services, Ukiah, Calif., 1964-65; chief profl. edn. Porterville (Calif.) State Hosp., 1965-66; dir. Tuolumne County Mental Health Services, Sonora, Calif., 1966-70; practice medicine, specializing in psychiatry, Turlock, Calif., 1970-73, Modesto, Calif., 1972—; mem. staff Sonora Community Hosp., Emanuel Hosp., Turlock, Modesto City Hosp., Doctors, Meml. Scenic Gen. hosps., Modesto; alienist Superior Ct. Stanislaus County. Served as capt. M.C., U.S. Army, 1944-46. Diplomate Am. Bd. Psychiatry and Neurology. Fellow Am. Psychiat. Assn. (life), Internat. Biog. Assn.; mem. AMA, Calif. Med. Assn., Am. Psychiat. Assn., Am. Med. Women's Assn., Central Calif. Psychiat. Soc., Stanislaus County Med. Soc., Am. Legion, Phi Beta Kappa, Sigma Xi, Phi Kappa Phi, Nu Sigma Phi, Phi Delta Gamma. Club: Soroptimist. Home: 2001 LaJolla Ct Modesto CA 95350 Office: 1130 Coffee Rd #8-B Modesto CA 95355

THOMAS, JANET KENNEDY, educator, account executive; b. Mpls., July 23, 1939; d. Gordon Douglas and Florence Otelia (Nelson) Kennedy; B.S., U. Minn., 1960, M.A., 1964; postgrad. U. Calif. (Santa Cruz and Riverside), Stanislaus State Coll., Calif. State Coll. (Fresno and San Bernadino); postgrad. Calif. Coast U., 1982—; m. Irven Earl Michael Thomas, Feb. 12, 1960. Tchr., Edina, Minn., 1960-61, Hermantown Sch., Duluth, Minn., 1961-65, Pleasant Valley Sch. Dist., Camarillo, Calif., 1966-68, Dept. of Def. Schs., Philippines, 1968-69, Atwater (Calif.) Sch. Dist., 1969-73, Moreno Valley Sch. Dist., Riverside, Calif., 1973-76; sch. site adminstr., prin. Pleasant Valley Sch. Dist., Camarillo, 1976-81; account exec. TMI Equities, Inc., 1981—; pvt. tutor, reading specialist, 1981—; owner Academics Plus, Camarillo. Asst. to state field dir. Calif., Pet Pride, 1969-81, dir. Philippines, 1968-69. Mem. Assn. Calif. Sch. Adminstrs. (conf. leader), Assn. Supervision and Curriculum Devel., Calif. Reading Assn., Internat. Reading Assn., AAUW, Nat. Assn. Securities Dealers, Ventura County Profl. Women's Network (charter). Author series of books on teaching and adminstering classes for the mentally retarded, 1969; author pamphlets and handbooks. Home: 2545 N Temple Ave Camarillo CA 93010 Office: 600 Temple Ave Camarillo CA 93010 also 601 Daily Dr Suite 132 Camarillo CA 93010

THOMAS, JOE CARL, city agency administrator; b. Adams, Tenn., Oct. 24, 1935; s. Charles Berry and Hattie (Kimbrough) T.; B.S. in Edn., Tuskegee Inst. (Ala.), 1958; M.A. in Guidance and Counselling, Rider Coll., Trenton, N.J., 1975; m. Marjorie Ann Thomas, Jan. 16, 1970. Commd. 2d lt. Adj. Gen. Corps, U.S. Army, 1958, advanced through grades to lt. col., 1976, ret., 1979; served at Presidio of San Francisco, 1959-61, 76-79, Fort Lewis, Wash., 1961-62, Japan, 1962-64, Def. Intelligence Agy., Washington, 1965-68, Thailand, 1968-69, Army Material Command, Washington, 1969-70, Vietnam, 1970-71, Fort Dix, N.J., 1971-76; exec. dir. Econ. Opportunity Council of San Francisco, 1979—. Chmn. membership com. San Francisco Black Leadership Forum; mem. Vallejo (Calif.) Choral Soc.; moderator Hillcrest Congl. Ch., Pleasant Hill, Calif.; mem. City of Benicia (Calif.) Planning Commn.; bd. dirs. United Way Bay Area; charter mem. Pres.'s Assocs. Pacific Sch. Religion, Berkeley, Calif. Decorated Legion of Merit, Meritorious Service medal, Army Commendation medal (3), Vietnam Service medal. Mem. NAACP, Calif.-Nev. Community Action Assn., Nat. Community Action Exec. Dirs. Assn., Alpha Phi Alpha (pres. Gamma Chi Lambda chpt., dir. No. Calif. region 1979—). Democrat. Home: 208 Chadwick Way Benicia CA 94510 Office: 730 Polk St San Francisco CA 94109

THOMAS, JOHN RICHARD, oil company executive; b. Anchorage, Ky., Aug. 26, 1921; s. John R. and Mildred (Woods) T.; m. Beatrice Ann Davidson, Dec. 7, 1944; children—Jonnie Sue Thomas Jacobs, Richard G. B.S., U. Calif., 1943, Ph.D., 1946. Research chemist Chevron Research Co., Richmond, Calif., 1948-49, sr. research assoc., 1951-60, sr. research scientist, 1961-67, mgr. research and devel. Ortho div., 1967-68, pres., 1970—; mem. AEC, 1949-51; asst. sec. Standard Oil Co. Calif., 1968-70; dir. Cetus Corp., Chevron Chem. Co., Chevron Environ. Health Ctr. Mem. vis. com. U. Wash. Coll. Engring.; mem. vis. com. Calif. Inst. Tech.; mem. Caltech Indsl. Assocs.; mem. indsl. adv. com. U. Calif.-San Diego. Mem. Am. Chem. Soc., AAAS, Indsl. Research Inst., Soc. Automotive Engrs. Republican. Contbr. articles to profl. jours. Patentee in field. Office: 576 Standard Ave Richmond CA 94802

THOMAS, KEITH RICHARD, marketing company executive; b. San Francisco, Feb. 11, 1953; s. Richard Cody and Janet Marie (Cope) T.; m. Marcia Hatch, Apr. 15, 1978; children—Cody Shipley, Adam Hatch. B.A. in Mktg., San Francisco State U., 1977. Pres. Joint Connection, San Francisco, 1971-73; ptnr. Pereira, Thomas & Assocs., San Francisco, 1973-78; pres. Keith R. Thomas and Co., Inc., San Francisco and N.Y.C., 1978—; cons. on internat mktg. Bd. dirs. Jr. Achievement of Bay Area, Inc. Mem. Am. Advt. Fedn. (nat. chmn. 1977-78) Sales and Mktg. Execs. Assn., Am. Mktg. Assn., San Francisco Advt. Club. Republican. Presbyterian. Club: San Francisco Press. Home: 1049 Pine Ln Lafayette CA 94549 Office: 153 Maiden Ln San Francisco CA 94108 also 15 Maiden Ln Suite 1500 New York NY 10038

THOMAS, LINDA IRENE, accounting executive; b. Seattle, Mar. 14, 1944; d. Donald and Lavada Irene (Doran) Craig; m. Robert Keith Reed Jr., Jan. 9, 1968; m. 2d, Alfred Richard Thomas, Feb. 16, 1972; children—Yvonne Michelle, Sherri Ellen. Student U. Wash., 1962, Tacoma Community Coll., 1968-78. Acctg. clk. Steven Motor Co., Tacoma, 1967-68; office mgr., rate clk. Tacoma Moving and Storage, 1969-72; dist. acct. Fife (Wash.) Sch. Dist., 1973-76; staff acct. Nelson, Johnson & Barlow, Federal Way, Wash., 1976-78; pres. Thomas Acctg. and Bookkeeping Services Inc., Gig Harbor, Wash., 1978—; tchr. SBA classes area community colls. Mem. adv. bd. Steilacoom High Sch.; bd. dirs. Tacoma Area Coalition Individuals with Disabilities. Mem. Home Builders Assn. Tacoma (chmn. edn. com., mem. legis. and membership service coms.), Tacoma C. of C. (energy task force), Puget Sound Mgrs. Council (past pres.), Nat. Accts. Assn., Nat. Assn. Female Execs., Greater Gig Harbor Bus. Assn., Nat. Fedn. Ind. Bus., Assn. Wash. Bus., LWV, University Place C. of C. (bd. dirs.). Democrat. Author: Payroll Taxes without Tears, 1981. Office: 7108A Pioneer Way W Gig Harbor WA 98335

THOMAS, LYNDIE MCHENRY, association executive; b. Corvallis, Oreg., Nov. 3, 1951; d. Walter B. and Lillian (Hosken) McHenry. B.S. in Anthropology, U. Calif.-Santa Barbara, 1974. Office mgr. Blue Ribbon Services, San Diego, 1976-77; med. asst. San Diego, 1977-78; office mgr. Ellsworth Harrold Co., Sacramento, 1978-79; ops. mgr. C. Brent Scott & Assocs., Sacramento, 1979-81; bus. mgr., exec. dir. Am. Soc. Enologists, Davis, Calif., 1981—, bd. dirs. ex-officio. Office: PO Box 411 Davis CA 95617

THOMAS, MARY RITA, nutritionist; b. Elizabethtown, Ky., Jan. 19, 1949; d. Francis Bruno and Mary Rosalene (McCamish) T. B.S., Eastern Ky. U., 1971; M.S., Purdue U., 1972, Ph.D., 1975. Asst. prof. nutrition and food sci. Tex. Woman's U., Denton, 1975-78; research asst. prof. dept. pediatrics U. Utah, 1980—, asst. prof. Coll. Health, 1978-81, assoc. prof., 1981—; vis. prof. Baylor Coll. Medicine, 1981—. Gen. Foods Co. fellow, 1973; David Ross predoctoral fellow, 1974; David P. Gardner research fellow, 1982. Mem. Am. Inst. Nutrition, Am. Soc. Clin. Nutrition, Am. Dietetics Assn., Soc. Nutrition Edn., Nat. Nutrition Consortium, Utah Nutrition Council pres. 1980-81), Sigma Xi. Democrat. Roman Catholic. Author papers in field. Clin. work in teenage pregnancy and lactation, also high risk infants. Office: HPER N-239 Univ Utah Salt Lake City UT 84112

THOMAS, OWEN FOSTER, physicist; b. Cave City, Ky., June 18, 1926; s. Warren and Ruth Katherine (Van Nort) T.; A.B., San Francisco State Coll., 1955; m. Nina LaRaye Williams, June 19, 1949; children—Zane, Vanc, Teri; m. 2d, Margaret E. Atkey, Feb. 14, 1973. Physicist, Naval Undersea Center, San Diego, 1955-77, sr. physicist, 1959-77; pres. Hetero-Sapiens, Inc., La Jolla, Calif., 1975—; sec. Vanlumar Corp., Los Angeles, 1974—. Served with AUS, 1943-46. Patentee digital camera. Home: 1949 Hypatia Way La Jolla CA 92037

THOMAS, PEGGY RUTH, railroad exec.; b. Granite, Okla., Dec. 19, 1933; d. Sidney Durrell and Ruth Mae (Tuley) Coffman; student U. Okla., 1951-52, Southwestern State Coll., Okla., 1952-53; m. Donald Edward Thomas, Feb. 26, 1969; children—Gene Lowell Gustafson, Richard Lynn Gustafson. Procurement specialist U.S. Air Force, Altus AFB, Okla., 1953-55, contract specialist, 1962-66; procurement specialist U.S. Air Force, Dyess AFB, Tex., 1955-58, Clinton-Sherman AFB, Okla., 1960-61, chief supply procurement br. Altus AFB, Okla. and Mountain Home AFB, Idaho, 1966-71; dep. chief base procurement div. Mountain Home AFB, 1972-76, chief services and constrn. contracts div. Alaskan Air Command, Elmendorf AFB, Alaska, 1976-78; chief contracting and gen. services div. U.S. Fish and Wildlife Service, Anchorage, 1978-79; chief purchasing div. Municipality of Anchorage, 1979; mgr. supply and procurement div. Alaska R.R., Anchorage, 1979—. Recipient Air Force Civilian Service award, 1966, 75; Air Force Incentive award, 1967, 72; Air Force Cert. of Achievement for Resources Conservation, 1968, 75, 76; Military Airlift Command Personal Achievement award, 1971; Tactical Air Command Personal Achievement award, 1973; Gov.'s Disting. Public Service award State of Idaho, 1973; nat. program award for Keeping Am. Beautiful, 1973. Mem. Nat. Assn. Female Execs., Am. Bus. Women's Assn., Nat. Fedn. Bus. and Profl. Women, Fed. Exec. Assn. Home: Star Route A Box 85T Anchorage AK 99507 Office: Supply Management Division Alaska Railroad Pouch 7-2111 Anchorage AK 99510

THOMAS, RICHARD CRAWFORD, configuration mgmt. engr.; b. Washington, May 14, 1930; s. Walter Austin and Stella (Crawford) T.; B.S. in Bus. Adminstrn., U. Fla., 1952; grad. numerous USAF schs.; cert. configuration mgmt. George Washington U., 1973; m. Martha Barrington, Dec. 22, 1952; children—Terry Lee, Richard Crawford, Steve Craig. Commd. 2d lt. USAF, 1952, advanced through grades to lt. col., 1968; service in Japan, Korea, Thailand, Spain; ret., 1972; configuration mgmt. engr. Raytheon Corp., Arlington, Va., 1973-79; div. configuration mgr. Ordnance div. FMC Corp., San Jose, Calif., 1980—. Decorated Meritorious Service medal, Air medal with 2 oak leaf clusters, Air Force Commendation medal. Mem. AIAA, Res. Officers Assn., Ret. Officers Assn., Phi Kappa Phi. Republican. Presbyterian. Office: 1105 Coleman Ave San Jose CA 95112

THOMAS, RICHARD VAN, justice Wyo. Supreme Ct.; b. Superior, Wyo., Oct. 11, 1932; s. John William and Gertrude M. (McCloskey) T.; B.S. with honors in Bus. Adminstrn., U. Wyo., 1954, LL.B. with honors, 1956; postgrad. N.Y. U. Sch. Law, 1956-57, LL.M. in Taxation, 1961; m. Lesley Arlene Ekman, June 23, 1956; children—Tara Lynn, Richard Ross, Laura Lee, Sidney Marie. Admitted to Wyo. bar, 1956, U.S. Supreme Ct. bar, 1960, U.S. Ct. Appeals for 10th circuit, 1960; teaching fellow N.Y. U. Sch. Law, 1956-57; law clk. to judge 10th Circuit Ct. Appeals, 1960-63; asso. firm Hirst & Applegate, Cheyenne, Wyo., 1963-64; partner firm Hirst, Applegate & Thomas, Cheyenne, 1964-69; U.S. atty. Dist. Wyo., Cheyenne, 1969-75; justice Wyo. Supreme Ct., 1975—. Chmn., Laramie County Health Planning Commn., 1980—; vestryman Episcopal Ch., sr. warden, 1973-75, exec. council Episcopal Diocese of Wyo., 1970—, diocesan chancellor, 1972—, lay dep. gen. conv., 1973—, chmn. search evaluation nomination com., 1976-77, lay reader, 1965—; pres. Laramie County (Wyo.) United Way, 1972, trustee, 1973-74, chmn., 1973; bd. dirs. Community Action Laramie County, 1977-82, Goodwill Industries of Wyo., Inc., 1974-77; chmn. Cheyenne dist. council Boy Scouts Am., 1977-79, pres. Longs Peak council, 1981—, mem. Nat. council, 1982—, v.p. membership/relationships, 1979—; mem. exec. com. Crusade for Christ, Cheyenne, 1974; bd. dirs. Cheyenne Youth for Christ, 1978-81. Served with JAGC, USAF, 1957-60. Named Civil Servant of Yr., Cheyenne Assn. Govt. Employees, 1973; Vol. of Yr., Cheyenne Office of Youth Alternatives, 1979; Boss of Yr., Nat. Secs. Assn., 1974; St. George Episcopal award, 1982. Mem. Am., Fed., Laramie County bar assns., Wyo. State Bar, Phi Kappa Phi, Omicron Delta Kappa, Sigma Nu. Lodges: Masons (33 deg.; past master), Shriners, Nat. Sojourners, Kiwanis (disting. pres. 1980-81, program com. 1969-70, dir. 1970-72, chmn. Key Club com. 1973-76). Office: Supreme Ct Bldg Cheyenne WY 82002

THOMAS, ROBERT BRUCE, advertising agency executive; b. Santa Monica, Calif., Apr. 2, 1951; s. Clifton Bruce and Zedna Virginia (Chapman) T.; m. Donna Marie Tonini, July 3, 1971 (div.); 1 son, Christopher Kalo. Ptnr. Cliff Assocs., Los Angeles, 1973-77; account exec. Boylhart, Lovett & Dean, Los Angeles, 1977-80; pres. Robert B. Thomas & Assocs., Los Angeles, 1980—. Mem. Los Angeles Advt. Club, Bus. Profl. Advt. Assn. (dir. Los Angeles chpt.), Western States Advt. Agy. Assn. Office: 2330 W 3d St Los Angeles CA 90057

THOMAS, ROBERT CHESTER, sculptor, art educator; b. Wichita, Kans., Apr. 19, 1924; s. Chester and Alma (Mead) T.; m. Eleanor Louise Brand, July 15, 1944; children—Robin Louise, Elizabeth Catherine. Studies with Ossip Zadkine, Paris, 1948-49; B.A., U. Calif.-Santa Barbara, 1951; M.F.A., Calif. Coll. Arts and Crafts, 1952. Prof. sculpture U. Calif., Santa Barbara, 1954—, executed life size bronze figure U. Calif., Santa Barbara, 1967, sculpture J. Magnin store, Century City, 1966, fountain, Montecito, 1968; represented in permanent collection Hirshhorn Mus., Washington, Whatcom Mus., Bellingham, Wash., Santa Barbara Mus., U. Calif., Santa Barbara. Served with USAAF, 1943-46; ETO. Recipient Bronze medal City of Los Angeles, 1949, Silver medal Calif. State Fair, 1954. Home: 38 San Mateo Ave Goleta CA 93117 Office: Dept Art U Calif Santa Barbara CA 93106

THOMAS, ROBERT EDWIN, ecumenical executive, clergyman; b. Cleve., Apr. 23, 1937; s. Reese E. and Ruth Augusta (Rossow) T.; m. Judith Ann Milano, May 27; children—Christopher Agape, Stephen Davar, Teresa Adonai. Student U.S. Mil. Acad., 1956-60; A.B., Boston U., 1961; B.D., Oberlin Coll., 1966; M.Div., Vanderbilt U., 1973; postgrad. United Theol. Sem., 1970-76. Ordained to ministry United Ch. of Christ, 1966. Pastor Highland Congregational Ch., Cleve., 1966-70; chaplain St. Paul (Minn.) Council of Chs., 1970-76; coordinator Dakota County (Minn.) Mental Health Ctr., 1976-78; pastor St. Paul's United Ch. of Christ, Sidney, Ohio, 1978-82; exec. Wyo. Ch. Coalition, Casper, 1982—. Mem. Am. Assn. Clin. Pastoral Edn., Nat. Assn. Ecumenical Staff. Club: Kiwanis. Author: Offenders Commentary (in Greek and English), 1976. Office: 1601 S Melrose Casper WY 82601

THOMAS, ROGER PARRY, interior designer, art consultant; b. Salt Lake City, Nov. 4, 1951; s. E. Parry and Peggy Chatterton T.; m. Marilyn Harris Hite, Nov. 21, 1976 (div. Apr. 1979); m. H. Andrea Wahn, Nov. 20, 1982. Student Interlochen Arts Acad., 1969; B.F.A., Tufts U., 1975. Pres. Miller-Thomas, Inc., Las Vegas, 1975-77; v.p. Yates-Silverman, Inc., Las Vegas, 1976-81; exec. designer Golden Nugget Hotels, Atlandia Design and Furnishings, Inc., Las Vegas, 1981—. Treas. bd. trustees Nev. Mus. Fine Art; bd. dirs. Nev. Dance Theatre, Wheelwright Mus., Santa Fe. Republican. Mem. Ch. of Jesus Christ of Latter-day Saints. Clubs: Sporting House, Country (Las Vegas). Office: 3380 Arville St Las Vegas NV 89102

THOMAS, SAMUEL FINLEY, physician; b. Paris, France, Oct. 2, 1913 (parents Am. citizens); s. Edward Russell and Elisabeth (Finley) T.; A.B., Princeton, 1935; M.D., Columbia, 1940; m. Ruth Larson, May 21, 1976; 1 dau. by previous marriage, Susan Faith. Intern St. Lukes Hosp., N.Y.C., 1940-41, resident 1941-42, Neurol. Inst. N.Y., 1942-43; practice medicine specializing in neurology and psychiatry, N.Y.C., 1946—; mem. staff Neurol. Inst., N.Y.C., 1946—, attending neurologist, 1975-80, cons. emeritus, 1980—, clin. prof. neurology, 1975-80; mem. staff St. Luke's Hosp., N.Y.C., 1946-80, attending physician neurology, 1955-80, attending psychiatrist, 1975; cons. physician and psychiatrist emeritus, 1980—. Served to maj., M.C., USAAF, 1943-46. Mem. A.M.A., N.Y. County Med. Soc., Am. Psychiat. Assn., N.Y. Neurol. Soc., N.Y. Acad. Medicine. Republican. Episcopalian. Clubs: Ambassador Athletic (Salt Lake City); Am. Alpine (N.Y.C.); Wasatch Mountain (Salt Lake City). Contbr. articles to med. jours., poetry to popular mags. and newspapers. Address: 123 2d Ave Salt Lake City UT 84103

THOMAS, SANDRA ELAINE WILSON, engineer; b. Kansas City, Kans., Feb. 11, 1943; d. Harry and Aline (Sloan) Jackson; B.A. in Bus., Kansas City Jr. Coll., 1962; B.G.S. in Psychology, U. Kans., 1979, B.S. in Bus. Law, 1964; m. A.D. Thomas; children—Vincent Charles, Michael DeWayne. Fgn. affairs supr. Nat. Bellas Hess Inc., Kansas City, Mo., 1962-63; file clk. AT&T, Kansas City, 1963-64, mktg. asso., 1964-66, sr. engring. clk., 1966-69, sr. engring. asso., 1970-79; circuit designer Pacific Tel. & Tel., Los Angeles, 1979—. Mem. Pasadena (Calif.) Sch. Bd., 1979-82; mem. women's aux. Pasadena Boys' Club, 1979-82; chairperson Pasadena/Altadena Consol. Funding Bd., 1978-81; music coordinator Lincoln Ave. Baptist Ch., Pasadena, 1980—, youth counselor, 1980—. Recipient cert. United Way Calif., Pasadena Sch. Bd. Mem. Profl. Women Calif., Exec. Females Am., Nat. Assn. Female Execs. Democrat. Club: Daus. of Elks. Home: 95 W Calaveras Altadena CA 91001 Office: 3525 W 8th St Los Angeles CA 90005

THOMAS, SCOTT ALAN, electronics company executive; b. Quincy, Mass., Apr. 21, 1947; s. Philip Brewster and Ruth Jeanne T.; B.S., U. Detroit, 1969; M.B.A., Eastern Mich. U., 1973; m. Robyn Celeste Geffel, Aug. 1, 1981; children—Zachary David, Jennifer Robin. Br. mgr. Gen. Electric Co., Detroit, 1968-72; mgr. cost budget and planning Xerox Corp., Ann Arbor, Mich., 1974-75; program control mgr., contract adminstr. Ford Aerospace and Communications, Palo Alto, Calif., 1975-78; group controller Signetics Corps., Sunnyvale, Calif., 1978-79; corp. controller, asst. treas. Siltec Corp., Menlo Park, Calif., 1979-81;

chief fin. officer, v.p. fin. and adminstrn. Fortune Systems, Belmont, Calif., 1981—; dir. Fortune Internat. Corp., Fortune Internat. Sales Corp., Fortune GmbH, Fortune, Ltd. Mem. Am. Electronics Assn., Am. Mgmt. Assn., Fin. Execs. Inst. Republican. Home: 75 Joaquin Rd Portola Valley CA 94025 Office: 300 Harbor Blvd Belmont CA 94002

THOMAS, TAMARA B., fine arts consultant; b. Oakland, Calif., July 24, 1940; d. Bruce E. and Elaine (Hudspeth) Eldridge; m. Hardy L. Thomas, May 20, 1972; 1 dau., Tara. Student U. Calif.-Berkeley, 1957-61. Founder, pres. Fine Arts Services, Inc., Los Angeles, 1971—, Fine Arts Assocs., Inc., 1975—. Trustee, Inst. Art and Urban Resources, N.Y.C., 1980; mem. exec. com. dean's council UCLA Grad. Sch. Architecture and Urban Planning. Mem. Assn. Profl. Art Advisers (founding, dir.). Office: 107 S Irving Blvd Los Angeles CA 90004

THOMAS, TERESA ANN, biologist, educator, consultant; b. Wilkes-Barre, Pa., Oct. 17, 1939; d. Sam Charles and Edna Grace Thomas. B.S. cum laude, Coll. Misericordia, 1961; M.S. in Biology, Am. U. Beirut, 1965; M.S. in Microbiology, U. So. Calif., 1973. Tchr., sci. supr., curriculum coordinator Meyers High Sch., Wilkes-Barre, 1962-64, Wilkes-Barre Area Public Schs., 1961-66; research asso. Proctor Found. for Research in Ophthalmology U. Calif. Med. Center, San Francisco, 1966-68; instr. Robert Coll. of Istanbul (Turkey), 1968-71, Am. Edn. in Luxembourg, 1971-72, Bosco Tech. Inst., Rosemead, Calif., 1973-74, San Diego Community Coll. Dist., 1974-80; instr. natural/social sci. div. Southwestern Coll., Chula Vista, Calif., 1980—, chmn.-elect acad. senate, 1983-84; adj. asst. prof. Chapman Coll., San Diego, 1974-83; asst. prof. San Diego State U., 1977-79; chmn. Am. Colls. Istanbul Sci. Week, 1969-71; mem. adv. bd. Chapman Coll. Community Center, 1979-80. Pres. Internat. Relations Club 1959-61; mem. San Francisco World Affairs Council, 1966-68; mem. exec. bd. U.S. Orgn. Med. and Ednl. Needs No. Calif., 1967-68; chmn. land use, energy and wildlife com. Congressman Duncan Hunter's Environ. Adv. Council, 1982—. NSF fellow, 1965; USPHS fellow, 1972-73; Pa. Heart Assn. research grantee, 1962. Mem. Am. Soc. Microbiology, Nat. Sci. Tchrs. Assn. (internat. com.), Nat. Assn. Biology Tchrs. San Diego Natural History Mus., S.D. Zool. Soc., Calif. Tchrs. Assn., NEA, MENSA, Arab Am. Med. Assn., Arab Am. Univ. Grads., San Diego Ecology Center, Am.-Lebanese Assn. San Diego (chmn. scholarship com.), Kappa Gamma Pi (pres. Wilkes-Barre chpt. 1963-64, San Francisco chpt. 1967-68), Sigma Phi Sigma. Club: Am. Lebanese Syrian Ladies (pres. 1982-84). Office: Southwestern College 900 Otay Lakes Rd Chula Vista CA 92010

THOMAS, WILLIAM JENNINGS, physician, pub. health adminstr.; b. Washington County, Va., Dec. 1, 1930; s. William W. and Novella (Eden) T.; B.S., Emory and Henry Coll., 1952; M.D., U. Va., 1956; m. Shirley Mae Conway, Sept. 14, 1954; children—Cheryl Wynne, William Jennings, Sharon Lynn, Douglas Eugene. Intern Watts Hosp., Durham, N.C., 1956-57; pub. health trainee Va. Dept. Health, 1959, dist. health dir., 1959-62; practice medicine specializing in preventive medicine and pub. health, Virgilina, Va., 1962-63, Flagstaff, Ariz., 1963—; mem. clin. staff Flagstaff Community Hosp., 1963-68, cons. staff pub. health and preventive medicine, 1968—; dir. Coconino County (Ariz.) Dept. Pub. Health, Flagstaff, 1967—; asst. coordinator Ariz. Regional Med. Program, 1969-73; mem. Ariz. State Cervical Cancer Screening Adv. Council, 1974-75. Mem. social health adv. council Flagstaff Pub. Schs., 1970-73; Gov.'s Emergency Med. Service Com., Ariz., 1968-73, Ariz. Alcoholism Adv. Com., 1972-75, Ariz. Family Planning Adv. Council, 1970-72; mem. child services mgmt. No. Ariz. U., 1976—; bd. dirs. Coconino Council on Alcoholism, 1971-72, No. Ariz. Comprehensive Guidance Centers, Inc., 1969-70, No. Ariz. Med. Evaluation Systems, 1980; bd. govs. No. Ariz. Health Systems Agy., 1979—. Served to lt. M.C., USN, 1957-59, to comdr. M.C., Res., 1959-80; col. Army N.G., 1980—. Fellow Am. Acad. Family Physicians, Royal Soc. Health; mem. Am., Ariz. med. assns., Coconino County Med. Soc., Am., Ariz. pub. health assns., Am., Ariz. acads. family physicians, Ariz. Health Officers Assn., Flagstaff C. of C. (mem. sci. and environ. adv. com. 1971). Methodist. Elk. Home: 2045 N Crescent Dr Flagstaff AZ 86001 Office: 2500 N Fort Valley Rd Flagstaff AZ 86001

THOMAS, WILLIAM M., congressman; b. Wallace, Idaho, Dec. 6, 1941; s. Virgil and Gertrude (White) T.; A.A., Santa Ana Community Coll., 1961; B.A., San Francisco State U., 1963; M.A., 1965; m. Sharon Lynn Hamilton, 1967; children—Christopher, Amelia. Prof. polit. sci. Bakersfield (Calif.) Coll., 1965-74; mem. Calif. Assembly, 1974-78, sec. Republican Caucus, 1974-76; mem. 96th Congress from 18th Dist. Calif., 98th Congress from 20th Dist. Calif. Chmn., Kern County (Calif.) Rep. Central Com., 1973; mem. Calif. Rep. Central Com., 1972—; bd. dirs. San Joaquin chpt. March of Dimes. Mem. Calif. Tchrs. Assn., Calif. State Employees Assn. Office: 324 Cannon House Office Bldg Washington DC 20515

THOMAS, WILLIAM (WILL) ELWOOD, newspaper editor; b. Willows, Calif., Feb. 5, 1932; s. Ralph E. and Bertha A. (Adam) T.; B.S. in Agrl. Journalism, Calif. State Poly. U., 1956; m. Nancy Rae Eisenbeiss, Aug. 27, 1955; children—William Scott, Brian Edward, Bradley Westlund, Karen Jessica. Reporter, Merced (Calif.) Sun-Star, 1956-57; patrolman-clk. Willows (Calif.) Police Dept., 1957-58; staff announcer, news dir. KHSL-TV and Radio Sta., Chico, Calif., 1958-60; editor Lakeport (Calif.) Record-Bee, 1960-66, North County Publs., San Mateo Times Newspaper Group, South San Francisco, 1966—. Active San Mateo council Boy Scouts Am., 1970-71; pres. Benjamin Franklin Jr. High Sch. PTA, 1971-72, del. state conv., 1971, 76; pres. Broadmoor Property Owners Assn., 1976-77. Served with U.S. Army, 1953-55. Recipient Hon. Service award Jefferson Council of PTA, 1976. Mem. Peninsula Press Club, South San Francisco C. of C. (bd. dirs.). Republican. Home: 723 87th St Colma CA 94015 Office: 1331 San Mateo Ave South San Francisco CA 94080

THOMASON, BURKE CURTIS, sociology educator; b. Aberdeen, Wash., Mar. 4, 1943; s. Karl M. and Helen E. (Hansen) T.; m. Sharon F. Backer, July 6, 1964; children—Cal M., Aaron J. B.A., U. Oreg., 1967; M.A., Simon Fraser U., 1970; D.Phil., U. Sussex, 1978. Instr. continuing edn. in sociology U. B.C., 1970; asst. prof. sociology Eastern Oreg. State Coll., La Grande, 1970-79, assoc. prof., 1979—, coordinator program of student-initiated courses, dir. honors program, 1972-74. Mem. adv. bd. Union County Mental Health Services, 1973-76. Mem. Internat. Sociol. Assn., Am. Sociol. Assn., Soc. for Study of Symbolic Interaction, Soc. for Phenomenology and Human Studies, Brit. Soc. for Phenomenology. Author: Making Sense of Reification: Alfred Schutz and Constructionist Theory, 1982. Home: 1207 Oak St La Grande OR 97850 Office: Eastern Oreg State Coll 8th and K Aves La Grande OR 97850

THOMASON, IVAN JAMES, nematologist, educator, agricultural research scientist; b. Burney, Calif., June 27, 1925; s. Boris John and Ellen Carolina (Greer) T.; m. Harriet Braun, Dec. 21, 1950; children—David, Eric, Alan, Martha, Will. B.S. in Plant Sci., U. Calif., 1950; M.S. in Plant Pathology, U. Wis., 1952, Ph.D. in Plant Pathology, 1954. Research asst. dept. plant pathology U. Wis., 1950-54; asst. and assoc. nematologist U. Calif.-Riverside, 1954—, chmn. dept. nematology, 1962-68; asst. dir., pest mgmt. program dir. Coop. Extension, U. Calif. Div. Agr., 1976-81; dir. U. Calif. statewide integrated pest mgmt. project, 1980-82; cons. U.S. Dept. Agr., U.S. AID, pest mgmt. SE Asia, 1971; mem. U.S. Dept. Agr. sponsored revs. plant pathology programs Cornell U., Tex. A&M U., U. Ariz. Tucson. Active Common Cause. Served with C.E. U.S. Army, 1943-46. Fellow Soc. Nematologists; mem. Am. Phytopathol. Soc., Soc. Nematologists, European Soc. Nematologists, Sigma Xi, Alpha Zeta. Democrat. Congregationalist. Clubs: University (Riverside), Kiwanis. Contbr. sci. papers to profl. publs. Office: Dept Nematology U Calif Riverside CA 92521

THOMASON, STEPHEN CLYDE, unemployment/workers compensation cons.; b. Ft. Lupton, Colo., June 3, 1947; s. Max J. and Dora C. (Priest) T.; B. Asso. Computer Sci., Colo. State U., 1965; B.A., Metro. State Coll., 1967, postgrad. 1967-77; m. Nancy Dittmer, Sept. 20, 1963; children—John, William, Thomas. Clk., State of Colo., Div. Employment, Denver, 1966-67, mgr. computer ops., 1967-74, chief unemployment ins. tax, 1974-75, chief unemployment ins. benefits, 1975-77; with Employers Unity, Inc., Westminster, Colo., 1977—, now chief exec. officer. Colo. state lobbyist. Recipient Testimony of Achievement, State of Colo., 1977. Democrat. Baptist. Clubs: Masons, Shriners. Home: 7521 Meade Way Westminster CO 80030 Office: PO Box 782 Westminster CO 80030

THOMASON, TOM WILLIAM, artist/jeweler, gallery operator; b. Shawnee, Okla., Oct. 28, 1934; s. William Wesley and Ogreta (Fox) T.; m. Celia Jo Failor. B.F.A., U. N.Mex., Albuquerque. Artist/jeweler, 1963—; mgr. Studio Gallery, fine arts, crafts, 1963-79; adv. to Zuni Indian Crafts Co-op, 1968-69, 1970-73; instr. in jewelry, New Mex. U. Community Coll., 1969-74; crafts adv. to Nat. Endowment Arts, 1972; owner, operator Studio of Tom W. Thomason; cons.-lectr. on designing and making jewelry, art gallery ops. Served in USN, 1953-57. Decorated Korean medal. Recipient award Craftsman of N.Mex., 1966, 68, Corrales Art Assn., 1965, 66, Tulsa Gallery Fine Arts, 1973, N.Mex. Contemporary Crafts, 1973; grantee Am. Specialist Abroad (Madagascar), 1973. Mem. World Crafts Council, Albuquerque Gallery Assn., Am. Crafts Council, N. Mex. Crafts Council. Democrat. Uniterarian. Clubs: Masons, Rosicrucian Order. Designer fountain, Albert Ussery Home, Albuquerque. Home/Gallery-Studio: 615 16th NW Albuquerque NM 87104

THOMPSEN, DOLORES IRENE, educator; b. Murray, Utah, Mar. 6, 1935; d. Walter Delbert and Afton Irene (Ronneburg) Jensen; B.S., U. Utah, 1970; m. Fergus C. Thompsen, Nov. 6, 1953; children—Pamela, Byron, Candace, Elizabeth. Jewelry examiner O.C. Tanner Co., 1953-54; tchr. schs. in Utah, 1970-73; tchr. home econs. West High Sch., Salt Lake City, 1973—. Pres., Young Women's Mut. Assn., Kearns, Utah, 1963-66, 72-73; chmn. fin. com. Mormon Ch., Kearns, 1980-81. Grantee U. Utah. Mem. Am. Home Econs. Assn., Am. Vocat. Assn., Utah Tchrs. Assn., Utah Home Econs. Assn., Utah Vocat. Assn., Salt Lake Tchrs. Assn. Republican. Author curriculum guides. Home: 4421 West 5480 S Kearns UT 84118 Office: 241 North 3d W Salt Lake City UT 84103

THOMPSON, ANNE MARIE, newspaper publisher; b. Des Moines, Feb. 7, 1920; d. George Horace and Esther Mayer Sheely; m. J. Ross Thompson, July 31, 1949; children—Annette McOracken, James Ross, Dana Hipp. B.A., U. Iowa, 1940; postgrad. U. Colo., 1971. Co-pub. Baca County Banner, Springfield, Colo., 1951-54; pub. Rocky Ford (Colo.) Daily Gazette, 1954—. Mem. Colo. Ho. of Reps., 1957-61; Colo. presdl. elector, 1972; chmn. Colo. adv. com. SBA, 1979-81. Recipient Community Service award Rocky Ford C. of C., 1975; named Colo. Woman of Achievement in Journalism, 1959; Colo. Bus. Person of Yr., Future Bus. Leaders of Am., 1981; elected to Colo. Community Journalism Hall of Fame, 1981. Mem. Nat. Fedn. Press Women (dir. 1971-81), Nat. Newspaper Assn., Inland Daily Press Assn., Colo. Press Assn. (dir. 1981-83), Colo. Press Women, PEO, Bus. and Profl. Women's Club, AAUW. Republican. Methodist.

THOMPSON, BRUCE RUTHERFORD, judge; b. Reno, July 31, 1911; s. Reuben Cyril and Mabel (McLeran) T.; A.B., U. Nev., 1932; LL.B., Stanford, 1936; m. Frances Ellen Creek, Sept. 11, 1938; children—Jeffrey, Judith, Harold. Admitted to Nev. bar, 1936; since practiced in Reno; asst. U.S. atty. Dist. Nev., 1942-52; spl. master U.S. Dist. Ct., Reno, 1952-53; U.S. dist. judge Dist. Nev., Reno, 1963—. Mem. Nev. State Planning Bd., 1959—, chmn., 1960-61. Regent, U. Nev. Mem. Am. Judicature Soc. (dir.), Am. Bar Assn., Bar of Nev., Am. Coll. Trial Lawyers, Am. Law Inst., Alpha Tau Omega. Democrat. Baptist. Elk. Home: 1550 Plumb Ln Reno NV 89502 Office: Fed Bldg 300 Booth St Reno NV 89109

THOMPSON, BRYAN EARNEST, JR., communications/electronics firm exec.; b. Kansas City Mo., Nov. 23, 1922; s. Bryan Earnest and Odia May (Gibson) T.; m. Margie Louise Ware, May 6, 1944. Student Wichita State U., 1959; Mgr. contracts adminstrn. LTV, Dallas, 1955-61; mgr. contracts adminstrn. ITT/VAFB Projects, Calif., 1961-70; pres., chmn. board, chief exec. officer Quintron Systems, Inc., Santa Maria, Calif., 1970—; dir. Mesa Microwave, Inc.; pres., chief exec. officer MTM Contractor Assocs., Quintron Telephone System, Quintron Internat. Corp. Names Small Bus. Prime Contractor of Yr. SBA, 1976. Mem. AIAA, Am. Mgmt. Assn., Santa Maria C. of C., Santa Maria Valley Developers. Clubs: Masons, Elks.

THOMPSON, CHARLES EDWARD, avionics exec.; b. Memphis, Jan. 3, 1933; s. Robert Henry and Nellie Agnes (Johns) T.; m. Beverly Ann Aughey, Sept. 1, 1951; children—Valerie Lynn Hall, Stephanie Lee Hanners. B.S., Tulane U., 1954; B.S. in Aero. Engring., Naval Postgrad. Sch., 1966; M.B.A., Auburn U., 1973. Commd. 2d lt. U.S. Marine Corps, 1954; advanced through grades to col., 1976; ret., 1981; prodn. mgr. comml. div. Sperry Flight Systems, Phoenix, 1981—. Mem. adv. bd. Ariz. Vietnam Vets. Leadership Program Inc.; speaker Full Gospel Businessmen's Fellowship Internat. Decorated Legion of Merit, Air medal with gold star, Purple Heart, others. Mem. AIAA (chmn. tech. com. aerospace maintenance), Am. Helicopter Soc., Marine Corps Assn. Republican. Mem. Assembly of God Ch. Contbr. articles to tech. jours. Home: 205 E Acapulco Ln Phoenix AZ 85022 Office: 21111 N 19th Ave Phoenix AZ 85027

THOMPSON, CHARLES HILARY, JR., helicopter manufacturing co. exec.; b. Englewood, N.J., Jan. 6, 1939; m. Mercedes Arisso, June 8, 1960; children—Lynmarie Kim, Mark Randall. B.S. in Engring., Air Force Acad., 1960; M.S. in Aero. Engring., U. Colo., 1968; M.B.A., Calif. State U., 1975. Commd. 2d lt. U.S. Air Force, 1960, advanced through grades to lt. col., 1976; pilot, strategic airlift aircraft comdr., ops. staff officer, 1960-66; test-devel. mgr., program mgr. H-53 and Pave Low project Air Force Helicopter Systems, 1968-72; engring. mgr. Air Force Contract Mgmt. div. Hughes Aircraft Co., Culver City, Calif., 1972-76; project mgr., developer automated info. mgmt. techniques for systems acquisition, Space Shuttle Program Office, USAF Space Div., 1976-80; ret., 1980; spl. asst. to v.p. materiel for advanced attack helicopter, project mgr. AH-64A prodn. program Hughes Helicopters, Inc., Culver City, 1980—; guest lectr. project planning and control systems UCLA, Los Alamos Sci. Labs., 1979-80. Decorated Legion of Merit, Air medal, Air Force Commendation medal. Recipient Best Paper award Air Force Mgmt. Info. Seminar, 1979. Mem. Am. Helicopter Soc., Project Mgmt. Inst., AIAA, Am. Mgmt. Assn., Am. Security Council. Author: (monograph) Evolving Acquisition Information Management Systems, 1979. Office: Hughes Helicopters Inc Centinela and Teale Sts Culver City CA 90230

THOMPSON, DANIEL EMERSON, vending company executive; b. Fairbanks, Alaska, Jan. 24, 1947; s. George Edmond and Emma Jean (Burns) T.; student U. Notre Dame, 1965-67; m. Yvette C. Brazeau, Aug. 16, 1980. Vice-pres., dir. Polaris Investments, Fairbanks, 1969-72; v.p. Music, Inc., dba Alaska Music, Fairbanks, 1965, pres., dir., 1967-81, v.p., dir. Music Inc. dba TLC Vend and Alaska Music, 1981—; partner Thompson Investment Co., Fairbanks, 1976—. Bd. dirs. Alaska State Devel. Corp., 1970-82; bd. trustees Hipow. Recipient Cert. of Appreciation, Fairbanks Kiwanis, 1973. Mem. Nat. Automatic Merchandising Assn., Amusement and Music Operators Am., Alaska Retail Assn., N.W. Automatic Retailers Council (bd. govs.), Alaska Coin-Machine Assn. (sec.), Fairbanks C. of C. (mem. legislative com.). Roman Catholic. Club: Elks. Office: 1890 Marika St Fairbanks AK 99701 also 6136 MacKay St Anchorage AK 99502

THOMPSON, DAVID ALFRED, industrial engineer, educator; b. Chgo., Sept. 9, 1929; s. Clifford James and Christobel Eliza (Sawin) T.; B.M.E., U. Va., 1951; B.S. in Indsl. Engring., U. Fla., 1955, M.S. in Engring., 1956; Ph.D., Stanford U., 1961; children—Nancy, Brooke, Lynda, Diane, Kristy. Research asst. U. Fla. Engring. and Industries Expt. Sta., Gainesville, 1955-56; instr. indsl. engring. Stanford (Calif.) U., 1956-58, acting asst. prof., 1958-61, asst. prof., 1961-64, assoc. prof., 1964-72, prof., 1972—; asso. chmn. dept. indsl. engring., 1972-74; prin. investigator NASA Ames Research Center, Moffatt Field, Calif., 1974-76, 81-82; cons. U.S. Dept. State, fed. EEO Commn., major U.S. and fgn. cos.; cons. emergency communications center design Santa Clara County Criminal Justice Bd., 1975, Bay Area Rapid Transit Control Center, 1977. Served to lt. USN, 1951-54. HEW grantee, 1967-70; registered profl. engr., Calif. Mem. Am. Inst. Indsl. Engrs., Human Factors Soc., IEEE, Am. Soc. Info. Sci., MTM Assn. Standards and Research, Am. Robotics Soc., Soc. Info. Display. Dir., editor documentary film Rapid Answers for Rapid Transit, U.S. Dept. Transp., 1974; contbr. articles to profl. jours.; mem. editorial adv. bd. Computers and Graphics, 1970—; reviewer Indsl. Engring. and IEEE Transactions, 1972—. Home: PO Box 7606 Stanford CA 94305 Office: Dept Indsl Engring and Engring Mgmt Stanford U Stanford CA 94305

THOMPSON, DENNIS PETERS, plastic surgeon; b. Chgo., Mar. 18, 1937; s. David John and Ruth Dorothy (Peters) T.; B.S., U. Ill., 1957, B.S., Coll. Medicine, 1959, M.S., 1961, M.D., 1961; m. Virginia Louise Williams, June 17, 1961; children—Laura Faye, Victoria Ruth, Elizabeth Jan. Intern, Presbyn.-St. Lukes Hosp., Chgo., 1961-62; resident in gen. surgery Mayo Clinic, Rochester, Minn., 1964-66, fellow in gen. surgery, 1964-66; resident in gen. surgery Harbor Gen. Hosp., Los Angeles, 1968-70; resident in plastic surgery UCLA, 1971-73, clin. instr. plastic surgery, 1975-82, asst. clin. prof. surgery, 1982—; practice medicine specializing in plastic and reconstructive surgery, Los Angeles, 1974-78, Santa Monica, Calif., 1978—; mem. staff St. John's Hosp., Santa Monica Hosp., UCLA Ctr. Health Scis., Brotman Med. Ctr., chmn. dept. surgery Beverly Glen Hosp., 1978-79. Moderator, Congregational Ch. of Northridge (Calif.), 1975-76; pres. Coop. of Am. Physicians Credit Union, 1978-80. Am. Tobacco Inst. research grantee, 1959-60. Diplomate Am. Bd. Surgery, Am. Bd. Plastic Surgery. Fellow ACS; mem. AMA (Physicians Recognition award 1971, 74, 77, 81), Calif., Los Angeles County (sec.-tres. dist. 5, 1982-83), Pan-Pacific med. assns., Am., Calif., Los Angeles socs. plastic and reconstructive surgeons, Los Angeles Soc. Plastic Surgeons (sec. 1980-81, pres. 1982-83), Am. Soc. Aesthetic Plastic Surgery, Western Los Angeles Regional C. of C. (dir., chmn. legis. action com. 1979—), Santa Monica C. of C., Phi Beta Kappa, Alpha Omega Alpha, Nu Sigma Nu, Phi Kappa Phi. Republican. Contbr. articles to med. jours. Office: 2001 Santa Monica Blvd Santa Monica CA 90404

THOMPSON, DENNIS ROY, information management executive; b. Chgo., Apr. 11, 1939; s. Roy Gustav and Charlotte Rose (Schultz) T.; B.S. with honors in Elec. Engring., U. Ill., 1964; M.S. in Bus. Adminstrn., UCLA, 1967. Ops. research cons. Dart Industries, Los Angeles, 1969-70; pres. Seahill, Inc., Los Angeles, 1971-72; dir. credit analysis Comml. Credit Co., Balt., 1973-77; pres. Epicom, Inc., San Diego, 1978—. Sec., Annapolis (Md.) Libertarians, 1975. Served with U.S. Army, 1959-61. Mem. Ops. Research Soc. Am., Assn. Computing Machinery, Mensa. Patentee matchbook. Office: 3647 Fairmount Ave San Diego CA 92105

THOMPSON, DOROTHY A., educator; b. Lemmon, S.D., July 1, 1928; d. Alexander Noble and Mary (Gallagher) Thomson; B.A., U. Wash., 1951, secondary teaching certificate, 1954; postgrad. Western Wash. U., 1970-74; m. Theodore B. Thompson, Aug. 1, 1953; children—Sandi, Todd, Timothy. Tchr., Shelton Sch. Dist., 1951-52, Fed. Way Sch. Dist., Federal Way, Wash., 1952-57, Burlington-Edison (Wash.) Sch. Dist., 1971-78; substitute sch. tchr. Skagit County, Wash., 1979—. Coordinating chmn. Berry-Dairy Days, City of Burlington; mem. Community Accountability Bd.; councilwoman, City of Burlington (Wash.), 1970-74, 76-80, Bicentennial chmn., 1976; City of Burlington rep. to Skagit County Fair Bd., 1981-83. Mem. NEA, Wash. Edn. Assn., Burlington-Edison Edn. Assn. Home: 500 S Gardner Rd Burlington WA 98233 Office: 102 Pine St Burlington WA 98233

THOMPSON, DOYLE FRANKLIN, residential bldg. co. exec.; b. Cadiz, Ohio, Mar. 2, 1928; s. Doyle W. and Famie V. (Russell) T.; diploma archtl. design Chgo. Tech. Coll., 1949; m. Helen E. Law, Sept., 1949 (div. 1976); children—Gregory, Patricia, Sandra; m. 2d, Gloria Mae Boyd, Aug. 20, 1977. Draftsman, Ventura County, Calif., 1953-57, jr. civil engr., 1957, asst. civil engr., 1958, chief subdiv. engr., 1958-63; chief engr. Goldberg Devel. Co., 1963, Sanitation Inc., 1963; pres., co-propr. Madera Engring. & Planning Co., Simi Valley, Calif., 1963-66; v.p. Jensen & Thompson Assos., Simi Valley and Ventura, 1966-70; v.p. Los Angeles div. McKeon Constrn. Co., Thousand Oaks, Calif., 1970-72; v.p. W & B Builders, Inc., Santa Monica, Calif., 1972-78, exec. v.p., 1978-80, pres., 1980—; pres. Ventura County Employees Fed. Credit Union, 1962-63. Mem. adv. bd. Ventura County Flood Control Dist., 1966-72, chmn., 1970-72; chmn. Constrn. Bond Issue Dr., Simi Valley Dist., 1967; mem. Ventura County Grand Jury, 1969. Served with inf., U.S. Army, 1946-47. Recipient Carnegie Bronze Hero medal, 1958; Civic Service award Ventura County Bd. Suprs., 1967, 70, 72. Mem. Calif. Council Civil Engrs. and Land Surveyors (dir. 1969-70), Internat. Union Operating Engrs. (dir. surveyors apprenticeship program 1969-70), Engrs. Club Ventura County (pres. 1961), Ventura County Econ. Devel. Assn. (dir. 1968-71). Club: Rotary (dir. Simi Valley 1970-71). Home: 4848 Alatar Dr Woodland Hills CA 91364 Office: 1666 9th St Santa Monica CA 90404

THOMPSON, EDWIN L(EE), educator; b. Alameda, Calif., Aug. 22, 1929; s. Charles Wesley and Gertrude Jeannette (Moehlman) T.; m. Doris May Goguen, July 6, 1952; children—Diane De Hollander, Linda Tracy, Denise. B.A., U. Calif.-Berkeley, 1952; M.A. in Adminstrn., Calif. State U.-Long Beach, 1963. Tchr. social studies pub. schs., Laton, Calif., 1953-55, Hayward, Calif., 1955-59, La Habra, Calif., 1959-63, Moraga, Calif., 1963-68; cons. in secondary curriculum Mt. Diablo Unified Sch. Dist., 1968-73; prin. Concord (Calif.) Summer High Sch., 1971-72; dir. secondary edn. Livermore (Calif.) Valley Unified Sch. Dist., 1973-79, dir. instructional services, 1979-81, dir. spl. edn., 1981-82; cons. social studies, div. curriculum and instr. Los Angeles County Office Edn., 1982—; chmn. Calif. Curriculum Alliance, 1981—; vice chmn. exec. com. Curriculum and Futures Conf., 1981—. Vice pres. bd. dirs. Children's Theatre Workshop, 1981-82; mem. Community TV Adv. Com., 1980-81; mem. scholarship adv. com. Valley Meml. Hosp., 1979-80; chmn. Livermore Lecture Forum Series, 1977-78; area coordinator Fgn. Study League, 1974; mem. Citizens Adv. Com. Drug Rehab., 1970-72. NSF fellow, 1972-73, 75; NDEA fellow, 1965. Mem.

Assn. Calif. Sch. Adminstrs., Assn. for Supervision and Curriculum Devel., World Future Soc., Calif. Council for the Social Studies, Nat. Council for the Social Studies (mem. ethics com. 1979-82, curriculum com. 1976-79). Author: Educational Simulations and Games, 1970; contbr. articles to profl. jours. Office: 9300 E Imperial Hwy Downey CA 90242

THOMPSON, FRANCISCO ARAPIZ, secondary school guidance administrator; b. Nogales, Ariz., Aug. 17, 1946; s. Frank A. and Maria (Arapiz) T.; div.; 1 son, Frankie R. A.A., Ariz. Western Coll., 1969; B.S., U. Ariz., 1972, M.S., 1974, postgrad., 1976—. Counselor, Nogales High Sch., 1972-73; guidance dir., asst. prin. Carpenter Jr. High Sch., Nogales, 1973—; coordinator Pima Community Coll., Nogales, 1972—; coordinator summer employment youth programs, Nogales, summers, 1972—. Bd. dirs. Santa Cruz Family Guidance Ctr. Mem. Assn. Supervision and Curriculum Devel., NEA, Nat. Rifle Assn., Phi Delta Kappa. Democrat. Roman Catholic.

THOMPSON, HERBERT ERNEST, tool and die co. exec.; b. Jamaica, N.Y., Sept. 8, 1923; s. Walter and Louise (Joly) T.; student Stevens Inst. Tech., 1949-51; m. Patricia Elaine Osborn, Aug. 2, 1968; children—Robert Steven, Debra Lynn. Foreman, Conner Tool Co., 1961-62, Eason & Waller Grinding Corp., 1962-63; owner Endco Machined Products, 1966-67, Thompson Enterprises, 1974—; pres. Method Machined Products, Phoenix, 1967; pres., owner Quality Tool, Inc., 1967—. Served to capt. USAAF, 1942-46. Decorated D.F.C., Air medal with cluster. Home: 14009 N 42d Ave Phoenix AZ 85023 Office: 4223 W Clarendon Ave Phoenix AZ 85019

THOMPSON, JACKLYN GENE, educator; b. Kans. City, Mo., Nov. 10, 1944; d. Keith McVae and Norvella (Jackson) Thompson; m. Kenrick Ronald Skinner, Aug. 6, 1973 (div.). B.A. in Edn., Fisk U., 1966; M.A. in Edn., Pepperdine U., 1971. Elem., reading, lang. arts tchr. Calif. Pub. Schs., 1967-77; adv. transp. permits Los Angeles Unified Sch. Dist., 1977-79; adv. integration 1st-12th grades Filmore Fundamental Magnet Sch., Los Angeles, 1979-82, coordinator 4th-6th grades, 1982-83; coordinator English oral lang. devel. 1st-6th grades Broadous Elem. Sch., Pacoima, Calif., 1983—; curriculum coordinator Hooper Elem. Sch., Los Angeles, 1983—; cons. Desegration Inst. Calif. State U., 1981-82; inservice leader Los Angeles Unified Sch. Dist., 1970-83. Mem. NAACP. Recipient Instruction Leadership cert. Los Angeles Unified Sch. Dist., 1977-78; Instructional Leadership in Integration award, 1978-79; Speakers Trophy, Toastmasters Inc., 1981; Valuable Service award Los Angeles Alliance Black Sch. Educators, 1982. Mem. Caucus Black Educators, Los Angeles Alliance Black Sch. Educators, Phi Delta Kappa, Delta Sigma Theta. Democrat. Baptist. Presenter workshops in ednl. field. Home: 5045 W 58th Pl Los Angeles CA 90056 Office: Hooper Sch 1225 E 52d St Los Angeles CA 90011

THOMPSON, JAMES HOMER, insurance agent, educator; b. Henrietta, Tex., Sept. 11, 1926; s. James Hite and Virginia (Marberry) T.; student U. Okla., 1944-45; Ph.B., U. Chgo., 1947, M.B.A., 1950; M.S. in Fin. Services, Am. Coll., Bryn Mawr, Pa., 1980; m. Ilene Kriss, Mar. 17, 1979; children by previous marriage—Julie A., Laurie J. Dist. sales mgr. Studebaker Corp., South Bend, Ind., 1951-55; assoc. gen. agt. State Mut. Life Assurance Co. Am., Denver, 1955—; instr. U. Colo. 1964—; mem. bd. nat. C.L.U. Inst. Mem. cabinet U. Chgo.; mem. Colo. Ins. Adv. Bd., 1980—. C.L.U., C.P.C.U. Bd. dirs. Adult Edn. Council of Met. Denver, 1977. Mem. Am. Soc. C.L.U.s (v.p. Rocky Mountain chpt 1967, pres. 1968-69, regional v.p. 1972-73), Denver Assn. Life Underwriters (dir. 1963-66). Home: 180 Ivanhoe Denver CO 80220 Office: 252 Clayton Denver CO 80206

THOMPSON, JAMES OSCAR, hotel/casino executive; b. Evanston, Ill., June 30, 1923; s. Oscar I. and Ellen S. (Anderson) T.; m. Rosemary Costanzo, Apr. 28, 1961; children—Jennifer Thompson Olson, Cheryl. B.S. in Journalism, U. Ill., 1949. Vice pres. Harris, Harland & Ward, Los Angeles, 1962-64; v.p., gen. mgr. Sta. KCBN, Reno, 1966-67; nat. sales mgr. Sta. KOLO-TV, Reno, 1967-68; v.p. of entertainment John Ascuaga's Nugget, Sparks, Nev., 1968—. chmn. bd. trustees Nugget PAC. Trustee Airport Authority Washoe County. Served with U.S. Army 1943-45. 2nd lt. USAR. Mem. Reno Advt. Club (pres.), Greater Reno/Sparks C. of C., Sigma Delta Chi. Home: 6445 Pebble Beach Dr Reno NV 89502 Office: Sparks Nugget PO Box 797 Sparks NV 89431

THOMPSON, JAMES WILLIAM, lawyer; b. Dallas, Oct. 22, 1936; s. John Charles and Frances (Van Slyke) T.; B.S., U. Mont., 1958, J.D., 1962; m. Marie Hertz, June 26, 1965; children—Elizabeth, Margaret, John. Accountant, Arthur Young & Co., N.Y.C., summer 1959; instr. bus. adminstrn. Eastern Mont. Coll., Billings, 1959-60, U. Mont., Missoula, 1960-61; admitted to Mont. bar, 1962; asso. firm. Cooke, Moulton, Bellingham & Longo, Billings, 1962-64, James R. Felt, Billings, 1964-65; asst. atty. City of Billings, 1963-64, atty., 1964-66; partner firm Felt, Speare & Thompson, Billings, 1966-72; partner firm McNamer, Thompson & Cashmore, 1973—. Mem. Billings Zoning Commn., 1966-69; v.p. Billings Community Action Program (now Dist. 7 Human Resources Devel. Council), 1968-70, pres., 1970-75, trustee, 1975—; mem. Yellowstone County Legal Services Bd., 1969-70; City-County Air Pollution Control Bd., 1969-70; pres. Billings Symphony Soc., 1970-71; bd. dirs. Billings Studio Theatre, 1967-73; mem. Diocesan exec. council, 1972-75; mem. Billings Transit Commn., 1971-73; mem. City Devel. Agy., 1972-73; bd. dirs. United Way, Billings, 1973-81. C.P.A., Mont. Mem. Am., Mont., Yellowstone County bar assns., Mont. Soc. C.P.A.s, C. of C., Sigma Chi (pres. Billings alumni assn. 1963-65). Clubs: Elks, Kiwanis. Episcopalian. Home: 123 Lewis Ave Billings MT 59101 Office: First Bank Bldg Billings MT 59101

THOMPSON, JANET MARIE, interior designer; b. Springlake, N.J., May 12, 1931; d. Norris Nelson and Margaret Mary (Hoey) Place; m. George Hobson Thompson, Jan. 19, 1954 (dec.); children—John Robert, George Douglas, David Henry, Constance Marie. Student South Tex. Jr. Coll., Houston, 1952-53, U. Houston, 1951, Orange Coast Coll., Costa Mesa, Calif., 1979, U. Calif.-Irvine, 1982. Personnel adminstr. Prudential Ins. Co., Newark, 1948-50, Houston, 1950-53; tchr. kindergarten Westbury Sch., Irving, Tex., 1963-65; personnel and ops. mgr. W.T. Grant Co., Huntington Beach, Calif., 1968-71, dist. trainer for new store openings, 1971; pres., owner Jan Thompson Interiors, Huntington Beach, 1972—. Leader Santiago council Girl Scouts U.S.A., 1969-71; mem. Little Mermaid Guild, Children's Hosp. Orange County, 1982—. Mem. Huntington Beach C. of C. Home: 20831 Skimmer Ln Huntington Beach CA 92646 Office: 5462 Oceanus St Suite G Huntington Beach CA 92649

THOMPSON, JOANNE, artist; b. Chgo., Nov. 2, 1922; d. George Augustus and Mary Louise (Glader) Thompson; student Colo. U., Boulder, 1942; divorced; children—Barry Gottula, Marc Gottula, Stacy Rymas. Exhibited in group shows: Nat. Arts Club Gallery, N.Y.C., 1965-69, Mus. Fine Arts, Springfield, Mass., 1965-70, Am. Artists Profl. League, N.Y.C., 1966-70, Hammond Mus., Westchester, N.Y., 1968, Am. West Mus., Los Angeles, 1976; tchr. watercolor, oil, drawing; porcelain designer. Mem. Am. Artists Profl. League, Artists Guild Chgo., Acad. Artists, Catherine Lorillard Wolfe Profl. Women's Club. Contbg. illustrator, author: Fun to Sketch with Pencil and Crayon, 1973; illustrator: Love Circles, 1978. Home: PO Box 4042 Scottsdale AZ 85261

THOMPSON, JOHN BROWN, physician; b. Eugene, Oreg., Mar. 18, 1929; s. Kenneth Guy and Alta Mae (Brown) T.; A.B. in Chemistry, Willamette U., 1951; M.D., U. Oreg., 1956; children—Sheri, Mark. Intern, Salt Lake City Gen. Hosp., 1956-57; resident Denver VA Hosp., 1957-60; practice medicine specializing in gastroenterology, Oklahoma City, 1962-75, Fargo, N.D., 1975-78, Fresno, Calif., 1978—; instr. medicine U. Okla., Oklahoma City, 1962-67, asst. prof., 1967-72, asso. prof., 1972-75, co-dir. NIH Gastroenterology Traineeship Program, 1967-71, co-dir. research and edn. VA, 1968-72; prof. medicine U. N.D., Fargo, 1975-78, chief div. gastroenterology, 1975-78; chief gastroenterology sect. VA Hosp., Oklahoma City, 1966-74, Fargo, 1975-78; chief of staff VA Med. Center, Fresno, 1978—. Served with USAF, 1960-62. Diplomate Am. Bd. Internal Medicine. Fellow A.C.P.; mem. Am. Gastroenterol. Assn., N.Y. Acad. Scis., Am. Fedn. Clin. Research, Am. Digestive Disease Soc., Nat. Assn. VA Chiefs of Staff. Contbr. articles to profl. jours. Office: VA Med Center 2615 E Clinton St Fresno CA 93703

THOMPSON, JOHN LESTER, bishop; b. Youngstown, Ohio, May 11, 1926; s. John Lester and Irene (Brown) T.; B.A., Youngstown Coll., 1948; S.T.B., Episcopal Theol. Sch., Cambridge, Mass., 1951; m. Shirley Amanda Scott, Aug. 1, 1951; children—Amanda, Ian. Ordained priest Episcopal Ch., 1951; curate, then rector chs. in Ohio, Oreg. and Calif., 1951-78; bishop Episcopal Diocese No. Calif., Sacramento, 1978—. Pres. Oreg. Shakespeare Festival, 1955-56, chmn. bldg. com. for outdoor theatre, 1957-58. Served with USNR, 1943-46. Office: PO Box 161268 Sacramento CA 95816

THOMPSON, JON WILLIAM, sales and marketing executive; b. Vancouver, Wash., Jan. 5, 1950; s. William Richard and Rozella Valentine (Olson) T. A.A.S., Everett Community Coll., 1970; B.A. in Bus., U. Wash., 1972; M.B.A., U. Mont., 1975. Mktg. asst. Ga. Pacific Corp., Portland, Oreg., 1975-77; product mgr. Armour-Dial Co., Phoenix, 1977-78; mktg. mgr. Minnetonka, Inc. (Minn.), 1978-79; gen. mgr. Aeroceuticals, Inc., Southport, Conn., 1979-80; v.p. Epic Research, Inc., Gt. Falls, Mont., 1980-81; ptnr., v.p. sales and mktg. Measuronics Corp., Gt. Falls, 1981—; dir. Olds Ltd., Gt. Falls. Served to 1st lt. USAF, 1972-75. Mem. Am. Mktg. Assn., Am. Advt. Fedn., Am. Assn. M.B.A.s, Am. Entrepreneurs Assn. Republican. Clubs: Universal Racquet, Meadowlark Country (Gt. Falls). Office: Measuronics Corp 4241 2d Ave N Great Falls MT 59401

THOMPSON, JULIA ELIZABETH, correctional counselor; b. Phila., June 14, 1949; d. Jacob Peter and Helena Leota (Caruthers) Hemmert; m. George C. Thompson, July 5, 1969 (div.); 1 son, George C. A.A., Solano Community Coll., 1971; postgrad. Calif. State U.-Sacramento, U. Calif.-Berkeley Extension. Group counselor I, Solano County Probation Dept., Solano County Welfare Dept., Fairfield, Calif., 1971-72, group counselor II, Solano County Welfare Dept., 1973-76; correctional officer Calif. Med. Facility, Vacaville, Calif., 1976-78, corectional sgt., 1981-82; correctional program supr. I, Calif. Correctional Ctr., Susanville, 1978-80; correctional sgt. Calif. State Prison, San Quentin, 1980-81; correctional counselor I, Correctional Tng. Facility, Soledad, Calif., 1982-83, No. Reception Ctr., Vacaville, 1983—. Mem. Calif. Correctional Counselors Assn., Calif. Correctional Peace Officers Assn., Chicano Correctional Workers Assn., Nat. Assn. Exec. Females, Calif. Human Services Orgn. (past pres. Solano County chpt., past state bd. rep.). Republican. Office: PO Box 2000 Vacaville CA 95696

THOMPSON, LARRY DEAN, accountant; b. Salt Lake City, Aug. 16, 1951; s. Lawrence James and Wanda (Layton) T.; m. Jane Hurst, Feb. 15, 1974; children—Philip, Jacob, Scott, Dean, Abby. B.S., Utah State U. 1976. C.P.A., Utah. Staff acct. James G. Drollinger & Assocs., Vernal, Utah, 1976-77; ptnr. Lyman and Thompson, C.P.A.s, Blanding, Utah, 1977—; tchr. community schs., Coll. Eastern Utah. Precinct chmn. S.W. Blanding Republican party, 1981-83. Mem. Am. Inst. C.P.A.s, Utah Assn. C.P.A.s, Nat. Assn. C.P.A.s, Blanding C. of C., Vernal Jaycees. Mormon. Home: 588 S 300W 60-3 Blanding UT 84511 Office: 261 S Main Blanding UT 84511

THOMPSON, LARRY EDWARD, laboratory manager; b. San Jose, Calif., May 2, 1943; s. James Edward and Lowie B. (Thompson) T.; student Calif. Poly. Coll., 1961-65, Foothill Coll., 1974-77. Animal technician Syntex Corp., Palo Alto, Calif., 1967-70, conf. coordinator, 1970-77; mgr. facilities and capital equipment Cooper Labs., Mountain View, Calif., 1977-80, mgr. corp. office services, Palo Alto, 1980—. Served with U.S. Army, 1964-66. Mem. Adminstrv. Mgmt. Soc. (pres., mem. arms com. of 500, Sequoia chpt. 1981—). Home: 1140 Calboro Dr San Jose CA 95117 Office: Cooper Labs Inc 3145 Porter Dr Palo Alto CA 94304

THOMPSON, LAURENCE CASSIUS, linguistics educator, researcher, consultant; b. Manchester, N.H., Mar. 11, 1926; s. Laurence Cassius and Marion Gertrude (Hayes) T.; m. Maranell Lewise Terry, May 8, 1964. A.B., Middlebury Coll., 1949; M.A., Yale U., 1950, Ph.D., 1954. Asst. instr. Vietnamese, Yale U., New Haven, 1953-54; asst. dean U.S. Army Lang. Sch., Monterey, Calif., 1954-56; instr. English, U. Wash., Seattle, 1957-59, asst. prof. linguistics, Russian, 1959-62, assoc. prof., 1962-66, coordinator Russian lang. program, 1959-65; vis. prof. linguistics U. Hawaii-Manoa, 1966-67, prof., 1967—; chmn. bd. trustees Melville Jacobs Collection, U. Wash. Archives, 1971—; mem. exec. bd. Melville and Elizabeth Jacobs Research Fund, Whatcom Mus., Bellingham, Wash., 1972—, chmn., 1972-80; Served with U.S. Army, 1944-46. Jr. Sterling fellow, Yale U., 1949-53; Ford Found. Fgn. Area fellow, 1952-53; Am. Council Learned Socs. fellow, 1951-54; Guggenheim fellow, 1979-80, NSF grantee, 1962-79; NEH grantee, 1979-84. Mem. Linguistic Soc. Am., Am. Oriental Soc., Internat. Linguistic Circle, Am. Anthrop. Assn., Am. Folklore Soc., Soc. for Study of Indigenous Langs. of the Americas, AAUP. Author: A Vietnamese Reader, 1961; A Vietnamese Grammar, 1965; Ballada o Soldate, 1966; Austroasiatic Studies, 1976. Guest issue editor Internat. Jour. Am. Linguistics, 1966, 68, 80, mem. editorial bd., 1982—; established (with M.T. Thompson and M. Dale Kinkade) Ann. Internat Conf. on Salish Langs., 1966, (with M.T. Thompson) Northwest Linguistic Collection, U. Wash. Archives, 1971. Home: 959 Koae St Honolulu HI 96816 Office: U Hawaii 1890 East-West Rd Room 569 Honolulu HI 96822

THOMPSON, LOHREN MATTHEW, oil co. exec.; b. Sutherland, Nebr., Jan. 21, 1926; s. John M. and Anna (Ecklund) T.; ed. U. Denver; m. Ruth A. Stammer, Jan. 2, 1959; children—Terence M., Sheila M., Clark M. Spl. rep. Standard Oil Co., Omaha, 1948-56; gen. sales mgr. Frontier Refining Co., Denver, 1956-68, v.p. mktg., 1967-68; mgr. mktg. U.S. region Husky Oil Co., Denver, 1968-72; v.p. Westar Stas., Inc., Denver, 1967-70; pres., chmn. bd. Colo. Petroleum, Denver, 1971—. Served with USAAF, 1944-46. Mem. Denver Petroleum Club, Colo. Petroleum Council, Am. Petroleum Inst., Denver Oilman's Club, Am. Legion. Democrat. Lutheran. Lion. Home: 10161 Melody Dr North Glenn CO 80221 Office: 4080 Globeville Rd Denver CO 80216

THOMPSON, LOIS JEAN, industrial psychologist; b. Chgo., Feb. 22, 1933; d. Harold William and Ethel Rose (Neumann) Heidke; m. Henry Thomas Ore, Aug. 28, 1954; children—Christopher, Douglas; m. 2d, Joseph Lippard Thompson, Aug. 3, 1972; children—Scott, Les, Melanie. B.A., Cornell Coll., 1955; M.A. in Secondary Edn. and History, Idaho State U., 1964, Ph.D. in Counselor Edn. and Counseling, 1981. Cert. tchr., counselor, Idaho. Tchr. pub. schs., Iowa, Wash., Wyo., Idaho, 1956-58, 61-63, 66-67; instr. Idaho State U., Pocatello, 1967-60, 71-72; orgn./employee devel. specialist Los Alamos Nat. Lab., 1981—; dir. Idaho State U. Parent and Family Edn. Ctr., 1981; speaker, cons. to pub. sch. tchrs., parent study groups. Mem. edn. com. LWV; pres. Welcome Wagon Newcomers Club, Pocatello. Mem. AAUW (edn. com.), Idaho State U. Faculty Women's Club (pres. 1966-67), Am. Personnel and Guidance Assn., Assn. Counselor Edn. and Supervision, N.Am. Soc. Adlerion Psychology, Women in Sci. (Los Alamos and N.Mex. chpts.), Los Alamos Ski Assn. Clubs: Los Alamos Tennis, Image de Los Alamos. Home: 340 Aragon Los Alamos NM 87544 Office: Los Alamos Nat Lab PO Box 1663 MS P-232 Los Alamos NM 87545

THOMPSON, MALCOLM FRANCIS, elec. engr.; b. Charleston, S.C., Sept. 2, 1921; s. Allen R. and Lydia (Brunson) T.; B.S., Ga. Inst. Tech., 1943, M.S., 1947; postgrad. Mass. Inst. Tech., 1947-49; m. Ada Rose O'Quinn, Jan. 20, 1943; children—Rose Mary, Nancy Belle, Susan Elizabeth, Frances Josephine. Instr. dept. elec. engring. Mass. Inst. Tech., 1947-49; research engr. Autonetics Co., Anaheim, Calif., 1949-70; tech. dir. SRC div. Moxon, Inc., Irvine, Calif., 1970-73; engring. mgr., mgr. computers and armament controls. Northrop Aircraft Div., Hawthorne, Calif., 1973—. Served to capt. AUS, 1943-46. Mem. IEEE, Nat. Geog. Soc., Nat. Rifle Assn., Am. Ordnance Assn., Eta Kappa Nu. Patentee in field. Home: 1602 Indus St Santa Ana CA 92707 Office: Northrop Aircraft Div Dept 3567/83 One Northrop Ave Hawthorne CA 90250

THOMPSON, MARGARET THERESE, nurse; b. Fontana, Calif., Jan. 26, 1950; d. Joseph Robert and Margaret Mary (McKinney) Benchwick; m. Jeffrey Lee Thompson, Sept. 8, 1973; children—Kristen Ashley, Cara Lauren. A.A., Moorpark Jr. Coll., 1970; B.S. in Nursing, B.A. in Psychology, Calif. State U.-Los Angeles, 1974; M.S. in Health Adminstrn., Calif. State U.-Northridge, 1981. Research asst. Los Angeles County Probation Dept., 1972-74; head nurse, group counselor Glendale (Calif.) Adventist Med. Ctr., 1974-76, quality assurance coordinator, 1976-80, nursing unit coordinator, definitive observation unit, 1980—; cons. West Coast Med. Mgmt. Assocs., Westlake Village, Calif., 1979—. NIMH scholar, 1972-74. Mem. Am. Assn. Critical Care Nurses, Calif. Soc. Nursing Service Adminstrs., Nat. Assn. Female Execs., Calif. Bus. Womens Network. Home: 9510 Haines Canyon Ave Tujunga CA 91042 Office: 1509 Wilson Terr Glendale CA 91206

THOMPSON, MARILYN L., library dir.; b. Portland, Oreg., Nov. 22, 1939; d. Guy S. and LaVon Thompson; B.A., Portland State U., 1961; M.L.S., U. Portland, 1964; M.L.S., McGill U., Montreal, Que., Can., 1971. Children's book reviewer San Francisco Pub. Library, 1967-70; cons. children and young adults Mass. Bd. Library Commrs., Boston, 1971-73; asst. mgr. Green Dolphin Bookshop, Portland, 1974-75; head collection devel., cons. Wyo. State Library, Cheyenne, 1975-78; dir. Ledding Library of Milwaukie (Oreg.), 1978—; mem. Cable TV communications adv. bd., Milwaukie, Oreg. U. Portland fellow, 1963. Mem. Oreg. Library Assn., Clackamas County Council Librarians (sec. 1981-82), Spl. Library Group of Portland. Office: 10660 SE 21st St Milwaukie OR 97222

THOMPSON, MARY JEAN, interior designer, lectr.; b. Salem, Oreg., Aug. 6, 1935; d. Lester Wayne and Bernis Laverne (Nelson) Shrenk; m. Newton L. Thompson, July 5, 1962 (div.); children—Craig L., Brooks D., K. Inga, Heidi A. B.A. cum laude in Music, Lewis and Clark Coll., 1957; B.A. cum laude in Interior Design, U. Utah, 1969. Designer, Clark Leaming Co., Salt Lake City, 1967-69; pres. Thompson Design Assocs., Inc., Reno, 1970—. Bd. dirs. Community Concerts, 1975-76, Washoe Landmark Preservation, 1976-82, Sierra Nev. Mus. of Art, 1980—. Recipient McGraw Edison Lighting Excellence award, 1978; AIA honor award, 1981. Mem. Am. Soc. Interior Designers (cert. 1970, Merit award ASID/Wilson design competition 1983), AIA (affiliate mem., dir. No. Nev. chpt. 1981-82). Interiors include: Western Nev. Community Coll., 1976, Reno Internat. Airport, 1981, Sparks Family Hosp., 1982. Office: 751 Marsh Ave Reno NV 89509

THOMPSON, ORVAL NATHAN, lawyer; b. Shedd, Oreg., Nov. 29, 1914; s. Otto M. and Laura L. (Halverson) T.; m. Jessie Mila Jackson, Nov. 24, 1938 (dec. 1983); children Kathleen Persons, Richard, Marion. B.S., U. Oreg., 1935, J.D., 1937, LL.M., Northwestern U., 1939. Bar: Oreg., 1937, U.S. Ct. Appeals, 1949, U.S. Supreme Ct., 1945. Practiced, Albany, Oreg., 1938—, pres. firm Weatherford, Thompson, Brickey & Powers, P.C., 1972—, dir. Citizens Valley Bank, 1956 ; sec. Oreg. Metall. Corp., 1955—. Mem. Oreg. Ho. of Reps., 1941-42; mem. Oreg. Senate, 1947-50. Served to lt. USN, 1942-46. Mem. ABA, Oreg. Bar Assn., Linn County Bar Assn. Democrat. Clubs: Masons, Springhill Country, Elks. Home: 605 Erin Crest NW Albany OR 97321 Office: Weatherford Thompson Brickey & Powers PC 130 W 1st Ave PO Box 667 Albany OR 97321

THOMPSON, PAUL RICHARDS, pathologist; b. Northville, S.D., Apr. 21, 1918; s. John Richards and Luzetta Winona (Dittes) T.; B.A., Union Coll., 1942; postgrad. UCLA, 1942-43; M.D., U. So. Calif., 1952; children—Deborah Ann, John Paul, Brett Richard. Intern, Los Angeles County Hosp., 1951-52, resident in internal medicine, 1952, resident in pathology, 1952-56, dir. blood bank, 1956-75; asso. pathologist St. Luke Hosp., Pasadena, 1957-75, St. Joseph Hosp., Burbank, Calif., 1975-76; med. dir. regional blood services ARC, Los Angeles, 1976—; asst. clin. prof. pathology U. So. Calif., Los Angeles, 1961-64, asso. clin. prof. pathology, 1964-70, clin. prof. pathology, 1970—; med. adv. com. on blood and blood derivatives Calif. Dept. Health, 1977—; mem. AIDS task force Calif. Dept. Health, 1983—; bd. dirs. Calif. Blood Bank System, 1978-81. Served with U.S. Army, 1942-46. Diplomate Am. Bd. Pathology. Mem. Los Angeles County Med. Assn., AAAS, Am. Assn. Blood Banks, Am. Assn. Phys. Anthropologists, Am. Assn. Tissue Banks, AMA, Am. Soc. Clin. Pathologists (fellow), Internat. Soc. Blood Transfusion, Calif. Blood Bank System, Calif. Med. Assn., Geneal. Soc. So. Calif., Los Angeles County Med. Assn., Los Angeles Soc. Pathologists, Profl. Staff Assn. of Los Angeles County and So. Calif. Med. Center, Grad. Soc. Pathology (bd. dirs.), Serum Cell Soc. Republican. Contbr. articles to profl. jours. Office: 1130 S Vermont Ave Los Angeles CA 90006

THOMPSON, RANDI EILEEN, public relations executive; b. Summit, N.J., June 25, 1952; d. Henry Gilbert and Betty Jane (Fritz) T.; m. Harry G. Wiles, June 30, 1979; 1 stepdau., Heather Ann. B.A. in Arts and Humanities, U. Md., 1973, M.A. in Communications, 1975. Radio intern Democratic Nat. Com., Washington, 1974; newsletter intern Marriott Corp., Washington, 1974; instr. interpersonal communication U. Md., College Park, 1974-75; assoc. Porter, Novelli & Assocs., Washington, 1975-78, sr. assoc., 1978-80, v.p., research dir., 1980-81, v.p., gen. mgr., Los Angeles, 1981-83, sr v.p., gen. mgr., 1983—, mem. exec. com., 1981—. Active Town Hall Calif., 1982, Performing Tree, 1982. Mem. Pub. Relations Soc. Am., Am. Assn. Bus. Communicators, Am. Mktg. Assn., Am. Pub. Health Assn., Los Angeles Advt. Women. Democrat. Office: 10889 Wilshire Blvd 1135 Los Angeles CA 90024

THOMPSON, RICHARD EARL, artist; b. Oak Park, Ill., Sept. 26, 1914; s. Abijah Snyder and Vera (Koster) T.; m. Mary Munn, June 25, 1937; children—Richard Earl, Bruce, Daniel. Student Chgo. Acad. Fine Arts, 1930-31, Am. Acad. Art, Chgo., 1932-33, Chgo. Art Inst., 1944. Instr., Am. Acad. Art, Chgo., 1935-37; comml. artist Coca Cola, Anheuser-Busch, Standard Oil and Miller Brewing Co., 1937-59; artist in residence U. Wis.-Rhinelander, 1980; numerous one-man exhibits include: Veldman Galleries, Milw., 1970-71, 73, 75, 77, Wild Life Art Gallery, Minocqua, Wis., 1971, John P. Klep Galley, Houston, 1971-74, Richard Thompson Gallery, San Francisco, 1977, 79, 81; group exhbns.

include: Vincent Price Collection Fine Art, 1965, Peter Darro Galleries, Chgo., 1969; mus. shows include: Berstorm Art Ctr., Neenah, Wis., 1965, Leigh Yawkey Woodson Art Mus., Wausau, Wis., 1979, R.W. Norton Art Gallery, Shreveport, La., 1982; represented in mus. and corp. collections: Continental Ill. Bank, Chgo., de Sasset Art Gallery and Mus. of U. Santa Clara, Calif., Leigh Yawkey Woodson Art Mus., Lewer Agy., Kansas City, Mo., Marquette U. Collection, Mills Coll., Milw. Jour., Naval Art Collection of Pentagon, Washington, New Britain Mus. Am. Art, R.W. Norton Art Gallery, Robert Louis Stevenson Acad. Collection, Carmel, Calif., Southland Fin. Corp., Irving, Tex., Southland Corp., Dallas, Wis. Meml. Park, Milw., Wood County Nat. Bank, Wisconsin Rapids, Wis. Recipient 1st hon. mention award Salmagundi Club, N.Y.C., 1981. Club: Salmagundi. Subject of book: Richard Earl Thompson—American Impressionist, a Prophetic Odyssey in Paint (Patricia Jobe Pierce), 1982. Office: Richard Thompson Gallery 80 Maiden Ln San Francisco CA 94108

THOMPSON, RICHARD FREDERICK, psychologist, educator; b. Portland, Oreg., Sept. 6, 1930; s. Frederick Albert and Margaret St. Clair (Marr) T.; m. Judith K. Pedersen, May 22, 1960; children—Kathryn M., Elizabeth K., Virginia St. Clair. B.A., Reed Coll., 1952; M.S., U. Wis., 1953, Ph.D., 1956. Asst. prof. med. psychology U. Oreg. Med. Sch., 1959-63, assoc. prof., 1963-65, prof., 1965-67; prof. psychobiology U. Calif.-Irvine, 1967-73, 75-80; Lashley chair Harvard U., 1973, prof. psychology, 1973-74; prof. psychology, Bing prof. human biology Stanford U., 1980—, chmn. human biology program. Fellow AAAS; mem. Am. Psychol. Assn. (Disting. Sci. Contbn. award, mem. Governing Council 1974—), Soc. Neurosci. (past counciilor), Nat. Acad. Sci., Internat. Brain Research Orgn., Psychonomic Soc. (mem. governing bd. 1972-77, chmn. bd., 1976), Soc. Exptl. Psychologists. Author: Foundations of Physiological Psychology, 1967; (with others) Psychology, 1971; Introduction to Physiological Psychology, 1975; psychology editor W. H. Freeman & Co. publs.; editor Jour. Comparative and Physiol. Psychology, 1981—; regional editor Physiology and Behavior. Home: 1097 Cathcart Way Stanford CA 94305 Office: Dept Psychology Stanford U Stanford CA 94305

THOMPSON, ROBERT HOWARD, publisher; b. San Jose, Calif., Jan. 10, 1947; s. William Howard and Violet Eleanor (Davis) T.; m. Roxane Rae Provence, May 14, 1983; 1 son by previous marriage, Jeffrey Robert; stepchildren—Robert, Trevor, and Rochelle Green. B.A., San Jose State U., 1974. Radio announcer Sta. KPLX, San Jose, 1968-69; sales/mktg. mgr. San Jose Mercury News, 1969-81; publisher, pres. Thompson Media Group, Inc., San Jose, 1981—; communications cons. Chmn. Santa Clara County Drug Abuse Commn., 1981-83; chmn. City of San Jose Housing Commn., 1983-84. Served with Army N.G., 1965-70. Mem. Santa Clara County Bar Assn. (fee arbitration panel), San Jose C. of C., Nat. Women's Polit. Caucus, Am. Assn. Ret. Persons. Democrat. Office: 12 S First St Suite 720 San Jose CA 95113

THOMPSON, ROBERT SAMUEL, lawyer, municipal judge; b. Cleve., Nov. 2, 1930; s. Wayne Charles and Cornelia Irene (Anderson) T.; m. JoAnne Courtney, Dec. 20, 1958; children—Robert Dale, Richard Wayne. B.A., Hamilton Coll., 1953; J.D., U. Mich., 1956; grad. Air Force Command and Staff Coll., 1978. Bar: Mich. 1956, U.S. Supreme Ct. 1961, Ohio 1965, Oreg. 1973, U.S. Patent and Trademark Office 1977. Patent examiner, U.S. Patent Office, 1956-57; commd. 1st lt. U.S. Air Force, 1957, advanced through grades to maj., 1977; chief mil. justice, Hdqrs. 7th Air Force, Vietnam, 1969-70, Alaskan Air Command, 1975-77; ret., 1977; sole practice law, McMinnville, Oreg., 1977—; mcpl. ct. judge, McMinnville, Newberg and Sheridan, Oreg., 1977—. Decorated Bronze Star. Mem. Oreg. Mcpl. Judges Assn. (dir.), Am. Legion. Clubs: Rotary (dir.), Masons, Elks. Home: 127 W 19th St McMinnville OR 97128 Office: PO Box 753 McMinnville OR 97128

THOMPSON, RONALD EDWARD, lawyer; b. Bremerton, Wash., May 24, 1931; s. Melville Herbert and Clara Mildred (Griggs) T.; B.A., U. Wash., 1953, J.D., 1958; m. Marilyn Christine Woods, Dec. 15, 1956; children—Donald Jeffery, Karen, Susan, Nancy, Sally, Claire. Admitted to Wash. bar, 1959; practiced in Tacoma, 1960—; asst. city atty., City of Tacoma, 1960-61; pres. Thompson, Krilich & LaPorte, P.S., Tacoma, 1961—. Judge pro tem Municipal Ct., City of Tacoma, Pierce County Justice Ct., 1972—; dir. Air Gemini, Inc. Chmn. housing and social welfare com., City of Tacoma, 1965-69; mem. Bd. Adjustment, Tacoma, 1967-71, chmn., 1968; mem. Com. for Future Devel., Tacoma, 1961-64. Mem. Tacoma Planning Commn., 1971-72. Bd. dirs., pres. Municipal League, Tacoma; bd. dirs. Tacoma-Pierce County Cancer Soc., Tacoma-Pierce County Heart Assn., Tacoma-Pierce County Council of the Arts, Econ. Devel. Council of Puget Sound, Tacoma Youth Symphony, Kleiner Group Home. Precinct committeeman Republican party, 1969-73. Served with AUS, 1953-55; col. Res. Recipient Internat. Community Service award Optimist Club, 1970; Patriotism award Am. Fedn. Police, 1974; citation for community service HUD, 1974, Meritorious Service medal, 1981. Mem. Am. Arbitration Assn. (panel of arbitrators), Am., Wash. State (mem. unauthorized practice com. 1970-73), Tacoma-Pierce County (sec. 1964, pres. 1979, mem. cts. and judiciary com. 1981-82) bar assns., Am. Trial Lawyers Assn., Wash. State Trial Lawyers Assn., Tacoma-Pierce County C. of C. (dir., exec. com., v.p., chmn.), Phi Delta Phi, Sigma Nu. Roman Catholic. Clubs: Variety (Seattle); Lawn Tennis, Tacoma, Optimist (internat. pres. 1973-74) (Tacoma). Home: 817 N Yakima Ave Tacoma WA 98403 Office: 524 Tacoma Ave S Tacoma WA 98402

THOMPSON, SUSAN KATHLEEN, home economics teacher; b. Seattle, Oct. 9, 1951; d. Frederick James and Vivian Lucille (Wood) T. B.S., Wash. State U., 1973; M.S., U. Nev., 1981. Tchr. home econs. White Pine High Sch., Ely, Nev., 1973-76; clk. Weinstock's Dept. Store, Reno, 1976-80; teller new accounts Nev. Nat. Bank, Reno, 1978-80; home econs. tchr. Carson Jr. High Sch., Carson City, Nev., 1980—. Sunday Sch. tchr. First Presbyn. Ch. Mem. Nev. State Edn. Assn. Republican. Home: 3351 S Carson St Apt 204 Carson City NV 89701 Office: Richmond and W King Sts Carson City NV 89701

THOMPSON, THEODORE JOSEPH, statistician; b. Buffalo, June 7, 1953; s. Theodore Ralph and Regina Cecelia (Weber) T.; m. Cheryl Edyth Aitken, June 28, 1975; m. 2d, Elisa DelMar Sims, Feb. 6, 1983. B.A. cum laude in Math., SUNY-Buffalo, 1975, M.S. in Statis. Sci., 1978. Statistician, David F. Herring Inc., LaJolla, Calif., 1978-81; math. statistician Navy Personnel Research and Devel. Ctr., San Diego, 1981—. Mem. Am. Statis. Assn., Biometric Soc. Club: Elks (North Tonawanda, N.Y.). Home: 1852 Chalcenody St San Diego CA 92109 Office: Navy Personnel Research and Devel Ctr Code 11 San Diego CA 92152

THOMPSON, VIRGINIA LOU, agricultural products supplier and importer; b. Malcolm, Iowa, July 15, 1928; d. Isaac Cleveland and Viola (Montgomery) Griffin; m. Alfred Thompson, Mar. 1, 1946; children—Michael Duane, Cathryn Lynn, Steven Curtis, Laura Lue. Student Phoenix Coll., 1962, Phoenix-Scottsdale Jr. Coll., 1973-74. With sales dept. Trend House, Phoenix, 1962-67; importer World Wide Imports, Ft. Collins, Colo., 1974-79; owner, mgr. Windsor Elevator Inc. (Colo.), 1979—; participant in trade shows, seminars. Mem. Nat. Grain and Feed Assn., Colo. Grain and Feed Assn., Rocky Mountain Beun Dealers, Colo. Cattle Feeders Assn., Western U.S. Agrl. Assn., Rice Millers Assn. Democrat. Lutheran. Clubs: Christian Women (Greeley, Colo.); Order of Eastern Star (Iowa).

THOMPSON, WALTER WILLIAM, financial executive; b. S.I., N.Y., June 29, 1927; s. Walter Harold and Rose Veronica (Dugan) T.; B.S. magna cum laude, Wagner Coll., 1950; m. Margaret Ellen Coulson, Mar. 5, 1956; 1 dau., Kathleen. Commd. officer USAF, 1951, advanced through grades to lt. col., 1967, ret., 1970; govt. bond salesman Merrill Lynch Pierce Fenner & Smith, Salt Lake City, 1970-73; staff Blythe, Eastman & Dillon, Salt Lake City, 1973-74, v.p., office mgr., 1974; v.p., mgr. Dean Witter & Co., Spokane, Wash., 1974; sr. govt. bond specialist Merrill Lynch Pierce Fenner & Smith, Seattle, 1975-76; v.p. sales Bache & Co., Seattle, 1976, sr. govt. bond specialist Loeb Rhodes Hornblower, Phoenix, 1976—; treas. Creative Realty, Salt Lake City, 1974—; sec.-treas. M & W Indsl. Enterprises, Salt Lake City, 1974—; pres., chmn. Thompson Fin. Cons., 1978—; v.p. Instnl. Networks Corp.; apptd. to Com. to Amend the Investment Laws, Utah, 1973, Ariz., 1979. Mem. Ret. Officers Assn., Air Force Assn. Republican. Roman Catholic. Home: 8667 Via del Palacio Scottsdale AZ 85258 Office: 8030 E Morgan Trail Suite 5 Scottsdale AZ 85258

THOMPSON, WESLEY BRUCE, health care exec.; b. Salt Lake City, June 22, 1948; s. Clyde LeRoy and Alice Arlene (Rohrbach) T.; m. Rebecca Landward, Mar. 15, 1974; children—Ryan, Kristin, Spencer. B.A. in Psychology, U. Utah, 1974, M.B.A. 1977. Dir. planning Latter Day Saints Hosp., Salt Lake City 1976-79, asst. adminstr. 1979-82; dir. ambulatory surgery Profl. Services Corp. subs. Intermountain Health Care, Salt Lake City 1982—. Served with USAR, 1966-72. Mem. Am. Coll. Hosp. Adminstrs., Am. Soc. Hosp. Planning, Freestanding Ambulatory Surgery Assn. Republican. Mormon.

THOMSON, DONALD BROWNLEE, theatrical producer, mktg. cons.; b. Cleve., Feb. 6, 1932; s. Dennis Alexander and Elizabeth Brownlie (Cusick) T.; student Balboa Jr. Coll., 1949-50, U. Md., 1950-51, Johann Wilhelm von Goethe U., Frankfurt am Main, Germany, 1951-52; B.A. in English, Kent State U., 1957; postgrad. U. Mich., 1958-60; m. Jane Caroline Fleishman, Mar. 24, 1956 (dec. Feb. 1974); children—Christopher, Miranda, Benjamin; m. 2d, Toni McDonald, Oct. 11, 1980. Editor, Bendix Aero., Ann Arbor, Mich., 1958-61; mgr. mktg. services Motorola Aero., Scottsdale, Ariz., 1961-65; pres. E Pluribus Unum Advt. Agy., Phoenix, 1962-66; pres. and gen. mgr. KPAZ-TV, Phoenix, 1964-69; pres. Continental Urban TV and gen. mgr. KGSC-TV, San Jose, Calif., 1969-71; gen. mgr. San Jose Symphony Assn., 1971-75; dir. mktg. Suburban Newspaper Publs., Inc., Cupertino, Calif., 1975-76; producer San Francisco Ballet in San Jose, Calif., 1975-76; exec. producer San Jose Theatre Guild, 1976-80; pres. The Theater Group, Inc., Los Gatos, Calif., 1980—; owner Sta. KXLV-TV, San Jose, Calif., 1981—. Mem. adv. com. FCC, 1964-70; arbitrator Santa Clara County Bar Assn.; bd. dirs. San Jose Police Activities League; bd. dirs. Santa Clara County Heart Assn., chmn., 1981. Served with U.S. Army, 1949-52. Club: Rotary. Home: 302 Los Gatos Blvd Los Gatos CA 95030 Office: Box 66 Charles St Los Gatos CA 95030

THOMSON, DONALD STEVEN, research engineer; b. Woodland, Calif., Apr. 29, 1951; s. Donald Frederick and Olivia Alicia (Sotelo) T. B.S. with honors in Aerospace Engring, Calif. State Poly. U., Pomona, 1973; M.S. in Biomed. Engring., U. Calif.-Berkeley, 1975. Assoc. engr., research and devel. engr., Edwards Pacemaker Systems, Irvine, Calif., 1975-77; research and devel. engr. Edwards Labs., Santa Ana, Calif., 1977-78; sr. project engr., mgr. new product planning, mgr. electromech. research and devel. Shiley Inc., Irvine, Calif., 1978—. Mem. ASME (nat. com. med. device standards), Assn. Advancement Med. Instrumentation (standards com.), AAAS, Tau Beta Pi. Contbr. articles to profl. jours. Office: 17600 Gillette Ave Irvine CA 92714

THOMSON, JOHN RANKIN, city manager; b. Oakland, Calif., Nov. 1, 1935; s. John Stalker and Mary Josephine (Estes) T.; children—Diane Mary (dec.), John Christopher, Deborah Ann. B.A., San Diego State U., 1960, M.P.A., 1973. Asst. utilities supt. City of San Diego, Calif., 1960-69; city mgr. City of Chula Vista, Calif., 1969-75; city mgr. City of Lawton, Okla., 1975-76; city mgr. City of Medford, Oreg., 1976—; instr. San Diego State U., 1974-75. Served with USMC, 1954-56. Mem. Internat. City Mgmt. Assn., Am. Soc. Pub. Adminstrn. (Civic Contbn. award 1975), Am. Mgmt. Assn., Mensa. Club: Kiwanis. Office: City Hall 411 W 8th St Medford OR 97501

THOMSON, THYRA GODFREY, state ofcl.; b. Florence, Colo., July 30, 1916; d. John and Rosalie (Altman) Godfrey; B.A. cum laude, U. Wyo., 1939; m. Keith Thomson, Aug. 6, 1939 (dec. Dec. 1960); children—William John II, Bruce Godfrey, Keith Coffey. With dept. agronomy and agrl. econs. U. Wyo., 1938-39; writer weekly column Watching Washington pub. in 14 papers, Wyo., 1955-60; planning chmn. Nat. Fedn. Republican Women, Washington, 1961; sec. state Wyo., Cheyenne, 1962—, also ex-officio lt. gov. Mem. Marshall Scholarships Com. for Pacific Region, 1964-68; del. 72d Wilton Park Conf., Eng., 1965; mem. youth commn. UNESCO, 1970-71, Allied Health Professions Council HEW, 1971-72; participant Internat. Women's Yr., Ger., 1975. Recipient Disting. Alumni award U. Wyo., 1969; named Internat. Woman of Distinction, Alpha Delta Kappa; citation Omicron Delta Epsilon, 1965, Beta Gamma Sigma, 1968, Delta Kappa Gamma, 1973. Mem. N.Am. Securities Adminstrs. (pres. 1973-74), Nat. Assn. Secs. of State, Council State Govts. (chmn. natural resources com. Western States 1966-68), Nat. Conf. Lt. Govs. (exec. com. 1976—), AAUW, Wyo. Press Women, Spurs, P.E.O., Pi Beta Phi, Alpha Kappa Psi, Psi Chi. Home: 3102 Sunrise Rd Cheyenne WY 82001 Office: Capitol Bldg Cheyenne WY 82002

THON, DAVID ERWIN, electronics company executive; b. Elmhurst, Ill., June 1, 1950; s. Erwin William and Dorothy Alice (Bartz) T.; B.A., Valparaiso U., 1973; B.S.E.E., Valparaiso Tech. Inst., 1976. Tech. editor communications products Motorola Co., Schaumburg, Ill., 1976-78, product planner, 1978-79, product cons., communications and electronics, Foster City, Calif., 1979-82, tng. mgr., 1982—. Nat. Merit scholar, 1968-72. Mem. IEEE, Am. Soc. for Tng. and Devel. Home: 123 Anita Rd No 12 Burlingame CA 94010 Office: Motorola C & E 1170 Chess Dr Foster City CA 94404

THONET, THEODORE ANDREW, consulting firm executive; b. Patchogue, N.Y., Oct. 25, 1931; s. Theodore Henry and Helen Conn (Appelgate) T.; B.S. in Chemistry, U. Miami, 1957; M.S. in Systems Mgmt., U. So. Calif., 1971; children—Sandra Linn, Deborah Susan, Cynthia Eileen, Theodore Andrew II, Christine Annette. Chemist, lab. mgr. Continental Filling Corp., 1957-59; dir. research Puritan Aerosol Corp., Boston, 1959-62; engr., scientist, chief engr's. office McDonnell Douglas Astronautics, Huntington Beach, Calif., 1962-75; dir. ops. Internat. Tech., Westminster, Calif., 1975-81; owner Thonet Cons., Irvine, Calif., 1972—. Ednl. advisor; active PTA. Served with USAF, 1950-53. Recipient awards Inst. Food Technologists, 1960, Soc. Cosmetic Chemists, 1960, Am. Pharm. Assn., 1961; recipient TRW Performance award, 1974. Mem. Soc. Automotive Engrs., Nat. Soc. Profl. Engrs., Am. Chem. Soc., Am. Rocket Soc., Nat. Mgmt. Assn. (cert.). Republican. Contbr. articles to publs. Office: 15 Hawthorn Irvine CA 92715

THOR, LINDA MARIA, college administrator; b. Los Angeles, Feb. 21, 1950; d. Karl Gustav and Mildred Dorrine (Hofius) T.; m. Robert Paul Huntsinger, Nov. 22, 1974; 1 son, Erik Thor. B.A. in Journalism magna cum laude, Pepperdine U., 1971; M.P.A., Calif. State U.-Los Angeles, 1980; postgrad. Pepperdine U., 1982. Pub. info. officer Los Angeles Community Coll. Dist., 1974-75, dir. communications services, 1975-81, dir. ednl. services, 1981-82, dir. high tech. ctrs. and services, 1982-83, sr. dir. occupational and tech. edn., 1983—. Recipient 2 awards, So. Calif. Sch. Pub. Relations Assn., 1978. Mem. Calif. Community and Jr. Coll. Assn. (PRO award 1977, 78), Women in Communications, Council Advancement and Support of Edn., Calif. Community Coll. Adminstrs. for Occupational Edn. Club: Soroptimists (cert. of achievement 1977). Editor: Curriculum Design and Development for Effective Learning, 1973; contbr. chpt. in book. Office: 617 W 7th St Los Angeles CA 90017

THORNE, ALISON COMISH, economist, writer; b. Chgo. May 9, 1914; d. Newel Howland and Louise (Larson) Comish; m. David Wynne Thorne Aug. 3, 1937 (dec.) children—Kip Stephen, Barrie, Sandra, Avril, Lance Gaylord. Instr. consumption econs. Colo. State U. 1936, Iowa State U. 1937; lectr. sociology and home econs. Utah State U. 1965—, coordinator Women and Internat. Devel. 1981—. Mem. adv. council Utah Dept. Employment Security 1965-82, chmn. 1974-82; mem. Utah State Bldg. Bd. 1965-77; mem. Logan Bd. Edn. 1959-71, pres. 1965-69; bd. trustees No. Utah Community Action Program 1966-71. Recipient Utah State U. Coll. Family Life Community Service award, 1965, Utah Sch. Bds. Assn. Disting. Service award, 1965; Utah Fedn. Bus. and Profl. Women's Clubs Woman of Achievement award, 1979; Gov. Community Service award, 1980. Mem. Am. Econ. Assn., Internat. Assn. Agrl. Economists, AAAS, Nat. Women's Studies Assn., AAUW, LWV. Democrat. Contbr. chpts. to books and articles to profl. jours. Home: 365 E 300 N Logan UT 84321

THORNE, DARLENE HAYNES, association executive, writer; b. San Francisco, June 15, 1937; d. William Robert and Genevieve Edith (Sylvestri) H.; div.; children—Vicki Leers, Dena, William. A.A. in Speech Pathology, DeAnza Coll., Cupertino, Calif., 1974; postgrad. Edinburgh (Scotland) U., 1976-77; B.A. in Journalism, San Jose State U., 1979. Pub. relations asst. DeAnza Coll., Cupertino, Calif., 1973-74; assoc. editor U.S. Vets. Mag., Sunnyvale, Calif., 1975-76; editor Peninsula Graphitti Mag., Los Altos, Calif., 1978-79; exec. mgr. Milpitas (Calif.) C. of C., 1979—; creator, editor Trianon Reflections newsletter, Calif. History Ctr., 1975; contbg. author Cupertino Chronicles, 1976; Author, editor Welcome to Edinburgh Manual, 1977; columnist Milpitas Post; writer Santa Clara County Bus. Mag. Bank of America home econs. scholar, 1955; recipient Nat. PTA lifetime hon. service award, 1973. Mem. Santa Clara County Assn. C. of C. Execs. (pres.), Calif. Press Women, Calif. Assn. C. of C. Execs. Office: 1 N Main St Milpitas CA 95035

THORNOCK, JOHN RICHMOND, army officer, lawyer; b. Idaho Falls, Idaho, Jan. 11, 1935; s. Roland Thomas and Don Ann (Goar) T.; m. Rochelle Henderson, June 17, 1955; children—Andrea, Mark, J. Michael, Kristalyn. B.A. in Polit. Sci., U. Idaho, 1957, J.D., 1960; M.S., U.S. Army Command and Gen. Staff Coll., 1971; LL.M., U.S. Army Judge Adv. Gen. Sch., 1968. Bar: Idaho 1960. Commd. 2d lt. U.S. Army, 1960, advanced through grades to col., 1979; trial counsel, 1960-64, Command Judge Adv., 1962-63; chief publs. div. JAG's Sch., 1964-66, dir. plans and publs. dept., 1968-70; chief mil. justice, Vietnam, 1966-67; staff judge adv. 3d Armor Div., Germany, 1971-74; exec. officer Judge Adv. U.S. Army Europe, 1974-76; exec. officer Def. Appellate Div., Washington, 1976-77; staff judge adv., Ft. Belvoir, 1977-78; appellate judge, Washington, 1978-79; staff judge adv., sr. legal officer, Ft. Carson, Colo., 1979—. Active Boy Scouts Am.; lay leader Ch. of Jesus Christ of Latter-day Saints. Decorated Bronze Star, Meritorious Service Medal (3), Army Commendation Medal (2). Recipient Young Fed. Lawyer award, 1969. Home: 3755 Inspiration Dr Colorado Springs CO 80917 Office: Staff Judge Advocate Fort Carson CO 80913

THORNTON, DAN PERKINS, marketing executive; b. Oakland, Calif., Nov. 24, 1931; s. Wayne H. and Dorothy P. (Perkins) T.; m. Elizabeth Prueher, Nov. 27, 1975; children—Peter, Nancy. A.B., U. of Pacific, 1953; postgrad. Golden Gate U., 1956-60. Advt. mgr. Folger Coffee Co., San Francisco, 1955-64; mktg. mgr. Spreckels Sugar Co., San Francisco, 1964-80; dir. mktg. Calif. Prune Bd., San Francisco, 1980—. Served with USNR, 1948-55. Mem. Merchandising Execs. Club of San Francisco (past pres.), San Francisco Advt. Club (past dir.). Republican. Home: 2741 Elmwood Ave Berkeley CA 94705

THORNTON, JACK NELSON, publishing company executive; b. Columbia, Mo., Nov. 9, 1932; s. Samuel Calvin and Mary Elizabeth T.; m. Susan Sylvester, July 1, 1955; children—Gray Nelson, Elizabeth Susan; m. Patricia Helmke, Sept. 15, 1973. A.B. U. Mo., 1954. Field rep., field supr., regional mgr. Wadsworth Pub. Co., Inc., Monterey, Calif., 1957-60, assoc. editor, 1960-62, editor, 1962-64, mng. editor, 1964-66, v.p., 1970—, sr. group exec., 1980—; dir. Wadsworth, Inc., Lange Med. Publ., Inc., Anaheim Pub. Co., Inc.; mng. editor Brooks/Cole Pub. Co., Monterey, 1966-70, exec. editor, 1970, pres., 1977-80. Served to capt. USAFR, 1954-57. Mem. Assn. Am. Pubs., Math. Assn. Am., Am. Rocket Soc., Knights of Vine, Nat. Council Tchrs. Math. Democrat. Home: PO Box 107 Carmel CA 93921 Office: 555 Abrego St Monterey CA 93940

THORNTON, JOHN IRVIN, forensic scientist, educator; b. Sacramento, Calif., Jan. 11, 1941; s. Lewis T. and Zilpha G. (Bowman) T.; B.S. in Criminology, U. Calif., Berkeley, 1962, M.S. in Criminology, 1968, D. Criminology, 1974; m. Kim Stanchfield Wildman, May 22, 1976; children—Edward Lewis, Christian John, Chad Wildman. Criminalist, Contra Costa County (Calif.) Sheriff's Dept., Martinez, 1963-72, supervising criminalist, 1970-72, lab. dir., 1969-70; asst. prof. forensic sci. U. Calif., Berkeley, 1972-76, asso. prof. forensic sci. Sch. Public Health, 1976-82, prof., 1982—; cons. to Law Enforcement Assistance Adminstrn., U.S. Dept. Justice, 1974, 75, 78, Calif. Council on Criminal Justice, 1970-71, Am. Council on Edn., 1978, Internal Review Bur., Dept. Transp. and Public Facilities, State of Alaska, 1978, various police agys., public defender's offices and attys., 1972—; mem. project adv. com. Nationwide Crime Lab. Proficiency Testing Project, Forensic Sci. Found., 1974-77. Bd. dirs. Friends Outside, 1973-74. Served with USAF, 1962-63. Recipient Award of Merit, Forensic Scis. Found., 1979. Mem. Am. Acad. Forensic Scis. (Criminalistics Sect. award 1979, sec. criminalistics sect. 1979, mem. council 1979-81., chmn. sect. 1980). Am. Chem. Soc., Calif. Assn. of Criminalists (pres. 1974-75, editorial sec. 1967-70), Academie Internationale de Medecine Legale et de Medecine Sociale, Forensic Sci. Soc. England, Sigma Xi, Mem. Society of Friends. Contbr. numerous articles to jours. in forensic sci. Home: 1093 Lokoya Rd Napa CA 94558 Office: School of Public Health Univ of California Berkeley CA 94720

THORP, EDWARD OAKLEY, investment management company executive; b. Chgo., Aug. 14, 1932; s. Oakley Glenn and Josephine (Gebert) T.; B.A. in Physics, UCLA, 1953, M.A. (NSF fellow 1954-55), 1955, Ph.D., 1958; m. Vivian Sinetar, Jan. 27, 1956; children—Raun, Karen, Jeffrey. Instr., UCLA, 1958-59, C.L.E. Moore instr. MIT, 1959-61; asst. prof., then assoc. prof. math. N.Mex. State U., 1961-65; mem. faculty U. Calif., Irvine, 1965—, prof. math., 1967-78, prof. mgmt., 1978-82; pres. Oakley Sutton Mgmt. Corp., investments, 1972—; v.p. Oakley Sutton Securities Corp., 1972—; gen. ptnr. Dorchester Govt. Securities Co. Grantee NSF, 1962-64, Air Force Office Sci. Research, 1964-74. Fellow Inst. Math. Stats.; mem. Am. Econ. Assn., Am. Fin. Assn., Am. Inst. Decision Scis., Am. Math. Soc., Am. Statis. Assn., Math. Assn. Am., Western Econ. Assn., Phi Deta Kappa, Sigma Xi. Author: Beat The Dealer: A Winning Strategy for the Game of Twenty-One, rev. edit., 1966; Elementary Probability, 1966; co-author:

Beat The Market, 1967; columnist Gambling Times, 1979—. Office: 901 Dover Dr Suite 250 Newport Beach CA 92660

THORPE, JAMES, literary scholar; b. Aiken, S.C., Aug. 17, 1915; s. James Ernest and Ruby Estelle (Holloway) T.; A.B., The Citadel, 1936; M.A., U. N.C., 1937; Ph.D., Harvard U., 1941; Litt.D., Occidental Coll., 1968; L.H.D., Claremont Grad. Sch., 1968; H.H.D., U. Toledo, 1977; LL.D., The Citadel, 1971; m. Elizabeth McLean Daniells, July 19, 1941; children—James, John D., Sarah Jans-Thorpe. Mem. faculty dept. English, Princeton U., 1946-66; dir. Huntington Library, Art Gallery and Bot. Gardens, San Marino, Calif., 1966-83, sr. research assoc. Huntington Library, 1966—. Bd. fellows Claremont Univ. Center. Served to col. USAF, 1941-46. Decorated Bronze Star; Guggenheim fellow, 1949-50, 65-66. Fellow Am. Acad. Arts and Scis., Am. Antiquarian Soc.; mem. MLA, Am. Philos. Soc. Democrat. Episcopalian. Clubs: Twilight, Zamarano. Author: Bibliography of Writings of George Lyman Kittredge, 1948; Milton Criticism, 1950, Rochester's Poems, 1950; Poems of Sir George Etherge, 1963; Aims and Methods of Scholarship, 1963, 70; Principles of Textual Criticism, 1972, 79; Use of Manuscripts in Literary Research, 1974, 79; Gifts of Genius, 1980; A Word to the Wise, 1982; John Milton: The Inner Life, 1983. Office: Huntington Library San Marino CA 91108

THORPE, JOHN NATHAN, electrical contractor; b. Oakland, Calif., May 18, 1934; s. Carl V. and Margaret B. Thorpe; m. Betty J. Stout, Mar. 9, 1967; children—Nathan Wade, Matthew John. B.A., Ohio State U., 1958. Lic. contractor Calif. Pres., Kutz-Hall-Thorpe Contractors, Chico, Calif., 1966-83; pres. Agri Electric, Chico, 1983—. Bd. dirs., chmn. Durham Parks & Recreation. Office: 11011 Midway Chico CA 95926

THORSEN, JAMES HUGH, dir. aviation, airport mgr.; b. Evanston, Ill., Feb. 5, 1943; s. Chester A. and Mary Jane (Currie) T.; B.A., Ripon Coll., 1965; m. Nancy Dain, May 30, 1980. Asst. dean of admissions Ripon (Wis.) Coll., 1965-69: adminstrv. asst. Greater Rockford (Ill.) Airport Authority, 1969-70; airport mgr. Bowman Field, Louisville, 1970-71; asst. dir. St. Louis Met. Airport Authority, 1971-80; dir. aviation, airport mgr. City of Idaho Falls (Idaho), 1980—. Named hon. citizen, State of Ill. Legislature, 1976; FAA cert. comml. pilot, flight instr. airplanes and instruments. Mem. Am. Assn. Airport Execs. (dir., accredited airport exec.), Internat. NW Aviation Council (dir.). Club: Sigma Alpha Epsilon. Home: 1270 First St Idaho Falls ID 83401 Office: Mcpl Airport Idaho Falls ID 83401

THORUP, JAMES TAT, agronomist; b. Salt Lake City, Dec. 20, 1930; s. James Berg and Agnes LaPreal (Maxwell) T.; m. Clara Beth Smith, June 9, 1958; children—Crystle, Jim, Tom, Dan. Carolynn. B.A., Brigham Young U., 1955; M.S., N.C. State Coll., 1957; Ph.D., U. Calif.-Davis, 1961. Profl. agronomist, soil scientist, Calif. Agronomist, Ortho div., Chevron Chem. Co., Dallas, 1966, regional agronomist, Fresno, Calif., 1967-81, mgr. mktg. devel., Dallas, 1981-82, San Francisco, 1983—. Charter mem. Republican. Presdl. Task Force. Mem. Am. Soc. Agronomy, Soil Sci. Soc. Mormon. Contbr. articles to profl. publs. Office: 575 Market St San Francisco CA 94104

THORUP, RICHARD MAXWELL, agronomist; b. Salt Lake City, Dec. 20, 1930; s. James Berg and Agnes LaPreal (Maxwell) T.; m. Evelyn Faye McKinney, Jan. 26, 1980; children—Teria Tribett, Christine Brownfield, Deanna McCallum, Terry, Margaret Ferrin, Troy. Cert. profl. agronomist, Calif. Agronomist Chevron Chem. Co., Phoenix, 1960-61, field agronomist, Fresno, Calif., 1961-66, regional agronomist, Ft. Madison, Iowa, 1967-75, nat. mgr. agronomy, San Francisco, 1975—. Mem. Am. Soc. Agronomy (v.p. Calif. chpt.), Soil Sci. Soc. Am., Crop Sci. Soc. Am. Republican. Mormon. Contbr. numerous articles to soil publs. and popular publs.

THRAILKILL, MARGARET ANN (PEGGY), property manager; b. Davenport, Iowa, Jan. 15, 1943; d. John Eugene and Margaret Marie (Driel) Raynoha; m. William Curtis Thrailkill, Oct. 17, 1964. B.A., U. San Diego, 1965; postgrad. U. Calif.-San Diego, 1971-75. Cert. tchr., Calif. Tchr., chmn. dept., counselor Our Lady of Peace Acad., San Diego, 1965-77; ops. mgr. Tyler Mall, Riverside, Calif., 1978; ops. mgr. Fashion Valley Shopping Ctr., San Diego, 1978-82, tchr. San Diego Community Coll., 1982; gen. mgr. Grossmont Land Co., ops. mgr. Grossmont Shopping Ctr. Co., La Mesa, Calif., 1982—. Mem. Specific Plan Com., La Mesa-Grossmont, 1982-83; trustee, Angels Unaware Found. Recipient Tribute to Women and Industry award YWCA, 1982. Mem. Internat. Council Shopping Ctrs., Bldg. Owners and Mgrs., AAUW. Republican. Roman Catholic. Home: 15616 Oak Valley Rd Ramona CA 92065 Office: 5500 Grossmont Center Dr La Mesa CA 92041

THRASHER, BOB ODELL, school administrator; b. Gila Bend, Ariz., Jan. 26, 1939; s. Otis and Ovelle (Bragg) T.; m. Mara Lynne Cyphers, Sept. 10, 1965; children—Bobby O., Laura Lynne. B.A. in Secondary Edn., Ariz. State U., 1970; M.A. in Indsl. Edn., No. Ariz. U., 1972. Cert. secondary tchr., secondary prin., supr., supt., Ariz. Police patrolman City of Phoenix, 1964-70; tchr. Sunnyslope High Sch., Phoenix, 1970-73; asst. dir. purchasing Glendale Union High Sch. Dist., Phoenix, 1974; dean of students Cortez High Sch., Phoenix, 1974-78; asst. prin. student activities Thunderbird High Sch., Phoenix, 1978—; affiliate Educator Tng. Ctr., Long Beach, Calif. Coach, mgr. Al-Villa Little League, 1980-83. Served with U.S. Army, 1960-63. Mem. Nat. Assn. Secondary Sch. Prins., Assn. Supervision and Curriculum Devel., Ariz. Interscholastic Athletic Adminstrs. Assn., Nat. Interscholastic Athletic Adminstrs. Assn., Phi Delta Kappa. Lodge: Masons. Devel. alternative programs for student dropouts, behavioral problems. Home: 6806 N 38th Dr Phoenix AZ 85019 Office: Thunderbird High School 1750 W Thunderbird Rd Phoenix AZ 85023

THRASHER, LINDA JACQUELINE, copier supplies company executive; b. Detroit, May 9, 1946; d. Nolan and Jeannette Leach; m. Paul Cameron Thrasher, Sept. 11, 1965; children—Laura Linda, Matthew Michael. Grad. Pontiac Bus. Inst., 1965. Sales rep. Bliss Supplies, Inc., Troy, Mich., 1975-78; pres. Cactus Copier Supplies, Inc., 1978—. Mem. NOW. Democrat. Quaker. Office: Cactus Copier Supplies Inc 10605 E Cactus Rd Scottsdale AZ 85260

THRONSON, RODERICK MORRIS, educational administrator, air force officer; b. Helena, Mont., July 22, 1949; s. Rolan Morris and Marjorie Dolores (Gregor) T.; m. Carolyn Claudia Miller, May 26, 1972; children—Kirsten Ann, Paul Roderick. B.S. in Botany, Montana State U., 1971, M.Ed. in Secondary Curriculum and Instrn., 1979; degree in Elem. Edn. Conversion, Carroll Coll., 1977. Class I teaching cert., class III adminstrn. cert., Mont. Commd. 2d lt. U.S. Air Force, 1971, advanced through grades to 1st lt., 1974; wing intelligence officer, Cannon AFB, N.Mex., 1972-74; tchr. middle sch. interdisciplinary team C.R. Anderson Sch., Dist. 1, Helena, 1974-79; tchr. 5th grade, 1979-81; supt. schs. Turner (Mont.) Sch. Dist. #43, 1981—; mem. Mont. planning com. Energy and Man's Environment; pub. affairs officer for Mont., liason officer Air Force Acad. Mem. Sch. Adminstrs. Mont., Am. Assn. Sch. Adminstrs., Hi-Line Adminstrs. Assn., Assn. Supervision and Curriculum Devel., Mont. Ofcls. Assn. Democrat. Lutheran. Contbg. author: Energy-Environment Simulator Montana Schools, 1980. Home: PO Box 151 Turner MT 59542 Office: Turner Sch Dist 43 PO Box 40 Turner MT 59542

THURBER, STEVEN DAVID, psychologist, educator; b. Boise, Idaho, June 9, 1941; s. Erin Butler and Afton May (Crowley) T.; m. Joyce Fay Feighner, June 21, 1963; children—David Edmund, Janean Alice, Eric Steven. B.S., Brigham Young U., 1965, M.S. (NDEA fellow), 1968; Ph.D. (Henderson fellow), U. Tex.-Austin, 1970; postdoctoral cert. (Bush Found. grantee) U. Minn., 1978; postdoctoral cert. U. Okla. Med. Sch., 1980. Lic. psychologist, Idaho. Asst. in psychology Calif. Instn. for Women, Frontera, 1965-66; grad. teaching asst. Brigham Young U., 1966-68; teaching asst. U. Tex., 1969-70; predoctoral intern Austin Child Guidance Ctr., 1969-70; asst. prof. psychology Boise State U., 1970-74, assoc. prof., 1974-77, prof., 1977—; dir. psychol. services Raleigh Hills Hosp., Boise, Idaho, 1982—, cons., 1982—; interim dir. adolescent treatment programs Intermountain Hosp., Boise, 1981-82, dir. youth treatment program, 1981—; research coordinator Nat. Inst. Edn. study, Boise, 1974; psychologist Idaho Crippled Children's Services, 1974-75, Boise Police Dept., 1975-79; assoc. dir. Behavior Change Inst., 1975—; mem. adv. bd. Desert Industries, 1975-76, Idaho Health Systems, 1976; mem. mental health adv. bd. Region IV, Idaho Dept. Health and Welfare, 1975-79, pres. bd., 1977-78; postdoctoral fellow U. Okla. Med. Sch., 1979-80; spl. instr. coll., univ. courses, 1973, 74, 76. Schmidt Edn. Found. research grantee, 1967-68. Mem. Idaho Psychol. Assn., Rocky Mountain Psychol. Assn., Soc. Advancement Social Psychology, Southwestern Psychol. Assn., Soc. Pediatric Psychology, Am. Psychol. Assn. Author: Mid-life adjustments and motivation, 1980; contbr. articles to profl. jours.; author profl. papers. Home: 7226 Cedarwood Dr Boise ID 83709 Office: 303 N Allumbaugh Boise ID 83704

THURSTON, CRAIG ROANE, real estate exec.; b. Fortuna, Calif., July 28, 1942; s. Harry R., Jr. and Maxine M. (Maxwell) T.; B.A. in Econs., Humboldt State Coll., Arcata, Calif., 1965; m. Barbara Pickle, Sept. 8, 1964; children—Scott, Matthew. Right-of-way agt. Calif. Dept. Transp., 1966-75; land agt. Calif. Dept. Gen. Services, 1975-76; owner Thurston Co., real estate investment, counseling, brokerage, appraisal and mgmt., Sacramento, 1976—. Treas. Greenhaven Soccer Club, 1981, 82, Sacramento Youth Soccer League, 1981, 82. Served with USAR, 1966-72. Mem. Am. Inst. Real Estate Appraisers, Sacramento Bd. Realtors, Sacramento Apt. Assn. Club: Southland 6000 Racket (Sacramento). Office: 2210 K St Sacramento CA 95816

THURSTON, RONALD CHARLES, psychiatrist; b. Cleve., Mar. 29, 1939; s. Charles George and June Hazel (Burton) T.; B.S., Wayne State U., 1963, M.D., 1968; M.Social Psychiatry, UCLA, 1974; m. Lynne May Thurston— children—Benjamin Ronald, Stephanie Lyn. Rotating intern Henry Ford Hosp., Detroit, 1968-69; resident psychiatry U. Calif. Sch. Medicine, Los Angeles, 1969-72, Académie de Paris, Université René Descartes, Faculté de Médecine Cochin Port-Royal, Centre Psychiatrique Ste-Anne, Paris, 1971-72; practice medicine specializing in psychiatry, Ventura, Calif., 1972—; chief of staff, dept. psychiatry Ventura County Gen. Hosp., 1977, 82; psychiatrist County Los Angeles, 1972-75; mem. staff Ventura County Gen., Community Meml. hosps. (both Ventura); cons. Ventura County Sheriff, Dept. Corrections, 1974-75, Calif. State Dept. Rehab., 1974—. Diplomate Am. Bd. Psychiatry and Neurology. Mem. Am. Psychiat. Assn., So. Calif. Psychiat. Soc., AMA, Psi Chi, Alpha Omega Alpha, Sierra Club. Home: 237 Barnard Way Ventura CA 93001 Office: 970 S Petit Ave Ventura CA 93004

THWAITES, JEANNE CAMBRAI, photographer, author; b. Kandy, Sri Lanka, Dec. 6, 1929; d. Reginald Young and Bertha (Van Langenberg) Daniel; m. James S. Thwaites, Nov. 29, 1952; children—Josephine Mary, Michael James Stamers, Daniel James. Licenciate Trinity Coll. Music, Eng., 1943. Self-employed photographer, freelance writer, San Luis Obispo, Calif., 1965—; tchr., lectr. in field. Mem. Profl. Photographers Assn. Democrat. Author: Mother and Child, 1967; Horses of the West, 1968; San Francisco After Dark, 1971; Once is Enough, 1972; How to Turn a Woman On and Off, 1973; Danger in Ceylon, 1981. Home and office: San Luis Obispo CA 93401

TIBBITTS, KENT D., educator; b. Rexburg, Idaho, Sept. 21, 1937; s. Don Woodrow and Nora (Grant) T.; B.S. in Music Edn., U. Utah, 1964, M.S. in Ednl. Adminstrn., 1969; ednl. specialist Brigham Young U., 1978; m. Cecelia Ann Marcroft, Aug. 15, 1963; children—ViAnn, Don, Ernest, Ruth. Band dir. San Juan High Sch., Blanding, Utah, 1964-69; work and tng. specialist Utah Dept. Employment Security Blanding, 1969-70; Navajo Curriculum Center dir. San Juan Sch. Dist., Blanding, 1970-76, Navajo bilingual Title I dir., 1976-79, Title I media dir., 1979—; bilingual/bicultural cons.; instr. coll. music, media. Chmn., San Juan County (Utah) Travel Council, 1970-74; bd. dirs. Utah Dept. Parks and Recreation, 1975—; treas. Kigalia Fine Arts Council, Blanding, 1976—; mem. Blanding City Council, 1976. Served with U.S. Army, 1961-62. Recipient Creative Uses of Ednl. Tech. regional award AVID Corp., 1975, 1 of 10 Top Media Projects award Stanford U., 1974. Mem. Assn. Supervision and Curriculum Devel. Democrat. Mormon. Club: Lions (pres. club 1976-77) (Blanding). Author booklets, instructional kits on Navajo culture, lang.; producer films, filmstrips on Navajo lang. and cultures. Home: 574 W 100 S Blanding UT 84511 Office: 28 W 200 N Blanding UT 84511

TICHY, GEORGE JOSEPH, II, lawyer; b. Longview, Wash., Nov. 11, 1942; s. George Joseph and Charlotte Marie (Hewitt) T.; B.A., U. Oreg., 1964; J.D., U. Minn., 1967; m. Sheila Marie Garvey, June 15, 1968; children—Shannon Marie, Megan Ann, Daniel George. Admitted to Calif. bar, 1967; assoc. Littler, Mendelson & Fastiff, 1968-70; mem. firm Littler, Mendelson, Fastiff & Tichy, 1970—. Calif. rep. U. Minn. Partnership in Excellence, 1972—. Bd. visitors U. Minn. Law Sch. Served with USCGR, 1967-68. Mem. AM., Wash., Calif., San Francisco bar assns., U. Minn. Law Alumni Assn., Greater San Francisco C. of C., Kappa Sigma, Alpha Kappa Psi, Delta Theta Phi. Republican. Home: Hillsborough CA 94010 Office: 650 California St 20th Floor San Francisco CA 94108

TIEDEMAN, DAVID VALENTINE, educator; b. Americus, Ga., Aug. 12, 1919; s. Walter Dohlen and Edna Marie (Komfort) T.; m. Marjorie Ida Denman, Sept. 26, 1942 (div. Jan. 1973); children—David Michael, Jeffrey Denman; m. 2d, Anna Louise Miller, Jan. 6, 1973. A.B., Union Coll., Schenectady, 1941; A.M., U. Rochester, 1943; Ed.M., Harvard U., 1948, Ed.D., 1949. Mem. staff NRC com. selection and tng. aircraft pilots U. Rochester, 1941-43; with dept. constrn. Coll. Entrance Exam. Bd., 1943-44; assoc. head stats. div. Manhattan Project, 1944-46; Milton teaching fellow, instr. edn. Harvard U. Grad. Sch. Edn., 1946-48, Sheldon travelling fellow, 1948-49, instr. edn., 1949-51, asst. prof. edn., 1951-52, lectr. edn., 1952-55, assoc. prof., 1955-59, prof., 1959-71, assoc. dir. Ctr. for Research in Careers, 1963-66, research assoc., also chmn. exec. com., info. system for vocat. decisions, 1966-69; prin. research scientist Palo Alto (Calif.) office Am. Insts. for Research, 1971-73; prof. edn. No. Ill. U., 1973-80, dir. ERIC Clearinghouse in Career Edn., 1973-76, coordinator Office Vocat., Tech., and Career Edn., 1978-80; prof. career and edn. U. So. Calif., 1981—; mem. Adv. Council on Guidance, Mass. Dept. Edn., 1957-63; chmn. commn. on tests Coll. Entrance Exam. Bd., 1967-70; mem. adv. screening com. in edn. Council Internat. Exchange Scholars, 1975-79, chmn., 1978-79. Bd. dirs. Mass. Com. Children and Youth, 1961-63. Ctr. for Advanced Study in Behavioral Scis., 1963-64; NIMH spl. fellow, 1963-64. Mem. Am. Ednl. Research Assn., Am. Personnel and Guidance Assn., Nat. Vocat. Guidance Assn. (pres. 1965-66, Eminent Career award 1979), Am. Psychol. Assn. (pres. div. counseling psychology 1965-66), Nat. Council on Measurement in Edn. (pres. 1962-63), NEA, Phi Beta Kappa, Sigma Xi, Phi Delta Kappa, Phi Kappa Phi. Contbr. articles to profl. jours., chpts. to books; editorial assoc. Jour. Counseling Psychology, 1957-63, Personnel and Guidance Jour., 1960-63, Character Potential: A Record of Research, 1977-83, Jour. Career Edn., 1979—. Office: Nat Inst Advancement Career Edn U So Calif Univ Park-MC 0031 Los Angeles CA 90089

TIEDT, IRIS MCCLELLAN, language arts educator, author; b. Dayton, Ohio, Feb. 3, 1928; d. Raymond Hill and Ermalene (Swartzel) McClellan; m. Sidney Willis Tiedt, 1949 (div.); children—Pamela Lynn, Ryan Collay. B.S., Northwestern U., 1950; M.A., U. Oreg., 1961; Ph.D., Stanford U., 1972. Cert. tchr., supr., adminstr. Calif. pub. sch. tchr. Chgo., Anchorage, Eugene, Oreg., 1950-65; dir. tchr. edn. U. Santa Clara, Calif., 1968-76; dir. South Bay Writing Project, San Jose State U., Calif., 1977—; cons. in field. Mem. Nat. Women's Polit. Caucus, NOW, Women's Campaign Fund. Stanford U. AAUW grantee, 1966; Calif. Writing Project grantee 1980-82. Mem. Nat. Council Tchrs. English (editor Language Arts 1972-76), Internat. Reading Assn., Calif. Assn. Tchrs. English, Nat. Writing Project. Democrat. Author: Effective English, 1978; Language Arts Activities for the Classroom, 1978; exploring Books with Children, 1979; Multicultural Teaching, 1979; The Writing Process, 1981; Teaching Writing in K-8 Classrooms, 1983; The Language Arts Handbook, 1983. Home: 1654 Fairorchard Ave San Jose CA 95125 Office: English Dept San Jose State U San Jose CA 95192

TIEDT, SIDNEY WILLIS, educator; b. Chgo., Aug. 15, 1927. B.S., Northwestern U., 1950, M.A., 1953; Ed.D., U. Oreg., 1961. Elementary and jr. high sch. tchr., Chgo. and Alaska, 1951-57, adminstr., 1958-59; faculty U. Oreg., 1959-61; faculty San Jose (Calif.) State U., 1961—, now prof. edn.; vis. instr. U. Wash., 1967; vis. scholar Stanford U., 1981-82; extension instr. U. Calif., Santa Cruz, 1963; dir. NDEA English Inst., 1964. Mem. Am. Ednl. Research Assn., Nat. Council Tchrs. English (cons., com. mem.), Calif. Assn. Tchrs. English (cons., com. mem.), Internat. Platform Assn., Creative Edn. Found., Phi Delta Kappa. Co-editor: Contemporary Classroom Series; editor: Contemporary Education Foundations Series, 1974; contbr. articles in field to profl. jours. Office: San Jose State U San Jose CA 95192

TIEGEL, ELIOT LLOYD, journalist; b. Bklyn., Jan. 28, 1936; s. Harry and Helen (Hariton) T.; m. Fran Goldberg, Jan. 13, 1961; children—Scott, Blake, Alexis, Kenny; m. 2d, Bonnie Gail Kaplan, Apr. 21, 1972. Editorial reporter, asst. N.Y. Herald Tribune, N.Y.C., 1954-56; West Coast info. mgr. Columbia Records, Los Angeles, 1962-63; mng. editor Billboard mag., Los Angeles, 1974-81, spl. issues editor, 1972-74, West Coast bur. chief, 1963-74; freelance writer, Los Angeles Times, Rolling Stone, People mag., Calif. Bus., USA Today, Billboard, Santa Ana Register, Washington Times, 1981—. Served with AUS, 1958-60. Recipient Best Mag. Writing and Pub. Relations Assn., Las Vegas, 1973-74. Democrat.

TIEN, CHANG LIN, mechanical engineer, editor, educator; b. Wuhan, China, July 24, 1935; came to U.S., 1956, naturalized, 1969; married; 3 children. B.S., Nat. Taiwan U., 1955; M.M.E., U. Louisville, 1957; M.A., Princeton U., 1959, Ph.D., 1959. Mem. faculty U. Calif.-Berkeley, 1959—, prof. mech. engring., 1968—, chmn. mech. engring. dept., 1974-81, chmn. thermal systems div., 1969-72; hon., prof. engring. Huazhong Inst. Tech.-China, 1981; hon. research prof. Chinese Acad. Scis. Inst. Thermophysics, 1981; cons. in field. Chmn. exec. com. Internat. Ctr. Heat and Mass Transfer, Belgrade, Yugoslavia, 1980-82. Recipient Disting. Teaching award U. Calif., 1962, Excellence in Teaching award Pi Tau Sigma, 1972, Max Jakob Meml. award Am. Inst. Chem. Engrs.-ASME, 1981; Howard Crathrone Phillips fellow, 1958-59, Guggenheim fellow, 1965, Humboldt Sr. U.S. Scientist award, 1979, Japan Soc. Promotion Sci. Sr. U.S. Scientist fellow, 1980. Fellow ASME (Heat Transfer Meml. award 1974, Gustus L. Larson Meml. award 1975); mem. Nat. Acad. Engring., AIAA (Thermophysics award 1977). Adv. editor Mechanical Engineering Book Series, 1966-75; assoc. editor: Jour. Quantitative Spectroscopy and Radiative Transfer, 1971—, also monograph series, 1977—; editor: Internat. Jour. Heat and Mass Transfer, 1981—, International Communications in Heat and Mass Transfer, 1981—. Contbr. numerous sci. articles to profl. publs. Home: 1451 Olympus Ave Berkeley CA 94720 Office: U Calif Mech Engring Dept Berkeley CA 94720

TIENSVOLD, MELVIN ORVILLE, C.P.A.; b. Rushville, Nebr., July 10, 1951; s. Orville Odin and Darleen (Jackson) T.; m. Benna Kay Wolff, July 10, 1951; Student, Mont. State U., 1969-71; B.S., U. Mont., 1973. C.P.A., Mont. Ptnr., Colberg Fasching Mrachek & Tiensvold, Laurel, Mont., 1980—, also office mgr. Mem. Am. Inst. C.P.A.s, Mont. Soc. C.P.A.s, Yellowstone Valley Estate Planning Council. Republican. Lutheran. Clubs: Laurel Rotary, Laurel Jaycees. Home: 1105 8th Ave Laurel MT 59044 Office: 106 E 1st St PO Box 308 Laurel MT 59044

TIETYEN, DAVID EARL, advertising executive; b. Milw., May 3, 1940; s. Elben Edward and Viola T.; B.S. in Journalism, U. Wis., 1965; M.B.A., UCLA, 1982; m. Mary Hoban, Nov. 15, 1975. Account exec. Klau Van Pietersom-Dunlap, Milw., 1966-69; account supr. Ketchum, MacLoed & Grove, Pitts. and Los Angeles, 1969-71; sr. account exec. Burson-Marstellar, Los Angeles, 1971; pres. PR Mix, Los Angeles, 1972-75; dir. advt. Hal Leonard Pub. Co., Milw., 1975-77; freelance author, Los Angeles, 1977-78; v.p., creative dir. Darryl Lloyd, Inc., North Hollywood, Calif., 1978-81; pres. TCI Advt. & Pub. Relations, Sherman Oaks, Calif., 1981—. Served with USCGR, 1960. Mem. Public Relations Soc. Am., Los Angeles Ad Club. Author: The Illustrated Disney Songbook, 1979. Office: 13741 Ventura Blvd Sherman Oaks CA 91423

TIETZ, WILLIAM JOHN, JR., univ. pres.; b. Chgo., Mar. 6, 1927; s. William John and Irma (Neuman) T.; B.A., Swarthmore Coll., 1950; M.S., U. Wis., 1952; D.V.M., Colo. State U., 1957; Ph.D., Purdue U., 1961; m. Patricia Lane Wells, Apr. 25, 1953; children—Karen Elizabeth, William John, Julia Wells. Instr., then asso. prof. Purdue U., 1957-64; faculty Colo. State U., 1964-77, prof., chmn. physiology and biophysics, 1967-70, v.p. student and univ. relations, 1970-71, dean Coll. Vet. Medicine and Biomed. Scis., 1971-77, asso. dir. Agr. Expt. Sta., 1975-77; pres. Mont. State U., Bozeman, 1977—; dir. First Nat. Bank, Bozeman. Bd. dirs. Children's House, Montessori Sch., 1966-70, chmn., 1968-70; bd. dirs. Colo. State U. Found., 1970-71; treas. Mont. Energy Research and Devel. Inst., 1977-78, v.p., 1978-80, chmn. bd., 1980—; bd. dirs. Greater Mont. Found., 1979—; mem. Mont. Com. for Humanities, 1980-83; mem. div. resources adv. council NIH, 1979-82; trustee Yellowstone Park Library and Museum Bd., 1981—. Served with USNR, 1945-46. Recipient Service award Colo. Vet. Med. Assn., 1976. Mem. Larimer County Vet. Med. Assn. (pres. 1968-69), Am. Assn. Vet. Physiologists and Pharmacologists (pres. 1971-72), Am. Physiol. Soc., Assn. Am. Colls. Vet. Medicine (chmn. council of deans 1975-76), Bozeman C. of C. (dir. 1981—), Sigma Xi, Phi Zeta (sec.-treas. 1970-71), Phi Kappa Phi, Phi Sigma Kappa, Omicron Delta Kappa, Beta Beta Beta. Address: Office of Pres Mont State U Bozeman MT 59715

TIFFANY, FORREST FRASER, medical lab. exec.; b. Hoboken, N.J., Feb. 7, 1916; s. Joseph Raymond and Adeline (Ely) T.; student Charlottesville Sch. Bus, 1936, U. Va., 1938; also various profl. seminars; m. Margaret Watson Clark, Dec. 9, 1941; children—Gretchen Tiffany Gieg, Joseph Raymond II, Beverly Ann, Tyler Jamison. Jr. exec. Kingsport Press, Inc. (Tenn.), 1938-41; with Reynolds Metals Co., 1947-58, divisional sales mgr., Pitts., 1951-55, mktg. mgr., Louisville,

1955-58; with Aluminum div. Olin Mathieson Chem. Corp., 1958-66, asst. dir. sales, N.Y.C., 1962-63, dir. mktg. Olin Foil Packaging, San Francisco, 1963-66; v.p. mktg. Micro Magnetic Industries, Palo Alto, Calif., 1967-68; prin. Tiffany & Co., mktg. cons., Woodside, Calif., 1969; asst. to med. dir. MML/Solano Labs., Palo Alto, 1970-72, staff v.p. and gen. mgr., 1972-75, staff v.p., asst. to med. dir., Berkeley, Calif., 1975-78; dir. ops. Metpath Inc. (acquired MML/Solano Labs. 1978), Berkeley, 1978-79, legal and regulatory adv. for Calif. ops., 1979—. Mem. adv. com. to rate devel. sect. Calif. Dept. Health Services, Sacramento. Served with U.S. Army, 1941-45; ETO. Mem. Am. Arbitration Assn. (nat. bd. artibrators), Calif. Clin. Lab. Assn. (founder 1976, pres., chmn. bd. 1976-81, exec. dir. 1982-83), Am. Assn. Ret. Persons, Sigma Alpha Epsilon. Republican. Mem. Woodside Village Ch. Home: 315 Laning Dr Woodside CA 94062 Office: 890 Cowan Rd Burlingame CA 94010

TIFFANY, PAUL NELSON, info systems co. exec.; b. Hollywood, Calif., Apr. 26, 1946; s. Nelson Herbert and Barbara J. (McCasland) T.; B.S.E., UCLA, 1968, M.B.A., 1979; m. Martha G. McKinney, June 5, 1976. Analyst, chief of computer services, chief bus. systems Dept. Water Resources, State of Calif., Los Angeles and Sacramento, 1970-78; cons. engr., partner, gen. mgr. S T Engring., Studio City, Calif., 1969-78; sr. mem. tech. staff Transaction Technology Citicorp, Santa Monica, Calif., 1978, network performance mgr., 1979-80, project mgr., asst. v.p., 1980-81; dir. info. systems Haney & Assocs., Woodland Hills, Calif., 1981-82; chmn. bd., chief exec. officer Software Power Corp., West Los Angeles, Calif., 1982—; guest lectr. UCLA, 1975-77. Chmn. fin. com. Berean Ch.; trustee, treas. Berean Day Care Center, Los Angeles, 1980-82. Republican. Adventist. Club: Toastmasters. Home: Bel-Air Estates CA 90077 Office: 1901 Ave of Stars Suite 1774 Century City CA 90067 also PO Box 24C56 Los Angeles CA 90024

TIFFIN, JAMES L., community relations/marketing manager; b. Urbana Ill., Nov. 9, 1948; s. Jesse J. and Betty Auzelia (Bestor) T. B.A. in Communications/Pub. Relations, Calif. State U.-Fullerton, 1980. Pub. info. asst. Santa Ana (Calif.) Community Coll., 1979, Pub. Info. Dept., City of Cerritos (Calif.), 1980; mktg. dir. Desert Schs. Fed. Credit Union, Phoenix, 1980-83; community relations/mktg. mgr. Bapt. Hosps. and Health Systems, Inc., Phoenix, 1983—; freelance copy writer, 1978—; cons., lectr. pub. relations Phoenix Coll. Served with USAF, 1967-74. Mem. Internat. Assn. Bus. Communicators (recipient several awards), Credit Union Execs. Soc. (recipient several awards), Pub. Relations Soc. Am. Republican. Office: Bapt Hosps and Health Systems Inc 2040 W Bethany Home Rd Phoenix AZ 85015

TILLER, DANIEL LEE, optometrist; b. Nampa, Idaho, Oct. 30, 1953; s. Norman Edward and Carol Jean (Straubhaar) T.; m. Jamie Lynn Ford, July 18, 1975; children—Lyndsay Danielle. B.B.A., Boise State U., 1976; B.S., Pacific U., 1980, O.D., 1983. With Consumers Inc., Nampa, 1968-81, pvt. practice optometry, Nampa, 1983—. Mem. Student Optometric Assn., Am. Optometric Assn. (contact lens sect.). Club: Rotary. Home: 367 Winther Blvd Nampa ID 83651

TILLERY, BILL W., educator; b. Muskogee, Okla., Sept. 15, 1938; s. William Earnest and Bessie C. (Smith) Freeman; B.S., Northeastern U., 1960; M.A., U. No. Colo., 1965, Ed.D., 1967; m. Patricia Weeks Northrop, Aug. 1, 1981; children by previous marriage—Tonya Lynn, Lisa Gail. Tchr. physics and chemistry Guthrie (Okla.) schs., 1960-62; tchr. sci. Jefferson County (Colo.) schs., 1962-64; teaching asst. U. No. Colo., 1965-67; asst. prof. Fla. State U., 1967-69; asso. prof. U. Wyo., 1969-73, dir. Sci. and Math. Teaching Center, 1969-73; asso. prof. dept. physics Ariz. State U., 1973-75, prof., 1976—; cons. in field. Fellow AAAS; mem. Nat. Sci. Tchrs. Assn., Ariz. Sci. Tchrs. Assn., Assn. Edn. of Tchrs. in Sci., Nat. Assn. Research in Sci. Teaching. Republican. Episcopalian. Author: (with Ploutz) Basic Physical Science, 1964; (with Sund and Trowbridge) Elementary Science Activities, 1967; (with Sund and Trowbridge) Elementary Biological Science, 1970, Elementary Physical Science, 1970, Elementary Earth Science, 1970, Investigate and Discover, 1975; Space, Time, Energy and Matter: Activity Books, 1976; editor Arizona Science Teachers Jour., 1975—, Arizona Energy Education, 1978—. Home: 9103 S Kachina Dr Tempe AZ 85284 Office: Arizona State U Dept Physics Tempe AZ 85287

TILLETT, ROB ROY, aerospace engineer; b. Lowell, Wyo., Feb. 22, 1931; s. William Edmund and Besse Frances (Strong) T.; m. Geraldine Elaine Moore, Feb. 21, 1953; children—Robin Renee, Clay Kevin. B.S. in Physics, U. Wyo., 1955. Sr. flight test engr. G.D. Astronautics, San Diego, 1956-62; sr. engr. Thiokol Chem. Corp., Brigham City, Utah, 1962-63; aerospace engr. NASA, White Sands Test Facility, Las Cruces, N. Mex., 1963-68; chief Propulsion Test Office, 1969-81, mgr., 1981—. Mem. N.Mex. Gov's. Tech. Excellence Com. Served in U.S. Army, 1950-51. Recipient NASA cert. of commendation, 1969, exceptional service medal, 1973; Johnson Space Ctr. spl. achievement award, 1980. Mem. AIAA. Republican. Clubs: Masons. Home: 2140 Gladys St Las Cruces NM 88001 Office: PO Drawer MM Las Cruces NM 88004

TIMBERLAKE, EDWARD WRENNE, JR., public relations director; b. West Point, N.Y., Dec. 6, 1925; s. Edward Wrenne and Mary Ala (Pierce) T.; m. Audrey Ann Spannaus, July 7, 1929; children—Scott Wrenne, Teresa Ann. Student Cornell U., Syracuse U., U. Wis., U. Ariz., Am. U.; B.A. in Journalism, U. Colo., 1951; M.S. in Mass Communications, Am. U., Washington, 1971. News reporter Colorado Springs (Colo.) Gazette Telegraph, 1951-53; assoc. editor Colo. State U., Fort Collins, 1953-54; mktg. specialist Duncan Hines Foods Inc., Ithaca, N.Y., 1954-55; dir. pub. relations Mut. Fedn., Syracuse, N.Y., 1955-62; asst. to dir. info. AEC, Albuquerque, 1962-64; dir. pub. affairs office U.S. Army Communications Command, Fort Huachuca, Ariz., 1964—; guest lectr. pub. relations, journalism Am. U., Ariz. U., Cochise Coll.; instr. journalism Cochise Coll., Sierra Vista, Ariz. Publicity chmn. Cancer Crusade, Albuquerque, 1963; communications chmn. United Fund Campaign, Sierra Vista/Fort Huachuca, 1980-81. Served in U.S. Army, 1944-46. Decorated Bronze Star; recipient Two Orchids awards Tucson Press Club; medal of Valor, Navajo Nation. Mem. Pub. Relations Soc. Am. (Silver Anvil award, pres. citation, pres. So. Ariz. 1974, N.Y. 1960, N.Mex. 1963), Assn. U.S. Army (chpt. dir. 1974-76), U. Colo. Alumni Assn. (pres. chpt. 1975-80), Sigma Delta Chi, Nat. Press Photographers Assn., Golf Writers Assn. Am. Republican. Episcopalian. Clubs: Tucson Press, Syracuse Press, Colorado Springs Press. Contbr. articles to profl. jours. Home: 6342 Brian Kent Tucson AZ 85710 Office: Greely Hall US Army Communications Command Fort Huachuca AZ 85613

TIMM, PAUL ROY, educator, university dean; b. Buffalo, Nov. 29, 1943; s. Roy Charles and Ruth Eleanora (LaVere) T.; B.A., SUNY, Buffalo, 1968; M.A., Ohio U., 1969; Ph.D., Fla. State U., 1977; m. Helen Louise Bauer, Dec. 28, 1963; children—Jennifer, Roy Charles, Erika Susan, Monika Corey, James Thomas. Writer, editor Martin Marietta Corp., Orlando, Fla., 1969; comml. mgr. So. Bell Telephone Corp., Orlando, 1969-73; sr. sales rep. Xerox Corp., Tallahassee, 1973-76; assoc. prof. dept. info. mgmt. Brigham Young U., Provo, Utah, 1979—, asst. dean sch. mgmt., 1981—; cons. to numerous corps. and govt. agys. Served with U.S. Army, 1963-66. Mem. Am. Bus. Communication Assn., Acad. Mgmt. Republican. Mormon. Author: Managerial Communication, 1980; Functional Business Presentations, 1981; People at Work, 1982; Business Communication, 1983; contbr. articles to profl. jours. Home: 81 E 2000 S Orem UT 84057 Office: Brigham Young U 730 TNRB Provo UT 84602

TIMMINS, WILLIAM F., painter; b. Chgo.; s. Harry L. and Pauline (Beckford) T.; m. Marjorie Vail; children—Gary William, Dana Timmins Leane. Student Grand Central Art Sch., 1933-34, Art Students League, 1933-34. Freelance illustrator Street & Smith Pubs., 1933-75, Colliers, Western Pubs., Los Angeles, Family Circle, Rand McNally, Boy Scouts Am., Nat. Advt. Assn.; exhibited paintings in numerous shows and galleries, New Eng., 1943-65, Calif. and Western U.S., 1965—; works represented in pvt. and corp. collections. lectr. in field. Mem. Soc. W. Artists, Nat. Portrait Soc. Republican. Club: Carmel Valley Racquet. Address: PO Box 5685 Carmel CA 93921

TIMMONS, EVELYN DEERING, pharmacist; b. Durango, Colo., Sept. 29, 1926; d. Claude Elliot and Evelyn (Allen) Deering; B.S. in Pharmacy and Chemistry, U. Colo., 1948; children—Roderick Deering, Steven Palmer. Asst., chief pharmacy services Meml. Hosp., Phoenix, 1950-54; chief med. research librarian Roche Pharms., Inc., Nutley, N.J., 1956-58; staff pharmacist St. Joseph's Hosp., Phoenix, 1958-60; from asst. to mgr. Doctors Bldg. Pharmacy, Phoenix, 1968-72; pres. Ariz. Apothecaries, Ltd., Mt. View Pharmacy, Phoenix, 1972—; owner, mgr. Prescription Pharmacy, 1972—; med. pharm. (therapeutic) cons. to several physicians; part-time relief to retail profl. and nursing home econs., 1960-68; dir. Ariz. Pharm. Assocs., 1968-70; pres. Ariz. Med. Aux., 1966-68. Asst. sec. Nat. Young Republican League, 1963-65; pres. Civitan Wives, 1960; mem. Scottsdale Planning and Zoning Bd., 1960-61. Recipient pub. service award Maricopa County Med. Soc., 1965. Fellow Am. Coll. Apothecaries (pres. Ariz. chpt. 1979-81, state dir. 1981-83, nat. 1st. v.p. 1982-83, nat. pres.-elect 1983—); mem. Am., Ariz. (bd. dirs., dir. continuing edn., Service to Pharmacy award 1976, Pharmacist of Yr. 1981), Maricopa County (pres. 1977) pharm. assns., Am. Soc. Hosp. Pharmacists, Nat. Assn. Retail Druggists (cert. fitter), Soaring Soc. Am., Aircraft Owners and Pilots Assn., Air Safety Found., Nat. Rifle Assn., Nat. Platform Assn., Rho Chi, Iota Sigma Pi, Kappa Epsilon (nominee Career Achievement award 1983). Republican. Author: Good Emergency Mother Substitute Handbook, 1962; editor: Wacademy World, 1943-44; contributing scribe, Ariz. Pharmacist, 1976, 77; contbr. poem to publs., 1975. Home: PO Box 1389 Scottsdale AZ 85252 Office: 10565 N Tatum Blvd Suite B-118 Paradise Valley AZ 85253

TIMMRECK, JOE EDWARD, data processor; b. Longview, Wash., Oct. 8, 1950; s. Carmin C. and Betty (Snyder) T.; m. Janet Clipp; 1 dau., Jennifer. A.A. in Computer Sci., Lower Columbia Coll., 1970; student Weber State Coll., 1971-74. Engr. technician Ultrasystems, Ogden, Utah, 1973-75; system programmer St. Benedict's Hosp., Ogden, 1975-77; system analyst Jackson County (Oreg.), 1978-79; data processing mgr. Medford (Oreg.) Sch. Dist. 549C, 1979—. Founder, pres. Human Potentials Unltd., Medford, 1981—; pub. The Obelisk, Medford, 1982—. Mem. Am. Mgmt. Assn., Oreg. Assn. Ednl. Data Systems. Office: 500 Monroe Medford OR 97501

TIMON, JUDY LYN, educator, consultant; b. Syracuse, N.Y., Dec. 31, 1948; d. Paul Benedict and R. Diane Goldsmith; m. Perry Scott Timon, Mar. 26, 1972; children—Joshua Scott, Mckenzie Lyn. B.S. in Edn. and Sociology, SUNY-Brockport, 1970; M.A. in Counseling and Guidance, U. Colo., 1982. Cert. counselor,, tchr., Colo. Tchr. Douglas County Schs., Castle Rock, Colo., 1970-72, Jefferson County Schs., Lakewood, Colo., 1973—; instr. Met. State Coll., Denver, summer 1981; cons. in classroom mgmt., classroom counseling; instr. parenting class, Lakewood, Vol. Mt. Evans Hospice, Boy Scouts Am.; host family Am. Scandanavian Student Exchange. Recipient outstanding performance award Jefferson County Outdoor Edn. Lab. Sch. 1978. Mem. Am. Personnel and Guidance Assn., NEA, Colo. Personnel and Guidance Assn. Methodist. Contbr. articles to profl. jours.; developer Huddle counseling technique. Home: 8702 Gray Fox Dr Evergreen CO 80439 Office: 26663 N Turkey Creek Rd Evergreen CO 80439

TIMS, SUE MITCHELL, counselor, nurse; b. Grenada, Miss., Feb. 16, 1941; d. Lavern Howard and Martha Claudine (Lane) Mitchell; m. Frederick Curtis Tims, Sept. 4 1965; children—Curt, Emily Susan. R.N., Baptist Meml. Hosp., Memphis, 1962; B.A., Blue Mountain Coll., 1965; M.A., U. No. Colo., 1982. R.N., Colo. Acting dir. nursing Roosevelt Gen. Hosp., Portales, N.Mex., 1965-66; nurse, student health service Eastern N.Mex. U., Portales, 1966-69; nurse Community Mental Health Ctr., St. Lawrence Hosp., Lansing, Mich., 1969-70; head nurse Neuropsychiat. Inst., U. Mich., Ann Arbor, 1970-71; coordinator Infant Research Lab., dept. human devel. U. Kans., Lawrence, 1971-74; nurse psychiat. unit Poudre Valley Hosp., Ft. Collins, Colo., 1977-80; women's program coordinator Crossroads Safehouse for Battered Women, Ft. Collins, 1982—; mem. sexual assault adv. team. Active NOW. Mem. Am. Personnel and Guidance Assn., Am. Mental Health Counselors Assn. Democrat. Methodist. Home: 1300 Ash Dr Fort Collins CO 80521

TINCHER, WILLIAM R., corp. exec.; b. Wichita, Kans., 1926; B.S., Wichita U., 1950; J.D., Washburn U., 1953. Admitted to Kans. bar; individual practice law, Topeka; with FTC, Washington; with Purex Corp. Lakewood, Calif., 1961—, corp. v.p., 1963, chmn. corp. study group, 1962, sr. v.p., 1963-65, chmn. corp. devel. com., 1965, pres., chief exec. officer, 1965—, chmn. bd., chmn. exec. com., 1968—; dir. 1st Western Bank & Trust Co., C.H.B. Foods, Inc. Bd. dirs. Martin Luther Hosp.; bd. councilors Sch. Bus. Adminstrn., U. So. Calif. Mem. NAM (dir., mem. exec. com.), Soap and Detergent Assn. (dir.). Office: Purex Industries 5101 Clark Ave Lakewood CA 90712*

TINDALL, ROBERT JAMES, organizational development consultant; b. Salt Lake City, Jan. 10, 1948; s. Thomas Ducharme and Betty Nadine (Frazier) T. B.S. in Human Relation Organizational Behavior, U. San Francisco, 1981, M. Human Resource and Organizational Devel., 1983. Customer service rep. Pacific Gas & Electric Co., San Francisco, 1972-79; tng. devel. cons., San Francisco, 1979-82, human resource mgmt., organizational devel. cons., 1982—; intern Drake, Beam, Morin, Inc. Cons. Mgmt. Human Resources, San Francisco, 1982—. Mem. Am. Soc. Tng. and Devel. (steering com. organizational devel. local chptr.), Organizational Devel. Network. Republican. Home and Office: 25 Corwin St #1 San Francisco CA 94114

TINDALL-BECKER, PAMELA, marketing executive; b. Chester, Pa., June James Michael 1948; d. Rodger Arthur and Doris (Meyers) Tindall; m. James Becker, Dec. 26, 1981. B.A. in Sociology, Kutztown State Coll., 1970. Mktg. adminstr. Franklin Mint, Franklin Ctr., Pa., 1973-74; asst. advt. mgr. Pennwalt Corp., Phila., 1974-77; regional advt. supr. McDonald's Corp., Columbus Ohio, 1977-78, regional mktg. mgr., San Jose, Calif., 1978—. Recipient McDonald's Pres.'s award, 1982. Office: 2025 Gateway Pl Suite 330 San Jose CA 95110

TINDEL, CAROLYN JEANNE, sch. adminstr.; b. Sacramento, Mar. 20, 1946; d. Marvin Homer and Antonette Jeanne (Perez) T.; A.A., Yuba Coll., 1966; B.A., Calif. State U.-Chico, 1968, M.A. in Edn., 1983; postgrad. U. Calif. Extension, Berkeley, 1969-71, Davis, 1971-73, Sacramento State Coll. Extension, 1972-73, Calif. State U., Fullerton, 1975, Morelia (Mex.) Summer Inst., 1975, Yuba Community Coll., 1974, Calif. State U., Chico, 1978-80. Elem. sch. tchr. Palmermo (Calif.) Union Sch. Dist., 1969; tchr. Yuba County Juvenile Hall, Harry P.B. Carden Sch., Marysville, Calif., 1970-74, Cedar Ln. Elem. Sch., Marysville Joint Unified Sch., Dist., 1969-79; evaluator fed., spl. programs Marysville Joint Unified Sch. Dist., 1979—; supervising tchr. Neighborhood Youth Corps Classroom Vols., 1971-73; master tchr. Yuba Community Jr. Coll., Marysville, 1971-73, Calif. State U.-Chico, 1973-79; cons. fed., state compensatory edn. programs Calif. State Dept. Edn., 1979. Leader, Linda 4-H Club, 1969-71. Recipient various awards for work in ednl. field. Mem. Assn. Calif. Sch. Adminstrs.; AAUW, Assn. Mgmt. and Confidential Employees, Assn. Supervision and Curriculum Devel., Phi Delta Kappa, Delta Kappa Gamma. Democrat. Roman Catholic. Clubs: Western States Covette Council, Butte Valley Corvette. Co-illustrator; T.A. for Kids (Walter Wilson), 1974; researcher: Marysville Oral Language Assessment Handbook, 1973. Home: 2135 Ramirez St Marysville CA 95901 Office: Marysville Joint Unified Sch Dist 1919 B St Marysville CA 95901

TINDULA, ROY VERNON, metallurgical engineer, executive; b. Ticonderoga, N.Y., Aug. 19, 1941; s. Roy Walter and Frances Elizabeth (Keenan) T.; m. Linda Mayer, Aug. 21, 1965; 1 son, R. Stephen. B.S. in Metall. Engring., Va. Poly. Inst., 1964; postgrad. Case Inst. Tech., 1964-66; M.S. in Commerce, U. Richmond, 1972. Jr. engr. Union Carbide Nuclear Co., Oak Ridge, 1960-63; research, teaching asst. Case Inst., Cleve., 1964-66; sr. devel. engr. Reynolds Metals Co., Richmond, Va., 1966-71; engring. supr., sr. mfg. engr., Carrier Air Conditioning Co., Syracuse, N.Y., Collierville, Tenn., 1972-78; div. v.p., corp. engring. dir. Consol. Metco Inc., Portland, Oreg., 1978-81; gen. mgr. Futura Home Products, Clearfield, Utah, Interstate Metal Fabricators, Portland, 1981—; mem. adv. bd. Western Regional Home Ctr. Show, 1983—. Served with U.S. Army, 1967-68. Decorated Bronze Star. Grantee, Alcoa, 1963, 64, Alpha Sigma Mu, 1964; recipient student award ASTM 1964. Mem. Utah Mfrs. Assn., Richmond Jaycees, Aluminum Extenders Council. Methodist. Developer of fluxless soldering facilities for aluminum air conditioner coils, 3102-H111 aluminum tubing alloys. Home: #32 525 E Park Ogden UT 84401 Office: Futura Home Products 36 S Main St Clearfield UT 84015

TINGLEY, FRED HOLLIS, ednl. adminstr.; b. Brigham City, Utah, Feb. 3, 1923; s. Guy Anton and LaVerne (Korth) T.; m. Mary Bauman, Apr. 11, 1947; children—Kirk R., Terrel F., Joelie, Jay, Jason, Kristine. B.S., Utah State U., 1947; M.S., U. Wash., 1949, Ph.D., 1951; cert. nuclear materials safeguards specialist Inst. Nuclear Materials Mgmt., 1980. Asst. gen. mgr. Aerojet Nuclear, Idaho Falls, 1974-77, EG&G Idaho Inc., Idaho Falls, 1977-79; dir. ctr. higher edn. U. Idaho, Idaho Falls, 1979—; cons. to nuclear industry. Mem. Idaho Falls Recreation Commn. Served to capt. USAAF, 1943-46. Mem. Inst. Nuclear Materials Mgmt. Mormon. Club: Kiwanis (Idaho Falls). Contbr. numerous articles to profl. jours. Home: 1820 Sequoia Idaho Falls ID 83401 Office: 1776 Science Center Dr Idaho Falls ID 83402

TINKER, ROBERT EUGENE, clergyman, ednl. cons.; b. Lincoln, Kans., June 10, 1915; s. Eugene F. and Mildred Adelaide (Brown) T.; A.B., Am. U., 1937; M.Div., Garrett Theol. Sem., 1942; postgrad. Northwestern U., 1942-46; m. Anne Elizabeth Hall, June 13, 1942; children—Anne Terrill, Robert Bruce, MaryBeth. Ordained to ministry Methodist Ch., 1942, Congregational Ch., 1947, United Ch. Christ; minister Oxen Hill, Md., Tuxedo, Md., 1933-37, Evergreen Park, Ill., 1940-41; asso. minister 1st Presbyterian Ch., Evanston, Ill., 1942-44; minister Glenview Meth. Ch. (Ill.), 1944-46, Broadway Meth. Ch., Chgo., 1946-47; with Chgo. Theol. Sem., 1947-58, asst. sec., asst. treas., bd. dirs., 1947-58, asst. bus. mgr., 1947-50, bus. mgr., 1951-55, dir. devel., 1953-55, v.p. charge devel., 1955-58; assoc. Gonser and Gerber, 1958-64; ptnr. Gonser, Gerber, Tinker Stuhr, ednl. cons. in devel. and public relations, Chgo., 1964-82, cons., 1982—; pres. Tabco Corp., Chgo., 1983—; lectr. Creighton U., Omaha, summers 1978-80. N.J. State scholar, 1933; Larry Foster scholar, 1933; Howes Meml. scholar, 1939-42. Bd. dirs. Hyde Park YMCA, Chgo., Hyde Park Union Ch., Porter Found., U. Chgo., Bryn Mawr Community Ch., Chgo. Mem. Phi Sigma Kappa, Phi Beta Zeta, Pi Gamma Mu. Republican. Club: Astoria (Oreg.) Golf and Country. Contbr. articles to profl. books and jours. Home: 8250 Circle Dr Neah Kah Nie Nehalem OR 97131 also 63 Oro Pl Oro Valley AZ 85704 Office: 105 W Madison St Chicago IL 60602

TINOCO, EDWARD NORBERTO, aeronautical engineer; b. El Paso, Tex., Oct. 13, 1940; s. Ignacio and Laurencia (Aizpuru) T.; m. Sylvia Yarbrough, Jan. 4, 1964; children—Joseph I., Lauren M., E. Andrew. B.S. in Aerospace Engring., U. Tex., 1963; M.S. in Aeros. and Astronautics, Stanford U., 1964. With Boeing Co., Seattle, 1964—, sr. engring. specialist, 1979—; lectr. in field. Active, Pacific Mus. of Flight. Mem. AIAA, Air Force Assn., Friends of Planetarium, Internat. Plastic Modelers Soc. Roman Catholic. Clubs: Boeing Fencing, Astronomy, and Model Flying. Contbr. articles to profl. jours.; patentee in field. Office: Boeing Co PO Box 3707 Mail Stop 3N 29 Seattle WA 98124

TINSLEY, ANNE MARIE, nutrition and food science educator, consultant; b. Easton, Pa., May 25, 1933; d. Hurley Ottis and Leora E. (Dimon) Patterson; m. Gayle C. Tinsley, Dec. 27, 1955 (div.); children—Gaye Ann Tinsley Vaterlaus, Dawn Marie, Gaylen. B.S., Pa. State U., 1954; postgrad. Tex. Women's U., 1968; M.S., U. Ariz., 1973, Ph.D., 1978. Dietitian, Woodville (Pa.) State Hosp., 1953; dietetic intern Brooke Army Hosp., San Antonio, Tex., 1954-55; therapeutic dietitian Camp Chaffee Army Hosp., Ft. Smith, Ark., 1955-56; cons. dietitian, Dallas, 1968-71; dir. food service, dietitian Univ. Park United Methodist Ch., Dallas, 1969-71; dir. food service, caterer Catalina United Methodist Ch., Tucson, 1971-72; teaching asst. Sch. of Home Econs., U. Ariz., Tucson, 1972-73, instr. dept. nutrition and food sci. Coll. Agr., 1973-79, asst. prof., 1979—; cons. dietitian, nutritionist Tex. Council, Girl Scouts U.S.A., Dallas, 1967-71; cons. dietitian Ariz. Elks Extended Care Facility, Tucson, 1971-75; owner, mgr. AT Co.; dir. Fitness, Image and Nutrition, Inc.; cons. Tucson Cystic Fibrosis Found. Bd. dirs. Parents Without Ptnrs. Served to 1st lt. Women's Med. Specialist Corp., U.S. Army, 1954-56. Recipient New award Unicorn Village of Tucson, 1982-83; Food and Nutrition Service U.S. Dept. Agr. grantee, 1977-80; Ariz. Dept. Edn. grantee, 1978-79, 81-82; U. Ariz. grantee, 1979-80; Title XII grantee, 1981-83. Mem. Am. Dietetic Assn., Am. Home Econs. Assn., Am. Sch. Food Service Assn., Ariz. Soc. Food Technologists (sec. Cactus sect. 1982-84), Ariz. Dietetic Assn. (edn. chmn. 1977-79), Inst. Food Technologists, Nutrition Council Ariz. (treas. 1982-83), Soc. for Nutrition Edn., So. Ariz. Dist. Dietetic Assn., Omicron Nu, Phi Delta Kappa, Gamma Sigma Delta. Methodist. Contbr. articles to profl. jours. Office: U Ariz 308 Home Econs Bldg Tucson AZ 85721

TINTOCALIS, CHRIS ANASTASIOS, podiatric surgeon; b. Concord, N.H., Feb. 21, 1938; s. Frank Anastasios and Theodora (Ternas) T.; m. Rae Jean Hay, Dec. 7, 1968. B.A., Bowdoin Coll., 1966; D.P.M., Calif. Coll. Podiatric Medicine, 1969. Podiatric surg. resident Lincoln Community Hosp., Buena Park, Calif., 1969-70; practice podiatric medicine and surgery, Santa Barbara, Calif., 1970—; mem. podiatry examining com. Calif. State Med. Bd., 1978—. Del. State Democratic Central Com. Conv., 1980; bd. dirs. Arthritis Found. Santa Barbara County, 1979—; pres. Santa Barbara Comprehensive Health Planning Assn., 1976; bd. dirs. Channel Counties Comprehensive Health Planning Assn., 1976. Served with U.S. Army, 1961-63. Diplomate Am. Bd. Podiatric Surgery, Am. Bd. Podiatric Orthopedics. Fellow Am. Coll. Foot Orthopedists, Am. Coll. Foot Surgeons; mem. Am. Podiatry Assn., Calif. Podiatry Assn., Tri-Counties Podiatric Soc. (past pres.), Am. Acad. Podiatric Sports Medicine (assoc.). Greek Orthodox. Office: 2428 Castillo St D Santa Barbara CA 93105

TIPPETS, DENNIS WILCOCK, mining executive; b. Wheatland, Wyo., Dec. 30, 1938; s. Neff H. and Elizabeth W. Tippets; m. Dianne Barkley, June 11, 1961; children—Lynn Elizabeth, Kevin Craig, Bruce Barkley. B.A., U. Colo., 1962. Personnel adminstr. Lamb-Grays Harbor

Co., Inc., Hoquiam, Wash., 1965-67; mgmt. cons. Roy Jorgensen Assos., Gaithersberg, Md., 1967-71; v.p., dir. Stylhomes, Inc., Riverton, Wyo., 1971-76; pres. Tippets Appraisal Service, Riverton, 1976-80; pres. chmn. bd. Minex Resources, Inc., Riverton, 1980—; dir., chief exec. officer NASDAQ pub. mineral exploration co. Chmn. bd. trustees Fremont County (Wyo) Sch. Dist. 25, 1975-81; v.p. Fremont County Rep. party, 1978-80. Served to lt. USN, 1962-65. Mem. Rocky Mountain Oil and Gas Assn., Am. Mining Congress, Am. Inst. Real Estate Appraisers. Mormon. Club: Rotary (Riverton). Home: 1614 Gannett Dr Riverton WY 82501 Office: N Broadway and Park Riverton WY 82501

TIPTON, ANN BAUGH, phys. chemist; b. Freeport, Tex., Sept. 4, 1938; d. Dewey Lawrence and Ruth Elizabeth (Tipton) Baugh; B.S., Southwestern U., Georgetown, Tex., 1960; M.A., U. Tex., Austin, 1963, Ph.D., 1966; M.B.A., Pepperdine U., 1982; m. Van Collier Tipton, Jr., Jan. 30, 1963. Asst. prof. chemistry Southwestern U., 1964-67; tech. specialist chemistry research dept. Lockheed Propulsion Co., Redlands, Calif., 1969-75; sr. research chemist fuels desulfurization group Occidental Research Corp., Irvine, Calif., 1975-78, group head, 1978-80, sr. research scientist, geothermal energy research, 1980-81, phosphoric acid research, 1981-82; program devel. mgr. chem. tech. Rocketdyne div. Rockwell Internat. Corp., Canoga Park, Calif., 1983—; cons. tech. mgmt., 1979—; NSF research asst. U. Tex., Austin, 1961-63. Robert A. Welch fellow in chemistry U. Tex., Austin, 1963-66, Robert A. Welch postdoctoral fellow in chemistry, 1966-69; named Woman of Achievement, Irvine Bus. and Profl. Women's Club, 1980; Woman of Yr., San Orco Dist. Bus. and Profl. Women's Clubs, 1980. Fellow Am. Inst. Chemists, Assn. for Women in Sci.; mem. Am. Chem. Soc., Am. Inst. Chem. Engrs., Soc. Applied Spectroscopy, Lockheed Propulsion Mgmt. Assn. (treas. 1973-74), Nat. Mgmt. Assn., Am. Phys. Soc., AAAS, Univ. Law Wives, NOW, Bus. and Profl. Women's Club, Iota Sigma Pi, Delta Theta Phi Wives, Delta Delta Delta. Inventor process for coal desulfurization, process for hydrogen sulfide removal from geothermal steam. Contbr. articles to profl. jours., World Book Ency. Home: 1615 Butternut Way Diamond Bar CA 91765

TIPTON, GARY LEE, personal services co. exec.; b. Salem, Oreg., July 3, 1941; s. James Rains and Dorothy Velma (Dierks) T.; B.S., Oreg. Coll. Edn., 1964. Credit rep. Standard Oil Co. Calif., Portland, Oreg., 1964-67; credit mgr. Uniroyal Inc., Dallas, 1967-68; partner, mgr. bus. Tipton Barbers, Portland, 1968—. Mem. Republican Nat. Com., 1980—, Sen. Howard Baker's Presdl. Steering Com., 1980. Fellow Internat. Biog. Assn. (life) (U.K.); mem. Sunset Mall Mchts. Assn. (co-founder, treas. 1974-79, pres. 1982—), Internat. Platform Assn., Smithsonian Assos. Office: 1085 NW Murray Rd Portland OR 97229

TIPTON, HAROLD FORREST, JR., data processing exec., former naval officer; b. Southgate, Calif., Jan. 2, 1925; s. Harold Forest and Edna Vivian (Chambers) T.; B.S., U.S. Naval Acad., 1949; M.A., George Washington U., 1965; data processing cert. U. Calif. at Irvine, 1972; m. Margaret Ann Campsey, June 11, 1949; 1 son, Brian. Commd. ensign U.S. Navy, 1949, advanced through grades to comdr., 1964; naval aviator, 1950-69; adminstrv. officer utility squadron, 1950-53; project officer Ordnance Test Sta., China Lake, Calif., 1954-57; catapult/arresting gear officer USS Ticonderoga, 1957-59; ops. officer, fighter squadron, 1960-62; instr. U.S. Naval Acad., Annapolis, 1962-65; logistics officer with comdr.-in-chief Pacific Fleet Staff, 1966-69; ret., 1969; project mgr. Rockwell Internat. Corp., Calif., 1970-75, data systems mgr., Western region, 1975-76, program mgr. systems security, 1976—, ext. bus. account mgr., 1978-79; pres. HFT Assos., 1982—. Mem. planning commn. City of Villa Park, Calif., 1972-74, councilman, 1974-78, mayor, 1976-78, city treas., 1979—. Decorated Meritorious Service medal. Republican. Club: Masons. Home: 18862 Colony Circle Villa Park CA 92667

TIPTON, HARRY B., physician, state legislator; b. Salida, Colo., Mar. 14, 1927; s. Harry B. and Nina Belle (Hailey) T.; m. Dorothy Joan Alexander, Sept. 16, 1950; children—Leslie Louise, Harry B., Robert A. B.A., U. Colo., 1949, M.D., 1953. Diplomate Am. Bd. Family Practice. Intern, Good Samaritan Hosp., Phoenix, 1953-54; practice medicine specializing in ob-gyn, Lander, Wyo., 1954—; mem. staff Bishop Randall Hosp., Lander; cons. Indian Health Service, USPHS; mem. Wyo. Ho. of Reps., 1980—. Mem. Lander Sch. Bd., 1950-78. Served with M.C., USNR, 1945-46. Mem. AMA, Wyo. Med. Soc., Am. Acad. Family Physicians, Am. Fertility Soc. Republican. Club: Rotary. Office: 745 Buena Vista Lander WY 82520

TIPTON, JOHN BURKE, plastic surgeon; b. Tulsa, Mar. 10, 1928; s. Charles Vance and Cecil C. (Davis) T.; B.Music Edn., U. Mich., 1951, M.D., 1959; children—John David, Scott Alan, Daniel Reed. Intern, St. Joseph Mercy Hosp., Ann Arbor, Mich., 1959-60, resident gen. surgery, 1960-63, resident plastic surgery, 1963-64; resident plastic surgery U. Mich., Ann Arbor, 1964-65; practice medicine, specializing in plastic surgery, Ann Arbor, 1965-69, Palm Springs, Calif., 1969—; active staff Eisenhower Med. Center, Palm Desert, until 1976; cons. plastic surgery Angel View Crippled Children Found., Inc., Desert Hot Springs, Calif.; attending physician VA Hosp., Long Beach; pres. med. and dental staff Desert Hosp., Palm Springs, 1974-76, chief of surgery, 1980-82; clin. instr. surgery (plastic) U. Mich., Ann Arbor, 1965-69; asst. clin. prof. surgery (plastic) U. Calif. at Irvine, 1971-76, asso. clin. prof., 1976—. Vice chmn. Palm Springs Airport Commn., 1982—. Recipient 2d prize, F.A. Coller award Mich. chpt. ACS, 1962, 64. Diplomate Am. Bd. Plastic Surgery, Pan Am. Med. Assn. Fellow ACS; mem. Am. Soc. Plastic and Reconstructive Surgeons (ednl. found.), Am. Assn. Plastic Surgeons, Am. Cleft Palate Assn., Pan-Pacific Surg. Assn., Frederick A. Coller Surg. Soc., Reed Dingman Soc., Calif. Soc. Plastic Surgeons, Am. Soc. Aesthetic Plastic Surgery, Flying Physicians Assn., Galens Hon. Med. Soc. of U. Mich., Druids Hon. Lit. Soc. of U. Mich., Phi Mu Alpha Sinfonia, Kappa Kappa Psi, Alpha Sigma Phi. Office: 700 E Tanquitz-McCallum Way Palm Springs CA 92262

TIRET, HORACE MEDLIN, accountant; b. Pacific Grove, Calif., Oct. 23, 1915; s. Auguste Hubert and Annie Blaine (Eliot) T.; student Am. Inst. Banking, 1933-35; B.A., San Francisco Inst. Accountancy, 1941; postgrad. Golden Gate U., 1948-49; m. Elsie Christine Bleuss, Nov. 5, 1938; children—Sharon Lee, Jeffrey, Steven, Daniel, Michael. Bond cashier, Investment dept., Wells Fargo Bank, San Francisco, 1933-41; owner Tiret & Assos. (formerly Horace M. Tiret & Assos.), San Francisco, 1946—, pres., 1976-77, partner, 1977-80; pres. Concise Contact Lens Co., San Leandro, Calif., 1949-78, v.p., sec., 1978—, also dir. Chmn. troop com. Boy Scouts Am., San Francisco, 1955-60. Served with AUS, 1945-46. C.P.A., Calif. Mem. Calif. C.P.A. Soc., Am. Inst. C.P.A.'s, Am. Fuchsia Soc., Nat. Fuchsia Soc. Presbyn. Patentee in fuchsia field. Home: 168 Lunado Ct San Francisco CA 94127 Office: 2225 Taraval St San Francisco CA 94116

TIRRE, JOANNE PUMPHREY, educational administrator; b. Broseley, Mo., Feb. 3, 1937; d. Walter and Ola A. (Keener)(Rescetter) Pumphrey; m. Christian A. Tirre, Aug. 15, 1959; 1 foster son, Gary L. Wycuff. B.S. in Edn., S.E. Mo. U., 1959; M.Ed., Miami U., 1963; postgrad. Ohio State U., 1962-70, U. Hawaii, 1971-76. Tchr., sch. counselor pub. schs., Ohio, 1959-70; tchr. Kauai (Hawaii) Schs., 1970-76, vice prin. Kauai High Sch., 1977-79; dist. edn. specialist Kauai Dist. Office, State of Hawaii, 1979-83; prin. Eleele (Hawaii) Sch., 1983—; summer instr. U. Hawaii. Chmn. Kauai County Democratic Party, 1982—; bd. dirs. Child and Family Service, 1982—; mem. Kauai Chorale, 1970-83; pres. Kauai Assn. United Churches of Christ, 1983—. Mem. NEA, Am. Personnel and Guidance Assn., Hawaii Govt. Employees Assn. (steward 1979—), Kauaii Assn. Sch. Adminstrs. (treas. 1982—), Delta Kappa Gamma. Home: PO Box 3428 Lihue HI 96766 Office: PO Box 38 Eleele HI 96705

TIRRELL, JOHN ALBERT, management consultant, mission executive; b. Boston, Feb. 11, 1934; s. George Howard and Helen Sarah (Hitchings) T.; m. Helga Ruth Eisenhauer, Jan. 29, 1966; children—Steffanie Ruth, Sabina Lisette, Monica Susanne. B.A., King's Coll., 1961; M. Ed., U. Ariz., 1975. Research staff mem. IBM Research Ctr., Yorktown Heights, N.Y., 1957-62, 63-65; cons., tech. advisor Universidad Central, Facultad de Odontologia, Quito, Ecuador, 1962-63; cons. to v.p. time sharing C-E-I-R Inc., Washington, 1965-66; sr. cons., behavioral scientist Gen. Learning Corp. div. Gen. Electric Co., Washington and Morristown, N.J., 1966-69; analyst ednl./instructional systems Space div. Gen. Electric Co., Daytona Beach, Fla., 1969-72; dir. curriculum and program devel. Brookdale Community Coll., Lincroft, N.J., 1972; dir. learning and faculty resources Pima Community Coll., Tucson, 1972-76, assoc. faculty mem., 1973-75; dir. human resource planning and devel. Inspiration Consol. Copper Co., Claypool, Ariz., 1976-79; founder, pres. Jethro Consultancy, Tucson, 1979—; gen. dir. Calvary Missionary Fellowship, 1983—; mem. adv. bd. United Indian Missions, 1983—; adj. prof. Montclair (N.J.) State Coll., 1972; assoc. faculty mem. Gila Pueblo campus, Eastern Ariz. Coll., Globe, Ariz., 1978. Contbr. numerous articles to profl. publs. Elder First Evang. Free Ch., Tucson, 1979-82, chmn. gen. bd., 1979-81, supt. Sunday sch., 1975-77, 83—, del. nat. conf., 1978, S.W. Border Dist. confs., 1980, 81; v.p. Palo Verde Christian Sch. Parent-tchr. fellowship, 1980-81. Mem. Am. Soc. Profl. Cons., Am. Soc. Tng. and Devel. (treas. Old Pueblo chpt. 1982, dir. at large 1983, Human Resource Devel. award, Valley Sun chpt. 1977), Nat. Assn. Self-Employed. Home and Office: 6540 N Mesa View Dr Tucson AZ 85718

TISDALE, CHRISTINE MINOR, computer systems exec.; b. Iowa City, Iowa, May 28, 1949; d. Winston Douglas and Bette Lou (Wiseman) Minor; B.A. in Math. and Computer Sci., U. Oreg., 1970; M.S., Ohio State U., 1973; m. Ralph Christopher Tisdale, Aug. 24, 1980. Sr. systems analyst, project mgr. Corp. Info. Systems Center, Rockwell Internat., 1974-76; project leader for long range planning, mgmt. systems TRW Def. & Space Systems, Redondo Beach, Calif., 1976, mgr. planning systems devel., 1977-79; mgr. software quality AM Jacquard Systems, Santa Monica, Calif., 1979, dir. research and product devel, performance evalution, documentation and project mgmt., Manhattan Beach, Calif., 1979-82; systems planning and office automation productivity cons. TRW Electronics and Def., Redondo Beach, Calif., 1982—. Jr. Achievement Program advisor, Redondo Beach, 1976-78. Recipient TRW Good Neighbor award, 1978. Mem. Assn. Computing Machinery, Phi Beta Kappa. Republican. Office: One Space Park Redondo Beach CA 90278

TISON, DAVID LAWRENCE, microbiologist; b. Whittier, Calif., Sept. 26, 1952; s. George Lawrence and Phyllis Ilene (Davis) T.; B.S., U. Puget Sound, 1974; M.S., U. Idaho, 1976; Ph.D., Rensselaer Poly. Inst., 1980; m. Regina Ann Malinowski, Sept. 22, 1979. Botany lab. asst. U. Puget Sound, 1973; NSF summer fellow dept. microbiology U. Wash., Seattle, 1973; cell physiology lab. asst. U. Puget Sound., 1974; research technician dept. microbiology U. Wash., Seattle, 1974; research asst. dept. bacteriology U. Idaho, 1974-76; research asst. dept. biology Rensselaer Poly. Inst., 1976-77; teaching asst. dept. biology Rensselaer Poly. Inst., 1977-78; Oak Ridge Associated Univs./lab. grad. participation fellow Savannah River Lab., 1978-80; research assoc. dept. microbiology Oreg. State U., Corvallis, 1980—; cons. U.S. Army C.E., U.S. Forest Service, 1981-82. Mem. Am. Soc. Microbiology, Am. Soc. Limnology and Oceanography, AAAS, Sigma Xi, Phi Sigma. Democrat. Presbyterian. Contbr. articles in field to profl. jours. Home: 3207 SW Knollbrook Ave Corvallis OR 97333 Office: Dept Microbiology Oreg State U Corvallis OR 97331

TISS, GEORGE JOHN, pediatrician, educator; b. Welser, Idaho, Aug. 4, 1925; s. George Joseph and Mildred Gwendolyn (Barham) T.; m. Catherine Cassady, June 6, 1968; children—Randy, Carolyn, Danny, Mary, Andy. B.S., U. Oreg., 1950, M.D., 1954. Diplomate Am. Bd. Pediatrics. Intern, U. Oreg. Hosps. and Clinics, Portland, 1954-55, resident in pediatrics, 1955-57; practice medicine specializing in pediatrics Visalia (Calif.) Med. Clinic, 1957—, chmn. bd., 1959-70; vol. specialist Care Medico, Malaysia, 1969, Indonesia, 1976, specialist, Managua, Nicaragua, 1979; cons. Keweah Delta Dist. Hosp., Visalia, Tulare (Calif.) Dist. Hosp., Tulare County Hosp.; chmn. 1st Rubella mass immunization program in U.S., Tulare, 1969; chmn. Visalia Comprehensive Health Planning Bd., 1973-74; mem. bd. consortium San Joaquin Valley, 1975—; co-chmn. Calif. Immunization Adv. Com., 1973-76, chmn., 1976-77; asst. clin. prof. pediatrics U. Calif., San Francisco. Mem. sch. bd. Liberty Sch., 1980—. Served with USAAF, 1945-46. Recipient Lyda M. Smiley award Calif. Assn. Sch. Nurses, 1981. Mem. Am., Calif. med. assns., Tulare County Med. Soc. (pres. 1969-70), Am. Acad. Pediatrics, W. Coast Allergy Soc., Los Angeles Pediatric Soc., Calif. Thoracic Soc., Am. Legion. Office: 5400 W Hillsdale Rd Visalia CA 93277

TITCHENAL, CHARLES RALPH, business executive, educator; b. Seattle, Apr. 15, 1916; s. Charles Arthur and Hazel (Whisnand) T.; B.A. in Bus., U. Wash., 1956; M.B.A., 1960; m. Marcia Besse Titchenal, Feb. 14, 1950; children—Lewis Alden, Mary, Joel Edward. Head secretarial sci. dept. Western Coll. Commerce, Wenatchee, Wash., 1947-48; tng. officer Office of Naval Intelligence, U.S. Navy, Seattle, 1948-59; pres. Telemart, Inc., Seattle, 1959-60; instr. Fullerton Jr. Coll., 1960-61; assoc. in bus. UCLA, 1961-62; dir. Willis Reading Inst., Santa Monica, Calif., 1962-63; dir. pub. relations Peterson Sch. Bus., Seattle, 1963-64; instr. Highline Community Coll., Seattle, 1964-71, Spokane Falls Community Coll., 1971-81; pres. Synlube, Spokane, 1981—. Served with USCGR, 1942-46, USNR, 1948-49, 50-52. Mem. Wash. State Assn. Distributive Edn. Tchrs. (pres. 1975-76), Wash. Vocat. Assn. (exec. bd. 1974-76), Nat. Assn. Distributive Edn. Tchrs., Wash. Edn. Assn., NEA, Am. Vocat. Assn., Am. Bus. Communication Assn., Wash. Mid-Mgmt. Educators Assn. (chmn. 1970-71), Nat. Ret. Tchrs. Assn., Soc. Automotive Engrs. Republican. Presbyterian. Club: Rotary. Address: N 12203 Whitehouse St Spokane WA 99218

TJERANDSEN, THOMAS CARL, advertising agency executive; educator; b. Washington, May 30, 1942; s. Carl and Myrtle A. (Tully) T.; m. Ruth Appleton, Aug. 30, 1968; children—Craig, Carl. B.A., Hobart Coll., 1964; M.B.A., San Francisco State Coll., 1972. Asst. account exec. Botsford/Ketchum Co., San Francisco, 1968-70; advt. exec. D'arcy Advt., San Francisco, 1970-73; product mgr. MJB Co., San Francisco, 1973-74; mktg. mgr. Tri Valley Growers, San Francisco, 1974-77; account supr. McCann & Erickson, San Francisco, 1977-81; v.p., mgmt. supr. J. Walter Thompson Co., San Francisco, 1981—; adj. prof. Grad. Sch. Bus., Golden Gate U., San Francisco, 1973—. Served with U.S. Army, 1964-66. Mem. Am. Mktg. Assn., Miraloma Neighborhood Assn. (v.p. 1982-83). Democrat. Home: 19 Sherwood Ct San Francisco CA 94127 Office: J Walter Thompson Co 4 Embarcadero Ctr San Francisco CA 94111

TOCCOLI, BETTY JO A(NNE), cosmetics company executive; b. Caldwell, Idaho, Oct. 28, 1933; d. Robert Emmett and C. Lucille (Justus) McGuire; m. Ray P. Toccoli, Feb. 1, 1963; 1 dau., Gaylene. Student Coll. of Idaho, 1950-52, Grimms Bus. Coll., 1958-59, Idaho State U., 1961-63. Lic. esthetician, Calif. With Idaho Bank & Trust, Pocatello, 1953-55; adminstrv. asst. Bur. Indian Affairs, Dept. Interior, Ft. Hall, Idaho, 1955-57; v.p. sales, bd. dirs. Welcome Wagon Internat., Div. Gillette Co., Boston, 1957-78; chief exec. officer, pres., dir. Laura Lynn Cosmetics, Los Angeles, 1978—; condr. mgmt. seminars. Elder, trustee Pacific Palisades Presbyterian Ch. Recipient James Hill Meml. award in sales and pub. speaking Idaho State U., 1962. Mem. Nat. Assn. Women Bus. Owners (bd. dirs., pres.-elect), Nat. Assn. Female Execs. Republican. Office: 5456 McConnell Ave Suite 189 Los Angeles CA 90066

TOCKEY, SALLY ANN, editor; b. Omaha, June 10, 1935; d. Eugene Charles and Gertrude Margaret (Dendinger) Smith; A.A., Chabot Coll., 1974; B.A., Calif. State U., Hayward, 1976; m. Robert Jay Tockey, May 31, 1954; children—Deborah, Charles, Stephen, Barbara, Karen. Reporter, Tri-Valley News, Danville, Calif., 1976; reporter Tri-Valley Herald, Livermore, Calif., 1977, feature editor Today sect., 1979—. Recipient 1st Pl. award Contra Costa Press Club, 1977. Mem. Women in Communications, Inc., Sigma Delta Chi. Democrat. Roman Catholic. Club: East Bay Press. Home: 641 Del Sol Ave Pleasanton CA 94566 Office: 325 South I St Livermore CA 94550

TODD, JOHN ODELL, JR., insurance executive; b. Mpls., Sept. 7, 1928; s. John Odell and Katherine (Cone) T.; m. Ann Avery, Mar. 22, 1958; children—John, William. B.A. cum laude, Amherst Coll., 1950; M.B.A., U. Pa., 1952; C.L.U., Am. Coll., 1978. Research analyst Zischke Orgn., Inc., San Francisco, 1955-57; sales rep. IBM, 1957-60, spl. rep., 1960-61, advanced computer application mgr., 1961-64, San Francisco, 1957-60, Los Angeles, 1960-64; sr. assoc. Cresap, McCormick & Paget, Inc., Los Angeles, 1964-68, prin., 1968-73; pres. Todd Bus. Planning & Ins. Service Co., Pasadena, 1973—. Active Tournament of Roses, 1970—. Served to lt. (j.g.) USNR, 1952-55. Mem. Estate Planning Council San Gabriel. Republican. Episcopalian. Clubs: Valley Hunt, University, Pasadena Athletic. Home: 932 W Inverness Dr Flintridge CA 91011 Office: 260 S Los Robles Ave Pasadena CA 91101

TODD, RONALD ALLEN, architect; b. Lubbock, Tex., July 25, 1944; s. Robert Allen and Maxine (Beasley) T.; B.Arch. Tex. Tech. U., 1969; m. Laurie Ann Roberts, Apr. 4, 1970; children—Nicole, Tyler Dillon. Job capt. Roark & Assos., Denver, 1969-71; staff architect J.C. Constrn., Denver, 1971-72; project architect Design Spectrum, Englewood, Colo., 1972; project architect Telesis, Arvada, Colo., 1972-73; staff architect Sink & Assos., Denver, 1973-74; project architect Pierce Briner & Fitzhugh Scott, Vail, Colo., 1974-75; partner/prin. architect Morter/Todd Partnership, Vail, 1975-78; sole propr./architect Ronald A. Todd-Architect, Vail, 1979—; tchr. Colo. Mountain Coll., Vail, 1979. Mem. Vail Town Council, 1979-83; chmn. Vail Planning and Environ. Commn., 1977-79; mem. Vail Design Rev. Bd., 1976-77; mem. Bd. Bldg. Appeals, 1977-79; chmn. Eagle County Master Plan Com., 1979-80; precinct committeeman Democratic Party. Served with USAF, 1962-64. Mem. Delta Tau Delta. Democrat. Episcopalian. Office: PO Box 1753 Vail CO 81658

TOENJES, DON ALAN, agricultural scientist, consultant; b. Los Angeles, June 22, 1931; s. Frederick William and Hilda Marian (Williamson) T.; B.S., U. Calif.-Davis, 1955; m. Virginia Marie Gayaldo, July 17, 1960; children—Carol Ann, Helen Marie, Kurt Alan. Farm advisor U. Calif. Coop. Extension, 1957—; guest lectr. Chico State U. Mem. Republican Presdl. Task Force. Served with M.C., USN, 1956-57. Mem. Council Agrl. Sci. and Tech., Am. Inst. Biol. Scis., Am. Dairy Sci. Assn., Calif. Aggie Alumni Assn., N.Y. Acad. Sci., Alpha Gamma Rho. Club: Elks. Research on Calif. agr.; contbr. articles to profl. jours. Home: Route 1 Box 1551A Orland CA 95963 Office: PO Box 697 Orland CA 95963

TOFFEL, PAUL HASKELL, otolaryngologist, maxillofacial surgeon; b. Los Angeles, Mar. 3, 1943; s. Harry and Estelle Charlotte (Kandel) T.; m. Beverly Diane Peterson, June 12, 1965; children—Nicole, Hope, Erica. Student Stanford U., 1961-62; M.D., U. So. Calif., 1968. Intern, Los Angeles County-U. So. Calif. Med. Center, 1968-69, resident in otolaryngology, 1969-73; practice medicine specializing in otolaryngology and maxillofacial surgery, Los Angeles, 1975—; mem. staff Daniel Freeman Med. Center, Centinela Valley Med. Center, Orthopedic, Verdugo Hills hosps.; clin. asst. prof. U. So. Calif. Med. Sch., 1974—; mem. med. emergency team Los Angeles County Sheriff's Dept., 1973—; head facial plastics div., med. adv. com. Calif. Athletic Commn.; chief med. officer equestrian events 1984 Los Angeles Olympiad. Served to lt. comdr. M.C., USNR, 1973-75. Fellow Am. Acad. Otolaryngology, Soc. Mil. Otolaryngologists, A.C.S., Am. Acad. Facial, Plastic and Reconstructive Surgery; mem. AMA, Calif., Los Angeles County med. assns., Salerni Collegium. Office: 301 N Prairie Ave Suite 500 Inglewood CA 90301 also 1808 Verdugo Blvd Suite 420 Glendale CA 91208

TOGASAKI, SHINOBU, math. analyst; b. San Francisco, Aug. 17, 1932; s. Kikumatsu and Sugi (Hida) T.; B.S. in Math., Duke U., 1954; postgrad. Stanford, 1954-56; m. Toshiko Kawaguchi, Nov. 24, 1959;children—John Shinobu, Ann Mariko. Research asst. mem. faculty Stanford, 1954-56; math. programmer IBM, 1956-61; mgr. applications devel. Service Bur. Corp., Palo Alto, Calif., 1961-64, sr. analyst, 1964-68, systems architect, devel. lab., San Jose, Calif., 1968-70; sr. programmer IBM Corp., Palo Alto, 1970—; chief fin. officer Robin Hood Ranch, Inc., 1976—. Treas., Friends Outside Santa Clara County, now pres. elect. Mem. Am. Mgmt. Assn., AAAS, Am. Statis. Assn., Assn. Computing Machinery, Inst. Mgmt. Sci., Palo Alto C. of C., Sigma Pi Sigma. Home: 2367 Booksin Ave San Jose CA 95125 Office: 5600 Cattle Rd San Jose CA 95193

TOKIOKA, FRANKLIN MAKOTO, finance company executive; b. Honolulu, Nov 17, 1936; s. Masayuki and Harue (Fujiyoshi) T.; B.S., Williams Coll., 1958; M.B.A., Stanford U., 1960; m. Suzanne M. Sears, Dec. 11, 1965; children—Franklin Makoto, II, Dana M. Vice pres., sec. Nat. Mortgage & Fin. Co., Ltd., Honolulu, 1960-78, exec. v.p., dir., sec., 1978—; pres., dir. Nat. Securities and Investment, Inc., 1975—, Mut. Fin. Co., Ltd., 1971—; v.p., sec. Island Ins. Co. Ltd., 1969-78, sr. v.p., sec. 1979—, also dir.; dir. Am. Security Bank, Honolulu, Honolulu TV Communications Corp., Intelect, Inc., ANA Hotels Hawaii, Inc. Bd. dirs. Big Bros./Big Sisters Honolulu, v.p. fin. Aloha council Boy Scouts Am.; adv. Honolulu YWCA, Cancer Ctr. Hawaii. Clubs: Waialae Country, Peninsula Wildlife, Honolulu. Home: 925 Waiholo St Honolulu HI 96821 Office: 1022 Bethel St Honolulu HI 96813

TOLAND, KAREN ANN, marketing executive; b. Philadelphia, June 19, 1951; d. Hugh Norman and Rita Ann (Gifford) Boyd; m. John Francis Toland, Apr. 19, 1970 (div.). Student pub. schs., King of Prussia, Pa. Sales rep., mktg. mgr. Savin Corp., Phila., 1973-76; nat. mktg. mgr., 1976-79; product devel. mgr., 1979-82; mktg. dir. Convergent Technologies, Sunnyvale, Calif., 1982—; product devel. cons. Recipient Savin Corp. Mktg. and Sales Nat. award, 1974, 79. Mem. Assn. Women in Computing, Am. Mgmt. Assn., Nat. Republican Conservative Com. Roman Catholic. Patentee in field. Home: 10275 Parkwood Dr Apt 8 Cupertino CA 95014 Office: 795 Kifer Sunnyvale CA 94086

TOLBERT, MICHAEL LAWRENCE, educator; b. Houston, Mar. 8, 1949; s. Jack H. and Evelyn (Osman) T.; student Tex. Christian U., 1967-68, U. Hawaii, 1968; B.A., U. Tex., 1971, M.A., 1975, Ph.D., 1980. Supr. student teaching program U. Tex., Austin, 1976-79; dir. outreach activities Inst. Latin Am. Studies, Austin, 1979-80; asst. prof. elem. edn. Huston-Tillotson Coll., Austin, Tex., 1980; coordinator edn. and Latin

Am. Studies Stanford (Calif.) U., 1981—, dir. ednl. resources Latin Am., Center for Internat. Research, 1981—. Mem. Latin Am. Studies Assn., Calif. Council Social Studies, Pacific Coast Geographers, Nat. Council Social Studies, Save the Children Fedn. Democrat. Christian. Home: care Box 1185 San Marcos TX 78666 Office: Stanford Univ Center for Research in International Studies Stanford CA 94305

TOLBERT, WILLIAM AUSTIN, military engr.; b. Mexico City, Mar. 20, 1948; s. Merrill Augustus and Victoria Louise (Brown) T.; m. Christine Louise McCain, Mar. 27, 1947; children—Tara T., Timothy C., Heather L., Seth R. B.S. cum laude in C.E., U. Wyo. 1972; M.S., U. Tex., 1974. Registered profl. engr., Tex. Enlisted U.S. Air Force, 1966, advanced through grades to capt., 1977; engring. staff officer Air Force Acad., 1974-76, dep. chief ops. and maintenance div., 1976-78, chief Energy Research Office, Tyndall AFB, Fla., 1978-80, chief DOE-AF Research and Tech. Liaison Office, Golden, Colo., 1980—; cons. in field; lectr. in field. Active Boy Scouts Am.; bishop Arvada 3rd Ward, Ch. of Jesus Christ of Latter-day Saints., 1981—. Recipient Honor award Freedom Found. Valley Forge, 1976; Jr. Officer of Yr., U.S. Air Force Acad., 1976. Mem. Internat. Solar Energy Soc., Interagy. Advanced Power Group, Sigma Tau, Phi Kappa Phi. Republican. Contbr. articles to profl. jours. Home: 6762 Xenon Dr Arvada CO 80004 Office: 1617 Cole Blvd 15/3 Golden CO 80401

TOLEFREE, JESSE W., transp. firm owner; b. Pine Bluff, Ark., July 31, 1928; s. Climmie and Octavia M. (Sanders) T.; student Law Sch. La Salle U., Merrit Coll., 1961-63; 1 son, Demetrius. Owner trucking firm, Oakland, Calif., 1956—. Mem. Fairplay Council, Hayward, Calif. Republican. Club: Teamsters Local 70. Address: PO Box 5095 Oakland CA 94605

TOLENTINO, JEAN GOMOS, dietician; b. Manila, Philippines, Oct. 17, 1936; came to U.S., 1967, naturalized, 1974; d. Pedro Malonog and Crescencia (Maghinay) Gomos; m. Manolo M. Tolentino, Nov. 9, 1974; stepchildren—Ronald, Alan, Ferdinand, Manolo; 1 son, Jeff. B.S. in Foods and Nutrition, Philippine Women's U., 1962. Hotel adminstr. Sulo Hotel, Philippines, 1965-67; therapeutics dietitian Meth. Hosp., Indpls., 1967-69; food adminstr. U. Ill., Urbana, 1969-70; food adminstr. I, Vets. Home and Med. Ctr., Yountville, Calif., 1970-74, food adminstr. II, 1974-79, chief therapeutics and edn., 1979-82, dir. dietetics, 1982—. Mem. Calif. Food Task Force, 1975—. Mem. Am. Dietetic Assn., Am. Soc. Hosp. Food Service Adminstrs. Roman Catholic.

TOLES, GEORGE EDWARD, JR., advertising agency executive; b. Memphis, Jan. 9, 1939; s. George Edward and Annie Jane (Arnold) T.; m. Elizabeth Claire Wyngarden, Aug. 25, 1961; children—Anne, Laurie, Andy. B.A. in Speech, Wheaton Coll., 1961; M. TV, U. Ill., 1962. Disc jockey Sta. WOOD-AM-FM, Grand Rapids, Mich., 1964-65, Sta. WJBK-AM-FM-TV, Detroit, 1965-67, newscaster Sta. WWJ-AM-FM-TV, Detroit, 1967; program dir. Sta KBIQ-FM, Seattle, 1967-69, Sta. KIRO-AM-FM, Seattle, 1969-70; account exec. Sta. KJR, Seattle, 1970-73; gen. mgr. Kaye-Smith Prodns., Seattle, 1974; account exec. Sta. KISW-FM, Seattle, 1974-75; pres., owner Toles Co., Lynnwood, Wash., 1976—; pub. address announcer Detroit Pistons, profl. basketball team, 1965-66, Seattle Sonics, profl. basketball team, 1967—. Served to 1st lt., Signal Corps, U.S. Army, 1962-64. Mem. AFTRA, Fellowship of Christians in Arts, Media and Entertainment. Republican. Office: Toles Co 6905 191st Pl SW Lynnwood WA 98036

TOLIN, DONALD LEE, lawyer, steel co. exec.; b. Casper, Wyo., Aug. 29, 1953; s. Sidney and Cecelia (Baer) T.; A.A. in Social Sci., Casper Coll., 1973; B.S. in Acctg. with honors, U. Wyo., 1975, J.D., 1978; m. Vickie Lynn Davison, Sept. 4, 1977; children—Cecelia Anne, Sarah Dawn. Admitted to Wyo. bar, 1978, U.S. Tax Ct. bar, 1978, U.S. Circuit Ct. Appeals bar, 1978; practiced in Casper, 1978—; v.p., treas., corp. counsel, gen. mgr. Casper Iron & Metal, Inc., 1972—, also dir. Pres., dir. Temple Beth El, Casper, 1978—; mem. nat. council Am. Israel Pub. Affairs Com. C.P.A., Wyo. Mem. ABA (div. com. chmn. 1978, mem. council real property probate and trust div.), Wyo. State Bar, Wyo. Trial Lawyers Assn., Am. Inst. C.P.A.s, Wyo. Soc. C.P.A.s, Am. Assn. Attys.-C.P.A.s, Inst. Scrap Iron and Steel (sec.-treas. Rocky Mountain chpt. 1977-79, v.p., pres.-elect 1981-82, pres. 1982—, nat. bd. dirs., environ. and legis. chmn.), Steel Service Center Inst. Clubs: Shriners, Masons. Home: 561 Walsh Dr Casper WY 82601 Office: 3200 W 13th St Casper WY 82601

TOLLES, WILLIAM MARSHALL, university administrator; b. New Britain, Conn., June 30, 1937; s. Marshall H. and Lily Virginia (Calmbach) T.; m. Elizabeth Mae Blackman, July 31, 1937; children—Christopher, Laurie. B.A., U. Conn., 1958; Ph.D., U. Calif.-Berkeley, 1962. Mem. faculty Rice U., Houston, 1961-62; prof. sci. and engring. Naval Postgrad. Sch., Monterey, Calif., 1962—, dean of research, 1978—. Shell fellow. Mem. Am. Phys. Soc., Am. Chem. Soc., Am. Optical Soc., Am. Soc. Engring. Edn., Sigma Xi, Phi Beta Kappa. Presbyterian. Contbr. articles to profl. jours. Office: Naval Postgraduate School Monterey CA 93940

TOLSON, JON HART, holding co. exec.; b. San Francisco, Aug. 10, 1939; s. Herschel and Lois T.; children—Andrew, Leigh. B.S., U. Calif., Berkeley, 1961, LL.B., 1964; m. Linda Lew, Jan. 20, 1967. Acct., Arthur Young & Co., San Francisco and Oakland, 1965-68; chief fin. officer Sutro & Co., Inc., San Francisco, after 1968, 1st v.p., dir., to 1980; v.p. Barclay & Co., Inc., San Francisco, 1980—. Served with AUS, 1961. Office: Barclay & Co Inc 500 Sansome St San Francisco CA 94111

TOM, LAWRENCE, computer graphics engineering executive; b. Los Angeles, Jan. 21, 1950; s. Tommy Toy and May (Fong) T. B.S., Harvey Mudd Coll., 1972; J.D. Western State U., San Diego, 1978. Design engr. Rockwell Internat., Los Angeles, 1972-73; design engr. Rohr Industries, Inc., Chula Vista, Calif., 1973-76, sr. design engr., 1980, computer graphics engring. specialist, 1980—; pvt. practice design engring. cons., Los Angeles, 1975-77; sr. engr. Rohr Marine, Inc., Chula Vista, 1977-79; cons. in field. George H. Mayr Found. scholar, 1971; Bate Found. Aero. Edn. scholar, 1970-72. Mem. AIAA. Republican. Office: Foot of H St Chula Vista CA 92012

TOMASSON, RICHARD FINN, sociology educator, b. Bklyn., May 28, 1928; s. Solfest and Sigrun Helene (Egge) T.; m. Nancy Lensen, Aug. 16, 1958 (div.); children—Lars Lensen, Leif Lensen, Christopher Lensen. B.A., Gettysburg Coll., 1949; M.A., U. Ill., 1953; Ph.D., U. Pa, 1960. Asst. prof. Scripps Found. for Research in Population Problems, Miami U., Oxford, Ohio, 1959-61; asst. prof. sociology U. Ill., Urbana, 1961-66; assoc. prof., 1966-67; Fulbright lectr., Sweden, 1963-64; assoc. prof. U. N.Mex., Albuquerque, 1967-70, prof., 1970—. Served to 1st lt. U.S. Army, 1953-55. Fulbright fellow, 1964-65; Nat. Endowment for Humanities sr. fellow, 1970-71. Mem. Am. Sociol. Assn., Soc. Advancement Scandinavian Study, Internat. Union Sci. Study Population, Council European Studies, Internat. Studies Assn. Democrat. Author: Sweden: Prototype of Modern Society, 1970; Iceland: The First New Society, 1980; editor: Comparative Social Research, 1976—. Home: 1602 Sigma Chi Rd NE Albuquerque NM 87106 Office: Dept Sociology U NMex Albuquerque NM 87131

TOMBERLIN, GEORGE E., lawyer; b. Atlanta, Nov. 15, 1949; s. George E. and Sarah H. T.; m. Jennifer Hood, Aug. 4, 1973. A.B., Princeton U., 1971; J.D., U. Calif.-Berkeley, 1976. Bar: Calif., 1976. Assoc., Cotton, Seligman & Ray, San Francisco, 1976-79, Dinkelspiel, Pelavin, Steefel & Levitt, San Francisco, 1979-80, Pelavin, Norberg, Harlick & Beck, San Francisco, 1980-82; counsel Kaiser Found. Health Plan, Inc., Oakland, Calif., 1983—. Bd. dirs. Berkeley (Calif.) Symphony Orch., 1979—, v.p., 1980—. Nat. Merit scholar, 1967-71. Mem. ABA, Calif. State Bar Assn., San Francisco Bar Assn. Office: Ordway Bldg One Kaiser Plaza Oakland CA 94612

TOMICH, LILLIAN, lawyer; b. Los Angeles, Mar. 28, 1935; d. Peter S. and Yovanka P. (Ivanovic) T.; A.A., Pasadena City Coll., 1954; B.A. (LaVerne Noyes scholar 1955, 56), U. Calif. at Los Angeles, 1956, gen. secondary teaching credential (Charles Fletcher Scott fellow), 1957, M.A., 1958; J.D. (Univ. scholar), U. So. Calif., 1961. Admitted to Calif. bar, 1961; practice law, 1961-66, 67-68; mem. firm Hurley, Shaw & Tomich, San Marino, Calif., 1968-76, firm Driscoll & Tomich, San Marino, 1976—; counsel Mfrs. Bank, Los Angeles, 1966; dir. Continental Culture Specialists, Inc., Glendale, Calif. Recipient Nat. 1st award debating Phi Rho Pi, 1954, Pacific Coast 1st award debating, 1953, 54; Nat. 1st award debating Pi Kappa Delta, 1955. Mem. Calif. State Bar, Am., Los Angeles (arbitration com.) bar assns., Women Lawyers Assn., U. Calif. at Los Angeles Alumni Assn., Order Mast and Dagger, Los Angeles World Affairs Council, Iota Tau Tau, Alpha Gamma Sigma (life), Pi Kappa Delta (pres. 1955-56), Phi Rho Pi (pres. 1953-54), Pi Sigma Alpha (v.p. 1957). Mem. Serbian Orthodox Ch. (trustee). Club: Town Hall of Los Angeles. Home: 501 N Del Mar Ave San Gabriel CA 91775 Office: 2297 Huntington Dr San Marino CA 91108

TOMMEY, RICHARD JOSEPH, librarian; b. Carnegie, Pa., June 9, 1924; s. Michael Richard and Agnes Rita (Kaminski) T.; Ph.B., Loyola Coll., 1949; M.S., Cath. U. Am., 1951; m. Marie Antonia Wiedenbauer, June 18, 1949; children—Ann Marie, Stephen Richard. Young adult librarian Enoch Pratt Library, Balt., 1949-50; interlibrary loan John K. Mullen Library, Cath. U. Am., Washington, 1950-51; reference librarian CIA, Washington, 1951-57; librarian Olin Mathieson Co., New Haven, 1957-60, GA Technologies Inc. (formerly Gen. Atomic Co.), San Diego, 1960—; instr. San Diego Community Coll. Evening Coll., 1977—. Served with U.S. Army, 1943-46. Mem. Spl. Libraries Assn. (chpt. pres. 1964-65, bull. editor 1962-63), San Diego Library Metro (v.p. 1979-80), Nat. Mgmt. Assn., GA Technologies Mgmt. Club (sec. 1979-80). Home: 6073 Avenida Chamnez La Jolla CA 92037 Office: 10955 John Jay Hopkins Dr La Jolla CA 92037

TOMPKINS, ROBERT EUGENE, psychologist; b. Fruita, Colo., July 27, 1942; s. Earl W. and Eleanor P. (Reed) T.; B.S., Colo. State U., 1964; M.A., U. No. Colo., 1966; Ed.D., U. S.D., 1973; m. Gayle Walters, June 17, 1967; children—Kirstin, Joshua. Psychologist, Winona State Coll., Minn., 1967-70, Yonngdahl Human Relations Center, Owatonna, Minn., 1970-72, Scottsdale (Ariz.) Public Schs., 1973-75, Mental Health Center, Billings, Mont., 1975-79, Billings Clinic, 1979—; dir. Neighborhood Counseling Center, Mental Health Center. Lic. psychologist, Mont. Mem. Mont. Psychol. Assn. (dir.), Yellowstone County Psychol. Assn. (pres.), Am. Psychol. Assn. Democrat. Research on gifted child. Home: 3915 Laredo Pl Billings MT 59101 Office: Box 2555 Billings MT 59103

TOMPKINS, ROGER BARTON, insurance company executive; b. Bloomington, Ill., Dec. 17, 1932; s. Arthur W. and Dortha (Christofer) T.; m. Elinor Grace Bieneman, June 12, 1954; children—Paul, Katy Tompkins Sappington, Laura. B.S., U. Ill., 1954, LL.B., 1956. Auto claims adjuster State Farm Ins., Tampa, Fla., 1956-57, agt., Sarasota, Fla., 1957-60, agy. mgr., Miami, Fla., 1960-62, agy. dir., Pompano Beach and St. Petersburg, Fla., 1962-67, with agy. exec. office, Bloomington, Ill., 1967-74, regional v.p., Costa Mesa, Calif., 1974—; chmn. Wycliffe Assocs., Orange, Calif., Wycliffe Bible Translators, Inc. Mem. Orange County Transp. Coalition. Mem. Am. Soc. C.L.U.s, Am. Soc. Chartered Property and Casualty Underwriters. Republican. Presbyterian. Clubs: Masons, Shriners.

TOMPKINS, WALKER ALLISON, historian, biographer, radio commentator; b. Prosser, Wsh., July 10, 1909; s. Charles Edward and Bertha (Allison) T.; m. Grace Spear, June 28, 1941 (div. Apr. 1965); children—Reid Edward, Joyce Susan, Pamela Lynn; m. 2d Barbara Hathaway Wachner, May 5, 1975. Student Modesto Jr. Coll., 1930; B.A. in Journalism, U. Wash., 1934. Newspaper reporter, Turlock, Calif., 1927-29; author books of fiction, 1931-58, biographies and regional history books, specializing in Santa Barbara, Calif. and vicinity, 1955—; author numerous books, including: California Editor, 1958; Royal Rancho, 1960; Santa Barbara Yesterdays, 1962; California's Wonderful Corner, 1962; Little Giant of Signal Hill, 1964; Continuing Quest, 1970; It Happened in Old Santa Barbara, 1975; Stagecoach Days, 1982; Santa Barbara History Makers, 1983; commentator on Santa Barbara History, twice-daily program Sta.-KTMS, Santa Barbara, 1967—; staff historian Santa Barbara News-Press, 1966-76; bd. dirs. Santa Barbara Hist. Soc.; mem. Santa Barbara County Landmarks Com.; Bd. dirs. San Roque Improvement Assn., Santa Barbara. Served with U.S. Army, 1942-45; ETO. Recipient Commendation Resolution, Calif. State Legislature, 1975. Mem. Calif. Writers' Guild, Western Writers Am. Republican. Presbyterian. Home:

TOMSHECK, LYLA ETHEL, speech profl.; b. Conrad, Mont., Oct. 23, 1950; d. Robert Anton and Ethel Johanna (Wallewein) Tomsheck; B.S. in Home Econs., Mont. State U., 1972, postgrad., 1977-79; postgrad. U. Mont., 1977-79; M.S. in Speech Communication, U. Oreg., 1981. Ravalli County extension agt. Mont. Extension Service, Hamilton, 1973-80; grad. teaching fellow U. Oreg., Eugene, 1980-83. Sunday sch. and confirmation tchr., fin. sec. Faith Luth. Ch. Recipient Heisey Found. award, 1967; Florence Hall award, 1978; Holmes award for dress design, 1972; Farm Found. fellow, 1980; J.C. Penney Co. fellow, 1980. Mem. Mont. Assn. Extension Home Economists (chmn. public relations com. 1974-77, public affairs com. 1977-80, sec. 1978-80), Nat. Assn. Extension Home Economists, Mont. Home Econs. Assn. (nominating com. 1977-78, family and public policy com. 1978-79), Am. Home Econs. Assn., Mont. Coop. Extension Assn. (dir. 1974-77, sec. 1976-77, chmn. public relations com. 1975-77), Alpha Gamma Delta. Club: Soroptimist (program com. 1976-77, nominating com. 1975-76). Contbr. articles to profl. publs. Home: 1810 Harris St Apt 226 Eugene OR 97401 Office: Speech Dept U Oreg Eugene OR 97403

TONELLI, EDITH ANN, art museum director; b. Westfield, Mass., May 20, 1949; d. Albert Robert and Pearl (Grubert) T.; B.A., Vassar Coll., 1971; M.A., CUNY, 1973; Ph.D., Boston U., 1981. Curriculum coordinator Project Search, Millbrook, N.Y., 1972-74; curator DeCordova Mus., Lincoln, Mass., 1976-78; dir. Univ. Art Gallery, asst. prof. dept. art U. Md., College Park, 1979-82; dir. Frederick S. Wight Gallery, adj. asst. prof. dept. art UCLA, Los Angeles, 1982—; reviewer pub. programs Nat. Endowment for Humanities, 1977—; teaching fellow Boston U., 1974-76. Recipient Dissertation award Boston U., 1979; Smithsonian fellow, 1979, Helen Squier Townsend fellow Vassar Coll., 1971-72. Mem. Am. Studies Assn., Assn. Art Mus. Dirs. Am. Assn. Museums, Coll. Art Assn., Woman's Caucus for Art. Office: UCLA Frederick S Wight Gallery Los Angeles CA 90024

TONG, HARRY W., lawyer, acct.; b. Canton, China, Feb. 11, 1934; came to U.S., 1939, naturalized, 1954; s. Ting Lit and Koon Hai (Wong) T.; A.A., Wilson Coll., 1957; B.S.B.A., Roosevelt U., 1959, M.S., 1964; J.D., DePaul U., 1972; m. Mary Lou Lum, Sept. 14, 1958; children—Thomas Michael, Karen Joy, Sharon Marie, Carol Lynn, Galen Douglas. Admitted to Ill. bar, 1972, Calif. bar, 1980; acctg. clk. Peoples Gas, Light & Coke Co., Chgo., 1957-58; sr. acct. David Himmelblau & Co., 1959-63; controller McCain Machinery Corp., 1963-65; individual practice law, Chgo., 1972-73 San Francisco, 1980—, also pvt. practice accountancy, 1965-73, 75—; pres. Tong Accountancy Corp., 1975—; Realtor, 1978—; asso. prof. acctg. and law Mayfair Coll., Wilson Coll., Chgo. State Coll., Harper Coll., San Mateo Coll., West Valley Coll. Bd. dirs. Chinese for Affirmative Action, 1976—, Chinese Am. Civic Council, 1971-73; mem. San Mateo County Human Relations Com. Recipient David Himmelblau award Northwestern U., 1960. Mem. Nat. Assn. Asian Am. C.P.A.s (pres. 1979-80), Soc. Chinese Am. Accts. (sec. 1979-80), Assn. Attys. and C.P.A.s, Calif. Soc. C.P.A.s, Asian Am. Bar Assn. Democrat. Roman Catholic. Club: Chinese Am. Dems. Author: Discrimination in Public Housing and the Fourteenth Amendment, 1971; author C.P.A. rev. manuals; weekly contbr. tax articles to Foster City Islander, 1978—. Home: 621 Bainbridge St Foster City CA 94404 Office: 490 Winslow Dr Redwood City CA 94063

TONG, RICHARD DARE, anesthesiologist; b. Chgo., Oct. 20, 1930; s. George Dare and June (Jung) T.; student U. Calif., Berkeley, 1949-52; M.D., U. Calif., Irvine, 1956; postgrad. U. Calif., Los Angeles, 1965-67; m. Diane Helene Davies, Apr. 12, 1970; children—Erin, Jason. Intern, Phoenix Gen. Hosp., 1956-57; resident in anesthesiology U. Calif., Los Angeles, 1965-67; practice medicine specializing in anesthesiology, Lakewood, Calif., 1967—; clin. instr. U. Calif. Sch. Medicine, Los Angeles, 1968—. Dep. sheriff reserve med. emergency team, Los Angeles County. Served with USNR, 1947-53. Diplomate Am. Bd. Anesthesiology. Fellow Am. Coll. Anesthesiology; mem. Am. Soc. Anesthesiologists, AMA, Calif., Los Angeles County med. assns. Democrat. Home: Rancho Palos Verdes CA Office: 3700 South St Lakewood CA 90712

TONGUE, THOMAS H., state judge, arbitrator; b. Hillsboro, Oreg., Feb. 4, 1912; s. Thomas H. and Irene (Cadwell) T.; B.S., U. Oreg., 1934, J.D., 1937; J.S.D., Yale, 1938; m. Bernice M. Healy, Nov. 30, 1939; children—Thomas Healy, John Richard, James Cadwell. Admitted to Oreg. bar, 1937; practiced in Portland, Oreg., 1942-69; partner firm Hicks, Tongue, Dale & Strader, Portland, 1948-67; of counsel Mautz, Souther, Spaulding, Kinsey & Williamson, Portland, 1967-69; justice Oreg. Supreme Ct., 1969-82; chmn. Oreg. Com. on Jud. Fitness, 1968-69; chmn. Oreg. Labor Mgmt. Relations Bd., 1961-63; mem. arbitration panels Am. Arbitration Assn. and Fed. Mediation and Conciliation Service, 1982—. Mem. Am., Oreg. bar assns. Episcopalian. Contbr. articles to profl. jours. Home and Office: 3421 Country Club S Salem OR 97302

TONINI, LEON RICHARD, hotel exec.; b. Pittsfield, Mass., May 16, 1931; s. John Richard and Mabel Grayce (Rushbrook) T.; B.A. in Mgmt., U. Md., 1951; m. Helen Jo, Aug. 15, 1966; 1 son, John Richard, II. Enlisted in U.S. Army, 1947, advanced through grades to master sgt., 1968; service in W.Ger., Vietnam; ret., 1974; dir. vets. employment and assistance Non-Commd. Officers Assn., San Antonio, 1974-75; supr. security Pinkerton's Inc., Dallas, 1975-78; gen. mgr. civil center Travelodge Motor Hotel and Restaurant, San Francisco, 1978—. Chmn. San Francisco Vets. Employment Com., 1981. Decorated Bronze Star; Republic Vietnam Honor medal 2d class. Mem. San Francisco Hotel Assn. (dir.), Non-Commd. Officers Assn. (dir. Calif. chpt.), Am. Legion, Regular Vets. Assn., Amvets, Patrons of Husbandry. Republican. Baptist. Club: Masons. Home: 205 Collins St Apt 9 San Francisco CA 94118 Office: 655 Ellis St San Francisco CA 94109

TONKIN, DAVID IRVING, association executive, computer consultant; b. Cleve., Nov. 15, 1938; s. Samuel Richard and Betty Jane (Felsenthal) T.; m. Karen Christine Samuelson, May 5, 1982. B.A., Calif. State U.-Los Angeles, 1974. Cert. data processor, Calif. Programmer analyst, systems analyst, 1962-69; cons. AID, Saigon, S. Vietnam, 1969-71; planning analyst Pacific Health Resources, Los Angeles, 1975-76; supr. Auto Club So. Calif., Los Angeles, 1976—. Vice pres. Beverly Hills Democratic club, 1975-78; bd. dirs. Calif. Dem. Council, 1975-78; chmn. adv. com. Los Angeles Dept. Environ. Quality, 1974-75; chmn. adv. com. Los Angeles Transp. Commn., 1978; mem. ACLU, Common Cause. Served with USNR, 1959-61. Mem. Assn. Systems Mgmt. Home: 12062 Edinger Ave Space 34 Santa Ana CA 92704

TONN, SHERI JEANNE, chemistry educator, researcher; b. Dallas, Oreg., May 13, 1949; d. Harvey C. Bartel and Jeanne Marie (Siddall) Shelton; m. Jeffrey F. Tonn, Aug. 22, 1971. B.S. in Chemistry, Oreg. State U., 1971; Ph.D. in Chemistry, Northwestern U., 1976. Postdoctoral fellow U. Minn., St. Paul, 1976-79; asst. prof. Pacific Lutheran U., Tacoma, Wash., 1979-82, assoc. prof., 1982—. Mem. exec. com., sec. Cascade chpt. Sierra Club, 1983—; chmn. Citizen's Com. of Air, Water Quality, 1980—; bd. dirs. Wash. Environ. Council, 1983-85. Recipient Regency Advancement award Pacific Luth. U., 1981. Mem. Am. Chem. Soc., (alt. councillor Puget Sound Sect. 1983-85), Assn. Women in Sci., Univ. Scholars Assn. Pacific Lutheran U. (dir. 1980-83, pres. 1982-83), Iota Sigma Pi, Phi Lambda Upsilon, Sigma Xi. Contbr. articles to profl. jours. Home: 1201 S Garfield Tacoma WA 98444 Office: Dept of Chemistry Pacific Luth U Tacoma WA 98447

TONTZ, JAY LOGAN, university dean; b. Balt., July 20, 1938; s. E. Logan and Charlotte (Mullikin) T.; m. F. Anne Deams, 1982. B.A., Denison U., Granville, Ohio, 1960; M.S., Cornell U., 1962; Ph.D., U. N.C., Chapel Hill, 1966. Asst. prof. econs. USAF Acad., 1966-69; mem. faculty Calif. State U., Hayward, 1969—, prof. econs., 1977—, dean Sch. Bus. and Econs., 1974—. Chmn. trustees St. Rose Hosp., Hayward. Served with USAF, 1966-69. Decorated D.S.M. Mem. Am. Econs. Assn., Western Econs. Assn., Delta Sigma Pi. Clubs: Hayward Rotary (treas. 1979-80), Hayward Trade (dir. 1971—). Office: Sch Bus and Econs Calif State Univ Hayward CA 94524

TOOKEY, ROBERT CLARENCE, consulting actuary; b. Santa Monica, Calif., Mar. 21, 1925; s. Clarence Hall and Minerva Maconachie (Anderson) T.; B.S., Calif. Inst. Tech., 1945; M.S., U. Mich., 1947; m. Marcia Louise Hickman, Sept. 15, 1956; children—John Hall, Jennifer Louise, Thomas Anderson. Actuarial clk. Occidental Life Ins. Co., Los Angeles, 1945-46; with Prudential Ins. Co. Am., Newark, 1947-49; assoc. actuary in group Pacific Mut. Life Ins. Co., Los Angeles, 1949-55; asst. v.p. in charge reins. sales and service for 17 western states Lincoln Nat. Life Ins. Co., Ft. Wayne, Ind., 1955-61; dir. actuarial services Peat, Marwick, Mitchell & Co., Chgo., 1961-63; mng. partner So. Calif. office Milliman & Robertson, cons. actuaries, Pasadena, 1963-76; pres. Robert Tookey Assos., Inc., 1977—. Committeeman troop 501 Boy Scouts Am., 1969-72; assoc. mem. arts and scis. com. Republican State Central Com., 1972-74. Served to lt. (j.g.) USNR, 1943-45, 51-52. Fellow Soc. Actuaries, Conf. Actuaries in Pub. Practice; mem. Am. Acad. Actuaries, Pacific States Actuarial Club, Pacific Ins. Conf. Clubs: San Gabriel Country; Rotary (Pasadena); Union League (Chgo.). Home: 1249 Descanso Dr La Canada CA 91011 Office: 80 S Lake Ave Pasadena CA 91101

TOOLE, BRICE, JR., real estate developer; b. Washington, Mar. 31, 1928; s. Brice and Eleanor Ann (Hibbard) T.; B.A., U. Mont., 1953; cert. in investment banking, U. Pa., 1964; cert. in real estate So. Meth. U., 1975; m. Maxine E. Howes, Nov. 16, 1952; children—Tracey A., Jonathan H., Jeffery H. Corp. fin. ofcl. Merrill, Lynch, Hemphill-Noyes & Co., Mitchum Jones & Templeton and Oriole Investment Co., 1954-79; asst. to pres., ventures mgr. Upland Industries Corp. subs. Union Pacific Corp., Los Angeles, 1979-82; sr. v.p. corp. real estate group Charles Robert Lesser & Co., Beverly Hills, Calif., 1982-83; sr.

v.p. Security Realty Adv. Services, Security Pacific Corp., 1983—. Mem. met. council YMCA. Served with AUS, 1945-47. Mem. Indsl. and Office Park Devel. Council, Urban Land Inst., Soc. Indsl. Realtors. Republican. Episcopalian. Clubs: Civic, Los Angeles Rotary. Home: 1200 S Orange Grove Blvd Apt 6 Pasadena CA 91105 Office: 333 S Hope St Los Angeles CA 90071

TOOPER, VIRGINIA OLIPHANT, ednl. cons., public speaker; b. Nashville, June 25, 1928; d. Thomas Alfred and Catherine (Holt) Oliphant; B.S., La. State U., 1949; M.A., Columbia U., 1954; Ed.D., U. Cin., 1973; occupational therapist Tex. Woman's U., 1954; m. Edward Benjamin Tooper, Aug. 6, 1955; 1 son, Jon Edward. Occupational therapist VA Hosp., Hines, Ill., 1955-58; tchr. Child Guidance Home, Jewish Hosp. Spl. Edn., Cin., 1963-65; instr. Cleve. State U., 1970-72; asst. prof. spl. edn., counseling and guidance San Jose (Calif.) State U., 1972-80; ednl. cons., public speaker on use of humor in edn., 1980—. Dept. Mental Hygiene and Correction grantee; Rehab. Services Adminstrn. grantee, 1970-72; Nat. Tb Assn. grantee, 1952-54. Mem. Am. Occupational Therapy Assn., Nat. Assn. Profl. Saleswomen (pres. East Bay chpt.), Sales and Mktg. Execs. Assn., Nat. Speakers Assn. (dir. No. Calif. chpt.), Author: Motor Skills - A Handbook for Teachers of the Mentally Retarded, 1971; Communication Skills - A Handbook for Teachers of the Mentally Retarded, 1973. Home: 7953 Stonehurst Ct Pleasanton CA 94566

TOOR, JASWANT SINGH, aerospace scientist; b. Sowaddi, Punjab, India, Sept. 12, 1938; s. Naginder Singh and Ind (Kaur) T.; came to U.S., 1965, naturalized, 1972; B.S. in Math., Punjab U., 1957, B.S. in Mech. Engring., 1961; M.S., Purdue U., 1967, Ph.D., 1971; m. Marlene Spiess; 1 dau., Jasbir Andrea Kaur. Lectr. mech. engring. Punjab Poly., Nilokheri, India, 1961-62; design engr. BBDO Power Plant Design Orgn., Punjab, 1962-65; research asst. mech. engring. Purdue U., Lafayette, Ind., 1966-67, 68-71, David Ross fellow, 1971-72; project engr. Lau Blower Co., Dayton, Ohio, 1967-68; project mgr. Stewart Warner Corp., Indpls., 1968; program mgr. Systems, Sci. and Software, San Diego, 1972-75; sr. scientist Sci. Applications Inc., La Jolla, Calif., 1976-81; program mgr. advanced research and tech. devel. Convair div. Gen. Dynamics Co., San Diego, 1981—; cons. in field. Mem. AIAA, ASME, Soc. Advancement of Materials and Processing Engring., Combustion Inst. Registered profl. engr. Calif. Contbr. articles to sci. jours. on energy, energy conservation, devel. of new and renewable resources of energy, heat transfer and thermodynamics. Office: Gen Dynamics Convair Div 5001 Kearny Villa Rd San Diego CA 92123

TOORENAAR, JACALYN SUE, production director; b. San Jose, Calif., Aug. 31, 1949; d. Gerard Jacob and Theresa Aeke (Aalders) Toorenaar. A.A. in Liberal Arts, Can. Coll., Redwood City, Calif., 1971; B.A. in Journalism, San Francisco State U., 1973. Sec. Internat. Banking div. Crocker Nat. Bank, San Francisco, 1973-74, Hewlett-Packard Co., Santa Clara, Calif., 1974-76; asst. editor, copy editor, advt. traffic coordinator, prodn. mgr. EW Communications Inc., Palo Alto, Calif., 1977-80, prodn. dir., 1980—; speaker Face-To-Face Mag. Pub. Conf., N.Y.C., 1982. Mem. Calif. Press Women, Nat. Fedn. Press Women, Pub. Mfg. Exec. Assn. (bd. govs.). Presbyterian. Office: EW Communications Inc 1170 E Meadow Dr Palo Alto CA 94303

TOPLIFF, MICHAEL LEWIS, computer scientist, consultant; b. Superior, Nebr., June 8, 1948; s. Lewis Henry Topliff and Willa Irene (Statz) T.; m. Cynthia Fay Kramer, Aug. 6, 1972. B.S. in Math. Computer Sci., N.Mex. State U., 1969; M.S. in Computer Sci., U. Ariz., 1974, Ph.D. in Higher Edn. and Computer Sci, 1983. Mgr., programmer Computer Ctr., U. Ariz., Tucson, 1975-70, mgr. acad. services Computer Ctr., 1970-78; cons., 1970-78; dir. systems engring. Pincock, Allen & Holt, Inc. Tucson, 1978—. Active Young Leadership Club. Mem. Assn. Computing Machinery. Republican. Club: Genealogical. Home: 1620 W Montebella Dr Tucson AZ 85704 Office: 1750 E Benson Hwy Tucson AZ 85714

TOPP, ALPHONSO AXEL, JR., environmental scientist; b. Indpls., Oct. 15, 1920; s. Alphonso Axel and Emilia (Karlsen) T.; m. Mary Catherine Virtue, July 7, 1942; children—Karen, Susan, Linda, Sylvia, Peter, Astrid, Heidi, Eric, Megan, Katrina. B.S. in Chem. Engring., Purdue U., 1942; M.S., UCLA, 1948. Commd. 2d lt. U.S. Army, 1942, advanced through grades to col., 1966, ret., 1970; environ. scientist Radiation Protection Sect., State of N.Mex., Santa Fe, 1970, program mgr., licensing and registration sect., 1978, chief radiation protection bur., 1981—. Decorated Legion of Merit, Bronze Star with 2 oak leaf clusters. Mem. Health Physics Soc., Sigma Xi. Democrat. Presbyterian. Club: Rotary. Home: 123 Balboa Rd Santa Fe NM 87501 Office: PO Box 968 Santa Fe NM 87504

TOPPS, LE ROY (LEE), insurance claims executive; b. Kansas City, Mo., Nov. 14, 1948; s. John W. and Mary L. (Williams) T.; m. Mary N. Davis, Feb. 26, 1982. Casualty claim law assoc. Am. Ednl. Inst., Basking Ridge, N.J, 1977; B.A., Golden State U., Ins. Inst. Am., 1979. With N.W. Pacific Indemnity Co., Portland, Oreg., v.p. claims, 1980; formerly with Chubb & Son Inc., N.Y.C., sr. claims officer Chubb Group Ins. Cos. N.W. Region, Seattle, 1980—. Vice pres. Gospel Music Educators Seminar, Inc., Seattle. Served with USMC, 1967-70; Vietnam. Decorated Navy Achievement medal; named Black Achiever, Harlem YMCA, N.Y.C., 1982. Mem. Seattle Claim Mgrs. Council, Seattle Adjusters Assn., NAACP. Club: Young Democrats. Home: 11707 SE 210th Pl Kent WA 98031 Office: 720 Olive Way Suite 1100 Seattle WA 98101

TORCZYNER, JOSHUA, corp. exec.; b. Vienna, Austria, Sept. 29, 1910; s. Eisig and Sarah (Wolfgang) T.; student Acad. Commerce, Vienna, 1925-29; m. Juana Spitzer, Jan. 9, 1940; children—Jerome Dan, Judith Arlene. Came to U.S., 1941. Jewelry wholesaler, newspaper writer, Vienna, 1929-38; chmn. Austria Maccabi region, 1938-39; exec. dir. World Maccabi Aid Com., Geneva, Switzerland, 1939-40; underground leader Jewish activities, Belgium, 1940-41; co-founder Jewish Refugee Orgn., Havana, Cuba, 1941; pres. Hakoah A.C., N.Y.C., 1942-43, founder chpt., San Francisco, 1944, pres., 1945-50, 62-69; owner Pacific Diamond Co., San Francisco, 1948-83, pres., 1966-83. Vice pres. U.S. Maccabi Assn., 1942-43; pres. Nordau dist. Zionist Orgn. Am., 1948-50, Nordau-Peninsula dist., 1950-51, pres. San Francisco dist., 1951-52; v.p. Jewish Nat. Fund, San Francisco, 1954-55; v.p. Am. Zionist Council, 1954-55, pres., 1969-70; pres. Louis D. Brandeis House, 1956-62, No. Calif. Am. Zionist Fedn., 1966-71. Mem. No. Calif. Soccer Football Assn. (pres. 1950-51), Chess Friends No. Calif. (pres. 1951-52). Home: 3003 Hillside Dr Burlingame CA 94010

TOREN, ROBERT, photojournalist; b. Grand Rapids, Mich., Oct. 9, 1915; s. Clarence J. and Helen (Holcomb) T.; student Winona Sch. Profl. Photography, 1957, West Coast Sch. Photography, 1959-62; m. Miriam Jeanette Smith, July 17, 1940. Photographer, Harris and Ewing, Washington, 1938-39, Versluis Studios, Grand Rapids, Mich., 1939-43, prodn. mgr., 1940-43; owner, photographer Toren Galleries, San Francisco, 1946—; photographer Combat Tribes of World, Rich Lee Orgn., 1978—, Darien jungle expdn. Am. Motors, 1979; feature writer Auburn (Calif.) Jour., 1983—. One man shows various univs.; prints in permanent collections: Photog. Hall of Fame, Coyote Point Mus., San Mateo County Hist. Mus.; photog. column San Mateo Times; lectr. Am. Pres. Lines, Coll. San Mateo, Peninsula Art Assn., Mendicino Art Center. Historian City of Foster City; vice chmn. Art Commn. Foster City. Trustee, West Coast Sch.; bd. dirs. Foster City Art League, Hillbarn Theatre, San Mateo County Arts Council; mem. art com. San Mateo County Fair, 1979—; coordinator, dir. Georgetown (Calif.) Mountain Mus., 1982—. Served from pvt. to staff sgt. AUS, 1943-46. Mem. Calif. Writers (br. pres.), Profl. Photographers Am. Presbyn. Author: Peninsula Wilderness. Illustrator: The Tainted Tree, 1963. Editor: The Evolution of Portraiture, 1965; The Western Way of Portraiture, 1965. Home: 3140 Cascade Trail Cool CA 95614

TORGERSON, LESTER JOHN, university administrator; b. Gifford, Idaho, Apr. 14, 1924; s. Edward John and Meta Marie (Stelljes) T.; B.S., U. Idaho, 1947; M.A., Humboldt State U., 1971; m. Margaret Jean Corus, June 6, 1947; children—Terrill, Kurt, Eric. Acct., U. Idaho, Moscow, 1947-63; asst. comptroller U. Alaska, Fairbanks, 1963-66, dir. personnel, 1977—; budget officer, adminstrv. asst. to bus. mgr. Humboldt State U., Arcata, Calif., 1966-69, personnel officer, 1969-77. Mem. Humboldt County Employment and Tng. Council, Eureka, Calif., 1974-76; mem. credit com. Calif. State Employees Credit Union, Eureka, 1969-77; chmn. bd. govs. Luth. Community Services of Humboldt County, 1976-77. Served with USN, 1943-46. Mem. Coll. and Univ. Personnel Assn. (Alaska coordinator 1982-83). Lutheran. Home: 1499 Carr Ave Fairbanks AK 99701 Office: 110 Bunnell Bldg Univ of Alaska Fairbanks AK 99701

TORGERSON, LOIS GLOCK, hospital administrative dietitian; b. Appleton, Minn., July 3, 1928; d. Conrad F. and Hilda A. (Brodhagen) Glock; m. Glen O. Torgerson, Nov. 29, 1952. B.S., U. Wis., 1950. Intern Harborview Hosp., Seattle, 1951; diabetic dietitian Firland Sanitorium, Seattle, 1951-52; dir. women's residence halls dining room U. Idaho, Moscow, 1952-54; dietitian mgr. Wash. State U., Pullman, 1954-56; clinic dietitian Rockwood Clinic, Spokane, Wash., 1960-65; therapeutic dietitian Sacred Heart Med. Center, Spokane, 1959-61, chief clin. dietitian, asst. dir., 1961-72, dir. dietetic services, 1972—. Wis. Dietetic Assn. fellow, 1950. Mem. Am. Dietetic Assn. (registered dietitian), Wash. State Dietetic Assn. (past pres.), Greater Spokane Dietetic Assn. (past pres.), Am. Soc. Hosp. Food Service Adminstrs., Wis. Alumni Assn., Wis. Home Econs. Alumni Assn. Home: N 250 Raymond Rd C 12 Spokane WA 99206 Office: W 101 Eighth Ave Spokane WA 99220

TORIGOE, RODNEY YOSHITO, clin. psychologist; b. Honolulu, Feb. 1, 1945; s. Samuel Yoshio and Sueko Thelma (Inakazu) T.; B.A. (Hemenway scholar, star scholar), U. Hawaii, 1968; postgrad. Calif. State U., Los Angeles, 1969-71; M.A., U. Colo., 1973, Ph.D., 1976; m. Bessie M. Nakamura, Aug. 7, 1971. Social worker Dept. Public Social Services, Los Angeles, 1968-69; psychology technician Calif. State U., Los Angeles, 1971; teaching asst. U. Colo., Boulder, 1972-74; psychology asso. Ariz. State Hosp., Phoenix, 1975-76; clin. psychologist VA Med. Center, Phoenix, 1976-78, coordinator human sexuality clinic and co-coordinator biofeedback clinic, 1977-78, coordinator psychol. services for inpatient psychiatry, 1978; chief day treatment center, chief psychology service VA Outpatient Clinic, Honolulu, 1978—; asst. clin. prof. dept. psychology U. Hawaii, asst. clin. prof. dept. Psychiatry Sch. Medicine; cons. Western Interstate Commn. for Higher Edn., Boulder, 1973, affirmative action officer, 1973-74. Bd. dirs. The House, Inc., 1980-82, pres. bd. dirs., 1981-82. NIMH fellow, 1971-72; recipient awards Am. Legion, 1963, Western Interstate Commn. for Higher Edn., 1974; cert. psychologist, Hawaii, Ariz.; diplomate Am. Acad. Behavioral Medicine. Mem. Am. Psychol. Assn., Western Psychol. Assn., Rocky Mountain Psychol. Assn., Hawaii Psychol. Assn., Asian-Am. Psychol. Assn., Assn. for Advancement of Psychology, Assn. for Advancement of Psychotherapy, Assn. for Advancement of Behavior Therapy, Biofeedback Soc. Am., Am. Assn. Sex Educators, Counselors and Therapists, Internat. Council Psychologists, Internat. Imagery Assn., Nat. Register Health Service Providers in Psychology, Sigma Lambda. Contbr. article to profl. jour.; first Japanese-Am. to receive Ph.D. in Clin. Psychology, U. Colo., Boulder. Office: 300 Ala Moana Blvd Honolulu HI 96850

TORIO, MARY CAROL, dietitian; b. Bellevue, Iowa, Sept. 3, 1938; d. Robert A. and Marcella Frances (Even) Hayes; m. Louis F. Torio, Oct. 21, 1972. B.S., Iowa State U., 1960, M.S., Cornell U., 1964; M.P.A., U. So. Calif., 1978. Registered dietitian. Adminstrv. dietitian Stanford U. Hosp. (Calif.), 1964-66, edn. dir., 1966-67, dir. dietetics, 1967-75; asst. prof. Calif. State U. Los Angeles, 1975-78; dir. food services Mary's Help Hosp., Daly City, Calif. 1978—. Mem. Am. Dietetic Assn., Calif. Dietetic Assn. (Disting. Service award 1981, treas. 1969-71, pres. 1975-77). Roman Catholic. Home: 711 Bowhill Rd Hillsborough CA 94010

TORKELSON, GERALD M., educator; b. Merrill, Wis., Feb. 28, 1917; s. Carl G. and Johanna Maric (Odegard) T.; m. Emily Bobb, Dec. 28, 1943; children—Thomas C., Emily J. B.S., U. Wis.-Stevens Point, 1941; Ph.M. in History, U. Wis., 1945; Ed.D., Pa. State U., 1953. Tchr. history pub. high schs., Mosinee, Wis., 1941-42, Park Fall, Wis., 1942-43, Stevens Point, 1943-44, Marinette, Wis., 1945-46; instr. social scis. Drake U., Des Moines, 1946-49; prof. edn. Pa. State U., University Park, 1949-65; dir. project NDEA, U.S. Office Edn., Washington, 1963-64; prof. edn., chmn. dept. ednl. communications U. Wash., Seattle, 1965—; advisor in edn. Pacific Luth. U., Parkland, Wash., 1977—; mem. humanities adv. council Shoreline Community Coll., Seattle, 1981—; Fulbright lectr. and cons. Greek and Turkish Cypriot Ministries of Edn., Cyprus, 1979. Recipient Outstanding Services award Wash. Assn. for Ednl. Communications and Tech., 1975. Mem. Assn. for Ednl. Communications and Tech. (nat. pres. 1974-75), Am. Ednl. Research Assn., Wash. Library-Media Assn., Nat. Soc. for Study Edn., Fulbright Alumni Assn., World Affairs Council Seattle, Phi Delta Kappa. Democrat. Lutheran. Assoc. editor for theory Ednl. Communication and Tech. Jour., 1977—; contbr. articles to profl. jours. Office: 412 Miller Hall Univ Wash Seattle WA 98195

TORLAKSON, JAMES DANIEL, artist, educator; b. San Francisco, Feb. 19, 1951; s. Allen Daniel and Catharine Agnus T.; m. Kathleen B. Bodnar, Dec. 12, 1981; 1 dau., Elizabeth B. L. B.F.A., Calif. Coll. Arts and Crafts, 1973; M.A., San Francisco State U., 1974. Watercolorist, printmaker; works exhibited nat., internat. exhbns., 1973—; part time instr. Calif. Coll. Arts and Crafts and Skyline Coll. Recipient awards Boston Printmakers Exhbn., 1983, 7th U. Dallas Nat. Print Invitational, 1981, Intaglio, U. Louisville, 1981. Mem. Boston Printmakers, Calif. Soc. Printmaking.

TORME, MARGARET ANNE, public relations executive, communications consultant; b. Indpls., Apr. 5, 1943; d. Ira G. and Margaret Joy (Wright) Barker; children—Karen Anne, Leah Vanessa. Student Coll. San Mateo, 1961-65. Pub. relations mgr. Hoefer, Dieterich & Brown, San Francisco, 1964-73; v.p., co-founder, creative dir. Lowry & Ptnrs., San Francisco, 1975-83; pres., founder Torme & Co., San Francisco, 1983—; cons. in communications. Mem. Pub. Relations Soc. Am., San Francisco Advt. Club, North Bay Advt. Club (dir.), San Francisco C. of C. Office: 40 Gold St San Francisco CA 94111

TORRACA, LOUIS ANTHONY, JR., air force officer; b. New Haven, May 13, 1935; s. Louis Anthony and Mary Elizabeth (Pyle) T.; m. Beryl Joyce Conins, Mar. 15, 1963; children—Martin, Kent, David, Toni, Tracey. B.S. in Pub. Relations, Boston U., 1957, M.A. in Communications, U. Okla., 1971. Joined U.S. Air Force, 1958, advanced through grades to col.; air traffic control officer, Kans., Eng., Ill., 1958-70; chief internal info. and community relations programs, Tan Son Nhut AFB, Vietnam, 1971-72; spokesman Mil. Assistance Command, Vietnam, 1972; chief community relations div. Hdqrs. Pacific Air Forces, Hickam AFB, Hawaii and chief pub. affairs div., 1973-74, chief media and community relations div., U.S. Pacific Command, Camp H.M. Smith, Hawaii, 1974-76; dir. info. Hdqrs. Air Force Communications Service, Richards-Gebaur AFB, Mo., 1976-78; dir. pub. affairs Mil. Airlift Command, Scott AFB, Ill., 1978-80; dir. pub. affairs Pacific Command, Honolulu, 1980—; pub. relations cons. Bd. dirs. Armed Services YMCA; com. chmn. Boy Scouts Am. Decorated Legion of Merit, Bronze Star, Meritorious Service medal with one oak leaf cluster, others. Mem. Pub. Relations Soc. Am., Sigma Delta Chi, Kappa Tau Alpha, Kappa Sigma. Clubs: Officers, Press (Kans., Ill., Mo., Hawaii), Jaycees. Episcopalian. Contbr. to mil. publs.

TORRENS, WILLIAM JOHN, arbitrator, management consultant, educator; b. Glen Rock, N.J., Mar. 30, 1928; s. William John and Hazel Hoyt (Lockwood) T.; m. Esther Patricia DeGeeter, May 30, 1950; children—Mary Elizabeth Parker, Patricia Anne. A.B., Rutgers U., 1951; M.B.A., Ph.D., Pacific Coast U., 1983. Cert. tchr., arbitrator, Calif. Prof. mgmt. Sch. Bus. Adminstrn., Calif. State Coll.-Stanislaus, 1970—, coordinator dept. mgmt. and mktg., 1980—; dir. indsl. relations United Vintners Inc., San Francisco, 1974-79; mgr. indsl. relations E & J Gallo Winery Inc., Modesto, Calif., 1971-74; Western regional mgr. Internat. Paper Co., N.Y.C., 1960-71; factfinder, Calif. Pub. Employee Relations Bd., 1980-83; dir. George Washington Meml. Corp. Chmn. arbitration bd. Stanislaus County Mobile Homes; mem. labor panel State Bar Calif. Served with AUS, 1945-48. Mem. Am. Soc. Personnel Adminstrn., Am. Soc. Tng. and Devel., Am. Inst. Indsl. Engrs., Am. Arbitration Assn., Indsl. Personnel Council. Republican. Roman Catholic. Clubs: Colgate Alumni (Arrowhead), Lions, 12:10 (Turlock); Elks. Author, lectr. in field. Home: 623 Sunnybrook Circle PO Box 1938 Turlock CA 95381 Office: 801 E Monte Vista C207A Turlock CA 95380

TORRES, ART, state senator; b. Los Angeles, Sept. 24, 1946; s. Arthur and Julia (Alvarado) T.; m. Yolanda Nava, 1975; children—Joaquin Anthony. A.A., East Los Angeles, Coll., 1966; B.A., U. Calif.-Santa Cruz, 1968; J.D., U. Calif.-Davis, 1971. Mem. Calif. State Assembly, from 1974, former chmn. health com., now mem. Calif. State Senate. Del. Democratic Nat. Conv., 1980. John F. Kennedy -fellow Harvard U. Mem. Jaycees, Phi Delta Phi. Club: Harvard of So. Calif. Office: California State Senate Sacramento CA 95814*

TORREZ, ROSA LUCERO, copper mining co. ofcl.; b. Silver City, N.Mex., Apr. 25, 1941; d. Trinidad C. and Maria G. (Carrillo) Lucero; student public schs.; 1 son, Samuel L. Bookkeeper, Am. Nat. Bank, Silver City, 1959-61; with Kennecott Corp., Hurley, N.Mex., 1968—, procurement clk., 1977-79, buyer, 1979—; mem. supervisory com. Chino Employees Credit Union. Democrat. Roman Catholic. Home: Route 8 Box 89 Silver City NM 88061 Office: Purchasing Dept Kennecott Corp Hurley NM 88043

TORRINGTON, MARY CHRISTINE, international training consultant; b. Denver, July 20, 1949; d. Warren Rene and Inez Marie (Alexander) T.; B.S. in Zoology, Duke U., 1971; M.A., U.S. Internat. U., 1973, Ph.D. in Clin. Psychology, 1976. Postdoctoral fellow in psychology Devereux Found., Santa Barbara, Calif., 1976-77; psychol. cons. Alysan Ctr., Santa Clara, Calif., 1979; counselor/cons. employee assistance program Wells Fargo Bank, San Francisco, 1980; participant, intern Johnson Inst., Mpls., 1980; internat. tng. cons., employee assistance program Standard Oil of Calif., San Francisco, 1980-81; pres. M.C. Torrington & Assocs., San Francisco, 1981—. Mem. San Francisco C. of C., World Trade Assn., Internat. Trade Council (dir.), Soc. Intercultural Edn., Tng. and Research, World Affairs Council, Sell Overseas Am., U.S.-Arab C. of C., Japan Soc., Calif. Council Internat. Trade, Internat. Visitors Ctr., Am. Psychol. Assn., Calif. Psychol. Assn. Club: Commonwealth No. Calif. Home: 2200 Sacramento St #1505 San Francisco CA 94115 Office: 211 Sutter St Suite 318 San Francisco CA 94100

TOTH, ARTHUR, JR., federal agency administrator; b. Chgo., Feb. 19, 1936; s. Arthur John and Margaret Elizabeth T.; B.S., U. So. Miss., 1967, M.E., 1974; m. Aurora Jean Gibson, Oct. 5, 1974. Illustrator, USAF Air Ground Ops. Sch., Keesler AFB, Miss., 1960-62, illustrator TV graphics USAF, 1962-64, supr. TV graphics, 1964-70, supr. A/V asst., 1970-73, chief visual services br., 1973-76; tng. specialist Tng. and Audiovisual Support Center, U.S. Army, Fort Lewis, Wash., 1976-77, chief services br., 1977-78, dep. dir., 1978-82, dir., 1982—. Lic. lay reader St. Joseph and St. John's Episcopal Ch., 1979—, mem. bishop's com., 1977-80; mem. Preservation and Review Bd., Steilacoom, Wash., 1977—. Served with USAF, 1954-59. Mem. Armed Forces Communications and Electronics Assn., Nat. Assn. Govt. Communicators, Nat. Trust Historic Preservation, Internat. TV Assn. Episcopalian. Home: 1515 Lafayette St Box 1040 Steilacoom WA 98388 Office: Tng and Audiovisual Support Center Fort Lewis WA 98433

TOTH, EMERICK, elec. engr., writer; b. N.Y.C., June 27, 1905; s. Emerick and Vilma (Barcsay) T.; B.S. in Elec. Engring., Newark Coll. Engring. (now N.J. Inst. Tech.), 1927; m. Elma Istok Dittrich, July 15, 1934; children—Emerick William, Michael Allen, Nicholas Lee. Asst. research physicist Bakelite Corp., Bloomfield, N.J., 1927-29; research engr. Bell Telephone Labs., N.Y.C., 1930, Wired Radio Labs., Ampere, N.J., 1930-32; devel. engr. DeForest Radio Co., Passaic, N.J., 1932-33, Sylvania Corp., Clifton, N.J., 1934-35, Pilot Radio Corp., Long Island City, N.J., 1935-37, Bendix Radio Corp., Balt. and Chgo., 1937-38; electronic scientist U.S. Naval Research Lab., Washington, 1938-68, head radio techniques br., 1957-68; mem. Naval Communication Adv. Bd., 1959-69, U.S. Commn. 6, URSI, 1956-64, NASA Tech. Com. Communication Satellites, 1965-68; ind. researcher and writer, 1968—. Pres., Sunny Acres Residents Assn., 1977-79; mem. Takoma Park council Boy Scouts Am., 1945-49; Democratic committeeman Adams County (Colo.), 1976-83. Recipient Meritorious Civilian Service award U.S. Navy, 1946, Group Achievement award, 1961, Superior Civilian Service award U.S. Navy, 1968; elected to Hall of Fame, Newark Coll. Engring., 1960. Fellow IEEE (various profl. groups and coms. 1958-68). Unitarian. Contbr. numerous articles on radio communication systems to tech. jours.; designer 15 radio communication receivers; sonar and aircraft type direction finders; patentee in field. (22). Address: 6150 S Monroe Dr Littleton CO 80121

TOTH, FRANK LOUIS, microprocessors company executive; b. Inglewood, Calif., June 5, 1953; s. Louis Alois and Anna (Haijtas) T.; m. Jacqueline Eva Walton, July 9, 1977. B.S. in Bus., Calif. State Consortium, Long Beach; M.B.A., Don Bosco Tech. Inst., 1972. Engr., Datatapes, Bell & Howell, Pasadena, Calif., 1974-78; mktg. mgr. Microprocessors, Am. Microsystems, Santa Clara, Calif., 1978-81, dir. mktg., 1981—. Mem. IEEE, Aircraft Owners and Pilots Assn. Democrat.

TOTH, GISELLE MARTHA, research scientist; b. Komarom, Hungary, Feb. 6, 1941; came to U.S., June 2, 1970, naturalized, 1979; d. Joseph Istvan and Gizella Rose (Erdey) T.; M.Sc., U. Debrecen, Hungary, 1964, Ph.D. magna cum laude, 1970. Project engr., Hungary, 1964-70; research scientist New Brunswick Sci. Co., Edison, N.J., 1971-75; dir. research and devel. Pharmachem Co., Bethlehem, Pa., 1976-78; mgmt. cons. Hill Inst. Tech., San Francisco, 1978-80, also dir.; research asso. Stauffer Chem. Co., Richmond, Calif., 1980—. Mem. Am. Chem. Soc., Am. Inst. Chem. Engrs., Am. Soc. Metals, Am. Acad. Polit. and Social Sci., Tissue Culture Assn. Clubs: Corinthian Yacht, Tiburon Peninsula Tennis. Contbr. articles to profl. jours. Patentee in field.

Home: 45 Harbor Oak #32 Tiburon CA 94920 Office: 1200 S 47th St Richmond CA 94804

TOTH, STEPHEN JOSEPH, sci. co. exec.; b. N.Y.C., June 2, 1925; s. Stephen Joseph and Viola Caroline (Schaefer) T.; B.S. in M.E., M.I.T., 1950; m. Kathryn N. Davis, Feb. 10, 1979. With Honeywell, Inc., N.Y.C., Mpls. and London, 1960-64; v.p. mktg. ITT, Los Angeles, 1964-67; div. gen. mgr. Hughes Aircraft Co., Los Angeles, 1967-70; group v.p. Wyle Labs., Los Angeles, 1970-73; pres., chief exec. officer, dir. Pacific Sci. Co., Anaheim, Calif., 1973—. Served with USAAF, 1944-45. Mem. Am. Mgmt. Assn. Republican. Mormon. Clubs: Balboa Bay, Big Canyon, Calif. Home: 25 Lochmoor Ln Newport Beach CA 92660 Office: 1350 S State College Blvd Anaheim CA 92803

TOTTON, CARL ALLEN, II, rehabilitation counselor; b. Los Angeles, May 10, 1948; s. Carl Allen and Elva (Ezell) T. D.D. (Hon.) Calif. State U., 1976, B.S. in Rehab. Counseling, 1978, M.S., 1980. Cert. rehab. counselor, Calif., 1981. Faculty mem. counseling psychology Univ. Without Walls, Los Angeles, 1982—; dir., instr. martial arts and Chinese studies Taoist Inst., North Hollywood, Calif., 1981—; dir., counselor Rehab. Counseling Assocs., North Hollywood, 1981—, pres., 1983—; stress mgmt. cons., hypnotherapist. Recipient cert. of appreciation Los Angeles Pub. Library, 1975, Mcpl. Sports Program Los Angeles, 1976. Mem. Calif. Rehab Counseling Assn., Am. Rehab. Counseling Assn., Am. Mental Health Counseling Assn., Am. Orthopsychiat. Assn. Democrat. Taoist. Club: Chinese Physical Health (Los Angeles). Contbr. articles to mags. Office: Rehabilitation Counseling Assocs 10632 Burbank Blvd N Hollywood CA 91601

TOUBY, JUDITH BOONE, educator; b. Noblesville, Ind., Sept. 24, 1943; d. Albert F. and Annabel (Robb) Boone; m. David G. Touby, June 13, 1964 (div.); children—Lisa Michele, David Todd. B.S., Purdue U., 1966; M.A., Ariz. State U., 1977. Cert. home econs. tchr., vocat. coop. edn. coordinator. Tchr. English, home econs., phys. edn. North White Sch. Corp., Monon, Ind., 1967-68; tchr. home econs. Washington Twp. Schs., Indpls., 1968-71; foods service supr. Purdue U. Men's Residence Halls, 1966-67; cafeteria mgr. Scottsdale (Ariz.) High Sch., 1972, home econs. tchr., coordinator, chmn. dept., 1972-83; tchr. Saguaro High Sch., Scottsdale, 1983—; curriculum cons. Vol. civic agys. Mem. Ariz. Home Econs. Assn., Am. Home Econs. Assn., Scottsdale Edn. Assn., Ariz. Edn. Assn., NEA, Phi Delta Kappa, Phi Mu, Kappa Kappa Kappa. Mem. Christian Ch. Office: 6250 N 82d St Scottsdale AZ 85253

TOUR, ROBERT LOUIS, physician; b. Sheffield, Ala., Dec. 30, 1918; s. R.S. and Marguerite (Meyer) T.; Chem.E., U. Cin., 1942, M.D., 1950. Intern, U. Chgo. Clinics, 1950-51; resident U. Calif. Med. Center-San Francisco, 1951-54; practice medicine, specializing in ophthalmology, San Francisco, 1954-76, Fairbanks, Alaska, 1976-79, Phoenix, 1979—; mem. staff John C. Lincoln Hosp., Humana Hosp., Boswell Meml. Hosp.; clin. prof. ophthalmology U. Calif.-San Francisco, 1974-76. Served to maj. AUS, 1942-45. Diplomate Am. Bd. Ophthalmology. Fellow ACS, Am. Acad. Ophthalmology; mem. Phoenix Ophthal. Soc., Contact Lens Assn. Ophthalmologists, Pacific Coast Oto-Ophthal. Soc., Pan-Am. Assn. Ophthalmology, AMA, Ariz. Med. Assn., Maricopa County Med. Soc., Assn. Research in Vision and Ophthalmology, F.C. Cordes Eye Soc., Sigma Xi, Nu Sigma Nu, Alpha Tau Omega, Tau Beta Pi, Alpha Omega Alpha, Phi Lambda Upsilon, Omicron Delta Kappa, Kappa Kappa Psi. Clubs: Masons, K.T., Lions. Shriners. Home: 1016 E Lois Ln Phoenix AZ 85020 Office: 13000 N 103d Ave Sun City AZ 85351

TOURTELLOTTE, WALLACE WILLIAM, neurologist; b. Great Falls, Mont., Sept. 13, 1924; s. Nathaniel Mills and Frances Victoria (Charlton) T.; m. Jean Esther Toncray, Feb. 14, 1953; children—Wallace William, George Mills, James Millard, Warren Gerard. Ph.B., B.S., U. Chgo., 1945, Ph.D., 1948, M.D., 1951. Intern, Strong Meml. Hosp., U. Rochester (N.Y.) Sch. Medicine and Dentistry, 1951-52; resident in neurology U. Mich. Med. Center, Ann Arbor, 1954-57, asst. prof. neurology, 1957-59, asso. prof., 1959-66, prof., 1966-71; prof., vice chmn. dept. neurology UCLA, 1971—; chief neurology service VA Wadsworth Med. Center, Los Angeles, 1971—; vis. asso. prof. Washington U., St. Louis, 1963-64; mem. med. adv. bd. Nat. Multiple Sclerosis Soc., 1968—, So. Calif. Multiple Sclerosis Socs., 1972—; dir. Human Specimen Bank of Am., 1976—; cons. dept. consumer affairs Bd. of Med. Assurance, 1980—. Served to lt. USN, 1952-54. Fellow Am. Acad. Neurology; mem. Am. Neurol. Assn. (counsellor 1982—), World Fedn. Neurology (founding mem.), Am. Assn. Neuropathologists, Internat. Soc. Neurochemistry (founding mem.), World Assn. Neurol. Commns., Am. Soc. Pharmacology and Exptl. Therapeutics, Am. Therapeutic Soc., Am. Soc. Neurochemistry (founding mem.); Fedn. Western Socs. of Neurol. Sci. Assn. Am. Med. Colls., AAAS, AAUP, Soc. Neurosci., Assn. Univ. Profs. of Neurology, Western Assn. Physicians, Los Angeles Soc. Neurology and Psychiatry (pres. 1974, councilor 1976-78), Soc. Exptl. Biology and Medicine, Soc. Francaise de Neurologie, Sigma Xi. Republican. Presbyterian. Author textbook on multiple sclerosis and quantitation of neurol. function; editor Bull. Los Angeles Neurol. Socs., 1976, Revue Neurologica; Survey and Synthesis of Pathology Research; contbr. over 400 articles to med. jours. Home: 1140 Tellem Rd Pacific Palisades CA 90272 Office: VA Wadsworth Med Center Wilshire and Sawtelle Blvds Los Angeles CA 90073

TOWLERTON, ALAN LEE, civil engineer, public administrator; b. Miles City, Mont., Sept. 15, 1948; s. Albert John and Patricia Lois (Haggerty) T.; m. Judith Ann Daly, Sept. 12, 1970; children—Megan, Nathan. B.S. in Civil Engring., Mont. State U., 1971, M.S. in Civil Engring., 1972. Registered profl. engr., Oreg., Mont.; cert. plant operator water and wastewater, Mont. Project engr., project mgr. CH2M Hill, Portland and Corvallis, Oreg., 1972-77; project mgr. HKM Assocs., Billings, Mont., 1977-79; utilities engr., supt. systems ops. pub. utilities dept. City of Billings, 1979—. Chmn. parent adv. council Alkali Creek Sch., Billings, 1982-83; coach Little League Baseball, 1982-83. Mem. Water Pollution Control Fedn., Am. Pub. Works Assn., Am. Water Works Assn. (chmn. membership com. Mont. sect.), Chi Epsilon. Home: 275 Nubias Pl Billings MT 59105 Office: Pub Utilities Dept PO Box 30958 Billings MT 59111

TOWNE, DAVID LAWRENCE, management and planning consultant; b. Seattle, Dec. 1, 1931; s. Arthur Herbert and Myra Alene (Harbach) T.; m. Sally Jo Stevens, Aug. 25, 1955; children—Susan Alene, David Lawrence. B.A. in Bus. Adminstrn., U. Wash., 1956. Asst. dir. City of Renton (Wash.) Parks, 1956-59; recreation dir. State of Wash., Olympia, 1959-61; redevel. mgr. City of Seattle, 1962-67, supt. Seattle Parks and Recreation Dept., 1969-77; v.p. ECI Cons., Mercer Island, Wash., 1977-79; gen. mgr., prin. Jones & Jones, Seattle, 1979—; dir. ECI Seattle; speaker on parks, recreation, open space and its relationship to economy. Exec. bd. dirs. Seattle Museum History and Industry; trustee Seattle and King County Allied Arts Assn.; bd. dirs. Wash. Roadside Council; chmn. Wash. Park Found. Mem. Nat. Park and Recreation Assn. (trustee, sec.), Am. Planning Assn., Am. Mgmt. Assn., Seattle Hist. Soc., Seattle C. of C., Downtown Devel. Assn. Clubs: Kiwanis, Wash. Athletic, Olympic Manor. Contbr. articles to profl. jours. Office: 105 S Main St Seattle WA 98104

TOWNE, DONNA MARIE, retail executive; b. San Diego, July 29, 1944; d. Merle G. and Edith Marie (Folck) Smith; m. Earl James Towne, Nov. 26, 1969; 1 dau., Dena Marie. B.A. magna cum laude, Nat. U., 1980. Bus. mgr. Terry Allen Autos, Inc., El Cajon, Calif., 1976-83; v.p. Allen Leasing Inc., El Cajon, 1979-83; pres. Diversified Data Corp., Reno, 1983—; chief fin. officer Alta Sports Inc., San Gabriel, Calif., 1983—. Mem. Nat. Assn. Female Execs., Auto Dealers Bus. Mgrs. Assn., Nat. Notary Assn. Office: 9034 Huntington Dr San Gabriel CA 91775 also: 2205 Kietzke Ln Suite G Reno NV 89502

TOWNES, CHARLES HARD, physicist; b. Greenville, S.C., July 28, 1915; s. Henry Keith and Ellen Sumter (Hard) T.; B.A., B.S., Furman U., 1935, D.Litt. (hon.), 1960; M.A., Duke U., 1937; Ph.D., Calif. Inst. Tech., 1939; hon. degrees: Sc.D., Columbia U., 1963, NYU, 1967, Ph.D., Hebrew U., Jerusalem, 1966, D.Eng., Carnegie-Mellon U., 1969, also others; m. Frances H. Brown, May 4, 1941; children—Linda Lewis (Mrs. Rosenwein), Ellen Screven (Mrs. Anderson), Carla Keith (Mrs. Lumsden), Holly Robinson. Mem. tech. staff Bell Telephone Labs., 1939-47; asso. prof. physics Columbia U., 1948-50, prof. physics, 1950-61, exec. dir. Columbia Radiation Lab., 1950-52, chmn. physics dept., 1952-55; provost and prof. physics M.I.T., 1961-66, Inst. prof., 1966-67, v.p., dir. research Inst. Def. Analyses, Washington, 1959-61; Univ. prof. U. Calif. at Berkeley, 1967—; Guggenheim fellow, 1955-56; Fulbright lectr. U. Paris, 1955-56, U. Tokyo, 1956; dir. Enrico Fermi Internat. Sch. Physics, 1963, lectr., 1955, 60; Scott lectr. U. Cambridge, 1963; Centennial lectr. U. Toronto, 1967; Lincoln lectr., 1972-73; Halley lectr., 1976; Schiff Meml. lectr., 1982, Michelson Meml. lectr., 1982. dir. Perkin-Elmer Corp., Gen. Motors Corp.; mem. Pres.'s Sci. Adv. Com., 1966-70, vice chmn., 1967-69; chmn. sci. and tech. adv. com. manned space flight NASA, 1964-69; mem. Pres.'s Com. on Sci. and Tech., 1976. Trustee, Calif. Inst. Tech., Carnegie Instn., Washington, Pacific Sch. Religion; mem. corp. Woods Hole Oceanographic Instn. Recipient numerous hon. degrees and awards, including Nobel prize for physics, 1964; Comstock award Nat. Acad. Scis., 1959; Stuart Ballantine medal Franklin Inst., 1959, 62; Thomas Young medal and prize Inst. Physics and Phys. Soc. (Eng.), 1963, medal of Honor IEEE, 1967; Disting. service medal NASA, 1969; Wilhelm Exner award, Austria, 1970; Niels Bohr Internat. Gold medal, 1979, Nat. Medal Sci., 1982. Fellow Am. Phys. Soc. (council 1959-62, 65-71, pres. 1967; Plyler prize 1977), Optical Soc. Am. (hon.; C.E.K. medal 1968), IEEE; mem. Am. Assn. Physics Tchrs., Am. Philos. Soc., Am. Astron. Soc., Am. Acad. Arts and Scis., Nat. Acad. Scis., Royal Soc. (fgn.), Pontifical Acad. Author: (with A.L. Schawlow) Microwave Spectroscopy, 1955. Author, co-editor: Quantum Electronics, 1960; Quantum Electronics and Coherent Light, 1964. Editorial bd. Rev. Sci. Instrument, 1950-52, Phys. Rev., 1951-53, Jour. Molecular Spectroscopy, 1957-60, Proc. Nat. Acad. Scis., 1978—. Research and publs. on nuclear and molecular structure, quantum electronics, radio and infrared astrophysics. Patentee masers and (with Schawlow) lasers. Office: Dept Physics U Calif at Berkeley Berkeley CA

TOWNSEND, BETTINA SMITH, state official, artist; b. Fairbanks, Alaska, Aug. 11, 1949; d. Hugh Ignatious and Ethel Marie (Frolich) Smith; m. Homer Jay Townsend, Jr., Dec. 31, 1975. B.A. in History of Art, U. Calif.-Berkeley, 1971. With Calif. Dept. Parks and Recreation, 1973—, state park maintenance worker I, 1979—, women's program dir., 1980—; sexual harassment, equal employment counselor; free lance artist. Mem. Nature Conservancy So. Calif., Nat. Audubon Soc., Am. Waterworks Assn. Democrat. Home: 29653 Nuevo Rd Nuevo CA 92367 Office: Dept Parks and Recreation 32040 Riverside Dr Lake Elsinore CA 92330

TOWNSEND, CHARLES KIRKPATRICK, govt. ofcl.; b. Orrick, Mo., Nov. 7, 1936; s. Harold Bushnell and Helen (Kirkpatrick) T.; m. Caroline Dorst, Oct. 22, 1960; children—Karen Lynn, Allan Stuart. B.S.C.E., U. Mo., 1958. Ensign, U.S. Coast & Geodetic Survey, 1958, Ship Pioneer, San Francisco, 1959, chief La. low-water line survey party, Franklin, 1960, chief field party 603, Daytona Beach, Fla., 1962, chief satellite triangulation party, Aberdeen, Md., 1964, comdg. officer Ship Peirce, Jacksonville, Fla., 1966-69, chief mapping, charting and geodesy div., 1969-72, spl. asst. to assoc. adminstr. for marine resources, 1972-73, Dept. Commerce rep. OMB Fed. Mapping Task Force, 1972-73, exec. officer (name changed to NOAA) Ship Oceanographer, Seattle, 1973-74, comdg. officer Ship Rainier, 1974-76, dep. dir. Pacific Marine Ctr., Seattle, 1976, promoted to rear adm., 1980, dir., 1980—. Bd. dirs. Seafair, Seattle, 1981—. Recipient Karo award Soc. Am. Mil. Engrs., 1961; Silver medal Dept. Commerce, 1973; NOAA unit citation, 1977. Mem. Soc. Am. Mil. Engrs. Methodist. Clubs: Rainier, Seattle Yacht. Office: 1801 Fairview Ave E Seattle WA 98102

TOWNSEND, JOHN MILTON, educator; b. Nimrod, Tex., Aug. 31, 1921; s. Walter Lee and Eulah Violia (Gardner) T.; B.S. in Agr., N.Mex. State U., 1948; M.S. in Edn. and Adminstrn., Eastern N.Mex. U., 1971; m. Myrtice L. King, May 21, 1950; children—Tommy Lee, James Albert, Carol Eyvonne. Tchr. vocat. agr. Dora (N.Mex.) High Sch., 1948-53; owner, operator dairy farm, Clovis, N.Mex., 1953-62, Floyd, N.Mex., 1953-68; tchr. biology, chemistry, earth sci. and gen. sci., public schs., Melrose, N.Mex., 1968-71; dir., tchr. farm bus. mgmt., public schs., Portales, N.Mex., 1971—. Pres. Floyd PTA, 1964-65; deacon First Baptist Ch., Portales, 1975. Served with A.C., U.S. Navy, 1943-46. Named Tchr. of Yr., Melrose Tchrs. Assn., 1968; NSF fellow, 1968-69. Mem. N.Mex. Vocat. Agr. Assn., N.Mex. Vocat. Assn., Nat. Vocat. Assn. Democrat. Club: Lions (sec. club 1973-81) (Portales). Author Farm Mgmt. Analysis, ann. report and analysis history, 1971-81. Home: 1400 S Ave A Portales NM 88130 Office: PO Box 779 Portales NM 88130

TOWNSEND, JOHN STANLEY, research and devel. engr.; b. Fort Worth, July 13, 1952; s. John Joseph and Gertrude Maria (Ostaszewski) T.; m. Jeannette Carol Harbin, Aug. 23, 1974; children—Kelly Jo, Kerry Jeannette. Student USAF Acad., 1970-72; B.Civil Engring., Auburn U., 1974; postgrad. Ala. U., Birmingham, 1975; M.S., Auburn U., 1977; postgrad. Wash. State U., 1980—; Asst. engr. So. Services, Inc., Birmingham, 1974-75; research and devel. engr. Bethea/Nat. Co., Birmingham, 1977-80, supr. mech. testing lab. and metall. lab., 1977-80, cons., 1980—; research asst. Wash. State U., 1980-81. Ala. Power Co. grantee, 1976, Kaiser Aluminum Co. grantee, 1980—. Registered profl. engr., Ala. Mem. ASCE, IEEE, Ala. Soc. Profl. Engrs., Chi Epsilon. Republican. Baptist. Home: Apt 56-C N Fairway Pullman WA 99163 Office: Dept Mech Engring Wash State U Pullman WA 99164

TOWNSEND, JOSEPH J., safety professional; b. Loma Linda, Calif., July 21, 1941; s. Willard B. and Sara Bell (Denton) T.; m. Doris Marie Schack, Nov. 25, 1967; children—Cheryl Marie, Linda Elaine. A.A., Riverside City Coll., 1962; B.A. in Econs., San Jose State U., 1966; Asso. Mgmt., Ins. Inst. Am., 1977. Cert. safety profl., assoc. risk mgmt. Ins. Inst. Am., 1983. Loss control engr. Safeco Ins. Co., Seattle, 1970-73, loss control mgr., 1973-76, loss control tng. supr., 1976-78, loss control asst. mgr., 1978—. Served as lt., USN, 1967-70. Mem. Am. Soc. Safety Engrs. Republican. Office: Safeco Plaza (T-20) Seattle WA 98185

TOWNSEND, MARTIN ALSTYNE, soil scientist; b. Lebanon, N.H., Sept. 25, 1929; s. Hugh and Marie (Kuhre) T.; B.S., U. N.H., 1951, postgrad. in Agronomy, 1953-55; grad. Soil Sci. Inst., Iowa State U., 1981; children—Ellen M., Brenda J., Cheryl M. Grad. research asst. U. N.H., 1953-55; research technician in soils and agrl. chemistry Nev. Agrl. Expt. Sta., Reno, 1955-56; soil scientist, soil survey party leader Soil Conservation Service, Dept. Agr., Fallon, Nev., 1956-68, tech. support specialist State Office, Reno, 1968-69; asst. soil scientist U. Nev. Reconnaisance Soil Survey, Reno, 1969-70; dist. soil scientist Bur. Land Mgmt., Dept. Interior, Coos Bay, Oreg., 1970-76, state soil scientist, Sacramento, 1977—; sec. Calif. Soil Survey Com., 1979, vice chmn., 1980, chmn., 1981; instr. S.W. Oreg. Community Coll., 1976. Mgr. Fallon Mchts. State Semi-Pro Baseball Champions, 1959-67; state commr. for Nev., Nat. Baseball Congress, 1963-68. Served with USAF, 1951-53. Recipient Spl. Achievement award Bur. Land Mgmt. Landslide Study, Coos Bay, 1976. Mem. Soil Sci. Soc. Am., Internat. Soil Sci. Soc., Soil Conservation Soc. Am., Profl. Soil Scientists' Assn. Calif., Am. Registry Cert. Profls. in Agronomy, Crops, and Soils, Oreg. Soc. Soil Scientists, Calif. Forest Soils Council, Friends of the Pleistocene, Am. Legion (past comdr. post 16). Republican. Methodist. Author books, the most recent being: (with Pomerening and Thomas) Soil Inventory of the Coos Bay District, Oregon, 1977. Home: 2543 Fulton Ave Apt 109 Sacramento CA 95821 Office: 2800 Cottage Way Sacramento CA 95825

TOWNSEND, PETER LEE, lawyer; b. Glendale, Calif., July 21, 1926; s. Craig and Georgia (Barhyte) T.; m. Irma Mathilde Greisberger, Aug. 12, 1947; children—Ingrid P., Russell T., Dorothy Poole. J.D. summa cum laude, McGeorge Coll. Law, 1958. Bar: Calif. 1959, U.S. Supreme Ct. 1982. Dep. dist. atty., Stockton, Calif., 1959-60; litigation counsel Western Title Ins. Co. of San Francisco, 1960-68; ptnr. firm Garrison, Townsend & Orser, San Francisco, 1969—. Served to capt., inf., U.S. Army, 1944-54. Republican. Clubs: San Francisco Lawyers, San Rafael Yacht.

TOWSON, JOHN FREDERICK, manufacturing company executive, consultant; b. Monessen, Pa., Jan. 31, 1929; s. William Joseph and Ella Pearl (Cosby) T.; m. Edith Bronwyn Jones, 1952; children—Bronwyn, John; m. Sharon Lockhart, 1976; 1 stepson, Jeffery. Student U. Md., 1949-51. Reconnaissance and intelligence specialist U.S. Air Force, Dayton, Ohio, 1954-58; mgr. Autometric Corp. subs. Paramount Pictures, N.Y.C., 1958-63; v.p. Conductron Corp., Ann Arbor, Mich., 1963-67; corp. v.p. KMS Industries, Inc., Ann Arbor, 1967-70, pres. photo sci. div., 1968-70, v.p. Tech. Ctr., Irvine, Calif., 1970-74; ind. contractor real estate sales and investments, Newport Beach, Calif., 1974-83; chmn. bd., chief exec. officer Vard Newport Corp., Santa Ana, Calif., 1983—; dir. Daedalus Enterprises, Inc., Ann Arbor; cons. to high tech. industries, U.S. govt. Served with USAF, 1948-54. Mem. Assn. Corp. Growth, N.Am. Soc. Corp. Planning. Republican. Home: 43 Harbor Ridge Dr Newport Beach CA 92660 Office: Vard Newport Corp 3324 W Warner Ave Santa Ana CA 92704

TOYOMURA, DENNIS TAKESHI, architect; b. Honolulu, July 6, 1926; s. Sansuke and Take (Sata) T.; B.S., Chgo. Tech. Coll., 1949; postgrad. U. Ill. Extension, 1950, 53, 54, Ill. Inst. Tech., 1954-55, U. Hawaii/Dept. Defense, 1966-67, 73; m. Charlotte Akiko Nakamura, May 27, 1949; children—Wayne J., Gerald, Amy, Lyle. Designer draftsman James M. Turner, Hammond, Ind., 1950-51, Wimberly & Cook, Honolulu, 1952, Gregg & Briggs, Chgo., 1952-54; architect Holabird, Root and Burgee, Chgo., 1954-55, Loebl, Schlossman and Bennett, Chgo., 1955-62; individual archtl. practice, 1962—; sec., dir. Maiko of Hawaii, 1972; dir. Pacific Canal of Hawaii, Inc., 1972—; mem. Bd. Registration Profl. Engrs., Architects, Land Surveyors and Landscape Architects, State of Hawaii, 1974-82, Nat. Council Archtl. Registration Bds., 1974-82, Nat. Council Engring. Examiners, 1974-82; Western regional del. Nat. Council Archtl. Registration Bds., 1975-81, nat. del., 1976, 77, 78, 79, 80, 81 cons. Honolulu Redevel. Agy., 1967-71; fallout shelter analyst Dept. Def.; adv. com. drafting tech. Leeward Community Coll., U. Hawaii, 1965—. Del. commr. State Assembly, Synod of Ill. Presbyn. Ch. U.S.A., 1958, to Los Angeles Presbytery, 1965; bd. dirs. Lyon Arboretum Assn., U. Hawaii, 1975-77, treas., 1976; 1973, mem. Hawaii State Found. on Culture and Arts, 1982—, chmn. media arts, co-chmn. visual arts, 1982, co-chmn. budget com. Recipient Outstanding Citizen Recognition award Cons. Engrs. Council Hawaii, 1975; cert. of appreciation Gov. of Hawaii, 1982, commendation, 1983. Registered profl. architect, Ill., Hawaii; real estate broker, Ill. Served with AUS, 1945-46. Fellow AIA (dir. Hawaii 1973-74, treas. 1975, mem. fin. mgmt. adv. com. 1976-77, office mgmt. com. 1977, practice mgmt. com. 1978, Pres.'s Mahalo award Hawaii chpt. 1981); mem. Am. Concrete Inst., Acad. Polit. Sci. (life), Chgo. Natural History Mus. (life), Chgo. Art Inst. (life), Am. Acad. Polit. and Social Scis. (life), AAAS (life), Ill. Assn. Professions, Bldg. Research Inst. (bldg. research adv. bd. of Nat. Acad. Sci.), Honolulu Acad. Arts (life), Constrn. Specifications Inst., ASTM, Honolulu C. of C., Council Ednl. Facility Planners Internat. (bd. govs. N.W. region 1980, 81, 82, 83), Constrn. Industry Legis. Orgn. (dir. 1973-81, 83-84, treas. 1976-77), Alpha Lambda Rho, Kappa Sigma Kappa. Presbyn. (elder 1956, trustee 1958-62, bd. of session 1956-62, 64-72, 74-79, sec. 1965). Clubs: Malolo Mariners; Purser (treas. 1964); Skipper (pres. 1965). Home: 2602 Manoa Rd Honolulu HI 96822 Office: 1370 Kapiolani Blvd Honolulu HI 96814

TRAAEN-WHEELIS, TERESA JEAN, counselor; b. Greenbay, Wis., Aug. 31, 1956; s. Donald and Lucille Theresa T.-W.; m. Ben G. Wheelis, Aug. 12, 1977. B.A., U. Ariz., 1978; M.A. with honors, Wheaton Coll., 1980; postgrad. Ariz. State U. Family housing asst. U. Ariz., Tucson, 1977-78; banking services rep. Bank of Lisle (Ill.), 1979-80; counseling intern Scottsdale (Ariz.) Community Coll., 1980; acad. counselor Upward Bound Program, Central Ariz. Coll., Coolidge, 1980—. Mem. Am. Personnel and Guidance Assn. (polit. edn. program trainer), Ariz. Counselors Assn. (treas., membership chairperson), Am. Assn. for Women in Community and Jr. Colls., Women in Higher Edn. in Ariz. Republican. Lutheran. Home: 1770 Harvard Ave Casa Grande AZ 85222 Office: Central Ariz Coll Woodruff at Overfield Rd Coolidge AZ 85228

TRACHTENBERG, JOHN LEWIS, printing company executive; b. Portland, Oreg., Nov. 10, 1940; s. Isaac N. and Gladys (Goodman) T.; student Clark Coll., 1964-65, Portland Community Coll., 1975, 80-82, U. Portland, 1978, 79, 81, 83; m. Susan Elizabeth Smith, Nov. 26, 1978; 1 son, Timothy N. Prodn. mgr. Graphic Arts Center, Portland, Seattle, 1965-69; prodn. mgr. Taylor & Assos., Advt., Portland, 1969-71; dir. estimating/planning The Recorder Printing & Pub. Co., San Francisco, 1971-72; directory and comml. prodn. mgr. Norwest Pub. Co., Portland, 1972-74, dir. estimating, 1974-77; exec. v.p., gen. mgr. Rono Graphic Communications Co., Portland, 1977—; v.p. Hicks-Chatten Engraving Co., Portland, 1977—; adv. bd. graphic communications dept. Portland Community Coll., 1978—. Mem. Portland Graphic Arts Trade Apprenticeship Com., 1979—; trustee Graphic Arts Health and Welfare Fund Oreg., 1983. Served with USAF, 1958-62. Mem. Oreg. Printing Industries, Printing Industries of Pacific (dir., officer 1979-84, pres. 1981-83), Western States Photoplatemakers Assn. (dir. 1982—), Printing Industries Am. (dir. dept. market inf. and research 1983), Internat. Assn. Photoplatemakers (membership com. 1981—). Am. Fedn. Communications Group (dir. 1979—), Am. Mgmt. Assn. Clubs: Craftsmen's Litho, Tualatin Country, Temple Beth Israel Brotherhood, Portland Lithographers and Printing House Craftsmen, University. Office: 535 NW 16 Ave Portland OR 97209

TRACY, HARVEY A., hospital executive; b. Plymouth, Mass., May 27, 1915; s. Oscar H. and Johnena W. (MacAuley) T.; m. Jane K. Kinsman, June 10, 1950 (dec.); children—Barbara, Janet, Mark, Deborah, John; m. 2d, Irene F. Duckett, Jan. 6, 1979. R.N., McLean Hosp., Waverly, Mass., 1938; grad. Lowell Inst., Cambridge, 1946, Mass Gen X-Ray Sch., 1949; cert. R.N., Mass., 1958, Am. Registered Radiologic Technologists, 1950. Head nurse McLean Hosp., Waverly, Mass., 1947-48, staff technologist, 1949-50; sr. technologists dept. radiology, Swedish Hosp. Med Center, Seattle, 1951-58, chief technologist, 1958-70, tech. dir. dept., 1970—; radiology cons., adv. bd. radiology tech. program Bellevue City Coll. Mem. Am. Soc. Radiology Technicians,

Am. Hosp. Radiology Assn., Wash. Soc. Radiology Technicians. Club: Elks. Home: 15550 Palatine Seattle WA 98133 Office: 747 Summit Seattle WA 98104

TRAENKNER, ALAN RAY, industrial engineer, safety engineer; b. Massena, N.Y., Feb. 23, 1946; s. Fred and Helena (Glink) T.; m. Janet Stayton, July 6, 1968; children—Stacey Lynn, Wendy Rae. B.S. in Indsl. Mgmt., Purdue U., 1969; M.S. in Indsl. Engring., U. Iowa, Iowa City, 1972. Cert. safety profl., 1980. Indsl. engr. Fairfield Gear Mfg. Co., LaFayette, Ind., 1966-68, U.S. Army Rock Island Arsenal, Ill., 1969-73; supr. indsl. engr. Hawthorne Naval Dept., Nev., 1973-76; prin. safety engr. Nev. Dept. Occupational Safety and Health, Carson City, 1976-80, dir., 1980-83; asst. regional adminstr. OSHA, U.S. Dept. Labor, 1983—. Mem. Occupational Safety and Health State Plan Assn. (vice chmn. 1982-83), Am. Soc. Safety Engrs. Lutheran. Home: 26 Corte Aires Moraga CA 94556 Office: 450 Golden Gate Ave San Francisco CA

TRAFTON, RONALD MILTON, corporate executive; b. Los Angeles, Jan. 1, 1920; s. Roland Brunswick and Lola Montana (Mills) T.; B.Sc. in Law, U. Wash., 1947, J.D., 1949; m. Rose Marie Ray, Apr. 25, 1942; children—Roger Milton, Stephen John, David Roland, Byron Gardner, Dwight Elliott. Admitted to Wash. bar, 1950; pvt. practice accounting, 1946-49; sr. tax accountant Arthur Andersen & Co., Seattle, 1950-51; controller, counsel Jam Handy Orgn., Detroit, 1951-52; with SAFECO Corp., Seattle, 1952—, pres., dir., 1970-81, chmn., chief exec. officer, 1981—; dir. affiliated cos. Trustee, CAPRI Found., 1972—. Served with Q.M.C., U.S. Army, 1942-46. C.P.A., Wash. Mem. Wash. Bar Assn. Office: SAFECO Corp SAFECO Plaza Seattle WA 98185*

TRAN, DIEN THANH, editor; b. Vietnam, Nov. 18, 1938; came to U.S., 1975; s. Seng and Loanh Thi (Lam) T.; m. Thuan Thu, Sept. 16, 1961; children—Trang, Thanh, Giang, Long. Equivalent B.S. degree in Mil. Sci., Nha Trang Naval Acad., 1962; equivalent M.S. degree of Mil. Sci., Armed Forces Coll., Vietnam, 1974. Commd. officer Vietnamese Navy, 1967, advanced through grades to capt., 1975; chief of security Republic of Vietnam Presidency, 1970-75; systems operator Rinconada (Calif.) Water Plant, Los Gatos-Santa Clara County, 1980—; editor, pub. Martial Arts and Sports mag., San Jose, Calif., 1982—. Pres. Vietnamese Martial Arts Fedn., 1973—. Decorated 5d Nat. Order (Vietnam). Roman Catholic. Home: 705 Orkney Ave Santa Clara CA 95050 Office: Martial Arts and Sports Mag 198 W Julian St San Jose CA 95113

TRANKLE, NANCY KAVAL, computer co. exec.; b. Chgo., Mar. 29, 1938; d. Stanley and Gladys (Kordik) Kaval; student Northwestern U., 1972, Roosevelt U., 1972; B.S., U. San Francisco, 1980; 1 dau., Pamela J. Office positions, Chgo., 1955-62; mem. sales staff Am. Family Assn., Chgo., 1959-65; v.p., 1965-77; editor, exec. dir. Ill. Cemetery Assn., Chgo., 1973-77; mgr. spl. communications Tandem Computers Co., Cupertino, Calif., 1977—. Chmn. communications Family Services, LWV, Wilmette, Ill., 1975-77; mem. adv. bd. Big Bros. and Big Sisters, 1981-83. Mem. Santa Clara County Social Services Vols., Profl. Connections for Women (founder, chmn.), Nat. Assn. Female Execs. (network dir.), San Jose C. of C. (bd. dirs. 82—), Women in Bus., Am. Soc. Tng. and Devel., Meeting Planners Internat. (v.p. membership No. Calif. chpt. 1981-82), Am. Soc. Assn. Execs., Tandem Users Group (sec./treas., conf. dir. 1977-83). Unitarian. Office: 19333 Vallco Pky Cupertino CA 95014

TRANSPOTA, ROBERT PAUL, artist, teacher; b. Spokane, Wash., Nov. 15, 1923; s. Gerald Garrique and Eleanor Fredrika (Schultz) T.; m. Mary Anne Taylor, June 10, 1946; children—Mary Antia, Allen Paul, Christopher. Student Los Angeles City Coll, 1942-43, Monmouth Coll., 1943-44, Chgo. Acad. Fine Arts, 1949-50. Tech. and fine arts artist, Los Angeles, 1950-60; tchr., cons. in field; one man shows Freeman Galleries, Beverly Hills, Calif., 1965, Palace Art Gallery, Prescott, Ariz., 1971, House of Bronze, Prescott, 1973; exhibited in group shows Am. Savs. & Loan Assn., Beverly Hills, 1967, Files Gallery of Fine Arts, Big Bear City, Calif., 1980; San Bernardino County (Calif.) Mus., 1982; represented in permanent collection George Phippen Meml. Invitation Western Art Show, Prescott, Nat. Cowboy Hall of Fame, Oklahoma City; paintings include oil portrait of John Mullens, Cowboy, 1976. Bd. dirs. George Phippen Meml. Art Found., 1976. Served with USN, 1944-46, PTO. Recipient gold medals George Phippen Meml. Invitational Western Art Show, 1976, 77, Files Gallery of Fine Arts, 1980; merit cert. award for oils Am. Painters in Paris Exhbn., 1975. Mem. Portrait Club N.Y., Fine Arts Guild, Big Bear Art Assn. Office: PO Box 1716 Big Bear City CA 92314

TRAPANI, RALPH JAMES, highway engineer, consultant; b. Buffalo, May 21, 1952; s. Ralph James and Estelle (Silvaroli) T.; m. Barbara Hicks. B.S. in Archtl. Engring., U. Colo., 1974. Hwy. engr. field constrn. and claims mgmt. Colo. Dept. Hwys., 1975-80; project mgr. Glenwood Canyon I-70, Glenwood Springs, Colo., 1980—; cons. Hicks & Assoc. Pres. Glenwood Springs Soccer Assn., Inc. Mem. ASCE, Nat. Soc. Profl. Engrs. Contbr. article to profl. jour. Home: 1194 137th Rd Glenwood Springs CO 81601 Office: PO Box 1430 Glenwood Springs CO 81601

TRASK, OZELL MILLER, judge; b. Wakita, Okla., July 4, 1909; s. Ozell and Nina (Miller) T.; m. Barbara Draper, June 27, 1939; children—Deborah, Melinda. A.B. magna cum laude, Washburn Coll., 1931; LL.B., Harvard U., 1934. Bar: Ariz. 1935. Sole practice law, Phoenix, 1936-69; sr. judge U.S. Ct. Appeals, 9th cir., Phoenix, 1969—. Office: 7469 Federal Bldg Phoenix AZ 85025

TRASK, PHILIP ALAN, pediatric dentist; b. Los Angeles, Apr. 15, 1942; s. Morris and Jen (Joseph) T.; A.A., Los Angeles City Coll., 1963; student U. Calif. at Los Angeles, 1963-64; B.S., U. Calif. at San Francisco, 1967, D.D.S., 1968; M.S., U. So. Calif., 1970; m. Rosario Juanita Valadez, Aug. 29, 1974; children—Benjamin Michael, Sarah Ann, Laura Esther. Sr. dental resident Children's Hosp. Los Angeles, 1969-70, dir. dental resident hosp. tng. program, 1970; asst. clin. prof. advanced pedodontics U. So. Calif., 1972-74; asst. clin. prof. pediatrics U. Calif. at Los Angeles Schs. Dentistry and Medicine, 1970-79; pvt. practice pediatric dentistry, Santa Monica, Calif., 1970—; mem. profl. staff Los Angeles Children's Hosp., St. John's Hosp., Santa Monica, Calif.; lectr. dental sci. and pedodontics, Europe, Mex., Japan. Recipient numerous awards including Outstanding Clin. Faculty U. Calif. Los Angeles Dental Sch., 1973, Advancement of Dental Profession award U. So. Calif., 1972-73. Diplomate Am. Bd. Pedodontics. Mem. Am. Dental Assn., Assn. Pedodontic Diplomates, Am. Soc. Dentistry for Children, Calif. Soc. Pediatric Dentists. Contbr. articles to profl. jours. Home: 506 Adelaide Dr Santa Monica CA 90402 Office: 1243 7th St Suite C Santa Monica CA 90401

TRAUTMAN, GERALD HOUGH, transportation executive, lawyer; b. Petoskey, Mich., Aug. 27, 1912; s. Newton Ellsworth and Madeline (Hough) T.; B.A., Stanford, 1934; LL.B., Harvard, 1937. Admitted to Calif. bar, 1937, since practiced in San Francisco; partner firm McCutchen, Doyle, Brown, Trautman & Enersen, 1937-65; pres., chief exec. officer Greyhound Corp., 1966-70, chmn. exec. com., 1968—, chmn. bd., chief exec. officer, 1970-81, pres., 1977-79, chmn. bd., 1981-82, hon. chmn. bd. and chmn. exec. com., 1982—, also dir.; dir. Greyhound de Mexico, S.A. de C.V., Armour & Co., Armour-Dial, Inc., Greyhound Leasing & Financial Corp., Greyhound Financial & Leasing Corp., A G, Greyhound Computer Corp., Pinetop Ins. Co., Greyhound Food Mgmt., Inc., Greyhound Lines, Inc., Greyhound Lines Can. Ltd., Verex Corp., Lehman Corp. Bd. dirs. Salk Inst. Served to lt. USNR, 1944-46. Mem. Am. Bar Assn., U.S. C. of C. (dir.), Grocery Mfrs. Am. (dir.), Delta Kappa Epsilon. clubs: Golf (Camelback, Phoenix); Links (N.Y.C.); Ariz., Plaza (Phoenix). Office: Greyhound Corp Greyhound Tower Phoenix AZ 85077*

TRAVELSTEAD, TERRILL TIFFANY, personnel adminstr.; b. Cedar Rapids, Iowa, Nov. 5, 1940; d. Carl Allison and Theresa Louise (Budelier) Tiffany; B.S. in Bus., Skidmore Coll., 1962; m. Gooch Ware Travelstead, Sept. 9, 1961; m. 2d, Joseph Michael Murray, Nov. 24, 1977; children—Gregory, Timothy, Jason. Mem. staff Rapid City (S.D.) Regional Hosp., 1971-79, personnel dir., 1975-79; human resources dir. Idaho Statesman, 1980-81, staff services dir., 1982—; cons. in field. Clk. of vestry Emmanuel Episcopal Ch., Rapid City, 1975-78; mem. Boise Mayor's Com. to Hire the Handicapped and Older Worker; mem. adv. bd. Center for Employment Tng. Mem. Am. Soc. Hosp. Personnel Adminstrs., S.D. Hosp. Personnel Adminstrs. Assn. (pres. 1979), Rapid City Personnel Adminstrs. Assn. (pres. 1976). Republican.

TRAVERS, ARTHUR HOPKINS, JR., educator, lawyer; b. Gary, Ind., July 29, 1936; s. Arthur Hopkins and Nellie Mae (Martin) T.; m. Judith Ann Brean, Aug. 24, 1963 (div.); children—Constance Lynn, Anne Kimberly. B.A., Grinnell Coll., 1957; LL.B. magna cum laude, Harvard U., 1962. Bar: Ill. 1962, Colo. 1976. Asso. atty. Mayer, Brown & Platt, Chgo., 1962-65; asst. prof. U. Kans., Lawrence, 1965-68, assoc. prof., 1968-69, prof., 1969-71; prof. law, U. Colo., 1971—, acting dean, 1973-74, assoc. dean, 1974-75; cons. antitrust law and econs. Mem. ABA, Colo. Bar Assn., Am. Econ. Assn., Selden Soc. Democrat. Contbr. articles in field to profl. jours.

TRAVIS, CRAIG MARTIN, political consultant; b. San Jose, Calif., Aug. 17, 1953; s. Carl Rolland and Margaret Louise (Morehead) T.; m. Debra Jean Rubalcaba, July 17, 1976; children—Sara Nicole, Kristin, Louise Noelani. B.A. in Pub. Relations, San Jose State U., 1978. Polit. cons. Republican. Party Hawaii, Honolulu, 1978, exec. dir., 1981—, precinct pres., 1979-81, dist. chmn., 1979-81, del. state conv., 1979-83, del. county conv., 1979-83; mem. state central com., 1979—, mem. Honolulu County com., 1979-81, mem. state exec. com., 1981—, 4th vice chmn. state central com., 1981; account asst. Fawcett McDermott Cavanagh Advt. and Pub. Relations, Honolulu, 1979; account exec. Stryker-Weiner Assocs., pub. relations, Honolulu, 1979-80; adminstrv. asst. to minority floor leader Hawaii Ho. of Reps., 1980-81. Mem. Pub. Relations Soc. Am. Club: Hawaii Econ. Study. Home: 1011 Prospect St Apt 904 Honolulu HI 96822 Office: 1136 Union Mall Suite 203 Honolulu HI 96813

TRAVIS, ROBIN, computer conversion specialist, author: b. Bklyn., Dec. 20, 1949; d. Elias and Fay T.; m. Jeffrey Sanchez Hinkle, Dec. 9, 1972. B.A., Hunter Coll., 1971; M.A., CUNY, 1974. Chief exec. officer TLC Computer Services, 1976—. Mem. Nat. Assn. for Exec. Females, Ind. Assn. Computer Cons. Author novels: China Train, 1979; Entering the Middle Kingdom, 1981; (play) Red Flannel Murders, 1980. Office: TLC Computer Services 2424 Wilshire Blvd Los Angeles CA 90057

TRAVIS, STUART PETER, sales executive; b. St. Paul, Minn., July 3, 1943; s. James S. and Margaret (Laufenberg) T.; m. Stephanie G. Taver, June 18, 1966; children—James, Pamela, Michael. B.S., Coll. St. Thomas, 1965. With sales mgmt. staff packaged soap and detergent div. Procter & Gamble, Ga. and Fla., 1969-75; sales mgr. Transales Corp., Savannah, Ga., 1975-78; sales, mktg., phys. distbn. cons. to food product mfrs., Southeastern states; nat. sales mgr. Kern Foods, Inc., City of Industry, Calif., 1978—. Mem. task force Calif. Secondary Sch. Home Econ. Curriculum Devel. Program. Served to lt. Supply Corps, AUS, 1965-68. Mem. Am. Mgmt. Assn., Mktg. and Sales Execs. Club Los Angeles, Food Industry Sales Mgrs. Club Los Angeles, Western Assn. Food Chains (assoc.), Food Mktg. Inst. (assoc.), Calif. Grocers Assn. (assoc.). Republican. Roman Catholic.

TRAYLOR, CLAIRE GUTHRIE, state senator, teacher; b. Kansas City, Mo., Jan. 18, 1931; d. Frank and Janet Guthrie; m. Frank A. Traylor, 1954; children—Nancy, Frank, Susan, David. B.S., Northwestern U., 1952; M.A., Washington U., St. Louis, 1955. Primary sch. tchr., 1955-57; communications adminstr. Jefferson County (Mo.) Schs., 1978; mem. Colo. Ho. of Reps., 1978, majority caucus chmn., 1980-82; mem. Colo. State Senate, 1982—, chmn. senate services, vice chmn. fin., bus. affairs and labor, health environ., welfare and instns. coms. Active League Denver, mem. exec. com.; founding bd. dirs. Assn. Mus. Naturla History; active Arvada Ctr. Performing Arts; bd. dirs. Highland W. and Highland S. (sr. housing); mem. Jeffco GOP Women's Club, Clear Creek Med. Aux., Colo. Med. Aux., Valley Med. Aux.; chmn. Citizens for Better Wheat Ridge; area chmn. Cancer Soc.; vol. resource Jeffco Schs. Mem. Kappa Kappa Gamma. Presbyterian. Office: State Capitol Denver CO 80203*

TRAYLOR, JANET LOUISE, advertising and design firm executive; b. McCook, Nebr., Dec. 9, 1951; d. Thomas Leon and Marilyn Jean (Wagner) T. Student U. So. Colo., 1970-71; B.F.A. magna cum laude, Colo. State U., 1974; postgrad. Art and Archtl. History, Ariz. State U., 1974-75. Cert. Am. Inst. Graphic Arts. Advt. coordinator, retail advt. dept. Ft. Collins (Colo.) Coloradoan Newspaper, 1973-74; designer, dept. printing and publs. Colo. State U., Ft. Collins, 1974; designer Hales Design Group, Phoenix, 1975-76; art dir., prodn. mgr. Clark Pub. Group, Phoenix, 1976-78; product mgr., mktg. dept. Farnam Cos., Inc., Phoenix, 1978-79; sr. art dir. Bozell & Jacobs, Inc., Phoenix, 1979-80; owner, head Janet Traylor Advt. and Design, Phoenix, 1980—; grad. teaching asst. art dept. Ariz. State U., 1974-75. Bd. mgmt. Downtown YMCA, Phoenix. Performing arts scholar Colo. State U., 1971-74; recipient Commendation award Ariz. Soc. AIA, 1978; Gold and Silver awards Phoenix Art Dirs. Club Exhbn., 1981, Silver and Merit awards, 1982. Mem. Am. Inst. Graphic Arts, Communicating Arts Group Ariz. (Silver and Merit awards 1982), Women in Design Internat. (bd. dirs. 1980—), Women in Design/Phoenix (founder 1981, co-pres. 1981-83), NOW. Democrat. Clubs: First Thursday Book, Southwest Women's Investment Group. Exhibitor work Scottsdale (Ariz.) Ctr. for the Arts, Women in Design Show, 1981. Office: 329 W Vernon Ave Phoenix AZ 85000

TRAYLOR, NATALIE SMITH, pub. co. mgr., real estate asso., cons., news corr., assn. exec.; b. St. Paul, Feb. 15, 1938; d. Howard Ripley and Maxine L. (Johnson) Smith; B.S. in Polit. Sci. with spl. honors, Jacksonville State U., 1975; children—Drew Michael Jorgensen, Dacia Lyn Jorgensen, Dana Ann Jorgensen. News corr. Birmingham (Ala.) Post Herald, 1970-72; pub. relations dir. Anniston (Ala.) Acad., 1970-76; feature newspaper writer Anniston Star, 1970-75; news corr. Birmingham News, 1972-76; dir. Jefferson Shelby div. Ala. affiliate Am. Heart Assn., Birmingham, 1976-77; real estate agt., 1977-82; div. sales Blake Pub. Co., 1982—; pres. Traylor Mgmt. Inc., 1982—; mem. editorial bd. Grace Notes, Grace Ch., Anniston, 1974-76. Vice pres., program chmn. Weatherly Heights Elementary Sch. PTA, Huntsville, Ala., 1966-68; chmn. Panhellenic Assn. Scholarship Com., Huntsville, 1968-69; pres. Holy Apostles Episcopal Churchwomen, New Orleans, 1963-65, del. diocesan conv., 1975; bd. dirs. Catholic Charities, Huntsville, 1966-69; del.-at-large Republican Nat. Conv., 1964; Rep. senatorial campaign mgr. for North Ala., 1968; pres. Madison County Fedn. Rep. Women, 1967; co-chmn. exec. finance com. Madison County Rep. Exec. Com., 1966-69; vice chmn. New Orleans Republican Met. Dist., 1964-65. Recipient Key to City, Selma, Ala., 1971, 1st place newswriting award, AP, 1971, 72, 73, 2d place award Ala. Women's Press Assn., 1973; other awards. Mem. Am. Heart Assn. (sec.-treas. profl. staff), Women in Communication, Kappa Kappa Gamma. Republican. Episcopalian. Home: PO Box 5187 San Diego CA 92105 Office: PO Box 2606 El Cajon CA 92021

TREANOR, WALTER JOHN, physician; b. County Tyrone, No. Ireland, May 14, 1922; came to U.S., 1949, naturalized, 1954; s. Hugh and Marion (deVine) T.; M.D., Nat. U. Ireland, 1947; m. Mary Stewart, Dec. 29, 1971; children—James P., Wanden, Dona, June. Intern, St. Mary's Hosp., San Francisco, 1949-52; resident Mayo Found., Rochester, Minn.; practice medicine specializing in rehab. medicine, Reno; mem. staff Washoe Med. Center; asso. clin prof. medicine U. Nev., Reno, 1979—. Served to capt., M.C., U.S. Army, 1953-55. Fellow ACP, Royal Soc. Medicine; mem. Am. Acad. Neurology, Internat. Med. Soc. Paraplegia, Am. Acad. Phys. and Rehab. Medicine. Republican. Anglican. Contbr. articles to profl. jours. Home: 6555 Plumas Reno NV 89509 Office: 975 Ryland Ave Reno NV 89520

TREDWAY, MICHAEL ALVIN, loss control supervisor; b. Omak, Wash., Jan. 14, 1947; s. Edward Ellis and Betty Jean (Spencer) T.; A.A.S. in Nursing, North Idaho Coll., 1974, postgrad., 1974-75; B.S. in Occupation Safety and Health, Eastern Wash. U., 1978; m. Melvina Mae, Mar. 28, 1980; children—Spencer Miles, Michelle Renay. Relief charge nurse, emergency room Kootenai Meml. Hosp., Coeur d'Alene, Idaho, 1974-76; safety specialist Cedar Ridge Saw Mill, Carrywood, Idaho, 1978, Jacklin Seed Co., Post Falls, Idaho, 1978-79; mill safety supr. Western Nuclear, Inc., nr. Wellpinit, Wash., 1979-82; loss control supr. Square D Co., Airway Heights, Wash., 1983—; tchr. safety tng. Vol. for first aid and safety tng. Boy Scouts Am.; den father Inland Empire council Cub Scouts Am., Boy Scouts Am. Served with USN, 1966-70. R.N., Wash. Mem. Am. Soc. Safety Engrs. Cited for contbn. to over-all safety program at Western Nuclear in Mine Safety and Health jour., 1980. Home: W 2515 Francis Spokane WA 99208 Office: PO Box 367 Airway Heights WA 99001

TREESE, DARLENE ANN, special education educator, counselor, writer; b. Warren, Ohio, Nov. 27, 1946; d. Steven Andrew and Ruth Suomi (Uitto) Dubasik; m. Robert Edward Treese, Sept. 26, 1965 (div.); children—Eric Michael, Craig Allen. B.Ed., summa cum laude, Ariz. State U., 1975, M.Ed., 1979, M.Counseling, 1981. Teaching cert. Ariz. Tchr., Painesville (Ohio) Twp. Schs., 1968-72; staff instrnl. leader Washington Elem. Sch. Dist., Phoenix, 1976-81, resource tchr. for gifted children, 1982—; cons., condr. workshops. Active local polit. campaigns. Recipient various grants. Mem. NEA, Ariz. Edn. Assn., Washington Dist. Edn. Assn., Ariz. Assn. Gifted and Talented, Kappa Delta Pi, Pi Lambda Theta. Republican. Home: 1825 W Ocotillo Apt 40 Phoenix AZ 85015 Office: 8610 N 19th Ave Phoenix AZ 85021

TREESE, WILLIAM R., art librarian, artist, painter; b. Burlington, Wash., Dec. 7, 1932; s. Paul E. and Emma J. (Dobbins) T.; m. Carolyn J. Hahn, July 3, 1953; 1 son, Richard D.; B.A., Art Inst. Chgo., 1960; M.A., Stanford U., 1961; M.L.S., Drexel U., 1964. Art librarian, Free Library of Phila., 1961-64; now art librarian U. Calif.-Santa Barbara. Served with U.S. Army, 1953-55. Mem. LArt Libraries Soc. N.Am. Editor: Art Exhibition Catalog Subject Index, 1978—; Adv. Bd., Art Bibliographies Modern, 1969—. Office: Arts Library U Calif Santa Barbara CA 93106

TREGEAGLE, STEVEN QUENTON, advertising photographer; b. Salt Lake City, Jan. 24, 1940; s. Virgil Quenton and Christina (Stout) T.; m. Karen Maddox, Nov. 30, 1944; children—Wendy, Kimberlee, Kelli. Student U. Utah, 1958-61, Los Angeles Art Ctr. Coll., 1967-68. Illustrator Hercules, Inc., Salt Lake City, 1960-62; designer Tregeagle & Assoc. Engrs., Salt Lake City, 1963-64; freelance illustrator, Phoenix, 1964-65; mech. design engr., mgr. Sargent Industries, El Segundo, Calif., 1967-70; mech. designer Western div. EDO Corp., Salt Lake City, 1971-75; comml. photographer, prin. Steve Tregeagle Photography, Salt Lake City, 1975—. Active Utah Taxpayers Assn. Recipient numerous awards for photographs. Mem. Am. Soc. Mag. Photographers, Profl. Photographers Am. (cert.), Intermountain Profl. Photographers Assn., Salt Lake C. of C. Republican. Mormon. Contbr. to The Profl. Photographer. Home: 9656 Sleepy Hollow Circle Sandy UT 84070 Office: 2994 S Richards St Suite C Salt Lake City UT 84115

TREIMAN, JOYCE WAHL, artist; b. Evanston, Ill., May 29, 1922; d. Rene and Rose (Doppelt) Wahl; A.A., Stephens Coll., 1941; B.F.A. (grad. fellow 1943), State U. Iowa, 1943; m. Kenneth Treiman, Apr. 25, 1945; 1 son, Donald. One man shows Paul Theobald Gallery, Chgo., 1942, John Snowden Gallery, Chgo., 1945, Art Inst. Chgo., 1947, 79, North Shore Country Day Sch., Winnetka, Ill., 1947, Fairweather-Garnett Gallery, Evanston, Ill., 1950, Edwin Hewitt Gallery, N.Y.C., 1950, Palmer House Galleries, Chgo., 1952, Glencoe (Ill.) Library, 1953, Elizabeth Nelson Gallery, Chgo., 1953, Charles Feingarten Gallery, Chgo., 1955, Cliff Dwellers Club, Chgo., 1955, Fairweather-Hardin Gallery, Chgo., 1955, 58, 72, 78, Marlan Willard Gallery, N.Y.C., 1960, Felix Landau Gallery, Los Angeles, 1961, Adele Bedwarz Gallery, Los Angeles, 1969, 72, Forum Gallery, N.Y.C., 1971, Tortue Gallery, 1978; numerous exhbns. including Carnegie Internat., 1955, 57, Met. Mus., 1950, Whitney Mus., 1951, 52, 53, 58, Art Inst. Chgo., 1945-59, Library of Congress, 1954, Corcoran Gallery, 1957, Pa. Acad. Fine Arts, 1958, John Herron Art Inst., 1953, Mus. Modern Art, 1962, Nat. Acad., 1971, 73; 10 year retrospective La Jolla Mus., 1972; 25 year retrospective Mcpl. Art Gallery, Los Angeles, 1978; represented in permanent collections Denver Mus. Art, State U. Iowa, Ill. State Mus., Tupperware Art Mus., Orlando, Fla., Art Inst. Chgo., Utah State U., Abbott Labs., Oberlin Allen Art Mus., Long Beach Mus. Art, Whitney Mus. Am. Art, Internat. Mineral Corp., Pasadena Art Mus., Grunwald Found., UCLA, Oakland Mus. Artist in residence San Fernando Valley (Calif.) State Coll., 1968; vis. artist Art Center Sch., Los Angeles, 1968; lectr. U. Calif. at Los Angeles, 1969-70. Recipient numerous awards including Logan prize and purchase Art Inst. Chgo., 1951, Martin B. Cahn prize, 1959, 60. Pauline Palmer prize, 1953; Saratosa Am. Painting Exhbn. award, 1959; Ford Found. purchase prize, 1960; Purchase prize Ball State Coll., 1961; prize La Jolla Art Mus., 1961; Purchase prize Pasadena Art Mus., 1961; named Woman of the Year in Art, Los Angeles Times, 1963. Tiffany fellow, 1947; Tupperware Art Fund fellow, 1955; Tamenind Lithography fellow, 1961. Address: 712 Amalfi Dr Pacific Palisades CA 90272

TREINEN, SYLVESTER WILLIAM, bishop; b. Donnelly, Minn., Nov. 19, 1917; s. William John and Kathryn (Krausert) T.; student Crosier Sem., Onamia, Minn., 1935-41; B.A., St. Paul's Sem., 1943. Ordained priest Roman Cath. Ch., 1946; asst. pastor in Dickinson, N.D., 1946-50; sec. to bishops Ryan and Hoch, 1950-53; asst. pastor Cathedral Holy Spirit, Bismarck, N.D., 1950-57; chancellor Diocese Bismarck, 1953-59; asst. pastor St. Anne's Ch., Bismarck, 1957-59; pastor St. Joseph's Ch., Mandan, N.D., 1959-62; bishop of Boise, Idaho, 1962—. Office: PO Box 769 420 Idaho St Boise ID 83701*

TRELEASE, FRANK JOHNSON, III, water engineer, consultant; b. Boulder, Colo., May 24, 1937; s. Frank Johnson and Mary (Thayer) T.; m. Patricia Powers, June 6, 1959; children—Gail F., Anne L., Amy L. B.S. in Civil Engring., U. Wyo., 1959; M.S., Colo. State U., 1961. Registered profl. engr., Colo., Wyo., Mont. With U.S. Bur. Reclamation, 1956-59; research assoc. Colo. State U., 1959-61; hydrological engr. Wright Water Engrs., Cheyenne, Wyo., 1963-64, v.p., 1979—; hydraulic engr. Denver Water Bd., 1964; sr. water resources engr. Colo. Water Conservation Bd., Denver, 1965-66; water resources engr. Wyo. Natural Resources Bd., 1966-68, dir. water planning program, 1968-78; v.p. BRW/Noblitt, Cheyenne, 1978. Treas. Cole Community Ctr., Cheyenne. Served to 1st lt. U.S. Army, 1961-63. Mem. ASCE, Wyo. Engring. Soc., Wyo. Assn. Cons. Engrs. and Surveyors, U.S. Com. on Irrigation Drainage and Flood Control, Am. Water Works Assn., Sigma Xi, Phi Kappa Phi, Omicron Delta Kappa. Republican. Club: Rotary (Cheyenne). Contbr. numerous articles and reports to profl. jours. Home: 3228 Locust Dr Cheyenne WY 82001 Office: 3130 Menderson Dr Cheyenne WY 82001

TRELEASE, RICHARD MITCHELL, JR., bishop; b. Berkeley, Calif., Apr. 16, 1921; s. Richard Mitchell and Ruth (Walker) T.; B.A., U. Mo., 1943; B.D., Ch. Div. Sch. Pacific, 1945, D.D., 1966; D.S., U. of South, 1972; m. Jean Ronayne, July 2, 1943; children—Richard Mitchell III, Christopher, Phyllis Hope. Ordained priest Episcopal Ch., 1945; curate St. Andrew's Cathedral, Honolulu, 1945; vicar, rector St. Christopher's Ch., Kailua, St. John's-by-the-Sea, Keneohe, 1947-50; rector St. Andrew's Cathedral, Honolulu, 1950-54, dean, 1954, St. Andrew's, Wilmington, Del., 1954-61, St. Paul's Episcopal Ch., Akron, Ohio, 1962-71; bishop Diocese of Rio Grande (New Mexico and S.W. Tex.), 1971—. Pres. Akron Ministerial Alliance, pres. Inpost, Akron, 1966-68, Goodwill Industries Akron, 1965-68; chmn. Kent State Chaplaincy Com., 1963; adv. com. United Community Council Akron, 1968-70, Poverty Program Akron, 1968-70, Eye Bank Akron, 1965-71; pres. N.Mex. Inter-Ch. Agy., 1974—; mem. Nat. Coalition for Ordination Women, Episcopal Ch., 1975—; mem. Nat. Commn. Regional and Local Ecumenism Nat. Council Chs., 1975—; mem. N.M. Humanities Council, 1974—. Bd. dirs. Tb Soc., Multiple Sclerosis Soc., Planned Parenthood Soc., Youth Service Advisory; v.p. Newcastle County Council Chs.; pres. People's Settlement; trustee Ch. Div. Sch. Chs.; pres. People's Settlement; trustee Ch. Div. Sch. Pacific, 1969-75, Episcopal Radio TV Found.; mem. adv. bd. Bataan Hosp. and Lovelace Clinic; bd. dirs. Santa Fe Opera Guild, 1973-74; adv. bd. Episcopal Theol. Sem. of Southwest. Mem. Aloha Tau Omega, Psi Chi. Rotarian (asso. mem.; trustee 1961-71). Office: 120 E Vassar SE Suite 1-B PO Box 4130 Albuquerque NM 87106

TREMBLAY, RICHARD EMERY, urologist, medical consultant; b. Spokane, Wash., Nov. 17; s. Emery Joseph and Marguerite (Schacht) T.; m. Betty Ann Nordstrom, May 4, (div.); children—Eric Emery, Rolf Richard, Jon Joel. B.S. in Chemistry, U. Wash., 1950; M.D., 1957. Diplomate Am. Bd. Urology. Intern Johns Hopkins Hosp., Balt., 1957-58, resident, 1958-59; resident U. San Francisco, 1959-60, U. Wash. Hosps, Seattle, 1960-63; practice medicine specializing in urology, Bellevue, Wash., 1963-74, Everett and Snohomish, Wash., 1978-80; med. cons. State of Wash. Dept. Social Health Services, Olympia, 1980—; clin. assoc. in urology U. Wash. Sch. Medicine. Served to capt. USMC, 1950-53; Korea. Decorated UN medal. Mem. Northwest Urol. Assn., Am. Urol. Assn., Wash. State Med. Soc., Thurston County Med. Soc., Physicians for Social Responsibility, Scientists for Nuclear Freeze, Alpha Omega Alpha. Republican. Roman Catholic. Contbr. numerous articles to profl. jours. Home: Apt 14 1125 E State Ave Olympia WA 98506 Office: PO Box 9303 LK 11 Olympia WA 98503

TRENHOLME, NANCY JEAN CLARY, educator; b. Boulder, Colo., Dec. 19, 1948; d. James Earl and Julia (Quint) Clary; m. Arthur Kingsley Trenholme, July 18, 1981. B.A., U. No. Colo., 1970, Ed. S., 1975; M.A., U. Colo., 1974. With Denver Pub. Schs., 1970—, tchr. West High Sch., 1970-73, tchr. South High Sch., 1975-79, program evaluation specialist, 1979—. Mem. Am. Personnel and Guidance Assn., Council Exceptional Children, Council Learning Disabilities. Democrat. Home: 4567 S Fairplay St Aurora CO 80015 Office: 900 Grant St Room 503 Denver CO 80203

TRENT, BOBBYE JEAN, hardware distbn. co. mgr.; b. Lynchburg, Tenn., Sept. 16, 1931; d. Sam B. and Marguerite (Moorhead) L.; student Odessa Coll., 1949-51, Compton Coll., 1963-65; m. Walter Travis Trent, Jan. 12, 1952; children—Gerry Lynn, Paula Gail, Priscilla Gay, Samuel Thaddeus. Reporter, sec. Midland (Tex.) Reporter-Telegram, 1951-52; pvt. sec. Fry Cons.'s, Los Angeles, 1970-71; exec. sec. Colvett, Kapner & Wolfberg, Palos Verdes, Calif., 1972-73; adminstrv. asst. Long-Lok Fasteners Corp., Los Angeles, 1972-73, adminstrv. mgr., 1973-80; ops. mgr. Reliable Industries, Inc., South Gate, Calif., 1980—; v.p. SST-III Inc.; pres. Jefe Inc.; ptnr. Trent & Assos., Loan Brokers. Pres., PTA, 1965, 70. Mem. Credit Mgrs. Assn., Mchts. and Mfrs. Assn. Republican. Home: 805 Green Ln Redondo Beach CA 90278 Office: 10724 Garwick Pl South Gate CA 90280

TRENT, MICHAEL EDWARD, office supply co. exec.; b. Boulder, Colo., Sept. 17, 1949; s. Michael Collins and Geraldine Elise (Blaser) T.; B.A. in Bus., Hastings Coll., 1975; m. Victoria Bogenschutz, Jan. 16, 1971; children—Elizabeth Louise, Kristin Elise, Donna Michelle. Bookkeeper, Standard Office Supply Co., Boulder, 1972, furniture salesman, 1972-77, owner, pres., 1977—. Chmn., Colo. & Northwestern Preservation Com. Mem. Nat. Office Products Assn., Boulder Jaycees, Boulder Model R.R. Club (past pres.), Rocky Mountain R.R. Club, Nat. Ry. Hist. Soc. Republican. Presbyterian. Home: 330 Bates St Boulder CO 80303 Office: 1221 Spruce St Boulder CO 80302

TRENT, RICHARD JAMES, newspaper publisher; b. Logan, W.Va., Jan. 16, 1946; s. Herman C. and Lita (Mounts) T.; married. A.B., George Washington U., 1969; postgrad. Am. U., 1970-72. Coordinator, Neighborhood Youth Corps, Washington, 1968; salesman to mgr. sales devel. Washington Post, 1969-77; dir. advt. Seattle Post-Intelligencer, 1977-79, dir. sales and mktg., 1979-80, gen. mgr., 1980-82; pres. San Diego Urban Newspaper Group, pub. Chula Vista (Calif.) Star-News, 1982—. lectr. in field. Mem. Wash. State Spl. Olympics, 1980-82, bd. dirs., mem. vis. com. and adv. bd. U. Wash., 1979-82. Recipient Commendation for Saving Human Life, Nat. Red Cross; named one of 100 Newsmakers of Future, Time Mag., 1978. Mem. Seattle Advt. Fedn. (pres. 1979-80, chmn. bd. 1980-82), Internat. Newspaper Advt. Execs., Am. Press Inst., Am. Advt. Fedn. (gov. 1980-82, Silver medal 1980). Creator Time and Ter. Mgmt. for Newspaper Sales Industry, tng. device, 1974. Home: 18 Kingston Ct Coronado CA 92118 Office: PO Box 1207 Chula Vista CA 92012

TRESMONTAN, OLYMPIA DAVIS, psychotherapist, human relations cons.; b. Boston, Nov. 27, 1925; d. Peter Konstantin and Mary (Hazimanolis) Davis; B.S., Simmons Coll., 1946; M.A., Wayne State U., 1960; Ph.D., U. Calif. at Berkeley, 1971; m. Dion Marc Tresmontan, Sept. 15, 1957 (dec. Mar. 1961); m. 2d, Robert Baker Stitt, Mar. 21, 1974. Child welfare worker San Francisco Dept. Social Service, 1964-66; sensitivity trainer NSF Sci. Curriculum Improvement Project, U. Calif. at Berkeley, 1967-68; pvt. practice psychol. counseling, San Francisco, 1971—; dir. Studio Ten Services, San Francisco, 1971—, Promise for Children, San Francisco, 1981—; clin. cons. Childworth Learning Ctr., San Francisco, 1976-80; cons. Queen's Bench Found., San Francisco, 1976; instr. U. Calif. Extension, San Francisco, 1971-73, Chapman Coll. extension, Travis AFB, 1971-74. Mem. Internat. Hospitality Com. of Bay Area, 1972—; bd. dirs. Childworth Learning Center, San Francisco, 1976-80. Schaefer Found. grantee, 1970-71. Mem. Am. Psychol. Assn., Am. Orthopsychiat. Assn., Am. Assn. Marriage and Family Therapists, Calif. Assn. Marriage and Family Therapists, Friends of San Francisco Public Library, Pi Lambda Theta. Club: Commonwealth of San Francisco. Author: (with J. Morris) The Evaluation of a Compensatory Education Program, 1967; What Is Curriculum Evaluation, Six Answers, 1968. Home and office: 2611 Lake St San Francisco CA 94121

TRETHEWEY, JAMES ALGER, civil engr.; b. Miami, Ariz., Jan. 5, 1937; s. Alger Perry and Lorna Mary T.; B.S.C.E., U. Ariz., 1960; student law McGeorge Coll. Law, 1964-66, U. Santa Clara, 1973, U. Calif.-Davis, 1978. Sr. engr. Aerojet Solid Propulsion Co., 1961-67; sr. project engr., chief mfg. engr. Lockheed Propulsion Co., 1967-74; dir. engring. Aerojet Solid Propulsion Co., Sacramento, 1974—; v.p. ops. Aerojet Strategic Propulsion Co., Sacramento, 1979—. Bd. dirs. Civic Assn./Sch. Bd., 1963-65. Mem. Lockheed Propulsion Co. Mgmt. Assn. (pres. 1972-73), Nat. Rifle Assn. (life), Am. Mgmt. Assn., Air Force Assn., AIAA, Soc. Advancement Material and Process Engring., Calif. Rifle and Pistol Assn. (life), Sigma Xi. Republican. Office: PO Box 15699C Sacramento CA 95813

TREVEJO, CARLOS MISAEL, chemical engineer; b. Corongo, Peru, Dec. 16, 1927; came to U.S., 1962, naturalized, 1967; s. Patrocinio and Auristela (Garay) T.; B.S., San Marcos U., 1957; M.S., U. Mont., 1967; m. Emma Canepa, Jan. 21, 1977; children—Rosalie, Cecelia. Process engr. Allied Chem. Co., Los Angeles, 1964-67; plant engr. Cargill, Inc., Lynwood, Calif., 1968-81; sr. engr. Silmar div. Sohio Chem. Corp., Hawthorne, Calif., 1981—. Mem. Am. Inst. Chem. Engring. Roman Catholic. Home: 10435 San Vincente South Gate CA 90280 Office: 12333 S Van Ness Ave Hawthorne CA 90250

TREVILLYAN, TERRY TILLMAN, optometrist; b. Yankton, S.D., Dec. 18, 1933; s. John T. and Olga E. (Farus) T.; m. Alice E. Prestis, Aug. 21, 1961; children—Mike D., Sherri R. B.S., Pacific U., 1961, O.D., 1963. Gen. practice optometry, Hermiston, Oreg., 1968—. Served to capt. U.S. Army, 1965-68. Mem. Am. Optometric Assn., Oreg. Optometric Assn. Republican. Methodist. Cubs: Kiwanis (pres. 1971, sec. 1972) (Hermiston); Masons, Elks. Home: 845 W Quince St Hermiston OR 97838 Office: 945 Orchard St Hermiston OR 97838

TREVITHICK, RONALD JAMES, accountant; b. Portland, Oreg., Sept. 13, 1944; s. Clifford Vincent and Amy Lois (Turner) T.; B.B.A., U. Wash., 1966; m. Delberta Russell, Sept. 11, 1965; children—Pamela, Carmen, Marla, Sheryl. Mem. audit staff Ernst & Ernst, Anchorage, 1966, 68-70; pvt. practice acctg., Fairbanks, Alaska, 1970-73; with Touche Ross & Co., Anchorage, 1973-78, audit partner, 1976-78; exec. v.p., treas., dir. Veco Internat., Inc., 1978-82; pres., dir. Petroleum Contractors Ltd., 1980-82; dir. P.S. Contractors A/S, Norcon, Inc., OFC of Alaska, Inc., V.E. Systems Services, Inc., Veco Turbo Services, Inc., Veco Drilling, Inc., Vemar, Inc., 1978-82; with Coopers & Lybrand, Anchorage, 1982—; instr. acctg. U. Alaska, 1971-72; lectr. acctg. and taxation Am. Coll. Life Underwriters, 1972. Div. chmn. United Way, 1975-76, YMCA, 1979; bd. dirs., fin. chmn. Anchorage Arts Council, 1975-78. Served with U.S. Army, 1967-68. C.P.A., Alaska, N.C., Va., La. Mem. Alaska Soc. C.P.A.s, Am. Inst. C.P.A.s. Petroleum Accts. Soc. (dir. Alaska 1976; nat. tax com. 1978-80), Fin. Execs. Inst. (pres. Alaska chpt. 1981-82), Beta Alpha Psi. Clubs: Rotary, Commonwealth North, Tower, Petroleum (dir. 1980—); Rainier. Home: SRA Box 372 W Anchorage AK 99507 Office: 430 W 7th Ave Anchorage AK 99501

TRIBBLE, VICTORIA NERNEY, tourism executive; b. Los Angeles, June 1, 1944; d. Albert Alexis and Constance (Horn) Nerney; m. Thomas Alfred Tribble, Dec. 30, 1967 (div.); children—Brent, Shannon. B.B.A., Nat. U., 1976; J.D., Western State U., 1980. Adminstrv. asst. Univ. Extension U. Calif.-San Diego, La Jolla, 1974-76; adminstrv. asst. San Diego Conv. and Visitors Bur., 1976-80, dir. adminstrn., 1980—. Republican. Roman Catholic. Club: Soroptimist Internat. Office: San Diego Conv and Visitors Bur 1200 3d Ave Suite 824 San Diego CA 92101

TRIFF, JOSEPH DAVID, electronic service exec., clergyman; b. Los Angeles, Oct. 15, 1931; s. John George and Elizabeth (Tamok) T.; student RCA Inst., 1963; m. Brenda Evelyne Rettig, June 20, 1965; children—Belisa Dawn, Joy Amber. Ordained to ministry Jehovah's Witnesses, 1941; pioneer minister, 1955-69; pres. Woodcrest Congregation of Jehovah's Witnesses, 1966-70, San Pedro Congregation, 1970-72; Watchtower condr. West Congregation, 1981-82; pres., owner Triffic Mobile Electronics, Long Beach, Calif., 1977—. Recipient Am. Legion Citizenship award, 1946; Bank of Am. Vocational award, 1949; Sealbearer award, 1949. Club: Alignment.

TRIFFET, TERRY, coll. dean; b. Enid, Okla., June 10, 1922; B.A., U. Okla., 1945; B.S., U. Colo., 1948, M.S., 1950; Ph.D. in Structural Mechanics, Stanford U., 1957; married; 3 children. Instr. engring. U. Colo., 1947-50; gen. engr. rocket and guided missile research U.S. Naval Ordnance Test Sta., 1950-55; gen. engr. radiol. research, head radiol. effects br. U.S. Naval Radiol. Def. Lab., 1955-59; asso. prof., then prof. mech. and materials sci., 1959-76; asso. dean research Coll. Engring., U. Ariz., Tucson, 1976—; mem. apex com. U.S. Naval Research Labs., 1959-65; cons. to govt. and industry. Grantee Australian Research Grants Com., 1966-67, 72-73. Mem. Am. Phys. Soc., Am. Math. Soc., Soc. Engring. Sci., Soc. Industry and Applied Math., IEEE. Address: Coll Engring Univ Ariz Tucson AZ 85721

TRIGG, CHARLES WILDERMAN, writer; b. Balt., Feb. 7, 1898; s. Samuel Holland and Mary E. (Wilderman) T.; B.S. in Chem. Engring., U. Pitts., 1917; M.A., U. So. Calif., 1931, M.S., 1934, postgrad., 1950-55; postgrad. U. Calif. at Los Angeles, 1936-38; m. Ida Faye Conner, Dec. 17, 1932 (dec. Aug. 1973); m. 2d, Avetta Hoffman Danford, Jan. 11, 1975. Fellow Mellon Inst. Indsl. Research, Pitts., 1916-20; chemist, prodn. mgr. King Coffee Products Corp., Detroit, 1920-23; sales promotion mgr. John E. King Coffee Co., Detroit, 1923-24; with E.R. Bohan Paint Co., Los Angeles, 1924-27; tchr. Los Angeles Pvt. High Sch., 1927-30; asso. prof. chemistry Cumnock Coll., Los Angeles, 1930-36, dean men, 1936-38; tchr. Eagle Rock High Sch., Los Angeles, 1938; instr. Los Angeles City Coll., 1938-43, coordinator Air Corps Inst., 1941-43; instr. East Los Angeles Jr. Coll., 1945-46, Los Angeles City Coll., 1946-49; coordinator Los Angeles City Coll., 1949-50, asst. dean, 1950-55, dean instruction, 1955-63, dean emeritus, prof. emeritus, 1963—; lectr. U. So. Calif., 1946, 59-60. Served to lt. comdr. USNR, 1943-45. Mem. Math. Assn. Am. (sect. chmn. 1952-53; mem. nat. bd. govs. 1953-56), Nat. Council Tchrs. Math., Sch. Sci. and Math. Assn., Assn. Los Angeles Jr. Coll. Adminstrs. (pres. 1957-58), Sigma Xi, Alpha Chi Sigma, Phi Lambda Upsilon, Phi Delta Kappa, Pi Mu Epsilon, Alpha Mu Gamma. Author: Mathematical Quickies, 1967. Mem. editorial bd. Los Angeles Math. Newsletter, 1954, Jour. Recreational Math., 1971—. Mem. editorial staff Math. Mag., 1949-63. Contbr. numerous articles to profl. jours. Book reviewer, 1961—. Patentee in field of instant coffee. Address: 2404 Loring St San Diego CA 92109

TRIGG, OLIVER ALVIN, JR., distbn. co. exec.; b. Ft. Knox, Ky., Nov. 22, 1950; s. Oliver Alvin and Mary Louise (Brown) T.; B.S. in E.E. (Nat. Merit scholar), UCLA, 1972; M.B.A. (Congress on Grad. Mgmt. Edn. fellow), Harvard U., 1975; m. La Nette Hardiman, July 15, 1978; 1 son, Oliver Alvin, III. Asst. to controller ARCO, Los Angeles, 1974; research engr. Jet Propulsion Lab., Pasadena, Calif., 1972-73; divisional fin. analyst Xerox Corp., Pasadena, 1975-76, regional service analyst, 1976-77, field service mgr., 1977-78, mktg. support mgr., 1978, area sales mgr., 1978-79; bus. devel. mgr., mktg. mgr. Beckman Instruments, Fullerton, Calif., 1979-80; pres., dir. Trigg Enterprises, Inc., Los Angeles, 1980—. Mem. Am. Mgmt. Assn., Los Angeles Council Black Profls. Engrs., Harvard Bus. Sch. Alumni Assn., So. Calif. Harvard Bus. Sch. Alumni, Los Angeles C. of C. Office: 1321 W 11th St Los Angeles CA 90015

TRIGIANO, LUCIEN LEWIS, physician; b. Easton, Pa., Feb. 9, 1926; s. Nicholas and Angeline (Lewis) T.; student Tex. Christian U., 1944-45, Ohio U., 1943-44, 46-47, Milligan Coll., 1944, Northwestern U., 1945, Temple U., 1948-52; children—Lynn Anita, Glenn Larry, Robert Nicholas. Intern, Meml. Hosp., Johnstown, Pa., 1952-53; resident Lee Hosp., Johnstown, 1953-54; gen. practice, Johnstown, 1953-59; med. dir. Pa. Rehab. Center, Johnstown, 1959-62, chief phys. medicine and rehab., 1964-70; fellow phys. medicine and rehab. N.Y. Inst. Phys. Medicine and Rehab., 1962-64; dir. rehab. medicine Lee Hosp., 1964-71, Ralph K. Davies Med. Center, San Francisco, 1973-75, St. Joseph's Hosp., San Francisco, 1975-78, St. Francis Meml. Hosp., San Francisco, 1978-83; asst. prof. phys. medicine and rehab. Temple U. Sch. Medicine; founder Disability Alert. Served with USNR, 1944-46. Diplomate Am. Bd. Phys. Medicine and Rehab. Mem. AMA, A.C.P., Pa., San Francisco County Med. socs., Am. Acad. Phys. Medicine and Rehab., Am. Congress Phys. Medicine, Calif. Acad. Phys. Medicine, Nat. Rehab. Assn., Babcock Surg. Soc. Author various med. articles. Home: 1050 Northpoint St San Francisco CA 94109 Office: 1145 Bush St San Francisco CA 94109

TRIMBLE, SANKY, public relations executive, journalist, researcher; b. Clovis, N.Mex., Apr. 3, 1921; s. Jesse Howard and Oris (Myatt) T.; m. Virginia Maurer, Dec. 24, 1943; children—Terry, Sharyn Trimble Forkner, Michael. Student Tex. Tech. U., 1939, Okla. A&M U., 1940. With AP, 1945-63; regional dir. Distilled Spirits Council U.S., Albuquerque, 1963—. Served with USAAF, World War II; served to capt. USAF; Korean War. Decorated Bronze Star. Winner first place sport news writing E.H. Shaffer Meml. awards, N.Mex., 1948, 54, 59. Mem. Pub. Relations Soc. Am. (accredited, past pres. N.Mex. chpt., past dist. chmn.), N.Mex. Soc. Assn. Execs. (past dir.), Sigma Delta Chi (founder, past pres. N.Mex. chpt.). Democrat. Home and Office: 328 Enchanted Valley NW Albuquerque NM 87107

TRIMMER, JOSEPH FRANCIS, transportation executive, consultant; b. McCook, Nebr., Dec. 5, 1928; s. Joe F. and Izella R. Trimmer; m. Barbara J. Robinson, May 19, 1934; children—Bret A., Linda A., Stacey Jo. B.S. in Bus. Adminstrn., U. Denver, 1953, M.B.A., 1954, J.D., 1962. Bar: Colo. 1962. Various positions, personnel clk. to sr. v.p. indsl. relations Ringsby Truck Lines, Inc., Denver, 1954-76; v.p., exec. v.p., pres., chief exec. officer Salt Creek Freightways, Casper, Wyo., 1976—; instr. motor carrier transp. U. Denver, 1954-59. Mem. Motor Carrier Lawyers Assn., Colo. Motor Carriers Assn. (pres. 1973, dir. 1965—), Wyo. Trucking Assn. (dir. 1979—). Lodges: Rotary (Casper); Masons, Shriners (Denver). Office: 3333 W Yellowstone PO Box 39 Casper WY 82602

TRIPATHI, VIJAY SHANKAR, geochemist; b. Varanasi, India, Aug. 16, 1952; came to U.S., 1975; s. Rajkeshwar and Kesari T.; B.Sc. in Geology and Chemistry, Banaras Hindu U., India, 1971, M.Sc., 1973; M.S. in Geochemistry, Stanford U., 1976, M.S. in Stats., 1981, Ph.D. in Geochemistry, 1983; m. Utpala Shukla, June 29, 1974; children—Vandana, Vinay Shankar. Research asst. applied earth scis. Stanford U., 1979—. Mem. Internat. Assn. Geochemistry and Cosmochemistry, Geochem. Soc., AAAS, N.Y. Acad. Scis., Sigma Xi. Contbr. articles to sci. publs. Home: 120 C Escondido Village Stanford CA 94305 Office: Dept Applied Earth Sciences Stanford Univ CA 94305

TRIPP, MINOT WELD, JR., lawyer; b. Cambridge, Mass., June 18, 1939; s. Minot Weld and Martha Jane (Swanson) T.; A.B. cum laude (Nat. scholar), Harvard U., 1961; J.D., U. Calif., Berkeley, 1964; m. Mallory Ann Penfield, Oct. 3, 1964; children—Stephen Minot, John Penfield. Admitted to Calif. bar, 1965; asso. mem. firm Taylor & Winokur, San Francisco, 1964-66; partner firm Taylor, Winokur & Schoenberg, San Francisco, 1966-74; counsel Knox, Herron & Masterson, Richmond, Calif., 1975-79; individual practice law, San Francisco, 1974—; gen. counsel, part owner Dickinson Communications, Ltd., San Francisco, 1976—; lectr. John F. Kennedy Law Sch., 1974-76, Golden Gate U., 1974-77. Democratic candidate Calif. Senate, 1972; mem. Calif. Dem. Central Com., 1969—, exec. com., 1973-79, chmn. rules com., 1977-79; mem. Contra Costa Dem. County Central Com., 1972—, chmn., 1975-77. Mem. Am. Bar Assn., Bar Assn. San Francisco, Lawyers Club San Francisco, Harvard Club San Francisco, Order Coif. Roman Catholic. Club: Richmond Country. Editor, Calif. Law Rev., 1962-64; contbr. articles to profl. jours. Home: 725 Ocean Ave Point Richmond CA 94801 Office: 1 Embarcadero Center Suite 2212 San Francisco CA 94111

TRISKA, JAN FRANCIS, political science educator; b. Prague, Czechoslovakia, Jan. 26, 1922; s. Jan and Bozena (Kubiznak) T.; m. Carmel Lena Burastero, Aug. 26, 1951; children—Mark Lawrence, John William. J.U.D., Charles U., 1948; LL.M., J.S.D., Yale U., 1952; Ph.D. in Polit. Sci., Harvard U., 1957. Co-dir. Project Theory, Law and Policy of Soviet Treaties, Hoover Instn. Stanford (Calif.) U., 1956-58, assoc. prof., prof. polit. sci., 1960—, assoc. chmn. dept. polit. sci., 1965-66, 68-69, 71-72, 74-75; lectr. polit. sci. dept. U. Calif.-Berkeley, 1957-58; asst. prof. dept. govt. Cornell U., 1958-60. Sterling fellow Yale U. Law Sch., 1948-51; Ford pub. affairs research grantee, 1959; faculty research grantee Cornell U., 1960; Inter-Univ. Com. on Travel Grants awardee, 1960; Russian Research Ctr. fellow Harvard U., 1961-62; Ford Found. research grantee, 1963-68, fellow, 1966-67, research grantee summers 1969, 70; fellow Internat. Research and Exchanges Bd., 1973-74; Fulbright-Hays faculty research fellow, 1973-74; Am. Council Learned Socs. grantee, 1975; recipient AAAS award, 1959, Am. Philos. Soc. award, 1968, NSF grant, 1971-72, Ctr. for Research in Internat. Studies award, Stanford U., 1974, Dickinson Meml. Symposium Fund and Otis Castle Fund awards, Stanford U., 1979; Internat. Ladies' Garment Workers' Union and AFL-CIO grantee, 1980; fellow Woodrow Wilson Internat. Center for Scholars, Smithsonian Instn., 1980-81; fund honoring Jan Francis Triska established Stanford U., 1980. Mem. Am. Soc. Internat. Law (exec. council 1964-67), Soviet Statutes and Decisions (adv. com. 1964—), Western Slavic Assn. (pres. 1968-69), Am. Polit. Sci. Assn. (sect. chmn. confs. 1970, 75, pres. Conf. on Communist Studies 1974-75), Am. Assn. for Advancement of Slavic Studies (dir. 1975—, sect. chmn. conf. 1977), Czechoslovak Soc. Arts and Scis. (pres. 1978-80). Democrat. Club: Palo Alto Fly Fishers. Author: (with Robert M. Slusser) A Calendar of Soviet Treaties, 1917-1957, 1959, The Theory, Law and Policy of Soviet Treaties, 1962; (with David D. Finley) Soviet Foreign Policy, 1968; Pattern and Level of Risk in Soviet Foreign Policy-Making, 1945-1963, 1966; (with Paul M. Johnson) Political Development and Political Change in Eastern Europe, 1975; (with Ike and North) The World of Superpowers, 1981; editor: Soviet Communism: Programs and Rules, 1962; Constitutions of the Community Party-States, 1968; Communist Party-States: Comparative and International Studies, 1969; (with Charles Gati) Blue Collar Workers in Eastern Europe, 1981; bd. editors publs. including East European Quar., Comparative Politics, Internat. Jour. Sociology, Jour. Comparative Politics, Studies in Comparative Communism, Soviet Statutes and Decisions, Documents in Communist Affairs; author monographs in field. Home: 720 Vine St Menlo Park CA 94025 Office: 164K Political Science Dept Stanford Univ Stanford CA 94305

TROESCHER, LOREN CARL, public speaker, clergyman; b. Cleve., May 21, 1931; s. Wilburn Loren and Milda Evelyn T.; m. Dorothy Lee Jenkins, Sept. 1, 1951; 6 children; m. 2d, Bonnie Jean Roberts, June 30, 1974. B.S. in Commerce, Ohio U., 1955; M.B.A., Harvard U., 1959.

Ordained to ministry Ch. of Scientology, 1973. Economist, P.R. Devel. Agy., 1960; mem. mktg. staff Orbit Kitchen Cabinets, 1961-62; internal auditor Sun Oil Co., 1962-63; cons., mem. trade negotiations staff The White House, Washington, 1963-64; ptnr. Horrace J. DePodwin & Assocs., econs. cons., 1965; economist UN African Econ. Devel. Orgn., Ethiopia, 1965; cons. Nat. Investment Bank of Ghana, 1966-68; chief exec. officer Delgado Bros., Manila, 1969; chief fin. officer Trans Asia Engrng. Assocs., Manila, 1970-71; mem. staff Ch. of Scientology, 1972-74, dir. communications for ch. mgmt. orgn., Los Angeles, 1972-73, dir. pastoral counseling, 1973-74, minister, Burbank, Calif., 1982—; owner, operator Exec. Cleaning Service, 1975-82, cons., 1983—; founder, prin. Vibrant Life, public speaking, 1981—; founder Mark Point Assn. Fine Speakers, 1983—; minister weekly TV ch. service, 1981—; host TV interview show, 1982—; counselor Narconon, 1973—; lectr. on abuse of mental patients. Vol. exec. dir. Citizens Commn. on Human Rights, 1975-76. Served to 1st lt., inf. U.S. Army, 1955-57. Mem. Nat. Speaker's Assn., North Hollywood C. of C. (dir. 1976-79), Burbank C. of C. (chmn. monthly breakfast meeting 1981-82), Hollywood C. of C. (ambassador 1978-79). Republican. Club: Toastmasters (v.p. club, area gov.). Home and Office: 1210 W Chestnut St Burbank CA 91506

TROMBLE, JOHN MERRILL, research hydrologist; b. Lincoln, Kans., Jan. 26, 1932; s. Roy W. and Jane M. (Howell) T.; m. Ruby L. Wolf, Jan. 26, 1972. B.S., Utah State U.-Logan, 1961; M.S., U. Ariz.-Tucson, 1964, Ph.D., 1973. Research asst. U. Ariz.-Tucson, 1961-63, research assoc., 1963-66; hydrologist, asst. dir. S.W. Watershed Research Ctr., U.S. Dept. Agr., Tucson, 1967-73; hydrologist Jornada Experimental Range, Las Cruces, N.Mex., 1974—; Served to 1st lt. U.S. Army, 1953-55. Mem. Am. Geophys. Union, Am. Water Resources Assn., Soil Conservation Soc., Internat. Soil Sci. Soc. Contbr. articles to tech. jours. Home: 200 S Weinrich Rd Las Cruces NM 88005 Office: Jornada Exptl Range PO Box 3JER NMSU Las Cruces NM 88003

TRONE, CURVIN J., JR., financial cons.; b. York, Pa., May 15, 1921; s. Curvin J. and Velma (Geltz) T.; A.B., Brown U., 1948; M.A., Harvard, 1949; postgrad. U. Mich. Law Sch., 1949-50; m. Alice Louise Young, Sept. 9, 1950. Asst. to pres., ops. controller Whirlpool Corp., Benton Harbor, Mich., 1953-63, pres. S.A. Royal Corp. subs., Paris, 1961-62; dir. planning consumers group Westinghouse Electric Corp., Pitts., 1963; dir. corporate, fin. planning and control Hunt Foods & Industries, Fullerton, Calif., 1963-67; v.p. Allis-Chalmers Corp., Milw., 1967-71, v.p. finance, 1967-71, also group exec., v.p. Consumer Products Group, 1969-71; exec. v.p. Penn-Pacific Corp., Phoenix, 1971-74; pres. Trone & Co., Allis-Chalmers Credit Corp., Allis-Chalmers Internat. Credit Corp., Allis-Chalmers Leasing Corp.; dir. Brastemp, S.A., Sao Paulo, Brazil, S.A. Royal Corp., Paris, Allis-Chalmers U.K., Allis-Chalmers France, Allis-Chalmers Australia, Air Calif., Dyna-Shield, Inc., Milw. County Bank, Allis-Chalmers-Siemens Electric Products Corp.; trustee in reorg. for U.S. Dist. Ct. Westgate-Calif. Corp. Mem. pres.'s select com. Brown U., bd. dirs. 3d Century Fund; trustee Allis-Chalmers Found. Fellow Fin. Analysts Fedn.; mem. Phoenix Soc. Fin. Analysts, Nat. Assn. Accountants, Am. Inst. Indsl. Engrs. (sr.), Fin. Execs. Inst. Clubs: Arizona, Cuyamaca, Brown U. Home: 7343 E Marlette Ave Scottsdale AZ 85253 Office: 3020 E Camelback Rd Phoenix AZ 85016

TRONNES, STEVEN FRANCIS, optometrist; b. Mpls., May 9, 1949; s. Vernon Trygve and Esther Wilhelmina (Scott) T.; m. Mary Jo Harney, July 1, 1972; children—Arik, Carshena, Katrina. B.S. in Zoology, Mont. State U., 1975; O.D. Pacific U., 1975. Lic. optometrist, Oreg., Mont., Alaska, Hawaii. Pvt. practice optometry, Baker, Oreg., 1980—; owner, operator Baker Vision Clinic, 1980—. Bd. dirs. Baker Family YMCA. Served with U.S. Army, 1975-80; Korea. Decorated Army Commendation medal with oak leaf cluster. NSF scholar, 1966. Mem. Am. Optometric Assn., Optometric Extension Program Found., Am. Acad. Optometry, Oreg. Optometric Assn., Eastern Oreg. Optometric Soc. Clubs: Kiwanis (sec.-treas., Outstanding Kiwanian of Yr. 1981-82), Knife and Fork (pres. 1983-84) (Baker). Home: 2630 1st St Baker OR 97814 Office: PO Box 509 2150 3d St Baker OR 97814

TROUSIL, EDWARD GEORGE, research chemist; b. Ravinia, Ill., Nov. 12, 1930; s. Bohumil and Barbara (Marhoul) T.; m. Olga Maria Listik, Apr. 18, 1934; children—Edward, Paul, Renee. B.S. in Chem. Engring., High Indsl. Sch. Chemistry, 1951; B.S. in Chemistry, U. Colo., 1969. Indsl. coatings chemist, Armstrong Paint & Varnish Works, Chgo., 1951-55; indsl. coatings chemist appliance coatings Desoto Chem. Coatings, Chgo., 1951-61; tech. dir. Komac Paint Inc., Denver, 1961—. Served with mil. intelligence U.S. Army, 1952-54. Recipient A.F. Voss competition Am. Paint Jour. 2nd pl. award, 2972. Mem. Am. Chem. Soc., Rocky Mountain Soc. Coatings Tech. (chmn. tech. com., past pres.). Roman Catholic. Contbr. articles to profl. jours. Home: 6977 Dudley Dr Arvada CO 80004 Office: 1201 Osage St Denver CO 80201

TROUT, STEVEN SMITH, architect, designer; b. Twin Falls, Idaho, Dec. 15, 1952; s. Chalmer Edward and Darline Josephine T.; B.Arch., U. Idaho, 1977. With C. Ed Trout & Assos., Architects, Boise, Idaho, 1970-74, Anton Eder Architect, Moscow, Idaho, 1974-78; designer, v.p. McCall Design & Planning, Inc. (Idaho), 1978-81; sec.-treas. architect Trout Binning & Assos., Boise, 1981—. Home: PO Box 1776 McCall ID 83638 Office: PO Box 1552 Boise ID 83701

TROUT, WILLIAM HOLLIS, architect; b. Cleve., June 29, 1935; s. William Henry and Margaret Marie (Pauer) T.; B.S., Kent State U., 1960; m. Beverly Heather Law, June 17, 1961; children—William Hollis, Peter Dunsmore, Timothy Pauer. With Hellman & Wilson, Falmouth, Mass., 1959-60, Visnapuu & Gaede, Cleve., 1962, John Terrance Kelly, Cleve., 1962, Houston Assos., Mentor, Ohio, 1964, William B. Morris Assos., Shaker Heights, Ohio, 1965; prin. The Trout Creek Architects, Inc., Vail, Colo., 1981—; lectr. in field. Formerly mem. Eagle County Planning Commn.; mem. Vail Planning and Environ. Commn.; mem. Design Rev. Bd. of Beaver Creek. Served with Ohio N.G., 1954. Recipient Cleve. Arts prize, 1978; 1st honor award Architects Soc. Ohio, 1969; design award AIA, 1970, for Schubert House, for DeBenedetto House, Ocepek House, Moore House, The Little House, 1971, Child Day Care Center T. Celeste, 1971, Office Interior of Trout Architects, 1972, Pirates' Cove, 1972, The Trout House, 1976, The Sciangula House, 1976; Craftsmanship award, Cleve. Builders Exchange, 1976, 77; Record House of the Yr., Archtl. Record Mag., 1978; nat. design award Nat. Assn. Home Builders and Better Home & Gardens mag., 1979, 78; Design for Better Living award Am. Wood Council, 1979. Mem. AIA, Architects Soc. Ohio, Am. Underground Space Assn., Eagle Valley Home Builders Assn. (dir.), Delta Tau Delta. Republican. Episcopalian. Clubs: Cleve. Yachting, Midget Ocean Racing Class Assn., Dillon Yacht. Author: Solar Houses, 1978; Modern Houses in America, 1978; contbr. articles to profl. jours. Home: 232 Brige St Vail CO 81657 Office: The Clock Tower Vail CO 81657

TROVER, DENIS WILLIAM, microcomputer co. exec.; b. Columbus, Ohio, Feb. 1, 1945; s. Kenneth Harold and Virginia June (Denis) T.; B.S. in Physics, Mich. State U., 1967; M.B.A., Coll. William and Mary, 1972; M.S. in Physics, Vassar Coll., 1973; m. Florence Ellen Lloyd, June 12, 1971; 1 dau., Florence Emma. Optical physicist IBM, Fishkill, N.Y., 1967-71; staff assoc., systems programmer Rockwell Internat. Sci. Center, Thousand Oaks, Calif., 1974-78; pres., dir. Sonix Systems, Inc., Thousand Oaks, 1978—. Mem. energy task force Conejo Future Found., 1975—, chmn., 1980-81. Club: Vassar So. Calif. (bd. dirs. 1982—). Home: 11355 Presilla Rd Camarillo CA 93010 Office: 1107 E Thousand Oaks Blvd Thousand Oaks CA 91362

TROVER, ELLEN LLOYD, lawyer; b. Richmond, Va., Nov. 23, 1947; d. Robert Van Buren and Hazel Pauline (Urban) Lloyd; m. Denis William Trover, June 12, 1971; 1 dau., Florence Emma. A.B., Vassar Coll., 1969; J.D., Coll. William and Mary, 1972. Bar: Va. 1972, Calif. 1973. Assoc. editor Bancroft-Witney Co., San Francisco, 1973-74; sole practice, Thousand Oaks, Calif., 1974-82; v.p. Sonix Systems, Inc., 1980-82; ptnr. Trover & Fisher, Thousand Oaks, 1982—. Mem. Thousand Oaks Franchise Adv. Bd., 1976-81, Ventura County Democratic Central Com., 1977; trustee Conejo Future Found., 1979—, vice chmn., 1982-83; trustee Hydro Help for the Handicapped, 1981—, exec. com., 1981—. Mem. Conejo-Simi Bar Assn. (pres. 1979-80, dir. 1983—), Ventura County Bar Assn., Calif. Bar Assn., ABA, Phi Alpha Delta. Democrat. Presbyterian. Club: Magic Castle (North Hollywood). Editor: Handbooks of State Chronologies, 1972. Home: 11355 Presilla Rd Camarillo CA 93010 Office: 1107 E Thousand Oaks Blvd Thousand Oaks CA 91362

TROW, CLIFFORD WAYNE, state senator, educator; b. Topeka, Kans.; s. George E. and Rubena (Swift) T.; m. JoAnne Johnson, 1969. A.B., Kans. Wesleyan U., 1951; M.A., U. Colo., 1958, Ph.D., 1966. Assoc. prof. history Oreg. State U., 1965—; mem. Oreg. State Senate, 1975—. Co-chmn. Benton County Democratic Central Com., 1972-74. Mem. AAUP, Orgn. Am. Historians (Binkley-Stephenson award). Home: 1835 NW Juniper Pl Corvallis OR 97330 Office: Oregon State Senate Salem OR 97310*

TROY, ALICE LOUISE, marketing executive; b. Pitts., Mar. 9, 1956; d. Robert and Lila (Beggs) T. B.A. in Biology, Washington and Jefferson Coll., 1978; M.B.A., Pepperdine U., 1982. Mktg. rep. Pepperdine U., Los Angeles, 1980—; chem. technician Allegheny Power Systems, 1979-80. Mem. Nat. Assn. Female Execs., Assn. M.B.A. Execs., Greensburg Central Cath. Alumni Assn., Westmoreland Hunt Assn. (farmer's cup 1977). Office: 3415 Sepulveda St Los Angeles CA 90034

TROY, FREDERIC ARTHUR, II, educator; b. Evanston, Ill., Feb. 16, 1937; s. Charles McGregor and Virginia (Minto) T.; B.S., Washington U., St. Louis, 1961; Ph.D., Purdue U., 1966; postgrad. (postdoctoral fellow) Sch. Medicine, Johns Hopkins U., 1966-68; m. Linda Ann Price, Mar. 23, 1959; children—Karen M., Janet R. Asst. prof. biol. chemistry U. Calif. Sch. Medicine, Davis, 1968-74, asso. prof., 1974-80, prof., 1980—, co-prin. investigator tumor biol. tng. program, 1972—; vis. research prof. dept. tumor biology Karolinska Inst. Med. Sch., Stockholm, 1976-77; cons. NIH, 1975—. Research Career Devel. award, NIH, 1975-80; Am. Cancer Soc.-Eleanor Roosevelt Internat. Cancer fellow Union Internat. Centre le Cancer, Geneva, 1976-77; NIH grantee, 1968—. Mem. Am. Soc. Biol. Chemistry, Am. Soc. for Cancer Research, Biochem. Soc. (London), Am. Chem. Soc., Am. Soc. Microbiology, Am. Soc. Enologists, Soc. for Complex Carbohydrates, N.Y. Acad. Scis., AAAS, Biophys. Soc., Sigma Xi. Contbr. articles to profl. jours.; editorial reviewer Jour. Biol. Chemistry, 1974, Cancer Research, 1978 , Biochem., Biophys., Acta., 1978—, also others. Address: Dept Biol Chemistry Univ of Calif Sch Medicine Davis CA 95616

TROYER, WAYNE EDWARD, mfg. co. exec.; b. Milford, Nebr., Jan. 15, 1933; s. Melvin and Mary (Saltzman) T.; student Colo. Coll., 1952-53, Midland Coll., Fremont, Nebr., 1956-57; m. Doris M. Knuth, Mar. 29, 1957; children—Rick, Tami. With Denver Equipment div. Joy Mfg. Co., 1959—, mfg. mgr., 1971-73, plant mgr., Colorado Springs, 1973—; dir. Yell Gold Co. Cripple Creek. Served with AUS, 1954-56. Presbyterian. Home: 2535 Fairway Dr Colorado Springs CO 80909 Office: 621 S Sierra Madre St Colorado Springs CO 80901

TRUAX, DONALD ROBERT, mathematics educator; b. Mpls., Aug. 29, 1927; s. William Raymond and Hermina Wilhelmina (Sobolik) T.; m. Barbara June Eckton, Sept. 16, 1950; children—Mary, Catherine, Patricia, Gail. B.S., U. Wash., 1951, M.S., 1953; Ph.D., Stanford U., 1955. Research fellow Calif. Inst. Tech., 1955-56; asst. prof. math. U. Kans., 1956-59; asst. prof. math. U. Oreg., 1959-63, assoc. prof., 1963-69, prof., 1969—; instr. researcher, mng. editor Inst. Math. Statis., 1975-81. Served in USN, 1945-48. Inst. Math. Statis. fellow, 1982. Mem. Am. Statis. Assn., Inst. Math. Statis. Democrat. Contbr. research articles on math. statis. to profl. jours. Home: 2323 University St Eugene OR 97403 Office: Dept Math U Oreg Eugene OR 97403

TRUCHLIKOVA, DANICA EVA, architect; b. Bratislava, Czechoslovakia, Mar. 12, 1942; came to U.S., 1971, naturalized, 1976; d. Rudolf and Maria Truchlikova (Popekova) T.; Faculty of Arch. and Bldg. Constrn., Slovak Tech. U., Bratislava, 1959, M.S. with honors, 1965. Project architect Dopravoprajekt, Bratislava, 1965-68; architect Yorke, Rosenberg, Mardall, London, 1968-71; project designer, asso. Skidmore, Owings & Merrill, San Francisco, 1972—; faculty U. Calif., Berkeley, 1980-81. Mem. AIA, Nat. Trust Historic Preservation, Orgn. Women Architects. Democrat. Roman Catholic. Home: 1234 Jones St San Francisco CA 94109 Office: 1 Maritime Plaza San Francisco CA 94111

TRUDEL, JOHN DAVIS, electronics company executive; b. Trenton, N.J., Aug. 1, 1942; s. LeRoy Renee and Elizabeth Etta (Reading) T.; B.E.E. cum laude (Western Electric scholar, State of N.J. scholar, McLendon scholar), Ga. Inst. Tech., 1964; M.E.E. (NDEA grad. fellow), Kans. State U., 1966; m. Barbara Banks Beaty, Sept. 1, 1973; 1 stepson, Michael Gene Beaty. Research and devel. project engr. Collins Radio Co., Richardson, Tex., 1966-67; sr. engr. Sanders Assos., Inc., Nashua, N.H., 1967-68; sr. electronic system engr. LTV Electrosystems, Inc., Greenville, Tex., 1968-69; sr. engr. Collins Radio Co., Richardson, 1969-70; project engr. F & M Systems, Co., Dallas, 1970-71; pres. Sci. System Tech., Inc., Richardson, 1971-74; product mgr. portable oscilloscopes Tektronix, Inc., Beaverton, Oreg., 1974-82, mgr. applications mktg. Lab. Instrument Systems br., 1983—; v.p. mktg. Cable Bus. Systems Corp., Beaverton, 1982-83. Mem. nat. adv. bd. Am. Security Council, 1974—. Recipient Scholastic award Lambda Chi Alpha, 1963, 64. Mem. IEEE, Assn. Old Crows, Am. Mktg. Assn., Nat. Avionics Soc., Automatic R.F. Techniques Group, Am. Electronics Assn., Aircraft Owners and Pilots Assn., Tau Beta Pi, Eta Kappa Nu. Roman Catholic. Primary author of MAGIC, gen. purpose microwave computer aided design program; contbr. articles in field to profl. jours. Home: 14755 S W 144th St Tigard OR 97223 Office: MS 39-327 PO Box 500 Beaverton OR 97077

TRUE, DIEMER, state senator, trucking company executive; b. Cody, Wyo., Feb. 12, 1946; s. Henry Alfonso and Jean (Durland) T.; B.S., Northwestern U., 1968; m. Susie Lynn Niethammer, Aug. 28, 1967; children—Diemer Durland, Kyle Shawn, Tara Jeanine, Tracy Lynn. With Black Hills Trucking, Inc., Casper, Wyo., 1970—, v.p., 1974—; pres., chmn. bd. Midland Fin. Corp.; v.p. Toolpushers Supply Co., Casper, 1981—; dir. Hilltop Nat. Bank, Mountain Plaza Nat. Bank; mem. Wyo. Ho. of Reps., 1972-76; mem. Wyo. Senate, 1976—, mem. travel, recreation and wildlife com., 1983, chmn. mines, minerals and indsl. devel. com., 1979—; governing bd. Council State Govts., 1979—. Bd. dirs. Hwy. Users Fedn., 1975-82, Am. Legis. Exchange Council, 1974-76. Pres. Natrona County United Way, 1976. Served with AUS, 1968. Mem. Wyo. Trucking Assn. (dir. 1972-80, pres. 1983-84), Ind. Petroleum Assn. Am. Republican. Methodist. Address: PO Box 2360 Casper WY 82602

TRUELSEN, THORVALD IRVIN ANTONE, geographer, market research exec.; b. Honolulu, Mar. 5, 1939; s. James Thor and Faye Belle (Blankenship) T.; B.S., U. Oreg., 1963, M.A., 1968; 1 dau., Kristine. Various retail operation positions Portland (Oreg.) div. Safeway Stores, Inc., 1958-68, sr. market research analyst market research dept., Oakland, Calif., 1968-72; mgr. econ. research Albertson's Inc., Boise, Idaho, 1972-76; prin. location and market planning T.I. Truelsen Assos., Boise, 1977—. Adv., Jr. Achievement East Bay, Oakland, 1969-71. Served with USNR, 1961-63. Mem. Assn. Am. Geographers, Am. Mktg. Assn., Nat. Assn. Corp. Real Estate Execs., Am. Soc. Photogrammetry, Urban Land Inst., Assn. Pacific Coast Geographers, Sigma Nu, Alpha Phi Omega. Democrat. Home: 324 Bitteroot Dr Boise ID 83709

TRUEX, GEORGE ROBERT, JR., banker; b. Red Bank, N.J., May 29, 1924; s. George Robert and Elsie D. (White) T.; A.B. in Econs., Rutgers U., 1949; m. Nancy Carroll Burt, May 10, 1947; children—Peter Barclay, Amy Dinsmore. Sr. v.p. Irving Trust Co., N.Y.C., 1949-66; exec. v.p. Bank of Am., San Francisco, 1966-73, vice chmn. Small Bus. Enterprises Co. subsidiary, 1968-72; chmn., chief exec. officer Rainier Bancorp., Seattle, 1973—, chmn. bd., chief exec. Rainier Nat. Bank, 1973—; dir., mem. exec. com. Nat. Airlines, Inc., Miami, Fla., 1962-80, INA Life Ins. Co.-N.Y., 1965-68; dir. Universal Furniture Ltd., Hong Kong, Fed. Res. Bank, San Francisco, N.Y.C., Pan Am. World Airways, N.Y.C. Bd. dirs. Calif. Bankers Assn., 1969-73, Wash. State China Relations Council, 1979—. Fin. chmn. Calif. Gov.'s Task Force on Flood Relief, 1969-73; mem. fin. advisory com. CAB, 1970-71; mem. orthopaedic council Orthopaedic Hosp., Los Angeles, 1969-72; mem. adv. bd. Pacific Rim Bankers Program, 1977—, chmn. adv. bd., 1980-81; mem. regional adv. com. Thirteenth Nat. Bank Region. Trustee, Calif. Inst. Arts, Los Angeles, 1968-72; bd. dirs. Walt Disney Assos. for Calif. Inst. Arts, 1972-81, San Francisco Planning and Urban Renewal Assn., 1973; bd. dirs. Jr. Achievement So. Calif., 1967-72, pres., 1968-70, Western Regional bd. dirs., 1968-72; nat. bd. dirs. Jr. Achievement, Inc., 1968-75; bd. dirs. Jr. Achievement Greater Seattle, 1976-77; div. chmn. United Way, Inc., Los Angeles, 1970, 71; asso. gen. campaign chmn. United Way of King County, 1976-78, gen. chmn., 1979, bd. dirs., 1979—; bd. dirs. Virgina Mason Hosp., 1976—; bd. regents Seattle U., 1976-80, trustee, 1980—; trustee Bank of Am. Found., 1973; mem. adv. bd. Grad. Sch. Bus. Adminstrn., U. Wash., 1975—, chmn., 1978-80.; trustee Com. Econ. Devel., 1980—, Seattle Art Mus., 1978-80, bd. dirs., sec., treas. Wash. Roundtable, 1983—; co-chmn. fin. com. Republican State Com., 1983. Served to capt., cav. AUS, World War II; ETO. Mem. Assn. Res. City Bankers, Seattle C. of C. (trustee 1975-78). Clubs: Bankers, Bohemian (San Francisco); Seattle Golf, Wash. Athletic, Rainier, Broadmoor Golf (Seattle); Stock Exchange (v.p. 1972), One Hundred (Los Angeles). Athletic. Office: Rainier Nat Bank Box 3966 Seattle WA 98124

TRUEX, LEIGH PATRICIA, pickle company executive, real estate broker; b. N.Y.C., Jan. 18, 1926; d. Harry and Dorothy (Abrams) Mahl; m. Wendell R. Truex, Nov. 26, 1947 (dec. 1970); children—Wende Stewart, Timothy. B.A., U. Pacific, 1950. Owner, pres. Bubbies of San Francisco, 1981—, The Best Kosher Dill Pickle Co., San Francisco, 1981—. Judge, Marin County Fair. Named Pickle Queen, Pickle Packers Internat., 1963; recipient Blue Ribbon award Culinary Carnival, 1981. Mem. Nat. Acad. Sci., Junior Aid, Nat. Press Club, Nat. Assn. Specialty Food Trade, Inc. Democrat. Clubs: Golden Gateway Tennis (San Francisco); Profl. Women's. Patentee in field. Home: 405 Davis Ct Apt 1305 San Francisco CA 94111 Office: San Francisco CA

TRUJILLO, LINDA ANN, management consultant; b. Tulsa, Dec. 28, 1947; d. William C. Lagoni and Mildred A. (Campbell) Wasson; student Coll. Marin, 1965-66, Calif. State U., Long Beach 1978-82, Calif. State U., Dominiquez Hills, 1978-81; m. Allen H. Trujillo, Jan. 25, 1976, children—Rand B., Allison J., Shawn A., Curtis G. Adminstrv. asst. Kaiser Hosp., Bellflower, Calif., 1976-78; emergency services coordinator City of Long Beach, 1978, supr., 1978-79, mgr./adminstr. Emergency Communications Center, 1979-81; owner, mgr. Exec. Word Systems, Santa Ana, Calif., 1981—; mgmt. cons. Planning Research Corp., 1982—. Mem. Nat. Assn. Female Execs., WeCan Women's Network, Nat. Notary Assn. Republican. Adventist. Club: Racquetball World Health. Home: 10231 Wembley Circle Westminster CA 92683 Office: 185 Berry St Suite 3808 San Francisco CA 94701

TRUJILLO, ROLAND SIMON, railroad official; b. Laramie, Wyo., Mar. 27, 1950; s. Samuel and Rosemarie (Studer) T. B.A. in French, U. San Francisco, 1973; M.S. in Human Relations and Orgn. Devel., 1982. Gen. claim agt. Atchison, Topeka & Santa Fe Ry., San Francisco, 1974-79, employment supr., Chgo., 1979-80, pricing analyst import/export traffic, San Francisco, 1981—. Vol. English as a 2d lang. instr. San Francisco Adult Learning Ctr., 1981. U. San Francisco scholar, 1968-72. Mem. Am. Soc. Tng. and Devel., Am. Soc. Personnel Adminstrn., World Affairs Council, Oakland World Trade Club, Brotherhood of Ry., Airline and Steamship Clks. (past lodge pres.), Delta Nu Alpha. Home: 677 43rd Ave San Francisco CA 94121

TRULL, SAMUEL GEORGE, JR., educator; b. Buffalo, Nov. 26, 1922; s. Samuel G. and Angeline C. (Cummings) T.; m. Deniece B. Burnell, Feb. 17, 1979; children—Robert, Deborah, Pamela. B.S.E.E., Union Coll., 1944; M.S.E.E., Renesselar Poly. Inst., 1947; Ph.D., Cornell U., 1956; lic. profl. engr., N.Y. 1950. Lighting and power engr., sales supr. Central Hudson Gas and Electric, Poughkeepsie, N.Y., 1947-55; instr. U. Calif.-Berkeley, 1957-62; prof. San Francisco State U., 1964—; pres. Ednl. Mgmt., Inc., 1960—. Served to lt. USN, 1943-46. Mem. Acad. Mgmt. Contbr. numerous articles to profl. jours. Home: 49 Brookside Dr Orinda CA 94563 Office: 2831 7th St Berkeley CA 94710

TRUMAN, ROLLAND ALBERT, mcpl. hearing appeals officer; b. Loma Linda, Calif., Apr. 30, 1912; s. Archibald William and Daisy Ethel (Nary) T.; B.A., U. So. Calif., 1940, J.D., 1942; m. Iola LaVerne Gilbert, June 14, 1941 (div.); children—Rolland Gilbert, Norris Wesley; m. 2d, Laurel A. Weibel, Sept. 15, 1953; children—Tracy, Tamara, Trina, Trent, Tricia. Admitted to Calif. bar, 1942, U.S. Supreme Ct. bar, 1957, Mil. Ct. Appeals, 1978, U.S. Tax Ct., 1978, U.S. Ct. Customs and Patent Appeals, 1978; mem. legal staff Pacific Electric Ry. Co., 1942-44; practiced in Long Beach, Calif., 1945-51, South Gate, Calif., 1952-63; Superior Ct. commr., judge protem Los Angeles County, 1963-77, 80-81; appeals hearing officer, bd. retirement Los Angeles County, 1979-81, 82—; resident faculty mem. Western State U. Coll. Law, 1977-79. City chmn. Community Chest, 1952-53; mem. Long Beach City Coll. Adult Stage Band, 1966-79 Jerry Reilly and his Calif. Banjoliers, 1980—, Banjos-a-Plenty, 1980—. Mem. Los Angeles County Democratic Central Com., 1949-52; chmn. Young Dems. of Calif., 1947-48. Bd. dirs. Anaheim Meml. Hosp., 1959-63, White Meml. Med. Center, 1975-83, Ch. State Council, Western U.S., 1965—, Lynwood Adventist Acad., 1980-81, Adventist Union Sch., 1982—. Recipient various legis. resolutions. Fellow Am. Acad. Matrimonial Lawyers (dir. chpt. 1980—); mem. Am., Los Angeles County, Long Beach bar assns., Assn. Trial Lawyers Am., Supreme Ct. Hist. Soc. (bd. dirs. 1981—), Los Angeles County Employees Assn. (parliamentarian council cabinet 1965), State Bar Calif., Nat. Audubon Soc., Audubon Soc. Los Angeles (dir. 1951), Fallbrook Citrus Assn., Sunkist Growers, Inc., Calavo Growers of Calif., N.Am. Assn. Ventriloquists (life), U. So. Calif. Gen. Alumni Assn. (life), Delta Theta Phi. Seventh Day Adventist (masterguide 1935—, elder 1983—). Clubs: Agassiz Nature (pres. 1948-50), Angelus Nature (pres. 1950-51), Audubon Screen Tours (pres. 1950-51), Kiwanis (dir. 1954-57, 62, editor Star), Assn. Radio Amateurs of Long Beach, Pathfinder (assoc. dir. Bellflower, Calif. 1961-65). Author: Lyrics for Fun, 1968. Home: 4522 Greenmeadow Rd Long Beach CA 90808

TRUMBO, BRUCE EDWARD, statistics educator, educational software writer; b. Springfield, Ill., Dec. 12, 1937; s. Harry Edward and Lucille Amalie (Andreasen) T. A.B. in Math./Chemistry, Knox Coll., 1959; S.M. in Stats., U. Chgo., 1961, Ph.D., 1965. Asst. prof. math. San Jose State U., 1963-64, biostats. fellow Stanford U., 1964-65; asst., assoc., prof. stats. and math. Calif. State U.-Hayward, 1965—; program dir. stats. research NSF. Woodrow Wilson fellow; Am. Council Edn. fellow. Mem. Inst. Math. Stats. (treas.), Am. Statis. Assn., Phi Beta Kappa, Sigma Xi. Contbr. articles to profl. jours. Office: Dept Stats Calif State U Hayward CA 94542

TRUMBULL, ROY HOWARD, elec. engr.; b. San Francisco, Nov. 28, 1939; s. Lyman Burr and Sue Helen (Higgins) T.; B.S.E.E., Heald Engrng. Coll., 1959; A.A., Coll. of Marin, 1965; postgrad. San Francisco State U.; m. Patricia E. Pick, Aug. 28, 1965; children—Erica, David. Research engr. Autonetics, 1959-62; chief engr. Sundial Broadcasting, 1962-63, Apollo Broadcasting, 1963-66, Wright Broadcasting, 1966-68; engrng. supr. Metromedia, 1968-71, CBS, 1971-76; instr. Laney Coll., 1976-79; engrng. supr. Chronicle Broadcasting Co., 1979; owner, operator Trumbull Co., El Cerrito, Calif., 1972—. Adult leader Boy Scouts Am. Mem. Calif. Council Electronic Instrs. (pres.; Allan Maxwell award), Soc. Broadcast Engrs. (cert.); Richard T. Parks award chpt. 40), Soc. Motion Picture and TV Engrs. Jewish. Author: Printed Circuit Techniques for the Hobbyist, 1974; contbr. articles to profl. jours. Office: 1001 Van Ness St San Francisco CA 94109

TRUSCOTT, IDA PROUTY, psychologist; b. Council Bluffs, Iowa, Oct. 1, 1915; d. Shirley Brooks and Grace Elizabeth (McKenzie) Prouty; m. Harry Austin Truscott, Jan. 2, 1942; children—Leigh Berry, Al McKenzie. B.A., State U. Iowa, 1940; M.A., Harvard U., 1945; Ph.D., U. Cin., 1966. Staff psychologist NYU Testing and Advisement Ctr., N.Y.C., 1946; staff psychologist Longview State Hosp. for Mentally Ill, Cin., 1966-67; asst. prof. Xavier U., Cin., 1966-67; instr. U. Cin., 1961-65; cons. research-eval. psychotherapy Rollman Psychiat. Inst., Cin., 1967-75; pvt. practice psychology, Cin., 1975-77, Aspen, Colo., 1978—. Finkbine scholar State U. Iowa, 1940. Mem. Am. Psychol. Assn., Internat. Transactional Assn., NOW, LWV, Colo. Psychol. Assn. Democrat. Club: Women's Forum (Aspen). Adv. editor Jour. Cons. and Clin Psychology, 1974-75; contbr. articles to profl. jours. Home: 770 Oak Ridge Rd Box 5341 Snowmass Village CO 81615 Office: 605 E Main St #7 Aspen CO 81611

TRUXAW, KATHLEEN ROSE (O'HANLON), educational psychologist; b. Fullerton, Calif., d. Daniel and Margaret Alice (Cottam) O'Hanlon; m. John Edmund Truxaw, July 1947; children—John, Kathleen, Daniel, Margaret, Mary, Christopher, Matthew, Claire. B.A., Mt. St. Mary's Coll., Los Angeles, 1945; M.S., Calif. State U., Fullerton, 1968; Ph.D., U. So. Calif., 1973; postgrad. Loyola U. Law sch., 1982. Lic. ednl. psychologist, Calif., 1976, lic. real estate sales person, 1979. Tchr., Los Angeles schs., 1946-47, Downey Unified Sch. Dist., 1951-52, Whittier high schs. and adult sch., 1963-67, Fullerton high sch. dist., 1968-70; psychologist mental health team Fullerton Coll., 1971-72; sch. psychologist Los Angeles Unified Schs., 1972-77, behavior specialist, 1978-80, sr. sch. psychologist, 1977-78, 80—; lectr. Mt. St. Mary's Coll., 1970, Calif. State U., Calif. Lutheran Coll., 1976. Recipient Outstanding Vol. Award, Calif. Youth Authority, 1970. Mem. Am. Psychol. Assn, Los Angeles Assn. Sch. Psychologists. Democrat. Roman Catholic. Clubs: Buccaneer Yacht Club, San Pedro; Ladies Art and Culture Soc., Whittier. Author: Reading Differences Between Brain-Injured and non-Brain-Injured EH Students, 1968; Recidivism Differences Among Delinquent Teacher Aides to Handicapped, 1973.

TRYGSTAD, JOHN ERIC, coal mining co. exec.; b. Webster, S.D.; B.S. in Mining Engrng., S.D. Sch. Mines, 1975; m. Ruth Ann Starbuck; 1 son, Nels Erik. Union labor and engrng. positions Consolidation Coal Co., W.Va., 1970-74; prepration plant engr. Zapata Coal Co., Sharples, W.Va., 1975-76; research longwall engr. Colo. Sch. Mines at York Canyon Mine, Raton, N.Mex., 1976-77; preparation engr. Freeman United Coal, West Frankfort, Ill., 1977-81; preparation engr., ops. supt., GEX Colo., Inc., Palisade, 1981-82; ops. supt. Western Fuels-Utah, Inc., 1982—. Mem. Soc. Mining Engrs., AIME, Ill. Soc. Coal Preparation Engrs. (past pres.). Home: Box 389 Rangely CO 81648 Office: Box 1589 Rangely CO 8168

TRYNCHY, PETER, Canadian government official; b. Rochfort Bridge, Alta., Can., Aug. 22, 1931; s. Peter and Anna (Roszko) T.; m. Lorraine Mary Wilkinson, Oct. 29, 1952; children—Darlene Annette, Marlin Peter. Student public schs., Rochfort Bridge, Alta., Can. Mem. Mayerthorpe (Can.) Town Council, 19-; mem. Alta. Legis. Assembly, Edmonton, 1971—, minister Recreation and Parks, 1979—. Conservative. Clubs: Masons, Royal Can. Legion, Mayerthorne Curling.

TRZYNA, THADDEUS CHARLES, research institute director; b. Chgo., Oct. 26, 1939; s. Thaddeus Stephen and Irene Mary (Giese) T.; B.A., U. So. Calif., 1961; Ph.D., Claremont Grad. Sch., 1975; 1 dau., Jennifer. Fgn. service officer Dept. State, Washington and posts in Africa, 1962-69; pres., dir. Calif. Inst. Pub. Affairs, affiliate of Claremont Colls., 1969—; chmn. Calif. Farmlands Project, 1982—; cons. on natural resource policy to fed. and state agys.; mem. commn. on environ. planning Internat. Union for Conservation of Nature and Natural Resources, 1982—. Mem. Am. Fgn. Service Assn., Am. Planning Assn., Authors Guild, Royal Geog. Soc. (London), Sierra Club (v.p. 1975-77, Calif. legis. com. 1981—), Book Pubs. Assn. So. Calif. (pres. 1973-75). Democrat. Unitarian. Club: University (Claremont). Author: The California Handbook, 4th edit., 1981; The California Environmental Quality Act, 1974; World Directory of Environmental Organizations, 2d edit., 1976; Environmental Impact Requirements in the States, 1974. Office: 226 W Foothill Blvd Claremont CA 91711

TSANG, VICTOR WING-HONG, surgeon; b. Shanghai, China, May 8, 1934; s. Lawrence and Catherine (Ouyang) T.; student McMurry Coll., Abilene, Tex., 1956-58; M.D., M.S., Tulane U., 1962; m. Marie Wong, May 28, 1965; children—Stephen, Yvonne, Victoria. Intern, Detroit Meml. Hosp., 1962-63; resident in surgery Temple U. Hosp., Phila., 1963-65, Episcopal Hosp., Phila., 1965-66, Norfolk Gen. Hosp., 1966-67; practice medicine specializing in surgery, San Jose, Calif., 1971—; staff surgeon San Jose Hosp.,Alexian Bros. Hosp., Santa Teresa Hosp., O'Connor Hosp., Good Samaritan Hosp., Valley West Hosp., Los Gatos Hosp. Served to maj. M.C., U.S. Army, 1969-71. Decorated Bronze Star. Mem. San Jose Surg. Soc., Am. Soc. Abdominal Surgeons. Republican. Methodist. Home: 7192 Wooded Lake Dr San Jose CA 95120 Office: 2101 Alexian Dr Suite 105 San Jose CA 95116 also 275 Hospital Pkwy Suite 660 San Jose CA 95119

TSAU, WEN SHIUNG, civil engineer; b. Taiwan, July 22, 1946; came to U.S., 1973, naturalized, 1982; s. Chun Fu and Yu In (Yang) T. B.Archtl. Engrng., Tankang U., Taiwan, 1969; B.S.C.E., Northeastern U., 1978; M.S.C.E., U. Wyo., 1981. Civil engr. Taiwan Power Co., Taipei, 1970-73; project engr., insp. Johnson, Fermelia & Crank, Inc., Kemmerer, Wyo., 1981—; cons. served to 2d lt. Taiwanese Army Engrs. Sch., 1969-70. Mem. Nat. Soc. Profl. Engrs., ASCE, Concrete Reinforced Steel Inst., Sigma Xi, Tau Beta Pi. Home: PO Box 1552 Rock Springs WY 82901 Office: Johnson Fermelia & Crank Inc PO Box 631 722 Cedar Ave Kemmerer WY 83101

TSENG, GAN-TAI, aerospace corporation official; b. Chungking, China, Sept. 9, 1938; came to U.S., 1962, naturalized, 1973; s. Shao-hsuen and Yun-ying (Shieh) T.; B.S., Nat. Taiwan U., 1960; M.S., U. Calif., Berkeley, 1964; Engr. (univ. fellow), Stanford U., 1966; Ph.D. with distinction, UCLA, 1971; m. Joan J. Liu, Sept. 5, 1965; children—Carol, Michelle. Engrng. specialist, cons. Garrett-AiResearch, Los Angeles, 1966-72; postgrad. research engr. UCLA, 1969-70; sr. engrng. scientist RCA Astro-Electornics, Princeton, N.J., 1972-77; mgr. Aerospace Corp., El Segundo, Calif., 1977—; cons. Garrett Corp.; instr. UCLA; mem. tech. com. Def. Advanced Research Projects Agy. Recipient engrng. recognition award RCA, 1973; NASA Big Dipper award, 1974. Mem. AIAA, Am. Astronautical Soc., Sigma Xi. Reviewer for NSF, 1977-78; reviewer profl. jours. and confs.; contbr. articles on dynamics and control to profl. publs. Office: 2350 E El Segundo Blvd El Segundo CA 90245

TSOI, MANG-SO, immunologist; b. Hong Kong, Dec. 13, 1934; came to U.S., 1959, naturalized, 1972; d. Sui-Po and King-Chong (Chan) Leung; diploma Northcote Teachers Tng. Coll., Hong Kong, 1956; B.S. (scholar), Whitworth Coll., 1961; M.S., U. Wash., Seattle, 1963, Ph.D., 1966; children—Douglas, Kenneth. Tchr., sub-inspector schs. Edn. Dept., Hong Kong, 1956-59; trainee U. Wash., Seattle, 1961-66, research assoc. dept. microbiology, 1966-67, dept. medicine, 1972-75, research asst. prof. dept. medicine, 1975-79, research assoc. prof., 1979—; research assoc. Virginia Mason Research Center, Seattle, 1971-72; asso. mem. Fred Hutchinson Cancer Research Center, Seattle, 1979—. Research grantee Am. Cancer Soc., 1979—, Nat. Cancer Inst., 1974—. Mem. Am. Assn. Immunologists, Reticuloendothelial Soc., N.Y. Acad. Scis., AAUP, Sigma Xi. Contbr. research papers to profl. publs. Office: 1124 Columbia St Seattle WA 98104

TSUE, JOHN MASAICHI, optometrist; b. Hilo, Hawaii, Sept. 6, 1949; s. Jackson Masami and Susan (Tatsue) T. B.A. in Zoology, U. Hawaii, 1971; O.D., Pacific U., 1978. Cert. optometrist, Hawaii. Intern, Forest Grove, Oreg., 1977-78; sole practice optometry, Kailua-Kona, Hawaii, 1979—; cons., lectr. Served with U.S. Army, 1971-73. Recipient Nat. Eye Research Found. award, 1978; Western Interstate Commn. Higher Edn. grantee, 1974-78. Mem. Hawaii Optometric Assn. (dir. 1983), Kona Coast C. of C., Better Vision Inst., Am. Optometric Found., Am. Optometric Assn. (charter mem. contact lens sect.), Nat. Eye Research Found., Kona Jaycees (v.p. 1983), Phi Theta Upsilon. Baptist. Club: Hualalai Exchange (past dir., sec.).

TSUJIMOTO, HARRY Y., biologist; b. El Centro, Calif., Sept. 18, 1926; s. Roy R. and Miki (Hayashi) T.; B.S., Cornell U., 1951; M.S., U. Calif.-Berkeley, 1958; m. Grace Kase, Mar. 15, 1963. Asst. specialist expt. sta. U. Calif.-Berkeley, 1958-66, assoc. specialist, 1966-72, specialist in plant physiology, 1972—, lectr. photosynthesis, 1958—. Served with U.S. Army, 1945-46. Recipient Pres.'s and Regents' citation U. Calif., 1964. Mem. Am. Soc. Plant Physiologists, Am. Soc. Photobiology, DAV. Club: Marines Memorial. Contbr. numerous articles on plant physiology and photosynthesis to sci. jours. Office: Dept Molecular Plant Biology U Calif Berkeley CA 94720

TSUKAMOTO, DIANE YOKO, interior designer; b. San Jose, Calif., Nov. 16, 1951; d. Yoshimi Henry and Kikuko May (Fujita) T.; B.A. in Interior Design, San Jose State U., 1974. Interior designer Design Office Concepts, Inc., Santa Clara, Calif., 1974-77, Facilities Planning & Design, San Jose, 1977-80; designer Habitec Architecture & Planning, Santa Clara, 1978. dir. interior design Takamoto & Assos., San Jose, 1980—. Mem. Am. Soc. Interior Designers (sec. Calif. Peninsula Chpt.). Buddhist. Office: 12 S First St Suite 520 San Jose CA 95113

TSUKIJI, RICHARD ISAO, business exec., investment cons.; b. Salt Lake City, Jan. 31, 1946; s. Isamu and Mitsuie (Hayashi) T.; grad. Sacramento City Coll., 1966; A.A., U. Pacific, McGeorge Sch. Law, 1970-72; m. Laura Elaine Gomes, Aug. 1976; children—Angela Jo, Richard Michael. Grocery mgr. Food Mart, Inc., Sacramento, 1963-65; agy. supr. Takehara Ins. Agy., Sacramento, 1965-68; sales rep. Kraft Foods Co., Sacramento, 1969-71; sales mgr. Olivetti Corp., Sacramento, 1972-73; co-founder Mktg. Devel. and Mgmt. Coll., Sacramento, 1973, pres., 1973-74; pres. Richard Tsukiji Corp., Sacramento, 1974-77; chief exec. officer Assos. Investment Group, San Diego, 1978-80, chmn. bd., 1978-82; chmn. bd. RichColor Corp. Sacramento, 1978-80, E.J. Sub Factories, Inc., Elk Grove, Calif., 1978-80, Phoenix Industries, Las Vegas, 1981—, Phoenix Industries, Inc., Carson City, Nev., 1981—; dir. LeRich Enterprises, Databank, Inc., Roseburg, Oreg.; gen. agt. Comml. Bankers Life Ins. Co., Los Angeles, 1974-82; mem. area Adv. Council of Western Oreg. Health Systems Agy., 1981—. mem. exec. bd., 1981-82; Computer World, Sacramento Mem. Yolo County Oral Rev. Bd., 1975-76, Calif. Quality Appraisal Panel, 1978-79; bd. dirs. Valley Area Constrn. Opportunity Program, 1972-76, chmn., 1976-77; active ARC, Citizens for Community Involvement. Served with U.S. Army, 1962-63. Recipient commendation Calif. Senate, 1978. Mem. Internat. Assn. Fin. Planners, Associated Gen. Contractors, San Diego Jaycees (dir. 1977-78), Umpqua Valley Arts Assn., Oreg. Assn. Edn. of Young Children, Asian Alliance, Japanese Am. Citizens League. Democrat. Roman Catholic. Club: Moose. Office: 2527 N Carson St Suite 205 Carson City NV 89701

TUBBS, HAROLD EDWARD, interior designer; b. Rochester, N.Y., Mar. 5, 1949; s. Donald F. and Norma H. (Langridge) T.; B.F.A., Chapman Coll., 1971; m. Terese A. Guarnera, Dec. 20, 1970; 1 son, Ian D. Jr. designer Diversified Design, Orange, Calif., 1969-71; interior designer Environments, Newport Beach, Calif., 1971-72; pvt. practice interior design, Orange, 1972-73; prin. designer, interior planning and design Contract Design of Jackson Hole, Jackson, Wyo., 1973—. Bd. dirs. Elaena B. Hunt Art Found., 1980-81; active local sch. system. Mem. Am. Soc. Interior Design (profl.), AIA (profl. affiliate). Club: Rotary. Office: PO Box II 410 W Pearl St Jackson WY 83001

TUBBS, JOHN CHARLES, accountant, consultant; b. Bryan, Tex., July 29, 1939; s. Leo G. and Mildred L. (Perkins) T.; m. Marilyn J. Hayes, Aug. 29, 1960; children—Carol L., Penny J., John A., Stephen B. Student, Tex. A&M U., 1957-58; B.B.A. in Acctg., U. Houston, 1963. C.P.A., N.Mex., Tex. Acct. W.S. Bellows Constrn. Co., Houston, 1962-63; mng. ptnr. Santa Fe office Peat, Marwick, Mitchell & Co., 1964-81; pvt. practice acctg., cons., Santa Fe, 1981—; creator, gen. ptnr. Footsteps Across N.Mex. Hist. Theater. Bd. dirs. United Way, 1970-76; dir. Bapt. Found. of N.Mex., 1981-82; treas., Sunday Sch. tchr. First Bapt. Ch. of Santa Fe. Recipient Boss of Yr. award Santa Fe Jaycees, 1979. Mem. Am. Inst. C.P.A.s, N.Mex. Soc. C.P.A.s, Santa Fe C. of C. (treas. dir. 1979-82). Democrat. Club: Sangre de Cristo Racquet.

TUBIS, SEYMOUR, painter, printmaker, sculptor, educator; b. Phila., Sept. 20, 1919; student Temple U., 1937-39, Phila. Mus. Sch. Art, 1941-42, Art Students League of N.Y., 1946-49, Academie Grande-Chaumiere, Paris, 1949-50, Instituto d'Arte, Florence, Italy, 1950; student of Hans Hofmann, N.Y.C., 1951. Pvt. tchr. art, N.Y.C., Rockport, Mass., 1948-60; tchr. art, summerprogram Bd. Edn., Great Neck, N.Y., 1949; asst. instr. Art Students League of N.Y., 1948, 49, Bklyn. Mus. Sch. Art, 1950-51; instr. N.Y.C. Adult Edn. Program, 1950-52; head dept. fine arts, instr. printmaking, painting and design Inst. of Am. Indian Arts, Santa Fe, 1963-80. One-man shows at Galerie St. Placide, Paris, 1950, Lowe Found. Galleries, N.Y.C., 1953, 55, Taft Sch., Conn., 1953, La Chapelle Gallery, Santa Fe, 1960, Mus. N.Mex., Santa Fe, 1964, Accents Gallery, Cleve., 1966, U. Calgary (Alta., Can.), 1967, Jamison Galleries, Santa Fe, 1967, N.Mex. State Library, Santa Fe, 1968, Coll. of Santa Fe, 1969, The New West, Albuquerque, 1969, 71, 72, 73, Gallery Contemporary Art, Taos, 1969, Antioch Coll., Balt. and Washington, 1973, numerous others; exhibited in group shows at Library of Congress, Carnegie Inst., Bklyn. Mus., Pa. Acad. Fine Arts, Dallas Mus. Art, Syracuse U., Royal Soc., London, Eng., Hofstra Coll., Asso. Gallery Art, Detroit, Riverside Mus., N.Y.C., Met. Mus. Art, N.Y.C., Seattle Art Mus., Dept. Interior, Dept. State Embassies Program, Mus. Modern Art, N.Y.C., Mus. of N.Mex., St. John's Coll., Santa Fe, Mus. Internat. Folk Art, Santa Fe, Pa. State Coll., Wichita Art Assn., John F. Kennedy Center for Performing Arts, Washington, also others; represented in permanent collections Library of Congress, Soc. Am. Graphic Artists, Met. Mus. Art, Pa. State Coll., U. Ariz., U. Calgary, Joe and Emily Lowe Found., Art Students League N.Y., U.S. Dept. Interior, Antioch Coll., also numerous pvt. collections; artist-cons. N.Y. World-Telegram and Sun, 1955-59, St. John's Coll., 1960, Mus. of N.Mex., 1960, N.Y. Times, 1961-63; research grantee U. Ariz., U. Calif.-Santa Barbara. Recipient 4th purchase award in painting Joe and Emily Lowe Found., 1st prize in painting Newspaper Guild N.Y., purchase award Mus. of N.Mex.; Nat. Endowment Arts grantee, 1980. Mem. Soc. Am. Graphic Artists (1st prize in etching), Art Students League N.Y., Coll. Art Assn. Home: 164 E MacArthur St Sonoma CA 95476

TUCHMAN, RALPH GREGORY, clergyman, audio-visual consultant; b. N.Y.C., Sept. 21, 1919; s. Herman and Anna (Gregory) T.; m. Fran Harris, June 26, 1949. B.S., NYU, 1939; M.S., Northwestern U., 1941. Ordained to ministry United Ch. of Religious Sci., 1976; reporter, editor Broadcasting Mag., 1942-49; head Harris-Tuchman Prodns., Inc., Burbank, Calif., 1950—; minister Burbank-Toluca Lake 1st Ch. of Religious Sci., 1973—. Founding incorporator Big Bros. Greater Los Angeles, 1953, past dir., now mem. adv. council. Served to capt. USAAF, 1943-46. Mem. Profl. Journalists Soc.

TUCK, LARRY GEORGE, health and safety administrator, loss control consultant, industrial hygienist; b. Lyons, N.Y., Apr. 3, 1949; s. George Vivian and Muriel Mary (Borys) T.; m. Deborah Marie, Nov. 11, 1979; children—Chris, Danny, Troy. B.A. in Psychology and Econ., Calif. State U. Hayward, 1975; M.S. in Safety, U. So. Calif., 1980. Claims Examiner State Comprehensive Ins. Fund, San Jose, Calif., 1976-77; sr. safety engr. Amdahl Corp., Sunnyvale, Calif., 1977-79; sr. loss control cons. Western Employers Ins., San Bruno, Calif., 1979-80; health and safety mgr. TRW, E.S.L. and Aertech, Sunnyvale, 1980—. Instr. ARC, CPR and First Aid. Served with USAF, 1969-71. Mem. Am. Soc. Safety Engrs., Am. Indsl. Hygiene Assn., Nat. Safety Mgmt. Soc., Risk Ins. Mgmt. Soc., Nat. Safety Council, Nat. Fire Protection Assn. Republican. Home: 2691 Toy Ln San Jose CA 95121 Office: 495 Java Dr Sunnyvale CA 94086

TUCKER, DONALD M., musician, educator; b. Portland, Oreg., Mar. 23, 1947; s. John H. and Dorothy L. (McDonald) T.; B.A. in Music Edn., Portland State U., 1973; M.A. in Music Edn., Lewis and Clark Coll., 1979. Dir. music Mt. Scott Park Presbyn. Ch., Portland, 1966-71, Tigard United Meth. Ch., 1972-74, Moreland Presbyn. Ch., Portland, 1979—; high sch. vocal music tchr.; tenor soloist, 1964—; performances include: Portland Chamber Orch., 1968, Peter Britt Festival Orch., 1968, Oreg. Symphony Orch. and Portland Symphonic Choir, 1970, First Christian Ch., Portland, 1977-78; asst. choral condr. Peter Britt Music Festival, 1968; condr.-dir. Portland Civic Choralaires, 1972-73; performer mus. prodns. including: The Mikado, The Marriage of Figaro, Goyescas, Of Thee I Sing, Oklahoma, Ab Hassan; condr. mus. prodns. including: Schubert Mass in G, Missa Brevis in F Major, Music Man, Vivaldi Gloria, Messiah, Britten Ceremony of Carols, Hovhaness Glory to God; mus. compositions include: (introit) Praise the Lord Alleluia, (prayer response) Hear Our Prayer O Lord, (anthem) Psalm 150, (Christmas introit) Gloria Et in Excelsis Deo, (congregation hymn) Sing and Rejoice, Rondo in A Major for Handbells, Variations on a Theme for Handbells, benedictional and offertory responses, solo compositions for tenor. Cert. dir. of music United Meth. Ch. Mem. Am. Choral Dirs., Am. Guild of English Handbell Ringers, Choristers Guild, Fellowship of United Meth. Musicians, Music Educators Nat. Conf., Nat. Assns. Teachers of Singing (guest adjudicator state voice scholorship auditions, 1977-78; 79-80), Am. Hymn Soc., Assn. Supervision and Curriculum Devel., Nat. Retired Teachers Assn., Phi Mu Alpha Sinfonia. Democrat. Methodist. Club: Masons. Home and office: 1615 SE Malden St Portland OR 97202

TUCKER, GORDON CHARLES, JR., archaeologist; b. Seattle, Dec. 20, 1950; s. Gordon Charles and Maureen Theresa (Robbins) T.; B.A., Western Wash. State Coll., 1972; M.A., Idaho State U., 1976; Ph.D., U. Colo., 1981; m. Kathleen Anne Rhudy, May 31, 1980. Grad. and teaching asst. Idaho State U., 1974-76, U. Colo., 1977-80; sr. staff archaeologist Nickens & Assocs., Montrose, Colo., 1980—; tchr. Idaho State U., U. Colo. Museums. Mem. AAAS, N.Y. Acad. Scis., Soc. Am. Archaeology, Sigma Xi. Democrat. Contbr. articles to profl. jours. Research on archaeology of Pacific N.W., Great Basin and Am. S.W. Office: Nickens & Assocs PO Box 727 Montrose CO 81401

TUCKER, HOWARD GREGORY, mathematics educator; b. Lawrence, Kans., Oct. 3, 1922; s. Louis H. and Jeannette A. (Garbarsky) T. B.A., U. Calif.-Berkeley, 1948, M.A., 1949, Ph.D., 1955. Instr. math., Rutgers U., New Brunswick, N.J., 1952-53; assoc. in math. U. Calif.-Berkeley, 1953-55; asst. prof. U. Oreg., Eugene, 1955-56; from asst. prof. to prof. U. Calif.-Riverside, 1956-68; prof. math., U. Calif.-Irvine, 1968—; mem. Inst. for Advanced Study, Princeton, N.J., 1963-64. Served with USN, 1942-46. Fellow Inst. Math. Stats.; mem. Am. Math. Soc., Math. Assn. Am., Am. Statis. Assn., Biometrics Soc. Author: An Introduction to Probability and Mathematical Statistics, 1962; A Graduate Course in Probability, 1967; contbr. research papers in probability and math. stats. to profl. jours. Office: Dept Math U Calif Irvine CA 92717

TUCKER, JAMES DAVID, manufacturing company executive; b. Mpls., Jan. 24, 1937; s. Gordon and Margaret Ann (Pilney) T.; B.A. cum laude in Econs., U. Minn., 1960; M.B.A. in Fin., U. Pa., 1961; m. Katherine Ann Hart, Nov. 28, 1964; children—Molly, Scott, Kevin, Ryan. Mgmt. cons. A.T. Kearney, Inc., 1965-70; pres., chief exec. officer Nimrod Inc., 1970-74; mgmt. cons., 1975-76; gen. partner Mgmt. Partners, Newport Beach, Calif., 1977—; interim exec. spl. projects HammerBlow Corp., Wausau, Wis., 1977-80; chief exec. officer Dakota Bake N Serv, Jamestown, N.D., 1978-79; chmn. bd., chief exec. officer Laguna Mfg. Co., Irvine, Calif. 1980-83; v.p., dir. Taylor Chain Co., Hammond, Ind., 1980-83; sec.-treas., dir. Supreme Castings & Pattern Co., Anaheim, Calif., 1981—; chmn. bd. Newport Controls, Inc., Santa Ana, Calif., 1982—. Recipient Design citation Am. Iron and Steel Inst., 1973. Mem. Assn. Corp. Growth. Roman Catholic. Club: Balboa Yacht. Home 1824 Port Sheffield Pl Newport Beach CA 92660

TUCKER, JAMES STEPHEN, priest, psychotherapist, coll. dean; b. Detroit, Apr. 14, 1943; s. Joseph George and Mary (Perinovic) T.; B.A., St. John's Coll., 1965; M.A., Calif. State U., 1977; M.S., Pacific Grad. Sch. Psychology, 1981, Ph.D., 1983. Ordained priest Roman Catholic Ch., 1969; exec. dir. East Valley Family Services, Los Angeles, 1971-74; prof. psychology St. Mary's Sem. and Univ., Balt., 1974-77; psychotherapist Cath. Social Services Sacramento, 1977-78; chmn. dept. psychology and dean of admissions St. Joseph's Coll., Mountainview, Calif., 1978—; pvt. practice psychoanalysis, Mountainview, 1978—; clin. dir. Pastoral Services Center, 1981—. Lic. clin. hypnotist, family therapist, Calif.; diplomate Am. Inst. Clin. Psychology. Fellow Masters and Johnson

Inst.; mem. Santa Clara County Psychol. Assn., Christian Assn. Psychol. Studies, Am. Assn. Marriage and Family Therapy. Author: Marriage Encounter: Christian Ontology/Humanistic Psychology, 1977; A Demographic Study of the College Seminarian, 1978; Psychoanalytic Lectures, 1979; A Psychological Study of the College Seminarian, 1980; Countertransference with the Clergy Patient, 1980; Object Relations Theory and Clinical Dream Analysis, 1980; Demographic, Clinical and Personality Variables of the Effective Roman Catholic Seminary Student, 1982. Address: St Joseph's Coll PO Box 7009 Mountainview CA 94039

TUCKER, JOHN ELLIOT, social worker, psychologist; b. San Jose, Calif., Jan. 12, 1934; s. Ernest Hunigton and Mary (Ogrodnick) T.; B.A., San Jose State U.; M.A., U. Mich., 1972; Ph.D., U. Santo Tomas, 1978; m. Roselie Iccovetta, June 23, 1964; children—John Elliot, Margo Lynn. Sci. coordinator Alamo (Calif.) Sch. Dist., 1960-62; tchr. Dept. of Def. Schs., Germany, France, Japan, Philippines, 1962-78; ednl. social worker, psychologist Subic-San Miguel Public Schs., 1978-81; social worker family advocacy Subic-San Miguel Naval Dasc; tchr. clin. psychology U. Santo Tomas, Philippines, 1978-81; pastor Ch. of Superiority and Social Interest, Universal Life Ch. Served with AUS, 1956-58. Mem. Am. Psychol. Assn., Nat. Assn. Social Workers, NEA. Research on family constellation in large group psychol. edn., early recollections, creative behavior, delinquent thought. Home and Office: Box 70 K FPO San Francisco CA 96651

TUCKER, JOHN RICHARD, JR., archtl. rendering and design co. exec.; b. Brownsville, Tex., Nov. 12, 1949; s. John Richard T.; student Grossmont Coll., 1974-76. Sr. draftsman PRC Tech. Applications, San Diego, 1976-78; archtl. designer, draftsman Cubic Corp., San Diego, 1978-79; archtl. designer, engr., estimator Archtl. Engring. Products Co., San Diego, 1980-81; owner Archtl. Rendering & Design Co., El Cajon, Calif., 1981—. Served with USAF, 1969-73. Mem. Nat. Soc. Profl. Engrs., Calif. Soc. Profl. Engrs., Am. Inst. Design and Drafting, Am. Soc. Metals. Democrat. Methodist. Clubs: San Diego MG, San Diego MGA Register, San Diego MG —T— Register. Address: Archtl Rendering & Design Co 15420 Olde Hwy 80 SP153 El Cajon CA 92021

TUCKER, KERRY DENNIS, public relations agency executive; b. Oakland, Calif., June 6, 1947; s. Harold F. and Mary I. (Cooper) T.; m. Linda J. Morris, Nov. 11, 1972; children—Brannan, Blake. Student Am. River Coll., 1965-67; B.A. in Govt., Journalism, Calif. State U.-Sacramento, 1969, postgrad., 1969-70; postgrad. NYU, 1979. Dir. pub. relations Sacramento Capitols Football Team, 1969-70; dir. communications Calif. Trial Lawyers Assn., Sacramento, 1970-72, Dairy Council Calif., Sacramento, 1972-80; ptnr., exec. v.p. Nuffer/Smith Assocs., Inc. San Diego, 1980—; cons. Calif. Dairy Mus. and Ednl. Found.; mem. pres.'s council Bank Rancho Bernardo; instr. Calif. State U.-San Diego. Cons. Tweedt for Calif. Assembly campaign, 1974, Johnson for County Supr., Sacramento, 1978; bd. dirs. Notre Dame Sch. Patrons Club, 1979-80. Served with USAFR, 1966-71. Mem. Pub. Relations Soc. Am. (past local chpt. officer), Sacramento Press Club, Sigma Delta Chi (past chpt. officer). Republican. Roman Catholic. Developed public relations course for Calif. State U., Sacramento, 1972. Contbr. articles to profl. jours. and local mags. Home: 17717 Corazon Pl San Diego CA 92127 Office: Nuffer/Smith Assocs Inc 2560 1st Ave San Diego CA 92103

TUCKER, ROCKWELL GILBERT, counselor; b. Bismarck, N.D., Oct. 29, 1941; s. Paul McClure and Maxine Elaine (Gilbert) T.; divorced; 1 son, Randall Shawn. B.S. in Elec. Engring., U. Mo., 1965; M.S. in Oceanography, Tex. A&M U., 1972; B.S. in Indsl. Edn., Oreg. State U., 1976; M.S., Oreg. Coll. Edn., 1980. Elec. engr. Boeing Co., Seattle, 1965-69; research asst. dept. oceanography Tex. A&M Coll. Station, 1969-72, Oreg. State U. Coll. Oceanography, Corvallis, 1972-75; lab. aide Linn-Benton Community Coll., Albany, Oreg., 1975-76; project engr. Peabody Flomatcher, Corvallis, 1977-78; cons., counselor State of N.C. and Duke U. Marine Lab., Beaufort, N.C., 1978-79; counselor, counselor mgr. Cry of Love, Northwest Human Services, Salem, Oreg., 1980—. Mem. bd. Unity Ch., Salem. Mem. Audubon Soc. (past pres. Corvallis), Am. Personnel and Guidance Assn., Oreg. Personnel and Guidance Assn. Contbr. articles to profl. publs. Home: 776 B Lockhaven Dr NE Salem OR 97303 Office: 2303 Fairgrounds Rd NE Salem OR 97303

TUCKER, WANDA HALL, newspaper editor, columnist; b. Los Angeles, Feb. 6, 1921; d. Frank Walliston and Hazel Gladys (Smith) Hall; A.A., Citrus Coll., 1939; m. Frank R. Tucker, Apr. 16, 1943; children—Frank Robert, Nancy Irene. Society editor Azusa (Calif.) Herald, 1939-42, editor, 1942-43; city editor San Marino (Calif.) Tribune, 1943-45; editor Canyon City (Calif.) News, 1953; reporter Pasadena (Calif.) Star-News, 1953-73, city editor, 1973-75, day mng. editor, 1975, mng. editor, 1975-81, sr. mng. editor, 1981—, dir. internship program, 1976-79, mem. editorial bd., 1982—. Recipient writing award Calif. Newspaper Pubs. Assn., 1965; named Woman of Year, Pasadena Women's Civic League, 1974, Pasadena chpt. NAACP, 1977, Emer Bates Meml. award, 1981. Mem. Greater Los Angeles Press Club (writing awards 1971-72), Sigma Delta Chi. Office: 525 E Colorado Blvd Pasadena CA 91109

TUDDENHAM, WILLIAM MARVIN, chemist; b. Salt Lake City, July 8, 1924; s. William Calder and Laura (Pack) T.; B.A. in Chemistry, U. Utah, 1947, M.A. in Chemistry, 1948, Ph.D. in Fuels, 1954; m. Dorothy Evelyn Snelgrove, May 1, 1945; children—William Marvin, Mary Alice, Evelyn, Laurie. Research chemist color control dept. Eastman Kodak Co., Rochester, N.Y., 1948-50; sr. scientist Research Center Kennecott Copper Corp., Salt Lake City, 1953-59, research sect. chief, 1959-72, mgr. analytical techniques dept., 1972-78, dir. analytical services Utah Copper div., 1978-80; mgr. product quality projects and process tech. Kennecott Minerals Co., Salt Lake City, 1980-83, ret., 1983. Served with USNR, 1944-45. Recipient Silver Beaver award Great Salt Lake council Boy Scouts Am., 1978. Mem. Am. Chem. Soc. (sec.-treas. Salt Lake sect. 1957-58, chmn. 1961, councilor 1970-71, 73—, Utah award Salt Lake sect. 1973), AIME, Sigma Xi, Alpha Chi Sigma. Republican. Mormon. Contbr. articles to profl. jours. Home: 1828 Lincoln St Salt Lake City UT 84105

TUFTY, JAMES VAN WAGONER, advertising executive; b. Evanston, Ill., Mar. 11, 1929; s. Harold Guilford and Esther Ellen (Van Wagoner) T.; m. Mary Elizabeth White, June 3, 1967; children—Patti Alyn, James Jr., Valentina Ivern. B.A. in Journalism and Advt., Mich. State U., 1953; postgrad. Alliance Francaise, Paris, 1963. Field rep. Young and Rubicam, Inc., N.Y.C., 1956-58, asst. all-media buyer, Chgo., 1958-60, sr. all-media buyer, Los Angeles, 1960-62; journalist Tufty News Service, Paris, 1962-64, sec. treas., Washington, 1956—; media dir. Am. Bakers Coop, Teaneck N.J., 1964-65; supr., account rep. J. Walter Thompson Co., Washington, 1965-72; pres., chmn. bd. Ad Agy., Inc. Washington, 1971-81, Communications Sales, Inc., Washington, 1975-81; pres., chmn. bd. Aloha Advt. Inc., Honolulu, 1981—. Served with U.S. Army, 1953-56. Mem. Nat. Press Club. Presbyterian. Home: 6614 Kauna St Honolulu HI 96825 Office: Aloha Advt Inc PO Box 25310 Honolulu HI 96825

TUKEY, HAROLD BRADFORD, JR., horticultural science educator; b. Geneva, N.Y., May 29, 1934; s. Harold Bradford and Ruth Schweigert) T.; B.S., Mich. State U., 1955, M.S., 1956, Ph.D., 1958; m. Helen Dunbar Parker, June 25, 1955; children—Ruth Thurbon, Carol Cameron, Harold Bradford. Research asst. AEC, 1955-58; postdoctoral fellow NSF, 1958-59; asst. prof. dept. floriculture and ornamental horticulture Cornell U., 1959-64, asso. prof., 1964-70, prof., 1970-80; cons. P.R. Nuclear Ctr., 1965-66; vis. prof. U. Calif.-Davis, 1973; prof., dir. arboreta, dir. Ctr. Urban Hort., U. Wash., Seattle, 1980—; internat. lectr.; mem. various coms. NRC/Nat. Acad. Sci.; cons. Electric Power Research Inst., 1976-83; hort. cons. Internat. Bonsai, 1979—; with IAEA Radioisotope Sch., Hanover, W.Ger., 1968; exec. v.p. Arbor Fund, Seattle, 1982-83, pres., 1983—. Co-pres. Ithaca (N.Y.) PTA; mem. Ithaca Social Planning Council; active Tompkins County United Fund. Served to lt. U.S. Army, 1958. Recipient Travel awards Cornell U., 1962, 75; U. Nebr. vis. scholar, 1982; NSF postdoctoral fellow, 1958-59. Mem. Internat. Plant Propagators Soc. (internat. pres. 1976), Am. Soc. Hort. Sci. (exec. com. 1978-79), Am. Hort. Soc. (dir. 1972-81), Internat. Soc. Hort. Sci. (U.S. del. to council 1971—, exec. com. 1974—, v.p. 1978-82, pres. 1982-86), Bot. Soc. Am. (travel award 1964), Am. Soc. Plant Physiologists, N.W. Ornamental Hort. Soc. (hon. dir.), Pi Alpha Xi, Alpha Zeta, Sigma Xi. Club: Rotary (pres. 1973-74). Editor: Horticulture for the People, 1981; contbr. articles to profl. jours. Home: 3300 E Saint Andrews Way Seattle WA 98112 Office: Center Urban Hort U Wash AR-10 Seattle WA 98195

TULLER, WENDY JUDGE, oil co. ofcl.; b. Cranston, R.I., Dec. 17, 1943; d. Alfred Carmen and Anna Louise (Waterman) Judge. A.B., Brown U., 1965; M.L.S., U. R.I., 1969. Librarian, Providence Public Schs., 1965-69; mgr. various locations Xerox Corp., 1969-75; mgr. Carter Hawley Hale Stores, Inc., Los Angeles, 1976; cons. Sibson & Co., Inc., Princeton, N.J., 1976-78; coordinator Atlantic Richfield Co., Los Angeles, 1978—. Mem. Am. Soc. Personnel Adminstrn., Am. Soc. Tng. and Devel., Internat. Assn. Personnel Women, AAUW (v.p. local chpt. 1979-80). Club: Los Angeles Athletic. Home: 222 S Figueroa St Los Angeles CA 90012 Office: 515 S Flower St Los Angeles CA 90071

TULLIUS, MARILYN ADELE WINSLOW, mgmt. cons.; b. Grants Pass, Oreg., Sept. 10, 1937; d. Marion Blaine and Hilma Josephine (Hendrickson) Winslow; B.A., Lewis and Clark Coll., 1958; M.S. in Mktg., Grad. Sch. Mgmt., UCLA, 1967; m. James A. Tullius, July 11, 1969 (div. 1980); children—Marsten Elissa, Eden Erin. Market analyst, indsl. systems div. Hughes Aircraft Co., 1968-70; market research analyst Arcata Data Mgmt. Co., 1970-71; sr. cons. IMA, Inc., Sherman Oaks, Calif., 1971-72, Marcom Applied Systems, Inc., Sherman Oaks., 1972-73; prin. Tullius Assos., mgmt. cons., Los Angeles, 1974—; guest lectr. bus. planning topics; instr. mktg. Calif. State U., Long Beach, 1979. Mem. Assn. Corp. Growth, So. Calif. Corp. Planners Assn. (v.p. programs 1982-83, v.p. membership 1983-84), UCLA Sch. Mgmt. Alumni Assn., Tech. Opportunities Council (vice chmn. program devel.), Mu Phi Epsilon (pres. Beverly Hills chpt. 1969-71). Home: 234 Entrada Dr Santa Monica CA 90402 Office: Tullius and Assos 520 S Sepulveda Blvd Suite 307 Los Angeles CA 90049

TULLOCH, JAMES MACDONALD, ins. co. exec.; b. Racine, Wis., Mar. 5, 1924; s. Thomas MacDonald and Mabel (Peterson) T.; B.A., Carleton Coll., Minn., 1949; m. Shirley Jordan, May 19, 1943; children—Tara Nancy, Thomas Scott, Gail Jean. Underwriter, Federated Mut. Ins. Cos., Owatonna, Minn., 1949-53; casualty underwriting mgr. Integrity Mut. Casualty Ins. Co., Appleton, Wis., 1953-57; actuarial and underwriting mgr. Nat. Farmers Union Ins. Cos., Denver, 1957-67, dir. research and planning, 1967-68; actuary Dairyland Ins. Co., Madison, Wis., 1968-69, v.p. and actuary, 1969-71, pres., Scottsdale, Ariz., 1971—, also dir.; chmn. and dir. Dairyland County Mut. Ins. Co.; dir. Sentry Life Ins. Co., Sentry Indemnity, United Bank. Bd. dirs. Scottsdale YMCA, Dairyland Found., Scottsdale Baptist Ch. Served with USAF, 1942-46; PTO. Mem. Phoenix Met. C. of C. (dir.), Nat. Assn. Ind. Insurers (dir.), Am. Mgmt. Assn. Clubs: Rotary, Ariz. Country, Camelback Golf, Mesa Country. Office: 9501 E Shea Blvd Scottsdale AZ 85258

TULLOCH-REID, ELMA DEEN, consultant, educator; b. Erie, Pa., June 27, 1938; d. Theodore and Roberta (Hicks) Carlisle; children—Robynne and Stacey (twins). B.S., N.C. Agrl. and Tech. State U., 1960; M.A., Calif. State U., 1977; Ed.D., Nova U., 1981. Staff nurse Michael Reese Hosp., Chgo., 1960-62; instr. Cook County Sch. Nursing, Chgo., 1962-64; tchr. St. Joseph Convent, Trinidad, W.I., 1964-66; med.-surg. coordinator St. Vincent Coll. Nursing, Los Angeles, 1967-69, med.-surg. coordinator, 1967-69; charge nurse Century City Hosp., Los Angeles, 1971-72; tchr. Los Angeles Unified Schs., 1972-75; instr. inservice dept. St. Vincent Med. Ctr., Los Angeles, 1972-75; dir. edn. and tng. Imperial Hosp., Inglewood, Calif., 1977-79; pres. Elma Tulloch-Reid Assocs., Los Angeles, 1981—; asst. prof. dept. continuing edn. Calif. State U.-Long Beach, 1977-81, assoc. prof., 1982—; provider Advanced Life Support in Cardiopulmonary Resuscitation, Am. Heart Assn., 1982-84, community instr. cert. basic life support Los Angeles Cardio-Pulmonary Resuscitation Consortium, 1981-82. Mem. Nat. Assn. Profl. Cons., Nat. Orgn. Mothers of Twins, Am. Nurses Found., Nat. Assn. Female Execs., N.C. Agrl. and Tech. State U. Alumni Assn., AAUW, Phi Kappa Phi. Club: Westside Mothers Twins (pres. 1971-73). Home: 1056 Cochran Ave Los Angeles CA 90019 Office: Wilshire Blvd 36A47 Los Angeles CA 90036

TULLY, DARROW, publisher; b. Charleston, W.Va., Feb. 27, 1932; s. William Albert and Dora (McCann) T.; student Purdue U., 1951; B.A. in Journalism, St. Joseph's Coll., 1972; Ph.D. in Journalism (hon.), Calumet Coll., 1975; m. Patricia Ann Fellner, Oct. 11, 1974; children—Bonnie Tully Paul, Michael Andrew. Vice pres., gen. mgr. Sta.-WDSM-AM-FM-TV, Duluth, Minn., 1956-59; bus. mgr. Duluth Herald & News Tribune, 1960-62; gen. mgr. St. Paul Dispatch & Pioneer Press, 1962-66; pub. Gary (Ind.) Post-Tribune, 1966-73; v.p., pub. Wichita (Kans.) Eagle & Beacon, 1973-75; pres., San Francisco Newspaper Agy., 1975-78; exec. v.p., pub. Ariz. Republic & Phoenix Gazette, 1978—; trustee Calumet Coll., Am. Grad. Sch. Internat. Mgmt. Bd. dirs. Phoenix Art Mus., Ariz. State U. Found., COMPAS, Newspaper Advt. Bur., Indsl. Relations Bur.; trustee Pacific Basin Inst.; mem. Ariz.-Mex. Commn. Mem. Am. Newspaper Pubs. Assn. (vice chmn. labor and personnel com.), Am. Soc. Newspaper Editors, Ariz. Newspaper Assn., Council on Fgn. Relations, Com. on the Present Danger Inter-Am. Press Assn., Sigma Delta Chi. Author: Minority Representation in the Media, 1968. Home: 7201 N Redledge Dr Paradise Valley AZ 85253 Office: 120 E Van Buren St Phoenix AZ 85004

TULLY, WILLIAM JIRD, financial corporation executive; b. Angola, Ind., Aug. 27, 1929; s. Mark James and Vera D. (Dirrim) T.; m Luetta May Tesmer, Mar. 16, 1957; children—Kathleen, Patricia, William, Alice. B.S.E.E. and B.S.I.E., Bowie Coll. Engring., Tucson, 1954; B.A. in Econs., Calif. State U.-Los Angeles, 1960; B.A. in Acctg., Calif. State U.-Long Beach, 1961; B.A. in Fin., Calif. State U.-Fullerton, 1966; J.D., U. West Los Angeles, 1969; M.B.A. and Ph.D. in Bus. Adminstrn., All Am. U., San Bernardino, Calif., 1974, LL.D. (hon.), 1975; LL.B., La Salle Extension U., Chgo., 1962, Blackstone Coll. Law, 1962, Am. Extension Sch. Law, 1962. Founder, pres. All Am. Fin. Services, 1958, All Am. Mining Corp., 1968, All Am. U., 1970, All Am. Mfg. Corp., 1977, All Am. Fin. Corp., 1977. Served with N.G., 1948-50. Republican. Methodist. Club: Masons. Contbr. articles to profl. jours. Invented All Am. Diesel Engine Series. Address: 634 E Yale St Ontario CA 91764

TUPIN, ROHNNIE LYNN, training executive; b. Gorman, Tex., Mar. 30, 1946; d. Willie and Ernesteen (Matthews) T.; children—Tegan L., Eric P. B.S., N. Tex. State U., 1969, M.Ed., 1971. Tchr. pub. schs., Irving, Tex., 1969-71, Silverton, Tex., 1971-77; supr. Levi Strauss & Co., Amarillo, Tex., 1977-80, tng. mgr., 1980-81; tng. coordinator, Zia Co., Los Alamos, N.Mex., 1981—. Mem. Am. Soc. Tng. and Devel., Tex. State Tchrs. Assn. Baptist.

TURCHIK, STEVE PAUL, educator; b. Ashtabula, Ohio, Feb. 23, 1927; s. Michael and Magda (Kerkes) T.; B.S. in Bus. Adminstrn., Kent State U., 1954, B.S. in Edn., 1954; M.S. in Edn., U. So. Calif., 1956; m. Wilma, Oct. 4, 1958; 1 dau., Stephie Ann. Buyer trainee Carlisle-Allen Co., Ashtabula, 1955-56; tchr. bus. Twenty-nine Palms (Calif.) High Sch., 1956-57, Anaheim (Calif.) High Sch., 1957-60; instr. bus. Ventura (Calif.) Coll., 1960-65; tchr. bus. Santa Paula (Calif.) High Sch., 1963-82, treas., chmn. bus. dept., 1966-71. Bd. dirs. Boys Clubs of Santa Paula, 1967-71; vice chmn. Santa Paula Taxpayers Assn., 1976; trustee Santa Paula Sch. Dist., 1977-81. Recipient Edn. award Mexican-Am. Service Orgn., 1975; Best of Show, Venpex Philatelic Expn., 1973, 80, 82. Mem. Ventura County Bus. Tchrs. Assn. (co-founder 1967), Internat. Platform Assn., Delta Pi Epsilon, Theta Chi. Club: Optimist (disting. sec. 1962-63, co-knight of yr. 1973-74, optimist of yr. 1976-77). Pub. editor KC News, 1972-76, recipient state editor of yr. award 1976. Home: 727 E Pleasant St Santa Paula CA 93060

TURK, JUDITH LEAH, advertising, public relations and marketing firm executive; b. Long Beach, Calif., Oct. 9, 1950; d. Dan H. and Ruth E. (Ditty) T.; m. C. Lawrence Thomas III, Sept. 16, 1978. B.A. in Journalism, Calif. State U.-Long Beach, 1974. Pasteup artist Printing Co., Los Alamitos, Calif., 1970-73; editor/designer alumni publ. Calif. State U.-Long Beach, 1973-74; prodn. artist Pacific Ventures, Newport Beach, Calif., 1974-76; chmn. bd., creative dir., prin. Judy Turk & Assocs., Newport Beach, Calif., 1976—, also Laguna Hills, Calif. Recipient award of Excellence, Pub. Relations Soc. Am., 1980, Gold awards Am. Conf. on Dental Advt. and Pub. Relations, 1982. Mem. Orange County Advt. Fedn. (cert. excellence 1977, 80), Med. Mktg. Assn., Western States Advt. Assn. Office: 23151 Plaza Pointe Dr Suite 120 Laguna Hills CA 92653

TURK, RUDY HENRY, artist, museum administrator; b. Sheboygan, Wis., June 24, 1927; s. Rudolph Anton and Mary Ursula (Stanisha) T.; B.S., U. Wis., Madison, 1949; M.A., U. Tenn., 1951; postgrad. Ind. U., Bloomington, 1952-56, U. Paris, 1956-57; m. Wanda Borders, Aug. 4, 1956; children—Tracy Lynn, Maria Theresa, Andrew Borders, Jennifer Welles. One-man shows: The Store, Berkeley, Calif., 1965; Udinotti Gallery, Scottsdale, Ariz., 1979, 81, 82, 83; instr., gallery dir. U. Mont., 1957-60; dir. Richmond (Calif.) Art Center, 1960-65; asst. dir. San Diego Mus. Art, 1965-67; assoc. prof. art Ariz. State U., Tempe, 1967-70, prof., 1970-77, dir. Univ. Art Collection, 1967—; cons. Ariz. Commn. on Arts and Humanities, 1967-80, bd. dirs., 1980—. Served with USN, 1945-46. Fulbright scholar, 1956-57. Mem. Western Assn. Art Museums (recipient Golden Gate award), Am. Assn. Art Museums, Phi Kappa Phi, Phi Alpha Theta. Democrat. Roman Catholic. Author: (with others) The Search for Personal Freedom; Scholder/Indians, 1972, 6th edit., 1981; Merrill Mahaffey: Monumental Landscapes, 1979; (with others) Scholder, 1982; numerous exhbn. catalogs. Home: 2113 E Huntington Dr Tempe AZ 85282 Office: Matthews Center Ariz State U Tempe AZ 85287

TURK, THOMAS NORMAN, mfg. co. exec.; b. New Castle, Pa., Dec. 9, 1938; s. Charles Julian and May Matilda (Cowperthwaite) T.; A.A., Golden West Coll., 1973; B.A., Calif. State U., 1976, M.B.A., Nat. U., 1982; m. Coleen Budd, Dec. 28, 1969; children—Thomas Jeffrey, Casey Thomas, Tiffany Ann. With Eaton-Leonard Corp., Carlsbad, Calif., 1976—, prodn. control mgr., 1978—. Served with USMC, 1956-58. Cert. profl. in inventory mgmt. Mem. Am. Prodn. and Inventory Control Soc. (v.p. membership 1980-81, v.p. edn. 1981-82), Soc. Mfg. Engrs. (cert. mfg. engr.), Internat. Platform Assn. Democrat. Home: 31710 Oak Glen Rd Valley Center CA 92082 Office: 6305 El Camino Real Carlsbad CA 92008

TURLEY, KEITH L., utilities executive; b. Mesa, Ariz., June 16, 1923; s. Ora Elmer and Zella Exa (Thurman) T.; B.A., Ariz. State U., 1948; m. Dorothy Rae Welton, Sept. 2, 1950; children—Sue Ann, Cinda Jane, Nancy Lynn, Robert. With Central Ariz. Light & Power Co., Phoenix, 1948-51, Stanolind Oil & Gas Co., Okla., 1951; with Ariz. Pub. Service Co., Phoenix, 1952—, v.p. marketing, 1967-69, exec. v.p. customer services, 1969-72, exec. v.p., gen. mgr., dir., 1972-73, pres., chief exec. officer, 1974-81, pres., 1981-83, chmn. bd., 1981—, also chief exec. officer; dir. Ariz. Bank, Del E. Webb Corp., Western Energy Supply & Transmission Assos. Dir., Central Ariz. Project, 1971—; chmn. Phoenix Commn. on Housing, 1972. Trustee, Am. Grad. Sch. Internat. Mgmt., Heard Mus.; bd. dirs. Sun Angel Found.; mem. pres.'s adv. council Ariz. State U. Served to lt. (j.g.) USNR, 1943-47. Recipient Alumni Service award Ariz. State U., 1971. Mem. Pacific Coast Electric Assn. (dir.), Pacific Coast Gas Assn., Edison Electric Inst., Atomic Indsl. Forum (dir.), Ariz. State U. Alumni Assn. (pres. 1966). Clubs: Paradise Valley Country, Arizona. Office: Ariz Public Service Co PO Box 21666 Phoenix AZ 85036

TURLEY, STANLEY F., state senator; b. Snowflake, Ariz., Feb. 27, 1921; s. Fred A. and Wilma (Fillerup) T.; m. Cleo Fern Olson, 1944; children—Tauna Lee, Margo Yvonne, Jana, Fredrick C., Miriam K., Lisa, Leslie. Student Brigham Young U., 3 yrs. Mem. Ariz. Ho. of Reps., 1964-72, speaker, 1967-72; mem. Ariz. State Senate, 1973—. Served to pfc, USAAF, 1944-46. Mem. Ariz. Cotton Growers (dir.), Farm Bur., Ariz. Cattle Growers Assn. Republican. Mormon. Club: Rotary. Home: 2650 E Southern Ave Mesa AZ 85201 Office: Arizona State Senate Phoenix AZ 85007*

TURMAN, GEORGE FUGETT, lieutenant governor of Montana; b. Missoula, Mont., June 25, 1928; s. George F. and Corinne McDonald T.; B.A., U. Mont., 1951; m. Kathleen Hager, Mar. 3, 1951; children—Marcia, Linda, Douglas, John, Laura. Adminstr., research asso. Fed. Res. Bank San Francisco, 1954-63; in property mgmt., Missoula, 1964-70; mayor of Missoula, 1970-72; mem. Mont. Ho. of Reps., 1973-74; public service commr. State of Mont., Helena, 1975-80, lt. gov., 1981—. Served with inf. U.S. Army, 1951-53. Democrat. Office: State Capitol Helena MT 59620

TURMAN, ROBERT LEE, educator; b. Gadsden, Ala., Sept. 29, 1926; s. Arthur and Lillian (Long) T.; m. Maggie Dossie, June 29, 1950; children—Daphne, Gregory, Robert, Arthur, Oliver. B.S. in Edn., Tuskegee Inst., 1949; M.S. in Ednl. Adminstrn., U. N.C., 1962; postgrad. U. No. Colo., 1973-75, U. Colo., 1977. Lic. sch. adminstr. Colo. Commd. U.S. Army, 1949; advanced through grades to lt. col., 1966; ret. 1972; prin. Helen Hunt Sch., Colorado Springs, Colo., 1974-77, Mark Twain Sch., Colorado Springs, 1977—. Pres. bd. edn. Harrison Sch. Dist. 2, Colorado Springs; mem. El Paso County

Democratic Exec. Com. Decorated Legion of Merit, Purple Heart, Bronze Star, Commendation medal (2). Mem. Nat. Assn. Elem. Prins., Nat. Assn. Sch. Bds., Colo. Black Caucus, Assn. U.S. Army, Am. Assn. Sch. Adminstrs., Phi Delta Kappa, Omega Psi Phi (Educator of Yr. 1982). Home: 208 Chamberlin Ave Colorado Springs CO 80906 Office: 110 S Circle Dr Colorado Springs CO 80910

TURNAGE, JEAN ALLEN, lawyer, state senator; b. St. Ignatius, Mont., Mar. 10, 1926; s. Edward and Julia (Martin) T.; J.D., U. Mont., 1951; m. Eula Mae Johnson, Nov. 20, 1952; children—Patricia Ann, Lloyd Allen. Admitted to Mont. bar, 1951, since practiced in, Polson, Mont.; Lake County atty., 1953-63; mem. Mont. Ho. of Reps., 1963-65; mem. Mont. Senate, 1965—, pres., 1981—; sr. v.p. Security State Bank, Polson, 1980—. Served with USAAF, 1944-46. Mem. Am. Bar Assn., Mont. Bar Assn. Republican. Lutheran. Club: Masons. Office: 312 1st St E Polson MT 59860

TURNBULL, WILLIAM, JR., architect; b. N.Y.C., Apr. 1, 1935; s. William and Elizabeth (Howe) T.; A.B., Princeton U., 1956, M.F.A. in Architecture, 1959; student Ecole des Beaux Arts Fontainebleau, 1956. With Skidmore, Owings & Merrill, San Francisco, 1960-63; founding partner Moore, Lyndon, Turnbull, Whitaker, 1962, partner charge San Francisco office, 1965-69; mem. design group Pres.'s Adv. Council Pennsylvania Ave., 1963; lectr. U. Calif., Berkeley, 1965-69; vis. prof. U. Oreg., 1966-68, dir. MLTW-Turnbull Assos., 1970—; lectr. Stanford U., 1973-77; vis. design critic M.I.T., 1975, U. Calif., Berkeley, 1977—; design cons. Formica Corp., 1978—; prin. works include Sea Ranch Condominium I, 1965, Sea Ranch Swim Tennis Club, 1966; asso. architect Lovejoy Fountain Plaza, Portland, Faculty Club at U. Calif. at Santa Barbara, Kresge Coll. at U. Calif. at Santa Cruz, Biloxi (Miss.) Library. Mem. tech. adv. com. Calif. Legislature Joint Com. Open Space Lands, 1968-69; mem. regional honor awards (10) jury AIA, 1968—, nat. honor awards jury, 1969, chmn. jury, 1977; C.E. honor award, 1973, 79; mem. Progressive Architecture Honor Awards Jury, 1975. Served with AUS, 1959-60. Recipient Nat. honor award AIA, 1967, 68, 73, 79; Calif. Gov. award planned communities, 1966; award of merit, bay region honor awards AIA, 1963, 67, 78; citation Progressive Architecture Design awards, 1962-66, 68-70, 1st honor award, 1971; First honor award Homes for Better Living, 1963, Merit award, 1966; Honor award Western Home awards, 1961-62, 63, 66-67, Merit award, 1966-67; House of Year award Archtl. Record, 1961, 67, 69, 70, 72. Fellow AIA. Author: Global Architecture Series: Moore, Lyndon, Turnbull & Whitaker: The Sea Ranch, The Sea Ranch Details. Illustrator: The Place of Houses. Office: Pier 1 1/2 The Embarcadero San Francisco CA 94111

TURNER, ALAN ERNEST, architect; b. Youngstown, Ohio, Sept. 12, 1953; s. Robert Edward and Sarah Ann (D'Agostino) T.; B.Arch., U. Notre Dame, 1976; student U. Notre Dame, Rome, 1973-74; m. Pamela Ann Cerny. Designer, Banner Assos., Laramie, Wyo., 1976-78, design architect, 1979-80, asso., project architect, 1980—, asst. dir. mktg., 1981-83, head archtl. services, 1983—; co-founder Cloudlevel Assos., Laramie, 1978-79, pres., 1980—; cons. Downtown Merchants Assn., 1980—. HUD Solar Demonstration grantee, 1978. Mem. AIA. Home: 216 S Filmore St Laramie WY 82070 Office: PO Box 550 Laramie WY 82070

TURNER, ALICE ELIZABETH, librarian; b. Saskatoon, Sask., Can., Oct. 16, 1925; d. John Ross and Annie Louise (Jackson) Turner. B.A., U. Sask., 1946; B.L.S., McGill U., 1950. Librarian, U. Man. (Can.), Winnipeg, 1950-52; childrens librarian Saskatoon Pub. Library, 1952-53, head reference dept., 1953-61, asst. chief librarian, 1961-80, chief librarian, 1981—. Office: Saskatoon Public Library 311 23d St E Saskatoon SK S7K 0J6 Canada

TURNER, CARL JEANE, electronics engineer, international business development executive; b. Sevierville, Tenn., July 27, 1933; s. Kenneth Albert and Lenna Faye (Christopher) T.; B.S.Ed., B.S.E.E., M.B.A., Columbia Pacific U.; m. Flossie Pearl Ingram, Dec. 11, 1954; children—Marcia, Kenneth, Theresa, Christopher, Robin. Enlisted in Fla. Air N.G., 1948, active duty in USAF, 1950, advanced through ranks with service in Korea and Vietnam; ret., 1972; with Itek Corp., 1972-77, 78-81, program devel. mgr. Optical Systems div., Athens, Greece, 1978-79, resident program mgr. Applied Tech. div., Ulm, W. Ger., 1979-81, mgr. program planning and control, internat. ops. Applied Tech. div., Sunnyvale, Calif., 1981; mgr. export mktg. GTE Corp., Systems Group, Western Div., 1981-83; pres. C.J. Turner and Assoc. Co., 1983—; sr. engr. analyst, chief instr. E-Systems, Inc., Greenville, Tex., 1977-78. Recipient George Washington Honor medal Freedoms Found., 1965; Presdl. Achievement award, 1982; Pres.'s Medal of Merit, 1982. Mem. IEEE, Assn. Old Crows, Air Force Assn., Am. Entrepreneurs Assn., Nat. Writers Club, Armed Forces Communications and Electronics Assn., Am. Entrepreneurs Assn., Nat. Assn. Professions, Nat. Writers Club, Profl. and Tech. Cons. Assn., Internat. Platform Assn., Order Seasoned Weasels. Republican. Baptist. Author, editor electronic warfare mgmt. courses and internat. bus. books. Address: 1064 E Evelyn Ave Sunnyvale CA 94086

TURNER, ED C., engineer; b. Santa Monica, Calif., Apr. 15, 1939; s. Herbert Chan and Helen Naomi (Hahn) T.; children—Michael Edwin, Lynn Elizabeth, Jennifer Sue. A.A., Santa Monica City Coll., 1963. Registered profl. engr., land surveyor, Idaho. With Mt. Whitney Pack Trains, Lone Pine, Calif., 1956-59; pub. works engr. City of Los Angeles, 1962-69; design engr., traffic engr., city engr. Idaho Falls, 1969—. Co-chmn., Conf. on Children, 1978; appeared before U.S. Senate Subcom. on Parental Kidnapping, Los Angeles. Mem. Am. Pub. Works Assn., Inst. Transp. Engrs. Office: PO Box 220 Idaho Falls ID 83402

TURNER, FRED, JR., soil scientist; b. Paris Crossing, Ind., Jan. 13, 1920; s. Fred and Laura (Click) T.; student U. Ariz., 1937-40, B.S., 1948; M.S., Wash. State Coll., 1951; Ph.D., Mich. State U., 1958; m. Lillian Irene Clark, Dec. 31, 1976; 1 son by previous marriage, Fred Lynwood. Soil scientist, Irrigation Experiment Sta., agrl. research service, USDA, Prosser, Wash., 1950-51, No. Gt. Plains Field Sta., Mandan, N.D., 1953-54; asst. prof., asso. prof. agrl. chemistry and soils, U. Ariz., Tucson, 1957-61, soil scientist and extension soil specialist, soils, water and engring., 1980-83, instr. soils courses; ret., 1983; supt., extension soil specialist, Safford (Ariz.) Br. Experiment Sta., 1961-80; cons. in soils and water, Brazil, North Yemen, U.S. Chmn. Mt. Graham chpt. ARC, 1968-80, mem. Western Nat. Field Office Adv. Council, 1976-79; pres. Copper Council Boy Scouts Am., 1976-78, v.p. Theodore Roosevelt Council, 1978-79. Served with USAF, 1940-46, served to col., 1951-53, ret. 1980. Decorated Air Medal with oak leaf cluster. Recipient appreciation award U. Ariz. Alumni Assn., 1966; public service award Nat. Weather Service, 1976; certified weather observer, Nat. Weather Service, 1972—. Mem. Am. Soc. Agronomy, Soil Sci. Soc. Am., Internat. Soc. Soil Sci., Council for Agrl. Sci. and Tech., Air Force Assn., Sigma Xi, Alpha Zeta, Gamma Sigma Delta. Republican. Methodist. Clubs: Rotary (pres. Safford, 1976-77), Am. Legion. Contbr. tech. and popular articles in field to publs. Home and office: PO Box 805 Thatcher AZ 85552

TURNER, GARY LUND, manufacturing executive; b. Kansas City, Mo., July 12, 1947; s. Kenneth P. and Elma M. (Lund) T.; m. Kathleen J. Redenbaugh, July 30, 1971; children—Emily S., Derek L., Ryan P. B.A. in Math. and Econ., U. Kans., Lawrence, 1969, M.B.A., 1971. Ops. research analyst Teledyne Water Pik, Ft. Collins., Colo., 1976, mgr. ops. research, 1976-81, dir. quality assurance, 1981-82, v.p. quality assurance, 1982—; instr. Colo. State U. distribution class, 1981. Served to capt. USAF, 1972-76. Decorated USAF commendation medal; Air Force ROTC fin. assistance grantee, 1967-69; recipient U. Kans. John Ise econ. award, 1969; NDEA Title IV fellow, 1970-72. Mem. Am. Inst. Decision Scis, Inst. Mgmt. Sci./Ops. Soc. Am., Am. Soc. Quality Control, Phi Beta Kappa, Pi Mu Epsilon, Beta Gamma Sigma. Methodist. Contbr. articles to profl. jours. Office: 1730 E Prospect Fort Collins CO 80525

TURNER, JACK HENRY, constrn. co. exec.; b. Scottfield, Ill., Nov. 28, 1940; s. Jack H. and Mary F. (Welsh) T.; B.S., U. Oreg., 1962, M.B.A., 1975; M.A., U. Md., 1972; m. Nguyen Thi, June 1, 1968; children—Suzanne, Jonathan, Benjamin. Mgr. personnel scheduling Air Asia Thailand, 1969-73; mgr. indsl. relations Lockheed, Riyadh, Saudi Arabia, 1975-76; indsl. relations mgr. Far East, Sundt Internat., Manila, 1976-79; v.p. personnel and adminstrn. M.M. Sundt Internat., Tucson, 1979—; dir. Tierra Internat., Manila, Asian Exec. Resources, Inc., Permian Constructors (Tex.), Singapore; instr. Asian Inst. Mgmt., 1978-79. Dir., Vietnamese Refugee Relief Assn., 1973-80. Served with U.S. Army, 1963-68. Decorated Silver Star, Purple Heart. Recipient Service award Sec. of Labor, Philippines, 1977; Eva and Joseph Zimmerman fellow, 1973-75. Mem. Am. Mgmt. Assn., Asian Inst. Personnel Mgmt. Clubs: Fly Fisherman's Assn., Ariz. Back Trails. Author: Labor Migration in the Third World, 1975; Expatriate Asians, 1976; The Asian Worker in the Middle East, 1977; Bac Si, 1979; Petro Bodies, 1982; Reference Checks, 1982. constrn. co. exec.; b. Scottfield, Ill., Nov. 28, 1940; s. Jack H. and Mary F. (Welsh) T.; B.S., U. Oreg., 1962, M.B.A., 1975; M.A., U. Md., 1972; m. Nguyen Thi, June 1, 1968; children—Suzanne, Jonathan, Benjamin. Mgr. personnel scheduling Air Asia Thailand, 1969-73; mgr. indsl. relations Lockheed, Riyadh, Saudi Arabia, 1975-76; indsl. relations mgr. Far East, Sundt Internat., Manila, 1976-79; v.p. personnel and adminstrn. M.M. Sundt Internat., Tucson, 1979—; dir. Tierra Internat., Manila, Asian Exec. Resources, Inc., Permian Constructors (Tex.), Singapore; instr. Asian Inst. Mgmt., 1978-79. Dir., Vietnamese Refugee Relief Assn., 1973-80. Served with U.S. Army, 1963-68. Decorated Silver Star, Purple Heart. Recipient Service award Sec. of Labor, Philippines, 1977; Eva and Joseph Zimmerman fellow, 1973-75. Mem. Am. Mgmt. Assn., Asian Inst. Personnel Mgmt. Clubs: Fly Fisherman's Assn., Ariz. Back Trails. Author: Labor Migration in the Third World, 1975; Expatriate Asians, 1976; The Asian Worker in the Middle East, 1977; Bac Si, 1979; Petro Bodies, 1982; Reference Checks, 1982. Office: 4001 E Irvington St Tucson AZ 85710

TURNER, JANET E., artist; b. Kansas City, Mo., 1914; d. James Ernest and Hortense (Taylor) Turner; A.B., Stanford, 1936; diploma, postgrad. Kansas City Art Inst. (under Thomas H. Benton, John de Martelly), 5 years; student art Claremont Grad. Sch. (Millard Sheets, Henry McFee), 2 years, M.F.A., 1947; student serigraphy, Edward Landon; Ed.D., Columbia, 1960. Faculty, Girls Collegiate Sch., Claremont, Calif., 1942-47; asst. prof. art Stephen F. Austin State Coll., Nacogdoches, Tex., 1947-56; asst. prof. Chico State U., 1959-63, asso. prof., 1963-68, prof., 1968-80, emeritus, 1980—. Works have been shown in painting, water colors and prints exhbns. throughout U.S.; exhibited over 140 one-man shows in U.S., Israel, Japan; exhibited in Internat. Biannual of Graphics, Krakow, Poland, 1978, Internat. Exchange Exhbn., Seoul, Korea, Le Salon des Nations, Paris, 1983. Represented in collections in U.S., fgn. countries. Illustrator The Yazoo, F. Smith. Guggenheim fellow, 1952; Tupperware fellow, 1956—. Recipient prizes including: (painting) 1st prize Tex. Fine Arts Assn., 1948; Dealey purchase prize and Comini poplar prize 11th Tex. Gen. Exhbn.; R.D. Straus prize 13th Tex. Gen. Exhbn.; 3 prize oils 50th Anniversary Exhbn. Art Assn. New Orleans; S. Karasick prize 59th Ann. Nat. Assn. Women Artists; (water colors) purchase prize 2d Tex. Water Color Soc.; Sun Carnival prize 3d Ann. Southwestern Sun Carnival Fine Arts Exhbn., El Paso; purchase prize Smith Coll. Mus. Art, 37th Ann. Exhbn. Western Art, Denver; Marcia Tucker prize Nat. Assn. Women Artists; (prints) Nat. Assn. Women Artists 1950; (graphics) 1st prize Painters and Sculptors Soc. N.J., 32d Ann. Springfield (Mass.) Art League, Pen and Brush Black and White Exhbn., N.Y.C.; purchase prize Soc. Am. Graphic Artists 36th Ann. A.N.A., 2d prize, Springfield Art League, Mass., 1955, 1st prize, Pen and Brush, 1956, 8th ann. Boston Printmakers purchase prize; 6th Southwestern Dallas Mus. Fine Arts, 1st prize graphics, Painters Sculptors Soc. of N.J., Tupperware Art Fund Fellowship award for painting, Los Angeles County Nat. purchase prize, purchase prize Calif. State Fair, 1960, Cannon prize N.A.D., 1961; Medal of Honor and Alice S. Buell Meml. prize Nat. Assn. Women Artists, 1963, Katheryn Colton prize, Medal of Honor and Mabel M. Garner award, 1967; A.P. Hankins Meml. prize Print Club Pa., 1972, Rosenwald prize, 1975; Am. Artists prize, 1982; co-recipient Outstanding Prof. award Calif. State U. and Colls., 1975. Mem. League Am. Pen Women, Los Angeles Printmaking Soc. (Purchase prize 1971), Nat. Assn. Women Artists (medal of honor 1977) Audubon Artists, Am. Color Print Soc., Soc. Am. Graphic Artists, N.A.D. (academician), Nat. Art Edn. Assn., A.A.U.W., Calif. Soc. Printmakers, San Francisco Women Artists, Internat. Arts Guild, Centro Studie Scambi Internazionale, Delta Kappa Gamma, Alpha Omicron Pi, Kappa Delta Pi, Pi Lambda Theta. Home: 567 E Lassen St Sp 701 Chico CA 95926

TURNER, JOHN FREELAND, state senator, rancher; b. Jackson, Wyo., Mar. 3, 1942; s. John Charles and Mary Louise (Mapes) T.; m. Mary Kay Brady, 1969; children—John Francis, Kathy Mapes, Mark Freeland. B.S. in Biology, U. Notre Dame, 1964; postgrad. U. Innsbruck, 1964-65, U. Utah, 1965-66; M.S. in Ecology, U. Mich., 1968. Rancher, outfitter Triangle X Ranch, Moose, Wyo.; photo-journalist; formerly mem. Wyo. Ho. of Reps. from Teton County, now mem. Wyo. State Senate, chmn. travel, recreation and wildlife com., agr. com., select com. sch. fin. Mem. student council pollution and environ. Dept. Interior, 1969-70; dir. C-V. Sch. for Handicapped Children, Teton Sci. Sch., Wyo. Environ. Inst.; mem. Wyo. Health Systems Agy., State Energy Conservation Commn., Nat. Wildlife Assn., Nat. Audubon Soc. Recipient Wyo. Press award, 1972; named Outstanding Freshman Legislator, Wyo. Ho. of Reps., 1971. Mem. Nat. Parks and Conservation Assn. Author: The Magnificent Bald Eagle: Our National Bird, 1971. Republican. Roman Catholic. Home: Triangle X Ranch Moose WY 83012 Office: Wyoming State Senate Cheyenne WY 82002

TURNER, JOHN REDMOND, clinical psychologist, educator; b. Los Angeles, Mar. 8, 1937; s. Hirst and Lillian (Redmond) T.; m. Susan Bradley, Oct. 8, 1972. B.A., Yale U., 1959; M.A. U. Utah, 1968, Ph.D. 1972. Lic. psychologist, Wash., 1975. Asst. dir., staff psychologist Mental Health Clinic, U. Utah, 1968-72; dir. mental health clinic, co-ordinator com. services Asotin and Garfield counties, Wash., 1972-74; hosp. liaison, ct. evaluator Spokane (Wash.) Community Mental Health Center, 1974-77, coordinator transitional care programs, 1977—; cons., trainer nursing homes, 1978—, cardiac rehab. programs, 1982—; adj. faculty Wash. State U., 1972-74; Gonzaga U., 1982—. Served to capt. USAF, 1960-64. Mem. Am. Psychol. Assn., Inland Empire Soc. Profl. Psychologists. Office: South 106 Division St Spokane WA 99202

TURNER, KARYN DONNA, publisher; b. Denver, Sept. 16, 1945; d. Donald C. and Aldean E. (Rea) Lee; m. Michael D. Turner, Aug. 25, 1944; 1 son, Gary G. Student pub. schs., Denver. Bookkeeper, Turner Assocs., Inc., Denver, 1970-82; pres. Superfights, Inc., Arvada, Colo., 1980—, also fight promoter; regional dir. and ratings chmn. Pro Karate Assn., Beverly Hills, Calif., 1982—; pub. Footnotes mag., Arvada, 1982—. Named Woman of Year Pro Karate Assn., 1982. Mem. Denver Latin C. of C. Home and Office: 9751 Sierra Dr Arvada CO 80005

TURNER, LEAF, physicist; b. Bklyn., Mar. 23, 1943; s. Max and Florence Estelle (Tanenbaum) T.; m. Ruby Ann Sherman, Sept. 11, 1966; children—Alyssa Wendy, Lara Dawn, Ari Mark. A.B. with honors in Physics, Cornell U., 1963; M.S., U. Wis., Madison, 1964, Ph.D., 1969. Inst. postdoctoral fellow Weizmann Inst. Sci., 1969; postdoctoral fellow U. Toronto, 1969-71; asst. scientist Space Sci. and Engring. Center, U. Wis., Madison, 1971-72, project assoc. dept. physics, 1972-74; staff mem. Los Alamos (N.Mex.) Nat. Lab., 1974—; instr. physics Scarborough Coll., U. Toronto (Ont., Can.), 1970-71. NSF coop. grad. fellow, 1964-66; Summer Symposium fellow Niels Bohr Inst., 1969; NSF summer fellow Brandeis U. Summer Inst. in Theoretical Physics, 1970. Mem. Am. Phys. Soc., Sigma Xi, Phi Beta Kappa. Contbr. articles in field to profl. jours. Office: CTR-6 MS-F642 Los Alamos Nat Lab Los Alamos NM 87545

TURNER, MARY JANE, educator, educational evaluator, consultant; b. Colorado Springs, Colo., June 1, 1923; d. David Edward and Ina Mable (Campbell) Nickelson; m. Harold Adair Turner, Feb. 15, 1945; children—Mary Ann, Harold A. B.A., U. Colo., 1947, M.P.A., 1968, Ph.D., 1978. Staff assoc. Social Sci. Edn. Consortium, Inc., Boulder, Colo., 1971—; co-dir. citizenship devel. project Nat. Inst. Edn., 1978-80; co-dir. law-related edn. evaluation project Office Juvenile Justice and Delinquency Prevention, 1979—; mem. grad. faculty Sch. Edn., U. Colo., Boulder, 1979—. Mem. Am. Polit. Sci. Assn., Nat. Council Social Studies, Coll. and Univ. Faculty Assembly, Phi Delta Kappa. Democrat. Presbyterian. Author: (with K. Switzer and C. Redden) American Government: Principles and Practices, 1983; (with H. Sussmuth) A Comparative Study of Social Studies/Social Science Education in the FRG and USA, 1983; also various ednl. guides. Home: 3009 Madison St Apt II-201 Boulder CO 80303 Office: Social Sci Edn Consortium Inc 855 Broadway St Boulder CO 80302

TURNER, RALPH HERBERT, sociology educator; b. Effingham, Ill., Dec. 15, 1919; s. Herbert and Hilda Rearl (Bohn) T.; m. Christine Elizabeth Hanks, Nov. 2, 1943; children—Lowell Ralph, Cheryl Christine. B.A., U. So. Calif., 1941, M.A., 1942; postgrad. U. Wis., 1942-43; Ph.D., U. Chgo., 1948. Research assoc. Am. Council Race Relations, 1947-48; faculty UCLA, 1948—, prof. sociology and anthropology, 1959—, chmn. dept. sociology, 1963-68; vis. summer prof. U. Wash., 1960, U. Hawaii, 1962; vis. scholar Australian Nat. U., 1972; vis. prof. U. Ga., 1975; vis. fellow Nuffield Coll., Oxford U., 1980. Mem. behavioral scis. study sect. NIH, 1961-66, chmn., 1963-64; dir.-at-large Social Sci. Research Council, 1965-66; chmn. panel on pub. policy implications of earthquake prediction Nat. Acad. Scis., 1974-75. Mem. com. social edn. and action Los Angeles Presbytery, 1954-56. Served to lt. (j.g.) USNR, 1943-46. Social Sci. Research Council fellow, 1953-56; Sr. Fulbright scholar, Eng., 1956-57; Guggenheim fellow, 1964-65. Mem. Am. Sociol. Assn. (council 1959-64, chmn. social psychology sect. 1960-61, nat. pres. 1968-69; chmn. sect. theoretical sociology 1973-74, chmn. collective behavior sect. 1983-84), Pacific Sociol. Assn. (pres. 1957), Internat. Sociol. Assn. (council 1974-82, v.p. 1978-82), Soc. Study of Social Problems (exec. com. 1962-63), Soc. Study of Symbolic Interaction (Charles Horton Cooley award 1978, pres. 1982-83), AAUP. Author: (with L. Killian) Collective Behavior, 1957, 2d edit., 1972; The Social Context of Ambition, 1964; Robert Park on Social Control and Collective behavior, 1967; Family Interaction, 1970; Earthquake Prediction and Public Policy, 1975; (with J. Nigg, D. Paz, B. Young) Earthquake Threat: The Human Response in Southern Calif., 1980; editor Sociometry, 1962-64; editorial cons., 1959-62; acting editor Ann. Rev. Sociology, 1977-78, assoc. editor, 1978-79, editor, 1980—; adv. editor Am. Jour. Sociology, 1954-56, Sociology and Social Research, 1961-74; editorial staff Am. Sociol. Rev., 1955-56; assoc. editor Social Problems, 1959-62, 67-69; cons. editor Sociol. Inquiry, 1968-73, Western Sociol. Rev., 1975-79; editorial bd. Ann rev. Sociology, 1973—, Mass Emergencies, 1975-79, Internat. Jour. Critical Sociology, 1974—. Home: 1126 Chautauqua Blvd Pacific Palisades CA 90272 Office: 405 Hilgard Ave Los Angeles CA 90024

TURNER, REX W., psychologist, educator; b. Louisville, Aug. 19, 1949; s. Carl Ray and Kay W. Turner; m. Jane Jensen, Feb. 14, 1949; children—Vangie Star, Rachel Jane, Cassie Ambrose. B.S. in Psychology, U. Utah, 1973, M.S. in Clin. Psychology, 1977. Ph.D. in Clin. Psychology, 1980. Lic. psychologists, Utah. Chief drug and alcohol treatment VA Med. Ctr., Salt Lake City, 1980—; asst. clin. prof. psychology U. Utah, 1980— , mem. clin. faculty, dept. family and community medicine, sch. medicine, 1981—. Served to lt. USNR, 1982—. Recipient VA research adv. group award for research in depression and alcoholism, 1980; Associated Students U. Utah awards, 1974-75. Mem. Am. Psychol. Assn., Utah Psychol. Assn. Mem. adv. bd. Beehive Health Review, Intermountain Health Review. Contbr. articles to profl. jours. Home: 1669 E 9400 S Sandy UT 84092 Office: VA Medical Center 500 Foothill Blvd Salt Lake City UT 84148

TURNER, ROBERT HENRY, manufacturing executive; b. Oklahoma City, Apr. 21, 1930; s. Clayton Bryan and Lela Elva (Nichols) T.; M. Vertice Kinser, Sept. 11, 1949; children—Deborah Turner Sheaffer, Robert Lyndon. B.S.M.E. with spl. distinction, U. Okla., 1960. Registered profl. engr., Okla. Engr., Western Electric Co., Denver, 1960-64, dept. chief, 1964-67, asst. mgr., 1967-74, mgr., 1974-77, dir. engring., 1977—. Served with USAF, 1951-55. Mem. Tau Beta Pi, Pi Tau Sigma. Lutheran. Patentee automatic assembly device designs. Home: 6334 S Yates Ct Littleton CO 80123 Office: 1200 NW 120th St Denver CO 80234

TURNER, WILLIAM COCHRANE, internat. mgmt. cons.; b. Red Oak, Iowa, May 27, 1929; s. James Lyman and Josephine (Cochrane) T.; B.S., Northwestern U., 1952; m. Cynthia Dunbar, July 16, 1955; children—Scott Christopher, Craig Dunbar, Douglas Gordon. Pres., dir. Western Mgmt. Cons., Inc., Phoenix, 1960-74, Western Mgmt. Cons. Europe, S.A., Brussels, 1968-74; U.S. ambassador, permanent rep. OECD, Paris, 1974-77, vice chmn. exec. com., 1976-77, U.S. rep. Energy Policy Commn., 1976-77; mem. U.S. dels. internat. meetings, 1974-77; chmn. Argyle Atlantic Corp., Phoenix, 1977—; dir. Nabisco Brands, Inc., Energy Transition Corp., Goodyear Tire & Rubber Co., AT&T Internat., Phibro-Salomon, Inc., Sunbelt Holdings, S.A., Swensen's, Inc.; chmn. European adv. council, Asia Pacific adv. council AT&T Internat.; mem. European adv. com. IBM World Trade Europe, Africa, Middle East Corp., 1977-80; mem. Asia Pacific adv. council Am. Can Co., 1981—; mem. Gen. Electric of Brazil adv. council Gen. Electric Co., Coral Gables, Fla., 1979-80; mem. Caterpillar of Brazil adv. council Caterpillar Tractor Co., Peoria, Ill., 1979—; mem. Adv. Com. on Trade Negotiations, 1982—. Bd. dirs. Atlantic Council U.S., 1977-82, Am. Grad. Sch. Internat. Mgmt., 1970—; bd. govs. Atlantic Inst. Internat. Studies, Paris, 1977—; adv. bd. Center Strategic and Internat. Studies, Georgetown U., 1977-81; mem. European Community-U.S. Businessmen's Council, 1978-79; bd. govs. Am. Hosp. of Paris, 1974-77; trustee Nat. Symphony Orch. Assn., Washington, 1973—, Am. Sch., Paris, 1974-77, Orme Sch., Mayer, Ariz., 1970-74, Phoenix Country Day Sch.,

1971-74; mem. nat. councils Salk Inst., 1978-82; mem. U.S. Adv. Com. Internat. Edn. and Cultural Affairs, 1969-74; nat. rev. bd. Center Cultural and Tech. Interchange between East and West, 1970-74; mem. vestry Am. Cathedral, Paris, 1976-77; pres., bd. dirs. Phoenix Symphony Assn., 1969-70; chmn. Ariz. Joint Econ. Devel. Com., 1967-68; exec. com., bd. dirs. Ariz. Dept. Econ. Planning and Devel., 1968-70; chmn. bd. Ariz. Crippled Children's Services, 1964-65; treas. Ariz. Republican Com., 1956-57; chmn. Ariz. Young Republican League, 1955-56. Recipient East-West Center Disting. Service award, 1977. Mem. U.S. Council Internat. Bus. (trustee, exec. com. 1977—), Council Fgn. Relations, Phoenix 40. Episcopalian. Clubs: Travellers (Paris); Metropolitan, Links (N.Y.C.); Plaza (Phoenix); Paradise Valley (Ariz.) Country; Bucks (London). Home: Scottsdale AZ Office: 4350 E Camelback Rd Suite 240-B Phoenix AZ 85018

TURNIPSEED, STEVEN DUVALL, substance abuse services administrator; b. Balt., Nov. 16, 1941; s. James Duvall and Grace T.; m. Beverly June Johnson, Dec. 18, 1972; children—Cheri, Bridgett, Shaka. Medex grad. U. Wash., 1970, M.P.H., 1982; B.S., SUNY Saratoga Springs, 1972. Commd. Spl. Forces, U.S. Army, 1958, 1968; med. officer USPHS Hosp., Levenworth, Kans., 1968-70; physician asst. Group Health Puget Sound, Seattle, 1970-72, dir. substance abuse services, 1974—; asst. prof. SUNY-Stony Brook, 1972-74. Bd. dirs. Medex Communication Ctr., 1972, Central Area Youth Assn., 1979, Planned Parenthood of Seattle, 1980—. Fellow Am. Acad. Physicians (dir. 1973), Am. Pub. Health Assn., Am. Acad. Physician Assts., Wash. State Acad. Physician Asst. (pres. 1978), Wash. State Pub. Health; Mem. Wash. State Acad. Physicians (dir. 1977), U. Wash. Sch. Pub. Health Alumni Assn. (sec.-treas. 1979-81). Baptist. Club: Masons. Home: 9728 Arrow Smith St S Seattle WA 98118 Office: Group Health Puget Sound 1600 E John St Seattle WA 98112

TUROCZY, CHERYL LA RAE, educational adminstrator; b. Rupert, Idaho, Aug. 14, 1943; d. Arthur Ray and Dorothy LaBelle (Hart) Fike; 1 son, Richard. B.A., Whitman Coll., 1965; M.Ed. in Human Services, Boston U., 1979. Tchr., Sharpstein Elem. Sch., Walla Walla, Wash., 1965-68, Tyler Primary Sch., Naha AFB, Okinawa, Japan, 1968-69, Nurnburg (W.Ger.) Elem. Sch., 1969-70, Stuttgart (W.Ger.) Elem.-Jr. High Sch., 1977-81; program dir. Federally Funded Guardian Ad Litem Program, Twin Falls, Idaho, 1981—; cons., trainer child abuse prevention and treatment; therapist Abuse Treatment Group; mem. adv. com. N.W Resource Assocs. Chmn. Twin Falls (Idaho) Child Protection Team, 1982—; bd. dirs. Vols. Against Violence, 1982—. Mem. Nat. Humane Soc., Nat. Assn. Counsel for Children, Nat. Assn. Juvenile and Family Ct. Judges, Nat. Ct. Apptd. Spl. Advocates Orgn. Club: Toastmistress Internat. Home: 1975 Sherry Ln Twin Falls ID 83301 Office: 726 Shoshone St W PO Box 531 Twin Falls ID 83301

TURRENTINE, LYNDA GAYLE, interior designer; b. Carrizozo, N. Mex., April 12, 1941; d. Edward Franklyn and Lora Olive (Allen) Adams; m. Frank George Turrentine, Sept. 5, 1961 (div.); children—Teri Lynn. Student U. N.Mex., 1959-60, 61; B.F.A. in Interior Design, North Tex. State U., 1964. Interior designer Marsh & Assos., Denton, Tex., 1964-65; interior designer Stewart Office Supply, Dallas, 1965-66; interior designer, project mgr. The Paper Mill, Inc., Las Cruces, N.Mex., 1966-72; interior design mgr., general mgr. Design Plaza, Las Cruces, 1972-79; account rep. Cholla Bus. Interiors, Tucson, 1979-80; prin. Interior Concepts, Tucson, 1980—; interior designer Larry Hayden Furniture Galleries, Tucson, 1982—. Cons.; adv. interior design program Dean of Agr., U. Ariz. Bd. dirs. Eastern Heights Village Town house Assn.; trustee St. Paul's United Methodist Ch.; mem. Rio Grande council Girl Scouts U.S.A., 1979, Dona Ana Arts Council. Mem. Nat. Fedn. Small Bus. (Right to Work comm.), Am. Soc. Interior Designers (pres. chpt. 1981-82, nat. dir. 1981-83, chpt. treas. 1983), Tucson C. of C., Las Cruces C. of C. Republican. Club: Sahauro Breakfast (v.p.). Address: 812 N Crescent Ln Tucson AZ 85710

TUSSING, ARLON REX, economic consultant, educator; b. Portland, July 22, 1933; s. A. Rex and Mildred Carolyn (Johnson) T.; m. Sandra Canino, Sept. 28, 1966; children—Maya, Francesca. B.A. U. Chgo. 1950, B.S. in Secondary Edn., 1952; Ph.D. in Econs., Oreg. State Coll. 1962; postgrad. Hitotsubashi U. Inst. Econ. Research 1965, U. Wash. 1965. Chief economist U.S. Senate Com. on Interior and Insular Affairs 1971-76; pres. ARTA, Inc., Seattle and Juneau, Anchorage 1977—; with Inst. Social and Econ. research U. Alaska 1965—, prof. 1972—; dir. Alaska Offshore Marine Services, Inc.; dir. Econ. Adv. Bd. U.S. Dept. Commerce. Mem. Am. Econ. Assn., Royal Econ. Soc., Econ. History Assn., Internat. House Japan, Internat. Assn. Energy Economists. Clubs: Cosmos (Washington); Washington Athletic, Mountaineers (Seattle); Mercer Island Country, Alaska Conservation Soc. Contbr. to books and profl. jours. Home: 31 Holly Hill Dr Mercer Island WA 98040 Office: 2720 Rainier Bank Tower Seattle WA 98101

TUTT, RUSSELL THAYER, investment company executive; b. Coronado, Cal., July 27, 1913; s. Charles Leaming and Eleanor (Armit) T.; grad. Thacher Sch., 1931; B.S. in Engring., Princeton, 1935; m. Margaret Louise Honnen, Aug. 12, 1950 (dec. Nov. 1974); children—Margaret Honnen Tutt Steinegger, Russell Thayer. With buying dept. Halsey, Stuart & Co., Inc., N.Y.C., 1935-40; v.p., gen. mgr. Garden City (Kans.) Co., 1946-56; pres. S.W. Kans. Power, Inc., Garden City, 1946-56; v.p. El Pomar Investment Co., Colorado Springs, Colo., 1956-61, pres., from 1961; chmn. bd. Holly Sugar Corp., Colorado Springs, chmn. exec. com. Affiliated Bank Shares of Colo., Inc., Central Telephone & Utilities Corp.; pres. Garden City Co.; pres. Broadmoor Hotel, Inc.; chmn. bd. First Nat. Bank Colorado Springs. Trustee Cheyenne Mountain Mus. and Zool. Soc., 1956—, pres., 1963-74, chmn. bd., 1974-80, hon. chmn. bd., 1980—; pres., trustee El Pomar Found.; trustee Colo. Coll., 1957—, chmn., 1966—; trustee Fountain Valley Sch. of Colo., Nat. Park and Recreation Assn., Washington, Nat. Recreation Found., N.Y.C. Served to maj. AUS, 1940-45. Decorated Bronze Star. Republican. Episcopalian. Clubs: Cheyenne Mountain Country, Broadmoor Golf, El Paso, Country of Colo., Cooking (Colorado Springs). Office: Holly Sugar Corp Holly Sugar Bldg Colorado Springs CO 80903

TUTTLE, ALLEN H., ednl. adminstr.; b. St. Louis, Nov. 10, 1929; s. Ray Loomis and Clara Josephine (Nelson) T.; B.S., Brigham Young U., 1951; M.A., San Francisco State Coll., 1955; cert. ednl. adminstrn. U. Calif., Berkeley, 1960; grad. Nat. War Coll., 1977; m. Carmen Celia Measom, July 26, 1950; children—Shauna, Jeffery Allen, Pamela, Terry James, Gregory Kent, Markham Dean. Tchr., Richmond (Calif.) City Schs., 1954-60; vice prin. schs., Mt. Eden, S.D., also Calif., 1960-63; prin. Edwin Markham Sch., Placerville (Calif.) Union Sch. Dist., 1963-66; dir. fed. projects El Dorado County (Calif.) Office Edn., 1966-71, asst. supt. curriculum, 1971-76, asso. supt. schs., 1976—; chmn. ednl. resources agy. 10-County Elem. and Secondary Edn. Act. Title III project, 1970-72. Pres. El Dorado County Sch. Employees Credit Union, 1964-79; fin. chmn. El Dorado dist. Golden Empire council Boy Scouts Am., 1968-71; chmn. El Dorado County Health Fair, 1978—; chmn. Placerville Area Joint Recreation Commn., 1979—; chmn. tech. adv. com. drug abuse Placerville, 1974—; counselor Calif.-El Dorado stake Ch. Jesus Christ Latter-Day Saints, 1978—; mem. Placerville City Council, 1982—. Served with U.S. Army, 1951-54; col. Calif. Army N.G., comdt. Calif. Mil. Acad., 1978—. Mem. Assn. Calif. Sch. Adminstrs. (pres. El Dorado County chpt. 1973-74), N.G. Assn. U.S., Assn. U.S. Army. Republican. Home: 575 Fairview Dr Placerville CA 95667 Office: 337 Placerville Dr Placerville CA 95667

TUTTLE, JERRY, community education and devel. consultant; b. Long Beach, Calif., Sept. 5, 1926; s. Preston Lyons and Dorothy (Tuttle) Wilson; m. M. Joan Lee, Oct. 26, 1955; children—Jerry Lee, Jon Wilson, Jana Lyn, Jeffrey David. B.A., U. Utah, 1950; M.A., Northwestern U., 1951; Ph.D., U. Nebr., 1958. Instr. in geography U. Colo., Boulder, 1955-56; water rights and resources engr. Water Resource Devel. and Regulation Agy., Utah Engrs. Office, 1957-61; tech. writer, missile research and devel. and prodn. Hercules Powder Co., Salt Lake City, 1961-62, Magna, Utah, tech. asst., 1962-63; with Bur. Indian Affairs, Regulatory and Devel. Agy., Dept. Interior, 1964-80, community devel. officer Albuquerque area, 1973-76, with detail to Zuni as fed.-officer-in-charge, 1975-76, indsl. devel. specialist, Albuquerque area, 1976-78, with detail to Western Fed. Regional Council at San Francisco, 1977, and as Albuquerque area coordinator Youth Conservation Corps-Young Adult Conservation Corps, 1978, program analyst So. Pueblos Agy., 1978-80; research assoc. Olivarez & Bowman Assocs., Albuquerque, 1980-83; br. mgr., program developer, project dir. Western Energy Planners, Ltd., cons., Albuquerque, 1980-82; cons. community edn. and community devel., Albuquerque, 1980-83; cons. on leadership devel. of Indians, Ford Found.; NSF rep. to 8th Quadrennial Internat. Geog. Congress, 1960; speaker, presenter in field. Treas., N. Mex. Swimming Assn.; treas. N. Mex. Pageant of Bands. Served with USNR, 1947-50, 52-53; PTO, Atlantic, Korea, Japan, Philippines. Recipient Spl. Achievement award U.S. Bur. Indian Affairs, 1971, Superior Performance award, 1965. Mem. Internat. Community Educators Assn. (founding), Sigma Xi. Democrat. Methodist. Club: Kirtland Officers. Contbr. articles to profl. publs. Home and Office: 12305 Eastridge Dr NE Albuquerque NM 87112

TUTTLE, KENNETH, psychologist; b. Provo, Utah, Feb. 3, 1946; s. Clarence Eugene and Dorothy (Hoover) T.; B.S., Brigham Young U., 1971, M.A., 1973, Ph.D., 1977; m. Teri Jean Walker, May 26, 1972; children—Lori Ann, Brian. With LDS Social Services, Spokane, Wash. and Orem, Utah, 1973-79, chief psychologist Utah Valley Hosp. Mental Health Services, Provo, 1979-80, exec. dir., 1981—; adj. asst. prof. dept. clin. psychology Brigham Young U., 1981—, Diplomate Internat. Acad. Profl. Counseling and Psychotherapy. Mem. Am. Psychol. Assn., Utah Psychol. Assn., Utah Falconer's Assn. (past pres.). Republican. Mormon. Office: 388 W 1150 N Provo UT 84601

TUTTLE, KENNETH LEWIS, energy mgmt. cons.; b. Toledo, Oreg., Apr. 4, 1944; s. Martin Lewis and Norma Corine (Nichols) T.; B.S., U.S. Naval Acad., 1967; M.S. in Mech. Engring., Oreg. State U., 1974, Ph.D., 1978; m. Susanna Annamaria Woodworth, June 24, 1967; children—Stephanie, Meghan, Lewis. Founder, pres. Solid Fuel Energy Assocs., Federal Way, Wash., 1982—; mem. faculty U.S. Naval Acad., Annapolis, Md., 1983—; cons. energy conversion, Corvallis Oreg., 1972-77; energy research and devel. Weyerhaeuser Co., Tacoma, 1978-82. U.S. Naval Acad. info. officer, Oreg., 1973-77. Served with USN, 1962-71; Vietnam. Registered profl. engr., Oreg. Mem. ASME, Air Pollution Control Assn., Combustion Inst., Smithsonian Inst. Author: Analysis and Design of a Small Gas Sampling Pump, 1974; Combustion Mechanisms in Wood Fired Boilers, 1978; patentee method for combustion of wood fuels.

TUVIL, JANABAI GAYLE, publishing company executive; b. St. Louis, Nov. 25, 1940; d. John Allan and Esther Elizabeth (Nolting) Wooten; m. Robert Benard Tuvil (div.); 1 dau., Jentry Joy. Student pub. schs., St. Louis. Sales rep., makeup artist Bonne Bell Cosmetics, Chgo., 1966-68, nat. advt. dir. Allied Arts Corp., Chgo., 1968-72; sr. account exec. Penthouse Internat., Chgo., Los Angeles, 1972-81; western advt. dir. Us mag., Peters Pub. Co., Los Angeles, 1981—. Mem. Los Angeles Advt. Club, Mag. Reps. Club. Home: 19746 Pacific Coast Hwy Malibu CA 90265 Office: Us mag Peters Pub Co 9441 Wilshire Blvd Suite 316 Beverly Hills CA 90212

TVEIT, LARRY JOHN, farmer, rancher, state senator; b. Fairview, Mont., Apr. 25, 1935; student public schs., Fairview; m. Doris Tveit; 5 children. Farmer, rancher, Fairview, Mont.; mem. Mont. Senate, 1981— . Former mem. Fairview Sch. Bd. Recipient Outstanding Young Farmer award Jaycees, 1961. Mem. Mont. Sch. Bds. Assn. (past dir., pres.), N.E. Mont. Land and Mineral Owners Assn. (dir.). Republican. Club: Elks (past officer). Office: Route 1 Box 117 Fairview MT 59221*

TWIGG-SMITH, THURSTON, newspaper pub.; b. Honolulu, Aug. 17, 1921; s. William and Margaret Carter (Thurston) Twigg-S.; B.Engring., Yale U., 1942; m. Laila Roster, Feb. 22, 1983; children by previous marriage—Elizabeth, Thurston, William, Margaret, Evelyn. With Honolulu Advertiser, 1946—, mng. editor, 1954-60, asst. bus. mgr., 1960-61, pub., 1961—; pres., pub., dir. Honolulu Advertiser, Inc., 1962—; pres., dir. Peris Corp.; chmn. Asa Properties Hawaii, Asa Properties Vt., Asa Properties Mass., Shiny Rock Mining Corp.; dir. First Fed. Savs. & Loan Assn., Hawaiian Electric Co., Ltd., Tongg Pub. Co., Am. Trust Co., Kamehameha Investment Corp. Trustee, Punahou Sch., Old Sturbridge Inc., Honolulu Acad. Arts, Honolulu Symphony Orch. Served to maj. AUS, 1942-46. Mem. Honolulu C. of C. Clubs: Waialae, Pacific, Oahu (Honolulu). Home: Honolulu HI 96725 Office: PO Box 3110 Honolulu HI 96802

TWIGHT, CHARLOTTE AUGUSTA, economist, lawyer; b. N.Y.C., Mar. 7, 1944; d. Jack Russell and Helen Forster (Wever) Lewis; m. Richard Blackledge Twight, June 13, 1964. B.A. summa cum laude, Calif. State U., 1965; postgrad. U. Wash., 1965-66, J.D., 1973, M.A. in Econs. 1980, Ph.D., 1983. Bar: Wash. 1973. Computer programmer/analyst Naval Command Systems Support Activity, Washington 1966-70; lectr. law U. Wash. 1975-78, teaching assoc. dept. econs. 1981-83, vis. asst. prof. bus. econs., 1983—; speaker and cons. in field. Mem. Am. Econ. Assn., Wash. State Bar Assn., Phi Kappa Phi. Club: The Mountaineers. Author: America's Emerging Fascist Economy 1975; contbr. articles to profl. jours. Office: Dept Finance Bus Econs and Quantitative Methods DJ-10 U Wash Seattle WA 98195

TWILEGAR, RON JESS, fin. services co. exec.; b. Vancouver, Wash., Sept. 18, 1943; s. Roy H. and Dorothy (Brown) T.; B.S., U. Idaho, 1966; J.D., George Washington U., 1971; m. Elizabeth Ann Condon, May 13, 1967; children—Megan Cary, Any Elizabeth, Tyson Alexander. Pres. Fee Simple Ltd., 1971—; asst. atty. gen. State of Idaho, 1973-74; individual practice law, Boise, 1974-77; pres., chief exec. officer First Idaho Corp., 1977—; mem. Idaho Ho. of Reps., 1974-76, Idaho Senate, from 1976. Served with U.S. Army, 1967-69. Mem. Idaho State Bar Assn., Boise Bar Assn. Democrat. Roman Catholic. Clubs: Multnomah Athletic, Crane Creek Country, Arid. Office: 205 N 10th St Boise ID 83702*

TWIST, ROBERT LANPHIER, farmer, rancher, cattle feeder; b. Memphis, Dec. 27, 1926; s. Clarence C. and Edith G. Twist; student Springfield (Ill.) Jr. Coll., 1943; B.S. in Agr., U. Ill., 1950; postgrad. U. Edinburgh (Scotland); 1 dau., Marilyn Edith. Owner, operator farm lands, Twist, Ark., 1949—, Bow Fiddle Ranch, Laramie, Wyo., 1961—, Lost Creek Ranch, Masters, Colo., 1963, Rolling T Ranch, Ft. Morgan, Colo., 1965—, R.L. Twist Ranches Cattle Feeding Enterprises, Greeley, Colo. and Ft. Morgan, 1974—; prin. R.L. Twist Land & Investments, Paradise Valley, Ariz., 1974—; Rocker M Ranch, Douglas, Ariz., 1981—; cons. agrl. mgmt. Justice of Peace, Twist, Ark., 1954. Served with USAAF, 1944-46. Mem. Colo. Farm Bur., Wyo. Farm Bur., Nat. Cattlemen's Assn. (charter). Republican. Presbyterian. Home: 4612 E Sparkling Ln Paradise Valley AZ 85253

TYLCZAK, MARGARET ANN, advertising copywriter; b. Shelton, Wash., Mar. 4, 1952; d. Louis F. and Ruth L. (Hillier) Tylczak. A.A., Stephens Coll., 1972; B.A. in Communications, Wash. State U., 1974. In comml. and feature film prodn. Skylight Prodns., Seattle, 1975-77; with promotion office Seattle Times, 1977-78; copywriter Kraft-Smith Advt., Seattle, 1977-79, Cole & Weber, Seattle, 1980-82, Tathem-Laird Kudner, Chgo., 1982—. Dir. communications Wash. State Women's Soccer Assn., 1977. Recipient numerous awards for advt. copy. Roman Catholic.

TYLER, DARLENE JASMER, dietitian; b. Watford City, N.D., Jan. 26, 1939; d. Edwin Arthur and Leola Irene (Walker) Jasmer; B.S., Oreg. State U., 1961; m. Richard G. Tyler, Aug. 26, 1977; children—Ronald, Eric, Scott. Clin. dietitian Salem (Oreg.) Hosp., 1965-73; sales supr. Sysco Northwest, Tigard, Oreg., 1975-77; clin. dietitian Physicians & Surgeons Hosp., Portland, Oreg., 1977-79; food service dir. Meridian Park Hosp., Tualatin, Oreg., 1979—. Registered dietitian. Mem. Am. Dietetic Assn., Oreg. Dietetic Assn., Portland Dietetic Assn., Am. Soc. Hosp. Food Service Adminstrs. Episcopalian. Home: 12800 SE Nixon Ave Milwaukie OR 97222 Office: 19300 SW 65th St Tualatin OR 97062

TYLER, FORREST PUTNAM, pub. relations exec.; b. Portsmouth, Va., June 15, 1922; s. Erland James and Margaret Jane (Bowen) T.; student Rollins Coll., 1946-47, Austin Coll., 1948-49, Baylor U., 1955-56, Md. U., 1959-61; m. M. Dorothea Avery, June 18, 1949; children—Darlene, Cynthia, Virginia. Served as enlisted man arty. AUS, 1940-42; commd. 2d lt. USAAF, 1942, advanced through grades to lt. col. USAF, 1961; dir. info. U.S. Forces Azores, 1959-61; dir. community relations, exec. officer Directorate of Info., Mil. Air Transport Service, 1961-64; ret., 1964; rep. Douglas Aircraft Co., Long Beach, Calif., 1964-67, mgr. community relations, 1967—. Past chmn. Long Beach, Port Ambassadors; past pres. Lakewood YMCA Bd. Mgrs., Lakewood Pan Am. Festival Assn., Long Beach Ind. Businessmens Assn., Douglas Aircraft Co. Mgmt. Club, So. Calif. Coll. Pres.'s Council, Lakewood Rose Float Assn.; v.p. pub. relations Met. Long Beach YMCA; bd. dirs. So. Calif. Coll., Pacific Hosp., Long Beach chpt. March of Dimes, Long Beach Symphony Assn., Lakewood U.S.A. Am. Revolution Bicentennial Com., Big Bros.-Big Sisters Orange County, Long Beach Temple Salvation Army, Long Beach Chpt. Goodwill Industries; mem. nat. council Light for the Lost; mem. exec. com. Long Beach council Boy Scouts Am.; past chmn. Long Beach chpt. ARC; chmn. Long Beach chpt. NCCJ. Decorated D.F.C. with 4 oak leaf clusters, Air medal with 16 oak leaf clusters, Air Force Commendation medal with oak leaf cluster; named Man of Yr., Lakewood, 1968, Douglas Aircraft Co. Mgmt. Club, 1982. Mem. Pub. Relations Soc. Am., Nat. Mgmt. Assn. (Outstanding Service award 1969), Town Hall of Calif., Long Beach C. of C. (dir.), Lakewood C. of C. (past pres.). Republican. Mem. Assemblies of God. Club: Rotary (gov. dist. 532, Rotarian of Yr. award dist. 532). Home: 11732 Reagan St Los Alamitos CA 90720 Office: 3855 Lakewood Blvd Long Beach CA 90846

TYLER, NAOMI PRESTON, food company executive; b. Cleve., Mar. 30, 1955; d. Nicholas Norman and Mary Barbara Preston; m. Michael James Tyler, May 29, 1982. B.S., Denison U., 1977; postgrad. Western Mich. U., 1979-81. Mktg. research analyst YEE/Minard & Assocs., Lathrup Village, Mich., 1977-78; mktg. research analyst Kellogg Co., Battle Creek, Mich., 1978-80, sr. mktg. research analyst, 1980, asst. product mgr., 1980-81; asst. product mgr. Ore-Ida Foods, Boise, Idaho, 1981-82, product mgr., 1982—. Mem. Am. Mktg. Assn., Phi Beta Kappa, Pi Beta Phi. Office: PO Box 10 Boise ID 83707

TYMES, ELNA RODENHOUSE, consultant, technical writer; b. Seattle, May 29, 1939; d. Evert and Irma Martha (Zintheo) Rodenhouse; m. Christopher Edmondstone Prael, Sept. 1, 1961 (div.); 1 son, Charles Evert; m. LaRoy Wayne Tymes, Sept. 29, 1973 (div.); 1 son, Adrian Jeremy. B.A., Stanford U., 1961, postgrad. U. Wash., 1962-64, M.B.A., Pepperdine U., 1982. Tech. writer, 1969-73, 80—; tchr. Seattle Pub. Schs., 1962-66; newspaper editor, Seattle, 1964; pres. Tymes & Assocs., Poppy Day Care Ctrs., Santa Clara, Osborne User's Group, Palo Alto, Calif., 1983—. Pres., Community Assn., 1975; active LWV, 1978-80. Mem. Mensa. Co-author: SuperCalc: Home and Office Companion, 1983. Home and Office: 4018 Ben Lomond Dr Palo Alto CA 94306

TYNDALL, JEAN AVIS, school district administrator; b. Fruita, Colo., Aug. 5, 1924; d. Ivan Claire and Catherine Benoni (Foster) Whipple; m. Lester Alexander Hockney, Jan. 27, 1946; children—John Lester, Lisa Diane; m. 2d, Robert Edward Tyndall, Dec. 7, 1963. B.A., Long Beach State Coll., 1962; student U. So. Calif., 1955-58; M.A., Calif. State U., 1966. Secondary teaching, pupil personnel, sch. adminstrn. credentials, Calif. Tchr. choral music, Huntington Beach (Calif.) Union High Sch. Dist., 1963-73, fine arts coordinator, 1964-73, counselor, 1973-77, dean of attendance, 1977-79, asst. prin., 1979-80, dir. pupil personnel services, 1980—; cons. on ednl. planning, assertive discipline. Adv. bd. mem., Interval House, 1980—; area bd. mem. United Way, 1982—; mem. Huntington Beach City Cultural Commn., 1971-74. Mem. Assn. Calif. Sch. Adminstrs., Calif. Pupil Guidance Assn., Calif. Adminstrs. Spl. Edn., Nat. Pupil Personnel Adminstrs., Delta Kappa Gamma, Sigma Alpha Iota (past nat. v.p.). Office: Union High Sch Dist 10251 Yorktown St Huntington Beach CA 92646

TYRAN, BENJAMIN, business cons.; b. Little Falls, N.Y., Apr. 21, 1921; s. Harry and Rose (Hryb) T.; B.S. in Edn., Rider Coll., 1944; M.B.A., N.Y. U., 1950; postgrad. Am. U., 1952, 53; m. Jeanne Marie Deckman, July 12, 1947; children—Garry K., Cynthia J., Craig K. Acctg. supr. ARAMCO, Saudi Arabia and N.Y.C., 1945-50; economist Standard Oil Co. Calif., 1950-52; petroleum price economist MSA, Washington, 1952-54; gen. sales mgr. Am. Ind. Oil Co., 1954-60; founder, pres., dir. Ind. Petroleum Supply Co., San Francisco and N.Y.C., 1960-72; petroleum cons., Burlingame, Calif., 1973-77; chmn. dir. Isle of Man Petroleum, Ltd., U.K.; pres., dir. Natomas Internat. Corp., Natomas of Can., Ltd., Ind. Petroleum Supply—U.K., Ltd., London, Natomas of Arabia, Ltd., Ind. Petroleum Supply Eastern, Tokyo, 1965-72; sec.-treas., dir. Tarfa, Inc., Ashland, Oreg., 1976-79; v.p., dir. Natomas Co., San Francisco, 1963-72, Ind. Indonesian Am. Petroleum Co., 1966-72; chmn., pres., dir. Doorcraft, Inc., Harrisburg, Oreg., 1976—; exec. v.p. Clay-Jones Overseas Ltd., San Francisco, 1976—; dir., chmn. exec. com. West Indies Oil Co., Antigua, W.I., 1965-72; dir., mem. exec. com. Natomas Co., San Francisco, 1963-72; dir. Sunshine TV, Inc., Medford, Oreg. Mem. San Francisco Com. Fgn. Relations; trustee So. Oreg. State Coll. Found., 1976—, pres., 1979-83; bd. dirs. Council Econ. Devel. in Oreg., 1982—; chmn. Econ. Devel. Commn., Ashland, 1980—. Recipient award for disting. accomplishments in world of bus. Tau Kappa Epsilon, 1972, Disting. Alumnus award Rider Coll., Lawrenceville, N.J., 1972. Mem. Am. Econ. Assn., Acad. Polit. Sci., World Affairs Council, Tau Kappa Epsilon. Clubs: Rogue Valley Country (Medford, Oreg.); Family (San Francisco). Home and Office: 1120 Prospect St Ashland OR 97520

TYSON, WALTER MUIR, III, safety council manager; b. S.I., N.Y., Dec. 6, 1947; s. Walter Muir and Lorraine Winifred (Becker) T.; m. Wendy Wood, May 29, 1971; children—Tanya Nicole, Tarra Dawn. B.A. in Psychology, U. Colo., Boulder, 1977. Assoc. dist. exec. Longs Peak council Boy Scouts Am., Longmont, Colo., 1977-78, Cheyenne dist. exec., Wyo., 1978-80; asst. mgr. Wyo. Safety Council, Cheyenne, 1980—. Mem. Wyo. Gov.'s Adv. Council Vocat. Rehab., Cheyenne, 1979-81; pres. Neighborhood Housing Services, 1979—. Served with USN, 1967-70; Vietnam. Mem. Am. Soc. Safety Engrs. (chmn. chpt.).

Clubs: Kiwanis. Home: 307 E 9th Cheyenne WY 82007 Office: 805 B W 24th Cheyenne WY 82001

TZVETIN, IVAN DIMITROV, architect; b. Sofia, Bulgaria, Apr. 6, 1929; came to U.S., 1966, naturalized, 1975; s. Dimitri Ivanov and Elena (Velcheva) T.; B.Arch., State Poly. U., Sofia, 1953; student in design Ecole Nationale Superieure des Beaux Arts, Paris, 1964; m. Ellen Yamada, June 25, 1980. Sr. designer in architecture and urban design Itis & Glavproject, Sofia, 1953-63; designer, city planner Gravereaux & Denieul, Marti, Paoli, Paris, 1964-66; architect designer McCue, Boone, Tomsick, Architects, San Francisco, 1967-70; v.p. design Anshen & Allen, San Francisco, 1970-81, prin., 1982—; exhibited archtl. sketches, Sofia, 1956, Mexico City, 1964, San Francisco, 1972. Recipient 2d prize Internat. Design Competition for Monument, Museum and Plaza at Playa Giron, Cuba, 1963, 1st prize Internat. Design Competition for Civic Center Plaza, San Francisco, 1965, 1st prize Internat. Competition for Landmark of City of Melbourne (Australia), 1980. Mem. AIA (corp.). Republican. Greek Orthodox. Designer numerous urban design plans bldgs. for edn., medicine, sci./research, transp., housing, fin. Office 461 Bush St Francisco CA 94108

UBELL, TERRI HALE, consultant; b. Roanoke, Va., Sept. 28, 1954; d. George C. and Daroline D. Hale; m. Frank D. Ubell, July 10, 1982. B.S. in Computer Sci., Calif. State U., 1976. Systems analyst Burroughs, Mission Viejo, Calif., 1976-78; sr. systems analyst Harris Corp., Los Angeles, 1978-80; info. systems mgr. Dynatech Corp., Santa Ana, Calif., 1980—, acting materials mgr., 1981-83; cons., 1983—. Mem. Calif. Data Base Mgmt. Assn., Am. Prodn. and Inventory Control Soc. Home: 411 Irvine Ave Newport Beach CA 92663

UCHIDA, PRENTISS SUSUMU, computer electronics company executive; b. San Jose, Calif., Nov. 30, 1940; s. Fred Toshio and Elise Chioye (Kurasaki) U.; B.A., San Jose State U., 1963; postgrad. Santa Clara U. Bus. Sch., 1965; m. Patricia Ann White, Oct. 17, 1981; children—S. Akemi, Toshio C., Kamal K. P. Programmer, Lockheed Missiles & Space Co., Sunnyvale, Calif., 1963-66, Adage Inc., Los Angeles, 1966-69; founder, pres., chmn. Vector Gen. Inc., Woodland Hills, Calif., 1969-79; pres. InnerGame Corp., Los Angeles, 1979—. Mem. adv. com. Stanford U. Exec. Inst., 1975-76; bd. dirs. United Crusade/United Way, 1977-79. Mem. Assn. Computer Machinery, Am. Mgmt. Assn., Aircraft Owners and Pilots Assn. Democrat. Club: Te Ken Jutsu Kai. Office: InnerGame Corp 127 Barrington Pl Los Angeles CA 90049

UDA, ROBERT TAKEO, manufacturing company executive; b. Honolulu, Aug. 1, 1942; s. Masao and Irene Kuualoha (Waipa) U.; m. Karen Elizabeth Rowland, June 8, 1968; children—Atom Richard, Marc Edward, Heather Ann. B.S. in Aerospace Engring, U. Okla., Norman, 1966; M.S. in Astronautics, USAF Inst. of Tech., 1968. Cert. tchr. Calif. Community Colleges, 1974. Joined USAF, 1966, advanced through grades to capt., 1974; astronautical devel. engr., 1966-74; lead sr. design engr., Planning Research Corp., Kennedy Space Center, Fla., 1974-76, prin. engr.; 1976-77; sr. preliminary design engr. United Technologies Corp., Windsor Locks, Conn., 1977-78; project engr. TRW, Inc., Redondo Beach, Calif., 1978-79; program mgr. H. R. Textron, Inc., Valencia, Calif., 1979-80, product line mgr., 1980-82, gen. mgr., Accessory Products Group, 1982—. Decorated Meritorious Service Medal. Mem. Jaycees, 1968-78, local pres., 1971-72, dist. gov. 1972-73; nat. dir., 1973-74, state chaplain, 1979, state chmn. 1970-71). Fellow Brit. Interplanetary Soc., AIAA (assoc.); mem. Am. Astron. Soc., Air Force Assn., Am. Def. Preparedness Assn., Nat. Mgmt. Assn., Sigma Tau, Alpha Sigma Phi. Republican. Mormon. Clubs: H. R. Textron Mgt. (dir.). Author: reports, papers, articles to profl. jours. Home: 19544 Delight St Canyon Country CA 91351 Office: 10445 Glenoaks Blvd Pacoima CA 91331

UDALL, MORRIS KING, congressman; b. St. Johns, Ariz., June 15, 1922; s. Levi S. and Louise (Lee) U.; LL.B., with distinction, U. Ariz., Tucson, 1949. children—Mark, Randolph, Judith, Anne, Bradley, Kathryn. Admitted to Ariz. bar, 1949; partner firm Udall and Udall, Tucson, 1949-61; chief dep. county atty. Pima County, 1950-52; county atty. Pima County, 1953-54; lectr. labor law U. Ariz., 1955-56; mem. 87th-97th congresses, 2d Congl. dist. Ariz., chmn. interior and insular affairs com., vice chmn. Post Office and Civil Service com.; vice chmn. Office Tech. Assessment. Del. Dem. Nat. Conv., 1956, chmn. Ariz. delegation, 1972; chmn. Ariz. Vols. for Stevenson, 1956. Candidate for Dem. presidential nomination, 1976. Served to Capt. USAAF, 1942-46; PTO. Author: Arizona Law of Evidence, 1960; The Job of the Congressman, 1966; Education of A Congressman, 1972. Office: 235 Cannon House Office Bldg Washington DC 20515

UDELMAN, DONNA LOU, psychotherapist, researcher, educator; b. Cleve.; m. Harold D. Udelman, Aug. 26, 1956; children—Lisa Udelman Cohn, Tamara, Randall. B.A., Antioch U., 1977, M.A., 1979; Ph.D., Clayton U., 1981. Cert. clin. mental health counselor. Co-therapist adolescent unit Central State Hosp., Anchorage, Ky., 1963-64; co-therapist Baptist Home for Children, Glendale, Ky., 1963-64; co-therapist Rheumatology Group for In-Patients, Good Samaritan Hosp., Phoenix, 1973-77; co-therapist Rheumatology Group for Out-Patients, Phoenix Arthritis Center, 1973-78; pvt. practice psychotherapy, Phoenix; 1973—; mem. clin. faculty dept. psychiatry and human behavior U. Calif.-Irvine; external examiner Fielding Inst., Santa Barbara, Calif.; numerous profl. presentations. Fellow Acad. Psychosomatic Medicine, Am. Orthopsychit. Assn.; mem. Am. Psychol. Assn. (assoc.), Arthritis Found., Am. Personnel and Guidance Assn., Ariz. Personnel and Guidance Assn., AAAS, Soc. Behavioral Medicine, N.Y. Acad. Scis., Assn. Advancement Psychotherapy, Internat. Acad. Profl. Counselling and Psychotherapy (clin.). Contbr. articles to profl. jours.; manuscript reviewer Psychosomatics; research in antidepressant therapy and immunity, 1982. Office: 45 E Osborn Rd Phoenix AZ 85012

UDICK, ROBERT EDGAR, newspaper executive; b. Colorado Springs, Colo., May 27, 1922; s. Albert Earl and Edna (Young) U. Student Colo. Coll., 1947. Staff corr. Rocky Mountain News, Denver, 1947-49, United Press Denver and Santa Fe, 1950-51; war corr. Korea, 1951-53, later became mgr. Hong Kong and Manila burs., then mgr. for Southwest Asia, hdqrs. Singapore; editor, pub. Bangkok World, until 1967; now pub. Pacific Daily News, Agana, Guam. Mem. civilian adv. bd. 8th Air Force; mem. Navy League, Guam Stock Exchange. Bd. regents U. Guam. Served with Coast Arty., Inf., Signal Corps, World War II. Mem. Fgn. Corr. Assn. Thailand (pres.), Phi Delta Theta. Lodge: Rotary. Address: Pacific Daily News PO Box DN Agana GU 96910

UFER, WILLIAM REX, agronomist; b. Wooster, Ohio, Mar. 8, 1939; s. William S. and Elizabeth (Snook) U.; children—William R., R. Brent, Melanie R. Student Ohio State U., 1957-59; B.S., Mich. State U., 1960. Farm planner Soil Conservation Service, Ohio, Mich., 1956-64; gen. mgr. Ufer Cert. Seed Co., Stryker, Ohio, 1964-70; dist. sales mgr., sr. agronomist Sohio Chem. Co., Jackson, Mich., and Lima, Ohio, 1970—; owner, mgr. Ufer Farms, Stryker, 1961—. Served with U.S. Army, 1962. Mem. Am. Soc. Agronomy, Am. Registry Cert. Profls. in Agronomy, Crops and Soils. Home: 1475 Edgewood Dr 5F Lima OH 45805 Office: PO Box 628 Lima OH 45802

UGARTE, ABDON JOSE, newspaper executive; b. Cochabamba, Bolivia, July 30, 1928; s. Julio Cesar and Cinda Maria (Palacios) U.; m. Beatriz Alanes, Feb. 20, 1981; children—Ernesto, Lesly. M.A. in Law, U. Cochabamba, 1952, M.A. in Journalism, 1955. Bolivian congressman, 1958-62; Bolivian consul, San Francisco, 1963-65; editor El Mundo, San Francisco, 1969—; producer Revista de la Semana, Sta. KTVU, San Francisco; latin corr. San Francisco Chronicle, San Francisco Examiner; instr. journalism Merritt Coll., Oakland; lectr. Latin Am. politics. Mem. TV Workers Am. Clubs: El Camino Real Optimists (charter pres.), Lions, Press, Flying Samaritans (San Francisco). Author: Tinku, 1961.

UGGEN, JOHN FORREST, educator; b. Devil's Lake, N.D., Sept. 1, 1943; s. Carl Quentin and Gladys Joy (Evensizer) U.; B.A., U. Oreg., 1965; M.A., U. Miami, Coral Gables, Fla., 1970, Ph.D., (fellow), 1974; m. Martha Piedad Gabilanes, July 6, 1968; children—John Eric, Maria Angela. Vol., Peace Corps, Ecuador, 1965-67; Andean fellow Catholic U. Ecuador, Quito, 1970-71; Latin Am. teaching fellow U. Oriente, Cumana, Venezuela, 1975-76, asst. prof. English, 1976-79; No. coordinator Latin C. of C. of Nevada, Reno, 1979-80, also grant writer; Latin Am. export mgr. AMERX, Reno, 1979-80; asst. prof. Spanish and internat. studies Willamette U., Salem, Oreg., 1980—, chmn. dept. fgn. langs., 1982—; instr. Western Nev. Community Coll., 1979-80; Latin Am. teaching fellow Tufts U., 1975-76. Election campaign cons. to 2 Nev. candidates, 1980; mem. community services adv. bd. Western Nev. Community Coll., 1979-80. Recipient John Barrett prize U. Miami, 1976. Mem. Am. Assn. Tchrs. Spanish and Portuguese; Latin Am. Studies Assn., Nev. World Trade Assn. Republican. Lutheran. Club: Toastmasters. Home: 2330 Church St SE Salem OR 97302 Office: Dept Fgn Langs Willamette U Salem OR 97302

UGLUM, JOHN RICHARD, optometrist; b. Wonewoc, Wis., Nov. 26, 1909; s. John R. and May (Dewey) U.; B.S., Northwestern U., 1930; postgrad. Dakota Wesleyan U., 1946; O.D., No. Ill. Coll. Optometry, 1932; Sc.D. honoris causa, Internat. Coll. Visual Sci., 1962, Philathea Coll., 1971, Ind. No. U., 1972; m. Frances T. Wikholm, Jan. 20, 1940; children—Karen, Katherine. Practice optometry, Reno, 1961; exec. sec. Nat. Bd. Examiners in Optometry, Reno, 1951-64; practice optometry, Brookings, S.D., 1964—; asso. Watson Clinic, Brookings, 1964-72; tchr. developmental reading S.D. State U.; dir. Daktronics Inc., 1968—; sec., fellow Distinguished Service Found. of Optometry, Reno, 1959; contract med. care officer USPHS; mem. Eye Research Found. Pres., Washoe Assn. for Mental Health; bd. dirs. Brookings Area Guidance Center, S.D. Bapt. Conv.; trustee Sioux Falls Coll.; mem. Gov.'s Com. Employment Handicapped; mem. S.D. Bldg. Authority, 1972—; mem. S.D. Central Democratic Com., 1972—. Mem. Nat. Bd. Examiners in Optometry, Nat. Bd. Examiners in Podiatry, 1962-69. Recipient medal Order of St. John of Jerusalem, knight of Honor, 1965; officer Order of Crown of Thorns, France, 1965; grand cross Fundacion Internationale Eloy Alfaro (Panama), 1966. Mem. Am. Optometric Assn., Am. Acad. Optometry, AAAS, Internat. Assn. Bds. Examiners Optometry, Nev., S.D. (hon.), Ariz. (hon.), Central Ariz. (hon.) optometric assns., Am. Geriatrics Assn., Contact Lens Soc. Am., Nev. Soc. for Crippled Children (pres.), Nat. Soc. for Crippled Children and Adults (trustee), Illuminating Engrs. Soc., Safety Engring. Soc., Am. Orthopsychiat. Assn., Sons of Norway, Norske Stravangerlager, Soc. for Advancement Research in Ophthalmology, Soc. European Optometrics, Sigma Xi. Baptist (pres. ch. council, moderator). Mason (Shriner), Kiwanian (past pres.). Home: 9418 Manzanita Dr Sun City AZ 85373

UHL, DIANA BROWN, microbiologist; b. Eaton Rapids, Mich., Mar. 23, 1941; d. Alton Loren and Bette B. (Winters) Brown; m. Kenneth Uhl, Nov. 21, 1975; children by previous marriages—Alton, Lee, Rebecca. B.S. magna cum laude, Saginaw Valley State Coll., 1977; M.B.A., So. Ill. U.-Edwardsville, 1982. Microbiologist, Dow Cornning Corp., Midland, Mich., 1973-78; quality control, assurance mgr. Cordis Dow Corp., Concord, Calif., 1978—. Chmn. energy conservation com., Concord C. of C. Served with USNR, 1979—. Mem. Parenteral Drug Assn., Am. Soc. Quality Control, Nat. Assn. for Female Execs., Health Industries Mfrs. Assn. (com. to draft standards on ethylene oxide testing), Beta Gamma Sigma. Republican. Episcopalian. Home: 331 Seaview Dr Benicia CA 94510 Office: 2450 Bisso Ln Concord CA 94520

UHLAND, RUTH ELLEN, educator; b. Escondido, Calif., May 4, 1925; d. William and Ruth (Rooker) U.; A.A., Mira Costa Coll., 1945; B.A., San Diego State U., 1947, postgrad., 1948-49, 61, 62, 64, 70-72, San Jose State U., 1966-67, Fresno State U., 1956-57, U. San Diego, 1969, Internat. U., 1971—. Tchr. jr. high sch. Brawley (Calif.) Elem. Sch. Dist., 1947-50, 53-54, 56-64, elem. tchr., 1950-53, 55, 65—, chmn. health-phys. edn. dept., 1960. Active various community drives. Adv. bd. Rainbow Girls, 1972—. Mem. Internat. Reading Assn. (sch. rep. 1969-72), Nat. Ret. Tchrs. Assn., Calif. Ret. Tchrs. Assn., Internat. Platform Assn., Calif., Brawley tchrs. assns., Imperial Valley Girls Phys. Edn. Assn. (pres. 1967-68), Brawley Bus. and Profl. Women's Club (v.p. desert sect. 1968-69, pres. 1967, 75, pres.'s ecology citation 1972, Service award 1978), Desert Protective Council (life), Imperial Photog. Soc., Nat. Audubon Soc., Wilson Ornithol. Soc., Cooper Ornithol. Soc. (life), Sierra Club, AAUW, Delta Kappa Gamma. Mem. Order Eastern Star. Clubs: Venture (pres. 1954-55) (Brawley); White Shrine Jerusalem. Home: 158 G St Brawley CA 92227 Office: Brawley CA 92727

UHLANER, JULIUS EARL, psychologist; b. Vienna, Austria, Apr. 22, 1917; came to U.S., 1928, naturalized, 1928; s. Benjamin and Ethel U.; B.S., CUNY, 1938; M.S., Iowa State U., 1941; Ph.D., N.Y.U., 1947; m. Vera Kolar, Sept. 3, 1949; children—Carole Jean, Lorraine Marie Uhlaner Hendrickson, Robert Theodore. Indsl. psychology asst. Ford Motor Co., 1940-41; research asst. Iowa State U., 1940-41; research asso. N.Y. U., 1941-42; asst. dir. tng. N.Y. State Div. Vets. Affairs, with 1946-49; with U.S. Army Research Inst., Washington, 1947-78, tech. dir., 1964-78; chief psychologist U.S. Army, 1964-78; adj. prof. psychology George Washington U., 1971—; v.p. Perceptronics, Inc., Woodland Hills, Calif., 1978-81; pres. Uhlaner Cons., Encino, Calif., 1981—; dir. Starpak, Perceptronics, Inc. Served with USAAF, 1944-46. Recipient Presdl. Mgmt. Improvement award, 1978. Fellow Am. Psychol. Assn. (pres. div. mil. psychology 1969-70), Human Factors Soc., Washington Acad. Scis., Iowa Acad. Scis., Ops. Research Soc. Am.; mem. Psi Chi. Club: Cosmos (Washington). Author: Psychological Research in National Defense Today, 1964. Cons. editor Jour. Applied Psychology, 1970—. Contbr. articles to profl. jours. Home and Office: 4258 Bonavita Dr Encino CA 91436

UHLEMANN, WILLIAM RICHARD, real estate loan executive; b. Evanston, Ill., Aug. 14, 1943; s. Richard Colbert and Virginia (Troup) U.; B.A., Westminster Coll., 1966; grad. Am. Inst. Banking, 1968; postgrad. U. Colo., 1975, 77, 78. Dist. mgr. Readers Digest, Pitts., 1966-67; analyst No. Trust Co. Bank, Chgo., 1967-69; FM sales mgr. sta. KHOW, Denver, 1970-71; v.p. mktg. Mountain Investments Inc., Dillon, Colo., 1973-75; with various real estate cos., Colo., 1973, 76-77; loan officer Megapolitan Mortgage Co., Denver, 1976; v.p., mgr. comml./constrn. loan dept. Majestic Savings & Loan Assn., Denver, 1977-82; v.p. comml. loans Capitol Fed. Savs. and Loan, Denver, 1982-83; dist. mgr. real estate loans Gen. Electric Credit Corp., Denver, 1983—; cons. in field. Mem. Jefferson County Rep. Party Caucus. Mem. Colo. Mortgage Bankers Assn. (comml. com., co-chmn.), Evergreen Bd. Realtors, U.S. Power Squadron, Sigma Chi. Republican. Episcopalian. Clubs: Ducks Unltd., Denver Press, White Lake Yacht, Mt. Vernon Country, Friends of Forest Heights. Home: PO Box 369 Evergreen CO 80439 Office: GECC Comml Real Estate Financing 600 S Cherry St Suite 1105 Denver CO 80222

UHLER, JAMES WALTER, engineering company executive; b. Olympia, Wash., Jan. 30, 1931; s. Walter Vincent and Beatrice Isabelle (Dimmick) U.; student Portland State Coll., 1955-56; B.S. in Civil Engring. U. Ariz., 1958; m. Janice Margaret Cardwell, Mar. 3, 1952; children—Deborah Kay, Teresa Lee, Kathleen Cle, Lynn Marie; m. 2d, Alta Faye Cutsforth, May 14, 1973; Project engr. Western Pipe Line Co., Inc., La., Miss. and Pa., 1958-60; chief engr. Huico, Inc., Pasco, Wash., 1960-68; project engr., project mgr. reactor constrn. Howard S. Wright & Assos., Idaho Falls, Idaho, 1968-70; project field engr. Bechtel Corp., Richland, Wash., 1970-74; pres. Uhler & Assos., Inc., Pasco, 1974—. Mem., past chmn. Mid Columbia Bldg. Appeals Commn., 1974—; bd. dirs., v.p. United Way of Benton and Franklin Counties, 1978—; trustee Columbia Basin Devel. League. Served with U.S. Army, 1952-54. Registered profl. engr., Wash., Oreg., Idaho. Mem. Nat. Soc. Profl. Engrs., Profl. Engrs. in Pvt. Practice, Wash. State Water Resources Assn., Pasco C. of C. Republican. Methodist. Clubs: Elks, Tri City Country (pres.). Home: 419 W 30th Ave Kennewick WA 99336 Office: 1120 Rd 28 N Pasco WA 99302

UHRICH, AMY SUSAN, association executive; b. Holyoke, Colo., Sept. 28, 1943; d. Harold Ivan and Fern Ethel Dinnell; m. James Byron Uhrich, June 15, 1963; 1 dau., Jill Renae. Student U. No. Colo., 1962-63, Adams State Coll., 1980-81. With acctg. dept. Hewlett-Packard, Loveland, Colo., 1964-66; with LaPlanta County Assessor's Office, Durango, Colo., 1969-71; with acctg. dept. Rio Grande Savs. & Loan, Monte Vista, Colo., 1971-73; with Monte Vista C. of C., 1976—, now mgr. Chmn. Rio Grande Republican. Central Com., 1977-79; sec. 3d Congl. Dist., 1977-79; mem. 3d Congl. Dist. Vacancy Com., 1978. Mem. U.S. C. of C., Colo. C. of C. Execs., San Luis Valley Tourist and Resort Assn., Colo. C. of C. Execs. (bd. dirs. 1977-78), PEO (sec. 1982-83), Beta Sigma Phi. Methodist. Office: Monte Vista C of C 1125 Park Ave Monte Vista CO 81144

UHRICH, RICHARD BECKLEY, health services administrator; b. Pitts., June 11, 1932; s. Leroy Earl and Mabel Hoffer (Beckley) U.; m. Thelma Domenici, Jan. 1, 1977; children—Mark, Karen, Kimberly. B.S., Allegheny Coll., 1954; M.D., U. Pa., 1958; M.P.H., U. Calif.-Berkeley, 1966. Diplomate Am. Bd. Preventive Medicine. Intern Lancaster Gen. Hosp. (Pa.), 1958-59; resident in preventive medicine U. Calif., 1965-66; dir. div. program ops. Indian Health Service, USPHS, 1971-73; assoc. dir. div. profl. resources Office Internat. Health, Office of Asst. Sec. for Health, HEW, 1973-74, assoc. dir. program devel. and coordination, 1974-78; dir. Phoenix Indian Med. Ctr. and Phoenix Service Unit, 1978-81; sr. adminstr. Good Samaritan Med. Ctr., Phoenix, 1981-82, chief exec. officer, 1982—; U.S. del. World Health Assembly, 1975-76; advisor to U.S. mem. WHO; dir. Med. Ctr. Redevel. Corp., 1982-83; v.p. Samaritan Redevel. Corp., 1983. Recipient Meritorious Service medal USPHS, 1973, citation, 1973, Commd. Officers award, 1981. Mem. Am. Coll. Hosp. Adminstrs., Am. Hosp. Assn., Council Teaching Hosps. Am. Assn. Med. Colls., Ariz. Hosp. Assn. (dir., exec. com.), Phoenix Regional Hosp. Assn. (pres. 1981), Am. Pub. Health Assn. Clubs: Arizona, Kiva, Camelback Country (Phoenix). Office: 1111 E McDowell Rd Phoenix AZ 85006

UHRICK, GENE ALLEN, sales engineer; b. Decatur, Ind., Oct. 19, 1931; s. Luzern Francis and Helen (Schmitz) U.; m. Patricia S. Lasch, June 25, 1955 (div.); children—Lisa and Lisbeth (twins), Steven, Anthony; m. 2d, Ann E. Belote, Nov. 10. 1981. B.S., Ind. U., 1960; M.S., U. Calif.-Berkeley, 1961. Sanitarian, Allen County Health Dept., Ft. Wayne, Ind., 1956-58; lab. technician Marion County (Ind.) Health Dept., 1958-60; field sanitarian San Diego Health Dept., 1961-62; water dist. sect. mgr. Leucadia County (Calif.), 1962-65; v.p. Western regional mgr. sales Walker Process div. Chgo. Bridge and Iron, Pasadena, Calif., 1965-81; pres. Uhrick Process, Glendale, Calif., 1981—. Served to staff sgt. USAF, 1951-55. Mem. Am. Water Works Assn. Office: Uhrick Process 65 West Del Mar Ave Pasadena CA 91105

ULITT, LILLY ROSE, dietitian; b. Charleston, W.Va., June 11, 1936; d. Elias and Georgette Haddad; B.S. in Foods and Nutrition, W.Va. State U., 1960; B.B.A. in Mgmt., Ariz. State U., 1975; M.B.A., Pepperdine U., 1980; m. Carl Ulitt, Sept. 16, 1967; 1 dau., Karen Marie. Dietitian, Bethesda Hosp., Cin., 1962-64; food service mgr. U. Ariz., Tucson, 1968-70, Long Beach (Calif.) Unified Sch. Dist., 1977-78; food service dir. Chino (Calif.) Community Hosp., 1978-80, San Diego Naval Regional Med. Center, 1981—; vol. nutritionist ARC, Okinawa, Japan, 1971-72; nutrition cons. Title VII Sr. Nutrition Program, 1977-78; instr. instl. food service program Palomar Coll., San Marcos, Calif. Active Meals-On-Wheels, Chino. Served to capt. USAF, 1964-68. Recipient cert. of achievement U.S. Army Med. Center, Okinawa. Mem. Am. Dietetic Assn., Calif. Sch. Food Service Assn., Calif. Dietetic Assn., Am. Soc. Hosp. Food Service Adminstrs., Aircraft Owners and Pilots Assn., Civil Air Patrol. Home: PO Box 351 Coronado CA 92118 Office: Food Mgmt Services Naval Regional Med Center San Diego CA 92134

ULLMAN, CORNELIUS GUMBEL, conservation cons.; b. Cleve., Sept. 14, 1906; s. Lee J. and Daisy (Gumbel) U.; B.S. in Econs., U. Calif. at Berkeley, 1928; M.S. in Agr., U. Calif. at Davis, 1934; m. Robie Jenkins, Jan. 24, 1936; children—Cornell, Lorna, Maury. Area agronomist soil conservation service U.S. Dept. Agr., 1935-41, dist. conservationist, 1941-50; field rep. Calif. Soil Conservation Commn., Sacramento, 1950-57; program coordinator div. soil conservation Calif. Dept. Conservation, Ventura, 1957-68, resource conservationist, 1967-68; resource conservation cons., 1968—. Fellow Am. Geog. Soc.; mem. Am. Geophys. Union, AAAS, Western Soc. Soil Sci., Soil Conservation Soc. Am., Sigma Xi. Republican. Club: Commonwealth of Calif. Home and Office: 117 N Calle Vista Camarillo CA 93010

ULLMAN, EDWIN FISHER, research chemist; b. Chgo., July 19, 1930; s. Harold P. and Jane F. Ullman; m. Elizabeth J. Findlay, June 26, 1954; children—Becky L., Linda J. B.A., Reed Coll., Portland, Oreg., 1952; M.A., Harvard U., 1954, Ph.D., 1956. Research chemist Lederle Labs., Am. Cyanamid, Pearl River, N.Y., 1955-60; group leader central research div. Am. Cyanamid, Stamford, Conn., 1960-66; sci. dir. Synvar Research Inst., Palo Alto, Calif., 1966-70; v.p., dir. research Syva Co., Palo Alto, 1970—. NSF predoctoral fellow, 1952-53; U.S. Rubber Co. fellow, 1954-55. Recipient Clin. Ligand Assay Soc. Mallinckrodt award, 1981, Can. Soc. Clin. Chemists Health Group award, 1982. Mem. Am. Chem. Soc., Am. Assn. Clin. Chemists, AAAS, Chem. Soc., InterAm. Photochemistry Soc. Contbr. articles to sci. jours. Patentee in field. Office: Syva Co PO Box 10058 Palo Alto CA 94303

ULMER, HARRIET GLASS, health services adminstr.; b. St. Louis, June 7, 1940; d. Melvin Gabriel and Deenie Joy (Laskowitz) Shcolnik; m. Allen L. Glass, Sept. 4, 1956 (div.); children—Bonnie Glass Nielson, Bernard J., Laura L.; m. 2d, Raymond A. Ulmer, Feb. 26, 1980. A.B. in English, UCLA, 1976; M.P.A. in Health Services Adminstrn., U. So. Calif., 1980. Regional project coordinator Kaiser Found. Health Plan, Los Angeles, 1977-80; dir. planning and mktg. Hosp. of Good Samaritan, Los Angeles, 1981—; cons. Humana Corp., Los Angeles Health Planning and Devel. Agy. Mem. Coro Assocs.; mem. Los Angeles Area Planning Com. Mem. Am. Hosp. Assn., Am. Coll. Hosp. Adminstrs., Women in Health Adminstrn., Healthcare Execs. of So. Calif., So. Calif. Soc. for Hosp. Planners, Am. Soc. Hosp. Planning, Am. Mktg. Assn. Office: 616 S Witmer St Los Angeles CA 90017

ULRICH, PAUL GRAHAM, lawyer; b. Spokane, Wash., Nov. 29, 1938; s. Donald Gunn and Kathryn (Vandercook) U.; B.A. with high honors, U. Mont., 1961; J.D., Stanford U., 1964; m. Virginia Ragland, June 10, 1961; children—Kathleen Elizabeth, Marilee Rae, Michael Graham; m. 2d, Kathleen Nelson Smith, July 30, 1982. Admitted to Calif. bar, 1965, Ariz. bar, 1966; law clk. judge U.S. Ct. Appeals 9th Circuit, San Francisco, 1964-65; asso. firm Lewis and Roca, Phoenix, 1965-70, partner, 1970—; instr. Thunderbird Grad. Sch. Internat. Mgmt., 1968-69, Ariz. State U. Coll. Law, 1970-73, 1978, Scottsdale Community Coll., 1975-77, also continuing legal edn. seminars. Bd. visitors Stanford U. Law Sch., 1974-77. Served with U.S. Army, 1956. Recipient continuing legal edn. award State Bar Ariz., 1978. Mem. ABA (chmn. selection and utilization of staff personnel com., legal econs. sect. 1979-81, mem. standing com. legal assts. 1982— Ariz. Bar Assn. (chmn. econs. of law practice com. 1980-81, co-chmn. lower ct. improvement com. 1982—, co-chmn. joint project appellate hanbbooks 1983—), Maricopa County Bar Assn., Calif. Bar Assn., Am. Law Inst., Am. Judicature Soc., Phi Kappa Phi, Phi Alpha Delta. Republican. Club: Ariz. Co-chmn., editor, contbr. Ariz. State Bar Appellate Handbook Project, 1976—; editor, contbr.: Working with Legal Assistants, 1980, 81; Future Directions for Law Office Management, 1982; contbr. numerous articles to profl. jours. Home: 107 E El Caminito Rd Phoenix AZ 85020 Office: Lewis and Roca 100 W Washington St Phoenix AZ 85003

ULRICH, VERA ELIZABETH, educator; b. Chippewa Falls, Wis., July 1, 1922; d. Albion Myles and Wilhelmina Josephine (Johnson) Britten; m. William Viorel Ulrich, Feb. 8, 1946; children—Susanna Ulrich Barton, Cawley. B.S., Wis. State U., 1953; M.S. Pepperdine U., 1976; postgrad. U. Minn., UCLA, U. So. Calif. Cert. tchr., Calif., Minn.; cert. Miller Unruh Reading Specialist. Tchr. pub. schs., Glidden and Beloit, Wis., 1943-44, 46, South St. Paul, Minn., 1946-53; tchr. Enterprise Sch., Compton, Calif., 1953-69, reading specialist, 1966-77; condr. pvt. reading clinic, Torrance, Calif., 1973-82. Leader, neighborhood chmn. Girl Scouts U.S.A., 1947-64; active VFW Aux., Centinella Hosp. Aux. Served with WAC, U.S. Army, 1944-45. Named hon. life mem. Enterprise PTA. Mem. NEA, Calif. Tachers Assn., Compton Faculty Assn. (pres. 1966-67), Reading Specialists Calif. (state exec. bd. 1972—), Nat. Reading Assn., Calif. Reading Assn., Torrance Reading Assn., WAC Vets. Assn. Democrat. Lutheran. Club: Eastern Star. Author: Face Puppets, 1977; editor Reading Specialists Newsletter. Address: 3805 W 183d St Torrance CA 90504

ULVILA, DAN L., accountant, computer consultant; b. Red Lodge, Mont., Mar. 29, 1949; s. Matt O. and Dorothy L. U.; m. Pennie J. Morton, June 9, 1973; 1 son, Michael. B.A. in Zoology, U. Mont., 1971, B.S. in Acctg., 1975. C.P.A., Mont. Tchr. pub. schs., Dixon, Mont., 1972-73; with Jordahl & Sliter, C.P.A.s, Kalispell, Mont., 1976-80, ptnr., 1980—, ptnr. in charge data processing dept., 1982—, tax and computer cons. Bd. dirs., treas. Hockaday for Arts, 1981—. Mem. Am. Inst. C.P.A.s, Mont. Soc. C.P.A.s (dir. 1979-82). Mormon. Clubs: Internat. Brotherhood of Magicians, Jaycees (all offices including pres., Outstanding Jaycee of Yr. and Keyman awards, Outstanding Pres. award Mont. Jaycees, 1979). Clubs: Elks, Eagles. Office: PO Box 817 Kalispell MT 59901

UMANS, MEG, psychotherapist, writer; b. Bklyn., May 26, 1945; d. Sam and Eleanor (Stone) U.; m. Bernard Schainholtz, Aug. 23, 1964 (div.). B.A. in French, SUNY-Buffalo, 1967; M.S. in Library Service, Columbia U., 1972; M.C. in Counseling, Ariz. State U., 1981. Cert. Profl. Hypnosis Tng. Ctr. Probation officer City of Phoenix, 1975; coordinator vol. program Phoenix Pub. Library, 1975-77, librarian social scis., 1977-81; pvt. practice psychotherapy, Phoenix, 1982—; tchr.; editor, columnist profl. newsletters. Trainer, Crisis Line, Phoenix, 1979-82; mem. Maricopa County Task Force on Women and Behavioral Health, Phoenix, 1982—. Mem. Am. Psychol. Assn., Am. Personnel and Guidance Assn., Am. Mental Health Counselors Assn., Assn. to Advance Ethical Hypnosis, Mensa. Democrat. Jewish. Author: Counseling Papers, 1982; editor Phoenix Women's Ctr. newsletter, 1981—. Home and Office: 2730 E Belleview Apt 3 Phoenix AZ 85008

UMBRAGE, DONALD H., accountant, educator; b. Albuquerque, June 27, 1936; s. Jake L. and Anabel T. (Tischhauser) U.; m. Louise M. McGonagel, Feb. 13, 1971; children—Celeste, Christopher, Steven. B.S. in Bus. Adminstrn., U. N.Mex., 1971. C.P.A., N.Mex. Mgr. Rafter Four Ranch, Raton, N.Mex., 1963-66; salesman Umbrage Co., Inc., Albuquerque, 1967-70; staff acct. Rogoff & Youngblood, C.P.A.s, Albuquerque, 1971-74, Donald W. Reid, C.P.A., Albuquerque, 1974-79; pvt. practice acctg., Albuquerque, 1977—; instr. acctg. U. N.Mex., 1979—. Served with USN, 1959-63. Mem. Albuquerque C. of C., Am. Inst. C.P.A.s, Nat. Fedn. Ind. Bus., N.Mex. Soc. C.P.A.s (mgmt. adv. com.). Republican. Roman Catholic. Club: Elks. Office: 3420 Constitution Ave NE Suite C Albuquerque NM 87106

UNDERDOWN, ARTHUR WILLIAM, transp. exec.; b. Glendale, Calif., Nov. 3, 1933; s. Arthur John and Mary Wilhelmina (Jureziz) U.; B.A., Claremont Men's Coll., 1955; M.A., Claremont Grad. Sch., 1979; m. Joyce Ann Sims, June 24, 1955; children—Cynthia, Amy, Allison. Asst. corp. controller Flying Tiger Line, Los Angeles, 1968-74; controller Bekins Co., Los Angeles, 1974-78; v.p. internat. group, 1978-79; corp. v.p. Internat. Customs Service, Inc., Los Angeles, 1979—. Served to 1st lt. Inf., U.S. Army, 1955-56. Mem. Claremont C. of C., Glendale C. of C., Planning Execs. Inst., Nat. Assn. Accts. Office: 2730 Monterey St Torrance CA 90503

UNDERWOOD, JAMES WALTON, coast guard officer; b. Loma Linda, Calif., June 11, 1950; s. Donald Charles and Jacqueline Louise (Thibault) U.; m. Katherine Ann Vaverchak, Apr. 27, 1973; 1 dau., Katherine Louise. B.S., U.S. Coast Guard Acad., 1972; grad. Def. Info. Sch., 1976, Maritime Law Enforcement Sch., 1979. Commd. ensign U.S. Coast Guard, 1972; advanced through grades to lt. comdr., 1982; communications officer USCG Cutter Glacier, 1972-74; boating safety officer 11th Dist., Long Beach, Calif., 1974-76, pub. affairs officer, adm.'s aide, 1976-79; exec. officer USCG Cutter Citrus, Coos Bay, Oreg., 1979-81; comdg. officer USCG Tng. Team One, Alameda, Calif., 1981—; instr. Maritime Law Enforcement; tng. dir. Pacific Area operational mobile tng. unit; instr. adult edn. english and history, 1973-74. Mem. Clayton Valley Parent Pre-Sch. Coop. Assn. Decorated Commendation medal, Achievement medal, Antarctic and Arctic service medals. Mem. Am. Polar Soc., Internat. Assn. Chiefs Police, Am. Soc. Tng. and Devel., U.S. Coast Guard Acad. Alumni Assn. Republican. Roman Catholic. Office: Training Team One Government Island Alameda CA 94501

UNDERWOOD, NANCY MAE, occupational health and safety cons.; b. Vancouver, Wash., Dec. 29, 1944; d. Robert Izea and Jennie Mae (McWhorter) Espie; B.S. in Occupational Health and Safety, Calif. State U., 1974, now post grad.; cert. of proficiency-engring./occupational safety and health, Travelers Ins. Co., 1975, Textron, Inc., 1977; postgrad. U. San Francisco, 1978-81; 1 dau., Apryl. Safety engr. Travelers Ins. Co., Los Angeles, 1975-76; tchr. Los Angeles City Unified Sch. System, 1976; mgr. safety Hydraulic research subs. Textron, Inc., Valencia, Calif., 1977-78; mgr. safety Northrop Aircraft Group, Hawthorne, Calif., 1978—; operator, operator Nancy's Safety Tng. and Cons. firm. Recipient Performance-78-Monthly Cost Reduction/Recognition award, Northrop Aircraft Corp., 1978. Mem. Nat. Safety Council, Am. Soc. Safety Engrs., Am. Indsl. Hygiene Assn., Intersafe Safety Soc., Nat. Assn. Female Execs., Am. Soc. Profl. and Exec. Women, Calif. State Univ. Alumni Assn., Am. Mgmt. Assn. Christian Scientist; Clubs: Wilshire; Tiffanys Social; Eastern Star; Daughters of Isis Court. Home: 1637 Veteran Ave #9 Los Angeles CA 90024 Office: 3516 E Century Blvd Lynwood CA 90262

UNDERWOOD, NANCY VERNAE, health and safety training company executive; b. Vancouver, Wash., Dec. 29, 1944; d. Robert Izea and Jennie Mae (McWhorter) Espie; div.; 1 dau., Apryl D. B.S. in Occupational Safety and Health, Calif. State U.-Los Angeles, 1974, M.A., 1982; M.S. in Environ. and Occupational Toxicology, U. San Francisco, 1981; cert. in engring. and occupational safety and health Textron, Inc., Providence, 1977. Cert. tchr. accident prevention, pub. safety, drivers tng. and edn., Calif. Safety engr. Travelers Ins. Co., Los Angeles, 1975-76; tchr. health edn., driver edn. and tng. Los Angeles Unified Sch. System, 1976; safety mgr. Hydraulic Research subs. Textron, Inc., Valencia, Calif., 1977-78, Northrop Aircraft Group, Hawthorne, Calif., 1978-82; owner, operator Nancy's Safety Tng. and Consultation Firm, Lynwood, Calif., 1982—; part-time mem. faculty, cons. on staff Sch. Health and Safety Studies, Calif. State U.-Los Angeles, 1982—. Mem. Nat. Safety Council, Am. Soc. Safety Engrs., Am. Indsl. Hygiene Assn., Calif. State U. Alumni Assn. Los Angeles, Assn. Safety Profls., Nat. Assn. Female Execs. Inc., Am. Soc. Profl. and Exec. Women. Club: Order of Eastern Star. Home: 1637 Veteran Ave Apt 9 Westwood CA 90025 Office: Nancy's Safety Tng & Consultation Firm 3516 E Century Blvd Suite 10 Lynwood CA 90262

UNFRED, JOHN MANNING, optometrist; b. Holton, Kans., Mar. 7, 1936; s. Joseph Manning and Mildred Melissa (Berry) U.; m. Glenna Lee Ridenour, Sept. 30, 1960 (dec.); children—Michael, Kristina, Steven, Amy; m. 2d, Jeanne Antoinette Leisure, June 16, 1972. B.S., Pacific U., 1958, O.D., 1959. Mem. staff Coll. Optometry, Pacific U., 1959-60, 63-64; sole practice optometry, Springfield, Oreg., 1964—. Served to capt. USAF 1960-63. Mem. Springfield C. of C., Lane Optometric Soc., Am. Optometric Assn., Am. Acad. Optometry, Better Vision Inst. Democrat. United Methodist. Clubs Toastmasters, Rotary, Elks.

UNGAR, IRA HARVEY, physician; b. Wilkes-Barre, Pa., Apr. 29, 1948; s. Lawrence and Annette, U.; B.S., Pa. State U., 1970; M.D., U. Autonoma de Guadalajara, 1974; m. Gail Shupeck, Aug. 24, 1969; children—Loren, Scott, Heidi. Intern, Pathway Hosp., Wilkes-Barre Gen. Hosp., 1974-75; resident in family practice Hahnemann Med. Coll., Phila., Sacred Heart Hosp., Allentown, Pa., 1975-78; emergency physician John C. Lincoln Hosp., Phoenix, 1979, dir. computer medicine, 1982—; practice medicine specializing in critical care, Phoenix, 1980—; tchr. paramedics, flight nurses, 1978—. Mem. Maricopa County Sheriff's Adj. Posse, 1982—. Diplomate Am. Acad. Family Practice. Mem. Am. Coll. Emergency Physicians, Phoenix Rose Soc. Republican. Jewish. Club: Downtown Phoenix Medical.

UNGVARSKY, MICHELE, pharmacist; b. N.Y.C., May 8, 1956; d. John James and Donna Lee (Verry) U.; m. David Michael Read, Mar. 17, 1980 (div.). B.S. in Pharmacy, U. N.Mex., 1980. Registered pharmacist. Pharmacist, Skaggs Drug Ctrs., Albuquerque, 1978-80, St. Lukes Hosp., Denver, 1980, Gerald Champion Meml. Hosp., Alamogordo, N.Mex., 1981, Meml. Gen. Hosp., Las Cruces, N.Mex., 1981, Skaggs Drug Ctr., Las Cruces, N.Mex., 1982—. Mem. Am. Pharm. Assn. Republican. Roman Catholic. Home: 3924 Eastview Las Cruces NM 88005 Office: Skaggs Drug Ctr Inc 579 S Main St Las Cruces NM 88001

UNRUH, BARBARA JOANNE, educational administrator; b. Marysville, Kans., May 31, 1939; d. Joseph Albert and Moreen Lucille (Padgett) Slama; m. Stanley Roger Unruh, Apr. 1, 1961; 1 son, Scott Stanley. B.S., Phillips U., 1961, M.E., 1970; postgrad. U. No. Colo., 1976—. Cert. tchr., adminstr., Colo. Elem. tchr. Enid (Okla.) Pub. Schs., 1961-65; jr. high tchr. English, high sch. librarian Re-1 Pub. Sch. Dist., Sterling, Colo., 1965-68; jr. high tchr. English, dept. coordinator Vikan Jr. High Sch., Dist. 27J, Brighton, Colo., asst. prin., 1975-79, acting prin., 1978, asst. prin. Brighton High Sch., 1979-83, prin., 1983—. Named Adminstr. of Yr., Brighton Assn. Edn. Office Personnel, 1983; State Adminstr. of Yr., Colo. Assn. Ednl. Office Personnel, 1983. Mem. Assn. Supervision and Curriculum Devel., Colo. Assn. Sch. Execs., Nat. Assn. Secondary Sch. Prins., Kappa Delta Pi, Alpha Delta Kappa. Republican. Mem. Christian Ch. (Disciples of Christ). Editor newsletter for parents of high sch. students. Home: 728 S 10th Ave Brighton CO 80601 Office: Brighton High Sch 270 S 8th Ave Brighton CO 80601

UNRUH, JESSE MARVIN, state ofcl.; b. Newton, Kans., Sept. 30, 1922; s. Isaac P. and Nettie Laura (Kessler) U.; B.A., U. So. Calif., 1948, postgrad., 1949; LL.D., U. So. Calif., 1967; m. Virginia June Lemon, Nov. 2, 1943; children—Bruce, Bradley, Robert, Randall, Linda Lu. Dist. staff dir. Fed. Census, 1950; with Pacific Car DeMurrage Bur., 1950-54; mem. Calif. Assembly, 1954-70, chmn. com. fin. and ins., 1957-59, chmn. ways and means com., 1959-61, speaker of assembly, 1961-68, Democratic leader, 1968-70, mem. adv. commn. on intergovtl. relations, 1967-70; vis. prof. polit. sci. San Fernando Valley State Coll., 1970; vis. prof. U. So. Calif. Sch. Law, 1971-72; now treas. State of Calif.; cons., prof. polit. sci. Eagleton Inst. Politics, Rutgers U., 1965—; co-chmn. Seminar Young Legislators, Carnegie Corp.; Chubb fellow Yale U., 1962. Mem. Calif. Central Democratic Com., 1954—; So. Calif. mgr. John F. Kennedy presdl. campaign, 1960; So. Calif. co-chmn. gubernatorial campaign, 1962; statewide coordinator assembly, congl. campaigns, 1962; chmn. Robert F. Kennedy's Calif. presdl. campaign, 1968; chmn. Calif. del. Dem. Nat. Conv., 1968; pres. Nat. Conf. State Legis. Leaders, 1966; Dem. candidate for gov. Calif., 1970; bd. regents U. Calif., 1961-68; trustee Calif. State Colls., 1961-68, Inst. for Am. Univs., Citizens Conf. on State Legislatures, 1968—. Served with USNR, 1942-45. Home: 306 Bora Bora Way Marina Del Rey CA 90291 Office: State Capitol Sacramento CA 95814*

UNTRACHT, BARBARA EVE, school psychologist; b. Bklyn., May 24, 1948; d. Harold and Alice (Pollen) Untracht; m. Larry Bruce Oakner, July 3, 1978; 1 son, Jesse. B.A. in Theatre Arts, SUNY-Albany, 1970; M.A., U. Calif.-Northridge, 1978. Cert. tchr., Calif. Jr. high drama and English tchr. Los Angeles Unified Schs., 1972-74, sch. psychologist, 1978-80; psychologist Portland (Oreg.) Pub. Schs., 1980—; actress Los Angeles, N.Y.C., 1970-74; pvt. practice in psychology, Portland; lectr., cons. in field. Chmn. Multnomah County Day Care. Calif. State U. Found. grantee, 1978. Mem. Oreg. Sch. Psychologists Assn., Am. Personnel and Guidance Assn. Home: 3245 NE 17th Ave Portland OR 97212 Office: 531 SE 14th Portland OR 97214

UNWIN, GORDON DOUGLAS, civil engr.; b. Anchorage, Alaska, Oct. 22, 1943; s. Gordon R. and Stella L. U.; B.S. in Civil Engring., Lehigh U., 1965; m. Karen Cannon, Dec. 22, 1973; 1 son, Sloane G.W. Airport engr. Alaska Div. Aviation, Anchorage, 1963-69; civil engr. Dowl Engrs., Anchorage, 1970-72; pres. Unwin-Scheben-Korynta-Huettl, Architects and Engrs., Anchorage, 1972-83. Mem. Citizens Adv. Bd. Greater Anchorage Area Borough Comprehensive Plan, 1973; mem. Municipality Anchorage Geotech. Commn., 1977-79; mem. Gen. Services Adminstrn. Public Adv. Bd., 1978. Registered profl. engr., Alaska, Wash. Served to capt. Alaska Army N.G., 1966-75. Mem. Nat. Soc. Profl. Engrs., ASCE, Profl. Engrs. In Pvt. Practice (past state chmn.), Am. Arbitration Assn., Aircraft Owners and Pilots Assn., Alaska Bd. Registration Architects, Engrs. and Land Surveyors (v.p. 1976-81), Alaska Soc. Profl. Engrs., Alaska Profl. Design Council (past dir.), Alaska Soc. Profl. Land Surveyors. Office: 2515 A St Anchorage AK 99503

UPATISRINGA, VISUTDHI, mathematics educator, investor; b. Phuket, Thailand, Sept. 2, 1936; came to U.S., 1955; s. Hun Kwan and Kim Lien (Chun) Goh; m. Sally Lea Bailey, Aug. 20, 1966. B.A. in Chemistry, Oreg. State Coll., 1959; M.A. in Math., Oreg. State U., 1967, Ph.D., 1975. Instr. Linn-Benton Community Coll., Albany, Oreg., 1967-68; asst. prof. math. Humboldt State U., Arcata, Calif., 1969-80, assoc. prof., 1980—, bd. dirs. Univ. Ctr. Bd., 1975-78, chmn. personnel com. dept. math., 1983-84, chmn. placement examination rev. com., 1976-77, chmn. search com., 1982-83; vis. scholar UCLA, 1980-81. Chmn. Hun Kwan Goh Meml. Scholarship Fund, Humboldt Area Found. Mem. Am. Math. Assn., Math. Assn. Am., AAUP, Pi Mu Epsilon, Phi Eta Sigma. Club: Eureka Coin. Contbr. in field. Home: 3315 H St Eureka CA 95501 Office: Dept Math Humboldt State Univ Arcata CA 95521

UPDEGRAFF, DAVID MAULE, microbiologist; b. Woodstock, N.Y., Dec. 19, 1917; s. Alan and Florence (Maule) U.; A.B., UCLA, 1941; Ph.D., Scripps Instn. Oceanography, 1948; m. Betti Laurel Mitchell, July 24, 1943; children—Janice M., Jeffrey G., Wendy M. Grad. research asst. marine microbiology Scripps Inst. Oceanography, LaJolla, Calif., 1946-47; sr. research microbiologist Field Research Labs., Mobil Oil Co., Dallas, Tex., 1948-55, central research dept. 3M Co., St. Paul, Minn., 1955-68; research sect. leader chem. div. Denver Research Inst., U. Denver, 1968-72; leader research sect. Cawthron Inst., Nelson, N.Z., 1972-75; v.p. Resource Industries Internat., Ltd., Denver, 1975-77; prof. biogeochemistry dept. chemistry Colo. Sch. of Mines, Golden, 1977—; cons. geomicrobiology, 1977—; coordinator U.S./USSR Sci. and Info. Exchange Program, 1977—. Served with USN, 1942-46. Mem. Am. Soc. for Microbiology, Soc. for Indsl. Microbiology, AAAS, Sigma Xi. Unitarian. Contbr. articles on indsl. microbiology to sci. jours.; patentee in field. Home: 1834 Smith Rd Golden CO 80401 Office: Dept of Chemistry Colorado School of Mines Golden CO 80401

UPHAM, FRANK TRANSUE, elec. engr.; b. Half Moon Bay, Calif., Mar. 23, 1921; s. Frank Leslie and Sarah Elizabeth (Transue) U.; B.S., U. Calif., Berkeley, 1950; m. Elizabeth Marian Sturtevant, Aug. 21, 1948; children—Arthur F., Steven W. With Lawrence Berkeley Lab., U. Calif., Berkeley, 1950—, project engr., 1965—. Served with USAAF, 1943-45. Mem. IEEE, AAAS, AIAA. Contbr. articles to profl. jours. Home: 18 Ramona Dr Orinda CA 94563 Office: Univ of California Lawrence Berkeley Laboratory Berkeley CA 94720

UPHOFF, SHIRLEY ANN, psychologist; children—Joseph, Katherine. B.A., U. Iowa; B.S., N.Mex. Highlands U., 1974; Ph.D., U.S. Internat. U., 1978. Lic. psychologist, Calif. Staff psychologist San Diego County Mental Health Adolescent Inpatient Unit, 1980-81; clin. psychologist, La Jolla, Calif., 1981—; cons. Mercy Hosp., Mesa Vista Hosp., Clairmont Hosp., Scripps Hosp. Mem. Calif. State Psychol. Assn., Am. Psychol. Assn., Acad. San Diego Psychologists. Author: Ego Defenses in Dreams, 1978.

UPSHAW, MARIE B., home economist, teacher; b. Maschitti, N.Mex., Apr. 5, 1950; d. Nelson M. and Jannie B. (Bochinclonny) Francisco; m. Michael W. Upshaw, Oct. 26, 1976 (dec.); children—Byran M., Vernon B. B.A. in Home Econs., Western N.Mex. U., 1973. Home economist extension agt. in housing N.Mex. State U. Coop. Extension Service, 1973-75; interviewer I, N.Mex. Employment Service, 1976; home econs. tchr. Central Consol. Sch. Dist. 22, Shiprock, N.Mex., 1976-78; extension 4-H agt. U. Ariz. Extension Service, 1979-80; home econs. tchr. Window Rock Schs., Ft. Defiance, Ariz., 1980—. Mem. Am. Home Econs. Assn. Office: PO Box 559 Ft Defiance AZ 86504

UPTON, RUSSELL MERRITT, tax preparer; b. Canaan, Conn., June 4, 1932; s. Gerald Dower and Helen Merritt Upton; m. Eleanor Canfield Wingett; children—Jeffrey Dean, Bradley Alan. B.S. in Mgmt., Ariz. State U., 1961. Parts mgr. Halken Shaker Motors, Shaker Heights, 1955-59; newscaster, announcer Sta. KTVK-TV, Phoenix, 1961-72; area mgr. Tax Corp. Am., Phoenix, 1975-80; owner Tax Counselor Assn. Ariz., Scottsdale, 1980—; investment advisor. Served with U.S. Army, 1952-54. Mem. Nat. Assn. Enrolled Agts. Republican. Methodist. Club: Philatelist. Developed Computer software income tax program. Home: 8213 E Coolidge St Scottsdale AZ 85251 Office: 6730 E McDowell #103 Scottsdale AZ 85257

URBAN, RICHARD WILLIAM, immunologist, microbiologist; b. Newark, July 30, 1945; s. Adolph Joseph and Wilma E. (Ellis) U.; m. Judith Arlene Hollo, June 3, 1967; children—Sasha William, Akira Kamma. Student U. Ariz., 1963-64; B.S., Ariz. State U., 1970; M.A., U. Hartford, 1973; Ph.D., U. Colo. 1978; Research fellow dept. surgery U. Colo. Med. Center, Denver, 1978; research asst. prof. tumor immunology Utah State U., 1979-80; asst. prof. biology Met. State Coll., Denver, 1978-79, 80-81; research assoc. dept. environ., population and orgnl. biology U. Colo., 1980-81; research assoc. dept. urology U. Calif. Med. Center, San Diego, 1980-81; research assoc. surg. oncology U. Colo. Med. Center, Denver, 1980—; v.p. research and devel., dir. Cell Tech., Inc., Boulder, Colo., 1983—. Served with USCG, 1964-68. Am. Cancer Soc. grantee, 1976, 77; Alexander Med. Found. cancer research grantee, 1980-81. Mem. Am. Soc. for Microbiology, AAAS, N.Y. Acad. Scis., Sigma Xi. Home: 2655 S Crystal St Aurora CO 80014 Office: Cell Tech Inc Boulder CO 80306

URBANCZYK, ANDREW AUGUSTUS, explorer, author; b. Russia, Mar. 1, 1936; came to U.S., 1972, naturalized, 1982; s. Sigmund Michailowich and Monika Urbanczyk; M.S. in Chemistry and Physics, Tech. U. Gdansk (Poland), 1960; m. Saborowska Krystyna, Oct. 5, 1968. Instr., Tech. U. Gdansk, 1960-68; research cons. Am. Yachting Assn., 1965-70; licensed capt., skipper, organizer oceanic expdns., 1957—; mem. exam. bd. Amateur Yachting Assn., 1965—; author 15 books, 1957—, including Lonely Voyages, 1971; Raft Expeditions, 1973; Thank You Pacific, 1981; world champion transpacific record in singlehanding sailing, 1978. Named Meritorious Laborer of Seas, Baltic Soc., 1970; recipient various grants. Mem. Slocum Soc. Address: 367 11th St Montara CA 94037

URBELIS, KATHLEEN, computer exec.; b. Amsterdam, N.Y., May 20, 1946; d. Henry and Armida M. (Casline) Flesh. B.S. in Mgmt. Sci., U. Rochester, 1968, M.B.A., 1972. Programmer, Info. Assocs. Inc., Rochester, N.Y., 1971-72; co-founder, v.p. product devel., corp. sec. Integral Systems, Inc., Walnut Creek, Calif., 1972—. Home: PO Box 583 Diablo CA 94528 Office: 165 Lennon Ln Walnut Creek CA 94598

UREDA, KATHLEEN ANN, retail gift store chain executive; b. Los Angeles, Sept. 9, 1946; d. Norbert J. and Alyce (Whiteley) Mueller; m. William V. Ureda, Nov. 25, 1968; 1 son, Bradley. B.A., UCLA, 1968. Tchr. art Los Angeles City Schs., 1968-71, tchr. art secondary schs., 1971-76; owner, pres. Down Home Craft Show, San Francisco, 1976—; owner, pres. Creative Ventures Inc., Sacramento and Mountain View, Calif., 1979—. Mem. AAUW (chairperson money talks topic), Network Women Entrepreneurs, Women's Ednl. Services Assn. (area dir. 1983), Women Entrepreneurs, Nat. Speakers Assn., Nat. Speakers Team. Republican. Office: 2550 W El Camino Real Mountain View CA 94043

URI, GEORGE WOLFSOHN, accountant; b. San Francisco, Dec. 8, 1920; s. George Washington and Ruby (Wolfsohn) U.; A.B., Stanford, 1941, I.A., 1943, M.B.A., 1946; postgrad. U. Leeds (Eng.), 1945; m. Pamela Dorothy O'Keefe, May 15, 1961. Mem. accounting, econs. and statistics depts. Shell Oil Co., Inc., San Francisco, 1946-48; partner,

Irelan, Uri, Mayer & Sheppie, San Francisco; pres. F. Uri & Co., Inc., Athos Corp., Irelan Accountancy Corp.; instr. acctg. and econs. Golden Gate Coll., 1949-50. Chmn. San Rafael (Calif.) Redevel. Adv. Com., 1977-78, mem., 1978—; bd. dirs. San Francisco Planning and Urban Renewal Assn., 1958-60. Served with AUS, 1942-46, col. ret. Recipient Key Man award San Francisco Jr. C. of C.; Meritorious Service medal Sec. of Army, 1978. C.P.A., Calif. Mem. Inst. Mgmt. Scis. (treas. No. Cal. chpt. 1961-62), Am. Inst. C.P.A.s, Calif. Soc. C.P.A.s (sec.-treas. San Francisco chpt. 1956-57, dir. 1961-63, state dir. 1964-66, mem. Forbes medal com. 1968-69, chmn. 1969-71), Am. Econ. Assn., Nat. Assn. Accountants, San Francisco Estate Planning Council (dir. 1965-68), Am. Statis. Assn., Assn. Mil. Comptrollers, Execs. Assn. of San Francisco (pres. 1965-66), Inst. Mgmt. Acctg. (cert. mgmt. acctg.; Disting. Performance cert. 1978). Clubs: Engrs. of San Francisco, Commonwealth (quar. chmn. 1971), Stanford, Rafael Racquet; Army and Navy (Washington). Contbr. to profl. jours. Home: 11 McNear Dr San Rafael CA 94901 Office: 160 Sansome St San Francisco CA 94104

URKA, MARTIN CHARLES, agriculturist, government official; b. Brethren, Mich., Nov. 11, 1924; s. Anton and Anna U.; m. Peggy Jean Crane, Nov. 27, 1953; children—Meggen, Wendy, Preston, Polly. Cert. Inst. Agr., Mich. State U., 1948, student in agr. Mich. State U., 1954, 56-57, 75. Soil conservation aide Soil Conservation Service, USDA, Manistee, Mich., 1948-49, Stanton, Mich., 1949-53, St. Johns, Mich., 1954, soil conservation technician, Marshall, Mich., 1955-63, soil conservationist, Marshall, 1963-64, Suttons Bay, Mich., 1964-67, Adrian, Mich., 1967-69, Coldwater, Mich., 1970-71, dist. conservationist, Harrisville, Mich., 1971-75, soil scientist, Jackson, Mich., 1975-79; soil scientist Bur. Indian Affairs, Dept. Interior, Rosebud, S.D., 1979-81, land ops. officer, Owyhee, Nev., 1981—; cons. in field. Cons. mem. Alcona County (Mich.) Land Use Planning Com., 1974-75. Served to sgt. inf. U.S. Army, 1944-46; Italy; with Signal Corps and F.A. USAR, 1953-56. Recipient Outstanding Performance award Soil Conservation Service, 1962; Spl. Service award and plaque Calhoun Soil Conservation Dist., Marshall, 1964; spl. recognition James Watt, Sec. Dept. Interior, 1981, News Editor of Citizens Patriot, Jackson, Mich., 1982; Spl. Chpt. award Future Farmers Am., Stanton, Mich., 1952, Mission, S.D., 1980, Owyhee, Nev., 1982. Mem. Soil Conservation Soc. Am., Soil Sci. Soc. Am., Crop Sci. Soc. Am., Am. Soc. Agronomy. Home: 308 Bur Indian Affairs Complex Owyhee NV 89832 Office: 301 Bur Indian Affairs Complex Owyhee NV 89832

URMACHER, URI, computer scientist; b. Siedlce, Poland, Apr. 25, 1935; came to U.S., 1961, naturalized, 1965; s. Samuel and Chaia (Appelbaum) U.; M.B.A. in Computer Sci., Calif. Western U., 1977; postgrad. UCLA, 1978—; m. Glenda Eiss, June 11, 1961; children—Carrie Dawn, Bridget. With Uri's Esso, Am. Electronics Co., L.I., N.Y., 1961-68; sr. tech. advisor Honeywell, L.I., 1969-70, Los Angeles, 1970-80; mem. tech. staff Aerospace Corp., El Segundo, Calif., 1980—; pres. Global Solar Power, Los Angeles, 1976—. Recipient Honeywell Eastern Region field award, 1970, Western Region Staff System Specialist award, 1978. Mem. Assn. for Computing Machinery, San Diego Computer Soc., AEA Computer and Electronic Club. Author: Computer Privacy and Security, 1977; Micro-Flow Copywrite, 1981. Office: 2350 E El Segundo Blvd El Segundo CA 90245

URSIN, BJARNE ELLING, mfg. co. exec.; b. Bridgeport, Conn., Aug. 8, 1930; s. Bjarne and Esther (Schiott) U.; B.S. in Physics, Mass. Inst. Tech., 1957; m. Mary Elizabeth Locke, July 26, 1969; children—Stephanie, Lara, Matthew, Jonathan, Teri, Kristian. Project engr. Raytheon, Andover, Mass., 1957-60; prin. investigator Gen. Dynamics, San Diego, 1960-62; sr. scientist Philco-Ford, Newport Beach, Calif., 1962-67; with McDonnell Douglas Corp., Huntington Beach, Calif., 1967-76, sr. ops. project mgr., mgr. mfg., 1967-76; prodn. mgr. Eldec Corp., Lynnwood, Wash., 1976-78; v.p. mfg. TCS Inc., Redmond, Wash., 1978-80; chief exec. officer BJI, Mercer Island, Wash., 1968-81, Atex Inc., A Kodak Co., Westechnology, Bellevue, Wash., 1980—; assoc. Johns Co. Realtors, Mercer Island, 1981-82; assoc. Coldwell Banker Co., 1981—, W. Bruck Realty, 1982—; pres. Nor'West Reps., Bellevue, 1980—; prodn. mgr. Atex Corp., Redmond, Wash., 1982-83; co-owner Lighthouse Interiors, 1982—; dir. Data I/O Corp. Commn. chmn. City of Huntington Beach, 1975-76. Served with AUS, 1951-53. Mem. Am. Inst. Physics, IEEE, Am. Assn. Physics Tchrs., AIAA, AAAS, U.S. Internat. Sailing Assn., Mercer Island Jogging and Sculling Assn. (adm. 1978-83), Am. Mgmt. Assn. Republican. Roman Catholic. Clubs: Mercer Island Yacht (commodore 1977-83), dir. 1977-83), Mercer Island Jogging and Sculling Assn. (adm. 1978-83); Bahia Corinthian Yacht (dir. 1972-76, rear commodore 1974, vice commodore 1975, commodore 1976) (Corona Del Mar); Royal Norwegian Yacht (Oslo); M.I.T. of Puget Sound (dir. 1979—). Home: 9520 SE 61st Pl Mercer Island WA 98040 Office: PO Box 596 Mercer Island WA 98040 also PO Box 6968 Bellevue WA 98008

USHIJIMA, JEAN M., city ofcl.; b. San Francisco, Feb. 14, 1933; d. Toyoharu and Frances (Fujiko) Miwa; m. Tad E. Ushijima, Dec. 30, 1951; children—Carol M., Ellen T. B.S. magna cum laude, U. San Francisco, 1981. Cert. mcpl. clk., Internat. Mcpl. Clks. Assn., 1978. Legal sec. to atty., Santa Monica, Calif., 1965-70; legal sec. to city atty. Beverly Hills (Calif.), 1970-71, adminstrv. sec. to pub. works dir., 1971-73, city clk., 1973—. Mem. West Los Angeles Japanese Am. Citizens League (dir. 1978—), Acad. Advanced Edn., Internat. Inst. Mcpl. Clks., City Clks. Assn. Calif. (treas. 1980-82), Assn. Records Mgrs. and Adminstrs., Calif. Women in Govt. Methodist. Office: 450 N Crescent Dr Beverly Hills CA 90210

USINGER, EMMETT CALVIN, accountant; b. Clayton, N.J., Dec. 4, 1929; s. Emmett L. and Edna May (Campbell) U.; m. Patsy Bonds, July 2, 1955. B.S. in Bus. Adminstrn. magna cum laude, UCLA, 1951. C.P.A., Calif., N.Mex., Tex. Staff acct. Ira N. Frisbee & Co., Beverly Hills, Calif., 1951-54; sr. acct. Linder, Burke & Stephenson, Albuquerque, 1954-56; sr. acct. Peat, Marwick, Mitchell & Co., Farmington, N.Mex., 1956-58; ptnr. Usinger, Podmore, Stockton & Henry, Farmington, 1958-63; ptnr. Peat, Marwick, Mitchell & Co., Albuquerque and Midland, Tex., 1964—; mem. faculty Denver U., 1963; speaker in field. Chmn. profl. div. fund drive United Way, Midland, 1975; tax adviser Albuquerque Indsl. Devel. Service, 1976—. Mem. Am. Inst. C.P.A.s, N.Mex. Soc. C.P.A.s (pres. 1981-82), Albuquerque Petroleum Assn., Ind. Petroleum Assn. N.Mex. (sec.-treas.), N.Mex. Oil and Gas Assn. Republican. Presbyterian. Clubs: Albuquerque Petroleum, Albuquerque Country. Monthly columnist Bud Usinger on Financial Planning, N.Mex. Bus. Jour., 1978-81. Office: 20 1st Plaza NW Suite 500 Albuquerque NM 87102

USSERY, ALBERT TRAVIS, lawyer, banker; b. Gulfport, Miss., Mar. 12, 1928; s. Walter Travis and Rosamond (Sears) U.; m. Margaret Grosvenor Paine, Nov. 22, 1950; children—Margaret Rosamond, John Travis, Marilyn Ann, Meredith Lee. A.B., Washington U., St. Louis, 1950; LL.B., U. N.Mex., 1951, J.D., 1968; LL.M., Georgetown U., 1955. Admitted to N.Mex. bar, 1951, since practiced in Albuquerque; mem. firm Gallagher and Ussery, 1951-53, Threet, Ussery & Threet, 1957-60; assoc. with Alfred H. McRae, 1961-63; ptnr. McRae, Ussery, Mims, Ortega & Kitts, 1964-65; chmn. Am. Bank Commerce, 1966-70, pres., 1967-70; ptnr. Ussery, Burciaga & Parrish, 1969-79; pres. Ussery & Parrish, P.A., 1980—; spl. counsel to Albuquerque on water law, 1956-66; chmn. Rio Grande Valley Bank, Albuquerque, 1972—; pres. Albuquerque Small Bus. Investment Co., 1977—; dir. Bank of Southwest, Rio Rancho, 1980—; lectr. mil. law U. N.Mex., 1956, instr. corp. fin., 1956-57, lectr. bus. law, 1960-61. Chmn. water adv. com. Albuquerque Indsl. Devel. Service, 1960-66; vice chmn. N.Mex. Council on Econ. Edn., 1969-74; mem. Region VI-Albuquerque adv. council SBA, 1982—; mem. N.Mex. Regional Export Expansion Council, 1969-74; mem. Albuquerque Armed Forces Adv. Assn., 1977—; mem. SBA Region VI-Albuquerque Adv. Council, 1982—. Trustee Village Los Ranchos de Albuquerque, 1970-72; chmn. adv. bd. Lovelace-Bataan Med. Ctr., 1976-78, trustee, 1978—; bd. dirs. Goodwill Industries N.Mex., 1957-65, Albuquerque Travelers Assistance, 1956-66, Family Consultation Service, 1961-64, Albuquerque Symphony Assn., 1964-68; bd. dirs. N.Mex. Arthritis Found., 1969-74, pres., 1971. Mem. Am., Fed., Albuquerque (treas. 1957-60) bar assns., State Bar N.Mex., Estate Planning Council Albuquerque (pres. 1962), N.Mex. Zool. Soc. (dir., pres. 1977-78), Am. Legion (comdr. 1962-63), Lawyers Club. Kiwanian (dir. 1957-60). Home: Rio Grande at Eakes Rd NW Albuquerque NM 87107 Office: 200 Rio Grande Valley Bank Bldg 501 Tijeras Ave NW PO Box 487 Albuquerque NM 87103

USSERY, HARRY MACRAE, lawyer, construction contracts consultant; b. Rockingham, N.C., Jan. 27, 1920; s. Robert Roy and Maggie Estelle (MacRae) U.; m. Olive Dual Simmons, Mar. 19, 1949. A.A., Wake Forest U., 1947; J.D., George Washington U., 1950. Bar: D.C. 1950. Assoc. firm Geiger & Harmel, Washington, 1950-52; ptnr. firm McNeill & Ussery, Washington, 1952-53; gen. counsel, dir. Harry R. Byers, Inc., Washington and Denver, 1953-59; procurement counsel Martin Mariette Corp., Denver, 1959-62; authorized agt. RCA, Camden N.J., 1962-69; staff counsel, mgr. internat. subcontract ops. Burns and Roe Constrn. Corp., Paramus, N.J., 1969-74, legal counsel, 1975-78, asst. to pres., Oradell, N.J., 1978-81; pvt. cons. on constrn. contracts, investor, Santa Fe, 1981—; chief moderator, dir., Dist. Roundtable, Sta. WWDC, Washington, 1950-53. Served with USAAF, 1941-45. Recipient Community Chest campaign awards, 1951, 52. Mem. ABA, Am. Judicature Soc., Nat. Contract Mgmt. Assn., George Washington U. Law Assn., Wake Forest U. Alumni Assn., Geneal. Soc. Santa Fe, Council Scottish Clans Assns., St. Andrew's Soc., Clan MacRae Soc., Delta Theta Phi. Republican. Presbyterian. Clubs: Delaware Valley Jaguar, Colony (Medford Lakes, N.J.), Vintage Car (Santa Fe). Author: The Origin of the Surname of Ussery, 1983; contbr. articles to various publs. Address: 2953 Plaza Azul Santa Fe NM 87501

UTLEY, ANTHONY JOHN, stock brokerage executive; b. Altoona, Pa., Nov. 6, 1955; s. Edward George and Catherine Joan (Berrich) U.; m. Jennifer Anne Lapp, Apr. 21, 1979 (div.). B.A. in Am. History, Muhlenberg Coll., 1977. Assoc. Commodity Resources Inc., N.Y.C., 1978; registered rep. Merrill Lynch, Allentown, Pa., 1978-81; rep., trader Covey & Co., Park City, Utah, 1981; rep., trader White & Co., San Francisco, 1981-82; owner, trader, broker Penn-West Securities, Park City, Utah, 1982—. Mgr. polit. campaign State Assembly, Bethlehem, Pa., 1980; researcher, writer Republican Party, Bethlehem. Mem. Nat. Assn. Security Dealers, Securities Investors Protection Corp., Bethlehem C. of C. Democrat. Roman Catholic. Office: 363 Main St Park City UT 84060

UTLEY, DONNA LAVELLE, hosp. personnel adminstr.; b. Tulare, Calif., June 30, 1948; d. Donald Raymond and Vivian Lee (Baber) Rogers; B.S., Calif. State U., Fresno, 1970; postgrad. U. So. Calif., 1978—; m. July 23, 1970. Resources and devel. asst. Concentrated Employment Program, Fresno, Calif., 1970-72; personnel analyst Fresno County Personnel Dept., 1972-74; personnel mgr. Fresno County Health Dept., 1974-79; personnel dir. Merced (Calif.) Community Med. Center, 1979-81; dir. human resources Bay Area Hosp., Coos Bay, Oreg., 1981—. Mem. Oreg. Soc. Hosp. Personnel Adminstrn. (sec.-treas. 1982-83). Republican. Methodist. Club: Soroptimist (chmn. chpt. pub. relations com.). Office: 1775 Thompson Rd Coos Bay OR 97420

UTTER, ROBERT FRENCH, state supreme court justice; b. Seattle, June 19, 1930; s. John M. and Besse A. (French) U.; B.S., U. Wash., 1952, LL.B., 1955; m. Elizabeth J. Stevenson, Dec. 28, 1953; children—Kimberly, Kirk, John. Bar: Wash. 1954. Dep. pros. atty., King County, 1955-57; individual practice law, Seattle, 1957-59; ct. commr. King County Superior Ct., 1959-64; judge King County Superior Ct., 1964-69; judge Wash. Ct. of Appeals, 1969-71; justice Wash. Supreme Ct., Olympia, 1971—, chief justice, 1979-81; guest lectr. U. Wash. Law Sch., Seattle U., 1975-76. Co-founder, pres. Seattle Big Brother Assn., 1955-67, Job Therapy, Inc., 1963-71. Recipient Man of Yr. award Seattle Jaycees, 1964, Alumnus of Yr. award Linfield Coll., 1973. Mem. ABA, Am. Judicature Soc. (Herbert Hartley award 1983), Nat. Conf. Chief Justices (exec. com.). Baptist. Editor: Washington Real Property Deskbook, 1979, Appellate Practice Handbook. Office: Temple of Justice Olympia WA 98504

UTTERSTROM, JOHN RAYMOND, missiles systems executive; b. Vancouver, B.C., Can., Oct. 8, 1922; s. John and Gertrude Wilhemina (Hanson) U.; m. Mary Agnes Deffries, Sept. 24, 1947; children—Vicki Ann, Thomas Raymond, Mary Susan, Kathy Jo. B.S.E.E., U. Wash., 1948. With Boeing Co., Seattle, 1948—, successively analyst, successively group leader, dept. head, chief engr., dir. engring., program mgr., 1948-80, v.p. Missile Systems div., 1980-83; pres. Boeing Mgmt. Assn. Bd. dirs. Wash. State Spl. Olympics. Served to lt., USAAF, 1942-45. Recipient Ann. Honors, Aviation Week, 1961. Fellow AIAA (assoc. dir. Outstanding Aerospace Engring. award 1980); mem. Sigma Xi, Tau Beta Pi. Clubs: Overlake Golf and Country (Bellevue, Wash.); Seattle Yacht. Patentee AC modulation suppressor. Home: 9830 Shoreland Dr SE Bellevue WA 98004 Office: PO Box 3999 MS 84 30 Seattle WA 98124

UTZ, SARAH WINIFRED, nursing educator; b. San Diego, Nov. 2, 1921; d. Frederick R. and Margaret M. (Gibbons) U.; B.S., U. Portland, 1943, Ed.M., 1958; M.S., UCLA, 1970; Ph.D., U. So. Calif., 1979. Clin. instr. Providence Sch. Nursing, Portland, Oreg., 1946-50, edn. dir., 1950-62; edn. dir. Sacred Heart Sch. Nursing, Eugene, Oreg., 1963-67; asst. prof. nursing Calif. State U., Los Angeles, 1969-74, assoc. prof., 1974-81, prof., 1981—, assoc. chmn. dept. nursing, 1982—; cons. in nursing curriculum, 1978—; past chmn. ednl. adminstrs., cons., tchrs. sect. Oreg. Nurses Assn., past pres. Oreg. State Bd. Nursing; mem. research program Western Interstate Commn. on Higher Edn. in Nursing; chmn. liaison com. nursing edn. Articulation Council Calif. Served with Nurse Corps, USN, 1944-46. HEW grantee, 1970-74, Kellogg Found. grantee, 1974-76; R.N., Calif., Oreg. Mem. Am. Nurses Assn., Calif. Nurses Assn. Am. Ednl. Research Assn., AAUP, Town Hall Calif., Phi Delta Kappa, Alpha Tau Delta, Delta Kappa Gamma. Formerly editor Oreg. Nurse; reviewer Western Jour. Nursing Research. Home: 1409 Midvale Ave Los Angeles CA 90024 Office: 5151 State University Dr Los Angeles CA 90032

UWAINE, CLIFFORD T., educator, state senator; b. Honolulu, Jan. 15, 1951; A.A., Leeward Community Coll.; B.Ed., U. Hawaii, M.Ed.; married, 1 child. Mem. Hawaii Ho. of Reps., 1976-80; mem. Hawaii State Senate, 1981—. Trustee Hawaii chpt. Nat. Sudden Infant Death Syndrome Found.; active YMCA, ARC, Moiliili Community Center; del. Hawaii State Democratic Conv., 1974, 76, 78.

UYEDA, ARTHUR ASA, psychologist; b. San Bernardino, Calif., Sept. 26, 1925; s. Roy Fusajiro and Hide (Sawada) U.; m. Sumiko Kato, July 23, 1960; children—Stanley Kei, Susan Asako. B.A., San Diego State Coll., 1951; M.A., UCLA, 1958, Ph.D., 1960, fellow dept. psychiatry, 1960-62. Lic. Calif. Bd. Med. Quality Assurance. Research psychologist dept. psychiatry UCLA, 1962-68, dept. anatomy, 1968-70; research specialist Sonoma State Hosp., Eldridge, Calif., 1970-73; psychologist Napa State Hosp., Imola, Calif., 1973—. Served to cpl. U.S. Army, 1952-54. NSF grantee, 1958-60; NIMH grantee, 1960-62, 1962-67. Mem. Am. Psychol. Assn., Western Psychol. Assn., Neurosci. Assn. Democrat. Methodist. Contbr. articles to sci. jours.

UYEHARA, HARRY YOSHIMI, librarian, educator; b. Honolulu, Jan. 6, 1934; s. Saburo and Uto Uyehara; B.Ed., U. Hawaii, 1958; M.A. in L.S., U. Mich., 1965; M.A., Columbia U., 1970, D.Ed., 1978; Tchr., librarian Waiakea-Kai Elem. and Intermediate Sch., Hilo, Hawaii, 1960-61; traveling sch. librarian Central Oahu Sch. Dist., Wahiawa, Hawaii, 1961-62, librarian Wahiawa Intermediate Sch., 1962-64, 65-66; program specialist, sch. library services Hawaii Dept. Edn., Honolulu, 1966-69, 70-74, staff specialist, sch. library media services and coordinator ESEA title IV-B, Hawaii Dept. Edn., 1974-76; asst. prof. Grad. Sch. Library Studies, U. Hawaii, Honolulu, 1976—. Mem. ALA, Hawaii Library Assn. (pres. 1977-78), Assn. Ednl. Communications and Tech., Assn. Supervision and Curriculum Devel., Nat. Soc. Study Edn., Assn. Am.Library Schs., Internat. Assn. Sch. Librarianship, Hawaii Assn. Sch. Librarians (pres. 1982-83), Pacific Assn. Communications and Technology, Phi Delta Kappa, Kappa Delta Pi. Home: 710 Lunalilo St Apt 1208 Honolulu HI 96813 Office: Grad Sch Library Studies U Hawaii Honolulu HI 96822

VADLEJCH, JAN B., JR., nuclear engr.; b. Prague, Czechoslovakia, Apr. 27, 1944; came to U.S., 1979; s. Jan B. and Maria A. (Strakova) V.: M.S., Prague Tech. U., 1969; m. Natalia Borodin, Dec. 28, 1969. Scientist, Inst. of Thermomechanics, Prague, 1965-76; tech. dir. Nuclear Research Inst., Prague, 1976-77; sci. programmer World Computer Corp., Paris, France, 1977-78; sr. cons., mgr. mech. engring. Quadrex Corp., Campbell, Calif., 1979—. Mem. Am. Nuclear Soc., ASME. Republican. Contbr. articles to tech. and sci. publs. and confs. Home: 833-B San Tomas Aquino Rd Campbell CA 95008 Office: 1700 Dell Ave Campbell CA 95008

VAGNEUR, KATHRYN OTTO, accountant, rancher; b. Aurora, Ill., Feb. 23, 1946; d. Harold William and Afton (Bryner) Otto; m. Gerald Ronald Terwilliger, Oct. 19, 1968 (div. 1974); 1 dau., Jocelyn Marie; m. 2d, Clyde O. Vagneur, Aug. 24, 1979. B.S. in Math., U. Utah, 1968; M.S. in Agribus. Mgmt., Ariz. State U., 1979. C.P.A., Colo. Computer systems designer U. Utah Libraries, Salt Lake City, 1966-68; research asst. in computer systems Carnegie-Mellon U., 1968-70; owner, mgr. Evening at Arthurs Restaurant, Aspen, Colo., 1973-76; self-employed tax cons. Phoenix, 1977-78; with Touche Ross & Co., Colorado Springs, Colo., 1978-82; ptnr., fin. mgr. V Bar Lazy V Ranch, Peyton, Colo., 1978—; ptnr., dir. taxation Glenn & Vagneur, Colorado Springs, 1982—. Bd. dirs. Pikes Peak Ctr.; del. Republican State Conv., 1982; 4-H leader. Mem. Am. Inst. C.P.A.s, Nat. Soc. Accts. for Coops., Colo. Soc. C.P.A.s, Nat. Assn. Accts., Colorado Springs C. of C. (com. chmn.), Am. Quarter Horse Assn., Beta Alpha Psi, Alpha Zeta. Author: A Financial Analysis of Cooperative Livestock Marketing, 1978. Home: 14725 Jones Rd Peyton CO 80831 Office: 105 E Vermijo Suite 600 Colorado Springs CO 80903

VAIL, ILONA MARIA MAGDOLNA, clinical psychologist; b. Budapest, Hungary, Dec. 6, 1942; came to U.S., 1955, naturalized, 1961; d. Bela and Ilona M. R. (Nagy) Galther; m. Anthony Vail, June 24, 1967; 1 son, Christopher Anthony. B.A., Marymount Coll., 1965; M.A., Fordham U., 1967, Ph.D., 1973. Sr. clin. psychologist Coping Clinic, Phila. Psychiat. Ctr., 1969-73, Glenmore unit, Devereux Found., Glenmore, Pa., 1973-75, San Diego County Mental Health, San Diego, 1976-81; pvt. practice clin. psychology, Poway, Calif., 1977—. USPHS fellow, 1967-68. Mem. Am. Psychol. Assn., Calif. State Psychol. Assn., Acad. San Diego Psychology, Associated Psychologists North County, Psychotherapists Associated in North Inland County, Kappa Gamma Phi, NOW. Office: 12630 Monte Vista Ave Suite 202 Boulder Med Ctr Poway CA 92064

VAIL, SUSAN MARIE, social work adminstr.; b. Portland, Oreg., Feb. 17, 1943; d. Ralph Orville and Perla Cora Elisabeth (Dobberstein) Clave; B.A., Portland State U., 1965, M.S.W., 1972; children—Catherine Anastasia, Juliana Elisabeth. Caseworker, Multnomah County Welfare, Portland, 1968-69, 69-70; service worker Multnomah County Children's Services, Portland, 1971; social worker Bess Kaiser Hosp., Portland, 1972; med. social worker Emanuel Hosp., Portland, 1972-73; dir. social work St. Vincent Hosp. and Med. Center, Portland, 1974—. Bd. dirs. Regional Conf. Managerial and Profl. Women, 1978, N.E. Portland Mental Health Planning Council, 1973-74; mem. home care adv. com. St. Vincent Hosp. and Med. Center, 1978—; mem. Washington County Home Health Adv. Bd., 1974-77; chmn. Washington County Child Abuse Council, 1975-76. Mem. Nat. Assn. Social Workers (chmn. nominating com. Oreg. chpt. 1975-77, chmn. by-laws com. 1976-77, chmn. Met. Dist. 1977-78, Oreg. chpt. pres. 1980-81), Soc. Hosp. Social Work Dirs. (sec.-treas. Oreg. chpt. 1980-81), Acad. Cert. Social Workers, Am. Public Health Assn., Oreg. Women's Polit. Caucus, Nat. Assn. Female Execs., LWV, Alpha Chi Omega. Democrat. Roman Catholic. Club: City (Portland). Home: 3226 NE 19th Ave Portland OR 97212 Office: 9205 SW Barnes Rd Portland OR 97225

VAJK, J. PETER, physicist, consultant; b. Budapest, Hungary, Aug. 3, 1942 (mother Am. citizen); s. Raoul and Mary L. (Gillespie) V.; A.B. in Physics, Cornell U., 1963; M.A. in Physics, Princeton U., 1965, Ph.D., 1968; m. Helen T. O'Keeffe, July 5, 1970; children—Fiona C., Kevin M., Owen P., Stephen D. Research and teaching asst. dept. physics Princeton (N.J.) U., 1963-67; sr. physicist theoretical physics div. Lawrence Livermore Lab., Livermore, Calif., 1968-76; sr. scientist Sci. Applications, Inc., Pleasanton, Calif., 1976-83; consultant, 1983—. Mem. President's Council for a Nat. Curriculum, Antioch (Ohio) U., 1978-81; bd. dirs. L-5 Soc., Tucson, 1976—. Mem. Am. Phys. Soc., AIAA, Sigma Xi. Author: Doomsday Has Been Cancelled, 1978; contbr. articles on space tech., astrophysics and atmospheric physics to sci. jours.; research in space industrialization and space colonization. Office: Suite 104 1811 Santa Rita Rd Pleasanton CA 94566

VALCOV, ALLEN WILLIAM, clinical psychologist; b. Columbus, Ohio, Jan. 11, 1938; s. Samuel and Helen Valcov; B.A., Ohio State U., 1959, M.A., 1963, Ph.D., 1967; m. M. Eileen Leitner, Aug. 20, 1961; 1 dau., Jennifer. Postdoctoral fellow in psychology Yale Sch. Medicine, 1967-69; clin. psychologist San Mateo County Mental Health Services, 1969—; chief adult outpatient and crisis services Central County Mental Health Center, 1975—, affiliate mem. dept. psychiatry Peninsula Hosp. and Med. Center, Burlingame, Calif. Mem. Am. Psychol. Assn., San Mateo County Psychol. Assn. Office: 3700 Edison St San Mateo CA 94403 also 117 N San Mateo Dr San Mateo CA 94401

VALDEZ, JOEL DAVID, city official; b. Tucson, July 2, 1934; s. Luis F. and Miriam Valdez; B.S., U. Ariz., 1957; Exec. Inst., MIT, 1972; S.M.G., Harvard U., 1978; m. Mary Lee Jacobs, May 30, 1958; children—David E., Laura Lisa. Dir. detention service Pima County Juvenile Ct., Tucson, 1958-66; adminstrv. asst. City of Tucson Library, 1966-70; asst. city mgrs. office City of Tucson, 1970-71, asst. city mgr., 1971-74, city mgr., 1974—. Mem. governing bd. Catholic Diocese of Tucson, Ariz. Mem. Ariz. internat. city mgrs. assns. Roman Catholic. Club: K.C. Home: 2045 Calle Armenta Tucson AZ 85705 Office: PO Box 27210 Tucson AZ 85726

VALDOVINOS, LAURO, fin. exec.; b. Mexico City, Sept. 18, 1938; s. Jose Cruz and Milburga G. V.; came to U.S., 1948; B.B.A., Centro Universitario Mexico, 1955; M.B.A., U. Mex., 1963; children—Lauro Rogelio, Mario Ricardo. Internat. auditor Roberto Casas Alatriste, Mexico City, 1962-64; chief accountant Schrader Scovill Inc, Mexico City, 1964-65; controller Warnaco, Mexico City, 1965-69; controller ITT-Avis, Mexico City, 1969-71; asst. corporate controller Estee Lauder Inc., Melville, N.Y., 1972-78; asst. v.p. internat. devel. Am. Med. Internat., Inc., Beverly Hills, Calif., 1978-83; fin. cons. Lauro Valdovinos & Assocs., Beverly Hills, 1983—. C.P.A., Mex. Home: 5460 Las Virgenes Rd Calabasas CA 91302 Office: 8306 Wilshire Blvd Suite 313 Beverly Hills CA 90211

VALENTE, JACK JOHN, advertising agency executive; b. Yonkers, N.Y., Dec. 10, 1953; s. Oswald Francis and Ann Marie (Sarubbi) V.; m. Marcia Kolback, Mar. 15, 1980 (div.); m. Pamela Lea Huisman, Dec. 4, 1982. Media planner Wells, Rich, Greene, N.Y.C., 1975-76, media mgr., N.Y.C., Los Angeles, 1980-82; media supr. Young and Rubican, N.Y.C., Chgo., 1976-80; assoc. media dir. Needham, Harper & Steers, Los Angeles, 1982—. Roman Catholic. Home: 608 Idaho Ave Apt 3 Santa Monica CA 90403 Office: 10889 Wilshire Blvd Suite 500 Westwood CA 90024

VALENTINE, RALPH SCHUYLER, research director, chemical engineer; b. Seattle, Nov. 3, 1932; s. John Campbell and Elizabeth Florence (Patterson) V.; m. Jeanne Belanger, June 15, 1957; children—Susan, Jacqueline, John. Ph.D. in Chem. Engring., U. Wash., Seattle, 1963. Lic. profl. engr., Calif., Va., Wash. Research engr. Chevron Research Corp., Richmond, Calif., 1956-61; inst. U. Wash., 1961-63; mgr. fluid dynamics Aerojet-Gen. Corp., Sacramento, 1963-69; mgr. chem. tech., Atlantic Research Corp., Alexandria, Va., 1969-79; mgr. research and adv. tech., United Techs. Chem. Systems, San Jose, Calif., 1979—. Mem. San Pablo (Calif.) Planning Commn., 1957-61; chmn. Citizens Urban Renewal Adv. Com., 1960-61. Recipient 1st prize Scanning Electron Microscopy photography, Nat. Ceramographic Exhbn., 1974. Mem. AIAA, AM. Inst. Chem. Engrs., Society Advancement of Materials and Process Engring., Sigma Xi, Tau Beta Pi, Phi Lambda Upsilon, Zeta Mu Tau. Contbr. author: Liquid Propellant Rocket Combustion Instability, 1972; contbr. to tech. publs.; patentee in field. Home: 10430 Stokes Ave Cupertino CA 95014 Office: 600 Metcalf Rd San Jose CA 95150

VALENTINE, WILLIAM R., dentist, state senator; b. Warren, Pa., July 12, 1944; s. William R. and Helen S. (Bellus) V.; B.S. in Chemistry, U. Pitts., 1966, D.M.D., 1970. Pvt. practice dentistry, Albuquerque; pres. Valentine, McPherson Profl. Dental Assn.; mem. N.Mex. Senate. Elder, La Mesa Presbyn. Ch.; pres. U. Pitts. Y.R.'s, 1963-65; pres. Bernalillo County Young Republicans, 1974-76; chmn. N.Mex. Rep. Legis. Campaign Com., 1977. Served to lt. comdr. USPHS, 1970-72. Fellow Am. Endodontic Soc.; mem. ADA, N.Mex. Dental Assn., Albuquerque Dist. Dental Soc., Albuquerque Acad. Gen. Dentistry (pres. 1976), Am. Endodontic Soc., Internat. Assn. Orthodontics, Duk City Study Club, N.Mex. Wildlife Fedn., Psi Omega. Republican. Clubs: Elks; Sandia Toastmasters. Office: 6101 Candeleria NE Albuquerque NM 87110*

VALENZUELA, FRED JOSEPH, health care executive; b. Oceanside, Calif., Mar. 19, 1942; s. Jesus Rosales and Esperanza Maria (Heredia) V.; m. Catheryn Anne Valenzuela, July 1, 1972; children—Caroline, Joseph, Deborah, Matthew, Richard, Kathleen. B.S. in Phys. Therapy, U. So. Calif., 1967, M.A., 1970. Registered phys. therapist. Pvt. practice phys. therapy 1970-73; program asst. Porterville (Calif.) State Hosp. 1973-75, program dir. 1975-79; clin. dir. Patton (Calif.) State Hosp. 1979-80; exec. dir. Lanterman State Hosp., Pomona 1980—. Bd. dirs. Hispanic Youth Task Force; bd. dirs. El Arco Human Services Corp. Mem. Nat. Assn. Supts. Pub. Residential Facilities for Mentally Retarded, Am. Phys. Therapy Assn., Calif. Assn. Physically Handicapped. Democrat. Roman Catholic. Home: 3530 W Pomona Blvd #1 Pomona CA 91769 Office: PO Box 100 Pomona CA 91769

VALERA, MAURICIO MOSCOSO, JR., ret. elec. engr.; b. Kilauea, Hawaii, Nov. 9, 1922; s. Mauricio Moscoso and Rosalie Goles (Alba) V.; B.S. in Elec. Engring., U. Denver, 1950; m. Felicidad Adversalo, Mar. 15, 1952; children—Jonathan Jaime, Maurilei Ligaya, Janalei Estrellita. Asst. engr. Hilo Electric Light Co. (Hawaii), 1951-54, asst. transmission and distbn. engr., 1954-57, 58-70, supt. customer engring., 1970-72, supt. engring. design, 1972-83; engr. Pub. Service Co. Colo., 1957-58; instr. Hawaii Community Coll., 1968-69. Mem. County of Hawaii Bd. Water Supply, 1967-69; commr. County of Hawaii Planning Dept., 1970-73. Served with USNR, 1942-45. Sr. mem. IEEE. Mem. United Ch. of Christ. Clubs: Masons, Shriners. Home: 37 Pilialoha St Hilo HI 96720 Office: 1200 Kilauea St Hilo HI 96720

VALERO, FRANCISCO PEDRO JORGE, physicist; b. Cordoba, Argentina, Mar. 12, 1936; came to U.S., 1968, naturalized, 1973; s. Francisco C. and Antonina (Vaccaro) V.; M.S., U. LaPlata (Argentina), 1960, Ph.D., 1965; m. Ana Maria Ghio, Apr. 28, 1962; children—Jorge, Gustavo, Silvanna. Prof. physics Mil. Naval Acad., Argentina, 1960-63; asso. prof. U. LaPlata, 1966-67; research asso. Nat. Research Council-Nat. Acad. Scis., 1968-69; research scientist NASA Ames Research Center, Moffett Field, Calif., 1969—; cons. mem. com. line spectra of elements Nat. Acad. Scis., 1971-76. Recipient various research grants. Mem. Optical Soc. Am., Am. Phys. Soc. Contbr. articles to profl. jours. Home: 1678 Langport Dr Sunnyvale CA 94087 Office: NASA Ames Research Center MS 245 6 Moffett Field CA 94035

VALIERE, GARY MARK, business consultant; b. Valley City, N.D., Feb. 24, 1931; s. Eugene Anthony and Doris Lois (Keeler) V.; m. Delores Elaine Leick, Jan. 2, 1950; children—Steven Mark, Michael Gordon, Thomas Paul, Gary James. B.S., N.D. State Coll., Valley City, 1955; M.B.A., Calif. State U.-Fullerton, 1968; Ph.D., U.S. Internat. U., San Diego, 1980. Lab. foreman, research chemist Phillips Chem. Co., Borger, Tex., 1955-58; research design engr. Boeing Co., Seattle, 1958-61; sr. electronics engr., mgr. program mgmt. Raytheon Corp., Santa Barbara, Calif. 1961-62; project dir. Mgmt. Systems Corp., Boston and Newport Beach, Calif., 1962-65; dir. mgmt. analysis Douglas Aircraft, Santa Monica and Huntington Beach, Calif., 1965-68; asst. v.p., dir. program planning and control, mil. aircraft div. McDonnell Douglas Corp., Long Beach, Calif., 1968-69; mgr. cons. Peat, Marwick, Mitchell, Los Angeles, 1969-72; v.p., dir. Rex Land & Assocs., Los Angeles, 1972-77; pres., chmn. bd. Gary Valiere & Assocs., Irvine, Calif., 1977—, Office Word Processing, Irvine, 1982—, Astro Vista, Inc., Irvine, 1982—; dir. Cypress Internat., Dovaly, Inc., Garretson-Valiere & Assocs.; lectr. Am. Mgmt. Assn., Am. Inst. Indsl. Engrs., Nat. Contract Mgmt. Assn., UCLA, U. So. Calif. Active senatorial compaigns, 1960, 68. Served with U.S. Army, 1949-51. Mem. AIAA, Univ. Doctoral Soc., Am. Def. Preparedness Assn., Assn. U.S. Army, U.S. Air Force Assn., Nat. Contract Mgmt. Assn., World Affairs Council, Nat. Security Council (adv. council), Am. Legion. Clubs: Congressional, Senatorial, Elks. Author books, manuals, papers on orgn. and mgmt. Office: 2021 Business Center Dr Suite 211 Irvine CA 92715

VALLEE, HUBERT PRIOR RUDY, orchestra leader; b. Island Pond, Vt., July 28, 1901; s. Charles Alphonse and Katherine (Lynch) V.; m. Fay Webb, July 6, 1931 (dec. Nov. 1936); m. Bette Jane Greer, Dec. 1943 (div. 1944); m. Eleanor Kathleen Norris, Sept. 3, 1949. Student U. Maine, 1921; Ph.B., Yale U., 1927. Played with Savoy Havana Band at Hotel Savoy, London, 1924-25, broadcast and recorded while there; played with band at Yale U. and led Yale football band during sr. yr.; toured U.S. with coll. band; formed Conn. Yankees, 1928; 1st U.S. broadcasts, 1928; performed with orch. for 10 yrs. on NBC's Fleischmann Variety Hour; appeared at Paramount (N.Y.) and Paramount (Bklyn.) 10 weeks spring of 1929, returning in Oct. for run of nearly 2 yrs.; starred in motion picture Vagabond Lover, 1929, George White's Scandals, 1934, Sweet Music, 1935, Gold Diggers in Paris, 1938, Second Fiddle, 1939, Time Out for Rhythm and Too Many Blondes, 1941, also Man Alive, People Are Funny, It's in the Bag, The Fabulous Suzanne, I Remember Mamma, The Bachelor and the Bobby Soxer, Beautiful Blonde from Bashful Bend, Father Was a Fullback, Mother is a Freshman, The Admiral Was a Lady, Mad Wednesday, Ricochet Romance, Gentlemen Marry Brunettes, How To Succeed in Business Without Really Trying, Live a Little, Love a Little; appeared in stage show of George White's Scandals, 1931, 36; played Coronation Week engagement in London, 1937, Cocoanut Grove, Los Angeles, 1937, 38; broadcasted weekly for Standard Brands, 1929-39, for Nat. Dairies, Sealtest program, 1940-41, Drene Show, 1944-46, Philip Morris, 1946-47, Rudy Vallee Show, 1950; frequent night club appearances; appeared in musical comedy How To Succeed in Business Without Really Trying, N.Y.C., 1961-64; has appeared on TV variety shows; tours with one-man multi-media show; composer of sons and musical numbers; author: Vagabound Dreams Come True, 1930, Let the Chips Fall, 1975. Served with USN, World War I; with USCG, World War II. Recipient N.Y. Critics award 1962. Mem. Am. Fedn. Actors (pres. 1973), Am. Fedn. Musicians, Am. Soc. Authors and Composers, Acad. Motion Picture Arts and Scis., Amateur Cinema League, Nat. Assn. Performing Artists, Screen Actors Guild, Am. Arbitration Assn., 40 and 8, Am. Legion, Sigma Alpha Epsilon. Clubs: N.Y. Athletic, Lambs, Friars, Yale (N.Y.C.). Lodge: Elks. Office: 7430 Pyramid Pl Hollywood CA 90046

VALLEN, JEROME JAY, coll. dean; b. Phila., Oct. 2, 1928; s. Harry Lionel and Frances Sylvia V.; B.S., Cornell U., 1950, Ph.D., 1978; M.Ed., St. Lawrence U., Canton, N.Y., 1959; m. Florence L. Levinson, Nov. 12, 1950; children—Marc, Gary, Randy, Rebecca. Prof., chmn. dept. hotel and food service adminstrn. SUNY, Canton, 1954-67; prof., dean Coll. Hotel Adminstrn., U. Nev., Las Vegas, 1967—; v.p. Univ. Assos., Inc.; dir. Grandissimo Hotel, Las Vegas; pres., chmn. bd. Council Hotel, Restaurant and Instl. Edn., 1974-77. Served with C.E., Aus., 1951-52. Recipient H.B. Meek award ednl. excellence Council Hotel, Restaurant, Instl. Edn., 1980. Mem. Internat. Assn. Hospitality Accts., Internat. Food Service Execs. Assn., Hotel Sales Mgmt. Assn., Phi Kappa Phi, Phi Delta Kappa. Author: Art and Science of Modern Innkeeping, rev. edit., 1978; Check-in, Check-out, rev. edit., 1980; Readings in Hotel, Restaurant and Institutional Management, 1977. Office: 5400 Maryland Pkwy Las Vegas NV 89154

VALMASSY, RONALD LOUIS, podiatrist, educator; b. San Francisco, July 8, 1947; s. Louis R. and Gloria Marie (Menconi) V.; m. Helen Paxinos, June 8, 1974; 1 son, Paul Nicholas. B.S. in Biology, U. San Francisco, 1970; D.Podiatric Medicine, Calif. Coll. Podiatric Medicine, 1974, M.S. in Biomechanics, 1976. Diplomate Am. Bd. Podiatric Orthopedics. Assoc. prof., chmn. dept. biomechanics Calif. Coll. Podiatric Medicine, 1976—. Fellow Am. Coll. Podopediatrics; mem. Am. Coll. Foot Orthopedists (pres. 80), Am. Podiatry Assn. Author papers in field. Office: 450 Sutter St San Francisco CA 94108

VAMPOLA, ALFRED LUDVIK, space scientist; b. Dwight, Nebr., July 10, 1934; s. Ludvik Anton and Pauline (Trousil) V.; m. Karen Agnes Kirkwood, Apr. 7, 1956; children—Joseph, John, Elaine, Mary, Mark, Robert, James, Donald. B.S. in Math. and Physics, Creighton U., 1956; M.S., St. Louis U., 1958, Ph.D. in Physics, 1961. Sr. physicist Convair Co., San Diego, 1961-62; mem. tech. staff Aerospace Corp., Los Angeles, 1962-68, staff scientist, 1968-78, sr. scientist, 1978—. Mem. Am. Geophys. Union. Republican. Roman Catholic. Contbr. articles to profl. jours. Office: PO Box 92957 Los Angeles CA 90009

VANALLEN, WILLIAM GEORGE, educational administrator; b. New Brunswick, N.J., July 19, 1914; s. George and Emma May (Smith) VanA.; m. Victoria Dolores Caballero, Oct. 16, 1937. B.S. in Elec. Engring., Rutgers U., 1936; M.S. in Civil Engring., State U. Iowa, 1948; postgrad. Army War Coll., 1955. Registered profl. engr., Hawaii. Commd. 2d lt. C.E., U.S. Army, 1936, advanced through grades to col., 1952, ret., 1965; dir. land div. Kamehameha Schs./Bishop Estate, Honolulu, 1965—. Decorated Legion of Merit with 2 oak leaf clusters, Bronze Star medal with 2 oak leaf clusters, Army Commendation medal with oak leaf cluster; Croix de Guerre with palm. Mem. Hawaii Soc. Profl. Engrs. (pres. 1969-70), Soc. Am. Mil. Engrs. (pres. Honolulu chpt. 1963-64), Engrs. Assn. Hawaii, Hawaii Council Engring. Socs., Honolulu C. of C., Oahu Devel. Conf., Phi Beta Kappa, Tau Beta Pi. Club: Plaza. Home: 4340 Pahoa Ave Apt 14A Honolulu HI 96816 Office: 567 South St Honolulu HI 96813

VAN ALSTYNE, ARVO, commissioner of higher education, legal educator; b. Beechhurst, N.Y., May 4, 1922; s. Guy Chase and Alli (Luoma) Van A.; m. Ruth Lamb, May 21, 1945; children—David, Peter, Laura Van Alstyne Rowland, Philip, Sara, Kristina. B.A., Yale U., 1943, J.D., 1949. Bar: Calif. 1949. Dep. county counsel, Los Angeles, 1951-53; prof. law, UCLA, 1953-66; prof. law U. Utah, Salt Lake City, 1966-73, v.p., exec. asst., 1973-81; commr. higher edn. State of Utah, Salt Lake City, 1981—; lectr., cons. in field. Mem. Edn. Commn. on the States, 1981—, Western Interstate Commn. on Higher Edn., 1981—, Utah State Job Tng. Coordinating Council, 1983, Utah State Adv. Council on Sci. and Tech., 1981—. Served with USNR, 1943-45. Ford Found. faculty fellow, 1959-60; recipient Disting. Tchr. award, U. Utah, 1972. Mem. Calif. State Bar, State Higher Edn. Exec. Officers Assn. Mormon. Clubs: Rotary, Timpanogas, Four Seasons. Contbr. writings to publs. in field. Office: 807 E S Temple St Salt Lake City UT 84102

VAN BELLE, GERALD, biostatistics educator; b. Enschede, Overijsel, Netherlands, July 23, 1936; s. Willem Jan and Martha (Segers) van B.; m. Johanna P. Praamsma, Feb. 22, 1963; children—Eloise Petronella, William John, Gerard Theodore, Christine Eline, Louis Calvin. Student Calvin Coll., 1953-56, U. Mich., 1956-57; B.A., U. Toronto, 1962, M.A., 1964, Ph.D., 1967. Asst. prof. Fla. State U., 1967-72, assoc. prof., dir. Statis. Cons. Ctr., 1972-74; vis. assoc. prof. U. Wash., Seattle, 1974-75, assoc. prof., 1975-76; prof. biostats. 1976—. Bd. dirs. Watson Groen Christian Sch., 1975-80, 82—, pres. bd., 1978-80, 82—. Mary Beatty fellow, U. Toronto, 1965-67. Mem. Am. Statis. Assn. (pres. Fla. chpt. 1973), Biometric Soc. (pres. Western N.Am. region 1982), Am. Sci. Affiliation, Sigma Xi (pres. Fla. State chpt. 1974). Contbr. numerous articles to profl. jours. Home: 17210 25th Ave NE Seattle WA 98155 Office: Biostatistics SC-32 U Wash Seattle WA 98195

VAN BELLEHEM, HARRY BRYCE, former municipal recreation ofcl.; b. St. Louis, Dec. 23, 1915; s. Engelbert and Harriet Elizabeth (Brice) Van B.; B.S. in Public Adminstrn., U. So. Calif., 1956; m. Marguerite Leonora Tucciarone, Sept. 14, 1935; children—Linda B. Van Bellehem Buffington, Judy Van Bellehem Castronovo. Recreator, Long Beach (Calif.) Recreation Commn., 1939-42; supr. Los Angeles County Parks and Recreation, 1947-53; recreation dir. City of Torrance (Calif.), 1953-72, park and recreation dir., 1972-77; ret., 1977; mem. Calif. Bd. Park and Recreation Personnel, 1963-67, 74-78, chmn., 1966-67; trustee South Bay Botanic Garden Found., 1981-82; bd. dirs. Redondo Beach Boating Council, 1980-82. Served with USNR, 1945-46. Mem. Calif. Parks and Recreation Soc. (pres. 1973; citation honor award 1967, Fellowship award 1977), Am. Park and Recreation Soc. (chmn. com. on registration 1969-72), Internat. Recreation Assn., Nat. Recreation and Park Assn. (chmn. nat. registration bd. 1970-72), U. So. Calif. Alumni Assn. Club: King Harbor Yacht. Author articles in field. former municipal recreation ofcl.; b. St. Louis, Dec. 23, 1915; s. Engelbert and Harriet Elizabeth (Brice) Van B.; B.S. in Public Adminstrn., U. So. Calif., 1956; m. Marguerite Leonora Tucciarone, Sept. 14, 1935; children—Linda B. Van Bellehem Buffington, Judy Van Bellehem Castronovo. Recreator, Long Beach (Calif.) Recreation Commn., 1939-42; supr. Los Angeles County Parks and Recreation, 1947-53; recreation dir. City of Torrance (Calif.), 1953-72, park and recreation dir., 1972-77; ret., 1977; mem. Calif. Bd. Park and Recreation Personnel, 1963-67, 74-78, chmn., 1966-67; trustee South Bay Botanic Garden Found., 1981-82; bd. dirs. Redondo Beach Boating Council, 1980-82. Served with USNR, 1945-46. Mem. Calif. Parks and Recreation Soc. (pres. 1973; citation honor award 1967, Fellowship award 1977), Am. Park and Recreation Soc. (chmn. com. on registration 1969-72), Internat. Recreation Assn., Nat. Recreation and Park Assn. (chmn. nat. registration bd. 1970-72), U. So. Calif. Alumni Assn. Club: King Harbor Yacht. Author articles in field. Home: 239 Paseo De Las Delicias Redondo Beach CA 90277

VAN BLARCOM, KENDALL EARL, human resource executive; b. Swampscott, Mass., June 25, 1935; s. Herman Kendall and Ruth Evelyn (Ladd) Van B.; m. Evelyn Leona Green, July 5, 1957; children—Deborah A., Mark Kendall, Eric Harold, Jeffrey Scott; m. 2d, Patricia Irene Bernadsky, Dec. 26, 1979. A.S., Berkshire Community Coll., 1972; B.A., U. Mass., 1974; M.A., U. San Francisco, 1976; doctoral candidate Walden U., Mpls. Cert. community coll. instr. and counselor; lic. marriage, family and child counselor, Calif. Counselor, family therapist San Rafael, Calif., 1974-77; co-owner, pres. Counseling Service Network, Daly City, Calif., 1978-82; owner, pres. Ken Van Blarcom & Assocs., San Francisco, 1982—. Supt. sts. Washington (Mass.), 1963-65, selectman, 1965-68. Mem. Am. Soc. Tng. and Devel., Am. Mgmt. Assn., Assn. Labor-Mgmt. and Cons. on Alcoholism. Author newsletter for human resource profls. Office: 533 Sutter St Suite 822 San Francisco CA 94102

VAN BLARICOM, DONALD PERRY, police chief; b. Seattle, Apr. 3, 1935; s. Donald Van B.; m. Janice Lee Ortolf, Mar. 25, 1978. With Bellevue (Wash.) Police Dept., 1956—, chief of police, 1975—. Trustee, Statewide City Employees Retirement System; mem. City of Bellevue Disability Bd.; mem. Mcpl. Employees Benefit Trust Retirement Com.; mem. adv. com. Wash. State Bd. Community Coll. Edn. Law Enforcement; mem. steering com. Wash. Criminal Justice Edn. and Tng. Center; chmn. Bellevue Police Dept. Minority Recruitment Com., 1974-77; mem. Wash. Atty. Gen.'s Com. on Security and Privacy; mem. Wash. State CAP Citizens Adv. Council; cons. U.S. Dept. Justice Community Relations Service; intern 94th Congress; mem. Gov.'s Community Task Force for Corrections Devel.; mem. search and screening com. Selection of Bellevue Community Coll. Pres.; mem. adult criminal policy com. Wash. State Council on Crime and Delinquency, mem. ad hoc com. on bd. prison terms and paroles; guest lectr. U. Wash., Seattle U., Northwestern U., Simon Fraser U.; mem. adv. council Bellevue Art Mus.; trustee Youth Eastside Services; mem. Gov.'s Select Com. for Police-Fire Pension Rev. Served with USMC, 1953-56. Mem. Internat. Assn. Chiefs of Police, Wash. Assn. Sheriffs and Police Chiefs, King County Chiefs Assn., Wash. State Council on Crime and Delinquency, Bellevue Police Officers Guild, Aircraft Owners and Pilots Assn. Republican. Club: Rotary. Office: PO Box 1768 Bellevue WA 98009

VAN BRONKHORST, EDWIN E., electronics company executive; b. Rio Linda, Calif., Feb. 21, 1924; s. Klaas and Ethel (Diebold) van B.; m. Russella Diane Ball, Feb. 16, 1957; children—Kort, Jon, Derek. B.S., U. Calif., 1944. Acct., ptnr. F.W. Larentz & Co., San Francisco, 1950-53, internal auditor Hewlett-Packard Co., Palo Alto, Calif., 1953-57, sec. treas., 1957-63, v.p., treas., dir., 1963-81, sr. v.p., treas., chief fin. officer, 1981—; dir. Rolm Corp., Santa Clara, Calif., Triad Systems Corp., Sunnyvale, Calif. Former dir. Palo Alto C. of C., Portola Valley Sch. Dist., Children's Health Council, Palo Alto Community Chest. Home: Portola Valley CA Office: 3000 Hanover St Palo Alto CA 94304

VAN BRUNT, EDMUND EWING, physician; b. Oakland Calif., Apr. 28, 1926; s. Adrian Wilbur and Kathryn Anne (Shattuck) Van B.; B.A., U. Calif., Berkeley, 1952, M.D., San Francisco, 1959; D.Sc. (hon.), U. Toulouse (France), 1978; m. Claire Monod, Feb. 28, 1949; children—Karin, Deryk, Jahn. Intern, Kaiser Found. Hosp., San Francisco, 1959-60, resident, 1960-62, staff physician internal medicine, 1964—; dir. dept. med. methods research The Permanente Med. Group, Oakland, Calif., 1979—; research assoc. physiology U. Calif. Med. Center, San Francisco, 1963-67; adj. prof. med. info. sci. U. Calif. Sch. Medicine, 1975—; mem. sci. com. Inst. Research in Info. and Automation, Paris, 1970-77. Served with AUS, 1944-46; ETO. NIH fellow, 1961-63. Mem. AAAS, ACP, Am. Heart Assn., Biomed. Engring. Soc. (charter), Calif. Med. Assn., San Francisco County Med. Assn., Sigma Xi; Editorial bd. Computers in Biomedicine, Med. Informatics. contbr. articles to profl. jours. physician; b. Oakland Calif., Apr. 28, 1926; s. Adrian Wilbur and Kathryn Anne (Shattuck) Van B.; B.A., U. Calif., Berkeley, 1952, M.D., San Francisco, 1959; D.Sc. (hon.), U. Toulouse (France), 1978; m. Claire Monod, Feb. 28, 1949; children—Karin, Deryk, Jahn. Intern, Kaiser Found. Hosp., San Francisco, 1959-60, resident, 1960-62, staff physician internal medicine, 1964—; dir. dept. med. methods research The Permanente Med. Group, Oakland, Calif., 1979—; research assoc. physiology U. Calif. Med. Center, San Francisco, 1963-67; adj. prof. med. info. sci. U. Calif. Sch. Medicine, 1975—; mem. sci. com. Inst. Research in Info. and Automation, Paris, 1970-77. Served with AUS, 1944-46; ETO. NIH fellow, 1961-63. Mem. AAAS, ACP, Am. Heart Assn., Biomed. Engring. Soc. (charter), Calif. Med. Assn., San Francisco County Med. Assn., Sigma Xi; Editorial bd. Computers in Biomedicine, Med. Informatics. contbr. articles to profl. jours. Office: 3451 Piedmont Oakland CA 94611

VAN BUSKIRK, ANNE MARIE, comml. printing co. exec.; b. Paris, May 29, 1927; came to U.S., 1933; d. Theodore and Georgette (Raphael) Burns; B.A., Los Angeles State Coll., 1949; m. Edward R. Van Buskirk, Nov. 23, 1949 (div.); children—James Edward, John Riley. Owner mgr. Rainbow Printing, Inc., Seattle, 1977—. Recipient various certs. appreciation. Mem. Seattle C. of C., Network Exec. Women, Career Network, Women & Bus., Women's Bus. Exchange, Seattle Women Bus. Owners, Sales and Mktg. Execs., Seattle Mut. Bus. Club, Winners Circle. Mem. Ch. of Religious Sci. Club: Swedish. Home: Northgate Plaza Apt 414 9416 1st Ave NE Seattle WA 98115 Office: Rainbow Printing Inc 2917 1st Ave Seattle WA 98121

VANCE, DON L., accountant; b. Peoria, Ill., June 29, 1947; s. Donald M. and Martha E. (Baer) V.; m. Kathy J. Robbins, July 13, 1972; children—Cheryl Kathryn, William Garrett. B.S., Ill. State U., 1969, M.S., 1970. Tchr., coach Cissna Park (Ill.) Sch. Dist., 1970-71; tchr. St. Charles (Ill.) Sch. Dist., 1971-80; tax cons., Tucson, 1980—. Pres., Marana chpt. Ariz. Assn. Gifted and Talented, 1981-83; mem. Marana Sch. Bd., 1983-86. Democrat. Mem. Ch. of Christ.

VAN CLEAVE, PHILIP FORD, naturalist; b. Urbana, Ill., Aug. 14, 1920; s. Harley Jones and Bernice (Ford) Van C; student U. Ill., 1938-40, U. Ariz., 1942; m. Winifred Louise Evans, May 21, 1950; children—Kent Bowen, Katherine Mary Van Cleave Parris, Lorna Louise. Acting custodian Wupatki Nat. Monument, Ariz., Nat. Park Service Dept. Interior, 1943-46, park ranger Lake Mead Recreation Area, Nev., 1946-47, archeologist Mesa Verde Nat. Park, Colo., 1947-56, chief park naturalist Petrified Forest Nat. Park, Ariz., 1956-64, chief park naturalist Carlsbad Caverns Nat. Park, N.Mex., 1964-68, chief interpretation and resource mgmt., 1968-71, chief tech. services, 1971-73, staff interpretive and environ. specialist, 1973-76, ret. Bd. advisers S.E. N.Mex. Regional Library. Recipient Meritorious Service award Dept. Interior, 1977. Mem. Southeastern N.Mex. Hist. Soc. (pres. 1971, 78-79, treas. 1980-82), Carlsbad Arts and Humanities Alliance (v.p. 1977-81), Early Am. Coppers Club, Am. Numismatic Assn., Internat. Platform Assn., Cave Research Found. (hon.). Author: (with Lancaster, Pinkley and Watson) Archeological Excavations in Mesa Verde National Park, Colorado, 1950, 54; Contbg. author The Arms of Ethan Allen and Associates. Home: 1505 Westridge Rd Carlsbad NM 88220

VAN DE KAMP, JOHN KALAR, state attorney general; b. Pasadena, Calif., Feb. 7, 1936; s. Harry and Georgie (Kalar) Van de K.; m. Andrea Fisher, Mar. 11, 1978; 1 dau., Diana. B.A., Dartmouth Coll., 1956; J.D., Stanford U., 1959. Bar: Calif. 1960. Asst. U.S. atty., chief of criminal div., chief asst. U.S. atty., Los Angeles, 1960-66; U.S. atty., Los Angeles, 1966-67; dep. dir., then dir. Exec. Office for U.S. Attys., Washington, 1967-69; spl. asst. Pres.'s Commn. on Campus Unrest, 1970; 1st fed. pub. defender City of Los Angeles, 1971-75; dist. atty. Los Angeles County, 1975-82; atty. gen. State of Calif., Los Angeles, 1982—. Mem. Nat. Dist. Attys. Assn., Calif. Dist. Attys. Assn., Peace Officers Assn. Los Angeles County, Peace Officers Standards and Tng. Commn. Democrat. Office: Office of the Attorney General 3580 Wilshire Blvd Suite 800 Los Angeles CA 90010

VANDE KEMP, HENDRIKA, psychology, educator; b. Voorthuizen, Gelderland, Netherlands, Dec. 13, 1948; d. Hendrik and Petronella (Van Peursem) Vande K.; B.A., Hope Coll., 1971; M.S., U. Mass., Amherst, 1974, Ph.D., 1977. Predoctoral intern Topeka State Hosp., 1975-76; instr. Fuller Theol. Sem., Pasadena, Calif., 1976-77, asst. prof., 1977-81, assoc. prof. psychology, 1981—. Elder, Sil Presbyn. Ch., 1981—. Mem. Am. Psychol. Assn., Am. Assn. for Marriage and Family Theraphy, Am. Acad. Religion, Calif. State Psychol. Assn., Internat. Soc. for History of Behavioral and Social Scis., Soc. for Sci. Study of Religion. Contbr. articles to profl. jours. Office: 177 N Madison St Pasadena CA 91101

VAN DEN BERGHE, PIERRE LOUIS, sociology and anthropology educator; b. Lubumbashi, Zaire, Jan. 30, 1933; s. Louis Samuel and Denise (Caullery) van den B.; m. Irmgard Cornelia Niehuis, Jan. 21, 1956; children—Eric, Oliver, Marc. B.A., Stanford U., 1952, M.A., 1953; M.A., Harvard U., 1959, Ph.D., 1960. Asst. prof. Wesleyan U., Middletown, Conn., 1962-63; assoc. prof. SUNY-Buffalo, 1963-65; prof. U.Wash., Seattle, 1965—. Served with M.C., U.S. Army, 1954-56. Rockefeller Found. vis. prof., 1967-69; NIMH grantee, 1972-73. Mem. Am. Sociol. Assn. (Spivak award 1980), Am. Anthropol. Assn. Author: South Africa, A Study in Conflict, 1965; Race and Racism, 1967; Race and Ethnicity, 1970; Academic Gamesmanship, 1970; Man in Society, 1978; Human Family Systems, 1979; The Ethnic Phenomenon, 1981; others. Home: 2006 19th Ave E Seattle WA 98112 Office: Dept Sociology DK-40 U Wash Seattle WA 98195

VANDENBERGHE, RONALD GUSTAVE, accountant; b. Oakland, Calif., July 1, 1937; s. Anselm Henri and Margaret B. (Bygum) V.; B.A. with honors, San Jose State Coll., 1959; postgrad. U. Calif. at Berkeley Extension, 1959-60, Golden Gate Coll., 1961-63; m. Patricia W. Dufour, Aug. 18, 1957; children—Camille, Mark, Matthew. Real estate investor, Pleasanton, Calif., 1964—. Instr. accounting U. Cal., Berkeley, 1963-70; C.P.A., Pleasanton, 1963—. Served with USAF. C.P.A., Calif. Mem. Calif. Soc. C.P.A.'s. Republican. Presbyn. Mason (Shriner). Home: PO Box 803 Danville CA 94526 Office: 20 Happy Valley Rd Pleasanton CA 94566

VANDENBURGH, WILLIAM GEORGE, university dean, physical education educator; b. Seattle, July 24, 1924; s. George Henry and Eva Mae (Wenger) V.; m. Rita Chillingworth Simon, Aug. 22, 1953; 1 dau., Laura Katherine. B.S., U. Wash., 1949, M.S., 1950; Ed.D., Columbia U., 1953. Asst. prof., basketball coach Fresno (Calif.) State Coll., 1953-56, assoc. prof., 1956-60; prof. phys. edn. Calif. State U., Hayward, 1960—, assoc. dean instrn., 1964-65, exec. dean, 1966—. Dir. C. of C.; chmn. Democratic Assembly; treas. Eden Housing; active grand jury commn, 1981-82. Served to capt. USMC, 1942-46, 52-53. Mem. AAHPER, N.Am. Soc. for Sport History, Internat. Council Health, Phys. Edn. and Recreation, Nat. Assn. Phys. Edn. in Higher Edn. Office: Exec Dean Calif State U Hayward CA 94542

VAN DER BIJL, WILLEM, educator; b. Alphen, The Netherlands, Aug. 15, 1920; s. Coenraad Johannes and Hillegonda Maria (Evenbly) Van der B.; came to U.S., 1956, naturalized, 1961; m. Godefrieda Judith Lemkes, Sept. 24, 1946; children—Joan Elizabeth, Bouwe Jan. B.Sc., Free U. Amsterdam, 1941, M.Sc., 1943; Ph.D., State U. Utrecht, 1952. Research assoc. Royal Netherlands Meteorol. Inst., 1946-56; assoc. prof. physics Kans. State U., Manhattan, 1956-61; assoc. prof. meteorology Naval Postgrad. Sch., Monterey, Calif., 1961—. U. Chgo. fellow, 1954-55. Mem. Am. Geophys. Union, Am. Meteorol. Soc., Sigma Xi. Author: Long Range Weather Forecasts, 1954; Statistical Applications in Climatology, 1952.

VANDER HOUWEN, BOYD ALBERT, bank communications officer; b. Yakima, Wash., Jan. 17, 1946; s. John W. and Elsie W. (Lanfear) V.; m. Loma Alene Madsen, June 27, 1970; children—Garth John, Dana Madsen. B.A. in Journalism, U. Mont., 1968; B.A. in Econs., U. Wash., 1971, M.A. in Communications/Bus., 1978. Edn., city hall reporter Idaho Falls (Idaho) Post-Register, 1971-72; farm bus. writer Tri-City Herald, Kennewick, Wash., 1973-74; bur. mgr., editor Yakima Valley Tri-City Herald, Sunnyside, Wash., 1974-76; editor Jour. Contemporary Bus., mgr. bus. publs. Grad. Sch. Bus. Adminstrn. U. Wash., Seattle, 1978-81; communications officer Rainier Nat. Bank, Seattle, 1981—. Mem. publs. redesign com. Hist. Seattle, 1982; mem. selection com. merit scholarship Rainier Nat. Bank, 1983; publicity chmn. United Way One to One Program, 1983, United Way Cabinet, 1982. Served with U.S. Army, 1969-71. NEH awardee summer seminar for journalists, 1979; recipient Excellence in Publs. award Soc. Tech. Publs., 1979, 81. Mem. Pub. Relations Soc. Am., Internat. Assn. Bus. Communicators (Pacesetter awards com. 1981-83 internal communications award of excellence Pacific N.W. chpt. 1982), Sigma Delta Chi (bus. writing editing awards 1971, 73, 74). Home: 7545 12th Ave NW Seattle WA 98117 Office: Rainier Nat Bank PO Box 3966 Seattle WA 98124

VANDERKOLK, BARBARA ANNE, management consultant; b. Phila., Jan. 5, 1949; d. Walter William and Barbara (Jackson) Schwarz. B.A., Calvin Coll., 1970; student U. Montpelier (France), 1967-68; postgrad. Central Wash. U. Tchr. high sch. English, Rochester, Wash., 1970-71; speechwriter Speaker of House, Wash. Ho. of Reps., Olympia, 1972-73; lobbyist, polit. action dir. Wash. Edn. Assn., Olympia, 1974-78; pres., owner Barbara Vanderkolk & Assocs., Inc., Seattle, 1978—. Pres., Women's Polit. Caucus, 1978; dir. Seattle Voice mag., 1981-82. Recipient B'nai B'rith award, 1966; Creative Leadership in Womens Rights award Wash. Edn. Assn., 1977; named to Seattle Times 81 Newsmakers of 1981. Mem. Nat. Assn. Female Execs., Seattle C. of C., Nat. Fedn. Ind. Bus., Nat. Women's Polit. Caucus, World Affairs Council. Clubs: Seattle Athletic, City. Office: 1305 3d Ave Suite 510 Seattle WA 98101

VAN DER MOLEN, KLAAS WILLEM, safety profl.; b. Zijpe, Netherlands, Mar. 4, 1938; came to U.S., 1962, naturalized, 1965; s. Jan and Johanna Hendrika (Schermer) van der M.; grad. Instituut voor Radiotechniek, Rotterdam, Netherlands, 1956, Calif. Mil. Acad., 1965, U.S. Army Command and Gen. Staff Coll., 1978; B.S. in Organizational Behavior, U. San Francisco, 1982; m. Cherie Ann Tracy, Nov. 5, 1977; children—Janine, Robert, Kelly, Bradley. Radio officer Dutch Mcht. Marine, 1956-62; with IBM Corp., 1962—, engr., San Jose, Calif., 1972—. Served to lt. col. U.S. Army Res., 1965-80. Mem. Am. Soc. Safety Engrs. (pres. chpt. 1975-76), Res. Officers Assn. U.S. (2d v.p. dept. Calif. 1978). Home: 6146 Escondido Ct San Jose CA 95119 Office: IBM 725/124 5600 Cottle Rd San Jose CA 95193

VANDERPLAATS, GARRET NIEL, mechanical engineer, educator; b. Modesto, Calif., Feb. 14, 1944; s. Fred and Annie (Hekman) V.; m. Virginia Vera Scott, Dec. 29, 1979. B.C.E., Ariz. State U., Tempe, 1967, M.C.E., 1968; Ph.D., Case Western Res. U., 1971. Research scientist Army Air Mobility Research lab., Moffett Field, Calif., 1971-74, NASA Ames Research Ctr., 1974-76, 78-79; adj. research prof. mech. engring. Naval Postgrad. Sch., Monterey, Calif., 1976-77, assoc. prof. mech. engring., 1979—; research scientist NASA liaison David Tayler Naval Ship Research and Devel. Ctr., Bethesda, Md., 1977-78; cons. in field. Recipient Wright Bros. medal Soc. Automotive Engrs., 1977. Fellow AIAA (assoc.); mem. ASME, ASCE. Republican. Presbyterian. Contbr. numerous articles to tech. jours. Home: 676 Van Buren Circle Monterey CA 93940 Office: Code 69Vn Naval Postgrad School Monterey CA 93940

VANDERSTAY, OTTO RANDOLPH, electronic engineer; b. Houston, Jan. 17, 1933; s. Otto Randolph, Sr. and Addie Byrd (Wallingford) V.; m. Jacqueline Paulette Douchet, Oct. 6, 1968; children—Natalie Michelle, Rachelle Monique. Student U. Tex., 1950-51, U. Houston, 1957. Engr. various cos., Ger. and Calif., 1956-68; owner, mfr.'s rep. Van Ness Assocs., Glendale, Calif., 1968-74; br. service mgr. Honeywell, Inc., Los Angeles, 1974-76; owner, mfr. Evaporation Apparatus Inc., Los Angeles, 1976-77; nat. service mgr. Vitek Systems, Pasadena, Calif., 1977-78; sr. engr. DuPont Instruments, Pasadena, 1978-79; dir. electronic engring. Children's Hosp. Los Angeles, 1980—; cons. analytical instrumentation Jet Propulsion Labs., DuPont Instruments, Pasadena. Mem. U.S. Congressional Adv. Bd., 1983; sustaining mem. Republican Nat. Com., 1982-83. Served with USAF, 1953-61; to capt. Calif. State Mil. Res., 1981—. Mem. Res. Officers Assn. U.S., N.G. Assn. Calif., Assn. Advancement Med. Instrumentation, Assn. Field Service Mgrs., Alliance Francaise, French War Vets. Designed Air Force temp. hangar, Anchorage. Home: 443 Edwards Pl Glendale CA 91206 Office: Children's Hospital Los Angeles 4650 Sunset Blvd Los Angeles CA 90027

VANDERVEST, JAN ANN, association executive; b. Casco, Wis., July 25, 1934; d. Emil and Mabel (Gigot) V.; B.S., U. Wis., Stevens Point, 1959; M.S.W., Cath. U. Am., 1968. With YWCA, 1961-83, exec. dir., San Jose, Calif., 1977-83; treas. United Way Execs., 1978-80; adv. bd. Women's Residence Center, San Jose, 1978-81, Career Outreach for Women, 1978-81. Mem. Nat. Assn. Social Workers, Am. Soc. Tng. and Devel., Bus. and Profl. Women's Club, Nat. Wilderness Soc., Quota Club of San Jose (v.p. 1981-82), AAUW, Sierra Club. Office: YWCA 375 S 3d St San Jose CA 95112

VANDERWILT, JOHN W, geology cons.; b. Oskaloosa, Iowa, May 3, 1898; s. William Jan and Margaret Johanna (Kempkes) V.; A.B., U. Mich., 1922, M.S., 1923; Ph.D., Harvard U., 1927; m. Charlotte Keating, Sept. 6, 1922; children—William Keating, Christine Vanderwilt Rundall, Joanna Knudsen Vanderwilt. Instr. geology U. Colo., 1923-25, asst. prof., 1928-29; jr. geologist U.S. Geol. Survey, 1927-28, asst. geologist, 1929-34; geol. cons., Denver, 1934-70, Sun City, Calif., 1970—; cons. geologist Climax Molybdenum Co., Denver, 1934-68; pres. Colo. Sch. Mines, Golden, 1950-63, pres. emeritus, 1963—; bd. cons. U.S. Bur. Reclamation, 1946-47, 57-63; mem. Nat. Mineral Adv. Council to Sec. Interior, 1947-51; dir. Jefferson Fed. Savs. & Loan Assn., Arvada, Colo., 1961-69. Bd. dirs. Resources for Future, Washington, 1958-68, hon. dir., 1968—. Mem. Soc. Econ. Geology, Geol. Soc. Am., Am. Geol. Inst., Am. Assn. Petroleum Geologists, AIME (dir. 1955-58), Mining and Metall. Soc. Am., Rocky Mountain Assn. Geologists (pres. 1946), Phi Beta Kappa, Sigma Xi. Mason (Shriner), Kiwanian. Contbr. articles to profl. jours. Address: 25830 Morgantown Way Sun City CA 92381

VAN DER WYK, JACK ALEX, musician; b. Los Angeles, Sept. 12, 1929; s. Sally Moritz and Hortense Hannah (Solomon) Van der W.; m. Lucille Anne Gewinner, Dec. 24, 1966; children—Eric, Karl, Amy, Julia. A.B., U. So. Calif., 1952, postgrad., 1952-53. Timpanist, Pasadena (Calif.) Symphony, 1945-53; percussionist San Antonio Symphony, 1955-56; timpanist San Francisco Ballet Co., 1958-71; timpanist Oakland (Calif.) Symphony, 1964-71, percussionist, 1972—; mem. faculty Holy Names Coll., Oakland; tchr. percussion Music and Arts Inst. San Francisco. Served with U.S. Army, 1953-55. Mem. Percussive Arts Soc. Composer of numerous pieces for percussion. Office: Music and Arts Institute of San Francisco Dept Percussion 2622 Jackson St San Francisco CA 94115

VAN DER ZALM, WILLIAM NICK, Canadian provincial government official; b. Nordwykerhout, Holland, May 29, 1934; s. Wilhelmus Antonius and Agatha C. (Warmerdam) Van der Z.; m. Lillian B. Mihalick, June 27, 1956; children—Jeffrey, Juanita, Wim, Lucia. ed. St. Josephs Noordwykerhout, Holland, Bradner and Mt. Lehman, B.C., Phillip Sheffield, Abbotsford, B.C. Minister human resources B.C., 1975-78, minister mcpl. affairs, 1978-82, minister edn., Victoria, 1982—; pres. Art Knapp Nurseries Ltd. Alderman Surrey (B.C.), 4 yrs., mayor 6 yrs. Mem. C. of C. Mem. Social Credit Party. Roman Catholic. Lodges: K.C., Lions. Office: Legis Bldgs Victoria BC V8V 1X4 Canada*

VANDEVENTER, JANICE LEIGH, cartographer, orgn. adminstr.; b. Long Beach, Calif., Aug. 10, 1944; d. Owen Jerome and Laurence Elizabeth (Monninger) V.; B.A. in Geography, UCLA, 1966. Cartographer, Automobile Club So. Calif., Los Angeles, 1966-70, sr. cartographer, 1970-72, research coordinator, 1972-74, chief cartographer, 1974—; flight instr. Falcon Air, Long Beach, 1975—. Recipient FAA Safety Pin, 1974; named Gen. Aviation Girl of Month, Aviation jour., Apr. 1979. Mem. Am. Congress Surveying and Mapping, Pilots Internat. Assn., Aircraft Owners and Pilots Assn., Internat. Platform Assn., UCLA Alumni Assn., Sweet Adelines Internat., Los Angeles C. of C. (aerospace com.), Alpha Xi Delta (pres. alumnae chpt. 1981-82). Home: 3626 Country Club Dr Long Beach CA 90807 Office: 2601 S Figueroa St Los Angeles CA 90007

VANDEVER, LOIS ARLENE, nurse, company executive; b. Milw., Apr. 17, 1931; d. Russell Dana Laycock and Thelma Elizabeth (Strodthoff) L.; 1 son, Vincent James Vandever. B.S.N., U. Denver, 1959; Pediatric Nurse Practioner, U. Colo., 1970. Staff nurse Denver Pub. Schs., 1959-64; coordinator health services Cherry Creek Schs., 1970-73; cons. U. Colo. Sch. Nursing, 1973-79, Colo. State Bd. Nursing, 1975-79; mem. Nurse Practice Act Rewrite Com., 1977-79; pres. Invest in Yourself Inc., Littleton, Colo., 1980—; presenter wellness seminars; guest lectr. Mem. adv. bd. Jefferson County Wellness; bd. dirs. U. Denver Assocs., Denver U. Friends of Nursing, Recipient Pediatric Nurse Practitioner award 1974. Mem. Am. Nurses Assn., Colo. Nurses Assn., Nat. Assn. Female Execs., Exec. Profl. Women's Council, Centennial C. of C. (com. mem.). Republican. Episcopalian. Clubs: Colo. Columbine Dollology (Denver); Zonta (dir.). Developed 1st wellness program in U.S.; co-author: Invest in Yourself; columnist; contbr. articles to profl. jours. Home: 835 W Geddes Circle Littleton CO 80120 Office: PO Box 3473 Littleton CO 80161

VAN DE VYVERE, JULES ROCEE, meat processing company executive; b. St. Boniface, Man., Can., May 2, 1923; s. Albert Achille and Irma Barbara (Brabant) Van de V.; m. Florence Ellen Shatford, Dec. 2, 1923; children—Albert William, James Lawrence, Brian Jules, Robert Thomas. Diploma in bus. St. Boniface Coll., 1940, Man. Commerce Coll., 1945. Acctg. clk. Anglo-Canadian Oils, 1940-42; with Can. Packers Inc., 1946—, area mgr. poultry, Winnipeg, 1976-78, Edmonton, Alta., 1978—. Served with Royal Canadian Navy, 1942-45. Mem. Canadian Egg and Poultry Assn. (sec. 1975—). Roman Catholic. Club: K.C. Office: 2619 91st Ave Edmonton AB T6P 1S3 Canada

VAN DORN, PETER DOUGLAS, accountant; b. Craig, Colo., June 28, 1941; s. Perry Douglas and Gloria Marjorie (Miller) Van D.; m. Joyce Lucille Swanson, Aug. 9, 1964; children—Douglas, Stephen, Marsha. Student Colo. State U., 1959-60; B.S., U. Colo., 1969. C.P.A., Wyo., La., N.C. With Touche Ross & Co., Denver, 1969—, ptnr., 1978—, nat. dir. banking, 1979—. Treas., Westlake Water and Sanitation Dist.; mem. dinner com. Nat. Jewish Hosp./Nat. Asthma Ctr., 1963-69. Served with Army NG, 1963-69. Mem. Colo. Soc. C.P.A.s, Wyo. Soc. C.P.A.s, Am. Inst. C.P.A.s. Republican. Baptist. Clubs: Ranch Country (Westminister); 26 (Denver); U. Colo. Alumni Dirs. Home: 4280 Creek Dr Broomfield CO 80020 Office: 400 United Bank Center Denver CO 80290

VAN DYCK, WAYNE KENNETH, wind energy company executive; b. Rochester, N.Y., Dec. 18, 1941; s. Kenneth Arthur and Ruth Amer Van D. B.A. in Econs., Franklin and Marshall Coll., 1965; postgrad. U. Miami, 1965-66, N.Y.U., 1968-69. Asst. mktg. mgr., project mgr. Marine Acoustical Services, Inc., Miami, Fla., 1965; gen. mgr. Bertram Electronics, Inc., Miami, 1966; cons. exec. recruiting D.R. Fagin & Assos., mgmt. cons., Dallas, 1967; v.p. DLJ Alliance Corp., asso. Donaldson, Lufkin & Jenrette, Inc., N.Y.C., 1967-70; v.p. Rock Island Corp., San Francisco, 1970-75; founder, pres., dir. Cosmic Communications Inc., Los Angeles, 1972-77; founder, pres., dir. Windfarms, Ltd., San Francisco, 1978—; dir. Sigma Resources, Inc., N.Y.C., Smith & Hawken Tool Co., Palo Alto, Calif. Bd. dirs. Golden Gate Energy Center, San Francisco. Mem. Alliance for Am. Innovation (dir.). Author: How to Save Your Divorce, 1978. Home: 56 Sunshine Ave Sausalito CA 94965 Office: Windfarms Ltd 639 Front St San Francisco CA 94111

VANESS, MARGARET HELEN, artist, illustrator; b. Seattle; d. Paul Edward and Alma Magdalena Lauch; B.F.A., U. Wash., Seattle, 1970, 71, M.F.A., 1973; cert. bus. Drexel U., Phila., 1975; m. Gerard Vaness; children—Bette, Bruce, Barbara, Helen-Cathleen. Teaching asst. Sch. Art, U. Wash., 1971-73; illustrator DuPont Co., Wilmington, Del., 1973-74, Boeing Vertol Co., Phila., 1974-75; illustrator, program mgr. Boeing Co., Seattle, 1978-83; judge art shows, 1969—; executed mural for Dr. L. Mellon-Boeing Vertol Med. Center, 1974; commd. by USIA, 1973. Mem. Soc. Tech. Communication, Coll. Art Assn., U. Wash. Alumni Assn., U. Wash. Arboretum Found. (unit pres. 1981-83), Pratt Graphics Manhattan, Soc. Tech. Communication, Lambda Rho (past pres.). Address: 17128 2d St SW Seattle WA 98166

VAN ETTEN, DAVID HOYT, training consultant; b. Boston, Feb. 13, 1948; s. Royal Cornelius and Peggy June (Walbridge) V.; B.A., Amherst Coll., 1970; M.B.A., Boston U., 1979; m. Janet U'Ren, June 26, 1976; children—Matthew Hoyt, Andrew Cornelius, Todd Schryver. Pub. rep. Little, Brown & Co., San Francisco, 1972-75, nat. sales mgr., Boston, 1975-77; product mgr. Forum Corp., Boston, 1978-81, tng. cons., San Francisco, 1981—. Mem. Am. Soc. Tng. and Devel., Holland Soc. N.Y. Home: 3430 Blackhawk Rd Lafayette CA 94549 Office: 44 Montgomery St San Francisco CA 94104

VAN FLEET, WILLIAM MABRY, architect; b. Point Richmond, Calif., Jan. 22, 1915; s. Harvey Lorenz and Allie O'Dell (Taylor) Van F.; A.B., U. Calif., Berkeley, 1938; m. Colette Sims, Apr. 26, 1940; children—Christine, Ellen, Peter. Pvt. practice architecture, Eureka, Calif., 1951—; lectr. design Humboldt (Calif.) State U., 1965-66; ptnr. William & Colette Van Fleet, 1954—; prin. works include: Del Norte County Courthouse and Library, Crescent City, Calif., 1957, Freshwater (Calif.) Elementary Sch., 1954, Lee residence, Sunnybrae, Calif., 1962, Zane Jr. High Sch., Eureka, 1965, offices for Brooks-Scanlon Lumber Co., Bend, Oreg., 1967. Chmn., No. Humboldt Vocat. Council, 1964-65, Humboldt County Scenic Resources Com., 1965; pres. Humboldt-Del Norte Mental Health Soc., 1970-71; mem. Humboldt County Community Services Ctr. 1970, Humboldt Arts Council, 1970, Humboldt County Energy Adv. Com., 1979; chmn. Eureka Beautification Com., 1969, Humboldt Sr. Retirement Homes Com., 1979—; bd. dirs. Humboldt County Assn. Retarded Children, 1960-68, Humboldt Family Service Ctr., 1970, Redwoods United Workshop, 1973, Open Door Clinic, 1973, Coordinating Council Human Services Humboldt County, 1976, Calif.-Oreg. Community Devel. Soc., 1980—; mem. Humboldt Energy Adv. Com., 1980—, Eureka City Housing Adv. Bd., 1982. Recipient Merit award HHFA, 1964, 1st Honor award Pub. Housing Adminstrn., 1964, Gov. Calif. Design award, 1966, Outstanding Service award Far West Indian Hist. Soc., 1973, Man of Year award Redwood region Nat. Audubon Soc., 1976, resolutions of commendation Calif. State Senate and Assembly, 1982. Mem. AIA, Net Energy Assn. (dir.), Humboldt Native Plant Soc., Redwood Art Assn. (pres. 1970), Sierra Club (dir. 1972), Fifty-Plus Runners Assn. (1st place in age group Nat. Fifty-Plus Runners Meet 1981). Unitarian. Clubs: Kiwanis (pres. Eureka 1976-77; Disting. Service award 1968); Six Rivers Running (dirs.). Home: Route 1 Box 108 Eureka CA 95501 Office: 818 3d St Eureka CA 95501

VAN FOSSEN, GORDON WAGNER, petroleum engineer; b. Tulsa, July 31, 1929; s. Clarence M. and Helen G. (Wagner) Van F.; m. Patricia A. Gladson, Mar. 26, 1948; children—Susan Iacopini, Steven, Shevin Stewart. B.S. in Petroleum Engring., U. Tulsa, 1953. Sr. prodn. geologist Shell Oil Co., Okla., Tex., Wyo., Mont., 1953-64; v.p. exploration and prodn. Gt. North Drilling Co., Billings, Mont., 1965-67; cons. geologist, engr. Prenalta Co., Billings, 1967-70, v.p. prodn., Casper, Wyo., 1970-75; mgr. reservoir engring. and acquisitions CENEX, Billings, 1975—. Scoutmaster, bd. chmn. Boy Scouts Am., 1961-82. Recipient speakers awards Mont. Geol. Soc., 1966, 69, Wyo. Geol. Soc., 1970. Mem. AIME, Soc. Petroleum Engrs., Mont. Geol. Assn., Wyo. Geol. Assn. Methodist. Clubs: Billings Petroleum. Home: 3215 Parkhill Dr Billings MT 59102 Office: 1601 Lewis PO Box 21479 Billings MT 59104

VAN HALDEREN, LAUREL LYNN, dietitian, administrator; b. Milw., June 27, 1951; d. Verne Leroy and Elisabeth (Siegel) Johnson; m. Robert John Van Halderen, Aug. 7, 1971; 1 son, Nickolas James. A.A., Phoenix Jr. Coll., 1971; B.S. in Foods and Human Nutrition, U. Ariz., 1973, postgrad., 1977; postgrad. Fla. Internat. U., 75. Registered dietitian. Dietetic intern Houston VA Med. Center, 1973-74; clin. dietitian Miami (Fla.) VA Med. Center, 1974-76; ambulatory care dietitian Tucson VA Med. Center, 1976-78; clin. dietitian, research technician U. Ariz. Med. Center Hosp., Tucson, 1977-78; chief nutrition therapy, edn. and research Battle Creek (Mich.) Va Med. Center, 1978-79; chief program mgmt. and planning, 1979-81; chief dietetic service Am. Lake VA Med. Center, Tacoma, 1981—. Recipient

Medallion of Merit Ariz. State U. Alumni Assn., 1971. Mem. Am. Dietetic Assn., Wash. State Dietetic Assn. Lutheran. Office: Dietetic Service (120) Am Lake VA Med Center Tacoma WA 98493

VAN HOESEN, BETH MARIE, printmaker; b. Boise, Idaho, June 27, 1926; d. Enderse G. and Freda Marie (Soulen) Van H.; student Escuela Esmaralda, Mexico City, 1945, San Francisco Art Inst., 1946, 47, 51, 52. Fountainbleau (France) Ecole des Arts, Acad. Julian and Acad. Grande Chaumier, Paris, 1948-51; B.A., Stanford U., 1948; postgrad. San Francisco State U., 1957-58; m. Mark Adams, Sept. 12, 1953. One-woman shows include: De Young Mus., San Francisco, 1959, E.B. Crocker Art Gallery, Sacramento, 1966, Achenbach Found., Calif. Palace Legion of Honor, San Francisco, 1961, 74, Santa Barbara (Calif.) Mus., 1963, 74, 76, Hansen/Fuller/Goldeen Gallery, San Francisco, 1966, 77, 80, Oakland (Calif.) Mus., 1980, Stanford U., 1983; group shows include: Calif. State Fair, Sacramento (award), 1951, Library of Congress, Washington, 1956, 57, San Francisco Mus. Modern Art, 1956 (award), 59 (award), 61 (award), 70 (award), Boston Mus. Fine Arts, 1959, 60, 62, Pa. Acad. Fine Arts, Phila., 1959, 61, 63, 65, Achenbach Found., 1961 (award), Bklyn. Mus., 1962, 66, 68, 77, Continuing Am. Graphics, Osaka, Japan, 1970, Hawaii Nat. Print. Exhbn., Honolulu, 1971 (award), 1980 (award), Oakland Mus., 1975 (award); traveling exhibit Am. Mus. Assn., 1983—, represented in permanent collections, including: Achenbach Found., San Francisco, Bklyn. Mus., Mus. Modern Art, N.Y.C., Oakland Mus., Pasadena (Calif.) Mus., San Francisco Mus. Modern Art, Victoria and Albert Mus., London, Chgo. Art Inst., Cin. Mus., Portland (Oreg.) Art Mus. Recipient award of Honor, San Francisco Art Commn., 1981. Mem. Calif. Soc. Printmakers, San Francisco Women Artists. Book: Collection of Wonderful Things, 1972. Address: care John Berggruen 228 Grant 3d Floor San Francisco CA 94108

VAN HOLE, MILDRED MAE, manufacturer's representative; b. Littleton, Colo., Aug. 14, 1920; d. William and Ruth Belle (Pearman) DeKoevend; m. Joseph L. Van Hole, Dec. 13, 1941; children—Larry M., William R., Melanie An, Patricia L. Student Central Bus. Coll., 1938. Exec. sec. to pres. O.K. Rubber Co., 1939-45; exec. sec. The Thorson Co., Denver, 1960-80; pres. V-H Tech. Inc., Denver, 1981—. Bd. dirs. Englewood Sch., 1964-73, pres., 1971-73; mem. Southeast Met. Bd. Coop. Services, 1968-73; mem. Arapahoe County Sch. Planning commn., 1964-66; mem. Colo. State Bd. Community Colls. and Occupational Edn., 1983—. Named Bus. and Profl. Woman of Yr., Colo. Bus. and Profl. Women, 1973. Mem. Christian Ch. (Disciples of Christ). Office: V-H Tech Inc 2785 Speer Blvd Denver CO 80211

VAN HORNE, PETER ERIC, priest, school administrator; b. Caldwell, Idaho, Dec. 28, 1944; s. Robert Negley and Elizabeth Louise (Kaylor) V.; m. Beverly Jean Dew, June 12, 1970; children—Samuel Alexander, Michael James. B.A., U. Idaho, 1967; M.Div., Ch. Div. Sch. of Pacific, 1970; M.A. in History, Grad. Theol. Union, 1970. Assoc. rector All Saints Episcopal Ch., Boise, Idaho, 1970-71; priest-in-charge All Souls' Episc. Ch., Berkeley, Calif., 1972; Episc. chaplain Calif. State U.-Fresno, 1972-73; rector St. John's Episc. Ch., Kula, Hawaii, 1973-78; instr. Seabury Hall, Makawao, Hawaii, 1974-77; rector Epiphany Episc. Ch., Honolulu, 1978—; prin. Epiphany Sch., Honolulu, 1978—. Bd. dirs. Episc. Diocese of Hawaii, 1975-77, 81—, chmn. Commn. Ministry, 1978—; pres. Mental Health Assn. Maui, 1976-78; bd. dirs., treas. Mental Health Assn. Hawaii, 1978-81. Recipient cert. recognition Mental Health Assn. Hawaii 1981. Mem. Am. Soc. Ch. History, Nat. Assn. Elem. Sch. Prins., Assn. Supervision and Curriculum Devel., Hawaii Assn. Ind. Schs. Book reviewer. Office: Epiphany Episcopal Ch 1041 10th Ave Honolulu HI 96816

VAN HOUTEN, GENE STEVEN, industrial engineering company executive; b. Chgo., June 18, 1946; s. Eugene Kazimier and Ann Geraldine (Durica) V.; m. Ellen Marie Meister, June 15, 1974; children—Steven, Heather, Kristopher. A.A., Riverside (Calif.) City Coll., 1973; student Calif. Poly. U., 1979-81; B.S., U. Redlands, 1982, M.A. in Bus. Adminstrn/Mgmt., 1983. Spl. equipment design and assembley engr. Deutsch Co., Banning, Calif., 1967-74; mgr. indsl. engring. Sunkist Growers Inc., Ontario, Calif., 1974—. Recipient So. Calif. Edison Energy Mgmt. award, 1982; cert. of appreciation Productivity Council of S.W., 1982. Mem. Am. Concrete Inst., IEEE, Presdl. Energy Adv. Council, Am. Inst. Indsl. Engrs. (pres. Inland Empire chpt.), Nat. Council of Farmer Co-ops (rep.), Sunkist Growers Suprs. Club (pres.), Internat. Assn. Quality Circles, Assn. Standards and Research. Club: Kiwanis (Ontario, Calif.). Democrat. Home: 5042 Red Bluff Rd Riverside CA 92503 Office: 616 E Sunkist St Ontario CA 91761

VANKEPPEL, BAREND, aerospace engineer; b. Amsterdam, Netherlands, Nov. 10, 1951; s. Niek and Dien (Doornbos) V.; M.S. in Aerospace, U. Kans., 1978; M.S. in Aerospace, U. Delft, 1979. Engr., Cessna Aircraft Co., Wichita, Kans., 1979-80; specialist engr. Boeing Co., Seattle, 1980—. Recipient Best Preliminary Airplane Design award U. Delft, 1976; Pride in Excellence award Boeing Co., 1982. Mem. AIAA, Royal Dutch Guild Engrs. Club: Holland-America (Seattle). Home: 9710 NE 27th St Bellevue WA 98004 Office: Boeing Co Seattle WA 98204

VAN KIRK, RICHARD LEE, management consultant; b. Omaha, Sept. 23, 1936; s. Reo P. and Rose R. (Turco) Van K.; B.S. in Mech. Engring. (F.W. Hinrichs award), Calif. Inst. Tech., 1958; postgrad. Long Beach State Coll., 1960-62, Los Angeles State Coll., 1964-65; M.B.E.-cons., Claremont Grad. Sch., 1971; m. Janet Carol Labory, July 12, 1959; children—Richard Lee, Karen Evelyn, Douglas Harley. Indsl. engr., prodn. mgr. Procter & Gamble Mfg. Co., Long Beach, Calif., 1958-63; assoc. dir. devel. Calif. Inst. Tech., Pasadena, 1963-65; prodn. supt. Riverside (Calif.) Cement Co., 1965-67; cons. Arthur Young & Co., Los Angeles, 1967-76, dir. mgmt. services, Los Angeles office, 1976-78, dir. mgmt. services West Region, 1978—. Trustee Woodbury U., 1979—, chmn. bd. trustees, 1982—; mem. Los Angeles County Productivity Adv. Com., 1981—, vice chmn., 1982-83. Mem. Am. Inst. Indsl. Engrs., Inst. Mgmt. Consultants (cert.), Am. Mgmt. Assn., Calif. Soc. C.P.A.s (mgmt. adv. services com. 1979-81), Caltech Alumni Assn. (pres., 1977-78). Republican. Methodist. Club: Jonathan (Los Angeles). Contbr. articles to tech. jours. Office: 515 S Flower St Los Angeles CA 90071

VAN KREGTEN, ANTHONY GERARD LODEWYK WILLEM, JR., aerospace engineer, real estate broker; b. Middelburg, Netherlands, Dec. 7, 1906; s. Anthony Gerard Lodewyk Willem and Anna Hermanna (Rompelman) Van K.; came to U.S., 1953, naturalized, 1959; m. Lucille Plantenga, Sept. 26, 1935; children—Ronald, Fitzgerald. B.S., Holland Poly. U., Arnhem, 1930, M.S. in Aero. Engring., 1942. Mem. staff preliminary design Fokker Aircraft, Holland, 1931-45; asst. prof. aero. div. Delft (Holland) U., 1945-53; staff engr. Lockheed Aircraft Corp., Burbank, Calif., 1953-57, research specialist Lockheed Missile and Space Co., Sunnyvale, Calif., 1957-66; staff cons. engr., Lockheed Missile and Space Co. and Lockheed Ga. div., San Jose, Calif., 1966—; v.p. Pacific Tech. Inst., San Jose. Lic. aircraft pilot. Fellow AIAA (asso.); mem. ASTM, Am. Ordnance Assn., Aircraft Owners and Pilots Assn., Airmen's Assn. Santa Clara. Presbyn. Author: Directions Aircraft Design, 1953; Reliability Engineering Missile Systems, 1961; contbg. author Tech. Engring. Ency., 1948—; patentee antitank missile, 1965. Home: 258 Cronin Dr Santa Clara CA 95051 Office: 100 N Winchester Blvd Suite 380 San Jose CA 95128

VAN LEIRSBURG, DEAN ALLEN, chemist; b. Chicago Heights, Ill., May 24, 1940; s. Julius and Regina Van Leirsburg; B.A., St. Joseph's Coll., Rensselaer, Ind., 1962; M.S., Iowa State U., 1969; Ph.D., Oreg. State U., 1973. Chemist, Oreg. Grad. Center, 1974-79, Chevron Research Co., Richmond, Calif., 1979—. Soviet-Am. exchange fellow, 1974. Mem. Am. Chem. Soc., Sigma Xi. Roman Catholic. Home: 1047 Helen Ct Petaluma CA 94952 Office: Chevron Research Co Richmond CA 94804

VAN LOO, M. FRANCES, educator; b. Grand Rapids, Mich., June 27, 1942; d. Jacob R. and Mary Louise (Mosher) V. B.A. U. Mich. 1964; M.A. U. Calif.-Berkeley, 1967, Ph.D., 1971. Economist, Office Planning and Systems Analysis U.S. Post Office Dept., Washington 1966, Bur. Budget, Washington 1967; asst. prof. econs. U. Ill., Chgo. 1970-75; vis. asst. prof. Sch. Bus. Adminstrn. U. Calif.-Berkeley 1975-76, lectr. 1976-79, asst. prof. 1979—. Mem. Am. Econs. Assn., Population Assn. Am., Assn. Pub. Policy Analysis and Mgmt. Contbr. articles to profl. jours. Office: School Bus Adminstrn University of California Berkeley CA 94720

VAN MICHAELS, CHRISTOPHER, research engr.; b. Bulgaria, Feb. 14, 1924; came to U.S., 1967, naturalized, 1972; s. Miho and Dragana (Ivanova-Dragneva) Van M.; student theoretical and nuclear physics U. Paris, 1962-66; diploma in physics, geophysics, chemistry U. Sofia (Bulgaria), 1949; M.Sci. Research, Acad. of Scis., Sohia, 1955; m. Anna Atanasova Vakarelyisky, Apr. 24, 1955; children—Diana Michaels, Julien Michaels. Research engr., physicist and geochemist Sci. Research Inst. Bulgaria Acad. of Scis., Sofia, 1949-60; research engr. ESCOA Corp., Phoenix, 1967-73; pres. Montex Corp., Los Angeles, 1964—; cons. in indsl. chemistry, geophysics. Recipient Magnavox award in semi conductors, 1974. Mem. Internat. Physics Assn. Patentee in field; contbr. articles to profl. jours. Office: 1817 1/2 N Las Palmas Ave Los Angeles CA 90028

VAN MOLS, BRIAN, publisher; b. Los Angeles, July 1, 1931; s. Pierre Matthias and Frieda Carthyl (MacArthur) M.; m. Barbara Jane Rose, Oct. 1, 1953 (dec.); children—Cynthia, Matthew, Brian; m. 2d, Nancy Joan Martell, June 11, 1977. A.B. in English, Miami U., Oxford, Ohio, 1953. Media supr. McCann-Erickson Inc., 1955-58; salesman Kelly Smith Co., 1959; with sales Million Market Newspapers Inc., 1959-63; sales mgr. Autoproducts Mag., 1964; sr. salesman True Mag., 1965-68, Look Mag., 1969-70; regional advt. dir. Petersen Pub. Co., Los Angeles, 1971-74, pub. Motor Trend, 1982—; assoc. pub., advt. dir. Cycle World CBS, Inc., Newport Beach, Calif., 1974-80, pub., 1981. Served with U.S. Army, 1953-55. Mem. Los Angeles Advt. Club, Adcraft Club Detroit, Am. Motorcycle Assn. Republican. Episcopalian. Home: 5 Odyssey St Newport Beach CA 92663 Office: Motor Trend Mag 8490 Sunset Blvd Los Angeles CA 90069

VANN, BARRY LEONARD, economist; b. San Francisco, Oct. 10, 1950; s. Homer Raymond and Marcella (Haber) V. A.B., U. Calif.-Berkeley, 1972; M.A., U. Mich., 1975, Ph.D., 1979. Staff economist Com. on the Judiciary, U.S. Ho. of Reps., 1975-78; analyst U.S. Dept. of Energy, 1978-79; economist Standard Oil Co. of Calif., 1979—, analyst Work Process Improvement Program, subs. Chevron U.S.A. Inc. San Francisco. Mem. Am. Econs. Assn. Republican. Jewish.

VAN PELT, W(ESLEY) AUSTIN, clergyman, educator; b. Rahway, N.J., Aug. 24, 1930; s. Charles Wesley and Grace Elizabeth (DeHart) Van P.; B.A., Maryville Coll., 1952; M.Div., Louisville Presbyn. Sem., 1955; M.A., U. Denver, 1964, Ph.D., 1970; m. Elenor Kramer, June 11, 1952; children—Mary, Anne, Peter, David. Ordained to ministry United Presbyn. Ch., mem. faculty Maryville (Tenn.) Coll., 1954-57, Sheldon Jackson Jr. Coll., Sitka, Alaska, 1957-59; gen. mgr. Sta. KSEW, 1959-61; pastor, New Castle, Pa., 1961-63; asst. prof. sociology Peru State Coll., 1964-68; dean Arapahoe Community Coll., Littleton, Colo., 1969-75, instr. sociology, 1976—; interim pastor chs., Colo.; adj. prof. U. Denver, 1976, McCormick Theol. Sem., Chgo., 1979-81. Mem. NEA, Colo. Edn. Assn., Am. Fedn. Tchrs., Colo. Fedn. Tchrs. Office: 5900 S Santa Fe Dr Littleton CO 80120

VAN POPPELEN, F. JOSEPH, electronics manufacturing co. executive; b. Detroit, July 30, 1927; s. Francis J. and Josephine (Hannon) Van P.; m. Marianne Suzanne Sullivan, Sept. 2, 1958; children—Linda, Lauren, David, Eric, Gretchen. B.S., Cornell U., 1949. Vice pres., gen. mgr. Signetics Corp., Sunnyvale, Calif., 1962-65; pres. ITT Semiconductors, West Palm Beach, Fla., 1965-68; v.p., gen. mgr. Fairchild Semiconductor, Mountain View, Calif., 1968-73; pres. Van Poppelen Assocs., Menlo Park, Calif., 1973-75; v.p. semiconductor mktg. Nat. Semiconductor Corp., Santa Clara, Calif., 1975—. Mem. IEEE. Republican. Roman Catholic. Clubs: Sharon Heights Golf (Menlo Park). Home: 46 Flood Circle Atherton CA 94025 Office: 2900 Semiconductor Dr M/S D3689 Santa Clara CA 95051

VAN REMMEN, ROGER, advertising executive; b. Los Angeles, Sept. 30, 1950; s. Thomas J. and Elizabeth (Vincent) V.; m. Mary Anne Montague, Sept. 11, 1976. B.S. in Bus., U. So. Calif., 1972. Account mgr. BBDO, Los Angeles, 1972-78; account mgr. Dailey & Assocs. Advt., Los Angeles, 1978—, v.p. account supr., 1980—; dir. Aux. Aids Inc., Energy Savers Inc. Mem. Univ. So. Calif. Alumni Assn., Advt. Club of Los Angeles. Roman Catholic. Home: 441 2d St Manhattan Beach CA 90266 Office: Dailey & Assocs 3055 Wilshire Blvd 2nd floor Los Angeles CA 90010

VAN SCHAIK, PETER HENDRIK, agronomist, agricultural research administrator; b. Arnhem, Netherlands, Apr. 18, 1927; s. Steven Theodore and Wilhelmina (van Berckel) van S.; m. Barbara Anne van Schaik, June 28, 1954; children—Carolyn, Barbara, Claire, Susanne, Peter. B.S.A., Ont. Agrl. Coll., Guelph, Can., 1952; M.S.A. in Plant Breeding and Genetics, U. Toronto, Can., 1954; Ph.D. in Plant Breeding and Genetics, Purdue U., Lafayette, Ind., 1957. With U.S. Dept. Agr., 1957—, research agronomist, Holland, Va., 1970-72, assoc. CA-HI area dir., Fresno, Calif., 1972-80, CA-HI area dir., Fresno, 1982—; cons. in field. Mem. AAAS, Am. Soc. Agronomy, Crop Sci. Soc. Am., Council for Agrl. Sci. and Tech., Orgn. Profl. Employees of Dept. Agr. Club: Optimist Internat. (life). Office: 2021 S Peach Ave PO Box 8143 Fresno CA 93747

VAN SCHILFGAARDE, JAN, agricultural engineer; b. The Hauge, Netherlands, Feb. 7, 1929; came to U.S., 1946, naturalized, 1957; s. Paul and Johanna Hendrika (Mijs) Van S.; m. Roberta Jean Hansen, Sept. 22, 1951; children—Paul, Mark, Craig. B.S., Iowa State U., 1949, M.S., 1950, Ph.D., 1954. Registered profl. engr., Iowa. Asst. prof. agrl. engring. N.C. State U., 1954-57, assoc. prof., 1957-62, prof., 1962-64; chief water mgmt. engr., soil and water conservation research div. Agrl. Research Service, Dept. Agr., Beltsville, Md., 1964-67, assoc. dir. div., 1967-71, dir. div., 1971-72, dir. U.S. Salinity Lab., Riverside, Calif., 1972—. Named to Drainage Hall of Fame, Ohio State U., 1980. Fellow Am. Soc. Agronomy; mem. Am. Soc. Agrl. Engrs. (John Deere Gold medal 1977), ASCE (Walter C. Huber Civil Engring. Research prize 1970), Soil Conservation Soc. Am. Contbr. numerous articles to profl. publs.; editor: Drainage for Agriculture, 1974. Office: 4500 Glenwood Dr Riverside CA 92501

VAN TASSEL, LOWELL THOMAS, mathematician, educator; b. Mpls., Jan. 31, 1932; s. Evan Thomas and Sophia Anna (Huebner) Van T.; B.S., U. Minn., 1952, M.A., 1962; m. Diane Laura Diedrich, June 14, 1953; children—Thomas Alan, Laurie Jean, Karin Lee. Teaching asst. in math. U. Minn., Mpls., 1951-52, research asst. Bur. Edn. Research, 1955-56; tchr. math. sr. high sch., San Diego, 1956-65; mem. staff dept. math. San Diego City Coll., 1965—, chmn. dept., 1971-72, 74-75; instr. USN Sci. Program, 1962-66; cons. engring. cos.; proctor profl. engring. exams., Calif. Served to 1st lt. USMC, 1952-54. Manuscript referee Math. Tchr., 1971—; editor Exponent, Greater San Diego Math. Council, 1960-61; author, contbr., cons. various math. publs. Home: 5550 Lodi St San Diego CA 92117 Office: 1313 12th Ave San Diego CA 92101

VAN VALER, BETTY CAROLYN, Realtor; b. Delhi, Calif., May 22, 1936; d. Harold Arthur and Joie Madeline (Harp) Sibell; student West Contra Costa Jr. Coll., 1954-55; m. Richard C. Van Valer, Dec. 1, 1962; children—Jeffrey David, Julia Catherine, John Buchanan. Escrow officer N.Am. Title Guaranty Corp., Richmond, Calif., 1954-58; loan officer/escrow officer Joe B. Powell, realtor, Richmond, Calif., 1958; Jones Mortgage Co., Oakland, Calif., 1959; office mgr./escrow officer Surety Title & Guaranty Co., San Jose, Calif., 1959-63; pres., dir. Redwood Escrow Co., San Jose, 1969—; dir. Van Vleck Real Estate, San Jose, 1966-79, pres., 1979—; owner VV Thrusts, Real Estate Mktg. Service; designer, home builder; adv. bd. Pacific Valley Bank, 1979—. Mem. Calif. Real Estate Polit. Action Com., 1973—; regent Bellarmine Coll. Prep., San Jose, 1980—; trustee Med. Found. of Santa Clara County (Calif.), 1980—; San Francisco met. chmn. Relo Inter-City Recreation Service, 1979—. Mem. San Jose, Los Gatos-Saratoga-San Benito, Sunnyvale bds. Realtors, Nat., Calif. assns. Realtors, Internat. Real Estate Fedn. Home: 19753 Farwell Ave Saratoga CA 95070 Office: 4950 Hamilton Ave San Jose CA 95130

VAN VALIN, CHARLES CARROLL, research chemist; b. Wakefield, Nebr., Aug. 10, 1929; s. Carroll D. and May E. (Brodersen) Van V.; B.A., Nebr. State Tchrs. Coll., Wayne, 1951; M.S., U. Colo., Boulder, 1958; m. Ann E. Tichy, June 3, 1954. Chemist, Shell Chem. Co., Denver, 1957-58; research chemist Great Western Sugar Co., Denver, 1958-60, Bur. Sport Fisheries and Wildlife, Dept. of Interior, Denver, 1961-66, Air Resources Labs., NOAA, Dept. of Commerce, Boulder, 1966—; abstractor Chem. Abstracts Service of Am. Chem. Soc., 1962-64. Served with AUS, 1951-53. Mem. Am. Chem. Soc., AAAS, Am. Geophys. Union, Sigma Xi. Research and publs. on chem. and phys. processes of precipitation formation, inadvertent weather modification, air pollution research, atmos. chemistry, pesticide chemistry. Home: 925 Gilbert St Boulder CO 80302 Office: 325 Broadway Boulder CO 80303

VAN VELDHUIZEN, PHILIP A(NDROCLES), mathematics and statistics educator; b. Hospers, Iowa, Nov. 6, 1930; s. Andrew and Elizabeth (Oordt) VanV.; m. Ruth Jooly; (div.); children—Robert M., Jay A., Varina Veronica. B.S., Central Coll., Pella, Iowa, 1952; M.S., U. Iowa, 1960; postgrad. Iowa State U., 1965-66. Instr., Central Coll., 1956-60; asst. prof. Calif. State U., Sacramento, 1960-63; prof. math. U. Alaska, Fairbanks, 1963—, chmn. statis. program, 1981—; cons. Alaska Dept. Edn. Mem. Sch. Bd. Fairbanks, 1978-81; bd. dirs. Alaska State Fair, 1978-82. Served with AUS, 1954-56. Recipient Gov.'s Outstanding Vol. Service to Alaska award, 1978. Mem. Am. Statis. Assn., Math. Assn. Am., Nat. Council Tchrs. Math. Presbyterian. Club: Kiwanis. Office: Dept Math U Alaska Fairbanks AK 99701

VAN VELZER, VERNA JEAN, librarian; b. State College, Pa., Jan. 22, 1929; d. Harry Leland and Golda Lillian (Cline) Van V.; B.S. in L.S., U. Ill., 1950; M.L.S., Syracuse U., 1957. Head librarian Gen. Electric Microwave Lab., Palo Alto, Calif., 1958-64, Research and Devel. Lab., Fairchild Semicondr. Products Co., Palo Alto, 1964-65; intelligence librarian Sylvania Electronic Products Co., Mountain View, Calif., 1965-66; research librarian ESL Inc., Sunnyvale, Calif., 1966—. Mem. Spl. Libraries Assn., Assn. for Computing Machinery, IEEE, Am. Def. Preparedness Assn.,AIAA, Assn. of Old Crows, Beta Phi Mu. Home: 4048 Laguna Way Palo Alto CA 94306 Office: ESL Inc 495 Java Dr Sunnyvale CA 94088

VAN VOORHIS, THOMAS, lawyer; b. Great Falls, Mont., Feb. 24, 1930; s. George E. and Ruthe (Williams) V.; A.A., U. Calif. at Berkeley, 1955, LL.B., J.D., Hastings Coll. Law, 1959, m. Eleanor Cooper, Mar. 21, 1958; children—Kevin, Karen, Thomas. Admitted to Calif. bar, 1960; pres. Campbell & Van Voorhis, Walnut Creek, Calif., 1960-82, of counsel Van Voorhis & Skaggs, 1982—; judge pro tem Walnut Creek-Danville Municipal Ct., 1974-82; pres. Domino II Cattle Co., Walnut Creek, 1971—; v.p. Blackhawk Devel. Co., Danville, Calif., 1972-75; v.p., dir. RWC Calif. Co., Danville, 1975—, RWC Nev. Co., Reno; sec., dir. Woodhill Devel. Co., Danville, 1976—. Pres. Republican Assembly, Walnut Creek, 1964. Bd. dirs. Walnut Creek (Cal.) Action for Beauty Council. Served with USAF, 1950-54. Decorated oakleaf clusters (3). Mem. State Bar Calif., ABA (com. on devel. and mgmt. real estate 1975—), Mt. Diablo Bar Assn., Internat. Assn. Fin. Planning, Contra Costa Bar, Lawyers Pilots Bar Assn., Assoc. Home Builders. Club: Lions. Home: 31 Julianne Ct Walnut Creek CA 94595 Office: 1855 Olympic Blvd Walnut Creek CA 94596

VAN VOROUS, TED, mfg. exec.; b. Billings, Mont., Jan. 6, 1929; s. Benjamin and Gladys (Yeager) Van V.; B.S. in Chemistry, Mont. State Coll., 1953, M.S. in Chemistry, 1954; m. Mary Pauline Tuttle, June 18, 1951; children—David, James, Paul, Peter, Lisa. Analytical chemist Dow Chem. Co., Midland, Mich., 1953-55, analytical chemist to research group mgr., Rocky Flats, Colo., 1955-69; pres., founder VTA, Inc., Boulder, Colo., 1969-75; pres., chmn. bd., founder Vac-Tec Systems, Boulder, 1976-81; founder, pres. Van Vorous Cons., Inc. and Vacuum, Inc., Boulder, 1981—. Served with USAAF, 1946-49. Mem. Am. Vacuum Soc., Am. Metall. Soc., Kappa Sigma. Episcopalian. Home: 992 Sycamore St Boulder CO 80303 Office: 5547 Central Ave Boulder CO 80301

VAN VORST, ROBERT BROBERG, psychologist, state ofcl.; b. Whitesalmon, Wash., June 15, 1913; s. Melvin J. and Martha Theodora (Broberg) Van V.; B.A., U. Ariz., 1935; M.A., Stanford U., 1938; postgrad. UCLA, 1947-48; m. Lucy Prescott Hale, May 28, 1936; children—Elizabeth (Mrs. Peter R. Phillips), Robert Broberg. Instr., clin. psychologist Ariz. State Indsl. Sch., Ft. Grant, 1935-36; asst. probation officer, psychologist Pima County Probation Office, Tucson, 1936-37; intern Calif. Bur. Juvenile Research, Stanford, 1938-39; jr. clin. psychologist Fred C. Nelles Sch., Whittier, Calif., 1939-41, sr. clin. psychologist, 1947-54; sr. clin. psychologist Preston Sch. Industry, Ione, Calif., 1941-46, Calif. Vocat. Instn., 1946-47, Calif. Instn. for Women, Frontera, 1954-69, Youth Tng. Sch., Ontario, Calif., summer 1960; psychol. cons. San Francisco State Coll., summers 1949-52; instr. UCLA Extension, spring 1953; vis. lectr. child psychology Whittier (Calif.) Coll., 1955; part time pvt. practice, Claremont, Calif., 1963-68, sr. supervising psychologist So. reception center Calif. Youth Authority, 1969-73, sr. cons. psychologist, 1973-78; cons. psychologist Episc. Community Service, San Diego. mem. faculty Golden West Coll., 1968-72; clin. assoc. U. So. Calif., Los Angeles, 1972; cons. San Diego County Probation. Pres., Amador County Mental Hygiene Soc., 1943-44; chmn. Profls. United for Meditation and Action, 1975. Chmn. bd. dirs. Whittier Mental Health Assn., 1957-58; bd. dirs. Los Tules Mut. Water Assn., 1962-68, pres., 1974-76, v.p., 1976-82, pres., 1982-83; mem. San Diego County-Warner Springs Planning Group, 1983. Diplomate Am. Bd. Profl. Psychology. Mem. Am., Western, Calif., San Diego County psychol. assns., Am. Assn. Correctional Psychologists (sec. 1957-58), Assn. Clin. Psychologists in Calif. Civil Services (pres.

1953-54), Calif. State Employees Assn. (pres. chpt. 30, 1953), So. Calif. Group Psychotherapy Assn., Sigma Xi, Psi Chi, Delta Sigma Lambda, Phi Delta Kappa. Republican. Episcopalian. Clubs: Warner Springs Lions (pres. 1975-76), Warner Springs Mens, Whittier U. (charter), Episc. Churchmen's. Contbr. articles to profl. jours. Home: Los Tules Rancho Camino Moro PO Box 415 Warner Springs CA 92086 Office: Episc Community Service San Diego CA 92103 also San Diego County Adult Honor Camp Westfork Warner Springs CA 92086

VAQUER, ARMAND MERLE, ins. co. exec.; b. Los Angeles, Feb. 4, 1954; s. Armand Manual and Mary Kathryn (Charleston) V.; B.A. in Polit. Sci., Calif. State U., Long Beach, 1979. Sales rep. Dialamerica Mktg. Co., Torrance, Calif., 1978-79; claims service rep. United Pacific/Reliance Ins. Co., Los Angeles, 1979—. First v.p. Los Angeles County Young Republicans, 1976-77; chmn. 53d Assembly Dist. Rep. Central Com., 1979—. Mem. Calif. Rep. Assembly, Young Americans for Freedom, Delta Phi Sigma. Home: 4923 W 129th St Hawthorne CA 90250

VARE, GEORGE AUGUSTUS, JR., winery executive; b. Phila., Dec. 29, 1936; s. George A. and Lucille Francis (Townsend) V.; children—Catherine C., Andrew T., Michael K. A.B., Williams Coll., 1958; M.B.A., Harvard U., 1966. Asst. controller Jos. Schlitz Brewing Co., Milw., 1968-72; chmn., pres. Geyser Peak Winery, Geyserville, Calif., 1972-79; owner George Vare & Assos., San Francisco, 1979—; owner Winedata, San Francisco, 1979—; owner Shadow Creek Champagne Cellars, Graton, Calif., 1980—. Exec. dir. Am. Vineyard Found. Served to lt. USCGR, 1958-59. Clubs: Harvard Bus. Sch. Club of No. Calif., San Francisco Yacht. Author: Partners for Profits, 1966. Home: 33 Vandewater St #103 San Francisco CA 94133 Office: 331B World Trade Center San Francisco CA 94133

VARGAS, ARMANDO, JR., university official; b. El Paso, Tex., Feb. 27, 1954; s. José Armando Rodriguez and Romelia (Matamoros) V. B.A. in Elem. Edn., U. Ariz., 1976, postgrad. 1977—. Clk. U. Ariz. Student Union, Tucson, 1976-77, program aide, 1977-79, adminstrv. asst., 1980-82, supr., mgr. recreational services, 1983—, also mem. activities bd. Bd. dirs., com. mem. Una Noche Plateada, 1977—, Open-Inn Inc., 1977-80; Active Friends of Tucson Pub. Library, 1982—. Mem. Assn. Coll. Unions Internat., Am. Personnel and Guidance Assn., Am. Coll. Personnel Assn., Smithsonian Assocs. Democrat. Home: 4232 E Fairmount Ave Apt 6 Tucson AZ 85712 Office: U Ariz Student Union SUPO 10,000 Tucson AZ 85720

VARGAS, RICHARD MARTIN, mfg. co. ofcl.; b. Albuquerque, Dec. 13, 1946; s. David H. and Mary Dolores (Baca) V.; B.A. (univ. grantee 1973, HUD grantee 1974-75), U. Albuquerque, 1975; postgrad. U. N.Mex., 1975; M.B.A., Highlands U., 1980, postgrad., 1980—; m. Dorothy J. Lowe, Feb. 15, 1969; children—Anjeanette, Joseph, Brian, Elizabeth. With Antonios, Albuquerque, 1965-70; owner, mgr. Three Fountains, Inc., Albuquerque, 1970-72; adminstrv. officer Bernalillo County Govt., Albuquerque, 1972-78; mgr. adminstrv. group Falcon Research and Devel. Co., Albuquerque, 1978-81; mgr. procurement and materials Eberline Corp., Albuquerque, 1981—; fin. cons. Active ARC, 1964-66, Kidney Found., 1968-72, St. Anthony's Orphange, 1968-70, Boys Ranch, 1969-71, Albuquerque Civic Light Opera, 1970-73, Albuquerque Little Theatre, 1971-73; mem. Mil. Acad. Selection Bd. Served with USN, 1963-64, Recipient Cert. of Award, Middle Rio Grande Council of Govts., 1975; Achievement award, Bernalillo County Commrs., 1975. Mem. Cosmetology Assn. (pres. 1969-71), Albuquerque Greater C. of C., Community Devel. Assn., Nat. Assn. Purchasing Mgrs., N.Mex. Minority Purchasing Council. Democrat. Clubs: Optimist, Lions. Home: 2825 Cuervo St NE Albuquerque NM 87110 Office: 3807 Academy Pkwy S NE Albuquerque NM 87109

VARLEY, ARTHUR JOSEPH, JR., condominium and resort development conversion co. exec.; b. Jacksonville, Fla., June 21, 1949; s. Arthur Joseph and Ula Mary (Maville) V. B.S. with honors, San Diego State U., 1971; M.D., U. Fla., 1975. Intern, U. Calif., San Diego, 1975-76; resident in orthopedic surgery U. So. Calif., Orthopedic Hosp., 1976-80; founder, pres. Varley Enterprises, San Diego, 1977—; prin. Kopple-Varley Properties, Los Angeles, 1979—, also dir.; pres. Grass Mountain Ski Parks of Am., Inc., Los Angeles, 1980—; v.p. Alutra Enterprises, Inc., San Diego, 1975—; dir. Southland Orthopedic Med. Assocs., San Diego, 1982—; med. advisor Nat. Ski Patrol, Far West Region, 1980-81. Mem. AMA, San Diego County Med. Soc. Roman Catholic. Office: PO Box 2319 Vista CA 92083

VARNER, WILLARD CHARLES, sales exec.; b. Columbus, Ohio, Nov. 4, 1940; s. Wilbur Willard and Helen Mae (Green) V.; m. Sandra Kay Winjum, July 3, 1969; children—Cathryn Ann, Lance Douglas, Jason Winjum; B.A. in Econs., Otterbein Coll., 1966; M.B.A., Pepperdine U., 1968; M.A. in Econs., Calif. State U.-Long Beach, 1973; M.S. in Fin., U. So. Calif., 1979. Market research analyst, Rockwell Internat., Los Angeles, 1967-69; sr. market research analyst, Douglas Aircraft Co., 1969-73; aviation systems cons., Daniel, Mann, Johnson & Mendenhall, Los Angeles, 1973-76; airline planning specialist Lockheed Aircraft Co., Burbank, 1977-79; sales mgr. Douglas Aircraft Co., 1979—. Mem. ASCE (past chmn. air transport group Los Angeles sect.), AIAA. Republican. Home: Office: Douglas Aircraft 3855 Lakewood Blvd Long Beach CA 90846

VARNI, JAMES WALTER, psychologist, hospital administrator, educator; b. San Francisco, Dec. 22, 1948; s. James Walter and Theresa Catherine (Leveroni) V. A.A. in Zoology, Coll. San Mateo, 1969; B.A. in Psychology with high honors, U. Calif.-Santa Barbara, 1972; M.A. in Psychology, UCLA, 1974, Ph.D. in Psychology (Chancellor's Patent Fund dissertation grantee), 1976. Research asst. dept. psychology and Inst. for Applied Behavioral Sci., U. Calif.-Santa Barbara, 1971-72; research asst. Camarillo State Hosp. Neuropsychiat. Inst. research program UCLA Sch. Medicine, 1972-73, research asst. dept. psychiatry Sex Dysfunction Clinic, 1974, research asst. dept. psychology, 1973-74, research assoc., 1974-75, teaching assoc., 1975-76; predoctoral trainee Center for Behavior Therapy, Beverly Hills, Calif., 1975; mem. staff dept. psychiatry and behavioral scis. Sch. Medicine and instr. Evening Coll., Johns Hopkins U., 1976-78, dir. tng. Div. Behavioral Psychology, John F. Kennedy Inst., 1977, mem. staff Pediatric Pain Clinic, 1977-78, instr. div. med. psychology, 1977-78, dir. Behavior Therapy Clinic, Behavioral Medicine Center, 1977-78; sr. psychologist psychosocial program div. hematology-oncology, Children's Hosp. Los Angeles, 1978-81; mem. staff Hemophilia Rehab. Center, Orthopaedic Hosp., Los Angeles, 1978—, co-dir. behavioral pediatrics program, 1980—; asst. clin. prof. pediatrics U. So. Calif., 1978-81, clin. assoc. prof. pediatrics, psychology, psychiatry and behavioral scis., 1982—; mem. pain adv. bd. Sickle Cell Disease br. Nat. Heart, Lung, and Blood Inst., NIH, Bethesda, Md., 1982. Mem. Soc. Behavioral Medicine, (chmn. nominations com. bd. dirs. 1980-83), Assn. Advancement Behavior Therapy, Am. Psychol. Assn. Soc. Pediatric Psychology. Author: Clinical Behavioral Pediatrics. An Interdisciplinary Biobehavioral Approach, 1983; contbr. chpts., articles to profl. publs.; editor (with D. C. Russo), contbg. author: Behavioral Pediatrics: Research and Practice, 1982; bd. editors, editor hematology-oncology area Behavioral Medicine Abstracts, 1980-81; bd. editors, editor arthritis and rheumatism area, 1981—; bd. editors, cons. editor: Jour. Pediatric Psychology, 1982—; guest reviewer for profl. jours. Office: Orthopaedic Hosp 2400 S Flower St Los Angeles CA 90007

VARON, ISAAC HARRY, optometrist; b. Seattle, Dec. 2, 1951; s. Harry Isaac and Rachel (Israel) V.; m. Lucille Joyce Benvenists, Aug. 14, 1951; children—Hezkiah, Hayyim. Student U. Wash., 1974; D.O. cum laude, So. Calif. Coll. Optometry, 1978. Optometrist, Optometrist Ctr., Seattle, 1978-79; pvt. practice optometry, Seattle, 1979—; cons. nursing homes, Lions Low Vision Clinic; staff optometrist Caroline Kline Galland Home, Seattle. Mem. Wash. Optometric Assn., Am. Optometric Assn. Jewish. Club: Toastmasters Internat. (Tukwila, Wash.). Office: 411 Strawder Blvd Suite 303 Tukwila WA 98188

VARON, MICHAEL NATHAN, spacecraft thermal control engineer; b. Bklyn., July 27, 1950; s. Jack and Ann (Cassuto) V.; m. Jane Renee Felland, June 21, 1981. B.E. in Mech. Engring., CCNY, 1973; M.S. in Mech. Engring., U. So. Calif., 1978. Staff engr. dept. thermophysics Space and Communications group, Hughes Aircraft Co., El Segundo, Calif., 1973—. Second v.p. Bodger Park Community Assn., 1982—. Mem. ASME (assoc.), AIAA. Democrat. Contbr. articles to profl. jours. Home: 15011 Kornblum Ave Hawthorne CA 90250 Office: 1950 E Imperial Hwy El Segundo CA 90245

VARZALY, LAIRD ALAN, trade co. exec.; b. Pitts., Jan. 31, 1947; s. George and Mildred (Tishko) V.; B.S. in Elec. Engring., U. Pitts., 1968; M.S. in Nuclear Engring., Purdue U., 1970; M.B.A., U. Santa Clara, 1975; m. Afsaneh Mavaddat, July 5, 1974; 1 dau., Jenifer Arezu. Project engr. Gen. Electric Nuclear Div., San Jose, 1972-76; pres. Ataollah Mavaddat Co., 1976—. Served to lt. USAF, 1970-72. Mem. San Jose C. of C. Club: Santa Clara Valley World Trade. Home: 706 Albanese Circle San Jose CA 95111 Office: 111 W Saint John St #724 San Jose CA 95113

VASELS, NICHOLAS CHARLES, lawyer; b. Evanston, Ill., Dec. 25, 1950; s. Homer Robert and Eugenia Artemis (Bookidis) V.; m. Dana Christine Ryan, Aug. 21, 1982. B.A., U. Calif.-Riverside, 1973; J.D., Loyola U., 1978. Bar: Calif. 1979. Ptnr. Vasels & Haguewood, Costa Mesa, Calif., 1981—; former pres., chmn. bd. Brian Head Corp. (Utah); ptnr. Worldview Internat. Democrat. Home: 1971 Cypress Point Dr Corona CA 91720 Office: 695 Town Center Dr Suite 1000 Costa Mesa CA 92626

VASH, CAROLYN LEE (MRS. R.P. VASH), psychologist; b. Oil City, Pa., Oct. 11, 1934; d. Roberto Carlos Conine and Sibyl Elizabeth (Baum) C.; m. Richard Paul Vash, Nov. 9, 1969. M.A. in Psychology, UCLA, 1961, Ph.D., 1964; lic. psychologist, Calif., 19. Clin. psychologist Rancho Los Amigos Hosp., Downey, Calif., 1963-67, chief vocat. services, 1967-73; chief dep. dir. Calif. Dept. Rehab., Sacramento, 1973-77; v.p. Inst. for Info. Studies, Falls Church Va. and Altadena Calif., 1978—. Active Los Angeles County Commn. on Disabilities. Mem. Am. Psychol. Assn. Unitarian. Author: The Burnt Out Administrator, 1979; The Psychology of Disability, 1981. Office: 35 E Las Flores Dr Altadena CA 91001

VASQUEZ, EDMUNDO EUSEBIO, ins. cons. and agt.; b. Chacon, N.Mex., May 14, 1932; s. Eusebio and Dora (Ortiz) V.; B.A., N.Mex. Highlands U., 1953; postgrad. U. Colo., 1958, Brigham Young U., 1959; M.A., Stanford U., 1961; postgrad. U. Costa Rica, 1966; m. Carol Vallendar, June 16, 1957; children—Amarante, Daniel, Amalio. With Sta. KFUN, 1949-53; dean Wasatch Acad., Mt. Pleasant, Utah, 1955-65; dean Colegio Americano, Ibagué, Colombia, 1966-71; pres. Menaul Sch., (Albuquerque, 1971-78; agt. Nat. Life of Vt. and Northwestern Mut. Life, Albuquerque, 1978—, cons. in field; lectr., cons. Hispanic affairs; cons. multicultural edn. Bd. dirs. United Presbyn. Health, Edn. and Welfare Assn., 1975-78, March of Dimes, 1976-79, ARC, 1979—; trustee San Francisco Theol. Sem., San Anselmo, Calif., 1982—; dir. So. Calif. Found., 1981—; rep. United Presbyn. Found., 1981—. fundraiser charitable and polit. orgns. Served with USAF, 1953-55. Mem. Assn. Supervision and Curriculum Devel., Nat. Assn. Life Underwriters. Clubs: Rotary, Lions, Masons. Office: 1501 Wilshire Blvd Los Angeles CA 90017

VAUDRIN, DONNA MARIE, university administrator, consultant; b. Akron, Ohio, July 26, 1946; d. Lyman Jerome and Helen Mary (Bruno) V. B.S. in Psychology, Murray State U., 1968; M.A. in Counseling Psychology, Ohio State U., 1970; postgrad. Seattle U., 1977—. Asst. dir. student devel., instr. SW Minn. State U., Marshall, 1970-72, assoc. dir., 1972-73, counselor admissions and spl. programs, 1973-74; dean women Seattle U., 1974-77, dean students, 1977—; pvt. practice human resources devel. cons. and tng., Seattle, 1975—. Bd. dirs. Univ. YWCA, Seattle, 1974-76; mem. Title I Career Mobility Project team, U. Wash., 1975-76. Mem. Am. Soc. Tng. and Devel., Am. Coll. Personnel Assn., Am. Personnel and Guidance Assn., Nat. Assn. Women Deans, Adminstrs., and Counselors. Contbr. articles to profl. jours.; author material on conflict mgmt., assertiveness tng., supervisory skills, communication skills. Home: 14217 12th Ave SW Seattle WA 98166 Office: Dean for Students Seattle U Seattle WA 98166

VAUGHAN, ARTHUR HARRIS, JR., astronomer, engring physicist; b. Salem, Ohio, July 19, 1934; s. Arthur Harris and Julia Helen (Higley) V.; B.Engring. Physics, Cornell U., 1958; Ph.D. in Physics and Astronomy, U. Rochester, 1965; m. Anne Elizabeth Montgomery, July 23, 1976; 1 son by previous marriage, Erik Brewster; step-children—William Morrison, Christopher Morrison, Elizabeth Morrison. Jr. scientist Avco-Everett Research Lab., Everett, Mass., 1958-59; Carnegie postdoctoral fellow Mt. Wilson & Palomar Obs. (now Mt. Wilson & Las Campanas Observatories), Pasadena, Calif., 1964-65, staff asso., 1965-67, staff mem., 1967-81; mgr. programs Astronomical Systems, Applied Optics Div., Perkin-Elmer Corp., 1981—, cons. Jet Propulsion Lab., Perkin-Elmer Corp.; vis. scientist European So. Obs., Geneva, 1979. Recipient Eastman Kodak sci. award, 1964; James Arthur prize Smithsonian Instn., 1981; NASA and NSF research grantee, 1974, 1980-81; Nat. Geog. Soc. grantee, 1982. Mem. Am. Astron. Soc., Internat. Astron. Union, Astron. Soc. of the Pacific. Co-designer telescope for Las Campanas Obs., 1970-76; optical designer wide field camera for space telescope. Author numerous articles in field. Home: 470 Fairview Ave Sierra Madra CA 91024 Office: 7421 Orangewood Ave PO Box 3115 Garden Grove CA 92642

VAUGHAN, EARLE RUSSELL, lawyer, apt. exec.; b. Denver, July 7, 1912; s. Russell U. and Harriette (Seaver) V.; student Antioch Coll., 1930-31, Loyola U., 1931-34; LL.B., Am. U., 1935; m. Virginia Healey, Sept. 3, 1977; children—Russell G., Robert P., Charles J., Charaline P. Commd. Page Mil. Acad., 1936-60; pres. bd. dirs. Page Schs., 1939-78, pres. emeritus, 1978—; admitted to Calif. bar, 1936; pvt. practice, 1936; nat. pres. United Motor Courts, 1951—. Pres. Bldg. and Safety Commn., Los Angeles, 1961-65; bd. dirs. United Cerebral Palsy Fund, 1957-59, 70-71. Served from ensign to lt. USNR, 1943-45. Mem. State Bar Calif., Apt. Assn. Los Angeles County (pres. 1957, 68-69), Calif. Rental Owners Assn. (pres. 1958-59), Nat. Apt. Owners Assn. (pres. 1960-61), Calif. Motel Assn. (dir. 1952), Wilshire C. of C. (dir. 1959, v.p. 1962, pres. 1963), Ret. Officers Assn., Am. Legion (post comdr. 1969-70), Delta Sigma Phi. Republican. Episcopalian (vestry 1951-53). Clubs: Masons (32 deg.), K.T., Shriners, Balboa Bay, Army and Navy, Rotary, Hi-12 (pres. 1979), Thursday Luncheon. Home: 11602 Town and Country Dr Garden Grove CA 92641 Office: 419 S Robertson Blvd Beverly Hills CA 90212 also 12111 Buaro St Garden Grove CA 92640

VAUGHAN, JAMES ARTHUR, JR., physician, surgeon; b. Sherman, Tex., Aug. 16, 1914; s. James Arthur and Nola Beatrice (Lawrence) V.; B.S., East Tex. State Coll., 1947, M.S., 1950; D.O., Chgo. Coll. Osteopathy, 1951; M.D., Calif. Coll. Medicine, 1962; m. Betty Ruth Brecheen, June 19, 1942 (dec.); children—J.A., James A. III; m. 2d, Betty Jo Stewart, Nov. 14, 1958 (div.); 1 dau., Karen. Intern Dallas Osteo. Hosp., 1951-52; pvt. practice, Dallas, 1952-63; assoc. Antelope Valley Med. Clinic, 1963-77; practice medicine, 1977—; vice chief staff Lancaster Community Hosp., 1968, chief of staff, 1980—; staff mem. Antelope Valley Hosp.; bd. dirs. Dallas Osteo. Hosp. until 1963; mem. adv. com. LVN Sch. Nursing until 1963. Served from seaman 2d class to lt. comdr. USNR, 1941-46, now lt. comdr. ret. Decorated Air medal with 1 gold star; recipient Disting. Service award CAP. Mem. AMA, Los Angeles County Med. Assn., Ret. Officers Assn. (life), Nat. Aero. Assn., Flying Doctors Soc. Africa (life), D.A.V. (life), Am. Legion (life), VFW (life), Sigma Tau Gamma, Iota Tau Sigma, Sigma Sigma Phi. Mason (32 deg., Shriner); mem. Order Eastern Star, Amaranth. Democrat. Episcopalian. Club: Caterpillar. Home: 45800 N 10th St E Lancaster CA 93535 Office: 43847 N Heaton St Lancaster CA 93534 also Box 2988 Lancaster CA 93539

VAUGHAN, LYNDA DIANE JULIEN, education administrator; b. Turlock, Calif., Apr. 8, 1941; d. Ronald Lyndon and Evelyn Gertrude (Eastman) Julien; m. Richard James Vaughan, Jan. 30, 1960; children—Lance Richard, Brent Alan, Brannan Paul, Julien Kristin. B.A., Calif. State Coll.-Stanislaus, 1961; M.A. in Ednl. Adminstrn., St. Mary's Coll., 1983. Cert. tchr., adminstr. Calif. Tchr. Turlock (Calif.) High Sch., 1961-62; tchr., adminstr. Waterford (Calif.) Sch. Dist., 1966-82; project specialist, coordinator Stanislaus County Dept. Edn., Modesto, Calif., 1982—. Mem. Family Service League, local C. of C. edn. com.; coordinator Stanislaus County Indsl. Edn. Council; past pres. Friends of Waterford Library, Waterford Tri-W; past dir. local heart assn. Recipient Bank of Am. Achievement award, Math. Assn. Am. award, Bausch and Lomb sci. award, 1958; Kettering Found. fellow, 1983. Mem. Assn. Calif. Sch. Adminstrs., Calif. Assn. for Gifted, Nat. Council Tchrs. Math., Nat. Sci. Tchrs. Assn., Calif. Scholarship Fedn. (life), P.E.O. Phi Delta Kappa. Home: Waterford CA 95386 Office: 801 County Center 111 Ct Modesto CA 95355

VAUGHAN, THOMAS JAMES GREGORY, historian; b. Seattle, Oct. 13, 1924; s. Daniel George and Kathryn Genevieve (Browne) V.; B.A., Yale U., 1948; M.A., U. Wis., 1950, doctoral residence, 1951-53; Litt.D., Pacific U., 1969; LL.D., Reed Coll., 1975; m. Elizabeth Ann Perpetua Crownhart, June 16, 1951; children—Meagan, Margot, Stephen, Cameron. Dir., Rock County (Wis.) Hist. Soc., 1953-54; exec. dir. Oreg. Hist. Soc., Portland, 1954—, editor-in-chief Oreg. Hist. Quar., 1954—; adj. prof. Portland State U., 1968—; pres., chmn. bd. Salar Enterprises, Ltd.; film producer, 1958-76; cons. Oreg. Am. Revolution Bicentennial Commn. First chmn. Oreg. State Com. for Humanities, Nat. Endowment for Humanities, 1969—; 1st chmn. Gov.'s Adv. Com. on Historic Preservation Oreg., 1970—, Oreg. Profl. Com. on Teaching of History; sec. Oreg. Geog. Names Bd., 1958—; adviser 1000 Friends of Oreg., 1972—; lay mem. Oreg. State Bar Disciplinary Rev. Bd., 1975—; vice chmn. adv. panel Nat. Endowment for Arts, 1975—; mem. Nat. Hist. Publs. and Records Commn. Matrix, 1975-76. Served with USMC, 1942-45. Decorated comdr. Order Brit. Empire; recipient Aubrey Watzek award Lewis and Clark Coll., 1975; Edith Knight Hill award, 1977; Tom McCall Broadcasting award, 1981; English Speaking Union grantee, 1961. Mem. Am. Assn. State and Local History (dir. 1955-74, pres. 1976—), Am. Assn. Museums (council), Nat. Trust Historic Preservation (adv. council). Clubs: City (bd. govs.), Univ. (bd. govs.) (Portland). Author: A Bibliography of Pacific Northwest History, 1958; A Century of Portland Architecture, 1967; Captain Cook, R.N., The Resolute Mariner: An International Record of Oceanic Discovery, 1974; Portland, A Historical Sketch and Guide, 1976; Now and Forever, 1976; Voyage of Enlightenment, Malaspina on the Northwest Coast, 1977; editor; Space, Style and Structure: Building in Northwest America, 2 vols., 1974; The Western Shore, 1975; numerous others; mem. adv. bd. Am. Heritage Mag., 1977—; producer films. Home: 1634 SW Myrtle St Portland OR 97201 Office: 1230 SW Park Ave Portland OR 97205

VAUGHN, DONALD ALLEN, advertising executive; b. San Mateo Calif., Aug. 6, 1930; s. Edgar Allen and Flora May (Allen) V.; m. Cheryl Ann Lindsay, Jan. 31, 1970; children—Diana, Gregory, Jeffry, Jennifer, Meghan. Student Long Beach City Coll., 1952-54; B.F.A., Art. Ctr. Coll of Design, Pasadena, Calif., 1957. Sr. art dir. Young and Rubicam, N.Y.C., 1957-69; assoc. creative dir. McCann-Marshalk, N.Y.C., and Atlanta, 1969-70; creative dir. Adams and Assocs., Compton, Calif., 1970-73, Glenn Advt., Burlingame Calif., 1973-75; sr. art. dir. Doyle Dane, Bernbach, Honolulu, 1975-77; v.p. creative dir. Tom, Vaughn, Hayashi Advt., Honolulu, 1977-78; sr. art dir. J. Walter Thompson, San Francisco, 1978—. Served to sgt. USMCR, 1950-51; Korea. Recipient Clio Advt. awards, 1977; Andy award, 1980. Mem. Art Ctr. Coll. of Design Alumni Assoc., Japanese-Am. Inst. Mgmt. Soc. Republican. Contbr. articles to profl. jours. Home: 1841 Trestle Glen Rd Piedmont CA 94610

VAUGHN, (OLIVE) RUTH, author, playwright; b. Wellington, Tex., Aug. 31, 1935; d. S.L. and Nora Norris (Knowles) Wood; B.A., M.A., U. Kans.; Ph.D., Am. U.; m. Bill Vaughn, Feb. 14, 1955; children—Billy, Ron. Author 35 books, including: Fun for Christian Youth, 1960, Dreams Can Come True, 1964, Portrait in a Nursery, 1965, What I Will Tell My Children About God, 1966, Skits that Win, 1967, No Matter the Weather, 1968, Hey! Have You Heard?, 1969, Playlets and Skits, 1970, Baby's Album, 1973, Even When I Cry, 1975, Proclaiming Christ in the Caribbean, 1976, More Skits that Win, 1977, Celebrate with Words, 1979, What's a Mother to Say?, 1980, Write to Discover Yourself, 1980, To Be a Girl—To Be a Woman, 1982, My God! My God!, 1982; author 46 plays, including: The Living Last Supper, The Man on the Center Cross, Behold a New World!, Lions Can't Eat Truth, Morning Comes at Sunrise, Catherine Marshall's Christy, Eugenia Price's The Beloved Invader; musical stageplays include: God's Dream, To Touch a Rainbow, Once Upon a Hill: The Coward and the Cut-Throat, Please Be King!, Shadow of the Almighty; prof. drama/creative writing Bethany Nazarene Coll., 1968-76; pvt. practice counseling; author numerous short stories and articles. Mem. Women in Communication Internat., Internat. Platform Assn., Pi Lambda Theta, Theta Sigma Phi. Republican. Nazarene. Home: 6151 W Fremont Dr Littleton CO 80123

VAUGHN, RONALD BRENT, advertising agency executive; b. Calif., July 8, 1936; s. Basil C. and Marjorie L. Vaughn; m. Merle Elizabeth Wierman, Nov. 28, 1957; children—Vicki, Debbie, Suzanne, Renee, Ronald Brent, Gregory. Area mgr. H & M Pub., Los Angeles, 1966-68; sales mgr. Sta. KFRE, Fresno, Calif., 1968-70, Sta. KYNO, Inc., Fresno, 1970-79; v.p. sales The Ad Works, Fresno, 1979—; guest lectr., cons. in field. Mem. adv. bd. Salvation Army, Fresno, 1973—; bd. dirs. Calif. Assn. Phys. Handicapped, 1981—; trustee Bulldog Found., Fresno, 1982—. Served with USN, 1954-57. Mem. Fresno Advt. Fedn. Republican. Seventh-day Adventist. Home: 6950 E McKenzie Fresno CA 93727 Office: 5110 E Clinton Way Suite 221 Frenso CA 93727

VAUGHT, KENNETH DARRYL, hydrologist; b. Ft. Worth, June 28, 1950; s. J.G. and Mary Francis (Baskin) V.; m. Martha Merle, Aug. 14, 1976; 1 son, John Thomas. B.S. in Agr., Tarleton State U., Stephenville, Tex., 1972. Hydrologic technician U.S. Geol. Survey, Houston and Denver, 1973-77; field hydrologist Leonard Rice Cons. Water Engrs., Denver, 1978-79; water resource specialist Adolph Coors Co., Golden, Colo., 1979—. Mem. Am. Soc. Agronomy, Soil Sci. Soc. Am., Trout

Unltd. Contbr. articles to profl. jours. Home: 8000 W 18th Ave Lakewood CO 80215 Office: Adolph Coors Company Mail Suite 309 Golden CO 80401

VEALE, JOHN EDMOND (JACK), business exec.; b. Winchester, Mass., July 12, 1954; s. Edmond John and Margaret Louise V.; B.S. in Bus. Adminstrn., Norwich U., 1976; m. Laurie Jean Howard, Apr. 29, 1978. With Southwest Hide Co., Boise, Idaho, 1976—, acct., 1977-78, office mgr., corp. office, 1978-79, corp. controller, 1979-81, chief fin. officer, 1981—. Mem. Idaho Assn. Commerce and Industry, Alpha Kappa Psi. Republican. Clubs: Full Gospel Businessmen's Internat., Nat. Ski Patrol. Home: 4062 Patton St Boise ID 83704 Office: Box 7946 Boise ID 83707

VEALE, WARREN LORNE, neuroscientist, educator; b. Antler, Sask., Can., Mar. 13, 1943; s. Lorne Elgin and Loletta Eleanor (Sawyer) V.; B.S., U. Man., 1965; M.S., Purdue U., 1968, Ph.D., 1971; m. Maureen Eola Fearns, Aug. 27, 1966; children—Pamela Margaret, Jeffrey Lorne. Lectr. Brandon U. (Man.), 1965-66; vis. scientist Inst. Med. Research, London, Eng., 1969; asst. prof. medicine U. Calgary, Alta., 1970-72, assoc. prof., 1972-76, prof., 1976—, head dept. med. physiology, 1979—, asso. dean research, 1974-80, adminstr. grad. program medicine, 1974-80. Research adv. com. Health and Welfare Can., Med. Research Council, 1973-74, mem. council, 1977—, exec., 1980—, v.p. Med. Research Council, 1981—; chmn. sci. adv. com. behavioural research, 1974-77; mem. research com. of bd. Alta. Cancer Hosp., 1978-83; mem. sci. adv. council Alta. Heritage Found. for Med. Research, also chmn. sci. rev. com. Mem. N.Y. Acad. Scis., Am. Physiol. Soc. Can. Physiol Soc. (council 1977—, v.p. 1983-84), Neurosci., Can., Midwestern psychol. assns., Collegium Internationale Neuro-Psychopharmacologicum, AAAS, Neurobiology Group of Can. Biochem. Soc., Internat. Brain Research Orgn. Regional editor Pharmacology Biochemistry and Behavior, 1973—; editorial adv. bd. Progress in Neuro-Psychopharmacology, 1976—. Contbr. chpts. to books, articles on central nervous system mechanisms regulating body temperature, prodn. fever, and origin of febrile convulsion to profl. publs.

VEGA, JOSE GUADALUPE, psychologist, consultant; b. San Benito, Tex., June 4, 1953; s. Jose Guadalupe and Bertha (Saenz) V.; m. Beth Susan Brimmer, Aug. 20, 1979; 1 dau., Lilian Anna. B.A., Pan. Am. U., Edinburg, Tex., 1975; M.A., U. Denver, 1976, Ph.D., 1979. Lic. psychologist, Colo., 1983; lic. profl. counselor, Tex., 1983. With Oasis of Chandala, Denver, 1978-79, Maytag-Emrick Clinic, Aurora, Colo., 1979; psychologist Spanish Peaks Mental Health Ctr., Pueblo, Colo., 1980—. Active Colo. Inst. Chicano Mental Health Community Youth Orgn., Boys Club Pueblo. Mem. Am. Psychol. Assn., Am. Personnel and Guidance Assn., Colo. Psychol. Assn., Phi Delta Kappa, Kappa Delta Pi. Democrat. Roman Catholic. Office: 310 Colorado St Pueblo CO 81004

VEGA, ROY DAVID, community official; b. San Jose, Calif., Dec. 6, 1946; s. Gabriel and Eloise (Osuna) V.; B.A. in Polit. Sci., U. Santa Clara, 1968; m. Kathy Marie Mestas, June 29, 1974; children—Angelene, David. Pub. safety dir. Pagosa (Colo.), 1974—, also County civil def. dir.; civil preparedness coordinator. Served to capt., M.P. U.S. Army, 1969-74. Decorated Bronze Star. Mem. S.W. Colo. Firemen's Tng. Assn., Emergency Med. Technicians Assn. Colo., Nat. Registry Emergency Med. Technicians, Nat. Sheriffs Assn., Nat. Fire Protection Assn., Internat. Assn. Chiefs of Police, Nat. Assn. Emergency Med. Technicians. Republican. Nat. Sheriffs Assn., Upper San Juan Emergency Med. Technicians Assn., Upper San Juan Peace Officers Assn. Roman Catholic. Office: 191 N Pagosa Blvd Pagosa Springs CO 81157

VEIR, CAROLE ANITA, educator; b. N.Y.C., Oct. 5, 1948; d. Frank Eakman and Mildred Olga (Krueger) Wilson. Student Colo. State U., 1966-68, U. Guadalajara (Mex.), 1969-70; B.A. with honors, U. Utah, 1971, M.Ed., 1975, Ed.D., 1980. Program dir., community edn. tchr., Salt Lake City, 1970-74; program developer, counselor, tchr. Clearfield (Utah) Job Corps, 1971-74; adminstr., tchr., reading specialist Granite Sch. Dist., Salt Lake City, 1974-79; asst. prof., U. Utah, 1979-80; dir., prof. adult vocat. edn. Mesa (Ariz.) Community Coll., 1980-81; asst. prof. bilingualmulticultural spl. edn. Ariz. State U., Tempe, 1981-82; program mgr. Alaska State Dept. Edn., Div. Exceptional Children, Div. Career and Vocat. Edn., 1982—; cons. in field. Public relations chairperson LWV, 1980-82; bd. dirs. Tempe Community Council, 1980-82. Mem. TESOL, Am. Vocat. Assn., Council Exceptional Children, Internat. Reading Assn., Women in Higher Edn. in Ariz., Phi Delta Kappa, Sigma Delta Pi, Pi Lambda Theta. (treas.). Contbr. articles to profl. jours. Home: 3-6000 Suite 163 Juneau AK 99801 Office: Pouch F Goldbelt Pl Alaska Dept Edn Juneau AK 99811

VEITCH, STEPHEN WILLIAM, investment counselor; b. Albuquerque, Aug. 19, 1927; s. Kenneth Easton and Edna (Miller) V.; B.A., U. N.Mex., 1949; LL.B., Stanford, 1957; student U. Nacional, Mex., 1949; m. Nancy Baker, June 28, 1951; children—Christopher Oxnard, Julia Blair. Admitted to Calif. bar, 1958; probate adminstr. Wells Fargo Bank, San Francisco, 1957-59; sr. v.p. Van Strum & Towne, Inc., San Francisco, 1959-76, sr. v.p., 1976-82, pres., 1982—; dir. Anza-Pacific Corp., Burlingame, Calif., 1964—, exec. com., 1965—. Mem. Guardsman, San Francisco, 1960—. Served with USNR, 1945-46; served to 1st lt. USAF, 1950-54. Mem. Am., San Francisco bar assns., Delta Theta Phi, Sigma Chi. Republican. Episcopalian. Clubs: Commonwealth, Pacific Union, University (San Francisco); Menlo Circus (Atherton, Calif.). Home: 33 Spencer Ln Atherton CA 94025 Office: 505 Sansone St Suite 1001 San Francisco CA 94111

VEITH-RIDEAU, KARYN LOREEN, personnel executive; b. Pasadena, Calif., Oct. 12, 1955; d. William Bernard and Mary Alice (Herrera) Veith; m. Andre A. Rideau, Mar. 29, 1980. B.S. in Bus. Adminstrn. and Personnel Mgmt., Calif. State U.-Fullerton, 1983. Bank ops. staff Valley Nat. Bank, Scottsdale, Ariz., 1973-75; bank ops. staff Lloyds Bank, Los Angeles, 1977, consumer fin. officer, 1977-78, asst. mgr., 1978, asst. v.p., mgmt. devel. adminstr., 1979-82, v.p., dir. human resources devel., 1982—. Mem. Los Angeles NAACP. Mem. Am. Soc. Tng. and Devel., Am. Inst. Banking (instr.). Democrat. Roman Catholic. Contbr. articles to profl. publs. Home: 5 Greenleaf Pomona CA 91766 Office: 612 S Flower St Suite 8411 Los Angeles CA 90017

VELASQUEZ, RALPH GILBERT, city ofcl.; b. Riverside, Calif. Oct. 24, 1921; s. Raymond Paul and Mary (Garcia) V.; student pub. schs. San Bernardino; m. Concepcion Santiago, Dec. 24, 1939; children—Gilbert Ralph, Veronica Ann. Meter repairman City of San Bernardino, 1947-60; sales mgr. LaTolteca Wholesale Foods, San Bernardino, 1960-65; ins. agt. Am. Nat. Ins. Co., San Bernardino, 1965-70; chief examiner, sec. Civil Service Bd., City of San Bernardino, 1970—, commr., 1965-70. Pres. bd. dirs. Family Service Agy., 1965—, Cath. Social Service, 1968-69; commr. Housing Authority County San Bernardino, 1971—, chmn., 1976, 77; mem. Juvenile Justice Commn. County San Bernardino, 1972-75. Served with U.S. Army, 1944-46. Recipient Good Citizen award Rotary, 1975; Paternal Apostolic blessing Pope Paul VI, 1970; Naturalization Program award Am. Legion, 1955; Nat. Civil Service League fellow, 1971. Mem. Internat. Personnel Mgmt. Assn., Nat. Civil Service League, Family Service Assn. Am., Nat. Assn. Housing and Redevel. Ofcls., Nat. Assn. Life Underwriters, Personnel and Indsl. Relations Assn., Am. Legion. Democrat. Roman Catholic. Clubs: Rotary, K.C. Home: 1307 Perris St San Bernardino CA 92411 Office: 300 North D St San Bernardino CA 92418

VELDE, JOHN ERNEST, JR., investor; b. Pekin, Ill., June 15, 1917; s. John Ernest and Alga (Anderson) V.; A.B., U. Ill., 1938; m. Shirley Margaret Walker, July 29, 1940 (dec. Dec. 1969); 1 dau., Drew; m. 2d, Gail Patrick, Sept. 28, 1974 (dec. July 1980); m. 3d, Gretchen Swanson Pullen, Nov. 7, 1981. Pres., Velde, Roelfs & Co., Pekin, 1955-60, Paisano Prodns., Inc., 1980—. Regional v.p. Am. Library Trustee Assn., Chgo., 1970-72, chmn. internat. relations com., 1973-76; hon. chmn. Nat. Library Week in Ill., 1973; mem. Nat. Commn. on Libraries and Info. Sci., 1970-79; mem. adv. bd. White House Conf. on Libraries, 1976-80; chmn. Am. Library Trustee Assn. Found., 1976; trustee ALA Endowment, 1976-82; chmn. bd. trustees Bd. Dirs. Center Ulcer Research and Edn. Found., Los Angeles, 1977-82; mem. bd. councilors Brain Research Inst. UCLA, 1977-82; trustee Center for Am. Archaeology, Evanston, Ill., 1978—, Joint Council Econ. Edn., N.Y.C., 1977—, Lakeview Center Arts and Scis., Peoria, 1964-72; mem. adv. com. Innovative Design Fund, N.Y.C., 1978-82; trustee Pekin Meml. Hosp., 1950-69, pres., 1951-55, 68-69; trustee Pekin Public Library, 1948-69, pres., 1955-69; trustee Ill. Valley Library System, 1966-69, pres., 1966-68; mem. Nat. Book Com., 1970-75; bd. dirs. U. Ill. Found., 1977—; vice chmn. U. Ill. Pres.'s Council, 1977-79, chmn., 1979-81; vice chmn. Fin. Resources Council Steering Com., 1976-78; mem. adv. council UCLA Grad. Sch. Library and Info. Sci., 1981-82. Served as lt. (j.g.) USNR, World War II. Mem. Kappa Sigma. Republican. Clubs: Internat., Chgo. Yacht (Chgo.); Country of Peoria, Creve Coeur (Peoria, Ill.); Capitol Hill (Washington); Chaine des Rotisseurs, Chevaliers du Tastevin, California (Los Angeles); Outrigger Canoe (Honolulu); Thunderbird Country (Rancho Mirage, Calif.); Omaha Country, Omaha (Omaha); Circumnavigators (N.Y.C.). Home: 2003 La Brea Terr Hollywood CA 90046 also 8405 Indian Hills Dr Omaha NE 68114

VELIE, GARY WAYNE, lawyer; b. Olympia, Wash., Dec. 7, 1941; s. Claude Richard and Dorothy Amelia (Sturges) V.; m. Elizabeth Anne Barlow, Sept. 15, 1962; children—Steven Richard, Charles Fredrick. Student Centralia Jr. Coll., 1960-61; B.S. in Forest Mgmt., U. Wash., 1964; J.D., Gonzaga U., 1974. Bar: Wash. 1974. Sole practice, Port Angeles, Wash., 1974—. Served with USNR, 1961-81. Recipient Air medal. Mem. Assn. Trial Lawyers Am., ABA, Wash. Bar Assn., Clallam County Bar Assn. Clubs: U.S. Yacht Racing Union, Yacht Club (Port Angeles), Eagles. Office: 101 W Front St Suite 102 Port Angeles WA 98362

VELONA, CHARLES SANTO, television executive; b. Jersey City, N.J., Feb. 1, 1941; s. Domenick N. and Rose V. (Impal) V.; m. Mary Kay Wathen, July 1, 1961; children—Gerard, Carrie, David, Christopher. Student, Tulane U., 1958-59, Local sales mgr. Sta.-KTLA-TV Los Angeles, 1959-71; salesman Sta-KHJ-TV, Los Angeles, 1972-74, sales mgr., 1974-80, v.p., gen. mgr., 1980—. Mem. Calif. Broadcasters, So. Calif. Broadcasters, Acad. TV Arts and Scis., Nat. Assn. TV Programming Execs., Assn. Ind. TV Stas. Office: Sta KHJ-TV 5515 Melrose Ave Los Angeles CA 90038

VELTRI, MARIO FRANK, accountant; b. N.Y.C., Dec. 23, 1941; s. Frank Mario and Maria (Castalano) V.; B.A., Woodbury Coll., 1962; m. Alice Jane Hoosan, June 2, 1962; children—Allyson Carol, Christopher Frank, Jennifer Marie. Acct., Lauter, Gaynor & Edison, C.P.A.s, Los Angeles, 1962-63, Joseph S. Herbert & Co., C.P.A.s, Beverly Hills, Calif., 1963-64, John F. Varela & Co., C.P.A.s, Los Angeles, 1964-69, Mario F. Veltri & Co., C.P.A.s, Los Angeles, 1970—; dir. Santa Ana State Bank, Pan Am. Nat. Bank. Bd. dirs. Manuscript Soc., 1974-75, v.p., 1975—; trustee Ramona's Mexican Food Products Scholarship Found. Served with USCG, 1959-67. Mem. Am. Inst. C.P.A.s, Calif. Soc. C.P.A.s. Democrat. Home: 236 24th St Santa Monica CA 90402 Office: 3345 Wilshire Blvd Los Angeles CA 90010

VENABLE, DOUGLAS, consulting physicist; b. Charleston, W. Va., Aug. 17, 1920; s. Ernest Haymond and Elizabeth Ross (Dabney) V.; B.S., Hampden-Sydney Coll., 1942, M.S., U. Va., 1947, Ph.D., 1950; m. Jessie Ann Mix, June 26, 1943; 1 son, Douglas Gordon. Design engr. Westinghouse Electric Corp., Balt., 1942-46; staff mem. U. Calif. Los Alamos Sci. Lab., 1950-57, alt. group leader, 1957-65, group leader, 1965-72, alt. div. leader, 1972-76, dep. asst. dir. weapons planning and coordination, 1976-79, program mgr., 1979-81, dep. assoc. dir. weapons research and devel., 1981-82; cons., 1982—. Bd. dirs. United Fund Los Alamos, 1972. Adj. prof. elec. engring. U. N.Mex., Los Alamos, 1957-58, physics, 1958-59, 61-62. Fellow AAAS, Am. Phys. Soc.; mem. Phi Beta Kappa, Sigma Xi, Omicron Delta Kappa. Contbg. author: Industrial Electronics Reference Book, 1948; contbr. articles to profl. jours. Research in shock hydrodynamics, flash radiography, electron accelerators. Home: 118 Aztec Ave Los Alamos NM 87544

VENABLE, HARLAN DEAN, welding equipment mfr.; b. Morrilton, Ark., Dec. 13, 1938; s. Elmer Bryan and Grace Elizabeth (McArthur) V.; B.S.E.E., Lehigh U., 1960; M.B.A., U. So. Calif., 1972; m. Joanne Ilene Lantz, May 4, 1969. Project engr. Aero Geo Astro Corp., College Park, Md., 1960-64; mgr. electronic equipment dept. Fairchild-Hilton Corp., Germantown, Md., 1964-66; applications engr. TRW Semicondrs., 1966-70; product specialist Gulton Industries, Hawthorne, Calif., 1970-71; sr. scientist Hughes Aircraft, Torrance, Calif., 1971-80; pres. Venable Industries, Inc., Rancho Palos Verdes, Calif., 1980—; tchr. computer programming; cons. power systems design. Recipient best paper award Powercon 7 Conf., 1980. Mem. Am. Welding Soc., IEEE, Internat. Power Conversion Soc. (dir.). Republican. Presbyterian. Club: Toastmasters. Contbr. articles on power conversion and stability analysis to profl. jours. Patentee high efficiency power conversion circuit. Home: 4968 Silver Arrow Dr Rancho Palos Verdes CA 90274

VENERABLE, DELBERT-GRANT, chemist; b. Los Angeles, Aug. 31, 1942; s. Grant D. and Thelma Lorraine (Scott) V.; B.S., UCLA, 1965; M.S., U. Chgo., 1967, Ph.D., 1970. AEC postdoctoral fellow in radiation biology UCLA Lab. Nuclear Medicine, 1970-71; instr. chemistry and biology Duarte (Calif.) High Sch., 1971; assoc. prof. dept. chemistry Calif. Poly. State U., San Luis Obispo, 1972-78; Sloan lectr. in chemistry U. Calif., Santa Cruz, 1978-80; ptnr. Omnitron Assocs., Mill Valley, Calif., 1982—. Recipient Disting. Teaching award, Calif. Poly. State U., 1977; NEH grantee, Mich. State U., 1978. Mem. Am. Chem. Soc., AAUP, Am. Soc. Tng. and Devel., AAAS, Sigma Xi, Alpha Chi Sigma. Unitarian/Congregationalist. Author: The Natu'l Flow, An Alchemy of Mind, 1975; The Gemini Conspiracy: A Compu-Math Survival Kit, 1981; inventor Calculus of Transformations (algebraic symbolization of abstract process, a mapping technique of problem solving), 1974; various maj. oil paintings commd. by sci. acads. in U.S., France, W. Ger. and E. Ger., Can., USSR. Office: 950 Duncan St Suite E305 San Francisco CA 94131

VENHUIZEN, BRADLEY AUSTIN, insurance company executive, lawyer; b. Hannaford, N.D., Dec. 19, 1944; s. Raymond Arthur and Valborg Alfreda (Tweit) VenH.; m. Linda Arlene Beveridge, Mar. 30, 1972; 1 son, Jason. B.S., U. N.D., 1966; M.Sc., U. B.C., 1970; J.D., U. Oreg. 1976. Bar: Wash. 1976. Instr. biology Capilano Community Coll., Vancouver, B.C., 1969-73; govt. affairs coordinator N.W. Pulp and Paper Assn., 1976-78; advanced underwriting cons., dir. advanced underwriting Sunset Life Ins. Co., Olympia, Wash., 1978—; dir. Sunset Fin. Services, Inc. Mem. ABA, Wash. State Bar Assn. Republican. Lutheran. Club: Tumwater (Wash.) Kiwanis. Home: 2860A Crosby Blvd Tumwater WA 98502 Office: 3200 Capitol Blvd Olympia WA 98507

VENKATESWARAN, KALYANA SUNDARAM, electrical engineer; b. Ravanasamudram, India, Sept. 13, 1943; came to U.S., 1972; s. Kalyanasundaram and Gomathi (Rajangam) V.; B.Tech., Indian Inst. Tech., Bombay, 1964, M. Tech., 1966; Ph.D., U. Waterloo (Ont., Can.), 1972; m. Shyamala Chandrasekhar, Jan. 17, 1971; children—Swapna, Nitya, Anoradha. Postdoctoral fellow UCLA, 1962-73; mem. tech. staff Rockwell Internat. Corp., Anaheim, Calif., 1972-76; sr. design engr., then design supr. Fairchild Semicondr. Co., San Jose, 1976-79, design engring. mgr., 1979-82; sr. design engr. VLSI Design, Inc., San Jose, 1982—; cons. in field. Treas. Bay Area chpt. S. India Fine Arts Assn., 1979-80. Recipient Tech. Achievement award Fairchild Semicondr. Co., 1980. Mem. IEEE, South India Cultural Soc. (pres. Los Angeles chpt. 1975-76). Author, patentee in field. Home: 138 Sweet Berry Ct San Jose CA 95136 Office: 4010 Moorepara Ave San Jose CA 95117

VER HEY, JAMES MATTHEW, architect; b. Albert Lea, Minn., Feb. 27, 1950; s. Cornelius William and Donna Faye Ver H.; B.Arch., U. Minn., 1976. Designer, Pope Assos., Mpls., 1976-77; designer, job capt. The Hodne/Stageberg Partners, Mpls., 1977-79; project designer Welton Becket Assos., Los Angeles, 1979—. Registered architect, Minn., Calif. Mem. AIA. Home: 400 N Mansfield Ave Los Angeles CA 90036 Office: 2900 31st St Santa Monica CA 90405

VERHEY, JOSEPH WILLIAM, physician/psychiatrist; b. Oakland, Calif., Sept. 28, 1928; s. Joseph Bernard and Anne (Hanken) V.; B.S. summa cum laude, Seattle U., 1954; M.D., U. Wash., 1958; m. Darlene Helen Seiler, July 21, 1956. Intern, King County Hosp., Seattle, 1958-59; resident Payne Whitney Psychiatric Clinic, N.Y. Hosp., Cornell Med. Center, N.Y.C., 1959-62, U. Wash. Hosp., Seattle, 1962-63; practice medicine, specializing in psychiatry, Seattle, 1963—; mem. staff U. Hosp., Providence Hosp., Fairfax Hosp., VA Med. Center, Tacoma; clin. instr. psychiatry U. Wash. Med. Sch., 1963-68, clin. asst. prof. psychiatry, 1968-82, clin. assoc. prof., 1982—; cons. psychiatry U.S. Dept. Def., Wash. State Bur. Juvenile Rehab.; examiner Am. Bd. Psychiatry and Neurology. Diplomate Am. Bd. Psychiatry and Neurology. Fellow N. Pacific Soc. Psychiatry and Neurology, Am. Psychiat. Assn.; mem. AMA, Am. Fedn. Clin. Research, World Fedn. Mental Health, Soc. Mil. Surgeons of U.S. Home: 1100 University St Seattle WA 98101 Office: VA Med Center Tacoma WA 98493

VERLOT, FRANK OSCAR, aerospace company executive; b. Ghent, Belgium, Oct. 18, 1941; s. Maximilian Gustave and Eva Emily (Danilevits) V.; m. Marian Berkner, June 24, 1967; children—Nancy, Susanne. B.S. in Mech. Engring., MIT, 1963; M.S. in Mech. Engring., Stanford U., 1964, postgrad., 1964-66. Thermodynamics engr. Grumman Aerospace Engring. Corp., Bethpage, N.Y., 1963-65; thermodynamics engr. Lockheed Missiles and Space Co., Sunnyvale, Calif., 1966-68, project engr. Chem. Systems div. United Technologies, Sunnyvale, 1968-71, mgr. procurement liaison, 1971-81, mgr. strategic and bus. planning, 1981—. Mayor, councilman City of Los Altos (Calif.), 1982-83; mem. Planning Commn. City of Sunnyvale, 1973-76, chmn., 1974-75; chmn. Republican Central Com. Santa Clara County, 1971-72; mem. exec. com. Rep. State Central Com. Calif., 1971-76; Rep. state precinct chmn., 1973-74; del. Rep. Nat. Conv., 1972. Mem. AIAA. Roman Catholic. Home: 634 S Springer Rd Los Altos CA 94022 Office: 600 Metcalf Rd San Jose CA 95138

VERNON, ROBERT WILLIAM, accountant; b. Youngstown, Ohio, May 25, 1931; s. Maynard William and Betty Zeigler (Snyder) V., m. Edith Christine Johnson, Mar. 28, 1929. B.S. in Bus. Adminstrn., Miami U., Oxford, Ohio, 1954. C.P.A., Idaho, Calif. With Ernst & Whinney, Youngstown, Ohio, 1956-57, Los Angeles, 1957-64, Santa Ana, Calif., 1964-79, Newport Beach, Calif., 1979-81, Boise, Idaho, 1981—, ptnr., 1971—, ptnr. in charge auditing Boise office, 1981—. Bd. dirs. Children's Home Soc. Calif., 1975-80, 1st v.p., 1980. Mem. Am. Inst. C.P.A.s., Idaho Soc. C.P.A.s., Calif. Soc. C.P.A.s., Nat. Assn. Accts. (pres. Orange Coast chpt. 1971-72, nat. bd. dirs. 1975-77), Boise C. of C., Sales and Mktg. Execs. Republican. Presbyterian. Clubs: Crane Creek Country, Shriners (Boise). Home: 1287 Candleridge Dr Boise ID 83702 Office: 999 Main St Suite 900 Boise ID 83702

VERRAN, JOYCE ANN, nurse, researcher, educator; b. Detroit, Nov 25, 1941; d. Melvin Roy and Dorothy Lucille (Rowe) V. Diploma, Sch. Nursing Los Angeles County-U. So. Calif. Med. Ctr., 1963; B.S., U. Ariz., 1969, M.S., 1970, Ph.D., 1982. Staff nurse Los Angeles County-U. So. Calif. Med. Ctr., Los Angeles, 1963-65, head nurse, 1965-69; asst. dir. med. nursing Ariz. Health Scis. Ctr. Univ. Hosp., Tucson, 1970-73, assoc. dir. clin. nursing, 1973-78, asst. dir., div. coordinator med.-surg. nursing Coll. Nursing, 1978—. Trustee Kino Community Hosp., 1975-77. Recipient Nat. Research Service award Div. Nursing, HHS, 1979-82. Mem. Am. Nurses Assn., Nat. League for Nursing, Am. Statis. Assn., Sigma Xi, Sigma Theta Tau, Inc. Developed ambulatory care client classification instrument; contbr. articles to profl. jours. Office: Coll Nursing U Ariz Tucson AZ 85721

VERSTRATEN, CHAROLETTE, accountant, fin. planner; b. Memphis, Sept. 20, 1942; d. Aaron Loyd and Elsie Elizabeth (Asher) Richardson; student Boise State Coll., 1965-68, Grossmont Community Coll., 1973; children—Rusty Driscoll, Robin Driscoll, Quint Driscoll. Jr. acct., Don W. McDougal, C.P.A., Emmett, Idaho, 1964-67; service rep. Pacific Telephone Co., Boise, 1967-68; acctg. clk. Security Industries, Boise, 1968-69; jr. acct. Charles O. Brady, C.P.A., Boise, 1969-70; sr. acct. M. Kornfeld & Co., San Diego, 1971-73; mgr. small bus. dept. Moody & Bucher, C.P.A.s, San Diego, 1973-79; owner, mgr. Charolette Verstraten, Enrolled Agt., comprehensive fin. bookkeeping and tax service, San Diego, 1979—; enrolled to practice before IRS; registered prin., real estate agt. Mem. Am. Soc. Women Accts., Nat. Assn. Enrolled Agts., Internat. Assn. Fin. Planners, Nat. Assn. Accts., Calif. Soc. Enrolled Agts., Am. Bus. Women's Assn. Office: 3505 Camino del Rio S Suite 220 San Diego CA 92108

VERTREES, SUSAN JANE, educator; b. Champaign, Ill., Apr. 26, 1950; d. Luther Roenoke and Helen Jane (Baird) Paulson; m. Billy Gene Vertrees, July 2, 1977; children—Jennifer Susan, Shannon Marie. B.S. in Home Econs. Edn., Wash. State U., 1972; 5th yr. degree in Edn., Central Wash. U., 1976. Tchr. home econs. Frontier Jr. High Sch., Moses Lake, Wash., 1972-73; tchr. home econs. Whitaker-Columbia Middle Sch., Portland, Oreg., 1973—. Republican. Lutheran.

VERZINO, WILLIAM JOHN, JR., chemist; b. Easton, Pa., Oct. 28, 1940; s. William John and Regina Margaret (Noti) V.; m. Judith Ann Massey, June 27, 1964; children—William John, Robert Lee, Anthony James, Patricia Margaret. B.S., Muhlenberg Coll., 1962; M.S., John Carroll U., 1967; Ph.D. in Chemistry, Colo. State U., 1970. Sr. research chemist Am. Enka Corp. (N.C.), 1970-74, exchange research chemist Enka-Glanzstoff, A.G., Obernburg, W.Ger., 1972-73; mem. tech. staff Aerospace Corp., El Segundo, Calif., 1974-78; acting assoc. group leader Los Alamos Nat. Lab., 1978-82; served as ensign U.S. Naval Res., 1962-65, commd. comdr., 1982; assoc. prof. chemistry U.S. Naval Acad., 1982—; fossil fuel/mil. cons. Los Alamos Cons., 1981—. Bd. dirs. Los Alamos YMCA, 1981-82. Fellow Am. Inst. Chemists (cert.); mem. Am. Chem. Soc., Royal Soc. Chemistry (chartered chemist) (London), N. Mex. Acad. Scis., Naval Res. Assn. (life), Res. Officers' Assn. (life), Sigma Xi, Phi Kappa Phi. Club: K.C. Author numerous govt. reports. Office: Dept Chemistry US Naval Acad Annapolis MD 21402

VEST, FEARN ROLLA, soil scientist, agronomist; b. Payson, Utah, July 29, 1935; s. John Rolla and Ruby Emilie (Olsen) V.; m. Ann Venone Cegler, Apr. 16, 1959; children—Kerry, Noreen, Mark, JoAnna, Michael, George, Julene, Karalie. B.A. in Agronomy, Brigham Young U., 1958, postgrad., 1959-60. Cert. profl. agronomist, soil scientist. Soil scientist Tuba City (Ariz.) Agy. of Bur. Indian Affairs, 1960-74, Ariz. div. Peabody Coal Co., Black Mesa, 1979—; cons. soil scientist, agronomist Williams Brother Engrng. Co., Tulsa, 1974-78. Active Boy Scouts Am., 1971-82; vol. fire chief Tuba City, 1972-74; pres. Tuba City PTA, 1973-74; mem. Kayenta (Ariz.) Planning and Zoning Bd., 1981-82. Served with U.S. Army, 1954-56. Recipient incentive awards U.S. Bur. Indian Affairs, 1964. Mem. Am. Soc. Agronomy, Soil Sci. Soc. Am., Internat. Soc. Soil Sci. (U.S. com. on irrigation drainage and flood control). Mormon. Co-author numerous U.S. govt. tech. reports and map atlases in field. Home: PO Box 3041 Page AZ 86040 Office: Peabody Coal Co Ariz Div PO Box 605 Kayenta AZ 86033

VESTAL, ROBERT, III, real estate executive; b. Elyria, Ohio, July 7, 1933; s. Robert and Frances A. (Whiteley) V.; m. Judith C. Herbert, Aug. 14, 1965; children—Paul, Debra, Janice, William. B.A., U. Denver, 1957. Editor Shell Oil Co., Denver, 1957-62; pub. relations rep. AT&T, N.Y.C. and Denver, 1962-67; mgr. Botsford-Ketchum Co., Denver, 1971-76; mktg. dir. Potato Bd., Denver, 1976-81; v.p. advt. and pub. relations Fuller & Co., Denver, 1981—. Mem. Denver Press Club, Denver Advt. Club. Office: Fuller & Co 1515 Arapahoe St Denver CO 80202

VESTER, DICK L., optometrist; b. Forest Grove, Oreg., July 24, 1946; s. Lyall F. and Clarice L. (Darnielle) V. Student U. Idaho, 1964-67; B.S., Pacific U., Forest Grove, 1974; D.O., 1976. Assoc. Dr. Rich and Assocs., Vancouver, Wash., 1976-81; pvt. practice optometry, Wallace, Idaho, 1981—. Pres. Greater Wallace Community Devel. Corp., 1981—, Wallace Youth Athletic Found., 1981—. Served with U.S. Army, 1971-73. Mem. Am. Optometric Assn., Idaho Optometric Assn., Wash. Optometric Assn., North Idaho Optometric Assn. Clubs: Shoshone Golf and Tennis (dir.) (Wallace); Oxford Athletic (Vancouver); Elks. Office: 608 Cedar St Wallace ID 83873

VESTRE, NORRIS DONALD, psychologist, educator, researcher; b. Mpls., Dec. 17, 1927; s. Nick and Dagny Magdalena (Moen) V.; 1 dau., Lori Denise. B.A., U. Minn., 1955, Ph.D., 1959. Research psychologist VA, St. Cloud, Minn., 1959-62; research assoc. U. Minn., Mpls., 1962-68; assoc. prof. Ind. State U., 1968-69; prof. Wash. State U., 1969-72; prof. psychology Ariz. State U., Tempe, 1972—. Mem. Am. Psychol. Assn., Western Psychol. Assn., Rocky Mountain Psychol. Assn. Contbr. numerous articles to profl. publs. Home: 119 E Fairmont Dr Tempe AZ 85282 Office: Dept Psychology Ariz State U Tempe AZ 85287

VIALPANDO, MICHAEL ANTHONY, educator; b. Santa Fe, Sept. 28, 1952; s. Issac J. and Mary C. (Martinez) V. B.B.A. in Bus. Edn., Coll. Santa Fe, 1974; postgrad. in vocat. edn. Eastern N.Mex. U., U. N.Mex. Cert. tchr., N.Mex. Tchr. mktg. Santa Fe Pub. Schs., 1972—; dir. Summer Youth Employment Programs, 1980, 81; counselor N.Mex. Boys State, 1978—; dir. Youth Employment Programs for Handicapped. Named Young Tchr. of Yr., Santa Fe Jaycees, 1978; Michael Lewis Jr. scholar, 1974. Mem. N.Mex. Vocat. Assn. (lobbyist 1983), Am. Vocat. Assn., Mktg. and Distributive Edn. Assn., N.Mex. Retailing Assn. Democrat. Roman Catholic. Clubs: Caballeros de Vaugas, Elks, Eagles (Santa Fe). Home: 2594 Camino Chueco Santa Fe NM 87501 Office: 2201 W Zia Rd Santa Fe NM 87501

VICENZI, RICHARD ANTHONY, exec. search cons.; b. Milw., Jan. 25, 1947; s. Reno Louis and Bernice Eleanor (Barsch) V.; B.A. in Econs. and Polit. Sci., U. Calif., Riverside, 1968; M.B.A. in Gen. Mgmt., UCLA, 1973; m. Susan Linda Interrante, July 15, 1972. Store mgr. Thrifty Corp., 1969-71; indsl. devel. cons. James F. Hays & Assos., Long Beach, Calif., 1973-74; cons. Engrng. Agy., Los Angeles, 1974-76; partner Proctor & Davis, Santa Monica, Calif., 1976—. Bd. dirs. Los Angeles Free Clinic, 1982—; Ill. State dir. Student Vote, 1972. Served with USAR, 1968-74. Mem. Soc. Petroleum Engrs., Center for Non-Profit Mgmt., UCLA Grad. Sch. Mgmt. Alumni Assn. (bd. dirs. 1982—). Office: 2811 Wilshire Blvd Santa Monica CA 90403

VICIAN, THOMAS ALLEN, SR., educator; b. Mason City, Iowa, Jan. 31, 1935; s. Stephen Roy and Blanche (Lucas) V.; A.B., Luther Coll., 1957; B.D., Luther Theol. Sem., 1961; postgrad. San Jose State Coll., 1963-64; Ph.D., Claremont Grad. Sch., 1971; m. Elizabeth Ann Overgaard, Aug. 11, 1957; 1 son, Thomas Allen, Jr. Ordained minister Luth. Ch., 1961; asso. minister Gloria Dei Luth. Ch., Rochester, Minn., 1961-62, Grace Luth. Ch., Palo Alto, Calif., 1962-64; asst. prof. philosophy Calif. State Coll., Hayward, 1966-67, U. Nev., Reno, 1967-68; prof. philosophy De Anza Coll., Cupertino, Calif., 1968—, also chmn. dept.; philos.-religious cons., Palo Alto, Calif. Woodrow Wilson fellow, 1964-65, Nat. Endowment Humanities fellow, 1973. Mem. AAUP, Philosophy of Sci. Assn., Bay Area Ednl. TV Assn., World Future Soc., Sierra Club, Smithsonian Assos., Center Study Democratic Instns., Am. Philos. Assn. Home: 3718 Redwood Circle Palo Alto CA 94306 Office: 21250 Stevens Creek Blvd Cupertino CA 95014

VICK, AUSTIN LAFAYETTE, civil engineer; b. Cedervale, N.Mex., Jan. 28, 1929; s. Louis Lafayette and Mota Imon (Austin) V.; B.S.C.E., N.Mex. State U., 1950, M.S.C.E., 1961; m. Norine E. Melton, July 18, 1948; children—Larry A., Margaret J., David A. Commd. 2d lt. U.S. Air Force, 1950, advanced through grades to capt., 1959, ret., 1970; ordnance engr. Ballistics Research Lab., White Sands Proving Ground, Las Cruces, N.Mex., 1950-51, civil engr., 1951-55, gen. engr. White Sands Missile Range, 1957-73, phys. scientist adminstr., 1955-57, 73—; owner A.V. Constrn., Las Cruces, 1979—; realtor Campbell Agy., Las Cruces, 1979—. Mem. outstanding alumni awards com. N.Mex. State U., 1980. Recipient Outstanding Performance award Dept. Army, White Sands Missile Range, 1972, Spl. Act awards, 1967, 71, 75. Mem. Mil. Ops. Research Soc. (chmn. logistics group 1968-69), Am. Def. Preparedness Assn. (pres. 1970-72), Assn. U.S. Army (v.p. 1970-71), Am. Soc. Photogrametry, Am. Astronautical Soc. (sr. mem.). Contbr. articles to profl. jours. Home: 4568 Spanish Dagger Las Cruces NM 88001 Office: Data Collection Div White Sands Missile Range NM 88002

VICKERS, GROVER WILLIAM, data processing administrator; b. Tyner, Ky., Jan. 16, 1927; s. Clifton Henry and Etta Mae (Cook) V.; m. Nancy Elizabeth Sanford, June 6, 1953; children—Elizabeth Ann Oliver, Donald William. B.S. in Commerce, U. Ky., 1951; grad. profl. mil. comptroller course, Air U., 1971. Commd. U.S. Air Force, 1951; advanced through grades to lt. col., 1968; mgr. data processing audit, 1954-59; mgmt. analyst, 1959-61; systems analyst USAF Hdqrs., Washington, 1967-70; mgr. systems analysis and programming, Colorado Springs, Colo., 1964-65; mgr. computer ctr. ops., various locations 1962, 63, 66, 71; dir. data automation, mgr. automated data processing, AFAFC, 1972-76; ret. 1976; dir. computer services Metropolitan State Coll., Denver, 1978—. Bd. dirs. Chateau Claire, Inc., condominium complex. Decorated Legion of Merit, Commendation medal, Bronze Star, Vietnam Service medal, Republic of Vietnam medal. Mem. ACM, Data Processing Mgmt. Assn., Colls. and Univs. Systems Exchange. Republican. Baptist. Office: 1006 11th St Box 15 Denver CO 80204

VICKERS, MARK STEPHEN, association executive; b. Vallejo, Calif., Sept. 11, 1957; s. John Frederick and Anna Ruth (Boschell) V. B.A. in Bus. Adminstrn., Azusa Pacific U., 1979. Dir. public relations Azusa Pacific div. Bus., 1977-78; copywriter Pennington, Inc., Fullerton, Calif., 1978; dir. communications Glendora (Calif.) C. of C., 1979; asst. mgr., dir. public relations Burbank (Calif.) C. of C., 1979-82, exec. dir., 1982—. Bd. dirs. Friends of Burbank Airport; coordinator Burbank Trade Fair Festival, Burbank Visitors Bur. Recipient Eagle Scout award Boy Scouts Am., 1971; Bus. award Bank of Am., 1975. Mem. Am. Chamber Execs. Assn., Calif. Chamber Execs. Assn., Los Angeles Public Interest Radio and TV Ednl. Soc. Clubs: Toastmasters (Burbank); San Fernando Valley Press (dir.). Pub. Burbank Bus. Today monthly, 1979—; columnist, poet and contbg. editor Calif. Chamber Execs. Assn. Newsletter and Greater Burbank Vis. Guide. Office: 200 W Magnolia Blvd Burbank CA 91502

VICKERY, BYRDEAN EYVONNE HUGHES, ednl. adminstr.; b. Belleview, Mo., Apr. 18, 1928; d. Roy Franklin and Margaret Cordelia (Wood) Hughes; student Flat River (Mo.) Jr. Coll., 1946-48; B.S. in Edn., S.E. Mo. State Coll., 1954; M.L.S., U. Wash., 1964; postgrad. Wash. State U., 1969-70, U. Wash., 1981-83; m. Charles Everett Vickery, Jr., Nov. 5, 1948; 1 dau., Camille Vickery Flaten (Mrs. Wayne Loren). Tchr., Ironton (Mo.) Pub. Schs., 1948-56; elem. tchr. Pasco (Wash.) Sch. Dist. 1, 1956-61, jr. high sch. librarian, 1961-68, coordinator libraries, 1968-69; asst. librarian Columbia Basin Community Coll., Pasco, 1969-70, head librarian, dir. Instructional Resources Center, 1970-78, dir. library services, 1978—; chmn. S.E. Wash. Library Service Area, 1977-78. Pres., Pasco-Kennewick Community Concert Assn., 1980-81; trustee Wash. Commn. Humanities, 1982—, Mid-Columbia Symphony Bd., 1983—. Recipient Woman of Achievement award Pasco Bus. and Profl. Women's Club, 1976. Mem. AAUW (2d v.p. 1966-68, corr. sec. 1969), Wash. Dept. Audio-Visual Instrn., ALA, Wash. Library Assn. (state conf. local arrangements chmn. 1979), Am., Wash. assns. higher edn., Wash. State Assn. Sch. Librarians (state conf. chmn. 1971-72), Tri-Cities Librarians Assn., Am. Assn. Research Libraries, Soroptimist Internat. Assn. (rec. sec. Pasco-Kennewick chpt. 1971-72, treas. 1973-74), Columbia Basin Coll. Adminstrs. Assn. (sec.-treas. 1973-74), Pacific N.W. Assn. Ch. Libraries, Women in Communications, Beta Sigma Phi, Delta Kappa Gamma, Phi Delta Kappa (sec. 1981-82 Outstanding Educator award 1983). Clubs: Pasco Bus. and Profl. Women's; Soroptimist (pres. Pasco-Kennewick chpt. 1978-80), PEO. Author, editor: Library and Research Skills Curriculum Guides for the Pasco School District, 1967; author: (with Jean Thompson), also editor Learning Resources Handbook for Teachers, 1969. Home: 4016 W Park St Pasco WA 99301 Office: 2600 N 20th Ave Pasco WA 99301

VIDAL, LINDA CADIZ, dietetics adminstr.; b. Manila, Philippines, Nov. 7, 1941; d. Jose R. and Consolacion (Lacson) Cadiz; m. Rusty L. Vidal, Mar. 9, 1969. B.S. in Foods and Nutrition, Philippines Women's U., 1962; M.P.A., Consortium of Calif. State Colls. and Univs., 1981. Registered dietitian. Food adminstr. I Napa (Calif.) State Hosp., 1970-77, dir. dietetics, 1977—. Mem. Am. Dietetic Assn., Calif. Dietetic Assn., Bay Area Dietetic Assn. Home: 3311 Scenic Dr Napa CA 94558 Office: PO Box A Imola CA 94558

VIDONI, DENNIS OSCAR, psychologist, college administrator, educator; b. Chgo., Mar. 22, 1945; s. Oscar and Fides (Forte) V.; m. Mary, Vidoni, June 7, 1975; 1 son, Eric. B.S. in Edn., Eastern Ill. U., 1968; M.A., Roosevelt U., 1972; Ph.D., Marquette U., 1975. High sch. social sci. tchr., pub. schs., Athens, Ill., 1968-70; tchr. history Farragut High Sch., Chgo., 1970-71; counseling psychologist U. Wis.-Oshkosh, 1975-76; dir. counseling, asst. prof. psychology Benedictine Coll., 1976-79; dir. Counseling Ctr., asst. prof. psychology Regis Coll., 1979—; clin. affiliate Denver U. Sch. Profl. Psychology. Mem. Common Cause. Mem. Am. Psychol. Assn. Author: Psychological Reports, 1976; Educational and Psychological Measurement, 1977; Counseling and Values, 1977; Psychology in the Schools, 1983. Home: 1376 S Clayton St Denver CO 80210 Office: Regis Coll 50th and Lowell Denver CO 80221

VIDUGIRIS, VICTOR-VYTAUTAS PETER, engineering executive; b. Raguva, Lithuania, July 3, 1930; came to U.S., 1949, naturalized, 1953; s. Paul P. and Alexandra (Kojelis) V.; m. Helen Agnes Vidugiris, June 26, 1955; 1 dau., Dianne J. A.T., Temple U., 1953; B.S.M.E., Ill. Inst. Tech., 1960; postgrad. U. Mich., 1960-61. Registered profl. engr., Calif. Design engr. Bendix Corp., St. Joseph, Mich., 1959-60; research engr. Lockheed Missiles & Space Co., Sunnyvale, Calif., 1960-61; missile test site supr. AMF, Chico, Calif., 1961-62; sr. devel. engr. Garrett AeResearch, Los Angeles, 1962-67; staff engr., sect. head TRW/Def. & Space Systems, Redondo, Beach, Calif., 1967-81; dept. mgr. TRW, 1981—; cons. in field. Chief scout Lithuanian Boy Scouts; pres. Am. Lithuanian Community, Inc., 1976-79; bd. dirs. Nat. Republican Heritage Group Council, 1978-82. Served with U.S. Army, 1952-54. Recipient Chgo. Tribune award, 1959; TRW Good Neighbor Award, 1978; Medal of Merit. Lithuanian Boy Scouts, 1978. Mem. ASME, AIAA, Am. Soc. Quality Control, World Am. Lithuanian Engrs. and Architects Soc. (past pres.), Am. Legion. Republican. Roman Catholic. Clubs: Luncheon, Elks. Contbr. articles to profl. jours. Home: 27923 San Nicholas Dr Rancho Palos Verdes CA 90274 Office: One Space Park Redondo Beach CA 90278

VIEGLAIS, NIKOLAJS, clergyman; b. Dundaga, Latvia, Mar. 31, 1907; s. Andrew P. and Eugenia (Jakobson) V.; grad. Theol. Sem., Latvia, 1928, Music Sch., 1932; baccalaureate Theol. Faculty, U. Latvia, 1940; m. Natalija Calders, Oct. 18, 1931; children—Natalija, Marina (Mrs. Alfredo Alva), Alexis, Olga (Mrs. J. Kuhlman), Tatjana (Mrs. T. Pardini); came to U.S., 1949, naturalized, 1955. Ch. choir dir., Cesis, Latvia, 1928-34; deacon cathedral, Riga, Latvia, 1934-37; ordained priest Eastern Orthodox Ch., Latvia, 1937; priest, Riga, 1937-44; priest refugee camps, Germany, 1944-49; apptd. priest Am.-Russian Orthodox Ch., 1949; priest, Lykens, Pa., 1949-51, Berkeley, Calif., 1952—. Editor, pub. ch. books and music, Latvia, 1935-40, 41-44, Germany, 1946-49, U.S.A., 1950-79; dean No. Calif., Am.-Russian Orthodox Ch., 1955-74, 75-76; sec. Exarchate for Baltic States, 1942-44; sec. San Francisco Diocese, 1960-72, mem. council, 1952-76; spiritual adviser local chpt. Federated Russian Orthodox Clubs, 1964-70, Pacific-Alaska Dist., 1967-68. Home: 1908 Essex St Berkeley CA 94703 Office: 1900 Essex St Berkeley CA 94703

VIELEHR, WILLIAM R., sculptor, curator; b. Chgo., Jan. 6, 1945; s. Charles Conrad and Jane Ruth (Kingsley) V.; m. Pauline Marie Bustamante, Nov. 27, 1975; children—William Nathan Bustamante. B.F.A., Colo. State U., 1969. One man shows: Gilman Gallery, Chgo., 1972, 74, 76, 80; group exhbns. include: Joslyn Art Mus., Omaha, 13th, 14th Midwest Biennial, Denver Art Mus., 1974, N.Am. Sculpture Exhibit, Foothills Art Ctr., Golden, Colo., 1980, Boulder (Colo.) Sculpture Symposium, 1982, Shidoni Sculpture Show N. Mex., 1980, 81, Denver Botanic Gardens, 1983; scupture commns. include Mace Rich Corp., Boulder, Park Place Bldg., Boulder; dir., Form Inc., 1981-83; curator Vail sculpture exhibits; art show juror, lectr. contemporary sculpture, 1979—. Bd. dirs. Boulder Ctr. Visual Arts, 1979, 81; curator, coordinator Sculpture in the Park, Boulder, 1979—. City of Boulder arts grantee, 1981.

VIERRA, MANUEL N., judge, lawyer; b. Hanford, Calif., Nov. 29, 1943; s. Manuel N. and Helen Frances (Kochevar) V.; A.A., Coll. of Sequoias, 1963; B.A., Fresno State U., 1965; postgrad. Humphrey's Sch. Law; J.D., U. Pacific, 1972; m. Maureen F. Vierra, Sept. 11, 1976 (div. Jan. 1980). Admitted to Calif. bar, 1972, U.S. Dist. Ct. bar, 1972, U.S. Ct. of Appeals bar, 1972; practiced in Hanford, Kings County, Calif., 1972—; asso. firm Clarence H. Wilson, 1972-77; judge Justice Ct., Lemoore Jud. Dist., Kings County, Calif., 1977—. Mem. Am. Bar Assn., Kings County Bar Assn. (v.p. 1975, pres. 1976), Calif. Judge's Assn., Phi Alpha Delta. Republican. Roman Catholic. Home: PO Box 132 Hanford CA 93230 Office: 449 C St PO Box 549 Lemoore CA 93245

VIESTI, CARL R., JR., psychologist; b. Bronx, N.Y., July 9, 1934; s. Carl R. and Madeline L. (Cafarelli) V. B.A., Catholic U. of Am., Washington, 1956; M.S., U. Bridgeport, 1965; Ph.D., U. Oreg., 1969, 80. Lic. clin. psychologist, Calif. Tchr. Conn. pub. schs., 1961-65; asst. prof. U. Victoria, B.C., Can., 1969-73; pres. VST Corp., Bronx, N.Y., 1973-76; clin. psychologist Atascadero (Calif.) State Hosp., 1981—; cons., tchr., researcher, pvt. practice psychology. Mem. Am. Psychol. Assn., Western Psychol. Assn., San Luis Obispo Psychol. Assn. Contbr. chpts. to profl. books. Office: Atascadero State Hosp Drawer A Atascadero CA 93422

VIGER, DAVID NATHAN, JR., management consultant; b. Denver, Oct. 8, 1942; s. David Nathan and Mary Louise (Kern) V.; student U. Mich., 1962-66; B.S. in Engrng., Ariz. State U., 1969; m. Marcia Lynn Hummel, Aug. 10, 1968; children—Davis Lynn, Kern Louise, David Nathan III, Carrie Margarite, Michael Charles. Indsl. engr., Motorola Semi-Condr., Phoenix, 1966-69; plant and mfg. engr. Alcoa Aluminum, Vernon works, Los Angeles, 1969-70; pres. Nat. Cons. Services, Vista, Calif., 1970—, Exec. Counseling subs., 1970—. Mem. Huntington Beach Res. Police Force, 1969-72; mem. high council Ch. Jesus Christ Latter-day Saints; Explorer Scout advisor, 1969—. Mem. Soc. Automotive Engrs. Republican. Home: 2323 Via Subria Vista CA 92083 Office: 846 Williamston Suites 201 and 202 Vista CA 92083

VIGNES, SUSAN MARIE, educational administrator; b. Los Angeles, July 9, 1943; d. Charles E. and Vera R. (Riolo) Vignes. B.A., U. Santa Clara, 1968; M.A., San Jose State U., 1975; M.A. with honors, San Francisco State U., 1983. Tchr. La Entrada and La Loma Schs., Menlo Park, Calif., 1969-80; asst. supt. for instrn. Archdiocese of San Francisco, 1980—; media specialist, photographer, 1974—. Chairperson San Mateo County Art Com., Redwood City, Calif., 1972-79. Mem. Assn. Calif. Schs. Adminstrs., Calif. Reading Assn., Assn. Supervision and Curriculum Devel., Instructional Assn. North (bd. dirs.), San Mateo County Reading Assn. (bd. dirs.). Republican. Roman Catholic. Office: Archdiocese of San Francisco 443 Church St San Francisco CA 94114

VIJAYAN, NAZHIYATH, neurologist, educator; b. Kerala, India, Feb. 27, 1941; came to U.S., 1968; s. Gopalan and Parukutty (Amma) Nair; M.B. B.S., Trivandrum Med. Coll., India, 1964, M.D., 1967; m. Vijayakumari, Feb. 6, 1966; children—Suju, Shalini. Resident physician in internal medicine, Trivandrum Med. Coll., India, 1964-67; sr. house officer Regional Neurology Center, Newcastle, Eng., 1967-68; resident in neurology, U. Calif., Davis., 1968-71, asst. prof., dept. neurology, 1971-81, dir. headache clinic U. Calif. at Davis Sacramento Med. Center; dir. Sacramento Headache and Neurology Clinic, 1981—. Mem. Am. Acad. Neurology, Am. Assn. for Study of Headaches, Calif. Med. Assn., Am. EEG Soc., Am. Epilepsy Soc., Internat. Cluster Headache Research Group. contbr. articles to profl. publs.; research on headaches. Office: 2600 Capitol Ave Suite 211 Sacramento CA 95816

VILARDI, AGNES FRANCINE, real estate broker; b. Monson, Mass., Sept. 29, 1918; d. Paul and Adelina (Mastrioanni) Vetti; m. Frank S. Vilardi, Dec. 2, 1939; children—Valerie, Paul. Cert. of dental assisting Pasadena Jr. Coll., 1954. Lic. real estate broker. Dental asst. Dr. Koontz, Alhombra, Calif., 1955-60; real estate broker, owner Vilardi Realty, Yorba Linda, Calif., Plocentia, Calif., Fullerton, Calif., 1968—; cons. in property mgmt. Mem. Am. Dental Asst. Assn., North Orange County Bd. Realtors (sec./treas. 1972). Club: Yorba Linda Country. Home and Office: 18982 Vila Terr Yorba Linda CA 92686

VILAS, CLARK DARRELL, advt. exec.; b. Taft, Calif., Apr. 17, 1932; s. Walter Clark and Grace Mae (Smith) V.; student UCLA, 1953-54; B.A., U. So. Calif., 1955, postgrad., 1955-60; m. Linda Lou O'Day, Feb. 22, 1959; children—Catharine Janine, Lise Anne. Account exec. Ward Griffith Co., Los Angeles, 1959-62; adminstr. advt. sta. NBC/KNBC-TV, Los Angeles, 1962-67; account exec. Dancer, Fitzgerald & Sample, San Francisco, 1967-68; advt. mgr. sta. CBS/KCBS, San Francisco, 1969-70; pres. Vilas Advt. Inc., Oakland, Calif., 1970—. Mem. task force fund raising com. Aid to Adoption of Spl. Kids. Served with U.S. Army, 1956-58. Mem. Advt. and Mktg. Assn. East Bay (dir.), No. Calif. Advt. Agy. Assn. (pres. 1976-77), Western States Advt. Agy. Assns., Sales and Mktg. Council, Audit Bur. Circulation, Bldg. Industry Assn., Am. Advt. Fedn. (exec. com. western region conf.), Press Club San Francisco, Sigma Nu, Alpha Epsilon Rho. Republican. Christian Scientist. Clubs: Clairemont Country, Commonwealth of Calif. Home: 41 Corte de Rosas Moraga CA 94556 Office: Vilas Bldg 3530 Grand Ave Oakland CA 94610

VILLHARD, VICTOR JOSEPH, aerospace engineer; b. St. Louis, Sept. 26, 1957; s. Vincent L. and Ann B. (Ackerman) V.; m. Diane L. Reitz, July 10, 1982. Commd. 2d lt. USAF, 1979, advanced through grades to capt., 1983; chief mechanics div. Frank J. Seiler Research Lab., U.S. Air Force Acad., Colo., 1981—. Mem. AIAA, Pi Mu Epsilon. Roman Catholic. Home: 4743 Daybreak Circle S Colorado Springs CO 80917 Office: Frank J Seiler Research Lab/NHM US Air Force Acad Colorado Springs CO 80840

VINCENT, ALBERT VERNON, real estate exec.; b. Rector, Ark., Sept. 4, 1921; s. Albert Wesley and Helen (Wilcher) V.; student pub. schs.; m. Kay Tokie Nagata, Sept. 4, 1960; children—Armond Vernon, Linda Carol, Sharon Lynn, Albert Vernon, Wendi Vernelle. Supr., Naval Supply Center, Pearl Harbor, 1942-48; div. mgr. Century Metalcraft Corp., 1948-54; gen. mgr. Saladmaster of Hawaii, 1954-56; realtor, 1957-60; pres. Tropic Shores Realty, Ltd., 1960—. Named Hawaii Realtor of Yr. Mem. Nat. (dir., v.p. 1970), Hawaii (pres. 1978) assns. realtors, Nat. Inst. Real Estate Brokers (gov.), Honolulu Bd. Realtors (pres.), Inst. Real Estate Mgmt., Nat. Inst. Farm and Land Brokers, Internat. Real Estate Fedn., Calif. Real Estate Assn., Realtors Nat. Mktg. Inst. (gov.), Real Estate Securities and Syndication Inst. (gov. 1973), Am. Soc. Real Estate Counselors (gov.), Internat. Platform Assn., Honolulu Press Club. Clubs: Pacific, Plaza, Honolulu. Home: 1517 Makiki St #1007 Honolulu HI 96822 Office: 33 S King St Honolulu HI 96813

VINCENT, CRAIG TYLER, lawyer; b. Salt Lake City, May 23, 1932; s. Tyler Richard and Edith (Anderson) V.; m. Patricia M. Marwede, June 28, 1962; children—Jeffrey C., Shaunalee, Stephen T., Suzanne, Kristen. B.A., U. Utah, 1956, J.D., 1959. Bar: Utah 1959. Sole practice, 1959-60; asst. U.S. atty. Dist. Utah, 1960-63; assoc. Kipp & Chavlier, Salt Lake City, 1963-65; ptnr. Beaslin, Nygaard, Cole & Vincent, Salt Lake City, 1965—; reference atty. Utah State Legislature, 1961-62. Mem. deferred gifts com. Primary Children's Hosp., 1980-81; mem. com. United Way, 1978. Mem. ABA, Fed. Bar Assn., Utah State Bar Assn., Phi Delta Phi, Delta Phi Kappa. Democrat. Mem. Ch. of Jesus Christ of Latter-day Saints. Home: 1917 E 5685 S Salt Lake City UT 84121 Office: 1100 Boston Bldg Salt Lake City UT 84111

VINCENT, DAVID RIDGELY, information executive; b. Detroit, Aug. 9, 1941; s. Charles Ridgely and Charlotte Jane (McCarroll) V.; m. Margaret Helen Anderson, Aug. 25, 1962 (div. 1973); children—Sandra Lee, Cheryl Ann; m. 2d, Judith Ann Gomez, July 2, 1978; 1 dau., Amber; stepsons—Michael Jr., Jesse Joseph Flores. B.S., B.A., Calif. State

U.-Sacramento, 1964; M.B.A., Calif. State U.-Hayward, 1971. Sr. ops. analyst Aerojet Gen. Corp., Sacramento, 1960-66; controller Hexcel Corp., Dublin, Calif., 1966-70; mng. dir. Memorex, Austria, 1970-74; sales mgr. Ampex World Ops., Switzerland, 1974-76; dir. product mgmt. NCR, Sunnyvale, Calif., 1976-79; v.p. Boole & Babbage Inc., gen. mgr. Inst. Software Engrng., Sunnyvale, Calif., 1979—. Mem. Republican Nat. Task Force; deacon Union Ch. Cupertino, Calif.; NCAA soccer referee. Mem. Football Assn. Fedn. Internat., European Computer Measurement Assn., Computer Mgmt. Group, Guide, Share, Assn. Computing Machinery. Club: Decathelon (Sunnyvale). Author: Perspectives in Information Management, Information Economics, Discovery of Concept, 1983; contbr. monographs and papers to profl. jours. Home: 617 Bancroft St Santa Clara CA 95051 Office: 510 Oakmead Pkwy Sunnyvale CA 94086

VINEYARD, C L, lawyer; b. Petersburg, Tex., Nov. 9, 1927; s. Clarence Calvin and Louella (Ray) V.; m. Nora Crawford; children—John, Paul, Anne. A.A., San Bernardino Valley Coll., 1953; B.A., Claremont Men's Coll., 1955; J.D., UCLA, 1959. Bar: Calif. 1960. Police officer, San Bernardino, Calif., 1950-56; claims rep. Farmers Ins., Los Angeles, 1958-60; partner King & Mussell, San Bernardino, 1960-71; sole practice, San Bernardino, 1971-74, 76—; mem. Eckhardt, Youmans & Vineyard, San Bernardino, 1974-75, Sprague, Milligan & Beswick, San Bernardino, 1975-76; instr. law and police sci. San Bernardino Valley Coll., 1961-62; arbitrator for claims, comml., constrn. and med. malpractice Am. Arbitration Assn.; judge pro tem San Bernardino Superior Ct. and San Bernardino Mcpl. Ct.; arbitrator personal injury panel San Bernardino Superior Ct. Commr., sec. San Bernardino Police Commn., 1960-65. Served with USN, 1944-48. Mem. Am. Bd. Trial Advocates, Internat. Assn. Ins. Counsel, ABA San Bernardino County Bar Assn. (judiciary com. 1967-79, bench-bar com., jud. selection and rev. com.), Calif. State Bar (prin. referee state bar ct.), Calif. Trial Lawyers Assn. Clubs: Lions, Masons, Shriners, Elks. Home: 3850 Atlantic Apt 123 Highland CA 92346 Office: Pacific Fed Plaza 330 N D St Suite 430 San Bernardino CA 92401

VINEYARD, DAVID JESS, automobile club ofcl.; b. Hollywood, Calif., Feb. 12, 1926; s. Owen and Lucille (McKee) V.; student Oreg. State U., 1945-49. Asst. to divisional credit mgr. Comml. Credit Corp., Portland, Oreg., 1949-51; field investigator Fed. Res. Bank of San Francisco, Portland, 1951-52; zone mgr. Anglo-Calif. Nat. Bank, San Francisco, 1953-54; credit mgr. Calif. Electric Supply Co., San Francisco, 1954-57; sr. supr. collection sect. Calif. State Automobile Assn., San Francisco, 1957-64; field insp. Approved Accommodations, Restaurants, San Francisco, 1964-69, mgr. market research dept., 1969—; pres. Vigilantia, Inc., San Francisco, 1961-62, dir., 1959-62; pres. CSAA Employees Fed. Credit Union, San Francisco, 1973, treas., mgr., 1975-82; v.p., dir. Credit Union Assn. No. Calif., San Francisco, 1978—. Mem. adv. bd. Eugene S. Elkus Found., San Francisco, 1961-62. Served with USNR, 1944-46. Mem. Am. Mktg. Assn., Real Estate Research Council No. Calif. Club: Commonwealth. Office: 150 Van Ness Ave San Francisco CA 94102

VINGO, J. RAY, airline executive; b. Oakland, Calif., Aug. 16, 1938; s. James S. and Pauline G. (Isbell) V.; m. Margaret J. Sheridan, Oct. 26, 1969; children—Andrea C., Michael A., Paul M. B.S. in Bus. Adminstrn., U. Calif., 1960. Sr. casualty underwriter Firemans Fund Ins. Co., San Jose, Calif., 1963-66; asst. treas. Western Temporary Services, San Francisco, 1966-69; casualty mgr. CNA Ins. Group, San Francisco, 1969-70; treas. Flying Tiger Line, Inc., Los Angeles, 1970-77; treas. Shaklee Corp., San Francisco, 1977-83; v.p. fin. Alaska Airlines, Inc., Seattle, 1983—. Served with U.S. Army, 1960-61. Office: Alaska Airlines Inc PO Box 68900 Seattle WA

VINICH, JOHN PAUL, state senator; b. Lander, Wyo., June 13, 1950; s. Mike M. and Mabel R. (Petro) V. B.S. in Social Work, U. Wyo., 1972. Mgr. Union Bar and Lounge, Hudson, Wyo., 1973-75; mem. Wyo. Ho. of Reps., from 1975, mem. revenue com., 1975-83; mem. Wyo. State Senate, 1983—. Mem. Wyo. Human Resources Council; dir. Casper (Wyo.) Big Bros., 1972-73; mgr. Hudson Youth Ctr., Hudson, 1974-75; mem. Hudson Vol. Firemen. Democrat. Roman Catholic. Clubs: Eagles, Elks. Home: Main St Box 67 Hudson WY 82515 Office: Wyoming State Senate Cheyenne WY 82002*

VINING, DAUNINE HAGMAN (MRS. W.H. VINING, JR.), interior designer, educator; b. Long Beach, Calif., Oct. 30, 1937; d. Robert Charles and Lois Isabell (Lamb) Hagman; m. William Henry Vining, Jr., Aug. 10, 1957; 1 son, William Henry. B.A. in Interior Design, Calif. State U.-Long Beach, 1966. Cert. Nat. Council Interior Designers. Interior designer, Orange County, 1966-68; dir. design staff Sage Environ. Interiors, Fullerton, Calif., 1968-72; instr. Santa Ana Community Coll., 1973; instr. interior design Calif. State U.-Fullerton, 1975; prin. Daunine Vining and Assocs., Orange, Calif., 1972—, Fashion Inst. Design and Merchandising, Los Angeles, 1981—; cons. Mem. Am. Inst. Interior Designers, Am. Soc. Interior Designers (pres. Orange County chpt.), Archtl. Guild, Interior Designers Educators Council. Contbr. articles to mags. Home: 3844 East Casselle Ave Orange CA 92669 Office: 1118 E 17th St Santa Ana CA 92701

VINSO, JOSEPH DAVID, economics educator; b. Wilkes-Barre, Pa., Dec. 20, 1941; s. Joseph David and Linda Marie (Castellani) V.; m. Helga Marie Vinso, Sept. 5, 1964; children—Kimberley, Joseph. B.Chem.Engrng., Cornell U., 1964; Ph.D., U. Mich., 1973. With Dow Chem. Co., Midland, Mich., 1964-70; asst. prof. Wharton Sch., U. Pa., Phila., 1973-79; assoc. prof. U. So. Calif., Los Angeles, 1979—; pres. Fin. Resources Mgmt., Inc.; cons., lectr. in field. Active Boy Scouts Am. NSF grantee, 1977. Mem. Am. Fin. Assn., Am. Econs. Assn., Am. Soc. Appraisers. Author numerous articles to profl. jours.; patentee in field. Home: 26805 Hawkhurst Dr Rancho Palos Verdes CA 90274 Office: Univ So Calif Los Angeles CA 90089

VINTON, BOBBY (STANLEY ROBERT), entertainer; b. Canonsburg, Pa., Apr. 16; s. Stanley and Dorothy (Studzenski) V.; student Duquesne U., Pitts.; m. Dolly Dobbin, Dec. 17, 1962; children—Robert, Kristin, Christopher, Jennifer, Rebecca. Leader own band, singer, night club entertainer; appearances on TV in Bobby Vinton Show, 1975—, also numerous guest appearances; single Gold records include Roses Are Red, Blue on Blue, Blue Velvet, Mr. Lonely, I Love How You Love Me, My Melody of Love; rec. artist Epic; dramatic roles in films Surf Party, Big Jake, 1971, The Train Robbers, 1973, also on TV; owner Tapestry Record Co., Feather Music Publishing Co., Acacia Music Pub. Co.; partner Vinton-Klein Film Prodn. Co. Served with U.S. Army. Named Number One Male Vocalist, Cash Box mag., 1965; Most Played Rec. Artist, Billboard mag., 1965; author: (autobiography) Polish Prince. Address: PO Box 49690 Los Angeles CA 90049

VIOLA, MICHAEL JAMES, city official; b. Rock Hill, S.C., Feb. 22, 1949; s. Archie E. and Mary E. (Stair) V. A.S., Kings Coll., Charlotte, N.C., 1968; B.S., Dyke Coll., 1970; postgrad. Calif. State U.-Fullerton, 1982—. Asst. buyer Higbee Co., Cleve., 1970-72; acct. Sealtest Dairy Co., Charlotte, 1972-75, Fairchild Industry Corp., Winston-Salem, N.C., 1975-77; credit officer City of Pasadena (Calif.), 1977-78, mcpl. services supr., 1978-79, mcpl. services adminstr., 1979—. Mem. Am. Mgmt. Assn., Pasadena Mgmt. Assn. (social and edn. chmn. 1980), Am. Water Works Assn., No. Utilities Credit Assn. (Calif. pres. 1981), Am. Soc. for Pub. Adminstrn. Republican. Mem. Unity Ch. Office: Mcpl Services Dept Room 121 100 N Garfield Ave Pasadena CA 91109

VIOLET, WOODROW WILSON, JR., chiropractor; b. Columbus, Ohio, Sept. 19, 1937; s. Woodrow Wilson and Alice Katherine (Woods) V.; student Ventura Coll., 1961-62; grad. Los Angeles Coll. Chiropractic, 1966; m. Judith Jane Thatcher, June 15, 1963; children—Woodina Lonize Violet Bentley, Leslie Alice. Pvt. practice chiropractic medicine, Santa Barbara, Calif., 1966-73, London, 1973-74, Carpinteria, Calif., 1974—; past mem. council roentgenology Am. Chiropractic Assn. Former mem. Parker Chiropractic Research Found., Ft. Worth. Served with USAF, 1955-63. Recipient award merit Calif. Chiropractic Colls., Inc., 1975, cert. of appreciation Nat. Chiropractic Antitrust Com., 1977. Mem. Nat. Geog. Soc., Los Angeles Coll. Chiropractic Alumni Assn., Delta Sigma. Patentee surg. instrument. Office: 1007 Casitas Pass Rd Carpinteria CA 93013

VIREDAY, PIERRE FRANCOIS, exec. chef; b. Lausanne, Switzerland, May 21, 1931; s. Francois Ulysses and Marie-Louise Maria (Ferrari) Viredaz; came to U.S., 1955, naturalized, 1961; ed. trade schs., Zurich, Switzerland; m. Claire Muhlberg, Apr. 24, 1954; children—Carol, Richard, Diane. Apprentice cook, Switzerland, journeyman France, Italy, Luxembourg, 1955-57; chef Beverly Hilton Hotel, Beverly Hills, Calif., 1957-59; chef Romanoff's, Beverly Hills, 1959-61, San Bernardino, Calif., 1961-62; chef Tropicana Hotel, Las Vegas, 1963-66; chef Caesar's Palace, Las Vegas, 1966-67; chef Stardust Hotel, Las Vegas, 1967-70; chef Landmark Hotel, Las Vegas, 1970-71; chef Bonanza Hotel, Las Vegas, 1971-72; exec. chef MGM Grand Hotel, Las Vegas, 1972—; culinary adviser Clark County Sch. Dist., Area Tech. Trade Sch., Las Vegas. Served with inf. Swiss Army, 1951-53. Recipient Grand Prize Gold medal Hospes, Lucerne, 1953; named Chef of Yr., Las Vegas Frat. of Exec. Chefs, 1975; cert. exec. chef. Mem. Fraternity Exec. Chefs Las Vegas (dir. 1974—, trustee food service 1974—), Am. Culinary Fedn. (conv. chmn. 1980, mem. industry council), Am. Acad. Chefs, Food Service Execs Assn., Am. Mgmt. Assn. Republican. Presbyterian. Author (with others) Wine and Dine with the Chefs of Las Vegas, 1980. Address: MGM Grand Hotel PO Box 11087 Las Vegas NV 89119

VIRNOCHE, KEITH PETER, marketing executive; b. Two Rivers, Wis., May 4, 1952; s. Gordon Joseph and Marie Mary (Kornely) V; m. Lynn Deck, Aug. 19, 1979. B.A., U. Wis., 1974; M.B.A., U. Evansville, 1976. Prod. planning mgr. Litton Microwave Cooking Products, Mpls., 1976-81; dir. mktg. Anova div. Dart & Kraft, Inc., San Mateo, Calif., 1981—. Office: 3 Waters Park Dr San Mateo CA 94403

VISCONTI, RON MICHAEL, vocational counselor, educator, career consultant; b. Redwood City, Calif., Feb. 23, 1952; s. George Louis and Josephine (Abate) V.; m. Eve Young, Dec. 16, 1978. B.A. in Sociology, U. San Francisco, 1973; postgrad. San Francisco State U., 1978-80. Social services worker County San Mateo Social Services, Calif., 1974-80; adult tchr., San Mateo, 1978—, De Anza Coll., Foothill Coll., San Mateo Adult Schs., 1980-81, Mideast Am. Corp., Burlingame, Calif., 1981-82; salesman Haines & Co., San Mateo, Calif., 1982—; vocat. counselor Tng. Employment Ctr., 1983—; career cons. Bd. dirs. Vol. Bur. No. Santa Clara County, also chmn. fundraising. Mem. Am. Personnel and Guidance Assn., Am. Mktg. Assn., Am. Soc. for Tng. and Devel., Alpha Sigma Nu. Author: Is There Work after College? Career Planning from A to Z, 1983.

VISHER, EMILY BROWNING, psychologist; workshop leader; b. Norwich, Conn., May 21, 1918; d. Carleton Perkins and Mary Rudd (Gibbs) Browning; m. Shirley Seavey Philbrick, Aug. 9, 1941 (div.); children—Sharon Carol, Wendy Joan, David Alan, Loren King; m. 2d, John Sargent Visher, Dec. 31, 1959. B.A. with honors (Durant scholar), Wellesley Coll., 1940, postgrad. (Anne Louise Barrett fellow), 1953-54; Ph.D. in Psychology (AAUW nat. fellow), U. Calif.-Berkeley, 1958. Lic. psychologist, Calif. Research chemist Nutrition Clinic, Birmingham, Ala. and Cin., 1940-41; pvt. practice clin. psychology, Palo Alto, Calif.; staff psychologist VA Hosp., Menlo Park, Calif., 1966-68, Kasier Found. Hosp., Redwood City, Calif., 1970 77; lectr. and workshop leader on working with stepfamilies, co-founder, v.p. Stepfamily Found. Calif., Inc., 1977-78, pres., 1979-80; pres., co-founder Stepfamily Assn. Am., Inc., 1979—. Mem. Wellesley Coll. Alumnae Assn., Am. Psychol. Assn., Phi Beta Kappa, Sigma Xi. Author: (with John S. Visher) Stepfamilies: A Guide To Working With Stepparents and Stepchildren, 1979, How To Win As A Stepfamily, 1982; contbr. articles to profl. publs.; assoc. editor Stepfamily Bull., 1980-82. Home: 10475 Albertsworth Ln Los Altos Hills CA 94022

VISSCHER, ENGBERTUS HENDERIKUS, missile and space co. exec.; b. Smilde, Netherlands, Jan. 29, 1922; came to U.S., 1956, naturalized, 1963; s. Eise and Aaltien (deVroome) V.; B.S., Tech. Evening Coll., Amsterdam, 1943; m. Lambertha Wiskerke, Dec. 30, 1949; children—Eise Jan, Francoise Janna, Irene Carol. Draftsman/designer Fokker Aircraft Co., Amsterdam, 1938-43, design engr., 1945-56; design engr. Messerschmitt Aircraft Co., Augsburg, Germany, 1943-45; design specialist Lockheed Missiles & Space Co., Sunnyvale, Calif., 1956-65, advanced systems staff engr., 1968-78, metric coordinator, 1978—, chmn. metric adv. com., 1978—; staff cons. Lockheed Aircr Deutschland, Munich, Germany, 1966-67. Mem. AIAA, U.S. Metric Assn. (chmn. cert. metrication specialist program bd.). Presbyterian. Patentee in field. Home: 1922 Serge Ave San Jose CA 95130 Office: 1111 Lockheed Way Sunnyvale CA 94086

VITALE, ELENA PERSIS, audio-visual production specialist, writer, producer; b. Santa Monica, Calif., Jan. 29, 1949; d. James and Ada (Tourtas) V. B.A. in Filmwriting, UCLA, 1970. Sect. supr. Becker & Hayes, 1971; clk./typist Comarco Engrng Co., Ridgecrest, Calif., 1972-73; engrng. technician Naval Weapons Ctr., China Lake, Calif., 1974-75, writer, editor, 1975-79, audio-visual prodn. specialist, 1979—. Mem. Community Light Opera and Theater Assn. (pres. 1981, 82); charter mem., by-laws originating com. High Desert Council for Arts, Ridgecrest. Named Woman of Yr., Fed. Women's Program Naval Weapons Ctr., 1982; recipient Order Golden Sword, Am. Cancer Soc., 1981; Best actress award Community Light Opera and Theater Assn., 1974, 75, Best Supporting Actress award, 1977, 1980, Best Tech. Dir., 1980, Best Dir., 1978, 79; Comdr.'s award Naval Weapons Ctr., 1983. Mem. Nat. Assn. Female Execs. Lutheran. Clubs: China Lake Players, Entertainers Network of Desert. Home: 231 Perdew St Ridgecrest CA 93555 Office: Code 3444 Naval Weapons Ctr China Lake CA 93555

VITALE-ROHLWING, JOAN, photographer; b. N.Y.C., Mar. 3, 1953; d. John Baptist Vitale and Felicia Josephine Cerasuolo; m. Gary Lee Rohlwing, July 31, 1977. B.F.A. in Fine Arts, U. Ariz., 1975, B.F.A. in Art Edn., 1977, M.A. in Journalism, 1980. Art instr. Boy's Club Am., Bayside, N.Y., 1972-74; photographer Ariz. Daily Wildcat, U. Ariz., 1974-77; instr. photography Pima Coll., Tucson, 1977-78; chief photographer, mgr. U. Ariz. Photo Service, 1978-82; instr. Bisbee Color Photo Workshop, 1979-80. Recipient Tucson Firefighters Media award in photography, 1979. Mem. Profl. Photographers Assn. Am., Kappa Tau Alpha. Work appears in Sports Illustrated, Touchdown Mag., Ariz. Republic, Tucson Citizen, Ariz. Daily Star, Associated Press, Tombstone Epitaph, Wildcat Country. Home: 948 E Devonshire Apt 129 Phoenix AZ 85014 Office: 202-18 46 Rd Bayside NY 11361

VITALIE, CARL LYNN, pharmacist, lawyer; b. Clinton, Ind., Aug. 31, 1937; s. Paul Gilman and Martha Irrydell (Heidrick) V. D.Pharmacy, U. So. Calif., 1961, J.D., 1965; postgrad. mgmt. U. Calif., Los Angeles, 1977. Community pharmacy practice, various pharmacies, So. Calif., 1961-65; admitted to Va., bar, 1966, Calif. bar, 1967; staff atty. Am. Pharm. Assn., Washington, 1965-66; staff pharmacist Sav-On-Drugs, Inc., Anaheim, Calif., 1966-69, asst. dir. indsl. and pub. relations, 1969-71, dir. pharmacies, 1971-74, v.p. pharmacy ops., 1974—; lectr. pharmacy law and ethics U. So. Calif., Los Angeles, 1968-70; mem. Calif. Bd. Pharmacy, 1968-76; nat. pres. Student Am. Pharm. Assn., 1958-59; U.S. liaison sec. Internat. Pharm. Students' Fedn., 1959-62. Mem. heart attack intervention system com. Am. Heart Assn. Served with USAF, 1961-62, Calif. Air N.G., 1962-68. Licensed pharmacist, Calif., Nev., Tex.; diplomate Am. Bd. Diplomates in Pharmacy. Mem. Am. Bar Assn., Va. State Bar, State Bar Calif., Am. Mgmt. Assn., Soc. for Advancement Mgmt., Am. Soc. Pharmacy Law, Am., Calif. pharm. assns., Nat. Assn. Bds. Pharmacy, Acad. Gen. Practice Pharmacy, Town Hall Calif., Delta Theta Phi, Phi Delta Chi. Club: Masons. Author: (with Nancy J. Wolff) Establishment and Maintenance of Membership Standards in Professional Societies of Pharmacists, 1967; mem. editorial adv. bd. Legal Aspects of Pharmacy Practice, 1978-80; also articles in profl. jours. Office: 1500 S Anaheim Blvd Anaheim CA 92805

VIXIE, ANNE CHRISTINE, librarian; b. Whittier, Calif., Jan. 3, 1943; d. Orvin Leroy and Jean Viola (Sharp) V.; m. Gordon Allred Isbell, Apr. 20, 1960 (div.); children—Shannon, Gordon Jr., Allison. M.L.S., Calif. State U., 1975. Acquisitions librarian Longview (Wash.) Pub. Library, 1974-76; communications specialist Northwest Pub. Power Assn., Vancouver, Wash., 1977-78; bus. research supr. Lamb-Weston, Inc., Portland, Oreg., 1978—. Spl. libraries rep. Washington County Coop. Library Services Bd., 1982-83. Mem. Spl. Libraries Assn. (sec., treas. Oreg. chpt. 1982-83), Women in Communications. Office: PO Box 23517 Portland OR 97223

VLACHOS, ANGIE, manufacturing company executive, importer; b. Kalamazoo, Feb. 15, 1935; s. Nick and Katine (Moritou) V.; m. Jeanne Lambros, June 15, 1966 (div.). B.A., Kalamazoo Coll., 1956. Formerly with Brunswick Corp., Cleve. Pneumatic Co., Water Lift Co., U.S. Industries, Allen Electric Co., Chgo. Threaded Fastners Co., Hanson-Hawk Co.; with Cal Custom Accessories, 1969-75; pres. N.M.I. Industries, Inc., Marina Del Rey, Calif., 1975—. Served with USNR, 1952-60. Republican. Greek Orthodox. Club: Marina City (Marina Del Rey). Office: PO Box 9177 Marina Del Rey CA 90291

VLAD, ADRIAN AUREL, aerospace architect; b. Transylvania, Rumania, Feb. 10, 1943; came to U.S., 1978; s. Aurel C. and Elisabeth M. (Kovacs) V., M.Aerospace Engring., Bucharest Inst. Tech., 1965. Mem. mgmt. team TAROM Airlines, until 1970; mem. design team of advanced attack helicopter AAH-64, Hughes Helicopter Co., Culver City, Calif.; mem. design team of space shuttles Columbia and Challenger, Space div. Rockwell Internat., Downey, Calif., 1979-81; design engr. Adams Rite Products Inc., Glendale, Calif., 1982—; mem. design team IS29D, IS28B, IS29E, IS28M2 high performace sailplanes, also IAR-822, IAR-823 and IAR-824 aircraft; interior and exterior designer of Allouette III-316 B and Puma IAR-SA330 helicopters. Recipient spl. award for 2-stage satellite booster Bucharest Inst. Tech., 1966. Mem. AIAA. Club: Langlaufers (Downey, Calif). Author: French-Romanian Aerospace Dictionary, 1973; designer liquid rocket engine AV-1. Home: 10520 Stamps Rd Downey CA 90241

VLAY, GEORGE JOHN, engrng. exec.; b. Buffalo, Dec. 1, 1927; s. John and Victoria (Mili) V.; B.S. in Elec. Engring., U. Buffalo, 1953, postgrad., 1954-56; m. Betty Jo Wayland, July 21, 1949; children—Vanessa Michelle, Susan Victoria, George John. Project engr. electronics R.B. Warman, Buffalo, 1954-56, Aero Comdr. Corp., Norman, Okla., 1956-61, GTE/Sylvania, Williamsville, N.Y., 1961-66; mgr. advanced communications systems Philco-Ford, Palo Alto, Calif., 1966-78; dir. bus. devel. and planning Ford Aerospace Corp., Palo Alto, 1978-82; dir. tech. affairs Ford Aerospace and Communications Corp., Palo Alto, 1982—. Served with USAF, 1946-49. Registered profl. engr., Okla. Mem. Air Force Assn., Armed Forces Communications and Electronics Assn., IEEE (sr.), AIAA, Pi Mu Epsilon. Republican. Methodist. Home: 32 Yerba Buena Ave Los Altos CA 94022 Office: 3939 Fabian Way Palo Alto CA 94303

VOBEJDA, WILLIAM FRANK, aerospace engineer; b. Lodgepole, S.D., Dec. 5, 1918; s. Robert and Lydia (Stefek) V.; m. Virginia Parker, Oct. 24, 1942; children—William N., Margaret, Mary Joan, Barbara, Lori. B.C.E., S.D. Sch. Mines and Tech., 1942. Registered profl. engr., Colo. Stress analyst Curtiss Wright Corp., Columbus, Ohio, 1942-45; civil/hydraulic engr. Bur. Reclamation, Denver, 1945-54; mech. supr. Stearns Roger Corp., Denver, 1954-62; mgr. Martin Marietta Corp., Denver, 1962—, mgr. engring. M-X Program, 1978—. Active Boy Scouts Am. Recipient Silver Beaver award. Mem. AIAA. Democrat. Roman Catholic. Clubs: St. Louis Men's, K.C., Martin Marietta Chess.

VOEGELIN, ERIC, political scientist; b. Cologne, Germany, Jan. 3, 1901; came to U.S., 1938; s. Otto and Elisabeth (Ruehl) V.; m. Lissy Onken, July 30, 1932. Dr. rer. pol., U. Vienna, 1922, Habilitation, 1928; hon. doctorate Marquette U., Notre Dame U., Colo. Coll., 1980, U. Augsburg, (W. Ger.), 1981, Dominican Sch. Philosophy and Theology, 1982, Emory U., 1983. Asst. in law faculty, Vienna, 1923-24; privatdozent, 1929; extraordinarius, 1936; dismissed by Nazis 1938; instr., tutor, Harvard, 1938-39, Bennington Coll., 1939; asst. prof. U. Ala., 1939-42; assoc. prof. La. State U., 1942-46, prof., 1946-52, Boyd prof., 1952-58; prof. polit. sci., U. Munich (W. Ger.), 1958-68; Henry Salvatori disting. scholar Hoover Instn., Stanford U. (Calif.), 1968-74, sr. research fellow, 1974—. Recipient Gold medal of City of Munich, 1981. Mem. Am. Polit. Sci. Assn. Author The Science of Politics, 1952; Order and History, Vol. I, 1956, Vol. II, 1957, Vol. III, 1957, Vol. IV, 1974; Anamnesis, 1966; From Enlightenment to Revolution, 1975; also texts in German.

VOELKEL, AUGUST GENE, cardiologist; b. Huntingburg, Ind., Dec. 26, 1945; s. August Andrew and Lois Evelyn (Thacker) V.; B.S. in Mech. Engring., Purdue U., 1968; M.D., Ind. U., 1973; m. Virginia Kay Anderson, June 28, 1969; children—Marna Ann, Laura Kay. Instr. elec. engring. Purdue U., 1969; intern Meth. Hosp of Ind., Indpls., 1973-74; Harvard fellow, resident in internal medicine New Eng. Deaconess, Peter Bent Brigham hosps., Boston, 1974-76; cardiology fellow Harvard-W. Roxbury VA Hosp., Boston, 1976-78; practice medicine specializing in cardiology, Walnut Creek, Calif., 1978—; staff cardiologist John Muir Hosp., Walnut Creek, 1978—; asst. clin. prof. medicine U. Calif., Davis, 1979—. Diplomate Am. Bd. Internal Medicine, Bd. Cardiovascular Diseases. Fellow Am. Coll. Chest Physicians, Am. Coll. Cardiology, ACP; mem. Am. Heart Assn. Club: Rotary (Concord, Calif.). Contbr. articles to profl. jours. Office: 130 La Casa Via Walnut Creek CA 94598 also 2600 Park Ave Concord CA 94520

VOGEL, LAURENCE, lawyer; b. N.Y.C., Dec. 17, 1936; s. Moe and Sylvia (Miller) V.; A.B. cum laude, CUNY, 1957; J.D., U. Va., 1960; LL.M., NYU, 1964; m. Anna Lise Andreasen, May 24, 1973; children—Peter Andrew, Carsten Dyhr. Bar: N.Y. 1961. Assoc. firm Cadwalader, Wickersham & Taft, N.Y.C., 1960-64; asst. U.S. atty., chief civil div. So. Dist. N.Y., 1964-69; mem. Schaeffer, Dale & Vogel, N.Y.C., 1970-75, Greenbaum, Wolff & Ernst, N.Y.C., 1976-82; pres. DFS Group Ltd., 1979—. Bd. dirs. Palama Settlement; trustee U. Va. Law Sch. Found., U. Hawaii Found., Rehab. Hosp. of Pacific; chmn. bd. dirs. Honolulu Symphony, Hawaii Pub. Radio, Aloha Bowl, Served with U.S. Army., 1960-61. Mem. Am. Bar Assn., Fed. Bar Council (pres. 1968-70, chmn. bd. dirs. 1970-72), Honolulu C. of C. (bd. dirs.), Order of Coif, Phi Delta Phi. Jewish. Clubs: University (N.Y.C.); Farmington Country (Charlottesville, Va.); Honolulu Internat. Country, Pacific, Waialae Country (Honolulu). Assoc. editor U. Va. Law Rev.; contbr. articles to profl. jours. Home: 3056 La Pietra Circle Honolulu HI 96815 Office: 2255 Kuhio Ave Honolulu HI 96815

VOGEL, VIRGIL WILLIAM, film dir.; b. Peoria, Ill.; s. William James and Maude C. (Stark) V.; student public schs., Pekin, Ill.; children—James Francis, Kenneth Lee. With Universal Pictures, Universal City, Calif., 1940-59, film editor, 1956-57, producer-dir., 1957-59; dir. M.C.A., Hollywood, Calif., 1959—; free-lance dir., 1965—; dir. feature films, including: Mole People, 1956, Sword of Ali Baba, 1965; dir. numerous TV films, shows, including: Wagon Train, Bonanza, Streets of San Francisco, Police Story, Centennial. Served with USAAF, 1942-45. Decorated D.F.C., Air medal with 2 oak leaf clusters; recipient Eddie award as Best TV Dir. of Yr. for Bonanza, 1965. Democrat. Christian Scientist. Author TV stories for Wagon Train series. Office: 5550 Colbath Ave Van Nuys CA 91401

VOGELSANG, ROBERT FREDERICK, scientific instrument company official; b. Pekin, Ill., Nov. 9, 1930; s. Louis Ralph and Gladys Manila (Frederickson) V.; B.S. in Chemistry, Bradley U., 1954; grad. U.S. Air Force ground electronics officers course, 1956; postgrad. in bus. law U. Miss., 1955-56; postgrad. in chemistry Calif. State U., Long Beach, 1958-59; m. Shirley Ann McGlenn, June 23, 1957; children—Stephen Kurt, Mark Richard. Research chemist Dept. Agr., Peoria, Ill., 1955; with Beckman Instruments Inc., 1957-71, 76-79, mgr. sci. essentials div., fgn. dept. mgr. for Latin Am., Pacific ops. mgr. Internat. div., v.p. Internat div. Beckman de Mex., nat. accounts mgr. Process Instruments div., Fullerton, Calif.; dir. mktg. Ultra-Violet Products Inc., San Gabriel, Calif., 1972-75; procurement exec. for instruments and control systems Fluor Engrs. & Constructors, Inc., Irvine, Calif., 1980-82; mktg. adminstr. Horiba Instruments, Irvine, Calif., 1982—. Active YMCA Indian Guides, Whittier, Calif., 1965-66; bd. dirs. troop 530 and 337C Pioneer council Boy Scouts Am., 1967-72; bd. dirs. La Mirada (Calif.) Football League, 1973-74; trees. Maverick Little League baseball, Whittier, 1975-76. Served to 1st lt. USAF, 1955-57; capt. Res. Mem. So. Calif. Meter Assn., Instrument Soc. Am. (treas. Orange County chpt.), Am. Mgmt. Assn. Republican. Roman Catholic. Inventor in field. Home: 15282 Woodcrest Dr Whittier CA 90604 Office: 333 Michelson Dr Irvine CA 92730

VOGET, JANE J., public policy planner, mediator; b. Montreal, Que., Can., Jan. 2, 1949; d. Fred W. and Mary Kay (Mee) Voget; B.A. in German and Anthropology, So. Ill. U., 1971, M.S. in Planning and Community Devel., 1977. Program mgr. State of Ill. Dept. Commerce and Community Affairs, Springfield, 1975-78, HUD, Washington, 1978; mem. White House Staff, Office of Asst. to Pres. for Intergovtl. Affairs, Washington, 1979-80; exec. dir. Ctr. for Collaborative Problem Solving, San Francisco, 1981—. Mem. admissions com. United Way Bay Area, 1983. Mem. Am. Arbitration Assn., Community Dispute Services Panel. Democrat. Roman Catholic.

VOGLER, GEORGE MICHAEL, accountant, consultant, educator; b. San Diego, Calif., July 12, 1946; s. George Lester, Jr., and Frances Evelyn (Clarke) V.; m. Patience Elaine Hupp, Aug. 23, 1969; children—George Michael, Amy Rebecca. B.S., U. Colo., 1969; M.S.B.A., U. No. Colo., 1982; postgrad. U. Denver, 1982. C.P.A., Colo. Acctg. mgr. Miller Internat., Inc., Denver, 1969-71; acctg. mgr. Gerry div. OSI, Denver, 1971-73; asst. corp. controller Rocky Mountain Prestress, Inc., Sheridan, Colo., 1973-77; sec.-treas., dir. Libraries, Unltd., Inc., Englewood, Colo., 1977—, also asst. corp. controller A.R. Wilfley & Sons, Englewood, 1978—; tchr. C.P.A. rev. courses; cons. to small bus.; guest speaker SBA seminar, 1980. Mem. Colo. Soc. C.P.A.s, Nat. Assn. Accts. Republican. Methodist. Contbr. book revs. to Am. Ref. Books Ann., 1978-83. Home: 5774 S Lansing Ct Englewood CO 80111 Office: 6931 S Yosemite St Englewood CO 80112

VOGNILD, LARRY LEE, state senator; b. Spokane, Jan. 21, 1932; s. James Howard and Helen Mildred (Pinkerton) V.; children—Valeria Ann, Margo Elaine. Mem. City of Everett (Wash.) Fire Dept., 1954-78, bn. chief, 1976-78; mem. Wash. Senate, 1979—. Served with USN, 1951-54. Democrat. Lutheran.

VOGT, DANIEL JOHN, ecosystem ecologist; b. Brisbane, Australia, Dec. 14, 1945; came to U.S., 1946, naturalized, 1960; s. Harry Frank and Noeleen May (Lowry) V.; m. Kristiina Ann Besmond, Dec. 22, 1973. B.S. in Biology, N.Mex. State U., 1968, M.S. in Agronomy, 1976; Ph.D. in Forestry, U. Wash., 1983. Asst. plant propagation supr. North Haven Gardens, Dallas, 1971-72; range aide Rocky Mountain Forest and Range Expt. Sta., Albuquerque, 1973; research asst. agronomy dept. N.Mex. State U., Las Cruces, 1973-75; research asst. Coll. Forest Resources, U. Wash., Seattle, 1976—; assoc. mem. World Devel. Cons., Inc. Served with F.A., U.S. Army, 1968-70. Decorated Air medal, Bronze Star. Mem. Am. Inst. Biol. Scis., Am. Soc. Agronomy, Can. Jour. of Forest Research, Ecol. Soc. Am., Internat. Soc. Soil Sci., Soil Sci. Soc. Am., Sigma Xi. Home: 10042 9th Ave NW Seattle WA 98177 Office: Coll Forest Resources AR-10 U Wash Seattle WA 98195

VOGT, PETER KLAUS, scientist; b. Braunau, Germany, Mar. 10, 1932; came to U.S., 1959; naturalized, 1968; s. Joseph M. and Elizabeth J. (Thiemann) V.; B.S., U. Würzburg (Germany), 1955; Ph.D., U. Tübingen (Germany), 1959; postgrad. U. Calif., Berkeley, 1959-62. Asst. prof. pathology U. Colo., 1962-66, asso. prof., 1966-67; asso. prof. microbiology U. Wash., Seattle, 1967-69, prof., 1970-71; Hastings prof. microbiology U. So. Calif., 1971-77, Hastings Disting. prof., 1978—, chmn. dept., 1980—. Named Calif. Scientist of Yr., 1975; recipient Vogeler prize Max-Planck Soc., 1976. Mem. Am. Soc. Microbiology, Nat. Acad. Scis., AAAS, N.Y. Acad. Scis. Roman Catholic. Editor, Virology, 1965—, Current Topics in Microbiology and Immunology, 1966—; mem. editorial bd. Jour. of Virology, 1966-72, Intervirology, 1973-75. Office: 2011 Zonal Ave Los Angeles CA 90033

VOIGHT, FRANK EDWARD, service orgn. exec.; b. Redlands, Calif., Dec. 28, 1915; s. Julius Edward and Mary Lucille (Cordero) V.; B.A. in Polit. Sch., U. Redlands, 1949; M.S. in Public Adminstrn., U. So. Calif., 1950; m. Betty Lou Collins, June 15, 1947; children—Susan Lynn Voight Stoney, Steven E. (dec.), Cynthia L. With Allied Trades & Fire Prevention, 1935-43; with CSC, 1950-76, communications staff officer San Bernardino Air Materiel Area, Norton AFB, Calif., 1960-63, chief resources info. Space and Missile Systems Orgn., Los Angeles Air Force Sta., 1966-76; dir. community services Goodwill Industries of Inland Counties, Inc., San Bernardino, Calif., 1976-77. Chmn. heritage com. Bicentennial Commn., Rialto, Calif., 1975-76; chmn. adv. bd. ARC, San Bernardino County, 1982—; bd. dirs. Am. Lung Assn., San Bernardino County, 1982-84; interim exec. dir., 1982; pres. Cerebral Palsy Assn., City of Hope; mem. nat. adv. bd. Am. Security Council; elder Seventh-Day Adventist Ch., Fontana, Calif.; chmn. lay adv. com. SE Calif. Conf., Seventh-Day Adventist Ch.; mem. Republican Nat. Com., Rep. Nat. Congressional Com., Rep. Presdl. Task Force, 1981-82. Served with M.C., U.S. Army, 1943-44. Recipient certificate of appreciation local lung assn., 1965-67, Cerebral Palsy Assn., 1963-64, City of Hope, 1964; named Citizen of Year, Rialto (Calif.) Inter-Service Club Council, 1961. Mem. Pub. Relations Soc. Am. (treas. Calif. Inland Empire chpt. 1978-79), Hist. Soc. Rialto, Am. Legion. Republican. Adventist. Club: Kiwanis (pres. local club 1976-77) (Rialto). Co-author: A History of Rialto, rev. edit., 1976.

VOIGT, ROBERT LEE, plant science educator, plant breeder; b. Hebron, Neb., Nov. 23, 1924; s. John Lorenzo and Cleo Libby (Heller) V.; m. Jane Carol Bridgman, June 9, 1951; children—David Robert, Carol Lee, Ann Elizabeth, Janice Marie. B.S., U. Nebr., 1949, M.S., 1955; Ph.D., Iowa State U., 1959. Cert. profl. agronomist. Fieldman, First Trust Co., Lincoln, Neb., 1949-52; instr. Iowa State U., Ames, 1955-59; asst. prof. plant sci. U. Ariz., Tucson, 1959-64, assoc. prof., 1964-69, prof., 1969—. Chmn. Ft. Lowell dist., Catalina council Boy Scouts Am. Served with USN, 1943-46, 1952-53. Mem. Am. Soc. Agronomy, Crop Sci. Soc. Am., Western Soc. Crop Sci., Ariz.-Nev. Acad. Sci., Sorghum Improvement Conf. N. Am. (bd. dirs., editor Sorghum Newsletter), Alpha Gamma Rho Alumni Corp. (past pres. Ariz. chpt.), Gamma Sigma Delta (past pres. Ariz. chpt.), Sigma XI. Republican. Methodist. Contbr. numerous articles to profl. jours. Home: 2131 E La Madera Dr Tucson AZ 85719 Office: Dept Plant Scis U Ariz Tucson AZ 85721

VOIGT, WILLIAM FREDERICK, state official; b. Washington, Oct. 29, 1928; s. Charles Sebastian and Mary Aelese (Glover) V.; m. Dolores Catherine Voigt, Apr. 21, 1959; children—Deborah C., Geoffrey B. B.S. in Polit. Sci., U. Md., 1960; postgrad. Kans. State U., 1972-73. Commd. officer U.S. Air Force, 1950, advanced through grades to lt. col., ret., 1974; mgr., account rep. Internat. Coin, Inc., Phoenix, 1974-76; dir. adminstrn. Ariz. Gov.'s Office of Econ. Planning and Devel., Phoenix, 1976-83. Mem. adv. com. Maricopa County Skill Ctr., 1981—. Decorated Bronze Star, Air medal. Mem. Mesa C. of C., Air Force Assn., Ret. Officers Assn., Am. Soc. Pub. Adminstrn., Ariz. Assn. Indsl. Devel., Am. Aviation Hist. Soc. Clubs: U.S. Naval Acad. Parent's, Order of Daedalians.

VOISENAT, FRANCIS (FRANK) WILLIAM, quality assurance engr.; b. Englewood, N.J., Aug. 21, 1935; s. Frank and Mary (Unalt) V.; B.S., Manhattan Coll., 1957; postgrad. U. Calif., Santa Barbara, 1969-71; m. Jan. 8, 1966 (div. Apr. 1972); children—Michelle Marie, Melissa Rene. Human engring. analyst Boeing A/C Co., Vandenberg AFB, Calif., 1965-66; sr. cngr. scientist Manned Orbital Lab., McDonnel Douglas Co., Vandenberg AFB, 1966-70; sr. quality control engr. Lunar Rover, Gen. Motors Co., Goleta, Calif., 1970-71; sr. project quality assurance engr. Infra red Components Santa Barbara Research Center, subs. Hughes Aircraft Co., Goleta, Calif., 1971—. Instr., supply officer U.S. Power Squadron, Santa Barbara, Calif. Served with USAFR, 1957-77. Mem. Am. Soc. Quality Control, Human Factors Soc., Pen and Sword Soc., Apt. Owners Assn. Club: Elks. Home: 415 Alameda Padre Serra Santa Barbara CA 93103 Office: 75 Coromar Goleta CA 93017

VOISINE, JOAN MARY, opera assn. exec.; b. London, Nov. 29, 1937; d. William Charles and Emily Rebecca (Pavitt) Day; m. Gerald Voisine, Sept. 6, 1968. Student pub. schs., London. Personal asst. to tech. dir. Royal Opera House, Covent Garden, London, 1960-67; exec. sec. to comptroller O'Keefe Centre Theatre, Toronto, Can., 1967-68; adminstr. Burlington Office Centre, Ont., Can., 1968-70; artistic adminstr. Vancouver (B.C., Can.) Opera Assn., 1971—. Office: Vancouver Opera Assn 548 Cambie St Vancouver BC V6B 2N7 Canada

VOLAK, JO ANNE, contract engring. co. exec.; b. Norway, Iowa, May 5, 1939; d. Carl Edward and Carmelita (Jayne) Miller; student Kirkwood Community Coll., Cedar Rapids, Iowa, 1960-62; divorced; children—Diane Lee Volak Knuckles, David James, Donald Todd, Deborah Anne. Clk., U.S. Postal Service, Cedar Rapids, 1967-69; sales sec. Best Barber Supply Co., Cedar Rapids, 1969-71, Electronics Communications, Ltd., St. Louis, 1971-72; exec. sec. B'nai B'rith Hillel Found., St. Louis, 1973-76; personnel mgr., office mgr., saleswomen Butler Service Group, Inc., St. Louis, 1976-79; sr. recruiter Collins-Phoenix Co., Tempe, Ariz., 1979-80; br. mgr. Lehigh Design Co., Scottsdale, Ariz., 1980—. Mem. Phoenix Mayor's Com. on Hiring Handicapped. Mem. Am. Bus. Women's Assn., Phoenix Personnel Mgrs. Assn., Nat. Tech. Services Assn. (past chpt. sec., past chpt. pres.; nat. dir.), Western Fraternal Life Assn. Mormon. Office: 4130 N Marshall Way #1 Scottsdale AZ 85251

VOLK, VERIL VAN, soil chemist, educator; b. Montgomery, Ala., Nov. 18, 1938; s. Garth William and Alice Marie (Peters) V.; m. Doris Mangum, Sept. 7, 1968. B.S., Ohio State U., 1960, M.S., 1961; Ph.D., U. Wis., 1965. Research assoc. U. Wis., Madison, 1965-66; asst. prof. soil sci. Oreg. State U., Corvallis, 1966-70, assoc. prof., 1970-79, prof., 1979—; asst. dir. Oreg. Agrl. Expt. Sta., Corvallis, 1980—. Served with Air N.G., 1956-62. Danforth fellow, 1960; Mershon Nat. Scholar, 1958-60. Mem. Am. Soc. Agronomists, Soil Sci. Soc. Am., Weed Sci. Soc., Council Agrl. Sci. and Tech. Lutheran. Club: Kiwanis. Office: Dept Soil Sci Oreg State U Corvallis OR 97331

VOLLMAYER, KARL A., librarian; b. Toledo, Ohio; s. George John and Ruth (Coles) V.; m. Catherine Zarri, Sept. 6, 1954; children—Carla, Anne, Mary. B.A., U. San Francisco, 1950; M.L.S., U. Wash., 1951. Reference librarian Washoe County Library, Reno, Nev., 1951-53; asst. librarian Richmond (Calif.) Pub. Library, 1953-60; city librarian Redwood City (Calif.) Pub. Library, 1960—. Served with USAF, 1941-48. Mem. ALA, Calif. Library Assn., San Mateo County Hist. Soc. Club: Book of Calif. Home: 286 Fulton St Redwood City CA 94062 Office: 881 Jefferson Ave Redwood City CA 94063

VOLLMER, WILLIAM MARION, biostatistician, educator, consultant; b. Balt., May 6, 1954; s. Frederick Joseph and Margaret Helen (Kennedy) V.; m. Jean Mary Moore, June 30, 1979; children—Adam Patrick, Eric Thomas, B.S. magna cum laude, U. Notre Dame, 1976; Ph.D., U. Wash., 1981. Postdoctoral fellow dept. stats. U. Waterloo (Ont., Can.), 1980-82; research instr. depts. physiology, psychiatry Oreg. Health Scis. U., Portland, 1982—; biostatistician Ctr. Study Biologic Effects Volcanic Ash. Mem. Am. Statis. Assn., Biometric Soc. Contbr. articles to profl. jours. Office: Dept Physiology L334 Oreg Health Scis U Portland OR 97201

VOLLUM, HOWARD, business executive; b. 1913; B.A., Reed Coll., 1936; married. With Murdock Radio & Appliance Co., 1936-41; a founder, chmn. Tektronix, Inc., 1946—; dir. U.S. Nat. Bank Oreg., Pacific Power & Light Co. Served with U.S. Signal Corps, 1941-45. Office: Tektronix Inc 4900 SW Griffith Dr Beaverton OR 97005*

VOLPERT, DON WAYNE, photographer; b. Denison, Tex., Oct. 8, 1944; s. James Charles and Eda Louise (Mooney) V.; student Austin Coll., 1959-60, So. Meth. U., 1960-61, Tex. Christian U., 1962-63, North Tex. State U., 1963-67, U. Nev., 1975-78, U. San Diego, 1979-80, U. Calif., 1979, Los Angeles City Coll., 1981-82; m. Helene Micki Ho-Tack, Feb. 9, 1976. Asst. shift boss Del Webb, Las Vegas, Nev., 1968-69; dist. mgr. POTW, Inc., Las Vegas, 1969-72; asst. v.p., mgr. sales Title Ins. & Trust Co., Las Vegas, 1972-78; asst. v.p. Nat. Title Services/Ticor, Los Angeles, 1978-80; mgr. Wall-Maes, 1981; pres., ASP, 1981—; with Am. Bell, Inc., 1982-83; photographer, 1967—. Counselor, Boy Scouts Am., Las Vegas, 1969—; fund raising coordinator United Way, Las Vegas, 1972-77; vol. handicapped program dir. YMCA, Las Vegas, 1968-73, swim program dir., 1969-70; program cons. Lorenzi Park Handicapped Center, 1972-73; vol. Helen J. Stewart Sch. for Handicapped, 1968—, dir. swim program, 1968-72, swim program cons., 1973—; bd. dirs. Girl Scouts U.S.A., 1974-75; founder, dir. Aquarian Swim Club for Underprivileged, 1972-75; 1st vice chmn. ARC, 1975, water safety instr. trainer, 1972—; bd. mem. A Silent Works; mem. Presdl. Task Force, 1981—, U.S. Senatorial Club, 1983—. Served with USN, 1967-69. Recipient Humanitarian award ARC, 1973, Bd. Mem. of Year award, 1974, Vol. of Year award, 1972; Aquarian's Citizen award, 1974, Good Samaritan award, 1974. Mem. Calif. Surveyors Assn., So. Nev. Mortgage Bankers Assn. (sec.-treas.), So. Nev. Homebuilders Assn. (polit. action com.), Nev. Land Title Assn., Kern County Bd. Realtors, Las Vegas Bd. Realtors, Profl. Businessmen's Assn., Greater Los Angeles C. of C., Latin C. of C., Las Vegas C. of C., Henderson C. of C., Bakersfield C. of C., Town Hall Assn., Am. Arts Soc., Guild for Preservation Arts, Writers Guild, ANA Film Soc., Nat. Trust Hist. Preservation, Internat. Platform Assn., Phi Kappa Sigma (Grand Delta 1981—), Beta Eta (chpt. pres. 1965-66). Republican. Anglican Catholic. Clubs: Exchange, Kern Trade. Ltd. edit. publs.; Reflexions; Close Images; Foreign Matter; Dennis and Friends. Home: PO Box 2177 Las Vegas NV 89101 Office: PO Box 2177 Las Vegas NV 89101

VOLPERT, RICHARD SIDNEY, lawyer; b. Cambridge, Mass., Feb. 16, 1935; s. Samuel Abbot and Julia (Fogel) V.; B.A., Amherst Coll., 1956; LL.B., Columbia U., 1959; m. Marcia Flaster, June 11, 1958; children—Barry, Sandy, Linda, Nancy. Admitted to Calif., bar, 1960; mem. firm O'Melveny & Myers, Los Angeles, 1959—, partner, 1967—; lectr. in field. Bd. dirs. Jewish Fedn. Council of Los Angeles, 1976—, v.p., 1978-81, chmn. community relations com., 1977-80; pres. Los Angeles County Natural History Mus. Found., 1978—, trustee, 1974—, bd. govs., 1980—; bd. councilors, chmn. U. So. Calif. Law Center, 1979—; vice chmn. Nat. Jewish Community Relations Adv. Council, 1981—, exec. com., 1978—; bd. govs., bd. dirs. U. Judaism, 1973—, chmn. Center on Contemporary Jewish Life, 1975—; chmn. bd. dirs. Valley Beth Shalom, Encino, Calif., 1972-75, named Man of Yr., 1978, dir., 1964—; mem. capital program major gifts com. Amherst Coll., 1978—; v.p., bd. dirs. Los Angeles Wholesale Produce Market Devel. Corp., 1978—; exec. bd. Am. Jewish Com., Los Angeles, 1967—, mem. nat. exec. council, 1977—; mem., vice chmn. Los Angeles County Econ. Devel. Council, 1978-82; bd. dirs. Jewish Community Found., 1981—, others. Mem. Los Angeles Area C. of C., Am. Bar Assn., Am. Bar Found. (fellow), Los Angeles County Bar Assn. (bd. trustees 1968-70, chmn. real property sect. 1974-75), Calif. Bar Assn., Urban Land Inst., Am. Soc. Planning Ofcls., Central City Assn. Jewish. Club: Univ. Editor, chmn. Calif. State Bar Jour., 1972-73; editor, chmn. Los Angeles Bar Jour., 1965, 66, 67; contbr. articles to profl. jours. Home: 4001 Stansbury Ave Sherman Oaks CA 91423 Office: O'Melveny and Myers 400 S Hope St Los Angeles CA 90071

VOLZ, MICHAEL GEORGE, chemist; b. Long Beach, Calif., Nov. 30, 1945; s. Edgar Louis and Fannie Rae (Young) V.; m. Adrienne Jane Machado, Mar. 17, 1968; children—Carla Marie, Eric Michael, Raphael Francis. B.S., U. Calif.-Berkeley, 1967, Ph.D., 1972. Cert. profl. soil scientist. Asst. research biochemist U. Calif.-Berkeley, 1973-75; asst. plant physiologist Conn. Agrl. Expt. Sta., New Haven, 1975-77; assoc. san. microbiologist State of Calif., Berkeley, 1977-82, pub. health chemist, 1982—; cons. characterization of toxic material dumpsites, influence pub. health and environ. quality, State of Calif.; reviewer jours. in field. Mem. AAAS, Assn. Ofcl. Analytical Chemists, Am. Soc. Agronomy, Crop Sci. Soc. Am., Internat. Humic Substances Soc., Soil Sci. Soc. Am. Democrat. Roman Catholic. Contbr. articles to profl. jours. Office: HMLS/DOHS 2151 Berkeley Way Berkeley CA 94704

VOMHOF, DANIEL WILLIAM, forensic consultant; b. Grant, Nebr., Apr. 19, 1938; s. Milton W. and Viola H. (Louis) V.; m. Lula B. James, Feb. 14, 1977; children—Daniel William, Tanya, Lisa. B.S., Augsburg Coll., 1962; M.S., U. Ariz., 1966, Ph.D., 1967. Research asst. Ariz. Expt. Sta., Tucson, 1962-67, Nat. Bur. Standards, Washington, 1967-69; dir. U.S. Customs Lab., Chgo., 1969-72; forensic scientist, San Diego, 1972-73; pres. Expert Witness Services, Inc., La Mesa, Calif., 1974—. Recipient Spl. Achievement award U.S. Treasury, 1971, 73, 74; citation Nat. Bur. Standards. Fellow Am. Inst. Chemists (cert.); mem. N.Y. Acad. Scis., AAAS, Am. Chem. Soc., ASTM, Nat. Fire Protection Assn., Ind. Assn. Questioned Document Examiners, Evidence Photographers Internat., Forensic Cons. Assn., Sigma Xi. Contbr. articles to profl. jours. Home: 8387 University Ave La Mesa CA 92041 Office: 8381 University Ave La Mesa CA 92041

VON BLENK-SCHMIDT, LOTHAR, engr.; b. Germany, Nov. 1, 1919; s. Hans Karl and Elfride Victoria (von Blenk) S.; came to U.S., 1952, naturalized, 1957; Mech. Engr., Tech. U. Berlin, 1943; postgrad. UCLA, 1963, U. So. Calif., 1966, U.S. Army Indsl. Coll., 1971; M.S. in Engring., Columbia Pacific U., 1981, Dr.Engring., 1982; m. Topper Wilson, July 23, 1959. Sr. engr. design and devel. of weapons and equipment Exptl. Proving Ground, Berlin, 1941-45; design powerplant control heavy duty Muehlen-Industrie-Aktiengesellschaft, Frankfurt/Main, Germany, 1949-52; engr. Hallett, Inglewood, Calif., 1952-54; test engr. Mpls./Honeywell Indsl. Co., Gardena, Calif., 1954-57; mil. flight safety specialist Lockheed Air Co., Los Angeles, 1959—. Mem. nat. adv. bd. Am. Security Council, 1973—; dep. sheriff Los Angeles County, 1973—. Served to comdr. German Army, 1940-45; prisoner-of-war, 1945-48. Named to Aviation Hall of Fame, 1977. Fellow Am. Inst. Aeros. and Astronautics (asso.); mem. U.S. Naval Inst., Soc. Airsafety Investigators, Solar Inst., Soc. Automotive Engrs., Am. Ordnance Assn., Epsilon Delta Chi. Mem. Divine Sci. Phd. Internat. Clubs: Cave des Roys, Trojan, Mach 2, Beverly Wilshire Shrine. Patentee in field. Home: 1246 Daniels Dr Los Angeles CA 90035

VONDERHEID, ARDA ELIZABETH, nursing administrator; b. Pitts., June 19, 1925; d. Louis Adolf and Hilda Barbara (Gerstacker) V.; diploma Allegheny Gen. Hosp. Sch. Nursing, 1946; B.S. in Nursing Edn., Coll. Holy Names, Oakland, Calif., 1956; M.S. in Nursing Adminstrn., UCLA, 1960. Head nurse Allegheny Gen. Hosp., Pitts., 1946-48; staff nurse Highland-Alameda County Hosp., Oakland, Calif., 1948-51, staff nurse poliomyelitis units, 1953-55; pvt. duty nurse Directory Registered Nurses Alameda County, Oakland, 1951-53; adminstrv. supervising nurse Poliomyelitis Respiratory and Rehab. Center, Fairmont, Alameda County Hosp., Oakland, 1955-58; night supr., relief asst. dir. nursing Peninsula Hosp., Burlingame, Calif., 1960, adminstrv. supr., 1961-62, inservice educator, 1963-69; staff nurse San Francisco Gen. Hosp., 1969, asst. dir. nurses, 1969-72; mem. faculty continuing edn. U. Calif., San Francisco, 1969-71; dir. nursing services Kaiser Permanente Med. Center, S. San Francisco, 1973-1982, asst. adminstr. Med. Center Nursing Services, 1982—. Chmn. edn. com. San Mateo County (Calif.) Cancer Soc., 1962-69; bd. dirs. San Mateo County Heart Assn., 1968-71; mem., foreman pro tem San Mateo County Civil Grand Jury, 1982-83. Cert. advanced nursing adminstrn. Mem. San Mateo County (dir. 1964-69, pres. elect 1967-68, pres. 1968-70), Golden Gate (1st v.p. 1974-78, dir. 1974-78), Calif., Am. nurses assns., Nat. League Nursing, Soc. for Nursing Service Adminstrs., State Practice and Edn. Council, AAUW, San Mateo County Grand Jury Assn., Calif. Grand Jury Assn., Sigma Theta Tau. Republican. Lutheran. Club: Kai-Perm. Contbr. articles in field to profl. jours. Home: 1047 Aragon Ct Pacifica CA 94044 Office: 1200 El Camino Real South San Francisco CA 94080

VON DER HEYDT, JAMES A(RNOLD), judge; b. Miles City, Mont., July 15, 1919; s. Harry Karl and Alice S. (Arnold) von der H.; A.B., Albion (Mich.) Coll., 1942; J.D., Northwestern U., 1951; m. Verna E. Johnson, May 21, 1952. Admitted to Alaska bar, 1951; pvt. law practice, Nome, 1953-59; judge Superior Ct., Juneau, Alaska, 1959-66; judge U.S. Dist. Ct., Alaska, 1966-73, chief judge, 1973—; U.S. commr., Nome, Alaska, 1951—; U.S. atty. div. 2, Dist. Alaska, 1951-53; mem. Ho. of Reps., Alaska Legislature, 1957-59. Pres. Anchorage Fine Arts Mus. Assn., 1969-72. Mem. Alaska Bar Assn. (bd. govs. 1955-59, pres.

1959-60), Wilson Ornithologists Soc., Sigma Nu, Phi Delta Phi. Clubs: Masons (32 deg.), Shriners. Specializing study Artic bird life. Office: US Courthouse and Fed Bldg Box 40 701 C St Anchorage AK 99513 also PO Box 1080 Anchorage AK 99510

VONDRICK, ART FRANK, environmental engineer, consultant; b. Chgo. Nov. 6, 1923; s. Frank J. and Antoinette (Pelikan) V.; m. Iva O. Fletcher, Dec. 23, 1978; children—Dean (dec.), Glen D. B.C.E., U. Wis., 1949. Cert. value specialist; registered profl. engr. Ill., Ariz., Calif., N. Mex., Tex., Utah. San. engr. Ind. State Bd. Health, Indpls., 1949-50; san. engr. Cook County (Ill.) Health Dept., Chgo., 1950-54; dist. engr. Chgo. Pump Co., 1954-58; dir. water and sewers dept. City of Phoenix, 1958-78; exec. v.p. Arthur Beard Engrs., Phoenix, 1978—. Chmn. Gov.'s Task Force on Emergency Planning for Water, 1966. Recipient Disting. Service Award in environ. control Nat. Clay Pipe Inst., 1972. Mem. Am. Water Works Assn. (utility Man of Yr. 1972), Water Pollution Control Fedn. (past pres., bd. dirs., Sidney Bedell award 1960), Am. Assn. Environ. Engrs. (diplomate), ASCE, Soc. Value Engrs., Central Ariz. Project Assn. (dir.), Ariz. Water and Pollution Control, Airz. Water Resources Com. (bd. dirs.). Episcopalian. Contbr. articles to profl. jours. Office: 4628 N 17th St Suite H-105 Phoenix AZ 85016

VON HOFFMANN, CHRISTINE ELVERA, educator; b. San Francisco, July 29, 1951; d. Emmet Morris and June Rose Carlson; B.A., teaching cert., U. Wash., Seattle, 1973, M.Ed. in Learning Disabilities (Orton Soc. scholar 1975), 1979; m. Ronald Steve Von Hoffman, Aug. 7, 1976; 1 son, Brett Jason. Pre-sch. tchr. Seattle Day Nursery Assn., 1969-73; spl. edn. tchr. severe and profoundly retarded Shoreline Sch. Dist., Seattle, 1973-76, curriculum editor and writer, 1975, learning disability tchr., 1976—; editorial bd. Wash. Coop. Curriculum Bd., 1975. Mem. Council Exceptional Children (chpt. v.p. 1979-80), Assn. Supervision and Curriculum Devel., Shoreline Sch. Ednl. Assn. Presbyterian. Author articles in field. Home: 5004 NE 188th St Seattle WA 98155 Office: 1815 N 155th St Seattle WA 98133

VON KOHORN, JEFFREY, clin. psychologist; b. N.Y.C., Mar. 31, 1949; s. Henry and Marcy Von K.; B.A., Northwestern U., 1971; M.A., Calif. Sch. Profl. Psychology, 1974, Ph.D., 1976; m. Nancy K. Lakeman, June 12, 1971; children—Daniel Adam, Jonathan Edward. Dir. client services Crisis House Work Devel. Center, El Cajon, Calif., 1976-78; cons. psychologist Mesa Vista Hosp., San Diego, 1980—; mem. faculty Edwards Inst. for Advanced Study, San Diego, 1980—; dir. clin. psychology Tri-Community Service Systems, San Diego, 1978—; sr. v.p., dir. Grid Research Corp., 1982—. Treas., bd. dirs. Crisis House, Inc., 1979-82. Mem. Am. Psychol. Assn., Assn. Advancement Psychology, Calif. State Psychol. Assn., Acad. San Diego Psychologists, San Diego Psychology and Law Soc. Office: 9619 Chesapeake Dr Suite 305 San Diego CA 92123

VON KRENNER, WALTHER GEORGE, artist, writer, art consultant and appraiser; b. W. Ger., June 26, 1940; s. Frederick and Anna-Marie (von Wolfrath) von K.; m. Hana Renate Geue, 1960; children—Michael P., Karen P. Privately educated by Swiss and English tutors; student of Asian studies, Japan, 1965-68; student of Southeast Asia studies, Buddhist U., Bankok, Thailand, Cambodia. Curator, v.p. Gallery Lahaina, Maui, Hawaii; pres. Internat. Valuation, Honolulu, 1974—; researcher culture of Indians of the No. Plains, Kalispell, Mont., 1980—. Mem. Am. Soc. Appraisers (pres., dir.). Author books on Oriental art. Office: 60 N Beretania Suite 2408 Honolulu HI 96817

VON RHEINWALD, EVA, psychologist; b. Prague, Czechoslovakia, Nov. 17, 1932; came to U.S., 1968, naturalized, 1975; d. Frantisek and Ludmila (Stara) Reinwald; m. Jaromir Otto Karel, July 17, 1956 (div.); 1 dau., Michaela Karlova. B.A. in Psychology summa cum laude (Univ. grantee), UCLA, 1975; M.A. in Psychology (J. Hovorkasscholar), Pepperdine U., 1976; Ph.D. in Profl. Psychology, U.S. Internat. U., 1979. Lic. marriage and family counselor, Nev. Author musicals, lyrics, move and TV scrips, short stories, translator, Prague, U.S., Can., 1952—; ballerina Nat. Theatre, Kosice Czechoslovakia, 1952-54, County Theatre, Pilsen, Czechoslovakia, 1954-61, Theatre of Prague, 1961-67, also TV appearances and European tours; vol. dance and movement therapist St. John's Hosp., Santa Monica, Calif., 1971-74; companion, community psychology project Ocean Side Residential Setting, Santa Monica, 1974; psychol. therapist trainee South Bay Therapeutic Clinic, Hawthorne, Calif., 1975-76; psychol. counselor trainee Clinic, Pepperdine U., 1975-76; psychol. counselor-trainee therapist Manhattan Beach (Calif.) Free Clinic, 1975-76; psychol. asst. Anxiety Treatment Center, San Diego, 1976-78; movement therapist Alvarado Convalescent and Rehab. Hosp., San Diego, 1977-78; clin. intern Las Vegas (Nev.) Mental Health Center, 1978-79; pvt. practice psychotherapy, marriage and family counseling, Las Vegas, 1979—; psychologist V, Las Vegas Mental Health Center, 1979-82; instr. U. Humanistic Studies, 1980—; condr. workshops in field; lectr. in field. Mem. Am. Psychol. Assn., Calif. State Psychol. Assn., Soc. Clin. Hypnosis San Diego, Am. Dance Therapist Assn., Am.-Czechoslovak Art and Sci. Orgn., AAUW, Acad. San Diego Psychologists, Assn. Humanistic Psychology. Clubs: Ski, Las Vegas, Club Med. Office: 2300 S Rancho Dr Suite 214 Las Vegas NV 89102

VON RIESEN, RICHARD DALE, ednl. adminstr.; b. Topeka, Apr. 8, 1935; s. Emil and Marian Virginia (Gregg) Von R.; B.B.A., Washburn U., 1960; M.S., U. Ill., 1962, Ph.D., 1968; m. Catherine Elizabeth Kanatzar, June 21, 1958; children—Gregory D., Michael A., Karen S. Asst. prof. bus. Colo. State U., 1964-66; asst. prof. to asso. prof. bus. Wichita State U., 1966-71; asso. prof. grad. program U. Wyo./AF Inst. Tech., Warren AFB, 1971—, resident adminstr., 1973-81; cons. mktg. and mktg. research. Bd. dirs. Cheyenne (Wyo.) Animal Shelter, 1973. Served with AUS, 1957. U. Ill. fellow in mktg., 1963-64. Mem. Am. Mktg. Assn., Am. Inst. Decision Scis., Phi Kappa Phi, Beta Gamma Sigma, Alpha Iota Delta. Clubs: Cheyenne Country, Cheyenne Execs. Author: Wyoming Market Data, 1975; Cheyenne Survey of Consumer Opinions and Buying Habits, 1974. Home: 5503 Syracuse Rd Cheyenne WY 82009 Office: AFIT Grad Program and Cheyenne MBA Program FE Warren AFB WY 82005

VON STROH, GORDON E., economist; b. Lockwood, Mo., Jan. 21, 1943; s. Edward C. and Hulda A. (Mein) V.; m. S. Patrice Von Stroh, Mar. 12, 1977; children—Christina M., Jonathan C., Justin E. B.A., Southwestern Coll., 1963; M.A., Kans. State U., 1964; Ph.D., U. Okla., 1967. Asst. prof. mgmt. U. Denver, 1967-71, assoc. prof., 1972-79, prof., 1979—; policy analyst and planner U.S. Dept. Transp., 1971-72. Chmn. bd. advisors St. John's Coll., 1980—; treas. Central City Opera House Assn., 1981—. Nat. Assn. Schs. of Pub. Adminstrn./Affairs fellow, 1971-72. Mem. Acad. Mgmt., Am. Econs. Assn., Am. Soc. Pub. Adminstrn. Republican. Lutheran. Clubs: City, Idea. Contbr. in field. Office: Grad Sch Bus Pub Mgmt U Denver Denver CO 80208

VON THADEN, ARTHUR GREGG, real estate exec.; b. Washington, Mar. 23, 1932; s. Arthur Herman and Helen Louise (Gregg) Von T.; m. Janis Newcomb Warren, June 11, 1983; children—Paul Gregg, Brinton. B.A., Trinity Coll., Hartford, Conn., 1954. Mgr. real estate fin. div. Mct. Life Ins. Co., N.Y.C., 1968-70; sr. v.p., then pres. BankAm. Realty Services, Inc., San Francisco, 1970-76, chmn. bd., pres., 1976—; trustee BankAm. Realty Investors. Bd. dirs. Calif. Housing Council. Served to capt. USAF, 1954-57. Recipient Commendation award San Francisco Bd. Edn., 1981. Mem. Nat. Assn. Real Estate Investment Trusts (pres. 1977-78, bd. govs.), Urban Land Inst., Internat. Council Shopping Ctrs. Republican. Episcopalian. Clubs: Bankers, Commonwealth (San Francisco). Office: 555 California St San Francisco CA 94104

VOORHEES, DONALD SHIRLEY, judge; b. Leavenworth, Kans., July 30, 1916; s. Ephraim and Edna Mary (Oliphint) V.; A.B., U. Kans., 1938; LL.B., Harvard U., 1946; m. Anne Elizabeth Spillers, June 21, 1946; children—Stephen, Spillers, David Todd, John Lawrence, Diane Patricia, Richard Gordon. Admitted to Okla. bar, 1947, Wash. State bar, 1948; practiced law, Tulsa, 1946-47, Seattle, 1947-74; partner firm Riddell, Williams, Voorhees, Ivie, & Bullitt, Seattle, 1952-74; judge U.S. Dist. Ct., Western dist. Wash., 1974—. Bd. dirs. Fed. Jud. Center. Served with USN, 1942-46. Mem. Am., Washington State, Seattle-King County bar assns., Maritime Law Assn., Am. Judicature Soc., Phi Beta Kappa. Democrat. Unitarian. Office: 502 US Courthouse Seattle WA 98104

VORIES, EUGENE CAPPS, plumbing and heating executive, cattle rancher; b. Walsenburg, Colo., Jan. 19, 1923; s. Eugene Stark and Ruby Leon (Capps) V. m. Eunice Marks, Sept. 20, 1942; children—Rebecca, Kimery, Nancy, Carol, Dan. Student Mesa Coll., 1941-42, Xavier U., 1943-44. Clk. Biggs-Kurtz Co., Grand Junction, Colo., 1946-49; warehouse foreman Colorado Springs (Colo.) Supply, 1949-51; mgr. Lasater Ranch, Matheson, Colo., 1951-54; salesman Warner Co., Denver, 1954-59; sales mgr., br. mgr. Southwest Supply Co., Pueblo and Grand Junction, 1959-66; pres., gen. mgr. Top Line Supply Co., Grand Junction, 1966—; owner Vories Cattle Co.; pres., dir. Found. Beefmaster Assn. Author: Arrowhead Ranch, 1959, The Man from Colorado, 1960, The La Veta Posse, 1976. Chmn. Mesa County Reagan for Pres., del. Nat. Republican Conv., 1976, mem. Colo. adv. com. Reagan for Pres., 1980. Served with AUS, 1943-46. Baptist. Club: Rotary (past pres., Dist. 547 gov. 1979-80, Paul Harris fellow 1980) (Grand Junction) Mason. Home: PO Box 2201 Grand Junction CO 81502 Office: PO Box 1236 Grand Junction CO 81502

VORIS, CHARLES WILLIAM, ednl. adminstr.; b. Neoga, Ill., Mar. 20, 1924; s. Louis K. and Faye (Hancock) V.; B.S., U. So. Calif., 1947, M.B.A., 1948; Ph.D., Ohio State U., 1951; LL.D., Sung Kyun Kwan U. (Korea), 1972, Eastern Ill. U., 1976; m. Mavis Marie Myre, Mar. 20, 1949; children—Charles William II, Michael K. Teaching asst. Ohio State U., Columbus, 1948-50; prof. mgmt. Wash. State U., Pullman, 1950-52; prof., head dept. mgmt. Los Angeles State Coll., 1952-58, 60-63; dean Coll. Bus. and Pub. Adminstrn., U. Ariz., Tucson, 1963-71; pres. Am. Grad. Sch. Internat. Mgmt., Glendale, Ariz., 1971—. Ford Found. research grantee Los Angeles State Coll., 1956; prof. U. Tehran (Iran), 1958-59; Ford Found. fellow Carnegie Inst. Tech., Pitts., 1961; prof. Am. U., Beirut, Lebanon, 1961, 62; cons. Hughes Aircraft Co., Los Angeles, Rheem Mfg. Co., Los Angeles, Northrop Aircraft Co., Palmdale, Calif., Harwood Co., Alhambra, Calif., ICA, Govt. Iran. Served with USNR, 1942-45. Fellow Acad. Mgmt.; mem. Ariz. Acad., Beta Gamma Sigma, Alpha Kappa Psi, Phi Delta Theta. Author: Production Control, Text and Cases, 1956, 3d edit., 1966; Management of Production, 1960. Research in indsl. future of Iran, mgmt. devel. in Middle East. Home: Thunderbird Campus Glendale AZ 85306

VORREITER, PATRICIA JOAN, lawyer; b. Savanna, Ill., July 5, 1940; d. Harry and Florence Kathryn (Fitzpatrick) Wolfe. B.A., Colo. State U., 1962; J.D., U. Santa Clara, 1980. Bar: Calif. 1980. Law clk. to William Steven Jarvis, Palo Alto, Calif., 1977-78; law clk. Mackey & Friedland, San Jose, Calif., 1978-80, assoc., 1981-82; sole practice, Cupertino, Calif., 1982—. Mem. ABA, State Bar Calif., Sunnyvale-Cupertino Bar Assn., Santa Clara County Bar Assn. Democrat. Presbyterian. Home: 937 Aster Ct Sunnyvale CA 94086 Office: 20440 Town Center Ln Suite D Cupertino CA 95014

VOSS, HAROLD JEFFREY, business executive; b. Ashtabula, Ohio, June 6, 1950; s. Harold Clayton and Dorothy Dee (Whittle) V.; B.A. in Psychology, U. So. Colo., 1972. Program dir. Teleprompter Cable TV, Greenville, S.C., 1972-73; bus. devel. mgr. Pacific-Atlantic Devel., Inc., Denver, 1973-77; western regional mgr. Property Mgmt. Cons., Inc., Fountain Valley, Calif., 1977-79; regional dir. Realty World, Bellevue, Wash., 1979-80; v.p., sec., treas. VP Enterprises, Inc., Garden Grove, Calif., 1980-81; pres. Money Market Check Cashing Centers, Anaheim, Calif., 1982—; cons. Property Protectors, Seattle, 1975-76, Solar Saver Co., Ft. Collins, Colo., 1977, L.J. Pontiac/Fiat Co., Pueblo, Colo.; instr. sales tng. Werner Investments, Inc., Los Angeles, 1977-79, co-owner Rentex Funny Car Dragster, Edmonton, Alta., Can., 1976-77. Recipient Nat. award (Realty World Internat., 1979. Home: 1707 S Brookhurst Anaheim CA 92604 Office: 12441 Haster St Garden Grove CA 92640

VOSS, JUDITH ANN, mgmt. co. exec.; b. Milford, Ill., Aug. 10, 1939; d. Lawrence Martin and Dorothy Estella (Fleming) Henke; student schs. Milford; m. Robert Clifford Voss, May 26, 1957; children—Dawn Ann, Sharon Sue. Clk. typist, hwy. div. State of Ill., Springfield, 1961-63; credit and personnel reporter, asst. mgr. Fond du Lac (Wis.) Credit Bur., 1966-68; sec., asst. to pres., purchasing agt. Delft Blue-Provimi, Inc., Watertown, Wis., 1969-77, gen. mgr., Concord, Calif., 1977-79; adminstrv. mgr. Bay Area div. EkoTek, Inc., Oakland, Calif., 1979-80; exec. v.p. Diablo Mgmt., Inc., Walnut Creek, Calif., 1980; office adminstr. Camp Dresser & Mc Kee Inc., Walnut Creek, 1981—. Home: 1790 Getoun Ct Concord CA 94518 Office: Camp Dresser & McKee Inc 710 S Broadway Suite 201 Walnut Creek CA 94596

VOSS, WILLIAM.BAKER, retired systems engineer; b. Rockwell City, Iowa, July 17, 1915; s. Enoch George and Lulu Moore (Porter) V.; B.A. in Physics and Math., Willamette U., 1936; postgrad. Calif. Inst. Tech., 1937-38; m. Dorothy Frances Nourse, Sept. 19, 1942; 1 son, Richard; m. 2d, Ernestine Elinore Shook Hobba, June 15, 1958; 1 dau., Virginia Anne. Chemist, Cinecolor Corp., Burbank, Calif., 1947-49; mem. tech. staff, research physicist Hughes Aircraft Co., Culver City, Calif., 1946-47, 49-56; group head Hughes Aircraft Co., Culver City, 1956-65, systems engr., El Segundo, Calif., 1965-67, Culver City, 1967-75, Canoga Park, Calif., 1975-82, ret., 1982. Treas. Westchester Republican Club, Los Angeles, 1954-55; mem. Citizens Planning Council, Los Angeles County Regional Planning Dept., 1977-81; pres., founder Malibu Highlands Property Owners Assn., 1978—. Served to capt. U.S. Army, 1942-43, USAAF, 1943-46. Mem. Sierra Club (life). Republican. Presbyterian. Patentee in field. Home: 387 N Kenter Ave Los Angeles CA 90049

VOTE, FREDERICK C., mechanical engineer; b. Denver, June 18, 1933; s. Fred Harry and Arminta Viola (Reynolds) V.; B.S. in M.E., U. Denver, 1955; M.S. in Engring., UCLA, 1965; m. Judith Gay Harvey, June 17, 1956; children—Kurt Frederic, Erika Christine. Research engr. Rocketdyne, Canoga Park, Calif., 1955-66; supr. liquid propulsion sect. Jet. Propulsion Lab., Pasadena, Calif., 1966-77, dep. sect. mgr. propulsion systems sect., 1977-81, mgr. elec. power and propulsion sect., 1981-82; dep. mgr. air/land battle advanced tech. project, 1982—; chmn. Vintage Fundamental Magnet Site Council, 1979-80. Served with U.S. Army, 1956-58. Recipient Exceptional Service medal NASA, 1976. Mem. AIAA. Office: 4800 Oak Grove Dr Pasadena CA 91109

VOTH, ANDREW CHARLES, museum director; artist; b. Akron, Ohio, Aug. 4, 1947; s. Roland L. and Dorothy Jane (Fynn) V.; student Madison (Conn.) Sch. Art, 1965-66; B.A., Ambassador Coll., 1970. Chmn. art dept. Imperial High Sch., Pasadena, Calif., 1970-73; lectr. art, art dir. Ambassador Coll., Pasadena, 1973-76, dir. publs., dir. fine arts and dir. galleries; dir. Pinewood Abbey, Tehachapi, Calif.; conservator paintings Pasadena Hist. Soc., 1977-81; chmn. traditional painting Pasadena Festival of Arts, 1975-79, dir., 1980; dir. exhbts. Ambassador Internat. Cultural Found., 1975-80; dir. fine arts Ambassador Coll., 1978-80; pres. Pasadena Inst. Arts, 1978—; cultural arts coordinator City of Oxnard (Calif.), 1981—; dir. Carnegie Cultural Arts Center, Oxnard, 1981—; v.p. Pasadena Arts Council, also bd. dirs.; dir. Pasadena Festival of Arts and Scis., 1980; mem. San Gabriel Fine Arts Club; trustee Aldrich Found., Pasadena Hist. Soc.; one-man shows: Ambassador Coll., 1968, 70, 72, 76, Republic Fed. Savs., Altadena, Calif., 1971, 74, Glendale Fed. Savs., Pasadena, 1970, Longpre Gallery, La Canada, Calif., 1976, Huntington-Sheraton Galleries, Pasadena, 1974, San Gabriel (Calif.) Fine Arts Show, 1976, Pasadena Festival of Arts, 1976, Holiday Inn, Pasadena, 1976-77; represented in permanent collections. Recipient best of show award San Gabriel Art Assn., 1978. Address: 424 South C St Oxnard CA 93030

VOURGOURAKIS, EMMANUEL JOHN, electronics engr.; b. Athens, Greece; came to U.S., 1956, naturalized, 1965; s. John Emmanuel and Toula J. (Skouras) V.; ensign R.H.N., Naval Cadet Coll., Piraeus, Greece, 1949; B.S.E.E., U. Pa., Phila., 1958; M.S.E.E. (Univ. fellow), U. Ill., Urbana, 1959; Ph.D. (Howard Hughes fellow), UCLA, 1967; m. Mary C. Bartnik, May 5, 1961; children—Matina, Jana, Yanni. Mem. tech. staff AVCO-RAD Corp., Wilmington. Mass., 1959-61, Hughes Aircraft Co., Culver City, Calif., 1962-67, mem. sr. staff space and communications group, 1967-76, program mgr. electo-optical and data processing group, 1976—; adj. asso. prof. UCLA, 1974-75; adv. com. sci. and tech. Greek Govt., 1977; dir. GETEN, Greece, 1975. Bd. dirs. Save Cyprus Council, 1974—. Served as ensign, Greek Navy, 1949-52, as lt., 1952-56. Patentee in field. Home: 1475 N Kenter Ave Los Angeles CA 90049 Office: Hughes Aircraft Co PO Box 902 El Segundo CA 90245

VRADENBURG, BEATRICE WHITE, symphony orchestra manager; b. Manhattan, Kans., Nov. 1, 1922; d. Richard Peregrine and Marian (Tyler) White; m. George Albert Vradenburg, Jr., Sept. 10; 1 son, George Albert. Student Oberlin Coll., to 1944. Mgr. Colorado Springs (Colo.) Symphony Orch., 1954—. Active Colo. Council on the Arts, 1965-71; pres. Spring-spree. Recipient Gov.'s award for Excellence in the Arts, 1978, Mayor's award, Colorado Springs, 1979. Mem. Am. Symphony Orch. League (Louis Sudler award 1980), Nat. Endowment for the Arts (music panel 1979-82). Republican. Episcopalian. Clubs: El Paso, Garden of the Gods. Office: PO Box 1692 Colorado Springs CO 80901

VRAJICH, NICK, manufacturing engineer, educator, consultant, educator; b. Botos, Yugoslavia, Oct. 21, 1938; s. Ilija and Zagorka (Onjin) V.; came to U.S., 1967, naturalized, 1974; m. Carla Roberta Howarth, May 11, 1973; children—Sasha, Michael. B. Vocat. Edn., Calif. State U.-Los Angeles, 1976, M.A., 1978; Ph.D. in Indsl. Tech., Colo. State U., 1983. Instr. credential, Calif. Community Colls. Apprentice machinist LZTK, Kikinda, Yugoslavia, 1954-57; journey level machinist/tool maker, Yugoslavia, 1957-64, W.Ger., 1964-65, Toronto, and Windsor, Ont. Can., 1965-67, Los Angeles, 1967-73; instr. assoc. engring. and tech. div. Orange Coast Coll., Costa Mesa, Calif., 1973-75; instr. engring. tech. div. Cuesta Coll., San Luis Obispo, Calif., 1975—; lectr. engring. tech. dept. Calif. Poly. State U., San Luis Obispo; prof. indsl. and tech. edn. MSC, Ada, Yugoslavia, 1978-79; corp. rep. mktg. ops. LSB Industries, Bucharest, Rumania, 1979-80; pres. Am. R&D Engring. Co.; cons. mfg. engring. Served Yugoslav Armed Forces, 1957-59. Mem. Am. Vocat. Edn. Assn., Soc. Mfg. Engrs. (sr.), Smithsonian Inst., Iota Lambda Sigma. Democrat. Serbian-Orthodox. Home: 745 Evans Rd San Luis Obispo CA 93401 Office: Cuesta Coll PO Box J San Luis Obispo CA 93406

VREDEVOE, DONNA LOU, medical educator, researcher; b. Ann Arbor, Mich., Jan. 11, 1938; d. Lawrence E. and Verna (Brower) V.; B.A. in Bacteriology, UCLA, 1959, Ph.D. in Microbiology (Univ. fellow, USPHS fellow), 1963; m. John Porter, Aug. 22, 1962; 1 dau., Verna. USPHS postdoctoral fellow Stanford, 1963-64; instr. dept. bacteriology UCLA, 1963, postgrad. research immunologist dept. surgery Center for Health Scis., 1964-65, asst. research immunologist dept. surgery, 1965-67, asst. research immunologist Sch. Nursing, 1967, asst. prof. Sch. Nursing, Center Health Scis., 1967-70, assoc. prof., 1970-76, prof., 1976—, assoc. dean Sch. Nursing, 1976-70, asst. dir. for space planning Cancer Center, 1976-78, dir. for space planning, 1978—, cons. to lab. nuclear medicine and radiation biology, 1967-80. Post-doctoral fellow USPHS, 1963-64; Mabel Wilson Richards scholar UCLA, 1960-61; research grantee Calif. Inst. Cancer Research, 1967-69, 72, 75-77, Calif. div. Am. Cancer Soc., 1968-69, 69-70, 72, USPHS, 1969—, Am. Nurses Found., 1968, Cancer Research Coordinating Com. of U. Calif., 1967-68, 75-76, Dept. Energy, 1977-80, Am. Cancer Soc., 1980—. Mem. Am. Soc. Microbiology, Am. Assn. Immunologists, Am. Assn. Cancer Research, Nat. League Nursing (2d v.p. 1979-81), Sigma Xi, Alpha Gamma Sigma, Sigma Theta Tau. Contbr. articles to profl. publs.; author book, 1981. Home: 355 21st Pl Santa Monica CA 90402 Office: Sch Nursing UCLA Los Angeles CA 90024

VREELAND, ROBERT WILDER, electronics engr.; b. Glen Ridge, N.J., Mar. 4, 1923; s. Frederick King and Elizabeth Leonora (Wilder) V.; B.S., U. Calif., Berkeley, 1947; m. Jean Gay Fullerton, Jan. 21, 1967; 1 son, Robert Wilder. Electronics engr. Litton Industries, San Carlos, Calif., 1948-55; sr. devel. electronics engr. U. Calif. Med. Center, San Francisco, 1955—; cons. electronics engr. Recipient Chancellor's award U. Calif., San Francisco, 1979; certified clin. engr. Nat. Bd. Examiners Clin. Engring. Mem. IEEE, Assn. Advancement Med. Instrumentation (bd. examiner), Am. Radio Relay League (Public Service award 1962). Contbr. articles to profl. jours., also to internat. meetings and symposiums; patentee in field. Home: 45 Maywood Dr San Francisco CA 94127 Office: Univ Calif Med Center 4th and Parnassus Sts San Francisco CA 94143

VRTAR, ROSE MARIE, constrn. co. exec.; b. Jamesburg, N.J., Nov. 30, 1946; d. John C. and Florence (Kesead) Gruca; B.A. in Edn., Trenton State Coll., 1968; postgrad. Calif. State U., Los Angeles, 1976—; m. Jacob Vrtar, Apr. 24, 1972. Cashier/bookkeeper Howard Johnson Restaurant, Cranbury, N.J., 1963-68; clk. McGraw Hill Inc., Hightstown, N.J., 1968-71, car plan adminstr., 1971-72; accounts payable clk. Fla. Realty Bldg. Co., West Palm Beach, Fla., 1972-73, full charge bookkeeper/supr. acct., 1973-75; accounts payable clk. Majestic Realty Co./Commerce Constrn. Co., Inc., Los Angeles, 1975-76, acctg. supr., 1976-78, controller, 1978—; co-owner Forever Green Garden Service. Sec. Pastoral Council, Archdiocese of Los Angeles, 1982-83. Mem. Soc. Am. Exec. and Profl. Women, Am. Rose Soc., Pacific Rose Soc. (corr. sec.), Greater Los Angeles Rose Council, Inland Valley Rose Soc. (sec.), San Gabriel Valley Rose and Hort. Soc. Roman Catholic. Club: El Monte Rose/Garden (editor newsletter 1977-78). Office: 6252 E Telegraph Rd Los Angeles CA 90040

VRYONIS, SPEROS, JR., historian, educator; b. Memphis, July 18, 1928; s. Speros Panayis, Sr., and Helen (Touliatou) V.; children—Speros Basil, Demetrios, Nikolas. B.A., Southwestern U., Memphis, 1950; M.A., Harvard U., 1952, Ph.D., 1956. Instr. history Harvard U., 1956-60; prof. history UCLA, 1960—, dir. G.E. von Grunebaum Ctr. of UCLA, 1972-75, 79-82; vis. prof. U. Chgo., 1966-67; fellow Dumbarton Oaks, Harvard U., 1979—; chmn. medieval and modern history U. Athens, 1976—. Recipient Kokkinos award Acad. Athens, 1974. Fellow Am. Mediaeval Acad. (Haskins medal); mem. Am. Philos. Soc., Am. Acad. Arts and Scis., Soc. Macedonian Studies. Author: Byzantium and Europe, 1967; Byzantium: Its Internal History and Relations with

Muslim World, 1971; Decline of Medieval Hellenism in Asia Minor, Process of Islamization, 1971; Studies on Byzantium, Seljuks, Ottomans, 1981; Istoria ton valkanikon laon, 1979; Readings in Medieval Historiography, 1968; The Balkans: Continuity and Change, 1972; The Role of the —Past— in Medieval and Modern Greek Culture, 1978; editor: (with others Islam and Cultural Change in the Middle Ages, 1975; contbr. articles to profl. jours. Office: Dept History UCLA 405 Hilgard Ave Los Angeles CA 90024

VUONG, SIU, ins. co. mgr.; b. Hai-Ninh, Vietnam, Feb. 8, 1945; s. Hai Phuc and Tran Duc (An) V.; student public schs. Cholon, Vietnam; m. Sydinh San, Apr. 15, 1968; children—Vaygi, Nhavan, Taivan, Kietvan, Boigi, Nancy. Sales engr. Universal World Trade Co., Saigon, 1972-73; v.p. ARINCO Advt., Printing Decorating Co., Saigon, 1973-75; sales rep. Met. Life Ins. Co., Los Angeles, 1978-79, sales mgr., 1979—. Mem. Glendale Burbank Assn. Life Underwriters, Nat. Assn. Life Underwriters, Ind. Ins. Brokers and Agts. U.S.A., Am. Vietnamese Chinese Friendship Assn. (v.p.). Mem. Indo Chinese refugee program adv. com. Pasadena Community Coll. Office: 840 North Hill St Suite 205 Los Angeles CA 90012

WACHNER, LINDA JOY, cosmetics executive; b. N.Y.C., Feb. 3, 1946; d. Herman and Shirley Wachner; B.S. in Econs. and Bus., U. Buffalo, 1966; m. Seymour Appelbaum, Dec. 21, 1973. Buyer, Foley's Federated Dept. Store, Houston, 1968-69; sr. buyer R.H. Macy's, N.Y.C., 1969-74; v.p. Warner div. Warnaco, Bridgeport, Conn., 1974-77; v.p. corp. mktg. Caron Internat., N.Y.C., 1977-79; pres. U.S. div. Max Factor & Co., Hollywood, Calif., 1979—; pres. Missoni Profumi S.p.A., Hollywood, 1980—. Named Outstanding Woman in Bus., Women's Equity Action League, 1980. Mem. Young Presidents Orgn. Republican. Jewish. Office: Max Factor & Co 1655 N McCadden Pl Hollywood CA 90028*

WACHTELL, THOMAS, petroleum company executive, lawyer; b. Crestwood, N.Y., Mar. 27, 1928; s. Theodore and Carolyn (Satz) W.; grad. Choate Sch., 1946; B.S., Syracuse U., 1950; LL.B., Cornell U., 1958; m. Esther Carole Pickard, Jan. 27, 1957; children—Roger Bruce, Wendy Ann, Peter James. Bar: N.Y. 1958. Assoc. Livingston, Wachtell & Co., C.P.A.s, N.Y.C., 1958-60; pres. Allied Homeowners Assn., Inc., White Plains, N.Y., 1960-63; pres. Gen. Factoring Co., White Plains, N.Y., 1960-63; exec. asst. to pres. Occidental Petroleum Corp., Los Angeles, 1963-65, v.p., exec. asst., chmn. bd., 1965-72, exec. v.p., 1972-73, officer, dir. numerous subsidiaries; pres. Hydrocarbon Resources Corp., 1973-81; chmn. Oriental Petroleum Corp., 1982—; pres., chief exec. officer, dir. NMR Ctrs., Inc., 1982—; pres., dir. Cayman Petroleum Corp., 1974-75, Ridgecrest Energy Corp., 1979; dir. Tanglewood Consol. Resources, 1982—. Panelist, lectr. Nat. Indsl. Conf. Bd.; bd. govs., performing arts council Los Angeles Music Center, 1973—; bd. dirs. Los Angeles Music Center Opera Assn., 1972—, pres., chief exec. officer, 1981—; trustee Good Hope Med. Found., Los Angeles, 1974—. Served to lt. Office Naval Intelligence, USNR, 1952-56. Mem. Am. Mgmt. Assn., Los Angeles World Affairs Council, Choate Alumni Assn. So. Cal. (chmn. 1969—), Confrerie des Chevaliers du Tastevin, Beta Theta Pi, Phi Delta Phi. Office: 10900 Wilshire Blvd Suite 1220 Los Angeles CA 90024

WACHTER, JOSEPH PAUL, thermodynamicist; b. Crown Point, Ind., Dec. 24, 1943; s. Sylvester Edward and Anna (Juricek) W.; m. Elizabeth Jean Stevenson, Mar. 30, 1972; children—Alyson, Lisa, Adam, Kimberly, Nathan. B.S. in Mech. Engring., Purdue U., 1965, M.S. in Mech. Engring., 1967; postgrad. in aerospace engring., U. Tenn. Space Inst., 1971-73. Rocket propulsion engr. Martin Marietta Aerospace, Denver, 1967-71; aerodynamics research asst. U Tenn. Space Inst., Tullahoma, 1971-73; sr. spacecraft thermodynamicist Lockheed Missiles and Space Corp., Sunnyvale, Calif., 1973-78; staff mech. engr. Amdahl Corp., Sunnyvale, 1978—. Mem. AIAA, ASHRAE, Am. Orchid Soc., Sigma Xi. Contbr. articles to profl. jours. Home: 769 Mahogany Ln Sunnyvale CA 94086 Office: PO Box 470 Sunnyvale CA 94086

WACHTER, KENNETH WILLCOX, statistician, demographer, educator; b. Bklyn., Jan. 13, 1947; s. John Henry and Evelyn Ardelle (Sidman) W.; m. Bernadette Bell, Aug. 27, 1982. A.B., Harvard U., 1968; M.A., Oxford U., 1971; Ph.D., Cambridge U., 1974. Assoc. mem. tech. staff Bell Labs., Murray Hill, N.J., 1968-69; research fellow St. Catherine's Coll., Oxford, Eng., 1971-74; asst. prof., then assoc. prof. Harvard U., 1974-78; assoc. prof. demography and stats. U. Calif.-Berkeley, 1979—; mem. panel on immigration stats. NRC; research assoc. Nat. Bur. Econ. Research. Presdl. Scholar, 1964; Miller fellow, 1977. Mem. Am. Statis. Assn., Population Assn. Am., Internat. Union for Sci. Study of Population (com. on family and life cycle). Author: Statistical Studies of Historical Social Structure, 1978. Home: 115 Black Point Reach Sea Ranch CA 95497 Office: 2234 Piedmont Ave Berkeley CA 94720

WACHTMANN, KIRK ROBERT, psychologist; b. Santa Maria, Calif., Sep. 4, 1949; s. Henry Arthur and Becca Jean (Conrad) W.; m. Angela Marie Adrignola, July 22, 1978; 1 dau., Amanda Marie. B.A., U. Pacific, 1971; M.A., Calif. Poly. State U., San Luis Obispo, 1972; Ph.D., Calif. Sch. Profl. Psychology, San Diego, 1977. Lic. psychologist, Calif.; diplomate Am. Acad. Behavioral Medicine; cert. Biofeedback Cert. Inst. Am. Pre-doctoral intern Mercy Hosp. and Med. Ctr., San Diego, 1976-77, postdoctoral fellow, 1977-78; ptnr., staff psychologist Biofeedback Inst. San Diego, 1979—. Mem. Am. Psychol. Assn., Acad. Behavioral Medicine, Biofeedback Soc. Calif., Alpha Kappa Lambda. Democrat. Episcopalian.

WADDOUPS, RAY OWEN, research engineer; b. Rigby, Idaho, Mar. 9, 1939; s. Ralph Owen and Nancy Fern (Whiting) W.; m. JoAnne Marie Brough, June 7, 1963; children—Wayne, Wendy, Vicki, Laurel, Rand. B.S., Utah State U., Logan, 1963, M.S., 1964, Ph.D. in Physics, 1968; postgrad., U. Chgo., 1964-65. Sr. engr. Goodyear Aerospace, Litchfield Park, Ariz., 1968-70; sr. mem. tech. staff ITT Gilfillan, Van Nuys, Calif., 1970-77; chief engr. tactical systems office Motorola Govt. Electronics Group, Scottsdale, Ariz., 1977—; tchr. evening div. Maricopa Community Coll. Bishop Valencia Ward Ch. of Jesus Christ of Latter Day Saints, 1975-77; mem. Mesa dist. com. Boy Scouts Am., 1978-80. Utah State U. research grantee, 1963. Mem. AIAA, AAAS, Sigma Xi. Contbr. articles to tech. jours.; patentee in field. Home: 1510 E Gable Mesa AZ 85204 Office: 8201 E McDowell Suite 1120 Scottsdale AZ 85252

WADE, JAMES EDGAR, former educator, bus. cons.; b. Tulsa, Dec. 8, 1910; s. James Eugene and Edith Mary (Norton) W.; B.A., U. Notre Dame, 1933, M.A., 1935; Ph.D., St. Louis U., 1942; m. Mary Hennessy, June 1, 1940; children—Edith Ann, Maureen; m. 2d, Lorraine Kirchoff Gardiner, July 31, 1971. Instr. St. John's U., Bklyn., 1939-40; asst. prof. U. San Francisco, 1940-48; asst. prof., asso. prof., prof., U. Santa Clara, Calif., 1948-60; specialist in edn. and tng. Gen. Electric Co., Richland, Wash., 1960-64; prof. bus. San Jose (Calif.) State U., 1964-80, prof. emeritus, 1980—; bus. cons., San Jose, 1964—. Mem. AAUP, Am. Bus. Communication Assn., Coll. English Assn., Adminstrv. Mgmt. Soc., Renaissance Soc. No Calif., COF. Republican. Roman Catholic. Club: ELks. Home: 5133 Glentree Dr San Jose CA 95129

WADE, NEIL HOWARD, geotechnical engineer; b. Fredericton, N.B., Can., Apr. 11, 1936; s. Paul Randal and Alma Elizabeth (McCracken) W.; B.Sc. in Civil Engring., U. N.B., 1959; Ph.D. in Soil Mechanics (Athlone fellow 1959-61, NRC scholar 1961-63), Imperial Coll., U. London, 1963; m. Louise Marie Nygren, May 15, 1981. Asst. prof. civil engring. U. Calif., Berkeley, 1963-64; asso. prof. Ga. Inst. Tech., 1964-68; sr. geotech. engr. Tippetts-Abbott-McCarthy-Stratton, N.Y.C., 1968-69, Tarbela, Pakistan, 1969-71; sr. geotech. engr. B.C. Hydro, Vancouver, 1971-74; exec. engr. Klohn Leonoff Cons., Vancouver, 1974-76; head geotech. engr. B.C. Hydro & Power Authority, Vancouver, 1976-80; head geotech. dept. Montreal Engring., Calgary, Alta., Can., 1980—; vis. lectr. U. Calif., Davis and U. B.C., Vancouver, 1976-80, U. Alta., Edmonton and U. Calgary, 1981-83; lectr. B.C. Inst. Tech., 1977-80; cons. in field. NSF grantee, 1965-69; Ford Found. fellow, 1968-69. Mem. Assn. Profl. Engrs. B.C., Assn. Profl. Engrs. Atla., Engring. Inst. Can., Canadian Geotech. Soc., ASCE, Internat. Soc. Soil Mechanics and Found. Engring. geotechnical engineer; b. Fredericton, N.B., Can., Apr. 11, 1936; s. Paul Randal and Alma Elizabeth (McCracken) W.; B.Sc. in Civil Engring., U. N.B., 1959; Ph.D. in Soil Mechanics (Athlone fellow 1959-61, NRC scholar 1961-63), Imperial Coll., U. London, 1963; m. Louise Marie Nygren, May 15, 1981. Asst. prof. civil engring. U. Calif., Berkeley, 1963-64; asso. prof. Ga. Inst. Tech., 1964-68; sr. geotech. engr. Tippetts-Abbott-McCarthy-Stratton, N.Y.C., 1968-69, Tarbela, Pakistan, 1969-71; sr. geotech. engr. B.C. Hydro, Vancouver, 1971-74; exec. engr. Klohn Leonoff Cons., Vancouver, 1974-76; head geotech. engr. B.C. Hydro & Power Authority, Vancouver, 1976-80; head geotech. dept. Montreal Engring., Calgary, Alta., Can., 1980—; vis. lectr. U. Calif., Davis and U. B.C., Vancouver, 1976-80, U. Alta., Edmonton and U. Calgary, 1981-83; lectr. B.C. Inst. Tech., 1977-80; cons. in field. NSF grantee, 1965-69; Ford Found. fellow, 1968-69. Mem. Assn. Profl. Engrs. B.C., Assn. Profl. Engrs. Atla., Engring. Inst. Can., Canadian Geotech. Soc., ASCE, Internat. Soc. Soil Mechanics and Found. Engring. Home: 240 Valhalla Crescent Calgary AB T3A 2A1 Canada Office: 400 Monenco Pl 801 6th Ave SW Calgary AB T2P 3W3 Canada

WADMAN, WILLIAM WOOD, III, health physicist; b. Oakland, Calif., Nov. 13, 1936; s. William Wood, Jr., and Lula Fae (Raisner) W.; M.A., U. Calif., Irvine, 1978; children—Roxanne Alyce, Raymond Alan. Radiation safety specialist, accelerator health physicist U. Calif. Lawrence Berkeley Lab., 1957-68; campus radiation safety officer U. Calif., Irvine, 1968-79; dir. ops., radiation safety officer Radiation Sterilizers, Inc., Tustin, Calif., 1979-80; prin. Wm. Wadman & Assos., 1980—; mem. team No. 1, health physics appraisal program NRC, 1980-81; cons. health physicist to industry; lectr. dept. community and environ. medicine U. Calif., Irvine, 1979-80, Orange Coast Coll. Active Cub Scouts; chief umpire Mission Viejo Little League, 1973. Served with USNR, 1955-56. Recipient award for profl. achievement U. Calif. Alumni Assn., 1972, Outstanding Performance award U. Calif., Irvine, 1973. Mem. Health Physics Soc. (treas. 1979-81, editor proc. 11th symposium, pres. So. Calif. chpt. 1977, Professionalism award 1975), Internat. Radiation Protection Assn. (U.S. del. 4th Congress 1977), Am. Nuclear Soc., Am. Public Health Assn. (chmn. program 1978, chmn. radiol. health sect. 1979-80), Campus Radiation Safety Officers (chmn. 1975, editor proc. 5th conf. 1975), Acad. Polit. Sci. Club: UCI Univ. (dir. 1976, sec. 1977, treas. 1978). Contbr. articles to tech. jours. Home: PO Box 4085 Irvine CA 92716 Office: 1400 W Edgehill Dr Suite 35 San Bernardino CA 92405

WAGER-BROWN, LOLA BENTON, vocational educator, educational administrator; b. Nogales, Ariz., May 19, 1920; d. Hugh Samuel and Dolores M. (Quintero) Benton; m. George Vincent Wager, Dec. 27, 1945 (dec.); children—Joseph B., Eric B., Dolores Wager Steele, Jorj Wager Goss; m. 2d, James Henry Brown, Apr. 2, 1982. Student, U. Ariz., 1942; postgrad. U. Minn., 1944, U. Mich., 1946; M.A., Ariz. State U., 1946; postgrad. Mich. State U., 1967, 68, No. Ariz. U., 1974; Ed.D., Utah State U., 1982. Cert. jr. coll., secondary sch., profl. guidance and counseling, coordinator coop. edn., vocat. edn. Tchr. bus., Spanish high schs. in Jerome, Tempe, and San Simon, Ariz., 1942-46; homebound tchr., vol., Phoenix, 1950-62; mem. faculty Glendale Coll., 1970-74; coop. work experience coordinator, bus. edn. instr. Phoenix Union High Sch. System, 1963-75; state supr. bus. edn. Oreg. Dept. Edn., Salem, 1977-81; instr. bus. developing bilingual program Cochise Coll., Douglas, Ariz., 1982-83; developer curriculum, writing materials for competency skills in office edn. Active Future Bus. Leaders Am. for Ariz. and Oreg., adviser, state chmn. 1963-83; chmn. Girls State, 1960-63; life mem. Hosp. Aux., Glendale, Ariz. Recipient Cardinal Newman Gold Key and Plaque, U. Ariz., 1942; Am. Cancer Soc. fellow, 1944; Nat. Tb Found. fellow, 1946; Ariz. Dept. Edn. fellow, 1975, 76; Utah Dept. Edn. grantee, 1975. Mem. Am. Vocat. Assn. (life mem.), Nat. Bus. Edn. Assn., Western Assn. for Coop. Work Experience, Future Bus. Leaders from Oreg. (life mem.), Women Adminstrs. in Vocat. Edn., Phi Delta Kappa, Delta Pi Epsilon. Democrat. Roman Catholic. Developer tng. plans, manuals, curriculum guides, model office for education clerical workers used as model by other schs. Office: Cochise Coll Douglas Hwy Douglas AZ 85607

WAGGENER, PAT VANDEVER, interior designer; b. Tulsa, June 26, 1928; d. Voris Vincent and May (Harris) Vandever; div.; children—Candi Rogers, Leslee Waggener. Student Bradford Jr. Coll., Mass., 1946, U. Okla., 1946-49 U. Tulsa, Okla., 1949, Oral Roberts U., Tulsa, 1964, Pasadena (Calif.) City Coll., 1965; U. Denver, 1969-73; Met. State Coll., Denver, 1973. Interior decorator (part-time) Vandevers Dept. Store, Tulsa, 1952-65; rep. St. Johns Mil. Acad., Camps St. John and Nagawicka, Delafield, Wis., 1950-69; interior decorator Karl Vogel Interiors, Denver, 1969-70; freelance custom designer, Denver, 1970-74; prin. Pat V. Waggener Interiors, Denver, 1975—. Bd. dirs. Tulsa Civic Ballet, 1959-64. Mem. Jr. League Denver, Denver City Ballet, Home Fashion League, Am. Soc. Interior Designers (assoc.). Republican. Episcopalian. Club: Inverness Golf 19 (Englewood, Colo.). Address: 3625 S Forest Way Denver CO 80237

WAGMAN, MICHAEL WILLIAM, advertising agency executive; b. Newark, July 13, 1941; s. Meyer and Nancy (Fidel) W.; m. Jan Oane; children—Nikki, Coby. Student (scholar) Juilliard Sch. Music, N.Y.C., 1960-65. Concert pianist, 1945-65; TV producer Doyle/Dane/Bernbach, N.Y.C., 1965-67; TV producer Papert Koenig Lois, N.Y.C., 1967-68; co-creative group head J. Walter Thompson, N.Y.C., 1969-71; TV prodn. head Daniel & Charles, N.Y.C., 1971-72; ind. writer, producer documentaries, N.Y.C. and Los Angeles, 1972-75; creative group head Foote, Cone, Belding, Los Angeles, 1975-79, exec. v.p., exec. creative dir., 1979—; lectr. on advt.; tchr. advt. in seminars, workshops. Mem. exec. pub. relations com. United Way So. Calif. William Kapell music scholar, 1947; Venice, Cork, Chgo., N.Y., Atlanta Film Festival awards; numerous other advt. awards. Author: The Far Horizons, 1980. Office: Foote Cone & Belding 2727 W 6th St Los Angeles CA 90057

WAGNER, CARLOS EDWARD, accountant; b. Dodgeville, Wis., Nov. 8, 1947; s. Charles E. and E. Elois (Cordts) W.; m. Ann Catherine Pierick, Jan. 11, 1969; children—Peter, Jennifer. B.B.A., U. Wis.-Whitewater, 1971. C.P.A., Ariz. Staff acct. Lester Witte & Co., Phoenix, 1971-75, ptnr., 1975-77; co-owner Miller Wagner & Co. Ltd., Phoenix, 1977—, dir. personnel, mgmt. services, 1977—. Bd. dirs. Scottsdale Arts Ctr. Assn., Planned Parenthood of Central and No. Ariz.; mem. profl. adv. com. Valley Big Bros., Phoenix. Served with AUS 1968-74. Mem. Am. Inst. C.P.A.s, Ariz. Soc. C.P.A.s. Roman Catholic. Office: 5225 N Central Ave Suite 220 Phoenix AZ 85012

WAGNER, GREGORY ALAN, psychologist; b. Madison, Wis., July 12, 1953; s. Frederic Hamilton and Marilyn Christine (Christensen) W. B.A., Colo. Coll., 1975; M.A., Kans. U., 1980, Ph.D., 1982. Research asst. Colo. Coll., 1972-75; behavior specialist Salt Lake City Pub. Schs., 1976; teaching and research asst. Kans. U., 1978-80; psychologist Sonoma State Hosp., Eldridge, Calif., 1980—; behavioral cons. Mem. Am. Psychol. Assn., Am. Assn. Mental Deficiency, Assn. Behavior Analysis, Assn. Advancement Behavior Therapy. Office: Sonoma State Hosp Eldridge CA 95431

WAGNER, HOLLY CLYDE, consulting geologist; b. Selma, Calif., Aug. 13, 1918; s. Hugh E. and Ethel Nina (McKinlay) W.; A.B. in Geology, UCLA, 1941, M.A., 1947; postgrad. U. Kans., 1951-56; m. Leslie Charlotte Newton, Aug. 29, 1942; children—Holiday, Hugh McKinlay, Rebecca. Asst. engring. aide U.S. Engr. Office, Los Angeles, 1941-42; jr. geologist U.S. Geol. Survey, geology of mining dists. in N.Mex. and Utah, 1942-44; lab. instr. geology UCLA, 1946-47; geologist fuels br. U.S. Geol. Survey, Alaska, 1947, Pa., 1947-50, fuels br., Kans., 1950-55, asst. br. chief fuels br., Washington, 1955-58, sr. geologist fuel br., Calif., 1958-60, sr. geologist Pacific Coast br., Oreg., Wash., 1960-66, research geologist Pacific Coast br., Calif., 1966-69, research geologist Office of Marine Geology, Calif., 1969-76; project chief offshore geology So. and South-Central Calif., also cons. to Calif. Nuclear Reactor Commn., 1974-76, 78-82; instr. geology Inst. Internat. Mineral Resources Devel., Japan, 1977; research geologist Office Marine Geology, U.S. Geol. Survey, Calif., Oreg., Wash., 1978-83, ret., 1983; cons., 1983—. Scoutmaster, Santa Clara (Calif.) council Boy Scouts Am., 1962-63, geology merit badge counselor, 1960-63. Served with C.E., U.S. Army, 1944-46. Fellow Geol. Soc. Am., AAAS; mem. Am. Assn. Petroleum Geologists, Geol. Soc. Wash., Sigma Xi, Sigma Gamma Epsilon. Democrat. Methodist. Contbr. numerous articles on mineral deposits, stratigraphic, structural and marine geology to sci. and govt. jours. Home: 1135 Lisa Ln Los Altos CA 94022

WAGNER, JANE TIFFANY, home economist; b. Kalamazoo, Nov. 5, 1904; d. Arthur Bennett and Helen Nellie May (Little) W.; B.S., Iowa State U., 1927; M.A., Columbia U., 1932; postgrad. Art Inst. Chgo., 1924-25, Simmons Coll., Boston, 1926; m. Albert R. Perkins, July 12, 1944; children by previous marriage—Diane Tiffany, Sarah Elizabeth; stepchildren—John, Nancy. Instr. home econs., Audubon, Iowa, 1928; field supr. Certo Corp., Rochester, N.Y., 1929; home service dir. Consol. Gas Co. and affiliated cos., N.Y.C., 1929-32; dir. Home Service Servel Corp., Inc., 1935-41; dir. Women's Service Center, Chgo. Daily News, 1941; dir. home econs. public relations div. Standard Brands, 1942; dir. women's war activities; dir. That They Might Live, Now Is the Time, UN Series, Home is What You Make It, dir. edn. NBC, 1942-50; food editor Am. Home mag., N.Y.C., 1950; home service editor Gas Appliance Mfrs. Assn. account Carl Byoir & Assos. Public Relations, N.Y.C., 1950-57; free-lance home economist, La Jolla, Calif., 1957—. Recipient Centennial award Iowa State U., 1957. Mem. Am. Home Econs. Assn., Home Economists in Bus. (chmn. N.Y.C. 1937), United Council Ch. Women (radio chmn. 1943-50), Advt. Women's Club (dir. N.Y.C.), Internat. Platform Assn., Women's Press Club, Pi Beta Phi. Episcopalian. Clubs: Zonta Internat.; Orienta Beach and Tennis (Mamaroneck, N.Y.); La Jolla Beach and Tennis. Home: 8205 Camino del Oro La Jolla CA 92037

WAGNER, MICHAEL JACK, human resources exec.; b. Brockton, Mass., Sept. 22, 1943; s. Selwyn and Estelle Eunice W.; B.A., Columbia Coll., 1966; M.B.A., Calif. Western U., 1979; m. Michele Scott; children—Tiffany, Jordan. Controller, Acurex Corp., Mountain View, Calif., 1973-76, Redken Labs. Inc., Canoga Park, Calif., 1976-78; pres. DiMaggio-Wagner Investment Corp., Monterey, Calif., 1978-82; human resource dir. Rolm Corp., Santa Clara, Calif., 1982—; real estate broker. Petitioner, Nat. Tax Limitation Com., 1978-79. Recipient cert. of merit Am. Mgmt. Assn., 1978. Mem. N.Y. Opera Assn. (life), San Francisco Opera Assn. Democrat. Mem. Ch. Religious Science. Club: Norred Riding. Office: 4900 Old Ironsides Dr Santa Clara CA 95050

WAGNER, RANDALL LEE, infosystems specialist; b. Kalamazoo, Jan. 6, 1954; s. Walter William and Marcy Lu (Van Alstyne) W.; m. Sheila Irene Ronan, Dec. 30, 1976. B.S., Ariz. State U., 1975, M.A., 1977. Sci. programmer Ariz. State U., Tempe, 1977-80; systems programmer Republic Airlines, Phoenix, 1980-82; sr. systems programmer Ramada Inns, Phoenix, 1982—. Mem. Am. Statis. Assn., Phi Beta Kappa.

WAGNER, RICHARD ELLIS, artist, educator; b. Trotwood, Ohio, June 18, 1923; s. Warren William and Myrtle Marie (Bowser) W.; m. Evelyn Ruth Fisher, Sept. 24, 1944; children—Scott David, Gail Louise. Student Antioch Coll., Yellow Springs, Ohio, 1941-42, Manchester Coll., North Manchester, Ind., 1942-43, Dayton Art Inst., Ohio, 1946-47; B.A., U. Colo., 1950, M.F.A., 1952. Instr. U. Colo., 1952-53; asst. prof. Dartmouth Coll., Hanover, N.H., 1953-63, assoc. prof., chmn. dept., 1963-66; vis. prof. U. Colo., 1955; tchr. painting workshops, Naples, Fla. and Telluride, Colo., 1966-69; juror art shows, 1955—; represented by Saks Gallery, Denver, Thackery Gallery, San Diego, Southwestern Arts, Carmel, Calif., Darvish Collection, Naples, Fla., Telluride Gallery, Telluride, Colo., Gallerie Marguerite, Durango, Colo. Illustrator 20 paintings for Ford Times Mag., 1958-72; author: Sketches in the San Juans 1976, Sketches in Southwest Seasons, 1982. Office: Wagner Art Gallery 27885 Hwy 160 Cortez CO 81321

WAGNER, RICHARD PHILIP, door contractor; b. Ft. Lewis, Wash., Jan. 27, 1942; s. Richard Paul and Helen Sybil (Carkin) W.; B.S., U. Nev., 1977; grad. U.S. Army Command and Gen. Staff Coll., 1976; m. Anne Irene Evans, Jan. 11, 1980; children—Paul, Thomas, Leah, Amy, Rachel, John. Self-employed contractor, ironworker, Reno, 1970-80; demographer, statistician U.S. Army, San Francisco, 1981; cons. elec., mech. Standard Oil, Richmond, Calif., 1981; ironwork contractor, Reno, 1981—. Mem. Washoe County Republican Central Com., 1974—; mem. Nev. Rep. Central Com., 1978—. Served with U.S. Army, 1965-70; maj. Res. Decorated Bronze Star with oak leaf cluster, Air medal. Mem. Assn. U.S. Army (2d v.p. Westmorland chpt. 1977-81). Republican. Mormon. Inventor door safety device, 1980. Home and office: 825 Casa Loma Dr Reno NV 89503

WAGNER, ROGER JAMES, structural engring. cons.; b. Kansas City, Mo., Jan. 17, 1949; s. Richard John and Joan Margaret (Shippee) W.; B.S. in Mech. Engring. cum laude and with honors, U. Mo., 1971; M.S. in Aeros. and Astronautics, Purdue U., 1972, Ph.D., 1974; m. Jonell Faye Franz, Aug. 28, 1971. Mem. tech. staff space and communications group Hughes Aircraft Co., El Segundo, Calif., 1974-77, staff engr., 1977-79, sect. head, 1979-80; sr. staff engr. Applied Research, Inc., Los Angeles, 1980; v.p., dir. engring. Structural Dynamics Consultants, Inc., Pacific Palisades, Calif., 1980-81; pres. Applied Structural Analysis, Inc., Northridge, Calif., 1981—; instr. U. So. Calif. David Ross fellow, 1973-74; recipient div. invention award Hughes Aircraft Co., 1978, Order of Engr., 1974; cert. in C.P.R. Mem. ASME, AIAA, U. Mo. Alumni Assn., Purdue U. Alumni Assn., Tau Beta Pi, Pi Tau Sigma, Omicron Delta Kappa, Phi Kappa Phi. Episcopalian. Inventor 3 point attachment for an ejectable spacecraft; contbr. articles to profl. jours. Office: 11741 Avenida Del Sol Northridge CA 91326

WAGNER, RONALD LEO, fin. exec.; b. Nacogdoches, Tex., Sept. 21, 1948; s. Leo and Maxine Ray (Pantalion) W.; B.S. in Bus. Adminstrn., S.W. Tex. State Coll., San Marcos, 1971. Owner, mgr. various collection agys., 1972-77; cons. hosp. collection, 1977-80; adminstr. firm Peter C. Rank, Los Angeles, 1978-81; pres. Calif. Agys., 1981—; leader seminars in field. Mem. Hosp. Fin. Mgmt. Assn., Am. Guild Patient Accounts Mgrs., Tau Kappa Epsilon. Republican. Home: 330 Marie Ave Los Angeles CA 90042 Office: 187 North Hill Ave Pasadena CA 91106

WAGNER, SHARON LEE SPENCE, rancher; b. Thermopolis, Wyo., Sept. 7, 1931; d. Henry Grant and Beulah Sue (Harris) Spence; student Eastern Mont. Coll., 1949-51; m. William R. Wagner, May 31, 1952 (div. 1974); children—Vicki Lee, Cindy Jo, Sheri Lynn, Kathleen Marie. Sec.-treas. Western States Constrn. Co., Inc., Loveland, Colo., 1964-69, v.p., 1969-72; sec.-treas. Rocky Mountain Concrete and Constrn., Inc., Estes Park, Colo., 1967-73; rancher, Thermopolis; artist. Mem. Am. Murray Grey Assn. Home: Lucerne Route 90A Thermopolis WY 82443

WAGNER, SHELLEY ELIZABETH, radio station executive, manufacturing company executive; b. Lewiston, Idaho, June 6, 1953; d. Shelton Brown and Mary Oberlander (Alford) W.; m. Harvey Irving Mednick, Oct. 3, 1981. B.A. in Sociology, Colo. Women's Coll., 1975; postgrad. Harvard U., 1975. With Ladies' Home Jour., N.Y.C., 1975-76; publicist Holt Rinehart & Winston, N.Y.C., 1976-79; freelance publicist, advt. dir. RKO Radio, Los Angeles, 1979; creative services asst. dir. Sta. KABC, Los Angeles, 1979—; owner, pres. Equi-Pac Mfg. Co., Los Angeles, 1982—; tchr. pub. relations, promotion local univs., seminars. Recipient Community award Girl Scouts Am., 1982.

WAGNER, SUE, state senator; b. Portland, Maine, Jan. 6, 1940; d. Raymond and Kathryn (Hooper) Pooler; B.A., U. Ariz., 1962; M.A., Northwestern U., 1964; m. Peter B. Wagner, Aug. 8, 1964 (dec. 1980); children—Kirk, Kristina. Asst. to dean women Ohio State U., Columbus, 1963-64; reporter Tucson Daily Citizen, 1964; tchr. Am. govt. and history Catalina High Sch., Tucson, 1965-68; mem. Nev. Ho. of Reps., 1975-79; mem. Nev. Senate, 1981—; tchr. Nev. Community Coll., 1976; mem. Nev. Legis. Commn., 1975-79; del. social services com. Council State Govts. Mem. Nev. Republican Central Com., Washoe County Rep. Central Com.; bd. dirs. Sierra Arts Found.; v.p. bd. dirs. Am. Field Service, 1972-73. Named Outstanding Legislator, Nev. Young Republicans, 1976; One of 10 Outstanding Young Women in Am., 1976; Legislator of Yr., Nev. Orgn. Wildlife, 1979, Nev. V.F.W., 1979, Nev. Trial Lawyers, 1981. Mem. AAUW (legis. chmn. chpt. 1974, community chmn. 1975), Bus. and Profl. Women's Club (Woman of Year Reno chpt. 1975). Episcopalian. Address: 845 Tamarack Dr Reno NV 89509

WAGONER, DAVID EVERETT, lawyer; b. Pottstown, Pa., May 16, 1928; s. Claude Brower and Mary Kathryn (Groff) W.; B.A., Yale U., 1950; LL.B., U. Pa., 1953; m. Landon Jensen; children—Paul R., Colin H., Elon D., Peter B. Admitted to D.C., Pa., Wash. bars, 1953; clk. to judge 3d Circuit U.S. Ct. Appeals, Pa., 1955-56, to justice U.S. Supreme Ct., Washington, 1956-57; ptnr. Perkins, Coie, Stone, Olsen & Williams, Seattle, 1957—. Mem. sch. com. Mcpl. League Seattle and King County, 1958—, chmn., 1962-65; mem. Seattle schs. citizens coms. on equal ednl. opportunity and adult vocat. edn., 1963-64, mem. Nat. Com. for Support Pub. Schs.; mem. adv. com. on community colls. to 1965 legislature interim com. on edn., 1964-65; mem. community coll. adv. com. to state supt. pub. instrn., 1965; chmn. edn. com. Forward Thrust, 1968; mem. Univ. Congl. Ch. Council Seattle, 1968-70; bd. dirs. Met. YMCA Seattle, 1968; bd. dirs. Seattle Pub. Schs., 1965-73, v.p., 1966-67, 72-73, pres., 1968, 73. Served to 1st lt. Med. Service Corps, AUS, 1953-55. Fellow Am. Coll. Trial Lawyers; mem. English Speaking Union (v.p. Seattle 1961-62), ABA (chmn. appellate advocacy com.), Wash. State, Seattle-King County bar assns., Nat. Sch. Bds. Assn. (bd. dirs.; chmn. Council Big City Bds. Edn. 1971-72), Chi Phi. Home: 1150 22d Ave E Seattle WA 98112 Office: Washington Bldg Seattle WA 98101

WAGONER, DEAN KAY, water utility executive; b. Kansas City, Mo., Aug. 12, 1918; s. John D. and Marion H. (Berry) W.; m. Pagene Mason, Feb. 14, 1939; children—Dee Louise, Lynn Page. Student pub. schs., Los Angeles. Field service rep. Lockheed Aircraft Co., Burbank, Calif., 1939-49; staff Calif. Water Service Co., Chico, 1951-62, Salinas, 1962-69, dist. mgr., Salinas, 1969—. Bd. dirs. Oldtown Salinas Assn., active local chpt. ARC, Heart Fund of Salinas; bd. govs. Salinas Valley Memorial Hosp. Served with USN, 1944-46. Named Salinas Outstanding Citizen of Yr., C. of C., 1980. Mem. Am. Water Works Assn., Monterey Bay Water Works Assn., Am. Pub. Works Assn. Baptist. Lodges: Lions, Elks. Office: Calif Water Service Co 254 Commission St Salinas CA 93901

WAHI, KRISHAN KISHORE, physicist; b. Hardwar, India, Oct. 20, 1948; came to U.S., 1967, naturalized, 1980; s. Wazir Chand and Raj Karni (Malhotra) W.; B.S. (tuition scholarship 1968-69), U. Wash., Seattle, 1969, M.S. (grad. asst. 1970-74), 1971, Ph.D. in Mech. Engring., 1974; m. Natalie R. Todd, June 5, 1974; children—Rajeev K., Nikhil D., Arun K. Sr. physicist Physics Internat. Co., San Leandro, Calif., 1974-75; with Sci. Applications, Inc., 1975—, sr. scientist, Fort Collins, Colo., 1979-80, Albuquerque, 1980—; cons. in field. Mem. ASME, Sigma Xi. Author papers in field. Home: 1312 Michael Hughes St NE Albuquerque NM 87112 Office: Western Bank Bldg 505 Marquette St NW Albuquerque NM 87102

WAHL, DALE FRANKLYN, safety engineering administrator; b. Crystal, Minn., Aug. 30, 1931; s. Rudolph J. and Leona E. Wahl; m. Sarah J. Nash, Aug. 4, 1956; children—Leisha Ann, Alison Andria. B.S., Stout State U., 1959. Safety engr. Aetna Life & Casualty Co., Mpls., 1959-67, engring. supt., Spokane, Wash., 1967-72, engring. mgr., 1972—. Mem. Mayor's Com. to Eliminate Archtl. Barriers to Handicapped, Spokane, 1974. Served with U.S. Army, 1952-54. Mem. Bd. Cert. Safety Profls., Am. Soc. Safety Engrs. (past pres. Inland Empire chpt.). Republican. Lutheran. Clubs: Spokane, Masons, Shriners. Designer sidewalk wheelchair ramps throughout City of Spokane. Home: W 2912 Weile St Spokane WA Office: W 601 Main Suite 1000 Spokane WA 99201

WAHL, DAVID PETER, flight dynamics and control engr.; b. N.Y.C., Jan. 7, 1940; s. Herbert John and Juliette Jenny (Noyer) W.; B.S. in Elec. Engring. Pa. State U., 1961; M.S. in Elec. Engring., U. So. Calif., 1966; m. Linda Louise Dennison, Feb. 10, 1962; children—Lori Lee, Darrin David. Electronics engr. Gen. Dynamics Co., San Diego, 1961-62; flight controls engr. N.Am. Aviation, Downey, Calif., 1962-66; sr. dynamics engr. Northrop Corp., Anaheim, Calif., 1966-78; mem. tech. staff Aerospace Corp., El Segundo, Calif., 1978-79; sr. staff engr. Hughes Aircraft Co., Fullerton, Calif., 1979—. Trustee, Lowell Joint Sch. Dist. Bd., 1979—, also v.p.; chmn. advancement com. troop 493 Boy Scouts Am., Whittier, 1978-80. Mem. AIAA, Soc. for Computer Simulation. Republican. Patentee in roll reference system for vehicles utilizing optical beam control. Home: 12318 Cullman Ave Whittier CA 90604 Office: B691/MS B220 1901 Malvern Ave Fullerton CA 92633

WAHL, FRANK BERNARD, JR., editor; b. St. Louis, Sept. 13, 1948; s. Frank Bernard and Lorraine Catherine (Hug) W.; B.S. in Systems Engring., U.S. Naval Acad., 1970; M.B.A., Nat. U., 1977; M.S. in Systems Mgmt., U. So. Calif., 1981; m. Barbara Ellen Kostlan, Apr. 24, 1971; children—Michael, Christina, Timothy. Commd. ensign U.S. Navy, 1970, advanced through grades to lt. comdr. USNR; served Vietnam; site mgr. SAI Comsystems, San Diego, 1975-76; project engr. ARINC Research, San Diego, 1976-77; corp. planner Gen. Dynamics, San Diego, 1977-79; editor-in-chief D.A.T.A. Book Series, San Diego, 1979—; dir. San Diego Navy Fed. Credit Union. Recipient Colts award for most original projects in systems engring., 1970. Mem. IEEE. Roman Catholic. Author: Microprocessor Software, Make or Buy: What are the Factors?Home: 11767 Papagallo Ct San Diego CA 92124 Office: 9889 Willow Creek Rd San Diego CA 92131

WAHL, IVER WILLIAM, aerospace co. exec.; b. Denver, Aug. 26, 1923; s. Iver William and Pearl Geneva (Warriner) W.; student U. Wichita, 1941-43; B.S. in Mech. Engring., U. Colo., 1949; m. Clayta Winifred Davis, June 23, 1945; children—Michael Dan, Eileen Annette. Stores supr. Cessna Aircraft Co., Wichita, Kans., 1941-43; tool design engr. Maytag Co., Newton, Iowa, 1949-51; insp. supr. Heckethorn Mfg. Co., Littleton, Colo., 1951-57; acting chief quality planning Martin-Marietta, Denver, 1957-64; quality assurance and property adminstrn. mgr. Ball Aerospace Systems Div., Boulder, 1964—. Bd. dirs. Littleton YMCA, 1952-55; mem. adv. council Met. State Coll., 1972-77. Served with USAAF, 1943-45. Recipient Skylab achievement award NASA; registered profl. engr., Calif. Fellow Am. Soc. Quality Control (officer, testimonial award); mem. Nat. Security Industries Assn. (com. chmn., Outstanding Achievement award), Electronics Industries Assn., Nat. Property Mgmt. Assn. (chpt. Officer-of-Yr. award). Presbyterian. Clubs: Elks, Knife and Fork (regional dir.), D.A.V. Home: 1205 Eastridge Boulder CO 80303 Office: PO Box 1062 Boulder CO 80306

WAHL, JOAN CONSTANCE, tech. writer, editor; b. Phila., Dec. 23, 1921; d. Frank L. and Sara E. (Timoney) O'Brien; B.A., Rosemont Coll., 1943; postgrad. U. Calif., Los Angeles, 1960-61; m. John Carl Wahl, Jr., Dec. 31, 1943 (div. 1959); children—John, Mark, David, Lawrence, Thomas, Jeanne Wahl Pearring, Madeleine Sophie, Eugene. Substitute tchr. Los Angeles City Bd. Edn., 1961; editor, proofreader Renner/Cal-Data Corp., Los Angeles, 1962-63; editor, tech. writer Volt Tech. Corp., 1964-66; sr. tech. editor, writer, project editor Aerospace Corp., El Segundo, Calif., 1966—. Sect. chmn. United Way, Los Angeles, 1963-64; mem. communications com. St. Paul the Apostle Roman Cath. Ch., Westwood, Calif., 1976-78. Recipient Outstanding Service award United Way, 1964. Mem. Soc. Tech. Communications (sr.), Aerospace Women's Com., Mental Health Assn. Los Angeles County, Kistler Honor Soc. Contbr. articles to profl. jours. Office: Aerospace Corp M3/377 2350 El Segundo Blvd El Segundo CA 90245

WAHLGREN, ERIK, educator; b. Chgo., Nov. 2, 1911; s. Oscar G. and Marion I. (Wilkins) W.; Ph.B., U. Chgo., 1933, Ph.D., 1938; M.A., U. Nebr., 1936; m. Dorothy Sly, Nov. 9, 1939 (div. 1951); children—Nils, Arvid; m. 2d, Beverly Pont, Dec. 18, 1952 (div. 1969); children—Siri, Thor; m. 3d, Helen Gilchrist-Wottring, July 2, 1971; 2 stepchildren Faculty, UCLA, 1938—, prof. Scandinavian langs., 1955-70, prof. Scandinavian and Germanic langs., 1970-77, prof. emeritus, 1977—; dir. study centers U. Bergen (Norway) and U. Lund (Sweden), 1972-74, vice chmn. dept. Germanic langs., 1963-69; lectr. Uppsala U., also vis. prof. Stockholm Sch. Econs., 1947-48; exchange instr. U. B.C., summer 1940; vis. prof. Augustana Coll., summer 1946; vis. prof. U. Calif.-Berkeley, 1968, U. Wash., 1970; sr. fellow Monterey Inst. Fgn. Studies, 1977-78; adj. prof. Portland State U., 1979-80; advisor NEH, 1978—. Mem. Mayor's Community Adv. Com., 1964-73; Am. mem. Commn. Ednl. Exchange U.S. and Sweden, 1973-74; advisor Gov.'s Commn. on Fgn. Langs. and Internat. Studies, 1980—; German lang. dir. Army Specialized Tng. Program, 1943-44. Am.-Scandinavian Found. fellow, Sweden, 1946-47; Am. Philos. Soc. grantee, 1954-55; Guggenheim Meml. Found. fellow, Scandinavia, 1961-62; pub. citation Icelandic Community Los Angeles, 1964; decorated knight Royal Swedish Order of Polar Star; knight Order of Lion (Finland), Order of Falcon (Iceland). Fellow Internat. Inst. Arts and Letters (life); mem. Swedish Cultural Soc. Am. (dir. 1940-48, pres. Los Angeles 1941-46), MLA So. Calif. (exec. bd. 1950-53), Am.-Scandinavian Found. (pres. Los Angeles chpt. 1958-60, Gold medal 1975), Leif Erikson Found. (dir. 1957-66), MLA (chmn. Scandinavian sect. 1955, 67), Soc. Advancement of Scandinavian Study (assoc. editor 1947-58, 70-73, assoc. mng. editor 1957-69), Am. Assn. Tchrs. German (nat. exec. council 1957-59, 60-63), Mediaeval Acad. Am., Finlandia Found., Am. Swedish Hist. Mus., Swedish-Am. Hist. Assn. Calif., World Affairs Council Oreg., Internat. Council Oreg.; Tau Kappa Epsilon, Delta Sigma Rho, Delta Phi Alpha. Author: The Kensington Stone: A Mystery Solved, 1958; Fact and Fancy in the Vinland Sagas, 1969, also several other books, translations, and numerous articles on Scandinavian philology. Home and Office: 1501 NW 12 St Corvallis OR 97330

WAHLKE, JOHN CHARLES, political science educator; b. Cin., Oct. 29, 1917; s. Albert B.C. and Clara J. (Ernst) W.; m. Virginia Joan Higgins, Dec. 1, 1943; children—Janet Wahlke Parmely, Dale. A.B., Harvard U., 1939, M.A., 1947, Ph.D., 1952. Asst. prof. polit. sci. Amherst (Mass.) Coll., 1949-53; prof. Vanderbilt U., 1953-63, SUNY-Buffalo, 1963-66, U. Iowa, 1966-71, 72-79, SUNY-Stony Brook, 1971-72; prof. polit. sci. U. Ariz., Tucson, 1979—. Served to capt. AUS, 1942-46. Decorated Air medal. Mem. Am. Polit. Sci. Assn. (past pres.), Midwest Polit. Sci. Assn. (past pres.), Western Polit. Sci. Assn., So. Polit. Sci. Assn., Southwestern Polit. Sci. Assn., Assn. for Politics and Life Scis., Soc. for Psychophysiol. Research, Internat. Soc. Polit. Psychology. Author: (with others) The Legislative System, 1962; Government and Politics, 1966; The Politics of Representation, 1978. Editor: Causes of the American Revolution, 1950; Loyalty in a Democratic State, 1952; co-editor: Legislative Behavior, 1959; The American Political System, 1967; Comparative Legislative Behavior, 1973. Office: Dept Polit Sci U Ariz Tucson AZ 85721

WAHLROOS, SVEN F. W., psychologist, author; b. Abo, Finland, May 6, 1931; s. Thure W. and Inga Alice (Juselius) W.; m. Eva Edit Terezia Adam; children—Ingalill, Sven-Erik. Ph.D. in Clin. Psychology, UCLA, 1955. Diplomate in clin. psychology Am. Bd. Profl. Psychology; diplomate in marital and family psychology Am. Bd. Family Psychology. Staff psychologist Los Angeles Psychiat. Service, 1955-58; pvt. practice, Van Nuys, Calif., 1958—; cons.; lectr.; supr. trainees. Trustee Finlandia Found. Mem. Am. Psychol. Assn., Los Angeles County Psychol. Assn., San Fernando Valley Psychol. Assn., Am. Acad. Family Psychologists. Lutheran. Author: Family Communication, 1974; Excuses: How to Spot Them, Deal with Them, and Stop Using Them, 1981; (cassette) Improving Family Communication, 1978. Office: 15243 Vanowen St Suite 200 Van Nuys CA 91405

WAIHEE, JOHN DAVID, III, state lieutenant governor; b. Honokaa, Hawaii, May 19, 1946; m. Lynne Kobashigawa; children—John David, Jennifer. B.A. with honors in History/Bus., Andrews U., 1968; M.A., Central Mich. U., 1973; J.D., U. Hawaii, 1976. Coordinator community edn. City of Benton Harbor (Mich.), 1968-70, asst. dir., 1970-71; program evaluator, adminstrv. asst. to dir., planner Honolulu Model Cities Program, 1971-73; sr. planner Office Human Resources, City and County of Honolulu, 1973-74, program mgr., 1974-75; assoc. firm Shim, Sigal, Tam & Naito, Honolulu, 1975-79; ptnr. firm Waihee, Manuia, Yap, Pablo & Hoe, Honolulu, 1979-82; mem. Hawaii Ho. of Reps., 1980-82; lt. gov. State of Hawaii, 1982—. Del., Hawaii Democratic Conv., 1972, 74, 76, 78, 82; del. Hawaii Constl. Conv., 1978; mem. Kalihi-Palama Hawaiian Civic Club; mem. bd. Alu Like; cons. Kaloko-Honokohau Study Commn.; past dir. Hawaii Sr. Citizens Travel Bd.; dir., past pres. Kalihi-Palama Community Council; mem. steering com. Goals for Hawaii Orgn. Named Outstanding Young Person, Hawaii Jr. C. of C., 1978. Mem. Filipino C. of C., ABA, Hawaii Bar Assn. (chmn. law com. 1979, legis. com. 1980), U. Hawaii Law Sch. Alumni Assn., Legal Aid Soc. Hawaii (past dir.). Lodge: Lions. Office: Office of the Lieutenant Governor Hawaii State Capitol Honolulu HI 96813

WAINER, STANLEY ALLEN, diversified industry exec.; b. Los Angeles, May 10, 1926; s. Calman and Katherine (Copeland) W.; B.S., U. Calif. at Los Angeles, 1950, grad. exec. program, 1958; m. Shirlene Joy Goldberg, Feb. 3, 1949; 1 son, William Edward. Accountant, Price Waterhouse & Co., Los Angeles, 1950-55; chief financial and adminstrv. officer Paramount Pictures Corp. and subsidiaries, 1955-60; v.p., sec.-treas. Royal Industries, Pasadena, Calif., 1960-61; with Wyle Labs., El Segundo, Calif., 1962—, pres., 1970—, chief exec. officer, 1979—; dir. Redwing Carriers, Inc., Elmar Electronics, Inc. Pres., dir. UCLA Bus. Sch. Alumni Assn., 1968-69; trustee UCLA Found., 1970—, dir. bd. overseers, 1972—; mem. dean's mgmt. council UCLA Grad. Sch. Mgmt.; bd. dirs. NCCJ, 1973—, Los Angeles Urban League, 1979—; regent U. Calif., 1980—; trustee Orthopaedic Hosp., Los Angeles, 1975—. Served with USNR, 1944-46. Mem. Financial Execs. Inst., Am. Inst. C.P.A.'s, Calif. Soc. C.P.A.'s, C. of C. of U.S., Calif. C. of C., Los Angeles C. of C. (dir. 1980—), UCLA Alumni Assn. (pres. 1980—), Soc. Order Blue Shield, Town Hall, Beta Gamma Sigma. Office: Wyle Labs 128 Maryland St El Segundo CA 90245

WAINWRIGHT, LEAH CHRISTINE, accountant, auditor; b. Oakland, Calif., Jan. 21, 1954; s. James Theodore and Marilyn Rose Wainwright; 1 dau., Elizabeth Rose. B.A., Columbia Coll., Mo., 1977; M.S. in Acctg., SUNY-Albany, 1981. Music instr. Bob Cummins Music, Hayward, Calif., 1968-70; bookkeeper Sutter's Mining Co., Inc., Albany, N.Y., 1978-81; auditor/acct. Bray, Burke, Waterman, Cockrill & Carter, C.P.A.s, Hayward, 1981—; tchr. bus. law Coll. St. Rose, Albany, 1980-81; tchr. acctg. Columbia Greene Community Coll., Hudson, N.Y., 1980. Served with U.S. Army, 1972-78. Mem. Beta Gamma Sigma. Home: 24823 2d St Hayward CA 94541 Office: 22300 Foothill Blvd Suite 509 Hayward CA 94541

WAITE, WENDELL LEROY, accountant; b. Los Angeles, July 24, 1941; s. William Noble and Anna Louisa June (Harriman) W.; m. Kathleen Christensen, Aug. 26, 1965. B.S. in Stats. and Math., Brigham Young U., 1965, M.B.A., 1967. C.P.A., Nev., Calif. Controller oil and gas exploration co., Los Angeles, 1968-71, motor home mfg. co., 1971-73; sr. cons. Coopers & Lybrand, 1973-75; mgr. in charge mgmt. adv. services Alexander Grant & Co., Reno, 1975-78; founder, pres. W.L. Waite & Assocs., C.P.A.s, Reno, 1978—; former instr. acctg. Los Angeles Coll., Harbor Coll., El Camino Coll., Sacramento State U. Founder Informed Voters League, Los Angeles; past chmn. Mt. Rose dist. Boy Scouts Am., Reno. Mem. Am. Inst. C.P.A.s, Nev. Soc. C.P.A.s, Calif. Soc. C.P.A.s, Data Processing Mgrs. Assn. Republican. Mormon. Club: Cougar. Contbr. articles to profl. jours. Office: 100 W Grove St Suite 250 Reno NV 89509

WAITON, RUDOLPH O., physician; b. Monessen, Pa., June 11, 1922; s. Lawrence and Anna (Ostrander) W.; B.S., U. Pitts., 1949; M.A., Stanford U., 1954, Ph.D., 1956; D.O., Kirksville Coll., 1965; M.D., U. Oreg., 1974; m. Marilyn Earle, Dec. 8, 1979; children—Richard, CorryAnn, Melanie, Thomas. Intern, Standring Meml. Hosp., Seattle, 1965-66; resident in rehab. medicine VA Hosp., Portland, Oreg., 1972-74; practice osteo. medicine and rehab. and phys. medicine, Los Gatos, Calif., 1975—; mem. staff Valley West Gen. Hosp. Served with USAAF, World War II, Korea. Decorated D.F.C. with oak leaf cluster, Air medal with three oak leaf clusters, Purple Heart. Diplomate Am. Bd. Osteo. Medicine, Am. Osteo. Coll. Rehab. Medicine. Fellow Am. Acad. Med. Preventics, Internat. Coll. Gen. Practice (charter), Internat. Coll. Applied Nutrition; mem. AMA, Calif. Med. Assn., Am. Acad. Family Physicians, Am. Acad. Osteopathy, Santa Clara County Med. Assn., Osteo. Physicians and Surgeons Calif., Fed. Aviation Med. Assn., Am. Osteo. Assn., Am. Coll. Rehab. Medicine, Internat. Acad. Preventive Medicine, Orthomolecular Med. Soc. Clubs: Elks, Rotary, Masons. physician; b. Monessen, Pa., June 11, 1922; s. Lawrence and Anna (Ostrander) W.; B.S., U. Pitts., 1949; M.A., Stanford U., 1954, Ph.D., 1956; D.O., Kirksville Coll., 1965; M.D., U. Oreg., 1974; m. Marilyn Earle, Dec. 8, 1979; children—Richard, CorryAnn, Melanie, Thomas. Intern, Standring Meml. Hosp., Seattle, 1965-66; resident in rehab. medicine VA Hosp., Portland, Oreg., 1972-74; practice osteo. medicine and rehab. and phys. medicine, Los Gatos, Calif., 1975—; mem. staff Valley West Gen. Hosp. Served with USAAF, World War II, Korea. Decorated D.F.C. with oak leaf cluster, Air medal with three oak leaf clusters, Purple Heart. Diplomate Am. Bd. Osteo. Medicine, Am. Osteo. Coll. Rehab. Medicine. Fellow Am. Acad. Med. Preventics, Internat. Coll. Gen. Practice (charter), Internat. Coll. Applied Nutrition; mem. AMA, Calif. Med. Assn., Am. Acad. Family Physicians, Am. Acad. Osteopathy, Santa Clara County Med. Assn., Osteo. Physicians and Surgeons Calif., Fed. Aviation Med. Assn., Am. Osteo. Assn., Am. Coll. Rehab. Medicine, Internat. Acad. Preventive Medicine, Orthomolecular Med. Soc. Clubs: Elks, Rotary, Masons. Home: 120 Carlton #54 Los Gatos CA 95030 Office: 221 Almendra Ave Los Gatos CA 95030

WAITS, ANITA MARY, accountant; b. Bakersfield, Calif., July 6, 1948; d. John and Josephine (Lorenzetti) Lencioni; m. Mark Waits, Aug. 1, 1970; children—Michael David, Jennifer Michele. A.A., Bakersfield Jr. Coll., 1968; B.S. in Acctg., Fresno State U., 1970. C.P.A., Calif. Internal auditor County of Fresno (Calif.), 1970-72; staff acct. Roberts Farms, Inc., McFarland, Calif., 1972-73, Smith Romiller, C.P.A., Bakersfield, 1973-74; sr. acct. Peter C. Brown Accountancy Corp., Bakersfield, 1974-79, supr., 1979-81, prin., 1981—. Mem. Am. Inst. C.P.A.s, Calif. Soc. of C.P.A.s, Delta Theta Tau, Phi Chi Theta (pres. 1980-81, award for scholastic achievement 1970). Republican. Roman Catholic. Club: Toastmasters (pres. 1983-84). Office: Peter C Brown Accountancy Corp 5700 Stockdale Hwy Suite 301 Bakersfield CA 93309

WAITZ, MARY LOUISE, educator; b. Telluride, Colo., Feb. 8, 1940; d. John Wesley and Kathrine Rose (Penasa) Dabney; m. Edward Koehler waitz, Jan. 25, 1964. B.S., Colo. State U., 1962, M.S., 1969. Tchr. vocat. home econs. Tehachapi (Calif.) Jr. High Sch., 1962-63, Frederick (Colo.) Jr. High Sch., 1964-67; tchr. home econs. Lyons (Colo) Jr. Sr. High Sch., 1967—. Mem. Am. Home Econs. Assn. (named Colo. Home Econs. Tchr. of yr. with Family Circle mag. 1980), Nat. Home Econs. Tchrs. Assn. (state membership chmn. 1982—), Colo. Home Econs. Assn. (chmn. family relations child devel. com. 1982—), Am. Vocat. Assn., Colo. Vocat. Assn., Colo. Assn. Vocat. Home Econs. Tchrs. (chmn. edn. exhbns. com. 1982-83), NEA, Colo. Edn. Assn., St. Vrain Valley Edn. Assn., Colo. Public Sch. Health Assn., Delta Kappa Gamma (treas. 1982-83). Republican. Methodist. Clubs: Order Eastern Star, Odd Fellows, Rebekahs. Home: 13820 N 95th St Longmont CO 80501 Office: PO Box 619 Lyons CO 80540

WAKABAYASHI, RONALD KAORU, association executive; b. Reno, Nev., Nov. 13, 1944; s. Fred Shinsuke and Edith Kimiko (Yamadera) W.; m. Jean Wong, July 10, 1976; 1 son, Jay Shin. B.A., Calif. State U., 1969. Nat. youth dir. Japanese Am. Citizens League, Los Angeles, 1969-72, nat. dir., 1981—; project dir. Japanese Sightless Inst., 1972-73; exec. dir. Asian Am. Drug Abuse Program, 1973-81. Democrat. Buddhist. Office: Japanese American Citizens League 1765 Sutter St San Francisco CA 94115

WAKEHAM, T. DAVID, insurance company executive; b. Orange, Calif., Sept. 10, 1945; s. Terry David and Dawn Patricia (Cornett) W.; B.A., Calif. State U., Fullerton, 1968; A.A., Fullerton Jr. Coll., 1966; student UCLA, 1967-68; m. Karen Louise McAdam, Feb. 10, 1973; 1 dau., Sarah. Claims rep. Hartford Ins. Co., San Francisco, 1972-73; claims adjuster Calif. Casualty Mgmt. Co., Los Angeles, 1974; claims examiner Wilshire Ins. Co., Los Angeles, 1974-75; claims supr. United

Pacific/Reliance Ins., Los Angeles, 1975-78, Republic Indemnity, 1978-80; field rep. Reagan Bush Com., Calif., 1980; claims supr. ESIS, Inc., Los Angeles, 1980-81; sr. account mgr. Marsh & McLennan, Inc., Los Angeles, 1981-82; adminstrv. asst. state legislature State of Calif., Bakersfield, 1982-83; adminstr. Alpha Beta Co., La Habra, 1983—. Alt. del. Rep. Nat. Com., 1976; nat. vice chmn. Young Rep. Nat. Fedn., 1975-77; mem. Calif. Rep. Central Com., 1978—. Served to 1st lt. U.S. Army, 1968-71; Vietnam. Mem. Calif. State U. Alumni Assn. Home: 615 W Palm St Monrovia CA 91016 Office: 777 S Harbor Blvd La Habra CA 90631

WAKEMAN, FREDERIC EVANS, JR., historian; b. Kansas City, Kans., Dec. 12, 1937; s. Frederic Evans and Margaret Ruth (Keyes) W.; B.A., Harvard U., 1959; postgrad. Institut d'Etudes Politiques, U. Paris, 1959-60; M.A., U. Calif., Berkeley, 1962, Ph.D., 1965; m. Carolyn Huntley, Dec. 31, 1974; children—Frederic Evans, III, Matthew Clark. Asst. prof. history U. Calif., Berkeley, 1965-67, asso. prof., 1968-70, prof., 1970—, chmn. Center for Chinese Studies, 1972-78; humanities research prof., vis. scholar Corpus Christi Coll., U. Cambridge (Eng.), 1976-77; nat. research scholar, vis. scholar Beijing U., 1980-81; acad. adviser U.S. Ednl. Del. for Study in China, 1979-81, chmn. joint com. on Chinese Studies. Harvard Nat. scholar, 1955-59; Tower fellow, 1959-60; Fgn. Area fellow, 1963-65; Am. Council Learned Socs. fellow, 1967-68; Guggenheim fellow, 1973-74. Mem. Am. Hist. Assn., Assn. Asian Studies. Author: Strangers at the Gate, 1966; History and Will, 1973; The Fall of Imperial China, 1975; Conflict and Control in Late Imperial China, 1976. Editor: Ming and Qing Historical Studies in the People's Republic of China. Home: 56 Arlington Ct Kensington CA 94707 Office: 460 Stephens St U Calif Berkeley CA 94720

WAKEMAN, THOMAS HERBERT, III, environmental engineer; b. Pasadena, Calif., Apr. 20, 1946; s. Thomas Herbert and Katherine Virginia (Stafford) W., II; B.S. in Biology, Calif. Poly. State U., 1970; M.A. in Marine Biology, San Francisco State U., 1975; m. Rosemary J. Mangiaracina, July 12, 1980; 1 dau., Gabrielle Georginne. Civilian with C.E., U.S. Army, San Francisco, 1973-82, biol. oceanographer, 1973-80, supervisory civil engr., 1980-82, research hydraulic engr. Hydrologic Engring. Ctr., Davis, Calif., 1983—. Served with USAR, 1970-73. Decorated Army Commendation medal; recipient Sustained Superior Performance award Dept. Army, 1975, Spl. Service award, 1982; Dept. Army Civil Works fellow, 1976-77. Mem. Soc. Wetland Scientists, Oceanic Soc. (water quality instr. 1975), Sigma Xi. Author papers in field. Office: 609 2d St Davis CA 95616

WALDEN, CAROLYN ELIZABETH, statistician; b. Houston, Dec. 2, 1948; d. William George and Angeline Elizabeth (Casey) Walker; m. Stanley John Walden, June 3, 1972. Student Tex. Tech. U.-Lubbock, 1967-69; B.S. in Fisheries Biology, U. Wash.-Seattle, 1971, M.S. in Biomathematics, 1976. Research technologist Ctr. for Quantitative Scis., U. Wash., 1971-72, statistician dept. biostatistics, 1972-78, research assoc., 1978—; statistician energy and technology div. Boeing Computer Services, Seattle, 1978; cons. in field of med. research. Bd. dirs. Northwest br. Childrens' Home Soc. Wash., 1980—; basketball referee Kirkland (Wash.) Parks Dept., 1979-82. M.K. Brown Found. grantee, 1969. Mem. Am. Statis. Assn., Biometric Soc. Lutheran. Contbr. articles in field to profl. jours. Home: 11443 110th Ave NE Kirkland WA 98033 Office: Department Biostatistics University of Washington Seattle WA 98195

WALDEN, KAREN FAYE, motel chain executive; b. Wausau, Wis., Dec. 24, 1950; d. Floyd Frederick and Lucille (Hetzel) Miller; m. Gary Rollin Walden, May 17, 1981; children—Cheri Michael, Kimberly Ann; m. 2d, Dennis Robert Meeker, Dec. 27, 1946. Dental asst., Billings, Mont., 1973-74; receptionist Husky Oil Co., Cody, Wyo., 1974-77; dir. sales Holiday Inn, Cody, 1977-78, regional sales mgr. various locations, 1978-81, Cheyenne, Wyo., 1981—. Exec. dir. Am. Cancer Soc., 1977-78. Mem. Cheyenne C. of C. (dir.), Beta Sigma Phi. Republican. Lutheran. Club: Toastmasters.

WALDEN, RICHARD KEITH, agri-business executive; b. Santa Paula, Calif., July 4, 1913; s. Arthur Frisbie and Eva Juanita (Southwick) W.; m. Barbara Eldredge Culbertson, Sept. 25, 1938 (div.); 1 son, Richard Sheffield; m. 2d, Dorothy Dayton Beck, July 5, 1967. B.A., Pomona Coll., 1936; postgrad. UCLA, 1934, 39. With Limoneira Ranch Co., Santa Paula, 1936-40; mgr. Ford-Craig Ranch Co., San Fernando, Calif., 1940-46; founder, pres., chmn. bd. Farmers Investment Co., Calif., Ariz. and Fla., 1946—; dir. Ariz. Feeds Co., 1950-74, 1st Interstate Bank, 1962—, Cotton, Inc., 1961-73; cons. Ford Found., Pakistan, 1969; dir. agr. adv. com. Stanford Research Inst., 1960-66; chmn. Pima County Agr. and Stblzn. Com., 1956-61. Bd. trustees Pomona Coll., 1978-81, Continental Sch. Bd., 1950-67; bd. dirs. Tucson C. of C.; chmn. Ariz. Oil and Gas Commn., 1960-66, Green Valley Community Health Ctr., 1981—; mem. Gov.'s Emergency Resources Planning Com. Recipient Disting. Citizen award U. Ariz. Alumni Assn., 1973; named Citizen of Yr., Rotary Club, 1980. Mem. Nat. Pecan Council, Ariz. Cotton Growers, Nat. Cotton Council (dir. 1960), Western Pecan Growers Assn. (dir. 1972-82), Ariz. Cattle Growers Assn. (dir. 1954-60), Cotton Council Internat. (chmn., pres. 1961-66), Town Hall Ariz. Republican. Clubs: Balboa (Mazatlan, Sinaloa, Mex.), Old Pueblo (Tucson), Plaza (Phoenix), Green Valley (Ariz.) Country. Home: 635 W Twin Buttes Rd PO Box 504 Green Valley AZ 85614 Office: PO Box 7 Sahuarita AZ 85629

WALDER, ROBERT ALAN, biomedical engineer, consultant; b. Alhambra, Calif., June 13, 1952; s. Irvin and Alice (Myronick) W.; m. Kelli Suzanne Cason, Aug. 18, 1973; children—Suzanne, James, Jonathan. Student East Los Angeles Coll., 1970-71; A.A. in Elec. Engring., Los Angeles Tech. Coll., 1972; cert. in elec. engring. Foothill Coll., 1977; cert. in supervision and mgmt. Mission Coll., 1981; M.S. cert. in Clin. Engring. (hon.), U. So. Calif., 1972. Cert. clin. engr., Calif. Chief biomed. engr. Amber Med., Culver City, Calif., 1971-73; field service mgr. Med. Life Systems, Mountain View, Calif., 1973-77; supr. clin. engring. Good Samaritan Med. Equipment Services, San Jose, Calif., 1977—; owner Samaritan Med. Equipment Services, 1977—; cons. in field. Served with USNR, 1970-71. Mem. Assn. Advancement Med. Instrumentation, Calif. Med. Instrumentation Assn. Democrat. Home: 6432 Ramblewood Dr San Jose CA 95124 Office: 2425 Samaritan Dr San Jose CA 95120

WALDMAN, LARRY FOSTER, child psychologist; b. Milw., Dec. 5, 1946; s. David and Rose (Driss) W.; m. Nan Ridberg, Aug. 15, 1971; children—Joshua, Chad. B.S., U. Wis., 1970, M.S. in Ednl. Psychology, 1973; Ph.D. in Ednl. Psychology, Ariz. State U., 1979. Lic. psychologist, Ariz., 1980; lic. sch. psychologist, Ariz., 1975. Tchr.-counselor The Acad., Racine, Wis., 1970-71; child care counselor Witt Hall for Boys, Milw., 1971-72; counselor Milw. Children's Hosp., 1972-73; tchr.-counselor Riverside High Sch., Milw., 1972-73; sch. psychologist Scottsdale (Ariz.) Pub. Schs., 1973-80; child psychologist The Family Ctr., Phoenix, 1980—; part-time lectr., counselor, prof. various other instns. in Wis. and Ariz. Mem. Nat. Assn. Sch. Psychologists, Am. Psychol. Assn., Council Exceptional Children, Ariz. Assn. Sch. Psychologists, Ariz. Assn. Children with Learning Disabilities, Ariz. Psychol. Assn., Employee Assistance Resources of Ariz., Maricopa Soc. Clin. Psychologists. Democrat. Jewish. Contbr. papers to profl. meetings. Home: 5061 E Cortez Scottsdale AZ 85254 Office: 525 N 18th St Phoenix AZ 85006

WALDO, BRUCE STONE, parks and recreation director; b. Hays, Kans., Dec. 14, 1933; s. Charles Stone and Doris Henryetta (Schwaller) W.; m. Gwendolyn Waggoner, Oct. 25, 1958; children—Kelli Denise, Juli Ann; m. 2d, Diana Lynn Tancher, Aug. 22, 1981. B.S., N. Tex. State U., 1956. Dir. parks and recreation, Fremont, Nebr., 1961-63, Irving, Tex., 1963-69, Westminster, Colo., 1969-72, Aurora, Colo., 1972—. Served with AUS, 1956-58. Fellow Tex. Parks and Recreation Soc., Colo. Parks and Recreation Soc.; mem. Westminster C. of C. (pres. 1971), Nat. Recreation and Parks Assn. Republican. Methodist. Office: 1470 S Havana St Suite 502 Aurora CO 80012

WALDO, SALLY, real estate, ins. broker; b. Seattle, Jan. 8, 1903; d. Hyman and Lena (Kaplan) Rosenstein; student Modesto Jr. Coll., 1930; m. Claude A Waldo, Nov. 6, 1925 (dec. June 1969). Exec. sec., co-owner firm Claude A. Waldo, land surveyor, Martinez, Calif., 1945-69; bus. opportunity broker, real estate broker, 1949—, ins. broker, 1950—. Mem. Calif. 50-50 Bill Com., 1937; mem. constn. revision com. nat. conv. Young Democratic Clubs Am., 1937, nat committeewoman, 1937-39, 1st v.p., 1936-37, chmn. woman's activities, 1936; Calif. chmn. circulation Nat. Young Dem. Paper, 1937; adv. bd. women's div. Calif. Dem. Central Com., 1936-38; organizer three young Dem. clubs in Stanislaus County, 1935; mem. Calif. Dem. Campaign Com., 1936; v.p. San Joaquin dist. Fed. Dem. Women's Study Clubs, 1940. Asso. mem. AIM; mem. San Joaquin Dist. Conv. Fedn. Women's Clubs (pub. chmn. 1935, legislation chmn. Stanislaus County 1934), Women's Improvement Club Modesto (Calif., sec. 1933), Women's Progressive Club (charter Modesto, sec. 1933), Tres Artes (organizer 1935), Modesto Art League (charter), Martinez Grange, Irish-Israeli-Italian Soc. San Francisco, Toastmistress Club (charter Modesto), Town Hall Forum Los Angeles. Mem. Order Eastern Star. Clubs: City Commons, Polit. Sci. (Berkeley); San Francisco Press (San Francisco). Office: PO Box 1023 Lafayette CA 94549

WALDORF, JEAN MOSELEY, newspaper executive; b. Montgomery, Ala., Mar. 15, 1942; d. Max H. and Lillian (Campbell) Moseley; m. Ronald C. Waldorf, May 1983; children—Kathleen, Michael and Patrick Kotecki. Student U. Ala., 1959, U. Ill., 1960-63, Troy State U., 1972-74. Supr. dept. advt./layout Champaign-Urbana (Ill.) Courier, 1959-63; freelance advt. promotional work, 1963-68; freelance advt., Memphis, 1968-70; owner, operator Books-N-Things, Montgomery, 1970-73; advt. mgr. Daily Sentinel Star, Grenada, Miss., 1974-76; advt sales mgr. Sta. WRIL-FM, Grenada, 1977; owner, publisher, editor The Copper Era, Greenlee County, Ariz., 1977—. County chmn. March of Dimes, Grenada; bd. dirs. Downtown Prescott Bus. Assn., Prescott, Ariz., 1982. Recipient Jaycee's Disting. Young Woman award, Montgomery, 1972, State of Ala., 1972; Nat. Found. March of Dimes Vol. Appreciation award, 1973. Mem. Miss. Presswomens Assn., Nat. Press Women's Assn., Miss. Advt. Execs., Nat. Advt. Execs. Assn., Ariz. Newspapers Assn., Nat. Press Assn. Republican. Roman Catholic. Clubs: Ala. Fedn. Women's, Soroptimist Internat. Home: 704 Laine Blvd Clifton AZ 85533 Office: 1 Park Ave Clifton AZ 85533

WALDWYN, MICHAEL ROBERT, real estate investment sales representative; b. Kidderminster, Eng., Sept. 24, 1944; came to U.S., 1965, naturalized, 1972; s. Robert and Margret E. (Evans) W.; A.A., San Jose City Coll., 1978. Sales rep. Nature's Best, 1971-73; air traffic controller San Jose (Calif.) Mcpl. Airport, 1973-81; real estate investment advisor, sales rep. Re/Max Realtors, San Jose, 1977—. Served with U.S. Army, 1969-71; Vietnam. Decorated Army Commendation Medal, Bronze Star. Mem. San Jose Real Estate Bd., Profl. Air Traffic Controller Orgn., North Valley Real Estate Assn. (past chmn.). Democrat. Home: 1108 Waterton Ln San Jose CA 95131 Office: 2690 Berreyessa Rd San Jose CA 95132

WALKER, ARNELL R., insurance executive; b. American Fork, Utah, Dec. 15, 1941; s. Thomas A. and Lucile (Allen) W.; m. Jaleen Jensen Walker, Nov. 20, 1962; children—J. Wallace. B.S., Utah State U., 1965. Tchr. Joint Sch. Dist. 150, Soda Springs, Idaho, 1966-72; safety mgr. B H & I Constrn. Co., Soda Springs, 1972-73; ins. agt., owner, mgr. Walker Ins., Soda Springs, 1973—. Mem. Soda Springs Bd. Edn., 1976-79, chmn., 1977-79; mem. Idaho Textbook Adoption Com., 1977—, chmn., 1983. v.p. programs Tendoy council Boy Scouts Am., 1982—. Mormon.

WALKER, BURTON LEITH, engineering writer, psychotherapist; b. Mt. Morris Twp., Mich., Oct. 23, 1927; s. Dalton Hugh and Muriel Joyce (Black) W.; m. Norva Jean Trochman, June 28, 1949; children—Paul, Cynthia, Halverson, Mark; m. 2d, Carol Jean DeAndrea, July 31, 1982. Cert. psychology. tchr., lic. psychotherapist, hypnotherapist, Calif. A.A., Allan Hancock Coll., 1971; B.A., Chapman Coll., 1974, M.A., 1975. From stock clk. to contract estimator Ryan Aeronaut., San Diego, 1949-59; logistics rep. GD/A, San Diego, 1960-62; systems engr., cons. fgn. service Ralph M. Parsons, Los Angeles, 1962-68; lead engring. writer Fed. Electric, Vandenberg AFB, Calif., 1969—; psychotherapist St. Mary's Counseling Ctr., Lompoc, Calif.; part time prof. Allan Hancock Coll., Santa Maria, Calif. Active Santa Ynez Valley Presbyn. Ch. Served with USN, 1946-48. Mem. Nat. Mgmt. Assn. (Outstanding Service award 1982), Fed. Electric Mgmt. Assn., Am. Profl. Guidance Assn., Solvang Bus. Assn. Republican. Forester. Home: 3149 Hwy 246 E Santa Ynez CA 93460 Office: 209 E Central PO Box 1082 Lompoc CA 93436

WALKER, DAVID LEE, training and development coordinator, educator; b. Stillwater, Okla., Dec. 27, 1946; s. Morris Seals and Winnifred Oleta (Fagg) W.; m. Viola Sue Wright, May 3, 1968; children—John, Michael, Joshua. B.A. with honors, Calif. Poly. State U., 1973, M.A., 1978. Vocat. tchr. Humboldt County Schs., Eureka, Calif., 1974-79; apprenticeship coordinator Louisanna Pacific, Samoa, Calif., 1974-79; tng. supr. ITT Rayonier, Port Angeles, Wash., 1979-82, tng. and devel. coordinator, 1982—; adj. prof. City U., Port Angeles, 1981—. Edn. and tng. coordinator United Way Campaign, 1983; pres. Port Angeles chpt. Full Gospel Bus. Men's Fellowship. Mem. Am. Soc. Tng. and Devel. (conv. coordinator 1983). Republican. Mem. Assembly of God Ch. Author audiovisual safety and indsl. relations programs.

WALKER, DOLORES ANN, chemical company executive; b. Dodge City, Kans., Feb. 8, 1935; d. Elwin Eugene and Sarah Frances (Moore) Lewis; m. Donald Carlos Bardwell, Dec. 2, 1955; children—Valerie Bardwell Herndon, Yvette Bardwell Graham, Sabrina Bardwell Alston, Donald; m. 2d, Earl Oscar Walker, Dec. 13, 1960; children—Darren, Darcel. B.A., Wichita State U., 1973. Dir., YWCA, Wichita, Kans., 1973; with indsl. engring. dept. NCR Corp., Wichita, 1974-76, buyer, 1976-77, personnel rep., 1977-78; personnel rep. Stauffer Chem. Co., San Francisco, 1978-80, personnel mgr., 1980—. Named Outstanding Sr. Woman Wichita State U., 1973. Roman Catholic. Club: Roscicrusian.

WALKER, DONALD IRVING, chemist, association executive; b. Lombard, Ill., Jan. 13, 1922; s. George B. and Grace (Patrick) W.; B.S., U. Ill., 1948; Ph.D., U. Colo., 1956; m. Ruth Ellen Rouley, Feb. 15, 1944; children—Judith Elyn, Marc Stephen, David Lee. Research chemist Los Alamos Sci. Lab., 1950-53; teaching asst. U. Colo., 1953-56; dep. dir. health and safety div. AEC, Idaho Falls, Idaho, 1956-57, dir. licensee compliance div., 1957-62, dir. region IV div. compliance, Denver, 1957-62, dir. region IV div. compliance, 1962-70, dir. health services lab., Idaho Falls, 1970-76; exec. dir. Associated Western Univs., Inc., Salt Lake City, 1976—. Served with C.E., AUS, 1942-46. Mem. Am. Chem. Soc., Internat. Health Physics Soc., Am. Inst. Chemists. Home: 2609 E Sundance Dr Sandy UT 84092 Office: 142 East 200 South Salt Lake City UT 84111

WALKER, DUANE DENNIS, nursing adminstr., educator; b. Waterloo, Iowa, July 28, 1938; s. Robert T. and Margery E. (Hoppe) W.; children—Geoffrey, Robyn, Troy. B.S., Weber State Coll., 1969; M.S. in Psycho-Social Nursing, U. Utah, 1977. R.N., 1963. Instr., Weber State Coll., 1968-70, clin. instr. nursing, 1972-78; dir. clin. services Weber County Hosp., Roy, Utah, 1968-70; asst. adminstr., dir. nursing service Holy Cross Hosp., Salt Lake City, 1970-75; asst. adminstr., patient care service U. Utah Med. Ctr., 1975-78; assoc. clin. prof. dept. biol. dysfunctions U. Calif.-San Francisco, 1979—; assoc. adminstr. hosp. clinics, dir. nursing service Stanford U., 1978—, lectr. dept. family, community and preventive medicine, 1979—. Bd. dirs. Lytton Gardens, 1981-82. Served with Nurse Corps, U.S. Army, 1966-68. Fellow Am. Acad. Nursing; mem. Nat. League Nursing, Am. Nurses Assn., Am. Hosp. Assn., Sigma Theta Tau. Republican. Roman Catholic. Contbr. articles to profl. jours. Home: 57 Wilburn Ave Atherton CA 94025 Office: 300 Pasteur Dr Stanford CA 94305

WALKER, E. CARDON, film company executive; b. Rexburg, Idaho, Jan. 9, 1916; s. Edmond Levier and Violet Walker; B.A. in Econs., UCLA, 1938; D.Sc. (hon.), Fla. Inst. Tech., 1976; m. Winifred L. Watkins, June 28, 1946; children—Mignonne, Marnie, John Cardon. With Walt Disney Prodns., Burbank, Calif., 1938—, v.p. advt. and sales, 1956-65, v.p. mktg., 1965-68, exec. v.p., chief operating officer, 1968-71, pres., 1971-76, pres., chief exec. officer, 1976-80, chmn. bd., chief exec. officer, 1980—. Trustee UCLA Found., Verdugo Hills Hosp., Calif. Inst. Arts; dir. San Gabriel Valley Council Boy Scouts Am., Bleitz Wildlife Found.; mem. exec. com., bd. dirs., chmn. licensing and merchandising adv. comm. Los Angeles 1984 Olympic Organizing Com. Served to lt. U.S. Navy, World War II. Recipient Parlin award Am. Mktg. Assn., 1974; Achievement in Mktg. award; Golden Plate award Am. Acad. Achievement, 1974; Pioneer of Yr. award Found. Motion Picture Pioneers, 1975; Disting. Alumni award Los Angeles Unified Sch. Dist.; Edward A. Dickson Alumnus of Yr. award UCLA, 1977. Mem. Am. Film Inst., Calif. C. of C. (dir.). Clubs: Oakmont Country, Pauma Valley Country. Office: Walt Disney Productions 500 S Buena Vista St Burbank CA 91521

WALKER, EDWARD DONALD, artist; b. Danville, Ill., Oct. 31, 1946; s. Edward Glennen and Hazel Mary Walker; m. Elizabeth Anne Walker, Oct. 1, 1977; children—Melody Robin, Courtney Elizabeth. Student Queensland Inst. Tech., Brisbane, Australia, 1966. One man shows: Jalisco State Mus., Guadalajara, Mex., 1975, Ligoa Duncan Gallery, N.Y.C., 1976, Galeries Raymond Duncan, Paris, 1976, Scott Gallery, Orinda, Calif., 1974-81, John Pence Gallery, San Francisco, 1982; works represented in permanent collections San Francisco Mus. Modern Art, Charles and Emma Frye Mus., Seattle, Stanford U., others; instr. oil and watercolor Asilomar Workshops, Monterey, Calif., 1977-80; juror awards various art assns., including Calif. State Fair, 1973. Served with USAF, 1967-71. Recipient 1st award Laguna Gloria Mus., Austin, Tex., 1976; Emily Lowe award Am. Watercolor Soc., Nat. Acad. N.Y., others. Mem. Am. Watercolor Soc., West Coast Watercolor Soc. (v.p. 1980-81). Illustrator note cards Nat. Assn. Visually Handicapped, 1978—; calendar Bankers Life Nebr., 1979. Address: 550 Sutter St San Francisco CA 94108

WALKER, ELJANA M. DU VALL, civic worker; b. France, Jan. 18, 1924; came to U.S., 1948; naturalized, 1954; student Med. Inst., U. Paris, 1942-47; m. John S. Walker, Jr., Dec. 31, 1947; children—John, Peter, Barbara. Pres., Loyola Sch. PTA, 1958-59; bd. dirs. Santa Calus shop, 1959-73; treas. Archdiocese Denver Catholic Women, 1962-64; rep. Cath. Parent-Tchr League, 1962-65; pres. Aux. Denver Gen. Hosp., 1966-69; precinct committeewoman Arapahoe County Republican Women's Com., 1973-74; mem. re-election com. Arapahoe County Rep. Party, 1973-78, Reagan election com., 1980; block worker Arapahoe County March of Dimes, Heart Assn., Hemophilia Drive, Muscular Dystrophy and Multiple Sclerosis Drive, 1978-81. Recipient Distinguished Service award Am.-by-choice, 1966; named to Honor Roll, ARC, 1971. Mem. Cherry Hills Symphony, Lyric Opera Guild, Alliance Franciase (life mem.), ARC, Civic Ballet Guild (life mem.), Needlework Guild Am. (v.p. 1980-82), Kidney Found. (life), Denver Art Mus., U. Denver Art and Conservation Assns. (chmn. 1980-82), U. Denver Women's Library Assn. Roman Catholic. Clubs: Union (Chgo.); Denver Athletic, 26 (Denver); Welcome to Colo. Internat. Address: 6185 S Columbine Way Littleton CO 80121

WALKER, FRANCIS JOSEPH, lawyer; b. Tacoma, Aug. 5, 1922; s. John M. and Veronica (Meehan) W.; A.B., St. Martin's Coll., 1947; J.D., U. Wash., 1950; m. Julia C. O'Brien, Jan. 27, 1951; children—Vincent, Monica, Jill, John, Michael, Thomas. Admitted to Wash. bar, 1950; asst. atty. gen. State of Wash., 1950-51; individual practice law, 1951—; gen. counsel Wash. Catholic Conf., 1967-76. Served with USNR, 1943-46. Mem. Wash. Bar Assn. Home: 2723 Hillside Dr Olympia WA 98501 Office: 301 Security Bldg Olympia WA 98501

WALKER, GAIL JUANICE, electrologist; b. Bosque County, Tex., Sept. 3, 1937; d. Hiram Otis and Hazel Ruth (Carmichael) Gunter; cert. Shults Inst. Electrolysis, 1971; children—Lillian Ruth, Deborah Lynn. In quality control Johnson & Johnson, San Angelo, Tex., 1962-70; owner, pres., electrologist Ariz. Inst. Electrolysis, Scottsdale, 1979—; ednl. cons. Gail Walker's Internat. Sch. Electrolysis, Tokyo, 1980; area corr. Hair Route mag., 1981; participant continuing edn. program in electrology Shelby State Coll., 1981. Editor Electrolysis World. Cert., Pvt. Bus. and Tech. Schs., State of Ariz. Mem. Ariz. Assn. Electrologists (pres. 1980—), Am. Electrolysis Assn., Internat. Guild Profl. Electrologists, Nat. Fedn. Ind. Businessmen, Ariz. Assn. Electrologists (organizer 1980). Republican. Baptist. Club: Order of Eastern Star. Office: 7033 E Indian Sch Rd 2 Scottsdale AZ 85251

WALKER, GLENN MILTON, accounting firm executive; b. Lewellen, Nebr., Feb. 17, 1928; s. Jonathan Seibert and Mary Hester (McKune) W.; m. Mildred Montague, Mar. 15, 1958 (div.); children—Kirk Montague Kimball, Richard Huntington Kimball. B.S. in Bus. Adminstrn., U. Denver, 1951, M.B.A., 1953. C.P.A., Colo. Ptnr.-in-charge Pannell Kerr Forster, Denver, 1961—. Served to lt. U.S. Army, 1946-59. Mem. Am. Inst. C.P.A.s (council 1978-79) (auditing standards bd. 1978-81), Colo. Soc. C.P.A.s (bd. dirs. 1978-81) (pres. 1979-80). Republican. Mem. Religious Science Ch. Clubs: Denver C. of C., Denver Athletic; Garden of the Gods (Colorado Springs). Author: Assertion I: Income Tax Simplification 1979. Office: 720 S Colorado Blvd Suite 1300 Denver CO 80222

WALKER, HENRY ALEXANDER A., JR., corp. exec.; b. Honolulu, Mar. 5, 1922; s. Henry Alexander and Una (Craig) W.; student Harvard, 1940-42, Columbia, 1946-47; m. Nancy Johnston, Mar. 10, 1946; children—Henry Alexander III, Susan Walker Kowen. With AMFAC, Inc., Honolulu, 1947—, v.p., operations, 1966, exec. v.p., 1966-67, pres., 1967, also chief exec. officer, chmn. bd., 1974—; dir. BanCal Tri-State Corp., Bank of Calif., Calif. & Hawaiian Sugar Co., Gulf and Western Industries, Inc., Hawaii Public Radio, Hawaiian Telephone Co., Hawaiian Trust Co., Bd. dirs. Opera Players Hawaii, Straub Clinic and Hosp. Served with USNR, 1944-46. Mem. Jud. Council Hawaii, Hawaiian Sugar Planters Assn. Clubs: Oahu Country, Pacific (Honolulu); Kaneohe Yacht; Pacific Union (San Francisco); Phoenix S.K.; Harvard; Chicago; The 200. Office: Amfac Inc PO Box 3230 Honolulu HI 96801

WALKER, JENEPHER, editor; b. Cedar Grove, N.J., Apr. 12, 1933; d. William Stevenson and Eloise (Rockhold) Walker; A.A., Principia Coll., 1952; B.S., U. San Francisco, 1977; m. Paul Sannar Smith, June 7, 1975; stepchildren—Robert G. Smith, Hoyt Austin Smith, Jennifer Joy Smith. Service rep. N.J. Bell Telephone Co., Pompton Lakes, 1953-54; exec. sec., researcher, asst. editor House & Home, Time, Inc., N.Y.C., 1955-64; asso. editor, products editor House & Home, McGraw-Hill, N.Y.C., 1964-72; mng. editor, editor Small Bus. Reporter, Bank of Am., San Francisco, 1972-78; editor Hudson Home mag., Los Altos, Calif., 1978-80, western editor Home, Foster City, Calif., 1980—; Kitchen designer, 1982—. Recipient Maggie award Western Pubs. Assn., 1979. Mem. Nat. Home Fashions League. Christian Scientist. Editor: Small Business Profiles and Operations, 1978; Author: How to Design and Remodel Kitchens, 1982; The Kitchen, 1982. Address: 902 Beachpark Blvd Foster City CA 94404

WALKER, JOHN A., aerospace co. exec.; b. Earlville, Iowa, July 20, 1930; s. John L. and Wilma F. W.; B.A., Coe Coll., 1953; postgrad. Chgo. Teachers Coll., 1957; m. Mary Ann Hunter, July 8, 1951; children—Michael, Jeff, Mark, Suzanne. Base mgr. Strategic Weapons Facility, Lockheed Missiles and Space Co., Submarine Base Bangor, Wash., 1979—. Bd. dirs. United Way of Kitsap County, Santa Clara County Diabetes Soc.; hon. life mem. PTA; active Boy Scouts Am. Served with USAF, 1952-57; Korea. Mem. Nat. Mgmt. Assn. (Silver Knight of Mgmt., 1980), Soc. Logistics Engrs., Navy League, Naval Inst. Presbyterian. Home: 591 Ludlow Bay Rd Port Ludlow WA 98365 Office: PO Box 6429 Naval Submarine Base Bangor WA 98315

WALKER, JOHN DAVIES, agronomy educator, researcher, consultant; b. Logan, Utah, Apr. 26, 1941; s. Rudger Harper and Fawn Lucile (Davies) W.; m. Sharon Lee Powers, Sept. 12, 1961; children—Suzanne Rachel, Michael Powers. B.S., Brigham Young U., 1963; Ph.D., U. Ill.-Urbana, 1973. Tchr. sci., pub. high schs., Salt Lake City, 1965-69; asst. prof. agronomy Ohio State U., 1973-76; prof. agronomy, chmn. dept. farm crops mgmt. Ricks Coll., 1976—; adj. prof. agronomy Brigham Young U., 1981—; seasonal researcher on range revegetation U.S. Forest Service, Utah, 1961-69; cons. in field; bd. dirs. Eastern Idaho Agrl. Hall of Fame, 1977—; producer, dir. ann. Idaho Field Days on Reduced Tillage Techniques; nat. and internat. speaker on reduced tillage. Served with U.S. Army N.G., 1963. Recipient teaching award Ohio State U. Agrl. Tech. Inst., 1976, Ricks Coll., 1979; Farmer Merchant Speaker award Rexburg (Idaho) C. of C., 1977; agrl. chem. cos. grantee, 1974—; Idaho Wheat Commn. grantee, 1979—. Mem. Am. Soc. Agronomy, Soil Sci. Soc. Am., Crop Sci. Soc. Am., Weed Sci. Soc. Am. Republican. Mormon. Author papers on practical and profitable agronomic techniques and procedures for widespread adoption of minimum tillage wheat and barley prodn. Office: Dept Farm Crops Mgmt Ricks Coll Rexburg ID 83440

WALKER, JOHN MARSHALL, structural engr.; b. Tulsa, Aug. 29, 1955; s. Donald Field and Joyce Ione W.; m. Sonja Ann Emery, July 14, 1979. B.S.C.E., B. Environ. Design, U. Colo., 1978, postgrad., 1978—. Registered profl. engr., Colo. Teaching asst. U. Colo., Boulder, 1977, 78, resident advisor, 1977-78; draftsman/solar homes designer Energy Systems Corp., 1977; structural engr., draftsman, adminstr. Lonco, Inc., Denver, 1978-79; sr. project engr. Borman/Smith & Ptnrs., Inc., Denver, 1979—; bldg. designs include: Borman/Smith Plaza 7000, Writer's Center V, 1981, Paragon Bldg., Writer's Center V, others. Treas. bd. mgrs. Club Valencia Condominim Assn., 1981—, mem. budget and fin. com., 1979—, mem. archtl. and maintenance com., 1980-81. Home: 1306 S Parker Rd Apt 280 Denver CO 80231 Office: Borman Smith & Partners Inc 789 Sherman St Suite 640 Denver CO 80203

WALKER, JOHN WALLACE, computer manufacturing company executive; b. Balt., May 16, 1949; s. William Wallace and Bertha Garnet (Bailey) W.; B.S. in Engring., Case Inst. Tech., 1971; m. Roxie Dawne Smail, May 19, 1973. Systems programmer Chi Corp., Cleve., 1969-72; programmer Sperry Vickers, Troy, Mich., 1972; mgr. software support Axicom Systems, Paramus, N.J., 1972-73; mgr. data communications Info. Systems Design, Santa Clara, Calif., 1973-77; pres. Marinchip Systems, Mill Valley, Calif., 1977—, Autodesk, Inc., Mill Valley, 1982—. Named Outstanding Tech. Contbr. for Year, Info. Systems Design, 1976. Mem. IEEE, Mensa. Inventor means to interface new microcomputer hardware to existing systems, 1977. Office: 16 St Jude Rd Mill Valley CA 94941

WALKER, KEITH ALLEN, plant genetics company executive; b. Cleve., Oct. 17, 1948; s. Joseph Fordun and Audrey Marie (Brindley) W.; m. Marguerite Joyce Ming, Aug. 29, 1970; children—Kenneth Alec, Andrew Fordun. B.A., Coll. of Wooster, 1970; Ph.D., Yale U., 1974. Sr. research biologist Monsanto Chem. Co., St. Louis, 1974-76, research group leader, 1976-79, sr. research group leader, 1979-81; dir. product devel. Plant Genetics, Inc., Davis, Calif., 1981-82, v.p. research, 1982—. Mem. Am. Soc. Plant Physiologists, Am. Soc. Agronomy, Soc. Devel. Biology, Am. Bot. Soc., Sigma Xi. Contbr. articles, chpts. to tech. jours., books. Office: Plant Genetics Inc 1930 5th St Davis CA 95616

WALKER, LINDA KATHRYN, vocational rehabilitation counselor; b. Butte, Mont., June 13, 1952; d. James Robert and Eleanor Delores (Miller) Dowling; m. Philip Duane Walker, Aug. 10, 1974. B.S. in Vocat. Rehab., Eastern Mont. Coll., 1979. Epilepsy medications cert.; developmental disabilities client programming tech. cert., 1982. Counselor, Children's Receiving Home, Billings, Mont., 1979-80; child devel. technician Yellowstone Boys Ranch, Billings, 1980; prodn. foreman, counselor, Billings Workshop, 1982—. Bd. dirs. Postal Customers Council, 1982—. Mem. Am. Personnel and Guidance Assn., Am. Rehab. Counseling Assn., Pub. Offender Counseling Assn., AAUW. Home: 1109 Dorothy Ln Billings MT 59105 Office: Billngs Workshop 200 S 24th St Billings MT 59101

WALKER, MARJORIE LOUISE, advt. exec., writer; b. Los Angeles, June 7, 1923; d. Joseph Bailey and Marjorie Warfield (Ward) W.; student U. So. Calif., 1940-41, UCLA, 1941-44; m. Douglas D. Coppin, July 12, 1944 (div.); 1 son, Gary Walker; m. 2d, Earl C. Kennedy, Sept. 2, 1955 (div.); 1 dau., Cynthia Walker. Model, actress, Hollywood, Calif., 1941-48; with program and promotion div. ABC, Los Angeles, 1948; co-founder, v.p. Kennedy, Walker and Wooten, Inc., Los Angeles, 1955—; owner, pres. Walker and Assos., Los Angeles, 1971—; weekly columnist Beverly Hills Courier; monthly columnist Club and Sports Mag. Mem. Hollywood Women's Press Club, Screen Smart Set, Los Angeles Orphanage Guild. Home: 8569 Burton Way Los Angeles CA 90048 Office: 8230 Beverly Blvd Los Angeles CA 90048

WALKER, MAXINE CANFIELD, real estate broker and developer; b. Boise, Idaho, June 29, 1933; d. Max M. and Alice Irene (Chamberlin) Armstrong; student Willamette U., 1950-51, Sacramento Jr. Coll., 1951-52; m. Jordan C. Walker, Aug. 4, 1967; children—Karen Joanne Walker Scott, Mark A. Canfield, Leslie Canfield. Real estate salesman MacBride Realty, Sacramento, 1961-63; propr., broker Canfield and Assos. Realtors, Sacramento, 1963-66; partner Canfield Hurst & Walker Realtors, Sacramento, 1966-67; propr., broker Canfield & Assos. Realtors, Sacramento, 1968—; pres. Jordan Devel. Co. Inc., 1976—; dir. Reliance Bancorp, Nat. Bancorp, Sierra Resources Corp., Courtesy Thrift and Loan. Bd. regents Christian Bros. High Sch.; trustee Gateway Found. Mem. Calif. Real Estate Assn., Nat. Assn. Real Estate Bds., Sacramento Bd. Realtors. Home: 4330 Sierra Madre Dr Sacramento CA 95825 Office: Jordan Development Co Inc/Canfield and Associates Realtors 1721 Eastern Ave Suite 8 Sacramento CA 95825

WALKER, PATRICIA SEARS CHALLENDER, govt. ofcl.; b. Sunfield, Mich., Apr. 7, 1934; d. Verle Eugene and Rhoda Leora (Sweet) Sears; B.A. magna cum laude, Golden Gate U., 1976, M.B.A., 1978; m. Wilford J. Challender, Apr. 17, 1952 (dec. Oct. 1960); children—Wilford, Patricia; m. 2d Russell E. Walker, Sept. 28, 1963 (dec. May 1971); 1 son, Russell. Contract specialist U.S. Army, Presidio of San Francisco, 1956-63; contracting officer Naval Supply Center, U.S. Navy, Oakland, Calif., 1964—, now supervisory contract negotiator. Mem. Nat. Contract Mgmt. Assn. (pres. Golden Gate chpt. 1978, dir. 1979-80, v.p. N.W. region 1981-83), Federally Employed Women, NOW, ACLU, Nat. Women's Polit. Caucus. Democrat. Unitarian. Clubs: Bridge, Toastmistress. Home: 14 Cheyenne Way Corte Madera CA 94925 Office: Code 201 A Naval Supply Center Oakland CA 94625

WALKER, PAUL ALLEN, psychologist; b. Balt., Sept. 29, 1946; s. Harry Lee and Augusta Marie (Kramer) W. Ph.D., U. Rochester, 1976. Lic. psychologist, Calif., Tex. Asst. prof. psychology U. Balt., 1973-76; asst. prof. med. psychology Johns Hopkins Med. Sch., Balt., 1976-80; asst. prof. psychiatry and pediatrics U. Tex. Med. Br., 1976-80; pres. Harry Benjamin Internat. Gender Dysphoria Assn. Inc., San Francisco, 1979-81; pvt. practice San Francisco, 1980—; sr. staff psychologist Pacific Profl. Assocs.; chmn. clin. studies dept. The One Inst. Grad. Sch. Bd. dirs. San Francisco Child Abuse Council, Inst. Study Human Resources. Mem. San Francisco Bay Area Psychol. Assn. (sec.). Columnist Gay Wellness, 1980-82. Contbr. articles to profl. jours. Office: 1952 Union St San Francisco CA 94123

WALKER, PHILIP CHAMBERLAIN, II, organization executive; b. Big Spring, Tex., July 7, 1944; s. Philip C. and Mary C. (St. John) W.; m. Linda Jane Holsclaw, Jan. 21, 1978. B.A. in Geography, Central Wash. State Coll., 1971, B.A. in Psychology, 1971; M.S. in Geography, U. Idaho, 1972. Chief exec. officer Profl. Rev. Orgn. for Wash., Seattle, 1981—; exec. dir. Wash. State PSRO, Seattle, 1981—; pres. T.D. Livestock Co., Ellensburg, Wash., 1982—; cons. in field. Served with USAF, 1962-66; Vietnam. Mem. Am. Assn. Profl. Rev. Orgns. (bd. dirs. 1979-81, chmn., exec. dir. sect. 1979-81). Democrat. Contbr. articles to profl. jours. Home: 418 N 157th Ct Seattle WA 98133 Office: Wash State PSRO 2150 N 107th St Suite 220 Seattle WA 98133

WALKER, PRISCILLA BOWMAN, cable television executive; b. Palisade, Colo., May 2, 1949; d. Marion G. and Helen E. (Maher) Bowman; m. Bruce A. Walker, Dec. 20, 1970. B.A., U. Denver, 1970. Acct. exec. Piper & Assocs., Denver, 1971-75; mktg. assoc., nat. mktg. services mgr. Am. TV & Communications Corp., Englewood, Colo., 1975-79, dir. communications, 1979-82, dir. field pub. affairs, 1982-83, dir. cable devel., 1983—. Mem. Citizens Action Com., Regional Transp. Dist., Denver, 1975. Mem. Women in Cable (Accolade award 1981, pres. Rocky Mountain chpt. 1983), Pub. Relations Soc. Am. Office: 160 Inverness Dr W Englewood CO 80112

WALKER, RAYMOND FRANCIS, bus., fin. cons. co. exec.; b. Medicine Lake, Mont., Nov. 9, 1914; s. Dennis Owen and Rose (Long) W.; grad. pub. schs.; student Edison Vocat. Sch., 1935-39; m. Patricia K. Blakey, May 15, 1951; children—Richard A., Mark D., Maxie R. Forest, Victoria L. Le Huray, Suzanne J. Adkins, Tracy A. McLemore. Truck mgr. Pacific Food Products, Seattle, 1939-42; machinist Todd Shipyard, Seattle, 1942-45; owner Delbridge Auto Sales, Seattle, 1945-48; pres. Pacific Coast Acceptance Corp., 1949-60; v.p. West Coast Mortgage, Seattle, 1960-67, United Equities Corp., Seattle, 1965-69; pres. Income Mgmt. Corp., Seattle, 1970-82; cons. Life Ins. Co. Am., Consumer Loan Service. Mem. Nat. Assn. Security Dealers. Methodist. Club: Elks. Home: 16510 Brickyard Rd Bothel WA 98011

WALKER, RICHARD F., utility company executive; b. 1924. B.S. in Elec. Engring., U. Colo., 1949. With Pub. Service Co. of Colo., Denver, 1949—, mgr. planning and analysis, 1964, asst. v.p. engring., 1967, v.p. engring. and planning elec. dept., 1968, pres., chief operating officer, 1976, pres., chief exec. officer, 1978—, also dir. Office: Pub Service Co of Colo 550 15th St PO Box 840 Denver CO 80201*

WALKER, SANDRA KAY, nurse; b. Whittier, Calif., Apr. 15, 1942; d. John Franklin and Alice Joyce (Kelsey) Summers; m. Lawrence Neil Walker, Aug. 15, 1964; children—Bradley Neil, Cynthia Kay, Matthew John. Grad. Good Samaritan Hosp. Sch. of Nursing, Portland, Oreg., 1963. Registered nurse, Oreg. Instr., Good Samaritan Hosp. Sch. Nursing, Portland, 1963-67; health coordinator Regional Health Planning, Medford, Oreg., 1967-69; inservice dir. Providence Hosp., Medford, 1969-71; health occupations tchr. Grants Pass (Oreg.) High Sch., 1971-75; health coordinator Jackson County Intermediate Edn. Dist., Medford, 1975-76; health occupation coordinator Rogue Community Coll., Grants Pass, 1976-82; inservice dir. Cascade Community Hosp., Central Point, Oreg., 1983—; cons. Oreg. Bd. Edn., 1972-81. Mem. Nurses Assn., Am. Vocat. Assn. Roman Catholic. Club: Soroptimist.

WALKER, SYLVIA CHRISTINE, chemist; b. Orange, Calif., July 4, 1954; d. Clarence Loring and Dorothy Mary (Greenwood) Hall; B.S., Calif. State Poly. U., 1974, M.S. in Chemistry, 1979, M.B.A., 1983; m. Ronald Raymond Walker, Sept. 9, 1978. Chem. technician Occidental Research Corp., LaVerne, Calif., 1974-76; lectr. Calif. State Poly. U., Pomona, 1978; chemist Lockheed Aircraft Service Co., Carlsbad, Calif., 1979-81; sr. research engr. Lockheed Missiles and Space Co., Sunnyvale, Calif., 1981-82; corrosion engr. Ameron, South Gate, Calif., 1983—. Mem. Am. Chem. Soc., Nat. Assn. Corrosion Engrs., Gamma Sigma Delta, Phi Kappa Phi. Home: 10034 Olive St Bloomington CA 92316

WALKER, THOMAS JEROME, environmental health and safety consultant; b. Springfield, Ohio, Sept. 23, 1932; s. Albert Rinehart and Mary Agnes (Kuss) W.; A.B., Athenaeum of Ohio, Norwood, 1955; M.Ed., Xavier U., Cin., 1959; M.S. (U.S. Dept. Health fellow in Indsl. Hygiene), U. Cin., 1969; m. Patricia Ann O'Leary, Oct. 27, 1956; children—Jerome Thomas, Stephen Martin, Sharon Lynn. Biology tchr. Loveland (Ohio) Pub. Schs., 1958-59; chemistry tchr. Oak Hills (Ohio) Pub. Schs., 1959-62, Aiken High Sch., Cin., 1962-68; mgr. indsl. hygiene Kaiser Aluminum & Chem. Corp., Oakland, Calif., 1969-82; pres. Thomas J. Walker, Inc., 1982—; clin. assoc. U. Calif., San Francisco and Berkeley. Served with U.S. Army, 1956-58. Indsl. participant in first U.S. Dept. Labor and Internat. Communications Agy. Program on Occupational Health for Spanish Govt., 1979. Registered profl. engr., Calif. Fellow Am. Acad. Indsl. Hygiene, Acad. Kettering Fellows-U. Cin. (pres. 1978-80), Am. Bd. Cert. Safety Profls.; mem. Am. Indsl. Hygiene Assn. (dir. 1979-82, pres. No. Calif. 1975-76), Am. Soc. Safety Engrs. Democrat. Roman Catholic. Asso. editor Jour. Am. Indsl. Hygiene Assn., 1977-79; contbr. to books and jours. Home and Office: 1678 Lower Grand Ave Piedmont CA 94611

WALKER, TIMOTHY CRAIG, automotive products company executive; b. Huntington, W.Va., Jan. 16, 1945; s. John Paul and Marjorie Frances (Withers) W.; B.A., Northwestern U., 1967; B.F.T., Am. Grad. Sch. Internat. Mgmt., 1968. Mgmt. trainee to dir. OIM/internat. mktg. ops. NCR Corp., Dayton, Ohio, 1968-79; v.p. mktg. Do-Ray Lamp Co., Inc., Colorado City, Colo., 1979—, dir., 1982—; recruiter Am. Grad. Sch. Internat. Mgmt., 1971—. Bd. dirs. Valley Human Resources, United Way agy., 1980—; mem. transp. com. Pueblo (Colo.) Area C. of C., 1981—. Recipient Pres.'s award (1st alumnus) Am. Grad. Sch. Internat. Mgmt., 1976, award for excellence in internat. advt., 1968; named to Automobile Hall of Fame, 1983. Mem. Truck Safety Equipment Inst. N.Am. (chmn. mktg. and statis. com. 1980-82). Republican. Presbyterian. Clubs: 500 Automotive Execs., Colo. City Country. Home: PO Box 54 Colorado City CO 81019 Office: PO Box 20 Colorado City CO 81019

WALKER, TIMOTHY WADE, public relations agency executive, educator; b. San Bernardino, Calif., Mar. 16, 1956; s. Byron Oliver and Janet Yvonne (Doubenmeir) W.; m. Carie Macdonald, May 17, 1979; children—Kelly, Michelle. B.A. in Pub. Relations, Brigham Young U., 1979. Cert. community coll. tchr. Research asst. David O McKay Inst. Instructional Scis., Brigham Young U., Provo, Utah, 1977-79; info. specialist mktg. U-Haul Internat., Phoenix, 1980-81, publicity dir. A & M Assocs. Advt. Inc. U-Haul, Phoenix, 1981—; publicity cons. Theodore Roosevelt council Boy Scouts Am. Sustaining mem. Republican Nat. Com., 1980—. Recipient award Merit One Sheet Publs. Internat. Assn. Bus. Communicators, 1980. Mem. Pub. Relations Soc. Am. Mormon. Home: 4032 W Sweetwater Phoenix AZ 85029 Office: A & M Assocs Inc 2727 N Central St Phoenix AZ 85004

WALKER, U. OWEN, government official; b. Huffman, Ark., Oct. 9, 1925; s. James Nathaniel and Amy Pricie (Wimberly) W. B.E., Yale U., 1946; cert. in plant layout and facilities planning U. Kans.-Lawrence, 1967; postgrad. U. N.Mex., 1981. Registered profl. engr., Miss., Ark. Office engr., field engr., project mgr., estimator, appraiser S & W Constrn. Co., Inc., Memphis, 1946-53, 70-72; dep. facilities engr., chief engring. plans and real property Def. Depot Memphis, Def. Logistics Agy., Memphis, 1953-70; civil engr. plan formulation sect. Engring. div. C.E., U.S. Army, Memphis, 1973-76; dir. engring. div. dept. pub. works U.S. Naval Sta., Mayport, Fla., 1976-79; dep. dir. facilities and services div. Marine Corps Logistics Base, Barstow, Calif., 1979-81; asst. regional mgr. programs and resources U.S. Dept. Interior, Albuquerque, 1981—. Served to lt. (j.g.) USN, 1943-46; mem. Res., 1946-59. Recipient Mr. Industry award Indsl. Maintenance and Plant Ops. mag. 1969. Fellow ASCE; mem. Am. Inst. Plant Engrs. (Engr. of Yr. medal 1968), Assn. Energy Engrs., Inst. Cert. Profl. Mgrs., Inst. Cert. Records Mgrs., Assn. Records Mgrs. and Adminstrs., Adminstrv. Mgmt. Soc., Soc. Advancement of Mgmt. Baptist. Club: Yale. Office: PO Box 1224 Albuquerque NM 87103

WALKER, WALTER WYRICK, metallurgical engineer; b. Winslow, Ariz., Jan. 14, 1924; s. John Edward and Sadie Theresa (Moore) W.; B.S., U. Ariz., 1950, M.Sc. (NDEA fellow 1959-62), 1962, Ph.D. (NSF fellow 1966-67), 1968; Ph.D. (hon.), U. Phys. Sci., 1958; m. Frances Ellen Sprawls, Jan. 16, 1952. Metall. engr., chemist in automotive, nuclear energy and aerospace field, 30 yrs.; group leader metall. tech. Hughes Aircraft Co., Tucson, 1978-82, staff engr., 1982—; mem. part-time and full-time faculty various univs. Mem. Pima County Pollution Control Hearing Bd., 1979—, Tucson Adv. Com. on Air Pollution, 1970-72. Served with USNR, World War II. Registered profl. engr., Ariz., Calif. Fellow Am. Inst. Chemists, AIME, Am. Soc. Metals, Nat. Soc. Profl. Engrs., AAAS, ASTM, Am. Geophys. Union, Am. Optical Soc., Nat. Assn. Corrosion Engrs., Ariz. Acad. Scis., N.Y. Acad. Scis., Brit. Inst. Metals, Mensa. German Shepherd Dog Club, So. Ariz. Rescue Assn., Sigma Xi. Democrat. Club: So. Ariz. Hiking. Author papers in field. metallurgical engineer; b. Winslow, Ariz., Jan. 14, 1924; s. John Edward and Sadie Theresa (Moore) W.; B.S., U. Ariz., 1950, M.Sc. (NDEA fellow 1959-62), 1962, Ph.D. (NSF fellow 1966-67), 1968; Ph.D. (hon.), U. Phys. Sci., 1958; m. Frances Ellen Sprawls, Jan. 16, 1952. Metall. engr., chemist in automotive, nuclear energy and aerospace field, 30 yrs.; group leader metall. tech. Hughes Aircraft Co., Tucson, 1978-82, staff engr., 1982—; mem. part-time and full-time faculty various univs. Mem. Pima County Pollution Control Hearing Bd., 1979—, Tucson Adv. Com. on Air Pollution, 1970-72. Served with USNR, World War II. Registered profl. engr., Ariz., Calif. Fellow Am. Inst. Chemists, AIME, Am. Soc. Metals, Nat. Soc. Profl. Engrs., AAAS, ASTM, Am. Geophys. Union, Am. Optical Soc., Nat. Assn. Corrosion Engrs., Ariz. Acad. Scis., N.Y. Acad. Scis., Brit. Inst. Metals, Mensa. German Shepherd Dog Club, So. Ariz. Rescue Assn., Sigma Xi. Democrat. Club: So. Ariz. Hiking. Author papers in field. Home: 5643 E 7th St Bldg 808 Tucson AZ 85711 Office: Hughes Aircraft Co Bldg 202-807 M/S MN Tucson AZ 85734

WALKER, WELDON JOSEPH, cardiologist, educator, former army officer; b. Garland, Kans., Jan. 14, 1916; s. Joe Shelton and Laura Nora (Humphrey) W.; B.S., Walla Walla Coll., 1937; M.D., Loma Linda U., 1940; m. Shirley Danae Nicola, Dec. 25, 1968; children—Elizabeth Carol, Tracy Dean, Scott Alan, Jamie Joel, Randy Quint. Commd. 1st lt. M.C., U.S. Army, 1940, advanced through grades to col., 1953; asso. prof. mil. medicine Harvard Med. Sch., 1950-52; chief of cardiology Brooke Army Hosp., San Antonio, 1953-57; cons. cardiology Walter Reed Gen. Hosp., Washington, 1960-64; mem. staff, Europe, 1957-60; cons. cardiology Office of Surgeon Gen., Washington, 1960-64; asso. prof. clin. medicine Baylor Med. Sch., Houston, 1954-57; asso. prof. clin. medicine Loma Linda Sch. Medicine (Calif.), 1964-66, clin. prof. medicine, 1966-77, clin. prof. medicine emeritus, 1977—; clin. prof. medicine U. So. Calif. Sch. Medicine, 1974-77; dir. cardiovascular lab. White Meml. Med. Center, Los Angeles, 1964-77; mem. cardiovascular study sect. Nat. Heart Inst., 1962-64. Decorated Bronze Star, Legion of Merit; recipient Maj. Louis Livingston Seaman prize U.S. Army, 1962; diplomate Am. Bd. Internal Medicine, Am. Bd. Cardiology. Fellow A.C.P., Am. Heart Assn., Am. Coll. Cardiology. Republican. Editorial bd. Jour. AMA, 1973-76; contbr. articles to med. jours. and chpts. to textbooks. Home: 6378 Pioneer Rd Medford OR 97501

WALKINGTON, DAVID LEO, biology educator; b. Waukegan, Ill., July 20, 1930; m. Loraine Walkington; 1 dau., Lori. B.A. in Chemistry, Ariz. State U., 1957, M.S. in Biology, 1959; Ph.D. in Botany, Claremont Grad. Sch., 1965. Instr. Ariz. State U., 1955-59, lectr. gen. botany, 1957-59, instr. botany, 1959-60, lectr. cell biology, summers 1966-71; asst. prof. biology Calif. State U.-Fullerton, 1963-66, assoc. prof., 1967-72, prof., 1972—, research assoc. Calif. State Coll. Found., Fullerton, various adminstrv. positions including assoc. dean Sch. Math., Sci. and Engring., 1976, acting assoc. v.p. for extended edn., 1978-80, assoc. v.p. for extended edn., 1980—. Served with USNR, 1948-50; with USN, 1950-54. Mem. Orange County Industry Edn. Council, 1975—, chmn. sci. resource task force, 1982-83; founder, treas. Career Guidance Inst. of Orange County, 1977-81; mem. Community Services Commn., City of Fullerton, 1982—; bd. dirs. Vol. Bur. of North Orange County, 1978, 79, treas., 1980, pres., 1981—; trustee Fullerton Mus. Assn., 1970-73, v.p., 1972-74; trustee, dir. edn. Mus. Assn. of North Orange County, 1974, pres., 1975-76, dir. spl. programs, 1977, v.p., 1978-79, 82; bd. dirs. Youth Sci. Ctr. of North Orange County,

1968-74, v.p., 1969-70, pres., 1971-72; head sci. council Greater Ariz. chpt. Allergy Found. of Am., 1959-60; mem. alumni bd. dirs. Claremont Grad. Sch., 1978-81. Mem. Soc. Calif. Botanists (sec.-treas. 1964-68, pres. 1968-69, bd. govs. 1970-71), So. Calif. Acad. Scis. (mem. adv. bd. 1966-68, program chmn. 1968-69, 73-74, bd. dirs. 1971-73), Cactus and Succulent Soc., Orange County Sci. Tchrs. Assn. (pres. elect 1967-68, pres. 1968-69, bd. dirs. 1970-71; bd. dirs. internat. sci. and engring. fair, v.p. 1976, 77, 78), Am. Inst. Biol. Scis., Western Soc. Naturalists (exec. officer-mem.-at-large 1970, program com. 57th ann. meeting 1976), Nat. Assn. Biology Tchrs. (nat. conv. program coordinator 1977), Faculty Ctr. Assn. Calif. State-Fullerton (v.p. 1968-69, pres. 1970, bd. dirs. 1971-75), Beta Beta Beta, Phi Delta Kappa. Recipient 50th Yr. V.I.P. Hon. Service award Fullerton High Sch. PTA. Contbr. articles to profl. jours. Office: Dept Biology Calif State U Fullerton CA 92634

WALL, ALIN HERNANDEZ, accountant; b. Los Angeles, Apr. 14, 1951; d. Frank Victor and Rose Parra (Miranda) H.; m. Robert Wall, Sept. 2, 1981. B.A., UCLA, 1974. C.P.A., Calif. Supr. auditing Laventhol & Horwath, C.P.A.s, Los Angeles, 1973-77; controller Michael Keele Enterprises, Santa Monica, Calif., 1977-79; sole practice Alin Hernandez, C.P.A., Los Angeles, 1980; ptnr. Cohen & Bender, C.P.A.s, Los Angeles, 1981—. Mem. Am. Inst. C.P.A.s, Calif. Soc. C.P.A.s, NOW. Office: 1801 Ave of Stars Suite 507 Los Angeles CA 90067

WALL, DONALD ARTHUR, lawyer; b. Lafayette, Ind., Mar. 17, 1946; s. Dwight Arthur and Myra Virginia (Peavey) W.; m. Cheryn Lynn Heinen, Aug. 29, 1970; children—Sarah Lynn, Michael Donald. B.A., Butler U., Indpls., 1968; J.D., Northwestern U., 1971. Bar: Ohio 1971, U.S. Dist. Ct. (no. dist.) Ohio 1973, U.S. Supreme Ct. 1980, Ariz. 1982, U.S. Dist. Ct. (no. dist.) W.Va. 1982, U.S. Ct. Appeals (6th cir.) 1982, U.S. Dist. Ct. Ariz. 1983. Assoc., Squire, Sanders & Dempsey, Cleve., 1971-80, ptnr., 1980-82, Phoenix, 1983—; speaker in field. Mem. adminstrv. bd. Ch. of the Saviour, Cleve., 1980-82, trustee Day Care Ctr., 1979-82; bd. dirs. Epilepsy Found. Northeast Ohio, 1976-82, pres. 1981-82. Mem. ABA (chmn. R.R. law com. 1982-83), Ariz. Bar Assn., Maricopa County Bar Assn., Nat. Assn. R.R. Trial Lawyers, Def. Research Inst., Ariz. Trial Lawyers Assn., Am. Judicature Soc. Methodist. Contbr. articles to law jours. Home: 5424 E Yucca St Scottsdale AZ 85254 Office: Valley Bank Center Phoenix AZ 85073

WALL, GARTON EVANS, physician; b. Honolulu, June 2, 1906; s. Walter Eugene and Edith Louise (Dietz) W.; m. Ellabelle Seagrave, Apr. 12, 1934; children—Walter Douglas, Martha Louise, Dominick, Mary Mary Alice Dias, Lawrence Alexander. M.D., Northwestern U., 1933. Intern, Evanston (Ill.) Hosp., 1931; intern Queens Med. Ctr., Honolulu, 1932-33, resident in surgery, 1934; med. dir. Ewa Plantation Co. (Hawaii), 1934-64, also govt., city, county physician Ewa Dist.; practice family medicine, Honolulu, 1964—; mem. staff Queens Med. Ctr. Served with USNR, 1942-47; PTO. Rotary Found. fellow, 1981. Fellow Am. Acad. Family Practice; mem. Hawaii Med. Assn., Honolulu County Med. Assn., AMA, Am. Acad. Family Practice, Hawaii Acad. Family Practice. Republican. Episcopalian. Clubs: Rotary (past pres.).

WALL, GENEVIEVE, lawyer; b. N.Y.C., Aug. 17, 1950; d. Philip J. and Catherine C. (Mohr) Wall; m. Michael Wolff, Sept. 7, 1974; children—Megan Elizabeth. B.A., UCLA, 1973; J.D., Western State U.-Fullerton, 1981. Bar: Calif. 1981, U.S. Dist. Ct. (cen. dist.) Calif. 1982. Paralegal, Nancy Boxley Tepper, Inc., Laguna Hills, Calif., 1977-81, assoc. atty., 1981-82; assoc. Lord & Ross, Laguna Hills, 1982—. Mem. ABA, Calif. Bar Assn., Orange County Bar Assn., So. Orange County Bar Assn. Club: Soroptimists. Office: Lord & Ross 23521 Paseo de Valencia Suite 201-B Laguna Hills CA 92653

WALL, LINDA, home economics educator; b. Provo, Utah, Dec. 20, 1951; d. Dale Clyne and LaRue (Gammell) W. A.S., Snow Coll., 1972; B.S., Brigham Young U., 1974. Home econs. tchr. Roosevelt (Utah) Jr. High Sch., 1974—. Republican. Mormon. Office: PO Box 160 Roosevelt UT 84066

WALLACE, BARBARA JEAN, educator, consultant; b. St. Marys, Pa., Dec. 30, 1947; d. Robert Russell and Marjorie Frances (Schreiber) Wilson; m. Michael H. Wallace, Oct. 20, 1976. B.S. cum laude, Old Dominion U., 1969; M.A., Calif. State U., 1977; Ed.D., U. So. Calif., 1981. Tchr. English, First Colonial High Sch., Virginia Beach, Va., 1969-70; tchr., team leader grades 4-6, Conejo Valley Unified Sch., Newbury Park, Calif., 1972-76, coordinator early childhood edn. project, 1976-79; supr. student tchrs. Calif. Poly. State U., San Luis Obispo, 1979—; evaluator pre-delinquent intervention program Paso Robles (Calif.) Schs. Trustee Paso Robles Joint Union High Sch. Dist.; pres. Paso Robles br. Calif. Fedn. Republican Women, 1983—. Mem. Assn. Calif. Sch. Adminstrs., Assn. Supervision and Curriculum Devel., Calif. Sch. Bds. Assn., AAUW. Home: Shandon Star Route Paso Robles CA 93446 Office: PO Box 276 Paso Robles CA 93446

WALLACE, FRAN ANDRON, personnel executive, career consultant; b. Oceanside, N.Y., July 3, 1955; s. Arnold I. and Shirley A. (Andron) W.; B.S., Cornell U., 1977; M.Ed., Harvard U., 1978. Career intern Harvard U., Cambridge, Mass., 1977-78; asst. dir. career plans Ithaca (N.Y.) Coll., 1978-79, dir., 1979-81; staff Nat. Career Devel. Project, Walnut Creek, Calif., 1981-82; asst. dean students Mills Coll., Oakland, Calif., 1981-82; personnel mgr. Remac Systems, Inc., Campbell, Calif., 1982; employee relations mgr. Bay View Fed. Savs., San Mateo, Calif., 1983—; cons. burnout and wellness. Mem. Com. for Prevention Child Abuse, Anorexia Nervosa and Related Eating Disorders Com. Recipient Campus Life award, 1981. Mem. Nat. Employment Counselors Assn., Am. Personnel and Guidance Assn., Am. Coll. Personnel Assn. (dir.), Alpha Lambda Delta, Omicron Nu, Phi Kappa Phi, Phi Delta Kappa. Contbr. articles to profl. jours. Home: 1431 Beach Park Blvd Foster City CA 94404 Office: Bay View Fed Savs Suite 815 San Mateo CA 94403

WALLACE, GARY ROE, army officer; b. Mercedes, Tex., Oct. 31, 1954; Russell Farrell and Beadie Pearl (Hand) W.; B.S., Tarleton State U., 1977; m. Karol Louise Thompson, July 15, 1978; 1 dau., Sarah Elaine. Commd. 2d lt. U.S. Army, 1977, advanced through grades to capt., 1981—; inf. officer Basic & Inf. Mortar Platoon Courses, Ft. Benning, Ga., 1978; platoon leader 24th Inf. Div., 2nd Battalion, 34th Inf., Ft. Stewart, Ga., 1977-79, ordnance officer Explosive Ordnance Disposal Sch., Indian Head, Md., 1979-80; Comdr. Escort & Disposal Detachment, Dugway Proving Ground, Utah, 1980—. Mem. Assn. of U.S. Army. Club: Masons. Home: 502 Bexfield Dugway UT 84022 Office: Escort and Disposal Detachment Dugway Proving Ground UT 84022

WALLACE, J. CLIFFORD, judge; b. San Diego, Dec. 11, 1928. A.B., San Diego State U., 1952; LL.B., U. Calif.-Berkeley, 1955. Bar: Calif. 1955. Practiced in San Diego; former judge U.S. Dist. Ct.; judge U.S. Ct. Appeals, 9th Circuit. Mem. ABA, Am. Bd. Trial Advocates, Am. Law Inst. Bd. editors Calif. Law Rev., 1954-55.

WALLACE, KENNETH ALAN, real estate devel. exec.; b. Gallup, N.Mex., Feb. 23, 1938; s. Charles Garrett and Elizabeth Eleanor (Jones) W.; A.B. in Philosophy, Cornell U., 1960; postgrad. U. N.Mex., 1960-61; m. Rebecca Marie Odell, July 11, 1980; children—Andrew McMillan, Aaron Blue, Susanna Garrett. Comml. loan officer Bank of N.Mex., Albuquerque, 1961-64; asst. cashier Ariz. Bank, Phoenix, 1964-67; comml. loan officer Valley Nat. Bank, Phoenix, 1967-70; pres. WWW, Inc., Houston, 1970-72; v.p. fin. Hometels of Am., Phoenix, 1972-77, Precision Mech. Co., Inc., 1972-77; partner Schroeder-Wallace, 1977—; mng. partner Pala Partners, San Diego; pres. Blackhawk, Inc., Phoenix, 1977—; pres., dir. Kloron Corp., Johannesburg, South Africa; exec. v.p. South African BMX; dir. Schroeder Constrn. Co., Inc., Phoenix; v.p., dir. C.G. Wallace Co., Albuquerque; gen. partner Diamond W Ranch, Ltd., Sanders, Ariz., Wallco Enterprises, Ltd., Mobile, Ala. Loaned exec. Phoenix United Way, 1966, Tucson United Way, 1967; mem. Valley Big Bros., 1970—; mem. Alhambra Village Planning Com.; fin. dir. Ret. Sr. Vol. Program, 1973—; mem. Phoenix Men's Arts Council, 1974—, Phoenix Symphony Council. Campaign committeeman Republican gubernatorial race, N.Mex., 1964; treas. Phoenix Young Reps., 1966; bd. dirs. Devel. Authority for Tucson, 1967. Mem. Soaring Soc. Am. (Silver badge), Am. Rifle Assn. (life), Nat. Mktg. Assn. (Mktg. Performance of Year award 1966), S.W. Profl. Geog. Assn., Nat. Assn. Skin Diving Schs., Pima County Jr. C. of C. (dir. 1967), Phoenix Little Theatre, Phoenix Musical Theatre, S.W. Ensemble Theatre (dir.), Alpha Tau Omega. Mason (Shriner). Clubs: Univ., Plaza (Phoenix). Home: 409 E Keim Dr Phoenix AZ 85012 Office: Schroeder-Wallace PO Box 7703 Phoenix AZ 85011

WALLACE, LEIGH ALLEN, JR., bishop; b. Norman, Okla., Feb. 5, 1927; s. Leigh Allen and Nellie Elizabeth (Whittemore) W.; B.A., U. Mont., 1950; M.Div., Va. Theol. Sem., 1962, D.Div., 1979; m. Alvira Kinney, Sept. 2, 1949; children—Jenny Leigh, Richard Kinney, William Paul. Ordained priest Episcopal Ch.; vicar chs., Sheridan, Virginia City, Jeffers, Mont., 1962-65; rector St. Luke's Ch., Billings, Mont., 1965-71; rector Holy Spirit Parish, Missoula, Mont., 1971-78; bishop of Spokane, 1979—. Served with USNR, 1945-46. Address: E 245 13th Ave Spokane WA 99202

WALLACE, MARIETTA MAE, ret. aircraft co. ofcl., consultant; b. Los Angeles, Jan. 18, 1926; d. Sanford H. and Rena (Van Vlack) Weeks; student Glendale (Calif.) Coll., 1965-72, Fullerton (Calif.) Coll., 1979-80; m. Frederick W. Wallace, Oct. 16, 1974; 1 son, Sanford Swallow. Dir. data processing Glendale Unified Sch. Dist., 1960-75; data processing cons., Fullerton, 1975-77; coordinator data processing Garden Grove (Calif.) Community Ch., 1977-79; chief fin. officer Abwal Avionics, Inc., Hemet, Calif., 1980-82; v.p. Wallace & Wallace, Cons., 1982—. Adminstrv. asst. to minister Reformed Ch. of Hemet Valley. Mem. Hemet C. of C., Hemet Aviation Club. Republican. Home: 41368 Stetson Ave Hemet CA 92343

WALLACE, ROBERT CHARLES, educator, administrator; b. Corning, Calif., Mar. 3, 1946; s. Robert Campbell and Ethel Irene (House) W.; m. Mary Kathleen O'Brien, Aug. 27, 1966; children—Mary Ann, Robert Patrick. B.S., Chico State Coll., 1968; M.S., Chapman Coll., 1978. Teaching credential, Calif. Tchr., coach East Union High Sch. Golden West Elem. Sch. and Lincoln Elem. Sch., Manteca, Calif., 1969-79; vice prin. Golden West Sch. 1979-81; prin. El Portal Middle Sch., Escalon, Calif., 1981—. Active in City Youth Soccer League. Recipient Manteca Outstanding Educator award, 1976; San Joaquin County Outstanding Elem. Special Edn. Tchr. award, 1976; PTA Honorary Service award, Lifetime Membership award, 1981. Mem. Assn. Calif. Sch. Adminstrs., Assn. for Supervision and Curriculum Devel. Republican.

WALLAR, ROBERT EDWARD, urban planner, realtor, Indian land claims specialist; b. St. Louis, Jan. 13, 1942; s. Robert E. and Anita E. (Krueger) W.; A.A., Santa Barbara City Coll., 1967; B.A., San Francisco State Coll., 1969; m. Kathleen A. Yett, Apr. 12, 1975; children by previous marriage—Jane, Lynn, Andrew. Assoc. planner City of Bellevue (Wash.), 1969-71, planning dir., 1971-73; v.p. Bert McNae, Inc., Bellevue, 1973-75; pres. Robert E. Wallar Assocs., 1973-74, Bryant/Wallar Assocs., 1974-76; pres. Robert E. Wallar Real Estate, 1975-79, 83—, The Wallar Assocs., 1976—; gen. mgr., chief exec. officer Puyallup Tribal Enterprises, Tacoma, 1978-80; chief staff dept. planning and community devel. Puyallup Nation, Tacoma, 1980—; exec. dir. Puyallup Nation Port Authority, Tacoma, 1980-82; instr. urban planning Bellevue Community Coll., 1970-71. Mem. King County Agrl. Preservation Task Force, 1977-78, King County Growth Mgmt. Forum, 1978-80; mem. Commencement Bay Environ. Impact Com., U.S.A.C.E., 1978-82. Served with AUS, 1962-65. Mem. Puget Sound C. of C. (chmn. land use com. 1973-75), Seattle C. of C. (chmn. agrl. preservation com. 1977-78), Tacoma C. of C., Tacoma-Pierce County Bd. Realtors, Downtown Tacoma Assn. Episcopalian. Home: 1356 Bellefield Ln Bellevue WA 98004 Office: Perkins Bldg Suite 540 Tacoma WA 98402

WALLENIUS, DALE KARL, communications executive; b. Maywood, Calif., Dec. 17, 1951; s. John S. and Maxine L. (Connelly) W.; m. Joan M. Stenger, Jan. 27, 1979. B.A., San Diego State U., 1975; M.A., Azusa Pacific U., 1978. Pres. Resources Unlimited, San Diego, 1978-79; co-founder, pres. Am. Media, San Diego, 1983—; pres. Pro Communications, San Diego, 1979—; instr. Club: Entrepreneur (founder, dir.). Office: Pro Communications 3200 Adams Ave Suite 201 San Diego CA 92116

WALLERICH, PETER KENNETH, banker; b. Tacoma, Mar. 4, 1931; s. Clarence W. and Ellen (Hansen) W.; B.A.A., U. Wash., 1953; m. Marylu Ann Oakland, July 9, 1954; children—Karen, Kristen, Karla, Kaari. Investment officer N. Pacific Bank, Tacoma, 1956-59, exec. v.p., 1959-71, chmn. bd., 1971-73, pres., 1973—; gen. mgr. South Tacoma Motor Co., 1959-68, pres., 1968-71; dir. N. Pacific Bank, Western Finance Co., Mountain View Devel. Co. Pres., Design for Progress, 1970-71. Bd. dirs. Goodwill Industries, Wash. Research Council; trustee, treas. U. Puget Sound; chmn. bd. trustees Mary Bridge Children's Hosp.; trustee Lakewood Gen. Hosp.; bd. visitors Sch. Law U. Puget Sound. Mem. Wash. Bankers Assn. (dir., treas.), Am. Bankers Assn. (nat. exec. planning com.), C. of C. (dir.), Mensa. Home: 12111 Gravelly Lake Dr SW Tacoma WA 98499 Office: 5448 S Tacoma Way Tacoma WA 98409

WALLIN, NORMAN ELROY, state legislator, auto dealer; b. Hannaford, N.D., Oct. 4, 1914; s. Eric Olaf and Cora Elvina (Fogderud) W.; m. Clarice Geneva, Oct. 17, 1953; children—David Allen, Eileen Clarice. B.A., Concordia Coll., 1936. With Universal Credit Corp., Detroit, 1937-42; pres. Bozeman (Mont.) Ford, Inc., 1946—; dir. Mont. Bank Bozeman; mem. Mont. Ho. of Reps., 1981—. Regent Concordia Coll., Moorhead, Minn., 1955-65. Served with USN, 1942-46; PTO. Mem. Mont. State Automobile Dealer's Assn. (past pres.), Bozeman C. of C. (pres. 1963). Republican. Lutheran. Club: Kiwanis (Bozeman). Home: 2422 Springcreek Dr Bozeman MT 59715 Office: 1800 W Main St Bozeman MT 59715

WALLIS, LYNN RUEL, electric mfg. co. cons.; b. Portland, Oreg., Mar. 14, 1934; s. Lynn R. and Monttie M. (Scott) W.; B.S. in Physics, U. Oreg.; postgrad. in Physics, Oreg. State U., 1960-65; m. Joan Smith, Aug. 30, 1954; children—Kathleen, Kim. With Gen. Electric Co., 1959—, mem. managerial engring. staff Vallecitos Nuclear Center, Pleasanton, Calif., 1967-71, mem. engring. and communication staff Nuclear Energy Bus. Group, San Jose, Calif., 1971—; instr. U. Calif., Berkeley, 1967, 68, 69; participant public service radio series on energy, atom, plutonium Am. Nuclear Soc., 1975, 77; contact for U.S. media on nuclear energy matters U.S. Atomic Indsl. Forum, Washington, 1977—; lectr. politics of nuclear power J.F. Kennedy Sch. Govt., Harvard U., 1977; mem. nat. steering com. public info. program Am. Nuclear Soc., U.S. del. Uranium Inst., London, 1982; chmn. Atomic Indsl. Forum Radiation Com. lectr. Mem. Calif. Legis. Adv. Com. Radioactive Waste. Registered profl. engr., Calif.; hon. Ky. Col. Home: 2326 Fairfield Pleasanton CA 94566

WALLMANN, JEFFREY MINER, author; b. Seattle, Dec. 5, 1941; s. George Rudolph and Elizabeth (Biggs) W.; B.S., Portland State U., 1962; m. Helga Reidun Eikefet, Dec. 1, 1974. Pvt. investigator Dale Systems, N.Y.C., 1962-63; asst. buyer, mgr. public money bidder Dohrmann Co., San Francisco, 1964-66; mfrs. rep. electronics industry, San Francisco, 1966-69; dir. public relations London Films, Cinelux-Universal and Trans-European Publs., 1970-75; editor-in-chief Riviera Life mag., 1975-77; books include: The Spiral Web, 1969, Judas Cross, 1974, Clean Sweep, 1976, Jamaica, 1977, Deathtrek, 1980, Blood and Passion, 1980; Brand of the Damned, 1981; The Manipulator, 1982; (under pseudonym Leon DaSilva) Green Hell, 1976, Breakout in Angola, 1977; (pseudonym Nick Carter) Hour of the Wolf, 1973, Ice Trap Terror, 1974; (pseudonym Peter Jensen) The Virgin Couple, 1970, Ravished, 1971; (pseudonmy Jackson Robard) Gang Initiation, 1971, Present for Teacher, 1972, Teacher's Lounge, 1972; (pseudonym Grant Roberts) The Reluctant Couple, 1969, Wayward Wives, 1970; (pseudonym Gregory St. Germain) Resistance #1: Night and Fog, 1982, Resistance #2: Maygar Massacre, 1983; (pseudonym Wesley Ellis) Lonestar on the Treachery Trail, 1982, Lonestar and the Hardrock Payoff, 1983, Lonestar and the Gold Raiders, 1983; also many other pseudonyms and titles; contbr. articles and short stories to Argosy, Ellery Queen's Mystery Mag., Alfred Hitchcock's Mystery Mag., Mike Shayne's Mystery Mag., Zane Grey Western, Venture Sci. Fiction, Oui, TV Guide; also (under pseudonym William Jeffrey in collaboration with Bill Pronzini) Dual at Gold Buttes, 1980, Border Fever, 1982, Day of the Moon, 1983. Mem. Mystery Writers of Am., Sci. Fiction Writers Am., Western Writers Am., Crime Writers Assn. Office: care Richard Curtis 164 E 64th St New York NY 10021

WALLOP, MALCOLM, senator, rancher; b. N.Y.C., Feb. 27, 1933; B.A., Yale U., 1954; children—Malcolm, Matthew, Amy, Paul. Owner, pres. Polo Land and Livestock, Big Horn, Wyo., 1957—; pres. Polo Ranch, Inc., Big Horn, 1976—; mem. U.S. Senate from Wyo., 1977—; mem. Senate coms. on Energy and Natural Resources, Fin., Intelligence. Served to 1st lt. U.S. Army, 1955-57. Mem. Wyo. Stockgrowers Assn., Nat. Cattleman's Assn., Am. Legion. Republican. Episcopalian. Home: Polo Ranch Big Horn WY 82833 Office: US Senate Washington DC 20510

WALLSTROM, WESLEY DONALD, bank exec.; b. Turlock, Calif., Oct. 4, 1929; s. Emil Reinhold and Edith Katherine (Lindberg) W.; student Modesto Jr. Coll., 1955-64; certificate Pacific Coast Banking Sch., U. Wash., 1974; m. Marilyn Irene Hallmark, May 12, 1951; children—Marc Gordon, Wendy Diane. Bookkeeper, teller First Nat. Bank, Turlock, 1947-50; v.p. Gordon Hallmark, Inc., Turlock, 1950-53; asst. cashier United Calif. Bank, Turlock, 1953-68, regional v.p., Fresno, 1968-72, v.p., mgr., Turlock, 1972-76; founding pres., dir. Golden Valley Bank, Turlock, 1976—. Campaign chmn. United Crusade, Turlock, 1971; chmn., founding dir. Covenant Village, retirement home, Turlock, 1973—; founding pres. Turlock Regional Arts Council, 1974, dir., 1975-76. Served with U.S. N.G., 1948-56. Mem. Nat. Soc. Accts. for Coops., Ind. Bankers No. Calif., Am. Bankers Assn., U.S. Yacht Racing Union, No. Calif. Golf Assn., Turlock C. of C. (dir. 1973-75), Stanislaus Sailing Soc. (commodore 1980-81), Republican. Mem. Covenant Ch. Clubs: Turlock Golf and Country (pres. 1975-76, v.p., 1977, dir. 1977, 83), 1977), Masons, Rotary. Home: 1720 Hammond Dr Turlock CA 95380 Office: 301 E Main St Turlock CA 95380

WALRATH, HARRY RIENZI, clergyman; b. Alameda, Calif., Mar. 7, 1926; s. Frank Rienzi and Cathren (Michlar) W.; A.A., City Coll. San Francisco, 1950; B.A., U. Calif. at Berkeley, 1952; M.Div., Ch. Div. Sch. of Pacific, 1959; m. Dorothy M. Baxter, June 24, 1961; 1 son, Gregory Rienzi. Dist. exec. San Mateo area council Boy Scouts Am., 1952-55; ordained deacon Episcopal Ch., 1959, priest, 1960; curate All Souls Parish, Berkeley, Calif., 1959-61; vicar St. Luke's, Atascadero, Calif., 1961-63, St. Andrew's, Garberville, Calif., 1963-64; asso. rector St. Luke's Ch., Los Gatos, 1964-65, Holy Spirit Parish, Missoula, Mont., 1965-67; vicar St. Peter's Ch., also headmaster St. Peter's Schs., Litchfield Park, Ariz., 1967-69; chaplain U. Mont., 1965-67; asst. rector Trinity Parish, Reno, 1969-72; coordinator counciling services Washoe County Council Alcoholism, Reno, 1972-74; adminstr. Cons. Assistance Services, Inc., Reno, 1974-76; pastoral counselor, contract chaplain Nev. Mental Health Inst., 1976-78; contract mental health chaplain VA Hosp., Reno, 1976-78, mental health chaplain VA Med. Center, 1978—, also triage coordinator for mental health; dir. youth Paso Robles Presbytery; chmn. Diocesan Commn. on Alcoholism; cons. teen-age problems Berkeley Presbytery; mem. clergy team Episcopal Marriage Encounter, 1979—, also Episc. Engaged Encounter. Mem. at large Washoe dist. Nev. area council Boy Scouts Am., scoutmaster troop 73, 1976, troop 585, 1979—, asst. scoutmaster troop 35, 1982—, also advisor Tannu Lodge 346; South Humboldt County chmn. Am. Cancer Soc. Trustee Community Youth Center, Reno. Served with USNR, 1944-46. Decorated Pacific Theater medal with star, Am. Theater medal, Victory medal, Fleet Unit Commendation medal; certified substance abuse counselor, Nev. Mem. Ch. Hist. Soc., U. Calif. Alumni Assn., Nat. Model R.R. Assn. (life), Sierra Club Calif., Missoula Council Chs. (pres.), Alpha Phi Omega. Democrat. Club: Rotary. Home: 580 Huffaker Ln E Reno NV 89511 Office: 1000 Locust St Reno NV 89520

WALSH, EDWARD JOSEPH, food company executive; b. Mt. Vernon, N.Y., Mar. 18, 1932; s. Edward Aloysius and Charlotte Cecilia (Borup) W.; m. Patricia Ann Farrell, Sept. 16, 1961; children—Edward Jr., Megan, John, Robert. B.B.A., Iona Coll., 1953; M.B.A., NYU, 1958. With Armour & Co., Phoenix, 1961-73; v.p. Toiletries div. Armour Dial Co., Phoenix, 1973-76; exec. v.p. Armour Dial Co., Phoenix, 1976—; pres. Armour Internat. Co., Phoenix, 1978—. Past pres. Mems. Assn. Mt. Vernon (N.Y.) Fire Dept. With U.S. Army, 1953-55. Mem. Am. Mgmt. Assn., Nat. Meat Canner Assn. (past pres.). Republican. Roman Catholic. Home: 5925 E Joshua Tree Ln Paradise Valley AZ 85253 Office: Greyhound Tower Sta 4102 Phoenix AZ 85077

WALSH, MARY D., civic worker; b. Whitewright, Tex., Oct. 29, 1913; d. William Fleming and Anna Maud (Lewis) Fleming; B.A., So. Meth. U., 1934; LL.D. (hon.), Tex. Christian U., 1979; m. F. Howard Walsh, Mar. 13, 1937; children—Richard, Howard, D'Ann (Mrs. Wm. F. Bonnell), Maudi Walsh Willson, William Lloyd. Pres. Fleming Found.; v.p. Walsh Found.; partner Walsh Co.; mem. Lloyd Shaw Found., Colorado Springs, Big Bros. Tarrant County, Colo. Guarantor Fort Worth Arts Council, Fort Worth Opera, Fort Worth Ballet, Tex. Boys' Choir, Fort Worth Theatre; hon. v.p. Opera Bd., 1960-81; co-founder Am. Field Service in Ft. Worth; mem. Tex. Commn. for Arts and Humanities, 1968-72, mem. adv. council, 1972-82; bd. dirs. Van Cliburn Internat. Piano Competition, Wm. Edrington Scott Theatre, 1977-82, Colorado Springs Day Nursery, Colorado Springs Symphony, Ft. Worth Symphony, 1974-81; hon. chmn. Opera Ball, 1975, Opera Guild Internat. Conf., 1976. Recipient numerous awards, including Altrusa Civic award as 1st Lady of Ft. Worth, 1968; (with husband) Disting. Service award So. Bapt. Radio and Television Commn., 1972; Opera award Girl Scouts, 1977-79; award Streams and Valleys, 1976-80; named (with husband) Patron of Arts in Ft. Worth, 1970, Edna Gladney Internat. Grandparents of 1972; Mary D. and Howard Walsh Meml. Organ dedicated Bapt. Radio and TV Commn., 1967; Mary D. and Howard Walsh Med. Bldg., Southwestern Bapt. Theol. Sem.; Brotherhood citation Tarrant County chpt. NCCJ, 1978; Spl. Recognition award Ft. Worth Ballet Assn.;

Royal Purple award Tex. Christian U., 1979; Friends of Tex. Boys Choir award, 1981; appreciation award Southwestern Bapt. Theol. Sem., 1981, B. H. Carroll Founders award, 1982. Mem. Ft. Worth Boys Club, Ft. Worth Children's Hosp., Jewel Charity Ball, Ft. Worth Pan Hellenic (pres. 1940), Opera Guild, Fine Arts Found. Guild, Girl's Service League, AAUW, Goodwill Industries Aux., Child Study Center, Tarrant County Aux. of Edna Gladney Home, YWCA (life), Ft. Worth Art Assn., Ft. Worth Ballet Assn., Tex. Boys Choir Aux., Friends of Tex. Boys Choir, Round Table, Colorado Springs Fine Art Center, Am. Automobile Assn., Nat. Assn. Cowbelles, Ft. Worth Arts Council, Rae Reimers Bible Study Class (pres. 1968), Tex. League Composers (hon. life), Chi Omega (pres. 1935-36), others. Baptist. Clubs: Kappa Sigma Wives and Mothers, The Woman's (Club Fidelite), Colorado Springs Country, Garden of Gods, Colonial Country, Ridglea Country, Shady Oaks Country, Chi Omega Mothers. Home: 2425 Stadium Dr Fort Worth TX 76109 also 1801 Culebra Ave Colorado Springs CO 80907

WALSH, RICHARD GEORGE, economist, educator; b. Seward, Nebr., Aug. 16, 1930; s. Thomas George and Francis Kathryn (Pape) W.; B.S., U. Nebr., 1952, M.A., 1955; Ph.D., U. Wis., 1961; m. Patricia Burke Bard, 1976; children by previous marriage—Cathryn M., Susan E., Thomas R., Robert J. From asst. prof. to prof. dept. agrl. econs. U. Nebr., 1958-68; prof. dept. econs. Colo. State U., Ft. Collins, 1968—; intergovt. exchange EPA, 1973-74. Cons., FTC, 1965-66, 72, 78-79, U. P.R., 1967, Justice Dept., 1971, U.S. Forest Service, 1972, Colo. Wildlife Div., 1972, Bur. Land Mgmt., 1973, Nat. Park Service, 1975-80; vis. prof. U. Md., 1965, Stanford Research Inst., 1971. Bd. dirs. No. Ft. Collins Sanitation Dist., 1971-73. Served to lt. (j.g.) USNR, 1952-54. Mem. Am. Econs. Assn., Am. Agrl. Econs. Assn. (Outstanding Pub. Research award 1964). Author: Economics of the Baking Industry, 1963; Market Structure of the Agricultural Industries, 1966; The Structure of Food Manufacturing, 1966; Organization and Competition in Food Retailing, 1966; Some Costs and Benefits of Strip Mining Western Coal, 1974; Efficiency of Wastewater Disposal in Mountain Areas, 1977; Economic Benefits of Improved Water Quality, 1982; Recreation Economic Decisions, 1982; Wilderness Resource Economics: Recreation Use and Preservation Values, 1982; also articles in profl. jours. Office: Dept Econs Colo State U Fort Collins CO 80523

WALSH, WILLIAM DESMOND, investment company executive, lawyer; b. N.Y.C., Aug. 4, 1930; s. William J. and Catherine G. (Desmond) W.; m. Mary Jane Gordon, Apr. 5, 1951; children—Deborah Walsh Hirsch, Caroline, Michael, Suzanne, Tara, Peter. B.A., Fordham U., 1951; J.D., Harvard U., 1955. Bar: N.Y. 1955. Asst. U.S. atty. So. Dist. N.Y., 1955-58; counsel N.Y. State Crime Commn., N.Y.C., 1958-61; mgmt. cons. McKinsey & Co., N.Y.C., 1961-67; sr. v.p. Arcata Corp., Menlo Park, Calif., 1967-82; gen. ptnr. Sequoia Assocs., Menlo Park, 1982—; chmn. Evergreen Assn.; dir. Interstate Bakeries, Advanced Systems, Inc., Natural Resources Mgmt. Mem. adv. council Peninsula Open Space Trust. Mem. N.Y. State Bar Assn., ABA. Clubs: Lincoln No. Calif.; Athletic, Harvard (N.Y.C.). Author: Syndicated Gambling in New York State, 1961. Home: 279 Park Ln Atherton CA 94025 Office: Sequoia Assocs 3000 Sand Hill Rd 140 Bldg 2 Menlo Park CA 94025

WALSH, WILLIAM E., profl. football club exec.; b. Los Angeles, Nov. 30, 1931; s. William A. and Ruth E. (Mathers) W.; B.A. in Edn., San Jose U., 1955, M.A., 1959; m. Geraldine Nardini, June 13, 1955; children—Steven, Craig, Elizabeth. Asst. football coach U. Calif., Berkeley, 1960-62, Stanford U., 1963-65, head coach, 1977-78; asst. coach Oakland (Calif.) Raiders, 1966-67, Cin. Bengals, 1968-75, San Diego Chargers, 1976; coach, gen. mgr. San Francisco 49ers, 1979—; pres., owner Bill Walsh Enterprises. Served with U.S. Army, 1956-57. Named Coach of the Year, Pacific Coast, 1977. Appearances on radio and TV shows; contbr. articles to profl. jours. Office: 711 Nevada St Redwood City CA 94061

WALSMITH, CHARLES RODGER, psychology educator; b. Denver, May 19, 1926; s. Joseph Francis and Florence Ophelia (Smith) W.; B.A. (Chancellor's Ednl. scholar), U. Denver, 1956, M.A., 1962; postgrad. U. Wash., 1968-76; Ph.D., Stanton U., 1976; children—Karen Frances, Cynthia Ann, Erik Konrad. Research psychologist Personnel Tng. and Research Center, Maintenance Lab., USAF Lowery AFB, Denver, 1956; research asst. U. Colo. Med. Center, Denver, 1956-57, research asso., 1957-64; asst. prof. psychology North Park Coll., Chgo., 1965-66; sr. human engring. analyst, psychoacoustics Boeing Co., Seattle, 1965-68; instr. psychology, dept. behavioral scis. Bellevue (Wash.) Community Coll., 1968—, chmn. dept., 1968-70, 80-84, Phi Theta Kappa adviser, 1981—. Resident trainer Gestalt Inst. of Can., Lake Cowichan, B.C., summers 1969, 71, assoc., 1969—; dir. Gestalt Inst. of Wash., Bellevue, 1970—. Democratic precinct chmn., Renton, Wash., 1966-68; patron BCC Found. Served with USNR, 1944-46. Mem. Wash. State, Psychol. Assn., Phi Beta Kappa, Psi Chi. Home: Gestalt House 14909 SE 44th Pl Bellevue WA 98006

WALSTON, FREDERICK, advertising executive; b. San Francisco, Mar. 30, 1939; s. Carl O. and Winona Ellis (Johnson) W.; m. Ortrud Elisabeth Behre, Aug. 30, 1970; 1 son, Kai Frederick. A.B. in Journalism and English, U. Calif.-Berkeley, 1963. Copywriter, N.Y., Germany, 1963-68; creative dir. Jennings & Thompson/Foote Cone & Belding, Phoenix, 1970-75; creative supr. Larson/Bateman/McAllister, Santa Barbara, Calif., 1976-80; creative dir. Walston & Co., Santa Barbara, 1980—. Served with USMCR, 1958-64. Winner Silver Statue Cannes TV Festival, 1966; recipient 1st place Best in the West Am. Advt. Fedn., 1971. Mem. Sigma Alpha Epsilon. Office: 108 Chapala St Santa Barbara CA 93101

WALTA, GREG, lawyer; b. Volga, S.D., June 5, 1941; s. Jack and Betty W.; B.A., St. John's U., 1964; J.D., Notre Dame U., 1967; children—Mark, Jason, Michael. Admitted to Colo. bar, 1967; with Pikes Peak Legal Services, Colorado Springs, Colo., 1968-70; mem. law firm Walta, Cross, Gadais & Kin, Colorado Springs, 1970-78; public defender State of Colo., Denver, 1978-82; sole practice, Colorado Springs, 1982—. Mem. Colo. Criminal Def. Bar, ACLU, NAACP. Roman Catholic. Home: 30 Clubridge Pl Coronado Springs CO 80906 Office: 105 E Vermijo Colorado Springs CO

WALTAR, ALAN EDWARD, nuclear engr.; b. Chehalis, Wash., July 10, 1939; s. Vaino Ensio and Doris Elmina (Panush) W.; A.A., Centralia Coll., 1959; B.S.E.E. magna cum laude, U. Wash., 1961; M.S. in Nuclear Engring. (AEC spl. fellow), MIT, 1962; Ph.D. in Engring. Sci. (AEC spl. fellow), U. Calif., Berkeley, 1966; m. Anna Ethel Geiszler, June 11, 1961; children—Stephen Michael, Douglas Brian, Karen Louise, Bruce Jonathan. Engr., Battelle-N.W., Richland, Wash., 1966-70; sr. engr. Westinghouse Hanford Co., Richland, 1970-72, mgr. reactor dynamics, 1972-76, adv. engr., 1977-79, mgr. fast reactor safety devel., 1979—; mem. U.S. team tour of selected European nuclear labs., 1972; vis. asso. prof. nuclear engring. U. Va., 1976-77; mem. faculty Joint Center for Grad. Studies Richland. Bd. dirs. Lower Columbia Basin YMCA, Richland, 1970-72, pres. bd., 1972; pres. Tri-Cities Assn., 1973; vol. United Way, Richland; Presbyn. del. World Council Chs. Conf. in Faith, Sci. and Future, M.I.T., 1979; mem. Richland Light Opera Co. Named Disting. Alumnus, Centralia Coll., 1980; Engr. of Yr., Tri Cities chpt. Nat. Soc. Profl. Engrs., 1981. Mem. Am. Nuclear Soc. (chmn. nuclear safety div. 1977-79, mem. exec. bd. nuclear reactor safety div. 1978-81, asso. tech. program chmn. 1979 Internat. Conf. Fast Reactor Safety Tech., chmn. Richland sect. public info. com. 1980, 82), AAAS. Author: (with A.B. Reynolds) Fast Breeder Reactors, 1981; contbr. articles to profl. jours. Home: 1617 Sunset St Richland WA 99352 Office: PO Box 1979 Richland WA 99352

WALTER, ANN LORAINE, educator; b. Scotland County, N.C., Aug. 22, 1945; d. John Francis and Loraine Amelia Stanek; B.A., Colo. State Coll., 1966; grad. (univ. spl. edn. stipend) Norfolk State U., 1981; m. Gary Lee Walter, Dec. 18, 1966; children—Lynda, Gregory. Primary tchr. educable mentally retarded, West Springfield, Mass., 1967; elem. tchr., Briggsdale, Colo., 1967-68, Fife, Wash., 1968-72, Panama, C.Z., 1972-76, Ft. Kobbe Army Edn. Center, C.Z., 1973-74; tchr. emotionally disturbed, Hampton, Va., 1976-80, tchr. learning disabled, 1980-81, grade chmn., 1978, 80, cooperating tchr., 1970, 71, 80, faculty participation com., 1980-81; spl. edn. tchr. jr./sr. high sch. Ellicott (Colo.) Sch., 1981-83; cons. confs. Norfolk State U., 1980; bd. advisors Mallory Elem. Sch., 1979-80; mem. math. book adoption com. Hampton City Schs., 1980-81; student council advisor, 1978-80. Sunday sch. tchr. Luth. Ch., 1977-81; leader Tidewater council Girl Scouts U.S.A., 1979; vol. civic activities including United Cerebral Palsy Telethon, Sarah Bonwell Hudgins Regional Center annual fair for handicapped individuals, Hilton Jr. Women's Club fund raising for juvenile diabetes, Ronald McDonald House and Home for Battered Women, Infant Stimulation Program; mem. PTA, Soc. for Battered Women. March of Dimes summer sch. grantee, 1968. Mem. NEA, Va. Edn. Assn., Hampton Edn. Assn., Council for Exceptional Children, Internat. Reading Assn., Nat. Council Math. Tchrs., Assn. for Supervision and Curriculum Devel. Clubs: Hilton Jr. Women's, VFW Aux., Beta Sigma Phi, Alpha Sigma Tau Alumni. Home: 7611 Safari Circle Colorado Springs CO 80918 Office: Ellicott High Sch Calhan CO 80808

WALTER, BRUCE ALEXANDER, physician, educator; b. Seattle, Apr. 15, 1922; s. Ernest R. and Marion (Alexander) W.; B.A., U. Wash., 1944, B.S., 1948, M.D., 1951; M.P.H., UCLA, 1962; m. Gloria Helen Parry, Feb. 4, 1956; children—Maia Marion, Wendy Diane, Shelley Kathleen, Allison Ann. Intern Los Angeles County Gen. Hosp., 1951-52; resident internal medicine Wadsworth Hosp., U. Calif., 1952-54; dir. grad. program hosp., health facilities adminstrn. UCLA, 1965-68; attending staff Salt Lake County Hosp., 1954-55; fellow medicine U. Utah, 1954-55; fellow medicine U. So. Calif., 1955-56, mem. faculty, 1956-65; attending staff Los Angeles County Hosp., 1956-65; physician internal medicine, Palm Springs, Calif., 1956-61; chief staff Desert Hosp., 1960-61; dir. med. care studies Calif. Dept. Pub. Health, Berkeley, 1962-65; dir. Med. Care Services, State of Utah, 1969-71, dep. dir. health, 1971-79, acting dir. health, 1979; cons. Newport Med. Group and Advanced Health Systems, Inc., Newport Beach, Calif., 1979—; asst. prof. community and family medicine U. Utah Sch. Medicine, Salt Lake City, 1969-79; mem. Utah State Bd. Aging; bd. dirs. Blue Shield of Utah, Utah Profl. Standards Rev. Orgn. Served to 1st lt. Signal Corps, AUS, 1943-46. Mem. AMA, Calif. Med. Assn., Nat. Assn. Health Facility Licensing and Certification Dirs. (pres. 1975-76), Orange County Med. Soc., Alpha Delta Phi, Alpha Kappa Kappa, Alpha Delta Sigma. Clubs: Balboa Bay. Home: 2821 Blue Water Dr Corona del Mar CA 92625 Office: 1300 Bristol St N Newport Beach CA 92660

WALTER, WILLIAM JACOB, JR., photographer; b. South Bend, Ind., Mar. 29, 1945; s. William Jacob and Adeline Louise W.; B.A., Miami U., Oxford, Ohio, 1967; M.B.A., U. So. Calif., Dominguez Hills, 1976; children—Kimberly Ann, Holly Kay. Pharm. salesman Parke-Davis & Co., Torrance, Calif., 1968-73, dist. sales mgr. So. Calif., 1973-77; free-lance photographer and writer, 1977-78; photographer, owner Keepsake Portraits, Torrance, 1978—. Mem. Profl. Photographers Am. Republican. Mem. Christian Ch. Club: King Harbor Yacht. Home: 104 S Francisca Redondo Beach CA 90277 Office: 133 Del Amo Fashion Sq Torrance CA 90503

WALTERMIRE, JIM, state govt. ofcl.; b. Choteau, Mont., Feb. 15, 1949; s. Robert and Anne Waltermire; B.A. in Bus. Adminstrn., U. Mont., 1971; m. Coy Davidson, June 1970. Engaged in real estate, ranching, constrn. and banking, 1972-75; partner Waltermire & Wicks, investments, Missoula, Mont., 1975-77; commr. Missoula County (Mont.), 1977-80; sec. of state State of Mont., 1980—. Union Bank & Trust fellow, 1970. Mem. Nat. Assn. Secs. State. Republican. Office: Room 202 State Capitol Helena MT 59620

WALTERS, ANNA LEE, writer; b. Pawnee, Okla., Sept. 9, 1946; d. Luther and Juanita Mae (Taylor) McGlaslin; student U. N.Mex., 1977—; m. Harry Walters, June 1965; children—Anthony, Daniel. Dir. Navajo Community Coll. Press, Tsaile (Navajo Nation), Ariz., 1977—; freelance writer, 1973—; contbg. author: The Man to Send Rainclouds, 1974, Warriors of the Rainbow, 1975, Shantih, 1976, The Third Woman, 1979; Remembered Earth, 1979. co-author textbook: The Sacred Ways of Knowledge, Sources of Life, 1977; guest editor Frauen Offensive, 1978; author: The Otoe-Missoneria Tribe: Centennial Memories, 1881-1981; contbr. articles to jours. Office: Navajo Community Coll Press Tsaile AZ 86556

WALTERS, J(OSPEH) BERK, advertising executive; b. Sewickley, Pa., May 5, 1923; s. Joseph William and Edith Pearl (Berkshire) W.; m. Evelyn Grace Mothersole, Aug. 31, 1946; children—Carole Louise, Gail Evelyn, Wayne Berk. B.A. cum laude, U. Pitts., 1955. With A. P. Hill Co., Pitts., 1946-50; prodn. mgr. Walker & Downing Agy., Pitts., 1950-63; account supr. Tolle Co., San Diego, 1963-65; owner, gen. mgr. Walters & Co., La Jolla, Calif., 1965—. Served in U.S. Army, 1943-45. Republican. Methodist. Clubs: Rotary (pres. elect 1983-84), Toastmasters (La Jolla). Home: 8984 Caminito Fresco La Jolla CA 92037 Office: 1020 Prospect St La Jolla CA 92037

WALTI, JOHN ALAN, mechanical engineer; b. Detroit, Apr. 22, 1944; s. John Walter and Dorothy Anne (Wilhelm) W.; m. Ann Marie Cloutier, Aug. 2, 1969; 1 son, Ian Alan. B.S. in Mech. Engring., Calif. Poly. U., San Luis Obispo, 1968; M.S. in Engring., U. So. Calif., 1973. Lic. profl. engr., Calif. Chief facilities design engr. mech. engring. sect. Los Angeles Dept. Water and Power, 1968—; air conditioning and solar systems cons. State of Calif.; cons. in field. Mem. ASME, ASHRAE, Am. Soc. Plumbing Engrs. Republican. Home: 209 Ave D Redondo Beach CA 90277 Office: 111 N Hope St Los Angeles CA 90051

WALTON, DIANA CLAIRE, security manager, law enforcement/crime prevention consultant; b. Portland, Oreg., Aug. 27, 1953; d. Lowell Clair and Teresina Marie (Bifano) Walton. B.A. in Polit. Sci., Seattle U., 1977, B. in Police Sci. and Adminstrn., 1977. Dir. Crime Prevention unit Kirkland Police Dept. (Wash.), 1977-80; branch mgr. Stanley Smith Security, Ranier, Oreg., 1980-82; private cons. loss prevention, Everett, Wash., 1982—; cert. instr. Pacific Northwest Crime Prevention Inst. Mem. Am. Soc. Indsl. Security, Wash. State Crime Prevention Assn., Pacific Northwest Security Assn. Roman Catholic. Address: 6030 Manor Pl Everett WA 98203

WALTON, JAMES NOBLE, architect; b. Alameda, Calif., Sept. 25, 1947; s. James Winfred and Jean S. (Mundie) W.; A.A., Diablo Valley Coll., 1968; B.A., U. Calif.-Berkeley, 1971, M.Arch., 1973; m. Kathleen Taylor, 1965; 1 dau., Christine. Architect, Skidmore Owings and Merrill, San Francisco, 1973-77; architect Oakland Unified Sch. Dist., 1977-79; prin. James Noble Walton, A.R.A., Architect and Gen. Contractor, Alameda, Calif., 1979-83; project mgr. Designed Bldg. Systems, Inc., Newark, Calif., 1982—; v.p. Fed. Bldg. Co., 1981-82. Lic. architect, Calif., Wash. Mem. Soc. Am. Registered Architects. Clubs: Masons (past master), Shriners. Home: 2826 Central Ave Alameda CA 94501 Office: PO Box 913 Newark CA 94560

WALTZ, KENNETH NEAL, educator, consultant; b. Ann Arbor, Mich., June 8, 1924; s. Christian Benjamin and Luella (Braun) W.; m. Helen Elizabeth Lindsley, June 4, 1949; children—Kenneth, Thomas, Daniel. A.B., Oberlin Coll., 1948; M.A., Columbia U., 1950, Ph.D., 1954. Instr., Columbia U., N.Y.C., 1953-55, asst. prof., 1955-57; assoc. prof. Swarthmore Coll., 1957-64, prof. politics, 1964-66; research assoc. Ctr. Internat. Affairs, Harvard U., 1963-64, 68-69, 72; prof. politics Brandeis U., Waltham, Mass., 1966-71, Adlai E. Stevenson prof. internat. politics, 1967-71; Ford prof. polit. sci. U. Calif.-Berkeley, 1971—. NSF grantee, 1968-71; Guggenheim fellow, 1976-77; Woodrow Wilson Ctr. fellow, 1979-80; vis. scholar Peking U., 1982. Mem. Am. Polit. Sci. Assn., Internat. Studies Assn., Council Fgn. Relations, Phi Beta Kappa. Author: Man, the State and War, 1959; Foreign Policy and Democratic Politics, 1967; Theory of International Politics, 1979; The Spread of Nuclear Weapons, 1981; co-author, co-editor: Conflict in World Politics, 1971; The Use of Force, 2d edit., 1983. Home: 70 Oak Ridge Rd Berkeley CA 94705 Office: Polit Sci Dept U Calif 210 Barrows Hall Berkeley CA 94720

WALZER, HAROLD LAURENCE, computer co. exec.; b. Mpls., June 6, 1955; s. Sam Israel and Barbara Bonnie (Lehman) W.; B.S. in Computer Info. Systems, Ariz. State U., 1977; m. Chris Johannsen. Programmer, Computer Software, Inc., Tempe, Ariz., 1977-78, systems analyst, 1978-79, v.p., 1979-80, pres., 1980—; asst. prof. communications Ariz. State Univ., Tempe, 1976-77. Mem. Jewish Community Ctr. Named Optimist of Yr., Tempe Optimists, 1976. Mem. Assn. Computer Machinery. Republican. Club: Phoenix Chess. Designer over 40 computer software systems on mini-computers; developer industry standards for mini-computer data-base mgmt. systems, 1979. Home: 5008 E Thomas Rd Apt 609 Phoenix AZ 85018 Office: 2121 S Priest St Suite 110 Tempe AZ 85282

WAMPLER, VANCE DELVEN, advertising executive; b. San Francisco, Sept. 9, 1935; s. Vance H. and Lillian (Miller) W.; m. Pauline Cecelia Andrade, Feb. 14, 1959; 1 son, Ryan James. B.A., Ariz. State U., 1958; postgrad. U. Mexico City, 1958-59. Pres., Vance Wmapler Advt., Phoenix and Tucson, 1970-78, The Ad Agy., Inc., Phoenix, 1978-80, Nanny Hooten's Inc., Phoenix, 1978—, Media Resources, Inc., Phoenix, 1980—; cons. in field. Committeeman, Ariz. Republican Party, 1970-74. Served With U.S. Army, 1954-56. Recipient Newspaper Bur. of Am. Best Ad Copy award, 1968, others. Author: SCAMCO, 1980; Kirkland, 1983. Home: 4035 E Fanfol Dr Phoenix AZ 85028 Office: 7700 E McCormick Pkwy Scottsdale AZ 85258

WANDER, JACK LELAND, water and wastewater equipment manufacturing company executive; b. Kansas City, Mo., Aug. 22, 1926; s. George Fredrich and Gladys May (Robinson) W.; m. Sally Louise Perry, Nov. 26, 1962; children—Julie Ann, Barbara Lee. B.S. in Civil Engring., U. Colo., 1954. Registered profl. engr., Tex., La. With Dorr-Oliver, Inc., Emeryville, Calif., 1956—, regional mgr., 1969-78, resident mgr., 1978—. Served to lt. comdr. USNR, 1943-49, 50-52. Decorated D.F.C. Mem. Am. Water Works Assn., ASCE, Water Pollution Control Fedn., Nat. Soc. Profl. Engrs., Colo. Water Pollution Control Assn., U.S. Power Squadron, Phi Kappa Psi. Democrat. Presbyterian.

WANER, FRANCES GREIFF, psychologist; b. N.Y.C., Aug. 22, 1923; d. Harry and Rebecca (Vogel) Greiff; m. Norman S. Waner, Sept. 16, 1944; children—Jonathan, Janet. M.A. in Pyschology, State U. Iowa, 1944. Lic. psychologist, Calif. Psychologist, Phila. Sch. Dist., 1944-45, Woods Sch. Psychology Clinic, 1945-46; psychologist U. Calif.-Berkeley, 1946—; pvt. practice psychology, Berkeley, 1974—. Mem. Am. Psychol. Assn., Am. Personnel and Guidance Assn. Home: 1023 Middlefield Rd Berkeley CA 94708 Office: 2140 Shattuck Ave Suite 904 Berkeley CA 94704

WANG, CHEN CHI, electronics co. exec., real estate exec., fin. corp. exec., b. Taipei, Taiwan, Aug. 10, 1932; s. Chin-Ting and Chen-Kim (Chen) W.; came to U.S., 1959, naturalized, 1970; B.A., Nat. Taiwan U., 1955; B.S.E.E., San Jose State U., 1965; M.B.A., U. Calif. at Berkeley, 1961; m. Victoria Rebisoff, Mar. 5, 1965; children—Katherine Kim, Gregory Chen, John Christopher, Michael Edward. With IBM, San Jose, Calif., 1965-72; founder, chief operative EIC Group, Woodside, Calif., 1968—; dir. Systek Electronics Corp., Santa Clara, Calif., 1970-73; founder, sr. partner Wang Enterprises, Santa Clara, 1974—; founder, chmn. Hanson & Wang Devel. Corp., Woodside, 1977—, Golden Alpha Enterprises, Hillsborough, Calif., 1979—; mng. partner Woodside Acres-Las Pulgas Estate, Woodside, 1980—; founder, sr. partner DeVine & Wang, Oakland, Calif., 1977—, Van Heal & Wang, West Village, Calif., 1981—; founder, chmn. EIC Bankcorp., Redwood City, Calif., 1982—. Served to 2d lt. Nationalist Chinese Army, 1955-56. Mem. Internat. Platform Assn., Tau Beta Pi. Mem. Christian Ch. Author: Monetary and Banking System of Taiwan, 1955; The Small Car Market in the U.S., 1961. Home: 195 Brookwood Rd Woodside CA 94062 Office: PO Box 4082 Woodside CA 94062

WANG, CHING CHUNG, chemistry educator; b. Peking, China, Feb. 10, 1936; came to U.S., 1960, naturalized, 1973; s. Shou Kang and Frances (Taao) W.; m. Alice Lee, Apr. 6, 1963; children—Charlotte, Felix. B.Sc. in Chemistry, Nat. Taiwan U., 1958; Ph.D., U. Calif., Berkeley, 1966. Research assoc. Coll. Physicians and Surgeons, Columbia U., N.Y.C., 1966-67; research assoc. Princeton (N.J.) U., 1967-1979; sr. research biochemist Merck Inst. for Therapeutic Research, Rahway, N.J., 1969-72, research fellow, 1972-75, sr. research fellow, 1975-78, sr. investigator, 1978-81; prof. dept. pharm. chemistry Sch. Pharmacy, U. Calif., San Francisco, 1981—. Bd. trustees Golden Gate Regional Ctrs. for Developmentally Disabled, San Francisco, 1982—. Grantee NIH, WHO, Merck Co., U. Calif.; recipient Burroughs Wellcome molecular parisitology award, 1983. Mem. Am. Soc. Biol. Chemists, Am. Chem. Soc., Soc. Neurosci., AAAS, N.Y. Acad. Sci., Am. Soc. Parasitologists, Am. Soc. Protozoologists. Patentee in field; contbr. articles to profl. jours.; editor Molecular and Biochem. Parasitology, 1980—. Home: 22 Miraloma Dr San Francisco CA 94127 Office: Dept Pharm Chemistry Sch Pharmacy Univ Calif San Francisco CA 94143

WANG, GEORGE CHUNG, economist, educator; b. Shanghai China, June 26, 1926; s. Tonghkwan and Shucheng; m. Jo Anne Lee, April 14, 1954. M.A., Columbia U., Ph.D., 1970; M.B.A., St. John's U. Asst. prof. U. So. Calif., Los Angeles, 1967-70; assoc. prof. U. Tenn., 1970-71; prof. econs. and mgmt. Calif. State U.-Carson, 1971—; cons. Pacific Internat. Corp. Fulbright sr. fellow, 1979-80. Mem. Am. Econ. Assn., Western Econ. Assn. Author: Fundamentals of Political Economy, 1977; editor Chinese Econ. Studies, 1964—; contbr. articles to profl. jours. Home: 1609 Via Zurita Palos Verdes Estates CA 90274 Office: Dept Econs Calif State U Carson CA 90747

WANG, JAMES CHIA-FANG, polit. scientist, educator; b. Nanling, China, Apr. 4, 1928; s. Chien-Yu and Lilian Wang; came to U.S., 1946, naturalized, 1962; B.A. in Polit. Sci., Oberlin Coll., 1950; postgrad. N.Y. U., 1951; Ph.D. in Polit. Sci., U. Hawaii, 1971; m. Sarah Cutter, May 7, 1960; children—Sarah, Eric. Research asst. Brookings Instn., 1951-53; adminstrv. and tng. officer UN Secretariat, N.Y.C., 1953-57; editor-in-charge UN Documents Edition, Readex Corp., N.Y.C., 1957-60; lectr. far eastern politics N.Y. U., N.Y.C., 1957-59; instr. Asian history and econs. Funahou Sch., Honolulu, 1960-64; program officer Inst. for

Student Interchange, East-West Center, Honolulu, 1964-69, acting dir. participant services, 1970, adminstrv. officer admissions, 1969-70; dir. freshmen integrated program Hilo (Hawaii) Coll., 1971-72; asst. prof. polit. sci. and internat. studies U. Hawaii at Hilo, 1971-72, assoc. prof., 1973-76, prof., 1976—, mem. Contemporary China Study Group, 1971—, chmn. dept. polit. sci., 1973-75; profl. assoc. East-West Communications Inst., Honolulu, 1978; cons. World Polit. Risk Forecast Project, Frost & Sullivan, N.Y.C.; adviser to AAUW, Hawaii, 1978—. Mem. Hawaii County Bicentennial Commn., 1975-76; vice chmn. Democratic Com., County Hawaii, 1972-76, chmn., 1982—, mem. Hawaii State Dem. Party Central Com., 1982—. U. Hawaii Research Found. grantee, 1972, 73, 75, 76, 78. Mem. Assn. Asian Studes, Assn. Chinese Lang. Tchrs., Am. Polit. Sci. Assn., Internat. Studies Assn. Democrat. Author: The Cultural Revolution in China: An Annotated Bibliography, 1976; Contemporary Chinese Politics: Political Institutions and Process, 1980; Hawaii State and Local Politics, 1981; Study Guide for Power in Hawaii (radio course); contbr. articles on Asian studies to scholarly jours. Home: PO Box 13 Hilo HI 96720 Office: Political Science Dept College Arts and Scis Univ Hawaii Hilo HI 96720

WANG, JOHN TING-KUAN, physician; b. Kwangton, China, Aug. 15, 1935; came to U.S., 1971, naturalized, 1980; s. Shee-check Wong and Wun-chun Chang; M.B., Nat. Taiwan U., 1964; m. Sally S.H., Nov. 12, 1967; children—Ian, Tricia, Joseph. Rotating intern, Victoria Gen. Hosp., Halifax, N.S., Can., 1965-66; asst. resident in internal medicine Ottawa (Ont., Can.) Gen. Hosp., 1966-67, asst. resident in pathology, 1968-71; asst. resident in pathology, Kingston (Ont., Can.) Gen. Hosp., 1967-68; resident in pathology Rochester (N.Y.) Gen. Hosp., 1971-73; asst. research pathologist Sch. Medicine, U. Calif., Davis, 1974-75; asst. pathologist Sacred Heart Hosp., Ft. Madison, Iowa, 1975-76; practice medicine specializing in medicine and pathology, Phoenix, 1976—; med. dir. Cyto-Lab, Phoenix, 1980—. Diplomate Am. Bd. Pathology. Fellow Coll. Am. Pathologists; mem. AMA, Ariz. Med. Assn., Maricopa County Med. Soc., Ariz. Soc. Pathologists.

WANG, JON YI, scientist; b. Taiwan, June 22, 1943; came to U.S., 1966, naturalized, 1974; s. Ko-Ming and Ming-Huey (Lai) W.; B.S., Nat. Taiwan U., 1965; M.S., MIT, 1968; Ph.D., Purdue U., 1971; m. Barbara C. Hwang, Aug. 21, 1971; 1 son, Eric. Sr. research engr. Convair div. Gen. Dynamics, San Diego, 1971-73, staff scientist, 1975-81, engring. staff scientist, 1981—; scientist Sci. Applications, Inc., La Jolla, Calif., 1973-75. Mem. Optical Soc. Am., Optical Soc. San Diego. Contbr. articles to profl. jours. Home: 2665 San Clemente Terrace San Diego CA 92122 Office: PO Box 5357 San Diego CA 92138

WANG, SHING CHUNG, electrical engineer; b. Hsinchu, Taiwan, Nov. 20, 1934; s. Wan Jen and Yu (Chen) W.; B.S., Taiwan U., 1957; M.S., Tohoku U., 1965; Ph.D. (scholar), Stanford U., 1971; m. Chu Mei Kuo, Jan. 21, 1958; children—Jean, Philip, Fanny, Charlie. Assoc. prof. elec. engring. Chiao Tung U., Hsinchu, Taiwan, 1965-67; research asso. Stanford (Calif.) U., 1971-74; sr. research scientist Xerox Corp., Pasadena, Calif., 1974—. Japanese Govt. scholar, 1963-65. Mem. So. Calif. Taiwanese Assn. (chmn. bd. 1979-80), Optical Soc. Am., IEEE, Quantum Electronics and Application Soc., Sigma Xi. Buddhist. Patentee in field. Contbr articles to profl. jours. Office: 250 N Halstead St Pasadena CA 91107

WANG, TONG-ENG, economist; b. Kaohsiung, Taiwan, May 20, 1933; came to U.S., 1960, naturalized, 1974; s. Shiao-mu and Yun-tai (Wu) W. B.A., Nat. Taiwan U., 1956; M.S., Auburn U., 1963; Ph.D., Iowa State U., 1966. Research asst. Auburn (Ala.) U., 1960-62; research asst. and assoc. dept. econs. Iowa State U., Ames, 1962-71; prof. Edward Waters Coll., Jacksonville, Fla., 1967-68; vis. asst. prof. econs. Central Mich. U., Mt. Pleasant, 1968; economist Md. Planning Dept., Balt., 1968; asst. prof. bus. adminstrn. Marshall U., Huntington, W.Va., 1969; cons. economist Dept. Hawaii Planning and Econ. Devel., Honolulu; economist Econ. Research Ctr., U. Hawaii, 1971-72; research assoc. Chinese Studies and econ. dept., asst. economist Ctr. for Chinese Studies, U. Calif.-Berkeley, 1972—; Guide prof. World Open U., Orange, Calif., 1981—. NSF grantee, 1973, 75. Mem. Am. Econ. Assn. Contbr. articles to profl. jours. Office: Ctr Chinese Studies U Calif Berkeley CA 94720

WANGENSTEEN, STEPHEN LIGHTNER, physician, surgeon; b. Mpls., Aug. 30, 1933; s. Owen Harding and Sarah D. (Davidson) W.; B.A., U. Minn., 1954, B.S., 1955; M.D., Harvard U., 1958; m. Lita L. Lindley, Oct. 1, 1977; children by previous marriage—Christine, Stephen, Philip, William. Intern, Columbia-Presbyn. Hosp., N.Y.C., 1958, resident, 1959-65, instr., 1965; asst. prof. U. Va., Charlottesville, 1967-69, assoc. prof., 1970-71, prof. surgery, 1972-76; prof., head dept. surgery U. Ariz., Tucson, 1976—; practice medicine specializing in surgery, Tucson, 1976—; mem. staff Ariz. Health Scis. Center, Tucson, 1976—; cons. VA Med. Center, Tucson, Phoenix, 1976—. Served with U.S. Army, 1965-66. Decorated Army Commendation medal. NIH grantee. Mem. Am. Surg. Assn., Halsted Soc., So. Surg. Assn., Western Surg. Assn., Soc. Univ. Surgeons, Assn. Acad. Surgery, Soc. for Surgery Alimentary Tract. Club: Mountain Oyster (Tucson). Contbr. articles to various publs. Office: Ariz Health Scis Center 1501 N Campbell St Tucson AZ 85724

WANLASS, STANLEY GLEN, sculptor, painter, art educator; b. Am. Fork, Utah, Apr. 3, 1941; s. L. Glen and Alta (Butler) W.; m. Joy Erikson, Feb. 17, 1966; children—Lincoln Stanley, Amber Joy, Britton Stanley, Brandy Joy, Brandon Stanley. B.F.A., Brigham Young U., 1966, M.A., 1968. Instr. Brigham Young U., Provo, Utah, 1965-70; art dir. Artifacts Design, Ogden, 1965-67; instr. European Art Acad., Paris, summer 1966; prof. Université de Grenoble (France), 1969-70; dir. art programs Study Guild Internat., Salt Lake City, 1970-71; prof. Clatsop Coll., Astoria, Oreg., 1971—; owner, painter, sculptor Stanley Wanlass Studios, Astoria, 1971—; paintings and sculptures represented in collections including: Des Arts Graphiques, Palais Congres, Paris, Cour de Maison, Université de Grenoble; design cons. for corps. and architects. Served with U.S. Army, 1959-60. Recipient Merrill award Brigham Young U., 1965; Brock Bank award, 1966; Art Dirs. Design of Excellence award Magic Mill Inc., 1979; St. Regis Paper Co. award, 1980; Grand Sweepstakes award Oreg. Trail Nat. Show, 1981; 1st place Bronze award, 1981; Silver medal Springfield Mus. Art, 1981. Mormon. Author Dictionary of America's Early Automobiles and Their Radiator Emblems, 1974. Home: 907 5th St Astoria OR 97103 Office: 16th and Jerome St Astoria OR 97103

WANTA, JOYCE ELAYNE, educator; b. Wausau, Wis., Apr. 3, 1926; d. Fred Burnett and Madge Zennetta (Narron) Nauta; grad. Kansas City Sch. Nursing, 1947; B.S.N., U. Utah, 1961, Ed.S., 1980; m. George J. Wanta, Sept. 11, 1948; children—Kristine, Georgine, Victoria. Public health nurse Salt Lake County Bd. Health, 1956-60; nurse, supr. Salt Lake County Gen. Hosp., 1960-62; dir. respiratory therapy Salt Lake County Hosp. and Univ. Hosp., 1962-69; dir. respiratory therapy edn. program Weber State Coll., Ogden, Utah, 1969—. Mem. Am. Assn. Respiratory Therapy, Utah Soc. Respiratory Therapy, Intermountain Thoracic Soc., AAUP, Utah Assn. Acad. Professionals, Utah Lung Assn., Epsilon Sigma Alpha. Roman Catholic. Club: Elks. Home: 3920 Lee Maur Salt Lake City UT 84119 Office: Weber State Coll Ogden UT 84408

WANTLAND, EARL, electronics executive; b. 1931; student Portland State Coll.; married. With Tektronix Inc., 1955—, exec. v.p., 1969-71, pres., 1971—, chief exec. officer, 1974—, also dir.; dir. Portland Gen. Electric Co., U.S. Bancorp., U.S. Nat. Bank Oreg., Floating Point Systems Inc. Bd. dirs. Portland State U. Found.; trustee Lewis and Clark Coll., Portland. Served with USNR, 1950-54. Office: Tektronix Inc 4900 SW Griffith Dr Beaverton OR 97005*

WANTUCHOWICZ, CAROL LOU, educational administrator; b. Chgo., Dec. 24, 1948; d. Leo and Victoria (Pivout) W.; m. Matthew W. Peters, Dec. 23, 1971 (div.). Student Coll. of Santa Fe, 1983. Office mgr. Lewis E. Thompson Advt., Santa Fe, 1972-76; owner, operator Payroll Service Bur., Santa Fe, 1976-78; adminstrv. asst. to atty. gen. State of N.Mex., Santa Fe, 1978-82; mgr. bus. affairs Coll. of Santa Fe, 1982—. Treas. for U.S. Senate campaign; mem. N.Mex. Kidney Found.; active Santa Fe County March of Dimes. Mem. LWY. Democrat. Roman Catholic. Home: PO Box 2458 Santa Fe NM 87501

WARD, ANTHONY JOHN, lawyer; b. Los Angeles, Sept. 25, 1931; s. John P. and Helen C. (Harris) W.; A.B., U. So. Calif., 1953; LL.B., U. Calif. at Berkeley, 1956; m. Marianne Edle von Graeve, Feb. 20, 1960 (div. 1977); 1 son, Mark Joachim; m. 2d, Julia Norby Credell, Nov. 4, 1978. Admitted to Calif. bar, 1957; asso. firm Ives, Kirwan & Dibble, Los Angeles, 1958-61; partner firm Marapese and Ward, Hawthorne, Calif., 1961-69; individual practice law, Torrance, Calif., 1969-76; partner firm Ward, Dodd & Gaunt, 1976—. Mem. Los Angeles World Affairs Council. Served to 1st lt. USAF, 1956-58. Mem. Am., Los Angeles County bar assns., Blue Key, Lambda Chi Alpha. Democrat. Home: 6085 Woodfern Rancho Palos Verdes CA 90274 Office: Pavilion A 21525 Hawthorne Blvd Torrance CA 90503

WARD, ARTHUR ALLEN, JR., educator, neurol. surgeon; b. Manipay, Ceylon, Feb. 4, 1916; s. Arthur A. and Alice (Bookwalter) W.; B.A., Yale, 1938, M.D., 1942; m. Janet L. Miller, Dec. 20, 1941; children—Sally L., Linda A. Intern, Mary Imogene Bassett Hosp., Cooperstown, N.Y., 1942-43; neuropathol. fellow McGill U., 1943, neurosurg. instern, 1944, resident neurology and neurosurgery, 1944-45; research asst. physiology Yale, 1945; instr. neurosurgery U. Louisville Sch. Medicine, 1946-47; faculty U. Wash. Sch. Medicine, 1948 , prof. neurol. surgery, 1965—, chmn. dept., 1965—; chief neurol. service Univ. Hosp., Harborview Med. Center; cons. VA Hosp. (all Seattle). Cons. Dept. Health, Edn. and Welfare, NIH, NSF. Diplomate Am. Bd. Neurol. Surgery, Nat. Bd. Med. Examiners. Mem. Harvey Cushing Soc., Am. Acad. Neurol. Surgery (pres. 1977-78), Am. Neurol. Assn. (v.p. 1972-73), Am. Acad. Neurology, Am. Electroencephalographic Soc. (pres. 1960), Am. Physiol. Soc., Assn. Research Nervous and Mental Disease, Soc. Neurol. Surgery (pres. 1974-75), Am. Bd. Neurol. Surgery, Am. Epilepsy Soc. (pres. 1971-72), Western Inst. Epilepsy, AAAS, Western Neurosurg. Soc. (pres. 1966), Western Soc. Electroencephalography (pres. 1957), N.W. Soc. Neurology and Psychiatry, Seattle Neurol. Soc., Seattle Surg. Soc., Research Soc. Neurol. Surgeons, Sigma Xi, Alpha Omega Alpha. Editor-in-chief Epilepsia; mem. adv. bd. Jour. Neurosurgery, Neurology, Rev. Surgery. Home: 4001 NE Belvoir Pl Seattle WA 98105

WARD, BREWER WINTON, JR., biomedical engineer, educator; b. Long Beach, Calif., July 9, 1948; s. Brewer Winton and Fern D. (Ostland) W.; m. Nancy L. Hjorth, June 20, 1971; children—Bill, John, Annie. B.S.E.E., Calif. State U.-Long Beach, 1971, M.S.E.E., 1973. Biomed. engr. St. Mary Med. Ctr., Long Beach, 1973—, mgr. dept. biomed. engring., 1978—; instr. Calif. State U., Long Beach, part-time 1973—. Mem. Assn. for Advancement Med. Instrumentation, Digital Equipment Computer Users Soc. Republican. Contbr. articles to profl. jours. Home: 3176 Oak Knoll Los Alamitos CA 90720 Office: 1050 Linden Ave Long Beach CA 90801

WARD, CAROL ESTHER, ceramic supply co. exec.; b. Phoenix, Oct. 14, 1930; d. Stephen Raymond and Marjorie Edith (Taylor) Brooks; student public schs.; divorced; children—Eileen Shepherd, Elaine Asmus, Stephen Hieb, Leslie Speissegger, Dawn Ward. With Marjon Ceramic, Inc., Phoenix, 1957—, now pres., owner; pres. Different Strokes, seminars for women in bus.; dir. Phoenix Nat. Bank; cons. in field; del. White Conf. Small Bus., 1980; mem. White House Task Force on Small Bus. Continuity; moderator weekly bus. roundtable, 1978-79. Mem. Mayor Phoenix Com. Future Budget and Fin., 1980, Gov. Ariz. Blue Ribbon Com. Edn., 1979; mem steering com., moderator Ariz. Small Bus. Conf. Mem. Ariz. C. of C. (Small Bus. Person of Yr. 1982), Ariz. Small Bus. Council (pres. 1979), Ariz. Ceramic Assn. (pres. 1964), Ariz. Bus. Alliance (pres. 1982), Ceramic Distbrs. Am. (pres. 1969), Nat. Ceramic Tchrs. Assn., Nat. Speakers Assn., Nat. Assn. Female Execs., Sales and Mktg. Execs. Assn., Bus. and Profl. Women. Republican. Club: Toastmasters. Author: Original Designs by Carol, 1968, Ceramic Business Survival Kit, 1976; contbr. articles to profl. jours. Office: 3434 W Earll Dr Phoenix AZ 85017

WARD, DIANE KOROSY, lawyer, educator; b. Cleve., Oct. 17, 1939; d. Theodore Louis and Edith (Bogar) Korosy; m. S. Mortimer Ward, IV, July 2, 1960; children—Christopher LaBruce, Samantha Martha; m. 2d, R. Michael Walters, June 30, 1979. A.B., Heidelberg Coll., 1961; J.D., U. San Diego, 1974. Bar: Calif. 1977. Ptnr., Ward & Howell, San Diego, 1978-79, Walters, Howell & Ward, APC, San Diego, 1979-81; mng. ptnr. Walters & Wards APC, San Diego, 1981—; v.p., dir. Oak Broadcasting Systems, Inc., Glendale, Calif.; instr. Ctr. Continuing Edn. of Rancho Bernando. Pres., Green Valley Civil Assn., 1979-80; founding pres. Profl. and Exec. Women of the Ranch, 1982-83; pres. Los Amados Aux. Childrens Home Soc. Calif. Mem. ABA, Calif. Bar Assn., San Diego Bar Assn., Rancho Bernardo Bar Assn. (chmn. 1982). Republican. Episcopalian. Clubs: Rancho Bernando Toastmasters, Soroptimist (pres. 1979-80). Home: 16503 Avenida Florencia Poway CA 92064 Office: 16776 Bernardo Center Dr Suite 214 San Diego CA 92128

WARD, FRANK ALAN, economist, educator, consultant; b. San Francisco, Oct. 8, 1948; s. John Martin and Jane (Ingley) W.; m. Deborah Louise Valverde, Aug. 21, 1982. B.S., Colo. State U., 1970, M.S., 1974, Ph.D. in Econs., 1977. Instr. econs. William Jewell Coll., Liberty, Mo., 1975-78; asst. prof. resource econs., N.Mex. State U., Las Cruces, 1978—; cons. in resource econs. Recipient Ph.D. dissertation award Am. Agrl. Econs. Assn. Mem. Am. Econs. Assn., Am. Agrl. Econs. Assn., Assn. Environ. and Resource Economists. Contbr. articles to profl. jours. Office: Box 3169 N Mex State U Las Cruces NM 88003

WARD, GORDON A(RTHUR), college president; b. Edgeley, N.D., May 22, 1926; s. Charles William and Eleanor Grace (Whitman) W.; B.S. in Edn., No. State Coll., 1950; M.A. in History, U. Wyo., 1958, Ph.D. in Higher Edn., 1969; postgrad. in econs. (Gen. Electrics fellow) Stanford U., 1961; m. Betty Lou Butler, Aug. 27, 1958; children—Cheryl Denise (dec.), Kimberly Ann. Adminstr. pub. schs., Casper, Wyo., N.D. and S.D., 1950-67; adminstrv. asst. to pres. Casper Coll., 1967; dean instrn. Central Wyo. Coll., 1968; chmn. Wyo. Pres.'s Council, 1982-83; pres. Wyo. Community Coll. Athletic Conf., 1977. Mem. Wyo. Ho. of Reps., 1964-66; exec. sec. No. Wyo. Community Found., 1973—; chmn. Legis.-Exec. Commn. on Reorgn. State Govt. Wyo., 1974-76, mem., 1974-78; mem. Wyo. Gov.'s Task Force on Nondiscrimination on Basis of Handicap, 1976-77; v.p. Salvation Army Adv. Bd., Sheridan, 1977—; mem. adv. bd. N.G., 1977—. Served with USN, 1944-45; PTO. Recipient Most Creative award Community Coll. Seminar, U. Wyo., 1967; Coe fellow, 1959. Mem. Am. Assn. Community and Jr. Colls., Am. Council Edn., Wyo. Taxpayers Assn., Mountain States Assn. Community Colls. (pres. 1982-83), Mountain Plains Adult Edn. Assn., Phi Delta Kappa, Delta Kappa Pi. Presbyterian (ruling elder). Club: Rotary Home: 1740 S Mountain View Dr Sheridan WY 82801 Office: PO Box 1500 Sheridan WY 82801

WARD, JAMES ALLEN, educator; b. Greeley, Colo., June 18, 1948; s. Frank and Bertha M. (Allen) W.; student Colo. State U., 1966-68; B.S., Wyo. U., 1970, M.S., 1978; m. Marilynn Gail Lowry, Mar. 26, 1970; children—Joye Ellen, Jill Eileen. Tchr. Vocat. agr. Greybull (Wyo.) High Sch., 1972-74; tchr. vocat. agr. Gillette (Wyo.) High Sch., 1974—, vocat. dept. head, 1979—. Bd. dirs. Stampede Drive Homeowners Assn., 1982—. Served with U.S. Army, 1970-72. Mem. Wyo. Vo-Ag Tchrs. Assn. (pres. 1979-80), Nat. Vo-Ag Tchrs. Assn., Am. Vocat. Assn., Wyo. Vocat. Assn., Greybull Tchrs. Assn. (pres. 1973-74), Campbell County Young Farmers, Gillette FFA Alumni Assn. Republican. Episcopalian. Club: Lions (pres. 1979-80, zone chmn. 1981-82). Home: Box 5036 Gillette WY 82716 Office: 1000 Camel Dr Gillette WY 82716

WARD, KAREN GRAFF, private security company executive, consultant; b. Phoenix, Nov. 14, 1948; d. Charles Wesley and Doris Mae (Walker) Graff; m. Raymond Edward List, Sept. 2, 1972; m. 2d, Forrest Herndon Ward, Aug. 8, 1982. B.S., Ohio U., 1970; cert. in French, Italian, Internat. House, Rome, 1972; postgrad. U. Calif.-Berkeley, 1974, 1978. Lic. ins. agent, Pa., 1975. Bilingual personnel agt. Kaiser Engrs. of Italy, Sardinia and Rome, 1970-74; agt. Lincoln Nat. Life Ins., Harrisburg, Pa., 1975-76; adminstrv. mgr. Peabody Office Furniture, Boston, 1976-78; mktg. dir., commd. sales Western Contract Furnishers, San Francisco, 1978-81; free lance cons. interior design and comml. Furnishings, San Francisco, 1981-82; dir. sales, mktg. Romex Sentinel Systems, Stockton, Calif., 1982—; cons., lectr. in field. Mem. Nat. Fedn. Bus. and Profl. Women, Adminstrv. Mgmt. Soc., Am. Mktg. Assn., Stockton C. of C., Chi Omega Alumnae. Republican. Presbyterian. Home: 4777 Grouse Run Dr Apt 155 Stockton CA 95207 Office: Romex Sentinel Systems 3416 Newton Rd Stockton CA 95205

WARD, LAETITIA, psychologist; b. Paris, Aug. 4, 1951; d. John and Jean (Bruce) Ward; m. Paul Eric Buehrens, Mar. 2, 1952. B.A., Lewis and Clark Coll., 1973; Ph.D., Case Western Res. U., 1977. Psychologist, Charleston (S.C.) Area Mental Health Ctr., 1979; cons. psychologist Oakgrove Children's Ctr., Charleston, 1978-81, Tacoma Child Study and Guidance Ctr., 1982—; staff psychologist Good Samaritan Hosp., Pullallup, Wash., 1982—. Vol., Sante Fe Chamber Music Festival. Mem. Am. Psychol. Assn., Nat. Register of Health Care Providers in Psychology, Am. Soc. Clin. Hypnosis, Wash. Acad. Clin. Hypnosis, Soc. Pediatric Psychology. Contbr. articles to profl. jours. Address: 1606 37th Ave Seattle WA 98122

WARD, LESTER LOWE, JR., lawyer; b. Pueblo, Colo., Dec. 21, 1930; s. Lester Lowe and Alysmai (Pfeffer) W.; A.B. cum laude, Harvard U., 1952; LL.B., 1955; m. Rosalind H. Felps, Apr. 18, 1964; children—Ann Marie, Alison, Lester Lowe. Admitted to Colo. bar, 1955; pvt. practice law, Pueblo, 1957—; partner firm Predovich, Ward & Banner, Pueblo, 1974—. Trustee, Thatcher Found., Frank I. Lamb Found.; pres. bd. trustees Pueblo Pub. Library, 1960-66; trustee St. Mary-Corwin Hosp., 1972—, pres., 1979-80. Served with U.S. Army, 1955-57. Recipient Outstanding Young Lawyer award Pueblo County Bar Assn., 1965, 67; named Outstanding Young Man of Yr., Pueblo Jaycees, 1964. Fellow Am. Coll. Probate Counsel; mem. Am. Bar Assn., Colo. Bar Assn. (bd. govs. 1977-79, pres. 1983-84), Pueblo County Bar Assn. (pres. 1976-77), Harvard Law Sch. Assn. Colo. (pres. 1972). Democrat. Roman Catholic. Club: Kiwanis (pres. 1969). Home: 118 Baylor St Pueblo CO 81005 Office: 727 Thatcher Bldg Pueblo CO 81003

WARD, ORVILLE ELVIN, insurance company executive; b. Topeka, May 6, 1926; s. John Edward and Sylvia (Anderson) W.; m. Dorothy Kathryn Brainard, Jan. 8, 1949; children—Claudia Ward McGrath, Virginia Ward Klevjer, Dona Ward Tindall, Jay. Student U. Wash., 1944-45. Ind. ins. agt., Seattle, 1955-62; field rep. SAFECO Life Ins. Co., Seattle, 1962-64, ins. educator, 1964-65, div. life mgr., 1965-69, v.p., dir. pensions, 1969—; dir. Sound Bank, Federal Way, Wash.; lectr. in field. Bd. dirs. Seattle-King County ARC; chairperson Ret. Sr. Vol. Program King County. Served with USAF, 1944-45. Mem. C.L.U. (cert. 1966). Contbr. articles to profl. mags. Home: 35790 27th Ave S Federal Way WA 98003 Office: SAFECO Life Ins Co SAFECO Plaza Seattle WA 98185

WARD, PATRICIA ANN, author; b. Cin., Mar. 24, 1932; d. Victor Clark and Anna Laura (Reutepohler) Searle; B.S. in Edn., U. Southwestern La., 1954; M.S. in Secondary Edn., Ft. Hays (Kans.) State U., 1971, Ed.S., 1977; m. William Haskins Ward, Oct. 18, 1952; children—Kathryn Barbara, William Holden. Tchr. schs. in La. and Kans., 1954-55, 66-80; freelance writer and photographer, Casper, Wyo., 1980—; co-author: Learning Packets: New Approach to Individualizing Instruction, 1976; creator simulation game Sanga, 1974; tchr. summer workshops Ft. Hays State U.; mem. Kans. Profl. Teaching Standards Adv. Bd., 1974-80; v.p. Russell County Ednl. Assn., 1979-80. Title III Elem. and Secondary Edn. Act mini-grantee, 1970, 75. Mem. NEA, Nat. Writers Club, Phi Kappa Phi, Phi Delta Kappa. Address: 3570 Big Horn St Casper WY 82609

WARD, PHILLIP JAMES, optometrist, researcher; b. Seattle, Dec. 9, 1946; s. Phillip Joseph and Elizabeth Beaulah (Bagguley) W.; m. Susan Lee Cavalle, July 19, 1965; m. 2d, Linda Carol Madewell, Nov. 15, 1975; children—Phillip James, Jason Matthew. A.A., Peninsula Jr. Coll., Port Angeles, Wash., 1967; B.S., Pacific U., 1969, O.D., 1971. Cert. optometrist, Nev. Optometrist, 1978-80; pvt. practice optometry, Reno, Nev., 1980—; cons. vision safety program U.S. Army Hawthorne Army Ammunition Depot. Served to capt. U.S. Army, 1971-77. Mem. Am. Optometric Assn., Nev. Optometric Assn. Democrat. Research in contact lenses. Home: 4140 Snow Shoe Ln Reno NV 89502 Office: 919 S Wells Ave Reno NV 89502

WARD, WILLIAM ANDREW, JR., air force officer; b. Balt., Jan. 13, 1953; s. William Andrew and Geneva Cecelia (Richardson) W.; B.A., U. Md., 1975; grad. Air Force Squadron Officers Sch., 1980; postgrad., Chapman Coll., 1980—; m. Elizabeth Foster, July 5, 1975; 1 son, William Andrew III. Commd. 2d lt. U.S. Air Force, 1975, advanced through grades to capt. 1980; dep. missile combat crew comdr., Malmstrom AFB, Mont., 1975-77, instr., 1978; missile combat crew comdr., 1979; instr. ICBM ops., Vandenberg AFB, Calif., 1979—. Recipient Excellence award 15th Air Force Combat Crew, 1979. Mem. Air Force Assn., Res. Officers Assn. (Appreciation award Mont. chpt. 1978), Alpha Phi Alpha. Episcopalian. Clubs: Masons, Order of Eastern Star. Home: 413 Baywood St Vandenberg AFB CA 93437 Office: 4315 CCTS/CMMB Vandenberg AFB CA 93437

WARD, WILLIAM OGDEN, finance co. exec.; b. Bismarck, N.D., Oct. 10, 1944; s. William O. and Kathryn C. Ward; B.A. in Econs., Wash. State U., 1966; M.B.A., U. Wash., 1969; postgrad. (fellow) U. Mich., 1970-71; M.B.A. in Taxation, Golden Gate U., 1973; m. Patricia E. Maffit, June 24, 1967. Nat. bank examiner U.S. Treasury Dept., Seattle, 1966-68; acct. Peat, Marwick, Mitchell & Co., San Francisco, 1971-74; div. v.p., dir. taxes Itel Corp., San Francisco, 1975-79; pres. Belvedere Equipment Fin. Co., San Francisco, 1979-82; ptnr. Ward Holmes & Co., Marin County, Calif., 1983—; dir. Belvedere Holdings Ltd., Bermuda; mem. faculty Golden Gate U., 1974-75. Bd. dirs., pres. Greenbrae Property Owners Assn., Marin County Service Area #16. Named Outstanding Alumni, Golden Gate U. Sch. Taxation, 1979; C.P.A., Calif., Wash. Mem. Am. Inst. C.P.A.s, Calif. Soc. C.P.A.s, Wash. Soc.

C.P.A.s, Beta Alpha Psi. Roman Catholic. Clubs: San Francisco Yacht, Elks. Office: 21 Tamai Vista Blvd Suite 186 Corte Madera CA 94925

WARDE, IBRAHIM ANTOINE, investment co. exec.; b. Beirut, Lebanon, July 3, 1953; came to U.S., 1977, naturalized, 1981; s. Antoine Ibrahim and Denise Abdallah (Zehil) W.; B.B.A., U. St. Joseph, Lebanon, 1975; Diplome de L'Ecole des Hautes Etudes Commerciales, France, 1977; M.A., U. Calif., Berkeley, 1981. Pres., I.B.P.C., Inc., San Francisco, 1979—; pres. A. I. Warde, Inc., San Francisco, 1980—. Roman Catholic. Author: Foreign Banking in the U.S., 1980; Foreign Investment in American Real Estate, 1981. Home: 720 2d Ave San Francisco CA 94118 Office: 419 Presidio Ave San Francisco CA 94115

WARDEN, IVAN LEIGH, clergyman, educator; b. N.Y.C., Aug. 18, 1943; s. Charles Lee and Miriam (Burgess) W.; m. Jean Scantlebury, Feb. 17, 1968; children—Ariel Jeanine, Angela Jeanice. B.A. in Theolory, Oakwood Coll., 1967; M.R.E., N.Y. Theol. Sem., 1970, M.S.T., 1974; postgrad. Princeton U. Theol. Sem., 1974—. Ordained to ministry Seventh-day Adventist Ch., 1972. Asst. minister Bethel Seventh-day Adventist Ch., Bklyn., 1967-70; minister S.I. (N.Y.) Seventh-day Adventist Ch., 1970-73, Beth-El Seventh-day Adventist Ch., Jersey City, 1973-75; asst. prof. urban ministries Andrews U., Berrien Springs, Mich., 1976-81, adj. prof., 1981—; dir. urban ministries and community services So. Calif. Conf. Seventh-day Adventists, Glendale, 1981—; facilitator call to city program Coll. Continuing Edn. Inst. Changing Ministries, U. So. Calif. Mem. adv. bd. Vols. in Probation of 5th Dist. Ct., State of Mich., 1977-81. Recipient award Concerned Citizens Alliance, Jersey City, 1975; faculty award Andrews U., 1979. Office: 1535 E Chevy Chase Dr PO Box 969 Glendale CA 91209

WARDLE, NORVAL JUNIUS, agricultural engineering educator, safety consultant; b. Victor, Idaho, Mar. 21, 1909; s. William Haston and Annie Serena (Sorensen) W.; m. Delsa Taysom, Aug. 30, 1935; children—Ronald William, Norval Leon, Carole Annette, Ilene Wardle Lyons, Theron J., Michael T., Robert B. B.S. in Agr., U. Idaho, 1937, M.S. in Agr., 1946; Ph.D. in Agr. Engring., Iowa State U., 1949; registered engr. Calif.; cert. safety profl. Farm operator, Rockland, Idaho, 1929-33; sec. entomology dept. U. Idaho, 1934-37; tchr. Vocat. Agrl. High Sch., Midway, Salmon and Preston, Idaho, 1937-44; critic tchr. agrl. ed. U. Idaho, 1944-45; instr. agrl. engring. Iowa State U., 1945-47, asst. prof. agrl. engring. safety, 1947-50; asso. prof., 1950-70; agrl. safety cons., Ames, Iowa, 1970-73, Logan, Utah, 1973—; exec. sec. Iowa State U. Safety Council, 1947-70; exec. Iowa Farm Safety Council, 1947-72. Mem. Govs. Com. (Iowa) 100 Public Safety, 1961-68; adv. Iowa State Com. sub-com. Law Enforcement on Fraud, Credit, Personal Purchases; bd. dirs. Iowa Pub. Health Assn., 1950-64, pres. 1962; bd. dirs. Iowa Geneal. Soc., 1964-68. Mem. Nat. Inst. Farm Safety (charter pres.), Nat. Safety Council, Nat. Fire Protection Assn., Am. Soc. Agrl. Engrs., Am. Soc. Safety Engrs., Veterans of Safety, Alpha Zeta, Epsilon Sigma Phi, Phi Delta Kappa, Delta Psi Omega, Gamma Sigma Delta. Club. Solare Social. Author: Operating Farm Tractors and Machinery, 1969; contbr. articles to jours. in field. Home: 220 N 400 E Logan UT 84321 Office: 220 N 400 E Logan UT 84321

WARD-STEINMAN, DAVID, composer, educator; b. Alexandria, La., Nov. 6, 1936; s. Irving and Daisy Leila (Ward) Ward-S.; B.Mus. cum laude (Dohnanyi award 1965, Outstanding Alumnus award 1976), Fla. State U., 1957; Mus.M., U. Ill., 1958, D.M.A., 1961; postdoctoral vis. fellow Princeton U., 1970; m. Susan Diana Lucas, Dec. 28, 1956; children—Jenna, Matthew. Grad. instr. U. Ill., 1957-58; mem. faculty San Diego State U., 1961—, prof. music, 1968—, dir. comprehensive musicianship program, 1972—, composer-in-residence, 1961—; mem. summer faculty Eastman Sch. Music Workshop, 1969; Ford Found. composer-in-residence, Tampa Bay (Fla.) Area, 1970-72; mus. adv. Calif. Ballet Co.; curriculum cons. U. North Sumatra (Indonesia); composer: Symphony, 1959, (ballet) Western Orpheus, 1964; Cello Concerto, 1966; Antares, 1971; Arcturus, 1972, The Tracker, 1976; Brancusi's Brass Beds, 1977; (oratorio) Song of Moses, 1964, Jazz Tangents, 1967, Childs Play, 1968, (2 act opera) Tamar, 1977; And in These Times, Christmas Cantata, 1979-81; Golden Apples, 1981; Of Wind and Water, choral suite, 1982; co-author: Comparative Anthology of Musical Forms, 2 vols., 1976; performed new music concerts in Java and Sumatra (sponsored by ICA); recs. include Fragments from Sappho, 1969, Duo for cello and piano, 1974, Childs Play for bassoon and piano, 1974. Kinley Meml. fellow, Paris, 1958-59; recipient Bearns prize Columbia U., 1961; SAI Am. Music award, 1962; Broadcast Music prize, 1954, 55, 60, 61; named Outstanding Prof., Calif. State Univs. and Colls., 1968; commd. by Chgo. Symphony, Joffrey Ballet, numerous others. Mem. Broadcast Music Inc., Am. Soc. U. Composers, Coll. Music Soc., Am. Music Center. Presbyterian. Club: Golden State Flying. Office: Music Dept San Diego State Univ San Diego CA 92182

WARE, PATRICIA LUCILLE, educator; b. Salt Lake City, Sept. 4, 1941; d. Daniel Beville Searcy (dec.) and Dorothy Melton Adkison; m. Willett Ware III; children—Kenton Daniel, Kimberly, Rebecca. Student Northwestern U., 1959-60; A.B., U. Calif.-Berkeley, 1963; M.A., Calif. State U.-Chico, 1978; postgrad. U. Calif.-Santa Barbara, 1966-67, U. Calif.-Santa Cruz, Calif. State U.-San Jose, La. State U. Cert. secondary and community coll. tchr., Calif. Tchr. Santa Barbara (Calif.) High Sch. Dist., 1967-69, Santa Cruz (Calif.) City Schs., 1969-73, Pajaro Valley (Calif.) Unified Schs., 1973-76; cons. Shasta County (Calif.) supt. schs., 1977-78; English tchr. Paradise (Calif.) Unified Sch. Dist., 1979—. Active Chico (Calif.) Unified Dist. PTA. Recipient Genevieve Haight award, 1967; No. Calif. Writing Project fellow, 1977. Mem. Nat. Council Tchrs. English, Calif. Assn. Tchrs. English, Calif. Tchrs. Assn. (state mem. at large), AAUW, Calif. Reading Assn., Phi Delta Kappa, Delta Kappa Gamma. Democrat. Club: Calif. State U.-Chico Faculty Wives. Home: 1710 Citrus Ave Chico CA 95926 Office: 5911 Maxwell Dr Paradise CA 95969

WARGO, WILLIAM GEORGE, former counselor, coll. adminstr.; b. McKeesport, Pa., Sept. 18, 1942; s. George Regis and Katherine Marie (Kaftanich) W.; A.A., Victor Valley Coll., 1969; B.A., Calif. State Coll., San Bernardino, 1971; M.A., Chapman Coll., 1974; postgrad. U.S. Internat. U., 1978—; m. Elizabeth Ann Nelson, Apr. 14, 1973 (div. 1979); children—Charles Raymond, Sherrie Marie. Tchr. sci. and math. grades 7-10, Penn Mil. Acad., Hesperia, Calif., 1969-70; instr. gen. ednl. devel. Edn. Office, George AFB, Calif., 1970-72; adult edn. counselor, coll. adminstr. Chapman Coll., Orange, Calif., 1972-83, established San Diego Community Edn. Center as part of coll., 1977; ednl. cons. and child adv., 1979—; counseling intern Family Counseling Service, San Diego, 1976-77, also abusive substance control dept. Cath. Community Service, San Diego; founder, dir. Career Change Club, 1979, Lifework Tng., San Diego, 1980; instr. San Diego Mesa Coll., Nat. U., 1980-82; researcher, tchr., cons. Burnout Prevention and Intervention, 1981—. Served with USAF, 1960-68. Mem. Am. Soc. Tng. and Devel., San Diego Career Guidance Assn. Democrat. Roman Catholic. Club: Internat. of Calif. State Coll. (San Bernardino). Author: Jobs/Careers That Work for You, 1981. Home: 8626 Longwood St San Diego CA 92126

WARLICK, MICHAEL DAVID, cosmetic company sales executive; b. Dallas, Dec. 5, 1949; s. Homer Elvy and Betty Jane (Ware) W.; A.A., North Tex. State U., 1974. Field rep. Redken Labs., San Francisco, 1975, asst. dist. mgr., So. Calif., 1975-76, dist. mgr., 1976-79, regional mgr., Western U.S., 1979—. Republican. Mem. Churches of Christ.

WARNATH, CHARLES FREDERICK, psychology educator, psychologist; b. Phila., Apr. 17, 1925; s. Oscar J. and Ruth H. (Juers) W.; m. Maxine Ammer, Aug. 20, 1952; children—Stephen, Cindy. B.A., Princeton U., 1949; M.A., Tchrs. Coll. Columbia U., 1951, Ph.D., 1954. Teaching asst. Tchrs. Coll., Columbia U., 1951-52, counseling asst., 1953-54, research assoc. Horace Mann-Lincoln Inst. Sch. Experimentation, 1954-55, research asst., 1952-54; asst. prof. family life, gen. counselor Univ. Counseling Ctr., U. Nebr., 1955-57; asst. prof. guidance and counseling U. Calif.-Berkeley, summer, 1961; cons. in counseling psychology VA Hosps., Roseburg, Oreg., Portland, Oreg. and Vancouver, Wash., 1957-61; asst. prof. psychology, counselor Univ. Counseling Ctr., U. Oreg., 1957-61; prof. guidance Anchorage (Alaska) Community Coll., summer 1963; prof. psychology Oreg. State U., Corvallis, 1961—, dir. Univ. Counseling Ctr., 1961-71; cons. in field; mem. Oreg. Bd. Psychologist Examiners, 1963-65, chmn., 1963-65; mem. adv. bd. Beton County Mental Health Clinic, 1970-73, Benton County Coop. Services Bldg., 1972; mem. Joint Commn. on Cert. Psychologists, Calif., Wash. and Oreg., 1964. Served with USMC, 1944-47. Fellow Am. Psychol. Assn. (chmn. com. on teaching awards div. teaching 1960-61, mem. edn. and tng. com. 1966-68); mem. Oreg. Psychol. Assn. (chmn. state bd. exam. for profl. psychologists 1959-62, corr. newsletter, 1959-62, mem. pub. relations com. 1960-61, coordinator legis. com. 1962-63), Nat. Vocat. Guidance Assn. (chmn. commn. on econ. opportunities 1966-68, editorial bd. quar. 1958-61), Am. Coll. Personnel Assn. (mem. ethical standards com. 1957, publs. com. 1958-60, state membership chmn. 1960-61, program chmn. meeting 1960, 62, mem. commn. on counseling 1964), N.W. Coll. Personnel Assn. (v.p. 1960-61), Western Psychol. Assn. (program com. Portland chpt. 1964). Author: (with Lawrence Stewart) The Counselor and Society: A Cultural Approach, 1965; New Myths and Old Realities: College Counseling in Transition, 1971; New Directions for College Counselors, 1973; contbr. articles to profl. jours. Home: 124 NW 30th St Corvallis OR 97330 Office: 208 Moreland Oreg State U Corvallis OR 97331

WARNE, WILLIAM ELMO, cons. irrigationist; b. nr. Seafield, Ind., Sept. 2, 1905; s. William Rufus and Nettie Jane (Williams) W.; m. Edith Margaret Peterson, July 9, 1929; children—Jane Ingrid Warne Beeder, William Robert, Margaret Edith Warne Monroe. A.B., U. Calif., 1927; D.Econs., Yonsei U., Seoul, 1959; LL.D., Seoul Nat. U., 1959. Reporter, San Francisco Bull. and Oakland (Calif.) Post-Enquirer, 1925-27; news editor Brawley (Calif.) News, 1927, Calexico (Calif.) Chronicle, 1927-28; editor and night mgr. Los Angeles bur. AP, 1928-31, corr. San Diego bur., 1931-33, Washington corr., 1933-35; editor Bur. Reclamation, Dept. Interior, 1935-37; staff Third World Power Conf., 1936; asso. to reviewing com. Nat. Resources Com. on Preparation of Drainage Basin Problems and Programs, 1936, mem. editorial com. for revision, 1937; chief of info. Bur. Reclamation, 1937-42; co-dir. (with late Harlan H. Barrows) Columbia Basin Joint Investigations, 1939-42; chief of staff, war prodn. dr. WPB, 1942; asst. dir. div. of power Dept. Interior, 1942-43, dir. info. Dept. Interior, 1943, asst. commr. Bur. Reclamation, 1943-47, apptd. asst. sec. interior, 1947, asst. sec. water and power devel., 1950-51; U.S. minister in charge tech. cooperation for Iran, 1951-55, Brazil, 1955-56; U.S. minister and econ. coordinator for Korea, 1956-59; dir. Calif. Dept. Fish and Game, 1959-60, Dept. Agr., 1960-61, Dept. Water Resources, 1961-67; v.p. water resources Devel. & Resources Corp., 1967-69, cons., 1969—; rep. Orange County Water Dist., 1972—; Phase I team leader, diagnostic study of Iranian ministry of energy for Purdue U. and U. So. Calif., 1975; disting. practitioner in residence Sch. Public Adminstrn., Sacramento campus U. So. Calif., 1975-78; mem. U.S. adv. group desalination and agr. Saudi Arabia, 1982; cons. for Internat. Exec. Service Corps to Egypt on water resource in Western desert, 1977; adminstr. Resources Agy. Calif., 1961-62. Chmn., Pres.'s Com. on San Diego Water Supply, 1944-46, chmn. Fed. Inter-Agency River Basin Com., 1948, Fed. Com. on Alaskan Devel., 1948; pres. Group Health Assn., Inc., 1947-51; chmn. U.S. del. 2d Inter-Am. Conf. Indian Life, Cuzco, Peru, 1949; U.S. del. 4th World Power Conf., London, 1950; mem. bd. Near East Found., 1956-58, 59-64; mem. Calif. Water Pollution Control Bd., 1959-67, Commn. Interstate Co-operation, 1960-67; mem. adv. bd. Fed. Water Pollution Control, 1962-65; Regents lectr. U. Calif. at Davis, 1967; mem. Gov.'s cabinet, 1961, U.S. com. Internat. Commn Large Dams, U.S. com. of Internat. Com. Irrigation, Flood Control and Drainage; bd. dirs. Nat. Water Supply Improvement Assn., 1973-81, pres., 1978-80; bd. dirs. No. Calif. Symphony Found., 1978—, v.p., 1979-82. Served as 2d lt. O.R.C., 1927-37. Recipient Disting. Service award Dept. Interior, 1951; Disting. Pub. Service Honor award FOA, 1955; Order of Crown, Shah of Iran, 1955; Outstanding Service citation UN Command, 1959; award of achievement Lambda Chi Alpha, 1963. Mem. Nat. Acad. Public Adminstrn. (chmn. standing com. on environ. and resource mgmt. 1971-78), Sacramento World Affairs Council (pres. 1975-76), Sacramento Symphony Assn. (v.p. 1978-79), Sigma Delta Chi, Lambda Chi Alpha. Clubs: Nat. Press (Washington); Explorers (N.Y.C.); Sutter (Sacramento). Author: Mission for Peace—Point 4 in Iran, 1956; The Bureau of Reclamation, 1973; How the Colorado River Was Spent, 1975; Mass Transfer of Water over Long Distances—The California Experience, 1978; Transfering Desalting Technology, 1979. Home: 2090 8th Ave Sacramento CA 95818

WARNER, CARYL ROWLAND, lawyer; b. Los Angeles, Jan. 5, 1908; s. Rowland Moseley and Emily Caryl (Clark) W.; m. Carol McGinnis, July 13, 1978; children—Caryl Christopher; Rick, Lynn, James, John; 1 stepdau., Amy Rubin. Bar: Calif. 1929. Sole practice, Los Angeles, 1929—. Served to lt. comdr. USNR, 1943-45. Mem. Phi Alpha Delta. Episcopalian. Clubs: Masons, Elks, First Families Los Angeles. Office: 6922 Hollywood Blvd Suite 418 Los Angeles CA 90028

WARNER, DONALD DODGE, aircraft manufacturing executive; b. Mpls., Dec. 24, 1918; s. Fred Garfield and Mary Alice (Swan) W.; m. Suzanne Baker; children—Laurie, Douglas, Kathryn, Wendy. B.S. in Aero. Engring., U. Minn., 1940; A.M.P., Harvard U., 1977. Structures engr. Glenn L. Martin Co., Balt., 1940-46; structures supr. N.Am. Aviation, Los Angeles, 1946-51, supr. structures, program mgr., 1951-70; v.p. engring. Northrop Corp., Hawthorne, Calif., 1970-77, v.p. materiel, facilities and services, 1978—. Bd. dirs. Am. Cancer Soc., 1981-83, Century City C. of C., 1978-83. Assoc. fellow AIAA; mem. Am. Mgmt. Assn., Am. Def. Preparedness Assn., Soc. Automotive Engrs., Nat. Aero. Assn. Presbyterian (elder). Club: Palos Verdes Golf. Home: 888 Via Del Monte Palos Verdes Estates CA 90274 Office: Northrop Corp 1800 Century Park E Los Angeles CA 90067

WARNER, FREDERICK W., fin. cons.; b. Scranton, Pa., June 15, 1942; s. Frederick W., Jr. and Anita C. (Clark) W.; B.S. in Acctg., U. Miss., 1963; M.B.A. in Fin., U. Ariz., 1965. Plant controller Aerovox Corp., Burbank, Calif., 1965-67; asst. div. controller Singer Co., Los Angeles, 1968-69; corp. controller Graphic Arts Packaging Corp., Gardena, Calif., 1969-72; corp. controller, chief fin. officer Brentwood Originals, Inc., Torrance, Calif., 1972-76; pres. Hartford Cons., Los Angeles, 1976—, also Warner/Rhoades Real Estate Devel.; v.p. Hugh A. Bell & Assos., Inc., SBH Industries, Inc. Office: Hartford Cons 3600 Wilshire Blvd Suite 1830 Los Angeles CA 90010

WARNER, PETER DERYK, psychotherapist, clinical director; b. Urmstom, Lancachire, Eng., Feb. 20, 1938; s. Hugh Francis and Belinda (Jones) W.; m. Valerie Elaine Gunning, June 17, 1961; children—Andrew Peter, Sharon Ruth. Student Liverpool Sch. Architecture, 1954-56; Th.D., Handsworth Coll., 1961; postgrad. Liverpool U. and U. West Indies, 1961-66. Diplomate Am. Inst. Counseling and Psychotherapy. Mgr., Norman Hurst Hotel, Rhyl, Wales, 1954; draftsman Jim Porter & Co., Colwyn Bay, Wales, 1954-56; pastor, supt. schs. Jamaica, W.I., 1961-68; pastor Harrisburg Methodist Ch., Harrisburg, 1968-71; sr. pastor Park Rose Meth. Ch., Portland, Oreg., 1971-78; psychotherapist N.W. Counseling Assocs., Portland, 1971-78; gen. mgr. La. Pacific Corp., Portland, 1978-81; pvt. practice psychotherapy, Portland, Oreg., 1981—; clin. dir. Ctr. Marriage and Family, Vancouver, Wash.; dir. E. Portland Clinic, 1982—; dir. N.W. Counseling Assn., 1975—. Bd. dirs. Park Rose Sch. Dist., 1974-78, chmn. bd., 1977-78; Oreg. soccer commr., 1975-79; sec. Jamaica Council Chs., 1963-67; active Multnomah County Juvenile Services Commn., 1980-81. Served with Royal Air Force, 1956-58. Recipient NCCJ award, 1978. Fellow Am. Orthopsychiat. Assn.; mem. Am. Assn. Marriage and Family Therapy, Am. Mental Health Counselors Assn., Acad. Orthomolecular Psychiatry (assoc). Republican. Office: 7218 NE Sandy Blvd Portland OR 97213

WARNER, ROBERT CHARLES, advertising executive; b. Portland, Oreg., Feb. 7, 1944; s. Henry Pat and Lorraine (Docktor) W.; m. Sharon Lee Prentice, July 11, 1970; m. 2d, Elizabeth Ann Brewer, Nov. 5, 1976; 1 dau., Anne Elizabeth. B.S. in Journalism, U. Oreg., 1969. Supr. advt. and pub. relations White Motor Corp., Portland, 1970-72; advt. and pub. relations mgr. Peterbilt Motors Co., San Francisco, 1972-76; dir. mktg. communications Freightliner Corp., Portland, 1976-83, dir. advt. and sales promotion, 1983—. Served with Army N.G., 1963-69. Mem. Portland Advt. Assn (past pres.), Chi Psi. Home: 6411 SE 32nd Portland OR 97202 Office: 4747 N Channel Portland OR 97208

WARNER, RONALD, lawyer; b. N.Y.C., Apr. 15, 1944; s. Harry and Lorraine (Goodrich) W.; B.A., Tulane U., 1965; J.D., N.Y. U., 1968; m. Michele Elen Dressler, Sept. 28, 1968; children—Stephen Harlan, Bradley Douglas. Admitted to N.Y. bar, 1969, Calif. bar, 1972, D.C. bar, 1978; assoc. firm Debevoise & Plimpton, N.Y.C., 1968-72; asso. firm Troy, Malin & Pottinger, Los Angeles, 1973-75, partner firm, 1975-80; founding partner firm Prince, Littenberg & Warner, Los Angeles, 1980-81; partner firm Kindel & Anderson, Los Angeles, 1981—; dir. Dynamic Sciences, Inc., Los Angeles. Chmn., So. Calif. alumni admissions com. Tulane U. Mem. Assn. Bar City N.Y., Am. Bar Assn., Los Angeles County Bar Assn. Editor N.Y. U. Law Rev., 1967-68. Home: 2394 Nalin Dr Los Angeles CA 90024 Office: 555 S Flower St 26th Fl Los Angeles CA 90071

WARNER, SUSAN ANN, soil scientist; b. Stockton, Calif., Jan. 26, 1947; d. Lincoln Eugene and Velva Viola (Hayford) W. B.A., U. Pacific, 1969; M.S. in Soil Sci., Oreg. State U., 1977. With Calif. Dept. Fish and Game, Stockton, 1969; chemist Shell Devel. Co., Modesto, Shell Chem. Co., N.Y.C., San Ramon, Calif., 1970-74; instr. San Joaquin Delta Coll., Stockton, 1976-77; soil scientist Calif. Central Valley Water Quality Control Bd., 1977, Calif. N. Coast Water Quality Control Bd., 1978—; cons., lectr. in field. Active Commn. on Status of Women, Poets of Vineyard, Sonoma County Arts Commn. Mem. Am. Soc. Agronomy, Crop Sci. Soc. Am., Soil Sci. Soc. Am. Contbr. articles to profl. publs. Home: 3651 Banyan Pl Santa Rosa CA 95401 Office: 1000 Coddingtown Center Santa Rosa CA 95401

WARNER, WILLIS LEE, consulting company executive; b. Endicott, N.Y., Jan. 28, 1930; s. Willis Eugene and Eva Mae (Zimmerman) W.; B.A., Syracuse U., 1950; M.D., SUNY, Syracuse, 1960. Intern, San Francisco Gen. Hosp., 1960-61; resident St. Mary's Hosp., San Francisco; asso. clin. researcher Baxter Labs., Morton Grove, Ill., 1963-66, asso. dir. clin. research, 1966-71; dir. clin. research, biologics Hoechst Pharm., Somerville, N.J., 1971-75; dir. med. ops. Cutter Labs., Berkeley, Calif., 1975-79; pres. Cons. for Health Care, San Rafael, Calif., 1979—, also dir. Served with U.S. Navy, 1950-55. Mem. Am. Soc. Hematology, World Fedn. Hemophilia, Am. Soc. Clin. Pharmacology and Therapeutics, Am. Assn. Blood Banks, Am. Heart Assn. Editor: Plasma Forum, 1979-82; contbr. articles to profl. jours.; patentee in field. Home: 39 Bret Harte Rd San Rafael CA 94901

WARNER, WILSON KEITH, sociology educator; b. Heyburn, Idaho, Sept. 6, 1930; s. Wilson A. and Eva L. (Pratt) W.; m. Vila Jenks, Sept. 1, 1950; children—Karen, Janice, Randall, Neil. B.S., Utah. State U., 1958, M.S., 1959; Ph.D., Cornell U., 1960. Asst. prof. rural sociology U. Wis.-Madison, 1960-66, assoc. prof., 1966-69, prof., 1969-71; prof. sociology Brigham Young U., Provo, Utah, 1971—, assoc. dir. univ. honors program, 1978-79, mem. steering com. for community progress program, 1973. Served with U.S. Army, 1953-55. Named Outstanding Educator of Am., 1972, 1974-75. Mem. Am. Sociol. Assn., Rural Sociol. Soc. (pres. 1973-74), Utah Acad. Scis., Arts and Letters. Contbr. articles to profl. jours.; editor Jour. Rural Sociology, 1968-69. Office: Dept Sociology Brigham Young U Provo UT 84602

WARNES, PHILIP GEORGE, consulting facilities engineer; b. Tuscola, Ill., Dec. 1, 1940; s. Everett Francis and Elrena Dorothy (Scider) W.; B.S., San Diego State U., 1963; married. Dir. corp. real estate and facilities Raychem Corp., Menlo Park, Calif, 1967-78; dir. corp. real estate and facilities Spectra Physics, San Jose, Calif., 1979-81; pres. Sigmatech, Santa Clara, Calif., 1982—. Mem. vice mayor's adv. com. on industry City of San Jose (Calif.). Served with USN, 1963-67, to comdr. USNR, 1967-81. Mem. Santa Clara Valley Mfrs. Group, Indsl. Devel. Research Council (bd. dirs. 1982-85). Republican. Mem. Ch. Religious Sci. Home: 10 Valmar Pl San Carlos CA 94070 Office: 3333 N 1st St San Jose CA 95134

WARNICK, JOHN WILLARD, psychologist; b. Kansas City, Mo., Aug. 22, 1944; s. Roy Willard and Helen Muriel (Martinson) W.; m. Sharon Kay Williams, June 15, 1966 (div.). B.A., Humboldt State U., 1975; M.A., 1976; Ed.D., U. San Francisco, 1982. Personal counselor, Open Door Clinic, Arcata, Calif., 1972-76; sch. psychologist, Arcata, 1975-76; dir. Trona (Calif.) Mental Health Clinic, 1979-81; pvt. practice counseling psychologist cancer research, hypnosis, San Bernardino, Calif., 1982. Mem. Am. Psychol. Assn., Calif. Psychol. Assn., San Francisco Acad. Hypnosis. Democrat. Roman Catholic. Home: 5341 No H St San Bernardino CA 92407

WARNKE, FRANK J., state senator; b. Havre, Mont., 1933. Student Central Wash. Coll. Edn., 3 yrs., U. Wash. Mem. Wash. Ho. of Reps., 1966-68, 75-83, Wash. State Senate, 1983—; exec. dir. Pub. Sch. Employees. Served with USCG, 3 yrs. Mem. Jaycees. Democrat. Club: Kiwanis. Home: 29457 51st St S Auburn WA 98002 Office: Washington State Senate Olympia WA 98504*

WARNKEN, VIRGINIA MURIEL THOMPSON, social worker; b. Anadarko, Okla., Aug. 13, 1927; d. Sam Monroe and Ruth L. (McAllister) Thompson; A.B., Okla. U., 1946; M.S.W., Washington U., 1949; m. Douglas Richard Warnken, Sept. 16, 1957; 1 son, William Monroe. Med. social cons. Crippled Children's Services, Little Rock, 1950-54; supr. VA Hosp., Little Rock, 1954-55; asst. prof. U. Tenn. Sch. Social Work, Nashville, 1955-57; dir. social services N.Y. State Rehab. Hosp., Rockland County, 1957-58; asst. prof. U. Chgo. Sch. Social Service Adminstrn., 1958-59; free lance editor, 1960—; instr. evening div. Coll. of Notre Dame, Belmont, Calif., 1967-68; asso. Mills Hosp., San Mateo, Calif., 1978—; med. aux. Community Hosp., Pacific Grove, Calif., 1980—. Com. mem. C. of C. Miss Belmont Pageant, 1971—, co-chmn., 1975-78. U.S. Children's Bur. scholar, 1947-49. Mem. Assn. Crippled Children and Adults (dir. 1952-55), Assn. Mentally Retarded (dir. 1953-55), Am. Assn. Med. Social Workers (practice chmn. 1954-55), Nat. Assn. Social Workers (dir. 1962-66), Acad. Cert. Social

Workers, Am. Assn. Med. Social Workers, Nat. Rehab. Assn., Am. Psychol. Assn., Am. Orthopsychiat. Assn., Council Social Work Edn. Democrat. Presbyterian. Clubs: Carmel Valley Golf and Country, Peninsula Golf and Country. Author: Annotated Bibliography of Medical Information and Terminology, 1956. Address: 1399 Bel Aire Rd San Mateo CA 94402

WAROBIEW, DENIS ALAN, optometrist, editor, publisher; b. Sharon, Pa., July 19, 1956; s. John and Alice Margaret (Cole) W. Student Youngstown State U., 1974-77; O.D., Ohio State U., 1981. Practice optometry, Delta, Colo., 1981—; optometrist Child Find Vision Screening, sr. citizens glaucoma screening. Mem. Colo. Optometric Assn., Am. Optometric Assn. (nat. recognition for work done for Save Your Vision Week 1982). Methodist. Club: Lions (Delta). Pub., editor Living Single on the Western Slope mag., 1982—. Home: 823 1/2 Main St Delta CO 81416 Office: 823 Main St Delta CO 81416

WARONKER, LENNY, record company executive; s. Si Waronker. Grad. U. So. Calif. Profl. mgr. Metric Music, 1960s; later promoter Liberty Records; artist and repertoire staff Warner Bros. Records, from 1966, later dir. artists and repertoire, v.p., dir. artists and repertoire, sr. v.p., dir. artists and repertoire, 1978-82, pres., 1982—. Office: Warner Bros Records 3330 Warner Blvd Burbank CA 91510*

WARR, ROBERT OSCAR, advertising agency executive; b. Montgomery, Ala., Oct. 15, 1937; s. Gilbert Henry and Grace (Hood) W.; m. Patricia Perlich, May 4, 1963; children—Kristin Ann, Darby Ann. B.S., U. Oreg., 1961. Copywriter, Allen de St. Maurice & Scroggin, San Francisco, 1964-66; creative dir. Pacific Nat. Advt., Portland, Oreg., 1966-68, Martel Scroggin Advt., San Francisco, 1968-70; account supr. Paul Pease Advt., Palo Alto, Calif., 1970-71; ptnr. Hommel Stanko Warr, Palo Alto, 1971; owner Warr Dept., Los Altos, 1972-74; pres., bd. chmn. Warr, Foote & Rose, Los Altos and Eugene, Oreg., 1974—; chmn. Pehaco Corp., Los Altos, 1975-80; pres. Warr Sports, Inc., Eugene, 1979—; dir. Forte Data Systems, Inc., San Jose, Calif. Promotion chmn. IEEE Computer Soc. Internat. Confs., 1971-75. Served with AUS, 1957-58. Mem. Sigma Chi. Republican. Clubs: U. Oreg. No. Calif. Alumni (pres. 1977-78), Oregon. Writer numerous print advts., broadcast commls., mag. articles.

WARREN, ARTHUR RANDOLPH, JR., real estate broker; b. Torrance, Calif., Nov. 19, 1940; s. Arthur Randolph and Mary Ann (Imig) W.; m. Marvel Rita Lankford, May 11, 1963; children—Kelly Jean, Arthur Randolph III, Robert Arthur II. Student San Diego Coll., 1960-62, Southwestern Coll., 1962-64, Coll. of San Mateo, 1970-71, Golden Gate U., 1979-80; grad. Realtors Inst. With Stanley C. Swartz Co., Redwood Shores, Calif., 1970-71, Am. Housing Guild, Redwood Shores and San Jose, 1971-73, L.B. Nelson Corp., Foster City, Calif., 1973-74, Shapell Industries, San Jose, 1974-76, Western Brokers Association, Mountain View, Calif., 1977-78, Grubb & Ellis Comml. Brokerage, 1978-80, The English Co., real estate investments, Los Altos, Calif., 1980-82; prin. Arthur R. Warren Jr., real estate brokerage, San Mateo, Calif., 1982—; owner Ski & Sports Ctr., San Mateo. Mem. Am. Soc. Real Estate Counselors, AIA, Calif. Assn. Realtors, East Bay Mktg. Group, South Bay Brokers. Republican. Congregationalist. Home: 1519 Shoal Dr PO Box 1555 San Mateo CA 94404 Office: PO Box 1555 San Mateo CA 94401

WARREN, CHARLES DEWEY, mgmt. cons.; b. Gill, Colo., Oct. 2, 1938; s. Charles Laybourn and Edna M. (Dewey) W.; B.A. in Econs., U. Denver, 1968; M.Human Resources Devel., Univ. Assocs., 1983; m. Judith Bryant, June 22, 1963. Tng. systems analyst LTV Aerospace Corp., Dallas, 1968-70; curriculum design mgr. Philco-Ford Corp., Pasadena, Calif., 1971-72; dir. mgmt. and organizational devel., internal cons. Host Internat., Santa Monica, Calif., 1972—; cons. to businesses and non-profit orgns.; lectr. on free-enterprise economics. Chpt. leader W. Los Angeles chpt. Com. for Freedom of Choice in Cancer Therapy, 1975-76; climb leader Valdez Glacier Expdn., Alaska, 1959, 80, Chilkoot Range Expdn., Alaska, 1968, Chilkat Range Expdn., Alaska, 1973. Served with USAF, 1956-60. Mem. Am. Soc. Tng. and Devel., Am. Mgmt. Assn. Author mgmt. models. Home: 11206 Woolford St Culver City CA 90230 Office: 3402 Pico Blvd Santa Monica CA 90406

WARREN, DALE EUGENE, big game hunter; b. Phillips, Wis., Apr. 14, 1927; s. Neal and Ethel (LaVarnay) W.; 1 son, Craig. Lumberjack, Ely, Minn., 1947-52; govt. trapper, Ely, 1947-59; profl. big game guide and hunter, Dubois, Wyo., 1959—; pres., owner Dale Warren's Wildlife Exhibit, Inc., Dubois, Wyo., 1962—. Served with USN, 1945-47. Mem. Nat. rifle Assn. Club: Safari. Home and Office: 20 Stalnaker St Dubois WY 82513

WARREN, EVELYN HELEN, educator, consultant; b. Muskogee, Okla., May 21, 1919; d. Alfred and Biana Blanch (Duff) Henry; m. William O. Warren; 1 son, William Henry. B.A. in Home Econs., Ariz. State U., 1944, M.A. in Early Childhood Edn., 1952. Adminstrn. cert.; Smith Hughes cert. Instr. to prof. early childhood edn., Mesa (Ariz.) Community Coll., dir. home econs. dept.; cons. in field; elem. tchr., Phoenix, 1944-70; tchr. Phoenix Union High Sch., 1971-76. Active Jack and Jill of Am. Named Outstanding Far West Regional Dir. Jack and Jill of Am., 1974. Mem. NEA, Ariz. Edn. Assn., Maricopa Community Coll. Tchrs. Assn., Phi Theta Kappa, Delta Sigma Theta. Democrat. Methodist. Office: 1833 W Southern St Mesa AZ 85022

WARREN, GERALD LEE, newspaper editor; b. Hastings, Nebr., Aug. 17, 1930; s. Hie Elias and Linnie (Williamson) W.; A.B., U. Nebr., 1952; m. Euphemia Florence Brownell, Nov. 20, 1965 (div.); children—Gerald Benjamin, Euphemia Brownell. Reporter Lincoln (Nebr.) Star, 1951-52; reporter, asst. city editor San Diego Union, 1956-61; bus. rep. Copley News Service, 1961-63; city editor San Deigo Union, 1963-68, asst. mng. editor, 1968-69, editor, 1975—; dep. press sec. to Pres. Nixon, 1969-74, Pres. Ford, 1974-75. Served to lt. (j.g.) USNR, 1952-56. Mem. Am. Soc. Newspaper Editors, Sigma Delta Chi, Sigma Nu. Republican. Episcopalian. Home: 1390 Park Row La Jolla CA 92037 Office: PO Box 191 San Diego CA 92112

WARREN, JAMES ANDERSON, III, investment banker; b. Lexington, Ky., Dec. 23, 1931; s. James Anderson and Madalyne A. Warren; B.S. in Mech. Engring., U. Calif.-Berkeley, 1953, M.B.A., 1955; children—Barbara A., Robert J. Mfg. engring. mgr. Gen. Electric Co., 1955-60; sr. assoc. Booz-Allen & Hamilton, Inc., Chgo., 1960-66; exec. v.p. Giltech Corp., Mpls., 1966-69; sr. assoc. Dean Witter & Co., Inc., San Francisco, 1969-74; ptnr. Peninsula Investors, Menlo Park, Calif., 1973-75; v.p. Kelso & Co., Inc., San Francisco, 1975-78; pres. ESOP, Inc., Mountain View, Calif., 1978—; dir. several tech. product cos. Served with USN, 1947-48, with U.S. Army, 1952-54. Mem. Am. Mgmt. Assn., ESOP Assn. Am. Contbr. articles on long range planning, ops. research, valuation closely held businesses to profl. publs. Office: 2680 Bayshore Frontage Rd Suite 210 Mountain View CA 94043

WARREN, JAMES RONALD, museum dir.; b. Goldendale, Wash., May 25, 1925; s. B.E. Chappell and Dorothy H. (Rodgers) Chappell Warren; stepson H.S. Warren; B.A., Wash. State U., 1949; M.A., U. Wash., 1953, Ph.D., 1963; m. Gwen Davis, June 25, 1949; children—Gail, Jeffrey. Adminstrv. v.p. Seattle Community Coll., 1965-69; pres. Edmonds Community Coll., Lynnwood, Wash., 1969-79; dir. Mus. of History and Industry, Seattle, 1979—. Served with U.S. Army, 1943-45. Mem. Am. Assn. Museum. Club: Rotary (Seattle). Columnist, Seattle Post Intelligencer, 1979—, Seattle Bus. News, 1980—. Home: 3235 99th NE St Bellevue WA 98004 Office: 2161 E Hamlin Seattle WA 98112

WARREN, JEFFRY CLARY, clin. psychologist; b. Burbank, Calif., Nov. 1, 1949; s. Bernard W. and Florence S. W.; student Valley Coll., 1967-79; B.A., U. Calif.-Santa Barbara, 1971; Ph.D. in Clin. Psychology, Calif. Sch. of Profl. Psychology, 1976; m. April Sue Yarbrough, Dec. 29, 1979; 1 son, Adam Bernard. Registered psychologist Tech. Research, San Diego, 1976-78; developer, coordinator grad. tng. program Edwards Inst. for Advanced Studies, San Diego, 1980, dir. profl. and acad. tng., 1980; clin. psychologist TRI-Community Service Systems, San Diego, 1979-83; pvt. practice, La Jolla, Calif., 1983—; sr. v.p., dir. Grid Research Corp., 1982—; cons. and educator in family therapy and child abuse. Developer task force on child abuse, San Diego, 1978-80. Mem. Am. Psychol. Assn., Nat. Register of Health Service Providers in Psychology, Calif. State Psychol. Assn., Acad. San Diego Psychologists, Western Psychol. Assn. Jewish. Contbr. papers to profl. assn. confs. Office: 1150 Silverado Suite 131 La Jolla CA 92037

WARREN, MERRITT CHARLES, pediatric cardiologist; b. Chungking, China, Nov. 24, 1923; s. Merritt Connick and Wilma Lane (Landis) W.; B.A., Pacific Union Coll., 1945; M.D., Loma Linda U., 1956; m. Shirley Rey Tamka, Aug. 27, 1944; children—Lawrence Charles, Judy Rey. Intern, Letterman Army Hosp., San Francisco, 1956-57; resident in pediatrics Fresno (Calif.) Gen. Hosp., 1961-63; physician Pediatric Med. Group, Fresno, 1963-64; individual practice medicine specializing in pediatrics, Tracy, Calif., 1964-65; fellow in pediatric cardiology Stanford (Calif.) U., 1965-67; asst. prof. pediatrics Loma Linda (Calif.) U., 1967; sub chief pediatric cardiology Permanente Med. Group, Sacramento, 1967—; chief med. edn. Kaiser Found. Hosp., Sacramento, 1968—; asst. clin. prof. pediatrics U. Calif. Med. Sch., Davis, 1973—; mem. regional edn. com. Permanente Med. Group No. Calif., 1968—; interfacility auditor Kaiser Hosps. No. Calif., 1972-79. Served to capt. M.C., AUS, 1956-59. Diplomate Am. Bd. Pediatrics, Am. Bd. Pediatric Cardiology. Fellow Am. Coll. Cardiology, Am. Acad. Pediatrics; mem. Calif. Med. Assn. (hosp. staff surveyor 1977-79), Sacramento County Med. Soc., Calif. Soc. Pediatric Cardiology. Office: 2025 Morse Ave Sacramento CA 95825

WARREN, RICHARD WAYNE, obstetrician and gynecologist; b. Puxico, Mo., Nov. 26, 1935; s. Martin R. and Sarah E. (Crump) W.; B.A., U. Calif., Berkeley, 1957; M.D., Stanford, 1961; m. Rosalie J. Franzola, Aug. 16, 1959; children—Lani Marie, Richard W., Paul D. Intern, Oakland (Calif.) Naval Hosp., 1961-62; resident in obstetrics and gynecology Stanford Med. Center (Calif.), 1964-67; practice medicine specializing in obstetrics and gynecology, Mountain View, Calif., 1967—; mem. staff Stanford and El Camino hosps.; pres. Reeves and Warren Med. Corp.; asst. clin. prof. obstetrics and gynecology Stanford Sch. Medicine. Served with USN, 1961-64. Diplomate Am. Bd. Ob-Gyn. Fellow Am. Coll. Obstetrics and Gynecology; mem. AMA, Calif. Med. Assn., San Francisco Gynecol. Soc., Peninsula Gynecol. Soc., Am. Assn. Gynecologic Laparoscopists, Assn. Profs. Gynecology and Obstetrics, Royal Soc. Medicine. Contbr. articles to profl. jours. Home: 102 Atherton Ave Atherton CA 94025 Office: 2500 Hospital Dr Mountain View CA 94040

WARRICK, DON D., educator, author, cons.; b. Alva, Okla., Feb. 23, 1940; s. Hollis E. and Ruth (Stringer) W.; B.B.A., U. Okla., 1963, M.B.A., 1964; D.B.A., U. So. Calif., 1972; m. Anna F. Kirchoff, Nov. 19, 1977; children—Troy Donovan, Shannon Kathleen, Ryan Matthew. Asst. to v.p. mktg. Continental Plastics, Oklahoma City, 1963-64; comml. mgr. Pacific Telephone Co., 1967-68; mgr. middle mgmt. devel. Hughes Aircraft, Culver City, Calif., 1968-70; mem. faculty U. Colo., Colorado Springs, 1971—; cons. numerous orgns.; internat. speaker; editor Acad. Mgmt. Orgn. Devel. Newsletter, 1978-83. Served as officer USAF, 1964-67. Recipient Outstanding Tchr. award (6) U. Colo.; named Outstanding OD Practitioner of Yr., 1982. Mem. Acad. Mgmt., Am. Soc. Tng. and Devel., Am. Mgmt. Assn., Orgn. Devel. Network, Assn. Bus. Simuation and Exptl. Learning. Republican. Presbyterian. Contbr. articles to profl. jours.; author 3 books. Home: 1370 Rangely Dr Colorado Springs CO 80908 Office: Bus Coll U Colo Colorado Springs CO 80908

WARSAVAGE, BARBARA, statistician; b. Denver, Sept. 30, 1942; d. Joseph and Margaret (Riley) W. Ph.D., Stanford U., 1982. Sci. programmer Stanford U., 1967-73; statistician SRO Assocs., San Francisco, 1980; computer cons. Stanford U., 1980-81; statistician CTB/McGraw-Hill, Monterey, Calif., 1981—; former mem. faculty Calif. State U.-Haywood. Mem. Am. Ednl. Research Assn., Am. Statis. Assn. Mem. Ch. of Religious Science. Home: 30 Monte Vista Apt 2107 Monterey CA 93940 Office: CTB/McGraw-Hill 2500 Garden Rd Monterey CA 93940

WARSHAWSKY, IVAN, advertising agency executive; b. Los Angeles, Oct. 20, 1931; s. Alexander and Berthe (Lushing) W.; m. Monique Helene Loisel, Feb. 7, 1954; m. Carol Laurain Larson, Sept. 13, 1968. B.A. in English and Theatre, UCLA, 1954. Media buyer Erwin Wasey Inc., Los Angeles, 1957-61, media supr., 1965-66; media dir. Coleman-Parr, Beverly Hills, Calif., 1961-65; assoc. media dir. Carson/Roberts Inc., Los Angeles, 1966-69; v.p. media Grey Advt. Inc., Los Angeles, 1969-82; dir. media services Ramey Communications, Los Angeles, 1983—. Mem. allocations com. Permanent Charities Com. of Entertainment Industries, Los Angeles. Served to 1st lt. U.S. Army, 1954-56. Mem. Los Angeles Media Dirs. Council, Los Angeles County Mus. Art (charter). Home: 2433 Solar Dr Los Angeles CA 90046 Office: 3008 Wilshire Blvd Los Angeles CA 90010

WARSINSKE, NORMAN GEORGE, designer, sculptor, painter; b. Wichita, Kans., Mar. 1929; s. Norman George and Gladys Elmira (Thompson) W. B.A. in Journalism, U. Mont., 1949; B.A. in Art, U. Wash., 1958; student Kunstwerk Schule Darmstadt, Ger., 1951-52. Ptnr. Miller-Pollard Interiors, Seattle, 1958—; sculptures commd. by numerous pub. and pvt. corps. Vice pres. Seattle Art Commn., 1956-57. Served with USAF, 1951-54. Home: 3823 94th St NE Bellevue WA 98004 Office: 4538 University Way NE Seattle WA 98105

WARTHEN, JOHN EDWARD, leasing and finance co. exec.; b. Cedar City, Utah, May 8, 1922; s. Mark Tew and Emma (Simkins) W.; student Branch Agrl. Coll. So. Utah, Cedar City, 1940-41; m. Norma Jane Hansen, June 22, 1943; children—Russel Edward, John Merrill, Judith Warthen Lally, Linda Fahringer, Carla Jean Warthen Thompson Lauri J. Warthen Sherratt. Pres., mgr. St. George Service, Inc. (Utah), 1945-61, Warthen Constrn. Co., Las Vegas, 1961—, Warthen Buick, 1961—. Councilman, City of St. George, 1950-54; nat. dir. Liberty Amendment Com.; state chmn. Dealer Election Action Com.; dist. dir. Freeman Inst.; trustee treas. Latter Day Saint Br. Geneal. Library, Las Vegas, 1964—. Fellow Internat. Biog. Assn. (life); mem. Nat. Fedn. Ind. Bus. (action council), S.A.R. Mormon (bishop 1957-61). Clubs: Rotary, Kiwanis. Home: 2475 Viking St Las Vegas NV 89121 Office: 3025 E Sahara Ave Las Vegas NV 89104

WASHBURN, JERRY MARTIN, accountant, company executive; b. Powell, Wyo., Dec. 31, 1943; s. Roland and Lavon (Martin) W.; B.S., Brigham Young U., 1969; m. Pamela Ruth Palmer, June 11, 1965; children—Garth, Gavin, Kristina. Staff acct. Arthur Andersen & Co., Seattle, 1969-71, sr. auditor, Boise, Idaho, 1971-73, audit mgr., Portland, Oreg., 1976-79; controller Washburn Musicland, Inc., Phoenix, 1979—; prin. Washburn Enterprises; Phoenix, 1979—; pres., gen. mgr. Total Info. Systems, Inc., Phoenix, 1982—. C.P.A., Wash., Idaho, Oreg. Mem. Inst. Internal Auditors (past pres. Boise, dir. Boise and Portland), Am. Mgmt. Assn., Am. Inst. C.P.A.'s, Idaho, Wash. socs. C.P.A.'s. Republican Mem. Ch. Jesus Christ of Latter-day Saints. Home: 4830 E Altadena Scottsdale AZ 85254 Office: 3333 E Indian School Rd Suite 106 Phoenix AZ 85018

WASHINGTON, CARLANE JOYCE HAMILTON, educational administrator; b. Port Arthur, Tex., Oct. 23, 1946; d. Robert George and Wilma (Dorsey) Hamilton; m. James Edward Ollee, Dec. 27, 1969; 1 son, James Edward; m. Joe Washington, Jan. 21, 1979. B.S. in Social Sci. Edn., Grambling State U., 1969; M.S. in Ednl. Vocat. Adminstrn., Eastern Wash. U., 1981. Cert. vocat. ednl. adminstr. Jr. high sch. tchr. Gilford Jr. High Sch., Racine, Wis., 1969-70; program developer Manpower Agy., Tacoma, 1971-72; ednl. tng. coordinator City of Tacoma, 1972-73; program supr. spl. needs State Supt. Pub. Instrn., Olympia, Wash., 1973—; profl. cons. Eastern Wash. U., Ednl. Innovators, Inc., Richardson, Tex. Mem. Gov.'s Com. for Employment of Handicapped, 1981—, Olympia Ind. Sch. Devel. Com., 1982. Recipient Region V State Supr. award Nat. Assn. Vocat. Edn. Spl. Needs Personnel, 1982; cert. of recognition Outstanding Direct Vocat. Support Person of Year, 1983; Ednl. Orientation Recognition USN, 1983; ann. award Wash. Assn. Vocat. Spl. Needs Personnel, 1980. Mem. Wash. Vocat. Assn. (life), Nat. Assn. Advancement of Black Ams. in Vocat. Edn. (charter), Am. Vocat. Assn., Nat. Assn. Vocat. Spl. Needs Personnel, Wash. Assn. Vocat. Needs Personnel. African Methodist. Club: Mary Kay Cosmetics Pace Setters. Author: Human Resource Development, 1982; Leadership Development for Special Populations, 1980; Problem Solving for Vocational Achievement, 1979; Diversified Occupations for Disadvantaged Students, 1978; Vocational Education for Handicapped Students in Agriculture, 1977. Office: Old Capitol Bldg MS FG-11 Olympia WA 98504

WASHINGTON, CHARLES EDWARD, educator; b. Little Rock, Nov. 27, 1933; s. David D. and Hazel M. Washington; B.A., Philander Smith Coll., Little Rock, 1958; M.Ed., U. Okla., 1962; postgrad. U. So. Calif.; m. Ruby N. Jones, Sept. 4, 1956 (div. 1965); 1 dau., Toni Regail. Tchr. pub. schs., Fort Smith, Ark., 1958-60, Oklahoma City, 1960-69, Los Angeles, 1979—; registered rep. ITT Hamilton Mgmt. Corp., 1963-70; fin. counselor Fin. Congeneric Corp., 1971-74, Am. Inst. Property and Liability Underwriters; spl. agt. Welsh & Assocs., Ins. Services, Walnut, Calif., 1979—. Mem. Crenshaw Christian Ctr. Served with USMC, 1951-54; Korea. Mem. NEA, Calif. Tchrs. Assn., Ind. Ins. Assn. Calif., United Tchrs. Los Angeles, U. Okla. Alumni Assn. (class rep. 1964-67), Nat. Dunbar Alumni Assn., Philander Smith Coll. Alumni Assn., Nat. Notary Assn., Omega Psi Phi. Democrat. Office: 959 Fairway Dr Walnut CA 91789

WASHINGTON, EDDIE MAE, internal revenue exec.; b. Austin, Tex.; d. Louis Charles and Olivia Henrietta (Slaughter) Clemons; student public schs.; m. Frank Washington, Jr., Mar. 23, 1958; children—Carlton Lynn, Sandra Rene, Quincy Ray, Karen Richelle, Kelvin Leslie. With IRS, 1965—, card punch operator transcription div., Austin, 1965-68, microfilm-tax examiner taxpayer service div., 1968-70, tax examiner analysis and control unit, 1970-71, tax examiner adjustment br., 1971-75, supr. exam. br. processing div., Fresno, Calif., 1975, supr. document services processing div., 1975-76, supr. taxpayer service div., 1976-77, supr., 1977-80, sect. chief tax accounts div., 1979-80, program analyst mgmt. staff, 1980, processing div. quality rev. mgr., 1980-81, program analyst mgmt. staff, 1981—. Spl. assignment chmn. Fresno County Grand Jury, 1978-79; bd. dirs. United Cerebral Palsy of Central Calif., 1979-80, treas., 1981-82. Mem. Am. Bus. Women (corr. sec., pres., treas., Woman of Yr.), Nat. Council Negro Women. Democrat. Baptist. Home: 1636 S Delno St #114 Fresno CA 93706 Office: 5045 E Butler St Fresno CA 93888

WASHINGTON, GENE EDWARD, fin. exec.; b. Birmingham, Ala., Aug. 12, 1931; s. Horace Webster and Dorothy Grace (Henderson) W.; B.S., Okla. State U., 1952; M.B.A., U. Chgo., 1970; m. Jacqualin Ann Kaiser, Jan. 26, 1952; children—Robert Todd, James Allen, Steven Lee, Darren Scott. Sr. mktg. rep. IBM, Dallas, 1956-63, mktg. mgr., Detroit, 1963-67; v.p. Greyhound Computer Corp., Chgo., 1967-68, exec. v.p., 1969-70; v.p. Boothe Computer Corp., San Francisco, 1970-71, sr. v.p., group exec., 1971-74; chmn., pres. and chief exec. officer Environ. Chemic Systems, Inc., Novato, Calif., 1975-80; chmn., pres. Systems Assurance & Fin. Corp., Novato, 1981—; dir. Systems Assurance & Fin. Corp., Environ. Chemic Systems, Inc., Greyhound Computer Corp., Greyhound Time-Sharing Corp., Greyhound Computer of Can., Ltd., Computer Personnel Cons., Inc., Boothe Computer of Can., Ltd., Boothe Mgmt. Systems, Inc., Boothe Computer Mktg., Inc., Boothe, A.G. (Zurich), Computer Leasing Services, Ltd. of S. Africa. Dir., Jr. Achievement, Dallas, 1958; precinct treas. Republican Party, 1965-66; mem. Pop Warner Com., 1976-80. Served to capt. USAF, 1952-56. Named Mgr. of Yr., IBM Dist., 1964, Industry Leader, 1962, Regional Mgrs. award, 1963. Mem. Arnold Air Soc. (treas. 1951-52), Data Processing Mgmt. Assn., Computer Lessors Assn., Blue Key, Mu Kappa Tau, Gamma Theta Psi, Alpha Kappa Psi, Sigma Chi (treas. 1951-52), Scabbard and Blade. Republican. Presbyterian. Clubs: Marin Country, Commonwealth. Home: 1427 Buchanan St Novato CA 94947 Office: 46A Hamilton Dr Novato CA 94947

WASHINGTON, KENNETH STRICKLAND, coll. chancellor; b. Chgo., Oct. 19, 1922; s. Louis C. and Velma (Strickland) W.; B.S., Roosevelt U., 1948; M.A., Calif. State U., Los Angeles, 1954; Ph.D., U. So. Calif., 1970; m. Henrietta Dunn, Oct. 5, 1974; children—Lori, Marcella, Henry, Coreen, Kim, Kent. Successively social worker, Los Angeles; head counselor, public schs., Los Angeles; asst. to chancellor UCLA; asst. dean for ednl. opportunities Calif. State Univs. and Colls.; asst. supt. public instrn., San Francisco; pres. City Coll. San Francisco; now vice chancellor edn. services Los Angeles Community Coll. Dist. Bd. dirs. Western Regional Council on Black Am. Affairs. Served with U.S. Army, 1944-46. Mem. Assn. Calif. Community Coll. Adminstrs., NAACP. Office: 617 W 7th St Los Angeles CA 90017

WASHINGTON, NAPOLEON, JR., insurance agent, clergyman; b. Ft. Baker, Calif., Apr. 12, 1948; s. Napoleon and Annie D. (Carter) W.; A.A., Merced Coll., 1976; student Stanislaus State Coll., 1976-77; m. Nadine Reed, Nov. 6, 1968; children—Gregory D., Kimberlee N., Geoffrey N. Lic. Baptist minister. Agt., Met. Life Ins. Co., Merced, Calif., 1970-72, sr. sales rep., 1972—; broker Gen. Ins. Brokers, Merced, 1973—; owner Washington Assocs. Fin. Services; tchr. salesmanship Merced Coll., 1979—. Chmn. bd. trustees St. Matthew Baptist Ch., 1978—, ordained deacon, lic. minister, assoc. minister, 1982—. vice-chmn. Merced County Pvt. Industries Council, 1981—; mem. ins. adv. council City of Merced Schs. Served with U.S. Army, 1968-70. Recipient Nat. Quality award Nat. Assn. Life Underwriters, 1979, Nat. Sales Achievement award, 1979, Health Ins. Quality award, 1977; mem.

Million Dollar Round Table, 1973, 74, 75, 76, 77, 78; teaching cert. Calif. community colls. Mem. Nat. Assn. Life Underwriters, Calif. Assn. Life Underwriters (dir. 1975-76), Merced County Assn. Life Underwriters (pres. 1976-77), Merced County Estate Planning Council (dir.), Merced County Pvt. Industries Council, NAACP, Phi Beta Lambda. Democrat. Club: Rotary (dir. 1974-76). Home: 1960 Cedar Crest Dr Merced CA 95340 Office: 1960 Cedar Crest Dr Merced CA 95340

WASICK, RANDOLPH ROBERT, engring. draftsman; b. Buffalo, Sept. 17, 1951; s. Charles Thomas and Louise (Turaj) W.; A.S., Erie Community Coll., 1972; m. Andrea Garcia, Apr. 1, 1978. With Lancaster Sales, Inc. (N.Y.), 1970; delivery supr. Shercen, Inc., Cheectowaga, N.Y., 1972-75; engring. technician N.Y. State Dept. Transp., Buffalo, 1975-76; chief draftsman Calabasas Engring. Corp. (Calif.), 1977-80; engring. draftsman Found. Engring. Co., Inc., Tarzana, Calif., 1980—. Reserve dep. sheriff Los Angeles County, 1978—. Republican. Baptist. Home: 22106 Kittridge St Canoga Park CA 91303 Office: 18344 Oxnard St Tarzana CA 91356

WASOWICZ, LIDIA, editor, reporter; b. Krakow, Poland, Apr. 3, 1951: d. Kazimierz and Janina (Wronska) W.; came to U.S., 1960, naturalized, 1967; m. Douglas Hall Pringle, Nov. 13, 1982. B.A. with honors, U. Utah, 1973. Reporter, Deseret News, 1970-72; intern Salt Lake City Tribune, 1972, copy editor, 1972-73; UPI reporter, Salt Lake City, 1973-75; news reporter, broadcast editor Pacific div. UPI, San Francisco, 1975-78, news reporter, editor, 1978—. Named Outstanding Journalist, 1979; Outstanding News Coverage 3d place award, 1980, 2d place, 1980, 81; 1st place feature writing award Peninsula Press Club, 1981; Rotary Club scholar, 1969; Russel S. Marriott scholar, 1969-73; Westminster Coll. Honors at Entrance scholar, 1969-70; Minute Women scholar, 1970-71; Maude May Babcock scholar, 1971-72; Sherwood Music Sch. scholar, 1969-73; Profl. Journalism fellow Stanford U., 1981-82. Mem. Am. Soc. Profl. and Exec. Women, Women in Communications, Internat. Platform Assn., Mortar Board, Smithsonian Instn., Phi Beta Kappa, Kappa Tau Alpha, Sigma Delta Chi. Democrat. Roman Catholic. Author: (with others) Violence in the 60's, 1972. Home: 535 Everett St #415 Palo Alto CA 94301 Office: 1390 Market St San Francisco CA 94102

WASSERMAN, ISAAC MILES, vocat. evaluator; b. Richmond, Va., Sept. 25, 1932; s. Joseph Benjamin and Eva W.; A.B.A., Nichols Jr. Coll., 1956; student in bus. adminstrn. Lynchburg Coll., 1953-55; B.S. in Edn., Boston U., 1958, M.Ed., 1959; 1 dau., Erica Jacqueline. Tutorial and remedial tchr. White Plains (N.Y.) Public Schs., 1959-60; tchr. English and geography Newton (Mass.) Public Schs., 1960; instr. psychology and public speaking Cambridge Jr. Coll., 1961-62; vocat. counselor Jewish Vocat. Service, Boston, 1962-63; guidance counselor jr. high schs. Winthrop (Mass.) Public Schs., 1963-68; elem. counselor, sch. psychologist Andover (Mass.) Public Schs., 1968-76; sch. psychologist Lawrence (Mass.) Pub. Schs., 1977, Greater Lowell (Mass.) Regional Vocat. Tech. Sch., 1976-77; vocat. evaluator/rehab. counselor Goodwill Industries, San Jose, Calif., 1977-81, vocat. evaluator, 1982—; Vocat. evaluator Westcom Industries, Richmond Calif., 1981; psychol. cons. Lawrence Public Schs. Recipient Dr. Quincy Merrill award Nichols Jr. Coll., 1959 Mem. Am. Personnel and Guidance Assn., Nat. Vocat. Guidance Assn., Am. Sch. Counselors Assn. Club: Masons (Richmond, Va.). Home: 38601 Royal Ann Common Fremont CA 94536 Office: 1080 N 7th St San Jose CA 95112

WASSERMAN, LEW R., entertainment industry executive; b. Cleve., Mar. 15, 1913; m. Edith Beckerman, July 5, 1936; 1 dau., Lynne Kay. Nat. dir. advt. and publicity Music Corp. Am., 1936-38, v.p., 1938-39, became v.p. charge motion picture div., 1940; now chmn. bd., dir., chief exec. officer, mem. exec. com. MCA, Inc., also chmn. bd., chief exec. officer, dir. subsidiary corps.; dir. Am. Airlines. Chmn. emeritus Assn. Motion Picture and TV Producers. Trustee John F. Kennedy Library, John F. Kennedy Center Performing Arts, Cal. Inst. Tech.; hon. chmn. bd. Center Theatre Group Los Angeles Music Center; bd. dirs. Research to Prevent Blindness; mem. nat. com. Lyndon Baines Johnson Meml. Grove on Potomac; mem. Rockefeller U. Council; mem. adv. bd. Presdl. Election Campaign Fund; mem. Radio Free Europe Com.; bd. dirs. Lyndon Baines Johnson Found. Recipient Jean Hersholt Humanitarian award Acad. Motion Picture Arts and Scis., 1973. Democrat. Office: MCA Inc 100 Universal City Plaza Universal City CA 91608*

WASSERMAN, LINDA MORGAN, psychologist, educator; b. Los Angeles, Apr. 3, 1943; d. Albert William and Mildred Emma (Lloyd) Morgan; m. Stephen Ira Wasserman, Aug. 22, 1964; children—Matthew William, Zachary Jacob. B.A., Stanford U., 1964; Ph.D., UCLA, 1968. Diplomate Am. Board Profl. Psychology. Staff psychologist dept. psychiatry, Mass. Gen. Hosp., Boston, 1968-70, 1972-79; psychologist Soland County Mental Health Services, Fairfield, Calif., 1970-72, San Diego County Mental Health Services, 1979-81; asst. prof. Calif. Sch. Profl. Psychology, San Diego, 1981—; instr. dept. psychiatry, Harvard U., 1972-74; asst. clin. prof. U. Calif.-San Diego, 1982. Mem. Am. Psychol. Assn., Mass. Psychol. Assn., Phi Beta Kappa. Contbr. articles to profl. jours. Home: 8420 Cliffridge Ln La Jolla CA 92037 Office: 3974 Sorrento Valley Rd San Diego CA 92122

WASSERMAN, PAUL ZACHARY, psychologist, research and planning consultant; b. N.Y.C., Mar. 28, 1943; s. Norman Zachary and Nina Naomi (Serxner) W.; m. Christine Callahan, Jan. 27, 1980; children—Adam Zachary, Daniel K. Student Antioch Coll., 1959-61; B.A., NYU, 1965; M.S. (scholar), U. Pitts., 1969. Cert. sch. psychologist, Pa. Psychologist, Woodville State Hosp., Pitts., 1969-70, McGill U. Guidance Center, Montreal, Que., Can., 1970-71, No. Communities Mental Health Services, Pitts., 1972-75; program coordinator Alaska State Office Alcoholism and Drug Abuse, Juneau, 1975-76; pvt. practice human services consulting, Juneau, 1977-78; program mgr. Municipality of Anchorage Dept. Health, 1978-79; program devel. coordinator, substance abuse counselor tng. curriculum coordinator Ctr. Alcohol and Addiction Studies, U. Alaska, 1979-81; owner, prin. Wasserman Consulting Services, Anchorage, 1981—. Mem. South Addition Community Council, Anchorage, 1980—, pres., 1980-82; mem. Downtown Devel. Adv. Com., Anchorage, 1982. Saul Brodsky Found. scholar, 1959-63; VA trainee, 1966-68. Mem. Alcohol and Drug Abuse Program Assn. Alaska (co-founder, coordinator 1980-81), Am. Psychol. Assn., Alaska Pub. Health Assn. Author govt. reports, profl. publs. in field. Home: 1421 N St Anchorage AK 99501 Office: Paul Z Wasserman Consulting Services 1421 N St Anchorage AK 99501

WASSERMAN, ROBERT, city ofcl.; b. Gary, Ind., Jan. 12, 1934; s. Morris K. and Alice W.; B.S., Calif. State U., 1963; M.P.A., U. So. Calif., 1975; m. Mary Linda Galantin, Sept. 13, 1958; children—Daniel Joseph, Jill Marie. Chief of police City of San Carlos (Calif.), 1969-72, City of Brea and Yorba Linda (Calif.), 1972-76, City of Fremont (Calif.), 1976—; chmn. adv. com. Calif. Commn. on Peace Officer Stds. and Tng., 1979—; mem. Pres.'s Adv. Com. Law Enforcement; cons. to police agys. Bd. mgrs. Fremont-Newark YMCA, 1978—. Served with U.S. Army, 1950-52. Mem. Calif. Peace Officers Assn. (pres. 1980), Internat. Assn. Chiefs of Police, Police Exec. Research Forum. Club: Rotary. Contbr. articles to profl. jours. Office: 39710 Civic Center Dr Fremont CA 94536

WASYLUKA, GEORGE MICHAEL, budget analyst and researcher; b. St. Louis, Oct. 3, 1946; s. William and Anna Margaret (Bartosz) W.; children—Christina Lynne, G. Michael. B.A. in Polit. Sci., St. Louis U., 1968, M.A. in Urban Affairs, 1972; M.P.A. in Exec. Mgmt., U. Denver, 1982. Lic. real estate salesperson, Colo. Adminstr., Hwy. safety Colo. Dept. Hwys., Denver, 1975-77; planner water quality Colo. Dept. Health, Denver, 1977-79; project mgr. The Pinery/Terracor, Inc., Parker, Colo., 1979-81; research dir. City of Thornton (Colo.), 1981-82; property mgr. N.W. Capital Mgmt., Inc., Olympia, Wash., 1982—; budget analyst Snohomish County, Everett, Wash., 1983—; cons. land use; real estate salesman; profl. musician. Chmn. Aurora (Colo.) Gateway Daze and Parade, 1974-76; loaned exec. Denver Mile High United Way, 1974-76; sec. Aurora Jaycees, 1975, v.p. community affairs, 1976, state dir., 1977; bd. dirs. Aurora Hist. Soc., 1975-77; mem. Aurora Planning and Zoning Commn., 1975-78; pres. Aurora Scholarship and Loan Trust, 1977. Served to capt. Intelligence, USAF, 1968-75; Vietnam. Decorated Bronze Star, Air medal; named Outstanding Young Man of Aurora, Aurora C. of C., 1976; Dept. def. fellow, 1971-72. Mem. Colo. Bd. Realtors. Democrat. Club: Pinery Country (Parker). Home and Office: PO Box 6081 Federal Way WA 98003

WAT, MAY KAM-MEI, computer programmer; b. Hong Kong, Mar. 22, 1956; came to U.S., 1975, Biu Wat and Yuk Ping Tang. B.S., Calif. State U.-Sacramento, 1979, M.S., 1982. Sci. programmer ADAC Labs, Sunnyvale, Calif., 1979-80; mem. tech. staff, system analyst Computer Scis. Corp., Long Beach, Calif., 1981—. Mem. Assn. System Mgmt. Office: Computer Scis Corp 2100 E Grand Ave A301 El Segundo CA 90245

WATANABE, RONALD KENICHI, resort management executive; b. Wailuku, Hawaii, Apr. 9, 1940; s. Paul Kenji and Bertha Shizuko (Oshiro) W.; B.Ed., U. Hawaii, 1963; B.S., Cornell U., 1969; children—Lynn Reiko, Brian Ken. Cons., mgr. Laventhol & Horwath, C.P.A.'s, Tampa, Fla., Miami, Fla. and Los Angeles, 1969-75; controller Hospitality Group, Amfac, Inc., Honolulu, 1975-79; pres. Mid Pacific Resorts Mgmt., Inc., 1979—. Served with U.S. Army, 1963-66. Mem. Hawaii Hotel Assn. (v.p. Maui chpt. 1981, pres. 1982), Maui County Visitors Assn., Maui C. of C., Pacific Area Travel Assn., Cornell Soc. Hotelmen, Maui County Bd. Realtors. Clubs: Waikiki Rotary, Lahaina Yacht, Cornell of Hawaii. Home: PO Box 327 Lahaina HI 96761 Office: 4242 Lower Honoapiilani Hwy Lahaina HI 96761

WATASE, KINICHI, real estate broker; b. Waimea, Hawaii, June 12, 1926; s. Katsuto George and Masako (Nakamaru) W.; m. Tomiko Okada, June 1944; children—Cheryl Lynn, Kenneth Dean, Christopher John; m. 2d, Maureen Catherin Dreyfus, Dec. 15, 1974. A.A., Los Angeles City Coll., 1953. Real estate broker, Calif. Real estate salesman Jones and Goodglick and Assocs., Inglewood, Calif., 1964-68; real estate broker Kenland Devel. Inc., Torrance, Calif., 1968-74; pres. Santa Barbara Land Co., Inc., 1974—. Hearing examiner Los Angeles Police Commn.; neighborhood commr. Hollywood-Wilshire Area council Boy Scouts Am.; mem. vestry St. Mary's Episcopal Ch., Los Angeles. Served with AUS, 1945-47. Office: 116 W Cook St Santa Maria CA 93454

WATENPAUGH, KEITH DONALD, chemist, educator; b. Amarillo, Tex., Sept. 3, 1939; s. Howard Norbert and Jean (Thompson) W.; B.S. in Chemistry, U. Idaho, 1962; Ph.D. in Chemistry, Mont. State U., 1967; m. Joyce Alice Fischer, Aug. 27, 1963; children—K. David, Brian E., Sharon J. Sr. fellow U. Wash., Seattle, 1966-69, research asso., 1969-72, research asst. prof., 1972-78, research asso. prof. dept. biol. structure, 1978—; cons. in field. Dist. Cub Scout chmn. Chief Seattle council Boy Scouts Am., 1980, dist. tng. chmn., 1981, dist. vice chmn., 1982. Mem. Am. Chem. Soc., Am. Crystallographic Assn. (program chmn. 1982, chmn. crystallographic computing com.), AAAS. Office: Dept Biol Structure SM20 Univ Washington Seattle WA 98195

WATERER, BONNIE LOUISE CLAUSING, educator, educational administrator; b. Toledo, Sept. 25, 1940; d. Kermit Henry and Helen Ethel (Waggoner) Clausing; m. Louis Phillipp Waterer, June 17, 1961, children—Ryan Frederick, Reid Louis. B.S. in Home Econs. Edn., Ohio State U., 1962; M.A. in Home Econs. Edn., San Jose State U., 1966. Cert. tchr., Calif. Tchr. James Lick High Sch., San Jose, Calif., 1963-67, 1973-76; adult edn. instr. San Jose Met. Adult Edn. Program, 1969-75; instructional team leader consumer homemaking edn. Independence High Sch., San Jose, 1976-80; subject area coordinator consumer homemaking edn. East Side Union High Sch. Dist., San Jose, 1980—. Com. chmn. Alum Rock United Methodist Ch., San Jose. Mem. Home Econs. Tchrs. Assn. Calif. (Region 4 pres.), Calif. Home Econs. Assn., Am. Home Econs. Assn., Assn. Calif. Sch. Adminstrs., Omicron Nu, Phi Upsilon Omicron, Republican. Home: 3836 Suncrest Ave San Jose CA 95132 Office: Independence High School 1776 Educational Park Dr San Jose CA 95133

WATERLAND, THOMAS MANVILLE, government official; b. Anyox, B.C., Can., Dec. 15, 1933; m. Donalda Stewart, Aug. 18, 1956; children—Teresa, Patricia, Elizabeth. B.S., S.D. Sch. Mines, 1957. Mining engr., supr. Craigmont Mines, Merritt, B.C., 1961-66; resident engr., inspector B.C. Dept. Mines, 1966-68; M.P., Victoria, B.C., 1968—, minister of mines and minister of forests, 1975-76, minister of forests, 1976—. Mem. Can. Inst. Mining and Metallurgy, B.C. Assn. Profl. Engrs. Club: Masons. Office: Minister of Forests #323 Parliament Bldgs Victoria BC V8W 1X4 Canada

WATERMAN, BARBARA ANN, clinical psychologist; b. Gainesville, Fla., Nov. 19, 1948; d. Arthur and Rosuritha Waterman. B.S. in Math., Duke U., 1970; M.A. in Social Psychology, Harvard U., 1973, Ph.D., 1975. Lic. psychologist, Calif. Teaching fellow Harvard U., Boston, 1971; instr. sociology Stanford U., 1975; asst. prof. dept. sociology U. Vt., Burlington, 1975-77; instr. dept. sociology Boston State Coll., 1977-78; clin. psychologist children and Adolescent Services, Richmond (Calif.) Mental Health, 1979—; pvt. practice clin. psychology, Oakland, Calif., 1981—; adj. faculty Calif. Sch. Profl. Psychology, Berkeley, 1983; lectr. John F. Kennedy U., 1982-83. NIMH trainee, 1970-74, predoctoral fellow, 1974-75; Comparative Internat. Studies grantee, 1971; U. Vt. grantee, 1976. Fellow AAUW; mem. Phi Beta Kappa, Sigma Pi Sigma, Pi Mu Epsilon. Office: 465 34th St Oakland CA 94609

WATERMAN, JILL MARCIA, psychologist, educator; b. Los Angeles, Apr. 22, 1945; d. Tod and Ada Ruth (Meyer) Waterman; m. Robert I. Janovici, Aug. 21, 1966; m. 2d Robert Burdick, June 27, 1981. Student U. Calif.-Berkeley, 1962-64; B.A., UCLA, 1965, M.A., 1966, Ph.D., 1972. Lic. psychologist, Calif. USPHS trainee, 1965-66, 68-72; asst. prof. psychiatry U. Calif.-Davis Med. Ctr., 1972-74; asst. prof. psychiatry, dir. tng. J.F.K. Child Devel. Ctr., U. Colo. Med. Ctr., Denver, 1974-79; staff psychologist Permanente Med. Ctr., Hayward, Calif., 1979-81; adj. assoc. prof. psychology, asst. coordinator UCLA Psychology Clinic, 1981—; pvt. practice psychology, also cons. in splty. areas of infant devel., child and family therapy, Los Angeles, 1981—. Mem. Am. Psychol. Assn., Soc. for Research in Child Devel., Phi Beta Kappa. Democrat. Contbr. articles to profl. jours. Office: Dept Psychology UCLA 405 Hilgard Ave Los Angeles CA 90024

WATERMAN, SHEREEN HUMES, educational adminstrator; b. Seward, Alaska, Feb. 20, 1949; d. William E. and Barbara (McAdam) Humes; m. Robert D. Waterman, Aug. 22, 1975; children—Craig, David. B.A., Wash. State U., 1971; M.A., N.Mex. State U., 1976, Ed.S. in Curriculum 1977-82. Tchr., Alamogordo (N.Mex.) public schs., 1971-82; counselor Southwestern Coll. Life Scis., Santa Fe, 1976—, also registrar, curriculum dir., instr. Minister, Movement of Spiritual Inner Awareness. NEA scholar, 1967. Mem. Assn. Supervision and Curriculum Devel. Author: The Fairy Kingdom: A Curriculum Guide, 1979. Office: 1418 Luisa St #1 and 2 Santa Fe NM 87501

WATERS, ALFRED ARVIN, counselor, university administrator; b. Pontiac, Mich., June 11, 1937; s. Arvin Franklin and Matilda Alfreda (Nichols) W.; m. Judith Louise Robertson, Aug. 30, 1958; children—James, Brent, Greg, Deborah, Denise; m. 2d, Jacqueline Sue Focht, Dec. 23, 1978; 1 dau., Erin. B.S., Mich. State U., 1959, M.A., 1963. Lic. social worker, Mich. Dir. admissions testing and counseling Monroe County Community Coll., 1975-78; br. mgr. Kellermeyer Bldg. Service, Columbus, Ohio, 1978-80; dir. coop. programs, instr. Ferris State Coll., Big Rapids, Mich., 1980-82; dir. placement and career plan U. Alaska, Anchorage, 1982—. Mem. Pacific N.W. Personnel Mgmt. Assn., Am. Soc. Personnel Adminstrn, Coll. Placement Council, Am. Personnel and Guidance Assn.

WATERS, LAUGHLIN EDWARD, fed. judge; b. Los Angeles, Aug. 16, 1914; s. Frank J. and Ida (Bauman) W.; A.B., U. Calif., Los Angeles, 1939; J.D., U. So. Calif., 1946; m. Voula Davanis, Aug. 22, 1953; children—Laughlin Edward, Maura Kathleen, Deirdre Mary, Megan Ann, Eileen Brigid. Admitted to Calif. bar, 1946; dep. atty. gen. Calif., Los Angeles, 1946; individual practice law, Los Angeles, 1947-53, 61-76; U.S. atty. So. Dist. Calif., 1953-61; judge U.S. Dist. Ct. for Calif. Central Dist., 1976—. Mem. Calif. Legislature, 1947-53. Served as capt. U.S. Army, 1942-46. Decorated Bronze Star medal, Purple Heart with oak leaf cluster, Combat Inf. badge. Fellow Am. Bar Found., Am. Coll. Trial Lawyers; mem. Am. Judicature Soc., U. So. Calif., U. Calif. at Los Angeles law assns., Am. Legion, U. So. Calif. Legion Lex, Order Blue Shield, Town Hall, Soc. Friendly Sons St. Patrick. Republican. Roman Catholic. Clubs: Knights of Malta, Anchor, Calif. Office: 243 US Courthouse 312 N Spring St Los Angeles CA 90012

WATERS, RODNEY LEWIS, manufacturing executive; b. Long Beach, Calif., July 13, 1936; s. Harris Eades and Gladys Edna (Lippy) W.; B.A. in Physics, UCLA, 1963; M.B.A., Pepperdine U., 1979; children—Julie Anna, Danae Lynn, John Davis. Research engr. N. Am. Rockwell, Downey, Calif., 1963-65; product mgr. Korad dept. Union Carbide Corp., 1965-73; mktg. mgr. Quantrad Corp., El Segundo, Calif., 1973-74; pres. Florod Corp., Hawthorne, Calif., 1974—; Pres. Gifted Childrens Assn., Hawthorne, 1971-72. Served with U.S. Army, 1958-60. Mem. Internat. Soc. Hybrid Microelectronics, Soc. Photog. Instrumentation Engrs. Republican. Contbr. articles to profl. jours. Office: 3341 W El Segundo Blvd Hawthorne CA 90250

WATERS, RUSSEL DEAN, auto parts retail executive; b. Rock Springs, Wyo., Sept. 14, 1939; s. Cecil Bruce and Carmen Marcella (Aurberger) W.; m. Lavanetta Pearl Forbes, Sept. 20, 1960; children—Timothy M., Jackson B., Dale D., Jerry L. Student U.S. Navy Electronic Sch., 1958-59. Counterman Auto Parts Co., 1964-67; parts mgr. Whisler Chevrolet, 1967-69; mgr. Adams' Auto Supply, 1969-80; owner, mgr. Adams Big A Auto Parts, all Rock Springs, Wyo., 1980—; mem. dist. adv. bd. Big A Auto Parts System. Capt. Sweetwater County (Wyo.) Search and Rescue, 1973—; bd. dirs. Little League Baseball and Football, Babe Ruth Baseball, ARC, all Rock Springs. Served with USN, 1957-64; Cuba. Mem. Wyo. Peace Officers Assn. Democrat. Congregationalist. Clubs: Shriners, Masons, Order Eastern Star, Order Demolay (chmn. chpt.), Jobs Daus. (assoc. guardian). Home: 1324 Liberty Dr Rock Springs WY 82901 Office: 1300 Dewar Dr Rock Springs WY 82901

WATHEN, JAMES ANDREW, hosp. adminstr.; b. San Pedro, Calif., Aug. 27, 1947; s. Raymond Andrew and Jeanne Marie (Kelahan) W.; B.S., J. San Francisco, 1969; M.H.A., U. Wash., 1978; m. Mary Jane Lucich, June 26, 1971; children—David, Theresa, Katie, Danny. Admintrv. asst. Rogue Valley Meml. Hosp., Medford, Oreg., 1978, asst. adminstr., 1979-80, asst. adminstr. planning and profl. services, 1980-81; asso. adminstr. Bay Area Hosp., Coos Bay, Oreg., 1981—. Served with AUS, 1970-76. Mem. Am. Coll. Hosp. Adminstrs., Hosp. Fin. Mgmt. Assn., Am. Assn. Hosp. Planners, Am. Hosp. Assn., Assn. Western Hosps., Oreg. Assn. Hosps., Healthcare Fin. Mgmt. Assn. (advanced). Republican. Roman Catholic. Office: 1775 Thompson Rd Coos Bay OR 97420

WATIA, TARMO, artist, educator; b. Detroit, May 11, 1938; s. Oiva and Mildred (Saari) W.; children—Paula Ann, Erik Talvi, Talvi Oiva. B.S. in Design, U. Mich., 1960, M.F.A., 1962. Asst. prof. Minot (N.D.) State U., 1964, Mont. State U., Bozeman, 1965, So. Oreg. State Coll., 1966-69; assoc. prof. art Boise State U., 1969—; traveling exhibn. Great Falls, Miles City and Butte, Mont., exhbn. for Idaho artists, Boise, 1981; two man show Herrett Mus., Twin Falls. Recipient award for works on paper Coll. So. Idaho, Twin Falls. Republican. Lutheran.

WATKINS, ANN ESTHER, mathematics educator; b. Los Angeles, Jan. 10, 1949; d. Rex Devere and Burnice Gordine (Duckworth) Hamilton; m. William E. Watkins, Oct. 5, 1973; children—Mary Ann, Barbara Lee. B.A. in Math., Calif. State U.-Northridge, 1970, M.S. in Math., 1972; Ph.D. in Edn., UCLA, 1977. Asst. prof. math. Calif. State U.-Northridge, 1977-79; assoc. prof. Los Angeles Pierce Coll., Woodland Hills, Calif., 1979—. Calif. State U.-Northridge Found. grantee, 1978. Mem. Nat. Council Tchrs. Math. (curriculum in stats. and probability com.), Am. Statis. Assn., Math. Assn. Am. Contbr. articles to Math. Tchr.; author math. cassette tapes. Office: Los Angeles Pierce Coll Woodland Hills CA 91371

WATKINS, BRUCE ALAN, nutritionist; b. Omaha, Nebr., Apr. 21, 1953; s. Jack Oliver and Eveln Neil (Thompson) W.; B.S., Colo. State U., 1976, M.S., 1981; Ph.D. candidate U. Calif., Davis, 1981—; m. Cynthia. Research assistantship Colo. State Univ., Fort Collins, 1976-79; nutritionist Fermented Products, Inc., Mason City, Iowa, 1979-80; research asst. in avian scis., nutrition U. Calif., Davis, 1981—; cons. growth promoting microbial products, 1981—. Recipient John L. Robbins award, 1980. PePa scholar, 1977, 80; Jake Kellogg Meml. scholar, 1977; Hubbard scholar, 1980. Mem. Poultry Sci. Assn. (cert. of excellence 1979, 82), Am. Assn. Lab. Animal Sci., Am. Assn. Animal Sci., Sigma Xi, Gamma Sigma Delta. Republican. Baptist. Home: 2219 Regis Dr Davis CA 95616 Office: Dept Avian Sci Univ of Calif Davis CA 95616

WATKINS, DANE HANSEN, state senator; b. Idaho Falls, Idaho, Aug. 24, 1943; s. George W. and Hope C. (Hansen) W.; B.S., U. Utah, 1965; m. Sherry McNamara, Aug. 8, 1964; children—Tory, Tracey, Dane Hansen, Damond, Taryn, David, Tiffany. Sec., treas. Snake River Equipment Co., Idaho Falls, Ida., 1965—; mem. Idaho Senate, Idaho Falls, 1971—, chmn. local govt. and taxation com., 1980-81, mem. agrl. affairs com. and fin. com., 1974-80. Pres. Idaho Employees Council, 1978-80; dir. Blue Cross Idaho, 1974-80; mem. Eastern Idaho Spl. Services Agy., 1981—, Bonneville County Home Health Agy., 1980-81; v.p. Teton Peaks Boy Scout Council, 1976-80; treas. Idaho Gasohol Commn., 1979—; mem. Nat. Gasohol Commn., 1978—; bd. dirs. Bonneville County United Way, 1968-74, YMCA, 1968-78; chmn. Bonneville County Republican Central Com., 1968-71; pres. Eastern Idaho Lincoln Day Assn., 1970-71. Mormon. Home: 2975 Fieldstream Ln Idaho Falls ID 83401 Office: PO Box 781 Idaho Falls ID 83402

WATKINS, GEORGE THOMAS, III, American studies educator; b. Durham, N.C., July 26, 1920; s. George Thomas and Lettie Edith (May) W.; m. Jennie Marie Strike, Apr. 20, 1946; (div. 1972); children—G.

Thomas IV, Sheila Marie, Clifford Strike; m. June Lenore Salvail, Jan. 5, 1973. Instr. dept. English, Wash. State U., Pullman, 1957-60, asst. prof., 1960-65, assoc. prof., 1965-74, prof., 1974—; lectr. on early Am. West. Served with USN, 1942-45. Mem. Oreg.-Calif. Trails Assn. (charter), AAUP, Am. Studies Assn., Pi Kappa Alpha (nat. sec. 1962-64, 66-68). Congregationalist. Assoc. editor Abstracts of English Studies, 1960-62, Pacific Northwesterner, 1962-65; contbr. numerous articles to profl. jours. Home: 1531 Lydon Ct Clarkson WA 99403 Office: Washington State U Dept English Pullman WA 99164

WATKINS, HELEN HUTH, psychologist; b. Augsburg, Germany; B.A., Pa. State U., 1946; M.A., U. Denver, 1949; m. John G. Watkins, Dec. 28, 1971; children from previous marriage—Marvin Huth, Karen Huth Eiblmayr. Psychologist, Center for Student Devel., U. Mont., 1959—; adj. prof. psychology Fla. Inst. Tech., 1979—; instr. workshops. Lic. psychologist, Mont. Mem. Am. Psychol. Assn., Soc. Clin. and Exptl. Hypnosis, Internat. Soc. Hypnosis, Am. Personnel and Guidance Assn., Phi Beta Kappa, Phi Kappa Phi, Psi Chi. Democrat. Contbr. articles to profl. jours. Home: 413 Evans Missoula MT 59801 Office: Univ of Mont Missoula MT 59812

WATKINS, ROBERT FRED, communications and electronics co. exec.; b. Pueblo, Colo., May 20, 1927; s. Robert F. and Ida C. (McDermott) W.; B.S., Calif. Western U., 1976, M.B.A., 1977, Ph.D. in Bus. Adminstrn., 1979; LL.B., LaSalle Law U., 1977; m. Janice Tising, Nov. 7, 1948; children—James Leland, Jody Lynn, Julia Louise. Sr. tech. instr. Philco Corp., 1953-55; liaison engr. Boeing Aircraft Co., 1955-56; sr. engr. Bendix Corp., Balt., 1956-61; regional mgr. bus. devel. data systems div. Litton Industries, Boston and Rome, N.Y., 1961-63, Dayton, Ohio, 1963-66, Colorado Springs, 1966-68, Red Bank, N.J., 1967—, Van Nuys, Calif., 1968-71; mgr. advance systems and mktg. F&M Systems Co., Dallas, 1971-75; bus. devel. mgr. Electrospace Systems, Inc., Richardson, Tex., 1975-83, strategic bus. planner, 1983—; cons. bus. planning and devel., 1979—; co-founder Integrated Mgmt. Tech., Inc., Colorado Springs, Colo., 1978. Bd. dirs. Continental Ministries Inc., Thousand Oaks, Calif., 1981—. Served with USN, 1944-46, 48-49, USAF, 1951-53; PTO, Korea. Mem. Soc. Applied Learning (charter), Armed Forces Communications Electronics Assn., LaSalle U. Alumni Assn. Republican. Mem. Calvary Community Ch., Thousand Oaks, Calif. Author: Move Ahead in Selling, 1974; The Marketing Audit: A Positive and Dynamic Method for Directing the Company's Total Marketing Program, 1977; The Marketing Audit: A Major Step Toward Successful Marketing Control, 1979. Home: 57 La Palma Newbury Park CA 91320

WATKINS, W. LAMARR, mgmt. cons.; b. Huntington, Ind., July 9, 1923; s. Floyd LaMarr and Ann (Dimmitt) W.; B.S., U. Detroit, 1952; certificate U. Pa., 1977; postgrad. Durham Coll., 1969; certificate in fin. analysis U. Tex., 1973; M.B.A., London Grad. Sch. Bus., 1981; m. Lorraine Napoles, Sept. 15, 1943; children—Michael, Reid, Rolando, Chaun. Gen. mgr. Detroit Credit & Service Bur., 1947-56; pres., mgr. Credit Clearing Interchange, Detroit, 1956-67; instr. Durham Coll., El Paso, Tex., 1968-69; adminstrv. mgr. Cummins Rio Grande, Albuquerque, 1969-82; pres. W. L. Watkins & Assos., mgmt. cons., Albuquerque, 1982—; fin. cons. Retirement fin. commr., Lincoln Park, Mich., 1953-67; civil service commr., El Paso, 1972-74; mem. U.S. Trade Commn. to Can., 1959. Served with U.S. Army, 1942-46. Decorated Bronze Star; recipient Disting. Service award U.S. Jr. C. of C., 1958. Fellow Nat. Inst. Credit; mem. Adminstrv. Mgmt. Soc., Western States Distbrs. Assn., Hi Way Credit Mgrs. Assn., Credit Research Found. Republican. Roman Catholic. Author: Investigators Handbook, 1960. Office: PO Box 6186 Albuquerque NM 87197

WATLER, JOHN FRANKLIN, JR., aerospace technical executive; b. Port Arthur, Tex., Jan. 14, 1928; s. John Franklin and Sarah Isabel W.; student Ga. Inst. Tech., 1949-50; B.S. in Engring., UCLA, 1958, M.S. in Engring., 1963; m. Carolyn Mae Cable, Sept. 3, 1949; children—Carolyn Anita, Deborah Ann, John Franklin III, Elaine Louise. Design engr. Douglas Aircraft Co., El Segundo, Calif., 1952-63, design specialist, Long Beach, Calif., 1963-64; design specialist Douglas Missile & Space Systems div., Santa Monica, Calif., 1964-65; br. mgr. Douglas Space Systems Center, Huntington Beach, Calif., 1965-68, McDonnell Douglas Astronautics Co., Culver City, Calif., 1968-69; dept. mgr. Douglas Aircraft Co., Long Beach, 1969-70; self-employed, Hawthorne, Calif., 1970-74; engring. specialist Northrop Corp., 1974-75, tech. mgr., Hawthorne, 1975—. Served with USMC, 1945-49, 50-52. Registered profl. engr., Calif. Mem. Aircraft Owners and Pilots Assn., Assn. Naval Aviation, AIAA, UCLA Alumni Assn., Northrop Mgmt. Club. Presbyterian. Home: 5403 W 142d Pl Hawthorne CA 90250 Office: One Northrop Ave Hawthorne CA 90250

WATNE, DONALD ARTHUR, accountant, educator; b. Gt. Falls, Mont., Jan. 18, 1939; s. Arthur Leonard and Anne (Salo) W.; m. Patricia Elaine Schick, Aug. 12, 1961; children—Elizabeth Anne, Michael Arthur. B.A. with high honors, U. Mont., 1960, M.A., 1961; Ph.D., U. Calif.-Berkeley, 1977. C.P.A., Oreg. Acct., Piquet & Minihan, Eugene, Oreg., 1961-65; mgr. capital investment analysis Weyerhaeuser Co., Tacoma, 1965-68; mktg. rep. IBM Corp., Portland, Oreg., 1968-70; dir. EDP Ctr. in Concejo Mcpl., Barquisimeto, Venezuela, 1971-72; prof. acctg. Portland State U., 1976—; cons. in field. Mem. Am. Inst. C.P.A.s, Am. Acctg. Assn., Oreg. Soc. C.P.A.s, Oreg. Soc. Individual Psychology (dir. 1977—). Author: (with Peter B.B. Turney) Auditing EDP Systems, 1984; contbr. articles in field, chpts. in handbooks. Home: 2826 NE 26th Ave Portland OR 97212 Office: Sch Bus Adminstrn Portland State U PO Box 751 Portland OR 97207

WATRY, C(HARLES) NICHOLAS, III, archlt. engr.; b. Oakland, Calif., Apr. 21, 1941; s. Charles Nicholas and Dorothy Celest (Hunt) W.; B.S., Calif. Poly. Inst., 1964; children—Lisa, John. Designer, H.N. Krull Co., Palo Alto, Calif., 1964-67, H. Neil Warren, 1967-68; div. mgr. Atlas Prestressing Co., Burlingame, Calif., 1969-70, Honolulu, 1970-74; owner, pres. Watry Engring., Inc., Redwood City, Calif., 1975—. Registered profl. engr. Calif., Nev. Mem. Structural Engring. Assn. Calif., Am. Concrete Inst., Prestressed Concrete Inst. Mem. Covenant Ch. Patentee in precast concrete panel bldg. constrn. Home: 1050 Lakeview Way Redwood City CA 94062 Office: Watry Engring Broadway at Main Redwood City CA 94063

WATSON, ADELE LOUISE, city librarian; b. Yonkers, N.Y., Sept. 10, 1929; d. James Albert and Beatrice Adele (Glover) W.; B.A., U.S. Internat. U., 1973; M.A., U. Denver, 1975; Ph.D., Columbia Pacific U., 1980; children—James Watson MacFarland, Laurie Adele MacFarland, Thalia Ann MacFarland. Office mgr. Calif. State Senator L.M. Backstrand, 1950-65; real estate appraiser L.I. Backstrand, 1965-69; librarian Denver Pub. Library, 1975; reference coordinator Serra Coop. Library System, San Diego, 1977-78; dir. Coalinga (Calif.)-Huron Dist. Libraries, 1978—. Speechwriter, active polit. campaigns Republican Party, 1950-65. Mem. Am. Humanist Assn., ALA, Women Library Works, AAUW, NOW, Calif. Library Assn., Nature Conservancy, Wilderness Soc. Unitarian. Clubs: Sierra, Toastmasters, Federated Women. Home: 405-B W Polk St Coalinga CA 93210 Office: Coalinga-Huron Dist Libraries 305 N 4th St Coalinga CA 93210

WATSON, ANDREA LOUISE, economist; b. Plymouth, Mass., Apr. 22, 1947; d. John Charles and Julia Louise (Avery) W.; B.A., U. Mass., 1969; M.A., Johns Hopkins U., 1972. Officer internat. staff Citibank, N.A., 1972-74; research assoc. Internat. Research & Tech., 1974-78; sr. analyst Bechtel, San Francisco, 1978-80, economist-fin., 1980—. Mem. Nat. Assn. Bus. Economists, World Affairs Council No. Calif., Soc. Internat. Devel., Corp. Planners Assn. Democrat. Unitarian. Club: Commonwealth of Calif. Home: 1380 Sacramento St San Francisco CA 94109 Office: PO Box 3965 San Francisco CA 94119

WATSON, DAVID COLQUITT, elec. engr.; b. Linden, Tex., Feb. 9, 1936; s. Colvin Colquitt and Nelena Gertrude (Keasler) W.; B.S.E.E., U. Utah, 1964, Ph.D. in Elec. Engring. (NASA fellow), 1968; m. Flora Janet Thayn, Nov. 10, 1959; children—Flora Janeen, Melanie Beth, Lorrie Gaylene, Cheralyn Gail, Nathan David, Amy Melissa, Brian Colvin. Electronic technician Hercules Powder Co., Magna, Utah, 1961-62; research fellow U. Utah, 1964-65, research asst. microwave devices and phys. electronics lab., 1964-68; sr. mem. tech. staff ESL, Inc., Sunnyvale, Calif., 1968-78, head dept. Communications, 1969-70; sr. engring. specialist Probe Systems, Inc., Sunnyvale, 1978-79; sr. mem. tech. staff ARGOSystems, Inc., Sunnyvale, 1979—; mem. faculty U. Santa Clara, 1978—, San Jose State U., 1981—. Served with USAF, 1956-60. Mem. IEEE, Phi Kappa Phi, Tau Beta Pi, Eta Kappa Nu. Mormon. Contbr. articles to IEEE Transactions, 1965-78; co-inventor cyclotron-wave rectifier. Office: 884 Hermosa Ct Sunnyvale CA 94086

WATSON, DENISE ANN, state correctional department official, consultant; b. Baxter Springs, Kans., Aug. 6, 1952; d. James Oliver and Mamie Jewell (Reynolds) Watson; 1 son, Tige O'Dare. Student (scholar) San Francisco Sch. Ballet, 1969-70, (scholar) Harlem Ballet Theatre, N.Y.C., 1972; B.A. in Psychology, U. N.Mex., 1974. Profl. dancer Ashton-Kochmann Prodn., N.Y.C., 1972-73; research asst. Checkerboard Area Health System, Cuba, N. Mex., 1974-75; counselor Opportunities Industrialization Center, Albuquerque, 1975-76; diagnostic eval. specialist Penitentiary of N. Mex., Santa Fe, 1975-76; probation, parole officer N. Mex. Dept. Corrections, Albuquerque, 1976-78, trouble employee adviser, Santa Fe, 1978-80, tng. specialist, 1978-81, chief employee devel. bur., edn. and tng. div., 1981—; cons. human resources devel. and tng. acad. devel. Coordinator Gov.'s Ann. Women's Career Conf., 1980; active Black Leadership Council, 1982; active Gt. SW council Boy Scouts Am. Served to 1st lt. USAR, 1972—. Mem. N.Mex. Criminal Justice Profls. Assn., Western Correctional Assn., Am. Correctional Assn., Criminal Justice Trainers Assn., Am. Jail Assn., Nat. Council Crime and Delinquency, Res. Officers Assn., Alpha Kappa Alpha. Democrat. Baptist. Home: 7912 Southern SE Albuquerque NM 87108 Office: 113 Washington Ave Santa Fe NM 87501

WATSON, DIANE EDITH, sch. psychologist, state senator; b. Los Angeles, Nov. 12, 1933; d. William Alan Louis and Dorothy Elizabeth W.; B.A., UCLA, 1956; M.S., Calif. State U., Los Angeles, 1967; postgrad. Claremont Grad. Sch., 1976—. Dep. dir. secondary schs. allied health project UCLA Div. Vocat. Edn., 1969-71; health occupations specialist Bur. Indsl. Edn., Calif. State Dept. Edn., 1971-73; sch. psychologist Area K, Los Angeles City Schs., 1973-74; mem. Los Angeles City Bd. Edn., 1975-78; mem. Calif. State Senate, 1978—; trustee Blue Shield. Mem. Los Angeles City Coll. Pres.'s Adv. Council, 1974-76; vice chmn. human resources com. Nat. Council of State Legislatures. Recipient Urban League Achievement award, 1976; Nat. Communications award Nat. Assn. Media Women, 1977; Senator of Yr., Calif. Trial Lawyers Assn., 1982; Alumnus of Yr., UCLA, 1982. Mem. Nat. Sch. Bds. Assn., Calif. Sch. Bds. Assn., Calif. Tchrs. Assn., Golden State Friends Found. (exec. bd.), Calif. Commn. on Status of Women, Urban League, NAACP, Alpha Kappa Alpha. Democrat. Roman Catholic. Author works in field. Office: Rm 4040 State Capitol Sacramento CA 95814

WATSON, DOUGLAS, winery company executive, engineering and financial consultant; b. Redwood City, Calif., Dec. 18, 1916; s. Douglas Sloane and Mai deBeau (Moody) W.; m. Marie Knauer Latshaw, June 16, 1941; children—Margaret, Douglas, Jorane, Thomas, Wade, Hanalee. A.B. in Engring., Stanford U., 1938, M.B.A., 1940. Registered profl. engr., Calif. Job study engr. Procter & Gamble, Ivorydale, Ohio and Long Beach, Calif., 1940-42; asst. chief indsl. engr. Columbia Steel Co., San Francisco, 1942-44; dir. McKinsey & Co., Inc., San Francisco, 1944-75; chmn., chief exec. officer C. Mondavi & Sons, St. Helena, Calif., 1977-78; pres., chief exec. officer Vichon Winery, Oakville, Calif., 1980—; dir. Calif. Casualty Ins. Group. Mem. ASME. Republican. Clubs: Bohemian (San Francisco); Meadowood (St. Helena). Office: 1595 Oakville Grade Oakville CA 94562

WATSON, HAROLD GEORGE, ordnance company executive, mechanical engineer; b. Phoenix, Oct. 19, 1931; s. Clarence Elmer and Eunice A. (Record) W.; m. Ruth May Thomas, Aug. 30, 1951; children—Patricia Ruth, Linda Darlene, Harold George. B.S., U. Ariz., 1954. Engr., Shell Oil Co., Los Angeles, 1954; project engr. Talco Engring. Co., Hamden Conn., 1956, area mgr., Mesa, Ariz., 1956-57, chief engr. rocket power, 1958-61, dir. engring., 1961-64; dir. engring. Space Ordnance Systems, El Segundo, Calif., 1964-68; dir. engring. Universal Propulsion Co., Riverside, Calif., 1968-70, gen. mgr., v.p. engring., Tempe, Ariz., 1970-76, v.p., mgr., 1976-77, pres., gen. mgr., Phoenix, 1977—. Served to 1st lt. USAR, 1954-56. Mem. Am. Ordnance Assn., SAFE Assn. (pres.), AIAA, Air Force Assn., Internat. Pyronetics Soc., Am. Def. Preparedness Assn. Patentee aircraft escape systems. Office: Universal Propulsion Co Inc Box 1140 Black Canyon Stage Number 1 Phoenix AZ 85029

WATSON, JAMES OLIVER, investment co. exec.; b. Berwyn, Ill., Sept. 25, 1942; s. Bernard C. and Betty Watson; B.A., UCLA, 1964; M.B.A., U. So. Calif., 1966; m. Susan Katz, Sept. 2, 1972. Vice-pres. Bank of Calif., Los Angeles, 1973-75; investment salesman Coldwell Banker, Los Angeles, 1975-77; project officer U.S. Dept. State, AID, Africa, Egypt, Jordan, Israel, Syria, 1977-81; pres. Quest 7 Investment Corp., Mission Viejo, Calif., 1981—; instr. Los Angeles City Coll., Santa Monica Coll. Bd. dirs. Los Angeles Apt. Owners Assn.; assoc. dir. Peace Corps, Africa. Served with AUS, 1966-72. Cannon Electric fellow, 1960-64. Mem. Calif. Real Estate Assn., Los Angeles Jaycees, Am. Fgn. Service Assn., Saddleback Valley C. of C. Clubs: Rotary, Mission Viejo Nadadores Booster. Office: 22481 El Toro Rd El Toro CA 92630

WATSON, JOHN WILLARD, architect; b. Pasadena, Calif., Mar. 28, 1949; s. Thomas E. and Mary Nau Watson; student Boston U., 1967-69, Boston Archtl. Center, 1971-73; B.Arch. summa cum laude, U. Tex., 1976. Founder, Archtl. Computer Software, Santa Barbara, Calif., 1979—; partner Bob Easton Design Assos., architects, Santa Barbara, 1980—. Office: 600 Colina Ln Santa Barbara CA 93103

WATSON, LITA LEA, employment co. exec.; b. Lovettsville, Va., May 28, 1931; grad. public schs., Lovettsville; m. Robert J. Watson, Jan. 20, 1951; children—Jeannine Roberta, Robert Neal, James Kevin, Mary Elizabeth, Frederick Michael. Sec., Household Finance Co., Silver Spring, Md., 1948-52, El Paso Natural Gas Co. (Tex.), 1956-59; mem. sales staff, sales mgr. Sarah Coventry Jewelry, Newark, 1959-67; Calif. regional mgr. Snelling and Snelling Employment Agy., 1967-71; owner, mgr. Dennis & Dennis Personnel Service, Anaheim, Santa Ana, Irvine, Huntington Beach and Cerritos, Calif., 1971—, now franchising in State of Calif. Mem. Calif. Employment Assn. (dir.), Orange County C. of C., Better Bus. Bur., Nat. Employment Assn., Am. Soc. for Personnel Adminstrn., Am. Mgmt. Assn., Internat. Platform Assn. Republican. Roman Catholic. Home: 594 Turnabout Rd Orange CA 92669 Office: 1600 N Broadway Suite 110 Santa Ana CA 92706

WATSON, RAYMOND LESLIE, architect; b. Seattle, Oct. 4, 1926; s. Leslie Alexander and Olive (Lorentzen) W.; B.A., U. Calif. at Berkeley, 1951, M.A., 1953; m. Elsa Constance Coito, Sept. 18, 1954; children—Kathy Ann, Bryan Frederich, Lisa Marie, David John. Architect firm Donald Haines & Assos., San Francisco, 1955-60; mgr. planning The Irvine Co., Newport Beach, Calif., 1960-64, v.p. planning, 1964-66, sr. v.p. land devel., 1966-70, exec. v.p., 1970-73, pres., 1973-77; pres., partner Newport Devel. Co., 1977-83; chmn. bd. Walt Disney Prodns., 1983—; dir. Disney Corp., Pacific Mut. Life Ins. Co., Mitchell Energy and Devel. Co., Irvine Co. Trustee Occidental Coll. Served with USAAF, 1944-45. Fellow AIA. Home: 2501 Alta Vista Dr Newport Beach CA 92660 Office: 900 Cagney Ln Newport Beach CA 92663

WATSON, SHARON GITIN, psychologist; b. N.Y.C., Oct. 21, 1943; d. Louis Leonard and Miriam (Myers) G.; B.A., Cornell U., 1965; M.A., U. Ill., 1968, Ph.D., 1971; m. Eric Watson, Oct. 31, 1969; 1 dau., Carrie. Psychologist, City N.Y. Prison Mental Health, Riker's Island, 1973-74, Youth Services Center, County of Los Angeles Dept. Public Social Services, Los Angeles, 1975-77, dir. clin. services, 1978, dir. youth services center, 1978-80; exec. dir. Crittenton Ctr. for Young Women and Infants, Los Angeles, 1980—. USPHS fellow, 1965-68. Mem. Am. Psychol. Assn., Calif. Assn. Services for Children (sec.-treas.), So. Calif. Assn. Children's Instns. and Agys. (pres.-elect), Am. Mgmt. Assn. Home: 4056 Camino Real Los Angeles CA 90065 Office: 234 East Ave 33 Los Angeles CA 90031

WATSON, VELVIN RICHARD, research physicist; b. Streator, Ill., June 2, 1932; s. Jotham Richard and Ruth Adeline (Trovillo) W.; m. Cassandra Watson, June 14, 1958; children—Melanie (Bruner), Mark, Amy. B.S., U. Calif.-Berkeley, 1959, M.S. in Aero. Engring., 1961; Ph.D. in Aeros. and Astronautics, Stanford U., 1969. Research scientist computational fluid dynamics NASA Ames Research Ctr., Moffett Field, Calif., 1961—; part time instr. computer sci. DeAnza Coll., Cupertino, Calif., 1977—; part-time instr. mech. engring. Santa Clara (Calif.) U., 1983—; cons. on microcomputers. Served to capt. U.S. Army, 1953-57. Mem. AIAA, IEEE, Am. Soc. Engring. Edn., Assn. Computing Machinery. Contbr. articles to sci. jours. Inventor of plasma generator (Nasa Invention Award, 1965); patentee of constricted electric arcs. Home: 21366 Amulet Dr Cupertino CA 95014 Office: Mail Stop 202A-1 NASA-Ames Research Ctr Moffett Field CA 94035

WATSON, WILLIAM KEITH ROSS, research scientist; b. Lowestoft, Eng., Nov. 8, 1930; s. William Ross and Elizabeth Margaret (Wood) W.; came to U.S., 1953, naturalized, 1957; student Corpus Christi Coll., 1950-53; B.A., Cambridge (Eng.) U., 1953; M.A., U. Calif. at Berkeley, 1955, Ph.D., 1957; children—Christine Margaret, Cynthia Kathryn, Carolyn Elizabeth. Research asso., lectr. U. Calif. at Berkeley, 1957; Sloane fellow Calif. Inst. Tech., 1957-59; asst. prof. U. So. Calif., Los Angeles, 1959-61; asst. prof. physics U. Calif. at Riverside, 1961-64; v.p. Winston Research Corp., Los Angeles, 1962-63, dir., 1962-67; v.p. Highland Research Corp., Riverside, 1963-64, pres., 1964-66; corporate staff Astrodata, Inc., 1964-66; v.p. research Medical Electronics div. Becton Dickinson & Co., East Rutherford, N.J., 1966-69; dir. CALSEIA, Neuro-Psychiat. and Health Care Services, S.W. Energy Mgmt.; sr. cons. Technicolor Corp. Sci.; cons. Abbott Labs., 1972-76, Kay Labs., 1972-76, U.S. Navy, 1976—, Dept. Energy, 1977—; solar cons. Calif. Gov.'s Office, 1980—. Mem. sci. adv. U.S. Senate Com. Energy and Natural Resources, 1977—, U.S. Dept. Def., 1977—, U.S. Senate Fin. Com., 1980—. Adv., Calif. Central Republican Com.; sci. advisor Carter Presdl. Campaign, 1976-76; mem. adv. bd. Energetics Systems Inc., Washington, 1981—; chmn. So. Calif.-San Diego County Desalination Com., 1983—; chmn. R.S.F. Energy Corp., 1983—; dir. Riverside Fin. Corp.; coordinator tech. steering com. UN Decade of Water Global Communication Forum, Mex., 1983. Fellow Am. Math. Soc.; mem. Am. Phys. Soc., Am. Inst. Aeros. and Astronautics, Bassetlaw Young Conservative Assn. (sec. 1950-52), Internat. Solar Energy Soc., Calif. Solar Energy Assn. (dir. 1975-80), Sigma Xi. Club: Rancho Santa Fe Tennis. Contbr. articles to sci. publs. Patentee med. instruments and renewable energy resources. Home: PO Box 1537 Rancho Santa Fe CA 92067

WATSON, WILLIAM MARK, hotel computer system executive; b. N.Y.C., Feb. 4, 1937; s. Eugene and Miriam (Shaw) W.; m. Donna Kirschner, Feb. 11, 1965; children—Randy Meg, Leslie Sue, Eric Scott. B.S., Ohio State U., 1958. Cert. in data processing Inst. Cert. Computer Profls. Sr. analyst Pan Am. World Airways, N.Y.C., 1960-65, Mobil Oil Corp., N.Y.C., 1966-68; project mgr. ABC, N.Y.C., 1969-71; dir. mgmt. info. systems MGM Grand Hotel, Las Vegas, 1972—. Served with USAF, 1958-59. Mem. Data Processing Mgmt. Assn., Assn. Systems Mgmt., Hotel Accts. Assn. Office: MGM Grand Hotel Las Vegas NV 89109

WATT, JOAN DUFFY, university dean; b. Battle Creek, Mich., Sept. 28, 1947; d. James Patrick and Idris Bell (Wyatt) Duffy; B.A. with distinction in Polit. Sci., U. Wash., 1969; m. John William Watt, Nov. 20, 1978; children—Kathleen Suzanne, Jennifer Joan. Nat. field cons. Delta Gamma, 1969-70; reporter Seattle Post-Intelligencer, 1969; dir. public info. U. Puget Sound, Tacoma, 1970-74, dir. public relations, 1974-80, asst. dean for admissions and law sch. relations, 1980—; cons. pub. relations to non-profit groups. Bd. dirs. Red Cross, 1982-83, chmn. pub. relations com., 1982-83; mem. activities council, chmn. publicity com. Tacoma Art Mus., 1981-83; bd. dirs. Jr. League Tacoma, 1979—, chmn. mktg. council, 1982-83, mem. exec. com., 1983—. Mem. Council for Advancement and Support of Edn. (N.W. Conf. planning com.), Pub. Relations Soc. Am., Phi Beta Kappa, Phi Kappa Phi. Republican. Roman Catholic. Contbr. articles to Seattle Times, Seattle Post-Intelligencer, Tacoma News Tribune and ednl. publs., editor U. Puget Sound Lawyer. Office: 950 Broadway Plaza Tacoma WA 98402

WATTENBERG, MARTIN PAUL, political science educator; b. Washington, June 6, 1956; s. Leonard and Frances Anna (Marans) W. B.A., Hampshire Coll., 1977; Ph.D., U. Mich., 1982. Asst. prof. polit. sci. UCLA, 1982-83, U. Calif.-Irvine, 1983—; lectr. polit. sci. U. Mich., Ann Arbor, summer 1982, teaching asst., 1979-82. Mem. Am. Polit. Sci. Assn., Mich. Polit. Sci. Assn. Jewish. Contbr. articles to profl. jours. Home: 240 Nice Ln 105 Newport Beach CA 92663 Office: Sch Social Scis U Calif Irvine CA 92717

WATTERSON, JON CRAIG, plant pathologist; b. Kalamazoo, Nov. 25, 1944; s. Donald Everett and Virginia Jean (Hewitt) W.; m. Peggy J. Day, Aug. 19, 1967; children—Kristin J., Nicholas B. B.A. with honors in Biology, Carleton Coll., 1966; M.S. in Plant Pathology, U. Wis., 1971. Research assoc. U. Wis., 1971-72; with Petoseed Co., Inc., Woodland, Calif., 1972—, head plant pathology dept., 1972—. Mem. Am. Phytopathol. Soc., Internat. Phytopathol. Soc., Soc. Nematologists. Home: 2319 Poppy Ln Davis CA 95616 Office: Petoseed Co Inc Route 4 Box 1255 Woodland CA 95695

WATTLES, GURDON HOWARD, cons. engr., surveyor; b. Glendale, Calif., May 24, 1910; s. William Charles and Amelia (Howard) W.; m. Daisy Forbes, Aug. 13, 1966. Subdiv. engr. Beverly Crest Realty Co., Beverly Hills, Calif., 1936-38; survey dir. Gen. Engring. Co., Los Angeles, 1938-41; asst. architect, Contractors Pacific Naval Air Bases, Wake Island, 1940; owner, mgr. Wattles Constrn. Co., Hemet, Calif., 1946-51; asst. v.p., cons. engr. all offices of Title Ins. & Trust Co. and Pioneer Nat. Title Ins. Co. hdqrs., Los Angeles, 1951-75; cons.-specialist, land-water boundaries and legal descriptions, Orange, Calif.,

1975—; condr. seminars and workshops for pvt. industry, govt. agys., tchr., also nat. lectr.; creator GW's Workshop, 1976. Mem. engring. aide adv. com. Orange Coast Coll.; mem. staff, counselor N.Am. Sch. of Surveying and Mapping; coordinating chmn. Inst. for Advancement Engring., 1970—; mem. survey tech. adv. com. Santa Ana Coll.; mem. Am. Bar Found. Project Adv. Com. Land Records Improvements, 1972-73. Mem. planning commn. City of Hemet, 1949-51, surveyed and created master plan, 1948. Pres. Ramona council Boy Scouts Am., 1951. Prisoner of war, Japan, 1941-45. Recipient numerous profl. assn. certs. appreciation, including ASCE Merit award. Fellow ASCE (nat. chmn. land survey com. 1970, 83); mem. Am. Congress on Surveying and Mapping (life mem., nat. chmn. com. for improvement nat. land title records 1970-72), Am. Right of Way Assn., Orange County Engring. Council (pres. 1970-71). Designed and contracted golddomed I AM Temple in Long Beach, 1961-64. Author: Subdivider's Guide, 1936; Surveying Field Handbook, 1972; Writing Legal Descriptions, 1975; (co-author): Land Survey Descriptions, 1974; Survey Drafting, 1977; GW's Workshop Exercise Book, 1980. Contbr. articles to nat. and internat. mags. Address: PO Box 5702 Orange CA 92667

WATTS, BARBARA KIMBALL, computer marketing executive; b. Ithaca, N.Y., Oct. 27, 1946; d. Everett L. and Gertrude Aileen (Palmer) Kimball; m. James J. Watts, Sept. 9, 1967; children—Aileen, Geoffrey, Jamie Kathryn. B.A., Pa. State U., 1967, M.A., 1973. Instr., Pa. State U., University Park, 1967-72; mktg. dir. AM Mgmt., Ft. Collins, Colo., 1973-74; dir. TeenAge Parent Program, State of Pa., 1972-73; owner, mgr. WOC Gift Wholesales, Ft. Collins, 1973-77, Vail (Colo.) Printing Services, 1975-78; owner, mgr., pres. Watts Computer Systems, Vail, 1976—; lectr. Vail Mgmt. Inst., Rocky Mountain Bus. Conf.; instr. Colo. Mountain Coll., 1979-81. Mem. Internat. Alpha Micro Computer Dealers Assn. (dir., founder, pub. relations officer). Republican. Address: 143 E Meadow Dr Suite 496 Vail CO 81657

WATTS, BARRY ALLEN, psychologist; b. Payette, Idaho, Nov. 15, 1943; s. Dale E. and Juanita Ruth (Amick) W.; B.A. magna cum laude, Pepperdine U., 1968; M.S., Eastern Wash. U., 1972; m. Bonnie Lee McKean, Dec. 28, 1965; children—Kelly Dale, Robert Allen. Ednl. dir., psychologist, program dir. Warm Springs Center, Boise, Idaho, 1971-74, exec. dir., 1974—; spl. lectr. psychology Boise State U., 1978, 79, 81. Pres., bd. dirs. Eagle Citizens Assn.; cubmaster Cub Scout Pack. Served with AUS, 1963-65. Mem. Am. Personnel and Guidance Assn., Idaho Personnel and Guidance Assn., Am. Mental Health Counselors Assn., Assn. Mental Health Adminstrs. (dep. gov. Idaho), Christian Assn. Psychol. Studies. Home: Route 1 Ballantyne Ln Eagle ID 83616 Office: 740 Warm Springs Ave Boise ID 83702

WATTS, BOBBY THOMAS, civil engineer; b. Danville, Ky., Sept. 19, 1948; s. Thomas Benton and Sally (Brown) W.; m. Donna Lynn Justice, June 2, 1973; 1 dau., Hanna Leah. B.S. in Civil Engring., U. Ky., 1972. Registered profl. engr., Ky., Colo. Traffic engr. Hensley-Schmidt Inc., Chattanooga, 1972-74, City of Louisville, 1974-77; civil engr. Atlantic Richfield Co., Denver, 1977-83; Design Assocs., Denver, 1983—; operator water and sewer dist. City of Wright (Wyo.), 1977-83. Mem. ASCE, Am. Water Works Assn., Nat. Fedn. Pollution Control. Home: 9952 W Florida Pl Lakewood CO 80226 Office: Design Assoc Cherry Creek Ctr 360 S Monroe St Suite 500 Denver CO 80209

WATTS, CURTIS R., engineer, consultant; B.S. in Engring., UCLA, 1965. Prin. C.R. Watts Assocs., Redondo Beach, Calif. Contbr. articles to profl. jours. Address: C R Watts Assocs PO Box 3539 Redondo Beach CA 90277

WATTS, JACK KING, computer programmer; b. Oklahoma City, June 11, 1927; s. Columbus David and Vera Mae (King) W.; grad. Air Force Navigator Sch., 1951, Pilot Tng. Sch., 1953, Day Fighter Sch., 1953, Indsl. Coll. Armed Forces, 1964, Pacific Air Force Jungle Survival Sch., 1968, Air War Coll., 1972; B.S., William Carey Coll., 1973; Command pilot, U.S. Air Force, 1950, advanced through grades to lt. col.; ret., 1976; self-employed computer programmer, Honolulu, 19[illegible]. Decorated Silver Star, D.F.C. with oak leaf cluster, Air medal with 0 oak leaf clusters. Mem. Air Force Assn., Ret. Officers Assn., Pen and Sword Soc., Phi Beta Lambda, Kappa Mu Epsilon. Republican. Episcopalian. Address: 1925 Kalakaua Ave Apt 2703 Honolulu HI 96815

WATTS, JOHN MCCLEAVE, ins. and investment co. exec.; b. Salt Lake City, July 20, 1933; s. Newell Edward and Mildred (McCleave) W.; B.S., Mass. Inst. Tech., 1956; m. Janis Marie Duncan, July 4, 1971; children—John McCleave, Christopher A., Kelly Lee; 1 stepson, Kenneth D. McCoy. Engaged in ins. bus., 1957—; dir. life ins. mktg. Channing Cos., Inc., Houston, 1968-71; dir. mktg. Waddell & Reed, Inc., Kansas City, Mo., 1971-74, exec. v.p., dir., 1974-79; exec. v.p., dir. subs. Research Mgmt. Assos., Inc., Kansas City, 1974-79; v.p. nat. ins. dept. E. F. Hutton & Co., N.Y.C., 1979—, pres. 19 mktg. subs., 1979—. Councilman, City of Leawood, Kans., 1973-78, public safety commr., 1973-79; chmn. Nueces County (Tex.) Republican Party, 1962-65; bd. govs. Nat. Ctr. Fin. Edn. Served to capt. AUS, 1957. Recipient Life Ins. Mktg. Inst. Achievement award Purdue U., 1960; C.L.U. Mem. Nat. Assn. Securities Dealers (registered prin.), Internat. Platform Assn., Am. Soc. Pension Actuaries, Internat. Assn. Fin. Planners, Nat. Assn. Life Underwriters, Internat. Found. Employee Benefit Plans. Republican. Club: Torrey (LaJolla, Calif.). Contbr. articles to profl. jours. Home: 16307 Woodson View Rd Poway CA 92064 Office: 11011 N Torrey Pines Rd Box 2700 LaJolla CA 92038

WATTS, MARVIN LEE, chemist, educator, rancher; b. Portales, N.Mex., Apr. 6, 1932; s. William Ellis and Jewel Reata (Holder) W.; B.S. in Chemistry and Math., Eastern N.Mex. U., 1959, M.S. in Chemistry, 1960; postgrad. U. Okla., 1966, U. Kans., 1967; m. Mary Myrtle Kiker, July 25, 1952; children—Marvin Lee, Mark Dwight, Wesley Lyle. Analytical chemist Dow Chem. Co., Midland, Mich., 1960-62; instr. chemistry N.Mex. Mil. Inst., Roswell, 1962-65, asst. prof., 1965-67; chief chemist AMAX Chem. Corp., Carlsbad, N.Mex., 1967-78, gen. surface supt., 1978—; chem. cons. Western Soils Lab., Roswell, 1962-67; instr. chemistry N.Mex. State U., Carlsbad, 1967—; owner, operator cattle ranch, Carlsbad and Loving, N.Mex., 1969—; dir. Soil Conservation Service; mem. Roswell dist. adv. bd. Bur. Land Mgmt. Bd. dirs. Southeastern N.Mex. Regional Sci. Fair, 1966; mem. adv. bd. Roswell dist. Bur. Land Mgmt.; mem. Eddy County Fair Bd., 1976—, chmn., 1978, 82; bd. dirs. Carlsbad Regional Med. Center, 1976-78; pres. bd. Carlsbad Found., 1979-82; adv. bd. N.Mex. State U. at Carlsbad, 1976—; vice chmn. bd. Guadalupe Med. Center; bd. dirs. N.Mex. State U. Found. Mem. Republican State Exec. com., 1972—; Rep. chmn. Eddy County (N.Mex.), 1970-74, 78-82. dirs. Conquistador council Boy Scouts Am., Regional Environ. Ednl. Research and Improvement Orgn. Served with Mil. Police Corps, AUS, 1953-55; Germany. Recipient Albert K. Mitchell award as outstanding Rep. in N.Mex., 1976; hon. state farmer N.Mex. Future Farmers Am.; hon. mem. 4-H. Fellow N.Mex. Acad. Sci.; mem. Am. Chem. Soc. (chmn. subsect.), Carlsbad C. of C. (dir. 1979—), N.Mex. Mining Assn. (dir.), AIME (chmn. Carlsbad potash sect. 1975), Am. Angus Assn., Am. Quarter Horse Assn., N.Mex. Cattle Growers Assn., Carlsbad Farm and Ranch Assn., Nat. Cattleman's Assn. Baptist. Kiwanis (Disting. lt. gov.), Elks. Home: PO Box 56 Carlsbad NM 88220 Office: Box 279 Carlsbad NM 88220

WATTS, OLIVER EDWARD, cons. engr.; b. Hayden, Colo., Sept. 22, 1939; s. Oliver Easton and Vera Irene (Hockett) W.; B.S., Colo. State U., 1962; m. Charla Ann French, Aug. 12, 1962; children—Erik Sean, Oliver Eron, Sherilyn. Crew chief Colo. State U. Research Found., Ft. Collins, 1962; with Calif. Dept. Water Resources, Gustine and Castaic, 1964-70; land and water engr. CF & I Steel Corp., Pueblo, Colo., 1970-71; engring. dir. United Western Engrs., Colorado Springs, Colo., 1971-76; partner United Planning & Engring. Co., Colorado Springs, 1976-79; owner Oliver E. Watts, cons. engr., 1979—. Served to 1st lt. C.E., AUS, 1962-64. Registered profl. engr., Colo., Calif.; recipient Individual Achievement award Colo. State U. Coll. Engring., 1981. Fellow ASCE (v.p. Colorado Springs br. 1975, pres. 1978); mem. Nat. Soc. Profl. Engrs. (pres. Pikes Peak chpt. 1975, sec. Colo. sect. 1976, v.p. 1977, pres. 1979, 1978, Young Engr. 1976, Pres.'s award 1979), Cons. Engrs. Council Colo. (cert.; dir. 1981-83), Am. Cons. Engrs. Council, Profl. Land Surveyors Colo., Colorado Springs Homebuilders Assn., Colo. Water Congress, U.S. Com. Irrigation and Drainage, Colo. Engrs. Council (del. 1980—), Colo. State U. Alumni Assn. (v.p., dir. Pike's Peak chpt. 1972-76), Lancers, Lambda Chi Alpha. Mem. Ch. of Christ (dir. edn. 1969-71, deacon 1977—). Home: 7195 Dark Horse Pl Colorado Springs CO 80919 Office: 300 Garden of Gods Rd Suite 103 Colorado Springs CO 80907

WAXMAN, HENRY A., congressman; b. Los Angeles, Sept. 12, 1939; B.A. in Polit. Sci., UCLA, 1961, J.D., 1965; m. Janet Kessler, 1971; children—Carol Lynn, Michael David. Admitted to Calif. bar, 1965; mem. Calif. State Assembly, 3 terms; mem. 94th-96th Congresses from 24th Calif. dist. Office: 2418 Rayburn House Office Bldg Washington DC 20515*

WAY, H(AROLD) FRANK, political science educator; b. Chillicothe, Mo., Mar. 29, 1929; s. Harold Frank and Lola Irene (Porter) W; children—David, Madeline, Deborah. B.S., N.E. Mo. State U., 1951; M.A., Okla. State U., 1952; Ph.D., Cornell U., 1957. Asst. prof. political sci. U. Calif.-Riverside, 1957-64, assoc. prof., 1964-69, prof. 1969—, divisional dean social scis., 1968-70, asst. vice chancellor Acad. Affairs, 1969-73, chmn. dept. polit. sci., 1977—; referee Calif. State Bar Ct. Mem. Am. Polit. Sci. Assn., So. Calif. Polit. Sci. Assn. Democrat. Author: Criminal Justice and the American Constitution, 1980; Liberty in the Balance, 5th edit., 1980; editor (with others) Politics, 1971-72. Office: Dept Polit Sci U Calif Riverside CA 92521

WAYLAND, L. C. NEWTON, pub. health pediatrician; b. Plainview, Tex., May 4, 1909; s. Levi Clarence and Connie Onita (Newton) W.; student Wayland Coll., Plainview, 1925-26, West Tex. State Tchrs. Coll., 1926-30; A.B., Stanford U., 1932, M.D., 1936; postgrad. U. Calif. Med. Sch., Children's, Gen. hosps., Los Angeles; m. Helen Hart, June 18, 1938 (div. 1966); children—Newton, Elizabeth (Mrs. John Runnette), Constance. Intern, San Francisco City and County Hosp., Stanford Service, 1936; house officer San Mateo County Hosp., 1937, Children's Hosp., Los Angeles, 1938; dir. maternal and child health Santa Barbara (Calif.) County Health Dept., 1938-44; dir. health Santa Barbara City Schs., 1944-74; dir. health Santa Barbara City Coll., 1946-74; pvt. practice medicine specializing in pediatrics, 1955-70; ret. mem. pediatric staffs Santa Barbara Gen., St. Francis, Cottage, Goleta Valley hosps.; ret. med. cons. Calif. State Dept. Rehab., 1974-78; emeritus mem. med. staff Calif. State Prison at Soledad. Past non-nurse dir. exec. com., sch. nursing sect. Nat. Orgn. Pub. Health Nurses; past chmn. subcom. on legislation and enforcement Santa Barbara County Interagy. on Smoking and Health; past mem. adv. com. Calif. Dept. Edn. on Pub. Sch. Health; mem. Pub. Citizen Inc. Past 1st bd. dirs. Get Oil Out!; mem. vol. staff. Santa Barbara Zool. Gardens. Recipient award Calif. Sch. Nurses Orgn., 1965, 71. Fellow Am. Sch. Health Assn. (past pres. Calif. div., past mem. legis. com., past chmn. coms. Calif. div.), Am. Pub. Health Assn. (mem. com. on health standard for sch. personnel); mem. NEA (ret.), Calif. Tchrs. Assn., Calif. Med. Assn., Santa Barbara County Med. Soc., Am. Acad. Pediatrics, Santa Barbara, Los Angeles pediatric socs., World Council Chs., Nat. Council Chs. (founding mem. laymen's commn.), UN Assn. (past pres. Santa Barbara chpt.), Ams. for Democratic Action, NAACP, ACLU, So. Christian Leadership Conf., Calif. Congress Parents and Tchrs. (hon. life), Scholastic Socs. South, Assn. Am. Indian Affairs, Santa Barbara Democratic League (founding), Nat. Audubon Soc., Save the Redwoods League, Wilderness Soc., Isaac Walton League, Nat. Parks Assn., Sierra Club, So. Christian Leadership Conf., Cousteau Soc., Planned Parenthood Fedn. Am., Environ. Protective Assn., Trustees for Alaska, Fellowship Reconciliation, Inst. for Am. Democracy, Com. for Improvement Med. Care, SANE, Ams. for Indian Opportunity, Nat. Indian Youth Council, Am. Soc. Contemporary Medicine and Surgery, Nat. Wildlife Assn., Intern at Wildlife Assn., Riviera Assn. (past pres.), Common Cause, Episcopal Peace Fellowship, Fund for Peace, Nature Conservancy, Scenic Shoreline Preservation Conf., Nat. Trust for Historic Preservation, Santa Barbara Mus. Natural History, Friends of the Earth, Green Peace, Gray Panthers, Defenders of Wildlife, Internat. Physicians for Prevention of Nuclear War, Physicians for Social Responsibility, Nat. Urban League, Nat. Abortion Rights Action League, Freedom from Hunger Found., Alliance for Survival, Inst. Aerobic Research, Calif. Wilderness Coalition, Center War/Peace Studies, Action for Children's TV, Am. Farmland Trust, NOW, So. Poverty Law Center, United World Federalists, Zero Population Growth, Amnesty Internat., Council for Livable World, Clergymen and Laymen Concerned, Community Environ. Council, Am. Horse Protection Assn., Am. Fedn. Scientists, Planning and Conservation League Calif., Am. Indian Fund, Humane Soc. U.S., numerous others. Democrat. Episcopalian. Contbr. articles to ednl. and other profl. jours. Home: 1807 Paterna Rd Santa Barbara CA 93103

WAYMAN, LANCE RICHARD, computer systems executive; b. Sussex, Eng., Sept. 15, 1938; came to U.S., 1968, naturalized, 1974; m. Nien-Ling Tung, Dec. 17, 1966; children—Thomas, Peter. B.S., U. Melbourne (Australia), 1963; M.B.A., U. So. Calif., 1971. Indsl. engr. State Electricity Commn., Melbourne, 1964-66; works mgr. Humes Ltd., Melbourne, 1966-68; project engr. United Concrete Pipe, Baldwin Park, Calif., 1968-70; chief engr. Tecklenborg Corp., Signal Hill, Calif., 1970; cons. Theodore Barry & Assocs., Los Angeles, 1971-72, A.T. Kearney, Inc., Chgo., 1972-77; pres. Wayman & Assocs., Inc., Redondo Beach, Calif., 1977—. Mem. Inst. Engrs. Australia, Los Angeles C. of C. (indsl. devel. com.). Address: 217 S Pacific Coast Hwy Redondo Beach CA 90277

WAYNE, JUNE C., artist; b. Chgo., Mar. 8, 1918; d. Albert and Dorothy Alice (Kline) LaVine; D.F.A. (hon.), 1976. Indsl. designer, N.Y.C., 1939-41; radio writer, mem. staff sta. WGN, Chgo., 1942-43; founder, 1959, since dir. Tamarind Lithography Workshop, Inc., funded by Ford Found., Los Angeles; adviser Tamarind Inst., U. N.Mex., 1970—; mem. vis. com. Sch. Visual and Environ. Studies, Harvard, 1972-74; mem. chancellors adv. com., arts mgmt. program Grad. Sch. Adminstrn., UCLA 1969—. Numerous one-woman exhbns., 1935—, latest being Art Mus., U. N.Mex., 1968, Cin. Art Mus., 1969, Iowa Art Mus., U. Iowa, 1970, Grunwald Graphics Arts Found., UCLA, 1971, Municipal Art Gallery, Barnsdale Park, Los Angeles, 1973, Van Doren Gallery, San Francisco, 1974, La Demeure, Paris, 1974, Musée de Brest (France), 1976, Montgomery Gallery, Pomona Colls., Calif., 1978, 83, Ariz. State U. Galleries, 1978, ICA travelling exhbn., Rennes, 1976, Nancy, 1977, Brussels, 1978, Reims, 1978, Lyons, 1979, San Diego Mus. Art, 1981, Jewish Mus., N.Y.C., 1982, Frederick S. Wright Gallery, UCLA, 1982, Des Moines Art Ctr., 1982, Crocker Mus., Sacramento, 1982, Visual Arts Gallery, U. Ala., 1982, San Jose Inst. Contemporary Art, 1983; rep. permanent collections Library of Congress, Mus. Modern Art, N.Y.C., Art Inst. Chgo., Houghton Library at Harvard, Smithsonian Instn., Rosenwald Collection, Nat. Gallery Art, N.Y. Pub. Library, Cin. Art. Mus., Pasadena (Cal.) Mus. Art, Phila. Mus. Art, Phila. Print Club, Walker Art Center, Mpls.; bd. dirs. Grunwald Center Graphic Arts, 1965—. Recipient numerous prizes, 1950—, latest being Prix de la Biennal Internat. de L'Estampe d'Epinal, France, 1971, Purchase prize Biennal d'Epinal, 1973; Golden Eagle Cine award and Acad. award nomination for film Four Stones for Kanemitzu, 1974. Mem. Writers Guild Am., Women in Film, AFTRA, Women's Caucus for Art, Soc. Am. Graphic Artists, Soc. Washington Printmakers, Los Angeles Printmakers Soc. Contbr. articles to profl. publs.; subject TV programs. Address: 1108 N Tamarind Ave Los Angeles CA 90038

WEASE, GARLAND BRADLEY, city ofcl.; b. Aruba, Netherlands Antilles, July 1, 1939; s. Ivan John and Gladys Mae (Bradley) W. B.S., So. Ill. U., 1962; M.B.A., U. San Francisco, 1973. Employee relations analyst Bechtel Corp., San Francisco, 1969-70; mgmt. asst. Bur. Bldg. Repair, San Francisco, 1972-73; sr. mgmt. asst. Mission Mental Health Center, San Francisco, 1973-77; departmental personnel officer San Francisco Internat. Airport, 1977-78; sr. mgmt. asst. Bur. Street Cleaning, San Francisco, 1978-82. Mem. youth services budget panel United Way, 1976; mem. Nat. Republican Congl. Com., Rep. Nat. Com., U.S. Def. Com. Served with USAF, 1962-68; capt. Res. (ret.). Mem. Res. Officers Assn., Air Force Assn., Am. Bowling Congress. U.S. Democrat. Home: 1169 Market St Apt 347 San Francisco CA 94103

WEATHERFORD, SYVILA, elec. engr.; b. Los Angeles, Dec. 2, 1951; d. James Emmett and Berniece W.; B.S.E.E., MIT, 1973; M.S.E.E., U. So. Calif., 1975; postgrad. Loyola-Marymount. Engring. instr. Howard U., Washington, 1975-76; digital design engr. Hughes Aircraft, Culver City, Calif., 1973-75; mgr. engring. project office Xerox, El Segundo, Calif., 1976—; lectr. profl. devel. seminar Bd. dirs. Ebonics, v.p., 1982-83. Hughes fellow, 1973-75; Delta Sigma Theta scholar, 1967-73. Mem. Los Angeles Council Black Profl. Engrs. (pres. 1980-82), IEEE, Black Women's Forum, Los Angeles Leadership Coalition, Western Regional Black Engring. and Sci. Council (chmn. 1983-84). Methodist Episcopal. Office: Xerox 830 Nash St N1-01 El Segundo CA 90245

WEATHERILL, ANNE SHARON, historical society executive; b. Ft. Lewis, Wash., Sept. 22, 1945; d. Kenneth M. and Mary H. (Smith) Roberts; m. James Vincent Weatherill, Dec. 20, 1966; children—Maryanne Marie, Christine Rose. B.A., U. Calif.-Riverside, 1969. Adminstrv. asst. Nez Perce County Hist. Soc., 1980-81, exec. dir., 1981—. Recipient Wakan Camp Fire award for exceptional and imaginative leadership and service to youth, 1980. Mem. Am. Assn. Museums, Hellsgate Graphics Assn. Home: 2178 23d St Clarkston WA 99403 Office: 3d and C Sts Lewiston ID 83501

WEATHERS, DANIEL JOSEPH, business exec.; b. Kansas City, Mo., Oct. 14, 1945; s. James Arthur and Lorraine Verdun (Moberly) W.; B.A., Central Mo. State U., 1971, M.S., 1972; children—Kari Beth, Tad Daniel. Grad. asst. Central Mo. State U., Warrensburg, 1970-71, instr. indsl. hygiene and indsl. safety, 1972-73; safety engr. chasis and automotive assembly div. Ford Motor Co., Detroit, 1973-75; corp. sr. safety engr. Kerr McGee Corp., Oklahoma City, 1975-79; mgr. corp. safety Utah Internat. Inc., San Francisco, 1979—. Served with USAF, 1966-70. Cert. safety profl. and hazard control mgr. master level. Mem. Am. Soc. Safety Engrs. (profl.), Mine Insps. Inst. Am. (bd. dirs.), N.W. Mining Assn., World Safety Orgn., Am. Mining Congress (coal mine safety com., metal and nonmetallic mine safety com., cons. resolution com.), Nat. Safety Council (exec. com. mining sect., William H. Cameron cert. of recognition 1976-77, William H. Cameron award 1978-79, 81-82), Phi Kappa Phi. Clubs: No. Calif. Golf Assn., Toastmasters Internat. (competent Toastmaster, community service award 1974). Author articles. Home: 350 Arbullo Dr San Francisco CA 94132 Office: 550 California San Francisco CA 94104

WEAVER, CYNTHIA LOUISE, biostatistician; b. Monterey Park, Calif., May 8, 1956; d. Thomas Lewis and Evon Jeannette (Frederickson) W. B.A. cum laude in Math., U. Calif.-Irvine, 1978; M.S. in Biostats., UCLA, 1980. Biostatistician, Sch. Pub. Health, UCLA, 1980—. Mem. Planetary Soc., Cousteau Soc., Am. Statis. Assn.

WEAVER, ELLSWORTH ELIAS, educator; b. Los Angeles, July 12, 1903; s. Ellsworth J. and Eliza (Culley) W.; student Weber Coll., Ogden, Utah, 1921-23; B.S., U. Utah, 1937, M.S., 1938; Ph.D., N.Y. U., 1953; m. Bessie Mickelson, Aug. 30, 1939; children—John, Ruth, Jared, Mary Lou, Joe. Grad. asst. N.Y. U., 1937-40; lectr. U. Utah, 1947-48, asst. prof., 1948-53, field rep. Inst. Govt., 1948-61, dir., 1961-72, asso. prof., 1953-57, prof., 1957-72, prof. emeritus, 1972—, chmn. dept. polit. sci., 1966-68; cons. Interstate Assn. Public Lands Counties, 1970-80; mem. exec. com. Conf. Univ. Burs. Govtl. Research. Cons. Utah Mcpl. League, 1950-58, 62-72, Utah Assn. County Ofcls., 1950-68, mem. Local Govt. Survey Commn. State Utah, 1955-57; mem. Com. Local Govt. Utah Legislative Council, 1957-59. Sec., Weber County Democratic Com., 1928-31. Served with AUS, 1933-35, 40-47; mil. gov., Korea, 1946-47. Mem. Am. Soc. Pub. Adminstrn., Am., Western polit. sci. assns., Utah Acad. Sci., Arts and Letters, Govtl. Research Assn., Tau Kappa Alpha. Delta Phi. Mormon (missionary 1923-25). Author: Revised Ordinances Midvale City, 1951; Legislative Apportionment in Utah, 1951; Revised Ordinances Town of Loa, 1955. Mng. editor: Western Polit. Quar., 1956-71. Home: 1370 Gilmer Dr Salt Lake City UT 84105

WEAVER, JAMES, congressman; b. Brookings, S.D., Aug. 8, 1927; s. Leo C. and Alice (Flittie) W.; B.S. in Polit. Sci., U. Oreg., 1952; m. Sally Cummins, June 11, 1955; children—Regan, Allison, Sarah; m. 2d, Jane Seegal, Apr. 1981. Pub.'s rep., 1954-58; staff dir. Oreg. Legis. Interim Com. Agr., 1959-60; builder, developer office and apt. bldg. complexes, 1960—; mem. 94th-98th Congresses from 4th Oreg. dist., chmn. forests subcom., 1977-83, chmn. House interior com. on investigation Three Mile Island nuclear mishap, chmn. subcom. on mining, forest mgmt., and Bonneville Power Adminstrn., 1983 active supporter Wilderness and environ. protection legislation. Del. Democratic Nat. Conv., 1960, 64. Served with USN, World War II. Recipient Neuberger award for service to environment Oreg. Environ. Council; Champion of West award for promotion alt. energy devel. Wood Energy Inst. Office: 1226 Longworth House Office Bldg Washington DC 20515

WEAVER, JOHN CARRIER, univ. pres. emeritus; b. Evanston, Ill., May 21, 1915; s. Andrew Thomas and Cornelia Myrta (Carrier) W.; A.B., U. Wis., 1936, A.M., 1937, Ph.D., 1942; LL.D., Mercer U., 1972, L.H.D., St. Scholastica, 1973; Litt.D., Drury Coll., 1973; m. Ruberta Louise Harwell, Aug. 8, 1940; children—Andrew Bennett, Thomas Harwell. Mem. editorial and research staff Am. Geog. Soc. of N.Y., 1940-42; mem. research staff Office of Geographer, U.S. Dept. State, 1942-44; asst. prof. dept. geography U. Minn., 1946-47, assoc. prof., 1947-48, prof., 1948-55; prof. geography, dean Sch. Arts and Sci., Kans. State U., 1955-57; prof. geography, dean grad. coll. U. Nebr., 1957-61, v.p. research, dean grad. coll., prof. geography State U. Iowa, 1961-64; v.p. acad. affairs, dean faculties, prof. geography Ohio State U., Columbus, 1964-66; pres., prof. geography U. Mo., 1966-70, U. Wis., 71; pres. U. Wis. System, 1971-77, emeritus, 1977—; prof. geography U. Wis. Milw., Madison, Green Bay, 1971-78; hon. prof. geography U. Wis. at Oshkosh; Disting. prof. U. So. Calif., 1977—, exec. dir. Center for Study of Am. Experience, 1978-81; research cons. Midwest Barley Improvement Assn., Milw., 1946-50; expert cons. to Com. on Geophysics and Geography, Research and Devel. Bd., Washington, 1947-53; mem. adv. com. on geography Office Naval Research, NRC, 1949-52, chmn., 1951-52; vis. prof. U. Oreg., summer 1951, Harvard U., summer

1954; cons. editor McGraw-Hill series in geography, 1951-67; mem. adv. com. to sec. HEW, 1958-62; mem. Mid-Am. State U. Assn., 1959-70, chmn., 1959-61, 70-71; chmn. Council Grad. Schs. U.S., 1961-62; mem. Woodrow Wilson fellow selection com., 1961-70; mem. com. instl. coop. Univs. Western Conf. and Chgo., 1962-66, chmn., 1964-66; pres. Assn. Grad. Schs. in Assn. Am. Univs., 1963-64; Wilton Park fellow Brit. Fgn. Office, 1965, 67, 70, 74, 76; mem. Am. Council on Pharm. Edn., 1964-77; mem. Mo. Commn. of Higher Edn., 1966-70; mem. White House Task Force on Priorities in Higher Edn., 1969-70; mem. Edn. Commn. of States, 1971-77. Bd. dirs. Harry S. Truman Library Inst. Nat. and Internat. Affairs, 1967-70, trustee Nat. Com. on Accreditation, 1966-76, Johnson Found., Racine, Wis., 1971-77, 80-83. Am. Univs. Field Service, 1971-75, Nat. Merit Scholarship Corp., 1971-77, 80-82; mem. Postmaster Gen.'s Citizen's Stamp Adv. Com., Washington, 1981—; chmn. Nat. Task Force on Pharmacy Edn., Am. Pharm. Assn., 1981—. Served as lt. (j.g.) USNR, 1944-46; assigned specialist Hydrographic Office, Office of Chief of Naval Ops., Washington. Recipient Vilas medal U. Wis., 1936, Letter Commendation from Chief of Naval Ops., 1946; Carnegie Found. adminstrv. fellow, 1957-58. Fellow Am. Geog. Soc. (trustee 1974—), AAAS; mem Assn. Am. Geographers (council 1949-51, Nat. Research award 1955), Am. Geophys. Union, Arctic Inst. N.Am. (charter asso.) Am. Polar Soc., Internat. Geog. Union, Am. Pharm. Assn. (hon.), Wis. Hist. Soc., Am. Friends of Wilton Park (pres. 1979-80), Phi Beta Kappa, Sigma Xi, Phi Kappa Phi, Delta Sigma Rho, Phi Eta Sigma, Chi Phi, Alpha Kappa Psi. Congregationalist. Author: Ice Atlas of the Northern Hemisphere, 1946; American Barley Production; A Study in Agricultural Geography 1950; A Statistical World Survey of Commercial Production; A Geographical Sourcebook (with Fred E. Lukerman), 1953; The American Railroads, 1958; Minnesota and Wisconsin, 1961; illustrator: Quiet Thoughts, 1972; contbr. articles to books and profl. periodicals; contbg. editor Geog. Rev., 1955-70. Home: 2978 Crownview Dr Rancho Palos Verdes CA 90274

WEAVER, JOSEPH WALTER, JR., real estate investments executive, physician; b. Atlanta, Sept. 4, 1913; s. Joseph Walter and Zana Valrie (Crumley) W.; m. Mary Price Woodroe, July 3, 1934; children—Joseph William, James Woodroe. B.S., Duke U., 1936; M.D., Tulane U., 1937. Intern, resident in internal medicine U. Hosp., Augusta, Ga., 1937-41; commd. lt. (j.g.) M.C., U.S. Navy, 1941, advanced through grades to capt., 1955; comdg. officer Naval Aerospace Med. Inst., Pensacola, Fla., 1967-69, force surgeon Naval Air Force, Pacific Fleet, 1969-72, ret., 1972; pres. PSW Enterprises, Coronado, Calif., 1972—. Del., Calif. State Republican Conv., 1980. Fellow Aerospace Med. Assn. (exec. council 1964-65). Club: Coronado Rotary (pres. 1981-82, Paul Harris fellow 1978—). Home: 821 Country Club Ln Coronado CA 92118 Office: PSW Enterprises PO Box 712 Coronado CA 92118

WEAVER, ROBIN BALES, social services administrator; b. Kansas City, Mo., Jan. 10, 1935; d. Harold Matthews and Dorothy Elizabeth (Rodgers) Bales; children—Brian Durant, Mark Allison, Kent Patterson, Stuart Graham. B.S. in Sci. Health Edn. magna cum laude, Utah State U. Ops. supr./programmer Hesston Corp., Logan, Utah, 1972-76; agt., asst. dist. mgr. Equitable Life Assurance, Logan, 1976-79; program dir. Tri-County Planned Parenthood Facility, Logan, 1979-82; dir., educator Bear River div. Utah Alcoholism Found., Logan 1982—. Chmn., Council on Alcoholism, 1979-80; adv. bd. Voluntary Action Ctr., 1980-82; mem. Hospice Tng. Team, Human Resources Council. Recipient West Central Div. Champion award Equitable Life; Women Leaders Round Table award Nat. Assn. Life Underwriters. Mem. Am. Sch. Health., Logan Bus. and Profl. Women. Democrat. Mormon.

WEBB, ALBERT DINSMOOR, enologist; b. Victorville, Calif., Oct. 10, 1917; s. Ralph Hough and Harriet Vida (Dinsmoor) W.; m. Nancy May Mathews, Sept. 5, 1943; children—Robert, Bradford. Ph.D., U. Calif.-Berkeley, 1948; Docteur h.c., U. Bordeaux, 1982. From asst. prof. to prof., from asst. chemist to chemist Experiment Sta., U. Calif.-Davis, chmn. dept. viticulture and enology, 1973-81, prof. emeritus, 1982—. Mem. Am. Soc. Enologists, Am. Chem. Soc., AAAS, Phytochem. Soc. N.Am., Med. Friends of Wine, Sigma Xi.

WEBB, JOHN FRANKLIN, JR., lawyer; b. Houston, Sept. 7, 1933; s. John Franklin and Newell Ann (Bretherton) W.; m. Kathleen Ewing, Nov. 10, 1956; children—Antonia Elizabeth, Leslie Kaa. B.A., J.D., Baylor U., 1956. Bar: Tex. 1956, Colo. 1977, U.S. Supreme Ct. 1964. Enlisted U.S. Army, 1956; advanced through grades to lt. col., 1969; judge advocate U.S., Europe, Asia, 1956-77; ret. 1977; assoc. J.E. Kuttler, P.C., Aurora, Colo., 1977-79; ptnr. Treece, Zbar and Webb, P.C., Littleton, Colo., 1979-82; individual practice law, Littleton, 1982—. Decorated Legion of Merit with 3 oak leaf clusters, Bronze Star, Army Commendation medal with oak leaf cluster. Republican. Mem. Disciples Christ. Home: 6313 E Emporia Circle Englewood CO 80111 Office: 2060 W Littleton Blvd Littleton CO 80120

WEBB, JUANITA IRENE FOGELSTROM, assistant principal, management consultant; b. Albany, Calif., May 8, 1952; d. James Carl and Mildred I. (McDougal) Fogelstrom; m. Thomas J. Webb, July 11, 1981. A.A., Skyline Coll., San Bruno, Calif., 1972; B.S. in Bus. Adminstrn., Biola Coll., La Mirada, Calif., 1976; postgrad., Talbot Theol. Sem., La Mirada, 1978—. Personnel interviewer, tng. mgr. Broadway Dept. Stores, So. Calif., 1976-79; asst. prin. Whittier (Calif.) Christian High Sch., 1979—; condr. leadership tng. seminars; cons. women's groups. Recipient Edn. award Bank of Am., 1970. Baptist. Office: Whittier Christian High Sch PO Box 1307 Whittier CA 90609

WEBB, LEONARD LEON, education evaluation systems executive; author; b. Larned, Kans., Sept. 10, 1937; s. Leonard Scott and Almyra Lovica (Goalden) W.; m. LuAnna Leavitt, Sept. 14, 1963; children—Lynnette, Layne, Leslie, Lee, LeAnn, Lance, Lynne. A.S., Dixie Coll., 1961; B.S., U. Utah, 1964, M.S. in Edn., 1965; postgrad. Stanford U., 1968; Ph.D. in Edn., Brigham Young U., 1969. Math and sci. tchr., Mesquite, Nev., 1964-67; Ford Found. fellow, 1967-68; dir. research and evaluation Scottsdale (Ariz.) Schs., 1969-73; dir. Ariz. Consortium Individualized Learning, 1973—; pres. Ednl. Evaluation Systems, Inc., Mesa, Ariz., 1977—, Ednl. Diffusion Systems, Inc., Mesa, 1977—, dir. Ariz. State Facilitator Project, U.S. Dept. Edn., Mesa, 1977—; pres. Webb Enterprises, Mesa, 1981—, Sun Internat., Mesa, 1983—, Computer Directions Inc., Mesa, 1983—; dir. Conceptually Oriented Math Program, U.S. Dept. Edn., 1982—. Active Boy Scouts Am., YMCA, other youth groups. Served with USN, 1955-58. NSF fellow 1964. Mem. Nev. Edn. Assn. (legis. chmn. 1965-68), Valley Ednl. Research Assn. (pres. 1971-73), Nat. Dissemination Study Group (pres. 1981—), Ariz. Assn. Supervision and Curriculum Devel., Assn. Supervision and Curriculum Devel., Nat. Council Tchrs. Math, Ariz. Assn. Sch. Adminstrs. Republican. Mormon. Contbr. research monographs, numerous articles to nat. jours. Office: 161 E 1st St #5 Mesa AZ 85201

WEBB, PATRICIA SHIRLEY, journalist, public relations counselor; b. Southampton, N.Y., Dec. 9, 1949; d. Frank A. and Leona C. (Deegan) Belson; m. James F. Webb, Jr., Mar. 22, 1969; children—Michelle M., James P. A.A., Honolulu Community Coll., 1980; B.A. in Journalism, U. Hawaii-Manoa, 1982. Asst. to sports info. dir., women's athletics dept. U. Hawaii-Manoa, 1981; account asst. in pub. relations Fawcett McDermott Cavanagh, Inc., 1981—; journal intern Hawaii Statewide Vol. Services, 1982. Carol Burnett Fund for Responsible Journalism grantee, 1983. Mem. Pub. Relations Soc. Am., Sigma Delta Chi. Roman Catholic.

WEBB, RUTH THEA, talent agent; b. N.Y.C., Mar. 17; d. Harry A. and Helen (Dentler) Ford; m. John Cother Webb, Jan. 15, 1942 (div. 1948); m. 2d, Richard Ober, July 1, 1948 (div. 1950); m. 3d, Albert Benjamin, Oct. 17, 1953 (div. 1958); m. 4th, Robert Cosden (div.); children—Jack Webb, Mike Webb. Student St. Petersburg Jr. Coll.; studied acting with Mary Ann Dentler, Lorna Carroll, St. Petersburg; studied singing with Helen Ford, N.Y.C., Leon Rothier, N.Y.C., 1942, Thelma Gainsborough, N.Y.C., 1961, Robert Kobin, N.Y.C., 1962. Profl. actress, singer, 1935-62; talent rep. Laura Arnold Agy., N.Y.C., 1962; prin. Ruth Webb Agy., N.Y.C., 1963; ptnr. Webb-Cosden Agy., N.Y.C., 1963-71; owner, operator Ruth Webb Enterprises Inc., Hollywood, Calif., 1971—. Mem. Actors' Equity Assn., AFTRA, AGVA Screen Actors Guild Associated Talent Agts. Mem. Ch. of Religious Science. Exclusive agt. for Mickey Rooney, other clients include Martha Raye, Robert Alda, Gene Barry, Terry Moore, Miame Van Doren and Kathryn Grayson. Home and Office: 7500 Devista Dr Los Angeles CA 90046

WEBB, VALORIS, social worker, educator; b. Riverton, Utah, June 21, 1926; d. Vernal Charles and Margaret Ellen (Niemann) Webb. B.S., U. Utah, 1949. Cert. elem. tchr., supr. social work, adminstr., Utah; lic. clin., cert. social worker, marriage and family counselor. Elem. tchr., 1952-54; tchr. homebound, hospitalized students, 1954-55; remedial reading tchr., 1955-57; social worker, 1958-65; supervising social worker, 1965-69; dir. guidance services Jordan Sch. Dist., Sandy, Utah, 1969-76, curriculum cons., 1976-77, dir. chpt. 1 programs, 1977—; field instr. Grad. Sch. Social Work, U. Utah, 1960-69. Chmn. mental health Utah Congress PTA; former pres. Utah chpt. Sch. Social Workers; mem. adv. bd. Murray Jordan Mental Health Centro. Mem. Nat. Assn. Supervision and Curriculum Devel., Nat. Assn. Social Workers, Internat. Reading Assn., NEA, AAUW, Delta Gamma, Phi Kappa Phi, Alpha Delta Kappa, Delta Kappa Gamma, Phi Delta Kappa. Mormon. Club: Wasatch Br. Office: Jordan Sch Dist 9361 S Fourth St E Sandy UT 84070

WEBB, WILLIAM CLEMENT, clergyman; b. Aransas Pass, Tex., Aug. 14, 1963; s. William Vernon and Maxine (Jordan) W.; B.A., Belmont Coll., 1968; M.Div., Midwestern Baptist Theol. Sem., 1971; M.A., U. No. Colo., 1976; m. Debra Ann Keenan, Dec. 15, 1972; children—Melinda Joy, Kristi Lin. Dir. transp. Kemmerer (Wyo.) Sch. Dist. 1, 1973-74; ordained to ministry So. Bapt. Ch., 1964; pastor First Bapt. Ch., Kemmerer, 1973-74, First Bapt. Ch., Bamberg, W.Ger., 1974, Meml. Bapt. Ch., Wheatland, Wyo., 1975-76; social worker Platte County Dept. Social Services, Wheatland, 1975-76; counselor, chaplain Union Mission Settlement, Charleston, W.Va., 1976-77; dir. Nome (Alaska) Bapt. Ministries, 1977-83; clin. services dir. Alaska Bapt. Family Service Ctr., Anchorage, 1983—. Publicity chmn. Wyo. Human Resouces Confedn., 1975-76; bd. dirs. Nome chpt. ARC, 1978. Mem. Am. Personnel and Guidance Assn., Am. Assn. Rehab. Counselors, Assn. Counselor Edn. and Supervision, Am. Assn. Specialists in Group Work, Am. Council on Alcohol Problems. Democrat. Clubs: Rotary, Masons. Home: SRA Box 4106H Anchorage AK 99502 Office: SRA Box 1791-A Anchorage AK 99507

WEBBER, KIKANZA NURI, educator; b. Boston, Jan. 3, 1950; d. Winston Hersley Robins and Barbara Estelle (Latimer) Brown; B.A., M.A., Occidental Coll., 1972; Ed.D., U. So. Calif., 1982. m. John Arthur Webber. Head tchr. Kawaida Ednl. and Devel. Ctr., Los Angeles, 1972-75; coordinator Los Angeles Semester program Sch. Pub. Adminstrn. U. So. Calif., 1976-79; adj. prof. edn. U. Redlands, 1977; cons. Desegregation Tng. Inst., Calif. State U., Northridge, 1978-82; lectr. ethnic studies U. So. Calif., 1978-82; owner Nuri Webber Assocs. Cons. Services; cons. in field. Pres. bd. dirs. People Coordinated Services, Los Angeles. Mem. Am. Speech and Hearing Assn., Sociology of Edn. Assn., Nat. Soc. Study of Edn., Assn. Supervision and Curriculum Devel., Nat. Alliance Black Sch. Educators, Los Angeles Alliance Black Sch. Educators (pres.), Phi Delta Kappa. Contbr. articles to profl. jours., confs. Office: PO Box 35096 Los Angeles CA 90035

WEBBER, LURANCE MARCINE, chemist; b. Oroville, Calif., Oct. 20, 1931; s. Herbert Earl and Lura Uldine (Bethel) W.; B.A., Calif. State U., Chico, 1956; M.S., Ill. Inst. Tech., 1962; Ph.D., U. Calif., Santa Barbara, 1970. Chemist, Thiokol Corp., Brigham City, Utah, 1961-63, U. Calif., Santa Barbara, 1970-72, Wadsworth VA Hosp., Los Angeles, 1972-73; research asso. U. New Orleans, 1974-77; public health chemist Calif. Dept. Health Services, Berkeley, 1978—. Served with U.S. Army, 1953-55. Vis. scholar, U. Calif., Berkeley, 1979. Mem. Am. Chem. Soc. Condr. research on pollution analysis. Office: 2151 Berkeley Way Berkeley CA 94709

WEBBER, MUKTA MALA MAINI, cancer research scientist; b. Abbottabad, India, Dec. 5, 1937; d. Hari Singh and Inder (Kahai) Maini; B.Sc., Agra. U., India, 1957, M.Sc., 1959; Ph.D., U. Sask and Queen's U., Kingston, Ont., 1963; diploma in electron microscopy, U. Toronto, 1968; m. Patrick J. Webber, Sept. 28, 1963; 1 dau., Michelle. Cancer research scientist Roswell Park Meml. Inst., Buffalo, 1962-63; lectr. histology and embryology Queen's U., 1963-65, research assoc. urogenital oncology, 1965-68; sr. instr. urology U. Colo. Sch. Medicine, Denver, 1971, asst. prof., dir. research, 1972-78, asst. prof. biochemistry, biophysics and genetics, 1977-79, assoc. prof., dir. research div. urology, 1978—; cadre mem. Nat. Prostatic Cancer Project, Nat Cancer Inst., NIH, HEW, 1979—; co-convener workshop on environ. monitoring of radiation with biol. systems, 1978; mem. council Boulder Centennial/Bicentennial Council on Cancer Prevention, Colo. div. Am. Cancer Soc., 1976. Recipient research award Am. Urol. Assn., 1966, 1st prize for sci. exhibit, 1973, 74, 75; Internat. Union Against Cancer, Cancer Research Tech. Transfer grantee, 1980; Am. Cancer Soc. research grantee, 1973-78; Nat. Cancer Inst. grantee, 1976—. Mem. AAAS, Am. Assn. Cancer Research, Am. Soc. Cell Biology, Electron Microscopy Soc. Am., N.Y. Acad. Scis., Tissue Culture Assn., AAUP, Sigma Xi. Reviewing editor In Vitro, Jour. Tissue Culture Assn., 1980-81; contbr. articles and revs. to profl. jours., chpts. to books; research on etiology and prevention of benign and malignant tumors of prostate in man, in vitro cell models for studies on aging, carcinogenesis and growth control, role of hormones, vitamins and polyamines in growth regulation, health hazards of metals as environ. pollutants. Office: Div of Urology Box C 319 U Colo Health Scis Center 4200 E 9th Ave Denver CO 80262

WEBER, FRANK ALBERT, aluminum extrusion company executive; b. Peoria, Ill., July 27, 1918; s. Frank Albert and Mildred Alice Weber; B.S. in Gen. Engring., U. Ill., 1942; m. Betty Louise Seffer, Nov. 2, 1940; children—David, Barbara, Frank Albert III. Engr., Firestone Tire Corp., 1942-47; product devel. mgr. Weather Seal Co., Barberton, Ohio, 1947-55; with Reynolds Metals Co., Louisville, 1955-65, Olin Aluminum Co., City of Industry, Calif., 1965-73; v.p., gen. mgr. Extrusions Unltd., Perris, Calif., 1973-82, ret., 1982. Active Jr. Achievement, 1943-54, United Fund, 1970. Republican. Home: 1532 N Mountain St Claremont CA 91711

WEBER, GEORGE RICHARD, accountant, author; b. The Dalles, Oreg., Feb. 7, 1929; s. Richard Merle and Maud (Winchell) W.; B.S., Oreg. State U., 1950; M.B.A., U. Oreg., 1962; m. Nadine Hanson, Oct. 12, 1957; children—Elizabeth Ann Weber Katooli, Karen Louise, Linda Marie. Sr. trainee U.S. Nat. Bank of Portland (Oreg.), 1950-51; jr. acct. Ben Musa, C.P.A., The Dalles, 1954; tax and audit asst. Price Waterhouse, Portland, 1955-59; sr. acct. Burton M. Smith, C.P.A., Portland, 1959-62; pvt. C.P.A. practice, Portland, 1962—; lectr. acctg. Portland State Coll. Sec.-treas. Mt. Hood Kiwanis Camp, Inc., 1965. Exec. counselor SBA; mem. fin. com. U.S. Powerlifting Fedn. Served with AUS, 1951-53. Decorated Bronze Star; C.P.A., Oreg. Mem. Am. Inst. C.P.A.s, Internat. Platform Assn., Beta Alpha Psi, Pi Kappa Alpha. Republican. Episcopalian. Clubs: Kiwanis, Portland Track, City (Portland); Multnomah Athletic; Sunrise Toastmasters. Contbr. to profl. publs. and poetry jours. Home: 2603 NE 32d Ave Portland OR 97212 Office: 5520 SW Macadam St Portland OR 97201

WEBER, HAROLD CHRISTIAN, emeritus chemical engineering educator; b. Boston, Mar. 20, 1895; s. Christian and Ellen (Arnold) W.; B.S., MIT, 1918; Sc.D., Eidgenossische Technische Hochschule, Zurich, Switzerland, 1935; Sc.D., Suffolk U., 1963; m. Madeleine A. Duffy, Nov. 14, 1931 (dec. Apr. 1960); m. 2d, Marian F. Shaughness, Apr. 18, 1963. Cons., Walker, Lewis, McAdams & Knowland, Boston, 1919-20; prof. chem. engring. Mass. Inst. Tech., 1920-65, prof. emeritus, 1965—; cons. in oil, textiles, paper, mech. and electronic equipment, 1925—. Tech. adviser Chem. Warfare Service, 1941-45; chief sci. adviser U.S. Army, 1958-66; mem. Army Sci. Adv. Panel, 1954-74. Served as 2d lt. Chem. Warfare Service, U.S. Army, 1918-19. Recipient Presdl. certificate of merit for work in World War II, 1947, Chem. Corps certificate of merit, 1958, Army Meritorious Civilian Service award, 1959, Army Distinguished Service award, 1966. Fellow AAAS, Am. Acad. Arts and Scis., Am. Inst. Chem. Engrs.; mem. Am. Chem. Soc., Sigma Xi, Tau Beta Pi. Roman Catholic. Author: Thermodynamics for Chemical Engineers, 1939, 2d edit., 1958; also thermodynamics sect. in Marks' Mechanical Engineers Handbook, 1950. Patentee in field of electronics and petroleum. Home: La Hacienda Apt F179 10333 W Olive Peoria AZ 85345

WEBER, HERSCHEL L., automobile agy. exec.; b. Madison, Wis., Oct. 7, 1943; s. Louis A. and Nellie I. W.; student U. Wis., Whitewater, 1961-62, Madison Area Tech. Coll., 1967-69. Ins. salesman, 1971-75; portrait salesman, 1975-76; fin. and ins. mgr. Don Sharp Motor Imports Inc., Carlsbad, Calif., 1976—. Served with Army NG, 1964-70. Mem. Ind. Order Foresters. Home: 2155 Manchester Ave Cardiff by the Sea CA 92007 Office: 5500 Paseo del Norte Carlsbad CA 92008

WEBER, JEAN MACPHAIL, museum director; b. Boston, Apr. 2, 1933; d. Harold and Dorothy (Mutch) MacPhail; children—Julia Lee, Karin MacPhail, Laurie Stewart. A.B. in Art History magna cum laude, Brown U., 1954; student R.I. Sch. Design, 1950-52, Edinburgh (Scotland) U., 1952-53; postgrad. U. Iowa, 1954-55. Dir., Jr. Art Galley, Louisville, 1965-69, Parrish Art Mus., Southampton, N.Y., Rochester (N.Y.) Mus., 1978-80, Mus. of N.Mex., Santa Fe, 1981—; adj. prof. Southampton Coll., 1971-76; co-dir. Mus. Mgmt. Inst., U. Calif.-Berkeley, 1981. Vice pres. N.E. Museums Conf., pres., 1976-78; pres. L.I. Mus. Assn., 1977-78. Bd. dirs. Inter Pueblo Cultural Ctr., 1981-82; mem. Nat. Mus. Art Adv. Council, 1980—; del State Dept. Cultural Exchange to China, 1981. Trustee Brown U., 1983—. Mem. Assn. Am. Museums (mem. accreditation commn. 1976—, chmn. 1982), Mountain Plains Mus. Assn., N.Mex. Mus. Assn. Contbr. articles to profl. jours. Address: Mus of New Mexico Box 2087 Santa Fe NM 87503

WEBER, JOSEPH JAMES, management consultant; b. Lorain, Ohio, Aug. 12, 1942; s. Joseph Sylvester and Loyola Ruth (Oberst) W.; m. Cherla Dee Kellogg, Jan. 29, 1966; 1 son, Shane Joseph Jack; m. 2d, Joanne Carol Kenagy, Oct. 18, 1975. B.S., Bowling Green U., 1964, M.A., 1966. Lic. psychologist, Ill. Mental health counselor Ill. Dept. Mental Health, 1968-70; psychologist, dir. clin. services, asst. dir., resdl. dir. Ill. Dept. Corrections, 1970-80; mgmt. cons. Contact, Inc., Tucson, 1980—. Served to lt. USAR, 1966-68. Mem. Am. Psychol. Assn. Home: 7700 N Lundberg Dr Tucson AZ 85741 Office: N Country Club Tucson AZ 85716

WEBER, LARRY GLENN, sales and marketing company executive, real estate sales company executive; b. Los Angeles, July 5, 1951; s. Carl and Frances Helene (Tullius) W. B.A., U. So. Calif., 1973, M.B.A., 1976. Salesman, Mktg. West, Inc., North Hollywood, Calif., 1976-78, product mgr., 1978-79, sales mgr., 1979-80, sec.-treas., 1980—; sec.-treas., owner/ptnr. Ind. Rep. Sales, Inc., North Hollywood, Calif., 1980—, Premium Sales & Distbg., Inc., North Hollywood, 1980—; v.p. Weber & Assocs. Real Estate, Inc., Gardena, Calif., 1978—. Mem. Los Solteros, 1981—, v.p., 1983. Named Salesman of Year, Mktg. West, Inc., 1976, 77, Millionare's Club, 1980, 81, Multi-Millionaire's Club, 1982, Mgr. of Year, 1982; Sales Performance award Sanyo Electric Inc., 1981. Mem. Calif. Assn. Realtors, Gardena Bd. Realtors, U. So. Calif. M.B.A. Alumni Assn., U. So. Calif. Gen. Alumni Assn., Mensa, Theta Xi. Democrat. Roman Catholic. Club: U.S. Ski Assn. Office: 13333 Saticoy St North Hollywood CA 91605

WEBER, LAVERN JOHN, marine scientist, educator; b. Isabel, S.D., June 7, 1933; s. Jacob and Irene (Bock) W.; m. Shirley Jean Carlson, June 19, 1959; children—Timothy, Peter, Pamela, Elizabeth. B.A. Pacific Luth. U., 1958; M.S., U. Wash., 1962, Ph.D., 1964. Asst. prof., U. Wash., 1967-69; assoc. prof. Oreg. State U., Corvallis, 1969-75, prof., 1976—, asst. dean grad. sch., 1974-77, dir. Marine Sci. Ctr., Newport, 1977—. Mem. Am. Soc. Pharmacology and Exptl. Therapeutics, Soc. Toxicology, Soc. Exptl. Biology and Medicine. Club: Rotary Internat. Editor Aquatic Toxicology, Vol. I, 1982. Contbr. numerous articles to profl. jours.

WEBER, ROBERT SYCKS, naval officer; b. Cin., Mar. 16, 1944; s. Robert Herman and Maya (Sycks) W.; m. Melody Myers, Oct. 19, 1977; children—Ashley, Holly, Susan. B.S. in Mgmt. Analysis, U. W. Fla., 1976; M.B.A., Chapman Coll., 1979. Enlisted in U.S. Navy, 1963, commd. ensign, 1965, advanced through grades to comdr.; maintenance officer, ops. officer VAQ131, 1977-79, exec. officer, comdg. officer VAQ132, 1981—. Instr. organizational psychology U. W. Fla. Adviser Air Explorers, Boy Scouts Am., Penscola, Fla.; mem. safety com. FAA; coordinator events Oak Harbor Spl. Olympics. Decorated Air medal with 7 gold stars, Navy Commendation medal; Vietnamese Air Cross of Gallantry; named Instr. of Yr., Tng. Squadron 4, 1974. Mem. Assn. Naval Aviation. Clubs: Oak Harbor Men's Golf (pres.), Pensacole Flying (instr. flight ops. 1975-76). Contbr. articles to profl. jours. Address: 739 E S Greenoch Dr Oak Harbor WA 98277

WEBER, ROBERTA (BOBBIE) BARSOTTI, educator; b. Portland, Nov. 21, 1944; d. Bruno Peter and Catherine Irene (Hart) Barsotti; m. Burce Alan Weber, Nov. 25, 1967; children—Rachael Catherine, Peter Joseph, Michael Goutam. B.A. in Polit. Sci., Seattle U., 1966; M.S. in Child Devel., U. Wis., 1975. Dir., Middleton Day Care Ctr., 1968-69; bd. dirs. Child Devel. Inc., Madison, Wis., 1969-71, v.p., 1970-71; co-dir. Day Care Apprenticeship project State of Wis., Madison, 1972-73; project assoc. family day care home demonstration Community Coordinated Child Care, Madison, 1973-74; parent edn. coordinator Linn Benton Community Coll., Albany, Oreg., 1977—. Bd. dirs. Council of Children, Corvallis, Oreg., 1978—, v.p., 1980—; bd. dirs. LWV, Corvallis, 1977-79. Christian Leadership scholar, 1962; named to Outstanding Young Women of Am., 1970, 80. Mem. Oreg. Assn. Edn. Young Children. Contbr. articles to profl. jours. Home: 236 NW 28th St Corvallis OR 97330 Office: 6500 SW Pacific Blvd Albany OR 97321

WEBSTER, GARY WARREN, chamber of commerce exec.; b. Yakima, Wash., July 11, 1940; s. Gordon I. and Dorothy M. (Dawson) W.; m. Phyllis Nadine Shinpaugh, Mar. 14, 1969; children—Michael John, Carol, Kristal. Grad. Yakima Valley Community Coll., 1960, Inst. Organizational Mgmt., U.S. C. of C., 1976. Gen. mgr. Walla Walla C.

of C., 1971-77; asst. mgr. Greater Yakima C. of C., 1968-71, chief exec., gen. mgr., 1977—; dir. Yakima chpt. ARC, chmn., 1982-83; bd. dirs. Assn. Wash. Bus., 1978-79. Served with Army N.G., 1960-66. Mem. Wash. C. of C. Execs. (pres. 1977-78), C. of C. Execs. Oreg., Washington, Idaho, Alaska, (pres. 1976-77). Lodge: Elks. Home: 6 S 36th Ave Yakima WA 98902 Office: PO Box 1490 10 N 9th St Yakima WA 98907

WEBSTER, ROY CLYDE, communications specialist, public relations consultant; b. Skykomish, Wash., Dec. 13, 1938; s. Clyde Arthur and Letha Hope (Eckert) W.; m. Virginia G. Herron, May 6, 1961; m. 2d, Judith Elaine Thoemke, Sept. 15, 1980; children—Elaine Patrice, Shane Monroe. B.A. in Journalism, U. Wash., 1960; postgrad. Boston U., 1963, San Jose State U., 1972. Reporter, news editor, photographer various newspapers, Wash., 1957-65; pub. relations mgr. various cos., Wash., 1966-74; exec. v.p. Pacific Northwest Waterways Assn., Walla Walla and Vancouver, Wash., 1976; pub. relations cons., Tucson, 1980; founder, pres. Webster Pub. Relations, Santa Cruz, Calif., 1982—; editor Elks Lodge publ., Tucson, 1982. Served with USAF, 1962-65. Recipient Bob Doble Scholastic award for journalism U. Wash., 1955, cert. appreciation Nat. Waterways Conf. Inc., 1979. Mem. Pub. Relations Soc. Am., Internat. Assn. Bus. Communicators, Sigma Delta Chi. Republican. Clubs: Lions (past pres.), Jaycees (past v.p.). Contbg. author, editor various publs. Home and Office: 309 Lee St Santa Cruz CA 95060

WEDEL, MILLIE REDMOND, educator; b. Harrisburg, Pa., Aug. 18, 1939; d. Clair L. and Florence (Heiges) Aungst; B.A., Alaska Meth. U., 1966; M.Ed., U. Alaska, Anchorage, 1972; postgrad. in communications Stanford U., 1975-76; m. Frederick L. Wedel, Jr., Nov. 2, 1974; 1 son, Tom Redmond. Profl. model Charming Models & Models Guild of Phila., 1954-61; public relations staff Haverford (Pa.) Sch., 1959-61; asst. dir. devel. in charge public relations Alaska Meth. U., Anchorage, 1966, part-time lectr., 1966-73; communications tchr. Anchorage Sch. Dist., 1967—; owner Wedel Prodns., Anchorage, 1976—; public relations staff Alaska Purchase Centennial Exhibit, U.S. Dept. Commerce, 1967; writer gubernatorial campaign, 1971; part-time instr. U. Alaska, Anchorage, 1976-79; cons. Cook Inlet Native Assn., 1978, No. Inst., 1979. Bd. dirs. Sta. KAKM, Alaska Public TV, membership chmn., 1978-80, elected nat. lay rep. to Public Broadcasting Service and Nat. Assn. Public TV Stas., 1979; bd. dirs. Ednl. Telecommunications Consortium for Alaska, 1979, Mid-Hillside Community Council, Municipality of Anchorage, 1979-80, research writer, legal asst. Vinson & Elkins, Houston, 1981. Recipient awards for newspapers, lit. mags.; award Nat. Scholastic Press Assn., 1968, 74, 77, Am. Scholastic Press Assn., 1981, 82, 83; Alaska Council Econs., 1982; lic. third class broadcasting, FCC. Mem. Assn. Public Broadcasting (charter mem., nat. lay del. 1980), Indsl. TV Assn. (San Francisco), Alaska Press Club (chmn. high sch. journalism workshops, 1968, 69, 73, awards for sch. newspapers, 1972, 74, 77), Alaska Fedn. Press Women (dir. 1978—, youth projects dir., award for brochures, 1978), NEA, Am. Educators in Communications Tech., World Affairs Council, Alaska Council Tchrs. of English, Houston Legal Assts. Assn., Delta Kappa Gamma. Presbyterian. Clubs: Stanford Alumni (pres. 1982-84) Capt. Cook Athletic (Anchorage). Home: Box 2196 Star Route A Anchorage AK 99507 Office: PO Box 8169 Anchorage AK 99508

WEDEMEYER, ROLAND CHRISTIAN, real estate developer; b. Palo Alto, Calif., Feb. 28, 1932; s. Roland Crofts and Ettha Marie (Jacobsen) W.; m. Harriet Ann Beaudoin, July 26, 1958; children—Robert E., Christine M. B.S. in Petroleum Engring., U. Calif.-Berkeley, 1954. Petroleum engr., Signal Oil & Gas Co., Tex. and La., 1954-60, asst. mgr. constrn., 1961-62; real property adminstr., 1962-73; v.p. indsl. Signal Landmark Properties, Inc., Irvine, Calif., 1973-1980, sr. v.p., 1980—, pres. Signal Devel. Corp., 1980—, also dir.; dir. Shoreland Escrow Co.; real estate broker. Bd. dirs., sec. Pacific Hosp. Long Beach; exec. com. So. Calif. Econ. and Job Devel. Council. Recipient Herb Nash Meml. award Los Angeles Area C. of C., 1979. Mem. Am. Econ. Devel. Council, Nat. Assn. Indsl. and Office Parks, Signal Hill C. of C. (dir. past pres.), Internat. Council of Shopping Ctrs., Lambda Alpha, Delta Sigma Phi, Theta Tau. Republican. Presbyterian. Clubs: Masons (Long Beach). Office: 17890 Skypark Circle Irvine CA 92714

WEED, ROGER OREN, vocat. planning mgmt. cons.; b. Bend, Oreg. Feb. 2, 1944; s. Chester E. and Ruth Marie (Urie) W.; B.S., U. Oreg., 1967, M.S., 1969, postgrad., 1969; postgrad. UCLA, 1978, U. Kans., 1979—; children—Nicholette, Andrew. Rehab. counselor State of Alaska, Anchorage, 1969-71; counselor Langdon Psychiat. Clinic, Anchorage, 1971-74; dep. and exec. dir. Hope Cottages, Inc., Anchorage, 1974-79; dir. Alaska Profl. Resources Group, Anchorage, 1978—, Winslow Enterprises; mng. partner Collins, Weed & Assos., 1980—; instr. U. Alaska, Anchorage, 1971-75; bd. dirs. Community Enterprise Devel. Corp., 1982—. Mem. exec. com. Gov. Council for Handicapped and Gifted, 1976-78; chmn. Govt. Com. on Employment of Handicapped, 1975-78; bd. dirs. Pres. Com. on Employment of Handicapped, 1976-77, Tanaina Child Devel. Corp., 1980-83, Employment and Tng. Center Alaska, 1981—. chmn. Gov. Task Force on Employment of Handicapped, 1973. Recipient Service award Govt. Council on Employment of Handicapped, 1978, cert. of appreciation, 1982; NSF grantee, 1966-67; Vocat. Rehab. Adminstrn. grantee, 1967-69. Fellow Nat. Rehab. Counselors Assn.; mem. Nat. Assn. of Pvt. Facilities Residential (bd. dirs. 1975-78), Alaska Rehab. Assn. (bd. dirs. 1971-76, pres. 1974-76), Nat. Rehab. Assn. (pres.-elect Pacific region), Am. Assn. Mental Deficiency (nat. planning council 1981—), Nat. Assn. Pvt. Residential Facilities for Mentally Retarded, Assn. Advancement of Behavior Therapy, Am. Mgmt. Assn. Republican. Methodist. Office: Denali Towers S Suite 501 2600 Denali St Anchorage AK 99503

WEEDA, SHELBY GALEN, bakery company executive; b. Hollywood, Calif., July 15, 1948; s. Thomas Galen and Ruth Doris (North) W.; m. Christine Ann Taylor, June 22, 1975. B.A., Long Beach State U., 1973. Sales rep. E & J Gallo Wine Co., Los Angeles, 1973-75; dist. sales mgr. Standard Brands Foods Co., Chgo., 1975-79; regional sales mgr. Plus Products, Irvine Calif., 1979-81; v.p. sales and mktg. Kings Hawaiian Bakery, Torrance, Calif., 1981—; cons. in mktg. and sales. Mem. Calif. Grocers Assn., Food Mktg. Inst., Nat. Food Brokers Assn. Office: 18655 S Western Ave Torrance CA 90504

WEEDIN, KENNETH RAYMOND, real estate broker; b. Fairfax, Mo., Apr. 27, 1923; s. Clarence R. and Lulu E. (Hedrick) W. Teller, Exchange Bank of Fairfax (Mo.), 1946-48; engaged in real estate and ins., Mo., 1947-56; pvt. practice real estate, Loveland, Colo., 1956—; Loveland agt. Midland Fed. Savings & Loan Assn., 1969-77. Bd. dirs. Loveland Devel. Fund; mem. Loveland Recreation Commn., 1961-66; mem. Loveland City Council, 1961-62, 70-71; mem. Loveland Planning Commn., 1970-71, mayor pro-tem, 1970-71. Mem. Nat. (membership chmn. 1977), Colo. (Realtor of Year 1976) assns. Realtors, Loveland C. of C. (indsl. com.), Colo. Assn. Real Estate Bds. (pres. 1974), V.F.W., Am. Legion, Loveland Bd. Realtors (v.p. 1973), Colo. (dir. 1964-67), Loveland (pres. 1963) insurors assns. Clubs: Rotary (pres. 1980-81), Elks (Loveland). Office: 1601 E Eisenhower Blvd Loveland CO 80537

WEEKES, MICHAEL MANNING, clergyman, lawyer; b. Leon, Iowa, July 12, 1938; s. Pearl W. and Marie (Manning) W. B.S., Drake U., 1960, J.D., 1963; M.Div., Fuller Theol. Sem., 1979. Bars: Iowa. 1963, Calif. 1964. Assoc. Dillavou and Cox (later Dillavou, Cox, Castle and Nicholson), Los Angeles, 1964-68, Cox, Castle & Nicholson, Los Angeles, 1968-71; partner Cox, Castle, Nicholson & Weekes, Los Angeles, 1972-76; asst. pastor Immanuel Presbyn. Ch., Los Angeles, 1980—; lectr. Christian Legal Soc., 1977-78, Oral Roberts U. Seminar, 1978. Bd. dirs. Wilshire Center Community Involvement Assn., Inc., 1980—; bd. dirs. Hollywood Presbyn. Med. Center, 1976—, chmn. spiritual emphasis com., 1977—. Mem. Calif. Bar Assn., Delta Theta Phi, Beta Gamma Sigma. Author: Manual for Application of Uniform Commercial Code for Surety Industry, 1964; editor: Words to Live By, 1969; Bibles Riches, 1970; author: Christian Mediation, 1977. Home: 691 S Irolo St Apt 903 Los Angeles CA 90005 Office: 3300 Wilshire Blvd Los Angeles CA 90010

WEEKS, THELMA EVANS, personnel adminstr., linguist; b. Portland, Oreg., Jan. 15, 1921; d. Harry E. and Clarissa B. (Marshall) Evans; m. Robert L. Weeks, Jan. 7, 1940 (dec. 1981); children—Barbara Weeks Patton, John Robert. A.B. cum laude, San Diego State U., 1962; Ph.D. in Linguistics, Stanford U., 1973. Sta. mgr. Sta. KUFM, San Diego, 1958-62; research asst. Stanford U., 1963-66; v.p. Weeks Research Assos., Indsl. Cons., Palo Alto, Calif., 1975-81; personnel mgr. Adaptec, Inc., Milpitas, Calif., 1981—; dir. Ctr. for Cross-Cultural Research, Palo Alto, 1974-79; dir. Inst. for Literacy Devel., Morgan Hill, Calif., 1979—; lectr. Calif. State U.-Hayward, 1977, 78; instr. San Jose State U., 1976, U. Calif.-Berkeley, 1974. Fellow Am. Anthrop. Assn.; mem. Am. Dialect Soc., Am. Psychol. Assn., Internat. Communication Assn., Internat. Reading Assn., Linguistic Soc. Am., Nat. Council Tchrs. English. Author: The Slow Speech Development of a Bright Child, 1974; Born to Talk, 1979; contbr. articles to profl. jours. Home: PO Box 1387 Morgan Hill CA 95037 Office: 1625 McCarthy Blvd Milpitas CA 95035

WEGMAN, RALPH SHUFRO, electronics systems engr.; b. Boston, May 31, 1922; s. Max Jacob and Jennie Libby (Shufro) W.; student Northeastern U., 1943-45; B.E., U. So. Calif., 1947; m. Sybil Clare Mager, Nov. 7, 1948; children—Barry Roger, Debra Jane, Melissa Joan. Design engr. Raytheon, 1948, U.S. Navy, 1949; instrumentation engr. Marquardt Corp., 1951-52; guided missile research and devel. engr. Hughes Aircraft Co., 1952-56, Radioplane, 1956; mem. tech. staff Ramo-Wooldridge, 1956-59; West Coast mgr. communications systems research and devel. Kellogg div. ITT, 1959-60; mem. tech. staff Aerospace Corp., 1960-67; sr. staff engr. TRW Systems, Redondo Beach, Calif., 1967-73, 80—; owner, pres. Minisec Systems, Van Nuys, Calif., 1973-78; security cons. to aerospace industry, 1978-80. Pres. bd. dirs. Pacific Hills Sch., Santa Monica, Calif., 1974; asso. founder Careers for Handicapped Inst., 1977. Served with USAAF, 1940-43. Mem. IEEE (sr.), AIAA, Associated Security Cons. Contbr. articles to profl. jours. Office: TRW Systems 1 Space Park Redondo Beach CA 90278

WEHMEYER, LILLIAN BIERMANN, educator; b. Milw., Oct. 29, 1933; s. William Alfred and Mabel (Knippel) Biermann; m. Gerald C. Edson, Aug. 29, 1953 (div. 1957); 1 dau., Paula; m. 2d, Werner F. Wehmeyer, Aug. 28, 1962. B.A., U. Calif.-Berkeley, 1965, M.L.S., 1969, Ph.D., 1978. Librarian, Pilgrim Park Jr. High Sch., Oak Grove, Wis., 1959-62; pub. health research asst., 1962-64; librarian Lafayette Sch. Dist., Calif., 1965-69, dist. librarian, 1969-73; part-time instr. U. Calif., Berkeley, 1977-80; asst. supt. instrn. Lafayette (Calif.) Sch. Dist., 1973-79, San Mateo (Calif.) City Sch. Dist., 1979—. Mem. Calif. Network for Ednl. Futures (chmn. 1981-82), World Future Soc., Assn. Supervision and Curriculum Devel., ALA, Nat. Council Tchrs. English. Lutheran (past choir dir., mem. council, chmn. edn. com.), Phi Beta Kappa, Phi Delta Kappa. Author: Images in a Crystal Ball; World Futures Portrayed in Fiction for Young People, 1981; The School Librarian as Educator, 1976; The School Library Volunteer, 1975. Contbr. articles to profl. jours. Home: 1333 37th Ave San Francisco CA 94122 Office: 300 28th Ave San Mateo CA 94403

WEHNER, ALFRED PETER, biomedical scientist; b. Wiesbaden, Germany, Oct. 23, 1926; s. Paul Heinrich and Irma (Schulze) W.; cand. med. Johannes Gutenberg U., 1949, Zahnarzt, 1951, D.M.D., 1953; m. Ingeborg Hella Miller, Aug. 30, 1955; children—Patricia Ingeborg, Alfred Peter, Jackie Diane, Peter Hermann. Came to U.S., 1953, naturalized, 1958. Individual practice dentistry, Wiesbaden, 1951-53; fellow clin. pedodontia Guggenheim Dental Clinic, N.Y.C., 1953-54, dentist 7100th Hosp., USAF, 1954-56; research asst. Mobil Oil Co., Dallas, 1957-62; sr. research scientist Biometrics Instrument Corp., Plano, Tex., 1962-64; pres. Electro-Aerosol Inst., Plano, Tex., dir. electro-aerosol therapy center, 1964-67, chmn. dept. sci. U. Plano, Tex., 1966-67; sr. research scientist, biology dept. Battelle Pacific NW Labs., Richland, Wash., 1967-70, research asso., 1970-77, staff scientist, 1977-78, mgr. environ. and indsl. toxicology, 1978-80, task leader, indsl. toxicology, 1980—; cons. VA Hosp., McKinney, Tex., 1963-65; chmn. various internat. sci. congresses and symposia. Fellow Internat. Soc. Med. Hydrology, Tex. Acad. Sci.; mem. AAAS, Am. Inst. Med. Climatology (dir. 1972—, sec. 1972—), Internat. Soc. Biometeorology (U.S. rep. 1972-80), Sci. Research Soc. Am., Soc. Exptl. Biology and Medicine, Internat. Soc. Aerosols in Medicine (mem. exec. bd. 1970-81), Dallas County Dental Soc. (hon.), Am. Physicians Fellowship, N.Y. Acad. Sci., Internat. Center for Lacustrine Environment Study (Como, Italy). Patentee in field. Author: From Hitler Youth to U.S. Citizenship, 1972. Author numerous sci. publs. Office: Battelle Biology Dept PO Box 999 Richland WA 99352

WEHR, HERBERT MICHAEL, agrl. specialist; b. San Francisco, Feb. 15, 1943; s. Carl Henry and Rosemary (Angelo) W.; student U. Calif.-Davis, 1961-63; B.S., U. Calif.-Berkeley, 1966; M.S., Oreg. State U., 1968, Ph.D., 1972; m. Nancy Briggs, Dec. 19, 1967; 1 dau., Anne Michelle. Supr., food sci.-microbiology lab. services Oreg. Dept. Agr., Salem, 1971-74, asst. adminstr. lab. services, 1974-78, adminstr., dir. lab. services, 1978—; chmn. Oreg. Adv. Com. on Synthetic Chems. in the Environment; chmn. Oreg. Interagy. Pesticides Com., 1980—, Oreg. State Agy. Lab. Consortium, 1979—. Mem. Assn. Ofcl. Analytical Chemists (planning com., internat. rep., chmn. ofcl. methods bd.), Inst. Food Technologists, Am. Public Health Assn. (com. standard methods for exam. of dairy products), Nat. Conf. Interstate Milk Shipments (lab. com.), Am. Chem. Soc., Internat. Assn. Milk, Food and Environ. Sanitarians, Council Agrl. Sci. and Tech. Republican. Episcopalian. Club: Rotary. Contbr. articles to profl. jours. Home: 2180 Irene Ct S Salem OR 97302 Office: 635 Capitol NE Salem OR 97310

WEHR, WESLEY CONRAD, paleontologist, artist; b. Everett, Wash., Apr. 17, 1929; s. Conrad John and Ingeborg (Hall) W.; B.A., U. Wash., 1951, M.A., 1954. Affiliate curator of paleobotany Wash. State Mus., U. Wash., Seattle, 1979—, research assoc. in paleontology, 1979—; exhibited in group shows U.S., Switzerland and Germany. Recipient numerous art awards and hon. citations. Mem. Pres.' Club U. Wash., Internat. Soc. Angiosperm Paleobotany. Author articles and papers on paleontology and paleobotany; composer. Home: Box 45221 University Station Seattle WA 98105 Office: Wash State Mus U Wash Seattle WA 98145

WEHRLY, JOSEPH MALACHI, mfg. co. exec.; b. County Armagh, Ireland, Oct. 2, 1915; s. Albert and Mary Josephine (Gribbon) W.; came to U.S., 1931, naturalized, 1938; student Los Angeles City Coll., evenings 1947-49; certificate indsl. relations U. Calif. at Berkeley Extension, 1957; m. Margaret Elizabeth Banks, July 3, 1946; children—Joseph Michael, Kathleen Margaret, Stephen Patrick. Mgr. interplant relations Goodyear Tire & Rubber Co., Los Angeles, 1935-42; dir. indsl. relations Whittaker Corp., Los Angeles, 1946-60, Meletron Corp., Los Angeles, 1960-61; asst. indsl. relations mgr. Pacific Airmotive Corp., Burbank, Calif., 1961-63; personnel mgr. Menasco Mfg. Co., Burbank, 1963-66; indsl. relations adminstr. Internat. Electronic Research, Burbank, 1966; dir. indsl. relations Adams Rite Industries, Inc., Glendale, Calif., 1966-75, cons., 1975-76; personnel mgr. TOTCO div. Baker Internat. Corp., Glendale, 1975-80; instr. indsl. relations and supervision Los Angeles Pierce Coll., 1949-76. Served with U.S. Army, 1942-46. Mem. Personnel and Indsl. Relations Assn., Mchts. and Mfrs. Assn. Republican. Roman Catholic. mfg. co. exec.; b. County Armagh, Ireland, Oct. 2, 1915; s. Albert and Mary Josephine (Gribbon) W.; came to U.S., 1931, naturalized, 1938; student Los Angeles City Coll., evenings 1947-49; certificate indsl. relations U. Calif. at Berkeley Extension, 1957; m. Margaret Elizabeth Banks, July 3, 1946; children—Joseph Michael, Kathleen Margaret, Stephen Patrick. Mgr. interplant relations Goodyear Tire & Rubber Co., Los Angeles, 1935-42; dir. indsl. relations Whittaker Corp., Los Angeles, 1946-60, Meletron Corp., Los Angeles, 1960-61; asst. indsl. relations mgr. Pacific Airmotive Corp., Burbank, Calif., 1961-63; personnel mgr. Menasco Mfg. Co., Burbank, 1963-66; indsl. relations adminstr. Internat. Electronic Research, Burbank, 1966; dir. indsl. relations Adams Rite Industries, Inc., Glendale, Calif., 1966-75, cons., 1975-76; personnel mgr. TOTCO div. Baker Internat. Corp., Glendale, 1975-80; instr. indsl. relations and supervision Los Angeles Pierce Coll., 1949-76. Served with U.S. Army, 1942-46. Mem. Personnel and Indsl. Relations Assn., Mchts. and Mfrs. Assn. Republican. Roman Catholic. Home: 4925 Swinton Ave Encino CA 91436

WEICK, RODNEY JAY, engineering geologist, consultant; b. Los Angeles, May 25, 1947; s. Walter Lawrence and Virginia Jane (Knopf) W.; m. Jeani Crichlow, Sept. 14, 1980. B.S., Calif. State U.-Los Angeles, 1974; postgrad. U. Nev., 1981. Registered geologist, Calif.; registered engring. geologist, Calif. From staff geologist to project mgr., ops. mgr. corp. office Leighton and Assocs., Inc., Irvine, Calif., 1974-81; cons. engring. geologist Reno, Nev., 1981—. Served with USN 1967-71. Recipient award Calif. State U. Alumni Assn., 1974; Aaron Waters award, dept. geol. scis. Calif. State U., 1974. Mem. Assn. Engring. Geologists, Geol. Soc. Am., South Coast Geol. Soc., Geol. Soc. Nev., Sigma Xi. Republican. Contbr. articles to profl. jours. Office: PO Box 8011 Reno NV 89507

WEIDA, DONNA LEE, computer co. exec.; b. Logansport, Ind., Oct. 29, 1939; d. Donald L. and Leila J. (Sweet) Kleckner; A.A., Orange Coast Coll. and Saddleback Coll., Mission Viejo, Calif., 1980; student Calif. State U.-Fullerton, 1983—; children—Mark, Traci, Teri, Sec., K.L.K. Mfg. Co., Logansport, 1957-60, 63-65; sec. Sch. Edn., Mich. State U., 1962-63; sec. Sch. Fine Arts, U. Calif., Irvine, 1966-69; co-organizer Plaza Vet. Clinic, Upland, Calif., 1969-70; mgr. Bob Bondurant Sch. High Performance Driving, Ontario (Calif.) Motor Speedway, 1970-73; mgr./pub. relations exec. Chuck Jones Racing, Costa Mesa, Calif., 1973; exec. sec. Dana Steel, Newport Beach, Calif., 1974; estimator/office mgr. Hardy & Harper, Tustin, Calif., 1975-76; controller/mgr. Gillen/Kloss Advt., Newport Beach, 1977-78; purchasing adminstr. Butler Housing, Irvine, 1979; controller/mgr. XMark Corp., Costa Mesa, 1980-81, adminstrv. mgr. concept devel., 1981; corp. sec. Personal Systems Tech., Inc., Irvine, Calif., 1982, founder/owner Numbers & Words, Irvine, 1982—. Mem. Nat. Assn. Female Execs., Am. Soc. Profl. and Exec. Women, Beta Sigma Phi. Republican. Episcopalian. Home: 14241 Utrillo Dr Irvine CA 92714 Office: Personal Systems Technology Inc 15801 Rockfield Blvd Suite A Irvine CA 92714

WEIDMAN, MARY LOU LOHMAN, business educator; Mo., Apr. 25, 1921; d. Herman Peter and La Vyca Alice (Peppard) Lohman; m. James Matthew Weidman, Aug. 18, 1944; children—James Matthew, Lynn. B.S. in Bus. Adminstrn., U. Kans., 1943; M.A. in Edn., U. Calif.-Long Beach, 1968. Prof. Cerritos Community Coll., Norwalk, Calif., 1962—. Mem. Nat. Bus. Edn. Assn., Calif. Bus. Edn. Assn., Internat. Soc. Bus. Edn., NEA, Theta Alpha Delta. Congregationalist. Author: Hedman Stenotype Theory, 1979; editor of textbooks. Home: 9905 Norlain Ave Downey CA 90240 Office: Cerritos Community Coll 5529/11110 Alondin Blvd Norwalk CA 90650

WEIDNER, CHARLES KENNETH, consulting engineer; b. Narcissa, Pa., Sept. 25, 1904; s. Charles Leonard and Sarah (MacNair) W.; ed. pub. schs.; m. Garnett Valentine Leyman, June 22, 1929; children—Wynn, Charles Leyman, Sarah Weidner Byrd. Constrn. foreman, then supt. heavy constrn. Wills Constrn. Co. and N.P. Ry., 1925-31; designer, engring. dept. Boeing Aircraft Co., 1931-34; instr. physics, supt. bldgs. and grounds Whitman Coll., 1934-36, asst. supt. bldgs. and grounds U. Wash., 1936-41; cons. engr., prof. U. Oreg., 1946-47; chief engr. charge design and constrn. Argonne Nat. Nuclear Research Lab., U. Chgo., 1947-51; prof. engring., also dean Sch. Engring. and Architecture, Am. U. Beirut, 1951-62, emeritus, 1962; gen. mgr. African ops. Contracting & Trading Co., 1962-65; pres. Am. Internat. Constrn. Co., 1965-67; cons. engr., 1967—; dir. Middle East Export Press, 1956-66. Devel. cons., Jordan, Syria, Saudia Arabia, 1952-60, Haiti, 1966—; edn. and tng. cons. U.S. Navy, 1947, U.S. Air Force, 1947, Aramco, Bapco, 1952-60. Vice pres. restoration Whitman Historic Sites, Walla Walla, Wash., 1934-36; v.p. West Surburban Symphony Assn., LaGrange, Ill., 1947-50. Served from lt. to capt. USNR, 1941-46. Decorated Bronze Star (2), medal Edn. Order of Cedars (Lebanon), Hashemite Order Independence; recipient George Washington Honor medal. Fellow ASCE (life), AAAS; mem. ASME, IEEE, Nat. Soc. Profl. Engrs., Soc. Am. Mil. Engrs., Am. Soc. Naval Engrs. (life). Address: 6005 Applewood Ridge Circle Colorado Springs CO 80907

WEIG, DAVID WILLIAM, economist; b. New Brunswick, N.J., Mar. 12, 1943; s. Walter Willis and Gwendolyn Whistler (Eichhorn) W.; m. Elizabeth Louise Wells, June 19, 1965; children—Lara Katherine, Erica Yvonne. B.A., U. N.Mex., 1965, M.A., 1967. Mathematician, Air Force Weapons Lab., Albuquerque, 1963-66; research asst. Office Fin. Mgmt., State Wash., 1969-73, chief economist Dept. Revenue, 1973-77, Office Fin. Mgmt., 1977—. Commd. health service officer USPHS, 1967-69. Nominated Exec. of Yr., Fed. Exec. Inst. Alumni Assn., 1982. Mem. Olympia Econs. Club (pres. 1982), Nat. Assn. Bus. Economists. Am. Econs. Assn., Pacific N.W. Econ. Conf. (dir.). Episcopalian. Contbr. articles to jours. in field.

WEIGAND, MARK WARREN, sociologist; b. Wichita, Kans., Dec. 15, 1950; s. Matthew Warren and Edith Mae (Stodard) W.; m. Karen Sue Brunmeier, Sept. 1, 1973. B.A. in Sociology, Colo. State U., 1973, M.A., 1975; Ph.D., U. Utah, 1980. Teaching asst. dept. sociology Colo. State U., Ft. Collins, 1974-75; instr. dept. sociology U. Utah, Salt Lake City, 1975-80; assoc. instr. Granite Community Mental Health Ctr., Salt Lake City, 1979; program adminstr., Jefferson County Dept. Social Services, Denver, 1981—; mem. exec. bd. Colo IV-D Dirs. Assn. Mem. Am. Sociol., ACLU, Common Cause, Sigma Phi Epsilon. Contbr. articles to profl. jours. Office: Jefferson County Dept of Social Services 8550 W 14th Ave Lakewood CO 80215

WEIGAND, WILLIAM KEITH, bishop; b. Bend, Oreg., May 23, 1937; ed. Mt. Angel Sem., St. Benedict, Oreg., St. Edward's Sem. and St. Thomas Sem., Kenmore, Wash. Ordained priest, Roman Cath. Ch., 1963; ordained bishop of Salt Lake City, 1980. Office: Pastoral Center 27 C St Salt Lake City UT 84103

WEIGEL, STANLEY ALEXANDER, U.S. judge; b. Helena, Mont., Dec. 9, 1905; s. Louis and Jennie (Hepner) W.; A.B., Stanford, 1926, J.D., 1928; M. Anne Kauffman, Apr. 21, 1940; children—Jane Anne, Susan Mary. Admitted to Calif. bar, 1928; practice in San Francisco, 1928-62; U.S. judge No. Dist. Calif., from 1962, now sr. judge; non-resident lectr. Stanford Law Sch., 1952—. Mem. Jud. Panel on

Multidist, Litigation, 1968-79; mem. temporary emergency Ct. Appeals of U.S., 1980—. Pres. Internat. Hospitality Center Bay Area, 1959-68, Nat. Council for Community Services to Internat. Visitors, 1972-73; adv. gov. Calif. on Automobile Accident Commn., 1959. Chmn. bd. visitors Stanford Law Sch., 1958-63; trustee World Affairs Council No. Calif., 1960—, pres., 1973-74; chmn. Ford Found. vis. com. to study behavioral sci. depts. Stanford, 1956-57. Served to lt. USNR, 1943-45. Decorated chevalier Order Leopold II (Belgium). Mem. Delta Sigma Rho, Phi Alpha Delta, Sigma Delta Chi. Office: US Dist Court San Francisco CA 94102

WEIGEND, GUIDO GUSTAV, coll. dean, geographer; b. Zeltweg, Austria, Jan. 2, 1920; s. Gustav F. and Paula (Sorgo) W.; came to U.S., 1939, naturalized, 1943; B.S., U. Chgo., 1942, M.S., 1946, Ph.D., 1949; m. Areta Kelble, June 26, 1947; children—Nina, Cynthia, Kenneth. With OSS, 1943-45, mil. intelligence, War Dept., 1946; instr. geography U. Ill., 1946-47; instr., then asst. prof. geography Beloit Coll., 1947-49; asst. prof. geography Rutgers U., 1949-51, asso. prof., 1951-57, prof., 1957-76, acting chmn. dept., chmn., 1951-67, asso. dean Rutgers Coll., 1972-76; dean Coll. Liberal Arts, prof. geography Ariz. State U., Tempe, 1976—; Fulbright lectr. U. Barcelona, 1960-61; vis. prof. geography Columbia, 1965-67, N.Y.U., 1967, U. Colo., summer 1968, U. Hawaii, summer 1969. Liaison rep. Rutgers U. to UN, 1950-52; chmn. Conf. on Polit. and Social Geography, 1968-69. Bd. adjustment Franklin Twp., N.J., 1959; mem. Bd. Edn., Highland Park, N.J., 1973-75, v.p., 1975; mem. exec. bd. Commn. on Instns. Higher Edn., N. Central Assn. Colls. and Schs., 1980—; mem. Ariz. Humanities Council, 1976-80; bd. dirs. Fedn. Pub. Programs in Humanities 1977-82. Served with OSS, U.S. Army, 1943-45. Research for study European ports Office Naval Research, 1952-55; Social Science Research Council grantee, 1956; Ford Found. grantee, 1966; Rutgers Research Council fellow, 1970-71; Fulbright travel grantee, Netherlands, 1970-71; grantee Am. Philos. Soc., 1970-71. Mem. Internat. Geog. Union (U.S. nat. com. 1951-58, 61-65), Assn. Am. Geographers (chmn. N.Y. Met. div. 1955-56, editorial bd. annals 1955-59, mem. council 1965-66; chmn. N.Y.-N.J. div. 1965-66), Assn. Pacific Coast Geographers, Phoenix Com. Fgn. Relations (chmn. 1979-81), Western Assn. German Studies, Council Colls. Arts and Scis. (bd. dirs. 1980—), Sigma Xi (chpt. pres. 1965-66). Author articles profl. jours., also monograph, bulls.; co-author: A Geography of Europe, 4th edit., 1977. Geog. editor-in-chief Odyssey World Atlas, 1966. Home: 2094 E Golf Ave Tempe AZ 85282 Office: College of Liberal Arts Ariz State U Tempe AZ 85287

WEIGLE, WILLIAM OLIVER, immunologist; b. Monaca, Pa., Apr. 28, 1927; s. Oliver James and Caroline Ellen (Alsing) W.; B.S., U. Pitts., 1950, M.S., 1951, Ph.D., 1956; m. Kathryn May Lotz, Sept. 4, 1948 (div. May 1980); children—William James, Cynthia Kay. Research asso. pathology U. Pitts., 1955-58, asst. prof. immunochemistry, 1959-61; asso. div. exptl. pathology Scripps Clinic and Research Found., LaJolla, Calif., 1961-62, asso. mem. div., 1962-63, mem. dept. exptl. pathology, 1963-74, mem. dept. immunopathology, 1974-82, chmn. dept., 1980-82, mem., vice chmn. dept. immunology, 1982—; adj. prof. dept. biology U. Calif., San Diego; cons. NIH, Am. Cancer Soc., Nat. Multiple Sclerosis Soc., Council Soc. Exptl. Biology and Medicine; adv. com. Nat. Research Council; McLaughlin vis. prof. U. Tex., 1977. Served with USNR, 1945-46. Public Health research fellow Nat. Inst. Neurol. Diseases and Blindness, 1956-59; sr. research fellow NIH, 1959-61, Research Career award, 1962. Mem. Am. Assn. Immunologists, Am. Soc. Exptl. Pathology (Parke, Davis award 1967), Am. Soc. Microbiology, N.Y. Acad. Scis., Am. Acad. Allergy, Western Assn. Clin. Research, Am. Assn. Pathologists, Soc. Exptl. Biology and Medicine. Author: Natural and Acquired Immunologic Unresponsiveness, 1967; asso. editor Clin. and Exptl. Immunology, 1972-79, Jour. Exptl. Medicine, 1974—, Immunochemistry, 1964-71, Procs. Soc. Exptl. Biology and Medicine, 1967-72, Jour. Immunology, 1967-71, Infection and Immunity, 1969—; sect. editor Jour. Immunology, 1971-75; editorial bd. Contemporary Topics in Immunobiology, 1971—, Cellular Immunology, 1983—; contbr. articles to sci. jours. Home: 13750 Ruette Le Parc Apt C Del Mar CA 92014 Office: Dept of Immunopathology Scripps Clinic and Research Foundation 10666 N Torrey Pines Rd LaJolla CA 92037

WEIHER, RICHARD G., clinical psychologist, educator, cons.; b. Ladysmith, Wis., June 23, 1946; s. Robert John Henry and Idella Mae (Williams) W.; m. Marilynn Lois Wexlor, Aug. 10, 1968; children—Andrew Robert, Todd Randall. B.A., U. Wis.-Oshkosh, 1971; M.S. Eastern Wash. State U. Cheney, 1973; Ph.D., Utah State U., 1975. Cert. psychologist, Nev. Outpatient dir. Reno Mental Health Center, 1975-77; dir. outpatient, residential services Children's Behavioral Services, Reno, 1977-79; dir. Carson (Nev.) Mental Health Center, 1979-81; adj. asst. prof. psychology, U. Nev., Reno, 1976—; clin. asst. prof. psychiatry, Sch. Med. U. Nev., 1979—; pvt. practice, 1980—; cons. in field. Bd. dirs. Campfire Girls, 1977-80; mem. Nev. Task Force on Child Abuse, 1975-80. Title XX grantee 1977. Mem. Am. Psychol. Assn., Northern Nev. Assn. Cert. Psychologists, Nat. Register Health Service Providers. Author: Behavior Therapy, 1975; Breakthrough, 1977. Office: 755 Forest St Reno NV 89509

WEIL, DEBRA SUE, food service co. exec.; b. Denver, June 28, 1933; d. Nelson and Carolyn Maxine (Meyer) New; student U. Colo., 1951-52; m. Robert Leonard Weil, Dec. 6, 1952; children—Ronald Leon, Richard Floyd, Linda Marie. Sec.-treas., dir. Westman Commn. Co., Denver, 1952—; contest judge HERO, DECA. Mem. bd. Temple Micah Sisterhood, Denver, treas., 1960-62; leader Girl Scouts, Denver, 1964-68; sec. Young Am. League, 1963-69; vol. Head Start, Public TV, Muscular Dystrophy, March of Dimes, Am. Cancer Soc., United Way, Four Mile Hist. Park, Children's Hosp. Aux.; Denver Area chairperson Children's Hosp. Outreach Program. Mem. Colo.-Wyo. Restaurant Assn. (dir., treas. aux. bd., recipient disting. service award 1975-76), Nat. Restaurant Assn., Denver C. of C., Denver and Colo. Conv. and Visitors Bur., Foodservice Orgn. Distbrs., Colo. Chefs de Cuisine Assn., Colo.-Wyo. Hotel and Motel Assn. Republican. Clubs: Tennis World Racquet World, Town (dir., treas.), Mile High Stadium. Home: 3766 S Jersey St Denver CO 80237 Office: 4450 Lipan St Denver CO 80211

WEIL, MARVIN LEE, child neurologist, educator; b. Gainesville, Fla., Sept. 28, 1924; s. Joseph and Anna (Abrams) W.; B.S., U. Fla., 1943; M.D., Johns Hopkins U., 1946; m. Joyce Sari Zimmerman, May 2, 1954; children—Daniel I., Clifford F., Meredith. Intern, Duke Hosp., Durham, N.C., 1946, resident pediatrics, 1947-48; resident in pediatrics Cin. Children's Hosp., 1950-52; instr. pediatrics U. Cin., 1953; practice medicine specializing in pediatrics, Miami, Fla., 1954-65; asst. prof. pediatrics and neurology UCLA, from 1968, then asso. prof., prof., 1978—; chief div. pediatric neurology Harbor-UCLA Med. Center, Torrance, Calif., 1968—. Served from 1st lt. to capt., M.C., AUS, 1948-50. Nat. Inst. Neurol. Diseases and Blindness spl. fellow, 1965-68, Fogarty internat. scholar, 1976-77. Mem. Am. Pediatric Soc., Am. Acad. Neurology, Am. Acad. Pediatrics, Am. Assn. Mental Deficiency (past regional chmn.), Child Neurology Soc. (councilor western region 1980-82), Los Angeles Soc. Neurol. Psychiatry (pres. 1981). Jewish. Contbr. articles to profl. jours. Home: 7030 Starstone Dr Rancho Palos Verdes CA 90274 Office: Harbor UCLA Med Center 1000 W Carson St Torrance CA 90509

WEIL, ROBERT LEONARD, food service distbn. co. exec.; b. Denver, Oct. 13, 1922; s. Felix Leon and Frances Bernice (Levy) W.; B.S. in Bus., U. Colo., 1947; m. Debra Sue New, Dec. 6, 1952; children—Ronald Leon, Richard Floyd, Linda Marie. Ind. ins. agt., Denver, 1947-52; pres., dir. Westman Commn. Co., Denver, 1952—; pres., dir. Continental Orgn. Distbr. Enterprises, Inc., Pitts., 1979—; treas., dir. Colo.-Wyo. Restaurant Assn.; dir., exec. com. Nat. Cooking Inst., 1976-80; pres. Food Service Industry Gourmet Soc., Denver, 1977-79; treas., dir. Foodservice Orgn. of Distbrs., 1979-81; dir. Internat. Foodservice Distbrs. Assn., Denver, 1981—. Bd. dirs. Children's Asthma Research Inst. and Hosp., Denver, 1965-74. Served with USN, 1943-46. Recipient Disting. Service award Colo.-Wyo. Restaurant Assn., 1972. Mem. Nat. Restaurant Assn., Denver C. of C., Denver and Colo. Conv. and Visitors Bus. (dir. 1979—), Colo. Chefs de Cuisine Assn., Colo.-Wyo. Hotel and Motel Assn., Zeta Beta Tau (past chpt. pres.; citation of merit 1960, 81). Clubs: Town (pres. 1973-75), Mile-Hi Stadium (dir. 1979), Optimist, Lowry Field Commd. Officers (Denver). Office: 4450 Lipan St Denver CO 80217

WEILER, CHARLES DAVID, program analyst; b. Palmer, Alaska, Apr. 26, 1937; s. Nick T. and Elsa E. (Bartelt) W.; m. Dolores G. Bagoy, Sept. 7, 1974; 1 dau., Tisa. Tour dir. Wien Alaska Airlines, Kotzebue, 1963; cost acct. RCA Service Co., Clear, Alaska, 1964-66; tech. data analyst RCA Service Co., Clear, 1966-69; data analyst Ballistic Missile Early Warning System, Clear, 1969—. Dir., City of Anderson (Alaska) Airport Com., 1974-80; search/rescue pilot CAP, 1971—, plans and programs officer, 1980—; chmn. Interior Alaska Dem. Party, 1978-80; mem. Alaska State Dem. Com., 1978—, precinct chmn., 1970—; mem. Joint Dem./Rep. Election Reform State Com., 1978—; bd. dirs. Alaska Civil Liberties Union, 1982-84. Served with U.S. Army, 1960-62. Recipient Lions Club Outstanding Contribution award, 1972; Civil Air Patrol Saving and Preservation of Human Life award, 1975. Democrat. Club: Lions (pres. 1969-70). Address: PO Box 441 Clear AK 99704

WEILER, DOROTHY ESSER, librarian; b. Hartford, Wis., Feb. 21, 1914; d. Henry Hugo and Agatha Christina (Dopp) Esser; A.B. in Fgn. Langs., Wash. State U., 1935; B.A.L., Grad. Library Sch., U. Wash., 1936; postgrad. U. Ariz., 1956-57, Ariz. State U., 1957-58, Grad. Sch. Librarianship, U. Denver, 1971; m. Henry C. Weiler, Aug. 30, 1937; children—Robert William, Kurt Walter. Tchr.-librarian Roosevelt Elem. Schs., Dist. #66, Phoenix, 1956-59; extension librarian Ariz. Dept. Library and Archives, Phoenix, 1959-67; library dir. City of Tempe (Ariz.), 1967-79; asso. prof., dept. library sci. Ariz. State U., 1968; vis. faculty Mesa Community Coll., 1980—. Mem. public relations com. United Fund; treas. Desert Samaritan Hosp. and Health Center Aux., 1981, v.p. community relations Hosp., 1982. Named Ariz. Librarian of Yr., 1971; recipient Silver Book award Library Binding Inst., 1963. Mem. Tempe Hist. Soc., Ariz. Pioneers Hist. Soc., Am. Radio Relay League, Am. Bus. Women's Assn., ALA, Southwestern Library Assn., Ariz. State Library Assn. (pres. 1973-74). Roman Catholic. Clubs: Our Lady of Mt. Carmel Ladies' Sodality, Soroptimist Internat. Founder, editor Roadrunner, Tumbling Tumbleweed; author Ency. Americana article on Tempe. Home: PO Box 26018 Tempe AZ 85282

WEILER, ROBERT JOSEPH, physician; b. Menomonie, Wis., May 18, 1932; s. William Joseph and Margaret (Eggers) W.; B.S., U. Notre Dame, 1954; M.D., U. Chgo., 1958; m. Patricia Anne Langan, July 12, 1975; children—Erik, Thomas. Intern, U. Chgo. Hosps. and Clinics, 1958-59, resident in medicine, 1959-62; fellow in hematology U. So. Calif. Sch. Medicine, Los Angeles, 1966-68, instr., asst. prof., 1968-71; practice medicine specializing in hematology and med. oncology, Albuquerque, 1971—; mem. staff Lovelace Med. Center, Albuquerque, 1971—, staff chmn., 1977; clin. asso. prof. U. N. Mex. Sch. Medicine. Served with USN, 1962-66. USPHS fellow, 1966-68. Diplomate Am. Bd. Internal Medicine. Mem. ACP, Am. Soc. Hematology, Am. Soc. Clin. Oncology, Sigma Xi. Democrat. Roman Catholic. Club: N.Mex. Mountain. Office: 5400 Gibson Blvd SE Albuquerque NM 87108

WEILL, SAMUEL, JR., automobile company executive; b. Rochester, N.Y., Dec. 22, 1916; s. Samuel and Bertha (Stein) W.; student U. Buffalo, 1934-35; m. Mercedes Weil, May 20, 1939 (div. Aug. 1943); children—Rita and Eric (twins); m. 2d, Cléanthe Kimball Carr, Aug. 12, 1960 (div. 1982); m. 3d, Jacqueline Natalie Bateman, Jan. 5, 1983. Co-owner, Brayton Air Coll., St. Louis, 1937-42; assos. editor, advt. mgr., bus. mgr. Road and Track Mag., Los Angeles, 1951-53; pres. Volkswagen Pacific, Inc., Culver City, Calif., 1953-73, Porsche Audi Pacific, Culver City, 1953-73; chmn. bd. Minto Internat., Inc., London; v.p. fin. Chieftain Oil Co., Ojai, Calif. Recipient Tom May award Jewish Hosp. and Research Center, 1971. Served with USAAF, 1943-45. Home: 305 Palomar Rd Ojai CA 93023 Office: 11300 Playa St Culver City CA 90230

WEINBAUM, JEAN DAVID, painter, sculptor, stained-glass artist; b. Zurich, Switzerland, Sept. 20, 1926; naturalized Am. citizen, 1974; s. Fritz Ismar and Gisele (Kahn) W.; student Sch. Arts and Crafts, Zurich, 1942-46. Exhibited on one-man shows: Galerie Weiller, Paris, 1955, Galerie Beno, Zurich, 1960, Galerie d'Art du Faubourg, Paris, 1960, 61, U. Calif. Med. Center, San Francisco, 1968, Stanford U., 1968, Triton Museum, Santa Clara, Calif., 1969, Galerie Smith-Andersen, Palo Alto, Calif., 1970, 71, 73, 79, Calif. Palace Legion of Honor, San Francisco, 1971, Musee des Arts Decoratifs, Lausanne, Switzerland, 1972, Bildungszentrum, Gelsenkirchen, Germany, 1972, Humboldt Galleries, San Francisco, 1973, Heimatmuseum, Bottrop, Germany, 1973, Lantern Gallery, Ann Arbor, Mich., 1973, Galerie Numaga, Auvernier, Switzerland, 1974, Linda Farris Gallery, Seattle, 1974, 75, Humboldt Galleries, N.Y.C., 1976, Galerie Smith-Andersen, San Francisco, 1976, Pasquale Iannetti, San Francisco, 1979, San Francisco Mus. Modern Art, 1981; exhibited in group shows; Palais de Tokyo, Paris, 1949, Galerie de France, Paris, 1959, Mus. Modern Art, Paris, 1961, 62, 63, 65, Galerie Weiller, Paris, 1961, Gallery Robert Elkon, N.Y.C., 1962, Gallerie Lutece, Paris, 1966, San Francisco Mus., 1971-72, Calif. Palace of Legion of Honor, San Francisco, 1971, and numerous others; represented in permanent collections: Mus. Modern Art, Paris, U. Art Mus. Berkeley, Calif., Nat. Collection Fine Arts, Washington, U. Mich., Ann Arbor, others; works include: stained-glass windows for Chapelle de Mosloy, Ferte Milon, France, 1951, Rosette window for Catholic ch. at Berne Sur Oise, 1955, St. Pieree du Regard Catholic ch., Calvados, France, 1957, Escherange, Moselle, France, 1962, Ailly for Catholic ch., Normandy, France, 1963, Lycee des Jeunes Filles, Bayonne, France, 1966. Home: PO Box 40291 San Francisco CA 94140

WEINBERG, WILLIAM LAWRENCE, clinical psychologist; b. N.Y.C., Oct. 30, 1927; s. Samuel H. and Rose (Stecker) W.; m. Arden K. Kamins, Dec. 24, 1950; children—Stephen, Wendy. A.B., U. Calif.-Berkeley, 1950; M.A., U. Oreg., 1952; Ph.D. Calif. Sch. Profl. Psychology, 1972; lic. psychologist, Calif. USPHS fellow in clin. psychology Stanford U., 1953; clin. psychologist Dept. Child Guidance Service, San Francisco Schs., 1953-58; sr. clin. psychologist San Mateo Mental Health Div., 1958-70; pvt. practice clin. psychology, Burlingame, Calif., 1956—. Served with USAAF, 1945-46. Mem. Am. Psychol. Assn., Calif. Psychol. Assn., San Mateo County Psychol. Assn. (pres. 1979). Office: 1750 El Camino Real Suite 201 Burlingame CA 94010

WEINER, KENNETH LAWRENCE, optometrist; b. Bronx, N.Y., June 6, 1934; s. Albert J. and Hilda (Kasindorf) W.; m. Lynne Cecele Greisler, Dec. 22, 1957; children—David Joseph, Karen Susan. Student CCNY, 1952-54; O.D., Pa. State Coll. Optometry, 1958. Pvt. practice optometry, Canyon Country, Calif., 1970—. Chmn., William S. Hart High Sch. Dist. Scholarship Com.; co-chmn. optometric sect. Bonds For Israel, Los Angeles. Served as 1st lt. Med. Service Corps, U.S. Army, 1958-61. Subject of resolutions Los Angeles City Council, 1977, Calif. Senate, 1977, Calif. Assembly, 1977; named Disting. Alumnus, Pa. Coll. Optometry, 1982. Mem. Am. Optometric Found., Council Sports Vision, Coll. Optometric Vision Devel. (assoc.), Optometric Extension Program, Am. Pub. Health Assn., So. Calif. Pub. Health Assn., Am. Optometric Assn., Calif. Optometric Assn. (chmn. members div. 1980-82, trustee 1982-84), San Fernando Valley Optometric Assn. (dir. 1971-78, chmn. dept. pub. info. 1973-74, pres. 1977), Optometric Care Council So. Calif. (pres. 1978), Gamma Omega Phi. Jewish. Home: 19611 Rosita St Tarzana CA 91356 Office: 19172 Soledad Canyon Rd Canyon Country CA 91351

WEINER, LEONARD, periodontist; b. N.Y.C., Aug. 4, 1913; s. Harris and Eva (Ossen) W.; A.B., Yale U., 1936; D.M.D., Harvard U., 1940; m. Doris E. Goldman, Dec. 14, 1940; children—Charles Lewis, Elizabeth J. Practice dentistry specializing in periodontics, Hartford, Conn., 1940, Tucson, 1946—; pres. Assos. in Periodontics and Endodontics, P.C., 1964-79; dir. Med. Square, Inc., Tucson, 1974-77, pres., 1977-80, treas., 1979-80; asso. U. Ariz. Med. Sch. Chmn., Combined Jewish Appeal, 1949; pres. Tucson chpt. Am. Friends Hebrew U., 1956-58; dir., v.p. Temple Emanu-El, 1947-57. Served with U.S. Army, 1940-46. Recipient Chai award, 1966, Maimonides award, 1978, Outstanding Citizen of Tucson award, 1978. Fellow Am. Assn. Endodontists, Am. Coll. Dentists; mem. Western Soc. Periodontology (pres. 1967), Nat. Fedn. Regional Peridontal Orgns. (pres. 1967-68), ADA, Ariz. Dental Assn., So. Ariz. Dental Soc., Sigma Xi, Alpha Omega. Clubs: President's (U. Ariz.), B'nai B'rith; Prime Minister's (Israel). Office: 12C Medical Sq 1601 N Tucson Blvd Tucson AZ 85716

WEINER, RICHARD ALLEN, TV sta. exec., producer; b. N.Y.C., Nov. 9, 1942; s. Alfred Kenneth and Martha Barbara (Debrest) W.; B.A., Allegheny Coll., 1963; J.D., St. Johns U. Sch. Law, 1965. Admitted to N.Y. bar, 1968, Calif. bar, 1973; atty. ABC-N.Y.-ABC-TV and Radio-ABC Radio Network, 1969-72; asst. resident counsel Paramount TV, Hollywood, Calif., 1972-73; exec. v.p. Heftel Broadcasting Co., Honolulu, 1975-77; gen. mgr. Sta. KGMB-TV, Honolulu, 1975—; producer Christmas in Hawaii, 1981; The Perfumed Handkerchief, 1981; Tahiti Holiday, 1982; Beyond the Great Wall: Journey to the End of China, 1982. Mem. Hawaii Energy Conservation Council, 1978; media cons. Hawaii Savs. Bond Vol. Com., 1979, 80-81. Served with USNR, 1968. Mem. N.Y. Bar Assn., Calif. Bar Assn., Assn. Bar City N.Y., Hawaiian Assn. Broadcasters (pres. 1978, v.p. TV 1981). Club: Plaza (gov. Honolulu). Office: 1534 Kapiolani Blvd Honolulu HI 96814

WEINER, SANDRA SAMUEL, critical care nurse; b. N.Y.C., Jan. 12, 1947; d. Herbert A. and Ruth (Wallerstein) Samuel; m. Neil D. Weiner, June 15, 1969 (div. June 1980); 1 dau., Jaime Michelle. B.S. in Nursing, SUNY-Buffalo, 1968; postgrad. UCLA. Registered nurse. Staff nurse N.Y. Hosp.-Cornell Med. Ctr., 1968-69; head nurse med.-surg. nursing Abington (Pa.) Hosp., 1969; asso. prof. Sch. Nursing, U.Pa., Phila., 1970; nursing instr. Coll. of Med. Assts., Long Beach, Calif., 1971-72; surg. nurse Med. Ctr. of Tarzana and Cedar Sinai, Los Angeles, 1976-80; supr. recovery room Beverly Hills (Calif.) Med. Ctr., 1981—; instr. C.P.R. Mem. Am. Nursing Assn., Am. Assn. Critical Care Nursing, Heart and Lung Assn., U.S. Ski Assn., AAU. Democrat. Jewish. Home: 2757 Anchor Ave Los Angeles CA 90064 Office: 1177 S Beverly Dr Los Angeles CA

WEINGARTEN, SAUL MYER, lawyer; b. Los Angeles, Dec. 19, 1921; s. Louis and Lillian Dorothy (Alter) W.; A.A., Antelope Valley Coll., 1940; A.B., UCLA, 1942; J.D., U. So. Calif., 1949, postgrad. (Coro Found. fellow, Marie Baker Carter scholar), 1950; m. Miriam E. Moore, Jan. 20, 1949; children—David Steven, Lawrence, Bruce. Bar: Calif. 1950; U.S. Supreme Ct. 1961. Legal counsel State of Calif., 1950; sole practice, 1954—, pres. Saul M. Weingarten, Inc., Seaside and Carmel Calif., 1952—; legal counsel Security Nat. Bank of Monterey County, Pacific Grove, Calif.; dir. Frontier Nat. Bank, Cheyenne Wyo.; writer, tech. dir. 5 films on law, 1952; City atty. City of Gonzales (Calif.), 1954-73, City of Seaside (Calif.), 1955-71; legal counsel Seaside Redevel. Agy., 1958-76. Bd. dirs. Alliance of Aging, 1968—, pres., 1974; bd. dirs. ARC, 1964—, United Way, 1965—, Monterey County Symphony Assn., 1974-82, Lyceum, 1968—; bd. dirs. Monterey Peninsula Shakespeare Festival, pres., 1973; trustee Clark Found., Monterey, Calif., 1980-82. Served to comdr. USNR, 1942-46, 50-54. Mem. Monterey County Bar Assn. Democrat. Jewish. Club: Rotary (pres. 1972, 81-82), Commonwealth. Home: 4135 Crest Rd Pebble Beach CA 93953 Office: Saul M Weingarten Inc Fremont Profl Center Suite 4 Seaside CA 93955 also Suite 101 3855 Via Nona Marie Carmel CA 93922

WEINHOLD, BARRY KERN, counselor educator, psychologist, writer; b. Ephrata, Pa., June 23, 1937; s. Kern G. and Betty R. W.; m. Mary Frances Johnstone, Nov. 21, 1959; m. 2d, Barbara N. MacDougald, May 14, 1980 (dec. 1983); children—Michael, Brian, Bill, Teresa, Siena, Marjorie, Mark. B.S., Millersville State Coll., 1959; Ph.D., U. Minn., 1968. Lic. psychologist, Colo. Asst. prof. Ohio U., 1968-69; dir. counseling, asst. prof. U. Wis.-Green Bay, 1969-71; assoc. prof. edn., guidance and counseling U. Colo.-Colorado Springs, 1971-78, prof., 1978—. Mem. Am. Personnel and Guidance Assn., Assn. Counselor Educators and Suprs., Assn. Transpersonal Psychology, Rocky Mountain Assn. Counselors Educators and Suprs., El Paso County Psychol. Soc. Author books including: Transpersonal Approaches to Counselor Education, 1982; Transpersonal Approaches to Counseling and Psychotherapy, 1982. Home: 11030 Thomas Rd Colorado Springs CO 80908 Office: Austin Bluffs Pkwy Colorado Springs CO 80907

WEINMANN, RICHARD ALAN, manufacturing company executive; b. Los Angeles, Nov. 23, 1934; s. Alonzo Bernard and Irene (Ferrao) W.; m. Mary Elizabeth Dickson, Aug. 31, 1956; children—Paul Alan, Mark Edward, Steven Andrew. B.B.A., Claremont McKenna Coll., 1956. Acct., Price, Waterhouse & Co., Los Angeles, 1956-58; sr. acct. Leach Corp., Long Beach, Calif., 1958-60; cost. acct. Cosmodyne Corp., Torrance, Calif., 1960-64, controller, 1964-71; controller TRE Corp., Santa Ana, Calif., 1971-78, Sierra Electric, Gardena, Calif., 1979-80; v.p., gen. mgr. Sierra Electric div Pass & Seymour Inc., Gardena, 1980—. Counselor Boy Scouts Am., 1975—; treas. local Episcopal Ch., 1972-77. Mem. Nat. Assn. Accts. (Orange Coast chpt.). Republican. Home: 4086 Germainder Way Irvine CA 92715 Office: 15100 S Figueroa St Gardena CA 90248

WEINRACH, ROY SYLVAN, oncologist; b. Phila., Apr. 24, 1930; s. Lewis Samuel and Jeannette Edith (Weintraub) W.; m. Judith Marcie Borens, Jan. 1, 1967; children—Jonathan Saul, David Marshall, Joshua Saul. A.B., Temple U., 1951, M.A., 1954; Ph.D., U. Chgo., 1957; M.D., Northwestern U., 1961. Diplomate Am. Bd. Internal Medicine. Intern, Phila. Gen. Hosp., 1962-63; resident Univ. Hosp., Ann Arbor, Mich., 1962-63, Mt. Sinai Hosp., N.Y.C., 1965-67; asst. prof. hematology/oncology Med. Coll. Pa., Phila., 1967-68; practice medicine specializing in med. oncology, Phoenix, 1968—. Served with USPHS, 1963-65. Fellow Am. Coll. Physicians; mem. AMA, Ariz. Med. Assn., Maricopa County Med. Soc., Am. Soc. Clin. Oncology, Am. Soc. Hematology, Galens Med. Soc. Jewish. Contbr. articles in field to med. jours. Office: 333 E Virginia St Suite 113 Phoenix AZ 85004

WEINSHIENK, ZITA LEESON (MRS. HUBERT TROY WEINSHIENK), judge; b. St. Paul, Apr. 3, 1933; d. Louis and Ada (Dubov) Leeson; student U. Colo., 1952-53; B.A. magna cum laude, U. Ariz., 1955; J.D. cum laude, Harvard, 1958; Fulbright grantee U. Copenhagen (Denmark), 1959; m. Hubert Troy Weinshienk, July 8, 1956; children—Edith Blair, Kay Anne, Darcy Jill. Admitted to Colo.

bar, 1959; probation counselor, legal adviser, referee Denver Juvenile Ct., 1959-64; judge Denver County Ct., 1964-71; Denver dist. judge, 1972-79; U.S. dist. judge for dist. Colo., 1979—. Mem. Denver Anti-Crime Council; vis. com. Harvard Law Sch.; Precinct com.-woman Denver Democratic Com., 1963-64. Named One of 100 Women in Touch with Our Time, Harper's Bazaar Mag., 1971. Mem. Am. Colo., Denver bar assns., Nat. Conf. Fed. Trial Judges, Colo. Women's Bar Assn., Women's Forum of Colo., Harvard Law Sch. Assn., Denver League Women Voters, Soroptimist Club Denver, Bus. and Profl. Women's Club Denver (Woman of Yr. 1969), Order of Coif (hon. Colo. chpt.). Home: 1881 S Niagara Way Denver CO 80224 Office: US Courthouse 1929 Stout St Denver CO 80294

WEINSTEIN, JUDITH, art cons.; b. Chgo., Feb. 11, 1927; d. Julius and Charlotte (Brandau) Braun; B.S. in Psychology, U. Wis., 1950; m. Irwin Weinstein, Jan. 20, 1951; children—James, David. Tchr., N.Y. State Child Care Center, N.Y.C., 1950-52, U. Chgo., 1952-53; interior designer, color cons. Paul Bennett & Assos., 1953-58; mem. polit campaign coms. for U.S. Senate, mayor of Los Angeles, 1958-63; dir. Ethnic Arts Shop, Bookshop and George Page Mus. Shop, Los Angeles County Mus. Natural History, also producer ethnic art shows and research asst. dept. anthropology, 1971-77; dir., continuing edn. specialist Artsreach program UCLA Extension, also bd. dirs. Los Angeles Mcpl. Art Gallery Assos. and Los Angeles Art Showcase, 1978—; project developer Zev Braun Pictures; spl. adv. for art U.S. Sen. Alan Cranston. Planning com. Democratic Nat. Telethon, 1960; bd. dirs. Calif. Chamber Symphony, 1960-71; v.p. Pacific chpt. UN Assn., 1963-69, adv. bd., 1969-71; organizer, developer UN Center, Westwood, Calif., 1963-71; del. 1st women's conf. Dem. Nat. Com., 1971-77; bd. dirs. Mus. Alliance, 1971-77; adv. com. Los Angeles Children's Mus., 1978; mem. com. Corp. Disabilities and Telecommunication, 1981—; bd. dirs. Alternative Living for Aging, Artsreach.

WEINSTEIN, MICHAEL GORDON, sociology educator; b. Detroit, July 19, 1941; s. Philip R. and Anne (Yetz) W. Ph.B., Wayne State U., 1963; A.M., Harvard U., 1966, Ph.D., 1968. Asst. prof. sociology U. Hawaii, 1967-80, assoc. prof. sociology, 1980—; editor Social Process in Hawaii, 1979—. Mem. Am. Sociol. Assn., Pacific Sociol. Assn., Hawaii Sociol. Assn. Home: 3350 Sierra Dr Apt 404 Honolulu HI 96816 Office: 2424 Maile Way Room 239 Honolulu HI 96822

WEINSTEIN, PAUL A(NDREW), psychologist; b. N.Y.C., Dec. 8, 1941; s. Herman H. and Lilian (Arnoff) W.; m. Susan E. Woodward, Aug. 23, 1944; 1 dau., Katharine Elizabeth. Area coordinator Am. Field Service, U. Wis., 1960-64, 64-66; vol. Peace Corps, Karnataka, India, 1966-68, trainer, Calif., 1968-69, India, 1971-72; cross-cultural coordinator Internat. Inst. Edn., N.Y.C., 1969-70; intern in psychology Seattle VA, 1975-76; pvt. practice psychology for adolescent, family and marriage counseling, Silverdale, Wash., 1976—; cons., tchr. in field. Mem. Am. Psychol. Assn. Home: 14216 Thomas Dr NW Silverdale WA 98383

WEINSTOCK, HELENE SUZETTE, psychotherapist, marriage, family and child counselor; b. Chgo., Apr. 26, 1935; d. Bernard L. and Betty E. (Balter) Karlin; m. Donald Jay Weinstock, Sept. 1, 1955. A.A., UCLA, 1954, A.B. in Polit. Sci., 1955, M.A., 1958, C.Phil. in History, 1969; M.A. in Psychology, Calif. State U.-Los Angeles, 1980. Lic. marriage, family and child counselor, Calif.; cert. sch. counselor, tchr., Calif. Tchr. Mt. Vernon Jr. High Sch., Los Angeles, 1958-61; edn. coordinator Riverside (Calif.) Mental Health Assn., 1967-73; psychol. asst. Leonard Schneider Ph.D. & Assocs., Newport Beach, Calif., 1976-78; psychol. counselor Huntington Beach (Calif.) Community Clinic, 1978-80, West County Counseling Ctr., Huntington Beach, 1980-81; pvt. practice as cons. psychotherapist, marriage, family and child counselor, Huntington Beach, 1981—; cons. and supr. interns West County Counseling Ctr., Huntington Beach, 1981—; pub. service adv. bds. Riverside County, 1967-73. Nat. Def. Fgn. Lang. Fellow, 1964-66; Mabel Wilson Richards grad. scholar UCLA, 1955-56. Mem. Am. Assn. Marriage and Family Therapy, Calif. Assn. of Marriage and Family Therapists, Western Psychol. Assn., Calif. State Psychol. Assn., Am. Psychol. Assn., Phi Beta Kappa, Alpha Lambda Delta, Alpha Mu Gamma, Pi Sigma Alpha, Phi Alpha Theta, Pi Gamma Mu, Psi Chi. Democrat. Jewish. Contbr. articles to profl. jours. Office: PO Box 2051 Huntington Beach CA 92647

WEINTRAUB, DEBORA SHARON, electrical engineer; b. N.Y.C., Nov. 12, 1953; d. David Weintraub and Norme Weintraub Fritz. B.S. in Microbiology, Ariz. State U., now postgrad. in indsl. engring. Assoc. programmer analyst Motorola GEG, Scottsdale, Ariz., 1979-81, programmer/analyst, 1981-82, sr. engr., electronics, 1982—. Mem. Assn. Computing Machinery. Club: Ariz. Road Racers.

WEIR, ALEXANDER, JR., utilities executive; b. Crossett, Ark., Dec. 19, 1922; s. Alexander and Mary Eloise (Feild) W.; B.S. in Chem. Engring., U. Ark., 1943; M.Ch.E., Poly. Inst. Bklyn., 1946; Ph.D., U. Mich., 1954; cert. U. So. Calif. Grad. Sch. Bus. Adminstrn., 1968; m. Florence Forschner, Dec. 28, 1946; children—Alexander III, Carol Jean, Bruce Richard. Analyst, chemist Am. Cyanamid and Chem. Corp., summers 1941, 42, chem. engr. Am. Cyanamid Co., Stanford Research Labs., 1943-47; with U. Mich., 1948-58, as research asso., project supr. Engring. Research Inst., 1948-57, lectr. chem. and metall. engring. dept., 1954-56, asst. prof., 1956-58; cons. Ramo-Wooldridge Corp., Los Angeles, 1956-57, mem. tech. staff, sect. head, asst. mgr., 1957-60, in charge Atlas Missile Captive test program, 1956-60; various tech. adv. positions Northrop Corp. Corporate Office, Beverly Hills, Calif., 1960-70; prin. scientist for air quality So. Calif. Edison Co., Los Angeles, 1970-76, mgr. chem. systems research and devel., 1976—; rep. Am. Rocket Soc. to Detroit Nuclear Council, 1954-57; chmn. session on chem. reactions Nuclear Sci. and Engring. Congress, Cleve., 1955; U.S. del. AGARD (NATO) Combustion Colloquium, Liege, Belgium, 1955; Western U.S. rep. task force on environmental research and devel. goals Electric Research Council, 1971. Bd. govs., past pres. Civic Union Playa del Rey, chmn. sch., police and fire, nominating, civil def., army liaison coms.; mem. Senate, Westchester YMCA, chmn. Dads sponsoring com., active fund raising; chmn. nominating com. Paseo del Rey Sch. P.T.A., 1961; mem. Los Angeles Mayors Community Adv. Com.; asst. chmn. advancement com., merit badge dean Centinella dist. Los Angeles Area council Boy Scouts Am. Mem. Am. Geophys. Union, Navy League U.S. (v.p. Palos Verdes Peninsula council 1961-62), N.Y. Acad. Scis., Sci. Research Soc. Am., Am. Chem. Soc., Am. Inst. Chem. Engrs., AAAS, Combustion Inst., Air Pollution Control Assn., Assn. U.S. Army, U.S. Power Squadron, Sigma Xi, Phi Kappa Phi, Phi Lambda Upsilon, Alpha Chi Sigma, Lambda Chi Alpha. Club: Santa Monica Yacht. Author: Two and Three Dimensional Flow of Air through Square-Edged Sonic Orifices, 1954; (with R. B. Morrison and T. C. Anderson) Notes on Combustion 1955; also tech. papers. Inventor Weir power plant stack scrubber. Office: So Calif Edison Co PO Box 800 Rosemead CA 91770

WEIR, ROBERT H., lawyer; b. Boston, Dec. 7, 1922; s. Abraham and Beatrice (Stern) W.; A.B., Harvard U., 1944, LL.B., 1948; m. Ruth Hirsch, July 2, 1954 (dec. Nov. 1965); children—Anthony, David, Michael H.; m. 2d, Sylvia T. Frias; children—Nicole F., Daniella F. Admitted to Mass. bar, 1948, Wash. bar, 1952, Calif. bar, 1957; spl. asst. to atty. gen. U.S. Dept. Justice, Seattle, 1948-53, Washington, 1953-56; practiced in San Jose, also Palo Alto, Calif., 1957—. Instr. taxation of real estate U. Calif. at San Jose and San Francisco, 1957—; lectr. U. So. Calif. Tax Inst. Mem. prison com. Am. Friends Service Com. Bd. dirs. San Jose Light Opera Assn., Inc. Served with U.S. Army, 1942-45. Mem. Am., Santa Clara County bar assns., State Bar Calif., Am. Judicature Soc. Author: Advantages in Taxes, 1960. Tax columnist Rural Realtor, Chgo., 1959—. Speaker taxation annual meetings Nat. Assn. Real Estate Bds., 1958-60. Author: Taxes Working for You, 1966; How to Make the Most of Depreciation Write Off. Contbr. articles to profl. jours. Address: PO Box 5764 San Jose CA 95150

WEIS, CARYL CHRISTINE, real estate broker; b. Kelseyville, Calif., Dec. 25, 1921; d. Fred W. and Maria Charlotte (Staheli) Flodberg; A.B., U. Calif.-Berkeley, 1943; m. Aug. 31, 1947. Realtor, owner Properties Unltd., Santa Rosa, Calif., 1966—; with Aames Employment Agy., Los Angeles, Wes Employment Agy., Whittier, Calif., 1955-60; staff Stanford Research Inst., South Pasadena, Calif., 1956-57. Served with USMC, 1944-46. Mem. ad hoc com. Econ. Devel. Bd. of Sonoma County (Calif.), 1966, Sonoma County Planning Dept., 1968-69; bd. dirs., vice chmn. Redwood Empire chpt. ARC, 1971-72, bd. dirs., 1974-81; chmn. Realtors Fund Drive, United Way, 1969, others. Mem. Sonoma County Bd. Realtors (dir. 1967-74, pres. 1973), Sonoma County Multiple Listing Service (dir., pres. 1969-70), Calif. Assn. Realtors (regional v.p. Div. IV 1977), Realtors Nat. Mktg. Inst., Nat. Assn. Realtors (exec. com. 1981, women's council), Santa Rosa C. of C., Execs. Assn. Realtors of Sonoma County. Club: Commonwealth of Calif., Newcomers, Zonta, Bus. and Profl. Women's. Address: 2001 4th St Santa Rosa CA 95404

WEISS, CHARLES FREDERICK, motion picture co. exec.; b. Los Angeles, Nov. 9, 1939; s. Walter E. and Marie E. W.; B.S., Calif. State U., Los Angeles, 1963; M.B.A., U. So. Calif., 1965; m. Katherine Joyce Weiss, June 26, 1959; children—Bryan Scott, Michael Craig. Vice pres. Great Western Savs. and Loan Assn., Los Angeles, 1963-69; corp. dir. orgn. devel. Republic Corp., Los Angeles, 1969-72; corp. v.p. Beverly Hills (Calif.) Bancorp, 1972-75; corp. v.p. 20th Century Fox Film Corp., Los Angeles, 1975—. Club: Los Angeles Turf. Home: 1542 Moreno Dr Glendale CA 91207 Office: PO Box 9276 Glendale CA 91206

WEISS, HARVEY MORTON, mgmt. cons., author, lectr.; b. St. Louis, Jan. 9, 1938; s. Isador and Lillian W.; B.S., Washington U., St. Louis, 1960; m. Beverly Lynn Miller, June 21, 1964; children—Stephen David, Mark Joel. Supr. methods IBM, St. Louis, Kansas City, 1960-63; systems supr. RCA, St. Louis, 1964-66; br. data base mgr. Gen. Electric/Honeywell, Denver, 1969-74; sr. cons. Touche Ross, Denver, 1966-69; prin. cons. Weiss & Assos., Inc., Denver, 1974—; lectr. database tech., data processing bus. planning, and data processing organizational structures. Pres., Pine Ridge Park Vista Home Owners Assn., 1970—; cubmaster Denver council Boy Scouts Am., 1975-76. Recipient Disting. Service award Assn. Systems Mgmt., 1974. Mem. Assn. Computing Machinery, Data Processing Mgmt. Assn., Profl. and Tech. Cons. Assn., Ind. Computer Cons. Assn. Contbg. editor Mini-Micro Systems; contbr. articles to profl. jours. Home: 3958 S Syracuse Way Denver CO 80237 Office: 2950 S Jamaica Ct #100 Aurora CO 80014

WEISS, HERBERT KLEMM, aeronautical engr.; b. Lawrence, Mass., June 22, 1917; s. Herbert Julius and Louise (Klemm) W.; B.S., Mass. Inst. Tech., 1937, M.S., 1938; m. Ethel Celesta Giltner, May 14, 1945; children—Janet Elaine, Jack Klemm (dec.). Engr., U.S. Army Arty. Bds., Ft. Monroe, Va., Camp Davis, N.C., Ft. Bliss, Tex., 1938-46; chief WPN Systems Lab., Ballistic Research Labs., Aberdeen Proving Grounds, Md., 1946-53; chief WPN systems analysis dept. Northrop Aircraft Corp., 1953-58; mgr. advanced systems devel. mil. systems planning aeronutronic div. Ford Motor Co., Newport Beach, Calif., 1958-61; group dir., plans devel. and analysis, staff to gen. mgr. for long range planning Aerospace Corp., El Segundo, Calif., 1961-65; with Litton Industries, Van Nuys, Calif., 1965-82, now cons. mil. systems analysis; cons. Office Dir. Def., Research and Engring., 1954-64. Mem. Army Sci. Adv. Panel, 1965-74; mem. sci. adv. commn. Army Ball Research Labs., 1973-77; adv. Pres. Commn. Law Enforcement and Adminstrn. Justice, 1966. Commendation for meritorious civilian service USAF, 1964. Fellow AAAS, Am. Inst. Aeros. and Astronautics (asso.); mem. Operations Research Soc. Am., IEEE, Inst. Mgmt. Scis. Republican. Presbyn. Club: Cosmos. Patentee in field. Contbr. articles in field to profl. jours. Home: PO Box 2668 Palos Verdes Peninsula CA 90274

WEISS, LAWRENCE ROBERT, venture capital co. exec.; b. Pasadena, Mar. 8, 1937; s. Joseph B. and Elsie (Shaw) W.; B.S. in Applied Physics, UCLA, 1959; M.S. in Mgmt. Sci., U. So. Calif., 1974; m. Elaine Saxon, June 23, 1963; children—Jeffrey Arthur, Jason Ashley. Electronic systems engr., N.Am. Aviation, Inc., Los Angeles, 1960-62, Litton Systems, Inc., 1962-63; group head Hughes Aircraft Co., Culver City, Calif., 1963-67, group head, sales rep., br. sales mgr. 1967-70; with Sci. Data Systems, Systems Engring. Labs., Gen. Automation, Inc., Inter-data Corp., Applied Digital Data Systems, Inc., 1973-80; co-founder, chmn., pres. Health-tronics Labs. Inc., Rochester, N.Y., 1970-72, Cal-trend Personality Systems, Inc., Los Angeles, 1973—; co-founder, chmn. bd., v.p. Evolution Computer Systems Corp., (name changed to Evolution Techs., Inc. 1981), Irvine, Calif., 1980-82; co-founder, chmn., pres. Capital Tech. Group Inc., Irvine, 1982—. Mem. Mensa. Home: 22706 Islamare Ln El Toro CA 92630 Office: 18003-L Sky Park S Irvine CA 92714

WEISS, LOUIS ISRAEL, marketing research executive; b. Bklyn., May 7, 1948; s. Lipman Leo and Frances (Markowitz) W.; m. Naomi F. Weiss, July 19, 1970; 1 son, Elan Stephen. B.S., Bklyn. Coll., 1969; M.B.A., Baruch Coll., 1972. Mktg. research supr. Gen. Foods Corp., White Plains, N.Y., 1970-72; exec. v.p. Peter Honig Assocs. Inc., White Plains, 1973-78; sr. v.p. Yankelovich, Skelly & White Inc., Newport Beach, Calif., 1978-80; pres. Am. Mktg. Services Inc., Newport Beach, 1980—; lectr., speaker. Bd. dirs. Jewish Community Ctr. of South Orange County, Portafina Assn.; mem. leadership council Chabad of Irvine. Mem. Mktg. Research Assn. So. Calif. (pres.), Am. Mktg. Assn. Democrat. Jewish. Home: 784 Barracuda Way Laguna Beach CA 92651 Office: Am Mktg Services 3822 Campus Dr Suite 220 Newport Beach CA 92660

WEISS, MAURICE S., marketing executive; b. N.Y.C., Jan. 3, 1928; s. Jacob and Sarah (Friedman) W.; m. Barbara Lee Curley, Sept. 15, 1938; 1 dau., Jane Weiss Schriber; 2d, Norma C. Gambert, Oct. 21, 1956; children—John, Regan, Kate, Maryann. A.B. CUNY-Bklyn., 1948. Advt. mgr., Kayser Roth Corp., N.Y.C., 1955-59; co-owner Sta. WHOO Orlando Fla., 1959-61, Sta. WBIC, Long Island, N.Y. 1961-63; mktg. dir. Revlon Cosmetics, N.Y.C., 1964-73, Clairol Co., N.Y.C., 1973-75; v.p. mktg. and advt. Maybelline Co., Memphis, 1975-79; v.p. mktg., world-wide Max Factor, Hollywood Calif., 1979—. Office: Max Factor Co 1655 No McCadden Pl Hollywood CA 90028

WEISS, RHODA ELAINE, public relations executive, consultant; b. Detroit, Oct. 8, 1949; d. Harold and Mildred (Million) W. B.A. in Communications and Journalism, Mich. State U., 1971; M.A. in Psychology and Health Mgmt., Antioch U., 1980. Cert. Western Network for Health Care Execs., U. Calif.-Berkeley. Cons. mktg. group, 1977-78; part-time counselor Elizabeth Seton Coll., Yonkers, N.Y., 1971-72; reporter Gannett Newspapers, 1971-72; part-time reporter Detroit-Suburban Newspapers, 1963-71; publs. editor Pacific Health Resources, Los Angeles, 1973; pub. relations specialist St. John's Hosp., Santa Monica, Calif., 1974-75; pub. relations rep. Rand Corp., Santa Monica, 1975-76; community relations dir. Torrance (Calif.) Meml. Hosp., 1976-78; pub. relations dir. St. Joseph Med. Ctr., Burbank, Calif., 1978—; mgmt. cons., 1976—; instr. South Bay U., 1975-80. Trustee, adv. bd.; Hosp. Home Health Care; bd. dirs., mem. com. Nat. Hospice Orgn. Hosp. Research and Edn. Kellogg Found. fellow, 1979-83; recipient pub. relations casebook awards, Sandoz Med. Journalism award, Desi award. Mem. women in Health Adminstrn. (officer, charter bd. dirs.), Internat. Assn. Bus. Communicators (Gold Quill 1981, 82, 83, 33 other awards), Pub. Relations Soc. Am. (8 awards), Radio and TV News Assn., Am. Hosp. Assn., Assn. Western Hosps. (10 awards), Acad. Hosp. Pub. Relations (11 awards), Women in Communications (Clarion awards 1982), Los Angeles Ad Women (7 awards), Am. Soc. Hosp. Pub. Relations (2 awards), Calif. Soc. Hosp. Pub. Relations (officer, 8 awards), Soc. for Profl. Journalists, Calif. Hosp. Assn., Alpha Delta Pi (pres. chpt. adviser U. So. Calif., named outstanding alumna). Clubs: Publicity (5 awards), Pacific Coast Press. Contbr. articles on hosp. and health care to profl. jours.; producer award winning film Day By Day, 1980.

WEISS, ROGER ALLAN, psychologist; b. Bklyn., Dec. 14, 1945; s. David and Helen (Garber) W.; m. Lydia Adjemian, June 26, 1982. B.A., with honors in Psychology, U. Buffalo, 1967; M.A., Hofstra U., 1970, Ph.D., 1973. Chief psychologist Roosevelt Community Mental Health Ctr., L.I., N.Y., 1975-78; co-founder The Health Project, 1981-82; coordinator psychol. services Patchogue Medford Pub. Schs., L.I., 1978-82; psychologist, pres. cons. Roger A. Weiss, P.C., Kailua-Kona, Hawaii, 1983—; instr. family medicine Glen Cove Hosp., 1973-77; lectr. in field. Mem. Nat. Register of Health Service Providers in Psychology, Am. Psychol. Assn. Author: Weiss Responsibility Scale (test), 1973. Address: PO Box 3178 Kailua-Kona HI 96740

WEISS, STEVEN ALAN, communications co. exec.; b. Glendale, Calif., Oct. 19, 1944; s. Adrian and Ethel (Long) W.; A.A., Los Angeles City Coll., 1964; B.S., U. So. Calif., 1966; M.S., Northwestern U., 1967; m. Laurie Charmak, Nov. 9, 1967; children—Ara Simon, Zachary Adam. Gen. mgr. Adrian Weiss Prodns., Beverly Hills, Calif., 1971-74; v.p., treas. Weiss Global Enterprises, Beverly Hills, 1974-76, sec.-treas., 1976—, dir., 1974—; sec.-treas. Film Investment Corp., Oxnard, Calif., 1975—. Charter mem. Republican Presdl. Task Force, U.S. Senatorial Club, Nat. Rep. Senatorial Com.; sustaining mem. Rep. Nat. Com. Served with USN, 1966-71. Mem. Nat. Cable TV Assn., Nat. Assn. TV Program Execs. Internat., Am. Film Inst. Jewish. Clubs: Masons, B'nai B'rith. Home: 4137 N Sunset Ln Hollywood Beach CA 93030 Office: 2055 S Saviers Rd Suite 12 Oxnard CA 93033

WEISS, THEODORE JOEL, chemist; b. Rochester, N.Y., Aug. 16, 1919; s. Edmond A. and Bella (Rady) W.; A.B., Syracuse (N.Y.) U., 1940, Ph.D. (Univ. fellow), 1953; m. Jane V. Goldberg, Nov. 20, 1941; children—Andree T. Weiss Norris, Bonnie N. Weiss Felter. Asst. chemist State of Md., 1941-43; research chemist Borden Co., Syracuse, 1944-49; chemist Dairymen's League Coop., Syracuse, 1949-52; research chemist, head edible fats and oils research div. Swift & Co., Chgo., 1952-63; tech. dir. Capital City Products Co., Columbus, Ohio, 1963-64; sr. project leader fats and oils lab. Hunt-Wesson Foods Inc., Fullerton, Calif., 1964-68; research chemist Agrl. Research Service, Dept. Agr., New Orleans, 1968-70, Agrl. Research Service, Washington, 1970-73; tech. mgr. indsl. sales dept. Hunt-Wesson Foods, Inc., 1972—. Served with U.S. Army, 1943-44. Mem. Am. Oil Chemists Soc., Am. Chem. Soc., Inst. Food Technologists, AAAS, Sigma Xi, Phi Beta Kappa, Pi Mu Epsilon, Sigma Pi Sigma. Jewish. Author: Food Oils and Their Uses, 1970, 2d edit., 1983, also articles, chpts. in books. Patentee in field. Home: 16775 Lake Terrace Way Yorba Linda CA 92686 Office: 1645 W Valencia Dr Fullerton CA 92634

WEISSBLUTH, MITCHEL, physics educator; b. Russia, Jan. 7, 1915; s. Elias and Miriam W.; m. Margaret Hochhauser, Feb. 25, 1940; children—Stephen, Marc, Thomas. B.A., Bklyn. Coll., 1936; M.A., George Washington U., 1941; Ph.D., U. Calif.-Berkeley, 1950. Metallurgist, U.S. Navy, Washington, 1937-41; radio engr. Crosley Radio Corp., Cin., 1942-43; sr. research engr., jet propulsion lab. Calif. Inst. Tech., Pasadena, 1943-45; teaching asst. U. Calif.-Berkeley, 1945-49, lectr., 1950; research assoc. Stanford (Calif.) U., 1950-51, instr., 1951-54, asst. prof. radiol. physics, 1954-66, assoc. prof. applied physics, 1966-75, prof., 1976—, dir. biophysics lab., 1964-67; Fulbright research awardee Weizmann Inst., Israel, 1960-66; liaison scientist office Naval Research, London, 1967-68, sr. liaison scientist, Tokyo, 1978-79. Mem. Am. Phys. Soc., Internat. Soc. Quantum Biology (pres. 1973-75). Author: Free Radicals in Biological Systems, 1961; Quantum Aspects of Polypeptides and Polynucleotides, 1964; Molecular Biophysics, 1965; Hemoglobin: Cooperativity and Electronic Properties, 1974; Atoms and Molecules, 1978. Home: 820 Pine Hill Rd Stanford CA 94305 Office: Dept Applied Physics Stanford U Stanford CA 94305

WEISS-EDWARDS, LINDA, jewelry designer; b. Detroit, Dec. 6, 1951; d. Albert and Edith (Warshawsky) Weiss; m. John Lyman Edwards, Dec. 12, 1979. B.F.A. magna cum laude, Central Mich. U., Mt. Pleasant, 1973; B.F.A., U. Wash., 1975; M.F.A., Cranbrook Acad. Art, Bloomfield Hills, Mich., 1977; postgrad. Gemological Instn. Am., Santa Monica, Calif., 1980. Instr. jewelry and metalsmithing U. Mich., Ann Arbor, 1977; designer, goldsmith, mgr. G.D. McLean & Co., Goldsmiths, Sausalito and Mill Valley, Calif., 1978-81; instr. Calif. Coll. Arts and Crafts, Oakland, 1979-80; ptnr., designer jewelry Weiss/Edwards Design Assocs., Mill Valley, 1979—; instr. Acad. of Art. Coll., San Francisco, 1981; group shows: San Jose Mus. Art, 1980, Farmington Valley Arts Ctr., Avon, Conn., 1980, Precious Arts Gallery, Los Gatos, Calif., 1980, 81, Cranbrook Art Mus., 1982, Palo Alto Cultural Ctr., others; works represented in pvt. collections. Mem. Soc. N. Am. Goldsmiths, Am. Crafts Council, Coll. Art Assn., Marin Arts Council, Mich. Silversmiths Guild (dir. 1977-78). Contbr. articles on jewelry making health hazards to periodicals. Office: PO Box 1032 Sausalito CA 94966

WEISSMAN, CLARK, computer co. exec.; b. Bklyn., June 12, 1934; s. Max and Ella Dorothy (Vogel) W.; B.S. in Aero. Engring., M.I.T., 1956; postgrad. U. So. Calif., 1956-57, UCLA, 1957-58, 61-63; m. Elaine C. Weissman; children—Ellin, Hillary, Wendy, Philip, Suzanne, Eric. Systems analyst N.Am. Aviation, Los Angeles, 1956-58; project leader System Devel. Corp., Paramus, N.J., 1958-60, mem. computer research staff, Santa Monica, Calif. 1960-69, mgr. research and devel. dept., 1969-71, chief technologist, 1971-73, 76—, mgr. computer security dept., 1973-76, dep. mgr. research and devel., 1976—; pres. bd. dirs. Songmakers, 1979-80; instr. UCLA, 1966-71; cons. U.S. Govt., 1971-72, 79-80; mem. adv. com. to sec. commerce on computer security, 1974-77; mem. organizing com., subchmn. Air Force summer study on data base mgmt. system security Nat. Acad. Scis., 1982. Mem. Assn. Computing Machinery (editor operating systems dept. of commn. 1973-75), Fedn. Am. Scientists, AAAS, Research Soc. Am., IEEE, L.A. Songmakers (dir. 1977-80, pres. 1979-80), Am. Fedn. Info. Processing Socs. (Best Paper 1964, 69), Calif. Traditional Music Soc. (founder, treas. 1982—). Author: Lisp 1.5 Primer, 1967, Japanese edit., 1971. Home: 4401 Trancas Pl Tarzana CA 91356 Office: 2500 Colorado Ave Santa Monica CA 90406

WEISSMANN, ROBIN CHARLOTTE, producer, researcher; b. N.Y.C., Aug. 4, 1956; d. Lwon Jeffrey and Sonja Karon (Stern) W. A.A., UCLA, 1976. Asst. dir. Unicom Internat., Guam, 1977; assoc. producer Alan Neuman Prodns., Inc., and Postscript Prodns., Inc., Los Angeles, 1978—. Office: 6725 Sunset Blvd #505 Los Angeles CA 90028

WEISZ, ROBERT, psychologist; b. Lima, Peru, June 24, 1944; came to U.S., 1957; naturalized, 1963; s. Herbert Michael and Anne Marie (Ehrmann) W.; m. Mary Anne Harvey, Aug. 30, 1969 (div. 1976). A.B. in Psychology, U. S.D., 1966; M.A., U.Wyo., 1968, Ph.D. in Clin. Psychology, 1972. Lic. psychologist, Wyo. Cert. psychologist, N.Mex. Teaching asst. U.Wyo., Laramie, 1967-70; clin. psychology intern Sedgwick County Mental Health Ctr., Wichita (Kans.) Guidance Ctr., 1970-71; county coordinator, clin. psychologist No. Wyo. Mental Health Ctr., Gillette, 1972-79; researcher U.S. Dept. Interior, Cuba, N.Mex., 1980-81; prin. investigator U.S. Bur. Land Mgmt., Alaska, 1981-82; dir. Milton Erickson Inst., Albuquerque, 1982—; asst. prof. Webster U., St. Louis, 1980—. Served with Med. Service Corps, USAR, 1966-76. Mem. Am. Psychol. Assn., Soc. for Psychol. Study of Social Issues, N.Mex. Soc. for Clin. Hypnosis, Soc. Clin. and Exptl. Hypnosis.

WEITZEL, ALLEN, indsl. engr., mgmt. cons.; b. Joliet, Ill., Feb. 28, 1943; s. Henry A. and Opal F. Weitzel; B.S. in Indsl. Engring., So. Ill. U., 1968; M.B.A., DePaul U., Chgo., 1973. Indsl. engr. A.E. Staley Mfg. Co., Decatur, Ill., 1968-69, Borden Chem. Co., Northfield, Ill., 1969-71; distbn. planning engr. Walgreen Co., Chgo., 1971-72, mgr. distbn. planning, 1973-75; asst. nat. distbn. mgr. Cotter & Co., Chgo., 1975-77; dir. materials mgmt. Hills Brothers Coffee Co., Inc., San Francisco, 1977-81; mgmt. cons. Am. Software, San Francisco, 1981—; partner Golden State Distbn. Services, San Francisco; owner Joseph-Allen Ltd., San Francisco; instr. Sch. of Bus., U. San Francisco, 1979—; mem. faculty San Francisco State U., 1980—. Mem. Am. Inst. Indsl. Engrs., Am. Material Mgmt. Soc., Grocery Mfrs. Am., Nat. Council of Phys. Distbn. Mgmt., Golden Gate Bus. Assn., Am. Mgmt. Assn. (seminar leader and instr. fundamentals of traffic 1977—). Presbyterian. Home: 576 Wisconsin St San Francisco CA 94142 Office: 44 Montgomery St San Francisco CA 94119

WEITZEN, JED HARRY, clinical psychologist; b. N.Y.C., Jan. 14, 1953; s. Hyman Grover and Jeanne N. (Vermette) W.; m. Ruana Starer, Oct. 27, 1979; 1 son, Jason Seth. M.A., Calif. Sch. Profl. Psychology, 1977, Ph.D. in Clin. Psychology, 1981. Emergency services caseworker I Didi Hirsch Community Mental Health Ctr., Culver City, Calif., 1977-79; psychol. asst. in pvt. practice, Upland, Calif., 1979; psychol. asst. Hillside Learning Ctr., Long Beach, Calif., 1979-80, staff psychologist Verdugo Mental Health Ctr., Glendale, Calif., 1980-82; pvt. practice clin. psychology, 1983—. Mem. Am. Psychol. Assn. Office: 417 Arden Ave Glendale CA 91203

WELCH, BARBARA LOUISE, business management executive; b. Wolf Point, Mont., Aug. 3, 1941; d. E.A. and Lona Belle (Vest) Fiske; m. Charles E. Welch, Apr. 9, 1970; children—Charles II, Barry, Randall, Tamara Martin. Bus. mgr. Glacier Route Toyota, Malta, Mont., 1974-80; bus. mgr. E.A. Fiske Enterprises, Malta, 1976-81; bus. mgr. Jansen Enterprises, Wolf Point, Mont., 1960-70; grantsperson City of Malta, 1981-82, Phillips County, Mont., 1981-82; pres. Bus. Services, Inc., Malta, 1981—. Roman Catholic. Club: Soroptimists. Office: 173 S Central St Drawer CC Malta MT 59538

WELCH, C. DEAN, newspaper official; b. Prairie Grove, Ark., May 23, 1949; s. William C. and Lois Louise (Hudson) W.; m. Linda Marie Stephens, Dec. 23, 1977; children—John Kraig, Brandon Tyler. Student Abilene Christian Coll., 1967-68; A.A. in Bus. Adminstrn., Coll. of Sequoias, 1975. Sales rep. Tulare (Calif.) Advance Register, 1971-72; sales rep. Visalia (Calif.) Times Delta, 1972-73, classified mgr., 1973-76; retail mgr., 1976-78; classified mgr. Sioux Falls (S.D.) Argus Leader, 1978-80; owner, operator Comml. Printing Co., Visalia, 1980-81; sales mgr. The Orange County Register, Santa Ana, Calif., 1981-82, mgr. classified advt., 1982—. Served in U.S. Army, 1968-71; Vietnam. Decorated Purple Heart, Bronze Star. Mem. Orange County Advt. Fedn., So. Calif. Classified Mgrs. Assn., Western Classified Mgrs., Nat. Assn. Classified Advt. Mgrs., Los Angeles Advt. Club, Orange County Auto Dealers Assn., Visalia Jaycees (pres. 1976-77). Republican. Southern Baptist. Clubs: Lions, Elks (Visalia). Home: Condo F 12838 Timber Dr Garden Grove CA 92680 Office: 625 N Grand Ave Santa Ana CA 92711

WELCH, CHARLES ARNOLD, psychologist, educator; b. Richgrove, Calif., Dec. 26, 1926; s. William Arleigh and Sallie (Harper Robinson) W.; B.A., Sacramento State U., 1958, M.A., 1966; Ph.D., U.S. Internat. U., 1972; postgrad U. Calif., Davis, 1967-68, Stanford U., 1964-67; m. Tamara Lee Dolin, Mar. 21, 1970. Tchr. elem. schs., 1954-59, secondary schs., 1959; prin. San Juan Unified Schs., 1960-70; prin. Chula Vista (Calif.) Schs., 1971-77, coordinator spl. project, 1977—; pvt. practice psychology, cons. ednl. behavior, La Jolla, Calif., 1973—; mem. faculty U.S. Internat. U., 1974-75, U. San Diego, 1977-78. Pres. Sacramento Symphony Orch., 1964-65. Served with USN, 1944-46. Cert. diamond grading Gem Inst. Am., 1977. Mem. Calif. Fedn. Poets (pres. 1974-75), Assn. Calif. Sch. Adminstrs., Assn. Supervision and Curriculum Devel. Columnist arts critic Sacramento Union, San Juan Record, 1964-69; contbr. poetry to mags.

WELCH, DAVID FITE, association executive; b. Fort Wayne, Ind., Sept. 5, 1918; s. Frederick Christian and Bessie Mae (Fifte) W.; A.B., Franklin Coll. Ind., 1940; M.A., George Washington U., 1961; Ed.D., Am. U., 1976; LL.D. Franklin Coll., 1969; m. Mary Spaulding Stewart, Dec. 7, 1949. Commd. ensign U.S. Navy, 1942, advanced through grades to rear adm., 1967; dir. amphibian tng. and edn., 1967-68; chief operating officer amphibious group, 1968-69; sr. exec. Operation Deep Freeze, 1969-71; asst. dep. chief naval ops., 1971-72, ret., 1972; asst. sec., treas., adminstrv. exec. Assn. Univs. Research in Astronomy, Inc., Tucson, Ariz., 1978—; lectr. Am. U., 1976-78. Decorated Legion of Merit, Bronze Star medal. Diplomate Coll. de la Defense del'Otan, Paris. Mem. NATO Def. Coll. Anciens, Naval Inst., Naval League, Antarctica Soc. Washington, Phi Delta Kappa. Clubs: Explorers; Army and Navy, Old Pueblo, Masons (Tucson, Ariz.), Shriners. Home: 5022 E Camino Alisa Tucson AZ 85718 Office: 1002 N Warren Ave Tucson AZ 85719

WELCH, FERN STEWART, public relations consultant; b. Redford, Mo., Aug. 13, 1934; d. Elza L. and Ruby I. (Bounds) DeMente; m. John M. Stewart III, May 24, 1954; children—Joni Stewart Olsen, Susan Stewart Caldwell, John D.; m. 2d, Kenneth A. Welch, Apr. 25, 1981. A.A. in Computer Programming, Phoenix Coll., 1953; student Ariz. State U., 1965, Bellevue Community Coll., 1967, Lake Washington Community Coll., 1968. Writer/reporter, columnist Sammamish Valley News, Redmond Wash., 1967-71; staff writer, asst. to pub. relations dir. First Nat. Bank Oreg., Portland, 1971-72; asst. pub. relations dir. The Ariz. Bank, Phoenix, 1972-73, pub. relations dir., 1973-77; founder, prin. Fern Stewart and Assocs., Ltd., Phoenix, 1977—; lectr. pub. relations. Bd. dirs. Central Ariz. chpt. ARC, 1976—, Combined Met. Arts and Scis.; mem. Arizonans for Cultural Devel., Scottsdale (Ariz.) Art Ctr. Assn., Valley Shakespeare Co. Recipient awards of merit and excellence Internat. Assn. Bus. Communicators, 1975-77. Mem. Pub. Relations Soc. Am., Women in Communications. Republican. Clubs: Phoenix Country, Plaza (Phoenix). Contbr. numerous articles to local and regional mags. Office: Fern Stewart and Assocs Ltd 4707 N 12th St Suite C Phoenix AZ 85014

WELCH, GARTH LARRY, college administrator; b. Brigham City, Utah, Feb. 14, 1937; s. Samuel and Minnie Jane (Hughes) W.; m. Melba Lael Coombs, Sept. 9, 1960; children—Larry K., Kathryn L., Richard S., G. Edward, Robert I., David J. B.S., U. Utah, 1959, Ph.D., 1963. Postdoctoral fellow UCLA, 1962-64; asst. prof. chemistry Weber State Coll., Ogden, Utah, 1964-68, assoc. prof., 1968-72, prof., 1972—, dean Sch. Natural Scis., 1974-83, exec. dir. for bus. affairs, 1983—; vis. prof. Brigham Young U., 1980. Mem. Am. Chem. Soc., Sigma Xi, Phi Kappa Phi. Mormon. Club: Ogden Rotary. Home: 3910 N 800 W Ogden UT 84404

WELCH, JASPER ARTHUR, III, printing co. executive; b. San Francisco, Calif., Mar. 1, 1954; s. Jasper Arthur, Jr., and Carroll (Wright) W.; m. Susan Louis, Nov. 1, 1975; children—Corrie Anna, Aaron Jasper. B.S. with distinction, U. Colo., 1975. Coordinator, counselor Colvig Silver Camps, Durango, Colo., summers 1975, 76; asst. mgr. Durango Office Products, 1976-79; mgr. Durango C. of C., 1979—1979-83; pres. Basin Reproduction and Printing Co., 1983—. Mem. La Plata County Republican Central Com. Mem. Colo. C. of C. Execs., Full Gospel Businessmen's Fellowship Internat. Four Corners Tourism Council (chmn., 1981), Early Bird Toastmasters. Home: 1831 W Third Ave Durango CO 81301 Office: PO Box 2587 Durango CO 81301

WELCH, KEVIN WILLIAM, sociologist; b. Janesville, Wis., Apr. 7, 1953; s. Richard Claire and Charlotte Agnes Welch; m. Diane Marie Samdahl, Sept. 8, 1979. B.A., U. Wis., 1975; M.A., U. Wash., 1978, Ph.D., 1983. NIMH trainee dept. sociology U. Wash., Seattle, 1976-77, teaching asst., 1977-78, staff cons. Center for Quantitative Studies, 1978-82. Cornell U. fellow, 1975. Mem. Am. Sociol. Assn., Soc. Scientific Study Religion, Phi Beta Kappa. Contbr. articles to profl. jours. Office: Department of Sociology University of Washington Seattle WA 98195

WELCH, LAWRENCE H., bishop; b. Winton, Wyo., Feb. 1, 1935; student U. Wyo., St. John's Sem., Collegeville, Minn., Cath. U. Am. Ordained priest, Roman Catholic Ch., 1962, ordained bishop of Spokane, 1978. Office: N 709 Cedar St Spokane WA 99210

WELCH, PETER FRANCIS, food vending and catering co. exec.; b. Portland, Oreg., July 24, 1930; s. Peter W. and Mary M. (Kelley) W.; student Multnomah Coll., 1949-50, DeAnza Coll., 1980-81, Wharton Sch., U. Pa., 1980; m. Ruby Mendicki, Apr. 18, 1953; children—Steven, Kevin, Sandra, Janice, Valerie. Salesman, Rawson Drug Co., San Jose, Calif., 1953-57; pres. dePaul Service Co., Santa Clara, Calif., 1957—, dePaul Catering Services, 1971-82 Diversified Coffee Services, 1974—, P.F.W. Distbg. Co. Inc., 1981—; dir. Autoviable Service Co. Served with U.S. Army, 1951-53. Mem. Nat. Automatic Merchandising Assn., Calif. Automatic Vendors Council (past dir.). Republican. Roman Catholic. Club: Rotary. Home: 19502 Miller Ct Saratoga CA 95070 Office: 2375 de la Cruz Blvd Santa Clara CA 95050

WELCH, WALTER ANDREW, JR., lawyer, commercial pilot; b. Melrose Park, Ill., Dec. 13, 1948; s. Walter Andrew and Myrtle M. (Kunzmann) W.; B.S.A.S., So. Ill. U., 1974; J.D., Pepperdine Law Sch., 1980. Bar: Calif., N.J., U.S. Ct. Internat. Trade, U.S. Ct. Customs and Patent Appeals, U.S. Ct. Claims, U.S. Ct. Appeals, U.S. Tax Ct., U.S. Ct. Mil. Appeals, other fed. cts.; cert. comml. pilot, tchr., real estate broker. Sole practice, Marina del Rey, Calif., 1981—. Del., Calif. Bar Conv. Served with USMC, 1974-77. Mem. AIAA, Lawyer-Pilot Bar Assn, Assn. Naval Aviation, Assn. Trial Lawyers Am., Christian Legal Soc., Malibu Hist. Soc., Tau Kappa Episilon, Phi Alpha Delta. Roman Catholic. Contbr. articles to profl. jours. Home: PO Box 133 Malibu CA 90265 Office: PO Box 9606 Marina del Rey CA 90291

WELCH, WILLIAM FRANCIS, mining engr.; b. Monarch, Wyo., Mar. 12, 1909; s. Frank and Mary Ellen (Scullen) W.; student Regis Coll., Denver, 1928-29; Engring. degree in metallurgy Colo. Sch. Mines, 1933; m. Lorene Elizabeth Wondra, Dec. 31, 1952. Mining engr. Sheridan-Wyo. Coal Co., Monarch, 1933-40; ranching and pvt. engring. practice, Acme, Wyo., 1940-48; supt. Welch Coal Co., Sheridan, 1948—, dir., 1948—; pres. Tongue River Ditch Co., 1951—; dir. Rocky Mountain Fed. Savs. and Loan, Steel Creek Producers, Ranchester State Bank, Capital Savs.; v.p. Wymo Oil Co. Treas. Sch. Dist. 24, 1955-58; pres., 1958-65; treas. Tongue River Soil Conservation Dist., 1949-60. Bd. dirs. Whitney Benefits Ednl. Found., 1964-69; pres. bd. Tongue River Fire Dist., 1954-78; bd. dirs. Billings (Mont.) Deaconess Hosp. Found. Life mem. Nat. Cowboy Hall of Fame; Paul Harris fellow; William F. Welch Mining Ctr. at Sheridan Coll. named for him; Welch Regional Heart Ctr., Billings Deaconess Hosp. named for him. Mem. Wyo. Mining Assn., Wyo. Stockgrowers, Wyo. Sch. Trustees Assn. AIME, Wyo. Water Resources Assn., Rocky Mountain Coal Mining Inst., Soc. Mining Engrs., Alpha Tau Omega, Theta Tau. Clubs: Elks, Rotary. Roman Catholic. Address: 155 Scott Dr Sheridan WY 82801

WELCOME, DENNIS PALMER, surgeon; b. Mpls., Apr. 25, 1936; s. Marcel Henry and Lillian (Kannenberg) W.; B.A., U. Minn., 1957, B.S., 1959, M.D., 1961; m. Mary Kathleen Freed, Mar. 21, 1958; children—Richard, Michael, Gregory. Intern, Riverside County (Calif.) Hosp., 1961-62; resident Kaiser Found. Hosp., Oakland, Calif., 1962-66; practice medicine, specializing in surgery Drummond Med. Group, Ridgecrest, Calif., 1968—; staff Ridgecrest Community Hosp., bd. dirs., 1974—. Bd. dirs. Drummond Med. Center, 1971—. Served with USAF, 1966-68. Diplomate Am. Bd. Surgery. Fellow Am. Coll. Angiology, A.C.S.; mem. Am. Soc. Abdominal Surgery, Southwestern Surg. Congress, Bakersfield Surg. Soc., AMA, Calif. Med. Assn., Kern County Med. Assn. (dir. 1981). Republican. Lutheran. Club: Exchange. Home: 1509 Welcome Way Ridgecrest CA 93555 Office: 1111 N China Lake Blvd Ridgecrest CA 93555

WELKER, JOAN ELIZABETH, business cons.; b. Gary, Ind., Oct. 15, 1940; d. Thomas Franklin and Dorothy Jane (Hogenfeld) Taylor; B.S., Ohio State U., 1972, M.S.W., 1973; m. John G. Welker, Dec. 18, 1971 (dec.). Psychiat. social worker Columbus (Ohio) State Hosp., 1973-74; psychiat. social worker Columbus Area Mental Health Center, 1974-75, coordinator intermediate care program, 1975-78, chief day treatment programs, 1976-78; clin. social worker KernView Mental Health Center and Hosp., Bakersfield, Calif., 1978-80, chief extended services to adults, 1980-81; co-founder, prin. therapist Bakersfield Community Rape Treatment Program, 1980; pvt. practice human relations cons., EAP Cons. for Bus. and Industry, 1981—; adj. instr. Coll. Social Work Ohio State U., 1975-78, Capital U., 1976-77. Lic. clin. social worker, Calif. Mem. Acad. Certified Social Workers, Nat. Assn. Social Workers, Nat. Registry Clin. Social Workers, AAUW. Democrat. Episcopalian. Home: 820 Bunting Dr Bakersfield CA 93307 Office: 5401 Business Park S Suite 123 Bakersfield CA 93309

WELLER, STEVEN, consultant; b. Cambridge, Mass. Oct. 28, 1942; s. Alfred and Gertrude (Ziegler) W.; m. Emily C. Guth, June 15, 1969; children—John B., Molly G. B.A., Yale U., 1964; J.D., 1967; Ph.D. in Polit. Sci., Cornell U., 1979. Bar: N.Y. 1968, Colo. 1980. Individual practice law, N.Y.C., 1967-70; mem. polit. sci. faculty SUNY, Albany, 1973-75; sr. staff atty., project dir. Nat. Ctr. State Courts, Denver, 1975-78; sole practice, Boulder, Colo., 1978—; cons. to small claims courts and in court reform; mem. faculty Nat. Jud. Coll., Reno. Mem. Am. Polit. Sci. Assn., Law and Society Assn., Colo. Bar Assn. Author numerous articles on court process. Home: 1300 Bear Mountain Ct Boulder CO 80303 Office: 1906 13th St Suite 205 Boulder CO 80302

WELLHAUSEN, JAMES RICHARD, agriculturist, consultant; b. Burley, Idaho, Sept. 13, 1951; s. Melvin Richard and Marian Louise (Neumann) W.; m. Brenda Lorene Dugger, Oct. 24, 1981; 1 dau., Rochelle Darlene. B.A. in Agrl. Bus., Coll. So. Idaho, 1971; diploma in indsl. psychology Internat. Corr. Sch., 1972; registered med technician. Vice pres. Coll. So. Idaho Vocat. Tech. Trade Sch., 1970; chmn. grievance com. Idaho Frozen Foods, 1971-72, pres. leaders council and fatstock sale com., 1973-79. Founding mem., pres., med. technician Richfield Quick Response Unit, 1976—; vice chmn. Lincoln County Fair bd., 1980-83, chmn., 1983; 4-H leader, 1972-79; chmn. Richfield Sch. bd. 1976—; spl. dep. sherriff Lincoln County, 1980—. Recipient Am. Legion Americanism award, 1969.

WELLMAN, DENNIS LEE, electronics engineer; b. Freeport, Ill., Mar. 18, 1942; s. Grant L. and Irene E. (Sicher) W.; m. Kathleen G. Markwell, June 8, 1968; children—Jennifer Lee, Timothy Sean. B.S. in Elec. Engring., U. Colo., 1971; postgrad. Colo. State U., 1980-81. Electronic engr. Ball Bros. Research Corp., Boulder, Colo., 1972, NOAA/Environ. Research Labs., Boulder, 1973—. Served with USAF, 1961-66. Recipient Spl. Achievement award NOAA, 1973, 77, cert. of recognition, 1978. Mem. Am. Geophys. Union. Office: NOAA/Environ Research Labs 3100 Marine St Boulder CO 80303

WELLS, CECIL HAROLD, JR., cons. engr.; b. San Mateo, Calif., Apr. 21, 1927; s. Cecil H. and Bertha (Teeter) W.; student Menlo Coll., 1948; B. C.E., U. Santa Clara, 1951, U. Calif., 1949, San Jose State Coll., 1948, U. Calif., 1952; m. Elizabeth Anne O'Leary (dec.); children—Cecilia E., A. Timothy; m. 2d, Christina Maria Poelzl; children—Kristy-Sue, Jeff-Dean. Engr., Hall & Pregnoff, San Francisco, 1951-56, Graham & Hayes, San Francisco, 1956-58; cons. engr. on bldgs. and structures Cecil H. Wells, Jr. & Assos., San Mateo, Calif., 1953—; pres. 20th Ave. Catering Corp., 1971-72, 2031 Pioneer Ct. Corp, 1958-70; tchr. engring. Menlo Coll., 1948-62; lectr. lateral design of bldgs. Stanford U., 1956-59. Mem. San Mateo County Regional Planning Bd., pres., 1964-65; mem. San Francisco, San Mateo, Santa Clara Tri County Planning Bd., pres., 1959-60; chmn. Elks Charity, 1964-65; mem. Calif. Bay Conservation and Devel. Commn., 1965-67, Internat. Conf. World Planners, Mexico City, 1964; commr. San Mateo City Planning, 1956-67, chmn., 1958-59, 61-62, 64-67; mem. San Mateo City Govtl. Efficiency Commn., chmn., 1970-72; engr. San Mateo County Harbor Dist., 1969-82; active Boy Scouts Am., mem. exec. bd. county council, 1969— county v.p., exec. bd., 1972-75, chmn. Explorers, 1969-74; pres. Menlo Alumni Council, 1967-68; mem. men's adv. com. LWV, 1970-71, 73-74; bd. dirs. Purissima Mut. Water Dist., 1968-71, San Mateo County Devel. Assn., 1964—; trustee Drew Sch., 1972-73; bd. dirs. San Mateo County Growth Policy Council, 1982—. Served with Submarine Service, USNR, World War II. Named Citizen of Day, Radio Sta. KABL, 1970, 74; recipient 1st place award in apt. design City of Fremont Environ. Design Com., 1973; Silver Beaver award Boy Scouts Am., 1975; Paul Harris fellow Rotary Internat., 1980; registered profl. engr., Calif., Alaska, Ariz., Colo., Mont., Nev., Oreg., Tex., Utah, Wash. Fellow ASCE; mem. Structural Engring. Assn. Calif. (sec. 1954-58), Seismol. Soc. Am., Am. Concrete Inst., ASTM, San Mateo C. of C. (dir. 1965—, pres. 1969-72), Nat. Soc. Profl. Engrs., Am. Soc. Mil. Engrs., Am. Inst. Timber Constrn., Prestressed Concrete Inst., Nat. Rifle Assn. Clubs: Elks (exalted ruler 1966-67, bd. trustees 1967-72, chmn. 1971-72), Rotary (pres. 1972-73), Peninsula Golf and Country. Author: Structural Engineering Design for Architects and Design of Buildings for Earthquakes and Wind. Office: 2031 Pioneer Ct Suite 12 San Mateo CA 94403

WELLS, CHERYL ANN, home economics teacher; b. Portland, Oreg., Sept. 27, 1955; d. James Edward and Carol Ann Wells. B.S., Oreg. State U., 1978. Home econs. tchr. Reynolds High Sch., Portland, 1978-82, H.B. Lee Middle Sch., Portland, 1982—. Mem. NEA, Oreg. Edn. Assn., Am. Home Econ. Assn., Tchrs. Home Econ. Oreg. (sec.), Oreg. Vocat. Assn., Sigma Kappa (sec. 1980-82). Democrat. Roman Catholic. Office: 1121 NE 172d St Portland OR 97230

WELLS, CHRISTOPHER POWERS, lawyer; b. Washington, Sept. 25, 1954; s. William Wellington and Leilani Tryon (Brink) W. B.A., U. Rochester, 1975; M.B.A., UCLA, 1979, J.D., 1979. Bar: Calif. 1979. Law clk. Gulf Oil Corp., Los Angeles, 1977-78; mem. Graham & James, Los Angeles, 1979-81, O'Melveny & Myers, Los Angeles, 1981—. Mem. C. of C. (Los Angeles com. vice chmn.), Los Angeles County Bar Assn., ABA. Republican. Editor: UCLA Alaska Law Rev., 1977-78; Federal Communications Law Jour., 1978-79. Office: 400 S Hope St 17th Floor Los Angeles CA 90071

WELLS, DOROTHY VIOLA, librarian; b. Boulder, Colo., Feb. 6, 1916; d. Harold Merton and Laura Belle (McCardie) Wells. A.B., U. Wyo., 1938; B.S. in Library Sci., U. Ill., 1939. Asst. librarian documents Ft. Hays (Kans.) State Coll., 1939-42; librarian Inst. of Govt. and Pub. Affairs, John Randolph Haynes and Dora Haynes Found., 1942-70; asst. dept. head and local documents librarian Pub. Affairs Service, U. Research Library, UCLA, 1971—. Mem. Spl. Library Assn., Council of Planning Librarians, Internat. City Mgmt. Assn., Western Govtl. Research Assn. Democrat. Presbyterian. Home: PO Box 24711 Los Angeles CA 90024 Office: Pub Affairs Service/Local U Research Library U Calif 405 Hilgard Ave Los Angeles CA 90024

WELLS, FRANK G., lawyer, film studio exec.; b. 1932; B.A. summa cum laude, Pomona Coll., 1953; M.A. in Law (Rhodes scholar), Oxford U., (Eng.), 1955; LL.B., Stanford U., 1959. Vice-chmn., Warner Bros. Inc. Mem. Phi Beta Kappa. Office: Warner Bros Inc 4000 Warner Blvd Burbank CA 91505*

WELLS, GLEN WALDEMAR, water treatment manager; b. Aberdeen, Wash., Nov. 21, 1920; s. Matts Arvid and Maria Alina (Anderson) W.; m. Jean Ruth Butterfield, July 7, 1945; children—Alina Louise Rossano, Bruce Arnold. B.S. in Mech. Engring., Wash. State U., 1943. Mgr. power ops. Gen. Electric Co., Hanford Atomics Works, 1947-65, sr. engr. Douglas United Nuclear, 1965-71; water prodn. supt. City of Phoenix, 1971—; tchr. water treatment courses Phoenix, Rio Salada jr. colls. Served to lt. USN, 1943-46. Mem. Ariz. Water and Pollution Control Assn. (past dir., sec.-treas. 1979-82), Am. Water Works Assn. (Fuller award 1978). Republican. Contbr. articles to tech. jours. Office: 5204 E Thomas Rd Phoenix AZ 85018

WELLS, J. GORDON, educator; b. Salt Lake City, Sept. 18, 1918; s. William Albert and Mable Grace (Taylor) W.; B.S., Pepperdine U., 1946; Ph.D., U. So. Calif., 1951; married; 1 child. Mem. faculty phys. edn. Pepperdine Coll., 1946-48; asst. aviation physiologist U. So. Calif., Los Angeles, 1948-49; aviation physiologist (med.) U.S. Air Force Sch. Aviation Medicine, 1949-56; supr. human engring. Norair div. Northrop Corp., 1956-61; asst. dir. life sci. Applied Sci. Space and Info. Systems div. N.Am. Aviation, Inc., 1961-62, mgr. Apollo engring. Apollo Crew Systems, 1962-66, asst. to v.p., gen. mgr. life sci. ops., 1966-67, dir. space programs, 1967, mgr. life sci. and systems, 1967-68, mgr. life sci. and systems, 1968-71, supr. life sci. systems engring. and tech., research and engring. and testing Space div., 1971-75; assoc. dean adminstrn. Grad. Sch. Edn. and Psychology, Pepperdine U., 1975-83, mem. faculty, 1983—. Fellow AIAA (assoc.), Aerospace Med. Assn. (v.p. 1959-60); mem. AAAS, Human Factors Soc., Am. Astron. Soc., others. Contbr. articles to profl. jours. Address: 11 La Vista Verde Dr Rancho Palos Verdes CA 90274

WELLS, JEFFREY M., state senator, lawyer; b. Springfield, Mass., Sept. 26, 1948; s. William and Pauline Wells; m. Sherri; children—Pamela, Kimberly, Tommy. B.A., Duke U., 1970; M.B.A., Fla. State U., 1972, J.D., 1974. Assoc. Wilder & Wells, P.C., Colorado Springs, Colo.;

mem. Colo. State Senate, 1982—. Mem. El Paso Bar Assn., Colo. Bar Assn., Fla. Bar Assn., Assn. Trial Lawyers Am. Republican. Presbyterian. Club: Moose. Office: State Capitol Denver CO 80203*

WELLS, JOHN ALLEN, aerospace engr.; b. Springville, Iowa, Apr. 7, 1925; s. Claude Cheyenne and Hazel Grace (Allen) W.; student Iowa State Coll., 1942-43, Cal-Aero Tech. Inst., 1951-53; m. Sharon Margaret Yelle, Mar. 14, 1979; children—Robin, Sandy, Thomas, Bret. Engring. specialist Ventura div. Northrop Corp., Newbury Park, Calif., 1967-69; sr. project engr. Space Ordnance Systems, Newhall, Calif., 1969-70; applications engr. Hi-Shear Corp., Torrance, Calif., 1970-73; sr. devel. engr. Meteorology Research, Inc., Altadena, Calif., 1973-79; sr. project engr. Irvin Industries, Inc., Gardena, Calif., 1979—. Served with U.S. Army, 1943-46. Recipient Apollo Program Snoopy award, 1969. Republican. Patentee in field. Home: 2052 Glentree Dr Lomita CA 90717 Office: 15001 S Figueroa St Gardena CA 90247

WELLS, KEN, social worker; b. Deming, N.Mex., July 5, 1935; s. Jack and Frances (Salsbury) W. B.A., U. N.Mex., 1961; M.A., Internat. Coll. Los Angeles, 1981. Cert. in social services, Calif. Organizer 1st outpatient program for alcohol abusers State of N.Mex., 1965; social worker dept. psychiatry, U. N.Mex. Med. Sch., 1965; social worker, Albuquerque, 1961-69; dir. Community Mental Health substance abuse program, Albuquerque, 1971-79; founder, dir. N.Mex. Community Services, 1979—; cons. in field. Founder Pueblo of Laguna Pub. Library; cantor, music dir. Reform Jewish Congregation, Albuquerque. Mem. Nat. Congress Am. Indians, Reform Zionist Assn., Rocky Mountain Jewish Hist. Soc., Internat. Transactional Analysis Assn., Am. Mental Health Counselors Assn., N.Mex. Mental Health Counselors Assn., Guild of Temple Musicians. Democrat. Contbr. poems and articles to regional and gen. interest mags. Home: 1814 Slate St NW Albuquerque NM 87104 Office: 619 San Mateo NE Albuquerque NM 87108

WELLS, KENNETH, botany educator; b. Portsmouth, Ohio, July 24, 1927; s. Roland and Pauline (Fay) W.; m. Ellinor Kirschner, Feb. 27, 1954; children—Henry K., Heidi K. B.S., U. Ky., 1950; M.S., U. Iowa, 1957, Ph.D., 1957. Teaching asst. U. Iowa, Iowa City, 1954-57; instr. botany U. Calif., Davis, 1957-59, asst. prof., 1959-65, assoc. prof., 1965-72, prof., 1972—, dept. chmn., 1978-82. Served with USN, 1945-46; 1st lt. inf. U.S. Army, 1951-54. Mem. Mycol. Soc. Am., British Mycol. Soc., Mycol. Soc. Japan, Mycol. Soc. San Francisco. Contbr. articles to profl. jours. Office: U Calif Botany Dept Davis CA 95616

WELLS, MERLE WILLIAM, historian, state archivist; b. Lethbridge, Alta., Can., Dec. 1, 1918; s. Norman Danby and Minnie Muir (Huckett) W.; student Boise Jr. Coll., 1937-39; A.B., Coll. Idaho, 1941, L.H.D. (hon.), 1981; M.A., U. Calif., 1947, Ph.D., 1950. Instr. history Coll. Idaho, Caldwell, 1942-46; asso. prof. history Alliance Coll., Cambridge Springs, Pa., 1950-56, 58, dean students, 1955-56; cons. historian Idaho Hist. Soc., Boise, 1956-58, historian and archivist, 1959—; hist. preservation officer, archivist State of Idaho, Boise, 1968—. Treas., So. Idaho Migrant Ministry, 1960-64, chmn., 1964-67, 70—; nat. migrant adv. com. Nat. Council Chs., 1964-67, gen. bd. Idaho council, 1967-75; bd. dirs. Idaho State Employees Credit Union, 1964-67, treas., 1966-67; mem. Idaho Commn. Arts and Humanities, 1966-67; mem. Idaho Lewis and Clark Trail Commn., 1968-70; mem. Idaho Bicentennial Commn., 1971-76; bd. dirs. Sawtooth Interpretive Assn., 1972—, Dept: History, United Presbyn. Ch., 1978—. Fellow Soc. Am. Archivists; mem. Nat. Conf. State Hist. Preservation Officers (dir. 1976-81, chmn. Western states council on geog. names 1982-83), Am. Hist. Assn., Western History Assn. (council 1973-76), AAUP, Am. Assn. State and Local History (council 1973-77), Soc. Am. Archivists, others. Author: Anti-Mormonism in Idaho, 1978; Boise: An Illustrated History, 1982. Office: 610 N Julia Davis Dr Boise ID 83702

WELLS, PATRICIA ANN, educator; b. Park River, N.D., Mar. 25, 1935; d. Benjamin Beekman Bennett, Jr. and Alice Catherine (Peerboom) Bennett Breckenridge; A.A., Allan Hancock Coll., 1964; B.S. magna cum laude, Coll. Great Falls, 1966; M.S., U. N.D., 1967, Ph.D., 1971; children—Bruce Bennett, Barbara Lea. Fiscal accountant Internat. Motion Picture Service, USIA, Washington, 1954-56; med. services accounts officer U.S. Air Force, 1962-64; instr. bus. adminstrn. Western New Eng. Coll., 1967-69; instr. econs. Yuba Coll., 1970-71, Chapman Coll., 1971-72; vis. prof. systems analysis masters program U. So. Calif., Rome, N.Y. extension, 1972-73; assoc. prof. Va. State U., Petersburg, 1973-74; prof. bus. adminstrn. Coll., Bus., Oreg. State U., Corvallis, 1974—; pres., chmn. bd. Adminstrv. Orgnl. Services, Inc., Corvallis, 1976—; cons. Digital Equipment Corp., Andover, Mass. Cert. adminstrv. mgr. Mem. Adminstrv. Mgmt. Soc., AAUP (pres. Oreg. conf. 1983—), Am. Bus. Women's Assn. (named Top Businesswoman in Nation 1980-81), Am. Bus. Communication Assn. (2d v.p. 1982-83), Internat. Word Processing Assn. (past chpt. pres.), Nat. Assn. Tchrs. in Bus. and Office Edn. (pres. 1976-77), Western Bus. Edn. Assn., Oreg. State Employees Assn. (exec. council 1978-80), Delta Pi Epsilon, Delta Epsilon Sigma, Delta Kappa Gamma, Phi Kappa Phi. Contbr. numerous articles to profl. jours. Office: 108 Bexell Hall Coll Bus Oreg State U Corvallis OR 97331

WELLS, THEODORA WESTMONT, communications cons.; b. Niagara Falls, N.Y., Apr. 18, 1926; d. Oscar B. and Marjorie Wells (Fraser) Westmont; B.S., U. Calif., Berkeley, 1947; M.B.A., U. So. Calif., 1965; divorced; children—David Kuettel, Steven Kuettel; 1 stepdau., Deanna Molina. Fin. dir. Los Angeles Council Girl Scouts U.S., 1954-58; asst. v.p., project coordinator, customer relations dir. Lytton Savs. & Loan Assn., Hollywood, Calif., 1961-68; tng. and customer relations mgr. First Charter Fin. Corp., Beverly Hills, Calif., 1968-69; partner Wells-Christie Assos., 1970-72; propr. Wells Assos., Beverly Hills, 1970—; extension tchr. mgmt. devel. for women UCLA, 1968—. Adv. bd. Los Angeles Commn. on Assaults Against Women. Mem. Acad. Mgmt., Am. Soc. Tng. and Devel., World Future Soc., Assn. Humanistic Psychology, Delta Gamma, Beta Gamma Sigma. Author: Woman—Which Includes Man, of Course, 1970; (with Rosalind K. Loring) Breakthrough: Women into Management (Edn. award Delta Kappa Gamma 1973, Profl. Achievement award Phi Chi Theta 1974), 1972; Keeping Your Cool Under Fire: Communicating Non-Defensively, 1980; also chpts. in books on non-defensive communication, psychology of women. Home: 341 S Swall Beverly Hills CA 90211 Office: Box 3392 Beverly Hills CA 90212

WELSCH, JAMES LESTER, realty specialist; b. Catskill, N.Y., Oct. 2, 1917; s. Wolfgang Frederick and Hazel Juene (Lester) W.; m. Grace Warner, Oct. 23, 1963. B.S., Purdue U., 1942; M.A., Los Angeles State Coll., 1954; D. Naturopathy, Golden State U., 1956. Lic. edul. adminstr., N. Mex., Ariz., Colo. real estate broker, N.Mex. Personnel mgr. Nat. Cash Register Co. electronics div., Hawthorne, Calif., 1952-55; dir. indsl. relations Mercast Mfg. Corp., LaVerne, Calif., 1955-57; asst. prof. mgmt. Eastern N.Mex. U., Portales, 1957-58; asst. prof. indsl. mgmt. Calif. Western U., San Diego, 1958-63; dir. Montelores Multicultural Ctr., Cortez, Colo., 1967-68; guidance counselor Dzilth-Na-o-dith-hle Sch., Bur. Indian Affairs, Bloomfield, N.Mex., 1974-76, supervisory guidance counselor, Huerfano, N.Mex., 1976-80, realty specialist, rights protection, Juneau, Alaska, 1980, supervisory realty specialist, Anchorage, 1981—. Chmn. San Juan County (N.Mex.) planning and zoning commn., 1973; bd. dirs. San Juan County Mus. Assn., 1978-79, San Juan County chpt. ARC, 1980; del. N.Mex., State Republican Conv., 1974, 76; sustaining mem. Rep. Nat. Com. Served to lt. USN, 1942-46, 51-52. Mem. Am. Soc. Safety Engrs., Phi Delta Kappa (pres. Mesa Verde, Colo. chpt., 1979), Am. Legion, VFW. Clubs: Elks, Masons, Red Cross Constantine. Home: 226 Salmon Dr Bloomfield NM 87413 Office: 1675 C St Suite 235 Anchorage AK 99502

WELSH, JOHN JOSEPH, civil engineer; b. Santa Barbara, Calif., Sept. 12, 1952; s. John James and Elizabeth Hilda (McMahon) W.; m. Katharine Krater, Apr. 25, 1980; children—Jeannette and Jessica (twins), Samantha. Student Modesto Jr. Coll., 1970-71; B.S. in Civil Engring., U. Nev., 1975. Registered profl. engr., Calif., Nev.; registered land surveyor, Calif.; state water rights surveyor, Nev. Water quality planner Environ. Protection Service, State of Nev., Carson City, 1976-77; staff engr. Sharp Krater & Assocs., Reno, 1977-79, sr. engr., 1979—. Mem. ASCE, Nat. Soc. Profl. Engrs., Nev. Soc. Profl. Engrs., Am. Water Works Assn., Nat. Home Builders Assn. (sec. Nev.), U. Nev. Engring. Alumni Assn., Tau Beta Pi. Roman Catholic. Home: 2715 Knob Hill Dr Reno NV 89506 Office: 3195 Mill St Reno NV 89510

WELSH, LAWRENCE H., bishop; b. Winton, Wyo., 1935. Ed. U. Wyo.-Laramie, St. John's Sem., Collegeville, Minn., Cath. U., Washington. Ordained priest, Roman Cath. Ch., 1962; bishop Archdiocese of Spokane, 1978—. Address: N 709 Cedar St Spokane WA 99210*

WELSH, M(ARY) CATHERINE, vocational home economics education administrator; b. Williamsburg, Iowa, Nov. 21, 1921; d. George Walker and Jane Ann (Williams) W.; B.S., Iowa State U.-Ames, 1943; M.Ed., Calif. State U.-Long Beach, 1957. Cert. secondary tchr., gen. adminstr., Calif. Assoc. prof. home econs., chairperson dept. Chapman Coll., Orange, Calif., 1955-60; cons. in nutrition edn. Los Angeles County Schs., 1960-64; program officer Region IX Office of Edn., San Francisco, 1964-67; supr. home econs. Long Beach (Calif.) Unified Sch. Dist., 1967-68; program mgr. home econs. edn. programs Calif. State Dept. Edn., Sacramento, 1968—. Ruling elder United Presbyterian Ch. in U.S.A., Sacramento; bd. dirs. YMCA. Recipient Home Econs. Disting. Alumni award Calif. State U., Long Beach 1977. Mem. Am. Home Econs. Assn., Calif. Home Econs. Assn. (named Outstanding Home Economist 1983), Am. Vocat. Assn., Nat. Assn. State Suprs. Home Econs., Calif. Assn. Future Homemakers Am. (hon.), AAUW, Delta Kappa Gamma. Republican. Club: PEO. Home: 781 Parklin Ave Sacramento CA 95831 Office: 721 Capitol Mall Sacramento CA 95814

WELSH, MARY MCANAW, educator; b. Cameron, Mo., Dec. 7, 1920; d. Francis Louis and Mary Matilda (Moore) McA.; m. Alvin F. Welsh, Feb. 10, 1944; children—Mary Celia, Clinton F., M. Ann. A.B., U. Kans., 1942; M.A., Seton Hall U., 1960; Ed.D., Columbia U., 1971. Reporter, Hutchinson (Kans.) News Herald, 1942-43; house editor Worthington Pump & Machine Corp., Harrison, N.J., 1943-44; tchr., housemaster, coordinator Summit (N.J.) Pub. Schs., 1960-68; prof. family studies N.Mex. State U., Las Cruces, 1972—; adj. faculty dept. family practice Tex. Tech. Regional Acad. Health Ctr., El Paso, 1978-82. Mem. AAUW (pres. N.Mex. 1981-83), AAUP, N.Mex. Council Women's Orgn. (founder, chmn. 1982-83), LWV, Nat. Council Family Relationships, Am. Home Econs. Assn., Western Gerontol. Soc., Theta Sigma Phi, Delta Kappa Gamma, Kappa Alpha Theta. Democrat. Roman Catholic. Author: A Good Family is Hard to Found, 1972; Parent, Child and Sex, 1970; contbr. articles to profl. jours.; writer, presenter home econs. and family study series KRWG-TV, 1974; moderator TV series The Changing Family in N.Mex./LWV, 1976. Home: PO Box 3483 University Park Las Cruces NM 88003 Office: PO Box 3470 NMex State U Las Cruces NM 88003

WELSH, WILLIAM ALLEN, political scientist, educator; b. Salina, Kans., Feb. 5, 1940; s. Robert Allen and Adelaide Catherine (Neilson) W.; m. Helga Hundegger; children—Gregory Allen, Wendy Joan. B.S., Northwestern U., 1961, M.A., 1962, Ph.D., 1965. Asst. prof. U. Ga., 1964-68, assoc. prof., 1968-69; assoc. prof. polit. sci. U. Iowa, Iowa City, 1969-74, prof., 1974-81; prof. polit. sci. Ariz. State U., Tempe, 1981—; research scholar U. Munich (W.Ger.), 1967-68; vis. prof. U. Istanbul (Turkey), 1973, guest research scholar Internat. Inst. for Applied Systems Analysis, Laxenburg, Austria, 1975, 76; research scholor Internat. Inst. Mgmt., West Berlin, 1979. Recipient grants, fellowships Ford Found., NSF, Alexander von Humboldt Found., Earhart Found., U.S. Internat. Communication Agy. Mem. Am. Polit. Sci. Assn., AAAS, Bulgarian Studies Assn., Internat. Polit. Sci. Assn., Southeastern Europe Studies Soc. Author: A Methodological Primer for Political Scientists, 1969; Comparative Communist Political Leadership, 1973; Studying Politics, 1973; Leaders and Elites, 1979; Survey Research and Public Attitudes in Eastern Europe and the Soviet Union, 1981; contbr. articles to profl. jours. Office: Dept Polit Sci Ariz State U Tempe AZ 85281

WELTE, MARILYN ELIZABETH, telephone company executive; b. Erie, Pa., Nov. 12, 1940; d. John Edward and Mary Dundon W. Student Loyola U., Balt., 1959-61, Notre Dame Coll., 1961-64; B.A., Gannon U., 1967; M.A., Calif. State U., 1971. Cert. tchr., Calif. Mem. religious community, 1958-64; editor, writer, 1965-68; tchr. St. Benedict's Acad., Erie, Pa., St. Anthony's High Sch., Long Beach, Calif., Los Amigos High Sch., Fountain Valley, Calif., 1965-72; dir. pub. relations San Diego council Girl Scouts U.S.A., 1972-73; writer, cons. Retson Assocs., St. Pierre Assocs., San Diego, 1973-74, mgmt. cons. solar turbines Internat. Harvester, San Diego, 1975-79; mgr. employee and orgn. devel., Western region GTE, Los Gatos, Calif., 1979-80; dir. edn. and tng. and Pacific Basin programs Hawaiian Telephone Co.-GTE, Honolulu, 1980—; cons., guest lectr. Active Girl Scouts, Jr. Achievement; bd. dirs. Kapiolani Children's Hosp., Sexual Abuse Clinic. Mem. Am. Soc. Tng. and Devel., Orgn. Devel. Network, Nat. Soc. for Performance and Instrn. Club: Lima KuKua.

WELWOOD, JOHN, clinical psychologist; b. Boston, Mar. 12, 1943; s. Arthur and Barbara (Aborn) W.; m. Carol McCarthy, June 15, 1967. B.A., Bowdoin Coll., Brunswick, Maine, 1964; Ph.D. (NIMH fellow), U. Chgo., 1974. Coordinator, Focusing Tng. Network, San Francisco, 1979—; staff assoc. Interface Counseling Assocs., San Francisco, 1979-81; dir. psychology program Calif. Inst. Integral Studies, San Francisco, 1981—. Mem. Am. Psychol. Assn., Assn. for Transpersonal Psychology, Phi Beta Kappa. Democrat. Author: The Meeting of the Ways: Explorations in East/West Psychology, 1979; Awakening the Heart: East/West Approaches to Psychotherapy and the Healing Relationship, 1983. Assoc. editor Jour. Transpersonal Psychology, 1977—. Office: 3494 21st St San Francisco CA 94110

WEN, LIANG-CHI, mech. engr.; b. China, Oct. 20, 1940; s. Chung-Chieh and Chong-Sung (Fan) W.; came to U.S., 1962, naturalized, 1975; B.S. in Mech.Engring., Cheng Kung U., Taiwan, 1961; Ph.D., Purdue U., 1969; m. Stella Chen, July 24, 1970. Postdoctoral research asst., dept. anatomy and physiology Ind. U., Bloomington, 1968-69; mem. tech. staff jet Propulsion Lab., Pasadena, Calif., 1969—. Mem. AIAA, Sigma Xi, Pi Tau Sigma. Contbr. articles on solar energy, heat transfer, temperature control and wave propagation to profl. jours. Home: 4701 Hampton Rd LaCanada CA 91011 Office: 4800 Oak Grove Dr Pasadena CA 91103

WENDEL, PHILIP J., III, personnel mgr.; b. Phila., June 9, 1948; s. Philip J. and Eileen B. (Banzhof) W.; m. Barbara K. McLaughlin, May 29, 1971; children—Jennifer, Philip. B.B.A., U. Tex., 1971. Prodn. supr., personnel adminstr. Johnson & Johnson, Sherman, Tex., 1971-77; personnel mgr. Frito-Lay, Inc., Los Angeles, 1977-80; personnel rep. Discovision Assocs., Carson, Calif., 1980-81; personnel mgr. Yamaha Motor Corp. U.S.A., Cypress, Calif., 1981—; guest speaker local univs. and colls. Vice pres. St. Joseph Sch. Parent's Guild, Long Beach, Calif., 1982—. Mem. Personnel and Indsl. Relations Assn., Am. Soc. Tng. and Devel. Republican. Roman Catholic. Office: Yamaha Motor Corp USA 6555 Katella Cypress CA 90630

WENDT, ANN CARLSON, univ. adminstr., hearing officer, educator; b. Holmquist, S.D., Sept. 11, 1937; d. Albin C. Carlson and Agnes Johnson Carlson Hillgren; student Gustavus Adolphus Coll., 1955-56, U. Minn., Mpls., 1963-66; B.S. in Polit. Sci. magna cum laude, B.S. in Psychology magna cum laude, U. Utah, 1977, M.S. in Human Resource Mgmt. (Allied Printing Trades scholar), 1980, Ph.D., 1984; m. Roderick N. Wendt, Apr. 20, 1957; children—LeAnn Corinne and LuAnn Victoria Wendt Brigham (twins). Labor relations and compensation analyst N.W. Orient Airlines, Inc., Mpls., 1956-61; exec. sec. to pres. G. M. Stewart Lumber Co., Mpls., 1961-62; adminstrv. asst. to dir. instl. market research Pillsbury Co., Mpls., 1962-63; asst. personnel mgr. Data Products Corp., St. Paul, 1963-64; adminstrv. asst. to v.p. personnel Brown & Bigelow, St. Paul, 1964-66; corp. officer, sec. Applied Mgmt. Sci., Inc., Mpls., 1964-66; adminstrv. asst. to v.p. pub. relations First Bank System, Mpls., 1966-70; human resource mgmt. program coordinator Inst. for Human Resource Mgmt., U. Utah, 1982—, teaching asst. dept. polit. sci., 1976-77, Coll. Bus., 1977-80, teaching fellow Coll. Bus., 1980—; Hearing examiner Utah Personnel Rev. Bd., Salt Lake City, 1982—; personnel cons., 1978—. Vol., Murry-Allen Center for Blind, Salt Lake City; active local, dist. and synod levels Lutheran Ch. in Am. Mem. Am. Soc. Personnel Adminstrn., Soc. Profls. in Dispute Resolution, AAUW, Acad. Mgmt., Indsl. Relations Research Assn. Research on arbitration. Home: 4823 Naniloa Dr Salt Lake City UT 84117 Office: U Utah 412 Coll Bus Salt Lake City UT 84112

WENK, JENNY, advt. exec.; b. Pitts., Dec. 29, 1942; d. Samuel Augustine and Jean Lois (Barnes) W.; B.A., U. Calif., Berkeley, 1964; M.B.A., Golden Gate U., 1980; m. Paul R. Allman, Dec. 31, 1981. Advt. promotion and research asst. Richmond (Calif.) Independent, 1965-67; sales promotion writer Dow Jones & Co., Inc., N.Y.C., 1968-70; mem. advt. sales staff Nat. Observer, San Francisco, 1970-74, advt. mgr. Pacific coast, 1974-77; advt. sales rep. Wall Street Jour., San Francisco, 1977—. Mem. San Francisco Women in Advt. (hon. mem., past pres.), San Francisco Advt. Club (dir. 1979-80), Seattle Women in Advt. (hon.). Presbyterian. Office: 220 Battery St San Francisco CA 94111

WENNERBERG, GUNNAR, electrical engineer, scientist; b. Stockholm, June 3, 1918; s. Gustaf Alfred and Elin Ida Kristina (Wennerberg) Gustafsson; m. Elsie Christina Forzelius, July 9, 1949; children—Leif, Kim, Ingrid Wennerberg Quigley, Stefan, Monica Wennerberg Johnston. M.S.E.E., Royal Inst. Tech., Stockholm, 1942. Cert. profl. engr., Calif. Teaching and research asst. Royal Inst. Tech., 1941-42; devel. engr. ITT, Stockholm, 1942-47; project engr. Lear, Inc., Santa Monica, Calif., 1947-59; devel. engr., mgr. Lockheed, Los Angeles and Sunnyvale, Calif., 1959-69; sr. staff scientist Measurex Corp., Cupertino, Calif., 1970—. Mem. IEEE (sr.), Instrument Soc. Am. (past pres. Santa Clara Valley sect.), AAAS. Patentee in field. Home: 8129 Park Villa Circle Cupertino CA 95014 Office: Measurex Corp 1 Results Way Cupertino CA 95014

WENTWORTH, THEODORE SUMNER, lawyer; b. Bklyn., July 18, 1938; s. Theodore Sumner and Alice Ruth (Wortmann) W.; A.A., Am. River Coll., 1958; J.D., Hastings Coll. Law, San Francisco, 1962; m. Sharon Linelle Arkush, Mar. 26, 1965; children—Christina Linn, Kathryn Allison. Admitted to Calif. bar, 1963; asso. Adams, Hunt & Martin, Santa Ana, Calif., 1963-66; partner Hunt, Liljestrom & Wentworth, Santa Ana, 1967-77; pres. Solabs Corp.; chmn. bd., exec. v.p. Plant Warehouse, Inc., Hawaii; prin. Law Offices of Theodore S. Wentworth, specializing in personal injury and malpractice litigation, Irvine, Calif. Pres., bd. dirs. Santa Ana-Tustin Community Chest, 1972; v.p., trustee South Orange County United Way, 1973-75; pres. Orange County Fedn. Funds, 1972-73; bd. dirs. Orange County Mental Health Assn. Diplomate Nat. Bd. Trial Advocacy. Mem. State Bar Calif., Am., Orange County (dir. 1972-76), San Francisco bar assns., Am. (judge pro tem superior ct. attys. panel), Calif. (bd. govs. 1968-70), Orange County (pres. 1967-68) trial lawyers assns., Lawyer-Pilots Bar Assn., Aircraft Owners and Pilots Assn. Clubs: Bahia Corinthian Yacht, Balboa Bay (Newport Beach, Calif.); Lincoln of Orange County. Research in vedic prins., natural law, metaphysics. Home: 3 Malibu Circle Corona Del Mar CA 92625 Office: 2112 Business Center Dr Suite 220 Irvine CA 92715

WERBACH, MELVYN ROY, psychiatrist; b. N.Y.C., Nov. 11, 1940; s. Samuel and Martha (Robbins) W.; B.A., Columbia U., 1962; M.D., Tufts U., 1966; m. Gail Beth Leibsohn, Feb. 12, 1967; children—Kevin Daniel, Adam Michael. Intern, VA Hosp., Bklyn., 1966-67; resident Cedars-Sinai Med. Center, Los Angeles, 1969-71; practice medicine, specializing in psychiatry, Tarzana, Calif., 1971—; chmn. dept. mental health Ross-Loos Med. Group, Los Angeles, 1972-75; dir. Biofeedback Med. Clinic, Los Angeles, 1971—; dir. clin. biofeedback and psychol. services Pain Control Unit, UCLA, 1976-80, asst. clin. prof. psychiatry, 1978—, asst. clin. prof. anesthesiology, 1980—. Served with USPHS, 1967-69. Diplomate Am. Bd. Psychiatry and Neurology. Mem. Am. Psychiat. Assn., Internat. Assn. Study of Pain, Biofeedback Soc. Am., Biofeedback Soc. Calif. (pres. 1976-77). Contbr. articles to profl. jours. Office: 18411 Clark St Tarzana CA 91356

WERKHEISER, STEVEN LAWRENCE, securities co. exec.; b. Mankato, Minn., Oct. 6, 1945; s. Laverne Eugene and Dorothy M. Werkheiser; student L.A. Pierce Coll., 1964-66, Oreg. State U., 1963-64; B.A., UCLA, 1970, M.S., 1971; m. Adrienne Lee Hayes, Apr. 26, 1969; children—Steven Lawrence, Kirsten Elizabeth. Mcpl. bond trader/underwriter Blyth & Co., Los Angeles, 1971-72, Blyth Eastman Dillon, 1972-73, mgr. mcpl. bond dept., 1974; fin. analyst Northrop Corp., Hawthorne, Calif., 1974-75, fin. planning analyst, 1976-80; v.p. trading R.H. Moulton & Co., Los Angeles, 1980-82; div. fin. specialist Northrop Corp., Hawthorne, Calif., 1982—; fin. cons., 1975—. Served with AUS, 1966-68. Mem. Los Angeles Bond Club, Assn. M.B.A.s, UCLA Alumni Assn. Republican. Methodist. Home: 27541 Diane Marie Circle Saugus CA 91350 Office: 523 W 6th St Los Angeles CA 90014

WERNER, DANIEL H., construction company executive; b. Billings, Mont., Apr. 24, 1937; s. David and Vera Mae W.; A.B. in Clin. Psychology, Brandeis U., 1960; postgrad. Harvard U., U. Colo., San Francisco State U.; m. Judith Grossenbacher, Jan. 1, 1977; children—Jordan, Jessia, Jacob. Employee relations mgr. Raychem Corp., Menlo Park, Calif., 1967-70; asso. dir. orgn. devel. Kaiser-Permanente Med. Care Program, Oakland, Calif., 1970-75; prin. Werner Assos., Carmel Valley, Calif. and Medford, Oreg., 1974-78; corp. dir. human resources devel Morrison-Knudsen Co., Inc., Boise, Idaho, 1978—; guest lectr. univ. schs. of bus. Mem. N.Am. Soc. Corp. Planning, Orgn. Devel. Network, Am. Soc. Tng. and Devel., Acad. Mgmt., Soc. Intercultural Edn., Tng. and Research, Am. Soc. Personnel Adminstrn., Human Resource Planning Soc. Office: Morrison-Knudsen Co Inc PO Box 7808 Boise ID 83729

WERNER, FRITZ, artist; b. Vienna, Austria, Apr. 7, 1898; came to U.S., 1932, naturalized, 1935; s. Louis and Elisabeth (Klem) W.; student fine art acads., Vienna, Munich, Ger., Paris and Rome; m. Emmy Smetzka, June 13, 1935. One-man exhbns. include: Wildenstein Art Gallery, N.Y.C., Closson Gallery, Cin., Stendahl Gallery, Los Angeles, Courvoisier Gallery, San Francisco, Bryant Gallery, Jackson, Miss., also in Munich, Ger., Alexandria and Cairo, Egypt, Buenos Aires, Argentina;

group exhbns. include: Terzia Biennale, Rome, Le Salon, Paris, Cin. Mus. Art, NAD, N.Y.C.; represented in permanent collections: Princeton U., art museums of Phoenix, Oklahoma City and Syracuse, N.Y., Supreme Ct., Ohio, Mayo Clinic, Rochester, Minn., Sloan-Kettering Meml. Hosp., N.Y.C., Chgo. Circuit Ct. Appeals, Christ Hosp., Cin., St. Luke's Hosp., Kansas City, Mo., Vt. State House, Montpelier, Okla. Heritage Assn., Oklahoma City; executed numerous portraits of prominent persons, including Pres. William H. Taft, Senator Robert A. Taft, Senator Warren R. Austin, Prince Barbu Stirbey, prime minister of Romania, Ahmed Ziwar Pasha, prime minister of Egypt. Recipient Austrian State prize in portraiture, 1918. Address: 1001 Genter St Apt 9-D La Jolla CA 92037

WERNER, JOHN ALVA, printer; b. Alamosa, Colo., May 13, 1940; s. Charles Alwyn and Cecelia Inez (Lorimer) W.; student Adams State Coll., 1959-61, 65-67, B.A., 1967; m. Marla R. Holden; children—Katheryn Eileen, Douglas Charles, Cynthia Louise; 1 stepdau., Michele Lee Holden. Miner, Am. Metals Climax, Climax, Colo., 1963-64, W.S. Moore Co., Summitville, Colo., 1964-65; tchr. Moffat (Colo.) Consol. Schs., 1966-68, Stanislaus County Schs., Riverbank, Calif., 1968; packaging analyst Fibreboard Corp., San Francisco, 1968-70; mine safety instr. and edn. specialist Mine Safety and Health Adminstrn., Alameda, Calif., Albany, Oreg., and Boise, Idaho, 1971-80; sr. safety rep. Bechtel Inc., Tonopah, Nev., 1980-81, Bechtel Civil & Minerals Inc., Bayard, N.Mex., 1981-83, Bechtel Power Corp., Richland, Wash., 1982-83; owner, Affordable Printing & Typing, Pasco, Wash., 1983—; mine safety cons.; mine safety trainer. Den parent Cub Scouts, Cascade area council Boy Scouts Am., 1979; emergency med. technician, Tonopah, 1980; instr. trainer Am. Heart Assn., Boise, 1977; chmn. Boise Field Fed. Safety and Health Council, 1977. Served with U.S. Army, 1958. Recipient Joseph A. Holmes medal of honor, 1972; citation for valor, Dept. Interior, 1972; Recognition award Sec. of Labor, 1979; Cert. of Appreciation, Dept. Labor, 1979; Mem. Am. Soc. Safety Engrs. (cert. hazard control mgr., cert. safety profl.). Illustrator Dept. Interior annual report, 1973, booklet: 60 Surface Mine Fatalities, 1974; painter mural for Bur. of Mines office, Alameda, Calif., 1971. Home: 1918 W 36th Ave Kennewick WA 99336 Office: Affordable Printing & Typing 1600 N 20th St Suite F-1 Pasco WA 99301

WERT, JAMES EDWARD, economist, educator, consultant; b. Clayton, Ohio, Jan. 28, 1923; s. Mark H. and Susan (Reed) W.; m. Janice F. Brendle, Sept. 14, 1952; children—Nora J., Martin J., Stacia M. Asst. prof. acctg. Lehigh U., 1954-57; sr. fin. economist Fed. Res. Bank, Cleve., 1957-59; prof. fin., chmn. dept. SUNY-Buffalo, 1959-67; prof. fin. U. Ariz., Tucson, 1967—, chmn. dept., 1967-78. Mem. investment council Ariz. Retirement System, 1983—. Served with USAF 1942-45. Mem. Am. Fin. Assn., Western Fin. Assn. (dir., 1968-70, pres., 1973-74), Fin. Mgmt. Assn. (dir., 1976-78). Author: (with others) Financing Bus. Firms, 6th edit., 1979, An Introduction to Financial Management, 1984.

WERTHEIM, ROBERT HALLEY, aerospace executive; former navy officer; b. Carlsbad, N.Mex., Nov. 9, 1922; s. Joseph and Emma (Vorenberg) W.; m. Barbara Louise Selig, Dec. 26, 1946; children—Joseph Howard, David Andrew. Student N.Mex. Mil. Inst., 1940-42; B.S. in Naval Sci., U.S. Naval Acad., 1945; M.S. in Physics, MIT, 1954; grad. Advanced Mgmt. Program, Harvard U., 1969-70. Commd. ensign U.S. Navy, 1945, advanced through grades to rear adm., 1972; head Polaris rentry vehicle research and devel., 1956-61, weapon system devel. Naval Ordnance Test Sta., 1961-62; mil. asst. to asst. dir. def. research and engring., 1962-65; missile br. head Strategic Systems Project Office, 1965-67, dep. tech. dir., 1967-68, tech. dir., 1968-77, dir., 1977-80, ret., 1980; sr. v.p. sci. and engring. Lockheed Corp., Burbank, Calif., 1981—; cons. Office Under Sec. of Def. for Research and Engring.; sci. adv. group Joint Strategic Target Planning Staff, Joint Chiefs of Staff; nat. security adv. bd. Los Alamos Nat. Lab.; mem. Charles Stark Draper Lab., Inc.; sci. adv. group Def. Nuclear Agy. Decorated Legion of Merit, D.S.M.; recipient Rear Adm. William S. Parsons award Navy League U.S., 1971. Fellow AIAA; mem. Nat. Acad. Engring., Am. Soc. Naval Engrs. (hon., Gold medal), Sigma Xi. Club: Woodland Hills Country. Office: Lockheed Corp PO Box 551 Burbank CA 91520

WERTHEIMER, MICHAEL, psychology educator, writer; b. Berlin, Mar. 20, 1927; s. Max and Anna (Caro) W.; m. Nancy MacKaye, Sept. 7, 1952; children—Karellynne Wertheimer Watkins, Mark David, Benjamin Gould; m. 2d, Marilyn Lou Schuman, Sept. 12, 1970. B.A., Swarthmore Coll., 1947; M.A., Johns Hopkins U., 1949; M.A., Harvard U., 1951, Ph.D., 1952. Instr. psychology Wesleyan U., Middletown, Conn., 1952-53, asst. prof. psychology, 1953-55; asst. prof. U. Colo., Boulder, 1955-57, assoc. prof., 1957-61, prof. psychology, 1961—; Mem. Rocky Mountain Rescue Group, 1956—. Recipient award for Disting. Teaching, Am. Psychol. Found., 1983. Mem. Am. Psychol. Assn. (past pres. several divs. acting adminstrv. officer ednl. affairs 1970-71), Am. Assn. State Psychology Bds. (exam. com., chmn. 1979-81), Rocky Mountain Psychol. Assn. (pres. 1981), Phi Beta Kappa, Sigma Xi. Club: Colo. Mountain. Author: A Brief History of Psychology, 1970, 2d edit., 1979; History of Psychology: A guide to information sources, 1979; Psychology: An Introduction, 1973, 3d edit., 1979; co-author, editor, co-editor numerous books and monographs; contbr. numerous articles to profl. jours. Home: 546 Geneva Ave Boulder CO 80302 Office: Dept Psychology U Colo Boulder CO 80309

WESLEY, PHILLIP, librarian; b. Los Angeles, June 3, 1930; s. George Gregor and Olive Vessie (Barnette) W.; A.A., Glendale, Coll., 1950; B.A., U. Calif. at Los Angeles, 1956; M.S., U. So. Calif., 1959. Sr. library asst. U. Calif. at Los Angeles Law Library, 1955-58; bindery clk., acquisitions librarian, cataloger Los Angeles County Law Library, 1958-59; ltd. loan and serials librarian Calif. State U. at Los Angeles Library, 1959-60; acquisitions librarian Los Angeles County Law Library, 1960-61, reference librarian, 1961-62, head catalog librarian, 1961-66; head catalog librarian Calif. State U., Northridge, 1966-67, chief tech. services, 1967-69, acting coll. librarian, 1969; dir. ednl. resources center Calif. State U., Dominguez Hills, 1969-77, dean ednl. resources, 1977—. Mem. Am. Assn. Law Libraries, So. Calif. Assn. Law Libraries (pres. 1964-65), Spl. Libraries Assn. (chpt. treas. 1969-70), So. Calif. Tech. Processes Group (pres. 1972-74), Am., Calif. library assns. Home: 2287 Panorama Terr Los Angeles CA 90039 Office: 1000 E Victoria St Carson CA 90747

WESNICK, RICHARD JAMES, newspaper editor; b. Racine, Wis., Oct. 14, 1938; s. John and Julia (Kassa) W.; m. Elaine Apoline Smith, Sept. 30, 1967; children—Catherine Elaine, Julie Ann. B.A., U. Houston, 1961. Staff writer Racine (Wis.) Jour. Times, 1965-76; mng. editor Helena (Mont.) Ind. Record, 1976-80; news editor Billings (Mont.) Gazette, 1980, editor, 1980—. Served with USMC, 1961-64. Mem. Am. Soc. Newspaper Editors, Soc. Newspaper Design, Assoc. Press Mng. Editors Assn. Roman Catholic. Clubs: Billings Petroleum, Kiwanis. Office: Billings Gazette 401 N Broadway Billings MT 59103

WESSLER, MELVIN DEAN, farmer, rancher; b. Dodge City, Kan., Feb. 11, 1932; s. Oscar Lewis and Clara (Reiss) W.; grad. high sch.; m. Laura Ethel Arbuthnot, Aug. 23, 1951; children—Monty Dean, Charla Cay, Virgil Lewis. Farmer-rancher, Springfield, Colo., 1950—; dir., sec. bd. Springfield Co-op. Sales Co., 1964-80, pres. bd., 1980—. Pres., Arkansas Valley Co-op. Council, S.E. Colo. Area, 1965—, Colo. Co-op. Council, 1969-72; community com. chmn. Baca County, Agr. Stablzn. and Conservation Service, Springfield, 1961-73, 79—, vice chmn. Baca County Com., 1980—; mem. spl. com. on grain mktg. Far-Mar-Co. Mem. Colo. Cattlemen's Assn., Colo. Wheat Growers Assn., Big Rock Grange (treas. 1964-76, master 1976-82). Baptist. Address: Route 2 Box 24 Springfield CO 81073

WESSON, ROBERT GALE, political scientist; b. Washington, Mar. 11, 1920; s. Laurence Goddard and Elizabeth Davis (Matthews) W.; A.B., U. Ariz., 1940; M.A., Fletcher Sch. Law and Diplomacy, 1941; Ph.D., Columbia U., 1961. Asst. prof. govt. Bates Coll., 1961-62, 63-64; asst. prof. polit. sci. U. Calif.-Santa Barbara, 1964-66, asso. prof., 1966-71, prof., 1971—; sr. research fellow Hoover Instn., Stanford U., 1978—. Served with U.S. Navy, 1944-46. Author: The Imperial Order; State Systems; The U.S. and Brazil: Limits of Influence; Democracy in Latin America; others; contbr. articles to Current History, N.Y. Times, Los Angeles Times, Survey, Slavic Rev., Orbis, Bus. Week, others. Office: Dept Polit Sci U Calif Santa Barbara CA 93106

WEST, ANDREW ERNEST, wheat farmer; b. Chgo., June 26, 1918; s. James Andrew and Minnie Elizabeth (Franklin) W.; m. Merietta B. Ball, Aug. 13, 1951; children—Riat Dee, James Edward. Student pub. schs., Briggsdale, Colo., 1923-32. Farmer Briggsdale, Colo., 1931-39, farm owner, 1939—; mem. Am. Soil Conservation Bd.; mem. Briggsdale Co-op. Bd. Mem. Briggsdale Bd. Edn., 1967-79; active Boy Scouts Am., 1942-44. Recipient outstanding community service award, 1979; named hon. mem. Nat. Honor Soc., 1981. Democrat. Mem. Union Congregational Ch. Clubs: Lions, Elks.

WEST, BARBARA JO, food company executive; b. Bishop, Calif., Apr. 10, 1945; d. James J. and Inez E. (Fackrell) Carberry; m. Robert M. West, Oct. 1, 1972 (div.); children—N. Dion, W. Todd. B.B.A., Boise State U. Mktg. asst. H.J. Heinz Co., Boise, Idaho, 1973-74, asst. product mgr., 1975-78, product mgr., 1978-80, sr. product mgr. new products Ore-Ida Brand div., 1980-81, sr. product mgr. product devel. dept. Weight Watchers div., 1981-83; sr. product mgr. Am. Home Products, 1983—. Advisor Jr. Achievement, Boise, 1976-77; pub. relations dir. Idaho chpt. Cystic Fibrosis, 1979-80. Recipient Mktg. Achievement award Sales and Mktg. Execs., 1979; Jr. Achievement scholar, 1964. Mem. Am. Mktg. Assn., Idaho Advt. Fedn., Assn. Nat. Advertisers. Roman Catholic.

WEST, BILLY GENE, public relations and mktg. co. exec.; b. Richmond, Ind., Nov. 22, 1946; s. Billy D. and Jean C. (Cox) W.; A.A., Cerritos Coll., 1966; B.A., U. So. Calif., 1969; M.A., U. Minn., 1971. Salesman, Marina Art Products, Los Angeles, 1967-73; v.p. Am. Telecon Network, Dallas, 1974-77; gen. mgr. Phoenix Publs., Houston, 1977-78; pres. San Dark, Inc., San Francisco, 1978—; also dir. Vice pres. Calif. Young Republican Coll. Fedn., 1966-67; exec. dir. Young Ams. for Freedom, Minn. and Wis., 1970-72; pres. S.F.P.A., San Francisco, 1982-83. Mem. Assn. M.B.A. Execs. Mem. Am. Ref. Ch. Office: PO Box 14583 San Francisco CA 94114

WEST, C(HARLES) KEITH, oil company executive; b. Rock Springs, Wyo., Apr. 7, 1931; s. Owen W. and Blanch L. (Samon) W.; m. Margene Hansen, June 14, 1952; children—Charles Keith II, Steven Paul, Kenneth Lee, Jan Marie, Neil Lenord. B.B.A., Brigham Young U., 1953. With Desert Oil Co., Rock Springs, 1953—, pres., 1955—; dir. First Security Bank. Mayor, City of Rock Springs, 1979—. Mem. Wyo. Assn. Municipalities, Rock Springs. C. of C. Democrat. Mormon. Office: Desert Oil Co Inc PO Box 1030 Rock Springs WY 82901

WEST, DARBY LINDSEY, mfg. co. exec.; b. Melrose, N.Mex., Jan. 13, 1938; s. Wayne Burton and Mildred Minnie (Lindsey) W.; grad. high sch.; m. Angelina Loomis, Feb. 9, 1980; children—Rebecca, Darby, Jr., Johnny Wayne. Well attendant El Paso Natural Gas Co., Farmington, N.Mex., 1957-65, instrument technician, 1965-67, dehydrator man, 1967-77; v.p., partner Natural Gas Prodn. Equipment P & A, Inc., Farmington, 1977—. Republican. Baptist. Home: PO Box 2648 Bloomfield NM 87413 Office: Route 3 Box 711 Farmington NM 87401

WEST, FRED DWAYNE, electronics engineer; b. Ft. Bell, Bermuda, Sept. 20, 1947; s. Fred Gamble and Trudy Aleva (Price) W.; B.S.E.E., U. Tex., 1972, M.S.E.E., 1978; m. Karen Sue Wilkinson, Apr. 25, 1970; children—David Michael, James Gamble. With Tex. Instruments, Austin, 1972-73; field engring. mgr. Dresser Industries, Dallas, 1973-77; electronics engr. flight test YAH-64 Hughes Helicopters, Yuma, Ariz., 1979-81; prin. engr. Boeing Co., 1981; data communications fiber optic cons. U.S. Army Elec. Proving Grounds, Ft. Huachaca, Ariz., 1983—; cons. control systems, theory. Served with USN, 1967-71. Mem. Profl. Scientists and Engrs., Am. Mgmt. Assn. Democrat. Author: Basic Radar Principles; contbr. articles to profl. jours.; patentee variable wavelength laser diode, tapered layer tech., particle pump, solar power plant, particle beam weapon. Home: 7503 Carriage St Austin TX 78752 Office: Comdr Yuma Proving Grounds Yuma AZ 85364

WEST, HUGH STERLING, aircraft leasing co. exec.; b. Kansas City, Kans., Apr. 5, 1930; s. Gilbert Eugene and Dorothy (Johnson) W.; B.S., U. Va., 1952; B.S. Aero., U. Md., 1959; grad. U.S. Naval Test Pilot Sch., 1959; m. Willa Alden Reed, Jan. 16, 1954; children—Karen, Phillip, Susan. Commd. 2d lt. U.S. Marine Corps., 1948, advanced through grades to maj., 1961; exptl. flight test pilot, U.S. Naval Air Test Center, Patuxent River, Md.; resigned, 1961; program mgr. Boeing Aircraft Co., Seattle and Phila., 1961-66, dir. airworthiness, comml. airplane div., 1969-71; dir. aircraft sales Am. Airlines, Tulsa, 1971-76; v.p. equipment mgmt. GATX Leasing Corp., San Francisco, 1976-80; v.p. tech., partner Polaris Aircraft Leasing Corp., San Francisco, 1980—; aircraft cons. Mem. Soc. Exptl. Test Pilots. Republican. Episcopalian. Club: Army Navy Country. Home: 387 Darrell Rd Hillsborough CA 94010 Office: 600 Montgomery St San Francisco CA 94111

WEST, JERRY ALAN, professional basketball team general manager; b. Chelyan, W.Va., May 28, 1938; s. Howard Stewart and Cecil Sue (Creasey) W.; m. Martha Jane Kane, May 1960 (div. 1977); children—David, Michael, Mark; m. 2d Karen Christine Bua, May 28, 1978; 1 son, Ryan. B.S., W.Va. U.; L.H.D. (hon.), W.Va. Wesleyan Coll. Mem. Los Angeles Lakers, prof. basketball team, 1960-74, coach, 1976-79, spl. cons., to from, 1979, gen. mgr., 1982—; played in NBA All-Star games; capt. U.S. Olympic Basketball team (Gold medal), Rome, 1960. Sixth all-time basketball scorer with 25,192 points; 2d all-time leader in free throws (7,160); 6th all-time leader in field goals (9,016); 5th all-time leader in assists (6,238); inducted into. NBA Hall of Fame, 1980.

WEST, JOHN LEROY, aerospace engineer; b. Los Angeles, Calif., June 18, 1947; s. John LeRoy and Margaret (Jones) W. B.S. in Aerospace Engring., U. So. Calif., 1970, M.S. in Mech. Engring., 1973. Engring. research asst. Air Force Rocket Propulsion Lab., Edwards AFB, Calif., summer 1968; systems engr. hdqrs. Air Force Satellite Control Facility, El Segundo, Calif., 1970-73; engring. research asst., Jet Propulsion Lab., Pasadena, Calif., summer 1969, systems engr., 1975—. Mem. AIAA. Mormon. Club: Corvair Soc. Am. Contbr. publs. in field of aerospace tech. Office: 4800 Oak Grove Dr Pasadena CA 91103

WEST, KENNETH LAFE, mining company owner, lecturer; b. Pocatello, Idaho, Aug. 15, 1939; s. Samual Lafe and Maxine Elliot (McKenzie) W.; m. Linda Mary Shaub, Oct. 19, 1969 (div.); 1 dau., Jeri Diane. A.A. in Counseling, Otereo Jr. Coll., 1979; A.A. in Electronics, Coll. So. Idaho, 1971; postgrad. in Sociology, Idaho State U., 1958-81. Gen. mgr., dir. Attitude Awareness Ctr., Idaho Falls, 1979-81; planner Custer County, Idaho, 1974; recreation dir. A.R.A., Inc., Idaho Falls, 1978-79; gen. mgr. Moonwalker, Inc., Mackay, Idaho, 1981—; county probation officer; host radio show; educator Idaho State U., 1980; fed. grant writer. Sec. Moonwalker Found., Mackay. Served with U.S. Army, 1957-58, USAF, 1962-65. Mem. Am. Legion. Republican. Seventh-day Adventist. Clubs: Lions, Masons. Columnist Idaho State Jour., Post Register. Home: PO Box 446 Mackay ID 83251 Office: 407 Pine Mackay ID 83251

WEST, LAWRENCE HOLLIS, educator; b. Glendale, Calif., Dec. 14, 1924; s. Walter Lawrence and Martha Lois (Taylor) W.; B.A., Pomona Coll., 1949; M.A., Stanford U., 1951; m. Callie Pershing Kaufman, Aug. 3, 1947; children—Peter Taylor, Richard Austing, Hollis Louise West Pifer. Clk., typist Stanford U. Press, 1952-54; tchr. Julia C. Lathrop Jr. High Sch., Santa Ana, Calif., 1954-56; tchr., dept. chmn., counselor Santa Ana Sr. high Sch., 1956-65; prof. history Santa Ana Coll., 1965—. Legal explorer post advisor Orange Empire council Boy Scouts Am., 1957-63; clk. St. Matthews Episcopal Mission, Santa Ana, 1963-65, bishop's warden, 1966; life mem. Western Med. Center Assn., 1979—. Served with U.S. Army, 1943-46. John Hay fellow, 1965; Fulbright-Hays fellow, 1968; Nat. Endowment for the Humanities fellow, 1973-74. Mem. Latin Am. Studies Assn., Conf. Latin Am. History, Phi Alpha Theta, Sigma Delta Pi. Republican. Author: A History of Ecuadorian Regionalism, 1809-1830, 1951. Home: 559 Oak St Laguna Beach CA 92651 Office: Dunlap Hall #415 Santa Ana College 17th St and Bristol St Santa Ana CA 92706

WEST, LOUIS JOLYON, psychiatrist; b. N.Y.C., Oct. 6, 1924; s. Albert Jerome and Anna (Rosenberg) W.; student U. Wis., 1941-42, State U. Iowa, 1943-44; B.S., U. Minn., 1946, M.B., 1948, M.D., 1949; m. Kathryn Louise Hopkirk, Apr. 29, 1944; children—Anne Kathryn, Mary Elizabeth, John Stuart. Intern, U. Minn. Hosps., 1948-49; resident in psychiatry Payne Whitney Clinic, N.Y.C., 1949-52; asst. in psychiatry Cornell U. Med. Coll., 1950-52; prof., head dept. psychiatry, neurology and behavioral scis. U. Okla., 1954-69; prof., chmn. dept. psychiatry and biobehavioral scis. UCLA, 1969—; psychiatrist-in-chief UCLA Hosp. and Clinics, 1969—, dir. Neuropsychiat. Inst., 1969—; cons. psychiatry VA Center Psychosocial Medicine at Brentwood, 1969—, VA Hosp., Sepulveda, Calif., 1969—; research adv. com. Gateways Hosp., Los Angeles, 1971—; Am. prof. adv. com. Jerusalem Mental Health Center, Tel Aviv, 1971—; attending staff Harbor Gen. Hosp., Torrance, Calif.; mem. med. staff St. John's Hosp. and Med. Center; Sommer Meml. lectr., Portland, Oreg., 1968; Dr. Gustav Bychowski Meml. lectr. Mt. Sinai Sch. Medicine, N.Y.C., 1974; H.B. Williams Meml. Travelling prof. Royal Australian and N.Z. Coll. Psychiatrists, 1979; dir. Inst. Research in Hypnosis, 1958-66; cons. USAF Aerospace Med. Center, 1961-66, Peace Corps, 1962-63, Bur. Social Research, Inc., 1965-68, Surgeon Gen. U.S. Army, 1974-77, VA health care com. NRC div. med. scis., Assembly of Life Scis., 1975-76; internat. bd. dirs. Kittay Sci. Found., 1972-77; Am. adv. bd. Jerusalem Mental Health Center, 1972—; internat. adv. bd. Israeli Center Psychobiology, 1974—. Served with inf., AUS, 1942-46, to maj., USAF, 1948-56. Fellow Center Advanced Study in Behavioral Scis., Stanford, Calif., 1966-67; diplomate Nat. Bd. Med. Examiners, Am. Bd. Psychiatry and Neurology. Fellow AAAS, Am. Coll. Psychiatrists, Am. Psychiat. Assn. (Benjamin Rush gold medal 1973); mem. Am. Acad. Psychiatry and Law, Am. Acad. Psychoanalysis, Am. Assn. Chairmen of Depts. Psychiatry (sec.-treas. 1970), AMA, Am. Orthopsychiat. Assn., Am. Psychol. Assn., Am. Psychopath. Assn., Am. Psychosomatic Soc., Antarctican Soc., Assn. Psychophysiol. Study of Sleep, Assn. Am. Med. Colls., Assn. Research in Nerous and Mental Diseases, Nat. Com. Against Mental Illness, Assn. Acad. Psychiatry, Pan Am. Med. Assn. (pres. sect. clin. hypnosis 1962-64, N.Am. co-chmn. sect. clin. hypnosis 1966-68), Pavlovian Soc. (pres. 1975), Soc. Biol. Psychiatry, Soc. Clin. and Exptl. Hypnosis, Soc. Med. Consultants to Armed Forces, Soc. Psychophysiol. Research, Alpha Omega Alpha. Author: (with Farber and Meyers) Prisoners of War, 1958; Hallucinations, 1962; editor: (with Greenblatt) Explorations in the Physiology of Emotions, 1960; (with Siegel) Hallucinations: Behavior, Experience Theory, 1975; (with Flinn) Treatment of Schizophrenia: Progress and Prospects, 1976; (with Stein) Critical Issues in Behavioral Medicine, 1982; adv. editor Internat. Jour. Clin. and Exptl. Hypnosis, 1958-66; adv. editorial bd. Jour. Nervous and Mental Disease, 1961-66; cons. editor Med. Aspects of Human Sexuality, 1967—; editorial bd. Jour. Existential Psychiatry, 1970-71, Psychiat. Annals, 1971-77, Weekly Psychiatry Update Series, 1976—, Psychiat. Books, 1979—, A Critical Guide to Psychiat. Lit., 1979—; adv. editorial bd. Med. Update, 1978—; contbr. numerous articles to profl. jours., chpts. in books. Office: University of California Neuropsychiatric Institute 760 Westwood Plaza Los Angeles CA 90024

WEST, MICHAEL ELDO, service company executive, consultant; b. Fullerton, Calif., Dec. 24, 1941; s. Merle E. and Elizabeth L. (Keeler) W.; m. Kathleen Andrews, July 6, 1967; 1 son, Joshua Allworth. A.A., Fullerton Coll., 1962; B.S., San Jose State U., 1966. Vice-pres., gen. mgr. Merle West, Inc., Whittier, Calif., 1969-82, pres., 1982—; expert examiner Calif. Bd. Fabric Care. Bd. dirs. Boy's and Girl's Club of Whittier. Served to 1st lt. QMC, U.S. Army, 1966-69. Mem. Assn. Interior Decor Specialists (divisional pres. 1980-82), Carpet Cleaners Inst. (pres. 1978-79, Joe Laurino Meml.-Carpet Cleaner of Yr. 1975, 77, Bill Bailey Meml. award 1977), Internat. Inst. Carpet and Upholstery Cleaners (trustee), Internat. Dry Cleaner Congress, Internat. Fabricare Inst. Republican. Mem. Soc. of Friends. Lodge: Kiwanis (pres. 1981-82) (Whittier Rio Hondo, Calif.). Editor Western Carpet Cleaner Trade Jour., 1974-78; contbr. articles in field to trade jours.

WEST, RICHARD VINCENT, art mus. ofcl.; b. Prague, Czechoslovakia, Nov. 26, 1934; s. Jan Josef and Katherine Frieda (Mayer) Vyslouzil; came to U.S., 1938, naturalized, 1947; student UCLA, 1952-55; B.A. with highest honors, U. Calif., Santa Barbara, 1961; postgrad. Akademie der Bildenden Kuenste, Vienna, 1961-62; M.A., U. Calif., Berkeley, 1965; m. Emily Ann Pagenhart, June 26, 1961; 1 dau., Jessica Katherine. Curatorial intern Cleve. Art Mus., 1965-66, Albright-Knox Art Gallery, Buffalo, 1966-67; curator Bowdoin Coll. Mus. Art, 1967-69, dir., 1969-72; dir. Crocker Art Mus., Sacramento, 1973-83, Santa Barbara (Calif.) Mus. Art, 1983—. Mem. Joint Yugoslav-Am. Excavations at Sirmium, 1971; bd. dirs., Sacramento Regional Art Council, 1973-77, Calif. Assn. Museums, 1980-82. Served with USN, 1956-57. Ford Found. fellow, 1965-67; Smithsonian fellow, 1971. Mem. Assn. Art Mus. Dirs., Am. Assn. Museums, Coll. Art Assn., Internat. Council Museums, Western Assn. Art Museums (pres. 1975-78). Club: Rotary Internat. Author: Language of the Print, 1968; The Walker Art Building Murals, 1972, also various monographs and articles on Am. art and artists. Office: Santa Barbara Mus Art 1130 State St Santa Barbara CA 93101

WEST, WILLIAM GEORGE, medical center manager; b. Devils Lake, N.D., July 3, 1948; s. James Donald and Cecelia Marie (Bryl) W.; m. Patricia Margaret Yuzna, Oct. 17, 1980; children—Christopher, Genevieve. B.A., U. N.D., 1971; student U.Paris, 1978; M.A., U. Minn., 1979. Processing supr. U. Minn. Hosps., Mpls., 1975-77, equipment supr., 1977-79; process equipment mgr. U. Calif. Med. Ctr., San Francisco, 1979—. Recipient Assn. for Advancement Med. Studies award, 1979. Mem. Golden Gate Assn. of Central Services Personnel (treas.), Am. Hosp. Assn. Democrat. Roman Catholic. Contbr. articles to profl. jours. Home: 219 Parnassus San Francisco CA 94117 Office: 505 Parnassus M-01 San Francisco CA 94122

WESTBERG, KARL ROGERS, chemist; b. Norwalk, Conn., Dec. 17, 1939; s. Arnold Karl and Bernice (Glanz) W.; B.A., Bowdoin Coll., 1961; Ph.D., Brown U., 1969; m. Carole Shirley Best, Dec. 19, 1971; children—Melissa, Brent, Gavin. Mem. tech. staff Aerospace Corp., El Segundo, Calif., 1968—. Served with U.S. Army, 1966-68. Mem. Am. Chem. Soc. Contbr. profl. jours. Co-discoverer role of carbon monoxide in photochem. smog formation. Home: 4436 Lucera Circle Palos Verdes Estates CA 90274 Office: PO Box 92957 Los Angeles CA 90009

WESTBO, LEONARD ARCHIBALD, JR., electronics engr.; b. Tacoma, Wash., Dec. 4, 1931; s. Leonard Archibald and Agnes (Martinson) W.; B.A. in Gen. Studies, U. Wash., 1958. Electronics engr. FAA, Seattle Air Route Traffic Control Center, Auburn, Wash., 1961-72; asst. br. chief electronics engring. br. 13th Coast Guard Dist., Seattle, 1972—. Served with USCG, 1951-54, 1958-61. Registered profl. engr., Wash. Mem. Aircraft Owners and Pilots Assn., I.E.E.E., Am. Radio Relay League. Home: 10528 SE 323d St Auburn WA 98002 Office: Comdr 13th Coast Guard Dist Fed Bldg 915 2d Ave Seattle WA 98174

WESTBROOK, PATRICK ALAN DE LUJAN, anthropologist; b. Laredo, Tex., Nov. 24, 1924; s. Samuel Albert and Mary Jo (de Lujan) W.; student No. Ariz. U., 1942-43; B.S., Ariz. State U., 1950; M.A., Vanderbilt U., 1952; M.S., U. Oreg., 1959; M.A., San Francisco State U., 1963. News editor State Press, Tempe, Ariz., 1949-50; curator anthropology, lectr. Mus. of Man, San Diego, 1953; curator anthropology, preparator Nashville Children's Mus., 1953-54; resident fellow So. Ill. U., 1954; anthrop. research, No. Sonora, Mex., 1954—; mus. preparator Mus. Anthropology, U. Calif., Berkeley, 1955—; curator and mus. preparator San Mateo Mus., 1955—; asst. curator Mus. Oriental Art, U. Oreg., 1958-59; lectr. southwestern anthropology; prof. sociology, coordinator anthropology and sociology, dept. behavioral studies City Coll. San Francisco, 1968—; cons. analyst U. Utah project, 1980—. Served with USNR, 1942-46. Mem. AAUP, Am. Anthrop. Assn., Am. Mus. Assn., F.B. Turner Welfare Soc., Archaeol. Inst. Am., AAAS, Am. Geog. Soc., Oceanic Soc., Alliance Francaise, Goethe Inst. (Neue Ulm, Germany), Mediaeval Acad. Am., Western Assn. Univs. and Colls. (accrediting commn. 1968—), Delta Phi Alpha, Alpha Psi Omega, Kappa Alpha. Club: Vanderbilt (San Francisco). Home: PO Box 5050 San Francisco CA 94101

WESTENDORF, DAVID RICHARD, produce sales co. exec.; b. Twin Falls, Idaho, May 6, 1945; s. Richard Henry and Berniece (Brandon) W.; B.Agr., U. Idaho, 1967; M.Agr., U. Calif., Davis, 1968; m. Carolyn D. Casebolt, Sept. 3, 1965; children—David, Eric, Ryan. Salesman, Albers Milling Co., Stockton, Calif., 1968-69, Boise Cascade Co., Sunnyvale, Calif., 1969-72; account exec. corrugated div. Continental Can Co., Los Angeles, 1972-76; sales mgr. produce packaging Continental Forest Industries (formerly Continental Can Co.), Los Angeles, 1976-78; co-founder G&W Produce Sales Co., Santa Ana, Calif., 1978-79; owner, pres. Dave Westendorf Produce Sales, Inc., Oceanside, Calif., 1979—. Vice pres. Westlake Hills Sch. PTA, Westlake Village, Calif., 1973; bd. dirs. Westlake Hills Property Owners Assn., v.p., 1976. Club: Rotary. Home: 105 Via Zapata San Clemente CA 92672 Office: 2521 Oceanside Blvd PO Box 2297 Oceanside CA 92054

WESTERBERG, ERIC NORMAN, consulting engineer; b. Detroit, Feb. 10, 1929; s. Sven Eric and Hellin Mathilda (Mattsson) W.; m. Benita Ingegard Eklund, Dec. 23, 1950; children—Dan, Christine, Kenneth. M.S. in Chem. Engring., Abo Akademi, Finland, 1953; M.S. In Nuclear Engring., Oak Ridge Sch. Reactor Tech., 1961. Lic. profl. engr., Ohio, Wash. Research engr. Dahle Cons., Allentown, Pa., 1954; process engr. Diamond Alkali Co., Cleve., 1956-58; dept. mgr. Ekono Oy, Helsinki, Finland, 1958-70, sr. v.p., 1971—; pres. Ekono Inc., Bellevue, Wash., 1981—; chmn. com. dist. heating, cogeneration and heat pumps World Energy Conf. Served with U.S. Army, 1954-56. Knighted Order of Lions (Finland). Mem. Finnish Assn. Cons. Firms (chmn. 1976-79), Finnish Am. C. of C. N.W. (pres.). Contbr. numerous articles to profl. jours. Office: 410 Bellevue Way SE Bellevue WA 98004

WESTERFIELD, WILLIAM, educator; b. Balt., Mar. 1, 1947; s. Richard Alfred and LaValle Marie (Slater) W.; student U. S.C., 1968; B.A., U. Md., 1970, M.A., 1971; Ph.D. (fellow), Wayne State U., 1976. Dir. pub. relations U. Md. Theatre, 1970-71; instr. jr. stage Washington Theatre Club, 1971-72; instr. Balt. Children's Theatre Assn., Balt., 1972, Marjorie Webster Jr. Coll., Washington, 1972; stage mgr., actor Villa Rosa Dinner Theater, Silver Spring, Md., 1971-72; model Cappa Chell Agy., Washington, 1971-72; instr. creative drama, asst. dir. pub. relations, theatre dept. Wayne State U., Detroit, 1972-74; founder, coordinator All City Arts Program, Detroit, 1972-74; assoc. prof. theatre arts San Francisco State U., 1974—, chairperson theatre arts dept., 1983—; founder, pres. BOWEST Talent and Modeling Agy., San Francisco, 1979-81; coordinator children's theatre Santa Rosa Summer Repertory Theatre, 1976; instr. Am. Conservatory Theatre, Young Conservatory, summer 1978; stage dir. San Francisco New Conservatory, 1982. Mem. Am. Children's Theatre Assn. (bd. govs. Region VIII, 1978-80), Internat. Children's Theatre Assn., Am. Theatre Assn. (chpt. bd. govs. 1978-80), Quill and Scroll, Pi Epsilon Delta. Lutheran. Author: Theatre Public Relations Manual, 1979; (with others) A Kid's Summer Night's Dream (play), 1978; Training the Actor for Participation Theatre (tape), 1978; The Emergence of an Americanized Form of Theatre-in-Education, (tape), 1977. Contbr. to How to Produce a Successful Children's Theatre Festival, 1976. Assoc. editor Children's Theatre Rev., 1980—. Home: 269 Gateway Dr Apt 221 Pacifica CA 94044 Office: Theatre Arts Dept 1600 Holloway Ave San Francisco CA 94132

WESTERGARD, ROLAND DEXTER, state official; b. Lovelock, Nev., Apr. 6, 1934; s. Hans and Mary (Christensen) W.; B.S. in Civil Engring., U. Nev., 1956; m. Dixie O. Sturges, Dec. 2, 1956; children—Laurie P., Tricia O., Todd N., Wendy J. Civil engr. Bur. of Reclamation, Carson City, Nev., 1958-60; civil engr. State of Nev., Carson City, 1960-67, state engr., 1967-79, dir. Dept. Conservation and Natural Resources, 1979—. Served with U.S. Army, 1956-58. Registered profl. engr., Nev. Mem. Carson City Profl. Engrs. (pres. 1965), Assn. Western State Engrs. (pres. 1970). Democrat. Club: Carson Booster (pres. 1974). Office: 201 S Fall St Carson City NV 89710

WESTERMAN, ARNE SOLOMON, painter; b. Portland, Oreg., Mar. 24, 1927; s. Simon and Sonia (Kutz) W.; children—Martin, Alan, Judy. Student Reed Coll., 1944; B.A. in Journalism, U. Oreg., 1950; studied art under George Hamilton, Charles Reid, William Reese. One-man shows include: White Gallery, Portland (Oreg.) State U., 1979, Galerie De Tours, San Francisco, 1981, 82, Galerie De Tours, Carmel, Calif., 1981, 82, Trails End Gallery, Portland, 1982; group shows include: Trails End Gallery, Lakewood Ctr. Gallery, Portland, Oreg., Galerie De Tours, San Francisco, Pebble Beach, Calif. and Carmel, 1980, 81, 82; represented in permanent collections: Mills Coll., Oakland, Calif., Robert Louis Stevenson Sch. Bd. dirs. Hillel Acad., Portland, 1979. Served with AUS, World War II. Recipient Grand prize N.W. Watercolor Soc., 1980, 81. Mem. Portland Assn. Advt. Agys. (past pres.). Democrat. Jewish. Clubs: Portland City, B'nai B'rith (past lodge pres.). Address: 2481 SW Sherwood Dr Portland OR 97201

WESTIN, WILLIAM S., corporate controller; b. Boston, Dec. 31, 1948; s. G. Wilbur and Lilian H. (Alexander) W.; m. Marlyn M. Fisher, Aug. 23, 1976; children—Kimberly, Cameron. B.S. in Computers, San Diego State U., 1971, M.B.A., 1974. Asst. v.p., comml. lending officer Union Bank, Los Angeles, 1975-79; corp. mgr., controller Clover Enterprises, Santa Fe Springs, Calif., 1979—. Mem. Am. Mgmt. Assn. Republican. Office: 13701 Excelsior Dr Santa Fe Springs CA 90670

WESTLUND, BERNARD JOHN, II, investment company executive, rancher; b. Long Beach, Calif., Sept. 3, 1949; s. Bernard John and Dorothy (Reynolds) W. B.A. in History, Whitman Coll., 1972; postgrad. U. Oreg., 1973. Corp. sec. Mgmt. Mktg. Assocs., Inc., Portland, Oreg., 1973-77; corp. sec. Am. Fossil, Portland, 1977-78; pres. Westlund Wood, Republic, Wash., 1980—; owner Juniper Butte Ranch, Mitchell, Oreg., 1980—; ptnr. Westlund Investment Co., Lake Oswego, Oreg., 1980—. Mem. Young Republicans, Sigma Chi. Club: Multnomah Athletic (Portland). Home and Office: Juniper Butte Ranch Mitchell OR 97750

WESTON, JAMES JOLLIFF, educator; b. Prescott, Ariz., Nov. 10, 1929; s. Omer Austin and Eloine (Osment) W.; B.S., No. Ariz. U., 1951; M.A., George Peabody Coll. Tchrs., Vanderbilt U., 1956; Ed.D., U. Ariz., 1961. Tchr. jr. high sch., Kingman, Ariz., 1953-55; tchr. high sch., Litchfield Park, Ariz., 1955-56, Avondale, Ariz., 1956-59; grad. asst., instr. U. Ariz., 1959-62, asst. prof., 1962-63; asst. prof. U. Tex., 1963-68; asso. prof. orgnl. behavior and environ. Calif. State U., Sacramento, 1968-75, prof., 1975—; vis. asso. prof. No. Ariz. U., summer 1971; cons. Calif. Dept. Edn., 1969-75. Served with U.S. Army, 1951-53. Mem. Calif. Bus. Edn. Assn., Am. Bus. Communication Assn., Pi Omega Pi, Delta Pi Epsilon. Democrat. Contbr. articles to profl. jours. Home: 8289 La Riviera Dr Sacramento CA 95826 Office: 6000 J St Sacramento CA 95819

WESTPHAL, EVERETT AUGUST, alarm company executive; b. Hankinson, N.D., May 4, 1914; s. Herman Charles and Minnie Ida (Tiegs) W.; m. Marjorie Viola Jensen, Jan. 13, 1939; children—Bruce, Roger, Linda, Chris. With Leach & Gamble, Wahpeton, N.D., 1936-37, Standard Fence Co., Los Angeles, 1937-38, U.S. Alarm Co., Los Angeles, 1938-44; ptnr. Driess Alarm Co., 1944-45; founder Bay Alarm Co., Oakland, Calif., 1946, chmn., 1973—; founder Alarm Equipment Co., Oakland, 1961, pres., 1968—; pres. Balco Real Estate Co., Oakland, 1978—; chmn. Security Alarm Service, Oxnard, Calif., 1980—. Chmn. troop Boy Scouts Am., Oakland, 1954-55. Mem. Nat. Burglar and Fire Alarm Assn. (v.p. 1952), ASTM, Western Burglar and Fire Alarm Assn. (pres. 1975). Republican. Clubs: Masons; Shriners (Oakland); Rotary (Oakland); Contra Costa Country (Concord, Calif.). Patentee alarm signalling devices. Office: 325 7th St Oakland CA 94607

WETHERWAX, RITCHIE JEAN, hospital administrator; b. Belleville, Ill., July 28, 1928; d. Richard and Viola L. (Davis) Grossner; m. Richard R. Wills, Jan. 23, 1948; children—Valann M. Kampf, Sheila L. Wills; m. Lawrence G. Wetherwax, June 29, 1974. A.A., Crafton Hills Coll., 1976; B.A., Redlands U., 1977. Lic. nursing home adminstr., Calif. Patient service rep. Loma Linda U. Hosp., 1968-72; office mgr. Canyon Crest Convalescent Hosp., Colton, Calif., 1972-74, Highland House Health-care (Calif.), 1974-76; adminstr. Beverly Manor Convalescent Hosp., Riverside, Calif., 1977-79, Terracina Convalescent Hosp., Redlands, Calif., 1979—. Mem. Am. Coll. Nursing Home Adminstrs. Nat. Assn. Female Execs., AAUW, Redlands C. of C. Republican. Adventist. Lodge: Order Eastern Star.

WETLE, LORRAINE MAY, union official; b. Chenango Forks, N.Y., Nov. 10, 1931; d. David Walter and Mildred Madeleine (Horton) Robinson; m. Jerome Edward Wetle, Aug. 1, 1953; children—Michael, David. Student pub. schs., Binghamton, N.Y. Clerical asst. Ansco Co., Binghamton, N.Y., 1950-52; reports clk. Pacific Tel. & Tel., San Francisco, 1952-55, reports clk., dial office clk., San Jose, Calif., 1968-82; pres. Communications Workers Am., local 9423, San Jose, 1976-83, rep. dist. 9, 1983—; 1st v.p. Santa Clara County Central Labor Council. Mem. allocations com. United Way. Named Communications Workers Am. Dist. 9, Woman of Yr., 1981. Mem. Coalition Labor Women. Democrat.

WETZEL, CHERIE LALAINE RIVERS, biologist; b. Lewiston, Idaho, June 20, 1930; d. Edwin Bagnal and Mary Elizabeth (Rose) Rivers; A.A., Chabot Coll., 1966; B.A. in Biology, Stanford U., 1968, M.A., 1970; Ph.D. in Botany, U. Calif., Berkeley, 1979; m. Herbert Don Wetzel, July 3, 1948; children—Margaret Elizabeth, Don Louis. Asst. curator Dudley Herbarium, Stanford U. (Calif.), 1968-70; instr. Calif. flora U. Calif., Berkeley, summer 1977, instr. U. Calif. Extension, 1977—, vis. assoc. prof., summer sessions 1981-83; instr. gen. biology, ecology and microbiology Chabot Coll., Hayward, Calif., 1970-71, 74-77; instr. botany, field ecology and biology San Francisco City Coll., 1977—, chmn. dept. biol. scis., 1980-83; participant various profl. meetings. Recipient Outstanding Scholarship Faculty award Chabot Coll., 1966, Gordon Ferris $1,000 award Stanford U., 1969; NIH grantee, 1976. Mem. AAAS, Am. Soc. Cell Biology, Bot. Soc. Am., Calif. Bot. Soc. (treas.), Calif. Native Plant Soc., Electron Microscope Soc. Am., Friends of U. Calif. Bot. Garden, No. Calif. Electron Microscope Soc., Sigma Xi. Contbr. bot and electron microscopie articles to profl. jours. Home: 48 Starview Dr Oakland CA 94618 Office: Dept Biol Scis San Francisco City Coll 50 Phelan Ave San Francisco CA 94112

WEWER, DEE J., sporting goods company executive; b. Mobile, Ala., Apr. 27, 1948; d. Gene B. and Juanita F. (Schmeckenbecher) Wewer; m. Ira Eliot Litke, Sept. 5, 1982. B.S., U. Miss., 1970; M.A., Am. U., 1974; postgrad. Georgetown U., 1980-81, Union for Experimenting Colls. and Univ., 1983—. Tchr., St. Martin Pub. Schs., Biloxi, Miss., 1970-71; newspaper editor Nat. Coll. of the Mil., Washington, 1971; press asst. Republican Nat. Com., Washington, 1972-73; media dir. Bailey Deardourff Agy., Washington, 1973-74; mktg. dir. Weitzman Advt., Washington, 1974-77; dir. mktg., creative dir. Britches of Georgetown, Washington, 1978-79; v.p. pub. affairs AMF Head Sportswear, Columbia, Md., 1979-81; instr. U. Md., Balt., 1978-82; exec. v.p. Sport-Obermeyer, Aspen, Colo., 1982—. Bd. dirs. Aspen Family Inst. Recipient numerous advt. awards including two Clios, 20 Andy Merit awards. Mem. Ski Industries Am., Advt. Club N.Y.C., Women in TV and Radio (mktg. com.), Washington Advt. Club, Am. Mgmt. Assn., Here and There Design Group. Club: Aspen Raquet. Contbr. numerous articles to profl. jours., poetry to mags. Home: 0226 Kings Row Carbondale CO 81623 Office: Sport Obermeyer 92 Atlantic Ave Aspen CO 81611

WEXLER, ARTHUR, food marketing executive; b. Bridgeport, Conn., Nov. 3, 1923; s. Morris Harry and Sarah (Berezin) W.; m. Trudy C. Strauss, Dec. 22, 1951; children—Anthony Howard, Donald Paul, Wendy Joy. A.A., Jr. Coll. Conn., 1947; M.B.A., U. Chgo., 1949. Salesman Hunt-Wesson Foods, 1950-53, sales supr., 1953-57, asst. dist. mgr., No. Calif., 1957-59, dist. mgr., New Eng. and Met. N.Y. area, 1959-65, N.E. regional sales mgr., 1965-67; corp. dir. sales Buitoni Foods Corp., South Hackensack, N.J., 1967-71; founder, pres. Consummate Mktg. Co. Inc., Oakland, Calif., 1972—. Pres. Casitas de Moraga Homeowners Assn., 1981-82. Mem. Nat. Food Brokers Assn., No. Calif. Food Brokers Assn., Pvt. Label Mfrs. Assn. Office: PO Box 2007 Oakland CA 94604

WEXLER, JUDIE GAFFIN, sociologist, educator; b. Bklyn. Apr. 15, 1945; d. Isaac and Sara (Widensky) Pearlman; m. Howard M. Wexler, Mar. 11, 1973; children—Robyn, Matthew. B.A., Russell Sage Coll., 1965; M.A. U. Pa., 1966; Ph.D., U. Calif.-Berkeley, 1975. Dir. Mental Retardation Research Unit, Office of Stats., N.Y. State Dept. Mental Hygiene, Albany, 1966-67; demographer/urban sociologist San Francisco Dept. City Planning, 1967-68; research asst. Inst. Planning & Urban Research, Berkeley, Calif., 1970; assoc. prof. sociology Holy Names Coll., Oakland, Calif., 1974—; cons., researcher in field. Population Council fellow, 1968-69, 70-71; NDEA fellow, 1968-69; recipient Millhouse award in Sociology, 1965. Mem. Am. Sociol. Assn. Contbr. articles to profl. jours. Office: Holy Names Coll Oakland CA 94619

WEYGAND, LAWRENCE RAY, insurance broker; b. South Haven, Mich., Jan. 5, 1940; s. Ray and Lorraine (Berkins) W.; B.A., Drake U., 1962, postgrad., 1962-63; 1 son, Chad C. Comml. multi-peril ins. underwriter Aetna Casualty & Surety Co., Mpls., also Indpls., 1964-66, Safeco Ins. Co., Denver, 1966-69; pres., chmn. bd. Weygand & Co., ins. agts., brokers and consultants, Denver, 1969—; pres. Homeowners Ins. Agy., Inc., Scottsdale, Ariz., Homeowners Ins., Inc., Denver, Weygand & Co. of Ariz., Inc., Scottsdale, Transatlantic Underwriters, Inc.; owner U.S. Insurors, Inc., Ariz. Dealers Ins. Services, Inc., Colo. Dealers Ins. Services, Inc., Denver, Storage Pak Ins., Inc.; owner, pres. mng. gen. agy. serving Colo., Ariz., Nev., Utah and N.Mex.; asst. to Gov. State of Iowa, 1961-62. Mem. bus. community adv. council Regis Coll., 1976—. Mem. Ind. Ins. Agts. Colo. (chmn. fair and ethical practice com.), Ind. Ins. Agts. Am., Profl. Ins. Agts. Colo., Profl. Ins. Agts. Am., Alpha Tau Omega. Republican. Congregationalist. Clubs: Denver Athletic. Home: 10703 E Crestline Ave Englewood CO 80110 also 8415 E San Candido Dr Scottsdale AZ

WEYGAND, LEROY CHARLES, security cons.; b. Webster Park, Ill., May 17, 1926; s. Xaver William and Marie Caroline (Hoffert) W.; B.A. in Sociology cum laude, U. Md., 1964; m. Helen V. Bishop, Aug. 28, 1977; children—Linda M. Weygand Vance (dec.), Leroy Charles, Cynthia R., Janine P. Enlisted in U.S. Army, 1944, commd. 2d lt., 1950, advanced through grades to lt. col., 1966; service in Korea, 1950; chief phys. security U.S. Army, 1965-70; ret., 1970; pres. Weygand Security Cons. Services, Anaheim, Calif., 1970—, W & W Devel. Corp., 1979—; security dir. Jefferies Banknote Co., 1972-78; dir. Mind Psi-Biotics, Inc. Bd. dirs. Nat. Assn. Control Narcotics and Dangerous Drugs. Decorated Legion of Merit. Mem. Am. Soc. Indsl. Security. Contbr. articles profl. jours. Patentee office equipment locking device. Home: Star Route 1 Box 800-89 Tehachapi CA 93561 Office: Star Route #1 Box 800-89 Tehachapi CA 93561

WHALEN, MARGARET L., accountant; b. Jerome, Ariz., Sept. 18, 1944; d. Salvador Pina and Mercedes (Lopez) Rodriguez; m. Ronald Lee Ledesma, June 29, 1963; children—Ronnette M.; m. Daniel Peter Whalen, Aug. 26, 1972; children—Tara L., Daniel Peter, Salvador. Student Calif. State U.-Los Angeles, 1978-79, E. Los Angeles Coll., 1966-72, U. Calif.-Riverside, 1962-63. C.P.A., Calif. Accounts payable clk. Byron Jackson, Vernon, Calif., 1965-66; accounts payable clk., to acctg. analyst Holly div. LSI, South Gate, Calif., 1966-69; staff acct. Maginnis, Bell, Knechtel & McIntyre, C.P.A.s, Pasadena, 1969-76; staff acct. Bell, Goehner & Isham, Pasadena, 1976-78; prin. Whalen's Bookkeeping & Tax Service, Glendora, Calif., 1978-81, Margaret L. Whalen, C.P.A. Azusa, Calif., 1981—. Mem. Am. Inst. C.P.A.s, Calif. Soc. C.P.A.s, Enrolled Agts. Republican. Roman Catholic. Club: Jerome Verde Valley (pres.). Home: 136 S Sandalwood Pl Glendora CA 91740 Office: 16517 E Arrow Hwy Azusa CA 91702

WHALEN, PAULINE KATHERINE, librarian; b. Boulder, Colo., May 11, 1921; d. William C. and Naoma S. (Ward) Malzahn; B.A., U. Colo., 1942, M.A., 1946; M.A., U. Denver, 1950. Asst. documents librarian U. Colo. Libraries, Boulder, 1950-51, order librarian, 1955-64; base librarian Ent AFB, Colorado Springs, Colo., 1951-53; documents librarian Colo. Sch. of Mines Library, Golden, 1953-55; sr. reference librarian Santa Rosa (Calif.) Library, 1965-66; humanities bibliographer U. Calif. San Diego Library, La Jolla, 1966-67; sr. librarian Salk Inst. for Biol. Studies, La Jolla, 1968—. Mem. Am., Spl., Med. library assns. Democrat. Home: 12988 Via Esperia Del Mar CA 92014 Office: Salk Institute PO Box 85800 San Diego CA 92138

WHANG, JINJOO, engineering specialist; b. Jinnampo, Korea, Jan. 1, 1940; s. Kiwha and Siha (Kim) W.; m. Soohyang Lee, Apr. 30, 1968; children—Theresa, Julie, Harry. B.S. in Engring., Seoul Nat. U., 1963; M.S.M.E., SUNY-Buffalo, 1971, M.S. in Engring. Sci., 1974. Registered profl. engr., Calif. Engring. surveyor Korean Devel. Corp., 1966-68; product engr. Houdaille Industries, Inc., Buffalo, 1970-76; engring. mgr. Greer Hydraulics, Commerce, Calif., 1976-82; engring. specialist Ford Aerospace, Newport Beach, Calif., 1982—. Served to lt. Korean Navy, 1963-66. Mem. ASME, Nat. Soc. Profl. Engrs. Author: Survey of Turbulent Flow in Diffusers, 1971. Office: Ford Aerospace Ford Rd Newport Beach CA 92660

WHARTON, CHARLES DENNIS, hosp. ofcl.; b. New Castle, Pa., Dec. 9, 1941; s. Charles L. and Opal (Allison) W.; student U. Ariz., 1959-69; m. Margaret Ann States, July 16, 1966; children—Lisa Marie, Anne Elliot, Susanna Leigh. Asst. to exec. dir. Nat. Found. for Asthmatic Children, Tucson, 1961-69; adminstrv. asst. Nat. Jewish Hosp., Denver, 1969-71; adminstrv. coordinator U. Ariz. Hosp., Tucson, 1971-74; regional dir. Browndale Arizona, Inc., Tucson, 1974-75; cons. Browndale Internat. Ltd., Toronto, Ont., Can., 1975-76; propr., mechanic Pro Tech Industries, Tucson, 1976-77, 79—; adminstrv. asst. phys. plant resources U. Ariz., Tucson, 1977-79; safety and security dir. St. Josephs Hosp., Tucson, 1979-80, dir. personnel services, 1980—. Mem. Am. Soc. Safety Engrs., Am. Indsl. Hygiene Assn. Republican. Methodist. Home: 1501 W Pomona Pl Tucson AZ 85704 Office: 350 N Wilmot Tucson AZ 85711

WHARTON, WARREN LINDBERGH, collection agy. exec.; b. Duncan, Okla., Sept. 25, 1929; s. Tillman D. and Willie (Johns) W.; student Hartwell Coll.; m. Lucy; children—Linda, Warren Lindbergh, Keith, Chris, Danny. With No. Calif. Relay Center Dept. Justice, Sacramento, 1952; credit mgr. Hirsch Jewelers, Carmel, Calif., 1953-54; asst. mgr. Credit Bur., Antioch, Calif., 1954-58; mgr. Salinas Collection Co. (Calif.), 1958—; owner Lindy's Collection Service, Salinas, 1958—, Central Calif. Collection Service, Modesto, 1971-72; pres. Cascade Credit Bureau Corp., 1972—; pres. Lindy's Collection Service, Inc.; organizer, pres. Credit Bur. Central Calif., Inc., 1965—; regional credit and collection mgr. Utility Trailer Sales Co., 1973—; owner Sun Creditors Bur., Palm Springs, Calif.; pres. Palm Springs Fin. & Investment Services, Inc., Central Calif. Collection Service, Inc., Salinas. Profl. collector dist. com. Boy Scouts, Monterey County, 1955—; mem. Monterey County Sheriff's Posse, Inc., 1962—; mem. adv. bd. Civil Defense, 1960-63. Served with USN, 1948-52. Mem. Am. Collectors Assn., Calif. Assn. Collectors (past unit pres.), Alisal C. of C. (past pres.). Seventh Day Adventist. Lion, Elk. Home: 2800 Golf Club Dr Apt 20-H Palm Springs CA 92264

WHATLEY, EL DUANE, educational administrator; b. Muldrow, Okla., Feb. 17, 1937; s. Loyd Eugene and Eunice Marie W.; m. Thelma Jean Lydic; children—Wendy Whatley Garner, Sherry Whatley Eddy,

Brenda, Jonathan. B.A., Pepperdine U., 1961; M.Ed., U. Oreg., 1967. Cert. tchr., prin., Wash.; cert. tchr., supt., Oreg. Elem. tchr., Longview, Wash., 1961-69; elem. prin., Mossyrock, Wash., 1971-78; tchr., prin., Huntington, Oreg., 1978-81; supt. Schs. Mt. Vernon (Oreg.) Sch. Dist., 1981—; mcpl. judge, Toledo, Wash., 1968-71, Mossyrock, Wash., 1973-78; minister Ch. of Christ, Toledo, Wash., 1963-71. Mem. Am. Assn. Sch. Adminstrs., Conf. Oreg. Sch. Adminstrs. Office: Mount Vernon Sch Dist PO Box 8 Mt Vernon OR 97865

WHATLEY, NORMAN, JR., budget and accounting analyst; b. Chattanooga, Nov. 13, 1934; s. Norman and Willie Mae (Vaughn) W.; A.A., SUNY, 1973; B.A., Columbia Coll., 1977; m. Naomi Winnifred Taylor, Jan. 4, 1956; children—Michael Douglas, Norma, Steven Wade. Enlisted USAF, 1953, U.S. Army, 1966, advanced through grades to chief warrant officer, 1966; acctg. and fin. technician, supr., 1953-64; spl. agt. criminal and counterintelligence investigator, 1964-66; spl. agt. mil. intelligence, intelligence officer, 1966-73; ret., 1973; staff acct. Info. Handling Services Co., 1973-74; fin. mgr. Bur. Land Mgmt., 1974-75; budget and acctg. analyst, U.S. Fish and Wildlife Service, 1975—. Decorated Meritorious Service medal, Army Commendation medal, Air Force Commendation medal. Mem. Ret. Officers Assn. Democrat. Patentee in field. Office: 134 Union Blvd Lakewood CO 80228

WHEABLE, BERT LOWELL, JR., corporate safety executive, chiropractor; b. Salt Lake City, June 1, 1922; s. Bert Lowell and Eva Christina (Holm) W.; m. Iona Finch, Aug. 12, 1946; children—Michael, Melodee Wheable Kennedy, Barbara Wheable Sarrica, Kit Wheable Barlow. D. Chiropractic, Calif. Chiropractic Coll., 1951, philosopher chiropractic (hon.), 1954. Lic. chiropractor, Calif. Route mgr. Pepsi Cola Co., Oakland, Calif., 1967-72, area mgr., 1972-74, merchandising and tng. coordinator, 1974-77, corp. safety dir., 1977—. Active Boy Scouts Am., 1942—, including cubmaster, scoutmaster, council tng. chmn., dist. and council coms. Recipient Scouting Dist. award Merit, Oakland Area council, Mt. Diablo council; Nat. award Boy Scouts Am., Silver Beaver. Mem. Am. Soc. Safety Engrs., Calif. Chiropractic Assn. Mormon. Home: 201 Powell Ave Pleasant Hill CA 94523 Office: 940 81st Ave Oakland CA 94621

WHEASLER, LOIS JEAN SHAW, educator; b. Indpls., Oct. 28, 1927; d. William Edward and Pauline Martha (Laufer) Shaw; B.A. with honors, U. Wyo., 1967, M.Ed., 1972, Ph.D., 1977; postgrad. U. Okla., summer 1975; m. Robert Arthur Wheasler, Feb. 16, 1946; children—Christy Anne Wheasler Davis, Ray Stanton. Tchr., A.A. Slade Elem. Sch., Albany County Sch. Dist. No. 1, Laramie, Wyo., 1967—; vis. asst. prof. English, U.S. Naval Acad., Annapolis, Md., 1982-83; condr. workshops Albany County Writing Project. Active LWV, 1959-62, exec. bd., editor newsletter, 1960-62. Mem. NEA, Albany County Edn. Assn. (treas. 1973-74, chmn. negotiations com. 1973-74), Internat. Reading Assn. (pres. Snowy Range Council, 1978-79), Assn. Supervision and Curriculum Devel., Kappa Delta Pi (life, Bicentennial Compatriot in Edn., 1976), Phi Kappa Phi, Delta Kappa Gamma, Phi Delta Kappa. Lutheran. Home: 1008 Park Ave Laramie WY 82070 Office: Slade Elementary School Laramie WY 82070

WHEATLEY, ROBERT BUCHANAN, public relations company executive; b. Edinburgh, Oct. 21, 1952; s. Robert Cottington and Isabella (Buchanan) W.; m. Marilyn Lorraine Welch, Mar. 17, 1979. B.A., Central Wash. U., 1976. Programming coordinator Central Wash. U., Ellensburg, 1975-76; pub. info. officer, King County, Wash., 1977-79; account mgr. Cole & Weber, Seattle, 1979-81, v.p., dir. pub. relations, 1981—. Mem. pub. relations adv. com. Nat. Multiple Sclerosis Soc., 1982; mem. pub. affairs com. Seattle Conv. and Visitors Bur., 1980-81. Recipient Seattle Salute, Seattle Conv. and Visitors Bur., 1982. Mem. Am. Advt. Fedn. (dir., mem. seminars com. Seattle chpt.), Pub. Relations Soc. Am., Seattle Advt. Fedn. Club: Ad (Seattle). Office: Cole & Weber 16040 Christensen Rd S Seattle WA 98188

WHEATON, JOHN SOUTHWORTH, wholesale company executive; b. Balt., Dec. 26, 1928; s. Ezra Almon and Ruth Adelaide (Otis) W.; B.A., Stanford U. 1951; M.B.A. (Seabord and Western Airlines 1953), Columbia U., 1953; m. Joy Lorriane Thuresson, Dec. 16, 1950; children—Sandra, Jason, Christopher. Mgr. finance TRW, Inc., Redondo Beach, Calif., 1956-60; v.p. ops. Bissett-Berman Corp., Santa Monica, Calif., 1960-71; v.p. ops. control Foremost-McKesson Corp., San Francisco, 1971-74, v.p. planning and analysis, 1974—. Served to lt. USNR, 1953-56. Club: Portuguese Bend (Los Angeles); Olympic (San Francisco). Home: 1723 Spyglass Ln Moraga CA 94556 Office: 1 Post St San Francisco CA 94104

WHEELER, BONNIE G., author; b. Charleston, W.Va., July 12, 1943; d. Earnest A. and Virginia F. (Barker) Lindner; m. Dennis R. Wheeler, June 14, 1961; children—Julie Lynn, Timothy Dennis, Robert Grant; adopted children—Rebecca Anne, Benjamin Joel, Jonathan. Student pub. schs., Ft. Lauderdale, Fla. Free-lance writer, 1977—; tchr. and workshop leader Writers' Workshops and Confs.; co-founder No. Calif. Christian Writers Ann. Workshop; co-founder and pres. Sutter-Buttes Christian Writers Fellowship. Mem. Colusa County Children's Health Adv. Bd., 1980—; chmn. Colusa County Spl. Edn. Adv. Bd., 1981-83; mem. Williams Sch. Site Council, 1981-83, Colusa County Mother and Child Adv. Commn., 1983—; dir. Mary, Martha & Me Time Stewardship Workshops; mem. Nat. Right to Life Com.; cons. editor The Caring Congregation; task force del. Christian and Missionary Alliance. Recipient Inspiration award Mt. Hermon Christian Writers Conf., 1982. Mem. Christian Writers Guild. Republican. Author: Of Braces and Blessings, 1980; Challenged Parenting, 1983; contbr.: Chosen Children, 1978; contbr. articles to religious publs.

WHEELER, DONALD WILLIAM, union business representative; b. Centralia, Wash., May 18, 1940; s. Earl Agustine and Ethel Irene (Ostrom) W.; m. Iris Arnold Gage, May 2, 1960; m. 2d, Joyce Francis Wheeler, Aug. 24, 1963; children—Mark S., Michael L., Brent R., Wade L., Michelle R. Grad. Labor Edn. and Research Center U. Oreg., 1980. Laborer, textile union negotiator Pendleton Woolen Mills, Washougal, Wash., 1962-66; journeyman machinist Columbia Machine Inc., Vancouver, Wash., 1966-70; sec. treas. Internat. Assn. Machinist and Aerospace Worker local 1374, Vancouver, 1970-74, business rep., Portland, Oreg., 1974—; mem. Portland Area Automotive Apprenticeship Com., 1975; mem. Vancouver Machinist and Automotive Apprenticeship Com., 1971. Democrat. Mem. Ch. of Christ. Home: 26112 SE 15th St Camas WA 98607 Office: 3645 SE 32d Ave Portland OR 97202

WHEELER, GLORIA EILEEN, business management educator, psychologist; b. Twin Falls, Idaho, June 6, 1943; d. William Edwin and Lida Jane (Mulliner) W. B.S. in Math., Mont. State Coll., Bozeman, 1961-65; M.A. in Psychology, U. Mich., 1966, M.S. in Math., 1968, Ph.D. in Math. Psychology, 1972. Research asst. Engring. Psychol. Lab., U. Mich., 1965-70; research assoc. Rensis Likert Assocs. Inc., Ann Arbor, 1971-78; asst prof. bus. mgmt. Brigham Young U., Provo, Utah, 1978-82, assoc. prof. bus. mgmt., 1982—. Active local youth groups. Nat. Assn. Schs. Pub. Affairs and Adminstrn. fed. faculty fellow, 1980-81. Mem. Am. Inst. Decision Scis., Am. Psychol. Assn. (div. indsl. and organizational psychology). Republican. Mormon. Contbr. articles to profl. jours. Office: 684 TNRB Brigham Young U Provo UT 84602

WHEELER, KENNETH RAY, metallurgist; b. Ogden, Utah, Dec. 16, 1921; s. Russell Clair and Maude Ellen W.; B.S., U. Mich., 1950, U. Calif., Berkeley, 1957; M.S., Wash. State U., 1968; m. Pauline Owen, June 20, 1950; children—Jody, Jennifer, Kirk, Darren. With Gen. Electric Co., 1957-65; sr. research scientist materials application to energy prodn. and med. orthopedics Battelle Meml. Inst. Hanford Labs., Richland, Wash., 1965—. Scoutmaster, Boy Scouts Am., 1972-75. Served with USAAF, 1942-45, with USAF, 1951-52. Decorated D.F.C., Air medal with 2 oak leaf clusters; co-recipient Jacquet-Lucas award in metallography, 1977; I.R. 100 award for new product devel., 1972; research grantee. Mormon. Contbr. articles to tech. jours. Patentee in field. Home: 110 Skyline Dr Richland WA 99352 Office: Battelle Northwest Labs 314 Bldg 300 Area Richland WA 99352

WHEELER, LARRY RICHARD, accountant; b. Greybull, Wyo., Nov. 30, 1940; s. Richard F. and Olive B. (Fredrickson) W.; m. Marjorie A. Frady, Dec. 20, 1961; m. 2d Patricia C. Marturanu, Dec. 3, 1977; children—Anthony, Richard, Teresa, Kara. B.S., U. Wyo., 1965. C.P.A. Staff acct. H. Greger C.P.A., Ft. Collins, Colo., 1965-66, sr. acct. Lester Draney & Wickham, Colorado Springs, Colo., 1966-67; acct., controller/treas., J.D. Adams Co., Colorado Springs, 1967-74; ptnr. Wheeler Pierce & Hurd, Inc., Colorado Springs, 1974-80; gen. mgr., v.p. Schneebeck's, Inc., Colorado Springs, 1980-81; prin. L.R. Wheeler & Co., P.C., Colorado Springs, 1981—; dir. Schneebeck's Industries, Williams Printing, Inc. Paul Stock Found. grantee, 1962. Mem. Am. Inst. C.P.A.s, Colo. Soc. C.P.A.s. Club: Rocky Mountain (Colorado Springs). Office: Suite 101 4570 Hilton Pkwy Colorado Springs CO 80907

WHEELER, MARILYN LEE, accountant, tax consultant; b. Inman, Nebr., May 15, 1936; d. Warren J. and Delia E. (Allyn) McClurg; m. Lee D. Wheeler, July 17, 1955 (div.); children—Linda Wheeler Tarpeh-Doe, Steven, David. Student Nebr. Wesleyan U., 1953-55, U. Wyo., 1955-57; B.S., U. Colo., 1972; M.T., U. Denver, 1980. C.P.A., Colo. Acct. Hurdman & Cranstoun (name later changed to Main Hurdman), Denver, 1973-82, ptnr., 1982—. Treas. Colo. affiliate Am. Diabetes Assn. Mem. Am. Inst. C.P.A.s, Colo. Soc. C.P.A.s, Am. Women's Soc. C.P.A.s (nat. dir.), Am. Soc. Women Accts. (pres. Denver chpt.). Republican. Methodist. Club: Petroleum (Denver). Office: 1675 Broadway Suite 1800 Denver CO 80202

WHEELER, RUSSELL LEONARD, geologist; b. Freeport, N.Y., June 12, 1943; s. Leonard Gallop and Dorothy Rose (Lehnen) W.; m. Peggy Anne Lentz, Sept. 3, 1979. B.S., Yale U., 1966; Ph.D., Princeton U., 1973. Asst. prof. geology W.Va. U., Morgantown, 1971-77, assoc. prof., 1977-79; geologist U.S. Geol. Survey, Morgantown, 1975-77, Denver, 1979—.

WHEELER, TREASURE ANN, optometrist; b. Phoenix, May 1, 1945; d. Charles Landis and Bette Jane (Oyler) Sullivan; m. Gary Hale Wheeler, May 13, 1968. B.S., Pacific U., 1968, O.D., 1969. Lic. optometrist Oreg. Assoc. Dr. Tole Greenstein, Oregon City, Oreg., 1968; civilian optometrist Bliss Army Hosp., Ft. Huachuca, Ariz., 1969-70; pvt. practice optometry, Medford, Oreg., 1970—; dir. Oreg. Optometric Extension Program, 1975-78, sponsor Northwest Optometric Assts. Program, 1975-80; mem. Oreg. Bd. Optometry; lectr., advisor, cons. in field. Mem. Nat. Adv. Bd., Biosocial Med. Ctr.; charter mem., mem. at large Parents for Better Nutrition; vol. Community Bus. Edn. Resource; mem. Gov's. Commn. for Women, Juvenile Services Commn., 1981-82. Fellow Coll. Optometrists in Vision Devel. (Oreg. dir. 1974-75); mem. Am. Optometric Assn. (edn. and manpower div. career guidance com.), Oreg. Optometric Assn. (chmn. Task Force Vision Screening, pres. 1979-80), So. Oreg. Optometric Soc. (Former v.p.), So. Oreg. Soc. Preventive Medicine, Phi Theta Upsilon. Contbr. articles to profl. publs. Home: 303 Gennessee St Medford OR 97504 Office: 309 Genessee St Medford OR 97504

WHEELON, ALBERT DEWELL, physicist; b. Moline, Ill., Jan. 18, 1929; s. Orville Albert and Alice Geltz (Dewell) W.; B.Sc., Stanford U., 1949; Ph.D., MIT, 1952; m. Nancy Helen Hermanson, Feb. 28, 1953 (dec.); children—Elizabeth Anne, Cynthia Helen. Teaching fellow, then research asso. physics M.I.T., 1949-52; with Douglas Aircraft Co., 1952-53, Ramo-Wooldridge Corp., 1953-62; dep. dir. sci. and tech. CIA, 1962-66; with Hughes Aircraft Co., 1966—, v.p., group exec. space and communications group, El Segundo, Calif., from 1970, now sr. v.p.; ; mem. Def. Sci. Bd., 1967-77; cons. President's Sci. Adv. Council, 1961-74, NSC, 1974—; Recipient Disting. Intelligence medal CIA, 1966. Fellow IEEE; mem. Nat. Acad. Engring., Am. Phys. Soc., Internat. Union Radio Sci., Sigma Chi. Republican. Episcopalian. Club: Cosmos (Washington). Author 30 papers on radiowaves propagation and guidance systems. Office: PO Box 92919 Los Angeles CA 90009

WHELAN, ROBERT LOUIS, bishop; b. Wallace, Idaho, 1912. Ed. St. Michael's Coll., Spokane, Alma (Calif.) Coll. Mem. Soc. of Jesus; ordained priest Roman Cath. Ch., 1944; titular bishop of Sicilibba and coadjutor bishop Fairbanks, Alaska, 1967-68; bishop of Fairbanks, 1968—. Address: 1316 Peger Rd Fairbanks AK 99701*

WHELAN, WILLIAM ANTHONY, forest products co. exec.; b. Bklyn., Aug. 18, 1921; s. Daniel and Catherine (Pugh) W.; B.S.M.E., U. Calif., Berkeley; m. Marcia M. McCorkle, Nov. 14, 1948; children—Michael, Greer, Danie, Ann. Vice pres. Klamath Machine & Locomotive Works, 1948-58; plant and dist. mgr. U.S. Plywood, 1959-68; v.p. West Coast ops. Champion Internat., 1968-74; exec. v.p. Roseburg Lumber Co., 1975-77; exec. v.p. Pope & Talbot, Inc., Portland, Oreg., 1978, pres., 1979—, also dir. Mem. Western Wood Products Assn. (dir. 1979—, pres. 1983—), Nat. Forest Products Assn. (dir. and mem. exec. com. 1980-83). Served with U.S. Army, 3 years; Okinawa. Club: Arlington. Office: Pope & Talbot Inc 1500 SW 1st Ave Portland OR 97201

WHELCHEL, SANDRA JANE, writer; b. Denver, May 31, 1944; d. Ralph Earl and Janette Isabelle (March) Everitt; m. Andrew Jackson Whelchel, June 27, 1965; children—Andrew Jackson, Anita Earlyn. B.A. in Elem. Edn., U. No. Colo., 1966; postgrad. Pepperdine Coll., 1971, UCLA, 1971. Elem. tchr. Douglas County Schs., Castle Rock, Colo., 1966-68, El Monte (Calif.) schs., 1968-72; br. librarian Douglas County Libraries, Parker, Colo., 1973-78; zone writer Denver Post, 1979-81; reporter The Express newspapers, Castle Rock, 1979-81; contbr. short stories and articles to various publs. including: Empire mag., Calif. Horse Rev., Jack and Jill, Child Life, Children's Digest; non-fiction book: Your Air Force Academy, 1982; lectr. on writing. Mem. Internat. Order of Foresters, Nat. Writers Club.

WHIPPLE, GEORGE STEPHENSON, architect, contractor; b. Evanston, Ill., Sept. 21, 1950; s. Taggart and Katharine (Brewster) W.; m. Lydia Buckley, May 30, 1981; 1 dau., Katherine Elizabeth. B.A., Harvard U., 1974; student Boston Architectural Ctr., 1975-76. Vice-pres., Call Us Inc., Edgartown, Mass., 1970-74; pres. Cattle Creek Assocs., Carbondale, Colo., 1976—, Earthworks Constrn., Carbondale, 1978—. Chmn., Redstone Hist. Preservation Commn., Colo. Mem. Rocky Mountain Harvard Club. Office: 3335 County Rd 113 Carbondale CO 81623

WHIPPLE, WALTER LEIGHTON, computer scientist, electrical engineer, educator; b. Washington, June 23, 1940; s. Walter Jones and Marian Katherine (Leighton) W.; m. Jean Anne Ewer, Sept. 11, 1965; children—Kathryn Ann, Sara Marie. B.S. Harvey Mudd Coll., Claremont, Calif., 1962; postgrad. U. Calif.-Berkeley, 1965-66; M.S.E., U. Mich., 1974. Engring. aide Vidya div. Itek Corp., Palo Alto, Calif., 1961; field service rep. Gen. Electric Co., Pittsfield, Mass., 1962-65; engr. Space and Info. Systems div. Raytheon Co., Sudbury, Mass., 1967-69; sr. elec. engr. Profl. Services div. Control Data Corp., Waltham, Mass., 1969-73, Detroit, 1973-78; design specialist weapon computer dynamics Gen. Dynamics, Pomona, Calif., 1978-83; prin. elec. engr. Electromagnetic Systems div. Raytheon Co., Goleta, Calif., 1983—; vis. prof. computer sci. Harvey Mudd Coll., Calif. State Poly. U., Pomona, 1978-81. Gen. Electric fellow, U. Mich., 1973-78. Mem. AIAA (assoc. fellow), Assn. Computing Machinery, IEEE (sr. mem.), Nat. Soc. Profl. Engrs., Soc. Computer Simulation, Armed Forces Communication Electronics Assn., Nat. Mgmt. Assn., Assn. Old Crows. Republican. Contbr. articles to profl. jours. Home: 770 Mariquita Dr Santa Barbara CA 93111 Office: Dept 9284 Electromagnetic Systems Div Raytheon Co Goleta CA 93117

WHISTLER, JAMES EDWIN, life ins. underwriter; b. Independence, Kans., Apr. 20, 1948; s. Olen J. and Donna Lucile (Lightner) W.; B.B.A., U. Idaho, 1970, J.D., 1973; M.Fin., Am. Coll., 1979; m. Kathryn Anne Skok, July 4, 1969; 1 son, James Michael. Spl. agt. Northwestern Mut. Life Ins. Co., Moscow, Idaho, 1969-73, agy. supr., San Francisco, 1973-75, asst. regional dir., Milw., 1975-80, gen. agt., San Diego, 1980—; admitted to Idaho bar, 1973, Calif. bar, 1974; instr. Milw. Stratton Bus. Coll., 1975-78. C.L.U. Mem. Nat. Assn. Life Underwriters, Am. Soc. C.L.U.s, Calif. Bar Assn., Idaho Bar Assn., Am. Bar Assn., Gen. Agts. and Mgrs. Assn., Phi Alpha Delta, Phi Gamma Delta. Republican. Club: Univ. of San Diego. Contbr. to legal and ins. publs. Home: 11435 Fuerte Farms Rd El Cajon CA 92020 Office: 233 A St Suite 800 San Diego CA 92101

WHITAKER, CORRINE COOPER, brokerage executive; b. Stamford, Conn., Aug. 31, 1934; d. Samuel and Natalie Gordon; m. Alan B. Cooper, Sept. 4, 1956; children—Nanette Cooper McGuinness, Robin; m. Don C. Whitaker, Aug. 31, 1979. B.A., Wellesley Coll., 1956; postgrad. N.Y. Inst. Fin., 1972-73, U. Houston, 1974. Sr. account exec. Eppler, Guerin & Turner, Inc., Houston, 1972-76; fixed income liaison Loeb, Rhodes & Co., Los Angeles, 1976-77; cons. Edward T. Watkins & Co., Houston, 1977; assoc. v.p., account exec. Bateman Eichler, Hill Richards, Los Angeles, 1977-79; chmn. bd., chief adminstrv. officer Don C. Whitaker, Inc., Los Angeles, 1980—, adminstr., co-trustee Don C. Whitaker, Inc., Defined Benefit Pension Plan, Don C. Whitaker, Inc., Money Purchase Pension Plan. Lectr., docent leader African art Rice U. Media Ctr. Art to Schs. Program, 1974-75; mem. Inner Quad, Stanford U., 1982; mem. pres.'s circle Los Angeles County Mus. Art, 1981-82; bd. dirs. women's div., nat. publicity chmn. Aerospace Med. Assn., 1964; mem. equity floor trading com. Pacific Stock Exchange, 1983. Durant scholar; recipient John Mansfield award Wellesley Coll., 1956, Katherine Lee Bates award, 1956; Rookie of Yr., Eppler, Guerin & Turner, 1973; commendation Houston Jaycees, 1975; others. Mem. Los Angeles Floor Brokers Assn. (founding), Los Angeles Area C. of C. (bus. and industry com. of women's council 1978), Phi Beta Kappa. Office: 618 S Spring St Los Angeles CA 90014

WHITAKER, JANET LOUISE, educational technologist; b. Terre Haute, Ind., Sept. 7, 1953; d. Joseph William and Marguerite Ella Whitaker. B.S., Ind. State U., Terre Haute, 1974, M.S., 1976; postgrad U. Iowa, Ariz. State U. Choral dir. Rochester (Ind.) Community High Sch., 1975; adj. faculty Ind. State U., Terre Haute, 1977; instructional designer W.Va. State Coll., Institute, 1979-80, Rio Salado Community Coll., Phoenix, 1981—; cons. computers in edn., instr. evaluation, program evaluation. Okoboji fellow Assn. Ednl. Communications and Tech., 1978. Mem. Assn. Ednl. Communications and Tech., Am. Soc. Supervision and Curriculum Devel. Office: 135 N 2d Ave Phoenix AZ 85003

WHITAKER, KERRY MARTIN, mathematical statistician; b. Oakland, Calif., Sept. 5, 1952; s. Sherrill Martin and Marjorie Louise (Miller) W.; m. Linda Louise Achziger, Mar. 17, 1979; 1 son, Brandon Martin. Student, U.S. Air Force Acad., 1970-72; B.S. in Math. Stats., U. Wash., 1973, M.S. in Biostats., 1976. Math. statistician Mining Safety and Health Adminstrn., U.S. Dept. Labor, Denver, 1977-78; cons. Boeing Computer Services, Renton, Wash., 1978-82, statistician energy tech. applications, Tukwila, Wash., 1982—. Recipient Citizens award Elks Club, 1970. Mem. Am. Statis. Assn., Biometric Soc. Democrat. Baptist. Contbr. articles to profl. jours. Office: 565 Andover Park West Tukwila WA 98188

WHITE, ANTHONY GENE, govt. ofcl., educator; b. Eugene, Oreg., Nov. 8, 1946; s. Wallace Eugene and Vivian Arlene (Thomson) W.; B.S., Oreg. State U., 1967; M.S., Portland (Oreg.) State U., 1971, M. Pub. Adminstrn., 1977; m. Carole Ann Price, May 17, 1969. Research asst. div. urban affairs U. Del., Newark, 1968-69; research assoc. City-County Charter Commn., Portland, 1972-74; property control officer Multnomah County, Portland, 1974-75; adminstrv. analyst/researcher Local Govt. Boundary Commn., Portland, 1975-76; evaluator, researcher Dist. Atty.'s Office, Portland, 1976-77; dir. public mgmt. programs Marylhurst (Oreg.) Coll., 1978-79; program coordinator Oreg. Public Utility Commn., Salem, 1979—. Bd. dirs. Oreg. Assn. for Children with Learning Disabilities, 1978-80; precinct committeeman Multnomah County Democratic central com., 1974-76; mem. Clackamas County Dem. central com., 1979—; mem. West Linn Comprehensive Plan Rev. Com., 1980; chmn. adminstrn. com., mem. ch. council West Linn Lutheran Ch., 1980-83, v.p. ch. council, 1982-83. Served with AUS, 1969-72; maj. Oreg. N.G. Res., 1978—. Decorated Joint Services Commendation medal, Gov.'s Unit citation. Mem. AAAS, Am. Math. Soc., Am. Acad. Polit. and Social Scis., Nat. Mcpl. League, Western, Pacific N.W. polit. sci. assns., World Future Soc. Author: Reforming Metropolitan Governments, Municipal Bonding and Taxation; also book chpt., monographs, papers, articles, reports. Home: 3270 Forest Ct West Linn OR 97068

WHITE, BARBARA J., educational administrator, consultant; b. Wausau, Wis., Sept. 21, 1944; d. Elmer A. and Delores M. (Braatz) Hoeft. B.Ed., U. Wash., 1966, M.Ed., 1970; Ed.D., U. Hawaii, 1983. Tchr. Lake Washington Sch. Dist., Kirkland, Wash., 1966-71; instr. Wenatchie Valley Coll., Wenatchie, Wash., 1972-73; program supr. State of Wash. Dept. Edn., Olympia, 1973-75; coordinator spl. services office of State Dir. Vocat. Edn., U. Hawaii, Honolulu, 1977-80, coordinator research and devel., 1980—; cons. No. Marianas, Guam, Hawaii Dept. Edn., N.Mex. U., Far West Lab, U. Calif.; chmn. Honolulu Employment and Tng. Adv. Council; mem. Oahu Pvt. Industry Council. Edn. Profl. Devel. Act fellow, 1975-77; named Outstanding Educator, State of Wash., 1971. Mem. Am. Vocat. Assn., Hawaii Vocat. Assn., Vocat. Edn. Equity Council, Oahu Pvt. Industry Council, Honolulu Symphony. Club: Alii Ski (Honolulu). Home: 625 Iolani St Honolulu HI 96813 Office: 2327 Dole St Honolulu HI 96822

WHITE, CHARLES OLDS, aeronautical engineer, b. Beirut, Apr. 2, 1931; s. Frank Laurence and Dorothy Alice (Olds) W.; m. Mary Carolyn Liechty, Sept. 3, 1955; children—Charles Cameron, Bruce Blair. B.S. in Aero. Engring., MIT, 1953, M.S., 1954. Aero. engr. Douglas Aircraft Long Beach, 1954-60, aero. engr. Ford Aerospace & Communication

Corp., Calif., 1960-79, sr. engr. specialist, 1979-80, staff office of gen. mgr. DIVAD div., 1980-81, tech. mgr. DIVAD Fuzes, 1981-82, supr. design and analysis DIVAD div., 1982—. Mem. AIAA, Nat. Mgmt. Assn., Am. Aviation Hist. Soc., Sigma Gamma Tau. Republican. Presbyterian. Clubs: Masters Swimming, Newport Beach Tennis. Contbr. articles to profl. jours.

WHITE, CHARLES RADCLIFFE, fish behavior researcher; b. Pitts., July 7, 1925; s. Charles Conley and Mary Louise (Radcliffe) W.; m. Anne Preston Anderson; children—Charles Leland, Kevin Radcliffe, David Radcliffe. B.S. in Civil Engring., Cornell U., 1946. Sales engr. Aluminum Co. of Am., Cleve., 1946-49; biologist, photographer Oreg. Fish Commn., 1950-52; exec. TV stas. KPTV, KLEW, CHEK, Portland, Oreg., Lewiston, Idaho, Victoria, B.C., Can., 1952-57; researcher Saltaire Products Ltd., Victoria, 1958-61; owner, operator Undersea Gardens Marine Exhibits, Can., U.S., 1962-69; writer, lectr. on marine life, 1970-73; fish behavior researcher for TV, films; lectr., 1974—; dir. B.C. TV Broadcasting Ltd.; lectr. Camosun Coll., Victoria, 1971—. Served with USN, 1944-46. Recipient Bartlett Cup, Bay of Island's Billfish Club, 1972. Author: How To Catch Salmon, 1971; contbr. numerous books on fish and marine life; patentee facility for viewing marine life, self extinguishing portable cooking unit, developer numerous fishing devices and remotely controlled underwater TV; camera system for studying fish behavior.

WHITE, CHARLES RAYMOND, psychologist; b. Milw., Apr. 14, 1934; s. Harold Villars and Dorothy Irene (Speer) W.; m. Marjorie JoHann Rider, Apr. 13, 1960; children—Carrie Rae White Hanson, Curtis Daniel, Craig Eugene. Ph.B., U. N.D., 1956, Ph.D., 1962. Registered psychologist, Wash. Clin. psychology intern Jamestown State Hosp. (N.D.), 1957-58, EEG technician, 1958-59; instr. psychology U. N.D., 1961-62, asst. prof., 1962-64; asst. prof. psychology Eastern Wash. U., Cheney, 1964-66; psychologist, dir. living skills ctr. Eastern State Hosp., Medical Lake, Wash., 1966—. Mem. Am. Psychol. Assn., Am. Personnel and Guidance Assn., Assn. Counselor Educators and Suprs., Inland Empire Assn. Profl. Psychologists, Silver Lake Property Owners Assn. Methodist. Club: Masons. Home: Route 1 PO Box 259 Medical Lake WA 99022 Office: Eastern State Hosp PO Box A Medical Lake WA 99022

WHITE, CHERYL ANN, educational adminstrator; b. Kalamazoo, Nov. 30, 1948; d. Byron Edward and Jean Alice (Hitzfield) W. B.A., Mich. State U., 1971, M.A., 1977; Ed.S. in Adminstrn. and Curriculum, Colo. State U., 1983. Tchr. 6th grade Flushing (Mich.) Sch. Dist., 1971-76; tchr. 6th and 7th grade, coach Thompson Sch. Dist., Loveland, Colo., 1976-79; elem. adminstr. St. Vrain Valley Sch. Dist., Longmont, Colo., 1980—. Bd. dirs Loveland YMCA, 1982—, Wilderness Adventures for Youth Program, 1980-82, Help Line, 1981-82. Mem. Assn. Supervision and Curriculum Devel., Nat. Assn. Elem. Sch. Prins., Colo. Assn. Sch. Execs., Bo-La-Weld, St. Vrain Adminstrv. Group, Phi Delta Kappa. Democrat. Methodist. Home: 1727 E 16th St Loveland CO 80537 Office: 820 Main St Longmont CO 80501

WHITE, DALE EDWARD, social service orgn. exec.; b. Spokane, Oct. 10, 1947; s. Charles Russell and Dolores (Grounds) W.; A.A., A.A.S., Spokane Falls Community Coll., 1975; m. Rhonda Jean Niles, Aug. 9, 1971; children—Margo Marie, Jennifer Lee, Charles Edward. Liaison officer Spokane Sch. Dist. 81, 1971-75; nat. service officer DAV, Seattle, 1975—, supr. Seattle office, also coordinator Vietnam Veterans Outreach, State of Wash., 1980—, chmn. publicity dept., 1978-79, commdr. Chpt. 10, Everett, Wash., bd. dirs. Snohomish Vets. Action Center, Everett. Served with USN, 1967-69. Office: 915 2d Ave Federal Bldg Seattle WA 98174

WHITE, DARCIE HOMER, utility executive; b. Goshen, Utah, Sept 20, 1926; s. Samuel D. H. and Mary Genevieve (Gagon) W.; m. Melva E. O'Very, Sept. 1, 1948; children—Terry, Steven, Linda. B.S.E.E., U. Utah, 1950. Registered profl. engr., Utah. Various positions Utah Power & Light, Salt Lake City, 1952-68, dir. pub. relations, 1968-69, employee affairs mgr., v.p. employee affairs, 1969-80, v.p. pub. and corp. relations, 1980—; dir. Electric Mut. Benefit Assn., Electric Life Ins. Co., Energy Mut. Ins. Co., Intermountain Mut. Benefit Assn., Salt Palace Complex; mem. Indsl. Commn. Bd. Rev. Utah Safety Council. Pres. West Valley Police Hon. Cols. Assn. Served with USN, 1944-46. Mem. Pub. Relations Soc. Am., Edison Electric Inst. (communications com.). Republican. Mormon. Clubs: Kiwanis, Ambassador Athletic. Home: 2817 Cherry Blossom Ln Salt Lake City UT 84117 Office: Utah Power & Light 1407 W North Temple Salt Lake City UT 84116

WHITE, EARL HARVEY, management consultant; b. Muskogee, Okla., Apr. 8, 1934; s. Earl Harvey and Mahtoltoya (Johnson) W.; B.S., U. San Francisco, 1963; M.B.A., Pepperdine U., Los Angeles, 1975; m. Doris Johnson, Feb. 19, 1960; children—Jean-Pierre, Jacques. Mgmt. trainee IBM Corp., 1961-63; probation officer Marin County (Calif.), 1963-66, Redwood City, Calif., 1966-67; cons. to City of San Francisco, 1967-69; ind. cons., 1969—; pres. E.H. White & Co., Inc., San Francisco; lectr. U. Calif. Served with USNR, 1953-57. Mem. U.S. Black C. of C. (pres. 1980-81), Am. Mgmt. Assn., Am. Soc. Bus. and Mgmt. Cons., NAACP. Club: Masons. Home: 399 Melrose Ave San Francisco CA 94127 Office: 245 Clement St San Francisco CA 94118

WHITE, EDMUND LAWRENCE, manufacturing company executive; b. N.Y.C., Sept. 27, 1932; s. Edmund W. and Catherine E. White; B.S. cum laude, U. Notre Dame, 1954, LL.B., 1956; M.B.A., N.Y.U., 1958; diploma in econs. of nat. security Indsl. Coll. Armed Forces, 1958; m. Priscilla C. Iannuzzi, July 1, 1961; children—Allison and Leslie (twins), Douglas. Mgmt. trainee Chase Manhattan Bank, 1956-57, investment analyst, 1957-58; mktg. research analyst Royal McBee Corp., 1958-61; mgr. market and acquisition research Smith Corona Marchant (SCM) Corp., N.Y.C., 1961-63; market economist IBM, Armonk, N.Y., 1963-64, sr. market economist, 1964-66, advisory forecaster, 1966-68, bus. program analyst, 1968-70, mgr. goals planning, 1970-72, asst. dir. bus. evaluation, 1972-73, mgr. market analysis, 1973-74; exec. v.p. Bus. & Investment Consultants Internat., Phoenix, 1974-76; sr. v.p. adminstrn., sec. Empire Gen. Corp., Los Angeles, 1976-78; treas. Empire Gen. Life Ins. Co. of Calif., Ohio and Tex., Los Angeles, 1977-78; v.p., gen. mgr. Pacific Furniture Mfg. Co., Compton, Calif., 1978—; pres. Artesia Mfg. Co., Compton, 1979—. Clubs: Pasadena Athletic, Notre Dame of Los Angeles (pres., dir. 1980—). Home: 1661 Lombardy Rd Pasadena CA 91106 Office: 1965 E Vista Bella Compton CA 90220

WHITE, EVAN DALZELL, economist; b. N.Y.C., Oct. 25, 1939; s. Calvin Stuart and Margaret Elizabeth (Dalzell) W.; m. Kaaren Horsley, Oct. 26, 1968; m. 2d, Patricia Anne White, June 13, 1982; children—Calvin S., Conrad, Karen Sylvester. B.A., Claremont Mckenna Coll., 1961; M.A. in Econs., U. Calif.-Berkeley, 1964; M.B.A. in Fin., U. Pa., 1970. With trust investment Wells Fargo Bank, San Francisco, 1967-68; econ. analyst Evans Products Co., Portland, 1969-72; with Pub. Utility Commn. Oreg., Salem, 1972—, adminstr. econ. research and fin. analysis div., 1972—; cons. and lectr. in field. Served to 1st lt. U.S. Army, 1964-66. H.B. Earhart fellow, 1961-62. Mem. Am. Econ. Assn. Episcopalian. Home: 1787 Joseph St S Salem OR 97302 Office: Labor and Industries Bldg Salem 97310

WHITE, FRISCO, architect; b. Kakura City, Japan, Dec. 10, 1950; came to U.S., 1955, naturalized, 1960; s. Willie L. and Mineko (Sato) W. B.Arch., Calif. Poly. State U., 1974. Assoc. Paul Thoryk & Assocs., Inc., San Diego, v.p. design and planning, 1974-80, exec. v.p., chief operating officer, 1980-81, pres., chief exec. officer, 1981—, also dir. Mem. AIA. Democrat. Baptist. Office: 1157 Columbia St San Diego CA 92101

WHITE, GEORGE HARVEY, supt. schs.; b. Durango, Colo., Feb. 5, 1939; s. Loyd Oscar and Sally Beatrice (Mullenix) W.; m. Janice Pope, Sept. 30, 1960. B.A. in History, U. Alaska, 1964; M.Ed. in Adminstrn., Eastern Wash. State Coll., 1969. Supt., div. regional schs. Beltz Regional High Sch., Nome, Alaska, 1968-69; regional supt. N.W. Region Div. State Operated Schs., Nome, 1970-71; assoc. supt. Alaska State Operated Sch. System, Anchorage, 1971-75; supt. Alaska Unorganized Borough Sch. Dist., Anchorage, 1975-76; dist. supt. N.W. Arctic Sch. Dist., 1976-82; supt. Kake (Alaska) City Sch. Dist., 1982—; vice chmn. Alaska Profl. Teaching Practices Commn., 1977-80; mem. Alaska Public Offices Commn., 1980—; mem. adv. bd. Alaska Airlines, vice chmn., 1980-81. Ex-officio mem. U. Alaska adv. council Kotzebue Community Coll., 1976-82; instl. rep. Boy Scouts Am., 1968-69; mem. Juvenile Adv. Com. to Superior Ct., Nome, 1968-69; mem. exec. com. N.W. Alaska Regional Strategy Planning Council, 1977-82; mem. Cross-Cultural Edn. Program Consortium, to 1980; bd. dirs. S.E. Regional Resource Center. Mem. State Operated Schs. Adminstrs. Assn., Am. Assn. Sch. Adminstrs., Rural Edn. Assn., Alaska Assn. Sch. Adminstrs. (pres.-elect, mem. exec. bd.; sec.-treas. 1979-80). Cert. prin., tchr., supt., Alaska. Home: Box 317 Kake AK 99830 Office: Box 450 Kake AK 99830

WHITE, HOWARD ASHLEY, univ. pres.; b. Cleverdale, Ala., Sept. 28, 1913; s. John Parker and Mabel Clara (Hipp) W.; B.A., Tulane U., 1946, M.A., 1952, Ph.D., 1956; m. Maxcine Feltman, June 17, 1952 (dec.); children—Ashley Feltman, Howard Elliott. Ordained to ministry, Ch. of Christ, 1930; pastor chs., New Orleans, 1941-53; prof. history, chmn. dept. David Lipscomb Coll., Nashville, 1953-58; chmn. social sci. dept. Pepperdine U., Malibu, Calif., 1958-63, dean grad. studies, dean undergrad. studies, 1963-71, exec. v.p., 1971-78, pres., 1978—. Mem. Am. Assn. Presidents of Ind. Colls. and Univs. (bd. dirs.), Ind. Colls. So. Calif. (bd. dirs.), Am. Hist. Assn., Orgn. Am. Historians, So. Hist. Assn. Club: Rotary. Author: Freedmen's Bureau in Louisiana, 1970. Address: 24255 Pacific Coast Hwy Malibu CA 90265

WHITE, IAN MCKIBBIN, museum administrator; b. Honolulu, May 10, 1929; s. Osborne and Alice Aileen (Dowsett) W.; B.A. in Architecture, Harvard U., 1951, postgrad., 1951-52; postgrad. in indsl. design, U. Calif. at Los Angeles, 1957-58; D.F.A. (hon.), Bowdoin Coll., 1977; m. Florence Hildreth, June 27, 1959; children—Peter, Daniel, Susanna. Adminstrv. asst. Bklyn. Botanic Garden, N.Y.C., 1959-60; supt. Bklyn. Mus., N.Y.C., 1961-63, asst. dir., 1964-67; dir. Cal. Palace of Legion of Honor, San Francisco, 1968—, M.H. de Young Meml. Mus., San Francisco, 1970—; adv. Archives of Am. Art; mem. mus. adv. panel Nat. Endowment Arts, 1973-76. Trustee, Louise A. Boyd Natural Sci. Mus., Marin County, Calif., 1969-70, Corning Mus. of Glass, 1977—. Served with USNR, 1953-56. Decorated Order of Rep. of Egypt. Mem. Am. Assn. Museums (adv. council 1980-83), Am. Fedn. Arts (trustee 1971—), Internat. Council Museums (U.S. nat. com. 1971-73, 83—, internat. com. on fine arts 1981—), Am. Assn. Mus. Dirs. (councilor, trustee, 1st v.p. 1975-76, pres. 1976-77), Mcpl. Art Soc. N.Y.C. (bd. dirs. 1966), Victorian Soc. Am. (adv. com. 1970). Clubs: Rembrandt (Bklyn.); Bohemian (San Francisco). Designed Frieda Shiff Warburg Sculpture Garden, Bklyn. Mus., 1966, Peary-MacMillan Arctice Mus. at Bowdoin Coll., Brunswick, Maine, 1967. Home: 2 Lagunitas Rd Ross CA 94957 Office: Calif Palace Legion Honor Lincoln Park San Francisco CA 94121

WHITE, JOHN MARK, conceptual artist; b. San Francisco, May 10, 1937; s. John T. and Betty Jeanne (LaVelle) W.; M.F.A., Otis Art Inst., Los Angeles, 1969; m. Sylvia Haimoff, Mar. 24, 1975. One-man shows: Betty Gold Gallery, Los Angeles, 1974, Gallerie Doyle, Paris, 1975, Okum Thomas Gallery, St. Louis, 1977, Jan Baum Gallery, Los Angeles, 1978, 81, Roy Boyd Gallery Chgo., 1981; group shows include: Contemporary Mus. Art, 1973, Los Angeles County Mus. Art, 1971, Newport Harbor Art Mus., 1975, Los Angeles Inst. Contemporary Art, 1975, St. Louis Mus. Art, 1977, U. B.C., 1977, Indspl. Mus. Art, 1979, Guggenheim Mus., N.Y.C., 1981; represented in permanent collections: Los Angeles County Mus. Art, St. Louis Mus. Contemporary Art, Smithsonian Archives of Am. Art, Indpls. Mus. Modern Art, Guggenheim Mus. Nat. Endowment for Arts fellow, 1975, 78. Office: Jan Baum Gallery 170 S La Brea Los Angeles CA 90036

WHITE, JUDITH ANNE, vocational consultant, rehabilitation counselor, career counselor; b. Los Angeles, May 26, 1948. B.A. in Social Anthropology, San Francisco State U., 1973, M.S. in Rehab. Counseling, 1976. Cert. rehab. counselor. Rehab. counseling intern Pacific Med. Ctr., San Francisco, 1974-75, San Francisco State U., 1975-76; counselor Stroke Activity Ctr., Cabrillo Coll., Aptos, Calif., 1977-78; counselor, coordinator Work Info. Ctr., YWCA, Santa Cruz, Calif., 1978; vocat. cons., Santa Cruz, 1978—; career counselor U. Calif.-Santa Cruz, 1980—. Bd. dirs., chmn. personnel com. Santa Cruz YWCA, 1980-82; mem. adv. bd. Goodwill Industries, 1979-80. Mem. Am. Personnel and Guidance Assn. Office: 513 Water St Suite 3 Santa Cruz CA 95060

WHITE, KENNETH DEWAN, computer consulting firm executive; b. Caruthers, Calif., Aug. 31, 1937; s. Walter Bert and Josie Mae (Jones) W.; student Am. U., 1963, San Diego State U., 1970; m. Virginia Mae Kizer, Aug. 6, 1966; children—Kenneth, Connie, Terry, Paula. Enlisted U.S. Navy, 1955, advanced through grades to lt., 1977, ret., 1979; with Rehab. Group, Inc., Falls Church, Va., 1979, mgr. West Coast Ops., San Diego, 1980—, v.p. Western div., 1981—; computerized adaptive testing cons. Decorated Meritorious Service medal, Navy Commendation medal. Recipient Lions Internat. State Achievement award, 1980, 100% pres. award, 1980, Dist. Gov.'s Outstanding Leadership award, 1980; named Lion of Yr., 1979. Mem. Ops. Research Soc. Am., Airplane Owners and Pilots Assn. Republican. Baptist. Club: Lions (pres. 1978-80). Author: Computerized Adaptive Testing Assessment of Requirements, 1980; Cost Target for a Computerized Adaptive Testing System, 1980. Office: 1360 Rosecrans St San Diego CA 92106

WHITE, LELIA CAYNE, librarian; b. Berkeley, Calif., Feb. 22, 1921; d. James Lloyd and Eulalia Fulton (Douglass) Cayne; B.A., U. Calif., Berkeley, 1943, M.L.S., 1969; children by previous marriage—Douglass Fulton, Cameron Jane. Bibliographer, lectr., asso. U. Calif., Berkeley Sch. Library and Info. Studies, 1969-72; reference librarian Berkeley-Oakland (Calif.) Service Systems, 1970-76, supervising librarian, 1973-76; dir. Oakland Public Library, 1976—; Mem. adv. council Bay Area Reference Ctr.; mem. adv. council Citizens for Better Nursing Home Care. Mem. ALA, Calif. Library Assn. (council), Calif. Inst. of Libraries (pres.), Urban Libraries Council, Pub. Library Assn. (pres. Met. Libraries sect.), Bay Area Libraries and Info. Systems (adminstrv. council), Oakland Pub Library Assn. (bd. dirs.), Oakland/Dalian (China) Friendship City Soc. (pres.), East Bay Negro Hist. Soc. (bd. dirs.), Calif. Spanish Lang. Data Base (bd. dirs.), LWV, Asian Shared Info. and Acquisitions (bd. dirs.). Home: 1927 Napa Ave Berkeley CA 94707 Office: 125 14th St Oakland CA 94612

WHITE, LOIS CARYL MANCE, educator; b. Denver, May 26, 1942; d. Henry Turner and Millie Turner (Green) Mance; m. Robert Lee Johnson, July 20, 1962; 1 son, Jason Deland; m. 2d, Ronnie Wayne White, Oct. 30, 1970; 1 dau., Ayana LaRon. A.A., So. Colo. State Coll., 1962; B.A. in Elem. Edn., U. Denver, 1964; postgrad. U. Colo., 1968-69. Cert. tchr., adminstr., Colo. Tchr., Denver Pub. Schs., 1965-75; tchr. asst. to prin. McMeen Elem. Sch., Denver, 1975-78; project specialist Elem. Schs. Assistance Project, Denver Pub. Schs., 1979-80, project mgr., 1980-82; diagnostician East Diagnostic Teaching Ctr., Denver, 1982—. Active Girl Scouts U.S.A.; sec. Aurora Human Relations Commn., 1976-82, bd. mgrs. Aurora YMCA, 1981-83. Recipient Working Women's award NOW, 1982. Mem. Denver Classroom Tchrs. Assn., Colo. Edn. Assn., NEA, Colo. Assn. Sch. Execs., Assn. Supervision and Curriculum Devel., Delta Sigma Theta. Democrat. African Methodist Episcopal.

WHITE, MARY GERALDINE, govt. ofcl.; b. Austin, Tex., Aug. 2, 1924; d. Clarice Pierce and Mary Rosalie (Roy) Rumph; B.S., U. N.Mex., 1960, M.S., 1964; m. Robert B. Mayes, June 23, 1945 (div.); children—Mary Lynn, Robert Charles. Radiation chemist Sandia Corp., Albuquerque, 1960-63; radiation biologist Lovelace Fission Products Lab., Albuquerque, 1963-65; research radiation biologist USPHS, Las Vegas, Nev., 1965-73; mgr. sci. environ. research program U.S. Dept. Energy, Las Vegas, 1973-78, Richland, Wash., 1978-81, program mgr. remedial action programs, nuclear waste mgmt., Washington, 1981—; mem. adj. faculty U. Nev., Las Vegas; speaker in field. Recipient Silver Medallion leadership award Camp Fire Girls, 1956; hon. life mem. N.Mex. PTA. Mem. Am. Nuclear Soc. (nat. tech. program chmn. 1980, dir., exec. com. 1982-83), Internat. Platform Assn., Health Physics Soc., AAUW, N.Mex. Acad. Sci., Phi Theta Kappa, Phi Kappa Phi, Phi Sigma, Pi Lambda Theta. Democrat. Author, editor papers, research documents. Home: Box 11146 Las Vegas NV 89111 Office: Dept Energy Germantown MD 20545

WHITE, NANCY JOANNE, librarian; b. Sharon, Pa., Oct. 1, 1953; d. William Roy and Lorraine Irene (Taylor) Aggers; m. Christopher White, June 27, 1975; 1 dau., Samantha Rae. B.A. in Latin, Oberlin Coll., 1975; M.L.S., U. Calif.-Berkeley, 1980. Library asst. Case Western Res. U., Cleve., 1976; adminstrv. asst., clk. treas. Cleve. Area Met. Library System, 1976-78; med. library asst. Letterman Army Med. Ctr., San Francisco, 1978-79; research asst. Sta. KRON-TV, San Francisco, 1980; reference librarian Standard Oil Co. of Calif., San Francisco, 1980; library asst. Pacific Gas and Electric Co., San Francisco, 1980-81, info. specialist, 1981, dir. corp. library, 1981-83, adminstrv. asst., 1983—. Pres. alumni bd. dirs. Grad. Sch. of Library and Info. Sci., U. Calif.-Berkeley. Mem. Associated Info. Mgrs., ALA, Spl. Library Assn., Am. Soc. Info. Scientists. Office: Pacific Gas and Electric Co 77 Beale St Suite 1096 San Francisco CA 94106

WHITE, RICHARD JAMES, training manager; b. Lynxville, Wis., May 12, 1937; s. Donald Jay and Lucille (Haville) W.; m. Mary Ellen Runkel, June 11, 1960; children—Michael Richard, Christopher Edward, Gregory James. B.S. in Naval Sci., U. Wis., 1960; M.S. in Mgmt., U.S. Naval Postgrad. Sch., 1971. Commd. ensign U.S. Navy, 1960, advanced through grades to lt. comdr., 1980; v.p. ops. Curriculum Devel. & Cons. Inc., San Diego, 1981—. Decorated Bronze Star. Mem. Am. Soc. Tng. and Devel., Nat. Soc. Performance and Instrn., Navy League of U.S. Home: 6497 Park Ridge Blvd San Diego CA 92120 Office: 7525 Mission Gorge Rd San Diego CA 92120

WHITE, ROLAND JAMES, aeronautical engineer; b. Missoula, Mont., Dec. 13, 1910; s. Roland John and Mamie (Jacobsen) W.; m. Mary Cleeton, Feb. 10, 1948; children—Roland, Glenna. B.S., U. Calif., 1933; M.S. in Mech. Engring., Calif. Inst. Tech., 1934, M.S. in Aero Engring., 1935. Engr. Curtiss Wright, St. Louis, 1935-36, Lockheed Aircraft, Burbank, Calif., 1937-38; instr. U. Wash., Seattle, 1938-40; engr. Curtiss Wright Corp., St. Louis, 1940-45; unit chief transport div. Boeing, Seattle, 1945-71; engr. Aerophysics Research Corp., Bellevue, Wash., 1971, Bell Aerospace Co., New Orleans, 1972-76, Analytical Methods, Bellevue, 1976, Rohr Industries, San Diego, 1976, Gates LearJet, Wichita, Kans., 1977-81, Canadair Ltd., Mojave, Calif., 1982. Served as lt. (j.g.) USNR, 1937-57. Mem. AIAA. Patentee (12); contbr. articles to profl. jours. Home and Office: 4670 95th Ave NE Bellevue WA 98004

WHITE, RONALD KURT, educator; b. Hooper, Colo., Nov. 13, 1938; s. Wesley Curtis and Edith (Commbs) W.; m. Elva Lafawn Jones, Feb. 7, 1964; children—Abby, Lisa, Kurt, Paula, LaNette, Scott, Mira, Brent, Carl. B.S., Brigham Young U., 1968, M.S., 1970; postgrad. No. Ariz. U., 1976, Ariz. State U., 1977; Ed.S., Nova U., 1981. Ednl. adminstrn. cert., Ariz. Instr. archtl. drafting Brigham Young U., Provo, Utah, 1968-70; tchr. woods and crafts Uintah High Sch., Vernal, Utah, 1970-71; career edn. hands-on specialist, tchr. indls. arts St. Johns (Ariz.) High Sch., 1971-73; career edn. specialist Appache and Navajo Counties, Ariz., 1973-81, coordinator career and vocat. edn., 1982—; asst. prin. Smiley Jr. High Sch., Durango, Colo., 1981-82. Mgr. Apache County Fair, 1978-81; chmn. Apache dist. Boy Scouts Am., 1976-80. Served with USMC, 1956-59. Recipient Dist. award of Merit, Apache Dist., Grand Canyon council Boy Scouts Am., 1976, Silver Beaver award Grand Canyon council, 1981; St. Johns Recognition award St. Johns C. of C., 1979. Mem. Am. Vocat. Assn., Ariz. Council Vocat. Adminstrs. Democrat. Mormon. Home: PO Box 959 160 W 100 N Saint Johns AZ 85936 Office: PO Box 749 Saint Johns AZ 85936

WHITE, RUTH S., composer, producer, publisher; b. Pitts., Sept. 1, 1925; d. Leon H. and Rose (Stevenson) W. B.F.A. in Piano, Carnegie Mellon U., 1948, B.F.A. in Composition, 1948, M.F.A. in Composition, 1949. Cert. tchr., Calif. Supr. UCLA Demonstration Sch., 1952-59; owner, pres. Rhythms Prodns., Los Angeles, 1955—; pres. Cheviot Corp., Los Angeles, 1961—; lectr. Recipient 1st prize in composition Nat. Soc. Arts and Letters, 1950; 1st prize for movie score Atlanta Film Festival, 1970; producer Notable Rec. for Children, ALA selection, 1982; Huntington Hartford Found. fellow, 1965. Mem. Am. Fedn. Musicians, ASCAP, Nat. Acad. Rec. Arts and Scis. (past bd. govs. and nat. trustee, past v.p. NARAS Inst.), Nat. Assn. Am. Composers, Music Educators Nat. Conf., Audio Engring. Soc., Sigma Alpha Iota. Author text and reference books; composer electronic music works, also albums of music for children; film scores. Office: Cheviot Corp Box 34485 Los Angeles CA 90034

WHITE, SANDRA ALINE, psychotherapist, educator; b. N.Y.C., Jan. 14, 1937; d. Louis and Molly Ruth (Singer) Schiffman. B.A., Calif. State U.-Los Angeles, 1972, M.A. in Psychology, 1974; Ph.D. in Psychology, Calif. Grad. Inst., 1983. Lic. marriage, family and child therapist, Calif. Sr. staff counselor F.R.E.E. Found., Beverly Hills, Calif., 1976-78; staff counselor Coldwater Counseling Center, Van Nuys, Calif., 1976-77; field faculty Goddard Coll., Los Angeles, 1976; lectr. Immaculate Heart Coll., Los Angeles, 1978; pvt. practice psychotherapy, Los Angeles, 1975—; founder, dir. Center for Applied Counseling, Los Angeles, 1982—. Mem. Calif. Assn. Marriage and Family Therapists (sec. Westside Los Angeles chpt.), Internat. Transactional Analysis Assn., Am. Personnel and Guidance Assn. Democrat. Jewish. Office: 8170 Beverly Blvd Suite 200 Los Angeles CA 90048

WHITE, SHERYL ZENZ, acct.; b. San Diego, Dec. 5, 1945; d. William Donald and Monica Jean (Herney) Zenz; B.S. in Bus. Adminstrn., Calif.

State U., San Diego, 1969; m. Don R. White, Apr. 26, 1970 (dec.). Departmental acct. water utilities City of San Diego, 1969-74, asst. coordinator, pub. employment program, 1974-75, fiscal analyst gen. services dept., 1976-77, investment officer treasury dept., 1977-78; owner, operator Fireside Manor Apts., Ontario, Calif., 1977—; prin acct. Sowell & Forsythe, La Jolla, Calif., 1979—; adj. instr. San Diego Community Coll., 1976-77. Bd. dirs. Law Center for Equal Rights, 1979-81. Mem. Young Ams. for Freedom (treas. San Diego chpt. 1965-66, v.p., 1966-67), Young Republicans, Mcpl. Fin. Officers' Assn. (pres. San Diego chpt. 1974), Calif. Women in Govt. (chmn. San Diego chpt. 1979-80), NOW, Ninety-Nines. Home: 8886 Caminito Primavera La Jolla CA 92037 Office: 1141-D W D St Ontario CA 91762 also 8950 Villa La Jolla Dr Suite 2241 La Jolla CA 92037

WHITE, STEPHEN HALLEY, biophysicist; b. Wewoka, Okla., May 14, 1940; s. James HalleY and Gertrude June (Wyatt) W.; B.A. in Physics, U. Colo., Boulder, 1963; M.S. in Physics, U. Wash., Seattle, 1965, Ph.D. in Biophysics, 1969; m. Buff Ertl, Aug. 20, 1961 (div. 1983); children—Saill, Shell, Storn, Sharr, Skye, Sunde. USPHS postdoctoral fellow in biochemistry U. Va., 1971-72; asst. prof. physiology and biophysics U. Calif., Irvine, 1972-75, assoc. prof., 1975-78, prof., 1979—, dept. vice chmn., 1974-75, chmn., 1977—; guest assoc. physiologist Brookhaven Nat. Labs. Served to capt. Chem. Corps, USAR, 1969-71. Recipient Kaiser-Permanente award for excellence in teaching, 1975; Research Career Devel. award NIH, 1975-80; NIH and NSF research grantee. Mem. Biophys. Soc. (council), Am. Assn. Med. Colls., N.Y. Acad. Scis., Am. Physiol. Soc., Am. Chem. Soc., Assn. Chairmen Depts. of Physiology (council), Internat. Union Pure and Applied Biophysics, Council of Acad. Socs. Editorial bd. Am. Jour. Physiology, 1981—; contbr. articles to profl. jours. Research on biophysics and phys. chemistry of cellular membranes. Office: Dept Physiology and Biophysics Univ Calif Irvine CA 92717

WHITE, THOMAS GENE, latex products mfg. ofcl.; b. Wapakoneta, Ohio, Aug. 19, 1936; s. Howard Leland and Hope Maude (Meeks) W.; m. Mai Thi-Huyn Le, July 20, 1980; children by previous marriage—Thomas Gene, Carolyn Renee. B.Sc., Ohio State U., 1958, 59; postgrad. U. Vt., 1960-61, Ohio State U., 1961-63; M.A., Bowling Green State U., 1968; postgrad. U. Akron, 1970-71; M.B.A., Pepperdine U., 1982. Mgr. new products research and devel. Sherwood Med. Industries, Willard, Ohio, 1967-73; sr. research chemist Internat. Playtex Corp., Paramus, N.J., 1973-74; v.p. research and devel. Seiberling Latex Products, Oklahoma City, 1974-79; dir. latex products Am. Pharmaseal, Glendale, Calif., 1979—; dir. SSUNOL, Inc.; cons. rubber products; tchr. chemistry. Pres. Willard Schs. PTA, 1971-72; trustee Willard United Fund, 1972-73; dist. chmn. Boy Scouts Am., 1972-73, exec. bd. council, 1972-73, 76-79, program dir., 1980—, dist. com., 1980—; pres. bd. dirs. Jr. Achievement of Willard, 1972-73, Central Region adv. council, 1972-73. NSF grantee, 1966-68; Bowling Green State U. grantee, 1966-68. Mem. Am. Chem. Soc., N.Y. Acad. Scis., AAAS, Soc. Plastics Engrs. Republican. Home: 2959 Fairbanks St Simi Valley CA 93063 Office: 1015 Grandview Ave Glendale CA 91201

WHITE, VIRGINIA JOYCELYN, interior designer, consultant; b. Des Moines, April 25, 1924; d. William Wood White and Alwilda (Denning) W. Student, Art Inst. Chgo., 1942-43; B.F.A., Choinard Sch. Art, 1947; postgrad. Woodbury Coll. Design, 1947-48, UCLA, 1948-50, Southwestern U. Law, 1954-56. Designer Martin Young Furniture Mfg. Co., Los Angeles, 1947-52; owner, designer Virginia White Interiors Co., Los Angeles, 1952-57, Studio City, 1966-80, Palm Desert, 1980—; dir. design Gen. Fireproofing Co., Los Angeles 1957-63, Barker Bros. Co., Los Angeles, 1963-66; instr. design Woman's Workshop, Northridge, Calif., 1973-79; cons. to furniture mfrs. Bd. dirs. Spastic Children's Fund, Los Angeles, 1952-56. Recipient Nat. Instn. Mag. design award, 1958; McCall Mag. design award, 1963. Mem. Calif. Fedn. Bus. and Profl. Women (charter pres. Los Angeles chpt. 1957-58), Am. Soc. Interior Designers (cert. 1974) Sigma Tau Psi (chpt. pres. 1945-46, nat. pres. 1946-48). Republican. Mem. Ch. Religious Sci. Patentee in furniture field; contbr. articles to publs.

WHITE, WILLARD WORSTER, III, physicist; b. Perth Amboy, N.J., July 6, 1944; s. Willard Worster and Josephine Wanda W.; m. Kathleen Mary Reilly, Aug. 5, 1972; 1 dau., Elizabeth. B.S. in Physics with distinction, U. Del., 1966; Ph.D. in Physics, Rensselaer Poly. Inst., 1970. Research assoc. Rensselaer Poly. Inst., 1970-72; staff scientist Mission Research Corp., Santa Barbara, Calif., 1972-78, sr. scientist, alt. phenomenology div. leader, 1978-82, MHD group leader, laser physics group leader, 1982—. Mem. Am. Phys. Soc., Am. Optical Soc., AAAS. Research, numerous publs. in physics of ionospheric/magnetospheric phenomena, physics of laser propagation phenomena. Office: 735 State St Santa Barbara CA 93101

WHITEHAIR, CHESTER LOUIS, aerospace engineering executive; b. Clarksburg, W.Va., Jan. 28, 1936; s. Berry Morgan and Margaret Beatrice (Fairfax) W.; m. Mary Kathryn Horsney, Aug. 16, 1958; children—Anne Michelle, Robert Scott. B.S. in Aero. Engring., W.Va. U., 1959. Design engr. various cos. W.Va., Calif., 1956-62; chief design engr. Metals div. Supertemp Corp., Santa Fe Springs, Calif., 1962-63; tech., mgmt. positions space launch vehicles Aerospace Corp., El Segundo, Calif., 1963-78, prin. dir. inertial upper stage, 1978—. Served with USMCR, 1956-62. Recipient Air Force Systems Command Outstanding Achievement award, 1966, Air Force Commendation Letters 1975, 78, 80, 81, 82. Mem. AIAA. Republican. Roman Catholic. Home: 8681 Shannon River Circle Fountain Valley CA 92708 Office: Aerospace Corp 2350 E El Segundo Blvd El Segundo CA 90245

WHITEHEAD, BARRY, thoroughbred racing ofcl.; b. San Francisco, Dec. 26, 1910; s. Samuel Barry II and Norine Imelda (Conway) W.; student U. San Francisco, 1929-33; m. Fritzi-Beth Bowman, Nov. 10, 1935; children—Peter Barry, David Barry. Corr. to Thoroughbred Record, Lexington, Ky., 1930; thoroughbred owner and breeder, 1932-36; racing ofcl. tracks, 1934—; dir. Sullivan-Greely Corp., Weightform Corp. Asst. sec. Calif. Thoroughbred Breeders Assn., 1937; dir. Soc. N.Am. Racing Ofcls., 1955. Col., a.d.c. gov.'s staff State of La. Bd. dirs. Calif. Racing Hall of Fame, 1968, also bd. dirs. found.; bd. dirs., v.p. William P. Kyne Meml. Library, 1974. Served with AUS, World War II. Mem. Friends Bancroft Library, Calif. Hist. Soc., Thoroughbred Club of Am. Club: Press of San Francisco. Contbr. to thoroughbred publs., chiefly on hist. or tech. background of racing. Has racing library. Address: PO Box 488 Monte Rio CA 95462

WHITEHEAD, PAUL LEON, psychiatrist; b. Salt Lake City, May 23, 1936; s. Rolland Nixon and Marva (Bullock) W.; B.S., U. Utah, 1957, M.D., 1960; m. Marilyn Davis, Sept. 5, 1964; children—Anne, Paul, Kathryn, Emily. Intern, Cin. Gen. Hosp., 1960-61; resident psychiatry and child psychiatry U. Cin., 1963-67; practice medicine, specializing in child psychiatry, Salt Lake City, 1967—; dir. Children's Psychiat. Center, 1967-76; chmn. dept. child psychiatry Primary Children's Med. Center, 1975-81; asst. prof. psychiatry U. Utah Coll. Medicine, 1967-77, clin. prof., 1977—, dir. div. child and adolescent psychiatry, 1977-78; cons. child psychiatry Utah Dept. Health, 1968—; chmn. Adv. Council for Children and Youth, Utah Div. Mental Health, 1968-73; mem. Utah Mental Health Task Force, 1970-71. Served as capt. M.C., USAF, 1961-63. Diplomate Am. Bd. Psychiatry and Neurology, also in child psychiatry. Fellow Am. Acad. Child Psychiatry; mem. AMA, Utah Med. Assn., Am., Utah (pres. 1977-78) psychiat. assns., Intermountain Acad. Child Psychiatry (pres. 1969), Phi Beta Kappa, Phi Kappa Phi, Alpha Omega Alpha. Editor, contbr. Primarily for Parents, 1970; contbr. articles to profl. jours. Home: 4650 Hugo Ave Salt Lake City UT 84117 Office: 1580 E 3900 S Salt Lake City UT 84117

WHITEHURST, DANIEL, mayor City of Fresno (Calif.); m. Kathleen McCann; children—Keenan, Jamie. Vice pres. Stephens & Bean, Inc.; mayor City of Fresno. Mem. U.S. Conf. Mayors, State Bar Calif. Club: Rotary. Address: City Hall 2326 Fresno Fresno CA 93721

WHITEHURST, WILLIAM EDWARD, educator; b. Bradenton, Fla., Feb. 2, 1953; s. Joseph Edward and Delores Martha (Moore) E. B.A., Ariz. State U., 1974, M.A., 1976, postgrad., 1976-83. Cert. secondary edn., elem. edn., reading specialist, adult edn., supervision. Tchr. reading and English, Phoenix Union High Sch. Dist., 1975-77; Title I reading specialist Picacho (Ariz.) Sch., 1977-78, spl. edn. tchr., 1978-79; jr. high lang. arts tchr. Laveen (Ariz.) Sch., 1979-81, reading and curriculum dir., 1981-83; curriculum dir. Cath. Diocese Phoenix, 1983—; instr. Ariz. State U., 1981-82. Mem. Assn. Supervision and Curriculum Devel., Ariz. State Reading Council, Ariz. Sch. Adminstrs. Republican. Roman Catholic. Home: 1628 W Osborn Phoenix AZ 85015 Office: 400 E Monroe St Phoenix AZ 85003

WHITE-THOMSON, IAN LEONARD, marketing executive; b. Halstead, Eng., May 3, 1936; s. Walter Norman and Leonore Jorgensen (Turney) (W.T.); m. Fiona McCarthy, Oct. 7, 1961; m. 2d, Barbara Ellyn Merola, Nov. 24, 1971; children—Capri Montgomery, Christopher Montgomery, Timothy Montgomery, Patrick. B.A. with 1st class honors, New Coll., Oxford U., 1960, M.A., 1969. Mgmt. trainee Borax Consol. Ltd., London, 1960-61, asst. to sales mgr., 1961-64, asst. to sales dir., 1964; comml. dir. Hardman & Holden Ltd., Manchester, 1965-67, joint mng. dir., 1967-69; v.p. mktg. dept. Borax & Chem. Corp., Los Angeles, 1969-73, exec. v.p. mktg., 1973—, also dir. Served to 2nd lt. Brit. Army, 1954-56. Mem. Chem. Industry Council Calif., (dir., vice chmn. 1982). Club: Los Angeles. Home: 1234 Wellington Ave Pasadena CA 91103 Office: 3075 Wilshire Blvd Los Angeles CA 90010

WHITFIELD, BENJAMIN HATCH, JR., ins. agt.; b. Jackson, Miss., Jan. 10, 1947; s. Benjamin Hatch and Lucy (Sellers) W.; B.A., Ambassador Coll., Pasadena, Calif., 1969, M.A. in Edn., 1973; m. Mary-Pat Whitfield. June 1, 1969; children—Benjamin Michael, John Gregory. Tchr., Imperial Schs., Pasadena, 1969-74; minister Worldwide Ch. of God, 1975-77, now elder; marriage counselor Carbon County (Wyo.) Counseling Center, Rawlins, 1977-78; agt. State Farm Ins., Rawlins, 1979—. Bd. dirs. Family Planning of Southwest Wyo., City of Rawlins Recreation Dept., Carbon County Recreation Bd.; committeeman Boy Scouts Am. Mem. Nat. Assn. Life Underwriters, Nat. Assn. Health Underwriters. Club: Rotary. Home: 1315 Date St Rawlins WY 82301 Office: PO Box 639 416 6th St Rawlins WY 82301

WHITFIELD, FREDRICK HAROLD, civil engineer; b. Portland, Oreg., Oct. 18, 1941; s. Harold T. and Sarah Eula (Marvin) W.; m. Sheila Ann Olson, July 12, 1963; children—Timothy, Wendy. B.S. in Civil Engring., Oreg. State U., 1963. Registered profl. engr., land surveyor, Oreg. Engr., M.B. Hinds, Co., Beaverton, Oreg., 1963-66, Port of Portland, 1966-71; gen. mgr. Clackamas (Oreg.) Water Dist., 1971-74; engr., project mgr. various large diameter water transmission mains, reservoirs Portland Water Bur., 1974-81, dir. ops., 1981—. Mem. Am. Water Works Assn., Am. Pub. Works Assn. Club: Small Yacht Sailing (Oreg.). Contbr. articles to profl. jours. Home: 12462 SE Winston Rd Boring OR 97009 Office: Water Bur 1900 N Interstate Ave Portland OR 97227

WHITFIELD, VALLIE JO, Realtor, writer, publisher; b. Nashville, Mar. 18, 1922; d. Joseph Edward and Valley (Schiefer) Fox; m. Robert E. Whitfield, Mar. 26, 1943; children—Christa, Robert E. II (dec.), James David, Joanne. A.A., Diablo Valley Coll., 1963; student Belmont Coll., 1940-41, U. Tenn., 1941-43, Rutgers U., 1949-51, Holy Names Coll., 1962. Chem. sci. technician Shell Devel. Co., Emeryville, Calif., 1943-45; operator, trustee Whitfield Farm, Pleasant Hill, Calif., 1952-62; real estate agt. Wells Realty, 1968-71, Pyramid Realty, 1972, J.N. Smith Realty, 1973-77; Realtor, Whitfield Realty, Pleasant Hill, 1978—; author books, including: Virginia History and Whitfield Biographies, 1976; History of Pleasant Hill, California, 1981; pub. Whitfield Books, Pleasant Hill, 1977—. Sec., Friends of Library, Pleasant Hill, 1982; regional v.p. Conf. Calif. Hist. Socs., 1982; rep. Pleasant Hill Community Action Network, 1982. Recipient cert. appreciation City of Pleasant Hill, 1976, 78. Mem. Nat. Assn. Realtors, Calif. Realtors Assn. Democrat. Roman Catholic. Home: 1841 Pleasant Hill Rd Pleasant Hill CA 94523

WHITLEY, MICHAEL PAUL, social service administrator; b. Tacoma, Wash., Nov. 15, 1944; s. Zerman Glynn and Ann Mary (Marko) W. B.A. in Sociology, St. Martin's Coll., 1967; M.A. in Sociology, Cath. U. Am., 1972, Ph.D. in Sociology, 1977. Instr. to asst. prof. sociology and community services St. Martin's Coll., Lacey, Wash., 1971-78, head behavioral sci. area, 1977-78; assoc. prof. sociology and youth in soc. Sterling (Kans.) Coll., 1978-79; evaluation research project dir. Statewide Alcohol Treatment Programs, Marymount Coll. and Kans. Dept. Social and Health Services, Salinas, 1980; dir. Cath. Community Services In-Home Maintenance Program, Seattle, 1980—, legislative forum coordinator King County. Sec., treas. Wash. State Coalition Chore Service Dirs./Mgrs.; mem. Sr. Citizens Communications Network King County, Social Services Outreach Com., Downtown Human Services Council. Mem. Am. Sociol. Assn., Pi Gamma Mu, Alpha Kappa Delta. Contbr. articles to profl. publs. Office: PO Box 22043 1715 E Cherry St Seattle WA 98122

WHITLEY, WALKER, consultant; b. Evanston, Ill., June 7, 1927; s. William Richard and Margaret Lillian (Sullivan) W.; m. Nancy Ann Brickbauer, Nov. 16, 1957; children—William Walker, Virginia Lyn. B.A., Grinnell Coll., 1950; postgrad. Northwestern U., 1958-59. Appraiser, asst. br. mgr. Cadillac Motor Car div. Gen. Motors Corp., Evanston, Ill., 1950-53; investment banker, statistician Betts, Borland & Co., Chgo., 1953-58; auto fin. and wholesale credit mgr. Southeastern U.S. Gen. Fin. Corp., Evanston, 1958-59; instl. bond salesman, govt. bond trader N.Y. Hanseatic Corp., Chgo., 1959-63; recognition rep. O. C. Tanner Co., Chgo., 1963-65; regional rep. L. G. Balfour Co., Mpls., 1966-76; cons. Walker Whitley Co., Scottsdale, Ariz., 1976—. Mem. Edina Sch. Dist. Citizens Adv. Task Force, 1975-77. Served with USNR, PTO, 1945-46. Mem. Nat. Assn. Securities Dealers. Club: Rotary (chmn. community projects com.). Home and Office: 5943 N 83d St Scottsdale AZ 85253

WHITMAN, DAVID LYNN, educator; b. Torrington, Wyo., Nov. 10, 1952; s. Donald Ray and Patricia Ann (Wilson) W.; m. Ellen Marie Griffith, Dec. 19, 1971; children—Andrea, Angela, Ashlee. B.S. in Elec. Engring., U. Wyo., 1975, Ph.D. in Mineral Engring., 1978. Registered profl. engr., Wyo. Vice pres. research and devel. World Energy, Inc., Laramie, Wyo., 1978—; asst. prof. petroleum engring. U. Wyo., Laramie, 1981—. No. Natural Gas fellow, 1975. Mem. Nat. Soc. Profl. Engrs., Sigma Xi, Phi Kappa Phi, Tau Beta Pi, Sigma Tau, Pi Epsilon Tau. Republican. Methodist. Contbr. articles to profl. jours. Home: 1666 N 23d St Laramie WY 82070 Office: PO Box 3295 University Station Laramie WY 82071

WHITNELL, DOUGLAS JEROME, engring. co. exec.; b. Flagstaff, Ariz., Oct. 21, 1935; s. Jerome Douglas and Ethel (Cardon) W.; B.S. in Elec. Engring., U. Ariz., 1958; children—Jerome, Robert, Patrick. Engr., Vitro Labs., Silver Spring, Md., 1960-62; project engr., test dir. Hughes Aircraft Co., Fullerton, Calif., 1962-67; sr. engr. Librascope, Glendale, Calif., 1968-69; electronics engr., project mgr. ARINC Research Co., Honolulu, 1971-73, San Diego, 1973-74; site adminstr., support br. mgr. PRC Tech. Applications, San Diego, 1974-79; logistics group supr. PRC Ridgecrest (Calif.) Engring. Co., 1979-83; cons. specialist COMAKCO, Inc., Ridgecrest, Calif., 1983—. Dist. vice chmn. United Republicans. Calif., 1964-66; asso. mem. Calif. Republican Central Com., 1966-67; senator Jr. Chamber Internat., 1969—. Served with U.S. Army, 1958-60. Named to Outstanding Young Men Am., U.S. Jaycees, 1970. Mem. IEEE, U.S. Naval Inst., Soc. Logistics Engrs., Am. Soc. Naval Engrs., Marine Tech. Soc., Am. Def. Preparedness Assn., Scabbard and Blade, Sigma Pi Sigma. Home: 424 N Warner Ridgecrest CA 93555 Office: 1417 B N Norma St Ridgecrest CA 93555

WHITNEY, ARTHUR SHELDON, agronomist; b. Oberlin, Ohio, Oct. 31, 1933; s. Arthur Emerson and Lois Deborah (Brown) W.; m. Mildred Ellen Mark, Aug. 1, 1964; children—Lois Leinani, Mark Kealoha. B.S., Ohio State U., 1955; M.S., Cornell U., 1958; Ph.D., U. Hawaii, 1966. Research asst. Cornell U., 1956-57; research instr. U. Philippines, Los Banos, 1960; East-West Ctr. scholar U. Hawaii, Honolulu, 1961-64; asst. agronomist U. Hawaii, Kula, 1965-71, assoc. agrnomist, 1971-76, agronomist, 1976—. Mem. Am. Soc. Agronomy, Crop Sci. Soc., Tropical Grassland Soc. of Australia. Contbr. articles to profl. jours. Office: PO Box 269 Kula HI 96790

WHITNEY, BERNARD, lawyer, accountant; b. Zaltbommel, Netherlands, Dec. 12, 1918; s. Heiman and Julia (Horn) Wolf; came to U.S., 1939, naturalized, 1944; student U. So. Calif., 1951-58, U. Calif., Los Angeles, 1942-44; J.D., Southwestern U., Los Angeles, 1947-51; m. Isolde Abas, Sept. 2, 1948; children—Cassandra, Carina. Admitted to Calif. bar, 1952; individual practice law; pvt. practice accounting; pres. Am. Land Program, Inc., Los Angeles, 1977-81, U.S. Shopping Centers, Inc., Los Angeles, 1978—, Intercontinental Investment Corp., Los Angeles, 1978—. Bd. dirs. Southwestern U., 1949-51. C.P.A., Calif. Mem. Coll. Measurement in Mgmt. (co—founder 1954), Los Angeles C.P.A. Soc., Los Angeles Realty Bd., Assn. Attys.—C.P.A.'s, Am. Math. Assn., Internat. Real Estate Fedn. Contbr. articles to accounting and mathematics jours. Office: 10850 Wilshire Blvd Suite 750 Los Angeles CA 90024

WHITNEY, EDWIN KENNETH, accountant; b. Louisville, Dec. 9, 1929; s. Edwin O. and Lotte Mae (Roberts) W.; m. Charlotte Geneva Silcox, June 8, 1931; children—Leah, Leisa, Bryan, Bradley, Erin. B.S., U. Louisville, 1951, LL.B., 1953. C.P.A., Ky. Bar: Ky. Acct., Ernst & Whitney, Charleston, W.Va., 1956-58; supr. internal audit, then asst. controller fibers div. Celanese Corp., N.Y.C., 1959-68; sr. ptnr. Anderson & Whitney, C.P.A.s, Greeley, Colo., 1968—; lectr. U. No. Colo., 1970-79. Pres., Greeley Philharmonic Soc., 1979, United Way Weld County, 1983; chmn. fin. U. No. Colo. Found., 1982. Served with U.S. Army, 1954-56; Korea. Mem. ABA (past chmn. agrl. sect. sub-com.), Am. Inst. C.P.A.s. Greeley C. of C. (pres. 1977-78). Democrat. Wesleyan. Lodges: Rotary, Masons. Contbr. articles to profl. jours. Office: 760 Greeley National Plaza Greeley CO 80631

WHITNEY, LEE ADRIAN, III, constrn. co. exec.; b. Darien, Conn., June 30, 1946; s. Lee Adrian II and Agnes Emma (Littlejohn) W.; student Colo. U., 1965-66, York Coll., Pa., 1969; m. Jeanne Susan Gillespie, Apr. 5, 1968; children—Jack, Katherine, Susan. Prodn. mgr. Cyro Flo Corp., Boulder, Colo., 1964-66; v.p. Chillers, Inc., Scotch Plains, N.J., 1966-68; plant mgr. Packless Metal Hose, Inc., York, Pa., 1969-70; v.p. Delta Engring. & Devel., Boulder, 1970-71; builder, Boulder, 1972-75; pres. Structures Co., Inc., Rifle, Colo., 1975—; dir. Mercury Molding Co., Structures Co., Inc.; designer solar heated and cooled office bldg., 1981. Mem. Nat. Assn. Home Builders, Colo. Assn. Housing and Bldg., N.W. Colo. Three Rivers home builders assns. Republican. Research on liquid base rotational molding machine. Home: 0413 Road 250 New Castle CO 81647 Office: PO Box 908 Rifle CO 81650

WHITNEY, MYRNA-LYNNE, system safety engineer; b. Montreal, Que., Can., May 27, 1942; came to U.S., 1949, naturalized, 1962; d. Edmund W. and Florence S. (Richardson) Prasloski; B.A. magna cum laude, Calif. State U.-Northridge, 1971; M.S., Central Mo. State U., 1975; m. Richard A. Whitney, Jan. 2, 1977. Sec., Rockwell Internat., Canoga Park, Calif., 1962-69, methods and procedures analyst, 1976-77, environ. health and safety engr., 1977-79, system safety engr., 1979—, developer missile support plan, 1981—. Served with USAF, 1971-74; maj. Res., 1975—. Recipient Meritorious Service medal USAF, 1974. Mem. Am. Soc. Safety Engrs., System Safety Soc., Phi Kappa Phi. Office: Rocketdyne 6633 Canoga Ave Canoga Park CA 91304

WHITNEY, STEPHEN LOUIS, librarian; b. Chgo., July 18, 1943; s. Walter Robert and Emma Agnes (Whitney) m. Gloria Jean Lujan, June 5, 1965; children—Laura Ann, Stephen Christopher, Mark Andrew. A.B., Rockhurst Coll., 1965; M.S.L.S., Case Western Res. U., 1966. Adult services librarian St. Louis Pub. Library, 1966-67; coordinator Mcpl. Library Coop. of St. Louis County, Kirkwood, Mo., 1967-70; adminstrv. asst. to the dir., St. Louis County Library, Ladue, Mo., 1970-74; county librarian Broward County Library, Ft. Lauderdale, Fla., 1974-76; city librarian San Bernardino (Calif.) Pub. Library, 1977—. Librarian, San Bernadino City Hist. Soc., 1978—; pres. Am. Lung Assn., 1982—. Mem. ALA, Calif. Library Assn., So. Calif. Library Film Circuit. Club: Rotary. Contbr. articles to profl. jours. Office: San Bernardino Pub Library 401 N Arrowhead Ave San Bernardino CA 92401

WHITSEL, RICHARD HARRY, biologist; b. Denver, Feb. 23, 1931; s. Richard Elstun and Edith Muriel (Harry) W.; B.A., U. Calif., Berkeley, 1954; M.A., San Jose State Coll., 1962; m. Joanne Elissa Cox, June 26, 1982; 1 son, Russell David; children by previous marriage—Robert Alan, Michael Dale, Steven Deane. Sr. research biologist San Mateo County Mosquito Abatement Dist., Burlingame, Calif., 1959-72; environ. program mgr., chief of planning Calif. Regional Water Quality Control Bd., Oakland, 1972—. Served with Med. Service Corps, U.S. Army, 1954-56. Mem. Entomol. Soc. Am., Entomol. Soc. Wash., Am. Mosquito Control Assn., Calif. Alumni Assn., Sierra Club. Democrat. Episcopalian. Contbr. articles to profl. jours. Home: 4331 Blenheim Way Concord CA 94521 Office: 1111 Jackson St Oakland CA 94607

WHITSON, NANCY LEE MILLER, sch. adminstr.; b. Columbia City, Ind., Oct. 7, 1936; d. DeLoss Herbert and Mary Elizabeth (Willits) Miller; B.S. in Edn., Ind. U., 1958; M.S. in Edn., Seattle Pacific U., 1974; postgrad. Ind. U., U. Idaho, Central Wash. U., Seattle Pacific U., UCLA, 1959—; m. Leslie B. Whitson, Oct. 7, 1971; stepchildren—Rick, Gregory, Gary; children by previous marriage—Robert, Timothy. Elem. tchr., Calif., Ind., Idaho and Wash., 1958-66, 71-76; dist. reading coordinator, Snoqualmie, Wash., 1968-71; elem. sch. prin., Snohomish, Wash., 1976-78, adminstrv. asst. curriculum and instrn., 1978-81, elem. sch. prin., 1981—; nat. reading cons. Economy Co. Ednl. Pubs., 1963-70, 75-76; adj. prof. reading and instrnl. improvement colls. and univs.,

1964—; adminstrv. asst. for curriculum and instrn. Snohomish Sch. Dist., 1978-81; cons. reading improvement and cons. programs for improvement of instructional skills of tchrs., supervisory skills of adminstrs., classroom mgmt. skills of tchrs. and learning styles, 1964—. Mem. Wash. Assn. Sch. Adminstrs., Nat. Assn. Elem. Sch. Prins., Assn. Wash. Sch. Prins., Snohomish County Prins. Assn., Snohomish Prins. Assn., Assn. Supervision and Curriculum Devel., Wash. Assn. Supervision and Curriculum Devel. (Educator of Yr. 1979), Internat. Reading Assn., Wash. Orgn. Reading Devel., Nat. Staff Devel. Council, Nat. Council Tchrs. of English. Republican. Mormon. Home: 14202 92d St SE Snohomish WA 98290 Office: 1103 Pine St Snohomish WA 98290

WHITSON, (PETER WHITSON WARREN), artist, educator; b. Concord, Mass., Sept. 7, 1941; s. Richard and Dorothy Esther (Brown) Warren; m. Dawn Lee Cannon, Apr. 23, 1975; 1 son, Jonathan Mark Whitson. B.A., U. N.H., 1963; M.A., U. Iowa, 1967, M.F.A., 1967. Grad. teaching asst. U. Iowa, 1965-67; instr. art Eastern Mont. Coll., 1967-69, asst. prof. art, 1969-77, assoc. prof. art, 1977-82, prof. art, 1982—; one-man shows: U. Iowa, 1965, 67, U. Buffalo, 1970, Scalping Gallery, Regina, Sask., Can., 1975, Eastern Mont. Coll., 1979, Yellowstone Art Center, Billings, Mont., 1980, Billings Clinic, 1980; group shows: Eastern Mont. Coll., 1969, 1973, 81, Colby Coll., New London, N.H., 1974, SUNY-Fredonia, 1975, U. N.H., 1981, Sheridan (Wyo.) Coll., also exhbns. in Poland, Brazil, France, Eng., New Zealand, Australia, Uruguay, Italy, Netherlands, Sweden, Argentina, Japan, East Germany, West Germany, Belgium, Spain, Mexico, South Africa, Yugoslavia, Peru, others. Recipient numerous art awards. Mem. Mont. Miniature Art Soc., Yellowstone Art Center, Nat. Acad. Conceptualists, Academie Neodada, others. Author: (poems and drawings) Al's Ham-'n'-Egger & Body Shop Again, 1974; The SLUJ Book, 1976; contbr. numerous articles to various publs. Office: Dept Art Eastern Mont Coll Billings MT 59101

WHITTAM, JAMES HENRY, business executive; b. N.Y.C., Apr. 23, 1949; s. Henry James and Barbara Pauline (Kipker) W.; B.Chem. Engring. CCNY, 1972; Ph.D., City U. N.Y., 1975; M.B.A., Boston U., 1978; m. Sybille Josette Rosano, Nov. 25, 1980. Cons., Gen. Foods Corp., White Plains, N.Y., 1972-75; sr. research scientist Gillette Co., Boston, 1975-78; dir. research Shaklee Corp., San Francisco, 1978—. Mem. sports medicine council U.S. Olympic Ski Team, 1981. Mem. Am. Coll. Sports Medicine, Am. Chem. Soc., Inst. Food Tech., Soc. Cosmetic Chemists, Am. Oil Chemists Soc., Am. Inst. Chem. Engrs., Sigma Xi, Tau Beta Pi. Mem. adv. bd. Cosmetic Technology, 1978—; editor text: Cosmetic Safety, 1984; Nutritional Determinants in Athletic Performance. Office: 959 Shoreline Dr San Mateo CA 94404

WHITTEMORE, CHRISTINE CHENAULT, hospital administrator; b. LaGrande, Oreg., Feb. 2, 1953; d. Donald L. and Mildred E. (Hadden) Chenault; m. Stephen Roy Whittemore, Oct. 11, 1975. B.A., Eastern Oreg. State Coll., 1975. Unemployment ins. aide Oreg. State Employment Div., 1971-75, claims adjuster, 1975-79; dir. personnel Grande Ronde Hosp., La Grande, 1979—. Mem. State of Oreg. Fair Dismissal Appeals Bd., 1982—; chmn. Union County March of Dimes, 1982—; trustee Eastern Oreg. State Coll., 1983—; mem. Grande Ronde Symphony. Mem. Am. Soc. Hosp. Personnel Adminstrn., Oreg. Soc. Hosp. Personnel Adminstrn. Republican. Presbyterian. Office: 900 Sunset Dr La Grande OR 97850

WHITTIER, EDWARD JAMES, insurance company executive; b. Superior, Wis., Aug. 12, 1928; s. Edward Joseph and Ann Marie (Haglund) W.; m. Marilyn Diane Grodwell, June 27, 1959; children—Michael James, Mary Diane. B.S. with honors, U. Wis.-Superior, 1952. Chartered Life Underwriter. With Pacific Mutual Life Ins. Co., Los Angeles and Newport Beach, Calif., 1954—, asst. v.p. agency adminstrn., 1969, 2d v.p., 1967-69, 2d v.p. individual adminstrn., 1969-70, v.p. mgmt. devel., 1971-80, v.p. group MET ops., Newport Beach, Calif., 1980—, pres. PM Mgmt. Services Co. subs. Pacific Mutual, Newport Beach, 1980—. Served with U.S. Army, 1946-48. Fellow Life Office Mgmt. Assn. Club: Balboa Bay. Home: 1301 Seacrest Dr PO Box 7010 Newport Beach CA 92660

WHITTIER, JAMES LEROY, psychologist; b. Portland, Oreg., Sept. 15, 1938; s. Charles Wilton and Dorothy Matilda (Morgan) W. B.A., Whitman Coll., 1960; M.A. with honors, U. Oreg., 1963, Ph.D., 1966; postgrad. Pendle Hill, Wallingford, Pa., 1969-70. lic. psychologist, Wash. Psychology trainee VA Hosp., Palo Alto, Calif., 1962-63; intern in psychology Modesto (Calif.) State Hosp., 1966-67; staff psychologist VA Hosp., Roseburg, Oreg., 1967-69; vol. Counselor White Bird Clinic, Eugene, Oreg., 197; participant Stillpoint Found. Meditation Center, 1971, Mountain Grove, Glendale, Oreg., 1972; clin. psychologist Baker County Mental Health Clinic, Baker, Oreg., 1973; psychologist II, Eastern Oreg. Hosp. and Tng. Center, Pendleton, 1973-80; trainee Inst. for Movement Therapy, Seattle, 1980—; pvt. practice clin. psychology, Seattle, 1981—; tchr. creative dance/movement Blue Mountain Community Coll., Pendleton, 1980. Mem. Am. Psychol. Assn., Western Psychol. Assn., Wash. State Psychol. Assn., N.W. Family Tng. Inst., Oreg. Psychol. Assn., Sigma Xi. Quaker. Contbr. articles to profl. jours. Home and Office: 7705 22d Ave NE Seattle WA 98115 Office: Inst Movement Therapy 1607 13th Ave Seattle WA 98122

WHITTINGTON, MARGARET ANN, business executive; b. Radford, Va., Aug. 3, 1948; d. David Kelsey and Margaret Ann (Kerns) W.; m. Edward Albert Wagner, Jr., Feb. 14, 1977. Student Blackburn Coll., 1967-68, Community Coll. Allegheny County, Pitts., 1971-72. Student employment coordinator Carneige Mellon U., Pitts., 1975-77; admissions asst. Calif. Inst. Arts, Valencia, 1977-80; adminstrv. mgr. G.W. Smith & Assocs., Inc., Valencia, 1980-82; v.p. U.S. Fin. Cons., Inc., Valencia, 1983—. Trustee, Calif. Inst. Arts, 1978-80. Mem. Career Women's Network (2d v.p. 1983-84), NOW. Office: 23929 W Valencia Blvd #205 Valencia CA 91355

WHITTINGTON, ROBERT BRUCE, foundation exec.; b. Oakland, Calif., Mar. 5, 1927; s. Edward and Loretta (Edalgo) W.; student Stockton Jr. Coll., 1946-48; B.A. in Journalism and Polit. Sci. (Friend W. Richardson fellow), U. Calif., Berkeley, 1950; m. Marie D. Sanguinetti, June 18, 1950; children—Mark, Lynn. Reporter, Stockton (Calif.) Record, 1950-60, exec. news editor, 1965-68, asso. pub., 1968-69, pub., 1969-72; v.p. Speidel Newspapers, Reno, 1972-77; pres. Speidel Newspapers, 1977-82, Gannett West Newspaper Group, 1978-82; pub. Reno Newspapers, 1980-82; dir. Gannett Co., Inc., Rochester, N.Y., 1977-82; v.p., trustee Gannett Found., 1982—; juror Pulitzer Prize, 1977; pres. Speidel Newspapers Charitable Found., 1977. Bd. dirs. United Way of No. Nev., 1977-82. Served with USN, 1944-46; PTO. Roman Catholic. Home: 2000 Del Rio Ln Reno NV 89509 Office: 350 S Center St Reno NV 89501

WHYTE, NORMAN JAMES, civil engr.; b. Denver, Feb. 2, 1917; s. Paul and Elizabeth (Milne) W.; B.S., Colo. U., 1942; M.S., Calif. State U. at Long Beach, 1969; m. Elizabeth Clarissa Schwaebe, Mar. 6, 1942; children—Betty Jo, Susan Ann. Jr. engr. Colo. Fuel & Iron Corp., Pueblo, 1942-43; detail engr. Boeing Aircraft Co., Seattle, 1943-45; reinforced concrete designer Stearns-Roger Mfg. Co., Colorado Springs, Colo., 1945; civil engr., outlet works sect., earth dam design div., chief engrs. office Bur. Reclamation, Denver, 1945-47, supervisory constrn. mgmt. engr. Trenton Dam project (Nebr.), 1947-54, supervisory civil engr., chief of engring. div., Ainsworth (Neb.) planning office, 1954-55, supervisory civil engr., head civil engring. br., pub. works dept. Pearl Harbor Naval Shipyard, Oahu, Hawaii, 1956-58; supervisory civil engr., dir. maintenance control div., pub. works dept. Long Beach Naval Shipyard, 1958-65, Long Beach Naval Base, 1965-73; civil engr. William F. Lever & Assos., cons. engrs., Long Beach, 1974-75; civil engr. dept. bldg. and safety City of Long Beach, 1975-76, sr. civil engr. environ. engring. dept., 1977-80; engring. cons., 1981—; instr. port engring. mgmt. and urban engring., Calif. State U. at Long Beach, 1974—. Guest lectr. Calif. State U. at Long Beach, 1969, 71. Bd. dirs. Wardlow Park Improvement Assn., Long Beach, 1969, 70. Served with USAAF, 1946-47. Registered profl. engr., Colo., Hawaii, Calif. Mem. Nat., Calif. (state dir. 1965-66, chpt. pres. 1964-65) socs. profl. engrs., ASCE, Shipyard Engrs. and Architects Assn. (dir. 1965, 68, 69; pres. 1964), Phi Kappa Phi. Elk. Home and office: 3437 Montair Ave Long Beach CA 90808

WIBORG, JAMES HOOKER, corporate executive; b. Seattle, Aug. 26, 1924; s. John R. and Hazel (Hooker) W.; B.A., U. Wash., 1946; m. Ann Rogers, July 1948; children—Katherine Ann, Mary Ellen, Caroline Joan, John Stewart. Owner Wiborg Mfg. Co., Tacoma, 1946-50; securities analyst Pacific N.W. Co., Seattle, 1950-53; founder Western Plastics Corp., Tacoma, 1953, pres., 1935-55, chmn. bd., dir., ret.; exec. v.p. Wash. Steel Products Co., Tacoma, 1955-58; mgmt. cons., Tacoma, 1958-60; v.p. United Pacific Corp., Seattle, 1960; pres. Pacific Small Bus. Investment Corp., Seattle, 1961-63; sr. v.p. indsl. div. United Pacific Corp., Seattle, 1963-65, pres., chief exec. officer, dir., 1965; pres., chief exec. officer, dir. Univar Corp. (formerly VWR United Corp.), Seattle, 1966—; dir. Seattle, Seafirst Corp., PACCAR Inc., Seattle-First Nat. Bank, Gensco Inc., Tacoma, Westin Hotel Co., Seattle, Northern Life Ins. Co., Seattle. Trustee U. Puget Sound. Clubs: Tacoma Country and Golf, Tacoma, Tacoma Yacht; Rainier, Harbor (Seattle). Home: 6608 N 46th St Tacoma WA 98407 Office: Norton Bldg Seattle WA 98104

WICHERS, DONNA LYNN, environmental engineer, consultant; b. Ada., Okla., Aug. 23, 1953; d. Donald Austin and Mary Nell (Coffee) Ledford; B.S. with honors, U. Wyo. 1975, M.S., 1978; m. William Frank Wichers, Aug. 14, 1976. Environ. engr. Wyo. Mineral Corp., Buffalo, 1978-79, sr. environ. projects engr., 1979-80, mgr. licensing and environ. projects, Buffalo, Wyo., 1980-82; ind. environ. cons., 1982—. U. Wyo. grad. research fellow, 1977; Office Water Research and Tech., State Engr.'s Office and Wyo. Game and Fish Dept. grantee, 1977. Mem. Am. Fisherics Soc., Am. Inst. Mining Engrs., Sigma Xi, Phi Kappa Phi, Alpha Zeta, Gamma Sigma Delta. Republican. Home: PO Box 837 Buffalo WY 82834

WICHMAN, HERMAN LEE, III, lawyer, financial consultant; b. St. Louis, July 3, 1919; s. Herman Lee and Pearl (Wilson) W.; m. Betty Morse, Oct. 16, 1961 (div. 1982); children by previous marriage—Dwight Lloyd, Susan. B.S. in Bus. Adminstrn., Washington U., St. Louis, 1942, M.B.A., 1943, LL.B., 1942, J.D., 1945. Bar: Mo. 1941. Assoc. Buder & Buder, St. Louis, 1941-42; with McDonnell-Douglas Co., St. Louis, 1942-52, asst. sec., 1946-51, sec., 1951-52, v.p., gen. counsel, 1949-52; corp. fin. cons., Dallas, 1952-56; founder, pres. Wickfield, Inc., Dallas, 1956-59; founder, dir., chmn. bd. Union Fin. Corp. (name now Transohio Co.), Cleve., 1959-62; founder, exec. v.p., chmn. exec. com. Republic Nat. Corp., Cleve., 1962-65; pres. Wichman Assocs., Inc., corp. fin. cons., San Francisco, Los Angeles and Indian Wells, Calif., 1965—; dir. Platt-LePage Aircraft Corp., Phila., Rotary Research Corp., Phila.; chmn. legal com. Aerospace Industries, Washington. Vice chmn. campaign ARC, St. Louis, 1950, chmn., 1951; chmn. Greater Bay area Washington U. Alumni Council, San Francisco, 1967-68, chmn. fund campaign, 1968; chmn. bd. trustees Calvary Presbyn. Ch., San Francisco. Mem. ABA, Mo. Bar, St. Louis Bar Assn. (chmn. ethics com. 1940-50), Tex. Bar Assn., Dallas Bar Assn., Phi Delta Phi, Sigma Nu. Republican. Clubs: Olympic, Eldorado Country. Home: 77-670 Cherokee Rd Indian Wells CA 92260 Office: 2035 Westwood Blvd Los Angeles CA 90025

WICHT, SCOTT FRANKLIN, mechanical engineer; b. San Rafael, Calif., June 26, 1957; s. Laffayette Alfred and Ruth (Eslinger) W. Student U. Calif.-Santa Barbara, 1975-76; B.S.M.E., Calif. Poly. State U., San Luis Obispo, 1979; M.S.E.M., Stanford U., 1982. With Pacific Gas & Electric Co., San Ramon, Calif., summer 1978; mech. engr. Hewlett-Packard, Santa Rosa, Calif., 1979—. Mem. ASME, Phi Kappa Phi, Tau Beta Pi.

WICK, JOHN ARTHUR, communications system engr.; b. Lincoln, Nebr., Sept. 14, 1942; s. Loren Adair and Mildred Marie W.; B.S.E.E. with high distinction, U. Nebr., 1965, M.S.E.E., 1966; Ph.D. in Elec. Engring., U. Wis., Madison, 1972; m. Gail Ellen Olson, Aug. 24, 1968; children—Christopher J., Matthew J. Engr., Collins Radio Co., Cedar Rapids, Iowa, 1964-70, Calspan Corp., Cornell Aero. Lab., Buffalo, 1972-74; leader Transmission Systems Test Group, MITRE Corp., Bedford, Mass., 1974-78, Ft. Huachuca, Ariz., 1978—. Mem. Am. Radio Relay League, Assn. Old Crows, Sigma Xi. Home: 1033 El Camino Real Sierra Vista AZ 85635 Office: Mitre Corp Drawer S Fort Huachuca AZ 85613

WICKE, DALLAS CLYDE, aerospace engineer; b. Atwood, Kans., Nov. 18, 1940; s. Ernest William and Edith (Wimer) W. B.S. in Aerospace Engring., U. Kans., 1962; M.S. in Aerospace Engring., U. So. Calif., 1968. Assoc. engr. McDonnell Douglas Corp., Huntington Beach, Calif., 1962-66, engr., 1966-67, engr. specialist, 1967-72, sr. engr., 1972-73, supr., 1973-75, sect. chief, 1975—. Mem. AIAA (adv. bd., sect. tech. com. for guidance, navigation, dynamics and control), U. Kans. Alumni Assn., U.S. Ski Assn. Republican. Contbr. articles to profl. jours. Home: 6877 Danvers Dr Garden Grove CA 92645 Office: 5301 Bolsa Ave Huntington Beach CA 92647

WICKLUND, LEE ARTHUR, school administrator; b. Ft. Atkinson, Wis., Aug. 10, 1938; s. Verner F. and Ellen V. (Anderson); m. Georganne Emilie Trumbull, June 27, 1964; children—Eric Trumbull, Lance Frederick. B.Ed., Chgo. State U., 1961; M.Ed., Loyola U., Chgo., 1964; Ed.D., U. Oreg., 1969. Elem., secondary and adult edn. tchr., asst. prin. Chgo. Bd. Edn., 1961-67; research asst. U. Oreg., 1967-69; dir. Lab. Sch., asst. prof. edn. Idaho State U., 1969-71; research and devel. specialist Northwest Regional Educational Lab., Portland, Oreg., 1971-72; assoc. prof. ednl. adminstrn. U. Wis., Superior, 1972-75; dir. curriculum and instruction North Bend Sch. Dist. 13, Oreg., 1975—; chmn. Oreg. State Textbook Commn. 1979—. Bd. dirs. Salvation Army, Music Enrichment Assn.; mem. exec. com., past sec. United Way of Coos County; v.p. Bay Area Christian Businessmen; mem. Lutheran Commn. Continuing Edn. in Northwest. Sr. fellow Kettering Found.; presenter Nat. Acad. Sch. Execs., Am. Assn. Sch. Adminstrs. Mem. Am. Assn. Sch. Adminstrs., Assn. Supervision and Curriculum Devel., Am. Ednl. Research Assn., Council for Basic Edn., Nat. Soc. Study Edn., Council Educational Facility Planners Internat., Confederation Oreg. Sch. Adminstrs., Oreg. Assn. Sch. Execs. (dir.), Oreg. Assn. Supervision and Curriculum Devel. Lutheran. Lodges: North Bend Kiwanis, Coquille Valley Elks. Co-author/author numerous mgmt. studies, funded proposals. Home: 206 Hillcrest Dr North Bend OR 97459 Office: North Bend School District 1313 Airport Ln North Bend OR 97459

WICKMAN, PAUL EVERETT, public relations executive; b. Bisbee, Ariz., Aug. 21, 1912; s. Julius and Hilda Wilhelmina (Soderholm) W.; student La Sierra Coll., Arlington, Calif., 1928-30, Pacific Union Coll., Angwin, Cal., 1931-32; spl. student Am. U., 1946; m. Evelyn Gorman, Nov. 22, 1969; children by previous marriage—Robert Bruce, Bette Jane, Marilyn Faye. Internat. traveler, lectr., writer, 1937-44; assoc. sec Internat. Religious Liberty Assn., 1944-46; travel lectr. Nat. Lecture Bur., 1944-55; exec. sec., dir. internat. radio and TV prodns. Voice of Prophecy Corp., Faith for Today Corp., 1946-53; v.p. Western Advt. Agy., Los Angeles, 1953-55; dir. devel. Nat. Soc. Crippled Children and Adults, Inc., Chgo., 1955-56; exec. v.p. Pub. Relations Soc. Am., Inc., N.Y.C., 1956-57; dir. corp. pub. relations Schering Corps., Bloomfield, N.J., 1957-83; pres. Wickman Pharm. Co., Inc., Calif.; mem. adv. bd. Eldorado Bank, Tustin, Calif. Past mem. Newport Beach CSC; bd. dirs. U. Calif. at Irvine Found., also mem. Chancellor's Club. Mem. Newcomen Soc., Pub. Relations Soc. Am. (accredited), Am., Calif. pharm. assns., Am. Hosp. Assn. Clubs: Masons (32 deg.), Shriners (pres. El Bandito 1982), Jesters; Swedish (past pres.) (Los Angeles); Kiwanis (past pres.), Irvine Coast Country (Newport Beach, Calif.); Vikings; 552 Hoag Hospital; Balboa Bay. Home: 28 Point Loma Dr Corona Del Mar CA 92625 Office: 14451 Franklin Ave Tustin CA 92680

WICKSTROM, BILL WARREN, mine and mill safety training supervisor, b. Riverton, Wyo., Sept. 17, 1949; s. Lee Worth and Emma Edith (Krone) W.; m. Christine Elizabeth Peterson, Aug. 28, 1971; children—Heather, James, Sara. B.S., U. Wyo., 1972. Asst. mgr. Hudson Oil Co., Laramie, Wyo., 1972-73; laborer J.H. Baxter & Co., Laramie, 1973-74; laborer Continental Oil Co., Frannie, Wyo., 1974-75; chemist Western Nuclear Inc., Jeffrey, Wyo., 1975-76, safety supr., 1976—. Pres. Jeffrey City Vol. Ambulance Service, 1979—. Mem. Am. Soc. Safety Engrs. Lutheran. Home: 822 C St S Box 41 Jeffrey City WY 82310 Office: Box 630 Jeffrey WY 82310

WICKWIRE, PATRICIA JOANNE NELLOR, psychologist, school administrator; b. Sioux City, Iowa; d. William McKinley and Clara Rose (Pautsch) Nellor; m. Robert James Wickwire, Sept. 7, 1957; 1 son, William James. B.A. cum laude, U. No. Iowa, 1951; M.A., U. Iowa, 1959; Ph.D., U. Tex., 1971. Tchr. Ricketts Ind. Schs., Iowa, 1946-48, Waverly-Shell Rock Ind. Schs., Iowa, 1951-55; reading cons., head dormitory counselor U. Iowa, Iowa City, 1955-57; tchr., sch. psychologist, dir. student services and spl. edn. South Bay Union High Sch. Dist., Hermosa Beach, Calif., 1962—; cons. in mgmt. and edn.; chmn. Calif. State U., Dominquez Hills. Exec. bd. Calif. Interagy. Mental Health Council, 1968-72; exec. bd., v.p. Beach Cities Symphony Assn., 1970-82. Mem. Los Angeles County Dirs. Pupil Services (pres. 1974-79), Los Angeles County Adminstrs. Spl. Edn., Los Angeles County Personnel and Guidance Assn., Calif. Personnel and Guidance Assn. (exec. bd. 1977-78), Assn. Calif. Sch. Adminstrs., Calif. Assn. Measurement and Edn. in Guidance (exec. bd.), Calif. Assn. Sch. Psychologists (exec. bd.), Am. Psychol. Assn., Am. Personnel and Guidance Assn., Nat. Assn. Sch. Adminstrs., World Future Soc., Psi Chi, Sigma Alpha Iota, Pi Lambda Theta, Alpha Phi Gamma, Kappa Delta Pi. Author numerous articles in profl. jours. Home: 2900 Amby Pl Hermosa Beach CA 90254

WIDDER, BETTE WIENBERG, nursing adminstr.; b. Lafayette County, Mo., June 20, 1929; d. Elmer Arthur and Lorene Mathilda (Bodenstab) Wienberg; m. John Arthur Widder, July 7, 1953; children—John A., Anne Whiteley, Susan Jane, Scott Kevin. B.S. cum laude, Linfield Coll., 1976. R.N., Oreg., N.Y. Acting supr. U. Mo. Hosps., 1951-52; mem. staff Arlington (Va.) Community Hosp., 1960-61, W. Jefferson Gen. Hosp., Marrero, La., 1965, dispensary 8th Naval Dist., 1965; mem. rehab. staff A. Holly Patterson Home, Uniondale, N.Y., 1969-70; mem. staff St. Vincent Hosp. and Med. Ctr., Portland, Oreg., 1972-78, asst. dir. nursing services, 1978—. Mem. Portland Women's Union, Oreg. Women's Polit. Caucus; leader Girl Scouts U.S.A., Virginia Beach, Va., 1963-64. Mem. AAUW, NOW, SEE Internat., Am. Hosp. Assn., Oreg. Hosp. Assn., Am. Soc. Nurse Adminstrs., Oreg. Soc. Nurse Adminstrs. (legis. com.). Founder, editor St. Vincent Nursing Newsletter. Home: 15095 NW Oakmont Loop Beaverton OR 97006 Office: 9205 SW Barnes Rd Portland OR 97225

WIDELOCK, MARGARET, marketing research executive; b. Hollister, Calif., Sept. 9, 1944; d. Charles James and Alice Leah (Southworth) Hawkins; student U. Pacific, 1962-63, U. Vienna, 1964-65; B.A., York U., 1967, M.A., 1969, student NYU, 1969-72; m. John Foster Widelock, May 10, 1969. Research asst. Inst. Behavioral Research, Toronto, Ont., Can., 1967-68; sr. analyst Asso. Merchandising Corp., N.Y.C., 1968-70; sr. asso. Yankelovich, Skelly & White, N.Y.C., 1971-75; v.p., mng. dir. NOVA Research Group, San Francisco, 1975—; vis. lectr. York U. Mem. standards com. ARC, 1973, water safety tchr., 1970-74. Can. Council fellow, 1969-72; Govt. Ont. Grad. fellow, 1967, 68. Mem. Am. Sociol. Assn., Am. Mktg. Assn., Am. Acad. Polit. and Social Sci. Office: 575 Sutter St San Francisco CA 94102

WIDENER, DON, writer, film producer; b. Holdenville, Okla., Mar. 13, 1930; s. Carl James and Lucile Victoria (Cole) W.; A.A. in Journalism, Compton (Calif.) Coll., 1950; m. Veda Rose Pannell, June 13, 1953; children—Jeffrey, Christopher. Newspaper reporter, editor Herald Pub. Co., Los Angeles, 1954-58; aerospace writer various cos., 1958-64; press relations ofcl., producer, writer NBC-TV, 1964-70; ind. film producer, writer, Calif., 1970—; lectr. in field. Active environ. groups. Founding mem. adv. bd. Calif. Mus. Sci. and Industry. Served with USAF, 1950-53. Recipient Hugo award Chgo. Film Festival, 1967, A.I. duPont-Columbia U. Broadcast Journalism award, 1969, Silver award N.Y. Film Festival, 1969, Broadcast Media award San Francisco State Coll., 1970, Emmy awards Acad. TV Arts and Scis. (3). Methodist. Author: Timetable for Disaster, 1970; N.U.K.E.E., 1974; Lemmon (biography of Jack Lemmon), 1975; (screenplays) Night of the 'Possum, 1978, N.U.K.E.E., 1982, Perks, 1983. Patentee nuclear warning system. Address: PO Box 247 Lake Arrowhead CA 92352

WIDENER, THOMAS ANDREW, JR., research psychologist; b. Los Angeles, Sept. 2, 1935; s. Thomas Andrew and Maudia Lee (James) W.; B.A., UCLA, 1959; M.A., Calif. State U., Los Angeles, 1965; divorced; 1 son, Robert Andrew. Engr., Northrop Corp., 1962-63; sr. engr. Litton Industries, 1963-65; mem. tech. staff TRW Systems, 1965-68; engring. specialist Litton Industries, 1968-70; human factors scientist Lockheed Calif., Co., 1970-72; staff scientist, program mgr. Manned Systems Scis. Co., 1972-74; navy program mgr. E-Tech, Inc., San Diego, 1975-80; mgr. personnel subsystems Aerojet Electro-Systems, Azuza, Calif., 1980—. Served to 1st lt. U.S. Army, 1959-60. Mem. Human Factors Soc. Republican. Home: 17144 Sherman Way Van Nuys CA 91406

WIDMER, ELMER ANDREAS, parasitologist, zoologist; b. Dodge, N.D., Apr. 27, 1925; s. Reinhold A. and Josephine (Ammon) W.; m. Eunice O. Olson, Dec. 25, 1952; children—Andrea Laura Barker, Owen Kristian. B.A. in Biology, Union Coll., 1951; M.A., U. Colo., 1956; Ph.D. in Zoology, U. Colo. State, 1965; M.P.H. in Parasitology, U. N.C., 1974. Sci. instr. DeWitt (N.B.) Coll. High Sch., 1952-53; instr. biology Coll. Arts and Scis., Loma Linda (Calif.) U., La Sierra Campus, 1953-58, asst. prof., 1958-65, assoc. prof., 1965-67, asst. prof. dept. environ. and tropical health Sch. Health, Loma Linda Campus, 1967-68, assoc. prof., 1968-71, prof., 1971—, chmn., 1967-78, interim assoc. dean acad. affairs, 1978-80, assoc. dean, 1980-82; mem. Riverside Environ. Protection Com., 1972-73. La. State U., Sch. Med. fellow, 1966; WHO fellow, 1971. Mem. Am. Inst. Biol. Scis., Nat. Environ. Health Assn., Am. Soc. Parasitologists, Am. Soc. Tropical Med. and Hygiene, Royal Soc. Tropical Med. and Hygiene, So. Calif. Parasitologists, Wildlife Disease Assn., Delta Omega, Phi Sigma, Sigma Xi. Seventh-day Adventist. Contbr. numerous tech. and non-tech. publs. to profl. jours.

WIDMOYER, FRED BIXLER, horticulturist, educator; b. Grandfield, Okla., Nov. 25, 1920; s. Fred B. and Sara D. (Popham) W.; B.A., Tex. Tech. U., 1942, M.S., 1950; Ph.D., Mich. State U., 1954; m. Genevieve Jean Jonas, June 26, 1961; children—Cathryn Jean, Timothy Fred, Ann Louise. Biology asst. Tex. Tech. U., Lubbock, 1940-42, instr. botany, 1946-50; adviser program instr. Philmont Scout Ranch, Cimarron, N.Mex., 1951-53; greenhouse asst. Iowa State U., Ames, 1951-53; asst. prof. Mich. State U., East Lansing, 1954-60; asso. prof. U. Conn., Storrs, 1960-63; prof. horticulture, head dept. N.Mex. State U., Las Cruces, 1963—; prin. horticulturist Dept. Agr., Sci. and Edn. Adminstrn. Co-op Research, Washington, 1977-78; adv. council Nat. Arboretum, 1970-80. Mem. Republican County Central Com., Dona Ana County, Las Cruces, 1975-77; trustee Town of Mesilla; western regional program dir. Nat. Jr. Hort. Assn. Served with USNR, 1942-46; PTO. Fellow Am. Soc. Hort. Sci.; mem. Soc. Am. Florists, Garden Writers Assn., Am. Assn. Bot. Gardens and Arboretums (hon.), Am. Hort. Soc., Nat. Council Therapy Through Horticulture, N.Mex. Landscape Assn., N.Mex. Nursery Industries. Roman Catholic. Contbr. articles on hort. sci. to profl. jours.; author, editor manuals and guides in field. Home: 1387 Snow Rd Las Cruces NM 88005 Office: Box 3530 NMex State Univ Las Cruces NM 88003

WIDNER, JERRI LYNNE, accountant; b. Walla Walla, Wash., Jan. 27, 1949; d. William Warren and Mildred Arlene (Blakely) W. Student Western Wash. State Coll.-Bellingham, 1967-69, Blue Mt. Community Coll., Pendleton, Oreg., 1969; B.S. in Bus. Adminstrn., So. Oreg. Coll., Ashland, 1971; M.B.A., U. Portland, 1977. Acct. Adult Student Housing, Inc., Portland, 1972-74; asst. to treas. UniserviceCorp., Portland, 1974-76; acct. Sleep Unlimited, Inc., Portland, 1976-77; gen. acct. Kaiser Found. Health Plan of Oreg., Portland, 1977-78; fin. dir., city recorder City of Troutdale, Oreg., 1978-81; mgr. acctg. Met. Service Dist., Portland, 1981; fin. services mgr. Multnomah County Rural Fire Protection Dist. 10, Portland, 1982-83; fin. dir. City of Tigard, Oreg., 1983—; instr. Mt. Hood Community Coll., 1979-82. Mem. Nat. Assn. Female Execs., Mcpl. Fin. Officers Assn., Nature Conservancy. Republican. Lutheran. Lodge: Eastern Star. Office: 12755 SW Ash St Tigard OR 97223

WIEBE, LEONARD IRVING, radiopharmacist, educator; b. Swift Current, Sask., Can., Oct. 14, 1941; s. Cornelius C. and Margaret (Teichroeb) W.; B.S.P., U. Sask., 1963, M.Sc., 1966; Ph.D., U. Sydney (Australia), 1970; m. Grace E. McIntyre, Sept. 5, 1964; children—Glenis, Kirsten, Megan. Pharmacist, Swift Current Union Hosp., 1963-64; sessional lectr. U. Sask., 1965-66; asst. prof. U. Alta., 1970-73, prof., 1978—, dir. Slowpoke Reactor Facility, 1975—, research asso. Cross Cancer Inst., 1978—; sessional lectr. U. Sydney, 1973; sec. Internat. Bionucleonics Cons. Ltd., 1975—. Commonwealth Univs. Exchange grantee, 1966; Alexander von Humboldt fellow, 1976-79, 82. Mem. Pharm. Bd. of N.S.W., Sask. Pharm. Assn., Soc. Nuclear Medicine, Assn. Faculties of Pharmacy of Can., Canadian Radiation Protection Assn., Canadian Radio Pharm. Scientists. Editor: Liquid Scintillation: Science and Technology, 1976; guest editor Jour. of Radioanalytical Chemistry, 1981. Office: Univ Alberta Edmonton AB T6G 2N8 Canada

WIEDERHOLT, WIGBERT C., neurologist, educator; b. Germany, Apr. 22, 1931; came to U.S., 1956, naturalized, 1966; m. Carl and Anna-Maria (Hoffmann) W.; student (Med. Sch. scholar), U. Berlin, 1952-53; M.D., U. Freiburg, 1955; M.S., U. Minn., 1965; children—Sven, Karen, Kristin. Intern in Ob-Gyn, Schleswig (W. Ger.) City Hosp., 1955-56; rotating intern Sacred Heart Hosp., Spokane, Wash., 1956-57; resident in medicine Cleve. Clinic, 1957-58, 61-62, U.S. Army Hosp., Frankfurt, W. Ger., 1958-59; resident in neurology Mayo Clinic, Rochester, Minn., 1962-65; asso. prof. medicine, dir. clin. neurophysiology Ohio State U. Med. Sch., Columbus, 1965-72; prof. neuroscis., neurologist-in-chief U. Calif. Med. Sch., San Diego, 1972—, chmn. dept. and group in neuroscis. 1978—; chief neurology VA Hosp., San Diego, 1972-79. Fulbright scholar, 1956-58. Diplomate Am. Bd. Psychiatry and Neurology. Fellow Am. Acad. Neurology (S. Weir Mitchell award 1965); mem. Internat. Brain Research Orgn., Am. Assn. EEG and Electrodiagnosis (sec.-treas. 1971-76, pres. 1977-78), AAAS, Soc. for Neurosci., Am. Neurol. Assn., Am. EGG Soc., Assn. U. Profs. Neurology, Western EEG Soc., Calif. Neurol. Soc., San Diego Neurol. Soc., N.Y. Acad. Scis., AMA, Calif. Med. Assn., San Diego County Med. Soc. Club: La Jolla Tennis. Contbr. numerous articles to med. jours. Home: 6683 La Jolla Scenic Dr La Jolla CA 92037 Office: Dept Neuroscis M-008 Univ Calif at San Diego La Jolla CA 92093

WIEDEWITSCH, LEWIS GRANT, safety administrator; b. Hillsboro, Oreg., Oct. 8, 1947; s. Lloyd Lewis and Viola Evelyn (Schlee) W.; m. Lonamae Tamee Baker, Jan. 23, 1982. B.A. in Chemistry, Linfield Coll., 1971. Chief chemist and safety dir. N.L. Industries, Portland, Oreg., 1971-72; lab. tech. Pennwalt Corp., Portland, 1972-75, plant chemist, 1975-81, safety supr., 1981—. Mem. Newberg Police Res. Served with USAR, 1967—. Mem. Am. Chem. Soc., Am. Soc. Safety Engrs. Republican. Club: Shriners. Home: Rt 3 Box 563 Newberg OR 97132 Office: PO Box 4102 Portland OR 97208

WIEFELS, PAUL HAROLD, computer company executive; b. Los Angeles, Jan. 20, 1954; s. Frank Leonard and Nancy Jean (Allen) W.; B.S., U. So. Calif., 1975, M.B.A., 1977. Assoc. product mgr. Nissan Motor Corp., Gardena, Calif., 1977-79; account exec., Foote, Cone and Belding, Los Angeles, 1979-80; account supr. SSC & B:Lintas, Los Angeles, 1980-81; account supr. Ketchum Communications, San Francisco, 1981-82; mgr. production advt. Apple Computer, Inc., Cupertino, Calif., 1982—; lectr. Calif. State U.-Long Beach. Mem. Los Angeles Advt. Club, Am. Mktg. Assn., Commerce Assocs. U. So. Calif. Office: Apple Computer Inc 20525 Mariani Ave Cupertino CA 95014

WIEGAND, VIRGINIA ANN KEISTER, computer co. exec.; b. Buffalo, July 21, 1928; d. Forest Glen and Bess Katherine (Baughman) Keister; B.A., U. Calif., Berkeley, 1962, M.A., 1966, Ph.D., 1969; m. William Charles Wiegand, Jr., Feb. 20, 1947; children—William, Cort, Ronn, James, Carley, Scott, Wenden. Asso. dir. Jack and Jill Nursery Sch., Walnut Creek, Calif., 1960-62; tchr. Lafayette (Calif.) Sch. Dist., 1963-64; teaching asst. U. Calif., 1965-69, research asst., 1964-69; asst. prof. ednl. psychology Calif. State U., Hayward, 1969-71; research psychologist Stanford Research Inst., Menlo Park, Calif., 1971-75; pvt. practice cons. psychology, Walnut Creek, 1975-77; pres. Wiegand System Design, Walnut Creek, 1977—; instr. computer sci. Diablo Valley Coll., Pleasant Hill, Calif., 1980. Mem. Am. Psychol. Assn., Western Psychol. Assn., Am. Ednl. Research Assn., AAAS, Assn. Computing Machinery. Democrat. Club: Commonwealth. Author: Social Inquiry: An Overview, 1979; contbr. articles to profl. jours.

WIEGLER, BARRY ALLAN, management consulting company executive; b. Newark, June 17, 1938; s. Paul Louis and Marie B. W.; m. Nancy Kathleen Kammerdiener, Jan. 26, 1961; m. 2d Deanna Mae Miller, Mar. 20, 1976; children—Laurie, David, Michael, Lisa, Shera. Student Santa Monica City Coll., 1956-59; B.B.A., Woodbury U., 1965; postgrad. in bus. adminstrn. Calif. State U.-Los Angeles, 1965-67. Cert. jr. coll. tchr., Calif. Asst. v.p. Security Pacific Nat. Bank, Los Angeles, 1961-69; mgr. fin. industry planning Computer div. Gen. Electric Co., Phoenix, 1969-71; dir. research and planning MSI Data Corp., Costa Mesa, Calif., 1971-72; v.p. Gottfried Cons., Inc., San Francisco, 1973-80, Los Angeles, 1980-81, sr. v.p., 1981-82; pres., co-founder Key Cons. Group, Inc., Santa Monica, Calif., 1982—; trustee, chmn. bd.'s EDP steering com., mem. office automation adv. com. Woodbury U.; instr., mem. curriculum adv. com. El Camino Coll., 1965-67. Served with USAFR, 1959-65. Mem. Data Processing Mgmt. Assn. (cert. data processor). Clubs: Warner Center (Woodland Hills, Calif.); Rotary (San Francisco). Office: 2850 Ocean Park Blvd Suite 300 Santa Monica CA 90405

WIELAND, MARY PAULETTE, nurse, nursing educator; b. N.Y.C., July 17, 1950; d. George Barrett and Mary Regina (Hirshka) W. B.S. in Nursing, Hunter-Bellevue Sch. Nursing, N.Y.C., 1972; M.S., U. Hawaii, 1976. Staff nurse Bellevue Hosp., N.Y.C., 1972-74; nurse Camp Seascape, Cape Cod, Mass., 1974; instr. Hawaii Med. Assn. Emergency Med. Services, 1976-78; emergency room/spl. services nurse coordinator Kuakini Med. Ctr., Honolulu, 1979-80, emergency room/critical care clin. nurse specialist, 1980-81; assoc. dir. emergency nursing/critical care U. Oreg., 1981—, asst. prof. nursing, 1981—; instr. basic and advanced cardiac life support. Mem. Am. Nurses Assn., Emergency Dept. Nurses Assn., Am. Assn. Critical Care Nurses, Sigma Theta Tau, Roman Catholic. Contbr. chpts. to books. Home: 7000 SW Vermont Ct Apt 1002 Portland OR 97223 Office: 3181 SW Sam Jackson Park Rd Portland OR 97201

WIEMAN, TERRY LYNN, lawyer; b. Montrose, Colo., Oct. 9, 1951; s. Simon William and Martha Elizabeth W.; m. Diane A. Vondra, May 27, 1982; 1 son, Jason. B.S. cum laude, Wichita State U., 1974; J.D., Washburn U., 1981. Bar: Colo. 1982, U.S. Dist. Ct. Colo. 1982. Propr., Smith & Co. Realty, Inc., Wichita, Kans., 1974-75; job supr. Thousand Oaks Enterprises, Inc., Ltd., Wichita, 1975-79; jr. ptnr. Colo. Law Ctrs. of Falcone and Alexander, Colorado Springs, 1981—. Mem. ABA, Colo. Bar Assn., El Paso County Bar Assn., Delta Theta Phi, Phi Delta Theta. Republican. Methodist.

WIENS, FRANK BERNHARD, engring. co. exec.; b. Hoover, Okla., Sept. 19, 1917; s. Bernhard Edward and Margaret (Jantzen) W.; A.A., Pasadena City Coll., 1960; B.S., UCLA, 1962; m. Ella Toews, Sept. 2, 1950; children—Franklin J., Dennis J., Denise S. Mgr. engring. services Bell & Howell Research, Pasadena, Calif., 1950-67; planetary sci. expt. engr. Martin Marietta, Denver, 1967-75; adminstrv. and fin. v.p. Custom Engring., Englewood, Colo., 1975—, also dir.; dir. Bell & Howell Profit Sharing Retirement Trust, 1967. Recipient citation Def. Atomic Support Agy., 1962. Mem. ASME, Am. Vacuum Soc., Am. Soc. Mass Spectrometry, AAAS. Patentee in field. Home: 2571 S Jersey St Denver CO 80222 Office: 2805 S Tejon St Englewood CO 80110

WIENS, RUTH HELEN, nurse, educator; b. Danbury, Conn., Aug. 9, 1923; d. Ralph Edward and Elizabeth Pauline (Meister) Avery; diploma Lucy Webb Hayes Sch. Nursing, Washington, 1949; B.S. in Nursing, U. Oreg., 1964, M.S. in Nursing Edn., 1965; cert. in community mental health U. Wash., 1979; m. Arthur Nicholai Wiens, June 11, 1949; children—Barbara Ann, Bradley Allen, Donald Avery. Supr., dir. nursing Topeka State Hosp., 1949-53; mem. faculty U. Oreg., Portland, 1963-68, clin. asso. faculty, 1968-72, asst. dean, 1972-75, dean pro-tem, 1975-76, asso. prof. psychiat.-mental health nursing, 1977—; dir. nursing St. Vincent Hosp. and Med. Center, Portland, 1968-72; clin. asso. faculty Portland VA Hosp.; clin. specialist in mental health nursing VA Med. Ctr., Portland, 1982—; cons. William Temple House, Portland. Mem. Am. Nurses Assn., Nat. League Nursing, Western Interstate Commn. Higher Edn. in Nursing, AAUW, Sigma Theta Tau. Home: 74 Condolea Way Lake Oswego OR 97034 Office: Oreg Health Scis Univ 3181 SW S Jackson Park Rd Portland OR 97201

WIERE, ROGER JAMES, psychologist, mental health administr.; b. Hollywood, Calif., June 30, 1943; s. Herbert and Jocelyn McLean (Wion) W.; m. Sandra Jean Atkisson, June 30, 1966; children—Roger Bryan, William Herbert. B.A., San Francisco State Coll., 1966, M.S., 1968; Ph.D., U. Okla., Norman, 1972. Lic. psychologist, Calif. Psychologist El Reno (Okla.) Fed. Reformatory, 1970-72; psychologist Regional Community Treatment Ctr., 1972-73; dir. Paseo (Okla.), Ctr., 1973-74; chief office of forensic services Calif. Dept. Mental Health Sacramento, 1979-80; chief spl. services Solano County (Calif.) Mental Health, 1976—; pvt. practice forensic psychology, 1979—; tng. faculty Calif. Sch. of Profl. Psychology. Mem. Am. Psychol. Assn. (divs. clin., forensic psychology), Calif. State Psychol. Assn. (divs. pvt., pub. practice). Office: 1147 Ohio St Fairfield CA 94533

WIERER, OTTO, lawyer, lectr., translator, univ. librarian; b. Prague, Czechoslovakia, Jan. 8, 1912; s. Alois and Emilie (Prokop) W.; Dipl. Sc. Pol., Free Sch. Polit. Sci., Prague, 1934; Dr. iuris, Charles U. Fac. Law, Prague, 1938, postgrad. 1932-41; postgrad. Maximilian U., Munich, 1945-46; M.L.S., Columbia U., 1958, postgrad. (A.V.W. Jackson fellow Indo-Iranian studies), 1958-60; m. Maria-Magdalena Rohrer, May 17, 1958. Came to U.S., 1956, naturalized, 1962. Sec., Central European Press, Prague, 1933-37; asst. Czech Charles U. Fac. Law, 1937-39; editor, head transl. dept. Melantrich publ. house, Prague, 1937-41; legal adviser, prosecutor U.S. High Commn. Cts. for Germany, Munich, 1946-51; external researcher RFE, Munich, 1951-54; export-import RMT, Rio de Janeiro, Brazil, 1955; legal collaborator, translator Internat. Commn. Jurists, Munich br., 1956; cataloguer EIS N.Y. Pub. Library, 1956-60; asst. head lang. div. Queens Borough Pub. Library, 1960-65; cataloguer Gibb Coll., Harvard U., 1965-66; head Internat. Info. Center, SUNY, Oyster Bay, 1966-68; univ. librarian, lectr. U.S. Internat. U., San Diego, 1968-76; lectr., librarian San Diego Community Coll., 1976-77; vis. prof. LATF, 1977-79; mem. faculty La Jolla U., 1978-79; adj. instr. human resources mgmt. Pepperdine U., 1978-79; instr. U. for Humanistic Studies, San Diego, 1982—; long-term care ombudsman Calif. Dept. Aging, 1982—. Mem. Spl. Libraries Assn., Am. Oriental Soc., Am. Soc. Info. Sci., Assn. Holistic Health (founding). Home: 1815 Magdalene Way San Diego CA 92110

WIERSMA, GEORGE BRUCE, ecologist; b. Paterson, N.J., Oct. 26, 1942; s. George and Marjorie W.; B.S., U. Maine, 1964; M.S. (fellow), Yale U., 1965; Ph.D. (fellow), Syracuse U., 1968; m. Ann Elizabeth Becker, Aug. 15, 1964; children—Heather Carol, Robin Kathryn, Jennifer Marjorie, Joshua Bruce. Chief ecol. monitoring br. EPA, 1970-74, chief pollutant pathways br. environ. monitoring systems lab., 1974-80; mgr. Office of Earth and Life Scis., EG & G Idaho, Idaho Falls, 1980—; expert cons. Global Environ. Monitoring Systems, UN Environ. Program, World Meteorol. Orgn., WHO, UNESCO; mem. U.S. USSR Bilateral Team on Biosphere Res., chmn. man and biosphere com. on pollution. Chmn. spiritual and parish life, Christian edn. United Ch. of Christ. Served with AUS, 1968-70. Decorated Army Commendation medal; vis. research fellow U. London, 1978. Mem. AAAS. Editor Jour. Environ. Monitoring and Assessment, 1980—; editorial adv. bd. Pesticides Monitoring Jour., 1970—; contbr. articles on environ. monitoring and assessment to profl. jours. Office: EG & G Idaho Inc PO Box 1625 Idaho Falls ID 83415

WIESE, WALTER RODNEY, retail co. exec.; b. Glendale, Calif., Feb. 28, 1937; s. Walter H. and Dorothy Jean W.; B.S. in Fin., Calif. State U., 1969; m. Margaret Ann Munford, June 23, 1962; children—Clark M., Brett N. With Bon Marche Co., Seattle, 1969—, dir. loss prevention, 1975—, v.p., 1982—; speaker loss prevention seminars Nat. Retail Mchts. Assn., 1973, 75, 77, 80. Organizer, pres. Consumer Awareness Council, Seattle, 1970, chmn., 1970-78; chmn. Seattle Retail Mchts. Loss Prevention Conf., adv. Wash. Crime Watch Anti-Shoplifting Program, 1977-78; pres. Sno-King Amateur Hockey Assn., 1979-80; bd. dirs., treas. Citizens Council Against Crime, Seattle, 1981—; bd. dirs. Issaquah Boosters Club. Recipient Seattle Downtown Devel. Assn. New Look award, 1973. Mem. Inst. Internal Auditors, Computer Auditors Assn., Sigma Chi. Office: Bon Marche 3d and Pine Sts Seattle WA 98111

WIESENFELD, IRVING HAROLD, otolaryngologist; b. San Francisco, June 14, 1912; s. Louis and Ann (Berke) W.; A.B., U. Calif., 1934, M.D., 1938, C.P.H. (Calif. State fellow), 1939, M.S., 1941, Dr.P.H., 1947; m. Betsey Ramsay Straub, May 11, 1939; children—Stephen Lee, Ramsay. Intern, U. Calif. Hosp., San Francisco, 1937-38; chief bur. maternal and child health Calif. Dept. Health, San Francisco, 1939-41; resident in otolaryngology Los Angeles County Hosp. on U. So. Calif. Service, 1941-42; chief otolaryngology service Kaiser Found. Hosp., Oakland, Calif., 1942-46; practice medicine specializing in otolaryngology, Oakland, 1946—; mem. staffs Herrick Meml. Hosp., Berkeley, Calif., Providence Hosp., Oakland, Children's Hosp., Oakland, Cowell Hosp., Berkeley; med. dir. Oakland Unified Sch. Dist., 1949—. Diplomate Am. Bd. Otolaryngology, Internat. Bd. Surgery. Fellow ACS, Internat. Coll. Surgeons; mem. AMA, Calif., Alameda-Contra Costa med. assns., Am. Med. Tennis Assn., Phi Beta Kappa, Sigma Xi, Alpha Omega Alpha. Republican. Jewish. Club: Oakland Athletic. Home: 120 Monte Ave Piedmont CA 94611 Office: 400 30th St Suite 206 Oakland CA 94609

WIGAL, IRIS SELIGMAN, educator; b. Madison, Wis., Aug. 7, 1947; d. Daniel Samuel and Birdie (Ginsburg) Seligman; m. Dennis Dean Wigal, Aug. 13, 1974; 1 dau., Amanda Michele. B.A. in Elem. Edn., Ariz. State U., 1969, M.A. in Spl. Edn., 1971. Cert. tchr., Ariz. Tchr., Cartwright Sch. Dist., Phoenix, 1969—. Mem. Valley Leadership; treas., bd. dirs. Valley Leadership Alumni Assn., 1982-84; rec. sec. Women's Orgn. for Rehab. Tng., 1979-80, v.p., 1980-81; mem. Maricopa County Child Services Task Force, 1981. Mem. NEA, Ariz. Edn. Assn., Cartwright Edn. Assn. (bldg. rep. 1970-74), AAUW, Ariz. State U Alumni Assn. (homecoming steering com., editorial adv. bd.), Phoenix Panhellenic, Alpha Lambda Housing Corp. (sec. 1983-84), Alpha Epsilon Phi (nat. rush chmn. 1979-81, nat. province supr. 1981-83, nat. alumnae sec. 1983-84; Phoenix Alumni pres. 1975-77). Democrat. Jewish. Home: 1735 W Seldon Ln Phoenix AZ 85021 Office: 2252 N 55th Ave Phoenix AZ

WIGGINS, ALICE TOLBERT, public transportation company official, Los Angeles, July 18, 1946; d. Edmund Howard and Flores (Payne) Tolbert; B.A. in Creative Writing, Wayne State U., 1969; m. Reginald Keith Wiggins, Jan. 1, 1977. Owner, mgr. Natral Artists' Enterprises, Inc., Los Angeles, 1975-77; freelance writer, 1970-71; reporter Chgo. Daily Defender, 1973-74; news bur. rep. So. Calif. Rapid Transit Dist., Los Angeles, 1974-78, sr. news bur. rep., 1978-80, supr. promotions, 1980-81, mgr. spl. promotional programs, 1981—; local access producer Valley Cable TV. Mem. Assn. Equal Representation in Mass Communications, Nat. Assn. Media Women, Los Angeles Jaycees, Publicity Club Los Angeles, Women's Community, Women in Cable. Office: 425 S Main St Los Angeles CA 90013

WIGGINS, WALTON WRAY, publisher; b. Roswell, N.Mex., May 13, 1924; s. Miles Burgess and Mona Cecil (Brown) W.; grad. Motion Picture Cameraman Sch., Astoria, N.Y., 1945; m. Roynel Fitzgerald, Apr. 30, 1963; children—Walton Wray, Kimberly Douglas, Lisa Renee. Free-lance photo-journalist for nat. mags., 1948-60; dir. public relations Ruidoso Racing Assn., Ruidoso Downs, N.Mex., 1960-69, v.p., 1967-68; founder, pub. Speedhorse Publs., Roswell, N.Mex. and Norman, Okla., 1969-78; owner/operator Wiggins Galleries Fine Art, 1978—; pres. Quarter Racing World, 1970-78, Am. Horse Publs., Washington, 1978; del. leader People to People, Internat. Served with U.S. Army, 1943-46. Recipient Detroit Art Dirs. award, 1955, Greatest Contbr. award Quarter Racing Owners Am., 1974. Mem. Overseas Press Club, Am. Soc. Mag. Photographers, Am. Horse Publs. Republican. Author: The Great American Speedhorse, 1978; Cockleburs and Cowchips, 1975; Alfred Morang-A Neglected Master, 1979; Ernest Berke-Paintings and Sculptures of the Old West, 1980; Juan Dell-The First Lady of Western Bronze, 1981; Go Man Go-The Legendary Speedhorse, 1982. Office: 209 W First St Roswell NM 88201

WIGGLESWORTH, DAVID CUNNINGHAM, bus. and mgmt. cons.; b. Passaic, N.J., Sept. 23, 1927; s. Walter Frederick and Janet (Cunningham) W.; B.A., Occidental Coll., 1950, M.A., 1953; postgrad. U. de las Ams., 1954-56; Ph.D., U. East Fla., 1957; L.H.D. (hon.), Arubaanse Handels Academie, 1969; m. Rita Dominguez, Mar. 15, 1956 (dec.); children—Mitchell Murray, Marc David, Miles Frederick, Janet Rose; m. 2d, Gayle Coates, Aug. 1, 1981; 1 dau., Danielle Coates. Dir., Spoken English Inst., Mexico City, also lectr. Mexico City Coll., 1954-56; headmaster Harding Acad., Glendale, Calif., also lectr. Citrus Jr. Coll., 1956-58; dir. Burma-Am. Inst., Rangoon, 1958-60; project dir. Washington Ednl. Research Assos., Washington, Conakry, Guinea, Benghazi, Libya, Carbondale, Ill., 1960-64; mng. editor linguistics div. T. Y. Crowell Pub. Co., N.Y.C., 1964-66; dir. linguistic studies Behavioral Research Labs., Palo Alto, Calif., 1966-67; pres. D.C.W. Research Assocs. Internat., Foster City, Calif., 1976—; mem. faculty external degree program St. Mary's Coll., Moraga, Calif., 1979—. Trustee, City U. Los Angeles; mem. adv. bd. Martin Luther King Reading Acad., Los Angeles; ordained minister Universal Life Ch., 1969. Served with U.S. Army, 1945-46, 52-54. Mem. Am. Mgmt. Assn., Orgn. Devel. Network, Am. Soc. Tng. and Devel., Soc. Internat. Edn. Tng. and Research, 1st World Congress Internat. Orgn. Devel., Orgn. Devel. Forum, Peninsula Orgn. Devel. Support, Mideast Am. Bus. Conf., World Future Soc. Clubs: Peninsula Exec. (Los Altos); SEDUMEX (Mexico City); Benghazi Sailing; Orient (Rangoon). Author: PI/LT-Programmed Instruction/Language Teaching, 1967; Career Education, 1976; ASTD in China, 1981; contbr. articles to profl. publs. Home: PO Box 4400 1320 Fibbon St Foster City CA 94404

WIGHT, LEE DAVIS, dentist; b. Midvale, Utah, Apr. 28, 1929; s. Guy Horton and Florence Alice (Davis) W.; B.S., U. Utah, 1951; postgrad. U. Wash., 1951-52; D.D.S., U. Kansas City, 1956; m. Marjorie Ann Alexander, July 19, 1953; children—Anna Lee, Wendy Vallene, Guy Alexander, Alice Francine. Pvt. practice dentistry, Colfax, Calif., 1960—; pres., chmn. bd. Royal Benevolent Seals Corp., Sacramento, 1963-65, Park Sutter Corp., Sacramento, 1967-68; v.p. Auburn Aviation Co., Inc., Calif., 1968-70; pres. Wight & Assos., Colfax, 1978—; Amway voting mem. direct distbr., 1979—. Served to lt. Dental Corps, USNR, 1956-60. Fellow Acad. Gen. Dentistry, Acad. Dentistry Internat.; mem. No. Calif. Acad. Gen. Dentistry (treas. 1981, v.p. 1983-84), Sacramento Dist. Dental Soc. (dir. 1975-79), ADA, Calif. Dental Assn., Central Assn. Dentists and Physicians, Am. Acad. Implant Dentistry (pres. Western dist. 1978-79), So. Calif. Acad. Nutritional Research, Kappa Sigma, Kappa Kappa Psi, Xi Psi Phi. Libertarian. Episcopalian. Home: 2685 Plumbago Ct Rocklin CA 95677 Office: 3015 Grass Valley St Colfax CA 95713

WIITA, THOMAS ARVO, medical equipment company executive; b. Fitchburg, Mass., Jan. 14, 1950; s. Arvo Lemmikki and Marie (Ahola) W. A.B. in Econs., Harvard U., 1971, M.B.A., 1975. Market research analyst The Gillette Co., Boston, 1971-73; ultrasound mktg. mgr. med. systems div. Gen. Electric Co., Milw., 1975-82; pres. Motion Control, Inc., Salt Lake City, 1982—. Clubs: Harvard, Harvard Bus. Sch. Office: Motion Control Inc 1005 S 300 W Salt Lake City UT 84101

WIK, MARGURETTE EUGENIA, greyhound racetrack clubhouse manager, businesswoman; b. Long Beach, Calif., May 17, 1952; d. Durward Tilden and Martha Jean (Walker) Dickens; m. Nils M. Wik, Jan. 19, 1970; children—James Matthew, Loretta Lynn. Detention officer, Pima (Ariz.) County Sheriffs Dept., 1976-78; clubhouse mgr. Gillet Greyhound Racing, Inc., Tucson, 1970—; owner, mgr. Maggie's Blankets, Inc., Tucson, 1978—; owner, mgr. Maggie's Dog Grooming, Tucson, 1983—. Active Multiple Sclerosis Found.; Democratic Party Politics. Home: 2500 East Calle Bacardi Vail AZ 85641 Office: Tucson Greyhound Park 2601 S 3d St Tucson AZ 85713

WIKE, GARVEL WAYNE, fund raiser; b. Galax, Va., June 27, 1940; s. Homer Jefferson and Blanche Victoria (Duncan) W.; m. Phyllis Rae Ball, June 12, 1961 (div. Dec. 1973); children—Robin Kathleen, Michael David; m. 2d Iris Dorothy Boyd, Feb. 26, 1983. Grad. high sch. With Salvation Army, Lynchburg, Va., 1967-68, New Orleans, 1968-70, exec. dir., Sheridan, Wyo., 1970-72; asst. dir. United Way, Washington, 1972-81; asst. dir. community relations and devel. dept. Salvation Army, Los Angeles, 1981-83; dir. devel. Greater Long Beach (Calif.) chpt. ARC, 1983—. Cons. Served with USAF, 1959-67. Mem. Nat. Soc. Fund Raising Execs., Christian Ministries Mgmt. Assn. Republican. Salvation Army. Club: Kiwanis. Office: 3150 E 29th St Long Beach CA 90806

WIKMAN, CARL HERMAN, video producer, cons.; b. N.Y.C., Apr. 20, 1950; s. Roy Eric and Virpi Lea (Koistinen) W. Student in journalism and speech Oreg. State U., 1970, in radio and TV, Mt. Hood Coll., Gresham, Oreg., 1972. Cable snake Wide World of Sports, ABC-TV, 1972-74; free lance TV producer, cons. Carl Wikman Video Tape, Portland, Oreg., 1974-82; program dir. Yakima (Wash.) Comml. TV, 1983—. Served with U.S. Army, 1969. Recipient Chicago Film Festival gold medal for best TV show, 1980; Radio TV News Dir. Assn. award for best regional story coverage, 1980, best internat. coverage award, 1981; N.W. Film Festival outstanding documentary award, 1981; Am. Scandinavian Found. cultural achievement for TV award, 1981. Mem. Am. Scandinavian Found. (dir.), Nat. Fedn. Local Comml. Programmers, Am. Film Inst., Internat. Alliance Theatrical Stage Employees. Office: Yakima Comml TV 129 N 2d St Yakima WA 98901

WILBEE, ROBERT HOBBS, surgeon; b. Edmonton, Alta., Can., Sept. 14, 1929; s. Thomas Judson and Edith (Powell) W.; B.A., Dartmouth Coll., 1951; M.D., SUNY at Buffalo Sch. Medicine, 1959; m. Shirley Rees, June 25, 1960; children—Lauren, Richard, Bruce. Intern U. Calif. at San Francisco, 1959-60; resident Buffalo Gen. Hosp., 1960-64; asso. plant surgeon Bethlehem Steel Co., Lackawanna, N.Y., 1964-68; asst. prof. surgery, asst. dean Suny at Buffalo Sch. Medicine, 1968-71; asso. dir. E. J. Meyer Hosp., Buffalo, 1970-71; pvt. practice medicine specializing in surgery, Las Cruces, N.Mex., 1971—; clin. asso. prof. surgery, Tex. Tech. Med. Sch., El Paso, 1978-81; mem. staffs Meml. Gen. Hosp., Las Cruces. Served with C.I.C., U.S. Army, 1952-54. Diplomate Am. Bd. Surgery. Fellow A.C.S., Southwestern Surg. Congress; mem. N.Mex. Med. Soc. (pres. 1979-80), Assn. Am. Physicians and Surgeons. Episcopalian. Contbr. articles to various publs. Home: 1790 Imperial Ridge Las Cruces NM 88001 Office: 2435 Telshor Blvd Las Cruces NM 88001

WILBER, CLARE MARIE O'KEEFE, musician, educator; b. Denver, Mar. 21, 1928; d. Thomas A. and Kathleen M. (Brennan) O'Keefe; A.B., Loretto Heights Coll., 1948; M.S., Fordham U., 1950; M.M., Colo. State U., 1972; m. Charles Grady Wilber, June 14, 1952; children—Maureen, Charles, Michael, Thomas (dec.), Kathleen, Aileen, John Joseph. Instr. biology Webster (Mo.) Coll., 1951-52, Loyola Coll., Balt., 1957-61; instr. music Colo. State U., Ft. Collins, 1972-82, mgr. Ft. Collins Symphony Orch., 1961-81, dir., 1969-77, exec. dir., 1981—; adjudicator Stars of Tomorrow, 1970; v.p. Elite Music Co., Ft. Collins, 1975—, dir., 1975—; piano adjudicator Rocky Mountain region, 1976—. Mem. adv. council Ft. Collins High Sch., 1972-74; mem. com. Designing Tomorrow Today, 1972-74; adminstr. grants Colo. State Council on the Arts and Humanities, 1974-75. Mem. adv. bd. Children's Sch. of Sci., Woods Hole, Mass., 1965—. Recipient Spl. Service award Delta Omicron, 1974; AT&T Crystal Clef award, 1982. Mem. Music Tchrs. Nat. Assn., Colo. State Music Tchrs. Assn. (co-chmn. cert. bd. 1980-81), Am. Symphony Orch. League, Delta Omicron, Kappa Gamma Pi. Roman Catholic. Clubs: Colo. State U. Women's Assn., Women's Guild of the Ft. Collins Symphony. Composer: musical composition for two pianos; Fantasie Romantique, 1972; Mass in D, 1981. Home: 900 Edwards St Fort Collins CO 80524 Office: Ft Collins Symphony PO Box 1963 Fort Collins CO 80522

WILBER, DONALD BLAINE, clergyman, counselor; b. Albuquerque, Oct. 5, 1952; s. M. Blaine and S. June (Warren) W.; m. Janet Marie Scott, Sept. 14, 1973; children—Eric, Casey, Ty. B.A. in Religion, N.W. Nazarene Coll., 1976; M.A. in Gen. Counseling, Coll. Idaho, 1980; Ph.D. in Counseling Psychology, Columbia Pacific U., 1982. Ordained to ministry Ch. of the Nazarene, 1978; pastor marriage and family counselor Ch. of the Nazarene, Harper, Oreg., 1976-79; intern, health counselor, Mountain State Tumor Inst., Boise, 1980; dir., therapist Treasure Valley Counseling, Ontario, Oreg., 1980-82; pastor Ch. of the Nazarene, Prosser, Wash., 1983—; pvt. practice counseling, Prosser, 1983—. Mem. Christian Assn. Psychol. Studies, Am. Orthopsychiat. Assn., Nat. Council Family Relations, Am. Mental Health Counselors Assn., Am. Personnel and Guidance Assn., Prosser Ministerial Assn. Democrat. Contbr. articles to profl. jours. Home: 1006 Burgundy Pl Prosser WA 99350 Office: Ch of the Nazarene 1937 Highland Dr Prosser WA 99350

WILBORN, SANDRA ELAINE, business machines manufacturing company executive; b. Columbus, Tex., Nov. 11, 1949; d. Thomas Earl Wilborn and Doris Elaine Smith Williams; B.B.A. in Acctg., U. Houston, 1972. Cost acctg. assoc. Am. Can Co., St. Louis, 1972-74; systems engr. IBM, Seattle, 1974-81, adv. market support rep., San Francisco, 1981—. Mem. Alpha Kappa Alpha. Democrat. Mem. African Methodist Episcopal Ch. Home: 1538 Trestle Glen Rd Oakland CA 94610 Office: 425 Market St San Francisco CA 94105

WILBOURN-LINGLE, GALE ANN, trusts executive; b. Long Beach, Calif., Nov. 7, 1946; d. Thomas Robin and Nada Jean Jones (Richards) Young; B.A., Mills Coll., 1968; postgrad. Ohio State U., 1968-70; m. Ted R. Lingle, Sept. 21, 1980; 1 son by previous marriage, Christopher Bradley Wilbourn. Spl. edn. tchr. Johnstown (Ohio) Elem. Sch., 1968-70; substitute tchr. San Diego (Calif.) Pub. Schs., 1970-71; trustee, portfolio mgr. assets of individual trusts, Long Beach, Calif., 1976—. Mem. Long Beach Traffic Mgmt. Com.; active P.T.A., Vols. in Pub. Schs., Rick Rackers; sec.-treas. Catalina 38 Fleet. Featured in Hearth and Home sect. Long Beach Rev., 1979. Republican. Home and Office: 131 Bay Shore Ave Long Beach CA 90803

WILBUR, PAUL JAMES, mechanical engineer, educator; b. Ogden, Utah, Nov. 8, 1937; s. Earl Burton and Ada Lucille (James) W.; m. Twyla Ann Beck, June 8, 1960; children—Wendy Lee, Dagny Ann. B.Sc. in Mech. Engring., U. Utah, 1960, Ph.D. in Aerospace and Mech. Sci., Princeton U., 1968. Nuclear power engr. AEC, 1960-64; research asst. aerospace and mech. sci. Princeton U., 1964-68; prof. mech. engring. Colo. State U., Ft. Collins, 1968—; dir. Ion Tech. Inc., Ft. Collins; cons. Hughes Research Labs., Jet Propulsion Lab. Served to lt. USN, 1960-64. Recipient Haliburton Teaching award Colo. State U., 1982. Mem. ASME, AIAA, Sigma Xi. Contbr. numerous articles to profl. jours. Home: 1500 Teakwood Ct Fort Collins CO 80525 Office: Dept Mech Engring Colo State U Fort Collins CO 80523

WILCOTT, J. CURTIS, computer scientist; b. Decatur, Ill., Oct. 25, 1940; s. Jack Lewis and Ruth Ada (Ramsey) W.; B.A., U. Tex., Austin, 1962; M.S. in Physics, U. N.Mex., 1965; postgrad. (NSF fellow) U. Ariz., 1965-70; Ph.D. in Systems Ecology, Utah State U., 1973; m. Sandra Louise Molesworth, Jan. 28, 1969; children—Daniel, Elijah, Isaac. Computer modeler U.S. Internat. Biol. Program, Desert Biome Project, Logan, Utah, 1970-73; asst. prof. landscape architecture U. Wis., Madison, 1973-77; phys. scientist Western Energy and Land Use Team, U.S. Fish and Wildlife Service, Ft. Collins, Colo., 1977-82; dir. software devel. 3CI, Ft. Collins, Colo., 1982—. Mem. Assn. Computing Machinery, Phi Beta Kappa. Evangelical. Author InfoCen, computerized database mgmt. system. Office: 363 W Drake Rd Fort Collins CO 80526

WILCOX, COLLEEN BRIDGET, speech pathologist; b. Rock Island, Ill., July 24, 1949; d. Wayne Eugene and Virginia Mae (Dewrose) W. B.S., U. Iowa, 1971; M.S., U. Ariz., 1974; doctoral candidate U. So. Calif., 1981-83; ednl. adminstrn. credential U. So. Calif. Asst. dir. parks and recreation City of Moline (Ill.), 1969-74; dir. speech pathology Instituto Guatemalteca Sequiridad, Peace Corps., Guatemala City, 1971-72; speech and lang. specialist Tucson Sch. Dist., 1974-75; aphasia tchr. specialist, itinerant specialist Los Angeles County Schs., 1975-77; program specialist in severe lang. disorder/aphasia Los Angeles County Supt. Schs., 1977-79, program adminstr./communication disorders, Baldwin Park, 1979—, mem. budget standards com. 1979-82; mem. credential adv. bd., communications dept. Calif. State U., Los Angeles, 1978, asst. prof., 1977—, chmn. sabbatical rev. com.; art dir. the Great Stampede, 1981—. Recipient Harriett Rutherford Johnstown award Pi Beta Phi, 1971; Barnes Drill award U. Iowa, 1971; lic. speech pathologist, cert. tchr. speech and hearing therapy, severely handicapped credential, learning handicapped credential, Calif.; cert. speech and lang. therapist, kindergarten-12th grades, Ariz. Mem. Calif. Speech and Hearing Assn., Am. Speech and Hearing Assn. (cert. clin. competence in speech pathology, conv. com. 1979, com. on manpower 1982-83), Council Exceptional Children, Assn. Calif. Sch. Adminstrs., UN Assn., Pi Beta Phi Alumnae, Phi Delta Kappa. Co-author, illustrator: Let's Share, 1983. Home: 1167 S Orange Grove Blvd Pasadena CA 91105

WILCOX, DANIEL EDWARD, III, air force personnel technician; b. Bryn Mawr, Pa., Dec. 27, 1946; s. Daniel Edward and Laura Elsie (Church) W.; m. Anita Leah Warwick, July 7, 1949; children—Crystal, Heather, Daniel. B.S. in Occupational Edn., So. Ill. U., 1982. Enlisted U.S. Air Force, 1966; adminstrv. technician, McChord AFB, Tacoma, Wash., 1966-71; edn./tng. supt. Fairchild AFB, Spokane, Wash., 1971-82; personnel supt. Travis AFB, Calif., 1982—. Decorated Meritorious Service medal, Air Force Commendation medal with oak leaf cluster. Mem. Am. Vocat. Assn., Noncommd. Officer Acad. Grad. Assn., Air Force Assn., Nat. Thespian Soc. Democrat. Methodist.

WILCOX, DAVID ALBERTSON, urban planner, economics consultant; b. Grand Rapids, Mich., Aug. 11, 1938; s. David Albertson and Florence Sanfield (McDonell) W.; m. Carol Francis Brian, Aug. 26, 1967; children—Wendy, Michele, Wilcox. B.A., U. Mich., 1961, M.A., 1961; M.R.P., Harvard U. Grad. Sch. Design, 1967. Vol., U.S. Peace Corps, 1962-64; planning asst. City of Lynn (Mass.), 1965-66; mgmt. analyst, urban planner U.S. Bur. Budget, Washington, 1966-68; planning dir., dep. administr. Community Redevel. Agy., City of Los Angeles, 1968-76; ptnr., v.p. Econ. Research Assocs., Los Angeles, 1977—; instr. community redevel. Sch. Urban and Regional Planning, U. So. Calif., 1977—. Bd. dir. Los Angeles Beautiful, 1978—; adv. com. Calif. Urban Forestry Program, Calif. Dept. Forestry, 1979—. Mem. Am. Inst. Cert. Planners (Lasker fellow 1964-66), Nat. Assn. Housing Redevel. Ofcls. Democrat. Roman Catholic. Office: 10960 Wilshire Blvd Suite 2400 Los Angeles CA 90024

WILCOX, DENNIS LEE, public relations educator, consultant; b. Rapid City, S.D., Mar. 31, 1941; s. Herbert D. and Star A. (Polhemus) W.; m. Marianne M. Milstead, May 24, 1969. B.A., U. Denver, 1963; M.A., U. Iowa, 1966; Ph.D., U. Mo., 1974. Accredited in pub. relations Pub. Relations Soc. Am. With Grand Junction (Colo.) Daily Sentinel, 1963-64; editor Ohio State Univ. Publs., 1966-68; pub. relations dir. Ketchum Inc., Pitts., 1968-70, Chapman Coll. World Campus Afloat, 1971; prof. San Jose (Calif.) State U., 1974—; vis. prof. pub. relations Rhodes U., South Africa, 1983. Faculty fellow Found. Pub. Relations Research and Edn., 1981; recipient Rex Harlow award for profl. achievement, 1982. Mem. Pub. Relations Soc. Am., Assn. Edn. in Journalism, Internat. Assn. Bus. Communicators. Republican. Episcopalian. Club: San Jose Athletic. Author publs. in field. Office: San Jose State University San Jose CA 95192

WILCOX, JOHN HYLAND, JR., restaurant chain executive; b. Lansdown, Pa., Apr. 6, 1954; s. John Hyland and Mary Evelyn (Foucart) W.; m. Ann Hellesmark, Apr. 7, 1979. B.S. in Advt., U. Fla., 1976; postgrad. Eastern Mont. Coll., 1979—. Prodn. mgr. Bailey Campell, Ft. Lauderdale, Fla., 1976; supr. Wendy's of Portland, Oreg., 1976-77; loan officer Empire Fed. Savs. & Loan, Livingston, Mont., 1977-79; v.p. Wendy's of Mont., Billings, 1979—. Bd. dirs. Billings Downtown Mchts. Assn. Mem. Billings Advt. and Mktg. Assn. (dir.), Mont. Bd. Realtors, Billings Ad Club, Savs. Inst. Mktg. Soc. Am., Am. Advt. Fedn., Sigma Alpha Epsilon. Clubs: Yellowstone Country, Billings Petroleum. Office: 2906 2nd Ave N Billings MT 59101

WILCOX, RAND ROGER, psychologist, educator; b. Niagara Falls, N.Y., July 6, 1946; s. Howard Clinton and Phyllis Hope (Stevens) W.; m. Judy Barbara Allen, July 12, 1969; m. 2d, Joan S. Murray, July 18, 1980. Ph.D., U. Calif., 1976. Sr. research assoc. UCLA, 1976-81; asst. prof. U. So. Calif., Los Angeles, 1981—. Nat. Inst. Edn. grantee; Psychometric Soc. travel grantee. Mem. Am. Ednl. Research Assn., Am. Stats. Assn., Biometric Soc., Inst. Math. Stats., Psychometric Soc., Am. Psychol. Assn., Nat. Council Measurement in Edn. Mem. editorial bd. Am. Jour. of Math. and Mgmt. Scis., Applied Psychol. Measurement, Jour. of Ednl. Measurement; contbr. articles to profl. jours. Office: Dept Psychology U So Calif Los Angeles CA 90007

WILCOX, WILLIAM WAYNE, engineer; b. Wausau, Wis., Jan. 28, 1942; s. Roy James and Leah Avis (Dery) W.; student U. Santa Clara, 1960-63; B.S., U. San Francisco, 1980; m. Donna Kay Dunham, Aug. 16, 1963; children—William Richard, David Wayne. Environ. test technician Sandia Corp., Livermore, Calif., 1963-65; with Lawrence Livermore Lab. (Calif.), 1965—, sr. engring. asso., 1981—; cons. mech. engring. dept. Oreg. State U. Recipient Significant Contbn. award in materials sci. and tech. Am. Nuclear Soc., 1981. Mem. Soc. Exptl. Stress Analysis. Contbr. articles to profl. jours. Office: PO Box 808 Livermore CA 94550

WILDE, CHARLES BROADWATER, investment banker, oil company executive; b. Oakland, Calif., July 22, 1940; s. Willard Henry and Elizabeth M. (Broadwater) W.; A.B., U. Calif. at Berkeley, 1962; m. Molly Burnett, June 23, 1962; children—Charles Broadwater, Stephen Burnett. Salesman Procter & Gamble, San Francisco, 1963-64, dist. head salesman, 1964-65, unit mgr., 1965-67; account exec. Dean Witter Reynolds, Inc., Hayward, Calif., 1967-70, asst. v.p., divisional syndicate mgr., 1972-74, v.p., nat. dir. tax advantaged investments, 1974-79; v.p. Winthrop Fin. Co., Inc., San Francisco, 1979—; sr. v.p. Winthrop Securities Co., Inc., 1979—; exec. v.p. Peregrine Oil & Gas Co., Burlingame, Calif., 1982—, Western Dominion Capital Corp., Denver; exec. v.p., chief fin. officer, dir. splty. Shelton Orgn. Inc., Walnut Creek, Calif., 1983—; dir. Allen & Dorward Advt.; cons. indsl. solar energy conversions Dept. Energy; co-founder, dir., exec. v.p. Interflight Corp., Long Beach, Calif., 1970-72. Vice pres. Tahoe Pines Assn., 1968-71. Fin. chmn. No. Calif. com. for Brian Van Camp, candidate Calif. sec. state, 1974. Bd. dirs. Golden Bear Athletic Found.; pres. No. Calif. chpt. Nat. Multiple Sclerosis Soc., 1980. Mem. Big C Soc. (dir. 1972-77, fin. chmn. 1973-77), U. Calif. Young Alumni Assn. (dir. 1968-70). Clubs: Bohemian (San Francisco); Claremont Country (Oakland). Home: 67 Lynwood Pl Moraga CA 94556 Office: 1440 Maria Ln Suite 200 Walnut Creek CA 94596

WILDER, ARTHUR GRAVES, metallurgist; b. Presque Isle, Maine, June 11, 1917; s. Daniel Webster and Margaret Letitia (McLean) W.; B.S., Bates Coll., 1939; M.A., Stanford U., 1946; m. Virginia Sawyer Parker, Dec. 20, 1941; children—Carol Ann, Arthur Graves, Margaret Susan. Chemist, Lever Bros., Cambridge, Mass., 1940-41, Permanente Metals, Los Altos, Calif., 1946-48; metallurgist Stanford Research Inst., Menlo Park, Calif., 1948-61, Astrotemp, Inc., Mountain View, Calif., 1961-63; sr. metallurgist Jersey Prodn. Research Co., Mountain View, 1963-64; research scientist Lockheed Missiles & Space Co., Palo Alto, Calif., 1964-69; chief metallurgist Christensen, Inc., Salt Lake City, 1969-82; cons., 1982—. Served with U.S. Army, 1941, with USAF, 1941-45. Mem. Am. Soc. Metals, Am. Welding Soc., Internat. Metallog. Soc., Sigma Xi. Republican. Presbyterian. Project leader of team developing super alloys, 1955-61; patented alloys, composites, diamond tools. Home: 3578 Kingshill Circle Salt Lake City UT 84121

WILDER, RAYMOND LEIGH, statistician, management consultant; b. Tacoma, Aug. 19, 1927; s. Raymond Dabney and Edna Mabel (Leigh) W.; m. Marion Shirley Champagne, Jan. 22, 1972; children—Michael Jon, Leslie Ann. B.S. in Math., Oreg. State U., 1952; postgrad. U. Wash., 1952-53, 55, U. Oreg., 1956-57, U. Del., 1958-59; M.S. in Quantitative Bus. Analysis, U. So. Calif., 1965. Applied statistician U. Wash. Pub. Opinion Lab., Seattle, 1953; computing analyst Douglas Aircraft Co., Long Beach, Calif., 1953-55; computing engr. N.W. Natural Gas Co., Portland, Oreg., 1956, 57; cons. statistician E.I. du Pont de Nemours & Co., Wilmington, Del., 1957-59, Niagara Falls, N.Y., 1959-60; group engr. McDonnell Douglas Corp., Culver City, Calif., 1960-63, Huntington Beach, Calif., 1972-74, asst. to dir., Santa Monica, Calif., 1963-72; sr. assoc. Wilder Assocs., Sunset Beach, Calif. and Seal Rock, Oreg., 1974—; cons., tchr. in field. Mem. adv. com. Waldport (Oreg.) Sch., 1978-79; treas., bd. dirs. Seal Rock Rural Fire Protection, 1979—; mem. Beaver Creek Citizens Adv. Com., Oreg. Land Conservation Devel. Commn., 1980-81; mem. endowment com. YMCA, Newport, Oreg., 1983—. Served with USN, 1945-48. Mem. Am. Statis. Assn. Phi Kappa Phi, Pi Mu Epsilon. Democrat. Episcopalian. Home and office: SR 3 Box 100 Seal Rock OR 97376

WILEY, RICHARD EDWIN, photographer; b. Marion, Ind., July 8, 1933; s. William Emmett and Laura Elizabeth (Williams) W.; m. Michael Ann Cater, Dec. 21, 1963. B.S. in Geology, Ind. U., 1958. Photographer, 1959—; pres. Wiley, Inc. 1974—. Served in USN, 1951-54. Recipient numerous awards including recognition of service and photographic excellence award Profl. Photographers of Am. Mem. Hawaii Profl. Photographers Assn. (dir., past pres.), Hawaii C. of C., Profl. Photographers of Am. Republican. Clubs: Honolulu, Honolulu Exec. Assn. Home: 920 Ward Ave 4-G Honolulu HI 96814 Office: 841 Bishop St B-2 Honolulu HI 96813

WILF, BOYCE LEONARD, JR., optometrist, marketing consultant; b. Colorado Springs, Colo., June 3, 1943; s. Boyce Leonard, Sr. and Doris Jean (Barrett) W.; m. Gail Sachicko Miyazono, Nov. 23, 1973; 1 dau., Erin Kimiko. Student U. Puget Sound, 1961-65; B.S., Pacific U., 1970, O.D., 1972. Prin. Grandview Vision Clinic (Wash.), 1972—; mktg. cons. Mem. Wash. Optometric Assn., Am. Optometric Assn., Yakima Valley Optometric Soc. (pres. 1981-82), Grandview C. of C. (v.p. 1975). Republican. Methodist. Lodges: Rotary, Elks. Home: Route 3 Box 3847 Grandview WA 98930 Office: Grandview Vision Clinic 147 Division St Grandview WA 98930

WILFLEY, GEORGE MERRITT, mfg. co. exec.; b. Denver, May 23, 1924; s. Elmer R. and Margaret W., B.A. U. Colo., 1950, postgrad., 1977; m. Eleanore Breitenstein; children—George Michael, John Frederick. With A.R. Wilfley & Sons, Inc., Denver, 1950—, pres., 1958—, also dir.; pres., dir. Western Foundries, Inc.; chmn. bd., dir. Conveying Industries, Inc.; dir. First Nat. Bank of Denver, Olson Industries. Vice pres. bd. trustees U. Denver, chmn. bd. Boys Club of Denver, Inc. Served with F.A., AUS, 1943-46. Mem. AIME, Nat. Assn. Corrosion Engrs., Colo. Mining Assn., NAM (dir.). Home: 34 Polo Club Circle Denver CO 80209 Office: PO Box 2330 Denver CO 80201

WILHELM, ROBERT OSCAR, lawyer, civil engineer; b. Balt., July 7, 1918; s. Clarence Oscar and Agnes Virginia (Grimm) W.; B.S.C.E., Ga. Inst. Tech., 1947, M.S., 1948; J.D., Stanford U., 1951; m. Grace Sanborn Luckie, Apr. 4, 1959. Admitted to Calif. bar, 1952, practiced in Redwood City, 1952—; mem. firm Wilhelm, Thompson, Wentholt and Gibbs, Redwood City, 1952—; gen. counsel Bay Counties Gen. Contractors, Peninsula Builders Exchange, Engring. and Grading Contractors Calif.; self-employed as civil engr., Redwood City, 1952—; pres. Bay Counties Builders Escrow, Inc., 1972—. Served with C.E., AUS, 1942-46. Mem. Bay Counties Civil Engrs. (pres. 1957), Peninsula Builders Exchange (pres. 1958-71, dir.), Calif. State Builders Exchange (treas. 1971). Clubs: Masons, Odd Fellows, Eagles, Elks. Author: The Manual of Procedures for the Construction Industry. 1971. Columnist Law and You in Daily Pacific Builder, 1954—; author: Construction Law for Contractors, Architects and Engineers. Home: 463 Raymondo Dr Woodside CA 94062 Office: 600 Allerton Redwood City CA 94063

WILHELM, WILLA METTA, ednl. media specialist; b. Jasper, Oreg., Sept. 10, 1912; d. Charles Elzie and Margaret Sephronia (Jacoby) Logsdon; B.S., U. Oreg., 1933, M.S., 1941; m. George August Wilhelm, June 21, 1941; 1 son, Daren Lyle. Instr. jr. high sch., Sprague River, Oreg., 1934-35, Canyonville (Oreg.) High Sch., 1935-37, Junction City (Oreg.) High Sch., 1937-41; mem. staff bus. office Convair Corp., San Diego, 1942-45; instr. Riddle (Oreg.) Sch. System, 1945-47, supt., 1946-47; instr. Lowell (Oreg.) High Sch., 1947-61, media specialist, 1961—, dir. high sch. paper, 1947-60. Recipient Internat. 1st Place award Lowell High Sch. Newspaper, Broadcaster, Quill and Scroll, 1948-49, 49-50. Republican. Home: 85501 Jasper Park Rd Pleasant Hill OR 97401

WILKENFELD, JEROME, oil co. exec.; b. Bklyn., Oct. 25, 1920; s. Elias and Pauline (Nadel) W.; m. Rhoda B. Barandes, Dec. 21, 1969; children—Richard S., Robert M. B.Chem. Engring., CCNY, 1943. Successively operating and tech. assignments, dir. process engring. group, quality control and product specification, mgr. research and control Hooker Chems. & Plastics Corp., 1943-65, dir. corp. program environ. health, 1966-78, dir. environ. health, 1970-78; dir. health, environ. and safety, Occidental Petroleum Corp., Los Angeles, 1978—; mem. N.Y. State Air Pollution Control Bd., 1958-70, N.Y. State Environ. Bd., 1970-80, N.Y. State Health Planning Adv. Council, 1972-76; adv. com. Calif. Occupational Health Ctrs., 1982; solvents adv. com. EPA, 1970-72. Bd. dirs. Am. Lung Assn., 1971-78. Mem. Mfg. Chemists Assn. (chmn. environ. coms.), Am. Petroleum Inst., Chlorine Inst., Air Pollution Control Assn. (chmn. Niagara Frontier sect., Outstanding Contbn. award for air pollution control 1964), Environ. Health Commn. (chmn.), N.Y. State Chem. Industries Council, Am. Inst. Chem. Engrs., Am. Chem. Soc., Water Pollution Control Fedn. Clubs: Youngstown Yacht, Niagara. Contbg. author: Waste Management and Control, 1966; Industrial Pollution Control Handbook, 1971;

Occupational Safety and Health Handbook. Office: 10889 Wilshire Blvd Los Angeles CA 90024

WILKENING, MARVIN H., physicist, educator; b. Oak Ridge, Mo., Mar. 13, 1918; s. Theodore C. and Myrtle V. (Lang) W.; B.S. in Edn., S.E. Mo. State U., 1939; M.S., Ill. Inst. Tech., 1943, Ph.D. in Physics, 1949; m. Ruby Alma Barks, Nov. 14, 1942; children—Laurel Lynn, J. Wes. High sch. sci. tchr., Jackson, Mo., 1939-41; physicist Manhattan Project, Chgo., Oak Ridge, Richland and Los Alamos, 1942-45; instr. physics Ill. Inst. Tech., 1945-48; asso. prof. N.Mex. Inst. Mining and Tech., Socorro, 1948-52, prof., head dept. physics, 1953-68, dean grad. studies, prof. physics, 1968—; participant symposia on natural radiation environ.; mem. com. radon measurements Nat. Council Radiation Protection, 1980—; mem. Fermi group for 1st nuclear reactor, 1942. State pres. N.Mex. Wildlife Fedn. Fellow Am. Phys. Soc., AAAS, N.Mex. Acad. Sci.; mem. Soc. Nuclear Medicine (named Nuclear Pioneer), Am. Assn. Physics Tchrs., Am. Geophys. Union, AAUP, Am. Meteorol. Soc., Health Physics Soc., N.Y. Acad. Scis., Sigma Xi. Methodist. Club: Socorro Rotary (past pres.). Contbr. articles to profl. jours.; research on natural atmospheric radioactivity. Home: 1218 South Dr Socorro NM 87801

WILKENS, LEONARD RANDOLPH, professional basketball coach; b. Bklyn., Oct. 28, 1937; m. Marilyn; children—Leesha, Jamee, Randy. Student Providence Coll., 1960, H.H.D. (hon.). Basketball player St. Louis Hawks, 1960-68, Seattle Supersonics, 1968-72; coach Seattle Supersonics, 1969-72; basketball player Cleve. Cavaliers, 1972-73; player-coach Portland Trailblazers, 1974-75, coach, 1975-76; coach Seattle Supersonics, 1977—, also dir. player personnel. Coach Nat. Basketball championship team Seattle Supersonics, 1979; Nat. Basketball Assn. All-Star Game Most Valuable Player award, 1971; recipient Whitney Young Jr. award; Coach of Yr. award, 1977-78; Congressional Black Caucus Coach of Yr. award, 1978-79; Sportsman of Yr. award City of Hope Research Ctr. Office: Seattle Supersonics Call Box 14102 Seattle WA 98114*

WILKER, LEONARD BERNARD, computer co. exec.; b. Boston, Jan. 8, 1931; s. Harry and Ida Bessie (Deckelbaum) W.; B.S. in Elec. Engring., Northeastern U., 1954; M.S. in Systems Engring., West Coast U., 1964; m. Margaret Joyce Stark, Apr. 9, 1961; children—Gregory Isaac, Leah Anne, Aaron Paul, Rivka Patrice. Sales rep. Xerox Data Systems, El Segundo, Calif., 1969-71; regional sales mgr. Computer Automation, Irvine, Calif., 1971-74; nat. sales mgr. Qume, Hayward, Calif., 1974-77; sales dir. Xycom, Hayward, 1977-79; chmn. bd. Wilker Inc., Hayward, 1979-83; v.p. sales and mktg. CXi Inc., Cupertino, Calif., 1983—; instr. minicomputer course Pasadena Jr. Coll.; cons. Taft Electrosystems. Program chmn. Jr. C. of C., 1958-62; Indian Guide leader YMCA, 1967-68; Webelo Scout Leader, San Francisco Bay Area Boy Scouts Am., 1970-71, scoutmaster troop 807, 1979—; pres. Share-Our-Selves, Cath. Relief Agy., 1973-74; active Hayward Area Planning Assn., 1979-80, Hayward Ahead, 1980; active Holiday Project, Common Cause Ballet Folklorico Mexicano, Mus. Soc., San Francisco; mem. Temple Beth Shalom, San Leandro, Calif. Served with U.S. Army, 1954-56. Named to Xerox Pro Club, 1971. Mem. IEEE (sr.), Nat. Fedn. Ind. Bus., Cousteau Soc., Solar Lobby. Jewish. Contbr. paper to profl. conf. Home: 26999 Parkside Dr Hayward CA 94542 Office: 10011 N Foothill Blvd Cupertino CA 95014

WILKIE, DONALD WALTER, museum director; b. Vancouver, B.C., Can., June 20, 1931; s. Otway James and Jessie Margaret (McLeod) W.; m. Frances Elizabeth Turner, June 25, 1955; children—Linda Wilkie Butterfield, Douglas William Gordon, Susanne Marie; m. 2d, Patricia Ann Archer, May 18, 1980. B.A., U. B.C., 1960, M.Sc. with 1st class honors, 1966. Cert. tchr., B.C. Curator, Vancouver Pub. Aquarium, 1961-63, Phila. Aquarama, 1963-65; dir. T-Wayland Vaughan Aquarium,-Mus., Scripps Instn. Oceanography, LaJolla, Calif., 1965—; aquatic cons.; dir. Univ. and State Employees Credit Union. Fellow San Diego Zool. Soc., San Diego Mus. Natural History; mem. Internat. Assn.-Aquatic Animal Medicine, Western Regional Conf. of Am. Assn. Mus. Contbr. articles to profl. jours. Home: 4548 Cather Ave San Diego CA 92122 Office: 8602 LaJolla Shores Dr La Jolla CA 92093

WILKINS, FLOYD, JR., lawyer; b. Fowler, Calif., Sept. 8, 1925; s. Floyd and Kathryn (Springborg) W.; m. Sybil Ann Perrault, Feb. 22, 1964; children—Douglas B., Janet H. B.S., U. Calif., 1946; LL.B., Harvard U., 1952. Bar: N.Y. 1953, Calif. 1959. Assoc. Dwight, Royal Harris, Koegel & Caskey, N.Y.C., 1952-58; v.p., trust officer San Diego Trust & Savs. Bank, 1958-63; assoc. then ptnr., prin. Seltzer Caplan Wilkins & McMahon, PC, and predecessors, San Diego, 1963—; lectr. U. So. Calif. Tax Inst., 1975, Calif. Continuing Edn. of Bar, 1975—. Bd. dirs., pres. San Diego County Citizens Scholarship Found. Served with USN, 1944-46. Mem. ABA, State Bar Calif., San Diego County Bar Assn. Republican. Home: 2005 Soledad Ave La Jolla CA 92037 Office: Seltzer Caplan Wilkins & McMahon PC 3003 4th Ave San Diego CA 92103

WILKINS, PHILIP CHARLES, judge; b. Jan. 27, 1913; student Sacramento Jr. Coll.; LL.B., U. Calif., San Francisco, 1939; m. Sue Wilkins, Aug. 9, 1941. Bar: Calif. 1939. Mem. firm A.D. McDougall, Sacramento, 1940-42, Rowland & Craven, Sacramento, 1946-54; individual practice law, Sacramento, 1954-59; ptnr. firm Wilkins, Little & Mix, Sacramento, 1959-65, Wilkins & Mix, Sacramento, 1966-69; now sr. judge U.S. Dist. Ct., Eastern Dist. Calif., Sacramento. Office: US Dist Ct 2020 US Courthouse 650 Capitol Mall Sacramento CA 95814

WILKINS, ROBERT MASON, physician, rancher; b. Durham, N.C., Apr. 18, 1937; s. Robert Bruce and Lillian Marguerite (Mason) W.; m. Gloria Charlotte Heil, Feb. 13, 1968; children—Marguerite Davis, Robert Bruce. A.B. in English, U. N.C., 1959; M.D., Wake Forest U., 1963. Diplomate Am. Bd. Internal Medicine. Intern, U. Colo. Med. Ctr., Denver, 1963-64; fellow in gastroenterology Duke U. Med. Ctr., Durham, 1964-65, resident in internal medicine, 1967-68, fellow in gastroenterology, 1968-69; practice medicine specializing in gastroenterology Croasdaile Clinic, Durham, 1969-72; practice medicine specializing in gastroenterology, Nampa, Idaho, 1972—; assoc. med. staff Watts Hosp., Durham, cons. gastroenterology VA Hosp., Fayetteville; clin. assoc. community health scis. Duke U. Med. Ctr.; mem. staff Mercy Med. Ctr., Nampa, 1972—; clin. asst. prof. medicine U. Wash., 1977—. Served with USN, 1965-67. Fellow Am. Coll. Physicians (gov.-elect Idaho), Am. Coll. Gastroenterology; mem. Am. Soc. Gastrointestinal Endoscopy, Am. Gastroent. Assn., AMA, Am. Soc. Internal Medicine, Idaho Med. Assn., Idaho Soc. Internal Medicine, Idaho Angus Assn. (pres. 1980-82), Western States Angus Assn. (pres. 1981-83). Episcopalian. Contbr. articles to med. jours. Home: Route 4 Dry Lake Rd Nampa ID 83651 Office: Med Ctr Physicians 215 E Hawaii St Nampa ID 83651

WILKINSON, DAVID LAWRENCE, lawyer, state attorney general; b. Washington, Dec. 6, 1936; s. Ernest LeRoy and Alice Valora (Ludlow) W.; B.A. with honors in History, Brigham Young U., 1961; B.A. (Rhodes scholar), Oxford (Eng.) U., 1964, M.A., 1971; J.D., U. Calif.-Berkeley, 1966; m. Patricia Anne Thomas, Dec. 30, 1976; children—David Andrew, Calvin Holiday (foster son), Julene Holiday (foster dau.). Bar: Calif. 1967. Assoc. Lawler, Felix and Hall, Los Angeles, 1966-71; ptnr. Cook and Wilkinson, Los Angeles, 1971-72; asst. atty. gen. State of Utah, Salt Lake City, 1972-78, chief justice div., 1974-76, chief transp. div., 1977-79; chief dep. Salt Lake County Atty., 1979-80; atty. gen. State of Utah, 1981—; spl. instr. J. Reuben Clark Sch. of Law, Brigham Young U., Provo, Utah, 1975-76. Del. to Republican State Conv., 1980; missionary Ch. of Jesus Christ of Latter-day Saints, W. Ger., 1957-59. Served with Intelligence Corps, U.S. Army, 1961-62. Hon. Woodrow Wilson fellow, 1961-64. Mem. ABA, Utah Bar Assn., Salt Lake County Bar Assn., Nat. Assn. Attys. Gen. Contbr. articles to legal jours. Home: 2081 Marwood Dr Salt Lake City UT 84117 Office: 236 State Capitol Salt Lake City UT 84114

WILKINSON, MICHAEL CHARLES, cons. engr.; b. Milw., Dec. 14, 1935; s. Joseph Henry and Lauretta (Larson) W.; B.S.C.E., U. Minn., 1958; m. Barbara Jean Jones, July 16, 1960 (div.); children—Lisa Ann, Katherine Jane, Megan Gail; m. 2d, Mary Evelyn Moras, Dec. 6, 1979. Structural test engr. Boeing Airplane Co., Seattle, 1958-60; project engr. Morrison-Knudsen, Honolulu, 1960-64; estimator, project engr., tunnel supt. Al Johnson Constrn. Co., Mpls., 1964-70; project mgr. Mich. Sewer Constrn. Co., Detroit, 1970; mgr. contract disputes div. Kellogg Corp., Denver, 1970-82, v.p., dir., 1982—; guest lectr. Stanford U., Assn. Gen. Contractors of Am., Am. Subcontractors Assn., Nat. Assn. Surety Bond Producers; mem. nat. panel of comml. arbitrators Am. Arbitration Assn., 1978—. Recipient Bausch & Lomb Sci. award, 1953. Mem. ASCE (chmn. com. on inspection 1975-78), Nat. Soc. Profl. Engrs. (chmn. com. on Denver Rapid Transit 1975), Brit. Tunnelling Soc., Am. Inst. Contractors, Am. Underground Space Assn., Nat. Ski Patrol, Beta Theta Pi. Republican. Lutheran. Author: Handbook of Highway Engring., Sect. 18, 1975; contbr. articles to profl. jours. Home: 8896 W Roxbury Dr Littleton CO 80123 Office: 5601 S Broadway Littleton CO 80121

WILKINSON, ROBERT SHIRLEY, health care adminstr.; b. Columbia, Mo., Jan. 19, 1931; s. Hugh Leonidas and Lydia Hulda (VonMeyer) W.; M.H.A., Dallas State U., 1974; m. Marcia Jean Gribble, May 21, 1950; children—Bob, Barry, Brent, Debra. Adminstr., Quintard Gen. Hosp., San Diego, 1955-61; bus. mgr. Pkwy. Med. Group & Clinic, San Diego, 1961-71; exec. dir. to Senator John Harmer, Rep. Caucus, Sacramento, 1971-73; adminstr. Crestwood Convalescent and Rehab. Hosp., Fremont, Calif., 1973; exec. adminstr. Carrolls Health Care Facilities, El Cajon, Calif., 1973-76; gen. mgr. Regency Retirement Homes, La Mesa, Calif. 1976-81; adminstr. Pacific Home Retirement Residences and Health Care Facilities, Chula Vista, Calif., 1981—; pres. Deseret Homes, Inc., El Cajon, 1954—; sec.-treas. Technetics, Inc., El Cajon, 1966-70; gen. mgr. Regency Retirement Homes, 1976-81; dir. Pkwy. Med. Group, 1960-70. Chmn., San Diego chpt. Am. Cancer Soc., 1967-70; active Boy Scouts Am.; ch. adminstr. Ch. of Jesus Christ of Latter-day Saints., 1953-81; exec. dir. spl. legis. Rep. Caucus, Calif. Senate, 1971-73. Lic. notary public, Calif.; lic. health care adminstr. Mem. Cajon Valley Sch. Dist. Personnel Commn., Am. Coll. Nursing Home Adminstrs., Am. Med. Mgmt. Assn., Calif. Assn. Home for Aged, Am. Restaurant Assn. (adv. com. 1981-82). Clubs: Rotary, Optimist, U.S. Mormon Battalion, Army of West. Home: 1336 Flamingo Pl El Cajon CA 92021 Office: 111 3d Ave Chula Vista CA 92010

WILL, OTTO ALLEN, JR., psychiatrist; b. Caldwell, Kans., Apr. 26, 1910; s. Otto August and Florence Sarah (Keeling) W.; A.B. with gt. distinction in Econs. and Sociology, Stanford U., 1933, M.D., 1940; grad. Washington Sch. Psychiatry, 1950, Washington Psychoanalytic Inst., 1953; m. Beulah Parker, Oct. 23, 1980; children by previous marriage—Patrick Terence, Deirdre Gwen. Intern, Stanford Lane Hosps., San Francisco, 1939-40, asst. resident in pediatrics, 1940-41, asst. resident in internal medicine, 1941-42; practice medicine specializing in psychiatry, Washington, 1943-67, Rockville, Md., 1947-67, Stockbridge, Mass., 1967-78, San Francisco and Richmond, Calif., 1978—; staff psychiatrist Chestnut Lodge, Rockville, 1947-54, dir. psychotherapy, 1954-67; mem. faculty Washington Sch. Psychiatry, 1950-67, trustee, 1953—; mem. faculty Washington Psychoanalytic Inst., 1953-67, tng. analyst, 1958-67; asso. clin. prof. dept. psychiatry, U. Md. Sch. Medicine, Balt., 1956-64, clin. prof., 1964-67; part-time lectr. dept. psychiatry Johns Hopkins U., Balt., 1962-67; vis. prof. dept. psychiatry U. Chgo. Sch. Medicine, 1963-64; clin. prof. dept. psychiatry Cornell U., N.Y.C., 1967-75; med. dir. Austen Riggs Center, Inc., Stockbridge, 1967-78; vis. prof. dept. psychiatry U. Cin., 1972; mem. faculty U. Mass. Sch. Medicine, Amherst, 1976-78; clin. dir. adolescent and young adult sect. dept. psychiatry Mt. Zion Hosp., San Francisco, 1978-79. Trustee, Austen Riggs Center, 1967—. Served to lt. comdr., M.C., USN, 1942-47. Life fellow Am. Psychiat. Assn., Am. Acad. Psychoanalysis; life mem. Washington Psychoanalytic Soc., Western Mass. Psychiat. Soc., Am. Psychoanalytic Assn., Internat. Psychoanalytic Assn.; mem. No. Calif. Psychiat. Soc., William Alanson White Psychoanalytic Soc. (hon. mem.), Am. Psychosomatic Soc., AAAS, Med. Soc. of St. Elizabeth's Hosp., Phi Beta Kappa, Alpha Omega Alpha. Contbr. articles on psychotherapy and psychiat. illness to prof. jours. Address: 307 Western Dr Richmond CA 94801

WILLAIMS, WIRT ALFRED, JR. (WIRT WILLIAMS), novelist, literary critic; b. Goodman, Miss., Aug. 21, 1921; s. Wirt A. and Nina Randolph (Rayner) W.; m. Anne Norene Meredith, Apr. 10, 1954; 1 dau., Meredith Van Ness Williams Bricken. B.A., Delta Coll., 1940. M.A., La. State U., 1941; Ph.D., U. Iowa, 1953; Corr., AP, Cleveland, Miss., 1938-40; news editor Shreveport (La.) Times, 1941-42; staff writer New Orleans Item, 1946-49; instr. U. Iowa, Iowa City, 1952-53; asst. prof. English, Calif. State U., Los Angeles, 1953, prof. English, 1961—, dir. Pacific Coast Writers Workshop, 1955-58, author: (novels) The Enemy, 1951, Love in a Windy Space, 1956, Ada Dallas, 1959, A Passage of Hawks, 1963, The Trojans, 1966, The Far Side, 1972; The Tragic Art of Ernest Hemingway, 1982; contbr. articles on lit. criticism to various scholarly jours.; field editor Little Brown & Co., 1966-70; guest lit. editor Los Angeles Times, 1960-61, 68. Served with USN, 1942-46; ret. lt. comdr. Res. Nominated for Pulitzer prize, 1952, 60, 73; Huntington Hartford Found. grantee, 1958. Mem. Authors Guild, AAUP, Nat. Book Critics Circle, PEN, Philological Assn. Pacific Coast. Democrat. Episcopalian. Office: Calif State U Dept English 5151 State University Dr Los Angeles CA 90032

WILLARD, H(ARRISON) ROBERT, elec. engr.; b. Seattle, May 31, 1933; s. Harrison Eugene and Florence Linea (Chelquist) W.; B.S.E.E., U. Wash., 1955, M.S.E.E., 1957, Ph.D., 1971. Staff asso. Boeing Sci. Research Labs., Seattle, 1959-64; research asso. U. Wash., 1968-72, sr. engr. and research prof. applied physics lab., 1972-81; sr. engr. Boeing Aerospace Co., Seattle, 1981—. Served with AUS, 1957-59. Lic. profl. engr., Wash. Mem. IEEE, Am. Geophys. Union, Phi Beta Kappa, Sigma Xi, Tau Beta Pi. Contbr. articles to tech. jours. Patentee in field. Office: PO Box 39 Seattle WA 98124

WILLE, GLENN RAYMOND, chem. co. ofcl.; b. Milw., July 7, 1935; s. Herbert G. and Florence (Keller) W.; B.S., Elmhurst Coll., 1957; M.S., U. Wis., 1969; m. Judith I. Wetzel; children—Amy, Kent, Ann. Dir. employee relations Koehring Farm Div., Appleton, Wis., 1969-74; dir. personnel Patrick Cudahy, Inc., Milw., 1975-77; mgr. labor and employee relations Teledyne Wis. Motor Co., Milw., 1977-80; employee relations rep., western region Stauffer Chem. Co., San Francisco, 1980—. Mem. vocat. adv. com. Milw. Sch. Bd., 1978-80; bd. dirs. Appleton C. of C. Served with U.S. Army, 1959-61. Mem. Am. Mgmt. Assn., Am. Soc. Personnel Adminstrn., San Francisco C. of C., Am. Soc. Tng. and Devel., Nat. Safety Council. Clubs: Kiwanis (sec. 1963-71), Masons. Home: 1265 Pinecrest Dr Concord CA 94521 Office: 636 California St San Francisco CA 94108

WILLE, JERALD ROBERT, electronics company official; b. Mesa, Ariz., Sept. 28, 1943; s. Jerald D. and Virginia Edith (Newell) W.; m. Carole Jean Robinson, Oct. 13, 1946; children—Kirsten, Robert. B.S. in Math., Oreg. State U., 1966, Ph.D. in Stats., 1975. Indsl. statistician Teledyne Wah Chang Albany (Oreg.), 1971-74, quality assurance mgr., 1974-77, quality control dir., 1977—. Chmn., Corvallis (Oreg.) Aquatic team; chmn. cabinet First Baptist Ch.; chmn. Benton County Child Evangelism Bd.; mem. West Linn Water Bd. NDEA fellow, 1968; recipient Benton County YMCA Service award, 1969. Mem. Am. Soc. Quality Control, Am. Statis. Soc., Sigma Nu. Republican. Home: 4383 NE Pheasant Dr Corvallis OR 97333 Office: PO Box 460 Albany OR 97321

WILLEMS, ARNOLD LEE, educator; b. Millersburg, Ohio, Sept. 16, 1942; s. Abe Lincoln and Ruth Esther (Miller) W.; B.A., Goshen (Ind.) Coll., 1964; M.A., Western Mich. U., 1968; Ed.D. (univ. fellow 1970-71), Ind. U., 1971; m. Wanda Lucille Mast, June 5, 1964; children—Emily Marie, David Arnold. Tchr., Goshen community schs., 1964-69; assoc. instr. Ind. U., 1970-71; mem. faculty U. Wyo., Laramie, 1971—, prof. curriculum and instrn., 1980—, acting chmn. dept. curriculum and instrn., 1982—; cons. to public schs. Mem. Assn. Supervision and Curriculum Devel., Assn. Tchr. Educators, Internat. Reading Assn., Nat. Council Tchrs. English, Nat. Sci. Tchrs. Assn., Phi Delta Kappa, Kappa Delta Pi. Presbyterian. Author, editor papers and books in field. Home: 1810 Barratt St Laramie WY 82070 Office: Room 114 Mc Whinnie Hall Univ Wyo Laramie WY 82071

WILLI, EDWARD FREDERICK, fire protection equipment company executive; b. Sacramento, July 20, 1920; s. Edward Frederick and Elsie Eleanor (Orr) W.; B.S., U. Calif.-Berkeley, 1942; M.B.A., Harvard U., 1949; m. Helena Wendy Carey, May 20, 1950; children—Wendy, Leslie. Adminstrv. asst. to pres. Avoset Co., Oakland, Calif., 1949-60; pres. Wilkirk Inc., Redwood City, Calif., 1961—, also chmn. bd.; founding stockholder Bay Area Bank, Redwood City, 1979; dir. Bell Plaza Travel Inc., 1981. Mem. adv. bd. Assistance League Santa Clara County. Served to lt. USN, 1942-47. Kiwanis Clubs scholar, 1937. Mem. Nat. Fire Protection Assn., Harvard U. Bus. Sch. Assn., U. Calif.-Berkeley Alumni Assn., Phi Delta Theta (pres. 1941). Republican. Episcopalian. Clubs: Kiwanis, Masons, Elks. Office: 2831 Spring St Redwood City CA 94063

WILLIAMS, AL, state senator, architect; b. Beach, N.D., Dec. 28, 1930; s. Nolan and Gudrun (Fosjord) W.; m. Leslie Scott, 1974; children—Erin, Brock, Hilary. Student architecture and urban planning U. Wash. Practicing architect; formerly mem. Wash. Ho. of Reps., now mem. Wash. State Senate. Mem. Seattle Design Commn., Ballard Ave Hist. Dist. Bd.; past chmn. Lake Union Adv. Commn.; past pres. Wallingford Community Council. Served with USMC. Democrat. Home: 4801 Fremont St N Seattle WA 98103 Office: Washington State Senate Olympia WA 98504*

WILLIAMS, ALBERT PAINE, economist; b. Elgin, Texas, Mar. 5, 1935; s. Albert Paine and Mary Dempes (Hudler) W.; m. Elizabeth Ann Whitaker, June 22, 1957; children—Albert, Robert, John. B.S., U.S. Naval Acad., 1957; M.A., Fletcher Sch., Tufts U., 1963, M.A. in Law and Diplomacy, 1964, Ph.D., 1967. Budget examiner and internat. economist Bur. Budget, Washington, 1965-67; advisor fgn. assistance strategy, econ. policy, White House staff, 1967-68; economist Rand Corp., Santa Monica, Calif., 1968-72, sr. economist, 1972—, dir. health scis. program, 1976—; dir. Rand/UCLA Ctr. for Health Policy Study, 1982—. Active Boy Scouts Am. Recipient Profl. Achievement award Exec. Office of the Pres., 1967. Mem. AAAS, Am. Econ. Assn., Assn. Pub. Policy Analysis and Mgmt. Unitarian. Home: 508 12th St Santa Monica CA 90402 Office: 1700 Main St Santa Monica CA 90406

WILLIAMS, ANNIE RUTH, rehab. corp. exec.; b. Gadsden, Ala., Dec. 24, 1934; d. Erwin and Rosie L. (Sturns) Stevens; B.S. in Nursing Edn., Fresno State U., 1971, M.S. in Mental Health, 1972; M.S. in Counseling, Calif. State U., Los Angeles, 1976. Psychiat. nurse VA Hosp., Denver, 1965-69; supervising counselor Valley Med. Center, Fresno, Calif., 1969-70; asst. prof. Fresno State U., 1971-72; instr. for in-service edn. VA Hosp., Long Beach, Calif., 1972-75; asst. prof. Calif. State U., Los Angeles, 1975-78, also dir. tutorial program for minority students; rehab. counselor Profl. Counselors Inc., Santa Monica, Calif., 1978; pres., owner Rehab. Mgmt. Specialist, Inc., Long Beach, 1978—; cons. Los Angeles Regional Family Planning Council, Inc.; ednl. com. for ednl. seminar Calif. Assn. Rehab. Program, 1980-81. Registered nurse; cert. credentials rehab. counselor, pupil personnel counselor, community coll. instr., coll. counselor, student personnel worker. Mem. Am. Personnel and Guidance Assn., Calif. Personnel and Guidance Assn., Assn. Black Faculty and Staff of So. Calif., Nat. Rehab. Assn., Calif. Assn. Rehab. Profls., Council of Nurses Assn., NAACP, Alpha Nu (pres.), Theta Alpha Omega (rec. sec., com. chmn.). Democrat. Home: 13068 Sutton Cerritos CA 90701 Office: 3605 Long Beach Blvd Suite 201 Long Beach CA 90807

WILLIAMS, BARBARA IVORY, educational evaluator; b. Detroit, Apr. 28, 1936; d. Henry Oliver and Willa Mae (Frazier) Ivory; m. Lee Andrew Thompson, May 22, 1982. B.S., Wayne State U., 1953, M.Ed., 1960; Ph.D., U. Wash., 1973. Tchr. Detroit Pub. Schs., 1957-68; inservice specialist Mich.-Ohio Regional Ednl. Lab., Detroit, 1968-70; coordinator tchr. tng. U. Mich., Ann Arbor, 1969-70; coordinator trainers of tchr. trainers project U. Wash., Seattle, 1970-73; program assoc. Far West Lab. for Ednl. Research and Devel., San Francisco, 1973-76; sr. cons. E.H. White & Co., San Francisco, 1976-77; asst. dir. tech. assistance ctrs. N.W. Regional Ednl. Lab., Portland, Oreg., 1977—. Mem. Am. Psychol. Assn., Am. Ednl. Research Assn., Assn. Black Psychologists, NAACP, Urban League, Alpha Kappa Alpha (pres. Portland chpt. 1981—). Democrat. Baptist. Home: 3425 NE Ainsworth Portland OR 97211 Office: 300 SW 6th Ave Portland OR 97204

WILLIAMS, BENJAMIN GEORGE, lawyer; b. Windsor, Eng., Oct. 11, 1943; came to U.S., 1955, naturalized, 1962. A.B., UCLA, 1967, J.D., 1971. Bar: Calif. 1972, U.S. Dist. Ct. (cen. dist.) Calif. 1972, U.S. Tax Ct. 1973, U.S. Supreme Ct. 1979; Practice law, Los Angeles, 1972—. Mem. ABA, Calif. Bar Assn., Los Angeles County Bar Assn. Office: Suite 1900 10880 Wilshire Blvd Los Angeles CA 90024-4173

WILLIAMS, CAL ROBERTSON, consumer educator; b. Ruleville, Miss., June 16, 1949; d. Willie Junior and Louise (Fuller) Robertson; m. Harold Cleophas Williams, June 21, 1975; children—Harold, Anthony Olympus D. B.S. in Home Econs. Edn., Alcorn State U., Lorman, Miss., 1973; M.Counseling, Portland State U., 1982. County extension home economist Wash., Clackamas and Multnomah, Counties, Oreg., 1973—, extension home economist Multnomah County, 1973—; asst. prof. Oreg. State U.; arbitrator Better Bus. Bur.; clothing cons.; numerous appearances TV and radio. Mem. Multnomah County Correction Commn., 1980—, Met. Youth Commn., 1980—. Recipient Outstanding Performance as a counseling intern award Portland State U., 1982; named Citizen of Week, Portland Observer/Pacific Power & Light, 1980; Rockefeller scholastic scholar, 1973; Sears Roebuck Found. scholar, 1969. Mem. Am. Home Econs. Assn., Nat. Extension Assn. Home Econs., Oreg. Personnel and Guidance Assn., Black Colls. Com., Portland Jr. League, Alpha Kappa Alpha. Methodist. Club: Portland City. Writer Pamphlets for consumer edn.; contbr. articles to newsletters and newspapers; weekly columnist Portland Observer, Skanner. Patentee in fashion design. Home: 6124 NE 11th St Portland OR 97211 Office: Multnomah County Extension PO Box 1261 Portland OR 97207

WILLIAMS, CARMEN BRAUN, clinical psychologist; b. Mannheim, Germany, Aug. 16, 1949; came to U.S., 1952; d. Frank Emerson and Emilie Wilma (Braun) W. M.A., U. No. Colo., 1974; M.S., Pa. State U., State College, 1977, Ph.D., 1980. Therapist, Pa. State U. Mental Health Ctr., State College, 1975-77, intake supr. Psychol. Clinic, 1977-78; clin. intern U. Colo. Health Scis. Ctr., Denver, 1978-79, clin. psychologist Counseling Ctr., Boulder, 1980—. Mem. Am. Psychol. Assn. (minority fellow 1978), Assn. Black Psychologists, Colo. Psychol. Assn. Office: Counseling Ctr U Colo Box 103 Boulder CO 80309

WILLIAMS, CECIL LEROY, civil disaster planner; b. Manning, S.C., Sept. 29, 1940; s. Jake and Ophelia Malissa (McKnight) W.; B.B.A., U. Redlands, 1980; A.A., Skyline Coll., 1973; div.; 1 son, Cecil LeRoy. Ops. analyst San Francisco Public Utilities Commn., 1973-75; adminstrv. asst. to dep. gen. mgr. San Francisco Mcpl. Ry., 1975-77, exec. asst. to gen. mgr., 1977-78; asst. area adminstr. San Mateo (Calif.) Area Disaster Office, 1978-82, dir. Contra Costa County Office Emergency Services, 1982—. Bd. dirs. Diablo chpt. ARC, 1982—; region bd. dirs., trustee Lighthouse Full Gospel Ch. Mem. Calif. Emergency Services Assn. (1st v.p.), Am. Mgmt. Assn., Am. Soc. Profl. Emergency Planners., San Francisco Black Leadership Forum, CAMINAR (pres. bd. dirs.). Club: Commonwealth of Calif. Office: 50 Glacier Dr Martinez CA 94553

WILLIAMS, CHRISTIAN RICHARD, clergyman; b. Memphis, Feb. 11, 1952; s. Louie Eugene and Anne Kathleen (Lewis) W.; grad. Holy Family Sem., St. Louis, 1970; cert. human services profl. Acad. Human Service Scis., N. Central Coll., 1973; in-service edn., mental health tech. Tenn. State Psychiat. Hosp. and Ill. State Psychiat. Research Inst., 1971-74; ordained priest Western Rite, Holy Orthodox Ch., Archdiocese of Nashville, 1976, elevated to archpriest as archdiocesan chamberlain, 1978; dir. archdiocesan dept. mission/parish expansion, 1978-80; asst. master of novices Holy Cross Monastery, Chgo., 1972-74; founding guardian Little Portion Monastery, Chgo., 1974-75; regional coordinator Nat. Worker-Priest Movement, San Francisco, 1975-78; exec. dir. Office for Peace and Justice, Am. Conf. Orthodox Bishops, San Francisco, 1978—; instr./lectr. Open Edn. Exchange, Oakland, Calif., 1976-78; staff chaplain St. Thomas Team Ministry. Ecumenical Center and Chapel, San Francisco Council Chs., 1978-79; research staff Jesuit U. San Francisco, Sch. Ednl. Psychology and Inst. Cath. Ednl. Leadership. Mem. Soc. St. Basil (Basilian Fathers) (professed mem. 1976), No. Calif. Ecumenical Council, San Francisco Council Chs., World Conf. on Religion and Peace, Acad. World Studies, UN Assn., World Affairs Council, Am. Council Counselors, Therapists and Educators, N.Am. Forum on Catecumenate. Editor-in-chief Holy Cross mag., 1973-74; editor, pub. Ad Forum Publs. and Nat. Religious Classifieds, 1982—; contbg. editor The Orthodox Am.; author and lectr. Office: Box 160 UN Plaza San Francisco CA 94101

WILLIAMS, DAVID ALLEN, supt. schs.; b. Carthage, Miss., Feb. 27, 1936; s. Albert F. and M. Aline (Hardy) W.; B.S., Ariz. State Coll., 1961, M.A., 1964; Ed.S., No. Ariz. U., 1968, Ed.D., 1980; m. Bobbie Beth Roberts, Feb. 24, 1955; children—David M., Elizabeth M., Phillip A. Tchr., Flagstaff (Ariz.) Unified Sch. Dist. I, 1961-64, asst. prin., 1964-66, prin., 1966-68, dir. curriculum, 1968-69, asst. supt. schs., 1969-71, supt. schs., 1971—; lectr.; mgmt. cons.; public speaker. Bd. dirs. Mus. No. Ariz., Flagstaff Festival of Arts, Center for Law Related Edn. Served with USAF, 1954-58. Named One of 100 Top Sch. Execs. of N. Am., Executive Educator Mag. Mem. Am. Assn. Sch. Adminstrs., Ariz. Sch. Adminstrs., Flagstaff C. of C. (dir., pres.-elect), Am. Legion, Phi Kappa Phi, Phi Delta Kappa. Lutheran. Club: Flagstaff Rotary. Contbr. articles to ednl. jours. Home: 1730 N Kutch Dr Flagstaff AZ 86001 Office: 701 N Kendrick St Flagstaff AZ 86001

WILLIAMS, DAVID CARY, nuclear power safety analyst; b. Santa Monica, Calif., June 22, 1935; s. Donald Cary and Katherine Priestley (Adams) W.; A.B. in Chemistry, Harvard Coll., 1957; Ph.D. in Nuclear Chemistry, M.I.T., 1962. Postdoctoral research fellow nuclear chemistry Princeton U., 1962-64, Los Alamos Sci. Lab., 1964-66; mem. tech. staff Saudia Nat. Labs., Albuquerque, 1966—, safety analyst nuclear power reactors, 1975—. Chmn. nuclear div. Americans for Rational Energy Alternatives, 1978—, bd. dirs., 1980—. Mem. Am. Nuclear Soc., Am. Phys. Soc., Am. Chem. Soc., AAAS, Sigma Xi. Republican. Clubs: N.Mex. Mountain, Sitzmarkers Ski. Home: 1300 Espanola St NE Albuquerque NM 87110 Office: Div 9424 Sandia Nat Labs Albuquerque NM 87185

WILLIAMS, DENNIS BEALL, reinsurance company executive; b. Los Angeles, June 14, 1943; s. Raymond Henry and Miriam C. (Beall) W.; m. Elizabeth A. Hayes, Apr. 24, 1976; children—Darcy Elizabeth, Seana Claire, Casey Anne. B.A., U. Calif.-Santa Barbara, 1966; M.B.A., Calif. State U.-Long Beach, 1971. With Gen. Reins. Corp., 1971—, sr. facultative underwriter, San Francisco, 1972-78, casualty facultative br. mgr., Seattle, 1978—. Served to 1st lt. USAR, 1966-69. Home: 312 W Comstock St Seattle WA 98119 Office: 1111 3d Ave Seattle WA 98101

WILLIAMS, DOLORES RAE, state administrator; b. Portland, Oreg., Jan. 12, 1933; d. Ray and Lois Dorothy (Cornell) Gallucci; m. Robert Nash Williams, Dec. 10, 1955; children—Bruce Marshall, Brian Nash. Owner, mgr. House of Hopper, Salt Lake City, 1959-76, Mountain West Cycle Supply, Salt Lake City, 1970-76; consumer services rep. Tracy Collins Bank & Trust, Salt Lake City, 1976-79, br. mgr., 1979-80; dir. advt. and public relations Utah Econ. and Indsl. Devel. Div., Salt Lake City, 1980—. Mem. adv. bd. U. Utah Coll. Nursing, 1980—. Mem. Utah Advt. Fedn., Pub. Relations Soc. Am. Democrat. Contbr. to mag. fin. column. Home: 4626 Brookwood Circle Salt Lake City UT 84117 Office: 200 S Main St Suite 620 Salt Lake City UT 84101

WILLIAMS, DONALD SPENCER, scientist; b. Pasadena, Calif., May 28, 1939; s. Charles Gardner and Delia Ruth (Spencer) W.; B.S., Harvey Mudd Coll., 1961; M.S., Carnegie Inst. Tech., 1962; Ph.D., Carnegie-Mellon U., 1969. Asst. project dir. Learning Research and Devel. Ctr., Pitts., 1965-67; cons. system design, Pitts., 1967-69; mem. tech. staff RCA Corp., Palo Alto, Calif., 1969-72; prin. investigator robot vision Jet Propulsion Lab., Calif. Inst. Tech., Pasadena, 1972-80; scientist user interface TRW Corp., Redondo Beach, Calif., 1980—; producer indsl. shows and films, 1970—; lectr. advanced computer applications, 1973—. Mem. Am. Assn. Artificial Intelligence, AAAS, Assn. Computing Machinery, Audio Engring. Soc., Fedn. Am. Scientists, Nat. Fire Protection Assn., IEEE, Robotics Internat. Assn., Soc. Motion Picture and TV Engrs., Soc. Preservation Variety Arts, Town Hall of Calif. Contbr. articles to profl. jours. Home: 1210 N Allen Ave Pasadena CA 91104 Office: One Space Park Redondo Beach CA 90278

WILLIAMS, DOUGLAS, management consultant; b. Newburgh, N.Y., Oct. 13, 1912; s. Everett Frank and Marjorie Tuthill W.; m. Esther Grant, Sept. 23, 1939; children—Penelope Williams Winters, Grant. A.B., Cornell U., 1934; M.B.A., Harvard U., 1936. With Air Reduction Co., 1936-37, Am. Inst. Pub. Opinion, 1938, Elmo Roper Co., 1939-40; assoc. dir. Nat. Opinion Research Ctr., U. Denver, 1940-42; pres. Douglas Williams Assos., Carefree, Ariz. and N.Y.C., 1948—. Pres. Community Chest, Larchmont, N.Y., 1959; bd. mgrs. West Side YMCA, N.Y.C., 1957-60. Served to lt. col. U.S. Army, 1942-45. Republican. Episcopalian. Clubs: Larchmont Yacht, Univ. (pres.) (Larchmont); Harvard, Union League, Cornell. Home: 7612 E Horizon Dr PO Box 941 Carefree AZ 85377 Office: Executive Center PO Box 941 Carefree AZ 85377

WILLIAMS, DOUGLAS GEORGE, seminary adminstrator, religious educator; b. Provo, Utah, Oct. 28, 1940; s. William V. and Mary Faye (Fail) Johnson; m. Nancy Taggart, June 24, 1963; children—Steven, Darrin, Noelle, Reven, Suzanne, Jeffrey, Tyler, Bradley. B.S., Weber State Coll., 1967; M.A., Brigham Young U., 1970; Ed.D., Utah State U., 1983. Cert. tchr., Utah. Tchr. chemistry and biology Bonneville High Sch., Ogden, Utah, 1966-67; tchr. Latter-day Saints Sem., Montpelier, Idaho, 1967-68, Ogden, 1968-70; religious educator Tonga Latter-day Saints Ch. Schs., 1970-71, adminstr. ch. schs., 1971-72; area dir. Religious Edn. Programs, Queensland, Australia, 1972-74; prin. Latter-day Saints Sem., Afton, Wyo., 1974-78, Smithfield, Utah, 1978—. Mem. Smithfield City Library Bd., 1980-82. Served with USMCR, 1959-60. Mem. Assn. Supervision and Curriculum Devel., Mormon History Assn. Home: 44 Chestnut Ln Smithfield UT 84335 Office: 470 S 250 E Smithfield UT 84335

WILLIAMS, EDWARD RAYMOND, safety engineer; b. Chgo., Dec. 12, 1932; s. Arthur Raymond and Edith Marie (Lindgren) W.; m. Mary Ann Rushing, May 29, 1957; children—David E., Megan E., Amy S. Douglas E. B.S. in Indsl. Mgmt., So. Ill. U., 1957-59; B.S. in Occupational Safety and Health, Utah State U., Logan, 1974-76. Commd. officer, U.S. Air Force, 1960, advanced through grades to maj., 1972, ret. 1976; helicopter instr., safety engr. Thiokol/Wasatch Div., Brigham City, Utah, 1976-80, adminstr. employee motivation programs, 1980—. Decorated D.F.C., Air medal; recipient NASA Group Achievement award. Mem. Am. Soc. Safety Engrs. Clubs: Elks. Home: 1888 27th St Ogden UT 84403 Office: PO Box 524 Brigham City UT 84302

WILLIAMS, EVELYN METOYER, educator; b. Evergreen, La., May 27, 1937; d. Steven and Alnetter T. Metoyer; B.S., Tex. So. U., 1959; M.Ed., So. U., 1965; Reading Specialist degree, U. So. Calif., 1979; m. Lindbergh Williams, Feb. 2, 1975. Master tchr. E. Baton Rouge Parish Sch. Dist., 1966-71; supr. aids and tchrs. Southeastern La. U. Lab. Sch., Hammond, 1971-73; asso. prof. So. Univ., New Orleans, 1973-74; Children's Center tchr., Los Angeles Unified Sch. Dist., 1977—, cons., tchr. in field. Com. mem. Calif. Tchrs. State Council; life mem. NAACP. Mem. NEA (Los Angeles Chpt.), Assn. for Supervision and Curriculum Devel., United Tchrs. Los Angeles; Internat. Reading Assn., Calif. Reading Assn., United Tchrs. Los Angeles. Roman Catholic.

WILLIAMS, GAIL WILSON, oil refining and marketing company executive; b. Roswell, N.Mex., Dec. 8, 1943; d. Don E. and Bettie (Core) Wilson; m. James E. Williams, Dec. 10, 1964. Student Ringling Sch., Sarasota, Fla., 1962-63; B.S. in Mgmt., Ga. State U., 1979; postgrad. Antioch Law Sch., 1981—. Adminstrv. services supr. Austin Industries, Dallas, 1968-76, personnel asst., 1972-76, asst. EEO adminstr., 1973-76; sr. sec. Ga. State U., 1976-79, adminstrv. mgr. Plateau, Inc., Albuquerque and Bloomfield, N.Mex., 1979—. Mem. Bloomfield C. of C., Profl. Orgn. Women, Nat. Assn. Female Execs., Desk and Derrick Clubs Am. (dir. 1981—). Republican. Unitarian. Office: PO Box 159 Bloomfield NM 87413

WILLIAMS, GEORGE ROBERT, energy co. exec.; b. Los Angeles, Feb. 19, 1948; s. Robert Thomas and Flora Francis (Froman) W.; B.A., Whittier Coll., 1970, M.P.A., 1971; Ph.D., UCLA, 1979. Writer, Los Angeles Herald Examiner, 1966-68; labor negotiator Am. Newspaper Guild, 1968-70; instr. Calif. State Poly. U., 1970-73; asso. dean internat. ops. UCLA, 1973-76; dir. corp. planning, dir. Rocky Mountain ops. System Devel. Corp., Santa Monica, Calif., 1976-81; pres., chief exec. officer Core Mgmt. Group, Denver, 1981—; adj. prof. bus. U. Colo. Chmn., Consortium on Energy Devel., State of Colo. Mem. Internat. Conf. on Energy Use Mgmt. (bd. dirs.). Author: American Labor Movement: A Study in Crisis, 1971; Jerry Brown: In a Plain Brown Wrapper, 1978; American Political Corruption, 1979. Home: 7433 Crannell Dr Boulder CO 80303

WILLIAMS, GERALD WALTER, sociologist; b. Eugene, Oreg., June 30, 1945; s. Jack and Gladys N. Williams; m. Ellen Spencer Credle, Aug. 11, 1979. Student Diablo Valley Coll., 1963-65, 1968-69; B.S. in Sociology, So. Oreg. State Coll., 1971, M.S. in Gen. Studies Social Sci., 1972; Ph.D. in Sociology, Wash. State U., 1976. Asst. prof. sociology Ind. State U., Terre Haute, 1975-77; dir. Community Needs Assessment Project, Eugene, Oreg., 1978, research contractor Eugene Parks and Recreation Dept., 1978-79; sociologist Umpqua Nat. Forest, Roseburg, Oreg., 1979—; lectr. Mem. Friends of Lane County Mus., Friends of Springfield Library. Served with U.S. Army, 1965-68. Mem. Am. Assn. State and Local History, Am. Name Soc., Am. Sociol. Assn., Forest History Soc., Lane County Hist. Soc., Oreg. Hist. Soc., Pacific Sociol. Assn., Soc. History in Fed. Govt., Umpqua Hist. Preservation Soc. Democrat. Unitarian. Contbr. articles on sociology and history to profl. jours. Home: 3972 Oak St Eugene OR 97405 Office: PO Box 1008 Roseburg OR 97470

WILLIAMS, GORDON FREDERICK, physician; b. Istanbul, Turkey, June 15, 1917; s. Frederick James and Leslie (Conner) W.; B.A., Stanford U., 1938, M.D., 1942; m. Sylvia Berry, Mar. 26, 1965; children—Sally, Melissa; came to U.S., 1921, naturalized, 1938. Intern, Stanford Univ. Hosp., San Francisco, 1941-42, resident pediatrics, 1946-48; practice medicine specializing in pediatrics Menlo Med. Clinic, Menlo Park, Calif., 1948-54, co-founder, 1948; med. dir. Stanford Children's Convalescent Hosp., Palo Alto, Calif., 1954-63; chief pediatrics San Mateo County Gen. Hosp., San Mateo, Calif., 1963-69; med. dir. East Palo Alto Neighborhood Health Center, 1970-71, Alviso (Calif.) Family Health Center, 1971-74; chief pediatrics Natividad Med. Center, Salinas, Calif., 1974-78; cons. pediatric rheumatology, mem. staff Children's Hosp. at Stanford, Palo Alto, 1978—; clin. prof. pediatrics Stanford U. Sch. Medicine, 1978—; mem. cons. staff Children's Hosp. Med. Center, Oakland, Calif. Served to maj., M.C., AUS, 1942-46. Fellow Am. Acad. Pediatrics; mem. Am. Rheumatism Assn., AAAS, Western Soc. Pediatric Research, N.Y. Acad. Scis., Sigma Xi, Alpha Omega Alpha. Democrat. Author: Children with Chronic Arthritis: A Manual for Patients and Parents, 1981. Home: 47 View St Los Altos CA 94022 Office: Children's Hosp at Stanford 520 Willow Rd Palo Alto CA 94304

WILLIAMS, HAROLD CURTIS, civil engineer, city official; b. New Orleans, Oct. 31, 1940; s. John B. and Rosetta E. Williams; m. Carolyn Lee, June 20, 1969; children—Michelle, Kevin; A.A., Los Angeles Trade Tech. Coll., 1965; B.S., Calif. State U.-Los Angeles, 1973; M.C.E., Calif. State U.-Long Beach, 1976, postgrad., 1977-78; postgrad. UCLA, 1979. Registered profl. engr., Calif. Civil engr. City of Long Beach, 1979-80; dir. pub. works, city engr. City of Lynwood (Calif.), 1980—. Served with AUS, 1960-63. Mem. ASCE, Inst. Transp. Engrs., Am. Pub. Works Assn., Inst. Mcpl. Engring., Los Angeles Council Black Profl. Engrs. Democrat. Lutheran. Office: 11330 Bullis Rd Lynwood CA 90262

WILLIAMS, HAROLD MCNEAL, psychiatrist; b. Trenton, N.J., Feb. 21, 1932; s. McNeal and Elizabeth (Carroll) W.; B.S. in Chemistry, Howard U., 1954, M.D., 1958; m. Beverly Arlene Eason, Sept. 19, 1959; children—Harold Michael, Steven Craig, Timothy Martin, Robert Matthew, Elizabeth Carroll Ann. Intern, Northwestern Hosp., Mpls., 1958-59; resident psychiatry N.J. State Hosp., Trenton, 1959-62; organizer, a developer Fresno (Calif.) County Dept. Mental Health, 1964—; with Fresno County Gen. Hosp., 1964—; chief psychiatry Fresno County Dept. Mental Health, 1964-65, program chief, 1964-65, acting dir., 1966-67, chief outpatient psychiat. services, 1967—; pvt. practice medicine specializing in psychiatry, Fresno, 1969—; mem. staffs Fresno Community Hosp., Valley Med. Center, Fresno. Acting mil. cons. psychiatry March AFB, 1963-64; cons. psychiatry VA Hosp., Fresno, 1969—, Westview Convalescent Hosp., Fresno, 1969—; vis. lectr. Grad. Sch. Social Work Fresno State Coll., 1965-68. Mem. interfaith adv. council Fresno Community Hosp., 1965—; mem. profl. adv. com. Fresno County Mental Health Assn., 1965-66; mem. adv. bd. KJEO TV, 1969—; v.p. Profl. Services Exchange Corp., 1980—. Bd. dirs. Goodwill Industries San Joaquin Valley, adv. com., Fresno, 1970-78; bd. dirs. Family Service Center Fresno, Central Calif. Blood Bank, 1981—; trustee Fresno Found. Med. Care, 1977—, Central Calif. Health Systems Agy., 1977-78; exec. bd. Bullard High Sch. PTA, 1977—. Served to capt. M.C., USAF, 1962-64. Recipient Outstanding Achievement award in psychiatry Howard U. Med. Coll., 1958. Fellow AAAS, Acad. Psychosomatic Medicine; mem. Am. Psychiat. Assn., Central Calif. Psychiat. Soc., AMA, Calif. (alt. del. ann. conv. 1979-80, del. 1980-82, 82-84), Nat. med. assns., N.Y. Acad. Scis., Am. Geriatrics Soc., Fresno Madera Med. Soc. (gov. 1975-77, pres. 1979), Golden State Med. Assn., Calif. Psychiat. Assn., Kappa Alpha Psi, Beta Kappa Chi. Methodist. Home: 2070 W San Ramon Ave Fresno CA 93711 Office: Fresno County Dept Mental Health 4441 E Kings Canyon Rd Fresno CA 93702 also 1300 N Fresno St Fresno CA 93703

WILLIAMS, HARRIETTE FLOWERS, ednl. adminstr.; b. Los Angeles, July 18; d. Orlando and Virginia (Carter) Flowers; B.S., UCLA, 1952, Ed.D., (HEW fellow), 1973; M.A., Calif. State U.-Los Angeles, 1956; m. Irvin F. Williams, Apr. 9, 1960; children—Lorin Finley, Lori Virginia. Tchr., Los Angeles Unified Sch. Dist., 1952-59, counselor, 1954-59; psychometrist, 1958-62, faculty chmn., 1956-57, student activities coordinator, 1955-59, leader insts. and workshops, 1952-76, dir. counseling, 1960-65, supr. Title I programs Elem. Secondary Edn. Act, 1965-68, asst. prin., 1968-76, prin., 1976-82, dir. instrn. sr. high sch. div., 1982-83; asst. dir. HEW project for high sch. adminstrn. UCLA, 1971-72; adj. prof. in Masters in Sch. Adminstrn. program Pepperdine U., Los Angeles, 1974-78. Recipient Sojourner Truth award Nat. Assn. Negro Bus. and Profl. Women's Clubs, Los Angeles, 1968; Life Membership Service award Los Angeles PTA, 1975; Los Angeles Mayor's Golden Apple award for ednl. excellence. Mem. Los Angeles Assn. Secondary Sch. Adminstrs., Assn. Calif. Sch. Adminstrs., Nat. Assn. Secondary Sch. Prins., Sr. High Sch. Asst. Prins. Assn. of Los Angeles (dir. 1974-76), Sr. High Sch. Prins. Orgn., Nat. Council of Negro Women (life mem.), Lullaby Guild of Children's Home Soc. Los Angeles, Los Angeles PTA, NAACP, Urban League, Jack and Jill of Am., Inc., Delta Sigma Theta (pres. Los Angeles chpt. 1964-66, regional dir. 1968-72, nat. committeewoman 1966—), Pi Lambda Theta, Kappa Delta Pi, Delta Kappa Gamma. Baptist. Office: 644 W 17th St Los Angeles CA 90015

WILLIAMS, J. MARSDEN, state senator, realtor, farmer; m. Phyllis Williams; 8 children. Student Utah State Agrl. Coll. Savs. rep., realtor, farmer; mem. Idaho State Senate; chmn. resources and environ. coms.; co-chmn. interim com. on energy devel. Republican. Mormon. Office: Idaho State Senate Boise ID 83720*

WILLIAMS, JAMES DOUGLAS, sociology educator, consultant; b. Anderson, Ind., June 13, 1951; s. David Francis and Anne (Daugherty) W.; m. Karen Lowe, Nov. 24, 1982; 1 stepdau., Emily Lowry. B.S., U. Iowa, 1973; M.A., Ball State U., 1975; Ph.D., U. Ill. 1978. Research asst. U. Ill.-Urbana, 1974-78, research assoc., 1978-79; asst. prof. sociology N.Mex. State U., 1979—; cons. demography. Mem. Population Assn. Am., Am. Sociol. Assn., Rural Sociol. Soc. Contbr. articles to profl. publs.; editor: (with Andrew Sofranto) Rebirth of Rural America, 1980; (with A. Sofranto and C. Roseman) Population Redistribution in the Midwest, 1980; research in field. Home: 645 W Las Cruces Ave Las Cruces NM 88005 Office: Dept Sociology NMex State U Box 3BC Las Cruces NM 88003

WILLIAMS, JEAN CARLSON, financial planning company executive; b. Chgo., July 19, 1928; d. Claes Berger and Thora Otilia (Johnson) Carlson; children—Gwen Ann, Grant Thomas. B.S., Syracuse (N.Y.) U., 1950, M.A., 1953. Dir. mdsg. Coll. Home Econs., Syracuse U., 1951-55; dir. women's div., N.Y. State Fair, Demonstration Kitchen, 1960-62; ins. agt., 1973; owner JCW Fin. Planning, Agoura, Calif., 1975—. Mem. Nat. Assn. Life Underwriters, San Fernando Valley Life Underwriters Assn. (past v.p., dir.), Women Leaders Round Table, Nat. Assn. Women Bus. Owners (v.p.), Am. Soc. Women Accts. (dir.), Calif. Women in Higher Edn., Women in Bus., Women's Equity Action League (pres. 1977, 78), Agoura Valley C. of C. (pres. 1978), Los Angeles County Mus. (costume council), Omicron Nu, Kappa Alpha Theta. Republican. Methodist. Home: 5853 Lake Lindero Dr Agoura CA 91301 Office: 28900 Roadside Dr Agoura CA 91301

WILLIAMS, JEFFREY LYNN, chem. co. exec.; b. Marysville, Kans., Mar. 25, 1943; s. Royal Farnsworth and Ella Mae (Lake) W.; B.S. in Phys. Edn., U. N.Mex., 1968; m. Karen Kay Keller, Dec. 28, 1968; children—Kari Lynn, Kimberly Anne. Operator, Cardinal Chem. Co., Hobbs, N.Mex., 1968; program dir. Boys Club of Hobbs, 1969; recreation playground leader City of Hobbs, 1970, recreation supt., 1970, parks and recreation dir., 1971-82; safety engr. Climax Chem. Co., 1982—. Small bus. chmn. United Fund, Hobbs, 1974, edn. div. chmn., 1980-81; chmn. bd. dirs. Hobbs Employee Fed. Credit Union, 1980; chmn. bd. dirs. Boys Club of Hobbs, 1977, pres., 1978. Served with U.S. Army, 1968. Recipient Meritorious Service award City of Hobbs, 1973. Mem. N.Mex. Parks and Recreation Assn. (Outstanding Profl. award 1975, pres. 1980—), Nat. Recreation and Park Assn., Soc. Safety Engrs. (sec. chpt.). Democrat. United Methodist. Club: Lions (Lion of Yr. 1978-79). Home: 421 W Clearfork Circle Hobbs NM 88240 Office: Monument NM

WILLIAMS, JEROME JACK, JR., city official; b. Beaumont, Tex., Nov. 15, 1936; s. Jerome Jack and Helen (Herum) W.; m. Margaret Elspeth Strachan, Mar. 7, 1959; children—Richard, Robin, Elizabeth, Jonathan. B.A., San Jose State U., 1968; postgrad. Calif. State U., 1976-78. Pub. works insp., City of Milpitas, Calif., 1959-63, chief insp., 1963-68, contract compliance officer, 1968-78, pub. facilities mgr., 1978-79, community services mgr., 1979—; tchr., cons. Mem. Am. Pub. Works Assn., Calif. Park and Recreation Assn., Milpitas C. of C., Delta Sigma Phi. Home: 3584 Vista del Valle San Jose CA 95132

WILLIAMS, JUDITH, public relations executive, art gallery director; b. Chgo., Nov. 4, 1929; d. Max and Ella (Santa) Friedman; m. Robert Francis Williams, Apr. 28, 1950; m. 2d, William Carlisle Scott VII, Dec. 26, 1964; children—William C. Scott VIII, Kirk Scott Cookson, Kevin Scott Besore, Christopher Scott, Gillian Scott, Bryan Scott. Student U.

Ariz., 1947-50. Reporter, Ariz. Daily Star, 1949-53; promotion dir. Tucson Newspapers, Inc., 1953-57; editor, employee publs. Missile div., Hughes Aircraft Co., Tucson, 1957-62; owner, JW Organisation, pub. relations, Tucson, 1962—; owner, dir. Rosequist Galleries, Tucson, 1982—; v.p. Sta. KGVY-AM, Green Valley, Ariz., 1981—; part owner Tucson Toros baseball team, 1976—; sec. JW Devel. Co., Tucson; instr. mktg. U. Ariz., 1976-78. Mem. Ariz. State Lottery Commn., 1983—; mem. City Tucson Bd. Adjustment, 1979—; treas. sr. Now Generation; bd. dirs. Tucson Trade Bur.; mem. adv. bd. Green Fields Country Day Sch. Mem. Pub. Relations Soc. Am. (nat. dir. 1976-77, 77-78). Democrat. Methodist. Office: PO Box 40756 Tucson AZ 85717

WILLIAMS, KENNETH JAMES, county ofcl.; b. Eureka, Calif., Apr. 28, 1924; s. E. J. and Thelma (Hall) W.; student Humboldt State Coll., 1942-43; B.S., U. Oreg., 1949, M.Ed., 1952; m. Mary Patricia Warring, Sept. 3, 1949; children—James Clayton, Susan May, Christopher Kenneth. Engaged as mountain triangulation observer with U.S. Coast and Geodetic Survey, 1942; instr. bus. and geography Boise (Idaho) Jr. Coll., 1949-51; tchr. Prospect High Sch., 1952-54; prin. Oakland (Oreg.) High Sch., 1954-58; supt. prin. Coburg Public Schs., 1958-64; supt. Yoncalla (Oreg.) Public Schs., 1964-66, Amity (Oreg.) Public Schs., 1966-72; adminstr. Yamhill County, McMinnville, Oreg., 1974—; county liaison officer Land and Water Conservation Fund, 1977. Dist. lay leader Oreg.-Idaho ann. conf. United Methodist Ch., 1968-80, bd. dirs. western dist. Ch. Extension Soc., 1976; mem. Mid-Willamette Manpower Council, 1974—; bd. dirs. Lafayette Noble Homes, 1970-72; mem. adv. com. local budget law sect. State of Oreg. Served with AUS, 1943-46. Recipient Purple Heart, Good Conduct medal, battle stars. Mem. NEA, Oreg. Edn. Assn., Oreg. Assn. Secondary Prins., Nat. Assn. Secondary Prins., AAUP, Oreg., Am. assns. sch. adminstrs., Assn. Supervision and Curriculum Devel., Nat. Sch. Pub. Relations Assn., Phi Delta Kappa. Mason (Shriner), Lion. Home: Route 2 Box 75 Dayton OR 97114

WILLIAMS, KNOX, water conditioning company executive; b. Grandfield, Okla., Aug. 9, 1928; s. Knox B. and Clara Mae (Butler) W.; m. Juanita June Wood, Sept. 9, 1951; children—Jodi Ann and Feri Ruth (twins), Drue Knox. B.A., UCLA, 1951. With Wilson-McMahan Furniture Stores, Santa Barbara, Calif., 1951-61; prin., pres. Rayne of North San Diego County, Vista, Calif., 1961—, Aqua Fresh Drinking Water Systems, Inc., San Diego, 1980—. Served with USNR, 1947-48. Mem. Carlsbad C. of C., Pacific Water Quality Assn. (pres. 1975-76), Water Quality Assn. (bd. dirs. 1980-83). Republican. Presbyterian. Clubs: El Camino Rotary (Oceanside, Calif.), Masons (Santa Barbara). Office: Rayne of North San Diego County 2011 W Vista Way Vista CA 92083 also Aqua Fresh Drinking Water Systems 7370 Opportunity Rd Suite I San Diego CA 92111

WILLIAMS, LOUIS ALLAN, attorney general Canadian province; b. Glenavon, Sask., Can., May 22, 1922; s. Louis Pomerine and Eula Belle (MacPherson) W.; m. Marjorie Ruth Lake, June 25, 1948; children—Louis Ryder, Leslie Ruth, Susan Jane. LL.B., U. B.C. Created queen's counsel. Mem. Legis. Assembly B.C. for West Vancouver-Howe Sound, 1966—, minister of labor, 1975, atty. gen. B.C., 1979—. Served to flight lt. RCAF. Mem. Social Credit Party. Office: Legis Bldgs Victoria BC V8V 1X4 Canada*

WILLIAMS, LYNNE HUIE, psychiatrist; b. Evanston, Ill., Aug. 23, 1943; d. Virgil Clifford and Vivian (Brown) W.; B.A., U. Mich., 1965; M.D., Wayne State U., 1969; children—Tavis Randall, Shepherd Subhan. Intern, Bronx Mcpl. Hosp., 1969-70, resident in pediatrics, 1970-72; resident in psychiatry U. Miami (Fla.), 1973-74, fellow developmental pediatrics, 1972-73; practice medicine, specializing in developmental pediatrics, gestalt therapy, Asheville, N.C., 1974-79; med. dir. Devel. Evaluation Center, Asheville, 1976-79; fellow in child and adolescent psychiatry U. Miami, 1979-81; practice medicine specializing in infant, child, adolescent and adult psychiatry, Spokane, Wash., 1981—. Diplomate Am. Bd. Pediatrics. Mem. Human Potential Inst. Gt. Smokies (dir. 1975—), Am. Soc. Adolescent Psychiatry, Gestalt Therapy Inst. Fla. (asso.), Am. Psychiat. Assn., Am. Orthopsychiat. Assn., N.C. Group Behavior Soc. Research on developmental effects of early parent-infant interactions. Home: E4518 Silver Pine Rd Colbert WA 99005 Office: E 12 5th Spokane WA 99207

WILLIAMS, MARK R(OSS), artist, publisher; b. Portland, Oreg., July 25, 1947; s. James L. and Norma F. (Beam) W.; m. Eunice Maldonado, May 22, 1972; children—Oliver Evan, Morgan James. A.A., Pasadena City Coll., 1972; student Art Ctr. Coll. Design, Los Angeles, 1972-74. Truck driver Donoghue's, Los Angeles, 1974-76; art dir. French Graphics, Burbank, Calif., 1976-82; pres. Mark Williams Advt., South Pasadena, Calif., 1982—; founder Tortilla Press, South Pasadena, 1979—; paintings exhibited: Pasadena Painting Exhbn., 1979, Redlands Painting Exhbn., 1975; represented in pvt. collections. Home: 1729 Virginia Pl South Pasadena CA 91030

WILLIAMS, MARSHALL MACKENZIE, utilities co. exec.; b. Londonderry, N.S., Can., Dec. 11, 1923; s. Millard Fillmore and Gladys Christine (MacKenzie) W.; B.Engring., Tech. U.N.S., 1947, M.Engring., 1949, D.Engring. (hon.), 1978; postgrad. Banff Sch. Advanced Mgmt., 1955; m. Joan Atlee Ross, Sept. 6, 1952; children—Peter, Alex, Stephen, Margot. Engr., Montreal Engring. Co. Ltd., 1948-54; with TransAlta Utilities Corp. (formerly Calgary Power Ltd.), Calgary, Alta., Can., 1954—, asst. to gen. mgr., 1954-60, exec. asst., 1960-66, asst. gen. mgr., 1966-68, exec. v.p., 1968-73, pres., 1973—, dir., 1972—, chief exec. officer, 1980—; chmn. bd. TransAlta Resources Corp., 1981—; dir. Pan Canadian Petroleum Ltd., Royal Trust Corp. Can., Royal Trustco Ltd., Nfld. Light & Power Co. Ltd., AEC Power Ltd., Sun Life Assurance Co. Can. Mem. Royal Trust Adv. Bd., Calgary; mem. Alta. Research Council; bd. dirs. Canadian Energy Research Inst., Soc., Environment and Energy Devel. Studies Found. Mem. Assn. Profl. Engrs., Geologists and Geophysicists Alta., Canadian Elec. Assn. (past pres.), N.W. Electric Light and Power Assn. (past pres.), Calgary C. of C. (dir.). Presbyterian. Club: Ranchmen's (Calgary). Office: 110 12th Ave SW Box 1900 Calgary AB T2P 2M1 Canada

WILLIAMS, MARY IRENE, educator; b. Hugo, Okla., June 30, 1944; d. Primer and Hylar B. (Tarkington) Jackson; B.Bus. Edn., Langston U., 1967; M.S. in Bus. Edn., Emporia State U., 1973; postgrad. U. Nev., 1975-77; m. Lee A. Williams, Feb. 10, 1973; 1 dau., Monica Ariane. Bus. instr. Spokane (Wash.) Community Coll., 1967-69; Topeka West High Sch., 1970-71, tchr. bus. Highland Park High Sch., Topeka, Kans., 1972-73; instr. Clark County Community Coll., North Las Vegas, Nev., 1973-78, dir. bus. div., 1978—; cons. Scott Foresman Pub. Co., 1977-80; condr. seminars for Las Vegas C. of C., 1980. Mem. NEA, Am. Bus. Communication Assn., Nat. Bus. Edn. Assn., Am. Assn. Women in Community and Jr. Colls., Internat. Assn. Bus. Communicators, Am. Assn. Female Execs. Office: 3200 E Cheyenne Ave North Las Vegas NV 89030

WILLIAMS, MARY YOUNG, educator, educational consultant; b. St. Marys, Pa., Nov. 29, 1949; d. Charles Bradford and Mary Amelia (Andrus) Young; m. Daniel Patrick Williams, Apr. 14, 1973; children—Ryan Daniel, Nicole Marie. B.S., Edinboro State Coll., 1971, M.Ed., 1974. Tchr. English, Warren (Pa.) Area High Sch., 1971-76, Franklin McKinley Sch. Dist., San Jose, Calif., 1976—; assoc. dir. South Bay Writing Project, San Jose State U., 1981—; mem. Calif. State Rev. Team, 1981. Named Tchr. of Yr., Fair Intermediate Sch., 1979. Mem. Nat. Council Tchrs. English, Internat. Reading Assn., Assn. Supervision and Curriculum Devel., Calif. Assn. Tchrs. English, Calif. Reading Assn., Central Calif. Council Tchrs. English (exec. bd.), Santa Clara County Reading Assn., Santa Clara County Com. on Writing, Nat. Writers Club, Phi Delta Kappa. Author: (with others) Teaching Writing in K-8 Classrooms, 1983. Home: 483 Cestaric Ave Milpitas CA 95035 Office: Box 943 Milpitas CA 95035

WILLIAMS, MICHAEL EARL, industrial hygienist, safety and health exec.; b. Hanford, Calif., Nov. 24, 1949; s. Robert D. and Evelyn E. (Whitman) W.; m. Patricia M. Mazzoni, Mar. 3, 1974; m. 2d, Danielle Y. Hall, Jun. 25, 1980. B.A., Calif. State U.-Fresno, 1972; M.P.H., U. Calif.-Berkeley, 1973, M.S., 1975. Cert. indsl. hygienist, Calif. Research assoc. U. Calif.-Berkeley, 1973-74; indsl. hygienist OSHA, U.S. Dept. Labor, 1975-76; asst. dep. chief div. occupational safety and health Calif. Dept. Indsl. Relations, 1977-81; safety and health mgr. Am. Microsystems, Inc., Santa Clara, Calif., 1981—. Mem. Am. Indsl Hygiene Assn., Am. Conf. Govtl. Indsl. Hygienists, Nat. Environ. Health Assn., Am. Electronics Assn. Democrat. Methodist. Contbr. articles to profl. jours. Office: 3800 Homestead Rd m/s 896 Santa Clara CA 95051

WILLIAMS, PAT, congressman; b. Helena, Mont., Oct. 30, 1937; student U. Mont., 1956-57; student William Jewell U.; B.A., U. Denver, 1961; postgrad. Western Mont. Coll. m. Carol Griffith, 1965; children—Griff, Erin, Whitney. Mem. Mont. Ho. of Reps., 1967, 69; exec. dir. Hubert Humphrey Presdl. campaign, Mont., 1968; exec. asst. to U.S. Rep. John Melcher, 1969-71; mem. Gov.'s Employment and Tng. Council, 1972-78; mem. Mont. Legis. Reapportionment Commn., 1973; co-chmn. Jimmy Carter Presdl. campaign, Mont., 1976; mem. 96th-98th Congresses from 1st Mont. dist.; coordinator Mont. Family Edn. Program, 1971-78. Served with U.S. Army, 1960-61, Army N.G., 1962-69. Mem. Mont. Fedn. Tchrs. Democrat. Club: Elks. Office: 1512 Longworth House Office Bldg Washington DC 20515

WILLIAMS, PHILLIP BROCK CARL, research immunologist; b. Cheyenne, Wyo., July 15, 1942; s. Russell Irenus and Carleen (Steckelberg) W.; B.S. in Zoology and Chemistry, U. Wyo., 1967; M.S. in Biophysics and Microbiology, U. Colo., 1969; Ph.D. in Exptl. Pathology, U. Utah, 1975. Research fellow San Diego Biomed. Research Inst., 1969-70; teaching and research fellow U. Colo. Med. Center, 1967-68; mem. faculty U. Calif., San Diego, 1970-71, U. Utah Med. Center, 1973-75; postdoctoral research fellow Nat. Jewish Hosp. and Research Center, Denver, 1976-78, research immunobiologist, 1980—; pres., dir. Applied Med. Systems, Inc.; asst. prof. U. Lausanne-Sur-Epalinges, Epalinges, Switzerland, 1979-80; research advisor, editor Am. Acad. Otolaryngic Allergy, Soc. Clin. Ecology. USPHS fellow, 1971; grantee NSF, 1976-78. Mem. AAUP, Tissue Culture Soc., AAAS, Swiss Soc. Allergy and Immunology, Sigma Xi, Phi Beta Phi, Signa Nu, Alpha Epsilon Delta. Republican. Presbyterian. Author research papers, reports in field. Editor-in-Chief Allergy Rev. Address: 3740 McComb Ave Cheyenne WY 82001

WILLIAMS, RALPH LEROY, JR., safety administrator, consultant; b. Kansas City, Mo., May 20, 1938; s. Ralph Leroy, Sr. and Edna Ruth (Cox) W.; m. Lanora Williams, Jan. 21, 1960; children—Suzette Williams Hains, Cheryl, Ralph. A.S., Modesto Jr. Coll., 1978. Cert. healthcare safety profl. With Meml. Hosps., Modesto, Calif., 1970-80; safety specialist County of Merced, Calif., 1980—; cons.; dist. mgr. Profl. Healthcare Safety Assn. Bd. dirs./past pres. Stanislaus County Safety Council. Served with USAF, 1956-59. Mem. Calif. Soc. Hosp. Risk Mgmt., Profl. Healthcare Safety Assn., Am. Soc. Safety Engrs., Stanislaus Safety Council. Republican. Baptist. Club: Kiwanis. Home: 305 N Santa Ana Modesto CA 95354 Office: 2222 M St Merced CA 95340

WILLIAMS, RICHARD CLAYTON, behavioral scientist; b. Colorado Springs, Colo., Mar. 31, 1931; s. Oliver Morton and Myrtle Edith (Wheeler) W.; children—Richard Charles, Donna Louise. B.A. in Music, UCLA, 1952; M.Div., Boston U., 1955; S.T.M., Harvard U., 1956; M.A., New Sch. Social Research, 1969; Ph.D., U. Colo.-Boulder, 1978. Pastor various United Methodist chs., Boston, Conn., N.Y.C., L.I., 1952-70; mem. fac. sociology dept. Adelphi U., 1970-71; mem. faculty behavioral sci. dept. N.Y. Inst. Tech., 1971-73; research assoc. Nat. Ctr. Higher Edn. Mgmt. Systems, Boulder, Colo., 1973-76; founder, pres. Social and Econ. Analysis Corp., Denver, 1976-82; research assoc. Behavioral Sci. Inst., Boulder, 1978-79; dir. research Pain Control Ctr., Boulder, 1978—; dir. Internat. Chronic Pain Soc.; cons. Nat. Chronic Pain Data Base; instr. sociology U. Colo., Boulder; adj. prof. ethics, theology Iliff Sch. Theology, Denver. Chmn. Community Action Program, Naugatuck, Conn., 1966-68; personnel dir. Boulder Philharm. Orch., Boulder, 1975-80; mem., music dir. Broomfield (Colo.) Community Orch., 1980-82. Recipient Harvard Ch. History award Harvard U., 1956; Disting. Service award Greater N.Y. Girl Scout Council, 1960; Community Mission cert. Metro Urban Tng. Inst. N.Y., 1968; Meritorious Service award Nat. Ctr. Higher Edn. Mgmt. Systems, 1977. Mem. Am. Pain Soc. (chpt. Internat. Assn. Study of Pain), Am. Sociol. Assn., Am. Statis. Assn., Am. Classification Soc., Holistic Health Network. Methodist. Author: Impact of Federal Grant Programs on Enrollment in Postsecondary Education, 1975; contbr. articles to edn., med. jours.

WILLIAMS, RICHARD HIRSHFIELD, professional baseball team manager; b. St. Louis, May 7, 1929; s. Harvey Grote and Kathryn Louise (Rohde) W.; m. Norma Marie Mussato, Oct. 23, 1954; children—Kathi, Richard Anthony, Marc Edmund. Student Pasadena City Coll., 1946-47. Profl. baseball player, 1947-64, mem. Bklyn. Dodgers, 1951-56, Balt. Orioles, 1956-58, 61, 62, Cleve. Indians, 1957, Kansas City Athletics, 1959-60, Boston Red Sox, 1963-63; baseball mgr. Toronto Mapleleafs, 1965-66, Boston Red Sox, 1967-69, Oakland A's, 1971-73, Calif. Angels, 1974-76, Montreal Expos, 1977-81, San Diego Padres, 1982—. Served with U.S. Army, 1951. Played in World Series, 1952-53, managed teams in World Series, 1967, 72-73; named All-Star Mgr., 1968, 73-74; Nat. League Mgr. of Yr., AP, 1979. Mem. Baseball Players Assn. Am. Roman Catholic. Office: San Diego Padres PO Box 2000 San Diego CA 92120*

WILLIAMS, RICHARD THOMAS, lawyer; b. Evergreen Park, Ill., Jan. 14, 1945; s. Raymond T. and Elizabeth W. A.B., Stanford U., 1967, J.D., M.B.A., 1972. Bar: Calif. 1972. Ptnr. Kadison, Pfaelzer, Woodard, Quinn and Rossi, Los Angeles, 1979—. Mem. Los Angeles County Bar Assn. (chmn. energy law com.), ABA, Fed. Energy Bar Assn. Contbg. editor Oil and Gas Price Regulation Analyst, 1978—. Office: 707 Wilshire Blvd Los Angeles CA 90017

WILLIAMS, ROBERT JOSEPH, psychologist, educator; b. Durango, Colo., Feb. 14, 1948; s. Owen Clement and Florence Kathryn (Fairchild) W.; B.A., U. Colo., 1970; M.A., U. No. Colo., 1976; Ph.D., U. Minn., 1979; m. Kay Lynn Noda, Mar. 24, 1973; children—Robin, Matthew, Nicholas. Tchr., adminstr. Jefferson County Public Schs., Lakewood, Colo., 1970-76; research asst. to chmn. dept. psychology U. Minn., Mpls., 1976-77; psychology intern VA Med. Center, Mpls., 1977-79; psychologist, clin. dir. Pikes Peak Mental Health Center, Colorado Springs, Colo., 1979—; asst. prof. counseling psychology U. Denver. Mem. Am. Psychol. Assn., El Paso County Psychol. Soc., Phi Kappa Phi. Democrat. Presbyterian. Club: Masons. Office: 875 W Moreno Colorado Springs CO 80905

WILLIAMS, RONALD OSCAR, systems engineer; b. Denver, May 10, 1940; s. Oscar H. and Evelyn (Johnson) W. B.S. in Applied Math., U. Colo. Coll. Engring., 1964, postgrad. U. Colo., U. Denver. Computer programmer Apollo Systems dept., missile and space div. Gen. Electric Co., Kennedy Space Center, Fla., 1965-67, Manned Spacecraft Center, Houston, 1967-68; computer programmer U. Colo., Boulder, 1968-73; computer programmer analyst def. systems div. System Devel. Corp. for NORAD, Colorado Springs, 1974-75; engr. def. systems and command-and-info. systems Martin Marietta Aerospace, Denver, 1976-80; systems engr. space and communications group, def. systems div. Hughes Aircraft Co., Aurora, Colo., 1980—. Vol. fireman Clear Lake City (Tex.) Fire Dept., 1968; officer Boulder Emergency Squad, 1969-76, rescue squadman, 1969-76, liaison to cadets, 1971, personnel officer, 1971-76, exec. bd., 1971-76, award of merit, 1971, 72, emergency med. technician 1973—; spl. police officer Boulder Police Dept., 1970-75; spl. dep. sheriff Boulder County Sheriff's Dept., 1970-71; nat. adv. bd. Am. Security Council, 1979—, Coalition of Peace through Strength, 1979—; mem. Republican Nat. Com., Nat. Rep. Senatorial Com. Served with USMCR, 1958-66. Decorated Organized Res. medal; recipient Cost Improvement Program award Hughes Aircraft Co., 1982, Systems Improvement award, 1982, Top Cost Improvement Program award, 1983. Mem. AAAS, Math. Assn. Am., Am. Math. Soc., Soc. Indsl. and Applied Math., AIAA, Armed Forces Communications and Electronics Assn., Assn. Old Crows, Am. Def. Preparedness Assn., Marine Corps Assn., Air Force Assn., Nat. Geog. Soc., Smithsonian Instn. (assoc.), Met. Opera Guild, Colo. Hist. Soc., Hist. Denver, Inc., Historic Boulder, Denver Art Mus., Denver Botanic Gardens, Denver Mus. Natural History, Denver Zool. Found., Am. Mensa Ltd., Denver Mile Hi Mensa. Republican. Lutheran. Home: 7504 W Quarto Ave Littleton CO 80123 Office: PO Box 31979 Aurora CO 80041

WILLIAMS, SAMUEL, real estate exec.; b. Newark, Apr. 4, 1934; s. Warren Prince and Helma Irene (Davis) W.; B.S., Central State U., 1957; M.S., Cornell U., 1965; postgrad. U. Tex., 1975—; m. Gladys Roberta Gantt, Oct. 26, 1956; children—Weslyn L., Glynis S. Commd. U.S. Army, 1957; advanced through grades to lt. col.; comdr. So. Germany Army and Air Force Exchange Service, 1973; ret., 1977; broker, owner Internat Traders, Breckenridge, Colo., 1977—. Mem. Breckenridge Town Council, 1977-80; v.p. Summit County (Colo.) Home Rule Charter Commn., 1980—. Decorated Bronze Star with Oak Leaf, Air medal, Legion of Merit. Mem. Nat. Assn. Realtors, Summit County Bd. Realtors, Breckenridge C. of C., Alpha Kappa Mu, Omega Psi Phi. Home: PO Box 2236 Breckenridge CO 80424 Office: PO Box 2463 325 S Main St Breckenridge CO 80424

WILLIAMS, SAMUEL MOSHER, broadcast co. exec.; b. Log Angeles, Sept. 18, 1948; s. Arthur Powell and Virginia Lee (Mosher) W.; B.A., U. Calif., Santa Barbara, 1971; postgrad. Centro Lingusitico Dante Alighieri, Florence, Italy, 1972; m. Shelley Thomas, Apr. 21, 1979; children—Walker Thomas, Hart Arthur. Sr. ops. supr. Flying Tiger Line, Inc., Los Angeles, 1970-72; asst. to.v.p. The Signal Cos., Washington, 1973; congressional liaison rep. Am. Gas Assn., Washington, 1973-75; asst. mgr. corp. relations Chem. Mfrs. Assn., Washington, 1975-77; v.p. broadcast div. Sta. KWMS, Salt Lake City, 1977-82; pres. WMS FAMCO, 1980—; dir. Channel 13, Las Vegas. Mem. Salt Lake Area C. of C., Nat. Assn. Broadcasters, Radio Assn. Broadcasters. Roman Catholic. Office: 1042 S 700 W Salt Lake City UT 84104

WILLIAMS, SONNY JIM, magazine editor; b. Ft. Knox, Ky., Nov. 20, 1946; s. Woodrow Thomas and Pauline Ann (Livingston) W.; B.A. in Polit. Sci., U. Richmond, 1969; B.A. in English, U. Idaho, 1973, M.A. in English, 1976. Instructional asst. dept. English, U. Idaho, Moscow, 1973-76; asso. editor CB Guide, Jess Pub. Co., Van Nuys, Calif., 1977; articles editor Treasure Mag. and asso. editor Treasure Search and Treasure Found. Mags., Van Nuys, Calif., 1978, editor, 1978—; prodn. and circulation mgr. Jess Pub. Co., Van Nuys, 1978—. Cert. scuba diver. Mem. Western Fulfillment Mgmt. Assn., Calif. Assn. Token Collectors, Los Angeles County Mus. of Art, Eta Sigma Phi. Presbyterian. Contbr. articles to profl. jours. Home: 71842 Sunnyslope Twenty-nine Palms CA 92277 Office: 6280 Adobe Rd Twenty-nine Palms CA 92277

WILLIAMS, SPENCER MORTIMER, federal judge; b. Reading, Mass., Feb. 24, 1922; s. Theodore Ryder and Anabel Lee (Hutchison) W.; A.B., UCLA, 1943; LL.B., J.D., Boalt Hall, 1948; m. Kathryn Bramlage, Aug. 20, 1943; children—Carol (Mrs. James Garvey), Peter, Spencer, Clark, Janice, Diane Williams Quinn. Admitted to Calif. bar, 1948; individual practice in San Jose, 1948-49, 70-71, Sacramento, 1970-71; with Office of County Counsel, Santa Clara County, 1949-50, 52-55, county counsel, 1955-67; adminstr. Calif. Health and Welfare Agy., Sacramento, 1967-69; sec. Human Relations Agy., 1969-70; U.S. dist. judge No. Dist. Calif., San Francisco, 1971—. Served with USNR, 1943-46, to lt. comdr. JAG Office, 1950-52. Named San Jose Young Man of Year, 1954. Mem. Nat. Assn. County Civil Attys. (pres. 1963-64), Calif. Dist. Attys. Assn. (pres. 1963-64), Calif., Santa Clara County bar assns., Calif. 9th Circuit Dist. Judges Assn. (pres. 1981-83), Fed. Judges Assn. (pres. 1982-83), Theta Delta Chi. Kiwanian. Address: PO Box 36060 San Francisco CA 94102

WILLIAMS, TALMAGE THEODORE, JR., physicist; b. Atlanta, Jan. 20, 1933; s. Talmage Theodore and Maye (Lamb) W.; m. Judy Ann Bain, Dec. 15, 1964; children—Angelyn Patricia, Patrick Dewey. B.S. in Physics, Ga. Inst. Tech., 1955; postgrad. Fla. Inst. Tech., 1965-71, U. So. Calif., 1976-77. Physicist, E.I. DuPont Co., Aiken, S.C., 1958-62; leader RCA Apollo Ships Evaluation, Patrick AFB, Fla., 1962-68, staff physicist, chief scientist's office RCA Missile Test Project, 1968-72, mgr. land and air systems analysis, 1972; mgr. sci. analysis dept. ITT Fed. Electric Corp., 1972-75, dep. dir. for plans and analysis, 1975-79, dir. advanced systems, 1979-83, div. ops. and evaluation, 1983—. Served to lt. (j.g.) USN, 1955-58. Mem. AAAS, Am. Phys. Soc., Am. Inst. Physics, Inst. Nav., AIAA (nat. flight test com.), Sigma Pi Sigma. Contbr. articles to profl. jours. Home: 725 Doverlee Dr Santa Maria CA 93454 Office: ITT Fed Electric Corp Vandenberg AFB CA 93437

WILLIAMS, VERLE ALVIN, cons. engr.; b. New Virginia, Iowa, Apr. 8, 1933; s. Donald Oliver and Josephine Emily (Read) W.; A.A., Pueblo Jr. Coll., 1957; B.S. in M.E., B.S. in Bus., Colo. U., 1960; m. Mary Sue Earley, June 2, 1957; children—Steven Lee, Randall Joe, LeAnne Sue. Sales engr. Johnson Controls, Inc., Portland, Oreg., 1960-67, Los Angeles, 1967-68, San Diego, 1968-69, br. mgr., 1970-79; asso. in charge of energy conservation systems dept. Dunn-Lee-Smith-Klein & Assos., National City, Calif., 1979-81; owner Verle A. Williams & Assos., profl. energy and control cons., San Diego, 1981—; lectr. in field. Founding mem. Rancho Bernardo Bapt. Ch., chmn., treas., 1970—. Served with U.S. Army, 1953-55. Registered profl. engr., Calif.; cert. energy auditor, Calif. Mem. Am. Mgmt. Assn., ASHRAE (chmn. energy mgmt. com. 1979-81, past pres., v.p., bd. govs.), Soc. Level Tech. Com. on Automatic Control Systems, Assn. Energy Engrs. (founding pres. San Diego chpt. 1981; Engr. of Yr. 1982), Energy Monitoring and Control Soc. Clubs: Rancho Bernardo Bowleros (pres. 1969-71). Home: 12561 Perla Ct San Diego CA 92128 Office: 8369 Vickers St Suite M San Diego CA 92111

WILLIAMS, WALTER HARRISON, scientist, physician; b. Topeka, Mar. 28, 1941; s. Walter and Marjorie Louise (McCord) W.; B.S. in Chemistry, U. Mo., Kansas City, 1963; Ph.D. in Chemistry, Purdue U., 1969; M.D., Yale U., 1980; m. Patricia Ann Edwards, Aug. 17, 1968; children—Steven Harrison, David Anthony. Teaching asst. organic chemistry U. Mo., Kansas City, 1960-63; teaching asst. chemistry Purdue U., 1963-65, research fellow molecular beam scattering, 1965-68; sr. scientist Jet Propulsion Lab., Calif. Inst. Tech., 1968-74, mem. tech.

staff, 1974-79, exptl. rep. ultraviolet spectrometer aboard Voyager Jupiter-Saturn, 1977, mem. com. on high vacuum safety, 1975, tuition support com., 1975; asst. prof. chemistry Calif. State U., Los Angeles, 1971; Nat. Urban League vis. prof. physics Black exec. exchange program N.C. A&T, Greensboro, 1972, So. U., New Orleans, 1976; resident Good Samaritan Med. Center, Portland, Oreg., 1980-82; resident in nuclear medicine Portland VA Hosp., 1982—. Victor Wilson fellow, 1979-80. Mem. Nat. Med. Assn., Sigma Xi. Research and publs. in field; built 1st electron-metal vapor impact spectrometer. Office: 3710 SW US Veterans Hospital Rd Portland OR 97207

WILLIAMS, WILLA ETTA MITCHELL, educator; b. Steubenville, Ohio, Apr. 17, 1934; d. Alex and Lucille Ida (Marbury) Mitchell. A.A., Los Angeles City Coll., 1954; B.A., Calif. State U.-Los Angeles, 1957; M.A., Azusa Pacific U., 1979. Cert. tchr., adminstr., Calif. Tchr., Los Angeles Unified Sch. Dist., 1957—, tchr. 4th grade, bi-lingual edn. Marvin Ave. Sch., 1983—, grade level chairperson, integration coordinator, 1983—, elem. intern dist. adminstrv. internship program, 1982. Mem. community adv. council Marvin Ave. Sch.; chairperson Project Esteam, United Way; mem. adminstrv. council, bd. dirs. St. Mark's United Methodist Ch., Los Angeles. Recipient Outstanding Service award Marvin Ave. PTA, 1982; United Way Service award, 1982. Mem. United Tchrs. Los Angeles, Calif. Tchrs. Assn., NEA, Assn. Supervision and Curriculum Devel., Nat. Assn. Coll. Women, Las Comunicadores, Black Educators of United Tchrs. Los Angeles, Smithsonian Assocs., Alpha Kappa Alpha, Phi Delta Kappa. Democrat. Club: Toastmistresses. Home: 7900 Crenshaw Blvd Apt D Inglewood CA 90305 Office: 2411 Marvin Ave Los Angeles CA 90016

WILLIAMS, WILLIAM ARNOLD, agronomy educator; b. Johnson City, N.Y., Aug. 2, 1922; s. William Truesdall and Nellie Viola (Tompkins) W.; m. Madeline P. Moore, Nov. 27, 1943; children—David, Kathleen, Andrew. B.S., Cornell U., 1947, M.S., 1948, Ph.D., 1951. Instr., U. Calif.-Davis, 1951-53, asst. prof., 1954-64, prof. 1965—. Mem. staff Res. Vessel Alpha Helix, Amaion Expdn., 1967. Rockefeller fellow, 1966; Fulbright scholar, Australia, 1960. Mem. Am. Soc. Agronomy, Crop Sci. Soc. Am., Soil Sci. Soc. Am., Am. Soc. Plant Physiology, Ecol. Soc. Am. Office: Dept Agronomy and Range Sci U Calif Davis CA 95616

WILLIAMS, WILLIAM HENRY, state supreme court justice; b. Spokane, Apr. 27, 1922; s. Ralph David and Ruth Grace Williams; m. Ruth Bernice Bevers, 1955. B.A. in Polit. Sci., U. Idaho, 1948; J.D., Gonzaga U., 1951. Bar: Wash. 1951. Dep. prosecutor Spokane County, 1954-57; sole practice law, 1954-57; judge Superior Ct., 1958-79; justice Wash. State Supreme Ct., Olympia, 1979—, chief justice, 1983—. Recipient law medal Gonzaga U. Sch. Law. Office: Temple of Justice Olympia WA 98504*

WILLIAMS, WILLIAM ROSS, real estate broker, investment adviser, investor and developer; b. Grand Junction, Colo., Sept. 7, 1950; s. Wilbur Deloss and Theresa Louise (Turman) W.; student Colo. State U., 1968-69; m. Deborah Ann Plass, July 23, 1971 (div.); children—William Ryan, Amy Marie, Trevor Patrick. Machinery salesman Schloss and Shubart Co., Denver, 1970-72; land salesman The Pinery, Denver, 1972-73; real estate salesman Greater Denver Properties, 1974, Grubb and Ellis, 1975; pres. Property Resources, Inc., Denver, 1975—; v.p. Devel. Resources Inc., Denver; prin. William R. Williams Investments; cons. real estate investment, apt. mgmt. Mem. Nat. Assn. Realtors. Republican. Episcopalian. Club: Masons. Home: 6495 Happy Canyon Rd Denver CO 80237 Office: 720 S Colorado Blvd Suite 860 Denver CO 80222

WILLIAMS, YVONNE ELAINE, home economist, teacher; b. Colorado Springs, Colo., Oct. 13, 1944; d. William Dean and Martha LaVerna (Golding) Sames; m. Lawrence Richard Williams, Dec. 22, 1967; 1 son, Jeremy Za. B.S., Bob Jones U., 1966; M.A., U. No. Colo., 1968, postgrad. U. Colo., 1980, 83. Cert. tchr. Colo. Tchr. home econs., phys. edn. Kit Carson (Colo.) Sch. Dist., 1966-68, tchr. home econs. Elkhart (Kans.) High Sch., 1968-73, Russell Jr. High Sch., Colorado Springs, Colo., 1974-75; home econs. tchr. Doherty High Sch., Colorado Springs, 1975—, chmn. home econs. dept., cheerleader sponsor, 1975-76; mem. curriculum writing com. Colorado Springs Sch. Dist. 11; tchr. adult edn. classes in sewing and tailoring; judge Colo. Beef Cook-off, local and dist. clothing exhibits El Paso County Fair. Mem. Gifted and Talented Parent Group Lincoln Elem. Sch., 1980-83; asst. cub scout den mother local Boy Scouts Am., 1981-83; Bible sch. tchr. Calvary Bible Ch., 1982-83. Recipient Bob Jones U. Outstanding Achievement in Home Econs. award, 1966; named Young Career Woman of Elkhart, Kans., 1969. Mem. Bob Jones U. Alumni Assn. (2d v.p.), Delta Kappa Gamma. Republican. Home: 1720 Applewood Ridge Ct Colorado Springs CO 80907 Office: 4515 Barnes Rd Colorado Springs CO 80917

WILLIAMSON, CONNIE MCDANIEL, home economics educator; b. Kent, Iowa, Dec. 15, 1943; d. John N. and Marjorie G. (Chandler) Davenport; 1 dau., Kerstin Ann McDaniel. B.S., Iowa State U., 1965, M.S., 1970; postgrad. U. Tenn., 1975, Colo. State U., 1982. Cert. occupational-vocat. home econs. tchr., Iowa, Kans., Tenn. Tchr. home econs. numerous pub. schs. in Iowa, Kans., Tenn., 1965-78; extension agt. Colo. State U., Fort Collins, 1978—; asst. supt. Colo. State Fair, 1983; rep. Nutrition Forum, Washington, 1983. Mem. NEA, Nat. Assn. Extension Home Economists, Nat. Home Econs. Assn., Nat. Assn. Female Execs., Bus. and Profl. Women Am. Republican. Methodist. Clubs: Atlantic Golf and Country, Fort Morgan Country, Order Eastern Star. Author instrnl. materials; contbr. articles to profl. jours. Home: PO Box 745 Montrose CO 81402 Office: Extension Office Friendship Hall 1001 N 2d St Montrose CO 81401

WILLIAMSON, DORIS, business educator; b. Salt Lake City, July 1, 1937; d. Frank Farrow and Ruby Dean (Andersen) W. A.S., Coll. So. Utah, Cedar City, 1957; B.S. in Bus. Edn., Brigham Young U., 1959; M.S. in Bus. Edn., Utah State U., 1974. Cert. secondary tchr., Utah. Tchr., Salt Lake City Schs., 1959-64; tchr. typewriting Granite Sch. Dist., Salt Lake City, 1964-70; lectr. bus. edn. Idaho State U., 1973-76; assoc. prof. So. Utah State Coll., Cedar City, 1976—; lectr. workshops in teaching methodology and secretarial sci. EDPA fellow, 1971-73; recipient Leadership award Delta Pi Epsilon, 1976; Outstanding Tchr.-Bus. Edn. award Utah Bus. Edn. and Utah Vocat. Assns. 1979; Disting. Educator award So. Utah State Coll., 1983. Mem. Utah Bus. Edn. Assn., Utah Vocat. Edn. Assn., Nat. Bus. Edn. Assn., Am. Vocat. Assn., Bus. and Profl. Women Internat. (Woman of Achievement award Cedar City 1983), Cedar City C. of C. (dir. 1977-83, pres. 1982-83), Western Bus. Edn. Assn., Classroom Edn. of Bus. Assn., Delta Pi Epsilon, Delta Kappa Gamma, Phi Kappa Phi. Mormon. Home: 17 W Robbers Roost Ln Cedar City UT 84720 Office: Bus So Utah State Coll Cedar City UT 84720

WILLIAMSON, JACKSON ARIEL, JR., safety engineer; b. Kingstree, S.C., Dec. 2, 1958; s. Jackson Ariel and Sylvia Margaret (Hodge) W. B.S. in Adminstrv. Mgmt., Clemson U., 1981. Loss prevention cons. Factory Mut. Engring., Charlotte, N.C., 1981; loss control rep. Aspen Indemnity Corp., Englewood, Colo., 1981—. Mem. Am. Soc. Safety Engrs. Methodist. Office: 5200 S Quebec St Suite 306 Englewood CO 80111

WILLIAMSON, JAMES DONALD, city purchasing mgr.; b. Buenos Aires, Argentina, Sept. 13, 1949; s. James Morrison and Heather Jessie (Kirkwood) W.; m. Susan Molay, Nov. 25, 1978; 1 son, Andrew Lewis. B.S., San Jose State U., 1971, M.P.A., 1980. Personnel intern City of Mountain View (Calif.), 1970-71, adminstrv. aide police dept., 1971-74, staff asst. fire dept., 1974-75, purchasing mgr., 1975—. Mem. Calif. Assn. Pub. Purchasing Officers, Nat. Assn. Purchasing Mgmt. (cert.), Delta Sigma Phi.

WILLIAMSON, JEAN MARIE, savings and loan association executive; b. Manila, Philippines, Oct. 28, 1935; d. William F. and Jane E. (Nowotny) Wendt; m. Delbert C. Williamson, Sept. 28, 1957; children—Sandra J., Joseph W. Student Crafton Hills Coll., 1979-80; cert. Exec. Devel. Program, U. Ga., 1981. Adminstrv. asst. Norton AFB, San Bernardino Calif., 1955-61; with Redlands Fed. Savs. & Loan (Calif.), 1961—, sr. v.p., dir. mktg., research and devel., 1981—. Bd. dirs. Redlands YMCA; mem. Republican Women's Orgn.; mem. communications com. Redlands United Way; past chmn. Redlands Bus. Improvement Dist. Mem. Savs. Instns. Mktg. Soc. Am., Beta Sigma Phi. Lutheran. Club: Soroptimist. Office: Redlands Fed Savs & Loan 300 E State St Redlands CA 92373

WILLIAMSON, MAX DONALD, forester; b. Williamsport, Pa., Nov. 1, 1915; s. William Harvey and Laura Belle (Corson) W.; B.S., Pa. State U., 1937; children—Nancy Gallagher, Carlef, Mitchel, Thomas Terkildsen, Sherman Williamson. Subdist. supr. New Eng. Timber Salvage Adminstrn., Keene, N.H., 1937-41; timber mgmt. asst. Shasta Nat. Forest, Mt. Shasta, Calif., 1941-43; asst. dist. ranger Shasta Nat. Forest, Dunsmuir, Calif., 1943-45; dist. ranger Tahoe Nat. Forest, Soda Springs, Calif., 1945-56; gen. mgr., treas. Soda Springs Ski Corp. (Calif.), 1956-66; timber mgmt. specialist Tahoe Nat. Forest, Soda Springs, Calif., 1960-66; forest silviculturist Tahoe Nat. Forest, Nevada City, Calif., 1967-73; forester Bohemia, Inc., Grass Valley, Calif., 1973-79; cons., 1979—. Bd. dirs. Donner Summit Pub. Utility Dist., 1957-67, pres., 1958-67; mem. Tahoe Truckee Sch. Bd., 1961-67, chmn., 1964-65. Mem. Soc. Am. Foresters (chmn. Sacramento-Tahoe chpt. 1970-71), Associated Calif. Loggers, Western Timber Assn., Calif. Lic. Foresters Assn. (dir. 1982-84), Calif. Forest Protective Assn. Republican. Methodist. Clubs: Masons (Dutch Flat, Calif.); Elks (Nevada City, Calif.); Donner Summit Community. Home and office: 10981 Glen Meadow Dr Grass Valley CA 95945

WILLIAMSON, RAYMOND CRAMER, JR., city transp. mgr.; b. Phila., May 2, 1946; s. Raymond Cramer and Angelina Vienna (Cavalli) W.; m. Mary Louise Ertell, Aug. 24, 1968; children—Jeffrey Allen, Melissa Kim; m. 2d, Susan Kay Mehlhop, Nov. 22, 1980. Student Drexel U., 1964-67, Temple U., 1967-68; B.A. in Math., U. Md., 1973; postgrad. Ariz. State U., 1974; transp. cert. Northwestern U., 1975. Statis. support supr., project engr. Simpson & Curtin Transp. Engrs., Phila., 1968-74; traffic engring. mgr. City of Scottsdale (Ariz.), 1974-80; city traffic engr., Sunnyvale, Calif., 1980—, mgr. city transp., 1981—; cons. Served with USNG, 1967-73. Mem. Sunnyvale C. of C., Santa Clara County Mfg. Group, Inst. Transp. Engrs. (past pres. Ariz. sect.), Am. Pub. Works Assn., South Bay Transp. Ofcls. Assn. (sec.-treas.). Home: 480 Madera Ave Sunnyvale CA 94086 Office: 456 W Olive Ave Sunnyvale CA 94086

WILLIAMSON, RICHARD SCOTT, water resources engineer; b. Oxnard, Calif., Apr. 26, 1954; s. John Arthur and Mari Louise (Richards) W. m. Teresa Marie Dematteis, Mar. 22, 1975 (div.). B.S. in Water Resources Engring., UCLA, 1975; postgrad. in mgmt. Golden Gate U., 1978. Registered profl. engr., Calif., Ariz. San. engr. region IX, EPA, San Francisco, 1975-79; mgr. safe drinking water program Ariz. Dept. Health Services, Phoenix, 1979-81; prin. Williamson & Assocs., Environ. Engring., Phoenix, 1981—; gen. mgr. Payson (Ariz.) San. Dist., 1982—; mem. Ariz. Water and Sewer Commn. Mem. Am. Water Works Assn., Water Pollution Control Fedn., Ariz. Water and Pollution Control Assn. Presbyterian. Club: Rotary (Payson). Home: 2711 W Nicklaus Dr Payson AZ 85541 Office: Payson Sanitary Dist PO Box 591 Payson AZ 85541

WILLIAMSON, ROBERT PAUL, computer company executive; b. Perth Amboy, N.J., June 6, 1956; s. Michael Abraham and Beatrice (Trachtenberg) W. Student, U. Idaho; B.S.B.A., Syracuse U., 1978. Pres., Unicomm, Inc., Tarzana, Calif., 1979—; market research project dir. Lieberman Research, Century City, Calif., 1979-80. Mem. Direct mktg. Assn., Los Angeles Advt. Club. Home: 949 Lincoln Blvd Apt 4 Santa Monica CA 90403 Office: Unicomm Inc 18639 1/2 Ventura Blvd Tarzana CA 91356

WILLIAMSON, STEPHEN VICTOR, state government official; b. Tulare, Calif., May 20, 1950; s. Grady Edgar and June Bernice (Gragg) W.; m. Heidi Laemmle Hilb, Sept. 8, 1974. B.A., U. Calif.-Davis, 1971. Sr. coordinator U. Calif. Statewide Student Body Presidents Council-Student Lobby, 1971-73; cons. budget div. Calif. Dept. Fin., 1973-74, Systems Research Inc., Los Angeles, 1974-76, Calif. Research, Sacramento, Calif., 1976-78; dir. Calif. State Clearinghouse, Gov.'s. Office Planning and Research, Sacramento, 1978—. Mem. Assn. Environ. Professionals, Data Processing Mgmt. Assn., Chi Phi. Club: Sierra. Home: 325 Claydon Way Sacramento CA 95825 Office: 1400 10th St Sacramento CA 95814

WILLIE, ELVIN, JR., Indian tribal executive; b. Schurz, Nev., Sept. 15, 1953; s. Elvin and Rosalie Irene (McKay) W.; 1 son, James X. II. B.A., U. Calif.-Berkeley, 1976. Media coordinator native Am. studies U. Calif.-Berkeley, 1973-76; curriculum devel. coordinator tribal edn. program Walker River Paiute Tribe, Schurz, Nev., 1976-77, tribal chmn., 1979—; smokeshop mgr. Walker River Tribal Enterprise, 1977-79. Election bd. chmn. precinct 12, Mineral County, Nev., 1980-83. Mem. Western Nev. Dirt Track Racing Assn.

WILLIS, HAROLD WENDT, dairy and gas sta. chain exec.; b. Marion, Ala., Oct. 7, 1927; s. Robert James and Della (Wendt) W.; student Loma Linda U., 1960, various courses San Bernardino Valley Coll.; m. Patsy Gay Bacon, Aug. 2, 1947 (div. Jan. 1975); children—Harold Wendt II, Timothy Gay, April Ann, Brian Tad, Suzanne Gail; m. 2d, Vernette Jacobson, Mar. 30, 1980. Partner, Victoria Guernsey, San Bernardino, Calif., 1950-63, co-pres., 1963-74, pres., 1974—; owner Quik-Save, 1966—, K-Mart Shopping Center, San Bernardino, 1969—; pres. Food N' Fuel Inc., 1978—, Energy Delivery Systems, 1978—. San Bernardino City water commr., 1965—; bd. councillors Loma Linda (Calif.) U., 1968—, pres., 1971-74; bd. dirs. Liga Internat., Inc., 1962—, pres., 1982, 83. Served as officer U.S. Mcht. Marine, 1945-46. Recipient Silver medal Sr. Olympics, U. So. Calif., 1979, 81, 82. Mem. Calif. Dairy Industries Assn. (pres. 1963, 64). Seventh-day Adventist (deacon 1950-67). Pvt. pilot. Home: 1155 E Ponderosa San Bernardino CA 92404 Office: PO Box 5607 San Bernardino CA 92412

WILLIS, JAY S., sculptor; b. Oct. 22, 1940; B.F.A. in Sculpture, U. Ill.-Urbana, 1964; M.A. in Sculpture, U. Calif.-Berkeley, 1966. Instr. sculpture U. Ariz., Tucson, 1966-69; assoc. prof. arts U. So. Calif., Los Angeles, 1969—; one man shows include: Hank Baum Gallery, San Francisco, 1969, 71, Cirrus Gallery, Los Angeles, 1972, 73, 74, 75, 78, 81, 83, Boehm Gallery, Palomar Coll., San Marcos, Calif., 1973, Fisher Art Gallery, U. So. Calif., Los Angeles, 1978; group shows include: Smithsonian Instn. traveling Exhbn., Washington, 1969-71, So. Assn. Sculptors, Traveling Exhbn., 1969-71, San Francisco Mus. Art, 1969, Los Angeles Inst. Contemporary Art, 1975, 78, Calif. Inst. Tech., Pasadena, 1981, Los Angeles Mcpl. Art Mus., 1982; represented in permanent collections including: Met. Mus. Art, N.Y.C., Hirshhorn Mus. Smithsonian Instn., Washington. Grantee U. Ariz., 1969, U. So. Calif. 1970, 71, 75. Recipient numerous purchase awards and honorable mentions. Home: PO Box 50101 Pasadena CA 91105

WILLIS, JOANN WILLIAMS, psychologist, educator; b. Portland, Oreg., Nov. 1, 1944; d. Alvin and Lydia (Obermiller) Williams; m. James D. Willis, Aug. 1, 1964; children—Lori Ann, James Robert. B.A., N.W. Nazarene Coll., Nampa, Idaho, 1963; M.A., U. Mo., Kansas City, 1970; Ph.D., Oreg. State U., Corvallis, 1976. Lic. psychologist Idaho, cert. sch. psychologist, Idaho. Tchr. Portland (Oreg.) Pub. Schs., 1965-66; asst. dean of women, N.W. Nazarene Coll., Nampa, Idaho, 1969-70, dean of women, 1970-74, assoc. acad. dean, 1975—. Mem. Am. Psychol. Assn. Office: Northwest Nazarene Coll Box H Nampa ID 83651

WILLIS, LEE FRANK, accountant; b. Rockwood, Tenn., Aug. 30, 1922; s. John William and Cora Harriett (Lee) W.; m. Lillian Russell Otto, Oct. 16, 1960; m. 2d, Janet Honeyman Hirsch, Jan. 1, 1973; children—Phyllis, Erwin. Student U. Tenn., 1946; A.A., Bakersfield Coll., 1948; student Knoxville Coll., 1949. C.P.A., Calif. Controller, Rocky Hill, Inc., Visalia, Calif., 1952-59, Donald Shanedling, Inc., Beverly Hills, Calif., 1961-62; pvt. practice acctg., Salinas, Calif., 1963-71; acct. Wain Samuel & Co., C.P.A.s, San Mateo, Calif., 1972-75; ptnr. Clow Accountancy Corp., San Francisco, 1975-76; pvt. practice acctg., San Rafael, Calif., 1976—; expert witness state and fed. cts. Served with USN, 1942-45. Mem. Calif. Soc. C.P.A.s. Republican. Clubs: Rotary, Kiwanis, Lions. Office: Lee Willis CPA 1010 B St Suite 329 San Rafael CA 94901

WILLISCROFT, BEVERLY R., lawyer; b. Conrad, Mont., Feb. 24, 1945; d. Paul A. and Gladys L. (Buck) W.; B.A., So. Calif. Coll., 1967; postgrad. San Jose State U., 1968-72; J.D., John F. Kennedy U., 1977. Tchr. pvt. sch., Sunnyvale, Calif., 1968-72; admitted to Calif. bar, 1977; with Reid & Axelrod, Inc., San Francisco, 1977-79; individual practice law, real estate broker, lectr., Concord, Calif., 1979—. Producer, v.p. Contra Costa Musical Theatre, 1981-82, v.p. adminstrn., 1980-81. Mem. exec. bd. Mt. Diablo Council Boy Scouts Am., 1981—; trustee Mt. Diablo Health Care Found., 1982-83; bd. dirs. 337 Club, Mt. Diablo Health Care Found., 1982—. Mem. Am. Bar Assn., Calif. Bar Assn., Contra Costa County Bar Assn., Contra Costa Barristers Assn., Calif. Women Lawyers, Concord C. of C. (dir.), Todos Santos Bus. and Profl. Women (pres. 1983-84; Woman of Achievement 1981). Office: 2108 Grant St Concord CA 94520

WILLMS, JAMES ALTON, marketing executive; b. Gooding, Idaho, Feb. 23, 1947; s. Alton William and Harriet (Lamb) W.; m. Paula Jean Cruikshank, Aug. 17, 1975; children—David James, Ashley Ann. B.S.M.E., U. Idaho, 1970; M.B.A., Harvard U., 1972. Brand asst. Procter and Gamble Co., Cin., 1972-73, asst. brand mgr., 1973-75, brand mgr., 1976-77, sr. brand mgr., 1978-80; gen. mgr. mktg. and product mgmt. Unicover Corp., Cheyenne, Wyo., 1980, v.p. mktg. and product mgmt., 1980-81, exec. v.p., 1982—, pres., dir. Unicover World Trade Corp., 1982—; lectr. U. Wyo., Laramie. Mem. bus. adv. com. U. Wyo. Active Cheyenne Symphony and Choral Soc., fund raising chmn., 1981-82; mem. City of Cheyenne Water Info. Commn., chmn. pub. info. com. Mem. ASME. Republican. Roman Catholic. Club: Rotary (Cheyenne). Home: 114 Ponderosa Trail Cheyenne WY 82009 Office: Unicover Corp One Unicover Ctr Cheyenne WY 82008

WILLNER, ROBERT FRANKLIN, hospital administrator; b. Cobleskill, N.Y., Aug. 13, 1942; s. Charles Benjamin and Catherine Spencer (McNeil) W.; m. Marie Angela Muchiarone, Apr. 15, 1972; children—Karen Marie, Stephanie Agnes. A.B., Franklin and Marshall Coll., 1964; M.H.A., Med. Coll. Va., 1966; D.Ministry, Chgo. Theol. Sem., 1979. Adminstrv. resident Washington (Pa.) Hosp., 1965-66; asst. adminstrv. officer USPHS Hosp., Carville, La., 1966-68; asst. adminstr./acting adminstr. Nat. Orthopedic and Rehab. Hosp., Arlington, Va., 1968-69, adminstr., 1969-72; assoc. adminstr. Cook County Hosp., Chgo., 1972, Oak Forest (Ill.) Hosp., 1973-79; pres. Billings (Mont.) Deaconess Hosp., 1979—; vice chmn. South Suburban Adv. Council, Suburban Cook County, Dupage County Health Systems Agy., 1977-79; bd. dirs. South Suburban Council on Aging, 1977-79; community profl. Sch. Health Scis., Govs. State U., 1978-79; chmn. Big Sky Hospice, Billings, 1980—; bd. dirs. Dist. 6 Commd. Officers Assn. of USPHS Learning Ctr. Mem. health and fitness com. Billings YMCA, 1981—; mem. exec. com., chmn. Christian Action com. Leighton Ford Billings Crusade, 1982; mem. health and welfare com. Yellowstone Conf., United Methodist Ch.; disconal minister United Meth. Ch.; bd. dirs., chmn. worship for worship planning Grace United Meth. Ch., Billings. Served with USPHS, 1966-68. Recipient Spl. Appreciation Recognition, Med. Staff Oak Forest Hosp., 1979, cert. and recognition for services rendered in field of rehab., 1979; lic. nursing home adminstr., Ill. Fellow Am. Coll. Hosp. Adminstrs. (regent); mem. Am. Hosp. Assn., United Wesleyan Hosp. Assn. Dist. 6 Hosp. Assn. (vice chmn.), Mont. Hosp. Assn., Am. Protestant Hosp. Assn. (health and religious values council). Club: Rotary. Office: PO Box 2547 Billings MT 59103

WILLSON, GARY EDWARD, broadcasting co. exec.; b. Royal Oak, Mich., Oct. 29, 1929; s. Staryl and Winifred W.; student Wayne State U., 1947-50; m. Martha-Mary Palmer, Sept. 6, 1952; children—Mark Allen, Nancy Ann, Constance Anne. Announcer, various radio stas., 1947-59, Sta.-KXOA, Sacramento, 1959-62; sales mgr. Sta.-KROY, Sacramento, 1962-64; account exec. Sta.-KXTV-TV, Sacramento, 1964-66, Sta.-KRON-TV, San Francisco, 1966-76; pres., gen. mgr. Sta.-KIOY-FM, Willson Broadcasting Co., Fresno, Calif., 1976-81; media broker Gammon, Camfield & Ninowski, San Francisco, 1981; pres. Gary Wilson Broadcast Cons./Media Brokers, Belvedere, Calif., 1981—. Democrat. Methodist.

WILLSON, KAY LILLIAN, counselor; b. Billings, Mont., May 23, 1949; d. Hugh H. and Izola M. (Albrecht) W. B.A. in Sociology, U. Mont., 1972; M.Ed. in Counseling, Mont. State U., 1981. Cert. sch. counselor, Mont. Tchr. sociology and psychology Libby High Sch., Libby, Mont., 1972-73; residence supr., guidance counselor Vashti Ctr., Thomasville, Ga., 1973-76; co-dir. Nuestra Casa, San Diego, 1976-77; adminstr. Southeastern Mont. Group Home, Miles City, 1977-79; bookkeeper Kindred, Holland & Lindberg C.P.A.s, Helena, Mont., 1980; dir. Madison County Christians, Sheridan, Mont., 1980-81; sch. counselor Frazer Pub. Schs. (Mont.), 1981—. Committeewoman Miles City Democratic Precinct Com., 1978. Mem. Am. Personnal and Guidance Assn., Mont. Personnel and Guidance Assn., Am. Sch. Counselors Assn., Assn. Humanistic Educ. and Devel., Assn. Religious and Values Issues in Counseling. Episcopalian. Home: PO Box 504 Frazer MT 59225 Office: PO Box 488 Frazer MT 59225

WILMETH, ERNEST WILLIAM, II, painter; b. Perryton, Tex., Dec. 21, 1952; s. Ernest William and Doris Jean W. Student, W. Tex. State U., 1971-72; B.F.A., No. Ariz. U., 1976. One-man shows: Statesman's Club, Albuquerque, 1982; represented in permanent collection Hansford County Library, Spearman, Tex. Recipient 1st place award in oil painting Tri-State Fair, Amarillo, Tex., 1979, hon. mention in watercolors, 1979. Mem. Royal Soc. Arts Gt. Britain (life), N.Mex. Watercolor Soc. Democrat. Methodist. Home: 1521 Bryn Mawr Dr NE Albuquerque NM 87106

WILMOTH, GARY LOU, ins. co. exec.; b. Beaver City, Okla., July 7, 1944; s. Victor Ray and Vera Lenor (Davis) W.; B.S. in Edn., U. Kans., 1966; m. Margaret Ann O'Hearn, July 11, 1965; children—Laura Rae,

Alena Kae. Tchr., dept. chmn. Public Schs. Great Bend (Kans.), 1966-69; sales rep. sales Met. Life Ins. Co., Denver, 1969-70; with Nat. Farmers Union Ins. Co., Denver, 1970—, personal lines underwriter, 1970-71, unit supr., 1971-74, tng. asst., 1974-76, dir. property and casualty tng., 1976-80, adminstr. career agt. devel. program, 1980-83, asst. v.p. career agt. devel., 1981—, dist. sales mgr., 1983—; guest speaker, tng. cons. to various cos. Recipient Ins. Inst. Am.-Gen. Cert., Asso. Risk Mgmt., 1977. Mem. North Central Tng. Dirs. Assn. (sec. 1981, pres. 1982). Office: 4605 Paris St PO Box 39628 Denver CO 80239

WILSON, ALEXANDER MURRAY, mining co. exec.; b. Tulane, Calif., May 17, 1922; s. Alexander Murray and Grace Ethel (Creech) W.; B.S. in Metall. Engring., U. Calif., Berkeley, 1948; m. Beverlee Elayne Forsblad, Jan. 4, 1948; children—Shelley Wilson Popuis, Kristin Wilson Keyes, Alexis Wilson Kjellstrom. With Bradley Mining Co., Stibnite, Idaho, 1948-51, Molybdenum Corp. Am., Nipton, Calif., 1951-54; with Utah Internat., Inc. (formerly Utah Constrn. and Mining Co.) subs. Gen. Electric Co., San Francisco, 1954—, dir., 1968—, pres., 1971-79, chief exec. officer, 1978—, chmn., 1979—; chmn., dir. Utah Devel. Co.; dir. Fireman's Fund Ins. Co., First Security Corp. Served with U.S. Army, 1944-46; CBI. Mem. Am. Mining Congress (dir.), Nat. Coal Assn., Soc. Mining Engrs., Mining and Metall. Soc. Am., Pacific Basin Econ. Council (chmn. U.S. nat. com.). Office: 550 California St San Francisco CA 94104

WILSON, ALVIN FREDERICK, automotive engr.; b. Cambridge, Ohio, June 6, 1929; s. Freeman D. and Phyllis R. (McGlaughlin) W.; B.S.E., Ohio State U., 1952; 1 son, Kevin P. With Chrysler Corp., Detroit, 1952-69; with U.S. Suzuki Motor Corp., Brea, Calif., 1969—, now nat. mgr. consumer affairs and product liability litigation. Mem. Soc. Automotive Engrs., Motorcycle Industry Council, Sporting Goods Mfrs. Assn. Calif. Home: 27551 Soncillo Mission Viejo CA 92691 Office: 3251 E Imperial Brea CA 92621

WILSON, ANN, singer, recording artist; b. 1950; d. John and Lou Wilson; ed. Sammamish High Sch., Bellevue, Wash. Lead singer with rock group Heart, 1975—; albums include: Dreamboat Annie, 1975, Magazine, 1975, Little Queen, 1977, Dog and Butterfly, 1978, Bebe le Strange, 1980, Heart Live/Gr, Private Audition, 1982, Passionworks, 1983; single recs. include: Magic Man, 1976, Barracuda, 1977, Crazy on You, 1976, Straight On, 1978, Even It Up, 1980, Sweet Darlin, 1980, Tell It Like It Is, 1981, Unchained Melody, 1981; This Man is Mine, 1982, City's Burning, 1982, Bright Light Girl, 1982, How Can I Refuse, 1983, Sleep Alone, 1983. Office: care Albatross Mgmt Inc 6300 Southcenter Blvd Suite 200 Seattle WA 98188

WILSON, ARNOLD JESSE, city manager; b. St. Louis, Oct. 18, 1941; s. Arnold J. and Eleanor I. (Zinn) W.; m. Sara Ann Roscoe, Aug. 29, 1970; children—Mark Wilson, Mary Beth; stepchildren—Kristin, Jesse. A.A., Southwest Bapt. Coll., 1961; B.A., William Jewell Coll., 1963; B.D., Yale U., 1967. Ordained to ministry Congregational Ch., 1966; dir. human resources City of University City (Mo.), 1968-70; dir. St. Louis County Mcpl. League, 1970-71; exec. asst. to the mayor City of St. Louis, 1971-76; city mgr. City of Portland (Maine), 1976-80, City of Santa Ana (Calif.), 1980—. Bd. dirs. Orange County Employment and Tng. Commn., 1980-83, Santa Ana Ambassadors, 1982-83; trustee Bowers Mus., 1982-83; mem. adv. bd. Pub. Tech., Inc., Washington, 1978-82. Mem. Internat. City Mgmt. Assn., Nat. Mcpl. Fin. Officers Assn. Club: Kiwanis. Contbr. articles in field to profl. jours. Office: Santa Ana City Hall 20 Civic Center Plaza Santa Ana CA 92701

WILSON, CARL ARTHUR, real estate broker; b. Manhasset, N.Y., Sept. 29, 1947; s. Archie and Florence (Hefner) W.; m. Mary Elizabeth Coppes. Student UCLA, 1966-68, 70-71. Tournament bridge dir. North Hollywood (Calif.) Bridge Club, 1967-68, 70-71; computer operator IBM, Los Angeles, 1967-68, 70-71; bus. devel. mgr. Walker & Lee Real Estate, Anaheim, Calif., 1972-76; v.p. sales and mktg. The Estes Co., Phoenix, 1976-82, Continental Homes Inc., 1982—. Mem. adv. com. Homebuilders Assn. and State Real Estate Dept., 1979—; mem. bd. adjustments City of Glendale, 1976-81, chmn., 1980-81, mem. bond council, 1981—; planning and zoning commr. City of Glendale, 1981—; mem. real estate edn. adv. council State Bd. Community Coll., 1981—; precinct committeeman, dep. registrar, 1980-81. Served with U.S. Army, 1968-70. Mem. Glendale C. of C. (dir. 1980-83), Sales and Mktg. Council (chmn. edn. com. 1980, chmn. council 1981—). Home: PO Box 10141 Phoenix AZ 85064 Office: PO Box 29099 Phoenix AZ 85038

WILSON, CAROL LYNN, investment company executive; b. San Jose, Calif., Aug. 12, 1935; d. Leonard Joseph and Frances Odessa (Foster) Pritchard; children—Darelyn K. Carpenter Christmon, Kevin G. Carpenter; m. Richard M. Wilson, Dec. 3, 1980. A.A. with high honors, Foothill Coll., 1975; student in journalism and pub. relations San Jose State U., 1976-81. Accredited bus. communicator. Various communications positions Saga Corp., Menlo Park, Calif., 1967-79, dir. corp. communications, 1979-82; v.p. investor services Fox & Carskadon Fin. Corp., San Mateo, Calif., 1982—. Named Disting. Woman, Mid-Peninsula Girls' Club; Mentor, Dept. Journalism and Mass Communications, San Jose State U.; recipient 26 awards for achievements in communications. Mem. Internat. Assn. Bus. Communicators, Calif. Press Women, Nat. Fedn. Press Women, Pub. Relations Soc. Am., Nat. Investor Relations Inst. Club: Los Altos Golf and Country. Developed slide presentation for seminars. Home: 2331 Hastings Dr Belmont CA 94002 Office: 2755 Campus Dr Suite 225 San Mateo CA 94403

WILSON, CHARLES WILLIAM, psychiatrist, parapsychologist; b. St. Joseph, Mo., Aug. 12, 1916; s. Jacob Resor and Estella (Cherrie) W.; B.A., Wichita U., 1938; M.D., U. Kans., 1942; m. Frances Preshia Stephenson, June 20, 1942; children—Charles William, Walter Stephen, Cherrie, James Robin. Intern, Harper Hosp., Detroit, 1942-43; resident in neurology U. Hosps., Iowa City, 1946-47; resident in psychiatry Griffin Meml. Central State Hosp., Norman, Okla., 1964-67; gen. practice medicine and surgery, St. Francis, Kans., 1947-62, LaCrosse, Kans., 1962-64; dir., psychiatrist Mental Health Clinic for Students, Okla. State U., Stillwater, 1968-71; staff psychiatrist Santa Barbasa County Mental Health Services, Santa Maria, Calif., 1971-72, San Luis Obispo (Calif.) Community Mental Health Services, 1973-75, Atascadero (Calif.) State Hosp., 1975-79; practice medicine specializing in psychiatry and hypnosis, Ponca City, Okla., 1967-71, Santa Maria, 1971—. Active Boy Scouts Am., 1928-33, 64-70. Mem. St. Francis Elem. Sch. Bd., 1959-62. Served to lt. USNR, 1943-46. Recipient Eagle Scout award, Explorer Silver award, Scout Master's Key, Boy Scouts Am., 1958, Wood Badge, 1960. NIMH grantee, 1964-67. Mem. Am. Soc. Clin. Hypnosis (charter), Soc. Clin. and Exptl. Hypnosis, Internat. Soc. Hypnosis, So. Calif. Psychiat. Soc., Am. Psychiat. Assn., Acad. Parapsychology and Medicine, Internat. Platform Assn., Phi Beta Pi, Delta Upsilon. Methodist (lay leader). Mason. Author: Stop Bedwetting and Help Your Child, 1979. Developer body image therapy-programmed personality integration, sleep-teach therapy, indirect remote psychotherapy, reality insight therapy; researcher in practical function and treatment of unconscious mind. Home: 4655 Basque Dr Santa Maria CA 93455

WILSON, CHRISTINE LOUISE, health administrator, consultant; b. Meyersdale, Pa., Apr. 27, 1953; d. Edmund George and Annemarie Jenny (Bohm) W. B.A., U. Pitts., 1975, M.P.H., 1977. Edn./Outreach supr. Planned Parenthood of Cambria Somerset, Johnstown, Pa., 1977-79; community organizer Family Planning Council Western Pa., Pitts., 1979; youth counselor VisonQuest Inc., Colorado Springs, Colo., 1980; staff asst. Colo. Med. Polit. Action Com., Colo. Profl. Liability Trust, Colo. Med. Soc., Denver, 1981; coordinator Colo. Jail Health Care Project, Colo. Med. Soc., 1981—; site survey cons. Am. Health Care Cons. Inc. Recipient hon. mention Gold Key awards Colo. chpt. Bus./Profl. Advt. Assn., 1981. Mem. Am. Correction Assn., Am. Correctional Health Services Assn., Am. Jail Assn., Am. Pub. Health Assn., Rocky Mountain Correctional Health Assn. (charter). Editor Jail Health Care Newsletter. Home: 2737 E 13th Ave Apt 1 Denver CO 80206 Office: Colo Jail Health Care Project 6825 E Tennessee Bldg 2 Suite 500 Denver CO 80224

WILSON, DAVID ALLEN, political science educator, university administrator; b. Rockford, Ill., May 1, 1926; s. Allen C. and Margaret M. W.; m. Marie M. Mannes, 1952; children—Elizabeth, Stephen. B.A., U. Toledo, 1948; Ph.D., Cornell U., 1960. Mem. faculty dept. polit. sci. UCLA, 1959—, prof., 1969—, exec. asst. to the pres. of Univ., 1977—; cons. U.S. govt., Rand Corp.; mem. Nat. Commn. on Higher Edn. Issues. NSF grantee, 1966; Ford Found. fgn. Area fellow, 1956; Fulbright grantee, 1952; Rockefeller Found. grantee, 1967. Mem. Am. Polit. Sci. Assn., Assn. Asian Studies. Author: Politics in Thailand, 1962; United States and the Future of Thailand, 1970; contbr. numerous articles and essays to profl. jours. Office: 2200 University Ave Suite 721 Berkeley CA 94720

WILSON, DAVID LEE, clinical psychologist, consultant; b. Mooresville, N.C., July 5, 1941; s. W.J. Mack and Joyce Evelyn (Evans) W.; m. Barbara Ann Klepter, April 22, 1960 (div.); children—Cheryl, Lisa, David L.; m. Cheryl Andersen, May 22, 1983. A.B. in Psychology, Davidson (N.C.) Coll., 1963; Ph.D. in Clin. Psychology, U. N.C.-Chapel Hill, 1967. Lic. clin. psychologist, Calif. Career teaching fellow U. N.C., 1964-65; intern clin. psychology Letterman Hosp., San Francisco, 1966-67, supervising psychologist, 1967-70; sr. psychologist Kaiser Hosp., Hayward, Calif., 1970-72; staff psychologist Far North Regional Ctr., 1972-74; pvt. practice clin. psychology, Redding, Calif., 1974—; dir. Ctr. for Growth; cons. Family Protection Act Bd., 1978—, Stepping Stones, 1982—. Mem. Shasta County Criminal Justice Adv. Bd., 1978—, chmn., 1983—; mem. Youth and Family Counseling Ctr. Bd., 1982—. Served to capt. U.S. Army, 1965-70. Dana scholar, 1960-63; Woodrow Wilson fellow, 1963-64. Mem. Am. Psychol. Assn., Western Psychol. Assn., Calif. State Psychol. Assn. Democrat. Methodist. Home: 275 Hilltop St Apt 29 Redding CA 96001 Office: 1864 South St Redding CA 06001

WILSON, DIERDRE, theatre and dance educator, therapist, choreographer, author, researcher, performer; b. La Mesa, Calif., Feb. 21, 1945; d. Joseph Herbert Wilson and Audrie Ilene (Branin) W.; m. Douglas John Hammel, Aug. 18, 1978; 1 son, Devon. A.A., Grossmont Coll., 1977; B.A. in Clin. Psychology, Antioch U., 1979; M.Ed. in Counseling Psychology, Wash. State U., 1983, M.A. in Theatre, 1983; dance and theatre tng. Agnes Moorehead Actor's Workshop, Los Angeles, 1967, Lee Strasberg Inst., Los Angeles, 1969, Odyssey Improvisation Theatre, Los Angeles, 1969, Theatre East Actor's Workshop, Los Angeles, 1969, Am. Conservatory Theatre, San Francisco, 1970-71; City Coll. San Francisco, 1975; dance tng. San Francisco Ballet, San Francisco Dance Spectrum, San Francisco Dance Theatre, Margueritte Ellicot Sch. Ballet, Pacific Ballet Acad., Gene Maranaccio Sch. Ballet, Roland Dupree Dance Acad., Wash. State U. Ballet instr. Ed Mock Studios, San Francisco, 1974-75, San Francisco Dance Theatre, 1974-75; tchr. creative dramatics Ballet Folk, Moscow, Idaho, 1980; instr., curriculum designer creative arts for handicapped Wash. State U., Pullman, 1980, instr. ballet, 1980, instr. acting, 1982-83, mem. senate, 1981; dir., owner, adminstr. Acad. Ballet, Pullman; dance cons., choreographer; appeared in numerous musicals, with various ballet cos., in several films. Chmn. disabled services adv. council San Diego Parks and Recreation Dept., 1978. San Diego Theatre for Disabled grantee, 1978; Wash. State U. grantee, 1982; Wash. Commn. for Humanities grantee, 1983. Mem. Actor's Equity Assn., Am. Guild Musical Artists, Nat. Assn. Drama Therapists, Am. Personnel and Guidance Assn., Phi Delta Kappa. Author: Introduction to Theatre for the Aged Disabled, 1977. Office: Acad of Ballet 115 State St Suite 204 Pullman WA 99163

WILSON, DORIS LOUISE, educator; b. Bend, Oreg., Feb. 27, 1933; d. Charles Henry and Minnie Louise (Hanneman) Whitman; m. Melvin Lewis, May 14, 1927. B.S., Oreg. State U., 1973. Health and home econs. tchr. Ponderosa Jr. High Sch., Klamath Falls, Oreg., 1973—. Democrat. Office: Home Econs Dept Ponderosa Jr High Sch 2554 Main St Klamath Falls OR 97601

WILSON, DOUGLAS ALLEN, consulting group executive; b. Dayton, Ohio, Sept. 9, 1948; s. Leonard E. and Mary L. (Hubbard) W.; m. Karen Lee Hellinga, June 2, 1972; children—Bryan D., Kayleigh L. B.A., So. Meth. U., 1971; Th.M., Dallas Theol. Sem., 1975; Ph.D., North Tex. State U., 1980. Dir. singles' seminars Christian Family Life, Dallas, 1972-75; counselor Christian Counseling Services, Dallas, 1975-77; dir. counseling ctr. Maximum Life Communications, Newport Beach, Calif., 1977-79; pres., owner CORE: Counseling and Organizational Resources, Newport Beach, 1979—; lectr. organizational behavior U. So. Calif. Grad. Sch., 1981—. Mem. Republican Presdl. Task Force, 1982; chmn. Newport Harbor Christian Leadership Week, Newport Beach. Mem. Am. Soc. Tng. and Devel., Am. Personnel and Guidance Assn., Am. Assn. Marriage and Family Therapists. Club: Balboa Bay (Newport Beach). Author: The Style of Influence Inventory, 1981; Profiles of Leadership, 1983; author tape series: Quest for Intimacy, 1977; contbr. articles to various mags. Office: 260 Newport Center Dr Suite 250 Newport Beach CA 92660

WILSON, DOUGLAS EDWIN, lawyer; b. Sacramento, Apr. 23, 1917; s. Richard Matthew and Ruth (O'Brien) W.; A.B., U. of Pacific, 1940; J.D., U. Calif. at San Francisco, 1948; m. Helen Marie Lewis, Apr. 5, 1942; children—Sandra Jane (Mrs. Kenneth Arthur Olds), Kent Lewis, Jay Douglas. Admitted to Calif. bar, 1949; partner Forslund & Wilson, Stockton, 1949-83, Wilson & Wison, 1983—; U.S. magistrate Stockton, Eastern Dist. of Calif., 1962-76. Mem. San Joaquin County Retirement Bd., 1952-72. Served to capt. AUS, 1941-46. Recipient Silver Beaver award Boy Scouts, 1955, Distinguished Eagle Scout award, 1971. Mem. San Joaquin County, Calif. State bars, Am. Legion. Republican. Methodist. Mason (Shriner, K.T.), Elk, Rotarian. Club: Commonwealth (San Francisco). Home: 2134 Gardena Ave Stockton CA 95204 Office: Bank of Am Bldg Stockton CA 95202

WILSON, EMILY MARIE, manufacturing company sales executive; b. Aberdeen, Wash., Mar. 24, 1951; d. Charles Robert and Alice Adele (Robinson) W.; student U. Puget Sound. 1969-71, Austro Am. Inst., Vienna, 1971; B.A. in Polit. Sci., U. Wash., Seattle, 1973; m. Michael A. Rich, July 1, 1976. Tour counselor, documents and receipts, air reservationist Princess Cruises and Tours, Seattle, 1973-75; with Clairol, Inc., Seattle, 1975—, sales rep. N.W. Wash., drug-mass mdse. div., 1975-77, sales rep. Met. Seattle, 1977-78, dist. mgr. sales western Wash., 1978-81, trainer territorial sales reps., mgr. dist. dollar sales; dist. sales mgr. of Wash., Oreg., Idaho and Mont., Clorox Inc., Seattle, 1981-82, assoc. regional mgr. Western div. Clorox spl. markets, 1982-83, regional mgr. Olympic Stain Co. div., Bellevue, Wash., 1983—. Mem. Transcendental Meditation Soc., Oreg. Hist. Soc., Sons and Daus. of Oreg. Pioneers, Pioneer Assn. Wash., Seattle Hist. Soc., Sidha of the Age of Enlightenment World Govt. Assn., Grad. Sci. of Creative Intelligence. Club: Zonta (Seattle). Office: 4417 54th Ave NE Seattle WA 98105

WILSON, EVIE CHRISTINA, county data processing manager; b. Ft. Hood, Tex., Jan. 5, 1953; d. John and Wanda (Filinsky) Barnett; m. Scott Lange Wilson, Nov. 4, 1978. Student City Coll. San Francisco, 1971-73, U. Calif.-Berkeley, 1973. Ops. mgr. C.I.C.S.-Pacific, San Francisco, 1977-79; data processing ops. mgr. Victoria Sta., Greenbrae, Calif., 1975-77; data processing ops. mgr., div. chief County of Marin, San Rafael, Calif., 1979—. Recipient Resolution of Commendation County of Marin, Commn. on Status of Women, 1981. Mem. Nat. Assn. Female Execs. Home: 11 Taurus Dr Novato CA 94947 Office: Civic Center Room 215 San Rafael CA 94903

WILSON, FRANCES GEORGINE, biologist, educator; b. Chariton, Iowa, Feb. 14, 1915; d. Elmer Ellsworth and Georgia Annice (McDonnell) Wilson; B.S., Drake U., Des Moines, 1936, M.S., 1937. Mem. faculty dept. biology East Los Angeles Coll., Monterey Park, Calif., 1949—, now. prof. Served as cpl. WAC, 1943-45. Mem. Am. Fedn. Tchrs., Pi Lambda Theta, Phi Sigma, Phi Delta Gamma, Psi Chi, Delta Sigma Epsilon. Democrat. Presbyterian. Contbr. articles to profl. jours. Office: Dept Life Sci East Los Angeles Coll 1301 E Brooklyn Ave Monterey Park PA 91754

WILSON, FRANK HENRY, electronics engineer; b. Dinuba, Calif., Dec. 4, 1935; s. Frank Henry and Lurene (Copley) W.; m. Carol Greening, Mar. 28, 1964; children—Frank Henry, Scott Edward. B.S., Oreg. State Coll., 1957. Electronics engr. Varian Assos., 1960-61; with Dept. Pharmacology, Stanford Sch. Medicine, Palo Alto, 1961-68, U. Calif., Davis, 1968-77; design engr. Litronix, Cupertino, Calif., 1978-81, Quantel, Santa Clara, Calif., 1981—. Tchr. handicapped children Vol. Swim Tchrs. for Handicapped Children, Inc., v.p., 1963-65, pres., 1965. Served with Signal Corps, AUS, 1958-60. Mem. IEEE. Home: 3826 Nathan Way Palo Alto CA 94303 Office: Quantel 385 Reed St Santa Clara CA 98050

WILSON, HAROLD EDWARD, hospital business manager; b. Lexington, Ky., Jan. 19, 1932; s. Daniel and Lillie Mae (Reed) W.; m. Sandra R. Sterling, Sept. 6, 1958; children—Stephen, Christopher, Joy, Michael. B.S. in Personnel Mgmt. and Acctg., U. Louisville, 1953; M.B.A., E. Wash. U., 1982. Commd. officer U.S. Air Force, 1953, advanced through grades to col., 1973; instr. pilot, 1953-69; mem. staff Pentagon, 1969-73; insp. gen. SAC, 1975-78; chief staff 1st Air Div., 1978-80; ret., 1980; bus. mgr. Eastern State Hosp., Medical Lake, Wash., 1980—. Decorated Legion of Merit, D.F.C. Mem. Air Force Assn., Ky. Cols. Home: N 7214 Valerie St Spokane WA 99208 Office: Box A Eastern State Hosp Medical Lake WA 99022

WILSON, JAMES LLOYD, marketing consultant; b. Portland, Oreg., Jan. 10, 1949; s. Harold Lloyd and Mary Lou (Schlaugh) W.; student Portland Community Coll., 1970-71, Clackamas Community Coll., 1974-75, City Coll. Seattle, 1974-76; m. Donna Rae Fishbaugh, Aug. 26, 1967; children—Mark James, Ian James. Sales rep. Am. Broadcasting Co., 1971-73; purchasing agt. G.I. Joes, Inc., Portland, 1973-75; mfr.'s rep. J.B. Sales Co., Portland, 1975-78; mfr.'s rep. Premier Autoware, Inc., Portland, 1977-79; prin., mfr.'s rep. Profl. Mktg. Assocs., rep. home center, hardware, automotive, nutritional food supplement items, Scappoose, Oreg., 1979—. Co-sponsor Mr. Am. Candidate. Served with USNR, 1968-77. Mem. Sales and Mktg. Execs. Internat., Asso. Electronics Industry Services. Democrat. Office: 27001 NW Columbia River Hwy Scappoose OR 97056

WILSON, JAMES ROBIN, educator; b. Goodland, Kans., June 20, 1951; s. Charles William and Frances Preshia (Stephenson) W.; B.A., Wichita State U., 1974; postgrad. U. Calif., Santa Barbara, 1974-75. Environ. edn. naturalist Santa Barbara (Calif.) County Public Schs., 1972-73; camp counselor Camp Lorr, Santa Barbara, summers, 1973-75; tchr. mentally gifted, tchr. phys. edn. Ralph Dunlap Sch., Orcutt, Calif., 1975-76; early childhood edn. tchr. Black Butte Elem. Sch., Shingletown, Calif., 1976-77; tchr. Pine Grove Sch., Orcutt, 1977-78; tchr. 2d grade Reliance (Wyo.) Sch., 1978-81; tchr. Overland Sch., Rock Springs, Wyo., 1981—; project dir., program developer and coordinator Title IV-C Project, Sweetwater County Sch. Dist. 1, Rock Springs, 1980-83, Desert View Elem. Sch., 1983—; condr. tchr. workshops. Chmn. Rock Springs March of Dimes Walk Am., 1983. Recipient Indian Lore award for outstanding counselor of yr. Camp Lorr, 1975. Mem. Assn. Supervision and Curriculum Devel., Rock Springs Classroom Tchrs. Assn., Wyo. Edn. Assn., NEA, Assn. Experiential Edn., Expdn. Research Inc., Delta Upsilon. Club: Kiwanis (v.p., membership chmn.) (Rock Springs). Address: PO Box 1223 Rock Springs WY 82901

WILSON, JAMES ROSS, broadcasting instructor; b. Petaluma, Calif., Nov. 25, 1939; s. Stanley Thomas and Cora Arville (Ross) W.; B.A., Fresno State Coll., 1961; M.A. in Mass Communications, Calif. State U.-Fresno, 1976; children—Jay Gregory, Thomas Jeffrey. News reporter Sta. KMJ, Fresno, Calif., 1966-67, news dir., 1967-71, program dir., 1971-78, v.p., gen. mgr. Sta. KMJ-AM, KNAX-FM, 1978-82; instr. Fresno State U., 1978—. Bd. dirs. Sta. KVPR, public radio sta., 1980-82. Served with U.S. Army, 1962-65. Mem. Central Calif. Broadcasters Assn., Sigma Delta Chi, Alpha Epsilon Rho. Office: Calif State U Dept Radio-TV-Cinema Fresno CA 93740

WILSON, JOHN HART, constrn. co. exec.; b. Seattle, June 11, 1922; s. Richard Hagan and Agnes Josephine (Hart) W.; student Stanford, 1940-43; B.S.C.E., Calif. Inst. Tech., 1944; m. Barbara Elizabeth Wells, Jan. 22, 1949; 1 dau., Wendy Wilson Smull. Engr., supt. Harms Bros. Co., Sacramento, 1946-52; dist. engr. Morrison-Knudsen Co., Inc., Los Angeles, 1960-64, dist. mgr., Los Angeles, 1964-67, chief engr., 1968-69, v.p. engring., 1970-74, v.p. spl. assignment, 1975—. Served with Civil Engrs. Corps, USN, 1943-46. Mem. ASCE, Am. Inst. Constructors, Soc. Am. Mil. Engrs., Beavers, Delta Kappa Epsilon. Republican. Club: Hillcrest Country. Home: 3904 Hillcrest Dr Boise ID 83705 Office: 1 Morrison-Knudsen Plaza Boise ID 83729

WILSON, JOHN LEWIS, economist, management consultant, educator; b. Columbus, Ohio, Mar. 18, 1943; s. John Robert and Betty Marie (Barker) W.; m. Linda Patricia Kiernan, Apr. 23, 1966; 1 dau., Heidi Annette. B.A. in Internat. Relations, Am. U., 1969, M.A. in Econs., 1973, Ph.D. in Econs., 1977. Staff asst. Congressman Paul N. McCloskey, Jr., Washington, 1968-72; sr. research and tng. assoc. Govtl. Affairs Inst., Washington, 1973-77; pres. Experience Devel. Inc., Tucson, Ariz., 1978—; prof. econs. U. Phoenix. Pres. Sabino Vista Recreation Assn., 1981-82. Served to 1st lt. U.S. Army, 1964-68. Decorated Bronze Star with oak leaf cluster. Mem. Am. Soc. Tng. and Devel., Am. Econ. Assn. Democrat. Clubs: Toastmasters Internat., Roadrunners in Tucson. Author: Managing Planned Agricultural Development, 1976; Solving Management Problems in the World Bank: A Casebook.

WILSON, JOHN ROBERT, physician; b. Jamaica, N.Y., Dec. 20, 1938; s. Wallace Monroe and Frances Gertrude (Wernery) W.; A.B., Cornell U., 1960, M.D., 1964; children—Jennifer, Emilie; m. 2d, Elise S. Richter, June 16, 1977. Intern, resident in medicine SUNY, Upstate Med. Center, Syracuse, 1964-66; resident in neurology Stanford U. Hosp., 1968-72; hon. clin. fellow Nat. Hosp. Queen Sq., London, 1970; practice medicine specializing in neurology San Jose, Calif., 1972-75, Palo Alto, Calif., 1975—; asst. clin. prof. neurology Stanford U. Med. Center, 1975—; dep. chief dept. neurology Stanford U. Hosp., 1979-81, dep. dir. electromyography lab., 1978—; cons. physician VA Med. Center, Palo Alto, 1975—. Served to capt. M.C., U.S. Army, 1966-68. Diplomate Am. Bd. Psychiatry and Neurology, Am. Bd. EEG. Mem.

Am. Acad. Neurology, AMA, Calif. Med. Assn., Am. Electroencephalographic Soc., Am. Assn. Electromyography and Electrodiagnosis, Western EEG Soc., San Francisco Neurol. Soc., Santa Clara Med. Soc., San Mateo Med. Soc. physician; b. Jamaica, N.Y., Dec. 20, 1938; s. Wallace Monroe and Frances Gertrude (Wernery) W.; A.B., Cornell U., 1960, M.D., 1964; children—Jennifer, Emilie; m. 2d, Elise S. Richter, June 16, 1977. Intern, resident in medicine SUNY, Upstate Med. Center, Syracuse, 1964-66; resident in neurology Stanford U. Hosp., 1968-72; hon. clin. fellow Nat. Hosp. Queen Sq., London, 1970; practice medicine specializing in neurology San Jose, Calif., 1972-75, Palo Alto, Calif., 1975—; asst. clin. prof. neurology Stanford U. Med. Center, 1975—; dep. chief dept. neurology Stanford U. Hosp., 1979-81, dep. dir. electromyography lab., 1978—; cons. physician VA Med. Center, Palo Alto, 1975—. Served to capt. M.C., U.S. Army, 1966-68. Diplomate Am. Bd. Psychiatry and Neurology, Am. Bd. EEG. Mem. Am. Acad. Neurology, AMA, Calif. Med. Assn., Am. Electroencephalographic Soc., Am. Assn. Electromyography and Electrodiagnosis, Western EEG Soc., San Francisco Neurol. Soc., Santa Clara Med. Soc., San Mateo Med. Soc. Office: 1101 Welch Rd Palo Alto CA 94304 also 2950 Whipple Ave Redwood City CA 94062

WILSON, LEE, hydrologist, consultant; b. Wichita Falls, Tex., Apr. 15, 1942; s. William Haynie and Sidney Jean (Main) W.; m. Gladys Danielle Freudmann, June 26, 1969; 1 dau., Dana. B.A., Yale U., 1964; Ph.D. (Faculty fellow), Columbia U., 1971. Tchr. geology Briarcliff Coll., Briarcliff Manor, N.Y., 1968-69; Brock U., St. Catherine, Ont., Can., summers 1969-70; cons. Le Nickel, N.Y.C., 1971-72; sr. scientist Environment Cons., Dallas, 1972-73; pres. Lee Wilson and Assocs., Santa Fe, 1973—. Fellow Geol. Soc. Am. Democrat. Author more than 30 environ. impact statements and documents. Contbr. articles to profl. jours. Home and Office: Box 931 Santa Fe NM 87501

WILSON, LEROY EDWARD, mech. engr., ofcl. Dept. Air Force; b. Lusk, Wyo., July 19, 1936; s. Tevis Albert and Velma Elizabeth (Mosier) W.; B.S., U. Wyo., 1959, M.S., 1962; Ph.D. (NDEA fellow), U. N.Mex., 1969; m. Audrey Ellen Bostrom; children—Cynthia Renee, Leroy Michael, Keith Edward. Research engr. Boeing Aircraft Co., Seattle, from 1962, research engr. USAF Shock Tube Facility, Albuquerque, 1964, 66-69; asst. dir. Mechanics Research Inc., Albuquerque br., Los Angeles, 1971-79; chief chem. lasers tech., Kirtland AFB, N.Mex., 1971—; mem. faculty mech. engring. dept. U. Wyo., 1959-62, mech. engring. dept. U. N.Mex., 1962-65, 68-69; organizer internat. colloquium electronic transition lasers; originator internat. bi-ann. chem. laser symposium. Div. dir. Rocky Mountain Nat. Ski Patrol System, 1974—; bd. dirs. AAU Swimming, 1974-76. Mem. ASME, AIAA. Lutheran. Club: Hobie Yacht (commodore, dir. 1976-79). Author: Electronic Transition Lasers, 3 vols.; contbr. tech. articles in field. Home: 7013 Carriage Rd NE Albuquerque NM 87109 Office: US Air Force Weapons Laboratory ARA Kirtland AFB NM 87117

WILSON, LIONEL JOSEPH, mayor, lawyer; b. New Orleans,; B.A. in Econs., U. Calif., Berkeley, 1939; J.D., U. Calif., Hastings Coll. Law, San Francisco, 1949; m. Dorothy; children—Robin and Lionel (twins), Steven. Admitted to Calif. bar, 1950; presiding judge Oakland (Calif.)-Piedmont mcpl. Ct. 1964, Alameda County (Calif.) Superior Ct., from 1973; chmn. presiding judges Calif. Superior Cts., 1973; presiding judge criminal div. Alameda County Superior Cts., Oakland, 1969, 72, 75, Apellate Dept., 1976; mayor City of Oakland, 1977—; part-owner Sta. KJAZ, Alameda, Calif., 1980—. Mem. adv. com. Alameda County Council Alcholism, Alameda County Mental Health Assn.; cons. Far West Sch.; chmn., pres. Oakland Econ. Devel. Council, Inc., 1961-69; chmn., pres. Oakland Men of Tomorrow, Charles Houston Law Club; chmn. Oakland's Anti Poverty Bd., Oakland Bail Project, 1964-65. Recipient awards including West Coast Region Merit award NAACP, 1960; award for outstanding profl. service No. Calif. Med., Dental, and Pharm. Assn., 1975; Man of Yr. award Oakland Lodge B'nai B'rith, 1977-78; Leadership award Chinese-Am. Citizens Alliance, 1979. Mem. NAACP (dir.), Nat. League of Cities, League of Calif. Cities (dir.), U.S. Conf. of Mayors. Democrat. Office: Room 302 City Hall Oakland CA 94612

WILSON, LOCKRIDGE WARD, real estate cons.; b. Roswell, N.Mex., Jan. 14, 1919; s. William Lockridge and Freda (Brough) W.; M.S., U. So. Calif., 1953; m. Fern B. Wilson, Mar. 14, 1942; children—Larry Ward, David Brown. Tchr., adminstr. Los Angeles Unified Sch. Dist., 1942-73; investment cons., pres. Am. Bus. Corp. Nev., Carlsbad, Calif., 1973—. Served to lt. USNR, 1942-46; Philippines. Cert. sch. adminstr., Calif. Mem. Delta Upsilon. Club: Kiwanis (pres. local club 1963). Home: 4798 Hillside Dr Carlsbad CA 92008

WILSON, LYALL STEVEN, hospital management executive; b. San Gabriel, Calif., Apr. 3, 1951; s. George Lyall and Marlene (Nielson) W.; m. Catherine Ann Coles, Aug. 14, 1976; children—Jaime Lea, Brooke Marlene, Bryan Lyall. B.S., Brigham Young U., 1976, M.P.A. in Health Services Adminstrn., 1978. Adminstrv. asst. Winslow (Ariz.) Indian Hosp., 1975; clerkship Utah State Health Planning and Devel. Agy., Salt Lake City, 1977; adminstrv. resident Orem (Utah) Community Hosp., 1977-78; fellow in hosp. adminstrn. U. Iowa, 1978-79; dir. planning McKay-Dee Hosp. Ctr., Ogden, Utah, 1979-80, asst. adminstr., 1980—; mem. adj. faculty Grad. Sch. Mgmt., Brigham Young U. Bd. dirs. Hospice No. Utah; mem. Com. Internat. Yr. Disabled Persons. Mem. Am. Soc. Hosp. Planning, Utah Hosp. Assn., Am. Hosp. Assn., Layton C. of C. Republican. Mem. Ch. of Jesus Christ of Latter-day Saints. Club: Mt. Ogden Rotary. Contbr. articles to profl. jours. Home: 244 E 600 North Kaysville UT 84037 Office: 3939 Harrison Blvd Ogden UT 84409

WILSON, MAURICE NORMAN, administrator; b. Harvey, Ill., Nov. 22, 1927; s. Harold Clifford and Hazel Rocella (Everman) W.; children—Russell, Richard, Catherine, Carol, Cheryl. Student Clark Coll., 1976-77. Served as enlisted man U.S. Navy, 1945-48, U.S. Air Force, 1950-67; retired 1967; with Portland Traffic Safety Commn., 1968—, dir., 1976—. Mem. Am. Soc. Safety Engrs., Am. Soc. Assn. Execs., Oreg. Council Safety Suprs., Oreg. Assn. D.D.C. Instrs. (sec.), Western Region Safety Council Mgrs. Assn. (chmn.). Club: Portland Rainmakers (pres.). Home: 7008 NE 57th St Vancouver WA 98661 Office: 1120 SW 5th Ave Room 902 Portland OR 97204

WILSON, NICHOLAS JON, wildlife artist; b. Seattle, June 7, 1947; s. Cecil Clark and Hazel Louise (Longon) W.; m. Laura Elaine Trost, Apr. 20, 1968; children—Stefan, Elliott. Curator of exhibits Ariz.-Sonora Desert Mus., Tucson, 1970-72; exhibited various shows in galleries, 1972—; producer ltd. edition prints for Mill Pond Press, Venice, Fla., 1978—; cons. on zoo and mus. projects. Mem. Soc. Animal Artists. Work appears in Wildlife Artists at Work, 1982. Address: 1600 W Mesa Dr Payson AZ 85541

WILSON, PAUL JAMES, optometrist; b. Jacksonville, Fla., July 18, 1949; s. James Ivan and Evelyn Josephine (Hutyra) W.; m. Rosanne Williamson, June 12, 1976; children—Nicholas Paul, Angela Carole, Jane Marie. Student Cabrillo Coll., 1967-68; A.S., Sheridan Coll., 1969; student U. San Francisco, 1969-70, San Jose State U., 1970—; B.S., U. Calif., 1972, O.D., 1974. Pvt. practice optometry, Los Gatos, Calif., 1974—; tchr. optometric asst. tng., 1974; visual cons. U.S. Geol. Survey, 1974—. Fellow Am. Acad. Optometry and Physiol. Optics (Julius Newmueller award 1974); mem. Am. Optometric Assn., Santa Clara County Optometric Soc. (dir., dir.-at-large 1980—), Am. Optometric Found., Los Gatos C. of C. Republican. Roman Catholic. Clubs: Almaden Bicycle Touring (San Jose), Am. Motorcycle Assn., Calif. Enduro and Cross Country Motorcycle Racing, Lions.

WILSON, RANDY ALLEN, safety consultant; b. Forrest City, Ark., Oct. 21, 1947; s. Jesse Pierce and Mildred Mae (Riggs) W.; m. Margaret Lash, Sept. 8, 1948; children—Mark Pierce, Jennifer Lash. B.S., U.S. Mil. Acad., 1969; M.B.A., U. Scranton, 1981. Environ. engr. Procter and Gamble, Mehoopany, Pa., 1974-81; safety and environ. mgr. Arco Solar, Inc., Camarillo, Calif., 1981-82, planning and analysis cons., Chatsworth, Calif., 1982—. Served as capt. U.S. Army, 1969-74. Decorated Bronze Star, Air medal. Mem. Am. Soc. Safety Engrs., Jaycees (dir., sec.). Presbyterian. Home: 415 Pacific Circle Newbury Park CA 91320 Office: 20554 Plummer St Chatsworth CA 91311

WILSON, ROBERT CHARLES, gen. contractor; b. Udall, Kans., Jan. 8, 1925; s. Clarence Short and Jennie Alice (Lusk) W.; B.C.E., Oreg. State U., 1950; m. Patricia McEwan, July 12, 1947; children—Patricia, Nancy, Susan, Cynthia. Owner Robert C. Wilson, Gen. Contractor, Corvallis, Oreg., 1950—; ptnr. Clothes Tree, Inc., Corvallis, 1950—; owner, mgr. Circle Nine Shopping Ctr., Corvallis, 1961—; dir. Citizens Bank of Corvallis, 1975—, chmn. bd., 1979—. Trustee Oreg. State U. Found., 1974—; bd. dirs. Benton County Found., 1968-74, pres. 1971-72; mem. Corvallis Planning Commn., 1958-59; chmn. Downtown Redevel. Commn., 1979-80. Served with U.S. Army, 1943-46. Mem. Assoc. Gen. Contractors (chpt. pres.). Republican. Methodist. Clubs: Rotary, Masons, Shriners, Oreg. State U. Pres.'. Home: 1400 NW Vista Pl Corvallis OR 97330 Office: PO Box 638 Corvallis OR 97339

WILSON, ROBIN SCOTT, university president; b. Columbus, Ohio, Sept. 19, 1928; married 1951; 4 children. B.A., Ohio State U., 1950; M.A., U. Ill., 1951, Ph.D. in English, 1959. Asst. instr. English, U. Ill., 1957-59; intelligence officer CIA, 1959-67; prof. English, Clarion State Coll., 1967-70; assoc. dir. Com. Instnl. Cooperation, 1970-77; assoc. provost Ohio State U., 1977-80; pres. Calif. State U.-Chico, 1980—; vis. lectr. Tulane U., 1971, Mich. State U., 1972-74, 76-81. Mem. Sci. Fiction Writers Am., MLA, Am. Assn. Higher Edn. Author: (with others) To the Sound of Freedom, 1973; editor: Clarion Experiment, 1971; Clarion II, 1972, Clarion III, 1973; Those Who Can: A Science Fiction Reader, 1973. Office: California State University Office of the President 1st and Normal Sts Chico CA 95929*

WILSON, ROGER LAVERN, agronomist; b. Siloam Springs, Ark., Oct. 22, 1936; s. Frank L. and Naomi A. W.; student (scholar) Mesa Jr. Coll., 1956; B.S., Utah State U., 1958; M.S., Mont. State U., 1963, Ph.D., 1970; m. Orma Ann Griffith, Sept. 14, 1956; children—Randall Allen, Lorna Jean, Loren Dale. Soil scientist Soil Conservation Service, Philipsburg, Mont., 1958-62; county agt. Coop. Extension Service, Mont., 1963-67, grad. asst. to county agt., 1967-70, extension soil specialist, Mont. rep. on conservation tillage, 1970-79; Pacific N.W. area dir. TVA, Pullman, Wash., 1979—; chmn. Wash. Soil Improvement Com., 1979—. Mem. Am. Soc. Agronomy, Crop Sci. Soc. Am., Soil Conservation Soc., Range Mgmt. Soc., Sigma Xi. Mem. Christian Ch. (deacon, elder, chmn. bd.). Contbr. agrl. articles to profl. jours.; author handbook on soil fertility. Home: SE 305 Bellevue Pullman WA 99163 Office: Pacific NW Area TVA 169 Johnson Hall Pullman WA 99164

WILSON, ROSEMARY DIANE NEWHOUSER LITTRELL, communications counselor; b. Fremont, Nebr., June 14, 1939; d. Lawrence Emerson and Rosemary Ann (Check) Littrell; m. Marc Anthony Wilson, Apr. 7, 1961; children—Charles Christopher, Alexandria Michelle, Roger Huntington. Student Colo. Womans Coll., 1958-59, Mills Coll., 1959-60, U. Hawaii, 1960-65. In radio and television prodn. and sales, Honolulu, 1961-66; radio salesperson stas. KZEL, KASH, KEED, KORE, Eugene, Oreg., 1967-74; media buyer Cochrane Chase & Co., Newport Beach, Calif., 1974-76; pub. relations cons. Cook Communications Services, Inc., Newport Beach, 1976-81; account exec. Five Star Mktg., Santa Ana, Calif., 1981-82, communications counselor Wilson/Creative Assocs., Irvine, Calif., 1982—; instr. Golden West Coll., Huntington Beach, Calif. Past pub. relations dir. Orange County Philharmonic Soc.; women's coms. promotion and publicity dir. Tri-County chpt. Leukemia Soc. Am. Super Swim Classic. Mem. Pub. Relations Soc. Am. (Orange County chpt.). Republican. Office: 5232 Michelson Dr Ste 20D Irvine CA 92715

WILSON, ROY WOODROW, computer consultant; b. Milw., Oct. 2, 1950; s. LeRoy Woodrow and Rosemary Agnes (Lee) W.; m. Diane Lieb, Apr. 2, 1976. M.A. in Math., Denver U., 1978; M.S. in Computer Sci., 1983. Instr. computer sci. Denver U., 1978; research assoc. Denver Research Inst., 1978-80; assoc. programming engr. Burroughs Corp., Northglenn, Colo., 1980-81; prin. Computer Skills Co., Denver, 1982—. Mem. ACM, Soc. Actuaries, Ind. Computer Cons. Assn. Home and Office: PO Box 24532 Denver CO 80224

WILSON, SETH JACKSON, air force officer; b. Madera, Calif., June 9, 1948; s. Jack B. and Barbara C. (Fain) W.; m. Judith L. Deis, Sept. 18, 1971; children—Kendra, Jared. B.S. in Criminology, Calif. State U.-Fresno, 1971; M.A. in Pub. Adminstrn./Justice Adminstrn. summa cum laude, 1977. Commd. 2d lt. U.S. Air Force, 1971, advanced through grades to capt., 1983; missile crew comdr. McConnell AFB, Wichita, Kans., 1972-74; missile instr., briefer Vanderberg AFB, Calif., 1974-78; ROTC instr. No. Ariz. U., Flagstaff, 1978-79; missile maintenance officer, squadron comdr. 390th Strategic Missile Wing hdqrs. Davis-Monthan AFB, Tucson, 1979-83; mem. Cruise missile deployment team, RAF Base, Greenham Common, Eng., 1983—. Decorated Air Force Commendation medal with 1 oak leaf cluster. Mem. Air Force Assn., Theta Chi Alumni Club. Democrat. Methodist. Home: 7814 E 34th St Tucson AZ 85710 Office: RAF Base Greenham Common England

WILSON, SODONIA MAE, psychologist; b. Galveston, Tex., Feb. 25; d. Jasper and Willie Mae (Reed) Moore; m. James Wilson, Jr., Mar. 24, 1957; 1 son, Demetrius D. R.N., French Hosp. Sch. Nursing; A.S., City Coll. San Francisco; B.A., M.A., San Francisco State U.; Ph.D., Calif. Sch. Profl. Psychology. Staff nurse French Hosp., San Francisco, 1956-57, Ft. Miley VA Hosp., San Francisco, 1957-60; counselor San Francisco Youth Guidance Ctr., 1966, probation officer, 1967; head start analyst Office Econ. Opportunity, San Francisco, 1968; social service rep. San Francisco Redevel. Agy., 1969; coll. counseling coordinator Sequoia Union High Sch. Dist., Redwood City, Calif., 1969-72; counselor Contra Costa Coll., San Pablo, Calif., 1972-73, dir. spl. programs and services, 1973—. Mem. Student Aid Commn., State of Calif., 1982—; commr. San Francisco Bd. Edn., 1982—. Mem. Am. Psychol. Assn., Assn. Calif. Community Coll. Adminstrs., Calif. Community Coll. Extended Opportunity Programs and Services Assn. (pres. 1977-78), Women in Higher Edn. Assn., NAACP, Nat. Black Caucus, Bay Area Black Women United, Nat. Women's Polit. Club, Black Women Organized for Action, Bus. and Profl. Women's Club, Nat. Assn. Negro Bus. and Profl. Women's Club. Democrat. Baptist. Home: 540 Darien Way San Francisco CA 94127 Office: 2600 Mission Bell Dr San Pablo CA 94806

WILSON, STEPHEN ROLAND, financial consultant; b. Toronto, Ont., Can., Jan. 14, 1941; came to U.S., 1981; s. Roland Frederick and Bernice Sill (Langrill) W. B.A., U. Western Ont., London, 1963; LL.B., Osgoode Hall Law Sch., Toronto, 1966; M.B.A., Stanford U., 1969. Chartered acct. Inst. Chartered Accts. of Ont., 1972. Auditor, Price Waterhouse, Toronto, 1966-67, 69-71; exec. asst. Toronto Dominion Bank, 1971-77; sr. mng. project fin. Bank of Montreal, Toronto, 1977-79; v.p. spl. financing Bank of Montreal Trust Co., N.Y.C., 1979-81; v.p. Bechtel Financing Services Inc., San Francisco, 1981—; lectr. Grad. Sch. Internat. Affairs Columbia U. Mem. Inst. Chartered Accts. of Ont., Toronto Soc. Fin. Analysts. Clubs: Met. (N.Y.C.); Univ. (Toronto). Home: 55F Red Hill Circle Tiburon CA 94920 Office: 50 Beale St San Francisco CA 94105

WILSON, STEVEN ALEXANDER, soil scientist; b. Tacoma, Wash., Apr. 12, 1952; s. Alexander and Lilliam May (Johnson) W.; m. Linda Hammond, Aug. 28, 1976. B.A. in Environ. Studies, Whitman Coll., 1974; M.S. in Soils, Wash. State U., 1977. Research asst. Wash. State U., Pullman, 1975-78; soil scientist Oreg. Dept. Environ. Quality, Portland, 1978-81; soil scientist, ptnr. Cascades Earth Scis., Ltd., Corbett, Oreg., 1981—; mem. EPA Nat. Tech. Rev. Com. Past master Columbia Grange 267, 1981; pres. Dist. 14 Vol. Firemans Assn., 1983. Mem. Oreg. Soil Sci. Soc., Pacific N.W. Pollution Control Assn., Soil Sci. Soc. Am. Libertarian. Office: Cascade Earth PO Box 137 Corbett OR 97019

WILSON, TED LEWIS, mayor Salt Lake City; b. Salt Lake City, May 18, 1939; s. Robert L. and Eva (Simpson) W.; B.S., U. Utah, 1964; M.Ed. (NSF fellow), U. Wash., 1969; m. Kathryn Carling, June 10, 1963; children—Benjamin, Jennifer, Melissa, Jessica, Joseph. Tchr., Granite Sch. Dist., Salt Lake City, 1966-73; adminstrv. asst. to a congressman, 1973-75; social services dir. Salt Lake County, Utah, 1975-76; mayor of Salt Lake City, 1976—. Bd. dirs. Intermountain Health Care, Inc. Served with U.S. Army, 1957-62, Utah N.G., 1957-63. Recipient Valor award Dept. of Interior, 1968. Mem. U.S. Conf. Mayors (adv. bd., trustee, chmn. energy and environ. com.), Nat. League Cities and Towns (dir.), Am. Soc. Public Adminstrs., Common Cause. Democrat. Mormon. Contbr. articles to profl. jours. Office: Room 300 City and County Bldg Salt Lake City UT 84111

WILSON, THOMAS CAVE, advertising executive; b. Phoenix, Nov. 11, 1907; s. Frederick Weston and Claire (Cave) W.; m. Ina Winters, Sept., 1933; children—Thomas R.C. II, Mary Elizabeth Vlaming. B.A., U. Nev., 1930. Reporter Santa Monica (Calif.) Evening Outlook, 1928-30; reporter, advt. salesman Humboldt Star, Winnemucca, Nev., 1930-32; advt. mgr., reporter Las Vegas Morning Age, 1932-33, Monterey County (Calif.) Post, 1933; advt. salesman San Pedro (Calif.) News-Pilot, 1933-34; advt. mgr. San Mateo (Calif.) Times, 1934-35; owner, pres. Thomas C. Wilson advt. agy., Reno, 1936—. Chmn. Nev. State Bd. Mus. and History; lt. col. naval wing CAP. Served with inf. USAR, 1933-43. Recipient U. Nev. Disting. Nevadan award, 1981. Mem. Reno C. of C., Affiliated Advt. Agys. Internat. (dir.), Advt. Fedn. Am. (silver medal, 1980), Advt. Assn. West (bd. govs.), Nev. State Press Assn. Democrat. Episcopalian. Clubs: Masons, Rotary, Prospectors, San Francisco Press, Reno Advt. (founding pres.). Author: Pioneer Nevada, 2 vols., 1950. Home: 99 Rancho Manor Dr Reno NV 89509 Office: 241 Ridge St Reno NV 89504

WILSON, THOMAS R. C., state senator, lawyer; b. San Francisco, Apr. 15, 1935; grad. Stanford U., Georgetown U. Law Sch.; m. Sandra Opsahl; children—Ann Louise, Ina Marie, Thomas R. C., John Weston. Sole practice law, Reno; asst. U.S. atty., 1961-64; mem. Nev. Senate from 1st dist., 1971—, mem. Legis. Commn., 1975-77, 79—, asst. majority leader, 1977-79, 81. Served with U.S. Army, 1957-58. Mem. Washoe County Bar Assn., Nev. Bar Assn., ABA. Democrat. Roman Catholic. Office: PO Box 2670 Reno NV 89505*

WILSON, THORNTON ARNOLD, airplane co. exec.; b. Sikeston, Mo., Feb. 8, 1921; s. Thornton Arnold and Daffodil (Allen) W.; student Jefferson City (Mo.) Jr. Coll., 1938-40; B.S., Iowa State Coll., 1943; M.S., Calif. Inst. Tech., 1948; Sloan fellow M.I.T., 1952-53; m. Grace Miller, Aug. 5, 1944; children—Thornton Arnold III, Daniel Allen, Sarah Louise. With Boeing Co., Seattle, 1943—, asst. chief tech. staff, project engring. mgr., 1957-58, v.p., mgr. Minuteman br. aerospace div., 1962-64, v.p. ops. and planning, 1964-65, exec. v.p., then pres., 1966-72, chmn. bd., chief exec. officer, 1972—, also dir.; dir. U.S. Steel, PACCAR, Inc., Seattle-First Nat. Bank, Weyerhaeuser Co. Bd. govs. Iowa State U. Found., mem. corp. M.I.T.; mem. Trilateral Commn. Fellow AIAA (hon.); mem. Aerospace Industries Assn. (bd. govs.), The Bus. Council Beta Theta Pi. Clubs: Rainier, Seattle Golf. Home: 126 SW 171st St Seattle WA 98166 Office: The Boeing Co PO Box 3707 Seattle WA 98124

WILSON, TOM PATRICK, fire chief; b. Miami, Okla., May 28, 1944; s. Tom Lyon and Virginia Lee (Patrick) W.; m. Virginia Carole Manning, Oct. 8, 1966; children—Virginia Elizabeth, Tom Lyon. A.A. with honors, Fullerton Coll., 1973; B.A., Calif. State U.-Fullerton, 1975. Ambulance supr. Crane Ambulance Service, Fullerton, Calif., 1965, 66; police officer City of San Jacinto (Calif.), 1967-70, City of La Palma (Calif.), 1971; firefighter Riverside County, Calif., 1967-71; fire. engr. Calif. Dept. Forestry, 1971, 75; fire chief City of Needles (Calif.), 1975, 78; fire capt., fire crew supr. Calif. Dept. Forestry, 1978, 80; fire chief City of Manhattan Beach (Calif.), 1980—; adj. instr. Nat. Fire Acad., Emmitsburg, Md. Served with USNR, 1970-72; USCGR. Mem. Calif. Fire Chiefs Assn. (labor relations com.). Clubs: Masons, Elks. Office: 400 15th St Manhattan Beach CA 90266

WILSON, WARREN BINGHAM, artist, art educator; b. Farmington, Utah, Nov. 4, 1920; s. Alma L. and Pearl E. (Bingham) W.; B.S. in Edn., Utah State U., 1943; M.F.A., Iowa State U., 1949; m. Donna Myrle VanWagenen, Dec. 22, 1948; children—Vaughn Warren, Michael Alma, Annette, Pauline, Douglas George, Craig Aaron, Robert Kevin. Asst. prof. art Utah State U., Logan, 1949-54; vis. instr. Salt Lake Art Center, Utah, 1952-53; prof. art and edn. Brigham Young U., Provo, Utah, 1954-83; ret., 1983 vis. lectr. ceramics U. Calif., Davis, 1968; fellow in residence Huntington Hartford Found., Pacific Palisades, Calif., 1960-61; vis. instr. Pioneer Crafthouse, Salt Lake City, 1969-70; one-man shows of paintings and/or sculpture include: Salt Lake Art Center, 1951, Yakima Valley Coll., 1962, UCLA, 1962, Mont. State U., Bozeman, 1963, Stanford U., 1963, Wash. State U., Pullman, 1964, Central Wash. State Coll., Ellensburg, 1964, Nev. So. U., Las Vegas, 1967, Ricks Coll., Rexburg, Idaho, 1976, 80, Brigham Young U., Provo, Utah, 1970, 75, 79, 82; group shows include: Denver Art Mus., 1951, Colorado Springs (Colo.) Fine Arts Center, 1951, Santa Fe Art Mus., 1953, Madison Sq. Gardens, N.Y.C., 1958, Wichita Art Center, 1960, Ceramic Conjunction Invitational, Glendale, Calif., 1973; represented in permanent collections: Utah State Inst. Fine Arts Salt Lake City, Utah State U., Logan, Utah State Fair Assn., Utah Dixie Coll., St. George, Coll. So. Utah, Cedar City, Brigham Young U., also numerous pvt. collections. Asst. dist. commr. Boy Scouts Am., 1975-80; counselor in Ward Bishopric, Ch. of Jesus Christ of Latter-day Saints, 1981—. Served with USAAF, 1943-46. Recipient Am. Craftsman Council merit award, 1964; Silver Beaver award Boy Scouts Am. Mem. Nat. Council for Edn. in Ceramic Arts. Republican. Home: 1000 Briar Ave Provo UT 84601

WILSON, WYVETTA CASTOR, community development specialist, urban planner; b. New Boston, Ohio, July 12, 1929; d. William Hugh and Merle (Monk) Castor; m. Robert J. Wilson, July 7, 1956. Student Merced Coll., 1971-72, Fresno State Coll., 1973-74, Muskingum Coll., 1977; B.A. in Psychology, Imperial Valley Coll., 1979; cert. in mgmt. Am. Mgmt. Sch., Fresno, Calif., 1973. Mgr. Anita Dress Shops, Merced, Calif., 1965-70; supr. Dept. Human Resources Merced County (Calif.), 1970-77; dir. Scioto County Programs on Aging, Portsmouth, Ohio, 1977-79; dir. Community Devel. Dept., City of Brawley (Calif.), 1979—.

Bd. dirs. Imperial Valley Indsl. Corp.; mem. governing body Health Systems Agy.; bd. dirs. Charlee Homes; past pres. Merced County Social Workers Orgn. Recipient award Ret. Sr. Vol. Program, 1978. Mem. Nat. Assn. Female Execs. (dir.). Republican. Episcopalian. Club: Soroptimist (Brawley). Wrote City of Brawley's Housing Plan Element and Community Devel. Manual.

WILTSE, CHLORYCE JERENE, home economics and computer science educator; b. Arnolds Park, Iowa, Nov. 25, 1933; d. Carl J. and Leila L. (Gibbs) Ode; m. Gary L. Wiltse, June 9, 1957; children—Mark, Lynn Wiltse Braswell. B.S., U. Nebr., 1955; postgrad. Iowa State, 1982, Mont. State U., 1968-81, U. Mont., 1967-72, Eastern Mont. Coll., 1965. Cert. secondary tchr., Mont. Tchr. home econs. Osceola (Nebr.) High Sch., 1955-57; rural tchr. Billup Sch., Powder River County, Mont., 1957-58; tchr. home econs., computer sci. Powder River High Sch., Broadus, Mont., 1964-83; lectr. computers in home econs. edn. Named Mont. Home Econs. Tchr. of Yr., Mont. Home Econs. Assn. and Family Circle mag., 1975. Mem. Am. Home Econs. Assn., Mont. Home Econs. Assn., NEA, Mont. Edn. Assn., Broadus Edn. Assn., Mortar Bd., Delta Kappa Gamma, Phi Upsilon Omicron, Omicron Nu, Gamma Alpha Chi, Alpha Lambda Delta, Phi Sigma Chi, Kappa Delta, Women in Farm Econs. Republican. Lutheran. Clubs: Apple Addicts Computer (Broadus), Order of Eastern Star. Author publs. in field. Home: Volborg MT 59351

WILTSHIRE, RAYMOND STANLEY, electrical engineer; b. West Portsmouth, Ohio, Dec. 17, 1929; s. Arley Hayes and Elizabeth Jane (Redden) W.; m. Mary Louise Mahan, Oct. 10, 1954; children—Blaine J., Brenda Jane. B.E.E., Ohio State U., 1952; M.B.A., Denver U., 1976. Registered profl. engr., Ohio, Colo. Sr. field engr. Nat. Cash Register Co., 1952-55; nuclear project engr. White Sands Missile Range, 1955-57; systems test engr. RCA, 1957-58; with Martin Marietta Corp., Denver, 1958—, mgr. Viking systems integration, 1969-71, dir. research and tech. programs, 1973-78, corp. dir. engring., 1978-81, dir. tech. ops., 1981—. Bd. dirs. Castlewood Fire Dept., 1968-70; troop chmn. Boy Scouts Am., 1968-73; mem. Greenwood Greenbelt Commn., 1973-75, Gov. Colo. Com. to obtain Solar Energy Research Inst., 1975—; mem. tech. com. Denver Urban Obs., 1976—; mem. adv. panel Denver Research Inst.; mem. adv. bd. exec. M.B.A. program U. Denver. Served with AUS, 1955-57. Fellow AIAA; mem. Am. Astron. Soc. (charter chmn. Rocky Mountain Sect.), Am. Radio Relay League. Author publs. in field. Home: 6387 S Saulsbury St Littleton CO 80123 Office: Martin Marietta Aerospace PO Box 179 Denver CO 80201

WIMBERLEY, JACK ERSKINE, systems engr.; b. Hattiesburg, Miss., Apr. 25, 1933; s. James Riley and Margaret Theodora (Skousgard) W.; B.S., M.I.T., 1954, M.S., 1955; m. Betty Jean Long, Oct. 8, 1960; children—Mark, John, Diane. Group engr. A-4 flight controls analysis Douglas Aircraft Co., El Segundo, Calif., 1955-59; systems specialist, program devel. mgr. System Devel. Corp., Santa Monica, Calif., 1959-76, sr. project engr. Emergency Command Control Communications System Program Office, 1976—. Vice pres. Sunset Mesa Property Owners Assn., Malibu, Calif., 1975-76, pres., 1976-78. Mem. AIAA, Assn. Unmanned Vehicle Systems, Sigma Xi. Republican. Club: Malibu Republican (pres. 1980). Home: 3607 Shoreheights Dr Malibu CA 90265 Office: 2500 Colorado Ave Santa Monica CA 90406

WIMMER, GLEN E., engineer, management consultant; b. Creston, Iowa, Feb. 16, 1903; s. Frank Elbert and Carrie Elizabeth (Autenreith) W.; m. Mildred G. McCullough, May 18, 1936; 1 son, Frank Thomas. B.S. in M.E., Iowa State U., 1925, M.S. in Mech. Engring., 1933; M.B.A., Northwestern U., 1935. Cert. profl. engr. Nat. Bur. Engring. Registration. Instr. mech. engring. Mich. Coll. Mining and Tech., Houghton, 1936-37; machine designer Firestone Tire & Rubber Co., Akron, Ohio, 1937-38; engr. charge of design Ditto, Inc., Chgo., 1938-39; asst. to chief engr. Victograph Corp., Chgo., 1939-40; designer, checker, supr. Detroit Engring. Co., 1940-43; head devel. dept. Cummins Perforator Co., Chgo., 1943-45; staff engr. charge design and devel. Tammen & Denison, Inc., Chgo., 1945-58; staff engr. Barnes & Reinecke, Inc., Chgo., 1961-68; mgmt. cons., Oceanside, Calif., 1968—; instr. cost analysis Ill. Inst. Tech. Evening Div., 1946-47. Fellow Am. Biog. Inst., Intercontinental Biog. Assn. (life); mem. Soc. Automotive Engrs., Soc. Mfg. Engrs., Nat., Ill. socs. profl. engrs., Am. Def. Preparedness Assn., Internat. Platform Assn., Iowa State U. Alumni Assn., Northwestern U. Alumni Assn., Delta Chi. Republican. Methodist. Patentee in field. Home: 3839 48 Vista Campana S Oceanside CA 92056

WIMMER, JOHN CHARLES, home bldg. co. exec.; b. Albany, Calif., May 25, 1944; s. Herbert Fredrick and Cornelia Marie (Rothove) W.; B.S. in B.A. with gt. distinction, San Jose (Calif.) State U., 1974; M.B.A. (Earnest A. Arbuckle fellow 1977, Grad. award Calif. Assn. Real Estate 1976), Stanford U., 1977. Chief pilot Diablo Aviation, Concord, Calif., 1970-71; real estate salesman Security Pacific Real Estate Co., Walnut Creek, Calif., 1971-73; adminstrv. asst. to pres. Anthony Sch. of Santa Clara Valley, Inc., 1973-75, v.p., dir., 1977-81; pres. Lifestyle Homes Inc., Santa Clara, Calif., 1977-81; v.p. constrn. The Meads Group, 1981-82, Heflin Corp., Palo Alto, Calif., 1982—. Served with USAF, 1968-70. Mem. Nat. Assn. Realtors, Nat. Assn. Home Builders, Calif. Assn. Realtors, San Jose Real Estate Bd., Bldg. Industry Assn. No. Calif. (dir. So. div. 1981). Republican. Home: PO Box 77 Palo Alto CA 94302 Office: 525 University Ave Suite 21 Palo Alto CA 94301

WIMMER, LARRY TURLEY, economics educator; b. Snowflake, Ariz., Dec. 8, 1935; s. James Ivan and Corinne (Turley) W.; m. Louise Johnson, Nov. 26, 1958; children—Brian, Greg, Kendall, Eric, Brett. B.S., Brigham Young U., 1960; M.A., U. Chgo., 1962, Ph.D., 1968. Faculty, Brigham Young U., Provo, Utah, 1963—, chmn., prof. econs., 1979—. Fulbright fellow, Taiwan, 1972-73; named Maeser Disting. Tchr., Brigham Young U., 1979; recipient Freedom Found. award, 1979. Mem. Am. Econs. Assn., Econ. History Assn., Social Sci. History Assn., Mormon History Assn., Mont Pelerin Soc. Mormon. Contbr. articles to profl. jours. Office: 700 Kimball Tower Dept Econs Brigham Young U Provo UT 84602

WINANS, GARY ALBERT, zoologist, genetics researcher, educator; b. Battle Creek, Mich., Mar. 12, 1951; s. Russell E. and Marilyn Virginia (Mauder) W.; m. Katherine Ann Kellogg, Dec. 18, 1976; 1 son, Jeremy Starr. B.S. with honors, Mich. State U., 1973; M.S. in Oceanography, Fla. Inst. Tech., 1975; Ph.D. in Zoology, U. Hawaii, 1980. Teaching asst. in oceanography Fla. Inst. Tech., 1973-75; part-time tchr. Calhoun County (Mich.) Pub. Schs., from 1980; NRC research assoc. NOAA, Seattle, 1981-82; with N.W. and Alaskan Fisheries Ctr., Seattle. Sigma Xi grantee, 1978-79; Jessie Smith Noyes fellow U. Hawaii. Mem. Soc. Study Evolution, Soc. Systematic Zoology, Sigma Xi. Contbr. articles to profl. jours. Office: NW and Alaskan Fisheries Ctr 2725 Montlake Blvd E Seattle WA 98112

WINANT, ETHEL WALD, broadcasting exec.; b. Worcester, Mass., Aug. 5; d. William and Janice (Woolson) Wald; A.A., Yuba Coll.; B.A., U. Calif., Berkeley; M.T.A., Whittier Coll.; children—William, Scott, Bruce. Dir. casting Talent Assocs., N.Y.C., 1953-56; assoc. producer Playhouse '90, CBS, Hollywood, Calif., 1956-60, All Fall Down, MGM, Calif., 1960-61; producer Gt. Adventure, DBS, Hollywood, 1961-62; v.p. talent, dir. program devel. CBS, Hollywood, 1962-75; exec. producer Best of Families, PBS, N.Y.C., 1975-77; v.p. talent NBC, Burbank, Calif., 1978—, v.p. mini-series and novels for TV, 1979; sr. v.p. creative affairs Metromedia Producers Corp., Hollywood, 1981—; assoc. artistic dir. theatre group UCLA; bd. govs. Nat. Acad. TV Arts and Scis.; bd. dirs. Circle Reperatory Theatre; mem. Pres.'s Commn. for Women; mem. Calif. Arts Council; adv. bd. Ctr. for Advanced Film Studies; cons. in field. Recipient Emmy award Nat. Acad. TV Arts and Scis., 1960; named TV Woman of Yr., Conf. Personal Mgrs., 1974. Mem. Acad. TV Arts and Scis., John Tracy Clinic, Women in Film (Crystal award 1979), Hollywood Radio and TV Soc. Office: 5746 Sunset Blvd Hollywood CA 90028

WINARSKI, DANIEL JAMES, mechanical engineer; b. Toledo, Dec. 16, 1948; s. Daniel Edward and Marguerite (Pietersien) W.; B.S. in Engring., U. Mich., 1970, Ph.D. (NSF fellow), 1976; M.S., U. Colo., 1973; m. Donna Ilene Robinson, Oct. 10, 1970; 1 son, Tyson York. Mech. engr. Libbey Owens Ford Co., Toledo, summers 1968, 69, 72; petroleum engr. Exxon Production Research, Houston, 1976-77; staff engr. mech. engring. sect. IBM, Tucson, 1977—; assoc. prof. dept. mechanics U.S. Mil. Acad., 1980—; instr. minority computer edn. No. Ariz. U., 1983—. Served to 1st lt. U.S. Army, 1970-72; capt. Res., 1977. Registered profl. engr., Ariz., Colo. Mem. ASME (pub. chmn. U. Mich. 1974), Am. Inst. Aeros., Assn. Lunar and Planetary Observers, Mus. No. Ariz., Phi Eta Sigma, Pi Tau Sigma, Tau Beta Pi. Republican. Methodist. Club: So. Ariz. Rd. Runners. Designer adjustable artificial leg; patentee tape reel hub, tape loose-wrap check, tape reel sizing, tape reel-cartridge. Home: 647 S Woodstock Tucson AZ 85710 Office: 64L/071-2 IBM Tucson AZ 85744

WINBERG, CARL DAVIS, pathologist; b. Detroit, Apr. 15, 1948; s. Carl A. and Marian Winberg; B.A., U. Mich., 1970; M.D., Wayne State U., 1974. Intern, Stanford U. Med. Ctr., Palo Alto, Calif., 1974-75, resident, 1975-77; practice medicine, specializing in pathology, 1980—; pathologist, assoc. chair div. anatomic pathology City of Hope Nat. Med. Ctr., Duarte, Calif., 1980—. Mem. Internat. Acad. Pathology. Office: City of Hope Med Center Duarte CA 91010

WINCHELL, ROBERT ALLEN, govt. ofcl., acct.; b. Ft. Monmouth, N.J., Oct. 28, 1945; s. Robert Winslow Winchell; B.A., U. Calif., Santa Barbara, 1967; M.B.A., U. Pa., 1969. Auditor, Air Force Audit Agy., El Segundo, Calif., 1972-73; accountant Scholefield, Bellanca & Co., W. Los Angeles, 1974-75, So. Calif. Gas Co., Los Angeles, 1975-76; auditor Def. Contract Audit Agy., Dept. Def., Los Angeles, 1976—. Served with AUS, 1969-71; Vietnam. Decorated Bronze Star. Mem. Assn. Govt. Accountants, Am. Inst. C.P.A.'s, Alpha Kappa Psi. Republican. Presbyterian. Club: Los Angeles Country. Home: 2008 California Ave Santa Monica CA 90403 Office: DCAA Resident Office Hughes Aircraft Co 909 N Sepulveda Blvd El Segundo CA 90245

WINCKEL, AUGUST, physician; b. Veendam, Netherlands, May 17, 1916; came to U.S., 1953, naturalized, 1959; s. August and Josephine Aleida (Van Heest) W.; M.D., U. Amsterdam, 1946; m. Joanne Kozlowski, July 29, 1975; children—August Henry, Paul, Joy, Michele. Resident in internal medicine and rheumatology U. Utrecht (Netherlands), 1949-53; rotating intern Seaside Meml. Hosp., Long Beach, Calif., 1954, Santa Monica (Calif.) Hosp., 1954-55; resident in emergency medicine Daniel Freeman Hosp., Inglewood, Calif., 1955-56; pvt. practice medicine, specializing in family practice, Santa Monica, 1956—; mem. staff Santa Monica Hosp., 1956-66, sr. staff, 1966—, mem. tumor bd., 1976—. Diplomate Am. Bd. Family Practice. Fellow Am. Acad. Family Physicians; mem. Loa Angeles County Med. Assn., AMA, Calif. Med. Assn. Republican. Presbyterian. Office: 2216 Santa Monica Blvd Santa Monica CA 90404

WINDER, DAVID KENT, U.S. dist. judge; b. Salt Lake City, June 8, 1932; s. Edwin Kent and Alma Eliza (Cannon) W.; B.A., U. Utah, 1955; LL.B., Stanford U., 1958; m. Pamela Martin, June 24, 1955; children—Ann, Kay, James. Admitted to Utah bar, 1958, Calif. bar, 1958; asso. firm Clyde, Mecham & Pratt, Salt Lake City, 1958-66; law clk. to chief justice Utah Supreme Ct., 1958-59; dep. county atty. Salt Lake County, 1959-63, chief dep. dist. atty., 1965-66; asst. U.S. atty., Salt Lake City, 1963-65; partner firm Strong & Hanni, Salt Lake City, 1966-77; judge Utah Dist. Ct., 1977-79, U.S. Dist. Ct., Dist. Utah, Salt Lake City, 1979—; examiner Utah Bar Examiners, 1975-79, chmn., 1977-79. Served with USAF, 1951-52. Mem. Am. Bd. Trial Advocates, Utah State Bar (Judge of Yr. award 1978), Salt Lake County Bar Assn., Calif. State Bar. Democrat. Office: US Courthouse Salt Lake City UT 84101

WINDER, WILLIAM BURCH, investment company executive; b. Hayden, Colo., Sept. 13, 1928; s. George Norman and Mary (Burch) W.; m. Jeanne Wells, June 26, 1954; children—Cameron Brooks, Paige Normandy. S.B., MIT, 1950. Engr., Am. Tel.&Tel. Co., Denver, 1953-56; mgr. power sources div. Whittaker Corp., Denver, 1956-66; pres. Mate Sales Co., Denver, 1966-74; regional mgr. The PACE Orgn., Denver, 1968-74; pres. Blue Mountain Corp., Denver, 1972-80; pres. Two Bar Ranch Co., Denver, 1977-79, dir., 1950-79; mgmt. cons., 1974-83; pres. The Winder Corp., Denver, 1983—. Chmn. men's task force Denver Art Mus., 1969-71. Served to 1st lt. U.S. Army, 1951-53. Mem. Am. Soc. Profl. Cons., Sales and Mktg. Execs., Phi Gamma Delta. Republican. Clubs: Athletic, City, Toastmasters (Denver). Editor: Mineral Resources in Wilderness, 1982. Home: 2672 S Jackson St Denver CO 80210

WINEGARNER, DOROTHY FRANCES, bus. services co. exec.; b. Marion, Ill., Mar. 29, 1940; d. Windell Kenneth and Helen Clara (Kirshman) W.; student U. Tenn., 1959-64. With Dun & Bradstreet, Inc., various locations, 1959—, mgr. ops. div., Van Nuys, Calif., 1980—. Mem. Nat. Assn. Female Execs. Republican. Methodist. Home: 8030 Langdon St #3 Van Nuys CA 91406 Office: 16600 Sherman Way Van Nuys CA 91406

WINETROBE, MAURY, film editor; b. Chelsea, Mass., July 6, 1922. Dir. music editing Columbia Pictures, Hollywood, Calif., 1961-67; free-lance film editor for major motion picture studios, 1968—, films include Funny Girl (Acad. Award nominee), Cactus Flower, Mame, Twilights Last Gleaming, Getting Straight, Ice-Castles, From Noon Til Three, Last of the Red-Hot Lovers, The Frisco Kid, The Black Marble, The Jazz Singer, Taps. Served with USN, 1942-45. Mem. Acad. Motion Picture Arts and Scis., Acad. TV Arts and Scis., Am. Cinema Editors, Calif. Thoroughbred Breeders Assn., Horsemen's Benevolent and Protective Assn. Clubs: U. So. Calif. Trojan, Masons (32 deg., Scottish Rite).

WINFIELD, ARMAND GORDON, internat. plastics cons.; b. Chgo., Dec. 28, 1919; s. Benjamin L. and Helen (Oscar) W.; B.S., Franklin and Marshall Coll., 1941; postgrad. U. N.Mex., 1941, State U. Iowa, 1944, Washington U., St. Louis, 1948-50; m. Lillian Tsukea Kubota, June 8, 1951 (dec. Dec. 1965); m. 2d, Barbara Jane La Barge, July 23, 1966. Owner, Winfield Fine Art in Jewelry, N.Y.C., 1946-48; research dir. Hanley Plastics Co. div. Wallace Pencil Co., St. Louis, 1955-57; plastic cons. engr. DeBell & Richardson, Inc., Hazardville, Conn., 1957-64; pres. Armand G. Winfield Inc., Santa Fe, 1964—; also lectr., writer; mem. faculty Harris Tchrs. Coll., 1950, Washington U., 1956; guest lectr. Yale U., 1960-61; adviser USIA on plastics show to tour USSR, 1960-61; exec. v.p. Crystopal, Ltd., Hazardville, Conn., 1963; vis. critic in plastics Sch. Architecture, CCNY, 1968-69; plastics cons. indsl. design dept., faculty Pratt Inst., Bklyn., 1964-70, instr. prodn. methods, 1968-70; lectr. U. Hartford, U. Kans., 1970, U. Ariz., 1978; adj. prof. plastics engring. U. Lowell (Mass.), 1978-81, Calif. Poly. State U., 1980. Bd. dirs. Santa Fe Crime Stoppers, also chmn. carnival, 1983, 84. U.S. State Dept. grantee to USSR, 1961; UN grantee for study plastics in low cost housing for developing countries, 1968-69; UN grantee, Vienna, Austria, 1971; UNIDO expert in newer fibers and composites, India, 1977, cons. glass fibers and composites, Colombia, 1979. Fellow Plastics and Rubber Inst. (Eng.); mem. Soc. Plastics Engrs. (pres. Western New Eng. sect. 1963-64, v.p. N.Y. sect. 1968-69, chmn. regional tech. conf. 1967, historian ann. tech. conf. 1968), Soc. Plastic Industry, Plastics Inst. Australia, Internat. Assn. Housing Sci. (charter), Santa Fe C. of C., Santa Fe Press Club. Author: The Alexian Brothers, 1951; The Merchants Exchange of St. Louis, 1953; Plastics For Architects, Artists and Interior Designers, 1961; 100 Years Young, 1968; also chpts. in books, monthly column in Display World Mag., 1965-68, Designer Mag., 1971-72, Museum Scope, 1976-77; numerous articles on plastics. Patentee in field. Office: 2879 All Trades Rd PO Box 1296 Santa Fe NM 87501

WINFIELD, THEODORE PAUL, JR., biol. cons.; b. Oakland, Calif., Jan. 3, 1944; s. Theodore Paul and Elizabeth Mae (Hopper) W.; B.S., Brigham Young U., Provo, Utah, 1967, M.S., 1971; Ph.D., U. Calif.-Riverside, 1980; m. Rosemary Keppen, Sept. 12, 1965; children—Timothy John, Jeffrey Thomas, Lawrence Wayne, Lisa Eileen. Biol. cons. specializing in marine ecology Woodward-Clyde Cons., San Diego, 1972—. Coach for youth soccer, 1977—. Named to All-Am. track team, 1965; NSF grantee summer 1967. Mem. Am. Soc. Limnology and Oceanography, Audubon Soc., Ecol. Soc. Am., Estuarine and Brackish-Water Scis. Assn., Estuarine Research Fedn., Internat. Assn. Aquatic Vascular Plant Biologists, Soc. Wetlands Scientists, Western Soc. Naturalists, Sigma Xi. Club: El Cajon Hotspurs Soccer (officer). Author papers in field. Home: 576 Ann St El Cajon CA 92021 Office: 3489 Kurtz St San Diego CA 92110

WING, HAROLD RAY, businessman; b. Springville, Utah, Mar. 5, 1940; s. Arthur and Mary Marguerite (Falkner) W.; student Springville public schs.; m. Brigitte Mayer, Dec. 23, 1960; children—Dennis, Harold, Michael, Michelle, Douglas, Christina, Heidi. Asst. mgr. Carson's Market, Provo, Utah, 1961-63; mem. quality control staff Munz Castings, Heilbronn, W. Ger., 1963-65; mem. prodn. control staff Hercules, Inc., 1965-70; agt. Beneficial Life Ins. Co., 1970-74; owner, pres., dir. Little Giant Industries, Provo, Utah, 1974—; owner, pres. Wing Enterprises, Springville, Utah; chmn. bd. CRW Specialties; vol. cons. small bus. Dist. pres., high councilman Ch. of Jesus Christ of Latter-day Saints. Served with U.S. Army, 1958-61. Mem. Am. Ladder Inst. Patentee in field. Home: 1185 E 225 N Springville UT 84663 Office: 2241 S Larsen Pkwy Provo UT 84601

WING, RICHARD CHOW, restaurateur; b. Hanford, Calif., June 20, 1921; s. Chow Gong and Shee Chan W.; B.A., U. So. Calif., 1953; m. Mary Lo, Jan. 25, 1965. Import-export rep. Fook Wah Co., Hong Kong, 1956-57; owner, operator, chef Imperial Dynasty 2, Hanford, 1957—; cons. in field. Recipient Man of Yr. award Chinese-Am. Citizen Alliance, 1960, Calif. Wine Patrons award, 1978. Mem. Chefs de Cuisine Assn. Calif., Am. Culinary Fedn., Am. Acad. Chefs, Les Amis d'Escoffier, Internat. Wine and Food Soc. (Cordon Bleu award 1960, 64), Chinese Hist. Soc., Confrerie Des Chevaliers du Tastevin, Soc. Bacchus, Calif. Wine Patrons. Democrat. Home: 854 Laurence Ln Hanford CA 93230 Office: Imperial Dynasty 2 China Alley Hanford CA 93230

WING, SARAH W., psychologist; b. Buffalo, N.Y., Feb. 11, 1932; d. Charles H. and Constance (Cook) W. B.A. in Psychology, Conn. Coll., 1953; M.A. in Human Relations, Ohio U., 1956; Ph.D. in Psychology, U. Oreg., 1966; M.P.A., Pacific Luth. U., 1979. Lic. psychologist Wash.; diplomate in sch. psychology Am. Bd. Profl. Psychology. Psychologist Wash. Corrections Ctr., 1970-72, mental health unit Wash. State Reformatory, 1972-77; staff psychologist legal offender program Western State Hosp., Ft. Steilacoom, Wash., 1977—; mem. human research rev. bd. Wash. State Dept. Social and Health Services. Sec. bd. trustees Pacific Luth. Theol. Sem.; sec. ct. adjudication Luth. Ch. Am. Fellow Am. Orthopsychiat. Assn.; mem. Am. Psychol. Assn., Am. Assn. Correctional Psychologists, Am. Counseling and Devel. Assn. Club: Evergreen Toastmistress (Council 13, Pacific N.W. region community service award, 1980). Home: 12956 SE 23d St Bellevue WA 98005 Office: Legal Offender Unit Western State Hospital Ft Steilacoom WA 98494

WING, THOMAS, micrometrologist, engineer; b. Shanghai, China, Mar. 12, 1929; came to U.S., 1930, naturalized, 1950; s. Lim and Fong Shee W.; B.S. in Engring. cum laude, Purdue U., 1953, postgrad., 1957-60; postgrad. CCNY, 1953-55; m Catherine Amajelia Scambia, Nov. 27, 1954; children—Karen Elyse, Thomas Scambia, Robert Frank Joseph, David Anthony. Sr. project mgr. Gulton Industries, Metuchen, N.J., 1960-63; adv. engr. IBM, Lexington, Ky., 1963-65; with guidance and control systems div. Litton Industries, Woodland Hills, Calif., 1966-69, mem. tech. staff, 1976—; staff cons. Devel. Consultants, Cin., 1965-66; image tech. mgr. Fairchild Semiconductor, Mountain View, Calif., 1969-71; gen. mgr. research and devel., v.p., Jade Corp., HLC Mfg. Co., Willow Grove, Pa., 1971-75; pres. Photronic Engring. Labs., Inc., Danbury, Conn., 1975-76; lectr. in micro-photo lithography, Inst. Graphic Communication, Boston; cons. engr. in micro image tech. and metrology; founding mem. Thermo Phys. Properties Research Center, Purdue U.; staff cons. Zantec Inc., North Hollywood, Calif., 1981—, Kasper Instruments, Sunnyvale, Calif., 1977-79, Quintel Corp., San Jose, Calif., 1979—. Coach, v.p. Roadrunners Hockey Club, 1972-75, founder, 1972, Bristol, Pa.; founder, pres. Eastridge Jr. Hockey Club, San Jose, Calif., 1970-71; coach Belmont (Calif.) Jr. Hockey Club, 1969; v.p. Greater Los Angeles Minor Hockey Assn., 1968-69; v.p., coach West Valley Minor Hockey Club, Tarzana, Calif., 1968-69; coach Topanga Plaza Jr. Hockey Club, 1967. Mem. ASME, ASTM (mem. F-1 com. on microelectronics 1972-75), Soc. Photog. Instrumentation Engrs., Soc. Photog. Scientists and Engrs., Tau Beta Pi, Pi Tau Sigma, Phi Eta Sigma. Organizer first internat. lecture series on micro photo lithography, Boston, 1974; contbr. articles to profl. publs.; patentee currency counter, trimming inductor, damped high frequency accelerometer, three phase dithered pivot, auto focus for step and repeat camera, temperature compensated dither drive for laser gyro, proximity printing mechanism. Home: 6261 Jumilla Ave Woodland Hills CA 91367 Office: 5500 Canoga Ave Woodland Hills CA 91367

WINGATE, MARCEL EDWARD, speech educator, researcher; b. New Castle, Pa., Feb. 27, 1923; s. Morton Harvey and Elizabeth (Martin) W.; m. Cicely Ann Johnston, June 7, 1969; children—Nancy, Amy, Jennifer, Marcel, Cicely; B.A., Grinnell (Iowa) Coll., 1948; M.A., U. Wash., 1952, Ph.D., 1956. Psychologist, Children's Hosp. and State Cerebral Palsy Ctr., Seattle, 1953-57; asst. prof. U. Wash., Seattle, 1957-65, assoc. prof., 1965-68; prof. SUNY-Buffalo, 1968-73; prof. U. Ariz., Tucson, 1973-75; prof. speech and hearing sci. Wash. State U., Pullman, 1975—. Served with U.S. Army, 1943-45. Fellow Am. Speech, Lang. and Hearing Assn. (cert.); mem. Am. Psychol. Assn., Am. Speech, Lang., and Hearing Assn., Wash. State Grange. Club: Spokane Country, City. Author: Stuttering: Theory and Treatment, 1976; contbr. articles to profl. jours. Home: Route 2 Box 102 Pullman WA 99163 Office: 314 Daggy Hall Washington State U Pullman WA 99164

WINGET, CHARLOTTE LOUISE, association executive; b. Northwood, N.D., Mar. 19, 1939; d. Franklin Woodrow and Margaret Christina (Egland) Hagert; m. William Peter Winget, Sept. 17, 1960; children—William Brian, Marcelle Denise, David Matthew. B.A., U. Minn., 1962; B.A., Baldwin-Wallace Coll., Berea, Ohio, 1977; M.A., Mills Coll., 1973. Dir. movement therapy Ellen K. Raskob Learning

Inst., Oakland, Calif., 1974; dir. student tax clinic Baldwin-Wallace Coll., Berea, 1977; jr. acct. Aloha Hawaii Travel, Ltd., Honolulu, 1978; membership/exhibits coordinator Pan-Pacific Surg. Assn., Honolulu, 1978-79; controller, 1979-80, controller-office mgr. 1980-82, exec. dir., 1982—. Mem. Hawaii Visitors Bur., 1980—. Mem. Nat. Assn. Accts., Nat. Assn. Female Execs., C. of C., Delta Zeta. Republican.

WINKENBACH, MICHELE MARIE, aircraft company executive, systems analyst; b. Alameda, Calif., Jan. 18, 1956; d. Raymond Patrick and Marian Frances (Werle) Winkenbach. Student U. Calif., 1974-76; B.S. in Bus. Adminstrn., Calif. State U.-Hayward, 1979. Analyst systems and procedure Hughes Aircraft Co., El Segundo, Calif., 1979—. Active Angeles council Girl Scouts U.S.A.; pres. New Sounds Hawthorne (Calif.). Mem. AAUW, Am. Prodn. and Inventory Control Soc., Sierra Club. Office: Hughes Aircraft Co EDS G Bldg E4/Mail Station M113 El Segundo CA 90245

WINKENWERDER, RICHARD ALAN, actuary; b. Yakima, Wash., Sept. 10, 1930; s. Clarence F. and Helmi (Sandberg) W.; m. Bonnie G. Olsen, June 23, 1974; children—Duff, Jill, Lynn, John, David, Heidi. B.A. in Math., Wash. State U., 1952; postgrad. U. Wash., 1952-53; B.S. in Meteorology, Pa. State U., 1955. Enrolled actuary. Actuary No. Life Ins. Co., Seattle, 1958-60; prin., cons. actuary Milliman & Robertson, Inc., Seattle, 1960—. Served to 1st lt. USAF, 1953-58. Fellow Soc. Actuaries, Conf. Actuaries Pub. Practice; mem. Am. Acad. Actuaries, Actuarial Club Pacific States, Seattle Actuarial Club, Internat. Found. Employee Benefit Plans, Internat. Assn. Cons. Actuaries, Assn. Pvt. Pension and Welfare Plans, Seattle C. of C. Republican. Clubs: Wash. Athletic, Harbor, Rainier (Seattle); Sahalee Country (Redmond). Office: 1301 5th Ave Suite 3600 Seattle WA 98101

WINKLER, AGNIESZKA M., advertising executive; b. Rome, Feb. 22, 1946; d. Wojciech A. and Halina Z. (Owsiany) W.; children—Renata G., Dana C. B.A., Coll. Holy Names, 1967; M.A., San Jose State U., 1971; M.B.A., U. Santa Clara, 1981. In-house sales rep. Sci. Products, Menlo Park, Calif., 1971; account exec. Graphic Assocs., Palo Alto, Calif., 1972; pres., chief exec. officer Commart Advt., Inc., Santa Clara, 1973—; teaching asst. San Jose State U.; guest lectr. Santa Clara U. grad. bus. program; chmn. bus. edn. program Stanford Bus. Wives, 1971; cons. Eastern European bus. Trustee Mid Peninsula Family Service Assn. Coll. Holy Names Pres.' scholar, 1964-66; Bill Raskob Found. grantee for study in USSR, 1965; recipient Lester-Tinneman award in history, 1966. Mem. Women in Advt., Women's Network, Bus./Profl. Assn., Direct Mail Assn., San Jose Ad Club, Polish Am. Congress, Pi Gamma Mu, Pi Delta Phi. Author: Underground Parliament: Creation of the Council of National Unity in Poland, 1939-44, 71. Office: 4701 Patrick Henry Dr Bldg 7 and 8 Santa Clara CA 95050

WINKLER, IRWIN, motion picture producer; b. N.Y.C., May 28, 1931; s. Sol and Anna W.; B.A., N.Y. U., 1955. Mailroom messenger William Morris Agy., N.Y.C., 1955-62; co-founder Chartoff-Winkler Prodns., Culver City, Calif., 1964; producer Rocky (10 Acad. award nominations, winner 3 including best picture, winner Los Angeles Film Critics best picture award), 1976, They Shoot Horses Don't They (9 Acad. award nominations), 1969, Nickelodeon, 1976, The Gambler, 1974, Up the Sandbox, 1972, The New Centurions, 1972, Point Blank, 1967, Double Trouble, 1967, Leo the Last (Best Dir. award Cannes Film Festival 1970, Belgrade Film Festival 1970), The Strawberry Statement (Jury prize Cannes Film Festival 1970), The Split, 1968, Breakout, 1975, Believe in Me, 1971, The Gang That Couldn't Shoot Straight, 1971, The Mechanic, 1972, Busting, 1974, SPYS, 1974, Peeper, 1975, New York, New York, 1977, Valentino, 1977, Uncle Joe Shannon, 1978, Comes A Horseman, 1978, Rocky II, 1979, Raging Bull (8 Acad. Award nominations, 2 Acad. awards, winner Los Angeles Film Critics award), 1980; Rocky III, 1981; Author, Author, The Right Stuff, 1982. Served with U.S. Army, 1951-53. Office: 10125 W Washington Blvd Culver City CA 90230

WINKLER, JOE, state senator, rancher, businessman; b. Denver, Apr. 23, 1928; s. Josef and Rose Winkler; m. Lois Simon. B.S., Colo. State U. Rancher and businessman Winkler Ltd.; mem. Colo. Ho. of Reps., 1976-82; mem. Colo. State Senate, 1982—, vice-chmn. appropriations con., mem. joint budget com. Republican county sec., chmn. 40th Dist. Served with U.S. Army. Roman Catholic. Office: State Capitol Denver CO 80203*

WINKLEY, LILLIAN VERONICA, social worker; b. St. Louis, May 5, 1926; d. Harry Francis and Lillian Veronica (Coleman) Winkley; A.A., Orange Coast Coll., 1973; B.A. cum laude, Calif. State U., Long Beach, 1976; M.S.W., U. So. Calif., 1979; m. Carl D. Jesch, Feb. 20, 1946 (div. Jan., 1978); children—H. Nicholas, Katherine Anne, Mary Margaret, Kevin G., Timothy G., Michael C., Philip and David (twins), Nora M. Case aide Cath. Social Services, Santa Ana, Calif., 1976-78; social worker Ray of Hope, Tustin, Calif., 1978-79; community worker Regional Center of Orange County, Orange, Calif., 1979-80, counselor, 1980, program evaluation specialist, 1980—; cons. co-parenting groups, div. Catholics, battered wives. Treas., NOW Orange County, 1976-78. Mem. Nat. Assn. Social Workers, Orange County Geneal. Soc., Social Work Aux. of Calif. State U.-Long Beach Alumni Assn. (life), U. So. Calif. Alumni Assn. (life). Roman Catholic. Clubs: Soc. for Creative Anachronism, Gyldenholt Barony. Office: Regional Center of Orange County Union Bank Sq Central Tower 500 S Main St Orange CA 92668

WINN, CHARLOTTE ANN, home economist, educator; b. Boise, Idaho, Sept. 27, 1955; d. Samuel Rockway and Laverne (Powell) Winn. B.S. in Home Econs., Whitworth Coll., 1977; M.Ed., U. Idaho, 1981. Tchr. home econs. Pub. Schs. Mountain Home (Idaho), 1977-79; cast mem. Up with People, 1979-80; ter. mgr. Homemakers Sch., Madison, Wis., 1980—. Mem. Am. Home Econs. Assn., Home Economists in Bus., Phi Delta Kappa. Presbyterian.

WINN, CYNTHIA, b. Hayden Colo., Mar. 4, 1950; d. Gordon C. and Caroline (Winder) Winn. B.S. in Vocat. Home Econs. Edn., Oreg. State U., 1972; M.A. in Home Econs. Edn., U. No. Colo., 1976. Cert. tchr., Colo. Tchr. home econs. and bus., McKenzie High Sch., Blue River, Oreg., 1972-73; tchr. home econs. Helen McCune Jr. High Sch., Pendleton, Oreg., 1973-76, Isaac Newton Jr. High Sch., Littleton, Colo., 1976-78; chmn. home econs. dept., tchr. Powell Jr. High Sch., Littleton, 1981—, chain dist. writing team, mem. dist. steering com., 1983—. Steering com. mem. Bethany Lutheran Ch. Singles, 1979—. Mem. NEA, Littleton Edn. Assn., Am. Home Econs. Assn., Colo. Home Econs. Assn., AAUW. Republican. Club: Colo. Mountain (Denver). Office: Home Econs Dept Powell Jr High Sch Littleton CO 80122

WINN, FLORA BELLE, reading educator; b. Burnet, Tex., Feb. 25, 1940; d. Russell and Grace Marian (Ferguson) Schraeder; m. Luther Allen Winn, June 14, 1958; children—Cindy Ann, Gregory Hunter. A.A. (hon.), Yavapai Coll., 1978; B.S. summa cum laude, No. Ariz. U., 1981. Cert. secondary sch. tchr., Ariz. Para profl. Page (Ariz.) High Sch., 1967-78, reading tchr., 1979—; reading cons. Mem. NEA, Ariz. Edn. Assn., Page Edn. Assn., Ariz. Council Reading, Assn. Supervision and Curriculum Devel. Democrat. Mem. Ch. of Christ. Clubs: Para Recreational, Tennis Racquet, Seasonal (Page). Home: 324 Elm St PO Box 374 Page AZ 86040 Office: Page High Sch PO Box 1927 Page AZ 86040

WINN, WILLIAM EDWIN, JR., educator; b. Kansas City, Mo., Apr. 4, 1935; s. William Edwin and Margaret (Goss) W.; student Merritt Coll., 1955-56, U. Minn., 1956-57; B.A. in Polit. Sci., U. Calif. at Berkeley, 1968, M.A. in Pub. Policy Formation, 1970, Ph.D. in Polit. Sci., 1973; m. Shirley Ann Anderson; children—Pearl, Aliah, Daniel, Ronald, Patricia. With employee benefits and workmen's compensation Algoma Steel Corp., Sault Sainte Marie, Ont., Can., 1959-63; with Crown Life Ins., Sault Ste. Marie, 1963-64, Dept. Fisheries, 1964, Lake Superior Cable TV, 1964, Ottawa (Ont.) Pub. Library, 1964-65, St. Pius X Sem., 1964-65, Capwell Dept. Store, 1965-66, St. Elizabeth High Sch., Oakland, Calif., 1966; tchr. St. Patrick High Sch., Vancouver, B.C., Can., 1966-67; cons. McClymonts Summer Project, Job and Study Oakland, 1968; head resident Smyth Hall, Univ. Housing, U. Calif. at Berkeley, 1968-70, Deutsch Hall, 1970-71, Davidson Hall, 1971-72, Smyth-Fernwald Married Student Housing, 1972-73, univ. guest lectr., 1970, minority rights and econ. devel., 1970, 71, lectr. Afro-Am. studies 1973-75; lectr. mil. sci., 1974, asso. prof., 1974-75; lectr. San Francisco State U., 1974; dir. grad. program pub. policy Lincoln U., 1974-79, also prof., chmn. dept. polit. sci., 1974-79, dir. univ. planning and devel., 1975-79, dean of students, 1976-79, supr. Sunday phys. edn. program, 1976; pres. Universal Systems Assos., 1973—; commentator Cablevision, 1974-75; observor III Sino-Am. Conf. Mainland China Affairs, 1973; designer learning systems San Francisco Unified Sch. Dist., 1979—. Faculty fellow U. Calif. at Berkeley Common Cause-Center Study Dem. Instns., 1973-75; founder Campus Democracy Now student orgn., 1968-70; pub. Golden Bear Weekly, 1969; asso. mem. Republican State Central Com. Calif.; founding mem. Concerned Reps. for Individual Rights, San Francisco, 1978; pres. Futures Found., 1979—. Mem. Am. Acad. Polit. and Social Scis. Clubs: Order Golden Bear (U. Calif. at Berkeley); Commonwealth of Calif. (San Francisco). Author: The Diefenbaker Achievement: Vision and Struggle: Canadian Politics, 1957-67; New Images for Old Lies: Struggles for Racial Equality; producer plays and film; contbr. articles to jours., mags. Home: PO Box 4411 Sather Gate Sta Berkeley CA 94704

WINNER, FRED M., judge; b. Denver, Apr. 8, 1912; s. Frank N. and Clara (Morse) W.; B.A., U. Colo., 1933, B.S., 1933, LL.B., 1936; m. Frankie R. Winner, Sept. 2, 1933; children—Claire Winner March, Margi Winner Raley. Bar: Colo. Practiced in Denver, 1936-70; U.S. dist. judge, Denver, 1970—, former chief judge, now sr. judge; instr. Westminister Law Sch., 1951-54; mem. jud. selection commn. Colo. Supreme Ct. Served with USNR, 1942-46. Mem. Am. Coll. Trial Lawyers, Internat. Acad. Trial Lawyers. Office: Room C-550 US Courthouse Denver CO 80294*

WINNING, CYNTHIA ANN, cable TV co. exec.; b. Marietta, Ohio, Apr. 13, 1951; d. Theodore Charles and Ruth E. (Valentine) Bauer; student Marietta Coll., 1969-71; m. Theodore P. Winning, Sept. 18, 1975. Art dir. Jour. Am. Newspaper, Myrtle Beach, S.C., 1973-75; local origination dir. Channel II TV, Surfside Beach, S.C., 1975; media dir. Catalina Advt. Agy., Tucson, 1977-78; dir. Winning Advt., Tucson, 1979; dir. advt. Levitz Furniture, Tucson, 1978-79; mktg. product mgr. Citicorp, Denver, 1979-81; dir. mktg. Capital Cities Cable, Denver, 1981—. Recipient AdMaster Nat. Advt. award, 1973. Mem. Direct Mktg. Assn., Women in Cable, CTAM, Sports Car Club Am. (events dir.). Republican. Roman Catholic. Home: 1331 S Victor St Aurora CO 80012 Office: 8800 E Arapahoe Rd Englewood CO 80112

WINSOR, TRAVIS WALTER, physician; b. San Francisco, Dec. 1, 1914; s. Samuel Wiley and Mabel Edna (Mc Carthy) W.; B.A., Stanford U., 1937, M.D., 1941; m. Elizabeth Adams, Sept. 1, 1939; children—David Wiley, Susan Elizabeth. Intern, Alameda County Hosp., Oakland, Calif., 1940-41; asso. fellow and instr. in medicine and cardiology Tulane U. Sch. Medicine, New Orleans, 1941-45; practice medicine specializing in cardiovascular disease; mem. staff Los Angeles County Hosp., Hosp. of Good Samaritan (hon.), St. Vincent's Med. Center, Los Angeles; clin. instr. in medicine U. So. Calif., Los Angeles, 1945-47, asst. clin. prof. medicine, 1947-61, asso. clin. prof. medicine, 1961-75, clin. prof. medicine, 1975—; dir. Meml. Heart Research Found., Inc., Los Angeles, 1957—. Diplomate Am. Bd. Internal Medicine. Fellow ACP, Am. Coll. Cardiology, Am. Coll. Chest Physicians, Internat. Coll. Angiology, Am. Coll. Angiology (pres. 1982-83), AMA, Am. Heart Assn.; mem. Am. Therapeutic Soc., Calif. Med. Assn., Los Angeles County Med. Assn., Calif. Soc. Internal Medicine, Los Angeles Soc. Internal Medicine, Am. Thermographic Soc. (pres. 1968-69), Royal Soc. Medicine London, Calif. Heart Assn., Internat. Cardiovascular Soc., Sigma Xi. Club: Los Angeles. Author: (with George E. Burch) A Primer of Electrocardiography, 1944; (with C. Hyman) A Primer of Peripheral Vascular Diseases, 1965; A Primer of Vectorcardiography, 1972; (with A. Kappert) Diagnosis of Peripheral Vascular Diseases, 1972; contbr. articles on cardiology to profl. jours. Home: 541 S Lorraine Blvd Los Angeles CA 90020 Office: 4041 Wilshire Blvd Los Angeles CA 90010

WINSTON, BRUCE EDWARD, printing co. exec.; b. Fairbanks, Alaska, July 19, 1950; s. William Barrett and Hulda Louise (Goodfellow) W.; student Wayne State Coll., 1968-69; B.S. in Psychology, U. Alaska, 1973; B.S. with highest honors in Printing Mgmt. and Tech. Rochester Inst. Tech., 1975; m. Kristie Sybil Collyer, Aug. 29, 1970; children—Kenneth Wray, Adam Collyer, Alexander Edward. With Ken Wray's Print Shop, Inc., Anchorage, 1971—, now pres. Mem. Wash.-Alaska Printing Industries Assn. (dir. 1976-77), Printing Industries Am. (prodn. mgmt. com.), Nat. Assn. Printers and Lithographers, Graphic Arts Tech. Found., Tech. Assn. Graphic Arts, Am. Mgmt. Assn., Aircraft Owners and Pilots Assn., Phi Kappa Phi. Club: Rotary (dir. 1978-81). Home: 3421 Purdue St Anchorage AK 99504 Office: 323 E Fireweed Ln Anchorage AK 99503

WINSTON, MORTON MANUEL, oil co. exec.; b. N.Y.C., Dec. 9, 1930; s. Myron Hugh and Minna (Schneller) W.; A.B., U. Vt., 1951; M.A., U. Conn., 1953; LL.B. magna cum laude, Harvard U., 1958; m. Katherine Tupper Winn, Feb. 3, 1979; children by previous marriages—Gregory Winston, Livia Winston; stepchildren—Wesley Hudson, Laura Hudson. Admitted to D.C. bar, 1961; law clk. to Justice Frankfurter, Supreme Ct. U.S., 1959-60; asso. firm Cleary, Gottlieb, Steen & Hamilton, N.Y.C., Washington, 1960-67; v.p. Tosco Corp., 1964-67, exec. v.p., 1967-71, pres., 1971—, chief exec. officer, 1976—; dir. Baker Internat. Corp., 1976—. Chmn. bd. trustees Craft and Folk Art Mus., Los Angeles, 1976—; trustee Mus. Contemporary Art, Los Angeles, 1977—; bd. dirs. Center Theatre Group Los Angeles. Served to lt. (j.g.) USCGR, 1953-55. Office: Tosco Corp 10100 Santa Monica Blvd Los Angeles CA 90067

WINTER, DAVID KENNETH, college president; b. South Pasadena, Calif., Sept. 15, 1930; s. Hugo H. and Hazel C. (Patterson) W.; m. L. Diane Fischer, June 28, 1960; children—Laura, Ruth, Bruce. B.A., UCLA, 1953, M.A., 1956; Ph.D. in Anthropology and Sociology, Mich. State U., 1968. Instr., Wheaton (Ill.) Coll., 1959-62; asst. prof., then assoc. prof. Mich. State U., 1965-70, dean of faculty, then exec. v.p. Whitworth Coll., Spokane, Wash., 1970-76; pres. Westmont Coll., Santa Barbara, Calif., 1976—. Bd. dirs. Cottage Hosp., Montecito Assn. Served to lt. USNR, 1955-59. Midwestern Univs. Consortium grantee, 1964-65. Fellow Am. Anthrop. Assn.; mem. Christian Coll. Consortium (chmn., dir.), Christian Coll. Coalition, Ind. Colls. So. Calif. (dir.), Council Ind. Colls. Republican. Presbyterian. Clubs: Santa Barbara, Montecito Rotary (bd. dirs.). Home: 985 La Paz Rd Santa Barbara CA 93108 Office: 955 La Paz Rd Santa Barbara CA 93108

WINTER, IRWIN FLOYD, radiologist; b. Parkston, S.D., June 12, 1914; s. John G. and Aline Louise (Jaton) W.; B.A., Huron (S.D.) Coll., 1935; B.S., U. S.D., 1937; M.D., Rush Med. Sch., Chgo., 1939; M.S. in Radiology, U. Minn., 1945; m. Leona LaVon Luchsinger, June 23, 1939; children—Kathleen Dee, Brian Irwin, Kent Louis. Intern, Washington Blvd. Hosp., Chgo., 1939-40; resident St. Mary's and Pima County hosps., Tucson, 1940-41; fellow in radiology Mayo Clinic, Rochester, Minn., 1941-44, jr. staff dept. radiology, 1944-46; practice medicine specializing in radiology, Seattle, 1946-48; radiologist Swedish Hosp., Seattle, 1946-48; radiologist Salt Lake Clinic, Salt Lake City, 1948-51; instr. radiology U. Utah, 1948-50; practice medicine specializing in radiology, Salt Lake City, 1948—. Mem. Utah, Salt Lake County med. socs., Am. Coll. Radiology, Utah Radiol. Soc. Clubs: Safari Internat., Masons. Home: 900 Donner Way #508 Salt Lake City UT 84108 Office: 508 E S Temple St Salt Lake City UT 84102

WINTER, WILLIAM ORVILLE, political scientist, educator; b. Richmond, Mo., Oct. 1, 1918; s. William Emmett and Lucy Deborah (Hauser) W.; m. Mary Mildred Crossland, Feb. 10, 1939; m. 2d, Alice Beardslee, Sept. 12, 1956; children—William Steven, Sharon Johnson, Susan Ann, Lucy Emily. B.A., U. Mo., 1942, M.A., 1947; Ph.D., U. Mich., 1950. Research assoc. U. Mich., Ann Arbor, 1949-50; asst. prof. So. Ill. U., Carbondale, 1950-56, assoc. prof. to prof., 1957-63; prof. polit. sci. U. Colo., Boulder, 1963—; Fulbright prof. Am. politics, U. Vienna (Austria), 1956-57. Author: The Special Assessment Today, 1952; The Urban Polity, 1968; State and Local Government in a Decentralized Republic, 1981. Served with USN, 1943-46, USNR, 1946-66. Mem. Am. Polit. Sci. Assn., Nat. Mcpl. League. Democrat. Congregationlist. Office: Campus Box 333 U Colo Boulder CO 80309

WINTERBOTTOM, GRETA STRAIN, educator; b. Alley Springs, Mo., Feb. 23, 1929; d. Frank and Julia (Ellerman) Strain; m. Richard Winterbottom, Dec. 12, 1953; 1 dau., Pegi. B.S. in Elem. Edn., So. Oreg. State Coll., 1959; M.Ed., U. Oreg. Cert. tchr., reading specialist, handicapped, Oreg. Reading Specialist Rogue River (Oreg.) Elementary Sch. Mem. Josephine County Art Assn., Rogue Valley Symphony, AAUW, Assn. Children Learning Disabilities, Assn. Supervision and Curriculum Devel., Internat. Reading Assn. Republican. Methodist.

WIPF, DEANA LYN, employment agency executive; b. Corning, Calif., Oct. 15, 1947; d. Leonard William and Clara May (Gwartney) Wirtz; m. Randolph Floris Banovich, Nov. 13, 1965; children—RanDee Lyn, Mathew Lain; m. David Edward Wipf, Oct. 7, 1982; stepchildren—Cheryl, Heidi. Student Western Nev. Coll., U. Nev., U. Alaska, Anchorage Community Coll. Adminstrv. asst. Anaconda Co., Weed Heights, Nev., 1970-77, bus. mgr., Anchorage, 1977-78; owner, mgr. Offices Unlimited Inc., Anchorage, 1978—; ptnr. B&D Bus. Services, Sparks, Nev., 1983—; lectr. Anchorage Bus. Coll., U. Anchorage, Human Resources Ctr., North Pacific Bus. Inst.; cons. employee counseling pub. relations. Active 4-H. Mem. Nat. Assn. Female Exec., Assn. Profl. Placement Services (v.p.), Anchorage Women in Bus., Anchorage C. of C., Alaska C. of C., Reno C. of C. Republican. Club: Toastmasters. Author tng. manual. Office: 2600 Denali St Anchorage AK 99503

WIREMAN, DON L., tech. support co. exec.; b. Grace, Idaho, Aug. 6, 1938; s. Joseph and Ethel Ellen (Stalker) W.; student Lee Coll., 1961-62, student U. Nev., 1969—; m. Rita Acasia Chong Onofre, Feb. 2, 1965; children—Don L., Sonja Marie. Radiol. lab. analysis technician Reynolds Elec. & Engring. Co., Inc., Las Vegas, Nev., 1964-73, radiol. services coodinator, 1974-77, dosimetry liaison officer, 1978—; radiol. emergency response instr. U.S. NRC Tng. Courses, Las Vegas, 1978-79. Democratic precinct campaign leader, Indian Springs, Nev., 1972. Served with U.S. Army, 1958-61. Mem. Health Physics Soc., Smithsonian Assos., Nat. Geog. Soc. Contbr. articles on radiation exposure to profl. publs.

WIRTH, TIMOTHY ENDICOTT, Congressman; b. Santa Fe, Sept. 22, 1939; s. Cecil and Virginia Maude (Davis) W.; B.A., Harvard U., 1961, M.Ed., 1964, Ph.D., Stanford U., 1973; m. Wren Winslow, Nov. 26, 1965; children—Christopher, Kelsey. White House fellow, spl. asst. to sec. HEW, Washington, 1967; asst. to chmn. Nat. Urban Coalition, Washington, 1968; dep. asst. sec. for edn. HEW, Washington, 1969; v.p. Great Western United Corp., Denver, 1970; mgr. Rocky Mountain office Arthur D. Little, Inc., cons. firm, Denver, 1971-73; mem. 94th-97th congresses from 2d Dist. Colo., mem. energy and commerce com., sci. and tech. com., budget com. Mem. Gov.'s Task Force on Returned Vietnam Vets., 1970-73; mem. bd. visitors U.S. Air Force Acad., 1978—; advisor Pres.'s Commn. on the 80's, 1979-80; trustee Planned Parenthood, Denver Head Start. Recipient Disting. Service award HEW, 1969. Ford Found. fellow, 1964-66. Mem. White House Fellows Assn. (pres. 1968-69), Denver Council Fgn. Relations (exec. com. 1974-75). Home: 3215 35th St NW Washington DC 20016 Office: 2454 Rayburn House Office Bldg Washington DC 20515

WIRTHLIN, DAVID BITNER, hosp. adminstr.; b. Salt Lake City, Sept. 19, 1935; s. Joseph L. and Madeline (Bitner) W.; B.S. in Bus. Adminstrn. cum laude, U. Utah, 1960; M.H.A., U. Minn., 1963; m. Anne Goalen, Apr. 26, 1961; children—Kimberly, Jennifer, David, Deborah, John, Marianne. Asst. adminstr. Idaho Falls (Idaho) Latter Day Saints Hosp., 1963-66; asst. to adminstr. Latter Day Saints Hosp., Salt Lake City, 1966-67, 1st asst. adminstr., 1967-70, asso. adminstr., 1970-73, adminstr., 1973—, adminstr. Primary Children's Med. Center, 1973-75; trustee Utah State Hosps.; mem. rev. com. Great Salt Lake Health Planning Agy., 1974; mem. Comprehensive Health Planning Rev. Com., 1975; chmn. Met. Hosp. Council, 1975; mem. Bd. Utah Profl. Rev., 1975-77; Utah regent Am. Coll. Hosp. Adminstrs. Mem. Am., Utah (pres.) hosp. assns., Western Assn. Hosps., Council Teaching Hosps., Am. Coll. Hosp. Adminstrs. Republican. Mormon. Clubs: Kiwanis, Timpanogos. Home: 2757 Saint Marys Way Salt Lake City UT 84108 Office: 325 8th Ave Salt Lake City UT 84143

WIRTZ, M(ARGARET) VIRGINIA, museum director, research librarian; b. Eleele, Kauai, Hawaii, May 20, 1916; d. Richard Lyon and Margaret (Scott) Hughes; m. Cable Ambrose Wirtz, June 17, 1937; children—Richard Paul, Sheila Marie Wirtz Kelly. A.B., Vassar Coll., 1937. Asst. librarian Maui County Library, Hawaii, 1955-56; mus. dir., vol. Maui Hist. Soc., 1958-73, mus. dir. Hale Hoikeike Mus., Wailuku, Hawaii, 1973—; pres. Lahaina Restoration Found. Friends. Recipient Vol. award Am. Cancer Soc., 1974; Thanks Badge and Statuette Pacific Council Girls Scouts U.S., 1968. Mem. Am. Assn. for State and Local History, Nat. Trust for Hist. Preservation, Hist. Hawaii Found., Hawaii Mus. Assn. Democrat. Episcopalian. Author: Hattie, 1975; author booklet: Hale Hoikeike, A House and Its People, 1975.

WIRTZ, SHARON COLLEEN, guidance counselor; b. Great Falls, Mont., Aug. 18, 1934; d. Thomas Day and Ann Marie (Jorgensen) Pearson; m. Richard Andrew Tomcheck, June 7, 1958; 1 dau., Tracie Jo; m. 2d, Ronald LeRoy Wirtz, July 27, 1979. B.S., Mont. State U., 1956, M.Ed. in Guidance and Counseling, 1969; postgrad. U. Mont., Caroll Coll. Tchr., Great Falls High Sch., 1956-58; tchr., counselor Helena (Mont.) Sr. High Sch., 1959-69, counselor, 1969-74; dir. guidance Capital High Sch., Helena, 1974—; workshop presenter; dir. Helena Industries, Helena Family Teaching Ctr./Achievement Home. Publicity chmn. St. Peter's Hosp. Charity Ball; mem. adv. bd. Mont., Am. Coll. Testing; bd. dirs. Helena Symphony Soc.; sci. scholarship judge Mont. high schs. Helena Scottish Rite Educators scholar, 1968; Newspaper Fund Journalism fellow, 1965. Mem. Mont. Personnel and Guidance Assn., NEA, Mont. Edn. Assn., Helena Edn. Assn., Helena Mental

Health Assn., Am. Personnel and Guidance Assn., Am. Sch. Counselors Assn., Alpha Omicron Pi, Delta Kappa Gamma. Clubs: Helena Soroptimist (past pres.), Green Meadows Country. Home: 1552 Beaverhead Rd Helena MT 59601 Office: 100 Valley Dr Helena MT 59601

WISE, JAMES CURTIS, bank executive; b. Elizabeth City, Va., July 17, 1941; s. Bennie Lee and Thelma (Sexton) W.; m. Jerra Barksdale, Mar. 17, 1962; children—Benee, Geoffrey, Micheline. Student Va. Poly. Inst. and State U.; B.A. in Bus., Upper Iowa U.; postgrad. Sch. Bank Mgmt., U. Va., 1973, Sch. Bank Mktg., U. Colo., 1979. Mktg. dir. Colonial Am. Bankshares, Roanoke, Va., 1966-80; v.p. 1st Nat. Bank, Lubbock, Tex., 1980-82; v.p., mktg. dir. 1st Interstate Bank Santa Fe, 1982—. Recipient award of excellence Nat. Research Bur. 1979; Bank Advt. award for fin. advt. excellence in radio, 1978. Mem. Bank Mktg. Assn., Am. Inst. Banking (pres. Roanoke chpt. 1978, mem. dist. council 1978-80). Presbyterian. Club: Santa Fe Country. Home: 2504 Calle des los Ninos Santa Fe NM 87501 Office: 1st Interstate Bank Santa Fe 124 E Marcy Santa Fe NM 87501

WISE, LESLIE EUGENE, emergency room physician; b. Bath, N.Y., Apr. 26, 1938; s. Beryl and Martha (Bailey) W.; m. Arlene Pellet, Aug. 26, 1976; 1 child, Ostin Moon. B.A., U. Calif., San Diego, 1973; M.D., SUNY, 1976. With Aeroflex Labs., Plainview, L.I., 1961-68, Gen. Dynamics Convair, 1969-71; intern Pacific Med. Ctr., San Francisco, 1977; emergency room physician San Bernardino (Calif.) Community Hosp., 1979—; chmn. bd. Wycor Industries, Inc. Mem. AMA, Undersea Med. Soc., Am. Coll. Emergency Physicians, Family Motor Coach Assn. Home: 3 Stone Pine Irvine CA 92714

WISE, MARSHALL, consultant; b. Revere, Mass., Jan. 1, 1935; s. Isadore and Mary Amy (Steinberg) W.; B.S.E.E., UCLA, 1960; m. Edythe Sandra Pearl, June 16, 1956; children—Randi Susan, Diane Aileen. Pres., Metrovonics, Inc., Los Alamitos, Calif., 1969-72; gen. mgr. Moxon, Inc., Irvine, Calif., 1972-74; cons. in communications and electronics Motorola, El Segundo, Calif., 1974-77; pres. U-Tel Service Co., Anaheim, Calif., 1977-82, also dir.; cons., 1982—. Served with U.S. Army, 1953-55. Mem. IEEE. Office: 2600 Broken Feather Lane Diamond Bar CA 91765

WISE, MYRLE KENT, fire chief; b. Hinton, Okla., Mar. 14, 1918; s. John Bon and Ida Ellen (Kent) W.; student Colo. State U., Purdue U.; m. Evelyn Louise Holland, July 12, 1938; children—Alan K., Diane E. Wise Bonnell. Chief ice cream maker O.P. Baurs Co., Denver, 1936-38; fan belt builder Gates Rubber Co., Denver, 1938-43; with Denver Fire Dept., 1943—, fire chief, 1970—; instr. firefighting Colo. State Vocat. Tng. Sch. Bd. dirs. Denver chpt. Am. Cancer Soc., 1968—, treas., 1979—; bd. dirs. Salvation Army, Denver, 1960—, chmn., 1968-72. Served with USN, 1944-46. Mem. Internat. Assn. Fire Chiefs (pres. 1975-76). Democrat. Clubs: Masons, Shriners, Jesters. Office: Denver Fire Dept 745 W Colfax Ave Denver CO 80204

WISEMAN, JAY DONALD, photographer, heating contractor; b. Salt Lake City, Dec. 23, 1952; s. Donald Thomas and Reva (Stewart) W.; m. Barbara Helen Taylor, June 25, 1977; children—Jill Reva, Steve Jay. Ed. Utah State U., Logan, U. Utah. Cert. profl. photographer. Vice pres. A & T Heating; pres. Jay Wiesman Photography. Recipient numerous Rocky Mountain Profl. Photographers, 1981, 82. Intermountain Profl. Photographers awards, 1980, 81 including Master's Trophy-Best of Show award. Mem. Profl. Photographers Assn. Am., Rocky Mountain Profl. Photographers, Inter-Mountain Photographers Assn. Mormon. Photographs pub. profl. jours. Office: 540 West 600 South Bountiful UT 84010

WISEMAN, STANLEY FRED, political science educator, author, researcher, company executive; b. Denver, Aug. 20, 1925; s. Fred Byron and Thora Rhondina (Miller) W.; m. Jacqueline Pindell, June 19, 1949; children—Scott Lee, Dana Allison. B.A., Denver U., 1950; LL.B., Golden Gate U., 1962; M.A., Calif. State U.-Hayward, 1974; Ph.D., U. Calif.-Riverside, 1982. Reporter, Denver Post, 1946-48, Colorado Springs Free Press, 1949-50, AP, 1948, San Francisco Examiner, 1950-51; reporter, editor Times, San Mateo, Calif., 1951-62; adminstrn. aid State Calif. Senate, 1972-75; editor, writer Systems Sci. div. Stanford Research Inst., 1965-70; mgr. Winter Music Festival No. Calif., 1972-73; lectr. U. Calif.-San Diego, 1976-77, Calif. State U.-Fullerton, 1975-76; research assoc. U. Strathclyde, Glasgow, 1980-81; mem. U. Calif. Inst. Global Conflict and Corp., Riverside; cons. immigration policy, urban problems and politics. Candidate Calif. Assembly, 26th dist., 1976. Served with USMC, 1943-45, Decorated Purple Heart. Recipient resource person award Smithsonian Conf., 1976; Chancellor's Patent award U. Calif., 1980. Mem. Am. Polit. Sci. Assn., Western Polit. Sci. Assn., Policy Studies Orgn., Brit. Politics Study Assn., Am. Acad. Social and Polit. Sci., Am. Newspaper Guild, Calif. Ski Writers Assn., Sigma Phi Epsilon. Democrat. Episcopalian. Clubs: Redwood City Democratic, Elks. Contbr. numerous articles to profl. jours. and confs. Home: 8039 La Jolla Shores Dr La Jolla CA 92037 Office: U Calif Riverside CA

WISEMAN, T. JAN, association executive, educator, consultant; b. Prairie du Chien, Wis., Mar. 26, 1941; s. E. Edward and Gertrude Jeanette (Roth) W. J.B.S., U. Wis., 1964; M.S.Ed., No. Ill. U., 1968, C.A.S., 1979. Journalism tchr. Glenbrook North High Sch., Northbrook, Ill., 1966-68; dean community edn. Kishwaukee Coll., Malta, Ill., 1968-79; staff v.p., dir. edn., mktg. Farm and Land Inst., Nat. Assn. Realtors, Chgo., 1979-81; exec. v.p. Am. Soc. Farm Mgrs. and Rural Appraisers, Denver, 1982—; dir. Profl. Devel. Inst., Denver, 1982—; human devel. cons. Bd. dirs. DeKalb-Kane County (Ill.) CETA, 1976-77, Nat. Scholastic Press Assn., 1974-79; co-founder Community Enrichment Assn., 1975. Mem. Am. Soc. Assn. Execs., Am. Soc. Tng. and Devel., Nat. Assn. Realtors, Journalism Edn. Assn. (nat. pres. 1973-75 Carl Towley award 1977). Author: Creative Communications: Teaching Mass Media, 1971, 74. Office: 360 S Monroe St Suite 460 Denver CO 80209

WISHON, JOHN ALBERT, lawyer, hotel executive; b. Los Angeles, Jan. 17, 1945; s. Frank R. and Dorothy (Woodhouse) W.; A.B. in Acctg., San Diego State U., 1968, A.B. in Psychology, 1968; J.D., U. San Diego, 1971; m. Connie J. Ray, Apr. 17, 1980; 2 children. Admitted to Calif. bar, 1972; sr. partner firm Lieb, Wishon, Catterlin and Gay, San Diego, 1972-76; gen. counsel Hotel del Coronado, Coronado, Calif., 1976-83, sr. v.p., 1976—, mgr., 1983—. Mem. San Diego County Beach Erosion Com., 1980—; bd. dirs. Calif. Coastal Council, 1979—, ARC, 1982—. Mem. Am. Bar Assn., San Diego Bar Assn., Coronado C. of C. (dir. 1978-83), San Diego C. of C. (local govt. affairs com. 1978-80), Navy League, Sigma Alpha Epsilon, Phi Delta Phi (pres. 1970-71, Outstanding Service Cert. 1970). Clubs: San Diego Marlin (judge adv. 1976—), Rotary; West Atwood Yacht (vice adm. 1972-73); Coronado Yacht. Home: 1620 Miguel Ave Coronado CA 92118 Office: Hotel del Coronado Coronado CA 92118

WISNER, JOAN VERONICA, hospital administrator; b. Lakeland, Fla., Jan. 31; d. John and Vera Beaden (Grant) Glover; m. James Harold Dotson, March 21, 1959; m. David Roland Schultz, Feb. 8, 1963; 1 son, John; m. William Louis Wisner, Sr., June 16, 1973. Student A.V. Jr. Coll., Lancaster, Calif., Upper Iowa U., Fayette. Telephone operator Gen. Telephone Co., San Bernardino, Calif., 1961-63; telephone operator, teller, gen. ledger bookkeeper, vault teller Bank of Am., Lancaster, 1964-69; telephone operator Mira Loma Hosp., Los Angeles County, Lancaster 1969-73, patient fin. services worker, 1973—, supervising patient fin. services worker, 1973-76, dir. patient fin. services, 1976—. Mem. Nat. Assn. Female Execs., Nat. Assn. Hosp. Admitting Mgrs., Calif. Assn. Hosp. Admitting Mgrs. Club: Order Eastern Star. Office: 44900 N 60th St W Lancaster CA 93534

WISOTSKY, JERRY JOSEPH, graphic arts company executive; b. N.Y.C., Oct. 22, 1928; s. Abraham I. and Anna P. (Slipoy) W.; student CCNY, 1946-48; m. Helen E. Lerner, Nov. 12, 1949; children—Pearle Eve Wisotsky Marr, Ronald Ian. Apprentice, Triplex Lithographic Corp., N.Y.C., 1949-51; pres. Kwik Offset Plate Inc., N.Y.C., 1952-59; pres. Imperial Lithographers Inc., Phoenix, 1959-69, chmn. bd., 1970-82, pres., chmn. bd., 1982—; ptnr. M.J. Enterprises, Phoenix, 1959—. Mem. bd. appeals, Phoenix, 1974-76; pres. Ariz. Found. for Handicapped, 1976—; campaign chmn. corp. div. United Way, 1975, gen. campaign chmn., 1977; trustee St. Luke's Hosp. Med. Center; pres. Phoenix Jewish Community Center, 1970-71; v.p. bd. dirs. United Way; pres. United Way Phoenix-Scottsdale, 1981; chmn. Valley of Sun United Way, 1981; chmn. Ariz. bd. dirs. Anti-Defamation League, also nat. commr.; active NCCJ; pres. Metro-Phoenix Citizens Council; bd. dirs. Boys' Clubs Phoenix, Combined Health Resources, 1982-83; mem. dean's adv. council Coll. Bus. Adminstrn., Ariz. State U., 1980-81; chmn. bd. dirs. St. Luke's Hosp., Phoenix, 1981—; bd. dirs. Combined Health Resources, 1982-83. Recipient Torch of Liberty award Anti-Defamation League, 1977; 12 Who Care Hon Kachina award, 1980. Mem. Phoenix Met. C. of C. (intercity com.). Home: 7520 N 1st St Phoenix AZ 85020 Office: 210 S 4th Ave Phoenix AZ 85003

WISSING, NEIL PHILLIP, company executive; b. Grants Pass, Oreg., Sept. 30, 1931; s. Virginia (Russell) W.; m. Donna Lee, Sept. 5, 1952; children—Kim, Jeff, Greg. B.S., Oreg. State U., 1953; B.B.A., U. Oreg., 1958; A.M.P., Harvard U., 1976. Tex. acct. Weyerhaeuser Co., Tacoma, Wash., 1957-63, mgr. tax research, 1963-68, asst. dir. taxes, 1968-73, dir. taxes, 1973-80, v.p., dir. taxes, 1980—. Trustee Wash. State Research Council. Served as 1st lt. USAF, 1953-55. Mem. Tax Execs. Com. (pres. Seattle chpt., nat. officer, exec. com.), Am. Paper Inst. (tax com.), Nat. Forest Products Assn. (bd. dirs.), Nat. Tax Assn. Home: 670 Monterey Ln Tacoma WA 98466 Office: Weyerhaeuser Co Tacoma WA 98477

WISSLER, STANLEY GEBHART, cons. geologist; b. N.Y.C., Mar. 31, 1900; s. Clark and Viola (Gebhart) W.; B.S., Earlham Coll., 1922; M.A., Columbia U., 1923; m. Agnes Elizabeth Meerhoff, Oct. 26, 1926; children—Ann Elizabeth Wissler Malcolm, Clark William, John Benjamin. Grad. asst. in geology and paleontology Columbia U., 1923-25; various positions oil and gas exploration and research and adminstrn., Alaska, contiguous U.S., Can., Mex., Costa Rica, Philippines, Indonesia, Malaysia, Thailand, Burma, Pakistan, Ecuador, Union Oil Co. Calif., 1925-65; oil and gas cons., 1965-68; cons. Internat. Resources Co., S.E. Asia, 1969-70; partner Hazzard, Morris & Assos., Los Angeles, 1970-73; cons. geologist, Long Beach, Calif., 1973—. Registered geologist, Calif. Fellow Geol. Soc. Am., AAAS; mem. Am. Assn. Petroleum Geologists (cert. petroleum geologist, hon. life mem. Pacific sect.), Soc. Econ. Paleontologists and Mineralgists (hon. life mem. pres. 1937, pres. Pacific sect., 1928), Am. Inst. Profl. Geologists (cert.), Geol. Soc. Malaysia, Am. Security Council, Sigma Xi. Republican. Congregationalist. Clubs: Petroleum of Los Angeles, Retired Oil Man's. Contbr. sci. papers to profl. publs. in field. Home: 4245 Chestnut Ave Long Beach CA 90807

WISTISEN, MARTIN J., agribusiness executive; b. Bancroft, Idaho, May 30, 1938; s. Raoul and Cora (Johnson) W.; m. Katherine Callister, Dec. 28, 1960; children—Kevin, Diane, Kaeleen, Janette, Richard, Michelle, R. Brent, N. Gregg. B.S., Brigham Young U., 1962; M.B.A., Northwestern U., 1964; Ph.D., Columbia U., 1976. Fin. analyst Esso Internat., Inc., 1964-65; dir. fin. analysis and mgr. econ. analysis TWA, 1968-70; dir. Ctr. Bus. and Econ. Research, asst. dean Grad. Sch. Mgmt., assoc. prof. bus. mgmt./bus. econs. and dir. M.B.A. program Brigham Young U., Provo, Utah, 1971-80; v.p. mktg. U and I Inc., Kennewick, Wash., 1980-82, sr. v.p., 1982—; pres. U & I Farms, 1982—. Bd. dirs. United Way, 1983. Mem. Tri-Cities C. of C., Phi Kappa Phi, Beta Gamma Sigma. Republican. Mem. Ch. Jesus Christ of Latter-day Saints. Club: Rotary. Office: PO Box 2308 Tri-Cities WA 99302

WISZINCKAS, EVELYN, psychologist; b. Balt., July 4, 1942; d. Vincent J. and Mildred A. (Janonis) Wiszinckas. B.A., Cath. U. Am., 1964; M.S., U. Pitts., 1970, Ph.D., 1974. Lic. psychologist, Pa., Alaska. Psychologist Arsenal Family and Children's Ctr., Pitts., 1970-77; pvt. practice psychology, Pitts., 1975-80; clin. psychologist St. Francis Gen. Hosp., Pitts., 1977-80, project dir. tng. program in primary prevention of childhood mental disorders, 1979-80; program dir./psychologist Upper Yukon Behavioral Health Service, Ft. Yukon, Alaska, 1980—. Mem. Am. Psychol. Assn., Alaska Psychol. Assn., Pa. Psychol. Assn., Greater Pitts. Psychol. Assn. Contbr. articles to profl. jours. Address: PO Box 237 Fort Yukon AK 99740

WITCHER, JOHN EDGAR, manufacturing company executive; b. Indpls., May 11, 1938; s. Edgar and Grace L. (Shrum) W.; m. Marilyn Jean Minor, Mar. 26, 1942; children—John M., Mark A. B.S., Ind. U.-Bloomington, 1961; LL.B. Blackstone Sch. Law, 1969. Quality engr. Cummins Engine Co., Inc., Columbus, Ind. and divs., 1961-70, materials dir., 1969-70; ops. mgr., v.p. ops. Remcom Systems, Inc., Garland, Tex., 1970-72; v.p., pres. Transtronics Corp., Garland, 1972-74; dir. purchasing, dir. materials Mitsubishi Aircraft Internat., Inc., San Angelo, Tex., 1975-80; dir. material Weber Aircraft div. Kidde, Inc., Burbank, Calif., 1980-82; dir. ops. control, 1982—. Mem. Am. Statis. Assn., Am. Prodn. and Inventory Control Soc. Club: Masons. Office: Weber Aircraft Div 2820 Ontario St Burbank CA 91510

WITCHER, JOHN REX, interior designer; b. Honey Grove, Tex., June 11, 1927; s. John Lee and Claude Elizabeth (Johnson) W.; m. Martha Lou Snow, June 4, 1957; 1 son, John Mark. B.S., U.S. Naval Postgrad. Sch., 1965; B.A., So. Methodist U., 1966. Mgr. design dept. Raymar Textiles, Colorado Springs, Colo., 1970-74; head designer Designers Depot, Colorado Springs, 1974—. Served as lt. comdr. USN, 1945-47, 51-69. Decorated Air medal. Mem. Am. Soc. Interior Designers (assoc.). Republican. Episcopalian. Club: Broadmoor Rotary (Colorado Springs.). Home: 1214 La Paloma Way Colorado Springs CO 80906 Office: Designers Depot 30 S Sierra Madre Colorado Springs CO 80903

WITHAM, RODNEY ARTHUR, retail executive; b. Medfored, Oreg., May 8, 1924; s. Harlan Clay and A. Violet (Grove) W.; student pub. schs. Medford; m. Joyce Hazel Wooldridge, Mar. 22, 1975; children—Robert, Alan, John. With Witham Parts Equipment Co., Medford, Oreg., 1940—, pres., 1972—, owner, 1978—. Served with AUS, 1942-44. Decorated Purple Heart (2). Republican. Clubs: Rogue Valley Country, Masons, Order Eastern Star, Shriners, Elks, Rolls Royce Owners. Office: 2343 Biddle Rd Medford OR 97501

WITHER, ROSS PLUMMER, chemist; b. Portland, Oreg., Dec. 29, 1922; s. William Matthew and Hildegarde (Plummer) W.; student U. Oreg., 1940-43, B.S., 1945, B.S., 1947, M.A., 1949; postgrad. Stanford U., 1948-51, 54, Ph.D., 1956; m. Alice Louise Allen, June 22, 1944; children—William A., Janice L., Bonnie A. Research chemist Crown Zellerbach Corp., Camas, Wash., 1955-65, sr. research chemist, 1965—; teaching asst. U. Oreg., 1947-48, Stanford U., 1948-49. Committeeman Columbia Pacific Council Boy Scouts Am., Camas, 1958-63; deacon, elder St. John's Presbyn. Ch., Camas, 1966—. Served with USN, 1943-46, 52-54. Mem. Am. Chem. Soc., TAPPI, Sigma Xi, Phi Lambda Upsilon. Republican. Clubs: Officers' Open Mess Portland AFB; Masons (Camas). Contbr. articles in field to tech. jours. Home: 1526 NE 4th Ave Camas WA 98607 Office: Crown Zellerbach Central Research Camas WA 98607

WITHERELL, CHARLES EICHHORN, metall. research engr.; b. Bayonne, N.J., Mar. 25, 1928; s. Charles Peter and Eva St. Clair (Wheeler) W.; B.S. in Mech. Engring., N.J. Inst. Tech., 1957; postgrad. N.Y. Law Sch., 1962-65; m. Jane Adair Wydeman, Nov. 11, 1950; children—Charles Victor, Glenn Edward, Carolyn Eva. Successively prin. investigator welding research, supr. welding research, group leader process metallurgy research, research mgr. process and mech. metallurgy Internat. Nickel Co., Suffern, N.Y., 1957-74; dir. research, v.p. research and devel. Eutectic Corp., Flushing, N.Y., 1974-76; dir. fabrication tech. Lawrence Livermore (Calif.) Nat. Lab., 1976—; cons. engr.; lectr. welding, mech. metallurgy, metall. research. Served with C.E., U.S. Army, 1950-52. Decorated Republic of Korea Presdl. Citation; registered profl. engr. various states. Mem. Am. Welding Soc. (A. F. Davis silver medal 1962, R. Wasserman award, J. F. Lincoln Gold medal 1980), Metall. Soc. of AIME, ASME, Am. Soc. Metals, Am. Powder Metallurgy Inst., ASTM, Sigma Xi, Tau Beta Pi, Pi Tau Sigma. U.S. and fgn. patentee in field; contbr. papers to tech. publs. Home: 7426 Hillview Ct Pleasanton CA 94566 Office: PO Box 808 L-332 Livermore CA 94550

WITKIN, JOEL-PETER, photographer; b. Bklyn., Sept. 13, 1939; s. Max and Mary (Pellegrino) W.; B.F.A., Cooper Union, 1974; M.F.A., U. N.Mex.; student (fellow) Columbia U., 1973-74; m. Cynthia Jean Bency, June 30, 1978; one child. Free-lance still photographer; one-man shows of photography include: Moore Coll. Art, Phila., 1969, Cooper Union Sch. Fine Art, N.Y.C., 1972, Lake Erie Coll. Art, Cleve., 1973, U. N.Mex., Albuquerque, 1976, Robert Samuel Gallery, N.Y.C., 1981, Photographer as Printmaker, Arts Council Gt. Brit., London, 1981; group shows, 1959—, latest being: Mus. Modern Art, N.Y.C., 1959, Robert Samuel Gallery, 1980, Ariz. State U., Tempe, 1980, U. N.Mex., Albuquerque, 1981, San Francisco Mus. Modern Art, 1981; represented in permanent collections: Mus. Modern Art, N.Y.C., San Francisco Mus. Modern Art, 1980, Lake Erie Coll. Art, Cleve., Andromeda Gallery, Buffalo, Ariz. State U., Tempe. Served with U.S. Army, 1960-64. Ford Found. grantee, 1977, 78, Nat. Endowment in Photography grantee, 1980, 81. Address: 222 Amherst St NE Albuquerque NM 87106

WITKOW, ELLIOT BRUCE, retail chain executive; b. Worcester, Mass., Dec. 26, 1948; s. Alexander and Le Verne A. (Schulman) W.; B.A. in Econs., UCLA, 1970; M.B.A., U. So. Calif., 1971; m. Bonnie G. Owen, Aug. 13, 1949; children—Brandon, Bryan. Gen. mgr. Eddan div. Cetec, Los Angeles, 1969-77; v.p. EBK Enterprises, Los Angeles, 1978-80; pres. Witkow Enterprises, Los Angeles, 1981—. Active Am. Cancer Soc., 1970-80. Mem. U. So. Calif. M.B.A.s Assn., Am. Floral Services Assn. Democrat. Jewish. Office: Witkow Enterprises 316 Omar St Los Angeles CA 90013

WITSMEER, ARTHUR JAMES, aerospace engineer; b. Chgo., Feb. 20, 1938; s. Edward Jacob and Charlotte Lois (Zwart) W.; m. Ruth Evelyn Andriese, July 9, 1965; children—Joan, Kirk, Laura, Nancy. B.S.E.E., Ill. Inst. Tech., 1959; M.S.E.E., U. So. Calif., 1965; D.Engring. in Aerospace and Astronautics, Stanford U., 1968. Lic. profl. engr., Wash. Research engr. Rockwell, Downey, Calif., 1962-65; research engr. Boeing Aerospace, Seattle, 1968-71, mgr. guidance and nav. tech., 1974—; mem. tech. staff Aerospace Corp., El Segundo, Calif., 1971-74; cons., China, 1982. Bd. dirs. Wash. chpt. Nat. Sudden Infant Death Soc., 1977-80. Served to lt. USN, 1959-62. Assoc. fellow AIAA. Republican. Mem. Christian Reformed Ch. Contbr. articles to tech. jours. Home: 1928 Sullivan Dr Gig Harbor WA 98335 Office: PO Box 3999 Seattle WA 98124

WITT, NEIL ORAND, educator; b. Milw., Oct. 30, 1941; s. Orand A. and Ruth E. W.; A.S., Clark County Community Coll., 1974; B.S., U. Nev., 1976; M.B.A., Golden Gate U., 1980; student Nev. So. U., 1965. Radiol. tech. So. Nev. Meml. Hosp., Las Vegas, 1965-79; instr. in mgmt. Clark County Community Coll., North Las Vegas, 1976—, instr. CETA program, 1979-80; tech. cons. Lincoln County Hosp., Caliente, Nev., 1974; mgmt. cons. MCS Assos., 1979—; coordinator bus. lab. Clark County Community Coll.; instr. bus. mgmt. Nev. State Prison, 1980-82; public relations Radio Sta. KVEG, Las Vegas, 1980-82; owner Neil O. Witt & Assocs., Mgmt. and Tng. Consultants. Mem. Nat. Bus. Edn. Assn., AAUP, Am. Registry Radiologic Techs., Am. Soc. Radiologic Techs., Am. Mgmt. Assn. Home: 5809 Granada Ave Las Vegas NV 89107 Office: 3200 E Cheyenne Ave North Las Vegas NV 89030

WITT, SHIRLEY HILL, state ofcl.; b. Whittier, Calif., Apr. 17, 1934; d. Melvin Ward and Cordelia B. (Beardsley) Hill; B.A., U. Mich., 1965, M.A., 1966; Ph.D., U. N.Mex., 1969; children—Randall Jacobs, Hilary. Vis. asst. prof. anthropology U. N.C., Chapel Hill, 1970-72; asso. prof. anthropology Colo. Coll., Colorado Springs, 1972-75; regional dir. Rocky Mountain Regional Office, U.S. Commn. on Civil Rights, Denver, 1975-82; cabinet sec. N.Mex. Dept. Natural Resources, Santa Fe, 1983—; mem. panel of experts U.S. Nat. Commn. for UNESCO, 1978. Commr. City and County of Denver Commn. on Community Relations, 1975—; del. Internat. Women's Year Conf., Mexico, 1974; del.-at-large Nat. Commn. on Observance of Internat. Women's Year, Houston, 1977; human rights expert U.S. Mission NGO, Conf. on Discrimination Against Indigenes of Ams., Geneva, 1977; mem. Indians Rights Com., ACLU; bd. dirs. Rural Am. Women, Inc. Recipient Anisfield-Wolf award for race relations Am. Indian Today, 1968. Fellow Am. Anthrop. Assn., Am. Assn. Phys. Anthropologists. Editor: (with Stan Steiner) The Way: An Anthology of American Indian Literature, 1972; (TV shows) Silent Heritage: The American Indian, 1966-67; contbr. articles to profl. jours. Office: Dept Natural Resources Villagra Bldg Santa Fe NM 87503

WITTELES, ELEONORA MEIRA, physicist; b. Jerusalem, July 14, 1938; d. Salomon and Rivka (Komornik) W.; B.S., Fordham U., 1962, M.S., 1963; M.S., N.Y.U., 1965; Ph.D. (research fellow), Yeshiva U., 1969. Postdoctoral fellow Bar-Ilan U., Israel, 1969-70, asst. prof., 1970-72; ind. cons., 1972-80; sr. research scientist Atlantic Richfield Co., Los Angeles, 1980—. Mem. Am. Phys. Soc., AAAS, IEEE, IEEE Engring. in Medicine and Biology Soc., IEEE Magnetics Soc., Com. on Status of Women in Physics. Research on solid state physics, superconductivity, applied material scis., inventor med. instrumentation and cryogenic instrumentation. Home: 4714 Browndeer Ln Palos Verdes CA 90274 Office: 515 S Flower St Los Angeles CA 90071

WITTENBERG, ERICA, psychotherapist; b. N.Y.C., Sept. 17, 1933; d. Charles L. and Edith (Wittenberg) Weis; children—Meredith, Laura, Jonathan. B.A. with honors in French, Swarthmore Coll., 1955; M.C., Ariz. State U., 1975. Lic. marriage family counselor, Calif.; cert. therapist, Gestalt Inst. Phoenix. Staff counselor Synergy, Phoenix, 1972-73; staff therapist Terros, Phoenix, 1975-80; dir. Terros Counseling Service, 1980-82; pvt. practice psychotherapy, Phoenix, 1982—; counselor technician, substance abuse counselor, programs tchr. Maricopa County Community Colls.; staff trainer, quality assurance cons. for community agys. Mem. Am. Personnel and Guidance Assn., Am. Assn. Marriage and Family Therapists (clin. mem.), Phoenix Psychoanalytic Study Group. Club: Mensa (Greater Phoenix chpt.). Author: Drug Abuse: A Handbook for Parents, 1983. Office: 2701 E Camelback Rd Suite 323 Phoenix AZ 85016

WITTER, THOMAS WINSHIP, investment banker and broker; b. Oakland, Calif., Nov. 12, 1928; s. Jean Carter and Catharine (Maurer) W.; m. Barbara Rogers, June 22, 1951; children—Jane Witter Raymond, Susan Witter Phillips, Nancy Witter Harrison, Barbara Witter Harden, Thomas K. B.S., U. Calif., 1951. Account exec. Dean Witter & Co., 1953-58, ptnr., 1958-68, exec. v.p., 1968-78; exec. v.p. Dean Witter Reynolds, Inc., San Francisco, 1978—. Pres. The Guardsmen, San Francisco, 1960-61; bd. dirs. Samuel Merritt Hosp., Oakland, Calif., 1961-76; regent U. of the Pacific, 1974—; past bd. dirs. San Francisco Boys Club, Hunters Point Boys Club. Served to capt. USMC, 1951-53. Mem. San Francisco Bond Club. Clubs: Pacific-Union, Bohemian (San Francisco); Claremont Country (Oakland). Office: 101 California St San Francisco CA 94111

WITZKE, DONALD BRUCE, psychologist; b. San Francisco, June 5, 1938; s. Otto Clarence and Helmi Hilja (Poutanen) W.; m. Hazel Everlyn Pittman, Mar. 3, 1972; children—Deborah S. DeShong, Kimberly N. DeShong, Wayne O. B.A., U. Tex., Austin, 1967, Ph.D., 1975. Head statis. services Survey Research Ctr., Inst. Social Sci. Research, UCLA, 1976-78, lectr. dept. edn., 1977; coordinator health sci. edn. research Office Ednl. Resources, Sch. Medicine, U. S.D., Vermillion, 1978-80, co-dir. Office Ednl. Evaluation, Research and Services, 1980-82; research assoc. Office Med. Edn., Coll. Med., U. Ariz., Tucson, 1982—. Served with USAF, 1961-65. Henderson fellow, 1968. Mem. Am. Psychol. Assn., Midwestern Psychol. Assn., S.D. Psychol. Assn., Assn. Am. Med. Colls. Author: (with others) Personality Development in Two Cultures, 1976. Home: 8905 N Hickory Dr Tucson AZ 85704 Office: Coll Medicine U Ariz Tucson AZ 85724

WOBKER, THOMAS FREEMAN, electronic company executive, lawyer; b. Bartlesville, Okla., June 11, 1944; s. Burle Freeman and Elizabeth (Ensch) W.; children—Scott, Joshua, Jill; m. Sharon Reynolds, June 24, 1977. B.S. in Journalism, U. Kans., 1967, J.D., 1974. Bar: Kans. 1974, Mo. 1976, Mich. 1977, Idaho 1981. Asst. state atty. gen., Topeka, 1973-75; asst. area atty. A.T.&T. Long Lines, Kansas City, Mo., 1975-76; corp. counsel Dalby Corp., Detroit, 1976-80; v.p. Gallagher Constrn., Inc., Coeur d'Alene, Idaho, 1980-81; v.p., corp. counsel Transtector Systems, Post Falls, Idaho, 1981—; dir. Gallagher Constrn., Inc.; asst. pros. atty., Kootenai County, Idaho, 1980-81. Served to capt. USAF, 1967-71. Recipient Disting. Service citation. Mem. Kans. Bar Assn., Mich. Bar Assn., Idaho Bar Assn., Mo. Bar, Audubon Soc. Republican. Club: Sierra. Home: 1606 Plaza Dr Post Falls ID 83854

WODTLI, GERALD LEWIS, optometrist; b. Sweet Home, Oreg., Feb. 11, 1947; s. John E. and Verna M. (Pittsley) W.; m. Shirley Rae Lamphear, June 21, 1969; children—Jeremy Jonathan, Jill Jennifer. B.A. in Biology, U. Oreg., 1969; O.D., Pacific U., 1973. Prin., Pasco (Wash.) Vision Clinic, 1975—. Served to 1st lt. USAF, 1973-75. Fellow Coll. Vision Devel.; mem. Am. Optometric Assn., Wash. Optometric Assn. (Young O.D. of Year, 1980-81), Optometric Extension Program Found. (asst. state dir.), Tri-Cities Optometric Soc. Lutheran. Club: Rotary (Pasco-Kennewick). Office: Pasco Vision Clinic 1906 N 20th St Pasco WA 99302

WOECKENER, JANE MARIE, dietitian; b. Chicago Heights, Ill., Dec. 15, 1949; d. Edward Peter and Helen (Grabski) Pachura; m. Michael Charles Woeckener, Aug. 17, 1974. B.S. in Food, Nutrition, Food Service Adminstrn., U. Wis.-Stevens Point, 1972; M.S. in Human Nutrition, U. Iowa, 1976. Registered dietitian, 1973. Dietetic intern U. Iowa Hosps. and Clinics, Iowa City, 1972-73, adminstrv. dietitian, 1973-76; clin. instr. dietetics U. Wis., Stevens Point, 1976-77; food service adminstr. and dir. dietetic internship program U. Wis. Hosp. and Clinics, Madison, 1977-80; asst. dir. dietetics and nutritional services Stanford U. Hosp., 1980—. HEW grantee, 1973-76. Mem. Am. Soc. Parenteral and Enternal Nutrition, Am. Dietetic Assn., Calif. Dietetic Assn., San-Jose-Peninsula Dist. Dietetic Assn., Am. Soc. Hosp. Food Service Adminstrs., Omicron Nu, Sigma Zeta. Democrat. Roman Catholic. Home: 3405 La Selva Dr San Mateo CA 94403 Office: Dept Dietetics Stanford Univ Hosp C108 300 Pasteur Dr Stanford CA 94305

WOELFEL, ROBERT WILLIAM, radio station manager, city official; b. Los Angeles, Nov. 5, 1944; s. William Herman and Mary Jane (Hiatt) W. A.A., Mt. San Antonio Coll., 1965; B.S. in Bus., Calif. State U.-Los Angeles, 1969; M.B.A., U. So. Calif., 1972. Salesman, Burroughs Corp., El Monte, Calif., 1969-71; radio announcer sta. KDAC, Ft. Bragg, Calif., 1973; sales mgr., announcer Sta. KMFB/KPMO, Mendocino, Calif., 1973-81; gen. mgr. Sta. KOZT, Ft. Bragg, 1981—; instr. advt. community coll.; advt. cons. Vice mayor City of Ft. Bragg, 1982—; mem. City Council, 1977—; v.p. bd. dirs. Mendocino Coast Ednl. TV Assn., 1983—. Served with USN, 1966-68. Presbyterian. Contbr. articles to photog. jour.

WOELPER, ALEXANDER ELLIOTT, environmental engineer; b. El Paso, Nov. 8, 1957; s. Walter E. and Elvira O. (Lopez) W. B.S. in Civil Engring., Va. Mil. Inst., 1980; M.A. in Edn., Mich. State U., 1983. Supt./engrs. asst. Borsberry Constrn. Co., El Paso, 1977-78; commd. 2d lt. U.S. Army, 1980; engr. project officer U.S. Army Pacific Environ. Health Engring. Agy., 1980-81, engr. officer, supply officer, 1981-83. Va. vol. firefighter, 1979-80. Named Outstanding Young Man, U.S. Jaycees, 1982. Mem. ASCE, Soc. Am. Mil. Engrs., Am. Water Works Assn. Republican. Methodist. Club: Tokyo Pegasus Running. Home: 4506 Frankfort Ave El Paso TX 79903 Office: USA-EHEA APO San Francisco CA 96343

WOHLFORTH, ERIC EVANS, lawyer; b. N.Y.C., Apr. 17, 1932; s. Robert Martin and Mildred Campbell (Evans) W.; A.B., Princeton, 1954; LL.B., U. Va., 1957; m. Caroline Barbour Penniman, May 9, 1932; children—Eric Evans, Charles P. Admitted to N.Y. State bar, 1957, Alaska bar; practiced in N.Y.C., 1957-66, Anchorage, 1966-70, 72—; asso. firm Hawkins, Delafield & Wood, N.Y.C., 1957-66; mem. firm McGrath & Wohlforth, Anchorage, 1966-70, McGrath, Wohlforth & Flint, Anchorage, 1972-74, Wohlforth & Flint, 1974—. Commr. revenue State of Alaska, 1970-72; mem. Alaska Investment com., 1972-80. Episcopalian (vestryman 1968-70, 71-72, sr. warden 1979, chancellor Diocese of Alaska 1972—). Home: 2226 Arbor Circle Anchorage AK 99503 Office: 900 W 5th Ave Anchorage AK 99501

WOHLMUT, THOMAS ARTHUR, communications exec.; b. Perth, Australia, Feb. 19, 1953; came to U.S., 1957, naturalized, 1963; s. Arthur John and Georgina Elfreida (Pipek) W.; B.A. cum laude, UCLA, 1975; m. Debra Lynn Hansen, Aug. 1, 1979. TV prodn. asst. CBS, Hollywood, Calif., 1971-74; video disc producer I/O Metrics Corp., Sunnyvale, Calif., 1975-77; dir., writer Innovative Media Inc., Menlo Park, Calif., 1977-78; pres. Wohlmut Media Services, Sunnyvale, 1978—; cons. Bechtel Power Corp., Sunset Mag., Xerox-Diablo Systems, Varian Assos., Atari. Mem. Internat. TV Assn. (pres. San Francisco chpt.), Interactive Communications Soc. (founder, pres.), Am. Soc. Tng. and Devel., Am. Film Inst. Office: 3503 Ryder St Santa Clara CA 95051

WOISH, MARK STANLEY, astronautical engineer, air force officer; b. Boston, Oct. 29, 1956; s. Stanley J. and Wanda F. (Woisnis) W.; m. Patricia L. Cucuzza, Aug. 16, 1980. B.S. in Astronautical Engring., U.S. Air Force Acad., 1979; M.S. in Systems Mgmt., U. So. Calif., 1982. Commd. 2d lt. U.S. Air Force, 1979, advanced through grades to capt., 1983; space vehicle field program engr. 6595 ATG/ASP, Vandenberg AFB, Calif., 1979, NAVSTAR GPS Payload systems engr., 1979-82, ABSAD field program mgr., 1982—. Mem. AIAA, Am. Astronautical Soc. Office: Bldg 7000 13th St Vandenberg AFB CA 93437

WOITASZEWSKI, DONNA MARIE, county extension agent; b. Kimball, Nebr., Apr. 30, 1952; d. Donald George and Elizabeth Ann (Janesofsky) Shandera; m. Ronald Paul Woitaszewski, May 29, 1982; 1 son, Andrew Paul. B.S. in Home Econs., Chadron State Coll., 1974; postgrad Mid-Plains Community Coll., 1978-79, U. Wyo., 1981, 82. Extension home economist Central Sandhills Area U. Nebr., Thedford, 1974-79, Natrona County, Casper, Wyo., 1979—. Mem. Nat. Assn. Extension 4-H Agts. (Disting. Service award 1983), Wyo. Assn. Extension 4-H Agts. (Disting. Service award 1982). Roman Catholic. Office: 100 West B St Casper WY 82601

WOJDA, RAYMOND GEORGE, college public information director; b. Alpena, Mich., Jan. 6, 1946; s. Raymond John and Ruth Nelly (Dinsmore) W.; m. Grace Lois Davenport, Mar. 25, 1967; children—Winston, James. B.A., U. Mich., 1972. Loan officer U.S. Nat. Bank of Oreg., Klamath Falls, 1972-74; assoc. editor Garden State Pub. Co., Sea Isle, N.J., 1975; pub. info. dir. Treasure Valley Community Coll., Ontario, Oreg., 1976—; coll. liaison Oreg. Com. Humanities; mem. publs. com. Oreg. Community Coll. Assn., 1980-81. Youth leader Quaker Ch., 1976; publicity chmn. Am. Cancer Soc., 1976. Served with USN, 1966-69. Mem. Nat. Council for Community Relations, Assn. Edn. in Journalism and Mass Communication, Ontario C. of C. Democrat. Quaker.

WOJNICH, ELEANOR MAE BENSON (MRS. WILLIAM WOJNICH), photojournalist, gerontologist; b. Louisville, July 7, 1917; d. Andy T. and Jennie Mae (Venable) Benson; A.B., Allegheny Coll., 1939; postgrad. Boston U., 1947; M.Ed., U. Ark., 1967; m. William Wojnich, June 20, 1946. Social worker Pitts. Assn. for Improvement of Poor, 1940-43; counselor Fla. Employment Service, Miami, 1950-54; asst. dir. Mpls. council Camp Fire Girls, 1954-57; case worker Minn. Div. Child Welfare, St. Paul, 1957-60, University Mound Sch., San Francisco, 1961-63; social worker Ark. Rehab. Services, Little Rock, 1966-67; counselor Minn. Div. Vocat. Rehab., St. Paul, 1967-69; counselor, tchr. Berryville (Ark.) High Sch., 1970-73; photojournalist Elliam Photography, Index, Wash., 1974—; coordinator social services The Source, Seattle, 1974-76; community outreach developer Sr. Services of Snohomish County, Everett, Wash., 1976-83. Served as 1st lt. WAC, 1943-46. Mem. Western Gerontol. Soc., Photog. Soc. Am., AAUW, Am. Personnel and Guidance Assn. Home: PO Box 166 Index WA 98256 Office: Elliam Photography Index WA 98256

WOLCHOK, ROBERT LLOYD, civil engineer; b. N.Y.C., Oct. 18, 1954; s. Sidney S. and Silkaly M. (Moskowitz) W. B.S. in Civil Engring. magna cum laude, Tufts U., 1977; M.S. in Civil/Water Resources Engring., Stanford U., 1978. Registered profl. engr., Calif. Assoc. civil engr. Boyle Engring. Corp., Newport Beach, Calif., 1978-82; civil/water resources engr. Kennedy/Jenks Engrs., Irvine, Calif., 1982—; cons. civil engr. Vol. operating room U. Calif.-Irvine Med. Center, 1982. Mem. ASCE (William P. Morse scholar Boston sect. 1977), Am. Water Works Assn., Orange County Water Assn., Calif. Water Pollution Control Assn., Tau Beta Pi. Home: 21661 Brookhurst St Apt 271 Huntington Beach CA 92646 Office: 2041 Business Center Dr Suite 207 Irvine CA 92715

WOLD, ROBERT MILES, optometrist; b. Devils Lake, N.D., Dec. 5, 1942; s. Anton Miles and Florence (Strommen) W.; m. Margery Ann Wilson, July 23, 1944; children—Peter Anthony, Dawn Marie. A.A., Devils Lake Jr. Coll., 1961; B.S., Pacific U., 1963, O.D., 1964, M.S., 1966. Pvt. practice optometry, Los Altos, Calif., 1965-69, Chula Vista, Calif., 1969—; lectr., cons. profl. assns., sch. dists. Diplomate Nat. Bd. Optometry. Fellow Am. Acad. Optometry, Coll. Optometrists in Vision Devel., Internat. Coll. Applied Nutrition; mem. Santa Clara County Optometric Soc. (past dir. depts. group vision, profl. affairs, past chmn. forum on vision and reading), San Diego County Optometric Soc. (pres. 1975, 80; Optometrist of Yr.), Calif. Optometric Assn. (jud. council 1981—, mem. edn. services com. 1983—; Young Optometrist of Yr. 1970), Nat. Soc. Vision and Perception Tng. (past v.p.), Coll. Optometrists in Vision Devel. (nat. sec. 1971—, chmn. peer rev. com. 1972-73; A.M. Skeffington award 1974), Am. Optometric Assn. (del. 1975, 76, 78, 79, 81, 82, 83), Am. Optometric Found. (dir. 1981—). Editor: Visual and Perceptual Aspects for the Achieving and Underachieving Child, 1969; Screening Tests to be Used by the Classroom Teacher, 1970; co-editor: In-Office Vision Therapy Manual, 1971. Contbr. numerous articles to profl. jours. Home: 627 Mission Ct Chula Vista CA 92010 Office: 353 H St Suite C Chula Vista 92010

WOLDE-TSADIK, GIRMA, educator, statistical consultant; b. Addis Ababa, Ethiopia, Dec. 15, 1940; came to U.S., 1969; s. Wolde-Kidan and Mahider (Bizuneh) W.; m. Mary Christine Hansen, Oct. 25, 1966; m. 2d, Aster Teshome, Oct. 4, 1980; children—Tsion, Tseday, Seshah. B.S., H.S.I. U., Ethiopia, 1963, M.S., 1966; Ph.D., UCLA, 1973. Lectr. H.S.I. U., 1963-64, 66-67; head statis. sect. Ministry of Health, Ethiopia, 1967-69; asst. prof. C.R. Drew Med. Sch., Los Angeles, 1973-79, assoc. prof. internal medicine, 1979—; dir. biostats. and data processing UCLA, 1973-79; stats. cons. numerous agys. WHO fellow. 1968; AID scholar, 1964-66. Mem. Biometric Soc., Am. Statis. Assn., Am. Pub. Health Assn. Author numerus publs. in field. Home: 126 Wavecrest Ave Venice CA 90291 Office: Drew Medical School 1621 E 129th St Los Angeles CA 90059

WOLF, ARON S., psychiatrist; b. Newark, Aug. 25, 1937; B.A., Dartmouth Coll., 1959; M.D., U. Md., 1963; married; children—Jon, Lisa, Laurie. Intern, U. Md. Hosp., Balt., 1963-64; resident in psychiatry Psychiat. Inst., U. Md. Hosp., Balt., 1964-67, chief resident, 1966-67; practice medicine specializing in psychiatry, Anchorage, 1967—; dir. Springfield Hosp. Alcoholic Clinic, Balt., 1966-67; psychiat. cons. Levindale Hebrew Home and Infirmary, Balt., 1966-67, McLaughlin Yough Center, Anchorage, 1969-72; mem. staff Providence Hosp., chief psychiatry sect., 1977-81; mem. staff Humana Hosp., Alaska, Kodiak Island Hosp., Palmer Valley Hosp., Valdez Community Hosp., Bethel Community Hosp., Cordova Alaska Hosp.; staff psychiatrist Langdon Psychiat. Clinic, 1970-71; partner Langdon Clinic, Anchorage, 1971—, clinic pres., 1981; med. dir. Cordova Community Mental Health Center, 1976-80; cons. Alaska Native Med. Center, 1975-77, Woman's Resource Center, Anchorage, 1977-81; instr. dept. psychology U. Alaska, Anchorage, 1968-75; asso. prof. psychiatry U. Alaska, Fairbanks, 1974—; asso. prof. U. Wash., 1974—; participant weekly mental health TV talk show, Anchorage, 1970—; guest lectr. to various profl. and civic groups, 1967—. Vice pres. Greater Anchorage Area Borough Sch. Bd., 1971-72, pres., 1973-74; pres. Chugach Optional Sch. Parent Adv. Bd., 1976-77; mem. med. adv. com. Alaska Kidney Found., 1977-82; mem. Alaska Gov.'s Mental Health Adv. Bd., 1976—, chmn., 1983; mem. Gov.'s Task Force on Criminally Committed Patients, 1980—; bd. dirs. Greater Anchorage Drug Mgmt. Group, 1972-73. Served with M.C., USAF, 1967-70. Recipient Wendell-Muncie award Md. Med. Soc., 1967; diplomate Am. Bd. Psychiatry and Neurology, Am. Bd. Forensic Psychiatry. Fellow Am. Psychiat. Assn. (pres. Alaska dist. br. 1975, del. assembly 1975-81, area III vice-chmn. assembly procedures com. 1981—, chmn. 1982—; nat. planning com. 1981, nat. membership com. 1981—); mem. Am. Acad. Psychiatry and Law, Am. Soc. Law and Medicine, Soc. Air Force Psychiatrists, ACLU, AMA (chmn. mental health com. 1971-75, medicine and law com. 1980-81), Alaska Med. Assn., N.Y. Acad. Scis. Contbr. articles on psychiatry to profl. jours. Home: 8133 Sundi Dr Anchorage AK 99502 Office: 4001 Dale St Anchorage AK 99504

WOLF, ARTHUR HENRY, museum director; b. New Rockford, N.D., June 18, 1953; s. Louis Irvin and Vivian Joyce (Grinde) W. B.A., U. Nebr., 1975; M.A., U. Ariz., 1977. Lab. asst. U. Nebr. State Mus., Lincoln, 1973-75; research asst. Ariz. State U., Tucson, 1975-77; curator of collections Sch. Am. Research, Santa Fe, 1977-79; dir. Millicent Rogers Mus., Taos, N.Mex., 1979—. Mem. Internat. Council Mus., Am. Assn. Mus., Mountain-Plains Mus. Assn., N.Mex. Assn. Mus. (pres. 1981-83), Council Mus. Anthropology. Democrat. Contbr. articles to profl. jours. Office: Millicent Rogers Mus PO Box A Taos NM 87571

WOLF, CHARLES, JR., economist, educator; b. N.Y.C., Aug. 1, 1924; s. Charles and Rosalie (Zeemans) W.; m. Theresa Van de Wint, Mar. 1, 1947; children—Charles Theodore, Timothy van de Wint. B.S., Harvard U., 1943, M.P.A., 1948, Ph.D. in Econs., 1949. Economist, fgn. service officer Dept. of State, 1945-47, 49-53; mem. faculty Cornell U., 1953-54, U. Calif.-Berkeley, 1954-55; sr. economist Rand Corp., Santa Monica, Calif., 1956-67, head econs. dept., 1967-8; dean Rand Grad. Inst., Santa Monica, 1970—, dir. internat. econ. policy program, 1981—; co-chmn., mem. exec. com. Calif. Seminar on Internat. Security and Fgn. Policy; lectr. econs. UCLA, 1960-72. Bd. visitors Inst. Pub. Policy Scis. and Pub. Affairs, Duke U; Mayor's Adv. Com. Rapid Transit, Los Angeles, 1973-74. Served with AUS, 1943-45. Mem. Am. Econ. Assn., Econometric Soc., Inst. Strategic Studies London, Council Fgn. Relations, Assn. Pub. Policy Analysis and Mgmt. (pres. policy council 1980-81), Phi Beta Kappa. Clubs: Riviera Tennis (Los Angeles); Cosmos (Washington). Author: Foreign Aid: Theory and Practice in Southern Asia, 1960; United States Policy and the Third World: Problems and Analysis, 1967; Rebellion and Authority: An Analytical Essay on Insurgent Conflicts, 1970; editorial bd. Internat. Security, 1976—, Jour. Policy Analysis and Mgmt., 1981—; contbr. articles to profl. jours. Office: 1700 Main St Santa Monica CA 90406

WOLF, DIANA PEARL, educational administrator; b. Denver, Dec. 23, 1942; d. Melbourne Courtland and Pearl Catherine (VanWestenberg) Reeves; m. Jerry R. Wolf, Oct. 1, 1960; children—Thomas Courtland, Kimberly Michelle. B.S., U. Colo., 1974, M.A., 1982. Cert. type A tchr., type D Adminstrv., Colo. Tchr. Jefferson County (Colo.) Pub. Schs., 1974-77; adminstrv. supr. social studies programs dist. elem. schs., 1977—; bd. dirs. Jefferson County Adminstrs. Assn., 1981—; coordinator Rocky Mountain Regional Social Studies conf., 1983; creator curriculum guides social studies for elem. grades Jefferson County Pub. Schs. Recipient Acad. Excellence award U. Colo., 1972; Japan Inst. Social and Econ. Affairs fellow, 1983. Mem. Nat. Council Social Studies, Social Studies Suprs. Assn., Colo. Council Social Studies (bd. dirs. 1981, 82, v.p. 1983, pres. 1984), Assn. Supervision and Curriculum Devel., Delta Kappa Gamma, Kappa Delta Pi, Beta Sigma Phi (past pres.), Beta Omega (chpt. adviser). Office: 1209 Quail St Lakewood CO 80215

WOLF, FRANK L(EWELLYN), accountant; b. N.Y.C., Mar. 15, 1928; s. Morris and Pearl (Falk) W.; m. Judy Efron, Aug. 23, 1953; children—Arthur, Madeline, Phyllis. B.B.A., U. Mich., 1949, M.B.A., 1950. C.P.A., N.Y., Calif. Ptnr. Ernst & Whinney (formerly S.D. Leidesdorf & Co.,), N.Y.C., 1950-74, Los Angeles, 1975—; vis. lectr. UCLA Grad. Sch. Mgmt. Bd. dirs. Block & Hexter Vacation Ctr. for Aged, N.Y.C., 1970-75; mem. adv. bd. Concern Found., Los Angeles, 1982—. Served to sgt. U.S. Army, 1950-52. Mem. Am. Inst. C.P.A.s., Calif. Soc. C.P.A.s. Jewish. Home: 2336 Banyan Dr Los Angeles CA 90049 Office: 1875 Century Park E Suite 2200 Los Angeles CA 90067

WOLF, FREDERICK EARL, educational administrator; b. St. Louis, Sept. 28, 1936; s. Frederick Beardsley and Elizabeth Ann (Combs) W.; student U. Nancy (France), 1958, U. Addis Ababa (Ethiopia), 1959-60; B.A., Pomona Coll., 1962, M.A., Calif. State Coll., Los Angeles, 1967; postgrad. Calif. Luth. Coll., 1967-70, Calif. Poly. State U., San Luis Obispo, 1971-76; m. Kristen St. Johns, Apr. 4, 1964; children—Jessica Lynn, Frederick Bogart, Robin Ann Kirk, Hilary Noel. Letter of credit writer French-Am. Bank, 1962; theatre technician Claremont Colls., Calif. State U., Los Angeles, 1964-67; drama instr., activities coordinator Calif. Luth. Coll., Thousand Oaks, 1967-70; coordinator spl. services and publs. Calif. Poly. State U., San Luis Obispo, 1971-82, dir. ann. giving, 1982-83. Mem. Arroyo Grande Lands Commn., 1976; leader 4-H, 1977—; mem. Harvest Festival Com., Calif. Measurement Sci. Adv. Bd.; vestryman St. Barnabas Episcopal Ch.; lic. lay reader, chalice bearer Episc. Diocese of El Camino Real. Served with U.S. Army, 1958-61. Mem. Audio Engring. Soc., Am. Theatre Assn., U.S. Inst. Theatre Tech., Calif. State Employees Assn. (past chpt. pres.). Democrat. Editor Cal Poly Report/Dateline, 1973-82. Home: 540 Gaynfair Terr Arroyo Grande CA 93420

WOLF, GERRIT, psychologist, educator; b. Evanston, Ill., Oct. 9, 1941; s. Carl Edwin and Helen (Sprietsma) W.; m. Suzanne Oko; children—Gabrielle, Christopher. B.A. Hope Coll., 1963; Ph.D., Cornell U., 1967. Asst. prof. adminstrv. scis. and psychology Yale U., later asso. prof.; prof. orgnl. behavior Ga. Sch. Tech., 1976-81; prof. orgnl. behavior U. Ariz, Tucson, 1981—, head mgmt. dept., 1981—. NSF grantee, 1969-72, 81-83. Mem. Am. Psychol. Assn., Acad. Mgmt., Am. Inst. Decision Scis. Contbr. articles to profl. jours. Home: 6114 E San Cristobal Tucson AZ 85715 Office: Management Dept U Ariz Tucson AZ 85721

WOLF, HELEN(E) COLLINS, govt. import specialist; b. Uniontown, Ala., Mar. 4, 1934; d. Willie and Katie Collins; A.A., Peters Coll., 1956; student San Diego Coll., 1976-78, Western State U., 1979—; m. Joseph Wolf; 1 son, Joseph III. Sec., IRS, Chgo., 1955-56, U.S. Army Fin. Center, Chgo., 1956-58, U.S. Marine Corps, San Diego, 1958-64, U.S. Navy Bur Yards and Docks, San Diego, 1964; with U.S. Customs Service, San Diego, 1964—, tng. officer, 1974-78, fed. women's program mgr., 1974-78, import specialist, 1970—. Vice pres. local PTA, 1975-78; vice chmn. fed. women's program div. San Diego County Equal Opportunity Council, 1977-78; mem. 4th dist. adv. com. 1978—; mem. community edn. com. Urban League, 1979-80; pres. adv. council Colina del Sol Recreation Center, 1980—; mem. San Diego Mayor's Adv. Com. on Women, 1980; mem. Children's Home Soc., 1980—; mem. central adv. bd. Salvation Army, 1981—; mem. adv. council on sr. citizen affairs to Congressman D. Hunter, 1982—. Recipient Service award Boy Scouts Am., 1971; Commendation letter U.S. Custom's Fed. Women's Program Mgr., 1977; Appreciation letter Southwestern Coll., 1978; Outstanding Performance award Equal Opportunity Com., 1979; Equal Opportunity award U.S. Customs, 1979; Appreciation cert. San Diego Unified Sch. Dist., 1980; recognition awards third Coll., U. Calif.-San Diego, 1980, 82. Mem. Presidents Council Women's Services, Bus. and Profl. Women (legis. chmn. San Diego 1979), UN Assn. (edn. com. 1982), Pacific S.W. Univ. Women's Studies Assn., Am. Mgmt. Assn., Career Devel. Assn., Nat. Council Negro Women (pres. San Diego sect. 1979-80, Woman of Yr. award 1979, Woman in Community Service, nat. bd. dirs.), Career Devel. Assn., Govt. Coll. Assn., LWV. Republican. Roman Catholic. Clubs: Lawyers of San Diego, Soroptimist Internat.

WOLF, JOAN SILVERMAN, psychologist, educator; b. Boston, Aug. 28, 1936; d. Isaac and Rose (Berman) Silverman; m. Harold H. Wolf, Aug. 11, 1957; children—Gary, David. B. Jewish Edn. with distinction, Hebrew Coll., 1957; B.S. cum laude, U. Utah, 1960; M.A., Ohio State U., 1971, Ph.D., 1976. Cert. sch. psychologist, Utah. Grad. research assoc. Ohio State U., Columbus, 1974-76; asst. prof. dept. spl. edn. U.

Utah, Salt Lake City, 1977—; cons. in field. U. Utah research com. grantee, 1982. Mem. Am. Psychol. Assn., Council Exceptional Children, Nat. Assn. for Gifted, Nat. Assn. Sch. Psychologists, Phi Delta Kappa. Contbr. numerous articles to profl. jours. Office: 214 MBH U Utah Salt Lake City UT 84112

WOLF, JUDITH CLARE, school administrator, teacher educator; b. Dothan, Ala., Mar. 6, 1945; d. Alfred and Miriam Jean (Office) Wolf. B.A., UCLA, 1966; M.S. in Sch. Adminstrn., Pepperdine U., 1977. Elem tchr. credential (life); adminstrv. K-12 credential (life), Calif. Tchr., elem. schs., Los Angeles Unified Sch. Dist., 1967-76; acad. tchr. adviser Area F & 5 1976-78, Emergency Sch. Aid Act magnet sch. adviser, 1979-80, asst. prin. Arlington Heights Elem. Sch., Los Angeles, 1980—; tchr. in-service classes, 1973-78; supr. K-3 and student tchrs. K-12 Magnin Sch. Religious Edn., 1974—; instr. continuing edn. Calif. State U.-Los Angeles, 1978—; mem. supt. field mgmt. adv. com. Sec. Vill D'Rosa Homeowners Assn.; active ARC, Wilshire Blvd. Temple and Camp Commn. Area H mini-grant student enrichment class grantee Los Angeles Unified Sch. Dist., 1973; PTA Life Membership award, 1975. Mem. Elem. Assn. Prins. Orgn. (pres.), Calif. Assn. for Gifted, EDUCARE (U. So. Calif.), UCLA Alumni Assn., PTA, Calif. Math. Council, Assoc. Adminstrs. Los Angeles, Assn. Calif. Sch. Adminstrs., Phi Delta Kappa. Club: East Valley Bruins. Author: fed. proposals to fund Dist. Magnet schs. and programs; contbr. articles in field to profl. jours. Office: 1717 Seventh Ave Los Angeles CA 90019

WOLF, MONICA THERESIA, procedures analyst; b. Germany, Apr. 26, 1943; came to U.S., 1953, naturalized, 1959; d. Otto and Hildegard Maria (Heim) Bellemann; m. Henry Wolf (div.); children—Clinton, Danielle. Student U. Albuquerque, 1981. Developer Word Processing Ctr., Pub. Service of N.Mex., Albuquerque, 1971-74, word processing supr., 1974-78, budget coordinator, 1978-80, lead procedures analyst, 1980—; mem. adv. bd., student trainer APS Career Enrichment Ctr. Instr. firearm safety and pistol marksmanship. Mem. Internat. Word Processing Assn. (founder N.Mex. chpt.), Nat. Assn. Female Execs., Nat. Rifle Assn., N.Mex. Shooting Sports Assn. Republican. Club. Sandia Gun (adv. bd., coach). Home: 912 Washington Ave NE Albuquerque NM 87110 Office: 414 Silver Ave SW Albuquerque NM 87103

WOLF, ROSE BARRY, bus. and tax cons.; b. Colchester, Conn., Apr. 27, 1921; d. Samuel S. and Lena S. (Hoffman) Barry; grad. Pace Coll., 1946; student Post Coll. Tax Inst., 1968-73; m. Lester Wolf, Sept. 28, 1946; children—Beverly Wolf Tillett, Perry. Office mgr. Hy & D Agar Realty, 1946; acct. B. Passilia, C.P.A., N.Y.C., 1948-66; sr. tax acct. Columbia Pictures Industries, Inc., N.Y.C., 1968-73; controller Alexander & Friends, Los Angeles, 1974-76; bus. and tax cons. Pennrose Assocs., Tarzana, Calif., 1976—; treas. Travel Group, Inc., Anaheim, Calif., Midway Energy, Inc., Los Angeles; pres. Group Services Internat. Inc. Mem. Am. Bus. Women's Assn. (treas. 1977-78), Canoga Park C. of C. (mem. polit. action com. 1975-76), Nat. Soc. Public Accountants, Assn. Enrolled Agts., Am. Soc. Women Accountants (corr. sec. chpt., bull. chmn. and editor 1980-81), Tarzana C. of C. Columnist, Weekend mag., 1978—. Office: 13615 Victory Blvd #205 Van Nuys CA 91401

WOLF, STEVEN ROBERT, educational administrator; b. Seattle, Jan. 1, 1942; s. Floyd and Georgia (Hayden) Woodbury; m. Elizabeth Ann Pilling Isley, Sept. 21, 1964 (div.); 1 dau., Laura. B.A., U. Wash., 1966, M.Ed., 1973; Ph.D., U. Tex., 1979. Resource tchr. Juneau (Alaska) Bur. Sch. Dist., 1973-75; cons. Round Rock (Tex.) Sch. Dist., 1978-79; research asst. U. Tex. Research and Devel. Ctr., 1978-79; dir. Alaska Spl. Edn. Inservice Tng. Ctr., Soldotna, 1979—. Pres. bd. Women's Resource and Crisis Ctr., Soldotna, 1982-83, bd. mem., 1979—; mem. central com. Alaska Democratic party. U. Wash. Dept. Edn. fellow, 1972-73; U. Tex.-Austin fellow, 1975-79; U.S. Dept. Edn. grantee, 1979—. Mem. Council Exceptional Children, Council Learning Disabilities, Internat. Reading Assn., Assn. Severely Handicapped, Assn. Supervision and Curriculum Devel. Democrat. Jewish. Home: Box 1123 Soldotna AK 99669 Office: Box 1200 Soldotna AK 99669

WOLFE, CURTIS LEE, mgmt. cons. co. exec.; b. Plainwell, Mich., Apr. 29, 1942; s. Gordon Lee and Velma Paulene (Hunt) W.; B.S., U.S. Air Force Acad., 1965; postgrad. Loyola U. Sch. Law, Los Angeles, 1967-69; m. Sharon Jeanne Gafford, June 9, 1965; children—Lisa Marie, Jeffrey Allan. Mgr. mgmt. services Arthur Young & Co., Los Angeles, 1969-74; prin. Wolfe & Assos., Anchorage, 1974-77; pres. Wolfe & Assos., mgmt. cons., Albuquerque, 1977—; speaker in field. Served with USAF, 1960-69. Mem. Inst. Mgmt. Cons. (cert. mgmt. cons.), Data Processing Mgmt. Assn. (cert. data processing). Home: 7500 American Heritage St NE Albuquerque NM 87109 Office: 5345 Wyoming St NE Suite 203 Albuquerque NM 87109

WOLFE, DAVID ARTHUR, SR., safety administrator; b. Ewen, Mich., Aug. 12, 1944; s. Oscar Anthony and Ida Margaret (Malnar) W.; m. JoAnne Elaine Ridgdill, Nov. 21, 1964; children—David Arthur, Michelle, Melissa. Student Nat. Sch. Constrn., 1962, MSHA Acads., 1975-77. Miner/former White Pine Copper Co., Mich., 1965-75; mine insp. MSHA, Geneva, N.Y., 1975-77; safety engr. Harrison Western Corp., Mt. Taylor, 1977-80; dir. safety and plant protection Gulf Mineral Resources Co., Mt. Taylor and Marino Lake, N.Mex., 1980-83; cons. to fire chief McMillian Twp., 1972-75; trustee McMillian Twp., 1974-75. Mem. Am. Soc. Safety Engrs., Uranium Operators Safety Council, Mine Rescue Team. Home: 3605 Zia Dr Gallup NM 87301

WOLFE, EDWARD CLARE, ret. investment co. account exec.; b. Horton, Kans., Feb. 16, 1922; s. Roland John and Mary Clella (Braley) W.; student pub. schs., Lincoln, Nebr.; m. Julia Teran, Apr. 12, 1965. Tool and die maker, designer Boeing Co., Wichita, Kans. and Seattle, 1947-52, Torrington Mfg. Co., Van Nuys, Calif., 1952-60; registered rep. Dempsey-Tegeler & Co., Glendale, Calif., 1960-70, Mitchum Jones & Templeton, Pasadena, Calif., 1970-71, Wagenseller & Durst, Pasadena, Calif., 1971-72; registered rep. Schumacher & Assos., Glendale, Calif., 1975—; account exec., Universal Stock Transfer, Woodland Hills, Calif., 1976-78; loan officer Sutro Mortgage, Inc., Los Angeles, 1978-79. Served with USNR, 1944-46. Republican. Home: 21315 Kingsbury St Chatsworth CA 91311

WOLFE, JOHN HENRY, space scientist; b. Lakewood, Ohio, July 13, 1933; s. Francis J. and Lucy (Nord) W.; B.A., Ohio Wesleyan U., 1955; Ph.D. in Physics, U. Ill., 1960; children by previous marriage—James N., Janet M., Nancy W. Mem. staff extraterrestrial research div. Ames Research Center, NASA, Moffett Field, Calif., 1960—, asst. chief electrodynamics br. space sci. div., 1965-71, chief space physics br., 1971-76, investigator Pioneer Venus orbiter mission, 1978; dep. chief Extraterrestrial Intelligence program team, 1976-80, program scientist extraterrestrial research div., 1980—; project scientist for pioneer interplanetary and Jupiter/Saturn flyby missions, 1963-80. Recipient Exceptional Sci. Achievement medal NASA, 1971; Space Sci. award AIAA, 1974. Mem. Am. Astron. Soc. Contbr. articles on interplanetary physics to sci. jours. Home: 457 Oliver St Milpitas CA 95035 Office: NASA Ames Research Center Moffett Field CA 94035

WOLFE, LAWRENCE IRVING, physician; b. Duluth, Minn., Mar. 31, 1924; s. Joseph and Edith (Kremen) W.; B.S., U. Minn., 1944, M.B., 1946, M.D., 1947; m. Charlotte Ione Avrick, Dec. 16, 1945; children—Jonathan, Douglas, Lori Allison. Intern, Ancker Hosp., St. Paul, 1947; postgrad. U. Minn. Hosp., Mpls., 1947-48; resident So. Pacific Gen. Hosp., San Francisco, 1948-50, Permanente Hosp., Oakland, Calif., 1950-51; pvt. practice specializing in internal medicine, San Carlos, Calif., 1951—; mem. staff Sequoia, San Mateo County Gen., Stanford-Palo Alto, Belmont Hills hosps.; faculty dept. medicine Stanford U., 1958—, now clin. asso. prof. Served with USNR, 1943-45, 1953-55. Diplomate Am. Bd. Internal Medicine, Pan Am. Med. Assn. Mem. Am., Calif. med. assns., San Mateo County Med. Soc., Am. Geriatrics Soc., Royal Soc. Medicine, A.C.P., Am., Calif. socs. internal medicine, Am. Heart Assn. Clubs: Stanford Faculty, Menlo Circus. Home: 180 Elena Ave Atherton CA 94025 Office: 1100 Laurel St San Carlos CA 94070

WOLFE, MAURICE G., manufacturing company executive; b. Chgo., May 11, 1931; s. Wolf and Rita (Rosenberg) Ghitzis; B.A., U. So. Calif., 1958; A.A., Los Angeles City Coll., 1955; m. Marilyn Frank, Jan. 11, 1978; 1 son, Mark D.; 1 stepdau., Heather Byer. Asst. sales mgr. Am. handicrafts Tandy Corp., Los Angeles, 1958; v.p. Vivitar Corp., Santa Monica, Calif., 1959-70; pres. Personapac Co., Los Angeles, 1970-71; mgmt. cons. Technicolor Corp., Pacific Coast Farms, 20th Century Plastics, Photo Plastics, Wein Corp., Los Angeles, 1971-75; pres. Great Am. Corp., Laguna Hills, Calif. 1975—. Served with U.S. Army, 1951-53. Mem. Printing Industry Am., Nat. Assn. Printers and Lithographers, Soc. Motion Picture and TV Engrs. Home: 779 Balboa Ave Laguna Beach CA 92651 Office: 23015 Del Lago Dr Laguna Hills CA 92653

WOLFE, SEBASTIAN ANDREW, architect; b. Chgo., Aug. 14, 1930; s. Sebastian Frank and Theresa Helen (DuMelle) W.; m. Sandra Ann Wells, Aug. 25, 1956; children—Cynthia Lynn, Sharron Leigh. Student, Inst. Design, Chgo., 1950-51, Ill. Inst. Tech., 1952-53. Lic. architect, Ill., Ariz., Tex., Calif., Colo.; cert. fallout shelter analyst. Apprentice and architect-in-tng. Shaw Metz & Dolio, Chgo., 1948-53, job capt., 1954-56; job capt. Herbert Sobel, AIA, Chgo., 1956-57; project architect Shaw Metz & Dolio, 1958-67; project mgr. Metz Train Olson Youngren, Chgo., 1967-73; project mgr. health facilities div. Caudill, Rowlett, Scott, Houston, 1969-73, assoc., 1970; v.p., architect-of-record MTOY & Sholder, Phoenix, 1973-75, also dir.; v.p., architect-of-record MTOY Of Ariz., 1975-79, pres., 1977, also dir.; prin., dir. Metz Train Youngren of Ariz., Inc., Phoenix, 1980—; assoc. prof. Coll. Architecture, Ariz. State U., 1981-82. Regatta dir. CYO, Chgo., 1951; fund raiser Community Chest, Chgo., 1968, United Way Camp, Phoenix, 1979-80; bd. dirs. Phoenix Dept. Parks and Recreation, 1980—, Valley Forward Assn., 1980—, chmn. environ. quality com., 1981-82; bd. dirs. Camelback Mental Health Found., Phoenix, 1982—. Recipient Merit award Western Mountain region AIA, 1981; Community Service award Mayor's Com. on Employment of Handicapped, 1981; Design award Desert Samaritan Hosp. and Health Ctr., Tex. Soc. Architects, 1973. Mem. Ariz. Soc. Architects, Ariz. Assn. Indsl. Devel., AIA, Constrn. Specifications Inst., Am. Correctional Assn. Republican. Mem. Christian Ch. Prin. works include: Desert Samaritan Hosp. and Med. Ctr., Mesa, Ariz., Elizabeth Arden Bldg., Chgo., Karsten Mfg. Corp., Phoenix, Oakbrook (Ill.) Exec. Towers, Mt. Sinai Med. Ctr., Milw., Phoenix Mt. Nursing Ctr., 3950 Marine Dr. Apts., Chgo., Mile Sq. Health Ctr., Chgo., Phoenix Day Sch. for Deaf, Zenith Radio Corp., Plant #6, Chgo. Office: 2721 N Central Ave Suite 1102 Phoenix AZ 85004

WOLFE, STEPHEN DOUGLAS, rancher; b. Enterprise, Oreg., July 23, 1947; s. Bill E. and Fern (Stein) W.; student Eastern Oreg. Coll., Okla. State U., 1966-68; B.S., Oreg. State U., 1970; m. Laidee Ann Bissinger, Sept. 13, 1969; children—Deve Ann, Carlynn, Woody. Partner, mgr. Wolfe Hereford Ranch, Wallowa, Oreg., 1970—; v.p. Bill Wolfe Ranches, Inc., Wallowa, 1970—; involved in registered polled Hereford sales mgmt. Committeeman Wallowa County Agrl. Stabilization and Conservation Service; mem. adv. council Wallowa County Extension Service. Served with Oreg. N.G., 1968-74. Mem. Wallowa County Jaycees, Wallowa County Stockgrowers, Oreg. Cattlemen's Assn. (chmn. beef improvement com.), Nat. Cattlemen's Assn., Wallowa County C. of C. (bd. dirs.), Oreg. Wheat League. Clubs: Elks, Masons, Lions. Address: Route 1 Box 135A Wallowa OR 97885

WOLFINGER, RAYMOND EDWIN, political science educator; b. San Francisco, June 29, 1931; s. Raymond Edwin and Hilda (Holm) W.; m. Barbara Kaye, Aug. 8, 1960; 1 son, Nicholas Holm. A.B., U. Calif.-Berkeley, 1951; M.A., U. Ill., 1955; Ph.D., Yale U., 1961. From vis. asst. prof. to prof. Stanford U., 1961-71; prof. dept. polit. sci. U. Calif.-Berkeley, 1971—, dir. State Data Program, 1980—; chmn. bd. overseers Nat. Election Studies, Ctr. Polit. Studies, U. Mich., 1982—. Served to 1st lt. U.S. Army, 1951-53. Ctr. Advanced Study Behavioral Scis. fellow, 1960-61; Guggenheim fellow, 1965; Ford Found. Faculty Research fellow, 1970-71. Fellow Am. Acad. Arts and Scis.; mem. Am. Polit. Sci. Assn. (sec. 1981-82), Western Polit. Sci. Assn. (exec. council), Midwest Polit. Sci. Assn., AAUP (pres. Calif. conf. 1976-77, mem. council 1981-84). Democrat. Author: The Politics of Progress, 1974; co-author: Who Votes?, 1980; Dynamics of American Politics, 1976; editor: Readings in American Political Behavior, 1966; Readings on Congress, 1971; contbr. articles to profl. jours. and newspapers. Office Dept Polit Sci U Calif Berkeley CA 94720

WOLFORD, RICHARD HOWARD, lawyer; b. Chgo., Aug. 12, 1922; s. Darwin H. and Lila (Ferguson) W.; LL.B., Harvard U., 1948; m. Helen Moore, Feb. 13, 1943; children—Richard George, Felicia Jane, Peter Arlington. Admitted to Calif. bar, 1949; law clk. U.S. Ct. of Appeals for 9th Circuit, San Francisco, 1948-49; pres. Los Angeles Jr. Bar Assn., 1957-58; mem. Calif. Law Revision Commn., Los Angeles, 1968-70; sr. partner Gibson, Dunn & Crutcher, Los Angeles, 1963-80, of counsel, 1981—; adj. prof. law (antitrust) U. Hawaii Law Sch., 1983. Mem. Los Angeles County Bar Assn. (trustee 1957-58), Am. Bar Assn., Internat. Bar Assn., Am. Judicature Soc. Clubs: Los Angeles Country, California. Home: 751 E Pulehuiki Rd Kula Maui HI 96790

WOLFORD, WILLIAM GRANE, banker; b. Ashland, Oreg., Apr. 15, 1926; s. Benjamin Edward and Anna Dorthia (Grane) W.; m. Adele J. Schmidt, Sept. 6, 1975; children by previous marriage—Douglas, Bruce, Monica. A.A., So. Oreg. Coll. 1948; B.S. Oreg. State U., 1950. Credit reporter Dun & Bradstreet, Inc., Portland, Oreg., 1950-51; bank examiner Fed. Deposit Ins. Corp., Seattle, 1952-58; v.p. Security State Bank, Ephrata, Wash., 1958-68; pres., chmn. bd. Security Bank Wash., Ephrata, 1968—. Bd. dirs. Wash. State Water Resources, 1973, Wash. State Energy Council, 1974; commr. Wash. State Dept. Ecology, 1975-77. Served with USN, 1944-46; PTO. Mem. Community Banks Wash. (pres. 1976), Wash. Bankers Assn. (pres. 1977-78), Am. Bankers Assn. (governing council 1979-80, govt. relations council 1981—), Columbia Basin Devel. League (pres. 1972-73, hon. life mem.), Western Ind. Bankers (exec. council, legis. chmn. 1981—), Ephrata C. of C., Am. Legion. Republican. Lutheran. Club: Elks. Office: PO Box 1177 Ephrata WA 98823

WOLFSON, MURRAY, economics educator; b. N.Y.C., Sept. 14, 1927; s. William and Bertha (Finkelstein) W.; m. Betty Ann Goessel, July 22, 1950; children—Paul G., Susan D., Deborah R. B.S. cum laude, CCNY, 1948; M.S., U. Wis., 1951, Ph.D., 1964; postgrad. Marquette U., 1959. Tchr. math. Montrose (Mich.) High Sch., 1959-61; faculty Thornton Jr. Coll., Harvey, Ill., 1961-63; faculty Oreg. State U., Corvallis, 1963—, prof. econs., 1971—; vis. prof. Ahmadu Bello U., Nigeria, 1969-70, U. Canterbury (N.Z.), 1970, U. Durham (U.K.), 1971-72; Fulbright sr. lectr. Japan, 1976-77, U. Wis.-Milw., 1969, U. Wis., Madison, 1969, U. So. Calif., 1980-81; Intercountry lectr., Korea, 1970. Active, Beit Am Jewish Community Ctr. Served with USN, 1945-46. N.Y. State Regents scholar, 1943; recipient first prize for excellence in coll. teaching of econs. Joint Council Econ. Edn., 1970. Mem. Am. Econ. Assn., Western Econ. Assn., Peace Sci. Assn., AAUP, History of Econs. Soc. Author: A Reappraisal of Marxian Economics, 1966; Karl Marx, 1972; A Textbook of Economics, 1977; Marx: Economist, Philosopher, Jew, 1982; contbr. articles to profl. jours. Office: Dept Econs Ore State U Corvallis OR 97331

WOLIVER, ROBERT EDWARD, college president, psychologist; b. Hanalei, Kauai, Hawaii, May 29, 1947; s. Edward Charles and Esther (Cottingham) W. B.S., Georgetown U., 1969; M.A., U. Hawaii, 1976, Ph.D., 1979. Lic. clin. psychologist, Hawaii. Master shipwright Yacht Repair Ctr., Marina Del Ray, Calif., 1969-73; head tennis profl. Club Med. Hanalei, 1973-75; charter boat capt. Hawaii Yacht Charters, Hanalei, 1975-78; cons. clinic psychologist Queen's Med. Ctr., Honolulu, 1978—; pvt. practice psychology, Honolulu, 1978—; pres. Hawaii Sch. Profl. Psychology, Honolulu, 1980—. Mem. Am. Psychol. Assn., Western Psychol. Assn., Hawaii Psychol. Assn. Club: Hawaii Yacht. Founder dynamic assessment therapy. Office: 2424 Pali Hwy Honolulu HI 96817

WOLK, ROCHELLE BREINDEL, clinical psychologist; b. N.Y.C., May 8, 1941; d. Benjamin Breindel and Ida (Rosen) B.; m. Robert L. Wolk, May 24, 1968. M.S. in Psychology, Pa. State U., 1963; Ph.D., Fordham U., 1970. Lic. psychologist N.Y., Calif. Sr. Clin. psychologist N.Y.C. Bur. Child Welfare, 1968-71; supervising psychologist So. Ulster Mental Health Clinic, Ellenville, N.Y., 1972-76; cons. psychologist United Cerebral Palsy Assn. Sullivan County (N.Y.), 1977-81; project dir. early intervention program Human Devel. Services Ctr., Liberty, N.Y., 1980-81, ind. practice, Piedmont, Calif., 1981—; clin. child psychologist, dept. pediatrics U. Calif.-San Francisco, 1982—. Grantee, N.Y. State Bur. Devel. Disabilities, 1980-81. Mem. Am. Psychol. Assn., Alameda County Psychol. Assn. (pres.-elect 1982), Phi Beta Kappa. Contbr. several to profl. jours.; author Gerontological Apperception Test, 1972. Office: 335 La Salle Ave Piedmont CA 94610

WOLKOVITS, PAUL DENNIS, bank executive; b. N.J., Dec. 22, 1948; s. Paul A. Wolkovitsch and Virginia V. Lauro. B.A., Columbia U., 1975; M. Div., Harvard U., 1978. Asst. v.p., dir. coll. relations and tng. adminstrn., sr. recruitment officer Mitsui Mfrs. Bank, Los Angeles, 1980—. Mem. Am. Soc. Tng. and Devel., Western Coll. Placement Assn., Am. Inst. Banking (chmn. instr. com. 1983-84). Office: 515 S Figueroa Los Angeles CA 90071

WOLLARD, DOUGLAS KENT, hospital administrator; b. Lamar, Colo., Mar. 4, 1947; s. Young Lowe and Gladys Eva (Mosher) W.; m. Mary Annes, Dec. 11, 1969; children—Eric Douglas, Sara Nicole. B.A., Southwestern Coll., Winfield, Kans., 1969; M.A. in Hosp. Adminstrn., U. Iowa, 1972. Asst. dir. Sweetwater Health Services, Rock Springs, Wyo., 1972-73; adminstrv. assoc. Midtown Hosp. Assn., Denver, 1973-76; v.p. Luth. Med. Ctr., Wheat Ridge, Colo. 1976—; pres. Luth. Med. Office Bldg. Corp., 1979—. Mem. regional council Jefferson County United Way, 1979—, chmn., 1982. Recipient United Way Recognition award, 1980. Mem. Am. Hosp. Assn., Nat. Facilities Mgmt. Assn. (Denver chpt.). Democrat. Methodist. Home and Office: 8320 W 38th Ave Wheat Ridge CO 80033

WOLLENBERG, RICHARD PETER, paper mfr.; b. Juneau, Alaska, Aug. 1, 1915; s. Harry L. and Gertrude (Arnstein) W.; B.S. in Mech. Engring., U. Calif. at Berkeley, 1936; M.B.A., Harvard U., 1938; grad. Army Indsl. Coll., 1941; D.Pub. Affairs (hon.), U. Puget Sound, 1977; m. Leone Bonney, Dec. 22, 1940; children—Kenneth Roger, David Arthur, Keith Kermit, Richard Harry, Carol Lynne. Prodn. control Bethlehem Ship, Quincy, Mass., 1938-39; with Longview Fibre Co. (Wash.), 1939—, safety engr., asst. chief engr., chief engr., mgr. container operations, 1951-57, v.p., 1953-57, v.p. operations, 1957-60, exec. v.p., 1960-69, pres., 1969-78, pres., chief exec. officer, 1978—, also dir. Mem. Wash. State Council for Postsecondary Edn., 1969-79, chmn., 1970-73. Bassoonist S.W. Washington Symphony. Trustee Reed Coll., Portland, 1962—, chmn., 1982. Served from 2d lt. to lt. col. USAAF, 1941-45. Mem. NAM (dir. 1981—). Home: 1632 Kessler Blvd Longview WA 98632 Office: PO Box 606 Longview WA 98632

WOLPA, RONALD BRUCE, med. device mfg. co. mktg. exec.; b. Omaha, Dec. 16, 1947; s. Jack and Ruth Jane (Nepomnick) W.; student (univ. basketball scholar) Pan Am. U., 1966-68; B.B.A., U. Houston, 1971; M.B.A., Pepperdine U., 1978. Personnel asst. Baker Oil Tools (now Baker Internat.), Houston, 1971-74; med. rep. Arnar-Stone Labs., Mt. Prospect, Ill., 1974-77; area mgr. Hydrocurve, Inc., San Diego, 1977-78; product mgr. cardiopulmonary products Shiley, Inc., Irvine, Calif., 1979-83, Home Health Care Am., 1983—. Mem. Am. Mgmt. Assn., Am. Mktg. Assn., Am. Soc. Extracorporeal Tech. Club: Toastmasters (pres. club 1979-80). Home: 71 Pergola Irvine CA 92715 Office: 4340 Von Karman Newport Beach CA 92660

WOLSEY, THOMAS MARK, accountant; b. Cardston, Alberta, Can., July 29, 1935; s. Thomas A. and Ida (Coombs) W.; m. Lynetta M. Bennett, Apr. 28, 1961; children—DeVere, Brian, Kristine, Melissa. B.A., Brigham Young U., 1960. C.P.A., Utah. Staff acct. Gardner, Hawkins and Borup, C.P.A., Provo, Utah, 1966-73. Owner T. Mark Wolsey, C.P.A., Orem, Utah, 1973-76; ptnr. Anderson, Wolsey, White & Cavanaugh, C.P.A.s, 1976—. Neighborhood chmn. Republican party, 1967-68, state del., 1968; leader, coordinating com. Boy Scouts Am. Served with USAR, 1958-64. Mem. Am. Inst. C.P.A.s, Utah Assn. C.P.A.s (exec. com.) officer, So. Utah chpt.). Mormon (mem. French mission 1955-58, bishopric counsellor 1974-81, High Councillor, 1972-74, 81—). Home: 147 E 1700 Orem UT 84057 Office: 1178 S State Orem UT 84057

WOLTER, MARY LOU(ISE), distbg. co. exec.; b. Prairie du Chien, Wis., Nov. 24, 1926; d. Ralph Waldo and Dessa May (Brownlee) Lathrop; m. Charles Thomas Wolter, Jan. 20, 1946; children—Thomas Quinn, David Ralph, Cynthia Louise, Martin Bryce. Free lance journalist; producer radio and cable TV shows; co-owner distributorship Amway Corp., Tucson and LaQuinta, Calif., 1969—; pres. Caml'lot Corp., Tucson and LaQuinta, 1976—; founder Tucson Learning Center, Tucson Bus. Center, 1976-80; owner, mgr. Pima Supply, Tucson; founder, creator Diamond Flock System and Center, 1980, 81. Mem. Amway Distbrs. Assn. U.S. Clubs: Amway Diamond, Order Eastern Star, Daus. of Nile. Author newspaper and mag. articles, bus.-related materials. Home: Box 985 54-950 Ramirez LaQuinta CA 92253 also 5160 E Pima Tucson AZ 85712

WOLTERSDORF, LEONARD OSCAR, naval officer; b. Laramie, Wyo., Mar. 10, 1939; s. Howard Henry and Donna Jane (Burtsfield) W.; m. Ruthann Barnicoat, Mar. 5, 1961; children—Kurt, Keith. B.S., Naval Postgrad. Sch., 1970; postgrad. Naval War Coll., 1975-76. Commd. ensign U.S. Navy, 1961, advanced through grades to capt., 1982; air dept. officer, 1970-72; exec./command officer helicopter anti-submarine squadron, San Diego, 1979-81; exec. officer USS New Orleans, San Diego, 1981-82. Active Boy Scouts Am., 1973-75, mem. troop com., 1975-80. Decorated D.F.C.; recipient Capt. A.J. Isbell Trophy, Lockheed Aircraft Corp., 1979. Mem. Navy Helicopter Assn. (trustee). Club: Masons. Office: USS New Orleans FPO San Francisco CA 96627

WOMACK, SHARON GENNELLE, library adminstr.; b. Flora, Ill., June 13, 1940; d. Teddy Roosevelt and Mary Martha (Sale) Martin; B.S. in Bus. Adminstrn., U. Ariz., 1972, M.L.S., 1976; m. Robert Darrol Womack, Jan. 29, 1960. Librarian, Phoenix Union High Sch. Dist., 1958-61, Yuma City-County Library, 1962-63, Ariz. State Library Extension Service, Phoenix, 1963-67, U. Ariz., 1967-69, Miami Meml.-Gila County, Ariz., 1972-76, Maricopa County Library, Phoenix, 1976-77; dir. Ariz. Dept. Library, Archives and Public Records, Phoenix, 1977—; vice chairperson State Adv. Council on Libraries, 1974-77. Chairperson steering com. Gila County Community Coll., 1975; mem. technician adv. com. Mesa Community Coll. Library, 1977—. Mem. ALA, Southwestern Library Assn. (chairperson state assn. 1977-78), Ariz. Library Assn. (pres. 1977-78). Office: Ariz State Library 3d Floor State Capitol 1700 W Washington St Phoenix AZ 85007

WOMELDORF, MARDIE GAIL, film director; b. Morristown, N.J., Apr. 11, 1950; s. William Benjamin and Marguerite (Heipertz) Womeldorf. B.A., Stetson U., 1972; M.A., U. Maine, 1974. Film and videotape editor Sta. KMPH-TV, Visalia, Calif., 1976-80; service rep. Pacific Telephone Co., Tulare, Calif., 1980-82; curator Tulare County Mus., Visalia, 1982; local origination dir. Sequoia Cablevision, Tulare, 1983; film dir. Sta. KDVR-TV, Denver, 1983—. Active Visalia Community Players; mem. adv. council R.S.V.P. Office: 100 Speer Blvd Denver CO 80231

WON, KYUNG-SOO, symphony conductor, director; b. Korea, Dec. 4, 1928; m. Hae-Ja (Won). Nov. 18, 1965; children—Alisa, Justin. Mus.M., Cin. Conservatory, 1957; postgrad. Ind. U. Cert. tchr., Calif. Formerly prof. Seoul (Korea) Nat. U., music dir. Modesto (Calif.) Symphony, Seoul Philharmonic Orch.; currently music dir., condr. Stockton (Calif.) Symphony; guest condr. orchs., London, Berlin, Paris, Vienna, Austria, Mexico City, S. Am. cities, Orient. Served with Korean Navy. Recipient Bartok award, Emeel Hermann award. Mem. Am. Symphony League. Home: 8034 Heather Dr Stockton CA 95209 Office: PO Box 4273 Stockton CA 95204

WONDERLING, LAWRENCE VERNON, psychologist, cons.; b. Chgo., Mar. 29, 1930; s. Lawrence and Betty (McNeal) W. B.A. in Sociology, San Francisco State U., 1953; M.S. in Psychology, San Diego State U., 1963; Ph.D. in Psychology, Calif. Sch. Profl. Psychology, 1974. Lic. psychologist, lic. marriage, family and child counselor, Calif. Psychologists, Minn. State Prison, Stillwater, 1964-65; cons. psychologist Sacramento Probation Dept., 1965-68; psychologist, tng. cons. Peace Corps, Washington with assignments in P.R., Swaziland, Afghanistan, Ghana and Paraguay, 1969-76; co-dir. Ctr. for Assessment, Psychotherapy and Edn., San Francisco, 1976—; cons. human relations, program evaluation to pvt. and govtl. agys. Served with U.S. Army, 1952-53. Mem. Am. Psychol. Assn., Calif. State Psychol. Assn. Democrat. Methodist. Office: 4444 Geary Blvd San Francisco CA 94102

WONG, ALFRED MUN KONG, lawyer; b. Honolulu, Sept. 12, 1930; s. Inn and Mew Kung (Choy) W.; student U. Hawaii, 1948-50; B.S., Marquette U., 1953; J.D., U. Calif., Hastings Coll. Law, San Francisco, 1964; m. Laureen Hong, Nov. 20, 1965; children—Peter Maron On, Julie Li Sharn. Hawaii bar, 1964; contract atty. Honolulu Redevel. Agy., 1968-71; mng. dir. Okumura Takushi Funaki & Wee, Law Corp., Honolulu, 1964—; adj. prof. U. Hawaii Law Sch., 1980-82; mem. bd. bar examiners State of Hawaii, 1968-79; mem. Hawaii Jud. Selection Commn., 1979—, chmn., 1983-85. Bd. dirs. Niu Valley Community Assn., 1974, 76, 77, pres., 1975, bd. dirs. Pacific council Girl Scouts U.S.A., 1973-78. Served with AUS, 1953-61. Recipient medal Chgo. Tribune, 1953, Am. Soc. Mil. Engrs., 1953; Outstanding Service award Girl Scouts U.S.A., 1978. Mem. Hawaii Bar Assn. (bd. dirs.), ABA, Hastings Coll. Law Alumni Assn. (bd. govs.), Am. Judicature Soc. Clubs: Waialae Country, Honolulu (founding dir.). Home: 5701 Haleola St Honolulu HI 96821 Office: 733 Bishop St Suite 1400 Honolulu HI 96813

WONG, BENEDICT NORBERT, marketing design consultant; b. Fresno, Calif., Jan. 1, 1943; s. Hon Way and Nellie Sue (Lee) W.; B.A., UCLA, 1964; postgrad. Calif. State U.-Los Angeles, 1967-68; m. Virginia Joyce Joke, Mar. 16, 1968; children—Cara Lisa, Matthew Jason. Graphics designer Autonetics, Anaheim, Calif., 1967-68; art dir. Bostelman Advt. Inc., Newport Beach, Calif., 1968-69; sr. art dir. Reach, McClinton & Co., Inc., Los Angeles, 1969-70; creative supr. Barnes-Champ Advt., Los Angeles, 1970-71; creative dir. Wenger-Michael Inc., San Francisco, 1971-75; owner, creative dir. Benedict Norbert Wong Mktg. Design, San Francisco, 1975—. Vol. cons. Big Bros., Girl Scouts, Coll. Notre Dame. Served with USN, 1964-66; Vietnam. Recipient awards N.Y. Art Dirs. Club, Communication Arts Soc. of Los Angeles, others. Mem. San Francisco Soc. Communicating Arts. Democrat. Roman Catholic. Clubs: San Francisco Tennis, Les Amis du Vin. Designer catalogs, Asian Art Mus. San Francisco, 1976-77; designs in Graphis, Communications Arts, Print, Art Dir. mags.; designer books: Guatemala: Faces of the Earth, 1976, Inflation Tax Planning, 1980; We Need a Cook, 1980. Home: 1719 Monticello Rd San Mateo CA 94402 Office: 369 Broadway San Francisco CA 94133

WONG, BENJAMIN YAU-CHEUNG, med. care delivery exec.; b. Hong Kong, July 15, 1943; s. Hung and Ku (Yip) W.; came to U.S., 1964, naturalized, 1979; B.C.E., Hong Kong Bapt. Coll., 1964; postgrad in Math., Baylor U., 1965; Ph.D. in C.E., Vanderbilt U., 1968; m. Beatrice Loh, Nov. 15, 1969; children—Carolyn, Jeffrey. Sr. structural engr. Smith, Hinchman & Grylls Assos., Inc., 1968-72; research fellow computer based tech. transfer Carnegie Mellon U., 1972-74; mgr. bldg. systems and computer applications devel. Architecture/Engring. Services, Kaiser Permanente Med. Care Program, Kaiser Found. Hosps., Inc., Oakland, Calif., 1974—. Recipient Scholastic award Hong Kong Bapt. Coll., 1964. Mem. Nat., Calif. (v.p. East Bay chpt., Achievement award) socs. profl. engrs., AAUP, ASCE, Am. Soc. Engring. Edn., Earthquake Engring. Research Inst., Structural Engring Assn. No. Calif., Med. Entities Mgmt. Assn., Tau Beta Pi. Contbr. articles on engring., bldg. systems, computer application, tech. transfer and health care delivery systems to profl. jours. Office: PO Box 12916 Oakland CA 94604

WONG, CHUEN Y., optometrist; b. Canton, China, Sept. 19, 1933; came to U.S., 1933, naturalized, 1953; s. Fong G. and Shee Y. (Yee) W.; m. Rosanna Y. L. Poon, Dec. 21, 1963; 1 son, Lance. B.S., Pacific U., 1955, O.D., 1956. Practice optometry, Winlock, Wash., 1957-58, 62—; mem. Wash. State Bd. Examiners in Optometry, 1982. Mem. Wash. State Comprehensive Health Planning Adv. Council, 1971-78. Served to capt. AUS, 1959-61. Decorated Army Commendation medal. Mem. Wash. Optometric Assn. (trustee 1968-71, chmn. pub. health div. 1970-71), Olympic Optometric Soc. (pres. 1968-70; Optometrist of Yr. 1973), Am. Optometric Assn., Am. Optometric Found., Am. Pub. Health Assn., Nat. Eye Reseach Found., Assn. Mil. Optometrists. Club: Lions. Home: 105 Walnut St Winlock WA 95896 Office: Optometry Clinic Bldg 118 SE First St Winlock WA 98596

WONG, DONA LEE, biochemist; b. San Francisco, Dec. 12, 1946; s. Donald Sam and Mary (Lee) W.; B.S. in Chemistry, Stanford U., 1968; M.A. in Biochemistry, U. Calif., Berkeley, 1971; Ph.D. in Neurosci., Stanford U., 1983; m. Kym Francis Faull, July 21, 1979. Teaching asst. dept. biochemistry U. Calif., Berkeley, 1969-70; research asst. dept. neuropathology, dept. neurosci. Harvard Med. Sch./Children's Hosp. Med. Center, Boston, 1971-74; sr. research asst. dept. psychiatry Stanford (Calif.) Med. Center, 1974-83, research assoc., 1983—. Mem. Soc. for Neurosci., Am. Chem. Soc., AAAS, N.Y. Acad. Sci., Iota Sigma Pi. Contbr. articles in field to profl. jours. Home: 2982 Louis Rd Palo Alta CA 94303 Office: Dept Psychiatry Stanford Medical Center Stanford CA 94305

WONG, DONALD HERBERT SIU KAU, veterinarian; b. Honolulu, Apr. 9, 1926; s. Herbert Y. and Rose Gertrude (Akina) W.; B.S., Wash. State U., 1948, D.V.M., 1949; m. Gyneve Maile Andrews, Mar. 3, 1951; children—Ryan A.M., Donnita L.K. Asso., Blue Cross Animal Hosp., Honolulu, 1949-51; pvt. practice as veterinarian, Honolulu, 1951-53; state veterinarian for Hawaii, 1955-59; owner, practitioner Kailua (Hawaii) Vet. Hosp., 1959—. Dir., v.p. Bay View Golf Center, 1963—; v.p. Arian Investment Co., Honolulu, 1972—, Furuya & Wong Investment Co., Honolulu, 1971—; partner Foreland Investment Co., 1977—. Served to capt. USAF, 1953-55. Mem. Bd. Vet. Examiners, 1965-71, chmn., 1968-71. Mem. Honolulu Vet. Soc. (pres. 1960-61). Rotarian. Club: Mid Pacific Country (dir. 1962-65, pres. 1963-64). Home: 46-307 Haiku Plantations Dr Kaneohe HI 96744 Office: 70 Kihapai St Kailua HI 96734

WONG, HARRY CHOW, anesthesiologist; b. Beloit, Wis., June 26, 1933; s. Charles T. and Yee S. Wong; B.S., U. Wis., 1955, M.D., 1958; m. Jean A. Nagahiro, June 21, 1958; children—Jeffrey, Stacey, Daphne, Steven. Intern, Providence Hosp., Portland, Oreg., 1959; resident in anesthesiology U. Wis. Hosps., 1959-61; practice medicine specializing in anesthesiology, Salt Lake City, 1961—; chmn. anesthesia dept. Latter-day Saints Hosp., Salt Lake City, 1966-67, 74-76; pres. med. staff Salt Lake Surg. Center, 1976—; clin. prof. anesthesia U. Utah Med. Sch., Salt Lake City, 1975—. Diplomate Am. Bd. Anesthesiology. Mem. AMA (Physician Recognition awards 1973, 76, 79), Utah State Soc. Anesthesiologists (pres. 1966), Am. Soc. Anesthesiologists (dir. 1977—), Am. Coll. Anesthesiology, Freestanding Ambulatory Surg. Assn. (dir. 1979, v.p. 1980-81), Utah Med. Assn., Internat. Anesthesia Research Soc., Soc. Critical Care Medicine. Office: 617 East 3900 South Salt Lake City UT 84107

WONG, HERBERT Z., clinical and organizational psychologist, mental health exec.; b. San Francisco; s. John K. and Fong H. Wong; B.A., San Francisco State U., 1968; M.A., U. Mich., 1973, Ph.D., 1976. Research asso. Research Center for Group Dynamics, U. Mich., 1972-73, clin. intern, 1972-74, project dir. Drug Edn. Program, 1973-74, research and evaluation cons., 1974-76; exec. dir. Richmond Area Multi-Services and Dist. V Mental Health Center, San Francisco, 1975—; prin. investigator Bay Area Indochinese Mental Health Project, San Francisco; program dir. Nat. Asian Am. Psychology Tng. Center, San Francisco, 1979—; prin. faculty The Staff Coll. NIMH, 1980—; prin. cons. Herbert Z. Wong and Assocs., cons. in field. USPHS fellow, 1973-74, Danforth Found. fellow, 1970-71. Mem. Am. Psychol. Assn., Am. Orthopsychiat. Assn., Western Psychol. Assn., Asian Am. Psychol. Assn., Am. Personnel and Guidance Assn. Am. Mgmt. Assn., All Japan Shorin-Ryu Karate-Do Internat. Assn. (7th degree black belt). Contbr. articles to profl. jours. Office: 3626 Balboa St San Francisco CA 94121

WONG, JAMES BOK, economist, engr., technologist; b. Canton, China, Dec. 9, 1922; s. Gen Ham and Chen (Yee) W.; came to U.S., 1938, naturalized, 1962; B.S. in Agr., U. Md., 1949, B.S. in Chem. Engring., 1950; M.S., U. Ill., 1951, Ph.D., 1954; m. Wai Ping Lim, Aug. 3, 1946;children—John, Jane Doris, Julia Ann. Research asst. U. Ill. at Urbana, 1950-53; chem. engr. Standard Oil of Ind., Whiting, 1953-55; process design engr., research engr. Shell Devel. Co., Emeryville, Calif., 1955-61; sr. planning engr., prin. planning engr. Chem.-Plastics Group, Dart Industries Inc. (formerly Rexall Drug & Chem. Co.), Los Angeles, 1961-66, supr. planning and econs., 1966-67, mgr. long range planning and econs., 1967, chief economist, 1967-72, dir. econs. and ops. analysis, 1972-78, dir. internat. technologies, 1978-81; pres. James B. Wong Assos., Inc., 1981—, chmn. exec. com., dir. United Pacific Bank; tech. cons. various corps. Named to Exec. Order Ohio Commodores. Mem. Asian Am. Edn. Commn.; bd. dirs., pres. Chinese Am. Citizens Alliance Found. Served with USAAF, 1943-46. Mem. Am. Inst. Chem. Engrs., Am. Chem. Soc., VFW (vice comdr. 1959), Sigma Xi, Tau Beta Pi, Phi Kappa Phi, Pi Mu Epsilon, Phi Lambda Upsilon, Phi Eta Sigma. Contbr. articles to profl. jours. Home: 2460 Venus Dr Los Angeles CA 90046

WONG, JEFFREY JOSEPH, lawyer; b. San Francisco, July 24, 1943; s. Joe Bing and Lili Phyllis (Jew) W.; A.B. in Politics, Princeton U., 1965; J.D., U. Calif., San Francisco, 1968; m. Julianne Bryant, Mar. 30, 1980. Admitted to Calif. bar, 1969; asso. firm Dinkelspiel & Dinkelspiel, San Francisco, 1969-75, partner, 1975—; mem. attys. com. Am. Assn. Equipment Lessors, 1978-82, chmn. attys. com., 1980—, participant legal seminars on equipment leasing law, 1978—; participant seminar on uniform comml. code Calif. Bus. Law Inst., 1979; instr. workshop leader Coll. Advocacy, Hastings Coll. Law, U. Calif., San Francisco, 1976. Mem. housing and urban devel. com. Human Rights Commn. San Francisco, 1976-79; dir. San Francisco Lawyers Com. for Urban Affairs, 1974—; bd. dirs. Golden Gate chpt. ARC, 1972-78, Vis. Nurse Assn. San Francisco, 1975—, Charilla Found., 1977—. Mem. ABA (subcom. personal property leasing sect. corp., banking and bus. law), State Bar Calif., Bar Assn. San Francisco (editor In Re newsletter 1976-78, del. to state bar convs. 1976, 77), Western Assn. Equipment Lessors (dir.). Democrat. Clubs: Princeton U. Canon; Bohemian, Presidio Golf, 20-30 (pres. 1969) Princeton of No. Calif. (pres. 1982—) (San Francisco). Office: care Dinkelspiel & Dinkelspiel One Market Plaza 1800 Stewart St Tower San Francisco CA 94105

WONG, KAM LEUNG, design engineer; b. Canton, China, Sept. 18, 1924; s. Som Quong and Yuet Ha (Tang) W.; m. Beatrice Johnson, July 18, 1953; children—LeRoy, Elaine, Edith, Elizabeth. B.S.E.E., Calif. Inst. Tech., 1950; M.S.E.E., U. So. Calif., 1954, postgrad., 1954-60. Mgr. product analysis lab. Hughes Aircraft Co., Culver City, Calif., 1951—. Recipient Chinese Engrs. and Scientists Assn. resource mgmt. achievement award, 1976. Mem. IEEE (reliability soc. P.K. McElroy award, 1981), Inst. Environ. Scis., AIAA. Republican. Co-author book; contbr. articles to tech. jours. Office: Hughes Aircraft Co 2000 E El Segundo Blvd El Segundo CA 90245

WONG, LAWRENCE JAMES, music educator, pianist, accompanist; b. Los Angeles, June 21, 1948; s. Harry and Violet (Ginn) W. B.A. in Music, Claremont Mem's Coll., 1970; M.Mus. in Accompanying, U. So. Calif., 1976. Prof. music Los Angeles Harbor Coll., adj. faculty mem. U. So. Calif., Calif. State U.-Dominguez Hills; appeared throughout U.S. and Europe accompanying artists including Judith Blegan, Justino Diaz, Elizabeth Hynes, Spiro Malas, James McCracken, Robert Merrill; accompanist for Leona Mitchell; appeared on TV shows: Merv Griffin, Mike Douglas, Tonight; performed for Pres. Gerald R. Ford 1976, Pres. James E. Carter, 1979. Mem. Pi Lambda Kappa. Office: 1111 Figueroa Pl Wilmington CA

WONG, MARY KAMM, rental company executive; b. Honolulu, Feb. 11, 1904; d. Charles Seu and Kim Kyau (Goo) Kamm; B.S., U. Hawaii, 1927; M.A. (scholar), Boston U., 1930; m. Duke Bung Yai Wong, July 12, 1945. With Pineapple Research Lab., U. Honolulu, 1927; lab. technician Children's Hosp., 1930; tchr. pub. schs. Hawaii Dept. Pub. Instrn., 1930-65; v.p., treas. Ala Moana Broadcasting Co., Inc., 1957-59; pres., treas. Polynesian Broadcasting Co. Inc., 1960-66, Rural Broadcasting Co. Inc., 1969-72, Leilani Enterprises, 1968— (all Honolulu); dir. Kam Travel Agy., Inc., Big 88. Mem. NEA, AAUW, Boston U. Alumni Assn., Am. Legion Aux., Theta Upsilon. Episcopalian.

WONG, OTTO, epidemiologist, biostatistician; b. Canton, China, Nov. 14, 1947; came to U.S., 1967, naturalized, 1976; s. Kui and Foon (Chow) W.; m. Betty Yeung, Feb. 14, 1970; children—Elaine, Jonathan. B.S., U. Ariz., 1970, M.S., Carnegie Mellon U., 1972; M.S., U. Pitts., 1973, Sc.D., 1975. Cert. epidemiologist, Am. Coll. Epidemiology, 1982. USPHS fellow U. Pitts., 1972-75; asst. prof. epidemiology Georgetown U. Med. Sch., 1975-78; mgr. epidemiology Equitable Environ. Health Inc., Rockville, Md., 1977-78; dir. epidemiology Tabershaw Occupational Med. Assocs., Rockville, 1978-80; dir. occupational research Biometric Research Inst., Washington, 1980-81; v.p., sr. epidemiologist Environ. Health Assocs., Inc., Berkeley, Calif., 1981—; cons. Nat. Cancer Inst., Nat. Inst. Occupational Safety and Health, Fairfax Hosp., Va. U. Ariz. scholar, 1967-68. Fellow Am. Coll. Epidemiology; mem. Am. Pub. Health Assn., Biometric Soc., Soc. Epidemiologic Research, Phi Beta Kappa, Pi Mu Epsilon. Democrat. Contbr. articles to profl. jours. Home: 111 Clyde Dr Walnut Creek CA 94598 Office: 2150 Shattuck Ave Suite 414 Berkeley CA 94704

WONG, PENELOPE LYNN, advertising agency executive, marketing communications consultant, writer; b. Salinas, Calif., May 22, 1945; d. Gung Jue and Nellie Sue (Lee) W.; m. Jeffrey Allen Berner, Jan. 27, 1968; m. 2d, Stephen Timothy Kochis, June 27, 1981. A.B. with highest honors, U. Calif.-Berkeley, 1967, postgrad., 1967-68. Founder pub. and mktg. cons. firms, 1967—; writer mag. articles, 1968—; with Interaction Assocs., 1970-73; creative dir. Ogilvy & Mather Direct, San Francisco, 1982—; cons. mktg. communications Chase Manhattan Bank, N.Y.C., 1979-80, govt. banking div., also internat. pvt. banking, 1978-80; employee benefits cons. FinanceAm., Allentown, Pa., 1978, Bank of Am., San Francisco, 1976-78; mktg. and tng. communications cons. interactive corp. services Bank of Am., 1976-77, communications cons., 1974-77; researcher Kaiser News mag.; program copy chief Franklin Mint, Phila., 1977-79, concept and product devel. cons., 1979-82, copy cons., 1979-82; mng. dir. Jennifer Wong, Ltd., N.Y.C., San Francisco and Hong Kong, 1979-80; research cons. Inst. Sci. Analysis, San Francisco, 1977. Vol. advt. cons. Oakland Symphony, Save the Cable Cars. Recipient copywriting awards Phila. Ad Club; spl. career fellow English doctoral program U. Calif.-Berkeley, 1968. Mem. San Francisco Ad Club, Women in Advt., AAUW. Democrat. Author: (as Vanessa Sing) Lift for Life, 1977; assoc. editor Stolen Paper Editions, 1966-68; editor, writer Interaction Assocs. newsletters, 1972-74; editor Wilderness Sch. Newsletter, 1972, The Innerspace Project (Jeff Berner), 1972; assoc. editor San Francisco, Reel, 1970; contbr. articles to popular mags. and profl. jours. Office: 735 Battery St San Francisco CA 94111

WONG, RONALD JAMES, pediatric dental surgeon; b. Fresno, Calif., Dec. 21, 1931; s. Raymond Arthur and Ruth (Moe) W.; B.S., U. So. Calif., 1954, D.D.S., 1956; m. Edith Mok, June 21, 1962; children—Gary Hunter, Julie, Christy, Carina, Lara, Sabrina. Intern, P.T.A. Clinic, Los Angeles Sch. Dist., 1956-57; resident Greenpark Sch. dental clinic, Chofu, Japan, 1958-59; practice dentistry specializing in pediatric dental surgery, Hollywood, Calif., 1959—; mem. staff Hollywood Presbyn. Hosp.; asst. clin. prof. pedodontics U. So. Calif., Los Angeles, 1959-68, 1973—; cons. Children's Hosp. Los Angeles, 1960-73, head dental div., 1973-78. Served to capt. USAF, 1957-59. First place winner 25 KG class U.S. Nat. Archery Flight Championship, 1982, Silver Wescott medal No. 2 amateur flight archer in U.S., 1983. Mem. Hollywood, Los Angeles dental socs., Hollywood Acad. Medicine, Am. Stomatological Soc. Japan, Am. Analgesia Soc., Am. Acad. Pedodontics, Am. So. Calif. (pres. 1968-69) socs. dentistry for children, So. Calif., Am. dental assns., Calif. Pedodontic Research Group, Western Pedodontic and Odontic Soc., Am. Endodontic Soc., Am. Hypnodontic Soc., Acad. of Dentistry for the Handicapped, Chinese Am. Citizen's Alliance, Delta Sigma Delta, Alpha Tau Omega. Rotarian. Author: Pedodontic Dental Preparations, 1961. Home: 2415 N Commonwealth Ave Los Feliz CA 90027 Office: 1616 Hillhurst Ave Hollywood CA 90027

WONG, SANDRA MARIA JOSEPHINE, aerospace company executive; b. Canton, China, June 15, 1948; came to U.S., 1957, naturalized, 1964; d. Herbert C. M. and Patricia C. (Joe) W.; m. Robert W. Visini, Sept. 2, 1978; 1 dau., Teresa S. B.A. in Asian Studies, San Diego State U., 1973, M.A., Stanford U., 1975, M.A. in Cultural Anthropology, 1977, postgrad., 1977—. Ind. cons., 1970-80; employee relations specialist U.S. Forest Service, San Francisco, 1976-78, employee devel. specialist, 1978-80; edn. and tng. specialist Ford Aerospace & Communications Corp., Palo Alto, Calif., 1980-81, supr. personnel planning and devel., 1982—; cons., tchr. in field. Mem. policy bd. Center for Research on Women, Stanford U., 1975-76. Nat. Def. Fgn. Lang. fellow, 1975-76, summer 1972; Nat. Inst. Gen. Med. Scis. fellow, 1976-78. Mem. Am. Soc. Tng. and Devel., Internat. Assn. for Quality Circles, Nat. Assn. Female Execs., Stanford U. Alumni Assn. Roman Catholic. Office: Ford Aerospace & Communications Corp 3939 Fabian Way Palo Alto CA 94303

WONG, STEVEN WYMANN, social service and economic development consultant; b. Honolulu, Oct. 24, 1946; s. Gerald Y.K. and Amy (Gwendolyn (Chun) W.; B.A., Claremont McKenna Coll., 1968; M.A., San Diego State U., 1969; M.B.A., So. Ill. U., Edwardsville, 1976. Exec. asst. to exec. dept. Pacific Fruit Express div. So. Pacific Industries, San Francisco, 1970; actuarial analyst Judson Branch Research Center, Menlo Park, Calif., 1971; econ. devel./manpower coordinator Oakland (Calif.) Model Cities Program, 1972-73; econ. cons. Marshall Kaplan, Gans & Kahn, San Francisco, 1973; econ. devel. dir. Econ. and Social Opportunities, Inc., San Jose, Calif., 1974-76; cons. to bus. and social services on fin. and mgmt., 1976—; prof. accountancy Merritt Coll., Oakland, Calif.; mem. faculty U. San Francisco, 1976—, Vista Coll., 1979—, Berkeley, Calif., Chapman Coll., Orange, Calif., 1980—. Home: 3808 Quail Ridge Rd Lafayette CA 94549 Office: 12500 Campus Dr Oakland CA 94618

WONG, WILLIAM LAWRENCE, accountant, financial consultant, educator; b. Hilo, Hawaii, Mar. 19, 1949; s. William F.K. and Doris Y. (Haraguchi) W.; m. Iris A. Matsumoto, Mar. 26, 1949. B.B.A. in Fin., U. Hawaii, 1971, postgrad., 1972. C.P.A., Hawaii. Comml. loan analyst Central Pacific Bank, Honolulu, 1971-72; in-charge acct. Ernst & Whinney, Honolulu, 1972-74; bus. mgr. Hilo Med. Group, Inc. (Hawaii), 1974-76; lectr. U. Hawaii-Kailua, 1976; owner, operator, pres. William L. Wong, C.P.A., Kailua, 1976—; condr. seminars for convs.; adviser, cons. to politicians. Dir. Kona Jaycees, 1978-83; sponsor softball team, Kailua; active Kona C. of C. Mem. Hawaii Soc. C.P.A.s, Am. Inst. C.P.A.s. Republican. Club: Hualalai Exchange.

WONG, WILLIAM MARTIN, devel. engr.; b. San Rafael, Calif., June 17, 1957; s. William and Josephine (Lum) W.; B.S. in Elec. Engring. and Computer Sci., U. Calif., Berkeley, 1978, B.A. in Econs., 1978. Devel. engr., research and devel. lab Destop Computer div. Hewlett-Packard Co., Ft. Collins, Colo., 1978-81; software quality assurance mgr., digital telephone systems div. Harris Corp., Novato, Calif., 1981—. Registered profl. engr., Calif. Mem. Am. Prodn. and Inventory Control Soc., IEEE, U. Calif. Soc. Elec. Engrs., Ft. Collins Bd. Realtors. Home: 2140 Elderberry Ln San Rafael CA 94903 Office: 1 Digital Dr Novato CA 94948

WONG, Y(ING) WOOD, real estate investment co. exec.; b. Hong Kong, Apr. 28, 1950; came to U.S.,1969; s. Loyee K. H. and Margaret

M. C. L. Wong; A.A. in Biology, Menlo Coll., 1971, B.S. in Bus. Adminstrn., 1974; B.A. in Zoology, U. Calif., Berkeley, 1972; M. Mgmt., Northwestern U., 1976; m. Leslie K. P. Chan, Dec. 18, 1977; children—Joshua H., Jonathan H. Auditor, Touche Ross & Co., C.P.A.s, San Francisco, 1976-78; instr. Golden Gate U., 1977; founder, mng. dir. Wong Properties, Menlo Park, Calif., 1976—. Mem. Internat. Platform Assn., Beta Alpha Psi. Office: PO Box 10737 Stanford CA 94305

WONG-McCARTHY, WILLIAM JAMES, research psychologist, consultant; b. Paris, May 20, 1951; s. John Robert and Helen Ruth (House) McC; m. Angela Wong, July 24, 1951. B.A., Columbia U., 1973; M.A., U. Ill., 1976; Ph.D., Yale U., 1980. Vis. asst. prof. Hampshire Coll., Amherst, Mass., 1978-79; lectr. Pepperdine U., Los Angeles, 1979-80; asst. research psychologist UCLA, 1980—. Mem. AAAS, Am. Psychol. Assn., Internat. Communication Assn., Am. Sociol. Assn. Democrat. Home: 1323 Carmelina Ave Apt 208 Los Angeles CA 90025 Office: 1282 Franz Hall Psychology Dept UCLA Los Angeles CA 90024

WONG-SING, JOSEPH, podiatrist; b. Trinidad, Feb. 20, 1946; immigrated to Can., 1968, naturalized, 1973; s. Edwin and Lily (Moo) Wong-S.; B.Sc., U. Toronto, 1973; D.Podiatric Medicine, Ohio Coll. Podiatric Medicine, 1977; m. Resela Assumpta Sham, Aug. 1, 1970; children—Aaron, Erline, Irwin. Teaching asst. histology Ohio Coll. Podiatric Medicine, 1974-77; resident in podiatry Vancouver (B.C., Can.) Hosp., 1977-78, mem. staff, 1978—, asst. dir. residency tng. in podiatry, 1978, dir. podiatry staff, 1983; staff podiatrist Saanich Peninsula Hosp., 1980. Recipient various service awards. Mem. Can. Podiatry Assn. (chmn. nat. bds. in podiatry 1981—), B.C. Assn. Podiatrists (council 1979-81, sec.-treas. 1981—), Vancouver Neurol. Soc., Can. Assn. Sports Medicine, Am. Podiatry Assn., Alumni Assn. Ohio Coll. Podiatric Medicine. Roman Catholic. Author papers, reports in field. Office: 203-2309 W 41st Ave Vancouver BC V6M 2A3 Canada

WOOD, BRIAN WALLACE, optometrist, consultant; b. Des Moines, May 1, 1951; s. Wallace Glen and Evelyn Irene W. B.S., U. Iowa, 1973; postgrad. Drake U., 1973; O.D., Ill. Coll. Optometry, 1977. Lab./teaching asst. Ill. Coll. Optometry, 1974-77; practice optometry, Denver, 1977—; mem. Eye Clinic staff Denver Gen. Hosp., 1977-81; cons., investigator mapping div. U.S. Geol. Survey; investigator explt. soft contact lenses FDA. Bd. dirs. Denver County (Colo.) Young Republicans, 1978-80. Merit scholar U. Iowa, 1969-70. Mem. Am. Optometric Assn., Lakewood C. of C., Colo. Optometric Assn., Jefferson County Optometric Soc., Phi Gamma Delta (bd. chpt. advs. 1982—), Beta Sigma Kappa. Republican. Club: Mt. Vernon Country (Golden, Colo.). Designer various optical aids for map makers Denver Fed. Center, U.S. Geol. Survey. Office: 8600 W 14th Ave Lakewood CO 80215

WOOD, CHARLES EARL, obstetrician, gynecologist; b. Sterling, Colo., Oct. 4, 1930; s. Walter Earl and Dorothy Nancy (Long) W.; m. Patricia Taylor, Nov. 1, 1960; children—Lecia, Spencer, Christine. B.A., Phillips U., 1959; M.D., U. Colo. 1963. Diplomate Am. Bd. Obstetrics and Gynecology. Intern, Denver Gen. Hosp., 1963-64, resident in ob-gyn, 1964-67, mem. staff, 1967—; practice medicine specializing in ob-gyn, Casper, Wyo., 1967—; mem. staff Natrona County Meml. Hosp., Casper, 1967—, chief of obstetrics, 1975, chmn. staff, 1981-83; mem. staff Converse County Hosp., Douglas, Wyo. 1967—, Carbon County Hosp., Rawline, Wyo., 1968—; mem. Wyo. Family Practice Residency program, 1978-83; clin. assoc. prof. family practice (ob-gyn) Univ. Hosp. of Wyo. Coll. Human Medicine, 1982-83. Mem. Natrona County Sch. Bd., 1974-80, vice chmn., 1976-77, chmn., 1978-79; pres. Casper YMCA, 1974-76, gen. chmn. fundraising campaign, 1976-77, mem. bldg. com. 1976-78; mem. Blue Envelope, 1970—; pres., charter mem. Wyo. Right to Life, 1970-75; T-Bird booster Casper Coll., 1970—. Served with USN, 1949-50. Mem. Internat. Soc. for Advancement of Humanistic Studies in Gyn. (charter), Am. Coll. Obstetricians and Gynecologists, Am. Fertility Soc. (charter), Wyo. Med. Soc., Denver Med. Soc., Natrona County Med. Soc. (pres. 1979-80), Audubon Soc., Casper Air Modelers Assn. (charter, pres. 1969-76), Wyo. Handball Assn., Wyo. Arabian Horse Assn., Irish Wolfhound Club Am., Wyo. Farm Bur. Club: Elks. Home: 5092 Alcova Rd Box 2 Casper WY 82604 Office: 167 S Conwell St Suite 5 Casper WY 82601

WOOD, CLYDE MATHESON, civil engr.; b. Macon, Ga., Apr. 26, 1890; s. Luther Hudson and Martha (Darracott) W.; B.S.C.E., Ga. Inst. Tech., 1915, C.E., 1930; m. Marion Christine Morris, June 11, 1917; 1 dau., Martha Eleanor Wood Becker. Draftsman, Pratt Engring. & Machine Co., Atlanta, 1910-12, 13; with Automatic Sprinkler Corp. Am., Atlanta, N.Y.C., Cleve., Cin., Youngstown, Ohio, Sao Paulo, Brazil, 1915-64, promotion mgr., 1928-31, 39-45, sales mgr., 1931-33, pres., dir. Automatic Sprinklers do Brasil, S.A. subs., 1945-57, cons. sales engring. and hydraulic research, 1957-64; researcher Nat. Fire Protection Assn., Soc. Fire Protection Engrs., 1964—. Chmn. Rossmoor-Las Trampas Map, 1972. Served to 1st lt. F.A., U.S. Army, 1917-19; AEF in France. Recipient Meritorious Civilian Service award Bur. Yards and Docks, U.S. Navy, 1944. Fellow Am. Geog. Soc., ASCE, Soc. Fire Protection Engrs. (publ. com. Fire Tech. 1964—); mem. Nat. Fire Protection Assn., Nat. Geog. Soc., Sociedade Geografica Brasileira (Marshall Candido Mariano da Silva Rondon medal 1959, Pedro Alvares Cabral medal 1972), Vets. World War I, Engrs. Club, Trails Club, Southeastern States Club of Rossmoor, Diablo Symphony and Rossmoor Music Assns., Pi Kappa Alpha. Methodist. Lodge: Rotary (Paul Harris fellow). Author: Automatic Sprinkler Hydraulic Data, 1944, 61, 64, 70, 72, 74 (transl. 5 langs.); contbr. to Fire Protection Handbook, 12th, 13th and 14th edits. Research on deluge sprinkler systems for airplane hangars, explosives, rocket powder mfg., hydraulics. Address: 2701 Pine Knoll Dr Apt 7 Walnut Creek CA 94595

WOOD, DAVID EXCEL, hospital administrator, consultant, educator; b. Wilmington, Del., Apr. 21, 1945; s. Ross A. and Sarah (Matthews) W.; m. Laura Vais, May 1, 1980; children—Christine, Nicholas. B.S., San Diego State U., 1971, M.B.A., 1976, M.P.A., 1981. Mgr. Health Care Systems Adminstrs., San Diego, 1972-74; v.p. fin. Calif. Med. Services, San Diego, 1974-76; asst. dir. fin. U. Calif. Med. Ctr., San Diego, 1976-81; assoc. dir., chief fin. officer Univ. Hosps., U. Colo. Health Ctr., Denver, 1981—, instr. sch. medicine, 1982. Mem. Hosp. Fin. Mgmt. Assn. (pres. San Diego chpt., William Folmer award 1981). Home: 6499 E Long Circle N Englewood CO 80112 Office: 4200 E 9th Ave Denver CO 80262

WOOD, DAVID MONTEL, engineering firm executive; b. Omaha, Nov. 12, 1937; s. Cledith Robert and Bertha Fransis (Phillips) W.; m. Mary Ann Sandoz, Aug. 20, 1962; m. 2d, Pamela Sue Wattier, June 15, 1975; children—Mark Montel, Wendy Doreen. A.A., Phoenix Community Coll., 1962; student Ariz. State U., 1962-72. Engr., designer Maddock & Assocs., Engrs., Phoenix, 1956-61, Moote, Kema Engrs., Phoenix, 1961-63; dir. planning Staggs Bilt Homes, Phoenix, 1963-69; gen. mgr. Skyline Homes, Phoenix, 1969-71; gen. mgr., exec. v.p. PRC Toups Phoenix, 1971—, also mem. exec. com. Mem. Scottsdale (Ariz.) Planning and Zoning Com., 1980—. Served with Ariz. NG, 1959-65, USAF, 1964-65. Mem. Urban League Inst., Homebuilders Assn., Ariz. Planners Assn. Republican. Home: 3323 N 82d Pl Scottsdale AZ 85258 Office: 4131 N 24th St Suite 110 Phoenix AZ 85016

WOOD, DAVID ROBERT, communications co. exec.; b. Worcester, Mass., Apr. 23, 1957; s. Robert Kendall and Patricia Joan (Mis) W.; B.S., U. Ariz., 1979. Dept. store sales rep. Hallmark Cards, No. Calif., 1980-81; asst. to pres. mktg. Am. West Telephone Co., Inc., Los Angeles, 1981-82; supply div. field sales rep. Centel Communications, Los Angeles, 1982—. Democrat. Roman Catholic. Address: 1745 Camino Palmero #418 Los Angeles CA 90046

WOOD, DENNIS PATRICK, clinical psychologist, educator; b. Oakland, Calif., Aug. 5, 1949; s. Donald James and Helen Winfred (Reimann) W.; m. Joan Anne Treinen, Feb. 14, 1971; children—Ross, Trevor, Megan. B.A. (Coll.-scholar 1967-71), St. Mary's Coll., Moraga, Calif., 1971; M.A. (Univ. scholar 1972-73), U. Nebr., 1973; Ph.D., Calif. Sch. Profl. Psychology, 1976. Lic. psychologist, Nev., Calif. Psychology intern In-Between Youth Ctr., San Diego, 1973-74, Golden State Community Mental Health Ctr. (now Hope Community Mental Health Ctr.), Lakeview Terrace, Calif., 1974-75, Alcohol Rehab. Ctr., Naval Sta., San Diego; co-dir. La Jolla (Calif.) Profl. Workshops, 1977—; pvt. practice clin. and health psychology, San Diego, 1980—; clin. instr. Sch. Medicine, U. Calif.-San Diego, 1979—; cons. to bus. and med. facilities. Vice pres. Donald James Wood Found., Oakland, Calif., 1971-77, trustee, 1977—. Served to lt. comdr. USNR, 1976-80. Recipient Outstanding Service cert. Commandant of 11th Naval Dist., 1975. Mem. Am. Psychol. Assn., Med. Psychology Network (program coordinator Western U.S.), Calif. Psychology Assn., Assn. for Advancement Psychology (assoc.) Democrat. Roman Catholic. Co-author: Clinical Hypnosis Primer, 1983 contbr. articles in psychology to profl. jours. Office: 550 Washington St Suite 104 San Diego CA 92103

WOOD, DIANE CLAIRE, training executive, consultant, researcher; b. Berkeley, Calif. Aug. 20, 1950; d. Kenneth Alvin and Jean Betty (Gristmacher) Fortenbery; m. James Dale Wood, Aug. 20, 1971. A.A., Foothill Jr. Coll., 1970; B.A. cum laude, Calif. State U.-Chico, 1972, M.A., 1974. Asst. mgr. Weinstocks, Modesto, Calif., 1978-80; store mgr. Friedmans Microwave Ovens, Modesto, 1980-82; franchise tng. mgr. Byte Industries, Hayward, Calif., 1982—. Mem. Am. Soc. Tng. Devel. Republican.

WOOD, DONALD FRANK, transportation educator, writer, consultant; b. Waukesha, Wis., Feb. 22, 1935; s. Frank Blaine and Vilah (Mathson) W.; m. Doreen Johnson, July 5, 1968; children—Tamara, Frank. B.A., U. Wis., 1957, M.A., 1958; Ph.D., Harvard U., 1970. Transp. planner State of Wis., Madison, 1960-70; mem. faculty San Francisco State U., 1970—, prof. transp., 1974—; cons. in field. Served with U.S. Army, 1958. Woodrow Wilson fellow, 1958-59. Mem. Am. Econ. Assn., Transp. Research Forum, Nat. Council Phys. Distbn. Mgmt., Am. Truck Hist. Soc. Presbyterian. Author: El Camino, 1982; co-author: Contemporary Physical Distribution and Logistics, 2d edit. 1982; Contemporary Transportation, 2d edit. 1982; Readings in Contemporary Physical Distribution, 4th edit. 1982; Readings in Contemporary Transportation, 1980. Home: 321 Riviera Circle Larkspur CA 94939 Office: Sch Bus San Francisco State U San Francisco CA 94132

WOOD, ERNEST WILLIAM, univ. adminstr.; b. West Point, Ill., Feb. 1, 1934; s. William E. and Martha E. (Hess) W.; B.S., Central Coll., 1957; M.A., San Jose State U., 1979; Ed.D., U. of Pacific, 1983; m. M. Ethylene Spence, Sept. 7, 1956; 1 dau., Tamara Dawn. Ordained to ministry Assemblies of God Ch., 1960; cert. fund raising exec. Assoc. pastor 1st Assembly of God Ch., Memphis, 1959-65; missionary, Philippines, 1965-72; exec. v.p., dir. devel. Bethany Bible Coll., Santa Cruz, Calif., 1972-79; asst. v.p. devel. U. of Pacific, Stockton, 1979—; cons. and lectr. in field. Republican. Mem. Nat. Soc. Fund Raising Execs. (bd. dirs. No. Calif. chpt.), Council for Advancement and Support of Edn., Phi Delta Kappa. Club: Rotary. Home: 5186 Gadwall Circle Stockton CA 95207 Office: Univ of the Pacific Stockton CA 95211

WOOD, FERGUS JAMES, geophys. cons.; b. London, Ont., Can., May 13, 1917; came to U.S., 1924, naturalized, 1932; s. Louis Aubrey and Dora Isabel (Elson) W.; student U. Oreg., 1934-36; A.B., U. Calif.-Berkeley, 1938, postgrad., 1938-39; postgrad. U. Chgo., 1939-40, U. Mich., 1940-42, Calif. Inst. Tech., 1946; m. Doris M. Hack, Sept. 14, 1946; children—Kathryn Celeste Wood Boulé, Bonnie Patricia Wood Ward. Teaching asst. U. Mich., 1940-42; instr. in physics and astronomy Pasadena City Coll., 1946-48, John Muir Coll., 1948-49; asst. prof. physics U. Md., 1949-50; assoc. physicist Johns Hopkins U. Applied Physics Lab., 1950-55; sci. editor Ency. Americana, N.Y.C., 1955-60; aero. and space research scientist, sci. asst. to dir. Office Space Flight Programs, Hdqrs., NASA, Washington, 1960-61; program dir. fgn. sci. info. NSF, Washington, 1961-62; phys. scientist, chief sci. and tech. info. staff U.S. Coast and Geodetic Survey (now Nat. Ocean Survey), Rockville, Md., 1962-66, phys. scientist Office of Dir., 1967-73, research asso. Office of Dir., 1973-77; cons. tidal dynamics, Bonita, Calif., 1978—. Served to capt. USAAF, 1942-46. Recipient Spl. Achievement award Dept. Commerce, NOAA, 1970, 74, 76, 77. Mem. Sigma Pi Sigma, Pi Mu Epsilon, Delta Phi Alpha. Democrat. Presbyterian. Author: The Strategic Role of Perigean Spring Tides in Nautical History and North American Coastal Flooding, 1635-1976, 1978; contbr. numerous articles to encys., reference sources, profl. jours.; writer, tech. dir. documentary film: Pathfinders from the Stars, 1967; editor-in-chief: The Prince William Sound, Alaska, Earthquake of 1964 and Aftershocks, vols. 1-2A and sci. coordinator vols. 2B, 2C and 3, 1966-69. Home: 3103 Casa Bonita Dr Bonita CA 92002

WOOD, GEORGE WILLIAM, hosp. adminstr.; b. Oakland, Calif., Mar. 11, 1927; s. George Uniac and Doris M. (Engle) W.; A.B., Stanford U., 1950; M.P.H., U. Calif., 1952; m. Mary Teresa Alexander, Jan. 10, 1951; children—Susan, Sandra, Shelly, George Uniac. Hosp. adminstrn. residence St. Francis Meml. Hosp., San Francisco, 1953; asst. adminstr. Washoe Med. Center, Reno, 1954; asst. adminstr. Brookside Hosp., San Pablo, Calif., 1955-62; owner, mgr. 1900 Corp., San Pablo, 1962-70; exec. dir. Oakland (Calif.) Hosp., 1970-81; owner Golden Years Guest Home, 1982—. Served with U.S. Navy, 1944-45. Fellow Am. Coll. Nursing Home Adminstrs.; mem. Am. Coll. Hosp. Adminstrs. Episcopalian. Club: Sequoyah Country (Oakland). Contbr. articles to profl. jours. Office: 931 San Anselmo Ave San Anselma CA 94960

WOOD, JAMES LESLIE, sociology educator; b. Oakland, Calif., Aug. 30, 1941; s. James Leslie and Maxine Edith (Butler) W.; m. Patricia Ann Taylor, June 13, 1964; children—Ann Marie, Jeffrey James. B.A. in Sociology, U. Calif.-Berkeley, 1963, M.A. in Sociology, 1964-66, Ph.D. in Sociology, 1966-73; postgrad. U. Calif.-San Francisco Sch. Law, 1963-64. Asst. prof. San Francisco State U., summer 1972; instr. sociology Holy Names Coll., 1971-73; lectr. U. Calif.-Riverside, 1973-75; lectr. San Diego State U., 1975-76, asst. prof., 1976-78, assoc. prof., 1978-81, prof. sociology, 1981—; lectr. San Diego State U. grantee; U. Calif.-Riverside grantee, 1975. Mem. Am. Sociol. Assn., Pacific Sociol. Assn., Alpha Kappa Delta. Author: (with Maurice Jackson) Social Movements: Development, Participation, and Dynamics, 1982; (with Howard J. Sherman) Sociology: Traditional and Radical Perspectives, 1979; The Sources of American Student Activism, 1974; also monographs; contbr. articles to profl. jours. Office: Dept Sociology San Diego State U San Diego CA 92182

WOOD, LARRY (MARY LAIRD WOOD), journalist, educator; b. Sandpoint, Idaho; d. Edward Hayes and Alice (McNeel) Small; B.A. magna cum laude, U. Wash., Seattle, 1938; M.A. with highest honors, 1940; postgrad. Stanford U., 1941-42; postgrad. U. Calif., Berkeley, 1943-44, certificate in photography, 1971; postgrad. journalism U. Wis., 1971-72, U. Minn., 1971-72, U. Ga., 1972-73; postgrad. in art, architecture and biology U. Calif., Santa Cruz, 1974-76, Stanford Hopkins Marine Sta.; children—Mary, Marcia, Barry. By-line columnist (home and gardens, archtl. editor) Oakland Tribune (Calif.), San Francisco Chronicle, 1946—, Parade mag., Chevron USA, Motorland, Westways, Accent; feature writer Western region Christian Sci. Monitor, CSM Radio Syndicate and Internat. News, 1973—, Register and Tribune Syndicate, Des Moines, 1975—, Calif. Today mag.; stringer Travelday mag., 1976—; No. Calif. contbg. editor Fashion Showcase, Dallas, Linguapress, Besancon, France, Parents Mag., 1950-68; regional corr. Spokane mag.; bylined feature writer Calif. Living and travel mag. San Jose Mercury News, 1978—, Oakland Calif C. of C., 1983—; photographer/feature writer Scholastic Publs., 1974—; Calif. corr. Seattle Times Sunday mag.; feature writer East/West Network, airline inflight mags., 1980—, Chevron USA, Times Mirror Syndicate and Knight Ridder Syndicate; freelance writer mag. including Parents', Sports Illus., Family Circle, Popular Mechanics, Family Handyman, House and Garden, Mechanix Illus., Oceans (award), Sea Frontiers (award), House Beautiful, Am. Home, Off-Duty, other nat. mags., 1946—; feature writer Meridian Publs., Ogden, Utah, Donnelley Publs., Oak Brook, Ill.; cons., reviewer for sci. textbooks, author sci. features on frontiers and scientists profiles Focus on Science Series Charles E. Merrill div. Bell & Howell Co., 1983— dir. pub. relations No. Calif. Assn. Phi Beta Kappa, 1969—; works used worldwide by USIA; cons., feature writer Met. Transp. Commn. No. Calif., 1970—; asst. prof. journalism San Diego State U., 1975—; prof. journalism San Jose State U., spring 1976; asst. prof. journalism Calif. State U., Hayward; prof. environ./sci. journalism U. Calif. Journalism Extension, 1979; prof. journalism U. of Pacific, spring 1979; keynote speaker Calif. State U. Women in Communications Conf., 1979, Nat. Assn. Edn. Journalism/Soc. Profl. Journalism Conf., 1979, Soc. Am. Travel Writers Conv., 1979; chmn. nat. travel writing contest for U.S. univ. journalism students Assn. for Edn. in Journalism/Soc. Am. Travel Writers, 1979—; dir. public relations/cons. in field of sci., environ. affairs and recreation to numerous, firms, instns., assns.; del. Nat. Press Photographers Flying Short Course, 1979, Asilomar Conf., FACS, Calif., 1982, 35th Nat. Conf. Public Relations Soc. Am., 1982, Nat. Trust for Historic Preservation nat. conf., 1982. Public Pub. relations dir. YWCA, YM-YW USO, Seattle, 1942-46, YWCA, Oakland, Calif., 1946-56, Children's Home Soc. Calif., 1946-56, Children's Med. Center No. Calif., 1946-70, Eastbay Regional Park Dist., 1946-58, Calif. Spring Garden Shows, 1946-58, Girl Scouts U.S.A., Oakland, 1948-56, others; speaker for ednl. insts., profl. groups, A.C.S., World Wildlife Fund, 1946—; sec. Jr. ctr. of Arts, Oakland, 1952—; vol. pub. relations Am. Cancer Soc., YMCA, Oakland, 1946-52; pub. relations writer ARC, 1946-56; judge Nat. Book Awards, 1980—, Nat. Assn. Real Estate Editors ann. real estate contest, 1982, 83; cons. Oakland Park Dept., YMCA, Seattle, Oakland; guest, press del. Govt. of Mexico, Mass. Dept. Econ. Devel. and City of Boston, Costa Rica, Wash., Oreg., Calif., Alaska, 1980-82, Fla., San Antonio, Atlanta, Chattanooga, Baton Rouge, Houston, Galveston, 1983. Bd. dirs. Camp Fire Girls, Oakland, Joaquin Miller PTA, Oakland; trustee Calif. State Parks Found., 1976—. Recipient citations U.S. Forest Service, 1975, citation for coverage 1st nat. historic preserve Ebey's Landing, San Juan Island, Wash., Nat. Park Service, 1976, Oakland Mus. Assn., 1978-79; named Calif. Woman of Achievement, 1979; co-recipient citation Oakland Mus., Nat. Headliners award numerous other citations; honoree for feature Oakland C. of C. and Standard Oil U.S.A., 1983. Mem. Pub. Relations Soc. Am., Nat. Sch. Public Relations Assn., Environ. Cons. N.Am., Internat. Environ. Cons., Oceanic Soc., Internat. Oceanographic Soc., Am. Assn. Edn. in Journalism (exec. bd. nat. mag. div. 1978—, newspaper div. 1974-77), U. Wash. Ocean Scis. Alumni Assn. (charter), Investigative Reporters and Editors, Soc. Travel Writers Am., Soc. Profl. Journalists, Women in Communications, Calif. Acad. Environ. News Writers, Am. Mgmt. Assn., AAAS, Nat. Press Photographers Assn., San Francisco Press Assn., Nat. Acad. TV Arts and Scis., council Advancement Sci. Writing, Inc., Eastbay Women's Press Club, Calif. Writers Club, Investigative Reporters and Editors Sigma Delta Chi, Theta Sigma Phi. Author/reviewer Focus on Science series, Bell & Howell. Author: Journalism Quar., 1978—; (with Charles Merrill) Principles of Science, 1982; (with Barry Wood) Fodor's California and San Francisco, 1983; Fodor Travel Guide. Pacific N.W. works in archives of U. Wash. Library, Calif. writings in archives of Oakland Pub. Library. Home: 6161 Castle Dr Oakland CA 94611

WOOD, LINCOLN JACKSON, aerospace engineer; b. Lyons, N.Y., Sept. 30, 1947; s. William Hulbert and Sarah Brock (Strumsky) W.; B.S. with distinction, Cornell U., 1968; M.S. (NSF trainee), Stanford U., 1969, Ph.D. (NSF trainee), 1972. Bechtel instr. engring. Calif. Inst. Tech., 1972-74, lectr. systems engring., 1975-76, vis. asst. prof. systems engring., 1976-78, vis. asso. prof. systems engring., 1978—; staff engr. Hughes Aircraft Co., El Segundo, Calif., 1974-77; mem. tech. staff Jet Propulsion Lab, Pasadena, Calif., 1977-81, tech. group supr., 1981—; cons. in field. Del., Calif. Democratic Council Conv., 1978. Mem. Am. Astronautical Soc. (sr.; space flight mechanics com. 1980—), AIAA (sr.), IEEE, AAAS, Seal and Serpent Soc. (pres. 1967-68), Sigma Xi, Tau Beta Pi, Phi Kappa Phi, Phi Eta Sigma. Club: Los Angeles Stanford Bachelors (v.p., dir.). Assoc. editor Jour. Astronautical Scis., 1980-83, Jour. Guidance, Control, and Dynamics, 1983—; contbr. articles on interplanetary nav., control theory and trajectory optimization to profl. jours. La Canada Flintridge CA Office: Jet Propulsion Lab 4800 Oak Grove Dr Pasadena CA 91109

WOOD, LINDA MAY, librarian; b. Fort Dodge, Iowa, Nov. 6, 1942; d. John Albert and Beth Ida (Riggs) Wiley; m. C. James Wood, Sept. 15, 1964. B.A., Portland State U., 1964; M.Librarianship, U. Wash., 1965. Reference librarian Library Assn. Portland (Oreg.), 1965-67, br. librarian, 1967-72, adminstrv. asst. to the librarian, 1972-73, asst. librarian, 1973-77; asst. city librarian Los Angeles Pub. Library, 1977-80; library dir. Riverside (Calif.) City and County Pub. Library, 1980—. Chmn. bd. dirs. Inland Library System, 1983—. Mem. AAUW, ALA, Pub. Library Assn., Library Adminstrn. and Mgmt. Assn., Calif. Library Assn., Pacific N.W. Library Assn., Calif. County Librarians Assn., LWV. Democrat. Club: Zonta. Office: Riverside City and County Public Library PO Box 468 Riverside CA 92502

WOOD, MARGARET ANN, advertising executive; b. Princes Risborough, Eng., May 20, 1934; d. Montague and Mary Anna (Hennessey) Jones; divorced; children—Mark, Michael, Peter. Vice pres., copy chief, creative dir. Lennen & Newell, Inc. advt., Honolulu, 1960-70; pres. Environ. Devel. Council, Inc., Honolulu, 1971-73; pres., chmn. bd. Margo Wood Advt., Inc., Honolulu, 1974—; chmn. bd. subs. Pacific Pub. Relations, 1979—. Trustee Hawaii Bound, Honolulu Jr. Acad.; bd. dirs. Hawaii Pub. Radio, Honolulu council Navy League U.S., Hawaii Visitors Bur., Honolulu chpt. ARC. Named Advt. Woman of Year, 1965. Mem. Sales and Mktg. Execs. Honolulu (past pres.), Am. Mktg. Assn. (v.p. Western region, pres. Honolulu 1979-80), Advt. Agy. Assn. Hawaii, Hawaii Hotel Assn., Pacific Area Travel Assn. (past chmn., internat. mktg. authority), Mensa, Honolulu C. of C. (dir.). Roman Catholic. Clubs: Oahu Country, Plaza. Contbr. articles to profl. jours. Home: 649 Ulili St Honolulu HI 96816 Office: 841 Bishop St Suite 1501 Honolulu HI 96813

WOOD, MARGARET MEEKS, agrl. co. exec.; b. Tipton, Okla., July 31, 1932; d. Fred Lionel Meeks and Josie Gladys (Alexander) Meeks Kennedy; A.A., Columbia Basin Coll., 1972, computer sci. cert., 1975; B.P.A., U. San Francisco; m. Leonard Herbert Wood, June 30, 1952 (div.); children—Regina Mary, Robin Theresa. With Burns & Roe, Inc., Richland, Wash., 1975-81, computer programmer, 1979-81; with Producters Cotton Oil Co., Fresno, Calif., 1981-82. Treas., Franklin County Democratic Central Com., 1978-80. Presbyterian.

WOOD, PETER OGDEN, architect; b. Ayer, Mass., Jan. 8, 1948; s. Howard Ogden and Sarah Jane (Fraser) W.; B.Arch., Ill. Inst. Tech., 1971; m. Joyce J. Hawley, Nov. 21, 1979; children—Russell, Geoffrey, Asa, Amanda. Pres., Energy Dynamics Corp., Colorado Springs, Colo., 1974-77; owner Engergy Equipment Co., Colorado Springs, 1977—; prin. GDA Designs, Colorado Springs, 1977-78; architect Wayne Browneller, Inc., Colorado Springs, 1978-79; prin. Starr/Wood, Inc., Colorado Springs, 1979-80; owner Counterpoint Studios, Colorado Springs, 1980—, Peter O. Wood, Architect, Colorado Springs, 1980—; partner Mac Wood Oil, 1980—; tech. cons. Sci. Sunsource, Inc., 1977—; owner Counterpoint Sch., 1983—; solar cons. Solar Service, Inc., 1977—. Mem. steering com. Libertarian Party El Paso County; mem. solar code review com. Regional Bldg. Dept., Colorado Springs, 1978. Cert. energy auditor, Colo. Dept. Energy. Mem. AIA, Home Builders Assn., Constrn. Specifications Inst., Am. Solar Energy Soc. Contbr. articles to profl. jours. Home: 927 N Royer St Colorado Springs CO 80903 Office: 815 N Nevada Ave Colorado Springs CO 80903

WOOD, PHILIP RAYMOND, advertising executive; b. Oakland, Calif., Apr. 22, 1937; s. Walter N. and Mildred (Schultze) W.; m. Donna Hunt, Mar. 28, 1972. B.A. in Journalism, San Jose State U., 1960. Mail clk. Lennen & Newell, Inc., San Francisco, 1960-61, account exec., 1962-65, Lennen & Newell, Honolulu, 1965-69, v.p., mgmt. supr., 1969-76; v.p., creative dir. Richardson Siegle Rolfs & McCoy, Inc., Honolulu, 1970-72; v.p., creative dir. Bozwell & Jacobs/Pacific, Honolulu, 1972-76; exec. v.p., creative dir., prin. Seigle Rolfs & Wood, Inc., Honolulu, 1976—. Served with USNR, 1955-63. Clubs: Pacific (Honolulu), Mid-Pacific Country (Kailua, Hawaii). Office: Seigle Rolfs & Wood Pioneer Plaza 900 Fort St Mall Suite 600 Honolulu HI 96813

WOOD, ROBERT EDWIN, insurance executive; b. Seattle, Nov. 20, 1904; s. Galen and Agnes (Irvine) W.; B.B.A., U. Wash., 1928; m. Marjorie May Kuhnley, June 19, 1935 (dec. 1959); 1 dau., Barbara L. Wood Acker; m. 2d, Esther Schelenberg, Aug. 6, 1966. Sec.-treas., buyer Gene Hatton, 1918-29; with Phoenix Mut. Life Ins. Co., 1929—, home office supr., San Francisco, Los Angeles, Cleve. and N.Y.C., 1936-40, br. mgr., San Francisco, 1940-44, personal prodn., 1944—; past pres. First San Francisco Planning Corp.; treas., dir. Royal Towers Corp.; lectr. in field; Calif. chmn. anti-inflation campaign Am. Council Life Ins., 1980; v.p. San Francisco Estate Planning Council, 1963-64, also dir. Treas., San Francisco Easter Seal Soc.; bd. dirs., sec. Million Dollar Round Table Found.; mem. nat. devel. com. Adventures Unltd.; v.p. bd. dirs. Woodman Property Owners; active Found. for Christian Living, Found. for Religion and Psychiatry; life mem. U.S. Olympic Games Hospitality Com. Recipient Orr award, 1948, Heron award for outstanding service to life ins. industry, 1956; charter mem. Phoenix Mut. Hall of Fame; C.L.U. Mem. Nat. (trustee, chmn. nominating com., recipient nat. quality com.), Calif. (past pres., award), San Francisco (past pres., nat. committeeman) assns. life underwriters, Am. Soc. C.L.U.s (past regional v.p.), Million Dollar Round Table (life mem., mem. organizing bd. Found.), U. Wash. Alumni Assn. (past pres. No. Calif. chpt.). Christian Scientist. Clubs: Masons (knight comdr. ct. of honor), Shriners (pres. Peninsula). Editorial bd. Leaders mag.; contbr. articles to profl. publs. Home and Office: Royal Towers 1750 Taylor St Apt 702 San Francisco CA 94133

WOOD, SHELTON EUGENE, army officer; b. Douglas, Ga., May 20, 1938; s. Shelton and Mae Lillie (Pheil) W.; A.A., St. Johns U., 1958; B.A., U. Nebr., 1959; M.Ed., Coll. William and Mary, 1971; Ph.D., Sussex U., 1973; Ed.D., Nova U., 1975; M.A., Central Mich. U., 1977; m. Edna Louise Tanner, Aug. 25, 1958; children—Shelton John, Deirdre Louise. Area mgr. Marshall Fields Corp., Fla., 1957-58, transp. supr. Greyhound Corp., Jacksonville, Fla., 1959-62; commd. lt. U.S. Army, 1963, advanced through grades to lt. col., 1977; with Redstone Readiness Group, 1977-80; chief studies and analysis div. Korean Inst. for Def. Analysis, 1981—. Active Boy Scouts Am., 1977—; lay leader United Meth. Ch., Falls Church, Va., 1977-79. Decorated Bronze Star with 2 oak leaf clusters, Air Medal with 3 oak leaf clusters, Purple Heart. Fellow Sussex Coll., 1969-70. Mem. Am. Soc. Trainers and Developers (pres. S.E. chpt. 1974-75), Am. Def. Preparedness Assn., NEA, Phi Kappa Delta, Phi Delta Kappa. Clubs: Masons, Shriners. Author: An Analysis of Incoming Freshmen at NSC, 1975; Choice of College Factors, 1976; 47 articles and handbooks in field of mil. tng. and mgmt. Address: Hdqrs JUSMAG-K Box 71 APO San Francisco CA 96302

WOOD, STEPHEN CRAIG, physiologist; b. Cleve., Sept. 28, 1942; s. Robert A. and Dorothy L. (Jewitt) W.; m. Linda Lou Gremer, June 15, 1967; children—Tracey, Stephen, Laura, Julia. B.S., Kent State U., 1964, M.A., 1966; Ph.D., U., 1970. Asst. Prof. Aarhus (Denmark) U., 1971-72, So. Ill. U., 1972-74; asst. prof. U. N.Mex. Sch. Medicine, 1974-78, assoc. prof. physiology, 1978—. NIH grantee, 1977-83, NSF grantee, 1978. Mem. Am. Physiol. Soc., Scandinavian Physiol. Soc., Am. Soc. Zoologists. Contbr. chpts. to profl. books and articles to profl. jours. Editorial bd. Am. Jour. Physiology, 1982—. Home: 4418 Avenida Manana NE Albuquerque NM 87110 Office: 915 Stanford NE Albuquerque NM 87131

WOOD, THOMAS JOSEPH, editor; b. Hoxie, Ark., Oct. 8, 1930; s. William Hubert and Lucy Blanch Woodyard; B.S. in Econs., Fla. State U., 1966; M.A. in Journalism, Ohio Christian Coll. Dayton, 1969; children—T.J., II, Jef von Lewis, Melanie Exeter. Served with USAF, 1947-60; freelance agr. pilot, 1960-78; editor, pub. Ag-Pilot Internat. mag., Milton Freewater, Oreg., 1978; editor IAAF Newsletter, Aviacion Tiempo mag., 1980-82. Recipient Safe Pilot award Nat. Pilots Assn., 1979. Mem. Aviation/Space Writers Assn., Am. Assn. Profl. Consultants, Nat. Rifle Assn., Am. Legion, VFW, Nat. Agrl. Aviation Assn., Agrl. Pilots Assn. Clubs: Elks, Rotary. Home: 1414 Topaz St Walla Walla WA 99362 Office: 10 NE 6th Ct Milton Freewater OR 97862

WOOD, VICTOR LOUIE, insurance consultant; b. Saint Jo, Tex., Nov. 9, 1913; s. Louie Edwin and Mary Emma (Foster) W.; student public schs.; m. Ida Mae Greer, June 20, 1935; children—Vern L., Charles Edward, Sue Eileen. Salesman, Pioneer Am. Life Ins. Co., Ft. Worth, 1938-47; organizer, operator Western Fidelity Life Ins. Co., Ft. Worth, 1947-52, N.Mex. Life Ins. Co., Albuquerque, 1952-64, Gt. Western Assurance Life Co., Albuquerque, 1964-70, Western Educators Life Ins. Co., Albuquerque, 1970-74, Future Security Life Ins. Co., Albuquerque, 1974-77; organizer, operator N.Mex. Investors Life Ins. Co., Albuquerque, 1977-81, cons., 1981—. Republican. Clubs: Four Hills Country, Masons. Home: 6400 Quemado Dr NE Albuquerque NM 87109 Office: N Mex Investors Life Ins Co Suite A 150 Louisiana St NE Albuquerque NM 87108

WOOD, W. WINSTON, marketing executive; b. Oakland, Calif., Aug. 8, 1941; s. Willsie Winston and Louise (Parcells) W.; m. Barbara Paskell, May 1, 1966; children—David Christopher, Jason Alan. B.A., Williams Coll., 1963; M.B.A., U. Santa Clara, 1978. With Time, Inc., 1964-68; mgr. mktg. research Harris Corp., 1968-69; with Arcata Corp., Menlo Park, Calif., 1969-80, mgr. mktg. research, 1977-80; mktg. dir. Wornick Co., Burlingame, Calif., 1980—. Mem. Las Lomitas Governing Bd., 1977-81, pres., 1979-80. Served with USCGR, 1963-71. Mem. Am. Mktg. Assn. (dir., pres. San Francisco chpt.), Peninsula Mktg. Assn., Assn. Corp. Growth. Democrat. Club: Ladera Tennis (Portola Valley). Home: 101 Coquito Way Portola Valley CA 94025

WOOD, WILLIS B., JR., natural gas company executive; b. Kansas City, Mo., 1934. Grad. U. Tulsa, 1957. Pres., chief exec. officer (gas supply, plan and acquisitions) Pacific Lighting Gas Supply Co., Los Angeles. Mem. Am. Gas Assn., Pacific Coast Gas Assn. (bd. dirs.), Pacific Energy Assn. Office: Pacific Lighting Gas Supply Co 720 W 8th St Los Angeles CA 90017*

WOODARD, DOROTHY MARIE, ins. broker; b. Houston, Feb. 7, 1932; d. Gerald Edgar and Bessie Katherine (Crain) Floeck; student N.Mex. State U., 1950; m. June 19, 1950 (dec.); m. Norman W. Libby, July 19, 1982. Partner, Western Oil Co., Tucumcari, N.Mex., 1950—; owner, mgr. Woodard & Co., Las Cruces, N.Mex., 1959-67; agt., dist. mgr. United Nations Ins. Co., Denver, 1968-74; agt. Western Nat. Life Ins. Co., Amarillo, Tex., 1976—. Exec. dir. Tucumcari Indsl. Commn., 1979—; dir. Bravo Dome Study Com., 1979—; regional bd. dirs. N.Mex., Eastern Plains Council Govts., 1979—. Mem. Tucumcari C. of C. Club: Mesa Country. Home: PO Box 823 Tucumcari NM 88401 Office: PO Box 1003 Tucumcari NM 88401

WOODARD, DUANE, state attorney general; b. Kansas City, Mo., Jan. 12, 1938; m. Thelma Hansen, Apr. 11, 1964; children—Elizabeth Anne, Mary Kathleen. B.A., U. Wyo., 1963; J.D., U. Okla., 1967. Bar: Okla., 1967, Colo., 1968, U.S. Supreme Ct., 1972; Dep. dist. atty. Larimer County, Ft. Collins, Colo., 1969-72; mcpl. judge Town of Windsor (Colo.), 1974-76; mem. firm Anderson, Dressel, Sommermeyer & Wooard, Ft. Collins, 1975-78; mem. Colo. State Senate, 1977-80; commr. Colo. Pub. Utilities, Denver, 1980-82; atty. gen. State of Colo., Denver, 1983—. Served with USMC, 1956-59. Mem. ABA. Republican. Episcopalian. Clubs: Rotary, Elks. Office: Office of Attorney General 1525 Sherman St Denver CO 80203

WOODBURY, JOHN BRYCE, accountant, educator; b. Hurricane, Utah, July 11, 1931; s. William Evans and Verda (Sullivan) W.; m. Ranae Raymond Strain, Dec. 21, 1957; children—John B., Bevan J., Denise, Michael S. B.S. in Acctg., Brigham Young U., 1953; M.B.A., U. Utah, 1966. C.P.A., Calif. Acct., John F. Forbes & Co., Sacramento, 1975-79; practice acctg., Sacramento, 1980—; instr. Calif. State U.-Sacramento, 1975—. Served to lt. col. USAF, 1953-75. Decorated Bronze Star. Mem. Am. Inst. C.P.A.s, Calif. Soc. C.P.A.s, Nat. Assn. Accts. (v.p. 1979-80, dir. 1977-80). Mormon. Club: Sacramento Suburban Kiwanis (dir., chmn. program and spiritual aims com. 1980-83). Home: 3405 Riverdale Way Carmichael CA 95608 Office: 2222 Sierra Blvd Suite 15 Sacramento CA 95825

WOODFIELD, FRANK WILLIAM, chemical engineer; b. Astoria, Oreg., Mar. 1, 1918; s. Francis William and Irta Luella (Page) W.; m. Joyce Elaine Gleeson, June 10, 1944; children—Susan, Dorothy, William. B.S.Ch.E., Oreg. State U., 1939; M.S.Ch.E., Columbia U., 1940. Chem. engr. process devel. E.I. duPont de Nemours, 1940-47; group leader to mgmt. engr. devel. Gen. Electric Co., Richland, Wash., 1947-64; dep. staff engrng. mgr., asst. lab. dir. tech. services Battelle Northwest, 1965-74; mgr. logistics Exxon Nuclear Co., Richland, 1974—. Mem. Richland Bd. Adjustments, 1959-75, Richland Planning Commn., 1963-64. Mem. Am. Chem. Soc., Am. Nuclear Soc., Am. Inst. Chem. Engrs., Sigma Xi, Tau Beta Pi, Phi Lambda Upsilon. Contbr. to Perry's Chemical Engineers Handbook, 1950; contbr. articles to profl. jours. Home: 81 McMurray St Richland WA 99352 Office: 2101 Horn Rapids Rd Richland WA 99352

WOODFIELD, WILLIAM READ, TV writer and producer; b. San Francisco, Jan. 21, 1928; s. William H. and Elizabeth Lylia Woodfield; student U. Calif., Berkeley, Golden Gate U.; m. Elizabeth Glinski, Dec. 17, 1966; children—Nancy Everett, William, Robert. Mag. journalist Life, Look, Esquire, Atlantic Monthly, Playboy, Time, Paris Match, N.Y. Times Mag.; writer, producer numerous TV series and movies including Mission: Impossible, Voyage to the Bottom of the Sea, Shaft, San Francisco Internat. Airport, Earth II, Satan's Triangle, Masquerade; writer, producer Timberley Co., Los Angeles, 1974—; v.p., 1976—; pres. Woodfield Co. Mem. Acad. Motion Picture Arts and Scis., Acad. TV Arts and Scis. (honored for outstanding dramatic series 1966-67, 67-68), Writers Guild Am. West. Author: Ninth Life, 1960. Address: Twentieth Century Fox 10201 W Pico Blvd Los Angeles CA 90035

WOODFIN, MARTHA CLOUD, interior designer; b. Georgetown, Tex., March 26, 1939; d. John Edward and Lenora (Beckmann) Cloud; m. Ronald Lynn Woodfin, Jan. 28, 1962; children—Alfred John, Edward Claude. B.S. in Interior Design, U. Tex., Austin, 1961. Interior designer R. Hall Interiors, Downey, Calif., 1963-64, Town House Interiors, South Gate, Calif., 1964-65, William L. Davis Sons Co., Seattle, 1965-72; prin. Martha Cloud Woodfin Interiors, Sandia Park, N. Mex., 1978—; instr. in interior design Seattle Community Coll., 1967-72, Cerro Coso Community Coll., 1973-78. Mem. Am. Soc. Interior Designers. Contbr. design work to profl. jours. Address: Box 55 Sandia Park NM 87047

WOODGER, ELIZABETH RUTH, archivist; b. Port Chester, N.Y., Mar. 22, 1957; d. Herbert Arthur and Carol (Magnusson) W. B.A. in History, SUNY-Binghamton, 1979; M.A. in History, Carnegie Mellon U., 1980. Project archivist Matthew G. Norton Co., Seattle, 1981-83; archivist Laird Norton Co., Seattle, 1983—. Mem. Soc. Am. Archivists, Am. Assn. State and Local History, N.W. Archivists. Office: Laird Norton Co 801 2d Ave 13th Floor Seattle WA 98104

WOODGER, MARY JANE, educator; b. Salt Lake City, June 4, 1958; d. Edward Winston and Norma (Taylor) W.; B.S., Brigham Young U., 1980. Recreational leader Utah State Tng. Sch., American Fork, 1974-76; dept. mgr. Zions Coop. Merc. Instn., Provo, Utah, 1976-80; with internat. vol. support services ACTION, Washington, 1981; tchr. Jordan Sch. Dist., Midvale, Utah, 1982—. Mem. Utah Home Econs. Assn., Am. Home Econs. Assn., Utah Vocat. Assn., Am. Vocat. Home Econs. Assn. Republican. Mormon. Home: 2033 N 650 W Provo UT 84601 Office: Jordan Sch Dist 138 Pioneer St Midvale UT 84047

WOODGRIFT, KENNETH EARL, aerospace co. exec.; b. Detroit, Oct. 13, 1934; s. George Elliot and Elvera Jenny (Reynolds) W.; m. Charleen E. Gray, Aug. 25, 1955; children—Randel W., Keriane Marie; m. 2d, Beverly D. Schoen, Sept. 7, 1968. B.S.M.E., Calif. Poly. State U. San Luis Obispo. With Marquardt Co., Van Nuys, Calif., 1957—, beginning as devel. engr., succesively group supr., program mgr., dir. engrng., v.p. and sr. v.p. engrng., exec. v.p. and chief operating officer, 1957-80, pres., chief exec. officer, 1980—. Mem. U.S. Senatorial Bus. Adv. Bd., Congl. Bus. Adv. Com. Named Alumnus of Yr., Calif. Poly. State U. Alumni Assn., 1981. Mem. Aerospace Industries Assn., Am. Def. Preparedness Assn. Home: 4517 Canoga Dr Woodland Hills CA 92364 Office: 16555 Saticoy St Van Nuys CA 91409

WOODHOUSE, ROSSALIND YVONNE, banker, state agency administrator; b. Detroit, June 7, 1940; d. Allen P. and Perediltha E. (Wright) Venable; B.A. in Sociology, U. Wash., 1963, M.S.W., 1970; m. Donald Woodhouse, July 19, 1958; children—Joycelyn, Justin. Program coordinator New Careers Project, Seattle, 1968; community orgn. specialist Seattle Housing Authority, 1969-70; exec. dir. Central Area Motivation Program, Seattle, 1971-73; instr./coordinator Edmonds Community Coll., Lynnwood, Wash., 1973-77; dir. Wash. State Dept. Licensing, Olympia, 1977—; v.p. Rainier Nat. Bank; adv. Nat. Accident Sampling System Com.; mem. Wash. State Minority and Women Bus. Enterprise Council; mem. states' task force U.S. Consumer Product Safety Commn. Pres. Seattle Women's Commn., 1971-72, 75-76. Recipient service award Iota Phi Lambda, 1979; named one of Ten Outstanding Young Women of Am., 1978; Nat. Fellowship Fund. fellow, 1976-77. Mem. Am. Assn. Motor Vehicle Adminstrs. (pres. western region), N.W. Conf. Black Public Ofcls. (pres. 1979-81), Wash. State Black Women Caucus, NAACP, Urban League, Alpha Kappa Alpha. Democrat. Office: Rainier Nat Bank Seattle WA

WOODIN, WILLIAM HARTMAN, III, lab. adminstr.; b. N.Y.C., Dec. 16, 1925; s. William Hartman and Carolyne Knowland (Hyde) W.; B.A., U. Ariz., 1950; M.A., U. Calif., Berkeley, 1956; m. Ann G. Snow, July 10, 1948; children—Peter H., John J., Michael S., W. Hugh; m. 2d, Elizabeth T. Leydon, May 28, 1977. Asst. dir. Ariz.-Sonora Desert Mus., Tucson, 1953-54, dir., 1954-71, dir. emeritus, 1972—; pres. Woodin Lab., Tucson, 1981—. Fellow AAAS, Ariz. Nev. Acad. Sci.; mem. Am. Def. Prepardness Assn., Am. Assn. Museums, Assn. Firearm and Tool Mark Examiners (tech. adv.). Author: (with F.W. Hackley and E.L. Scranton) History of Modern U.S. Military Small Arms Ammunition, 1967, Vol. 2, 1978; contbr. articles to profl. jours. Home and office: 3600 N Larrea Ln Tucson AZ 85715

WOODROME, HARVEY NILES, talent agent; b. Denver, June 17, 1949; s. Harvey George and Ilo Clara (Niles) W.; m. Susan Ferne Roesch. B.A., U. No. Colo., 1971, M.A., 1976; Ph.D., U. Denver, 1979. Dir. Vannoy Talent Agy., Colorado Springs, Colo., 1979—, sr. v.p., 1980—. Served USAF, 1971-79. Decorated USAF Commendation medal (2), USAF Longevity award 1977. Home: PO Box 126 USAF Acad CO 80840

WOODROOF, ERNEST AUBREY, sci. lab. exec.; b. Nashville, Mar. 12, 1939; s. Ernest Alonzo and Emogene (Perry) W.; B.S., San Diego State U., 1966; Ph.D. in Biochemistry (fellow), UCLA, 1970; M.S. in Fin. and Mgmt. Sci., West Coast U., 1975; m. Nancy Ward, July 20, 1962; children—Eric, Amy, Laurie. Biochemistry supr. Edwards Lab. Am. Hosp. Supply, 1970-75; project mgr. Shiley Labs., Irvine, Calif., 1975-78; pres., owner Woodroof Labs. Inc., Santa Ana, Calif., 1978—; pres., chmn. bd. Hall-Woodroof, Inc., Santa Ana, 1979—. Served with USAR, 1957-65. Mem. Am. Soc. Biomaterials, Internat. Soc. Artificial Organs, Am. Burn Assn., Am. Soc. Artificial Internal Organs, Am. Soc. Advancement of Med. Instrumentation, Western Connective Tissue Soc., N.Y. Acad. Sci. Contbr. articles to profl. jours.; developer synthetic skin substitute for use with burn victims; developer Bioflex foul-weather clothing. Office: 3100-7 Harvard St Santa Ana CA 92704

WOODRUM, DONALD, advertising and public relations executive; b. N.Y.C., Aug. 6, 1917; s. Donald and Gertrude (Conn) W.; A.B., U. Calif.-Berkeley, 1937; m. Mary Harvey, Mar. 18, 1944 (div. 1956); 1 dau., Mary Lynn; m. 2d, Dorothea Enzor, Nov. 27, 1957. Pres., Woodrum & Staff, Ltd., Honolulu, 1946—. Served with USNR, 1941-45, 50-53; now comdr. ret. Mem. Honolulu Advt. Fedn. (founding pres., award of distinction 1977), Honolulu C. of C., Advt. Assn. West (lt. gov. 1965-67), Advt. Agy. Assn. Hawaii (past pres.), Navy League, Bishop Mus., Alpha Sigma Phi. Republican. Club: Outrigger Canoe (Honolulu). Author: This is Hawaii, 1974. Home: 207 Kawaikui Pl Honolulu HI 96821 Office: 720 Kapiolani Blvd Honolulu HI 96813

WOODS, JAMES CHARLES, museum director; b. Twin Falls, Idaho, Oct. 23, 1953; s. Edwin Charles and Alyce Helen (Peyron) W.; A.A., Coll. So. Idaho, 1973; B.F.A., Boise State U., 1975; postgrad. Idaho State U., 1982; m. Cynthia Lou Kofoed, Aug. 23, 1975; children—Preston James, Kirsten Alyce. Dir., Herrett Mus., Coll. So. Idaho, Twin Falls, 1975—; tchr. anthropology program Idaho State U., 1982-83. Assn. Humanities in Idaho grantee, 1979, 80. Mem. Am. Assn. Mus., Idaho Assn. Mus., Idaho Archaeol. Soc. (bd. dirs.). Democrat. Roman Catholic. Editor: (with Plew and Pavesic) Essays in Honor of Don E. Crabtree, 1983. Home: 1287 Parkmeadows Dr Twin Falls ID 83301 Office: PO Box 1238 Coll So Idaho Twin Falls ID 83301

WOODS, JEROME BERRYMAN, banker; b. Wichita, Kans., July 10, 1937; s. Jerome B. and Mabel (Stokes) W.; m. Judith Ann Anderson, April 30, 1982; children—Lisa, Amy, Lainie, Jessica, Naomi. B.A. in Banking and Bus., Colo. Coll., 1960; student Grad. Sch. Banking, U. Wis., 1969-72. Owner J. B. Woods & Co., Colorado Springs, Colo., 1961-63; v.p. 1st Nat. Bank of Denver, 1963-76; exec. v.p., dir. Security Bank N.A., Billings, Mont., 1976—; dir. Rimrock Bank. Bd. dirs. Eastern Mont. Found., Salvation Army, YMCA Found. Mem. C. of C., Am. Inst. Banking. Clubs: Yellowstone Country, Yellowstone Kiwanis, Petroleum (Billings). Home: 5533 Bobby Jones Blvd Billings MT 59106 Office: PO Box 30918 Billings MT 59116

WOODS, JONATHAN CARL, protective coatings company executive, coating engineer, consultant; b. Cleve., Aug. 11, 1939; s. Carl Stoner and Ruth Louise (Class) W.; m. Sharon Elizabeth Starkey, July 17, 1965; m. 2d Janet Sue Parker, Apr. 8, 1975; children—Christine, Nicola, Jonathan. A.A., East Los Angeles Coll., 1962; cert. in paint tech. Los Angeles City Coll., 1962; B.S., U. Redlands, 1980. Registered corrosion engr., quality control engr., nuclear safety related coating engr., Calif. Formulating coating chemist Magna Corp., Santa Fe Springs, Calif., 1961-63, Mobil Chem. Corp., Azusa, Calif., 1963-65; founder, pres. Engard Coatings Corp., Huntington Beach, Calif., 1963—, chmn. bd., 1977—. Parish treas. St. Pauls Lutheran Ch., Laguna Beach, Calif. Served with USMC, 1962-63. Recipient Eagle Scout award Boy Scouts Am., 1954. Mem. Nat. Assn. Corrosion Engrs., ASTM, Utilities Nuclear Coating Work Com., Nat. Paint and Coatings Assn., Los Angeles Soc. Coating Tech., Am. Water Works Assn. Club: Poor Man's Poker of Laguna Beach. Office: 15541 Commerce Ln Huntington Beach CA 92649

WOODS, LESLIE VICTOR, optometrist; b. Los Angeles, Dec. 26, 1925; s. Kenneth Campbell and Ada Lucille (Meyers) W.; student U. B.C., 1944-46; B.S., Pacific U., 1948, O.D., 1949; m. Noreen Ellen Barry, Nov. 23, 1950; children—Deirdre Ann, Megan Louise. Individual practice optometry, Sedro Wooley, Wash., 1949, Spokane, 1950, 65—, Chelan, Wash., 1951-65; optometrist dept. ophthalmology Pacific Med. Ctr.; mem. faculty Columbia-Pacific U.; mem. optometric faculty Spokane Community Coll., 1975-78. Chmn. optometric affairs State and County CD, 1958-65; dir. Chelan CD, 1951; mem. Wash. Welfare Med. Care Com., 1958-66; councilman, Chelan, 1952; trustee Fort Wright Coll. of the Holy Names, Spokane; vice-chmn. bd. trustees Ft. Wright Coll., 1978-79. Mem. Wash. Optometric Assn. (pres. Inland soc. 1975-77), N. Central Wash. Optometric Soc. (pres. 1954-56, 63-64, state trustee 1954-56, 63-64), Omega Delta, Delta Upsilon. Democrat. Roman Catholic. Club: Lions (dir. N. Spokane 1975-76, v.p. 1976, pres. 1977-78). Home: 1979 Clay St San Francisco CA 94109 Office: 2340 Clay St Room 635 San Francisco CA 94115

WOODS, ROBERT LAWRENCE, life ins. exec., agy. mgmt. cons.; b. Los Angeles, May 17, 1911; s. Walter A. and Alice (Strang) W.; A.B., U. Calif. at Los Angeles, 1933; C.L.U., Am. Coll. Life Underwriters, 1937; m. Dorothy Welbourn, Oct. 10, 1942; children—Robert Lawrence, Susan Welbourn Woods. With Los Angeles agy. of Mass. Mut. Life Ins. Co., 1934—, asst. gen. agt., 1938-46, asso. gen. agt., 1946-49, gen. agt. in partnership, 1949-57, sole gen. agt., 1957-73. Fund raising chmn. Los Angeles chpt. ARC, 1961, dir., 1960-63. Trustee Am. Coll., 1958-61, 71-79. Served to lt. col., inf., AUS, 1941-46. Recipient John Newton Russell award Nat. Assn. Life Underwriters, 1971, Will G. Farrell award Los Angeles Life Ins. Assns., 1974; named to Mgmt. Hall of Fame, Nat. Gen. Agts. and Mgrs. Conf., 1974. Mem. Am. Soc. C.L.U.'s (pres. Los Angeles 1953-54, nat. pres. 1959-60), Mass. Mut. Gen. Agts. Assn. (pres.

1959-60), Gen. Agts. and Mgrs. Assn. (pres. Los Angeles 1957-58, nat. pres. 1967-68), Phi Gamma Delta. Home: 720 N Oakhurst Dr Beverly Hills CA 90210 Office: 4401 Wilshire Blvd Los Angeles CA 90010

WOODS, VIRGINIA M., home economist, educator; b. Clarkston, Wash., July 2, 1923; d. Ward L. and Gladys M. (Dissmore) Dempsey; m. Ivan D. Woods, Jan. 18, 1948 (div.); children—Stephen D., Mark B., Lee M. B.S. in Home Econs., U. Idaho, 1945, M.S., 1971. Asst. prof. home econs. Mont. State U., Bozeman, 1971-73; home econs. tchr. Grangeville (Idaho) High Sch., 1974-76; home econs. program coordinator Lewis Clark State Coll., Lewiston, Idaho, 1976-78; Asotin County extension agt. Wash. State U. Coop. Extension, Asotin, Wash., 1979—. Mem. Am. Assn. Extension Home Economists, Wash. Assn. Extension Home Economists, Kappa Alpha Theta. Home: PO Box 578 Asotin WA 99402 Office: PO Box 9 Asotin WA 99402

WOODSIDE, EDMUND RECTOR, Greek linguist, educator; b. Lodi, Calif., Nov. 22, 1921; s. Homer Henry and Mary Augusta (Rector) W.; B.A., U. Redlands, 1946, M.A., 1950; postgrad. U. So. Calif., 1950-52; Ph.D., Kensington U., 1977; m. Dorothy Ann Wells, Feb. 14, 1981. Freelance ednl. and acad. researcher linguistics, Bible and Bibl. Greek, Pasadena, Calif., 1952—; adj. prof. Bibl. Greek, Calif. Center for Bibl. Studies, Culver City, 1972—. Served with USAAF, 1942-45. Fellow Victoria Inst.; mem. Soc. Bibl. Lit., Internat. Orgn. for Septuagint and Cognate Studies, Am. Sci. Affiliation, AAAS, N.Y. Acad. Scis., Interdisciplinary Bibl. Research Inst., Phi Delta Kappa. Author: A Programmed Guide to Philippians, 1968; Matthew 13, 1971; Six Parables of the End, 1972; (with J.W. McMillan) Bible Doctrine, 1969, Earthly Life of the Lord Jesus, 1975. Home and Office: 3530 Damien Ave Apt 179 LaVerne CA 91750

WOODSON, WELDON DWIGHT, nature writer; b. Ft. Worth, Feb. 17, 1907; s. Neal William and Mary Margaret (Hooser) W.; B.S., Wheaton (Ill.) Coll., 1931; M.A., Columbia U., 1938; m. Eva Freada Husted, Sept. 15, 1943. Asso. editor Welcome News, Los Angeles, 1933-43; writer Make It With Leather (formerly The Craftsman), Ft. Worth, 1965—; stringer Modern People, Franklin Park, Ill., 1974-76; reviewer On Target With Books, AIM, Chgo., 1978-79; co-author: Black Widow, America's Most Poisonous Spider, 1945; author articles condensed in publs. including Magazine Digest, Science Digest, Everybody's Digest, World Digest, Restaurant Digest; writings included sci. and reference publs. including Ency. Britannica, Jour. AMA, Zoological Record, Bibliography of Animal Venoms, Herpetologica, Our Scientific World; free lance contbr. to publs. including Christian Sci. Monitor, Desert Mag., Westways, Natural History, American Forests, Travel, Scientific American, Audubon Mag., Pacific Discovery, Frontiers, A Magazine of Natural History; pvt. tutor in writing; nature counselor youth groups; author film scripts in field; lectr. writers week Redlands (Calif.) U., 1954, 55, 56. Mem. AAAS, Herpetologists League. Democrat. Baptist. Author: Natural History Roundup, 1934; Nature Writing —From Pliny to Peattie, 1935; Nutria — From Pen to Fur Salon, 1955; co-author: How to Make a Saddle, 1968; contbg. author Illustrated Library of the Natural Sciences, 1958; condr. research on poisonous reptiles, spiders, insects. Home and Office: 340 N Stoneman Ave Alhambra CA 91801

WOODSON, WILBERTA, documentation specialist; b. Tecumseh, Nebr., Sept. 7, 1939; d. Charles Wilber and Edith Mildred Woodson; student Coll. of Emporia, 1957-61; B.A., Wichita State U., 1963; M.A., U. Hawaii, 1966; postgrad. U. Conn., 1968, U. Ill., 1969-70; M.S., U. San Francisco, 1980; 1 dau., Rebecca Louise. Research asst., computer programmer U. Hawaii, Honolulu, 1964-66; computer programmer Newport News (Va.) Shipbldg., 1967; computer programmer econ. research U. Ill., Urbana, 1969-70; cons. Ventura County Mental Health, Ventura, Calif., 1973-78; tech. writer Mohawk Data Scis., Los Gatos, Calif., 1978-79; sr. tech. writer Tandem Computers, Cupertino, Calif., 1979-82, documentation specialist, 1982—. Mem. Nat. Assn. Female Execs., Soc. Tech. Communication. Democrat. Unitarian. Home: 1056 Queensbrook Dr San Jose CA 95129 Office: Tandem Computers 19333 Vallco Parkway Cupertino CA 95014

WOODWARD, OSCAR JAMES, III, lawyer, real estate developer; b. Oakland, Calif., Oct. 14, 1935; s. Oscar James II and Beatrice (Denke) W.; A.B., U. Calif., Berkeley, 1958, J.D., 1964; M.B.A., Stanford U., 1961; children—Baron James, Skye Lynne. Teaching asst. U. Calif., Berkeley, 1962-64; admitted to Calif. bar, 1965; asst. gen. counsel Regents of U. Calif., 1966-67; partner firm Gallagher, Baker, Manock & Woodward, Fresno, Calif., 1967-72; regional mgr., counsel Kaiser Aetna, Newport Beach, Calif., 1972-77; v.p., counsel 1st Savs. & Loan Assn., Fresno, also exec. v.p. Uniservice Corp., 1977-83; v.p. Central Savs. & Loan Assn., 1983—; lectr. Calif. State U., Fresno. Pres., Fresno Arts Center, 1968-69, Storyland of Fresno, 1970, Fresno County Taxpayers Assn., 1981-82; treas. United Crusade, 1972; bd. dirs. Urban Coalition, 1969-71, Community Theatre, 1969-72 Pub. Radio, 1979-80, Hist. Soc., 1983—; vice chmn. bd. trustees Fresno Regional Found., 1980—; trustee Fresno County Bd. Rev., 1980-82, St. Agnes Hosp. Found. Council, 1983—. Served to capt. U.S. Army, 1958-66. Cert. tchr. community coll., Calif. Mem. ABA, Urban Land Inst., Fresno C. of C., Fresno County Bar Assn., Estate Planning Council, Phi Delta Phi, Phi Delta Theta. Republican. Clubs: Sierra Sport and Racquet, Fig Garden Swim and Racquet, Stanford, Golden Bear, Commonwealth. Home: 5044 N Wishon Ave Fresno CA 93704 Office: 1515 E Shaw Ave Fresno CA 93710

WOODWORTH, JAN CAPLAN, educational consultant; b. Ithaca, N.Y., Jan. 15, 1944; d. Frank and Shirley E. (Rickard) Caplan; student Cornell U., 1961-63; B.S., Cornell U. Sch. Nursing, 1966; M.A. in Social Scis., Dartmouth Coll., 1974; postgrad. in med. care orgn. and adminstrn. Cornell U., 1973-76; children by previous marriage—Joshua, Gregory, Ginger. Instr. maternal nursing Mary Hitchcock Meml. Hosp. Sch. Nursing, Hanover, N.H., 1970-73; nurse coordinator Conception Control Clinic, Dartmouth Coll., Hanover, 1972-73; cons. to Women's Center, Ithaca, N.Y., 1975-76; head nurse USPHS Hosp. Clinic, Kotzebue, Alaska, 1976; fed. programs coordinator N.W. Arctic Sch. Dist., Alaska, 1976-78, dir. instructional programs, 1978-80; health, edn. and social services task force coordinator regional strategy planning process N.W. Alaska Native Assn., Kotzebue, 1979-82; dir. Kotzebue Tech. Center, 1980-82; cons. Arctic Instructional Devel. Inc., 1982—; utilization specialist U. Alaska Instructional Telecommunications Consortium, 1982—. Mem. Alaska Assn. Sch. Adminstrs., Alaskan Women in Ednl. Adminstrn., Sigma Theta Tau (corr. sec. Alpha Upsilon chpt. 1967-68). Home: 205 E 4th St Anchorage AK 99510

WOODYARD, LINDA WILSON, nursing educator, professional graphologist; b. Denver, June 11, 1952; d. John Rawles and Carmen Phyllis (Henry) Wilson; m. Michael William Woodyard, Oct. 17, 1982. Diploma, Presbyterian Sch. Nursing, Denver, 1974; B.S. in Nursing, Met. State Coll., Denver, 1978; M.S. (NIMH grantee), U. Colo.-Denver, 1980. Staff nurse Presbyn. Med. Ctr., Denver, 1974-80; instr. psychiat.-mental health nursing Presbyn./St. Luke's Sch. Nursing, Denver, 1980—; staff nurse Bethesda Hosp., Denver, 1981—. Mem. CAP, 1966—. Mem. Am. Nurses Assn., Am. Holistic Nurses Assn., Nat. League Nursing. Office: 2025 High St Denver CO 80217

WOOLEY, MARILYN JANE, clin. psychologist; b. Syracuse, N.Y., Aug. 20, 1951; d. Robert Lockard and Dorothy Forrester (McKay) W.; B.S., Ariz. State U., 1973; M.A., U. Ariz., 1975, Ph.D., 1977; 1 dau., Jessica Elaine. Teaching asst. U. Ariz., Tucson, 1973-75; NIMH research trainee, 1975-77; postdoctoral intern Long Beach (Calif.) VA Med. Center, 1977-78; postdoctoral trainee Switzer Center, Torrence, Calif., 1978; postdoctoral intern County of Orange Human Services Agy., Fullerton, Calif., 1978-79; coordinator psychol. services Breakthru Consultations, Long Beach, 1978-79; clin. psychologist Shasta County Mental Health Services, Redding, Calif., 1979-81; pvt. practice clin. psychology, Redding, 1981—; asst. clin. prof. family practice residency program U. Calif.-Davis, Shasta-Cascade Br., 1981—. Community vol. Parents United of Shasta County; bd. dirs. Group Foster Home, Inc., Shasta County, 1980—. Mem. Assn. for Advancement of Psychology, Am. Psychol. Assn., Mensa, Sigma Xi. Contbr. articles in field to profl. publs. Office: 1524 East St Redding CA 96001

WOOLFORD, WILLIAM ALLEN, civil engr.; b. Balt., Nov. 7, 1919; s. William Allen and Jeane (Hurst) W.; B.S.C.E., Colo. A&M Coll., 1951; m. Mary Jo Ryan, Feb. 21, 1950; children—Jean Marie, Julie Ann, Lisa Joan. Vice-pres. The Ken R. White Co., Denver, 1967-73, Tech. Service Co., Denver, 1973-75; dir. mktg. DMJM Cons. Engrs., Denver, 1975-77; prin. William Woolford & Assos., Denver, Pueblo, Colo., 1953—, pres., Denver, 1979—. Served with U.S. Army, 1940-46. Fellow ASCE; mem. Am. Inst. Real Estate Appraisers, Am. Soc. Appraisers. Democrat. Roman Catholic. Club: University (Denver). Home: 1735 Cherry St Denver CO 80220 Office: 155 S Madison St Suite 323 Denver CO 80209

WOOLHEATER, ROBERT L., consumer electronics company executive; b. Sioux Falls, S.D., May 17, 1930; s. Bernard L. and Adeline A (Lass) W.; m. Lorna Colquhoun, Feb. 11, 1956; children—Carol, Dale, Robert; 1 stepson, Richard Stellabotte. B.S. in Acctg., UCLA, 1952. Controller, Vernitron Corp., Torrance, Calif., 1960-64; mgr. of fin. FMA, Inc., Los Angeles, 1964-68; treas. Anthony Industries, Los Angeles, 1968-69; v.p., treas., controller Craig Corp., Compton Calif., 1969—; Mem. curriculum adv. council Calif. Colls. Served to sgt. U.S. Army, 1952-54. Named Citizen of Yr., Lomita, Calif., 1974. Mem. Nat. Assn. Accts. (past nat. v.p.), Fgn. Trade Assn. So. Calif. (sec.), Assn. Electronic Importers (pres.), Fin. Execs. Inst. Republican. Roman Catholic. Club: Internat. (Los Angeles). Home: 3821 Heather St Seal Beach CA 90740 Office: Craig Corp 921 W Artesia Blvd Compton CA 90220

WOOLLIAMS, KEITH RICHARD, botanical garden director; b. Chester, Eng., July 17, 1940; came to U.S., 1971; s. Gordon Frank and Margaret Caroline (Hobbs) W.; m. Akiko Narita, Apr. 12, 1969; children—Frank Hiromi, Angela Misako. Student Royal Bot. Gardens, Kew, Eng., 1961-63. Head research sta. U. London, 1963-65; horticulturist Hotel Group, Bermuda, 1965-67; curator bot. garden, dept. forests, botany div., Lae, Papua New Guinea, 1967-68; supt. bot. garden Pacific Tropical Bot. Garden, Kauai, Hawaii, 1971-74; horticulturist Waimea Arboretum and Bot. Garden, Haleiwa, Hawaii, 1974-80; dir. Waimea Arboretum and Bot. Garden, Haleiwa, 1980—; research affiliate botany Bishop Mus., Honolulu. Mem. Am. Assn. Bot. Gardens and Arboreta, Royal Hort. Soc., Am. Hort. Soc., Hawaiian Bot. Soc. (pres. 1980). Home: 47-722J Ahuimanu Loop Kaneohe HI 96744 Office: 59-864 Kamehameha Hwy Haleiwa HI 96712

WOOLSCHLAGER, LAURA TOTTEN, artist; b. Dallas, Sept. 1, 1932; d. Johns McCleave and Katherina Elizabeth Johanna (Smith) Totten; m. Hawley Lee Woolschlager, Apr. 16, 1931; children—Christy Nielsen, Layne, Wilson. Student Redlands U., 1950-51; B.A. magna cum laude, Syracuse U., 1954. Painter, etcher; represented in permanent collections Carnegie Library, Lewiston, Idaho, Mus. Native Am. Cultures, Spokane, Wash., Favelle Mus. Western Art, Klamath Falls, Oreg.; painting and drawing instr. Omak (Wash.) br. Wenatchee Valley Community Coll. Recipient awards Western Art Show, Western Art Assn.; named Wash. Best of Show, 1979, Artists of the Old West Best of Show, 1979. Mem. Am. Artists of Rockies (v.p.). Home and Studio: Route 1 Box 122H Omak WA 98841

WOOLSEY, JAMES ELMORE, clinical psychologist, consultant, educator; b. Evansville, Ind., July 29, 1940; s. Joseph Orval and Mary Lois (Bone) W.; m. Sandra Carolyn Fisher, Sept. 16, 1962; children—Sandra Darlene, James II, Kathleen, Sharlene. B.A. in Psychology, Fresno Pacific Coll., 1971; M.A. in Counseling, Calif. State U.-Fresno 1975; postgrad., Laurence U., 1981—. Cert. counselor-psychologist, N.Mex.; lic. tchr., Calif. Pastor Ch. of God, Fresno, Eureka, Napa, Calif., 1965-73; adminstr., coordinator Alcohol First Offender Programs, Silver City (N.Mex.) Area Human Resources, 1976-81; occupational program cons. State of N.Mex., Santa Fe, 1978-79; clin. psychologist, tng. dir. Ft. Bayard (N.Mex.) Med. Ctr., 1979—; also pvt. cons.; cons. N.Mex. Nurses Assn. Continuing Edn. Mem. SW Services to Handicapped; Civil Rights Com.; Gov.'s Council Criminal Justice. Served with USN, 1958. Named Disting. Citizen, N.Mex. Sec. State; First Offender Program grantee; Alcohol and Family Services grantee. Mem. Am. Soc. Tng. and Devel., N.Mex. Hosp. Adminstrs. Assn., Assn. Labor-Mgmt. Adminstrs and Cons. on Alcoholism. Democrat. Methodist. Clubs: Kiwanis, Rotary (Silver City), Masons. Home: 1015 Luck St Silver City NM 88061 Office: Ft Bayard Med Ctr PO Box 177 Fort Bayard NM 88036

WOOTEN, FREDERICK O., phys. chemist; b. Linwood, Pa., May 16, 1928; B.S. in Chemistry, M.I.T., 1950; Ph.D. in Chemistry, U. Del., 1955; m. Jane Watson MacPherson, Aug. 30, 1952; children—Donald, Bartley. Staff physicist All Am. Engring. Co., Wilmington, Del., 1953-57, Lawrence Livermore Nat. Lab., Livermore, Calif., 1957-72; prof. applied sci. U. Calif., Davis, 1972—, chmn. dept. applied sci., 1973—. Mem. Am. Phys. Soc., AAAS, Sigma Xi. Author: Optical Properties of Solids, 1972. Office: U Calif Davis CA 95616

WORDELL, EDWIN HOWLAND, artist, former government official; b. Phila., Aug. 27, 1927; s. Edwin Howland and Cathryn (Williams) W.; m. Laveta Rose Stehr, May 23, 1948; children—Cathryn Lynn, Thomas Allan; m. Marie Cunningham, Oct. 8, 1977. B.S. with honors, San Diego State U., 1961. Meat cutter, journeyman, 1949-61; spl. agt. criminal investigation div. IRS, San Diego, 1961-82; artist, 1956—; exhibited in group shows including Riverside Art Ctr. (Calif.), 1975, San Diego Mus. Fine Art, 1976, Fla. A&M Coll., Tallahassee, 1977, Calif. State U.-Northridge, 1977, Marietta Coll. (Ohio), 1977, Haste Gallery, Ipswich, Eng., 1978, Tacoma Art Mus., 1978, Loyola U., 1979, Purdue U., 1979, Foothills Art Ctr., Golden, Colo., 1980, Laguna Beach Mus. Art (Calif.), 1980, Sierra Nevada Mus. Art, Reno, 1980, Springville Mus. Art (Utah), 1981, N.Mex. U., Portales, 1981, Pueblo Grande Mus., Phoenix, 1982, Pueblo Grande Mus., Phoenix, 1982, Westmoreland County Mus. Art, Greensburg, Pa., 1982, San Bernardino County Mus., Redlands, Calif., 1982, Owensboro Mus. Fine Art (Ky.), 1983, Robert W. Woodruff Arts Ctr., Atlanta, 1983, Nat. Arts Club, N.Y.C., 1983; represented in permanent collections San Diego Trust & Savs. Bank, San Bernardino Valley Coll., Kaiser Hosp., Utah State U., San Diego Zool. Soc., Bank of Am., Wells Fargo Bank. Served with USN, 1945-49. Recipient Albert Gallatin award Dept. Treasury, 1982. Mem. Nat. Watercolor Soc., Rocky Mountain Watermedia Soc., Watercolor West, San Diego Art Inst. (pres. 1978-79), San Diego Watercolor Soc. (pres. 1975-76), Nat. Soc. Painters in Casein and Acrylic (assoc.), Beta Gamma Sigma. Home: 6251 Lorca Dr San Diego CA 92115

WORK, STEVE, metallurgical engineer, educator; b. Los Alamos, N.Mex., Jan. 19, 1954; s. John Gould and Marjorie Stevens (Peacock) W.; m. Christine Rae Musilek, Aug. 11, 1979 (div.). B.S. in Metall. Engring., N.Mex. Inst. Mining and Tech., 1977; M.B.A. in Fin. U. Phoenix, 1983. Metall. engr. Duval Corp., Sierrita, Ariz., 1977-81, Pinto Valley Copper Corp., Miami, Ariz., 1981—; tchr. phys. metallurgy Gila Pueblo Coll. Active Ariz. Desert Bighorn Sheep Soc., Y-Men's Assn., YMCA. Mem. AIME, Nat. Rifle Assn. (life), Alpha Sigma Mu. Republican. Episcopalian. Contbr. articles to profl. jour. Home: PO Box 881 Miami AZ 85539 Office: PO Box 100 Miami AZ 85539

WORKER, GEORGE FREDERICK, JR., agronomist; b. Ordway, Colo., June 1, 1923; s. George F. and Eleanor (Budde) W.; m. Donna Rae Pinkerton; children—Debbie (dec.), Kent, Stephanie Worker Shoup, Cathy, Melinda. B.S., Colo. State U., 1941; postgrad. Adams State Coll., 1941-43, 46; M.S., U. Nebr., 1953. Asst. county agt. U. Nebr., Holdridge, 1949-51, asst. in agronomy, Lincoln, 1951-53; agronomist and sta. supt. Imperial Valley Field Sta., U. Calif.-El Centro, 1953—; cons. in field; field trials mgr., Libya; agronomist, Iran, North Yemen. Bd. dirs. Meadows Union Sch., Holtville Unified Sch. Served with U.S. Army, 1943-47. Mem. Agronomy Soc. Am., Gamma Sigma Delta. Developed Meloland Grain sorphum and UC Signal barley; contbr. chpt. to book, numerous articles to profl. jours. Home: 1004 E Holton Rd El Centro CA 92243 Office: 1004 E Holton Rd El Centro CA 92243

WORKS, MADDEN TRAVIS, JR., manufacturing engineer, author, skydiving instructor; b. Harris County, Tex., Mar. 17, 1943; s. Madden Travis and Vivian Alle (Browning) W.; m. Janet Elaine Allen, Dec. 19, 1970. Student Tex. A&M U., 1962-64; B.A., U. Houston, 1967. Engr. in tng. Cameron Iron Works, Houston, 1963-65; promotion planner, supr. field advt. Procter & Gamble, Cin., 1967-70; mgr. sta. promotions Union Oil Co. Calif., Chgo., 1970-73; mgr. sales promotion Hunt Wesson Foods, Fullerton, Calif., 1973-76; mgr. promotions Knott's Berry Farm Holdings, 1976-77; owner RWU Parachuting Publs., Fullerton, 1975—; supr. mfg. engring., chmn. change bd. HITCO, ARMCO, Gardena, Calif., 1981—; cons. engr. D.A.R. Enterprises; instr. advanced freefall in 9 countries; pub. speaker. Nat. bd. dirs. U.S. Parachute Assn., 1980—. Served with Army NG, 1962. Recipient medal for merit Australian Parachute Fedn., 1972, Medal for Services French Nat. Team, 1972, certs. appreciation YMCA, 1980, 82, numerous awards and medals related to parachuting. Mem. AIAA, Computer and Automated Systems Assn. (sr., cert. systems engr.), Soc. Mfg. Engrs. (sr., cert. mfg. engr., BMW Owners Assn., Am. Motorcycle Assn., U.S. Parachute Assn. (dir. 1980—), Club: Toastmasters (v.p. 1977). Author: Parachuting, English, German, French and Spanish edits.; Parachuting: United We Fall, 1978; Theory of Freefall, 1979. Contbr. articles to parachuting publs. Inventor flight suit, parachute line knife; nat. champion Nat. Collegiate Parachuting League, 1967; nat. winner Point of Purchase Profl. Inst., 1974. Home: 1656 Beechwood Ave Fullerton CA 92636 Office: 1600 W 135th St HITCO Enginering Gardena CA 90249

WORLEY, EUGENE ROBERT, elec. engr.; b. San Bernardino, Calif., Dec. 6, 1947; s. Ernest Floyd and Frances Jenette (DeRoule) W.; B.S. in Elec. Engring., Calif. State U., Los Angeles, 1970; M.S., U. Calif., Berkeley, 1973; m. Pearl Niimi, Aug. 28, 1970; children—Eugene Robert, Christa. Engr., MOS tech. dept. Rockwell Internat. Corp., Newport Beach, Calif., 1974; staff engr. Newport Beach Research Center, Hughes Aircraft Co., 1976-80; v.p. engring., dir. Vari-Tronics Mfg., Inc., integrated circuits, Garden Grove, Calif., 1980—. Served with U.S. Army, 1971-73. Mem. Eta Kappa Nu, Tau Beta Pi, Phi Kappa Phi. Author papers on physics of silicon-on-sapphire electronic devices. Home: 11 Bowditch Ave Irvine CA 92714 Office: 11372 Trask St Suite 107 Garden Grove CA 92643

WORMAN, DAVID LEE, airline exec.; b. Abilene, Kans., Oct. 12, 1947; s. Russell E. and Maurine (Jessee) W.; B.S., Colo. State U., 1969; m. Dinah Gwen Kershner, June 6, 1970; children—Sarah Anne, Katherine Marie. Line capt. Air U.S., Denver, 1977—, dir. ops., 1978-80, v.p. corp. planning and devel., 1980—. Pres., homeowners assn., 1978-81. Served as officer USN, 1970-76. Mem. Aircraft Owners and Pilots Assn. Home: 7755 E Quincy Ave Apt T-71 Denver CO 80237 Office: Air US Box 38647 AMF Denver CO 80238

WORMLEY, LORENTZ ENGLEHART, SR., civil engineer; b. Savoy, Ill., Oct. 29, 1899; s. Edwin and Katherine (Grove) W.; m. Geneva A. Stillman, Mar. 9, 1921; children—Lorentz, Phyllis Jeanne (Mrs. Calvin Adams). B.S. in Mining Engring., U. Ill., 1921; postgrad. U. Calif., 1930-40; extension work U. Chgo., 1925-26, Purdue U., 1926-28, Stanford U., 1942-43. Mining engr. Roane Iron Co., Rockwood, Tenn., 1922-23; resident engr. Ill. Div. Hwys., East St. Louis, 1923-24; instr. and athletic coach Du Quoin (Ill.) Twp. High Sch., 1923-26; instr. and dept. head Hammond (Ind.) Tech. High Sch., 1926-28; constrn. and plant engr., field engring. unit Columbia Steel Corp., Pittsburg, Calif., 1928-29; asst. bridge engr., resident engr. Calif. State Hwy. Dept., Sacramento, 1929-30; constrn. engr., asst. to mgr. Austin Co. of Calif., Oakland, 1930; dir. adult edn. Monterey (Calif.) Union High Sch., 1930-40; asst. state supr. trade and indsl. edn. Bur. Trade and Indsl. Edn., State Dept. Edn., Sacramento, 1940-41; dir. trade and indsl. tng. Unified Sch. Dist., San Francisco, 1941-42; supervising engr. Def. Plant Corp., San Francisco, 1942-43; area tng. specialist, civilian personnel div. Office Sec. of War, San Francisco, 1943-46; tng. officer-in-charge VA, San Francisco, 1946-47; supr. edn. Calif. Dept. Corrections, Sacramento, 1947-69, ret.; sec. Calif. State Interagy. Com. Inmate Tng. and Parole Placement, 1955-69; mem. Statewide Com. for Equal Opportunity in Apprenticeship Tng. for Minority Groups, 1962-69. Mem. Calif. Assn. Adult Edn. Adminstrs., Am. Prison Assn. Correctional Ednl. Assn. (pres. 1958-60), Calif., Nat. ret. tchrs. assns., Alumni Assn. U. Ill., Vets. World War I (adj. barracks 2247 1979-82), AARP, SAR, Ret. Pub. Employees Assn. Calif. (dr. chpt. 4 1973-75), Pi Kappa Phi. Mason. Clubs: Sirs, Comstock. Author numerous articles on profl. subjects. Home: 2360 Purinton Dr Sacramento CA 95821 Dec. Jan. 1983

WORRALL, WILLIAM CHARLES, publisher; b. London, Ont., Can., Mar. 23, 1936; s. Winnett Irwin and Eloise Margaret (Brown) W.; ed. Long Beach City Coll., U. Calif. at Irvine and San Luis Obispo, extensions NYU, Notre Dame, N.H. Pub., Organist Mag. Keyboard World Mag.; founder Young Organists Assn.; dir. Home Organists Adventures; pres., chmn. bd. BW Prodns. Inc.; v.p. Distinctive Communications Corp.; organist, entertainer, concerts in U.S., Can., Mex., Australia; judge Yamaha Electone Festival Can., 1976, Liberace Talent Search, 1980. Active, Exceptional Children's Found. Served with RCAF, 1953-58. Mem. Nat. Assn. Organ Tchrs. (mem. bd.), Long Beach (pres. 1971-72), Los Angeles (pres. 1980) profl. organists clubs, Orange County Profl. Organists Guild (v.p. 1982, pres. 1983), Am. Theatre Organ Soc., Electronic Arts Found. (mem. bd.), Telephone Interconnect Assn. of Calif. (founder), Hollywood Comedy Club, Los Angeles World Affairs Council, Toastmasters. Home Address: 8525 S Passons Blvd Pico Rivera CA 90660

WORREST, ROBERT CHARLES, radiation biologist; b. Hartford, Conn., July 6, 1935; s. Ralph N. and Ruth E. (Shafer) W.; B.A., Williams Coll., 1957; M.A., Wesleyan U., Middletown, Conn., 1964; Ph.D. in Radiation Biology, Physiology and Zoology, Oreg. State U., 1975; m. Virginia Louise Peplaw, Aug. 24, 1957; 1 dau., Colleen Emilie. Tchr. biology, chemistry and math. Canterbury Sch., New Milford, Conn., 1957-59; tchr. biology and math. Belmont (Mass.) Hill Sch., 1959-70; teaching asst. biology Oreg. State U., Corvallis, 1970, instr., 1971-72, research assoc. dept. gen. sci., 1975-77, asst. prof. dept. gen. sci., 1977-81, assoc. prof., 1981—; project leader photobiology program EPA, Corvallis, 1980-82. Internat. Congress Radiation Research grantee, 1974; Internat. Congress on Photobiology travel grantee, 1976, 80. Mem. Am. Soc. Limnology and Oceanography, Ecol. Soc. Am., Am. Soc. Photobiology, AAAS, Radiation Research Soc., Soc. for Risk Analysis. Contbr. articles on photobiology and photochemistry to sci. jours. Office: Environmental Research Lab EPA 200 SW 35th St Corvallis OR 97333

WORTHEN, BLAINE RICHARD, psychology educator, consultant; b. Murray, Utah, Oct. 10, 1936; s. Donovan Hayden and Grace Viola (Middleton) W.; m. Barbara Allen, Jan. 16, 1959; children—Jeffrey Allen, Lynette, Bradley Wade. B.S., U. Utah, 1960, M.S., 1965; Ph.D., Ohio State U., 1968. Tchr. Jordan (Utah) Sch. Dist., 1960-62; instr. U. Utah Campus Sch., 1962-64, instr. Coll. Edn., 1964-65; asst. prof. Coll. Edn. Ohio State U., 1968-69; asst. prof. edn. U. Colo., 1969-71, assoc. prof., 1971-73; prof. dept. psychology Utah State U., 1978—, also head dept., 1978—; lectr. and cons. in field. Bd. dirs. Hospice of Cache Valley, Logan, Utah. Grantee in field; recipient Outstanding Evaluation Study award Am. Ednl. Research Assn., 1978; Nat. Curriculum Study Inst. Outstanding Cons. award Assn. for Supervision and Curriculum Devel., 1982. Mem. Am. Ednl. Research Assn., Nat. Soc. Profs. Ednl. Research, Am. Psychol. Assn., Nat. Council Measurement in Edn., Nat. Evaluation Network, Phi Delta Kappa. Mormon. Author: (with J.E. Sanders) Educational Evaluation: Theory and Practice, 1973; (with A.L. Roaden) The Research Assistantship: Recommendations for Colleges and Universities, 1975; editor: (with D.L. Clark) Preparing Research Personnel for Education, 1967; contbr. articles in field to profl. jours. Office: Department of Psychology UMC 28 Utah State University Logan UT 84322

WORTHEN, EDWARD MONTGOMERY, optometrist; b. Tacoma, Dec. 25, 1953; s. Fredrick Richard and Janet Briggs (Robbins) W.; m. Constance Lacey Hayden, Oct. 22, 1977. Student, Wash. State U., 1972-75; B.S., Pacific U., 1977, O.D., 1979. Lic. optometrist, Wash., Gen. practice optometry, Tacoma, 1979-82; assoc. optometrist Winslow Vision Clinic (Wash.), 1980-82; v.p. Gig Harbor Vision Ctr. (Wash.), 1982—. Active Girl Scouts U.S.A. Mem. Wash. Optometric Assn., Am. Optometric Assn., Contact Lens Soc. Am. Republican. Episcopalian. Club: Gig Harbor Sportsman. Office: PO Box 2020 Gig Harbor Profl Bldg Gig Harbor WA 98335

WOZNIAK, SAM, aerospace executive; b. Timblin, Pa., Mar. 6, 1931; s. John and Fenyi (Fedasz) W.; m. Shirley J. Johnson, Dec. 28, 1961; children—Vicki Lynn, John David. B.S., U. Tulsa, 1971, M.B.A., 1972; postgrad. in physics Carnegie Mellon U. Elec. engr. Douglas Aircraft, Long Beach, Calif., 1955; supr. Bell Aircraft, Cleve., 1955-58; engring. mgr. N.Am. Aviation, Rockwell Internat., 1958-73; tech. dir. Brunswick Corp., Skokie, Ill., 1973-82; program mgr. spl. projects Rockwell Internat., Lakewood, Calif., 1982—; adj. prof. U. Tulsa, 1971-73; adviser U.S. Air Force mission analysis on electronic warfare, 1971-74, sci. adviser low radar cross sect. and radar absorbing materials, 1978. Mem. admission council Carnegie Mellon U., 1968-70; vice chmn. YMCA, 1968-70; dist. chmn. Boy Scouts Am., 1970-72. Served with USAF, 1951-55. Mem. AAAS, Am. Mgmt. Assn., AIAA, IEEE, Assn. of Old Crows, Am. Def. Prepardness Assn., Pi Sigma Epsilon, Beta Gamma Sigma. Republican. Presbyterian. Co-author: Guided Missiles Fundamentals, 1953; Radar Systems Manual, 1954; Radar Absorbing Materials and Radar Cross Section Analysis on Electronic Warfare, 1972; Radar Camoflage Benefits, 1975; Army Camoflage Net Systems, 1975; Peenemunde Luftwaffe-Wehrmacht-Party Interaction and Development of V-2 Weapon System, 1979. Home: 1168 Princess Ct Costa Mesa CA 92626 Office: 2770 E Carson St Lakewood CA 90712

WRAY, KARL, newspaper pub.; b. Bishop, Tex., June 8, 1913; s. Ernest Paul and Gertrude (Garvin) W.; A.B., Columbia U., 1935; m. Flora-Lee Koepp, Aug. 11, 1951; children—Diana, Mark, Kenneth, Norman, Thomas. Auditor, U.S. Dept. Agr., Washington, Little Rock, 1935-37; salesman O'Mara & Ormsbee, Inc., N.Y.C., 1937-42; advt. mgr. Lompoc (Calif.) Record, 1947-54; owner and pub. San Clemente (Calif.) Daily Sun-Post, 1954-67, Coastline Dispatch, San Juan Capistrano, Calif., 1956-67, Dana Point (Calif.) Lamplighter, 1966-67; research cons. Lear Siegler, Inc., Washington, 1967-68; pub. Daily Star-Progress, La Habra-Brea, Calif., 1969-74, Anaheim (Calif.) Bulletin, 1974—. Mem. Calif. State Park Commn., 1960-64, vice chmn., 1961-62; mem. exec. bd. Orange County council Boy Scouts Am., 1961-64, 76-81; mem. citizens adv. com. Orange Coast Coll., 1963-66; bd. dirs. Calif. Newspaper Youth Found., 1978-80. Served to capt. USMCR, 1942-46. Mem. Calif. Newspaper Pubs. Assn. (dir. 1960-64), San Clemente (pres. 1956-57), La Habra (dir. 1970-74) chambers commerce, Calif. Newspaper Advt. Execs. Assn. (dir. 1949-54, pres. 1952-53), Am. Theatre Critics Assn., Football Writers Assn. Am., San Juan Capistrano (pres. 1966), Anaheim (dir. 1974—) chambers commerce. Presbyn. (elder). Home: 2420 S Ola Vista San Clemente CA 92672 Office: PO Box 351 1771 S Lewis St Anaheim CA 92805

WRIEDEN, JAMES ERIK, real estate broker; b. Bklyn., June 7, 1943; s. William and Isabel (Ryan) W.; B.S., San Diego State U., 1968; children—Wendy, Jamie. Owner, Mariposa Mgmt., Citrus Heights, Calif., 1979—, Antelope Properties, 1979—, James E. Wrieden & Assocs., Inc., 1969—. Served to lt. USN, 1968-71. Mem. Better Bus. Bur., Sacramento Real Estate Bd., Nat. Assn. Real Estate Brokers, Sacramento Apt. Assn. Office: 7715 Mariposa Ave Citrus Heights CA 95610

WRIGHT, BERNARD, artist; b. Pitts., Feb. 23, 1938; s. Garfield and Emma (Wesley) W.; m. Corrine Westley, Mar. 7, 1964; 1 son, Jeffrey. Student Otis Art Inst., Los Angeles, 1969-70, Los Angeles Trade Tech. Coll., 1971-73. Exhibited traveling art show Moscow, Baku, Leningrad, Alma Alta, USSR, European capitals, 1966, Los Angeles City Hall Rotunda Gallery, 1967, Calif. Lutheran Coll., Thousand Oaks, 1967, Alley Gallery, Beverly Hills, 1968, Florenz Art Gallery, Los Angeles, 1969, San Diego Mus., 1969, Phillip E. Freed Gallery of Fine Arts, Chgo., 1969, Art West Gallery, Los Angeles, 1973, N.J. State Mus., Trenton, Detroit Inst. Arts, Mich., 1974, U. So. Calif., Calif. Mus. Sci. and Industry, 1974, City Art Mus., St. Louis, 1976, N.Y.C. Pub. Library, 1977; represented in pvt. and pub. collections including Howard U., Library of Congress. collections past pres. co-founder Wright's & Westley Prodns., furniture and garment designers. Cited by U.S. Rep. Cardiss Collins, Ill., 1978, state senator Bill Greene, Calif, 1981, Mayor Richard S. Callguiri, Pitts., 1981, Mayor Coleman A. Young, Detroit, 1981, Mayor Tom Bradley, Los Angeles. bd. supr. Kenneth Hahn, Los Angeles, 1981. Mem. Art West Assn. (bd. dirs.). Contbr. articles to profl. jours. Home: PO Box 8990 Los Angeles CA 90008

WRIGHT, BESSIE MARGARET, landscape architect; b. Centralia, Kans., May 23, 1905; d. Onbey Roscoe and Sarah Elizabeth (Shrontz) Roberts; student pub. schs., Rupert, Idaho; m. Loyd K. Wright, Feb. 6, 1924; 1 son, John Robert. Partner, treas. Kimberly Nurseries, Inc., Twin Falls, Idaho, 1924—. Sunday sch. tchr., 1946-56. Mem. Nat. Fedn. Ind. Bus., Twin Falls C. of C., Am. Nurseryman, Idaho Nursery Assn., Hagerman Valley Hist. Soc., Nat. Assn. Watch and Clock Collectors, Twin Falls Fish and Wildlife Conservation Corp., Hagerman Valley Hist. Soc. (life), Twin Falls Hist. Soc. (dir.), Bibl. Archaeology Rev., Archaeol. Inst. Am., Smithsonian Assocs. Republican. Methodist. Club: Daus. of Nile (past pres. club). Author: (autobiography) Me and My Other Self. Home: PO Box L Kimberly ID 83341 Office: Kimberly Nurseries Inc Addison Ave E Twin Falls ID 83301

WRIGHT, BEVERLY ALGER, business exec.; b. Twin Falls, Idaho, June 10, 1932; d. James Irwin and Tessie Devota (Rainey) Alger; student U. Idaho, 1950-52; B.A. summa cum laude, U. Minn., 1972, postgrad., 1973-76; children—Thomas Lee, Daniel Lawrence, Lisa Anne, Kathleen Marie. Personnel adminstr. Control DATA Corp., Mpls., 1972-74; pres., treas. Encode Assos./Pennant Ednl. Materials, Mpls., 1974, San Diego, 1975-76; dir. tng. Greyhound Corp., Phoenix, 1977; pres. Western Ctr. Assocs., North Hollywood Calif., 1983—. Pres., Assn. for Retarded Children, Thousand Oaks, Calif., 1964. Mem. Am. Soc. for Tng. and Devel. (treas. Valley of Sun chpt. 1979, chpt. pres. 1980), Orgn. Devel. Network, Phoenix Women's Network, Women Emerging, Gamma Phi Beta. Democrat. Roman Catholic. Club: Toastmasters. Office: 1729 W Citrus Way Phoenix AZ 85015

WRIGHT, CHARLES LEE, software design and programming consultant; b. Dalton, Ga., Dec. 18, 1949; s. Charlie William and Catherine Christine (Quarles) W.; A.A. in Bus., Dalton Jr. Coll., 1971; B.S. in Bus., U. Tenn., Chattanooga, 1977; also numerous IBM classes on various machines and systems; m. Lora Langford, May 11, 1968; children—Charles Lee, Christina. Mgmt. trainee Ludlow Carpets, Dalton, 1971, EDP supr., 1971-73, EDP mgr., 1973-77; ops. mgr. Walten Carpet Mills, Industry, Calif., 1977-80; ptnr., cons. TCT Systems, San Dimas, Calif., 1978-81; ptnr. Williams, Wright & Assocs., San Dimas, 1981—. Served as sgt. U.S. Army, 1969-71; Vietnam, Cambodia. Decorated Bronze Star, Army Commendation medal with oak leaf and oak leaf cluster, Air medal. Mem. Data Processing Mgmt. Assn., Am. Mgmt. Assn., Small Systems User Group. Republican. Baptist. Home: 2410 Sandpiper Pl Ontario CA 91761 Office: 1575 Middleton Rd San Dimas CA 91773

WRIGHT, CHARLES LESTER, JR., scientific apparatus manufacturing company executive; b. Lubbock, Tex., Oct. 9, 1931; s. Charles Lester and Ellen Olivia (Blue) W.; B.S., Tex. Tech. U., 1957; M.S., U. Ariz., 1961; Ph.D., U. Tex., 1965; m. Jacqueline A. Jeffery, Nov. 11, 1976; children—Valerie Suzanne, Charles Lester, Gregory Wallace, Sally June, Dan Bruen, Mary Elizabeth. Sr. elec. engr. Gen. Dynamics Co., Pomona, Calif., 1965-66; tech. staff Tex. Instruments Co., Dallas, 1966-70; cons. Republic Nat. Bank, Dallas, 1970-71; pres., chmn. bd. Frontier Enterprises Inc., Albuquerque, 1971-79, Climatek Inc., Albuquerque, 1976-79; pres., dir. Dynatech Frontier Corp., 1979—; cons. mergers and acquisitions, 1983—; instr. elec. engring. U. Ariz., 1958-61; asst. prof. elec. engring. Tex. Tech U., 1961-62; adj. prof. elec. engring. So. Meth. U., Dallas, 1968-70. Active Boy Scouts Am. Served with USAF, 1950-54; Korea. Ford Found. fellow, 1962-65. Mem. Am. Mgmt. Assn. (Pres.'s Assn.), Assn. Contamination Control Mfrs. (v.p.). Republican. Home: 10004 Hendrix Ct NE Albuquerque NM 87111 Office: PO Box 30041 Albuquerque NM 87110

WRIGHT, CURTIS LYNN, advt. agy. exec.; b. Beloit, Wis., Sept. 16, 1944; s. Kenneth Archie and Lorraine Millicent (Hanamann) W.; student Purdue U., 1963-66; m. JoAnn Margaret Korn, Apr. 16, 1966; children—Christopher Michael, Bryan Edward. Advt. prodn. mgr. L.S. Ayres & Co., Indpls., 1962-66; advt. mgr. John Bean div. FMC Corp., Tipton, Ind., 1966-67, mktg. asst. Riverside (Calif.) div., 1967-68, asst. advt. mgr. ordnance div., San Jose, Calif., 1968-69; pres. Bergthold, Fillhardt & Wright, Inc., San Jose, 1969—. Bd. dirs. San Jose Symphony, 1971-72, Santa Clara (Calif.) County Performing Arts League, 1972, San Jose Community Theater, 1972, Santa Clara County Jr. Achievement, 1973—, Better Bus. Bur., 1977-78, Live Oaks Found., 1982—. Recipient Ad Man of Yr. award Am. Advt. Fedn., 1973, Andy award Advt. Club N.Y.C., 1973, 74, 75, 77, 79, 80, 81, 82, 1st pl. awards (21) San Francisco Soc. Communicating Arts, 1973, 75, 76, 77, 78, 79, 80, 81, 82, Western Art Dirs. competition award, 1973, 75, 76, 77, 78, 79, 80, 81, 82, Communication Arts competition award, 1974, 77, 79, 81, others. Mem. Am. Assn. Advt. Agys. (gov. No. Calif. council 1974-75), San Jose C. of C. (chmn. communications com. 1974-76), No. Calif. Assn. Indsl. Advertisers (dir. 1973-74), Santa Clara Valley Assn. Advt. Agys. (bd. dirs. 1982—), San Jose Advt. Club (pres. 1974-76). Home: 15080 Jackson Oaks Dr Morgan Hill CA 95037 Office: 190 Park Center Plaza San Jose CA 95113

WRIGHT, DAVID ALLEN, stockbroker; b. Norwood, Mass., May 5, 1939; s. Laurence S. and Marry Lou (Warren) W.; B.S. in Bus., U. Colo., 1961; m. Gavala F. Monahan, June 2, 1960; children—Kim Elizabeth, William Warren, Brook, Chris. Asst. to pres. ERC Internat., 1961-62; dir. mktg. Conf. Bd., 1962-71; v.p. mktg. Investors Mgmt. Scis., Inc. subs. Standard & Poors, Englewood, Colo., 1971-73; instl. sales Boettcher & Co., 1973-76; v.p. Dain Bosworth, Denver, 1976-81; gen. ptnr., dir. instnl. sales Boettcher & Co., Denver, 1981—. Dir., pres. sec.-treas. Castiewood Sanitation Dist. Republican. Presbyterian. Club: Union League (N.Y.C.). Home: 5816 S Florence Englewood CO 80111 Office: 828 17th St Denver CO 80202

WRIGHT, DAVID ARTHUR, architect; b. Salinas, Calif., Feb. 13, 1941; s. Stanley A. and Ruth H. (Collier) W.; A.A., Sierra Coll., 1960; B.S. in Archtl. Engring., Calif. Poly. State U., 1964; student U. Utah, 1964; m. Catherine Lee Hendel, Nov. 8, 1980; 1 dau., Megan Elizabeth. Peace Corps architect, Tunisia and Guinea, 1964-65, Guinea, 1965-66; naval architect Mare Island Naval Base, Vallejo, Calif., 1966-67; designer and draftsman with Donald Wexler, P.C., architect, Palm Springs, Calif., 1967-68; project chief with Linsey R. Lamberson, architect, La Selva Beach, Calif., 1968-69, James Ellmore, architect, Aptos, Calif., 1969-70; project architect with William Lumpkins, P.C., architect, Santa Fe, N.Mex., 1970-74; project architect Sun Mountain Design, Ltd., Santa Fe, 1972-74; prin. David Wright, environ. architect, Santa Fe, 1973-75, The Sea Ranch, Calif., 1976-78; prin. The SEAgroup, Nevada City, Calif., 1979-83, David Wright Assocs., AIA, Nevada City, 1983—; juror numerous AIA competitions. Major works include numerous residential bldgs., solar energy oriented residential bldgs.; spl. cons. Calif. Energy Resources Conservation and Devel. Commn., 1977, Dept. of Energy Natural Solar Program, 1977; lectr. Ecola Polytechnis, Lausanne, Switzerland, 1980. Bd. advs. Foothill Solar Exchange, 1979-81; active Tahoe council Boy Scouts Am., 1952-62. Named Alumnus of Yr., Calif. State Poly. U., 1983. Mem. AIA (Western Home award 1977), Internat. Solar Energy Assn., N.Mex. Solar Energy Assn., No. Calif. Solar Energy Assn. Author: Natural Solar Architecture: a Passive Primer, 1978; Passive Solar Architecture: Logic and Beauty, 1982; producer TV films on applications of solar energy. Home: 315 Park St Nevada City CA 95959 Office: 418 Broad St Nevada City CA 95959

WRIGHT, DONALD FRANKLIN, newspaper executive; b. St. Paul, July 10, 1934; s. Floyd Franklin and Helen Marie (Hansen) W.; B.M.E., U. Minn., 1957, M.B.A., 1958; m. Sharon Kathleen Fisher, Dec. 30, 1960; children—John, Dana, Kara, Patrick. With Mpls. Star & Tribune Co., 1958-77, research planning dir., then ops. dir., 1971-75, exec. editor, 1975-77; exec. v.p., gen. mgr. Newsday, Inc., L.I., N.Y., 1977-78, pres., chief operating officer, 1978-81; pres., chief operating officer Los Angeles Times, 1981—. City councilman, Mahtomedi, Minn., 1967-69, 71; chmn. Citizens Com. Sch. Dist. 832, Mahtomedi, 1970; vice chmn. Inter nat. Press Telecommunications Council; bd. dirs. United Way L.I. Mem. Am. Newspaper Pubs. Assn. (chmn. prodn. mgmt. com. 1975-77, vice chmn. telecommunications com.), L.I. Assn. Commerce and Industry (dir.), Nat. Soc. Profl. Engrs., ASME. Presbyterian. Clubs: U. Minn. Alumni; Huntington Country. Home: 19 Saint Marks Pl Huntington NY 11743 Office: Los Angeles Times Times Mirror Sq Los Angeles CA 90053

WRIGHT, EUGENE ALLEN, fed. judge; b. Seattle, Feb. 23, 1913; s. Elias Allen and Mary (Bailey) W.; A.B., U. Wash., 1935, J.D., 1937; m. Esther Ruth Ladley, Mar. 19, 1938; children—Gerald Allen, Meredith Ann Wright Morton. Admitted to Wash. bar, 1937; with firm Wright & Wright, Seattle, 1937-54; judge Superior Ct. King County (Wash.), 1954-66; v.p., sr. trust officer Pacific Nat. Bank Seattle, 1966-69; judge U.S. Ct. of Appeals 9th Circuit, Seattle, 1969—; acting municipal judge, Seattle, 1948-52; mem. faculty Nat. Jud. Coll., 1964-72; lectr. Sch. Communications, U. Wash., 1965-66, Law Sch., 1952-74; lectr. appellate judges' seminars, 1973-76, Nat. Law Clks. Inst., La. State U., 1973; chmn. Wash. State Com. on Law and Justice, 1968-69; mem. com. on appellate rules Jud. Conf., 1978—. Chmn. bd. visitors Sch. Law, U. Puget Sound; bd. dirs. Met. YMCA, Seattle, 1955-72. Served to lt. col., AUS, 1941-46; col. Res. (ret.). Recipient Disting. Service award U.S. Jr. C. of C., 1948, Disting. Service medal Am. Legion; decorated Combat Inf. Badge, Bronze Star, Army Commendation medal. Fellow Am. Bar Found.; mem. Am. (council div. jud. adminstrn. 1971-76), Wash., Seattle bar assns., Am. Judicature Soc., Appellate Judges Conf., Ret. Officers Assn., Order of Coif, Delta Upsilon, Phi Delta Phi. Episcopalian. (lay reader). Clubs: Masons (33 deg.), Shriners, Rainier, Broadmoor Golf, Harbor, Nat. Lawyers, Wash. Athletic. Author: (with others) The State Trial Judges Book, 1966; also articles; editor Trial Judges Jour., 1963-66; contbr. articles to profl. jours. Office: 902 US Courthouse Seattle WA 98104

WRIGHT, GEORGE RUSSELL, physician; b. Marshall, Mo., July 21, 1909; s. Alfred Lee and Carrie L. (Herndon) W.; student U. Colo., 1927-30, M.D., 1935; m. Myrle I. Benson, Feb. 16, 1935 (dec. 1955); 1 dau., Marjorie Lou; m. 2d, Edna J. Row, May 6, 1963. Intern, Gorgas Hosp., Ancon, C.Z., 1935-36, resident, 1936-37, ward surgeon urology, 1939-42, chief urol. service, 1942-49; physician Panama Canal, 1936-39; cons. urologist Colon Hosp., Cristobal, C.Z., Coco Solo Naval Hosp., Ft. Clayton Army Hosp., C.Z., 1949; chief urol. service VA Hosp., Moutain Home, Tenn., 1949-50; urologist Longmont (Colo.) Hosp. and Clinic, 1949-71; cons. urology Denver Clinic, 1972-81; emeritus staff Presbyn. Hosp., Denver; courtesy staff St. Joseph's Hosp., Denver; field staff A.C.S., 1968-75. Served from 1st lt. to lt. col., M.C., AUS, 1942-47. Diplomate Am. Bd. Urology. Fellow A.C.S. (pres. Colo. chpt. 1968), Southwestern Surg. Congress; mem. Am. Urol. Assn. (dir., mem. exec. com. south central sect.), AMA, Colo., Boulder County med. socs., Assn. Mil. Surgeons, Med. Assn. Isthmian C.Z. (past pres.), Rocky Mountain Urol. Soc. (past pres.), Alpha Omega Alpha, Nu Sigma Nu. Home and Office: 3236 S Heather Gardens Way Aurora CO 80014

WRIGHT, HAVILAND, business educator, consultant; b. Phila., July 21, 1948; s. Frederick G. and Sara A. (McCracken) W.; B.A., U. Pa., 1972, M.B.A., 1975, Ph.D., 1981. CPA. Asst. prof. mgt. info. systems U. Denver; cons. in field. Mem. Am. Econ. Assn., Am. Statis. Assn., Mind Assn., Inst. Mgmt. Sci., Art Alliance of Phila. Contbr. articles to profl. jours. Office: Coll Bus U Denver Denver CO 80208

WRIGHT, HENRY PRICE, rubber co. exec., trading co. exec.; b. Washington, Mar. 20, 1943; s. Henry Price and Margaret (Wall) W.; B.A. in Econs. and Anthropology, U. Calif., Santa Barbara, 1967; B. Fgn. Trade, Am. Grad. Sch. Internat. Mgmt., 1968; m. Marina Scafidas, Mar. 19, 1970. Vice pres. internat. ops. Frazar & Hansen Ltd., San Francisco, 1968-71, pres., gen. mgr. H&H Trading Corp., San Francisco, 1971—, Ro-Lab Rubber Co. Inc., Tracy, Calif., 1978—; cons. exports. Office: 16 California St San Francisco CA 94111

WRIGHT, HOWARD SPRAGUE, III, aviation executive; b. Seattle, May 2, 1953; s. Howard Sprague and Theiline A. (Pigott) W.; m. Katherine Ann Janeway, Apr. 9, 1983. Student George Washington U., 1973-74; B.A. in Polit. Sci. and B.A. in Spanish, Wash. State U., 1976; postgrad. Universidad de Valencia, 1976-77. With Seattle First Nat. Bank, 1978-81; owner, partner Renton (Wash.) Aviation, 1981—; dir. Wright Schuchart Inc., 1981—. Co-mgr. Paul Schell for Mayor, Seattle, 1977, Bruce Chapman for Gov., State of Wash., 1980—; trustee Intiman Theatre, Seattle Infant Devel. Center; trustee Amigos de las Americas, named outstanding bd. mem., 1974. Aircraft Owners and Pilots Assn., Am. Bankers Assn., Am. Mgmt. Assn. Clubs: Seattle Tennis, Central Park Tennis, Seattle Yacht, Washington Athletic. Office: 840 N Perimeter Rd Renton WA 98055

WRIGHT, JOHN GEORGE, JR., manufacturing company executive; b. Cleve., June 5, 1947; s. John George and Margaret Josephine (Laumer) W.; m. Isabelle H. Pasquier, Dec. 21, 1976; children—Daniel William, Marie-Christine, Nicholas Fernand. B.S., U. Pa., 1969; M.S. summa cum laude, U. Minn., 1970; M.B.A., Claremont Grad. Sch., 1982. With Columbia-Great Lakes Corp., Northridge, Calif., 1970—, corp. gen. mgr., 1973-80, v.p., 1980—, dir., 1978—. Mem. Data Processing Mgrs. Assn., U. Pa. Alumni Assn. (v.p., exec. com.), Beta Gamma Sigma, Delta Upsilon (life), Delta Sigma Pi (life). Office: Columbia-Great Lakes Corp 19414 Londelius St Northridge CA 91324

WRIGHT, KENNETH LYLE, psychologist; b. American Falls, Idaho, Sept. 11, 1911; s. Jesse Joshua and Martha Sophia (Dickenson) W. children—Anne Collins, Corrella Carmelette Brown, Sandra Lynne Sutherland. B.A., U. Wash., 1941; M.A., U. So. Calif., 1957; Ph.D., San Gabriel Coll., 1958. Coach State Tng. Sch. for Boys, Chehalis, Wash., 1941; dep. probation officer, Los Angeles County, Calif., 1954-56; vis. lectr. Whittier Coll. (Calif.), 1955-56; dist. sch. psychologist Anaheim Union High Sch. Dist. (Calif.); guidance counselor, vice prin. Orleans Am. High Sch., Dept. Army (France), also psychol. services and spl. edn. coordinator Dependent Edn. Group Hdqrs., Karlsruhe, W.Ger., 1959-62; edn. specialist U.S. Navy, San Diego, 1962-63; pvt. practice psychology, San Diego, 1963-64, 69—; psychol. cons. Clin. Bd. Speech Therapy, Children's Hosp., San Diego, 1963-64; vis. prof. U. Western Ont., lectr., sch. psychologist London Bd. Edn. (Ont., Can.), 1964-66; dir. psychol. services Niagara Falls Dist. Bd. Edn. (N.Y.), 1966-69; lectr. Syracuse U., 1968. Pres. Whittier Coordinating Council; a founder Can. Sch. Vol. Program; founder Niagara Inst. Human Devel., European Assns. Am. Personnel and Guidance and Speech and Hearing in Dependent Schs. Served with USNR, 1941-46. Recipient outstanding award San Diego County Assn. Retarded Children. Fellow San Diego Biomed. Research Inst. (past pres.); mem. Assn. Children with Learning Disabilities, Council Exceptional Children (past pres. Niagara Falls chpt.), Royal Soc. Medicine, Am. Psychol. Assn., Calif. Psychol. Assn., San Diego County Psychol. Assn., Am. Soc. Clin. Hypnosis, Calif. Soc. Clin. Hypnosis (sec.), San Diego County Soc. Clin Hypnosis (pres. 1975-76), San Diego Assn. Clin. Psychologists (past pres.), Mensa. Club: Koua Kai. Lodge: Masons. Author: My Name Is Kim; The American Symbol; The Fantastic Journey with Visualization and Imagery; The Psychological Effects of Allergy; Allergy and Learning Disabilities in Children. Home: 751 Amiford Dr San Diego CA 92107 Office: 3720 3d Ave San Diego CA 92103

WRIGHT, LAURENCE ALBERT, investment banker; b. Farmington, Wash., Apr. 5, 1925; s. Albert and Mary (Thompson) W.; B.A., U.

Wash., 1947, M.B.A., 1951. Instr. econs. Western Wash. Coll., 1950-52; asst. prof. finance U. Wash., 1954-59; sr. analyst Dean Witter & Co., San Francisco, 1959-63, dir. tng., 1963-74, also v.p.; adj. assoc. prof. finance Gonzaga U., Spokane, also exec.-in-residence Sch. of Bus., 1982—; Library fin. cons. Bd. dirs. Crosby Library Assocs. Served as lt. (j.g.) USNR, 1946. Mem. Newcomen Soc. N.Am., Pi Kappa Phi, Alpha Kappa Psi. Address: PO Box 103 Farmington WA 99128

WRIGHT, LEWIS JONES, corporation executive, consultant; b. Cuyahoga Falls, Ohio, Mar. 9, 1927; s. Charles Lewis and Margaret Phyllis (Jones) W.; m. Donna Lee Ritter, Nov. 30, 1952; children—John, Tom, Susan, Jim, Ted. B.A., Mt. Union Coll., 1950; postgrad. Am. Coll., Bryn Mawr, Pa., 1962. C.L.U. Methods engr. Hoover Co., North Canton, Ohio, 1950-53; gen. mgr. N.Y. Life, Chgo., 1953-68; exec. v.p. Tekton Corp., Oak Brook, Ill., 1968-74; chmn. bd., chief exec. officer NV-West Inc., Phoenix, 1974—; cons. Western Savs. and Loan; dir. W.R. Effingee Co., San Diego, NV-West Co., Calgary, Can., Gulfstream, Inc., Denver. Bd. dirs. Ariz. State U.; mem. nat. policy adv. bd. Joint Ctr. at Harvard and MIT; trustee Ariz. State Sch. Bus. Served with USAF, 1945-47. Named to Athletic Hall of Fame, Mt. Union Coll., 1980. Mem. Nat. Assn. Home Builders. Republican. Christian Scientist. Clubs: Paradise Valley Country, White Mountain Country. Home: 7113 N Tatum Blvd Scottsdale AZ 85253 Office: 2910 E Camelback Suite 200 Phoenix AZ 85064

WRIGHT, MARY LOU, communications executive; b. Washington, Mar. 30, 1940; d. Peery Brittain and Mary Curtis (Jordan) Greever; student Beaver Coll., 1957-59, Mich. State U., 1959-60; student in acctg. and fin. mgmt. American River Coll., 1980—; married; 3 children. Adminstrv. officer U.S. Dept. Def., Ft. Belvoir, Va., 1966-68; sales mgr. Litton/Bionetics, Inc., Falls Church, Va., 1968-72, Quality Control Med. Labs., Inc., Reading, Pa., 1972-73; People for People, Yakima, Wash., 1977-78, assoc. dir., 1978-79; corp. devel. cons. Decoto Aircraft, Inc., Yakima, 1979, GPM Corp., West Sacramento, Calif., 1979; owner, operator Autoworld/Lotus, Inc., Nashville, 1973-74; pres., gen. mgr. Video Design Industry, Inc., Nashville, 1974-77; franchise dir. United Cable TV of Sacramento, Inc. subs. United Cable TV Corp., 1981-82; sr. v.p. United-Tribune Cable of Sacramento, 1982-83; v.p. The ELRA Group and v.p., corp. officer Wander Research/Communications, San Francisco, 1983—. Chmn. adv. bd. Calif. Gov.'s Office Citizen Initiative and Voluntary Action, 1980-81; mem. corp. fundraising com. Planned Parenthood Sacramento, 1980-81; bd. dirs. Sacramento Regional Transit Dist., 1980—, mem. retirement bd., 1981—; bd. dirs. Sacramento Transit Devel. Agy., 1983—; trustee Community Action Against Drug Abuse, Sacramento, 1981—; bd. dirs. United Way; co-chmn. Community Task Force on Light Rail, Sacramento, 1980—. Recipient Meritorious award Dept. Labor Bur. Apprenticeship and Tng., 1979; named Sacramento Businesswoman of Yr., 1982. Mem. Sacramento Met. C. of C. (chmn. city govt. affairs com. 1980—, mem. women's council 1980—, mem. small bus. council 1980—). Presbyterian. Office: 2762 Octavia St San Francisco CA 94123

WRIGHT, OSCAR DEAN, III, advertising executive, photographer; b. Artesia, Calif., Feb. 27, 1948; s. Oscar Dean, Jr. and Ann Wells (Ruggles) W.; m. Elizabeth Anne Sidnam, May 22, 1982. B.F.A. in Graphic Design, Calif. State U.-Long Beach, 1977. Graphic designer Meredith Corp., Des Moines, 1977-78; dir. advt. Odetics Inc., Anaheim, Calif., 1978—. Served with USAF, 1968-72; Vietnam. Republican. Office: 1380 S Anaheim Blvd Anaheim CA 92805

WRIGHT, RONALD EDWARD, clergyman, educator; b. Port Elizabeth, S. Africa, Aug. 27, 1930; s. Cecil Valentine and Isabel Jacoba (Barnard) W.; came to U.S., 1970; diploma S. Africa Bible Coll., 1956; B.A., Central Bible Coll., Springfield, Mo., 1960; M.R.E., Central Bapt. Sem., 1963; M.Div., N.W. Bapt. Theol. Coll., 1967; m. Barbara Joy Kolo Colling, Feb. 4, 1956; 1 dau., Catherine Joy. Evangel. and pastoral ministry, S. Africa, 1946-58, England, 1958, U.S., 1958-60; ordained to ministry Assemblies of God, 1962; assoc. pastor, minister edn., Toronto, Ont., Can., 1960-63; dir. summer children's camps, Apsley, Ont., 1960-63; prof. religion, dean, v.p. Western Pentecostal Bible Coll., North Vancouver, B.C., Can., 1963-70; prof. N.T. lang. and lit. Central Bible Coll., Springfield, 1970-75; prof. religion So. Calif. Coll., Costa Mesa, 1975—; adj. faculty Melodyland Sch. Theology, Anaheim, Calif., 1976-82; sr. adj. in N.T., Am. Christian Theol. Sem., Anaheim, Calif., 1982—. Mem. Soc. Pentecostal Studies, Evang. Theol. Soc. Office: 55 Fair Dr Costa Mesa CA 92626

WRIGHT, ROSALIE MULLER, newspaper and mag. editor; b. Newark, June 20, 1942; d. Charles and Angela (Fortunata) Muller; B.A. in English, Temple U., Phila., 1965; m. Lynn Wright, Jan. 13, 1962 (div.); children—James Anthony Meador, Geoffrey Shepard. Mng. editor Suburban Life mag., Orange, N.J., 1960-62; assoc. editor Phila. mag., 1962-64, mng. editor, 1969-73; founding editor Womensports mag., San Mateo, Calif., 1973-75; editor scene sect. San Francisco Examiner, 1975-77; exec. editor New West mag., San Francisco and Beverly Hills, Calif., 1977-81; features and Sunday editor San Francisco Chronicle, 1981—; tchr. mag. writing U. Calif.-Berkeley, 1975-76; participant pub. procedures course Stanford U. 1977-79; chmn. mag. judges Council Advancement and Support Edn. Conf., 1980. Mem. Am. Assn. Sunday and Feature Editors. Author numerous mag. articles, critques, revs.; contbr. to Compton's Ency. Office: 901 Mission St San Francisco CA 94119

WRIGHT, WILBUR ERNEST, hospital social work administrator; b. Berkeley Twp., N.J., July 23, 1933; s. Wilbur Samuel and Marie Ernestine (Clarke) W.; m. Mary J. Lavelle (div.); children—Diane, Stephen, Brian, Jeanine. B.S., St. Peter's Coll., 1955; M.Social Sci., Fordham U., 1958; postgrad. U.S. Army Med. Service Sch., 1959, 61, Army Spl. Warfare Sch., 1963, U. Okla., 1964-65, Peninsula U. Coll. Law, 1983. Lic. clin. social worker, Calif. Family counselor United Family and Children's Soc., Plainfield, N.J., 1958-59; health service officer, cons. Bur. State Services, USPHS, Washington, 1962-65; sr. med. social worker U. Calif.-San Diego County Hosp., 1965-66; dir. social work Scripps Meml. Hosp., La Jolla, Calif., 1966-68; dir. service, rehab. Calif. div. Am. Cancer Soc., San Francisco, 1968-72; cons./dir. resource devel. Orgn. for Bus., Edn. and Community Advancement, Cath. Charities, Archdiocese San Francisco, 1972-73; dep. head dept. social work Fawkner Park Community Health Center, dept. preventive and social medicine Alfred-Monash U. Hosp., Prahran, Victoria, Australia, 1973-74; head dept. social work Royal Perth Hosp., Western Australia, 1974-75; exec. dir. Community Mental Health Bd. Central Fla., Orlando, 1975-78; sec. gen. Council Internat. Programs, Washington, 1978-80; pub. health social work cons. State of Calif. Dept. Health Services, Los Angeles, 1981-82; adminstr. mental health programs San Francisco Council Chs., 1980-81; dir. clin. social work Stanford U. Med. Center, 1982—; cons. Republic of Korea Ministry Health and Welfare, 1961-62; mem. internat. case com. San Diego-Tijuana (Mex.) Health Council, Pan-Am. Health Orgn., 1966-68; chmn. service com., mem. exec., budget coms. San Diego County unit Am. Cancer Soc., 1967-68, mem. social work edn., profl. edn. coms. Calif. div., 1967-68; mem. stroke com., regional med. program U. Calif.-San Diego, 1967-68; mem. legis. com. Calif. Pub. Health Assn., 1971-73; commr. Marinwood Community Service Dist. Calif., 1971-73; mem. Prahran Social Action Com., 1973-74; mem. Richmond fellowship bd. Western Australia Dept. Mental Hygiene Community Devel. Ctr., 1974-75; mem. Fla. Dept. Health and Rehab. Services Task Force on Emotionally Disturbed Children and Adolescents, 1976-78; exec. dir. rep. exec. com. Fla. Assn. Dist. Mental Health Bds., 1976-77; mem. Blue Ridge Inst., So. Community Services Execs., 1977; mem. adv. com. Fla. Mental Health/Health Systems Tng. Program, 1977-78; mem. exec. com. Council Internat. Fellowship, Bonn, W.Ger., 1978-80; Area V Developmental Disabilities Bd. Calif., 1983; lectr., instr. various univs., insts., seminars. Served to 1st lt. U.S. Army; comdr. USPHS. Fellow Am. Pub. Health Assn., Royal Soc. for Health (U.K.); mem. Nat. Assn. Social Workers (chmn. health council San Diego chpt. 1968), Internat. Conf. on Social Welfare (U.S. com.), Assn. Mental Health Adminstrs., Nat. Soc. Fund Raisers. Contbr. articles in field to profl. jours. Office: Dept Clin Social Work Stanford U Hosp Med Center Stanford CA 94305

WRIGLEY, ELIZABETH SPRINGER (MRS. OLIVER K. WRIGLEY), found. exec.; b. Pitts., Oct. 4, 1915; d. Charles Woodward and Sarah Maria (Roberts) Springer; B.A. U. Pitts., 1935; B.S., Carnegie Inst. Tech., 1936; m. Oliver Kenneth Wrigley, June 16, 1936 (dec. July 1978). Procedure analyst U.S. Steel Corp., Pitts., 1941-43; research asst. The Francis Bacon Found., Inc., Los Angeles, 1944, exec., 1945-50, trustee, 1950—, dir. research, 1951-53, pres., 1954—, dir. Francis Bacon Library. Mem. ALA, Calif. Library Assn., Renaissance Soc. Am., Modern Humanities Research Assn., Cryptogram Assn., Alpha Delta Pi. Presbyn. Mem. Order Eastern Star, Damascus Shrine. Editor: The Skeleton Text of the Shakespeare Folio L.A. (by W.C. Arensberg), 1952. Compiler: Short Title Catalogue Numbers in the Library of the Francis Bacon Foundation, 1958; Wing Numbers in the Library of the Francis Bacon Foundation, 1959; Supplement To Francis Bacon Library Holdings in the STC of English Books, 1967; (with David W. Davies) A Concordance to the Essays of Francis Bacon, 1973. Home: 4805 N Pal Mal Ave Temple City CA 91780 Office: 655 N Dartmouth Ave Claremont CA 91711

WROBLICKY, THEODORE PETER, management consultant; b. Harvey, Ill., Sept. 9, 1937; s. Nestor Peter and Helen Marie (Hajek) W.; B.S., No. Ill. U., 1963; M.B.A., Golden Gate U., 1970; m. Barbara Kathryn Bukowski, Aug. 12, 1961; children—Gregory, Peter, Nicholas, Alexander. Programmer, Sears Roebuck & Co., 1963; application engr. Gen. Electric Co., 1964-67; asst. dir. mgmt. services Western Pacific R.R., 1967-71; cons. Ill. Central Gulf R.R., 1971-73; mgr. Haskins & Sells, Chgo., 1973-77; prin. Arthur Young & Co., Sacramento, 1978-82, dir. EDP cons., dir. mgmt. cons. Touche, Ross & Co., Sacramento, 1982—; mem. faculty Calif. State U., Sacramento, 1980; data processing adv. Reagan-Bush Com., Arlington, Va., 1980, mem. transition team, Washington, 1980-81; mem. Calif. Govt. Efficiency Team, 1983. Served with U.S. Army, 1956-59. Mem. Assn. Computing Machinery, Data Processing Mgmt. Assn., EDP Auditors Assn. Republican. Byzantine Catholic. Clubs: Sutter, KC, Polish Am. Office: 100 Howe Ave Suite 100 S Sacramento CA 95825

WROOBEL, ART IRWIN, advertising executive, sales training consultant; b. Bklyn., June 1, 1932; s. Felix and Frances (Levine) W.; m. Marilyn Joyce Shanblum, Nov. 27, 1955; children—Julie, Barry. B.S. in Bus. Adminstrn., UCLA, 1955. Cert. tchr., Calif. Ptnr. Waldman & Wroobel, advt. agy., 1970—; account exec. Larry Courtney Co., Encino, Calif., 1970—. Served with U.S. Army, 1955-57.

WRUSCH, MICHAEL MANFRED, interior designer; b. Detroit, Oct. 26, 1957; s. Gerhard Werner and Margot Dora (Bergemann) W. B.A. summa cum laude in Interior Design, Mich. State U., 1980. Interior designer Martha Shinn Interiors, Okemos, Mich., 1978-80; sr. interior designer Carlton Wagner Designs, Palos Verdes, Calif., 1980-81; prin. designer, owner Michael Wrusch Designs, Palos Verdes Estates, Calif., 1981—; guest lectr. UCLA. Decorative arts and architecture scholar Mich. State U., 1979. Mem. Am. Soc. Interior Designers (profl.), Omicron Nu (leadership award 1979), Phi Kappa Phi. Lutheran. Contbr. Long Beach Corp. Arts Designhouse, 1981, Sandpiper Design House, Palos Verdes, 1982; Am. Soc. Interior Designers Design House West, 1982. Office: 27 Malaga Cove Plaza Palos Verdes CA 90274

WU, CHIALIN, elec. engr.; b. Nanking, China, June 23, 1947; s. Cheng-Hao and Jan (Pao) Wu; came to U.S., 1970, naturalized, 1980; B.S., Nat. Taiwan U., 1969; M.S., Purdue U., 1972, Ph.D., 1975; m. Yi-Ni Loh, Aug. 18, 1973; children—Emily, Michael. mem. tech. staff. group supr. Jet Populsion Lab., Calif. Inst. Tech., Pasadena, 1974—, supr. radar signal processing research group, 1980—. Served with Taiwan Air Force, 1969-70. Mem. IEEE, Sigma Xi, Sigma Pi Sigma. Contbr. articles to profl. jours.; pioneer in digital spacecraft imaging radar processor. Office: 4800 Oak Grove Dr Pasadena CA 91109

WU, I-CHEN, poet, artist, historian; b. Ochen, Hupeh, China, Nov. 25, 1927; s. Hsien-yuan and Yu-cheng (Tsai) Wu; came to U.S., naturalized, 1979; B.A. with highest honors, Chung Hsing U., China, 1958; postgrad. U. Mo., 1968; M.A., Calif. State U., San Jose, 1974; doctoral candidate in Chinese History, U. Ariz.; m. Hsiao-hua Huang, Feb. 14, 1963; children—Rao-hsien, Rao-kuo, Meiching. Instr., Chinese painting U. Calif., Berkeley, 1972-73, Mills Coll., Oakland, Calif., 1974, San Francisco Community Coll., 1974-75, U. Calif., Santa Barbara, 1976-77, U. Nev., Reno, summer 1976, 77, 81, 82, U. Ariz., 1979-82, Pima Community Coll., Tucson, 1981-82, U. Calif.-Berkeley Extension, San Francisco, 1983—, San Jose State U., 1984—; art insp. Taiwan Provincial Dept. Edn., 1953-66; mem. staff U.S. Armed Forces Interpreters Tng. Sch., 1955-56. Recipient Distinguished Service award Taiwan Provincial Govt., 1964. Mem. Internat. Soc. Chinese Philosopy, Art Soc. China, Chinese Calligraphers' Assn. Author: Chinese Political Set-Up, Taiwan, 1957; Introduction to Chinese Painting, 1967. Research in Yüan, Ming Paintings and the Eccentric School in Yang Chou. Home: 1683 Christopher St San Jose CA 95122

WU, LIN LION, agronomist, educator; b. Peking, China, Mar. 18, 1939; came to U.S., 1978; s. Jan-nan and Wen-in (Wu) Lee; B.S., Nat. Taiwan U., Taipei, 1966; Ph.D., U. Liverpool (Eng.), 1973. Research asst. Inst. Botany, Academia Sinica, Taipei, 1966-68, asst. research fellow, 1968-70; assoc. research fellow, 1975-78; research assoc. agronomy and range sci. U. Calif., Davis, 1978-79, asst. prof. environ. horticulture, 1979-83, assoc. prof., 1983—; research assoc. botany Duke U., 1973-75. Elvenia J. Slosson Endowment Fund research grantee. Mem. Bot. Soc. Am., Am. Soc. Agronomy, Crop Sci. Soc. Am. Research on ecol. and evolutionary genetics and metal tolerance in plants. Home: 1307 Champhor Ln Davis CA 95616 Office: Dept Environ Horticulture Univ Calif Davis CA 95616

WU, THEODORE YAO-TSU, engineering science educator; b. Changchow, Kiangsu, China, Mar. 20, 1924; s. Ren Fu and Gee Ing (Shu) W.; m. Chin-Hua Shih, June 17, 1950; children—Fonda, Melba. B.S., Chian-Tung U., Shanghai, 1946; M.S., Iowa State Coll., 1948; Ph.D., Calif. Inst. Tech., 1952. Research fellow Calif. Inst. Tech., Pasadena, 1952-55, asst. prof., 1955-57, assoc. prof., 1957-61, prof. engring. sci., 1961—; vis. prof. Hamburg (W.Ger.) U., 1964-65; lectr. Australian univs., 1976, Chinese univs., 1979; Russell Severance Springer vis. prof. mech. engring., U. Calif.-Berkeley, 1980; lectr. Chinese Acad. Sci., 1981. Guggenheim Found. fellow, 1964-65, Japan Soc. Promotion Sci. fellow, 1982. Fellow Am. Phys. Soc., AIAA (asso.); mem. Soc. Naval Architects and Marine Engrs., Nat. Acad. Engring., Sigma Xi, Phi Tau Phi, Pi Mu Epsilon. Contbr. chpts. to books and articles to profl. jours. Office: 1201 Calif St Calif Inst Tech Pasadena CA 91125

WULSIN, LUCIEN, lawyer, business executive; b. Cin., Sept. 21, 1916; s. Lucien and Margaret (Hager) W.; m. Eleanor Tubman, Jan. 9, 1944; children—Lucien III, Henry H., Jeanne P., Diane M.; m. Joan Friedlander, Dec. 30, 1959; 1 son, Winthrop H.; m. Pamela Pardee, May 6, 1977. A.B., Harvard U., 1939; LL.B., U. Va., 1947. Bar: Ohio 1948, Ark. 1958. Ptnr. firm Kyte, Conlan, Wulsin & Vogeler, Cin., 1952-62; pres. D.H. Baldwin Co. (name now Baldwin-United Corp.), Cin., 1962-74, chmn., chief exec. officer, 1974-81. Trustee Denver U. Mem. Ark. Bar Assn., Cin. Bar Assn. Clubs: Arapahoe Hunt; University (Denver); Queen City, Camargo (Cin.). Office: 3 Park Central Suite 1005 1515 Arapahoe St Denver CO 80202

WUNDER, BRUCE ARNOLD, zoologist, educator; b. Monterey Park, Calif., Feb. 10, 1942; s. Edwin Claude and Phyllis Viviene (Lehman) W.; m. Gayle Virginia Anderson, June 16, 1963; children—Michael Brent, Kristin Kathleen. B.A., Whittier Coll., 1963; Ph.D., UCLA, 1968. Teaching asst. in zoology UCLA, 1963-65, assoc. in zoology, 1965-66, USPHS trainee in cardiovascular zoophysiology, 1966-68; postdoctoral fellow NIH, 1968-69; asst. prof. zoology, 1969-76, assoc. prof. zoology and entomology, 1976—; small mammal and physiol. ecologist Ecology Cons., Inc., Biol. Research Assocs., Inc., Fort Collins, Thorne Ecol. Inst., Boulder, U.S. Army C.E., U.S. Fish and Wildlife Service; vis. investigator at biotron U. Wis., Madison, 1971; summer faculty Nat. Wildlife Fedn. Conservation Summit, Estes Park, Colo., 1972-77; summer faculty U. Mich. Biol. Sta., Douglas Lake, 1976, 78; Alexander von Humboldt Research fellow J.W. Goethe U., Frankfort, W.Ger., 1979-80; vis. prof. zoology U. Mont. Biol. Sta., Flathead Lake, 1981, 83. Mem. AAAS, Am. Soc. Zoologists, Am. Soc. Mammalogists, Am. Inst. Biol. Scis., Ecol. Soc. Am., Sigma Xi, Omicron Delta Kappa. Contbr. numerous articles to profl. jours. Home: 505 Canadian Pkwy Fort Collins CO 80524 Office: Dept Zoology-Entomology Colo State Univ Fort Collins CO 80523

WUNSCH, DORIS ANN, industrial hygienist; b. Newark, June 16, 1948; d. Rudolf George and Doris Rosemary (Myers) W. B.A. in Chemistry, Beaver Coll., 1970; M.S. in Environ. Health and Toxicology, Temple U., 1972; cert. in comprehensive practice Bd. Indsl. Hygiene. Research asst. U. Edinburgh (Scotland) Med. Sch., 1970-71; indsl. hygienist U.S. Dept. Labor, Portland, Oreg., 1972-74; indsl. hygienist, cons. State of Alaska, Anchorage, 1975-77; indsl. hygienist Atlantic Richfield Co., Cherry Point Refinery, Ferndale, Wash., 1977—. Mem. Am. Indsl. Hygiene Assn., Am. Bd. Indsl. Hygiene, Am. Conf. Govtl. Indsl. Hygiene, Am. Soc. Safety Engrs., Nature Conservancy, Oceanic Club. Office: ARCO Cherry Point Refinery PO Box 1127 Ferndale WA 98248

WURLITZER, FRED PABST, real estate executive, surgeon; b. San Francisco, Dec. 26, 1937; s. Raimund Billing and Pauline (Pabst) W.; m. Elliott Jones, Dec. 23, 1963; children—Ricky, Arnisha, Susan, Elena. B.A. in Biology, Stanford U., 1960; M.D., U. Cin., 1965. Diplomate Am. Bd. Surgery. Intern, Highland Hosp., Oakland, Calif., 1965-66, resident, 1966-67; resident Wadsworth VA Hosp., Los Angeles, 1967-70; U. Tex. fellow M.D. Anderson Hosp., Houston, 1970-71; clin. instr. surgery U. So. Calif., Los Angeles, 1972; assoc. Pasadena Tumor Inst., 1971-73; ptnr. San Mateo (Calif.) Med. Clinic, 1973-77; owner, pres. Wurlitzer Properties, Inc., Burlingame, Calif., 1976—. Served with U.S. Army, 1956. Fellow ACS; mem. AMA. Republican. Presbyterian. Clubs: Peninsula Tennis (Burlingame); Peninsula Gold and Country (San Mateo); Hollytree Country (Tyler, Tex.). Contbr. tech. articles to med. jours.

WURSTEN, HELMUT, child and adolescent clinical psychologist; b. Switzerland, Feb. 12, 1916; came to U.S., 1946, naturalized, 1947; s. Arnold and Flora W.; children—Christine, Eric. Ph.D. in Clin. Psychology, U. Geneva, 1946. Lic. psychologist, Calif. Chief clin. psychologist Children's Hosp., Los Angeles, 1947-60; dir. psychol. services Frostig Ctr. for Children with Learning Difficulties, Los Angeles, 1960-72; pvt. practice psychodiagnostic evaluation and psychotherapy of children and adolescents, Los Angeles, 1960—; assoc. clin. prof. psychiatry (child psychology), supr. child psychotherapy and lectr. dept. psychiatry U. So. Calif.; supr. child psychotherapy Didi Hirsch Mental Health Ctr., Los Angeles. Served with Swiss Anti-Aircraft Units, 1939-46. Diplomate Am. Bd. Profl. Psychology. Mem. Am. Psychol. Assn., Calif. Psychol. Assn., Los Angeles County Psychol. Assn. (pres. 1973-74), Am. Soc. Clin. Hypnosis. Contbr. articles on child psychology to profl. jours. Home: 633 Ocean Ave Apt 27 Santa Monica CA 90402 Office: 11665 W Olympic Blvd Suite 501 Los Angeles CA 90064

WURTELE, ZIVIA SYRKIN, statistician; b. N.Y.C., Apr. 1, 1921; d. Nachman and Mashe (Osnos) Syrkin; b. Morton Gaither Wurtele, Dec. 31, 1942; children—Eve Syrkin, Jonathan Syrkin. B.A., Hunter Coll., 1940; M.A., UCLA, 1944; Ph.D., Columbia U., 1954. Research fellow Harvard U. Econ. Research Project, 1956-58; asst. research statistician UCLA Grad. Sch. Bus. Adminstrn., 1959-62, assoc. research statistician, 1963-65; cons. in stats. and econ. U.S. and local govt. agys., Los Angeles, 1966-75; sr. statistician Pan Heuristics div. R&D Assocs., Marina del Rey, Calif., 1976—; lectr. Hebrew U., Jerusalem, 1975. Mem. Nat. Acad. Scis. Bd. Army Sci. and Tech. Columbia U. scholar, 1944-46; Fulbright scholar U. Paris, 1949-50. Mem. Inst. Math. Stats., Am. Statis. Assn. Contbr. articles to profl. publs. Office: PO Box 9695 Marina del Rey CA 90291

WUTZKE, BEVERLEY LORRAINE, interior designer; b. Melbourne, Australia, June 20, 1942; d. Russel Stewart and Ethel Jane (Rowley) Crabtree; m. Gerard Wutzke, Dec. 1, 1962 (div.); children—Wendy Nicole, Teresa Michele. B.A. in Sociology, San Francisco State U., 1962, M.B.A., 1983. Assoc. designer Edwin Smalle & Assocs., San Rafael, Calif., 1973-77; instr. in interior design Novato (Calif.) Unified Sch. District, 1974-78; prin. Designs Unltd., Novato, 1977-83, Decorum, Moraga, Calif., 1983—. Active Redwood Empire Cursillo Movement; 4-H Leader, campaigner McQuaide for Congress. Recipient Anne B. McDonald award, 1976. Mem. Novato C. of C., Am. Soc. Interior Designers, AAUW, Mensa. Paintings auctioned by sta. KQED, 1973, 74. Home and Office: 11 Doral Dr Moraga CA 94556

WYATT, CHRISTEN, state official; b. Inyokern, Calif., July 3, 1948; d. George Leon and Gladys Shane (Baker) Siders; m. Leonard Eugene Wyatt, Jan. 1, 1982; m. Harvey Parrott, Nov. 10, 1963; children—Julie, Mark, Erica, Brent, Christina. Student Fresno City Coll., 1972-74. Adminstrv. asst. Housing Authority, City of Madera, Calif., 1971-76; personnel asst. United Vintners, Madera, 1976-77; mgr. public relations Calif. Pistachio Commn., Fresno, 1981—. Baptist. Home: 5072 E Hedges St Fresno CA 93727

WYATT, JOHN CRITTENTON, ins. agy. exec.; b. Stinnett, Tex., Oct. 7, 1927; s. George Nicholas and Nellie Irene (Boone) W.; student Balboa U., 1948-49, San Diego State U., 1949-52; m. Ruth Lucille Asbury, Oct. 16, 1948; children—Joann Ruth, Maril yn Louise, Patricia Lee, Leslie Irene. Store mgr. Gamble-Skogmo, Inc., 1952-54; agt. Prudential Ins. Co., 1954-59; owner, operator Hart & Wyatt Ins. Agy., Brawley, Calif., 1959-64; brokerage mgr. Mfrs. Life Ins. Co., 1964-73; pres. Wyatt Ins. Agy., Inc., San Diego, 1973—; mem. adv. council San Diego Community Coll., 1974-81, instr. in ins., 1974-77. Trustee Brawley Sch. Dist.,

1960-64; trustee Brawley C. of C., 1960-64. Served with USN, 1945-48; PTO. Named Citizen of Yr., Brawley C. of C., 1962; recipient life cert. San Diego Community Coll., 1975. C.L.U. Mem. Ind. Ins. Agts. Assn., Western Assn. Ins. Brokers, San Diego State U. Alumni Assn., Aztec Athletic Found., Am. Soc. C.L.U.'s, Propeller Club U.S. Republican. Roman Catholic. Clubs: Lions (pres. club 1961-62, 78-79, chmn. bd. Welfare Found. 1980-81), Elks. Home: 7748 Cedar Lake Ave San Diego CA 92119 Office: 2831 Camino Del Rio S San Diego CA 92108

WYATT, JOSEPH LUCIAN, JR., lawyer, author, educator; b. Chgo., Feb. 21, 1924; s. Joseph Lucian and Cecile Gertrude (Zadico) W.; m. Marjorie Kathryn Simmons, Apr. 9, 1954; children—Daniel, Linn, Jonathan. A.B. in English Lit. with honors, Northwestern U., 1947; LL.B., Harvard U., 1949. Bar: Calif. 1950, U.S. Supreme Ct. 1965. Assoc., Brady, Nossaman & Walker, Los Angeles, 1950-58, ptnr., 1958-61; sole practice, Los Angeles, 1961-71; sr. mem. Cooper, Wyatt, Tepper & Plant, P.C., Los Angeles, 1971-79; of counsel Beardsley, Hufstedler & Kemble, Los Angeles, 1979-81; ptnr. Hufstedler, Miller, Carlson & Beardsley, Los Angeles, 1981—; mem. faculty Pacific Coast Banking Sch., Seattle, 1963—, lectr. Trustee Pacific Oaks Coll. and Children's Sch., 1969—; counsel, parliamentarian Calif. Democratic Party and presdl. conv. dels., 1971—; mem. Calif. State Personnel Bd., 1961-71, v.p., 1963-65, pres., 1965-67; bd. dirs. Calif. Pub. Employees Retirement System, 1963-71. Served to sgt. USAAF, 1943-45. Fellow Am. Coll. Probate Counsel; mem. ABA, Los Angeles Bar Assn. (trustee), Internat. Acad. Estate and Trust Law, Calif. State Bar (del. state bar conf. 1956, 1962-67). Democrat. Christian Scientist. Author: Trust Administration and Taxation, 4 vols., 1964—; editor: Trusts and Estates, 1962-74. Home: 1119 Armada Dr Pasadena CA 91103 Office: Hufstedler Miller et al 700 S Flower St Suite 1600 Los Angeles CA 90017

WYCKOFF, CHARLOTTE, ednl. adminstr.; b. Wichita, Kan., Oct. 8, 1934; d. Ray L. and Ruth Charlotte (McLain) Murphy; B.A. in Psychology, LaVerne Coll., 1974; M.A., Calif. State U., San Bernardino, 1977; postgrad. U.S. Internat. U., San Diego; m. Bill Wyckoff, Oct. 25, 1954; children—Robert, Shir, Paul, Brandy, Joseph. Founder, dir. Calif. Learning Centers, Rancho Cucamonga, 1967—; prof. Chaffey Community Coll., Rancho Cucamonga, 1973—; coordinator tng. program Casa Colina Hosp., Pomona, Calif., 1975-76. Mem. adv. bd. Bonita High Sch., San Dimas, Calif., 1975-77, Pomona High Sch., 1975-77; adminstr. Claremont (Calif.) Collegiate Sch., 1977—; mem. adv. bd. Pomona High Sch., Bonita High Sch. Mem. Am. Personnel and Guidance Assn., Nat. Soc. Autistic Children, Nat. Assn. Edn. of Young Children, Assn. Humanistic Psychologists, Calif. Assn. Spl. Schs., Nat. Assn. for Edn. Young Children, Pre-Sch. Assn., Calif. Assn. Sch. Psychologists and Psychometrists, Calif. State Psychol. Assn., Calif. Assn. Neurologically Handicapped Children, Doctorial Soc. Club: Altrusa. Home: 5333 Amethyst Alta Loma CA 91701 Office: 8736 Baker Ave Rancho Cucamonga CA 91730 Mailing Address: PO Box 190 Rancho Cucamonga CA 91730

WYCKOFF, THEODORE, political science educator; b. N.Y.C., Feb. 24, 1922; s. Wallace Hook and Helena (Schmid) W.; m. Ludmilla Dmitrieff, Apr. 22, 1945; children—Ann Wyckoff-Payne, Barbara Wuckoff-Siris, Cathryn. B.A., UCLA, 1942, M.A., M.P.A., Princeton U., 1957; Ph.D., Bonn, Germany, 1967. Commd. 2d lt. U.S. Army, 1942, advanced through grades to lt. col., 1960; ret., 1968; assoc. prof. polit. sci. No. Ariz. U., Flagstaff, 1968—; lectr. U. Md., 1958-60; prof. mil. sci. Ariz. State U., 1961-64; vis. scholar U. Mich., 1978-79. Active Mus. No. Ariz., Bd. Cert. Holders, Flagstaff Hosp. Mem. Internat. Polit. Sci. Assn., Am. Polit. Sci. Assn., Internat. Studies Assn., Phi Beta Kappa, Pi Sigma Alpha. Democrat. Episcopalian. Clubs: Wyckoff Assn. Am. (v.p.), Rotary (pres.-elect Flagstaff). Contbr. articles to publs. in U.S., Ger.; patnetee Wyckoff's automatic transmission. Home: 515 E David Dr Flagstaff AZ 86001 Office: Dept Polit Sci No Ariz Univ Flagstaff AZ 86011

WYDOSKI, RICHARD STANLEY, biologist; b. Nanticoke, Pa., Feb. 3, 1936; s. Stanley and Monica (Ludorf) W.; B.S., Bloomsburg State Coll., 1960; M.S., Pa. State U., 1962, Ph.D., 1965; m. Joy Anne Caley, May 23, 1959; children—Richard G., Duane S., Diane M., Susan G. Fishery biologist U.S. Fish and Wildlife Service, Sandusky, Ohio, 1965-66, Newport, Oreg., Seattle, Logan, Utah and Leetown, W.Va., 1966-81, chief br. fishery extension services, Washington, 1981-82, mgmt. devel. program, 1982—. Served with U.S. Army, 1953-56. Recipient Spl. Achievement award U.S. Fishery and Wildlife Service, 1973; Disting. Served award Am. Fisheries Soc., 1981; NSF teaching fellow, 1964. Mem. Am. Fisheries Soc., Am. Inst. Fishery Research Biologists, Pacific Fishery Biologists, Sigma Xi, Phi Sigma. Author: Inland Fishes of Washington, 1979. Office: Fish and Wildlife Service US Dept Interior Washington DC 20240

WYETH, HENRIETTE, artist; b. Wilmington, Del., Oct. 22, 1907; d. Newell Convers and Caroline (Bockius) W.; m. Peter Hurd, June 28, 1929; children—Peter Wyeth, Ann Carol, Michael. Student Pa. Acad. Fine Arts, 1922-25; pvt. study with N.C. Wyeth. One-man shows: Phila., 1932, Washington, 1934, Wilmington, Del., 1938, N.Y.C., 1942, Brandywine Mus., Chadds Ford, Pa., 1980, Santa Fe, 1982; exhibited in numerous group shows; represented in pvt. and pub. collections; commd. work includes portrait Pres. Richard Nixon, White House, 1979. Address: Sentinel Ranch San Patricio NM 88348

WYLE, EWART HERBERT, clergyman; b. London, Eng., Sept. 12, 1904; s. Edwin and Alice Louise (Durman) W.; B.A., U. Louisville, 1930; B.D., Lexington Theol. Sem., 1933; postgrad. Louisville Presbyn. Theol. Sem., Temple U., 1933-35; D.D., Tex. Christian U., 1953; m. Prudence Harper, June 12, 1959; 1 son, Ewart Herbert. Ordained to ministry Christian Ch., 1935; pastor First Ch., Palestine, Tex., 1935-37, First Ch., Birmingham, Ala., 1937-41, First Ch., Tyler, Tex., 1944-54, Country Club Ch., Kansas City, Mo., 1954-59; minister Torrey Pines Ch., La Jolla, Calif., 1959-79, minister emeritus, 1979—. Bd. dirs. Scripps Meml. Hosp., pres., 1980-81. Served as chaplain, maj., AUS, 1941-44. Mem. Mil. Order World Wars, Am. Legion, Tau Kappa Epsilon, Pi Kappa Delta. Clubs: Masons (32 deg.), Shriners, Rotary, LaJolla Beach and Tennis. Home: 8850 LaJolla Scenic Dr N La Jolla CA 92037

WYLIE, PAUL RICHTER, JR., lawyer; b. Livingston, Mont., Dec. 25, 1936; s. Paul R. and Alice H. Wylie; B.S. in Chem. Engring., Mont. State U., 1959; J.D., Am. U., 1965; married; 1 dau. Engr., Thiokol Chem. Co. and Hercules Powder Co., Utah, 1959-62; patent examiner U.S. Patent Office, Washington, 1962-64; patent agt. Phillips Petroleum Co., Washington, 1964-65; admitted to Utah bar, 1965, Calif. bar, 1970, Supreme Ct. bar, 1971; patent counsel The Eimco Corp., Salt Lake City, 1965-66; asst. gen. patent counsel Dart Industries Inc., Los Angeles, 1967-81; sole practice as Paul R. Wylie, P.C., 1981—. Lic. real estate broker. Mem. Am. Bar Assn., Licensing Exec. Soc., Internat. Patent and Trademark Assn., U.S. Trademark Assn., Am. Patent Law Assn., Patent Law Assn. Los Angeles, Inter-Am. Assn. Indsl. Property.

WYMAN, H. JACK, advertising executive; b. San Francisco, Aug. 27, 1921; s. Herbert S. and Ruth B. (Jacobs) W.; m. Barbara Voorshagen, Apr. 28, 1951 (div.); children—Gareth P., John G., Richard D., Jo Ann m. 2d Elaine J. Snay, Jan. 3, 1980. Student San Mateo (Calif.) Jr. Coll., 1939, San Francisco State Coll., 1942-43. A.A., San Francisco Jr. Coll., 1942; Account exec. Kirschner & Co., San Francisco, 1946-49; founder pres. Wyman Co., Inc., Mill Valley, Calif., 1950—. Past trustee Ross (Calif.) Sch. Dist., past pres. PTA. Served with USN, 1943-46. Mem. Am. Assn. Advt. Agys. (former chmn. No. Calif. council). Club: North Bay Advt. Contbr. articles to religious and govt. publs. Office: 650 E Blithedale Ave Mill Valley CA 94942

WYNHOFF, PATRICIA VERNON, theatrical business manager; b. N.Y.C., June 7, 1933; d. William Ward and Mary Carter (Graham) Vernon; m. G.E. Anderson, Apr. 13, 1958; children—Heather, Mark; m. F. James Wynhoff, Aug. 10, 1983. B.S. in Journalism (scholar), Northwestern U., 1954. Editor Celebrity Service, N.Y.C., 1954-55, Calif., 1955-57; writer-researcher N.Y. Herald Tribune and Joe Hyams, Calif., 1957-59; account supr. various C.P.A. firms, 1960-79; pvt. practice, 1979—. Treas., Calif. ERA campaign, Sepulveda Unitarian Universalist Soc. Mem. Am. Film Inst., Nat. Assn. Female Execs., Theta Sigma Phi, Acad. Magical Arts (Los Angeles). Office: 16027 Ventura Blvd Encino CA 91436

WYNN, CHARLES CHARTERS, engineering company executive; b. Phila., Feb. 2, 1929; s. Charters Redmond and Mary (Bliss) W.; B.A., U. Wash., Seattle, 1952; children—Charters, Christopher, Bruce, Bryan, David, Daniel. Vice pres., project mgr. Redwood Shores Devel. for Leslie Salt Co., San Francisco, 1967-72; v.p. Brown & Kauffman, land devel. and builders, Palo Alto, Calif., 1962-72; v.p. mktg. and project mgmt. Creegan & D'Angelo, cons. engrs., San Jose, Calif., 1972—. Active fund raising local YMCA. Served with AUS, 1946-48. Mem. Soc. Am. Mil. Engrs., Design Profls. Council, Nat. Assn. Home Builders. Home: 350 Sharon Park Dr Apt T-21 Menlo Park CA 94025 Office: 1046 Taylor St PO Box 26220 San Jose CA 95159

WYRO, JOHN LEE, land devel. co. exec.; b. Monterey, Calif., Dec. 18, 1945; s. Walter Edward and Muriel Eileen (Endicott) W.; B.S., Utah State U., 1968; M.P.A., San Jose State U., 1978; m. Evans Alice Mary Greenland, Nov. 30, 1968; children—Alice Endicott, Emily Goodwin. Adminstrv. asst. city of Milpitas (Calif.), 1973-75; asst. city mgr. City of Vacaville, Calif., 1975; dir. land acquisition and forward planning Shapell, Inc., Milpitas, 1979-80; v.p. Perma Bilt Homes, Walnut Creek, Calif., 1980—. lectr. Golden Gate U., San Francisco, 1978-79. Chmn., United Way, Vacaville, 1978, Sch. Bond Dr., Vacaville, 1975-76; seminar leader, bd. dirs. Solano County Mgmt. Devel. Center, 1975-79. Served with USN, 1968-73. Recipient Rotary Group Study Exchange award, 1978. Mem. Bldg. Industry Assn. (dir. eastern div. 1983). Home: 2 Bien Venida Orinda CA 94563 Office: 1660 Olympic Blvd Suite 320 Walnut Creek CA 94596

WYSE, JOHN PATRICK HENRY, anatomy educator; b. Kamloops, B.C., Can., July 28, 1948; s. Henry Clement and Anne Elizabeth (Leitch) W.; B.Sc., magna cum laude, U. B.C., 1971, M.D., 1975; Ph.D., U. Calgary, 1978; m. Betty Ann Advent, June 17, 1972; children—Heidi Christine, Mark Egan Douglas, Alexander Stephen Henry, Sarah Ann. Med. Research Council Can. fellow dept. anatomy U. Calgary, 1975-78, asst. prof. dept. anatomy, 1978-81, assoc. prof., 1981—. Med. Research Council Can. grantee, 1978—; Nat. Retinitis Pigmentosa Found. grantee, 1978-83; Alta. Mental Health grantee, 1980-82; Alta. Heritage Found. Med. Research grantee, 1981-82. Mem. Assn. Research in Vision and Ophthalmology, Soc. Neurosci., Can. Assn. Anatomists. Home: 111 Silver Ridge Rise NW Calgary AB T3B 4P6 Canada Office: 3330 Hospital Dr NW Calgary AB T2N 4N1 Canada

WYSZYNSKI, VALENTINE ADAM, graphics cons.; b. Chgo., Dec. 24, 1941; s. Anthony Marion and Genevieve Anne (Stabosz) W.; m. Joy Anne Halverson, Oct. 5, 1966 (div.); children—April Suzanne, Brian Matthew, Charlotte Lillian. Student, U.S. Air Force Inst., 1965-68; B.I.S., N.M. State U., 1981. With U.S. Post Office, Lyons, Ill., 1959-64, Mut. Trust Life Ins., Chgo., 1968-71, Circle News, Joliet, Ill., 1971-73, Combined Ins. Co. of Am., So. N.Mex., 1973-76; faculty drama dept., N.Mex. State U., Las Cruces, 1977-81; graphics cons., Las Cruces, 1982—; owner, pres. Tierra-com Systems, satellite and video equipment installations. Served with USAF, 1964-70. Mem. Soc. for Pvt. and Comml. Earth Stas., Soc. Broadcast Engrs., Electronic Music Engrs. Club: Convention (pres.). Contbr. articles to profl. jours. Home: 1340 Rayos de Luna Las Cruces NM 88005

YABUTANI, KOICHI MOLE, aerospace exec.; b. Brawley, Calif., Jan. 21, 1931; s. Shunzo K. and Toyoko (Kondo) Y.; B.S., U. Utah, 1958; M.Engring., U. Calif. at Los Angeles, 1975; m. Pauline T. Tanabe, Oct. 8, 1960. Equipment engr. RCA, Riverton, N.J., 1959-62; engr. Northrop Corp., Hawthorne, Calif., 1962-63; mem. tech. staff Hughes Aircraft Co., Culver City, 1958-59, group head, 1965-67, staff engr., 1967-68, sr. system engr., 1968-70, section head, 1970-72, asst. dept. mgr., 1972-79, asso. lab. mgr., 1979-82, lab. mgr., 1982—. Served with USAF, 1950-54. Mem. IEEE, Eta Kappa Nu, Tau Beta Pi, Phi Kappa Phi. Home: 4665 Guava St Seal Beach CA 90740 Office: MX 1088 Bldg R7 Hughes Aircraft Co PO Box 92426 Los Angeles CA 90009

YACCO, RICHARD ALAN, television executive; b. San Jose, Calif., Aug. 23, 1951; s. Samuel Thomas and Rose (lasus) Y.; m. Susan Joan Cole, May 30, 1976; 1 son, Cole Richard. A.A. in Liberal Arts, De Anza Coll., 1971; B.A. in Radio-TV, San Jose State U., 1974. Cert. adult edn. tchr. Calif. News anchor, program host, producer dir. Sunnyvale (Calif.) Cablevision, 1970-74; program mgr. Teleprompter Cable TV, Los Gatos, Calif., 1974, dist. dir. programming, Santa Clara, Calif., 1974-79; producer dir. Bay Area Interconnect (fomerly Gillcable Broadcast Div.), San Jose, Calif., 1979—; ind. cons., producer, tchr., writer. Democrat. Office: 1310 N 4th St San Jose CA 95112

YACKLE, ALBERT REUSTLE, aero. engr.; b. Phila., May 13, 1922; s. Albert Jacob and Marion Dorothy (Reustle) Y.; B.S. in Mech. Engring., Pa. State U., 1943; m. Ruth Elizabeth Everett, Sept. 18, 1948; children—Linda J., Tom Reustle, Brad Everett. Stress engr. Eastern Aircraft Corp., Trenton, 1943-44; stress engr. Kellett Aircraft, Willow Grove, Pa., 1946-49, program mgr., 1950-60; structures engr. Chase Aircraft, Trenton, 1949-50; div. engr. advanced design Lockheed Corp., Burbank, Calif., 1960—, advanced design program mgr., 1975—. Chmn. troop com. Boy Scouts Am., 1963-68. Served with USN, 1944-46. Recipient Spl. Achievements award Lockheed Corp., 1976, 77, 79; registered profl. engr., Calif. Mem. AIAA, Am. Helicopter Soc. Republican. Presbyterian. Patentee in field. Home: 5105 Quakertown Ave Woodland Hills CA 91364 Office: Lockheed Corp Burbank CA 91520

YACOUBI, M. ABDUH, agronomist; b. Oujda, Morocco, Feb. 26, 1945; s. Adelkader and Aicha (Yacoubi) Y.; m. Annette Gibson, Nov. 11, 1982. B.S. in Soil and Irrigation Engring., Am. U. Beirut, 1970; M.S. in Agronomy, U. Ariz., 1973, Ph.D., 1974. Asst. wheat project mgr. Govt. Morocco, 1970-75; assoc. prof. Agronomic Inst., Rabat, Morocco, 1975-82; agronomist research advisor U. Ariz., 1981-82; tng. officer Icarda, Aleppo, Syria, 1982-83; pres. Sedima Cons. Co. Internat., Tucson, 1983—. U.S. AID grantee, 1965-70, 72-73. Mem. Am. Soc. Agronomy, Soil Sci. Soc. Am., Internat. Soil Sci. Soc., Moroccan Soc. Soil Sci. (founding; pres.), Sigma Kappa Gamma, Assn. Moroccan Alumni, Orgn. African Students. Moslem. Club: Internat. (Tucson). Contbr. articles to profl. publs. Office: Box 3397 Tucson AZ 85722

YADAVALLI, SRIRAMAMURTI VENKATA, physicist; b. Secunderabad, India, May 12, 1924; came to U.S., 1948, naturalized, 1963; s. Sankara Somayajulu and Durgamba (Boddupalli) Y.; B.S., Andhra U., 1942, M.S., 1945; M.S., U. Calif., Berkeley, 1949, Ph.D., 1953; m. Suzan Sunel, Apr. 26, 1952. Research engr. Inst. Engring. Research, U. Calif., Berkeley, 1952-53; mem. tech. staff, cons. engr. Electric Co., Syracuse, 1953-59; N.Y. and Palo Alto, Calif., sr. math. physicist, staff scientist Stanford Research Inst., Menlo Park, Calif., 1959-77; pres., dir. research Shastra, Inc., Palo Alto, 1977—. Mem. IEEE (sr.), Am. Phys. Soc., AAAS, N.Y. Acad. Scis., Soc. Engring. Sci., AIAA, Sigma Xi. Contbr. articles to profl. jours. Home: 868 Thornwood Dr Palo Alto CA 94303 Office: Shastra Inc PO Box 1231 Palo Alto CA 94302

YADON, VERNAL LEE, museum director, artist; b. Exeter, Calif., Feb. 18, 1930; s. Jacob Nelson and Hazel Winifred (Miller) Y. B.S., Oreg. State U., 1952, M.S., 1954. Dir. Pacific Grove (Calif.) Mus. Natural History, 1957—. Active Calif. Native Plant Soc., Audubon Soc.; former chmn. Ventura Chpt. Sierra Club. Served with U.S. Army, 1954-56. Mem. Am. Assn. Mus. (sr. counselor accreditation commn.; former pres. Western Regional Conf.), Assn. Sci. Mus. Dirs., AAAS.

YAGER, EDWIN GEORGE HARLAND, mgmt. edn. cons.; b. Detroit, July 13, 1938; s. William Edwin and Myrtle Veronica (Harland) Y.; student U. Detroit, 1956-57, Brigham Young U., 1958-60; M.B.A., Mich. State U., 1966; m. Judith Mae Hartman, June 14, 1961; children—Julne Lambert, Lori, Jon, Suzanne, Carol, Karen. With J. L. Hudson Co., Detroit, 1960-68; corp. staff Ford Motor Co., Dearborn, Mich., 1968-73, dir. mgmt. devel., 1971-73; pres. Consulting Assocs., Inc., Novi, Mich., 1973-81; pres. Yager Assocs., 1981—; lectr. Brigham Young U., U. Pitts., U. Colo., U. Mich., Eastern Mich. U., Wayne State U. Cons. to urban groups through Profl. Skills Alliance, Detroit, 1967-73; active numerous civic coms., election campaigns, others. Mem. Am. Soc. Tng. Devel., Coll. Placement Council, Internat. Assn. Quality Circles, Orgn. Devel. Network. Mormon (former bishop). Club: Mich. Mormon Concert Choir (condr. 1975-80). Author: Making The Training Process Work, 1979; Organization Development for Managers, 1981; Is There Life After Assessment; contbr. articles on human resource devel. to profl. publs. Home and office: 3697 Wagon Wheel Park City UT 84060

YAMANE, STANLEY JOEL, optometrist, contact lens consultant; b. Lihue, Kauai, Hawaii, Mar. 13, 1943; s. Tooru and Yukiko (Miura) Y.; m. Joyce Mitsuko Tamura; children—Stanley Tooru Aiichi, Karen Margaret. B.S. in Optometry, Pacific U., 1966, O.D., 1966. Diplomate Am. Acad. Optometry. Practice optometry, Waipahu, Hawaii, 1967-73; ptnr. with Dr. Dennis M. Kuwabara, 1973-81, Drs. Kuwabara & Yamane, Optometrists, Inc., 1981—. Lectr., cons. in field; sec.-treas. Hawaii Bd. Examiners in Optometry, 1975-76, v.p., 76-78, pres., 78-80; mem. adj. faculty Coll. Optometry, Pacific U., 1977—, Pa. Coll. Optometry, 1981—, So. Coll. Optometry, 1982—. Bd. mgrs. Leeward Oahu Br. YMCA, 1967-70, Hi-Y advisor, 1967—, mem. Century Club, 1967—; bd. mgrs. W. Oahu Br., 1971-78, gen. chmn. sustaining membership, 1976; 2d v.p. August Ahrens Elem. Sch. PTA, 1969; mem. Leilani Community Assn.; mem. Leeward Mental Health Adv. Council, 1975-76, Friends of Waipahu Cultural Garden Park Found., 1976—, Aloha council Boy Scouts Am., 1976—; mem. bus. adv. council Waipahu High Sch., 1976-81, Parent-Tchr.-Community adv. council, 1978-80; dir. Central/Leeward unit Am. Cancer Soc., 1977-80 (Central/Leeward unit vol. of Yr. 1980), pub. edn. dir., 1978-79, v.p., 1979-80, founder, chmn. Celebrity Auction, 1980, dir. Oahu Baseline Survey, 1978; bd. dirs. Barbers Point council Navy League Am., 1981—. Recipient Merit award Nat. Eye Research Found., 1974, Disting. Service award, 1976. Fellow Am. Acad. Optometry (cornea and contact lens cert., corp. support for Jour. com. 1981—), AAAS, Am. Optometric Assn. (ann. congress del. 1978, pub. health com. 1978, optometric paraoptometric personnel com. 1978-79, contact lens project team 1979-80), Am. Optometric Found. (dir. 1981—, chmn. task force clin. research 1981—, nominations com. 1982), Am. Pub. Health Assn., Better Vision Inst., Coll. Optometrists in Vision Devel., Hawaii Optometric Assn., (corr. sec. 1968-70, state newsletter editor 1968-70, rec. sec. 1971, 2d v.p. 1972, pres.-elect 1973, pres. 1974-75; Man of Yr. 1975, Optometrist of Yr. 1979), Hawaii Vision Services, Japan Contact Lens Acad., Mut. Assn. Profl. Services, Nat. Assn. Professions, Nat. Eye Research Found. (fellow Internat. Orthokeratology sect.; editorial bd. Contacto Jour. 1979—, contact lens cert. com. 1981—), Nat. Fedn. Ind. Bus., Optometric Cons. in Contact Lens, Optometric Extension Program Found. (chmn. study group 1969-70, state dir. 1971-73), Optometric Hist. Soc., Optometric Polit. Action Coms., Soc. Contact Lens Specialists, Hawaii Assn. Children with Learning Disabilities, Hawaii Assn. Intellectually Gifted Children (pub. relations chmn. 1st Ann. State Conf. 1975, legis. lobbyist 1973-76), Waipahu Bus. Assn. (dir. 1974-78, chmn. pub. relations 1974-75, legis. lobbyist 1974-75, pres. 1974-75). Democrat. Baptist. Clubs: Leeward Oahu Jaycees (Disting. Service award 1969, Top Outstanding Young Man award 1975), Hawaii State Jaycees. Contbr. articles to profl. jours. Home: 98-336 Kaonohi St Apt 3 Aiea HI 96701 Office: 94-748 Hikimoe St Suite C Waipahu HI 96797

YAMASAKI, BARBARA LEE, nurse; b. Waipahu, Oahu, Hawaii, July 10, 1928; d. Bong Soo and Cha Ok (Hong) Lee; R.N., St. Francis Hosp., Honolulu, 1949; student Mpls. Gen Hosp. Sch. Anesthesia, 1953, Emergency Med. Service, 1974; m. George Shoji Yamasaki, Feb. 20, 1954; children—Cathy Lee, Stephen George. Staff nurse Wahiawa (Hawaii) Gen. Hosp., 1949, operating room nurse, 1951-52, evening supr., 1953; staff nurse Mpls. Gen. Hosp., 1952; ch. camp and indsl. nurse pineapple cannery, 1952; clin. nurse Barber's Point Clinic, 1956, Submarine Base Dispensary, 1966-70; indsl. nurse Pan Am. World Airways, 1970-71; clin. nurse Makalapa Dispensary, 1971-74; emergency room supr., central supply room supr., minor surgery supr., immunization supr., CPR coordinator, instr. Navy Regional Med. Clinic, Aiea, Hawaii, 1974—; affiliate faculty mem. basic cardiac life support, emergency services com., instr.-trainer basic life support Hawaii Heart Assn., recipient award, 1979. Mem. Hawaii Heart Assn., Emergency Dept. Nurses Assn., Am. Hosp. Assn., Am. Soc. Hosp. Central Service Personnel. Methodist. Home: 99 428 Kekoa Pl Aiea HI 96701 Office: Navy Regional Medical Clinic PO Box 121 Pearl Harbor HI 96860

YAMASAKI, MAMORU, state senator; b. Paia, Hawaii, Sept. 6, 1916. Marine terminal clk. Kahului R.R. Co.; asst. clk. Senate Ways and Mean Com., Territorial Legislature, 1959; mem. Hawaii Ho. of Reps., 1959-67, Hawaii Senate, 1968—. Mem. adv. bd. Maui County council Boy Scouts Am.; adv. bd. mem. Salvation Army; active Maui United Fund, Big Bros., J. Walter Cameron Center; mem. Hawaii Democratic Central Com., 1956-64, del. Dem. Nat. Conv., 1960. Office: Room 211 State Capitol Bldg Honolulu HI 96813*

YAMAUCHI, SHOYEI, surgeon; b. Okinawa, Japan, Dec. 19, 1904; came to U.S., 1913, naturalized, 1952; s. Shosei and Uto (Kameya) Y.; B.S., U. Hawaii, 1929; M.D., U. Mich., 1931; m. Erna B., Dec., 1934; children—Shoyei (Ernest), Shoji (Eric), Shosei (Chris). Intern in surgery, Sinai Hosp., Balt., 1931-32, chief surg. resident, 1934-35; teaching staff Kuakini Hosp., Honolulu, 1935-55, chief surgeon, 1941-55, cons. in urology, 1945-65, mem. governing bd., 1956-59, mem. bd. councillors, 1956-59; teaching staff St. Francis Hosp., 1942-47, chief of staff, 1946-47; teaching staff Queen's Hosp., 1946-48, cons. in surgery, 1948-52; cons. in surgery Children's Hosp.; med. dir. U. Hawaii Okinawa Med. Program, 1966; lectr., cons. in surgery Okinawa Med. Soc., 1964, cons., team leader, 1965; lectr. Peter Bent Brigham Hosp., Harvard Med. Sch., Boston, 1973, Centennial Med. Seminar, Sinai Hosp., Balt., 1966, U. Tex. Med. Br., Galveston, 1982. Chmn. health com. Hawaii State Commn. on Aging, 1960-64, del. confs., 1961; mem. Hawaii State Commn. on Aging, 1964-72, chmn. legis. com., 1965-66; bd. dirs. Kuakini Med. Research Inst., 1963-72; mem. research com. Kuakini

Med. Center, 1972—. Fellow Am. Coll. Cardiology, A.C.S. (pres. Hawaii chpt., 1965), Pan-Pacific Surg. Assn., Sci. Council of Collegium Internationale Angiologiae; mem. AAAS, AMA, Hawaii Med. Assn. (chmn. chronic illness and aging com. 1951-53, 60—), Sociedade Brasileira de Angiologia (corr. fgn. mem.), Internat. Soc. Lymphology, Royal Soc. Medicine (London, affiliate), Sigma Xi. Contbr. writings to publs. in field; speaker lymphology confs., U.S., Belgium, Italy, Brazil, Argentina, Japan, Czechoslovakia; hon. chmn. seminar VII Internat. Congress of Lymphology, Florence, Italy, Montreal, Can., 1981. Home: 1517 Makiki St Apt 1105 Honolulu HI 96822 Office: 321 N Kuakini St Room 304 Honolulu HI 96817

YANCEY, PAUL HERBERT, biology educator; b. Whittier, Calif., July 4, 1951; s. Herbert William and Sara Barbara (Druilard) Y.; m. Caroline Susan Weiler, Jan. 29, 1949. B.S. in Biology, with honors, Calif. Inst. Tech., 1973; Ph.D. in Marine Biology, Scripps Inst. Oceanography, 1978. Asst. prof. biology Whitman Coll., Walla Walla, Wash., 1981—. NATO fellow, 1978-79, U. St. Andrews, Scotland, 1978-81; Leverhulme fellow, 1979-80; recipient Eckart Dissertation prize, 1979. Mem. AAAS, Soc. Devel. Biology, Am. Inst. Biol. Scis. Contbr. articles to profl. jours. Office: Biology Dept Whitman Coll Walla Walla WA 99362

YANCY, EMMA ETTA, home economics educator; b. Humnoke, Ark., Dec. 22, 1949; d. Waymon and Elnora Beatrice (Bailey) Brooks; m. David Lewis Yancy, June 19, 1976 (div.); children—Johnny Dwayne, David Lewis. B.S. in Child Devel., Vocat. Home Econs., U. Ark., 1971; cert. Brooks Gen. Med. Ctr., Ft. Sam Houston, Tex., 1974; M.A. in Early Childhood Edn., Atlanta U., 1975. Various teaching positions, 1972-76; curriculum devel. coordinator follow-through program Ga. State U., Atlanta, 1975-76; project coordinator child and family resource program Econ. Opportunity Bd. Clark County (Nev.), Las Vegas, 1977-78; human devel. agent, expanded food and nutrition edn. supr. Coop. Extension Service, Las Vegas, 1978-82, asst. county agent-in-charge, 1982—; dir. Nev. Dept. Human Resources Youth Bd., Econ. Opportunity Bd. Clark County. Mem. ad hoc com. Women in Internat. Devel. Served to 1st lt. USAR, 1973-76; to lt. (s.g.) USAFR, 1981—. Mem. Am. Soc. Pub. Adminstrs., Nat. Child Devel. Assn., Nat. Assn. Edn. Young Children, Nat. Council Family Relations, Nat. Assn. Female Execs., Nat. Assn. Extension Home Economists (pres. Nev. chpt.). Democrat. Baptist.

YANG, CARY YUAN-WAI, physicist; b. Hong Kong, Dec. 17, 1948; s. James Tao-Yao and Anna Yuan-Kwan (Fung) Y.; m. Jean Akemi Tsukamoto, June 5, 1971; children—Elaine, Jocelyn. B.S.E.E., U. Pa., 1970, M.S.E.E., 1971, Ph.D., 1975. Postdoctoral fellow materials sci. and engring. MIT, 1975-76; NRC research assoc. NASA-Ames Research Cen., Moffett Field, Calif., 1976-78; research assoc. Stanford/NASA Ames Joint Inst. surface and microstructure research, materials sci. and engring. dept. Stanford U., 1978-79; pres., founder Surface Analytic Research, Inc., Mountain View, Calif., 1979—; lectr. U. Santa Clara, 1977, assoc. prof. elec. engring. and computer sci., 1983—. Recipient Albert P. Godsho Engring. prize, 1971, jr. merit award Engrs. Club Phila., 1971. Mem. Am. Phys. Soc., Sigma Xi (prize for grad. research 1975), Eta Kappa Nu, Tau Beta Pi. Contbr. articles profl. jours. Research on electronic structure calculations as applied to study of properties of solid surfaces and interfaces. Office: 465A Fairchild Dr Suite 128 Mountain View CA 94043

YANG, TIEN TSAI, laser scientist; b. Taiwan; came to U.S., 1961, naturalized, 1972; s. Shui Shung and Tao Mei (Chuang) Y.; m. Jane J.J. HSU, July 31, 1965; children—John, Davi. B.S.M.E., Nat. Taiwan Cheng Kung U., 1959; M.S.M.E., U. N.C., 1964; Ph.D. in Engring., UCLA, 1968. Sr. engring. specialist AiResearch/Garrett Corp., Los Angeles, 1968-71; postdoctoral scholar, reearch engr. UCLA, 1971-73; sr. staff scientist dept. physics and Ctr. Laser Studies, U. So. Calif., Los Angeles, 1973-75; prin. scientist advanced laser tech. dept. Rocketdyne/Rockwell Internat. Canoga Park, Calif., 1975—. Recipient Pres.'s Achievement award Rocketdyne, 1982. Mem. Am. Phys. Soc., Optical Soc. Am., AIAA, IEEE. Democrat. Contbr. articles to profl. jours. Home: 3224 Corinth Ave Los Angeles CA 90066 Office: D631-FA38 Rocketdyne/Rockwell Internat 6633 Canoga Ave Canoga Park CA 91304

YANG, YUNG YONG, economist, educator; b. South Korea, Mar. 2, 1942; s. Hoe Wu and Sun Im (Song) Y.; m. Choongja Jane Kim, Sept. 9, 1969; 1 son, Eugene. Ph.D., U. Oregon, 1974. Research assoc. Korea Inst. Sci. and Tech., Seoul, 1966-70; grad. teaching fellow U. Oregon, 1970-74; mem. faculty Calif. State U.-Sacramento, 1974—, assoc. prof., 1978—. Mem. Am. Econ. Assn., So. Econ. Assn. Contbr. articles to profl. jours.

YANNI, JOHN OLIVER, advertising copywriter, computer coordinator; b. Salt Lake City, July 26, 1951; s. Francis Joseph and Mary Catherine (Oliver) Y.; m. Gladys Elizabeth Limb, Feb. 24, 1979; 1 son, Timothy John. Student U. San Diego, 1969-70; B.S., U. Utah, 1975. Advt. copywriter George Assocs., Inc., Salt Lake City, 1977—. Active polit. campaigns. Democrat. Roman Catholic. Home: 3445 S Beehive Circle Salt Lake City UT 84119 Office: 139 E S Temple #6002 Salt Lake City UT 84111

YARBROUGH, IDA ELIZABETH, oil company official, financial consultant; b. Athens, Ala., July 16, 1952; d. Leard Leo and Margaret Louise (Allen) Yarbrough. B.A., Ala. A&M U., 1973; M.B.A., U. So. Calif., 1982. C.P.A. Calif. Sr. auditor Price Waterhouse & Co., Los Angeles, 1974-79; sr. analyst Atlantic Richfield Co., Los Angeles, 1979—. Mem. Am. Inst. C.P.A.s, Calif. Soc. C.P.A.s, Nat. Assn. Black Accts. (nat. dir. 1981-82, pres. Los Angeles chpt. 1980-82, Outstanding Mem. award), Nat. Urban League, Ala. A&M Alumni Assn., Black Women's Forum, NAACP, Nat. Assn. Female Execs. Democrat. Baptist. Office: Atlantic Richfield Co 515 S Flower St Suite AP-4321 Los Angeles CA 90071

YARBROUGH, WALTER H., state senator; m. Lucy Yarbrough; 4 children. Mem. Idaho State Senate, maj. caucus chmn. Past dir. Associated Taxpayers of Idaho, Farm Bur.; pres. Idaho State Fair and Rodeo Assn.; past comdr. post Am. Legion; past chmn. Owyhee County Fair Bd.; 4-H leader 10 yrs. Veteran of World War II. Republican. Congregationalist. Lodges: Masons, Shriners. Office: Idaho State Senate Boise ID 83720*

YARINGTON, CHARLES THOMAS, JR., surgeon; b. Sayre, Pa., Apr. 26, 1934; s. Charles Thomas and Florence Jane (Hutchinson) Y.; A.B., Princeton U., 1956; M.D., Hahnemann Med. Coll., 1960; m. Barbara Taylor Johnson, Sept. 28, 1963; children—Leslie Anne, Jennefer Lynne, Barbara Jane. Intern, Rochester Gen. Hosp., 1960-61; resident, Dartmouth Med. Sch. Hosp., 1961-65; resident, instr. U. Rochester, 1962-65; asst. prof. surgery W.Va. U. Med. Sch., 1967-68; assoc. prof., dept. head U. Nebr. Med. Sch., 1968-69, prof. otolaryngology, dept. head, 1969-74; prof. otolaryngology U. Wash. Sch. Medicine, Seattle, 1974—; chief ear, nose, throat and plastic surgery Mason Clinic, Seattle, 1974—; trustee Virginia Mason Research Ctr., mem. exec. com., 1978—, pres., 1983—; trustee Virginia Mason Med. Found., 1980—. Bd. dirs. King County Comprehensive Health Planning Council; mem. extramural council Fred Hitchinson Cancer Ctr.; trustee Seattle Opera. Served to maj. U.S. Army, 1965-67; to brig. gen. USAF Res., 1980—. Decorated Legion of Merit. Decorated knights cross Order of Constantini Magni; knight Order of St. Lazarus (Spain). Mem. Am. Acad. Otolaryngology (bd. govs. 1982—; honor award 1974, Barraquer Meml. award 1968), Am. Broncho-Esophogeal Assn. (treas. 1982—), Am. Soc. Head and Neck Surgery, Aerospace Med. Assn., Pacific Coast Oto-ophthalmol. Soc. (exec. council), N.W. Acad. Otolaryngology (sec.-treas.), AMA, Royal Soc. Medicine (London), Am. Laryngol. Assn., King County Med. Soc., Soc. Head and Neck Surgery, Soc. Med. Consultants to Armed Forces, Pan Pacific Surg. Assn., ACS, Sigma Xi. Clubs: Cosmos (Washington); RAF (London); College, Mercerwood Shore, Seattle Yacht. Mem. editorial bd. Jour. Continuing Edn. Otorhinolaryngology, Aviation, Space, Environ. Medicine, Otorhinolaryngologic Clinics of N.Am.; contbr. to books and sci. publs., motion pictures. Office: 1100 9th Ave Seattle WA 98101

YARLING, CHARLES BYRON, process engr.; b. El Paso, Tex., May 8, 1945; s. Byron Hendricks and Clara Catherine (Wingo) Y.; B.A. in Math., U. Tex., 1968, B.S.E.E., 1976. Field service engr. Welex, Beaumont, Tex., 1976-77; design engr. Accelerators, Inc., Austin, Tex., 1977-78; ion implant engr. Motorola, Austin, 1978-79, Mesa, Ariz., 1979-80, sect. mgr., Mesa, 1980-81; sect. mgr. ion implant metals Backlap & Goldback, 1980-81, sr. process engr., 1981—. Served with U.S. Army, 1968-70. Decorated Purple Heart, Army Commendation medal; recipient Motorola Engring. award, 1980. Mem. IEEE, Am. Vacuum Soc., Motorola Sci. and Tech. Soc., Am. Water Ski Assn., Pi Lambda Phi (nat. council 1973-76). Home: 1146 W Grandview St Mesa AZ 85201 Office: Box 20906 Phoenix AZ 85036

YAROS, RONALD MICHAEL, dentist, real estate developer; b. Gary, Ind., June 7, 1946; s. Michael G. and Mary (Lobo) Y.; student Loyola U., Chgo., 1964-66; D.D.S., Ind. U., 1970; m. Christine Hein, Aug. 10, 1968; children—Lisa, Craig. Dentist, pres. Ronald M. Yaros, DDS, P.C., Aurora, Colo., 1973—; treas. Affiliated Dental Mgmt. Co., 1980—; pres. R.M. Dental, Inc., 1979—. Served with USAF, 1970-73. Mem. ADA, Colo. Dental Assn., Met. Denver Dental Assn., Aurora Dental Soc. (pres. 1981), Acad. Gen. Dentistry, Am. Acad. Group Practice. Office: 11000 E Yale Ave Auroa CO 80014

YARYMOVYCH, MICHAEL IHOR, manufacturing company executive; b. Bialystok, Poland, Oct. 13, 1933; came to U.S., 1951, naturalized, 1956; s. Nicholas Joseph and Olga (Kruczowy) Y.; B.Aero. Engring., N.Y. U., 1955; M.S. in Engring. Mechanics, Columbia U., 1956, D.Engring. Sci., 1960; m. Roxolana Abramiuk, Nov. 21, 1959; children—Tatiana, Nicholas. Dep. asst. sec. research and devel. USAF, Washington, 1967-70; dir. AGARD, NATO, Paris, 1970-73; chief scientist USAF, 1973-75; asst. adminstr. field ops. ERDA, 1975-77; v.p. engring. N. Am. aerospace ops. Rockwell Internat. Corp., El Segundo, Calif., 1977-81, v.p. advanced systems devel. corp. engring., 1981—; cons. in field. Recipient Exceptional Civilian Service award Dept. Air Force, 1968, 73, 75, Disting. Service award ERDA, 1977; Guggenheim fellow, 1956-58. Fellow AIAA (dir., pres., gen. chmn. ann. meeting 1978), Air Force Assn., Nat. Mgmt. Assn., Nat. Security Industries Assn., AAAS, Am. Astronautical Soc., Aerospace Industry Assn. Author papers in field; translator Russian books and periodicals. Office: 2230 E Imperial Hwy El Segundo CA 90245

YASNYI, ALLAN DAVID, TV prodn. co. exec.; b. New Orleans, June 22, 1942; s. Ben Z. and Bertha R. (Michalove) Y.; B.B.A., Tulane U., 1964; m. Lesley E. Behrman, Dec. 8, 1968; children—Benjamin Charles, Evelyn Judith. Free-lance exec. producer, producer, writer, actor and designer for TV, motion picture and theatre, 1961-73; dir. fin. and adminstrn. Quinn Martin Prodns., Hollywood, Calif., 1973-76, v.p. fin., 1976-77, exec. v.p. fin. and corp. planning, 1977; vice chmn., chief exec. officer QM Prodns., Beverly Hills, Calif., 1977-78, chmn. bd., chief exec. officer, 1978-80; pres., chief exec. officer Vitrus Prodns., 1981—. Mem. adv. bd. Filmex; trustee Hollywood Arts Council; exec. v.p., trustee Hollywood Hist. Trust; bd. dirs. Am. Asthma and Allergy Found. Served with U.S. Army, 1964-66. Mem. Acad. TV Arts and Scis., Am. Advt. Fedn., Am. Mgmt. Assn., Hollywood Radio and TV Soc., Hollywood C. of C. (dir., vice-chmn.), Screen Actors Guild. Home: 3343 Laurel Canyon Blvd Studio City CA 91604

YASUE, ALLAN TSUTOMU, accountant; b. Honolulu, May 29, 1942; s. Morio and Martha C. (Komori) Y.; m. Incha Kang, Sept. 25, 1971; 1 son, Jim S. B.B.A., U. Hawaii, 1965. C.P.A., Hawaii. Ptnr., Coopers & Lybrand, Honolulu, 1965-76, ptnr., 1976—. Budget panel chmn. Aloha United Way, 1979—; bd. dirs., treas. Mohala Pua Sch., 1976-80. Mem. Am. Inst. C.P.A.s, Nat. Assn. Accts., Hosp. Fin. Mgmt. Assn., Internal Auditors Inst., Mcpl. Fin. Officers Assn., Hawaii Soc. C.P.A.s. Clubs: Oahu Country, Honolulu.

YATES, ADRIENNE GOLDBERG, child abuse therapist; b. St. Louis, Dec. 8, 1953; d. Ervin and Gertrude (Strauss) Goldberg; m. Scott A. Yates, Aug. 29, 1981. B.A. in Russian Studies, Grinnell Coll., 1976; M.Ed. in Community counseling, U. Alaska, 1983. Tchr., curriculum coordinator Grinnell Community Day Care Ctr., 1976-77; health extension agt. Peace Corps, West Africa, 1977-80; dir. Kinder Care Learning Ctr., Florrissant, Mo., 1980; counselor Women in Crisis Counseling and Assistance, Fairbanks, Alaska, 1980-81; child abuse specialist Resource Ctr. Parents and Children, Fairbanks, 1981—; mem. Fairbanks Interagy. Child Sexual Abuse Treatment Team. Mem. NOW, Am. Personnel and Guidance Assn., Assn. Specialists in Group Work, Am. Mental Health Counselors Assn., Nat. Assn. Edn. of Young Children, Phi Beta Kappa. Co-author: Everyone Needs a Parent, 1983. Home: 813 5th Ave Fairbanks AK 99701 Office: Resource Ctr 809 College Ave Fairbanks AK 99701

YATES, ALDEN PERRY, engineering executive; b. Los Angeles, July 12, 1928; s. John Perry and Sybil Norma (Kerr) Y.; m. Dawn Blacker, Dec. 16, 1950; children—Stephen, Michael, Karen Weiss, Jeffrey, Russell, Patricia. B.S. in Civil Engring., Stanford U., 1951. Field engr. Bechtel Corp., San Francisco, 1953-70, v.p., Bechtel Power Corp., San Francisco, 1970-75, v.p., dep. div. mgr. Internat. Bechtel Inc., Kuwait City, Kuwait, 1975-78, Bechtel Overseas Corp., London, 1978-80, pres. Bechtel Petroleum Inc., San Francisco, 1983—; dir. First City Bancorp. Tex. Inc., Houston. Served to lt. (j.g.) USCG, 1951-53. Republican. Clubs: Pacific Union, San Francisco Golf (San Francisco). Office: 50 Beale St San Francisco CA 94105

YATES, CHERYL ANN, home economist, teacher; b. Cheyenne, Wyo., Oct. 11, 1945; d. Robert Watson and Harriette Julia (Oberg) Y. B.S., U. Wyo., 1968. Cert. home econ. tchr., Ariz. Tchr., Carson Jr. High Sch., Mesa, Ariz., 1968-69; tchr., chmn. home econs. dept. Powell Jr. High Sch., Mesa, 1970-80, Mountain View High Sch., Mesa, 1980-81, Dobson High Sch., Mesa, 1981—. Active Friends of Channel 8. Mem. NEA, Ariz. Edn. Assn., Mesa Edn. Assn. Republican. Contbr. articles to mags. in field. Office: 1502 W Guadalupe Mesa AZ 85202

YATES, GEORGE MARTIN, oil co. exec.; Artesia, N.Mex., Aug. 26, 1946; s. Harvey Emmons and Louise (Davidson) Y.; B.B.A., U. Tex., Austin, 1969; m. Abby J. Harris, June 12, 1975; children—Laura S., Lindsey A. Pres., Harvey E. Yates Co., Roswell, N.Mex., 1981—, Explorers Petroleum Corp., Roswell, 1976—; dir. Security Nat. Bank, Roswell; state adv. Mountain States Tel. & Tel. Co. Bd. dirs. Mountain States Legal Found. Mem. Ind. Petroleum Assn. Am. (v.p.), Ind. Petroleum Assn. N.Mex. (v.p.). Office: Box 1933 Roswell NM 88201

YATES, HARVEY EMMONS, JR., energy co. exec.; b. Artesia, N.M., Mar. 4, 1942; s. Harvey Emmons and Louise (Davidson) Y.; B.A., U. Tex.; J.D., Cornell U., 1973; m. Janice Bader, Nov. 1976; children—Barrett Elizabeth, Whitney Mona-Wilson. Pres., Cibola Energy Corp., Albuquerque, 1978—. Vice-pres. adminstrn. Greater S.W. council Boy Scouts Am., 1982—. Served with USAR, 1964-70. Mem. Albuquerque Petroleum Assn. (pres. 1982-83). Office: 1005 Marquette St NW Albuquerque NM 87102

YATES, STEVEN A., curator, artist; b. Chgo., Nov. 14, 1949; s. Thomas A. and Phyllis E. (Wilson) Y.; m. Lynne A. Smith, Aug. 5, 1972; children—Kelsey, Victoria. B.F.A., U. Nebr., 1972; M.A., U. N.Mex., 1975, M.F.A., 1978. Faculty, Claremont (Calif.) Coll. and Pomona, 1976, U. N.Mex., Albuquerque, 1976-80; curator photography, prints and drawings Mus. of N.Mex., Santa Fe, 1980—; one man show: Sheldon Meml. Art Gallery, Lincoln, Nebr., 1978; group shows include: San Francisco Mus. Modern Art, 1980, 81, Sheldon Meml. Art Gallery, 1982-83; represented in permanent collections: San Francisco Mus.

YBARRA, EVA, tchr. bilingual edn.; b. Alma, Mich., Aug. 17, 1945; d. Pantaleon Belmares and Cesarea Rosario (Cortez) Ybarra; student Marymount-Loyola U., 1970-73, Calif. State U., Fullerton, 1972-73; B.A., Calif. State U., Los Angeles, 1978, M.A., 1981; postgrad. in ednl. adminstrn. Exec. sec. Boy Scouts Am., Yakima, Wash., 1965-67; exec. sec. Hops Extract Corp., Yakima, 1967-69; tch. St. Jeanne de Lestonnac Sch., Tustin, Calif., 1971-72, St. Antonio de Padua Sch., Los Angeles, 1973-76; tchr. Los Angeles Children's Mus., 1981; bilingual tchr. Franklin Sch., Pasadena, Calif., 1981, Magnola Ave. Sch., Los Angeles, 1982—; lectr. in field. BASIC Ednl. Opportunity grantee; Calif. State fellow, 1979-80. Mem. United Tchrs., Los Angeles, Mexican Am. Scholarship Com., Nat. Council Family Relations, Educare (U. So. Calif.) Roman Catholic. Home: 821 N Wilcox Apt A-204 Montebello CA 90640 Office: 1626 N Orchard Los Angeles CA 90006

YEAGER, KURT ERIC, research inst. ofcl.; b. Cleve., Sept. 11, 1939; s. Joseph Ellsworth and Karolyn Kristine (Pedersen) Y.; m. Rosalie Ann McMillan, Feb. 5, 1960; children—Geoffrey, Phillip; m. 2d, Regina Ursula Querfurt, May 12, 1970; 1 dau., Victoria. B.A. in Chemistry, Kenyon Coll., 1961; postgrad. Ohio State U., 1961-62; M.S. in Physics, U. Calif.-Davis, 1964. Teaching asst. Ohio State U., 1961-62; officer, program mgr. Air Force Tech. Applications Ctr., Alexandria, Va., 1962-68; assoc. dept. dir. Mitre Corp., McLean, Va., 1968-72; dir. energy research and devel. planning EPA, Washington, 1972-74; dir. fossil power plants dept. Electric Power Research Inst., Palo Alto, Calif., 1974-79, dir. coal combustion systems, 1979-83, v.p. coal combustion systems, 1983—; commerce tech. adv. bd., Oak Ridge fossil energy adv. bd. Nat. Acad. Engring. Pres. No. Va. Youth Football Assn., 1973-74; mem. Palo Alto C. of C. Served to capt. USAF, 1962-68. Decorated Air Force Commendation medals (2); recipient Outstanding Service award EPA, 1974. Mem. ASME (Research Policy Bd.), AAAS, Am. Chem. Soc. Republican. Episcopalian. Contbr. articles profl. jours.

YEAP, ARTHUR K., electronics co. exec.; b. Hong Kong, Feb. 15, 1956; s. Choong Yow and Alice Miu-Lan (Ko) Y.; came to U.S., 1963, naturalized, 1972; student U. Calif., Berkeley, 1973-74, Foothill Coll., 1975. Spl. programs engr. Hewlett Packard Central Research Labs., Palo Alto, Calif., 1974-75, cons. Hewlett Packard Studios, 1973; co founder, bd. chmn., pres. ADI-Audio Developments Internat., Palo Alto, 1975—; mng. dir. Alembic, Inc., Santa Rosa, Calif., 1979-80; v.p., dir. Shama Sound Corp., San Francisco, 1981—; cons. to TV and recording studios and recording groups; advisor spl. scis. Foothill Coll., 1975. Recipient contbns. to sci. awards NASA, USAF, USN, also 2d place Sci. Clubs Am., 1970. Bd. dirs. judges San Francisco/Bay Area Science Fair, 1975—. Mem. Audio Engring. Soc. (chmn. San Francisco sect., 1976-78, chmn. Internat. Conv. on Sound Reinforcement in New York, 1977). Evangelical. Asst. concertmaster San Francisco All City Orch., 1971-72. Contbr. articles to profl. jours., newspapers. Patentee in field. Home: 1722 38th Ave San Francisco CA 94122 Office: 3383 Lubich Dr Mountain View CA 94040

YEAP, JOHNNIE CHEE BENG, paint co. exec.; b. Rangoon, Burma, Oct. 21, 1943; s. Hock Tyan and Chye Lyan (Teoh) Y.; came to U.S., 1974, naturalized, 1979; B.A., U. Rangoon, 1965; m. Donata Mya Han, Dec. 21, 1969; children—Tricia, Allan. With import-export and mfg. bus., Burma, 1962-64; accounts mgr. Burmese Govt. Trade Corp., 1964-66; with Am. embassy, Rangoon, 1967-74, Synkoloid Co., Los Angeles, 1974-76; regional purchasing mgr. Glidden Coatings and Resins div. SCM Corp., San Francisco, 1976—. C.P.A., Burma. Mem. Nat., Golden Gate (dir.) paint and coatings assns. Rosicrucian. Home: 124 Catalina Ct Vallejo CA 94589

YEARIAN, FREDERICK ARTHUR, elec. engr.; b. Seattle, Jan. 2, 1941; s. Fred Abraham and Louise (Ziebell) Y.; B.S., U. Wash., 1963, M.S., 1967; m. Patricia Rae Gleason, Apr. 22, 1978. Owner Economy Data Processing, Renton, Wash., 1974—. Mem. Sigma Xi, Tau Beta Pi. Home: 16036 SE 172nd Place Renton WA 98055

YEARSLEY, KENNETH GEORGE, laboratory administrator; b. Ogden, Utah, July 18, 1929; s. Vernal E. and Ione S. (Slater) Y.; student Weber Jr. Coll., 1949-50, Thomas D. Dee Meml. Hosp. Sch. Med. Tech., 1953-54; B.S., Utah State U., 1961, M.S., 1968; m. Eleanor Harrison, Sept. 8, 1956 (dec.); children—Janet, Kenneth D., Carolyn, Allan V. Chemistry supr. lab. Thomas D. Dee Meml. Hosp., Ogden, 1954-57, chief technologist lab., 1957-69; chief technologist lab. McKay-Dee Hosp. Ctr., 1969-76, tech. coordinator lab., 1976—; clin. instr. Weber State Coll., Ogden, 1968-78; clin. faculty Utah State U., Logan, 1978—. Chmn., North Ogden Cherry Days, 1962-63; mem. fin. com. United Fund, 1959-60; mem. vocat. adv. com. Weber State Coll., 1971—. Mem. Am. Soc. for Med. Tech., Utah Soc. Med. Tech. (past pres.), Am. Soc. Clin. Pathologists (affiliate), Sigma Xi (assoc.). Mormon. Club: Kiwanis (pres. North Ogden 1963, 83-84). Home: 2931 North 150 West North Ogden UT 84404 Office: McKay-Dee Hosp Center 3939 Harrison Blvd Ogden UT 84409

YEGEN, PETER, JR., ins. and real estate exec.; b. Billings, Mont., July 12, 1896; s. Peter and Margaret (Trepp) Y.; grad. Inst. Dr. Schmidt., St. Gall, Switzerland, 1913; student U. Wis., 1915-17; m. Zellah Wilson Cardwell, Mar. 27, 1918; children—Peter, III, Edward Cardwell. Ins., real estate bus. as Peter Yegen, Jr., Billings, 1919—; pres. Yellowstone Ditch Co., 1935—, Arnold Drain Repair, 1955-70. Pres., Shiloh Drainage Dist., 1942—, Arnold Drainage Dist., 1965—; chmn. Urban Renewal, 1962-63. Chmn., Yellowstone County Tb Soc., 1948; chmn. Salvation Army Adv. Bd., 1949-66, hon. life mem., 1966—; chmn., pres. Yellowstone Mus. Bd., 1956—. Served to 2d lt. F.A., U.S. Army, 1918. Named hon. state fire marshall, hon. chief Billings Fire Dept.; mem. Nat. Cowboy Hall of Fame; 1st co-recipient with Zellah Realtors ann. Peter Yegen, Jr. award for outstanding community service, 1976; named Agri-Bus. Man of Yr., N. Internat. Livestock Expn., 1978. Mem. Billings Bd. Insurors (life, pres. 1936), Hartford Jonathan Trumbull Assn., Billings Bd. Realtors (life mem., pres. 1937), Mont. Assn. Realtors (life mem., pres. 1948-49, realtor emeritus), Mont. Assn. Ins. Agts. (life, pres. 1940-41), Pioneers of Eastern Mont. and their Sons and Daus. (pres. 1953, sec. 1960-81), Yellowstone Hist. Soc. (life, pres. 1960), Westerners Internat., Mont. Pioneer and Classic Auto Club, Mus. Assn. Mont. (pres. 1967-69), Am. Legion (life, comdr. 1933, comdr. emeritus 1977), Mont. Stockgrowers Assn., Range Riders. Episcopalian. Mason (life, past master, Shriner). Clubs: Saddle (pres. 1939, 41, 43), Yellowstone Corral, Goggles and Dusters, Yellowstone Country (pres. 1952-54), Kiwanis (life, pres. 1947, lt. gov. 1958, Kiwanian of Yr. 1979). Home:

306 N 30th St Billings MT 59101 Office: 211 N 30th St Billings MT 59101

YEGGE, ROBERT BERNARD, coll. dean, lawyer; b. Denver, June 17, 1934; s. Ronald Van Kirk and Fairy (Hill) Y.; A.B. magna cum laude, Princeton U., 1956; M.A. in Sociology, U. Denver, 1958, J.D., 1959. Bar: Colo. 1959. Assoc. Yegge, Hall and Evans, and predecessors, Denver, 1959-62, mem. firm, 1962-78; mng. ptnr. Nelson & Harding, 1979—; adj. assoc. prof. law U. Denver Coll. Law, 1962-65, dir. program in jud. adminstrn., 1962-65; prof. law, 1965—, dean Coll. Law, 1965-77, dean emeritus, 1977—; asst. to pres. Denver Post, 1971-75. Chmn. Colo. Council Arts and Humanities, 1967-80; mem. research application policy com. NSF; active nat. and local ARC; mem. Denver County Republican Central Com.; mem. Colo. Rep. Central Com., 1960-62; mng. trustee Denver Center for Performing Arts, 1972-76; trustee, sec. Denver Symphony Soc., 1959-80; trustee Inst. Ct. Mgmt.; trustee, vice-chmn. Mexican-Am. Legal Edn. and Def. Fund, 1970-76. Recipient Disting. Service award Denver Jr. C. of C., 1965. Mem. Am., Colo., (bd. govs. 1965-77), D.C., Denver bar assns., Am. Judicature Soc. (dir. 1968-72, 75—), Am. Sociol. Soc., Am. Acad. Polit. and Social Sci., Nat. Alumni Assn. Princeton, Assn. Bar City N.Y., Assn. Am. Law Schs., Order St. Ives, Phi Beta Kappa, Phi Delta Phi, Alpha Kappa Delta, Beta Theta Pi, Omicron Delta Kappa. Clubs: Denver (sec., v.p., dir.), Rocky Mountain Princeton (pres.), Denver Press, Denver Country, Mile High (Denver); Nat. Lawyers, Cosmos (Washington). Author: Colorado Negotiable Instruments Law, 1960; Some Goals, Some Tasks, 1965; The American Lawyer: 1976, 1966; New Careers in Law, 1969; The Law Graduate, 1972; Tomorrow's Lawyer: A Shortage and Challenge, 1974; Declaration of Independence for Legal Education, 1976. Home: 4209 W 38th Ave Denver CO 80212 Office: Law Center 200 W 14th Ave Denver CO 80204 also 2600 Energy Center Denver CO 80202

YEH, HSUEH-WEN CHANG, geochemist; b. Taiwan, Republic of China, May 18, 1940; came to U.S., 1970, naturalized, 1978; s. Tsan-Hsen Chang and Kan-Mei C. Yeh; Ph.D., Case Western Res. U., 1974; postdoctoral student chemistry Woods Hole (Mass.) Oceanographic Inst., 1974-75; m. Ivy Tai, Mar. 10, 1968; children—Heidi, Ryan. Research fellow div. geol. and planetary sci. Calif. Inst. Tech., Pasadena, 1975-77, sr. research fellow, 1977-78; asst. geochemist Inst. Geophysics, U. Hawaii, Honolulu, 1978-81, asso. geochemist, 1981—. Served to 2d lt. Army of Republic of China, 1968-69. Mem. Am. Geol. Soc., Am. Geophys. Union, Clays and Clay Minerals Soc., Sigma Xi. Contbr. articles on mineral. and chem. processes in sediments and sedimentary rocks to sci. jours. Home: 1040F Awawamalu Honolulu HI 96825 Office: 2525 Correa Rd Honolulu HI 96822

YEH, YEA-CHUAN MILTON, electronic engr.; b. Szu-Chuan, China, Apr. 16, 1943; s. Sing-min and Dah-chwen Y.; B.S., Nat. Taiwan U., 1965; M.S., UCLA, 1969, Ph.D., 1973; m. Grace Ching-Hsia, June 7, 1969; children—Caroline, Christopher; came to U.S., 1967, naturalized, 1977. Head radio multiplex relay sta., Peng-Ho, Taiwan, China, 1965-66, asst. instr. Nat. Taiwan U., Taipei, 1966-67; teaching asso. elec. engring. dept. UCLA, 1967-72; mem. tech. staff Jet Propulsion Lab., Pasadena, Calif., 1972-82; dir. advanced research Applied Solar Energy Corp., Industry, Calif., 1982—. Disting. fellow UCLA, 1969-70; NASA Major Monetary award, 1977; cert. of Recognition NASA, 1976, 77, 81. Mem. IEEE, Internat. Solar Energy Soc., Sigma Xi. Office: 15251 E Don Julian Rd Industry CA 91749

YELLEN, JANET LOUISE, educator; b. N.Y.C., Aug. 13, 1946; d. Julius and Anna Ruth (Blumenthal) Y.; m. George Arthur Akerlof, July 8, 1978; 1 son, Robert Joseph. A.B., Brown U., 1967, Ph.D., Yale U., 1971. Asst. prof. econs. Harvard U., 1971-76; economist Trade and Fin. Studies sect. div. Internat. Fin. Bd. Govs. Fed. Res. System, Washington, 1976-78; lectr. econs. London Sch. Econs. and Polit. Sci., 1978-80; asst. prof. bus. adminstrn. U. Calif.-Berkeley, 1980-82, assoc. prof., 1982—. Woodrow Wilson fellow, 1967; NSF fellow 1967-70. Mem. Am. Econs. Assn., Phi Beta Kappa. Contbr. articles to profl. jours. Home: 683 San Luis Rd Berkeley CA 94707 Office: 330 Barrows Hall Sch of Bus Adminstrn U Calif Berkeley CA 94720

YELLOWHAIR, STELLA, nurse; b. Chilchinbeto, Ariz., Dec. 4, 1941; d. Kitsillie and Lucy (Gilmore) Y.; children—Jeannine, Jeannette, Leonel. R.N., Mercy Hosp., 1963; B.S.N., Ariz. State U.-Tempe, 1982. Registered Nurse, Ariz. Staff nurse, night supr. Tuba City (Ariz.) Indian Hosp., 1963-70; maternal and child health nurse Winslow (Ariz.) Indian Hosp., 1970-76; clin. nurse supr. Kayenta (Ariz.) Health Center, 1976-79, dir. nurses, 1982—; nursing cons.; dir. several local med. coms. Recipient awards for nursing, 1975, 79. Mem. Ariz. Nurses Assn., Am. Nurses Assn., Am. Indian Alaska Native Nurses Assn., Sigma Theta Tau. Democrat. Mem. Native Am. Church. Office: Kayenta Health Center PO Box 368 Kayenta AZ 86033

YEN, KUO-HSIUNG, electrical engineer; b. Tainan, Taiwan, China, Sept. 8, 1941; came to U.S., 1967, naturalized, 1979; s. Tien-Su and Ching-Yeh Y.; B.S., Nat. Taiwan U., 1964; M.S., Nat. Chiao-Tung U., 1967; Ph.D., Poly. Inst. N.Y., 1972; m. Anna Yen, June 23, 1974; children—Jayme Lin-Lin, Leslie Yee-Tin. Research assoc. Poly. Inst. N.Y., 1972-74; head microwave tech. sect. system group research staff TRW Systems Group, Los Angeles, 1974-80, sr. tech. staff, head microwave acoustics sect. microelectronics ctr. Electronic System Group, TRW, 1981—. Mem. IEEE, Sigma Xi. Contbr. articles sci. jours.; patentee in field. Home: 1521 23d St Manhattan Beach CA 90266 Office: One Space Park Redondo Beach CA 90278

YEN, SAMUEL S. C., physician, scientist, educator; b. Peking, China, Feb. 22, 1927; s. K. Y. and E. K. Y.; B.S., Cheeloo U., China, 1949; M.D., U. Hong Kong, 1954; D.Sc., 1980; m. Kathryn Bachman, July 26, 1958; children—Carol Amanda, Dolores Amelia, Margaret Rae. Intern, Queen Mary Hosp., Hong Kong, 1954-55; resident Johns Hopkins U., 1956-60; chief dept. Ob-Gyn, Guam Meml. Hosp., 1960-62; asst. prof. dept. Ob-gyn., Case Western Res. U., 1962-67, asso. prof. dept. reproductive biology, 1967-70; asso. dir. obstetrics Univ. Hosps. Cleve., 1968-70; prof. Ob-gyn., U. Calif., San Diego, 1970-72, prof. dept. reproductive medicine, 1972—, chmn. dept., 1972—; examiner, dir. Am. Bd. Ob-Gyn; lectr. 42d Nobel Symposium, Stockholm, 1978; vis. prof. U. Melbourne, Flinders U., Royal Adelaide Hosp. U. Sidney, U. Hong Kong; Harrison Meml. lectr. Endocrine Soc. Australia, 1978. Recipient Wyeth awards, 1972, 75, 76; Green-Armytage award Royal Coll. Ob-gyn. Eng. Fellow Am. Coll. Obstetricians and Gynecologists; mem. Am. Gynecol. Soc. San Diego Gynecol. Soc., Soc. Gynecol. Investigation, The Endocrine Soc. (postgrad. com. 1978—), Perinatal Research Soc., Am. Diabetes Assn. Editor: Reproductive Endocrinology: Physiology, Pathophysiology and Clinical Management, 1978; editorial bd. Jour. Clin. Endocrinology and Metabolism, 1970-77, Neuroendocrinology, 1979—. Office: Dept Reproductive Medicine Sch Medicine U Calif San Diego La Jolla CA 92093

YEN, YEN-CHEN, chem. engr.; b. China, June 21, 1912; s. Chin-Chuen and (Pei) Y.; Dipl. Ing., Technische Hochschule Berlin, 1937; m. Er-Ying, Sept. 9, 1939; children—Martha (Mrs. Chin-I Meng), Madalena (Mrs. Louis Chu), Rosa (Mrs. Y.R. Chin), Margaret (Mrs. C.Y. Chu), Tien-Sze Benedict. Came to U.S., 1965, naturalized, 1972. Prof. several univs. in Taiwan and China, 1940-50; v.p. Taiwan Fertilizer Co., 1950-53; commr., chief chem. sect. Indsl. Devel. Commn., Taiwan, 1953-58; engring. cons., Singapore and Taiwan, 1959-65; sr. chem. engr. Stanford Research Inst., Menlo Park, Calif., 1965—. Mem. Am. Electrochem. Soc., Am. Inst. Chem. Engrs. Contbr. articles to profl. jours. Home: 3373 St Michael Palo Alto CA 94306 Office: 333 Ravenswood Ave Menlo Park CA 94025

YEO, RICHARD SWEE-CHYE, scientist, chem. engr.; b. Singapore, Aug. 18, 1945; s. Jwee Khiang and Chye Hong (Chia) Y.; came to U.S., 1976, naturalized, 1979; B.Sc., Ngee Ann Tech. Coll., Singapore, 1968; M.Sc., St. Francis Xavier U., Antigonish, N.S., Can., 1970; Ph.D., McGill U., Montreal, Que., Can., 1976; m. Mabel Yip-Bao Lee, June 29, 1977; children—Jason Chia-Sim, Sophie Hong-Gil. Research assoc. Brookhaven Nat. Lab., Upton, N.Y., 1976-79; staff scientist energy systems lab. The Continental Group Inc., Cupertino, Calif., 1979-81; dir. sci. Pinnacle Research Inst., Cupertino, 1982—; chmn. symposia in field. Mem. Am. Chem. Soc., Electrochem. Soc., Am. Inst. Chem. Engrs. Author: A Guide to Advanced Level Physics, 1966; author govt. publs.; contbr. chpts. to books, articles to profl. jours.; patentee field of battery energy storage. Home: 995 Blair Ave Sunnyvale CA 94087 Office: 10432 N Tantau Ave Cupertino CA 95014

YEO, RONALD FREDERICK, librarian; b. Woodstock, Ont., Can., Nov. 13, 1923; s. Frederick Thomas and Jugertha Aleda (Vansickle) Y.; B.A., U. Toronto, 1948, B.L.S., 1966; m. Margaret Elizabeth Horsley, Sept. 12, 1953; children—Joanne, Peter. Mgr. book dept. Am. News Co., Toronto, Ont., 1948-53; sales mgr., dir. Brit. Book Service, Toronto, 1953-63; mgr. trade div. Collier-Macmillan Can., Ltd., Toronto, 1963-65; pub. services coordinator North York (Ont.) Pub. Library, 1971; chief librarian Regina (Sask.) Pub. Library, 1971—. Served with RCAF, 1942-45. Recipient Silver Jubilee medal, 1977. Mem. Can. Library Assn. (pres. 1978-79), Sask. Library Assn., Can. Assn. Pub. Libraries (chmn. 1975-76), Adminstrs. of Large Pub. Libraries (chmn. 1973-74). Club: Regina Kiwanis. Office: 2311 12th Ave Regina SK S4P 0N3 Canada

YESIL, OKTAY, engineer, scientist; b. Turkey, Jan. 27, 1941; came to U.S., 1968; s. Omer and Emine Yesil; B.S., M.S., Istanbul Tech. U., 1965; M.S., M.I.T., 1970; Ph.D., U. Wash., 1978; m. Fatma Sevim Ornek, Nov. 27, 1965; children—Aysen, Meltem. Teaching and research staff Istanbul Tech. U., 1965-68; research asst. M.I.T., 1968-70; predoctoral, then postdoctoral research assoc. U. Wash., Seattle, 1970-72, 74-79; specialist engr. Boeing Comml. Airplane Co., Seattle, 1979—; chmn. internat. energy symposia. Mem. AIAA, Internat. Assn. Hydrogen Energy, Laser Inst. Am., Sigma Xi. Author papers in field. Office: PO Box 3707 M/S 9W-65 Seattle WA 98124

YESSIS, MICHAEL, physical education educator; b. Bklyn., June 16, 1932; s. Anton and Mary Petrovna (Honcharik) Y.; m. Edith Ruth Evans, July 8, 1979; 1 dau., Marissa Kay. B.S., NYU, 1954, M.A., 1956, Ph.D., 1963. Tchr. phys. edn. and sci. East N.Y. Vocat. High Sch., 1953-54; tchr. phys. edn. and sci., swimming coach Manual Tng. High Sch., 1955-56; instr. phys. edn. and health U. So. Calif., Los Angeles, 1958-61; assoc. prof. Tex. Woman's U., Denton, 1961-64; asst. prof. Chico (Calif.) State U., 1964-66; prof. Calif. State U.-Fullerton, 1966—; cons. sports tng. to profl. and Olympic teams. Served with Chem. Corps, U.S. Army. Boys' Club Am. scholar, 1952; Hack fellow, 1960. Mem. Nat. Strength and Conditioning Assn. (assoc. editor), AAHPER and Dance, Internat. Congress for Health, Am. Coll. Sports Medicine. Author: Handball, 3d edit., 1978; editor, pub. Soviet Sports Rev., 1966—; created gluteus-ham developing exercise machine, 1983. Home and Office: PO Box 2878 Escondido CA 92025

YETTER, ADRIENNE DERYL, federal agency administrator; b. San Jose, Calif., May 28, 1936; d. Adrian Reed and Elsa Rose (Jacop) Smith; student Heald Coll., 1954, U. San Francisco, 1975-76; m. Joseph Eugene Yetter, Dec. 31, 1955; children—Joseph Eugene, Wayne Adrian, Bonnie Marie. Sec. dist. driver edn. project Salinas (Calif.) Union High Sch. Dist., 1973-76, curriculum devel. sec., office mgr., 1973-75, career center asst., 1975-76; research asst. for doctoral candidate, 1973-74; sec. Army Research Inst., Dept. Def., Ft. Ord, Calif., 1977; sec. to dep. dir. Salinas Data Ops. Center, Social Security Adminstrn., 1977-78, employee devel. specialist, tech. and ops. tng. staff, 1978-81, acting dir. tech. and ops. tng. staff, 1980. Recipient Spl. Achievement award Social Security Adminstrn., 1979, 80, Commrs. citation, 1980. Mem. Am. Soc. Tng. and Devel. Republican. Roman Catholic. Home: 12881 Jasper Way Salinas CA 93906

YIH, MAE DUNN, state senator; b. Shanghai, China, May 24, 1928; d. Chung Woo and Fung Wen (Feng) Dunn; m. Stephen W.H. Yih, 1953; children—Donald, Daniel. B.A., Barnard Coll., 1951; postgrad. Columbia U., 1951-52. Mem. Oreg. Ho. of Reps. from Dist. 36, 1977-83, Oreg. State Senate, 1983—; asst. to bursar Barnard Coll., N.Y.C., 1952-53. Precinct person Oreg. Democratic Party; mem. Clover Ridge Elem. Sch. Bd., Albany, Oreg., 1969—; mem. Albany Union High Sch. Bd., 1975—; adv. com. Linn County Environ. Health Dept., 1977—; mem. LWV, Linn County Citizens for Retarded, Linn County Mental Health Assn., Oreg. Sch. Bd. Assn., AAUW. Democrat. Episcopalian. Home: Box 274 Route 2 Albany OR 97321 Office: Oregon State Senate Salem OR 97310*

YING, KUANG LIN, cytogeneticist; b. Kiangsu, China, June 12, 1927; s. Shao Chen and Suan (Sun) Y.; m. Sun Chyi, Mar. 5, 1954; children—May Ying Wong, Bonni, Edward. B.S., Nat. Taiwan U., 1952; Ph.D., U. Sask., 1961. Sr. specialist plant industry div. Sino-Am. Joint Commn. on Rural Reconstrn., Taipei, Taiwan, 1961-64; research assoc. dept. pediatrics U. Sask., 1964-67, asst. prof. div. med. genetics, 1967-73, assoc. prof., 1973-78; dir. cytogenetics and prenatal detection lab. Valley Childrens Hosp., Fresno, Calif., 1978-81; dir. sect. cytogenetics Med. Genetics div. dept. pediatrics Childrens Hosp. Los Angeles, 1981—; assoc. prof. dept. botany Nat. Taiwan U., 1962-63; asst. prof., dir. cytogenetics lab. Meharry Med. Coll., 1970-71; vis. research scientist div. med. genetics UCLA, 1977-78; assoc. research cytogeneticist U. Calif.-San Francisco, 1978-81; assoc. clin. prof. pediatrics U. So. Calif., 1981—. NRC Can. assistanship 1957-61. Mem. Genetics Soc. Can., Am. Soc. Human Genetics, Tissue Culture Assn. Contbr. articles to profl. jours. Office: 4650 Sunset Blvd PO Box 54700 Los Angeles CA 90054

YINGLING, JOHN, broadcasting executive; b. Los Angeles, July 3, 1939; s. Harold John and Elizabeth F. Yingling; m. Peggy Everett, Nov. 3, 1973; 2 children. B.S., U. So. Calif., 1961, M.A., 1964. Supr. network ops. CBS, Los Angeles, 1964-68; dir. prodn. KCET, Los Angeles, 1968-76; labor relations cons., Los Angeles, 1976-78; dir. bus. mgmt., asst. to v.p. adminstrn. ABC, Los Angeles, 1978—; dir. Commuter Computer, Inc., Los Angeles. Served with USNR, 1961-64. Mem. Acad. TV Arts and Scis., Nat. Assn. Broadcasters, Hollywood Radio and TV Soc. Home: 975 Winston Ave San Marino CA 91108 Office: 2040 Ave of Stars Suite 200 Los Angeles CA 90067

YOCAM, DELBERT WAYNE, electronic products mfg. co. exec.; b. Long Beach, Calif., Dec. 24, 1943; s. Royal Delbert and Mary Rose (Gross) Y.; B.A. in Bus. Adminstrn., Calif. State U., Fullerton, 1966; M.B.A., Calif. State U., Long Beach, 1971; m. Janet McVeigh, June 13, 1965; children—Eric Wayne, Christian Jeremy, Elizabeth Janelle. Mktg./supply changeover coordinator Automotive Assembly div. Ford Motor Co., Dearborn, Mich., 1966-72; prodn. control mgr. Control Data Corp., Hawthorne, Calif., 1972-74; prodn. and material control mgr. Bourns Inc., Riverside, Calif., 1974-76; corp. material mgr. Computer Automation Inc., Irvine, Calif., 1976-78; prodn. planning mgr. central staff ITT Cannon Electric Div., World hdqrs., Santa Ana, Calif., 1978-79; corp. v.p., gen. mgr. ops. div. Apple Computer Inc., Cupertino, Calif., 1979—; mem. faculty Cypress (Calif.) Coll., 1972-79; co-founder Control Data Corp. Mgmt. Assn., 1974. Active Los Angeles County Heart Assn., 1966. Mem. Am. Prodn. and Inventory Control Soc., Purchasing Mgmt. Assn. Republican. Methodist.

YOCOM, CHARLES FREDERICK, educator; b. Logan, Iowa, Oct. 21, 1914; s. Fred E. and Idabelle Y.; B.S., Iowa State U., 1939; M.S., Wash. State U., 1942; Ph.D., 1949; m. Iris Isabelle Graham, Aug. 27, 1939; children—Barbara June Yocom Simmons, Nancy Lyn Yocom Kamph, Cynthia Iris Yocom Dowling. Grad. asst. Wash. State U., 1940-42, asst. prof., 1947-53; prof. game mgmt. Humboldt State U., Arcata, Calif., 1953-78, emeritus prof. game mgmt., 1978—; with Wash. Game Dept., 1942-50; head div. natural resources, 1956-60; cons. U.S. Navy, various occasions, 1958-72, Nat. Park Service, 1951-52, 63, 66, Fish and Wildlife Service, Alaska, 1962; mem. Humboldt County Fish and Game adv. com., 1969-79, chmn., 1972-73. Served with USAAF, 1943-44, USN, 1944-46. Recipient various research grants. Mem. Wildlife Soc., Pacific NW Bird and Mamal Soc., Am. Ornithologists Union, Cooper Ornithol. Soc., Pacific Seabird Group, Sigma Xi. Republican. Author, co-author, illustrator books; contbr. sci. papers to profl. jours. Home: 1666 Charles Ave Arcata CA 95521 also 9907 Pleasant Valley Rd Sun City AZ 85351 Office: Humboldt State Univ Arcata CA 95521

YODER, DORIS ELAINE, food company executive; b. Los Angeles, Sept. 23, 1931; d. John Charles and Bertha (Koenig) Allen; m. Feb. 12, 1966; 1 son, Paul Thomas. Student East Los Angeles Coll., 1960-62, Woodbury Coll., 1965-66; B.S., U. Beverly Hills, 1981, M.S. in Acctg., 1983. Office adminstr. Northington, Inc., West Los Angeles, Calif., 1950-55, Bonded Products Co., Los Angeles, 1955-60; owner, operator C & D Plastics, Monterey Park, Calif., 1960-64; bookkeeper Kold Kist Foods, Los Angeles, 1964-76, office mgr., controller, 1976—. Violinist, All Cities Orch., 1947-50; 1st violinist Huntington Park Symphony Orch., 1950-53; 2d violinist San Gabriel Symphony Orch., 1953-56. Mem. Am. Mgmt. Assn. Lutheran. Home: 353 De La Fuente Monterey Park CA 91754 Office: 5356 Jillson St Los Angeles CA 90022

YODER, GENE FRANCIS, geologist; b. Washington, Iowa, May 17, 1934; s. Glenn Clayton and Elizabeth Margaret (Bauer) Y.; student U. Iowa, 1952-56; B.S. in Geology, Western State Coll. of Colo., 1959; m. Marilyn L. Scott, June 19, 1954; children—Christy Moore, Jene, Beth, David. Jr. geologist Pinnacle Exploration, Inc., Gunnison, Colo., 1956-60; asst. store mgr. oil field supply Franklin Supply Co., Moab, Utah, 1960-63; sr. geologist, mine supt. Homestake Mining Co., Kenedy, Tex., Casper, Wyo., Gunnison, Colo., and La Sal, Utah, 1963-74; land mgr. metals div. Union Carbide Corp., Grand Junction, Colo., 1974—; uranium cons., 1974. Mem. Grand Junction dist. adv. council Bur. Land Mgmt. Served with U.S. Army, 1954-56. Mem. Am. Mining Congress (public lands com. 1976—), Am. Assn. Petroleum Landmen (chmn. mining and geothermal com. 1979), Rocky Mountain Assn. Mineral Landmen, N.Mex. Mining Assn., Colo. Mining Assn., AIME, Soc. Mining Engrs. Republican. Lutheran. Home: 2813 Mesa Ave Grand Junction CO 81501 Office: PO Box 1029 Grand Junction CO 81502

YOHN, RICHARD VAN, clergyman; b. Lancaster, Pa., Apr. 16, 1937; s. Henry Martin and Ada (Dommel) Y.; student Franklin and Marshall Coll., 1956; B.S., Phila Coll. Bible, 1960; Th.M., Dallas Theol. Sem., 1964; D.Min., Talbot Theol. Sem., 1980; m. Linda Harriet Anderson, June 18, 1960; children—Richard Van, Steven Eric. Ordained to ministry Evang. Free Ch., 1971; dir. Christian edn. Oliver Presbyn. Ch., Mpls., 1964-67; pastor Windsor Park Evang. Free Ch., Winnipeg, Man., Can., 1967-71, Evang. Free Ch. of Fresno (Calif.), 1971—; originator radio program Living Word, 1980; pres. Contact Ministries Inc., 1980—; faculty Winnipeg Bible Coll., 1969-70. Recipient Mark of Excellence award Campus Life Mag., 1975. Mem. Nat. Assn. Evangelicals. Author: Discover Your Spiritual Gift and Use It, 1974; Now That I'm A Disciple, 1976; What Every Christian Should Know About God, 1976; God's Answers to Life's Problems, 1976; God's Holy Spirit for Christian Living, 1977; Getting Control of Your Life, 1978; God's Answer to Financial Problems, 1978; Getting Control of Your Inner Self, 1981; What Every Christian Should Know About Bible Prophecy, 1982; First-hand Joy, 1982. Office: 3438 E Ashlan St Fresno CA 93726

YOKELL, MICHAEL DAVID, economist; b. Plattsburgh, N.Y., Nov. 21, 1946; s. Stanley and Edith (Gersen) Y.; m. Jane Bunin, June 11, 1967. Ph.D. in Econs., U. Colo., 1975, M.A., 1973; B.S. in Physics, MIT, 1968. Prin. econs. and chief adminstrv. officer Energy & Resource Cons., Inc., Boulder, Colo., 1979—; pres. Document Control, Inc., Boulder, 1979—; mng. ptnr. RRR Leasing, 1979—; sr. economist Solar Energy Research Inst., Golden, Colo., 1977-79; faculty U. Calif.-Berkeley, 1976-77. Mem. Am. Econ. Assn., Nat. Assn. Bus. Economists, Fedn. Am. Scientists, Internat. Assn. Energy Economists, AAAS. Club: Am. Alpine (former chmn. fellowship com.). Author: The Environmental Benefits and Costs of Solar Energy, 1980; (with June Taylor) Yellowcake: The International Uranium Cartel, 1979; contbr. articles to profl. jours. Address: PO Drawer O Boulder CO 80306

YOKOTA, GLEN ISAO, wholesale co. exec.; b. Kyoto, Japan, Apr. 25, 1938; s. Aguru and Shizue Yokota; B.S. in Aero. Engring., Osaka Furitsu U., 1962; m. Yoko Hamano, Oct. 12, 1966; children—Osamu, Yumi, Jake. Supr., C. Itoh & Co., Tokyo, 1962-68, asst. mgr., N.Y.C., 1968-70, mgr., 1970-73; exec. v.p. C. Itoh Aviation, Inc., Los Angeles, 1973-74; pres. Nat. Dynamics Corp., Lomita, Calif., 1975—; pres. CTK Industries, Inc., Lomita, 1980—. Home: 26392 Via Conchita Mission Viejo CA 92691 Office: 3001 Redhill Ave Suite 5-104 Costa Mesa CA 92626

YORK, DAVID ALAN, safety manager; b. Sedilia, Mo., May 17, 1946; s. Raymond Arch and Mary Lucille (Hall) Y.; m. Lisa C. York, Dec. 28, 1982; children—Lori, Arch, Amy. B.S. in Indsl. Health and Safety, Central Wash. U., 1980; M.S. in Indsl. Safety, Colo. State U., 1981. Safety mgr. VA, 1971-80; corp. safety dir. Black & Veatch Engrs., 1980-81; pres., gen. mgr. Safety Mgmt. Systems Inc., 1981—. Served with U.S. Army, 1964-71; Vietnam. Mem. Am. Soc. Safety Engrs., Nat. Fire Protection Assn. (healthcare sect. charter mem.), Internat. Assn. Arson Investigators, Colo. Safety Assn., Nat. Safety Council, U.S. Submarine Vet. Assn. Republican. Club: Masons. Office: PO Box 8915 Fort Collins CO 80522

YORK, HERBERT FRANK, physicist, govt. ofcl., ednl. adminstr.; b. Rochester, N.Y., Nov. 24, 1921; s. Herbert Frank and Nellie Elizabeth (Lang) Y.; B.S., U. Rochester, 1942, M.S., 1943; Ph.D., U. Calif., Berkeley, 1949; D.H.L. (hon.), U. San Diego, 1962, Claremont Grad. Sch., 1972; D.Sc. (hon.), Case Western Res. U., 1960; m. Sybil Dunford, Sept., 1947; children—David Winters, Rachel, Cynthia. Physicist, U. Calif. Radiation Lab., 1943-52; asst. prof. physics, dir. Lawrence Livermore Lab., U. Calif., Livermore, 1952-58; chief scientist Def. Advanced Research Projects Agy., Office Sec. Def., Washington, 1958, dir. def. research and engring., 1958-61, mem. Pres.'s Sci. Adv. Com., 1957-58, 64-67, mem. Gen. Adv. Com. on Arms Control and Disarmament, 1962-69; chancellor U. Calif., San Diego, 1961-64, 70-72, dir. program on sci., tech., and public affairs, La Jolla, 1972—; U.S. ambassador Nuclear Test Ban Negotiations, 1979-81; trustee Aerospace Corp., 1961—, Inst. Def. Analyses, 1962—; Phi Beta Kappa lectr., 1978-79. Recipient E. O. Lawrence award AEC, 1964; Guggenheim fellow, 1972-73. Fellow Am. Phys. Soc., Internat. Acad. Astronautics, Am. Acad. Arts and Scis. Club: Cosmos (Washington). Author: Race to Oblivion, 1970; The Advisors, 1976; editor: Readings on Arms Control,

1973. Home: 6110 Camino De La Costa La Jolla CA 92037 Office: U Calif at San Diego La Jolla CA 92093

YORK, ROBERT FRANCIS, elec. engr.; b. Grove City, Pa., Sept. 12, 1943; s. Charles Walter and Dorothy Ruth (Reiter) Y.; B.S.E.E., Pa. State U., 1965; m. Anya Dehnart, July 14, 1979; 1 dau., Elizabeth. Communications test engr. Apollo Project Grumman Aerospace Co., Bethpage, N.Y., 1965-66, Kennedy Space Center, Fla., 1966-72; communications/software test engr. Viking Project, Martin Marietta Corp., Denver, 1972-76, Lander command lead Viking Mission Ops., Pasadena, Calif., 1976-78, Lander mission planning lead. 1976-77, dep. dir. Viking sci. analysis and mission planning, 1977-78; lead communications test engr., spl. programs Martin Marietta Aerospace Co., Denver, 1978-79, system test engr. Venus orbiting imaging radar study, 1980, system test mgr. def. systems, 1980; cons. software system design AYE, 1980—. Recipient Public Service award NASA, 1977. Mem. IEEE. Republican. Designed Viking Mission segments permitting Mars landers to survive Martian winter and return data through 1980's. Home: 30111 Peggy Ln Evergreen CO 80439

YOSHII, DAN OSAMU, optometrist, air force officer; b. Rohwer, Ark., Feb. 2, 1945; s. Gion and Hisayo (Muramoto) Y. A.B., UCLA, 1967; B.S., So. Calif. Coll. Optometry, 1969, O.D., 1971. Diplomate Nat. Bd. Examiners in Optometry. Commd. 1st lt. U.S. Army, 1971, interservice transfer to U.S. Air Force, 1975, advanced through grades to maj., 1980; chief optometry clinic, Izmir, Turkey, 1975-77, Nellis AFB, Nev., 1977-82, Hickam AFB, Hawaii, 1982—; adj. faculty Pa. Coll. Optometry. Fellow Am. Acad. Optometry; mem. Air Force Assn., Am. Acad. Optometry, Am. Optometric Assn., Armed Forces Optometric Soc., Assn. Mil. Surgeons U.S., UCLA Alumni Assn., Beta Sigma Kappa, Omega Delta. Democrat. Baptist. Office: Optometry Clinic US Air Force Clinic Hickam Hickam AFB HI 96853

YOSHIMURA, LEE, constrn. co. exec.; b. Warren, Ohio, Feb. 16, 1940; d. A. Monroe and Rebecca A. (Cross) Ohl; student Youngstown U., 1960-66, Metro Coll. Denver, 1980—. With Lauar's, Youngstown, Ohio, 1958-64; office mgr. Grimes Consol., Youngstown, 1964-67; tax and account exec. sec. William C. Mears, Akron, Ohio, 1967-69; exec. sec. U.S. Petroleum Co., Joplin, Mo., 1969-71; asst. comptroller Hessler Mfg., Denver, 1971-73; treas. Haco Contractors, Wheat Ridge, Colo., 1973—, equal employment opportunity officer, 1979—; pres. Title Constrn. Co., Inc., 1982—. Treas. Career Women's Symphony Guild. Mem. Nat. Assn. Women in Constrn. Office: 5075 Tabor St Wheat Ridge CO 80033

YOSHIOKA, VERNON TADAO, aerospace engineer; b. Hayward, Calif., Feb. 21, 1938; s. Giichi and June Noriko (Nishi) Y.; m. Shinobu Kobayashi, Sept. 18, 1965; children—Charles O. Bender, Carol A. Sainz, Linda L. Bender, Christine M. B.S. in Aero. and Astronautical Engring., MIT, 1960. Aero. engr. Ryan Aero. Co., San Diego, 1960-62; dynamics Gen. Dynamics Astronautics, San Diego, 1962-64; dynamics engr. Teledyne Ryan Aero. San Diego, 1964-68, tech. specialist, 1968—. Mem. San Diego Japanese-Am. Citizens League, 1960—, bd. dirs., 1970-80, 82—; v.p. membership and services, Nat. Japanese-Am. Citizens League, 1980—; founding chmn. Union of Pan Asian Communities, San Diego, 1973-76, bd. dirs., 1973—; mem. citizens adv. com. San Diego City Coll., 1974—; bd. dirs. Kiku Gardens Inc., San Diego, 1979—; chmn. San Diego Noise Abatement and Control Bd., 1980—. Mem. AIAA, Assn. of Unmanned Vehicle Systems. Republican. Mem. United Church of Christ. Home: 6968 Glenflora Ave San Diego CA 92119 Office: 2701 Harbor Dr San Diego CA 92138

YOSHIZUMI, DONALD TETSURO, dentist; b. Honolulu, Feb. 18, 1930; s. Richard Kiyoshi and Hatsue (Tanouye) Y.; B.S., U. Hawaii, 1952; D.D.S., U. Mo., 1960, M.S., 1963; m. Barbara Fujiko Iwashita, June 25, 1955; children—Beth Ann E., Cara Leigh S, Erin Yuri. Clin. instr. U. Mo. Sch. Dentistry, Kansas City, 1960-63; gen. practice dentistry Santa Clara, Calif., 1963-70, San Jose, Calif., 1970—. Served with USAF, 1952-56. Mem. Am., Calif. dental assns., Santa Clara County Dental Soc., Omicron Kappa Upsilon, Delta Sigma Delta. Contbr. articles to profl. jours. Home: 5054 Parkfield Ave San Jose CA 95129 Office: 2011 Forest Ave San Jose CA 95128

YOSHIZUMI, MARC OSAMU, retina and vitreous surgeon, ophthalmologist; b. Honolulu, Oct. 1, 1945; s. Richard Kiyoshi and Hatsue(Tanoue) Y.; M.D., Yale U., 1970. Knight meml. fellow in nervous diseases Oxford U. (Eng.), 1970-71; intern, fellow in medicine Johns Hopkins Med. Sch., Balt., 1971-72; resident in ophthalmology Harvard Med. Sch., Mass. Eye and Ear Infirmary, Boston, 1974-77; retina and vitreous fellow Retina Assos., Mass. Eye and Ear Infirmary, 1977-78; asst. prof. ophthalmology Jules Stein Eye Inst., UCLA, Los Angeles, 1978—, dir. eye trauma unit, 1982; commr. Bd. Med. Quality Assurance State of Calif., 1981; cons. U. Caracas, Venezuela, 1977-78. Recipient Disting. Service award, dept. ophthalmology U. Caracas, 1978. Fellow Am. Bd. Ophthalmology; mem. Am. Acad. Ophthalmology, Los Angeles Med. Soc., Los Angeles Ophthalmology Soc., Pan-Am. Assn. Ophthalmology, Retina Soc. '83. Contbr. articles to profl. jours. Office: 800 Westwood Plaza Jules Stein Eye Inst UCLA Los Angeles CA 90024

YOST, BARBARA JEANNE, arts council executive; b. Balt., Jan. 20, 1947; d. Paul Alton and Kathleen Annette (Barnhart) Beavin; m. Douglas Leighton Yost, July 20, 1968. B.A. in Speech, North Central Coll., Naperville, Ill., 1969. Cert. tchr., Ill., Colo; lic. real estate, Colo. Tchr. speech DeKalb (Ill.) Community Unit Schs., 1969-70; savs. counselor, savs. supr. Majestic Savs. and Loan Assn., Denver, 1972-75; realtor Mary Rae and Assocs., Denver, 1976; staff aide, press sec. U.S. Rep. Patricia Schroeder, Denver, 1977-80; fed. hazard mitigation coordinator Fed. Emergency Mgmt. Agy., Denver, 1981; adminstrv. coordinator, exec. dir. Met. Denver Arts Alliance, 1982—. Co-chmn. North Neighborhood Campus Concept Com., 1976-80; chmn. task force Regional Council of Govts. Citizen Adv. Com., 1976-80; mem. Colo. Blue Ribbon Task Force on Housing, 1977; bd. dirs., treas. Denver Mobility, Inc.; bd. dirs., sec. Colo. Dance Alliance. Recipient Dorothea Zehnder Seder Prose prize 1969. Mem. Am. Mgmt. Assn., Nat. Assn. Female Execs., Bus. and Profl. Women (sec. 1975-79). Democrat. Club: Denver Figure Skating. Contbr. artcles to profl. jours. Office: 1331 18th St Denver CO 80202

YOST, CAMILLE SULLIVAN, food service consultant; b. Bakersfield, Calif., June 15, 1944; d. Robert Michael and Anita Marie (Koehnke) Sullivan; m. Mark T. Yost, Dec. 26, 1973; children—Jeanine, Kevin. B.A. in Social Scis., St. Mary's Coll., Notre Dame, Ind., 1966. Trainee edn. div. Saga Corp., Ill., 1967, asst. mgr. corp., Cin., 1967; asst. mgr. Coll. Idaho, Caldwell, 1968, Seattle U., 1969, Temple Buell, Denver, 1970, Carroll Coll., Helena, Mont.; mgr. U. Calif.-Irvine, 1971, Calif. Baptist Coll., Riverside, 1972; food service dir. Syntex, Palo Alto, Calif., 1972-76, dist. mgr. San Francisco peninsula, 1976-78; food service cons., Mountain View, Calif., 1979—. Bd. dirs., treas. Crestview Homeowners Assn. Mem. St. Mary's Alumnae Assn., La Leche League. Democrat. Roman Catholic. Club: St. Simon's Women's. Home and Office: 1031 Crestview 307 Mountain View CA 94040

YOST, MEL E., lawyer; b. Newcastle, Ind., May 24, 1947; s. Melvin T. and Roberta Eileen Yost; A.B., Columbia U., 1969; J.D. summa cum laude, U. N.Mex., 1973; m. Barbara Ann Bookwalter, Jan. 28, 1978; 1 dau., Sarah. Admitted to N.Mex. bar, 1973; asso. firm Modrell, Sperling, Roehl, Harris and Sisk, Albuquerque, 1973-75; partner firm Yost, Felter, Barberousse, Yost & Silver, Santa Fe, 1975—; instr. Sch. Law, U. N.Mex., Albuquerque, 1973-75. Bd. dirs. Am. Heart Assn., 1978-81. Served with U.S. Army, 1969-75. Recipient Christine M. Jaeger Meml. award U. N.Mex. Sch. Law, 1972, 73. Mem. Am. Bar Assn., Am. Judicature Soc., Order of Coif. Democrat. Presbyterian. Home: 106 Calle Palomita Santa Fe NM 87501 Office: 320 Paseo de Peralta Santa Fe NM 87501

YOST, ROGER WILLIAM, apparel co. exec.; b. Wesson, Miss., Jan. 6, 1936; s. Paul Leslie and Mary (Hardcastle) Y.; B.S. in Journalism, Northwestern U., 1958; m. Barbara Helen Brown, Aug. 19, 1955; children—Kathryn Elizabeth, Douglas Roger. Reporter, copy editor, columnist Chgo. Sun-Times, 1954-59; account exec. Selz Orgn., Chgo., 1959-60; account supr. J. Walter Thompson Co., Chgo., 1960-65; mgr. advt., sales promotion and public relations Jantzen, Inc., Portland, Oreg., 1965—; producer TV programs on basketball star Jerry West, 1974, Boomer World Team Challenge on Surfing, 1981, 82; Windriders at Malibu, 1983; lyricist Boomer World Theme, Columbia Records, 1981; producer Packed in Surf, Columbia Records 1981. Pres. Ill. Jr. Miss Pageant, 1963-64. Recipient merit award for art direction Art Dirs. Club N.Y., 1981, 82 (2); named Oreg. Advt. Profl. of Yr., 1982-83. Mem. Portland Advt. Fedn. (dir., pres. 1979-80), Am. Advt. Fedn. (4 Best in West awards 1981 (3), 1982, Addy award of excellence for newspaper ad devel. 1981). Office: PO Box 3001 Portland OR 97208

YOTOPOULOS, PAN A., economist, educator; b. Athens, Greece, May 10, 1933; s. Konstantin and Theoni (Papaspyrou) Panayotopoulos; m. Mary Louise Kroos, Dec. 26, 1962; children—Kyvele-Rhea, Jason-Konstantin. Diploma in law and polit. sci., U. Athens, 1952; Ph.D. in Econs., UCLA, 1962. Prof., U. Wis.-Milw., 1961-63, 65-67; sr. assoc., dir. gen. Ctr. Planning and Econ. Research, Athens, 1963-65; prof., dir. econ. research ctr. U. Hawaii, 1967-68; prof. econs. Food Research Inst., Stanford U., 1968—; advisor UN FAO, 1975—; cons. World Bank, 1975—, Internat. Fund Agrl. Devel., 1979—. Pres. Demokritos Soc. Sr. fellow East-West Ctr., Hawaii, 1974. Mem. Am. Econ. Assn., Econometric Soc., Am. Agrl. Econs. Assn. (award profl. excellence 1969), Population Assn. Am. Author: 8 books including: Allocative Efficiency in Economic Development, 1968; Economics of Development: Empirical Investigations, 1976; The Population Problem and the Development Solution, 1977.

YOUMANS, PAUL EDWIN, investment banker; b. Fort Smith, Ark., June 1, 1902; s. Frank Abijah and Delia (Enroughty) Y.; B.S. in Bus. and Public Adminstrn., U. Mo., 1923; m. Katherine St. John Carter, June 7, 1928 (dec.); 1 dau., Anne Carter Youmans Mason. Entered investment banking through Nat. Bank of Commerce, St. Louis, 1923; joined Internat. Trust Co., Denver, 1927; with Nat. City Co., 1928-29; joined Sullivan & Co., 1930, partner 1941-46; chmn., dir. Bosworth, Sullivan & Co., Inc., Denver, mem. N.Y. Stock Exchange, 1952-74; exec. v.p. Dain, Bosworth, Inc., 1979-80; dir. emeritus Inter-Regional Fin. Group, Inc.; bd. govs. Midwest Stock Exchange, 1969-71. Trustee, Blue Shield Plan, Denver, 1962-70. Mem. Investment Bankers Assn. Am. (gov. 1952-55), Nat. Assn. Securities Dealers (gov. 1960-63), Assn. Stock Exchange Firms (gov. 1965-70), Phi Delta Theta. Episcopalian. Clubs: Univ., Rotary (Denver), 26, Mile High. Home: 480 S Marion St Pkwy Denver CO 80209 Office: 950 17th St Denver CO 80202

YOUNG, CHARLES EDWARD, polit. scientist, univ. chancellor; b. San Bernardino, Calif., Dec. 30, 1931; s. Clayton Charles and Eula May (Walters) Y. A.B., U. Calif., Riverside, 1955; M.A., UCLA, 1957, Ph.D., 1960; D.H.L. (hon.) U. Judaism, Los Angeles, 1969. Polit. Sci. Assn. Congressional fellow U.S. Senate, Washington, 1958-59; adminstrv. analyst, office of pres. U. Calif., Berkeley, 1959-60; asst. prof. polit. sci. U. Calif., Davis, 1960; asst. prof. UCLA, 1960-66, assoc. prof., 1966-69, prof., 1969—, asst. to chancellor, 1960-62, asst. chancellor, 1962-63, vice chancellor, adminstrn., 1963-68, chancellor, 1968—, trustee UCLA Found. mem. Chancellor's Assos., UCLA; dir. UMF Systems, Inc., Dir's. Capital Inc., Intel Corp., Carlsberg Corp., Fin. Corp. Am., Micro-Z Corp., State Savs. and Loan Assn. Mem. Nat. Com. on U.S.-China Relations, Inc.; v.p. Young Musicians Found.; bd. dirs. So. Calif. Theatre Assn., Los Angeles Olympic Organizing Com., Los Angeles Council for Internat. Visitors; founding com. mem. Mansfield Center for Pacific Affairs. Served with 116th Fighter Bomber Wing, USAF, 1951-52. Mem. Assn. Am. Univs. (exec. com., vice chmn.), Internat. Assn. Univs. (adminstrv. bd.). Contbr. articles to polit. sci. jours. Office: UCLA Chancellor's Office Los Angeles CA 90024

YOUNG, DON RAY, fire chief; b. Cedar City, Utah, Oct. 8, 1933; s. Edward Webb and Cora (Tanner) Y.; m. Madeleine Ebeling, Dec. 20, 1952; children—Cheryl Kajans, Suzanne Francis, Annette. Student U. Nev., Reno, 1951-52; A.S., Western Nev. Community Coll., 1972. Cert. vocat. edn. teaching, Nev., 1970. With Sparks (Nev.) Fire Dept., 1957-60, 62—, bn. chief, 1967-76, fire chief, 1976—; fire capt., asst. fire chief Washoe County (Nev.) Fire Dept., 1961-62; fire sci. instr. U. Nev., Reno, Western Nev. Community Coll. Mem. Internat. Assn. Fire Chiefs, Nat. Fire Protection Assn., Nev. Fire Chiefs Assn. Republican. Home: 845 Browning Dr Reno NV 89506 Office: 1605 B St Sparks NV 89431

YOUNG, DONALD E., congressman; b. Meridian, Calif., June 9, 1933; grad. Chico (Cal.) State Coll.; m. Lula Fredson; children—Joni, Dawn. Former educator, river boat capt.; mem. Fort Yukon (Alaska) City Council, then mayor; mem. Alaska Ho. of Reps., 1966-70, Alaska Senate, 1970-73; mem. 93d-97th Congress from Alaska. Republican. Office: US House of Representatives Washington DC 20515

YOUNG, DOUGLAS JANSEN, economist, educator; b. Portland, Oreg., July 13, 1946; s. George Wendell and Phyllis (Jansen) Y. B.A., U. Puget Sound, 1971; M.A., U. Wis., 1972, Ph.D., 1977. Asst. prof. econs. Mont. State U., 1977—, U. Wis.-Madison, 1982. Served with U.S. Army, 1967-70. Ford Found. fellow, 1974; Sloan Found. fellow, 1976-77; NIH grantee, 1980-81. Mem. Am. Econ. Assn., Western Econ. Assn., Econometric Soc., Pub. Choice Soc., Assn. Vol. Action Scholars. Contbr. articles to profl. jours. Office: Dept Econs Mont State U Bozeman MT 59717

YOUNG, EULALIE BARNES, social services cons.; b. New Orleans, Oct. 24, 1942; d. Roy and Lucille (Woods) Barnes; B.A., So. U., 1966; M.S., SUNY, Buffalo, 1976; m. Harris Samuel McGee, July 11, 1963; children—Shawn Arlene McGee, Darren Lance McGee; m. 2d, James Leonard Young, Mar. 24, 1970; 1 dau., Jayanna Lucille, Supervisory recreation specialist Dept. Army, Ft. Polk, La., 1967-72; program coordinator YMCA/Model Cities Teen Center, Buffalo, 1972-74; student intern VA Hosp., Buffalo, 1974-76; program coordinator BUILD Work Assessment Center, Buffalo, 1976-77; sr. rehab. counselor Calif. Dept. Rehab., Los Angeles, 1978-80; social services cons. Calif. Dept. Social Services, 1980—. Calif. coordinator Nat. Hook-up of Black Women, 1979—. Recipient Outstanding Achievement award Calif. State Dept. Rehab., 1980. Mem. Assn. Black Psychologists, Am. Personnel and Guidance Assn., Nat. Rehab. Assn. Aware of Women Orgn. Club: Rosicrucians. Address: 2165 E 19th St A San Bernardino CA 92404

YOUNG, FRANCIS ALLAN, psychologist, educator; b. Utica, N.Y., Dec. 29, 1918; s. Frank Allan and Julia Mae (McOwen) Y.; m. Judith Wadsworth Wright, Dec. 21, 1945; children—Francis Allan, Thomas Robert. B.S., U. Tampa, 1941; M.A., Western Res. U., 1945; Ph.D., Ohio State U., 1949. Lic. psychologist, Wash. Instr., Wash. State U., Pullman, 1948-50, asst. prof., 1950-56, assoc. prof., 1956-61, prof., 1961—, dir. Primate Research Ctr., 1957—; vis. prof. ophthalmology U. Oreg., Portland, 1964; vis. prof. pharmacology U. Uppsala (Sweden), 1971; vis. prof. optometry U. Houston, 1979-81. Recipient Paul Yarwood Meml. award Calif. Optometric Assn., 1978; Apollo award Am. Optometric Assn., 1980; Nat. Acad. Sci.-NRC postdoctoral fellow, 1956-57; NSF grantee, 1950-53; USAF grantee, 1965-72, NIH grantee, 1960-78. Mem. AAAS, Psychonomic Soc., Am. Psychol. Assn. (exec. officer div. 31, 1975—), Wash. State Psychol. Assn. (exec. sec. 1965-77), Western Psychol. Assn., N.Y. Acad. Sci., Assn. Research in Vision and Ophthalmology, Am. Acad. Optometry, Internat. Soc. Myopia Research (sec.-treas. 1978—), Common Cause, Ams. for Dem. Action, Sigma Xi, Psi Chi (nat. pres. 1968-70). Editor: (with Donald B. Lindsley) Early Experience and Visual Information Processing in Perceptual and Reading Disorders, 1970. Home: NW 344 Webb St Pullman WA 99163 Office: Wash State U Pullman WA 99164

YOUNG, FRANK SHARP, elec. engr.; b. Salt Lake City, Apr. 26, 1933; s. Frank Elbert and Gertrude (Sharp) Y.; B.S. in Elec. Engring., Stanford U., 1955; M.S. in Elec. Engring., U. Pitts., 1962; m. Roberta Pearl Crusan, Sept. 9, 1957; children—Kathy, Janette, Frank Robert, Susanne, John William. Engr., Westinghouse Electric Corp., East Pitts., 1955-63, sponsor engr., 1963-66; mgr. underground transmission test facility, Walt Mill, Pa., 1966-72, mgr. UHV Transmission Research, East Pittsburgh, Pa., 1972-75,; program mgr., high voltage transmission Electric Power Research Inst., Palo Alto, Calif., 1975-77, mgr. planning and strategic analysis, 1977—; instr. U. Pitts., 1964-66; cons., internat. power system planning. Served with AUS, 1957-58. Fellow IEEE; mem. Internat. Conf. Large HighVoltage Electric Systems, US/USSR Joint Commn. on High Voltage Transmission Technology, Tau Beta Pi. Republican. Mormon. Contbr. articles to profl. jours. Patentee in field. Office: 3412 Hillview Ave Palo Alto CA 94303

YOUNG, GEORGE WALTER, lawyer; b. Los Angeles, May 15, 1950; s. George Albert and Edna Margaret (Hill) Y.; m. Marian Eileen Bement, May 29, 1982. B.A., UCLA, 1972; J.D., Southwestern U., 1976. Bar: Calif. 1976, U.S. Supreme Ct. 1981. Mem. Young & Young, Los Angeles, 1976-82, Pepper, Hamilton & Scheetz, Los Angeles, 1982—. Mem. John Marshall High Sch. Alumni Assn. (pres.), UCLA Alumni Assn., UCLA Bruin Bench. Republican. Presbyterian. Clubs: Los Angeles Athletic, Masons. Office: Pepper Hamilton & Scheetz 606 S Olive St Suite 2000 Los Angeles CA 90014

YOUNG, HAROLD EUGENE, oral surgeon; b. Bowdoin, Mont., Dec. 22, 1922; s. Thomas Willis and Kittie Gertrude (Van Gordon) Y.; B.S., Mont. State U., 1948; postgrad. U. Oreg., 1948; D.D.S., U. Pacific, San Francisco, 1952; m. Judith Ann Mathews, Mar. 5, 1976; children—Laurel Diane, Robert Kenneth, Tracy Ann. Resident in oral surgery Herrick Meml. Hosp., 1952-53; partner in oral surgery with B.C. Kingsbury, Vallejo, Calif., 1953-60; individual practice oral surgery, El Cerrito, Calif., 1960—. Bd. dirs. Siduerado council Boy Scouts Am., 1959-63. Served with AUS, 1942-46; PTO. Named Man of Yr., Vallejo Jr. C. of C., 1956. Fellow Am. Coll. Dentists; mem. ADA (del. 1974-78), Calif. Dental Assn. (trustee 1969-80), Am. (chmn. com. pub. info. 1973-74, trustee 1980—), Western (past pres.) socs. oral and maxilofacial surgeons), No. Calif. Soc. Oral Surgeons (past pres.), Omicron Kappa Upsilon, Kappa Sigma, Delta Sigma Delta. Clubs: Kiwanis, Masons. Contbr. profl. jours. Home: 705 Augusta Dr Moraga CA 94556 Office: 111 Plaza Profl Bldg El Cerrito CA 94530

YOUNG, HOPE THREADGILL, counselor, university official; b. Wadesboro, N.C., July 5, 1953; d. Henry Frank and Audrey Ann (Carter) Threadgill; m. David Pingwah Young, Nov. 6, 1973; 1 son, Daniel Shungchi. Student Winthrop Coll., 1971-72; B.S. in Psychology, U. S.C., 1974; M.A. in Counseling and Student Personnel Psychology, U. Minn., 1982. Residential dir., clin. counselor Whitten Village Mental Retardation Inst., Clinton, S.C., 1974-76; coordinator patient services Muscular Dystrophy Assn., St. Paul, 1976-77; counselor, teaching asst. counseling and student personnel psychology U. Minn., Mpls., 1978-79; counselor, program dir. Women's Info. Ctr., U. Colo., Colorado Springs, 1980—, also staff advisor Internat. Club. Bd. dirs. Women's Resource Agy., Colorado Springs. Mem. Am. Psychol. Assn., Am. Personnel and Guidance Assn., Am. Soc. Tng. and Devel., Nat. Assn. Women Adminstrs. and Counselors, Colo.-Wyo. Assn. Women Adminstrs. and Counselors (dir., historian). Methodist. Office: Library 127 Austin Bluffs Colorado Springs CO 80933

YOUNG, J(IO) L(OWELL), soil chemist, biologist; b. Perry, Utah, Dec. 13, 1925; s. I. A. and Elzada (Nelson) Y.; B.S., Brigham Young U., 1953; Ph.D., Ohio State U., 1956; m. Ruth Ann Jones, Sept. 15, 1950; children—Gordon, LoAnn, Colene, Kathryn. Research asst. Ohio Agrl. Expt. Sta., Columbus, 1953-56; chemist Agrl. Research Service, U.S. Dept. Agr., Corvallis, Oreg., 1957-64, research chemist, 1964-78; asst. prof. Oreg. State U., Corvallis, 1957-63, assoc. prof., 1963-78, prof. soil sci., 1978—; research chemist ornamental/hort. plants unit Agrl. Research Service, U.S. Dept. Agr., Corvallis, 1978—. Served with USAAF, 1944-46. Ohio Agrl. Expt. Sta. postdoctoral fellow, 1956-57. Mem. Internat. Soil Sci. Soc., Internat. Clay Minerals Soc., U.S. Clay Minerals Soc., Soil Sci. Soc. Am., Am. Soc. Agronomy (officer western br. 1966-72), Soil Sci. Soc. Am. (assoc. editor jour. 1975-80), AAAS, Western Soc. Soil Sci. (officer 1966-71). Contbr. articles in field to profl. jours. Office: Soil Sci Dept Oreg State U Corvallis OR 97331

YOUNG, JOAN CRAWFORD, advertising executive; b. Hobbs, N.Mex., July 30, 1931; d. William Bill and Ora Maydelle (Boone) Crawford; m. Herchelle B. Young, Nov. 23, 1971 (div.). B.A., Hardin Simmons U., 1952; postgrad. Tex. Tech. U., 1953-54. Reporter, Lubbock (Tex.) Avalanche-Jour., 1952-54; promotion dir. KCBD-TV, Lubbock, 1954-62; account exec. Ward Hicks Advt., Albuquerque, 1962-70; v.p. Mellekas & Assocs., Advt., Albuquerque, 1970-78; pres. Young & Gallegly Advt., Albuquerque, 1978—. Bd. dirs. N.Mex. Symphony Orch., 1970-73. Recipient Silver medal N.Mex. Advt. Fedn., 1977. Mem. N.Mex. Advt. Fedn. (dir. 1975-76), Am. Advt. Fedn., Greater Albuquerque C. of C. (dir. 1983). Republican. Author: (with Louise Allen and Audre Lipscomb) Radio and TV Continuity Writing, 1962. Home: 3425 Avenida Charada NW Albuquerque NM 87107 Office: 303 Roma NW Albuquerque NM 87102

YOUNG, JOHN ALAN, electronics co. exec.; b. Nampa, Idaho, Apr. 24, 1932; s. Lloyd Arthur and Karen Eliza (Miller) Y.; B.S. in Elec. Engring., Oreg. State U., 1953; M.B.A., Stanford, 1958; m. Rosemary Murray, Aug. 1, 1954; children—Gregory, Peter, Diana. Various mktg. and finance positions Hewlett Packard Co. Inc., Palo Alto, Calif., 1958-63, gen. mgr. microwave div., 1963-68, v.p. electronic products group, 1968-74, exec. v.p., dir., 1974-77, pres., 1977—, chief exec. officer, 1978—, chmn. exec. com., 1983—; dir. Wells Fargo Bank, Dillingham Corp., SRI Internat. Chmn. ann. fund Stanford, 1969-73, nat. chmn. corp. gifts, 1973-77. Bd. dirs. Mid-Peninsula Urban Coalition, 1972-80, co-chmn., 1976-80; mem. adv. council Grad. Sch. Bus., Stanford U., 1968-73, 75-80, univ. trustee, 1977—. Served with USAF, 1954-56. Mem. Am. Electronics Assn. Office: Hewlett-Packard Co 3000 Hanover St Palo Alto CA 94304*

YOUNG, JOHN PAUL, newspaper editor; b. Denver, Dec. 31, 1952; s. Robert Bell and Helen Jo (Hundley) Y. B.A. in Tech. Journalism, Colo. State U., 1975. Sports editor Alamosa Valley Courier, Alamosa, Colo., 1975-78, news editor, 1978, editor, 1978—. Bd. dirs. San Luis Valley (Colo.) Am. Diabetes Assn. Recipient Nat. Weather Service Pub.

Service award, 1979; Am. Legion state media award, 1980; numerous Colo. Press Assn. awards. Mem. Sigma Delta Chi. Democrat. Home: PO Box 92 Alamosa CO 81101 Office: Valley Courier PO Box 1099 Alamosa CO 81101

YOUNG, JOSEPH EARNEST, art history educator; b. Los Angeles, Sept. 8, 1939; s. Joseph Milo and Henrietta Virginia (Johnson) Y.; M.A. in Art History, UCLA, 1978. West Coast editor Art Internat., 1970-71; asst. curator prints and drawings Los Angeles County Mus. Art, 1965-79; art critic The Ariz. Republic, 1979-80, Phoenix mag., 1980-81; assoc. prof. art history Ariz. State U., Tempe, 1979—, dir. Harry Wood Art Gallery, 1981—. Bd. dirs. Print Research Facility, Ariz. State U., 1979—. Mem. Nat. Print Council (dir. 1980—), Print Council Am. Editor, Jour. of the Theory and Criticism of the Visual Arts, 1981—. Office: Sch Art Ariz State Univ Tempe AZ 85281

YOUNG, LESLIE GORDON, Canadian provincial government official; b. Compton, Que., Can., Aug. 19, 1934; s. Gordon F. and Lena N. (Cairns) Y.; m. Helen G. McKirdy, June 28, 1958; children—Susan L., Mary A. Attended Park Bus. Coll., Hamilton; B.A., U. Montreal (Que.); M.S., U. Mass. Cons. econs., bus.; mem. Legis. Assembly Alta. (Can.), Edmonton, 1971—, minister of labor Alta., 1979—. Mem. Can. Inst. Pub. Adminstrn., Edmonton C. of C. Progressive Conservative. Presbyterian. Office: Legis Bldg 404 Edmonton AB T5K 2B7 Canada*

YOUNG, LOUISA FRANCES, interior designer; b. Dayton, Ohio, Mar. 12, 1907; d. William Frederick and Bertha Elizabeth (Kurtz) Kennell; m. Dallas M. Speer, Mar. 14, 1970. Student Ohio Tchr.'s Coll., Dayton, 1926-27, Heatherley's Art Sch., London, 1931-32, Sch. of Art Inst. Chgo., 1932-33. Illustrator, Aero-Med. Lab., Wright Field, Dayton, 1941-45; interior designer Rike's, Dayton, 1958-71. Sec. Women's Civic Group, Dayton, 1935-40. Recipient: Disting. Service award Am. Soc. Interior Designers, 1980. Mem. Am. Soc. Interior Designers, Dayton Painter and Sculptor Soc. Republican. Episcopalian. Clubs: Dayton Fedn. Women's Clubs. One woman show: U. Dayton, 1969; portrait: Martha, 1969. Address: 205 S Belardo Rd Palm Springs CA 92262

YOUNG, MARY LYNN, psychologist; b. DuBois, Pa., Apr. 24, 1941; d. Fredrick Frick and Gertrude Cruzan (Carns) Y.; m. Tom Spencer Allison, Jan. 2, 1975. B.A., Ariz. State U., Tempe, 1965, Ph.D. (NASA trainee), 1971; cert. in applied behavior analysis Ind. U., 1972. Lic. psychologist, Calif., 1976. Instr., Glendale (Ariz.) Community Coll., 1969-71; research specialist Calif. Youth Authority, Stockton, 1972-75; psychologist Stockton (Calif.) State Hosp., 1975-79, Calif. Youth Authority, Preston Sch., Ione, 1979-80; pvt. practice behavior therapy, Stockton, 1980—; part time instr. San Joaquin Delta Community Coll., Stockton, 1981-82; adj. prof. psychology U. Pacific, Stockton, 1973—. Sec., Human Services Projects, Inc., 1977-79. Mem. No. Calif. Behavior Analysis Assn. (pres. 1981-82), Assn. Behavior Analysis, Am. Psychol. Assn., ACLU (sec. 1982—). Contbr. articles to profl. jours. Address: 3216 Country Club Blvd Stockton CA 95204

YOUNG, MARY PENELOPE, school psychologist, educational consultant; b. Kuala Lumpar, Malaysia, Sept. 20, 1946; d. Christian R. and Harris Therese (Hare) Martin; m. David Anthony Young, Feb. 17, 1968; children—Anthony, Brian, In Soo. B.A. with honors in English, Univ. Coll., Dublin, 1967; M.A. in English, U. Wash., 1968; M.A. in Ednl. Psychology, Counseling and Guidance, Calif. State U., 1978. Cert. secondary tchr., pupil personnel services, sch. psychologist Calif. Research asst. English dept. U. Wash., Seattle, 1967-68; tchr. Our Lady of Lourdes Sch., Northridge, Calif., 1969-76, psychol. asst. Thomas Aquinas Clinic, Encino, Calif., 1980-82; high sch. counselor Alemany High Sch., Mission Hills, Calif., 1976—, also vice prin. personnel services; ednl. cons. pvt. elem. schs. Bd. dirs. Mission Hills C. of C.; tchr.-sponsor ARC; counselor Right to Life League So. Calif. Mem. Am. Personnel and Guidance Assn., Nat. Cath. Educators Assn., Calif. Assn Student Fin. Aid Adminstrs., San Fernando Valley Industry-Edn. Council. Roman Catholic. Contbr. numerous poems to poetry jours. Office: Alemany High Sch 15241 Rinaldi St Mission Hills CA 91345

YOUNG, MONIKA JANE, public relations executive, musician; b. Ft. Worth, Tex., Oct. 24, 1952; d. Robert Emerson and Katherine Ann (Frank) Young. Student Am. Inst. Mus. Studies, 1969, So. Meth. U., 1970-71, U. Tex., 1971-74, Mich. State U., 1976. Asst. adminstr. Dallas County Dental Soc., 1974-78; account supr. Helen Holmes and Assocs. Pub. Relations, Dallas, 1978-80; pub. relations dir. GSD&M Advt., Austin, 1980-82; pub. relations exec. Ruder Finn & Rotman, Los Angeles, 1982—. Active pub. broadcasting, Mus. Contemporary Art; co-founder renaissance mus. groups. Recipient Internat. Coll. Dentists Journalism Competition award, 1977. Mem. Pub. Relations Soc. Am., Am. Soc. Assn. Execs. Democrat. Methodist. Contbr. various publs. Office: Ruder Finn & Rotman 3345 Wilshire Blvd Suite 909 Los Angeles CA 90010

YOUNG, ROBERT ALTON, economist, educator; b. Minden, Nebr., Sept. 2, 1931; s. Alton and Frances Boardman (Jones) Y.; m. Lynn Laree Hamberger, Aug. 30, 1958; children—Wesley E., Douglas A., Brian, Kathryn E., Kristiana M. B.S. in Agr., U.Calif-Davis, 1954; Ph.D. in Agrl. Econs., Mich. State U., 1963. Research assoc. Mich. State U., 1961-63; asst. prof., then assoc. prof. U. Ariz., 1963-68; research assoc. Resources for the Future, Washington, 1968-70; prof. econs. Colo. State U., Ft. Collins, 1970—; cons. Natural Resource Econs. Served to lt. U.S. Army, 1954-56. Fulbright-Hayes sr. research fellow, N.Z., 1976; recipient research awards Western Agrl. Econ. Assn., 1966, 70, 82, Am. Agrl. Econs Assn., 1979. Mem. AAAS, Western Agrl. Econs. Assn. (pres. 1979-80), Am. Agrl. Econs. Assn., Am. Econs. Assn., Am. Water Resources Assn. Unitarian-Universalist. Contbr. articles to profl. jours. Home: 1601 Sheely Dr Fort Collins CO 80526 Office: Dept Econs Colo State U Fort Collins CO 80523

YOUNG, ROGER WAYNE, chamber of commerce executive; b. Carrington, N.D., Feb. 23, 1942; s. August and Alma Y.; m. Carol Rae Hansen, May 11, 1968; children—Steven, Patricia. B.S., N.D. State U., Fargo, 1964. Cert. C. of C. exec. Dept. mgr. pub. relations and govtl. affairs Rochester (Minn.) Area C. of C., 1966-69; exec. v.p. Moorhead (Minn.) Area C. of C., 1969-75, Great Falls (Mont.) Area C. of C., 1975—. Served with AUS, 1964-66. Mem. Am. C. of C. Execs. (dir. 1980—), Minn. C. of C. Execs. (pres. 1973), Mont. Assn. C. of C. Execs. (pres. 1977). Republican. Lutheran.

YOUNG, ROLAND HESEIK, design cons., art dir.; b. San Francisco, Apr. 15, 1938; s. Gene Wah and Lena See (Lum) Y.; B.A., Art Center Sch.; student Calif. Coll. Arts and Crafts, 1956, Chounard Art Inst., 1957; m. Kathi Sawyer, Mar. 30, 1980; children—Dirk, Ari, Dov. Jr. art dir. Fuller, Smith & Ross Systems Devel. Corp., 1961-62; free-lance photographer, 1964-70; cons. art dir.; art dir. Capitol Records, 1965-70, A & M. Records, Inc., Hollywood, Calif., 1971-80; design cons. Alfa Records, Inc. (Japan and U.S.), Qwest Records, Inc. (Quincy Jones, U.S.A.), Los Angeles County Mus. of Art; guest lectr. U. Calif., Santa Barbara, UCLA, Whittier Coll., Calif. Inst. Arts, Calif. State U., Long Beach; exhbns. photography and illustration Am. Inst. Graphic Arts. Recipient various awards. Mem. Am. Inst. Graphic Arts, Nat. Acad. Rec. Arts and Scis. Democrat. Jewish. Home: Home and Office: Encino CA 91316

YOUNG, ROY ROBERT, JR., bank official; b. Tucson, Oct. 16, 1944; s. Roy Robert and Jean (Maddox) Y.; m. Marilyn McVey, Sept. 6, 1969 (div.); children—Meredith, Christopher. B.S., No. Ariz. U., 1971. With Valley Nat. Bank of Ariz., Phoenix, 1971-77, 81—, comml. and agrl. loan officer, 1981—; with Charter Bank of London, 1977-78, Nev. State Bank, 1978-81; tchr. Ariz. Western Coll. Chmn. legis. com. Yuma C. of C.; mem. Yuma Planning and Zoning Commn., Yuma County Fair Commn. Served in U.S. Army, 1964-68. Recipient Var Dee's award United Way. Republican. Clubs: Yuma Kiwanis, Elks, Masons. Office: 100 W Main St Yuma AZ 85364

YOUNG, RUSSEL RAY, safety professional, insurance executive; b. Portland, Oreg., Dec. 14, 1934; s. Walton Meyers and Charlotte Francis (Bottemiller) Y.; m. Barbara Jean Koonce, Mar. 24, 1956; children—Russel Ray, Cheryl Lynne. B.S. in Mgmt., Golden Gate U., 1974. Cert. safety profl. Bd. Cert. Safety Profls. Commd. officer U.S. Air Force, 1954, advanced through grades to maj., 1966; transport pilot U.S. and Orient, 1955-61; acad. instr. aircraft maintenance, 1961-63; aircraft instrument pilot instr., 1963-65; aircraft comdr., Vietnam, 1965-66; chief command post European Hdqrs. Command and Control Ctr., 1966-70; chief flight safety br. Mather AFB, Calif., 1970-74, ret., 1974; loss control rep. Continental Ins. Co., Sacramento, Calif., 1974-76, loss control mgr., 1976-79; loss control mgr. Mission Ins. Co., Sacramento, 1979—. Decorated Bronze Star, D.F.C., Air medal with 8 clusters, Air Force Commendation medal with cluster, Meritorious Service medal, Air Force Expeditionary medal, Republic of Vietnam Service medal. Mem. Am. Soc. Safety Engrs. (chpt. v.p.), Exptl. Aircraft Assn. Home: Roseville CA 95678 Office: 655 University Ave Suite 100 Sacramento CA 95825

YOUNG, SHARON O'NAN, psychologist; b. Long Beach, Calif., Oct. 26, 1944; d. Elmo Erville and Maxine Gan (Roper) Y. B.A., Kans. U., Lawrence, 1965; M.A. tchrs. coll. Columbia U., 1970; Ph.D., So. Ill. U., Carbondale, 1974. Psychology intern Pa. State U., State College, 1967-69; psychologist HEW, Rockland, Md., 1969-70; psychologist counseling and placement ctr. So. Ill. U., Carbondale, 1970-73; psychologist counseling ctr. U. Va., Charlottesville, 1973-74; psychologist counseling and psychol. services U. Calif.-San Diego, 1975-78; psychologist Sharon Young Ph.D. and Assocs., La Jolla, Calif., 1978—; lectr. women's studies San Diego State U. Mem. Am. Psychol. Assn., Assn. Women in Psychology. Home: 1430 Felton St San Diego CA 92102 Office: 1129 Torrey Pines Rd Suite 8 La Jolla CA 92037

YOUNG, STEPHEN HENRY, educational administrator; b. Seattle, May 9, 1941; s. Richard T. and Frances F. (Finch) Y.; m. Lila M. Hagen, July 2, 1971; children—Dana, Melainee. B.A., U. Calif.-Riverside, 1963; M.A. Calif. State U.-Fresno, 1975. Cert. tchr., supr., Calif. Dept. mgr. Sears Roebuck & Co., San Bernardino, Calif., 1964-67; tchr. Terrace Sch., Cecil Ave Sch., Delano, Calif., 1969-75; sch. adminstr. Kern Ave. Sch., McFarland, Calif., 1975-77; prin. E.V. Cain School, Auburn, Calif., 1977—. Served with USAR, 1963-69. Mem. Calif. Tchrs. Assn., Assn. Supervision and Curriculum Devel., Nat. Soc. Study Edn., Assn. Calif. Sch. Adminstrs., Calif. Capital Aquatics (dir., past pres.). Club: Lions. Office: 150 Palm Ave Auburn CA 95603

YOUNG, WAYNE ROBERT, educator, coach; b. Westwood, Calif., June 1, 1952; s. Guard LeRoy and Christal Jane (Lister) Y. B.A., Brigham Young U., 1975; M.A., Pa. State U., 1983; m. Carol Broadhead, June 18, 1975; children—Jessica, Guard, Britney, Heather. Mem. faculty Brigham Young U., Provo, Utah, 1979—, gymnastics coach, 1977—. Mem. Nat. Judges Assn., Nat. Coll. Athletic Assn. (rules com., chmn. gymnastics com.), U.S. Gymnastics Fedn. (dir., men's program com.). Mormon. Home: 1128 E 435 N Orem UT 84057 Office: 229 Smith Field House Brigham Young Univ Provo UT 84602

YOUNG, YEE-WAH, interior designer; b. Hong Kong, Aug. 8, 1943, came to U.S. 1968; d. Kan Kowk; m. Jerry Shiu, June 23, 1969; 1 dau. Garmen. B.S. equivalent Hackney Hosp. Sch. Nursing, London, 1964; diploma, Inchbald Sch. Design, London, 1967; cert. Rudolph Schaeffer Sch. Design, San Francisco, 1969. R.N., London, 1965-66; profl. model and actress, 1966 , represented interior designer Graham Design Inc., London, 1966-68; sr. designer Duval Ltd., Hong Kong, 1969; designer W & J Sloane, San Francisco, 1970-78; owner, interior designer Yee-Wah Young Interiors, San Francisco and Oakland, Calif., 1970—. Mem. Am. Soc. Interior Designers (profl.), Internat. Soc. Interior Designers. Contbr. articles to design jours; work featured in House Beautiful, Better Homes and Gardens, Oakland Tribune, Asian Week. Home: 600 Prospect Ave Oakland CA 94610 Office: Yee-Wah Young Interiors 297C Kansans St San Francisco CA 94103

YOUNGBLOOD, RONALD FRED, theology educator, clergyman; b. Chgo., Aug. 10, 1931; s. William and Ethel (Arenz) Y.; m. Carolyn June Johnson, Aug. 16, 1952; children—Glenn Stuart, Wendy Sue. B.A. with highest honors, Valparaiso U., 1952; B.D. summa cum laude, Fuller Theol. Sem., 1955; Ph.D., Dropsie Coll., 1961; postgrad. NYU, 1966. Ordained to ministry Am. Baptist Ch., 1958. Prof. O.T., Bethel Theol. Sem., St. Paul, 1961-78; assoc. dean, prof. O.T., Wheaton (Ill.) Coll., 1978-80, dean, 1980-81; prof. O.T. and Semitic langs. Trinity Evang. Div. Sch., Deerfield, Ill., 1981-82; prof. O.T. and Hebrew, Bethel Sem. West, San Diego, 1982—; lectr., cons. in field. Owen D. Young fellow in Religion, Gen. Electric Corp., 1959-61; Hebrew Union Coll. fellow in archaeology, 1967-68. Mem. Evang. Theol. Soc., Soc. Bibl. Lit., Near East Archaeol. Soc. Republican. Author: Great Themes of the Old Testament, 1968; The Heart of the Old Testament, 1971; Special Day Sermons, 1973; Faith of Our Fathers, 1976; How It All Began, 1980; The Living and Active Word of God, 1982; Exodus, 1983. Office: Bethel Seminary West 4747 College Ave San Diego CA 92115

YOUNGDAHL, PAUL FREDERICK, mech. engr.; b. Brockway, Pa., Oct. 8, 1921; s. Harry Ludwig and Esther Marie (Carlson) Y.; student Pa. State U., 1938-40; B.S.E., U. Mich., 1942, M.S.E., 1949, Ph.D., 1962; m. Elinor Louise Jensen, Nov. 27, 1943; children—Mark Erik, Marcia Linnea, Melinda Louise. Indsl. and devel. engr. duPont, Bridgeport, Conn., 1942-43, Carneys Point, N.J., 1946-48; dir. research Mech. Handling Systems, Detroit, 1953-62; prof. U. Mich., Ann Arbor, 1962-74; cons. mech. engr., Palo Alto, Calif., 1974—; dir. Liquid Drive Corp., Holly, Mich. Served as officer USNR, 1943-46. Mem. Mich. Soc. Profl. Engrs., Nat. Soc. Profl. Engrs., ASME, Am. Soc. Engring. Edn., Mich. Assn. Professions, Sigma Xi, Tau Beta Pi, Phi Kappa Phi, Pi Tau Sigma. Methodist. Contbr. articles to profl. jours. Address: 501 Forest St 1002 Palo Alto CA 94301

YOUNGLOVE, RUTH ANN, watercolor painter; b. Chgo., Feb. 14, 1909; d. Roy Sylvander and Mary Ella (Peters) Y.; m. Benjamin Rhees Loxley, Mar. 8, 1935; 1 dau., Margaret Ann. B.A. in Edn., UCLA, 1932; pvt. studies with Orrin A. White and Marion Wachtel. Freelance watercolorist, block printer; exhibited one-woman shows. Named Red Cross Vol. of Yr., 1961. Mem. Nat. Watercolor Soc., Am. Watercolor Soc., Laguna Beach Art Assn., Pasadena Soc. Artists, Gamma Phi Beta. Republican. Presbyterian. Club: Mr. & Mrs. Address: 1180 Yocum St Pasadena CA 91103

YOUNGQUIST, TED NOWAK, mining engr.; b. Stockton, Calif., Sept. 5, 1947; s. Herbert John and May A. (Nowak) Y; student public schs., Stockton; m. Lillie Ellen Younquist, Jan. 16, 1967; children—Philip, Thad, Leif. Lic. state safety instr. Operator own mines, Calif., 1970—; miner El Dorado Limestone, Shingle Springs, Calif., 1970; foreman Alhambra Atlanta Gold Mines, El Dorado County, Calif., 1971, Am. Hill Mine, Placer County, Calif., 1974; cons. engr. French Corral Mine, Nevada County, Calif., 1974; core drilling engr. Mine Rite Corp., El Dorado, Calif., 1974; cons. engr., assayer Manzinita Mine, El Dorado County, 1974; cons. engr. Trail Claim Mine, El Dorado, 1974—; engr. Sergeant Jacobs Placer Mines, Nevada County, 1975; cons. engr. Pease Mining Co., 1976, Horseshoe Bar Mining Co., 1976-77, Glacier King Uranium Mine, Carson City, Nev., 1978, Rolfe Ranches, Coulterville, Calif., 1979, Troy Gold Industries, 1979, Superior Extension Mine, Placerville, Calif., 1980, Relief Silver mine, Asarco County, Nev., 1980; cons. Teritary, Inc., 1977—, Benchmark Mining, Bishop, Calif., 1978—; owner, operator Tungo Mine, El Dorado County, 1977—; owner Houston Mining & Resources, 1979—; cons. Bentley Internat., Liberia, 1980; owner Youngquist Assaying, Georgetown, Calif., 1980—; Calif. safety instr., 1978—. Mem. Dem. Central Com., 1972-73. Mem. AIME, ASME, Constrn. Specifications Inst. Liberian Fellowship of Mining Engrs. Lodge: Masons. Address: Star Route Georgetown CA 95634

YOUNGS, JOHN WILLIAM THEODORE, JR., historian; b. Columbus, Ohio, Feb. 18, 1941; s. John William Theodore and Marguerite Davenport (Strong) Y.; B.A., Harvard U., 1963; Ph.D., U. Calif.-Berkeley 1970; m. Linda Miller, June 24, 1967; children—John William Theodore, Hope Eleanor. Asst. prof. history Kenyon Coll., Gambier, Ohio, 1970-72; asst. prof. Eastern Wash. U., Cheney, 1972-76, assoc. prof., 1976-80, prof., 1980—; vis. asst. prof. U. Wash., 1974. Am. Philos. Soc. grantee, 1973; Nat. Endowment Humanities fellow, 1979-80; trustee Wash. Commn. for Humanities, 1980—. Mem. Am. Hist. Assn., Orgn. Am. Historians, Western Hist. Assn., Soc. History of Edn., Am. Soc. Ch. History. Author: God's Messengers: Religious Leadership in Colonial New England, 1700-1750 (Brewer prize Am. Soc. Ch. History), 1976; American Realities: Historical Episodes from the First Settlements to the Present, 2 vols., 1981; Eleanor Roosevelt, 1984; editor Pacific N.W. Forum, 1976—. Home: 10014 SE 16th St Bellevue WA 98004 Office: Dept History Eastern Wash U Cheney WA 99004

YOUNGSTRUM, DAVID MANSFIELD, actuary; b. Racine, Wis., Sept. 2, 1942; s. George Gustav and Marion Eloise (Lundberg) Y.; B.S. in Stats., Colo. State U., 1964; M.S. in Bus. Adminstrn., U. No. Colo., 1980. Cert. fin. examiner. Asst. actuary United Am. Life Ins. Co., Denver, 1964-73; asst. treas. United Am. Securities, Denver, 1973; chief actuary Colo. Div. Ins., Denver, 1973—. Recipient award Am. Math. Assn., 1964. Fellow Life Mgmt. Inst.; mem. Internat. Actuarial Assn., Am. Statis. Assn., Denver Soc. Security Analysts, Am. Pub. Health Assn., Soc. Fin. Examiners, Mensa, Nat. Eagle Scout Assn. Republican. Presbyterian. Clubs: Denver Execs., Denver Actuarial, Collie of Colo. Office: Div Ins State of Colo 201 E Colfax Ave Room 106 Denver CO 80203

YOUNGSWICK, FRED DONALD, podiatrist; b. N.Y.C., Oct. 28, 1949; s. Sol and Sylvia (Ondelman) Y.; student U. Okla., 1967-70; B.A., Richmond Coll., City U. N.Y., 1971; B.S., Calif. Coll. Podiatric Medicine, 1973, Dr. Podiatric Medicine, 1975; m. Catherine Kal Haas, Jan. 24, 1971; children—Robyn Brook, Ashley Haas. Intern, Calif. Podiatry Hosp., San Francisco, 1975-76, surg. resident, 1976-77; assoc. prof. dept. podiatric surgery Calif. Coll. Podiatric Medicine, San Francisco, 1978, bd. dirs., 1980—, dir. residency tng., 1978—, coordinator clin. tng., 1980—; pres. Cow Hollow Podiatry Group, Inc., San Francisco, 1980; chief of staff Calif. Podiatry Hosp., 1980—. Diplomate Am. Bd. Podiatric Surgery. Fellow Am. Coll. Foot Surgeons; mem. San Francisco/San Mateo Counties Podiatry Soc. (pres. 1979-81), Calif. Podiatry Assn., Am. Podiatry Assn., Calif. Podiatric Med. Assn. (dir.). Office: 2001 Union St San Francisco CA 94123

YOUNNEL, CREIGHTON CHARLES, advertising executive; b. Stockton, Calif., Jan. 10, 1948; s. George Michael and Gilda (Cima) Y.; m. Janet Lee Hench, Dec. 6, 1980. B.F.A., Calif. Coll. Arts and Crafts, 1972. Art dir. Bozell & Jacobs, Phoenix, 1972-74; owner, pres., art dir. Creighton Younnel Advt. Inc., Stockton, Calif., 1975—. Mem. Stockton C. of C., Full Gospel Businessmen's Fellowship. Mem. Sacramento Art Dirs. Club. Republican. Clubs: Yosemite, Comml. Exchange (Stockton). Office: 2502 Beverly Pl Stockton CA 95204

YOUNT, DAVID EUGENE, physicist; b. Prescott, Ariz., June 5, 1935; s. Robert Ephram and Jeannette Francis (Judson) Y.; B.S. in Physics, Calif. Inst. Tech., 1957; M.S. in Physics, Stanford U., 1959, Ph.D. in Physics, 1963; m. Christel Marlene Notz, Feb. 22, 1975; children—Laura Christine, Gregory Gordon, Steffen Jurgen Robert, Sonja Kate Jeannette. Instr., Princeton U., 1962-63, asst. prof. physics, 1963-64, Minn. Mining and Mfg. postdoctoral fellow, 1963; NSF postdoctoral fellow U. Paris, Orsay, France, 1964-65; research asso. Stanford Linear Accelerator Center, U. Stanford, 1965-69; asso. prof. U. Hawaii, 1969-73, prof., 1973—, chmn. dept. physics and astronomy, 1979—. Mem. Am. Phys. Soc., Undersea Med. Soc., Am. Chem. Soc., U.S. Tennis Assn., Sigma Xi. Republican. Lutheran. Research, numerous articles in elementary particle physics, undersea medicine, and acoustics, 1962—. Home: 5468 Opihi St Honolulu HI 96821 Office: 2505 Correa Rd Honolulu HI 96822

YOUNT, (GEORGE) STUART, paper converting company executive; b. Los Angeles, Mar. 4, 1949; s. Stanley G. and Agnes (Pratt) Y.; m. Geraldine Marie Silvio, July 18, 1970; children—Trisha Marie, Christopher George. Student U. Nev., 1968-69, UCLA, 1972, Calif. Inst. Tech., 1976, Harvard Grad. Sch. Bus., 1982-83. Salesman, Silverwood Co., 1968; with Fortifiber Corp., Los Angeles, 1969—, asst. to v.p. sales, 1969-72, asst. to v.p., 1972, asst. treas., 1973-74, treas. and v.p. adminstrn., 1974—, sec., 1975—; also dir.; dir. Stanwall Corp.; dir., past pres. Hollister Ranch Cattle Coop. Mem. Republican Assocs. Mem. Flexible Packaging Assn., Am. Paper Inst. Clubs: Rotary #5, Jonathan (Los Angeles); San Marino City. Office: Fortifiber Corp 4489 Bandini Blvd Los Angeles CA 90023

YOUNT, STANLEY GEORGE, paper co. exec.; b. Ketchum, Idaho, Feb. 15, 1903; s. George and Cansada (Smith) Y.; student U. Nev., 1924; m. Agnes Pratt, Feb. 17, 1944; children—Ann E., George S. Div. sales mgr. Crown Zellerbach Corp., 1926-40; pres. Southland Paper Converting Co., 1940-56; pres. Fortifiber Corp. and affiliates, Los Angeles, 1956-77, chmn., 1977—, also dir.; dir. Stanwall Corp. Served with U.S. Army, World War I; AEF in France. Mem. Nat. Flexible Packaging Assn. (pres. Indsl. Bag and Cover div. 1954-56), Am. Paper Inst. (spl. packaging and indsl. div.). Mason (Shriner). Clubs: Jonathan (Los Angeles), San Gabriel Country, Rotary. Home: 2260 Robles Ave San Marino CA 91108 Office: United Calif Bank Bldg Suite 4820 707 Wilshire Blvd Los Angeles CA 90017

YOUSEF, FATHI SALAAMA, communications educator, management consultant; b. Cairo, Jan. 2, 1934; came to U.S., 1968, naturalized, 1973; s. Salaama and Rose (Tadros) Y.; m. Caroline Droge, Nov. 27, 1969. B.A., Ain Shams U., Cairo, 1955; M.A., U. Minn., 1970, Ph.D., 1972. Service ctr. supt. Shell Oil Co., Cairo, 1955-61; indsl., mgmt. tng. instr. ARAMCO, Dhahran, Saudi Arabia, 1961-68; teaching assoc. U.-Minn., Mpls., 1968-72; speech communication prof. Calif. State U.-Long Beach, 1972—; with ARAMCO, 1978-80. Grantee NSF, 1981, 82, 83. Mem. Am. Mgmt. Assns., Internat. Communication Assn., Am. Soc. Tng. and Devel., Soc. Cross-Cultural Research, Speech Communication Assn., Communication Assn. Pacific. Democrat. Co-author: An Introduction to Intercultural Communication, 1975; contbr. articles to profl. jours. Office: Dept Speech Communication Calif State U Long Beach CA 90840

YOUSSEFZADEH, EMIL, research engr.; b. Tehran, Iran, Oct. 24, 1952; s. Alber and Valentine (Youssefmir) Y.; B.S.C.E., B.S.E.E., Catholic U. Am., 1974; M.S., Stanford U., 1975, Ed.D., 1976. Research assoc. Stanford U., 1975; chief satellite engr. Nat. Iranian Radio and TV, Tehran, 1976; satellite research engr. Hughes Aircraft Co., El Segundo, Calif., 1979-82; pres. Satellite Tech. Mgmt., Inc., Los Angeles, 1982—. Mem. IEEE, ASCE, Sigma Xi, Tau Beta Pi. Jewish. Home: 10611 Ahton Ave Unit 3 Los Angeles CA 90024 Office: 10100 Santa Monica Blvd Suite 1020 Los Angeles CA 90067

YOWELL, WILMA LEE, advt. exec.; b. Los Angeles, Dec. 25, 1944; d. W.O. and W.L. Y.; A.A., Santa Monica Coll., 1966; postgrad., UCLA, 1968. Prodn. coordinator Needham, Harper & Steers, Los Angeles, 1967-68, research asst., 1968-74, media asst., 1974-76, v.p., gen. mgr. recruitment advt., 1980-83; v.p. Deutsch, Shea & Evans, Inc., subs Foote, Cone & Belding, Los Angeles, 1983—; dist. sales mgr. Nat. Fedn. Ind. Bus., San Francisco, 1976-77; client service mgr. N. Am. Creative, Los Angeles, 1977-78; v.p., chief fin. officer F.K. Hubbard & Assos., Inc., Hermosa Beach, Calif., 1978-80. Home: 9643 Charleville Blvd Beverly Hills CA 90212 Office: 3727 W 6th St Los Angeles CA 90020

YU, DAVID U. L., cons. engr., physicist, corp. exec.; b. Hong Kong, Aug. 27, 1940; came to U.S., 1959, naturalized, 1968; s. Hsien Liang and Wei Ching (Leung) Y.; B.S., Seattle Pacific U., 1961; Ph.D., U. Wash., 1964; m. Carolyn Mattson, Dec. 27, 1965; children—Christine, Jonathan. Research asso. prof. Stanford U., 1964-66, U. Surrey, London, 1966-67; asso. prof. Seattle Pacific U., 1967-73, U. Wash., 1968-72; mgr. Computer Scis. Corp., Richland, Wash. and El Segundo, Calif., 1973-75; exec. v.p., dir. Basic Technology Inc., Manhattan Beach, Calif., 1975—. Ford Found. fellow, 1962-63; NASA fellow Jet Propulsion Lab., 1969-70; NSF fellow Ill. Inst. Tech., 1972; registered profl. engr., Calif. Mem. Am. Phys. Soc., ASME. Author tech. reports, sci. articles. Home: 1912 MacArthur St San Pedro CA 90732 Office: 806 Manhattan Beach Blvd Manhattan Beach CA 90266

YU, DONALD ROBERT, consumer electronics products executive; b. Shanghai, China, Sept. 12, 1937; came to U.S., 1955, naturalized, 1958; s. Robert and Lillian (King) Y.; m. Jean King, Nov. 25, 1963; children—David Richard, Jennifer Katherine. A.A., Menlo Coll., Menlo Park, Calif., 1959, B.S., 1961; postgrad. Hastings Coll. Law, 1961. With consumer products div. Sharp Electronics Corp., 1968-72; pres., chief exec. officer Sheen Industries Ltd., San Rafael, Calif., 1973-75; mem. Hutchison Internat. Ltd., Hong Kong, 1973-75; pres., chmn., chief exec. office Elint Semiconductors, Inc., Santa Clara, Calif., 1976—; pres., founder U.S. Games Corp., Santa Clara, 1980-82; chmn., chief exec. officer Torgo Tech. Corp., Santa Clara, 1982—; dir. Westin Internat. Corp. Office: 3150 Coronado Dr Santa Clara CA 95051

YU, KAR YUK, environ. engr.; b. Canton, China, Sept. 19, 1948; s. Wah Shek and Sui Fah (Ng) Y.; B.S., U. Calif., 1972; M.S., U. Wis., 1974; Ph.D., U. So. Calif., 1979; m. Cecilia L. Yu, May 12, 1974. Sr. environ. engr. Jacobs Co., Pasadena, Calif., 1978; mem. tech. staff TRW, Inc., Redondo Beach, Calif., 1978-80, project engr., 1980—, head tech. assessment sect., 1981—. Mem. Am. Water Works Assn., Water Pollution Control Fedn., Sigma Xi. Office: One Space Park TRW MS R4-1136 Redondo Beach CA 90078

YUEN, MOON HING, engineering firm executive, consultant; b. Canton, China, Sept. 10, 1922; came to U.S., 1939, naturalized, 1939; s. Yip S. and Oi (Chan) Y.; m. Ruby E. Fong, May 24, 1947; children—Carter, Bonnie, Breene. B.E.E. Healds Engring. Coll., 1948; bus. mgmt. cert. U. Calif. Extension, San Francisco, 1970. Cert. engr., 22 states, Can. Engr., asst. chief engr. Bechtel, Corp., San Francisco, 1948-65, project engr., 1975; pres., owner Yuen-Fenner, Inc., 1975-81, chmn. bd., 1981—; cons. power systems. Trustee Chinese Affirmative Action, 1982-84. Served with U.S. Army, 1942-46; Decorated Purple Heart. Mem. IEEE, Instrument Soc. Am., Chinese Am. Inst. Engrs., Scientists. Democrat. Baptist. Club: YMCA, San Francisco. Contr. articles to profl. jours.; patentee In-Line Motor Heating Circuit, 1973. Office: 1485 Bayshore Blvd Suite 328 San Francisco CA 94114

YUEN, WALTER WAH, mechanical engineering educator, cons.; b. China, Nov. 1, 1949; s. Wai and Diane S. (Pang) Y.; m. So-Le Hom, Aug. 1975; children—Rayna, Tritia. Ph.D., U. Calif.-Berkeley, 1977. Devel. engr. Gen. Electric Co., San Jose, Calif., 1977-78; asst. prof. U. Calif.-Santa Barbara, 1978-81, assoc. prof. mech. engring., 1981—. Mem. ASME, AIAA, Soc. Automotive Engrs. (R.A. Teetor award 1980), Am. Soc. Engring. Edn. Contbr. publs. to tech. jours. Office: Dept Mech Engring U Calif Santa Barbara CA 93106

YUNT, MARY LENA, union ofcl.; b. Monticello, Ky., Apr. 3, 1930; d. Millard Filmore and Minnie Pearl (Wright) Smith; student Eastern Ky. State Coll., 1947, U. Calif.-Irvine, 1971, UCLA Extension, 1972, El Camino Jr. Coll., 1974, Fullerton Jr. Coll., 1975; div.; children—A. James, Debra L., Terry L. Office mgr. Teamsters Local 180, operating engr. Engrs. #501, 1964-66; office mgr. Communications Workers Am. #9510, 1966-72; state coordinator Calif. Labor Fedn., AFL-CIO, San Francisco, 1972-74; state labor coordinator for Senator Alan Cranston Campaign, 1972-74; sec.-treas. Orange County Central Labor Council, Orange, Calif., 1979—. Bd. dirs. United Way, 1979—, Pvt. Industry Council, 1979—, Exploratory Learning Ctr., 1980—, Affordable Devel., 1980—, Orange County Indsl. Relations Research Assn., 1980—, Orange County Health Planning Council, 1981—, Turning Point, family counseling on drugs, alcohol abuse, 1981—; mem. labor com. of nat. disaster com. ARC, 1979—; mem. John Wayne Airport Master Plan Adv. Group, 1980—; chmn. accessibility subcom. Calif. Gov.'s Com. Employment of Handicapped, 1980—. Named Histadrut Labor Woman of Yr., 1980; Key Woman, Calif. Democratic Com., 1980; recipient cert. of appreciation City of Hope, 1980, U.S. Treasury Dept., 1979, U.S. Dept. Commerce, 1980; commendation Congressman Agustus Hawkins, 1972, Mayor of Los Angeles, 1972; commd. Ky. col., 1982. Mem. Am. Soc. Profl. Exec. Women. Democrat. Roman Catholic. Home: 27831 Calle Valdes Mission Viejo CA 92692 Office: 1124 W Chapman Ave Orange CA 92668

ZABALA, THOMAS MICHAEL, architect; b. Boise, Idaho, Feb. 7, 1946; s. Thomas Floyd and Conchita Juanita (Arostegui) Z.; m. Jayne Abbe McMillen, Sept. 15, 1972; 1 son, Jeffrey Mark. B.Arch., U. Oreg., 1969. Draftsman, N.W. Illustrations, 1967-68; architect intern Hamill/Shaw Assocs., 1968-69, Cline/Smull/Hamill/Shaw Assocs., 1969-72; architect Cline/Smull/Hamill Assocs., 1972-73; prin./ptnr. Zabala-Giltzow-Albanese, Boise, 1973—. Chmn., Boise City Design Rev. Com., 1976-80; mem. Citizens Adv. Com. on Downtown Renewal, 1979-80; mem. Idaho Hist. Preservation Council. Served with U.S. Army, 1969-76. Mem. AIA (merit award 1978, citation award 1982, chmn. design awards com. 1976, 78, 82, mem. legis. law com. 1973—), Nat. Council Archtl. Registration Bds. Democrat. Roman Catholic. Mem. editorial adv. bd. Symposia Mag., 1981-83, N.W. Architecture Mag., 1982—. Home: 3974 Oak Park Pl Boise ID 83703 Office: 110 W 31st St Boise ID 83704

ZABINSKY, JOSEPH MARVIN, aeronautical engineer; b. N.Y.C., July 31, 1924; s. Simon and Ruth (Primost) Z.; m. Helen Kava, Oct. 30; children—Steven, Zachary, Zelda. B.S., U. Ill., 1949, M.S., 1950. Registered profl. engr., Wash. Project aerodynamicist Bell Aircraft Co., Buffalo, 1950-61; prin. engr. Boeing Comml. Airplane Co., Seattle, 1961—. Served with U.S. Army, 1943-45. Decorated Air medal. Assoc. fellow Am. Inst. Aero. Scis. Contbr. articles to profl. jours.

ZACHAU, DENISE EILEEN, optometrist; b. Phoenix, Oct. 30, 1958; d. George Vernon and Nora Margaret (Lemas) Z. Student Colo. State U., 1976-78, Met. State Coll., Denver, 1977; O.D. magna cum laude, So. Calif. Coll. Optometry, 1982. Lic. optometrist, Colo. Gen. optometric and office asst., Los Alamitos, Calif., 1981-82; optometrist Seventh-Day Adventist Clinic-Eye Clinic, Tamuning, Guam, 1982; optometrist Lakewood (Colo.) Vision Clinic, 1982—. Mem. bus. and membership council, mem. membership involvement task force Lakewood C. of C. Colo. State U. Presdl. scholar, 1978. Mem. Am. Optometric Assn., Colo. Optometric Assn., Women Bus. Owners Assn., AAUW, Gold Key (pres. chpt. 1981-82), Alpha Lambda Delta, Phi Kappa Phi, Beta Sigma Kappa. Club: Lakewood Bus. and Profl. Women's (chpt. Young Career Woman 1983, sec. 1983-84). Home: 12484 W Nevada Pl #214 Lakewood CO 80228 Office: 2020 Wadsworth Blvd Suite 9 Lakewood CO 80215

ZACHRISSON, CARL UDDO, JR., political scientist, educator; b. San Francisco, Dec. 4, 1940; s. Carl Uddo and Erma Christiana (Luce) Z.; m. Adele Lee Hall, Dec. 30, 1971; children—Carl Frederick, Christopher Dawes. B.A., Stanford U., 1962; Lic. es Sci. Politiques U. Geneva (Switzerland) Grad. Inst. Internat. Studies; D.Phil., Oxford U. (Eng.), 1972. Instr. to asst. prof. polit. studies Pitzer Coll., Claremont, Calif., 1967-74; assoc. prof. internat. relations Pomona Coll., Claremont, 1974-81; asst. to vis. prof. govt. and internat. relations Claremont Grad. Sch., 1981—; dir. West Coast Region, Inst. Internat. Relations, San Francisco, 1983—; pres. Internat. Studies Assocs. Inc., 1981-83; lectr. USIS, West Africa, 1972; dir. Edn. Abroad, Pomona and Scripps Colls., 1973-81; v.p. edn. So. Calif. div. UN Assn., 1976-79; bd. dirs. Council Internat. Ednl. Exchange, 1978-81, So. Calif. Global Edn. task force, 1978-81; rapporteur Panel Internat. Exchanges, Pres.'s Commn. Fgn. Lang. and Internat. Studies, 1979; treas. Calif. Council UN U., 1979-81; bd. dirs. Acad. World Studies, Am. Com. East-West Accord; mem. liaison com. Internat. Studies, Articulation Council of Calif. Trustee Town Sch. Boys. Mem. African Studies Assn., Am. Polit. Sci Assn., Am. Soc. Internat. Law, Nat. Assn. Fgn. Student Affairs, Soc. Internat. Edn., Tng. and Research, Soc. Internat. Devel. Republican. Episcopalian. Clubs: Bohemian, Oxford Union Soc. Office: Inst Internat Edn 312 Sutter St Suite 610 San Francisco CA 94108

ZADOROZNY, EDWARD ALEXANDER, design engr.; b. Pitts., Dec. 24, 1956; s. Edward and Helen Catherine (Kurtaneck) Z.; B.S. in Mech. Engring., U. Pitts., 1978. Design engr., space div. Rockwell Internat., Downey, Calif., 1978—, involved in research and devel. of Space Shuttles Columbia, Challenger, Discovery, and Atlantis, also teaching asst. for computer aided design 1980-82; research on advanced carbon-carbon composite material devel., 1981—, on advanced thermal protection systems devel., 1982—. Mem. AIAA (chpt. pres. 1977-78), Planetary Soc., Tau Beta Pi, Phi Eta Sigma, Pi Tau Sigma. Democrat. Orthodox Catholic. Researcher on design for artificial heart, 1975, on ground effects aircraft design, 1978. Home: 2444 Daphne Pl Apt 210 Fullerton CA 92633 Office: 12214 Lakewood Blvd Downey CA 90241

ZADRA, PETER J., highway patrol officer; b. Nyssa, Oreg., Jan. 30, 1931; s. Peter and Cathrine A. (Gallager) Z.; m. Darlene J. Mello, Dec. 8, 1952; children—Vicki, Sharon. San Jose State U. With Nev. Hwy. Patrol, Carson City, 1955—, now chief. Served with USMC, 1948-52. Mem. Internat. Assn. Chiefs Police. Clubs: Masons, Shriners. Office: Nevada Highway Patrol 555 Wright Way Carson City NV 89711

ZAEBST, FRED (LONIUS), biologist; b. Cleve., Aug. 17, 1935; s. Ivan R. and Vivian G. (Lonius) Z.; B.S. in Zoology, San Diego State U., 1961, M.S. in Physiology, 1964; postgrad. in physiology (NIH fellow) U. Ill., 1964-67; m. Shirley Jones, Oct. 26, 1979; children—Mark Louis, Julia Kay. Instr., San Diego State U., 1963-64, So. Ill. U., 1967-68; chief physiol. research, bioengring. lab. U.S. Air Force Acad., 1968-72; pres. Biotechnology Applications, Monument, Colo., 1972-75; instr., sci. coordinator Pikes Peak Community Coll., 1975—; cons. devel. biomed. devices, environ. impact, local cos. Mem. AAAS, Colo. Assn. Sci. Tchrs., Colo. Biology Consortium, Sigma Xi, Phi Sigma. Devel. physiol. monitoring devices for manned spacecraft program. Home: 205 N Murray Blvd Apt 205 Colorado Springs CO 80916 Office: 5675 S Academy Blvd Colorado Springs CO 80906

ZAH, PETERSON, American Indian tribal executive; b. Low Mountain, Ariz., Dec. 2, 1937; s. Henry and Mae (Multine) Z.; m. Rosalind Begay; children—Elaine, Eileen, Kiiyonnie. B.A., Ariz. State U. Journeyman carpenter Vocat. Edn. Dept., State of Ariz., Phoenix, 1963-64; constrn. estimator, design and constrn. dept. Navajo Tribe, Fort Defiance, Ariz., 1964-65; field coordinator VISTA Indian Tng. Ctr., Ariz. State U., Tempe, 1965-67; exec. dir. DNA People's Legal Services, Inc., Window Rock, Ariz., 1967—; now chmn. Navajo Tribal Council. Mem. Ariz. adv. com. U.S. Civil Rights Commn., 1983—; pres. Window Rock Sch. Bd., 1973—. Mem. Nat. Assn. Indian Legal Services. Democrat. Office: Office of Chairman PO Box 308 Window Rock Navajo Nation AZ 86515

ZAHLER, LEONARD R., lawyer, insurance company executive; b. Coimbra, Portugal, May 11, 1937; s. Karl Alfred and Sarah H. (Sandoval-Ramses) Z.; M.S., U. So. Calif., 1969; J.D., John Marshall Sch. Law, 1973; m. Jean A. Lowe, Oct. 18, 1978; children—Nichole Alexandra Sarah, Aaron L. Bar: Ill., Calif. Atty., Legal Defender's Office Cook County, Chgo.; individual practice law, Chgo., also Calif.; counsel Gt.-Western Life Ins. Co., Chgo.; now. pres. Zenith Ins. Consol., Calif. Recipient Legal Defender award and citation Cook County, 1974-75. Mem. ABA, Ill. Bar Assn., Calif. Bar Assn., Orange County Bar Assn., Am. Soc. Life Underwriters, Golden Key Soc. Life Underwriters. Republican. Jewish. Clubs: Lions (membership chmn. 1974, 79, 80); World Racquetball; Masons (San Francisco). Home: Apt 214 2945 Harding Ave Carlsbad CA 92008

ZAISER, SALLY SOLEMMA VANN (MRS. FOSTER E. ZAISER), retail book co. exec.; b. Birmingham, Ala., Jan. 18, 1917; d. Carl Waldo and Einnan (Herndon) Vann; student Birmingham-So. Coll., 1933-36, Akron Coll. Bus., 1937; m. Foster E. Zaiser, Nov. 11, 1939. Acct., A. Simionato, San Francisco, 1958-65; head acctg. dept. Richard T. Clarke Co., San Francisco, 1966; acct. John Howell-Books, San Francisco, 1967-72, sec., treas., 1972-83, dir., 1982—; sec. Great Eastern Mines, Inc., Albuquerque, 1969-81, dir., 1980—. Braille transcriber for ARC, Kansas City, Mo. 1941-45; vol. worker ARC Hosp. Program, São Paulo, Brazil, 1952. Mem. Book Club Calif., Calif. Hist. Soc., Soc. Lit. and Arts, Nat. Notary Assn., Theta Upsilon. Republican. Episcopalian. Club: Capitol Hill. Home: 355 Serrano Dr San Francisco CA 94132 Office: 434 Post St San Francisco CA 94102

ZAITZ, JOHN, underwriter; b. Los Angeles, Feb. 3, 1943; s. Albert Anthony and Emma (Augustin) Z.; m. Cathy Wirtz, Oct. 11, 1980; 1 son, John Edward. Claims supr. Auto Club of So. Calif., Los Angeles, 1969-71, regional underwriting mgr., 1971-75, underwriting mgr., 1975—. Served as lt., M.P., U.S. Army, 1966-69. C.P.C.U. Republican. Home: 2230 Old Creek Ln Fullerton CA 92631 Office: 2601 S Figueroa St Los Angeles CA 90004

ZAJAC, JOHN, semiconductor equipment co. exec.; b. N.Y.C., July 21, 1946; s. John Andrew and Catherine (Canepa) Z.; A.A.S., U. N.Y., 1966; B.E.E., U. Ky., 1968; m. Vera Barbagallo, Jan. 13, 1973. Project engr. B.C.D. Computing, N.Y.C., 1968-70; v.p. Beacon Systems, Commack, N.Y., 1970-73, E.T. Systems, Santa Clara, Calif., 1973-77; v.p. research and devel. Eaton Corp., Sunnyvale, Calif., 1977-81; founder U.S. Alcohol, San Jose, Calif., 1980, Cono Labs., Deer Park, N.Y., 1969, Materials Processing Corp., 1980, D.D.S. Supplies, San Jose, 1981; pres. Semitech, San Jose, 1981-83; mgr. advanced product div. Tegal Corp., Novato, Calif., 1983—. Patentee in field. Home: 1137 Angmar Ct San Jose CA 95121

ZALEWSKI, WOJCIECH, librarian; b. Gdynia, Poland, Mar. 20, 1937; came to U.S., 1968, naturalized, 1977; m. Atanazy and Malgorzata Ch. (Sentkowska) Z.; M.A., Catholic U. Lublin, 1965; lic. Bibl. scis., Bibl. Inst. Rome, 1967; Th.D., Gregorianum U., Rome, 1968; M.A. in Librarianship, San Jose State U., 1971; m. Rosemarie Böhm, Aug. 31, 1968; children—Barbara, Marcus. Librarian, curator Russian and East European collections Stanford U., 1971—; lectr. in bibliography, dept. Slavic lang. and lit. Stanford U., 1973—; chmn. Slavic and East European sect. Assn. Coll. and Research Libraries, ALA, 1980-81. Mem. AIA, Am. Assn. Advancement Slavic Studies, Polish Inst. Arts and Scis. Am. Author: Russian-English Dictionaries with Aids for Translators, 1981; ann. survey reference materials in Russian-Soviet area studies for Russian Rev., 1975—; (with Rimma Yolynska-Bogert) Czeskaw Mi Kosz, An International Biography, 1930-80, 1983. Home: 162 Highland Ave San Carlos CA 94070 Office: Stanford U Libraries Stanford CA 94305

ZALLEN, DENNIS MICHAEL, combustion and environmental engineer; b. East Chicago, Ind., Dec. 6, 1943; s. Stanley George and Ann (Kloac) Z.; B.S.M.E., Purdue U., 1965, M.S.M.E., 1967, Ph.D. (David Ross fellow), 1973; postgrad. So. Meth. U., 1968-69. m. Sallie-White Harvey, May 14, 1977. Research engr. Gen. Dynamics Corp., Ft. Worth, 1967-70; asst. project engr. Pratt & Whitney Aircraft, East Hartford, Conn., 1973-75; asst. prof. N.Mex. State U., Las Cruces, 1975-76; group leader Inst. Mining and Minerals Research, Ky. Center Energy Research, Lexington, 1977-78; mgr. energy systems devel. Ultrasystems, Inc., Energy and Environ. Research Corp., Santa Ana, Calif., 1978-80; sr. research engr. N.Mex. Engring. Research Inst., U. N.Mex., Albuquerque, 1980—; cons. on environ. instrumentation Dept. of Energy. Registered profl. engr., Calif. Mem. Combustion Inst., Air Pollution Control Assn., ASME, Am. Phys. Soc., AIAA, Nat. Fire Protection Assn., Sigma Pi Sigma, Pi Tau Sigma. Club: Albuquerque Off-Roadrunners (sec.). Contbr. articles to profl. jours. Patentee in field. Home: 14216 Turner Ct NE Albuquerque NM 87123 Office: New Mexico

ZALTA, EDWARD, otorhinolaryngologist; b. Houston, Mar. 2, 1930; s. Nouri Louis and Marie Zahde (Lizmi) Z.; B.S., Tulane U., 1952, M.D., 1956; m. Carolyn Mary Gordon, Oct. 8, 1971; 1 son, Ryan David; children by previous marriage—Nouri Allan, Lori Ann, Barry Thomas, Marci Louise. Intern, Brooke Army Hosp., San Antonio, 1956-57; resident in otolaryngology U.S. Army Hosp., Ft. Campbell, Ky., 1957-60; practice medicine specializing; in otolaryngology, Glendora, West Covina and San Dimas, Calif., 1960—; ENT cons. City of Hope Med. Center, 1961-76; mem. staff Foothill Presbyn.; chmn. bd., pres. Calif. Preferred Profls. chmn., founder, dir. San Gabriel Valley ENT Med. Group, Inc.; chmn. bd. MDM, Inc.; bd. dirs. Foothill Presbyn. Hosp.; chmn. bd. Glendora Med. Investment Co.; pres. Los Angeles Found. Community Service, Los Angeles Poison Info. Center; pres. So. Calif. Physicians Council, Inc., Calif. Preferred Profls., Inc., mem. exec. com. Calif. Polit. Action Com.; founder Inter-Hosp. Council Continuing Med. Edn.; mem. Physicians Adv. Com. 1984 Olympics. Pres. bd. govs. Glendora Unified Sch. Dist., 1965-71; mem. Calif. Cancer Adv. Council, 1967-71. Served to capt. M.C., AUS, 1957-60. Recipient medal of Merit, Internat. Order of St. Lazarus, 1981. Mem. AMA, Calif. Med. Assn. (ho. of dels.), Los Angeles County Med. Assn. (chmn. bd.), Am. Council Otorhinolaryngology, Am. Council Otolaryngology, Am. Acad. Otolaryngology, Head and Neck Surgery, Kappa Nu, Phi Delta Epsilon. Republican. Jewish. Clubs: Glendora County, Centurion, Sea Bluff Beach and Racquet. Contbr. articles to profl. jours. Home: 207 Whispering Oaks Glendora CA 91740 Office: 427 W Carroll Ave Glendora CA 91740

ZALUTSKY, MORTON HERMAN, lawyer; b. Schenectady, Mar. 8, 1935; s. Albert and Gertrude (Daffner) Z.; m. Audrey Englebardt, June 16, 1957; children—Jane, Diane, Samuel. B.A., Yale U., 1957; J.D., U. Chgo., 1960. Bar: Oreg. 1961. Clk. Oreg. Supreme Ct., 1960-61; assoc. Hart, Davidson, Veazie & Hanlon, 1961-63, Veatch & Lovett, 1963-64, Morrison, Bailey, Dunn, Cohen & Miller, 1964-69; prin. Morton H. Zalutsky, P.C., 1970-76, 79—; ptnr. Dahl, Zalutsky, Nichols & Hinson, 1977-79, Zalutsky & Klarquist, P.C., Portland, 1980—; instr. Portland State U., 1961-64, Northwestern Sch. Law, 1969-70; assoc. prof. U. Miami Law Sch.; lectr. Practicing Law Inst., 1971—, Oreg. State Bar Continuing Legal Edn. Program, 1970, Am. Law Inst.-Am. Bar Assn., 1973—, 34th, 37th N.Y.U. ann. insts. fed. taxation, So. Fed. Tax Inst., U. Miami Inst. Estate Planning, Southwestern Legal Found., numerous other profl. orgns. Mem. ABA (tax sect., com. on taxation, chmn. com. on continuing legal edn. and research 1978-79, coordinator spl. programs 1980—), Multnomah County Bar Assn., Oreg. State Bar, Oreg. Estate Planning Council. Jewish. Author: (with others) The Professional Corporation in Oregon, 1970, 82; contbg. author: The Dentist and the Law, 3d. edit. Contbr. to numerous publs. in field. Home: 3118 SW Fairmount Blvd Portland OR 97201 Office: 1099 SW Columbia St Suite 300 Portland OR 97201

ZAMONSKI, STANLEY WALTER, mus. curator; b. Shenandoah, Pa., Aug. 7, 1919; s. Stanley Walter and Cecilia (Baleshewski) Z.; student New Eng. Aircraft-Wentworth Inst., 1940-42, Mass. Inst. Tech., 1940-42, Georgetown U., 1943. Engring. draftsman Colo. Dept. Hwys., 1947-54; free-lance photographer-writer, Denver, 1954-70; prof. photojournalism Instituto Allende, San Miguel Allende, Mexico, 1970-72; engring. draftsman Denver Planning Dept., 1973-78; curator Buffalo Bill Meml. Mus., Golden, Colo., 1978—. Dep. sheriff Denver Posse Westerners. Served to 2d lt. USAAF, 1939-45. Decorated Air medal with two oak leaf clusters; recipient Braum award Denver Art Dirs. and Advt. Assn., 1959; named Colo. Press Photographer of Year, 1965, 66, 67. Mem. Polish Am. Hist. Assn., Nat. Historic Assn., Am. Assn. State and Local History, Nat. Writers Club, Am. Assn. Tchrs. Slavic and East European Langs., Polish Inst. Arts and Scis. Am., Colo. Authors League, Colo. Hist. Assn., Colo.-Wyo. Assn. Mus., Western History Assn., Colo. Authors League, Denver Press Club, Denver Art Club, Industries Jefferson County, Lakewood C. of C. Clubs: Polish (Denver); Am. Council Polish Cultural. Author: The 59'ers, Roaring Denver, 1961; The Westernaires on the Gallop, 1967; Grunwald, 1981; Gentleman Rogue, 1982. Home: 800 S Vallejo St Denver CO 80223 Office: Box 950 Route 5 Golden CO 80401

ZAMZOW, CLAUDIA GOOCH, needle art designer; b. Day, Calif., Aug. 2, 1936; d. Rush Potter and Lila Adeline (Marvin) Gooch; m. Dale R. Zamzow, Dec. 15, 1962. Student Shasta Coll., 1954-56, Calif. Coll. Arts and Crafts, 1956-57. Profl. doll designer, Santa Clara, Calif., 1968—; tchr., lectr., workshop leader in needle arts and lacemaking, 1978—; founder The Lace Mus., Mountain View, Calif., 1980; curator Bear Force Mus., San Jose, Calif., 1982—; lace and needlework appraiser, 1976—; one-woman shows: Tapestry in Talent, San Jose, Calif., 1979, 80, Stanford Research Inst. Internat., 1974. Mem. United Fedn. Doll Clubs, Internat. Old Lacers, Nat. Assn. Miniature Enthusiasts, Embroiderers Guild Am., Peninsula Lace Mavericks (textbook reviewer 1980-81; founding), Contemporary Doll Artists Guild (founder; charter mem.), Santa Clara Doll Collectors (founder), Phelan City Miniaturists (founder; charter mem.), Doll Fashion Study Group (founder). Club: Lace Mus. Aux. Developer trademarks Needlemaid, P.W. Bear, U.S. Bear Force, 1979-82; commd. to design teddy bear for His Royal Highness Prince William of Wales. Office: PO Box 4610 Santa Clara CA 95054

ZAMZOW, DALE R., consultant; b. Beaver Dam, Wis., May 9, 1935; s. Alfred Eric and Viola I. (Dinkel) Z.; student U. Wis., 1953-54, Heidelberg U., 1959-60, Am. U. Beirut, 1960-61; m. Claudia Gooch, Dec. 15, 1962. Mgr. O/R Theatre Group, Milw., 1954-59; adminstrv. asst. Am. embassy, Lebanon, 1959-61; pres. IPC-Licensing, Santa Clara, Calif., 1962-81; exec. dir. U.S. Bear Force, Sunnyvale, Calif., 1982—, also chmn. bd.; cons. systems analyst, 1969-80. Founder, pres. Sunnyvale Art League, 1964; sec. Burbank Sanitary Dist., 1966-69; pub. relations dir. Lace Mus., 1979-81. Served with USAF, 1957-61. Decorated Award of Merit, Lebanese Air Force; recipient Presdl. Fitness awards, 1978, 79, U.S. Olympic Assn. award, 1980. Mem. Pub. Relations Roundtable, Vols. in Tech. Assistance, Nirvana Assn., Am. Soc. Systems Analysts (cert.). Clubs: Brit. Am., German Service, Good Bears of the World. Patentee packaging; designer 12 trademarks; author book and articles; Appropriate Tech. editor Vita News; pub. relations cons. Le Cav, Beirut, Lebanon; editor, publisher The Bear Force Times; cons. editor: Matchmaking News. Office: PO Box 4610 Santa Clara CA 95054

ZAMZOW, DENNIS ROBERT, podiatrist; b. Ripon, Wis., Apr. 30, 1944; s. Arthur Robert and Charlotte Gwendolyn Z.; student Coll. San Mateo, 1971-73; Dr. Podiatric Medicine, Calif. Podiatric Medicine, San Francisco, 1976. Pvt. practice podiatry, Mountain View, Calif., 1976—; instr. De Anza Coll., Cupertino, Calif., 1980-82. Adv., Calif. Gov.'s Council on Wellness and Phys. Fitness, also co-dir. San Jose chpt. Served with USN, 1962-70. Mem. Am. Podiatry Assn., Calif. Podiatry Assn., Am. Acad. Podiatric Sports Medicine. Club: California Road Runners Running (pres.). Author: (with W. P. Feigel) Runners World Foot Care Book. Office: 2500 Hospital Dr Bldg 9 Mountain View CA 94040

ZANE, GLENN ALAN, forester; b. Modesto, Calif., Sept. 21, 1939; s. Alan Mortimer and Lois Olive (Leach) Z.; B.S. in Forest Mgmt., U. Calif., Humboldt, 1967; m. Cora Charlotte Sanders, Apr. 10, 1960; children—Elaina Cora, Eric Alan, Tobe Glenn, Nancy Melissa, Diana Rosanna, Betsey Elaina. Fire control officer Calif. Div. Forestry, 1957-64; researcher U.S. Forest Service, 1964; indsl. forester Hollow Tree Lumber Co., Ukiah, Calif., 1965; resources mgr. Paul Bunyan Lumber Co., Anderson, Calif., 1966-74; partner Mason, Bruce & Girard, Cons. Foresters, Portland, Oreg. and Redding, Calif., 1974—. Mem. Redding Land Use Planning Bd. Mem. Soc. Am. Foresters (chmn. chpt. 1972-73, sect. officer 1969-74). Republican. Mem. Nazarene Ch. Office: PO Box 218 1005 Yuba St Redding CA 96001

ZANE, LAWRENCE F(AR) H(EONG), educator, consultant; b. Pauwela, Hawaii, Oct. 9, 1931; s. Gilbert Ting and Daisy (Ching) Z.; m. Aileen Yau Wan Au, May 15, 1954; children—Deborah, Renee, Jacqueline. B.S. in Agr., U. Hawaii, 1953, 5th Yr. Diploma in Vocat. Agr., 1954, M.Ed., 1963; Ph.D. in Indl. Edn., U. Md., 1968. Cert. tech. sch. profl. tchr. and secondary edn. Tchr. vocat. agr. Waipahu High Sch., 1954; tchr. McKinley High Sch., 1956-59; physics instr. Honolulu Community Coll., 1959-69; assoc. prof. trades and indl. edn. U. Hawaii, 1970-75, prof. vocat. edn. and community coll. edn., 1975—; staff specialist tchr. tng. and basic edn. manpower devel. and tng. State Dept. Vocat. Edn., 1966, program specialist indsl. arts edn., 1966-67; staff mem. Hawaii Community Coll. Systems Office, U. Hawaii and Hawaii Vocat.-Tech. Research Coordinating Unit, 1967-68; cons. U.S. Office Edn., U. Hawaii, N.Y. Tech. Inst., U. Hawaii-Am. Samoa, U.S. Office Edn., U. Hawaii, 1969, Dept. Edn. Trust Ter. Pacific Islands, Naha Ryukyuan-Am. Cultural Center, Okinawa, Kasetsart U., Thailand, U. Wash., Seattle, others. Bd. regents Coll. Micronesia, 1978—; active Kuhio dist. Boy Scouts Am. Served with U.S. Army, 1954-56, to lt. col. Res., 1968—. Recipient grants, contracts various agys. Mem. Am. Assn. Community and Jr. Colls., Nat. Assn. Indsl. and Tech. Tchr. Educators, Am. Council Indsl. Arts Tchr. Edn. (life), Am. Vocat. Assn. (life), Am. Indsl. Arts Assn. (life), Hawaii Practical Arts and Vocat. Assn., NEA, Hawaii Edn. Assn., Coll. and Univ. Profl. Assembly, Am. Tech. Edn. Assn. (life), Am. Soc. Tng. and Devel. (pres. Hawaii 1982), Council Occupational Edn., Council Univs. and Colls. (trustee), Hawaii Indsl. Arts Assn., Phi Delta Kappa. Lutheran. Contbr. articles to profl. publs. Home: 2831 Poelua St Honolulu HI 96822

ZANINOVICH, KAREN IRENE, telecommunications company executive; b. Bakersfield, Calif., Jan. 15, 1956; d. Jack Marion and Beatrice Carolyn (Perry) Zaninovich; m. Ray Earl Cunningham, May 28, 1976 (div.); 1 son, Jeremy. B.S. in Fin., San Jose State U., 1980; postgrad. U. Santa Clara, 1984—. Accounts payable coordinator SSI Container div. Itel Corp., San Francisco 1976-78; acct. Memorex Corp., Santa Clara, Calif., 1978-81, fin. analyst, 1981-82; fin. systems analyst ROLM Corp., Santa Clara, 1982—. Mem. Nat. Assn. Female Execs., AAUW, Assn. M.B.A. Execs. Home: 2201 The Alameda Apt 28 Santa Clara CA 95050 Office: ROLM Corp 4900 Old Ironside Dr Santa Clara CA 95050

ZAPEL, KAREN MARGARET, educational administrator; b. Chgo., Mar. 29, 1942; d. Nels Gustav and Ethel Amanda (Maximini) Lundgren; m. William Louis Zapel, Feb. 10, 1962 (div.); 1 dau., Johanna Lyn. B.S. in Edn., U. Colo., 1972, postgrad., 1979—. Cert. tchr., Colo. Exec. sec. Stral Advt. Co., Chgo., 1964-68; dir. Community Sch. Colorado Springs (Colo.), 1972-78; dir. lower sch. Colorado Springs Sch., 1978—; conf. coordinator, workshop leader. Mem. Colorado Springs Symphony Orch., Pikes Peak Task Force on Single Parenting. Mem. Assn. Curriculum Devel. and Supervision, Internat. Reading Assn., Nat. Assn Ind. Schs., Common Cause. Office: 21 Broadmoor Ave Colorado Springs CO 80906

ZARROW, SHEILA DICKMAN, psychotherapist, educator; b. Boston, Feb. 24, 1937; d. Archie C. and Anne Dickman; m. Stanton Harold Zarrow, June 15, 1958; children—Joshua, Julie, Joel, Aaron. B.S., Boston U., 1958; M.A., Calif. State U.—Northridge, 1976; Ph.D., Internat. Coll., Los Angeles, 1981. Lic. tchr., community coll. prof., marriage, family, child therapist, hypnotherapist, Calif. Pvt. practice psychotherapy, Encino, Calif., 1976—; clin. dir. Profl. Assoc. Psychologists and Counselor; tng. supr. San Fernando Valley Counseling Center; clin. dir. Community Psychol. Services; mem. Los Angeles Olympic Organizing Com. Med. Adv. Bd.; condr. profl. workshops. Active LWV, Fair Housing Council. Named New Tchr. of Year, NEA, 1958-59. Mem. Am. Psychol. Assn., Am. Personnel and Guidance Assn., Jung Inst., Calif. Assn. Marriage and Family Therapists, Internat. Assn. Sports Psychologists. Democrat. Jewish. Office: 5535 Balboa Blvd Suite 107 Encino CA 91316

ZARSKE, JOHN ALDEN, psychologist, educator; b. Milw., Jan. 30, 1951; s. Albert Alden and Marjorie Rose (Van Herke) Z.; m. Susan Ellen Michelson, Oct. 11, 1982. B.A. in Psychology, Marquette U., Milw., 1973; Ed.D. in Ednl. Psychology, No. Ariz. U., Flagstaff, 1980. Lic. psychologist, Ariz. Psychol. asso. No. Ariz. U., Inst. Human Devel., 1977-80; pvt. practice psychology No. Ariz. Psychol. Services, 1980—; adj. faculty U. B.C. (Can.), Vancouver, summer 1982; cons. Flagstaff Pilot Parents Program, Assn. Advancement of Psychology, Coconino County Assn. Retarded Citizens. Mem. Am. Psychol. Assn., Nat. Assn. Sch. Psychologists, Ariz. Psychol. Assn., Ariz. Assn. Sch. Psychologists. Democrat. Contbr. articles to profl. jours. Home: 10 W Dale Flagstaff AZ Office: Flagstaff Med Bldg 1355 N Beaver Flagstaff AZ 86001

ZARTMAN, DAVID LESTER, educator, farming corp. exec.; b. Albuquerque, July 6, 1940; s. Lester Grant and Mary Elizabeth (Kitchel) Z.; B.S. with honors, N.Mex. State U., 1962; M.S., Ohio State U., 1966, Ph.D., 1968; m. Micheal Aline Plemmons, July 6, 1963; children—Kami Renee, Dalan Lee. Research asst. Ohio State U., 1964-68; asst. prof. N.Mex. State U., Las Cruces, 1968-71, assoc. prof., 1971-78, prof. dept. animal and range scis., 1978—; pres. Mary K. Zartman, Inc., farming corp., Albuquerque, 1977—; chmn. N. Am. Symposia on Cytogenetics and Cell Biology of Domestic Animals, 1981, 83; lectr. in field. Judge, 4-H Fairs, Future Farmers Am. Fairs, N.Mex. Hay Festival; supt. dairy div. So. N.Mex. State Fair, 1978—; active Mesilla Valley Christian Ch.; leader sci. group Syn-Con Crime Prevention Program, 1976. Fellow AAAS; mem. Am. Dairy Sci. Assn., Am. Inst. Biol. Scis., Am. Soc. Animal Sci., N.Mex. Farm and Livestock Bur., Dairy Shrine Club, Sigma Xi (past chpt. sec.-treas., past pres.), Phi Kappa Phi, Alpha Gamma Rho, Alpha Zeta, Gamma Sigma Delta. Research in reproductive efficiency for livestock, automation of estrus detection and gen. dairy energy efficiency. Home: 1803 Debra St Las Cruces NM 88001 Office: Box 3-1 Dept Animal Sci New Mexico State U Las Cruces NM 88003

ZATIK-THIMIS, ALISON JOY, electric utility economist; m. Cleve., Sept. 28, 1956; d. Andrew John and Louisa Rose (Colleoni) Zatik; m. Nicholas T. Thimis, Sept., 1982. B.A. cum laude in Psychology, U. Cin., 1977; M.S. in Applied Econs., Wright State U., 1979. Cons. Hanselman-Eskew & Assocs., Dayton, Ohio, 1976-79; chief economist, rates specialist Plains Electric Generation & Transmission, Albuquerque, 1980—; cons., model builder for innovative analysis. Dept. Energy grantee, 1977. Mem. Am. Econs. Assn., Am. Statis. Assn., Am. Econometricians Assn. Roman Catholic. Contbr. articles in field to publs. Home: 1750 Pegasus Albuquerque NM 87124 Office: 2401 Aztec Rd NE Albuquerque NM 87107

ZAVALA, ALBERT, research psychologist; b. Chgo., Mar. 10, 1930; s. Edward and Maria Soledad (Herrejon) Z.; div.; children—Camille, Sally, Elena, Jenifer, Alexis. B.A., Willamette U., Salem, Oreg., 1959; M.A. Mich. State U., 1961; Ph.D., Kans. State U., 1966. Prof., head life scis. Calspan, Buffalo, 1967-73; prof. SUNY Coll. at Buffalo, 1968-78; exec. dir. Corp. IV, Cheektowaga, N.Y., 1973-77; dir. projects Inpsych, Cupertino, Calif., 1978-80; sr. research psychologist SRI Internat., Menlo Park, Calif., 1980—. Mem. Erie County (N.Y.) sheriff's sci. staff, 1972-78. Served with U.S. Army, 1955-57. Dunlap fellow, 1964; Greater Kans. City Mental Health Found. fellow, 1962-63. Mem. Am. Psychol. Assn., Human Factors Soc., Sigma Xi, Psi Chi, Phi Kappa Phi. Author: (with J.J. Paley) Personal Appearance Identification, 1972. Contbr. numerous articles to profl. jours. Office: 333 Ravenswood Menlo Park CA 94025

ZAWACKI, FRANCIS STULA, educator, fashion consultant; b. Colchester, Conn., Aug. 22, 1933; d. Ferdinand and Irene (Melnick) Stula; m. Henry A. Zawacki, July 21, 1956; children—Christine Marie and Wayne Henry. B.S. with high honors in Home Econs. Edn., U. Conn., 1956; M.S. in Edn., U. Alaska-Fairbanks, 1974, postgrad., 1974-82. Telephone operator, Conn., 1951-53; asst. underwriter Conn. Gen. Ins. Co., 1954; tchr. home econs. Jr./Sr. High Sch., Glastonbury, Conn., 1956-57; tchr. home econs., head dept. Lathrop High Sch., Fairbanks, Alaska, 1957—; fashions cons.; owner, operator Fielding Lake Lodge, 1982—. Mem. State Home Econs. Assn. (No. area rep.), Fairbanks Home Econs. Assn. (past pres.), NEA, Alaska Edn. Assn., Fairbanks Edn. Assn., Univ. Womens Assn., Alpha Delta Kappa (Alaska state pres.), Phi Omicron Nu. Roman Catholic. Developed first statewide home econs. curriculum for Alaska Schs. Home: 1038 Pedro St Fairbanks AK 99701 Office: 901 Airport Way Fairbanks AK 99701

ZAWACKI, GAIL MARIE, school principal; b. Bridgeport, Conn., Apr. 25, 1947; d. Raymond Walter and Marie Fausta (Homza) Z. B.A. in Psychology, Sacred Heart U., 1969. Tchr., Westport, Conn., 1969-74, San Marino, Calif., 1974-81; prin., San Marino, Calif., 1981-82, Montrose, Calif., 1982—. Mem. Nat. Catholic Ednl. Assn., Assn. Supervision and Curriculum Devel. Office: 2361 Del Mar Rd Montrose CA 91020

ZEAMAN, LAURA BETH, English and reading educator; b. N.Y.C., Mar. 8, 1946; d. Abraham and Edith Nettie (Cohen) Banner; m. Bernard James Zeaman, July 7, 1973 (dec.); stepchildren—Jon Becker, Rachel Anne; 1 dau., Sara Jane. B.A., Adelphi U., 1967. Tchr., English, Hicksville (N.Y.) High Sch., 1967-69; tchr. English/social studies Alta Vista Continuation High Sch., Vista, Calif., 1971-77; all subject tchr. opportunity program Washington Jr. High Sch., Vista, 1977-81; reading tchr. Washington Middle Sch., Vista, 1981—. N.Y. state scholar, 1962. Mem. NEA, Internat. Reading Assn., Nat. Assn. Tchrs. English, Calif. Tchrs. Assn., San Diego Reading Assn., Vista Tchrs. Assn. Democrat. Club: Centre City Optimist (hon.) (San Diego). Home: 14333 Range Park Rd Poway CA 92064 Office: 740 Olive St Vista CA 92083

ZECHER, ALBERT MICHAEL, lawyer; b. San Francisco, July 3, 1930; s. Albert Gustav and Mary M. (Hayes) Z.; B.S., U. San Francisco, 1953, J.D.; LL.B., Hastings Coll. Law, 1956; m. Marilyn Pestarino, Apr. 9, 1960; children—Vanessa Ann, Albert Michael, Jr., Eryth Z. Admitted to Calif. bar, 1956; dep. county counsel, San Joaquin, Calif., 1956-60; partner Zecher & Pestarino, San Jose, Calif., 1960-74; pvt. practice law, San Jose, 1974—. Served with U.S. Army, 1948-49. Mem. Santa Clara County Bar Assn. (trustee), Am. Bar Assn., Calif. Bar Assn., Assn. Bus. Trial Lawyers. Democrat. Clubs: Commonwealth, Olympic (San Francisco). Office: 111 N Market St 900 San Jose CA 95113

ZECHTER, LEE ALAN, architect; b. Phila., Feb. 5, 1953; s. Nathan and Dorothea (Schwarts). Student San Diego State U., 1971-72; B.Arch., U. Ariz., 1977. Lic. architect, Calif. Draftsman, designer Innis-Tennebaum Architects, San Diego, 1976; assoc. in charge Jerry L. Pollak, AIA & Assoc., Los Angeles, 1977-82; pres. Proptimal Internat., Beverly Hills, Calif., 1982—. Mem. AIA (past pres. Los Angeles chpt. 1980, Service award 1980, 81), Constrn. Specifications Inst., Author: In Your Own Backyard, 1976; designed residential, comml., indsl. and recreational projects in So. Calif., Mex. Office: 9454 Wilshire Blvd Penthouse Beverly Hills CA 90212

ZEE, CAROL ANN, communications system project manager; b. Los Angeles, June 24, 1951; d. Zygmund John and Helen (Brasky) Zee. B.A. in Chemistry, Occidental Coll., 1973. Analytical chemist, sect. head TRW Electronics and Def. Sector, Redondo Beach, Calif., 1974-78, project mgr., 1978-80, satellite project mgmt. team, 1980—; vice chmn. TRW's Women's Adv. Group, 1980, chmn., 1981. Patron Los Angeles County Mus. of Art, Greater Los Angeles Zoo Assn.; active local politics and civic issues, Manhattan Beach, Calif. Mem. AIAA, Am. Chem. Soc., Soc. Women Engrs. Contbr. articles to profl. jours. Home: 432 1st St Manhattan Beach CA 90266 Office: TRW One Space Park MI/2104 Redondo Beach CA 90278

ZEGLEN, MARIE ELAINA, university administrator; b. Phila., Aug. 26, 1950; d. Richard A. and Frances E. (Green) Z. B.A. magna cum laude in Anthropology, Ohio State U., 1972; M.A. in Sociology, Wash. State U., 1975, Ph.D. in Sociology, 1976. Head evaluator Wash.-Oreg.-Idaho Regional Program in Vet. Medicine, Wash. State U., Pullman, 1976-77, dir. biomed. communications, 1977—; cons. computer systems, communications, pet therapy. NIMH trainee, 1974-76; Adminstrn. Aging fellow, 1975-76. Mem. Am. Sociol. Assn., AAAS, Nat. Council Family Relations, Am. Vet. Computer Soc., People Pet Partnership, Delta Soc. Democrat. Contbr. articles to profl. publs. Home: 822 E 5th Moscow ID 83843 Office: College Veterinary Medicine VS 123 Wash State U Pullman WA 99164

ZEIG, JEFFREY KENNETH, clinical psychologist; b. N.Y.C., Nov. 6, 1947; s. Martin Joel and Ruth E. (Epstein) Z.; m. Sherron Sue Peters, Dec. 8, 1980. B.S., Mich. State U., 1969; M.S., San Francisco State U., 1973; Ph.D., Ga. State U., 1977. Lic. psychologist, Ariz., marriage family and child counselor, Calif. Staff psychologist Ariz. State Hosp., 1977-78; pvt. practice clin. psychology, 1979—; dir. Milton H. Erickson Found.; adj. asst. prof. clin. psychology Ariz. State U. Recipient Milton H. Erickson award Am. Jour. Clin. Hypnosis, 1981; Netherlands Soc. Clin. Hypnosis award, 1980. Mem. Am. Psychol. Assn., Am. Soc. Clin. Hypnosis, Phoenix Soc. Clin. Hypnosis (founding pres.). Editor: A Teaching Seminar with Milton H. Erickson, 1980; Ericksonian Approaches to Hypnosis and Psychotherapy, 1982; mem. editorial bd. Am. Jour. Clin. Hypnosis. Home and Office: 1935 East Aurelius Ave Phoenix AZ 85020

ZEIGER, DELBERT LEE, human services program adminstr.; b. Compton, Calif., Jan. 5, 1941; s. John Q. and Lois M. (Smith) Z.; B.A., Calif. State U., Los Angeles, 1964; M. Pub. Adminstrn., U. So. Calif., 1973; m. Pamela Earl, Aug. 26, 1962; children—Julie, Jennifer. Social worker San Bernardino County (Calif.) Dept. Public Social Services, 1966-68, ednl. tng. specialist, 1969, social service supr., 1970-71, program asst. to dep. dir., 1971-72, Ont. dist. supr., 1972-77, San Bernardino dist. mgr., 1977-79; program mgr. Yolo County (Calif.) Dept. Social Services, 1979-80, dir. Social Services div., 1980—; guest lectr., field instr., social services dept. Chaffey Coll. Co-chmn. Victor Valley Community Action Program; mem. San Bernardino County Dependency Prevention Commn.; coach Sunshine Soccer League, 1976; bd. dirs., mem. exec. com., treas. Mental Health Assn. San Bernardino, 1977-79; mem. dir.'s adv. bd. Ret. Sr. Vol. Program, City of San Bernardino, 1979; bd. dirs. Planned Parenthood of Yolo County, 1980. Recipient Key Man award Associated In Group Donors United Givers, 1971; Outstanding Service award City of Ontario, 1976. Mem. Am. Mgmt. Assn., San Bernardino, Apple Valley Victorville (sec., treas. 1966-68) jr. chambers commerce. Home: 99 California St Woodland CA 95695 Office: 120 W Main St Woodland CA 95695

ZEIGER, JUDITH ANN, educator; b. Waterloo, Iowa, May 25, 1938; d. James N. and Marguerite E. (Maring) Hinson; children—Jeffrey Keith, Anne Elizabeth. B.A., Wellesley Coll., 1960; M.Ed., Boston U., 1965; Ph.D., U. Colo., 1973. Counselor-tchr., U. Colo., Boulder, 1966-76; dir. study abroad program Expt. in Internat. Living, Oxford, Eng., 1976-80; dir. tng. and staff devel. Colo. Jud. Dept., Denver, 1980—; adj. prof. dept. pub. affairs, U. Colo., Denver; cons. pvt. industry, govt. agys. Mem. Boulder County Community Corrections Bd. Mem. Am. Assn. Tng. and Devel. Home: 2165 Dartmouth St Boulder CO 80303 Office: 2 E 14th Ave Denver CO 80203

ZEIGLER, SHERILYN KAY, marketing educator, marketing, advertising and public relations consultant; b. Evanston, Ill., June 4, 1943; d. Albert Howard and Madeline Louise (Lambert) Z. B.A., Mich. State U., East Lansing, 1965, M.A., 1966, Ph.D., 1969. Instr. mktg. communications Mich. State U., 1968-69, asst. prof., 1969-72, assoc. prof., 1972-73; assoc. prof. U. Tenn., 1974-77, prof., 1979-80; adj. prof. dept. mktg. U. Hawaii, 1980—; with Foote, Cone & Belding Advt., Chgo., 1965-67, Young & Rubicam Advt., Detroit, 1969, Sta. WKAR AM & FM, East Lansing, 1961-63, Sta. KITV-TV, Honolulu, 1972; vis. prof. Fla. Internat. U., Chaminade U., Honolulu; mktg., advt. dir. Ruchigami Advt., Honolulu, 1981—; publicity dir. Aloha Week Festival, Honolulu, 1980—, Kawaiahao Ch., Honolulu, 1982—, Hawaii Spl. Olympics, 1982—. Mem. Nat. Assn. Broadcasters, Am. Acad. Advt., Am. Assn. Advt. Agys., Direct Mail/Mktg. Assn., Sigma Delta Chi, Nat. Alumni U. Tenn. Author: Advertising, 5th edit., 1982; Creative Strategy & Tactics in Advertising, 1981; Broadcast Advertising, 2d edit., 1984; Perspectives on Advertising Education, 1974. Office: 1684 Ala Moana Blvd Suite 101 Honolulu HI 96815

ZEILINGER, ELNA RAE, educator; b. Tempe, Ariz., Mar. 24, 1937; d. Clayborn Eddie and Ruby Elna (Laird) Simpson; B.A. in Edn., Ariz. State U., 1958, M.A. in Edn., 1966, Ed.S., 1980; m. Philip Thomas Zeilinger, June 13, 1970; children—Shari, Chris. Bookkeeper, First Nat. Bank of Tempe, 1955-56; with registrar's office Ariz. State U., 1956-58; piano tchr., recreation dir. City of Tempe, tchr. Thew Sch., Tempe, 1958-61, elem. tchr. Mitchell Sch., 1962-74, intern prin., 1976, personnel intern, 1977; specialist in gifted edn. Tempe Elem. Schs., 1977—; grad. asst. ednl. adminstrn., Iota Workshop coordinator Ariz. State U., 1978; presenter Ariz. Gifted Conf., 1978-81; condr. survey of gifted programs, 1980; reporter public relations Tempe Sch. Dist., 1978-80, Access com. for gifted programs, 1981-83. Freedom Train com. Ariz. Bicentennial Commn., 1975-76. Named Outstanding Leader in Elem. and Secondary Schs., 1976' Ariz. Cattle Growers scholar, 1954-55; Elks scholar, 1954-55; recipient Judges award Tempe Art League, 1970, Best of Show, Scottsdale Art League, 1976. Mem. Council Exceptional Children, Ariz. Assn. Gifted and Talented, Ariz. Sch. Adminstrs., Tempe Hist. Assn. (liaison 1975), Scottsdale Artists League, Tempe Art League, Am. Bus. Women's Assn. (Woman of Yr. 1983), Phi Kappa Phi, Pi Lambda Theta, Kappa Delta Pi, Phi Delta Kappa, Kappa Delta. Democrat. Congregationalist. Club: Eastern Star. Author: Leadership Role of the Principal in Gifted Programs: A Handbook, 1980; Classified Personnel Handbook, 1977, also reports and monographs. Home: 610 E Colgate St Tempe AZ 85283 Office: 1975 E Cornell St Tempe AZ 85283

ZEIND, SAMIR MAURICE, medical librarian; b. Egypt, Oct. 1, 1939; s. Maurice R. and Georgette F. (Hag) Z.; m. Jeanne F., June 28, 1969; 1 dau., Rita Marie-Noelle. B.S. in Chemistry, Am. U., Cairo, 1967; M.L.S., U. So. Calif., 1976. Library asst. U. So. Calif. Sch. Dentistry, 1970-76; asst. mgr. library Huntington Meml. Hosp., Pasadena, Calif., 1976-80, mgr., 1980—. Mem. ALA, Med. Library Assn., Med. Library Group So. Calif. and Ariz. Home: 14610 Runnymede St Van Nuys CA 91405 Office: 100 Congress St Pasadena CA 91105

ZEITLER, BILL LORENZ, aviation engineer; b. Columbus, Ohio, July 14, 1920; s. Walter Andrew and Naomi Lee (Limes) Z.; B.S.C.E., Calif. State U.-Long Beach, 1965; m. Betty Eileen Thomas, Nov. 8, 1942; children—Eddie, Naomi Parker. Loftsman, Curtiss Wright Corp., Columbus, 1941-43, 44-46; linesman Lockheed Corp., Burbank, Calif., 1943-44; linesman N.Am. Rockwell (and predecessor firms), Inglewood, Calif., 1946-50, airframe designer, 1950-62, supr., 1962-65, project engr., 1965-69, mem. tech. staff, Downey, Calif., 1956—; mem. Space Shuttle Speakers Bur. Cert. vocat. tchr., Calif. Mem. AIAA, Nat. Geog. Soc., Smith Instn. Assocs. Republican. Clubs: Rockwell Mgmt., Toastmasters. Office: 12241 Lakewood Blvd AE47 Downey CA 92041

ZEITLER, JUDITH ELAINE, occupational therapist; b. Algoma, Wis., Sept. 25, 1957; d. Harold G. and Jeanette R. (Post) Zeitler. B.S. in Occupational Therapy, U. Wis.-Madison, 1979. Occupational therapist Brown County Mental Health Ctr., Green Bay, Wis., 1980, Stewart Rehabilitation Ctr. McKay-Dee Hosp. Ctr., Ogden, Utah, 1980-82, U. Utah Med. Ctr., Salt Lake City, 1982—. Mem. Utah Occupational Therapy Assn. (sec. 1982), Am. Occupational Therapy Assn., World

Fedn. Occupational Therapists, Assn. Drivers' Educators for Disabled. Lutheran. Office: Univ Utah Med Ctr 50 N Medical Dr Salt Lake City UT 84132

ZEITLIN, MAURICE, sociology educator, author; b. Detroit, Feb. 24, 1935; s. Albert J. and Rose (Goldberg) Z.; m. Marilyn Geller, Mar. 1, 1959; children—Michelle, Carla, Erica. B.A. cum laude, Wayne State U., 1957; M.A., U. Calif.-Berkeley, 1960, Ph.D., 1964. Instr. anthropology and sociology Princeton (N.J.) U., 1961-64, research assoc. Ctr. Internat. Studies, 1962-64; asst. prof. sociology U. Wis.-Madison, 1964-67, assoc. prof., 1967-70, prof., 1970-77, dir. Ctr. Social Orgn., 1974-76; prof. sociology UCLA, 1977—, also research assoc. Inst. Indsl. Relations; vis. prof. polit. sci. and sociology Hebrew U., Jerusalem, 1971-72. Chmn. Madison Citizens for a Vote on Vietnam, 1967-68; chmn. Am. Com. for Chile, 1973-75; mem. exec. bd. U.S. Com. for Justice to Latin Am. Polit. Prisoners, 1977—; mem. exec. com. Calif. Campaign for Econ. Democracy, 1983—. Ford Found. fellow, 1965-67, 70-71; Guggenheim fellow, 1981-82; NSF grantee, 1981-82; recipient Project Censored award Top Censored Story, 1981; Ten Best Censored list, 1978. Mem. Am. Sociol. Assn. (governing council 1977-80), Internat. Sociol. Assn. (editorial bd. 1977-81), Latin Am. Studies Assn., Orgn. Am. Historians. Democrat. Jewish. Author: (with R. Scheer) Cuba: An American Tragedy, 1964; Revolutionary Politics and the Cuban Working Class, 1967, 1970; editor-in-chief: Political Power and Social Theory, 1980—; editor: (with J. Petras) Latin America: Reform or Revolution?, 1968; American Society, Inc., 1970, 77; Classes, Class Conflict and the State, 1980. Office: Haines 264 UCLA 405 Hilgard Ave Los Angeles CA 90024

ZEITLIN, MICHAEL DONALD, accountant; b. Denver, Apr. 20, 1951; s. Eugene Louis and Sylvia Myra (Weiss) Z.; m. Cheryl Ann Scott, Aug. 3, 1975. B.S., U. Colo., 1976, M. Taxation, U. Denver, 1978. C.P.A. Colo., 1978. Staff acct. Arthur Andersen & Co., San Diego, 1978-79; sr. tax acct. Zaveral, Boosalis & Raisch, Denver, 1980; tax mgr. Louis L. Fox & Co., Denver, 1980-82; owner Michael D. Zeitlin, CPA, Denver, 1982—; pub. speaker. Mem. Am. Inst. C.P.A.s, Colo. Soc. C.P.A.s. Club: B'nai B'rith. Home: 4181 S Quebec St Denver CO 80237 Office: Michael D Zeitlin CPA 925 S Niagara St Suite 150 Denver CO 80224

ZELMAN, VLADIMIR, physician; b. Sckvira, U.S.S.R., Oct. 17, 1935; came to U.S., 1977, naturalized, 1977; s. Leyzo and Fanya (Gozodetsky) Z.; M.D., Novosibirsk State Med. Sch., 1959, Ph.D., 1965; m. Leah Ryabtseva, Feb. 23, 1958; 1 son, Michael. Resident, research asso. anesthesiology UCLA, 1977-80; asso. prof. anesthesiology and neurosurgery, dir. neuroanesthesia service U. So. Calif. Sch. Medicine, Los Angeles County Med. Center, 1981—; practice medicine specializing in anesthesiology; mem. staffs VA Med. Center, Sepulveda, Calif., UCLA Med. Center. Mem. Am. Soc. Anesthesia, Calif. Soc. Anesthesia. Jewish. Home: 1015 18th St #1 Apt 11 Santa Monica CA 90403 Office: USC-LAC Med Center 1200 N State St Los Angeles CA 90033

ZENZ, BARBARA ELIZABETH, advertising executive; b. Stockton, Calif., Jan. 24, 1956; d. Robert Lee and Patricia Frances (Lowdon) Zenz; m. Kim K. Yamaguchi Sept. 29, 1979. A.A., Sacramento City Coll., 1976; B.A., San Jose State U., 1979; postgrad. U. Santa Clara, 1979-80. Ops. mgr. Hotel Ste. Clair, San Jose, Calif., 1976-78; pub. relations specialist Santa Clara County Housing Authority, 1978-80; ptnr./account dir. The Stephenz Group, Campbell, Calif., 1980—; advt./mktg. communications cons. Mem. Project Area Com. for Redevel. of Downtown Campbell, 1983—. Republican. Roman Catholic. Club: Campbell Culture. Address: 145 Dillon Ave Bldg D Campbell CA 95008

ZEPEDA, SUSAN GHOZEIL, health program administrator; b. N.Y.C., Aug. 8, 1946; d. Harry S. and Anne (Golden) Kantor; B.A., Brown U., 1967; M.A., U. Ariz., 1971, postgrad., 1972—; children—Daniel Jacob, Adam Leo. Asst. dir. div. coll. and edn. Barron's Ednl. Series, Woodbury, N.Y., 1968; research asst. U. Ariz., 1969-73, programs evaluator Coll. Medicine, 1975-76, instr. psychology, 1975; asso. dir. Pima Alcoholism Consortium, Tucson, 1976-78, exec. dir., 1979-80; dep. dir. pub. health and med. services Orange County Health Care Agy., Santa Ana, Calif., 1980—; cons. research div. Tucson Sch Dist. 1, 1973-75; chmn. Ariz. Task Force on Women and Behavioral Health, 1978-80; mem. Tucson Women's Commn., 1978, Ariz. Women's Commn., 1978-80. Mem. Am. Pub. Health Assn., U.S.-Mex. Border Health Assn., LWV. Club: Soroptimists. Editor: (with L.R. Klein) Manpower Research Monograph No. 27, 1973, Twenty-One: A Popularization of 21 Federally-Funded Dissertation, 1978; editor Tucson Early Edn. Model Exchange, 1970-72. Contbr. column on grantsmanship to Drug Survival News. Home: 2619 Monterey Pl Fullerton CA 92633 Office: 515 N Sycamore Santa Ana CA 92701

ZEPEDA, VERONICA HUBBARD, educator; b. Tucson, June 15, 1939; s. Al and Julieta Ester (Zepeda) Hubbard; B.A., U. Ariz., 1961, M.A., 1964, Ph.D., 1972; m. John Beamer, May 29, 1978; 1 dau., Johanna Camille. Tchr. high schs. Oak Park and River Forest, Ill., 1962-65; lang. coordinator Peace Corps, U. Ariz., 1965-68; tchr. ESL, U. Ariz., Tucson, 1966-68; tchr., No. Ariz. U., Flagstaff, 1973-74; asst. prof. secondary edn. U. Ariz., 1975-78; coordinator statewide pupil achievement testing Ariz. Dept. Edn., Phoenix, 1978—; cons. bilingual edn., Asuncion, Paraguay, 1974. Mem. Ariz. Sch. Adminstrs., Assn. Supervision and Curriculum Devel., Nat. Assn. Bilingual Edn., Ariz. Assn. Bilingual Edn., Phi Beta Kappa, Phi Kappa Phi, Sigma Delta Pi, Pi Lambda Theta. Contbr. articles to profl. jours. Home: 7112 N 8th Ave Phoenix AZ 85021 Office: 1535 W Jefferson St Phoenix AZ 95007

ZERBE, RICHARD OLIS, JR., economics educator; b. Nitro, W. Va., Oct. 2, 1938; s. Richard O. and Fanny H. (Carter) Z.; m. E. Diane Husband, July 24, 1971; 1 son, R. Alexander; 1 son by previous marriage, Robert Riley. Ph.D., Duke U., 1969. Research fellow U. Chgo. Law Sch., 1969-70; scholar in residence, Am. Bar Found., 1971; assoc. prof. Roosevelt U., Chgo., 1972-74; vis. assoc. prof. dept. econs. Northwestern U., Evanston, Ill., 1975-76; prof. Sch. Pub. Affairs, U. Wash., Seattle, 1976—; cons. and pres. Econ. Evolution Assocs., 1975—. Mem. Am. Econ. Assn., Western Econ. Assn., Futures Soc. Editor: Research in Law and Economics, 1976; contbr. articles to profl. jours.; author: (with Kevin Croke) Urban Transportation for the Environment, 1974. Office: Sch Pub Affairs DP 30 Univ Wash Seattle WA 98195

ZERBST, ROBERT HOWARD, financial consulting company executive; b. Charleston, S.C., Nov. 16, 1946; s. Howard Cristel and Margaret (Seviour) Z.; B.A., Miami U., Oxford, Ohio, 1968; M.A., Ohio State U., 1971, M.B.A., 1972, Ph.D., 1974; m. Anne Kohr, Apr. 12, 1969; children—Aaron, Thomas, Sara Anne. Economist, Kohr & Royer, Inc., Columbus, Ohio, 1968-74; asst. prof. econs. U. B.C. (Can.), Vancouver, 1974-77; assoc. prof. econs. So. Meth. U., Dallas, 1977-80; pres. Pension Real Estate Services, Inc., San Francisco, 1980—. Real Estate Council B.C. research grantee, 1977-78; Tex. Real Estate Research Ctr. research grantee, 1979; U.S. Dept. Energy research grantee, 1980. Mem. Am. Real Estate and Urban Econs. Assn., Am. Fin. Assn., Am. Inst. Real Estate Appraisers, Soc. Real Estate Appraisers. Contbr. numerous articles and monographs on real estate fin., valuation and investments to profl. publs. Home: 201 Ricardo Ave Piedmont CA 94611 Office: 650 California St 31st Floor San Francisco CA 94108

ZERGA, JOSEPH FREDERICK, accountant, educator; b. Torrance, Calif., Apr. 28, 1942; s. Joseph Edmund and LaVerne Theresa (Piner) Z.; m. Elaine Masouras, July 15, 1970. B.B.A. summa cum laude, Pace U.-Westchester Campus, 1973. C.P.A., Nev. Sr. acct. Harris, Kerr, Forster & Co., C.P.A.s, 1973-75; sr. agt. Nev. Gaming Control Bd., 1976; mng. ptnr. Joseph F. Zerga, Ltd., C.P.A.s, Las Vegas, 1976—; instr. acctg. U. Nev.-Las Vegas, 1978-83. Dir. Nev. Spl. Olympics, 1979. Pace scholar, 1973. Mem. Am. Inst. C.P.A.s, Nev. Soc. C.P.A.s, Nat. Assn. Accts. Democrat. Office: 1785 E Sahara St Suite 380 Las Vegas NV 80104

ZERLAUT, GENE ARLIS, chemist; b. Bailey, Mich., June 23, 1930; s. George David and Glenna Mae (Palm) Z.; student Western Mich. U., 1948-49; B.S., U. Mich., 1956; m. Cecelia Gail McGukin, Mar. 4, 1961; children—Scott Michael, Christopher Robert. Chemist, U.S. Army Ballistic Missle Agy., Huntsville, Ala., 1958-60; aerospace technologist, chemist NASA, Huntsville, 1960-62; sr. chemist, mgr. polymer chemistry research Ill. Inst. Tech. Research Inst., Chgo., 1962-73; pres., tech. dir. DSET Labs., Inc., Phoenix, 1973—. Coach, Little League Baseball, 1974-76; bd. dirs., vice chmn. bd. Solar Energy Research and Edn. Found., 1978-79; commr. Ariz. Solar Commn., 1979-83. Served with U.S. Army, 1956-58. Recipient Invention awards NASA, 1968, Innovation award, 1973. Mem. Solar Energy Industries Assn. (bd. govs. 1976, v.p. 1978-79, exec. com. 1979-81, bd. dirs. 1981-83), Am. Inst. Chemists (dir. 1975), ASTM (nat. chmn. solar energy conversion com. 1978-83), Am. Council Ind. Labs., Am. Inst. Aeros. and Astronautics, Am. Nat. Standards Inst. (mem. solar energy standards coordinating com. 1979-83), Internat. Solar Energy Soc., Internat. Standards Orgn. (chmn. U.S. tech. adv. com. on solar energy), Soc. Plastics Engrs., Fedn. Paint Socs. Patentee in field. Contbr. articles to profl. jours. Research in spectral solar radiometry and accelerated environ. testing. Home: 346 W Pine Valley Dr Phoenix AZ 85023 Office: Box 1850 Black Canyon Stage I Phoenix AZ 85029

ZERZAN, CHARLES JOSEPH, JR., physician; b. Portland, Oreg., Dec. 1, 1921; s. Charles Joseph and Margaret Cecelia (Mahony) Z.; B.A., Wilamette U., 1948; M.D., Marquette U., 1951; m. Joan Margaret Kathan, Feb. 7, 1948; children—Charles Joseph, Michael, Kathryn, Paul, Joan, Margaret, Terrance, Phillip, Thomas, Rose, Kevin, Gregory. Commd. 2d. lt., U.S. Army, 1940, advanced through grades to capt., 1945, ret., 1946, re-enlisted, 1951, advanced through grades to lt. col., M.C., 1965; intern Madigan Gen. Hosp., Ft. Lewis, Wash., 1951-52; resident in internal medicine Letterman Gen. Hosp., San Francisco, 1953-56, Walter Reed Gen. Hosp., Washington, 1960-61; chief of medicine Rodriquez Army Hosp., 1957-60, U.S. Army Hosp., Fort Gordon, Calif., 1962-65; chief gastroenterology Fitzsimmons Gen. Hosp., Denver, 1965-66; chief profl. services U.S. Army Hosp., Ft. Carson, Colo., 1967-68; dir. continuing med. edn. U. Oreg., Portland, 1968-73; partner Permanente Clinic, Portland, 1973—; assoc. clin. prof. medicine U. Oreg., 1973—; individual practice medicine, specializing in gastroenterology, Portland, 1968—; staff Northwest Permanente, P.C.; dir., 1980-83. Decorated Legion of Merit, Army Commendation medal with oak leaf cluster. Diplomate Am. Bd. Internal Medicine. Fellow A.C.P.; mem. Am. Gastroenterol. Assn., Oreg. Med. Assn. (del. Clackamas County, mem. pub. policy com., mem. task force on alternative methods of health care delivery), Ret. Officers Assn. Republican. Roman Catholic. Home: 6364 SE McNary Rd Milwaukie OR 97222 Office: 10200 SE Sunnyside Rd Clackamas OR 97015

ZGUT, JO ELEN KATHERINE, college administrator; b. Walsenburg, Colo., Apr. 5, 1939; d. Joseph Thomas and Helen Z. B.S. in Vocat. Home Econs. Edn., Colo. Stat U., 1961, M.Ed. in Vocat. Adminstrn. and Supervision, 1967. Vocat. credential, Colo. Tchr. home econs. Aurora (Colo.) Pub. Schs., 1961-67; grad. research asst. Colo. State U., Ft. Collins, 1967-69; dir. community and personal service occupations Community Coll. Denver, 1969-75, dir. resource devel., 1975-82, dir. human resources and services div. Red Rocks campus, Golden, Colo., 1982—. Mem. Am. Vocat. Assn. (life; regional v.p., dir.), Colo. Vocat. Assn. (life; pres., mem. exec. bd.; Outstanding Service award), Nat. Council Local Adminstrs. (sec.), Colo. Council Local Adminstrs. (dir.), Colo. Assn. Vocation Adminstrs., Colo. Assn. Community/Jr. Colls., NEA, Colo. Edn. Assn., Aurora Edn. Assn. (sec.), Nat. Assn. Pub. Sch. Adult Edn., Colo. Assn. Continuing Adult Edn. (v.p.), Adult Edn. Assn. U.S.A., Mountain Plains Adult Edn. Assn., Nat. Assn., Vocat. Home Econs. Tchrs., Colo. Assn. Vocat. Home Econs. Tchrs., Nat. Environ. Educators Assn., Air Pollution Control Assn., Nat. Council Research Devel. (sec. region VIII), Delta Kappa Gamma. Roman Catholic. Club: Altrusa (dir.) (Denver). Office: 12600 W 6th Ave Golden CO 80401

ZIDEK, JAMES VICTOR, statistician; b. Acme, Alta., Can., Sept. 26, 1939; s. John and Anna Zidek; B.Sc. with honors, U. Alta., 1961; M.Sc., Stanford U., 1963, Ph.D., 1967; m. Patricia Lynne Donald, Aug. 5, 1961. Prof. stats. U. B.C., Vancouver, 1967—; hon. research fellow Univ. Coll., London, 1971-72; vis. profl. scientist Commonwealth Sci. and Indsl. Research Orgn., Canberra, Australia, 1976-77; cons. engrng. and law; mem. statis. sci. grant selection com. Natural Sci. and Engrng. Research Council of Can. Fellow Inst. Math. Stats.; mem. Statis. Soc. Can., Royal Statis. Soc., Am. Statis. Assn., Internat. Assn. Survey Statisticians, Internat. Statis. Inst. Sr. asso. editor Can. Jour. Statistics, 1980—, asso. editor, 1977-80; asso. editor Annals of Stats., 1975-80; contbr. articles to profl. jours. Home: 4100 Salish Dr 19 Vancouver BC V6N 3M2 Canada Office: Univ Brit Columbia 121 1984 Mathematics Rd Vancouver BC V6T 1Y4 Canada

ZIEGEL, CRISTOPHER CAYARD, biologist, educator; b. Long Beach, Calif., May 27, 1951; s. Dean E. and Wanda J. (Howey) Z.; B.A., Calif. State U., Long Beach, 1973, M.A., 1976; Ed.D., U. So. Calif., 1982. Tchr. sci. and math. Los Angeles Unified Sch. Dist., 1974—; adminstrv. coordinator D.W. Griffith/Calif. Inst. Tech. Magnet Ctr. for Enriched Studies in Sci. and Math., 1978—; mem. faculty Griffith Jr. High Sch., 1974—; ptnr. Ziegel Engrng. Co., Long Beach, 1977—. Mem. So. Calif. Acad. Sci., Natural History Museum Alliance, Friends of Am. Theatre Organ Soc. Author papers in field. Home: 2108 Lomina Ave Long Beach CA 90815 Office: 4765 E 4th St Los Angeles CA 90022

ZIEGEL, DEANE ELLSWORTH, JR., educator; b. Long Beach, Calif., Oct. 3, 1947; s. Deane Ellsworth and Wanda Jean (Howey) Z.; Asso. Sci., Long Beach City Coll., 1967; B.A. in Math. and Physics, Calif. State U., 1969, M.A. in Ednl. Adminstrn. and Secondary Edn., 1972; Ed.D. in Edn. Adminstrn., Curriculum and Instrn., U. So. Calif., 1977. Teaching asst. Long Beach Unified Sch. Dist., 1968-69; tchr. Bellflower (Calif.) Unified Sch. Dist., 1969-70; tchr. San Marino (Calif.) Unified Sch. Dist., 1970-78, chmn. sci. dept. 1972-78; ESEA Title I math. coordinator Los Angeles Unified Sch. Dist., 1978-80, student data system coordinator and registrar, 1980-81, work experience coordinator and R.O.P. adv., 1981-82, dean of students, 1982—. Active Boy Scouts Am., 1965—. Mem. Calif. Tchrs. Assn., NEA, Am. Theatre Organ Soc. Republican. Baptist. Author: The Proposed Voucher System for California Schools, 1972; The Perceptions of Teachers, Administrators and Board Members of Collective Bargaining, 1977. Home: 2108 Lomina Ave Long Beach CA 90815 Office: 450 N Grand Ave Los Angeles CA 90051

ZIEGLER, ANTOINETTE, telecommunications analyst; b. Portsmouth, Va., July 4, 1947; d. George Frederick and Antionette (Hudak) Z.; m. Elliot Scott Helfer, Oct. 28, 1974 (dec.); m. 2d, Eric Allen Morrison, June 21, 1981. B.A., U. Calif.-Berkeley, 1968; M.A. in Edn. and Human Devel., Holy Names Coll., 1981; M.A. in Communications Mgmt., Annenberg Sch., U. So. Calif., 1982. Instr. Alameda County Spl. Schs., San Leandro, Calif., 1974-79; pub. affairs cons. Contact Calif., Beverly Hills, 1980-81; communications planner TRW, Redondo Beach, Calif., 1981-82, sr. communications analyst, 1983—; mgr. office systems Paramount Studios, Los Angeles, 1982-83. Alameda County Regional Criminal Justice planning bd., 1979-80, Alameda County Children's Interest commn., 1979-80; mem. bd. behavioral sci. examiners Calif. Dept. Consumer Affairs. Democrat. Office: One Space Park E2B147 Redondo Beach CA 90278

ZIEGLER, DAVID WAYNE, graphic arts designer, executive; b. Denver, Feb. 12, 1950; s. Westley Wayne and Shirley LaVerne (Diehl) Z. Student Mesa Coll., 1967-68. Graphic designer Penny Pincher Publ., Grand Junction, Colo., 1968-70; designer Mut. Graphics & Typesmith, Denver, 1970-77; free-lance designer, Denver, 1977-79; pres., art dir. Sundance Studio Ltd., Denver, 1979—. Mem. Graphic Arts Prodn. Club, Art Dirs. Club. Office: Sundance Studio Ltd 14 Inverness Dr E Bldg H-236 Englewood CO 80112

ZIELINSKI, CASIMIR EDMUND, therapist, educator; b. Joliet, Ill., Nov. 3, 1923; s. Wincenty and Teofila (Lis) Z. Student Mt. Carmel Coll., 1944-48, Cath. U., 1948-52; A.M., U. Chgo., 1956; Ed.D., U. Houston, 1973. Lic. psychologist, Ill. Ordained priest Carmelite Order, Roman Catholic Ch., 1952. Vice prin. Joliet Cath. High Sch., 1953-54, dir. religion, 1956-64; vice prin. DeSales High Sch., Louisville, 1955-56; dir. counseling and guidance Mt. Carmel High Sch., Houston, 1964-69; instr. Carmelite Jr. Sem., 1965-69; teaching fellow U. Houston, 1969-72; dir., vocat. services Menard (Ill.) Correctional Ctr., 1973-74; asst. prof., counselor edn. So. Ill. U., Edwardsville, 1974-79; assoc. prof. Seattle U., 1979—; adj. prof. Eastern Wash. U., Cheney, 1979—. Mem. Am. Assn. Marriage and Family Therapists; Am. Psychol. Assn., Am. Assn. Counseling and Devel. (pres.-elect Wash. div. 1983-84), N.Am. Soc. Adlerian Psychology, N.W. Inst. Family Therapists, Phi Delta Kappa. Contbr. numerous articles to profl. jours. Home: 7045 120th Ave NE Kirkland WA 98033 Office: Sch Edn Seattle U Seattle WA 89122

ZIESENHENNE, DELORES MAE, pipeline company executive; b. Salt Lake City, Aug. 5, 1943; d. Paul and Gladys M. (Honn) Steed; m. R. H. Ziesenhenne, July 5, 1963. Student U. Utah, 1961-63; B.S. with highest honors, UCLA, 1966; postgrad. middle mgmt. course, Simmons Coll., 1978. C.P.A., Calif. Supervising sr. Peat Marwick Mitchell & Co., Los Angeles, 1966-72; mgr. internal audit Filmways, Inc., Los Angeles, 1972; analyst acctg. policy Atlantic Richfield Co., Los Angeles, 1974; controller, treas., sec., dir. Four Corners Pipe Line Co., Long Beach, 1976. Mem. Calif. C.P.A. Soc., Am. Inst. C.P.A.s, Am. Women Soc. C.P.A.s. Home: 3304 Shelby Dr Los Angeles CA 90034 Office: Four Corners Pipe Line Co 5900 Cherry Ave Long Beach CA 90805

ZIFFREN, PAUL, lawyer; b. Davenport, Iowa, July 18, 1913; s. Jacob and Bella Minnie (Rothenberg) Z.; m. Muriel Averett, May 20, 1948; children—Kenneth, Tony, Abbie, John. B.S., Northwestern U., 1935, J.D., 1938. Bar: Ill. 1938, Calif. 1944, U.S. Supreme Ct. 1951. Ptnr. Gottlieb & Schwartz, Chgo., 1942-46, Loeb & Loeb, Los Angeles, 1946; sr. ptnr. Swartz, Tannenbaum & Ziffren, Los Angeles, 1946-50, Ziffren & Ziffren, Los Angeles, 1950-79, Gibson, Dunn & Crutcher, Los Angeles, 1979—; dir. Pacific Mut. Life Inst. Co., Pacific Telephone and Telegraph Co.; lectr. fed. taxation Northwestern U. Sch. Law; spl. asst. to chief counsel Bur. Internal Revenue, Chgo.; asst. U.S. atty. in charge of tax div., Chgo. Bd. govs., mem. exec. council Performing Arts Council, Music Ctr., Los Angeles; bd. dirs. Music Ctr. Found.; trustee Brandeis U.; chmn. 1984 Los Angeles Olympic Games; trustee St. John's Hosp. and Health Ctr. Found.; bd. dirs. Community TV of So. Calif., KCET, Exec. Service Corps of So. Calif.; mem. Democratic Nat. Com., 1953-60, exec. com., 1956-60; mem. Dem. Nat. Adv. Council, 1957-60; chmn. Calif. Conv. Com. for 1960 Dem. Nat. Conv.; trustee Citizens' Research Found., Los Angeles; bd. dirs. William Holden Wildlife Found. Recipient CORO found. Pub. Affairs award, 1980; Northwestern U. Alumni Assn. Merit award, 1980; Earl Warren Legal Achievement award NAACP Legal Def. Fund, 1979; Mayor's Human Relations Trophy, 1983; named Alumnus of Yr. for Northwestern U., Big Ten Club of So. Calif., 1983; Headliner Greater Los Angeles Press Club, 1983. Mem. ABA, Calif. State Bar Assn., Los Angeles County Bar Assn., Order of Coif. Clubs: Regency, Hillcrest Country (Los Angeles). Office: 2029 Century Park E Suite 4100 Los Angeles CA 90067

ZIGMAN, PAUL EDMOND, environmental planning executive; b. Los Angeles, Mar. 10, 1924; s. Fernand and Rose (Orlijan) Z.; children—Andrea Karen, Eric Kenneth. B.S., UCLA, 1948. Head applied research br. U.S. Naval Radiol. Def. Lab., San Francisco, 1949-59, head tech. mgmt. office, 1961-69; supervisory analytical chemist Atomics Internat., Canoga Park, Calif., 1959-61; pres. Environ. Sci. Assocs., Inc., San Francisco, 1969—; subcom. radioactivity standards Nat. Acad. Scis.-NRC, 1964; instr. U. Calif. Extension, 1977-79. Planning com. San Francisco C. of C., 1981; San Francisco mayor's adv. com. bldg. permit processing, 1980. Served with AUS, 1943. Recipient Meritorious Civilian Service award U.S. Navy, 1968. Mem. Am. Chem. Soc., Assn. Environ. Profls. (pres. 1976-77, award for outstanding service 1977), Am. Planning Assn. Contbr. articles profl. jours. Home: 1191 Compass Ln 112 Foster City CA 94404 Office: 1390 Market St Suite 215 San Francisco CA 94102

ZIKMUND, JOSEPH, II, political scientist, educator; b. Chgo., Dec. 3, 1937; s. Joseph and Dorothy E. (Barlow) Z.; m. Barbara Brown, Aug. 26, 1961; 1 son, Brian Joseph. B.A., Beloit Coll., 1959; M.S., U. Wis., 1961; Ph.D., Duke U., 1965; M.U.P., Wayne State U., 1976. Instr. Duke U., 1964-65; asst. prof. Temple U., Phila., 1965-69; assoc. prof. Albion (Mich.) Coll., 1969-75, chmn. polit. sci. dept., 1972-75; assoc. prof. Ill. Inst. Tech., Chgo., 1975-81, chmn. social scis. dept., 1978-81; dean Sch. Letters and Scis., Menlo Coll., Menlo Park, Calif., 1981—. Woodrow Wilson fellow, 1959-60. Mem. Midwest Polit. Sci. Assn. (sec.-treas. 1979-81), Am. Polit. Sci. Assn. Congregationalist. Author (with D.E. Dennis): Suburbia: Guide to the Literature, 1979; co-editor Ecology of American Political Culture, 1975, Black Politics in Philadelphia, 1973; contbr. articles to profl. publs. Office: 1000 El Camino Real Atherton CA 94025

ZILBERBERG, NAHUM NORBERT, video and film prodn. exec., publisher; b. Manheim, Germany, Feb. 13, 1925; s. Mendel Max and Pasia Paula (Morgenstern) Z.; came to U.S., 1957, naturalized, 1961; grad. Sem. for Art Tchrs., Tel Aviv, 1952; B.F.A., Yale U., 1960, M.F.A., 1961; m. Rita Orechovsky, 1946 (div.); children—Oded, Doron; m. 2d, Barbara Cahn, 1968 (div.); children—Jedediah, Noah. Print shop apprentice, 1936; master of trade, lectr. on printing, 1940; prof. Sem. for Art Tchrs., Tel Aviv, also tchr. arts and crafts in elementary and high sch., 1952-57; teaching fellow Yale U., New Haven, 1958-61; designer Macmillan Pub. Co., Inc., 1963; asst. designer, Harcourt Brace & World (name changed to Harcourt Brace Jovanovich, Inc.), 1964-72, v.p. Center for Study of Instrn. div., San Francisco, 1972-73, pres. Harcourt Brace Jovanovich Films div., San Francisco, 1973-80; founder, pres. NZ Videodisc Prodns., Mill Valley, Calif., 1980—; adj. prof. edn. tech. San Francisco State U. Served with Israel Def. Forces, 1948-5. Recipient film and audio-visual awards including: Grand award Internat. Film and TV Festival N.Y., 1976, 80, Gold awards 1977, 78, 79, 80; Cindy award Info. Film Producers Am., 1976, Gold Camera award U.S. Indsl. Film Festival, 1977, Gold Camera award for videodisc U.S. Indsl. Film Festival, 1979, Gold Hugo award Chgo. Internat. Film Festival, 1980, Gold awards, 1977, 78; Gold award 10th Ann. Festival of Ams., 1977; Disting. Tech. Service awards Soc. Tech. Communication, 1979; Gold award Houston Internat. Film Festival, 1979. Mem. Bookbuilders West, Am. Inst. Graphic Arts, Calif. Humanities Assn., Assn. Ednl. Communications and Tech. (study com. on videodisc). Office: Harcourt Brace Jovanovich Films 1001 Polk St San Francisco CA 94109

ZIMDAHL, ROBERT LAWRENCE, botany educator; b. Buffalo, Feb. 28, 1935; s. Alfred F. and Mildred M. (Lawrence) Z.; m. Ann C. Osborn, Nov. 24, 1956; children—Randall, Jennifer, Robert, Thomas. B.S. in Dairy Husbandry, Agronomy, Cornell U., 1956, M.S. in Agronomy, Plant Physiology, 1966; Ph.D. in Agronomy, Agrl. Chemistry, Oreg. State U., 1968. Agrl. extension agt. State of N.Y., Hudson, 1958-61; with Genoa Farm Service (N.Y.), 1964-66; research assoc. Cornell U., Ithaca, N.Y., 1963-64; asst. prof. Colo. State U., Ft. Collins, 1968-72, assoc. prof., 1972-77, prof. botany and plant pathology dept., 1977—; dir. Internat. Edn., Colo. State U., 1977—. Chmn. bd. dirs. United Campus Ministry, Colo. State U. Danforth assoc., 1976. Mem. Weed Sci. Soc. Am., Western Soc. Weed Sci., Am. Soc. Agronomy, Am. Chem. Soc., AAAS, Sigma Xi. Methodist. Home: 1513 Whedbee St Fort Collins CO 80524 Office: 115 Weed Research Lab Colo State U Fort Collins CO 80523

ZIMMER, RAYMOND EUGENE, accountant; b. Youngstown, Ohio, Aug. 25, 1932; s. Joseph Ignatius and Cecelia Barbara Z.; m. Barbara Ann Langer, June 8, 1953; children—Mark, Kristina Zimmer Adkins, Karen Zimmer Knutson, Karl, Lisa, Paula. B.B.A., U. N.Mex., 1958. C.P.A., N.Mex. Mgr. Zimmer Hardware & Supply Co., Albuquerque, 1951-53; tax acct. Peat, Marwick, Mitchell & Co., Albuquerque, 1957-65, ptnr. in charge tax dept., 1965—. Bd. dirs. Sandia Prep. Sch., 1971—; pres. bd. dirs. Community Council of Albuquerque, 1974-76; treas. R.O. Anderson Sch. Mgmt. Found., 1975—; bd. dirs. St. Joseph Hosp., 1981—; pres. bd. dirs. Albuquerque Community Found., 1982—. Served with U.S. Army, 1953-55. Mem. Am. Inst. C.P.A.s (council 1966-67, 73-76), N.Mex. Soc. C.P.A.s, N.Mex. Estate Planning Council. Republican. Roman Catholic. Club: Albuquerque Petroleum. Office: Peat Marwick Mitchell & Co PO Box 1027 Albuquerque NM 87103

ZIMMERMAN, ANNE RYDER, librarian; b. Seattle, Mar. 20, 1939; d. John N. and M. Margaret (Dyer) R.; m. Gary A. Zimmerman, June 25, 1960; children—Teresa J., Thoams E. B.Econs. magna cum laude, Radcliffe Coll., 1960; postgrad. U. Wis., 1960-63; M.L.S., U. Wash., 1973. Cert. librarian, Wash. Bus. and econs. reference librarian Seattle Pub. Library, 1973-75; research librarian Fed. Home Loan Bank Seattle, 1975-80, asst. v.p., info. officer, 1980—. Bd. dirs. Seattle Zool. Soc., Bellevue (Wash.) Pub. Library; docent Woodland Park Zool. Gardens, Seattle. Seven Coll. Conf. scholar, 1956-60. Mem. Internat. Assn. Bus. Communicators, Pub. Relations Soc. Am., Seattle Bus. Economists, Spl. Libraries Assn., Am. Assn. Zool. Parks and Aquaria, LWV. Clubs: Bellevue Athletic; City (Seattle). Author: A Basic Library for Savings and Loan Associations, 1979. Home: 401-100 Ave NE Apt 323 Bellevue WA 98004 Office: 600 Stewart St Seattle WA 98101

ZIMMERMAN, CHESTER ARTHUR, astronautical engineer; b. San Francisco, Apr. 15, 1921; s. Phillip and Blanche (Sonneborn) Z.; children—Blanche, Joan, Douglas. B.S., U. Calif.-Berkeley 1942; B.S., U.S. Naval Postgrad. Sch., 1951; M.S., Lehigh U., 1952. Commd. ensign U.S. Navy, 1942, advanced through grades to capt., 1962; ret., 1962; dir. propulsion devel. Lockheed Corp., Sunnyvale, Calif., 1962—; pres. Air Cooled Motors, 1979-82. Mem. AIAA, Antique Auto Club Am. Contbr. articles to profl. jours. Home: 2081 Madelaine Ct Los Altos CA 94022 Office: Org 83-01 B/ 154 LMSC Sunnyvale CA 94086

ZIMMERMAN, DON HOWARD, sociology educator; b. Los Angeles, Oct. 16, 1937; s. George Robert and Mary Louise (Donnell) Z.; m. Siu Foo, June 17, 1961; children—Todd Young, Tracy Siu. B.A. in Sociology, UCLA, 1961, M.A., 1963, Ph.D., 1966. Acting asst. prof. sociology U. Calif.-Santa Barbara, 1965-66, asst. prof., 1966-72, assoc. prof., 1972-80, prof., 1980—, chairperson dept., 1980—. Served with USAR, 1961-64. Mem. Am. Sociol. Assn. Democrat. Mem. United Ch. of Christ. Contbr. to profl. jours. Office: Dept Sociology U Calif Santa Barbara CA 93106

ZIMMERMAN, HAROLD SAMUEL, newspaper executive, state senator; b. Valley City, N.D., June 1, 1923; s. Samuel Alwin and Lulu (Wylie) Z.; m. Julianne Williams, Sept. 12, 1946; children—Karen, Steven, Judi Jean (dec.). B.A., U. Wash., 1947. News editor Sedro-Woolley (Wash.) Courier Times, 1947-50, editor, pub. Advocate, Castle Rock, Wash., 1950-57; pub. Post-Record, Camas, Wash., 1957-80, assoc. pub., columnist, 1980; assoc. pub., columnist, dir. Eagle Publs., Camas, 1980—. Mem. Wash. Ho. of Reps., 1967-80; mem. Wash. Senate, 1981—. Served with USAAF, 1943-46. Mem. Grange, Sigma Delta Chi, Sigma Chi. Republican. Methodist. Clubs: Lions, Kiwanis.

ZIMMERMAN, HOWARD CLINTON, education educator, consultant; b. Quilcene, Wash., Jan. 16, 1926; s. William Truesdale and Malvina Elizabeth (Langworthy) Z.; m. Lydia Koch, July 14, 1956 (div.); children—Sylvia, Angela, Joan, Garth. B.A., N.W. Nazarene Coll., Nampa, Idaho, 1948; M.A., U. Oreg., 1954, D.Ed., 1967; postdoctoral NDEA Insts., Kellogg Found. Inst., Kellogg-West retreat. Tchr. English and drama Nampa Sr. High Sch., 1948, Collinsview Grade Sch., Portland, Oreg., 1948-49; tchr., chmn. dept. English, Willamette High Sch., Eugene, Oreg., 1950-65; teaching asst., doctoral fellow U. Oreg., 1949-50, 53-54, 61-62, 64-65; prof. edn. U. Toledo, 1965-70, Calif. State U.-Bakersfield, 1970—; assoc. vis. prof. English, Bowling Green State U., 1968; cons. Am. Book Co.; cons. tech. edn. Advisor, Calif. Democratic party; mem. Kern Philharm. Soc. Served with USNR, 1943-44. Mem. NEA, Calif. Tchrs. Assn. (Who award 1976), Oreg. Edn. Assn. (pres. Lane County), Bethel Edn. Assn. (pres.), Calif. Higher Edn. Assn. (pres.), Nat. Council Tchrs. of English, Assn. Supervision and Curriculum Devel., Calif. Poetry Soc., Calif. Assn. Tchrs. of English, Calif. Reading Assn., Congress Faculty Assns. (local pres., state dir.), Calif. Profs. Reading, Council Exceptional Children, Kern County Assn. Neurol. Handicapped Children (pres.), Calif. Coll. and Univ. Faculty Assn. (pres.), Phi Delta Kappa (Outstanding Man in Edn. 1965). Author: Dico Ergo sum: An Introduction to the Nature of Language, 1961; Ideal Designs for English Programs, 1968; contbr. poetry to Orpheus, 1971-83; contbr. articles profl. jours.

ZIMMERMAN, JACK LAWRENCE, clinical psychologist, educator; b. N.Y.C., Feb. 18, 1945; s. LeRoy Jerome and Rita (Sichelman) Z.; m. Syd Carol Tanner Jacobcik, Sept. 30, 1982; children—Scott Alan, David Brian. B.A. in Psychology, C.W. Post Coll., L.I. U., 1968; Ph.D., U. So. Calif., 1979. Lic. clin. psychologist, Utah. Tchr. emotionally disturbed children Bd. Coop. Ednl. Services, Nassau County, N.Y., 1968-71; recreational therapist Wallace Village for Children, Broomfield, Colo., 1971-72; pvt. practice clin. psychology, Los Angeles, 1975-79, Ogden, Utah, 1979—; dir. treatment alcohol and chem. dependency treatment program St. Benedict's Hosp., Ogden, 1979-81; clin. assoc. prof. nursing Weber State Coll., Ogden, 1979—. Recipient Richard P. Runyon award C.W. Post Coll., 1968; NIMH fellow, 1974. Mem. Am. Psychol. Assn. Jewish. Office: 425 E 5350 S Suite 265 Ogden UT 84403

ZIMMERMAN, RONALD WILLIAM, direct marketing executive; b. Gold Beach, Oreg., Mar. 9, 1948; s. William H. and Lola M. (Kammer) Z. B.A. in English, U. Wash., 1971; postgrad. in Mktg., NYU, 1981. With Eastside Air Conditioning Co., Seattle, 1966-70; salesman Seattle Pub. Market, 1971; owner, mgr. Bonefire Press, Seattle, 1971-72; ptnr. Andromeda Promotions, Seattle, 1971, Grand Central Concepts Co., 1972-73; v.p. mktg., ptnr. Early Winters, Ltd., Seattle, 1974—. Recipient Sci. and Arts Found. award Wash. State U., 1965; Best in Catalogs award Maxwell Sroge, 1982. Mem. Direct Mktg. Assn., Nat. Sporting Goods Assn., Am. Mgmt. Assn. Contbr. articles to Popular Sci. Mag., Assay Mag., Direct Mktg. Mag., others; developer new products in sporting good bus. Home: 153 McGraw St Seattle WA 98109 Office: Early Winters Ltd 110 Prefontaine Pl S Seattle WA 98104

ZIMMERMAN, THOMAS FLETCHER, III, psychologist, med. educator; b. South Bend, Ind., Feb. 11, 1938; s. Thomas Fletcher and Elizabeth Harriet (Price) Z; div.; children—Thomas Fletcher, Jeremy Adam. B.A., Evang. Coll., Springfield, Mo., 1959; M.S., U. Mo., 1961; Ph.D., U. Oreg., 1972. Lic. psychologist, Ill. Research assoc. Inst. Community Studies, Kansas City, Mo., 1966-68; dir. dept. health manpower AMA, Chgo., 1968-72; dean Coll. Associated Health Professions, U. Ill. Med. Ctr., Chgo., 1972-78, assoc. vice chancellor acad. affairs, 1978-81, assoc. prof. psychiatry Coll. Medicine, 1978-80; dir. Annenberg Ctr. Health Scis., Eisenhower Med. Ctr., Rancho Mirage, Calif., 1982—; lectr., cons. in field. Bd. govs. Continuing Edn. Exchange; mem. Council Med Adminstrn., pres., 1968; mem. bd. higher edn. Gen. Council Assemblies of God. NDEA fellow, 1965-66; Bob Hope chair med. edn. Mem. Am. Psychol. Assn., AAAS, Soc. Human Values Medicine. Republican. Contbr. articles to profl. jours. Home: PO Box 921 Rancho Mirage CA 92270 Office: 39000 Bob Hope Dr Rancho Mirage CA 92270

ZINK, LEWIS ELMER, airplane mfg. co. exec.; b. Toledo, Dec. 8, 1929; s. Elmer P. and Jeune M. Zink; B.S. in Econs., Purdue U., 1953; m. Betty Jean Bergheim, Aug. 27, 1955; children—Peter L., Randi E. With Boeing Co., 1956—, mil. mktg. mgr. Boeing Aerospace Co., 1972-83, sr. mgr. program mgmt. Everett div. (747 and 767) Boeing Comml. Airplane Co., Seattle, 1978—. Served with AUS, 1953-55. Mem. Am. Mgmt. Assn., Air Force Assn. Republican. Baptist. Home: 11666 SE 58th St Bellevue WA 98006 Office: Boeing Co PO Box 3707 Seattle WA 98124

ZINKLE, THOMAS EDWARD, clin. psychologist; b. Prairie du Chien, Wis., Feb. 22, 1944; s. Thomas Francis and Anne (Honzel) Z.; B.A., St. Louis U., 1968; M.A., U.S. Internat. U., San Diego, 1970, Ph.D., 1974. Lic. clin. psychologist, Calif. Intern, Community Mental Health Ctr., Pensacola, Fla., 1973-78; pvt. practice psychology, Riverside, Calif., 1978-79, Fontana, Calif., 1979—; clin. psychologist Kaiser Permanente, Fontana, 1979—. Mem. Am. Psychol. Assn., Calif. Psychol. Assn., Inland Counties Psychol. Assn., Nat. Registry Psychologists, Am. Contract Bridge League. Democrat. Home: 12125 Country Club Ln Grand Terrace CA 92324 Office: 9985 Sierra Ave Fontana CA 92335

ZINS, GEORGE BRIAN, assn. exec.; b. Great Falls, Mont., Sept. 26, 1942; s. Leo George and Marion Frances (O'Leary) Z.; m. Diana Mae Dirkson, June 7, 1969; children—Erica Ann, Kendra Lee, Ryan Leo, Scott Raymond. B.S., Coll. Great Falls, 1969. Account mgr. Mont. Deaconess Hosp., Great Falls, 1966-69; dir. bus. Central Mont. Hosp., Lewistown, 1969-70; exec. dir. Mont. Med. Assn., Helena, 1970—. Served with AUS, 1964-66. Mem. Am. Soc. Assn. Execs., Am. Assn. Med. Soc. Execs. Club: Lions. Home: 1055 Flathead Rd Helena MT 59601 Office: 2021 11th Ave Suite 12 Helena MT 59601

ZINT, WILLIAM LEROY, JR., air force officer; b. Denver, May 22, 1936; s. William L. and Anna Maud (Garnett) Z.; m. Jeanette Erickson, Aug. 3, 1963; children—William L. III, Todd M., Sharon C., Steven E. B.S., Colo. State U., 1959; M.A., U. Denver, 1969; postgrad. Armed Forces Staff Coll., 1973. Commd. lt. col. U.S. Air Force, 1959, advanced through grades to lt. col., 1975—, U.S. mil. spokesman for S.E. Asia, Bangkok, Thailand, 1975-76; pub. affairs officer U.S. Pacific Command, Hawaii, 1976-80, exec. asst. to comdr. insp. gen., instr. pilot Williams AFB, Ariz., 1980-83; cons. Pres., Mitchell Field Civic Assn., 1971-72. Decorated D.F.C. (2), Bronze Star, Air Medal (15), Air Force and Joint Services Commendation medal, Vietnamese Gallantry Cross with Silver Star. Mem. Air Force Assn., Aviation Space Writers, Pub. Relations Soc. Am., Order of Daedalians. Republican. Roman Catholic. Club: Toastmasters. Home: 2103 N Gentry St Mesa AZ 85203 Office: 82 FTW Williams AFB AZ 85224

ZIPPIN, CALVIN, epidemiologist, educator; b. Albany, N.Y., July 17, 1926; s. Samuel and Jennie (Perkel) Z.; m. Patricia Jayne Schubert, Feb. 9, 1964; children—David Benjamin, Jennifer Dorothy. A.B. magna cum laude, SUNY-Albany, 1947; Sc.D., Johns Hopkins U., 1953. Research asst. Sterling-Winthrop Research Inst., Rensselaer, N.Y., 1947-50; instr. biostats. Sch. Pub. Health, U. Calif.-Berkeley, 1953-55; vis. assoc. prof. stats. Stanford (Calif.) U., 1962; NIH postdoctoral fellow U. London, 1964-65; prof. epidemiology U. Calif. Sch. Medicine, San Francisco, 1967—; vis. research worker Middlesex Hosp. Med. Sch., London, 1975. Eleanor Roosevelt Am. Cancer Soc. Internat. Cancer fellow, 1975; recipient SUNY-Albany Disting. Alumnus award, 1969. Fellow Am. Statis. Assn., Royal Statis. Soc., Am. Coll. Epidemiology; mem. Am. Soc. Preventive Oncology, Biometric Soc. (pres. Western N.Am. region 1979), Sigma Xi, Phi Beta Kappa. Jewish. Club: B'nai B'rith (pres. Golden Gate Lodge 1970-71, pres. Greater San Francisco Bay Area council 1974-75). Contbr. numerous articles to profl. jours. Home: 4 Warren Ct Tiburon CA 94920 Office: Room U 585 U Calif San Francisco CA 94143

ZIPSER, EDWARD J., meteorologist; b. N.Y.C., Dec. 2, 1937; s. Samuel S. and Sylvia (Wiltsek) Z.; B.S.E., Princeton U., 1958; M.S., Fla. State U., 1960, Ph.D., 1965; m. Marelynn M. Weiss, Sept. 6, 1958; children—Geraldine M., J. Claire. Meteorologist, Nat. Center for Atmospheric Research, Boulder, Colo., 1966—, sr. scientist, 1976—. Mem. Colo. Air Pollution Control Commn., 1976-78. Recipient Nat. Center for Atmospheric Research pubs. prize, 1969; U.K. Nat. Environ. Research Council research fellow, 1974-75. Mem. Am. Meteorol. Soc. (Spl. award 1977) Nat. Acad. Sci. (mem. coms.), AAAS, Sigma Xi. Contbr. articles to profl. jours. Home: 1800 Sunset Blvd Boulder CO 80302 Office: NCAR PO Box 3000 Boulder CO 80307

ZIRKER, JOSEPH, artist, educator, lecturer; b. Los Angeles, Aug. 13, 1924; s. Clarence Harold and Lillian (Rappaport) Z.; m. Virginia Luth, 1947; m. 2d, Eva Meyer, Aug. 12, 1963; children—Daniel Gates, Lisa Zirker Moses, Nila. Student UCLA, 1943-44, 46-47; B.F.A., U. Denver, 1949; M.F.A., U. So. Calif., 1951. Printer and research fellow Tamarind Lithography Workshop, Los Angeles, 1961-63; lectr. U. So. Calif., Los Angeles, 1963; instr. Los Angeles County Art Inst., 1964, San Jose (Calif.) City Coll., 1966-80; lectr. Stanford (Calif.) U., 1981—; represented in permanent collections Syntex Corp., Palo Alto, Calif., Internat. Paper Corp., N.Y.C., Univ. Art Collection, Ariz. State U., Tempe. Served with USN, 1944-46.

ZISHKA, RONALD LOUIS, sociologist, clergyman, educator, marriage and family therapist; b. Sheldon, Iowa, Mar. 27, 1935; s. Louis Frank and Wilma Marie (Plantz) Z.; B.A., Capital U., 1958; M.Div., Trinity Theol. Sem., 1962; M.A., Case Western Res. U., 1965; Ph.D., Ohio State U., 1973; postdoctoral psychotherapy tng. Pastoral Counseling Services, Columbus, Ohio, 1973-75; children from previous marriage —Mary, John, Cathy. Asst. prof. sociology Ohio U., Athens, 1966-79; assoc. prof. sociology Christ Coll. of Irvine (Calif.), 1979—, dir. social work program, 1981—; pvt. practice marriage, family and child counseling and psychotherapy, Irvine, 1979—; ordained to ministry Luth. Ch., 1962. Lic. marriage, family and child counselor, Calif. Mem. Am. Assn. Marriage and Family and Child Counselors, Calif. Assn. Marriage, Family and Child Therapists, Am. Sociol. Assn., Pacific Sociol. Assn., Soc. Sci. Study Social Problems, Calif. Psychol. Assn. Address: 1530 Concordia Irvine CA 92715

ZISHKA, WILLIAM ALBERT, JR., marketing, financial exec.; b. Lawrence, Kan., Aug. 14, 1949; s. William Albert and Margaret (Foley) Z.; student Arapahoe Community Coll., 1968-71, U. Colo., 1971-74; certificate, U. Mich., 1978; m. Ann B. Gordon, Aug. 16, 1973. Journeyman clk. Safeway Stores, Inc., Denver, 1968-78; fin./mktg. dir. WJL Sound, Inc., Denver, 1975-81; v.p. mktg. Thompson, McPherson and Marx, 1981—; audio video instr.; audio video cons. Mem. Environ. Action Com., 1975-80. Mem. Nat. Geographic Soc., Soc. Audio Cons.,Guild of Audio Specialists. Democrat. Roman Catholic. Clubs: Optimist (bd. dirs. 1979—). Home: PO Box 2464 Littleton CO 80161 Office: PO Box 17484TA Denver CO 80217

ZISMAN, FRANK, optometrist, visual scientist; b. Los Angeles, July 18, 1948; s. Max and Celia (Kinsbursky) Z.; m. Katherina Rohanova, Nov. 9, 1977; children—Emily, Sarah, Celia. B.S., U. Calif-Berkeley, 1972, O.D., 1974; Ph.D., U. Manchester (Eng.), 1977. Cons. electrodiagnostics and color vision and diabetology Donnor Pavilion, Lawrence-Berkeley Labs., Calif., 1973-74; 78-80; demonstrator U. Manchester Inst. Sci. and Tech., 1975-77; individual practice optometry, Eng. and Calif., 1975—; mem. faculty U. Calif. Sch. Optometry-Berkeley, 1978—, asst. clin. prof. optometry, 1978—, assoc. research specialist, 1980—; cons. in field. Nikon scholar, 1971; Am. Optometric Found. fellow, 1974-75, Borish award, 1974. Fellow Am. Acad. Optometry; mem. Assn. Research in Vision and Ophthalmology, Calif. Optometric Assn., Alameda County Optometric Assn., Am. Optometric Assn., Internat. Research Group in Color Vision Deficiencies, AAAS. Contbr. numerous articles on vision to profl. publs. Office: Univ Calif Sch Optometry Berkeley CA 94720

ZIVIC, WILLIAM THOMAS, artist, sculptor, gallery owner; b. Ironwood, Mich., Aug. 31, 1930; s. Stephan and Anna Louise (Herbenar) Z.; m. Carol Jean Engebretsen, July 11, 1959; children—William, John. Student pub. schs., Ironwood, Mich. Mcht. seaman, Atlantic and Pacific oceans, 1948; surveyor, Canada-U.S. oil pipeline, 1949; mcht. seaman, Gt. Lakes; iron miner, Ironwood, 1958-61; detective, Tucson Police Dept., 1961-67; now owner, Trail Dust Gallery; art lectr. Bd. dirs. YMCA. Served in U.S. Army, 1950-52, 1954-58. Decorated Bronze Star. Awards include: 1st place in watercolor Huachuca Art Show, Ariz., 1973-75; best of show Internat. Fine Arts Exhbn., Palm Springs, Calif., 1977; 1st place in oil painting Wis. Art Festival, 1978. Roman Catholic. Author: Southwest Memories, 1975; painted official bicentennial painting for Ariz., 1976.

ZLOTLOW, SUSAN FRANCES, psychotherapist, educator; b. Huntington, N.Y., July 13, 1952; d. Moses Gideon and Guta (Friedman) Z.; B.A., U. Rochester, 1974; M.A., U. Conn., 1977, Ph.D., 1979; m. Kevin Edward O'Grady, Sept. 2, 1982. Asst. prof. dept. psychology Wheaton Coll., Norton, Mass., 1979-80; staff psychologist Albuquerque Child Guidance Center, Albuquerque, 1980—; lectr. dept. guidance and counseling U. N.Mex., Albuquerque, 1981—, clin. asst. prof. dept. psychiatry Med. Sch., 1982—; cons. Isleta Headstart, 1980; N.Mex. cons. Albuquerque Pub. Sch. Counselors, 1980. USPHS fellow U. Conn., 1974-76. Mem. Am. Psychol. Assn., Southwestern Psychol. Assn., Western Psychol. Assn., N.Mex. Psychol. Assn., Phi Beta Kappa, Phi Kappa Phi. Contbr. articles to profl. jours. Office: 117 Montclaire St SE Albuquerque NM 87108

ZOLBER, KATHLEEN KEEN, nutrition educator, mgmt. cons.; b. Walla Walla, Wash., Dec. 9, 1916; d. Wildie H. and Alice (Johnson) Keen; m. Melvin L. Zolber, Sept. 19, 1937. B.S. in Foods and Nutrition, Walla Walla Coll., 1941; M.A., Wash. State U., 1961; Ph.D., U. Wis., 1968. Registered dietitian. Dir. food service Walla Walla Coll., 1941-50, mgr. coll. store, 1951-59, asst. prof. food and nutrition, 1959-62, assoc. prof., 1962-64; assoc. prof. nutrition Loma Linda (Calif.) U., 1964-72, prof. nutrition, 1973—, dir. dietetic edn., 1967—, dir. dietetics Med. Ctr., 1972—. Mead Johnson grantee, 1965-67; recipient Alumna of Yr. award Walla Walla Coll., 1977; Delores Nyhus award Calif. Dietetic Assn., 1978. Mem. Am. Dietetic Assn. (pres. 1982—), Am. Pub. Health Assn., Am. Home Econs. Assn., Am. Mgmt. Assn., AAUP, Soc. Food Service Research, Soc. Personnel Adminstrn., Omicron Nu, Delta Omega. Home: PO Box 901 Loma Linda CA 92354 Office: Dept Nutrition Sch of Allied Health Loma Linda U Loma Linda CA 93354

ZOLL, JAMES GREGORY, school administrator; b. Buffalo, Sept. 25, 1947; s. John George and Mary Elizabeth (Griffen) Z.; m. Patricia Leslie Greblo, June 2, 1979; 1 son, James Patrick. B.A. in History and English, U. New Eng., 1969; M.Edn. of Deaf, Smith Coll., 1974; M.Ednl. Adminstrn., U. San Diego, 1978. Adminstrv. services credential, Ariz., Calif.; teaching credential, N.Y., Ariz., Mass., Calif. Instr., Rochester (N.Y.) Sch. of Deaf, 1974-77; elem. prin. Miami (Ariz.) Sch. Dist., 1978-80; prin. U. San Diego High Sch., 1980—; interpreter for deaf. Chmn. Mother's march Ariz. March of Dimes, 1979. Served to capt. U.S. Army, 1969-73. Decorated Bronze Star; Cross of Gallantry (Vietnam); recipient Ednl. Adminstrn. award U. San Diego, 1977; Winefred Witter fellow, 1973. Mem. Council Advancement and Support of Edn., Nat. Assn. Ind. Schs., Conv. Am. Instrs. of Deaf, Nat. Assn. Secondary Sch. Prins., Nat. Assn. Elem. Sch. Prins. Roman Catholic. Clubs: Exchange, Kiwanis (San Diego). Home: 2096 Ventana Way El Cajon CA 92020 Office: U San Diego High School 5961 Linda Vista Rd San Diego CA 92110

ZOLLINGER, BOYD J., manufacturing executive; b. Rexburg, Idaho, July 17, 1940; s. Vern W. and Ann (Johanson) Z.; m. Diane Sue Call, June 15, 1968; children—Leslie Ann, Christian, Richard, Jennifer, Melisa. B.A., Brigham Young U., 1965, M.S., 1967; M.B.A., Columbia U., 1969. In mgmt. tng. program First Nat. City Bank, N.Y.C., 1968; pres., owner Yellowstone Leather Products Inc., Idaho Falls, Idaho, 1969—. Chmn., Idaho Falls Consol. Hosp.; past pres. Bonneville County United Way. Mormon. Club: Rotary (Idaho Falls). Home: 2940 Redbarn Ln Idaho Falls ID 83401 Office: PO Box 26 Idaho Falls ID 83402

ZOMMERS, G. JURIS, interior designer, consultant; b. Riga, Latvia, Dec. 13, 1938; s. Hermanis Rudolfs Zommers and Milda (Makars) Z.; m. Dzintra Aina Zamelis, June 15, 1963 (div.); children—Andrejs Markus, Karlis Eduards, Pauls Hermanis; m. 2d, Stephanie Lee Harris, Dec. 23, 1982. B.S. in Interior Design, U. Wash., 1962. Designer, Aaron's Interiors Co., Bellevue, Wash., 1962-65, Western Internat. Hotels, Seattle, 1965-68; mgr. interior design dept. Allied Stores (The Bon Marche), Seattle, 1968-73; dir. design Mayer Baron Assos., Seattle, 1973; ptnr., operator Daina Design-Interior Design Studio, 1973—; advisor career seminars. Active Boy Scouts Am., Nat. Right to Work Found. Served with USAR 1962-68. Recipient Edward E. Carlson creativity award, 1972. Mem. Am. Soc. Interior Designers (cert. 1980). Republican. Lutheran. Club: American-Latvian, Seattle. Office: 126 Madrone Ln PO Box 10255 Bainbridge Island WA 98110

ZOMMICK, KENNETH, lawyer; b. Chester, Pa., June 21, 1938; s. Louis J. and Lee C. Zommick; m. Barbara V. Zommick, Dec. 22, 1963, children—Melinda, Jordan, Jason. B.A., UCLA, 1960; LL.B., U. Calif.-Berkeley, 1964. Bar: Calif. 1965, U.S. Supreme Ct. 1975. Legal aid City of Long Beach (Calif.), 1963; ptnr. firm. Blumberg & Zommick, Long Beach, 1964-77, Simon, McKinsey, Miller, Zommick, Sandor & Alban, Long Beach, 1977—. Mayor City of Los Alamitos (Calif.),

1978-83; mem. Los Alamitos City Council, 1977—. Served to 1st lt. USAR, 1960-68. Recipient recognition for service as bd. mem. for 15 yrs. Found. Ednl. and Behavioral Therapy, 1968, as charter asst. commr. Am. Youth Soccer Orgn. Region 159, 1974. Mem. Long Beach Bar Assn. (pres. 1981), Los Angeles Bar Assn. (trustee 1979-80), Calif. Bar Assn., Calif. trial Lawyers Assn. Democrat. Jewish. Office: 2750 Bellflower Blvd Suite 100 Long Beach CA 90815

ZONGKER, ELIZABETH KATHRYN, publication executive; b. McVille, N.D.; d. Harry Thomas and Beth Kathryn (Croskell) Hanson; m. Norman Thomas Wright, Sept. 8, 1961; children—Heather, Thomas; m. 2d, William Lee Zongker, Feb. 10, 1975. B.A. in English, San Diego State U., 1971. With San Diego Mag., 1972—, advt. dir., 1975—, assoc. pub., 1980—; organizer Sun Savs. & Loan, 1981; dir. Harvest Savs. & Loan. Trustee, Combo, San Diego, 1981-83; bd. dirs. Charter 100, San Diego, 1978-83. Club: Ad (San Diego). Home: 1221 Parker Pl San Diego CA 92109 Office: 3254 Rosecrans St San Diego CA 92110

ZONGOLOWICZ, HELEN MICHAELINE, school principal; b. Kenosha, Wis., July 22, 1936; d. Edmund S. and Helen (Ostrowski) Z.; Ed.B., Dominican Coll., 1966; M.A., Cardinal Stritch Coll., 1973; Ed.D., U. No. Colo., 1977. Tchr. elem. schs. Kenosha, 1956-58, Center Line, Mich., 1958-59, Taft, Calif., 1960-61, Lake Wales, Fla., 1962-63, Albuquerque, 1963-65; tchr., asst. prin. St. Mary's Sch., Taft, 1965-69; asst. sch. supt. Diocese of Fresno, Calif., 1969-70; tchr. primary grades Greasewood Boarding Sch., Ganado, Ariz., 1970-72, coordinator spl. projects, 1972-75, liaison to parent adv. council, 1972-75, tchr. supr., 1972-76; ednl. specialist Ft. Defiance Agy., Navajo Area, Ariz., 1974-75, ednl. diagnostician, 1979-80; vis. asst. prof. U. Colo., 1976; asst. prof. Auburn (Ala.) U., 1977-79; prin. Chuska Sch., Tohatchi, N.Mex., 1980—. Recipient Spl. Achievement award U.S. Dept. Interior, 1971, 73, Superior Performance award, 1982. Mem. Am. Assn. Mental Deficiency, Assn. for Supervision and Curriculum Devel., Council for Exceptional Children, Council for Basic Edn., Phi Delta Kappa. school principal; b. Kenosha, Wis., July 22, 1936; d. Edmund S. and Helen (Ostrowski) Z.; Ed.B., Dominican Coll., 1966; M.A., Cardinal Stritch Coll., 1973; Ed.D., U. No. Colo., 1977. Tchr. elem. schs. Kenosha, 1956-58, Center Line, Mich., 1958-59, Taft, Calif., 1960-61, Lake Wales, Fla., 1962-63, Albuquerque, 1963-65; tchr., asst. prin. St. Mary's Sch., Taft, 1965-69; asst. sch. supt. Diocese of Fresno, Calif., 1969-70; tchr. primary grades Greasewood Boarding Sch., Ganado, Ariz., 1970-72, coordinator spl. projects, 1972-75, liaison to parent adv. council, 1972-75, tchr. supr., 1972-76; ednl. specialist Ft. Defiance Agy., Navajo Area, Ariz., 1974-75, ednl. diagnostician, 1979-80; vis. asst. prof. U. Colo., 1976; asst. prof. Auburn (Ala.) U., 1977-79; prin. Chuska Sch., Tohatchi, N.Mex., 1980—. Recipient Spl. Achievement award U.S. Dept. Interior, 1971, 73, Superior Performance award, 1982. Mem. Am. Assn. Mental Deficiency, Assn. for Supervision and Curriculum Devel., Council for Exceptional Children, Council for Basic Edn., Phi Delta Kappa. Address: Chuska School Tohatchi NM 87325

ZOOK, DEAN ALVA, safety consultant; b. Los Angeles, Nov. 3, 1947; s. M. Alva and Caroline Claire (Erskine) Z., Jr.; m. Donna May Lento, Mar. 25, 1972. B.S. in Biology, Pepperdine Coll., 1968. Cert. assoc. safety profl. Shift supr. Micro-Mask Inc., Sunnyvale, Calif., 1974-75; loss prevention cons. Liberty Mut. Ins. Com., Fresno, Calif., 1975—. Served to capt. USAF, 1969-74. Decorated Air Medal (6). Mem. Am. Soc. Safety Engrs. Club: Fresno Model R.R. Office: PO Box 5014 Fresno CA 93784

ZOOLALIAN, EDWARD, electronics co. mgr.; b. Newburyport, Mass., May 4, 1934; s. Masis and Haygouhi (Sakayan) Z.; B.S., M.I.T., 1956; M.B.A., U. So. Calif., 1965; m. Denise Ruel, Oct. 17, 1959; children—James, Pamela, Linda. Mfg. mgr. Space Labs., Chatsworth, Calif., 1965-66, Neff Instrument Corp., Monrovia, Calif., 1966—. Mem. Monrovia City Council, 1979—. Served with U.S. Army, 1957-59. Republican. Presbyterian. Home: 981 Briarcliff Rd Monrovia CA 91016 Office: 700 S Myrtle Ave Monrovia CA 91016

ZSCHAU, ED, congressman, business executive; b. Omaha, Jan. 6, 1940; m. Jo Ann Wiedmann; children—Ed, Liz, Cameron. A.B. in Philosophy cum laude, Princeton U., 1961; M.B.A., Stanford U., 1963, M.S. in Stats., 1964, Ph.D. in Bus. Adminstrn., 1967. Asst. prof. Stanford (Calif.) Grad. Sch. Bus., 1965-69; vis. asst. prof. Harvard Bus. Sch., 1967-68; founder, pres. System Industries, Sunnyvale, Calif., 1968-82; mem. 98th Congress from 12th Calif. Dist., mem. Fgn. Affairs Com., chmn. Task Force on High Tech. for Research Com. House Republican Conf. Del. White House Conf. on Small Bus., 1980; dir. Am. Council for Capital Formation, 1979-82; chmn. bd. San Francisco Bay Area High Tech. Sci. Ctr., 1983; community advisor Jr. League of Palo Alto, 1981-82. Named Bus. Leader of Year, Santa Clara County Bus. Mag., 1978. Mem. Am. Electronics Assn. (dir. 1974-79, chmn. bd. 1978, chmn. Capital Formation Task Force 1978). Office: 505 W Olive Ave Suite 125 Sunnyvale CA 94086 also 429 Cannon Bldg Washington DC 20515

ZUCKER, ALFRED JOHN, educator, sch. adminstr.; b. Hartford, Sept. 25, 1940; s. Samuel and Rose (Zucker) Z.; A.A., Los Angeles Valley Coll., 1960; B.A., U. Calif. at Los Angeles, 1962, M.A., 1963, Ph.D., 1966; m. Sallie Lea Friedheim, Dec. 25, 1966; children—Mary Anne, John James, James Patrick, Patrick Jonathan, Anne-Marie Kathleen. Lectr. English, Los Angeles City Coll., 1963-68; prof. English, philosophy, chmn. div. humanities Los Angeles Southwest Coll., 1968-72, chmn. English dept., 1972-74, asst. dean instruction, 1974—. Mem. Los Angeles Jr. Coll. Dist. Senate, 1969—. Mem. Los Angeles Coll. Tchrs. Assn. (dir.), Calif. Jr. Coll. Assn., Calif. Tchrs. Assn., AAUP, Phi Beta Kappa, Phi Delta Kappa (pres. U. Calif. at Los Angeles chpt. 1966-67, v.p. 1967-68). Club: K.C. Contbr. articles to profl. jours. Home: 3009 Oakwood Torrance CA 90505

ZUCKER, DEVRA Z. HILL, author, radio commentator, nutritionist; b. Berkeley, Calif.. Aug. 26; d. James John and Giovana Z. (Muzio) Bolton; m. Irwin Zucker, Sept. 1, 1957; children—Lori Brana, Jodi Michele, Shari Lynne. B.A., Union U., Los Angeles, 1977; M.S. in Nutrition, Donsbach U., 1979; Ph.D. in Communications Golden State U., 1980. Radio communicator Sta. KSFO, San Francisco, 1955—, Sta. KJAY, Sacramento, 1978—, Sta. KMPC, Los Angeles, 1975—, Sta. KNBC, San Francisco, 1954—; lectr. in field. Recipient Humanitarian Bronze Halo award So. Calif. Motion Picture Council, 1982. Mem. Women in Bus. Author: Rejuvenate, 1982; How to Delay Wrinkles, 1980; biography: My Name is Leona Gage, 1964; novels: You Better Believe It, 1965; Three to Make Merry, 1966; contbr. articles to numerous mags. including Coronet, Modern Screen, Girl Talk; reporter Nat. Enquirer, 1976—; columnist So. Calif. News Syndicate, 1974—; author column What's Happening. Address: 714 N Crescent Dr Beverly Hills CA 90210

ZUCKERMAN, HAROLD FRED, school administrator; b. Hartford, Conn., Mar. 29, 1926; s. Frank and Anna (Arinowitz) Z.; m. Ilene Fay Tunick, July 15, 1933; children—Dori Alix, David Jason, Marne Erica. B.A., U. Calif., 1964, M.A., 1964. Cert. secondary and elem. adminstr., Calif. Elem. sch. tchr., 1949-65; middle sch., jr. high sch. prin. Whisman Sch. Dist., Mountain View, Calif., 1965-75; prin. Fremont High Sch., Oakland, Calif., 1967-82; dir. Schs. Organized for Acad. Revitalization, Oakland, 1982—; cons., speaker in field. Trustee San Ramon Valley Unified Sch. Dist., 1971-78; founder, past pres. Diablo Light Opera Co.; mem. adv. bd. Clark Found. Partnership. Kettering Found. fellow, 1970-83; recipient Calif. Tchrs. Assn. Creative Schs. award, 1969. Mem. Am. Mgmt. Assn., Am. Soc. Tng. and Devel., Assn. Supervision and Curriculum Devel., Nat. Acad. Sch. Execs., Nat. Assn. Secondary Sch. Prins., Assn. Calif. Sch. Adminstrs., Nat. Tchrs. English. Democrat. Jewish. Contbr. articles to profl. publs. Home: 302 Cameo Dr Danville CA 94526 Office: 1025 2nd Ave Oakland CA 94606

ZUCKERMAN, IRA LAURENCE, lawyer; b. N.Y.C., Apr. 14, 1947; s. William J. and Lillian (Skolnick) Z.; m. Ginger Senatore, Sept. 17, 1982; children—David, Jonathan. B.B.A., Temple U., 1968; J.D., St. John's U., 1974; postgrad. NYU, 1974-76; LL.M. in Taxation, U. Miami, 1978. Bar: N.Y. 1975, U.S. Tax Ct. 1975. Acct., Hanigsberg, Delson, Broser, N.Y.C., 1973-75; tax atty. Nabisco, Inc., East Hanover, N.J., 1975-76; tax mgr. Coulter Electronics, Inc., Hialeah, Fla., 1976-79; asst. controller taxes Storage Tech. Corp., Louisville, Colo., 1979—; speaker in field. Mem. ABA, N.Y. State Bar Assn., Internat. Fiscal Assn., Tax Execs. Inst., Denver Internat. Tax Group. Contbr. articles to profl. jours. Office: 2270 S 88th St MD45 Louisville CO 80028

ZUCKERMAN, MADELINE MARY, public relations and advertising executive; b. N.Y.C., Dec. 3, 1947; d. Sterling and Ann (Tunno) Bottenus; m. Leonard Zuckerman, Mar. 8, 1970; children—Jennifer, Matthew. B.A. in Journalism and Communications, NYU, 1969; cert. N.Y. Sch. Interior Design, 1970, Collegiate Bus. Sch., N.Y.C., 1967. Asst. to dir. corp. pub. relations Burlington Industries, N.Y.C., 1966-68; v.p., ptnr. Letitia Baldrige Enterprises, Inc., N.Y.C., 1968-75; owner, pres. Madeline Zuckerman Pub. Relations/Advt., Tustin, Calif., 1977—. Lectr., Orange Coast Coll., Golden West Coll., Calif. State U.-Fullerton. Mem. program com. Indsl. League Orange County; publicity vol. Orange County Child Gudiance Ctr., Jr. Assistance League, Newport Beach, Calif. Recipient N.Y. Young Achiever award Glamour mag., 1974. Mem. Pub. Relations Soc. Am., Exec. Women Internat., Women in Communications, Orange County Press. Club, Newport Harbor Area C. of C., Irvine C. of C. Contbr. articles to mags. Office: 14751 Plaza Dr Suite E Tustin CA 92680

ZUEHLKE, WILLIAM HENRY, financial consultant; b. Appleton, Wis., Apr. 19, 1915; s. William H. and Ina (Babcock) Z.; Ph.B., Lawrence U., 1936; m. Muriel Mae Heidemann, May 2, 1953. Trading and syndicate mgr. Harris, Hall & Co., investment bankers, Chgo. and N.Y.C., 1936-46; sr. v.p., dir. investments Aid Assn. for Lutherans, Appleton, 1946-77; pres., dir. Tunnel Springs Ranch Corp.; dir. emeritus Post Corp., Appleton, emeritus First Nat. Bank of Appleton. Bd. dirs., v.p. Santa Cruz County Fair and Rodeo Assn.; co-chmn. Santa Cruz County Fair, 1980-83; commr. Santa Cruz County Bd. Adjustment; bd. dirs. Santa Cruz County Better Govt. Assn.; trustee Lawrence U., Valparaiso U. Served to lt. comdr. USNR, 1941-46. Paul Harris fellow Rotary Internat. Mem. Chartered Fin. Analysts, Fraternal Investment Assn., Soc. Tympanuchus Cupido Pinnatus, Ariz.-Sonora Desert Mus., Ariz. Nature Conservancy, Los Charros del Desierto, Sigma Phi Epsilon. Republican. Lutheran. Clubs: Rotary, Old Pueblo (Tucson). Home: Tunnel Springs Ranch Sonoita AZ 85637 Office: PO Box 326 Sonoita AZ 85637

ZUELOW, MARGO JEANNE, educational administrator; b. Eau Claire, Wis., Mar. 8, 1938; d. Ivan Eugene and Alice May (Krause) Chamberlain; B.A., Bethel Coll., St. Paul, 1965; M.Ed., U. Alaska, 1973; Ph.D., U. Oreg., 1977; m. James F. Zuelow, Aug. 20, 1960 (div.); children—Cynthia Jeanne, James F. Tchr. elem. schs., Minn., Alaska, Oreg., 1965-71; instr. Koskokwim Community Coll., Bethel, Alaska, 1974-76; supr. adult vocat. edn. Alaska Dept. Edn., Juneau, 1977-79; dean instrn. Kenai Peninsula Community Coll., Soldotna, Alaska, 1979-82; mem. rural edn. research staff U. Alaska, Anchorage, 1982—; adj. prof. Alaska Pacific U.; active various state coms. and commns. Del., Alaska Dem. Conv. Mem. Am. Assn. Supervision and Curriculum Devel., Am. Assn. Ednl. Research, Nat. Assn. Exec. Females, Phi Delta Kappa. Lutheran. Club: Seraptomus. Author: Activities for Young Children, 1975; contbr. articles to profl. publs. Address: 3701 E 20th St Anchorage AK 99508

ZUKER, RAYMOND FREDERICK, college dean, philosophy educator; b. Dothan, Ala., Dec. 30, 1945; s. Raymond Francis and Naomi Amanda Z.; m. Su Young Lee, May 15, 1971; children—Sonya Lee, Juliana Marie. A.B., Duke U., 1967, M.Ed., 1975, Ph.D., 1982. Asst. dir. admission, scholarship officer Duke U., Durham, N.C., 1971-77; dir. admissions Tulane U., New Orleans, 1979-81; dean admissions and fin. aid, mem. faculty philosophy dept. Pomona Coll., Claremont, Calif., 1981—. Served with U.S. Army, 1968-71. Fellow N.C. Inst. Politics, 1974. Mem. Nat. Assn. Coll. Admissions Counselors (v.p.), Am. Assn. Collegiate Registrars and Admissions Officer, Nat. Assn. Fgn. Student Affairs, Am. Personnel and Guidance Assn., N.C. Psychol. Assn. (assoc.). Democrat. Roman Catholic. Author: (with Karen C. Hegener) Peterson's Guide to College Admissions: Getting into the College of Your Choice, 1976, 3d edit., 1983. Office: Pomona College 104 Sumner Hall Claremont CA 91711

ZUKOWSKI, LINDA MARIA, manager; b. Hackensack, N.J., July 11, 1952; d. Charles John and Helen Francis (Moticker) Zukowski. B.A., Jersey City State Coll., 1974; M.S., Central Conn. State, 1977; postgrad. Golden Gate U., 1982—. Cert. spl. edn. tchr., reading cons. Spl. edn. tchr., New London, Conn., 1974-77; dept. chmn. secondary spl. edn., 1977-79; high sch. spl. edn. tchr., Groton, Conn., 1979-80; frame supr. Pacific Telephone, Palo Alto, Calif., 1980-81, staff mgr., San Francisco, 1981-82, staff asst. to div. mgr., 1983—. Mem. New London Fedn. Tchrs. (v.p. 1975-76), Kappa Delta Pi. Home: 812 Camelback Pl Pleasant Hill CA 94523 Office: 666 Folsom St Ste 558 San Francisco CA 94107

ZUMBERGE, JAMES HERBERT, geologist, university president; b. Mpls., Dec. 27, 1923; s. Herbert Samuel and Helen (Reich) Z.; student Duke, 1943-44; B.A., U. Minn., 1946, Ph.D., 1950; LL.D., Grand Valley State Coll., 1970, Kwansei Gakuin U. (Japan), 1979; L.H.D., Nebr. Wesleyan U., 1972; m. Marilyn Edwards, June 21, 1947; children—John Edward, JoEllen, James Frederick, Mark Andrew. Instr., Duke U., 1946-47; mem. faculty U. Mich., 1950-62, prof. geology, 1960-62; pres. Grand Valley State Coll., Allendale, Mich., 1962-68; prof. geology, dean U. Ariz. Coll. Earth Sci., Tucson, 1968-72; chancellor U. Nebr. at Lincoln, 1972-75; pres. So. Meth. U., Dallas, 1975-80; pres. U. So. Calif., Los Angeles, 1980—. Cons. geologist ground water and non-metallic minerals, 1950-62; chief glaciologist Ross Ice Shelf Project, IGY, 1957-58; dir. Dresser Industries, Security Pacific Nat. Bank; chmn. vis. com. Gen. Motors Inst., 1977—; ofcl. del. Sci. Com. on Antarctic Research; mem. adv. com. on Antarctic affairs U.S. Dept. State; chmn. Ross Ice Shelf Project, 1970-73, NSF, also mem. steering group Greenland Ice Sheet Program; del. numerous internat. confs. on polar research, Moscow, 1958, Chamonix, 1958, Helsinki, 1960, Obergurgl, Austria, 1962, Poland, 1967, Oslo, 1970, Sydney, Australia, 1972, Mendoza, Argentina, 1976, Warsaw, 1978, New Zealand, 1980; mem. Nat. Sci. Bd., 1974—. Bd. overseers Hoover Instn. on War, Revolution and Peace, 1978—. Recipient Antarctic Service medal, 1966; Distinguished Alumni award U. Minn., 1972; James H. Zumberge Library, Grand Valley State Coll., named 1968; Cape Zumberge, Antarctica named 1960. Mem. Geol. Soc. Am., Am. Geophys. Union, Soc. Econ. Geologists, Internat. Glaciological Soc., AAAS, Mich. Acad. Scis. (pres. 1967), Sigma Xi (nat. lectr. 1978-80). Clubs: Cosmos (Washington); Calif.; Univ., Explorers (N.Y.C.). Author: The Lakes of Minnesota, 1952; Laboratory Manual for Physical Geology, 1967, 73, 80; Elements of Geology, 1963, 72; Elements of Physical Geology, 1976; also articles. Address: Office of Pres U Southern Calif Los Angeles CA 90007

ZUNKER, GEORGE ALLEN, lawyer; b. Spruce Center Twp., Minn., July 29, 1940; s. George William and Elda Louise (Wilke) Z.; m. Jo Patricia Rheingans, June 6, 1964; children—Karl Eric, Kurt Allen. B.S., St. Cloud State U., 1962; M.A. U. No. Colo., 1968; J.D., U. Wyo., 1975. Admitted to Wyo. bar, 1975; tchr., St. Charles, Minn., 1962-65, Central High Sch., Cheyenne, Wyo., 1965-72; law clk. to U.S. dist. judge, 1975-77; mem. firm Urbigkit & Whitehead, P.C., 1977—. Mem. Sch. Bd. Laramie County, 1973-79, pres., 1977-79. Served with U.S. Army N.G., 1957-62. Mem. ABA, Assn. Trial Lawyers Am., Wyo. Trial Lawyers Assn., Laramie county Bar Assn., Cheyenne C. of C. Democrat. Episcopalian.

ZUPAN, CRAIG F., architect, designer, structural engring. draftsman; b. N.Y.C., Dec. 29, 1950; s. Frank Matthew and Evelynn Corrine (Visteen) Z.; m. Elizabeth Ann Goss, Dec. 20, 1975 (div.). B.F.A., U. N.Mex., 1973. Lic. architect, N.Mex. Assoc., Christensen, Christensen and Assocs., Architects, Farmington, N.Mex., 1975-79; staff architect Robert L. Torres and Assocs., Albuquerque, 1979-80; structural engring. draftsman Engring. Assocs., Albuquerque, 1980-82; prin. Interior Concepts, Albuquerque, 1982—. Recipient Reynolds Aluminum prize for Archtl. Students. Mem. Am. Soc. Interior Designers (pres. N.Mex. chpt.). Episcopalian. Home: 4821 Crest Ave SE #5 Albuquerque NM 87108 Office: Interior Concepts 4821 Crest Ave SE #5 Albuquerque NM 87108

ZWEIG, ROBERT MORRIS, physician; b. Phila., July 1, 1924; s. Morris Leopold and Marguerite (Kunz) Z.; B.S., Ursinus Coll., 1948; M.D., Jefferson Med. Coll., 1952; m. Dolores Jean Reynolds, Dec. 21, 1946; children—Robert Laurence, Tracy, Peter Reynolds, Wendy, David James. Intern, Frankford Hosp., Phila., 1952-53; resident, Gen. Hosp. of Riverside County, Riverside, Calif., 1953-54; practice medicine, specializing in family practice, Riverside, 1954—; asst. clin. prof. dept. family practice Loma Linda Med. Coll., 1972—; mem. staff Parkview Community Hosp., Riverside, Gen. Hosp. of Riverside County. Pres., Clean Fuel Inst., Riverside, 1975—; pres. Hydrogenics, Inc., 1981—. Served with USN, 1942-46. Mem. AMA, Riverside County Med. Assn., Calif. Med. Assn., Acad. Family Practice, Am. Lung Assn. (pres. Riverside County chpt. 1977—). Home: 2936 McAllister St Riverside CA 92503 Office: 6391 Magnolia Ave Riverside CA 92506

ZWETSCHKE, EARL T(HEODORE), marriage and family counselor; b. Freeburg, Ill., Jan. 7, 1914; s. Fred H. and Lena W. (Krauss) Z.; B.S. in Edn., Wash. U., 1946; M.P.S., U. Colo., 1947; Ph.D. in Ednl. Psychology (fellow), U. Minn., 1953; m. Nadean K. Brown, June 26, 1947; children—Barbara Ann Zwetschke Willis, Kurt Arthur. Jr. high sch. tchr., Belleville, Ill., 1938-42; vocat. counselor U. Kansas City, 1947-49; counselor U. Minn., 1949-52; asst. prof. to asso. prof. psychology Long Beach (Calif.) State Coll., 1952-57; dir. counseling Colo. State Coll., 1957-60; dir. secondary counseling program Oakland (Calif.) Public Schs., 1960-62; asso. prof. to prof. psychology Portland State Coll., 1962-67; prof. counseling preparation Wright State U., Dayton, Ohio, 1967-79, dir. counseling center, 1971-74; marriage and family counselor, 1964—; speaker; vocat. expert Bur. Hearings and Appeals, 1963-79; speaker to community groups on psychology and mental health. Served to staff sgt. AUS, 1942-45. Lic. psychologist, Ohio; cert. Nat. Health Service Providers in Psychology. Mem. Acad. Psychologists in Marital and Family Therapy, Am. Assn. Marriage and Family Therapy, Am. Psychol. Assn., Am. Personnel and Guidance Assn., Nat. Vocat. Guidance Assn., Assn. Counselor Edn. and Supervision, Assn. Measurement and Evaluation in Guidance, Phi Delta Kappa. Democrat. Home and Office: 18050 NW Bartley Ct Beaverton OR 97006

ZYGIELBAUM, PAUL SOLOMON, mech. engr.; b. Los Angeles, July 1, 1950; s. Joseph Leonard and Adele Zygielbaum; B.S. in Engring. and Applied Sci., Calif. Inst. Tech., 1972, M.S. in Mech. Engring., 1973; m. Michelle Margolese, Oct. 29, 1972; children—Samuel M., Beth R., Joshua M. Tech. aide, engr. Jet Propulsion Lab., Pasadena, Calif., 1970-73; engr. AiResearch Mfg. Co. Los Angeles, Torrance, Calif., 1973; project mgr. Electric Power Research Inst., Palo Alto, Calif., 1973-81; on loan as engr. and generation planning cons. Portland Gen. Electric Co. (Oreg.), 1977-79; materials engr. Signal Analysis div. Hewlett-Packard Co., Santa Rosa, Calif., 1982—; interim dep. dir. for tech. Mont. Energy and Magnetohydrodynamics Research and Devel. Inst., Butte, 1977; dir. Symposia for Engring. Aspects of Magnetohydrodynamics, Washington, 1977-81; mem. ad hoc rev. com. magnetohydrodynamics program. Argonne Nat. Lab., 1981. Recipient Prize Paper award Power Generation com. IEEE, 1982. Registered profl. engr., Calif. Mem. ASME (chmn. papers review com. 1977-81, exec. com. advanced energy systems div. 1977-81), AIAA (tech. com. plasmadynamics 1976-78). Author: (with A.C. Dolbec) Magnetohydrodynamics: An Engineering Perspective, 1980; (with A. Lowenstein) A First-Generation Open-Cycle MHD Power Plant, 1979; contbr. numerous tech. papers, articles and reviews to profl. jours.

Who'sWho in America

Biographees of the West

The following biographees of the Western region have sketches appearing in the 42nd edition of *Who's Who in America.*

REGIONAL LISTING—WEST

Aagaard, George Nelson
Aaker, David A.
Aaron, Benjamin
Abben, Peer
Abbott, Bernard Cyril
Abbott, Donald Putnam
Abbott, Isabella Aiona
Abbott, Jeanne Montague
Abbott, Philip
Abbott, Stanley Eugene
Abbott, Woodrow Acton
Abboud, A. Robert
Abdul-Jabbar, Kareem (Lew Alcindor)
Abel, Brent Maxwell
Abel, Elie
Abel, Joseph K.
Abel, Willard Edward
Abell, George Ogden
Abell, Millicent Demmin
Abell, Thornton Montaigne
Abelson, Harold Herbert
Abercrombie, Lee Roy, Jr.
Abraham, Willard
Abrahams, Roger David
Abrahams, William Miller
Abrahamson, Stephen
Abram, John Charles
Abramovitz, Moses
Abramowitz, Morton I.
Abrams, Herbert Kerman
Abrams, Norman
Abrams, Richard Martin
Abramson, Norman
Abravanel, Maurice
Abroms, Edward Mackin
Abst, Raymond Christian
Ackerly, Robert Saunders, Jr.
Ackerman, Arthur Waldron, Jr.
Ackerman, Bettye Louise (Mrs. Sam Jaffe)
Ackerman, Harry S.
Ackerman, Helen Page
Ackerman, Wesley Ardmore
Acret, James Elvero
Acrivos, Andreas
Adams, Alice
Adams, Ansel
Adams, Brockman
Adams, Brooke
Adams, Charles J.
Adams, Charles Lynford
Adams, Clinton
Adams, Don
Adams, Donald Paul
Adams, Edie
Adams, Eva Bertrand
Adams, Everett Merle
Adams, Georgia S.
Adams, Hazard Simeon
Adams, John Coolidge
Adams, John R.
Adams, Margaret Bernice
Adams, Mark
Adams, Phelps Haviland
Adams, Philip
Adams, Richard Donald
Adams, Richard Miller
Adams, Robert Allan
Adams, Robert Hickman
Adams, Robert Pardee
Adams, Stephen
Adams, Thomas Merritt
Adams, William John, Jr.
Adams, William Mansfield
Adamson, Jack
Adamson, John William
Addison, John West, Jr.
Adel, Arthur
Adelberger, Eric George
Adelizzi, Robert Frederick
Adell, Hirsch
Adelman, Irma Glicman
Adels, Robert Mitchell
Adelson, Marvin
Adelson, Mervyn Lee
Adler, Fred Peter
Adler, Norman Abner
Adler, Norman Paul
Adlum, Merle Daniel
Adrian, Charles Raymond
Aduja, Peter Aquino
Agler, David
Agnew, Allen Francis
Agnew, Harold Melvin
Agnew, Spiro Theodore
Aguilar, Robert P.
Aguzzi-Barbagli, Danilo Lorenzo
Ahlem, Lloyd Harold
Ahlers, Eleanor Emily
Ahmanson, William Hayden
Aidman, Charles
Aikawa, Jerry Kazuo
Aitcheson, George A., Jr.
Akamatsu, Nimei
Akasofu, Syun-Ichi
Akesson, Norman Berndt
Akinaka, Asa Masayoshi
Akins, Claude
Akiyoshi, Toshiko
Akutagawa, Donald
Albee, Arden Leroy
Albersheim, Peter
Albert, Alfred Gerhardt
Albert, Eddie
Alberts, Bruce Michael
Albrecht, Paul Abraham
Albrecht, Richard Raymond
Albrecht, Robert Glenn
Albright, Lola (Jean)
Albritton, Robert Sanford
Albritton, Rogers Garland
Albuquerque, Lita
Alchian, Armen Albert
Alcorn, Gordon Dee
Alcott, Amy Strum
Alcott, John
Alda, Alan
Alden, Dauril
Alder, Berni Julian
Aldrich, Daniel Gaskill, Jr.
Aldrich, Joseph Coffin
Aldrich, Robert
Aldrich, Robert Anderson
Aldrich, Thomas Albert
Aldrich, Virgil Charles
Aldridge, Gordon James
Aldrin, Edwin Eugene, Jr.
Alessio, Ronald Joseph
Alexander, Alec Peter
Alexander, Denise
Alexander, Edward Russell
Alexander, George F.
Alexander, George Jonathon
Alexander, Harry Walter
Alexander, Herbert E.
Alexander, John David, Jr.
Alexander, John Harvey
Alexander, Kenneth Lewis
Alexander, Peter Houston
Alexander, Robert Evans
Alexanderson, Gerald Lee
Alfers, Gerald Junior
Alfin-Slater, Roslyn Berniece
Alford, Jack Leland
Alford, Robert Ross
Alfven, Hannes Olof Gosta
Algazi, Vidal Raphael
Alhadeff, David Albert
Alhadeff, Morris Jerome
Ali, Mir Kursheed
Ali, Muhammad (Cassius Marcellus Clay)
Alinder, James Gilbert
Alioto, Robert Franklyn
Aljian, James Donovan
Allan, Rupert Mortimer, Jr.
Allan, Willard
Allan, William George
Allard, Robert Wayne
Alldredge, Leroy Romney
Allegretti, Joseph Benedict
Allen, Ashael Lester
Allen, Charles William
Allen, Clarence Roderic
Allen, Dex (Claude Turner)
Allen, Gina
Allen, Harland Hill
Allen, Howard Pfeiffer
Allen, Irwin
Allen, J(oseph) Garrott
Allen, James Lovic, Jr.
Allen, James Sircom
Allen, John Eliot
Allen, Lucile
Allen, Merle Maeser, Jr.
Allen, Phillip Richard
Allen, Rex Whitaker
Allen, Richard Garrett
Allen, Sian Barbara
Allen, Stephen Valentine Patrick William
Allen, Toby
Allen, William M.
Allen, William Richard
Allen, William Stephen
Aller, Lawrence Hugh
Allery, Kenneth Edward
Allison, Gerald Lou
Alloway, James Alexander
Allred, Evan Leigh
Allred, John Caldwell
Allyson, June
Alm, Richard Sanford
Almeida, Laurindo
Almendros, Nestor
Almond, Gabriel Abraham
Alpen, Edward Lewis
Alpert, Herb
Alpert, Norman Joseph
Alps, Glen Earl
Alter, Robert B.
Altman, Ellen
Altman, Irwin
Altman, Robert B.
Alton, Bruce Taylor
Altus, William David
Alvarez, Luis W.
Alvarez, Robert Smyth
Alzado, Lyle Martin
Amberg, John Raymond
Amdahl, Gene Myron
Amerine, Maynard Andrew
Ames, Bruce N(athan)
Ames, Edmund Dantes (Ed)
Ames, Ralph Wolfley
Ames, Robert R.
Amioka, Shiro
Ammons, Robert Bruce
Amon, William Frederick, Jr.
Amos, John
Amrein, Yost Ursus Lucius
Amster, Harvey Jerome
Amundson, John Melvin, Jr.
Amyx, Darrell Arlynn
Anargyros, Spero
Anastos, Milton Vasil
Anaya, Richard Alfred, Jr.
Ancker, Clinton James, Jr.
Anderegg, Doyle Edward
Anders, Mariedi
Andersen, Niels Hjorth
Andersen, Richard
Anderson, Arthur G., Jr.
Anderson, Arthur Roland
Anderson, Arthur Salzner
Anderson, B(enard) Harold
Anderson, Bradley Jay
Anderson, Carl David
Anderson, Carl Leonard
Anderson, Charles Arthur
Anderson, Daryl
Anderson, Don Lynn
Anderson, Donald Bernard
Anderson, Donald Lorraine
Anderson, Donald Rene
Anderson, Ernest LeRoy
Anderson, Frederick Randolph, Jr.
Anderson, Grant Thralls
Anderson, Guy Irving
Anderson, Herbert D.
Anderson, Herbert E.
Anderson, Herschel Vincent
Anderson, Ivan Delos
Anderson, J. Blaine
Anderson, James Treat
Anderson, Jeremy R.
Anderson, John David
Anderson, John Edward
Anderson, John Firth
Anderson, John Richard
Anderson, John Robert
Anderson, John Robert
Anderson, Karl Herbert
Anderson, Kinsey A.
Anderson, LeMoyne W.
Anderson, Leo E.
Anderson, Loni
Anderson, Michael Joseph
Anderson, Orson Lamar
Anderson, Raymond Charles
Anderson, Richard William
Anderson, Robert E.
Anderson, Robert Gregg
Anderson, Robert Orville
Anderson, Ronald Delaine
Anderson, Ross Francis
Anderson, Roy Arnold
Anderson, Stanley Joseph
Anderson, Stuart LeRoy
Anderson, Theodore Wilbur
Anderson, Totton James
Andrews, Dale Walker
Andrews, Fred Charles
Andrews, J. David
Andrews, John Thomas
Andrews, Julie
Andrews, Marvin Arnold
Andrews, R. Bruce
Andrews, Tige (Tiger)
Andrews, William Stuart
Andriola, Alfred
Andros, Dee G.
Andrus, Cecil D.
Angel, James Roger Prior
Angelakos, Diogenes James
Angell, James Browne
Angell, Philip Harold
Anglemire, Kenneth Norton
Anjard, Ronald Paul, Sr.
Ann-Margret (Ann-Margret Olsson)
Ansara, Michael
Ansbacher, Charles Alexander
Ansell, Edward Orin
Anson, Fred Colvig
Anthony, Carl
Anthony, Harry Antoniades
Anthony, Joseph Garner
Anthony, Margery Stuart
Antin, David
Antin, Eleanor
Antle, Robert Victor
Anton, Susan
Antonio, Lou
Antonoff, Gary L.
Antosiewicz, Henry Albert
Antreasian, Garo Zareh
Apel, John Ralph
Applebee, William Robert
Appleby, Joyce Oldham
Applegate, Edward Timothy
Appleman, John Alan
Apt, Leonard
Aptheker, Herbert
Aragon, John Anthony
Aragonés, Sergio
Arant, Eugene Wesley
Arbiter, Nathaniel
Arbizu, Ray Lawrence
Arbuckle, Ernest Comings
Arce, Phillip William
Archer, Jerome Walter
Archer, Richard Allen
Archer, Richard Joseph
Archer, Stephen Hunt
Archibeck, Philip James
Arden, Eve (Eunice Quedens)
Arena, John I.
Arensberg, George Howard, Jr.
Ariyoshi, George Ryoichi
Arkin, Alan Wolf
Arkoff, Samuel Z.
Arledge, Charles Stone
Armentrout, Steven Alexander
Armitage, Richard
Armitage, William Barclay
Armour, Richard (Willard)
Arms, Brewster Lee
Armstrong, Dickwin Dill
Armstrong, Don L(eigh)
Armstrong, Gerald Stuart
Armstrong, Grant
Armstrong, Herbert W.
Armstrong, Robert Arnold
Armstrong, Warren Bruce
Arnaud, Claude Donald, Jr.
Arneson, Robert Carston
Arness, James
Arnold, Aerol
Arnold, Danny
Arnold, Harry Loren, Jr.
Arnold, James Richard
Arnold, John Bentley
Arnold, Marilyn
Arnold, Richard Monroe
Arnold, Robert Morris
Arnold, Stanley Richard
Arnon, Daniel I(srael)
Aron, William
Aronow, Wilbert Solomon
Aronson, David
Aroyan, Harry James
Arraj, Alfred Albert
Arrington, Leonard James
Arriola, Gus
Arrol, John
Arrow, Kenneth Joseph
Arthur, Beatrice
Arthur, Ransom James
Arveson, William Barnes
Arzube, Juan Alfredo
Asbury, William Fitts
Aschenbrenner, Karl
Ash, C. Neil
Ash, Roy Lawrence
Ashby, Hal
Ashel, Joyce Bulifant
Ashley, Elizabeth
Ashley, Holt
Ashmore, Harry Scott
Ashton, Geoffrey Cyril
Ashton, Wendell Jeremy
Asimow, Michael R.
Askevold, David Marius
Askin, Leon
Askin, Walter Miller
Asleson, Robert Freeman
Asling, Clarence Willet
Asmus, John Fredrich
Asner, Edward
Asper, Merle Willis, Jr.
Astaire, Fred
Astin, Alexander William
Astin, John Allen
Astin, Patty Duke (Anna Marie Duke)
Atchison, Richard Calvin
Athearn, James Lomen
Atherton, Alexander Simpson
Atiyeh, Victor George
Atkin, J. Myron
Atkin, Kenward Louis
Atkins, Dale Morrell
Atkins, Stuart (Pratt)
Atkinson, Arthur Sheridan
Atkinson, Daniel Edward
Atkinson, Richard Chatham
Atsumi, Takayori Paul
Attenborough, Sir Richard (Samuel)
Attneave, Carolyn (Adams) Lewis
Atwater, Tanya Maria
Atwood, Ann Margaret
Atwood, George Elliot
Atwood, Kenneth Ward, Jr.
Atwood, Robert Bruce
Auberjonois, René Murat
Auerback, Alfred
Augenstein, Bruno W.
Aumont, Jean Pierre
Aurner, Robert Ray
Ausfahl, William Friend
Austin, Donald Stafford
Austin, James Henry
Austin, James Willis
Austin, Ronald
Austin, Tracy Ann
Autry, Orvon Gene
Averill, Lloyd James, Jr.
Avery, Luther J.
Aweida, Jesse Issa
Aweida, Naim Saleh
Axelrad, Irving Irmas
Axelrod, Daniel Isaac
Axelrod, George
Axelson, Charles Frederic
Axton, Hoyt Wayne
Ayala, Francisco Jose
Aydelott, Alfred Lewis
Aydelott, Gale Benton
Ayers, Thomas Dudley
Ayllon, Cándido
Ayres, James Marx
Ayres, Lee Spencer
Ayres, Lew
Ayres, Samuel, III
Azar, Raymond George
Azzara, Candy
Azzolina, Ronald
Babb, Albert Leslie
Babbitt, Bruce Edward
Babbitt, John George
Babcock, Barbara Allen
Babcock, Horace Welcome
Baccigaluppi, Roger John
Bach, George Leland
Bach, Marcus
Bacharach, Burt
Bacharach, Melvin Lewis
Bachenheimer, Klaus G.
Bacher, Vernon Alfred
Bachman, David Christian
Bachrach, Ira Nathaniel
Bach-y-Rita, Paul
Backus, John
Backus, Standish, Jr.
Bacon, Ernst
Bacon, Wallace Alger
Baddeley, Hermione
Badgley, Theodore McBride
Badham, John MacDonald
Baeder, Donald Lee
Baer, Mark Homer
Baer, Max Adelbert, Jr.
Baer, Walter S., III
Baesel, Stuart Oliver
Baez, Joan
Bagby, John R., Jr.
Bagdikian, Ben Haig
Baggetta, Vincent
Bahm, Archie John
Bahr, Ehrhard
Bahr, Howard Miner
Bailey, Dana Kavanagh
Bailey, Exine Margaret Anderson
Bailey, Henry John, III
Bailey, John Cyril
Bailey, Richard Clayton
Bailey, Thomas Andrew
Bailin, Lionel J.
Baillie, Charles Douglas
Baily, Norman Arthur
Bain, Barbara (Mrs. Martin Landau)
Bain, Conrad Stafford
Bain, William James
Bain, William James, Jr.
Bainer, Philip La Vern
Bainer, Roy
Bair, William J.
Baird, Alexander Kennedy
Baird, Hugh Adamson
Baker, Alonzo L(afayette)
Baker, Alton Fletcher, Jr.
Baker, Bruce Robert
Baker, Charles William
Baker, Clifton Earl
Baker, David Kenneth
Baker, Diane (Gross)
Baker, Dick Barnard
Baker, Donald James, Jr.
Baker, Elbert Hall, II
Baker, Harvey Willis
Baker, Herbert
Baker, Herbert George
Baker, Jackson Arnold
Baker, Joe Don
Baker, Joseph Neil
Baker, Kendall Lee
Baker, Lawrence Colby, Jr.
Baker, Louis R.
Baker, Malcolm Frederic
Baker, Marilyn
Baker, Raymond Emerson
Baker, Richard Mark
Baker, Sheldon S.
Baker, Warren J(oseph)
Baker, William Dunlap
Baker, William Ernest
Baker, William Garrett, Jr.
Baker, William Kaufman
Baker-Batsel, John David
Bakes, Robert E.
Bakko, Orville Edwin
Bakshi, Ralph
Balabanian, David Mark
Balch, Glenn
Baldeschwieler, John Dickson
Baldessari, John Anthony
Baldridge, B. Bruce
Baldwin, George Curriden
Baldwin, John Edwin
Baldwin, Joseph Lyle
Baldwin, Lionel V.
Baldwin, Robert Lesh
Balin, Marty (Martyn Jerel Buchwald)
Ball, Fred Shelton
Ball, George Hudson
Ball, John Dudley, Jr.
Ball, Joyce
Ball, Lucille
Ball, William
Ballam, Joseph
Ballantine, Morley Cowles (Mrs. Arthur Atwood Ballantine)
Ballantyne, Arnold Paul
Ballard, Kaye
Ballard, Louis Wayne
Baller, Warren Robert
Balles, John Joseph
Ballhaus, William Francis
Ballmer, Ray Wayne
Balmer, Thomas James
Balmy, Alexis
Balow, Irving Henry
Balsam, Martin Henry
Balsiger, David Wayne
Baltz, Lewis
Bancroft, Anne (Mrs. Mel Brooks)
Bancroft, James Ramsey
Bander, Myron

Bandura, Albert
Banen, David Merton
Banfield, Armine Frederick
Bangert, Richard Elmer
Bangs, F(rank) Kendrick
Banks, David Russell
Banks, Harvey Oren
Banks, James Albert
Banks, Peter Morgan
Banks, Virginia
Bannan, Bernard Jerome (Barney)
Banner, Bob
Banning, Elizabeth (Mrs. Charles Perry Davies)
Bannister, Walter S.
Bannon, Jack
Barati, George
Barbagelata, Robert Dominic
Barber, Albert Alcide
Barbera, Joseph
Barbieri, Renolds John
Barbour, Ross
Barchas, Jack David
Bardach, Sheldon Gilbert
Bardeen, James Maxwell
Bare, Bruce
Bareuther, Ernst Ellis
Barger, Richards Dale, Sr.
Barich, Dewey Frederick
Barkan, Philip
Barker, Norman, Jr.
Barker, Robert William
Barker, Wiley Franklin
Barker, William Alfred
Barkey, Patrick Terrence
Barnard, Rollin Dwight
Barnard, William Calvert
Barnes, Barnard Paul
Barnes, Charles Andrew
Barnes, Frank Stephenson
Barnes, Hazel Estella
Barnes, Joanna
Barnes, Martin McRae
Barnes, Paul Howard
Barnes, Roger William
Barnes, Stanley Nelson
Barnes, William P.
Barnet, Robert Joseph
Barnett, Eugene Victor
Barnett, Ola Wilma
Barnewall, Gordon Gouverneur
Barnum, William Laird
Baron, Sidney
Barondes, Samuel Herbert
Barr, Roger Terry
Barraclough, William George
Barratt, Raymond William
Barrett, Arthur J., Jr.
Barrett, Charles Sanborn
Barrett, Edward Louis, Jr.
Barrett, James E.
Barrett, John Thomas
Barrett, Michael Henry
Barrett, Robert Daker
Barrett, Robert John, Jr.
Barrett, Samuel Cassell
Barrick, Paul Latrell
Barrie, Barbara Ann
Barringer, Anthony Rene
Barrio, Raymond
Barris, Chuck
Barron, Charles Irwin
Barron, Milton Leon
Barrone, Gerald Doran
Barrow, Frank Pearson, Jr.
Barrow, Gordon Milne
Barrow, Thomas Francis
Barry, Gene
Barry, Jack
Barry, Jeff
Barry, Philip Semple
Barry, Richard Francis, III
Barry, Robert Raymond
Barry, Roger Graham
Barry, Walter Russell, Jr.
Barselou, Paul Edgar
Bartalini, C. Richard
Bartel, Roland
Bartell, Lee
Bartha, Dennis Richard
Bartholomew, Allan Camp
Bartizal, Robert George
Bartkus, Richard Anthony
Bartlett, Albert Allen
Bartlett, Arthur Eugene
Bartlett, Hall
Bartlett, J(ames) Kenneth
Bartlett, James Lowell, III
Bartlett, Leonard Lee
Bartlett, Neil
Bartlett, Neil Riley
Bartlett, Scott
Bartley, William Warren, III
Bartnicki-Garcia, Salomon
Bartoe, Otto Edwin, Jr.
Bartolanzo, Leo Joseph
Barton, Babette B.
Barton, Brigid S.
Barton, Bruce Walter
Barton, Gerald Lee
Barton, Jay
Barton, John Selby
Bartosic, Florian
Barty, Billy John
Barut, Asim Orhan
Basehart, Richard
Bashkin, Stanley
Basil, Douglas Constantine
Basile, Richard Emanuel
Baskin, Herbert Bernard
Baskin, Ronald Joseph
Basri, Saul Abraham
Bass, Barbara DeJong
Bass, Joel Leonard
Bass, Louis Nelson
Bassett, Edward Powers
Bassetti, Frederick Forde
Bassingthwaighte, James Bucklin
Bassler, Robert Covey
Basye, Paul Edmond
Batastini, Ralph Charles
Batchelder, Ardern R.
Batdorf, Samuel B(urbridge)
Bate, Geoffrey
Bates, Charles Carpenter
Batiuk, Thomas Martin
Batjer, Cameron McVicar
Batlin, Robert Alfred
Batt, Philip E.
Battaglia, Frederick Camillo
Battan, Louis Joseph
Battin, James Franklin
Battisti, Paul Oreste
Batzel, Roger Elwood
Baucom, Sidney George
Bauer, Malcolm Clair
Bauer, Robert Oliver
Bauer, Roger Duane
Baughman, Fred Hubbard
Baughn, William Hubert
Baum, David Barry
Baum, Dwight Crouse
Baum, William Alvin
Bauman, Jon
Baumann, Richard Gordon
Baumgart, Norbert K.
Baumhefner, Clarence Herman
Bauml, Franz Heinrich
Baumrind, Diana
Baxter, Anne
Baxter, John Darling
Baxter, John Lincoln, Jr.
Baxter, Ralph Felix
Bayer, Herbert
Bayer, James Theodore
Bayley, David Hume
Bayley, Frank Sawyer
Baylor, Donald Edward
Bazemore, Thomas Clifford
Beach, Lee Roy
Beadle, Alfred Newman
Beagle, Peter Soyer
Beaird, Betty
Beal, George Melvin
Beal, Richard Sidney, Jr.
Beall, Burtch W., Jr.
Beall, Dennis Ray
Bean, Lowell John
Bean, Monte Lafayette
Bean, Orson (Dallas Frederick Burrows)
Bear, Stanley Herman
Beard, Rodney Rau
Beardall, James C.
Bearden, Alan Joyce
Beardmore, Glenn Everett
Beare, John Alan
Beasley, Bruce Miller
Beaton, Roy Howard
Beatty, John Cabeen, Jr.
Beatty, Ned
Beatty, Patricia Jean
Beatty, Warren
Beaver, Robert Pierce
Becher, John C.
Bechtel, Stephen Davison
Bechtel, Stephen Davison, Jr.
Beck, Edward William
Beck, Jay Vern
Beck, John Christian
Beck, Marilyn Mohr
Beckel, Charles Leroy
Beckenbach, Edwin Ford
Becker, George Joseph
Becker, Robert Richard
Becker, Walter
Becker, Wesley Clemence
Becket, MacDonald George
Beckett, John Raymond
Beckman, Arnold Orville
Beckman, Millard Warren
Beckmann, George M.
Beckmann, Jon Michael
Beckmann, Petr
Beckner, Morton Orvan
Beckwith, Charles Emilio
Bedelia, Bonnie
Bedford, Clay Patrick
Bedke, Ernest Alford
Bednar, James Edmund
Bedrosian, Edward
Bedrosian, John Charles
Bedrossian, Peter Stephen
Beebe, Mary Livingstone
Beebe, Robert Park
Beer, Clara Louise Johnson
Beer, Reinhard
Beery, Noah
Beesley, Kenneth Horace
Beeson, Paul Bruce
Begam, Robert George
Begelman, David
Beglarian, Grant
Begovich, Nicholas Anthony
Behler, Ernst Heitmar
Behlke, Charles Edward
Beise, Seth Clark
Beistline, Earl Hoover
Bekey, George Albert
Belanger, Frederick Belmar
Bell, Arthur Donald
Bell, Charles Greenleaf
Bell, Derrick Albert
Bell, Graydon Dee
Bell, Herbert Aubrey Frederick
Bell, Howard William
Bell, John James
Bell, Larry Stuart
Bell, Stoughton
Bellah, Robert Neelly
Bellamy, James Ernest
Bellamy, Ralph
Belli, Melvin Mouron
Bellinger, John Dooley
Bellis, Carroll Joseph
Belloni, Robert Clinton
Bellows, James Gilbert
Bellport, Bernard Philip
Belluschi, Pietro
Bellville, Ralph Earl
Bellwood, Sherman J.
Belnap, David Foster
Belnap, Norma Lee Madsen
Belok, Michael Victor
Beloof, Robert Lawrence
Benchimol, Alberto
Bender, Betty Wion
Bender, Richard
Bender, Welcome William
Benditt, Earl Philip
Benedict, Dirk
Benedict, Francis Ward
Benedict, Paul
Benford, Gregory Albert
Bengelsdorf, Irving Swem
Bengston, Billy Al
Bengston, Clarence William
Benham, James Mason
Benirschke, Kurt
Benjamin, Karl Stanley
Benjamin, Richard
Bennett, Charles Leo
Bennett, Donald William
Bennett, Edward Moore
Bennett, Grover Bryce
Bennett, Harve (Harve Fischman)
Bennett, James Austin
Bennett, Jim
Bennett, Joseph Clifford
Bennett, Richard Charles
Bennett, William Michael
Benning, Arthur E.
Bennion, Douglas Noel
Bennis, Warren
Bensch, Klaus George
Bensfield, Richard Edward
Benson, Andrew Alm
Benson, Arvid Leland
Benson, Charles Scott
Benson, David William
Benson, Edward M., Jr.
Benson, George
Benson, John Alexander, Jr.
Benson, John Edward
Benson, Lucille
Benson, Thomas Quentin
Bentel, Dwight
Bentley, Claude
Benton, Fletcher
Benton, John Frederic
Ben-Veniste, Richard
Benyo, Richard Stephen
Benzer, Seymour
Berdahl, Robert Max
Berentson, Duane Lyman
Berg, David
Berg, Jeffrey Spencer
Berg, Lloyd
Berg, Paul
Bergen, Candice
Bergen, Harold E.
Bergen, Julius
Bergen, Polly
Berger, Andrew John
Berger, Bennett Maurice
Berger, Clemens Rainer Anton
Berger, Evelyn Miller
Berger, John Hanus
Berger, Joseph
Berger, Martin
Berger, Michael
Bergeron, Charles Edward
Bergeron, Victor J.
Berges, Marshall William
Bergeson, Scott
Berghold, Joseph Philip
Bergholz, Richard Cady
Bergin, Daniel Timothy
Berglund, Robin Gunnar
Bergman, Alan
Bergman, (Ernst) Ingmar
Bergman, Marilyn Keith
Bergman, Robert George
Bergsma, William Laurence
Berk, Jack Edward
Berk, Morton Emmett
Berke, Nathan R.
Berl, Warren Harry
Berland, James Fred
Berlant, Anthony
Berle, Milton
Berlekamp, Elwyn Ralph
Berlin, Overton Brent
Berlinger, Warren
Berman, Baruch
Berman, Daniel Lewis
Berman, Martin M.
Berman, Neil Sheldon
Berman, Pandro Samuel
Berman, Ronald Stanley
Bermingham, Peter
Bernacchi, Richard Lloyd
Bernard, Charles Keith
Bernardi, Herschel
Bernauer, Edmund Michael
Berndt, Rexer
Bernfield, Merton Ronald
Bernheimer, Martin
Bernstein, Elmer
Bernstein, Eugene Felix
Bernstein, Florence Henderson
Bernstein, Sol
Berry, Charles Michael
Berry, William Benjamin Newell
Bersani, Leo
Bersi, Robert Marion
Bertain, G(eorge) Joseph, Jr.
Bertelsen, Thomas Elwood, Jr.
Bertke, Eldridge Melvin
Bertramson, B. Rodney
Bertrand, Watson Clark
Beshears, Robert Gene
Bessman, Samuel Paul
Best, Jacob Hilmer, Jr. (Jerry)
Best, James Knowland
Bettelheim, Bruno
Bettina, Albert Anthony
Betts, Bert A.
Beutel, Frederick Keating
Beutler, Ernest
Bevan, Donald Edward
Beyer, John Adrian
Beyer, Morten Sternoff
Bezzone, Albert Paul
Bhaumik, Mani Lal
Biaggini, Benjamin Franklin
Bianchi, George Roy
Biberstein, Ernst Ludwig
Bice, Max H.
Bice, Scott Haas
Bickel, Peter John
Bickley, Robert Charles
Bickmore, J. Grant
Bicknell, Joseph McCall
Bieler, Charles Linford
Bienenstock, Arthur Irwin
Bierbaum, J. Armin
Bierman, Charles Warren
Bierman, Edwin Lawrence
Bierschbach, Raymond Anton
Bierstedt, Peter Richard
Bigelow, William R.
Biggerstaff, Warren Richard
Biggs, Hugh Lawry
Bigliardi, Matthew Paul
Biglieri, Edward George
Bijou, Sidney William
Bilby, Ralph Willard
Bilby, Richard Mansfield
Biles, John Alexander
Bill, Tony
Billings, Bruce Hadley
Billings, Charles Edgar
Billingsley, William Allen
Billiter, William Overton, Jr.
Bils, Robert Frederick
Bilson, Bruce
Bimrose, Arthur Sylvanus, Jr.
Bimson, Carl Alfred
Binford, Thomas Oriel
Binford, Thomas Peter
Bingaman, Jeff
Bingel, Joe
Bingham, Woodbridge
Binkley, Max Arthur
Binnie, Arthur Alex
Binns, James Edward
Bird, Bruce
Bird, Jack Dee
Bird, Rose Elizabeth
Birdsall, Charles Kennedy
Bires, Joseph John
Birge, Robert Walsh
Birmingham, Bascom Wayne
Birn, Raymond Francis
Birnbaum, Henrik
Birnbaum, Zygmunt William
Birney, David Edwin
Birney, Meredith Baxter
Birney, William Joseph
Birnkrant, Norman Howard
Birren, James Emmett
Bischoff, William Norbert
Bishop, Anne
Bishop, Avery Alvin
Bishop, Joey (Joseph Abraham Gottlieb)
Bishop, Leo Kenneth
Bishop, Sidney Willard
Bisoglio, Val
Bissell, George
Bisset, Jacqueline
Bistline, Stephen
Bitter, Gehart Leonard
Bittle, Billy McMillan, Jr.
Bitts, Todd Michael
Bixby, Bill
Bjorkman, Olle Erik
Blachman, Nelson M(erle)
Black, Arthur Leo
Black, Charles Henry
Black, Donald Bruce
Black, Edwin Fahey
Black, John Woodland
Black, Karen
Black, Shirley Temple (Mrs. Charles A. Black)
Black, Thompson, Jr.
Blackburn, Jack Bailey
Blackman, Vernon Harold
Blackner, Boyd Atkins
Blackstone, George Arthur
Blackstone, Harry Bouton, Jr.
Blaesser, Willard William
Blahd, William Henry
Blaik, Earl Henry
Blaine, Vivian
Blair, Charles Melvin
Blair, George Simms
Blair, Linda Denise
Blake, Judith
Blake, Robert
Blakefield, William Henry
Blakely, Lawrence Mace
Blakemore, Claude Coulehan
Blakey, Richard Watson
Blakley, Ronee
Blalock, Hubert Morse, Jr.
Blandau, Richard Julius
Blankenbecler, Richard
Blankenhorn, David Henry
Blasingame, Benjamin Paul
Blatter, Frank Edward
Blauner, Bob
Blecher, Maxwell Michael
Bleck, Eugene Edmund
Bleibtreu, Hermann Karl
Bleitz, Donald Louis
Bleiweiss, Robert Morton
Blessing, Richard Allen
Blethen, John Alden
Blewett, Robert Noall
Bleymaier, Joseph Sylvester
Bliss, Carman Arthur
Bliss, Lawrence Carroll
Bliss, Robert Lewis
Blizzard, Alan
Bloch, E. Maurice
Bloch, Felix
Bloch, Richard L.
Bloch, Robert Albert
Block, Irving Alexander
Block, Melvin August
Bloland, Paul Anson
Blom, Daniel Charles
Blomgren, Paul Brown
Blonston, Gary Lee
Blood, Dwight Melvin
Blood, Howard Loran
Blood, W. Joseph
Bloom, Floyd Elliott
Bloom, Joseph Duitch
Bloomberg, Warner, Jr.
Bloomfield, Arthur John
Bloomingdale, Alfred S.
Blosl, Thomas Louis
Blouke, Peter S.
Blue, Linden Stanley
Blue, Vida Rochelle
Bluemle, Robert Louis
Blum, Fred Andrew
Blum, Gerald Saul
Blum, Richard Hosmer Adams
Blumberg, Grace Ganz
Blumberg, Mark Stuart
Blumberg, Nathan(iel) Bernard
Blume, John August
Blumel, Joseph Carlton
Blumer, Herbert
Blumofe, Robert Fulton
Blundell, Harry
Blundell, William Edward
Blunk, Forrest Stewart
Bluth, Elizabeth Jean Catherine
Boak, Ruth Alice
Boba, Imre
Boberschmidt, John Richard
Boccardo, James Frederick
Bock, Russell Samuel
Bodansky, David
Bodemer, Charles William
Bodily, David Martin
Bodkin, Henry Grattan, Jr.
Bodle, George Emery
Bodvarsson, Gunnar
Boehm, Eric Hartzell
Boehm, Felix Hans
Boehning, Joseph Frederick
Boettcher, Byron Kurth
Bogaard, William Joseph
Bogardus, John Robert
Bogart, Neil
Bogart, Paul
Bogdanovich, Joseph James
Bogdanovich, Peter
Boggess, William Randolph
Boggs, Sam, Jr.
Bogue, Philip Roberts
Bogy, David B(eauregard)
Bohannon, David D.
Bohm, Karl-Heinz Hermann
Bohmont, Dale Wendell
Bohn, Ralph Carl
Bohnett, Floyd Newell
Bok, Bart Jan
Bok, P. Dean
Boland, Edward Ward
Boland, John Francis, Jr.
Bolden, Connie Edward
Boldrey, Edwin Barkley
Bolender, David Francis
Boles, Forrest Howard
Boles, Roger
Bolger, Ray
Bolin, William Harvey
Bolinder, Robert Donald
Bolks, Ervin Jay
Bollay, William
Bollens, John Constantinus
Bolles, Richard Nelson
Bologna, Joseph
Bolomey, Roger Henry
Bolt, Bruce Alan
Bolt, Robert James
Boltinoff, Henry
Bolton, Earl Clinton
Bombeck, Erma Louise (Mrs. William Bombeck)
Bomberg, Thomas James
Bomberger, Russell Branson
Bonapart, Alan David
Bond, Frederick Edwin
Bond, Richard Randolph
Bone, Hugh Alvin, Jr.
Bone, Jack Norman
Bonerz, Peter
Bongart, Sergei
Bongiorno, James William
Bonham, Clifford Vernon
Bonhorst, Carl William
Boni, John Anthony
Bonica, John Joseph
Boniface, Robert Lee
Bonn, Paul Verne
Bonn, Robert Thomas
Bonner, Frank
Bonner, James
Bonney, George William
Bonney, John Dennis
Bono, Philip
Bono, Sonny Salvatore
Boochever, Robert
Booke, Sorrell
Booker, Henry George
Booker, Sue
Boone, Deborah Ann (Debby)
Boone, Pat
Boone, Philip Sandford
Boorman, John
Booth, Brian Geddes
Booth, Richard Earl
Booth, Shirley
Booth, Wallace Wray
Boothe, Dyas Power, Jr.
Borah, Woodrow Wilson
Borda, Richard Joseph
Boresi, Arthur Peter
Borg, Grant Kenneth
Borgatta, Edgar F.
Borhani, Nemat O.
Boris, Ruthanna
Borko, Harold
Borman, Burton
Bornstein, Paul
Borovoy, Roger Stuart
Borrowman, Merle L.
Borst, Philip West
Borthick, Mirvin D.
Borthwick, William Mendel, Jr.
Bortolazzo, Julio Lawrence
Bortz, Paul Isaac
Bossen, David August
Bossio, Salvatore
Bostwick, Richard Raymond
Bosustow, Stephen
Bosworth, Thomas Lawrence
Bothwell, Dorr
Botsai, Elmer Eugene
Bottel, Helen Alfea
Bottoms, Timothy
Boudart, Michel
Boulding, Kenneth Ewart
Bouman, Harry Daan
Bourgaize, Robert G.
Bourgholtzer, Frank
Bourne, Charles Percy
Bourns, Marlan E.
Bouwer, Herman
Bouwsma, William James
Bowart, Walter Howard
Bowden, William Darsie
Bowdoin, Robert Emanuel
Bowen, Albert Reeder
Bowen, Charles Clark
Bowen, Charles Corbin
Bowen, Charles Hugh, Jr.
Bowen, Don Leslie
Bowen, Edwin Anderson
Bowen, Howard Rothmann
Bowen, J(ean) Donald
Bowen, Jewell Ray
Bower, Allan Maxwell
Bower, Gordon Howard
Bower, Willis Herman
Bowers, Raymond Victor
Bowie, David (David Robert Jones)
Bowkett, Gerald Edson
Bowler, Duane Wilson
Bowles, John
Bowman, Alfred Connor
Bowman, David Bartholomew
Bowman, Dean Orlando
Bowman, John Wick
Bowman, Joseph Searles
Bowyer, (Charles) Stuart
Box, Thadis Wayne
Boyan, Norman John
Boyarsky, Benjamin William
Boyce-Smith, John, III
Boyd, Douglas Perry
Boyd, Harry Dalton
Boyd, James
Boyd, James Brown
Boyd, Landis Lee
Boyd, Malcolm
Boyd, Richard Hays
Boyd, William Richard
Boyden, Allen Marston
Boyer, Calvin James
Boyer, Herbert Wayne
Boyer, Paul D.
Boykin, Edward McCallum
Boyko, Edgar Paul
Boylan, John Patrick
Boylan, Merle Nelson
Boyle, Barbara Dorman
Boyle, Daniel Edward, Jr.
Boyles, Robert Michael
Boynton, Robert Merrill
Boysen, Harry
Bozich, Anthony Thomas
Brace, Clayton Henry
Brachtenbach, Robert F.
Brack, O M, Jr.
Bracken, Eddie (Edward Vincent)
Bracken, Peg
Bradburn, David Denison
Bradbury, Norris Edwin
Bradbury, Ray Douglas
Braden, Victor Kenneth
Bradfield, James McComb
Bradford, Howard
Bradford, Richard Roark
Bradford, William Parkinson
Bradley, Emmett Hughes
Bradley, Gilbert Francis
Bradley, John Edmund
Bradley, Lester Eugene
Bradley, Melvin L.

Bradley, Thomas (Tom)
Bradley, Van Allen
Bradley, William T.
Bradshaw, George Blair
Bradshaw, Richard John
Bradshaw, Richard Rotherwood
Brady, Carl Franklin
Brady, Hugh
Brady, Hugh Picken
Brady, James Joseph
Brady, Lynn Robert
Brady, Rodney Howard
Brady, Scott (Gerard Kenneth Tierney)
Bragdon, Paul Errol
Bragg, David Gordon
Bragg, Robert Henry
Brain, George Bernard
Brainard, Edward Axdal
Branch, Charles Henry Hardin
Branch, Clifford (Cliff)
Branch, Robert Lee
Brand, Neville
Brand, Stewart
Brandauer, Frederick Paul
Brandborg, Lloyd Leon
Brandenburg, Richard George
Brandes, Raymond Stewart
Brandin, Alf Elvin
Brando, Marlon, Jr.
Brandon, Donald Wayne
Brandow, George Everett
Brandt, Frederick William
Brandt, Harry
Brandt, Rexford Elson
Branham, William Thomas
Brannan, Charles Franklin
Brannen, Barry
Brantley, Lee Reed
Brathovde, James Robert
Bratt, Bengt Erik
Brattain, Walter Houser
Bratton, Howard Calvin
Brattstrom, Bayard Holmes
Braude, Abraham Isaac
Brauman, John I.
Braun, David Adlai
Braun, Jerome Irwin
Braun, John Gilbert
Braun, Theodore William
Braun, Zev
Braunstein, Rubin
Braverman, Charles Dell
Bravmann, Rene Aaron
Bray, Arthur Philip
Bray, R(obert) Bruce
Brayfield, Arthur Hills
Brazier, Mary A. B.
Break, George Farrington
Breck, Allen du Pont
Breckinridge, James Bernard
Breese, Charles Reagan
Breese, Melvin Wilson
Brega, Charles Franklin
Breidenbach, Francis Anthony
Breitenstein, Jean Sala
Breitrose, Henry S.
Breitwieser, Charles John
Bremser, George, Jr.
Brennan, Eileen Regina
Brennan, Francis W.
Brennen, Stephen Alfred
Brent, Paul Leslie
Brentano, Robert
Breslow, Lester
Bresnahan, Richard Anthony
Bressler, Richard Main
Brevik, J. Albert
Brew, William Daniel
Brewer, Charles Moulton
Brewer, Gerald Bernie
Brewer, John Charles
Brewer, Leo
Brewer, Richard George
Brewer, William Augustus, III
Brewer, William Dodd
Breyer, Charles Roberts
Brice, William Jules
Bricken, Gordon L.
Bricker, Neal S.
Bricker, Seymour Murray
Brico, Antonia
Bridenbaugh, William
Bridges, Albert Peyton
Bridges, B. Ried
Bridges, Beau (Lloyd Vernet III)
Bridges, James
Bridges, Lloyd
Bridges, Robert Lysle
Bridges, William Bruce
Bridgewater, Dee Dee
Brieger, Gert Henry
Brier, Warren Judson
Briggs, Edward Samuel
Briggs, Paul Warren
Briggs, Rodney Arthur
Briggs, William Egbert
Briggs, Winslow Russell
Brigham, Samuel Townsend Jack, III
Brigham, Thomas Myron
Bright, John Willis
Bright, William Oliver
Brill, Norman Quintus
Brillinger, David Ross
Brimmer, Clarence Addison
Brinckerhoff, Sidney Burr
Brinegar, Claude Stout
Brinkerhoff, Dericksen Morgan
Brinkman, Fred John
Brinkman, Fred Joseph
Brinner, William Michael
Brinsley, John Harrington
Brinton, Reed Wollerton
Briscoe, Ralph Owen
Briskey, Ernest Joseph
Briskin, Bernard
Bristow, Lonnie Robert
Britain, Radie
Britt, John Roy
Broad, Eli
Broadbent, Thomas Ray
Broadfoot, Albert Lyle
Broccoli, Albert Romolo
Brockhaus, William Lee
Brockman, Michael Stephen
Broderick, Carlfred Bartholomew
Broderson, Morris
Brodsky, Robert Fox
Brody, Jacob Jerome
Broen, William Ernest, Jr.
Brokaw, Charles Jacob
Brokaw, Norman Robert
Brolin, James
Brom, Libor
Bromage, Philip Raikes
Bromberg, Ben George
Bromberg, Robert
Bromberg, Walter
Bronski, Eugene William
Bronson, Charles (Charles Buchinsky)
Bronson, Edward D., Jr.
Bronstein, Gerald Morton
Brookes, Valentine
Brookhart, John Mills
Brookins, Douglas Gridley
Brooks, Albert
Brooks, Edward Howard
Brooks, Ellen Kay
Brooks, Harry William, Jr.
Brooks, James L.
Brooks, James Sprague
Brooks, Mel
Brooks, Norman Herrick
Brooks, Richard
Brooks, Richard M.
Brooks, Toney
Broome, John William
Brophy, James John
Brose, Raymond Edwin
Brosin, Henry Walter
Brosnahan, James Jerome
Brossman, Walter Robert
Brot, Ronald Franklin
Brotherton, David Legge
Broude, Richard Frederick
Brough, Kenneth James
Broughton, James Richard
Brouillet, Frank B.
Broussard, Thomas Rollins
Browder, Robert Paul
Brower, David Ross
Brown, Albert C.
Brown, Arthur Thomas
Brown, B. Mahlon, III
Brown, Benjamin Andrew
Brown, Byron William, Jr.
Brown, Cecil
Brown, Charles Stuart
Brown, Dennis Edward
Brown, Donald Downey
Brown, Edmund Gerald, Jr.
Brown, Edmund Gerald (Pat)
Brown, Edmund Randolph
Brown, Edward James
Brown, Edwin Garth
Brown, Edwin Garth
Brown, Esther Lucile
Brown, Eve (Schimpf)
Brown, Gail Nile
Brown, Garry Leslie
Brown, George Wallace
Brown, Gerald Ernest
Brown, Giles Tyler
Brown, Harrison Scott
Brown, Harry Peter McNab, Jr.
Brown, Harry S.
Brown, Herbert Joseph
Brown, Hermione Kopp
Brown, Jack Edward
Brown, James Isaac
Brown, James Moreau, III
Brown, James Wilson
Brown, Jim
Brown, Joe Robert
Brown, John Edward
Brown, Josiah
Brown, Kenneth Taylor
Brown, Louis M.
Brown, Lowell Severt
Brown, Robert Alfred
Brown, Robert Eugene
Brown, Robert Harold
Brown, Robert Henry
Brown, Robert McAfee
Brown, Robert Minge
Brown, Robert Wallace
Brown, Robert Wallace
Brown, Theodore Dana
Brown, Thomas Anthony
Brown, Thomas Paul
Brown, Victor Lee
Brown, Warren Allston, Jr.
Brown, Willet Henry
Browne, Alan Kingston
Browne, Jackson
Browne, Millard Child
Browne, Roscoe Lee
Browne, Walter Shawn
Brownell, John Arnold
Browning, Edmond Lee
Browning, Iben
Browning, James Robert
Browning, Norma Lee (Mrs. Russell Joyner Ogg)
Browning, Roderick Hanson
Browning, Val Allen
Browning, William Docker
Brownlee, Donald Eugene, II
Brownson, Jacques Calmon
Bruce, James Edmund
Bruck, Bella
Brucker, Gene Adam
Bruckner, Andrew Michael
Brueckner, Keith Allan
Brues, Alice Mossie
Bruestle, Beaumont
Bruhn, Soren Frederick
Bruinsma, Henry Allen
Bruinsma, Theodore August
Brumfield, John Richard
Brunet, Barrie Kirk
Brunk, Hugh Daniel
Brunton, Paul Edward
Brush, Robert Murray
Bruyn, Henry Bicker
Bryan, Jack Yeaman
Bryan, Richard H.
Bryan, Roderick Rae
Bryant, Edward Albert
Bryce, Graham Christopher
Bryson, Arthur Earl, Jr.
Bryson, Gary Spath
Brzeinski, Joseph Edward
Bubb, Harry Geiple
Bube, Richard Howard
Bublitz, Walter John, Jr.
Buchalter, Stuart David
Buchanan, James David
Buchanan, James Weddle
Buchanan, Jesse Everett
Buchanan, Mary Estill
Bucher, Charles Augustus
Buchheim, Robert William
Buchsbaum, Ralph
Buchwach, Buck Aaron
Buck, Robert Follette
Buckalew, James Kenneth
Buckels, Marvin Wayne
Buckingham, Lindsey
Buckland, Michael Keeble
Bucklew, Neil S.
Buckley, John Wilmer
Buckley, Richard Edward
Buckner, Elmer La Mar
Bucks, Charles Alan
Budge, Hamer Harold
Buell, Temple Hoyne
Buff, Conrad, III
Buffett, Jimmy
Bugental, Robert William Garish
Buggs, Charles Wesley
Bugliosi, Vincent T.
Buhler, Aaron
Buie, Robert Frank
Bukowski, Charles
Bull, Bergen Ira
Bull, Brian Stanley
Bull, David
Bull, Henrik Helkand
Bullock, Kenneth C.
Bullock, Theodore Holmes
Bullock, William Stephen
Bumgardner, Albert Orin
Bunker, John Birkbeck
Bunnett, Joseph Frederick
Bunting, Anne Evelyn (Eve)
Bunton, Clifford Allen
Buono, Victor Charles
Burbank, Howard Donald
Burbank, Ronald E.
Burbidge, Geoffrey
Burch, Robert Dale
Burciaga, Juan Guerrero
Burden, Chris
Burden, Jean (Prussing)
Burford, Robert Fitzpatrick
Burge, Henry Charles
Burger, Edmund Ganes
Burger, Othmar Joseph
Burger, Robert Eugene
Burgess, Charles Orville
Burgess, Lloyd Albert
Burgess, William Henry
Burghardt, Kurt Joseph
Burghoff, Gary
Burgoyne, Edward Eynon
Burke, Edmond Wayne
Burke, Edmund Charles
Burke, John Garrett
Burke, John James
Burke, Lloyd Hudson
Burke, Robert Eugene
Burke, William James
Burke, Yvonne Watson Brathwaite (Mrs. William A. Burke)
Burkett, William Andrew
Burkhardt, Hans Gustav
Burkhardt, Lawrence, III
Burkhart, Michael Joseph
Burleson, Paul Richard (Rick)
Burnam, Tom (Thomas Bond)
Burnett, Carol
Burnett, Lowell Jay
Burnett, William Riley
Burnette, Nancy Everitt
Burns, Allan P.
Burns, Brian Patrick
Burns, Dan
Burns, E(dward) Bradford
Burns, Hugh Allan
Burns, Kenneth Dean
Burns, Marvin Gerald
Burns, Richard Dean
Burns, Robert Ignatius
Burnside, Helen H.
Burnside, Waldo Howard
Burr, Raymond
Burr, Robert Edward
Burr, Robert Lyndon
Burress, James Russell, Jr.
Burrington, David Edson
Burrows, Abe
Burrows, Benjamin
Burrows, Frank Ferguson
Burrows, William Claude
Burrud, William James
Burt, Wayne Vincent
Burton, Al
Burton, Levardis Robert Martyn, Jr. (Levar Burton)
Burton, Richard (Richard Jenkins)
Bury, Thomas Lincoln
Busch, Niven
Buschman, Richard A.
Busey, Gary
Bush, Beverly
Bush, Charles Vernon
Bush, James Morton
Bush, Spencer Harrison
Bushacher, H.W.
Bushman, Victor Carl
Bushong, James William
Buss, Claude Albert
Buss, Jerry Hatten
Buss, Walter Richard
Bussard, Robert William
Busse, Friedrich Hermann
Bussman, John Wood
Buster, Edmond Bate
Butler, Edward Lee
Butler, James H.
Butler, John
Butler, Karla
Butow, Robert Joseph Charles
Butterfield, Alexander Porter
Butterfield, Jan Van Alstine (Mrs. Henry T. Hopkins)
Butterfield, Samuel Hale
Buttons, Red
Butz, Otto William
Buyse, Emile J.
Buzick, William Alonson, Jr.
Bye, Richard Earl
Byers, Lex J.
Byers, Nina
Byers, William Mitchell, III
Byrd, Milton Bruce
Byrne, Jerome Camillus
Byrne, William Matthew, Jr.
Byrnes, George Bartholomew
Byrnes, James Bernard
Byrns, Richard Howard
Cable, Donald Aubrey
Cades, Julius Russell
Cadwalader, Arthur Bruns
Caen, Herb
Caesar, Sid
Caesar, Vance Roy
Cagle, Fredric William, Jr.
Cagney, James
Cahalan, (John) Donald
Cahill, James Francis
Cahill, Thomas Andrew
Cahn, Sammy
Cahouet, Frank Vondell
Caillouette, James Clyde
Cain, Douglas Mylchreest
Cain, Edmund Joseph
Cain, Leo Francis
Cairns, Elton James
Calamar, Gloria
Calame, Alexandre Emil
Calame, Byron Edward
Caldwell, Erskine
Caldwell, Gaylon Loray
Caldwell, William Mackay, III
Calfee, Robert Chilton
Calhoun, Rory
Call, C. Lyle
Call, Osborne Jay
Callagan, Dwight A.
Callahan, Kenneth
Callant, Marcel Alphonse
Callaway, Ely Reeves, Jr.
Callaway, Howard Hollis
Calleton, Theodore Edward
Calley, John
Callies, David Lee
Callow, Keith McLean
Calvert, Jack George
Calvin, Allen David
Calvin, Lyle David
Calvin, Melvin
Cameron, Colin Campbell
Cameron, Eleanor Frances
Cameron, J. Elliot
Cameron, James Duke
Cameron, James William
Cameron, JoAnna
Camp, Wofford Benjamin
Campanella, Joseph Mario
Campanis, Alexander Sebastian
Campbell, Allan McCulloch
Campbell, Burnham Orlando, Jr.
Campbell, Charles Bryan
Campbell, Charles J.
Campbell, Donald Guy
Campbell, Glen
Campbell, Jack M.
Campbell, James Arthur
Campbell, John Richard
Campbell, Kenneth Eugene, Jr.
Campbell, Leonard Martin
Campbell, Milton Hugh
Campbell, Richard Alden
Campbell, Richard Arthur
Campbell, Robert Dale
Campbell, Robert Sanders, Jr.
Campbell, Wesley Glenn
Campion, Robert Thomas
Campos, Santiago E.
Camron, Roxanne
Canaga, Bruce Livingston, Jr.
Canby, William Cameron, Jr.
Candiotty, Max
Canin, Stuart Victor
Cann, William Hopson
Cannell, Stephen Joseph
Cannon, Charles Nibley
Cannon, Dyan
Cannon, George Quayle
Cannon, Helen Leighton
Cannon, J. D.
Cannon, Peter
Cannon, Robert Hamilton, Jr.
Cannon, Rowland Morrell
Canova, Judy
Cantlay, George Gordon
Cantor, David Geoffrey
Cantrell, James Randall
Cantwell, Kenneth Robert
Cantwell, William Patterson
Cape, Ronald Elliot
Capiaux, Raymond
Capice, Philip Charles
Capobianco, Tito
Caponigro, Paul
Capp, Michael Paul
Cappelletti, John Raymond
Capps, Gary Lee
Capra, Frank
Carapetyan, Armen
Carbone, John Vito
Cardenas, Robert Leon
Cardon, Marriner Paul
Cardoza, Norman Francis
Caren, Robert Poston
Caretto, Laurence Stephen
Carew, Rodney Cline
Carey, Ernestine Gilbreth (Mrs. Charles E. Carey)
Carey, Harry, Jr.
Carey, Macdonald
Carey, Ron (Ronald J. Cicenia)
Carey, Willard Keith
Cargo, David Francis
Cariaga, Marvellee Dyvonne (Moody)
Carley, James French
Carlsberg, Richard Presten
Carlsen, Albert
Carlsen, James Caldwell
Carlsmith, Carl Wendell
Carlsmith, James Merrill
Carlson, Dale Arvid
Carlson, DeVon McElvin
Carlson, Edward Elmer
Carlson, Frederick Paul
Carlson, George Arthur
Carlson, Roy Washington
Carlson, William Donald
Carlson, William Dwight
Carlton, Paul Kendall
Carlyle, Jack Webster
Carmack, John Kay
Carman, Hoy Fred
Carman, William Brainerd
Carmichael, David Burton
Carmichael, Ian Stuart Edward
Carmody, Martin Doan
Carnahan, Orville Darrell
Carner, Donald Charles
Carney, Arthur William Matthew
Carnochan, Walter Bliss
Carnoy, Martin
Caron, Leslie (Leslie Clare Margaret Caron)
Carpenter, James Edgar
Carpenter, John Howard
Carpenter, Karen Anne
Carpenter, Malcolm Scott
Carpenter, Richard Amon
Carpenter, Richard Lynn
Carr, Allan
Carr, Bernard Francis
Carr, John Howard
Carr, Lester
Carr, Michael Harold
Carr, Robert Allen
Carr, Vikki (Florencia Bisenta de Casillas Martinez Cardona)
Carradine, David
Carradine, John Richmond
Carradine, Keith Ian
Carrera, Joseph Anthony
Carrier, Estelle Stacy
Carrigan, Jim Richard
Carroll, Christina
Carroll, Clifford Andrew
Carroll, Diahann
Carroll, Jonathan Richard
Carroll, Pat
Carroll, Walter William
Carroll, William Jerome
Carruthers, John Robert
Carruthers, Peter Ambler
Carsey, Marcia Lee Peterson
Carson, Edward Mansfield
Carson, George Barr, Jr.
Carson, Hampton Lawrence
Carson, James Donald
Carson, Johnny
Carson, Robert
Carsten, Mary E.
Carstensen, Vernon
Carswell, Lloyd Brooks
Cartales, John August
Carter, Edward Walter, III
Carter, Edward William
Carter, Edwin Lee
Carter, Everitt A.
Carter, H. Lee
Carter, Herbert Edmund
Carter, Hugh Clendenin
Carter, James Larry
Carter, Launor Franklin
Carter, Lynda
Carter, Marshall Sylvester
Carter, Terry (John E. DeCoste)
Carterette, Edward Calvin Hayes
Cartwright, Philip Windsor
Cartwright, Robert Eugene
Carver, Loyce Cleo
Carver, Steven
Casals, Rosemary
Casanova, Aldo John
Casassa, Charles Stephen
Casassa, Charles Stephen
Case, Keith Edmond
Case, Williby Eugene, Jr.
Caselli, Virgil P.
Casey, James Vincent
Casey, John Thomas
Casey, John Wesley
Casey, Ralph Waldo
Cash, Johnny
Casida, John Edward
Caspary, Sister Anita
Casper, David John
Casper, William Earl, Jr.
Cassavetes, John
Cassell, John William, Jr.
Casserly, John Joseph
Cassiday, Benjamin Buckles, Jr.
Cassidy, Adrian Clyde
Cassidy, Paul James
Cassidy, Shaun
Castaldi, David Lawrence
Castaneda, Carlos
Castel, Jack
Castellano, Richard S.
Castellino, Ronald Augustus Dietrich
Castle, Marian Johnson
Castleberry, Donald Montgomery
Castleman, Albert Welford, Jr.
Castles, James B.
Castonquay, Thomas Tellsphore
Castro, Raul Hector
Catalfomo, Philip
Cates, Gilbert
Catlett, Mary Jo
Cattell, Raymond B.
Catton, Ivan
Catton, Jack Joseph
Caughlan, Georgeanne Robertson
Caulfield, George F.
Cavanagh, Harry Joseph
Cavanagh, John Charles
Cavanagh, John Edward
Cavanaugh, James Henry
Cavanaugh, Kenneth Clinton
Cazier, Stanford
Cecchetti, Giovanni
Cecil, John Lamont
Celentano, Francis Michael
Cenarrusa, Pete T.
Cermak, Jack Edward
Cey, Ronald Charles
Chadwick, Wallace Lacy
Chafe, Wallace L.
Chaffee, Walter Burns
Chafin, Charles Edmond
Chagall, David
Chahine, Moustafa Toufic
Chaille, Howard Elmer
Chakiris, George
Chall, Leo Paul
Chamberlain, Adrian Ramond
Chamberlain, Owen
Chamberlain, (George) Richard
Chambers, Jack A.
Chambers, Lawrence Cleveland
Chambers, Richard H.
Chambers, Robert Leroy
Chambers, Robert Rood
Chambré, Paul L.
Champion, Marge (Marjorie Celeste Belcher)
Champlin, Charles Davenport
Champlin, Malcolm McGregor
Chan, Shau Wing
Chan, Shu-Park
Chan, Sunney Ignatius
Chandler, John Herrick
Chandler, Otis
Chang, Chen Chung
Chang, Clarence Hoo Yuen
Chang, David Ping-Chung
Chang, Phil Zangfei
Chang, William Shen Chie
Channing, Carol
Channing, Stockard (Susan Stockard)
Chapin, Francis Stuart, Jr.
Chaplin, George
Chapman, Douglas George
Chapman, G. Arnold
Chapman, Loring
Chapman, Micheal Donald
Chapman, Orville Lamar
Chapman, Warren Howe
Chapman, William Cloud
Char, Kenneth Fook Chong
Charisse, Cyd (Tula Ellice Finklea)
Charles, Carol Morgan
Charles, E. Otis
Charles, Ernest
Charlson, Robert Jay
Chase, Allen
Chase, Chevy (Cornelius Crane)
Chase, Cochrane
Chase, Gerald
Chase, Goodwin
Chase, James Keller
Chase, James Richard

Chase, John David
Chase, Robert Arthur
Chassman, Leonard Fredric
Chatland, Harold
Chauncey, Tom
Chavannes, Albert Lyle
Chavez, Cesar
Chavez, Victor Edwin
Chaykin, Sterling
Cheatham, Julian North
Checkley, David Milton
Cheek, George C(urtin)
Cheit, Earl Frank
Chelapati, Chunduri Venkata
Chen, Chuan Fang
Chen, Joseph Tao
Ch'en, Kenneth Kuan-Sheng
Chen, Kenneth Yat-Yi
Cheney, Richard Bruce
Chenhall, Robert Gene
Chequer, John Hamilton
Cherberg, John Andrew
Chern, Shiing-Shen
Chernev, Irving
Chernev, Melvin
Cherniack, Reuben Mitchell
Chernoff, Daniel Paregol
Chernow, Fred
Cherrix, John Elder
Cherry, James Donald
Chertok, Jack
Chesarek, Ferdinand Joseph
Cheshire, Maxine (Mrs. Herbert W. Cheshire)
Chesney, Lee Roy, Jr.
Chetkovich, Michael N.
Chia, Pei-yuan
Chiang, Chin Long
Chiarella, Peter Ralph
Chiarelli, James Joseph
Chicago, Judy
Chickering, Allen Lawrence, Jr.
Chiesa, Donald Andrew
Chigos, David
Child, Frank Clayton
Childs, Morris Elsmere
Childs, Orlo Eckersley
Childs, Wylie Jones
Chillson, Charles White
Chilson, Olin Hatfield
Ching, Francis F. T.
Chisholm, Margaret Elizabeth Bergman
Cho, Lee-Jay
Choate, Joseph
Chodorow, Marvin
Choi, Byung Ho
Chomsky, Marvin
Chong, Thomas
Choper, Jesse Herbert
Chopra, Anil Kumar
Chorin, Alexandre Joel
Chow, Kao Liang
Choy, Herbert Young Cho
Choy, Wilbur Wong Yan
Christensen, Albert Sherman
Christensen, Clyde Martin
Christensen, Harold Graham
Christensen, Harvey DeVon
Christensen, Lew Farr
Christensen, Nikolas Ivan
Christensen, Ray Richards
Christensen, William Farr
Christensen, William Rozelle
Christian, Percy Willis
Christian, Winslow
Christiansen, Ernest Bert
Christiansen, John Rees
Christianson, Richard Lindbergh
Christie, Hans Frederick
Christoffersen, Ralph Earl
Christofides, Constantine George
Christol, Carl Quimby
Christopher, Warren Minor
Chruden, Herbert Jefferson
Chua, Leon Ong
Chuck, Walter G(oonsun)
Chung, Constance Yu-hwa
Chung, Dae Hyun
Chung, Kyung Cho
Chunn, Calvin Ellsworth
Church, Alonzo
Church, Foster
Churchill, Mac Milo
Churchman, Charles West
Ciampi, Mario Joseph
Cikovsky, Nicolai, Jr.
Cimino, Michael
Clairborne, Harry Eugene
Clampett, Bob
Clanon, Thomas Lawrence
Clapp, Norton
Clark, Alan Barthwell
Clark, Ann Nolan
Clark, Birge Malcolm
Clark, Bruce Budge
Clark, Burton Robert
Clark, Candy
Clark, Carroll Gordon
Clark, Chapin DeWitt
Clark, Charles Gilbert
Clark, Charles Lester
Clark, Dick
Clark, Earl
Clark, Earnest Hubert, Jr.
Clark, Edward
Clark, Glynn Alden
Clark, Henry Benjamin, Jr.
Clark, Hervey Parke
Clark, J. Kent
Clark, James Charles
Clark, James Henry
Clark, John Desmond
Clark, Kenneth Courtright
Clark, Kenneth Sears
Clark, Lynwood Edgerton
Clark, M(ary) Margaret
Clark, Martin
Clark, Petula
Clark, Susan (Nora Goulding)
Clark, Thomas Willard
Clarke, David Marshall
Clarke, Edmund Willcox
Clarke, James Thompson
Clarke, Kenneth Stevens
Clarke, Stanley Marvin
Clary, Everett Burton
Clary, Robert
Clasen, Claus-Peter
Class, Maurice Morrissey
Claus, Clyde Robert
Clausen, Henry Christian
Clausen, John Adam
Clauser, Francis H.
Claver, Robert E.
Clawson, Eldon Richard
Clawson, Roger Wayne
Claycomb, Cecil Keith
Clayton, James LeRoy
Clayton, Sharon
Cleary, Edward William
Cleary, James W.
Clebsch, William Anthony
Clecak, Peter Emmett
Clemente, Carmine Domenic
Clements, John Allen
Clements, Neal Woodson
Clements, Thomas
Clendenin, William Ritchie
Cleveland, Frank Allen
Clevenger, William Albert, Jr.
Clever, Linda Hawes
Clewett, Kenneth Vaughn
Clifford, Geraldine Marie Joncich (Mrs. William F. Clifford)
Clinard, Marshall Barron
Clinch, Harry Anselm
Cline, Martin Jay
Cline, Robert Stanley
Clinton, Frank Mark
Clinton, Gordon Stanley
Clinton, John Hart
Cloonan, Clifford B.
Cloud, Preston
Clough, John Ernest
Clough, Ray William, Jr.
Clough, Richard Hudson
Clow, John W.
Clubb, Louise George
Clubb, Merrel Dare, Jr.
Clumeck, Jack Reginald
Clute, John E.
Clyde, Larry Forbes
Cobb, Brian Eric
Cobb, Vincent
Cobb, William Ballinger
Cobble, James Wikle
Coben, William Allen
Coberly, William Bayley, Jr.
Cobham, William Emanuel, Jr.
Cobin, Martin Theodore
Coblentz, Stanton Arthur
Coblentz, William Kraemer
Cobley, George Gordon
Coburn, James
Coburn, Robert Craig
Cochnar, Robert John
Cochran, David Rea
Cochrane, Willard Wesley
Cockburn, John F.
Cockell, William Arthur, Jr.
Cockle, John Robinson
Cockrum, William Monroe, III
Cocks, George Gosson
Coco, Alfred Joseph
Codding, George Arthur, Jr.
Coddington, Earl Alexander
Code, Charles Frederick
Cody, Iron Eyes
Coe, Robert Campbell
Coe, William Charles
Cohagen, Chandler Carroll
Cohan, John Robert
Cohen, Albert
Cohen, Arthur LeRoy
Cohen, Donald Sussman
Cohen, Karl Paley
Cohen, Lawrence Joseph
Cohen, Lee J.
Cohen, Leonard
Cohen, Leonard (Norman)
Cohen, Marshall Harris
Cohen, Marvin Lou
Cohen, Moses Elias
Cohen, Paul Joseph
Cohen, Robert L.
Cohen, Sanford
Cohen, Sidney
Cohen, Stanley Norman
Cohen, William
Cohn, Seymour Bernard
Coke, Frank Van Deren
Coke, Frank Van Deren
Coladarci, Arthur Paul
Colangelo, Jerry John
Colbert, Edwin H.
Colburn, Philip William
Colburn, Richard Dunton
Colden, Herbert
Cole, Bruce Herman
Cole, Donald Willard
Cole, Kenneth S(tewart)
Cole, Michael
Cole, Natalie Maria
Cole, Olivia
Cole, Roger David
Cole, Victor Eugene
Cole, Wendell Gordon
Coleman, Charles Clyde
Coleman, James Covington
Coleman, Rexford Lee
Coleman, Sherman Smoot
Coles, Donald Earl
Coley, John Ford (John Edward Colley)
Colgate, Stirling A.
Colicos, John
Colin, Lawrence
Collen, Morris Frank
Colles, Alvin Robert
Colley, Nathaniel Sextus
Collier, Clarence Robert
Collier, Robert Percy
Collings, Charles LeRoy
Collins, Charles Roland
Collins, Clella Reeves
Collins, Ernest W., Jr.
Collins, Jack Dorr
Collins, James Arthur
Collins, Joan Henrietta
Collins, John Austin
Collins, Maribeth Wilson
Collins, Robert Emmet
Collins, Robert Oakley
Collman, James Paddock
Colson, Elizabeth Florence
Colton, Anita Belle (O'Day)
Colton, Stanton Benjamin
Colvin, Hugh Frank
Colvin, Jack
Colyar, Ardell Benton
Comarr, Avrom Estin
Combellack, Frederick Malcolm
Combes, James Homer
Combs, Harry Benjamin
Combs, William George
Come, Arnold Bruce
Comfort, Alexander
Comfort, John
Comings, David Edward
Commons, Kim Steven
Compton, James Randolph
Compton, Robert Ross
Comroe, Julius Hiram, Jr.
Comstock, Dale Robert
Comstock, Ralph J., Jr.
Conant, Howard Somers
Conant, Mary Placida
Conboy, John Joseph
Condon, Justin Jerome
Conger, Harry Milton
Conger, John Janeway
Conine, Ernest
Conklin, Marie Eckhardt
Conkling, Roger Linton
Conlan, John Bertrand
Conley, Philip James, Jr.
Conlin, Alfred Thomas
Conlon, Jack Martin
Conmy, Peter Thomas
Conn, James Patrick
Conn, Robert William
Connell, Evan Shelby, Jr.
Conner, Bruce
Connery, Sean
Connick, Charles Milo
Connick, Robert Elwell
Conniff, Ray
Connolly, David I.
Connolly, Thomas Arthur
Connolly, Thomas Joseph
Connor, Linda
Connor, Roger George
Connor, William Elliott
Connors, Chuck Kevin Joseph
Connors, Mike (Krekor Ohanian)
Conrad, Charles, Jr.
Conrad, Paul Francis
Conrad, Robert (Conrad Robert Falk)
Conrad, William
Conrat, Richard Fraenkel
Conron, John Phelan
Considine, John William, III
Constantine, Michael
Conta, Lewis Dalcin
Conti, Samuel
Contois, David Ely
Convy, Bert
Conway, James Valentine Patrick
Cooder, Ry
Coogan, John Leslie (Jackie)
Cook, Jean Louise
Cook, Jeffrey Ross
Cook, Lyle Edwards
Cook, Paul M.
Cook, Robert Donald
Cook, William Boyd
Cook, William Howard
Cooke, Kenneth Lloyd
Coolbaugh, Frank
Cooley, Richard Pierce
Coombe, George William, Jr.
Coombs, John Wendell
Coombs, Robert Holman
Coombs, Walter Paul
Cooney, Lloyd Everett
Coop, Frederick Robert
Cooper, Alice
Cooper, Charles Grafton
Cooper, Edwin Lowell
Cooper, Frank Evans
Cooper, Frank Richard
Cooper, Grant Burr
Cooper, Hal
Cooper, Jackie
Cooper, Jay Leslie
Cooper, John Joseph
Cooper, John Shepherd
Cooper, Kathleen Marie
Cooper, Leon Melvin
Cooper, Leroy Gordon, Jr.
Cooper, Ron
Coors, William K.
Cope, David Howell
Cope, Jackson Irving
Cope, Kenneth Wayne
Copi, Irving Marmer
Copley, Helen Kinney
Copley, Stephen Michael
Coppel, Alfred
Copple, William Perry
Coppola, Carmine
Coppola, Francis Ford
Corben, Herbert Charles
Corbet, Leo F., Jr.
Corbett, Gary Edward
Corbett, Gretchen
Corbin, Robert K.
Corbus, William
Corcoran, Barbara Asenath
Corcoran, William Harrison
Cord, Alex (Alexander Viespi)
Cord, Virginia Kirk Tharpe
Corday, Eliot
Cordingley, William Andrew
Cordova, Valdemar A.
Corea, (Armando) Chick
Corette, John E.
Corey, Jeff
Corey, Paul Frederick
Corker, Charles Edward
Corman, Eugene Harold
Corman, James Charles
Corman, Roger William
Cornelius, Charles Edward
Cornelius, Francis duPont
Cornell, Corwin David
Cornett, William Forrest, Jr.
Cornuelle, Herbert Cumming
Corona, Peter
Corrick, Ann Marjorie
Corrigan, Daniel
Corrigan, James John, Jr.
Corsini, Raymond Joseph
Cort, Bud
Corteway, Robert C.
Cortright, Edgar Maurice, Jr.
Corwin, Norman
Corwin, Stanley Joel
Coryell, Donald David
Coryell, Roger Charles
Cosand, Joseph Parker, Jr.
Cosby, Bill
Cosgriff, Stewart
Cosgrove, Frank Dennis
Cosgrove, Frank Peter
Cost, James Peter
Costa, Walter Henry
Costello, Edward Joseph, Jr.
Costigan, Giovanni
Cosway, Richard
Cota-Robles, Eugene Henry
Cotlar, Morton
Cotten, Joseph
Cotter, George Edward
Cotton, Aylett Borel
Cotton, John
Cotton, Richard Grant
Couger, James Daniel
Coughlan, Patrick Campbell
Coughlin, Bernard John
Coughlin, Magdalen
Coulson, Roy
Coulter, Myron Lee
Coulter, Myron Lee
Counts, James Curtis
Counts, Stanley Thomas
Coupe, Irene Fay
Coupland, Don
Courtenaye, Richard Hubert
Courtney, Howard Perry
Cousins, Norman
Cowan, James Douglas
Cowan, Michael Heath
Cowan, William Maxwell
Cowap, Charles Richardson
Cowee, John Widmer
Cowles, William Hutchinson, 3d
Cowley, John Maxwell
Cox, Allan V.
Cox, Alvin Joseph, Jr.
Cox, Clifton Benjamin
Cox, Exum Morris
Cox, Gilbert Edwin
Cox, John Paul
Cox, Thomas Richard
Crabbe, John Crozier
Crabill, Kenneth Kaye
Crabtree, James Alan
Craddock, Charles Granville
Crafts, James Spray
Craib, Ralph Grant
Craig, Glendon Brooks
Craig, Harmon
Craig, Larry Edwin
Craig, Stephen Wright
Craig, Walter Early
Crain, Charles Anthony
Crain, Cullen Malone
Cram, Donald James
Cramer, Douglas Schoolfield
Cramer, Morgan Joseph, Jr.
Cramer, Richard Louis
Crampton, Charles Gregory
Crandall, Kenneth Hartley
Crandall, Walter Ellis
Crane, Barry
Crane, Edward Harrison, III
Crane, Fenwick James
Crane, Michael Patrick
Crane, Richard A.
Crane, Richard Patrick, Jr.
Cranshaw, Patrick
Cranston, John Montgomery
Crasemann, Bernd
Craven, John Howard
Craven, John Pinna
Crawford, Broderick
Crawford, Charles McNeil
Crawford, Frank Stevens
Crawford, John, Jr.
Crawford, John Edward
Crawford, Norman
Crawford, William Howard, Jr.
Crawshaw, Ralph
Creager, Joe Scott
Crede, Robert Henry
Creighton, John Wallis, Jr.
Creighton, Thomas Hawk
Crenna, Richard
Crenshaw, George Webster
Creson, William T.
Cressey, Donald Ray
Cressman, Ralph Dwight
Creston, Paul
Crews, Frederick Campbell
Crichton, John Michael
Crilly, William Michael
Criminale, William Oliver, Jr.
Crimmins, Philip Patrick
Crinella, Francis Michael
Crispo, Lawrence Walter
Cristol, Stanley Jerome
Critchlow, B. Vaughn
Crittenden, James Nixon
Critzer, William Ernest
Crocker, Myron Donovan
Crockett, Clyll Webb
Crockett, Ethel Stacy
Crockett, J. Allan
Crockett, James Grover, III
Crockett, James Grover, III
Crofts, Dash
Crombie, Douglass Darnill
Cromwell, Florence Stevens
Cromwell, Leslie
Cronbach, Lee Joseph
Crone, Richard Irving
Cronemiller, Philip Douglas
Cronin, Gilbert Francis
Cronyn, Marshall William
Crosbie, Stanley Blandford
Crosby, David
Crosby, Gary Evan
Crosby, Joan Carew
Crosby, John O'Hea
Crosby, Kathryn Grandstaff (Grant)
Crosby, Norm
Crosby, Roger Joseph
Cross, Harry Maybury
Cross, Irvie Keil
Cross, Jennifer Mary (Mrs. Ellis M. Gans)
Cross, Richard John
Cross, Stuart Green
Crossan, Alexander
Crossland, Samuel Hess
Crossley, Frank Alphonso
Crossley, John Parshley, Jr.
Crossley, Randolph Allin
Crothers, Benjamin Sherman
Crouch, Andrae
Crouch, James Ensign
Crouch, Jordan Jones
Crouch, Paul Franklin
Crow, John Armstrong
Crowe, Charles Lawson
Crowell, Charles Monroe
Crowell, John B., Jr.
Crowell, John Chambers
Crowell, Russell Roland
Crowell, Warren H.
Crowley, Dorothy Marie
Crowley, Jerome Joseph, Jr.
Crowley, John Robert
Crowley, Joseph Neil
Crowley, Lawrence G.
Crowley, Mart
Crowley, Pat
Crull, Tim F.
Crum, James Davidson
Crump, Spencer
Cuadra, Carlos Albert
Cuddy, Daniel Hon
Cuddy, Lucy Hon
Cukor, George Dewey
Culhane, John Hubert
Culick, Fred Ellsworth Clow
Cullen, Bill
Cullenbine, Clair Stephens
Culler, Floyd LeRoy, Jr.
Culler, John Rutledge
Cullinan, Terrence
Cullinan, Vincent
Culp, Robert
Culver, Arthur Alan
Culver, Virginia Price
Culverwell, Albert Henry
Culwell, Charles Louis
Cumming, Gordon Robertson
Cumming, Theodore MacNeill
Cummings, Bob (Robert Orville Cummings)
Cummings, Charles William
Cummings, Nicholas Andrew
Cummins, John Stephen
Cummins, Joseph Hervey
Cundall, Donald Rogers
Cunha, Tony Joseph
Cunningham, Arthur Francis
Cunningham, Sister Catharine Julie
Cunningham, Julia Woolfolk
Cunningham, Melvin Eugene
Cunningham, Robert Louis
Cunningham, Ross Lee
Cupp, David Foster
Curb, Michael Charles
Curran, Darryl Joseph
Curran, Frank Earl
Curran, James Albert
Currie, Malcolm Roderick
Curry, Bill
Curry, Daniel Arthur
Curry, Francis John
Curry, James Trueman, Jr.
Curry, Jane Louise
Curtin, Jane Therese
Curtin, Richard Daniel
Curtis, Jesse William, Jr.
Curtis, Joseph Roger
Curtis, Keene Holbrook
Curtis, Orlie Lindsey, Jr.
Curtis, Philip C.
Curtis, Philip Chadsey, Jr.
Curtis, Tony (Bernard Schwartz)
Curtiss, Elden F.
Curtiss, Ursula Reilly (Mrs. John Curtiss, Jr.)
Cushing, Charles Cook
Cushman, Richard David
Cussler, Clive Eric
Cuthbertson, Kenneth McLean
Cutler, Cassius Chapin
Cutler, Howard Armstrong
Cutler, Leonard Samuel
Cutler, Max
Cutter, David Lee
Cutter, Edward Ahern, III
Cutter, James Arthur
Cuttle, Tracy Donald
Dabagia, Robert C.
D'Accone, Frank A.
Dackawich, S. John
Daggatt, Walter Russell
Dahl, Charles Raymond
Dahl, John Anton
Dahl, Robert Kenneth
Dahlberg, Eric John, Jr.
Dahlem, Maurice Jacob
Dahlquist, Arlen R.
Dahlquist, Eric Eugene
Dahlstrom, Donald Albert
Dailey, Peter Heath
Daines, William Purdie
Dale, Francis Lykins
Dale, Leon Andrew
Dalenberg, Robert Van Raalte
Dales, Richard Clark
Daley, Daniel Hayes
Dalis, Irene
Dallas, Jack Dorwin
Dallin, Alexander
Dallis, Nicholas Peter
Dallman, Peter Richard
Dalshaug, Allan Emory
Dalton, Douglas
Daltrey, Roger
Daly, Edward Joseph
Daly, Gene Benedict
Daly, Robert Anthony
Dames, Trent R.
Damm, Alexander
Dana, Bill
Dana, Edward Runkle
Dance, Francis Esburn Xavier
Dance, Maurice Eugene
Dandoy, Maxima Antonio
Dandoy, Suzanne Eggleston
Danelski, David Joseph
D'Angelo, Robert William
Dangerfield, George
Daniel, Elmer Leon
Daniel, Robert Edwin
Daniels, Alfred Harvey
Daniels, Arlene Kaplan
Daniels, Elmer Harland
Daniels, William David
Danner, Blythe Katharine (Mrs. Bruce W. Paltrow)
Danson, Edward Bridge
Dantley, Adrian
Danton, Joseph Periam
Danziger, Jerry
Dapples, Edward Charles
Darby, Kim
Darby, Michael Rucker
d'Arcambal, Thomas Radford
Darcy, John Francis
Darden, Edwin Speight, Jr.
Darden, Severn Teackle
Darmstandler, Harry Max
Dart, Justin
Dasmann, Raymond Fredric
Dassin, Jules
Daub, Guido Herman
Dauben, William Garfield
Dauer, Francis Watanabe
Dauer, William Eugene
Daugherty, Carroll Roop
Daugherty, Robert Melvin, Jr.
Davenport, Gerald Dale
Davern, Cedric Inglis
David, Paul Allan
David, Pedro Rubens
Davidson, Crow Girard
Davidson, Donald Herbert
Davidson, Eric Harris
Davidson, Ernest Roy
Davidson, Eugene Arthur
Davidson, Ezra C., Jr.
Davidson, Gordon
Davidson, Ian Bruce
Davidson, John
Davidson, Robert Meyer
Davies, Daniel R.
Davies, David George
Davies, David Lloyd
Davies, David William
Davies, James Chowning
Davies, John Sherrard
Davies, Paul Lewis, Jr.
Davies, Raymond Douglas
Davies, Thomas Mockett, Jr.
Davis, Allen

Davis, Ann Bradford
Davis, Craig Alphin
Davis, Daniel Edward
Davis, Don G.
Davis, Donald Cooke
Davis, Dwight M.
Davis, George Donald
Davis, Hamilton Seymour
Davis, J. Luther
Davis, James Robert
Davis, Jay Michael
Davis, Jerome Lewis, Jr.
Davis, Jerrold Calvin
Davis, John Donald
Davis, John MacDougall
Davis, John Rowland
Davis, Joseph Edward
Davis, Kenneth Culp
Davis, Lance Edwin
Davis, Leverett, Jr.
Davis, Mac
Davis, Richard Marden
Davis, Robert Troy
Davis, Ron
Davis, Roy Tasco, Jr.
Davis, Russell Leonard
Davis, Stanley Nelson
Davis, Stuart
Davis, Walter
Davis, William Eugene
Davis, William Gordon, Jr.
Davison, Beaumont
Dawes, Carol J.
Dawson, John Hallam
Dawson, John Hallam
Dawson, John Myrick
Day, Anthony
Day, Arthur Grove
Day, David Allen
Day, (Joseph) Dennis
Day, Frank E.
Day, James Lewis
Day, John Francis
Day, Robert Edgar
Day, Robert Winsor
Day, Timothy Townley
Daynard, John A.
Deal, Lanham
Dean, Charles Thomas
Dean, John Wilson, Jr.
Dean, Paul John
Deane, Thomas Andersen
Dearing, Vinton Adams
Dearmore, Thomas Lee
Deasy, Cornelius Michael
Deasy, William John
DeBra, Daniel B.
de Bretteville, Charles
Debreu, Gerard
DeCamp, Rosemary Shirley
De Castro, Hugo Daniel
Deck, Joseph Francis
Decker, Donald Gilmore
Decker, Gilbert Felton
Decker, John Peter
Decker, Robert Wayne
de Cordova, Frederick Timmins
Dedini, Eldon Lawrence
Dee, Ruby
Deering, Fred Arthur
Deever, Roy Merwin
De Felitta, Frank Paul
DeFeo, Vincent Joseph
deFord, Sara Whitcraft
De Forest, Roy D.
Deftos, Leonard John
Degenkolb, Henry John
Degler, Carl Neumann
Degnan, Thomas Leonard
deGooyer, Kirk Alan
DeHart, A. Robert
Dehmelt, Hans Georg
De Hoffmann, Frederic
De Hoffmann, Frederic
DeLamater, James Newton
De Lancie, Richard
De Land, Edward Charles
de la Ossa, Ernest George
Delap, Tony
Delaplane, Stanton Hill
Delawie, Homer Torrence
De Layo, Leonard Joseph
Del Chiaro, Mario Aldo
Deleeuw, Dianne Margaret
Delevie, Harold Jacob
De Lisio, Stephen Scott
Delliquadri, Pardo Frederick
Dellums, C.L.
deLuccia, Emil Robert
Delugach, Albert Lawrence
De Luise, Dom
del Valle, Juan
Demaris, Ovid (Ovide E. Desmarais)
deMatties, Nicholas Frank
De Ment, Jack (Andrew)
DeMieri, Joseph L.
Deming, Willis Riley
De Money, Fred William
Demorest, Jean-Jacques
Dempsey, Howard Stanley
Dempster, Richard Vreeland
DenBesten, Lawrence
Denecke, Arno Harry
Deneuve, Catherine (Catherine Dorleac)
DeNiro, Robert
Denlea, Leo Edward, Jr.
Denney, K. Duane
Denney, Reuel Nicholas
Denning, Richard (Louis Albert Denninger)
Dennis, Kenneth Ralph
Dennis, Richmond Bramwell
Dennis, Robert John
Dennis, Sandy
Dennis, Ward Brainerd
Dennison, David Short, Jr.
Dennison, Stanley Scott
Denniston, F. Edwin
Denny, Brewster Castberg
Denny, Frank Walter
Denton, Charles Mandaville
Denver, John (Henry John Deutschendorf Jr.)
DePatie, David Hudson
de Poix, Vincent Paul
De Prima, Charles Raymond
DePuy, Charles Herbert
Derbes, Daniel William
Dergarabedian, Paul
Dern, Bruce MacLeish
De Rosier, Arthur Henry, Jr.
Derr, K. T.
Derr, Robert James
Desai, Chandrakant S.
de Silva, Colin
Desoer, Charles Auguste
de Soto, Simon
Despres, Louis Richard
Determan, John David
Detert, Gunther Richard
Dethero, J. Hambright
de Tornyay, Rheba
Deukmejian, George
Dev, Vasu
Devlin, Michael Coles
Devol, Kenneth Stowe
DeVos, George Alphonse
de Vries, Jan
De Vries, Kenneth Lawrence
DeVries, William Castle
de Waart, Edo
DeWeese, David Downs
Dewey, Donald Odell
Dewey, Donald William
Dewey, Phelps
Dewitt, Charles Wayne
Dial, Oliver Eugene
Diamandopoulos, Peter
Diamond, Bernard Lee
Diamond, Isidore
Diamond, Jared Mason
Diamond, Neil
Diamond, Stanley Jay
Dibble, Charles Elliott
Dibble, John Rex
Dick, Bertram Gale, Jr.
Dick, Henry Henry
Dick, Nancy E.
Dickason, James Frank
Dickeman, Raymond Louis
Dickerson, Harvey
Dickeson, Robert Celmer.
Dickey, Glenn Ernest, Jr.
Dickey, William (Hobart)
Dickinson, Angie (Angeline Brown)
Dickinson, Charles Arthur
Dickinson, Eleanor Creekmore
Dickinson, Ernest Milton
Diehl, Digby Robert
Diehl, Richard Kurth
Diemer, Emma Lou
Dierker, Charles Torrance
Dierks, Donald Arthur
Dietrich, Marlene (Maria Magdalena von Losch)
Dietsch, Alfred John
di Furia, Giulio
DiGiorgio, Robert
Dignac, Geny (Bermudez, Eugenia M.)
Dignam, Robert Joseph
Dike, Phil
Dike, Sheldon Holland
Dill, Guy
Dill, Laddie John
Dillard, David Hugh
Diller, Barry
Dillhoff, J. Thomas
Dillman, Bradford
Dillon, John B.
Dillon, Paul Sanford
Dillon, Richard Hugh
Dimmick, Carolyn Reaber
DiMuccio, Mary Jo
Dini, Joseph E., Jr.
Dinkel, John George
Dinkelspiel, Richard Coleman
Dinnerstein, Leonard
diPrima, Diane
Diridon, Rodney John (Rod)
Dirks, John Edward
Dirksen, Charles Joseph
Distler, William Francis
Dixon, Albert George, Jr., III
Dixon, Frank James
Dixon, Harold Christopher
Dixon, Harvey Lewis
Dixon, Ivan N., III
Dixon, John Aldous
Dixon, Peter Lee
Dixon, Thomas Francis
Dixon, Wilfrid Joseph
Dixon, William Cornelius
di Zerega, Thomas William
Djerassi, Carl
Djordjevic, Dimitrije
Djordjevich, Michael
Doan, Cortland Charles
Dobbins, Harry Michael
Dobbs, Dan Byron
Dobey, James Kenneth
Dobler, Conrad Francis
Dobler, Donald William
Dobson, Herbert Gordon
Dockson, Robert Ray
Dodd, Paul A(lbert)
Dodds, Gordon Barlow
Dodge, Earl Farwell
Dodge, Peter Hampton
Dodgen, Harold Warren
Dodson, Edwin Stanton
Doe, Bruce Roger
Doi, James Isao
Dolan, Joseph Francis
Dolan, Mary Anne
Dolby, Ray Milton
Dole, Hollis Mathews
Dole, William
Dolley, Stephen Hayden
Dolliver, James Morgan
Dolph, Wilbert Emery
Dominick, David DeWitt
Donahoe, Francis Marion
Donahue, Elinor
Donahue, Kenneth
Donahue, Terrence Michael
Donaldson, Charles Russell
Donaldson, Lauren R.
Donaldson, Robert Charles
Donaldson, Stephen Reeder
Donavan, Neil Bernard
Donen, Stanley
Donnelly, Marian Card
Donnelly, Russell James
Donofrio, Francis Joseph
Donoghue, Mildred Ransdorf
Donohoe, Hugh Aloysius
Donovan, Allen Francis
Dooley, George Elijah
Doolittle, James Harold
Doran, Ann Lee
Dore, Fred H.
Dorfman, Ralph Isadore
Dorgan, John Joseph, Jr.
Dorius, Kermit Parrish
Dorkin, Frederic Eugene
Dorman, Albert A.
Dorn, Edward Merton
Dorn, Russell William, Jr.
Dornbusch, Sanford Maurice
Dorpat, Theodore Lorenz
Dorra, Henri
Dorrenbacher, Carl James
Dorsey, Dolores Florence
Dorsey, Eugene Carroll
Dorsey, Ray
Dorsey, Thomas Brookshier
Dougan, Robert Ormes
Dougherty, David Mitchell
Douglas, Donald Wills, Jr.
Douglas, George Marvin
Douglas, Gordon
Douglas, James
Douglas, John Jefferson
Douglas, Kirk
Douglas, Michael Kirk
Douglas, Mike
Dourif, Brad
Doutt, Richard Leroy
Dow, Daniel Gould
Dow, Frederick Warren
Dowd, Peter Jerome
Dowie, Mark
Dowlin, Kenneth Everett
Downer, Eugene Debs, Jr.
Downer, Joseph Platt
Downey, John Francis
Dows, David Alan
Doxsee, Lawrence Edward
Doyle, Morris McKnight
Doyle, William Edward
Doyle, William Thomas
Dozier, William
Drachkovitch, Milorad M.
Drachler, Norman
Drain, Albert Sterling
Drake, Charles Whitney
Drake, William Whiting, Jr.
Drake (Jurras), Sylvie
Drechsel, Edwin Jared
Drecksel, Calvin Otis
Drees, Thomas Clayton
Drell, Sidney David
Drell, William
Drennan, G(eorge) Eldon
Dresser, Jesse Dale
Drew, Clifford James
Drew, Paul
Drews, John George
Drexler, Fred
Dreyfus, Pierre Marc
Dreyfuss, John Alan
Dreyfuss, Richard Stephan
Driggs, Don Wallace
Driggs, Douglas Harmon
Driggs, Gary Harmon
Driggs, John Douglas
Driggs, Junius Elmarion
Driscoll, John Brian
Driscoll, Margaret Weyerhaeuser (Mrs. Walter Bridges Driscoll)
Drohan, Thomas Edward
Droz, Henry
Drucker, Peter Ferdinand
Drummond, Forrest Stuart
Dryden, Robert Eugene
Drysdale, Donald Scott
Du Bain, Myron
Dubberly, Ronald Alvah
Dubin, Robert
Dubofsky, Jean Eberhart
Du Bois, Edmund Louis
Du Bois, Ja'net
Du Bridge, Lee Alvin
Duckworth, Guy
Ducommun, Alan N.
Ducommun, Charles Emil
Dudenhoeffer, Frank Edward
Duecy, Charles Michael
Duff, Cloyd Edgar
Duff, George Alexander
Duff, William Leroy, Jr.
Duffie, Cornelius Roosevelt
Duffin, John Henry
Duffy, Patrick
Dufner, Max
Dugan, Hugh Patrick
Duggan, Andrew
Dugger, Edwin Ellsworth
Dugger, Willie Mack, Jr.
Duhl, Leonard J.
Duignan, Peter James
Duke, Donald Norman
Duke, Harold Benjamin, Jr.
Dukeminier, Jesse
Dukes, David
Dulbecco, Renato
Dullea, Keir
Dumke, Glenn S.
Dunaway, Faye
Dunbar, John Raine
Duncan, Donal Baker
Duncan, James Wendell
Duncan, Robert Edward
Duncan, Sandy
Duncan, Thomas William
Duncan, Verne Allen
Dundes, Alan
Dundes, Jules
Dunford, Max Patterson
Duniway, Benjamin Cushing
Dunlap, Marjorie Snyder
Dunlap, Richard Donovan
Dunlavey, Dean Carl
Dunn, Harry Lippincott
Dunn, Joseph McElroy
Dunn, Richard Brandner
Dunn, Robert Joseph
Dunnahoo, Terry (Mrs. Thomas William Dunnahoo)
Dunne, Philip
Dunnell, Robert Chester
Dunsire, Peter Kenneth
Du Pen, Everett George
Dupuy, Howard Moore, Jr.
Duran, Servet Ahmet
Durant, Bartley Sanders
Durham, George Homer
Durham, Robert Lewis
Durning, Charles
Durrenberger, Robert Warren
Durslag, Melvin
Dussault, Nancy Elizabeth
Dutton, John Maynard
Duvall, Shelley
Duwez, Pol Edgard
Dwan, Lois Smith
Dworkin, Samuel Franklin
Dworsky, Daniel Leonard
Dwyer, William Warren
Dwyre, William Raymond
Dyatt, Betty Marie
Dyer, Sister Mary Celestine
Dykinga, Jack William
Dykstra, Daniel James
Dysinger, Paul William
Dyson, Allan Judge
Dziura, Horst Wolfgang
Eades, Luis Eric
Eagleton, Robert Don
Eamer, Richard Keith
Eames, Alfred Warner, Jr.
Eames, Wilmer Ballou
Eardley, Richard Roy
Earle, Merie
Earle, Sylvia Alice
Earley, James Staintorth
Early, James Michael
Easley, Mack
East, William G.
Eastlake, William Derry
Eastlick, John Taylor
Eastman, Richard Hallenbeck
Easton, Anthony Terrence
Easton, William Heyden
Eastwood, Clint
Eaton, Ben H.
Eaton, Berrien Clark
Eaton, Francis Homer
Eaton, John Sisco
Eaton, Lewis Swift
Eaton, Robert Philip
Eaves, Ronald Weldon
Ebaugh, Franklin Gessford, Jr.
Ebeling, Alfred Wallace
Eberle, Robert William
Ebert, Paul Allen
Ebright, James Newton
Ebsen, Buddy (Christian Ebsen, Jr.)
Eby, George William
Eccles, George Stoddard
Eckbo, Garrett
Eckel, Edwin Butt
Eckhardt, August Gottlieb
Eckhart, Myron, Jr.
Eckles, Lucius Elkanah
Eddy, Charles P(hillips)
Edel, Joseph Leon
Edelbrock, Gary Ray
Edelman, Joel
Eden, Barbara Jean
Ediger, Robert Ike
Edington, Robert Van
Edmiston, Charles H.
Edmondson, Hugh Allen
Edmondson, W(allace) Thomas
Edmunds, Stahrl William
Edsall, Kenneth Richard
Edson, William Alden
Edwards, Blake
Edwards, Charles Cornell
Edwards, Donald Kenneth
Edwards, George Kent
Edwards, Howard Lee
Edwards, Jerome
Edwards, John Hamilton
Edwards, Ralph Livingstone
Edwards, Walter Meayers
Edwards, Ward Dennis
Edwards, Wayne Forrest
Edwards, William Cleveland
Edwards, William Foster
Edwards, William Sterling, III
Eekman, Thomas Adam
Effinger, Cecil
Eggar, Samantha (Victoria Louise Samantha Marie Elizabeth Therese Eggar)
Eggers, David Frank, Jr.
Eggert, Robert John
Eggleston, William Wallace
Ehricke, Krafft Arnold
Ehrlich, Paul Ralph
Ehrlichman, John Daniel
Eiberger, Carl Frederick, II
Eichelbaum, Stanley
Eicher, George John
Eickhoff, Theodore Carl
Eikenberry, Kenneth Otto
Einstein, Clifford Jay
Einstein, Elizabeth Roboz (Mrs. Hans Albert Einstein)
Eisaman, Josiah Reamer, III
Eisberg, Robert Martin
Eiseman, Ben
Eisgruber, Ludwig Maria
Eisner, Elliot Wayne
Eitel, Karl Emil
Eitzen, David Stanley
Ekelund, John Joseph
Eklund, Gordon Stewart
Eklund, Nils O., Jr.
Ekman, Paul
Elam, Jack
Elam, Stanley Munson
Elberg, Sanford Samuel
Elder, Lonne, III
Elder, Rex Alfred
Elderkin, Charles Edwin
Eldredge, Laurence Howard
Eldridge, Carl Wallace
Eldridge, Roy
Elgee, Neil Johnson
Eliassen, Rolf
Eliel, Leonard Paul
Elikann, Lawrence (Larry) S.
Elkind, Mortimer Murray
Elkins, Francis Clark
Elkins, Hillard
Elkus, Richard J.
Ellegood, Donald Russell
Eller, Charles Howe
Elliman, Yvonne
Ellingboe, Albert Harlan
Ellingson, Steve
Elliot, David Clephan
Elliot, Jeffrey M.
Elliott, Bruce Alan
Elliott, Edward Procter
Elliott, J. Randolph
Elliott, James Heyer
Elliott, William Hall
Elliott, William Michael
Ellis, Don A.
Ellis, Donald Howard
Ellis, James Reed
Ellis, John Martin
Ellis, John W.
Ellis, Ted Ellsworth
Ellis, Willis Hill
Ellison, David Ernest
Ellison, Harlan Jay
Ellison, Herbert Jay
Ellsberg, Daniel
Ellsworth, Frank L.
Ellsworth, Samuel George
Ellwood, Robert Scott, Jr.
Elmore, James Walter
Elms, James Cornelius, IV
Elorriaga, John A.
Elsen, Albert Edward
Elsener, Leonard Frank
Elsing, William Taddes
Elsner, Larry Edward
Elton, Robert Moffat
Ely, Paul C., Jr.
Ely, Paul C., Jr.
Ely, Walter Raleigh, Jr.
Emanuel, Irvin
Emberson, Richard Maury
Emch, Arnold Frederick
Emerson, David Winthrop
Emerson, Frederick George
Emerson, Gladys Anderson
Emmett, John Lester
Emmons, C.S.
Emmons, Donn
Emmons, Robert John
Emonds, Joseph Embley
Emory, Meade
Enarson, Harold L.
Endicott, William F.
Endress, Henry
Enelow, Allen Jay
Enersen, Burnham
Engbretson, William Earl
Engdahl, James Camerer
Engel, William Fremont
Engel, William King
Engelhardt, Albert George
Engelmann, Rudolf Jacob
Engen, Richard Bruce
Engle, Harold Martin
Englekirk, John Eugene
Engleman, Ephraim Philip
English, Lowell Edward
Enlow, Fred Clark
Enoch, Jay Martin
Enright, William Benner
Ensign, Richard Papworth
Ensminger, Marion Eugene
Enthoven, Alain Charles
Enzler, Ellen Rochelle
Epel, David
Epstein, Bernard
Epstein, Charles Joseph
Epstein, Emanuel
Epstein, John Howard
Epstein, Leon Joseph
Epstein, Seymour
Epstein, William Louis
Erasmus, Charles John
Erburu, Robert F.
Erdman, Paul Emil
Erdman, Robert Lee
Erhard, Werner
Erickson, James Harrison Miller
Erickson, Lawrence Wilhelm
Erickson, Richard Carl
Erickson, William Hurt
Eriksen, Otto Louis
Erikson, Erik Homburger
Erlandson, Theodore Roy
Erlicht, Lewis Howard
Erman, John
Ernst, Roger Charles
Ernst, Wallace Gary
Ernstrom, Carl Anthon
Eros, Peter
Erteszek, Jan Jakub
Ervin, John Wesley
Erwin, Robert Cecil
Erwin, William Carl
Escamilla, Roberto Francisco
Eschmeyer, William Neil
Eshleman, Clayton
Eshleman, Von Russel
Eshman, Aaron Richard
Esselman, Walter Henry
Essenburg, Franklin
Estes, Carroll Lynn
Estes, Walter Eugene
Estevez, Luis de Galvez
Estrada, Erik (born Enrique)
Etcheson, Warren Wade
Etheridge, Richard Emmet
Etkes, Raphael
Ettinger, Richard Prentice
Eu, March Kong Fong
Eulau, Heinz
Euster, Joanne Reed
Eustis, Alvin Allen, Jr.
Eustis, Robert Henry
Evanoff, George C.
Evans, Bernard William
Evans, Bill (James William)
Evans, Daniel Jackson
Evans, David Albert
Evans, David Woolley
Evans, Ellis Dale
Evans, Ersel Arthur
Evans, George Robert, Jr.
Evans, Gil
Evans, Harold J.
Evans, Harrison Silas
Evans, Howard Ensign
Evans, Jerry Lee
Evans, John Martin
Evans, John Martin
Evans, John Victor
Evans, John Wainwright, Jr.
Evans, Larry Melvyn
Evans, Lloyd Roberts
Evans, Michael Jonas
Evans, Norman Allen
Evans, Oakley Spencer
Evans, Orrin Bryan
Evans, Robert
Evans, Robley Dunglison
Evans, Trevor Heiser
Evenden, Frederick George
Evenson, Pattee Edward
Everett, Chad
Everhart, Edgar
Everote, Warren Peter
Evers, William Dohrmann
Eversley, Frederick John
Everson, William Oliver
Evigan, Gregory Ralph
Evitt, William Robert
Evons, Harry
Evoy, John Joseph
Ewald, Earl
Ewell, Tom (Yewell Tompkins)
Exum, Glenn
Eyman, Richard Kenneth
Eyring, Edward Marcus
Eyring, Henry
Eyring, LeRoy
Eyzaguirre, Carlos Edwards
Ezer, Mitchel Julian
Faas, Andrew Stanley
Faas, Larry Andrew
Fabeck, Joseph Edward
Fabian, Francis Gordon, Jr.
Fabian, Robert Hart
Fabray, Nanette
Factor, Ted H.
Fadiman, Clifton
Fagan, George Vincent
Fagen, Donald
Fagg, Fred Dow, III
Faggin, Federico
Fagin, Henry
Fagot, Joseph Burdell
Fahey, John Aloysius
Fahey, Walter John
Fahrenkopf, Frank Joseph, Jr.
Fahrney, Delmer Stater
Faibisoff, Sylvia
Faigin, Larry Bernard
Fain, Sammy
Fain, Samuel S.
Fairbank, William Martin
Fairbanks, Charles Leo
Fairley, Henry Barrie
Faison, Edmund Winston Jordan
Falcon, Walter Phillip

Falcone, Alfonso Benjamin
Falconer, Donald Pearson
Falconer, Neil Eugene
Falicov, Leopoldo Maximo
Falk, Karl L.
Falk, Peter
Falkner, Frank Tardrew
Falkow, Stanley
Faller, James Elliot
Falls, Edward Joseph
Falsone, Anne Marie McMahon
Fan, Ky
Fanestil, Darrell Dean
Fanning, Katherine Woodruff
Faragher, Thomas Robert
Farber, Bernard
Farber, Seymour Morgan
Farella, Frank Eugene
Fargo, Louis James
Farley, Eugene Shedden, Jr.
Farley, Philip Judson
Farmer, Crofton Bernard
Farmer, John David
Farmer, Robert Lindsay
Farner, Donald Sankey
Farnon, Christine Miller
Farnsworth, Raymond Bartlett
Farquhar, John William
Farr, Fredrick Sharon
Farr, Jamie
Farr, Lee Edward
Farr, Richard Claborn
Farr, Richard Studley
Farr, Walter Greene, Jr.
Farrar, Frederick M.
Farrell, Austin James
Farrell, Edward Joseph
Farrell, Frank Samuel
Farrell, Joseph
Farrell, Mike
Farrell, Sharon
Farrer, William Cameron
Farris, Jerome
Fasi, Frank Francis
Fassio, Virgil
Faul, George Johnson
Faulkner, Adele Lloyd
Faus, Warren Wilson
Faw, Duane Leslie
Fawcett, Farrah Leni
Fearn-Banks, Kathleen
Feather, Leonard Geoffrey
Feder, Harold A.
Federici, William R.
Federman, Irwin
Fee, Roger Dexter
Fehlberg, Robert Erick
Fehrenbacher, Don Edward
Feigenbaum, Edward Albert
Feigl, Eric Otto
Fein, Irving Ashley
Feinberg, Joel
Feinberg, Lawrence Bernard
Feingold, Benjamin Franklin
Feinstein, Allen Lewis
Feinstein, Dianne
Feinstein, Joseph
Felchlin, James Alois
Felciano, Richard James
Feld, Fritz
Felder, Donald William
Feldman, Julian
Feldman, Marty
Feldman, Philip
Feldman, Raymond
Feldman, Stanley George
Feliciano, Jose
Fell, John Louis
Fell, Norman
Feller, Jack Henry, Jr.
Fellows, George Harvey
Felt, Donald Linn
Felton, Jean Spencer
Felton, Norman
Felts, James Martin
Fendler, Miriam Olden (Mrs. Harold A. Fendler)
Fenimore, George Wiley
Fenn, Raymond Wolcott, Jr.
Fenno, Harold O.
Fenton, Lewis Lowry
Fenton, Martin
Fenton, Noel John
Fenwick, William Augustus
Ferderber, Joseph
Ferejohn, John Arthur
Ferguson, Eldon Earl
Ferguson, Lloyd Noel
Ferguson, Maynard
Ferguson, Neil Taylor
Ferguson, Robert Louis
Ferguson, Roger Nephi
Ferguson, Sybil Rae
Ferguson, Warren John
Fergusson, Robert George
Ferlinghetti, Lawrence
Fernald, Peter J.
Fernandez, Ferdinand Francis
Ferraro, Edward James
Ferreira, Armando Thomas
Ferrell, Conchata Galen
Ferril, Thomas Hornsby
Ferrin, Chariton Arnold, Jr.
Ferris, Arthur Leland
Ferris, Melton
Ferris, Raymond West
Ferris, Robert Albert
Ferroggiaro, F. A.
Fery, John Bruce
Feshbach, Seymour
Fest, Thorrel Brooks
Fetherling, Dale Singer
Fetter, Alexander Lees
Feucht, Donald Lee
Feuer, Stanley Burton
Feuerstein, Kathleen W.
Fey, Harold Edward
Feyerabend, Paul Karl
Feynman, Richard Philipps
Ficzere, Attila Gyorgy
Field, David McLucas
Field, John Louis
Field, Sally
Field, Thomas Walter, Jr.
Fielding, Gabriel (Alan Gabriel Barnsley)
Fielding, Jonathan Evan
Fields, Bertram Harris
Fields, Victor Alexander
Fielstra, Helen Adams (Mrs. Clarence Fielstra)
Fife, Austin Edwin
Fiflis, Ted J.
Figley, Melvin Morgan
Fike, Edward Lake
Filep, Robert Thomas
Filerman, Michael Herman
Filfillan, George William
Filiciotto, Jerome Joseph
Filippi, Frank Joseph
Fillius, Milton Franklin, Jr.
Filosa, Gary Fairmont Randolph de Marco, II
Finch, Clement A.
Finch, H(arold) Curtis
Finch, Stuart McIntyre
Finck, William Albert
Findly, Sarah Elizabeth
Fine, Jerry
Fine, Max
Fine, Richard Isaac
Fine, Timothy Herbert
Finegold, Sydney Martin
Finell, Marvin
Finesilver, Sherman Glenn
Finger, John Holden
Fink, Robert Morgan
Finley, Carmen Joyce
Finlinson, Burns Lyman
Finnell, Michael Hartman
Finnie, Iain
Finnman, Paul Gordon
Firestein, Chester
Firestone, Morton H.
Firmage, Edwin Brown
Firmin, Peter Arthur, Jr.
Firminger, Harlan Irwin
Firor, John William
Firth, Robert
Fischer, Dale Arnold
Fischthal, Glenn Jay
Fish, Barbara
Fisher, Carrie Frances
Fisher, Delbert Arthur
Fisher, Edison David
Fisher, Gerald Saul
Fisher, Jerome
Fisher, Kenneth Robinson
Fisher, Leon Harold
Fisher, Lucy Jane
Fisher, Marjorie
Fisher, Michael Robert
Fisher, Wayne H.
Fishman, Erwin
Fishman, Robert Allen
Fiske, Marjorie
Fisken, Alexander McEwan
Fitz, John Allen
Fitzgerald, Ella
Fitzgerald, James Martin
Fitz Patrick, George Albert
Fitzpatrick, Joseph Edward
Fitzpatrick, Kirby Ward
Fitzpatrick, Robert John
Fitzsimmons, John Robert
Fitzsimons, Patrick S.
Fitzwater, Bonnie
Fix, Wilbur James
Fixman, Marshall
Flach, Victor H.
Flanagan, Fionnula Manon
Flanagan, John Clemans
Flanders, Edward Paul
Flannery, Robert Gene
Flatt, Ernest Orville
Flatte, Stanley Martin
Flaum, Marshall Allen
Flax, Serene (Mrs. Donald Flax)
Fleagle, Robert Guthrie
Fleck, Raymond Anthony, Jr.
Fleetwood, Mick
Fleischer, Everly Borah
Fleischer, Richard O.
Fleischman, Albert Sidney
Fleischmann, Ernest Martin
Fleming, Brice Noel
Fleming, John Gunther
Fleming, Louis Brown
Fleming, Peggy Gale
Fleming, Rhonda
Fleming, Richard Carl Dunne
Fleming, Ruth
Fleming, Scott
Fleming, William David
Fletcher, Allen
Fletcher, Hon. Betty B.
Fletcher, Dean Charles
Fletcher, Douglas Baden
Fletcher, Homer Lee
Fletcher, Kim
Fletcher, Louise
Fletcher, Max Ellis
Fletcher, Robert Dawson
Fletcher, Thomas William
Flick, John Edmond
Flicker, Ted
Flickinger, Thomas L.
Flier, Michael Stephen
Flittie, Edwin Gilbert
Flodin, Harvey Curtis
Flood, James Joseph
Flood, John Etchells, Jr.
Florea, John Ted
Flores, Thomas R.
Flory, Paul John
Flournoy, Houston Irvine
Flowerree, Robert Edmund
Floyd, Robert W.
Fluke, John Maurice
Fluno, Robert Younger
Fluor, John Robert
Flynn, Thomas William
Flynt, Althea Sue
Flynt, Larry Claxton
Foch, Nina
Fogelberg, Daniel Grayling
Fogg, Philip Shearer
Foisie, Jack
Foley, Harry John Patrick
Foley, Roger D.
Foley, (Mary) Suzanne
Folsom, Franklin Brewster
Foltz, Richard Harry
Foltz, Rodger Lowell
Fonda, Henry
Fonda, Jane
Fonda, Peter
Fondahl, John Walker
Fong, Benson
Fong, Hiram L.
Fonkalsrud, Eric Walter
Fontaine, Armand Louis
Fontaine, Joan
Foonberg, Jay G.
Foos, William Franklin
Foote, Christopher Spencer
Forbes, Lorna Miriam (Mrs. Robert Chaney)
Forbes, Samuel Emery
Forbis, William Hunt
Ford, Carey Alford, Jr.
Ford, Cornelius William
Ford, Donald Hainline
Ford, Ernest Jennings
Ford, Gerald Rudolph, Jr.
Ford, Glenn (Gwyllyn Samuel Newton Ford)
Ford, Harrison
Ford, Harry Xavier
Ford, James Dayton
Ford, Kenneth William
Fordham, Jefferson Barnes
Forester, Russell
Forgatch, Joseph Thomas
Forkosch, Morris David
Forman, William N.
Forrest, John Russell
Forrest, Steve (William Forrest Andrews)
Forrester, Alvin Theodore
Forrester, Eugene Priest
Forsee, Aylesa
Forsen, Harold Kay
Forsen, Harold Kay
Forsham, Peter Hugh
Forster, Leslie Stewart
Forsythe, John
Forte, John Gaetano
Foss, Phillip Oliver
Foster, George McClelland, Jr.
Foster, Gerald Pentland
Foster, Jodie (Alicia Christian Foster)
Foster, Julian Francis Sherwood
Foster, Stephen Kent
Fouts, Daniel Francis
Fowler, Thomas Kenneth
Fowler, William Alfred
Fox, Bernard Mitchell
Fox, Charles Ira
Fox, Francis Thomas
Fox, James Joseph
Fox, Jean DeWitt
Fox, Loyd John
Fox, Robert August
Fox, William Walter
Foxley, William Coleman
Foxworthy, James Ernest
Foxx, Redd (John Elroy Sanford)
Foye, Laurance Vincent, Jr.
Fraenkel-Conrat, Heinz
Frampton, Merle Elbert
France, John Lyons
Franciosa, Anthony (Anthony Papaleo)
Francis, Merrill Richard
Francis, Sam
Franciscus, James Grover
Frank, Anthony Melchior
Frank, Floyd William
Frank, John Paul
Frank, Richard H(arvey)
Franke, Ernest August
Franke, William Augustus
Frankel, Jacob Porter
Franken, James Burton
Franken, Peter Alden
Frankenberger, James Gilwood
Frankenheimer, John Michael
Franklin, Bonnie Gail
Franklin, Carl Mason
Franklin, Charles Scothern
Franklin, Gene Farthing
Franklin, Joel Nicholas
Franklin, Marc Adam
Franklin, Michael Harold
Frankovich, Mike J.
Frantz, John Corydon
Frasier, S. Douglas
Fraunfelder, Frederick Theodore
Frautschi, Steven Clark
Frawley, Patrick Joseph, Jr.
Frazer, Jack Winfield
Frazer, William Robert
Frazier, J. Phillip
Frazier, Joe
Frazier, Kendrick Crosby
Freberg, Carl Roger
Frech, William Paul
Fredenburg, Robert Love
Fredericks, John Donnan
Fredericksen, Burton Baum
Frederickson, Harry Gray, Jr.
Frederickson, Horace George
Freed, Aaron David
Freed, Bert
Freedman, Jeffrey Charles
Freedman, Mervin Burton
Freedman, Theodore Murray
Freeh, Edward James
Freeman, Barry Victor
Freeman, Cynthia
Freeman, Harry Lynwood
Freeman, John George
Freeman, Kathleen
Freeman, Linton Clarke
Freeman, Mark Price, Jr.
Freeman, Roger Kaye
Freeman, Russell Adams
Freeman, Samuel Ralph
Freeman, Seth
Freidel, Frank Burt, Jr.
Freimark, Robert
Freitas, George Ernest
Frel, Jiri K.
French, Charles Stacy
French, Clarence Levi, Jr.
French, John Douglas
French, Robin Hugh
French, Victor
Frensdorff, Wesley
Frenz-Heckman, Faith
Fretter, William Bache
Freudenthal, Steven Franklin
Frey, Albert
Frey, Charles Frederick
Frey, Christian Miller
Frey, Glenn
Frey, William Carl
Freymuth, G. Russell
Fricano, Tom Salvatore
Frick, Fay Arrieh
Frick, Oscar Lionel
Fricker, Peter Racine
Fried, Burton David
Fried, John
Friedenberg, Richard Myron
Friedkin, Morris Enton
Friedkin, William
Friedlander, Sheldon Kay
Friedman, Alan Barry
Friedman, Albert Barron
Friedman, H. Harold
Friedman, K. Bruce
Friedman, Lawrence M.
Friedman, Meyer
Friedman, Milton
Friedman, Morton Lee
Friedman, Paul Jay
Friedman, Robert Lee
Friedman, William Foster
Friedman, William Gary
Friedmann, Herbert
Friedmann, Norman Ernest
Friendly, Ed
Friesen, Gilbert Bryan
Frietzsche, Arthur H.
Friou, George Jacob
Frisbee, Don Calvin
Frisch, Robert A.
Frischknecht, Lee Conrad
Fritts, Robert Ellery
Frizzell, William Kenneth
Frohnmayer, David Braden
Froines, John Radford
Fromer, Seymour
Fromkin, Victoria Alexandria
Fromm, Alfred
Fronk, William Joseph
Frost, Harold Maurice
Frost, Otis Lamont, Jr.
Fruechtenicht, Richard William
Frumkin, Paul
Fry, Donald Owen
Fry, Michael Graham
Fry, Robert Paul
Frye, Helen Jackson
Frye, John Chapman
Fryer, Robert Sherwood
Fryer, Thomas Waitt, Jr.
Fuchs, Jacob
Fuchs, Roland John
Fuchs, Victor Robert
Fudge, Alan
Fuelling, Thomas Norton
Fuerstenau, Douglas Winston
Fugate, Ivan Dee
Fuhrman, Frederick Alexander
Fuhrman, Harold George
Fuhrman, Robert Alexander
Fuhs, Allen Eugene
Fujimoto, Masakazu Jack
Fujiyama, Wallace Sachio
Fukuda, Nobuko
Fukunaga, George Joji
Fukuyama, Kimie
Fulco, Armand John
Fulco, Jose Roque
Fuller, Anne Elizabeth Havens
Fuller, Duane Wendell
Fuller, Samuel
Fuller, Wallace Hamilton
Fullerton, Bill Junior
Fullerton, Gail Jackson
Fullerton, Robert Victor
Fullmer, Daniel Warren
Fulton, Len
Fung, Yuan-Cheng Bertram
Funk, William Henry
Furbay, John Harvey
Furbee, Dick Waitman
Furgason, Robert Roy
Furnas, David William
Furst, Arthur
Furth, Alan Cowan
Furth, Frederick Paul
Furth, George
Fuster, Joaquin Maria
Gabbert, James Jeffery
Gable, Richard Walter
Gabor, Eva
Gabor, Zsa Zsa (Sari)
Gabriel, Earl A.
Gaburo, Kenneth Louis
Gaffney, Mason
Gaffney, Peter Charles
Gaffney, Thomas
Gage, Nathaniel Lees
Gagnon, Alfred Joseph
Gail, Maxwell Trowbridge, Jr.
Gaillard, Robert Louis
Gaines, Francis Pendleton, Jr.
Gaines, Howard Clarke
Galane, Morton Robert
Galanos, James
Galbraith, James Marshall
Galbraith, John Semple
Gale, Thomas Martin
Gales, Robert Sydney
Gallacci, Robert John
Gallagher, Charles Patrick
Gallagher, Edward Stephen
Gallagher, Gerald Raphael
Gallagher, James Stephen
Gallagher, James Wes
Gallagher, Joseph Francis
Gallagher, Marian Gould
Gallagher, Richard Hugo
Gallander, Cathleen Sparks
Gallivan, John William
Galloway, Don
Galloway, Joseph Lee, Jr.
Galt, John Kirtland
Galt, John Kirtland
Gamble, John Robert
Gamelin, Theodore William
Gamo, Hideya
Ganas, Perry Spiros
Gann, Ernest Kellogg
Ganong, William F(rancis)
Garas, Kazimer Saul
Garbarini, Edgar Joseph
Garbarino, Joseph William
Garcia, Jerome John (Jerry)
Garcia, Walter Manuel
Gardenia, Vincent
Gardiner, Henry Gilbert
Gardiner, John William
Gardiner, Peter Alexander Jack
Gardiner, Robert M.
Gardner, Ava
Gardner, David Pierpont
Gardner, Donald LaVere
Gardner, James Albert
Gardner, John Hale
Gardner, Leonard Burton, II
Gardner, Murray Briggs
Gardner, Peter D.
Gardner, Richard Kent
Garfias, Robert
Garfin, Louis
Garlid, Kermit Leroy
Garner, James (James Scott Bumgarner)
Garnett, William
Garoutte, Bill Charles
Garr, Teri
Garrett, Betty
Garrett, Donald Everett
Garrett, Lila
Garrett, Luther Weaver, Jr.
Garrett, Stephen George
Garrett, Thomas Leslie (Snuff)
Garrido, August Edmun, Jr.
Garrison, Clayton
Garrity, Donald Lee
Garrity, Rodman Fox
Garsh, Thomas Burton
Garstang, Roy Henry
Garstin, Michael Edward
Garvey, Joanne Marie
Garvey, Steven Patrick
Garwood, Victor Paul
Gary, James Frederick
Gary, James Hubert
Gary, Richard Neel
Gaskell, Robert Eugene
Gastil, Russell Gordon
Gatell, Frank Otto
Gates, Charles Cassius
Gates, Dillard Herbert
Gates, Mahlon Eugene
Gates, Mark Thomas, Jr.
Gatti, Richard Anthony
Gauer, Charlotte Edwina
Gaustad, Edwin Scott
Gaustad, John Eldon
Gautier, Dick
Gavalas, George R.
Gaver, Kenneth Darrel
Gavin, Herbert James
Gavin, John
Gavin, John Joseph
Gay, E. Laurence
Gay, James
Gaye, Marvin
Gayle, Crystal
Gaylord, Donald Andrew
Gaynor, Joseph
Geballe, Ronald
Geballe, Theodore Henry
Gebhard, David
Gebhart, Carl Grant
Geckler, Richard Delph
Geddes, Frank Michael, Jr.
Geehan, James
Geehan, Robert William
Geer, Stephen DuBois
Geffen, David
Gehry, Frank Owen
Geiduschek, E(rnest) Peter
Geiger, Louis George
Geiringer, Karl
Geis, Gilbert Lawrence
Geisel, Theodor Seuss (Dr. Seuss)
Geiser, Karl Frederick
Geissinger, James Donovan
Geist, Jerry Douglas
Gelbart, Larry
Gelfand, David H.
Gell-Mann, Murray
Gelly, George Balfour
Gelman, Larry
Gelpi, Albert Joseph
Gendlin, Frances O.
Gendron, John Wilbrod
Gengerelli, Joseph Anthony
Genn, Nancy
Gentile, Joseph F.
Geoffroy, Charles Henry
Geoghegan, Elmo Leon
George, Alexander Lawrence
George, Lynda Day
Gerace, Felix John
Gerard, Gil
Gerber, Austin James
Gerber, Sanford Edwin
Gerberding, William Passavant
Gerbode, Frank Leven Albert
Gerbosi, William A.
Gerdemann, James Wessel
Gerdes, Ingeborg
Gere, James Monroe
Gere, Richard
Gerhard, Lee Clarence
Gerhart, James Basil
Gerig, Jared Franklin
Gering, Willis G.
Gerken, Walter Bland
Gerking, Shelby Delos, Jr.
German, William
Germane, Gayton Elwood
Gernreich, Rudi
Gerson, Samuel Joseph
Gersten, Bernard
Gersten, Jerome William
Gerstenberger, Donna Lorine
Gerster, Robert Gibson
Gerstley, James Mack
Gert, Gerard Martin
Gerth, Donald Rogers
Gerwick, Ben Clifford, Jr.
Gerwig, A. Robert
Gettelman, Thomas Robert
Getting, Ivan Alexander
Getz, George Fulmer, Jr.
Geyman, John Payne
Ghirardo, Joseph Bernard
Ghiselin, Brewster
Ghose, Rabindra Nath
Ghostley, Alice
Gialanella, Philip Thomas
Giaudrone, Angelo
Giauque, William Francis
Gibaldi, Milo
Gibb, Richard Dean
Gibbens, Alfred Morton
Gibbons, Don Cary
Gibbons, Jerry Lee
Gibbs, Alan John
Gibbs, Marla (Margaret Gibbs)
Giblett, Eloise Rosalie
Gibor, Aharon
Gibson, Count Dillon, Jr.
Gibson, Daniel Eugene
Gibson, George
Gibson, Henry
Gibson, Melvin Roy
Gibson, Moses Carl
Gibson, Robert Lee
Gibson, Robert Valentine
Gibson, Robert Walter
Gibson, Weldon Bailey
Gicovate, Bernard
Gidwitz, John David
Giedt, Warren Harding
Giessner, William Richard
Giffin, Glenn Orlando, II
Gilberg, Arnold Larry
Gilbert, Benjamin Franklin
Gilbert, Fred Ivan, Jr.
Gilbert, John Baptiste
Gilbert, William Wayne
Gilchrist, James Beardslee
Gilderhus, Mark Theodore
Gildersleeve, Thomas Arthur
Giles, Frederic Thomas
Gilkeson, Murray Mack
Gilkey, Gordon Waverly
Gill, Mark Moreland
Gill, Stanley Jensen
Gillam, Isaac Thomas, IV
Gillam, Max Lee
Gillcrist, Paul Thomas
Gillespie, David Ellis
Gillespie, James J.
Gillette, Robert Emery
Gilliam, Jackson Earle
Gillis, Harvey Neal
Gillis, John Simon
Gilman, David Ward
Gilman, Richard Carleton
Gilmore, Art
Gilmore, Charles W.
Gilmore, Jesse Lee
Gimbel, Norman
Gimbutas, Marija
Gimlett, James Irwin

Ginsburg, Seymour
Ginzton, Edward Leonard
Giovenco, John Vincent
Gipson, Gordon
Gipson, James Herrick
Girard, Alexander Hayden
Girard, René Noel
Girardeau, Marvin Denham
Giraud, Raymond Dorner
Girvigian, Raymond
Githens, John Horace, Jr.
Giulini, Carlo Maria
Gius, Julius
Glad, Edward Newman
Gladman, Maurice
Gladstein, Robert David
Glantz, Mary Ann Danin
Glascock, Hardin Roads, Jr.
Glaser, Daniel
Glaser, Donald A(rthur)
Glaser, Edward Lewis
Glaser, Paul Michael
Glaser, Robert Joy
Glasgow, Lowell Alan
Glass, Herbert
Glass, Laurel
Glass, Ron
Glasser, William
Glassock, Richard James
Glazer, Barry
Glazer, Guilford
Gleason, Denis J.
Gleason, John F.
Glenny, Lyman Albert
Glick, David
Glickman, Harry
Glicksman, Frank Leonard
Glithero, Eleanor Ferguson
Glock, Charles Young
Glorfeld, Louis Earl
Glos, Karl Frederick
Glover, William Wayne
Gluck, Louis
Glynn, William Celester
Go, Mateo Lian Poa
Goble, George G.
Goddard, Samuel Pearson, Jr.
Goddard, Wesley Rawdon
Goddard, William Andrew
Godfrey, George Denton
Godfrey, Samuel Addison
Godunov, Alexander Boris
Goeddel, David Van Norman
Goeglein, Richard John
Goeldner, Charles Raymond
Goell, James Emanuel
Goering, Kenneth Justin
Goerlitz, Harvey Theodore
Goff, Abe McGregor
Goggin, Margaret Knox
Goheen, Harry Earl
Goin, John Morehead
Golbert, Albert Sidney
Gold, Arnold Henry
Gold, Carol Sapin
Gold, Herbert
Gold, Raymond L.
Goldberg, Edward David
Goldberg, Fred Sellmann
Goldberg, Gary David
Goldberg, Joseph B.
Goldberg, Leonard
Goldberger, Marvin L.
Golden, Charles Franklin
Golden, Milton M.
Golding, Charles William
Goldman, Bernard
Goldman, Bo
Goldman, Charles Remington
Goldman, Ralph
Goldreich, Peter Martin
Goldsboro, Bobby
Goldschmidt, Neil Edward
Goldschmidt, Walter R.
Goldsmith, Bram
Goldsmith, Claude Orville
Goldsmith, Ulrich Karl
Goldstein, Avram Shalom
Goldstein, Charles H.
Goldstein, Edward David
Goldstine, Abner Don
Goldstine, Stephen Joseph
Goldwater, Richard
Goldwhite, Harold
Goldwyn, Samuel John, Jr.
Golino, Carlo Luigi
Göllner, Marie Louise
Gonda, Thomas Andrew
Gonge, John Foster
Gonzales, Richard A. (Pancho)
Gonzalez, Michael Ibs
Gonzalez, Raymond
Emmanuel
Good, Charles E.
Goodall, Jackson Wallace, Jr.
Goodall, Leonard Edwin
Goode, William Josiah
Goodenow, Donald Irving
Goodfriend, Arthur
Goodin, Vernon Lee
Gooding, Charles Arthur
Goodlad, John Inkster
Goodman, Clark Drouillard
Goodman, Dody (Dolores)
Goodman, Joseph Wilfred
Goodman, Leon
Goodman, Linda (Mrs. Sam O. Goodman)
Goodman, Louis S.
Goodman, Max A.
Goodman, Michael A.
Goodman, Murray
Goodman, Sam Richard
Goodman, Steven Benjamin
Goodman, Thomas Leo
Goodnight, Scott H., Jr.
Goodrich, Hile Wayne
Goodrich, Norma Lorre (Mrs. John H. Howard)
Goodspeed, Stephen Spencer
Goodstein, David Louis
Goodwin, Alfred Theodore
Goodwin, Nancy Lee
Goodwin, Willard E.
Goodwin, William Richard
Goodyear, Alfred Wyman, III
Goorwitz, Allen
Goran, Michael J.
Gorans, Gerald Elmer
Gorbman, Aubrey
Gorchels, Clarence Clifford
Gordan, Gilbert Saul
Gordon, Arthur Ernest
Gordon, Basil
Gordon, Don
Gordon, Frank X., Jr.
Gordon, Horace Earl
Gordon, Irving
Gordon, John Lutz
Gordon, Joseph Harold
Gordon, Malcolm Stephen
Gordon, Margaret Shaughnessy
Gordon, Michael
Gordon, Milton G.
Gordon, Milton Paul
Gordon, Oakley Junior
Gordon, Seth (Edwin)
Gordon, Shirley Blom
Gordon, Walter
Gordy, Berry
Gores, Joseph Nicholas
Gorham, Frank DeVore, Jr.
Gorman, Mel
Gorman, Rudolph Carl
Gorney, Cynthia Elizabeth
Gorodezky, Eli
Gorrell, Robert Mark
Gorshin, Frank
Gorski, Roger Anthony
Gorsuch, John Elliott
Gortner, Marjoe (Hugh Marjoe Ross Gortner)
Gortner, Willis Alway
Gorton, Slade
Gose, Richard Vernie
Goss, Robert Francis
Goss, Wesley Perry
Gossage, Richard Michael
Gossett, Louis
Gottlieb, Abraham Mitchell
Gottschalk, Louis August
Gough, Harrison Gould
Goughlin, Magdalen
Gould, Alvin R.
Gould, Charles Lessington
Gould, Charles Perry
Gould, Elliott
Gould, Frank Nelson, Jr.
Gould, Harold
Gould, Morley David
Gould, Roy Walter
Gould, William Richard
Goulden, Stephen Arthur
Goulet, Robert Gerard
Goulian, Mehran
Gouraud, Jackson S.
Gourley, Ronald Robert
Gouterman, Martin Paul
Goyan, Jere Edwin
Goyen, Charles William
Graburn, Nelson Hayes Henry
Gradishar, Randy Charles
Grady, Edward Francis
Grady, Stafford R.
Graebner, James Herbert
Graetz, Rick
Graham, Alexander Steel
Graham, Bill
Graham, C(lyde) Benjamin, Jr.
Graham, Dee McDonald
Graham, Donald Andrew
Graham, Francis William
Graham, Hugh Jack, Jr.
Graham, Irwin Patton
Graham, Richard Harper
Graham, Robert Bruce
Grand, Richard D.
Grande, John Alphonse
Grandy, Fred
Grandy, Leonard A.
Grandy, Walter Thomas, Jr.
Granger, Marvin Frank
Grant, Alan J.
Grant, Brooke
Grant, Irving Maxwell
Grant, Lee (Lyova Haskell Rosenthal)
Grant, Merrill Alan
Grant, Perry James
Grant, Robert Yearington
Grant, Stanley Cameron
Grant, Thom
Grant, William
Grant, William West, III
Grantham, Richard Robert
Granz, Norman
Grasshof, Alex
Grassl, Theodore Peter
Grassle, Karen
Gratz, H. Tucker
Gravel, Mike
Graves, Charles Edward
Graves, Peter
Graves, Ray
Gray, Carl Albert
Gray, David Eugene
Gray, Frances M.
Gray, Harry Barkus
Gray, John Delton
Gray, John Justin
Gray, John Stephens
Gray, Linda
Gray, Paul Russell
Gray, Philip Howard
Gray, Robert Hugh
Gray, William Percival
Graysmith, Robert
Grayson, Kathryn
Grayston, J. Thomas
Greaver, Harry
Greb, Gordon Barry
Grebanier, Michael Peter
Grebene, Alan Bekir
Greeley, Paul Webb
Greely, Michael Truman
Green, Charles Walter
Green, Cyril Kenneth
Green, Dale Monte
Green, Edith
Green, Francis Joseph
Green, Guy
Green, Harold Francis
Green, Harry
Green, John Alden
Green, John Root
Green, Joshua, III
Green, Oliver Francis, Jr.
Green, William Porter
Greenbaum, James Richard
Greenberg, Arthur Norman
Greenberg, Byron Stanley
Greenberg, Carl
Greenberg, Daniel Ben
Greenberg, Joanne
Greenberg, Joseph H.
Greenberg, Maxwell Elfred
Greenberg, Paul Robert
Greenberger, Ellen
Greenblatt, Milton
Greene, A. Crawford, Jr.
Greene, Browne
Greene, Carla
Greene, David Lee
Greene, Donald Johnson
Greene, Herb
Greene, James Coffin
Greene, John Burkland
Greene, John Clifford
Greene, John Thomas, Jr.
Greene, Laurence Francis
Greene, Lorne
Greene, Robert Everist
Greene, Shecky
Greenfeld, Alexander
Greenlee, John Alden
Greenlick, Merwyn Ronald
Greenspan, Francis S.
Greenspun, Herman Milton
Greenstadt, Melvin
Greenstein, Jesse Leonard
Greenwald, Guy Preston, Jr.
Greenway, John Selmes
Greer, Howard Earl
Greer, Monte Arnold
Greever, William St. Clair
Gregg, Earl Clifford
Gregor, Howard Frank
Gregory, Arthur Stanley
Gregory, Bobby Lee
Gregory, Christopher
Gregory, Donald Munson
Gregory, Harold La Mar
Gregory, James
Gregory, Joseph Tracy
Gregory, Michael Strietmann
Gregory, Paul (Jason Gregory Lenhart)
Greig, William Taber, Jr.
Gremban, Joe Lawrence
Gressak, Anthony Raymond, Jr.
Grether, David Maclay
Grey, John R.
Grice, Harwood Vinson
Grich, Robert Anthony
Grider, James Bayard
Grier, Herbert Earl
Grier, Pamela Suzette
Gries, George Alexander
Griffen, William Bedford
Griffin, Charles Calvin
Griffin, DeWitt James
Griffin, F. O'Neil
Griffin, Gerald Duane
Griffin, Herschel Emmett
Griffin, Merv Edward
Griffin, Thomas Ward
Griffith, Ernest Ralph
Griffith, William Alexander
Griffiths, Iorwerth Davis Ace
Griggs, Gordon Phillip
Griggs, Harold Warner
Grigsby, John Lynn
Grill, Lawrence J.
Grimes, David Charles
Grimes, Tammy
Grimm, Edward Elias
Grings, William (Washburn)
Grisanti, Frank Anthony
Grisham, Jack Edwin
Griswold, Donald John
Griswold, Herbert Edward, Jr.
Griswold, Lyman Dwight
Grivas, Theodore
Grobe, Charles Stephen
Grobe, James Lester
Grobstein, Clifford
Grodin, Charles
Grodins, Fred Sherman
Grodsky, Gerold Morton
Groebli, Werner Fritz (Mr. Frick)
Groh, Clifford John
Groh, David Lawrence
Grohman, Robert T.
Grojean, Thomas Francis
Groman, Neal Benjamin
Grosenbaugh, Downey A.
Gross, Avrum Michael
Gross, Hal Raymond
Gross, Richard Edmund
Gross, Ruth Taubenhaus
Gross, Sidney W.
Grossinger, Richard Selig
Grossman, Arnold Joseph
Grossman, Lawrence Morton
Grossman, Marshall Bruce
Grossman, Morton Irvin
Grossman, Moses
Groussman, Raymond G.
Grover, Edward D.
Grover, Myron Roberts, Jr.
Grubbs, Glen Allen
Gruber, John Balsbaugh
Gruber, William Carl
Grumbach, Melvin Malcolm
Grundmann, Albert Wendell
Gruner, George Frank
Grutka, Andrew Gregory
Gryson, Joseph Anthony
Guard, Dave
Guarino, John Ralph
Guarrera, Frank
Guastaferro, Angelo
Gubser, Charles S.
Guedel, John
Guenther, Arthur Henry
Guerard, Albert Joseph
Guerrant, Edward Owings
Guggenhime, Richard Elias
Guilfoyle, Merlin Joseph
Guillemin, Roger
Guillermin, John
Guinn, Donald Eugene
Gulick, Sidney Lewis
Gullander, Werner Paul
Gumbel, Bryant Charles
Gunaji, Narendra Nagesh
Gund, George, III
Gunderson, Elmer Millard
Gunderson, Herbert Edmond
Gunn, Moses
Gunn, Thom(son William)
Gunst, Robert Allen
Gunther, Gerald
Guntheroth, Warren Gaden
Gurdin, Michael Meyer
Gurgin, Vonnie Ann
Gurney, Daniel Sexton
Gusfield, Joseph Robert
Gustavson, Dean Leonard
Gustlin, Philip Raymond
Gute, George Gaylord
Guthery, Peter Charles
Guthrie, Alfred Bertram, Jr.
Guthrie, Franklin Kirney
Guthrie, James Williams
Guthrie, Robert Val
Gutierrez, Max, Jr.
Gutknecht, Paul Herbert
Gutmann, John
Gutwillig, Robert Alan
Guyol, John Todd
Gwilliam, Gilbert Franklin
Gwinn, John L.
Gwinn, William Dulaney
Gwinner, Robert Fred, Jr.
Haag, James Norman
Haak, Harold Howard
Haas, Harold Murray
Haas, Peter E.
Habbe, Donald Edwin
Haber, Joyce
Habib, Philip Charles
Hack, Shelley
Hackett, Buddy
Hackett, Norbert Allen
Hackman, Gene
Haddad, Zack Haroun
Haddon, Harold Alan
Haddon, Sam Ellis
Haden, Charles
Haden, Clovis Roland
Haden, Patrick Capper (Pat)
Hadley, Gilbert Gordon
Hadley, Paul Ervin
Haeberlin, John Benjamin, Jr.
Haeckel, Gerald Burseth
Haehl, Harry Lewis
Hafen, LeRoy R.
Hageman, Warren Carl
Hagen, Ronald Henry
Hagenstein, William David
Hager, Robert Worth
Haggard, Merle Ronald
Haggerty, Dan
Hagiwara, Susumu
Hague, Donald Victor
Hague, William Edward, Jr.
Hahn, Betty
Hahn, Erwin Louis
Hahn, Roger
Hahn, Thomas Marshall, Jr.
Hahne, Henry Victor
Haight, Fulton Wilbur
Haight, James Theron
Haight, Warren Gazzam
Haile, Lawrence Barclay
Haile, Raymond Alderson, Jr.
Haines, Richard
Haines, William Wister
Haire, James
Hake, Robert Carruth
Halasz, Nicholas Alexis
Halbach, Edward Christian, Jr.
Halberg, Charles John August, Jr.
Halbert, Sherrill
Haldeman, Harry R. (Bob)
Hale, Charles Russell
Hale, Newton Johnston
Hale, Ralph Webster
Haley, Jack, Jr. (John J., Jr.)
Hall, Carl William
Hall, Carlyle Washington, Jr.
Hall, Charles Frederick
Hall, Clarence Albert, Jr.
Hall, Conrad
Hall, Cynthia Holcomb
Hall, Don Alan
Hall, Donald Keith
Hall, Edward Twitchell
Hall, Gary Curtis
Hall, Gordon R.
Hall, Henry Kingston, Jr.
Hall, Howard Tracy
Hall, Jack Gilbert
Hall, James Byron
Hall, Jerome
Hall, Marshall, Jr.
Hall, Monty
Hall, Nathan Albert
Hall, Perry Edwards, II
Hall, Richard Neal
Hall, Robert Thallon
Hall, Roy Charles
Hall, William Edward, Jr.
Hallenbeck, George Aaron
Halley, James Harvey
Halliday, William Ross
Hallier, Gerard Edouard
Hallock, C. Wiles, Jr.
Hallum, Jules Verne
Halperin, John William
Halperin, Robert Milton
Halprin, Anna Schuman (Mrs. Lawrence Halprin)
Halprin, Lawrence
Halseth, William Laibly
Halstead, Bruce Walter
Halstead, Harry Moore
Halstead, Scott Barker
Haltiner, George Joseph
Halver, John Emil
Halverson, George Clarence
Ham, Lee Edward
Hamblin, Richard Wallace
Hamill, Dorothy Stuart
Hamill, Mark
Hamilton, Calvin Sargent
Hamilton, Donald Bengtsson
Hamilton, Frederic Crawford
Hamilton, Joseph Henry Michael, Jr.
Hamilton, Paul Larnell
Hamilton, Randy Haskell
Hamilton, Richard Daniel
Hamilton, William Thorne
Hamister, Donald Bruce
Hamlin, Kenneth Eldred, Jr.
Hamlisch, Marvin
Hammer, Armand
Hammerbeck, Wanda Lee
Hammers, Oliver Bertrand
Hamming, Richard W.
Hammond, George Denman
Hammond, George Peter
Hammond, Jay Sterner
Hammond, R. Philip
Hamner, Earl Henry, Jr.
Hamner, Homer Howell
Hampe, Keith Robert
Hampton, Gordon Francis
Hampton, James C.
Hampton, James Wade
Hampton, Rex Herbert
Han, Yu-Shan
Hanafee, William
Hanauer, James Donald
Hanbury, Una
Hance, Margaret T.
Hanchett, William
Hancock, Ernest William
Hancock, Herbert Jeffrey
Hancock, John D.
Hancock, John Walker, III
Hancock, Ralph Lowell
Hancocks, David Morgan
Hand, Cadet Hammond, Jr.
Hand, Clifford Jay
Hand, Wayland Debs
Handelman, Lad
Handlery, Paul Robert
Handschumacher, Albert Gustave
Handy, Lyman Lee
Handy, Robert John
Handy, Robert Maxwell
Haneman, Vincent Siering, Jr.
Hanifen, Richard Charles
Hankin, Charles Donald
Hanlon, John Joseph
Hanna, John Paul
Hanna, Melvin Wesley
Hanna, Paul Robert
Hanna, Stanley Sweet
Hanna, Thomas Louis
Hanna, William Denby
Hanna, William Johnson
Hannaford, Mark Warren
Hannaford, Peter Dor
Hannay, N(orman) Bruce
Hansberger, Robert Vail
Hansch, Corwin Herman
Hansch, Theodor Wolfgang
Hansen, Arne Rae
Hansen, Elwood Leslie
Hansen, Grant Lewis
Hansen, Hugh Justin
Hansen, James Lee
Hansen, James V.
Hansen, Larry Lee
Hansen, Pete Ruse
Hansen, Richard King
Hansen, Richard W.
Hansen, Robert William
Hansen, Terry Dale
Hanson, Allan Morris
Hanson, Donald Norman
Hanson, Gaylord Heber
Hanson, Jo
Hanson, John J.
Hanson, Kenneth Ostlin
Hanson, Kermit Osmond
Hanson, Nels William
Hanson, Raymond Lester
Hanson, Robert Carl
Hanson, Roger Kvamme
Hanson, Virgil
Hanzlik, Rayburn DeMara
Hara, Ernest Hideo
Harbaugh, George Milton
Harcleroad, Fred Farley
Hardbeck, George William
Harden, Marvin
Harden, Patricia Lee
Harder, Virgil Eugene
Hardisty, Huntington
Hardman, John Maley
Hardy, Charles Leach
Hardy, D. Elmo
Hardy, David
Hardy, Thomas Austin
Hardy, Walter Lincoln
Hare, Nathan
Hare, Robert Lewis
Hargadon, Bernard Joseph, Jr.
Harlan, Neil Eugene
Harlin, Vivian Krause
Harlow, LeRoy Francis
Harmon, Harry William
Harmon, Mont Judd
Harmon, Myra Ruth Freed
Harmsen, Tyrus George
Harness, William Edward
Harnett, Daniel Joseph
Harnett, David Arthur
Harnish, Jay Dewey
Harper, Ashby Taylor
Harper, Harold Anthony
Harper, Jene
Harper, Lawrence Averell
Harper, Owen Howe
Harper, Valerie
Harrah, Robert Eugene
Harrangue, Renee Lorraine
Harrigan, John Frederick
Harriman, John Howland
Harrington, Donald Charles
Harrington, LaMar
Harrington, (Daniel) Patrick, Jr.
Harris, Aaron
Harris, Barbara
Harris, Burt Irving
Harris, Darryl Wayne
Harris, Ellen Gandy (Mrs. J. Ramsay Harris)
Harris, Emmylou
Harris, Frank Ephraim
Harris, Fred R.
Harris, George Thomas, Jr.
Harris, Grant Anderson
Harris, Ira Whitney
Harris, James Dexter
Harris, John Black
Harris, Julie
Harris, Mark
Harris, Markham
Harris, Milton M.
Harris, Morgan
Harris, N. Nell
Harris, Paul
Harris, Richard (St. John)
Harris, Robert Martin
Harris, Robert Norman
Harris, Stephen Ernest
Harris, Theodore Edward
Harris, Vincent Crockett
Harrison, Donald Carey
Harrison, Earle
Harrison, George
Harrison, Gregory
Harrison, James Thomas
Harrison, John Conway
Harrison, Mark I.
Harrison, Walter Ashley
Hart, Arthur Alvin
Hart, C. Allan
Hart, Donald Milton
Hart, Dwight Howard, Jr.
Hart, Edward LeRoy
Hart, Edwin James
Hart, Frederick Michael
Hart, Hubert J(oseph)
Hart, James David
Hart, John Lathrop Jerome
Hart, Joseph
Hart, Louis Ireland, Jr.
Hart, Maurice Arthur
Hart, N. Berne
Hart, Ray Lee
Harte, Joseph Meakin
Harter, Lafayette George, Jr.
Harter, Robert Jackson, Jr.
Hartford, John Cowan
Harth, Robert James
Hartinger, James V.
Hartke, Jan Alan
Hartl, Richard James
Hartley, Fred Lloyd
Hartley Boyriven, Mariette
Hartlieb, Gordon Wesley
Hartman, Ashley Powell
Hartman, Margaret Jane
Hartman, Robert Leroy
Hartnack, Carl Edward
Hartsough, Walter Douglas
Hartung, Ernest William, Jr.
Hartwick, Elbert Stuart
Hartz, J(ohn) Ernest, Jr.
Harvey, Bernard George
Harvey, James Ross
Harvey, Joseph Paul, Jr.
Harvey, Lawrence A.

Harvey, Van Austin
Haskell, Peter Abraham
Hassard, Howard
Hassett, Marilyn
Hassid, Sami
Hasslein, George Johann
Hastings, Albert Baird
Hastings, Edward Walton
Hastings, L(ois) Jane
Hastings, Robert Pusey
Hastorf, Albert Herman
Hastrich, Jerome Joseph
Haswell, Frank Irvin
Hatch, Calvin Shipley
Hatch, Eastman Nibley
Hatch, George Clinton
Hatch, Richard
Hatfield, Paul Gerhart
Hatt, Gunther Josef
Hatter, Terry Julius, Jr.
Hattox, John Stanley
Haugh, Robert Darrell
Haughey, James McCrea
Haughton, Kenneth Elwood
Hauk, A. Andrew
Haun, John Daniel
Haupt, George Edward, Jr.
Haurwitz, Bernhard
Haury, Emil Walter
Hauser, Emil Daniel William
Hauser, Robert Elmer
Hausman, Arthur Herbert
Havel, Richard Joseph
Haviland, James West
Hawke, Sharon Lynne
Hawkes, Thomas Frederick
Hawkins, Howard Gresham, Jr.
Hawkins, James Victor
Hawkins, Jasper Stillwell, Jr.
Hawkins, K(enneth) Courtenay, Jr.
Hawkins, Michael Daly
Hawkins, Neil Middleton
Hawkins, Oliver Jerry
Hawkins, Willis Moore, Jr.
Hawley, Donald Thomas
Hawley, Philip Metschan
Hawn, Goldie
Hawthorne, Betty Eileen
Hawthorne, Marion Frederick
Haxo, Francis Theodore
Hay, John Thomas
Hayden, Tom
Hayes, Denis Allen
Hayes, Janet Gray
Hayes, Peter Lind
Hayes, Robert Mayo
Hayes, Vertis Clemon
Hayes, William Frederick
Haynes, Harold Walter
Haynes, Howard Homer
Haynes, Moses Alfred
Haynes, Norman Ray
Hays, Daniel Mauger
Hays, Howard H (Tim)
Hays, Jack D.H.
Hays, Marguerite Thompson
Hays, Patrick Gregory
Hays, Peter L.
Hays, Peter L.
Haytin, Harold Alexander
Haywood, L. Julian
Hayworth, Rita (Margarita Carman Cansino)
Hazard, Robert Culver, Jr.
Hazeltine, Herbert Samuel, Jr.
Hazen, Paul Mandeville
Heacock, Raymond Leroy
Headlee, Rolland Dockeray
Headley, Sherman Knight
Heady, Ferrel
Heady, Harold Franklin
Heafey, Edwin Austin, Jr.
Healey, Derek Edward
Healy, Mary (Mrs. Peter Lind Hayes)
Healy, Otis McDowell
Heaman, William McPherson
Hearon, William Ray
Hearst, George Randolph, Jr.
Hearst, Joseph Albert, Jr.
Hearst, Randolph Apperson
Heartz, Daniel Leonard
Heath, George Ross
Heath, Richard Raymond
Heath, Stratton Rollins, Jr.
Heatherington, J. Scott
Heaton, Culver
Hebeler, Henry Koester
Hebert, Joseph Floyd
Hebner, Paul Chester
Hecht, Lee Martin
Heckel, John Louis
Heckler, George Earl
Heckman, William Robert
Hedison, David Albert
Hedley, Robert Olds
Hedrick, Donald Ward
Hedrick, Wally Bill
Hedrick, Walter Russell, Jr.
Heer, David Macalpine
Heetland, Gerald Charles
Hegarty, William Kevin
Heggland, Radoy Witt
Heidelberger, Charles
Heidenheim, Roger Stewart
Heidt, John Murray
Heifetz, Jascha
Heilbron, John L.
Heilbron, Louis Henry
Heilig, Louis Frank
Heilman, Gail Ellen
Heilman, Robert Bechtold
Hein, Leonard William
Heinecken, Robert Friedli
Heineman, Warner
Heinlein, Robert Anson
Heinrichs, William LeRoy
Heinselman, James L.
Heintzberger, Henry John
Heiserman, Richard Dean
Heistand, Joseph Thomas
Heitman, Hubert, Jr.
Helbling, Robert Eugene
Helburn, Nicholas
Helin, Frank Edward
Helinski, Donald Raymond
Heller, Jules
Heller, Paul Michael
Helliwell, Robert Arthur
Hellmann, Donald Charles
Hellwarth, Robert Willis
Hellyer, Clement David
Hellyer, George Maclean
Helmer, George Alfred
Helmericks, Harmon
Helmholz, August Carl
Helmond, Katherine
Helmond, Katherine
Helmstetter, C. W. (Shad)
Helphand, Ben J.
Helson, Henry Berge
Helzer, James Dennis
Hemingway, Richard Keith
Hemion, Dwight Arlington
Hempel, Valdemar
Hemphill, Bernice Monahan (Mrs. Charles D. Hemphill)
Hempler, Orval Frederick
Hemsley, Sherman
Hendee, William Richard
Hendel, Frank Joseph
Henderson, Dan Fenno
Henderson, Florence
Henderson, George Miller
Henderson, Girard Brown
Henderson, Maureen McGrath
Henderson, Thelton Eugene
Hendricks, Calvin
Hendricks, Charles Durrell, Jr.
Hendricks, John Carl
Hendricksen, Holmes
Hendy, Robert
Heneman, Herbert Gerhard, Jr.
Henkin, Leon Albert
Henley, Ernest Mark
Henley, William Ballentine
Hennessey, Alice Elizabeth
Hennessy, John James
Hennessy, Thomas Edward
Henning, Charles Nathaniel
Henning, John Frederick, Jr.
Henning, Paul William
Hennion, Reeve Lawrence
Henreid, Paul (Paul Georg Julius von Hernried Ritter von Wasel-Waldingau)
Henricks, John Dwaine
Henriksen, Melvin
Henry, Anthony Ray
Henry, Buck
Henry, Margaret
Henry, Marguerite
Henry, Nicholas Llewlyn
Henry, Rene Arthur, Jr.
Henry, Richard Charles
Henry, William Earl
Henshaw, Jere Coyle
Henshaw, Paul Carrington
Hensley, Pamela Gail
Henson, Ray David
Hepburn, Audrey
Hepler, Robert Sidney
Herberg, Roland Leo
Herberger, G. Robert
Herbert, Donald Jeffrey (Mr. Wizard)
Herbert, Frank Patrick
Herbert, Gavin Shearer
Herbert, James Hall
Herbert, James Keller
Herdrich, Norman Wesley
Hergenrather, Edmund Richard
Herman, James Richard
Herman, Robert Dunton
Hermann, Ernest Theodore
Hernandez, Aileen Clarke
Hernandez, Benigno Carlos
Hernstadt, William H.
Heron, David Winston
Herr, Richard
Herring, William Conyers
Herringer, Frank Casper
Herrmann, Christian, Jr.
Herrmann, Edward Kirk
Herrmann, George
Herron, Stephen House
Herschensohn, Bruce
Herschler, Ed
Herschler, Robert John
Hersh, LeRoy
Hershey, Barbara
Hershman, Lynn Lester
Hertzberg, Abraham
Herzberg, Frederick
Herzog, Bertram
Hess, David Fredric
Hess, Oleen
Hess, Robert Daniel
Hess, Wilford Moser
Hess, Wilmot Norton
Hesseman, Howard
Heston, Charlton
Hetland, John Robert
Hetzel, Ralph Dorn, Jr.
Hetzron, Robert
Hewitt, Edwin
Hewitt, James Orville
Hewitt, Robert Russell
Hewitt, William Lane
Hewlett, William (Redington)
Hewson, Edgar Wendell
Heyborne, Robert Linford
Heyler, David Baldwin, Jr.
Heyman, Ira Michael
Heyneman, Donald
Heyns, Roger William
Heywood, Stanley John
Hiaring, Robert Dale
Hiatt, Peter
Hiatt, Robert Worth
Hibbs, Loyal Robert
Hibler, Douglas Harry
Hickel, Walter Joseph
Hickerson, Glenn Lindsey
Hickey, Margaret A.
Hickman, Bert George, Jr.
Hickman, William Herbert
Hicks, Donald Alden
Hicks, Floyd V.
Higashi, Wilfred Hiroto
Higbee, David M.
Higgins, Colin
Higgins, James George
Higgins, William Henry Clay, III
Higgs, DeWitt A.
Hightower, John Murmann
Hilberry, Norman
Hilbert, Bernard Charles
Hilbert, Robert Backus
Hilbrecht, Norman Ty
Hilburn, (Charles) Robert
Hildebrand, George Herbert
Hildebrand, Joel Henry
Hilgard, Ernest Ropiequet
Hilgers, Gary Mike
Hilker, Walter Robert, Jr.
Hill, Arthur
Hill, Carrick Augustus
Hill, Douglas Green
Hill, Francis Frederick
Hill, Frank Whitney, Jr.
Hill, Fredric William
Hill, George Richard
Hill, George Roy
Hill, Hamlin Lewis, Jr.
Hill, Harold Eugene
Hill, Henry Allen
Hill, Irving
Hill, James Newlin
Hill, John deKoven
Hill, Orion Alvah, Jr.
Hill, Rey Marshall
Hill, Richard Anthony
Hill, Richard Johnson
Hill, Robert Raymond, II
Hill, Walter
Hillaire, Marcel
Hillbruner, Anthony
Hiller, Arthur
Hiller, Stanley, Jr.
Hillerman, John Benedict
Hillway, Tyrus
Hillyard, Ira William
Hillyer, Robert Morris
Hilton, Barron
Hilton, Peter John
Hilton, Ronald
Hilts, Margarete Louise
Hinchliffe, Stephen Freeman, Jr.
Hinchman, Roger Walworth
Hind, Harry William
Hinderaker, Ivan
Hine, Charles Henri, II
Hine, Robert Van Norden, Jr.
Hinerfeld, Robert Elliot
Hingle, Pat
Hinman, Frank, Jr.
Hinshaw, David Burdg
Hinshaw, Ernest Theodore, Jr.
Hinshaw, Horton Corwin
Hinshaw, Randall (Weston)
Hirsch, Harold Seller
Hirsch, Judd
Hirsch, Monroe Jerome
Hirsch, Werner Zvi
Hirschberg, Gert K.
Hirschfeld, Gerald J.
Hirschfeld, Tomas Beno
Hirschfield, Alan J.
Hitch, Charles Johnston
Hitch, Henry Atwood, Jr.
Hitch, Thomas Kemper
Hitchcock, George Parks
Hitchcock, Richard Elonzo
Hitchcock, Walter Anson
Hitchman, Robert Bruce
Hitchner, Dell Gillette
Hiteshew, Frank Melton
Hjortsberg, William Reinhold
Ho, Chinn
Hoadley, Walter Evans
Hoag, Arthur Allen
Hoag, Frank Stephen, Jr.
Hoagland, Albert Smiley
Hoagland, Donald Wright
Hoare, Tyler James
Hobbs, Carl Fredric
Hobbs, Linder Charlie
Hoch, Orion Lindel
Hochschild, Adam Marquand
Hodder, R(oland) Frederick, Jr.
Hoddick, Howard Kinsey
Hodgdon, Herbert James
Hodge, Paul William
Hodgen, Maurice Denzil
Hodges, David Albert
Hodges, Paul Vincent, Jr.
Hodgman, Joan Elizabeth
Hodgson, James Day
Hodson, William Alan
Hoefer, John Henry
Hoehn, William Edwin, Jr.
Hoel, Paul
Hoenig, William Charles
Hoenshell, Donald Junior
Hoerni, Jean Amédée
Hofer, William Jacob
Hofer, William Jacob
Hoff, David Daniel
Hoff, Marcian Edward, Jr.
Hoff, Nicholas John
Hoffer, Eric
Hoffman, Allan Sachs
Hoffman, Donald M.
Hoffman, Dustin
Hoffman, Hallock Brown
Hoffman, Jack Leroy
Hoffman, John Raleigh
Hoffman, Julien Ivor Ellis
Hoffman, Wayne Melvin
Hoffmann, William Frederick
Hofmann, Hans
Hofstadter, Robert
Hogan, Clarence Lester
Hogan, Curtis Jule
Hogan, Mark
Hogan, Mervin Booth
Hogan, William Walter
Hogenson, Galen Ray
Hogg, David Clarence
Hogg, Thomas Clark
Hogg, Tony Jefferson
Hogue, James Lawrence
Hoiland, Andrew Calvin
Holbrook, Donald Benson
Holbrook, Hal
Holcombe, William Jones
Holen, Harold Hampton
Holland, Jeffrey R.
Holland, Paul Deleval
Hollander, Jack M(arvin)
Holley, Lawrence Alvin
Holley, Robert William
Holliday, Malcolm Alexander
Holliday, Polly Dean
Holliman, Earl
Hollingsworth, Guilford Leroy
Hollingsworth, Robert Edgar
Hollister, Charles Warren
Hollon, William Eugene
Holloway, Edgar Austin
Holloway, Sterling Price
Holly, Edwin E.
Holly, James Francis
Holm, Richard William
Holman, Arthur Stearns
Holman, Francis Edwards
Holman, Harland Eugene
Holman, John Francis
Holman, Kermit Layton
Holman, Steele
Holmes, Darrell
Holmes, Fred Gillespie
Holmes, Harry Edward
Holmes, John Richard
Holmes, Richard Hugh Morris
Holmes, Robert William
Holmes, Thomas Hall
Holmquist, Carl Oreal
Holohan, William Andrew
Holstein, Theodore David
Holt, Edwin Graves
Holt, Maurice
Holtby, Kenneth Fraser
Holter, Norman Jefferis
Holton, Richard Henry
Holzer, Robert Edward
Holzman, D. Keith
Holzman, Jac Easton
Homme, Herbert Gordon
Honey, David Charles
Honey, Richard Churchill
Honeysett, William Lee
Hong, Charles Juay
Hood, Leroy Edward
Hook, Ralph Clifford, Jr.
Hook, Sidney
Hooker, John Lee
Hooks, Robert
Hookstratten, Edward Gregory
Hooley, James Robert
Hooper, Emmet Thurman, Jr.
Hooper, Frederick Richard
Hooper, John William
Hooper, Shirley
Hoopes, Donelson Farquhar
Hoopes, Lorenzo Neville
Hoover, Francis Louis
Hoover, Helen D. (Mrs. Adrian E. Hoover)
Hoover, Robert B.
Hoover, William Ray
Hope, Bob
Hopfield, John Joseph
Hopkins, Anthony
Hopkins, Carl Edward
Hopkins, Henry Tyler
Hoppe, Arthur Watterson
Hopper, Dennis
Hopping, Richard Lee
Horace, Charles Clay
Horkay, Thomas Edward, Jr.
Horn, Alan Frederick
Horn, Martin Robert
Horn, Stephen
Horn, Thomas Carl
Hornbein, Philip, Jr.
Hornbein, Thomas F.
Hornbein, Victor
Hornby, William Harry
Horne, Lena
Horner, Harry
Horner, Larry Dean
Horngren, Charles Thomas
Horowitz, Charles
Horowitz, David Charles
Horowitz, David Joel
Horowitz, Norman Harold
Horowitz, Stephen Irwin
Horsell, Mary Kay
Horsley, Andrew Burt
Horton, Aaron Wesley
Horton, Bernard Francis
Horton, Jack King
Horton, Philip G.
Hosford, Ray E.
Hosokawa, William K.
Hospers, John
Hosterman, Fred O.
Hostler, Charles Warren
Houck, John Candee
Houk, John Louis
Houlihan, Patrick Thomas
Housel, Jerry Winters
Houseman, John
Houser, Douglas Guy
Houseworth, Richard Court
Housner, George William
Houston, Ivan James
Houtchens, Barnard
Houts, Marshall Wilson
Hovet, Thomas, Jr.
Hovgard, Carl
Hovin, Arne William
Hovsepian, Vatche
Howard, Carl
Howard, David E.
Howard, Donald Roy
Howard, Hildegarde (Mrs. Henry Anson Wylde)
Howard, James Webb
Howard, Kenneth Joseph, Jr.
Howard, Robert Boardman
Howard, Robert Staples
Howard, Ron
Howard, Sandy
Howard, William Jack
Howard, Winston Stanley
Howe, Daniel Walker
Howe, Jack Homer
Howe, John Perry
Howe, Richard Cuddy
Howe, Richard Esmond, Jr.
Howell, James Edwin
Howell, John Stephen
Howell, Robert James
Howerton, Herman Hugh
Howes, Benjamin Durward
Howes, Benjamin Durward, III
Howland, Beth
Hsi, David Ching Heng
Hsu, Francis Lang Kwang
Hsu, Immanuel Chung Yueh
Hu, Chi Yu
Hu, Sze-Tsen
Huang, Francis Fu-Tse
Huang, George Wenhong
Hubbard, David Allan
Hubbard, Frederick Dewayne
Hubbard, Howard Leland
Hubbard, John Randolph
Hubbard, Lafayette Ronald
Hubbell, Wayne Lester
Hubenthal, Karl Samuel
Huber, William H., Jr.
Hubler, James T(errence)
Huck, Leonard William
Huckins, Charles Albert
Huckins, William Judd
Hudachek, John William
Huddle, Elizabeth Marguerite
Huddleson, Edwin Emmet, Jr.
Huddleston, David William
Hudson, Donald Ellis
Hudson, Harriet Dufresne
Hudson, Jerry E.
Hudson, John L.
Hudson, Leonard Dean
Hudson, Rock (Roy Fitzgerald)
Huebner, Harlan Pierce
Huenemann, Ruben Henry
Huff, Abner
Huff, Paul Emlyn
Huffman, James Thomas William
Hufschmidt, Maynard Michael
Hufstedler, Seth Martin
Hufstedler, Shirley Mount (Mrs. Seth M. Hufstedler)
Hug, Procter Ralph, Jr.
Huggins, Robert A(lan)
Huggins, Roy
Hughart, Stanley Parlett
Hughes, Author E., Jr.
Hughes, Charles Campbell
Hughes, David H.
Hughes, Eugene Morgan
Hughes, Everett Clark
Hughes, H(enry) Stuart
Hughes, James Paul
Hughes, Jay Melvin
Hughes, John Chamberlain
Hughes, Joseph P.
Hughes, Keith William
Hughes, Robert Harrison
Hughes, Roy Elward
Hughs, Richard Earl
Hugo, Richard Franklin
Hugstad, Paul Steven
Huizingh, William
Hulbert, Bruce Walker
Hulbert, William Glen, Jr.
Hulet, Ervin Kenneth
Hull, Cordell William
Hull, Herbert Mitchell
Hull, McAllister Hobart, Jr.
Hull, Robert Leslie
Hull, Suzanne White
Hulsbos, Cornie Leonard
Hulse, Jerry
Hulteng, John Linne
Hultgren, Herbert Nils
Hultquist, Paul Fredrick
Humbert, Richard Bernard
Hume, David Lang
Hummel, Fred Ernest
Hummer, David Graybill
Humperdinck, Engelbert (Arnold George Dorsey)
Humphrey, Fred A.
Humphrey, Lucie King
Hund, William Harrison
Hundley, Norris Cecil, Jr.
Hungerford, Gerald Fred
Hunkins, Francis Peter
Hunsaker, Harold Jeff
Hunt, Daniel Stockton
Hunt, Earl Busby
Hunt, Frank Bouldin
Hunt, Gordon
Hunt, Robert Lewis
Hunt, Robert Sherwood
Hunten, Donald Mount
Hunter, Celia Margaret
Hunter, Charles Bryan
Hunter, Dorian
Hunter, Duncan Lee
Hunter, E. Allan
Hunter, Howard William
Hunter, James M.
Hunter, John Harnden
Hunter, Paul Robinson
Hunter, Ross
Huntley, James Robert
Huntsinger, Fritz Roy
Hupp, Jack Scott
Hurd, Cuthbert C.
Hurd, Peter
Hurley, Francis T.
Hurley, Mark Joseph
Hurley, Morris Elmer, Jr.
Hurt, William
Hurt, William Holman
Huskey, Harry Douglas
Hussey, Ruth
Hussey, William Bertrand
Huston, John
Hutchens, Tyra Thornton
Hutchings, George Henry
Hutchinson, Leonard Reginald
Hutchinson, Robert Earl
Hutchinson, Thomas Eugene
Hutchison, John Alexander
Huth, Donald Earl
Huttenback, Robert Arthur
Hyams, Joe
Hyde, Dayton Ogden
Hyde, Earl K.
Hyde, Stuart Wallace
Hyde-White, Wilfrid
Hyer, Martha (Mrs. Hal Wallis)
Hyink, Bernard Lynn
Hyland, Lawrence A(vison)
Ian, Janis
Iberall, Arthur Saul
Ida, Shoichi
Ide, Chandler
Idriss, Izzat M.
Igl, Richard Franklin
Ihle, John Livingston
Ihrig, Judson La Moure
Ike, Nobutaka
Ikle, Frank William
Iliff, Warren Jolidon
Imagawa, David Tadashi
Imbrie, Andrew Welsh
Imhoff, Walter Francis
Imirie, Joseph Scott
Infanger, Carlton Adolph
Ingalls, Robert Lynn
Ingels, Marty
Ingersoll, Alfred Cajori
Ingle, John Ide
Ingraham, Rex
Ingram, William Austin
Ingwersen, Martin Lewis
Inkeles, Alex
Inlow, Edgar Burke
Innis, Robert Cecil
Inskeep, Gordon Charles
Inskeep, Richard Guy
Iorillo, Mario Angelo
Ipaktchian, Sidney
Ireland, Jill (Jill Dorothy Ireland Bronson)
Ireland, Robert Ellsworth
Irell, Lawrence E(lliott)
Ireson, William Grant
Irsfeld, James Balthazar, Jr.
Irvin, Robert Joseph
Irvine, F. Gerald
Irving, Jack Howard
Irwin, James Benson
Irwin, Joseph Augustus
Irwin, Richard Warren
Irwin, Robert Walter
Isaac, Robert Michael
Isbell, Marion William
Isenberg, Phillip L.
Isherwood, Christopher
Isom, Lloyd Warren
Israel, David
Issel, Dan
Itabashi, Hideo Henry
Itano, Harvey Akio
Ivans, William Stanley
Ives, John David (Jack)
Iwan, Wilfred Dean
Izenstark, Joseph Louis
Izutsu, Satoru
Jackson, Elmer Joseph
Jackson, Everett Gee
Jackson, Felix
Jackson, Gabriel
Jackson, Glenda
Jackson, Harry Andrew
Jackson, Henry Martin
Jackson, Kate
Jackson, Keith MacKenzie

Jackson, Mary
Jackson, Michael Joe
Jackson, Miles Merrill
Jackson, Milton (Bags Jackson)
Jackson, Peter Vorious, III
Jackson, William Turrentine
Jacob, Charles Waldemar
Jacob, Philip Ernest
Jacob, Stanley Wallace
Jacobi, Lee
Jacobs, Alma Smith
Jacobs, Clyde Edward
Jacobs, David
Jacobs, Donald Paul
Jacobs, Eugene Brown
Jacobs, Jody (Josephine C. Leason)
Jacobs, Joseph Donovan
Jacobs, Joseph John
Jacobs, Morris Elias
Jacobs, Wilbur Ripley
Jacobs, Winfred Oscar
Jacobsen, Adolf Marcelius Bergh
Jacobson, Alan Donald
Jacobson, Eino Matti
Jacobson, Marcus
Jacobson, Phillip Lee
Jacobson, Phyllis Colleen
Jacobson, Saul P.
Jacobstein, J(oseph) Myron
Jacquette, F. Lee
Jaffe, Frohm Filmore
Jaffe, Robert Benton
Jaffe, Sam
Jaffe, Sheldon Mayer
Jaffe, Sigmund
Jaffee, Robert Isaac
Jagger, Dean
Jahns, Richard Henry
Jahsman, William Edward
Jakobsen, Jakob Knudsen
Jakobson, Mark John
Jakstas, Alfred John
Jallow, Raymond
James, David Lee
James, George Barker, II
James, Leonard Gage
James, Rembert Faulkner
James, Robert Clarke
James, Sidney Lorraine
James, Wright Elwood
Jameson, Michael Hamilton
Jameson, William James
Jamieson, John Charles
Jamieson, Robert Gordon
Jamison, Max Killian
Jamison, Oliver Morton
Janich, George Peter
Janis, Conrad
Janis, Jay
Jankura, Donald Eugene
Janofsky, Leonard S.
Janowitz, Walter
Janowsky, David Steffan
Jans, James Patrick
Janss, William Cluff
Jantzen, J(ohn) Marc
Jaquette, John Joseph
Jaramillo, Mari-Luci
Jardetzky, Oleg
Jarreau, Al
Jarrott, Charles
Jarvik, Lissy F.
Jarvik, Murray Elias
Jarvis, Graham Powley
Jarvis, Joseph Boyer
Jarvis, Oscar T., Jr.
Jaunich, Robert, II
Jawetz, Ernest
Jedenoff, George Alexander
Jefferds, Vincent Harris
Jefferies, John Trevor
Jeffrey, Kirk
Jeffries, Carson Dunning
Jeffs, George W.
Jehorek, Steven Scott
Jelliffe, Roger Woodham
Jemelian, John Nazar
Jencks, Richard William
Jenden, Donald James
Jenkins, Bruce Sterling
Jenkins, Donald John
Jenkins, George
Jenkins, Margaret Ludmilla
Jenkins, William Maxwell
Jenks, George Schuyler
Jenner, Richard Howard
Jenni, Donald Alison
Jennings, Jesse David
Jennings, Richard Wormington
Jennings, William Howard (Harold)
Jensen, Arthur Milton
Jensen, Arthur Robert
Jensen, Clayne R.
Jensen, James Herbert
Jensen, John Eric
Jensen, Merle Harold
Jensen, Raylan Dee
Jensen, Robert Trygve
Jensen, Rue L.
Jensen, William August
Jeppson, Jay Herald
Jerome, Jerrold Vincent
Jeske, Howard Leigh
Jessup, Warren T.
Jeter, Wayburn Stewart
Jewell, William Sylvester
Jewett, Emelyn Knowland
Jewett, George Frederick, Jr.
Jewison, Norman F.
Joanning, Harold T.
Joanou, Phillip
Jobusch, Frederick Henry
Johanos, Donald
Johanson, Perry Bertil
Johncock, Gordon Walter
Johns, Albert Cameron
Johns, Christopher George
Johns, Claude Jackson, Jr.
Johns, Peter Richard
Johns, Varner Jay, Jr.
Johns, W(illiam) Lloyd
Johnson, Adolph Oscar
Johnson, Albert Willard
Johnson, Arte
Johnson, Bernard Thomas
Johnson, Bjarne
Johnson, Bruce
Johnson, Charles Bartlett
Johnson, Charles Harold
Johnson, Dale Gedge
Johnson, Dennis
Johnson, Diane Lain
Johnson, Donal Dabell
Johnson, Donald Milton
Johnson, Earl, Jr.
Johnson, Earvin (Magic)
Johnson, Eric Folke
Johnson, Ferd
Johnson, Francis Benjamin
Johnson, Frank H.
Johnson, Gardiner
Johnson, Horace Richard
Johnson, Joan D.
Johnson, John J.
Johnson, John Rauche
Johnson, Jonathan Edwin, II
Johnson, Judith Salter
Johnson, Kenneth Owen
Johnson, Lamont
Johnson, Lloyd Peter
Johnson, Marques Kevin
Johnson, Marvin Donald
Johnson, Oliver Adolph
Johnson, Paul Christian
Johnson, Rafer Lewis
Johnson, Ralph M.
Johnson, Reverdy
Johnson, Robert Britten
Johnson, Robert Curtis
Johnson, Robert Kellogg
Johnson, Robert Louis
Johnson, Robert Raymond
Johnson, Ronald
Johnson, Stanford Leland
Johnson, Wayne Eaton
Johnson, Wayne Harold
Johnson, Willard Lyon
Johnson, William Robert
Johnson, Wyatt Thomas, Jr.
Johnsrud, Russell Lloyd
Johnston, Bruce Gilbert
Johnston, David Cay Boyle
Johnston, Frank Evington
Johnston, George Palmer, Jr.
Johnston, Harold Sledge
Johnston, Harry Driscoll, Jr.
Johnston, Richard Wyckoff
Johnston, Ynez
Johnstone, James George
Jolley, Jack J.
Jolly, William Lee
Jonas, Federico Roque
Jonas, Peter Stephen
Jones, Allan Barry
Jones, Bobette LaVelle
Jones, Carolyn
Jones, Cedric Henry
Jones, Charles Martin (Chuck)
Jones, Charles Martin (Chuck)
Jones, Charles Williams
Jones, Clifford Aaron
Jones, Dean Carroll
Jones, Dorothy Cameron
Jones, Edgar Allan, Jr.
Jones, Edwin Donatus, Jr.
Jones, Frank William
Jones, Garth Nelson
Jones, Grant Richard
Jones, Greydon G.
Jones, H(arold) Gilbert, Jr.
Jones, Harold Henry
Jones, Hazel Lucile James
Jones, Henry
Jones, Jennifer
Jones, Jerry Lynn
Jones, Jesse Claude
Jones, Joie Pierce
Jones, Joseph Severn
Jones, Lee Bennett
Jones, Lincoln, III
Jones, Lynn Edwin
Jones, Malcolm David
Jones, Max LaMar, Jr.
Jones, Milton Wakefield
Jones, Orlo Dow
Jones, Pirkle
Jones, Quincy
Jones, Regina Nickerson
Jones, Reginald Lanier
Jones, Richard Hutton
Jones, Richard Theodore
Jones, Robert Eugene
Jones, Robert Thomas
Jones, Roger Clyde
Jones, Sheldon
Jones, Shirley
Jones, Thomas Victor
Jones, Tom
Jones, Tommy Lee
Jones, Tony Everett
Jones, Victor Emory
Jones, William Orville
Jones, William Thomas
Jones, Wyman H.
Jonsen, Albert R.
Jonsson, Jens Johannes
Joppa, Robert Glenn
Jordan, Daniel C(lyde)
Jordan, Glenn
Jordan, John Emory
Jordan, John Patrick
Jordan, Leonard Beck
Jorgensen, Earle Mogensen
Jorgensen, Joseph Gilbert
Jorgensen, Paul Alfred
Jorgensen, William Ernest
Jorgenson, Jack Duane
Jose, James Robert
Joseph, Allan Jay
Joseph, Marjory L.
Josephson, Joseph Paul
Joss, Robert L.
Jossey-Bass, Allen Quitman
Jourdan, Louis
Jourdonais, Leonard Francis
Joutz, Rainer Herbert Hans
Joy, Ned Vernon
Joyner, Conrad Francis
Judah, Jay Stillson
Judd, Dennis Ray
Judd, Howard Lund
Judd, Lewis Lund
Judge, Thomas Lee
Juell, Bruce Charles
Juenger, Friedrich Klaus
Juhl, John Harold
Jukes, Thomas Hughes
Julian, Ormand Clinkinbeard
Julien, Richard Edward Hale
Jumonville, Felix Joseph, Jr.
Jump, Gordon
Jungers, Francis
Jungkuntz, Richard Paul
Jurgens, Curt
Juvet, Richard Spalding, Jr.
Kaapcke, Wallace Letcher
Kac, Mark
Kachlein, George Frederick, Jr.
Kadish, Sanford Harold
Kadison, Stuart
Kado, Clarence Isao
Kagan, Jeremy Paul
Kahn, Jacob Philip
Kahn, Raymond Lee
Kahn, Richard
Kahn, Robert Irving
Kahn, Theodore Charles
Kailath, Thomas
Kaisel, Stanley Francis
Kaiser, Armin Dale
Kalina, Robert Edward
Kalish, Donald
Kallenberg, John Kenneth
Kaltinick, Paul R.
Kamar, Astrid Elaine Wennermark
Kamb, Walter Barclay
Kambara, George Kiyoshi
Kamemoto, Fred Isamu
Kamemoto, Haruyuki
Kamm, Thomas Allen
Kanaly, Steven Francis
Kanamori, Hiroo
Kanbara, Bertram Teruo
Kane, Carol
Kane, Eneas Dillon
Kane, Harry Joseph
Kane, John Lawrence, Jr.
Kane, Mary Kay
Kane, Robert Joseph
Kanemitsu, Matsumi
Kanin, Fay
Kanin, Michael
Kanter, Hal
Kantner, Paul
Kao, Shih-Kung
Kaplan, Alvin Irving
Kaplan, Gabriel
Kaplan, Henry Seymour
Kaplan, Jonathan Stewart
Kaplan, Marvin Wilbur
Kaplan, Nathan Oram
Kaplan, Oscar Joel
Kaplan, Solomon Alexander
Kappe, Raymond
Kaprielian, Zohrab Arakel
Karamardian, Stepan
Karawina, Erica
Karinen, Arthur Eli
Karlen, Gottfried Emanuel
Karlin, Myron D.
Karlinsky, Simon
Karlstrom, Paul Johnson
Karlton, Lawrence K.
Karma, Arthur
Karp, David
Karp, Nathan
Karp, Richard Manning
Karpf, Merrill Hugh
Karplus, Robert
Karplus, Walter J.
Karras, Alex
Karson, Burton Lewis
Karsten, Thomas Loren
Kartchner, Mark Martineau
Kasdan, Lawrence Edward
Kasha, Lawrence N.
Kashdan, Isaac
Kashiwahara, Ken
Kaslow, Arthur Louis
Kassander, Arno Richard, Jr.
Kassar, Raymond E.
Kast, Fremont Ellsworth
Kasten, Karl Albert
Katayama, Arthur Shoji
Katchadourian, Herant Aram
Katleman, Harris L.
Kattus, Albert Adolph
Katz, Hilliard Joel
Katz, Maurice Harry
Katz, Robert Lee
Katz, Ronald Lewis
Katz, Solomon
Kauderer, Bernard Marvin
Kauffman, George Bernard
Kauffman, Mark
Kaufman, Andy
Kaufman, Arnold Richard
Kaufman, Harold Richard
Kaufman, Irvin Sidney
Kaufman, Irving
Kaufman, Julian Mortimer
Kaufman, Phillip
Kaufman, Sanford Paul
Kaufold, Leroy
Kaula, William Mason
Kaus, Otto Michael
Kauvar, Abraham J.
Kavanagh, Ralph William
Kawano, Walter Masao
Kay, Dean
Kay, Douglas Casey
Kay, Herma Hill
Kay, Jerome Harold
Kay, John Stephen
Kaye, Danny
Kaye, Sylvia Fine
Kays, William Morrow
Kayser, Donald Robert
Kazan, Lainie (Lainie Levine)
Keach, Stacy, Jr.
Keach, Stacy, Sr.
Keady, Michael Jennings
Keala, Francis Ahloy
Kean, Joseph Andrew
Keane, Bil
Kearney, Joseph Laurence
Kearns, David Richard
Kearns, Henry
Keating, Eugene Kneeland
Keating, Thomas Arthur
Keating, William Cleveland, Jr.
Keatinge, Richard Harte
Keaton, Harry Joseph
Keats, Donald Howard
Kececioglu, Dimitri Basil
Keehn, Grant
Keely, George Clayton
Keene, Clifford Henry
Keene, Thomas Victor, Jr.
Keeney, Edmund Ludlow
Keepin, George Robert, Jr.
Keesling, Francis Valentine, Jr.
Kefford, Noel Price
Kegel, Charles Herbert
Kegley, Charles William
Keiser, John Howard
Keitel, Harvey
Keith, Brian Michael
Keithley, George Frederick
Keith-Spiegel, Patricia Cosette
Kelch, Ray Alden
Kellaway, Roger Warren
Kelleher, Robert Joseph
Keller, Alex Stephen
Keller, Edward Lowell
Keller, George Matthew
Keller, Harold Kefauver
Keller, John Francis
Keller, Joseph Bishop
Keller, Marthe
Keller, Robert Karl
Keller, William Martin
Kellerman, Sally Claire
Kelley, Donald E.
Kelley, Frank
Kelley, Harold Harding
Kelley, Jackson DeForest
Kelley, Robert Lloyd
Kelley, Vincent Charles
Kellogg, Ralph Henderson
Kellogg, William Welch
Kelly, Arthur Francis
Kelly, Aurel Maxey
Kelly, Crosby Moyer
Kelly, Edward James
Kelly, Gene Curran
Kelly, Henry Ansgar
Kelly, John Coleman
Kelly, John Patrick
Kelly, Raymond Francis
Kelly, William Harold
Kelsey, Floyd Lamar, Jr.
Kelsey, Linda
Kelso, Alec John (Jack)
Kelso, Louis Orth
Kelso, Robert Charles
Kemp, Arthur
Kemp, J. Robert
Kemp, Patrick Samuel
Kemper, H. Doug, Jr.
Kemper, John Dustin
Kemper, Robert Louis
Kemper, Victor Way
Kempf, Paul Stuart
Kempner, Jack Julian
Kempter, Charles Prentiss
Kendall, Glen Richard
Kendall, Robert McCutcheon
Kendall, William Denis
Kendig, Ellsworth Harold, Jr.
Kendler, Howard H.
Kendrick, James Blair, Jr.
Kendrick, Joseph Trotwood
Kenkel, Robert August
Kennedy, Anthony M.
Kennedy, Arthur
Kennedy, Bruce R.
Kennedy, Burt Raphael
Kennedy, David Michael
Kennedy, Donald
Kennedy, George
Kennedy, Harry Sherbourne
Kennedy, Jack Leland
Kennedy, Richard Jerome
Kennedy, Royal
Kennedy, Ruth Lee
Kennedy-Minott, Rodney
Kennel, Charles Frederick
Kennelly, Robert Andrew
Kenney, H(arry) Wesley, Jr.
Kenney, John William
Kenney, Louis Augustine
Kenny, Dumont Francis
Kenny, Michael H.
Kenny, Thomas Henry
Kent, Harold Winfield
Kent, Harry Christison
Kent, James Woodward
Keppel, Geoffrey
Kerby, Philip Pearce
Kercheval, Ken
Kerfoot, H(ubert) Potter
Kerins, Francis Joseph
Kerkorian, Kirk
Kerlinger, Fred Nichols
Kern, Fred, Jr.
Kern, Robert Bradford
Kerr, Clark
Kerr, Deborah
Kerr, Donald MacLean, Jr.
Kerr, Ewing Thomas
Kerr, John Fay
Kerr, John G.
Kerr, Malcolm Hooper
Kerschner, Lee R(onald)
Kersh, Bert Yarbrough
Kerth, Leroy T.
Kesey, Ken
Kesler, Alonzo Pratt
Kessel, Brina
Kessler, John Otto
Kester, Lenard
Kester, Randall Blair
Ketcham, Henry King
Ketchum, Milo Smith
Ketchum, Robert Glenn
Ketring, Vernon Vivian
Kettel, Louis John
Key, Mary Ritchie
Keyes, Cornelius Michael
Keyes, Paul William
Keyt, David
Khachigian, Kenneth Larry
Khan, Mohammad Asad
Kharasch, Norman
Kherdian, David
Kho, James Wang
Khosla, Ved Mitter
Kidd, Michael
Kieffer, William Franklinn
Kiely, John Roche
Kieran, James
Kieschnick, William Frederick
Kieser, Ellwood E.
Kilgore, Eugene Sterling, Jr.
Kilkenny, John Francis
Killam, Eva King
Killips, Danforth
Kimball, Edward Lawrence
Kimball, John Seymour
Kimball, Lorenzo Kent
Kimball, Spencer Woolley
Kimball, Thomas Lloyd
Kimbark, Edward Wilson
Kimberling, John Farrell
Kimble, William Earl
Kimmerle, Gerald William
Kimnach, Myron William
Kinariwala, Bharat
Kindel, James Horace, Jr.
Kinder, James S.
King, Alan
King, Bruce
King, Cary Judson, III
King, Charles Everett
King, David Joseph
King, Edward Louis
King, Hanford Langdon, Jr.
King, Harold Taft
King, Ivan Robert
King, James Bruce
King, James Claude
King, Jean Sadako
King, John Hugh
King, Kenneth Tyler
King, Leland W.
King, Paul Hamilton
King, Robert Leonard
King, Samuel Pailthorpe
King, Sheldon Selig
King, Stephen Scott
Kingdon, Henry Shannon
Kinghan, Charles Ross
Kingman, Alton (Hayward), Jr.
Kingman, Woodward
Kingrey, Burnell Wayne
Kingsley, Robert
Kingsley, Walter Ingalls
Kingston, Maxine Hong
Kinkle, George Phillip, Jr.
Kinnaird, Lawrence
Kinne, Morris Y., Jr.
Kinneberg, Arthur Hempton
Kinney, Gilbert Ford
Kinney, Harry Edwin
Kino, Gordon Stanley
Kinsinger, Floyd Elton
Kintzele, John A.
Kinzel, Augustus Braun
Kippenhan, Charles Jacob
Kirby, William Murray Maurice
Kirchheimer, Arthur Edward
Kirchhoff, Donald Joseph
Kirgis, Frederic L.
Kirk, Dudley
Kirk, Richard A.
Kirk, Samuel Alexander
Kirkham, Francis Robison
Kirkwood, Gene
Kirkwood, Roderick Richard
Kirman, Charles Gary
Kirschen, Borell
Kirsten, Richard Charles (Daiensai)
Kisslinger, Carl
Kistner, David Harold
Kitchel, Denison
Kitchell, Ralph Lloyd
Kitchen, Lawrence Oscar
Kitchener, Saul Laurence
Kjelland, Roland Arthur
Klag, Edwin James
Klauer, Raymond Louis
Klausen, Raymond
Klee, Victor La Rue, Jr.
Kleiman, Joseph
Klein, Burton Harold
Klein, Eugene Victor
Klein, Harold Paul
Klein, Herbert George
Klein, Joan Dempsey
Klein, Joseph Mark
Klein, Maurice J.
Kleinberg, Marvin H.
Kleindienst, Richard Gordon
Kleiner, Richard Arthur
Kleinholz, Lewis Hermann
Kleinjans, Everett
Kleinknecht, Kenneth Samuel
Kleinpell, Robert Minssen
Kleinrock, Leonard
Kleiser, John Randal
Klemme, Howard Charles
Klett, Gordon A.
Kline, Elliot Howard
Kline, Lee B.
Kline, Stephen Jay
Klinman, Norman Ralph
Klooster, Judson
Kloss, Gene (Mrs. Phillips Kloss, nee Alice Geneva Glasier)
Kloster, Frank Ellis
Klotz, Arthur Paul
Knaebel, John Ballantine
Knapp, Charles William
Knapp, Cleon T.
Knapp, James Rochester
Knecht, James Herbert
Knievel, Robert Craig (Evel Knievel)
Knight, Arthur
Knight, Claude Arthur
Knight, Ralph Morton
Knight, Ted (Tadeus Wladyslaw Konopka)
Knight, William J.
Knoblauch, Arthur Lewis
Knoebel, Betty Lou
Knoepfler, Peter Tamas
Knoles, George Harmon
Knopf, Kenyon Alfred
Knopoff, Leon
Knorr, Donald Robert
Knotts, Don
Knowles, Richard Thomas
Knowlton, Edgar Colby, Jr.
Knox, James Lester
Knudsen, James George
Knudsen, William Claire
Knudtzon, Halvor, Jr.
Knuth, Donald Ervin
Knuth, Eldon Luverne
Knutzen, Victor Francis
Kobayashi, Bert Takaaki
Kobayashi, Shiro
Kobayashi, Shoshichi
Koch, Carl Galland
Koch, Howard Winchel
Koch, Richard
Kochanski, Adrian Joseph
Kocher, Paul Harold
Koelsch, M. Oliver
Koelsche, Edward Giles
Koelzer, Victor Alvin
Koeppel, Donald Allen
Kofranek, Anton Miles
Kogovsek, Raymond Peter
Kohler, Karl Otto, Jr.
Kohloss, Frederick Henry
Kohn, Henry Irving
Kohn, Karl
Kohn, Misch Harris
Kohn, Walter
Kohne, Richard Edward
Koide, Frank Takayuki
Kojian, Varujan Haig
Kokaska, Charles James
Kolb, Theodore Alexander
Kole, Delbert Merrill
Kolender, William Barnett
Koler, Robert Donald
Kolff, Willem Johan
Komack, James
Komes, Jerome William
Konigsberg, Franklin Daniel
Kooken, John Frederick
Koontz, Harold
Kopell, Bernard Morton
Kopp, Charles Leo
Kopp, Eugene Howard
Kopp, Harriet Green
Koppett, Leonard
Koprowski, Eugene Joseph
Kordus, Henry
Korenman, Stanley George
Korg, Jacob
Korman, Harvey Herschel
Korman, Jess J.
Korn, David
Korn, Lester Bernard
Kornberg, Arthur
Kornblum, Guy Orville
Korngold, Alvin Leonard
Korpal, Eugene Stanley
Korson, Selig Morley
Korty, John Van Cleave
Kos, Paul Joseph
Koshalek, Richard H(ubert)
Kosheff, Martin Joel
Koshland, Daniel Edward, Jr.

Koshland, Marian Elliott
Kossel, Clifford George
Koster, Henry
Kostof, Spiro Konstantin
Kotch, Alex
Kotcheff, William Theodore (Ted)
Kotin, Paul
Kotrady, John
Kottler, Howard William
Kotto, Yaphet Fredrick
Kotzebue, Kenneth Lee
Koubourlis, Demetrius John
Kourkene, Jacques, II
Kovach, Ladis Daniel
Kovacs, Laszlo
Kowal, Charles Thomas
Kowalek, Jon W.
Kowalski, Bernard Louis
Krack, James Joseph
Krafft, Julia Steven
Kraft, Lisbeth Martha
Krag, Donald Richards
Kramer, Binnie Henrietta
Kramer, Stanley E.
Kramer, Steven Gregory
Krantz, Judith Tarcher
Krantz, Stephen Falk
Krapf, Lyle Vance
Krasno, Louis Richard
Krassowski, Witold
Kratzer, Frank Howard
Krause, Bernard Leo
Krause, Ernst Henry
Krause, LaVerne Erickson
Krauss, George
Krauss, Robert Wallfar
Kravetz, Nathan
Kravitz, Ellen King
Kreager, Henry Dewayne
Krebs, Edwin Gerhard
Krebs, John H.
Krebs, Robert Duncan
Kreisman, Arthur
Kreissman, Bernard
Krenek, Ernst
Krenkel, Peter Ashton
Krevans, Julius Richard
Krick, Irving Parkhurst
Krieger, Benjamin William
Krieger, Murray
Kriken, John Lund
Krikos, George Alexander
Krill, Arthur Melvin
Krinsky, Fred
Krinsley, David Henry
Kripke, Kenneth Norman
Krishnamurthy, Gerbail Thimmegowda
Krishnamurti, Jiddu
Kriss, Joseph Pincus
Kristof, Ladis Kris Donabed
Kristofferson, Kris
Krizek, Thomas Joseph
Kroc, Robert Louis
Kroener, William Frederick, Jr.
Kroger, Ferdinand Anne
Kroger, William Saul
Krohn, Duane Ronald
Kroll, Norman Myles K.
Krone, Lawrence James
Kruckeberg, Arthur Rice
Krueger, Eugene Rex
Krueger, Robert Blair
Krueger, Robert William
Kruger, Charles Herman, Jr.
Kruger, Fredrick Christian
Krugman, Stanley Lee
Krulak, Victor Harold
Krumboltz, John Dwight
Krumm, William Frederick
Krupp, Clarence William
Krupp, Edwin Charles
Krupp, Marcus Abraham
Krus, David James
Kruschke, Earl Roger
Kruse, Paul Robert
Kruse, Roland Robert
Kryter, Karl David
Kubler-Ross, Elisabeth
Kubly, Donald Raymond
Kubrick, Stanley
Kuby, Stephen Allen
Kuchel, Thomas Henry
Kuechler, Henry Norbury, Jr.
Kuentz, Frederick Paul
Kuhl, David Edmund
Kuhlman, Walter Egel
Kuhse, Harold H.
Kuklin, Jerome
Kulkarni, Hemant B.
Kullas, Albert John
Kulp, John Laurence
Kulp, Nancy Jane
Kulpa, John Edward, Jr.
Kumler, William Larence
Kummer, Wolfgang Helmut
Kummert, Richard Osborne
Kung, Shien Woo
Kunkel, Wulf Bernard
Kunz, Phillip Ray
Kuo, Ping-chia
Kupchick, Alan Charles
Kupel, Frederick John
Kuplan, Louis
Kuroda, Sige-Yuki
Kurtz, Francis Anthony
Kurtz, Gary Douglas
Kurtz, Lloyd Sherer, Jr.
Kurze, Theodore
Kuzdas, Anton Frank
Kuzell, William Charles
Kwan, Kian Moon
Kwiker, Louis A.
Kwiram, Alvin L.
Kyman, Alexander Leon
Laartz, Esther Elizabeth
Labinger, Albert L.
La Bonté, C(larence) Joseph
La Bounty, Hugh Orvice
Lacagnina, Michael Anthony
Lacayo, Carmela Gloria
Lachman, Morton
Lacitis, Erik
Lackey, Lawrence Bailis, Jr.
Lackey, Robert (Shields)
Lacy, Jerry (Gerald LeRoy)
Lacy, Peter Dempsey
Ladar, Jerrold Morton
Ladar, Samuel Abraham
Ladd, Alan Walbridge, Jr.
Ladd, Cheryl (Cheryl Stoppelmoor)
Ladefoged, Peter Nielsen
Laetsch, Watson McMillan
Laffer, Arthur
Laffoon, Carthrae Merrette
LaFollette, Charles Sanborn
La Force, James Clayburn, Jr.
Lagarias, John Samuel
Lagasse, Leo Darrell
Lagerstrom, Paco Axel
Lague, Richard Paul
Lahey, Marion Eugene
Lair, Jesse K.
Laird, Alan Douglas Kenneth
Laird, David
Laird, Jack
Laird, Wilbur David, Jr.
Lake, David S.
Lake, David S.
Lake, (Finley) Edward
Lake, Joseph Frank, Jr.
Lake, Meno Truman
Lake, Walter Benjamin
Lamas, Fernando
Lamb, George A.
Lamb, Ursula Schaefer
Lamb, Willis Eugene, Jr.
Lambert, Nadine Murphy
Lambert, Robert Lowell
Lamberti, N.A.
Lambiase, Vincent A.
Lambro, Phillip
Lamm, Michael
Lamm, Richard Douglas
Lamm, Robert William
Lammel, Jeanette Osborn
L'Amour, Louis Dearborn
Lamparski, Richard
Lamson, Baldwin Gaylord
Lancaster, Burt(on) (Stephen)
Lancaster, John Howard
Lanchester, Elsa
Landau, Ellis
Landau, Ely
Landau, Martin
Landau, Martin
Lander, Richard Leon
Landis, John David
Landow, Stanley
Landres, Morris M.
Lane, Homer Logan
Lane, Howard Raymond
Lane, Laurence William, Jr.
Lane, Marilyn Edith
Lane, Ralph, Jr.
Lane, Rembrandt Peale
Lane, Robert Casey
Lane, Rosemary Payne
Lane, Sylvia
Lane, Walter Byron
Lang, Jennings Bently
Lang, Margo Terzian
Lang, Philip David
Lang, Thompson Hughes
Langacker, Ronald Wayne
Langdon, Sue Ane
Lange, Charles Henry
Lange, Clifford E.
Lange, Hope
Lange, Lester Henry
Lange, Ted
Langella, Frank
Langen, Herbert John
Langer, Glenn Arthur
Langhans, Edward Allen
Langley, Ellis Bradford, Jr.
Langlois, Walter Gordon
Langmuir, Robert Vose
Langridge, Robert
Lanham, Richard Alan
Lanham, Urless Norton
Lanker, Brian Timothy
Lansing, Sherry Lee
Lantz, Walter
Lanzet, Monroe
La Piere, Richard Tracy
Lapin, Raymond Harold
La Plante, James Gamelin
Laporte, Leo Frederic
Lappen, Chester I.
Lark, Howard (Bill) William
Lark, Raymond
Larkin, Kenneth Vincent
Larkins, Gary Lee
Larner, Jeremy
Larsen, Allan Franklin
Larsen, Lyle Vernon
Larsen, Richard Lee
Larsen, Susan Carol
Larson, Charles Philip
Larson, Glen
Larson, James Alvin
Larson, John William
Larson, Martin Alfred
Larson, Milton B.
Larson, Nettabell Girard
Larson, Oliver C.
Larson, Robert Edward
Larson, Taft Alfred
La Scala, Anthony Charles
Lasch, Robert
Laser, Marvin
Lasker, Edward
Lasky, Moses
LaSor, William Sanford
Lasorda, Tom Charles
Lasser, Elliott Charles
Lasser, Louise
Lassick, Sydney
Lasswell, Marcia Lee
Lasswell, Mary Clyde Grayson Lubbock (Mrs. Dudley Winn Smith)
Lasswell, Thomas Ely
Laster, Leonard
Lastfogel, Abe
Laszlo, Ernest
Lathrop, Irvin Tunis
Lathrop, Kaye Don
Lathrop, Mitchell Lee
Latimer, Jonathan Wyatt
Latno, Arthur Clement, Jr.
Lattman, Laurence Harold
Laub, William Murray
Laube, Roger Gustav
Laughlin, Larry
Laurie, Piper (Rosetta Jacobs)
Laurila, Simo Heikki
Lauritzen, Peter Owen
Lauterbach, Robert Alan
Lauther, Samuel Edgar
Lautz, Lindsay Allan
LaVeck, Gerald DeLoss
Lavenson, James H.
Laver, Rodney George
Lavery, Emmet Godfrey
Lavin, David J.
Lavin, Linda
Lavine, Harold
Lavis, Rick Comstock
Law, David Hillis, IV
Law, John Manning
Law, John Philip
Lawford, Peter
Lawrence, Barry Howard
Lawrence, Hallett Thompson
Lawrence, Harold
Lawrence, Jacob
Lawrence, John Frederick
Lawrence, Les (Edwin)
Lawrence, Mark Howard
Lawrence, Steve
Lawrence, Vicki Ann
Lawrence, William Porter
Lawrenson, Thomas Richard
Lawroski, Harry
Lawson, Neils Vinton
Lawson, Ray Shepherd
Laxson, Russell William
Lay, S. Houston
Laybourne, Everett Broadstone
Layne, John Anthony
Layton, Jack Malcolm
Layton, Joe
Layton, Robert Lynn
Lazar, Alfred Leo
Lazar, Irving Paul
Lazarevich, Emil Robert
Lazarus, A(rnold) L(eslie)
Lazarus, Richard Stanley
Lazzaro, Anthony Derek
Leach, John Frank
Leachman, Cloris
Leaf, Paul
Leahy, John Jacob
Leake, Donald Lewis
Lear, Norman Milton
Learn, Elmer Warner
Learned, Michael
Leary, Robert Michael
Leary, Timothy
Leavitt, Christopher Pratt
Leavitt, Dana Gibson
Leavitt, Harold Jack
Leavitt, Jerome Edward
Leavitt, Myron E.
LeBaron, Francis Newton
LeBeau, Edward Charles
LeBerthon, Edward Lynch
LeBien, Robert Frank
Lebra, William Philip
LeCam, Lucien Marie
Le Claire, Harry Walter
Le Croissette, Dennis Harlow
Ledecky-Janecek, Emanuel V.A.
Lederer, Marion Irvine
Ledford, Jack C.
Lee, Bert Gentry
Lee, Burns Wells
Lee, Christopher Frank Carandini
Lee, Edward Matthew, Jr.
Lee, Eugene Canfield
Lee, Glenn Richard
Lee, Isaiah Chong-Pie
Lee, Joanna
Lee, Lawrence John
Lee, Rex E.
Lee, Robert
Lee, Robert Bartlett
Lee, Robert Edwin
Lee, Roger
Lee, Thomas Peter
Leedy, Robert Allan
Leefe, James Morrison
Lees, Lester
Lees, Martin Henry
Leestamper, Robert Eugene
Lefebvre d'Argencé, René-Yvon Marie Marc
Lefevre, George, Jr.
Leftwich, James Adolf
Legg, Robert Henry
Le Guin, Ursula Kroeber
Lehman, Ernest
Lehman, Israel Robert
Lehmann, Erich Leo
Lehmann, Justus F.
Lehmann, William Leonardo
Lehnert, Herbert Hermann
Lehrer, Keith Edward
Lehrer, Leonard
Leiber, Fritz, Jr.
Leibman, Ron
Leibson, Irving
Leiby, Paul D.
Leider, Gerald J.
Leigh, Janet (Jeanette Helen Morrison)
Leighton, Robert Benjamin
Lein, Allen
Lein, John Nave
Leinwand, Gerald
Leipper, Dale Frederick
Leisy, James Franklin
Leith, Cecil Eldon, Jr.
Leith, Roderick Gordon
Leitmann, George
Leitstein, Robert
Leland, David Dale
Leland, Joy Hanson
Lemert, James Bolton
Lemke, John Raymond
Lemmon, Jack
Lemon, Leslie Gene
Lemont, George William
Lenczowski, George
Lendrum, James Thoburn
Lengyel, Cornel Adam
Lenhoff, Howard Maer
Lenox, Glen Walter
Lent, Berkeley
Lents, John Eldon
Lentz, Robert Henry
Lenz, Kay
Leon, Dennis
Leonard, Allan Langdon, Jr.
Leonard, George Edmund
Leonard, Richard Manning
Leonard, Sheldon
Leone, William Charles
Leonhard, William Edward
Leopold, Aldo Starker
Leopold, Estella Bergere
Leopold, Irving Henry
Leopold, Luna Bergere
Lepawsky, Albert
Lepore, Albert
Leps, Thomas MacMaster
Lerch, Stanford Earl
Le Roy, Bruce Murdock
Leroy, David Henry
Le Roy, Mervyn
Lerude, Warren Leslie
Le Shana, David Charles
Lesher, Dean Stanley
Lesher, Donald Miles
Lesher, Robert Overton
Lesko, Leonard Henry
Leslie, Jacques Robert, Jr.
Leslie, William, Jr.
Lessler, Richard Sigmund
Lester, Robert Carlton
Lester, William Alexander, Jr.
Letiche, John Marion
Letofsky, Irvin Myles
Le Tourneau, Duane John
Lev, Daniel Saul
Leve, Alan Donald
Leven, Boris
Levenson, Alan Ira
Levenson, Milton
Levenstein, Robert
LeVere, Richard Craig
Leverich, Ivamay (Dennewill)
Levi, Julian Hirsch
Levin, Betsy
Levin, Irving Herbert
Levin, Morton D(avid)
Levin, Peter J.
Levine, Aaron
Levine, Arnold Milton
Levine, Joseph
Levine, Martin Lyon
Levine, Michael Elias
Levine, Norman Gene
Levine, Philip
Levine, Philip
Levine, Rachmiel
Levine, Robert Arthur
Levine, Sanford Norman
Levinson, David Lester
Levinson, Mark Lawrence
Levinson, Richard Leighton
Levit, Victor Bert
Leviton, Alan Edward
Levy, David
Levy, Leonard Williams
Levy, Louis
Levy, Norman
Levy, S. William
Lewenstein, Morris Robert
Lewin, Henri J.
Lewin, Werner S.
Lewine, Robert F.
Lewis, Al
Lewis, Bronson J.
Lewis, Charles Edwin
Lewis, David Thomas
Lewis, Donald Joseph
Lewis, Dudley Cushman
Lewis, Frank Harlan
Lewis, Geoffrey
Lewis, Goldy Sarah
Lewis, Harold Warren
Lewis, Harry Arthur
Lewis, Jack (Cecil Paul)
Lewis, Jerry
Lewis, John Aaron
Lewis, John Clark, Jr.
Lewis, John Wilson
Lewis, Norman
Lewis, Orme
Lewis, Peter Cushman
Lewis, Ralph Milton
Lewis, Richard Alan
Lewis, Richard Burton
Lewis, Richard Clayton
Lewis, Samella Sanders
Lewis, Shari
Lewis, Sheldon Noah
Lewis, Wilbur H.
Lewitzky, Bella
Leyden, Donald Elliott
Leyden, Norman Fowler
Leydorf, Frederick LeRoy
Lezak, Sidney Irving
Lhamon, George Marion
L'Heureux, John Clarke
Li, Choh Hao
Libby, Leona Marshall (Mrs. Willard Libby)
Liberace (Wlad ziu Valentino Liberace)
Liberatore, Nicholas Alfred
Liberman, Ira L.
Libott, Robert Yale
Lichstein, Jacob
Licht, Paul
Lichty, George M.
Lick, Wilbert James
Liddicoat, Richard Thomas, Jr.
Liddle, Alan Curtis
Lidicker, William Zander, Jr.
Lidow, Eric
Lidstone, Herrick Kenley
Lieb, Irwin Chester
Lieber, David Leo
Lieber, Edward Joseph
Lieberman, Gerald J.
Lieberson, Stanley
Lie-Injo, Luan Eng
Lien, Eric Jung-chi
Lieuallen, Roy Elwayne
Lieuwen, Edwin
Lifka, William Joseph
Liggett, Darwin Sligar
Liggett, Lawrence Melvin
Light, Kenneth Freeman
Lightstone, Ronald
Liker, Alan Donald
Lilienthal, James Richard
Lillevang, Omar Johansen
Lillie, John Mitchell
Lilly, James Alexander
Lilly, John Cunningham
Lilly, John Russell
Lillyman, William John
Lim, Robert Cheong, Jr.
Limbach, Karl Averell
Lin, Tung Yen
Lincoln, J(eannette) Virginia
Lind, David Arthur
Lind, James Forest
Lindauer, John Howard
Linde, Hans Arthur
Lindee, Robert Grant
Linden, Hal
Linden, Jeffrey Lee
Lindenberger, Herbert Samuel
Linder, Allan David
Lindh, Patricia Sullivan
Lindheim, Richard David
Lindholm, Dwight Henry
Lindholm, Richard Wadsworth
Lindley, Audra
Lindley, Curtis Price
Lindman, Erick LeRoy
Lindon, John Arnold
Lindquist, Raymond Irving
Lindsay, Dale Richard
Lindsay, Dennis John
Lindsay, Donald Parker
Lindsay, George Edmund
Lindsell, Harold
Lindsey, David
Lindsley, Donald Benjamin
Lindsley, Richard Graham
Lindzey, Gardner
Lingafelter, Edward Clay, Jr.
Link, Richard Meboldt
Link, William Theodore
Linkletter, Arthur Gordon
Linman, James William
Linn, Stuart Michael
Linnell, Robert Dale
Linnell, Robert Hartley
Linsley, Earle Gorton
Linsley, Ray Keyes
Linton, Frederick M.
Linvill, John Grimes
Linville, Larry Lavon
Lipetz, Milton Edward
Lipman, Howard Waldman
Lippincott, William Thomas
Lipscomb, Paul Rogers
Lipset, Seymour Martin
Lipson, Leslie Michael
Liskamm, William Hugo
List, Robert Frank
Lister, Robert Hill
Litfin, Richard Albert
Little, Bernard Harold
Little, Christopher Mark
Little, Cleavon Jake
Little, John Russell
Little, Richard Caruthers
Little, William Arthur
Littlefield, Edmund Wattis
Littler, Gene Alec
Littman, Lynne
Littman, Richard Anton
Littmann, Mark Evan
Litwack, Leon Frank
Liu, James Jo-Yü
Livermore, Joseph McMaster
Livingston, David Glenn
Livingston, James Prince, Jr.
Livingston, Johnston R.
Livingston, Myra Cohn
Livingston, R(ussell) Lynn
Livingston, Robert Burr
Lloyd, Christopher
Lloyd, David Pierce Caradoc
Lloyd, Don Keith
Lloyd, Jay William
Lloyd, Michael Jeffrey
Lobdell, Frank
Lobdell, Robert Charles
LoBianco, Tony
Lobitz, Walter Charles, Jr.
Lobner, Kneeland Harkness
Lockard, Thomas Swift, Jr.
Lockard, William Kirby
Locke, Hubert Gaylord
Locke, Sondra
Lockhart, Brooks Javins
Lockhart, James Blakely
Lockhart, June
Lockmiller, David Alexander
Lockwood, Gary
Lockwood, Robert W.
Loeb, William
Loeblich, Helen Nina Tappan
Loeffke, Bernard
Loeffler, Richard Harlan
Loeffler, Robert MenDelle
Loesch, Harrison
Loetterle, Francis Robert
Loewe, Frederick
Lofgren, Edward Joseph
Lofland, John Franklin
Löfstedt, Bengt Torkel Magnus
Loftis, John (Clyde Jr.)
Logan, Albert Boyd
Logan, Donald Chapman
Logan, Frank Anderson
Logan, Joseph Granville, Jr.
Logan, Richard Fink
Loganbill, G. Bruce
Loggia, Robert
Loggins, Kenny (Kenneth) Clarke
Lohnes, Walter F.
Lohrer, Richard Baker
Loiseaux, Pierre Roland
Lokke, William Anton
Lomax, Jerrold Ellsworth
Lombardi, Eugene Patsy
London, Jack
London, Marc (Albert F. Ruby)
Long, Durward
Long, Francis Mark
Long, James Cassidy
Long, James Edward
Long, Melvin Durward
Long, Robert Lyman John
Long, Robert Merrill
Longley, Bernique
Longmire, William Polk, Jr.
Longo, Lawrence Daniel
Longstreet, Stephen
Loomis, Ted Albert
Looney, Ralph Edwin
Loose, Arthur Joseph
Loper, Robert Bruce
Lopes, David Earl
Lopez, Trini
Loran, Erle
Lorber, Victor
Lord, Jack
Lord, Jere Johns
Lord, Samuel
Lorenz, Philip Manfred
Lorenz, Robert Milton
Loriaux, Maurice Lucien
Lorincz, Albert Bela
Loring, Gloria Jean
Lo Schiavo, John Joseph
Losse, John William, Jr.
Loth, David
Lothrop, Richard Alan
Lott, Leo Benjamin
Louch, Alfred Richard
Louden, Lynn Mansell
Loudon, Dorothy
Loughnane, Lee David
Louisell, William Henry
Louks, David Jerrold
Lounsbury, John Frederick
Love, Harold Oren
Love, Robert Merton
Love, William Edward
Lovelace, Jon B.
Loveland, Joseph Albert, Jr.
Loveless, Edward Eugene
Loveless, Norman Worth
Lovett, Wendell Harper
Lovewell, Paul Joseph
Low, Donald Gottlob
Low, Frank James
Low, Harry William
Low, Stephen
Lowe, Dewey Kwoc Kung
Lowe, Harry J.
Lowe, Robert Charles
Lowe, Robert Stanley
Lowell, Marcia
Lowenstam, Heinz A.
Lower, Frederick Joseph, Jr.
Lowney, Bruce Stark
Lowry, Edward Francis, Jr.
Lowy, Jay Stanton
Loy, Myrna
Lubenow, Gerald Charles
Lubin, Arthur
Lubner, Martin P.
Lucas, Clarence Bickford
Lucas, Donald Brooks
Lucas, George
Lucas, James Alfred
Lucas, Malcolm Millar

Luce, Clare Boothe
Luce, Gordon Coppard
Luchsinger, Wayne Wesley
Luckey, Eleanore Braun
Luckinbill, Laurence George
Luckman, Charles
Luckmann, Lloyd Detlef
Lude, Milo R.
Ludwig, George Harry
Ludwig, Harvey Fred
Ludwig, John Howard
Ludwig, William
Lueders, Edward George
Luepke, Gordon Maas
Luhring, John William
Lujan, Herman Damien Leilehua
Lukash, William Matthew
Lum, Bert Kwan Buck
Lum, Herman Tsui Fai
Lumsdaine, Arthur Allen
Lumsden, Marshall Edward
Lund, Ronald McMurray
Lundberg, Dan
Lundberg, George David
Lunde, Finn
Lunden, Samuel Eugene
Lungren, Daniel Edward
Lunt, Owen Raynal
Lupino, Ida
Lurie, Paul Raymond
Lusted, Lee Browning
Luter, John
Lutes, Donald Henry
Luther, Marylou Jacqueline
Luty, Fritz Wilhelm
Lutzky, Seymour Ezekiel
Luxemburg, Wilhelmus Anthonius Josephus
Lyden, Fremont James
Lydick, Lawrence Tupper
Lyford, Joseph Philip
Lyman, John
Lynberg, Charles Augustus
Lynch, Ben E.
Lynch, Charles Allen
Lynch, Charles Thomas
Lynch, Dale L.
Lynch, Frank William
Lynch, George Cotchett
Lynch, Gerald John
Lynch, Martin Andrew
Lynch, Peter John
Lynch, William Brennan, Jr.
Lynde, Stan
Lynds, Beverly Turner
Lyness, Robert Marron
Lynley, Carol Ann
Lynn, Fredric Michael
Lynne, Jeff
Lyon, David William
Lyon, Elijah Wilson
Lyon, Frederick Charles
Lyon, John David
Lyon, Richard
Lyon, Roger Adrian
Lyon, Waldo Kampmeier
Mabry, Harry Cooper
MacArthur, James
MacBride, Thomas Jamison
Maccoby, Eleanor Emmons
Maccoby, Nathan
MacCorquodale, Kenneth
Mac Cready, Paul Beattie
MacCurdy, Raymond Ralph, Jr.
Macdonald, J(ohn) Tyler P(erineau), Jr.
Macdougall, Iver Cameron
Mace, John Weldon
Macey, Robert Irwin
Macey, William Blackmore
MacFadden, Clifford Herbert
MacFarlane, David Dimling
Mac Farlane, John Dee
Macfarlane, Robert Stetson, Jr.
Mac Gowan, Mary Eugenia
MacGraw, Ali
MacGregor, (John) Geddes
MacGregor, George Lescher, Jr.
Macgregor, Wallace
Machle, Edward Johnstone
Mac Intyre, Donald John
Mack, Jerome David
Mack, John O.
MacKay, Gerald Wallace
Mac Kay, Pierre Antony
Mackenzie, Cosmo Glenn
MacKenzie, Gisele
MacKenzie, John Douglas
Mackenzie, Kenneth Victor
Mackie, Robert Gordon
MacKillop, Malcolm Andrew
Maclachlan, Douglas Lee
MacLaine, Shirley
Mac Laughlin, Douglas Earl
Mac Lean, Donald Drew
MacLeod, Gavin
MacLeod, Robert Fredric
MacMinn, Aleene Barnes
MacMurray, Frederick Martin
Macnee, (Daniel) Patrick
Macovski, Albert
Macpherson, James Lusk
Mac Queen, Robert Moffat
Macrae, Edwin Weir
Mac Rae, Frederick Edward
MacRae, Gordon
MacRae, Sheila Stephens
Mac Vicar, Robert William
Madden, Clifford John
Madden, Henry Miller
Madden, John William
Madden, Richard Blaine
Madera, Joseph J.
Madsen, Brigham Dwaine
Madsen, Douglas Fred
Maffie, Michael Otis
Magasinn, Arnold W.
Mager, Artur
Maggal, Moshe Morris
Magill, Frank Northen
Magnin, Cyril
Magnin, Edgar Fogel
Magnus, Bernd
Magnuson, Harold Joseph
Magnuson, Warren Grant
Magoon, John Henry, Jr.
Magor, Louis Roland
Magowan, Robert Anderson
Maguire, John David
Mahaffay, William Edward
Mahal, Taj (Henry St. Clair Fredericks)
Mahanthappa, Kalyana Thipperudraiah
Maher, Leo Thomas
Maibach, Howard I.
Maier, Cornell C.
Maier, Francis Xavier
Maier, Peter K.
Mailliard, John Ward, III
Maiman, Theodore Harold
Maines, Clifford Bruce
Mainwaring, William Lewis
Maisel, Sherman Joseph
Maison, George L.
Majdrakoff, Ivan
Major, Coleman Joseph
Majors, Lee
Maki, Kazumi
Maki, Robert Richard
Makowski, Edgar Leonard
Malarkey, Thomas B., Jr.
Malavasi, Ray
Malden, Karl (Malden Sekulovich)
Malecki, Edward Stanley, Jr.
Maley, Samuel Wayne
Malick, Terrence
Malkiel, Yakov
Mallen, Ronald Edward
Mallery, Richard
Mallon, Francis Bernard
Mallory, V(irgil) Standish
Mallory, John Michael
Malone, David Henry
Malone, Hugh Adrian
Maloney, James A.
Malott, James Raymond, Jr.
Malsh, William Ronald
Maltzman, Irving Myron
Malville, John McKim
Mamoulian, Rouben
Mancini, Henry
Mandan, Robert
Mandel, Siegfried
Mandelbaum, David Goodman
Mandell, Arnold Joseph
Mandino, Og
Mandler, Jean Matter
Manfred, Roger Lee
Mangels, John Donald
Mangual, Arthur Myron
Mangum, Garth Leroy
Mangum, Harvey Karl
Manley, Harry Stockwell
Manley, John Frederick
Mann, Abby
Mann, Alfred Eugene
Mann, Bruce Alan
Mann, Delbert
Mann, Maurice
Mann, Robert W.
Mann, Roderick
Manne, Alan Sussmann
Manne, Shelly
Manning, Duane
Manning, Karen Nerita
Manning, Reginald
Manning, Timothy
Manolis, Paul George
Manos, James Anthony
Manoukian, Noel Edwin
Mansfield, Michael Joseph
Manshardt, Clifford
Manson, Eddy Lawrence
Manson, Ira Rexon
Mansour, Tag Eldin
Mansure, Edmund F.
Mantle, John Edward
Manulis, Martin
Mapelli, Roland Lawrence
Maquet, Jacques Jerome Pierre
Mar, Brian Wayne
Marafino, Vincent Norman
March, George Patrick
March, James Gardner
March, Ralph Burton
Marchand, Ernest LeRoy
Marchant, Maurice Peterson
Marchioro, Thomas Louis
Marco, Guy Anthony
Marcovitz, Leonard Edward
Marcus, Frank Isadore
Marcus, Marvin
Marcus, Robert
Marcus, Rudolph Arthur
Mardian, Samuel, Jr.
Margol, Irving
Margolin, Ephraim
Margolin, Stuart
Margolis, Julius
Margutti, Victor Mario
Marin, Richard Anthony ("Cheech")
Marine, Gene
Marini, Frank
Mark, James B. D.
Mark, James Leland
Mark, Shelley M.
Markey, William Alan
Markle, George Bushar, IV
Marks, Arnold
Marks, Bruce
Markus, Norbert Williams, Jr.
Marlett, De Otis Loring
Marmor, Judd
Maron, Melvin Earl
Maronde, Robert Francis
Marquardt, Frederic Sylvester
Marquis, Harold Holliday, Jr.
Marquis, Robert B.
Marr, Allen Gerald
Marr, Clinton, Jr.
Marr, Jerome Soo Whan
Marr, Luther Reese
Marr, Sally K.
Marriner, David Richard
Marriott, David Daniel
Marsaglia, George
Marschalk, William John
Marsh, Donald Jay
Marsh, Jean Lyndsey Torren
Marshall, Anthony Wallace
Marshall, Arthur K.
Marshall, C. Penny
Marshall, Consuelo Bland
Marshall, Garry
Marshall, George Dwire
Marshall, Kneale Thomas
Marshall, Norman Sturgeon
Marshall, Robert Charles
Marshall, Robert Herman
Marshall, William Edward
Marsoobian, Edward Fred
Martel, John Sheldon
Marten, John Francis
Martin, Agnes
Martin, Alfred Manuel (Billy)
Martin, Ben
Martin, Bernard Lee
Martin, Bill
Martin, Boyd Archer
Martin, Dean
Martin, Fred
Martin, George Coleman
Martin, George Raymond Richard
Martin, Harry Victor
Martin, Henry H.
Martin, Jay Herbert
Martin, Jerry Chambers
Martin, Joan Callaham
Martin, John Hugh
Martin, Joseph, Jr.
Martin, Keith Justin
Martin, Marie Young
Martin, Morgan Graham
Martin, Quinn
Martin, Steve
Martin, Thomas Edward
Martin, Tony
Martin, Walter Edwin
Martin, Walter Patrick
Martin, Walter Tilford
Martindell, Anne Clark
Martines, Lauro René
Martini, Emil P., Jr.
Marumoto, Masaji
Marvel, John A.
Marvell, Elliot Nelson
Marvin, David Keith
Marvin, Lee
Marx, Arthur (Julius)
Marx, Wesley
Marylander, Stuart Jerome
Masiko, Peter, Jr.
Masket, Edward Seymour
Maslach, George James
Masner, Gary William
Mason, Arthur Winfred, Jr.
Mason, Dean Towle
Mason, Ellsworth Goodwin
Mason, George Robert
Mason, James Boyd
Mason, James Tate
Mason, Pamela Helen
Massey, Leon R.
Massey, Raymond
Massy, William Francis
Masursky, Harold
Matarazzo, Joseph Dominic
Matarazzo, Ruth Gadbois
Mateju, Joseph Frank
Matheny, Raymond Thomas
Mather, Allen Frederick
Mather, James Absolom
Matheson, Alan Adams
Matheson, Scott Milne
Mathews, Christopher King
Mathews, Edward Ray
Mathews, Warren Edward
Mathies, Allen Wray, Jr.
Mathis, Johnny
Matson, Wallace I.
Matsuda, Fujio
Matsumoto, George
Matsunaga, Ronald Shigeto
Matsushita, Sadami
Matteucci, Malcom Gene
Matteucig, Giacinto
Matthaei, Charles William Henry
Matthau, Walter
Matthews, Donald Rowe
Matthews, Eugene Edward
Matthews, G(eorge) Hubert
Matthews, John Roupee
Matthews, Lemuel Hatch
Matthews, Phillip Dean
Matthews, Robert Lloyd
Matthews, Wanda (Lee) Miller
Matthews, Warren Wayne, Jr.
Matthews, William Proctor
Mattson, Marcus
Mattson, Roy Henry
Mattson, Vernon Linnaeus
Mattsson, Carvel
Mau, Chuck
Mau, William Koon-Hee
Mauch, Gene W.
Maurer, James Richardson
Maurer, John Edward
Maurer, Walter Harding
Mauro, Andrew Emil
Maxeiner, Clarence William
Maxfield, Robert Roy
Maxson, William Burdette
Maxwell, Albert Leland
Maxwell, Art Vernon
Maxwell, Arthur Graham
Maxwell, David Samuel
Maxwell, Donald Stanley
Maxwell, Frank
Maxwell, Michael
Maxwell, Morton Harrison
Maxwell, Robert LeRoy
May, Adolf Darlington
May, Francis Hart, Jr.
May, Henry Farnham
May, Larry James
May, Melvin Arthur
May, Michael M.
May, Paul White
May, Robert A.
May, Rollo
Mayall, John Brumwell
Mayer, Edgar Nathan
Mayer, Frederick Rickard
Mayer, James B.
Mayer, Joseph E.
Mayer, Milton
Mayer, Steven Edward Max
Mayers, Eugene David
Mayers, Jean
Mayhew, Lawrence Lee
Mayhew, Leon Hinckley
Mayhew, Lewis Baltzell
Maynard, Harry Lee
Maynard, Robert Clyve
Mayo, Byron W.
Mayo, Frank Rea
Mays, Carl W., Jr.
Mays, Edward Everett
Maytham, Thomas Northrup
Mazia, Daniel
Mazo, Robert Marc
Mazursky, Paul
Mazzaferri, Ernest Louis
Mazzia, Valentino Don Bosco
Mazzocchi, Anthony
Mc Adams, Ronald Earl
Mc Allister, Decker Gordon
Mc Allister, James M.
McAllister, Robert John
Mc Atee, Patricia Anne Rooney
McAuley, Raymond Redden
Mc Auliffe, Frank Malachi
Mc Bain, LeRoy Doward
Mc Bath, James Harvey
Mc Bratney, William H.
Mc Bride, Guy Thornton, Jr.
McCabe, Charles Raymond
Mc Caffrey, Stanley Eugene
McCain, Warren Earl
Mc Callum, David
Mc Cambridge, Mercedes
McCamish, Harley Milton
Mc Cann, Cecile Nelken
McCann, Gilbert Donald, Jr.
Mc Cann, Leslie Coleman
McCann, William James
Mc Carroll, James Renwick
Mc Carthy, Dennis
Mc Carthy, Frank
Mc Carthy, Frank Martin
Mc Carthy, Fred
McCarthy, John
McCartney, Forrest Striplin
McCarty, Chester Earl
Mc Carty, Perry Lee
Mc Cauley, Bruce Gordon
Mc Chesney, Robert Pearson
McChrystal, William Richard
Mc Clain, Alice
Mc Clanahan, Rue (Eddi-Rue)
McClary, James Daly
McClatchy, Charles Kenny
McClatchy, James B.
McClave, Donald Silsbee
McCleary, Lloyd E(verald)
McClellan, Roger Orville
McClellan, Stan Leon
McClelland, Harold Franklin
Mc Clelland, John Peter
McClendon, Ernestine Epps
Mc Clennen, Louis
Mc Clintock, Archie Glenn
Mc Clintock, Ross Augustus
Mc Clory, Sean Joseph
Mc Cloud, James Ferdinand
McClure, Joel William, Jr.
Mc Clure, Michael Thomas
McClure, Thomas Fulton
Mc Cluskey, Edward Joseph
Mc Collum, Robert Stuart
McColpin, Carroll Warren
Mc Comic, Robert Barry
Mc Conkie, Bruce Redd
McConnell, Calvin Dale
Mc Connell, Robert Eastwood
Mc Connell, Thomas Raymond
Mc Connor, William S.
Mc Cool, Woodford Bethel
Mc Corkle, Chester Oliver, Jr.
McCorkle, Horace Jackson
McCormac, Billy Murray
Mc Cormack, Francis Xavier
McCormick, Floyd Guy, Jr.
Mc Cormick, Harold L.
Mc Cormick, Wilfred
McCosker, John Edward
Mc Covey, Willie Lee
McCoy, Craig Walpole
McCoy, George Thomas
Mc Coy, John Louis
Mc Coy, Robert Baker
Mc Cracken, Harold
McCracken, John Harvey
Mc Cracken, Philip Trafton
Mc Craken, Robert Stanton
Mc Cravey, Mary Alvaretta
Mc Craw, James Edward
Mc Cready, Albert Lee
Mc Crone, Alistair William
Mc Croskey, William James
McCulloch, Frank Walter
Mc Culloch, Samuel Clyde
McCullough, Edgar Joseph, Jr.
Mc Cullough, Helen Craig
McCullough, James Russell
Mc Cune, Bernard Edward
Mc Cune, Ellis E.
Mc Cune, George David
Mc Cune, Sara Miller (Mrs. George D. McCune)
Mc Curdy, Solomon Portious
Mc Cutchan, Joseph Wilson
Mc Cutcheon, Lawrence
Mc Daniel, Glen
Mc Daniel, Thomas M., Jr.
McDaniels, Eugene Lamar
Mc Dermott, John Francis, Jr.
Mc Dermott, Thomas Charles, Jr.
McDonald, Donald John
Mc Donald, James Michael, Jr.
Mc Donald, John Richard
Mc Donald, Lee Cameron
Mc Donald, Roy Joseph
McDonald, Warren George
Mc Donough, John Richard
Mc Dowall, Roddy
Mc Dowell, Frank
Mc Dowell, Jack Sherman
Mc Duffie, Malcolm
Mc Elroy, William David
Mc Elwain, Joseph A.
Mc Evilly, Thomas Vincent
Mc Ewan, Leonard
Mc Fadden, Frank William
Mc Fadden, Joseph James
Mc Fall, John
McFarland, Ernest William
Mc Farland, Norman Francis
Mc Feron, Dean Earl
Mc Gagh William Gilbert
Mc Gahan, Merritt Wilson
McGarry, Eugene L.
Mc Gaugh, James Lafayette
McGaughey, Emmett Connell
McGavin, Darren
McGee, Winston Eugene
Mc Ghan, William Frederick
Mc Gill, Esby Clifton
Mc Gill, William James
Mc Givern, William Peter
Mc Gonigle, Paul John
Mc Goohan, Patrick
Mc Govern, Maureen Therese
Mc Govern, Walter T.
Mc Govern, William Montgomery, Jr.
McGowan, Mark Gregory
Mc Grath, Earl James
Mc Greevy, Susan Brown
Mc Guane, Thomas Francis, III
McGuire, Delbert
Mc Guire, Dorothy Hackett
Mc Guire, Joseph William
McHale, Edward Robertson
Mc Hardy, Louis William
Mc Hendrie, Douglas
Mc Henry, Dean Eugene
McHugh, Helen Frances
Mc Hugh, Robert Clayton
McIlwain, Carl Edwin
Mc Innis, Donald Alan
Mc Innis, Edwin
Mc Intire, Junius M.
Mc Intosh, J(ohn) Richard
Mc Intyre, Donald B.
Mc Intyre, Doris Carter
Mc Intyre, Henry Langenberg
Mc Intyre, Lee Emerson
Mc Intyre, Vonda Neel
Mc Kaig, George David
McKay, Monroe Gunn
McKay, William Ivor
Mc Kean, Michael
McKean, Thomas Wayne
Mc Kechnie, Ian Donald Gray
Mc Kee, Edwin Dinwiddie
Mc Kell, Cyrus Milo
McKelvey, Judith Grant
Mc Kenna, David Loren
McKenna, J. Fenton
Mc Kenna, William Edward
McKenzie, James Basil
Mc Keown, Raymond Merll
McKiernan, John William
McKinlay, Donald Carl
Mc Kinley, David Alexander, Jr.
McKinley, Loren Dhue
Mc Kinley, Royce Baldwin
Mc Kinney, Alexis
Mc Kinney, John Adams
McKinney, Judson Thad
Mc Kinney, Montgomery Nelson
Mc Kinnon, Clinton D.
Mc Kinnon, Clinton Dan
McKirahan, Robert Roy
McKissock, Paul Kendrick
McKnight, Robert Kellogg
McKnight, Tom Lee
Mc Koy, Basil Vincent Charles
Mc Kuen, Rod
Mc Laglen, Andrew Victor
McLarnan, Donald Edward
McLaughlin, Glen
Mc Laughlin, Jerome Michael
Mc Laughlin, Joseph Mailey
Mc Laughlin, Leighton Bates, II
Mc Lean, Edward Barnard
McLean, Hugh
McLean, Richard Thorpe
Mc Lean, Robert Joseph
McLennan, Charles Ewart
Mc Lure, Charles E., Jr.
Mc Mahon, Ed
McMichen, Robert Sidney
Mc Millan, Claude, Jr.
Mc Millan, Edwin Mattison
Mc Millan, James Thomas
Mc Millan, John Robertson
Mc Millan, Kenneth
McMillian, John Guy
McMullen, Thomas Michael
Mc Murray, Paul Ray
McMurren, William Henry
Mc Murrin, Sterling Moss
McMurtry, Burton John
McNabb, Joe Bennett
Mc Nair, Barbara
McNally, Thomas Charles, III
Mc Namara, Joseph Donald
McNeal, Dale William, Jr.
Mc Near, Denman Kittredge
Mc Neely, E.L.
Mc Neil, Joseph Dennis
McNenny, Harold Francis
Mc Nichol, Kristy
Mc Nicholas, John Patrick, III
Mc Nichols, Ray
Mc Nichols, William Henry, Jr.
McNiel, James Robertson
Mc Nitt, Willard Charles
Mc Nulty, Frederick Charles
McNulty, John Kent
Mc Nulty, Kneeland
Mc Phee, Bruce Gordon
McPherson, Donald J.
Mc Pherson, John Dallas
Mc Pherson, Rolf Kennedy
Mc Quade, Henry Ford
Mc Quaid, Frank John
Mc Quarrie, Donald Allan
McQueen, Justice Ellis (also known as L.Q. Jones)
McRae, Carmen
Mc Raven, Dale Keith
McRuer, Duane Torrance
Mc Shann, Jay
Mc Tague, John Paul
McVay, John Edward
McWhirter, William Buford
McWilliams, Edwin Joseph
Mc Williams, Margaret Ann
Mc Williams, Robert Hugh
Meacham, Charles Harding
Meadows, Jack Edward
Meadows, Jayne
Meadows, Paul Dwain
Meaker, Gerald Henry
Meany, Herbert John
Meara, Anne
Mears, Rick Ravon
Mechem, Edwin Leard
Mecum, Dudley Clarke, II
Medavoy, Mike
Medberry, Chauncey Joseph, III
Medearis, Roger Norman
Meditch, James Stephen
Mednick, Murray
Medoff, Mark Howard
Medsger, Betty Louise
Mee, Lowell Edison
Meechan, Charles James
Meehan, Paula Kent
Meeker, William Everett
Mee-Lee, Denis
Meem, John Gaw
Meenaghan, James Joseph
Mefferd, George W.
Meggs, Brown Moore
Meier, Gerald Marvin
Meier, Richard Louis
Meighan, Clement Woodward
Meigs, Walter Berkeley
Meily, Harry S.
Meindl, James Donald
Meister, Charles Walter
Melbo, Irving Robert
Melby, Orville Erling
Melchert, James Frederick
Melchior, Kurt Werner
Melczer, Joseph Treuhaft, Jr.
Meldrum, Barbara Ruth Howard
Melendez, Jose Cuauhtemoc
Melendy, Howard Brett
Melican, James Patrick, Jr.
Melich, Mitchell
Melick, Dermont Wilson
Mellish, Donald Leroy
Mellor, James Robb
Melmon, Kenneth Lloyd
Melnick, Daniel
Meloan, Taylor Wells
Melsheimer, Mel P(owell)
Meltzer, David
Menard, Henry William, Jr.
Mendel, Dennis David
Mendel, Werner Max
Mendelsohn, Harold

Mendelsohn, Mortimer Lester
Mendelson, Lee M.
Mendicino, V. Frank
Mendoza, Stanley Atran
Mengers, Sue
Menk, Louis Wilson
Menn, Julius Joel
Mennis, Edmund Addi
Menon, Vijaya Bhaskar
Menor, Benjamin
Mensinger, Peggy Boothe
Mercer, Marian
Mercereau, James Edgar
Merdinger, Charles John
Meredith, Burgess
Meriam, James Lathrop
Merigan, Thomas Charles, Jr.
Meriwether, Lee
Merkel, John Condon
Merklin, Kenneth Edwin
Merlo, Harry Angelo
Merman, Ethel
Merrell, Brownell, Jr.
Merrick, George Boesch
Merrifield, Donald Paul
Merrill, Charles Merton
Merrill, Harvie Martin
Merrill, John Ogden, Jr.
Merrill, Reed Miller
Merrill, Richard James
Merritt, Evelyn Caroline
Merryman, Holt Wallace
Merryman, John Henry
Mersman, Scudder, Jr.
Merszei, Zoltan
Mertz, George Henry
Messer, Arnold William
Messinger, Sheldon L(eopold)
Messinger, William Henry
Metcalf, Frederic Thomas
Metcalf, Lawrence Vincent
Metcalfe, Burton Denis
Metcalfe, Darrel Seymour
Metschan, Joseph Emil
Metzger, H(owell) Peter
Meyer, Adolph Conrad, Jr.
Meyer, Barry Michael
Meyer, Edmond Gerald
Meyer, James Henry
Meyer, Kurt Werner
Meyer, Louis, Jr.
Meyer, Margaret Eleanor
Meyer, Milton Edward, Jr.
Meyer, Nicholas
Meyer, Russ
Meyer, William Danielson
Meyerhof, Walter Ernst
Meyers, Charles Jarvis
Miccio, Joseph V.
Michael, Edward Nelson
Michael, Ernest Arthur
Michael, Gary Linn
Michael, Jerrold Mark
Michael, Robert S.
Michaelis, George H.
Michaels, Leonard
Michals, George Francis
Michel, Lester Allen
Michel, Mary Ann Kedzuf
Michela, Bernard Joseph
Mickelson, Sig
Mickelwait, Lowell Pitzer
Middlebrook, Robert David
Middlebrooks, Eddie Joe
Middleton, James Arthur
Midkiff, Robert Richards
Midlarsky, Manus Issachar
Miedél, Rainer
Mielke, Frederick William, Jr.
Migden, Chester L.
Mihalas, Dimitri Manuel
Mihaly, Eugene Bramer
Mikalson, Roy Gale
Mikesell, Raymond Frech
Mikkelsen, Henning Dahl
Miklos, Jack C.
Miklowitz, Julius
Mikuta, Rudolf
Milander, Henry Martin
Miles, Franklin Everett
Miles, Joanna
Miles, John Wilder
Miles, Josephine
Miles, Vera
Milius, John Frederick
Milkis, Edward Kenneth
Milland, Ray(mond Alton)
Millar, Gregory
Millar, Kenneth (pseudonym Ross Macdonald)
Millar, Margaret Ellis
Millar, Richard William
Millard, George Richard
Miller, Ann (Lucille Ann Collier)
Miller, Arjay
Miller, Charles D.
Miller, Charles William
Miller, Dale Alworth
Miller, Don Robert
Miller, Donn Biddle
Miller, Dudley Eugene
Miller, Eldon Earl
Miller, Francis Don
Miller, G. Willard, Jr.
Miller, Gavin
Miller, George
Miller, Harriet Evelyn
Miller, Herman
Miller, Hiram Augustus
Miller, Irwin Robert
Miller, Jack Barnett
Miller, James Rumrill, III
Miller, James Vince
Miller, John Jose
Miller, Johnny Laurence
Miller, Jon Hamilton
Miller, Judson Frederick
Miller, Kenneth Larry
Miller, Louis Rice
Miller, Lyle Leslie
Miller, M. Hughes
Miller, Milton Howard
Miller, Paul James
Miller, Raymond Jarvis
Miller, Richard Alan
Miller, Richard Austin
Miller, Robert Fred
Miller, Robert Neil
Miller, Roger Dean
Miller, Ronald Thomas
Miller, Ronald William
Miller, Ross Franklin
Miller, Roy Andrew
Miller, Stanley Custer, Jr.
Miller, Stephen Herschel
Miller, Steve
Miller, Terrence Brent
Miller, Thomas Lee
Miller, Thormund Aubrey
Miller, Timothy Alden
Miller, William Charles
Miller, William Frederick
Miller, William Hughes
Millikan, Charles English (Brad)
Millikan, Clark Harold
Millikan, Roger Conant
Milliken, John Barnes
Milliken, John Gordon
Millis, Robert Lowell
Mills, Carrol
Mills, Eugene Sumner
Mills, Glen Earl
Mills, James Robert
Mills, Joseph William
Mills, Lorna Henrietta
Milne, David Spencer
Milne, Eric Nightingale Campbell
Milosz, Czeslaw
Milstein, Frederick
Milton, Charles Hamilton, III
Minami, Wayne
Minchin, Michael M., Jr.
Minckler, Robert Alan
Minde, Stefan Paul
Minear, Leon Pierson
Miner, John Ronald
Mink, Patsy Takemoto
Minnelli, Vincente
Minnick, Walter Clifford
Minor, Benton Lee
Mirisch, Marvin Elliot
Mirisch, Walter Mortimer
Mischel, Walter
Mischer, Donald Leo
Mishell, Daniel Randolph, Jr.
Mishkin, Paul J.
Misner, Arthur Jack
Misrach, Richard Laurence
Mitchell, Bruce Tyson
Mitchell, Cameron (Cameron Mizell)
Mitchell, David Lester
Mitchell, E. A.
Mitchell, Frederick Cleveland
Mitchell, Homer Irving
Mitchell, James Kenneth
Mitchell, John Clark, II
Mitchell, John H.
Mitchell, John Theodore
Mitchell, Joni (Roberta Joan Anderson)
Mitchell, Joseph Nathan
Mitchell, Leona Pearl
Mitchell, Lydell Douglas
Mitchell, Maurice B.
Mitchell, Ulyss S. Stanford
Mitchelson, Marvin M(orris)
Mitchum, Robert (Charles)
Mitford, Jessica
Mittman, Charles
Miwa, Ralph Makoto
Miyasaki, George Joji
Mnookin, Robert Harris
Moberly, David Lindsey
Moberly, Ralph Moon
Moch, Robert Gaston
Mock, David Clinton, Jr.
Mock, Henry Byron
Mock, Richard M.
Moe, Chesney Rudolph
Moe, Edward Owen
Moe, Lawrence Henry
Moeller, Therald
Moellering, John Henry
Moen, Donne Philip
Moench, Robert William
Moffat, Donald
Moffet, Alan Theodore
Moffitt, Donald Eugene
Mofford, Rose
Mogull, Arthur
Mohler, Ronald Rutt
Mohlie, Raymond Eugene
Mohney, Russell Earle
Mohr, John Luther
Mohr, Milton Ernst
Moir, Alfred Kummer
Mokrzycki, Andrew Gustav
Molina, Mario Jose
Molinaro, Al
Moll, John Lewis
Molloy, Peter Michael
Molzen, Dayton Frank
Momaday, Navarre Scott
Mommaerts, Wilfried Francis Henry Maria
Mommsen, Katharina
Monagan, Robert Timothy, Jr.
Monaghan, Eileen
Monaghan, Keith
Monagle, John Joseph
Monahan, Harry Edmund, Jr.
Moncrief, Ernest
Monday, John Christian
Mondragon, Roberto A.
Monge, Joseph Paul
Monger, Albert Jackson
Monie, Ian Whitelaw
Monin, Lawrence Owen
Monismith, Carl Leroy
Monsen, Elaine Ranker
Monsen, Raymond Joseph, Jr.
Monson, Arch, Jr.
Monson, David Smith
Monson, Forrest Truman
Monson, James Edward
Monson, Karen Ann
Monson, Thomas Spencer
Montagna, William
Montalban, Ricardo
Montana, Patsy (Mrs. Paul Edward Rose)
Montefusco, John Joseph, Jr.
Monteith, Robert
Montgomery, Belinda J.
Montgomery, David Bruce
Montgomery, Francis Rhodes
Montgomery, George Charles, II
Montgomery, James Fischer
Montgomery, Parker Gilbert
Montgomery, Theodore Ashton
Montgomery, Victor Ernest
Moody, Frank Gordon
Moody, George Franklin
Moody, Graham Blair
Moody, Ralph E.
Moon, Marjorie Ruth
Moon, Thomas Stanley
Mooney, Harold Alfred
Mooneyham, Walter Stanley
Moore, Benjamin
Moore, Brian
Moore, Calvin C.
Moore, Carleton Bryant
Moore, Charles Willard
Moore, Clayton Jack
Moore, Dale Grant
Moore, Daniel Charles
Moore, Dorotha (Mrs. Collis P. Moore)
Moore, Douglas Ross
Moore, Dudley Stuart John
Moore, Edythe
Moore, Emmett Burris
Moore, Emmett Burris, Jr.
Moore, George Eugene
Moore, Gordon E.
Moore, Hal G.
Moore, Hayden Albert
Moore, Hudson, Jr.
Moore, Jack William
Moore, James Collins
Moore, John Alexander
Moore, John Ashton
Moore, John George, Jr.
Moore, John H.
Moore, John Robert
Moore, Kenneth Ray
Moore, Laurence
Moore, Malcolm Arthur
Moore, Marc Anthony
Moore, Mary Tyler
Moore, Randolph Graves
Moore, Richard Donald
Moore, Robert James
Moore, Robert Madison
Moore, Thomas Carrol
Moore, Tom
Moore, Ward Frederick
Moore, Warren Carroll
Moore, Wesley Sanford
Moore, Wilbert Ellis
Moore, William Edwards
Moore, William Estill, Jr.
Moorhead, Jennelle Vandevort
Moorhead, Louis David, II
Moorhouse, Douglas Cecil
Moos, Rudolf H.
Morby, Edwin Seth
Morehouse, Harold Geddes
Morey, Walter Nelson
Morgan, Arthur Ivason, Jr.
Morgan, Beverly Carver
Morgan, Clarold Forrest
Morgan, Elmo Rich
Morgan, Hazel Nohavec
Morgan, Henry (Harry) (Harry Bratsburg)
Morgan, Jaye P.
Morgan, Joe Leonard
Morgan, Neil
Morgan, Sterling William
Morgan, William Robert
Morgenstern, Leon
Morgner, Aurelius
Morgridge, Howard Henry
Mori, Jun
Moriarty, Eugene Vincent
Moriarty, James Francis (Jay), Jr.
Morin, Joseph Marshall
Morison, William W.
Morita, James Masami
Moritz, Louisa Cira
Morphet, Edgar Leroy
Morrill, Richard Leland
Morrill, Thomas Clyde
Morrin, Thomas Harvey
Morris, Allen Ray
Morris, Bourne Gafill
Morris, Carl
Morris, Grant Harold
Morris, Greg
Morris, Henry Madison, Jr.
Morris, Herbert
Morris, Howard
Morris, Jack Austin, Jr.
Morris, Laval Sidney
Morris, Oswald
Morris, Richard Herbert
Morris, Robert Emuel
Morris, Stephen James Michael
Morris, Thomas Martin
Morris, William Joseph
Morris, William Lester
Morris, Wright
Morrison, Frank Brenner, Jr.
Morrison, Fred Beverly
Morrison, George Ivan (Van)
Morrison, Gilbert Caffall
Morrison, Lester Marvin
Morrison, Manley Glenn
Morrison, Martin Earl
Morrison, Perry David
Morrison, Robert Joseph
Morrison, Shelley
Morrison, Van
Morrissey, John Carroll
Morrow, Charles Paul
Morrow, Frederick Charles
Morrow, John Howard
Morrow, Winston Vaughan
Morse, Cynthia Brown
Morse, Gerry Elden
Morse, Richard
Morse, Richard McGee
Morse, True Delbert
Mortimer, Robert Keith
Morton, Larry Craig
Morton, Lawrence
Morton, Newton Ennis
Moscov, Alan Jay
Moseley, Robert David, Jr.
Moser, James Leland
Moser, Kenneth Miles
Moser, Leo John
Moser, Norman Calvin
Moser, Stephen Benjamin
Moses, Forrest (Lee, Jr.)
Moses, Gilbert
Moses, Lincoln E.
Moses, Raphael Jacob
Mosher, Harry Stone
Moshy, Raymond Joseph
Mosich, Anelis Nick
Mosier, Harry David, Jr.
Mosk, Richard Mitchell
Mosk, Stanley
Moss, Arthur J.
Moss, Claude Scott
Moss, Gary Elliot
Moss, Jerry
Moss, John Emerson
Moss, McKenzie, II
Moss, William Thomas
Mostofi, Khosrow
Moszkowski, Steven Alexander
Mote, Clayton Daniel, Jr.
Mothershead, John Leland, Jr.
Motulsky, Arno Gunther
Motz, Kenneth Lee
Moudy, Roark Virgil
Mount, Thomas H(enderson)
Mowbray, John Code
Moxley, John Howard, III
Moye, John Edward
Moyer, Alan Dean
Mrazek, Robert Vernon
Muchow, William Charles
Mucklestone, Robert Stanley
Mudd, Henry Thomas
Muecke, Charles (Carl) Andrew
Muedeking, George Herbert
Muehleisen, Gene Sylvester
Mueller, Fred Jack
Mueller, George E.
Mueller, Gerhard G(ottlob)
Mueth, Joseph Edward
Muetterties, Earl Leonard
Muhleman, Duane Owen
Muir, William Ker, Jr.
Mulcahy, Richard Edward
Muldaur, Diana Charlton (Mrs. James Mitchell Vickery)
Muldaur, Maria
Mulder, Donald Gerrit
Mulgrew, Kate
Mulhollan, Paige Elliott
Mulholland, Raymond Charles
Mulkern, Louis Joseph
Mull, Martin
Mullaley, Robert Charles
Mullane, L. Wayne
Mullavey, Greg
Mullen, Daniel Robert
Mullen, Thomas Michael
Mullen, Thomas Moore
Muller, Burton Harlowe
Muller, Nicholas Guthrie
Müller-Eberhard, Hans Joachim
Mulligan, Robert Patrick
Mullikin, Harry LaVerne
Mullineaux, Donal Ray
Mumford, Emily Hamilton
Mumford, Milton Christopher
Mumford, William Porter II
Munch, Christopher Henry
Mundell, David Edward
Munger, Charles Thomas
Munger, Edwin Stanton
Munk, Walter Heinrich
Munnecke, Donald Edwin
Munoz, John Joaquin
Munro, Alan Ross
Munro, Ralph Davies
Munro, Sanford Sterling, Jr.
Munson, Alexander Lee
Munson, Theodore Edward
Munzer, Rudolph James
Murdock, David Howard
Murdock, John Carey
Murkowski, Frank Hughes
Murphey, Bradford
Murphey, Byron Freeze
Murphey, Elwood
Murphey, Vera Edna Randle
Murphy, Barry Ames
Murphy, Benjamin Edward
Murphy, Franklin David
Murphy, James Emmett
Murphy, James Fredrick
Murphy, James Patrick
Murphy, Lewis Curtis
Murphy, Lorenzo Dow, Jr.
Murphy, Reg
Murphy, Richard Ernest
Murphy, Thomas Joseph
Murphy, William James
Murray, Anthony
Murray, Arthur
Murray, Bruce C.
Murray, Donald Patrick
Murray, Frank
Murray, J. Edward
Murray, J(oseph) Hartley
Murray, James D.
Murray, James Patrick
Murray, Jan
Murray, Joan Elizabeth
Murray, John Frederic
Murray, Kathryn Hazel
Murray, Raymond Carl
Murray, William Daniel
Murray, William Paul, Jr.
Murray, William Randolph
Murtha, Richard A.
Muscatine, Charles
Musgrave, Richard Abel
Mussen, Paul Henry
Musser, C. Walton
Mussman, William Edward
Mutschler, Herbert Frederick
Mycielski, Jan
Myers, Beverlee Ann Reardan
Myers, Clay
Myers, Dale DeHaven
Myers, John Thomas
Myers, John Wescott
Myers, Robert David
Myers, Smithmoore Paul
Myers, William Hardy
Myerson, Alan
Myhers, John
Myhre, Byron Arnold
Myshak, Richard John
Nachman, Gerald Weil
Nachmanoff, Arnold
Nacht, Daniel Joseph
Nack, Donald Henry
Nadel, Arthur Howard
Nadel, Jay Alan
Nagamura, Toshio
Nageotte, Francis Louis
Naghdi, Paul Mansour
Nagle, Robert John
Nagle, Robert Owen
Nagley, Winfield Eugene
Nagy, Bartholomew Stephen
Nahman, Norris Stanley
Nahstoll, Richardson Wadsworth
Najarian, Melvin Kenneth
Nakahodo, Henry T.
Nakamura, Mitsuru James
Nakatani, Roy Eiji
Namias, Jerome
Nanney, Herbert Boswell
Napolitano, Leonard Michael
Narath, Albert
Nardino, Gary
Narodick, Sally G.
Narver, John Colin
Nash, Frank Erwin
Nash, Gary Baring
Nash, Gerald David
Nash, Graham William
Nash, H. Richard
Nash, Merrill Lloyd
Nassi, Samuel
Natcher, Stephen Darlington
Nater, James Ronald
Nathan, Leonard Edward
Natzler, Otto
Navarre, Donald Casper
Navis, Herbert Albert
Naylor, Harry Brooks
Naylor, John Thomas
Neal, Fred Warner
Neal, Philip Mark, Jr.
Neame, Ronald
Nederlander, James Morton
Needham, Hal
Neff, Benjamin Clarence
Neff, Francine Irving (Mrs. Edward John Neff)
Neiburger, Morris
Neidert, Kalo Edward
Neighbors, William Donald
Neill, Warren Joseph
Neinas, Charles Merrill
Neiter, Gerald Irving
Nelles, Maurice
Nelligan, Michael Thomas
Nellis, Donald Owen
Nelp, Wil Borchers
Nelson, Alan Jan
Nelson, Alan Ray
Nelson, Arthur D.
Nelson, Charles Rowe
Nelson, Don Nichols
Nelson, Donald Kofoed
Nelson, Donald Lloyd
Nelson, Dorothy Wright (Mrs. James F. Nelson)
Nelson, Edward Humphrey
Nelson, Edwin Stafford
Nelson, Elmer Kingsholm (Kim), Jr.
Nelson, Eric Hilliard (Rick)
Nelson, George Leonard
Nelson, Harold Thorvald
Nelson, Harriet Hilliard
Nelson, Howard Joseph
Nelson, Jack Russell
Nelson, James Carmer, Jr.
Nelson, James Cecil
Nelson, John William
Nelson, Kay LeRoi
Nelson, Lawrence Olaf
Nelson, Lindsey
Nelson, Lyle Morgan
Nelson, Mark Bruce
Nelson, Philip Francis
Nelson, Ralph
Nelson, Rodney Ellsworth
Nelson, Roger Hugh
Nelson, Russell Marion
Nelson, Wendel Lane
Nemerovski, Howard Norman
Nemeth, Charlan Jeanne
Nemeth, Kathleen Nanette Lucas
Nerheim, Lawrence Eugene
Neri, Manuel
Nero, Peter
Nesen, Robert Dean
Nesvold, Betty Anne Krambuhl
Neubert, Richard Jacque
Neufeld, Mace Alvin
Neugebauer, Gerry
Neumann, Harry
Neustein, Harry B(ernard)
Neustein, Joseph
Neutra, Dion
Nevin, Edward Joseph
Nevius, Blake Reynolds
Newberry, Conrad Floyde
Newby, Idus Atwell
Newcombe, Richard Sumner
Newell, William Thrift
Newhall, Beaumont
Newhall, Scott
Newhart, Bob
Newhouse, Joseph Paul
Newkirk, Gordon Allen, Jr.
Newkirk, John Burt
Newley, Anthony
Newlin, Charles William
Newman, Barry Foster
Newman, Frank Cecil
Newman, John Scott
Newman, John V.
Newman, Joyce Kligerman
Newman, Laraine
Newman, Max Karl
Newman, Paul
Newman, Randy
Newman, William Louis
Newman-Gordon, Pauline
Newmarker, Michael Jon
Newsom, Melvin Max
Newsom, Will Roy
Newton, James Quigg, Jr.
Newton, Robert Eugene
Newton, Thomas Hans
Newton, Wayne
Newton-John, Olivia
Ney, James Walter Edward Colby
Nibley, Robert Ricks
Nicholls, Merrill Edgar
Nichols, Alan Hammond
Nichols, Charles August
Nichols, Robert Edmund
Nichols, William Ford, Jr.
Nicholson, Glen Ira
Nicholson, Henry B.
Nicholson, Jack
Nicholson, James Milton
Nicholson, Roy Stephen
Nicholson, Will Faust, Jr.
Nickelson, Donald Eugene
Nicks, Stevie
Nicolaides, John Dudley
Nicolaysen, Peter Smith
Nicoll, Charles Samuel
Nidetch, Jean
Niebauer, John Joseph, Jr.
Niedzielski, Henri Zygmunt
Nielsen, Emiel Theodore, Jr.
Nielsen, Lawrence Ernie
Nielsen, Leslie
Nielsen, Thomas Harold
Nielson, Howard Curtis
Nielson, James Edward
Nierenberg, William Aaron
Nigam, Bishan Perkash
Nightingale, Earl Clifford
Nikolaieff, George Alexander
Nilan, Robert Arthur
Niland, Edward John
Nilsson, A. Kenneth
Nimmo, Robert Powers
Nimoy, Leonard
Nininger, Harvey Harlow
Nishimura, Pete Hideo
Nishitani, Martha
Nishkian, Byron Levon
Niswender, Gordon Dean
Niven, David
Niven, Laurence Van Cott
Nivison, David Shepherd
Nix, William Dale
Nixon, Alan Charles
Nixon, John Erskine
Nixon, Marni

Nixon, Robert James
Nobe, Ken
Nobe, Kenneth Charles
Noble, James Van Petten
Noble, Richard Lloyd
Noe, Guy
Noe, Jerre Donald
Noehren, Robert
Noel, Michael Lee
Noerdlinger, Peter David
Noggle, Anne
Noguchi, Thomas Tsunetomi
Nokes, John Richard
Nolan, Kathleen
Nolan, William Francis
Noland, Robert LeRoy
Noll, Roger Gordon
Noltmann, Ernst August
Nong
Norby, Maurice Joseph
Norby, Rockford Douglas
Nord, Alan Andrew
Nord, Robert W(illiam)
Nordby, Gene Milo
Nordyke, James Walter
Norgren, C. Neil
Norian, Roger W.
Norman, Ralph David
Norris, Robert Matheson
Norris, William Albert
North, Alex
North, Douglass Cecil
North, Edmund Hall
North, Harper Qua
North, James Dennis
North, Judy
North, Wheeler James
Northrop, John Howard
Northrup, Laness Donald
Northup, George Warren
Norton, Clifford Charles
Norton, Delmar Lynn
Norton, Ken
Norton-Taylor, Judy
Nostrand, Howard Lee
Notari, Paul Celestin
Nothmann, Gerhard Adolf
Nova, Saul Harry
Novack, Alvin John
Novak, Maximillian Erwin
Novak, Milan Vaclav
Novak, Raymond Francis
Novak, Terry Lee
Novick, Aaron
Nowels, Richard Wright
Noyce, Donald Sterling
Noyce, Robert Norton
Noyes, H(enry) Pierre
Noyes, Richard Hall
Noyes, Richard Macy
Noyes, Robert Wallace
Nuber, Charles Norman
Nuckolls, Leonard Arnold
Nugent, Charles Arter
Nunes, Gordon Maxwell
Nunis, Doyce Blackman, Jr.
Nunis, Richard Arlen
Nunn, Warne Harry
Nutt, Jim Sutcliffe
Nutzle, Futzie (Bruce John Kleinsmith)
Nybakken, James Willard
Nyborg, Keith Foote
Nye, Harry Safford
Nye, William Allen
Nygaard, Henry Sigurd
Nyhan, William Leo
Nykiel, Ronald Alan
Nyman, Carl John, Jr.
Oaks, Dallin Harris
Oates, Gordon Cedric
Oates, Warren
Oberhelman, Harry Alvin, Jr.
Oblad, Alexander Golden
Oboler, Eli Martin
O'Boyle, James Bernard
O'Brian, Hugh
O'Brien, Edmond
O'Brien, Gerald James
O'Brien, Jack George
O'Brien, James Edward
O'Brien, Margaret (Angela Maxine O'Brien)
O'Brien, Raymond Francis
O'Brien, Richard Frank
O'Brien, Robert S.
O'Brien, Rosanne P.
O'Brien, William Martin
O'Byrne, Bryan Jay
Ocheltree, Richard Lawrence
O'Connell, Hugh Mellen, Jr.
O'Connell, Kenneth John
O'Connell, Kevin
O'Connor, Carroll
O'Connor, G(eorge) Richard
O'Connor, John Jay, III
Oda, Robert Colin
Odell, William Douglas
Oder, Frederic Carl Emil
Odishaw, Hugh
Odland, George Fisher
O'Donnell, Bryant
O'Donnell, Hugh
O'Donnell, Joseph Vincent
O'Donnell, Pierce Henry
O'Flaherty, Terrence
Ogata, Thomas Shoichi
Ogdon, Wilbur
Ogg, James Elvis
Ogier, Walter Thomas
Ogilvie, Lloyd John
O'Green, Frederick W.
Ogren, Carroll Woodrow
O'Hanlon, Richard E.
O'Hara, John Francis
O'Hare, James Raymond
O'Hare, Stephen Thomas
Ohkawa, Tihiro
Ohl, Donald Charles
Okamura, Arthur
Oke, John Beverley
O'Keefe, Donald L.
O'Keefe, Edward Franklin
O'Keeffe, Georgia
O'Konski, Chester Thomas
Okrent, David
Okuma, Thomas Masaji
Olafson, Frederick Arlan
Olah, George Andrew
Olander, Linda Marie Piskorski
Olds, Glenn Alvero
O'Leary, Robert Thomas
Olesen, Douglas Eugene
Olesen, Virginia Lee
Olfe, Daniel Burrhus
Oliansky, Joel
Oliphant, Oscar Dabney
Olitt, Arnold
Oliver, Bernard More
Oliver, Donald Lynn
Oliver, Robert Warner
Oliveros, Pauline
Olleman, Roger Dean
Ollman, Arthur Lee
Olmstead, Stephen Goodwin
Olmsted, Richard Williams
Olney, Daniel Clanton
Olscamp, Paul James
Olsen, Alfred Jon
Olsen, Alvin Gordon
Olsen, Edward Gustave
Olsen, Harold Fremont
Olsen, Jack
Olsen, Kurt H.
Olsen, Merlin Jay
Olsen, Tillie
Olsen, Viggo Norskov
Olson, David Henry
Olson, David John
Olson, Donald Ernest
Olson, Earl Eidswold
Olson, Elder James
Olson, Ernest LeRoy
Olson, H. Everett
Olson, Oscar Donald
Olson, Richard George
Olson, Russel Einar
Olson, Stanley Granville
Olson, Walter
Olsson, Harry Enoch
Olstad, Roger Gale
Olum, Paul
O'Malley, John G., Jr.
O'Malley, Peter
Oman, LaFel Earl
O'Meara, David Collow
O'Meara, Edward Francis
O'Melveny, John
Omenn, Gilbert Stanley
Omer, George Elbert, Jr.
Omura, Jimmy Kazuhiro
Onak, Thomas Philip
O'Neal, Adrain P.
O'Neal, Ryan
O'Neal, Tatum
O'Neil, Kitty Linn
O'Neill, Daniel Patrick
O'Neill, Edward Arthur
O'Neill, Russell Richard
Openshaw, Maynard Karl
Opotowsky, Maurice Leon
Oppen, George
Oppenheim, Antoni Kazimierz
Orbach, Jerry
Orbach, Raymond Lee
Orchard, Henry John
Ordin, Andrea Sheridan
Ordung, Philip Franklin
Orell, Bernard Leo
Orem, Charles Reace
Orgel, Leslie Eleazer
Orlando, Tony (Michael Anthony Orlando Cassavitis)
Orliss, Theodore Eugene
Orloff, Monford Arthur
Ornstein, Donald Samuel
O'Rourke, Dennis
Orr, Douglass Winnett
Orr, Jack Edward
Orr, John Berk
Orr, Robert Thomas
Orrick, William Horsley, Jr.
Ortega, Ruben Baptista
Orth, Frederick James
Orth, William Albert
Ortiz, Alfonso Alex
Ortlieb, Robert Eugene
Osborn, James Robert
Osborn, Leslie Andrewartha
Osborn, Ronald Edwin
Osmond, Cliff (Clifford O. Ebrahim)
Osmond, Donald Clark (Donny)
Osmond, Marie
Osmundson, Theodore Ole
Osserman, Robert
Ossipoff, Vladimir Nicholas
Oster, Richard McKay
Osterbrock, Donald Edward
Osterhaus, William Eric
Osterwald, Bibi (Margaret Virginia Osterwald)
Osthaus, Franz
Ostlund, Lyman Ellis
Ostroff, Peter Ivan
Ostrom, Donald Duane
Ostrow, Martin M.
O'Sullivan, William John
Oswald, William Joseph
Oswalt, Wendell Hillman
Ott, Wendell Lorenz
Ottenheimer, Miles Eldon
Ottensmeyer, David Joseph
Otth, Edward John, Jr.
Ottley, Jerold Don
Otto, George John
Ottoman, Richard Edward
Ouchi, William George
Ouzts, Johnie Melvin
Ovenfors, Carl-Olof Nils Sten
Overgaard, Willard Michele
Overman, Glenn Delbert
Overpeck, Lem Franklin
Owen, Fred Wynne
Owen, James Churchill
Owen, John
Owen, Lewis James
Owen, Ray David
Owen, Robert Roy
Owen, Thomas Walker
Owens, Buck (Alvis Edgar, Jr.)
Owens, Gary
Owens, J(ames) Cuthbert
Owens, Jack Byron
Owens, Marvin Franklin, Jr.
Owens, Warren Spencer
Owings, Margaret Wentworth
Owings, Nathaniel Alexander
Oxnard, Charles Ernest
Ozark, Daniel Leonard
Ozawa, Paul Masami
Pace, Charles Robert
Pace, R(alph) Wayne
Pachter, Martin Charles
Pacino, Frank George
Pack, Walter Frank
Packard, David
Packard, Richard Dean
Packard, Robert Charles
Packer, Robert Clyde
Padelford, Norman J.
Paderewski, Clarence Joseph
Padula, Fred David
Paffenbarger, Ralph Seal, Jr.
Page, John Boyd
Page, Patti
Page, Thomas Alexander
Paglia, Donald Edward
Paige, Glenn Durland
Paige, Lowell J.
Paine, Thomas Otten
Pake, George Edward
Pakiser, Louis Charles, Jr.
Pakula, Alan J.
Pal, Pratapaditya
Palance, Jack
Palaschak, Daniel John
Palevsky, Max
Paley, Martin Aaron
Pallin, Irving M.
Palm, Nancy Jane
Palmer, Alice Eugenia
Palmer, Claude Funston
Palmer, David Hamblin, Sr.
Palmer, Irene Sabelberg
Palmer, John Alfred
Palmer, John Mattern
Palmer, John Thomas
Palmer, Philip Edward Stephen
Palmer, Robert Lewis
Palmer, Samuel Copeland, III
Palmer, Ted Wayne
Palmer, William Ross
Palmore, James Andrew, Jr.
Palumbo, Nicholas Eugene
Pamperin, John Harry
Panic, Milan
Panico, Victor Gerarde
Pankey, Edgar Edward
Pankow, James Carter
Panofsky, Wolfgang Kurt Hermann
Panozzo, Charles Salvatore
Papas, Charles Herach
Papiano, Neil Leo
Pappagianis, Demosthenes
Pappas, Costas Ernest
Paquette, Robert George
Parac, Thomas J.
Parad, Howard Joseph
Paradise, Michael Emmanuel
Paradise, Philip Herschel
Parazaider, Walter Joseph
Parden, Robert James
Paredes, Alfonso
Parent, Judith Ellen
Paret, Peter
Parfrey, Sydney Woodrow
Paris, Gordon Daniel
Paris, Harold P.
Paris, Jerry
Parish, James Robert
Park, Roderic Bruce
Parker, Alfred Charles
Parker, David Stuart
Parker, Donald Henry
Parker, Earl Randall
Parker, George Earl
Parker, Harry E.
Parker, John Eger
Parker, Michael Leigh
Parker, Norman Francis
Parker, Pierson
Parker, Richard Alan
Parker, Richard Bennett
Parker, Robert Roy
Parker, Sydney Richard
Parkhurst, George Leigh
Parkhurst, John David
Parkhurst, Violet Kinney
Parkins, Barbara
Parkinson, Charles Jay
Parkinson, Thomas Francis
Parks, Bert
Parks, George Albert
Parks, John Emory
Parks, Robert Myers
Parlee, Norman Allen Devine
Parmelee, Arthur Hawley, Jr.
Parmenter, Robert Haley
Parmley, William Watts
Parnell, Francis William, Jr.
Parrish, Thomas Evert
Parry, Edward P.
Parry, Robert Troutt
Parry, Robert Walter
Parsons, Elmer Earl
Parsons, Harriet Oettinger
Parsons, James Jerome
Parsons, Theran Duane
Parsons, William Walter
Partch, Virgil Franklin, II
Parton, Dolly Rebecca
Parton, Walter Jeff
Partridge, David Mel
Partridge, Roi
Partridge, Wayne Earl
Partridge, William Schaubel
Pascale, Richard Tanner
Pascoe, William T., III
Pasinetti, Pier-Maria
Pask, Joseph Adam
Passaglia, Martin, Jr.
Passalaqua, Joseph Anthony
Passaro, Edward, Jr.
Pasternak, Joseph
Pastorius, Jaco
Pastreich, Peter
Patera, John Arlen
Pates, Gordon
Pati, Charles
Patrick, Dennis
Patten, Bebe Harrison
Patterson, Dick
Patterson, Kenneth Denton
Patterson, Richard Wallace
Pattison, William J.
Patton, Stuart
Patton, Warren L.
Paul, Benjamin David
Paul, Elias
Paul, Jack
Paul, Lee Gilmour
Paul, Rodman Wilson
Paulikas, George Algis
Pauling, Linus Carl
Paulsen, Albert
Paulsen, Frank Robert
Paulsen, Martin Raymond
Paulsen, Pat
Paulson, Stephen Jon
Paulus, Harold Edward
Paulus, Norma Jean Petersen
Paxton, Harold Denver
Payne, Ancil Horace
Payne, Harry Vern
Payne, Rose M.
Payne, (Orville) Thomas
Payonzeck, John August
Payton-Wright, Pamela
Peacher, Douglas John
Peairs, Richard Hope
Pearce, Morton Lee
Pearce, Ronald William
Pearce, Roy Harvey
Pearl, George Clayton
Pearlman, David Samuel
Pearlman, Sholom
Pearson, Donald Stuart
Pearson, Gerald Leondus
Pearson, Paul Brown
Pearson, Ralph Gottfrid
Pecaro, George Joseph
Peccorini, Francisco Letona
Peck, Austin H.
Peck, Clair Leverett, Jr.
Peck, Girvan
Peck, Gregory
Peck, LeRoy Eugene
Peck, Paul Arthur
Peck, Templeton
Peckham, Donald Eugene
Peckham, Robert Francis
Pecsok, Robert Louis
Peden, Irene Carswell
Pedersen, John Richard
Pederson, Donald Oscar
Pedrick, Willard Hiram
Peek, Merl Bicknell
Peeler, Joseph David
Peeler, Stuart Thorne
Peerce, Larry
Peetz, John Edward
Peever, Arthur Jay
Pefley, Richard Kramer
Pegis, Anton George
Pelandini, Thomas Francis
Pelly, Francis Justinian
Pemberton, John de Jarnette, Jr.
Pence, Martin
Pendleton, Austin
Pendleton, Robert Cecil
Penn, Robert Marvin
Penneman, Robert Allen
Penner, Stanford Solomon
Pennington, Chester Arthur
Pennington, Weldon Jerry
Penrod, James Wilford
Penuelas, Marcelino Company
Penzien, Joseph
Penzl, Herbert
Peppard, George
Pereira, William L.
Perella, Nicholas James
Perenchio, Andrew Jerrold
Perkins, Anthony
Perkins, Carroll Mason
Perkins, David D(exeter)
Perkins, DeForest
Perkins, Henry Crawford
Perkins, Herbert Asa
Perkins, Thomas James
Perl, Martin Lewis
Perlberger, Martin
Perlman, Clifford Seeley
Perlman, David
Perloff, Marjorie Gabrielle
Perret, Joseph Aloysius
Perrin, Edward Burton
Perrine, Richard Leroy
Perrine, Valerie
Perry, Jacquelin
Perry, John Richard
Perry, Lee Rowan
Perry, Louis Barnes
Perry, Mervyn F.
Perry, Ralph Barton, III
Perry, Richard Van
Perry, Robert Michael
Perry, William James
Persoff, Nehemiah
Person, Evert Bertil
Person, Robert John
Person, Robert Tallman
Pescow, Donna Gail
Peter, Frank Alfred
Peter, Laurence Johnston
Peterfreund, Herbert
Peters, Brock
Peters, Lynn Herman
Peters, Max Stone
Peters, Mitchell Thomas
Peters, Richard Morse
Peters, Virginia
Peters, William Wesley
Petersen, Eugene Edward
Petersen, John Chresten
Petersen, Marshall Arthur
Petersen, Martin Eugene
Petersen, Robert E.
Petersen, Robert V.
Petersen, Roland
Petersen, Sidney R.
Peterson, Ben
Peterson, Ben Anton
Peterson, Charles Loren
Peterson, Chase N.
Peterson, Conrad Alyn
Peterson, Courtland Harry
Peterson, Edwin J.
Peterson, Evan Tye
Peterson, George Harold
Peterson, Harries-Clichy
Peterson, James Algert
Peterson, John Eric
Peterson, John Willard
Peterson, Laurence E(lmer)
Peterson, Maurice Lewellen
Peterson, Nad A.
Peterson, Oscar Emmanuel
Peterson, Paul Ames
Peterson, Philip Everett
Peterson, Raymond MacDonald
Peterson, Richard Hamlin
Peterson, Robert Lewis
Peterson, Robin Tucker
Peterson, Roderick William
Peterson, Rodney Delos
Peterson, Rudolph A.
Peticolas, Warner Leland
Petrie, Daniel Mannix
Petrone, Rocco A.
Petry, Ray C.
Petterson, Donald K.
Pettigrew, Thomas Fraser
Pettis, Shirley Neil
Pettit, Lawrence Kay
Pettit, Thomas Henry
Pettitt, Roger Carlyle
Petty, Thomas Lee
Petzoldt, Paul Kiesow
Péwé, Troy Lewis
Peyton, Patrick Joseph
Peyton, Wesley Grant, Jr.
Pfaelzer, Mariana R.
Pfau, George Harold, Jr.
Pfau, John M(artin)
Pfeffer, J. Alan
Pfeiffer, John Stephen
Pfeiffer, John William
Pfeiffer, Robert John
Pfister, Alfred John
Pfnister, Allan Orel
Phalen, Francis Thomas
Phelan, Gladys Kathryn
Phelps, Mason
Phelps, Orme Wheelock
Phemister, Robert David
Phibbs, Harry Albert
Phibbs, Philip Monford
Philbrick, Ralph N.
Philip, Cornelius Becker
Philip, William Warren
Philipp, Robert Bernard
Philips, Irving
Phillippi, Edward Franklin
Phillips, Bernard (Barney)
Phillips, Edwin Allen
Phillips, Gifford
Phillips, James Emerson, Jr.
Phillips, Jeanne Shirley
Phillips, John Gardner
Phillips, John Pierson
Phillips, John Richard
Phillips, Josef Clayton
Phillips, Julia
Phillips, Michael Steven
Phillips, Norman Edgar
Phillips, Paul David
Phillips, Ralph Saul
Phillips, Randall Clinger
Phillips, Theodore Locke
Phillips, Thomas Porter
Phillips, Wallace Watts, Jr.
Phillips, William George
Phinney, Hartley Keith, Jr.
Phipps, Allan Rogers
Phipps, Gerald H.
Phister, Montgomery, Jr.
Phleger, Atherton Macondray
Phleger, Herman
Picard, Meredith Dane
Picchioni, Albert Louis
Pickens, Alexander Legrand
Pickens, Slim (Louis Bert Lindley, Jr.)
Pickerell, Albert George
Pickering, William Hayward
Pickett, Morris John
Pierce, Bruce John
Pierce, Gordon Barry
Pierce, John (Jack) B. L.
Pierce, John Grissim
Pierce, Thomas Hughes
Pierno, Anthony Robert
Pierotti, Roland
Pierson, Albert Chadwick
Pierson, Frank Romer
Pietsch, Charles Joseph, Jr.
Piette, Lawrence Hector
Pigford, Thomas Harrington
Pigott, Charles McGee
Pike, Frederick Ernest
Pike, Nelson
Pike, Thomas Potter
Pilch, Judah
Pilcher, George William
Pilla, Felix Mario
Pilz, Dale Francis
Pimentel, George Claude
Pinkerman, John Horton
Pinkerton, Clayton David
Pinkney, David Henry
Pinnell, George Lewis
Pinney, Edmund
Pinola, Joseph John
Pinsky, Robert Neal
Pinson, William Meredith, Jr.
Pintoff, Ernest
Pipal, George Henry
Pirofsky, Bernard
Pischel, Dohrmann Kaspar
Pister, Karl Stark
Pitcher, Tom Stephen
Pitelka, Frank Alois
Pitlik, Noam
Pitt, Carl Allen
Pitt, Paul Arthur
Pittendrigh, Colin Stephenson
Pitzer, Kenneth S.
Place, John Bassett Moore
Place, Mary Kay
Plane, Donald Ray
Plant, Forrest Albert
Platt, Donald Hewitt
Platt, Joseph Beaven
Platt, Kenneth Allan
Pleasence, Donald
Pleshette, Eugene
Pleshette, Suzanne
Plott, Charles R.
Plowman, Boyd Rex
Plugge, Wilfred Robert
Plumly, Stanley Ross
Plummer, Christopher
Plummer, Raymond Eugene
Plunkett, James William, Jr.
Plusk, Ronald Frank
Pocker, Yeshayau
Poe, Jerry B.
Poettmann, Fred Heinz
Poindexter, William Mersereau
Pois, Robert August
Poitier, Sidney
Polak, Elijah
Polan, Morris
Poland, Burdette Crawford
Polanski, Roman
Policoff, Leonard David
Polin, Albert Terrence
Politzer, Hugh David
Pollack, Gerald Harvey
Pollack, Sydney
Pollard, Desmond Laurence
Pollard, Henry
Pollard, William Sherman, Jr.
Pollock, James Valiant
Pollock, John Phleger
Polonis, Douglas Hugh
Polsby, Nelson Woolf
Pomeroy, Earl
Pomeroy, Wardell Baxter
Pomraning, Gerald Carlton
Pond, Calvin Parker
Ponder, Herman
Ponty, Jean-Luc
Poole, Cecil Avery
Poole, Cecil F.
Pope, Alexander H.
Pope, Bill Jordan
Popelka, Robert Joseph
Popják, George Joseph
Popov, Egor Paul
Poppa, Ryal Robert
Porcello, Leonard Joseph
Port, Sidney Charles
Porter, Blaine Robert Milton
Porter, Eliot Furness
Porter, Jack Easton
Porter, Julian Donald
Porter, Keith Roberts
Porter, Paul Berggren
Porter, Vernon L.
Portis, Alan Mark
Portnoff, Collice Henry
Posin, Daniel Q.
Post, Richard Freeman
Post, Ted
Postl, Anton
Postman, Leo Joseph
Poston, Tom
Postyn, Sol

Potter, Karl Harrington
Potthoff, Carl John
Potts, Erwin Rea
Pough, Frederick Harvey
Poulson, Robert Dean
Poulton, Charles Edgar
Pound, Glenn Simpson
Pound, Guy Marshall
Powell, Clinton Cobb
Powell, Colin Luther
Powell, Earl Alexander, III
Powell, George Van Tuyl
Powell, Jane (Suzanne Burce)
Powell, Philip Wayne
Powell, Randolph Marlin
Powell, Ray Bedenkapp
Powell, Stanley, Jr.
Powelson, John Palen
Power, Cornelius Michael
Power, Dennis Michael
Power, Jules
Power, Robert Harbison
Powers, David Price
Powers, Mala
Powers, Richard Ralph
Powers, William Shotwell
Prakash, Ravi
Prasad, Jagdish
Pratt, Charles Anderson
Pratt, Charles Dudley, Jr.
Pratt, Lawrence Arthur
Pratt, Matthew
Prausnitz, John Michael
Pregerson, Harry
Prehm, Herbert John
Preiser, Wolfgang Friedrich Ernst
Prelock, Edward Patrick
Prescott, David Marshall
Prescott, Norm
Present, Arthur Jerome
Press, Edward
Pressly, Thomas James
Prestele, Joseph Alan
Prestini, James Libero
Preston, Billy
Preston, David Bemis
Preston, Frederick Willard
Preston, George W., III
Previn, Dory Langan
Price, Frank
Price, Harrison Alan
Price, Karl S.
Price, Keith Murray
Price, Max
Price, Paul Buford
Price, Paxton (Pate)
Price, Roger Taylor
Price, Vincent
Price, Willis Joseph
Pricher, Lawrence Stadon, Jr.
Prideaux, Thomas Stephen
Prim, Wayne LaVerne
Prince, David Allan
Principal, Victoria
Prine, Andrew Louis
Prine, John
Pringle, Edward E.
Pringle, Henry Hudson
Prins, David
Prinster, John Howard
Priola, Donald Victor
Pritchard, Ross Joseph
Pritchard, William Roy
Pritchett, Charles Herman
Pritikin, Nathan
Pritzlaff, John Charles, Jr.
Privat, Jeannette Mary
Proctor, Harvey Albert
Proctor, Robert Swope
Pronzini, Bill (William) John
Prosterman, Roy L.
Prout, Ralph Eugene
Provost, Donald Edgar
Prowse, Juliet
Proyect, Martin H.
Prudhomme, Harry P
Prugh, Dane Gaskill
Prugh, George Shipley
Prunty, Bert Sherman, Jr.
Prusmack, John Jacob
Pryne, Phillip Donald
Pryor, Hubert
Pryor, Richard
Pucciani, Oreste Francesco
Puck, Theodore Thomas
Puckett, Allen Emerson
Pudney, Gary Laurence
Pugh, David Arthur
Pugnetti, Donald Anton
Puhvel, Jaan
Pundsack, Fred Leigh
Purcell, Kenneth
Purcell, Robert Laughlin
Purim, Flora
Purkiser, Westlake Taylor
Purl, O. Thomas
Purpura, Dominick Paul
Pursell, Carroll Wirth
Purves, William Kirkwood
Pusateri, C. Joseph
Putnam, Frederick Warren, Jr.
Putnam, George Endicott, Jr.
Putter, Irving
Pyle, Denver
Pyle, Kenneth Birger
Quackenbush, Justin Lowe
Quadt, Raymond Adolph
Quaid, Dennis William
Quaid, Randy
Quall, Alvin Bertrand
Qualley, Charles Albert
Quaresma, Edward Anthony
Quate, Calvin Forrest
Quiat, Gerald M.
Quilligan, Edward James
Quimby, George Irving
Quinn, Anthony Rudolph Oaxaca
Quinn, Francis A.
Quinn, Hugh Joseph
Quinn, John R.
Quinn, Joseph R.
Quinn, Brother Thomas Michael (Thomas Leo Quinn, Jr.)
Quinn, Wesley Marion
Quinn, William Francis
Quinn, William George
Quinsler, William Thomson
Raaf, John Elbert
Rabbitt, Edward Thomas
Rabineau, Louis
Rabinovitch, Benton Seymour
Rabinovitz, Jason
Rabinowitz, Jay Andrew
Rabinowitz, Jesse Charles
Raciti, Cherie
Radford, Wesley E.
Radock, Michael
Rae, Matthew Sanderson, Jr.
Rafelson, Bob
Raffael, Joseph
Raffin, Bennett Lyon
Rafton, Michael George
Ragent, Boris
Raggio, William John
Ragland, Jack Whitney
Ragosine, Victor Eugene
Rahimtoola, Shahbudin Hooseinally
Rahmig, William Conrad
Rainey, Charles Peter, Jr.
Rainis, Richard David
Raitt, Bonnie
Raitt, John Emmet
Ralls, Katherine
Ralston, Henry James, III
Ramadan, Paul Rafiq
Ramadanoff, David Dimitri
Ramage, Colin Stokes
Rambeck, LeRoy (Roy) Stanley
Ramer, Lawrence Jerome
Ramirez, Raul Anthony
Ramo, Simon
Ramsdell, Vittz-James
Ramsey, David Goggin
Rand, Robert Wheeler
Randall, William B.
Randolph, Carl Lowell
Randolph, John
Randolph, Thomas Frederick
Randolph, William Devine
Rangell, Leo
Rankin, Robert
Rankin, Robert Avran Michael
Ranney, Helen Margaret
Ransohoff, Martin
Ransom, Edward Duane
Ransom, William Michael
Rapaport, Samuel I.
Rapaport, Walter
Raper, John F., Jr.
Rapf, Matthew Wallace
Rasi, Humberto Mario
Raskin, Michael A.
Rasmuson, Elmer Edwin
Rasmussen, Aaron Frederick
Rasmussen, John Oscar, Jr.
Rasmussen, Leonard Elton
Rasmussen, Lyman Merrill
Rasmussen, Phipps Louis
Rathbun, John Wilbert
Rather, Lelland Joseph
Rattray, Maurice, Jr.
Rauch, Irmengard
Rauch, John Harold
Rauch, Lawrence Lee
Raulinaitis, Pranas Algis
Rautenstraus, Roland Curt
Raven, Robert Dunbar
Raventos, Antolin
Ravesies, Paul
Rawls, Lou
Rawls, Roy Martin
Rawson, Rulon Wells
Ray, Charles Kendall
Ray, Dixy Lee
Ray, Reid Hackett
Rayburn, George Marvin
Raye, Martha (Maggie Yvonne O'Reed)
Raymond, Gene
Raymond, Guy
Rea, Paul V.
Read, William Merritt
Reagan, Michael Daniel
Real, Manuel Lawrence
Ream, Norman Jacob
Reaney, Gilbert
Reardon, John
Reasons, George Hubert
Reay, Donald Patterson
Rebennack, Malcom John Michael Creaux, Jr. (Dr. John)
Rechard, Ottis William
Rechtin, Eberhardt
Rector, Floyd Clinton, Jr.
Rector, Richard Robert
Rector, Robert Wayman
Redden, James Anthony
Reddy, Helen
Redeker, Allan Grant
Redfield, Peter Scranton
Redgrave, Lynn
Redheffer, Raymond Moos
Rediess, Herman Arthur
Redig, Dale Francis
Redman, Dewey
Reed, Clarence C.
Reed, David Andrew
Reed, Doel
Reed, Donna
Reed, Eugene D.
Reed, Gregory William
Reed, H. Carlyle
Reed, H(orace) Curtis
Reed, Ishmael Scott
Reed, Kenneth G.
Reed, Richard John
Reed, Robert Daniel
Reed, Roy Marvin
Reed, Thomas Care
Reed, Wallace Allison
Reed, William Garrard
Rees, Rees Bynon
Reese, Della (Delloreese Patricia Early)
Reeve, Christopher
Reeve, George Washington
Reeves, Albert Lee
Reeves, Barbara Ann
Reeves, Robert Lloyd
Reeves, William Carlisle
Regensburg, Anthony Shepard
Rehder, Robert Richard
Rehfeld, Robert William
Rehme, Robert G.
Reich, Kenneth Irvin
Reich, Peter Maria
Reichek, Jesse
Reichert, Kurt
Reichler, Robert Jay
Reichman, Fredrick Thomas
Reid, Daniel Peter
Reid, Kate
Reid, Spencer Beal
Reif, Frederick
Reilly, Charles Nelson
Reilly, Philip Joseph
Reiner, Bernard Benjamin
Reiner, Carl
Reiner, Rob
Reines, Frederick
Reinhardt, Stephen Roy
Reinhardt, William Oscar
Reinhardt, William Parker
Reinwald, Arthur Burton
Reiss, Alvin
Reiss, Howard
Remer, Vernon Ralph
Remington, Jack Samuel
Remington, Paul Ellsworth
Rempel, Averno Milton
Remsen, Herbert B.
Rencher, Ronald L.
Renda, Dominic Phillip
Rendell-Baker, Leslie
Renehan, Robert Francis Xavier
Renfrew, Charles Byron
Renfrew, Malcolm MacKenzie
Rensch, Joseph Romaine
Rentschler, Frederick Brant
Renwick, Edward Shield
Renzetti, Attilio David
Repass, John Lawrence
Reres, Mary Epiphany
Reshetar, John Stephen, Jr.
Resko, John Allen
Resnikoff, George Joseph
Reuler, Maurice
Reuther, Ronald Theodore
Revel, John Chase
Revelle, Keith
Rewak, William John
Rexroth, Kenneth
Reynolds, Burt
Reynolds, Collins James, III
Reynolds, Donald Worthington
Reynolds, Frank Edward
Reynolds, Gardner Mead
Reynolds, Gene
Reynolds, Harry Lincoln
Reynolds, Jack
Reynolds, John Hamilton
Reynolds, William Craig
Reynolds, William Harold
Rhodes, Willard
Riasanovsky, Nicholas Valentine
Rice, Denis Timlin
Rice, Donald Blessing, Jr.
Rice, Edward Earl
Rice, Gene Edward
Rice, Kingsley Loring, Jr.
Rice, Lawrence Harvey
Rice, Philip Joseph, Jr.
Rice, Robert Maurice
Rice, Stanley Travis, Jr.
Rich, Alan
Rich, Frances Luther
Rich, John
Rich, Lee
Richards, Gale Lee
Richards, Herbert East
Richards, John Hall
Richards, Linden Jay
Richards, Lisle Frederick
Richards, Norman Blanchard
Richards, Paul Linford
Richards, Richard Kohn
Richards, Victor
Richardson, Frank Kellogg
Richardson, Harold Beland
Richardson, John Hamilton
Richardson, John Pratt
Richardson, L. Janette
Richardson, Robert Dale, Jr.
Richardson, Samuel Matthew
Richardson, William Chase
Richardson, William Shaw
Richey, Mary Anne Reimann
Richey, Phil Horace
Richley, Robert
Richman, Peter Mark
Richter, Burton
Richter, Charles Francis
Richter, George Robert, Jr.
Rick, Charles Madeira, Jr.
Rickard, Corwin Lloyd
Ricketson, Frank Henry, Jr.
Rickles, Don
Riddel, Joseph Neill
Riddell, James Gilmour
Riddell, Richard Harry
Ridder, Bernard J.
Ridder, Daniel Hickey
Ridder, Joseph Bernard
Ridder, Paul Anthony
Riddles, James Arnold
Rider, Morrette LeRoy
Ridge, Martin
Ridgley, Robert Louis
Ridker, Norman Lee
Riedel, Donald Carl
Rieke, William Betten
Rieke, William Oliver
Rienzi, Thomas Matthew Michael
Ries, Jane Silverstein
Riggs, Donald Eugene
Riggs, James Lear
Riggs, Robert Edwon
Riggs, Robert Larimore
Riker, William Kay
Riles, Wilson Camanza
Riley, Conrad Milton
Riley, Jack
Riley, Terry
Rimoin, David Lawrence
Riney, Hal Patrick
Ringkjob, Erik Tuxen
Rintels, David W.
Riordan, William F.
Ris, William Krakow
Risman, Michael
Ritcheson, Charles Ray
Ritchey, Samuel Donley, Jr.
Ritchie, Michael Brunswick
Ritt, Martin
Rittenhouse, Franklin Pierce Ross
Ritter, John (Johnathan Southworth)
Ritz, Dennis Walter
Rivera, Tomás
Rivera, Victor Manuel
Rivers, Joan
Rivers, William Lawrence
Rivkin, Allen
Roach, Barrett Browning
Roach, William Russell
Roane, Donald Patterson
Roark, James Joseph
Robb, John Donald
Robb, John Wesley
Robbins, Billy Alvin
Roberti, Mario Andrew
Roberts, Arthur
Roberts, Bradley House
Roberts, Doris
Roberts, Ernest Roth
Roberts, George Adam
Roberts, George Rosenberg
Roberts, Jack Earle
Roberts, James McGregor
Roberts, John D.
Roberts, Justin
Roberts, Lorin Watson
Roberts, Neil Fletcher
Roberts, Pernell
Roberts, Sidney
Roberts, Stephen
Roberts, Walter Herbert Beatty
Roberts, Walter Orr
Robertson, Armand James, II
Robertson, Gregg W.
Robertson, Jaime Robbie
Robertson, Lawrence Vernon, Jr.
Robertson, Paul Kenneth
Robertson, William Osborne
Robin, Eugene Debs
Robins, John Samuel
Robinson, Clark Shove
Robinson, Daniel Thomas
Robinson, Earl Hawley
Robinson, Frank
Robinson, Gwynn Herndon
Robinson, Hamilton Burrows Greaves
Robinson, Herbert William
Robinson, John Alexander
Robinson, John Minor
Robinson, Len (Truck)
Robinson, Mark Parker
Robinson, Martha Stewart
Robinson, Robert Blacque
Robinson, S. Monte
Robinson, William Franklin
Robison, Paul Frederick
Robkin, Maurice Abraham
Rochette, Edward Charles
Rock, Arthur
Rockefeller, W.C.
Rockoff, Neil Frederick
Rockrise, George Thomas
Rockwell, Alvin John
Rockwell, Bruce McKee
Rockwell, James Mitchell
Rodda, Peter Ulisse
Roddenberry, Eugene Wesley (Gene)
Roddey, Otha Charles
Roddis, Richard Stiles Law
Rodgers, John Barney
Rodgers, Robert Leroy
Rodman, Harry Eugene
Rodnick, Eliot Herman
Rodrigues, Percy
Rodriguez, Jaime Edmundo
Roe, Benson Bertheau
Roe, Charles Richard
Roedel, Philip Morgan
Roehl, Joseph E.
Roemer, Elizabeth
Roemer, Milton Irwin
Roesgen, William Newell
Rogers, Carl Ransom
Rogers, Conway Reid
Rogers, Dale Evans (Frances Octavia Smith)
Rogers, Ginger (Virginia Katherine McMath)
Rogers, Kenneth Ray
Rogers, Lawrence S.
Rogers, Robert Nicholas
Rogers, Robert William
Rogers, Robison Max
Rogers, Rosemary
Rogers, Roy
Rogers, Wayne
Rogger, Hans Jack
Rogliano, Aldo Thomas
Rohr, Ignatius Robert
Roker, Roxie
Roland, Gilbert
Rolle, Andrew F.
Roman, Herschel Lewis
Roman, Lawrence
Romberg, Paul F(rederick)
Rome, Bernard
Romeo, Luigi
Romine, Joanne Barbara
Romney, Marion George
Ronstadt, Linda Maria
Rood, James Leslie, Jr.
Rooney, Mickey (Joe Yule, Jr.)
Roos, Frederick Ried
Roosevelt, James
Roosevelt, Nicholas
Root, William Pitt
Rosaldo, Renato Ignacio
Rosberg, Carl Gustaf
Rosch, Stanley
Roscia, John J.
Roscoe, Stanley Nelson
Rose, Christopher Walcott
Rose, Mark Allen
Rose, Mason H., IV
Rose, Reva
Rose, Robert Leonard
Rose, Robert R., Jr.
Rose, Sidney Rudolph
Rose, William
Rose Marie
Rosen, James Mahlon
Rosen, Jerome
Rosen, Louis
Rosen, Ronald Stanley
Rosen, Stuart Martin
Rosenbaum, Edward E.
Rosenberg, Allen Leon
Rosenberg, Arthur James
Rosenberg, Barr Marvin
Rosenberg, Claude Newman, Jr.
Rosenberg, Richard Morris
Rosenberg, Saul Allen
Rosenberg, Stuart
Rosenberger, Carol
Rosenblatt, Paul
Rosencrans, Evan William
Rosenfelt, Frank Edward
Rosenheim, Donald Edwin
Rosenlicht, Maxwell Alexander
Rosenthal, Albert Harold
Rosenthal, Jack
Rosenthal, Joseph Aaron
Rosenthal, Julian Bernard
Rosenzweig, Mark Richard
Rosenzweig, Richard Stuart
Rosenzweig, Robert Myron
Rosett, Arthur Irwin
Roshkind, Michael
Roshko, Anatol
Rosky, Burton Seymour
Rosoff, Leonard
Ross, Diana
Ross, Floyd Hiatt
Ross, German Reed
Ross, Glynn
Ross, Herbert David
Ross, John, Jr.
Ross, John Raymond
Ross, Joseph Foster
Ross, Katharine
Ross, Marion
Ross, Michael
Ross, Russell
Ross, Stanley Ralph
Ross, Thurston Howard
Rossano, August Thomas
Rosser, James Milton
Rossi, Mario Alexander
Rossman, Ruth Scharff
Rosten, Irwin
Rostron, Robert Zeldon
Rostvold, Gerhard Norman
Roth, Edward Stanford
Roth, Henry
Roth, Henry Logan
Roth, William Matson
Rothell, George Edwin
Rothenberg, Jerome (Dennis)
Rothenberg, Leslie Steven
Rother, George Ulrich
Rothman, Stephanie
Rothschild, August Barnet
Rothschild, Loren Robert
Rothstein, Barbara Jacobs
Rotter, Paul Talbott
Rounds, Donald Edwin
Roundtree, Richard
Rouse, George E.
Rouse, Richard Hunter
Roush, David P.
Rouss, Ruth
Rousselot, John Harbin
Rovira, Luis Dario
Rowe, David Nelson
Rowe, Galen Otto
Rowe, John Howland
Rowe, Verald Keith
Rowe, William John
Rowinski, Ludwig Joseph
Rowland, Frank Sherwood
Rowland, Ivan Wendell
Rowlands, Gena
Roy, Radha Raman
Royden, Halsey Lawrence
Royer, Bill
Royer, Charles Theodore
Rozett, Walter Philip
Rubel, David Michael
Rubenstein, Edward
Rubin, Edward
Rubin, Harry
Rubin, Stanley Creamer
Rubinstein, John Arthur
Rubinstein, Moshe Fajwel
Rubright, Royal Cushing
Rucci, Eustine Paul
Ruckelshaus, William Doyle
Rucker, Winfred Ray
Ruder, Melvin Harvey
Rudhyar, Dane
Rudisill, Richard
Rudnick, Isadore
Rudolph, Abraham Morris
Rudolph, Richard Casper
Rudolph, Wallace Morton
Ruesch, Jurgen
Rufe, Redding Kane
Ruff, Howard Joseph
Ruffin, Roger Sherman
Ruge, Neil Marshall
Ruhlman, Terrell Louis
Ruibal, Rodolfo
Ruiz, Manuel, Jr.
Ruiz, Ramon Eduardo
Rummel, Robert Wiland
Rumsey, Victor Henry
Runge, Thomas Carl
Rupp, John Norris
Rusack, Robert Claflin
Ruscha, Edward
Rush, Alvin
Rush, Andrew Wilson
Rush, Donald Eugene
Rush, Herman E.
Rush, Richard
Rushmer, Robert Frazer
Rushworth, Robert Aitken
Rusk, David Patrick
Ruskin, Joseph Richard
Rusnell, Wesley Allen
Russ, Joanna
Russell, Charles Roberts
Russell, David Allison
Russell, Findlay Ewing
Russell, Francia
Russell, Jeffrey Burton
Russell, Ken
Russell, Kurt Von Vogel
Russell, Leon
Russell, R. Dana
Russell, Ray
Russell, William Fraser
Russin, Robert Isaiah
Russo, Joseph Frank
Rust, Clinton Albert
Rust, William Charles
Rutland, George Patrick
Rutledge, Gene Preston
Rutledge, John
Rutten, Timothy Calder
Ruttenberg, Joseph
Rutter, Marshall Anthony
Rutter, William J.
Ruvolo, Felix
Ryan, Arthur Norman
Ryan, James Edwin
Ryan, Martin Frederick
Ryan, Patrick Michael
Ryan, Stephen Joseph, Jr.
Ryan, William Joseph
Ryberg, H(erman) Theodore
Rydell, Mark
Ryder, Thomas O'Neal
Ryker, Charles Edwin
Ryland, Glen Leroy
Ryles, Gerald Fay
Ryser, Herbert John
Ryskind, Morrie
Saar, Betye (Irene)
Sabeck, Robert V.
Sabersky, Rolf Heinrich
Sabes, Harold
Sabharwal, Ranjit Singh
Sabins, Rolland Clifford
Sabloff, Jeremy Arac
Sachs, Bernice Cohen (Mrs. Allan Eli Sachs)
Sack, Ronald Lawrence
Sackett, Roger Winslow
Sacksteder, Frederick Henry
Sacksteder, William
Sackton, Frank Joseph
Sadis, Jerry
Sadler, Carl L.
Sadler, George Marion
Saenger, Theodore Jerome
Saffman, Philip G.
Sagawa, Yoneo
Sagness, Richard Lee
Sago, Paul Edward
Saint, Eva Marie
St.-Amand, Pierre
St. George, William Ross
St. Jacques, Raymond
Saint James, Susan
St. John, Jill

St. John, Sheldon Curtis
St. Johns, Richard Rogers
Sakurai, Jun John
Salah, Albert Anton
Salisbury, Douglas Lee
Salisbury, Frank Boyer
Salk, Jonas Edward
Salkin, David
Salkind, Milton
Salla, Salvatore
Saloutos, Theodore
Saltman, Paul David
Saltzman, Joseph
Saltzman, Philip
Salvatierra, Oscar, Jr.
Salveson, Melvin Erwin
Salzer, John M.
Salzman, David Elliot
Samilson, Robert Leblang
Sammons, Francis Edward, Jr.
Sample, Joseph Scanlon
Sampson, Roger Lee
Samson, Alvin
Sanazaro, Paul Joseph
Sanchez, Francisco Demetrio, Jr.
Sanchez, Robert Fortune
Sandage, Allan Rex
Sandberg, Robert Alexis
Sanders, Charles Franklin
Sanders, Daniel Selvarajah
Sanders, Fred Joseph
Sanders, Geoffrey Peter
Sanders, James Alvin
Sanders, John R.
Sanders, Joseph Stanley
Sanders, Richard Kinard
Sanders, Walter Jeremiah, III
Sanders, William George
Sandgren, Clyde Dahlman
Sandler, Herbert M.
Sandler, Marion Osher
Sandlin, Richard Mancel
Sandrich, Jay H.
Sands, Lester Bruton
Sands, Matthew Linzee
Sandy, Gary
Saner, Reginald Anthony
Sanford, Isabel Gwendolyn
Sanford, Nevitt
Sannwald, William Walter
Santana, Carlos
Santi, Maurice John
Santo, Henry Eugene
Santos, Joe
Saperstein, Henry Gahagan
Sappington, Lee Edward
Sarafian, Armen
Sarason, Irwin Gerald
Sargent, Dick
Sargent, Joseph Daniel
Sargent, Wallace Leslie William
Sargent, Wayne Cummings
Sargis, Joseph Eugene
Sarkisian, Paul
Sarkowsky, Herman
Sarnat, Bernard George
Sarnoff, Thomas Warren
Sarpkaya, Turgut
Sasaki, Robert Tasuku
Saslow, George
Sassoon, Vidal
Sato, Eunice Noda
Sato, Robert Yoichi
Sato, Tadashi
Satre, Wendell Julian
Sauer, Jonathan Deininger
Sauer, Kenneth
Sauer, Ralph Charles
Sauerbrey, Barbara Anne
Saul, John Woodruff, III
Saul, Peter
Saunders, Raymond Jennings
Saunders, Russell Joseph
Saunders, Sam Cundiff
Saunders, William Lockwood
Savage, Charles Francis
Savage, Edward Warren, Jr.
Savalas, Telly Aristoteles
Savoy, Douglas Eugene
Savoy, James C.
Sawiris, Milad Youssef
Sawyer, Charles Henry
Sawyer, Ed Curtis
Saxberg, Borje Osvald
Saxon, David Stephen
Sayers, George
Sayre, Robert H.
Scaggs, William Royce (Boz)
Scala, James
Scalapino, Robert Anthony
Scandling, William Fredric
Scanga, Italo
Scanlan, John J.
Scardina, Frank Joseph
Schaaf, Samuel Albert
Schaal, Richard Victor
Schaber, Gordon Duane
Schacher, John Fredrick
Schachman, Howard Kapnek
Schacht, Henry Mevis
Schaefer, Carl George Lewis
Schaefer, George Louis
Schaefer, Jack Warner
Schaefer, John Paul
Schaefer, W(illiam) Stanley
Schafer, Edward Hetzel
Schafer, Eldon (Guy)
Schaffner, Franklin James
Schaffner, Marlowe Harlan
Schaie, Klaus Warner
Schaller, Jane Green
Schallert, William Joseph
Schanes, Steven Eli
Scharfe, Hartmut Ewald Fritz
Scharffenberger, George Thomas
Schatz, Irwin Jacob
Schaugaard, Gary Lee
Schaumberg, William Lloyd
Schawlow, Arthur Leonard
Scheer, Carl
Scheerer, Robert Joseph
Scheibel, Arnold Bernard
Scheid, Vernon Edward
Scheidel, Thomas Maynard
Scheider, Roy Richard
Scheifly, John Edward
Scheimer, Louis
Schepman, Berne Adair
Scher, Allen Myron
Scheuer, Paul Josef
Schiller, Herbert I.
Schiller, Lawrence Julian
Schiller, Robert (Bob) Achille
Schilling, John Albert
Schimke, Robert Tod
Schimmel, S. Arthur
Schine, Gerard David
Schirmer, Howard August, Jr.
Schirra, Walter Marty, Jr.
Schlanger, Seymour Oscar
Schlegel, David Edward
Schleifer, Stephen
Schlein, Peter Eli
Schlesinger, Rudolf Berthold
Schmeckpeper, Charles Eugene
Schmid, Rudi Rudolf
Schmidhauser, John Richard
Schmidt, Chauncey Everett
Schmidt, Cyril James
Schmidt, David Gordon
Schmidt, Fred Henry
Schmidt, James Craig
Schmidt, Maarten
Schmidt, Robert A.
Schmidt, William Henry, Jr.
Schmit, Lucien André, Jr.
Schmit, Timothy Bruce
Schmitz, Dennis Mathew
Schmutz, Arthur Walter
Schnacke, Robert Howard
Schnaitter, Allene Flora
Schneck, Stuart Austin
Schneider, Arthur Paul
Schneider, Carl Glendon
Schneider, Charles I.
Schneider, David
Schneider, Herbert William
Schneider, Raymond Clinton
Schneider, Stephen Henry
Schnitzer, Leonard Elliott
Schoeck, Richard Joseph
Schoen, Max Howard
Schoendorf, Walter John
Schoener, Jason
Schoenfeld, Walter Edwin
Schoettger, Theodore Leo
Scholder, Fritz
Schomaker, Verner
Schooley, Elmer Wayne
Schopf, James William
Schorling, Horace Oren
Schorr, Alan Edward
Schort, Donald Reece, Jr.
Schottland, Charles Irwin
Schoultz, Robert Francis
Schrader, Harry Christian, Jr.
Schrader, Paul
Schrag, Peter
Schreiber, George Arthur
Schrier, Robert William
Schrock, Virgil Edwin
Schroeder, Mary Murphy
Schroeder, Walter Phelps
Schrum, Marion Margaret
Schubert, Glendon
Schubert, Paul Ervin
Schuck, Carl J.
Schuele, Carl L.
Schuller, Brice Willis
Schuller, Robert Harold
Schulman, Samuel
Schulte, William Dallas
Schultz, Michael
Schulze, Robert Oscar
Schumacher, Edward Walter
Schumm, Stanley Alfred
Schurman, Glenn August
Schutte, Charles Frederick
Schutz, John Adolph
Schutz, Richard Edward
Schuyler, Philip
Schuyler, Robert Len
Schwab, Joseph Jackson
Schwabe, Arthur David
Schwabe, Calvin Walter
Schwada, John
Schwadron, Abraham Abe
Schwartz, Donald
Schwartz, Douglas Wright
Schwartz, Edward J.
Schwartz, Herbert Charles
Schwartz, Leon
Schwartz, Melvin
Schwartz, Milton Lewis
Schwartz, Murray Louis
Schwartz, William Tanney
Schwarz, M. Roy
Schwarzer, William W
Schwegmann, Jack Carl
Schweickart, Russell L.
Schweikher, Paul
Schweppe, Alfred John
Schwinden, Ted
Schwinger, Julian
Scitovsky, Anne Aickelin
Scordelis, Alexander Costicas
Scorsese, Martin
Scott, Charles Ross
Scott, David R.
Scott, Donald Rector
Scott, Elizabeth Leonard
Scott, Frank Laurence
Scott, Franklin Daniel
Scott, Jack Alan
Scott, Kenneth Eugene
Scott, Lizabeth Virginia
Scott, Louis Edward
Scott, Martha Ellen
Scott, Michael Dennis
Scott, Robert Lane
Scott, Thomas Wright
Scott, Verne Harry
Scott, Walter Bruce
Scott, Walter Decker
Scott, William Richard
Scotti, Vito
Scripps, John P.
Scudder, Thayer
Seaborg, Glenn Theodore
Seabury, Paul
Seader, Junior DeVere
Seager, Daniel Albert
Seals, James
Seaman, Edwin
Searcy, Alan Winn
Searle, John Rogers
Sears, Robert Needham
Sears, Robert Richardson
Sears, William Rees
Sears, William Robert
Seaton, Lewis Hiram
Seawell, Donald Ray
Secunda, (Holland) Arthur
Sedgwick, Wallace Ernest
Seebass, Alfred Richard, III
Seed, Harry Bolton
Seegmiller, Jarvis Edwin
Seelenfreund, Alan
Seely, Lyman E.
Seeman, Melvin
Segal, D. Robert
Segal, Jack
Sege, Thomas Davis
Segelin, Bernard
Segrè, Emilio
Seib, Kenneth Allen
Seidenbaum, Art David
Seider, Harold
Seidlitz, George Richards
Seifert, Russell Jay
Seinfeld, John Hersh
Self, Edwin Forbes
Self, Kenneth W.
Seligman, Thomas Knowles
Seligson, Robert Allen
Sell, Wendell Burley
Seltzer, Leon Eugene
Seltzer, Leon Zee
Seltzer, Maryann Mauskopf
Selvin, Paul Phillip
Selz, Peter Howard
Selzer, Arthur
Selzer, Milton
Semel, Terry Steven
Semler, Dean Russell
Sensiper, Samuel
Seraphine, Danny Peter
Serisawa, Sueo
Serlis, Harry George
Serota, Herman Michael
Service, Elman Rogers
Sessler, Andrew M.
Sete, Bola (Djalma de Andrade)
Seth, Oliver
Setterberg, Carl
Severino, John C.
Sevier, Ernest Youle
Sevilla, Stanley
Seymour, Anne
Seymour, Jane
Seymour, Richard Kellogg
Sfreddo, Robert Louis
Shackelford, Barton Warren
Shackelford, Ted
Shadduck, Louise
Shafer, Joseph Ernest
Shafer, Robert Eugene
Shaffer, Richard James
Shaffer, Robert Nesbit
Shagan, Steve
Shahovskoy, John
Shaklee, Forrest Clell, Sr.
Shalkop, Robert Leroy
Shallenberger, Garvin Fletcher
Shames, Henry Joseph
Shanahan, Robert H.
Shanaman, Richard Lowell
Shane, Leonard
Shangraw, Clarence Frank
Shank, Russell
Shanks, Ann Zane
Shannon, Edfred L., Jr.
Shannon, James A.
Shannon, Melvin LeRoy
Shansby, John Gary
Shao, Otis Hung I
Shapell, Nathan
Shapiro, Howard Allen
Shapiro, Karl Jay
Shapiro, Mark Howard
Shapiro, Victor Lenard
Shapley, Lloyd Stowell
Sharif, Omar (born Michael Shalhoub)
Sharman, William
Sharpe, Dores Robinson
Sharpe, William Forsyth
Shastid, Jon Barton
Shatner, William
Shaughnessy, Daniel Robert, Jr.
Shavelson, Melville
Shaver, James Porter
Shaw, Arnold
Shaw, Artie
Shaw, George Robert
Shaw, Manford Avis
Shaw, Milton Clayton
Shaw, Richard
Shaw, Robert Nelson
Shaw, Stanford Jay
Shaw, William Vaughan
Shayne, Alan
Shea, Jack
Shea, James Gerard
Shea, John Martin, Jr.
Shea, William Francis, Sr.
Shearon, James Curtis
Shearouse, Henry Grady, Jr.
Sheats, Paul Henry
Shedd, Ben Alvin
Shedd, Milton C.
Sheehan, Joseph Green
Sheen, Jack Henry
Sheen, Martin (Ramon Estevez)
Shefelman, Harold S.
Sheffield, Gilbert (LeRoy)
Sheh, Robert Bardhyl
Sheinberg, Sidney Jay
Sheinfeld, David
Sheingold, Abraham
Sheinwold, Alfred
Sheldon, Charles Harvey
Sheldon, Richard Jay
Sheline, Glenn Elmer
Shell, Arthur (Art)
Shell, Billy Joe
Shelley, James LaMar
Shellhorn, Ruth Patricia
Shelton, Frank Harvey
Shelton, James Truesdall
Shelton, Mercel Joseph
Shelton, Richard Fottrell
Shelton, Turner Blair
Shenar, (Albert) Paul
Shenker, M(orris) Arthur, Jr.
Shenker, Morris Abraham
Shepard, Allan Guy
Shepard, Paul Howe
Shepard, Roger Newland
Shepard, Sam (Samuel Shepard Rogers)
Shepard, Thomas Hill
Shephard, Ronald William
Sheppard, Thomas Richard
Sheppard, William Jacob
Shepperson, Wilbur Stanley
Shera (Shapiro), Mark
Sherburne, James Wilson
Sherk, Kenneth John
Sherman, Edith Mary
Sherman, Howard
Sherman, John Clinton
Sherman, Lawrence M.
Sherman, Martin
Sherman, Richard Morton
Sherman, Robert Bernard
Sherman, Robert Jules
Sherman, Samuel S., Jr.
Shernoff, William M.
Sherriffs, Alex Carlton
Sherris, John Charles
Sherwin, Chalmers William
Sherwood, Donald
Sherwood, Richard Edwin
Shetterly, Robert Browne
Shettles, Landrum Brewer
Shields, Currin Vance
Shields, Robert
Shilling, Mayfield Raymond
Shimkin, Michael Boris
Shinefield, Henry Robert
Shipley, Kenneth Thomas
Shippey, David B.
Shire, David Lee
Shire, Talia Rose
Shirley, Michael James
Shirpser, Clara
Shneidman, Edwin S.
Shneour, Elie Alexis
Shnider, Sol Mervin
Shockley, Edward Julian
Shockley, William Bradford
Shoemaker, David Powell
Shoemaker, Eugene Merle
Shoemaker, Vaughn
Shoemaker, Willie (William Lee)
Shoen, Leonard Samuel
Shohet, Stephen Byron
Shor, George G., Jr.
Shor, Samuel Wendell Williston
Shore, Dinah (Frances Rose Shore)
Shore, James H(enry)
Shore, Samuel
Short, James Franklin, Jr.
Short, Robert Allen
Short, Robert Henry
Shorter, Wayne
Shott, Gerald Lee
Shreeve, Jean'ne Marie
Shreve, Ronald Lee
Shrodes, Caroline
Shrontz, Frank Anderson
Shropshire, Donald Gray
Shroyer, Frederick Benjamin
Shryock, Edwin Harold
Shubb, William B.
Shubert, Gustave Harry
Shuck, Emerson Clayton
Shugart, Howard Alan
Shuler, Kurt Egon
Shull, Harrison
Shulman, Irving
Shulman, Max
Shultz, George Pratt
Shumaker, Hugh Joseph
Shumway, Forrest Nelson
Shupe, John Wallace
Shurtleff, David Bertrand
Shurtliff, Marvin Karl
Shuster, Alvin
Shutan, Robert Harry
Shutler, Kenneth Eugene
Shwayder, King David
Siart, William Eric Baxter
Siatos, Thomas John
Sibley, William Austin
Siciliano, Rocco Carmine
Sickels, Robert Judd
Sicuro, Natale Anthony
Siddiqui, Wasim Ahmad
Siddoway, William Ralph
Sidjakov, Nicolas
Sidney, George
Sidwell, Robert William
Siebert, Charles Alan
Sieckmann, Everett Frederick
Siefermann, Valentine Andrew
Siegan, Bernard Herbert
Siegel, Alberta Engvall (Mrs. Sidney Siegel)
Siegel, Don
Siegel, Morris J.
Siegel, Sheldon C.
Siegman, Anthony Edward
Siegriest, Louis Lundy
Siemer, John William
Sievers, Allen Morris
Sigband, Norman Bruce
Sigler, William Franklin
Sikma, Jack
Sikula, Andrew Frank
Silbaugh, Preston Norwood
Silberman, Laurence Hirsch
Silberman, Lou Hackett
Silberman, Richard Theodore
Siler, Walter Orlando, Jr.
Sillars, Malcolm Osgood
Silliphant, Stirling Dale
Sills, Theodore Roosevelt
Silver, Henry K.
Silver, Howard Findlay
Silver, Joe
Silverberg, Charles D.
Silverberg, Robert
Silverman, Arnold
Silverman, Fred
Silverman, Frederic Noah
Silverman, Harold Irvin
Silverman, Jacob
Silverman, Lawrence F.
Silvers, Phil
Sime, Donald Rae
Simkin, Peter Anthony
Simmons, Daniel H.
Simmons, Forrest Wiemann
Simmons, Jean
Simmons, Norman Stanley
Simmons, Roy William
Simoens, Alvin Cosman
Simon, David Harold
Simon, Ernest Robert
Simon, Lee Will
Simon, Norton Winfred
Simon, William George
Simonds, John Edward
Simoni, John Peter
Simonsmeier, Larry Marvin
Simpson, David William
Simpson, George Gaylord
Simpson, O.J. (Orenthal James)
Simpson, Robert Leatham
Sims, Paul Kibler
Sinatra, Frank (Francis Albert Sinatra)
Sinay, Joseph
Singer, Kurt Deutsch
Singer, Margaret Thaler
Singer, S(eymour) J(onathan)
Singher, Martial
Singlaub, John Kirk
Singleton, Henry Earl
Sink, Charles Stanley
Sinsheimer, Robert Louis
Sipes, Donald
Siri, William Emil
Sirotkin, Phillip Leonard
Siscoe, George Leonard
Sisk, Daniel Arthur
Six, Robert Forman
Sixta, George
Sizemore, Herman Mason, Jr.
Sjostrand, Fritiof Stig
Sjostrom, George William
Skaff, Andrew Joseph
Skaggs, James Bonner
Skeen, Joseph Richard
Skelton, (Richard) Red
Skerritt, Thomas Roy
Skidmore, Rex Austin
Skilling, John Bower
Skinner, Carlton
Skinner, David Edward
Skinner, David Haven
Skinner, G(eorge) William
Skinner, Knute Rumsey
Skinner, Stanley Thayer
Skinsnes, Olaf Kristian
Sklar, George
Sklar, Richard Lawrence
Sklarek, Norma Merrick
Skogerboe, Gaylord Vincent
Skolsky, Sidney
Skopil, Otto Richard, Jr.
Skotheim, Robert Allen
Skurdahl, Dale Maynard
Skutch, Ira
Skylstad, William S.
Slade, Bernard Newbound
Slade, Hutton Davison
Slama, Murray Alfred
Slater, James Munro
Slater, Manning
Slatkin, Leonard
Slavenska, Mia
Slavitt, David Walton
Slayden, James Bragdon
Sleicher, Charles Albert
Sleisenger, Marvin Herbert
Slick, Grace Wing
Slipe, Walter James
Slivinsky, Cornell J.
Sloan, Lloyd Lawrence
Sloane, Robert Bruce
Sloane, Robert Bruce
Sloane, Robert Malcolm
Sloane, Thomas O.
Slocum, Ronald Arthur
Slonimsky, Nicolas
Sludikoff, Stanley Robert
Smales, Fred Benson
Small, Lawrence Farnsworth
Small, Milton Morris
Small, Roland E.
Smart, Charles Rich
Smart, Frederick Kellogg
Smart, William Buckwalter
Smathers, James Burton
Smedegaard, Norman H.
Smelser, Neil Joseph
Smelt, Ronald
Smiley, Robert W., Jr.
Smiley, Robert William
Smiley, Terah Leroy
Smith, Albert Charles
Smith, Andrew Vaughn
Smith, Arthur Henry
Smith, Arthur Mathews, Jr.
Smith, Ballard Flanders, Jr.
Smith, Barbara Barnard
Smith, Byron Owen
Smith, Carl Reginald (Reggie)
Smith, Cecil Howard, III
Smith, Chester Leo
Smith, Clifford Vaughn, Jr.
Smith, Dan Throop
Smith, Daniel Clayton
Smith, David Wayne
Smith, Dean Carlton
Smith, Delford Michael
Smith, Donald William
Smith, Doris Anita
Smith, Douglas Hill
Smith, Dwight Morrell
Smith, Earl William
Smith, Eldred Gee
Smith, Frederick Rutledge
Smith, G(odfrey) T(aylor)
Smith, George Foster
Smith, Gordon Paul
Smith, H. Pete
Smith, H. Russell
Smith, Hallett Darius
Smith, Herbert Bonnewell
Smith, Hobart Muir
Smith, Jack Clifford
Smith, James Lewis
Smith, Joe Mauk
Smith, Joel Pritchard
Smith, John Grady, Jr.
Smith, Joseph Benjamin
Smith, Kate (Kathryn Elizabeth)
Smith, Kenneth Acton
Smith, Leo Gilbert
Smith, Leslie Clark
Smith, Leslie Roper
Smith, Lester Martin
Smith, Lloyd Hollingsworth
Smith, Lloyd Preston
Smith, M(ahlon) Brewster
Smith, Maurice Edward
Smith, Moishe
Smith, Monroe G.
Smith, Mortimer Brewster
Smith, Nathan James
Smith, Nels Jensen
Smith, Orville Auverne
Smith, Paul, Jr.
Smith, Paul Lynge
Smith, Paul Samuel
Smith, Ralph Carlisle
Smith, Ralph Judson
Smith, Ray Fred
Smith, Reuben William, III
Smith, Robert Alan
Smith, Robert Bruce
Smith, Robert Bruce
Smith, Robert Gray
Smith, Robert Harold
Smith, Robert Howard
Smith, Robert John
Smith, Robert Junius
Smith, Robert London
Smith, Robert Nelson
Smith, Robert W. (Wolfman Jack)
Smith, Roberts Angus
Smith, Ross Wilbert
Smith, Russell Evans
Smith, Samuel David
Smith, Scott L.
Smith, Sid
Smith, Theodore Donley
Smith, Victor Joachim
Smith, Watson
Smith, Wayne Henry
Smith, William McFate
Smith, William Vick
Smolka, Fred Alois
Smoot, Leon Douglas
Smothers, Dick
Smothers, Tom
Smuckler, Edward Aaron
Smuin, Michael
Smyser, Adam Albert
Smyth, Bernard John

Smyth, Joel Douglas
Smythe, William Rodman
Snead, Samuel Jackson
Snedden, Charles Willis
Snedeker, John Haggner
Sneed, Joseph Tyree
Snell, Frank Linn
Snell, Richard
Snelson, Roy
Sneva, Thomas Edsol
Snidecor, John Clifton
Snodgress, Carrie
Snow, Donald Ray
Snow, Gordon Harold
Snow, Karl Nelson, Jr.
Snowden, Fredrick
Snyder, Clifford Charles
Snyder, Gary Sherman
Snyder, J. Herbert
Snyder, Richard Carlton
Snyder, Zilpha Keatley
Sobel, Eli
Soble, Ronald Norman
Soderblom, Laurence Albert
Sognnaes, Reidar Fauske
Sokolow, Maurice
Solberg, Carl Edward
Solberg, Morten Edward
Soldner, Paul Edmund
Soldwedel, Donald Norman
Soleri, Paolo
Solheim, Wilhelm Gerhard, II
Solie, Richard John
Sollenbarger, Lee R.
Solomon, David Harris
Solomon, Edward David
Solomon, Ezra
Solomon, George Edward
Solomon, George Freeman
Solomon, Gus J.
Solomon, Joseph Michael
Solomon, Margaret Claire Boyle
Solomon, Sidney
Somers, Harold Milton
Somers, Steven Mark
Somers, Suzanne (Suzanne Mahoney)
Somerset, Harold Richard
Sommer, Elke (Schletz, Elke)
Sommer, Frederick
Sommers, Bill
Sondergaard, Gale
Sonenshein, Nathan
Sonett, Charles Philip
Sonnenschein, Ralph Robert
Sontag, Frederick Earl
Sooy, Francis Adrian
Sorensen, Gladys Elaine
Sorensen, Neil Clifford
Sosa, Dan, Jr.
Sothern, Ann (formerly Harriette Lake)
Soul, David
Soule, John Dutcher
Sours, James Kingsley
Souter, Robert Taylor
South, Jerry Glover
Southwick, Charles Henry
Southwick, Linus Ely
Sowards, Glade M.
Sowder, Robert Robertson
Spacek, Leonard Paul
Spacek, Sissy (Mary Elizabeth)
Spangle, Clarence Wilbur
Spangler, Scott Michael
Spanier, Edwin Henry
Sparks, Morgan
Sparks, Richard Kingsley
Sparks, Robert William
Sparks, Thomas Lee
Sparks, Walter Chappel
Spaur, George
Specht, Harry
Spector, Phil
Speer, Paul Harold
Speers, Roland Root, II
Spelling, Aaron
Spellman, John Dennis
Spelts, Richard John
Spencer, Dick, III
Spencer, Lewis Neal
Spencer, Murlin Bertrand
Spencer, Vaino Hassan
Spencer, William Joseph
Sperber, William Henry, Jr.
Sperlich, Peter Werner
Sperling, George Elmer, Jr.
Sperling, James Evans
Spero, Stanley Leonard
Speroff, Leon
Speroni, Charles
Sperry, Roger Wolcott
Speziale, Angelo John
Spicer, Edward Holland
Spicer, William Edward, III
Spiegel, Edward Rozler
Spielberg, Steven
Spielman, John Russel
Spiess, Fred Noel
Spindler, George Dearborn
Spinks, John Lee
Spinrad, Bernard Israel
Spinrad, Hyron
Spinrad, Robert Joseph
Spiotta, Robert R.
Spiro, Benjamin Paul
Spiro, Melford Elliot
Spitz, Barbara Salomon
Spitz, Lewis William
Sponenburgh, Mark Ritter
Spooner, Thomas Clarence
Sprague, Norman Frederick, Jr.
Sprecher, David A.
Spriggs, Everett Lee

Springer, Charles Edward
Springer, Eustace Laurence
Sproul, John Allan
Sprouse, John Alwyn
Sprouse, Robert Allen, II
Spuhler, James Norman
Spyers-Duran, Peter
Squire, Alexander
Squires, James Radcliffe
Srivastava, Jaya Nidhi
Sroge, Maxwell Harold
Staar, Richard Felix
Stack, Robert Langford
Stacy, Gardner W.
Staehle, Robert L.
Stafford, Charles Frederick
Stafford, William Edgar
Stahmann, Robert F.
Stalder, Fred Collins
Stalker, Alfred Joseph
Stallone, Sylvester Enzio
Stambaugh, John Howland
Stamm, Alan
Stamper, Malcolm Theodore
Stamper, Willson Young, III
Stampp, Kenneth Milton
Stander, Richard Wright
Stanfill, Dennis Carothers
Stanford, Ann
Stanford, Melvin Joseph
Stanley, Lowell
Stans, Maurice Hubert
Stansky, Peter David Lyman
Stanton, William John, Jr.
Stanwyck, Barbara (Ruby Stevens)
Stapleton, Jean (Jeanne Murray)
Stapleton, Maureen
Stapp, John Paul
Starbuck, Jo Jo (Alicia Jo)
Starger, Martin
Stark, Franklin Culver
Stark, Herbert H.
Stark, John Edwin
Stark, Ronald William
Starr, Albert
Starr, Arnold
Starr, Chauncey
Starr, Eugene Carl
Starr, Richard William
Starr, Ringo (Richard Starkey)
Starr, Ross Marc
Stasack, Edward Armen
Stashower, Arthur Lewis
Staver, LeRoy Baldwin
Staw, Harold
Stea, David
Steadman, John Marcellus, III
Stebbins, George Ledyard
Steckel, Richard J.
Steckler, Phyllis Betty Schwartzbard
Steel, Geoffrey Arthur
Steele, Donald John, Jr.
Steele, Jack Donald
Steen, Paul J.
Steen, Peter
Steen, William Brooks
Steensma, Robert Charles
Stefano, Joseph
Stegemeier, Richard Joseph
Stegenga, Preston Jay
Stegner, Wallace Earle
Steidel, Robert Francis, Jr.
Steiger, Rod
Stein, Isaac
Steinberg, Charles Allan
Steinberg, Daniel
Steinberg, David
Steinberg, Howard
Steinberg, Michael
Steinberg, Morris Albert
Steiner, Herbert Max
Steiner, Kenneth Donald
Steiner, Kurt
Steiner, Richard Russell
Steiner, Stan
Steinhoff, Dan
Stell, James L.
Stenchever, Morton Albert
Stensrud, Russell Kenneth
Stent, Gunther Siegmund
Stephan, John Jason
Stephens, Bart Nelson
Stephens, William Leonard
Stephens, William Thomas
Stephenson, Arthur Emmet, Jr.
Stephenson, Herman Howard
Sterling, Donald Justus, Jr.
Sterling, John Ewart Wallace
Sterman, Irvin
Stern, Alfred Phillip
Stern, Daniel David
Stern, Edgar Bloom, Jr.
Stern, Edward Abraham
Stern, Jan Peter
Stern, Leonard Bernard
Stern, Marvin
Stern, Mort(imer) P(hillip)
Stern, Theodore
Stern, Thomas
Stern, Walter Eugene
Sternberg, Harry
Sternberg, Hilgard O'Reilly
Sternberg, Moshe M.
Sterner, James Hervi
Stetler, Russell Dearnley, Jr.
Steuben, Norton Leslie
Stevens, Andrew
Stevens, Arthur Wilber, Jr.
Stevens, Cat (Steven Demetre Georgiou)
Stevens, Connie
Stevens, Craig
Stevens, David

Stevens, Denis William
Stevens, Franklyn Edward
Stevens, Halsey
Stevens, Jack Gerald
Stevens, Norman E.
Stevens, Paul Irving
Stevens, Robert David
Stevens, Roy W.
Stevens, Warren
Stevenson, Donald Ross
Stevenson, Elmer Clark
Stevenson, Robert
Stevenson, Robert Murrell
Stevenson, Ward Barker
Stewart, Al
Stewart, George Franklin
Stewart, Homer Joseph
Stewart, Isaac Daniel, Jr.
Stewart, Isaac Mitton
Stewart, James Maitland
Stewart, James Paul
Stewart, John Lincoln
Stewart, John Mathews
Stewart, Omer Call
Stewart, Paul
Stewart, Reginald
Stewart, Samuel B.
Stickel, Frederick A.
Stiegelmeyer, Norman Earl
Stiehm, E. Richard
Stiers, David Ogden
Still, Stephen Allen
Stille, John Kenneth
Stillner, Verner
Stine, George Harry
Stivers, William Charles
Stockdale, James Bond
Stockham, Thomas Greenway, Jr.
Stocking, Clifford Ralph
Stocks, Chester Lee, Jr.
Stockton, David Knapp
Stockwell, Robert Paul
Stoddard, Brandon
Stoddard, George Edward
Stoddard, Stephen Davidson
Stokstad, Evan Ludwig Robert
Stoll, Forrest Duane
Stoller, Claude
Stoller, Robert Jesse
Stoltenberg, Carl Henry
Stoltzman, Richard Leslie
Stone, Charles Bertody, III
Stone, Edward Carroll, Jr.
Stone, Elmer L.
Stone, George William
Stone, Howard Francis
Stone, Irving
Stone, James Herbert
Stone, Martin
Stone, Nelson
Stone, Oliver
Stone, William Edward
Stoner, Bartine Albert, Jr.
Stoney, Ronald Joseph
Storey, Will Miller
Stork, Donald Harvey
Stork, Willis William
Storms, Lowell Hanson
Stotland, Ezra
Stotter, Lawrence Henry
Stoughton, Richard Baker
Stout, Fern Dale
Stout, Glyn Bob
Stout, Gregory Stansbury
Stoutenburg, Adrien (pseudonym Lace Kendall)
Stowell, Kent
Strack, Harold Arthur
Strahler, Arthur Newell
Strain, Douglas Campbell
Straka, Ronald Albert
Stralka, Albert R.
Strandjord, Paul Edphil
Strandness, Donald Eugene, Jr.
Strasberg, Susan
Straszewski, Thomas Martin
Stratton, Thomas Oliver
Strauch, Charles Scureman
Strauch, Donald William, Jr.
Strauss, Herbert Leopold
Strauss, John
Strauss, Peter
Strausz, Lawrence Eugene
Stream, Jay Wilson
Street, Dana Morris
Street, Robert Elliott
Street, Robert Lynnwood
Street, William Sherman
Streeter, Daniel Denison, Jr.
Streifer, William
Streisinger, George
Streitwieser, Andrew, Jr.
Strickland, Eugene Lee
Strogoff, Alfred
Strom, Stephen Eric
Stromberg, Arthur Harold
Strong, Charles Wilbur, Jr.
Strong, Gary Eugene
Strong, Leonell Clarence
Strong, William James
Strong, William Lee
Stroock, Daniel Wyler
Struckmeyer, Frederick Christian, Jr.
Struthers, Sally Anne
Strycula, Thomas Francis
Stryer, Lubert
Stuart, Dwight Lyman
Stuart, Mel
Stuart, Robert Marvin
Stubberud, Allen Roger
Stucki, Roland
Stucky, Ronald Leon
Stude, Everett Wilson, Jr.
Stufflebean, John Howard

Stuhr, Walter Martin
Stumpf, Paul Karl
Sturges, John Eliot
Sturman, Joseph Howard
Sturtevant, Judd
Styles, Margretta Madden
Sudarsky, Jerry M.
Suerstedt, Henry, Jr.
Sugar, Peter Frigyes
Sugaski, Lloyd John
Sugg, John Logan (Jack)
Sugihara, Thomas Tamotsu
Suhl, Harry
Suhr, Donald Carl
Suinn, Richard Michael
Sullivan, Barbara Boyle
Sullivan, Barry
Sullivan, Daniel Joseph
Sullivan, Edward Gerald
Sullivan, George Murray
Sullivan, James Francis
Sullivan, John Francis
Sullivan, John Francis
Sullivan, John Patrick
Sullivan, Joseph Edward
Sullivan, Kenneth James
Sullivan, Michael
Sullivan, Robert Edwin
Sullivan, Roger Michael
Sullivan, William James
Summer, Charles Edgar
Summer, Donna (La Donna Andrea Gaines)
Summers, Carol
Summit, Roger Kent
Sumner, James DuPre, Jr.
Sunderland, Thomas Elbert
Sunshine, Philip
Suppes, Patrick
Suppes, Robert William
Surbeck, Leighton Homer
Surtees, Robert Lee
Susman, Leland Stanford
Susskind, Charles
Sussman, Karl E.
Sutcliffe, Eric
Sutherland, Donald
Sutherland, Robert Louis
Sutro, John Alfred
Sutter, Carolyn Opthoff
Sutton, Albert Alton
Sutton, Charles Richard
Sutton, John Paul
Sutton, Robert Clive
Suyematsu, Toshiro
Suzuki, Noboru
Sveilis, Emil Rudolf
Swackhamer, William D.
Swain, Edward Parsons, Jr.
Swan, Bruce Thomas
Swan, Emerson Ward
Swan, Henry, II
Swan, Kenneth Carl
Swank, Roy Laver
Swanson, Alvin De Vern
Swanson, Glen Owen
Swanson, Gustav Adolph
Swanson, Guy Edwin
Swanson, Karl Thor Waldemar
Swanson, Phillip Dean
Swanson, Robert A.
Swanson, Robert Killen
Swarthout, Glendon Fred
Swartz, Roderick Gardner
Swartzburg, Gary Bennett
Swatek, Frank Edward
Swearingen, Rodger
Sweeney, Beatrice Marcy
Sweeney, Kevin Brendan
Sweeney, Stender Edward
Swenson, Harry William
Swenson, James Reed
Swift, Richard
Swig, Richard L.
Swigert, John Leonard, Jr.
Swinerton, William Arthur
Swinford, William Steele
Swinyard, Chester Allan
Swinyard, Ewart Ainslie
Swit, Loretta
Swofford, Edward Emery
Syapin, John James
Sypherd, Paul Starr
Syrkin, Marie
Syverson, LaVand Merlyn
Syvertson, Clarence Alfred
Szabo, Gabor
Szego, Clara Marian
Taagepera, Rein
Taapken, Albertus
Tabackin, Lewis Barry
Tabor, Doris Dee
Tafoya, Arthur N.
Takahashi, Yasundo
Takasugi, Robert Mitsuhiro
Talbert, Ernest William
Talbot, James Lawrence
Talbot, Matthew Joseph
Talbot, Walter D.
Talley, Robert Boyd
Talley, Warren Dennis Rick
Tallman, Johanna Eleonore
Tallman, Kenneth Lee
Talmadge, Marion Lyman
Talmage, David Wilson
Tam, Reuben
Tambs, Lewis Arthur
Tamkin, S. Jerome
Tanagho, Emil Abdelsayed
Tanaka, Kouichi Robert
Tanaka, Richard Isamu
Tanen, Ned Stone
Tanenbaum, Basil Samuel
Tanenbaum, Robert Karl
Tang, Thomas
Tanis, Norman Earl

Tanji, Kenneth Kazuo
Tannenbaum, Percy H.
Tannenbaum, Thomas David
Tanner, George Stephen
Tanner, William
Tanzer, Jacob
Taper, S. Mark
Tappan, David S., Jr.
Tarjan, George
Tarson, Herbert Harvey
Tarver, Ervin
Tashima, Atsushi Wallace
Tatarian, Hrach Roger
Tatum, Donn Benjamin
Taub, Abraham Haskel
Taub, Harald J.
Taube, Henry
Tavrow, Richard Lawrence
Taylor, Allan Ross
Taylor, Dermot Brownrigg
Taylor, Don
Taylor, Douglas Roy
Taylor, Dwight Davidson
Taylor, Edward Stewart
Taylor, Fred Monroe
Taylor, George E.
Taylor, Guy Watson
Taylor, Herbert Cecil, Jr.
Taylor, Hugh Pettingill, Jr.
Taylor, J. Mary
Taylor, James Vernon
Taylor, John David
Taylor, John Frank
Taylor, John Lockhart
Taylor, Keith Breden
Taylor, Leigh H.
Taylor, Raynor Dunham
Taylor, Rod
Taylor, Samuel
Taylor, Stuart Symington
Taylor, Theodore Langhans
Tchobanoglous, George
Teague, Donald
Teague, Elwood Andrew
Teal, John Jerome, Jr.
Tebet, David William
Tedesco, Ted
Teeguarden, Dennis Earl
Teets, John William
Teitsworth, Robert Allan
Telfer, James Gavin
Tellep, Daniel Michael
Teller, Edward
Tellez, Theresa Pino
Tellier, Richard Davis
Telmossé, Robert Dennis
Temes, Gabor Charles
Temianka, Henri
Temko, Allan Bernard
Tempelis, Constantine Harry
Temple, Arthur
Templeman, Edward John, II
Templeton, Benjamin John
Tenenbaum, Louis
Tenzer, Michael Leonard
Terkla, Louis Gabriel
Terman, Frederick Emmons
Terrell, Frederick Reynolds
Terrell, Glenn
Terry, Thomas Carlton, Jr.
Terry, Thomas Dutton
Terry, Walter English
Terry, William E.
Tesich, Steve
Testman, Thomas Robert
Tewkesbury, Joan F.
Thaler, Alan Maurice
Thaler, Robert Lee
Tharp, William Everett
Thatcher, George Alfred
Thayer, James Norris
Thedens, Edgar Otto
Thelen, Max, Jr.
Thiebaud, Wayne
Thiel, Philip
Thier, Herbert David
Thieriot, Richard Tobin
Thiessen, Cornie R.
Thimann, Kenneth Vivian
Thinnes, Roy
Thiry, Paul
Thode, Edward Frederick
Thomas, Blakemore Ewing
Thomas, Charles Allen, Jr.
Thomas, Danny (Amos Jacobs)
Thomas, David Phillip
Thomas, Edward Donnall
Thomas, Gareth
Thomas, George Edward
Thomas, Gerald Eustis
Thomas, Gerald Waylett
Thomas, Jess
Thomas, John Richard
Thomas, Joseph Allan
Thomas, Joseph Fleshman
Thomas, Joseph Henry
Thomas, Lowell, Jr.
Thomas, M. Donald
Thomas, Marlo
Thomas, Owen Daniel
Thomas, Paul Emery
Thomas, Sister Peter Claver
Thomas, Richard
Thomas, Richard Van
Thomas, Robert David
Thomas, Robert Harold
Thomas, Robert Joseph
Thomas, Robert Murray
Thomas, Ross Elmore
Thomas, Ruth Harrell
Thomas, William F.
Thomas, William Gordon
Thomas, William LeRoy
Thomas, William Marshall
Thomas, William Orvill, Jr.
Thomas, William Richard

Thomlinson, Ralph
Thompson, Alvin Jerome
Thompson, Bernie Eunie
Thompson, Bruce Rutherford
Thompson, Cliff F.
Thompson, David Alfred
Thompson, David O'Neal
Thompson, Earl Albert
Thompson, Elisabeth Kendall
Thompson, George Albert
Thompson, Gordon, Jr.
Thompson, Hale George
Thompson, Hugh Currie
Thompson, Hunter Stockton
Thompson, JB
Thompson, John Albert
Thompson, John Brown
Thompson, John Lester
Thompson, John Silvey, Jr.
Thompson, Jon F.
Thompson, Loring Moore
Thompson, Martin Christian
Thompson, Milton Orville
Thompson, R. E.
Thompson, Raymond Harris
Thompson, Richard Frederick
Thompson, Robert Carlysle
Thompson, Robert Elliott
Thompson, Robert Franklin
Thompson, Robert Marion
Thompson, Sada Carolyn
Thompson, Theodore Kvale
Thompson, Thomas Sanford
Thompson, Travis Loftin
Thompson, Truet Bradford
Thompson, Tyler
Thompson, Warren
Thompson, Wayne Edward
Thompson, William Bell
Thomson, Herman Otha
Thomson, Richard James
Thomson, Thyra Godfrey
Thon, J. George
Thorn, Robert Nicol
Thornbury, John Rousseau
Thorne, Kip Stephen
Thorne, Richard Mansergh
Thornton, Jack Nelson
Thornton, James Francis
Thornton, Judith Ann
Thorpe, James
Thorpe, James Alfred
Thouless, David James
Thrower, Norman Joseph William
Thulean, Donald Myron
Thulsan, Donald Myron
Thurber, Clarence Egbert
Thurman, Samuel David
Thurston, Alice Janet
Thurston, George Riley, Jr.
Thurston, Jacqueline Beverly
Tibbitts, Samuel John
Ticho, Harold Klein
Tidyman, Ernest
Tiedeman, Ardell Clifford
Tiedeman, David Valentine
Tiegs, Fay Adams
Tien, Chang Lin
Tierney, Donald Frank
Tietz, William John, Jr.
Tiffany, Lawrence Paul
Tift, Mary Louise
Tilbury, Roger Graydon
Tillinghast, Charles Carpenter, III
Tilton, David Lloyd
Timm, Jerry Roger
Timmerhaus, Klaus Dieter
Timothy, Robert Keller
Tincher, William R.
Tinker, Grant A.
Tinoco, Ignacio, Jr.
Tinsley, Walton Eugene
Tissot, Ernest Eugene, Jr.
Titus, Robert Farren
Tivy, Robert Clifford
Tobias, Charles William
Tobin, Ronald William
Tobis, Jerome Sanford
Tobriner, Mathew Oscar
Todd, Charles Gillett
Todd, David Keith
Todd, Harold Wade
Todd, John
Todd, Malcolm Clifford
Todd, Michael Cullen
Tokatyan, Leon Gabriel
Tolbert, Bert Mills
Toll, Jack Benjamin
Toll, Maynard Joy
Tollenaere, Lawrence Robert
Tolles, E. Leroy
Tom, Robert Mun Sung
Tomash, Erwin
Tomlin, Lily
Tompkins, Ronald K.
Tomsick, Frank
Tongue, Thomas H.
Toole, Allan H.
Toole, Bruce Ryan
Topkins, Katharine
Topping, Norman Hawkins
Torkelson, Dean John
Torme, Melvin Howard
Tormey, Thomas James
Torn, Rip (Elmore Torn, Jr.)
Tors, Ivan
Tostenrud, Donald Boyd
Totter, F Al
Toupin, Arthur Vernon
Towers, Bernard
Towers, Constance Mary
Towery, Hosia Malcolm, Jr.
Towey, Edward Bernard
Townes, Charles Hard

Townley, John Mark
Townsend, Claire Tracy
Townsend, G(eorge) Marshall
Townsend, Irving Joseph
Townsend, Ramon H.
Townsley, Edwin Stuart
Tozzi, Giorgio
Trachta, Stanley Willard
Tracy, James Jared, Jr.
Trafton, Roland Milton
Trapp, Gerald Bernard
Trapp, Jack Martin
Trappe, James Martin
Trautman, Gerald Hough
Travelstead, Chester Coleman
Travis, Albert Hartman
Travolta, John
Traylor, Frank Allen
Traynor, J. Michael
Treadgold, Donald Warren
Treadway, James Butler
Treanor, Walter Gladstone
Trefftzs, Kenneth Lewis
Treiman, Joyce Wahl
Treinen, Sylvester William
Treister, George Marvin
Trelease, Richard Mitchell, Jr.
Tremayne, Les
Trembly, Dennis Michael
Trent, Darrell M.
Trenton, Norman B.
Trever, John Paul
Trevor, Elleston
Trezek, George James
Trezevant, John Gray
Triem, Eve
Trimble, George Simpson
Trimborn, Harry
Trost, J. Ronald
Troxel, Bennie Wyatt
Troy, Joseph Freed
Trueblood, Harry Albert, Jr.
Trueblood, Kenneth Nyitray
Trueblood, Paul Graham
Truex, George Robert, Jr.
Trujillo, Arthur Ernest
Trumbull, Douglas
Trumbull, Robert
Trust, Samuel Smith
Trygstad, Lawrence Benson
Tsu, John B.
Tuan, San Fu
Tubis, Seymour
Tuck, Leo Dallas
Tucker, Forrest Meredith
Tucker, Richard Clive
Tucker, Tanya Denise
Tuddenham, Read Duncan
Tuell, Jack Marvin
Tull, Donald Stanley
Tully, Darrow
Tunks, Lehan Kent
Tunnell, Wallace Lee
Tunney, John Varick
Tuohy, William Klaus
Tupper, Charles John
Turetzky, Bertram Jay
Turin, George Lewis
Turk, Rudy Henry
Turley, Keith L.
Turman, George
Turnbull, William, Jr.
Turnbull, William Watson
Turner, Arthur Campbell
Turner, Burnett Coburn
Turner, Ike
Turner, Janet E.
Turner, Lana (Julia Jean Mildred Frances Turner)
Turner, Ralph Herbert
Turner, Richard Lee
Turner, Robert Wayne
Turner, Ross James
Turner, Wallace L.
Turrell, James Archie
Turrentine, Howard Boyd
Tusher, Thomas William
Tutt, Russell Thayer
Tutt, William Thayer
Tuttle, Albert Theodore
Tuveson, Ernest Lee
Tweedie, Eleanor Margaret
Twigg-Smith, Thurston
Twitty, Howard Allen
Twomey, William Peter
Tyler, Samuel Lyman
Tyndall, David Gordon
Tyne, George
Tyre, Norman Ronald
Tyson, Cicely
Tyson, Kenneth Robert Thomas
Tzimoulis, Paul James
Uberoi, Mahinder Singh
Udall, Calvin Hunt
Ueland, Kent
Uggams, Leslie
Uhlman, Wes Carl
Ukropina, James Robert
Ulene, Arthur Lawrence
Ullstrom, L. Berwyn
Ulrich, Paul Graham
Ulrich, Peter Henry
Ulyshen, Michael
Umbach, William Eckhard
Underwood, Jane Hainline Hammons
Underwood, Thomas Carroll
Unrue, John Calvin
Unruh, James Arlen
Unruh, Jesse Marvin
Unser, Al
Unser, Bobby
Unterecker, John Eugene
Upchurch, Rickie
Upson, Donald V.
Urich, Robert
Ushijima, John Takeji
Utlaut, William Frederick
Utter, Robert French
Utzinger, Robert Conde
Uzgalis, Robert Charles
Vaccaro, Brenda
Vail, Nathan Columbus
Valdez, Joel David
Valens, Evans Gladstone
Valente, Michael Feeney
Valentine, Dewain
Valentine, George Gordon
Vallee, Hubert Prior Rudy
Valli, Frankie (Frank Castelluccio)
van Bronkhorst, Edwin Earl
Van Buren, Abigail (Pauline Friedman Phillips)
Van Camp, Brian Ralph
Van Campen, Joseph Alfred
Vance, John Holbrook
Van Citters, Robert Lee
Van Cleave, William Robert
Van Cleef, Lee
van Dam, Heiman
van den Berghe, Pierre Louis
van-den-Noort, Stanley
Vanderbilt, Kermit
Van Der Meulen, Joseph Pierre
Vandervort, Lowell Miller
Van Der Zee, John Riley
Van Devere, Trish
Van de Wetering, Richard Lee
van Dreelen, John (Jacques Theodore van Drielen Gimberg)
Van Dreser, Merton Lawrence
Van Dyke, Dick
Van Dyke, Milton Denman
Van Gytenbeek, Richard Peter
Van Hoefen, Hari
Van Hoesen, Beth Marie
Van Holde, Kensal Edward
Van Horne, James Carter
Vanier, Kieran Francis
Van Lancker, Julien Leon
Van Leuven, Arthur Edwin, Jr.
Vann, John Daniel, III
Vanoni, Vito August
Van Pallandt, Nina Magdalene
Van Patten, Dick Vincent
Van Petten, Harry O, Jr.
Van Schilfgaarde, Jan
van Tamelen, Eugene Earle
van Vogt, Alfred Elton
Van Wagner, Albert Edwin
Van Young, Oscar
Vanzi, Max Bruno
Varanasi, Usha
Vargas, George Leland
Varley, John Herbert
Vaughan, Joseph Robert
Vaughan, Marilou Taylor
Vaughan, Richard Patrick
Vaughan, Sarah Lois
Vaughan, Thomas James Gregory
Vaughn, John Vernon
Vaughn, Kenneth Willard
Vaughn, Robert
Vaughn, Robert Lockard
Vaughn, William Weaver
Vaupel, Michael Christian
Vaux, Henry James
Vawter, Ralphe B.
Vazquez, Jacinto Jose
Veder, Sal
Vedros, Neylan Anthony
Veinott, Arthur Fales, Jr.
Veith, Ilza
Velde, John Ernest, Jr.
Velick, Sidney Frederick
Vendler, Zeno
Verger, Morris David
Verity, Maurice Anthony
Verleger, Philip King
Vermeulen, Theodore
Vernon, Glenn Morley
Vernon, Leo Preston
Vertlieb, Richard Harvey
Vesak, Norbert Franklin
Vesper, Karl Hampton
Vicker, Ray
Vickers, Roger Spencer
Victor, Janet Marshall (Mrs. Donald C. Victor)
Victor, Robert Eugene
Vidor, King Wallis
Vigil, Charles S.
Vigoda, Abe
Villard, Oswald Garrison, Jr.
Villechaize, Herve Jean Pierre
Vincent, Charles Ridgely
Vincent, Clark Edward
Vincent, Gerald Glenn
Vincent, Hal Wellman
Vincenti, Louis Rudolph
Vincenti, Walter Guido
Vinton, Bobby (Stanley Robert)
Viterbi, Andrew James
Voegelin, Harold Stanley
Voelkel, Robert T(ownsend)
Vogel, Charles Stimmel
Vogel, Orville Alvin
Vogt, James H.
Vogt, Peter Klaus
Vogt, Rochus Eugen
Vohs, James Arthur
Volchok, Zollie Marc
Volk, Harry J.
Volkart, Edmund Howell
Volkmann, Daniel George, Jr.
Vollum, Howard
Volman, David Herschel
Volpert, Richard Sidney
Volpp, Louis Donovan
Volwiler, Wade
von Ammon, Philip Ernst
von der Heydt, James Arnold
Von Flue, Frank Walter
von Furstenberg, Betsy
Von Harz, James Lyons
von Hippel, Peter Hans
von Hofe, Harold
von Kalinowski, Julian Onesime
von Leden, Hans Victor
von Sydow, Max Carl Adolf
Vook, Frederick Ludwig
Voorhees, Donald Shirley
Voorhees, William Delano, Jr.
Vosper, Robert Gordon
Voulkos, Peter
Vredevoe, Donna Lou
Vucinich, Wayne S.
Vuyleteke, Allen George
Vyas, Girish Narmadashankar
Wachner, Linda Joy
Waddingham, John Alfred
Wade, Glen
Wadlow, Joan Krueger
Wagener, Hobart Dean
Waggoner, James Norman
Wagner, Carruth John
Wagner, Christian Nikolaus Johann
Wagner, Lindsay J.
Wagner, Marjorie Coogan Downing
Wagner, Richard Lorraine, Jr.
Wagner, Robert
Wagner, William Gerard
Wagoner, David Russell
Wagoner, Robert Vernon
Wahler, William Albert
Wahlgren, Erik
Wahlke, John Charles
Wahlstrom, Ernest Eugene
Wainer, Stanley Allen
Wainwright, James
Wainwright, Paul Edward Blech
Wait, James Richard
Waite, Elin Jane
Waite, Ralph
Waiter, Serge-Albert
Wakatsuki, James Hiroji
Wakeman, Frederic Evans, Jr.
Wakerlin, George Earle
Walbot, Virginia
Walch, David Bean
Walden, Robert
Waldman, Martin Herbert
Waldman, Theodore
Waldron, Rodney K.
Waldschmidt, Paul Edward
Wales, Harold Webster
Wales, Hugh Gregory
Walker, Brooks, Jr.
Walker, Charles Montgomery
Walker, E. Cardon
Walker, E. Cardon
Walker, Henry Alexander A., Jr.
Walker, James Carter
Walker, Joseph
Walker, Leland Jasper
Walker, Nancy (Ann Myrtle Swoyer)
Walker, Theodore Roscoe
Walker, Timothy Blake
Walker, William Tidd, Jr.
Walkup, Bruce
Walkup, William Edmondson
Wall, Brian Arthur
Wall, Frederick Theodore
Wall, William Monroe
Wallace, Charles Edward
Wallace, Donald Sheridan
Wallace, Helen Margaret
Wallace, Irving
Wallace, J. Clifford
Wallace, James Ellis
Wallace, John Carleton
Wallace, John McChrystal
Wallace, Leigh Allen, Jr.
Wallace, Marcia
Wallace, Robert Ash
Wallace, Robert Fergus
wallach, e. robert (bob)
Waller, Thomas Edward
Waller, William Kelly
Waller, William Kelly, Jr.
Wallerstein, George
Wallerstein, Ralph Oliver
Wallerstein, Robert Solomon
Wallis, Earl L.
Wallis, Hal Brent
Walls, Forrest Wesley
Walpole, Ronald Noel
Walsh, Denny Jay
Walsh, Edward Joseph
Walsh, Frederick
Walsh, James A.
Walsh, James Starrak
Walsh, Joseph Fidler
Walsh, Mason
Walsh, Richard George
Walsh, William
Walsh, William Desmond
Walston, Ray
Walstrom, Milton Carl
Walt, Harold Richard
Walt, Martin
Walter, Jessica
Waltermire, Jim
Walters, Charles
Walters, Lee Joseph
Walters, Mary Dawson
Walthall, Wilson Jones, Jr.
Walton, Clyde Cameron
Walton, Harold Frederic
Walton, Jean B.
Walton, Robert Edward
Walton, William (Bill) Theodore
Waltz, Kenneth Neal
Walzer, Stuart Bernard
Wambaugh, Joseph
Wands, Alfred James
Wang, James Chia-Fang
Wang, Jaw-Kai
Wang, William Kai-Sheng
Wang, William Shi-Yuan
Wangsgard, Robert Louis
Wangsness, Roald Klinkenberg
Wann, Andrew Jackson
Wantland, Earl
Ward, Arthur Allen, Jr.
Ward, Baldwin Helfrich
Ward, David Schad
Ward, Donald Butler
Ward, Harold Gordon
Ward, John Robert
Ward, Joseph Simeon
Ward, Paul Hutchins
Ward, Richard Theodore
Ward, Thomas Martin, Jr.
Ward, William Reed
Ward, Yvette Hennig
Warden, Gail L.
Warden, Jack
Ward-Steinman, David
Ware, James Edwin
Ware, Marcus John
Ware, Willis Howard
Warf, James Curren
Wark, Robert Rodger
Warkentin, Benno Peter
Warne, John Llewellyn
Warne, William Elmo
Warnecke, John Carl
Warner, Carolyn
Warner, Harold Clay, Jr.
Warner, Jack, Jr.
Warner, Nancy Elizabeth
Warner, Richard Alan
Warner, Robert S.
Warnken, Douglas Richard
Warnock, William Kirkpatrick
Warns, Raymond H.
Warren, Charles Marquis
Warren, David Hardy
Warren, Edward Willard
Warren, James Ronald
Warren, Mark Edward
Warren, Robert Carlton
Warren, William David
Warrington, Richard Wayne
Warthan, John Willard
Washburn, Albert Lincoln
Washburn, Jack
Washburn, Stan
Washington, James Winston, Jr.
Washington, Kenneth Strickland
Washington, Warren Morton
Wasmuth, Carl Erwin
Wasserburg, Gerald Joseph
Wasserman, Arthur
Wasserman, Lew R.
Wasserstrom, Richard Alan
Watai, Takeo
Waterman, John Thomas
Waterman, Richard D.
Waterman, Ronald Frederick
Waters, Laughlin Edward
Waters, Lee
Watkin, Lawrence Edward
Watkins, Dean Allen
Watkins, Jack Lewis
Watkins, John Francis
Watkins, John Goodrich
Watkins, Stephen Edward
Watson, Arthel Lane (Doc)
Watson, Donald Stevenson
Watson, Glenn R.
Watson, Kenneth Marshall
Watson, Mills
Watson, Raymond Leslie
Watt, Ian Pierre
Watts, Malcolm S.M.
Watts, Vervon Orval
Wax, Stephen Martin
Way, E. Leong
Way, H(arold) Frank, II
Way, Walter Lee
Wayland, J(ames) Harold
Wayne, June C.
Wayne, Patrick John
Wear, James Smith
Weaver, Albert Bruce
Weaver, Dennis
Weaver, John Carrier
Weaver, Sylvester Laflin, Jr.
Weaver, Thomas
Weaver, William H.
Webb, Eugene
Webb, Eugene John
Webb, Jack
Webb, James Sidney, Jr.
Webb, Richard C.
Webb, Robert Wallace
Webber, Hugh E.
Webber, Robert
Weber, Arnold R.
Weber, Brom
Weber, Charles Joseph
Weber, David C(arter)
Weber, Eugen
Weber, Harold Christian
Webster, David Arthur
Webster, George Van O'Linda
Webster, Grady Linder, Jr.
Webster, Martin Haskell
Wedgeworth, Ann
Wedgwood, Ralph Josiah Patrick
Wedman, Elwood Edward
Weed, Frederic Augustus
Weed, Herbert M.
Weegar, Edwin Alexander, Jr.
Weekes, Michael Manning
Weems, Frank Taylor
Weems, Robert Cicero
Wehausen, John Vrooman
Wehner, Alfred Peter
Wehrli, Robert Louis
Weide, William Wolfe
Weidman, Jerome
Weidmann, Victor Hugo
Weigand, William Keith
Weigel, Stanley Alexander
Weigend, Guido Gustav
Weihaupt, John George
Weil, D(onald) Wallace
Weil, Leonard
Weil, Max Harry
Weimer, Robert Jay
Weinbaum, Jean David
Weinberg, Leonard Burton
Weinberg, Matthew Basil
Weinberg, William Henry
Weiner, Irving Bernard
Weiner, Leslie Philip
Weiner, Norman
Weinglass, Leonard Irving
Weinshienk, Zita Leeson (Mrs. Hubert Troy Weinshienk)
Weinstein, Boris
Weinstein, Irving Benjamin
Weinstein, Irwin Marshall
Weinstock, Harold
Weinstock, Herbert Frank
Weir, Thomas Charles
Weisbord, Sam
Weisbrod, Fred Edgar
Weisenfluh, Norman Donald
Weiser, Paul David
Weiss, Charles Frederick
Weiss, David Edward
Weiss, Lionel Edward
Weiss, Martin Harvey
Weiss, Max Tibor
Weiss, Thomas Michael
Weiss, Walter Stanley
Weitkamp, William George
Weitzner, David A.
Welch, Claude (Raymond)
Welch, Garth Larry
Welch, Raquel
Welch, William John
Weld, Tuesday Ker (Weld, Susan Ker)
Weldon, Edward Joseph, Jr.
Weldon, Scott Bryce
Welk, Lawrence
Weller, Herman Gayle
Wells, Edward Curtis
Wells, Frank G.
Wells, George Douglas
Welmers, William Evert
Welp, Theodore Martin
Welpott, Jack Warren
Welsh, Lawrence H.
Welty, James Richard
Welz, Carl John
Wengert, Norman Irving
Wenk, Edward, Jr.
Wenkert, Ernest
Werchick, Jack
Werckmeister, Otto Karl
Werman, Thomas Ehrlich
Werner, Emmy Elisabeth
Werner, Fritz
Werner, Mort
Werner, Robert Joseph
Werner, Sidney Charles
Werson, James Byrd
Wert, James Edward
Werth, Glenn Conrad
Wertheim, Robert Halley
Wesenberg, John Herman
Wessel, Henry, Jr.
Wessells, Norman Keith
Wesson, Robert Gale
West, Arleigh Burton
West, Barry George
West, Bernie
West, Henry George, Jr.
West, Howard Norton
West, Jessamyn
West, John Burnard
West, Louis Jolyon
West, Richard Vincent
West, Robert Seth
Westbrooks, Logan Hart
Westcott, Ralph Merrill
Westerfield, Putney
Westheimer, David Kaplan
Westheimer, Gerald
Westin, George Wilbur
Westman, William Leonard, II
Westmore, Michael George
Weston, Brett
Weston, John Frederick
Weston, William Lee
Westover, Harry Clay
Westphal, Paul
Wetzel, Harry Herman
Wexler, Haskell
Wexler, Norman
Weyerhaeuser, George Hunt
Whalen, Carol Kupers
Whalen, John Sydney
Wheat, Francis Millspaugh
Wheat, Joe Ben
Wheatley, Floyd Arthur
Wheatley, John Charles
Wheatley, Melvin Ernest, Jr.
Wheeler, John Harvey
Wheeler, Sessions Samuel
Wheeler, William Thornton
Wheelon, Albert Dewell
Whelan, Francis C.
Whelan, James Robert
Whelan, James Robert
Whelan, John William
Whelan, Robert Louis
Whelan, Thomas Joseph
Whelan, William Anthony
Whetten, John Theodore
Whetton, James Junior
Whinnery, John Roy
Whinston, Arthur Lewis
Whitaker, Clem, Jr.
Whitaker, Eileen Monaghan
Whitaker, Thomas Wallace
Whitaker, Urban George, Jr.
Whitcombe, John Alfred
White, Alvin Swauger
White, Betty
White, Donald Edward
White, Donald Keys
White, Gerald Taylor
White, Gilbert F(owler)
White, Homer
White, Howard Ashley
White, Ian McKibbin
White, James Edward
White, Jesse Marc
White, John Mark
White, John Patrick
White, John Patrick
White, John Sylvester
White, Larry Lee
White, Lelia Cayne
White, Leonard LeRoy
White, Maurice
White, Paul A.
White, Richard Stanley
White, Robb
White, Robert Lee
White, Stanley Archibald
White, Steven Virgil
White, Tim Douglas
White, William Allen
Whiteford, Andrew Hunter
Whitehead, Clay Thomas
Whitehurst, Daniel Keenan
Whitcker, Roy Archie
Whitesell, John Edwin
White-Thomson, Ian Leonard
Whitfield, Francis James
Whitlatch, Wayne Edward
Whitmore, James Allen
Whitmore, Ralph Ervin, Jr.
Whitmore, Sharp
Whitmore, William Francis
Whitney, Donald Eugene
Whitten, Charles Alexander, Jr.
Whittington, Floyd Leon
Whittington, Robert Bruce
Wibberley, Leonard Patrick O'Connor
Wiborg, James Hooker
Wick, William Quentin
Wickes, Mary Isabella
Wickham, John Adams, Jr.
Wickham, Kenneth Gregory
Wickman, Paul Everett
Widasky, Stanley William
Widmann, Chester Henry
Widmark, Richard
Widmoyer, Fred Bixler
Wiebe, O. Roy
Wiederholt, Wigbert C.
Wiegel, Robert Louis
Wiegman, Eugene William
Wiener, Herman
Wiens, Arthur Nicholai
Wiesen, David Stanley
Wiesler, James Ballard
Wiggs, Eugene Overbey
Wight, Frederick S.
Wilber, Charles Grady
Wilbur, Jordan Rockwood
Wilcox, Calvin Hayden
Wilcox, Collin M.
Wilcox, Howard Albert
Wilcox, Larry Dee
Wilcox, Raymond John
Wilcox, Robert Fraser
Wilcox, Thomas Robert
Wild, Nelson Hopkins
Wild, Peter
Wild, Robert Lee
Wilde, Cornel
Wilder, Billy
Wilder, Brooks
Wilder, Gene
Wildgen, John Jerome
Wiles, Eugene F.
Wilets, Lawrence
Wiley, Carl Ross
Wiley, Donovon Linn
Wiley, Richard Haven
Wiley, Thomas Glen
Wiley, William T.
Wilgus, D.K.
Wilhelm, Robert G.
Wilke, Charles Robert
Wilkens, Leonard Randolph (Lenny)
Wilkie, Donald Walter
Wilkie, Robert John
Wilkin, Eugene Welch
Wilkinson, Robert Neil
Will, John
Willard, Dean M.
Willard, Donna Carol Morris
Willard, Frederic Charles
Willard, Robert Edgar
Willeford, Jack Allen
Willens, Harold

Willerding, Margaret Frances
Williams, Albert Paine
Williams, Andy
Williams, Arthur Cozad
Williams, Ben Franklin, Jr.
Williams, Betty Leola
Williams, Billy Dee
Williams, Carl Harwell
Williams, Carlton Hinkle
Williams, Cynthia Jane
Williams, David Rogerson, Jr.
Williams, David Welford
Williams, Delwyn Charles
Williams, Donald John
Williams, Douglas George
Williams, George Abiah
Williams, George Arthur
Williams, George Zur
Williams, Gerald Alvin
Williams, Gordon Roland
Williams, Hal
Williams, Harold Marvin
Williams, Howard Russell
Williams, J(ohn) Tilman
Williams, J. Vernon
Williams, Joe
Williams, Joseph Richard
Williams, Lawrence Eugene
Williams, Oliver Joseph, Jr.
Williams, Olwen
Williams, Patrick Moody
Williams, Paul Hamilton
Williams, Ralph Chester, Jr.
Williams, Richard Edmund
Williams, Robert Luther
Williams, Robert Martin
Williams, Robert Walter
Williams, Robin
Williams, Roger
Williams, Ronald Lee
Williams, Samuel Leslie
Williams, Spencer M.
Williams, Stephen Fain
Williams, Theodore Earle
Williams, Tony
Williams, Walter Charles, Jr.
Williams, Walter Charles, Jr.
Williams, Wayne DeArmond
Williams, William Appleman
Williams, William Harrison
Williams, William Henry
Williamson, Laird
Williamson, Nicol
Willig, Karl Victor
Willis, Beverly A.
Willis, David Lee
Willis, Donald Sigurdson
Willis, Gordon
Willits, E. Joseph
Willoughby, Carroll Vernon
Willoughby, Rodney Erwin
Willson, James Douglas
Wilmot, Richard Wayne
Wilmoth, Evert Dale
Wilmsen, Harry Robert
Wilner, Daniel Murray
Wilson, Albert Eugene
Wilson, Alexander Murray
Wilson, Brian Douglas
Wilson, Carl Dean
Wilson, Charles Bryon
Wilson, Charles William
Wilson, Charles Zachary, Jr.
Wilson, Donald Grey
Wilson, Gabriel Henry
Wilson, Garff Bell
Wilson, George Andrew
Wilson, Hugh Hamilton, Jr.
Wilson, J. Robert
Wilson, James Caldwell
Wilson, John Long
Wilson, Lewis Kenneth
Wilson, Lionel J.
Wilson, Luther
Wilson, Miriam Geisendorfer
Wilson, Nancy
Wilson, Pete
Wilson, Ramon B.
Wilson, Raphael
Wilson, Robert Becker
Wilson, Ted Lewis
Wilson, Thornton Arnold
Wilson, Timothy Watson Burr
Wilson, William Jewell
Wiltshire, Raymond Stanley
Wimberly, George James
Winchell, Paul
Winchester, Albert McCombs
Winchester, Jesse James Ridout
Winder, David Kent
Windom, William
Winegar, Albert Lee
Winfield, Paul Edward
Wing, George Milton
Winkelstein, Warren, Jr.
Winkler, Henry Franklin
Winkler, Irwin
Winkler, Lee B.
Winner, Fred M.
Winogrand, Garry
Winokur, Robert M.
Winslow, Walter William
Winston, Morton Manuel
Winter, Donald Ferguson
Winter, Paul Theodore
Winters, Barbara Jo
Winters, Jonathan
Winters, Shelley
Wintrobe, Maxwell Myer
Wirth, John D(avis)
Wirthlin, David Bitner
Wischmeyer, Paul Alan
Wise, George Edward
Wise, Robert
Withington, Holden White
Witkin, Joel-Peter
Witt, Paul Junger
Wittbrodt, Edwin Stanley
Witte, Merlin Michael
Witter, Thomas Winship
Witter, William Maurer
Wittler, Shirley Joyce
Wittrock, Merlin C.
Woelffer, Emerson Seville
Wofsy, Leon
Wojcicki, Stanley George
Wolas, Herbert
Wolbrecht, Walter Frederick
Wolcott, Oliver Dwight
Wolcott, Robert Boynton, Jr.
Wold, John Schiller
Wolf, Alfred
Wolf, Charles, Jr.
Wolf, Hans Abraham
Wolf, Harold Herbert
Wolf, Joseph Albert
Wolf, Walter
Wolfe, Bertram
Wolfe, David K.
Wolfe, Douglas Arthur
Wolfe, James Digby
Wolfe, Kenneth Gilbert
Wolfe, Raymond Grover, Jr.
Wolfert, Richard Jerome
Wolff, Herbert Eric
Wolff, Manfred Ernst
Wolff, Sheldon
Wolfle, Dael Lee
Wolfman, Earl Frank, Jr.
Wolfsberg, Max
Wollenberg, Albert Charles
Wollenberg, Richard Peter
Wollert, Gerald Dale
Wollman, Nathaniel
Wolper, David Lloyd
Wolpert, Stanley Albert
Wolterstorff, Robert Munro
Wolvington, Winston Warren
Womack, John James
Wonder, John Paul
Wonder, Stevie (Stevland Morris)
Wong, Curtis F.
Wong, Edwin Sau Nin
Wong, Kuang Chung
Woo, Chia-Wei
Wood, David Alvra
Wood, David Kennedy Cornell
Wood, David Shotwell
Wood, Erskine Biddle
Wood, Evelyn Nielsen
Wood, Harry Emsley, Jr.
Wood, Larry (Marylaird Wood)
Wood, Mari Lou
Wood, Robert Dennis
Wood, William Barry, III
Woodard, Clarence James
Woodard, Earyle Dean
Woodard, George Sawyer, Jr.
Woodard, Lawrence Joseph
Woodberry, Robert Leonard
Woodbridge, John Marshall
Woodbury, Lael Jay
Woodbury, Rollin Edwin
Wooden, John Robert
Woodfill, William Stewart
Woodford, Charles Day
Woodhead, Robert Kenneth
Woodress, James Leslie, Jr.
Woodruff, Jeffrey Stuart
Woodruff, John Rowland
Woods, Geraldine Pittman
Woods, Gurdon Grant
Woods, John Arnold
Woods, Wilfred Rufus
Woodward, Daniel Holt
Woodward, Don Adcook
Woodward, Joanne Gignilliat
Woodward, M. Irene
Woodward, Richard Joseph, Jr.
Woodward, Thomas Morgan
Wooldridge, Dean Everett
Wooster, Warren S(criver)
Work, Martin Haverty
Work, Richard Nicholas
Workman, Thomas Edgar, Jr.
Worner, Lloyd Edson
Wornick, Ronald Charles
Worsley, John Clayton
Worth, Gary James
Wrather, John Deveraux, Jr.
Wray, Karl
Wren, Melvin Clarence
Wrenn, C. Gilbert
Wright, Amy
Wright, Andrew
Wright, Byron T.
Wright, Charles Edward
Wright, Charles Penzel, Jr.
Wright, Donald Franklin
Wright, Eugene Allen
Wright, Gordon
Wright, Gordon Brooks
Wright, Gordon Kennedy
Wright, Hamilton Mercer
Wright, Henry Lyman
Wright, James William
Wright, Joyce Mary
Wright, Kenneth Brooks
Wright, Leroy Augustus
Wright, Milburn Dockery
Wright, Olgivanna Lloyd
Wright, Philip Lincoln
Wright, S. Earl
Wright, Willard Jurey
Wu, Theodore Yao-Tsu
Wulf, Robert Findley
Wulk, Ned William
Wulsin, Lucien
Wunsch, William Fritz
Wurman, Richard Saul
Wurtele, Morton Gaither
Wyatt, James Luther
Wyatt, Jane
Wyckoff, Jean Bratton
Wydick, Richard Crews
Wyle, Frederick S.
Wyler, Leopold Samuel, Jr.
Wylie, Frank Winston
Wylie, Turrell Verl
Wyman, H. Jack
Wymore, A. Wayne
Wynar, Bohdan Stephen
Wyne, Jon Robbin
Wynn, Keenan
Wynter, Dana
Wyse, William Walker
Wyshak, Lillian Worthing
Wyshak, Robert Habeeb
Yablans, Frank
Yablonka, Hy J.
Yaffe, James
Yaklich, Frank Joseph, Jr.
Yamaguchi, Ralph Tadashi
Yamamoto, Joe
Yamato, Kei C.
Yandell, Lunsford P.
Yanofsky, Charles
Yantis, Phillip Alexander
Yantis, Richard William
Yaqub, Adil Mohamed
Yarington, Charles Thomas, Jr.
Yariv, Amnon
Yarrow, Peter
Yaru, Nicholas
Yates, Ronald Eugene
Yates, William Robert
Yates-Edwards, Ella (Mae) Gaines
Yeats, Robert Sheppard
Yee, Albert Hoy
Yegge, Robert Bernard
Yeh, Raymond Wei-Hwa
Yellon, Donald Jerome
Yellott, John Ingle
Yen, Samuel S. C.
Yeo, Ron
Yep, Laurence Michael
Yerke, Fredric Albert
Yerxa, Charles Tuttle
Yesson, Charles Joseph
Yockey, Samuel Delbert
York, Herbert Frank
York, Susannah
Yorkin, (Alan) Bud
Yorty, Samuel William
Youmans, Julian Ray
Young, Al (Albert James Young)
Young, Arthur Nichols
Young, Bryant Llewellyn
Young, Burt
Young, Charles Edward
Young, Francis Allan
Young, Herbert Jack
Young, James Arthur
Young, James Vincent
Young, John Alan
Young, John Willis
Young, Joseph Louis
Young, Leo Vernon
Young, Loretta (Gretchen)
Young, Matt Norvel, Jr.
Young, Matt Norvel, Jr.
Young, Neil
Young, Ralph Alden
Young, Robert (George)
Young, Robert Nelson
Young, Terence
Young, Theodore Charles
Youngblood, Herbert Jackson, III
Younger, Evelle Jansen
Youngman, Henny
Yount, David Eugene
Yu, Jason Chia-Hsin
Yue, Alfred Shui-choh
Yuen, George Ah Leong
Zabka, Stanley William
Zaenglein, William George
Zaenglein, William George, Jr.
Zaffaroni, Alejandro Cesar
Zajac, Jack Simon
Zall, Paul Maxwell
Zalta, Edward
Zammitt, Norman
Zanuck, Richard Darryl
Zapata, Carmen
Zappa, Frank
Zare, Richard Neil
Zarem, Abe Mordecai
Zarem, Harvey Alan
Zawinul, Josef
Zawodny, Janusz Kazimierz
Zeder, Fred Monroe, II
Zeis, Robert Herschel
Zeitlin, Herbert
Zelazny, Roger Joseph
Zelditch, Morris, Jr.
Zellerbach, William Joseph
Zemach, Margot (Mrs. Harvey Fischtrom)
Zemplenyi, Tibor Karol
Zenczak, Piotr
Zentmyer, George Aubrey, Jr.
Zerbe, Anthony
Zevon, Warren
Ziadeh, Farhat J.
Ziegler, Raymond Stewart
Ziegler, Robert Holton, Sr.
Ziemer, Gregor
Ziering, William Mark
Zifferblatt, Steven Michael
Zimbalist, Efrem, Jr.
Zimbardo, Philip George
Zimet, Carl Norman
Zimm, Bruno Hasbrouck
Zimmer, Karl Ernst
Zimmer, Norman Cunningham
Zimmerman, Bryant Kable
Zimmerman, Gary A(lan)
Zipper, Herbert
Zipser, Stanley
Zirin, Harold
Zirker, Jack Bernard
Zirpoli, Alfonso Joseph
Zisk, Richard Walter
Zolotow, Maurice
Zondag, Cornelius Henry
Zornes, Milford
Zsigmond, Vilmos
Zuckerman, Irwin
Zukoski, Edward Edom
Zumberge, James Herbert
Zumsteg, Rickard Lee
Zweig, George
Zwerdling, Alex